W9-APF-511

PRESENTED TO

____

BY

____

ON THE OCCASION OF

____

DATE

____

No eye has seen,
no ear has heard,
and no mind has imagined
what God has prepared
for those who love him.
1 CORINTHIANS 2:9

BOUND FOR GLORY

PARALLEL BIBLE

King James Version

presented side by side with the

Tyndale House Publishers, Inc.
Carol Stream, Illinois

Visit Tyndale's exciting Web sites at www.newlivingtranslation.com and www.tyndale.com.

ISBN 978-1-4143-4988-6 Hardcover
ISBN 978-1-4143-4989-3 LeatherLike Ebony/Heritage Tapestry

Printed in South Korea

18 17 16 15 14 13 12 11
8 7 6 5 4 3 2 1

Tyndale House Publishers and Wycliffe Bible Translators share the vision for an understandable, accurate translation of the Bible for every person in the world. Each sale of the *Holy Bible*, New Living Translation, benefits Wycliffe Bible Translators. Wycliffe is working with partners around the world to accomplish Vision 2025—an initiative to start a Bible translation program in every language group that needs it by the year 2025.

CONTENTS

THE OLD TESTAMENT

THE NEW TESTAMENT

Alphabetical Listing of Bible Books

Water cannot be squeezed from a stone. And the spirituals could never have been squeezed from a people who had not suffered deeply and who were not grounded in the Holy Scriptures. It was from these creative contexts that the spiritual songs of the African-American slave community sprang.

The words and music of spirituals have been one of the precious contributions of the African-American community to the church of Jesus Christ. Beyond the richness of their content and music, these songs point us to an important truth: Our deepest pain, in the context of faith, can be the soil from which profound and enduring beauty grows. These songs also show how the experience of suffering and injustice in this world can awaken our spiritual senses to hope for eternal life with God, while also inspiring and energizing the pursuit of justice and transformation in this life.

Just as Paul and Silas sang songs of praise while locked up in the Philippian prison (Acts 16:25), the slaves raised their voices in hope and praise as they worked the fields and struggled to find their identity in a land that degraded their humanity. When they heard the stories of God's deliverance of Israel from slavery and oppression, they knew that this was the One they wanted to worship. They came to believe in the God of the Bible, even while they worshiped from the balconies of their masters' churches and perhaps wondered at their masters' hypocrisy. And though they listened to their masters' sermons, they often caught a different message—a message that promised hope and freedom.

After the Civil War, as black believers began to separate from white churches to form their own congregations, the spirituals they had once sung at their work and as lullabies for their children now found expression in their church music. The spirituals, some of which were used as worship songs, also gave rise to a new gospel music, sung to the African rhythms that still echoed in their ears and trembled in their bones. All the while, newly ordained black preachers opened the same Bible as their former masters and told many of the same stories, but they found new messages for their people—now "free," but still facing the painful realities of oppression and prejudice. They often looked to eternal life in heaven as a source of hope, but not at the expense of concern for the here and now. Turning to the numerous Scriptures that call for justice for the poor and oppressed, they began to call for transformation in a society that had long accepted oppressive practices.

In time, the African-American church found its own voice in song and preaching. That voice now stands as a profound witness to their faith in the God of Scripture—the God of deliverance, who offered the ultimate sacrifice of his Son, Jesus, to bring eternal hope to all people. In Christ, they were bound for glory, no matter what their present sufferings.

This Bible has been created to celebrate the 400th anniversary of the *Holy Bible,* King James Version, first published in 1611. The King James Version was the common translation for English-speaking Christians from the era of slavery until as recently as 50 years ago, when more contemporary Bible translations became available. As black believers separated from white churches to form their own congregations in the late 1800s, the KJV was the only Bible translation available to them, and its flow and cadences are woven into the fabric of black preaching and Scripture reading to this day. In this edition of the *Holy Bible*, the New Living Translation is set alongside the King James Version. The NLT is an authoritative Bible translation, rendered faithfully into today's English from the ancient texts by 90 leading Bible scholars. For younger readers unfamiliar with the older language of the KJV, the NLT will provide a text that is clear, accurate, and understandable.

In addition to including the full text of two Bible translations, this edition also celebrates the spiritual songs that arose from the years of African-American slavery. These spirituals stand as a testimony to the enduring faith of the African-American people, as well as representing a slice of America's musical history that has stood the test of time as it is continually performed by many of today's symphonies and chorales. We have included artwork from the Bound for Glory collection by Timothy R. Botts celebrating 16 of the best-known spirituals through calligraphic artwork. Each one is paired with a Scripture passage that expresses the message of the song, allowing you to reflect further on its biblical roots. Below we include the complete lyrics of the 16 spirituals, since the art pieces often only include one or two stanzas. We also include a statement from the artist that will allow you to join him in experiencing this rich musical heritage of our great land and will provide helpful background for understanding his work.

LYRICS OF FEATURED SPIRITUALS

HE'S GOT THE WHOLE WORLD IN HIS HANDS

He's got the whole world in His hands.
He's got the big, round world in His hands.
He's got the whole world in His hands.
He's got the whole world in His hands.

He's got the wind and the rain in His hands. (4X)

He's got the tiny little baby in His hands. (4X)

He's got you and me, sister, in His hands. (4X)

He's got you and me, brother, in His hands. (4X)

He's got the whole world in His hands. (4X)

WE ARE CLIMBING JACOB'S LADDER

We are climbing Jacob's ladder. (3X)
Soldiers of the cross.

Every round goes higher, higher. (3X)
Soldiers of the cross.

Sinner, do you love my Jesus? (3X)
Soldiers of the cross.

If you love Him, why not serve Him? (3X)
Soldiers of the cross.

Rise, shine, give God glory! (3X)
Soldiers of the cross

JOSHUA FOUGHT THE BATTLE OF JERICHO

Joshua fought the battle of Jericho, Jericho, Jericho;
Joshua fought the battle of Jericho,
And the walls come a tumbling down.
You may talk about your king of Gideon,
You may talk about your man of Saul;
There's none like good old Joshua
At the battle of Jericho.

Up to the walls of Jericho,
He marched with spear in hand.
"God blow them ram horns," Joshua cried,
"'Cause the battle is in my hand."

Then the lamb ram sheep horns began to blow,
Trumpets begin to sound.
Joshua commanded the children to shout,
And the walls came a tumbling down.

DEEP RIVER

Deep river, my home is over Jordan.
Deep river, Lord, I want to cross over into campground.
Lord, I want to cross over into campground.

O don't you want to go to that Gospel feast,
That promised land where all is peace?
Lord, I want to cross over into campground.

I'll walk into heaven and take my seat,
And cast my crown at Jesus' feet.
Lord, I want to cross over into campground.

O when I get to heaven, I'll walk all about,
There's nobody there for to run me out.
Lord, I want to cross over into campground.

THERE IS A BALM IN GILEAD

There is a balm in Gilead
To make the wounded whole.
There is a balm in Gilead
To heal the sin-sick soul.

Sometimes I feel discouraged
And think my work's in vain,
But then the Holy Spirit
Revives my soul again.

Don't ever feel discouraged,
For Jesus is your friend,
And if you lack for knowledge,
He'll never refuse to lend.

If you cannot preach like Peter,
If you cannot pray like Paul,
You can tell the love of Jesus,
And say, "He died for all."

NOBODY KNOWS THE TROUBLE I'VE SEEN

Nobody knows the trouble I've seen,
Nobody knows but Jesus.
Nobody knows the trouble I've seen,
Glory, hallelujah!

Sometimes I'm up, sometimes I'm down,
oh, yes, Lord.
Sometimes I'm almost to the ground, oh, yes, Lord.

Although you see me going along so, oh, yes, Lord.
I have my troubles here below, oh, yes, Lord.

One day when I was walking along,
The elements opened, and His love came down.

I never shall forget that day
When Jesus washed my sins away.

AMEN

Amen, Amen, Amen, Amen, Amen

See the little baby, lying in a manger,
On Christmas morning, Amen, Amen, Amen.

See Him in the Temple, talking to the elders.
How they marveled at His wisdom, Amen,
Amen, Amen.

See Him in the garden, praying to His Father,
As Judas betrays Him, Amen, Amen, Amen.

See Him on Calvary, dying for our sins,
But He rose on Easter, Amen, Amen, Amen.

THIS LITTLE LIGHT OF MINE

This little light of mine, I'm going to let it shine.
This little light of mine, I'm going to let it shine,
let it shine, let it shine.

Down in my heart, I'm going to let it shine.
Down in my heart, I'm going to let it shine, let it shine,
let it shine.

All in my house, I'm going to let it shine.
All in my house, I'm going to let it shine, let it shine,
let it shine.

Everywhere I go, I'm going to let it shine.
Everywhere I go, I'm going to let it shine, let it shine,
let it shine.

Out in the dark, I'm going to let it shine.
Out in the dark, I'm going to let it shine, let it shine,
let it shine.

All through the night, I'm going to let it shine.
All through the night, I'm going to let it shine,
let it shine, let it shine.

I'M GOING TO LAY DOWN MY BURDEN

I'm going to lay down my burden,
Down by the riverside,
Down by the riverside,
Down by the riverside.
I'm going to lay down my burden,
Down by the riverside,
Down by the riverside.

I'm going to lay down my sword and shield,
Down by the riverside . . .

I ain't going to study war no more,
Down by the riverside . . .

I'm going to put on my long white robe,
Down by the riverside . . .

I'm going to talk to the Prince of Peace,
Down by the riverside . . .

LET US BREAK BREAD TOGETHER

Let us break bread together on our knees,
Let us break bread together on our knees,

When I fall on my knees,
With my face to the rising sun,
O Lord, have mercy on me.

Let us drink wine together on our knees,
Let us drink wine together on our knees, . . .

Let us praise God together on our knees,
Let us praise God together on our knees, . . .

LORD, I WANT TO BE A CHRISTIAN IN MY HEART

Lord, I want to be a Christian,
In-a-my heart, in-a-my heart.
Lord, I want to be a Christian,
In-a-my heart.

Lord, I want to be more loving,
In-a-my heart, in-a-my heart. . . .

Lord, I want to be more holy,
In-a-my heart, in-a-my heart. . . .

Lord, I want to be like Jesus,
In-a-my heart, in-a-my heart. . . .

WERE YOU THERE WHEN THEY CRUCIFIED MY LORD?

Were you there when they crucified my Lord?
Were you there when they crucified my Lord?
Sometimes it causes me to tremble, tremble, tremble.
Were you there when they crucified my Lord?

Were you there when they nailed Him to the tree? . . .

Were you there when they pierced Him in the side? . . .

Were you there when the sun refused to shine? . . .

Were you there when they laid him in the tomb? . . .

Were you there when He rose up from the grave?
Were you there when He rose up from the grave?
Sometimes I feel like shouting glory, glory, glory!
Were you there when He rose up from the grave?

ALL GOD'S CHILDREN GOT SHOES

I got shoes, you got shoes,
All God's children got shoes.
When I get to heaven, gonna put on my shoes.
Gonna walk all over God's heaven.

Heaven, heaven, everybody talking about heaven
ain't going there.
Heaven, heaven, gonna shout all over God's heaven.

I got a robe, you got a robe,
All God's children got a robe. . . .

I got a crown, you got a crown,
All God's children got a crown. . . .

I got a harp, you got a harp,
All God's children got a harp. . . .

I got wings, you got wings,
All God's children got wings. . . .

SWING LOW, SWEET CHARIOT

Swing low, sweet chariot,
Coming for to carry me home.
Swing low, sweet chariot,
Coming for to carry me home.

I looked over Jordan, and what did I see?
Coming for to carry me home.
A band of angels coming after me,
Coming for to carry me home.

If you get there before I do,
Coming for to carry me home.
Tell all my friends I'm a-coming too,
Coming for to carry me home.

The brightest day that ever I saw,
Coming for to carry me home.
When Jesus washed my sins away,
Coming for to carry me home.

I'm sometimes up, I'm sometimes down,
Coming for to carry me home.
But still my soul feels heavenly bound,
Coming for to carry me home.

THE GOSPEL TRAIN'S A-COMIN'

The Gospel train's a-comin'
The fare is cheap and all can go.
No second class aboard this train.
Get on board, little children
There's room for many-a-more.

WHEN THE SAINTS COME MARCHIN' IN

When the saints come marchin' in,
When the saints come marchin' in,
Lord, I want to be in that number
When the saints come marchin' in.

When they crown Him Lord of all,
When they crown Him Lord of all,
Lord, I want to be in that number
When they crown Him Lord of all.

When they gather 'round the throne,
When they gather 'round the throne,
Lord, I want to be in that number
When they gather 'round the throne.

ARTIST'S STATEMENT

I sang nearly half of the spirituals included here when I was growing up in the youth fellowship of my church. I also remember, as if it were yesterday, Ethel Waters singing "His Eye Is on the Sparrow" on our black-and-white television.

With this body of work, I want to celebrate the incredible gift of music that African-Americans gave to the church and to the whole world. It is especially amazing that these people, many of them enslaved by Christians, saw beyond their owners' hypocrisy and met the real Jesus. I pray that the visual interpretations of this spirit-filled music will be instruments of healing and reconciliation among us.

This has been the most difficult artwork I ever created. From my western, European calligraphic background, I have tried to make a bridge to a heritage different from my own. During a period of self-doubt, I heard a beautiful interpretation of a European Christmas carol by a black singer. That experience encouraged me to come from the opposite direction with my paints and proceed with the project.

You may notice influences from both traditional American quilts and the wonderful quilts of Gee's Bend. I have been inspired by traditional African art and writing systems as well as by the best of urban graffiti. I hope that my use of color and movement in these pieces helps you hear both the sorrow and joy of the music. The majority of the designs are written with a watercolor medium called gouache, using pens or brushes. Most of the colored papers are Canson MiTientes. The painted backgrounds are prepared with acrylic paint and wallpaper paste on Arches Text Wove. I also applied gold leaf to many of the works.

Listening to the music of The Fisk Jubilee Singers, Mahalia Jackson, Jessye Norman, Moses Hogan, Rollo Dilworth, and Wintley Phipps carried me through eight years of stewing, sketching, and calligraphic writing.

These works are dedicated to our three African-American grandchildren—Naomi, Miriam, and Moses—who are helping me to become color-blind.

Timothy R. Botts

ARTIST'S BIOGRAPHY

The work of Tim Botts reaches back to use letterforms as old as the first century and combines with them contemporary graphic design principles in order to express the meaning of great works.

Tim has a BFA in graphic design from Carnegie Mellon University, during which time he apprenticed in calligraphy with Arnold Bank. He spent three years in Japan teaching conversational English and was influenced by the rich tradition of their brush writing. He has designed more than 600 books for Tyndale House Publishers near Chicago where he is a Senior Art Director. Nine books of his own work have been published, including *Doorposts*, *Messiah,* and a Bible illustrated in his calligraphy.

In 2010, Tim completed a new body of work with the lyrics of African-American spirituals which were on display at the Billy Graham Center Museum in Wheaton, Illinois.

TYNDALE
BIBLE VERSE FINDER

ABORTION
God cares for the unborn (Exodus 21:22-25) *page 123*
We should protect the helpless (Psalm 82:3-4) *page 926*
Children are from God (Psalm 127:3) *page 968*
God forms every child (Psalm 139:13-16) *page 974*
God plans the future of every child (Jeremiah 1:5) *page 1154*

ABUSE
God cares about minorities (Exodus 22:21) *page 125*
God protects those who are helpless (Psalm 12:5) *page 862*
Jesus was abused (Matthew 26:67-68) *page 1528*
Abuse has no place in family relationships (Ephesians 5:21–6:4) *page 1808*

ACCOUNTABILITY
God will judge our work (2 Chronicles 19:5-10) *page 718*
Sin has consequences (Ezekiel 18:20) *page 1295*
God will hold us accountable for our sin (Ezekiel 18:30) *page 1295*
We are accountable for every word that we speak (Matthew 12:36) *page 1498*
Confronting others with their sins should be done in private (Matthew 18:15) *page 1509*
We should hold each other accountable (Luke 17:3) *page 1611*
We are accountable for what we believe (John 3:18) *page 1635*
God holds Christians accountable (Romans 14:11-12) *page 1750*
God will reward Christians for their good deeds (1 Corinthians 3:8) *page 1758*
God will examine our actions (2 Corinthians 5:10) *page 1783*

ACCUSATIONS
Satan accuses God's people of doing wrong (Zechariah 3:1) *page 1455*
Jesus was falsely accused (Matthew 26:59-60) *page 1528*
Christians' sins are forgiven (Colossians 1:22) *page 1817*
Accusations against church leaders must come from more than one person (1 Timothy 5:19) *page 1834*
Satan is known as the Accuser (Revelation 12:10) *page 1910*

ADOLESCENCE
Young people should worship God (1 Kings 18:12) *page 577*
God can give hope to young people (Psalm 71:5) *page 913*
Young people should remember God (Ecclesiastes 12:1) *page 1039*
Young people should be an example to others (1 Timothy 4:12) *page 1833*
Young people should run from their youthful lust (2 Timothy 2:22) *page 1839*

ADOPTION, SPIRITUAL
God helps his children grow (Deuteronomy 8:5) *page 304*
God's children should obey him (Deuteronomy 26:18) *page 332*
God disciplines his children (2 Samuel 7:14) *page 504*
Do not despise God's discipline (Proverbs 3:11-12) *page 986*
God is our Father (Matthew 6:9) *page 1485*
Christians are God's children (John 1:12) *page 1631*
God's Spirit leads his children (Romans 8:14-17) *page 1740*
Christians should be separate from the world (2 Corinthians 6:17-18) *page 1784*
All of God's children are equal in God's eyes (Galatians 3:28) *page 1797*
God's children will receive a spiritual inheritance (Galatians 4:4-7) *page 1797*

God chose us to be his children (Ephesians 1:4-5) *page 1802*
Jesus is our spiritual brother (Hebrews 2:11) *page 1848*

ADULTERY

God forbids adultery (Exodus 20:14) *page 121*
Adultery has consequences (Proverbs 6:26) *page 990*
Adultery is foolish (Proverbs 6:32) *page 991*
Adultery is disgusting to God (Jeremiah 7:9-10) *page 1168*
God considers lust as sinful as adultery (Matthew 5:27-28) *page 1484*
Divorce often leads to adultery (Mark 10:11-12) *page 1554*
God can forgive the adulterer (John 8:1-11) *page 1647*

ADVICE

Leaders should consider the advice of others (Exodus 18:13-26) *page 118*
Older people often give wise advice (1 Kings 12:1-11) *page 565*
Stay away from people who give wicked advice (Psalm 1:1) *page 855*
God's advice is best (Psalm 73:24) *page 916*
Wise people seek advice (Proverbs 1:5) *page 983*
Advice helps provide success (Proverbs 11:14) *page 997*
Foolish people do not listen to advice (Proverbs 12:15) *page 998*
Give advice to those in need (1 Thessalonians 5:14) *page 1826*

ALCOHOL

Being controlled by alcohol is foolish (Proverbs 20:1) *page 1009*
Becoming drunk is sin (Romans 13:13-14) *page 1749*
God hates drunkenness (Galatians 5:19-21) *page 1800*
Church leaders should not be controlled by alcohol (Titus 1:7) *page 1842*

ANGELS

Angels carry out God's judgment (2 Samuel 24:16-17) *page 537*
Angels serve God (Psalm 103:21) *page 942*
Angels praise God (Psalm 148:2) *page 980*
Angels are messengers (Daniel 4:17) *page 1363*
Angels protect God's people (Daniel 6:22) *page 1368*
Angels do not marry (Matthew 22:30) *page 1517*
Angels do not die (Luke 20:36) *page 1619*
Angels will be judged by people (1 Corinthians 6:3) *page 1761*
Satan disguises himself as an angel of light (2 Corinthians 11:14) *page 1789*
Angels encourage Christians (Hebrews 1:14) *page 1848*
Angels who sinned were thrown into hell (2 Peter 2:4) *page 1880*
Angels are holy (Jude 1:14) *page 1894*
Angels are in the presence of God (Revelation 4:8) *page 1901*
Angels should not be worshiped (Revelation 22:8-9) *page 1923*

ANGER

Anger can lead to murder (Genesis 4:3-8) *page 8*
Anger leads to evil actions (Psalm 37:8) *page 884*
Showing anger is foolish (Proverbs 12:16) *page 998*
Gentle words can soothe anger (Proverbs 15:1) *page 1002*
Being quick-tempered is foolish (Ecclesiastes 7:9) *page 1034*
God becomes angry when we are ruled by anger (Amos 1:11) *page 1405*
Anger is like murdering someone (Matthew 5:21-22) *page 1483*
Jesus grew angry at sin (John 2:13-17) *page 1634*
Anger can give Satan a place in your life (Ephesians 4:26-27) *page 1806*
Christians should get rid of anger (Colossians 3:8) *page 1819*
Leaders in the church should not be quick-tempered (Titus 1:7) *page 1842*
Be slow to become angry (James 1:19) *page 1867*

ANTICHRIST

Many will claim to be God's messenger (Matthew 24:5) *page 1521*
Many will have miraculous powers (Matthew 24:24) *page 1521*

Jesus died for sins (1 Corinthians 15:3) *page 1773*
Our atonement allows us to know God (Ephesians 2:13) *page 1804*
Jesus' death rescues us from eternal punishment (Colossians 1:13) *page 1816*
Christ's death purifies God's people (Titus 2:14) *page 1843*
Sin requires that a sacrifice be made (Hebrews 9:22) *page 1857*
Jesus' sacrifice was perfect (1 Peter 1:18-19) *page 1873*
Jesus took our punishment (1 Peter 2:21-24) *page 1875*
We cannot improve Jesus' sacrifice (1 Peter 3:18) *page 1876*

ATTITUDE

Bad attitudes hurt our relationship with God (Genesis 4:6-7) *page 8*
Bad attitudes lead to poor decisions (Numbers 14:1-4) *page 241*
Always trust God for your life (Proverbs 29:25) *page 1024*
Choose a positive attitude (Habakkuk 3:17-19) *page 1443*
God will reward the meek (Matthew 5:5) *page 1482*
God gives Christians a new attitude (Philippians 1:20-25) *page 1811*
We should imitate Jesus' attitude (Philippians 2:5) *page 1812*
Christians should always rejoice (Philippians 4:4) *page 1814*
Never be anxious (Philippians 4:6-7) *page 1814*

AUTHORITY *(see also Respect)*

God will hold people in authority accountable for their actions (Daniel 4:31) *page 1364*
Jesus is the highest authority (Matthew 28:18) *page 1533*
God gave government its authority (John 19:11) *page 1668*
Christians should obey the government (Romans 13:1-2) *page 1749*
Parents are authorities to their children (Ephesians 6:1) *page 1808*
The Bible is our authority (2 Timothy 3:16) *page 1840*
Church leaders are authoritative (Hebrews 13:17) *page 1864*

BAPTISM

Baptism signifies repentance (Matthew 3:11) *page 1480*
All followers of Jesus should be baptized (Matthew 28:19) *page 1533*
Jesus was baptized (Mark 1:9) *page 1534*
Jesus baptizes with the Holy Spirit (John 1:32-33) *page 1632*
Baptism is closely linked with a changed life (Acts 2:38) *page 1677*
New Christians should be baptized (Acts 8:12-17) *page 1688*
Entire families of the early church were baptized (Acts 16:33-34) *page 1706*
Baptism initiates us into Christ (Romans 6:3-8) *pages 1737-1738*
Salvation is identified with baptism (1 Peter 3:21) *page 1876*

BELIEF

Believing God makes us righteous (Genesis 15:6) *page 23*
Belief in God should be accompanied by action (Deuteronomy 27:10) *page 333*
Belief affects the way we live (Mark 1:15) *page 1534*
Right beliefs are important for salvation (Romans 10:9) *page 1744*
Believing is more than acknowledging (James 2:21) *page 1868*

BIBLE

The Bible is perfect (Psalm 18:30) *page 866*
The Bible is true (Psalm 33:4) *page 879*
The Bible will last forever (Psalm 119:89) *page 961*
The Bible gives us wisdom (Psalm 119:99) *page 962*
The Bible can be trusted (Psalm 119:138) *page 963*
The Bible reveals the truth (Acts 18:28) *page 1710*
The Bible is holy (Romans 1:2) *page 1730*
God's Holy Spirit helps us understand the Bible (1 Corinthians 2:12-16) *page 1757*
The Bible is authoritative (Galatians 3:10) *page 1796*
The Bible is a Christian's spiritual weapon (Ephesians 6:17) *page 1809*
The Bible is inspired by God (2 Timothy 3:16) *page 1840*

The Bible judges our life (Hebrews 4:12) *page 1851*
The Bible helps us grow spiritually (1 Peter 2:2) *page 1873*

BIRTH

God is the Life-Giver (Genesis 2:7) *page 5*
Children are a blessing from God (Psalm 127:3-5) *page 968*
God carefully creates each person (Psalm 139:13-14) *page 974*
God's Son was born (Isaiah 9:6) *page 1064*
God plans the lives of people before they are born (Jeremiah 1:5) *page 1154*
Jesus' birth (Luke 2:7) *page 1574*
God's children are reborn spiritually (John 1:12-13) *page 1631*
People must be reborn spiritually to enter heaven (John 3:3) *page 1635*

BLESSING

God blesses those who obey him (Leviticus 26:3-5) *page 207*
God blesses godly people (Psalm 5:12) *page 858*
We are blessed when we worship God (Psalm 24:3-6) *page 872*
Christians bless God through praise (Psalm 103:1) *page 941*
God will bless those who fear him (Psalm 112:1-3) *page 953*
God blesses us when we seek to please him (Matthew 6:33) *page 1487*
Christians should bless their enemies (Luke 6:28) *page 1585*
Salvation is our greatest blessing (Ephesians 1:3) *page 1802*
The Bible brings us blessing (James 1:25) *page 1867*

BLOOD

God hates the shedding of an innocent person's blood (Genesis 4:10) *page 8*
Jesus' blood seals God's relationship with his people (Matthew 26:28) *page 1526*
Jesus' blood allows us to have access to God (Romans 5:8-9) *page 1736*
Christians are redeemed by Jesus' blood (Ephesians 1:5-7) *page 1802*
Blood is required for forgiveness (Hebrews 9:22) *page 1857*

BODY OF CHRIST

The body of Christ has been given many gifts (Romans 12:3-6) *page 1748*
There are many parts, but one body (1 Corinthians 12:12-13) *page 1769*
Christians make up the body of Christ (1 Corinthians 12:27) *page 1770*
Christians of different nationalities form one body (Ephesians 3:6) *page 1804*
There must be unity in the body of Christ (Ephesians 4:3) *page 1805*
Different members of the body help each other grow (Ephesians 4:11-12) *page 1806*
Jesus is the head of the body (Colossians 1:18) *page 1817*

BOOK OF LIFE

God writes our names in his book (Psalm 87:6) *page 929*
The names of Christians are in the Book of Life (Philippians 4:3) *page 1814*
Our names cannot be removed from the Book of Life (Revelation 3:5) *page 1900*
People whose names are not written in the Book of Life will experience God's wrath (Revelation 20:15) *page 1921*
Only those whose names are in God's Book will enter heaven (Revelation 21:27) *page 1922*

BRIDE

God's children should be as pure as a bride (Isaiah 49:18) *page 1127*
We should be devoted to God as a bride is to her husband (Jeremiah 2:2) *page 1155*
The church is the bride of Christ (2 Corinthians 11:2-3) *page 1767*
The bride of Christ will be presented to Christ (Revelation 19:7) *page 1919*

BUSINESS

God's people should be good workers (Genesis 31:42) *page 53*
Work should not overrun your time with God (Exodus 16:23) *page 115*
God gives you the ability to work (Exodus 35:30-31) *page 150*
Workers should be trustworthy (Proverbs 25:13) *page 1017*
Do the best job you can (Ecclesiastes 9:10) *page 1037*

Work as though Jesus were your boss (Ephesians 6:6-7) *page 1808*
Christians should do their best at their job (Titus 2:9-10) *page 1843*

CARING

God cares for his people (Deuteronomy 7:9) *page 302*
God cares for underprivileged people (Psalm 68:5) *page 908*
Protect the needy (Psalm 82:3) *page 926*
God's people should help the oppressed (Isaiah 1:17) *page 1052*
Care for your enemies (Luke 6:27) *page 1585*
God's people should care for the needy (Luke 14:13-14) *page 1607*
God cares for his children (Romans 1:6-7) *page 1730*
Treat parents with care (Ephesians 6:2) *page 1808*
Treat coworkers with care (Colossians 4:1) *page 1820*
Care for the elderly (1 Timothy 5:1-4) *page 1833*
Christians need to care for the needy (James 1:27) *page 1867*

CHILDREN

God tells children to honor their parents (Exodus 20:12) *page 31*
Parents should teach their children to follow God (Deuteronomy 6:6-7) *page 301*
Christians are children of God (John 1:12) *page 1631*
Children of God should imitate God (Ephesians 5:1) *page 1807*
Parents should nurture their children (Ephesians 6:4) *page 1808*
Children must obey their parents (Colossians 3:20) *page 1820*

CHURCH *(see also Worship)*

Jesus is the cornerstone of the church (Psalm 118:22) *page 957*
We should have joy going to God's house (Psalm 122:1) *page 966*
Satan works against the church (Matthew 16:18) *page 1506*
Members of the church should take care of each other (Acts 2:44) *page 1677*
The church sends out missionaries (Acts 13:2) *page 1697*
The church is like a body (1 Corinthians 12:12-13) *page 1769*
The church is a family of Christians (Galatians 6:10) *page 1801*
God's children form the church (Ephesians 2:19-22) *page 1804*
The church should not allow immoral behavior by its members (Ephesians 5:3-4) *page 1807*
Christ is the head of the church (Colossians 1:18) *page 1817*
Many people groups form one universal church (Colossians 3:11) *page 1819*
Church leaders are qualified to lead by their character (Titus 1:6-9) *page 1842*
The church is made up of God's children (1 John 3:1) *page 1886*
The church is the bride of Christ (Revelation 19:7-8) *page 1919*

COMFORT

Friends should comfort each other (Job 2:12-13) *page 808*
God comforts us (Isaiah 40:1-11) *page 1108*
God promises to comfort those who mourn (Matthew 5:4) *page 1482*
God's Holy Spirit is our Comforter (John 14:16) *page 1661*
Jesus has overcome the world's troubles (John 16:33) *page 1664*
God comforts those who are hurting (2 Corinthians 1:3-11) *page 1778*
Christians should comfort each other (1 Thessalonians 4:18) *page 1825*
All pain will end (Revelation 21:3-4) *page 1921*

COMPLAIN

Bring your complaints to God (Psalm 142:1-2) *page 976*
Christians should not complain to each other (Philippians 2:14) *page 1812*
People complain because they want their own way (Jude 1:16) *page 1894*

COMPROMISE

Do not compromise your convictions (1 Kings 11:4) *page 562*
Compromise can be wise (Matthew 5:25) *page 1484*
Compromise can divide our loyalty (Matthew 6:24) *page 1486*

Jesus' death was a sacrifice (Colossians 1:20-22) *page 1817*
Jesus' death defeated Satan (Colossians 2:14-15) *page 1818*
Jesus' cross is an example for us (Hebrews 12:2) *page 1862*

CULT

God hates the occult (Leviticus 19:26) *page 195*
God judges those who wrongly claim to speak for him (Deuteronomy 18:20-22) *page 251*
God hates occult practices (2 Kings 17:17) *page 621*
God despises false prophets (Ezekiel 13:8-9) *page 1285*
False teachers will come (Matthew 7:15) *page 1487*
Only Jesus brings salvation (John 14:6) *page 1660*
Members of the occult will never enter God's Kingdom (Galatians 5:19-21) *page 1800*
Be careful in your spiritual life (1 Thessalonians 5:21) *page 1826*

DARKNESS, SPIRITUAL

God's Word enlightens us (Psalm 119:105) *page 962*
The way of wicked people is darkness (Proverbs 4:19) *page 988*
Jesus brings light to darkened lives (John 1:5) *page 1631*
Living without God is living in spiritual darkness (Acts 26:17-18) *page 1724*
Christians do not live in spiritual darkness (Ephesians 5:8) *page 1807*
God rescued us from eternal darkness (Colossians 1:13) *page 1816*
There is no darkness in Jesus (1 John 1:5) *page 1884*
Sinners' eternal punishment will be in darkness (Jude 1:4-13) *page 1893*

DEATH

Death is a result of sin (Genesis 3:17-19) *page 7*
Life is short (Job 7:6-7) *page 813*
Every person will face death (Psalm 89:48) *page 933*
Death of Christians is precious (Psalm 116:15) *page 956*
Christians enter perfect peace at death (Isaiah 57:1-2) *page 1137*
God has power over death (John 14:19) *page 1661*
The death of Christians brings fellowship with Jesus (Acts 7:59) *page 1687*
God provides eternal life (Romans 6:23) *page 1738*
Jesus will raise everyone who has died (1 Corinthians 15:20-23) *page 1774*
Living in heaven is better than living on earth (2 Corinthians 5:6-7) *page 1782*
Death is not the end of a person (1 Thessalonians 4:13-14) *page 1825*
Prepare your spiritual life for death (Hebrews 9:27-28) *page 1857*
We don't know how long we'll live (James 4:13-14) *page 1870*
God will destroy death (Revelation 21:4) *page 1921*

DECISIONS

Pray before making decisions (Nehemiah 1:4) *page 768*
Decide to do things that honor God (Job 1:8) *page 806*
God's Word helps us make decisions (Psalm 119:105) *page 962*
Get good advice before making decisions (Proverbs 18:15) *page 1006*
Ask God for wisdom before making decisions (James 1:2-8) *page 1866*

DEMONS *(see also Satan)*

Worship in false religions honors demons (Psalm 106:37) *page 948*
Demons try to hinder God's plan (Daniel 10:13) *page 1375*
Demons are no match for Jesus (Mark 1:34) *page 1535*
Demons want to destroy people (Mark 5:5) *page 1542*
Demons submit to the name of Jesus (Luke 10:17) *page 1596*
Demons can be driven out by Jesus' followers (Acts 16:16-18) *page 1705*
Demons are powerful (Acts 19:16) *page 1711*
Demons cannot separate people from God's love (Romans 8:38-39) *page 1742*
Demons deceive people (2 Corinthians 11:13-15) *page 1789*
Christians fight against the plans of demons (Ephesians 6:12) *page 1809*
Demons want to mislead people (1 Timothy 4:1-2) *page 1833*
Demons believe in God (James 2:19) *page 1868*

Demons are angels that have sinned (2 Peter 2:4) *page 1880*
God will judge demons (Jude 1:6) *page 1893*
Do not take demons lightly (Jude 1:8-9) *page 1893*
Demons can work miracles (Revelation 16:13-14) *page 1914*
In the last days, demons will be bound by God (Revelation 20:1-3) *page 1920*

DEPRESSION
Depression can follow exhausting times (Judges 15:18) *page 421*
God can encourage hurting people (2 Samuel 22:29-31) *page 532*
Depression can follow success (1 Kings 19:3-4) *page 580*
God helps those who feel crushed (Psalm 34:18) *page 881*
Abraham had hope when there was no reason to hope (Romans 4:18-22) *page 1736*
God will wipe away depression (Revelation 21:4) *page 1921*

DESIRES
You should not desire something that belongs to someone else (Exodus 20:17) *page 121*
Wicked people desire evil (Psalm 36:1-4) *page 883*
God gives those who fellowship with him what they desire (Psalm 37:4) *page 883*
Desire to know God (Psalm 42:1) *page 889*
Desire to worship God (Psalm 84:1-2) *page 927*
Desire to honor God (Psalm 86:12) *page 929*
Do not desire self-promotion (Psalm 119:36) *page 959*
Money doesn't satisfy desires (Ecclesiastes 5:10) *page 1033*
Christians should not give in to sinful desires (Ephesians 4:22) *page 1806*
Sinful desires should not have a home with God's children (1 Peter 1:14) *page 1873*
Desire to do God's will (1 Peter 4:2) *page 1877*
God's children desire to obey God (1 John 2:3-6) *page 1884*

DETERMINATION
Be determined to obey God (1 Samuel 7:3) *page 449*
Determine not to sin (Job 31:1) *page 839*
Determine to stand firm (Isaiah 7:9) *page 1061*
God helps us be determined (Isaiah 50:7) *page 1129*
Determine to follow Christ (Mark 8:34-38) *page 1550*

DEVOTION
Be fully devoted to God (1 Chronicles 28:9) *page 689*
Worship God with devotion (1 Chronicles 29:9) *page 690*
Be devoted to prayer (Psalm 5:3) *page 857*
Let your life be devoted to God (Romans 12:1-2) *page 1747*

DISCERNMENT
The Bible will help you discern bad teaching (Acts 17:11) *page 1707*
God grants discernment (1 Corinthians 12:10) *page 1769*
Discern between right and wrong behavior (Hebrews 5:14) *page 1852*
Ask God for help in discerning his will (James 1:5) *page 1866*

DISCIPLESHIP
Christians are to make disciples (Matthew 28:19-20) *page 1533*
Jesus' followers are known by their love (John 13:35) *page 1660*
Christians should help other Christians grow (Acts 14:21-22) *page 1701*

DISCIPLINE
Punishment is a consequence of sinful actions (Genesis 3:6-19) *page 6*
God's punishment does not change his love for us (Psalm 89:32-33) *page 931*
The Lord disciplines those he loves (Proverbs 3:11-12) *page 986*
Parents are responsible to discipline their children (Proverbs 13:24) *page 1000*
Punishment for sin may be swift and severe (Acts 5:1-11) *page 1681*
Paul commanded punishment for blatant sin in the church (1 Corinthians 5:1-5) *page 1760*

Punishment should lead to repentance (2 Corinthians 7:8-9) *page 1785*
Sometimes God punishes us to bring us back to himself (Hebrews 12:5-11) *page 1862*

DISCRIMINATION

Be fair in your judgment of others (Leviticus 19:15) *page 194*
Don't discriminate against someone who is not powerful (Deuteronomy 1:17) *page 290*
Do not oppress the disadvantaged (Malachi 3:5) *page 1472*
God does not discriminate among his people (Acts 10:34) *page 1694*
All Christians are equal in God's eyes (Galatians 3:28) *page 1797*
God will judge those who discriminate (Colossians 3:25) *page 1820*
Do not discriminate against the poor (James 2:1-9) *page 1867*

DISHONESTY

Dishonesty is listed in the Ten Commandments (Leviticus 19:11) *page 194*
Be honest in your business dealings (Leviticus 19:35-36) *page 195*
Do not lie for your own gain (Deuteronomy 19:14) *page 322*
Dishonest people cannot know God (Psalm 101:7) *page 940*
God hates deception (Proverbs 12:22) *page 998*
God will punish those who take advantage of others (1 Thessalonians 4:6) *page 1824*

DOCTRINE

Protect sound doctrine (2 Timothy 1:13-14) *page 1837*
Doctrine comes from the Bible (2 Timothy 3:16) *page 1840*
Leaders in the church must have sound doctrine (Titus 1:6-9) *page 1842*
Christians should teach correct beliefs (Titus 2:1) *page 1843*

DOUBT

God will help us overcome doubts (Psalm 42:5-6) *page 889*
God doesn't leave us during our time of doubt (Isaiah 40:27-28) *page 1111*
Help those who have spiritual doubts (Hebrews 3:12) *page 1850*
Doubt inhibits our prayers (James 1:5-7) *page 1866*

DRINKING

People controlled by alcohol are fools (Proverbs 20:1) *page 1009*
Alcohol can cause you to become poor (Proverbs 21:17) *page 1011*
Alcohol can destroy you (Proverbs 23:29-35) *page 1015*
God will judge those who are controlled by alcohol (Isaiah 5:22) *page 1059*
Becoming drunk is dangerous (Luke 21:34) *page 1621*
Drunkenness is not fitting for a Christian (Romans 13:11-14) *page 1749*
Drunkenness can cause immoral behavior (Ephesians 5:18) *page 1807*

EARTH

God created the earth (Genesis 1:1) *page 3*
People are the caretakers of the earth (Genesis 1:28) *page 4*
The earth was cursed because of sin (Genesis 3:17-19) *page 7*
The earth belongs to God (Psalm 89:11) *page 931*
The earth was created for God's glory (Colossians 1:16) *page 1817*
Jesus sustains the earth (Hebrews 1:3) *page 1847*

EDUCATION

Parents are responsible to teach their children (Deuteronomy 6:1-9) *page 300*
Train children to follow God (Proverbs 22:6) *page 1012*
Christians should always learn more about God (Ephesians 4:14-15) *page 1806*

EMBARRASSMENT

Be careful not to embarrass others (Ruth 2:15) *page 436*
Embarrassment can lead to rash actions (Matthew 14:1-12) *page 1502*
We should not be embarrassed about the gospel (Romans 1:16) *page 1731*
We should not be embarrassed by Jesus (Galatians 1:10) *page 1793*

EMOTIONS

Emotions can lead us to sin (Genesis 4:2-6) *page 8*
Emotions can lead to foolish promises (Judges 11:29-40) *page 415*
Emotions are a part of worship (Ezra 3:1-13) *page 753*
God heals those with broken hearts (Psalm 34:18) *page 881*
Carefully guard your emotions (Proverbs 4:23) *page 988*
Emotions can crush us (Proverbs 15:13) *page 1002*
Do not be led by emotions (Proverbs 19:2) *page 1007*
Jesus experienced emotions (John 11:35) *page 1655*
Emotions are not reliable guides (Galatians 5:1-17) *page 1799*
Some emotions can be sinful (Ephesians 4:31) *page 1807*

EMPLOYMENT

God's people should be good workers (Genesis 31:42) *page 53*
Work should not overrun your time with God (Exodus 16:23) *page 115*
God gives you the ability to work (Exodus 35:30-31) *page 150*
Workers should be trustworthy (Proverbs 25:13) *page 1017*
Do the best job you can (Ecclesiastes 9:10) *page 1037*
Work as though Jesus were your boss (Ephesians 6:6-7) *page 1808*
Christians should do their best at their job (Titus 2:9-10) *page 1843*

ENCOURAGEMENT

Encourage the underprivileged (Isaiah 1:17) *page 1052*
God encourages us (Isaiah 40:31) *page 1111*
The Holy Spirit encourages us (Acts 9:31) *page 1691*
Encourage your neighbor (Romans 15:2) *page 1751*
The Bible encourages us (Romans 15:4) *page 1751*
Our position in Christ encourages us (Philippians 2:1) *page 1811*
We should encourage each other (1 Thessalonians 4:18) *page 1825*
Encourage those who are weak and afraid (1 Thessalonians 5:14) *page 1825*
Encourage elderly people (1 Timothy 5:1-4) *page 1833*
Encourage others not to sin (Hebrews 3:13) *page 1850*
Encourage others to love (Hebrews 10:24) *page 1859*

ENVY

Envy can destroy someone (Job 5:2) *page 810*
Do not envy those who do wrong (Psalm 37:1) *page 883*
Do not envy the prosperity of wicked people (Psalm 73:2-3) *page 915*
Envy steals your peace (Proverbs 14:30) *page 1001*
Envy is a powerful enemy (Proverbs 27:4) *page 1020*
Being envious is foolish (Ecclesiastes 4:4) *page 1031*
Envy can cause you to act rashly (Acts 7:9) *page 1685*
Envy characterizes sinful people (Romans 1:29) *page 1731*
We should not envy other Christians (Galatians 5:26) *page 1800*
Envy has no place in a Christian's life (Titus 3:3) *page 1844*
Do not harbor envy (James 3:14-15) *page 1869*
Get rid of envy (1 Peter 2:1) *page 1872*

ETERNAL LIFE

Eternal life is only for those who do God's will (Matthew 7:21) *page 1488*
The righteous will receive eternal life (Matthew 25:46) *page 1525*
Belief in Jesus is required for eternal life (John 3:15-16) *page 1635*
Evil people will receive eternal punishment (John 5:28-29) *page 1640*
Jesus came to give life (John 10:10) *page 1652*
Jesus gives eternal life (John 11:25) *page 1654*
Jesus is eternal life (John 14:6) *page 1660*
Eternal life cannot be earned (Ephesians 2:8-9) *page 1803*
Eternal life comes from God (Titus 1:2) *page 1842*
Eternal life gives us hope (Titus 3:7) *page 1844*

EVANGELISM *(see also Witnessing)*

We are God's messengers (Isaiah 43:10-11) *page 1116*
Christians bring light to a spiritually dark world (Matthew 5:14-16) *page 1483*
Jesus made salvation available to all people (Matthew 9:9-13) *page 1490*
Be bold in your evangelism (Matthew 10:33) *page 1494*
Jesus sent his followers to make disciples (Matthew 28:18-20) *page 1533*
The Holy Spirit gives us power to evangelize (Acts 1:8) *page 1674*

EVIL

God will destroy evil people (Job 4:8) *page 809*
God helps keep his people from sin (Psalm 19:13) *page 868*
God hates people who do evil (Psalm 26:5) *page 874*
God permits evil (Romans 1:24-28) *page 1731*
God cannot coexist with evil (Galatians 5:16-17) *page 1800*
Christians should put away evil from their lives (Ephesians 4:22) *page 1806*
There are spiritual forces behind evil (Ephesians 6:12) *page 1809*

FAITH

Believing God takes faith (Genesis 15:6) *page 23*
Only a small amount of faith is needed (Luke 17:6) *page 1611*
Faith is needed for salvation (Romans 3:28) *page 1734*
Faith puts us in a right relationship with God (Romans 5:1) *page 1736*
Faith comes from hearing the Word of God (Romans 10:17) *page 1745*
Accept the person who has weak faith (Romans 14:1) *page 1749*
Christianity is the only true faith (Ephesians 4:5) *page 1805*
Faith is hoping in what is not seen (Hebrews 11:1) *page 1859*
Faith accompanies obedience to God (Hebrews 11:7-12) *page 1860*

FAMILY

The members of a family can teach each other about God (Deuteronomy 6:4-9) *page 301*
Do not let sin affect your family life (Psalm 101:2) *page 940*
Do not bring trouble to a family (Proverbs 11:29) *page 997*
Christian faith is of greater importance than family (Luke 12:51-53) *page 1604*
Christians are members of God's family (Ephesians 2:19) *page 1804*
Husbands and wives should love each other (Ephesians 5:21-33) *page 1808*
Children should obey their parents (Ephesians 6:1) *page 1808*
Church leaders must have a good family life (1 Timothy 3:4-5) *page 1832*
Families should take care of each other (1 Timothy 5:3-5) *page 1833*

FEAR

God will protect us (Genesis 15:1) *page 22*
God will not forget us (Genesis 46:3) *page 80*
We should fear God (Psalm 25:12) *page 873*
Christians do not need to fear anyone (Psalm 27:1) *page 874*
God strengthens us (Psalm 46:1-3) *page 892*
We do not need to fear darkness or violence (Psalm 91:5) *page 934*
We do not need to fear bad news (Psalm 112:7) *page 954*
Love drives fear away (1 John 4:18) *page 1888*

FOOLISHNESS

Being foolish is lacking discernment (Job 5:2) *page 810*
Fools do not acknowledge God (Psalm 14:1) *page 863*
Fools do not know God (Proverbs 1:7) *page 983*
Fools invite their own destruction (Proverbs 10:14) *page 995*
Fools enjoy evil (Proverbs 10:23) *page 995*
Fools show their annoyance (Proverbs 12:16) *page 998*
Stay away from foolish people (Proverbs 14:7) *page 1000*
A foolish person rejects discipline (Proverbs 15:5) *page 1002*
Fools return to their folly (Proverbs 26:11) *page 1019*

A foolish person gives in to anger (Proverbs 29:11) *page* 1023
A foolish person is lazy (Ecclesiastes 4:5) *page 1031*
The foolishness of God is wiser than man's wisdom (1 Corinthians 1:25) *page 1756*

FORGIVENESS
God forgives our many sins (Psalm 65:3) *page 906*
God forgives us because he loves us (Psalm 86:5) *page 928*
God makes us as clean as freshly fallen snow (Isaiah 1:18) *page 1052*
God removes our impurities (Ezekiel 36:25) *page 1330*
We must forgive others (Matthew 6:14-15) *page 1486*
Don't keep track of how many times you forgive (Matthew 18:21-35) *page 1509*
Freely forgive others as God has forgiven you (Colossians 3:13) *page 1819*
God will forgive our sins if we confess them (1 John 1:8-9) *page 1884*

FOUL LANGUAGE
Foul language is not fitting for a Christian (Ephesians 5:4) *page 1807*
Our speech reflects our relationship with God (Colossians 4:6) *page 1820*
Our speech should be an example to others (1 Timothy 4:12) *page 1833*

FREEDOM
Christians are spiritually free (John 8:36) *page 1648*
Christians are free from sin's power (Romans 5:21) *page 1737*
Christians are free in order to serve others (Galatians 5:1) *page 1799*

FRIENDSHIP *(see also Relationships)*
Friends can cause great pain (Psalm 55:12-14) *page 899*
Friends love during difficult times (Proverbs 17:17) *page 1006*
Faithful friends are not common (Proverbs 18:24) *page 1007*
Friends influence you (Proverbs 22:24-25) *page 1013*
Friendship is marked by sacrifice (John 15:13-15) *page 1662*
We can be friends with God (James 2:23) *page 1868*

FUTURE
God has plans for our future (Genesis 12:1-4) *page 19*
God will bless our future if we obey him (Deuteronomy 5:29) *page 300*
Do not plan your future like evil people do (Jeremiah 10:2-3) *page 1174*
God gives us hope for our future (Jeremiah 31:17) *page 1212*
God prepares a future for us (1 Corinthians 2:9) *page 1757*

GIVING
God is honored by our gifts (Exodus 35:22) *page 150*
Generous giving honors God (Ezra 2:68-69) *page 753*
God will reward us for giving to others (Mark 9:41) *page 1553*
Giving helps others live (Acts 2:44-45) *page* 1677
We should support Christian workers (Acts 28:10) *page 1728*
Wealthy people should give generously (1 Timothy 6:17-19) *page 1836*
God is pleased with our gifts (Hebrews 13:16) *page 1864*
Giving reflects God's love (1 John 3:17) *page 1887*

GOD
God created everything (Genesis 1:1) *page 3*
God is a warrior (Exodus 15:3) *page 112*
God is one (Deuteronomy 6:4) *page 301*
God is trustworthy (Deuteronomy 7:9) *page 302*
God is too great to be described (1 Kings 8:27) *page 556*
God is gracious and merciful (Nehemiah 9:31) *page 783*
God is good (Psalm 34:8) *page 880*
God helps his people when they are in trouble (Psalm 46:1) *page 892*
God is mighty (Psalm 50:1) *page 895*
God is our rock (Psalm 62:6) *page 905*

Hell was prepared for Satan and demons (Matthew 25:41) *page 1524*
Wicked people will receive punishment (Romans 1:18-20) *page 1731*
God will punish those who do not turn from their sin (2 Peter 2:4-9) *page 1880*
Hell is a place of eternal fire (Jude 1:7) *page 1893*
God will send to hell those who do not believe in him (Revelation 21:8) *page 1921*

HOLY

God is known for his holiness (Psalm 93:5) *page 935*
God cannot tolerate sin (Isaiah 59:2) *page 1140*
God uses his Word to make us holy (John 17:17) *page 1665*
Christians should try to be holy (1 Peter 1:15) *page 1873*
God is worthy of praise because he is holy (Revelation 4:8) *page 1901*

HOLY SPIRIT

The Holy Spirit was involved in Creation (Genesis 1:2) *page 3*
The Holy Spirit empowers leaders (Judges 3:10) *page 397*
The Holy Spirit teaches us (John 14:26) *page 1661*
The Holy Spirit guides us (John 16:13) *page 1663*
The Holy Spirit empowers us to be witnesses (Acts 1:8) *page 1674*
The Holy Spirit lives within us (Romans 8:11) *page 1740*
The Holy Spirit sanctifies us (Romans 15:16) *page 1752*
The Holy Spirit opens our spiritual eyes (1 Corinthians 2:10) *page 1757*
The Holy Spirit is involved in salvation (Titus 3:5) *page 1844*

HOMOSEXUALITY

God finds homosexual behavior detestable (Leviticus 18:22) *page 193*
God will judge those who practice homosexual behavior (Romans 1:18-32) *page 1731*
Homosexual behavior has no place among Christians (1 Corinthians 6:9-10) *page 1761*

HONESTY

Honesty is commanded by God (Exodus 20:16) *page 121*
Only honest people can worship God (Psalm 24:3-4) *page 872*
God is truth and desires truth (Psalm 51:6) *page 897*
God hates lies (Proverbs 6:16-17) *page 990*
Be honest (Proverbs 19:1) *page 1007*
Christians should be known by their honesty (Matthew 5:37) *page 1484*
Lies make someone unclean before God (Matthew 15:18-20) *page 1504*
Christians should put away dishonesty from their lives (Ephesians 4:25) *page 1806*

HOPE

God gives hope to the needy (Psalm 9:18) *page 860*
Hope gives us confidence (Psalm 25:3) *page 872*
The Bible gives us hope (Psalm 119:43) *page 959*
Christians always have hope (Romans 8:28) *page 1741*
Hope comes from the Holy Spirit (Romans 15:13) *page 1751*
Jesus' resurrection gives us hope (1 Corinthians 6:14) *page 1761*
We have hope in Jesus (1 Corinthians 15:19) *page 1774*
We have confidence of eternal life (Titus 1:1-2) *page 1842*

HOSPITALITY

Christians should take care of those in need (Matthew 25:34-40) *page 1524*
Hospitality brings heavenly reward (Mark 9:41) *page 1553*
Christians should be hospitable (Romans 12:13) *page 1748*
Christians should be hospitable to people they do not know well (Hebrews 13:2) *page 1863*
Be cheerful about being hospitable (1 Peter 4:9-11) *page 1877*
Hospitality reflects God's love (3 John 1:5-8) *page 1891*

HUMILITY

God humbles us for our own good (Deuteronomy 8:16) *page 304*
God hears the prayers of the humble (2 Chronicles 7:14) *page 1785*
God saves those who are humble (Psalm 18:27) *page 866*

God preserves the lives of humble people (Psalm 147:6) *page 980*
Those who are humble become wise (Proverbs 11:2) *page 996*
God cares for the humble (Isaiah 66:2) *page 1157*
God will exalt the humble (Luke 18:14) *page 1613*
Be humble in dealing with others (Philippians 2:1-11) *page 1811*
Humble yourself before God (James 4:10) *page 1870*

HYPOCRISY

Do not associate with hypocrites (Psalm 26:4) *page 873*
God hates hypocrisy in worship (Isaiah 29:13) *page 1092*
Hypocrites pretend to be devoted to God (Ezekiel 33:31-32) *page 1325*
God finds hypocrites repulsive (Matthew 23:27-28) *page 1520*
Beware of hypocrisy in your life (Luke 12:1-2) *page 1601*
God will punish hypocrisy (Luke 20:46-47) *page 1620*
Hypocrites are worthless (Titus 1:16) *page 1843*
Get rid of hypocrisy (1 Peter 2:1) *page 1873*

IDOLATRY

We should have no other gods (Exodus 20:3) *page 121*
Do not be devoted to anyone or anything more than God (Deuteronomy 4:23) *page 297*
Devote your heart to God (Joshua 24:14) *page 391*
Look to God for your security (Judges 10:13-16) *page 413*
We give in to idolatry when we forget God (Psalm 106:19-22) *page 947*
God will not share his glory with anything else (Isaiah 42:8) *page 1114*
Christians cannot serve both God and the things of this world (Luke 16:13) *page 1610*

IMMORALITY

Compromises can lead to immorality (Judges 3:1-11) *page 396*
Stay away from immoral Christians (1 Corinthians 5:9-11) *page 1760*
Practicing immorality treats God lightly (1 Corinthians 6:19-20) *page 1761*
Immorality should have no place among Christians (Ephesians 4:17-19) *page 1806*

INSULT

Respond properly to an insult (Proverbs 12:16) *page 998*
God will bless Christians who are insulted because of their faith (Luke 6:22) *page 1585*
Do not insult others (1 Peter 3:9) *page 1876*

INTEGRITY

Leaders should have integrity (Psalm 78:72) *page 923*
Integrity takes effort (Psalm 101:3-8) *page 940*
Leaders in the church should be full of integrity (Titus 1:7) *page 1842*
Maintain integrity in teaching others (Titus 2:7) *page 1843*

INTIMIDATION

God can help us overcome intimidation (Genesis 15:1) *page 22*
God does not forget us when we are intimidated (Genesis 46:3) *page 74*
We do not need to fear anyone (Psalm 27:1) *page 874*
God empowers us (Psalm 46:1-3) *page 892*
We do not need to be intimidated (Psalm 112:7-8) *page 954*
Jesus' strength can give us courage (John 16:33) *page 1664*
God will help us be bold (Acts 4:31) *page 1680*
Be on your guard against intimidation (1 Corinthians 16:13) *page 1777*
Pray for courage (Ephesians 6:19-20) *page 1809*
Christians can pray without being intimidated (Hebrews 4:16) *page 1851*

JEALOUSY

God doesn't want to share our devotion (Deuteronomy 4:24) *page 297*
Jealousy can destroy someone (Job 5:2) *page 810*
Do not envy those who do wrong (Psalm 37:1) *page 883*
Do not be jealous of wicked people (Psalm 73:2-3) *page 915*

Jealousy steals away peace (Proverbs 14:30) *page 1001*
Jealousy is a powerful enemy (Proverbs 27:4) *page 1020*
Jealousy is foolish (Ecclesiastes 4:4) *page 1031*
Jealousy can cause rash behavior (Acts 7:9) *page 1685*
We should not be jealous of other Christians (Galatians 5:26) *page 1800*
Jealousy has no place in a Christian's life (Titus 3:3-5) *page 1844*

JESUS CHRIST

Jesus is all-powerful (Isaiah 9:6) *page 1064*
Jesus has authority over demons (Mark 1:27) *page 1535*
Jesus is the Son of God (Luke 1:35) *page 1571*
Jesus is God (John 1:1-5) *page 1631*
Jesus is the Messiah (John 4:25-26) *page 1637*
Jesus is the Judge (John 5:22) *page 1640*
Jesus gives life (John 10:10) *page 1652*
Jesus is the Good Shepherd (John 10:11) *page 1652*
Jesus is the only way to God (John 14:6) *page 1660*
Jesus is the author of life (Acts 3:15) *page 1678*
Jesus is the wisdom of God (1 Corinthians 1:21-24) *page 1756*
Jesus is the head of the church (Ephesians 5:23) *page 1808*
Jesus is the highest authority (Philippians 2:9-10) *page 1812*
Jesus is the Creator (Colossians 1:15-16) *page 1817*
Jesus is faithful (2 Timothy 2:13) *page 1840*
Jesus is coming again (Titus 2:13) *page 1843*
Jesus is sinless (Hebrews 4:15) *page 1851*
Jesus is holy (Hebrews 7:26) *page 1854*
Jesus is the King of the ages (Revelation 15:3) *page 1913*
Jesus is the Lamb of God (Revelation 21:22) *page 1922*

JUDGMENT

God is able to judge (Job 34:23) *page 844*
God is the ultimate authority (Psalm 9:7) *page 860*
God will judge all people (Ecclesiastes 3:17) *page 1031*
God will judge people for their actions (Ecclesiastes 11:9) *page 1039*
God will judge everything done in secret (Ecclesiastes 12:14) *page 1040*
God will rule that wicked people are guilty (Malachi 3:5) *page 1472*
God will judge the words we speak (Matthew 12:36) *page 1498*
God does not judge by appearances (John 7:21-24) *page 1645*
God will judge Christians (Romans 14:10) *page 1750*
God will judge Christians for their actions (2 Corinthians 5:10) *page 1783*
God will judge all people (Hebrews 9:27) *page 1857*
People whose names are in God's Book of Life will enter heaven (Revelation 20:11-15) *page 1920*

JUSTICE

Justice should not be influenced by a crowd (Exodus 23:2) *page 126*
Protect the poor (Exodus 23:6) *page 126*
Do not hold back justice (Deuteronomy 27:19) *page 333*
God loves justice (Psalm 11:7) *page 862*
Jesus' death was justice for sin (Romans 3:25-26) *page 1734*

KINDNESS

Christians should be kind to each other (Ephesians 4:32) *page 1807*
Be kind to people who treat you wrongly (1 Thessalonians 5:15) *page 1826*
Choose to be kind rather than to argue (2 Timothy 2:24) *page 1839*
Being kind takes effort (2 Peter 1:5-7) *page 1879*

KINGDOM OF GOD/HEAVEN

You must turn from sin before you can enter God's Kingdom (Matthew 3:1-2) *page 1480*
Jesus describes members of God's Kingdom (Matthew 5:1-19) *page 1482*

Obeying God's commands yields great rewards in his Kingdom (Matthew 5:19) *page 1483*
Only righteous people will enter God's Kingdom (Matthew 5:20) *page 1483*
God's Kingdom is open to those who do his will (Matthew 7:21) *page 1488*
Healed lives are associated with God's Kingdom (Matthew 9:35-36) *page 1492*
Entering God's Kingdom costs someone everything (Matthew 13:44-45) *page 1501*
God's Kingdom is reserved for the humble (Matthew 18:2-3) *page 1508*
No one deserves God's Kingdom (Matthew 18:23-35) *page 1509*
God's Kingdom is within our hearts (Luke 17:20-21) *page 1612*
God's Kingdom will fully arrive in the future (Luke 21:25-31) *page 1621*
Only those who are spiritually reborn can enter God's Kingdom (John 3:3) *page 1635*
Entering God's Kingdom is not easy (Acts 14:22) *page 1702*
Christians should tell others about the Kingdom of God (Acts 28:31) *page 1729*
God's Kingdom affects our lives (Romans 14:17) *page 1750*
God's Kingdom is powerful (1 Corinthians 4:20) *page 1758*
No immoral person will be allowed into God's Kingdom (Ephesians 5:5) *page 1807*
Christians are members of God's Kingdom (Colossians 1:13) *page 1816*
Christians' lives should reflect their membership in God's Kingdom (1 Thessalonians 2:12) *page 1823*
God calls people into his Kingdom (1 Thessalonians 2:12) *page 1823*
God's Kingdom cannot be shaken (Hebrews 12:28) *page 1863*
God's Kingdom will one day be fully consummated (Revelation 11:15) *page 1909*

LAZINESS

Laziness can ruin you (Proverbs 6:6-11) *page 989*
Laziness can make you poor (Proverbs 10:4-5) *page 994*
Lazy people work for others (Proverbs 12:24) *page 999*
Lazy people make excuses (Proverbs 22:13) *page 1013*
Lazy people oversleep (Proverbs 26:14) *page 1019*
Encourage lazy people to work (1 Thessalonians 5:14) *page 1826*
Lazy people should not be allowed to be freeloaders (2 Thessalonians 3:10) *page 1829*

LEADERSHIP

Leaders should be trustworthy (Exodus 18:21) *page 119*
Leaders look out for the people's best interests (Numbers 27:16-17) *page 270*
Leaders should represent God in their decisions (2 Chronicles 19:5-7) *page 718*
Leaders should receive advice (Proverbs 11:14) *page 997*
Leaders must serve others (Matthew 20:26-28) *page 1513*
Leaders should sacrifice for others (John 10:11) *page 1652*
Leaders should be obeyed (Romans 13:1-4) *page 1749*
Leaders give an account to God for their actions (Hebrews 13:17) *page 1864*

LIFE

Life comes from God (Genesis 2:7) *page 5*
God carefully creates each person (Psalm 139:13-14) *page 974*
Life should be enjoyed (Ecclesiastes 9:9) *page 1037*
God plans the lives of people before they are born (Jeremiah 1:5) *page 1154*
People must be reborn spiritually to enter heaven (John 3:3) *page 1635*
Jesus came to give abundant life (John 10:10) *page 1652*
We should live lives worthy of our Christian calling (Ephesians 4:1) *page 1805*
Christ is the reason for life (Philippians 1:21) *page 1811*
Our lives should honor God (Colossians 3:17) *page 1820*

LIGHT

Light comes from God (Genesis 1:3) *page 3*
God is light (Psalm 27:1) *page 874*
God's Word enlightens our path (Psalm 119:105) *page 962*
God can turn darkness into light (Isaiah 42:16) *page 1114*
Christians are the light of the world (Matthew 5:14) *page 1483*
Jesus is the Light of the World (John 8:12) *page 1647*

Light shines in the hearts of Christians (2 Corinthians 4:6) *page 1781*
Christians are children of light (Ephesians 5:8) *page 1807*

LONELINESS

God is concerned about our loneliness (Genesis 2:18) *page 5*
God encourages the lonely (1 Kings 19:14-18) *page 581*
God takes care of lonely people (Psalm 68:6) *page 908*
Friends help in times of loneliness (Ecclesiastes 4:10-11) *page 1032*
God remains with us (Matthew 28:20) *page 1533*

LORD'S SUPPER

Jesus celebrated the Lord's Supper with his disciples (Matthew 26:26-29) *page 1526*
Christians should be thankful for the Lord's Supper (1 Corinthians 10:16) *page 1766*
Christians who celebrate the Lord's Supper together should be unified (1 Corinthians 11:20-34) *pages 1768-1769*

LOVE

Love in marriage is strong (Song of Songs 8:6-7) *page 1049*
Love your enemies (Matthew 5:43-44) *page 1485*
Loving God is the most important command (Mark 12:29-30) *page 1559*
Christians must love each other (John 13:34) *page 1660*
We cannot be separated from Jesus' love (Romans 8:35-39) *page 1742*
Love must be genuine (Romans 12:9) *page 1748*
Love never quits (1 Corinthians 13:4-8) *page 1771*
God's love for us is beyond our understanding (Ephesians 3:18) *page 1805*
Love helps you look past offenses (1 Peter 4:8) *page 1877*
God is love (1 John 4:16) *page 1888*
We must be known for our love (2 John 1:5) *page 1890*

LOYALTY

Friends are loyal (Proverbs 17:17) *page 1006*
We cannot divide our loyalty (Matthew 6:24) *page 1486*
There must be loyalty in marriage (Hebrews 13:4) *page 1864*

LUST

Lustful thoughts are sinful (Matthew 5:28) *page 1484*
Christians should not give in to lust (Colossians 3:5) *page 1819*
Christians should avoid lust (1 Thessalonians 4:3-5) *page 1824*
Godless people enjoy immorality (1 Peter 4:3) *page 1877*

LYING *(see Dishonesty)*

MARRIAGE

God hates divorce (Malachi 2:16) *page 1471*
Two people become one through marriage (Mark 10:2-12) *page 1553*
Angels do not get married (Mark 12:25) *page 1559*
Married partners should meet each other's needs (1 Corinthians 7:2-5) *page 1762*
Married partners are united to each other for life (1 Corinthians 7:39) *page 1763*
A Christian wife can witness to her non-Christian husband (1 Peter 3:1-6) *page 1875*

MERCY

God requires that we show mercy (Micah 6:8) *page 1430*
People who show mercy to others will be rewarded (Matthew 5:7) *page 1482*
We should imitate God's mercy (Luke 6:36) *page 1585*
Jesus is merciful (1 Timothy 1:2) *page 1830*
Mercy is from God (2 Timothy 1:2) *page 1837*

MESSIAH

The prophets prophesied about the Messiah (Genesis 3:15) *page 7*
The Messiah's mother would be a virgin (Isaiah 7:14) *page 1061*
The Messiah would be great (Isaiah 9:6-7) *page 1064*
The Messiah would suffer (Isaiah 53:2-12) *page 1132*

The Messiah would heal broken lives (Isaiah 61:1-3) *page 1144*
The Messiah would be born in Bethlehem (Micah 5:2) *page 1429*
Jesus' disciples knew he was the Messiah (Mark 8:27-29) *page 1550*
The Messiah will come again (Mark 14:61-62) *page 1565*
Jesus claimed to be the Messiah (John 4:25-42) *page 1637*
The Messiah brings salvation (Hebrews 2:10) *page 1848*

MIND
Keep away from mental sins (Matthew 5:27-30) *page 1484*
A Christian's thoughts should be holy (Romans 12:2) *page 1748*
Our fellowship with God helps us make decisions (1 Corinthians 2:6-16) *page 1757*
Christians should please God with their thoughts (Philippians 4:8) *page 1815*

MONEY
Greed brings trouble (Proverbs 15:27) *page 1003*
Do not make money the most important part of your life (Matthew 6:19) *page 1486*
Money can distract people from God (Mark 10:17-24) *page 1554*
You cannot serve both God and money (Luke 16:13) *page 1610*
Christians should share their resources with those in need (Acts 2:42-45) *page 1677*
Christians should not be lovers of money (1 Timothy 3:3) *page 1832*
We should look to God for security, not money (1 Timothy 6:17-19) *page 1836*
Do not love money (Hebrews 13:5) *page 1864*
Be careful to treat rich and poor equally (James 2:1-9) *page 1867*

MURDER
God has forbidden murder (Deuteronomy 5:17) *page 299*
Hateful anger is the same in God's eyes as murder (Matthew 5:21-22) *page 1483*

MUSIC
Music can be used to worship God (Exodus 15:1) *page 112*
Music is useful to focus our attention on God (Psalm 81:1-2) *page 925*
We should make music for God's glory (Colossians 3:16) *page 1820*

OBEDIENCE
Obeying is better than saying, "I'm sorry" (1 Samuel 15:22) *page 464*
People who obey God's Word will be blessed (Luke 11:28) *page 1599*
Christians should obey the government (Romans 13:1-4) *page 1749*
Children should obey their parents (Ephesians 6:1) *page 1808*
Christians obey God (1 John 2:3) *page 1884*

PAIN
God cares for his people (Deuteronomy 7:9) *page 302*
Friends should comfort each other (Job 2:12-13) *page 808*
God comforts us in our darkest times (Job 35:10) *page 845*
God watches over the weak (Psalm 12:5) *page 862*
God comforts us (Isaiah 40:9-11) *page 887*
God promises to comfort those who mourn (Matthew 5:4) *page 1482*
God's Holy Spirit is our Comforter (John 14:16) *page 1661*
Christians should comfort each other (1 Thessalonians 4:18) *page 1825*
All pain will end (Revelation 21:3-4) *page 1921*

PARENTS
Parents should teach children to follow God (Deuteronomy 6:6-7) *page 301*
Parents should nurture their children (Ephesians 6:4) *page 1808*
Children must obey their parents (Colossians 3:20) *page 1820*

PATIENCE
Be patient with God (Psalm 75:2) *page 917*
Patience is valuable (Proverbs 25:15) *page 1017*
Patience is better than pride (Ecclesiastes 7:8) *page 1034*
Patience demonstrates love (1 Corinthians 13:4) *page 1771*

The Holy Spirit allows believers to prophesy (Acts 2:17-18) *page 1676*
Prophecy is a spiritual gift (1 Corinthians 14:1-5) *page 1771*
We should listen to God's message (1 Thessalonians 5:20) *page 1826*
True prophets speak God's words (2 Peter 1:20-21) *page 1881*

PURITY

Only God can make us pure (Psalm 51:1-10) *page 897*
We can remain pure by following God's Word (Psalm 119:1-20) *page 958*
We cannot claim purity apart from God (Proverbs 20:9) *page 1009*
The pure in heart will see God (Matthew 5:8) *page 1482*
Purity begins in the heart (Matthew 5:27-30) *page 1484*
Outward purity cannot substitute for inner purity (Matthew 23:25-28) *page 1519*
Purity comes from God (John 17:17) *page 1665*
Purity ought to mark believers' lives (Ephesians 5:1-4) *page 1807*
Our minds should think about things that are pure (Philippians 4:8) *page 1815*
One day our purity will be like Christ's (1 John 3:1-3) *page 1886*

QUESTIONS

God may not always answer our questions (Job 42:1-3) *page 853*
God welcomes our sincere questions (Luke 7:18-23) *page 1587*
We need not be afraid when questioned about our faith (Luke 21:12-15) *page 1620*
We should be ready with answers when questioned about our faith (1 Peter 3:15) *page 1876*

RAPTURE *(see Second Coming of Christ)*

RELATIONSHIPS *(see also Friendship, Marriage)*

Our relationship with God is made possible through Jesus Christ (John 14:19-21) *page 1661*
Our relationships should not compromise our faith (2 Corinthians 6:14-18) *page 1784*
We are unified with all believers in God's family (Ephesians 2:21-22) *page 1804*
Our relationship with Christ is deep and abiding (2 Timothy 2:11-13) *page 1838*
Our relationship with Christ makes us children of God (1 John 3:1-3) *page 1886*

REPENTANCE *(see also Confession of Sin)*

Repentance of sin opens the way for a relationship with God (Luke 3:7-8) *page 1576*
Unless we repent of our sins, we will perish (Luke 13:3-5) *page 1604*
Angels rejoice when a sinner repents (Luke 15:7) *page 1608*
Forgive those who repent of wrongs done to you (Luke 17:4) *page 1611*
Repentance is essential for the Holy Spirit to work (Acts 2:38) *page 1677*
God can use difficulties to encourage us to repent (2 Corinthians 7:9-10) *page* 1785
God would like everyone to repent and believe (2 Peter 3:9) *page 1882*

REPUTATION

A good reputation can be built by obeying God's Word (Deuteronomy 4:1-14) *page 314*
Integrity builds a good reputation (Ruth 2:1-13) *page 435*
A bad reputation will follow you (Proverbs 25:9-10) *page 1017*
The Christians in Rome had a reputation for obedience (Romans 16:19) *page 1753*
Guard your reputation (2 Corinthians 8:18-24) *page 1786*
Maintain a good reputation among non-Christians (Colossians 4:5) *page 1820*

RESPECT *(see also Authority)*

God is worthy of our respect (Exodus 3:5) *page 91*
Our parents are worthy of respect (Leviticus 19:3) *page 193*
Those in authority should have our respect (1 Samuel 24:1-6) *page 480*
Husbands and wives should respect each other (Ephesians 5:33) *page 1808*
Those in leadership should have respectful children (1 Timothy 3:4) *page 1832*
Show respect to all people (1 Peter 2:17) *page 1881*

RESPONSIBILITY
Responsible people admit their wrongs (1 Chronicles 21:8) *page 676*
Responsible people are faithful with what they have been given (Matthew 25:14-30) *page 1523*
People are responsible for their decision about Christ (John 3:18-19) *page 1635*
Responsible people know their abilities and limitations (Acts 6:1-7) *page 1683*
People are responsible for their own actions (James 1:13-15) *page 1866*

REST
God gave us an example of and a command to rest (Genesis 2:3) *page 5*
Rest is important for worship (Exodus 20:8) *page 121*
God tells us to rest (Exodus 23:12) *page 126*
Jesus promises to give us rest from our burdens (Matthew 11:28-30) *page 1496*
Rest is a gift of God (Hebrews 4:9-11) *page 1851*
Heaven will be a place of rest (Revelation 14:13) *page 1912*

RESURRECTION
Christ's resurrection is a historical fact (Matthew 28:5-10) *page 1532*
All people will be resurrected (John 5:24-30) *page 1640*
Jesus promised to raise his followers (John 6:38-40) *page 1643*
We know we will be resurrected (John 11:24-26) *page 1654*
We will experience resurrection (Romans 6:3-11) *page 1737*
Jesus' resurrection is the foundation of Christianity (1 Corinthians 15:12-21) *page 1774*
Our resurrected bodies will be eternal bodies (1 Corinthians 15:51-53) *page 1776*

REVENGE
God's people should not seek revenge (Leviticus 19:18) *page 194*
Do not pay back evil for evil (Proverbs 24:29) *page 1016*
Believers ought to resist revenge (Matthew 5:38-42) *page 1484*
Leave revenge in God's hands (Romans 12:19) *page 1748*
Desire for revenge is not compatible with the Christian life (1 Thessalonians 5:15) *page 1826*
Jesus is our example (1 Peter 2:21-23) *page 1875*

RIGHTEOUS/RIGHTEOUSNESS
God is completely righteous (Isaiah 45:21-24) *page 1121*
We cannot attain righteousness on our own (Isaiah 64:6) *page 1148*
Human nature is the opposite of righteousness (Romans 3:10-18) *page 1733*
Righteousness is not attained by works (Romans 4:18-25) *page 1736*
Strict legalism cannot make us righteous (Galatians 3:11-21) *page 1796*
Our God-given righteousness is armor against Satan's attacks (Ephesians 6:14) *page 1809*
We become righteous through faith in Christ (Philippians 3:9) *page 1813*
Studying God's Word helps us grow in righteousness (2 Timothy 3:16) *page 1840*
Righteousness ought to characterize each believer's life (1 Peter 2:24) *page 1875*

SADNESS *(see Grief, Sorrow)*

SALVATION
Those who receive salvation become God's children (John 1:12-13) *page 1631*
Salvation is a work of the Holy Spirit in a person's life (John 3:1-16) *page 1634*
Belief and trust in Jesus Christ are the only way to be saved (John 14:6) *page 1660*
Salvation includes gaining a relationship with God (John 17:1-5) *page 1664*
Receiving salvation means we must turn from our sins (Acts 2:37-38) *page 1677*
Salvation cannot be earned; it is a gift of God (Romans 6:23) *page 1738*
Receiving salvation is simple and personal (Romans 10:8-10) *page 1744*
Salvation is by God's grace alone (Ephesians 2:1-9) *page 1803*
Salvation rescues us from Satan's dominion (Colossians 1:13-14) *page 1816*
Our salvation was obtained by Jesus' blood (1 Peter 1:18-19) *page 1873*

SATAN *(see also Demons)*

Satan is under God's authority (Job 1:6-12) *page 806*
Satan will tempt Jesus' followers (Matthew 4:1-11) *page 1481*
Satan is completely evil (John 8:44) *page 1649*
Satan is the temporary ruler over this world (Ephesians 2:1-2) *page 1803*
Satan and his demons are spiritual (Ephesians 6:12) *page 1809*
Satan works through an army of demons (1 Timothy 4:1) *page 1833*
Believers have the authority to resist Satan (James 4:1-10) *page 1869*
Satan is an enemy to Christians (1 Peter 5:8) *page 1878*
Jesus destroyed Satan's work with his death on the cross (1 John 3:7-8) *page 1886*
Satan is a defeated enemy (Revelation 20:10) *page 1920*

SECOND COMING OF CHRIST

We do not know when Jesus will return (Matthew 24:36) *page 1522*
Christ's return will be unmistakable (Mark 13:26-27) *page 1562*
Christ's return will be joyous for those who are ready (Luke 12:35-40) *page 1603*
The Second Coming will be a time of judgment on unbelievers (John 12:37-50) *page 1658*
At Christ's second coming we will be with him forever (John 14:1-3) *page 1660*
The promise of Christ's return (Acts 1:10-11) *page 1674*
Believers will be resurrected and given glorious bodies (1 Corinthians 15:51-57) *page 1776*
Christ's return will be visible and glorious (1 Thessalonians 4:16) *page 1825*
At Christ's return, Christians who are dead and alive will rise to meet him (1 Thessalonians 4:16-17) *page 1825*
Continue to serve God as you await the Second Coming (1 Peter 4:7-8) *page 1877*
Patiently await Christ's return (2 Peter 3:8-13) *page 1882*
Jesus is coming soon (Revelation 22:20-21) *page 1923*

SELF-ESTEEM *(see also Pride)*

We are made in God's image (Genesis 1:26-27) *page 4*
We are a little lower than the angels (Psalm 8:3-5) *page 859*
God took special care to create us (Psalm 139:1-18) *page 973*
We have been formed by God's loving hands (Isaiah 64:8) *page 1148*
We are of great value to God (Luke 12:4-12) *page 1601*
God gave his Son for us (John 3:16) *page 1635*
Our self-esteem is affected by our relationship with Christ (Romans 12:1-8) *page 1747*
Our self-esteem is based on God's approval (2 Corinthians 10:12-18) *page 1788*
We should not overestimate ourselves (Galatians 6:3-5) *page 1800*

SEX

Sex is God's gift to married people (Proverbs 5:15-21) *page 988*
Sex outside of marriage is foolish (Proverbs 6:23-35) *page 990*
Sex within marriage is meant to be a delight (Song of Songs 4:1-16) *page 1044*
Sexual sin begins in the mind (Matthew 5:27-30) *page 1484*
Sex is a powerful bond not meant to be taken lightly (1 Corinthians 6:13-20) *page 1762*
Sexual immorality has no place among Christians (Ephesians 5:1-3) *page 1807*
We are to have nothing to do with sexual immorality (Colossians 3:5) *page 1819*
God wants us to live in holiness, not lustful passion (1 Thessalonians 4:1-8) *page 1824*
Sex in marriage is honorable and pure (Hebrews 13:4) *page 1864*

SICKNESS

God cares for the sick (Psalm 41:1-13) *page 888*
A cheerful spirit can act as good medicine against sickness (Proverbs 17:22) *page 1006*
Jesus can heal sickness (Matthew 4:23-25) *page 1482*
Believers ought to have compassion on the sick (Matthew 25:34-40) *page 1524*
It is better to be physically crippled than spiritually crippled (Mark 9:43-48) *page 1553*
Paul had an infirmity that God would not remove (2 Corinthians 12:7-10) *page 1791*

SIN

Sin has consequences (Genesis 3:1-19) *page 6*
God must punish sin (Exodus 32:34) *page 145*
Our consciences can identify sin (2 Samuel 24:10-15) *page 536*
We should humbly confess our sins to God (Ezra 9:5-15) *page 764*
We should ask God to forgive our sins (Psalm 51:1-10) *page 896*
Stay away from people who lead you to sin (Proverbs 1:10-19) *page 983*
Sin begins in the mind (Matthew 5:27-28) *page 1484*
All people have sinned (Romans 3:23) *page 1734*
Sin leads to eternal death (Romans 6:23) *page 1738*
Jesus takes the penalty of our sin on himself (Romans 8:1-2) *page 1740*
Sin begins with temptation (James 1:15) *page 1866*
We can sin by avoiding something we should do (James 4:17) *page 1870*
God is willing to forgive our sins (1 John 1:8-9) *page 1884*

SINGLENESS

Some people remain single to work for God's Kingdom (Matthew 19:12) *page 1511*
Singleness is a gift from God (1 Corinthians 7:7-8) *page 1762*
Single people can serve God (1 Corinthians 7:25-31) *page 1763*
Single people have more time to focus on service for God (1 Corinthians 7:32-35) *page 1763*

SORROW *(see also Grief)*

Sorrow is often a necessary part of repentance (Judges 2:4-5) *page 395*
Weeping will be followed by joy (Psalm 30:5) *page 876*
Jesus understands sorrow (Isaiah 53:3-9) *page 1133*
God promises comfort to those who experience sorrow (Matthew 5:4) *page 1482*
God may use sorrow to point out sin and draw us back to him (2 Corinthians 7:10-11) *page 1785*
We sorrow over believers who die, but one day we will meet again (1 Thessalonians 4:13-18) *page 1825*
Sorrow will not exist in God's Kingdom (Revelation 21:3-4) *page 1921*

SOUL

People cannot destroy your soul (Matthew 10:28) *page 1493*
We are to love God with our whole being—heart, soul, and mind (Matthew 22:36-40) *page 1518*
It is of no value to gain the world but lose your soul (Mark 8:34-38) *page 1550*
We can place our soul under Christ's protection (John 10:27-29) *page 1652*
Believers are assured of immortality (1 Corinthians 15:46-53) *page 1775*

SPIRITUAL GIFTS

God expects us to use our gifts (Romans 12:3-8) *page 1748*
God gives us our spiritual gifts (1 Corinthians 12:4-11) *page 1769*
Spiritual gifts build up the body of Christ (Ephesians 4:11-13) *page 1806*
Spiritual gifts ought not be denied nor overemphasized (1 Thessalonians 5:19-22) *page 1826*
God distributes spiritual gifts according to his will (Hebrews 2:4) *page 1848*

STRESS

Delegating work can alleviate stress (Exodus 18:13-26) *page 118*
God is a refuge in times of stress (Psalm 62:1-8) *page 904*
Pray to God in times of stress (Psalm 69:1-36) *page 910*
Wait upon the Lord (Isaiah 40:30-31) *page 1111*
God is always with us (Romans 8:31-39) *page 1741*
God cares about our stress (2 Corinthians 4:8-12) *page 1782*
Don't let stress cause you to worry (Philippians 4:4-9) *page 1814*

SUBMISSION *(see also Obedience)*

Christ is our example of submission to the Father's will (Matthew 26:39, 42) *page 1577*
Following Christ requires submission to him (Luke 14:27) *page 1607*

God created lines of authority for harmonious relationships (1 Corinthians 11:2-16) *page 1767*
Marriage calls for mutual submission (Ephesians 5:21-33) *page 1808*
Submit to God (James 4:7-10) *page 1870*

SUFFERING *(see also Trials)*
Those who suffer need encouragement (Job 16:1-6) *page 823*
Christ's followers will face suffering (Matthew 16:21-26) *page 1506*
Our suffering helps us comfort others who are suffering (2 Corinthians 1:3-7) *page 1778*
Our suffering will end in glory (2 Corinthians 4:17-18) *page 1782*
Jesus can help us through suffering (Hebrews 2:11-18) *page 1848*
Christ showed how to handle suffering (1 Peter 2:21-24) *page 1875*
There will be no suffering in Christ's Kingdom (Revelation 21:4) *page 1921*

TEACHING *(see also Witnessing)*
Parents must teach their children about the Lord (Deuteronomy 6:4-9) *page 301*
Believers teach each other (2 Timothy 2:2) *page 1838*
Qualities of a good teacher (2 Timothy 2:22-26) *page 1839*
Instruction to those who teach God's Word (Titus 2:1-15) *page 1843*

TEMPTATION
Temptation comes from Satan (Genesis 3:1-6) *page 6*
How to avoid temptation (Proverbs 7:1-5) *page 991*
How to respond when tempted (Matthew 4:1-11) *page 1481*
God will provide a way of escape from every temptation (1 Corinthians 10:13) *page 1766*
Run from temptation (2 Timothy 2:22) *page 1839*
Christ can help us, for he, too, has faced temptation (Hebrews 4:15-16) *page 1851*
God never tempts people to sin (James 1:13-15) *page 1866*

THANKFULNESS
Thank the Lord because he is good (Psalm 107:1-3) *page 948*
Be thankful for answers to prayer (Psalm 138:1-5) *page 973*
Be thankful for salvation (Ephesians 2:4-10) *page 1803*
Our prayers should include words of thankfulness (Philippians 4:6) *page 1814*
Our life should be characterized by thankfulness to God (Colossians 3:15-17) *page 1819*
We are called to give thanks in all circumstances (1 Thessalonians 5:16-18) *page 1826*

TRIALS *(see also Suffering)*
Christ promises us rest from our trials (Matthew 11:28-30) *page 1496*
Jesus understands our struggles (John 15:18) *page 1662*
Have peace in trials (John 16:33) *page 1664*
Trials help us develop patience (Romans 5:1-5) *page 1736*
God knows what he is doing with our life (Romans 8:28) *page 1741*
Believers can expect to suffer for their faith (2 Corinthians 6:3-13) *page 1783*
Present trials fade in comparison to the joy of our relationship with Christ (Philippians 3:7-11) *page 1813*
God expects us to grow through our trials (James 1:2-4) *page 1866*

TRUST *(see Faith)*

TRUTH
God wants us to be true and righteous (Psalm 51:1-6) *page 896*
Truth never changes (Proverbs 12:19) *page 998*
Truth sets us free (John 8:31-32) *page 1648*
Truth is found in Jesus Christ (John 14:6) *page 1660*
God's Word is truth (John 17:17) *page 1665*
We must not only believe the truth but also live by it (1 John 1:5-7) *page 1884*

UNBELIEVERS
We must not imitate unbelievers (Psalm 26:5) *page 874*
We must share the gospel with unbelievers (John 17:14-19) *page 1665*

Unbelievers do not belong to Christ (Romans 8:9) *page 1740*
We should avoid situations that force us to compromise our beliefs (2 Corinthians 6:14-18) *page 1784*
Unbelievers will not enter heaven (1 John 5:10-12) *page 1889*

UNITY

Unity among believers pleases God (Psalm 133:1) *page 970*
Christians are not supposed to live in isolation (John 17:11) *page 1665*
Unity includes bearing one another's joys and burdens (Romans 12:9-16) *page 1748*
Believers must seek unity in all essentials (1 Corinthians 1:10) *page 1755*
There can be great unity even in great diversity (Ephesians 4:3-13) *page 1805*
The love Christ commanded should create unity among believers (Philippians 1:3-11) *page 1810*
Unity ought to be a distinctive mark among Christians (Philippians 2:1-2) *page 1811*

WISDOM

The fear of God is the beginning of wisdom (Proverbs 1:7) *page 983*
To find wisdom, first find God (Proverbs 2:6-12) *page 985*
Wise people accept advice (Proverbs 13:10) *page 999*
Wise people boast not in their wisdom but in knowing God (Jeremiah 9:23-24) *page 1174*
The wise understand God's ways and follow his guidance (Hosea 14:9) *page 1396*
Wise people build on the solid foundation of God and his Word (Matthew 7:24-27) *page 1488*
God's wisdom is different from the world's wisdom (1 Corinthians 2:1-16) *page 1756*
God will give us wisdom if we ask for it (James 1:5) *page 1866*

WITNESSING *(see also Evangelism, Teaching)*

Bringing the good news of Christ is a wonderful privilege (Isaiah 52:7) *page 1132*
God's message will accomplish what he desires wherever it is spoken (Isaiah 55:10-11) *page 1136*
God holds us accountable for avoiding a chance to witness for him (Ezekiel 3:18-19) *page 1272*
Let your light shine (Matthew 5:14-16) *page 1483*
Jesus commanded all believers to witness (Matthew 28:16-20) *page 1533*
If we acknowledge our faith before people, Jesus will acknowledge us (Luke 12:8-9) *page 1601*
Christians are called to spread the gospel across the world (Acts 1:8) *page 1674*
We plant or water the seed of faith, but only God makes it grow (1 Corinthians 3:5-9) *page 1758*
God has entrusted us with the message we need to share with others (2 Corinthians 5:18-21) *page 1783*
Always be ready to tell what God has done for you (1 Peter 3:15) *page 1876*

WOMEN

God's image is shared equally by women and men (Genesis 1:26-27) *page 4*
Women should fulfill their responsibilities well (Proverbs 31:10-31) *page 1026*
Women and men are equal before God (Galatians 3:28) *page 1797*
The church should care for widows who have no relatives (1 Timothy 5:3-16) *page 1833*

WORK

Hard work is honored by God (Genesis 31:38-42) *page 53*
Use your skills to honor God (Exodus 36:1) *page 151*
Hard work brings rewards (Proverbs 12:14) *page 998*
Hard work helps supply basic needs (Proverbs 28:19) *page 1022*
Our work for God is never wasted (1 Corinthians 15:58) *page 1774*
All work should be done as though we are working for God (Ephesians 6:5-9) *page 1808*

WORRY *(see Stress)*

WORSHIP *(see also Church)*

Worship is an encounter with the living and holy God (Exodus 3:1-6) *page 91*
Worship is reserved for God alone (Exodus 34:14) *page 147*
In worship, we ascribe to the Lord the glory due him (Psalm 29:1-2) *page 876*
We can worship because of Christ's sacrifice on our behalf (Hebrews 10:1-10) *page 1857*
We should worship with reverence for God (Hebrews 12:28) *page 1863*
When we draw near to God, he draws near to us (James 4:8) *page 1870*

YOUTH *(see Adolescence)*

365-DAY READING PLAN

This 365-day plan will give you a year-long guided tour of the Bible. Though it doesn't include every verse, it will lead you through all the most important passages. You might think of it as a "best parts" tour of the Scriptures. The calendar dates will help guide and discipline your reading. But if reading every day is too much for you, slow your pace and follow the "Day" numbers instead. Read at a pace you can manage and enjoy. Should you want to read through the entire Bible, you might try *The One Year Bible,* which leads you through the entire Bible in a year.

January 1 / Day 1: Genesis 1:1–2:3
January 2 / Day 2: Genesis 2:15–3:24
January 3 / Day 3: Genesis 4:1-16
January 4 / Day 4: Genesis 6:9-22
January 5 / Day 5: Genesis 7:1-24
January 6 / Day 6: Genesis 8:1-22
January 7 / Day 7: Genesis 9:1-17
January 8 / Day 8: Genesis 11:1-9
January 9 / Day 9: Genesis 12:1-9; 17:1-8
January 10 / Day 10: Genesis 18:1-15
January 11 / Day 11: Genesis 19:15-29
January 12 / Day 12: Genesis 21:8-21
January 13 / Day 13: Genesis 22:1-19
January 14 / Day 14: Genesis 24:1-27
January 15 / Day 15: Genesis 24:28-67
January 16 / Day 16: Genesis 25:19-34
January 17 / Day 17: Genesis 27:1-40
January 18 / Day 18: Genesis 28:10-22
January 19 / Day 19: Genesis 29:14-30
January 20 / Day 20: Genesis 32:1–33:16
January 21 / Day 21: Genesis 37:1-36
January 22 / Day 22: Genesis 39:1-23
January 23 / Day 23: Genesis 40:1-23
January 24 / Day 24: Genesis 41:1-36
January 25 / Day 25: Genesis 41:37-57
January 26 / Day 26: Genesis 42:1-38
January 27 / Day 27: Genesis 43:1-34
January 28 / Day 28: Genesis 44:1-34
January 29 / Day 29: Genesis 45:1-28
January 30 / Day 30: Genesis 49:1-33
January 31 / Day 31: Exodus 1:8–2:10

February 1 / Day 32: Exodus 2:11-25
February 2 / Day 33: Exodus 3:1-22
February 3 / Day 34: Exodus 4:1-17
February 4 / Day 35: Exodus 5:1-23
February 5 / Day 36: Exodus 6:1-13
February 6 / Day 37: Exodus 7:1-14
February 7 / Day 38: Exodus 7:15–9:7
February 8 / Day 39: Exodus 9:8–10:29
February 9 / Day 40: Exodus 11:1-10; 12:29-36
February 10 / Day 41: Exodus 13:17–14:31
February 11 / Day 42: Exodus 15:22-27; 17:1-7
February 12 / Day 43: Exodus 16:1-36
February 13 / Day 44: Exodus 18:1-27
February 14 / Day 45: Exodus 19:1-25
February 15 / Day 46: Exodus 20:1-22
February 16 / Day 47: Exodus 32:1-29
February 17 / Day 48: Exodus 40:1-38
February 18 / Day 49: Numbers 12:1-16
February 19 / Day 50: Numbers 13:1–14:4
February 20 / Day 51: Numbers 14:5-45
February 21 / Day 52: Numbers 21:4-9
February 22 / Day 53: Numbers 22:5-38
February 23 / Day 54: Deuteronomy 29:1-29
February 24 / Day 55: Deuteronomy 30:1-20
February 25 / Day 56: Deuteronomy 31:1-8
February 26 / Day 57: Deuteronomy 34:1-12
February 27 / Day 58: Joshua 1:1-18
February 28 / Day 59: Joshua 2:1-24

March 1 / Day 60: Joshua 3:1-17
March 2 / Day 61: Joshua 5:13–6:27
March 3 / Day 62: Joshua 7:1-26
March 4 / Day 63: Joshua 10:1-15
March 5 / Day 64: Joshua 23:1-16
March 6 / Day 65: Joshua 24:1-31
March 7 / Day 66: Judges 4:4-24
March 8 / Day 67: Judges 6:1-40
March 9 / Day 68: Judges 7:1-25
March 10 / Day 69: Judges 13:1-25
March 11 / Day 70: Judges 14:1-20
March 12 / Day 71: Judges 15:1-20
March 13 / Day 72: Judges 16:1-21
March 14 / Day 73: Judges 16:22-31
March 15 / Day 74: Ruth 1:1-22
March 16 / Day 75: Ruth 2:1-23
March 17 / Day 76: Ruth 3:1-18
March 18 / Day 77: Ruth 4:1-22
March 19 / Day 78: 1 Samuel 1:1-28
March 20 / Day 79: 1 Samuel 3:1-21
March 21 / Day 80: 1 Samuel 8:1-5
March 22 / Day 81: 1 Samuel 8:6-22
March 23 / Day 82: 1 Samuel 9:1-21
March 24 / Day 83: 1 Samuel 10:1-27
March 25 / Day 84: 1 Samuel 14:1-23
March 26 / Day 85: 1 Samuel 16:1-13
March 27 / Day 86: 1 Samuel 17:1-31
March 28 / Day 87: 1 Samuel 17:32-58
March 29 / Day 88: 1 Samuel 18:1-30

March 30 / Day 89: 1 Samuel 20:1-42
March 31 / Day 90: 1 Samuel 24:1-22

April 1 / Day 91: 1 Samuel 25:1-42
April 2 / Day 92: 1 Samuel 28:1-25
April 3 / Day 93: 2 Samuel 5:1-12
April 4 / Day 94: 2 Samuel 9:1-13
April 5 / Day 95: 2 Samuel 11:1-27
April 6 / Day 96: 2 Samuel 12:1-25
April 7 / Day 97: 2 Samuel 13:1-19
April 8 / Day 98: 2 Samuel 13:20-39
April 9 / Day 99: 2 Samuel 15:1-37
April 10 / Day 100: 2 Samuel 18:1-18
April 11 / Day 101: 1 Kings 1:5-27
April 12 / Day 102: 1 Kings 1:28-53
April 13 / Day 103: 1 Kings 3:1-15
April 14 / Day 104: 1 Kings 3:16-28
April 15 / Day 105: 1 Kings 6:1-38
April 16 / Day 106: 1 Kings 10:1-13
April 17 / Day 107: 1 Kings 12:1-24
April 18 / Day 108: 1 Kings 17:1-24
April 19 / Day 109: 1 Kings 18:16-46
April 20 / Day 110: 1 Kings 19:1-21
April 21 / Day 111: 1 Kings 21:1-29
April 22 / Day 112: 1 Kings 22:29-40
April 23 / Day 113: 2 Kings 2:1-12
April 24 / Day 114: 2 Kings 2:13-25
April 25 / Day 115: 2 Kings 5:1-27
April 26 / Day 116: 2 Kings 11:1-21
April 27 / Day 117: 2 Kings 22:1–23:3
April 28 / Day 118: Ezra 3:7-13
April 29 / Day 119: Nehemiah 2:1-20
April 30 / Day 120: Nehemiah 5:1-19

May 1 / Day 121: Nehemiah 8:1-18
May 2 / Day 122: Esther 1:1-22
May 3 / Day 123: Esther 2:1-23
May 4 / Day 124: Esther 3:1-15
May 5 / Day 125: Esther 4:1-17
May 6 / Day 126: Esther 5:1-14
May 7 / Day 127: Esther 6:1–7:10
May 8 / Day 128: Job 1:1-22
May 9 / Day 129: Job 2:1-13
May 10 / Day 130: Job 38:1-41
May 11 / Day 131: Job 42:1-17
May 12 / Day 132: Psalm 1:1-6
May 13 / Day 133: Psalm 8:1-9
May 14 / Day 134: Psalm 23:1-6
May 15 / Day 135: Psalm 51:1-19
May 16 / Day 136: Psalm 103:1-22
May 17 / Day 137: Psalm 139:1-24
May 18 / Day 138: Psalm 145:1-21
May 19 / Day 139: Proverbs 4:1-27
May 20 / Day 140: Proverbs 5:1-23
May 21 / Day 141: Ecclesiastes 12:1-14
May 22 / Day 142: Isaiah 6:1-13
May 23 / Day 143: Isaiah 53:1-12
May 24 / Day 144: Jeremiah 1:1-9
May 25 / Day 145: Jeremiah 36:1-32
May 26 / Day 146: Jeremiah 38:1-13
May 27 / Day 147: Ezekiel 37:1-14
May 28 / Day 148: Daniel 1:1-21
May 29 / Day 149: Daniel 2:1-24
May 30 / Day 150: Daniel 2:25-49
May 31 / Day 151: Daniel 3:1-30

June 1 / Day 152: Daniel 5:1-30
June 2 / Day 153: Daniel 6:1-28
June 3 / Day 154: Jonah 1:1-2:10
June 4 / Day 155: Jonah 3:1-4:11
June 5 / Day 156: John 1:1-18
June 6 / Day 157: Luke 1:5-25
June 7 / Day 158: Luke 1:26-56
June 8 / Day 159: Luke 1:57-80
June 9 / Day 160: Matthew 1:1-25
June 10 / Day 161: Luke 2:1-20
June 11 / Day 162: Luke 2:21-39
June 12 / Day 163: Matthew 2:1-12
June 13 / Day 164: Matthew 2:13-23
June 14 / Day 165: Luke 2:41-52
June 15 / Day 166: Mark 1:1-13
June 16 / Day 167: John 1:19-34
June 17 / Day 168: John 1:35-51
June 18 / Day 169: John 2:1-25
June 19 / Day 170: John 3:1-21
June 20 / Day 171: John 3:22-36
June 21 / Day 172: John 4:1-42
June 22 / Day 173: John 4:43-54
June 23 / Day 174: Luke 4:16-30
June 24 / Day 175: Mark 1:16-39
June 25 / Day 176: Luke 5:1-39
June 26 / Day 177: John 5:1-47
June 27 / Day 178: Mark 2:23–3:19
June 28 / Day 179: Matthew 5:1-16
June 29 / Day 180: Matthew 5:17-30
June 30 / Day 181: Matthew 5:31-48

July 1 / Day 182: Matthew 6:1-18
July 2 / Day 183: Matthew 6:19-34
July 3 / Day 184: Matthew 7:1-12
July 4 / Day 185: Matthew 7:13-29
July 5 / Day 186: Luke 7:1-17
July 6 / Day 187: Matthew 11:1-30
July 7 / Day 188: Luke 7:36-8:3
July 8 / Day 189: Matthew 12:22-50
July 9 / Day 190: Mark 4:1-29
July 10 / Day 191: Matthew 13:24-43
July 11 / Day 192: Matthew 13:44-52
July 12 / Day 193: Luke 8:22-56
July 13 / Day 194: Matthew 9:27-38
July 14 / Day 195: Mark 6:1-13
July 15 / Day 196: Matthew 10:16-42
July 16 / Day 197: Mark 6:14-29
July 17 / Day 198: Matthew 14:13-36
July 18 / Day 199: John 6:22-40
July 19 / Day 200: John 6:41-71
July 20 / Day 201: Mark 7:1-37
July 21 / Day 202: Matthew 15:32–16:12
July 22 / Day 203: Mark 8:22–9:1
July 23 / Day 204: Luke 9:28-45
July 24 / Day 205: Matthew 17:24–18:6
July 25 / Day 206: Mark 9:38-50

July 26 / Day 207: Matthew 18:10-22
July 27 / Day 208: John 7:1-31
July 28 / Day 209: John 7:32-53
July 29 / Day 210: John 8:1-20
July 30 / Day 211: John 8:21-59
July 31 / Day 212: Luke 10:1-24

August 1 / Day 213: Luke 10:25-42
August 2 / Day 214: Luke 11:1-13
August 3 / Day 215: Luke 11:14-32
August 4 / Day 216: Luke 11:33-54
August 5 / Day 217: Luke 12:1-21
August 6 / Day 218: Luke 12:22-48
August 7 / Day 219: Luke 12:49-59
August 8 / Day 220: Luke 13:1-21
August 9 / Day 221: John 9:1-41
August 10 / Day 222: John 10:1-18
August 11 / Day 223: Luke 13:22-35
August 12 / Day 224: Luke 14:1-14
August 13 / Day 225: Luke 14:15-35
August 14 / Day 226: Luke 15:1-10
August 15 / Day 227: Luke 15:11-32
August 16 / Day 228: Luke 16:1-18
August 17 / Day 229: Luke 16:19-31
August 18 / Day 230: John 11:1-36
August 19 / Day 231: John 11:37-57
August 20 / Day 232: Luke 17:1-19
August 21 / Day 233: Luke 17:20-37
August 22 / Day 234: Luke 18:1-14
August 23 / Day 235: Mark 10:1-16
August 24 / Day 236: Mark 10:17-31
August 25 / Day 237: Matthew 20:1-19
August 26 / Day 238: Mark 10:35-52
August 27 / Day 239: Luke 19:1-27
August 28 / Day 240: John 12:1-11
August 29 / Day 241: Matthew 21:1-17
August 30 / Day 242: John 12:20-36
August 31 / Day 243: John 12:37-50

September 1 / Day 244: Mark 11:20-33
September 2 / Day 245: Matthew 21:28-46
September 3 / Day 246: Matthew 22:1-14
September 4 / Day 247: Luke 20:20-40
September 5 / Day 248: Mark 12:28-37
September 6 / Day 249: Matthew 23:1-39
September 7 / Day 250: Luke 21:1-24
September 8 / Day 251: Luke 21:25-38
September 9 / Day 252: Matthew 25:1-30
September 10 / Day 253: Matthew 25:31-46
September 11 / Day 254: Luke 22:1-13
September 12 / Day 255: John 13:1-20
September 13 / Day 256: John 13:21-38
September 14 / Day 257: John 14:1-14
September 15 / Day 258: John 14:15-31
September 16 / Day 259: John 15:1-16
September 17 / Day 260: John 15:17–16:4
September 18 / Day 261: John 16:5-33
September 19 / Day 262: John 17:1-26
September 20 / Day 263: Mark 14:26-52
September 21 / Day 264: John 18:1-24
September 22 / Day 265: Matthew 26:57-75
September 23 / Day 266: Matthew 27:1-10
September 24 / Day 267: Luke 23:1-12
September 25 / Day 268: Mark 15:6-24
September 26 / Day 269: Luke 23:32-49
September 27 / Day 270: Matthew 27:57-66
September 28 / Day 271: John 20:1-18
September 29 / Day 272: Matthew 28:8-15
September 30 / Day 273: Luke 24:13-43

October 1 / Day 274: John 20:24–21:14
October 2 / Day 275: John 21:15-25
October 3 / Day 276: Matthew 28:16-20
October 4 / Day 277: Luke 24:44-53
October 5 / Day 278: Acts 1:1-11
October 6 / Day 279: Acts 1:12-26
October 7 / Day 280: Acts 2:1-13
October 8 / Day 281: Acts 2:14-40
October 9 / Day 282: Acts 2:41–3:11
October 10 / Day 283: Acts 3:12–4:4
October 11 / Day 284: Acts 4:5-22
October 12 / Day 285: Acts 4:23-37
October 13 / Day 286: Acts 5:1-16
October 14 / Day 287: Acts 5:17-42
October 15 / Day 288: Acts 6:1-15
October 16 / Day 289: Acts 7:1-29
October 17 / Day 290: Acts 7:30-60
October 18 / Day 291: Acts 8:1-25
October 19 / Day 292: Acts 8:26-40
October 20 / Day 293: Acts 9:1-19
October 21 / Day 294: Acts 9:20-31
October 22 / Day 295: Acts 9:32-42
October 23 / Day 296: Acts 10:1-23
October 24 / Day 297: Acts 10:24-48
October 25 / Day 298: Acts 11:1-18
October 26 / Day 299: Acts 11:19-29
October 27 / Day 300: Acts 12:1-25
October 28 / Day 301: Acts 13:1-12
October 29 / Day 302: Acts 14:1-28
October 30 / Day 303: Acts 15:1-21
October 31 / Day 304: Acts 15:22-41

November 1 / Day 305: Acts 16:1-15
November 2 / Day 306: Acts 16:16-40
November 3 / Day 307: Acts 17:1-15
November 4 / Day 308: Acts 17:16-34
November 5 / Day 309: Acts 19:1-20
November 6 / Day 310: Acts 19:21-41
November 7 / Day 311: Acts 20:1-12
November 8 / Day 312: Acts 20:13-38
November 9 / Day 313: Acts 21:1-17
November 10 / Day 314: Acts 21:18-36
November 11 / Day 315: Acts 21:37–22:29
November 12 / Day 316: Acts 22:30–23:22
November 13 / Day 317: Acts 23:23–24:27
November 14 / Day 318: Acts 25:1-27
November 15 / Day 319: Acts 26:1-32
November 16 / Day 320: Acts 27:1-26
November 17 / Day 321: Acts 27:27-44
November 18 / Day 322: Acts 28:1-14
November 19 / Day 323: Acts 28:15-31
November 20 / Day 324: Romans 5:1-11

November 21 / Day 325: Romans 8:1-18
November 22 / Day 326: Romans 8:19-39
November 23 / Day 327: Romans 12:1-21
November 24 / Day 328: 1 Corinthians 13:1-13
November 25 / Day 329: 1 Corinthians 15:1-20
November 26 / Day 330: 1 Corinthians 15:42-58
November 27 / Day 331: 2 Corinthians 4:1-18
November 28 / Day 332: Galatians 5:13-26
November 29 / Day 333: Ephesians 1:3-23
November 30 / Day 334: Ephesians 2:1-22

December 1 / Day 335: Ephesians 4:1-16
December 2 / Day 336: Ephesians 6:10-20
December 3 / Day 337: Philippians 2:1-18
December 4 / Day 338: Philippians 3:1-21
December 5 / Day 339: Colossians 2:1-15
December 6 / Day 340: Colossians 3:1-17
December 7 / Day 341: 1 Thessalonians 1:1-10
December 8 / Day 342: 1 Thessalonians 4:1-18
December 9 / Day 343: 2 Thessalonians 1:1-12
December 10 / Day 344: 2 Thessalonians 3:1-18
December 11 / Day 345: 1 Timothy 4:1-16
December 12 / Day 346: 1 Timothy 6:3-21
December 13 / Day 347: 2 Timothy 1:1-18
December 14 / Day 348: 2 Timothy 3:1-17
December 15 / Day 349: Titus 3:1-11
December 16 / Day 350: Hebrews 10:19-39
December 17 / Day 351: Hebrews 11:1-40
December 18 / Day 352: Hebrews 12:1-13
December 19 / Day 353: James 1:2-27
December 20 / Day 354: James 2:1-13
December 21 / Day 355: James 3:1-12
December 22 / Day 356: 1 Peter 2:1-25
December 23 / Day 357: 1 Peter 3:1-22
December 24 / Day 358: 2 Peter 1:2-21
December 25 / Day 359: 1 John 1:1-10
December 26 / Day 360: 1 John 3:1-24
December 27 / Day 361: 1 John 5:1-21
December 28 / Day 362: Jude 1:17-25
December 29 / Day 363: Revelation 1:1-20
December 30 / Day 364: Revelation 21:1-27
December 31 / Day 365: Revelation 22:1-21

A NOTE TO READERS

Nearly four hundred years ago, a committee of fifty scholars was commissioned by King James I to create a new translation of the Bible in English. Their work, now known as the Authorized Version or the King James Version, was to stand as a milestone in Christian history. It became a cornerstone of English-speaking cultures around the world and the standard of grace and elegance against which all other English translations are measured.

But time produces changes in language. And while these changes did not destroy the beauty of the King James Version, they created barriers that prevented many readers from clearly understanding the Scriptures. As a result, modern translations have been created to ensure that people can readily understand God's Word.

The *Holy Bible,* New Living Translation, was first published in 1996 and quickly became one of the most popular English translations of the Bible. The NLT Bible Translation Committee determined shortly after its initial publication that the text could still be improved, so they began an additional eight-year process with the purpose of increasing the level of the NLT's precision. This second-generation text was completed in 2004 and is reflected in this edition of the New Living Translation. An additional update with minor changes was subsequently introduced in 2007.

The goal of any Bible translation is to convey the meaning and content of the ancient Hebrew, Aramaic, and Greek texts as accurately as possible to contemporary readers. A central goal of the NLT translators was to create a text that would communicate as clearly and powerfully to today's readers as the original texts did to readers in the ancient biblical world. The resulting NLT text is easy to read and understand, while also accurately communicating the Bible's content and meaning.

Now these two monumental works are combined into one convenient volume. The classic beauty and grace of the King James Version is side by side with the contemporary, easy-to-understand New Living Translation. We present the Bound for Glory Parallel Bible with the prayer that God will use it to speak his timeless truth to the church and to the world in a fresh new way.

The Publishers
October 2010

INTRODUCTION TO THE KING JAMES VERSION

The King James Version of the Bible was published in 1611. However, it was not the first English Bible. The King James Version is indebted to several English versions that had been published in the previous century. At the head of the list is Tyndale's version of 1525. Following this monumental translation was Coverdale's version of 1537, the Great Bible of 1537, and the Bishops' Bible of 1568. Another translation of the sixteenth century, the Geneva Bible, was also instrumental in the formation of the King James Version. An understanding of these versions will deepen our understanding of and appreciation for the King James Version.

William Tyndale's Version

The story of the King James Version actually begins with William Tyndale, who was born in the age of the Renaissance. He graduated in 1515 from Oxford, where he had studied the Scriptures in Greek and in Hebrew—the Bible's original languages. By the time he was 30, Tyndale had committed his life to translating the Bible from the original languages into English. Tyndale argued against the view that only the clergy were qualified to read and correctly interpret the Scriptures. He expressed his heart's desire when he told a fellow clergyman, "If God spare my life, ere many years, I will cause a boy that driveth the plough to know more of the Scripture than thou dost."

In 1523 Tyndale went to London seeking a place to work on his translation. When the bishop of London would not give him hospitality, he was provided a place by Humphrey Monmouth, a cloth merchant. Then, in 1524, Tyndale left England for Germany because the English church, which was still under the pope's authority, strongly opposed putting the Bible into the hands of the laity. Tyndale first settled in Hamburg, Germany. Quite possibly, he met Luther in Wittenberg soon thereafter. Even if he didn't meet Luther, he was well acquainted with Luther's writings and Luther's German translation of the New Testament (published in 1522). Throughout his lifetime, Tyndale was harassed for propagating Luther's ideas. Both Luther and Tyndale used the same Greek text (one compiled by Erasmus in 1516) in making their translations.

Tyndale completed his translation of the New Testament in 1525. Fifteen thousand copies, in six editions, were smuggled into England between the years 1525 and 1530. Church authorities did their best to confiscate copies of Tyndale's translation and burn them, but they couldn't stop the flow of Bibles from Germany into England. Tyndale himself could not return to England because his life was in danger since his translation had been banned. However, he continued to work abroad—correcting, revising, and reissuing his translation until his final version appeared in 1535. Shortly thereafter, in May of 1535, Tyndale was arrested and carried off to a castle near Brussels. After being in prison for over a year, he was tried and condemned to death. He was strangled and burned at the stake on October 6, 1536. His final words were so very poignant: "Lord, open the king of England's eyes."

After finishing the New Testament, Tyndale had begun work on a translation of the Hebrew Old Testament, but he did not live long enough to complete the task. He had, however, translated the Pentateuch (the first five books of the Old Testament), Jonah, and some historical books. While Tyndale was in prison, an associate of his named Miles Coverdale (1488–1569) brought to completion an entire Bible in English—based largely on Tyndale's translation work. In other words, Coverdale finished what Tyndale had begun.

Miles Coverdale's Edition

Miles Coverdale was a Cambridge graduate who, like Tyndale, was forced to flee England because he was boldly preaching against Roman Catholic doctrine, also having been strongly influenced by Luther. While he was abroad, Coverdale met Tyndale and then served as an assistant—primarily helping Tyndale translate the Pentateuch. By the time Coverdale produced a complete translation (1537), the king of England, Henry VIII, had broken all ties with the pope and was ready to see an English Bible. Perhaps Tyndale's prayer had been answered—with a very ironic twist: The king gave his royal approval to Coverdale's translation, which was based on the work done by Tyndale, the man Henry VIII had earlier condemned.

The Great Bible

In the same year that Coverdale's Bible was endorsed by the king (1537), another Bible was published in England. This was the work of one called Thomas Matthew, a pseudonym for John Rogers (c. 1500–1555), a friend of Tyndale. Evidently, to form the entire Bible, Rogers used Tyndale's unpublished translation of the Old Testament historical books, other parts of Tyndale's translation, and still other parts of Coverdale's translation. This Bible also received the king's approval. Matthew's Bible was revised in 1538 and printed for distribution in the churches throughout England. This Bible, called the "Great Bible" because of its size and costliness, became the first English Bible authorized for public use.

Many editions of the Great Bible were printed in the early 1540s. However, its distribution was limited. Furthermore, King Henry's attitude about the new translation changed. As a result, the English Parliament passed a law in 1543 restricting the use of any English translation. It became a crime for any unlicensed person to read or explain the Scriptures in public. Many copies of Tyndale's New Testament and Coverdale's Bible were burned in London.

Greater repression was to follow. After a short period of leniency (during the reign of Edward VI, 1547–1553), severe persecution came from the hands of Queen Mary. As a Roman Catholic, she was determined to restore Catholicism to England and repress Protestantism. Many Protestants were executed, including John Rogers, the Bible translator. Coverdale was arrested, then released. He fled to Geneva, a sanctuary for English Protestants.

The Geneva Bible

When Coverdale arrived at Geneva, he discovered that the English exiles in Geneva had chosen William Whittingham (c. 1524–1579) to make an English translation of the New Testament for them. He used Theodore Beza's Latin translation and consulted the Greek text. This Bible (published in 1550) became very popular because it was small and moderately priced. For nearly two hundred years, it was the most popular English Bible—until it was superseded by the popularity of the King James Version in the mid-1700s. The Geneva Bible was the first English Bible to be used in America, brought by some of the Puritan passengers on the Mayflower (1620).

The preface to the Geneva Bible and its many annotations were affected by a strong evangelical influence, as well as by the teachings of John Calvin. Calvin was one of the greatest thinkers of the Reformation, a renowned biblical commentator, and the principal leader in Geneva during those days.

The Bishops' Bible

While the Geneva Bible was popular among many English men and women, it was not accepted among many leaders in the Church of England because of its Calvinistic notes. These leaders, recognizing that the Great Bible was inferior to the Geneva Bible in style and scholarship, initiated a revision of the Great Bible. This revised Bible, published in 1568, became known as the Bishops' Bible. It continued in use until it was superseded by the King James Version of 1611.

The King James Version

After James VI of Scotland became the king of England (known as James I), he invited several clergymen from Puritan and Anglican factions to meet together with the hope that differences could be reconciled. The meeting did not achieve this. However, during the meeting one of the Puritan leaders, John Reynolds, president of Corpus Christi College, Oxford, asked the king to authorize a new translation because Reynolds wanted to see a translation that was more accurate than previous translations.

King James liked this idea because he considered the notes in the widely used Geneva Bible to be subversive, and the Bishops' Bible had failed to replace it in popular usage. The king initiated the work and took an active part in planning the new translation. He suggested that university professors work on the translation to assure the best scholarship, and he strongly urged that they should not have any marginal notes besides those pertaining to literal renderings from the Hebrew and Greek. The absence of interpretive notes would help the translation be accepted by all the churches in England.

More than fifty scholars, trained in Hebrew and Greek, began the work in 1607. The translation went through several committees before it was finalized. The scholars were instructed to follow the Bishops' Bible as the basic version, as long as it adhered to the original text, and to consult the translations of Tyndale, Matthew, and Coverdale, as well as the Great Bible and the Geneva Bible when they appeared to contain more accurate renderings of the original languages. This dependence on other versions is expressed by the translators of the King James Version: "Truly, good Christian reader, we never thought from the beginning that we should need to make a new translation, nor yet to make of a bad one a good one . . . but to make a good one better, or out of many good ones one principal good one."

The King James Version captured the best of all the preceding English translations and exceeded all of them. Because it was authorized by the king, it became known in England as the Authorized Version. It was the culmination of all the previous English Bible translations. It united high scholarship with Christian devotion and piety. Furthermore, it came into being at a time when the English language was vigorous and beautiful—the age of Elizabethan English and Shakespearean English. This version has justifiably been called "the noblest monument of English prose." Indeed, the King James Version has become an enduring monument of English prose because of its gracious style, majestic language, and poetic rhythms. No other book has had such a tremendous influence on English literature, and no other translation has touched the lives of so many English-speaking people for centuries and centuries.

The King James Version became the most popular English translation in the seventeenth, eighteenth, and nineteenth centuries. As such, it acquired great stature as the standard English Bible. The King James Version has been revised several times in the past 100 years, but not one of its revisions has outsold it. It was first revised in 1881 in the English Revised Version, then in 1901 in the American Standard Version. Later, it was revised in the Revised Standard Version (1946, 1952), followed by the New Revised Standard Version in 1990. Another noteworthy revision is the New King James Version (1982), which provides updated language for the modern reader.

INTRODUCTION TO THE NEW LIVING TRANSLATION

Translation Philosophy and Methodology

English Bible translations tend to be governed by one of two general translation theories. The first theory has been called "formal-equivalence," "literal," or "word-for-word" translation. According to this theory, the translator attempts to render each word of the original language into English and seeks to preserve the original syntax and sentence structure as much as possible in translation. The second theory has been called "dynamic-equivalence," "functional-equivalence," or "thought-for-thought" translation. The goal of this translation theory is to produce in English the closest natural equivalent of the message expressed by the original-language text, both in meaning and in style.

Both of these translation theories have their strengths. A formal-equivalence translation preserves aspects of the original text—including ancient idioms, term consistency, and original-language syntax—that are valuable for scholars and professional study. It allows a reader to trace formal elements of the original-language text through the English translation. A dynamic-equivalence translation, on the other hand, focuses on translating the message of the original-language text. It ensures that the meaning of the text is readily apparent to the contemporary reader. This allows the message to come through with immediacy, without requiring the reader to struggle with foreign idioms and awkward syntax. It also facilitates serious study of the text's message and clarity in both devotional and public reading.

The pure application of either of these translation philosophies would create translations at opposite ends of the translation spectrum. But in reality, all translations contain a mixture of these two philosophies. A purely formal-equivalence translation would be unintelligible in English, and a purely dynamic-equivalence translation would risk being unfaithful to the original. That is why translations shaped by dynamic-equivalence theory are usually quite literal when the original text is relatively clear, and the translations shaped by formal-equivalence theory are sometimes quite dynamic when the original text is obscure.

The translators of the New Living Translation set out to render the message of the original texts of Scripture into clear, contemporary English. As they did so, they kept the concerns of both formal-equivalence and dynamic-equivalence in mind. On the one hand, they translated as simply and literally as possible when that approach yielded an accurate, clear, and natural English text. Many words and phrases were rendered literally and consistently into English, preserving essential literary and rhetorical devices, ancient metaphors, and word choices that give structure to the text and provide echoes of meaning from one passage to the next.

On the other hand, the translators rendered the message more dynamically when the literal rendering was hard to understand, was misleading, or yielded archaic or foreign wording. They clarified difficult metaphors and terms to aid in the reader's understanding. The translators first struggled with the meaning of the words and phrases in the ancient context; then they rendered the message into clear, natural English. Their goal was to be both faithful to the ancient texts and eminently readable. The result is a translation that is both exegetically accurate and idiomatically powerful.

Translation Process and Team

To produce an accurate translation of the Bible into contemporary English, the translation team needed the skills necessary to enter into the thought patterns of the ancient authors and then to render their ideas, connotations, and effects into clear, contemporary English. To begin this process, qualified biblical scholars were needed to interpret the meaning of the original text and to check it against our base English translation. In order to guard against personal and theological biases, the scholars needed to represent a diverse group of Evangelicals who would employ the best exegetical tools. Then to work alongside the scholars, skilled English stylists were needed to shape the text into clear, contemporary English.

With these concerns in mind, the Bible Translation Committee recruited teams of scholars that represented a broad spectrum of denominations, theological perspectives, and backgrounds within the worldwide Evangelical community. (These scholars are listed at the end of this introduction.) Each book of the Bible was assigned to three different scholars with proven expertise in the book or group of books to be reviewed. Each of these scholars made a thorough review of a base translation and submitted suggested revisions to the appropriate Senior Translator. The Senior Translator then reviewed and summarized these suggestions and proposed a first-draft revision of the base text. This draft served as the basis for several additional phases of exegetical and stylistic committee review. Then the Bible Translation Committee jointly reviewed and approved every verse of the final translation.

Throughout the translation and editing process, the Senior Translators and their scholar teams were given a chance to review the editing done by the team of stylists. This ensured that exegetical errors would not be introduced late in the process and that the entire Bible Translation Committee was happy with the final result. By choosing a team of qualified scholars and skilled stylists and by setting up a process that allowed their interaction throughout the process, the New Living Translation has been refined to preserve the essential formal elements of the original biblical texts, while also creating a clear, understandable English text.

The New Living Translation was first published in 1996. Shortly after its initial publication, the Bible Translation Committee began a process of further committee review and translation refinement. The purpose of this continued revision was to increase the level of precision without sacrificing the text's easy-to-understand quality. This second-edition text was completed in 2004, and an additional update with minor changes was subsequently introduced in 2007. This printing of the New Living Translation reflects the updated 2007 text.

Written to Be Read Aloud

It is evident in Scripture that the biblical documents were written to be read aloud, often in public worship (see Nehemiah 8; Luke 4:16-20; 1 Timothy 4:13; Revelation 1:3). It is still the case today that more people will hear the Bible read aloud in church than are likely to read it for themselves. Therefore, a new translation must communicate with clarity and power when it is read publicly. Clarity was a primary goal for the NLT translators, not only to facilitate private reading and understanding, but also to ensure that it would be excellent for public reading and make an immediate and powerful impact on any listener.

The Texts behind the New Living Translation

The Old Testament translators used the Masoretic Text of the Hebrew Bible as represented in *Biblia Hebraica Stuttgartensia* (1977), with its extensive system of textual notes; this is an update of Rudolf Kittel's *Biblia Hebraica* (Stuttgart, 1937). The translators also further compared the Dead Sea Scrolls, the Septuagint and other Greek manuscripts, the Samaritan Pentateuch, the Syriac Peshitta, the Latin Vulgate, and any other versions or manuscripts that shed light on the meaning of difficult passages.

The New Testament translators used the two standard editions of the Greek New Testament: the *Greek New Testament*, published by the United Bible Societies (UBS, fourth revised edition, 1993), and *Novum Testamentum Graece*, edited by Nestle and Aland (NA, twenty-seventh edition, 1993). These two editions, which have the same text but differ in punctuation and textual notes, represent, for the most part, the best in modern textual scholarship. However, in cases where strong textual or other scholarly evidence supported the decision, the translators sometimes chose to differ from the UBS and NA Greek texts and followed variant readings found in other ancient witnesses. Significant textual variants of this sort are always noted in the textual notes of the New Living Translation.

Translation Issues

The translators have made a conscious effort to provide a text that can be easily understood by the typical reader of modern English. To this end, we sought to use only vocabulary and language structures in common use today. We avoided using language likely to become quickly dated or that reflects only a narrow subdialect of English, with the goal of making the New Living Translation as broadly useful and timeless as possible.

But our concern for readability goes beyond the concerns of vocabulary and sentence structure. We are also concerned about historical and cultural barriers to understanding the Bible, and we have sought to translate terms shrouded in history and culture in ways that can be immediately understood. To this end:

- We have converted ancient weights and measures (for example, "ephah" [a unit of dry volume] or "cubit" [a unit of length]) to modern English (American) equivalents, since the ancient measures are not generally meaningful to today's readers. Then in the textual footnotes we offer the literal Hebrew, Aramaic, or Greek measures, along with modern metric equivalents.
- Instead of translating ancient currency values literally, we have expressed them in common terms that communicate the message. For example, in the Old Testament, "ten shekels of silver" becomes "ten pieces of silver" to convey the intended message. In the New Testament, we have often translated the "denarius" as "the normal daily wage" to facilitate understanding. Then a footnote offers: "Greek *a denarius,* the payment for a full day's wage." In general, we give a clear English rendering and then state the literal Hebrew, Aramaic, or Greek in a textual footnote.
- Since the names of Hebrew months are unknown to most contemporary readers, and since the Hebrew lunar calendar fluctuates from year to year in relation to the solar calendar used today, we have looked for clear ways to communicate the time of year the Hebrew months (such as Abib) refer to. When an expanded or interpretive rendering is given in the text, a textual note gives the literal rendering. Where it is possible to define a specific ancient date in terms of our modern calendar, we use modern dates in the text. A textual footnote then gives the literal Hebrew date and states the rationale for our rendering. For example, Ezra 6:15 pinpoints the date when the postexilic Temple was completed in Jerusalem: "the third day of the month Adar." This was during the sixth year of King Darius's reign (that is, 515 B.C.). We have translated that date as March 12, with a footnote giving the Hebrew and identifying the year as 515 B.C.
- Since ancient references to the time of day differ from our modern methods of denoting time, we have used renderings that are instantly understandable to the modern reader. Accordingly, we have rendered specific times of day by using approximate equivalents in terms of our common "o'clock" system. On occasion, translations such as "at dawn the next morning" or "as the sun was setting" have been used when the biblical reference is more general.
- When the meaning of a proper name (or a wordplay inherent in a proper name) is relevant to the message of the text, its meaning is often illuminated with a textual footnote. For example, in Exodus 2:10 the text reads: "The princess named him Moses, for she explained, 'I lifted him out of the water.' " The accompanying footnote reads: "*Moses* sounds like a Hebrew term that means 'to lift out.' "

  Sometimes, when the actual meaning of a name is clear, that meaning is included in parentheses within the text itself. For example, the text at Genesis 16:11 reads: "You are to name him Ishmael *(which means 'God hears'),* for the LORD has heard your cry of distress." Since the original hearers and readers would have instantly understood the meaning of the name "Ishmael," we have provided modern readers with the same information so they can experience the text in a similar way.
- Many words and phrases carry a great deal of cultural meaning that was obvious to the original readers but needs explanation in our own culture. For example, the phrase "they beat their breasts" (Luke 23:48) in ancient times meant that people were very upset, often in mourning. In our translation we chose to translate this phrase dynamically for clarity: "They went home *in deep sorrow.*" Then we included a

footnote with the literal Greek, which reads: "Greek *went home beating their breasts*." In other similar cases, however, we have sometimes chosen to illuminate the existing literal expression to make it immediately understandable. For example, here we might have expanded the literal Greek phrase to read: "They went home beating their breasts *in sorrow*." If we had done this, we would not have included a textual footnote, since the literal Greek clearly appears in translation.

- Metaphorical language is sometimes difficult for contemporary readers to understand, so at times we have chosen to translate or illuminate the meaning of a metaphor. For example, the ancient poet writes, "Your neck is *like* the tower of David" (Song of Songs 4:4). We have rendered it "Your neck is *as beautiful as* the tower of David" to clarify the intended positive meaning of the simile. Another example comes in Ecclesiastes 12:3, which can be literally rendered: "Remember him . . . when the grinding women cease because they are few, and the women who look through the windows see dimly." We have rendered it: "Remember him before your teeth—your few remaining servants—stop grinding; and before your eyes—the women looking through the windows—see dimly." We clarified such metaphors only when we believed a typical reader might be confused by the literal text.
- When the content of the original language text is poetic in character, we have rendered it in English poetic form. We sought to break lines in ways that clarify and highlight the relationships between phrases of the text. Hebrew poetry often uses parallelism, a literary form where a second phrase (or in some instances a third or fourth) echoes the initial phrase in some way. In Hebrew parallelism, the subsequent parallel phrases continue, while also furthering and sharpening, the thought expressed in the initial line or phrase. Whenever possible, we sought to represent these parallel phrases in natural poetic English.
- The Greek term *hoi Ioudaioi* is literally translated "the Jews" in many English translations. In the Gospel of John, however, this term doesn't always refer to the Jewish people generally. In some contexts, it refers more particularly to the Jewish religious leaders. We have attempted to capture the meaning in these different contexts by using terms such as "the people" (with a footnote: Greek *the Jewish people*) or "the religious leaders," where appropriate.
- One challenge we faced was how to translate accurately the ancient biblical text that was originally written in a context where male-oriented terms were used to refer to humanity generally. We needed to respect the nature of the ancient context while also trying to make the translation clear to a modern audience that tends to read male-oriented language as applying only to males. Often the original text, though using masculine nouns and pronouns, clearly intends that the message be applied to both men and women. A typical example is found in the New Testament letters, where the believers are called "brothers" (*adelphoi*). Yet it is clear from the content of these letters that they were addressed to all the believers—male and female. Thus, we have usually translated this Greek word as "brothers and sisters" in order to represent the historical situation more accurately.

We have also been sensitive to passages where the text applies generally to human beings or to the human condition. In some instances we have used plural pronouns (they, them) in place of the masculine singular (he, him). For example, a traditional rendering of Proverbs 22:6 is: "Train up a child in the way he should go, and when he is old he will not turn from it." We have rendered it: "Direct your children onto the right path, and when they are older, they will not leave it." At times, we have also replaced third person pronouns with the second person to ensure clarity. A traditional rendering of Proverbs 26:27 is: "He who digs a pit will fall into it, and he who rolls a stone, it will come back on him." We have rendered it: "If you set a trap for others, you will get caught in it yourself. If you roll a boulder down on others, it will crush you instead."

We should emphasize, however, that all masculine nouns and pronouns used to represent God (for example, "Father") have been maintained without exception. All decisions of this kind have been driven by the concern to reflect accurately the intended meaning of the original texts of Scripture.

Lexical Consistency in Terminology

For the sake of clarity, we have translated certain original-language terms consistently, especially within synoptic passages and for commonly repeated rhetorical phrases, and within certain word categories such as divine names and non-theological technical terminology (e.g., liturgical, legal, cultural, zoological, and botanical terms). For theological terms, we have allowed a greater semantic range of acceptable English words or phrases for a single Hebrew or Greek word. We have avoided some theological terms that are not readily understood by many modern readers. For example, we avoided using words such as "justification" and "sanctification," which are carryovers from Latin translations. In place of these words, we have provided renderings such as "made right with God" and "made holy."

The Spelling of Proper Names

Many individuals in the Bible, especially the Old Testament, are known by more than one name (e.g., Uzziah / Azariah). For the sake of clarity, we have tried to use a single spelling for any one individual, footnoting the literal spelling whenever we differ from it. This is especially helpful in delineating the kings of Israel and Judah. King Joash / Jehoash of Israel has been consistently called Jehoash, while King Joash / Jehoash of Judah is called Joash. A similar distinction has been used to distinguish between Joram / Jehoram of Israel and Joram / Jehoram of Judah. All such decisions were made with the goal of clarifying the text for the reader. When the ancient biblical writers clearly had a theological purpose in their choice of a variant name (e.g., Esh-baal / Ishbosheth), the different names have been maintained with an explanatory footnote.

For the names Jacob and Israel, which are used interchangeably for both the individual patriarch and the nation, we generally render it "Israel" when it refers to the nation and "Jacob" when it refers to the individual. When our rendering of the name differs from the underlying Hebrew text, we provide a textual footnote, which includes this explanation: "The names 'Jacob' and 'Israel' are often interchanged throughout the Old Testament, referring sometimes to the individual patriarch and sometimes to the nation."

The Rendering of Divine Names

All appearances of *'el, 'elohim,* or *'eloah* have been translated "God," except where the context demands the translation "god(s)." We have generally rendered the tetragrammaton (*YHWH*) consistently as "the LORD," utilizing a form with small capitals that is common among English translations. This will distinguish it from the name *'adonai,* which we render "Lord." When *'adonai* and *YHWH* appear together, we have rendered it "Sovereign LORD." This also distinguishes *'adonai YHWH* from cases where *YHWH* appears with *'elohim,* which is rendered "LORD God." When *YH* (the short form of *YHWH*) and *YHWH* appear together, we have rendered it "LORD GOD." When *YHWH* appears with the term *tseba'oth,* we have rendered it "LORD of Heaven's Armies" to translate the meaning of the name. In a few cases, we have utilized the transliteration, *Yahweh,* when the personal character of the name is being invoked in contrast to another divine name or the name of some other god (for example, see Exodus 3:15; 6:2-3).

In the New Testament, the Greek word *christos* has been translated as "Messiah" when the context assumes a Jewish audience. When a Gentile audience can be assumed, *christos* has been translated as "Christ." The Greek word *kurios* is consistently translated "Lord," except that it is translated "LORD" wherever the New Testament text explicitly quotes from the Old Testament, and the text there has it in small capitals.

Textual Footnotes

The New Living Translation provides several kinds of textual footnotes, all designated in the text with an asterisk:

- When for the sake of clarity the NLT renders a difficult or potentially confusing phrase dynamically, we generally give the literal rendering in a textual footnote. This allows the reader to see the literal source of our dynamic rendering and how our translation relates to other more literal translations. These notes are prefaced with "Hebrew," "Aramaic," or "Greek," identifying the language of the underlying source text. For example, in Acts 2:42 we translated the literal "breaking of bread" (from the Greek) as "the Lord's Supper" to clarify that this verse refers to the ceremonial practice of the church rather than just an ordinary meal. Then we attached a footnote to "the Lord's Supper," which reads: "Greek *the breaking of bread.*"

- Textual footnotes are also used to show alternative renderings, prefaced with the word "Or." These normally occur for passages where an aspect of the meaning is debated. On occasion, we also provide notes on words or phrases that represent a departure from long-standing tradition. These notes are prefaced with "Traditionally rendered." For example, the footnote to the translation "serious skin disease" at Leviticus 13:2 says: "Traditionally rendered *leprosy*. The Hebrew word used throughout this passage is used to describe various skin diseases."

- When our translators follow a textual variant that differs significantly from our standard Hebrew or Greek texts (listed earlier), we document that difference with a footnote. We also footnote cases when the NLT excludes a passage that is included in the Greek text known as the *Textus Receptus* (and familiar to readers through its translation in the King James Version). In such cases, we offer a translation of the excluded text in a footnote, even though it is generally recognized as a later addition to the Greek text and not part of the original Greek New Testament.

- All Old Testament passages that are quoted in the New Testament are identified by a textual footnote at the New Testament location. When the New Testament clearly quotes from the Greek translation of the Old Testament, and when it differs significantly in wording from the Hebrew text, we also place a textual footnote at the Old Testament location. This note includes a rendering of the Greek version, along with a cross-reference to the New Testament passage(s) where it is cited (for example, see notes on Psalms 8:2; 53:3; Proverbs 3:12).

- Some textual footnotes provide cultural and historical information on places, things, and people in the Bible that are probably obscure to modern readers. Such notes should aid the reader in understanding the message of the text. For example, in Acts 12:1, "King Herod" is named in this translation as "King Herod Agrippa" and is identified in a footnote as being "the nephew of Herod Antipas and a grandson of Herod the Great."

- When the meaning of a proper name (or a wordplay inherent in a proper name) is relevant to the meaning of the text, it is either illuminated with a textual footnote or included within parentheses in the text itself. For example, the footnote concerning the name "Eve" at Genesis 3:20 reads: "*Eve* sounds like a Hebrew term that means 'to give life.' " This wordplay in the Hebrew illuminates the meaning of the text, which goes on to say that Eve "would be the mother of all who live."

As we submit this translation for publication, we recognize that any translation of the Scriptures is subject to limitations and imperfections. Anyone who has attempted to communicate the richness of God's Word into another language will realize it is impossible to make a perfect translation. Recognizing these limitations, we sought God's guidance and wisdom throughout this project. Now we pray that he will accept our efforts and use this translation for the benefit of the church and of all people.

We pray that the New Living Translation will overcome some of the barriers of history, culture, and language that have kept people from reading and understanding God's Word. We hope that readers unfamiliar with the Bible will find the words clear and easy to understand and that readers well versed in the Scriptures will gain a fresh perspective. We pray that readers will gain insight and wisdom for living, but most of all that they will meet the God of the Bible and be forever changed by knowing him.

The Bible Translation Committee
October 2007

BIBLE TRANSLATION TEAM
Holy Bible, New Living Translation

PENTATEUCH
Daniel I. Block, Senior Translator
Wheaton College

GENESIS
Allen Ross, *Beeson Divinity School, Samford University*
Gordon Wenham, *Trinity Theological College, Bristol*

EXODUS
Robert Bergen, *Hannibal-LaGrange College*
Daniel I. Block, *Wheaton College*
Eugene Carpenter, *Bethel College, Mishawaka, Indiana*

LEVITICUS
David Baker, *Ashland Theological Seminary*
Victor Hamilton, *Asbury College*
Kenneth Mathews, *Beeson Divinity School, Samford University*

NUMBERS
Dale A. Brueggemann, *Assemblies of God Division of Foreign Missions*
R. K. Harrison (deceased), *Wycliffe College*
Paul R. House, *Beeson Divinity School, Samford University*
Gerald L. Mattingly, *Johnson Bible College*

DEUTERONOMY
J. Gordon McConville, *University of Gloucester*
Eugene H. Merrill, *Dallas Theological Seminary*
John A. Thompson (deceased), *University of Melbourne*

HISTORICAL BOOKS
Barry J. Beitzel, Senior Translator
Trinity Evangelical Divinity School

JOSHUA, JUDGES
Carl E. Armerding, *Schloss Mittersill Study Centre*
Barry J. Beitzel, *Trinity Evangelical Divinity School*
Lawson Stone, *Asbury Theological Seminary*

1 & 2 SAMUEL
Robert Gordon, *Cambridge University*
V. Philips Long, *Regent College*
J. Robert Vannoy, *Biblical Theological Seminary*

1 & 2 KINGS
Bill T. Arnold, *Asbury Theological Seminary*
William H. Barnes, *North Central University*
Frederic W. Bush, *Fuller Theological Seminary*

1 & 2 CHRONICLES
Raymond B. Dillard (deceased), *Westminster Theological Seminary*
David A. Dorsey, *Evangelical School of Theology*
Terry Eves, *Erskine College*

RUTH, EZRA—ESTHER
William C. Williams, *Vanguard University*
H. G. M. Williamson, *Oxford University*

WISDOM BOOKS
Tremper Longman III, Senior Translator
Westmont College

JOB
August Konkel, *Providence Theological Seminary*
Tremper Longman III, *Westmont College*
Al Wolters, *Redeemer College*

PSALMS 1–75
Mark D. Futato, *Reformed Theological Seminary*
Douglas Green, *Westminster Theological Seminary*
Richard Pratt, *Reformed Theological Seminary*

PSALMS 76–150
David M. Howard Jr., *Bethel Theological Seminary*
Raymond C. Ortlund Jr., *Immanuel Church, Nashville, Tennessee*
Willem VanGemeren, *Trinity Evangelical Divinity School*

PROVERBS
Ted Hildebrandt, *Gordon College*
Richard Schultz, *Wheaton College*
Raymond C. Van Leeuwen, *Eastern College*

ECCLESIASTES, SONG OF SONGS
Daniel C. Fredericks, *Belhaven College*
David Hubbard (deceased), *Fuller Theological Seminary*
Tremper Longman III, *Westmont College*

PROPHETS
John N. Oswalt, Senior Translator
Wesley Biblical Seminary

ISAIAH
John N. Oswalt, *Wesley Biblical Seminary*
Gary Smith, *Union University*
John Walton, *Wheaton College*

JEREMIAH, LAMENTATIONS
G. Herbert Livingston, *Asbury Theological Seminary*
Elmer A. Martens, *Mennonite Brethren Biblical Seminary*

EZEKIEL
Daniel I. Block, *Wheaton College*
David H. Engelhard, *Calvin Theological Seminary*
David Thompson, *Asbury Theological Seminary*

DANIEL, HAGGAI—MALACHI
Joyce Baldwin Caine (deceased), *Trinity College, Bristol*
Douglas Gropp, *Catholic University of America*
Roy Hayden, *Oral Roberts School of Theology*
Andrew Hill, *Wheaton College*
Tremper Longman III, *Westmont College*

HOSEA—ZEPHANIAH
Joseph Coleson, *Nazarene Theological Seminary*
Roy Hayden, *Oral Roberts School of Theology*
Andrew Hill, *Wheaton College*
Richard Patterson, *Liberty University*

GOSPELS AND ACTS
Grant R. Osborne, Senior Translator
Trinity Evangelical Divinity School

MATTHEW
Craig Blomberg, *Denver Seminary*
Donald A. Hagner, *Fuller Theological Seminary*
David Turner, *Grand Rapids Baptist Seminary*

MARK
Robert Guelich (deceased), *Fuller Theological Seminary*
George Guthrie, *Union University*
Grant R. Osborne, *Trinity Evangelical Divinity School*

LUKE
Darrell Bock, *Dallas Theological Seminary*
Scot McKnight, *North Park University*
Robert Stein, *The Southern Baptist Theological Seminary*

JOHN
Gary M. Burge, *Wheaton College*
Philip W. Comfort, *Coastal Carolina University*
Marianne Meye Thompson, *Fuller Theological Seminary*

ACTS
D. A. Carson, *Trinity Evangelical Divinity School*
William J. Larkin, *Columbia International University*
Roger Mohrlang, *Whitworth University*

LETTERS AND REVELATION
Norman R. Ericson, Senior Translator
Wheaton College

ROMANS, GALATIANS
Gerald Borchert, *Northern Baptist Theological Seminary*
Douglas J. Moo, *Wheaton College*
Thomas R. Schreiner, *The Southern Baptist Theological Seminary*

1 & 2 CORINTHIANS
Joseph Alexanian, *Trinity International University*
Linda Belleville, *Bethel College, Mishawaka, Indiana*
Douglas A. Oss, *Central Bible College*
Robert Sloan, *Houston Baptist University*

EPHESIANS—PHILEMON
Harold W. Hoehner (deceased), *Dallas Theological Seminary*
Moises Silva, *Gordon-Conwell Theological Seminary*
Klyne Snodgrass, *North Park Theological Seminary*

HEBREWS, JAMES, 1 & 2 PETER, JUDE
Peter Davids, *St. Stephen's University*
Norman R. Ericson, *Wheaton College*
William Lane (deceased), *Seattle Pacific University*
J. Ramsey Michaels, *S. W. Missouri State University*

1–3 JOHN, REVELATION
Greg Beale, *Westminster Theological Seminary*
Robert Mounce, *Whitworth University*
M. Robert Mulholland Jr., *Asbury Theological Seminary*

SPECIAL REVIEWERS
F. F. Bruce (deceased), *University of Manchester*
Kenneth N. Taylor (deceased), *Translator,* The Living Bible

COORDINATING TEAM
Mark D. Taylor, *Director and Chief Stylist*
Ronald A. Beers, *Executive Director and Stylist*
Mark R. Norton, *Managing Editor and O.T. Coordinating Editor*
Philip W. Comfort, *N.T. Coordinating Editor*
Daniel W. Taylor, *Bethel University, Senior Stylist*

OLD TESTAMENT

Genesis

KING JAMES VERSION

1 1In the beginning God created the heaven and the earth.

2And the earth was without form, and void; and darkness *was* upon the face of the deep. And the Spirit of God moved upon the face of the waters.

3And God said, Let there be light: and there was light.

4And God saw the light, that *it was* good: and God divided the light from the darkness.

5And God called the light Day, and the darkness he called Night. And the evening and the morning were the first day.

6And God said, Let there be a firmament in the midst of the waters, and let it divide the waters from the waters.

7And God made the firmament, and divided the waters which *were* under the firmament from the waters which *were* above the firmament: and it was so.

8And God called the firmament Heaven. And the evening and the morning were the second day.

9And God said, Let the waters under the heaven be gathered together unto one place, and let the dry *land* appear: and it was so.

10And God called the dry *land* Earth; and the gathering together of the waters called he Seas: and God saw that *it was* good.

11And God said, Let the earth bring forth grass, the herb yielding seed, *and* the fruit tree yielding fruit after his kind, whose seed *is* in itself, upon the earth: and it was so.

12And the earth brought forth grass, *and* herb yielding seed after his kind, and the tree yielding fruit, whose seed *was* in itself, after his kind: and God saw that *it was* good.

13And the evening and the morning were the third day.

14And God said, Let there be lights in the firmament of the heaven to divide the day from the night; and let them be for signs, and for seasons, and for days, and years:

15And let them be for lights in the firmament of the heaven to give light upon the earth: and it was so.

NEW LIVING TRANSLATION

The Account of Creation

1 In the beginning God created the heavens and the earth.* 2The earth was formless and empty, and darkness covered the deep waters. And the Spirit of God was hovering over the surface of the waters.

3Then God said, "Let there be light," and there was light. 4And God saw that the light was good. Then he separated the light from the darkness. 5God called the light "day" and the darkness "night."

And evening passed and morning came, marking the first day.

6Then God said, "Let there be a space between the waters, to separate the waters of the heavens from the waters of the earth." 7And that is what happened. God made this space to separate the waters of the earth from the waters of the heavens. 8God called the space "sky."

And evening passed and morning came, marking the second day.

9Then God said, "Let the waters beneath the sky flow together into one place, so dry ground may appear." And that is what happened. 10God called the dry ground "land" and the waters "seas." And God saw that it was good. 11Then God said, "Let the land sprout with vegetation—every sort of seed-bearing plant, and trees that grow seed-bearing fruit. These seeds will then produce the kinds of plants and trees from which they came." And that is what happened. 12The land produced vegetation—all sorts of seed-bearing plants, and trees with seed-bearing fruit. Their seeds produced plants and trees of the same kind. And God saw that it was good.

13And evening passed and morning came, marking the third day.

14Then God said, "Let lights appear in the sky to separate the day from the night. Let them be signs to mark the seasons, days, and years. 15Let these lights in the sky shine down on the earth."

1:1 Or *In the beginning when God created the heavens and the earth, . . .* Or *When God began to create the heavens and the earth, . . .*

KING JAMES VERSION

16 And God made two great lights; the greater light to rule the day, and the lesser light to rule the night: *he made* the stars also.

17 And God set them in the firmament of the heaven to give light upon the earth,

18 And to rule over the day and over the night, and to divide the light from the darkness: and God saw that *it was* good.

19 And the evening and the morning were the fourth day.

20 And God said, Let the waters bring forth abundantly the moving creature that hath life, and fowl *that* may fly above the earth in the open firmament of heaven.

21 And God created great whales, and every living creature that moveth, which the waters brought forth abundantly, after their kind, and every winged fowl after his kind: and God saw that *it was* good.

22 And God blessed them, saying, Be fruitful, and multiply, and fill the waters in the seas, and let fowl multiply in the earth.

23 And the evening and the morning were the fifth day.

24 And God said, Let the earth bring forth the living creature after his kind, cattle, and creeping thing, and beast of the earth after his kind: and it was so.

25 And God made the beast of the earth after his kind, and cattle after their kind, and every thing that creepeth upon the earth after his kind: and God saw that *it was* good.

26 And God said, Let us make man in our image, after our likeness: and let them have dominion over the fish of the sea, and over the fowl of the air, and over the cattle, and over all the earth, and over every creeping thing that creepeth upon the earth.

27 So God created man in his *own* image, in the image of God created he him; male and female created he them.

28 And God blessed them, and God said unto them, Be fruitful, and multiply, and replenish the earth, and subdue it: and have dominion over the fish of the sea, and over the fowl of the air, and over every living thing that moveth upon the earth.

29 And God said, Behold, I have given you every herb bearing seed, which *is* upon the face of all the earth, and every tree, in the which *is* the fruit of a tree yielding seed; to you it shall be for meat.

30 And to every beast of the earth, and to every fowl of the air, and to every thing that creepeth upon the earth, wherein *there is* life, *I have given* every green herb for meat: and it was so.

31 And God saw every thing that he had made, and, behold, *it was* very good. And the evening and the morning were the sixth day.

NEW LIVING TRANSLATION

And that is what happened. 16 God made two
great lights—the larger one to govern the day, and
the smaller one to govern the night. He also made
the stars. 17 God set these lights in the sky to light
the earth, 18 to govern the day and night, and to
separate the light from the darkness. And God
saw that it was good.

19 And evening passed and morning came,
marking the fourth day.

20 Then God said, "Let the waters swarm with fish
and other life. Let the skies be filled with birds of
every kind." 21 So God created great sea creatures
and every living thing that scurries and swarms in
the water, and every sort of bird—each producing
offspring of the same kind. And God saw that it
was good. 22 Then God blessed them, saying, "Be
fruitful and multiply. Let the fish fill the seas, and
let the birds multiply on the earth."

23 And evening passed and morning came,
marking the fifth day.

24 Then God said, "Let the earth produce every sort
of animal, each producing offspring of the same
kind—livestock, small animals that scurry along
the ground, and wild animals." And that is what
happened. 25 God made all sorts of wild animals,
livestock, and small animals, each able to
produce offspring of the same kind. And God
saw that it was good.

26 Then God said, "Let us make human beings*
in our image, to be like us. They will reign over
the fish in the sea, the birds in the sky, the
livestock, all the wild animals on the earth, and
the small animals that scurry along the ground."

27 So God created human beings* in his
own image.
In the image of God he created them;
male and female he created them.

28 Then God blessed them and said, "Be fruitful
and multiply. Fill the earth and govern it. Reign
over the fish in the sea, the birds in the sky, and
all the animals that scurry along the ground."

29 Then God said, "Look! I have given you every
seed-bearing plant throughout the earth and all
the fruit trees for your food. 30 And I have given
every green plant as food for all the wild animals,
the birds in the sky, and the small animals that
scurry along the ground—everything that has
life." And that is what happened.

31 Then God looked over all he had made, and
he saw that it was very good!

And evening passed and morning came,
marking the sixth day.

1:26 Or *man;* Hebrew reads *adam.* **1:27** Or *the man;* Hebrew reads *ha-adam.*

KING JAMES VERSION

2 1Thus the heavens and the earth were finished,
and all the host of them.
2And on the seventh day God ended his work
which he had made; and he rested on the seventh day
from all his work which he had made.
3And God blessed the seventh day, and sanctified
it: because that in it he had rested from all his work
which God created and made.
4These *are* the generations of the heavens and of
the earth when they were created, in the day that the
LORD God made the earth and the heavens,

5And every plant of the field before it was in the
earth, and every herb of the field before it grew: for
the LORD God had not caused it to rain upon the
earth, and *there was* not a man to till the ground.
6But there went up a mist from the earth, and
watered the whole face of the ground.
7And the LORD God formed man *of* the dust of the
ground, and breathed into his nostrils the breath of
life; and man became a living soul.
8And the LORD God planted a garden eastward
in Eden; and there he put the man whom he had
formed.
9And out of the ground made the LORD God to
grow every tree that is pleasant to the sight, and good
for food; the tree of life also in the midst of the garden, and the tree of knowledge of good and evil.
10And a river went out of Eden to water the garden;
and from thence it was parted, and became into four
heads.
11The name of the first *is* Pison: that *is* it which
compasseth the whole land of Havilah, where *there*
is gold;
12And the gold of that land *is* good: there *is*
bdellium and the onyx stone.
13And the name of the second river *is* Gihon:
the same *is* it that compasseth the whole land of
Ethiopia.
14And the name of the third river *is* Hiddekel: that
is it which goeth toward the east of Assyria. And the
fourth river *is* Euphrates.
15And the LORD God took the man, and put him
into the garden of Eden to dress it and to keep it.
16And the LORD God commanded the man, saying,
Of every tree of the garden thou mayest freely eat:
17But of the tree of the knowledge of good and
evil, thou shalt not eat of it: for in the day that thou
eatest thereof thou shalt surely die.
18And the LORD God said, *It is* not good that the
man should be alone; I will make him an help meet
for him.
19And out of the ground the LORD God formed
every beast of the field, and every fowl of the air; and
brought *them* unto Adam to see what he would call
them: and whatsoever Adam called every living creature, that *was* the name thereof.

NEW LIVING TRANSLATION

2 So the creation of the heavens and the earth
and everything in them was completed. 2On
the seventh day God had finished his work of
creation, so he rested* from all his work. 3And
God blessed the seventh day and declared it holy,
because it was the day when he rested from all his
work of creation.

4This is the account of the creation of the heavens
and the earth.

The Man and Woman in Eden

When the LORD God made the earth and the heavens,
5neither wild plants nor grains were growing on the
earth. For the LORD God had not yet sent rain to water
the earth, and there were no people to cultivate the
soil. 6Instead, springs* came up from the ground and
watered all the land. 7Then the LORD God formed the
man from the dust of the ground. He breathed the
breath of life into the man's nostrils, and the man
became a living person.
8Then the LORD God planted a garden in Eden in
the east, and there he placed the man he had made.
9The LORD God made all sorts of trees grow up from
the ground—trees that were beautiful and that produced delicious fruit. In the middle of the garden he
placed the tree of life and the tree of the knowledge
of good and evil.
10A river flowed from the land of Eden, watering
the garden and then dividing into four branches.
11The first branch, called the Pishon, flowed around
the entire land of Havilah, where gold is found.
12The gold of that land is exceptionally pure; aromatic resin and onyx stone are also found there.
13The second branch, called the Gihon, flowed
around the entire land of Cush. 14The third branch,
called the Tigris, flowed east of the land of Asshur.
The fourth branch is called the Euphrates.
15The LORD God placed the man in the Garden of
Eden to tend and watch over it. 16But the LORD God
warned him, "You may freely eat the fruit of every
tree in the garden—17except the tree of the knowledge of good and evil. If you eat its fruit, you are sure
to die."
18Then the LORD God said, "It is not good for the
man to be alone. I will make a helper who is just
right for him." 19So the LORD God formed from the
ground all the wild animals and all the birds of the
sky. He brought them to the man* to see what he
would call them, and the man chose a name for each

2:2 Or *ceased;* also in 2:3. **2:6** Or *mist.* **2:19** Or *Adam,* and so throughout the chapter.

KING JAMES VERSION

20 And Adam gave names to all cattle, and to the fowl of the air, and to every beast of the field; but for Adam there was not found an help meet for him.

21 And the LORD God caused a deep sleep to fall upon Adam, and he slept: and he took one of his ribs, and closed up the flesh instead thereof;

22 And the rib, which the LORD God had taken from man, made he a woman, and brought her unto the man.

23 And Adam said, This *is* now bone of my bones, and flesh of my flesh: she shall be called Woman, because she was taken out of Man.

24 Therefore shall a man leave his father and his mother, and shall cleave unto his wife: and they shall be one flesh.

25 And they were both naked, the man and his wife, and were not ashamed.

3 1 Now the serpent was more subtil than any beast of the field which the LORD God had made. And he said unto the woman, Yea, hath God said, Ye shall not eat of every tree of the garden?

2 And the woman said unto the serpent, We may eat of the fruit of the trees of the garden:

3 But of the fruit of the tree which *is* in the midst of the garden, God hath said, Ye shall not eat of it, neither shall ye touch it, lest ye die.

4 And the serpent said unto the woman, Ye shall not surely die:

5 For God doth know that in the day ye eat thereof, then your eyes shall be opened, and ye shall be as gods, knowing good and evil.

6 And when the woman saw that the tree *was* good for food, and that it *was* pleasant to the eyes, and a tree to be desired to make *one* wise, she took of the fruit thereof, and did eat, and gave also unto her husband with her; and he did eat.

7 And the eyes of them both were opened, and they knew that they *were* naked; and they sewed fig leaves together, and made themselves aprons.

8 And they heard the voice of the LORD God walking in the garden in the cool of the day: and Adam and his wife hid themselves from the presence of the LORD God amongst the trees of the garden.

9 And the LORD God called unto Adam, and said unto him, Where *art* thou?

10 And he said, I heard thy voice in the garden, and I was afraid, because I *was* naked; and I hid myself.

11 And he said, Who told thee that thou *wast* naked? Hast thou eaten of the tree, whereof I commanded thee that thou shouldest not eat?

12 And the man said, The woman whom thou gavest *to be* with me, she gave me of the tree, and I did eat.

NEW LIVING TRANSLATION

one. 20 He gave names to all the livestock, all the birds of the sky, and all the wild animals. But still there was no helper just right for him.

21 So the LORD God caused the man to fall into a deep sleep. While the man slept, the LORD God took out one of the man's ribs* and closed up the opening. 22 Then the LORD God made a woman from the rib, and he brought her to the man.

23 "At last!" the man exclaimed.

"This one is bone from my bone,
and flesh from my flesh!
She will be called 'woman,'
because she was taken from 'man.'"

24 This explains why a man leaves his father and mother and is joined to his wife, and the two are united into one.

25 Now the man and his wife were both naked, but they felt no shame.

The Man and Woman Sin

3 The serpent was the shrewdest of all the wild animals the LORD God had made. One day he asked the woman, "Did God really say you must not eat the fruit from any of the trees in the garden?"

2 "Of course we may eat fruit from the trees in the garden," the woman replied. 3 "It's only the fruit from the tree in the middle of the garden that we are not allowed to eat. God said, 'You must not eat it or even touch it; if you do, you will die.'"

4 "You won't die!" the serpent replied to the woman. 5 "God knows that your eyes will be opened as soon as you eat it, and you will be like God, knowing both good and evil."

6 The woman was convinced. She saw that the tree was beautiful and its fruit looked delicious, and she wanted the wisdom it would give her. So she took some of the fruit and ate it. Then she gave some to her husband, who was with her, and he ate it, too. 7 At that moment their eyes were opened, and they suddenly felt shame at their nakedness. So they sewed fig leaves together to cover themselves.

8 When the cool evening breezes were blowing, the man* and his wife heard the LORD God walking about in the garden. So they hid from the LORD God among the trees. 9 Then the LORD God called to the man, "Where are you?"

10 He replied, "I heard you walking in the garden, so I hid. I was afraid because I was naked."

11 "Who told you that you were naked?" the LORD God asked. "Have you eaten from the tree whose fruit I commanded you not to eat?"

12 The man replied, "It was the woman you gave me who gave me the fruit, and I ate it."

2:21 Or *took a part of the man's side.* **3:8** Or *Adam,* and so throughout the chapter.

KING JAMES VERSION

13 And the LORD God said unto the woman, What *is* this *that* thou hast done? And the woman said, The serpent beguiled me, and I did eat.

14 And the LORD God said unto the serpent, Because thou hast done this, thou *art* cursed above all cattle, and above every beast of the field; upon thy belly shalt thou go, and dust shalt thou eat all the days of thy life:

15 And I will put enmity between thee and the woman, and between thy seed and her seed; it shall bruise thy head, and thou shalt bruise his heel.

16 Unto the woman he said, I will greatly multiply thy sorrow and thy conception; in sorrow thou shalt bring forth children; and thy desire *shall be* to thy husband, and he shall rule over thee.

17 And unto Adam he said, Because thou hast hearkened unto the voice of thy wife, and hast eaten of the tree, of which I commanded thee, saying, Thou shalt not eat of it: cursed *is* the ground for thy sake; in sorrow shalt thou eat *of* it all the days of thy life;

18 Thorns also and thistles shall it bring forth to thee; and thou shalt eat the herb of the field;

19 In the sweat of thy face shalt thou eat bread, till thou return unto the ground; for out of it wast thou taken: for dust thou *art,* and unto dust shalt thou return.

20 And Adam called his wife's name Eve; because she was the mother of all living.

21 Unto Adam also and to his wife did the LORD God make coats of skins, and clothed them.

22 And the LORD God said, Behold, the man is become as one of us, to know good and evil: and now, lest he put forth his hand, and take also of the tree of life, and eat, and live for ever:

23 Therefore the LORD God sent him forth from the garden of Eden, to till the ground from whence he was taken.

24 So he drove out the man; and he placed at the east of the garden of Eden Cherubims, and a flaming sword which turned every way, to keep the way of the tree of life.

NEW LIVING TRANSLATION

13 Then the LORD God asked the woman, "What have you done?"

"The serpent deceived me," she replied. "That's why I ate it."

14 Then the LORD God said to the serpent,

"Because you have done this, you are cursed
more than all animals, domestic and wild.
You will crawl on your belly,
groveling in the dust as long as you live.
15 And I will cause hostility between you and the woman,
and between your offspring and her offspring.
He will strike* your head,
and you will strike his heel."

16 Then he said to the woman,

"I will sharpen the pain of your pregnancy,
and in pain you will give birth.
And you will desire to control your husband,
but he will rule over you.*"

17 And to the man he said,

"Since you listened to your wife and ate from the tree
whose fruit I commanded you not to eat,
the ground is cursed because of you.
All your life you will struggle to scratch a living from it.
18 It will grow thorns and thistles for you,
though you will eat of its grains.
19 By the sweat of your brow
will you have food to eat
until you return to the ground
from which you were made.
For you were made from dust,
and to dust you will return."

Paradise Lost: God's Judgment

20 Then the man—Adam—named his wife Eve, because she would be the mother of all who live.*
21 And the LORD God made clothing from animal skins for Adam and his wife.

22 Then the LORD God said, "Look, the human beings* have become like us, knowing both good and
evil. What if they reach out, take fruit from the tree
of life, and eat it? Then they will live forever!"
23 So the LORD God banished them from the Garden of
Eden, and he sent Adam out to cultivate the ground
from which he had been made.
24 After sending them
out, the LORD God stationed mighty cherubim to the
east of the Garden of Eden. And he placed a flaming
sword that flashed back and forth to guard the way
to the tree of life.

3:15 Or *bruise;* also in 3:15b. **3:16** Or *And though you will have desire for your husband, / he will rule over you.* **3:20** *Eve* sounds like a Hebrew term that means "to give life." **3:22** Or *the man;* Hebrew reads *ha-adam.*

KING JAMES VERSION

4 [1]And Adam knew Eve his wife; and she conceived, and bare Cain, and said, I have gotten a man from the LORD.

[2]And she again bare his brother Abel. And Abel was a keeper of sheep, but Cain was a tiller of the ground.

[3]And in process of time it came to pass, that Cain brought of the fruit of the ground an offering unto the LORD.

[4]And Abel, he also brought of the firstlings of his flock and of the fat thereof. And the LORD had respect unto Abel and to his offering:

[5]But unto Cain and to his offering he had not respect. And Cain was very wroth, and his countenance fell.

[6]And the LORD said unto Cain, Why art thou wroth? and why is thy countenance fallen?

[7]If thou doest well, shalt thou not be accepted? and if thou doest not well, sin lieth at the door. And unto thee *shall be* his desire, and thou shalt rule over him.

[8]And Cain talked with Abel his brother: and it came to pass, when they were in the field, that Cain rose up against Abel his brother, and slew him.

[9]And the LORD said unto Cain, Where *is* Abel thy brother? And he said, I know not: *Am* I my brother's keeper?

[10]And he said, What hast thou done? the voice of thy brother's blood crieth unto me from the ground.

[11]And now *art* thou cursed from the earth, which hath opened her mouth to receive thy brother's blood from thy hand;

[12]When thou tillest the ground, it shall not henceforth yield unto thee her strength; a fugitive and a vagabond shalt thou be in the earth.

[13]And Cain said unto the LORD, My punishment *is* greater than I can bear.

[14]Behold, thou hast driven me out this day from the face of the earth; and from thy face shall I be hid; and I shall be a fugitive and a vagabond in the earth; and it shall come to pass, *that* every one that findeth me shall slay me.

[15]And the LORD said unto him, Therefore whosoever slayeth Cain, vengeance shall be taken on him sevenfold. And the LORD set a mark upon Cain, lest any finding him should kill him.

[16]And Cain went out from the presence of the LORD, and dwelt in the land of Nod, on the east of Eden.

[17]And Cain knew his wife; and she conceived, and bare Enoch: and he builded a city, and called the name of the city, after the name of his son, Enoch.

[18]And unto Enoch was born Irad: and Irad begat Mehujael: and Mehujael begat Methusael: and Methusael begat Lamech.

NEW LIVING TRANSLATION

Cain and Abel

4 Now Adam* had sexual relations with his wife, Eve, and she became pregnant. When she gave birth to Cain, she said, "With the LORD's help, I have produced* a man!" [2]Later she gave birth to his brother and named him Abel.

When they grew up, Abel became a shepherd, while Cain cultivated the ground. [3]When it was time for the harvest, Cain presented some of his crops as a gift to the LORD. [4]Abel also brought a gift—the best of the firstborn lambs from his flock. The LORD accepted Abel and his gift, [5]but he did not accept Cain and his gift. This made Cain very angry, and he looked dejected.

[6]"Why are you so angry?" the LORD asked Cain. "Why do you look so dejected? [7]You will be accepted if you do what is right. But if you refuse to do what is right, then watch out! Sin is crouching at the door, eager to control you. But you must subdue it and be its master."

[8]One day Cain suggested to his brother, "Let's go out into the fields."* And while they were in the field, Cain attacked his brother, Abel, and killed him.

[9]Afterward the LORD asked Cain, "Where is your brother? Where is Abel?"

"I don't know," Cain responded. "Am I my brother's guardian?"

[10]But the LORD said, "What have you done? Listen! Your brother's blood cries out to me from the ground! [11]Now you are cursed and banished from the ground, which has swallowed your brother's blood. [12]No longer will the ground yield good crops for you, no matter how hard you work! From now on you will be a homeless wanderer on the earth."

[13]Cain replied to the LORD, "My punishment* is too great for me to bear! [14]You have banished me from the land and from your presence; you have made me a homeless wanderer. Anyone who finds me will kill me!"

[15]The LORD replied, "No, for I will give a sevenfold punishment to anyone who kills you." Then the LORD put a mark on Cain to warn anyone who might try to kill him. [16]So Cain left the LORD's presence and settled in the land of Nod,* east of Eden.

The Descendants of Cain

[17]Cain had sexual relations with his wife, and she became pregnant and gave birth to Enoch. Then Cain founded a city, which he named Enoch, after his son. [18]Enoch had a son named Irad. Irad became the

4:1a Or *the man;* also in 4:25. **4:1b** Or *I have acquired. Cain* sounds like a Hebrew term that can mean "produce" or "acquire." **4:8** As in Samaritan Pentateuch, Greek and Syriac versions, and Latin Vulgate; Masoretic Text lacks *"Let's go out into the fields."* **4:13** Or *My sin.* **4:16** *Nod* means "wandering."

KING JAMES VERSION

19And Lamech took unto him two wives: the name of the one *was* Adah, and the name of the other Zillah.

20And Adah bare Jabal: he was the father of such as dwell in tents, and *of such as have* cattle.

21And his brother's name *was* Jubal: he was the father of all such as handle the harp and organ.

22And Zillah, she also bare Tubal-cain, an instructor of every artificer in brass and iron: and the sister of Tubal-cain *was* Naamah.

23And Lamech said unto his wives, Adah and Zillah, Hear my voice; ye wives of Lamech, hearken unto my speech: for I have slain a man to my wounding, and a young man to my hurt.

24If Cain shall be avenged sevenfold, truly Lamech seventy and sevenfold.

25And Adam knew his wife again; and she bare a son, and called his name Seth: For God, *said she,* hath appointed me another seed instead of Abel, whom Cain slew.

26And to Seth, to him also there was born a son; and he called his name Enos: then began men to call upon the name of the LORD.

5 1This *is* the book of the generations of Adam. In the day that God created man, in the likeness of God made he him;

2Male and female created he them; and blessed them, and called their name Adam, in the day when they were created.

3And Adam lived an hundred and thirty years, and begat *a son* in his own likeness, after his image; and called his name Seth:

4And the days of Adam after he had begotten Seth were eight hundred years: and he begat sons and daughters:

5And all the days that Adam lived were nine hundred and thirty years: and he died.

6And Seth lived an hundred and five years, and begat Enos:

7And Seth lived after he begat Enos eight hundred and seven years, and begat sons and daughters:

8And all the days of Seth were nine hundred and twelve years: and he died.

9And Enos lived ninety years, and begat Cainan:

10And Enos lived after he begat Cainan eight hundred and fifteen years, and begat sons and daughters:

11And all the days of Enos were nine hundred and five years: and he died.

NEW LIVING TRANSLATION

father of* Mehujael. Mehujael became the father of
Methushael. Methushael became the father of
Lamech.

19Lamech married two women. The first was
named Adah, and the second was Zillah. 20Adah gave
birth to Jabal, who was the first of those who raise
livestock and live in tents. 21His brother's name was
Jubal, the first of all who play the harp and flute.
22Lamech's other wife, Zillah, gave birth to a son
named Tubal-cain. He became an expert in forging
tools of bronze and iron. Tubal-cain had a sister
named Naamah. 23One day Lamech said to his wives,

"Adah and Zillah, hear my voice;
listen to me, you wives of Lamech.
I have killed a man who attacked me,
a young man who wounded me.
24 If someone who kills Cain is punished
seven times,
then the one who kills me will be punished
seventy-seven times!"

The Birth of Seth

25Adam had sexual relations with his wife again, and
she gave birth to another son. She named him Seth,*
for she said, "God has granted me another son in
place of Abel, whom Cain killed." 26When Seth grew
up, he had a son and named him Enosh. At that time
people first began to worship the LORD by name.

The Descendants of Adam

5 This is the written account of the descendants
of Adam. When God created human beings,*
he made them to be like himself. 2He created them
male and female, and he blessed them and called
them "human."

3When Adam was 130 years old, he became the
father of a son who was just like him—in his very
image. He named his son Seth. 4After the birth of
Seth, Adam lived another 800 years, and he had
other sons and daughters. 5Adam lived 930 years,
and then he died.

6When Seth was 105 years old, he became the
father of* Enosh. 7After the birth of* Enosh, Seth
lived another 807 years, and he had other sons
and daughters. 8Seth lived 912 years, and then
he died.

9When Enosh was 90 years old, he became the
father of Kenan. 10After the birth of Kenan,
Enosh lived another 815 years, and he had other
sons and daughters. 11Enosh lived 905 years, and
then he died.

4:18 Or *the ancestor of,* and so throughout the verse. **4:25** *Seth* probably means "granted"; the name may also mean "appointed." **5:1** Or *man;* Hebrew reads *adam;* similarly in 5:2. **5:6** Or *the ancestor of;* also in 5:9, 12, 15, 18, 21, 25. **5:7** Or *the birth of this ancestor of;* also in 5:10, 13, 16, 19, 22, 26.

KING JAMES VERSION

12And Cainan lived seventy years, and begat Mahalaleel:

13And Cainan lived after he begat Mahalaleel eight hundred and forty years, and begat sons and daughters:

14And all the days of Cainan were nine hundred and ten years: and he died.

15And Mahalaleel lived sixty and five years, and begat Jared:

16And Mahalaleel lived after he begat Jared eight hundred and thirty years, and begat sons and daughters:

17And all the days of Mahalaleel were eight hundred ninety and five years: and he died.

18And Jared lived an hundred sixty and two years, and he begat Enoch:

19And Jared lived after he begat Enoch eight hundred years, and begat sons and daughters:

20And all the days of Jared were nine hundred sixty and two years: and he died.

21And Enoch lived sixty and five years, and begat Methuselah:

22And Enoch walked with God after he begat Methuselah three hundred years, and begat sons and daughters:

23And all the days of Enoch were three hundred sixty and five years:

24And Enoch walked with God: and he *was* not; for God took him.

25And Methuselah lived an hundred eighty and seven years, and begat Lamech:

26And Methuselah lived after he begat Lamech seven hundred eighty and two years, and begat sons and daughters:

27And all the days of Methuselah were nine hundred sixty and nine years: and he died.

28And Lamech lived an hundred eighty and two years, and begat a son:

29And he called his name Noah, saying, This *same* shall comfort us concerning our work and toil of our hands, because of the ground which the LORD hath cursed.

30And Lamech lived after he begat Noah five hundred ninety and five years, and begat sons and daughters:

31And all the days of Lamech were seven hundred seventy and seven years: and he died.

32And Noah was five hundred years old: and Noah begat Shem, Ham, and Japheth.

6 1And it came to pass, when men began to multiply on the face of the earth, and daughters were born unto them,

2That the sons of God saw the daughters of men that they *were* fair; and they took them wives of all which they chose.

3And the LORD said, My spirit shall not always

NEW LIVING TRANSLATION

12When Kenan was 70 years old, he became
the father of Mahalalel. 13After the birth of
Mahalalel, Kenan lived another 840 years, and
he had other sons and daughters. 14Kenan lived
910 years, and then he died.
15When Mahalalel was 65 years old, he became
the father of Jared. 16After the birth of Jared,
Mahalalel lived another 830 years, and he had
other sons and daughters. 17Mahalalel lived
895 years, and then he died.
18When Jared was 162 years old, he became the
father of Enoch. 19After the birth of Enoch, Jared
lived another 800 years, and he had other sons
and daughters. 20Jared lived 962 years, and then
he died.
21When Enoch was 65 years old, he became the
father of Methuselah. 22After the birth of
Methuselah, Enoch lived in close fellowship with
God for another 300 years, and he had other
sons and daughters. 23Enoch lived 365 years,
24walking in close fellowship with God. Then
one day he disappeared, because God took him.
25When Methuselah was 187 years old, he became
the father of Lamech. 26After the birth of
Lamech, Methuselah lived another 782 years,
and he had other sons and daughters.
27Methuselah lived 969 years, and then he died.
28When Lamech was 182 years old, he became the
father of a son. 29Lamech named his son Noah,
for he said, "May he bring us relief* from our
work and the painful labor of farming this
ground that the LORD has cursed." 30After the
birth of Noah, Lamech lived another 595 years,
and he had other sons and daughters. 31Lamech
lived 777 years, and then he died.
32By the time Noah was 500 years old, he was the
father of Shem, Ham, and Japheth.

A World Gone Wrong

6 Then the people began to multiply on the earth,
and daughters were born to them. 2The sons
of God saw the beautiful women* and took any they
wanted as their wives. 3Then the LORD said, "My
Spirit will not put up with* humans for such a long

5:29 *Noah* sounds like a Hebrew term that can mean "relief" or "comfort."
6:2 Hebrew *daughters of men;* also in 6:4. 6:3 Greek version reads *will not remain in.*

KING JAMES VERSION

strive with man, for that he also *is* flesh: yet his days shall be an hundred and twenty years.

4 There were giants in the earth in those days; and also after that, when the sons of God came in unto the daughters of men, and they bare *children* to them, the same *became* mighty men which *were* of old, men of renown.

5 And GOD saw that the wickedness of man *was* great in the earth, and *that* every imagination of the thoughts of his heart *was* only evil continually.

6 And it repented the LORD that he had made man on the earth, and it grieved him at his heart.

7 And the LORD said, I will destroy man whom I have created from the face of the earth; both man, and beast, and the creeping thing, and the fowls of the air; for it repenteth me that I have made them.

8 But Noah found grace in the eyes of the LORD.

9 These *are* the generations of Noah: Noah was a just man *and* perfect in his generations, *and* Noah walked with God.

10 And Noah begat three sons, Shem, Ham, and Japheth.

11 The earth also was corrupt before God, and the earth was filled with violence.

12 And God looked upon the earth, and, behold, it was corrupt; for all flesh had corrupted his way upon the earth.

13 And God said unto Noah, The end of all flesh is come before me; for the earth is filled with violence through them; and, behold, I will destroy them with the earth.

14 Make thee an ark of gopher wood; rooms shalt thou make in the ark, and shalt pitch it within and without with pitch.

15 And this *is the fashion* which thou shalt make it *of*: The length of the ark *shall be* three hundred cubits, the breadth of it fifty cubits, and the height of it thirty cubits.

16 A window shalt thou make to the ark, and in a cubit shalt thou finish it above; and the door of the ark shalt thou set in the side thereof; *with* lower, second, and third *stories* shalt thou make it.

17 And, behold, I, even I, do bring a flood of waters upon the earth, to destroy all flesh, wherein *is* the breath of life, from under heaven; *and* every thing that *is* in the earth shall die.

18 But with thee will I establish my covenant; and thou shalt come into the ark, thou, and thy sons, and thy wife, and thy sons' wives with thee.

19 And of every living thing of all flesh, two of every *sort* shalt thou bring into the ark, to keep *them* alive with thee; they shall be male and female.

NEW LIVING TRANSLATION

time, for they are only mortal flesh. In the future, their normal lifespan will be no more than 120 years."

4 In those days, and for some time after, giant Nephilites lived on the earth, for whenever the sons of God had intercourse with women, they gave birth to children who became the heroes and famous warriors of ancient times.

5 The LORD observed the extent of human wickedness on the earth, and he saw that everything they thought or imagined was consistently and totally evil. 6 So the LORD was sorry he had ever made them and put them on the earth. It broke his heart. 7 And the LORD said, "I will wipe this human race I have created from the face of the earth. Yes, and I will destroy every living thing—all the people, the large animals, the small animals that scurry along the ground, and even the birds of the sky. I am sorry I ever made them." 8 But Noah found favor with the LORD.

The Story of Noah

9 This is the account of Noah and his family. Noah was a righteous man, the only blameless person living on earth at the time, and he walked in close fellowship with God. 10 Noah was the father of three sons: Shem, Ham, and Japheth.

11 Now God saw that the earth had become corrupt and was filled with violence. 12 God observed all this corruption in the world, for everyone on earth was corrupt. 13 So God said to Noah, "I have decided to destroy all living creatures, for they have filled the earth with violence. Yes, I will wipe them all out along with the earth!

14 "Build a large boat* from cypress wood* and waterproof it with tar, inside and out. Then construct decks and stalls throughout its interior. 15 Make the boat 450 feet long, 75 feet wide, and 45 feet high.* 16 Leave an 18-inch opening* below the roof all the way around the boat. Put the door on the side, and build three decks inside the boat—lower, middle, and upper.

17 "Look! I am about to cover the earth with a flood that will destroy every living thing that breathes. Everything on earth will die. 18 But I will confirm my covenant with you. So enter the boat—you and your wife and your sons and their wives. 19 Bring a pair of every kind of animal—a male and a female—into the boat with you to keep them alive during the flood.

6:14a Traditionally rendered *an ark*. **6:14b** Or *gopher wood*. **6:15** Hebrew *300 cubits* [138 meters] *long, 50 cubits* [23 meters] *wide, and 30 cubits* [13.8 meters] *high*. **6:16** Hebrew *an opening of 1 cubit* [46 centimeters].

KING JAMES VERSION

20Of fowls after their kind, and of cattle after their kind, of every creeping thing of the earth after his kind, two of every *sort* shall come unto thee, to keep *them* alive.

21And take thou unto thee of all food that is eaten, and thou shalt gather *it* to thee; and it shall be for food for thee, and for them.

22Thus did Noah; according to all that God commanded him, so did he.

7 1And the LORD said unto Noah, Come thou and all thy house into the ark; for thee have I seen righteous before me in this generation.

2Of every clean beast thou shalt take to thee by sevens, the male and his female: and of beasts that *are* not clean by two, the male and his female.

3Of fowls also of the air by sevens, the male and the female; to keep seed alive upon the face of all the earth.

4For yet seven days, and I will cause it to rain upon the earth forty days and forty nights; and every living substance that I have made will I destroy from off the face of the earth.

5And Noah did according unto all that the LORD commanded him.

6And Noah *was* six hundred years old when the flood of waters was upon the earth.

7And Noah went in, and his sons, and his wife, and his sons' wives with him, into the ark, because of the waters of the flood.

8Of clean beasts, and of beasts that *are* not clean, and of fowls, and of every thing that creepeth upon the earth,

9There went in two and two unto Noah into the ark, the male and the female, as God had commanded Noah.

10And it came to pass after seven days, that the waters of the flood were upon the earth.

11In the six hundredth year of Noah's life, in the second month, the seventeenth day of the month, the same day were all the fountains of the great deep broken up, and the windows of heaven were opened.

12And the rain was upon the earth forty days and forty nights.

13In the selfsame day entered Noah, and Shem, and Ham, and Japheth, the sons of Noah, and Noah's wife, and the three wives of his sons with them, into the ark;

14They, and every beast after his kind, and all the cattle after their kind, and every creeping thing that creepeth upon the earth after his kind, and every fowl after his kind, every bird of every sort.

15And they went in unto Noah into the ark, two and two of all flesh, wherein *is* the breath of life.

16And they that went in, went in male and female of all flesh, as God had commanded him: and the LORD shut him in.

NEW LIVING TRANSLATION

20Pairs of every kind of bird, and every kind of animal, and every kind of small animal that scurries along the ground, will come to you to be kept alive. 21And be sure to take on board enough food for your family and for all the animals."

22So Noah did everything exactly as God had commanded him.

The Flood Covers the Earth

7 When everything was ready, the LORD said to Noah, "Go into the boat with all your family, for among all the people of the earth, I can see that you alone are righteous. 2Take with you seven pairs—male and female—of each animal I have approved for eating and for sacrifice,* and take one pair of each of the others. 3Also take seven pairs of every kind of bird. There must be a male and a female in each pair to ensure that all life will survive on the earth after the flood. 4Seven days from now I will make the rains pour down on the earth. And it will rain for forty days and forty nights, until I have wiped from the earth all the living things I have created."

5So Noah did everything as the LORD commanded him.

6Noah was 600 years old when the flood covered the earth. 7He went on board the boat to escape the flood—he and his wife and his sons and their wives. 8With them were all the various kinds of animals—those approved for eating and for sacrifice and those that were not—along with all the birds and the small animals that scurry along the ground. 9They entered the boat in pairs, male and female, just as God had commanded Noah. 10After seven days, the waters of the flood came and covered the earth.

11When Noah was 600 years old, on the seventeenth day of the second month, all the underground waters erupted from the earth, and the rain fell in mighty torrents from the sky. 12The rain continued to fall for forty days and forty nights.

13That very day Noah had gone into the boat with his wife and his sons—Shem, Ham, and Japheth—and their wives. 14With them in the boat were pairs of every kind of animal—domestic and wild, large and small—along with birds of every kind. 15Two by two they came into the boat, representing every living thing that breathes. 16A male and female of each kind entered, just as God had commanded Noah. Then the LORD closed the door behind them.

7:2 Hebrew *of each clean animal;* similarly in 7:8.

KING JAMES VERSION

17 And the flood was forty days upon the earth; and the waters increased, and bare up the ark, and it was lift up above the earth.

18 And the waters prevailed, and were increased greatly upon the earth; and the ark went upon the face of the waters.

19 And the waters prevailed exceedingly upon the earth; and all the high hills, that *were* under the whole heaven, were covered.

20 Fifteen cubits upward did the waters prevail; and the mountains were covered.

21 And all flesh died that moved upon the earth, both of fowl, and of cattle, and of beast, and of every creeping thing that creepeth upon the earth, and every man:

22 All in whose nostrils *was* the breath of life, of all that *was* in the dry *land,* died.

23 And every living substance was destroyed which was upon the face of the ground, both man, and cattle, and the creeping things, and the fowl of the heaven; and they were destroyed from the earth: and Noah only remained *alive,* and they that *were* with him in the ark.

24 And the waters prevailed upon the earth an hundred and fifty days.

8 1 And God remembered Noah, and every living thing, and all the cattle that *was* with him in the ark: and God made a wind to pass over the earth, and the waters asswaged;

2 The fountains also of the deep and the windows of heaven were stopped, and the rain from heaven was restrained;

3 And the waters returned from off the earth continually: and after the end of the hundred and fifty days the waters were abated.

4 And the ark rested in the seventh month, on the seventeenth day of the month, upon the mountains of Ararat.

5 And the waters decreased continually until the tenth month: in the tenth *month,* on the first *day* of the month, were the tops of the mountains seen.

6 And it came to pass at the end of forty days, that Noah opened the window of the ark which he had made:

7 And he sent forth a raven, which went forth to and fro, until the waters were dried up from off the earth.

8 Also he sent forth a dove from him, to see if the waters were abated from off the face of the ground;

9 But the dove found no rest for the sole of her foot, and she returned unto him into the ark, for the waters *were* on the face of the whole earth: then he put forth his hand, and took her, and pulled her in unto him into the ark.

10 And he stayed yet other seven days; and again he sent forth the dove out of the ark;

NEW LIVING TRANSLATION

17 For forty days the floodwaters grew deeper, covering the ground and lifting the boat high above the earth. 18 As the waters rose higher and higher above the ground, the boat floated safely on the surface. 19 Finally, the water covered even the highest mountains on the earth, 20 rising more than twenty-two feet* above the highest peaks. 21 All the living things on earth died—birds, domestic animals, wild animals, small animals that scurry along the ground, and all the people. 22 Everything that breathed and lived on dry land died. 23 God wiped out every living thing on the earth—people, livestock, small animals that scurry along the ground, and the birds of the sky. All were destroyed. The only people who survived were Noah and those with him in the boat. 24 And the floodwaters covered the earth for 150 days.

The Flood Recedes

8 But God remembered Noah and all the wild animals and livestock with him in the boat. He sent a wind to blow across the earth, and the floodwaters began to recede. 2 The underground waters stopped flowing, and the torrential rains from the sky were stopped. 3 So the floodwaters gradually receded from the earth. After 150 days, 4 exactly five months from the time the flood began,* the boat came to rest on the mountains of Ararat. 5 Two and a half months later,* as the waters continued to go down, other mountain peaks became visible.

6 After another forty days, Noah opened the window he had made in the boat 7 and released a raven. The bird flew back and forth until the floodwaters on the earth had dried up. 8 He also released a dove to see if the water had receded and it could find dry ground. 9 But the dove could find no place to land because the water still covered the ground. So it returned to the boat, and Noah held out his hand and drew the dove back inside. 10 After waiting another seven days, Noah

7:20 Hebrew *15 cubits* [6.9 meters]. **8:4** Hebrew *on the seventeenth day of the seventh month;* see 7:11. **8:5** Hebrew *On the first day of the tenth month;* see 7:11 and note on 8:4.

KING JAMES VERSION

11 And the dove came in to him in the evening; and, lo, in her mouth *was* an olive leaf plucked off: so Noah knew that the waters were abated from off the earth.

12 And he stayed yet other seven days; and sent forth the dove; which returned not again unto him any more.

13 And it came to pass in the six hundredth and first year, in the first *month,* the first *day* of the month, the waters were dried up from off the earth: and Noah removed the covering of the ark, and looked, and, behold, the face of the ground was dry.

14 And in the second month, on the seven and twentieth day of the month, was the earth dried.

15 And God spake unto Noah, saying,

16 Go forth of the ark, thou, and thy wife, and thy sons, and thy sons' wives with thee.

17 Bring forth with thee every living thing that *is* with thee, of all flesh, *both* of fowl, and of cattle, and of every creeping thing that creepeth upon the earth; that they may breed abundantly in the earth, and be fruitful, and multiply upon the earth.

18 And Noah went forth, and his sons, and his wife, and his sons' wives with him:

19 Every beast, every creeping thing, and every fowl, *and* whatsoever creepeth upon the earth, after their kinds, went forth out of the ark.

20 And Noah builded an altar unto the LORD; and took of every clean beast, and of every clean fowl, and offered burnt offerings on the altar.

21 And the LORD smelled a sweet savour; and the LORD said in his heart, I will not again curse the ground any more for man's sake; for the imagination of man's heart *is* evil from his youth; neither will I again smite any more every thing living, as I have done.

22 While the earth remaineth, seedtime and harvest, and cold and heat, and summer and winter, and day and night shall not cease.

9 1 And God blessed Noah and his sons, and said unto them, Be fruitful, and multiply, and replenish the earth.

2 And the fear of you and the dread of you shall be upon every beast of the earth, and upon every fowl of the air, upon all that moveth *upon* the earth, and upon all the fishes of the sea; into your hand are they delivered.

3 Every moving thing that liveth shall be meat for you; even as the green herb have I given you all things.

4 But flesh with the life thereof, *which is* the blood thereof, shall ye not eat.

5 And surely your blood of your lives will I require; at the hand of every beast will I require it, and at the hand of man; at the hand of every man's brother will I require the life of man.

NEW LIVING TRANSLATION

released the dove again. 11 This time the dove returned to him in the evening with a fresh olive leaf in its beak. Then Noah knew that the floodwaters were almost gone. 12 He waited another seven days and then released the dove again. This time it did not come back.

13 Noah was now 601 years old. On the first day of the new year, ten and a half months after the flood began,* the floodwaters had almost dried up from the earth. Noah lifted back the covering of the boat and saw that the surface of the ground was drying. 14 Two more months went by,* and at last the earth was dry!

15 Then God said to Noah, 16 "Leave the boat, all of you—you and your wife, and your sons and their wives. 17 Release all the animals—the birds, the livestock, and the small animals that scurry along the ground—so they can be fruitful and multiply throughout the earth."

18 So Noah, his wife, and his sons and their wives left the boat. 19 And all of the large and small animals and birds came out of the boat, pair by pair.

20 Then Noah built an altar to the LORD, and there he sacrificed as burnt offerings the animals and birds that had been approved for that purpose.* 21 And the LORD was pleased with the aroma of the sacrifice and said to himself, "I will never again curse the ground because of the human race, even though everything they think or imagine is bent toward evil from childhood. I will never again destroy all living things. 22 As long as the earth remains, there will be planting and harvest, cold and heat, summer and winter, day and night."

God Confirms His Covenant

9 Then God blessed Noah and his sons and told them, "Be fruitful and multiply. Fill the earth. 2 All the animals of the earth, all the birds of the sky, all the small animals that scurry along the ground, and all the fish in the sea will look on you with fear and terror. I have placed them in your power. 3 I have given them to you for food, just as I have given you grain and vegetables. 4 But you must never eat any meat that still has the lifeblood in it.

5 "And I will require the blood of anyone who takes another person's life. If a wild animal kills a person, it must die. And anyone who murders a fellow human

8:13 Hebrew *On the first day of the first month;* see 7:11. **8:14** Hebrew *The twenty-seventh day of the second month arrived;* see note on 8:13. **8:20** Hebrew *every clean animal and every clean bird.*

KING JAMES VERSION

6 Whoso sheddeth man's blood, by man shall his
blood be shed: for in the image of God made he man.
7 And you, be ye fruitful, and multiply; bring forth
abundantly in the earth, and multiply therein.
8 And God spake unto Noah, and to his sons with
him, saying,
9 And I, behold, I establish my covenant with you,
and with your seed after you;
10 And with every living creature that *is* with you, of
the fowl, of the cattle, and of every beast of the earth
with you; from all that go out of the ark, to every
beast of the earth.
11 And I will establish my covenant with you; neither shall all flesh be cut off any more by the waters
of a flood; neither shall there any more be a flood to
destroy the earth.
12 And God said, This *is* the token of the covenant
which I make between me and you and every living
creature that *is* with you, for perpetual generations:
13 I do set my bow in the cloud, and it shall be for a
token of a covenant between me and the earth.
14 And it shall come to pass, when I bring a cloud
over the earth, that the bow shall be seen in the
cloud:
15 And I will remember my covenant, which *is* between me and you and every living creature of all
flesh; and the waters shall no more become a flood
to destroy all flesh.
16 And the bow shall be in the cloud; and I will look
upon it, that I may remember the everlasting covenant between God and every living creature of all
flesh that *is* upon the earth.
17 And God said unto Noah, This *is* the token of the
covenant, which I have established between me and
all flesh that *is* upon the earth.
18 And the sons of Noah, that went forth of the ark,
were Shem, and Ham, and Japheth: and Ham *is* the
father of Canaan.
19 These *are* the three sons of Noah: and of them
was the whole earth overspread.
20 And Noah began *to be* an husbandman, and he
planted a vineyard:
21 And he drank of the wine, and was drunken; and
he was uncovered within his tent.
22 And Ham, the father of Canaan, saw the nakedness of his father, and told his two brethren without.
23 And Shem and Japheth took a garment, and laid
it upon both their shoulders, and went backward,
and covered the nakedness of their father; and their
faces *were* backward, and they saw not their father's
nakedness.
24 And Noah awoke from his wine, and knew what
his younger son had done unto him.
25 And he said, Cursed *be* Canaan; a servant of servants shall he be unto his brethren.

NEW LIVING TRANSLATION

must die. 6 If anyone takes a human life, that person's
life will also be taken by human hands. For God made
human beings* in his own image. 7 Now be fruitful
and multiply, and repopulate the earth."
8 Then God told Noah and his sons, 9 "I hereby confirm my covenant with you and your descendants,
10 and with all the animals that were on the boat with
you—the birds, the livestock, and all the wild animals—every living creature on earth. 11 Yes, I am
confirming my covenant with you. Never again will
floodwaters kill all living creatures; never again will a
flood destroy the earth."
12 Then God said, "I am giving you a sign of my
covenant with you and with all living creatures, for
all generations to come. 13 I have placed my rainbow
in the clouds. It is the sign of my covenant with you
and with all the earth. 14 When I send clouds over the
earth, the rainbow will appear in the clouds, 15 and I
will remember my covenant with you and with all
living creatures. Never again will the floodwaters
destroy all life. 16 When I see the rainbow in the
clouds, I will remember the eternal covenant between God and every living creature on earth."
17 Then God said to Noah, "Yes, this rainbow is the
sign of the covenant I am confirming with all the
creatures on earth."

Noah's Sons

18 The sons of Noah who came out of the boat with
their father were Shem, Ham, and Japheth. (Ham is
the father of Canaan.) 19 From these three sons of
Noah came all the people who now populate the
earth.
20 After the flood, Noah began to cultivate the
ground, and he planted a vineyard. 21 One day he
drank some wine he had made, and he became
drunk and lay naked inside his tent. 22 Ham, the father of Canaan, saw that his father was naked and
went outside and told his brothers. 23 Then Shem
and Japheth took a robe, held it over their shoulders,
and backed into the tent to cover their father. As
they did this, they looked the other way so they
would not see him naked.
24 When Noah woke up from his stupor, he learned
what Ham, his youngest son, had done. 25 Then he
cursed Canaan, the son of Ham:

"May Canaan be cursed!
May he be the lowest of servants
to his relatives."

9:6 Or *man;* Hebrew reads *ha-adam.*

KING JAMES VERSION

26And he said, Blessed *be* the LORD God of Shem;
and Canaan shall be his servant.
27God shall enlarge Japheth, and he shall dwell in
the tents of Shem; and Canaan shall be his servant.
28And Noah lived after the flood three hundred
and fifty years.
29And all the days of Noah were nine hundred and
fifty years: and he died.

10 1Now these *are* the generations of the sons
of Noah, Shem, Ham, and Japheth: and unto
them were sons born after the flood.

2The sons of Japheth; Gomer, and Magog, and
Madai, and Javan, and Tubal, and Meshech, and
Tiras.
3And the sons of Gomer; Ashkenaz, and Riphath,
and Togarmah.
4And the sons of Javan; Elishah, and Tarshish,
Kittim, and Dodanim.
5By these were the isles of the Gentiles divided in
their lands; every one after his tongue, after their
families, in their nations.

6And the sons of Ham; Cush, and Mizraim, and
Phut, and Canaan.
7And the sons of Cush; Seba, and Havilah, and
Sabtah, and Raamah, and Sabtechah: and the sons of
Raamah; Sheba, and Dedan.
8And Cush begat Nimrod: he began to be a mighty
one in the earth.
9He was a mighty hunter before the LORD: wherefore it is said, Even as Nimrod the mighty hunter before the LORD.
10And the beginning of his kingdom was Babel,
and Erech, and Accad, and Calneh, in the land of
Shinar.
11Out of that land went forth Asshur, and builded
Nineveh, and the city Rehoboth, and Calah,
12And Resen between Nineveh and Calah: the
same *is* a great city.
13And Mizraim begat Ludim, and Anamim, and
Lehabim, and Naphtuhim,
14And Pathrusim, and Casluhim, (out of whom
came Philistim,) and Caphtorim.
15And Canaan begat Sidon his firstborn, and Heth,
16And the Jebusite, and the Amorite, and the
Girgasite,
17And the Hivite, and the Arkite, and the Sinite,
18And the Arvadite, and the Zemarite, and the
Hamathite: and afterward were the families of the
Canaanites spread abroad.
19And the border of the Canaanites was from

NEW LIVING TRANSLATION

26Then Noah said,

"May the LORD, the God of Shem, be blessed,
and may Canaan be his servant!
27 May God expand the territory of Japheth!
May Japheth share the prosperity of Shem,*
and may Canaan be his servant."

28Noah lived another 350 years after the great
flood. 29He lived 950 years, and then he died.

10 This is the account of the families of Shem,
Ham, and Japheth, the three sons of Noah.
Many children were born to them after the great
flood.

Descendants of Japheth

2The descendants of Japheth were Gomer, Magog,
Madai, Javan, Tubal, Meshech, and Tiras.
3The descendants of Gomer were Ashkenaz,
Riphath, and Togarmah.
4The descendants of Javan were Elishah, Tarshish,
Kittim, and Rodanim.* 5Their descendants
became the seafaring peoples that spread out
to various lands, each identified by its own
language, clan, and national identity.

Descendants of Ham

6The descendants of Ham were Cush, Mizraim,
Put, and Canaan.
7The descendants of Cush were Seba, Havilah,
Sabtah, Raamah, and Sabteca. The descendants
of Raamah were Sheba and Dedan.
8Cush was also the ancestor of Nimrod, who
was the first heroic warrior on earth. 9Since he
was the greatest hunter in the world,* his name
became proverbial. People would say, "This man
is like Nimrod, the greatest hunter in the world."
10He built his kingdom in the land of Babylonia,*
with the cities of Babylon, Erech, Akkad, and
Calneh. 11From there he expanded his territory
to Assyria,* building the cities of Nineveh,
Rehoboth-ir, Calah, 12and Resen (the great city
located between Nineveh and Calah).
13Mizraim was the ancestor of the Ludites,
Anamites, Lehabites, Naphtuhites, 14Pathrusites,
Casluhites, and the Caphtorites, from whom the
Philistines came.*
15Canaan's oldest son was Sidon, the ancestor of the
Sidonians. Canaan was also the ancestor of the
Hittites,* 16Jebusites, Amorites, Girgashites,
17Hivites, Arkites, Sinites, 18Arvadites, Zemarites,
and Hamathites. The Canaanite clans eventually
spread out, 19and the territory of Canaan

9:27 Hebrew *May he live in the tents of Shem.* **10:4** As in some Hebrew manuscripts and Greek version (see also 1 Chr 1:7); most Hebrew manuscripts read *Dodanim.* **10:9** Hebrew *a great hunter before the LORD;* also in 10:9b. **10:10** Hebrew *Shinar.* **10:11** Or *From that land Assyria went out.* **10:14** Hebrew *Casluhites, from whom the Philistines came, and Caphtorites.* Compare Jer 47:4; Amos 9:7. **10:15** Hebrew *ancestor of Heth.*

KING JAMES VERSION

Sidon, as thou comest to Gerar, unto Gaza; as thou
goest, unto Sodom, and Gomorrah, and Admah, and
Zeboim, even unto Lasha.
20These *are* the sons of Ham, after their families,
after their tongues, in their countries, *and* in their
nations.

21Unto Shem also, the father of all the children of
Eber, the brother of Japheth the elder, even to him
were *children* born.
22The children of Shem; Elam, and Asshur, and
Arphaxad, and Lud, and Aram.
23And the children of Aram; Uz, and Hul, and
Gether, and Mash.
24And Arphaxad begat Salah; and Salah begat
Eber.
25And unto Eber were born two sons: the name of
one *was* Peleg; for in his days was the earth divided;
and his brother's name *was* Joktan.
26And Joktan begat Almodad, and Sheleph, and
Hazarmaveth, and Jerah,
27And Hadoram, and Uzal, and Diklah,
28And Obal, and Abimael, and Sheba,
29And Ophir, and Havilah, and Jobab: all these
were the sons of Joktan.
30And their dwelling was from Mesha, as thou
goest unto Sephar a mount of the east.
31These *are* the sons of Shem, after their families,
after their tongues, in their lands, after their nations.

32These *are* the families of the sons of Noah, after
their generations, in their nations: and by these were
the nations divided in the earth after the flood.

11 1And the whole earth was of one language, and
of one speech.
2And it came to pass, as they journeyed from the
east, that they found a plain in the land of Shinar; and
they dwelt there.
3And they said one to another, Go to, let us make
brick, and burn them throughly. And they had brick
for stone, and slime had they for mortar.
4And they said, Go to, let us build us a city and a
tower, whose top *may reach* unto heaven; and let us
make us a name, lest we be scattered abroad upon
the face of the whole earth.
5And the LORD came down to see the city and the
tower, which the children of men builded.
6And the LORD said, Behold, the people *is* one, and
they have all one language; and this they begin to do:
and now nothing will be restrained from them,
which they have imagined to do.
7Go to, let us go down, and there confound their

NEW LIVING TRANSLATION

extended from Sidon in the north to Gerar and
Gaza in the south, and east as far as Sodom,
Gomorrah, Admah, and Zeboiim, near Lasha.
20These were the descendants of Ham, identified
by clan, language, territory, and national identity.

Descendants of Shem

21Sons were also born to Shem, the older brother
of Japheth.* Shem was the ancestor of all the
descendants of Eber.
22The descendants of Shem were Elam, Asshur,
Arphaxad, Lud, and Aram.
23The descendants of Aram were Uz, Hul, Gether,
and Mash.
24Arphaxad was the father of Shelah,* and Shelah
was the father of Eber.
25Eber had two sons. The first was named Peleg
(which means "division"), for during his lifetime
the people of the world were divided into
different language groups. His brother's name
was Joktan.
26Joktan was the ancestor of Almodad, Sheleph,
Hazarmaveth, Jerah, 27Hadoram, Uzal, Diklah,
28Obal, Abimael, Sheba, 29Ophir, Havilah, and
Jobab. All these were descendants of Joktan.
30The territory they occupied extended from
Mesha all the way to Sephar in the eastern
mountains.
31These were the descendants of Shem, identified by
clan, language, territory, and national identity.

Conclusion

32These are the clans that descended from Noah's
sons, arranged by nation according to their lines of
descent. All the nations of the earth descended from
these clans after the great flood.

The Tower of Babel

11 At one time all the people of the world spoke
the same language and used the same words.
2As the people migrated to the east, they found a
plain in the land of Babylonia* and settled there.
3They began saying to each other, "Let's make
bricks and harden them with fire." (In this region
bricks were used instead of stone, and tar was used
for mortar.) 4Then they said, "Come, let's build a
great city for ourselves with a tower that reaches into
the sky. This will make us famous and keep us from
being scattered all over the world."
5But the LORD came down to look at the city and
the tower the people were building. 6"Look!" he said.
"The people are united, and they all speak the same
language. After this, nothing they set out to do will
be impossible for them! 7Come, let's go down and

10:21 Or *Shem, whose older brother was Japheth.* **10:24** Greek version reads *Arphaxad was the father of Cainan, Cainan was the father of Shelah.* Compare Luke 3:36. **11:2** Hebrew *Shinar.*

KING JAMES VERSION

language, that they may not understand one another's speech.
8So the LORD scattered them abroad from thence
upon the face of all the earth: and they left off to
build the city.
9Therefore is the name of it called Babel; because
the LORD did there confound the language of all the
earth: and from thence did the LORD scatter them
abroad upon the face of all the earth.

10These *are* the generations of Shem: Shem *was*
an hundred years old, and begat Arphaxad two years
after the flood:
11And Shem lived after he begat Arphaxad five
hundred years, and begat sons and daughters.
12And Arphaxad lived five and thirty years, and
begat Salah:
13And Arphaxad lived after he begat Salah four
hundred and three years, and begat sons and
daughters.
14And Salah lived thirty years, and begat Eber:
15And Salah lived after he begat Eber four hundred and three years, and begat sons and daughters.
16And Eber lived four and thirty years, and begat
Peleg:
17And Eber lived after he begat Peleg four hundred and thirty years, and begat sons and daughters.
18And Peleg lived thirty years, and begat Reu:
19And Peleg lived after he begat Reu two hundred
and nine years, and begat sons and daughters.
20And Reu lived two and thirty years, and begat
Serug:
21And Reu lived after he begat Serug two hundred
and seven years, and begat sons and daughters.
22And Serug lived thirty years, and begat Nahor:
23And Serug lived after he begat Nahor two hundred years, and begat sons and daughters.
24And Nahor lived nine and twenty years, and
begat Terah:
25And Nahor lived after he begat Terah an
hundred and nineteen years, and begat sons and
daughters.
26And Terah lived seventy years, and begat Abram,
Nahor, and Haran.

27Now these *are* the generations of Terah: Terah
begat Abram, Nahor, and Haran; and Haran begat
Lot.
28And Haran died before his father Terah in the
land of his nativity, in Ur of the Chaldees.

NEW LIVING TRANSLATION

confuse the people with different languages. Then
they won't be able to understand each other."
8In that way, the LORD scattered them all over the
world, and they stopped building the city. 9That is
why the city was called Babel,* because that is where
the LORD confused the people with different languages. In this way he scattered them all over the
world.

The Line of Descent from Shem to Abram
10This is the account of Shem's family.

Two years after the great flood, when Shem
was 100 years old, he became the father of*
Arphaxad. 11After the birth of* Arphaxad, Shem
lived another 500 years and had other sons and
daughters.
12When Arphaxad was 35 years old, he became
the father of Shelah. 13After the birth of Shelah,
Arphaxad lived another 403 years and had other
sons and daughters.*
14When Shelah was 30 years old, he became the
father of Eber. 15After the birth of Eber, Shelah
lived another 403 years and had other sons and
daughters.
16When Eber was 34 years old, he became the
father of Peleg. 17After the birth of Peleg, Eber
lived another 430 years and had other sons and
daughters.
18When Peleg was 30 years old, he became the
father of Reu. 19After the birth of Reu, Peleg lived
another 209 years and had other sons and
daughters.
20When Reu was 32 years old, he became the father
of Serug. 21After the birth of Serug, Reu lived
another 207 years and had other sons and
daughters.
22When Serug was 30 years old, he became the
father of Nahor. 23After the birth of Nahor, Serug
lived another 200 years and had other sons and
daughters.
24When Nahor was 29 years old, he became the
father of Terah. 25After the birth of Terah, Nahor
lived another 119 years and had other sons and
daughters.
26After Terah was 70 years old, he became the
father of Abram, Nahor, and Haran.

The Family of Terah
27This is the account of Terah's family. Terah was the
father of Abram, Nahor, and Haran; and Haran was
the father of Lot. 28But Haran died in Ur of the

11:9 Or *Babylon*. *Babel* sounds like a Hebrew term that means "confusion." **11:10** Or *the ancestor of;* also in 11:12, 14, 16, 18, 20, 22, 24. **11:11** Or *the birth of this ancestor of;* also in 11:13, 15, 17, 19, 21, 23, 25. **11:12-13** Greek version reads [12]*When Arphaxad was 135 years old, he became the father of Cainan.* [13]*After the birth of Cainan, Arphaxad lived another 430 years and had other sons and daughters, and then he died. When Cainan was 130 years old, he became the father of Shelah. After the birth of Shelah, Cainan lived another 330 years and had other sons and daughters, and then he died.* Compare Luke 3:35-36.

KING JAMES VERSION

29 And Abram and Nahor took them wives: the name of Abram's wife *was* Sarai; and the name of Nahor's wife, Milcah, the daughter of Haran, the father of Milcah, and the father of Iscah.

30 But Sarai was barren; she *had* no child.

31 And Terah took Abram his son, and Lot the son of Haran his son's son, and Sarai his daughter in law, his son Abram's wife; and they went forth with them from Ur of the Chaldees, to go into the land of Canaan; and they came unto Haran, and dwelt there.

32 And the days of Terah were two hundred and five years: and Terah died in Haran.

12 1 Now the LORD had said unto Abram, Get thee out of thy country, and from thy kindred, and from thy father's house, unto a land that I will shew thee:

2 And I will make of thee a great nation, and I will bless thee, and make thy name great; and thou shalt be a blessing:

3 And I will bless them that bless thee, and curse him that curseth thee: and in thee shall all families of the earth be blessed.

4 So Abram departed, as the LORD had spoken unto him; and Lot went with him: and Abram *was* seventy and five years old when he departed out of Haran.

5 And Abram took Sarai his wife, and Lot his brother's son, and all their substance that they had gathered, and the souls that they had gotten in Haran; and they went forth to go into the land of Canaan; and into the land of Canaan they came.

6 And Abram passed through the land unto the place of Sichem, unto the plain of Moreh. And the Canaanite *was* then in the land.

7 And the LORD appeared unto Abram, and said, Unto thy seed will I give this land: and there builded he an altar unto the LORD, who appeared unto him.

8 And he removed from thence unto a mountain on the east of Bethel, and pitched his tent, *having* Bethel on the west, and Hai on the east: and there he builded an altar unto the LORD, and called upon the name of the LORD.

9 And Abram journeyed, going on still toward the south.

10 And there was a famine in the land: and Abram went down into Egypt to sojourn there; for the famine *was* grievous in the land.

11 And it came to pass, when he was come near to enter into Egypt, that he said unto Sarai his wife, Behold now, I know that thou *art* a fair woman to look upon:

12 Therefore it shall come to pass, when the Egyptians shall see thee, that they shall say, This *is* his wife: and they will kill me, but they will save thee alive.

NEW LIVING TRANSLATION

Chaldeans, the land of his birth, while his father, Terah, was still living. 29 Meanwhile, Abram and Nahor both married. The name of Abram's wife was Sarai, and the name of Nahor's wife was Milcah. (Milcah and her sister Iscah were daughters of Nahor's brother Haran.) 30 But Sarai was unable to become pregnant and had no children.

31 One day Terah took his son Abram, his daughter-in-law Sarai (his son Abram's wife), and his grandson Lot (his son Haran's child) and moved away from Ur of the Chaldeans. He was headed for the land of Canaan, but they stopped at Haran and settled there. 32 Terah lived for 205 years* and died while still in Haran.

The Call of Abram

12 The LORD had said to Abram, "Leave your native country, your relatives, and your father's family, and go to the land that I will show you. 2 I will make you into a great nation. I will bless you and make you famous, and you will be a blessing to others. 3 I will bless those who bless you and curse those who treat you with contempt. All the families on earth will be blessed through you."

4 So Abram departed as the LORD had instructed, and Lot went with him. Abram was seventy-five years old when he left Haran. 5 He took his wife, Sarai, his nephew Lot, and all his wealth—his livestock and all the people he had taken into his household at Haran—and headed for the land of Canaan. When they arrived in Canaan, 6 Abram traveled through the land as far as Shechem. There he set up camp beside the oak of Moreh. At that time, the area was inhabited by Canaanites.

7 Then the LORD appeared to Abram and said, "I will give this land to your descendants.*" And Abram built an altar there and dedicated it to the LORD, who had appeared to him. 8 After that, Abram traveled south and set up camp in the hill country, with Bethel to the west and Ai to the east. There he built another altar and dedicated it to the LORD, and he worshiped the LORD. 9 Then Abram continued traveling south by stages toward the Negev.

Abram and Sarai in Egypt

10 At that time a severe famine struck the land of Canaan, forcing Abram to go down to Egypt, where he lived as a foreigner. 11 As he was approaching the border of Egypt, Abram said to his wife, Sarai, "Look, you are a very beautiful woman. 12 When the Egyptians see you, they will say, 'This is his wife. Let's kill

11:32 Some ancient versions read *145 years;* compare 11:26 and 12:4.
12:7 Hebrew *seed.*

KING JAMES VERSION

13 Say, I pray thee, thou *art* my sister: that it may be well with me for thy sake; and my soul shall live because of thee.

14 And it came to pass, that, when Abram was come into Egypt, the Egyptians beheld the woman that she *was* very fair.

15 The princes also of Pharaoh saw her, and commended her before Pharaoh: and the woman was taken into Pharaoh's house.

16 And he entreated Abram well for her sake: and he had sheep, and oxen, and he asses, and menservants, and maidservants, and she asses, and camels.

17 And the LORD plagued Pharaoh and his house with great plagues because of Sarai Abram's wife.

18 And Pharaoh called Abram, and said, What *is* this *that* thou hast done unto me? why didst thou not tell me that she *was* thy wife?

19 Why saidst thou, She *is* my sister? so I might have taken her to me to wife: now therefore behold thy wife, take *her*, and go thy way.

20 And Pharaoh commanded *his* men concerning him: and they sent him away, and his wife, and all that he had.

13 1 And Abram went up out of Egypt, he, and his wife, and all that he had, and Lot with him, into the south.

2 And Abram *was* very rich in cattle, in silver, and in gold.

3 And he went on his journeys from the south even to Bethel, unto the place where his tent had been at the beginning, between Bethel and Hai;

4 Unto the place of the altar, which he had made there at the first: and there Abram called on the name of the LORD.

5 And Lot also, which went with Abram, had flocks, and herds, and tents.

6 And the land was not able to bear them, that they might dwell together: for their substance was great, so that they could not dwell together.

7 And there was a strife between the herdmen of Abram's cattle and the herdmen of Lot's cattle: and the Canaanite and the Perizzite dwelled then in the land.

8 And Abram said unto Lot, Let there be no strife, I pray thee, between me and thee, and between my herdmen and thy herdmen; for we *be* brethren.

9 *Is* not the whole land before thee? separate thyself, I pray thee, from me: if *thou wilt take* the left hand, then I will go to the right; or if *thou depart* to the right hand, then I will go to the left.

10 And Lot lifted up his eyes, and beheld all the plain of Jordan, that it *was* well watered every where, before the LORD destroyed Sodom and Gomorrah, *even* as the garden of the LORD, like the land of Egypt, as thou comest unto Zoar.

11 Then Lot chose him all the plain of Jordan; and

NEW LIVING TRANSLATION

him; then we can have her!' 13 So please tell them you are my sister. Then they will spare my life and treat me well because of their interest in you."

14 And sure enough, when Abram arrived in Egypt, everyone noticed Sarai's beauty. 15 When the palace officials saw her, they sang her praises to Pharaoh, their king, and Sarai was taken into his palace. 16 Then Pharaoh gave Abram many gifts because of her—sheep, goats, cattle, male and female donkeys, male and female servants, and camels.

17 But the LORD sent terrible plagues upon Pharaoh and his household because of Sarai, Abram's wife. 18 So Pharaoh summoned Abram and accused him sharply. "What have you done to me?" he demanded. "Why didn't you tell me she was your wife? 19 Why did you say, 'She is my sister,' and allow me to take her as my wife? Now then, here is your wife. Take her and get out of here!" 20 Pharaoh ordered some of his men to escort them, and he sent Abram out of the country, along with his wife and all his possessions.

Abram and Lot Separate

13 So Abram left Egypt and traveled north into the Negev, along with his wife and Lot and all that they owned. 2 (Abram was very rich in livestock, silver, and gold.) 3 From the Negev, they continued traveling by stages toward Bethel, and they pitched their tents between Bethel and Ai, where they had camped before. 4 This was the same place where Abram had built the altar, and there he worshiped the LORD again.

5 Lot, who was traveling with Abram, had also become very wealthy with flocks of sheep and goats, herds of cattle, and many tents. 6 But the land could not support both Abram and Lot with all their flocks and herds living so close together. 7 So disputes broke out between the herdsmen of Abram and Lot. (At that time Canaanites and Perizzites were also living in the land.)

8 Finally Abram said to Lot, "Let's not allow this conflict to come between us or our herdsmen. After all, we are close relatives! 9 The whole countryside is open to you. Take your choice of any section of the land you want, and we will separate. If you want the land to the left, then I'll take the land on the right. If you prefer the land on the right, then I'll go to the left."

10 Lot took a long look at the fertile plains of the Jordan Valley in the direction of Zoar. The whole area was well watered everywhere, like the garden of the LORD or the beautiful land of Egypt. (This was before the LORD destroyed Sodom and Gomorrah.) 11 Lot chose for himself the whole Jordan Valley to

KING JAMES VERSION

Lot journeyed east: and they separated themselves
the one from the other.
12 Abram dwelled in the land of Canaan, and Lot
dwelled in the cities of the plain, and pitched *his* tent
toward Sodom.
13 But the men of Sodom *were* wicked and sinners
before the LORD exceedingly.
14 And the LORD said unto Abram, after that Lot
was separated from him, Lift up now thine eyes, and
look from the place where thou art northward, and
southward, and eastward, and westward:
15 For all the land which thou seest, to thee will I
give it, and to thy seed for ever.
16 And I will make thy seed as the dust of the earth:
so that if a man can number the dust of the earth,
then shall thy seed also be numbered.
17 Arise, walk through the land in the length of it
and in the breadth of it; for I will give it unto thee.
18 Then Abram removed *his* tent, and came and
dwelt in the plain of Mamre, which *is* in Hebron, and
built there an altar unto the LORD.

14 1 And it came to pass in the days of Amraphel
king of Shinar, Arioch king of Ellasar, Chedorlaomer king of Elam, and Tidal king of nations;
2 *That these* made war with Bera king of Sodom,
and with Birsha king of Gomorrah, Shinab king of
Admah, and Shemeber king of Zeboiim, and the king
of Bela, which is Zoar.
3 All these were joined together in the vale of
Siddim, which is the Salt Sea.
4 Twelve years they served Chedorlaomer, and in
the thirteenth year they rebelled.
5 And in the fourteenth year came Chedorlaomer,
and the kings that *were* with him, and smote the
Rephaims in Ashteroth Karnaim, and the Zuzims
in Ham, and the Emims in Shaveh Kiriathaim,
6 And the Horites in their mount Seir, unto El-
paran, which *is* by the wilderness.
7 And they returned, and came to En-mishpat,
which *is* Kadesh, and smote all the country of the
Amalekites, and also the Amorites, that dwelt in
Hazezon-tamar.
8 And there went out the king of Sodom, and the
king of Gomorrah, and the king of Admah, and the
king of Zeboiim, and the king of Bela (the same *is*
Zoar;) and they joined battle with them in the vale of
Siddim;
9 With Chedorlaomer the king of Elam, and with
Tidal king of nations, and Amraphel king of Shinar,
and Arioch king of Ellasar; four kings with five.
10 And the vale of Siddim *was full of* slimepits; and
the kings of Sodom and Gomorrah fled, and fell
there; and they that remained fled to the mountain.
11 And they took all the goods of Sodom and Gomorrah, and all their victuals, and went their way.

NEW LIVING TRANSLATION

the east of them. He went there with his flocks and
servants and parted company with his uncle Abram.
12 So Abram settled in the land of Canaan, and Lot
moved his tents to a place near Sodom and settled
among the cities of the plain. 13 But the people of this
area were extremely wicked and constantly sinned
against the LORD.
14 After Lot had gone, the LORD said to Abram,
"Look as far as you can see in every direction—north
and south, east and west. 15 I am giving all this land,
as far as you can see, to you and your descendants* as
a permanent possession. 16 And I will give you so
many descendants that, like the dust of the earth,
they cannot be counted! 17 Go and walk through the
land in every direction, for I am giving it to you."
18 So Abram moved his camp to Hebron and settled
near the oak grove belonging to Mamre. There he
built another altar to the LORD.

Abram Rescues Lot

14 About this time war broke out in the region.
King Amraphel of Babylonia,* King Arioch of
Ellasar, King Kedorlaomer of Elam, and King Tidal
of Goiim 2 fought against King Bera of Sodom, King
Birsha of Gomorrah, King Shinab of Admah, King
Shemeber of Zeboiim, and the king of Bela (also
called Zoar).
3 This second group of kings joined forces in
Siddim Valley (that is, the valley of the Dead Sea*).
4 For twelve years they had been subject to King
Kedorlaomer, but in the thirteenth year they rebelled
against him.
5 One year later Kedorlaomer and his allies arrived
and defeated the Rephaites at Ashteroth-karnaim,
the Zuzites at Ham, the Emites at Shaveh-kiriathaim,
6 and the Horites at Mount Seir, as far as El-paran at
the edge of the wilderness. 7 Then they turned back
and came to En-mishpat (now called Kadesh) and
conquered all the territory of the Amalekites, and
also the Amorites living in Hazazon-tamar.
8 Then the rebel kings of Sodom, Gomorrah,
Admah, Zeboiim, and Bela (also called Zoar) prepared for battle in the valley of the Dead Sea.* 9 They
fought against King Kedorlaomer of Elam, King
Tidal of Goiim, King Amraphel of Babylonia, and
King Arioch of Ellasar—four kings against five. 10 As
it happened, the valley of the Dead Sea was filled
with tar pits. And as the army of the kings of Sodom
and Gomorrah fled, some fell into the tar pits, while
the rest escaped into the mountains. 11 The victorious invaders then plundered Sodom and Gomorrah
and headed for home, taking with them all the spoils

13:15 Hebrew *seed;* also in 13:16. **14:1** Hebrew *Shinar;* also in 14:9.
14:3 Hebrew *Salt Sea.* **14:8** Hebrew *Siddim Valley* (see 14:3); also in 14:10.

KING JAMES VERSION

12 And they took Lot, Abram's brother's son, who dwelt in Sodom, and his goods, and departed.

13 And there came one that had escaped, and told Abram the Hebrew; for he dwelt in the plain of Mamre the Amorite, brother of Eshcol, and brother of Aner: and these *were* confederate with Abram.

14 And when Abram heard that his brother was taken captive, he armed his trained *servants,* born in his own house, three hundred and eighteen, and pursued *them* unto Dan.

15 And he divided himself against them, he and his servants, by night, and smote them, and pursued them unto Hobah, which *is* on the left hand of Damascus.

16 And he brought back all the goods, and also brought again his brother Lot, and his goods, and the women also, and the people.

17 And the king of Sodom went out to meet him after his return from the slaughter of Chedorlaomer, and of the kings that *were* with him, at the valley of Shaveh, which *is* the king's dale.

18 And Melchizedek king of Salem brought forth bread and wine: and he *was* the priest of the most high God.

19 And he blessed him, and said, Blessed *be* Abram of the most high God, possessor of heaven and earth:

20 And blessed be the most high God, which hath delivered thine enemies into thy hand. And he gave him tithes of all.

21 And the king of Sodom said unto Abram, Give me the persons, and take the goods to thyself.

22 And Abram said to the king of Sodom, I have lift up mine hand unto the LORD, the most high God, the possessor of heaven and earth,

23 That I will not *take* from a thread even to a shoelatchet, and that I will not take any thing that *is* thine, lest thou shouldest say, I have made Abram rich:

24 Save only that which the young men have eaten, and the portion of the men which went with me, Aner, Eshcol, and Mamre; let them take their portion.

15 1 After these things the word of the LORD came unto Abram in a vision, saying, Fear not, Abram: I *am* thy shield, *and* thy exceeding great reward.

2 And Abram said, Lord GOD, what wilt thou give me, seeing I go childless, and the steward of my house *is* this Eliezer of Damascus?

NEW LIVING TRANSLATION

of war and the food supplies. 12 They also captured Lot—Abram's nephew who lived in Sodom—and carried off everything he owned.

13 But one of Lot's men escaped and reported everything to Abram the Hebrew, who was living near the oak grove belonging to Mamre the Amorite. Mamre and his relatives, Eshcol and Aner, were Abram's allies.

14 When Abram heard that his nephew Lot had been captured, he mobilized the 318 trained men who had been born into his household. Then he pursued Kedorlaomer's army until he caught up with them at Dan. 15 There he divided his men and attacked during the night. Kedorlaomer's army fled, but Abram chased them as far as Hobah, north of Damascus. 16 Abram recovered all the goods that had been taken, and he brought back his nephew Lot with his possessions and all the women and other captives.

Melchizedek Blesses Abram

17 After Abram returned from his victory over Kedorlaomer and all his allies, the king of Sodom went out to meet him in the valley of Shaveh (that is, the King's Valley).

18 And Melchizedek, the king of Salem and a priest of God Most High,* brought Abram some bread and wine. 19 Melchizedek blessed Abram with this blessing:

"Blessed be Abram by God Most High,
Creator of heaven and earth.
20 And blessed be God Most High,
who has defeated your enemies for you."

Then Abram gave Melchizedek a tenth of all the goods he had recovered.

21 The king of Sodom said to Abram, "Give back my people who were captured. But you may keep for yourself all the goods you have recovered."

22 Abram replied to the king of Sodom, "I solemnly swear to the LORD, God Most High, Creator of heaven and earth, 23 that I will not take so much as a single thread or sandal thong from what belongs to you. Otherwise you might say, 'I am the one who made Abram rich.' 24 I will accept only what my young warriors have already eaten, and I request that you give a fair share of the goods to my allies—Aner, Eshcol, and Mamre."

The LORD's Covenant Promise to Abram

15 Some time later, the LORD spoke to Abram in a vision and said to him, "Do not be afraid, Abram, for I will protect you, and your reward will be great."

2 But Abram replied, "O Sovereign LORD, what good are all your blessings when I don't even have a

14:18 Hebrew *El-Elyon;* also in 14:19, 20, 22.

KING JAMES VERSION

3 And Abram said, Behold, to me thou hast given no seed: and, lo, one born in my house is mine heir.

4 And, behold, the word of the LORD *came* unto him, saying, This shall not be thine heir; but he that shall come forth out of thine own bowels shall be thine heir.

5 And he brought him forth abroad, and said, Look now toward heaven, and tell the stars, if thou be able to number them: and he said unto him, So shall thy seed be.

6 And he believed in the LORD; and he counted it to him for righteousness.

7 And he said unto him, I *am* the LORD that brought thee out of Ur of the Chaldees, to give thee this land to inherit it.

8 And he said, Lord GOD, whereby shall I know that I shall inherit it?

9 And he said unto him, Take me an heifer of three years old, and a she goat of three years old, and a ram of three years old, and a turtledove, and a young pigeon.

10 And he took unto him all these, and divided them in the midst, and laid each piece one against another: but the birds divided he not.

11 And when the fowls came down upon the carcases, Abram drove them away.

12 And when the sun was going down, a deep sleep fell upon Abram; and, lo, an horror of great darkness fell upon him.

13 And he said unto Abram, Know of a surety that thy seed shall be a stranger in a land *that is* not theirs, and shall serve them; and they shall afflict them four hundred years;

14 And also that nation, whom they shall serve, will I judge: and afterward shall they come out with great substance.

15 And thou shalt go to thy fathers in peace; thou shalt be buried in a good old age.

16 But in the fourth generation they shall come hither again: for the iniquity of the Amorites *is* not yet full.

17 And it came to pass, that, when the sun went down, and it was dark, behold a smoking furnace, and a burning lamp that passed between those pieces.

18 In the same day the LORD made a covenant with Abram, saying, Unto thy seed have I given this land, from the river of Egypt unto the great river, the river Euphrates:

19 The Kenites, and the Kenizzites, and the Kadmonites,

20 And the Hittites, and the Perizzites, and the Rephaims,

21 And the Amorites, and the Canaanites, and the Girgashites, and the Jebusites.

NEW LIVING TRANSLATION

son? Since you've given me no children, Eliezer of Damascus, a servant in my household, will inherit all my wealth. 3 You have given me no descendants of my own, so one of my servants will be my heir."

4 Then the LORD said to him, "No, your servant will not be your heir, for you will have a son of your own who will be your heir." 5 Then the LORD took Abram outside and said to him, "Look up into the sky and count the stars if you can. That's how many descendants you will have!"

6 And Abram believed the LORD, and the LORD counted him as righteous because of his faith.

7 Then the LORD told him, "I am the LORD who brought you out of Ur of the Chaldeans to give you this land as your possession."

8 But Abram replied, "O Sovereign LORD, how can I be sure that I will actually possess it?"

9 The LORD told him, "Bring me a three-year-old heifer, a three-year-old female goat, a three-year-old ram, a turtledove, and a young pigeon." 10 So Abram presented all these to him and killed them. Then he cut each animal down the middle and laid the halves side by side; he did not, however, cut the birds in half. 11 Some vultures swooped down to eat the carcasses, but Abram chased them away.

12 As the sun was going down, Abram fell into a deep sleep, and a terrifying darkness came down over him. 13 Then the LORD said to Abram, "You can be sure that your descendants will be strangers in a foreign land, where they will be oppressed as slaves for 400 years. 14 But I will punish the nation that enslaves them, and in the end they will come away with great wealth. 15 (As for you, you will die in peace and be buried at a ripe old age.) 16 After four generations your descendants will return here to this land, for the sins of the Amorites do not yet warrant their destruction."

17 After the sun went down and darkness fell, Abram saw a smoking firepot and a flaming torch pass between the halves of the carcasses. 18 So the LORD made a covenant with Abram that day and said, "I have given this land to your descendants, all the way from the border of Egypt* to the great Euphrates River—19 the land now occupied by the Kenites, Kenizzites, Kadmonites, 20 Hittites, Perizzites, Rephaites, 21 Amorites, Canaanites, Girgashites, and Jebusites."

15:18 Hebrew *the river of Egypt,* referring either to an eastern branch of the Nile River or to the Brook of Egypt in the Sinai (see Num 34:5).

KING JAMES VERSION

16 1 Now Sarai Abram's wife bare him no children: and she had an handmaid, an Egyptian, whose name *was* Hagar.

2 And Sarai said unto Abram, Behold now, the LORD hath restrained me from bearing: I pray thee, go in unto my maid; it may be that I may obtain children by her. And Abram hearkened to the voice of Sarai.

3 And Sarai Abram's wife took Hagar her maid the Egyptian, after Abram had dwelt ten years in the land of Canaan, and gave her to her husband Abram to be his wife.

4 And he went in unto Hagar, and she conceived: and when she saw that she had conceived, her mistress was despised in her eyes.

5 And Sarai said unto Abram, My wrong *be* upon thee: I have given my maid into thy bosom; and when she saw that she had conceived, I was despised in her eyes: the LORD judge between me and thee.

6 But Abram said unto Sarai, Behold, thy maid *is* in thy hand; do to her as it pleaseth thee. And when Sarai dealt hardly with her, she fled from her face.

7 And the angel of the LORD found her by a fountain of water in the wilderness, by the fountain in the way to Shur.

8 And he said, Hagar, Sarai's maid, whence camest thou? and whither wilt thou go? And she said, I flee from the face of my mistress Sarai.

9 And the angel of the LORD said unto her, Return to thy mistress, and submit thyself under her hands.

10 And the angel of the LORD said unto her, I will multiply thy seed exceedingly, that it shall not be numbered for multitude.

11 And the angel of the LORD said unto her, Behold, thou *art* with child, and shalt bear a son, and shalt call his name Ishmael; because the LORD hath heard thy affliction.

12 And he will be a wild man; his hand *will be* against every man, and every man's hand against him; and he shall dwell in the presence of all his brethren.

13 And she called the name of the LORD that spake unto her, Thou God seest me: for she said, Have I also here looked after him that seeth me?

14 Wherefore the well was called Beer-lahai-roi; behold, *it is* between Kadesh and Bered.

15 And Hagar bare Abram a son: and Abram called his son's name, which Hagar bare, Ishmael.

16 And Abram *was* fourscore and six years old, when Hagar bare Ishmael to Abram.

17 1 And when Abram was ninety years old and nine, the LORD appeared to Abram, and said unto him, I *am* the Almighty God; walk before me, and be thou perfect.

2 And I will make my covenant between me and thee, and will multiply thee exceedingly.

NEW LIVING TRANSLATION

The Birth of Ishmael

16 Now Sarai, Abram's wife, had not been able to
bear children for him. But she had an Egyptian servant named Hagar.
2 So Sarai said to Abram,
"The LORD has prevented me from having children.
Go and sleep with my servant. Perhaps I can have
children through her." And Abram agreed with
Sarai's proposal.
3 So Sarai, Abram's wife, took Hagar
the Egyptian servant and gave her to Abram as a wife.
(This happened ten years after Abram had settled in
the land of Canaan.)

4 So Abram had sexual relations with Hagar, and
she became pregnant. But when Hagar knew she was
pregnant, she began to treat her mistress, Sarai, with
contempt.
5 Then Sarai said to Abram, "This is all
your fault! I put my servant into your arms, but now
that she's pregnant she treats me with contempt. The
LORD will show who's wrong—you or me!"

6 Abram replied, "Look, she is your servant, so deal
with her as you see fit." Then Sarai treated Hagar so
harshly that she finally ran away.

7 The angel of the LORD found Hagar beside a
spring of water in the wilderness, along the road to
Shur.
8 The angel said to her, "Hagar, Sarai's servant,
where have you come from, and where are you
going?"

"I'm running away from my mistress, Sarai," she
replied.

9 The angel of the LORD said to her, "Return to your
mistress, and submit to her authority."
10 Then he
added, "I will give you more descendants than you
can count."

11 And the angel also said, "You are now pregnant
and will give birth to a son. You are to name him
Ishmael (which means 'God hears'), for the LORD has
heard your cry of distress.
12 This son of yours will be
a wild man, as untamed as a wild donkey! He will
raise his fist against everyone, and everyone will be
against him. Yes, he will live in open hostility against
all his relatives."

13 Thereafter, Hagar used another name to refer to
the LORD, who had spoken to her. She said, "You are
the God who sees me."* She also said, "Have I truly
seen the One who sees me?"
14 So that well was
named Beer-lahai-roi (which means "well of the Living One who sees me"). It can still be found between
Kadesh and Bered.

15 So Hagar gave Abram a son, and Abram named
him Ishmael.
16 Abram was eighty-six years old when
Ishmael was born.

Abram Is Named Abraham

17 When Abram was ninety-nine years old, the
LORD appeared to him and said, "I am El-
Shaddai—'God Almighty.' Serve me faithfully and
live a blameless life.
2 I will make a covenant with you,

16:13 Hebrew *El-roi*.

KING JAMES VERSION

3And Abram fell on his face: and God talked with him, saying,

4As for me, behold, my covenant *is* with thee, and thou shalt be a father of many nations.

5Neither shall thy name any more be called Abram, but thy name shall be Abraham; for a father of many nations have I made thee.

6And I will make thee exceeding fruitful, and I will make nations of thee, and kings shall come out of thee.

7And I will establish my covenant between me and thee and thy seed after thee in their generations for an everlasting covenant, to be a God unto thee, and to thy seed after thee.

8And I will give unto thee, and to thy seed after thee, the land wherein thou art a stranger, all the land of Canaan, for an everlasting possession; and I will be their God.

9And God said unto Abraham, Thou shalt keep my covenant therefore, thou, and thy seed after thee in their generations.

10This *is* my covenant, which ye shall keep, between me and you and thy seed after thee; Every man child among you shall be circumcised.

11And ye shall circumcise the flesh of your foreskin; and it shall be a token of the covenant betwixt me and you.

12And he that is eight days old shall be circumcised among you, every man child in your generations, he that is born in the house, or bought with money of any stranger, which *is* not of thy seed.

13He that is born in thy house, and he that is bought with thy money, must needs be circumcised: and my covenant shall be in your flesh for an everlasting covenant.

14And the uncircumcised man child whose flesh of his foreskin is not circumcised, that soul shall be cut off from his people; he hath broken my covenant.

15And God said unto Abraham, As for Sarai thy wife, thou shalt not call her name Sarai, but Sarah *shall* her name *be.*

16And I will bless her, and give thee a son also of her: yea, I will bless her, and she shall be *a mother* of nations; kings of people shall be of her.

17Then Abraham fell upon his face, and laughed, and said in his heart, Shall *a child* be born unto him that is an hundred years old? and shall Sarah, that is ninety years old, bear?

18And Abraham said unto God, O that Ishmael might live before thee!

19And God said, Sarah thy wife shall bear thee a son indeed; and thou shalt call his name Isaac: and

NEW LIVING TRANSLATION

by which I will guarantee to give you countless descendants."

3At this, Abram fell face down on the ground. Then God said to him, 4"This is my covenant with you: I will make you the father of a multitude of nations! 5What's more, I am changing your name. It will no longer be Abram. Instead, you will be called Abraham,* for you will be the father of many nations. 6I will make you extremely fruitful. Your descendants will become many nations, and kings will be among them!

7"I will confirm my covenant with you and your descendants* after you, from generation to generation. This is the everlasting covenant: I will always be your God and the God of your descendants after you. 8And I will give the entire land of Canaan, where you now live as a foreigner, to you and your descendants. It will be their possession forever, and I will be their God."

The Mark of the Covenant

9Then God said to Abraham, "Your responsibility is to obey the terms of the covenant. You and all your descendants have this continual responsibility. 10This is the covenant that you and your descendants must keep: Each male among you must be circumcised. 11You must cut off the flesh of your foreskin as a sign of the covenant between me and you. 12From generation to generation, every male child must be circumcised on the eighth day after his birth. This applies not only to members of your family but also to the servants born in your household and the foreign-born servants whom you have purchased. 13All must be circumcised. Your bodies will bear the mark of my everlasting covenant. 14Any male who fails to be circumcised will be cut off from the covenant family for breaking the covenant."

Sarai Is Named Sarah

15Then God said to Abraham, "Regarding Sarai, your wife—her name will no longer be Sarai. From now on her name will be Sarah.* 16And I will bless her and give you a son from her! Yes, I will bless her richly, and she will become the mother of many nations. Kings of nations will be among her descendants."

17Then Abraham bowed down to the ground, but he laughed to himself in disbelief. "How could I become a father at the age of 100?" he thought. "And how can Sarah have a baby when she is ninety years old?" 18So Abraham said to God, "May Ishmael live under your special blessing!"

19But God replied, "No—Sarah, your wife, will give birth to a son for you. You will name him Isaac,* and I

17:5 *Abram* means "exalted father"; *Abraham* sounds like a Hebrew term that means "father of many." **17:7** Hebrew *seed;* also in 17:7b, 8, 9, 10, 19. **17:15** *Sarai* and *Sarah* both mean "princess"; the change in spelling may reflect the difference in dialect between Ur and Canaan. **17:19** *Isaac* means "he laughs."

KING JAMES VERSION

I will establish my covenant with him for an everlasting covenant, *and* with his seed after him.
[20]And as for Ishmael, I have heard thee: Behold,
I have blessed him, and will make him fruitful, and
will multiply him exceedingly; twelve princes shall
he beget, and I will make him a great nation.
[21]But my covenant will I establish with Isaac,
which Sarah shall bear unto thee at this set time in
the next year.
[22]And he left off talking with him, and God went
up from Abraham.
[23]And Abraham took Ishmael his son, and all that
were born in his house, and all that were bought with
his money, every male among the men of Abraham's
house; and circumcised the flesh of their foreskin in
the selfsame day, as God had said unto him.
[24]And Abraham *was* ninety years old and nine,
when he was circumcised in the flesh of his foreskin.
[25]And Ishmael his son *was* thirteen years old,
when he was circumcised in the flesh of his foreskin.
[26]In the selfsame day was Abraham circumcised,
and Ishmael his son.
[27]And all the men of his house, born in the house,
and bought with money of the stranger, were circumcised with him.

18 [1]And the LORD appeared unto him in the
plains of Mamre: and he sat in the tent door
in the heat of the day;
[2]And he lift up his eyes and looked, and, lo, three
men stood by him: and when he saw *them,* he ran to
meet them from the tent door, and bowed himself
toward the ground,
[3]And said, My Lord, if now I have found favour in
thy sight, pass not away, I pray thee, from thy servant:
[4]Let a little water, I pray you, be fetched, and wash
your feet, and rest yourselves under the tree:
[5]And I will fetch a morsel of bread, and comfort ye
your hearts; after that ye shall pass on: for therefore
are ye come to your servant. And they said, So do, as
thou hast said.
[6]And Abraham hastened into the tent unto Sarah,
and said, Make ready quickly three measures of fine
meal, knead *it,* and make cakes upon the hearth.
[7]And Abraham ran unto the herd, and fetched a
calf tender and good, and gave *it* unto a young man;
and he hasted to dress it.
[8]And he took butter, and milk, and the calf which
he had dressed, and set *it* before them; and he stood
by them under the tree, and they did eat.
[9]And they said unto him, Where *is* Sarah thy wife?
And he said, Behold, in the tent.
[10]And he said, I will certainly return unto thee
according to the time of life; and, lo, Sarah thy wife
shall have a son. And Sarah heard *it* in the tent door,
which *was* behind him.
[11]Now Abraham and Sarah *were* old *and* well

NEW LIVING TRANSLATION

will confirm my covenant with him and his descendants as an everlasting covenant. [20]As for Ishmael, I
will bless him also, just as you have asked. I will make
him extremely fruitful and multiply his descendants. He will become the father of twelve princes,
and I will make him a great nation. [21]But my covenant will be confirmed with Isaac, who will be born
to you and Sarah about this time next year." [22]When
God had finished speaking, he left Abraham.
[23]On that very day Abraham took his son, Ishmael,
and every male in his household, including those
born there and those he had bought. Then he circumcised them, cutting off their foreskins, just as
God had told him. [24]Abraham was ninety-nine years
old when he was circumcised, [25]and Ishmael, his
son, was thirteen. [26]Both Abraham and his son,
Ishmael, were circumcised on that same day, [27]along
with all the other men and boys of the household,
whether they were born there or bought as servants.
All were circumcised with him.

A Son Is Promised to Sarah

18 The LORD appeared again to Abraham near
the oak grove belonging to Mamre. One day
Abraham was sitting at the entrance to his tent
during the hottest part of the day. [2]He looked up and
noticed three men standing nearby. When he saw
them, he ran to meet them and welcomed them,
bowing low to the ground.
[3]"My lord," he said, "if it pleases you, stop here for
a while. [4]Rest in the shade of this tree while water is
brought to wash your feet. [5]And since you've honored your servant with this visit, let me prepare some
food to refresh you before you continue on your
journey."
"All right," they said. "Do as you have said."
[6]So Abraham ran back to the tent and said to
Sarah, "Hurry! Get three large measures* of your best
flour, knead it into dough, and bake some bread."
[7]Then Abraham ran out to the herd and chose a tender calf and gave it to his servant, who quickly prepared it. [8]When the food was ready, Abraham took
some yogurt and milk and the roasted meat, and he
served it to the men. As they ate, Abraham waited on
them in the shade of the trees.
[9]"Where is Sarah, your wife?" the visitors asked.
"She's inside the tent," Abraham replied.
[10]Then one of them said, "I will return to you
about this time next year, and your wife, Sarah, will
have a son!"
Sarah was listening to this conversation from the
tent. [11]Abraham and Sarah were both very old by this

18:6 Hebrew *3 seahs,* about 15 quarts or 18 liters.

KING JAMES VERSION

stricken in age; *and* it ceased to be with Sarah after
the manner of women.
12 Therefore Sarah laughed within herself, saying,
After I am waxed old shall I have pleasure, my lord
being old also?
13 And the LORD said unto Abraham, Wherefore did
Sarah laugh, saying, Shall I of a surety bear a child,
which am old?
14 Is any thing too hard for the LORD? At the time
appointed I will return unto thee, according to the
time of life, and Sarah shall have a son.
15 Then Sarah denied, saying, I laughed not; for she
was afraid. And he said, Nay; but thou didst laugh.

16 And the men rose up from thence, and looked
toward Sodom: and Abraham went with them to
bring them on the way.
17 And the LORD said, Shall I hide from Abraham
that thing which I do;
18 Seeing that Abraham shall surely become a great
and mighty nation, and all the nations of the earth
shall be blessed in him?
19 For I know him, that he will command his children and his household after him, and they shall
keep the way of the LORD, to do justice and judgment;
that the LORD may bring upon Abraham that which
he hath spoken of him.
20 And the LORD said, Because the cry of Sodom
and Gomorrah is great, and because their sin is very
grievous;
21 I will go down now, and see whether they have
done altogether according to the cry of it, which is
come unto me; and if not, I will know.
22 And the men turned their faces from thence,
and went toward Sodom: but Abraham stood yet
before the LORD.
23 And Abraham drew near, and said, Wilt thou
also destroy the righteous with the wicked?
24 Peradventure there be fifty righteous within the
city: wilt thou also destroy and not spare the place
for the fifty righteous that *are* therein?
25 That be far from thee to do after this manner, to
slay the righteous with the wicked: and that the righteous should be as the wicked, that be far from thee:
Shall not the Judge of all the earth do right?
26 And the LORD said, If I find in Sodom fifty righteous within the city, then I will spare all the place for
their sakes.
27 And Abraham answered and said, Behold now, I
have taken upon me to speak unto the Lord, which
am but dust and ashes:
28 Peradventure there shall lack five of the fifty
righteous: wilt thou destroy all the city for *lack of*
five? And he said, If I find there forty and five, I will
not destroy *it*.
29 And he spake unto him yet again, and said,

NEW LIVING TRANSLATION

time, and Sarah was long past the age of having children. 12 So she laughed silently to herself and said,
"How could a worn-out woman like me enjoy such
pleasure, especially when my master—my husband—
is also so old?"
13 Then the LORD said to Abraham, "Why did Sarah
laugh? Why did she say, 'Can an old woman like me
have a baby?' 14 Is anything too hard for the LORD? I
will return about this time next year, and Sarah will
have a son."
15 Sarah was afraid, so she denied it, saying, "I
didn't laugh."
But the LORD said, "No, you did laugh."

Abraham Intercedes for Sodom

16 Then the men got up from their meal and looked
out toward Sodom. As they left, Abraham went with
them to send them on their way.
17 "Should I hide my plan from Abraham?" the
LORD asked. 18 "For Abraham will certainly become a
great and mighty nation, and all the nations of the
earth will be blessed through him. 19 I have singled
him out so that he will direct his sons and their families to keep the way of the LORD by doing what is
right and just. Then I will do for Abraham all that I
have promised."
20 So the LORD told Abraham, "I have heard a great
outcry from Sodom and Gomorrah, because their
sin is so flagrant. 21 I am going down to see if their actions are as wicked as I have heard. If not, I want
to know."
22 The other men turned and headed toward
Sodom, but the LORD remained with Abraham.
23 Abraham approached him and said, "Will you
sweep away both the righteous and the wicked?
24 Suppose you find fifty righteous people living
there in the city—will you still sweep it away and
not spare it for their sakes? 25 Surely you wouldn't do
such a thing, destroying the righteous along with
the wicked. Why, you would be treating the righteous and the wicked exactly the same! Surely you
wouldn't do that! Should not the Judge of all the
earth do what is right?"
26 And the LORD replied, "If I find fifty righteous
people in Sodom, I will spare the entire city for their
sake."
27 Then Abraham spoke again. "Since I have begun, let me speak further to my Lord, even though I
am but dust and ashes. 28 Suppose there are only
forty-five righteous people rather than fifty? Will
you destroy the whole city for lack of five?"
And the LORD said, "I will not destroy it if I find
forty-five righteous people there."
29 Then Abraham pressed his request further.
"Suppose there are only forty?"

KING JAMES VERSION

Peradventure there shall be forty found there. And
he said, I will not do *it* for forty's sake.
30And he said *unto him,* Oh let not the Lord be angry, and I will speak: Peradventure there shall thirty
be found there. And he said, I will not do *it,* if I find
thirty there.
31And he said, Behold now, I have taken upon me
to speak unto the Lord: Peradventure there shall be
twenty found there. And he said, I will not destroy *it*
for twenty's sake.
32And he said, Oh let not the Lord be angry, and I
will speak yet but this once: Peradventure ten shall
be found there. And he said, I will not destroy *it* for
ten's sake.
33And the LORD went his way, as soon as he had left
communing with Abraham: and Abraham returned
unto his place.

19 1And there came two angels to Sodom at
even; and Lot sat in the gate of Sodom: and
Lot seeing *them* rose up to meet them; and he bowed
himself with his face toward the ground;
2And he said, Behold now, my lords, turn in, I pray
you, into your servant's house, and tarry all night, and
wash your feet, and ye shall rise up early, and go on
your ways. And they said, Nay; but we will abide in
the street all night.
3And he pressed upon them greatly; and they
turned in unto him, and entered into his house; and
he made them a feast, and did bake unleavened
bread, and they did eat.
4But before they lay down, the men of the city,
even the men of Sodom, compassed the house
round, both old and young, all the people from every
quarter:
5And they called unto Lot, and said unto him,
Where *are* the men which came in to thee this night?
bring them out unto us, that we may know them.
6And Lot went out at the door unto them, and shut
the door after him,
7And said, I pray you, brethren, do not so wickedly.
8Behold now, I have two daughters which have not
known man; let me, I pray you, bring them out unto
you, and do ye to them as *is* good in your eyes: only
unto these men do nothing; for therefore came they
under the shadow of my roof.
9And they said, Stand back. And they said *again,*
This one *fellow* came in to sojourn, and he will needs
be a judge: now will we deal worse with thee, than
with them. And they pressed sore upon the man,
even Lot, and came near to break the door.
10But the men put forth their hand, and pulled Lot
into the house to them, and shut to the door.

NEW LIVING TRANSLATION

And the LORD replied, "I will not destroy it for the
sake of the forty."
30"Please don't be angry, my Lord," Abraham
pleaded. "Let me speak—suppose only thirty righteous people are found?"
And the LORD replied, "I will not destroy it if I find
thirty."
31Then Abraham said, "Since I have dared to speak
to the Lord, let me continue—suppose there are only
twenty?"
And the LORD replied, "Then I will not destroy it
for the sake of the twenty."
32Finally, Abraham said, "Lord, please don't be angry with me if I speak one more time. Suppose only
ten are found there?"
And the LORD replied, "Then I will not destroy it
for the sake of the ten."
33When the LORD had finished his conversation
with Abraham, he went on his way, and Abraham returned to his tent.

Sodom and Gomorrah Destroyed

19 That evening the two angels came to the entrance of the city of Sodom. Lot was sitting
there, and when he saw them, he stood up to meet
them. Then he welcomed them and bowed with his
face to the ground. 2"My lords," he said, "come to my
home to wash your feet, and be my guests for the
night. You may then get up early in the morning and
be on your way again."
"Oh no," they replied. "We'll just spend the night
out here in the city square."
3But Lot insisted, so at last they went home with
him. Lot prepared a feast for them, complete with
fresh bread made without yeast, and they ate. 4But
before they retired for the night, all the men of
Sodom, young and old, came from all over the city
and surrounded the house. 5They shouted to Lot,
"Where are the men who came to spend the night
with you? Bring them out to us so we can have sex
with them!"
6So Lot stepped outside to talk to them, shutting
the door behind him. 7"Please, my brothers," he
begged, "don't do such a wicked thing. 8Look, I have
two virgin daughters. Let me bring them out to you,
and you can do with them as you wish. But please,
leave these men alone, for they are my guests and are
under my protection."
9"Stand back!" they shouted. "This fellow came to
town as an outsider, and now he's acting like our
judge! We'll treat you far worse than those other
men!" And they lunged toward Lot to break down
the door.
10But the two angels* reached out, pulled Lot into

19:10 Hebrew *men;* also in 19:12, 16.

KING JAMES VERSION

11 And they smote the men that *were* at the door of
the house with blindness, both small and great: so
that they wearied themselves to find the door.
12 And the men said unto Lot, Hast thou here any
besides? son in law, and thy sons, and thy daughters,
and whatsoever thou hast in the city, bring *them* out
of this place:
13 For we will destroy this place, because the cry of
them is waxen great before the face of the LORD; and
the LORD hath sent us to destroy it.
14 And Lot went out, and spake unto his sons in law,
which married his daughters, and said, Up, get you out
of this place; for the LORD will destroy this city. But he
seemed as one that mocked unto his sons in law.
15 And when the morning arose, then the angels
hastened Lot, saying, Arise, take thy wife, and thy two
daughters, which are here; lest thou be consumed in
the iniquity of the city.
16 And while he lingered, the men laid hold upon
his hand, and upon the hand of his wife, and upon
the hand of his two daughters; the LORD being merciful unto him: and they brought him forth, and set
him without the city.
17 And it came to pass, when they had brought them
forth abroad, that he said, Escape for thy life; look not
behind thee, neither stay thou in all the plain; escape
to the mountain, lest thou be consumed.
18 And Lot said unto them, Oh, not so, my Lord:
19 Behold now, thy servant hath found grace in thy
sight, and thou hast magnified thy mercy, which
thou hast shewed unto me in saving my life; and I
cannot escape to the mountain, lest some evil take
me, and I die:
20 Behold now, this city *is* near to flee unto, and it *is*
a little one: Oh, let me escape thither, (*is* it not a little
one?) and my soul shall live.
21 And he said unto him, See, I have accepted thee
concerning this thing also, that I will not overthrow
this city, for the which thou hast spoken.
22 Haste thee, escape thither; for I cannot do any
thing till thou be come thither. Therefore the name
of the city was called Zoar.
23 The sun was risen upon the earth when Lot entered into Zoar.
24 Then the LORD rained upon Sodom and upon
Gomorrah brimstone and fire from the LORD out
of heaven;
25 And he overthrew those cities, and all the plain,
and all the inhabitants of the cities, and that which
grew upon the ground.
26 But his wife looked back from behind him, and
she became a pillar of salt.
27 And Abraham gat up early in the morning to the
place where he stood before the LORD:
28 And he looked toward Sodom and Gomorrah,
and toward all the land of the plain, and beheld, and,
lo, the smoke of the country went up as the smoke of
a furnace.

NEW LIVING TRANSLATION

the house, and bolted the door.
11 Then they blinded
all the men, young and old, who were at the door of
the house, so they gave up trying to get inside.
12 Meanwhile, the angels questioned Lot. "Do you
have any other relatives here in the city?" they asked.
"Get them out of this place—your sons-in-law, sons,
daughters, or anyone else.
13 For we are about to de-
stroy this city completely. The outcry against this
place is so great it has reached the LORD, and he has
sent us to destroy it."
14 So Lot rushed out to tell his daughters' fiancés,
"Quick, get out of the city! The LORD is about to destroy it." But the young men thought he was only
joking.
15 At dawn the next morning the angels became
insistent. "Hurry," they said to Lot. "Take your wife
and your two daughters who are here. Get out right
now, or you will be swept away in the destruction of
the city!"
16 When Lot still hesitated, the angels seized his
hand and the hands of his wife and two daughters
and rushed them to safety outside the city, for the
LORD was merciful.
17 When they were safely out of
the city, one of the angels ordered, "Run for your
lives! And don't look back or stop anywhere in the
valley! Escape to the mountains, or you will be swept
away!"
18 "Oh no, my lord!" Lot begged.
19 "You have been
so gracious to me and saved my life, and you have
shown such great kindness. But I cannot go to the
mountains. Disaster would catch up to me there, and
I would soon die.
20 See, there is a small village
nearby. Please let me go there instead; don't you see
how small it is? Then my life will be saved."
21 "All right," the angel said, "I will grant your request. I will not destroy the little village.
22 But hurry!
Escape to it, for I can do nothing until you arrive
there." (This explains why that village was known as
Zoar, which means "little place.")
23 Lot reached the village just as the sun was rising
over the horizon.
24 Then the LORD rained down fire
and burning sulfur from the sky on Sodom and Gomorrah.
25 He utterly destroyed them, along with the
other cities and villages of the plain, wiping out all
the people and every bit of vegetation.
26 But Lot's
wife looked back as she was following behind him,
and she turned into a pillar of salt.
27 Abraham got up early that morning and hurried
out to the place where he had stood in the LORD's
presence.
28 He looked out across the plain toward
Sodom and Gomorrah and watched as columns
of smoke rose from the cities like smoke from a
furnace.

KING JAMES VERSION

29 And it came to pass, when God destroyed the cities of the plain, that God remembered Abraham, and sent Lot out of the midst of the overthrow, when he overthrew the cities in the which Lot dwelt.

30 And Lot went up out of Zoar, and dwelt in the mountain, and his two daughters with him; for he feared to dwell in Zoar: and he dwelt in a cave, he and his two daughters.

31 And the firstborn said unto the younger, Our father *is* old, and *there is* not a man in the earth to come in unto us after the manner of all the earth:

32 Come, let us make our father drink wine, and we will lie with him, that we may preserve seed of our father.

33 And they made their father drink wine that night: and the firstborn went in, and lay with her father; and he perceived not when she lay down, nor when she arose.

34 And it came to pass on the morrow, that the firstborn said unto the younger, Behold, I lay yesternight with my father: let us make him drink wine this night also; and go thou in, *and* lie with him, that we may preserve seed of our father.

35 And they made their father drink wine that night also: and the younger arose, and lay with him; and he perceived not when she lay down, nor when she arose.

36 Thus were both the daughters of Lot with child by their father.

37 And the firstborn bare a son, and called his name Moab: the same *is* the father of the Moabites unto this day.

38 And the younger, she also bare a son, and called his name Ben-ammi: the same *is* the father of the children of Ammon unto this day.

20 1 And Abraham journeyed from thence toward the south country, and dwelled between Kadesh and Shur, and sojourned in Gerar.

2 And Abraham said of Sarah his wife, She *is* my sister: and Abimelech king of Gerar sent, and took Sarah.

3 But God came to Abimelech in a dream by night, and said to him, Behold, thou *art but* a dead man, for the woman which thou hast taken; for she *is* a man's wife.

4 But Abimelech had not come near her: and he said, Lord, wilt thou slay also a righteous nation?

5 Said he not unto me, She *is* my sister? and she, even she herself said, He *is* my brother: in the integrity of my heart and innocency of my hands have I done this.

6 And God said unto him in a dream, Yea, I know that thou didst this in the integrity of thy heart; for I

NEW LIVING TRANSLATION

29 But God had listened to Abraham's request and
kept Lot safe, removing him from the disaster that
engulfed the cities on the plain.

Lot and His Daughters

30 Afterward Lot left Zoar because he was afraid of
the people there, and he went to live in a cave in the
mountains with his two daughters. 31 One day the
older daughter said to her sister, "There are no men
left anywhere in this entire area, so we can't get married like everyone else. And our father will soon be
too old to have children. 32 Come, let's get him drunk
with wine, and then we will have sex with him. That
way we will preserve our family line through our
father."

33 So that night they got him drunk with wine, and
the older daughter went in and had intercourse with
her father. He was unaware of her lying down or getting up again.

34 The next morning the older daughter said to her
younger sister, "I had sex with our father last night.
Let's get him drunk with wine again tonight, and you
go in and have sex with him. That way we will preserve our family line through our father." 35 So that
night they got him drunk with wine again, and the
younger daughter went in and had intercourse with
him. As before, he was unaware of her lying down or
getting up again.

36 As a result, both of Lot's daughters became
pregnant by their own father. 37 When the older
daughter gave birth to a son, she named him Moab.*
He became the ancestor of the nation now known as
the Moabites. 38 When the younger daughter gave
birth to a son, she named him Ben-ammi.* He became the ancestor of the nation now known as the
Ammonites.

Abraham Deceives Abimelech

20 Abraham moved south to the Negev and
lived for a while between Kadesh and Shur,
and then he moved on to Gerar. While living there
as a foreigner, 2 Abraham introduced his wife, Sarah,
by saying, "She is my sister." So King Abimelech of
Gerar sent for Sarah and had her brought to him at
his palace.

3 But that night God came to Abimelech in a dream
and told him, "You are a dead man, for that woman
you have taken is already married!"

4 But Abimelech had not slept with her yet, so he
said, "Lord, will you destroy an innocent nation?
5 Didn't Abraham tell me, 'She is my sister'? And she
herself said, 'Yes, he is my brother.' I acted in complete innocence! My hands are clean."

6 In the dream God responded, "Yes, I know you
are innocent. That's why I kept you from sinning

19:37 *Moab* sounds like a Hebrew term that means "from father."
19:38 *Ben-ammi* means "son of my kinsman."

KING JAMES VERSION

also withheld thee from sinning against me: therefore suffered I thee not to touch her.

7 Now therefore restore the man *his* wife; for he *is* a prophet, and he shall pray for thee, and thou shalt live: and if thou restore *her* not, know thou that thou shalt surely die, thou, and all that *are* thine.

8 Therefore Abimelech rose early in the morning, and called all his servants, and told all these things in their ears: and the men were sore afraid.

9 Then Abimelech called Abraham, and said unto him, What hast thou done unto us? and what have I offended thee, that thou hast brought on me and on my kingdom a great sin? thou hast done deeds unto me that ought not to be done.

10 And Abimelech said unto Abraham, What sawest thou, that thou hast done this thing?

11 And Abraham said, Because I thought, Surely the fear of God *is* not in this place; and they will slay me for my wife's sake.

12 And yet indeed *she is* my sister; she *is* the daughter of my father, but not the daughter of my mother; and she became my wife.

13 And it came to pass, when God caused me to wander from my father's house, that I said unto her, This *is* thy kindness which thou shalt shew unto me; at every place whither we shall come, say of me, He *is* my brother.

14 And Abimelech took sheep, and oxen, and menservants, and womenservants, and gave *them* unto Abraham, and restored him Sarah his wife.

15 And Abimelech said, Behold, my land *is* before thee: dwell where it pleaseth thee.

16 And unto Sarah he said, Behold, I have given thy brother a thousand *pieces* of silver: behold, he *is* to thee a covering of the eyes, unto all that *are* with thee, and with all *other:* thus she was reproved.

17 So Abraham prayed unto God: and God healed Abimelech, and his wife, and his maidservants; and they bare *children.*

18 For the LORD had fast closed up all the wombs of the house of Abimelech, because of Sarah Abraham's wife.

21 1 And the LORD visited Sarah as he had said, and the LORD did unto Sarah as he had spoken.

2 For Sarah conceived, and bare Abraham a son in his old age, at the set time of which God had spoken to him.

3 And Abraham called the name of his son that was born unto him, whom Sarah bare to him, Isaac.

4 And Abraham circumcised his son Isaac being eight days old, as God had commanded him.

5 And Abraham was an hundred years old, when his son Isaac was born unto him.

6 And Sarah said, God hath made me to laugh, *so that* all that hear will laugh with me.

NEW LIVING TRANSLATION

against me, and why I did not let you touch her. 7 Now
return the woman to her husband, and he will pray
for you, for he is a prophet. Then you will live. But if
you don't return her to him, you can be sure that you
and all your people will die."

8 Abimelech got up early the next morning and
quickly called all his servants together. When he told
them what had happened, his men were terrified.
9 Then Abimelech called for Abraham. "What have
you done to us?" he demanded. "What crime have I
committed that deserves treatment like this, making
me and my kingdom guilty of this great sin? No one
should ever do what you have done! 10 Whatever possessed you to do such a thing?"

11 Abraham replied, "I thought, 'This is a godless
place. They will want my wife and will kill me to get
her.' 12 And she really is my sister, for we both have
the same father, but different mothers. And I married her. 13 When God called me to leave my father's
home and to travel from place to place, I told her, 'Do
me a favor. Wherever we go, tell the people that I am
your brother.'"

14 Then Abimelech took some of his sheep and
goats, cattle, and male and female servants, and he
presented them to Abraham. He also returned his
wife, Sarah, to him. 15 Then Abimelech said, "Look
over my land and choose any place where you would
like to live." 16 And he said to Sarah, "Look, I am giving
your 'brother' 1,000 pieces of silver* in the presence
of all these witnesses. This is to compensate you for
any wrong I may have done to you. This will settle any
claim against me, and your reputation is cleared."

17 Then Abraham prayed to God, and God healed
Abimelech, his wife, and his female servants, so they
could have children. 18 For the LORD had caused all
the women to be infertile because of what happened
with Abraham's wife, Sarah.

The Birth of Isaac

21 The LORD kept his word and did for Sarah
exactly what he had promised. 2 She became
pregnant, and she gave birth to a son for Abraham in
his old age. This happened at just the time God had
said it would. 3 And Abraham named their son Isaac.
4 Eight days after Isaac was born, Abraham circumcised him as God had commanded. 5 Abraham was
100 years old when Isaac was born.

6 And Sarah declared, "God has brought me laughter.* All who hear about this will laugh with me.

20:16 Hebrew *1,000 [shekels] of silver,* about 25 pounds or 11.4 kilograms in weight. **21:6** The name *Isaac* means "he laughs."

KING JAMES VERSION

7And she said, Who would have said unto Abraham, that Sarah should have given children suck? for
I have born *him* a son in his old age.
8And the child grew, and was weaned: and Abraham made a great feast the *same* day that Isaac was
weaned.
9And Sarah saw the son of Hagar the Egyptian,
which she had born unto Abraham, mocking.
10Wherefore she said unto Abraham, Cast out this
bondwoman and her son: for the son of this bondwoman shall not be heir with my son, *even* with
Isaac.
11And the thing was very grievous in Abraham's
sight because of his son.
12And God said unto Abraham, Let it not be grievous in thy sight because of the lad, and because of
thy bondwoman; in all that Sarah hath said unto
thee, hearken unto her voice; for in Isaac shall thy
seed be called.
13And also of the son of the bondwoman will I
make a nation, because he *is* thy seed.
14And Abraham rose up early in the morning, and
took bread, and a bottle of water, and gave *it* unto
Hagar, putting *it* on her shoulder, and the child, and
sent her away: and she departed, and wandered in
the wilderness of Beer-sheba.
15And the water was spent in the bottle, and she
cast the child under one of the shrubs.
16And she went, and sat her down over against *him*
a good way off, as it were a bowshot: for she said, Let
me not see the death of the child. And she sat over
against *him*, and lift up her voice, and wept.
17And God heard the voice of the lad; and the angel of God called to Hagar out of heaven, and said
unto her, What aileth thee, Hagar? fear not; for God
hath heard the voice of the lad where he *is*.
18Arise, lift up the lad, and hold him in thine hand;
for I will make him a great nation.
19And God opened her eyes, and she saw a well of
water; and she went, and filled the bottle with water,
and gave the lad drink.
20And God was with the lad; and he grew, and
dwelt in the wilderness, and became an archer.
21And he dwelt in the wilderness of Paran: and his
mother took him a wife out of the land of Egypt.
22And it came to pass at that time, that Abimelech
and Phichol the chief captain of his host spake unto
Abraham, saying, God *is* with thee in all that thou
doest:
23Now therefore swear unto me here by God that
thou wilt not deal falsely with me, nor with my son,
nor with my son's son: *but* according to the kindness
that I have done unto thee, thou shalt do unto me,
and to the land wherein thou hast sojourned.
24And Abraham said, I will swear.

NEW LIVING TRANSLATION

7Who would have said to Abraham that Sarah would
nurse a baby? Yet I have given Abraham a son in his
old age!"

Hagar and Ishmael Are Sent Away

8When Isaac grew up and was about to be weaned,
Abraham prepared a huge feast to celebrate the occasion. 9But Sarah saw Ishmael—the son of Abraham
and her Egyptian servant Hagar—making fun of her
son, Isaac.* 10So she turned to Abraham and demanded, "Get rid of that slave woman and her son.
He is not going to share the inheritance with my son,
Isaac. I won't have it!"
11This upset Abraham very much because Ishmael
was his son. 12But God told Abraham, "Do not be upset over the boy and your servant. Do whatever Sarah
tells you, for Isaac is the son through whom your descendants will be counted. 13But I will also make a
nation of the descendants of Hagar's son because he
is your son, too."
14So Abraham got up early the next morning, prepared food and a container of water, and strapped
them on Hagar's shoulders. Then he sent her away
with their son, and she wandered aimlessly in the
wilderness of Beersheba.
15When the water was gone, she put the boy in the
shade of a bush. 16Then she went and sat down by
herself about a hundred yards* away. "I don't want to
watch the boy die," she said, as she burst into tears.
17But God heard the boy crying, and the angel of
God called to Hagar from heaven, "Hagar, what's
wrong? Do not be afraid! God has heard the boy crying as he lies there. 18Go to him and comfort him, for
I will make a great nation from his descendants."
19Then God opened Hagar's eyes, and she saw a
well full of water. She quickly filled her water container and gave the boy a drink.
20And God was with the boy as he grew up in the
wilderness. He became a skillful archer, 21and he
settled in the wilderness of Paran. His mother arranged for him to marry a woman from the land
of Egypt.

Abraham's Covenant with Abimelech

22About this time, Abimelech came with Phicol, his
army commander, to visit Abraham. "God is obviously with you, helping you in everything you do,"
Abimelech said. 23"Swear to me in God's name that
you will never deceive me, my children, or any of my
descendants. I have been loyal to you, so now swear
that you will be loyal to me and to this country where
you are living as a foreigner."
24Abraham replied, "Yes, I swear to it!" 25Then

21:9 As in Greek version and Latin Vulgate; Hebrew lacks *of her son, Isaac.*
21:16 Hebrew *a bowshot.*

KING JAMES VERSION

25 And Abraham reproved Abimelech because of a well of water, which Abimelech's servants had violently taken away.

26 And Abimelech said, I wot not who hath done this thing: neither didst thou tell me, neither yet heard I *of it,* but today.

27 And Abraham took sheep and oxen, and gave them unto Abimelech; and both of them made a covenant.

28 And Abraham set seven ewe lambs of the flock by themselves.

29 And Abimelech said unto Abraham, What *mean* these seven ewe lambs which thou hast set by themselves?

30 And he said, For *these* seven ewe lambs shalt thou take of my hand, that they may be a witness unto me, that I have digged this well.

31 Wherefore he called that place Beer-sheba; because there they sware both of them.

32 Thus they made a covenant at Beer-sheba: then Abimelech rose up, and Phichol the chief captain of his host, and they returned into the land of the Philistines.

33 And *Abraham* planted a grove in Beer-sheba, and called there on the name of the LORD, the everlasting God.

34 And Abraham sojourned in the Philistines' land many days.

22 1 And it came to pass after these things, that God did tempt Abraham, and said unto him, Abraham: and he said, Behold, *here* I *am.*

2 And he said, Take now thy son, thine only *son* Isaac, whom thou lovest, and get thee into the land of Moriah; and offer him there for a burnt offering upon one of the mountains which I will tell thee of.

3 And Abraham rose up early in the morning, and saddled his ass, and took two of his young men with him, and Isaac his son, and clave the wood for the burnt offering, and rose up, and went unto the place of which God had told him.

4 Then on the third day Abraham lifted up his eyes, and saw the place afar off.

5 And Abraham said unto his young men, Abide ye here with the ass; and I and the lad will go yonder and worship, and come again to you.

6 And Abraham took the wood of the burnt offering, and laid *it* upon Isaac his son; and he took the fire in his hand, and a knife; and they went both of them together.

7 And Isaac spake unto Abraham his father, and said, My father: and he said, Here *am* I, my son. And he said, Behold the fire and the wood: but where *is* the lamb for a burnt offering?

8 And Abraham said, My son, God will provide himself a lamb for a burnt offering: so they went both of them together.

NEW LIVING TRANSLATION

Abraham complained to Abimelech about a well that Abimelech's servants had taken by force from Abraham's servants.

26 "This is the first I've heard of it," Abimelech answered. "I have no idea who is responsible. You have never complained about this before."

27 Abraham then gave some of his sheep, goats, and cattle to Abimelech, and they made a treaty.
28 But Abraham also took seven additional female lambs and set them off by themselves.
29 Abimelech asked, "Why have you set these seven apart from the others?"

30 Abraham replied, "Please accept these seven lambs to show your agreement that I dug this well."
31 Then he named the place Beersheba (which means "well of the oath"), because that was where they had sworn the oath.

32 After making their covenant at Beersheba, Abimelech left with Phicol, the commander of his army, and they returned home to the land of the Philistines.
33 Then Abraham planted a tamarisk tree at Beersheba, and there he worshiped the LORD, the Eternal God.*
34 And Abraham lived as a foreigner in Philistine country for a long time.

Abraham's Faith Tested

22 Some time later, God tested Abraham's faith. "Abraham!" God called.

"Yes," he replied. "Here I am."

2 "Take your son, your only son—yes, Isaac, whom you love so much—and go to the land of Moriah. Go and sacrifice him as a burnt offering on one of the mountains, which I will show you."

3 The next morning Abraham got up early. He saddled his donkey and took two of his servants with him, along with his son, Isaac. Then he chopped wood for a fire for a burnt offering and set out for the place God had told him about.
4 On the third day of their journey, Abraham looked up and saw the place in the distance.
5 "Stay here with the donkey," Abraham told the servants. "The boy and I will travel a little farther. We will worship there, and then we will come right back."

6 So Abraham placed the wood for the burnt offering on Isaac's shoulders, while he himself carried the fire and the knife. As the two of them walked on together,
7 Isaac turned to Abraham and said, "Father?"

"Yes, my son?" Abraham replied.

"We have the fire and the wood," the boy said, "but where is the sheep for the burnt offering?"

8 "God will provide a sheep for the burnt offering, my son," Abraham answered. And they both walked on together.

21:33 Hebrew *El-Olam.*

KING JAMES VERSION

9And they came to the place which God had told
him of; and Abraham built an altar there, and laid the
wood in order, and bound Isaac his son, and laid him
on the altar upon the wood.
10And Abraham stretched forth his hand, and took
the knife to slay his son.
11And the angel of the LORD called unto him out of
heaven, and said, Abraham, Abraham: and he said,
Here *am* I.
12And he said, Lay not thine hand upon the lad,
neither do thou any thing unto him: for now I know
that thou fearest God, seeing thou hast not withheld
thy son, thine only *son* from me.
13And Abraham lifted up his eyes, and looked, and
behold behind *him* a ram caught in a thicket by his
horns: and Abraham went and took the ram, and offered him up for a burnt offering in the stead of his
son.
14And Abraham called the name of that place
Jehovah-jireh: as it is said *to* this day, In the mount of
the LORD it shall be seen.
15And the angel of the LORD called unto Abraham
out of heaven the second time,
16And said, By myself have I sworn, saith the LORD,
for because thou hast done this thing, and hast not
withheld thy son, thine only *son:*
17That in blessing I will bless thee, and in multiplying I will multiply thy seed as the stars of the heaven,
and as the sand which *is* upon the sea shore; and thy
seed shall possess the gate of his enemies;
18And in thy seed shall all the nations of the earth
be blessed; because thou hast obeyed my voice.
19So Abraham returned unto his young men, and
they rose up and went together to Beer-sheba; and
Abraham dwelt at Beer-sheba.
20And it came to pass after these things, that it was
told Abraham, saying, Behold, Milcah, she hath also
born children unto thy brother Nahor;
21Huz his firstborn, and Buz his brother, and
Kemuel the father of Aram,
22And Chesed, and Hazo, and Pildash, and Jidlaph,
and Bethuel.
23And Bethuel begat Rebekah: these eight Milcah
did bear to Nahor, Abraham's brother.
24And his concubine, whose name *was* Reumah,
she bare also Tebah, and Gaham, and Thahash, and
Maachah.

23 1And Sarah was an hundred and seven and
twenty years old: *these were* the years of the
life of Sarah.
2And Sarah died in Kirjath-arba; the same *is* Hebron in the land of Canaan: and Abraham came to
mourn for Sarah, and to weep for her.
3And Abraham stood up from before his dead, and
spake unto the sons of Heth, saying,
4I *am* a stranger and a sojourner with you: give me

NEW LIVING TRANSLATION

9When they arrived at the place where God had
told him to go, Abraham built an altar and arranged
the wood on it. Then he tied his son, Isaac, and laid
him on the altar on top of the wood. 10And Abraham
picked up the knife to kill his son as a sacrifice. 11At
that moment the angel of the LORD called to him
from heaven, "Abraham! Abraham!"
"Yes," Abraham replied. "Here I am!"
12"Don't lay a hand on the boy!" the angel said. "Do
not hurt him in any way, for now I know that you truly
fear God. You have not withheld from me even your
son, your only son."
13Then Abraham looked up and saw a ram caught
by its horns in a thicket. So he took the ram and sacrificed it as a burnt offering in place of his son.
14Abraham named the place Yahweh-Yireh (which
means "the LORD will provide"). To this day, people
still use that name as a proverb: "On the mountain of
the LORD it will be provided."
15Then the angel of the LORD called again to
Abraham from heaven. 16"This is what the LORD
says: Because you have obeyed me and have not
withheld even your son, your only son, I swear by my
own name that 17I will certainly bless you. I will
multiply your descendants* beyond number, like
the stars in the sky and the sand on the seashore.
Your descendants will conquer the cities of their
enemies. 18And through your descendants all the
nations of the earth will be blessed—all because you
have obeyed me."
19Then they returned to the servants and traveled
back to Beersheba, where Abraham continued to
live.
20Soon after this, Abraham heard that Milcah, his
brother Nahor's wife, had borne Nahor eight sons.
21The oldest was named Uz, the next oldest was Buz,
followed by Kemuel (the ancestor of the Arameans),
22Kesed, Hazo, Pildash, Jidlaph, and Bethuel. 23(Bethuel became the father of Rebekah.) In addition to
these eight sons from Milcah, 24Nahor had four
other children from his concubine Reumah. Their
names were Tebah, Gaham, Tahash, and Maacah.

The Burial of Sarah

23 When Sarah was 127 years old, 2she died at
Kiriath-arba (now called Hebron) in the
land of Canaan. There Abraham mourned and wept
for her.
3Then, leaving her body, he said to the Hittite elders, 4"Here I am, a stranger and a foreigner among
you. Please sell me a piece of land so I can give my
wife a proper burial."

22:17 Hebrew *seed;* also in 22:17b, 18.

KING JAMES VERSION

a possession of a buryingplace with you, that I may bury my dead out of my sight.

5 And the children of Heth answered Abraham, saying unto him,

6 Hear us, my lord: thou *art* a mighty prince among us: in the choice of our sepulchres bury thy dead; none of us shall withhold from thee his sepulchre, but that thou mayest bury thy dead.

7 And Abraham stood up, and bowed himself to the people of the land, *even* to the children of Heth.

8 And he communed with them, saying, If it be your mind that I should bury my dead out of my sight; hear me, and intreat for me to Ephron the son of Zohar,

9 That he may give me the cave of Machpelah, which he hath, which *is* in the end of his field; for as much money as it is worth he shall give it me for a possession of a buryingplace amongst you.

10 And Ephron dwelt among the children of Heth: and Ephron the Hittite answered Abraham in the audience of the children of Heth, *even* of all that went in at the gate of his city, saying,

11 Nay, my lord, hear me: the field give I thee, and the cave that *is* therein, I give it thee; in the presence of the sons of my people give I it thee: bury thy dead.

12 And Abraham bowed down himself before the people of the land.

13 And he spake unto Ephron in the audience of the people of the land, saying, But if thou *wilt give it*, I pray thee, hear me: I will give thee money for the field; take *it* of me, and I will bury my dead there.

14 And Ephron answered Abraham, saying unto him,

15 My lord, hearken unto me: the land *is worth* four hundred shekels of silver; what *is* that betwixt me and thee? bury therefore thy dead.

16 And Abraham hearkened unto Ephron; and Abraham weighed to Ephron the silver, which he had named in the audience of the sons of Heth, four hundred shekels of silver, current *money* with the merchant.

17 And the field of Ephron, which *was* in Machpelah, which *was* before Mamre, the field, and the cave which *was* therein, and all the trees that *were* in the field, that *were* in all the borders round about, were made sure

18 Unto Abraham for a possession in the presence of the children of Heth, before all that went in at the gate of his city.

19 And after this, Abraham buried Sarah his wife in the cave of the field of Machpelah before Mamre: the same *is* Hebron in the land of Canaan.

20 And the field, and the cave that *is* therein, were made sure unto Abraham for a possession of a buryingplace by the sons of Heth.

NEW LIVING TRANSLATION

5 The Hittites replied to Abraham, 6 "Listen, my
lord, you are an honored prince among us. Choose
the finest of our tombs and bury her there. No one
here will refuse to help you in this way."

7 Then Abraham bowed low before the Hittites
8 and said, "Since you are willing to help me in this
way, be so kind as to ask Ephron son of Zohar 9 to let
me buy his cave at Machpelah, down at the end of his
field. I will pay the full price in the presence of witnesses, so I will have a permanent burial place for
my family."

10 Ephron was sitting there among the others, and
he answered Abraham as the others listened, speaking publicly before all the Hittite elders of the town.
11 "No, my lord," he said to Abraham, "please listen to
me. I will give you the field and the cave. Here in the
presence of my people, I give it to you. Go and bury
your dead."

12 Abraham again bowed low before the citizens of
the land, 13 and he replied to Ephron as everyone
listened. "No, listen to me. I will buy it from you. Let
me pay the full price for the field so I can bury my
dead there."

14 Ephron answered Abraham, 15 "My lord, please
listen to me. The land is worth 400 pieces* of silver,
but what is that between friends? Go ahead and bury
your dead."

16 So Abraham agreed to Ephron's price and paid
the amount he had suggested—400 pieces of silver,
weighed according to the market standard. The
Hittite elders witnessed the transaction.

17 So Abraham bought the plot of land belonging
to Ephron at Machpelah, near Mamre. This included
the field itself, the cave that was in it, and all the surrounding trees. 18 It was transferred to Abraham as
his permanent possession in the presence of the
Hittite elders at the city gate. 19 Then Abraham buried his wife, Sarah, there in Canaan, in the cave of
Machpelah, near Mamre (also called Hebron). 20 So
the field and the cave were transferred from the
Hittites to Abraham for use as a permanent burial
place.

23:15 Hebrew *400 shekels,* about 10 pounds or 4.6 kilograms in weight; also in 23:16.

KING JAMES VERSION

24 [1]And Abraham was old, *and* well stricken in
age: and the LORD had blessed Abraham in
all things.
[2]And Abraham said unto his eldest servant of his
house, that ruled over all that he had, Put, I pray thee,
thy hand under my thigh:
[3]And I will make thee swear by the LORD, the God
of heaven, and the God of the earth, that thou shalt
not take a wife unto my son of the daughters of the
Canaanites, among whom I dwell:
[4]But thou shalt go unto my country, and to my kindred, and take a wife unto my son Isaac.
[5]And the servant said unto him, Peradventure the
woman will not be willing to follow me unto this
land: must I needs bring thy son again unto the land
from whence thou camest?
[6]And Abraham said unto him, Beware thou that
thou bring not my son thither again.
[7]The LORD God of heaven, which took me from my
father's house, and from the land of my kindred, and
which spake unto me, and that sware unto me, saying, Unto thy seed will I give this land; he shall send
his angel before thee, and thou shalt take a wife unto
my son from thence.
[8]And if the woman will not be willing to follow
thee, then thou shalt be clear from this my oath: only
bring not my son thither again.
[9]And the servant put his hand under the thigh of
Abraham his master, and sware to him concerning
that matter.
[10]And the servant took ten camels of the camels of
his master, and departed; for all the goods of his
master *were* in his hand: and he arose, and went to
Mesopotamia, unto the city of Nahor.
[11]And he made his camels to kneel down without
the city by a well of water at the time of the evening,
even the time that women go out to draw *water*.
[12]And he said, O LORD God of my master Abraham,
I pray thee, send me good speed this day, and shew
kindness unto my master Abraham.
[13]Behold, I stand *here* by the well of water; and
the daughters of the men of the city come out to
draw water:
[14]And let it come to pass, that the damsel to whom I
shall say, Let down thy pitcher, I pray thee, that I may
drink; and she shall say, Drink, and I will give thy camels drink also: *let the same be* she *that* thou hast appointed for thy servant Isaac; and thereby shall I know
that thou hast shewed kindness unto my master.
[15]And it came to pass, before he had done speaking, that, behold, Rebekah came out, who was born
to Bethuel, son of Milcah, the wife of Nahor, Abraham's brother, with her pitcher upon her shoulder.
[16]And the damsel *was* very fair to look upon, a virgin, neither had any man known her: and she went
down to the well, and filled her pitcher, and came up.

NEW LIVING TRANSLATION

A Wife for Isaac

24 Abraham was now a very old man, and the
LORD had blessed him in every way. [2]One
day Abraham said to his oldest servant, the man in
charge of his household, "Take an oath by putting
your hand under my thigh. [3]Swear by the LORD, the
God of heaven and earth, that you will not allow my
son to marry one of these local Canaanite women.
[4]Go instead to my homeland, to my relatives, and
find a wife there for my son Isaac."
[5]The servant asked, "But what if I can't find a
young woman who is willing to travel so far from
home? Should I then take Isaac there to live among
your relatives in the land you came from?"
[6]"No!" Abraham responded. "Be careful never to
take my son there. [7]For the LORD, the God of heaven,
who took me from my father's house and my native
land, solemnly promised to give this land to my descendants.* He will send his angel ahead of you, and
he will see to it that you find a wife there for my son.
[8]If she is unwilling to come back with you, then you
are free from this oath of mine. But under no circumstances are you to take my son there."
[9]So the servant took an oath by putting his hand
under the thigh of his master, Abraham. He swore to
follow Abraham's instructions. [10]Then he loaded ten
of Abraham's camels with all kinds of expensive gifts
from his master, and he traveled to distant Aram-
naharaim. There he went to the town where Abraham's brother Nahor had settled. [11]He made the
camels kneel beside a well just outside the town. It
was evening, and the women were coming out to
draw water.
[12]"O LORD, God of my master, Abraham," he
prayed. "Please give me success today, and show unfailing love to my master, Abraham. [13]See, I am
standing here beside this spring, and the young
women of the town are coming out to draw water.
[14]This is my request. I will ask one of them, 'Please
give me a drink from your jug.' If she says, 'Yes, have a
drink, and I will water your camels, too!'—let her be
the one you have selected as Isaac's wife. This is how
I will know that you have shown unfailing love to
my master."
[15]Before he had finished praying, he saw a young
woman named Rebekah coming out with her water
jug on her shoulder. She was the daughter of
Bethuel, who was the son of Abraham's brother
Nahor and his wife, Milcah. [16]Rebekah was very
beautiful and old enough to be married, but she was
still a virgin. She went down to the spring, filled her

24:7 Hebrew *seed;* also in 24:60.

KING JAMES VERSION

17 And the servant ran to meet her, and said, Let me, I pray thee, drink a little water of thy pitcher.

18 And she said, Drink, my lord: and she hasted, and let down her pitcher upon her hand, and gave him drink.

19 And when she had done giving him drink, she said, I will draw *water* for thy camels also, until they have done drinking.

20 And she hasted, and emptied her pitcher into the trough, and ran again unto the well to draw *water*, and drew for all his camels.

21 And the man wondering at her held his peace, to wit whether the LORD had made his journey prosperous or not.

22 And it came to pass, as the camels had done drinking, that the man took a golden earring of half a shekel weight, and two bracelets for her hands of ten *shekels* weight of gold;

23 And said, Whose daughter *art* thou? tell me, I pray thee: is there room *in* thy father's house for us to lodge in?

24 And she said unto him, I *am* the daughter of Bethuel the son of Milcah, which she bare unto Nahor.

25 She said moreover unto him, We have both straw and provender enough, and room to lodge in.

26 And the man bowed down his head, and worshipped the LORD.

27 And he said, Blessed *be* the LORD God of my master Abraham, who hath not left destitute my master of his mercy and his truth: I *being* in the way, the LORD led me to the house of my master's brethren.

28 And the damsel ran, and told *them of* her mother's house these things.

29 And Rebekah had a brother, and his name *was* Laban: and Laban ran out unto the man, unto the well.

30 And it came to pass, when he saw the earring and bracelets upon his sister's hands, and when he heard the words of Rebekah his sister, saying, Thus spake the man unto me; that he came unto the man; and, behold, he stood by the camels at the well.

31 And he said, Come in, thou blessed of the LORD; wherefore standest thou without? for I have prepared the house, and room for the camels.

32 And the man came into the house: and he ungirded his camels, and gave straw and provender for the camels, and water to wash his feet, and the men's feet that *were* with him.

33 And there was set *meat* before him to eat: but he said, I will not eat, until I have told mine errand. And he said, Speak on.

34 And he said, I *am* Abraham's servant.

35 And the LORD hath blessed my master greatly; and he is become great: and he hath given him flocks, and herds, and silver, and gold, and menservants, and maidservants, and camels, and asses.

NEW LIVING TRANSLATION

jug, and came up again. 17 Running over to her, the servant said, "Please give me a little drink of water from your jug."

18 "Yes, my lord," she answered, "have a drink." And she quickly lowered her jug from her shoulder and gave him a drink. 19 When she had given him a drink, she said, "I'll draw water for your camels, too, until they have had enough to drink." 20 So she quickly emptied her jug into the watering trough and ran back to the well to draw water for all his camels.

21 The servant watched her in silence, wondering whether or not the LORD had given him success in his mission. 22 Then at last, when the camels had finished drinking, he took out a gold ring for her nose and two large gold bracelets* for her wrists.

23 "Whose daughter are you?" he asked. "And please tell me, would your father have any room to put us up for the night?"

24 "I am the daughter of Bethuel," she replied. "My grandparents are Nahor and Milcah. 25 Yes, we have plenty of straw and feed for the camels, and we have room for guests."

26 The man bowed low and worshiped the LORD. 27 "Praise the LORD, the God of my master, Abraham," he said. "The LORD has shown unfailing love and faithfulness to my master, for he has led me straight to my master's relatives."

28 The young woman ran home to tell her family everything that had happened. 29 Now Rebekah had a brother named Laban, who ran out to meet the man at the spring. 30 He had seen the nose-ring and the bracelets on his sister's wrists, and had heard Rebekah tell what the man had said. So he rushed out to the spring, where the man was still standing beside his camels. 31 Laban said to him, "Come and stay with us, you who are blessed by the LORD! Why are you standing here outside the town when I have a room all ready for you and a place prepared for the camels?"

32 So the man went home with Laban, and Laban unloaded the camels, gave him straw for their bedding, fed them, and provided water for the man and the camel drivers to wash their feet. 33 Then food was served. But Abraham's servant said, "I don't want to eat until I have told you why I have come."

"All right," Laban said, "tell us."

34 "I am Abraham's servant," he explained. 35 "And the LORD has greatly blessed my master; he has become a wealthy man. The LORD has given him flocks of sheep and goats, herds of cattle, a fortune in silver and gold, and many male and female servants and camels and donkeys.

24:22 Hebrew *a gold nose-ring weighing a half shekel* [0.2 ounces or 6 grams] *and two gold bracelets weighing 10 shekels* [4 ounces or 114 grams].

KING JAMES VERSION

36 And Sarah my master's wife bare a son to my master when she was old: and unto him hath he given all that he hath.

37 And my master made me swear, saying, Thou shalt not take a wife to my son of the daughters of the Canaanites, in whose land I dwell:

38 But thou shalt go unto my father's house, and to my kindred, and take a wife unto my son.

39 And I said unto my master, Peradventure the woman will not follow me.

40 And he said unto me, The LORD, before whom I walk, will send his angel with thee, and prosper thy way; and thou shalt take a wife for my son of my kindred, and of my father's house:

41 Then shalt thou be clear from *this* my oath, when thou comest to my kindred; and if they give not thee *one*, thou shalt be clear from my oath.

42 And I came this day unto the well, and said, O LORD God of my master Abraham, if now thou do prosper my way which I go:

43 Behold, I stand by the well of water; and it shall come to pass, that when the virgin cometh forth to draw *water*, and I say to her, Give me, I pray thee, a little water of thy pitcher to drink;

44 And she say to me, Both drink thou, and I will also draw for thy camels: *let* the same *be* the woman whom the LORD hath appointed out for my master's son.

45 And before I had done speaking in mine heart, behold, Rebekah came forth with her pitcher on her shoulder; and she went down unto the well, and drew *water:* and I said unto her, Let me drink, I pray thee.

46 And she made haste, and let down her pitcher from her *shoulder*, and said, Drink, and I will give thy camels drink also: so I drank, and she made the camels drink also.

47 And I asked her, and said, Whose daughter *art* thou? And she said, The daughter of Bethuel, Nahor's son, whom Milcah bare unto him: and I put the earring upon her face, and the bracelets upon her hands.

48 And I bowed down my head, and worshipped the LORD, and blessed the LORD God of my master Abraham, which had led me in the right way to take my master's brother's daughter unto his son.

49 And now if ye will deal kindly and truly with my master, tell me: and if not, tell me; that I may turn to the right hand, or to the left.

50 Then Laban and Bethuel answered and said, The thing proceedeth from the LORD: we cannot speak unto thee bad or good.

51 Behold, Rebekah *is* before thee, take *her*, and go, and let her be thy master's son's wife, as the LORD hath spoken.

52 And it came to pass, that, when Abraham's servant heard their words, he worshipped the LORD, *bowing himself* to the earth.

53 And the servant brought forth jewels of silver, and jewels of gold, and raiment, and gave *them* to

NEW LIVING TRANSLATION

36 "When Sarah, my master's wife, was very old, she gave birth to my master's son, and my master has given him everything he owns. 37 And my master made me take an oath. He said, 'Do not allow my son to marry one of these local Canaanite women. 38 Go instead to my father's house, to my relatives, and find a wife there for my son.'

39 "But I said to my master, 'What if I can't find a young woman who is willing to go back with me?' 40 He responded, 'The LORD, in whose presence I have lived, will send his angel with you and will make your mission successful. Yes, you must find a wife for my son from among my relatives, from my father's family. 41 Then you will have fulfilled your obligation. But if you go to my relatives and they refuse to let her go with you, you will be free from my oath.'

42 "So today when I came to the spring, I prayed this prayer: 'O LORD, God of my master, Abraham, please give me success on this mission. 43 See, I am standing here beside this spring. This is my request. When a young woman comes to draw water, I will say to her, "Please give me a little drink of water from your jug." 44 If she says, "Yes, have a drink, and I will draw water for your camels, too," let her be the one you have selected to be the wife of my master's son.'

45 "Before I had finished praying in my heart, I saw Rebekah coming out with her water jug on her shoulder. She went down to the spring and drew water. So I said to her, 'Please give me a drink.' 46 She quickly lowered her jug from her shoulder and said, 'Yes, have a drink, and I will water your camels, too!' So I drank, and then she watered the camels.

47 "Then I asked, 'Whose daughter are you?' She replied, 'I am the daughter of Bethuel, and my grandparents are Nahor and Milcah.' So I put the ring on her nose, and the bracelets on her wrists.

48 "Then I bowed low and worshiped the LORD. I praised the LORD, the God of my master, Abraham, because he had led me straight to my master's niece to be his son's wife. 49 So tell me—will you or won't you show unfailing love and faithfulness to my master? Please tell me yes or no, and then I'll know what to do next."

50 Then Laban and Bethuel replied, "The LORD has obviously brought you here, so there is nothing we can say. 51 Here is Rebekah; take her and go. Yes, let her be the wife of your master's son, as the LORD has directed."

52 When Abraham's servant heard their answer, he bowed down to the ground and worshiped the LORD. 53 Then he brought out silver and gold jewelry and clothing and presented them to Rebekah. He also

KING JAMES VERSION

Rebekah: he gave also to her brother and to her
mother precious things.
54 And they did eat and drink, he and the men that
were with him, and tarried all night; and they rose up
in the morning, and he said, Send me away unto
my master.
55 And her brother and her mother said, Let the
damsel abide with us *a few* days, at the least ten; after
that she shall go.
56 And he said unto them, Hinder me not, seeing
the LORD hath prospered my way; send me away that
I may go to my master.
57 And they said, We will call the damsel, and inquire at her mouth.
58 And they called Rebekah, and said unto her, Wilt
thou go with this man? And she said, I will go.
59 And they sent away Rebekah their sister, and her
nurse, and Abraham's servant, and his men.
60 And they blessed Rebekah, and said unto her,
Thou *art* our sister, be thou *the mother* of thousands
of millions, and let thy seed possess the gate of those
which hate them.
61 And Rebekah arose, and her damsels, and they
rode upon the camels, and followed the man: and the
servant took Rebekah, and went his way.
62 And Isaac came from the way of the well Lahai-
roi; for he dwelt in the south country.
63 And Isaac went out to meditate in the field at the
eventide: and he lifted up his eyes, and saw, and, behold, the camels *were* coming.
64 And Rebekah lifted up her eyes, and when she
saw Isaac, she lighted off the camel.
65 For she *had* said unto the servant, What man *is*
this that walketh in the field to meet us? And the servant *had* said, It *is* my master: therefore she took a
veil, and covered herself.
66 And the servant told Isaac all things that he
had done.
67 And Isaac brought her into his mother Sarah's
tent, and took Rebekah, and she became his wife;
and he loved her: and Isaac was comforted after his
mother's *death*.

25 1 Then again Abraham took a wife, and her
name *was* Keturah.
2 And she bare him Zimran, and Jokshan, and
Medan, and Midian, and Ishbak, and Shuah.
3 And Jokshan begat Sheba, and Dedan. And the
sons of Dedan were Asshurim, and Letushim, and
Leummim.
4 And the sons of Midian; Ephah, and Epher, and
Hanoch, and Abidah, and Eldaah. All these *were* the
children of Keturah.
5 And Abraham gave all that he had unto Isaac.
6 But unto the sons of the concubines, which Abraham had, Abraham gave gifts, and sent them away

NEW LIVING TRANSLATION

gave expensive presents to her brother and mother.
54 Then they ate their meal, and the servant and the
men with him stayed there overnight.
But early the next morning, Abraham's servant
said, "Send me back to my master."
55 "But we want Rebekah to stay with us at least
ten days," her brother and mother said. "Then she
can go."
56 But he said, "Don't delay me. The LORD has made
my mission successful; now send me back so I can
return to my master."
57 "Well," they said, "we'll call Rebekah and ask her
what she thinks." 58 So they called Rebekah. "Are you
willing to go with this man?" they asked her.
And she replied, "Yes, I will go."
59 So they said good-bye to Rebekah and sent her
away with Abraham's servant and his men. The
woman who had been Rebekah's childhood nurse
went along with her. 60 They gave her this blessing as
she parted:

"Our sister, may you become
the mother of many millions!
May your descendants be strong
and conquer the cities of their enemies."

61 Then Rebekah and her servant girls mounted the
camels and followed the man. So Abraham's servant
took Rebekah and went on his way.
62 Meanwhile, Isaac, whose home was in the Negev,
had returned from Beer-lahai-roi. 63 One evening as he
was walking and meditating in the fields, he looked up
and saw the camels coming. 64 When Rebekah looked
up and saw Isaac, she quickly dismounted from her
camel. 65 "Who is that man walking through the fields
to meet us?" she asked the servant.
And he replied, "It is my master." So Rebekah covered her face with her veil. 66 Then the servant told
Isaac everything he had done.
67 And Isaac brought Rebekah into his mother Sarah's tent, and she became his wife. He loved her
deeply, and she was a special comfort to him after
the death of his mother.

The Death of Abraham

25 Abraham married another wife, whose
name was Keturah. 2 She gave birth to
Zimran, Jokshan, Medan, Midian, Ishbak, and Shuah.
3 Jokshan was the father of Sheba and Dedan.
Dedan's descendants were the Asshurites, Letushites,
and Leummites. 4 Midian's sons were Ephah, Epher,
Hanoch, Abida, and Eldaah. These were all
descendants of Abraham through Keturah.
5 Abraham gave everything he owned to his son
Isaac. 6 But before he died, he gave gifts to the sons of

KING JAMES VERSION

from Isaac his son, while he yet lived, eastward, unto
the east country.
7And these *are* the days of the years of Abraham's
life which he lived, an hundred threescore and fifteen years.
8Then Abraham gave up the ghost, and died in a
good old age, an old man, and full *of years;* and was
gathered to his people.
9And his sons Isaac and Ishmael buried him in the
cave of Machpelah, in the field of Ephron the son of
Zohar the Hittite, which *is* before Mamre;
10The field which Abraham purchased of the sons
of Heth: there was Abraham buried, and Sarah his
wife.
11And it came to pass after the death of Abraham,
that God blessed his son Isaac; and Isaac dwelt by the
well Lahai-roi.
12Now these *are* the generations of Ishmael, Abraham's son, whom Hagar the Egyptian, Sarah's handmaid, bare unto Abraham:
13And these *are* the names of the sons of Ishmael,
by their names, according to their generations: the
firstborn of Ishmael, Nebajoth; and Kedar, and
Adbeel, and Mibsam,
14And Mishma, and Dumah, and Massa,
15Hadar, and Tema, Jetur, Naphish, and Kedemah:
16These *are* the sons of Ishmael, and these *are*
their names, by their towns, and by their castles;
twelve princes according to their nations.
17And these *are* the years of the life of Ishmael,
an hundred and thirty and seven years: and he gave
up the ghost and died; and was gathered unto his
people.
18And they dwelt from Havilah unto Shur, that *is*
before Egypt, as thou goest toward Assyria: *and* he
died in the presence of all his brethren.
19And these *are* the generations of Isaac, Abraham's son: Abraham begat Isaac:
20And Isaac was forty years old when he took
Rebekah to wife, the daughter of Bethuel the Syrian
of Padan-aram, the sister to Laban the Syrian.
21And Isaac intreated the LORD for his wife, because she *was* barren: and the LORD was intreated of
him, and Rebekah his wife conceived.
22And the children struggled together within her;
and she said, If *it be* so, why *am* I thus? And she went
to inquire of the LORD.
23And the LORD said unto her, Two nations *are* in
thy womb, and two manner of people shall be separated from thy bowels; and *the one* people shall be
stronger than *the other* people; and the elder shall
serve the younger.
24And when her days to be delivered were fulfilled, behold, *there were* twins in her womb.
25And the first came out red, all over like an hairy
garment; and they called his name Esau.

NEW LIVING TRANSLATION

his concubines and sent them off to a land in the
east, away from Isaac.
7Abraham lived for 175 years, 8and he died at a
ripe old age, having lived a long and satisfying life.
He breathed his last and joined his ancestors in
death. 9His sons Isaac and Ishmael buried him in the
cave of Machpelah, near Mamre, in the field of
Ephron son of Zohar the Hittite. 10This was the field
Abraham had purchased from the Hittites and where
he had buried his wife Sarah. 11After Abraham's
death, God blessed his son Isaac, who settled near
Beer-lahai-roi in the Negev.

Ishmael's Descendants

12This is the account of the family of Ishmael, the son
of Abraham through Hagar, Sarah's Egyptian servant.
13Here is a list, by their names and clans, of Ishmael's
descendants: The oldest was Nebaioth, followed by
Kedar, Adbeel, Mibsam, 14Mishma, Dumah, Massa,
15Hadad, Tema, Jetur, Naphish, and Kedemah.
16These twelve sons of Ishmael became the founders
of twelve tribes named after them, listed according
to the places they settled and camped. 17Ishmael
lived for 137 years. Then he breathed his last and
joined his ancestors in death. 18Ishmael's descendants occupied the region from Havilah to Shur,
which is east of Egypt in the direction of Asshur.
There they lived in open hostility toward all their
relatives.*

The Births of Esau and Jacob

19This is the account of the family of Isaac, the son
of Abraham. 20When Isaac was forty years old, he
married Rebekah, the daughter of Bethuel the Aramean from Paddan-aram and the sister of Laban the
Aramean.
21Isaac pleaded with the LORD on behalf of his
wife, because she was unable to have children. The
LORD answered Isaac's prayer, and Rebekah became
pregnant with twins. 22But the two children struggled
with each other in her womb. So she went to ask
the LORD about it. "Why is this happening to me?"
she asked.
23And the LORD told her, "The sons in your womb
will become two nations. From the very beginning,
the two nations will be rivals. One nation will be
stronger than the other; and your older son will serve
your younger son."
24And when the time came to give birth, Rebekah
discovered that she did indeed have twins! 25The
first one was very red at birth and covered with thick

25:18 The meaning of the Hebrew is uncertain.

KING JAMES VERSION

26 And after that came his brother out, and his
hand took hold on Esau's heel; and his name was
called Jacob: and Isaac *was* threescore years old
when she bare them.

27 And the boys grew: and Esau was a cunning
hunter, a man of the field; and Jacob *was* a plain man,
dwelling in tents.
28 And Isaac loved Esau, because he did eat of *his*
venison: but Rebekah loved Jacob.
29 And Jacob sod pottage: and Esau came from the
field, and he *was* faint:
30 And Esau said to Jacob, Feed me, I pray thee, with
that same red *pottage;* for I *am* faint: therefore was
his name called Edom.
31 And Jacob said, Sell me this day thy birthright.
32 And Esau said, Behold, I *am* at the point to die:
and what profit shall this birthright do to me?
33 And Jacob said, Swear to me this day; and he
sware unto him: and he sold his birthright unto
Jacob.
34 Then Jacob gave Esau bread and pottage of
lentiles; and he did eat and drink, and rose up, and
went his way: thus Esau despised *his* birthright.

26 1 And there was a famine in the land, beside
the first famine that was in the days of
Abraham. And Isaac went unto Abimelech king of
the Philistines unto Gerar.
2 And the LORD appeared unto him, and said, Go
not down into Egypt; dwell in the land which I shall
tell thee of:
3 Sojourn in this land, and I will be with thee, and
will bless thee; for unto thee, and unto thy seed, I will
give all these countries, and I will perform the oath
which I sware unto Abraham thy father;
4 And I will make thy seed to multiply as the stars
of heaven, and will give unto thy seed all these countries; and in thy seed shall all the nations of the earth
be blessed;
5 Because that Abraham obeyed my voice, and
kept my charge, my commandments, my statutes,
and my laws.
6 And Isaac dwelt in Gerar:
7 And the men of the place asked *him* of his wife;
and he said, She *is* my sister: for he feared to say, *She
is* my wife; lest, *said he,* the men of the place should
kill me for Rebekah; because she *was* fair to look
upon.
8 And it came to pass, when he had been there a
long time, that Abimelech king of the Philistines
looked out at a window, and saw, and, behold, Isaac
was sporting with Rebekah his wife.

NEW LIVING TRANSLATION

hair like a fur coat. So they named him Esau.* 26 Then
the other twin was born with his hand grasping
Esau's heel. So they named him Jacob.* Isaac was
sixty years old when the twins were born.

Esau Sells His Birthright

27 As the boys grew up, Esau became a skillful hunter.
He was an outdoorsman, but Jacob had a quiet tem-
perament, preferring to stay at home. 28 Isaac loved
Esau because he enjoyed eating the wild game Esau
brought home, but Rebekah loved Jacob.
29 One day when Jacob was cooking some stew,
Esau arrived home from the wilderness exhausted
and hungry. 30 Esau said to Jacob, "I'm starved! Give
me some of that red stew!" (This is how Esau got his
other name, Edom, which means "red.")
31 "All right," Jacob replied, "but trade me your
rights as the firstborn son."
32 "Look, I'm dying of starvation!" said Esau.
"What good is my birthright to me now?"
33 But Jacob said, "First you must swear that your
birthright is mine." So Esau swore an oath, thereby
selling all his rights as the firstborn to his brother,
Jacob.
34 Then Jacob gave Esau some bread and lentil
stew. Esau ate the meal, then got up and left. He
showed contempt for his rights as the firstborn.

Isaac Deceives Abimelech

26 A severe famine now struck the land, as had
happened before in Abraham's time. So
Isaac moved to Gerar, where Abimelech, king of the
Philistines, lived.
2 The LORD appeared to Isaac and said, "Do not go
down to Egypt, but do as I tell you. 3 Live here as a foreigner in this land, and I will be with you and bless
you. I hereby confirm that I will give all these lands to
you and your descendants,* just as I solemnly promised Abraham, your father. 4 I will cause your descendants to become as numerous as the stars of the sky,
and I will give them all these lands. And through your
descendants all the nations of the earth will be
blessed. 5 I will do this because Abraham listened to
me and obeyed all my requirements, commands, decrees, and instructions." 6 So Isaac stayed in Gerar.
7 When the men who lived there asked Isaac about
his wife, Rebekah, he said, "She is my sister." He was
afraid to say, "She is my wife." He thought, "They will
kill me to get her, because she is so beautiful." 8 But
some time later, Abimelech, king of the Philistines,
looked out his window and saw Isaac caressing
Rebekah.

25:25 *Esau* sounds like a Hebrew term that means "hair." **25:26** *Jacob* sounds like the Hebrew words for "heel" and "deceiver." **26:3** Hebrew *seed;* also in 26:4, 24.

KING JAMES VERSION

9 And Abimelech called Isaac, and said, Behold, of
a surety she *is* thy wife: and how saidst thou, She *is*
my sister? And Isaac said unto him, Because I said,
Lest I die for her.
10 And Abimelech said, What *is* this thou hast
done unto us? one of the people might lightly have
lien with thy wife, and thou shouldest have brought
guiltiness upon us.
11 And Abimelech charged all *his* people, saying,
He that toucheth this man or his wife shall surely be
put to death.

12 Then Isaac sowed in that land, and received in
the same year an hundredfold: and the LORD blessed
him.
13 And the man waxed great, and went forward,
and grew until he became very great:
14 For he had possession of flocks, and possession
of herds, and great store of servants: and the
Philistines envied him.
15 For all the wells which his father's servants had
digged in the days of Abraham his father, the Philistines had stopped them, and filled them with earth.
16 And Abimelech said unto Isaac, Go from us; for
thou art much mightier than we.
17 And Isaac departed thence, and pitched his tent
in the valley of Gerar, and dwelt there.
18 And Isaac digged again the wells of water, which
they had digged in the days of Abraham his father;
for the Philistines had stopped them after the death
of Abraham: and he called their names after the
names by which his father had called them.
19 And Isaac's servants digged in the valley, and
found there a well of springing water.
20 And the herdmen of Gerar did strive with Isaac's
herdmen, saying, The water *is* ours: and he called the
name of the well Esek; because they strove with him.
21 And they digged another well, and strove for that
also: and he called the name of it Sitnah.
22 And he removed from thence, and digged another well; and for that they strove not: and he called
the name of it Rehoboth; and he said, For now the
LORD hath made room for us, and we shall be fruitful
in the land.
23 And he went up from thence to Beer-sheba.
24 And the LORD appeared unto him the same
night, and said, I *am* the God of Abraham thy father:
fear not, for I *am* with thee, and will bless thee, and
multiply thy seed for my servant Abraham's sake.
25 And he builded an altar there, and called upon
the name of the LORD, and pitched his tent there: and
there Isaac's servants digged a well.

26 Then Abimelech went to him from Gerar, and
Ahuzzath one of his friends, and Phichol the chief
captain of his army.

NEW LIVING TRANSLATION

9 Immediately, Abimelech called for Isaac and exclaimed, "She is obviously your wife! Why did you
say, 'She is my sister'?"
"Because I was afraid someone would kill me to
get her from me," Isaac replied.
10 "How could you do this to us?" Abimelech exclaimed. "One of my people might easily have taken
your wife and slept with her, and you would have
made us guilty of great sin."
11 Then Abimelech issued a public proclamation:
"Anyone who touches this man or his wife will be put
to death!"

Conflict over Water Rights

12 When Isaac planted his crops that year, he harvested a hundred times more grain than he planted,
for the LORD blessed him. 13 He became a very rich
man, and his wealth continued to grow. 14 He acquired so many flocks of sheep and goats, herds of
cattle, and servants that the Philistines became jealous of him. 15 So the Philistines filled up all of Isaac's
wells with dirt. These were the wells that had been
dug by the servants of his father, Abraham.
16 Finally, Abimelech ordered Isaac to leave the
country. "Go somewhere else," he said, "for you have
become too powerful for us."
17 So Isaac moved away to the Gerar Valley, where
he set up their tents and settled down. 18 He reopened the wells his father had dug, which the
Philistines had filled in after Abraham's death. Isaac
also restored the names Abraham had given them.
19 Isaac's servants also dug in the Gerar Valley and
discovered a well of fresh water. 20 But then the shepherds from Gerar came and claimed the spring.
"This is our water," they said, and they argued over it
with Isaac's herdsmen. So Isaac named the well Esek
(which means "argument"). 21 Isaac's men then dug
another well, but again there was a dispute over it. So
Isaac named it Sitnah (which means "hostility").
22 Abandoning that one, Isaac moved on and dug another well. This time there was no dispute over it, so
Isaac named the place Rehoboth (which means
"open space"), for he said, "At last the LORD has created enough space for us to prosper in this land."
23 From there Isaac moved to Beersheba, 24 where
the LORD appeared to him on the night of his arrival.
"I am the God of your father, Abraham," he said. "Do
not be afraid, for I am with you and will bless you. I
will multiply your descendants, and they will become
a great nation. I will do this because of my promise to
Abraham, my servant." 25 Then Isaac built an altar
there and worshiped the LORD. He set up his camp at
that place, and his servants dug another well.

Isaac's Covenant with Abimelech

26 One day King Abimelech came from Gerar with
his adviser, Ahuzzath, and also Phicol, his army

KING JAMES VERSION

27 And Isaac said unto them, Wherefore come ye
to me, seeing ye hate me, and have sent me away
from you?
28 And they said, We saw certainly that the LORD
was with thee: and we said, Let there be now an oath
betwixt us, *even* betwixt us and thee, and let us make
a covenant with thee;
29 That thou wilt do us no hurt, as we have not
touched thee, and as we have done unto thee nothing
but good, and have sent thee away in peace: thou *art*
now the blessed of the LORD.
30 And he made them a feast, and they did eat and
drink.
31 And they rose up betimes in the morning, and
sware one to another: and Isaac sent them away, and
they departed from him in peace.
32 And it came to pass the same day, that Isaac's
servants came, and told him concerning the well
which they had digged, and said unto him, We have
found water.
33 And he called it Shebah: therefore the name of
the city *is* Beer-sheba unto this day.
34 And Esau was forty years old when he took to
wife Judith the daughter of Beeri the Hittite, and
Bashemath the daughter of Elon the Hittite:
35 Which were a grief of mind unto Isaac and to
Rebekah.

27 1 And it came to pass, that when Isaac was
old, and his eyes were dim, so that he could
not see, he called Esau his eldest son, and said unto
him, My son: and he said unto him, Behold, *here am* I.
2 And he said, Behold now, I am old, I know not the
day of my death:
3 Now therefore take, I pray thee, thy weapons, thy
quiver and thy bow, and go out to the field, and take
me *some* venison;
4 And make me savoury meat, such as I love, and
bring *it* to me, that I may eat; that my soul may bless
thee before I die.
5 And Rebekah heard when Isaac spake to Esau his
son. And Esau went to the field to hunt *for* venison,
and to bring *it*.
6 And Rebekah spake unto Jacob her son, saying,
Behold, I heard thy father speak unto Esau thy
brother, saying,
7 Bring me venison, and make me savoury meat,
that I may eat, and bless thee before the LORD before
my death.
8 Now therefore, my son, obey my voice according
to that which I command thee.
9 Go now to the flock, and fetch me from thence
two good kids of the goats; and I will make them savoury meat for thy father, such as he loveth:
10 And thou shalt bring *it* to thy father, that he may
eat, and that he may bless thee before his death.
11 And Jacob said to Rebekah his mother, Behold,

NEW LIVING TRANSLATION

commander. 27 "Why have you come here?" Isaac
asked. "You obviously hate me, since you kicked me
off your land."
28 They replied, "We can plainly see that the LORD
is with you. So we want to enter into a sworn treaty
with you. Let's make a covenant. 29 Swear that you
will not harm us, just as we have never troubled you.
We have always treated you well, and we sent you
away from us in peace. And now look how the LORD
has blessed you!"
30 So Isaac prepared a covenant feast to celebrate
the treaty, and they ate and drank together. 31 Early
the next morning, they each took a solemn oath not
to interfere with each other. Then Isaac sent them
home again, and they left him in peace.
32 That very day Isaac's servants came and told him
about a new well they had dug. "We've found water!"
they exclaimed. 33 So Isaac named the well Shibah
(which means "oath"). And to this day the town that
grew up there is called Beersheba (which means
"well of the oath").
34 At the age of forty, Esau married two Hittite
wives: Judith, the daughter of Beeri, and Basemath,
the daughter of Elon. 35 But Esau's wives made life
miserable for Isaac and Rebekah.

Jacob Steals Esau's Blessing

27 One day when Isaac was old and turning
blind, he called for Esau, his older son, and
said, "My son."
"Yes, Father?" Esau replied.
2 "I am an old man now," Isaac said, "and I don't
know when I may die. 3 Take your bow and a quiver
full of arrows, and go out into the open country to
hunt some wild game for me. 4 Prepare my favorite
dish, and bring it here for me to eat. Then I will pronounce the blessing that belongs to you, my firstborn son, before I die."
5 But Rebekah overheard what Isaac had said to
his son Esau. So when Esau left to hunt for the wild
game, 6 she said to her son Jacob, "Listen. I overheard
your father say to Esau, 7 'Bring me some wild game
and prepare me a delicious meal. Then I will bless
you in the LORD's presence before I die.' 8 Now, my
son, listen to me. Do exactly as I tell you. 9 Go out to
the flocks, and bring me two fine young goats. I'll use
them to prepare your father's favorite dish. 10 Then
take the food to your father so he can eat it and bless
you before he dies."
11 "But look," Jacob replied to Rebekah, "my
brother, Esau, is a hairy man, and my skin is smooth.

KING JAMES VERSION

Esau my brother *is* a hairy man, and I *am* a smooth man:

12 My father peradventure will feel me, and I shall seem to him as a deceiver; and I shall bring a curse upon me, and not a blessing.

13 And his mother said unto him, Upon me *be* thy curse, my son: only obey my voice, and go fetch me *them*.

14 And he went, and fetched, and brought *them* to his mother: and his mother made savoury meat, such as his father loved.

15 And Rebekah took goodly raiment of her eldest son Esau, which *were* with her in the house, and put them upon Jacob her younger son:

16 And she put the skins of the kids of the goats upon his hands, and upon the smooth of his neck:

17 And she gave the savoury meat and the bread, which she had prepared, into the hand of her son Jacob.

18 And he came unto his father, and said, My father: and he said, Here *am* I; who *art* thou, my son?

19 And Jacob said unto his father, I *am* Esau thy firstborn; I have done according as thou badest me: arise, I pray thee, sit and eat of my venison, that thy soul may bless me.

20 And Isaac said unto his son, How *is it* that thou hast found *it* so quickly, my son? And he said, Because the LORD thy God brought *it* to me.

21 And Isaac said unto Jacob, Come near, I pray thee, that I may feel thee, my son, whether thou *be* my very son Esau or not.

22 And Jacob went near unto Isaac his father; and he felt him, and said, The voice *is* Jacob's voice, but the hands *are* the hands of Esau.

23 And he discerned him not, because his hands were hairy, as his brother Esau's hands: so he blessed him.

24 And he said, *Art* thou my very son Esau? And he said, I *am*.

25 And he said, Bring *it* near to me, and I will eat of my son's venison, that my soul may bless thee. And he brought *it* near to him, and he did eat: and he brought him wine, and he drank.

26 And his father Isaac said unto him, Come near now, and kiss me, my son.

27 And he came near, and kissed him: and he smelled the smell of his raiment, and blessed him, and said, See, the smell of my son *is* as the smell of a field which the LORD hath blessed:

28 Therefore God give thee of the dew of heaven, and the fatness of the earth, and plenty of corn and wine:

29 Let people serve thee, and nations bow down to thee: be lord over thy brethren, and let thy mother's sons bow down to thee: cursed *be* every one that curseth thee, and blessed *be* he that blesseth thee.

NEW LIVING TRANSLATION

12 What if my father touches me? He'll see that I'm
trying to trick him, and then he'll curse me instead of
blessing me."

13 But his mother replied, "Then let the curse fall
on me, my son! Just do what I tell you. Go out and get
the goats for me!"

14 So Jacob went out and got the young goats for
his mother. Rebekah took them and prepared a delicious meal, just the way Isaac liked it. 15 Then she
took Esau's favorite clothes, which were there in the
house, and gave them to her younger son, Jacob.
16 She covered his arms and the smooth part of his
neck with the skin of the young goats. 17 Then she
gave Jacob the delicious meal, including freshly
baked bread.

18 So Jacob took the food to his father. "My father?" he said.

"Yes, my son," Isaac answered. "Who are you—
Esau or Jacob?"

19 Jacob replied, "It's Esau, your firstborn son. I've
done as you told me. Here is the wild game. Now sit
up and eat it so you can give me your blessing."

20 Isaac asked, "How did you find it so quickly,
my son?"

"The LORD your God put it in my path!" Jacob
replied.

21 Then Isaac said to Jacob, "Come closer so I can
touch you and make sure that you really are Esau."
22 So Jacob went closer to his father, and Isaac
touched him. "The voice is Jacob's, but the hands are
Esau's," Isaac said. 23 But he did not recognize Jacob,
because Jacob's hands felt hairy just like Esau's. So
Isaac prepared to bless Jacob. 24 "But are you really
my son Esau?" he asked.

"Yes, I am," Jacob replied.

25 Then Isaac said, "Now, my son, bring me the wild
game. Let me eat it, and then I will give you my blessing." So Jacob took the food to his father, and Isaac
ate it. He also drank the wine that Jacob served him.
26 Then Isaac said to Jacob, "Please come a little
closer and kiss me, my son."

27 So Jacob went over and kissed him. And when
Isaac caught the smell of his clothes, he was finally
convinced, and he blessed his son. He said, "Ah! The
smell of my son is like the smell of the outdoors,
which the LORD has blessed!

28 "From the dew of heaven
 and the richness of the earth,
may God always give you abundant harvests
 of grain
 and bountiful new wine.
29 May many nations become your servants,
 and may they bow down to you.
May you be the master over your brothers,
 and may your mother's sons bow down to you.
All who curse you will be cursed,
 and all who bless you will be blessed."

KING JAMES VERSION

30And it came to pass, as soon as Isaac had made
an end of blessing Jacob, and Jacob was yet scarce
gone out from the presence of Isaac his father, that
Esau his brother came in from his hunting.
31And he also had made savoury meat, and
brought it unto his father, and said unto his father,
Let my father arise, and eat of his son's venison, that
thy soul may bless me.
32And Isaac his father said unto him, Who *art*
thou? And he said, I *am* thy son, thy firstborn Esau.
33And Isaac trembled very exceedingly, and said,
Who? where *is* he that hath taken venison, and
brought *it* me, and I have eaten of all before thou
camest, and have blessed him? yea, *and* he shall be
blessed.
34And when Esau heard the words of his father, he
cried with a great and exceeding bitter cry, and said
unto his father, Bless me, *even* me also, O my father.
35And he said, Thy brother came with subtilty, and
hath taken away thy blessing.
36And he said, Is not he rightly named Jacob? for
he hath supplanted me these two times: he took away
my birthright; and, behold, now he hath taken away
my blessing. And he said, Hast thou not reserved a
blessing for me?
37And Isaac answered and said unto Esau, Behold,
I have made him thy lord, and all his brethren have I
given to him for servants; and with corn and wine
have I sustained him: and what shall I do now unto
thee, my son?
38And Esau said unto his father, Hast thou but one
blessing, my father? bless me, *even* me also, O my father. And Esau lifted up his voice, and wept.
39And Isaac his father answered and said unto
him, Behold, thy dwelling shall be the fatness of the
earth, and of the dew of heaven from above;
40And by thy sword shalt thou live, and shalt serve
thy brother; and it shall come to pass when thou
shalt have the dominion, that thou shalt break his
yoke from off thy neck.

41And Esau hated Jacob because of the blessing
wherewith his father blessed him: and Esau said in
his heart, The days of mourning for my father are at
hand; then will I slay my brother Jacob.
42And these words of Esau her elder son were told
to Rebekah: and she sent and called Jacob her younger son, and said unto him, Behold, thy brother Esau,
as touching thee, doth comfort himself, *purposing* to
kill thee.
43Now therefore, my son, obey my voice; and arise,
flee thou to Laban my brother to Haran;
44And tarry with him a few days, until thy brother's
fury turn away;
45Until thy brother's anger turn away from thee,
and he forget *that* which thou hast done to him: then
I will send, and fetch thee from thence: why should I
be deprived also of you both in one day?

NEW LIVING TRANSLATION

30As soon as Isaac had finished blessing Jacob,
and almost before Jacob had left his father, Esau returned from his hunt. 31Esau prepared a delicious
meal and brought it to his father. Then he said, "Sit
up, my father, and eat my wild game so you can give
me your blessing."
32But Isaac asked him, "Who are you?"
Esau replied, "It's your son, your firstborn son,
Esau."
33Isaac began to tremble uncontrollably and said,
"Then who just served me wild game? I have already
eaten it, and I blessed him just before you came. And
yes, that blessing must stand!"
34When Esau heard his father's words, he let out a
loud and bitter cry. "Oh my father, what about me?
Bless me, too!" he begged.
35But Isaac said, "Your brother was here, and he
tricked me. He has taken away your blessing."
36Esau exclaimed, "No wonder his name is Jacob,
for now he has cheated me twice.* First he took my
rights as the firstborn, and now he has stolen my
blessing. Oh, haven't you saved even one blessing
for me?"
37Isaac said to Esau, "I have made Jacob your master and have declared that all his brothers will be his
servants. I have guaranteed him an abundance of
grain and wine—what is left for me to give you, my
son?"
38Esau pleaded, "But do you have only one blessing? Oh my father, bless me, too!" Then Esau broke
down and wept.
39Finally, his father, Isaac, said to him,

"You will live away from the richness
of the earth,
and away from the dew of the heaven above.
40 You will live by your sword,
and you will serve your brother.
But when you decide to break free,
you will shake his yoke from your neck."

Jacob Flees to Paddan-Aram

41From that time on, Esau hated Jacob because their
father had given Jacob the blessing. And Esau began
to scheme: "I will soon be mourning my father's
death. Then I will kill my brother, Jacob."
42But Rebekah heard about Esau's plans. So she
sent for Jacob and told him, "Listen, Esau is consoling
himself by plotting to kill you. 43So listen carefully,
my son. Get ready and flee to my brother, Laban, in
Haran. 44Stay there with him until your brother cools
off. 45When he calms down and forgets what you
have done to him, I will send for you to come back.
Why should I lose both of you in one day?"

27:36 *Jacob* sounds like the Hebrew words for "heel" and "deceiver."

KING JAMES VERSION

46 And Rebekah said to Isaac, I am weary of my life because of the daughters of Heth: if Jacob take a wife of the daughters of Heth, such as these *which are* of the daughters of the land, what good shall my life do me?

28 1 And Isaac called Jacob, and blessed him, and charged him, and said unto him, Thou shalt not take a wife of the daughters of Canaan.

2 Arise, go to Padan-aram, to the house of Bethuel thy mother's father; and take thee a wife from thence of the daughters of Laban thy mother's brother.

3 And God Almighty bless thee, and make thee fruitful, and multiply thee, that thou mayest be a multitude of people;

4 And give thee the blessing of Abraham, to thee, and to thy seed with thee; that thou mayest inherit the land wherein thou art a stranger, which God gave unto Abraham.

5 And Isaac sent away Jacob: and he went to Padan-aram unto Laban, son of Bethuel the Syrian, the brother of Rebekah, Jacob's and Esau's mother.

6 When Esau saw that Isaac had blessed Jacob, and sent him away to Padan-aram, to take him a wife from thence; and that as he blessed him he gave him a charge, saying, Thou shalt not take a wife of the daughters of Canaan;

7 And that Jacob obeyed his father and his mother, and was gone to Padan-aram;

8 And Esau seeing that the daughters of Canaan pleased not Isaac his father;

9 Then went Esau unto Ishmael, and took unto the wives which he had Mahalath the daughter of Ishmael Abraham's son, the sister of Nebajoth, to be his wife.

10 And Jacob went out from Beer-sheba, and went toward Haran.

11 And he lighted upon a certain place, and tarried there all night, because the sun was set; and he took of the stones of that place, and put *them for* his pillows, and lay down in that place to sleep.

12 And he dreamed, and behold a ladder set up on the earth, and the top of it reached to heaven: and behold the angels of God ascending and descending on it.

13 And, behold, the LORD stood above it, and said, I *am* the LORD God of Abraham thy father, and the God of Isaac: the land whereon thou liest, to thee will I give it, and to thy seed;

14 And thy seed shall be as the dust of the earth, and thou shalt spread abroad to the west, and to the east, and to the north, and to the south: and in thee and in thy seed shall all the families of the earth be blessed.

15 And, behold, I *am* with thee, and will keep thee in all *places* whither thou goest, and will bring thee again into this land; for I will not leave thee, until I have done *that* which I have spoken to thee of.

NEW LIVING TRANSLATION

46 Then Rebekah said to Isaac, "I'm sick and tired
of these local Hittite women! I would rather die than
see Jacob marry one of them."

28 So Isaac called for Jacob, blessed him, and
said, "You must not marry any of these
Canaanite women. 2 Instead, go at once to Paddan-
aram, to the house of your grandfather Bethuel, and
marry one of your uncle Laban's daughters. 3 May
God Almighty* bless you and give you many children. And may your descendants multiply and become many nations! 4 May God pass on to you and
your descendants* the blessings he promised to
Abraham. May you own this land where you are
now living as a foreigner, for God gave this land to
Abraham."
5 So Isaac sent Jacob away, and he went to Paddan-
aram to stay with his uncle Laban, his mother's
brother, the son of Bethuel the Aramean.
6 Esau knew that his father, Isaac, had blessed
Jacob and sent him to Paddan-aram to find a wife,
and that he had warned Jacob, "You must not marry a
Canaanite woman." 7 He also knew that Jacob had
obeyed his parents and gone to Paddan-aram. 8 It was
now very clear to Esau that his father did not like the
local Canaanite women. 9 So Esau visited his uncle
Ishmael's family and married one of Ishmael's
daughters, in addition to the wives he already had.
His new wife's name was Mahalath. She was the
sister of Nebaioth and the daughter of Ishmael,
Abraham's son.

Jacob's Dream at Bethel

10 Meanwhile, Jacob left Beersheba and traveled toward Haran. 11 At sundown he arrived at a good place
to set up camp and stopped there for the night. Jacob
found a stone to rest his head against and lay down to
sleep. 12 As he slept, he dreamed of a stairway that
reached from the earth up to heaven. And he saw the
angels of God going up and down the stairway.
13 At the top of the stairway stood the LORD, and he
said, "I am the LORD, the God of your grandfather
Abraham, and the God of your father, Isaac. The
ground you are lying on belongs to you. I am giving it
to you and your descendants. 14 Your descendants
will be as numerous as the dust of the earth! They
will spread out in all directions—to the west and the
east, to the north and the south. And all the families
of the earth will be blessed through you and your descendants. 15 What's more, I am with you, and I will
protect you wherever you go. One day I will bring you
back to this land. I will not leave you until I have finished giving you everything I have promised you."

28:3 Hebrew *El-Shaddai.* **28:4** Hebrew *seed;* also in 28:13, 14.

KING JAMES VERSION

16And Jacob awaked out of his sleep, and he said,
Surely the LORD is in this place; and I knew *it* not.
17And he was afraid, and said, How dreadful *is* this
place! this *is* none other but the house of God, and
this *is* the gate of heaven.
18And Jacob rose up early in the morning, and took
the stone that he had put *for* his pillows, and set it up
for a pillar, and poured oil upon the top of it.
19And he called the name of that place Bethel: but
the name of that city *was called* Luz at the first.
20And Jacob vowed a vow, saying, If God will be
with me, and will keep me in this way that I go, and
will give me bread to eat, and raiment to put on,
21So that I come again to my father's house in
peace; then shall the LORD be my God:
22And this stone, which I have set *for* a pillar, shall
be God's house: and of all that thou shalt give me I
will surely give the tenth unto thee.

29 1Then Jacob went on his journey, and came
into the land of the people of the east.
2And he looked, and behold a well in the field, and,
lo, there *were* three flocks of sheep lying by it; for out
of that well they watered the flocks: and a great stone
was upon the well's mouth.
3And thither were all the flocks gathered: and they
rolled the stone from the well's mouth, and watered
the sheep, and put the stone again upon the well's
mouth in his place.
4And Jacob said unto them, My brethren, whence
be ye? And they said, Of Haran *are* we.
5And he said unto them, Know ye Laban the son of
Nahor? And they said, We know *him*.
6And he said unto them, *Is* he well? And they said,
He is well: and, behold, Rachel his daughter cometh
with the sheep.
7And he said, Lo, *it is* yet high day, neither *is it* time
that the cattle should be gathered together: water ye
the sheep, and go *and* feed *them*.
8And they said, We cannot, until all the flocks be
gathered together, and *till* they roll the stone from
the well's mouth; then we water the sheep.
9And while he yet spake with them, Rachel came
with her father's sheep: for she kept them.
10And it came to pass, when Jacob saw Rachel the
daughter of Laban his mother's brother, and the
sheep of Laban his mother's brother, that Jacob went
near, and rolled the stone from the well's mouth, and
watered the flock of Laban his mother's brother.
11And Jacob kissed Rachel, and lifted up his voice,
and wept.
12And Jacob told Rachel that he *was* her father's
brother, and that he *was* Rebekah's son: and she ran
and told her father.

NEW LIVING TRANSLATION

16Then Jacob awoke from his sleep and said,
"Surely the LORD is in this place, and I wasn't even
aware of it!" 17But he was also afraid and said, "What
an awesome place this is! It is none other than the
house of God, the very gateway to heaven!"
18The next morning Jacob got up very early. He
took the stone he had rested his head against, and he
set it upright as a memorial pillar. Then he poured
olive oil over it. 19He named that place Bethel (which
means "house of God"), although it was previously
called Luz.
20Then Jacob made this vow: "If God will indeed be
with me and protect me on this journey, and if he will
provide me with food and clothing, 21and if I return
safely to my father's home, then the LORD will certainly be my God. 22And this memorial pillar I have
set up will become a place for worshiping God, and I
will present to God a tenth of everything he gives me."

Jacob Arrives at Paddan-Aram

29 Then Jacob hurried on, finally arriving in
the land of the east. 2He saw a well in the
distance. Three flocks of sheep and goats lay in an
open field beside it, waiting to be watered. But a
heavy stone covered the mouth of the well.
3It was the custom there to wait for all the flocks to
arrive before removing the stone and watering the
animals. Afterward the stone would be placed back
over the mouth of the well. 4Jacob went over to the
shepherds and asked, "Where are you from, my
friends?"
"We are from Haran," they answered.
5"Do you know a man there named Laban, the
grandson of Nahor?" he asked.
"Yes, we do," they replied.
6"Is he doing well?" Jacob asked.
"Yes, he's well," they answered. "Look, here comes
his daughter Rachel with the flock now."
7Jacob said, "Look, it's still broad daylight—too
early to round up the animals. Why don't you water
the sheep and goats so they can get back out to
pasture?"
8"We can't water the animals until all the flocks
have arrived," they replied. "Then the shepherds
move the stone from the mouth of the well, and we
water all the sheep and goats."
9Jacob was still talking with them when Rachel arrived with her father's flock, for she was a shepherd.
10And because Rachel was his cousin—the daughter
of Laban, his mother's brother—and because the
sheep and goats belonged to his uncle Laban, Jacob
went over to the well and moved the stone from its
mouth and watered his uncle's flock. 11Then Jacob
kissed Rachel, and he wept aloud. 12He explained to
Rachel that he was her cousin on her father's side—
the son of her aunt Rebekah. So Rachel quickly ran
and told her father, Laban.

KING JAMES VERSION

13And it came to pass, when Laban heard the tidings of Jacob his sister's son, that he ran to meet him, and embraced him, and kissed him, and brought him to his house. And he told Laban all these things.

14And Laban said to him, Surely thou *art* my bone and my flesh. And he abode with him the space of a month.

15And Laban said unto Jacob, Because thou *art* my brother, shouldest thou therefore serve me for nought? tell me, what *shall* thy wages *be?*

16And Laban had two daughters: the name of the elder *was* Leah, and the name of the younger *was* Rachel.

17Leah *was* tender eyed; but Rachel was beautiful and well favoured.

18And Jacob loved Rachel; and said, I will serve thee seven years for Rachel thy younger daughter.

19And Laban said, *It is* better that I give her to thee, than that I should give her to another man: abide with me.

20And Jacob served seven years for Rachel; and they seemed unto him *but* a few days, for the love he had to her.

21And Jacob said unto Laban, Give *me* my wife, for my days are fulfilled, that I may go in unto her.

22And Laban gathered together all the men of the place, and made a feast.

23And it came to pass in the evening, that he took Leah his daughter, and brought her to him; and he went in unto her.

24And Laban gave unto his daughter Leah Zilpah his maid *for* an handmaid.

25And it came to pass, that in the morning, behold, it *was* Leah: and he said to Laban, What *is* this thou hast done unto me? did not I serve with thee for Rachel? wherefore then hast thou beguiled me?

26And Laban said, It must not be so done in our country, to give the younger before the firstborn.

27Fulfil her week, and we will give thee this also for the service which thou shalt serve with me yet seven other years.

28And Jacob did so, and fulfilled her week: and he gave him Rachel his daughter to wife also.

29And Laban gave to Rachel his daughter Bilhah his handmaid to be her maid.

30And he went in also unto Rachel, and he loved also Rachel more than Leah, and served with him yet seven other years.

31And when the LORD saw that Leah *was* hated, he opened her womb: but Rachel *was* barren.

32And Leah conceived, and bare a son, and she called his name Reuben: for she said, Surely the LORD hath looked upon my affliction; now therefore my husband will love me.

NEW LIVING TRANSLATION

13As soon as Laban heard that his nephew Jacob had arrived, he ran out to meet him. He embraced and kissed him and brought him home. When Jacob had told him his story, 14Laban exclaimed, "You really are my own flesh and blood!"

Jacob Marries Leah and Rachel

After Jacob had stayed with Laban for about a month, 15Laban said to him, "You shouldn't work for me without pay just because we are relatives. Tell me how much your wages should be."

16Now Laban had two daughters. The older daughter was named Leah, and the younger one was Rachel. 17There was no sparkle in Leah's eyes,* but Rachel had a beautiful figure and a lovely face. 18Since Jacob was in love with Rachel, he told her father, "I'll work for you for seven years if you'll give me Rachel, your younger daughter, as my wife."

19"Agreed!" Laban replied. "I'd rather give her to you than to anyone else. Stay and work with me." 20So Jacob worked seven years to pay for Rachel. But his love for her was so strong that it seemed to him but a few days.

21Finally, the time came for him to marry her. "I have fulfilled my agreement," Jacob said to Laban. "Now give me my wife so I can sleep with her."

22So Laban invited everyone in the neighborhood and prepared a wedding feast. 23But that night, when it was dark, Laban took Leah to Jacob, and he slept with her. 24(Laban had given Leah a servant, Zilpah, to be her maid.)

25But when Jacob woke up in the morning—it was Leah! "What have you done to me?" Jacob raged at Laban. "I worked seven years for Rachel! Why have you tricked me?"

26"It's not our custom here to marry off a younger daughter ahead of the firstborn," Laban replied. 27"But wait until the bridal week is over, then we'll give you Rachel, too—provided you promise to work another seven years for me."

28So Jacob agreed to work seven more years. A week after Jacob had married Leah, Laban gave him Rachel, too. 29(Laban gave Rachel a servant, Bilhah, to be her maid.) 30So Jacob slept with Rachel, too, and he loved her much more than Leah. He then stayed and worked for Laban the additional seven years.

Jacob's Many Children

31When the LORD saw that Leah was unloved, he enabled her to have children, but Rachel could not conceive. 32So Leah became pregnant and gave birth to a son. She named him Reuben,* for she said, "The LORD has noticed my misery, and now my husband will love me."

29:17 Or *Leah had dull eyes,* or *Leah had soft eyes.* The meaning of the Hebrew is uncertain. **29:32** *Reuben* means "Look, a son!" It also sounds like the Hebrew for "He has seen my misery."

KING JAMES VERSION

33 And she conceived again, and bare a son; and
said, Because the LORD hath heard that I *was* hated,
he hath therefore given me this *son* also: and she
called his name Simeon.
34 And she conceived again, and bare a son; and
said, Now this time will my husband be joined unto
me, because I have born him three sons: therefore
was his name called Levi.
35 And she conceived again, and bare a son: and
she said, Now will I praise the LORD: therefore she
called his name Judah; and left bearing.

30 1 And when Rachel saw that she bare Jacob
no children, Rachel envied her sister; and
said unto Jacob, Give me children, or else I die.
2 And Jacob's anger was kindled against Rachel:
and he said, *Am* I in God's stead, who hath withheld
from thee the fruit of the womb?
3 And she said, Behold my maid Bilhah, go in unto
her; and she shall bear upon my knees, that I may
also have children by her.
4 And she gave him Bilhah her handmaid to wife:
and Jacob went in unto her.
5 And Bilhah conceived, and bare Jacob a son.
6 And Rachel said, God hath judged me, and hath
also heard my voice, and hath given me a son: therefore called she his name Dan.
7 And Bilhah Rachel's maid conceived again, and
bare Jacob a second son.
8 And Rachel said, With great wrestlings have I
wrestled with my sister, and I have prevailed: and she
called his name Naphtali.
9 When Leah saw that she had left bearing, she
took Zilpah her maid, and gave her Jacob to wife.
10 And Zilpah Leah's maid bare Jacob a son.
11 And Leah said, A troop cometh: and she called
his name Gad.
12 And Zilpah Leah's maid bare Jacob a second son.
13 And Leah said, Happy am I, for the daughters
will call me blessed: and she called his name Asher.
14 And Reuben went in the days of wheat harvest,
and found mandrakes in the field, and brought them
unto his mother Leah. Then Rachel said to Leah, Give
me, I pray thee, of thy son's mandrakes.
15 And she said unto her, *Is it* a small matter that
thou hast taken my husband? and wouldest thou
take away my son's mandrakes also? And Rachel said,
Therefore he shall lie with thee to night for thy son's
mandrakes.
16 And Jacob came out of the field in the evening,
and Leah went out to meet him, and said, Thou must
come in unto me; for surely I have hired thee with my
son's mandrakes. And he lay with her that night.

NEW LIVING TRANSLATION

33 She soon became pregnant again and gave birth
to another son. She named him Simeon,* for she
said, "The LORD heard that I was unloved and has
given me another son."
34 Then she became pregnant a third time and gave
birth to another son. She named him Levi,* for she
said, "Surely this time my husband will feel affection
for me, since I have given him three sons!"
35 Once again Leah became pregnant and gave
birth to another son. She named him Judah,* for she
said, "Now I will praise the LORD!" And then she
stopped having children.

30 When Rachel saw that she wasn't having any
children for Jacob, she became jealous of
her sister. She pleaded with Jacob, "Give me children,
or I'll die!"
2 Then Jacob became furious with Rachel. "Am I
God?" he asked. "He's the one who has kept you from
having children!"
3 Then Rachel told him, "Take my maid, Bilhah,
and sleep with her. She will bear children for me,*
and through her I can have a family, too." 4 So Rachel
gave her servant, Bilhah, to Jacob as a wife, and he
slept with her. 5 Bilhah became pregnant and presented him with a son. 6 Rachel named him Dan,* for
she said, "God has vindicated me! He has heard my
request and given me a son." 7 Then Bilhah became
pregnant again and gave Jacob a second son. 8 Rachel
named him Naphtali,* for she said, "I have struggled
hard with my sister, and I'm winning!"
9 Meanwhile, Leah realized that she wasn't getting
pregnant anymore, so she took her servant, Zilpah,
and gave her to Jacob as a wife. 10 Soon Zilpah presented him with a son. 11 Leah named him Gad,* for
she said, "How fortunate I am!" 12 Then Zilpah gave
Jacob a second son. 13 And Leah named him Asher,*
for she said, "What joy is mine! Now the other
women will celebrate with me."
14 One day during the wheat harvest, Reuben
found some mandrakes growing in a field and
brought them to his mother, Leah. Rachel begged
Leah, "Please give me some of your son's mandrakes."
15 But Leah angrily replied, "Wasn't it enough that
you stole my husband? Now will you steal my son's
mandrakes, too?"
Rachel answered, "I will let Jacob sleep with you
tonight if you give me some of the mandrakes."
16 So that evening, as Jacob was coming home
from the fields, Leah went out to meet him. "You
must come and sleep with me tonight!" she said. "I
have paid for you with some mandrakes that my son

29:33 *Simeon* probably means "one who hears." **29:34** *Levi* sounds like a Hebrew term that means "being attached" or "feeling affection for." **29:35** *Judah* is related to the Hebrew term for "praise." **30:3** Hebrew *bear children on my knees.* **30:6** *Dan* means "he judged" or "he vindicated." **30:8** *Naphtali* means "my struggle." **30:11** *Gad* means "good fortune." **30:13** *Asher* means "happy."

KING JAMES VERSION

17 And God hearkened unto Leah, and she conceived, and bare Jacob the fifth son.

18 And Leah said, God hath given me my hire, because I have given my maiden to my husband: and she called his name Issachar.

19 And Leah conceived again, and bare Jacob the sixth son.

20 And Leah said, God hath endued me *with* a good dowry; now will my husband dwell with me, because I have born him six sons: and she called his name Zebulun.

21 And afterwards she bare a daughter, and called her name Dinah.

22 And God remembered Rachel, and God hearkened to her, and opened her womb.

23 And she conceived, and bare a son; and said, God hath taken away my reproach:

24 And she called his name Joseph; and said, The LORD shall add to me another son.

25 And it came to pass, when Rachel had born Joseph, that Jacob said unto Laban, Send me away, that I may go unto mine own place, and to my country.

26 Give *me* my wives and my children, for whom I have served thee, and let me go: for thou knowest my service which I have done thee.

27 And Laban said unto him, I pray thee, if I have found favour in thine eyes, *tarry: for* I have learned by experience that the LORD hath blessed me for thy sake.

28 And he said, Appoint me thy wages, and I will give *it*.

29 And he said unto him, Thou knowest how I have served thee, and how thy cattle was with me.

30 For *it was* little which thou hadst before I *came*, and it is *now* increased unto a multitude; and the LORD hath blessed thee since my coming: and now when shall I provide for mine own house also?

31 And he said, What shall I give thee? And Jacob said, Thou shalt not give me any thing: if thou wilt do this thing for me, I will again feed *and* keep thy flock.

32 I will pass through all thy flock today, removing from thence all the speckled and spotted cattle, and all the brown cattle among the sheep, and the spotted and speckled among the goats: and *of such* shall be my hire.

33 So shall my righteousness answer for me in time to come, when it shall come for my hire before thy face: every one that *is* not speckled and spotted among the goats, and brown among the sheep, that shall be counted stolen with me.

34 And Laban said, Behold, I would it might be according to thy word.

35 And he removed that day the he goats that were ringstraked and spotted, and all the she goats that were speckled and spotted, *and* every one that had *some* white in it, and all the brown among the sheep, and gave *them* into the hand of his sons.

NEW LIVING TRANSLATION

found." So that night he slept with Leah. 17 And God answered Leah's prayers. She became pregnant again and gave birth to a fifth son for Jacob. 18 She named him Issachar,* for she said, "God has rewarded me for giving my servant to my husband as a wife." 19 Then Leah became pregnant again and gave birth to a sixth son for Jacob. 20 She named him Zebulun,* for she said, "God has given me a good reward. Now my husband will treat me with respect, for I have given him six sons." 21 Later she gave birth to a daughter and named her Dinah.

22 Then God remembered Rachel's plight and answered her prayers by enabling her to have children. 23 She became pregnant and gave birth to a son. "God has removed my disgrace," she said. 24 And she named him Joseph,* for she said, "May the LORD add yet another son to my family."

Jacob's Wealth Increases

25 Soon after Rachel had given birth to Joseph, Jacob said to Laban, "Please release me so I can go home to my own country. 26 Let me take my wives and children, for I have earned them by serving you, and let me be on my way. You certainly know how hard I have worked for you."

27 "Please listen to me," Laban replied. "I have become wealthy, for* the LORD has blessed me because of you. 28 Tell me how much I owe you. Whatever it is, I'll pay it."

29 Jacob replied, "You know how hard I've worked for you, and how your flocks and herds have grown under my care. 30 You had little indeed before I came, but your wealth has increased enormously. The LORD has blessed you through everything I've done. But now, what about me? When can I start providing for my own family?"

31 "What wages do you want?" Laban asked again.

Jacob replied, "Don't give me anything. Just do this one thing, and I'll continue to tend and watch over your flocks. 32 Let me inspect your flocks today and remove all the sheep and goats that are speckled or spotted, along with all the black sheep. Give these to me as my wages. 33 In the future, when you check on the animals you have given me as my wages, you'll see that I have been honest. If you find in my flock any goats without speckles or spots, or any sheep that are not black, you will know that I have stolen them from you."

34 "All right," Laban replied. "It will be as you say." 35 But that very day Laban went out and removed the male goats that were streaked and spotted, all the female goats that were speckled and spotted or had white patches, and all the black sheep. He placed

30:18 *Issachar* sounds like a Hebrew term that means "reward." **30:20** *Zebulun* probably means "honor." **30:24** *Joseph* means "may he add." **30:27** Or *I have learned by divination that.*

KING JAMES VERSION

[36]And he set three days' journey betwixt himself and Jacob: and Jacob fed the rest of Laban's flocks.

[37]And Jacob took him rods of green poplar, and of the hazel and chestnut tree; and pilled white strakes in them, and made the white appear which *was* in the rods.

[38]And he set the rods which he had pilled before the flocks in the gutters in the watering troughs when the flocks came to drink, that they should conceive when they came to drink.

[39]And the flocks conceived before the rods, and brought forth cattle ringstraked, speckled, and spotted.

[40]And Jacob did separate the lambs, and set the faces of the flocks toward the ringstraked, and all the brown in the flock of Laban; and he put his own flocks by themselves, and put them not unto Laban's cattle.

[41]And it came to pass, whensoever the stronger cattle did conceive, that Jacob laid the rods before the eyes of the cattle in the gutters, that they might conceive among the rods.

[42]But when the cattle were feeble, he put *them* not in: so the feebler were Laban's, and the stronger Jacob's.

[43]And the man increased exceedingly, and had much cattle, and maidservants, and menservants, and camels, and asses.

31 [1]And he heard the words of Laban's sons, saying, Jacob hath taken away all that *was* our father's; and of *that* which *was* our father's hath he gotten all this glory.

[2]And Jacob beheld the countenance of Laban, and, behold, it *was* not toward him as before.

[3]And the LORD said unto Jacob, Return unto the land of thy fathers, and to thy kindred; and I will be with thee.

[4]And Jacob sent and called Rachel and Leah to the field unto his flock,

[5]And said unto them, I see your father's countenance, that it *is* not toward me as before; but the God of my father hath been with me.

[6]And ye know that with all my power I have served your father.

[7]And your father hath deceived me, and changed my wages ten times; but God suffered him not to hurt me.

[8]If he said thus, The speckled shall be thy wages; then all the cattle bare speckled: and if he said thus, The ringstraked shall be thy hire; then bare all the cattle ringstraked.

[9]Thus God hath taken away the cattle of your father, and given *them* to me.

[10]And it came to pass at the time that the cattle conceived, that I lifted up mine eyes, and saw in a dream, and, behold, the rams which leaped upon the cattle *were* ringstraked, speckled, and grisled.

NEW LIVING TRANSLATION

them in the care of his own sons, [36]who took them a three-days' journey from where Jacob was. Meanwhile, Jacob stayed and cared for the rest of Laban's flock.

[37]Then Jacob took some fresh branches from poplar, almond, and plane trees and peeled off strips of bark, making white streaks on them. [38]Then he placed these peeled branches in the watering troughs where the flocks came to drink, for that was where they mated. [39]And when they mated in front of the white-streaked branches, they gave birth to young that were streaked, speckled, and spotted. [40]Jacob separated those lambs from Laban's flock. And at mating time he turned the flock to face Laban's animals that were streaked or black. This is how he built his own flock instead of increasing Laban's.

[41]Whenever the stronger females were ready to mate, Jacob would place the peeled branches in the watering troughs in front of them. Then they would mate in front of the branches. [42]But he didn't do this with the weaker ones, so the weaker lambs belonged to Laban, and the stronger ones were Jacob's. [43]As a result, Jacob became very wealthy, with large flocks of sheep and goats, female and male servants, and many camels and donkeys.

Jacob Flees from Laban

31 But Jacob soon learned that Laban's sons were grumbling about him. "Jacob has robbed our father of everything!" they said. "He has gained all his wealth at our father's expense." [2]And Jacob began to notice a change in Laban's attitude toward him.

[3]Then the LORD said to Jacob, "Return to the land of your father and grandfather and to your relatives there, and I will be with you."

[4]So Jacob called Rachel and Leah out to the field where he was watching his flock. [5]He said to them, "I have noticed that your father's attitude toward me has changed. But the God of my father has been with me. [6]You know how hard I have worked for your father, [7]but he has cheated me, changing my wages ten times. But God has not allowed him to do me any harm. [8]For if he said, 'The speckled animals will be your wages,' the whole flock began to produce speckled young. And when he changed his mind and said, 'The striped animals will be your wages,' then the whole flock produced striped young. [9]In this way, God has taken your father's animals and given them to me.

[10]"One time during the mating season, I had a dream and saw that the male goats mating with the females were streaked, speckled, and spotted.

KING JAMES VERSION

11 And the angel of God spake unto me in a dream,
saying, Jacob: And I said, Here *am* I.
12 And he said, Lift up now thine eyes, and see, all
the rams which leap upon the cattle *are* ringstraked,
speckled, and grisled: for I have seen all that Laban
doeth unto thee.
13 I *am* the God of Bethel, where thou anointedst
the pillar, *and* where thou vowedst a vow unto me:
now arise, get thee out from this land, and return
unto the land of thy kindred.
14 And Rachel and Leah answered and said unto
him, *Is there* yet any portion or inheritance for us in
our father's house?
15 Are we not counted of him strangers? for he hath
sold us, and hath quite devoured also our money.
16 For all the riches which God hath taken from
our father, that *is* ours, and our children's: now then,
whatsoever God hath said unto thee, do.
17 Then Jacob rose up, and set his sons and his
wives upon camels;
18 And he carried away all his cattle, and all his
goods which he had gotten, the cattle of his getting,
which he had gotten in Padan-aram, for to go to Isaac
his father in the land of Canaan.
19 And Laban went to shear his sheep: and Rachel
had stolen the images that *were* her father's.
20 And Jacob stole away unawares to Laban the
Syrian, in that he told him not that he fled.
21 So he fled with all that he had; and he rose up,
and passed over the river, and set his face *toward* the
mount Gilead.

22 And it was told Laban on the third day that Jacob
was fled.
23 And he took his brethren with him, and pursued
after him seven days' journey; and they overtook him
in the mount Gilead.
24 And God came to Laban the Syrian in a dream by
night, and said unto him, Take heed that thou speak
not to Jacob either good or bad.
25 Then Laban overtook Jacob. Now Jacob had
pitched his tent in the mount: and Laban with his
brethren pitched in the mount of Gilead.
26 And Laban said to Jacob, What hast thou done,
that thou hast stolen away unawares to me, and
carried away my daughters, as captives *taken* with
the sword?
27 Wherefore didst thou flee away secretly, and
steal away from me; and didst not tell me, that I
might have sent thee away with mirth, and with
songs, with tabret, and with harp?
28 And hast not suffered me to kiss my sons and my
daughters? thou hast now done foolishly in *so* doing.
29 It is in the power of my hand to do you hurt: but
the God of your father spake unto me yesternight,
saying, Take thou heed that thou speak not to Jacob
either good or bad.

NEW LIVING TRANSLATION

11 Then in my dream, the angel of God said to me,
'Jacob!' And I replied, 'Yes, here I am.'
12 "The angel said, 'Look up, and you will see that
only the streaked, speckled, and spotted males are
mating with the females of your flock. For I have
seen how Laban has treated you.
13 I am the God who
appeared to you at Bethel,* the place where you
anointed the pillar of stone and made your vow to
me. Now get ready and leave this country and return
to the land of your birth.'"
14 Rachel and Leah responded, "That's fine with
us! We won't inherit any of our father's wealth anyway.
15 He has reduced our rights to those of foreign
women. And after he sold us, he wasted the money
you paid him for us.
16 All the wealth God has given
you from our father legally belongs to us and our
children. So go ahead and do whatever God has
told you."
17 So Jacob put his wives and children on camels,
18 and he drove all his livestock in front of him. He
packed all the belongings he had acquired in
Paddan-aram and set out for the land of Canaan,
where his father, Isaac, lived.
19 At the time they left,
Laban was some distance away, shearing his sheep.
Rachel stole her father's household idols and took
them with her.
20 Jacob outwitted Laban the Ara-
mean, for they set out secretly and never told Laban
they were leaving.
21 So Jacob took all his possessions
with him and crossed the Euphrates River,* heading
for the hill country of Gilead.

Laban Pursues Jacob

22 Three days later, Laban was told that Jacob had
fled.
23 So he gathered a group of his relatives and set
out in hot pursuit. He caught up with Jacob seven
days later in the hill country of Gilead.
24 But the pre-
vious night God had appeared to Laban the Aramean
in a dream and told him, "I'm warning you—leave
Jacob alone!"
25 Laban caught up with Jacob as he was camped in
the hill country of Gilead, and he set up his camp not
far from Jacob's.
26 "What do you mean by deceiving
me like this?" Laban demanded. "How dare you drag
my daughters away like prisoners of war?
27 Why did
you slip away secretly? Why did you deceive me? And
why didn't you say you wanted to leave? I would have
given you a farewell feast, with singing and music, accompanied by tambourines and harps.
28 Why didn't
you let me kiss my daughters and grandchildren and
tell them good-bye? You have acted very foolishly!
29 I could destroy you, but the God of your father appeared to me last night and warned me, 'Leave Jacob

31:13 As in Greek version and an Aramaic Targum; Hebrew reads *the God of Bethel*. **31:21** Hebrew *the river*.

KING JAMES VERSION

30 And now, *though* thou wouldest needs be gone, because thou sore longedst after thy father's house, *yet* wherefore hast thou stolen my gods?

31 And Jacob answered and said to Laban, Because I was afraid: for I said, Peradventure thou wouldest take by force thy daughters from me.

32 With whomsoever thou findest thy gods, let him not live: before our brethren discern thou what *is* thine with me, and take *it* to thee. For Jacob knew not that Rachel had stolen them.

33 And Laban went into Jacob's tent, and into Leah's tent, and into the two maidservants' tents; but he found *them* not. Then went he out of Leah's tent, and entered into Rachel's tent.

34 Now Rachel had taken the images, and put them in the camel's furniture, and sat upon them. And Laban searched all the tent, but found *them* not.

35 And she said to her father, Let it not displease my lord that I cannot rise up before thee; for the custom of women *is* upon me. And he searched, but found not the images.

36 And Jacob was wroth, and chode with Laban: and Jacob answered and said to Laban, What *is* my trespass? what *is* my sin, that thou hast so hotly pursued after me?

37 Whereas thou hast searched all my stuff, what hast thou found of all thy household stuff? set *it* here before my brethren and thy brethren, that they may judge betwixt us both.

38 This twenty years *have* I *been* with thee; thy ewes and thy she goats have not cast their young, and the rams of thy flock have I not eaten.

39 That which was torn *of beasts* I brought not unto thee; I bare the loss of it; of my hand didst thou require it, *whether* stolen by day, or stolen by night.

40 *Thus* I was; in the day the drought consumed me, and the frost by night; and my sleep departed from mine eyes.

41 Thus have I been twenty years in thy house; I served thee fourteen years for thy two daughters, and six years for thy cattle: and thou hast changed my wages ten times.

42 Except the God of my father, the God of Abraham, and the fear of Isaac, had been with me, surely thou hadst sent me away now empty. God hath seen mine affliction and the labour of my hands, and rebuked *thee* yesternight.

43 And Laban answered and said unto Jacob, *These* daughters *are* my daughters, and *these* children *are* my children, and *these* cattle *are* my cattle, and all that thou seest *is* mine: and what can I do this day unto these my daughters, or unto their children which they have born?

NEW LIVING TRANSLATION

alone!' 30 I can understand your feeling that you must
go, and your intense longing for your father's home.
But why have you stolen my gods?"

31 "I rushed away because I was afraid," Jacob answered. "I thought you would take your daughters
from me by force. 32 But as for your gods, see if you
can find them, and let the person who has taken
them die! And if you find anything else that belongs
to you, identify it before all these relatives of ours,
and I will give it back!" But Jacob did not know that
Rachel had stolen the household idols.

33 Laban went first into Jacob's tent to search there,
then into Leah's, and then the tents of the two servant wives—but he found nothing. Finally, he went
into Rachel's tent. 34 But Rachel had taken the household idols and hidden them in her camel saddle, and
now she was sitting on them. When Laban had thoroughly searched her tent without finding them,
35 she said to her father, "Please, sir, forgive me if I
don't get up for you. I'm having my monthly period."
So Laban continued his search, but he could not find
the household idols.

36 Then Jacob became very angry, and he challenged Laban. "What's my crime?" he demanded.
"What have I done wrong to make you chase after
me as though I were a criminal? 37 You have rum-
maged through everything I own. Now show me
what you found that belongs to you! Set it out here in
front of us, before our relatives, for all to see. Let
them judge between us!

38 "For twenty years I have been with you, caring
for your flocks. In all that time your sheep and goats
never miscarried. In all those years I never used a single ram of yours for food. 39 If any were attacked and
killed by wild animals, I never showed you the carcass and asked you to reduce the count of your flock.
No, I took the loss myself! You made me pay for every
stolen animal, whether it was taken in broad daylight
or in the dark of night.

40 "I worked for you through the scorching heat of
the day and through cold and sleepless nights. 41 Yes,
for twenty years I slaved in your house! I worked for
fourteen years earning your two daughters, and then
six more years for your flock. And you changed my
wages ten times! 42 In fact, if the God of my father had
not been on my side—the God of Abraham and the
fearsome God of Isaac*—you would have sent me
away empty-handed. But God has seen your abuse
and my hard work. That is why he appeared to you
last night and rebuked you!"

Jacob's Treaty with Laban

43 Then Laban replied to Jacob, "These women are
my daughters, these children are my grandchildren,
and these flocks are my flocks—in fact, everything
you see is mine. But what can I do now about my

31:42 Or *and the Fear of Isaac.*

KING JAMES VERSION

44Now therefore come thou, let us make a covenant, I and thou; and let it be for a witness between
me and thee.
45And Jacob took a stone, and set it up *for* a pillar.
46And Jacob said unto his brethren, Gather stones;
and they took stones, and made an heap: and they
did eat there upon the heap.
47And Laban called it Jegar-sahadutha: but Jacob
called it Galeed.
48And Laban said, This heap *is* a witness between
me and thee this day. Therefore was the name of it
called Galeed;
49And Mizpah; for he said, The LORD watch between me and thee, when we are absent one from
another.
50If thou shalt afflict my daughters, or if thou shalt
take *other* wives beside my daughters, no man *is*
with us; see, God *is* witness betwixt me and thee.
51And Laban said to Jacob, Behold this heap, and
behold *this* pillar, which I have cast betwixt me
and thee;
52This heap *be* witness, and *this* pillar *be* witness,
that I will not pass over this heap to thee, and that
thou shalt not pass over this heap and this pillar unto
me, for harm.
53The God of Abraham, and the God of Nahor, the
God of their father, judge betwixt us. And Jacob
sware by the fear of his father Isaac.
54Then Jacob offered sacrifice upon the mount,
and called his brethren to eat bread: and they did eat
bread, and tarried all night in the mount.
55And early in the morning Laban rose up, and
kissed his sons and his daughters, and blessed them:
and Laban departed, and returned unto his place.

32 1And Jacob went on his way, and the angels
of God met him.
2And when Jacob saw them, he said, This *is* God's
host: and he called the name of that place Mahanaim.

3And Jacob sent messengers before him to Esau
his brother unto the land of Seir, the country of
Edom.
4And he commanded them, saying, Thus shall ye
speak unto my lord Esau; Thy servant Jacob saith
thus, I have sojourned with Laban, and stayed there
until now:
5And I have oxen, and asses, flocks, and menservants, and womenservants: and I have sent to tell
my lord, that I may find grace in thy sight.

NEW LIVING TRANSLATION

daughters and their children? 44So come, let's make
a covenant, you and I, and it will be a witness to our
commitment."
45So Jacob took a stone and set it up as a monument. 46Then he told his family members, "Gather
some stones." So they gathered stones and piled
them in a heap. Then Jacob and Laban sat down beside the pile of stones to eat a covenant meal. 47To
commemorate the event, Laban called the place
Jegar-sahadutha (which means "witness pile" in Aramaic), and Jacob called it Galeed (which means "witness pile" in Hebrew).
48Then Laban declared, "This pile of stones will
stand as a witness to remind us of the covenant we
have made today." This explains why it was called
Galeed—"Witness Pile." 49But it was also called
Mizpah (which means "watchtower"), for Laban said,
"May the LORD keep watch between us to make sure
that we keep this covenant when we are out of each
other's sight. 50If you mistreat my daughters or if you
marry other wives, God will see it even if no one else
does. He is a witness to this covenant between us.
51"See this pile of stones," Laban continued, "and
see this monument I have set between us. 52They
stand between us as witnesses of our vows. I will
never pass this pile of stones to harm you, and you
must never pass these stones or this monument to
harm me. 53I call on the God of our ancestors—the
God of your grandfather Abraham and the God of my
grandfather Nahor—to serve as a judge between us."
So Jacob took an oath before the fearsome God
of his father, Isaac,* to respect the boundary line.
54Then Jacob offered a sacrifice to God there on the
mountain and invited everyone to a covenant feast.
After they had eaten, they spent the night on the
mountain.
55*Laban got up early the next morning, and he
kissed his grandchildren and his daughters and
blessed them. Then he left and returned home.

32 1*As Jacob started on his way again, angels
of God came to meet him. 2When Jacob saw
them, he exclaimed, "This is God's camp!" So he
named the place Mahanaim.*

Jacob Sends Gifts to Esau

3Then Jacob sent messengers ahead to his brother,
Esau, who was living in the region of Seir in the land
of Edom. 4He told them, "Give this message to my
master Esau: 'Humble greetings from your servant
Jacob. Until now I have been living with Uncle Laban,
5and now I own cattle, donkeys, flocks of sheep and
goats, and many servants, both men and women. I
have sent these messengers to inform my lord of my
coming, hoping that you will be friendly to me.'"

31:53 Or *the Fear of his father, Isaac.* **31:55** Verse 31:55 is numbered 32:1 in Hebrew text. **32:1** Verses 32:1-32 are numbered 32:2-33 in Hebrew text. **32:2** *Mahanaim* means "two camps."

KING JAMES VERSION

6 And the messengers returned to Jacob, saying,
We came to thy brother Esau, and also he cometh to
meet thee, and four hundred men with him.
7 Then Jacob was greatly afraid and distressed: and
he divided the people that *was* with him, and the
flocks, and herds, and the camels, into two bands;
8 And said, If Esau come to the one company, and
smite it, then the other company which is left shall
escape.
9 And Jacob said, O God of my father Abraham, and
God of my father Isaac, the LORD which saidst unto
me, Return unto thy country, and to thy kindred, and
I will deal well with thee:
10 I am not worthy of the least of all the mercies,
and of all the truth, which thou hast shewed unto thy
servant; for with my staff I passed over this Jordan;
and now I am become two bands.
11 Deliver me, I pray thee, from the hand of my
brother, from the hand of Esau: for I fear him, lest he
will come and smite me, *and* the mother with the
children.
12 And thou saidst, I will surely do thee good, and
make thy seed as the sand of the sea, which cannot
be numbered for multitude.
13 And he lodged there that same night; and took
of that which came to his hand a present for Esau his
brother;
14 Two hundred she goats, and twenty he goats,
two hundred ewes, and twenty rams,
15 Thirty milch camels with their colts, forty kine,
and ten bulls, twenty she asses, and ten foals.
16 And he delivered *them* into the hand of his servants, every drove by themselves; and said unto his
servants, Pass over before me, and put a space betwixt drove and drove.
17 And he commanded the foremost, saying, When
Esau my brother meeteth thee, and asketh thee, saying, Whose *art* thou? and whither goest thou? and
whose *are* these before thee?
18 Then thou shalt say, *They be* thy servant Jacob's;
it *is* a present sent unto my lord Esau: and, behold,
also he *is* behind us.
19 And so commanded he the second, and the
third, and all that followed the droves, saying, On this
manner shall ye speak unto Esau, when ye find him.
20 And say ye moreover, Behold, thy servant Jacob *is*
behind us. For he said, I will appease him with the
present that goeth before me, and afterward I will
see his face; peradventure he will accept of me.
21 So went the present over before him: and himself lodged that night in the company.
22 And he rose up that night, and took his two
wives, and his two womenservants, and his eleven
sons, and passed over the ford Jabbok.
23 And he took them, and sent them over the
brook, and sent over that he had.

NEW LIVING TRANSLATION

6 After delivering the message, the messengers returned to Jacob and reported, "We met your brother,
Esau, and he is already on his way to meet you—with
an army of 400 men!" 7 Jacob was terrified at the
news. He divided his household, along with the
flocks and herds and camels, into two groups. 8 He
thought, "If Esau meets one group and attacks it, perhaps the other group can escape."
9 Then Jacob prayed, "O God of my grandfather
Abraham, and God of my father, Isaac—O LORD, you
told me, 'Return to your own land and to your relatives.' And you promised me, 'I will treat you kindly.'
10 I am not worthy of all the unfailing love and faithfulness you have shown to me, your servant. When I
left home and crossed the Jordan River, I owned
nothing except a walking stick. Now my household
fills two large camps! 11 O LORD, please rescue me
from the hand of my brother, Esau. I am afraid that
he is coming to attack me, along with my wives and
children. 12 But you promised me, 'I will surely treat
you kindly, and I will multiply your descendants until
they become as numerous as the sands along the
seashore—too many to count.'"
13 Jacob stayed where he was for the night. Then
he selected these gifts from his possessions to present to his brother, Esau: 14 200 female goats,
20 male goats, 200 ewes, 20 rams, 15 30 female camels with their young, 40 cows, 10 bulls, 20 female
donkeys, and 10 male donkeys. 16 He divided these
animals into herds and assigned each to different
servants. Then he told his servants, "Go ahead of me
with the animals, but keep some distance between
the herds."
17 He gave these instructions to the men leading
the first group: "When my brother, Esau, meets you,
he will ask, 'Whose servants are you? Where are you
going? Who owns these animals?' 18 You must reply,
'They belong to your servant Jacob, but they are a
gift for his master Esau. Look, he is coming right behind us.'"
19 Jacob gave the same instructions to the second
and third herdsmen and to all who followed behind
the herds: "You must say the same thing to Esau
when you meet him. 20 And be sure to say, 'Look, your
servant Jacob is right behind us.'"
Jacob thought, "I will try to appease him by sending gifts ahead of me. When I see him in person, perhaps he will be friendly to me." 21 So the gifts were
sent on ahead, while Jacob himself spent that night
in the camp.

Jacob Wrestles with God

22 During the night Jacob got up and took his two
wives, his two servant wives, and his eleven sons
and crossed the Jabbok River with them. 23 After
taking them to the other side, he sent over all his
possessions.

KING JAMES VERSION

24And Jacob was left alone; and there wrestled a
man with him until the breaking of the day.
25And when he saw that he prevailed not against
him, he touched the hollow of his thigh; and the hollow of Jacob's thigh was out of joint, as he wrestled
with him.
26And he said, Let me go, for the day breaketh. And
he said, I will not let thee go, except thou bless me.
27And he said unto him, What *is* thy name? And he
said, Jacob.
28And he said, Thy name shall be called no more
Jacob, but Israel: for as a prince hast thou power with
God and with men, and hast prevailed.
29And Jacob asked *him,* and said, Tell *me,* I pray
thee, thy name. And he said, Wherefore *is* it *that*
thou dost ask after my name? And he blessed him
there.
30And Jacob called the name of the place Peniel:
for I have seen God face to face, and my life is
preserved.
31And as he passed over Penuel the sun rose upon
him, and he halted upon his thigh.
32Therefore the children of Israel eat not *of* the
sinew which shrank, which *is* upon the hollow of the
thigh, unto this day: because he touched the hollow
of Jacob's thigh in the sinew that shrank.

33 1And Jacob lifted up his eyes, and looked,
and, behold, Esau came, and with him four
hundred men. And he divided the children unto
Leah, and unto Rachel, and unto the two handmaids.
2And he put the handmaids and their children
foremost, and Leah and her children after, and Rachel and Joseph hindermost.
3And he passed over before them, and bowed himself to the ground seven times, until he came near to
his brother.
4And Esau ran to meet him, and embraced him,
and fell on his neck, and kissed him: and they wept.
5And he lifted up his eyes, and saw the women and
the children; and said, Who *are* those with thee? And
he said, The children which God hath graciously
given thy servant.
6Then the handmaidens came near, they and their
children, and they bowed themselves.
7And Leah also with her children came near, and
bowed themselves: and after came Joseph near and
Rachel, and they bowed themselves.
8And he said, What *meanest* thou by all this drove
which I met? And he said, *These are* to find grace in
the sight of my lord.
9And Esau said, I have enough, my brother; keep
that thou hast unto thyself.
10And Jacob said, Nay, I pray thee, if now I have
found grace in thy sight, then receive my present
at my hand: for therefore I have seen thy face, as
though I had seen the face of God, and thou wast
pleased with me.

NEW LIVING TRANSLATION

24This left Jacob all alone in the camp, and a man
came and wrestled with him until the dawn began to
break. 25When the man saw that he would not win
the match, he touched Jacob's hip and wrenched it
out of its socket. 26Then the man said, "Let me go, for
the dawn is breaking!"
But Jacob said, "I will not let you go unless you
bless me."
27"What is your name?" the man asked.
He replied, "Jacob."
28"Your name will no longer be Jacob," the man
told him. "From now on you will be called Israel,* because you have fought with God and with men and
have won."
29"Please tell me your name," Jacob said.
"Why do you want to know my name?" the man
replied. Then he blessed Jacob there.
30Jacob named the place Peniel (which means
"face of God"), for he said, "I have seen God face to
face, yet my life has been spared." 31The sun was rising as Jacob left Peniel,* and he was limping because
of the injury to his hip. 32(Even today the people of
Israel don't eat the tendon near the hip socket because of what happened that night when the man
strained the tendon of Jacob's hip.)

Jacob and Esau Make Peace

33 Then Jacob looked up and saw Esau coming
with his 400 men. So he divided the children among Leah, Rachel, and his two servant wives.
2He put the servant wives and their children at the
front, Leah and her children next, and Rachel and
Joseph last. 3Then Jacob went on ahead. As he approached his brother, he bowed to the ground seven
times before him. 4Then Esau ran to meet him and
embraced him, threw his arms around his neck, and
kissed him. And they both wept.
5Then Esau looked at the women and children
and asked, "Who are these people with you?"
"These are the children God has graciously given
to me, your servant," Jacob replied. 6Then the servant
wives came forward with their children and bowed
before him. 7Next came Leah with her children, and
they bowed before him. Finally, Joseph and Rachel
came forward and bowed before him.
8"And what were all the flocks and herds I met as I
came?" Esau asked.
Jacob replied, "They are a gift, my lord, to ensure
your friendship."
9"My brother, I have plenty," Esau answered. "Keep
what you have for yourself."
10But Jacob insisted, "No, if I have found favor with
you, please accept this gift from me. And what a relief to see your friendly smile. It is like seeing the

32:28 *Jacob* sounds like the Hebrew words for "heel" and "deceiver." *Israel* means "God fights." **32:31** Hebrew *Penuel,* a variant spelling of Peniel.

KING JAMES VERSION

11 Take, I pray thee, my blessing that is brought to thee; because God hath dealt graciously with me, and because I have enough. And he urged him, and he took *it*.

12 And he said, Let us take our journey, and let us go, and I will go before thee.

13 And he said unto him, My lord knoweth that the children *are* tender, and the flocks and herds with young *are* with me: and if men should overdrive them one day, all the flock will die.

14 Let my lord, I pray thee, pass over before his servant: and I will lead on softly, according as the cattle that goeth before me and the children be able to endure, until I come unto my lord unto Seir.

15 And Esau said, Let me now leave with thee *some* of the folk that *are* with me. And he said, What needeth it? let me find grace in the sight of my lord.

16 So Esau returned that day on his way unto Seir.

17 And Jacob journeyed to Succoth, and built him an house, and made booths for his cattle: therefore the name of the place is called Succoth.

18 And Jacob came to Shalem, a city of Shechem, which *is* in the land of Canaan, when he came from Padan-aram; and pitched his tent before the city.

19 And he bought a parcel of a field, where he had spread his tent, at the hand of the children of Hamor, Shechem's father, for an hundred pieces of money.

20 And he erected there an altar, and called it El-elohe-Israel.

34 1 And Dinah the daughter of Leah, which she bare unto Jacob, went out to see the daughters of the land.

2 And when Shechem the son of Hamor the Hivite, prince of the country, saw her, he took her, and lay with her, and defiled her.

3 And his soul clave unto Dinah the daughter of Jacob, and he loved the damsel, and spake kindly unto the damsel.

4 And Shechem spake unto his father Hamor, saying, Get me this damsel to wife.

5 And Jacob heard that he had defiled Dinah his daughter: now his sons were with his cattle in the field: and Jacob held his peace until they were come.

6 And Hamor the father of Shechem went out unto Jacob to commune with him.

7 And the sons of Jacob came out of the field when they heard *it*: and the men were grieved, and they were very wroth, because he had wrought folly in Israel in lying with Jacob's daughter; which thing ought not to be done.

8 And Hamor communed with them, saying, The soul of my son Shechem longeth for your daughter: I pray you give her him to wife.

NEW LIVING TRANSLATION

face of God! 11 Please take this gift I have brought you, for God has been very gracious to me. I have more than enough." And because Jacob insisted, Esau finally accepted the gift.

12 "Well," Esau said, "let's be going. I will lead the way."

13 But Jacob replied, "You can see, my lord, that some of the children are very young, and the flocks and herds have their young, too. If they are driven too hard, even for one day, all the animals could die. 14 Please, my lord, go ahead of your servant. We will follow slowly, at a pace that is comfortable for the livestock and the children. I will meet you at Seir."

15 "All right," Esau said, "but at least let me assign some of my men to guide and protect you."

Jacob responded, "That's not necessary. It's enough that you've received me warmly, my lord!"

16 So Esau turned around and started back to Seir that same day. 17 Jacob, on the other hand, traveled on to Succoth. There he built himself a house and made shelters for his livestock. That is why the place was named Succoth (which means "shelters").

18 Later, having traveled all the way from Paddan-aram, Jacob arrived safely at the town of Shechem, in the land of Canaan. There he set up camp outside the town. 19 Jacob bought the plot of land where he camped from the family of Hamor, the father of Shechem, for 100 pieces of silver.* 20 And there he built an altar and named it El-Elohe-Israel.*

Revenge against Shechem

34 One day Dinah, the daughter of Jacob and Leah, went to visit some of the young women who lived in the area. 2 But when the local prince, Shechem son of Hamor the Hivite, saw Dinah, he seized her and raped her. 3 But then he fell in love with her, and he tried to win her affection with tender words. 4 He said to his father, Hamor, "Get me this young girl. I want to marry her."

5 Soon Jacob heard that Shechem had defiled his daughter, Dinah. But since his sons were out in the fields herding his livestock, he said nothing until they returned. 6 Hamor, Shechem's father, came to discuss the matter with Jacob. 7 Meanwhile, Jacob's sons had come in from the field as soon as they heard what had happened. They were shocked and furious that their sister had been raped. Shechem had done a disgraceful thing against Jacob's family,* something that should never be done.

8 Hamor tried to speak with Jacob and his sons. "My son Shechem is truly in love with your daughter,"

33:19 Hebrew *100 kesitahs;* the value or weight of the kesitah is no longer known. **33:20** *El-Elohe-Israel* means "God, the God of Israel."
34:7 Hebrew *a disgraceful thing in Israel.*

KING JAMES VERSION

[9]And make ye marriages with us, *and* give your daughters unto us, and take our daughters unto you.

[10]And ye shall dwell with us: and the land shall be before you; dwell and trade ye therein, and get you possessions therein.

[11]And Shechem said unto her father and unto her brethren, Let me find grace in your eyes, and what ye shall say unto me I will give.

[12]Ask me never so much dowry and gift, and I will give according as ye shall say unto me: but give me the damsel to wife.

[13]And the sons of Jacob answered Shechem and Hamor his father deceitfully, and said, because he had defiled Dinah their sister:

[14]And they said unto them, We cannot do this thing, to give our sister to one that is uncircumcised; for that *were* a reproach unto us:

[15]But in this will we consent unto you: If ye will be as we *be,* that every male of you be circumcised;

[16]Then will we give our daughters unto you, and we will take your daughters to us, and we will dwell with you, and we will become one people.

[17]But if ye will not hearken unto us, to be circumcised; then will we take our daughter, and we will be gone.

[18]And their words pleased Hamor, and Shechem Hamor's son.

[19]And the young man deferred not to do the thing, because he had delight in Jacob's daughter: and he *was* more honourable than all the house of his father.

[20]And Hamor and Shechem his son came unto the gate of their city, and communed with the men of their city, saying,

[21]These men *are* peaceable with us; therefore let them dwell in the land, and trade therein; for the land, behold, *it is* large enough for them; let us take their daughters to us for wives, and let us give them our daughters.

[22]Only herein will the men consent unto us for to dwell with us, to be one people, if every male among us be circumcised, as they *are* circumcised.

[23]*Shall* not their cattle and their substance and every beast of theirs *be* ours? only let us consent unto them, and they will dwell with us.

[24]And unto Hamor and unto Shechem his son hearkened all that went out of the gate of his city; and every male was circumcised, all that went out of the gate of his city.

[25]And it came to pass on the third day, when they were sore, that two of the sons of Jacob, Simeon and Levi, Dinah's brethren, took each man his sword, and came upon the city boldly, and slew all the males.

[26]And they slew Hamor and Shechem his son with the edge of the sword, and took Dinah out of Shechem's house, and went out.

NEW LIVING TRANSLATION

he said. "Please let him marry her. [9]In fact, let's arrange other marriages, too. You give us your daughters for our sons, and we will give you our daughters for your sons. [10]And you may live among us; the land is open to you! Settle here and trade with us. And feel free to buy property in the area."

[11]Then Shechem himself spoke to Dinah's father and brothers. "Please be kind to me, and let me marry her," he begged. "I will give you whatever you ask. [12]No matter what dowry or gift you demand, I will gladly pay it—just give me the girl as my wife."

[13]But since Shechem had defiled their sister, Dinah, Jacob's sons responded deceitfully to Shechem and his father, Hamor. [14]They said to them, "We couldn't possibly allow this, because you're not circumcised. It would be a disgrace for our sister to marry a man like you! [15]But here is a solution. If every man among you will be circumcised like we are, [16]then we will give you our daughters, and we'll take your daughters for ourselves. We will live among you and become one people. [17]But if you don't agree to be circumcised, we will take her and be on our way."

[18]Hamor and his son Shechem agreed to their proposal. [19]Shechem wasted no time in acting on this request, for he wanted Jacob's daughter desperately. Shechem was a highly respected member of his family, [20]and he went with his father, Hamor, to present this proposal to the leaders at the town gate.

[21]"These men are our friends," they said. "Let's invite them to live here among us and trade freely. Look, the land is large enough to hold them. We can take their daughters as wives and let them marry ours. [22]But they will consider staying here and becoming one people with us only if all of our men are circumcised, just as they are. [23]But if we do this, all their livestock and possessions will eventually be ours. Come, let's agree to their terms and let them settle here among us."

[24]So all the men in the town council agreed with Hamor and Shechem, and every male in the town was circumcised. [25]But three days later, when their wounds were still sore, two of Jacob's sons, Simeon and Levi, who were Dinah's full brothers, took their swords and entered the town without opposition. Then they slaughtered every male there, [26]including Hamor and his son Shechem. They killed them with their swords, then took Dinah from Shechem's house and returned to their camp.

KING JAMES VERSION

27The sons of Jacob came upon the slain, and
spoiled the city, because they had defiled their sister.
28They took their sheep, and their oxen, and their
asses, and that which *was* in the city, and that which
was in the field,
29And all their wealth, and all their little ones, and
their wives took they captive, and spoiled even all
that *was* in the house.
30And Jacob said to Simeon and Levi, Ye have
troubled me to make me to stink among the inhabitants of the land, among the Canaanites and the
Perizzites: and I *being* few in number, they shall
gather themselves together against me, and slay me;
and I shall be destroyed, I and my house.
31And they said, Should he deal with our sister as
with an harlot?

35 1And God said unto Jacob, Arise, go up to
Bethel, and dwell there: and make there an
altar unto God, that appeared unto thee when thou
fleddest from the face of Esau thy brother.
2Then Jacob said unto his household, and to all that
were with him, Put away the strange gods that *are*
among you, and be clean, and change your garments:
3And let us arise, and go up to Bethel; and I will
make there an altar unto God, who answered me in
the day of my distress, and was with me in the way
which I went.
4And they gave unto Jacob all the strange gods
which *were* in their hand, and *all their* earrings
which *were* in their ears; and Jacob hid them under
the oak which *was* by Shechem.
5And they journeyed: and the terror of God was
upon the cities that *were* round about them, and they
did not pursue after the sons of Jacob.
6So Jacob came to Luz, which *is* in the land of Canaan, that *is,* Bethel, he and all the people that *were*
with him.
7And he built there an altar, and called the place
El-bethel: because there God appeared unto him,
when he fled from the face of his brother.
8But Deborah Rebekah's nurse died, and she was
buried beneath Bethel under an oak: and the name
of it was called Allon-bachuth.
9And God appeared unto Jacob again, when he
came out of Padan-aram, and blessed him.
10And God said unto him, Thy name *is* Jacob: thy
name shall not be called any more Jacob, but Israel
shall be thy name: and he called his name Israel.
11And God said unto him, I *am* God Almighty: be
fruitful and multiply; a nation and a company of
nations shall be of thee, and kings shall come out of
thy loins;
12And the land which I gave Abraham and Isaac, to

NEW LIVING TRANSLATION

27Meanwhile, the rest of Jacob's sons arrived.
Finding the men slaughtered, they plundered the
town because their sister had been defiled there.
28They seized all the flocks and herds and donkeys—
everything they could lay their hands on, both inside
the town and outside in the fields. 29They looted all
their wealth and plundered their houses. They also
took all their little children and wives and led them
away as captives.
30Afterward Jacob said to Simeon and Levi, "You
have ruined me! You've made me stink among all the
people of this land—among all the Canaanites and
Perizzites. We are so few that they will join forces
and crush us. I will be ruined, and my entire household will be wiped out!"
31"But why should we let him treat our sister like a
prostitute?" they retorted angrily.

Jacob's Return to Bethel

35 Then God said to Jacob, "Get ready and move
to Bethel and settle there. Build an altar
there to the God who appeared to you when you fled
from your brother, Esau."
2So Jacob told everyone in his household, "Get rid
of all your pagan idols, purify yourselves, and put on
clean clothing. 3We are now going to Bethel, where I
will build an altar to the God who answered my
prayers when I was in distress. He has been with me
wherever I have gone."
4So they gave Jacob all their pagan idols and earrings, and he buried them under the great tree near
Shechem. 5As they set out, a terror from God spread
over the people in all the towns of that area, so no
one attacked Jacob's family.
6Eventually, Jacob and his household arrived at
Luz (also called Bethel) in Canaan. 7Jacob built an
altar there and named the place El-bethel (which
means "God of Bethel"), because God had appeared
to him there when he was fleeing from his brother,
Esau.
8Soon after this, Rebekah's old nurse, Deborah,
died. She was buried beneath the oak tree in the valley below Bethel. Ever since, the tree has been called
Allon-bacuth (which means "oak of weeping").
9Now that Jacob had returned from Paddan-aram,
God appeared to him again at Bethel. God blessed
him, 10saying, "Your name is Jacob, but you will not
be called Jacob any longer. From now on your name
will be Israel."* So God renamed him Israel.
11Then God said, "I am El-Shaddai—'God Almighty.'
Be fruitful and multiply. You will become a great nation, even many nations. Kings will be among your descendants! 12And I will give you the land I once gave to

35:10 *Jacob* sounds like the Hebrew words for "heel" and "deceiver." *Israel* means "God fights."

KING JAMES VERSION

thee I will give it, and to thy seed after thee will I give
the land.
13 And God went up from him in the place where
he talked with him.
14 And Jacob set up a pillar in the place where he
talked with him, *even* a pillar of stone: and he poured
a drink offering thereon, and he poured oil thereon.
15 And Jacob called the name of the place where
God spake with him, Bethel.

16 And they journeyed from Bethel; and there was
but a little way to come to Ephrath: and Rachel travailed, and she had hard labour.
17 And it came to pass, when she was in hard labour, that the midwife said unto her, Fear not; thou
shalt have this son also.
18 And it came to pass, as her soul was in departing,
(for she died) that she called his name Ben-oni: but
his father called him Benjamin.
19 And Rachel died, and was buried in the way to
Ephrath, which *is* Bethlehem.
20 And Jacob set a pillar upon her grave: that *is* the
pillar of Rachel's grave unto this day.
21 And Israel journeyed, and spread his tent beyond the tower of Edar.
22 And it came to pass, when Israel dwelt in that
land, that Reuben went and lay with Bilhah his father's concubine: and Israel heard *it*. Now the sons of
Jacob were twelve:
23 The sons of Leah; Reuben, Jacob's firstborn, and
Simeon, and Levi, and Judah, and Issachar, and
Zebulun:
24 The sons of Rachel; Joseph, and Benjamin:
25 And the sons of Bilhah, Rachel's handmaid; Dan,
and Naphtali:
26 And the sons of Zilpah, Leah's handmaid; Gad,
and Asher: these *are* the sons of Jacob, which were
born to him in Padan-aram.
27 And Jacob came unto Isaac his father unto
Mamre, unto the city of Arbah, which *is* Hebron,
where Abraham and Isaac sojourned.
28 And the days of Isaac were an hundred and fourscore years.
29 And Isaac gave up the ghost, and died, and was
gathered unto his people, *being* old and full of days:
and his sons Esau and Jacob buried him.

36 1 Now these *are* the generations of Esau, who
is Edom.
2 Esau took his wives of the daughters of Canaan;
Adah the daughter of Elon the Hittite, and Aholibamah the daughter of Anah the daughter of Zibeon
the Hivite;
3 And Bashemath Ishmael's daughter, sister of
Nebajoth.

NEW LIVING TRANSLATION

Abraham and Isaac. Yes, I will give it to you and your
descendants after you." 13 Then God went up from the
place where he had spoken to Jacob.
14 Jacob set up a stone pillar to mark the place
where God had spoken to him. Then he poured wine
over it as an offering to God and anointed the pillar
with olive oil. 15 And Jacob named the place Bethel
(which means "house of God"), because God had
spoken to him there.

The Deaths of Rachel and Isaac

16 Leaving Bethel, Jacob and his clan moved on toward Ephrath. But Rachel went into labor while they
were still some distance away. Her labor pains were
intense. 17 After a very hard delivery, the midwife finally exclaimed, "Don't be afraid—you have another
son!" 18 Rachel was about to die, but with her last
breath she named the baby Ben-oni (which means
"son of my sorrow"). The baby's father, however,
called him Benjamin (which means "son of my right
hand"). 19 So Rachel died and was buried on the way
to Ephrath (that is, Bethlehem). 20 Jacob set up a stone
monument over Rachel's grave, and it can be seen
there to this day.
21 Then Jacob* traveled on and camped beyond
Migdal-eder. 22 While he was living there, Reuben
had intercourse with Bilhah, his father's concubine,
and Jacob soon heard about it.
These are the names of the twelve sons of Jacob:

23 The sons of Leah were Reuben (Jacob's oldest son),
Simeon, Levi, Judah, Issachar, and Zebulun.
24 The sons of Rachel were Joseph and Benjamin.
25 The sons of Bilhah, Rachel's servant, were Dan
and Naphtali.
26 The sons of Zilpah, Leah's servant, were Gad and
Asher.

These are the names of the sons who were born to
Jacob at Paddan-aram.

27 So Jacob returned to his father, Isaac, in Mamre,
which is near Kiriath-arba (now called Hebron),
where Abraham and Isaac had both lived as foreigners. 28 Isaac lived for 180 years. 29 Then he breathed
his last and died at a ripe old age, joining his ancestors in death. And his sons, Esau and Jacob,
buried him.

Descendants of Esau

36 This is the account of the descendants of
Esau (also known as Edom). 2 Esau married
two young women from Canaan: Adah, the daughter
of Elon the Hittite; and Oholibamah, the daughter of
Anah and granddaughter of Zibeon the Hivite. 3 He
also married his cousin Basemath, who was the
daughter of Ishmael and the sister of Nebaioth.

35:21 Hebrew *Israel;* also in 35:22a. The names "Jacob" and "Israel" are often interchanged throughout the Old Testament, referring sometimes to the individual patriarch and sometimes to the nation.

KING JAMES VERSION

4 And Adah bare to Esau Eliphaz; and Bashemath
bare Reuel;
5 And Aholibamah bare Jeush, and Jaalam, and
Korah: these *are* the sons of Esau, which were born
unto him in the land of Canaan.

6 And Esau took his wives, and his sons, and his
daughters, and all the persons of his house, and his
cattle, and all his beasts, and all his substance, which
he had got in the land of Canaan; and went into the
country from the face of his brother Jacob.

7 For their riches were more than that they might
dwell together; and the land wherein they were
strangers could not bear them because of their cattle.

8 Thus dwelt Esau in mount Seir: Esau *is* Edom.

9 And these *are* the generations of Esau the father
of the Edomites in mount Seir:
10 These *are* the names of Esau's sons; Eliphaz the
son of Adah the wife of Esau, Reuel the son of
Bashemath the wife of Esau.

11 And the sons of Eliphaz were Teman, Omar,
Zepho, and Gatam, and Kenaz.
12 And Timna was concubine to Eliphaz Esau's son;
and she bare to Eliphaz Amalek: these *were* the sons
of Adah Esau's wife.

13 And these *are* the sons of Reuel; Nahath, and
Zerah, Shammah, and Mizzah: these were the sons of
Bashemath Esau's wife.

14 And these were the sons of Aholibamah, the
daughter of Anah the daughter of Zibeon, Esau's
wife: and she bare to Esau Jeush, and Jaalam, and
Korah.

15 These *were* dukes of the sons of Esau: the sons
of Eliphaz the firstborn *son* of Esau; duke Teman,
duke Omar, duke Zepho, duke Kenaz,

16 Duke Korah, duke Gatam, *and* duke Amalek:
these *are* the dukes *that came* of Eliphaz in the land
of Edom; these *were* the sons of Adah.
17 And these *are* the sons of Reuel Esau's son; duke
Nahath, duke Zerah, duke Shammah, duke Mizzah:
these *are* the dukes *that came* of Reuel in the land of
Edom; these *are* the sons of Bashemath Esau's wife.

18 And these *are* the sons of Aholibamah Esau's
wife; duke Jeush, duke Jaalam, duke Korah: these
were the dukes *that came* of Aholibamah the daughter of Anah, Esau's wife.

19 These *are* the sons of Esau, who *is* Edom, and
these *are* their dukes.

20 These *are* the sons of Seir the Horite, who inhabited the land; Lotan, and Shobal, and Zibeon, and Anah,
21 And Dishon, and Ezer, and Dishan: these *are* the
dukes of the Horites, the children of Seir in the land
of Edom.

NEW LIVING TRANSLATION

4 Adah gave birth to a son named Eliphaz for Esau.
Basemath gave birth to a son named Reuel.
5 Oholibamah gave birth to sons named Jeush, Jalam,
and Korah. All these sons were born to Esau in the
land of Canaan.

6 Esau took his wives, his children, and his entire
household, along with his livestock and cattle—all
the wealth he had acquired in the land of Canaan—
and moved away from his brother, Jacob. 7 There was
not enough land to support them both because of all
the livestock and possessions they had acquired. 8 So
Esau (also known as Edom) settled in the hill country
of Seir.

9 This is the account of Esau's descendants, the
Edomites, who lived in the hill country of Seir.

10 These are the names of Esau's sons: Eliphaz, the
son of Esau's wife Adah; and Reuel, the son of
Esau's wife Basemath.
11 The descendants of Eliphaz were Teman, Omar,
Zepho, Gatam, and Kenaz. 12 Timna, the
concubine of Esau's son Eliphaz, gave birth to a
son named Amalek. These are the descendants
of Esau's wife Adah.
13 The descendants of Reuel were Nahath, Zerah,
Shammah, and Mizzah. These are the
descendants of Esau's wife Basemath.
14 Esau also had sons through Oholibamah, the
daughter of Anah and granddaughter of Zibeon.
Their names were Jeush, Jalam, and Korah.

15 These are the descendants of Esau who became
the leaders of various clans:

The descendants of Esau's oldest son, Eliphaz,
became the leaders of the clans of Teman, Omar,
Zepho, Kenaz, 16 Korah, Gatam, and Amalek.
These are the clan leaders in the land of Edom
who descended from Eliphaz. All these were
descendants of Esau's wife Adah.
17 The descendants of Esau's son Reuel became the
leaders of the clans of Nahath, Zerah, Shammah,
and Mizzah. These are the clan leaders in the
land of Edom who descended from Reuel. All
these were descendants of Esau's wife Basemath.
18 The descendants of Esau and his wife Oholibamah
became the leaders of the clans of Jeush, Jalam,
and Korah. These are the clan leaders who
descended from Esau's wife Oholibamah, the
daughter of Anah.
19 These are the clans descended from Esau (also
known as Edom), identified by their clan leaders.

Original Peoples of Edom

20 These are the names of the tribes that descended
from Seir the Horite. They lived in the land of Edom:
Lotan, Shobal, Zibeon, Anah, 21 Dishon, Ezer, and
Dishan. These were the Horite clan leaders, the descendants of Seir, who lived in the land of Edom.

KING JAMES VERSION

22 And the children of Lotan were Hori and Hemam; and Lotan's sister *was* Timna.

23 And the children of Shobal *were* these; Alvan, and Manahath, and Ebal, Shepho, and Onam.

24 And these *are* the children of Zibeon; both Ajah, and Anah: this *was that* Anah that found the mules in the wilderness, as he fed the asses of Zibeon his father.

25 And the children of Anah *were* these; Dishon, and Aholibamah the daughter of Anah.

26 And these *are* the children of Dishon; Hemdan, and Esh-ban, and Ithran, and Cheran.

27 The children of Ezer *are* these; Bilhan, and Zaavan, and Akan.

28 The children of Dishan *are* these; Uz, and Aran.

29 These *are* the dukes *that came* of the Horites; duke Lotan, duke Shobal, duke Zibeon, duke Anah,

30 Duke Dishon, duke Ezer, duke Dishan: these *are* the dukes *that came* of Hori, among their dukes in the land of Seir.

31 And these *are* the kings that reigned in the land of Edom, before there reigned any king over the children of Israel.

32 And Bela the son of Beor reigned in Edom: and the name of his city *was* Dinhabah.

33 And Bela died, and Jobab the son of Zerah of Bozrah reigned in his stead.

34 And Jobab died, and Husham of the land of Temani reigned in his stead.

35 And Husham died, and Hadad the son of Bedad, who smote Midian in the field of Moab, reigned in his stead: and the name of his city *was* Avith.

36 And Hadad died, and Samlah of Masrekah reigned in his stead.

37 And Samlah died, and Saul of Rehoboth *by* the river reigned in his stead.

38 And Saul died, and Baal-hanan the son of Achbor reigned in his stead.

39 And Baal-hanan the son of Achbor died, and Hadar reigned in his stead: and the name of his city *was* Pau; and his wife's name *was* Mehetabel, the daughter of Matred, the daughter of Mezahab.

40 And these *are* the names of the dukes *that came* of Esau, according to their families, after their places, by their names; duke Timnah, duke Alvah, duke Jetheth,

41 Duke Aholibamah, duke Elah, duke Pinon,

42 Duke Kenaz, duke Teman, duke Mibzar,

43 Duke Magdiel, duke Iram: these *be* the dukes of Edom, according to their habitations in the land of their possession: he *is* Esau the father of the Edomites.

NEW LIVING TRANSLATION

22 The descendants of Lotan were Hori and Hemam. Lotan's sister was named Timna.

23 The descendants of Shobal were Alvan, Manahath, Ebal, Shepho, and Onam.

24 The descendants of Zibeon were Aiah and Anah. (This is the Anah who discovered the hot springs in the wilderness while he was grazing his father's donkeys.)

25 The descendants of Anah were his son, Dishon, and his daughter, Oholibamah.

26 The descendants of Dishon* were Hemdan, Eshban, Ithran, and Keran.

27 The descendants of Ezer were Bilhan, Zaavan, and Akan.

28 The descendants of Dishan were Uz and Aran.

29 So these were the leaders of the Horite clans:
Lotan, Shobal, Zibeon, Anah, 30 Dishon, Ezer, and
Dishan. The Horite clans are named after their clan
leaders, who lived in the land of Seir.

Rulers of Edom

31 These are the kings who ruled in the land of Edom before any king ruled over the Israelites*:

32 Bela son of Beor, who ruled in Edom from his city of Dinhabah.

33 When Bela died, Jobab son of Zerah from Bozrah became king in his place.

34 When Jobab died, Husham from the land of the Temanites became king in his place.

35 When Husham died, Hadad son of Bedad became king in his place and ruled from the city of Avith. He was the one who defeated the Midianites in the land of Moab.

36 When Hadad died, Samlah from the city of Masrekah became king in his place.

37 When Samlah died, Shaul from the city of Rehoboth-on-the-River became king in his place.

38 When Shaul died, Baal-hanan son of Acbor became king in his place.

39 When Baal-hanan son of Acbor died, Hadad* became king in his place and ruled from the city of Pau. His wife was Mehetabel, the daughter of Matred and granddaughter of Me-zahab.

40 These are the names of the leaders of the clans
descended from Esau, who lived in the places named
for them: Timna, Alvah, Jetheth, 41 Oholibamah, Elah,
Pinon, 42 Kenaz, Teman, Mibzar, 43 Magdiel, and Iram.
These are the leaders of the clans of Edom, listed according to their settlements in the land they occupied. They all descended from Esau, the ancestor of the Edomites.

36:26 Hebrew *Dishan,* a variant spelling of Dishon; compare 36:21, 28. **36:31** Or *before an Israelite king ruled over them.* **36:39** As in some Hebrew manuscripts, Samaritan Pentateuch, and Syriac version (see also 1 Chr 1:50); most Hebrew manuscripts read *Hadar.*

KING JAMES VERSION

37 1And Jacob dwelt in the land wherein his father was a stranger, in the land of Canaan.
2These *are* the generations of Jacob. Joseph, *being*
seventeen years old, was feeding the flock with his
brethren; and the lad *was* with the sons of Bilhah,
and with the sons of Zilpah, his father's wives: and
Joseph brought unto his father their evil report.
3Now Israel loved Joseph more than all his children, because he *was* the son of his old age: and he
made him a coat of *many* colours.
4And when his brethren saw that their father
loved him more than all his brethren, they hated him,
and could not speak peaceably unto him.
5And Joseph dreamed a dream, and he told *it* his
brethren: and they hated him yet the more.
6And he said unto them, Hear, I pray you, this
dream which I have dreamed:
7For, behold, we *were* binding sheaves in the field,
and, lo, my sheaf arose, and also stood upright; and,
behold, your sheaves stood round about, and made
obeisance to my sheaf.
8And his brethren said to him, Shalt thou indeed
reign over us? or shalt thou indeed have dominion
over us? And they hated him yet the more for his
dreams, and for his words.
9And he dreamed yet another dream, and told it
his brethren, and said, Behold, I have dreamed a
dream more; and, behold, the sun and the moon and
the eleven stars made obeisance to me.
10And he told *it* to his father, and to his brethren:
and his father rebuked him, and said unto him, What
is this dream that thou hast dreamed? Shall I and thy
mother and thy brethren indeed come to bow down
ourselves to thee to the earth?
11And his brethren envied him; but his father observed the saying.
12And his brethren went to feed their father's
flock in Shechem.
13And Israel said unto Joseph, Do not thy brethren
feed *the flock* in Shechem? come, and I will send
thee unto them. And he said to him, Here *am I*.
14And he said to him, Go, I pray thee, see whether it
be well with thy brethren, and well with the flocks;
and bring me word again. So he sent him out of the
vale of Hebron, and he came to Shechem.
15And a certain man found him, and, behold, *he*
was wandering in the field: and the man asked him,
saying, What seekest thou?
16And he said, I seek my brethren: tell me, I pray
thee, where they feed *their flocks*.
17And the man said, They are departed hence; for I
heard them say, Let us go to Dothan. And Joseph
went after his brethren, and found them in Dothan.

NEW LIVING TRANSLATION

Joseph's Dreams

37 So Jacob settled again in the land of Canaan,
where his father had lived as a foreigner.
2This is the account of Jacob and his family. When
Joseph was seventeen years old, he often tended his
father's flocks. He worked for his half brothers,
the sons of his father's wives Bilhah and Zilpah. But
Joseph reported to his father some of the bad things
his brothers were doing.
3Jacob* loved Joseph more than any of his other
children because Joseph had been born to him in his
old age. So one day Jacob had a special gift made for
Joseph—a beautiful robe.* 4But his brothers hated
Joseph because their father loved him more than the
rest of them. They couldn't say a kind word to him.
5One night Joseph had a dream, and when he told
his brothers about it, they hated him more than ever.
6"Listen to this dream," he said. 7"We were out in the
field, tying up bundles of grain. Suddenly my bundle
stood up, and your bundles all gathered around and
bowed low before mine!"
8His brothers responded, "So you think you will be
our king, do you? Do you actually think you will reign
over us?" And they hated him all the more because of
his dreams and the way he talked about them.
9Soon Joseph had another dream, and again he
told his brothers about it. "Listen, I have had another
dream," he said. "The sun, moon, and eleven stars
bowed low before me!"
10This time he told the dream to his father as well
as to his brothers, but his father scolded him. "What
kind of dream is that?" he asked. "Will your mother
and I and your brothers actually come and bow to
the ground before you?" 11But while his brothers
were jealous of Joseph, his father wondered what the
dreams meant.
12Soon after this, Joseph's brothers went to pasture their father's flocks at Shechem. 13When they
had been gone for some time, Jacob said to Joseph,
"Your brothers are pasturing the sheep at Shechem.
Get ready, and I will send you to them."
"I'm ready to go," Joseph replied.
14"Go and see how your brothers and the flocks
are getting along," Jacob said. "Then come back and
bring me a report." So Jacob sent him on his way, and
Joseph traveled to Shechem from their home in the
valley of Hebron.
15When he arrived there, a man from the area noticed him wandering around the countryside. "What
are you looking for?" he asked.
16"I'm looking for my brothers," Joseph replied.
"Do you know where they are pasturing their sheep?"
17"Yes," the man told him. "They have moved on
from here, but I heard them say, 'Let's go on to
Dothan.'" So Joseph followed his brothers to Dothan
and found them there.

37:3a Hebrew *Israel;* also in 37:13. See note on 35:21. **37:3b** Traditionally rendered *a coat of many colors.* The exact meaning of the Hebrew is uncertain.

KING JAMES VERSION

18 And when they saw him afar off, even before he came near unto them, they conspired against him to slay him.

19 And they said one to another, Behold, this dreamer cometh.

20 Come now therefore, and let us slay him, and cast him into some pit, and we will say, Some evil beast hath devoured him: and we shall see what will become of his dreams.

21 And Reuben heard *it*, and he delivered him out of their hands; and said, Let us not kill him.

22 And Reuben said unto them, Shed no blood, *but* cast him into this pit that *is* in the wilderness, and lay no hand upon him; that he might rid him out of their hands, to deliver him to his father again.

23 And it came to pass, when Joseph was come unto his brethren, that they stripped Joseph out of his coat, *his* coat of *many* colours that *was* on him;

24 And they took him, and cast him into a pit: and the pit *was* empty, *there was* no water in it.

25 And they sat down to eat bread: and they lifted up their eyes and looked, and, behold, a company of Ishmeelites came from Gilead with their camels bearing spicery and balm and myrrh, going to carry *it* down to Egypt.

26 And Judah said unto his brethren, What profit *is it* if we slay our brother, and conceal his blood?

27 Come, and let us sell him to the Ishmeelites, and let not our hand be upon him; for he *is* our brother *and* our flesh. And his brethren were content.

28 Then there passed by Midianites merchantmen; and they drew and lifted up Joseph out of the pit, and sold Joseph to the Ishmeelites for twenty *pieces* of silver: and they brought Joseph into Egypt.

29 And Reuben returned unto the pit; and, behold, Joseph *was* not in the pit; and he rent his clothes.

30 And he returned unto his brethren, and said, The child *is* not; and I, whither shall I go?

31 And they took Joseph's coat, and killed a kid of the goats, and dipped the coat in the blood;

32 And they sent the coat of *many* colours, and they brought *it* to their father; and said, This have we found: know now whether it *be* thy son's coat or no.

33 And he knew it, and said, *It is* my son's coat; an evil beast hath devoured him; Joseph is without doubt rent in pieces.

34 And Jacob rent his clothes, and put sackcloth upon his loins, and mourned for his son many days.

35 And all his sons and all his daughters rose up to comfort him; but he refused to be comforted; and he said, For I will go down into the grave unto my son mourning. Thus his father wept for him.

36 And the Midianites sold him into Egypt unto Potiphar, an officer of Pharaoh's, *and* captain of the guard.

NEW LIVING TRANSLATION

Joseph Sold into Slavery

18 When Joseph's brothers saw him coming, they recognized him in the distance. As he approached, they
made plans to kill him. 19 "Here comes the dreamer!"
they said. 20 "Come on, let's kill him and throw him
into one of these cisterns. We can tell our father, 'A
wild animal has eaten him.' Then we'll see what becomes of his dreams!"
21 But when Reuben heard of their scheme, he
came to Joseph's rescue. "Let's not kill him," he said.
22 "Why should we shed any blood? Let's just throw
him into this empty cistern here in the wilderness.
Then he'll die without our laying a hand on him."
Reuben was secretly planning to rescue Joseph and
return him to his father.
23 So when Joseph arrived, his brothers ripped off
the beautiful robe he was wearing. 24 Then they
grabbed him and threw him into the cistern. Now
the cistern was empty; there was no water in it.
25 Then, just as they were sitting down to eat, they
looked up and saw a caravan of camels in the distance coming toward them. It was a group of
Ishmaelite traders taking a load of gum, balm, and
aromatic resin from Gilead down to Egypt.
26 Judah said to his brothers, "What will we gain by
killing our brother? We'd have to cover up the crime.*
27 Instead of hurting him, let's sell him to those
Ishmaelite traders. After all, he is our brother—our
own flesh and blood!" And his brothers agreed. 28 So
when the Ishmaelites, who were Midianite traders,
came by, Joseph's brothers pulled him out of the cistern and sold him to them for twenty pieces* of silver.
And the traders took him to Egypt.
29 Some time later, Reuben returned to get Joseph
out of the cistern. When he discovered that Joseph
was missing, he tore his clothes in grief. 30 Then he
went back to his brothers and lamented, "The boy is
gone! What will I do now?"
31 Then the brothers killed a young goat and dipped
Joseph's robe in its blood. 32 They sent the beautiful
robe to their father with this message: "Look at what
we found. Doesn't this robe belong to your son?"
33 Their father recognized it immediately. "Yes,"
he said, "it is my son's robe. A wild animal must have
eaten him. Joseph has clearly been torn to pieces!"
34 Then Jacob tore his clothes and dressed himself in
burlap. He mourned deeply for his son for a long
time. 35 His family all tried to comfort him, but he refused to be comforted. "I will go to my grave*
mourning for my son," he would say, and then he
would weep.
36 Meanwhile, the Midianite traders* arrived in
Egypt, where they sold Joseph to Potiphar, an officer
of Pharaoh, the king of Egypt. Potiphar was captain
of the palace guard.

37:26 Hebrew *cover his blood.* **37:28** Hebrew *20 shekels,* about 8 ounces or 228 grams in weight. **37:35** Hebrew *go down to Sheol.* **37:36** Hebrew *the Medanites.* The relationship between the Midianites and Medanites is unclear; compare 37:28. See also 25:2.

KING JAMES VERSION

38

1 And it came to pass at that time, that Judah went down from his brethren, and turned in to a certain Adullamite, whose name *was* Hirah.

2 And Judah saw there a daughter of a certain Canaanite, whose name *was* Shuah; and he took her, and went in unto her.

3 And she conceived, and bare a son; and he called his name Er.

4 And she conceived again, and bare a son; and she called his name Onan.

5 And she yet again conceived, and bare a son; and called his name Shelah: and he was at Chezib, when she bare him.

6 And Judah took a wife for Er his firstborn, whose name *was* Tamar.

7 And Er, Judah's firstborn, was wicked in the sight of the LORD; and the LORD slew him.

8 And Judah said unto Onan, Go in unto thy brother's wife, and marry her, and raise up seed to thy brother.

9 And Onan knew that the seed should not be his; and it came to pass, when he went in unto his brother's wife, that he spilled *it* on the ground, lest that he should give seed to his brother.

10 And the thing which he did displeased the LORD: wherefore he slew him also.

11 Then said Judah to Tamar his daughter in law, Remain a widow at thy father's house, till Shelah my son be grown: for he said, Lest peradventure he die also, as his brethren *did*. And Tamar went and dwelt in her father's house.

12 And in process of time the daughter of Shuah Judah's wife died; and Judah was comforted, and went up unto his sheepshearers to Timnath, he and his friend Hirah the Adullamite.

13 And it was told Tamar, saying, Behold thy father in law goeth up to Timnath to shear his sheep.

14 And she put her widow's garments off from her, and covered her with a veil, and wrapped herself, and sat in an open place, which *is* by the way to Timnath; for she saw that Shelah was grown, and she was not given unto him to wife.

15 When Judah saw her, he thought her *to be* an harlot; because she had covered her face.

16 And he turned unto her by the way, and said, Go to, I pray thee, let me come in unto thee; (for he knew not that she *was* his daughter in law.) And she said, What wilt thou give me, that thou mayest come in unto me?

17 And he said, I will send *thee* a kid from the flock. And she said, Wilt thou give *me* a pledge, till thou send *it?*

18 And he said, What pledge shall I give thee? And she said, Thy signet, and thy bracelets, and thy staff

NEW LIVING TRANSLATION

Judah and Tamar

38

About this time, Judah left home and moved to Adullam, where he stayed with a man named Hirah. 2 There he saw a Canaanite woman, the daughter of Shua, and he married her. When he slept with her, 3 she became pregnant and gave birth to a son, and he named the boy Er. 4 Then she became pregnant again and gave birth to another son, and she named him Onan. 5 And when she gave birth to a third son, she named him Shelah. At the time of Shelah's birth, they were living at Kezib.

6 In the course of time, Judah arranged for his firstborn son, Er, to marry a young woman named Tamar. 7 But Er was a wicked man in the LORD's sight, so the LORD took his life. 8 Then Judah said to Er's brother Onan, "Go and marry Tamar, as our law requires of the brother of a man who has died. You must produce an heir for your brother."

9 But Onan was not willing to have a child who would not be his own heir. So whenever he had intercourse with his brother's wife, he spilled the semen on the ground. This prevented her from having a child who would belong to his brother. 10 But the LORD considered it evil for Onan to deny a child to his dead brother. So the LORD took Onan's life, too.

11 Then Judah said to Tamar, his daughter-in-law, "Go back to your parents' home and remain a widow until my son Shelah is old enough to marry you." (But Judah didn't really intend to do this because he was afraid Shelah would also die, like his two brothers.) So Tamar went back to live in her father's home.

12 Some years later Judah's wife died. After the time of mourning was over, Judah and his friend Hirah the Adullamite went up to Timnah to supervise the shearing of his sheep. 13 Someone told Tamar, "Look, your father-in-law is going up to Timnah to shear his sheep."

14 Tamar was aware that Shelah had grown up, but no arrangements had been made for her to come and marry him. So she changed out of her widow's clothing and covered herself with a veil to disguise herself. Then she sat beside the road at the entrance to the village of Enaim, which is on the road to Timnah. 15 Judah noticed her and thought she was a prostitute, since she had covered her face. 16 So he stopped and propositioned her. "Let me have sex with you," he said, not realizing that she was his own daughter-in-law.

"How much will you pay to have sex with me?" Tamar asked.

17 "I'll send you a young goat from my flock," Judah promised.

"But what will you give me to guarantee that you will send the goat?" she asked.

18 "What kind of guarantee do you want?" he replied.

She answered, "Leave me your identification seal

KING JAMES VERSION

that *is* in thine hand. And he gave *it* her, and came in unto her, and she conceived by him.

19 And she arose, and went away, and laid by her veil from her, and put on the garments of her widowhood.

20 And Judah sent the kid by the hand of his friend the Adullamite, to receive *his* pledge from the woman's hand: but he found her not.

21 Then he asked the men of that place, saying, Where *is* the harlot, that *was* openly by the way side? And they said, There was no harlot in this *place*.

22 And he returned to Judah, and said, I cannot find her; and also the men of the place said, *that* there was no harlot in this *place*.

23 And Judah said, Let her take *it* to her, lest we be shamed: behold, I sent this kid, and thou hast not found her.

24 And it came to pass about three months after, that it was told Judah, saying, Tamar thy daughter in law hath played the harlot; and also, behold, she *is* with child by whoredom. And Judah said, Bring her forth, and let her be burnt.

25 When she *was* brought forth, she sent to her father in law, saying, By the man, whose these *are, am* I with child: and she said, Discern, I pray thee, whose *are* these, the signet, and bracelets, and staff.

26 And Judah acknowledged *them,* and said, She hath been more righteous than I; because that I gave her not to Shelah my son. And he knew her again no more.

27 And it came to pass in the time of her travail, that, behold, twins *were* in her womb.

28 And it came to pass, when she travailed, that *the one* put out *his* hand: and the midwife took and bound upon his hand a scarlet thread, saying, This came out first.

29 And it came to pass, as he drew back his hand, that, behold, his brother came out: and she said, How hast thou broken forth? *this* breach *be* upon thee: therefore his name was called Pharez.

30 And afterward came out his brother, that had the scarlet thread upon his hand: and his name was called Zarah.

39 1 And Joseph was brought down to Egypt; and Potiphar, an officer of Pharaoh, captain of the guard, an Egyptian, bought him of the hands of the Ishmeelites, which had brought him down thither.

2 And the LORD was with Joseph, and he was a prosperous man; and he was in the house of his master the Egyptian.

NEW LIVING TRANSLATION

and its cord and the walking stick you are carrying." So Judah gave them to her. Then he had intercourse with her, and she became pregnant. 19 Afterward she went back home, took off her veil, and put on her widow's clothing as usual.

20 Later Judah asked his friend Hirah the Adullamite to take the young goat to the woman and to pick up the things he had given her as his guarantee. But Hirah couldn't find her. 21 So he asked the men who lived there, "Where can I find the shrine prostitute who was sitting beside the road at the entrance to Enaim?"

"We've never had a shrine prostitute here," they replied.

22 So Hirah returned to Judah and told him, "I couldn't find her anywhere, and the men of the village claim they've never had a shrine prostitute there."

23 "Then let her keep the things I gave her," Judah said. "I sent the young goat as we agreed, but you couldn't find her. We'd be the laughingstock of the village if we went back again to look for her."

24 About three months later, Judah was told, "Tamar, your daughter-in-law, has acted like a prostitute. And now, because of this, she's pregnant."

"Bring her out, and let her be burned!" Judah demanded.

25 But as they were taking her out to kill her, she sent this message to her father-in-law: "The man who owns these things made me pregnant. Look closely. Whose seal and cord and walking stick are these?"

26 Judah recognized them immediately and said, "She is more righteous than I am, because I didn't arrange for her to marry my son Shelah." And Judah never slept with Tamar again.

27 When the time came for Tamar to give birth, it was discovered that she was carrying twins. 28 While she was in labor, one of the babies reached out his hand. The midwife grabbed it and tied a scarlet string around the child's wrist, announcing, "This one came out first." 29 But then he pulled back his hand, and out came his brother! "What!" the midwife exclaimed. "How did you break out first?" So he was named Perez.* 30 Then the baby with the scarlet string on his wrist was born, and he was named Zerah.*

Joseph in Potiphar's House

39 When Joseph was taken to Egypt by the Ishmaelite traders, he was purchased by Potiphar, an Egyptian officer. Potiphar was captain of the guard for Pharaoh, the king of Egypt.

2 The LORD was with Joseph, so he succeeded in everything he did as he served in the home of his

38:29 *Perez* means "breaking out." **38:30** *Zerah* means "scarlet" or "brightness."

KING JAMES VERSION

3 And his master saw that the LORD *was* with him,
and that the LORD made all that he did to prosper in
his hand.
4 And Joseph found grace in his sight, and he
served him: and he made him overseer over his
house, and all *that* he had he put into his hand.
5 And it came to pass from the time *that* he had
made him overseer in his house, and over all that he
had, that the LORD blessed the Egyptian's house for
Joseph's sake; and the blessing of the LORD was upon
all that he had in the house, and in the field.
6 And he left all that he had in Joseph's hand; and
he knew not aught he had, save the bread which he
did eat. And Joseph was *a* goodly *person*, and well
favoured.
7 And it came to pass after these things, that his
master's wife cast her eyes upon Joseph; and she
said, Lie with me.
8 But he refused, and said unto his master's wife,
Behold, my master wotteth not what *is* with me in the
house, and he hath committed all that he hath to my
hand;
9 *There is* none greater in this house than I; neither
hath he kept back any thing from me but thee, because thou *art* his wife: how then can I do this great
wickedness, and sin against God?
10 And it came to pass, as she spake to Joseph day
by day, that he hearkened not unto her, to lie by her,
or to be with her.
11 And it came to pass about this time, that *Joseph*
went into the house to do his business; and *there was*
none of the men of the house there within.
12 And she caught him by his garment, saying, Lie
with me: and he left his garment in her hand, and
fled, and got him out.
13 And it came to pass, when she saw that he had
left his garment in her hand, and was fled forth,
14 That she called unto the men of her house, and
spake unto them, saying, See, he hath brought in an
Hebrew unto us to mock us; he came in unto me to
lie with me, and I cried with a loud voice:
15 And it came to pass, when he heard that I lifted
up my voice and cried, that he left his garment with
me, and fled, and got him out.
16 And she laid up his garment by her, until his lord
came home.
17 And she spake unto him according to these
words, saying, The Hebrew servant, which thou hast
brought unto us, came in unto me to mock me:
18 And it came to pass, as I lifted up my voice and
cried, that he left his garment with me, and fled out.
19 And it came to pass, when his master heard the
words of his wife, which she spake unto him, saying,
After this manner did thy servant to me; that his
wrath was kindled.
20 And Joseph's master took him, and put him into
the prison, a place where the king's prisoners *were*
bound: and he was there in the prison.

NEW LIVING TRANSLATION

Egyptian master. 3 Potiphar noticed this and realized
that the LORD was with Joseph, giving him success in
everything he did. 4 This pleased Potiphar, so he soon
made Joseph his personal attendant. He put him in
charge of his entire household and everything he
owned. 5 From the day Joseph was put in charge of his
master's household and property, the LORD began to
bless Potiphar's household for Joseph's sake. All his
household affairs ran smoothly, and his crops and
livestock flourished. 6 So Potiphar gave Joseph complete administrative responsibility over everything
he owned. With Joseph there, he didn't worry about a
thing—except what kind of food to eat!
Joseph was a very handsome and well-built young
man, 7 and Potiphar's wife soon began to look at him
lustfully. "Come and sleep with me," she demanded.
8 But Joseph refused. "Look," he told her, "my master trusts me with everything in his entire household. 9 No one here has more authority than I do. He
has held back nothing from me except you, because
you are his wife. How could I do such a wicked thing?
It would be a great sin against God."
10 She kept putting pressure on Joseph day after
day, but he refused to sleep with her, and he kept out
of her way as much as possible. 11 One day, however,
no one else was around when he went in to do his
work. 12 She came and grabbed him by his cloak, demanding, "Come on, sleep with me!" Joseph tore
himself away, but he left his cloak in her hand as he
ran from the house.
13 When she saw that she was holding his cloak
and he had fled, 14 she called out to her servants.
Soon all the men came running. "Look!" she said.
"My husband has brought this Hebrew slave here to
make fools of us! He came into my room to rape me,
but I screamed. 15 When he heard me scream, he ran
outside and got away, but he left his cloak behind
with me."
16 She kept the cloak with her until her husband
came home. 17 Then she told him her story. "That
Hebrew slave you've brought into our house tried to
come in and fool around with me," she said. 18 "But
when I screamed, he ran outside, leaving his cloak
with me!"

Joseph Put in Prison

19 Potiphar was furious when he heard his wife's story
about how Joseph had treated her. 20 So he took
Joseph and threw him into the prison where the
king's prisoners were held, and there he remained.

KING JAMES VERSION

21 But the LORD was with Joseph, and shewed him mercy, and gave him favour in the sight of the keeper of the prison.

22 And the keeper of the prison committed to Joseph's hand all the prisoners that *were* in the prison; and whatsoever they did there, he was the doer *of it*.

23 The keeper of the prison looked not to any thing *that was* under his hand; because the LORD was with him, and *that* which he did, the LORD made *it* to prosper.

40 1 And it came to pass after these things, *that* the butler of the king of Egypt and *his* baker had offended their lord the king of Egypt.

2 And Pharaoh was wroth against two *of* his officers, against the chief of the butlers, and against the chief of the bakers.

3 And he put them in ward in the house of the captain of the guard, into the prison, the place where Joseph *was* bound.

4 And the captain of the guard charged Joseph with them, and he served them: and they continued a season in ward.

5 And they dreamed a dream both of them, each man his dream in one night, each man according to the interpretation of his dream, the butler and the baker of the king of Egypt, which *were* bound in the prison.

6 And Joseph came in unto them in the morning, and looked upon them, and, behold, they *were* sad.

7 And he asked Pharaoh's officers that *were* with him in the ward of his lord's house, saying, Wherefore look ye *so* sadly today?

8 And they said unto him, We have dreamed a dream, and *there is* no interpreter of it. And Joseph said unto them, *Do* not interpretations *belong* to God? tell me *them*, I pray you.

9 And the chief butler told his dream to Joseph, and said to him, In my dream, behold, a vine *was* before me;

10 And in the vine *were* three branches: and it *was* as though it budded, *and* her blossoms shot forth; and the clusters thereof brought forth ripe grapes:

11 And Pharaoh's cup *was* in my hand: and I took the grapes, and pressed them into Pharaoh's cup, and I gave the cup into Pharaoh's hand.

12 And Joseph said unto him, This *is* the interpretation of it: The three branches *are* three days:

13 Yet within three days shall Pharaoh lift up thine head, and restore thee unto thy place: and thou shalt deliver Pharaoh's cup into his hand, after the former manner when thou wast his butler.

14 But think on me when it shall be well with thee, and shew kindness, I pray thee, unto me, and make mention of me unto Pharaoh, and bring me out of this house:

NEW LIVING TRANSLATION

21 But the LORD was with Joseph in the prison and
showed him his faithful love. And the LORD made Joseph a favorite with the prison warden. 22 Before
long, the warden put Joseph in charge of all the other
prisoners and over everything that happened in the
prison. 23 The warden had no more worries, because
Joseph took care of everything. The LORD was with
him and caused everything he did to succeed.

Joseph Interprets Two Dreams

40 Some time later, Pharaoh's chief cup-
bearer and chief baker offended their royal
master. 2 Pharaoh became angry with these two officials, 3 and he put them in the prison where Joseph
was, in the palace of the captain of the guard. 4 They
remained in prison for quite some time, and the captain of the guard assigned them to Joseph, who
looked after them.

5 While they were in prison, Pharaoh's cup-bearer
and baker each had a dream one night, and each
dream had its own meaning. 6 When Joseph saw
them the next morning, he noticed that they both
looked upset. 7 "Why do you look so worried today?"
he asked them.

8 And they replied, "We both had dreams last
night, but no one can tell us what they mean."

"Interpreting dreams is God's business," Joseph
replied. "Go ahead and tell me your dreams."

9 So the chief cup-bearer told Joseph his dream
first. "In my dream," he said, "I saw a grapevine in
front of me. 10 The vine had three branches that began to bud and blossom, and soon it produced clusters of ripe grapes. 11 I was holding Pharaoh's wine
cup in my hand, so I took a cluster of grapes and
squeezed the juice into the cup. Then I placed the
cup in Pharaoh's hand."

12 "This is what the dream means," Joseph said.
"The three branches represent three days. 13 Within
three days Pharaoh will lift you up and restore you to
your position as his chief cup-bearer. 14 And please
remember me and do me a favor when things go well
for you. Mention me to Pharaoh, so he might let me

KING JAMES VERSION

15For indeed I was stolen away out of the land of
the Hebrews: and here also have I done nothing that
they should put me into the dungeon.
16When the chief baker saw that the interpretation was good, he said unto Joseph, I also *was* in my
dream, and, behold, *I had* three white baskets on
my head:
17And in the uppermost basket *there was* of all
manner of bakemeats for Pharaoh; and the birds did
eat them out of the basket upon my head.
18And Joseph answered and said, This *is* the interpretation thereof: The three baskets *are* three days:
19Yet within three days shall Pharaoh lift up thy
head from off thee, and shall hang thee on a tree; and
the birds shall eat thy flesh from off thee.
20And it came to pass the third day, *which was*
Pharaoh's birthday, that he made a feast unto all his
servants: and he lifted up the head of the chief butler
and of the chief baker among his servants.
21And he restored the chief butler unto his butler-
ship again; and he gave the cup into Pharaoh's hand:
22But he hanged the chief baker: as Joseph had
interpreted to them.
23Yet did not the chief butler remember Joseph,
but forgat him.

41 1And it came to pass at the end of two full
years, that Pharaoh dreamed: and, behold,
he stood by the river.
2And, behold, there came up out of the river seven
well favoured kine and fatfleshed; and they fed in a
meadow.
3And, behold, seven other kine came up after them
out of the river, ill favoured and leanfleshed; and
stood by the *other* kine upon the brink of the river.
4And the ill favoured and leanfleshed kine did eat
up the seven well favoured and fat kine. So Pharaoh
awoke.
5And he slept and dreamed the second time: and,
behold, seven ears of corn came up upon one stalk,
rank and good.
6And, behold, seven thin ears and blasted with the
east wind sprung up after them.
7And the seven thin ears devoured the seven rank
and full ears. And Pharaoh awoke, and, behold, *it was*
a dream.
8And it came to pass in the morning that his spirit
was troubled; and he sent and called for all the magicians of Egypt, and all the wise men thereof: and Pharaoh told them his dream; but *there was* none that
could interpret them unto Pharaoh.
9Then spake the chief butler unto Pharaoh, saying, I do remember my faults this day:
10Pharaoh was wroth with his servants, and put me
in ward in the captain of the guard's house, *both* me
and the chief baker:

NEW LIVING TRANSLATION

out of this place. 15For I was kidnapped from my
homeland, the land of the Hebrews, and now I'm
here in prison, but I did nothing to deserve it."
16When the chief baker saw that Joseph had given
the first dream such a positive interpretation, he said
to Joseph, "I had a dream, too. In my dream there
were three baskets of white pastries stacked on my
head. 17The top basket contained all kinds of pastries for Pharaoh, but the birds came and ate them
from the basket on my head."
18"This is what the dream means," Joseph told
him. "The three baskets also represent three days.
19Three days from now Pharaoh will lift you up and
impale your body on a pole. Then birds will come
and peck away at your flesh."
20Pharaoh's birthday came three days later, and he
prepared a banquet for all his officials and staff. He
summoned* his chief cup-bearer and chief baker to
join the other officials. 21He then restored the chief
cup-bearer to his former position, so he could again
hand Pharaoh his cup. 22But Pharaoh impaled the
chief baker, just as Joseph had predicted when he interpreted his dream. 23Pharaoh's chief cup-bearer,
however, forgot all about Joseph, never giving him
another thought.

Pharaoh's Dreams

41 Two full years later, Pharaoh dreamed that
he was standing on the bank of the Nile
River. 2In his dream he saw seven fat, healthy cows
come up out of the river and begin grazing in the
marsh grass. 3Then he saw seven more cows come
up behind them from the Nile, but these were
scrawny and thin. These cows stood beside the fat
cows on the riverbank. 4Then the scrawny, thin cows
ate the seven healthy, fat cows! At this point in the
dream, Pharaoh woke up.
5But he fell asleep again and had a second dream.
This time he saw seven heads of grain, plump and
beautiful, growing on a single stalk. 6Then seven
more heads of grain appeared, but these were shriveled and withered by the east wind. 7And these thin
heads swallowed up the seven plump, well-formed
heads! Then Pharaoh woke up again and realized it
was a dream.
8The next morning Pharaoh was very disturbed by
the dreams. So he called for all the magicians and
wise men of Egypt. When Pharaoh told them his
dreams, not one of them could tell him what they
meant.
9Finally, the king's chief cup-bearer spoke up.
"Today I have been reminded of my failure," he told
Pharaoh. 10"Some time ago, you were angry with the
chief baker and me, and you imprisoned us in the

40:20 Hebrew *He lifted up the head of.*

KING JAMES VERSION

11And we dreamed a dream in one night, I and he; we dreamed each man according to the interpretation of his dream.

12And *there was* there with us a young man, an Hebrew, servant to the captain of the guard; and we told him, and he interpreted to us our dreams; to each man according to his dream he did interpret.

13And it came to pass, as he interpreted to us, so it was; me he restored unto mine office, and him he hanged.

14Then Pharaoh sent and called Joseph, and they brought him hastily out of the dungeon: and he shaved *himself*, and changed his raiment, and came in unto Pharaoh.

15And Pharaoh said unto Joseph, I have dreamed a dream, and *there is* none that can interpret it: and I have heard say of thee, *that* thou canst understand a dream to interpret it.

16And Joseph answered Pharaoh, saying, *It is* not in me: God shall give Pharaoh an answer of peace.

17And Pharaoh said unto Joseph, In my dream, behold, I stood upon the bank of the river:

18And, behold, there came up out of the river seven kine, fatfleshed and well favoured; and they fed in a meadow:

19And, behold, seven other kine came up after them, poor and very ill favoured and leanfleshed, such as I never saw in all the land of Egypt for badness:

20And the lean and the ill favoured kine did eat up the first seven fat kine:

21And when they had eaten them up, it could not be known that they had eaten them; but they *were* still ill favoured, as at the beginning. So I awoke.

22And I saw in my dream, and, behold, seven ears came up in one stalk, full and good:

23And, behold, seven ears, withered, thin, *and* blasted with the east wind, sprung up after them:

24And the thin ears devoured the seven good ears: and I told *this* unto the magicians; but *there was* none that could declare *it* to me.

25And Joseph said unto Pharaoh, The dream of Pharaoh *is* one: God hath shewed Pharaoh what he *is* about to do.

26The seven good kine *are* seven years; and the seven good ears *are* seven years: the dream *is* one.

27And the seven thin and ill favoured kine that came up after them *are* seven years; and the seven empty ears blasted with the east wind shall be seven years of famine.

28This *is* the thing which I have spoken unto Pharaoh: What God *is* about to do he sheweth unto Pharaoh.

29Behold, there come seven years of great plenty throughout all the land of Egypt:

30And there shall arise after them seven years of famine; and all the plenty shall be forgotten in the land of Egypt; and the famine shall consume the land;

NEW LIVING TRANSLATION

palace of the captain of the guard. 11One night the chief baker and I each had a dream, and each dream had its own meaning. 12There was a young Hebrew man with us in the prison who was a slave of the captain of the guard. We told him our dreams, and he told us what each of our dreams meant. 13And everything happened just as he had predicted. I was restored to my position as cup-bearer, and the chief baker was executed and impaled on a pole."

14Pharaoh sent for Joseph at once, and he was quickly brought from the prison. After he shaved and changed his clothes, he went in and stood before Pharaoh. 15Then Pharaoh said to Joseph, "I had a dream last night, and no one here can tell me what it means. But I have heard that when you hear about a dream you can interpret it."

16"It is beyond my power to do this," Joseph replied. "But God can tell you what it means and set you at ease."

17So Pharaoh told Joseph his dream. "In my dream," he said, "I was standing on the bank of the Nile River, 18and I saw seven fat, healthy cows come up out of the river and begin grazing in the marsh grass. 19But then I saw seven sick-looking cows, scrawny and thin, come up after them. I've never seen such sorry-looking animals in all the land of Egypt. 20These thin, scrawny cows ate the seven fat cows. 21But afterward you wouldn't have known it, for they were still as thin and scrawny as before! Then I woke up.

22"Then I fell asleep again, and I had another dream. This time I saw seven heads of grain, full and beautiful, growing on a single stalk. 23Then seven more heads of grain appeared, but these were blighted, shriveled, and withered by the east wind. 24And the shriveled heads swallowed the seven healthy heads. I told these dreams to the magicians, but no one could tell me what they mean."

25Joseph responded, "Both of Pharaoh's dreams mean the same thing. God is telling Pharaoh in advance what he is about to do. 26The seven healthy cows and the seven healthy heads of grain both represent seven years of prosperity. 27The seven thin, scrawny cows that came up later and the seven thin heads of grain, withered by the east wind, represent seven years of famine.

28"This will happen just as I have described it, for God has revealed to Pharaoh in advance what he is about to do. 29The next seven years will be a period of great prosperity throughout the land of Egypt. 30But afterward there will be seven years of famine so great that all the prosperity will be forgotten in

KING JAMES VERSION

31 And the plenty shall not be known in the land by reason of that famine following; for it *shall be* very grievous.

32 And for that the dream was doubled unto Pharaoh twice; *it is* because the thing *is* established by God, and God will shortly bring it to pass.

33 Now therefore let Pharaoh look out a man discreet and wise, and set him over the land of Egypt.

34 Let Pharaoh do *this,* and let him appoint officers over the land, and take up the fifth part of the land of Egypt in the seven plenteous years.

35 And let them gather all the food of those good years that come, and lay up corn under the hand of Pharaoh, and let them keep food in the cities.

36 And that food shall be for store to the land against the seven years of famine, which shall be in the land of Egypt; that the land perish not through the famine.

37 And the thing was good in the eyes of Pharaoh, and in the eyes of all his servants.

38 And Pharaoh said unto his servants, Can we find *such a one* as this *is,* a man in whom the Spirit of God *is?*

39 And Pharaoh said unto Joseph, Forasmuch as God hath shewed thee all this, *there is* none so discreet and wise as thou *art:*

40 Thou shalt be over my house, and according unto thy word shall all my people be ruled: only in the throne will I be greater than thou.

41 And Pharaoh said unto Joseph, See, I have set thee over all the land of Egypt.

42 And Pharaoh took off his ring from his hand, and put it upon Joseph's hand, and arrayed him in vestures of fine linen, and put a gold chain about his neck;

43 And he made him to ride in the second chariot which he had; and they cried before him, Bow the knee: and he made him *ruler* over all the land of Egypt.

44 And Pharaoh said unto Joseph, I *am* Pharaoh, and without thee shall no man lift up his hand or foot in all the land of Egypt.

45 And Pharaoh called Joseph's name Zaphnath-paaneah; and he gave him to wife Asenath the daughter of Poti-pherah priest of On. And Joseph went out over *all* the land of Egypt.

46 And Joseph *was* thirty years old when he stood before Pharaoh king of Egypt. And Joseph went out from the presence of Pharaoh, and went throughout all the land of Egypt.

47 And in the seven plenteous years the earth brought forth by handfuls.

48 And he gathered up all the food of the seven years, which were in the land of Egypt, and laid up the food in the cities: the food of the field, which *was* round about every city, laid he up in the same.

NEW LIVING TRANSLATION

Egypt. Famine will destroy the land.
31 This famine will be so severe that even the memory of the good years will be erased.
32 As for having two similar dreams, it means that these events have been decreed by God, and he will soon make them happen.
33 "Therefore, Pharaoh should find an intelligent and wise man and put him in charge of the entire land of Egypt.
34 Then Pharaoh should appoint supervisors over the land and let them collect one-fifth of all the crops during the seven good years.
35 Have them gather all the food produced in the good years that are just ahead and bring it to Pharaoh's storehouses. Store it away, and guard it so there will be food in the cities.
36 That way there will be enough to eat when the seven years of famine come to the land of Egypt. Otherwise this famine will destroy the land."

Joseph Made Ruler of Egypt

37 Joseph's suggestions were well received by Pharaoh and his officials.
38 So Pharaoh asked his officials, "Can we find anyone else like this man so obviously filled with the spirit of God?"
39 Then Pharaoh said to Joseph, "Since God has revealed the meaning of the dreams to you, clearly no one else is as intelligent or wise as you are.
40 You will be in charge of my court, and all my people will take orders from you. Only I, sitting on my throne, will have a rank higher than yours."
41 Pharaoh said to Joseph, "I hereby put you in charge of the entire land of Egypt."
42 Then Pharaoh removed his signet ring from his hand and placed it on Joseph's finger. He dressed him in fine linen clothing and hung a gold chain around his neck.
43 Then he had Joseph ride in the chariot reserved for his second-in-command. And wherever Joseph went, the command was shouted, "Kneel down!" So Pharaoh put Joseph in charge of all Egypt.
44 And Pharaoh said to him, "I am Pharaoh, but no one will lift a hand or foot in the entire land of Egypt without your approval."
45 Then Pharaoh gave Joseph a new Egyptian name, Zaphenath-paneah.* He also gave him a wife, whose name was Asenath. She was the daughter of Potiphera, the priest of On.* So Joseph took charge of the entire land of Egypt.
46 He was thirty years old when he began serving in the court of Pharaoh, the king of Egypt. And when Joseph left Pharaoh's presence, he inspected the entire land of Egypt.
47 As predicted, for seven years the land produced bumper crops.
48 During those years, Joseph gathered all the crops grown in Egypt and stored the

41:45a *Zaphenath-paneah* probably means "God speaks and lives."
41:45b Greek version reads *of Heliopolis;* also in 41:50.

KING JAMES VERSION

[49]And Joseph gathered corn as the sand of the sea,
very much, until he left numbering; for *it was* without number.
[50]And unto Joseph were born two sons before the
years of famine came, which Asenath the daughter
of Poti-pherah priest of On bare unto him.
[51]And Joseph called the name of the firstborn
Manasseh: For God, *said he,* hath made me forget all
my toil, and all my father's house.
[52]And the name of the second called he Ephraim:
For God hath caused me to be fruitful in the land of
my affliction.
[53]And the seven years of plenteousness, that was
in the land of Egypt, were ended.
[54]And the seven years of dearth began to come, according as Joseph had said: and the dearth was in all
lands; but in all the land of Egypt there was bread.
[55]And when all the land of Egypt was famished,
the people cried to Pharaoh for bread: and Pharaoh
said unto all the Egyptians, Go unto Joseph; what he
saith to you, do.
[56]And the famine was over all the face of the earth:
And Joseph opened all the storehouses, and sold
unto the Egyptians; and the famine waxed sore in the
land of Egypt.
[57]And all countries came into Egypt to Joseph for
to buy *corn;* because that the famine was *so* sore in
all lands.

42 [1]Now when Jacob saw that there was corn in
Egypt, Jacob said unto his sons, Why do ye
look one upon another?
[2]And he said, Behold, I have heard that there is
corn in Egypt: get you down thither, and buy for us
from thence; that we may live, and not die.
[3]And Joseph's ten brethren went down to buy corn
in Egypt.
[4]But Benjamin, Joseph's brother, Jacob sent not
with his brethren; for he said, Lest peradventure mischief befall him.
[5]And the sons of Israel came to buy *corn* among
those that came: for the famine was in the land of
Canaan.
[6]And Joseph *was* the governor over the land, *and*
he *it was* that sold to all the people of the land: and
Joseph's brethren came, and bowed down themselves before him *with* their faces to the earth.
[7]And Joseph saw his brethren, and he knew them,
but made himself strange unto them, and spake
roughly unto them; and he said unto them, Whence
come ye? And they said, From the land of Canaan to
buy food.
[8]And Joseph knew his brethren, but they knew not
him.
[9]And Joseph remembered the dreams which he
dreamed of them, and said unto them, Ye *are* spies;
to see the nakedness of the land ye are come.

NEW LIVING TRANSLATION

grain from the surrounding fields in the cities. [49]He
piled up huge amounts of grain like sand on the seashore. Finally, he stopped keeping records because
there was too much to measure.
[50]During this time, before the first of the famine
years, two sons were born to Joseph and his wife,
Asenath, the daughter of Potiphera, the priest of On.
[51]Joseph named his older son Manasseh,* for he
said, "God has made me forget all my troubles and
everyone in my father's family." [52]Joseph named his
second son Ephraim,* for he said, "God has made me
fruitful in this land of my grief."
[53]At last the seven years of bumper crops throughout the land of Egypt came to an end. [54]Then the
seven years of famine began, just as Joseph had predicted. The famine also struck all the surrounding
countries, but throughout Egypt there was plenty of
food. [55]Eventually, however, the famine spread
throughout the land of Egypt as well. And when the
people cried out to Pharaoh for food, he told them,
"Go to Joseph, and do whatever he tells you." [56]So
with severe famine everywhere, Joseph opened up
the storehouses and distributed grain to the Egyptians, for the famine was severe throughout the land
of Egypt. [57]And people from all around came to
Egypt to buy grain from Joseph because the famine
was severe throughout the world.

Joseph's Brothers Go to Egypt

42 When Jacob heard that grain was available
in Egypt, he said to his sons, "Why are you
standing around looking at one another? [2]I have
heard there is grain in Egypt. Go down there, and buy
enough grain to keep us alive. Otherwise we'll die."
[3]So Joseph's ten older brothers went down to
Egypt to buy grain. [4]But Jacob wouldn't let Joseph's
younger brother, Benjamin, go with them, for fear
some harm might come to him. [5]So Jacob's* sons arrived in Egypt along with others to buy food, for the
famine was in Canaan as well.
[6]Since Joseph was governor of all Egypt and in
charge of selling grain to all the people, it was to him
that his brothers came. When they arrived, they
bowed before him with their faces to the ground.
[7]Joseph recognized his brothers instantly, but he
pretended to be a stranger and spoke harshly to
them. "Where are you from?" he demanded.
"From the land of Canaan," they replied. "We have
come to buy food."
[8]Although Joseph recognized his brothers, they
didn't recognize him. [9]And he remembered the
dreams he'd had about them many years before. He
said to them, "You are spies! You have come to see
how vulnerable our land has become."

41:51 *Manasseh* sounds like a Hebrew term that means "causing to forget."
41:52 *Ephraim* sounds like a Hebrew term that means "fruitful."
42:5 Hebrew *Israel's.* See note on 35:21.

KING JAMES VERSION

10And they said unto him, Nay, my lord, but to buy
food are thy servants come.
11We *are* all one man's sons; we *are* true *men,* thy
servants are no spies.
12And he said unto them, Nay, but to see the nakedness of the land ye are come.
13And they said, Thy servants *are* twelve brethren,
the sons of one man in the land of Canaan; and, behold, the youngest *is* this day with our father, and one
is not.
14And Joseph said unto them, That *is it* that I spake
unto you, saying, Ye *are* spies:
15Hereby ye shall be proved: By the life of Pharaoh
ye shall not go forth hence, except your youngest
brother come hither.
16Send one of you, and let him fetch your brother,
and ye shall be kept in prison, that your words may
be proved, whether *there be any* truth in you: or else
by the life of Pharaoh surely ye *are* spies.
17And he put them all together into ward three
days.
18And Joseph said unto them the third day, This
do, and live; *for* I fear God:
19If ye *be* true *men,* let one of your brethren be
bound in the house of your prison: go ye, carry corn
for the famine of your houses:
20But bring your youngest brother unto me; so
shall your words be verified, and ye shall not die. And
they did so.
21And they said one to another, We *are* verily
guilty concerning our brother, in that we saw the anguish of his soul, when he besought us, and we would
not hear; therefore is this distress come upon us.
22And Reuben answered them, saying, Spake I not
unto you, saying, Do not sin against the child; and ye
would not hear? therefore, behold, also his blood
is required.
23And they knew not that Joseph understood
them; for he spake unto them by an interpreter.
24And he turned himself about from them, and
wept; and returned to them again, and communed
with them, and took from them Simeon, and bound
him before their eyes.
25Then Joseph commanded to fill their sacks with
corn, and to restore every man's money into his sack,
and to give them provision for the way: and thus did
he unto them.
26And they laded their asses with the corn, and
departed thence.
27And as one of them opened his sack to give his
ass provender in the inn, he espied his money; for,
behold, it *was* in his sack's mouth.
28And he said unto his brethren, My money is restored; and, lo, *it is* even in my sack: and their heart
failed *them,* and they were afraid, saying one to another, What *is* this *that* God hath done unto us?

NEW LIVING TRANSLATION

10"No, my lord!" they exclaimed. "Your servants
have simply come to buy food. 11We are all brothers—members of the same family. We are honest
men, sir! We are not spies!"
12"Yes, you are!" Joseph insisted. "You have come
to see how vulnerable our land has become."
13"Sir," they said, "there are actually twelve of us.
We, your servants, are all brothers, sons of a man living in the land of Canaan. Our youngest brother is
back there with our father right now, and one of our
brothers is no longer with us."
14But Joseph insisted, "As I said, you are spies!
15This is how I will test your story. I swear by the life
of Pharaoh that you will never leave Egypt unless
your youngest brother comes here! 16One of you
must go and get your brother. I'll keep the rest of you
here in prison. Then we'll find out whether or not
your story is true. By the life of Pharaoh, if it turns out
that you don't have a younger brother, then I'll know
you are spies."
17So Joseph put them all in prison for three days.
18On the third day Joseph said to them, "I am a God-
fearing man. If you do as I say, you will live. 19If you
really are honest men, choose one of your brothers to
remain in prison. The rest of you may go home with
grain for your starving families. 20But you must bring
your youngest brother back to me. This will prove
that you are telling the truth, and you will not die." To
this they agreed.
21Speaking among themselves, they said, "Clearly
we are being punished because of what we did to Joseph long ago. We saw his anguish when he pleaded
for his life, but we wouldn't listen. That's why we're in
this trouble."
22"Didn't I tell you not to sin against the boy?"
Reuben asked. "But you wouldn't listen. And now we
have to answer for his blood!"
23Of course, they didn't know that Joseph understood them, for he had been speaking to them
through an interpreter. 24Now he turned away from
them and began to weep. When he regained his
composure, he spoke to them again. Then he chose
Simeon from among them and had him tied up right
before their eyes.
25Joseph then ordered his servants to fill the
men's sacks with grain, but he also gave secret instructions to return each brother's payment at the
top of his sack. He also gave them supplies for their
journey home. 26So the brothers loaded their donkeys with the grain and headed for home.
27But when they stopped for the night and one of
them opened his sack to get grain for his donkey, he
found his money in the top of his sack. 28"Look!" he
exclaimed to his brothers. "My money has been returned; it's here in my sack!" Then their hearts sank.
Trembling, they said to each other, "What has God
done to us?"

KING JAMES VERSION

29And they came unto Jacob their father unto the
land of Canaan, and told him all that befell unto
them; saying,
30The man, *who is* the lord of the land, spake
roughly to us, and took us for spies of the country.
31And we said unto him, We *are* true *men;* we are
no spies:
32We *be* twelve brethren, sons of our father; one *is*
not, and the youngest *is* this day with our father in
the land of Canaan.
33And the man, the lord of the country, said unto
us, Hereby shall I know that ye *are* true *men;* leave
one of your brethren *here* with me, and take *food for*
the famine of your households, and be gone:
34And bring your youngest brother unto me: then
shall I know that ye *are* no spies, but *that* ye *are* true
men: so will I deliver you your brother, and ye shall
traffick in the land.
35And it came to pass as they emptied their sacks,
that, behold, every man's bundle of money *was* in his
sack: and when *both* they and their father saw the
bundles of money, they were afraid.
36And Jacob their father said unto them, Me have
ye bereaved *of my children:* Joseph *is* not, and Simeon *is* not, and ye will take Benjamin *away:* all these
things are against me.
37And Reuben spake unto his father, saying, Slay
my two sons, if I bring him not to thee: deliver him
into my hand, and I will bring him to thee again.
38And he said, My son shall not go down with you;
for his brother is dead, and he is left alone: if mischief befall him by the way in the which ye go, then
shall ye bring down my gray hairs with sorrow to
the grave.

43 1And the famine *was* sore in the land.
2And it came to pass, when they had eaten
up the corn which they had brought out of Egypt,
their father said unto them, Go again, buy us a little
food.
3And Judah spake unto him, saying, The man did
solemnly protest unto us, saying, Ye shall not see my
face, except your brother *be* with you.
4If thou wilt send our brother with us, we will go
down and buy thee food:
5But if thou wilt not send *him,* we will not go
down: for the man said unto us, Ye shall not see my
face, except your brother *be* with you.
6And Israel said, Wherefore dealt ye *so* ill with me,
as to tell the man whether ye had yet a brother?
7And they said, The man asked us straitly of our
state, and of our kindred, saying, *Is* your father yet
alive? have ye *another* brother? and we told him according to the tenor of these words: could we certainly know that he would say, Bring your brother
down?
8And Judah said unto Israel his father, Send the

NEW LIVING TRANSLATION

29When the brothers came to their father, Jacob,
in the land of Canaan, they told him everything that
had happened to them. 30"The man who is governor
of the land spoke very harshly to us," they told him.
"He accused us of being spies scouting the land.
31But we said, 'We are honest men, not spies. 32We
are twelve brothers, sons of one father. One brother
is no longer with us, and the youngest is at home with
our father in the land of Canaan.'
33"Then the man who is governor of the land told
us, 'This is how I will find out if you are honest men.
Leave one of your brothers here with me, and take
grain for your starving families and go on home.
34But you must bring your youngest brother back to
me. Then I will know you are honest men and not
spies. Then I will give you back your brother, and you
may trade freely in the land.'"
35As they emptied out their sacks, there in each
man's sack was the bag of money he had paid for the
grain! The brothers and their father were terrified
when they saw the bags of money. 36Jacob exclaimed, "You are robbing me of my children! Joseph
is gone! Simeon is gone! And now you want to take
Benjamin, too. Everything is going against me!"
37Then Reuben said to his father, "You may kill my
two sons if I don't bring Benjamin back to you. I'll be
responsible for him, and I promise to bring him
back."
38But Jacob replied, "My son will not go down with
you. His brother Joseph is dead, and he is all I have
left. If anything should happen to him on your journey, you would send this grieving, white-haired man
to his grave.*"

The Brothers Return to Egypt

43 But the famine continued to ravage the land
of Canaan. 2When the grain they had
brought from Egypt was almost gone, Jacob said to
his sons, "Go back and buy us a little more food."
3But Judah said, "The man was serious when he
warned us, 'You won't see my face again unless your
brother is with you.' 4If you send Benjamin with us,
we will go down and buy more food. 5But if you don't
let Benjamin go, we won't go either. Remember, the
man said, 'You won't see my face again unless your
brother is with you.'"
6"Why were you so cruel to me?" Jacob* moaned.
"Why did you tell him you had another brother?"
7"The man kept asking us questions about our
family," they replied. "He asked, 'Is your father still
alive? Do you have another brother?' So we answered
his questions. How could we know he would say,
'Bring your brother down here'?"
8Judah said to his father, "Send the boy with me,

42:38 Hebrew *to Sheol.* **43:6** Hebrew *Israel;* also in 43:11. See note on 35:21.

lad with me, and we will arise and go; that we may
live, and not die, both we, and thou, *and* also our
little ones.

9 I will be surety for him; of my hand shalt thou require him: if I bring him not unto thee, and set him
before thee, then let me bear the blame for ever:

10 For except we had lingered, surely now we had
returned this second time.

11 And their father Israel said unto them, If *it must
be* so now, do this; take of the best fruits in the land
in your vessels, and carry down the man a present, a
little balm, and a little honey, spices, and myrrh, nuts,
and almonds:

12 And take double money in your hand; and the
money that was brought again in the mouth of your
sacks, carry *it* again in your hand; peradventure it
was an oversight:

13 Take also your brother, and arise, go again unto
the man:

14 And God Almighty give you mercy before the
man, that he may send away your other brother, and
Benjamin. If I be bereaved *of my children,* I am
bereaved.

15 And the men took that present, and they took
double money in their hand, and Benjamin; and rose
up, and went down to Egypt, and stood before Joseph.

16 And when Joseph saw Benjamin with them, he
said to the ruler of his house, Bring *these* men home,
and slay, and make ready; for *these* men shall dine
with me at noon.

17 And the man did as Joseph bade; and the man
brought the men into Joseph's house.

18 And the men were afraid, because they were
brought into Joseph's house; and they said, Because
of the money that was returned in our sacks at the
first time are we brought in; that he may seek occasion against us, and fall upon us, and take us for
bondmen, and our asses.

19 And they came near to the steward of Joseph's
house, and they communed with him at the door of
the house,

20 And said, O sir, we came indeed down at the first
time to buy food:

21 And it came to pass, when we came to the inn,
that we opened our sacks, and, behold, *every* man's
money *was* in the mouth of his sack, our money in
full weight: and we have brought it again in our hand.

22 And other money have we brought down in our
hands to buy food: we cannot tell who put our money
in our sacks.

23 And he said, Peace *be* to you, fear not: your God,
and the God of your father, hath given you treasure
in your sacks: I had your money. And he brought
Simeon out unto them.

24 And the man brought the men into Joseph's
house, and gave *them* water, and they washed their
feet; and he gave their asses provender.

and we will be on our way. Otherwise we will all die
of starvation—and not only we, but you and our little
ones.
9 I personally guarantee his safety. You may
hold me responsible if I don't bring him back to you.
Then let me bear the blame forever.
10 If we hadn't
wasted all this time, we could have gone and returned twice by now."

11 So their father, Jacob, finally said to them, "If it
can't be avoided, then at least do this. Pack your bags
with the best products of this land. Take them down
to the man as gifts—balm, honey, gum, aromatic
resin, pistachio nuts, and almonds.
12 Also take dou-
ble the money that was put back in your sacks, as it
was probably someone's mistake.
13 Then take your
brother, and go back to the man.
14 May God Al-
mighty* give you mercy as you go before the man, so
that he will release Simeon and let Benjamin return.
But if I must lose my children, so be it."

15 So the men packed Jacob's gifts and double the
money and headed off with Benjamin. They finally
arrived in Egypt and presented themselves to Joseph.
16 When Joseph saw Benjamin with them, he said to
the manager of his household, "These men will eat
with me this noon. Take them inside the palace.
Then go slaughter an animal, and prepare a big
feast."
17 So the man did as Joseph told him and took
them into Joseph's palace.

18 The brothers were terrified when they saw that
they were being taken into Joseph's house. "It's because of the money someone put in our sacks last
time we were here," they said. "He plans to pretend
that we stole it. Then he will seize us, make us slaves,
and take our donkeys."

A Feast at Joseph's Palace

19 The brothers approached the manager of Joseph's
household and spoke to him at the entrance to the
palace.
20 "Sir," they said, "we came to Egypt once before to buy food.
21 But as we were returning home, we
stopped for the night and opened our sacks. Then we
discovered that each man's money—the exact
amount paid—was in the top of his sack! Here it is;
we have brought it back with us.
22 We also have addi-
tional money to buy more food. We have no idea who
put our money in our sacks."

23 "Relax. Don't be afraid," the household manager
told them. "Your God, the God of your father, must
have put this treasure into your sacks. I know I received your payment." Then he released Simeon and
brought him out to them.

24 The manager then led the men into Joseph's
palace. He gave them water to wash their feet and

43:14 Hebrew *El-Shaddai.*

KING JAMES VERSION

25And they made ready the present against Joseph came at noon: for they heard that they should eat bread there.

26And when Joseph came home, they brought him the present which *was* in their hand into the house, and bowed themselves to him to the earth.

27And he asked them of *their* welfare, and said, *Is* your father well, the old man of whom ye spake? *Is* he yet alive?

28And they answered, Thy servant our father *is* in good health, he *is* yet alive. And they bowed down their heads, and made obeisance.

29And he lifted up his eyes, and saw his brother Benjamin, his mother's son, and said, *Is* this your younger brother, of whom ye spake unto me? And he said, God be gracious unto thee, my son.

30And Joseph made haste; for his bowels did yearn upon his brother: and he sought *where* to weep; and he entered into *his* chamber, and wept there.

31And he washed his face, and went out, and refrained himself, and said, Set on bread.

32And they set on for him by himself, and for them by themselves, and for the Egyptians, which did eat with him, by themselves: because the Egyptians might not eat bread with the Hebrews; for that *is* an abomination unto the Egyptians.

33And they sat before him, the firstborn according to his birthright, and the youngest according to his youth: and the men marvelled one at another.

34And he took *and sent* messes unto them from before him: but Benjamin's mess was five times so much as any of theirs. And they drank, and were merry with him.

44 1And he commanded the steward of his house, saying, Fill the men's sacks *with* food, as much as they can carry, and put every man's money in his sack's mouth.

2And put my cup, the silver cup, in the sack's mouth of the youngest, and his corn money. And he did according to the word that Joseph had spoken.

3As soon as the morning was light, the men were sent away, they and their asses.

4*And* when they were gone out of the city, *and* not *yet* far off, Joseph said unto his steward, Up, follow after the men; and when thou dost overtake them, say unto them, Wherefore have ye rewarded evil for good?

5*Is* not this *it* in which my lord drinketh, and whereby indeed he divineth? ye have done evil in *so* doing.

6And he overtook them, and he spake unto them these same words.

7And they said unto him, Wherefore saith my lord these words? God forbid that thy servants should do according to this thing:

8Behold, the money, which we found in our sacks' mouths, we brought again unto thee out of the land

NEW LIVING TRANSLATION

provided food for their donkeys. 25They were told they would be eating there, so they prepared their gifts for Joseph's arrival at noon.

26When Joseph came home, they gave him the gifts they had brought him, then bowed low to the ground before him. 27After greeting them, he asked, "How is your father, the old man you spoke about? Is he still alive?"

28"Yes," they replied. "Our father, your servant, is alive and well." And they bowed low again.

29Then Joseph looked at his brother Benjamin, the son of his own mother. "Is this your youngest brother, the one you told me about?" Joseph asked. "May God be gracious to you, my son." 30Then Joseph hurried from the room because he was overcome with emotion for his brother. He went into his private room, where he broke down and wept. 31After washing his face, he came back out, keeping himself under control. Then he ordered, "Bring out the food!"

32The waiters served Joseph at his own table, and his brothers were served at a separate table. The Egyptians who ate with Joseph sat at their own table, because Egyptians despise Hebrews and refuse to eat with them. 33Joseph told each of his brothers where to sit, and to their amazement, he seated them according to age, from oldest to youngest. 34And Joseph filled their plates with food from his own table, giving Benjamin five times as much as he gave the others. So they feasted and drank freely with him.

Joseph's Silver Cup

44 When his brothers were ready to leave, Joseph gave these instructions to his palace manager: "Fill each of their sacks with as much grain as they can carry, and put each man's money back into his sack. 2Then put my personal silver cup at the top of the youngest brother's sack, along with the money for his grain." So the manager did as Joseph instructed him.

3The brothers were up at dawn and were sent on their journey with their loaded donkeys. 4But when they had gone only a short distance and were barely out of the city, Joseph said to his palace manager, "Chase after them and stop them. When you catch up with them, ask them, 'Why have you repaid my kindness with such evil? 5Why have you stolen my master's silver cup,* which he uses to predict the future? What a wicked thing you have done!'"

6When the palace manager caught up with the men, he spoke to them as he had been instructed.

7"What are you talking about?" the brothers responded. "We are your servants and would never do such a thing! 8Didn't we return the money we found

44:5 As in Greek version; Hebrew lacks this phrase.

KING JAMES VERSION

of Canaan: how then should we steal out of thy lord's house silver or gold?

9 With whomsoever of thy servants it be found, both let him die, and we also will be my lord's bondmen.

10 And he said, Now also *let* it *be* according unto your words: he with whom it is found shall be my servant; and ye shall be blameless.

11 Then they speedily took down every man his sack to the ground, and opened every man his sack.

12 And he searched, *and* began at the eldest, and left at the youngest: and the cup was found in Benjamin's sack.

13 Then they rent their clothes, and laded every man his ass, and returned to the city.

14 And Judah and his brethren came to Joseph's house; for he *was* yet there: and they fell before him on the ground.

15 And Joseph said unto them, What deed *is* this that ye have done? wot ye not that such a man as I can certainly divine?

16 And Judah said, What shall we say unto my lord? what shall we speak? or how shall we clear ourselves? God hath found out the iniquity of thy servants: behold, we *are* my lord's servants, both we, and *he* also with whom the cup is found.

17 And he said, God forbid that I should do so: *but* the man in whose hand the cup is found, he shall be my servant; and as for you, get you up in peace unto your father.

18 Then Judah came near unto him, and said, Oh my lord, let thy servant, I pray thee, speak a word in my lord's ears, and let not thine anger burn against thy servant: for thou *art* even as Pharaoh.

19 My lord asked his servants, saying, Have ye a father, or a brother?

20 And we said unto my lord, We have a father, an old man, and a child of his old age, a little one; and his brother is dead, and he alone is left of his mother, and his father loveth him.

21 And thou saidst unto thy servants, Bring him down unto me, that I may set mine eyes upon him.

22 And we said unto my lord, The lad cannot leave his father: for *if* he should leave his father, *his father* would die.

23 And thou saidst unto thy servants, Except your youngest brother come down with you, ye shall see my face no more.

24 And it came to pass when we came up unto thy servant my father, we told him the words of my lord.

25 And our father said, Go again, *and* buy us a little food.

26 And we said, We cannot go down: if our youngest brother be with us, then will we go down: for we may not see the man's face, except our youngest brother *be* with us.

NEW LIVING TRANSLATION

in our sacks? We brought it back all the way from the land of Canaan. Why would we steal silver or gold from your master's house? 9 If you find his cup with any one of us, let that man die. And all the rest of us, my lord, will be your slaves."

10 "That's fair," the man replied. "But only the one who stole the cup will be my slave. The rest of you may go free."

11 They all quickly took their sacks from the backs of their donkeys and opened them. 12 The palace manager searched the brothers' sacks, from the oldest to the youngest. And the cup was found in Benjamin's sack! 13 When the brothers saw this, they tore their clothing in despair. Then they loaded their donkeys again and returned to the city.

14 Joseph was still in his palace when Judah and his brothers arrived, and they fell to the ground before him. 15 "What have you done?" Joseph demanded. "Don't you know that a man like me can predict the future?"

16 Judah answered, "Oh, my lord, what can we say to you? How can we explain this? How can we prove our innocence? God is punishing us for our sins. My lord, we have all returned to be your slaves—all of us, not just our brother who had your cup in his sack."

17 "No," Joseph said. "I would never do such a thing! Only the man who stole the cup will be my slave. The rest of you may go back to your father in peace."

Judah Speaks for His Brothers

18 Then Judah stepped forward and said, "Please, my lord, let your servant say just one word to you. Please, do not be angry with me, even though you are as powerful as Pharaoh himself.

19 "My lord, previously you asked us, your servants, 'Do you have a father or a brother?' 20 And we responded, 'Yes, my lord, we have a father who is an old man, and his youngest son is a child of his old age. His full brother is dead, and he alone is left of his mother's children, and his father loves him very much.'

21 "And you said to us, 'Bring him here so I can see him with my own eyes.' 22 But we said to you, 'My lord, the boy cannot leave his father, for his father would die.' 23 But you told us, 'Unless your youngest brother comes with you, you will never see my face again.'

24 "So we returned to your servant, our father, and told him what you had said. 25 Later, when he said, 'Go back again and buy us more food,' 26 we replied, 'We can't go unless you let our youngest brother go with us. We'll never get to see the man's face unless our youngest brother is with us.'

KING JAMES VERSION

27 And thy servant my father said unto us, Ye know that my wife bare me two *sons:*

28 And the one went out from me, and I said, Surely he is torn in pieces; and I saw him not since:

29 And if ye take this also from me, and mischief befall him, ye shall bring down my gray hairs with sorrow to the grave.

30 Now therefore when I come to thy servant my father, and the lad *be* not with us; seeing that his life is bound up in the lad's life;

31 It shall come to pass, when he seeth that the lad *is* not *with us,* that he will die: and thy servants shall bring down the gray hairs of thy servant our father with sorrow to the grave.

32 For thy servant became surety for the lad unto my father, saying, If I bring him not unto thee, then I shall bear the blame to my father for ever.

33 Now therefore, I pray thee, let thy servant abide instead of the lad a bondman to my lord; and let the lad go up with his brethren.

34 For how shall I go up to my father, and the lad *be* not with me? lest peradventure I see the evil that shall come on my father.

45 1 Then Joseph could not refrain himself before all them that stood by him; and he cried, Cause every man to go out from me. And there stood no man with him, while Joseph made himself known unto his brethren.

2 And he wept aloud: and the Egyptians and the house of Pharaoh heard.

3 And Joseph said unto his brethren, I *am* Joseph; doth my father yet live? And his brethren could not answer him; for they were troubled at his presence.

4 And Joseph said unto his brethren, Come near to me, I pray you. And they came near. And he said, I *am* Joseph your brother, whom ye sold into Egypt.

5 Now therefore be not grieved, nor angry with yourselves, that ye sold me hither: for God did send me before you to preserve life.

6 For these two years *hath* the famine *been* in the land: and yet *there are* five years, in the which *there shall* neither *be* earing nor harvest.

7 And God sent me before you to preserve you a posterity in the earth, and to save your lives by a great deliverance.

8 So now *it was* not you *that* sent me hither, but God: and he hath made me a father to Pharaoh, and lord of all his house, and a ruler throughout all the land of Egypt.

9 Haste ye, and go up to my father, and say unto him, Thus saith thy son Joseph, God hath made me lord of all Egypt: come down unto me, tarry not:

10 And thou shalt dwell in the land of Goshen, and thou shalt be near unto me, thou, and thy children, and thy children's children, and thy flocks, and thy herds, and all that thou hast:

NEW LIVING TRANSLATION

27 "Then my father said to us, 'As you know, my wife had two sons, 28 and one of them went away and never returned. Doubtless he was torn to pieces by some wild animal. I have never seen him since. 29 Now if you take his brother away from me, and any harm comes to him, you will send this grieving, white-haired man to his grave.*'

30 "And now, my lord, I cannot go back to my father without the boy. Our father's life is bound up in the boy's life. 31 If he sees that the boy is not with us, our father will die. We, your servants, will indeed be responsible for sending that grieving, white-haired man to his grave. 32 My lord, I guaranteed to my father that I would take care of the boy. I told him, 'If I don't bring him back to you, I will bear the blame forever.'

33 "So please, my lord, let me stay here as a slave instead of the boy, and let the boy return with his brothers. 34 For how can I return to my father if the boy is not with me? I couldn't bear to see the anguish this would cause my father!"

Joseph Reveals His Identity

45 Joseph could stand it no longer. There were many people in the room, and he said to his attendants, "Out, all of you!" So he was alone with his brothers when he told them who he was. 2 Then he broke down and wept. He wept so loudly the Egyptians could hear him, and word of it quickly carried to Pharaoh's palace.

3 "I am Joseph!" he said to his brothers. "Is my father still alive?" But his brothers were speechless! They were stunned to realize that Joseph was standing there in front of them. 4 "Please, come closer," he said to them. So they came closer. And he said again, "I am Joseph, your brother, whom you sold into slavery in Egypt. 5 But don't be upset, and don't be angry with yourselves for selling me to this place. It was God who sent me here ahead of you to preserve your lives. 6 This famine that has ravaged the land for two years will last five more years, and there will be neither plowing nor harvesting. 7 God has sent me ahead of you to keep you and your families alive and to preserve many survivors.* 8 So it was God who sent me here, not you! And he is the one who made me an adviser* to Pharaoh—the manager of his entire palace and the governor of all Egypt.

9 "Now hurry back to my father and tell him, 'This is what your son Joseph says: God has made me master over all the land of Egypt. So come down to me immediately! 10 You can live in the region of Goshen, where you can be near me with all your children and grandchildren, your flocks and herds, and everything

44:29 Hebrew *to Sheol;* also in 44:31. **45:7** Or *and to save you with an extraordinary rescue.* The meaning of the Hebrew is uncertain.
45:8 Hebrew *a father.*

KING JAMES VERSION

11And there will I nourish thee; for yet *there are* five years of famine; lest thou, and thy household, and all that thou hast, come to poverty.

12And, behold, your eyes see, and the eyes of my brother Benjamin, that *it is* my mouth that speaketh unto you.

13And ye shall tell my father of all my glory in Egypt, and of all that ye have seen; and ye shall haste and bring down my father hither.

14And he fell upon his brother Benjamin's neck, and wept; and Benjamin wept upon his neck.

15Moreover he kissed all his brethren, and wept upon them: and after that his brethren talked with him.

16And the fame thereof was heard in Pharaoh's house, saying, Joseph's brethren are come: and it pleased Pharaoh well, and his servants.

17And Pharaoh said unto Joseph, Say unto thy brethren, This do ye; lade your beasts, and go, get you unto the land of Canaan;

18And take your father and your households, and come unto me: and I will give you the good of the land of Egypt, and ye shall eat the fat of the land.

19Now thou art commanded, this do ye; take you wagons out of the land of Egypt for your little ones, and for your wives, and bring your father, and come.

20Also regard not your stuff; for the good of all the land of Egypt *is* yours.

21And the children of Israel did so: and Joseph gave them wagons, according to the commandment of Pharaoh, and gave them provision for the way.

22To all of them he gave each man changes of raiment; but to Benjamin he gave three hundred *pieces* of silver, and five changes of raiment.

23And to his father he sent after this *manner;* ten asses laden with the good things of Egypt, and ten she asses laden with corn and bread and meat for his father by the way.

24So he sent his brethren away, and they departed: and he said unto them, See that ye fall not out by the way.

25And they went up out of Egypt, and came into the land of Canaan unto Jacob their father,

26And told him, saying, Joseph *is* yet alive, and he *is* governor over all the land of Egypt. And Jacob's heart fainted, for he believed them not.

27And they told him all the words of Joseph, which he had said unto them: and when he saw the wagons which Joseph had sent to carry him, the spirit of Jacob their father revived:

28And Israel said, *It is* enough; Joseph my son *is* yet alive: I will go and see him before I die.

46 1And Israel took his journey with all that he had, and came to Beer-sheba, and offered sacrifices unto the God of his father Isaac.

NEW LIVING TRANSLATION

you own. 11I will take care of you there, for there are
still five years of famine ahead of us. Otherwise you,
your household, and all your animals will starve.'"
12Then Joseph added, "Look! You can see for yourselves, and so can my brother Benjamin, that I really
am Joseph! 13Go tell my father of my honored position here in Egypt. Describe for him everything you
have seen, and then bring my father here quickly."
14Weeping with joy, he embraced Benjamin, and
Benjamin did the same. 15Then Joseph kissed each
of his brothers and wept over them, and after that
they began talking freely with him.

Pharaoh Invites Jacob to Egypt

16The news soon reached Pharaoh's palace: "Joseph's
brothers have arrived!" Pharaoh and his officials
were all delighted to hear this.
17Pharaoh said to Joseph, "Tell your brothers,
'This is what you must do: Load your pack animals,
and hurry back to the land of Canaan. 18Then get
your father and all of your families, and return here
to me. I will give you the very best land in Egypt, and
you will eat from the best that the land produces.'"
19Then Pharaoh said to Joseph, "Tell your brothers, 'Take wagons from the land of Egypt to carry
your little children and your wives, and bring your father here. 20Don't worry about your personal belongings, for the best of all the land of Egypt is yours.'"
21So the sons of Jacob* did as they were told. Joseph
provided them with wagons, as Pharaoh had commanded, and he gave them supplies for the journey.
22And he gave each of them new clothes—but to
Benjamin he gave five changes of clothes and 300
pieces* of silver. 23He also sent his father ten male
donkeys loaded with the finest products of Egypt, and
ten female donkeys loaded with grain and bread and
other supplies he would need on his journey.
24So Joseph sent his brothers off, and as they left,
he called after them, "Don't quarrel about all this
along the way!" 25And they left Egypt and returned to
their father, Jacob, in the land of Canaan.
26"Joseph is still alive!" they told him. "And he is
governor of all the land of Egypt!" Jacob was stunned
at the news—he couldn't believe it. 27But when they
repeated to Jacob everything Joseph had told them,
and when he saw the wagons Joseph had sent to
carry him, their father's spirits revived.
28Then Jacob exclaimed, "It must be true! My son
Joseph is alive! I must go and see him before I die."

Jacob's Journey to Egypt

46 So Jacob* set out for Egypt with all his possessions. And when he came to Beersheba,

45:21 Hebrew *Israel;* also in 45:28. See note on 35:21. **45:22** Hebrew *300 shekels,* about 7.5 pounds or 3.4 kilograms in weight. **46:1** Hebrew *Israel;* also in 46:29, 30. See note on 35:21.

KING JAMES VERSION

2And God spake unto Israel in the visions of the
night, and said, Jacob, Jacob. And he said, Here *am* I.
3And he said, I *am* God, the God of thy father: fear
not to go down into Egypt; for I will there make of
thee a great nation:
4I will go down with thee into Egypt; and I will also
surely bring thee up *again:* and Joseph shall put his
hand upon thine eyes.
5And Jacob rose up from Beer-sheba: and the sons
of Israel carried Jacob their father, and their little
ones, and their wives, in the wagons which Pharaoh
had sent to carry him.
6And they took their cattle, and their goods, which
they had gotten in the land of Canaan, and came into
Egypt, Jacob, and all his seed with him:
7His sons, and his sons' sons with him, his daughters, and his sons' daughters, and all his seed brought
he with him into Egypt.
8And these *are* the names of the children of Israel,
which came into Egypt, Jacob and his sons: Reuben,
Jacob's firstborn.
9And the sons of Reuben; Hanoch, and Phallu, and
Hezron, and Carmi.
10And the sons of Simeon; Jemuel, and Jamin, and
Ohad, and Jachin, and Zohar, and Shaul the son of a
Canaanitish woman.
11And the sons of Levi; Gershon, Kohath, and
Merari.
12And the sons of Judah; Er, and Onan, and Shelah,
and Pharez, and Zarah: but Er and Onan died in the
land of Canaan. And the sons of Pharez were Hezron
and Hamul.
13And the sons of Issachar; Tola, and Phuvah, and
Job, and Shimron.
14And the sons of Zebulun; Sered, and Elon, and
Jahleel.
15These *be* the sons of Leah, which she bare unto
Jacob in Padan-aram, with his daughter Dinah: all the
souls of his sons and his daughters *were* thirty and
three.
16And the sons of Gad; Ziphion, and Haggi, Shuni,
and Ezbon, Eri, and Arodi, and Areli.
17And the sons of Asher; Jimnah, and Ishuah, and
Isui, and Beriah, and Serah their sister: and the sons
of Beriah; Heber, and Malchiel.
18These *are* the sons of Zilpah, whom Laban gave
to Leah his daughter, and these she bare unto Jacob,
even sixteen souls.
19The sons of Rachel Jacob's wife; Joseph, and
Benjamin.
20And unto Joseph in the land of Egypt were born
Manasseh and Ephraim, which Asenath the daughter of Poti-pherah priest of On bare unto him.

NEW LIVING TRANSLATION

he offered sacrifices to the God of his father, Isaac.
2During the night God spoke to him in a vision.
"Jacob! Jacob!" he called.

"Here I am," Jacob replied.

3"I am God,* the God of your father," the voice
said. "Do not be afraid to go down to Egypt, for there
I will make your family into a great nation. 4I will go
with you down to Egypt, and I will bring you back
again. You will die in Egypt, but Joseph will be with
you to close your eyes."
5So Jacob left Beersheba, and his sons took him to
Egypt. They carried him and their little ones and
their wives in the wagons Pharaoh had provided for
them. 6They also took all their livestock and all the
personal belongings they had acquired in the land of
Canaan. So Jacob and his entire family went to
Egypt—7sons and grandsons, daughters and grand-
daughters—all his descendants.
8These are the names of the descendants of
Israel—the sons of Jacob—who went to Egypt:

Reuben was Jacob's oldest son. 9The sons of Reuben
were Hanoch, Pallu, Hezron, and Carmi.
10The sons of Simeon were Jemuel, Jamin, Ohad,
Jakin, Zohar, and Shaul. (Shaul's mother was a
Canaanite woman.)
11The sons of Levi were Gershon, Kohath, and
Merari.
12The sons of Judah were Er, Onan, Shelah, Perez,
and Zerah (though Er and Onan had died in the
land of Canaan). The sons of Perez were Hezron
and Hamul.
13The sons of Issachar were Tola, Puah,* Jashub,*
and Shimron.
14The sons of Zebulun were Sered, Elon, and Jahleel.
15These were the sons of Leah and Jacob who were
born in Paddan-aram, in addition to their daughter,
Dinah. The number of Jacob's descendants (male
and female) through Leah was thirty-three.

16The sons of Gad were Zephon,* Haggi, Shuni,
Ezbon, Eri, Arodi, and Areli.
17The sons of Asher were Imnah, Ishvah, Ishvi, and
Beriah. Their sister was Serah. Beriah's sons were
Heber and Malkiel.
18These were the sons of Zilpah, the servant given to
Leah by her father, Laban. The number of Jacob's de-
scendants through Zilpah was sixteen.

19The sons of Jacob's wife Rachel were Joseph
and Benjamin.
20Joseph's sons, born in the land of Egypt, were
Manasseh and Ephraim. Their mother was
Asenath, daughter of Potiphera, the priest
of On.*

46:3 Hebrew *I am El.* **46:13a** As in Syriac version and Samaritan Pentateuch (see also 1 Chr 7:1); Hebrew reads *Puvah.* **46:13b** As in some Greek manuscripts and Samaritan Pentateuch (see also Num 26:24; 1 Chr 7:1); Hebrew reads *Iob.* **46:16** As in Greek version and Samaritan Pentateuch (see also Num 26:15); Hebrew reads *Ziphion.* **46:20** Greek version reads *of Heliopolis.*

KING JAMES VERSION

[21]And the sons of Benjamin *were* Belah, and
Becher, and Ashbel, Gera, and Naaman, Ehi, and
Rosh, Muppim, and Huppim, and Ard.
[22]These *are* the sons of Rachel, which were born
to Jacob: all the souls *were* fourteen.
[23]And the sons of Dan; Hushim.
[24]And the sons of Naphtali; Jahzeel, and Guni, and
Jezer, and Shillem.
[25]These *are* the sons of Bilhah, which Laban gave
unto Rachel his daughter, and she bare these unto
Jacob: all the souls *were* seven.
[26]All the souls that came with Jacob into Egypt,
which came out of his loins, besides Jacob's sons'
wives, all the souls *were* threescore and six;
[27]And the sons of Joseph, which were born him
in Egypt, *were* two souls: all the souls of the house
of Jacob, which came into Egypt, *were* threescore
and ten.

[28]And he sent Judah before him unto Joseph, to direct his face unto Goshen; and they came into the
land of Goshen.
[29]And Joseph made ready his chariot, and went up
to meet Israel his father, to Goshen, and presented
himself unto him; and he fell on his neck, and wept
on his neck a good while.
[30]And Israel said unto Joseph, Now let me die,
since I have seen thy face, because thou *art* yet alive.
[31]And Joseph said unto his brethren, and unto his
father's house, I will go up, and shew Pharaoh, and
say unto him, My brethren, and my father's house,
which *were* in the land of Canaan, are come unto me;
[32]And the men *are* shepherds, for their trade hath
been to feed cattle; and they have brought their
flocks, and their herds, and all that they have.
[33]And it shall come to pass, when Pharaoh shall
call you, and shall say, What *is* your occupation?
[34]That ye shall say, Thy servants' trade hath been
about cattle from our youth even until now, both we,
and also our fathers: that ye may dwell in the land of
Goshen; for every shepherd *is* an abomination unto
the Egyptians.

47 [1]Then Joseph came and told Pharaoh, and
said, My father and my brethren, and their
flocks, and their herds, and all that they have, are
come out of the land of Canaan; and, behold, they *are*
in the land of Goshen.
[2]And he took some of his brethren, *even* five men,
and presented them unto Pharaoh.
[3]And Pharaoh said unto his brethren, What *is* your
occupation? And they said unto Pharaoh, Thy servants *are* shepherds, both we, *and* also our fathers.
[4]They said moreover unto Pharaoh, For to sojourn
in the land are we come; for thy servants have no pasture for their flocks; for the famine *is* sore in the land

NEW LIVING TRANSLATION

[21]Benjamin's sons were Bela, Beker, Ashbel, Gera,
Naaman, Ehi, Rosh, Muppim, Huppim, and Ard.
[22]These were the sons of Rachel and Jacob. The
number of Jacob's descendants through Rachel was
fourteen.

[23]The son of Dan was Hushim.
[24]The sons of Naphtali were Jahzeel, Guni, Jezer, and
Shillem.
[25]These were the sons of Bilhah, the servant given to
Rachel by her father, Laban. The number of Jacob's
descendants through Bilhah was seven.

[26]The total number of Jacob's direct descendants
who went with him to Egypt, not counting his sons'
wives, was sixty-six. [27]In addition, Joseph had two
sons* who were born in Egypt. So altogether, there
were seventy* members of Jacob's family in the land
of Egypt.

Jacob's Family Arrives in Goshen

[28]As they neared their destination, Jacob sent Judah
ahead to meet Joseph and get directions to the region of Goshen. And when they finally arrived there,
[29]Joseph prepared his chariot and traveled to Goshen to meet his father, Jacob. When Joseph arrived,
he embraced his father and wept, holding him for a
long time. [30]Finally, Jacob said to Joseph, "Now I am
ready to die, since I have seen your face again and
know you are still alive."
[31]And Joseph said to his brothers and to his father's entire family, "I will go to Pharaoh and tell him,
'My brothers and my father's entire family have come
to me from the land of Canaan. [32]These men are
shepherds, and they raise livestock. They have
brought with them their flocks and herds and everything they own.'"
[33]Then he said, "When Pharaoh calls for you and
asks you about your occupation, [34]you must tell him,
'We, your servants, have raised livestock all our lives,
as our ancestors have always done.' When you tell
him this, he will let you live here in the region of
Goshen, for the Egyptians despise shepherds."

Jacob Blesses Pharaoh

47 Then Joseph went to see Pharaoh and told
him, "My father and my brothers have arrived from the land of Canaan. They have come with
all their flocks and herds and possessions, and they
are now in the region of Goshen."
[2]Joseph took five of his brothers with him and
presented them to Pharaoh. [3]And Pharaoh asked the
brothers, "What is your occupation?"

They replied, "We, your servants, are shepherds,
just like our ancestors. [4]We have come to live here
in Egypt for a while, for there is no pasture for our

46:27a Greek version reads *nine sons,* probably including Joseph's grandsons through Ephraim and Manasseh (see 1 Chr 7:14-20). **46:27b** Greek version reads *seventy-five;* see note on Exod 1:5.

KING JAMES VERSION

of Canaan: now therefore, we pray thee, let thy servants dwell in the land of Goshen.
5 And Pharaoh spake unto Joseph, saying, Thy father and thy brethren are come unto thee:
6 The land of Egypt *is* before thee; in the best of the
land make thy father and brethren to dwell; in the
land of Goshen let them dwell: and if thou knowest
any men of activity among them, then make them
rulers over my cattle.
7 And Joseph brought in Jacob his father, and set
him before Pharaoh: and Jacob blessed Pharaoh.
8 And Pharaoh said unto Jacob, How old *art* thou?
9 And Jacob said unto Pharaoh, The days of the
years of my pilgrimage *are* an hundred and thirty
years: few and evil have the days of the years of my
life been, and have not attained unto the days of the
years of the life of my fathers in the days of their
pilgrimage.
10 And Jacob blessed Pharaoh, and went out from
before Pharaoh.
11 And Joseph placed his father and his brethren,
and gave them a possession in the land of Egypt, in
the best of the land, in the land of Rameses, as Pharaoh had commanded.
12 And Joseph nourished his father, and his brethren, and all his father's household, with bread, according to *their* families.
13 And *there was* no bread in all the land; for the
famine *was* very sore, so that the land of Egypt and *all*
the land of Canaan fainted by reason of the famine.
14 And Joseph gathered up all the money that was
found in the land of Egypt, and in the land of Canaan,
for the corn which they bought: and Joseph brought
the money into Pharaoh's house.
15 And when money failed in the land of Egypt, and
in the land of Canaan, all the Egyptians came unto
Joseph, and said, Give us bread: for why should we
die in thy presence? for the money faileth.
16 And Joseph said, Give your cattle; and I will give
you for your cattle, if money fail.
17 And they brought their cattle unto Joseph: and
Joseph gave them bread *in exchange* for horses, and
for the flocks, and for the cattle of the herds, and for
the asses: and he fed them with bread for all their
cattle for that year.
18 When that year was ended, they came unto him
the second year, and said unto him, We will not hide
it from my lord, how that our money is spent; my lord
also hath our herds of cattle; there is not aught left in
the sight of my lord, but our bodies, and our lands:
19 Wherefore shall we die before thine eyes, both
we and our land? buy us and our land for bread, and
we and our land will be servants unto Pharaoh: and
give *us* seed, that we may live, and not die, that the
land be not desolate.
20 And Joseph bought all the land of Egypt for
Pharaoh; for the Egyptians sold every man his field,

NEW LIVING TRANSLATION

flocks in Canaan. The famine is very severe there. So
please, we request permission to live in the region of
Goshen."
5 Then Pharaoh said to Joseph, "Now that your father and brothers have joined you here, 6 choose any
place in the entire land of Egypt for them to live. Give
them the best land of Egypt. Let them live in the region of Goshen. And if any of them have special
skills, put them in charge of my livestock, too."
7 Then Joseph brought in his father, Jacob, and
presented him to Pharaoh. And Jacob blessed
Pharaoh.
8 "How old are you?" Pharaoh asked him.
9 Jacob replied, "I have traveled this earth for
130 hard years. But my life has been short compared
to the lives of my ancestors." 10 Then Jacob blessed
Pharaoh again before leaving his court.
11 So Joseph assigned the best land of Egypt—the
region of Rameses—to his father and his brothers,
and he settled them there, just as Pharaoh had commanded. 12 And Joseph provided food for his father
and his brothers in amounts appropriate to the
number of their dependents, including the smallest
children.

Joseph's Leadership in the Famine

13 Meanwhile, the famine became so severe that all
the food was used up, and people were starving
throughout the lands of Egypt and Canaan. 14 By selling grain to the people, Joseph eventually collected
all the money in Egypt and Canaan, and he put the
money in Pharaoh's treasury. 15 When the people of
Egypt and Canaan ran out of money, all the Egyptians
came to Joseph. "Our money is gone!" they cried.
"But please give us food, or we will die before your
very eyes!"
16 Joseph replied, "Since your money is gone, bring
me your livestock. I will give you food in exchange
for your livestock." 17 So they brought their livestock
to Joseph in exchange for food. In exchange for their
horses, flocks of sheep and goats, herds of cattle, and
donkeys, Joseph provided them with food for another year.
18 But that year ended, and the next year they came
again and said, "We cannot hide the truth from you,
my lord. Our money is gone, and all our livestock
and cattle are yours. We have nothing left to give but
our bodies and our land. 19 Why should we die before your very eyes? Buy us and our land in exchange
for food; we offer our land and ourselves as slaves
for Pharaoh. Just give us grain so we may live and
not die, and so the land does not become empty and
desolate."
20 So Joseph bought all the land of Egypt for Pharaoh. All the Egyptians sold him their fields because
the famine was so severe, and soon all the land

KING JAMES VERSION

because the famine prevailed over them: so the land
became Pharaoh's.
21 And as for the people, he removed them to cities
from *one* end of the borders of Egypt even to the
other end thereof.
22 Only the land of the priests bought he not; for
the priests had a portion *assigned them* of Pharaoh,
and did eat their portion which Pharaoh gave them:
wherefore they sold not their lands.
23 Then Joseph said unto the people, Behold, I have
bought you this day and your land for Pharaoh: lo,
here is seed for you, and ye shall sow the land.
24 And it shall come to pass in the increase, that ye
shall give the fifth *part* unto Pharaoh, and four parts
shall be your own, for seed of the field, and for your
food, and for them of your households, and for food
for your little ones.
25 And they said, Thou hast saved our lives: let us
find grace in the sight of my lord, and we will be Pharaoh's servants.
26 And Joseph made it a law over the land of Egypt
unto this day, *that* Pharaoh should have the fifth
part; except the land of the priests only, *which* became not Pharaoh's.
27 And Israel dwelt in the land of Egypt, in the country of Goshen; and they had possessions therein, and
grew, and multiplied exceedingly.
28 And Jacob lived in the land of Egypt seventeen
years: so the whole age of Jacob was an hundred forty
and seven years.
29 And the time drew nigh that Israel must die: and
he called his son Joseph, and said unto him, If now I
have found grace in thy sight, put, I pray thee, thy
hand under my thigh, and deal kindly and truly with
me; bury me not, I pray thee, in Egypt:
30 But I will lie with my fathers, and thou shalt
carry me out of Egypt, and bury me in their
buryingplace. And he said, I will do as thou hast said.
31 And he said, Swear unto me. And he sware unto
him. And Israel bowed himself upon the bed's head.

48 1 And it came to pass after these things, that
one told Joseph, Behold, thy father *is* sick:
and he took with him his two sons, Manasseh and
Ephraim.
2 And *one* told Jacob, and said, Behold, thy son Joseph cometh unto thee: and Israel strengthened
himself, and sat upon the bed.
3 And Jacob said unto Joseph, God Almighty appeared unto me at Luz in the land of Canaan, and
blessed me,
4 And said unto me, Behold, I will make thee fruitful, and multiply thee, and I will make of thee a
multitude of people; and will give this land to thy
seed after thee *for* an everlasting possession.

NEW LIVING TRANSLATION

belonged to Pharaoh. 21 As for the people, he made
them all slaves,* from one end of Egypt to the other.
22 The only land he did not buy was the land belonging to the priests. They received an allotment of food
directly from Pharaoh, so they didn't need to sell
their land.
23 Then Joseph said to the people, "Look, today I
have bought you and your land for Pharaoh. I will
provide you with seed so you can plant the fields.
24 Then when you harvest it, one-fifth of your crop
will belong to Pharaoh. You may keep the remaining
four-fifths as seed for your fields and as food for you,
your households, and your little ones."
25 "You have saved our lives!" they exclaimed.
"May it please you, my lord, to let us be Pharaoh's servants." 26 Joseph then issued a decree still in effect in
the land of Egypt, that Pharaoh should receive one-
fifth of all the crops grown on his land. Only the land
belonging to the priests was not given to Pharaoh.
27 Meanwhile, the people of Israel settled in the region of Goshen in Egypt. There they acquired property, and they were fruitful, and their population
grew rapidly. 28 Jacob lived for seventeen years after
his arrival in Egypt, so he lived 147 years in all.
29 As the time of his death drew near, Jacob* called
for his son Joseph and said to him, "Please do me this
favor. Put your hand under my thigh and swear that
you will treat me with unfailing love by honoring this
last request: Do not bury me in Egypt. 30 When I die,
please take my body out of Egypt and bury me with
my ancestors."
So Joseph promised, "I will do as you ask."
31 "Swear that you will do it," Jacob insisted. So
Joseph gave his oath, and Jacob bowed humbly at the
head of his bed.*

Jacob Blesses Manasseh and Ephraim

48 One day not long after this, word came to
Joseph, "Your father is failing rapidly." So
Joseph went to visit his father, and he took with him
his two sons, Manasseh and Ephraim.
2 When Joseph arrived, Jacob was told, "Your son
Joseph has come to see you." So Jacob* gathered his
strength and sat up in his bed.
3 Jacob said to Joseph, "God Almighty* appeared to
me at Luz in the land of Canaan and blessed me. 4 He
said to me, 'I will make you fruitful, and I will multiply your descendants. I will make you a multitude of
nations. And I will give this land of Canaan to your
descendants* after you as an everlasting possession.'

47:21 As in Greek version and Samaritan Pentateuch; Hebrew reads *he moved them all into the towns.* **47:29** Hebrew *Israel;* also in 47:31b. See note on 35:21. **47:31** Greek version reads *and Israel bowed in worship as he leaned on his staff.* Compare Heb 11:21. **48:2** Hebrew *Israel;* also in 48:8, 10, 11, 13, 14, 21. See note on 35:21. **48:3** Hebrew *El-Shaddai.* **48:4** Hebrew *seed;* also in 48:19.

KING JAMES VERSION

5And now thy two sons, Ephraim and Manasseh, which were born unto thee in the land of Egypt before I came unto thee into Egypt, *are* mine; as Reuben and Simeon, they shall be mine.

6And thy issue, which thou begettest after them, shall be thine, *and* shall be called after the name of their brethren in their inheritance.

7And as for me, when I came from Padan, Rachel died by me in the land of Canaan in the way, when yet *there was* but a little way to come unto Ephrath: and I buried her there in the way of Ephrath; the same *is* Bethlehem.

8And Israel beheld Joseph's sons, and said, Who *are* these?

9And Joseph said unto his father, They *are* my sons, whom God hath given me in this *place*. And he said, Bring them, I pray thee, unto me, and I will bless them.

10Now the eyes of Israel were dim for age, *so that* he could not see. And he brought them near unto him; and he kissed them, and embraced them.

11And Israel said unto Joseph, I had not thought to see thy face: and, lo, God hath shewed me also thy seed.

12And Joseph brought them out from between his knees, and he bowed himself with his face to the earth.

13And Joseph took them both, Ephraim in his right hand toward Israel's left hand, and Manasseh in his left hand toward Israel's right hand, and brought *them* near unto him.

14And Israel stretched out his right hand, and laid *it* upon Ephraim's head, who *was* the younger, and his left hand upon Manasseh's head, guiding his hands wittingly; for Manasseh *was* the firstborn.

15And he blessed Joseph, and said, God, before whom my fathers Abraham and Isaac did walk, the God which fed me all my life long unto this day,

16The Angel which redeemed me from all evil, bless the lads; and let my name be named on them, and the name of my fathers Abraham and Isaac; and let them grow into a multitude in the midst of the earth.

17And when Joseph saw that his father laid his right hand upon the head of Ephraim, it displeased him: and he held up his father's hand, to remove it from Ephraim's head unto Manasseh's head.

18And Joseph said unto his father, Not so, my father: for this *is* the firstborn; put thy right hand upon his head.

19And his father refused, and said, I know *it*, my son, I know *it*: he also shall become a people, and he also shall be great: but truly his younger brother shall be greater than he, and his seed shall become a multitude of nations.

NEW LIVING TRANSLATION

5"Now I am claiming as my own sons these two boys of yours, Ephraim and Manasseh, who were born here in the land of Egypt before I arrived. They will be my sons, just as Reuben and Simeon are.
6But any children born to you in the future will be your own, and they will inherit land within the territories of their brothers Ephraim and Manasseh.

7"Long ago, as I was returning from Paddan-aram, Rachel died in the land of Canaan. We were still on the way, some distance from Ephrath (that is, Bethlehem). So with great sorrow I buried her there beside the road to Ephrath."

8Then Jacob looked over at the two boys. "Are these your sons?" he asked.

9"Yes," Joseph told him, "these are the sons God has given me here in Egypt."

And Jacob said, "Bring them closer to me, so I can bless them."

10Jacob was half blind because of his age and could hardly see. So Joseph brought the boys close to him, and Jacob kissed and embraced them.
11Then Jacob said to Joseph, "I never thought I would see your face again, but now God has let me see your children, too!"

12Joseph moved the boys, who were at their grandfather's knees, and he bowed with his face to the ground.
13Then he positioned the boys in front of Jacob. With his right hand he directed Ephraim toward Jacob's left hand, and with his left hand he put Manasseh at Jacob's right hand.
14But Jacob crossed his arms as he reached out to lay his hands on the boys' heads. He put his right hand on the head of Ephraim, though he was the younger boy, and his left hand on the head of Manasseh, though he was the firstborn.
15Then he blessed Joseph and said,

"May the God before whom my grandfather Abraham
and my father, Isaac, walked—
the God who has been my shepherd
all my life, to this very day,
16 the Angel who has redeemed me from all harm—
may he bless these boys.
May they preserve my name
and the names of Abraham and Isaac.
And may their descendants multiply greatly
throughout the earth."

17But Joseph was upset when he saw that his father placed his right hand on Ephraim's head. So Joseph lifted it to move it from Ephraim's head to Manasseh's head.
18"No, my father," he said. "This one is the firstborn. Put your right hand on his head."

19But his father refused. "I know, my son; I know," he replied. "Manasseh will also become a great people, but his younger brother will become even greater. And his descendants will become a multitude of nations."

KING JAMES VERSION

20 And he blessed them that day, saying, In thee
shall Israel bless, saying, God make thee as Ephraim
and as Manasseh: and he set Ephraim before
Manasseh.
21 And Israel said unto Joseph, Behold, I die: but
God shall be with you, and bring you again unto the
land of your fathers.
22 Moreover I have given to thee one portion above
thy brethren, which I took out of the hand of the
Amorite with my sword and with my bow.

49

1 And Jacob called unto his sons, and said,
Gather yourselves together, that I may tell
you *that* which shall befall you in the last days.
2 Gather yourselves together, and hear, ye sons of
Jacob; and hearken unto Israel your father.
3 Reuben, thou *art* my firstborn, my might, and the
beginning of my strength, the excellency of dignity,
and the excellency of power:
4 Unstable as water, thou shalt not excel; because
thou wentest up to thy father's bed; then defiledst
thou *it:* he went up to my couch.
5 Simeon and Levi *are* brethren; instruments of
cruelty *are in* their habitations.
6 O my soul, come not thou into their secret; unto
their assembly, mine honour, be not thou united: for
in their anger they slew a man, and in their selfwill
they digged down a wall.
7 Cursed *be* their anger, for *it was* fierce; and their
wrath, for it was cruel: I will divide them in Jacob, and
scatter them in Israel.
8 Judah, thou *art he* whom thy brethren shall
praise: thy hand *shall be* in the neck of thine enemies; thy father's children shall bow down before
thee.
9 Judah *is* a lion's whelp: from the prey, my son,
thou art gone up: he stooped down, he couched as a
lion, and as an old lion; who shall rouse him up?
10 The sceptre shall not depart from Judah, nor a
lawgiver from between his feet, until Shiloh come;
and unto him *shall* the gathering of the people *be*.
11 Binding his foal unto the vine, and his ass's colt
unto the choice vine; he washed his garments in
wine, and his clothes in the blood of grapes:
12 His eyes *shall be* red with wine, and his teeth
white with milk.

NEW LIVING TRANSLATION

20 So Jacob blessed the boys that day with this
blessing: "The people of Israel will use your names
when they give a blessing. They will say, 'May God
make you as prosperous as Ephraim and Manasseh.'"
In this way, Jacob put Ephraim ahead of Manasseh.
21 Then Jacob said to Joseph, "Look, I am about to
die, but God will be with you and will take you back
to Canaan, the land of your ancestors. 22 And beyond
what I have given your brothers, I am giving you an
extra portion of the land* that I took from the
Amorites with my sword and bow."

Jacob's Last Words to His Sons

49

Then Jacob called together all his sons and
said, "Gather around me, and I will tell you
what will happen to each of you in the days to come.

2 "Come and listen, you sons of Jacob;
listen to Israel, your father.

3 "Reuben, you are my firstborn, my strength,
the child of my vigorous youth.
You are first in rank and first in power.
4 But you are as unruly as a flood,
and you will be first no longer.
For you went to bed with my wife;
you defiled my marriage couch.

5 "Simeon and Levi are two of a kind;
their weapons are instruments of violence.
6 May I never join in their meetings;
may I never be a party to their plans.
For in their anger they murdered men,
and they crippled oxen just for sport.
7 A curse on their anger, for it is fierce;
a curse on their wrath, for it is cruel.
I will scatter them among the descendants
of Jacob;
I will disperse them throughout Israel.

8 "Judah, your brothers will praise you.
You will grasp your enemies by the neck.
All your relatives will bow before you.
9 Judah, my son, is a young lion
that has finished eating its prey.
Like a lion he crouches and lies down;
like a lioness—who dares to rouse him?
10 The scepter will not depart from Judah,
nor the ruler's staff from his descendants,*
until the coming of the one to whom it belongs,*
the one whom all nations will honor.
11 He ties his foal to a grapevine,
the colt of his donkey to a choice vine.
He washes his clothes in wine,
his robes in the blood of grapes.
12 His eyes are darker than wine,
and his teeth are whiter than milk.

48:22 Or *an extra ridge of land.* The meaning of the Hebrew is uncertain.
49:10a Hebrew *from between his feet.* **49:10b** Or *until tribute is brought to him and the peoples obey;* traditionally rendered *until Shiloh comes.*

KING JAMES VERSION

13Zebulun shall dwell at the haven of the sea; and
he *shall be* for an haven of ships; and his border *shall*
be unto Zidon.
14Issachar *is* a strong ass couching down between
two burdens:
15And he saw that rest *was* good, and the land that
it was pleasant; and bowed his shoulder to bear, and
became a servant unto tribute.
16Dan shall judge his people, as one of the tribes
of Israel.
17Dan shall be a serpent by the way, an adder in the
path, that biteth the horse heels, so that his rider
shall fall backward.
18I have waited for thy salvation, O LORD.
19Gad, a troop shall overcome him: but he shall
overcome at the last.
20Out of Asher his bread *shall be* fat, and he shall
yield royal dainties.
21Naphtali *is* a hind let loose: he giveth goodly
words.
22Joseph *is* a fruitful bough, *even* a fruitful bough
by a well; *whose* branches run over the wall:
23The archers have sorely grieved him, and shot *at*
him, and hated him:
24But his bow abode in strength, and the arms of
his hands were made strong by the hands of the
mighty *God* of Jacob; (from thence *is* the shepherd,
the stone of Israel:)
25*Even* by the God of thy father, who shall help
thee; and by the Almighty, who shall bless thee with
blessings of heaven above, blessings of the deep that
lieth under, blessings of the breasts, and of the
womb:
26The blessings of thy father have prevailed above
the blessings of my progenitors unto the utmost
bound of the everlasting hills: they shall be on the
head of Joseph, and on the crown of the head of him
that was separate from his brethren.
27Benjamin shall ravin *as* a wolf: in the morning
he shall devour the prey, and at night he shall divide
the spoil.
28All these *are* the twelve tribes of Israel: and this
is it that their father spake unto them, and blessed
them; every one according to his blessing he blessed
them.
29And he charged them, and said unto them, I am
to be gathered unto my people: bury me with my
fathers in the cave that *is* in the field of Ephron
the Hittite,

NEW LIVING TRANSLATION

13 "Zebulun will settle by the seashore
and will be a harbor for ships;
his borders will extend to Sidon.

14 "Issachar is a sturdy donkey,
resting between two saddlepacks.*
15 When he sees how good the countryside is
and how pleasant the land,
he will bend his shoulder to the load
and submit himself to hard labor.

16 "Dan will govern his people,
like any other tribe in Israel.
17 Dan will be a snake beside the road,
a poisonous viper along the path
that bites the horse's hooves
so its rider is thrown off.
18 I trust in you for salvation, O LORD!

19 "Gad will be attacked by marauding bands,
but he will attack them when they retreat.

20 "Asher will dine on rich foods
and produce food fit for kings.

21 "Naphtali is a doe set free
that bears beautiful fawns.

22 "Joseph is the foal of a wild donkey,
the foal of a wild donkey at a spring—
one of the wild donkeys on the ridge.*
23 Archers attacked him savagely;
they shot at him and harassed him.
24 But his bow remained taut,
and his arms were strengthened
by the hands of the Mighty One of Jacob,
by the Shepherd, the Rock of Israel.
25 May the God of your father help you;
may the Almighty bless you
with the blessings of the heavens above,
and blessings of the watery depths below,
and blessings of the breasts and womb.
26 May the blessings of your father
surpass the blessings of the ancient
mountains,*
reaching to the heights of the eternal hills.
May these blessings rest on the head of Joseph,
who is a prince among his brothers.

27 "Benjamin is a ravenous wolf,
devouring his enemies in the morning
and dividing his plunder in the evening."

28These are the twelve tribes of Israel, and this is
what their father said as he told his sons good-bye.
He blessed each one with an appropriate message.

Jacob's Death and Burial

29Then Jacob instructed them, "Soon I will die and
join my ancestors. Bury me with my father and

49:14 Or *sheepfolds,* or *hearths.* 49:22 Or *Joseph is a fruitful tree, / a fruitful tree beside a spring. / His branches reach over the wall.* The meaning of the Hebrew is uncertain. 49:26 Or *of my ancestors.*

KING JAMES VERSION

30In the cave that *is* in the field of Machpelah,
which *is* before Mamre, in the land of Canaan, which
Abraham bought with the field of Ephron the Hittite
for a possession of a buryingplace.
31There they buried Abraham and Sarah his wife;
there they buried Isaac and Rebekah his wife; and
there I buried Leah.
32The purchase of the field and of the cave that *is*
therein *was* from the children of Heth.
33And when Jacob had made an end of commanding his sons, he gathered up his feet into the bed,
and yielded up the ghost, and was gathered unto his
people.

50 1And Joseph fell upon his father's face, and
wept upon him, and kissed him.
2And Joseph commanded his servants the physicians to embalm his father: and the physicians embalmed Israel.
3And forty days were fulfilled for him; for so are
fulfilled the days of those which are embalmed: and
the Egyptians mourned for him threescore and ten
days.
4And when the days of his mourning were past,
Joseph spake unto the house of Pharaoh, saying, If
now I have found grace in your eyes, speak, I pray
you, in the ears of Pharaoh, saying,
5My father made me swear, saying, Lo, I die: in my
grave which I have digged for me in the land of Canaan, there shalt thou bury me. Now therefore let
me go up, I pray thee, and bury my father, and I will
come again.
6And Pharaoh said, Go up, and bury thy father,
according as he made thee swear.
7And Joseph went up to bury his father: and with
him went up all the servants of Pharaoh, the elders of
his house, and all the elders of the land of Egypt,
8And all the house of Joseph, and his brethren, and
his father's house: only their little ones, and their
flocks, and their herds, they left in the land of Goshen.
9And there went up with him both chariots and
horsemen: and it was a very great company.
10And they came to the threshingfloor of Atad,
which *is* beyond Jordan, and there they mourned
with a great and very sore lamentation: and he made
a mourning for his father seven days.
11And when the inhabitants of the land, the
Canaanites, saw the mourning in the floor of Atad,
they said, This *is* a grievous mourning to the Egyptians: wherefore the name of it was called Abel-
mizraim, which *is* beyond Jordan.
12And his sons did unto him according as he commanded them:
13For his sons carried him into the land of Canaan,
and buried him in the cave of the field of Machpelah,
which Abraham bought with the field for a possession of a buryingplace of Ephron the Hittite, before
Mamre.

NEW LIVING TRANSLATION

grandfather in the cave in the field of Ephron the
Hittite. 30This is the cave in the field of Machpelah,
near Mamre in Canaan, that Abraham bought
from Ephron the Hittite as a permanent burial site.
31There Abraham and his wife Sarah are buried.
There Isaac and his wife, Rebekah, are buried. And
there I buried Leah. 32It is the plot of land and the
cave that my grandfather Abraham bought from the
Hittites."
33When Jacob had finished this charge to his sons,
he drew his feet into the bed, breathed his last, and
joined his ancestors in death.

50 Joseph threw himself on his father and wept
over him and kissed him. 2Then Joseph told
the physicians who served him to embalm his father's body; so Jacob* was embalmed. 3The embalm-
ing process took the usual forty days. And the
Egyptians mourned his death for seventy days.
4When the period of mourning was over, Joseph
approached Pharaoh's advisers and said, "Please do
me this favor and speak to Pharaoh on my behalf.
5Tell him that my father made me swear an oath. He
said to me, 'Listen, I am about to die. Take my body
back to the land of Canaan, and bury me in the tomb
I prepared for myself.' So please allow me to go and
bury my father. After his burial, I will return without
delay."
6Pharaoh agreed to Joseph's request. "Go and bury
your father, as he made you promise," he said. 7So
Joseph went up to bury his father. He was accompanied by all of Pharaoh's officials, all the senior members of Pharaoh's household, and all the senior
officers of Egypt. 8Joseph also took his entire household and his brothers and their households. But they
left their little children and flocks and herds in the
land of Goshen. 9A great number of chariots and
charioteers accompanied Joseph.
10When they arrived at the threshing floor of
Atad, near the Jordan River, they held a very great and
solemn memorial service, with a seven-day period of
mourning for Joseph's father. 11The local residents,
the Canaanites, watched them mourning at the
threshing floor of Atad. Then they renamed that
place (which is near the Jordan) Abel-mizraim,* for
they said, "This is a place of deep mourning for these
Egyptians."
12So Jacob's sons did as he had commanded them.
13They carried his body to the land of Canaan and
buried him in the cave in the field of Machpelah,
near Mamre. This is the cave that Abraham had
bought as a permanent burial site from Ephron the
Hittite.

50:2 Hebrew *Israel.* See note on 35:21. **50:11** *Abel-mizraim* means "mourning of the Egyptians."

KING JAMES VERSION

14 And Joseph returned into Egypt, he, and his
brethren, and all that went up with him to bury his
father, after he had buried his father.
15 And when Joseph's brethren saw that their father was dead, they said, Joseph will peradventure
hate us, and will certainly requite us all the evil
which we did unto him.
16 And they sent a messenger unto Joseph, saying,
Thy father did command before he died, saying,
17 So shall ye say unto Joseph, Forgive, I pray thee
now, the trespass of thy brethren, and their sin; for
they did unto thee evil: and now, we pray thee, forgive
the trespass of the servants of the God of thy father.
And Joseph wept when they spake unto him.
18 And his brethren also went and fell down before
his face; and they said, Behold, we *be* thy servants.
19 And Joseph said unto them, Fear not: for *am* I in
the place of God?
20 But as for you, ye thought evil against me; *but*
God meant it unto good, to bring to pass, as *it is* this
day, to save much people alive.
21 Now therefore fear ye not: I will nourish you, and
your little ones. And he comforted them, and spake
kindly unto them.
22 And Joseph dwelt in Egypt, he, and his father's
house: and Joseph lived an hundred and ten years.
23 And Joseph saw Ephraim's children of the third
generation: the children also of Machir the son of
Manasseh were brought up upon Joseph's knees.
24 And Joseph said unto his brethren, I die: and
God will surely visit you, and bring you out of this
land unto the land which he sware to Abraham, to
Isaac, and to Jacob.
25 And Joseph took an oath of the children of
Israel, saying, God will surely visit you, and ye shall
carry up my bones from hence.
26 So Joseph died, *being* an hundred and ten years
old: and they embalmed him, and he was put in a
coffin in Egypt.

NEW LIVING TRANSLATION

Joseph Reassures His Brothers

14 After burying Jacob, Joseph returned to Egypt with
his brothers and all who had accompanied him to his
father's burial. 15 But now that their father was dead,
Joseph's brothers became fearful. "Now Joseph will
show his anger and pay us back for all the wrong we
did to him," they said.
16 So they sent this message to Joseph: "Before
your father died, he instructed us 17 to say to you:
'Please forgive your brothers for the great wrong they
did to you—for their sin in treating you so cruelly.' So
we, the servants of the God of your father, beg you to
forgive our sin." When Joseph received the message,
he broke down and wept. 18 Then his brothers came
and threw themselves down before Joseph. "Look,
we are your slaves!" they said.
19 But Joseph replied, "Don't be afraid of me. Am I
God, that I can punish you? 20 You intended to harm
me, but God intended it all for good. He brought me
to this position so I could save the lives of many
people. 21 No, don't be afraid. I will continue to take
care of you and your children." So he reassured them
by speaking kindly to them.

The Death of Joseph

22 So Joseph and his brothers and their families continued to live in Egypt. Joseph lived to the age of 110.
23 He lived to see three generations of descendants of
his son Ephraim, and he lived to see the birth of the
children of Manasseh's son Makir, whom he claimed
as his own.*
24 "Soon I will die," Joseph told his brothers, "but
God will surely come to help you and lead you out of
this land of Egypt. He will bring you back to the land
he solemnly promised to give to Abraham, to Isaac,
and to Jacob."
25 Then Joseph made the sons of Israel swear an
oath, and he said, "When God comes to help you and
lead you back, you must take my bones with you."
26 So Joseph died at the age of 110. The Egyptians
embalmed him, and his body was placed in a coffin
in Egypt.

50:23 Hebrew *who were born on Joseph's knees.*

Exodus

KING JAMES VERSION

1 1Now these *are* the names of the children of Israel, which came into Egypt; every man and his household came with Jacob.

2Reuben, Simeon, Levi, and Judah,

3Issachar, Zebulun, and Benjamin,

4Dan, and Naphtali, Gad, and Asher.

5And all the souls that came out of the loins of Jacob were seventy souls: for Joseph was in Egypt *already*.

6And Joseph died, and all his brethren, and all that generation.

7And the children of Israel were fruitful, and increased abundantly, and multiplied, and waxed exceeding mighty; and the land was filled with them.

8Now there arose up a new king over Egypt, which knew not Joseph.

9And he said unto his people, Behold, the people of the children of Israel *are* more and mightier than we:

10Come on, let us deal wisely with them; lest they multiply, and it come to pass, that, when there falleth out any war, they join also unto our enemies, and fight against us, and *so* get them up out of the land.

11Therefore they did set over them taskmasters to afflict them with their burdens. And they built for Pharaoh treasure cities, Pithom and Raamses.

12But the more they afflicted them, the more they multiplied and grew. And they were grieved because of the children of Israel.

13And the Egyptians made the children of Israel to serve with rigour:

14And they made their lives bitter with hard bondage, in mortar, and in brick, and in all manner of service in the field: all their service, wherein they made them serve, *was* with rigour.

15And the king of Egypt spake to the Hebrew midwives, of which the name of the one *was* Shiphrah, and the name of the other Puah:

16And he said, When ye do the office of a midwife to the Hebrew women, and see *them* upon the stools; if it *be* a son, then ye shall kill him: but if it *be* a daughter, then she shall live.

17But the midwives feared God, and did not as the king of Egypt commanded them, but saved the men children alive.

NEW LIVING TRANSLATION

The Israelites in Egypt

1 These are the names of the sons of Israel (that is, Jacob) who moved to Egypt with their father, each with his family: 2Reuben, Simeon, Levi, Judah, 3Issachar, Zebulun, Benjamin, 4Dan, Naphtali, Gad, and Asher. 5In all, Jacob had seventy* descendants in Egypt, including Joseph, who was already there.

6In time, Joseph and all of his brothers died, ending that entire generation. 7But their descendants, the Israelites, had many children and grandchildren. In fact, they multiplied so greatly that they became extremely powerful and filled the land.

8Eventually, a new king came to power in Egypt who knew nothing about Joseph or what he had done. 9He said to his people, "Look, the people of Israel now outnumber us and are stronger than we are. 10We must make a plan to keep them from growing even more. If we don't, and if war breaks out, they will join our enemies and fight against us. Then they will escape from the country.*"

11So the Egyptians made the Israelites their slaves. They appointed brutal slave drivers over them, hoping to wear them down with crushing labor. They forced them to build the cities of Pithom and Rameses as supply centers for the king. 12But the more the Egyptians oppressed them, the more the Israelites multiplied and spread, and the more alarmed the Egyptians became. 13So the Egyptians worked the people of Israel without mercy. 14They made their lives bitter, forcing them to mix mortar and make bricks and do all the work in the fields. They were ruthless in all their demands.

15Then Pharaoh, the king of Egypt, gave this order to the Hebrew midwives, Shiphrah and Puah: 16"When you help the Hebrew women as they give birth, watch as they deliver.* If the baby is a boy, kill him; if it is a girl, let her live." 17But because the midwives feared God, they refused to obey the king's orders. They allowed the boys to live, too.

1:5 Dead Sea Scrolls and Greek version read *seventy-five;* see notes on Gen 46:27. 1:10 Or *will take the country.* 1:16 Hebrew *look upon the two stones;* perhaps the reference is to a birthstool.

KING JAMES VERSION

18And the king of Egypt called for the midwives,
and said unto them, Why have ye done this thing,
and have saved the men children alive?
19And the midwives said unto Pharaoh, Because
the Hebrew women *are* not as the Egyptian women;
for they *are* lively, and are delivered ere the midwives
come in unto them.
20Therefore God dealt well with the midwives: and
the people multiplied, and waxed very mighty.
21And it came to pass, because the midwives
feared God, that he made them houses.
22And Pharaoh charged all his people, saying,
Every son that is born ye shall cast into the river,
and every daughter ye shall save alive.

2 1And there went a man of the house of Levi, and
took *to wife* a daughter of Levi.
2And the woman conceived, and bare a son: and
when she saw him that he *was a* goodly *child,* she hid
him three months.
3And when she could not longer hide him, she
took for him an ark of bulrushes, and daubed it with
slime and with pitch, and put the child therein; and
she laid *it* in the flags by the river's brink.
4And his sister stood afar off, to wit what would be
done to him.
5And the daughter of Pharaoh came down to wash
herself at the river; and her maidens walked along by
the river's side; and when she saw the ark among the
flags, she sent her maid to fetch it.
6And when she had opened *it,* she saw the child:
and, behold, the babe wept. And she had compassion on him, and said, This *is one* of the Hebrews'
children.
7Then said his sister to Pharaoh's daughter, Shall I
go and call to thee a nurse of the Hebrew women,
that she may nurse the child for thee?
8And Pharaoh's daughter said to her, Go. And the
maid went and called the child's mother.
9And Pharaoh's daughter said unto her, Take this
child away, and nurse it for me, and I will give *thee*
thy wages. And the woman took the child, and
nursed it.
10And the child grew, and she brought him unto
Pharaoh's daughter, and he became her son. And she
called his name Moses: and she said, Because I drew
him out of the water.

11And it came to pass in those days, when Moses
was grown, that he went out unto his brethren, and
looked on their burdens: and he spied an Egyptian
smiting an Hebrew, one of his brethren.
12And he looked this way and that way, and when
he saw that *there was* no man, he slew the Egyptian,
and hid him in the sand.

NEW LIVING TRANSLATION

18So the king of Egypt called for the midwives.
"Why have you done this?" he demanded. "Why
have you allowed the boys to live?"
19"The Hebrew women are not like the Egyptian
women," the midwives replied. "They are more vigorous and have their babies so quickly that we cannot get there in time."
20So God was good to the midwives, and the Israelites continued to multiply, growing more and more
powerful. 21And because the midwives feared God,
he gave them families of their own.
22Then Pharaoh gave this order to all his people:
"Throw every newborn Hebrew boy into the Nile
River. But you may let the girls live."

The Birth of Moses

2 About this time, a man and woman from the
tribe of Levi got married. 2The woman became
pregnant and gave birth to a son. She saw that he
was a special baby and kept him hidden for three
months. 3But when she could no longer hide him,
she got a basket made of papyrus reeds and water-
proofed it with tar and pitch. She put the baby in the
basket and laid it among the reeds along the bank of
the Nile River. 4The baby's sister then stood at a distance, watching to see what would happen to him.
5Soon Pharaoh's daughter came down to bathe in
the river, and her attendants walked along the riverbank. When the princess saw the basket among the
reeds, she sent her maid to get it for her. 6When the
princess opened it, she saw the baby. The little boy
was crying, and she felt sorry for him. "This must be
one of the Hebrew children," she said.
7Then the baby's sister approached the princess.
"Should I go and find one of the Hebrew women to
nurse the baby for you?" she asked.
8"Yes, do!" the princess replied. So the girl went
and called the baby's mother.
9"Take this baby and nurse him for me," the princess told the baby's mother. "I will pay you for your
help." So the woman took her baby home and
nursed him.
10Later, when the boy was older, his mother
brought him back to Pharaoh's daughter, who
adopted him as her own son. The princess named
him Moses,* for she explained, "I lifted him out of
the water."

Moses Escapes to Midian

11Many years later, when Moses had grown up, he
went out to visit his own people, the Hebrews, and he
saw how hard they were forced to work. During his
visit, he saw an Egyptian beating one of his fellow
Hebrews. 12After looking in all directions to make
sure no one was watching, Moses killed the Egyptian
and hid the body in the sand.

2:10 *Moses* sounds like a Hebrew term that means "to lift out."

KING JAMES VERSION

13 And when he went out the second day, behold, two men of the Hebrews strove together: and he said to him that did the wrong, Wherefore smitest thou thy fellow?

14 And he said, Who made thee a prince and a judge over us? intendest thou to kill me, as thou killedst the Egyptian? And Moses feared, and said, Surely this thing is known.

15 Now when Pharaoh heard this thing, he sought to slay Moses. But Moses fled from the face of Pharaoh, and dwelt in the land of Midian: and he sat down by a well.

16 Now the priest of Midian had seven daughters: and they came and drew *water*, and filled the troughs to water their father's flock.

17 And the shepherds came and drove them away: but Moses stood up and helped them, and watered their flock.

18 And when they came to Reuel their father, he said, How *is it that* ye are come so soon today?

19 And they said, An Egyptian delivered us out of the hand of the shepherds, and also drew *water* enough for us, and watered the flock.

20 And he said unto his daughters, And where *is* he? why *is* it *that* ye have left the man? call him, that he may eat bread.

21 And Moses was content to dwell with the man: and he gave Moses Zipporah his daughter.

22 And she bare *him* a son, and he called his name Gershom: for he said, I have been a stranger in a strange land.

23 And it came to pass in process of time, that the king of Egypt died: and the children of Israel sighed by reason of the bondage, and they cried, and their cry came up unto God by reason of the bondage.

24 And God heard their groaning, and God remembered his covenant with Abraham, with Isaac, and with Jacob.

25 And God looked upon the children of Israel, and God had respect unto *them*.

3 1 Now Moses kept the flock of Jethro his father in law, the priest of Midian: and he led the flock to the backside of the desert, and came to the mountain of God, *even* to Horeb.

2 And the angel of the LORD appeared unto him in a flame of fire out of the midst of a bush: and he looked, and, behold, the bush burned with fire, and the bush *was* not consumed.

3 And Moses said, I will now turn aside, and see this great sight, why the bush is not burnt.

4 And when the LORD saw that he turned aside to see, God called unto him out of the midst of the bush, and said, Moses, Moses. And he said, Here *am* I.

5 And he said, Draw not nigh hither: put off thy shoes from off thy feet, for the place whereon thou standest *is* holy ground.

NEW LIVING TRANSLATION

13 The next day, when Moses went out to visit his people again, he saw two Hebrew men fighting. "Why are you beating up your friend?" Moses said to the one who had started the fight.

14 The man replied, "Who appointed you to be our prince and judge? Are you going to kill me as you killed that Egyptian yesterday?"

Then Moses was afraid, thinking, "Everyone knows what I did." 15 And sure enough, Pharaoh heard what had happened, and he tried to kill Moses. But Moses fled from Pharaoh and went to live in the land of Midian.

When Moses arrived in Midian, he sat down beside a well. 16 Now the priest of Midian had seven daughters who came as usual to draw water and fill the water troughs for their father's flocks. 17 But some other shepherds came and chased them away. So Moses jumped up and rescued the girls from the shepherds. Then he drew water for their flocks.

18 When the girls returned to Reuel, their father, he asked, "Why are you back so soon today?"

19 "An Egyptian rescued us from the shepherds," they answered. "And then he drew water for us and watered our flocks."

20 "Then where is he?" their father asked. "Why did you leave him there? Invite him to come and eat with us."

21 Moses accepted the invitation, and he settled there with him. In time, Reuel gave Moses his daughter Zipporah to be his wife. 22 Later she gave birth to a son, and Moses named him Gershom,* for he explained, "I have been a foreigner in a foreign land."

23 Years passed, and the king of Egypt died. But the Israelites continued to groan under their burden of slavery. They cried out for help, and their cry rose up to God. 24 God heard their groaning, and he remembered his covenant promise to Abraham, Isaac, and Jacob. 25 He looked down on the people of Israel and knew it was time to act.*

Moses and the Burning Bush

3 One day Moses was tending the flock of his father-in-law, Jethro,* the priest of Midian. He led the flock far into the wilderness and came to Sinai,* the mountain of God. 2 There the angel of the LORD appeared to him in a blazing fire from the middle of a bush. Moses stared in amazement. Though the bush was engulfed in flames, it didn't burn up. 3 "This is amazing," Moses said to himself. "Why isn't that bush burning up? I must go see it."

4 When the LORD saw Moses coming to take a closer look, God called to him from the middle of the bush, "Moses! Moses!"

"Here I am!" Moses replied.

5 "Do not come any closer," the LORD warned.

2:22 *Gershom* sounds like a Hebrew term that means "a foreigner there." **2:25** Or *and acknowledged his obligation to help them.* **3:1a** Moses' father-in-law went by two names, Jethro and Reuel. **3:1b** Hebrew *Horeb,* another name for Sinai.

KING JAMES VERSION

6 Moreover he said, I *am* the God of thy father, the
God of Abraham, the God of Isaac, and the God of
Jacob. And Moses hid his face; for he was afraid to
look upon God.
7 And the LORD said, I have surely seen the affliction of my people which *are* in Egypt, and have heard
their cry by reason of their taskmasters; for I know
their sorrows;
8 And I am come down to deliver them out of the
hand of the Egyptians, and to bring them up out of
that land unto a good land and a large, unto a land
flowing with milk and honey; unto the place of the
Canaanites, and the Hittites, and the Amorites, and
the Perizzites, and the Hivites, and the Jebusites.
9 Now therefore, behold, the cry of the children of
Israel is come unto me: and I have also seen the oppression wherewith the Egyptians oppress them.
10 Come now therefore, and I will send thee unto
Pharaoh, that thou mayest bring forth my people the
children of Israel out of Egypt.
11 And Moses said unto God, Who *am* I, that I
should go unto Pharaoh, and that I should bring
forth the children of Israel out of Egypt?
12 And he said, Certainly I will be with thee; and
this *shall be* a token unto thee, that I have sent thee:
When thou hast brought forth the people out of
Egypt, ye shall serve God upon this mountain.
13 And Moses said unto God, Behold, *when* I come
unto the children of Israel, and shall say unto them,
The God of your fathers hath sent me unto you; and
they shall say to me, What *is* his name? what shall
I say unto them?
14 And God said unto Moses, I AM THAT I AM: and
he said, Thus shalt thou say unto the children of Israel, I AM hath sent me unto you.
15 And God said moreover unto Moses, Thus shalt
thou say unto the children of Israel, The LORD God of
your fathers, the God of Abraham, the God of Isaac,
and the God of Jacob, hath sent me unto you: this *is*
my name for ever, and this *is* my memorial unto all
generations.
16 Go, and gather the elders of Israel together, and
say unto them, The LORD God of your fathers, the
God of Abraham, of Isaac, and of Jacob, appeared
unto me, saying, I have surely visited you, and *seen*
that which is done to you in Egypt:
17 And I have said, I will bring you up out of the affliction of Egypt unto the land of the Canaanites, and
the Hittites, and the Amorites, and the Perizzites,
and the Hivites, and the Jebusites, unto a land flowing with milk and honey.
18 And they shall hearken to thy voice: and thou
shalt come, thou and the elders of Israel, unto the king
of Egypt, and ye shall say unto him, The LORD God of
the Hebrews hath met with us: and now let us go,
we beseech thee, three days' journey into the wilderness, that we may sacrifice to the LORD our God.

NEW LIVING TRANSLATION

"Take off your sandals, for you are standing on holy
ground. 6 I am the God of your father*—the God of
Abraham, the God of Isaac, and the God of Jacob."
When Moses heard this, he covered his face because
he was afraid to look at God.
7 Then the LORD told him, "I have certainly seen
the oppression of my people in Egypt. I have heard
their cries of distress because of their harsh slave
drivers. Yes, I am aware of their suffering. 8 So I have
come down to rescue them from the power of the
Egyptians and lead them out of Egypt into their own
fertile and spacious land. It is a land flowing with
milk and honey—the land where the Canaanites, Hittites, Amorites, Perizzites, Hivites, and Jebusites now
live. 9 Look! The cry of the people of Israel has
reached me, and I have seen how harshly the Egyptians abuse them. 10 Now go, for I am sending you to
Pharaoh. You must lead my people Israel out of
Egypt."
11 But Moses protested to God, "Who am I to appear before Pharaoh? Who am I to lead the people of
Israel out of Egypt?"
12 God answered, "I will be with you. And this is
your sign that I am the one who has sent you: When
you have brought the people out of Egypt, you will
worship God at this very mountain."
13 But Moses protested, "If I go to the people of Israel and tell them, 'The God of your ancestors has
sent me to you,' they will ask me, 'What is his name?'
Then what should I tell them?"
14 God replied to Moses, "I AM WHO I AM.* Say this
to the people of Israel: I AM has sent me to you."
15 God also said to Moses, "Say this to the people of
Israel: Yahweh,* the God of your ancestors—the God
of Abraham, the God of Isaac, and the God of Jacob—
has sent me to you.

This is my eternal name,
my name to remember for all generations.

16 "Now go and call together all the elders of Israel.
Tell them, 'The LORD, the God of your ancestors—the
God of Abraham, Isaac, and Jacob—has appeared to
me. He told me, "I have been watching closely, and
I see how the Egyptians are treating you. 17 I have
promised to rescue you from your oppression in
Egypt. I will lead you to a land flowing with milk and
honey—the land where the Canaanites, Hittites, Amorites, Perizzites, Hivites, and Jebusites now live."'
18 "The elders of Israel will accept your message.
Then you and the elders must go to the king of Egypt
and tell him, 'The LORD, the God of the Hebrews, has
met with us. So please let us take a three-day journey
into the wilderness to offer sacrifices to the LORD,
our God.'

3:6 Greek version reads *your fathers*. 3:14 Or *I WILL BE WHAT I WILL BE*.
3:15 *Yahweh* is a transliteration of the proper name *YHWH* that is sometimes rendered "Jehovah"; in this translation it is usually rendered "the LORD" (note the use of small capitals).

19 And I am sure that the king of Egypt will not let you go, no, not by a mighty hand.

20 And I will stretch out my hand, and smite Egypt with all my wonders which I will do in the midst thereof: and after that he will let you go.

21 And I will give this people favour in the sight of the Egyptians: and it shall come to pass, that, when ye go, ye shall not go empty:

22 But every woman shall borrow of her neighbour, and of her that sojourneth in her house, jewels of silver, and jewels of gold, and raiment: and ye shall put *them* upon your sons, and upon your daughters; and ye shall spoil the Egyptians.

4 1 And Moses answered and said, But, behold, they will not believe me, nor hearken unto my voice: for they will say, The LORD hath not appeared unto thee.

2 And the LORD said unto him, What *is* that in thine hand? And he said, A rod.

3 And he said, Cast it on the ground. And he cast it on the ground, and it became a serpent; and Moses fled from before it.

4 And the LORD said unto Moses, Put forth thine hand, and take it by the tail. And he put forth his hand, and caught it, and it became a rod in his hand:

5 That they may believe that the LORD God of their fathers, the God of Abraham, the God of Isaac, and the God of Jacob, hath appeared unto thee.

6 And the LORD said furthermore unto him, Put now thine hand into thy bosom. And he put his hand into his bosom: and when he took it out, behold, his hand *was* leprous as snow.

7 And he said, Put thine hand into thy bosom again. And he put his hand into his bosom again; and plucked it out of his bosom, and, behold, it was turned again as his *other* flesh.

8 And it shall come to pass, if they will not believe thee, neither hearken to the voice of the first sign, that they will believe the voice of the latter sign.

9 And it shall come to pass, if they will not believe also these two signs, neither hearken unto thy voice, that thou shalt take of the water of the river, and pour *it* upon the dry *land:* and the water which thou takest out of the river shall become blood upon the dry *land.*

10 And Moses said unto the LORD, O my Lord, I *am* not eloquent, neither heretofore, nor since thou hast spoken unto thy servant: but I *am* slow of speech, and of a slow tongue.

11 And the LORD said unto him, Who hath made man's mouth? or who maketh the dumb, or deaf, or the seeing, or the blind? have not I the LORD?

12 Now therefore go, and I will be with thy mouth, and teach thee what thou shalt say.

19 "But I know that the king of Egypt will not let you go unless a mighty hand forces him.* 20 So I will raise my hand and strike the Egyptians, performing all kinds of miracles among them. Then at last he will let you go. 21 And I will cause the Egyptians to look favorably on you. They will give you gifts when you go so you will not leave empty-handed. 22 Every Israelite woman will ask for articles of silver and gold and fine clothing from her Egyptian neighbors and from the foreign women in their houses. You will dress your sons and daughters with these, stripping the Egyptians of their wealth."

Signs of the LORD's Power

4 But Moses protested again, "What if they won't believe me or listen to me? What if they say, 'The LORD never appeared to you'?"

2 Then the LORD asked him, "What is that in your hand?"

"A shepherd's staff," Moses replied.

3 "Throw it down on the ground," the LORD told him. So Moses threw down the staff, and it turned into a snake! Moses jumped back.

4 Then the LORD told him, "Reach out and grab its tail." So Moses reached out and grabbed it, and it turned back into a shepherd's staff in his hand.

5 "Perform this sign," the LORD told him. "Then they will believe that the LORD, the God of their ancestors—the God of Abraham, the God of Isaac, and the God of Jacob—really has appeared to you."

6 Then the LORD said to Moses, "Now put your hand inside your cloak." So Moses put his hand inside his cloak, and when he took it out again, his hand was white as snow with a severe skin disease.* 7 "Now put your hand back into your cloak," the LORD said. So Moses put his hand back in, and when he took it out again, it was as healthy as the rest of his body.

8 The LORD said to Moses, "If they do not believe you and are not convinced by the first miraculous sign, they will be convinced by the second sign. 9 And if they don't believe you or listen to you even after these two signs, then take some water from the Nile River and pour it out on the dry ground. When you do, the water from the Nile will turn to blood on the ground."

10 But Moses pleaded with the LORD, "O Lord, I'm not very good with words. I never have been, and I'm not now, even though you have spoken to me. I get tongue-tied, and my words get tangled."

11 Then the LORD asked Moses, "Who makes a person's mouth? Who decides whether people speak or do not speak, hear or do not hear, see or do not see? Is it not I, the LORD? 12 Now go! I will be with you as you speak, and I will instruct you in what to say."

3:19 As in Greek and Latin versions; Hebrew reads *will not let you go, not by a mighty hand.* **4:6** Or *with leprosy.* The Hebrew word used here can describe various skin diseases.

KING JAMES VERSION

13 And he said, O my LORD, send, I pray thee, by the hand *of him whom* thou wilt send.

14 And the anger of the LORD was kindled against Moses, and he said, *Is* not Aaron the Levite thy brother? I know that he can speak well. And also, behold, he cometh forth to meet thee: and when he seeth thee, he will be glad in his heart.

15 And thou shalt speak unto him, and put words in his mouth: and I will be with thy mouth, and with his mouth, and will teach you what ye shall do.

16 And he shall be thy spokesman unto the people: and he shall be, *even* he shall be to thee instead of a mouth, and thou shalt be to him instead of God.

17 And thou shalt take this rod in thine hand, wherewith thou shalt do signs.

18 And Moses went and returned to Jethro his father in law, and said unto him, Let me go, I pray thee, and return unto my brethren which *are* in Egypt, and see whether they be yet alive. And Jethro said to Moses, Go in peace.

19 And the LORD said unto Moses in Midian, Go, return into Egypt: for all the men are dead which sought thy life.

20 And Moses took his wife and his sons, and set them upon an ass, and he returned to the land of Egypt: and Moses took the rod of God in his hand.

21 And the LORD said unto Moses, When thou goest to return into Egypt, see that thou do all those wonders before Pharaoh, which I have put in thine hand: but I will harden his heart, that he shall not let the people go.

22 And thou shalt say unto Pharaoh, Thus saith the LORD, Israel *is* my son, *even* my firstborn:

23 And I say unto thee, Let my son go, that he may serve me: and if thou refuse to let him go, behold, I will slay thy son, *even* thy firstborn.

24 And it came to pass by the way in the inn, that the LORD met him, and sought to kill him.

25 Then Zipporah took a sharp stone, and cut off the foreskin of her son, and cast *it* at his feet, and said, Surely a bloody husband *art* thou to me.

26 So he let him go: then she said, A bloody husband *thou art,* because of the circumcision.

27 And the LORD said to Aaron, Go into the wilderness to meet Moses. And he went, and met him in the mount of God, and kissed him.

28 And Moses told Aaron all the words of the LORD who had sent him, and all the signs which he had commanded him.

29 And Moses and Aaron went and gathered together all the elders of the children of Israel:

30 And Aaron spake all the words which the LORD had spoken unto Moses, and did the signs in the sight of the people.

31 And the people believed: and when they heard that the LORD had visited the children of Israel, and

NEW LIVING TRANSLATION

13 But Moses again pleaded, "Lord, please! Send anyone else."

14 Then the LORD became angry with Moses. "All right," he said. "What about your brother, Aaron the Levite? I know he speaks well. And look! He is on his way to meet you now. He will be delighted to see you. 15 Talk to him, and put the words in his mouth. I will be with both of you as you speak, and I will instruct you both in what to do. 16 Aaron will be your spokesman to the people. He will be your mouthpiece, and you will stand in the place of God for him, telling him what to say. 17 And take your shepherd's staff with you, and use it to perform the miraculous signs I have shown you."

Moses Returns to Egypt

18 So Moses went back home to Jethro, his father-in-law. "Please let me return to my relatives in Egypt," Moses said. "I don't even know if they are still alive."

"Go in peace," Jethro replied.

19 Before Moses left Midian, the LORD said to him, "Return to Egypt, for all those who wanted to kill you have died."

20 So Moses took his wife and sons, put them on a donkey, and headed back to the land of Egypt. In his hand he carried the staff of God.

21 And the LORD told Moses, "When you arrive back in Egypt, go to Pharaoh and perform all the miracles I have empowered you to do. But I will harden his heart so he will refuse to let the people go. 22 Then you will tell him, 'This is what the LORD says: Israel is my firstborn son. 23 I commanded you, "Let my son go, so he can worship me." But since you have refused, I will now kill your firstborn son!'"

24 On the way to Egypt, at a place where Moses and his family had stopped for the night, the LORD confronted him and was about to kill him. 25 But Moses' wife, Zipporah, took a flint knife and circumcised her son. She touched his feet* with the foreskin and said, "Now you are a bridegroom of blood to me." 26 (When she said "a bridegroom of blood," she was referring to the circumcision.) After that, the LORD left him alone.

27 Now the LORD had said to Aaron, "Go out into the wilderness to meet Moses." So Aaron went and met Moses at the mountain of God, and he embraced him. 28 Moses then told Aaron everything the LORD had commanded him to say. And he told him about the miraculous signs the LORD had commanded him to perform.

29 Then Moses and Aaron returned to Egypt and called all the elders of Israel together. 30 Aaron told them everything the LORD had told Moses, and Moses performed the miraculous signs as they watched. 31 Then the people of Israel were convinced that the LORD had sent Moses and Aaron. When they heard

4:25 The Hebrew word for "feet" may refer here to the male sex organ.

KING JAMES VERSION

that he had looked upon their affliction, then they bowed their heads and worshipped.

5 1And afterward Moses and Aaron went in, and told Pharaoh, Thus saith the LORD God of Israel, Let my people go, that they may hold a feast unto me in the wilderness.

2And Pharaoh said, Who *is* the LORD, that I should obey his voice to let Israel go? I know not the LORD, neither will I let Israel go.

3And they said, The God of the Hebrews hath met with us: let us go, we pray thee, three days' journey into the desert, and sacrifice unto the LORD our God; lest he fall upon us with pestilence, or with the sword.

4And the king of Egypt said unto them, Wherefore do ye, Moses and Aaron, let the people from their works? get you unto your burdens.

5And Pharaoh said, Behold, the people of the land now *are* many, and ye make them rest from their burdens.

6And Pharaoh commanded the same day the taskmasters of the people, and their officers, saying,

7Ye shall no more give the people straw to make brick, as heretofore: let them go and gather straw for themselves.

8And the tale of the bricks, which they did make heretofore, ye shall lay upon them; ye shall not diminish *aught* thereof: for they *be* idle; therefore they cry, saying, Let us go *and* sacrifice to our God.

9Let there more work be laid upon the men, that they may labour therein; and let them not regard vain words.

10And the taskmasters of the people went out, and their officers, and they spake to the people, saying, Thus saith Pharaoh, I will not give you straw.

11Go ye, get you straw where ye can find it: yet not aught of your work shall be diminished.

12So the people were scattered abroad throughout all the land of Egypt to gather stubble instead of straw.

13And the taskmasters hasted *them*, saying, Fulfil your works, *your* daily tasks, as when there was straw.

14And the officers of the children of Israel, which Pharaoh's taskmasters had set over them, were beaten, *and* demanded, Wherefore have ye not fulfilled your task in making brick both yesterday and today, as heretofore?

15Then the officers of the children of Israel came and cried unto Pharaoh, saying, Wherefore dealest thou thus with thy servants?

16There is no straw given unto thy servants, and they say to us, Make brick: and, behold, thy servants *are* beaten; but the fault *is* in thine own people.

NEW LIVING TRANSLATION

that the LORD was concerned about them and had seen their misery, they bowed down and worshiped.

Moses and Aaron Speak to Pharaoh

5 After this presentation to Israel's leaders, Moses and Aaron went and spoke to Pharaoh. They told him, "This is what the LORD, the God of Israel, says: Let my people go so they may hold a festival in my honor in the wilderness."

2"Is that so?" retorted Pharaoh. "And who is the LORD? Why should I listen to him and let Israel go? I don't know the LORD, and I will not let Israel go."

3But Aaron and Moses persisted. "The God of the Hebrews has met with us," they declared. "So let us take a three-day journey into the wilderness so we can offer sacrifices to the LORD our God. If we don't, he will kill us with a plague or with the sword."

4Pharaoh replied, "Moses and Aaron, why are you distracting the people from their tasks? Get back to work! 5Look, there are many of your people in the land, and you are stopping them from their work."

Making Bricks without Straw

6That same day Pharaoh sent this order to the Egyptian slave drivers and the Israelite foremen: 7"Do not supply any more straw for making bricks. Make the people get it themselves! 8But still require them to make the same number of bricks as before. Don't reduce the quota. They are lazy. That's why they are crying out, 'Let us go and offer sacrifices to our God.' 9Load them down with more work. Make them sweat! That will teach them to listen to lies!"

10So the slave drivers and foremen went out and told the people: "This is what Pharaoh says: I will not provide any more straw for you. 11Go and get it yourselves. Find it wherever you can. But you must produce just as many bricks as before!" 12So the people scattered throughout the land of Egypt in search of stubble to use as straw.

13Meanwhile, the Egyptian slave drivers continued to push hard. "Meet your daily quota of bricks, just as you did when we provided you with straw!" they demanded. 14Then they whipped the Israelite foremen they had put in charge of the work crews. "Why haven't you met your quotas either yesterday or today?" they demanded.

15So the Israelite foremen went to Pharaoh and pleaded with him. "Please don't treat your servants like this," they begged. 16"We are given no straw, but the slave drivers still demand, 'Make bricks!' We are being beaten, but it isn't our fault! Your own people are to blame!"

KING JAMES VERSION

[17]But he said, Ye *are* idle, *ye are* idle: therefore ye
say, Let us go *and* do sacrifice to the LORD.
[18]Go therefore now, *and* work; for there shall no
straw be given you, yet shall ye deliver the tale of
bricks.
[19]And the officers of the children of Israel did see
that they *were* in evil *case*, after it was said, Ye shall
not minish *aught* from your bricks of your daily task.
[20]And they met Moses and Aaron, who stood in
the way, as they came forth from Pharaoh:
[21]And they said unto them, The LORD look upon
you, and judge; because ye have made our savour to
be abhorred in the eyes of Pharaoh, and in the eyes of
his servants, to put a sword in their hand to slay us.
[22]And Moses returned unto the LORD, and said,
LORD, wherefore hast thou *so* evil entreated this
people? why *is* it *that* thou hast sent me?
[23]For since I came to Pharaoh to speak in thy
name, he hath done evil to this people; neither hast
thou delivered thy people at all.

6 [1]Then the LORD said unto Moses, Now shalt
thou see what I will do to Pharaoh: for with a
strong hand shall he let them go, and with a strong
hand shall he drive them out of his land.
[2]And God spake unto Moses, and said unto him,
I *am* the LORD:
[3]And I appeared unto Abraham, unto Isaac, and
unto Jacob, by *the name of* God Almighty, but by my
name JEHOVAH was I not known to them.
[4]And I have also established my covenant with
them, to give them the land of Canaan, the land of
their pilgrimage, wherein they were strangers.
[5]And I have also heard the groaning of the children of Israel, whom the Egyptians keep in bondage;
and I have remembered my covenant.
[6]Wherefore say unto the children of Israel, I *am*
the LORD, and I will bring you out from under the
burdens of the Egyptians, and I will rid you out of
their bondage, and I will redeem you with a stretched
out arm, and with great judgments:
[7]And I will take you to me for a people, and I will
be to you a God: and ye shall know that I *am* the LORD
your God, which bringeth you out from under the
burdens of the Egyptians.
[8]And I will bring you in unto the land, concerning
the which I did swear to give it to Abraham, to Isaac,
and to Jacob; and I will give it you for an heritage:
I *am* the LORD.
[9]And Moses spake so unto the children of Israel:
but they hearkened not unto Moses for anguish of
spirit, and for cruel bondage.
[10]And the LORD spake unto Moses, saying,
[11]Go in, speak unto Pharaoh king of Egypt, that he
let the children of Israel go out of his land.
[12]And Moses spake before the LORD, saying,

NEW LIVING TRANSLATION

[17]But Pharaoh shouted, "You're just lazy! Lazy!
That's why you're saying, 'Let us go and offer sacrifices to the LORD.' [18]Now get back to work! No straw
will be given to you, but you must still produce the
full quota of bricks."
[19]The Israelite foremen could see that they were
in serious trouble when they were told, "You must
not reduce the number of bricks you make each day."
[20]As they left Pharaoh's court, they confronted
Moses and Aaron, who were waiting outside for
them. [21]The foremen said to them, "May the LORD
judge and punish you for making us stink before
Pharaoh and his officials. You have put a sword into
their hands, an excuse to kill us!"
[22]Then Moses went back to the LORD and protested, "Why have you brought all this trouble on
your own people, Lord? Why did you send me?
[23]Ever since I came to Pharaoh as your spokesman,
he has been even more brutal to your people. And
you have done nothing to rescue them!"

Promises of Deliverance

6 Then the LORD told Moses, "Now you will see
what I will do to Pharaoh. When he feels the
force of my strong hand, he will let the people go. In
fact, he will force them to leave his land!"
[2]And God said to Moses, "I am Yahweh—'the
LORD.'* [3]I appeared to Abraham, to Isaac, and to
Jacob as El-Shaddai—'God Almighty'*—but I did not
reveal my name, Yahweh, to them. [4]And I reaffirmed
my covenant with them. Under its terms, I promised
to give them the land of Canaan, where they were
living as foreigners. [5]You can be sure that I have
heard the groans of the people of Israel, who are
now slaves to the Egyptians. And I am well aware of
my covenant with them.
[6]"Therefore, say to the people of Israel: 'I am the
LORD. I will free you from your oppression and will
rescue you from your slavery in Egypt. I will redeem
you with a powerful arm and great acts of judgment.
[7]I will claim you as my own people, and I will be your
God. Then you will know that I am the LORD your
God who has freed you from your oppression in
Egypt. [8]I will bring you into the land I swore to give to
Abraham, Isaac, and Jacob. I will give it to you as your
very own possession. I am the LORD!'"
[9]So Moses told the people of Israel what the LORD
had said, but they refused to listen anymore. They
had become too discouraged by the brutality of
their slavery.
[10]Then the LORD said to Moses, [11]"Go back to Pharaoh, the king of Egypt, and tell him to let the people
of Israel leave his country."
[12]"But LORD!" Moses objected. "My own people

6:2 *Yahweh* is a transliteration of the proper name *YHWH* that is sometimes rendered "Jehovah"; in this translation it is usually rendered "the LORD" (note the use of small capitals). **6:3** *El-Shaddai,* which means "God Almighty," is the name for God used in Gen 17:1; 28:3; 35:11; 43:14; 48:3.

KING JAMES VERSION

Behold, the children of Israel have not hearkened
unto me; how then shall Pharaoh hear me, who *am* of
uncircumcised lips?
13 And the LORD spake unto Moses and unto Aaron,
and gave them a charge unto the children of Israel,
and unto Pharaoh king of Egypt, to bring the children of Israel out of the land of Egypt.

14 These *be* the heads of their fathers' houses: The
sons of Reuben the firstborn of Israel; Hanoch, and
Pallu, Hezron, and Carmi: these *be* the families of
Reuben.
15 And the sons of Simeon; Jemuel, and Jamin,
and Ohad, and Jachin, and Zohar, and Shaul the son
of a Canaanitish woman: these *are* the families of
Simeon.
16 And these *are* the names of the sons of Levi according to their generations; Gershon, and Kohath,
and Merari: and the years of the life of Levi *were* an
hundred thirty and seven years.
17 The sons of Gershon; Libni, and Shimi, according to their families.
18 And the sons of Kohath; Amram, and Izhar, and
Hebron, and Uzziel: and the years of the life of Kohath *were* an hundred thirty and three years.
19 And the sons of Merari; Mahali and Mushi:
these *are* the families of Levi according to their
generations.
20 And Amram took him Jochebed his father's sister to wife; and she bare him Aaron and Moses: and
the years of the life of Amram *were* an hundred and
thirty and seven years.
21 And the sons of Izhar; Korah, and Nepheg, and
Zichri.
22 And the sons of Uzziel; Mishael, and Elzaphan,
and Zithri.
23 And Aaron took him Elisheba, daughter of Amminadab, sister of Naashon, to wife; and she bare
him Nadab, and Abihu, Eleazar, and Ithamar.
24 And the sons of Korah; Assir, and Elkanah, and
Abiasaph: these *are* the families of the Korhites.
25 And Eleazar Aaron's son took him *one* of the
daughters of Putiel to wife; and she bare him Phinehas: these *are* the heads of the fathers of the Levites
according to their families.
26 These *are* that Aaron and Moses, to whom the
LORD said, Bring out the children of Israel from the
land of Egypt according to their armies.
27 These *are* they which spake to Pharaoh king of
Egypt, to bring out the children of Israel from Egypt:
these *are* that Moses and Aaron.

NEW LIVING TRANSLATION

won't listen to me anymore. How can I expect Pharaoh to listen? I'm such a clumsy speaker!*"
13 But the LORD spoke to Moses and Aaron and
gave them orders for the Israelites and for Pharaoh,
the king of Egypt. The LORD commanded Moses and
Aaron to lead the people of Israel out of Egypt.

The Ancestors of Moses and Aaron

14 These are the ancestors of some of the clans of
Israel:

The sons of Reuben, Israel's oldest son, were
Hanoch, Pallu, Hezron, and Carmi. Their
descendants became the clans of Reuben.
15 The sons of Simeon were Jemuel, Jamin, Ohad,
Jakin, Zohar, and Shaul. (Shaul's mother was a
Canaanite woman.) Their descendants became
the clans of Simeon.
16 These are the descendants of Levi, as listed in
their family records: The sons of Levi were
Gershon, Kohath, and Merari. (Levi lived to be
137 years old.)
17 The descendants of Gershon included Libni
and Shimei, each of whom became the ancestor
of a clan.
18 The descendants of Kohath included Amram,
Izhar, Hebron, and Uzziel. (Kohath lived to be
133 years old.)
19 The descendants of Merari included Mahli
and Mushi.

These are the clans of the Levites, as listed in their
family records.

20 Amram married his father's sister Jochebed, and
she gave birth to his sons, Aaron and Moses.
(Amram lived to be 137 years old.)
21 The sons of Izhar were Korah, Nepheg, and Zicri.
22 The sons of Uzziel were Mishael, Elzaphan, and
Sithri.
23 Aaron married Elisheba, the daughter of
Amminadab and sister of Nahshon, and she
gave birth to his sons, Nadab, Abihu, Eleazar,
and Ithamar.
24 The sons of Korah were Assir, Elkanah, and
Abiasaph. Their descendants became the clans
of Korah.
25 Eleazar son of Aaron married one of the
daughters of Putiel, and she gave birth to his son,
Phinehas.

These are the ancestors of the Levite families, listed
according to their clans.

26 The Aaron and Moses named in this list are the
same ones to whom the LORD said, "Lead the people of
Israel out of the land of Egypt like an army." 27 It was
Moses and Aaron who spoke to Pharaoh, the king of
Egypt, about leading the people of Israel out of Egypt.

6:12 Hebrew *I have uncircumcised lips;* also in 6:30.

KING JAMES VERSION

28And it came to pass on the day *when* the LORD
spake unto Moses in the land of Egypt,
29That the LORD spake unto Moses, saying, I *am*
the LORD: speak thou unto Pharaoh king of Egypt all
that I say unto thee.
30And Moses said before the LORD, Behold, I *am* of
uncircumcised lips, and how shall Pharaoh hearken
unto me?

7 1And the LORD said unto Moses, See, I have
made thee a god to Pharaoh: and Aaron thy
brother shall be thy prophet.
2Thou shalt speak all that I command thee: and
Aaron thy brother shall speak unto Pharaoh, that he
send the children of Israel out of his land.
3And I will harden Pharaoh's heart, and multiply
my signs and my wonders in the land of Egypt.
4But Pharaoh shall not hearken unto you, that I
may lay my hand upon Egypt, and bring forth mine
armies, *and* my people the children of Israel, out of
the land of Egypt by great judgments.
5And the Egyptians shall know that I *am* the LORD,
when I stretch forth mine hand upon Egypt, and
bring out the children of Israel from among them.
6And Moses and Aaron did as the LORD commanded them, so did they.
7And Moses *was* fourscore years old, and Aaron
fourscore and three years old, when they spake unto
Pharaoh.
8And the LORD spake unto Moses and unto Aaron,
saying,
9When Pharaoh shall speak unto you, saying,
Shew a miracle for you: then thou shalt say unto
Aaron, Take thy rod, and cast *it* before Pharaoh, *and*
it shall become a serpent.
10And Moses and Aaron went in unto Pharaoh, and
they did so as the LORD had commanded: and Aaron
cast down his rod before Pharaoh, and before his servants, and it became a serpent.
11Then Pharaoh also called the wise men and the
sorcerers: now the magicians of Egypt, they also did
in like manner with their enchantments.
12For they cast down every man his rod, and they
became serpents: but Aaron's rod swallowed up
their rods.
13And he hardened Pharaoh's heart, that he hearkened not unto them; as the LORD had said.
14And the LORD said unto Moses, Pharaoh's heart
is hardened, he refuseth to let the people go.
15Get thee unto Pharaoh in the morning; lo, he
goeth out unto the water; and thou shalt stand by the
river's brink against he come; and the rod which was
turned to a serpent shalt thou take in thine hand.
16And thou shalt say unto him, The LORD God of
the Hebrews hath sent me unto thee, saying, Let my
people go, that they may serve me in the wilderness:
and, behold, hitherto thou wouldest not hear.

NEW LIVING TRANSLATION

28When the LORD spoke to Moses in the land of
Egypt, 29he said to him, "I am the LORD! Tell Pharaoh,
the king of Egypt, everything I am telling you." 30But
Moses argued with the LORD, saying, "I can't do it! I'm
such a clumsy speaker! Why should Pharaoh listen
to me?"

Aaron's Staff Becomes a Serpent

7 Then the LORD said to Moses, "Pay close attention to this. I will make you seem like God to
Pharaoh, and your brother, Aaron, will be your
prophet. 2Tell Aaron everything I command you, and
Aaron must command Pharaoh to let the people of
Israel leave his country. 3But I will make Pharaoh's
heart stubborn so I can multiply my miraculous signs
and wonders in the land of Egypt. 4Even then Pharaoh will refuse to listen to you. So I will bring down
my fist on Egypt. Then I will rescue my forces—my
people, the Israelites—from the land of Egypt with
great acts of judgment. 5When I raise my powerful
hand and bring out the Israelites, the Egyptians will
know that I am the LORD."
6So Moses and Aaron did just as the LORD had
commanded them. 7Moses was eighty years old, and
Aaron was eighty-three when they made their demands to Pharaoh.
8Then the LORD said to Moses and Aaron, 9"Pharaoh will demand, 'Show me a miracle.' When he
does this, say to Aaron, 'Take your staff and throw
it down in front of Pharaoh, and it will become a
serpent.*'"
10So Moses and Aaron went to Pharaoh and did
what the LORD had commanded them. Aaron threw
down his staff before Pharaoh and his officials, and
it became a serpent! 11Then Pharaoh called in his
own wise men and sorcerers, and these Egyptian
magicians did the same thing with their magic.
12They threw down their staffs, which also became
serpents! But then Aaron's staff swallowed up their
staffs. 13Pharaoh's heart, however, remained hard.
He still refused to listen, just as the LORD had
predicted.

A Plague of Blood

14Then the LORD said to Moses, "Pharaoh's heart is
stubborn,* and he still refuses to let the people go.
15So go to Pharaoh in the morning as he goes down
to the river. Stand on the bank of the Nile and meet
him there. Be sure to take along the staff that turned
into a snake. 16Then announce to him, 'The LORD,
the God of the Hebrews, has sent me to tell you, "Let
my people go, so they can worship me in the wilderness." Until now, you have refused to listen to him.

7:9 Hebrew *tannin,* which elsewhere refers to a sea monster. Greek version translates it "dragon." **7:14** Hebrew *heavy.*

KING JAMES VERSION

17 Thus saith the LORD, In this thou shalt know that
I *am* the LORD: behold, I will smite with the rod that *is*
in mine hand upon the waters which *are* in the river,
and they shall be turned to blood.
18 And the fish that *is* in the river shall die, and the
river shall stink; and the Egyptians shall lothe to
drink of the water of the river.
19 And the LORD spake unto Moses, Say unto Aaron,
Take thy rod, and stretch out thine hand upon the
waters of Egypt, upon their streams, upon their
rivers, and upon their ponds, and upon all their pools
of water, that they may become blood; and *that* there
may be blood throughout all the land of Egypt, both
in *vessels of* wood, and in *vessels of* stone.
20 And Moses and Aaron did so, as the LORD commanded; and he lifted up the rod, and smote the waters that *were* in the river, in the sight of Pharaoh,
and in the sight of his servants; and all the waters
that *were* in the river were turned to blood.
21 And the fish that *was* in the river died; and the
river stank, and the Egyptians could not drink of the
water of the river; and there was blood throughout
all the land of Egypt.
22 And the magicians of Egypt did so with their enchantments: and Pharaoh's heart was hardened, neither did he hearken unto them; as the LORD had said.
23 And Pharaoh turned and went into his house,
neither did he set his heart to this also.
24 And all the Egyptians digged round about the
river for water to drink; for they could not drink of
the water of the river.
25 And seven days were fulfilled, after that the
LORD had smitten the river.

8 1 And the LORD spake unto Moses, Go unto Pharaoh, and say unto him, Thus saith the LORD, Let
my people go, that they may serve me.
2 And if thou refuse to let *them* go, behold, I will
smite all thy borders with frogs:
3 And the river shall bring forth frogs abundantly,
which shall go up and come into thine house, and
into thy bedchamber, and upon thy bed, and into the
house of thy servants, and upon thy people, and into
thine ovens, and into thy kneadingtroughs:
4 And the frogs shall come up both on thee, and
upon thy people, and upon all thy servants.
5 And the LORD spake unto Moses, Say unto Aaron,
Stretch forth thine hand with thy rod over the
streams, over the rivers, and over the ponds, and
cause frogs to come up upon the land of Egypt.
6 And Aaron stretched out his hand over the waters
of Egypt; and the frogs came up, and covered the land
of Egypt.
7 And the magicians did so with their enchantments, and brought up frogs upon the land of Egypt.
8 Then Pharaoh called for Moses and Aaron, and
said, Intreat the LORD, that he may take away the

NEW LIVING TRANSLATION

17 So this is what the LORD says: "I will show you that I
am the LORD." Look! I will strike the water of the Nile
with this staff in my hand, and the river will turn to
blood. 18 The fish in it will die, and the river will
stink. The Egyptians will not be able to drink any
water from the Nile.'"
19 Then the LORD said to Moses: "Tell Aaron, 'Take
your staff and raise your hand over the waters of
Egypt—all its rivers, canals, ponds, and all the reservoirs. Turn all the water to blood. Everywhere in
Egypt the water will turn to blood, even the water
stored in wooden bowls and stone pots.'"
20 So Moses and Aaron did just as the LORD commanded them. As Pharaoh and all of his officials
watched, Aaron raised his staff and struck the water
of the Nile. Suddenly, the whole river turned to
blood! 21 The fish in the river died, and the water became so foul that the Egyptians couldn't drink it.
There was blood everywhere throughout the land of
Egypt. 22 But again the magicians of Egypt used their
magic, and they, too, turned water into blood. So
Pharaoh's heart remained hard. He refused to listen
to Moses and Aaron, just as the LORD had predicted.
23 Pharaoh returned to his palace and put the whole
thing out of his mind. 24 Then all the Egyptians dug
along the riverbank to find drinking water, for they
couldn't drink the water from the Nile.
25 Seven days passed from the time the LORD
struck the Nile.

A Plague of Frogs

8 1* Then the LORD said to Moses, "Go back to
Pharaoh and announce to him, 'This is what the
LORD says: Let my people go, so they can worship me.
2 If you refuse to let them go, I will send a plague of
frogs across your entire land. 3 The Nile River will
swarm with frogs. They will come up out of the river
and into your palace, even into your bedroom and
onto your bed! They will enter the houses of your
officials and your people. They will even jump into
your ovens and your kneading bowls. 4 Frogs will
jump on you, your people, and all your officials.'"
5* Then the LORD said to Moses, "Tell Aaron, 'Raise
the staff in your hand over all the rivers, canals, and
ponds of Egypt, and bring up frogs over all the land.'"
6 So Aaron raised his hand over the waters of Egypt,
and frogs came up and covered the whole land! 7 But
the magicians were able to do the same thing with
their magic. They, too, caused frogs to come up on
the land of Egypt.
8 Then Pharaoh summoned Moses and Aaron and
begged, "Plead with the LORD to take the frogs away

8:1 Verses 8:1-4 are numbered 7:26-29 in Hebrew text. **8:5** Verses 8:5-32 are numbered 8:1-28 in Hebrew text.

KING JAMES VERSION

frogs from me, and from my people; and I will let the people go, that they may do sacrifice unto the LORD.

9And Moses said unto Pharaoh, Glory over me: when shall I intreat for thee, and for thy servants, and for thy people, to destroy the frogs from thee and thy houses, *that* they may remain in the river only?

10And he said, Tomorrow. And he said, *Be it* according to thy word: that thou mayest know that *there is* none like unto the LORD our God.

11And the frogs shall depart from thee, and from thy houses, and from thy servants, and from thy people; they shall remain in the river only.

12And Moses and Aaron went out from Pharaoh: and Moses cried unto the LORD because of the frogs which he had brought against Pharaoh.

13And the LORD did according to the word of Moses; and the frogs died out of the houses, out of the villages, and out of the fields.

14And they gathered them together upon heaps: and the land stank.

15But when Pharaoh saw that there was respite, he hardened his heart, and hearkened not unto them; as the LORD had said.

16And the LORD said unto Moses, Say unto Aaron, Stretch out thy rod, and smite the dust of the land, that it may become lice throughout all the land of Egypt.

17And they did so; for Aaron stretched out his hand with his rod, and smote the dust of the earth, and it became lice in man, and in beast; all the dust of the land became lice throughout all the land of Egypt.

18And the magicians did so with their enchantments to bring forth lice, but they could not: so there were lice upon man, and upon beast.

19Then the magicians said unto Pharaoh, This *is* the finger of God: and Pharaoh's heart was hardened, and he hearkened not unto them; as the LORD had said.

20And the LORD said unto Moses, Rise up early in the morning, and stand before Pharaoh; lo, he cometh forth to the water; and say unto him, Thus saith the LORD, Let my people go, that they may serve me.

21Else, if thou wilt not let my people go, behold, I will send swarms *of flies* upon thee, and upon thy servants, and upon thy people, and into thy houses: and the houses of the Egyptians shall be full of swarms *of flies,* and also the ground whereon they *are.*

22And I will sever in that day the land of Goshen, in which my people dwell, that no swarms *of flies* shall be there; to the end thou mayest know that I *am* the LORD in the midst of the earth.

23And I will put a division between my people and thy people: tomorrow shall this sign be.

NEW LIVING TRANSLATION

from me and my people. I will let your people go, so they can offer sacrifices to the LORD."

9"You set the time!" Moses replied. "Tell me when you want me to pray for you, your officials, and your people. Then you and your houses will be rid of the frogs. They will remain only in the Nile River."

10"Do it tomorrow," Pharaoh said.

"All right," Moses replied, "it will be as you have said. Then you will know that there is no one like the
LORD our God. 11The frogs will leave you and your houses, your officials, and your people. They will remain only in the Nile River."

12So Moses and Aaron left Pharaoh's palace, and Moses cried out to the LORD about the frogs he had
inflicted on Pharaoh. 13And the LORD did just what Moses had predicted. The frogs in the houses, the
courtyards, and the fields all died. 14The Egyptians piled them into great heaps, and a terrible stench
filled the land. 15But when Pharaoh saw that relief had come, he became stubborn.* He refused to listen to Moses and Aaron, just as the LORD had predicted.

A Plague of Gnats

16So the LORD said to Moses, "Tell Aaron, 'Raise your staff and strike the ground. The dust will turn into
swarms of gnats throughout the land of Egypt.'" 17So Moses and Aaron did just as the LORD had commanded them. When Aaron raised his hand and struck the ground with his staff, gnats infested the entire land, covering the Egyptians and their animals. All the dust in the land of Egypt turned into
gnats. 18Pharaoh's magicians tried to do the same thing with their secret arts, but this time they failed. And the gnats covered everyone, people and animals alike.

19"This is the finger of God!" the magicians exclaimed to Pharaoh. But Pharaoh's heart remained hard. He wouldn't listen to them, just as the LORD had predicted.

A Plague of Flies

20Then the LORD told Moses, "Get up early in the morning and stand in Pharaoh's way as he goes down to the river. Say to him, 'This is what the LORD says:
Let my people go, so they can worship me. 21If you refuse, then I will send swarms of flies on you, your officials, your people, and all the houses. The Egyptian homes will be filled with flies, and the ground will be
covered with them. 22But this time I will spare the region of Goshen, where my people live. No flies will be found there. Then you will know that I am the LORD and that I am present even in the heart of your land.
23I will make a clear distinction between* my people and your people. This miraculous sign will happen tomorrow.'"

8:15 Hebrew *made his heart heavy;* also in 8:32. **8:23** As in Greek and Latin versions; Hebrew reads *I will set redemption between.*

KING JAMES VERSION

24And the LORD did so; and there came a grievous swarm *of flies* into the house of Pharaoh, and *into* his servants' houses, and into all the land of Egypt: the land was corrupted by reason of the swarm *of flies*.

25And Pharaoh called for Moses and for Aaron, and said, Go ye, sacrifice to your God in the land.

26And Moses said, It is not meet so to do; for we shall sacrifice the abomination of the Egyptians to the LORD our God: lo, shall we sacrifice the abomination of the Egyptians before their eyes, and will they not stone us?

27We will go three days' journey into the wilderness, and sacrifice to the LORD our God, as he shall command us.

28And Pharaoh said, I will let you go, that ye may sacrifice to the LORD your God in the wilderness; only ye shall not go very far away: intreat for me.

29And Moses said, Behold, I go out from thee, and I will intreat the LORD that the swarms *of flies* may depart from Pharaoh, from his servants, and from his people, tomorrow: but let not Pharaoh deal deceitfully any more in not letting the people go to sacrifice to the LORD.

30And Moses went out from Pharaoh, and intreated the LORD.

31And the LORD did according to the word of Moses; and he removed the swarms *of flies* from Pharaoh, from his servants, and from his people; there remained not one.

32And Pharaoh hardened his heart at this time also, neither would he let the people go.

9 1Then the LORD said unto Moses, Go in unto Pharaoh, and tell him, Thus saith the LORD God of the Hebrews, Let my people go, that they may serve me.

2For if thou refuse to let *them* go, and wilt hold them still,

3Behold, the hand of the LORD is upon thy cattle which *is* in the field, upon the horses, upon the asses, upon the camels, upon the oxen, and upon the sheep: *there shall be* a very grievous murrain.

4And the LORD shall sever between the cattle of Israel and the cattle of Egypt: and there shall nothing die of all *that is* the children's of Israel.

5And the LORD appointed a set time, saying, Tomorrow the LORD shall do this thing in the land.

6And the LORD did that thing on the morrow, and all the cattle of Egypt died: but of the cattle of the children of Israel died not one.

7And Pharaoh sent, and, behold, there was not one of the cattle of the Israelites dead. And the heart of Pharaoh was hardened, and he did not let the people go.

8And the LORD said unto Moses and unto Aaron, Take to you handfuls of ashes of the furnace, and let Moses sprinkle it toward the heaven in the sight of Pharaoh.

NEW LIVING TRANSLATION

24And the LORD did just as he had said. A thick swarm of flies filled Pharaoh's palace and the houses of his officials. The whole land of Egypt was thrown into chaos by the flies.

25Pharaoh called for Moses and Aaron. "All right! Go ahead and offer sacrifices to your God," he said. "But do it here in this land."

26But Moses replied, "That wouldn't be right. The Egyptians detest the sacrifices that we offer to the LORD our God. Look, if we offer our sacrifices here where the Egyptians can see us, they will stone us.
27We must take a three-day trip into the wilderness to offer sacrifices to the LORD our God, just as he has commanded us."

28"All right, go ahead," Pharaoh replied. "I will let you go into the wilderness to offer sacrifices to the LORD your God. But don't go too far away. Now hurry and pray for me."

29Moses answered, "As soon as I leave you, I will pray to the LORD, and tomorrow the swarms of flies will disappear from you and your officials and all your people. But I am warning you, Pharaoh, don't lie to us again and refuse to let the people go to sacrifice to the LORD."

30So Moses left Pharaoh's palace and pleaded with
the LORD to remove all the flies. 31And the LORD did
as Moses asked and caused the swarms of flies to disappear from Pharaoh, his officials, and his people.
Not a single fly remained. 32But Pharaoh again be-
came stubborn and refused to let the people go.

A Plague against Livestock

9 "Go back to Pharaoh," the LORD commanded Moses. "Tell him, 'This is what the LORD, the God of the Hebrews, says: Let my people go, so they
can worship me. 2If you continue to hold them and
refuse to let them go, 3the hand of the LORD will
strike all your livestock—your horses, donkeys, camels, cattle, sheep, and goats—with a deadly plague.
4But the LORD will again make a distinction between the livestock of the Israelites and that of the Egyptians. Not a single one of Israel's animals will die!
5The LORD has already set the time for the plague to begin. He has declared that he will strike the land tomorrow.'"

6And the LORD did just as he had said. The next morning all the livestock of the Egyptians died, but
the Israelites didn't lose a single animal. 7Pharaoh
sent his officials to investigate, and they discovered that the Israelites had not lost a single animal! But even so, Pharaoh's heart remained stubborn,* and he still refused to let the people go.

A Plague of Festering Boils

8Then the LORD said to Moses and Aaron, "Take handfuls of soot from a brick kiln, and have Moses

9:7 Hebrew *heavy*.

KING JAMES VERSION

[9]And it shall become small dust in all the land of Egypt, and shall be a boil breaking forth *with* blains upon man, and upon beast, throughout all the land of Egypt.

[10]And they took ashes of the furnace, and stood before Pharaoh; and Moses sprinkled it up toward heaven; and it became a boil breaking forth *with* blains upon man, and upon beast.

[11]And the magicians could not stand before Moses because of the boils; for the boil was upon the magicians, and upon all the Egyptians.

[12]And the LORD hardened the heart of Pharaoh, and he hearkened not unto them; as the LORD had spoken unto Moses.

[13]And the LORD said unto Moses, Rise up early in the morning, and stand before Pharaoh, and say unto him, Thus saith the LORD God of the Hebrews, Let my people go, that they may serve me.

[14]For I will at this time send all my plagues upon thine heart, and upon thy servants, and upon thy people; that thou mayest know that *there is* none like me in all the earth.

[15]For now I will stretch out my hand, that I may smite thee and thy people with pestilence; and thou shalt be cut off from the earth.

[16]And in very deed for this *cause* have I raised thee up, for to shew *in* thee my power; and that my name may be declared throughout all the earth.

[17]As yet exaltest thou thyself against my people, that thou wilt not let them go?

[18]Behold, tomorrow about this time I will cause it to rain a very grievous hail, such as hath not been in Egypt since the foundation thereof even until now.

[19]Send therefore now, *and* gather thy cattle, and all that thou hast in the field; *for upon* every man and beast which shall be found in the field, and shall not be brought home, the hail shall come down upon them, and they shall die.

[20]He that feared the word of the LORD among the servants of Pharaoh made his servants and his cattle flee into the houses:

[21]And he that regarded not the word of the LORD left his servants and his cattle in the field.

[22]And the LORD said unto Moses, Stretch forth thine hand toward heaven, that there may be hail in all the land of Egypt, upon man, and upon beast, and upon every herb of the field, throughout the land of Egypt.

[23]And Moses stretched forth his rod toward heaven: and the LORD sent thunder and hail, and the fire ran along upon the ground; and the LORD rained hail upon the land of Egypt.

[24]So there was hail, and fire mingled with the hail, very grievous, such as there was none like it in all the land of Egypt since it became a nation.

NEW LIVING TRANSLATION

toss it into the air while Pharaoh watches. [9]The ashes will spread like fine dust over the whole land of Egypt, causing festering boils to break out on people and animals throughout the land."

[10]So they took soot from a brick kiln and went and stood before Pharaoh. As Pharaoh watched, Moses threw the soot into the air, and boils broke out on people and animals alike. [11]Even the magicians were unable to stand before Moses, because the boils had broken out on them and all the Egyptians. [12]But the LORD hardened Pharaoh's heart, and just as the LORD had predicted to Moses, Pharaoh refused to listen.

A Plague of Hail

[13]Then the LORD said to Moses, "Get up early in the morning and stand before Pharaoh. Tell him, 'This is what the LORD, the God of the Hebrews, says: Let my people go, so they can worship me. [14]If you don't, I will send more plagues on you* and your officials and your people. Then you will know that there is no one like me in all the earth. [15]By now I could have lifted my hand and struck you and your people with a plague to wipe you off the face of the earth. [16]But I have spared you for a purpose—to show you my power* and to spread my fame throughout the earth. [17]But you still lord it over my people and refuse to let them go. [18]So tomorrow at this time I will send a hailstorm more devastating than any in all the history of Egypt. [19]Quick! Order your livestock and servants to come in from the fields to find shelter. Any person or animal left outside will die when the hail falls.'"

[20]Some of Pharaoh's officials were afraid because of what the LORD had said. They quickly brought their servants and livestock in from the fields. [21]But those who paid no attention to the word of the LORD left theirs out in the open.

[22]Then the LORD said to Moses, "Lift your hand toward the sky so hail may fall on the people, the livestock, and all the plants throughout the land of Egypt."

[23]So Moses lifted his staff toward the sky, and the LORD sent thunder and hail, and lightning flashed toward the earth. The LORD sent a tremendous hailstorm against all the land of Egypt. [24]Never in all the history of Egypt had there been a storm like that, with such devastating hail and continuous lightning.

9:14 Hebrew *on your heart.* **9:16** Greek version reads *to display my power in you;* compare Rom 9:17.

KING JAMES VERSION

25 And the hail smote throughout all the land of Egypt all that *was* in the field, both man and beast; and the hail smote every herb of the field, and brake every tree of the field.

26 Only in the land of Goshen, where the children of Israel *were*, was there no hail.

27 And Pharaoh sent, and called for Moses and Aaron, and said unto them, I have sinned this time: the LORD *is* righteous, and I and my people *are* wicked.

28 Intreat the LORD (for *it is* enough) that there be no *more* mighty thunderings and hail; and I will let you go, and ye shall stay no longer.

29 And Moses said unto him, As soon as I am gone out of the city, I will spread abroad my hands unto the LORD; *and* the thunder shall cease, neither shall there be any more hail; that thou mayest know how that the earth *is* the LORD'S.

30 But as for thee and thy servants, I know that ye will not yet fear the LORD God.

31 And the flax and the barley was smitten: for the barley *was* in the ear, and the flax *was* bolled.

32 But the wheat and the rie were not smitten: for they *were* not grown up.

33 And Moses went out of the city from Pharaoh, and spread abroad his hands unto the LORD: and the thunders and hail ceased, and the rain was not poured upon the earth.

34 And when Pharaoh saw that the rain and the hail and the thunders were ceased, he sinned yet more, and hardened his heart, he and his servants.

35 And the heart of Pharaoh was hardened, neither would he let the children of Israel go; as the LORD had spoken by Moses.

10 1 And the LORD said unto Moses, Go in unto Pharaoh: for I have hardened his heart, and the heart of his servants, that I might shew these my signs before him:

2 And that thou mayest tell in the ears of thy son, and of thy son's son, what things I have wrought in Egypt, and my signs which I have done among them; that ye may know how that I *am* the LORD.

3 And Moses and Aaron came in unto Pharaoh, and said unto him, Thus saith the LORD God of the Hebrews, How long wilt thou refuse to humble thyself before me? let my people go, that they may serve me.

4 Else, if thou refuse to let my people go, behold, tomorrow will I bring the locusts into thy coast:

5 And they shall cover the face of the earth, that one cannot be able to see the earth: and they shall eat the residue of that which is escaped, which remaineth unto you from the hail, and shall eat every tree which groweth for you out of the field:

6 And they shall fill thy houses, and the houses of all thy servants, and the houses of all the Egyptians; which neither thy fathers, nor thy fathers' fathers

NEW LIVING TRANSLATION

25 It left all of Egypt in ruins. The hail struck down everything in the open field—people, animals, and plants alike. Even the trees were destroyed. 26 The only place without hail was the region of Goshen, where the people of Israel lived.

27 Then Pharaoh quickly summoned Moses and Aaron. "This time I have sinned," he confessed. "The LORD is the righteous one, and my people and I are wrong. 28 Please beg the LORD to end this terrifying thunder and hail. We've had enough. I will let you go; you don't need to stay any longer."

29 "All right," Moses replied. "As soon as I leave the city, I will lift my hands and pray to the LORD. Then the thunder and hail will stop, and you will know that the earth belongs to the LORD. 30 But I know that you and your officials still do not fear the LORD God."

31 (All the flax and barley were ruined by the hail, because the barley had formed heads and the flax was budding. 32 But the wheat and the emmer wheat were spared, because they had not yet sprouted from the ground.)

33 So Moses left Pharaoh's court and went out of the city. When he lifted his hands to the LORD, the thunder and hail stopped, and the downpour ceased. 34 But when Pharaoh saw that the rain, hail, and thunder had stopped, he and his officials sinned again, and Pharaoh again became stubborn.* 35 Because his heart was hard, Pharaoh refused to let the people leave, just as the LORD had predicted through Moses.

A Plague of Locusts

10 Then the LORD said to Moses, "Return to Pharaoh and make your demands again. I have made him and his officials stubborn* so I can display my miraculous signs among them. 2 I've also done it so you can tell your children and grandchildren about how I made a mockery of the Egyptians and about the signs I displayed among them—and so you will know that I am the LORD."

3 So Moses and Aaron went to Pharaoh and said, "This is what the LORD, the God of the Hebrews, says: How long will you refuse to submit to me? Let my people go, so they can worship me. 4 If you refuse, watch out! For tomorrow I will bring a swarm of locusts on your country. 5 They will cover the land so that you won't be able to see the ground. They will devour what little is left of your crops after the hailstorm, including all the trees growing in the fields. 6 They will overrun your palaces and the homes of your officials and all the houses in Egypt. Never in the history of Egypt have your ancestors seen a

9:34 Hebrew *made his heart heavy.* **10:1** Hebrew *have made his heart and his officials' hearts heavy.*

have seen, since the day that they were upon the earth unto this day. And he turned himself, and went out from Pharaoh.

7And Pharaoh's servants said unto him, How long shall this man be a snare unto us? let the men go, that they may serve the LORD their God: knowest thou not yet that Egypt is destroyed?

8And Moses and Aaron were brought again unto Pharaoh: and he said unto them, Go, serve the LORD your God: *but* who *are* they that shall go?

9And Moses said, We will go with our young and with our old, with our sons and with our daughters, with our flocks and with our herds will we go; for we *must hold* a feast unto the LORD.

10And he said unto them, Let the LORD be so with you, as I will let you go, and your little ones: look *to it;* for evil *is* before you.

11Not so: go now ye *that are* men, and serve the LORD; for that ye did desire. And they were driven out from Pharaoh's presence.

12And the LORD said unto Moses, Stretch out thine hand over the land of Egypt for the locusts, that they may come up upon the land of Egypt, and eat every herb of the land, *even* all that the hail hath left.

13And Moses stretched forth his rod over the land of Egypt, and the LORD brought an east wind upon the land all that day, and all *that* night; *and* when it was morning, the east wind brought the locusts.

14And the locusts went up over all the land of Egypt, and rested in all the coasts of Egypt: very grievous *were they;* before them there were no such locusts as they, neither after them shall be such.

15For they covered the face of the whole earth, so that the land was darkened; and they did eat every herb of the land, and all the fruit of the trees which the hail had left: and there remained not any green thing in the trees, or in the herbs of the field, through all the land of Egypt.

16Then Pharaoh called for Moses and Aaron in haste; and he said, I have sinned against the LORD your God, and against you.

17Now therefore forgive, I pray thee, my sin only this once, and intreat the LORD your God, that he may take away from me this death only.

18And he went out from Pharaoh, and intreated the LORD.

19And the LORD turned a mighty strong west wind, which took away the locusts, and cast them into the Red sea; there remained not one locust in all the coasts of Egypt.

20But the LORD hardened Pharaoh's heart, so that he would not let the children of Israel go.

21And the LORD said unto Moses, Stretch out thine hand toward heaven, that there may be darkness over the land of Egypt, even darkness *which* may be felt.

22And Moses stretched forth his hand toward

plague like this one!" And with that, Moses turned and left Pharaoh.

7Pharaoh's officials now came to Pharaoh and appealed to him. "How long will you let this man hold us hostage? Let the men go to worship the LORD their God! Don't you realize that Egypt lies in ruins?"

8So Moses and Aaron were brought back to Pharaoh. "All right," he told them, "go and worship the LORD your God. But who exactly will be going with you?"

9Moses replied, "We will all go—young and old, our sons and daughters, and our flocks and herds. We must all join together in celebrating a festival to the LORD."

10Pharaoh retorted, "The LORD will certainly need to be with you if I let you take your little ones! I can see through your evil plan. 11Never! Only the men may go and worship the LORD, since that is what you requested." And Pharaoh threw them out of the palace.

12Then the LORD said to Moses, "Raise your hand over the land of Egypt to bring on the locusts. Let them cover the land and devour every plant that survived the hailstorm."

13So Moses raised his staff over Egypt, and the LORD caused an east wind to blow over the land all that day and through the night. When morning arrived, the east wind had brought the locusts. 14And the locusts swarmed over the whole land of Egypt, settling in dense swarms from one end of the country to the other. It was the worst locust plague in Egyptian history, and there has never been another one like it. 15For the locusts covered the whole country and darkened the land. They devoured every plant in the fields and all the fruit on the trees that had survived the hailstorm. Not a single leaf was left on the trees and plants throughout the land of Egypt.

16Pharaoh quickly summoned Moses and Aaron. "I have sinned against the LORD your God and against you," he confessed. 17"Forgive my sin, just this once, and plead with the LORD your God to take away this death from me."

18So Moses left Pharaoh's court and pleaded with the LORD. 19The LORD responded by shifting the wind, and the strong west wind blew the locusts into the Red Sea.* Not a single locust remained in all the land of Egypt. 20But the LORD hardened Pharaoh's heart again, so he refused to let the people go.

A Plague of Darkness

21Then the LORD said to Moses, "Lift your hand toward heaven, and the land of Egypt will be covered with a darkness so thick you can feel it." 22So Moses

10:19 Hebrew *sea of reeds.*

KING JAMES VERSION

heaven; and there was a thick darkness in all the land
of Egypt three days:
23 They saw not one another, neither rose any from
his place for three days: but all the children of Israel
had light in their dwellings.
24 And Pharaoh called unto Moses, and said, Go ye,
serve the LORD; only let your flocks and your herds
be stayed: let your little ones also go with you.
25 And Moses said, Thou must give us also sacrifices and burnt offerings, that we may sacrifice unto
the LORD our God.
26 Our cattle also shall go with us; there shall not
an hoof be left behind; for thereof must we take to
serve the LORD our God; and we know not with what
we must serve the LORD, until we come thither.
27 But the LORD hardened Pharaoh's heart, and he
would not let them go.
28 And Pharaoh said unto him, Get thee from me,
take heed to thyself, see my face no more; for in *that*
day thou seest my face thou shalt die.
29 And Moses said, Thou hast spoken well, I will see
thy face again no more.

11 1 And the LORD said unto Moses, Yet will I
bring one plague *more* upon Pharaoh, and
upon Egypt; afterwards he will let you go hence:
when he shall let *you* go, he shall surely thrust you
out hence altogether.
2 Speak now in the ears of the people, and let every
man borrow of his neighbour, and every woman of
her neighbour, jewels of silver, and jewels of gold.
3 And the LORD gave the people favour in the sight
of the Egyptians. Moreover the man Moses *was* very
great in the land of Egypt, in the sight of Pharaoh's
servants, and in the sight of the people.
4 And Moses said, Thus saith the LORD, About midnight will I go out into the midst of Egypt:
5 And all the firstborn in the land of Egypt shall die,
from the firstborn of Pharaoh that sitteth upon his
throne, even unto the firstborn of the maidservant
that *is* behind the mill; and all the firstborn of beasts.
6 And there shall be a great cry throughout all the
land of Egypt, such as there was none like it, nor shall
be like it any more.
7 But against any of the children of Israel shall not
a dog move his tongue, against man or beast: that ye
may know how that the LORD doth put a difference
between the Egyptians and Israel.
8 And all these thy servants shall come down unto
me, and bow down themselves unto me, saying, Get
thee out, and all the people that follow thee: and after that I will go out. And he went out from Pharaoh
in a great anger.
9 And the LORD said unto Moses, Pharaoh shall not
hearken unto you; that my wonders may be multiplied in the land of Egypt.

NEW LIVING TRANSLATION

lifted his hand to the sky, and a deep darkness
covered the entire land of Egypt for three days.
23 During all that time the people could not see each
other, and no one moved. But there was light as
usual where the people of Israel lived.
24 Finally, Pharaoh called for Moses. "Go and
worship the LORD," he said. "But leave your flocks
and herds here. You may even take your little ones
with you."
25 "No," Moses said, "you must provide us with animals for sacrifices and burnt offerings to the LORD
our God. 26 All our livestock must go with us, too; not
a hoof can be left behind. We must choose our sacrifices for the LORD our God from among these animals. And we won't know how we are to worship the
LORD until we get there."
27 But the LORD hardened Pharaoh's heart once
more, and he would not let them go. 28 "Get out of
here!" Pharaoh shouted at Moses. "I'm warning you.
Never come back to see me again! The day you see
my face, you will die!"
29 "Very well," Moses replied. "I will never see your
face again."

Death for Egypt's Firstborn

11 Then the LORD said to Moses, "I will strike Pharaoh and the land of Egypt with one more
blow. After that, Pharaoh will let you leave this country. In fact, he will be so eager to get rid of you that he
will force you all to leave. 2 Tell all the Israelite men
and women to ask their Egyptian neighbors for
articles of silver and gold." 3 (Now the LORD had
caused the Egyptians to look favorably on the people
of Israel. And Moses was considered a very great man
in the land of Egypt, respected by Pharaoh's officials
and the Egyptian people alike.)
4 Moses had announced to Pharaoh, "This is what
the LORD says: At midnight tonight I will pass
through the heart of Egypt. 5 All the firstborn sons
will die in every family in Egypt, from the oldest son
of Pharaoh, who sits on his throne, to the oldest
son of his lowliest servant girl who grinds the flour.
Even the firstborn of all the livestock will die. 6 Then
a loud wail will rise throughout the land of Egypt, a
wail like no one has heard before or will ever hear
again. 7 But among the Israelites it will be so peaceful
that not even a dog will bark. Then you will know that
the LORD makes a distinction between the Egyptians
and the Israelites. 8 All the officials of Egypt will run
to me and fall to the ground before me. 'Please leave!'
they will beg. 'Hurry! And take all your followers with
you.' Only then will I go!" Then, burning with anger,
Moses left Pharaoh.
9 Now the LORD had told Moses earlier, "Pharaoh
will not listen to you, but then I will do even more

KING JAMES VERSION

10 And Moses and Aaron did all these wonders before Pharaoh: and the LORD hardened Pharaoh's heart, so that he would not let the children of Israel go out of his land.

12 1 And the LORD spake unto Moses and Aaron in the land of Egypt, saying,

2 This month *shall be* unto you the beginning of months: it *shall be* the first month of the year to you.

3 Speak ye unto all the congregation of Israel, saying, In the tenth *day* of this month they shall take to them every man a lamb, according to the house of *their* fathers, a lamb for an house:

4 And if the household be too little for the lamb, let him and his neighbour next unto his house take *it* according to the number of the souls; every man according to his eating shall make your count for the lamb.

5 Your lamb shall be without blemish, a male of the first year: ye shall take *it* out from the sheep, or from the goats:

6 And ye shall keep it up until the fourteenth day of the same month: and the whole assembly of the congregation of Israel shall kill it in the evening.

7 And they shall take of the blood, and strike *it* on the two side posts and on the upper door post of the houses, wherein they shall eat it.

8 And they shall eat the flesh in that night, roast with fire, and unleavened bread; *and* with bitter *herbs* they shall eat it.

9 Eat not of it raw, nor sodden at all with water, but roast *with* fire; his head with his legs, and with the purtenance thereof.

10 And ye shall let nothing of it remain until the morning; and that which remaineth of it until the morning ye shall burn with fire.

11 And thus shall ye eat it; *with* your loins girded, your shoes on your feet, and your staff in your hand; and ye shall eat it in haste: it *is* the LORD's passover.

12 For I will pass through the land of Egypt this night, and will smite all the firstborn in the land of Egypt, both man and beast; and against all the gods of Egypt I will execute judgment: I *am* the LORD.

13 And the blood shall be to you for a token upon the houses where ye *are*: and when I see the blood, I will pass over you, and the plague shall not be upon you to destroy *you*, when I smite the land of Egypt.

14 And this day shall be unto you for a memorial; and ye shall keep it a feast to the LORD throughout your generations; ye shall keep it a feast by an ordinance for ever.

15 Seven days shall ye eat unleavened bread; even the first day ye shall put away leaven out of your houses: for whosoever eateth leavened bread from the first day until the seventh day, that soul shall be cut off from Israel.

NEW LIVING TRANSLATION

mighty miracles in the land of Egypt." 10 Moses and
Aaron performed these miracles in Pharaoh's presence, but the LORD hardened Pharaoh's heart, and he
wouldn't let the Israelites leave the country.

The First Passover

12 While the Israelites were still in the land of
Egypt, the LORD gave the following instructions to Moses and Aaron: 2 "From now on, this
month will be the first month of the year for you.
3 Announce to the whole community of Israel that on
the tenth day of this month each family must choose
a lamb or a young goat for a sacrifice, one animal
for each household. 4 If a family is too small to eat a
whole animal, let them share with another family in
the neighborhood. Divide the animal according to
the size of each family and how much they can eat.
5 The animal you select must be a one-year-old male,
either a sheep or a goat, with no defects.

6 "Take special care of this chosen animal until the
evening of the fourteenth day of this first month.
Then the whole assembly of the community of Israel
must slaughter their lamb or young goat at twilight.
7 They are to take some of the blood and smear it on
the sides and top of the doorframes of the houses
where they eat the animal. 8 That same night they
must roast the meat over a fire and eat it along with
bitter salad greens and bread made without yeast.
9 Do not eat any of the meat raw or boiled in water.
The whole animal—including the head, legs, and internal organs—must be roasted over a fire. 10 Do not
leave any of it until the next morning. Burn whatever
is not eaten before morning.

11 "These are your instructions for eating this
meal: Be fully dressed,* wear your sandals, and carry
your walking stick in your hand. Eat the meal with
urgency, for this is the LORD's Passover. 12 On that
night I will pass through the land of Egypt and strike
down every firstborn son and firstborn male animal
in the land of Egypt. I will execute judgment against
all the gods of Egypt, for I am the LORD! 13 But the
blood on your doorposts will serve as a sign, marking
the houses where you are staying. When I see the
blood, I will pass over you. This plague of death will
not touch you when I strike the land of Egypt.

14 "This is a day to remember. Each year, from
generation to generation, you must celebrate it as a
special festival to the LORD. This is a law for all time.
15 For seven days the bread you eat must be made
without yeast. On the first day of the festival, remove
every trace of yeast from your homes. Anyone who
eats bread made with yeast during the seven days of
the festival will be cut off from the community of

12:11 Hebrew *Bind up your loins.*

KING JAMES VERSION

16And in the first day *there shall be* an holy convocation, and in the seventh day there shall be an holy
convocation to you; no manner of work shall be done
in them, save *that* which every man must eat, that
only may be done of you.
17And ye shall observe *the feast of* unleavened
bread; for in this selfsame day have I brought your
armies out of the land of Egypt: therefore shall ye
observe this day in your generations by an ordinance
for ever.
18In the first *month,* on the fourteenth day of the
month at even, ye shall eat unleavened bread, until
the one and twentieth day of the month at even.
19Seven days shall there be no leaven found in
your houses: for whosoever eateth that which is leavened, even that soul shall be cut off from the congregation of Israel, whether he be a stranger, or born in
the land.
20Ye shall eat nothing leavened; in all your habitations shall ye eat unleavened bread.
21Then Moses called for all the elders of Israel, and
said unto them, Draw out and take you a lamb according to your families, and kill the passover.
22And ye shall take a bunch of hyssop, and dip *it* in
the blood that *is* in the basin, and strike the lintel and
the two side posts with the blood that *is* in the basin;
and none of you shall go out at the door of his house
until the morning.
23For the LORD will pass through to smite the
Egyptians; and when he seeth the blood upon the lintel, and on the two side posts, the LORD will pass over
the door, and will not suffer the destroyer to come in
unto your houses to smite *you.*
24And ye shall observe this thing for an ordinance
to thee and to thy sons for ever.
25And it shall come to pass, when ye be come to
the land which the LORD will give you, according as
he hath promised, that ye shall keep this service.
26And it shall come to pass, when your children
shall say unto you, What mean ye by this service?
27That ye shall say, It *is* the sacrifice of the LORD's
passover, who passed over the houses of the children
of Israel in Egypt, when he smote the Egyptians, and
delivered our houses. And the people bowed the
head and worshipped.
28And the children of Israel went away, and did
as the LORD had commanded Moses and Aaron, so
did they.
29And it came to pass, that at midnight the LORD
smote all the firstborn in the land of Egypt, from the
firstborn of Pharaoh that sat on his throne unto the
firstborn of the captive that *was* in the dungeon; and
all the firstborn of cattle.
30And Pharaoh rose up in the night, he, and all his
servants, and all the Egyptians; and there was a great
cry in Egypt; for *there was* not a house where *there*
was not one dead.

NEW LIVING TRANSLATION

Israel. 16On the first day of the festival and again on
the seventh day, all the people must observe an official day for holy assembly. No work of any kind may
be done on these days except in the preparation
of food.
17"Celebrate this Festival of Unleavened Bread, for
it will remind you that I brought your forces out of
the land of Egypt on this very day. This festival will be
a permanent law for you; celebrate this day from
generation to generation. 18The bread you eat must
be made without yeast from the evening of the fourteenth day of the first month until the evening of the
twenty-first day of that month. 19During those seven
days, there must be no trace of yeast in your homes.
Anyone who eats anything made with yeast during
this week will be cut off from the community of Israel. These regulations apply both to the foreigners living among you and to the native-born Israelites.
20During those days you must not eat anything made
with yeast. Wherever you live, eat only bread made
without yeast."
21Then Moses called all the elders of Israel together and said to them, "Go, pick out a lamb or
young goat for each of your families, and slaughter
the Passover animal. 22Drain the blood into a basin.
Then take a bundle of hyssop branches and dip it
into the blood. Brush the hyssop across the top and
sides of the doorframes of your houses. And no one
may go out through the door until morning. 23For the
LORD will pass through the land to strike down the
Egyptians. But when he sees the blood on the top and
sides of the doorframe, the LORD will pass over your
home. He will not permit his death angel to enter
your house and strike you down.
24"Remember, these instructions are a permanent
law that you and your descendants must observe forever. 25When you enter the land the LORD has promised to give you, you will continue to observe this
ceremony. 26Then your children will ask, 'What does
this ceremony mean?' 27And you will reply, 'It is the
Passover sacrifice to the LORD, for he passed over
the houses of the Israelites in Egypt. And though he
struck the Egyptians, he spared our families.'" When
Moses had finished speaking, all the people bowed
down to the ground and worshiped.
28So the people of Israel did just as the LORD had
commanded through Moses and Aaron. 29And that
night at midnight, the LORD struck down all the firstborn sons in the land of Egypt, from the firstborn
son of Pharaoh, who sat on his throne, to the firstborn son of the prisoner in the dungeon. Even the
firstborn of their livestock were killed. 30Pharaoh
and all his officials and all the people of Egypt woke
up during the night, and loud wailing was heard
throughout the land of Egypt. There was not a single
house where someone had not died.

KING JAMES VERSION

31 And he called for Moses and Aaron by night, and said, Rise up, *and* get you forth from among my people, both ye and the children of Israel; and go, serve the LORD, as ye have said.

32 Also take your flocks and your herds, as ye have said, and be gone; and bless me also.

33 And the Egyptians were urgent upon the people, that they might send them out of the land in haste; for they said, We *be* all dead *men*.

34 And the people took their dough before it was leavened, their kneadingtroughs being bound up in their clothes upon their shoulders.

35 And the children of Israel did according to the word of Moses; and they borrowed of the Egyptians jewels of silver, and jewels of gold, and raiment:

36 And the LORD gave the people favour in the sight of the Egyptians, so that they lent unto them *such things as they required*. And they spoiled the Egyptians.

37 And the children of Israel journeyed from Rameses to Succoth, about six hundred thousand on foot *that were* men, beside children.

38 And a mixed multitude went up also with them; and flocks, and herds, *even* very much cattle.

39 And they baked unleavened cakes of the dough which they brought forth out of Egypt, for it was not leavened; because they were thrust out of Egypt, and could not tarry, neither had they prepared for themselves any victual.

40 Now the sojourning of the children of Israel, who dwelt in Egypt, *was* four hundred and thirty years.

41 And it came to pass at the end of the four hundred and thirty years, even the selfsame day it came to pass, that all the hosts of the LORD went out from the land of Egypt.

42 It *is* a night to be much observed unto the LORD for bringing them out from the land of Egypt: this *is* that night of the LORD to be observed of all the children of Israel in their generations.

43 And the LORD said unto Moses and Aaron, This *is* the ordinance of the passover: There shall no stranger eat thereof:

44 But every man's servant that is bought for money, when thou hast circumcised him, then shall he eat thereof.

45 A foreigner and an hired servant shall not eat thereof.

46 In one house shall it be eaten; thou shalt not carry forth aught of the flesh abroad out of the house; neither shall ye break a bone thereof.

47 All the congregation of Israel shall keep it.

48 And when a stranger shall sojourn with thee, and will keep the passover to the LORD, let all his males be circumcised, and then let him come near and keep it; and he shall be as one that is born in the land: for no uncircumcised person shall eat thereof.

NEW LIVING TRANSLATION

Israel's Exodus from Egypt

31 Pharaoh sent for Moses and Aaron during the
night. "Get out!" he ordered. "Leave my people—and
take the rest of the Israelites with you! Go and worship the LORD as you have requested. 32 Take your
flocks and herds, as you said, and be gone. Go, but
bless me as you leave." 33 All the Egyptians urged the
people of Israel to get out of the land as quickly as
possible, for they thought, "We will all die!"

34 The Israelites took their bread dough before
yeast was added. They wrapped their kneading
boards in their cloaks and carried them on their
shoulders. 35 And the people of Israel did as Moses
had instructed; they asked the Egyptians for clothing
and articles of silver and gold. 36 The LORD caused
the Egyptians to look favorably on the Israelites, and
they gave the Israelites whatever they asked for. So
they stripped the Egyptians of their wealth!

37 That night the people of Israel left Rameses and
started for Succoth. There were about 600,000
men,* plus all the women and children. 38 A rabble of
non-Israelites went with them, along with great
flocks and herds of livestock. 39 For bread they baked
flat cakes from the dough without yeast they had
brought from Egypt. It was made without yeast because the people were driven out of Egypt in such a
hurry that they had no time to prepare the bread or
other food.

40 The people of Israel had lived in Egypt* for
430 years. 41 In fact, it was on the last day of the
430th year that all the LORD's forces left the land.
42 On this night the LORD kept his promise to bring
his people out of the land of Egypt. So this night
belongs to him, and it must be commemorated
every year by all the Israelites, from generation to
generation.

Instructions for the Passover

43 Then the LORD said to Moses and Aaron, "These are
the instructions for the festival of Passover. No outsiders are allowed to eat the Passover meal. 44 But any
slave who has been purchased may eat it if he has
been circumcised. 45 Temporary residents and hired
servants may not eat it. 46 Each Passover lamb must
be eaten in one house. Do not carry any of its meat
outside, and do not break any of its bones. 47 The
whole community of Israel must celebrate this Passover festival.

48 "If there are foreigners living among you who
want to celebrate the LORD's Passover, let all their
males be circumcised. Only then may they celebrate the Passover with you like any native-born Israelite. But no uncircumcised male may ever eat the

12:37 Or *fighting men;* Hebrew reads *men on foot.* **12:40** Samaritan Pentateuch reads *in Canaan and Egypt;* Greek version reads *in Egypt and Canaan.*

KING JAMES VERSION

[49]One law shall be to him that is homeborn, and
unto the stranger that sojourneth among you.
[50]Thus did all the children of Israel; as the LORD
commanded Moses and Aaron, so did they.
[51]And it came to pass the selfsame day, *that* the
LORD did bring the children of Israel out of the land
of Egypt by their armies.

13 [1]And the LORD spake unto Moses, saying,
[2]Sanctify unto me all the firstborn, whatsoever openeth the womb among the children of Israel,
both of man and of beast: it *is* mine.
[3]And Moses said unto the people, Remember this
day, in which ye came out from Egypt, out of the
house of bondage; for by strength of hand the LORD
brought you out from this *place:* there shall no leavened bread be eaten.
[4]This day came ye out in the month Abib.
[5]And it shall be when the LORD shall bring thee
into the land of the Canaanites, and the Hittites, and
the Amorites, and the Hivites, and the Jebusites,
which he sware unto thy fathers to give thee, a land
flowing with milk and honey, that thou shalt keep
this service in this month.
[6]Seven days thou shalt eat unleavened bread, and
in the seventh day *shall be* a feast to the LORD.
[7]Unleavened bread shall be eaten seven days; and
there shall no leavened bread be seen with thee, neither shall there be leaven seen with thee in all thy
quarters.
[8]And thou shalt shew thy son in that day, saying,
This is done because of that *which* the LORD did unto
me when I came forth out of Egypt.
[9]And it shall be for a sign unto thee upon thine
hand, and for a memorial between thine eyes, that
the LORD's law may be in thy mouth: for with a strong
hand hath the LORD brought thee out of Egypt.
[10]Thou shalt therefore keep this ordinance in his
season from year to year.
[11]And it shall be when the LORD shall bring thee
into the land of the Canaanites, as he sware unto thee
and to thy fathers, and shall give it thee,
[12]That thou shalt set apart unto the LORD all that
openeth the matrix, and every firstling that cometh
of a beast which thou hast; the males *shall be* the
LORD's.
[13]And every firstling of an ass thou shalt redeem
with a lamb; and if thou wilt not redeem it, then thou
shalt break his neck: and all the firstborn of man
among thy children shalt thou redeem.
[14]And it shall be when thy son asketh thee in time
to come, saying, What *is* this? that thou shalt say unto
him, By strength of hand the LORD brought us out
from Egypt, from the house of bondage:
[15]And it came to pass, when Pharaoh would hardly
let us go, that the LORD slew all the firstborn in the

NEW LIVING TRANSLATION

Passover meal. [49]This instruction applies to everyone, whether a native-born Israelite or a foreigner
living among you."
[50]So all the people of Israel followed all the LORD's
commands to Moses and Aaron. [51]On that very day
the LORD brought the people of Israel out of the land
of Egypt like an army.

Dedication of the Firstborn

13 Then the LORD said to Moses, [2]"Dedicate to
me every firstborn among the Israelites. The
first offspring to be born, of both humans and animals, belongs to me."
[3]So Moses said to the people, "This is a day to remember forever—the day you left Egypt, the place of
your slavery. Today the LORD has brought you out by
the power of his mighty hand. (Remember, eat no
food containing yeast.) [4]On this day in early spring,
in the month of Abib,* you have been set free. [5]You
must celebrate this event in this month each year after the LORD brings you into the land of the Canaanites, Hittites, Amorites, Hivites, and Jebusites. (He
swore to your ancestors that he would give you this
land—a land flowing with milk and honey.) [6]For
seven days the bread you eat must be made without
yeast. Then on the seventh day, celebrate a feast to
the LORD. [7]Eat bread without yeast during those
seven days. In fact, there must be no yeast bread or
any yeast at all found within the borders of your land
during this time.
[8]"On the seventh day you must explain to your
children, 'I am celebrating what the LORD did for
me when I left Egypt.' [9]This annual festival will be a
visible sign to you, like a mark branded on your hand
or your forehead. Let it remind you always to recite
this teaching of the LORD: 'With a strong hand, the
LORD rescued you from Egypt.'* [10]So observe the decree of this festival at the appointed time each year.
[11]"This is what you must do when the LORD fulfills
the promise he swore to you and to your ancestors.
When he gives you the land where the Canaanites
now live, [12]you must present all firstborn sons and
firstborn male animals to the LORD, for they belong
to him. [13]A firstborn donkey may be bought back
from the LORD by presenting a lamb or young goat in
its place. But if you do not buy it back, you must
break its neck. However, you must buy back every
firstborn son.
[14]"And in the future, your children will ask you,
'What does all this mean?' Then you will tell them,
'With the power of his mighty hand, the LORD
brought us out of Egypt, the place of our slavery.
[15]Pharaoh stubbornly refused to let us go, so the
LORD killed all the firstborn males throughout the

13:4 Hebrew *On this day in the month of Abib.* This first month of the ancient Hebrew lunar calendar usually occurs within the months of March and April. **13:9** Or *Let it remind you always to keep the instructions of the LORD on the tip of your tongue, because with a strong hand, the LORD rescued you from Egypt.*

KING JAMES VERSION

land of Egypt, both the firstborn of man, and the firstborn of beast: therefore I sacrifice to the LORD all that openeth the matrix, being males; but all the firstborn of my children I redeem.

16And it shall be for a token upon thine hand, and for frontlets between thine eyes: for by strength of hand the LORD brought us forth out of Egypt.

17And it came to pass, when Pharaoh had let the people go, that God led them not *through* the way of the land of the Philistines, although that *was* near; for God said, Lest peradventure the people repent when they see war, and they return to Egypt:

18But God led the people about, *through* the way of the wilderness of the Red sea: and the children of Israel went up harnessed out of the land of Egypt.

19And Moses took the bones of Joseph with him: for he had straitly sworn the children of Israel, saying, God will surely visit you; and ye shall carry up my bones away hence with you.

20And they took their journey from Succoth, and encamped in Etham, in the edge of the wilderness.

21And the LORD went before them by day in a pillar of a cloud, to lead them the way; and by night in a pillar of fire, to give them light; to go by day and night:

22He took not away the pillar of the cloud by day, nor the pillar of fire by night, *from* before the people.

14 1And the LORD spake unto Moses, saying,

2Speak unto the children of Israel, that they turn and encamp before Pi-hahiroth, between Migdol and the sea, over against Baal-zephon: before it shall ye encamp by the sea.

3For Pharaoh will say of the children of Israel, They *are* entangled in the land, the wilderness hath shut them in.

4And I will harden Pharaoh's heart, that he shall follow after them; and I will be honoured upon Pharaoh, and upon all his host; that the Egyptians may know that I *am* the LORD. And they did so.

5And it was told the king of Egypt that the people fled: and the heart of Pharaoh and of his servants was turned against the people, and they said, Why have we done this, that we have let Israel go from serving us?

6And he made ready his chariot, and took his people with him:

7And he took six hundred chosen chariots, and all the chariots of Egypt, and captains over every one of them.

8And the LORD hardened the heart of Pharaoh king of Egypt, and he pursued after the children of

NEW LIVING TRANSLATION

land of Egypt, both people and animals. That is why I now sacrifice all the firstborn males to the LORD—except that the firstborn sons are always bought back.' 16This ceremony will be like a mark branded on your hand or your forehead. It is a reminder that the power of the LORD's mighty hand brought us out of Egypt."

Israel's Wilderness Detour

17When Pharaoh finally let the people go, God did not lead them along the main road that runs through Philistine territory, even though that was the shortest route to the Promised Land. God said, "If the people are faced with a battle, they might change their minds and return to Egypt." 18So God led them in a roundabout way through the wilderness toward the Red Sea.* Thus the Israelites left Egypt like an army ready for battle.*

19Moses took the bones of Joseph with him, for Joseph had made the sons of Israel swear to do this. He said, "God will certainly come to help you. When he does, you must take my bones with you from this place."

20The Israelites left Succoth and camped at Etham on the edge of the wilderness. 21The LORD went ahead of them. He guided them during the day with a pillar of cloud, and he provided light at night with a pillar of fire. This allowed them to travel by day or by night. 22And the LORD did not remove the pillar of cloud or pillar of fire from its place in front of the people.

14 Then the LORD gave these instructions to Moses: 2"Order the Israelites to turn back and camp by Pi-hahiroth between Migdol and the sea. Camp there along the shore, across from Baal-zephon. 3Then Pharaoh will think, 'The Israelites are confused. They are trapped in the wilderness!' 4And once again I will harden Pharaoh's heart, and he will chase after you.* I have planned this in order to display my glory through Pharaoh and his whole army. After this the Egyptians will know that I am the LORD!" So the Israelites camped there as they were told.

The Egyptians Pursue Israel

5When word reached the king of Egypt that the Israelites had fled, Pharaoh and his officials changed their minds. "What have we done, letting all those Israelite slaves get away?" they asked. 6So Pharaoh harnessed his chariot and called up his troops. 7He took with him 600 of Egypt's best chariots, along with the rest of the chariots of Egypt, each with its commander. 8The LORD hardened the heart of Pharaoh, the king of Egypt, so he chased after the people

13:18a Hebrew *sea of reeds.* **13:18b** Greek version reads *left Egypt in the fifth generation.* **14:4** Hebrew *after them.*

KING JAMES VERSION

Israel: and the children of Israel went out with an
high hand.
9 But the Egyptians pursued after them, all the
horses *and* chariots of Pharaoh, and his horsemen,
and his army, and overtook them encamping by the
sea, beside Pi-hahiroth, before Baal-zephon.
10 And when Pharaoh drew nigh, the children of Israel lifted up their eyes, and, behold, the Egyptians
marched after them; and they were sore afraid: and
the children of Israel cried out unto the LORD.
11 And they said unto Moses, Because *there were*
no graves in Egypt, hast thou taken us away to die in
the wilderness? wherefore hast thou dealt thus with
us, to carry us forth out of Egypt?
12 *Is* not this the word that we did tell thee in Egypt,
saying, Let us alone, that we may serve the Egyptians?
For *it had been* better for us to serve the Egyptians,
than that we should die in the wilderness.
13 And Moses said unto the people, Fear ye not,
stand still, and see the salvation of the LORD, which
he will shew to you today: for the Egyptians whom
ye have seen today, ye shall see them again no more
for ever.
14 The LORD shall fight for you, and ye shall hold
your peace.
15 And the LORD said unto Moses, Wherefore criest
thou unto me? speak unto the children of Israel, that
they go forward:
16 But lift thou up thy rod, and stretch out thine
hand over the sea, and divide it: and the children of
Israel shall go on dry *ground* through the midst of
the sea.
17 And I, behold, I will harden the hearts of the
Egyptians, and they shall follow them: and I will get
me honour upon Pharaoh, and upon all his host,
upon his chariots, and upon his horsemen.
18 And the Egyptians shall know that I *am* the
LORD, when I have gotten me honour upon Pharaoh,
upon his chariots, and upon his horsemen.
19 And the angel of God, which went before the
camp of Israel, removed and went behind them; and
the pillar of the cloud went from before their face,
and stood behind them:
20 And it came between the camp of the Egyptians
and the camp of Israel; and it was a cloud and darkness *to them,* but it gave light by night *to these:* so
that the one came not near the other all the night.
21 And Moses stretched out his hand over the sea;
and the LORD caused the sea to go *back* by a strong
east wind all that night, and made the sea dry *land,*
and the waters were divided.
22 And the children of Israel went into the midst of
the sea upon the dry *ground:* and the waters *were* a
wall unto them on their right hand, and on their left.
23 And the Egyptians pursued, and went in after
them to the midst of the sea, *even* all Pharaoh's
horses, his chariots, and his horsemen.
24 And it came to pass, that in the morning watch

NEW LIVING TRANSLATION

of Israel, who had left with fists raised in defiance.
9 The Egyptians chased after them with all the forces
in Pharaoh's army—all his horses and chariots, his
charioteers, and his troops. The Egyptians caught
up with the people of Israel as they were camped
beside the shore near Pi-hahiroth, across from Baal-
zephon.
10 As Pharaoh approached, the people of Israel
looked up and panicked when they saw the Egyptians overtaking them. They cried out to the LORD,
11 and they said to Moses, "Why did you bring us out
here to die in the wilderness? Weren't there enough
graves for us in Egypt? What have you done to us?
Why did you make us leave Egypt? 12 Didn't we tell
you this would happen while we were still in Egypt?
We said, 'Leave us alone! Let us be slaves to the Egyptians. It's better to be a slave in Egypt than a corpse in
the wilderness!'"
13 But Moses told the people, "Don't be afraid. Just
stand still and watch the LORD rescue you today. The
Egyptians you see today will never be seen again.
14 The LORD himself will fight for you. Just stay calm."

Escape through the Red Sea

15 Then the LORD said to Moses, "Why are you crying
out to me? Tell the people to get moving! 16 Pick up
your staff and raise your hand over the sea. Divide
the water so the Israelites can walk through the middle of the sea on dry ground. 17 And I will harden the
hearts of the Egyptians, and they will charge in after
the Israelites. My great glory will be displayed
through Pharaoh and his troops, his chariots, and his
charioteers. 18 When my glory is displayed through
them, all Egypt will see my glory and know that I am
the LORD!"
19 Then the angel of God, who had been leading
the people of Israel, moved to the rear of the camp.
The pillar of cloud also moved from the front and
stood behind them. 20 The cloud settled between
the Egyptian and Israelite camps. As darkness fell,
the cloud turned to fire, lighting up the night. But the
Egyptians and Israelites did not approach each other
all night.
21 Then Moses raised his hand over the sea, and
the LORD opened up a path through the water with a
strong east wind. The wind blew all that night, turning the seabed into dry land. 22 So the people of Israel
walked through the middle of the sea on dry ground,
with walls of water on each side!
23 Then the Egyptians—all of Pharaoh's horses,
chariots, and charioteers—chased them into the
middle of the sea. 24 But just before dawn the LORD

KING JAMES VERSION

the LORD looked unto the host of the Egyptians
through the pillar of fire and of the cloud, and
troubled the host of the Egyptians,
25 And took off their chariot wheels, that they
drave them heavily: so that the Egyptians said, Let us
flee from the face of Israel; for the LORD fighteth for
them against the Egyptians.
26 And the LORD said unto Moses, Stretch out thine
hand over the sea, that the waters may come again
upon the Egyptians, upon their chariots, and upon
their horsemen.
27 And Moses stretched forth his hand over the
sea, and the sea returned to his strength when the
morning appeared; and the Egyptians fled against it;
and the LORD overthrew the Egyptians in the midst
of the sea.
28 And the waters returned, and covered the chariots, and the horsemen, *and* all the host of Pharaoh
that came into the sea after them; there remained
not so much as one of them.
29 But the children of Israel walked upon dry *land*
in the midst of the sea; and the waters *were* a wall
unto them on their right hand, and on their left.
30 Thus the LORD saved Israel that day out of the
hand of the Egyptians; and Israel saw the Egyptians
dead upon the sea shore.
31 And Israel saw that great work which the LORD
did upon the Egyptians: and the people feared the
LORD, and believed the LORD, and his servant Moses.

15 1 Then sang Moses and the children of Israel
this song unto the LORD, and spake, saying, I
will sing unto the LORD, for he hath triumphed gloriously: the horse and his rider hath he thrown into
the sea.
2 The LORD *is* my strength and song, and he is
become my salvation: he *is* my God, and I will prepare him an habitation; my father's God, and I will
exalt him.
3 The LORD *is* a man of war: the LORD *is* his name.
4 Pharaoh's chariots and his host hath he cast into
the sea: his chosen captains also are drowned in the
Red sea.
5 The depths have covered them: they sank into
the bottom as a stone.
6 Thy right hand, O LORD, is become glorious in
power: thy right hand, O LORD, hath dashed in pieces
the enemy.

NEW LIVING TRANSLATION

looked down on the Egyptian army from the pillar of
fire and cloud, and he threw their forces into total
confusion. 25 He twisted* their chariot wheels, making their chariots difficult to drive. "Let's get out of
here—away from these Israelites!" the Egyptians
shouted. "The LORD is fighting for them against
Egypt!"
26 When all the Israelites had reached the other
side, the LORD said to Moses, "Raise your hand over
the sea again. Then the waters will rush back and
cover the Egyptians and their chariots and charioteers." 27 So as the sun began to rise, Moses raised
his hand over the sea, and the water rushed back into
its usual place. The Egyptians tried to escape, but the
LORD swept them into the sea. 28 Then the waters
returned and covered all the chariots and charioteers—the entire army of Pharaoh. Of all the Egyptians who had chased the Israelites into the sea, not
a single one survived.
29 But the people of Israel had walked through the
middle of the sea on dry ground, as the water stood
up like a wall on both sides. 30 That is how the LORD
rescued Israel from the hand of the Egyptians that
day. And the Israelites saw the bodies of the Egyptians washed up on the seashore. 31 When the people
of Israel saw the mighty power that the LORD had un-
leashed against the Egyptians, they were filled with
awe before him. They put their faith in the LORD and
in his servant Moses.

A Song of Deliverance

15 Then Moses and the people of Israel sang
this song to the LORD:

"I will sing to the LORD,
for he has triumphed gloriously;
he has hurled both horse and rider
into the sea.
2 The LORD is my strength and my song;
he has given me victory.
This is my God, and I will praise him—
my father's God, and I will exalt him!
3 The LORD is a warrior;
Yahweh* is his name!
4 Pharaoh's chariots and army
he has hurled into the sea.
The finest of Pharaoh's officers
are drowned in the Red Sea.*
5 The deep waters gushed over them;
they sank to the bottom like a stone.
6 "Your right hand, O LORD,
is glorious in power.
Your right hand, O LORD,
smashes the enemy.

14:25 As in Greek version, Samaritan Pentateuch, and Syriac version; Hebrew reads *He removed.* **15:3** *Yahweh* is a transliteration of the proper name *YHWH* that is sometimes rendered "Jehovah"; in this translation it is usually rendered "the LORD" (note the use of small capitals). **15:4** Hebrew *sea of reeds;* also in 15:22.

KING JAMES VERSION

7 And in the greatness of thine excellency thou hast overthrown them that rose up against thee: thou sentest forth thy wrath, *which* consumed them as stubble.

8 And with the blast of thy nostrils the waters were gathered together, the floods stood upright as an heap, *and* the depths were congealed in the heart of the sea.

9 The enemy said, I will pursue, I will overtake, I will divide the spoil; my lust shall be satisfied upon them; I will draw my sword, my hand shall destroy them.

10 Thou didst blow with thy wind, the sea covered them: they sank as lead in the mighty waters.

11 Who *is* like unto thee, O LORD, among the gods? who *is* like thee, glorious in holiness, fearful *in* praises, doing wonders?

12 Thou stretchedst out thy right hand, the earth swallowed them.

13 Thou in thy mercy hast led forth the people *which* thou hast redeemed: thou hast guided *them* in thy strength unto thy holy habitation.

14 The people shall hear, *and* be afraid: sorrow shall take hold on the inhabitants of Palestina.

15 Then the dukes of Edom shall be amazed; the mighty men of Moab, trembling shall take hold upon them; all the inhabitants of Canaan shall melt away.

16 Fear and dread shall fall upon them; by the greatness of thine arm they shall be *as* still as a stone; till thy people pass over, O LORD, till the people pass over, *which* thou hast purchased.

17 Thou shalt bring them in, and plant them in the mountain of thine inheritance, *in* the place, O LORD, *which* thou hast made for thee to dwell in, *in* the Sanctuary, O Lord, *which* thy hands have established.

18 The LORD shall reign for ever and ever.

19 For the horse of Pharaoh went in with his chariots and with his horsemen into the sea, and the LORD brought again the waters of the sea upon them; but the children of Israel went on dry *land* in the midst of the sea.

20 And Miriam the prophetess, the sister of Aaron, took a timbrel in her hand; and all the women went out after her with timbrels and with dances.

21 And Miriam answered them, Sing ye to the LORD,

NEW LIVING TRANSLATION

7 In the greatness of your majesty,
you overthrow those who rise against you.
You unleash your blazing fury;
it consumes them like straw.
8 At the blast of your breath,
the waters piled up!
The surging waters stood straight like a wall;
in the heart of the sea the deep waters
became hard.

9 "The enemy boasted, 'I will chase them
and catch up with them.
I will plunder them
and consume them.
I will flash my sword;
my powerful hand will destroy them.'
10 But you blew with your breath,
and the sea covered them.
They sank like lead
in the mighty waters.

11 "Who is like you among the gods, O LORD—
glorious in holiness,
awesome in splendor,
performing great wonders?
12 You raised your right hand,
and the earth swallowed our enemies.

13 "With your unfailing love you lead
the people you have redeemed.
In your might, you guide them
to your sacred home.
14 The peoples hear and tremble;
anguish grips those who live in Philistia.
15 The leaders of Edom are terrified;
the nobles of Moab tremble.
All who live in Canaan melt away;
16 terror and dread fall upon them.
The power of your arm
makes them lifeless as stone
until your people pass by, O LORD,
until the people you purchased pass by.
17 You will bring them in and plant them on
your own mountain—
the place, O LORD, reserved for your
own dwelling,
the sanctuary, O Lord, that your hands
have established.
18 The LORD will reign forever and ever!"

19 When Pharaoh's horses, chariots, and charioteers rushed into the sea, the LORD brought the water crashing down on them. But the people of Israel had walked through the middle of the sea on dry ground!

20 Then Miriam the prophet, Aaron's sister, took a
tambourine and led all the women as they played
their tambourines and danced. 21 And Miriam sang
this song:

for he hath triumphed gloriously; the horse and his rider hath he thrown into the sea.

22 So Moses brought Israel from the Red sea, and they went out into the wilderness of Shur; and they went three days in the wilderness, and found no water.

23 And when they came to Marah, they could not drink of the waters of Marah, for they *were* bitter: therefore the name of it was called Marah.

24 And the people murmured against Moses, saying, What shall we drink?

25 And he cried unto the LORD; and the LORD shewed him a tree, *which* when he had cast into the waters, the waters were made sweet: there he made for them a statute and an ordinance, and there he proved them,

26 And said, If thou wilt diligently hearken to the voice of the LORD thy God, and wilt do that which is right in his sight, and wilt give ear to his commandments, and keep all his statutes, I will put none of these diseases upon thee, which I have brought upon the Egyptians: for I *am* the LORD that healeth thee.

27 And they came to Elim, where *were* twelve wells of water, and threescore and ten palm trees: and they encamped there by the waters.

16 1 And they took their journey from Elim, and all the congregation of the children of Israel came unto the wilderness of Sin, which *is* between Elim and Sinai, on the fifteenth day of the second month after their departing out of the land of Egypt.

2 And the whole congregation of the children of Israel murmured against Moses and Aaron in the wilderness:

3 And the children of Israel said unto them, Would to God we had died by the hand of the LORD in the land of Egypt, when we sat by the flesh pots, *and* when we did eat bread to the full; for ye have brought us forth into this wilderness, to kill this whole assembly with hunger.

4 Then said the LORD unto Moses, Behold, I will rain bread from heaven for you; and the people shall go out and gather a certain rate every day, that I may prove them, whether they will walk in my law, or no.

5 And it shall come to pass, that on the sixth day they shall prepare *that* which they bring in; and it shall be twice as much as they gather daily.

6 And Moses and Aaron said unto all the children of Israel, At even, then ye shall know that the LORD hath brought you out from the land of Egypt:

7 And in the morning, then ye shall see the glory of the LORD; for that he heareth your murmurings

"Sing to the LORD,
for he has triumphed gloriously;
he has hurled both horse and rider
into the sea."

Bitter Water at Marah

22 Then Moses led the people of Israel away from the Red Sea, and they moved out into the desert of Shur. They traveled in this desert for three days without finding any water. 23 When they came to the oasis of Marah, the water was too bitter to drink. So they called the place Marah (which means "bitter").

24 Then the people complained and turned against Moses. "What are we going to drink?" they demanded. 25 So Moses cried out to the LORD for help, and the LORD showed him a piece of wood. Moses threw it into the water, and this made the water good to drink.

It was there at Marah that the LORD set before them the following decree as a standard to test their faithfulness to him. 26 He said, "If you will listen carefully to the voice of the LORD your God and do what is right in his sight, obeying his commands and keeping all his decrees, then I will not make you suffer any of the diseases I sent on the Egyptians; for I am the LORD who heals you."

27 After leaving Marah, the Israelites traveled on to the oasis of Elim, where they found twelve springs and seventy palm trees. They camped there beside the water.

Manna and Quail from Heaven

16 Then the whole community of Israel set out from Elim and journeyed into the wilderness of Sin,* between Elim and Mount Sinai. They arrived there on the fifteenth day of the second month, one month after leaving the land of Egypt.* 2 There, too, the whole community of Israel complained about Moses and Aaron.

3 "If only the LORD had killed us back in Egypt," they moaned. "There we sat around pots filled with meat and ate all the bread we wanted. But now you have brought us into this wilderness to starve us all to death."

4 Then the LORD said to Moses, "Look, I'm going to rain down food from heaven for you. Each day the people can go out and pick up as much food as they need for that day. I will test them in this to see whether or not they will follow my instructions. 5 On the sixth day they will gather food, and when they prepare it, there will be twice as much as usual."

6 So Moses and Aaron said to all the people of Israel, "By evening you will realize it was the LORD who brought you out of the land of Egypt. 7 In the morning you will see the glory of the LORD, because

16:1a The geographical name *Sin* is related to *Sinai* and should not be confused with the English word *sin*. **16:1b** The Exodus had occurred on the fifteenth day of the first month (see Num 33:3).

KING JAMES VERSION

against the LORD: and what *are* we, that ye murmur against us?

8And Moses said, *This shall be,* when the LORD shall give you in the evening flesh to eat, and in the morning bread to the full; for that the LORD heareth your murmurings which ye murmur against him: and what *are* we? your murmurings *are* not against us, but against the LORD.

9And Moses spake unto Aaron, Say unto all the congregation of the children of Israel, Come near before the LORD: for he hath heard your murmurings.

10And it came to pass, as Aaron spake unto the whole congregation of the children of Israel, that they looked toward the wilderness, and, behold, the glory of the LORD appeared in the cloud.

11And the LORD spake unto Moses, saying,

12I have heard the murmurings of the children of Israel: speak unto them, saying, At even ye shall eat flesh, and in the morning ye shall be filled with bread; and ye shall know that I *am* the LORD your God.

13And it came to pass, that at even the quails came up, and covered the camp: and in the morning the dew lay round about the host.

14And when the dew that lay was gone up, behold, upon the face of the wilderness *there lay* a small round thing, *as* small as the hoar frost on the ground.

15And when the children of Israel saw *it,* they said one to another, It *is* manna: for they wist not what it *was.* And Moses said unto them, This *is* the bread which the LORD hath given you to eat.

16This *is* the thing which the LORD hath commanded, Gather of it every man according to his eating, an omer for every man, *according to* the number of your persons; take ye every man for *them* which *are* in his tents.

17And the children of Israel did so, and gathered, some more, some less.

18And when they did mete *it* with an omer, he that gathered much had nothing over, and he that gathered little had no lack; they gathered every man according to his eating.

19And Moses said, Let no man leave of it till the morning.

20Notwithstanding they hearkened not unto Moses; but some of them left of it until the morning, and it bred worms, and stank: and Moses was wroth with them.

21And they gathered it every morning, every man according to his eating: and when the sun waxed hot, it melted.

22And it came to pass, *that* on the sixth day they gathered twice as much bread, two omers for one *man:* and all the rulers of the congregation came and told Moses.

23And he said unto them, This *is that* which the LORD hath said, Tomorrow *is* the rest of the holy sabbath unto the LORD: bake *that* which ye will bake *today,* and seethe that ye will seethe; and that which

NEW LIVING TRANSLATION

he has heard your complaints, which are against
him, not against us. What have we done that you
should complain about us?" 8Then Moses added,
"The LORD will give you meat to eat in the evening
and bread to satisfy you in the morning, for he has
heard all your complaints against him. What have
we done? Yes, your complaints are against the LORD,
not against us."

9Then Moses said to Aaron, "Announce this to the
entire community of Israel: 'Present yourselves before the LORD, for he has heard your complaining.'"
10And as Aaron spoke to the whole community of
Israel, they looked out toward the wilderness. There
they could see the awesome glory of the LORD in
the cloud.

11Then the LORD said to Moses, 12"I have heard the
Israelites' complaints. Now tell them, 'In the evening
you will have meat to eat, and in the morning you will
have all the bread you want. Then you will know that
I am the LORD your God.'"

13That evening vast numbers of quail flew in and
covered the camp. And the next morning the area
around the camp was wet with dew. 14When the dew
evaporated, a flaky substance as fine as frost blanketed the ground. 15The Israelites were puzzled
when they saw it. "What is it?" they asked each other.
They had no idea what it was.

And Moses told them, "It is the food the LORD has
given you to eat. 16These are the LORD's instructions:
Each household should gather as much as it needs.
Pick up two quarts* for each person in your tent."

17So the people of Israel did as they were told.
Some gathered a lot, some only a little. 18But when
they measured it out,* everyone had just enough.
Those who gathered a lot had nothing left over, and
those who gathered only a little had enough. Each
family had just what it needed.

19Then Moses told them, "Do not keep any of it
until morning." 20But some of them didn't listen and
kept some of it until morning. But by then it was full
of maggots and had a terrible smell. Moses was very
angry with them.

21After this the people gathered the food morning
by morning, each family according to its need. And
as the sun became hot, the flakes they had not picked
up melted and disappeared. 22On the sixth day, they
gathered twice as much as usual—four quarts* for
each person instead of two. Then all the leaders of
the community came and asked Moses for an explanation. 23He told them, "This is what the LORD commanded: Tomorrow will be a day of complete rest, a
holy Sabbath day set apart for the LORD. So bake or
boil as much as you want today, and set aside what is
left for tomorrow."

16:16 Hebrew *1 omer* [2 liters]; also in 16:32, 33. **16:18** Hebrew *measured it with an omer.* **16:22** Hebrew *2 omers* [4 liters].

KING JAMES VERSION

remaineth over lay up for you to be kept until the
morning.
24And they laid it up till the morning, as Moses
bade: and it did not stink, neither was there any
worm therein.
25And Moses said, Eat that today; for today *is* a
sabbath unto the LORD: today ye shall not find it in
the field.
26Six days ye shall gather it; but on the seventh day,
which is the sabbath, in it there shall be none.
27And it came to pass, *that* there went out *some* of
the people on the seventh day for to gather, and they
found none.
28And the LORD said unto Moses, How long refuse
ye to keep my commandments and my laws?
29See, for that the LORD hath given you the sabbath, therefore he giveth you on the sixth day the
bread of two days; abide ye every man in his place, let
no man go out of his place on the seventh day.
30So the people rested on the seventh day.
31And the house of Israel called the name thereof
Manna: and it *was* like coriander seed, white; and the
taste of it *was* like wafers *made* with honey.
32And Moses said, This *is* the thing which the
LORD commandeth, Fill an omer of it to be kept for
your generations; that they may see the bread wherewith I have fed you in the wilderness, when I brought
you forth from the land of Egypt.
33And Moses said unto Aaron, Take a pot, and put
an omer full of manna therein, and lay it up before
the LORD, to be kept for your generations.
34As the LORD commanded Moses, so Aaron laid it
up before the Testimony, to be kept.
35And the children of Israel did eat manna forty
years, until they came to a land inhabited; they did
eat manna, until they came unto the borders of the
land of Canaan.
36Now an omer *is* the tenth *part* of an ephah.

17 1And all the congregation of the children of
Israel journeyed from the wilderness of Sin,
after their journeys, according to the commandment
of the LORD, and pitched in Rephidim: and *there was*
no water for the people to drink.
2Wherefore the people did chide with Moses, and
said, Give us water that we may drink. And Moses
said unto them, Why chide ye with me? wherefore do
ye tempt the LORD?
3And the people thirsted there for water; and the
people murmured against Moses, and said, Wherefore *is* this *that* thou hast brought us up out of
Egypt, to kill us and our children and our cattle
with thirst?

NEW LIVING TRANSLATION

24So they put some aside until morning, just as
Moses had commanded. And in the morning the leftover food was wholesome and good, without maggots
or odor. 25Moses said, "Eat this food today, for today is
a Sabbath day dedicated to the LORD. There will be no
food on the ground today. 26You may gather the food
for six days, but the seventh day is the Sabbath. There
will be no food on the ground that day."
27Some of the people went out anyway on the seventh day, but they found no food. 28The LORD asked
Moses, "How long will these people refuse to obey
my commands and instructions? 29They must realize that the Sabbath is the LORD's gift to you. That is
why he gives you a two-day supply on the sixth day,
so there will be enough for two days. On the Sabbath
day you must each stay in your place. Do not go out to
pick up food on the seventh day." 30So the people did
not gather any food on the seventh day.
31The Israelites called the food manna.* It was
white like coriander seed, and it tasted like honey
wafers.
32Then Moses said, "This is what the LORD has
commanded: Fill a two-quart container with manna
to preserve it for your descendants. Then later generations will be able to see the food I gave you in the
wilderness when I set you free from Egypt."
33Moses said to Aaron, "Get a jar and fill it with two
quarts of manna. Then put it in a sacred place before
the LORD to preserve it for all future generations."
34Aaron did just as the LORD had commanded Moses.
He eventually placed it in the Ark of the Covenant—
in front of the stone tablets inscribed with the terms
of the covenant.* 35So the people of Israel ate manna
for forty years until they arrived at the land where
they would settle. They ate manna until they came to
the border of the land of Canaan.
36The container used to measure the manna was
an omer, which was one-tenth of an ephah; it held
about two quarts.*

Water from the Rock

17 At the LORD's command, the whole community of Israel left the wilderness of Sin* and
moved from place to place. Eventually they camped
at Rephidim, but there was no water there for the
people to drink. 2So once more the people complained against Moses. "Give us water to drink!" they
demanded.
"Quiet!" Moses replied. "Why are you complaining against me? And why are you testing the LORD?"
3But tormented by thirst, they continued to argue
with Moses. "Why did you bring us out of Egypt? Are
you trying to kill us, our children, and our livestock
with thirst?"

16:31 *Manna* means "What is it?" See 16:15. **16:34** Hebrew *He placed it in front of the Testimony;* see note on 25:16. **16:36** Hebrew *An omer is one-tenth of an ephah.* **17:1** The geographical name *Sin* is related to *Sinai* and should not be confused with the English word *sin.*

KING JAMES VERSION

4And Moses cried unto the LORD, saying, What
shall I do unto this people? they be almost ready to
stone me.
5And the LORD said unto Moses, Go on before the
people, and take with thee of the elders of Israel; and
thy rod, wherewith thou smotest the river, take in
thine hand, and go.
6Behold, I will stand before thee there upon the
rock in Horeb; and thou shalt smite the rock, and
there shall come water out of it, that the people may
drink. And Moses did so in the sight of the elders
of Israel.
7And he called the name of the place Massah, and
Meribah, because of the chiding of the children of
Israel, and because they tempted the LORD, saying,
Is the LORD among us, or not?

8Then came Amalek, and fought with Israel in
Rephidim.
9And Moses said unto Joshua, Choose us out men,
and go out, fight with Amalek: tomorrow I will stand
on the top of the hill with the rod of God in mine
hand.
10So Joshua did as Moses had said to him, and
fought with Amalek: and Moses, Aaron, and Hur
went up to the top of the hill.
11And it came to pass, when Moses held up his
hand, that Israel prevailed: and when he let down his
hand, Amalek prevailed.
12But Moses' hands *were* heavy; and they took a
stone, and put *it* under him, and he sat thereon; and
Aaron and Hur stayed up his hands, the one on the
one side, and the other on the other side; and his
hands were steady until the going down of the sun.
13And Joshua discomfited Amalek and his people
with the edge of the sword.
14And the LORD said unto Moses, Write this *for* a
memorial in a book, and rehearse *it* in the ears of
Joshua: for I will utterly put out the remembrance of
Amalek from under heaven.
15And Moses built an altar, and called the name of
it Jehovah-nissi:
16For he said, Because the LORD hath sworn *that*
the LORD *will have* war with Amalek from generation
to generation.

18 1When Jethro, the priest of Midian, Moses'
father in law, heard of all that God had done
for Moses, and for Israel his people, *and* that the
LORD had brought Israel out of Egypt;
2Then Jethro, Moses' father in law, took Zipporah,
Moses' wife, after he had sent her back,
3And her two sons; of which the name of the one
was Gershom; for he said, I have been an alien in a
strange land:

NEW LIVING TRANSLATION

4Then Moses cried out to the LORD, "What should
I do with these people? They are ready to stone me!"
5The LORD said to Moses, "Walk out in front of the
people. Take your staff, the one you used when you
struck the water of the Nile, and call some of the elders of Israel to join you. 6I will stand before you on
the rock at Mount Sinai.* Strike the rock, and water
will come gushing out. Then the people will be able
to drink." So Moses struck the rock as he was told,
and water gushed out as the elders looked on.
7Moses named the place Massah (which means
"test") and Meribah (which means "arguing") because the people of Israel argued with Moses and
tested the LORD by saying, "Is the LORD here with us
or not?"

Israel Defeats the Amalekites

8While the people of Israel were still at Rephidim,
the warriors of Amalek attacked them. 9Moses commanded Joshua, "Choose some men to go out and
fight the army of Amalek for us. Tomorrow, I will
stand at the top of the hill, holding the staff of God in
my hand."
10So Joshua did what Moses had commanded and
fought the army of Amalek. Meanwhile, Moses,
Aaron, and Hur climbed to the top of a nearby hill.
11As long as Moses held up the staff in his hand,
the Israelites had the advantage. But whenever he
dropped his hand, the Amalekites gained the advantage. 12Moses' arms soon became so tired he could
no longer hold them up. So Aaron and Hur found
a stone for him to sit on. Then they stood on each
side of Moses, holding up his hands. So his hands
held steady until sunset. 13As a result, Joshua overwhelmed the army of Amalek in battle.
14After the victory, the LORD instructed Moses,
"Write this down on a scroll as a permanent reminder, and read it aloud to Joshua: I will erase the
memory of Amalek from under heaven." 15Moses
built an altar there and named it Yahweh-Nissi
(which means "the LORD is my banner"). 16He said,
"They have raised their fist against the LORD's
throne, so now* the LORD will be at war with Amalek
generation after generation."

Jethro's Visit to Moses

18 Moses' father-in-law, Jethro, the priest of
Midian, heard about everything God had
done for Moses and his people, the Israelites. He
heard especially about how the LORD had rescued
them from Egypt.
2Earlier, Moses had sent his wife, Zipporah, and
his two sons back to Jethro, who had taken them in.
3(Moses' first son was named Gershom,* for Moses
had said when the boy was born, "I have been a

17:6 Hebrew *Horeb,* another name for Sinai. 17:16 Or *Hands have been lifted up to the LORD's throne, and now.* 18:3 *Gershom* sounds like a Hebrew term that means "a foreigner there."

KING JAMES VERSION

4 And the name of the other *was* Eliezer; for the
God of my father, *said he, was* mine help, and delivered me from the sword of Pharaoh:
5 And Jethro, Moses' father in law, came with his
sons and his wife unto Moses into the wilderness,
where he encamped at the mount of God:
6 And he said unto Moses, I thy father in law Jethro
am come unto thee, and thy wife, and her two sons
with her.
7 And Moses went out to meet his father in law, and
did obeisance, and kissed him; and they asked each
other of *their* welfare; and they came into the tent.
8 And Moses told his father in law all that the LORD
had done unto Pharaoh and to the Egyptians for Israel's sake, *and* all the travail that had come upon them
by the way, and *how* the LORD delivered them.
9 And Jethro rejoiced for all the goodness which
the LORD had done to Israel, whom he had delivered
out of the hand of the Egyptians.
10 And Jethro said, Blessed *be* the LORD, who hath
delivered you out of the hand of the Egyptians, and
out of the hand of Pharaoh, who hath delivered the
people from under the hand of the Egyptians.
11 Now I know that the LORD *is* greater than all
gods: for in the thing wherein they dealt proudly *he*
was above them.
12 And Jethro, Moses' father in law, took a burnt offering and sacrifices for God: and Aaron came, and
all the elders of Israel, to eat bread with Moses'
father in law before God.

13 And it came to pass on the morrow, that Moses
sat to judge the people: and the people stood by
Moses from the morning unto the evening.
14 And when Moses' father in law saw all that he
did to the people, he said, What *is* this thing that
thou doest to the people? why sittest thou thyself
alone, and all the people stand by thee from morning
unto even?
15 And Moses said unto his father in law, Because
the people come unto me to inquire of God:
16 When they have a matter, they come unto me;
and I judge between one and another, and I do make
them know the statutes of God, and his laws.
17 And Moses' father in law said unto him, The
thing that thou doest *is* not good.
18 Thou wilt surely wear away, both thou, and this
people that *is* with thee: for this thing *is* too heavy for
thee; thou art not able to perform it thyself alone.
19 Hearken now unto my voice, I will give thee
counsel, and God shall be with thee: Be thou for the
people to God-ward, that thou mayest bring the
causes unto God:
20 And thou shalt teach them ordinances and laws,

NEW LIVING TRANSLATION

foreigner in a foreign land." 4 His second son was
named Eliezer,* for Moses had said, "The God of my
ancestors was my helper; he rescued me from the
sword of Pharaoh.") 5 Jethro, Moses' father-in-law,
now came to visit Moses in the wilderness. He
brought Moses' wife and two sons with him, and
they arrived while Moses and the people were
camped near the mountain of God. 6 Jethro had sent
a message to Moses, saying, "I, Jethro, your father-
in-law, am coming to see you with your wife and
your two sons."
7 So Moses went out to meet his father-in-law. He
bowed low and kissed him. They asked about each
other's welfare and then went into Moses' tent.
8 Moses told his father-in-law everything the LORD
had done to Pharaoh and Egypt on behalf of Israel.
He also told about all the hardships they had experienced along the way and how the LORD had rescued
his people from all their troubles. 9 Jethro was delighted when he heard about all the good things the
LORD had done for Israel as he rescued them from
the hand of the Egyptians.
10 "Praise the LORD," Jethro said, "for he has rescued you from the Egyptians and from Pharaoh. Yes,
he has rescued Israel from the powerful hand of
Egypt! 11 I know now that the LORD is greater than all
other gods, because he rescued his people from the
oppression of the proud Egyptians."
12 Then Jethro, Moses' father-in-law, brought a
burnt offering and sacrifices to God. Aaron and all
the elders of Israel came out and joined him in a
sacrificial meal in God's presence.

Jethro's Wise Advice

13 The next day, Moses took his seat to hear the
people's disputes against each other. They waited
before him from morning till evening.
14 When Moses' father-in-law saw all that Moses
was doing for the people, he asked, "What are you
really accomplishing here? Why are you trying to do
all this alone while everyone stands around you from
morning till evening?"
15 Moses replied, "Because the people come to
me to get a ruling from God. 16 When a dispute
arises, they come to me, and I am the one who settles
the case between the quarreling parties. I inform
the people of God's decrees and give them his
instructions."
17 "This is not good!" Moses' father-in-law exclaimed. 18 "You're going to wear yourself out—and
the people, too. This job is too heavy a burden for you
to handle all by yourself. 19 Now listen to me, and let
me give you a word of advice, and may God be with
you. You should continue to be the people's representative before God, bringing their disputes to him.
20 Teach them God's decrees, and give them his

18:4 *Eliezer* means "God is my helper."

KING JAMES VERSION

and shalt shew them the way wherein they must
walk, and the work that they must do.
21Moreover thou shalt provide out of all the
people able men, such as fear God, men of truth,
hating covetousness; and place *such* over them, *to be*
rulers of thousands, *and* rulers of hundreds, rulers
of fifties, and rulers of tens:
22And let them judge the people at all seasons: and
it shall be, *that* every great matter they shall bring
unto thee, but every small matter they shall judge: so
shall it be easier for thyself, and they shall bear *the*
burden with thee.
23If thou shalt do this thing, and God command
thee *so*, then thou shalt be able to endure, and all this
people shall also go to their place in peace.
24So Moses hearkened to the voice of his father in
law, and did all that he had said.
25And Moses chose able men out of all Israel, and
made them heads over the people, rulers of thousands, rulers of hundreds, rulers of fifties, and rulers
of tens.
26And they judged the people at all seasons: the
hard causes they brought unto Moses, but every
small matter they judged themselves.
27And Moses let his father in law depart; and he
went his way into his own land.

19 1In the third month, when the children of Israel were gone forth out of the land of Egypt,
the same day came they *into* the wilderness of Sinai.
2For they were departed from Rephidim, and were
come *to* the desert of Sinai, and had pitched in the
wilderness; and there Israel camped before the
mount.
3And Moses went up unto God, and the LORD
called unto him out of the mountain, saying, Thus
shalt thou say to the house of Jacob, and tell the children of Israel;
4Ye have seen what I did unto the Egyptians, and
how I bare you on eagles' wings, and brought you
unto myself.
5Now therefore, if ye will obey my voice indeed,
and keep my covenant, then ye shall be a peculiar
treasure unto me above all people: for all the earth
is mine:
6And ye shall be unto me a kingdom of priests, and
an holy nation. These *are* the words which thou shalt
speak unto the children of Israel.
7And Moses came and called for the elders of the
people, and laid before their faces all these words
which the LORD commanded him.
8And all the people answered together, and said,
All that the LORD hath spoken we will do. And Moses
returned the words of the people unto the LORD.
9And the LORD said unto Moses, Lo, I come unto
thee in a thick cloud, that the people may hear when
I speak with thee, and believe thee for ever. And
Moses told the words of the people unto the LORD.

NEW LIVING TRANSLATION

instructions. Show them how to conduct their lives.
21But select from all the people some capable, honest
men who fear God and hate bribes. Appoint them as
leaders over groups of one thousand, one hundred,
fifty, and ten. 22They should always be available to
solve the people's common disputes, but have them
bring the major cases to you. Let the leaders decide
the smaller matters themselves. They will help you
carry the load, making the task easier for you. 23If
you follow this advice, and if God commands you to
do so, then you will be able to endure the pressures,
and all these people will go home in peace."
24Moses listened to his father-in-law's advice and
followed his suggestions. 25He chose capable men
from all over Israel and appointed them as leaders
over the people. He put them in charge of groups of
one thousand, one hundred, fifty, and ten. 26These
men were always available to solve the people's
common disputes. They brought the major cases to
Moses, but they took care of the smaller matters
themselves.
27Soon after this, Moses said good-bye to his
father-in-law, who returned to his own land.

The LORD Reveals Himself at Sinai

19 Exactly two months after the Israelites left
Egypt,* they arrived in the wilderness of Sinai. 2After breaking camp at Rephidim, they came to
the wilderness of Sinai and set up camp there at the
base of Mount Sinai.
3Then Moses climbed the mountain to appear before God. The LORD called to him from the mountain
and said, "Give these instructions to the family of
Jacob; announce it to the descendants of Israel: 4'You
have seen what I did to the Egyptians. You know how
I carried you on eagles' wings and brought you to
myself. 5Now if you will obey me and keep my covenant, you will be my own special treasure from
among all the peoples on earth; for all the earth belongs to me. 6And you will be my kingdom of priests,
my holy nation.' This is the message you must give to
the people of Israel."
7So Moses returned from the mountain and called
together the elders of the people and told them
everything the LORD had commanded him. 8And all
the people responded together, "We will do everything the LORD has commanded." So Moses brought
the people's answer back to the LORD.
9Then the LORD said to Moses, "I will come to you
in a thick cloud, Moses, so the people themselves can
hear me when I speak with you. Then they will always trust you."
Moses told the LORD what the people had said.

19:1 Hebrew *In the third month after the Israelites left Egypt, on the very day*, i.e., two lunar months to the day after leaving Egypt. Compare Num 33:3.

KING JAMES VERSION

10 And the LORD said unto Moses, Go unto the
people, and sanctify them today and tomorrow, and
let them wash their clothes,
11 And be ready against the third day: for the third
day the LORD will come down in the sight of all the
people upon mount Sinai.
12 And thou shalt set bounds unto the people round
about, saying, Take heed to yourselves, *that ye* go *not*
up into the mount, or touch the border of it: whosoever toucheth the mount shall be surely put to death:
13 There shall not an hand touch it, but he shall
surely be stoned, or shot through; whether *it be* beast
or man, it shall not live: when the trumpet soundeth
long, they shall come up to the mount.
14 And Moses went down from the mount unto the
people, and sanctified the people; and they washed
their clothes.
15 And he said unto the people, Be ready against
the third day: come not at *your* wives.
16 And it came to pass on the third day in the morning, that there were thunders and lightnings, and a
thick cloud upon the mount, and the voice of the
trumpet exceeding loud; so that all the people that
was in the camp trembled.
17 And Moses brought forth the people out of the
camp to meet with God; and they stood at the nether
part of the mount.
18 And mount Sinai was altogether on a smoke, because the LORD descended upon it in fire: and the
smoke thereof ascended as the smoke of a furnace,
and the whole mount quaked greatly.
19 And when the voice of the trumpet sounded
long, and waxed louder and louder, Moses spake, and
God answered him by a voice.
20 And the LORD came down upon mount Sinai, on
the top of the mount: and the LORD called Moses
up to the top of the mount; and Moses went up.
21 And the LORD said unto Moses, Go down, charge
the people, lest they break through unto the LORD to
gaze, and many of them perish.
22 And let the priests also, which come near to the
LORD, sanctify themselves, lest the LORD break forth
upon them.
23 And Moses said unto the LORD, The people cannot come up to mount Sinai: for thou chargedst us,
saying, Set bounds about the mount, and sanctify it.
24 And the LORD said unto him, Away, get thee
down, and thou shalt come up, thou, and Aaron with
thee: but let not the priests and the people break
through to come up unto the LORD, lest he break
forth upon them.
25 So Moses went down unto the people, and spake
unto them.

NEW LIVING TRANSLATION

10 Then the LORD told Moses, "Go down and prepare
the people for my arrival. Consecrate them today and
tomorrow, and have them wash their clothing. 11 Be
sure they are ready on the third day, for on that day
the LORD will come down on Mount Sinai as all the
people watch. 12 Mark off a boundary all around the
mountain. Warn the people, 'Be careful! Do not go up
on the mountain or even touch its boundaries. Anyone who touches the mountain will certainly be put
to death. 13 No hand may touch the person or animal
that crosses the boundary; instead, stone them or
shoot them with arrows. They must be put to death.'
However, when the ram's horn sounds a long blast,
then the people may go up on the mountain.*"
14 So Moses went down to the people. He consecrated them for worship, and they washed their
clothes. 15 He told them, "Get ready for the third day,
and until then abstain from having sexual intercourse."
16 On the morning of the third day, thunder roared
and lightning flashed, and a dense cloud came down
on the mountain. There was a long, loud blast from a
ram's horn, and all the people trembled. 17 Moses led
them out from the camp to meet with God, and they
stood at the foot of the mountain. 18 All of Mount Sinai was covered with smoke because the LORD had
descended on it in the form of fire. The smoke billowed into the sky like smoke from a brick kiln, and
the whole mountain shook violently. 19 As the blast
of the ram's horn grew louder and louder, Moses
spoke, and God thundered his reply. 20 The LORD
came down on the top of Mount Sinai and called
Moses to the top of the mountain. So Moses climbed
the mountain.
21 Then the LORD told Moses, "Go back down and
warn the people not to break through the boundaries to see the LORD, or they will die. 22 Even the
priests who regularly come near to the LORD must
purify themselves so that the LORD does not break
out and destroy them."
23 "But LORD," Moses protested, "the people cannot
come up to Mount Sinai. You already warned us. You
told me, 'Mark off a boundary all around the mountain to set it apart as holy.'"
24 But the LORD said, "Go down and bring Aaron
back up with you. In the meantime, do not let the
priests or the people break through to approach the
LORD, or he will break out and destroy them."
25 So Moses went down to the people and told
them what the LORD had said.

19:13 Or *up to the mountain.*

KING JAMES VERSION

20 1 And God spake all these words, saying,
2 I *am* the LORD thy God, which have brought
thee out of the land of Egypt, out of the house of
bondage.
3 Thou shalt have no other gods before me.
4 Thou shalt not make unto thee any graven image,
or any likeness *of any thing* that *is* in heaven above,
or that *is* in the earth beneath, or that *is* in the water
under the earth:
5 Thou shalt not bow down thyself to them, nor
serve them: for I the LORD thy God *am* a jealous God,
visiting the iniquity of the fathers upon the children
unto the third and fourth *generation* of them that
hate me;
6 And shewing mercy unto thousands of them that
love me, and keep my commandments.
7 Thou shalt not take the name of the LORD thy God
in vain; for the LORD will not hold him guiltless that
taketh his name in vain.
8 Remember the sabbath day, to keep it holy.
9 Six days shalt thou labour, and do all thy work:
10 But the seventh day *is* the sabbath of the LORD
thy God: *in it* thou shalt not do any work, thou, nor
thy son, nor thy daughter, thy manservant, nor thy
maidservant, nor thy cattle, nor thy stranger that *is*
within thy gates:
11 For *in* six days the LORD made heaven and earth,
the sea, and all that in them *is,* and rested the seventh
day: wherefore the LORD blessed the sabbath day, and
hallowed it.
12 Honour thy father and thy mother: that thy days
may be long upon the land which the LORD thy God
giveth thee.
13 Thou shalt not kill.
14 Thou shalt not commit adultery.
15 Thou shalt not steal.
16 Thou shalt not bear false witness against thy
neighbour.
17 Thou shalt not covet thy neighbour's house,
thou shalt not covet thy neighbour's wife, nor his
manservant, nor his maidservant, nor his ox, nor his
ass, nor any thing that *is* thy neighbour's.
18 And all the people saw the thunderings, and the
lightnings, and the noise of the trumpet, and the
mountain smoking: and when the people saw *it,* they
removed, and stood afar off.
19 And they said unto Moses, Speak thou with us,
and we will hear: but let not God speak with us, lest
we die.
20 And Moses said unto the people, Fear not: for
God is come to prove you, and that his fear may be
before your faces, that ye sin not.

NEW LIVING TRANSLATION

Ten Commandments for the Covenant Community

20 Then God gave the people all these instructions*:
2 "I am the LORD your God, who rescued you from
the land of Egypt, the place of your slavery.
3 "You must not have any other god but me.
4 "You must not make for yourself an idol of any
kind or an image of anything in the heavens or on
the earth or in the sea. 5 You must not bow down
to them or worship them, for I, the LORD your
God, am a jealous God who will not tolerate your
affection for any other gods. I lay the sins of the
parents upon their children; the entire family is
affected—even children in the third and fourth
generations of those who reject me. 6 But I lavish
unfailing love for a thousand generations on
those* who love me and obey my commands.
7 "You must not misuse the name of the LORD your
God. The LORD will not let you go unpunished if
you misuse his name.
8 "Remember to observe the Sabbath day by keeping
it holy. 9 You have six days each week for your
ordinary work, 10 but the seventh day is a Sabbath
day of rest dedicated to the LORD your God. On
that day no one in your household may do any
work. This includes you, your sons and daughters,
your male and female servants, your livestock,
and any foreigners living among you. 11 For in six
days the LORD made the heavens, the earth, the
sea, and everything in them; but on the seventh
day he rested. That is why the LORD blessed the
Sabbath day and set it apart as holy.
12 "Honor your father and mother. Then you will live
a long, full life in the land the LORD your God is
giving you.
13 "You must not murder.
14 "You must not commit adultery.
15 "You must not steal.
16 "You must not testify falsely against your
neighbor.
17 "You must not covet your neighbor's house.
You must not covet your neighbor's wife, male
or female servant, ox or donkey, or anything else
that belongs to your neighbor."

18 When the people heard the thunder and the
loud blast of the ram's horn, and when they saw the
flashes of lightning and the smoke billowing from
the mountain, they stood at a distance, trembling
with fear.
19 And they said to Moses, "You speak to us, and we
will listen. But don't let God speak directly to us, or
we will die!"
20 "Don't be afraid," Moses answered them, "for
God has come in this way to test you, and so that your
fear of him will keep you from sinning!"

20:1 Hebrew *all these words.* **20:6** Hebrew *for thousands of those.*

KING JAMES VERSION

21 And the people stood afar off, and Moses drew
near unto the thick darkness where God *was*.

22 And the LORD said unto Moses, Thus thou shalt
say unto the children of Israel, Ye have seen that I
have talked with you from heaven.
23 Ye shall not make with me gods of silver, neither
shall ye make unto you gods of gold.
24 An altar of earth thou shalt make unto me, and
shalt sacrifice thereon thy burnt offerings, and thy
peace offerings, thy sheep, and thine oxen: in all
places where I record my name I will come unto thee,
and I will bless thee.
25 And if thou wilt make me an altar of stone, thou
shalt not build it of hewn stone: for if thou lift up thy
tool upon it, thou hast polluted it.
26 Neither shalt thou go up by steps unto mine altar, that thy nakedness be not discovered thereon.

21 1 Now these *are* the judgments which thou
shalt set before them.
2 If thou buy an Hebrew servant, six years he shall
serve: and in the seventh he shall go out free for
nothing.
3 If he came in by himself, he shall go out by himself: if he were married, then his wife shall go out
with him.
4 If his master have given him a wife, and she have
born him sons or daughters; the wife and her children shall be her master's, and he shall go out by
himself.
5 And if the servant shall plainly say, I love my master, my wife, and my children; I will not go out free:
6 Then his master shall bring him unto the judges;
he shall also bring him to the door, or unto the door
post; and his master shall bore his ear through with
an awl; and he shall serve him for ever.
7 And if a man sell his daughter to be a maidservant, she shall not go out as the menservants do.
8 If she please not her master, who hath betrothed
her to himself, then shall he let her be redeemed: to
sell her unto a strange nation he shall have no power,
seeing he hath dealt deceitfully with her.
9 And if he have betrothed her unto his son, he
shall deal with her after the manner of daughters.
10 If he take him another *wife;* her food, her raiment, and her duty of marriage, shall he not diminish.
11 And if he do not these three unto her, then shall
she go out free without money.

12 He that smiteth a man, so that he die, shall be
surely put to death.
13 And if a man lie not in wait, but God deliver *him*

NEW LIVING TRANSLATION

21 As the people stood in the distance, Moses approached the dark cloud where God was.

Proper Use of Altars

22 And the LORD said to Moses, "Say this to the people
of Israel: You saw for yourselves that I spoke to you
from heaven. 23 Remember, you must not make any
idols of silver or gold to rival me.
24 "Build for me an altar made of earth, and offer
your sacrifices to me—your burnt offerings and
peace offerings, your sheep and goats, and your
cattle. Build my altar wherever I cause my name to
be remembered, and I will come to you and bless
you. 25 If you use stones to build my altar, use only
natural, uncut stones. Do not shape the stones with
a tool, for that would make the altar unfit for holy
use. 26 And do not approach my altar by going up
steps. If you do, someone might look up under your
clothing and see your nakedness.

Fair Treatment of Slaves

21 "These are the regulations you must present
to Israel.
2 "If you buy a Hebrew slave, he may serve for no
more than six years. Set him free in the seventh year,
and he will owe you nothing for his freedom. 3 If he
was single when he became your slave, he shall leave
single. But if he was married before he became a
slave, then his wife must be freed with him.
4 "If his master gave him a wife while he was a slave
and they had sons or daughters, then only the man
will be free in the seventh year, but his wife and children will still belong to his master. 5 But the slave may
declare, 'I love my master, my wife, and my children.
I don't want to go free.' 6 If he does this, his master
must present him before God.* Then his master
must take him to the door or doorpost and publicly
pierce his ear with an awl. After that, the slave will
serve his master for life.
7 "When a man sells his daughter as a slave, she
will not be freed at the end of six years as the men
are. 8 If she does not satisfy her owner, he must allow
her to be bought back again. But he is not allowed to
sell her to foreigners, since he is the one who broke
the contract with her. 9 But if the slave's owner arranges for her to marry his son, he may no longer
treat her as a slave but as a daughter.
10 "If a man who has married a slave wife takes another wife for himself, he must not neglect the rights
of the first wife to food, clothing, and sexual intimacy.
11 If he fails in any of these three obligations, she may
leave as a free woman without making any payment.

Cases of Personal Injury

12 "Anyone who assaults and kills another person
must be put to death. 13 But if it was simply an accident permitted by God, I will appoint a place of

21:6 Or *before the judges.*

into his hand; then I will appoint thee a place
whither he shall flee.
[14]But if a man come presumptuously upon his
neighbour, to slay him with guile; thou shalt take him
from mine altar, that he may die.
[15]And he that smiteth his father, or his mother,
shall be surely put to death.
[16]And he that stealeth a man, and selleth him, or if
he be found in his hand, he shall surely be put to
death.
[17]And he that curseth his father, or his mother,
shall surely be put to death.
[18]And if men strive together, and one smite another with a stone, or with *his* fist, and he die not, but
keepeth *his* bed:
[19]If he rise again, and walk abroad upon his staff,
then shall he that smote *him* be quit: only he shall
pay *for* the loss of his time, and shall cause *him* to be
thoroughly healed.
[20]And if a man smite his servant, or his maid, with
a rod, and he die under his hand; he shall be surely
punished.
[21]Notwithstanding, if he continue a day or two, he
shall not be punished: for he *is* his money.
[22]If men strive, and hurt a woman with child, so
that her fruit depart *from her,* and yet no mischief
follow: he shall be surely punished, according as the
woman's husband will lay upon him; and he shall pay
as the judges *determine.*
[23]And if *any* mischief follow, then thou shalt give
life for life,
[24]Eye for eye, tooth for tooth, hand for hand, foot
for foot,
[25]Burning for burning, wound for wound, stripe
for stripe.
[26]And if a man smite the eye of his servant, or the
eye of his maid, that it perish; he shall let him go free
for his eye's sake.
[27]And if he smite out his manservant's tooth, or
his maidservant's tooth; he shall let him go free for
his tooth's sake.
[28]If an ox gore a man or a woman, that they die:
then the ox shall be surely stoned, and his flesh shall
not be eaten; but the owner of the ox *shall be* quit.
[29]But if the ox were wont to push with his horn in
time past, and it hath been testified to his owner, and
he hath not kept him in, but that he hath killed a man
or a woman; the ox shall be stoned, and his owner
also shall be put to death.
[30]If there be laid on him a sum of money, then he
shall give for the ransom of his life whatsoever is laid
upon him.
[31]Whether he have gored a son, or have gored a
daughter, according to this judgment shall it be done
unto him.
[32]If the ox shall push a manservant or a maidservant; he shall give unto their master thirty shekels
of silver, and the ox shall be stoned.

refuge where the slayer can run for safety. [14]How-
ever, if someone deliberately kills another person,
then the slayer must be dragged even from my altar
and be put to death.
[15]"Anyone who strikes father or mother must be
put to death.
[16]"Kidnappers must be put to death, whether they
are caught in possession of their victims or have already sold them as slaves.
[17]"Anyone who dishonors* father or mother must
be put to death.
[18]"Now suppose two men quarrel, and one hits the
other with a stone or fist, and the injured person
does not die but is confined to bed. [19]If he is later
able to walk outside again, even with a crutch, the as-
sailant will not be punished but must compensate
his victim for lost wages and provide for his full
recovery.
[20]"If a man beats his male or female slave with a
club and the slave dies as a result, the owner must be
punished. [21]But if the slave recovers within a day or
two, then the owner shall not be punished, since the
slave is his property.
[22]"Now suppose two men are fighting, and in the
process they accidentally strike a pregnant woman so
she gives birth prematurely.* If no further injury results, the man who struck the woman must pay the
amount of compensation the woman's husband demands and the judges approve. [23]But if there is further injury, the punishment must match the injury:
a life for a life, [24]an eye for an eye, a tooth for a tooth,
a hand for a hand, a foot for a foot, [25]a burn for a burn,
a wound for a wound, a bruise for a bruise.
[26]"If a man hits his male or female slave in the eye
and the eye is blinded, he must let the slave go free to
compensate for the eye. [27]And if a man knocks out
the tooth of his male or female slave, he must let the
slave go free to compensate for the tooth.
[28]"If an ox* gores a man or woman to death, the ox
must be stoned, and its flesh may not be eaten. In
such a case, however, the owner will not be held lia-
ble. [29]But suppose the ox had a reputation for goring, and the owner had been informed but failed to
keep it under control. If the ox then kills someone, it
must be stoned, and the owner must also be put to
death. [30]However, the dead person's relatives may accept payment to compensate for the loss of life. The
owner of the ox may redeem his life by paying whatever is demanded.
[31]"The same regulation applies if the ox gores a
boy or a girl. [32]But if the ox gores a slave, either male
or female, the animal's owner must pay the slave's
owner thirty silver coins,* and the ox must be
stoned.

21:17 Greek version reads *Anyone who speaks disrespectfully of.* Compare Matt 15:4; Mark 7:10. **21:22** Or *so she has a miscarriage;* Hebrew reads *so her children come out.* **21:28** Or *bull,* or *cow;* also in 21:29-36.
21:32 Hebrew *30 shekels of silver,* about 12 ounces or 342 grams in weight.

KING JAMES VERSION

33And if a man shall open a pit, or if a man shall dig
a pit, and not cover it, and an ox or an ass fall therein;
34The owner of the pit shall make *it* good, *and* give
money unto the owner of them; and the dead *beast*
shall be his.
35And if one man's ox hurt another's, that he die;
then they shall sell the live ox, and divide the money
of it; and the dead *ox* also they shall divide.
36Or if it be known that the ox hath used to push in
time past, and his owner hath not kept him in;
he shall surely pay ox for ox; and the dead shall be
his own.

22 1If a man shall steal an ox, or a sheep, and
kill it, or sell it; he shall restore five oxen for
an ox, and four sheep for a sheep.
2If a thief be found breaking up, and be smitten
that he die, *there shall* no blood *be shed* for him.
3If the sun be risen upon him, *there shall be* blood
shed for him; *for* he should make full restitution; if
he have nothing, then he shall be sold for his theft.
4If the theft be certainly found in his hand alive,
whether it be ox, or ass, or sheep; he shall restore
double.
5If a man shall cause a field or vineyard to be
eaten, and shall put in his beast, and shall feed in
another man's field; of the best of his own field,
and of the best of his own vineyard, shall he make
restitution.
6If fire break out, and catch in thorns, so that the
stacks of corn, or the standing corn, or the field, be
consumed *therewith;* he that kindled the fire shall
surely make restitution.
7If a man shall deliver unto his neighbour money
or stuff to keep, and it be stolen out of the man's
house; if the thief be found, let him pay double.
8If the thief be not found, then the master of the
house shall be brought unto the judges, *to see*
whether he have put his hand unto his neighbour's
goods.
9For all manner of trespass, *whether it be* for ox,
for ass, for sheep, for raiment, *or* for any manner of
lost thing, which *another* challengeth to be his, the
cause of both parties shall come before the judges;
and whom the judges shall condemn, he shall pay
double unto his neighbour.
10If a man deliver unto his neighbour an ass, or an
ox, or a sheep, or any beast, to keep; and it die, or be
hurt, or driven away, no man seeing *it:*

NEW LIVING TRANSLATION

33"Suppose someone digs or uncovers a pit and
fails to cover it, and then an ox or a donkey falls into
it. 34The owner of the pit must pay full compensation to the owner of the animal, but then he gets to
keep the dead animal.
35"If someone's ox injures a neighbor's ox and the
injured ox dies, then the two owners must sell the
live ox and divide the price equally between them.
They must also divide the dead animal. 36But if the
ox had a reputation for goring, yet its owner failed to
keep it under control, he must pay full compensation—a live ox for the dead one—but he may keep the
dead ox.

Protection of Property

22 1*"If someone steals an ox* or sheep and
then kills or sells it, the thief must pay back
five oxen for each ox stolen, and four sheep for each
sheep stolen.
2*"If a thief is caught in the act of breaking into a
house and is struck and killed in the process, the person who killed the thief is not guilty of murder. 3But
if it happens in daylight, the one who killed the thief
is guilty of murder.
"A thief who is caught must pay in full for everything he stole. If he cannot pay, he must be sold as a
slave to pay for his theft. 4If someone steals an ox or a
donkey or a sheep and it is found in the thief's possession, then the thief must pay double the value of
the stolen animal.
5"If an animal is grazing in a field or vineyard and
the owner lets it stray into someone else's field to
graze, then the animal's owner must pay compensation from the best of his own grain or grapes.
6"If you are burning thornbushes and the fire gets
out of control and spreads into another person's
field, destroying the sheaves or the uncut grain or
the whole crop, the one who started the fire must pay
for the lost crop.
7"Suppose someone leaves money or goods with a
neighbor for safekeeping, and they are stolen from
the neighbor's house. If the thief is caught, the compensation is double the value of what was stolen.
8But if the thief is not caught, the neighbor must
appear before God,* who will determine if he stole
the property.
9"Suppose there is a dispute between two people
who both claim to own a particular ox, donkey,
sheep, article of clothing, or any lost property. Both
parties must come before God, and the person
whom God declares* guilty must pay double compensation to the other.
10"Now suppose someone leaves a donkey, ox,
sheep, or any other animal with a neighbor for safekeeping, but it dies or is injured or gets away, and no

22:1a Verse 22:1 is numbered 21:37 in Hebrew text. **22:1b** Or *bull,* or *cow;* also in 22:4, 9, 10. **22:2** Verses 22:2-31 are numbered 22:1-30 in Hebrew text. **22:8** Or *before the judges.* **22:9** Or *before the judges, and the person whom the judges declare.*

KING JAMES VERSION

11 *Then* shall an oath of the LORD be between them
both, that he hath not put his hand unto his neighbour's goods; and the owner of it shall accept
thereof, and he shall not make *it* good.
12 And if it be stolen from him, he shall make restitution unto the owner thereof.
13 If it be torn in pieces, *then* let him bring it *for*
witness, *and* he shall not make good that which
was torn.
14 And if a man borrow *aught* of his neighbour, and
it be hurt, or die, the owner thereof *being* not with it,
he shall surely make *it* good.
15 *But* if the owner thereof *be* with it, he shall
not make *it* good: if it *be* an hired *thing*, it came for
his hire.

16 And if a man entice a maid that is not betrothed,
and lie with her, he shall surely endow her to be his
wife.
17 If her father utterly refuse to give her unto him,
he shall pay money according to the dowry of virgins.
18 Thou shalt not suffer a witch to live.
19 Whosoever lieth with a beast shall surely be put
to death.
20 He that sacrificeth unto *any* god, save unto the
LORD only, he shall be utterly destroyed.
21 Thou shalt neither vex a stranger, nor oppress
him: for ye were strangers in the land of Egypt.
22 Ye shall not afflict any widow, or fatherless child.
23 If thou afflict them in any wise, and they cry at
all unto me, I will surely hear their cry;
24 And my wrath shall wax hot, and I will kill you
with the sword; and your wives shall be widows, and
your children fatherless.
25 If thou lend money to *any of* my people *that is*
poor by thee, thou shalt not be to him as an usurer,
neither shalt thou lay upon him usury.
26 If thou at all take thy neighbour's raiment to
pledge, thou shalt deliver it unto him by that the sun
goeth down:
27 For that *is* his covering only, it *is* his raiment for
his skin: wherein shall he sleep? and it shall come to
pass, when he crieth unto me, that I will hear; for I
am gracious.
28 Thou shalt not revile the gods, nor curse the
ruler of thy people.
29 Thou shalt not delay *to offer* the first of thy ripe
fruits, and of thy liquors: the firstborn of thy sons
shalt thou give unto me.
30 Likewise shalt thou do with thine oxen, *and* with
thy sheep: seven days it shall be with his dam; on the
eighth day thou shalt give it me.

NEW LIVING TRANSLATION

one sees what happened. 11 The neighbor must then
take an oath in the presence of the LORD. If the LORD
confirms that the neighbor did not steal the property, the owner must accept the verdict, and no payment will be required. 12 But if the animal was indeed
stolen, the guilty person must pay compensation to
the owner. 13 If it was torn to pieces by a wild animal,
the remains of the carcass must be shown as evidence, and no compensation will be required.
14 "If someone borrows an animal from a neighbor
and it is injured or dies when the owner is absent, the
person who borrowed it must pay full compensation. 15 But if the owner was present, no compensation is required. And no compensation is required if
the animal was rented, for this loss is covered by the
rental fee.

Social Responsibility

16 "If a man seduces a virgin who is not engaged to
anyone and has sex with her, he must pay the customary bride price and marry her. 17 But if her father
refuses to let him marry her, the man must still pay
him an amount equal to the bride price of a virgin.
18 "You must not allow a sorceress to live.
19 "Anyone who has sexual relations with an animal must certainly be put to death.
20 "Anyone who sacrifices to any god other than
the LORD must be destroyed.*
21 "You must not mistreat or oppress foreigners in
any way. Remember, you yourselves were once foreigners in the land of Egypt.
22 "You must not exploit a widow or an orphan. 23 If
you exploit them in any way and they cry out to me,
then I will certainly hear their cry. 24 My anger will
blaze against you, and I will kill you with the sword.
Then your wives will be widows and your children
fatherless.
25 "If you lend money to any of my people who are
in need, do not charge interest as a money lender
would. 26 If you take your neighbor's cloak as security
for a loan, you must return it before sunset. 27 This
coat may be the only blanket your neighbor has. How
can a person sleep without it? If you do not return it
and your neighbor cries out to me for help, then I will
hear, for I am merciful.
28 "You must not dishonor God or curse any of
your rulers.
29 "You must not hold anything back when you
give me offerings from your crops and your wine.
"You must give me your firstborn sons.
30 "You must also give me the firstborn of your
cattle, sheep, and goats. But leave the newborn animal with its mother for seven days; then give it to me
on the eighth day.

22:20 The Hebrew term used here refers to the complete consecration of things or people to the LORD, either by destroying them or by giving them as an offering.

KING JAMES VERSION

31 And ye shall be holy men unto me: neither shall
ye eat *any* flesh *that is* torn of beasts in the field; ye
shall cast it to the dogs.

23 1 Thou shalt not raise a false report: put not
thine hand with the wicked to be an unrighteous witness.
2 Thou shalt not follow a multitude to *do* evil; neither shalt thou speak in a cause to decline after many
to wrest *judgment*:
3 Neither shalt thou countenance a poor man in
his cause.
4 If thou meet thine enemy's ox or his ass going
astray, thou shalt surely bring it back to him again.
5 If thou see the ass of him that hateth thee lying
under his burden, and wouldest forbear to help him,
thou shalt surely help with him.
6 Thou shalt not wrest the judgment of thy poor in
his cause.
7 Keep thee far from a false matter; and the innocent and righteous slay thou not: for I will not justify
the wicked.
8 And thou shalt take no gift: for the gift blindeth
the wise, and perverteth the words of the righteous.
9 Also thou shalt not oppress a stranger: for ye
know the heart of a stranger, seeing ye were strangers in the land of Egypt.
10 And six years thou shalt sow thy land, and shalt
gather in the fruits thereof:
11 But the seventh *year* thou shalt let it rest and lie
still; that the poor of thy people may eat: and what
they leave the beasts of the field shall eat. In like
manner thou shalt deal with thy vineyard, *and* with
thy oliveyard.
12 Six days thou shalt do thy work, and on the seventh day thou shalt rest: that thine ox and thine ass
may rest, and the son of thy handmaid, and the
stranger, may be refreshed.
13 And in all *things* that I have said unto you be cir-
cumspect: and make no mention of the name of
other gods, neither let it be heard out of thy mouth.

14 Three times thou shalt keep a feast unto me in
the year.
15 Thou shalt keep the feast of unleavened bread:
(thou shalt eat unleavened bread seven days, as I
commanded thee, in the time appointed of the
month Abib; for in it thou camest out from Egypt:
and none shall appear before me empty:)

NEW LIVING TRANSLATION

31 "You must be my holy people. Therefore, do not
eat any animal that has been torn up and killed by
wild animals. Throw it to the dogs.

A Call for Justice

23 "You must not pass along false rumors. You
must not cooperate with evil people by
lying on the witness stand.
2 "You must not follow the crowd in doing wrong.
When you are called to testify in a dispute, do not be
swayed by the crowd to twist justice. 3 And do not
slant your testimony in favor of a person just because
that person is poor.
4 "If you come upon your enemy's ox or donkey
that has strayed away, take it back to its owner. 5 If
you see that the donkey of someone who hates you
has collapsed under its load, do not walk by. Instead,
stop and help.
6 "In a lawsuit, you must not deny justice to the
poor.
7 "Be sure never to charge anyone falsely with evil.
Never sentence an innocent or blameless person
to death, for I never declare a guilty person to be
innocent.
8 "Take no bribes, for a bribe makes you ignore
something that you clearly see. A bribe makes even a
righteous person twist the truth.
9 "You must not oppress foreigners. You know
what it's like to be a foreigner, for you yourselves
were once foreigners in the land of Egypt.
10 "Plant and harvest your crops for six years, 11 but
let the land be renewed and lie uncultivated during
the seventh year. Then let the poor among you harvest whatever grows on its own. Leave the rest for
wild animals to eat. The same applies to your vineyards and olive groves.
12 "You have six days each week for your ordinary
work, but on the seventh day you must stop working.
This gives your ox and your donkey a chance to rest.
It also allows your slaves and the foreigners living
among you to be refreshed.
13 "Pay close attention to all my instructions. You
must not call on the name of any other gods. Do not
even speak their names.

Three Annual Festivals

14 "Each year you must celebrate three festivals in my
honor. 15 First, celebrate the Festival of Unleavened
Bread. For seven days the bread you eat must be
made without yeast, just as I commanded you. Celebrate this festival annually at the appointed time in
early spring, in the month of Abib,* for that is the anniversary of your departure from Egypt. No one may
appear before me without an offering.

23:15 Hebrew *appointed time in the month of Abib.* This first month of the ancient Hebrew lunar calendar usually occurs within the months of March and April.

KING JAMES VERSION

16 And the feast of harvest, the firstfruits of thy labours, which thou hast sown in the field: and the feast of ingathering, *which is* in the end of the year, when thou hast gathered in thy labours out of the field.

17 Three times in the year all thy males shall appear before the Lord GOD.

18 Thou shalt not offer the blood of my sacrifice with leavened bread; neither shall the fat of my sacrifice remain until the morning.

19 The first of the firstfruits of thy land thou shalt bring into the house of the LORD thy God. Thou shalt not seethe a kid in his mother's milk.

20 Behold, I send an Angel before thee, to keep thee in the way, and to bring thee into the place which I have prepared.

21 Beware of him, and obey his voice, provoke him not; for he will not pardon your transgressions: for my name *is* in him.

22 But if thou shalt indeed obey his voice, and do all that I speak; then I will be an enemy unto thine enemies, and an adversary unto thine adversaries.

23 For mine Angel shall go before thee, and bring thee in unto the Amorites, and the Hittites, and the Perizzites, and the Canaanites, the Hivites, and the Jebusites: and I will cut them off.

24 Thou shalt not bow down to their gods, nor serve them, nor do after their works: but thou shalt utterly overthrow them, and quite break down their images.

25 And ye shall serve the LORD your God, and he shall bless thy bread, and thy water; and I will take sickness away from the midst of thee.

26 There shall nothing cast their young, nor be barren, in thy land: the number of thy days I will fulfil.

27 I will send my fear before thee, and will destroy all the people to whom thou shalt come, and I will make all thine enemies turn their backs unto thee.

28 And I will send hornets before thee, which shall drive out the Hivite, the Canaanite, and the Hittite, from before thee.

29 I will not drive them out from before thee in one year; lest the land become desolate, and the beast of the field multiply against thee.

30 By little and little I will drive them out from before thee, until thou be increased, and inherit the land.

31 And I will set thy bounds from the Red sea even unto the sea of the Philistines, and from the desert unto the river: for I will deliver the inhabitants of the land into your hand; and thou shalt drive them out before thee.

NEW LIVING TRANSLATION

16 "Second, celebrate the Festival of Harvest,*
when you bring me the first crops of your harvest.
"Finally, celebrate the Festival of the Final Harvest* at the end of the harvest season, when you have
harvested all the crops from your fields. 17 At these
three times each year, every man in Israel must appear before the Sovereign, the LORD.

18 "You must not offer the blood of my sacrificial offerings together with any baked goods containing yeast. And do not leave the fat from the festival offerings until the next morning.

19 "As you harvest your crops, bring the very best of the first harvest to the house of the LORD your God.
"You must not cook a young goat in its mother's milk.

A Promise of the LORD's Presence

20 "See, I am sending an angel before you to protect
you on your journey and lead you safely to the place I
have prepared for you. 21 Pay close attention to him,
and obey his instructions. Do not rebel against him,
for he is my representative, and he will not forgive
your rebellion. 22 But if you are careful to obey him,
following all my instructions, then I will be an enemy
to your enemies, and I will oppose those who oppose
you. 23 For my angel will go before you and bring you
into the land of the Amorites, Hittites, Perizzites, Canaanites, Hivites, and Jebusites, so you may live there.
And I will destroy them completely. 24 You must not
worship the gods of these nations or serve them in
any way or imitate their evil practices. Instead, you
must utterly destroy them and smash their sacred
pillars.

25 "You must serve only the LORD your God. If you
do, I* will bless you with food and water, and I will
protect you from illness. 26 There will be no mis-
carriages or infertility in your land, and I will give you
long, full lives.

27 "I will send my terror ahead of you and create
panic among all the people whose lands you invade. I
will make all your enemies turn and run. 28 I will send
terror* ahead of you to drive out the Hivites, Canaanites, and Hittites. 29 But I will not drive them out in a
single year, because the land would become desolate
and the wild animals would multiply and threaten
you. 30 I will drive them out a little at a time until your
population has increased enough to take possession
of the land. 31 And I will fix your boundaries from
the Red Sea to the Mediterranean Sea,* and from
the eastern wilderness to the Euphrates River.* I will
hand over to you the people now living in the land,
and you will drive them out ahead of you.

23:16a Or *Festival of Weeks*. This was later called the Festival of Pentecost (see Acts 2:1). It is celebrated today as Shavuot (or Shabuoth). **23:16b** Or *Festival of Ingathering*. This was later called the Festival of Shelters or Festival of Tabernacles (see Lev 23:33-36). It is celebrated today as Sukkot (or Succoth). **23:25** As in Greek and Latin versions; Hebrew reads *he*.
23:28 Often rendered *the hornet*. The meaning of the Hebrew is uncertain.
23:31a Hebrew *from the sea of reeds to the sea of the Philistines*.
23:31b Hebrew *from the wilderness to the river*.

KING JAMES VERSION

32 Thou shalt make no covenant with them, nor with their gods.

33 They shall not dwell in thy land, lest they make thee sin against me: for if thou serve their gods, it will surely be a snare unto thee.

24 1 And he said unto Moses, Come up unto the LORD, thou, and Aaron, Nadab, and Abihu, and seventy of the elders of Israel; and worship ye afar off.

2 And Moses alone shall come near the LORD: but they shall not come nigh; neither shall the people go up with him.

3 And Moses came and told the people all the words of the LORD, and all the judgments: and all the people answered with one voice, and said, All the words which the LORD hath said will we do.

4 And Moses wrote all the words of the LORD, and rose up early in the morning, and builded an altar under the hill, and twelve pillars, according to the twelve tribes of Israel.

5 And he sent young men of the children of Israel, which offered burnt offerings, and sacrificed peace offerings of oxen unto the LORD.

6 And Moses took half of the blood, and put *it* in basins; and half of the blood he sprinkled on the altar.

7 And he took the book of the covenant, and read in the audience of the people: and they said, All that the LORD hath said will we do, and be obedient.

8 And Moses took the blood, and sprinkled *it* on the people, and said, Behold the blood of the covenant, which the LORD hath made with you concerning all these words.

9 Then went up Moses, and Aaron, Nadab, and Abihu, and seventy of the elders of Israel:

10 And they saw the God of Israel: and *there was* under his feet as it were a paved work of a sapphire stone, and as it were the body of heaven in *his* clearness.

11 And upon the nobles of the children of Israel he laid not his hand: also they saw God, and did eat and drink.

12 And the LORD said unto Moses, Come up to me into the mount, and be there: and I will give thee tables of stone, and a law, and commandments which I have written; that thou mayest teach them.

13 And Moses rose up, and his minister Joshua: and Moses went up into the mount of God.

14 And he said unto the elders, Tarry ye here for us, until we come again unto you: and, behold, Aaron and Hur *are* with you: if any man have any matters to do, let him come unto them.

15 And Moses went up into the mount, and a cloud covered the mount.

16 And the glory of the LORD abode upon mount Sinai, and the cloud covered it six days: and the

NEW LIVING TRANSLATION

32 "Make no treaties with them or their gods. 33 They must not live in your land, or they will cause you to sin against me. If you serve their gods, you will be caught in the trap of idolatry."

Israel Accepts the LORD's Covenant

24 Then the LORD instructed Moses: "Come up here to me, and bring along Aaron, Nadab, Abihu, and seventy of Israel's elders. All of you must worship from a distance. 2 Only Moses is allowed to come near to the LORD. The others must not come near, and none of the other people are allowed to climb up the mountain with him."

3 Then Moses went down to the people and repeated all the instructions and regulations the LORD had given him. All the people answered with one voice, "We will do everything the LORD has commanded."

4 Then Moses carefully wrote down all the LORD's instructions. Early the next morning Moses got up and built an altar at the foot of the mountain. He also set up twelve pillars, one for each of the twelve tribes of Israel. 5 Then he sent some of the young Israelite men to present burnt offerings and to sacrifice bulls as peace offerings to the LORD. 6 Moses drained half the blood from these animals into basins. The other half he splattered against the altar.

7 Then he took the Book of the Covenant and read it aloud to the people. Again they all responded, "We will do everything the LORD has commanded. We will obey."

8 Then Moses took the blood from the basins and splattered it over the people, declaring, "Look, this blood confirms the covenant the LORD has made with you in giving you these instructions."

9 Then Moses, Aaron, Nadab, Abihu, and the seventy elders of Israel climbed up the mountain. 10 There they saw the God of Israel. Under his feet there seemed to be a surface of brilliant blue lapis lazuli, as clear as the sky itself. 11 And though these nobles of Israel gazed upon God, he did not destroy them. In fact, they ate a covenant meal, eating and drinking in his presence!

12 Then the LORD said to Moses, "Come up to me on the mountain. Stay there, and I will give you the tablets of stone on which I have inscribed the instructions and commands so you can teach the people." 13 So Moses and his assistant Joshua set out, and Moses climbed up the mountain of God.

14 Moses told the elders, "Stay here and wait for us until we come back. Aaron and Hur are here with you. If anyone has a dispute while I am gone, consult with them."

15 Then Moses climbed up the mountain, and the cloud covered it. 16 And the glory of the LORD settled down on Mount Sinai, and the cloud covered it for six days. On the seventh day the LORD called to

KING JAMES VERSION

seventh day he called unto Moses out of the midst of the cloud.

17 And the sight of the glory of the LORD *was* like devouring fire on the top of the mount in the eyes of the children of Israel.

18 And Moses went into the midst of the cloud, and gat him up into the mount: and Moses was in the mount forty days and forty nights.

25 1 And the LORD spake unto Moses, saying, 2 Speak unto the children of Israel, that they bring me an offering: of every man that giveth it willingly with his heart ye shall take my offering.

3 And this *is* the offering which ye shall take of them; gold, and silver, and brass,

4 And blue, and purple, and scarlet, and fine linen, and goats' *hair*,

5 And rams' skins dyed red, and badgers' skins, and shittim wood,

6 Oil for the light, spices for anointing oil, and for sweet incense,

7 Onyx stones, and stones to be set in the ephod, and in the breastplate.

8 And let them make me a sanctuary; that I may dwell among them.

9 According to all that I shew thee, *after* the pattern of the tabernacle, and the pattern of all the instruments thereof, even so shall ye make *it*.

10 And they shall make an ark *of* shittim wood: two cubits and a half *shall be* the length thereof, and a cubit and a half the breadth thereof, and a cubit and a half the height thereof.

11 And thou shalt overlay it with pure gold, within and without shalt thou overlay it, and shalt make upon it a crown of gold round about.

12 And thou shalt cast four rings of gold for it, and put *them* in the four corners thereof; and two rings *shall be* in the one side of it, and two rings in the other side of it.

13 And thou shalt make staves *of* shittim wood, and overlay them with gold.

14 And thou shalt put the staves into the rings by the sides of the ark, that the ark may be borne with them.

15 The staves shall be in the rings of the ark: they shall not be taken from it.

16 And thou shalt put into the ark the testimony which I shall give thee.

17 And thou shalt make a mercy seat *of* pure gold: two cubits and a half *shall be* the length thereof, and a cubit and a half the breadth thereof.

18 And thou shalt make two cherubims *of* gold, *of* beaten work shalt thou make them, in the two ends of the mercy seat.

NEW LIVING TRANSLATION

Moses from inside the cloud. 17 To the Israelites at the foot of the mountain, the glory of the LORD appeared at the summit like a consuming fire. 18 Then Moses disappeared into the cloud as he climbed higher up the mountain. He remained on the mountain forty days and forty nights.

Offerings for the Tabernacle

25 The LORD said to Moses, 2 "Tell the people of Israel to bring me their sacred offerings. Accept the contributions from all whose hearts are moved to offer them. 3 Here is a list of sacred offerings you may accept from them:

gold, silver, and bronze;
4 blue, purple, and scarlet thread;
fine linen and goat hair for cloth;
5 tanned ram skins and fine goatskin leather;
acacia wood;
6 olive oil for the lamps;
spices for the anointing oil and the fragrant incense;
7 onyx stones, and other gemstones to be set in the ephod and the priest's chestpiece.

8 "Have the people of Israel build me a holy sanctuary so I can live among them. 9 You must build this Tabernacle and its furnishings exactly according to the pattern I will show you.

Plans for the Ark of the Covenant

10 "Have the people make an Ark of acacia wood—a sacred chest 45 inches long, 27 inches wide, and 27 inches high.* 11 Overlay it inside and outside with pure gold, and run a molding of gold all around it. 12 Cast four gold rings and attach them to its four feet, two rings on each side. 13 Make poles from acacia wood, and overlay them with gold. 14 Insert the poles into the rings at the sides of the Ark to carry it. 15 These carrying poles must stay inside the rings; never remove them. 16 When the Ark is finished, place inside it the stone tablets inscribed with the terms of the covenant,* which I will give to you.

17 "Then make the Ark's cover—the place of atonement—from pure gold. It must be 45 inches long and 27 inches wide.* 18 Then make two cherubim from hammered gold, and place them on the two ends of

25:10 Hebrew *2.5 cubits* [115 centimeters] *long, 1.5 cubits* [69 centimeters] *wide, and 1.5 cubits high.* **25:16** Hebrew *Place inside the Ark the Testimony;* similarly in 25:21. The Hebrew word for "testimony" refers to the terms of the LORD's covenant with Israel as written on stone tablets, and also to the covenant itself. **25:17** Hebrew *2.5 cubits* [115 centimeters] *long and 1.5 cubits* [69 centimeters] *wide.*

KING JAMES VERSION

19 And make one cherub on the one end, and the other cherub on the other end: *even* of the mercy seat shall ye make the cherubims on the two ends thereof.

20 And the cherubims shall stretch forth *their* wings on high, covering the mercy seat with their wings, and their faces *shall look* one to another; toward the mercy seat shall the faces of the cherubims be.

21 And thou shalt put the mercy seat above upon the ark; and in the ark thou shalt put the testimony that I shall give thee.

22 And there I will meet with thee, and I will commune with thee from above the mercy seat, from between the two cherubims which *are* upon the ark of the testimony, of all *things* which I will give thee in commandment unto the children of Israel.

23 Thou shalt also make a table *of* shittim wood: two cubits *shall be* the length thereof, and a cubit the breadth thereof, and a cubit and a half the height thereof.

24 And thou shalt overlay it with pure gold, and make thereto a crown of gold round about.

25 And thou shalt make unto it a border of an hand breadth round about, and thou shalt make a golden crown to the border thereof round about.

26 And thou shalt make for it four rings of gold, and put the rings in the four corners that *are* on the four feet thereof.

27 Over against the border shall the rings be for places of the staves to bear the table.

28 And thou shalt make the staves *of* shittim wood, and overlay them with gold, that the table may be borne with them.

29 And thou shalt make the dishes thereof, and spoons thereof, and covers thereof, and bowls thereof, to cover withal: *of* pure gold shalt thou make them.

30 And thou shalt set upon the table shewbread before me alway.

31 And thou shalt make a candlestick *of* pure gold: *of* beaten work shall the candlestick be made: his shaft, and his branches, his bowls, his knops, and his flowers, shall be of the same.

32 And six branches shall come out of the sides of it; three branches of the candlestick out of the one side, and three branches of the candlestick out of the other side:

33 Three bowls made like unto almonds, *with* a knop and a flower in one branch; and three bowls made like almonds in the other branch, *with* a knop and a flower: so in the six branches that come out of the candlestick.

34 And in the candlestick *shall be* four bowls made like unto almonds, *with* their knops and their flowers.

35 And *there shall be* a knop under two branches of the same, and a knop under two branches of the

NEW LIVING TRANSLATION

the atonement cover.
19 Mold the cherubim on each end of the atonement cover, making it all of one piece of gold.
20 The cherubim will face each other and look down on the atonement cover. With their wings spread above it, they will protect it.
21 Place inside the Ark the stone tablets inscribed with the terms of the covenant, which I will give to you. Then put the atonement cover on top of the Ark.
22 I will meet with you there and talk to you from above the atonement cover between the gold cherubim that hover over the Ark of the Covenant.* From there I will give you my commands for the people of Israel.

Plans for the Table

23 "Then make a table of acacia wood, 36 inches long, 18 inches wide, and 27 inches high.*
24 Overlay it with pure gold and run a gold molding around the edge.
25 Decorate it with a 3-inch border* all around, and run a gold molding along the border.
26 Make four gold rings for the table and attach them at the four corners next to the four legs.
27 Attach the rings near the border to hold the poles that are used to carry the table.
28 Make these poles from acacia wood, and overlay them with gold.
29 Make special containers of pure gold for the table—bowls, pans, pitchers, and jars—to be used in pouring out liquid offerings.
30 Place the Bread of the Presence on the table to remain before me at all times.

Plans for the Lampstand

31 "Make a lampstand of pure, hammered gold. Make the entire lampstand and its decorations of one piece—the base, center stem, lamp cups, buds, and petals.
32 Make it with six branches going out from the center stem, three on each side.
33 Each of the six branches will have three lamp cups shaped like almond blossoms, complete with buds and petals.
34 Craft the center stem of the lampstand with four lamp cups shaped like almond blossoms, complete with buds and petals.
35 There will also be an almond

25:22 Or *Ark of the Testimony.* **25:23** Hebrew *2 cubits* [92 centimeters] *long, 1 cubit* [46 centimeters] *wide, and 1.5 cubits* [69 centimeters] *high.* **25:25** Hebrew *a border of a handbreadth* [8 centimeters].

KING JAMES VERSION

same, and a knop under two branches of the same, according to the six branches that proceed out of the candlestick.

36 Their knops and their branches shall be of the same: all it *shall be* one beaten work *of* pure gold.

37 And thou shalt make the seven lamps thereof: and they shall light the lamps thereof, that they may give light over against it.

38 And the tongs thereof, and the snuffdishes thereof, *shall be of* pure gold.

39 *Of* a talent of pure gold shall he make it, with all these vessels.

40 And look that thou make *them* after their pattern, which was shewed thee in the mount.

26 1 Moreover thou shalt make the tabernacle *with* ten curtains *of* fine twined linen, and blue, and purple, and scarlet: *with* cherubims of cunning work shalt thou make them.

2 The length of one curtain *shall be* eight and twenty cubits, and the breadth of one curtain four cubits: and every one of the curtains shall have one measure.

3 The five curtains shall be coupled together one to another; and *other* five curtains *shall be* coupled one to another.

4 And thou shalt make loops of blue upon the edge of the one curtain from the selvedge in the coupling; and likewise shalt thou make in the uttermost edge of *another* curtain, in the coupling of the second.

5 Fifty loops shalt thou make in the one curtain, and fifty loops shalt thou make in the edge of the curtain that *is* in the coupling of the second; that the loops may take hold one of another.

6 And thou shalt make fifty taches of gold, and couple the curtains together with the taches: and it shall be one tabernacle.

7 And thou shalt make curtains *of* goats' *hair* to be a covering upon the tabernacle: eleven curtains shalt thou make.

8 The length of one curtain *shall be* thirty cubits, and the breadth of one curtain four cubits: and the eleven curtains *shall be all* of one measure.

9 And thou shalt couple five curtains by themselves, and six curtains by themselves, and shalt double the sixth curtain in the forefront of the tabernacle.

10 And thou shalt make fifty loops on the edge of the one curtain *that is* outmost in the coupling, and fifty loops in the edge of the curtain which coupleth the second.

11 And thou shalt make fifty taches of brass, and put the taches into the loops, and couple the tent together, that it may be one.

12 And the remnant that remaineth of the curtains of the tent, the half curtain that remaineth, shall hang over the backside of the tabernacle.

NEW LIVING TRANSLATION

bud beneath each pair of branches where the six
branches extend from the center stem. 36 The almond buds and branches must all be of one piece
with the center stem, and they must be hammered
from pure gold. 37 Then make the seven lamps for
the lampstand, and set them so they reflect their
light forward. 38 The lamp snuffers and trays must
also be made of pure gold. 39 You will need seventy-
five pounds* of pure gold for the lampstand and its
accessories.

40 "Be sure that you make everything according to
the pattern I have shown you here on the mountain.

Plans for the Tabernacle

26 "Make the Tabernacle from ten curtains of
finely woven linen. Decorate the curtains
with blue, purple, and scarlet thread and with skillfully embroidered cherubim. 2 These ten curtains
must all be exactly the same size—42 feet long and
6 feet wide.* 3 Join five of these curtains together to
make one long curtain, then join the other five into a
second long curtain. 4 Put loops of blue yarn along
the edge of the last curtain in each set. 5 The fifty
loops along the edge of one curtain are to match the
fifty loops along the edge of the other curtain. 6 Then
make fifty gold clasps and fasten the long curtains
together with the clasps. In this way, the Tabernacle
will be made of one continuous piece.

7 "Make eleven curtains of goat-hair cloth to serve
as a tent covering for the Tabernacle. 8 These eleven
curtains must all be exactly the same size—45 feet
long and 6 feet wide.* 9 Join five of these curtains together to make one long curtain, and join the other
six into a second long curtain. Allow 3 feet of material from the second set of curtains to hang over
the front* of the sacred tent. 10 Make fifty loops for
one edge of each large curtain. 11 Then make fifty
bronze clasps, and fasten the loops of the long curtains with the clasps. In this way, the tent covering
will be made of one continuous piece. 12 The remaining 3 feet* of this tent covering will be left to hang

25:39 Hebrew *1 talent* [34 kilograms]. **26:2** Hebrew *28 cubits* [12.9 meters] *long and 4 cubits* [1.8 meters] *wide.* **26:8** Hebrew *30 cubits* [13.8 meters] *long and 4 cubits* [1.8 meters] *wide.* **26:9** Hebrew *Double over the sixth sheet at the front.* **26:12** Hebrew *The half sheet that is left over.*

KING JAMES VERSION

13 And a cubit on the one side, and a cubit on the other side of that which remaineth in the length of the curtains of the tent, it shall hang over the sides of the tabernacle on this side and on that side, to cover it.

14 And thou shalt make a covering for the tent *of* rams' skins dyed red, and a covering above *of* badgers' skins.

15 And thou shalt make boards for the tabernacle *of* shittim wood standing up.

16 Ten cubits *shall be* the length of a board, and a cubit and a half *shall be* the breadth of one board.

17 Two tenons *shall there be* in one board, set in order one against another: thus shalt thou make for all the boards of the tabernacle.

18 And thou shalt make the boards for the tabernacle, twenty boards on the south side southward.

19 And thou shalt make forty sockets of silver under the twenty boards; two sockets under one board for his two tenons, and two sockets under another board for his two tenons.

20 And for the second side of the tabernacle on the north side *there shall be* twenty boards:

21 And their forty sockets *of* silver; two sockets under one board, and two sockets under another board.

22 And for the sides of the tabernacle westward thou shalt make six boards.

23 And two boards shalt thou make for the corners of the tabernacle in the two sides.

24 And they shall be coupled together beneath, and they shall be coupled together above the head of it unto one ring: thus shall it be for them both; they shall be for the two corners.

25 And they shall be eight boards, and their sockets *of* silver, sixteen sockets; two sockets under one board, and two sockets under another board.

26 And thou shalt make bars *of* shittim wood; five for the boards of the one side of the tabernacle,

27 And five bars for the boards of the other side of the tabernacle, and five bars for the boards of the side of the tabernacle, for the two sides westward.

28 And the middle bar in the midst of the boards shall reach from end to end.

29 And thou shalt overlay the boards with gold, and make their rings *of* gold *for* places for the bars: and thou shalt overlay the bars with gold.

30 And thou shalt rear up the tabernacle according to the fashion thereof which was shewed thee in the mount.

31 And thou shalt make a veil *of* blue, and purple, and scarlet, and fine twined linen of cunning work: with cherubims shall it be made:

32 And thou shalt hang it upon four pillars of shittim *wood* overlaid with gold: their hooks *shall be of* gold, upon the four sockets of silver.

33 And thou shalt hang up the veil under the taches, that thou mayest bring in thither within the veil the

NEW LIVING TRANSLATION

over the back of the Tabernacle. 13 Allow 18 inches*
of remaining material to hang down over each side,
so the Tabernacle is completely covered. 14 Complete
the tent covering with a protective layer of tanned
ram skins and a layer of fine goatskin leather.

15 "For the framework of the Tabernacle, construct
frames of acacia wood. 16 Each frame must be 15 feet
high and 27 inches wide,* 17 with two pegs under
each frame. Make all the frames identical. 18 Make
twenty of these frames to support the curtains on the
south side of the Tabernacle. 19 Also make forty silver
bases—two bases under each frame, with the pegs
fitting securely into the bases. 20 For the north side of
the Tabernacle, make another twenty frames, 21 with
their forty silver bases, two bases under each frame.
22 Make six frames for the rear—the west side of the
Tabernacle—23 along with two additional frames to
reinforce the rear corners of the Tabernacle. 24 These
corner frames will be matched at the bottom and
firmly attached at the top with a single ring, forming
a single corner unit. Make both of these corner units
the same way. 25 So there will be eight frames at the
rear of the Tabernacle, set in sixteen silver bases—
two bases under each frame.

26 "Make crossbars of acacia wood to link the
frames, five crossbars for the north side of the Tabernacle 27 and five for the south side. Also make five
crossbars for the rear of the Tabernacle, which will
face west. 28 The middle crossbar, attached halfway
up the frames, will run all the way from one end of
the Tabernacle to the other. 29 Overlay the frames
with gold, and make gold rings to hold the crossbars.
Overlay the crossbars with gold as well.

30 "Set up this Tabernacle according to the pattern
you were shown on the mountain.

31 "For the inside of the Tabernacle, make a special
curtain of finely woven linen. Decorate it with blue,
purple, and scarlet thread and with skillfully embroidered cherubim. 32 Hang this curtain on gold
hooks attached to four posts of acacia wood. Overlay
the posts with gold, and set them in four silver bases.
33 Hang the inner curtain from clasps, and put the
Ark of the Covenant* in the room behind it. This

26:13 Hebrew *1 cubit* [46 centimeters]. **26:16** Hebrew *10 cubits* [4.6 meters] *high and 1.5 cubits* [69 centimeters] *wide.* **26:33** Or *Ark of the Testimony;* also in 26:34.

KING JAMES VERSION

ark of the testimony: and the veil shall divide unto you between the holy *place* and the most holy.

34 And thou shalt put the mercy seat upon the ark of the testimony in the most holy *place*.

35 And thou shalt set the table without the veil, and the candlestick over against the table on the side of the tabernacle toward the south: and thou shalt put the table on the north side.

36 And thou shalt make an hanging for the door of the tent, *of* blue, and purple, and scarlet, and fine twined linen, wrought with needlework.

37 And thou shalt make for the hanging five pillars *of* shittim *wood,* and overlay them with gold, *and* their hooks *shall be of* gold: and thou shalt cast five sockets of brass for them.

27 1 And thou shalt make an altar *of* shittim wood, five cubits long, and five cubits broad; the altar shall be foursquare: and the height thereof *shall be* three cubits.

2 And thou shalt make the horns of it upon the four corners thereof: his horns shall be of the same: and thou shalt overlay it with brass.

3 And thou shalt make his pans to receive his ashes, and his shovels, and his basins, and his fleshhooks, and his firepans: all the vessels thereof thou shalt make *of* brass.

4 And thou shalt make for it a grate of network *of* brass; and upon the net shalt thou make four brasen rings in the four corners thereof.

5 And thou shalt put it under the compass of the altar beneath, that the net may be even to the midst of the altar.

6 And thou shalt make staves for the altar, staves *of* shittim wood, and overlay them with brass.

7 And the staves shall be put into the rings, and the staves shall be upon the two sides of the altar, to bear it.

8 Hollow with boards shalt thou make it: as it was shewed thee in the mount, so shall they make *it*.

9 And thou shalt make the court of the tabernacle: for the south side southward *there shall be* hangings for the court *of* fine twined linen of an hundred cubits long for one side:

10 And the twenty pillars thereof and their twenty sockets *shall be of* brass; the hooks of the pillars and their fillets *shall be of* silver.

11 And likewise for the north side in length *there shall be* hangings of an hundred *cubits* long, and his twenty pillars and their twenty sockets *of* brass; the hooks of the pillars and their fillets *of* silver.

12 And *for* the breadth of the court on the west side *shall be* hangings of fifty cubits: their pillars ten, and their sockets ten.

13 And the breadth of the court on the east side eastward *shall be* fifty cubits.

14 The hangings of one side *of the gate shall be* fifteen cubits: their pillars three, and their sockets three.

NEW LIVING TRANSLATION

curtain will separate the Holy Place from the Most
Holy Place.
34 "Then put the Ark's cover—the place of atonement—on top of the Ark of the Covenant inside the
Most Holy Place.
35 Place the table outside the inner
curtain on the north side of the Tabernacle, and place
the lampstand across the room on the south side.
36 "Make another curtain for the entrance to the
sacred tent. Make it of finely woven linen and embroider it with exquisite designs, using blue, purple,
and scarlet thread.
37 Craft five posts from acacia
wood. Overlay them with gold, and hang the curtain
from them with gold hooks. Cast five bronze bases
for the posts.

Plans for the Altar of Burnt Offering

27 "Using acacia wood, construct a square altar 7½ feet wide, 7½ feet long, and 4½ feet
high.*
2 Make horns for each of its four corners so
that the horns and altar are all one piece. Overlay the
altar with bronze.
3 Make ash buckets, shovels, ba-
sins, meat forks, and firepans, all of bronze.
4 Make a
bronze grating for it, and attach four bronze rings at
its four corners.
5 Install the grating halfway down
the side of the altar, under the ledge.
6 For carrying
the altar, make poles from acacia wood, and overlay
them with bronze.
7 Insert the poles through the
rings on the two sides of the altar.
8 The altar must be
hollow, made from planks. Build it just as you were
shown on the mountain.

Plans for the Courtyard

9 "Then make the courtyard for the Tabernacle, enclosed with curtains made of finely woven linen. On
the south side, make the curtains 150 feet long.*
10 They will be held up by twenty posts set securely in
twenty bronze bases. Hang the curtains with silver
hooks and rings.
11 Make the curtains the same on
the north side—150 feet of curtains held up by
twenty posts set securely in bronze bases. Hang the
curtains with silver hooks and rings.
12 The curtains
on the west end of the courtyard will be 75 feet
long,* supported by ten posts set into ten bases.
13 The east end of the courtyard, the front, will also be
75 feet long.
14 The courtyard entrance will be on the
east end, flanked by two curtains. The curtain on the
right side will be 22½ feet long,* supported by three

27:1 Hebrew *5 cubits* [2.3 meters] *wide, 5 cubits long, a square, and 3 cubits* [1.4 meters] *high.* **27:9** Hebrew *100 cubits* [46 meters]; also in 27:11. **27:12** Hebrew *50 cubits* [23 meters]; also in 27:13. **27:14** Hebrew *15 cubits* [6.9 meters]; also in 27:15.

KING JAMES VERSION

15 And on the other side *shall be* hangings fifteen *cubits:* their pillars three, and their sockets three.

16 And for the gate of the court *shall be* an hanging of twenty cubits, *of* blue, and purple, and scarlet, and fine twined linen, wrought with needlework: *and* their pillars *shall be* four, and their sockets four.

17 All the pillars round about the court *shall be* filleted with silver; their hooks *shall be of* silver, and their sockets *of* brass.

18 The length of the court *shall be* an hundred cubits, and the breadth fifty every where, and the height five cubits *of* fine twined linen, and their sockets *of* brass.

19 All the vessels of the tabernacle in all the service thereof, and all the pins thereof, and all the pins of the court, *shall be of* brass.

20 And thou shalt command the children of Israel, that they bring thee pure oil olive beaten for the light, to cause the lamp to burn always.

21 In the tabernacle of the congregation without the veil, which *is* before the testimony, Aaron and his sons shall order it from evening to morning before the LORD: *it shall be* a statute for ever unto their generations on the behalf of the children of Israel.

28 1 And take thou unto thee Aaron thy brother, and his sons with him, from among the children of Israel, that he may minister unto me in the priest's office, *even* Aaron, Nadab and Abihu, Eleazar and Ithamar, Aaron's sons.

2 And thou shalt make holy garments for Aaron thy brother for glory and for beauty.

3 And thou shalt speak unto all *that are* wise hearted, whom I have filled with the spirit of wisdom, that they may make Aaron's garments to consecrate him, that he may minister unto me in the priest's office.

4 And these *are* the garments which they shall make; a breastplate, and an ephod, and a robe, and a broidered coat, a mitre, and a girdle: and they shall make holy garments for Aaron thy brother, and his sons, that he may minister unto me in the priest's office.

5 And they shall take gold, and blue, and purple, and scarlet, and fine linen.

6 And they shall make the ephod *of* gold, *of* blue, and *of* purple, *of* scarlet, and fine twined linen, with cunning work.

7 It shall have the two shoulder pieces thereof joined at the two edges thereof; and *so* it shall be joined together.

8 And the curious girdle of the ephod, which *is* upon it, shall be of the same, according to the work

NEW LIVING TRANSLATION

posts set into three bases. 15 The curtain on the left side will also be 22½ feet long, supported by three posts set into three bases.

16 "For the entrance to the courtyard, make a curtain that is 30 feet long.* Make it from finely woven linen, and decorate it with beautiful embroidery in blue, purple, and scarlet thread. Support it with four posts, each securely set in its own base. 17 All the posts around the courtyard must have silver rings and hooks and bronze bases. 18 So the entire courtyard will be 150 feet long and 75 feet wide, with curtain walls 7½ feet high,* made from finely woven linen. The bases for the posts will be made of bronze.

19 "All the articles used in the rituals of the Tabernacle, including all the tent pegs used to support the Tabernacle and the courtyard curtains, must be made of bronze.

Light for the Tabernacle

20 "Command the people of Israel to bring you pure oil of pressed olives for the light, to keep the lamps burning continually. 21 The lampstand will stand in the Tabernacle, in front of the inner curtain that shields the Ark of the Covenant.* Aaron and his sons must keep the lamps burning in the LORD's presence all night. This is a permanent law for the people of Israel, and it must be observed from generation to generation.

Clothing for the Priests

28 "Call for your brother, Aaron, and his sons, Nadab, Abihu, Eleazar, and Ithamar. Set them apart from the rest of the people of Israel so they may minister to me and be my priests. 2 Make sacred garments for Aaron that are glorious and beautiful. 3 Instruct all the skilled craftsmen whom I have filled with the spirit of wisdom. Have them make garments for Aaron that will distinguish him as a priest set apart for my service. 4 These are the garments they are to make: a chestpiece, an ephod, a robe, a patterned tunic, a turban, and a sash. They are to make these sacred garments for your brother, Aaron, and his sons to wear when they serve me as priests. 5 So give them fine linen cloth, gold thread, and blue, purple, and scarlet thread.

Design of the Ephod

6 "The craftsmen must make the ephod of finely woven linen and skillfully embroider it with gold and with blue, purple, and scarlet thread. 7 It will consist of two pieces, front and back, joined at the shoulders with two shoulder-pieces. 8 The decorative sash will be made of the same materials: finely woven linen

27:16 Hebrew *20 cubits* [9.2 meters]. **27:18** Hebrew *100 cubits* [46 meters] *long and 50 by 50* [23 meters] *wide and 5 cubits* [2.3 meters] *high.* **27:21** Hebrew *in the Tent of Meeting, outside the inner curtain that is in front of the Testimony.* See note on 25:16.

thereof; *even of* gold, *of* blue, and purple, and scarlet, and fine twined linen.

9 And thou shalt take two onyx stones, and grave on them the names of the children of Israel:

10 Six of their names on one stone, and *the other* six names of the rest on the other stone, according to their birth.

11 With the work of an engraver in stone, *like* the engravings of a signet, shalt thou engrave the two stones with the names of the children of Israel: thou shalt make them to be set in ouches of gold.

12 And thou shalt put the two stones upon the shoulders of the ephod *for* stones of memorial unto the children of Israel: and Aaron shall bear their names before the LORD upon his two shoulders for a memorial.

13 And thou shalt make ouches of gold;

14 And two chains *of* pure gold at the ends; *of* wreathen work shalt thou make them, and fasten the wreathen chains to the ouches.

15 And thou shalt make the breastplate of judgment with cunning work; after the work of the ephod thou shalt make it; *of* gold, *of* blue, and *of* purple, and *of* scarlet, and *of* fine twined linen, shalt thou make it.

16 Foursquare it shall be *being* doubled; a span *shall be* the length thereof, and a span *shall be* the breadth thereof.

17 And thou shalt set in it settings of stones, *even* four rows of stones: *the first* row *shall be* a sardius, a topaz, and a carbuncle: *this shall be* the first row.

18 And the second row *shall be* an emerald, a sapphire, and a diamond.

19 And the third row a ligure, an agate, and an amethyst.

20 And the fourth row a beryl, and an onyx, and a jasper: they shall be set in gold in their inclosings.

21 And the stones shall be with the names of the children of Israel, twelve, according to their names, *like* the engravings of a signet; every one with his name shall they be according to the twelve tribes.

22 And thou shalt make upon the breastplate chains at the ends *of* wreathen work *of* pure gold.

23 And thou shalt make upon the breastplate two rings of gold, and shalt put the two rings on the two ends of the breastplate.

24 And thou shalt put the two wreathen *chains* of gold in the two rings *which are* on the ends of the breastplate.

25 And *the other* two ends of the two wreathen *chains* thou shalt fasten in the two ouches, and put *them* on the shoulder pieces of the ephod before it.

26 And thou shalt make two rings of gold, and thou shalt put them upon the two ends of the breastplate in the border thereof, which *is* in the side of the ephod inward.

27 And two *other* rings of gold thou shalt make, and

embroidered with gold and with blue, purple, and
scarlet thread.
9 "Take two onyx stones, and engrave on them the
names of the tribes of Israel. 10 Six names will be on
each stone, arranged in the order of the births of the
original sons of Israel. 11 Engrave these names on the
two stones in the same way a jeweler engraves a seal.
Then mount the stones in settings of gold filigree.
12 Fasten the two stones on the shoulder-pieces of
the ephod as a reminder that Aaron represents the
people of Israel. Aaron will carry these names on his
shoulders as a constant reminder whenever he goes
before the LORD. 13 Make the settings of gold filigree,
14 then braid two cords of pure gold and attach them
to the filigree settings on the shoulders of the ephod.

Design of the Chestpiece

15 "Then, with great skill and care, make a chestpiece
to be worn for seeking a decision from God.* Make
it to match the ephod, using finely woven linen embroidered with gold and with blue, purple, and scarlet thread. 16 Make the chestpiece of a single piece of
cloth folded to form a pouch nine inches* square.
17 Mount four rows of gemstones* on it. The first row
will contain a red carnelian, a pale-green peridot, and
an emerald. 18 The second row will contain a turquoise, a blue lapis lazuli, and a white moonstone.
19 The third row will contain an orange jacinth, an
agate, and a purple amethyst. 20 The fourth row will
contain a blue-green beryl, an onyx, and a green
jasper. All these stones will be set in gold filigree.
21 Each stone will represent one of the twelve sons of
Israel, and the name of that tribe will be engraved on
it like a seal.
22 "To attach the chestpiece to the ephod, make
braided cords of pure gold thread. 23 Then make two
gold rings and attach them to the top corners of the
chestpiece. 24 Tie the two gold cords to the two rings
on the chestpiece. 25 Tie the other ends of the cords
to the gold settings on the shoulder-pieces of the
ephod. 26 Then make two more gold rings and attach
them to the inside edges of the chestpiece next to
the ephod. 27 And make two more gold rings and

28:15 Hebrew *a chestpiece for decision.* **28:16** Hebrew *1 span* [23 centimeters]. **28:17** The identification of some of these gemstones is uncertain.

KING JAMES VERSION

shalt put them on the two sides of the ephod underneath, toward the forepart thereof, over against the *other* coupling thereof, above the curious girdle of the ephod.

[28]And they shall bind the breastplate by the rings thereof unto the rings of the ephod with a lace of blue, that *it* may be above the curious girdle of the ephod, and that the breastplate be not loosed from the ephod.

[29]And Aaron shall bear the names of the children of Israel in the breastplate of judgment upon his heart, when he goeth in unto the holy *place,* for a memorial before the LORD continually.

[30]And thou shalt put in the breastplate of judgment the Urim and the Thummim; and they shall be upon Aaron's heart, when he goeth in before the LORD: and Aaron shall bear the judgment of the children of Israel upon his heart before the LORD continually.

[31]And thou shalt make the robe of the ephod all *of* blue.

[32]And there shall be an hole in the top of it, in the midst thereof: it shall have a binding of woven work round about the hole of it, as it were the hole of an habergeon, that it be not rent.

[33]And *beneath* upon the hem of it thou shalt make pomegranates *of* blue, and *of* purple, and *of* scarlet, round about the hem thereof; and bells of gold between them round about:

[34]A golden bell and a pomegranate, a golden bell and a pomegranate, upon the hem of the robe round about.

[35]And it shall be upon Aaron to minister: and his sound shall be heard when he goeth in unto the holy *place* before the LORD, and when he cometh out, that he die not.

[36]And thou shalt make a plate *of* pure gold, and grave upon it, *like* the engravings of a signet, HOLINESS TO THE LORD.

[37]And thou shalt put it on a blue lace, that it may be upon the mitre; upon the forefront of the mitre it shall be.

[38]And it shall be upon Aaron's forehead, that Aaron may bear the iniquity of the holy things, which the children of Israel shall hallow in all their holy gifts; and it shall be always upon his forehead, that they may be accepted before the LORD.

[39]And thou shalt embroider the coat of fine linen, and thou shalt make the mitre *of* fine linen, and thou shalt make the girdle *of* needlework.

[40]And for Aaron's sons thou shalt make coats, and thou shalt make for them girdles, and bonnets shalt thou make for them, for glory and for beauty.

[41]And thou shalt put them upon Aaron thy brother, and his sons with him; and shalt anoint them, and consecrate them, and sanctify them, that they may minister unto me in the priest's office.

NEW LIVING TRANSLATION

attach them to the front of the ephod, below the
shoulder-pieces, just above the knot where the decorative sash is fastened to the ephod. [28]Then attach
the bottom rings of the chestpiece to the rings on
the ephod with blue cords. This will hold the chestpiece securely to the ephod above the decorative
sash.

[29]"In this way, Aaron will carry the names of the
tribes of Israel on the sacred chestpiece* over his
heart when he goes into the Holy Place. This will be a
continual reminder that he represents the people
when he comes before the LORD. [30]Insert the Urim
and Thummim into the sacred chestpiece so they
will be carried over Aaron's heart when he goes into
the LORD's presence. In this way, Aaron will always
carry over his heart the objects used to determine
the LORD's will for his people whenever he goes in
before the LORD.

Additional Clothing for the Priests

[31]"Make the robe that is worn with the ephod from a
single piece of blue cloth, [32]with an opening for
Aaron's head in the middle of it. Reinforce the opening with a woven collar* so it will not tear. [33]Make
pomegranates out of blue, purple, and scarlet yarn,
and attach them to the hem of the robe, with gold
bells between them. [34]The gold bells and pomegranates are to alternate all around the hem. [35]Aaron will
wear this robe whenever he ministers before the
LORD, and the bells will tinkle as he goes in and out of
the LORD's presence in the Holy Place. If he wears it,
he will not die.

[36]"Next make a medallion of pure gold, and engrave it like a seal with these words: HOLY TO THE
LORD. [37]Attach the medallion with a blue cord to the
front of Aaron's turban, where it must remain.
[38]Aaron must wear it on his forehead so he may take
on himself any guilt of the people of Israel when they
consecrate their sacred offerings. He must always
wear it on his forehead so the LORD will accept the
people.

[39]"Weave Aaron's patterned tunic from fine linen
cloth. Fashion the turban from this linen as well.
Also make a sash, and decorate it with colorful
embroidery.

[40]"For Aaron's sons, make tunics, sashes, and
special head coverings that are glorious and beautiful. [41]Clothe your brother, Aaron, and his sons with
these garments, and then anoint and ordain them.
Consecrate them so they can serve as my priests.

28:29 Hebrew *the chestpiece for decision;* also in 28:30. See 28:15.
28:32 The meaning of the Hebrew is uncertain.

KING JAMES VERSION

[42]And thou shalt make them linen breeches to cover their nakedness; from the loins even unto the thighs they shall reach:
[43]And they shall be upon Aaron, and upon his sons, when they come in unto the tabernacle of the congregation, or when they come near unto the altar to minister in the holy *place;* that they bear not iniquity, and die: *it shall be* a statute for ever unto him and his seed after him.

29 [1]And this *is* the thing that thou shalt do unto them to hallow them, to minister unto me in the priest's office: Take one young bullock, and two rams without blemish,
[2]And unleavened bread, and cakes unleavened tempered with oil, and wafers unleavened anointed with oil: *of* wheaten flour shalt thou make them.
[3]And thou shalt put them into one basket, and bring them in the basket, with the bullock and the two rams.
[4]And Aaron and his sons thou shalt bring unto the door of the tabernacle of the congregation, and shalt wash them with water.
[5]And thou shalt take the garments, and put upon Aaron the coat, and the robe of the ephod, and the ephod, and the breastplate, and gird him with the curious girdle of the ephod:
[6]And thou shalt put the mitre upon his head, and put the holy crown upon the mitre.
[7]Then shalt thou take the anointing oil, and pour *it* upon his head, and anoint him.
[8]And thou shalt bring his sons, and put coats upon them.
[9]And thou shalt gird them with girdles, Aaron and his sons, and put the bonnets on them: and the priest's office shall be theirs for a perpetual statute: and thou shalt consecrate Aaron and his sons.
[10]And thou shalt cause a bullock to be brought before the tabernacle of the congregation: and Aaron and his sons shall put their hands upon the head of the bullock.
[11]And thou shalt kill the bullock before the LORD, *by* the door of the tabernacle of the congregation.
[12]And thou shalt take of the blood of the bullock, and put *it* upon the horns of the altar with thy finger, and pour all the blood beside the bottom of the altar.
[13]And thou shalt take all the fat that covereth the inwards, and the caul *that is* above the liver, and the two kidneys, and the fat that *is* upon them, and burn *them* upon the altar.
[14]But the flesh of the bullock, and his skin, and his dung, shalt thou burn with fire without the camp: it *is* a sin offering.
[15]Thou shalt also take one ram; and Aaron and his sons shall put their hands upon the head of the ram.
[16]And thou shalt slay the ram, and thou shalt take his blood, and sprinkle *it* round about upon the altar.

NEW LIVING TRANSLATION

[42]Also make linen undergarments for them, to be worn next to their bodies, reaching from their hips to their thighs. [43]These must be worn whenever Aaron and his sons enter the Tabernacle* or approach the altar in the Holy Place to perform their priestly duties. Then they will not incur guilt and die. This is a permanent law for Aaron and all his descendants after him.

Dedication of the Priests

29 "This is the ceremony you must follow when you consecrate Aaron and his sons to serve me as priests: Take a young bull and two rams with no defects. [2]Then, using choice wheat flour and no yeast, make loaves of bread, thin cakes mixed with olive oil, and wafers spread with oil. [3]Place them all in a single basket, and present them at the entrance of the Tabernacle, along with the young bull and the two rams.

[4]"Present Aaron and his sons at the entrance of the Tabernacle,* and wash them with water. [5]Dress Aaron in his priestly garments—the tunic, the robe worn with the ephod, the ephod itself, and the chestpiece. Then wrap the decorative sash of the ephod around him. [6]Place the turban on his head, and fasten the sacred medallion to the turban. [7]Then anoint him by pouring the anointing oil over his head. [8]Next present his sons, and dress them in their tunics. [9]Wrap the sashes around the waists of Aaron and his sons, and put their special head coverings on them. Then the right to the priesthood will be theirs by law forever. In this way, you will ordain Aaron and his sons.

[10]"Bring the young bull to the entrance of the Tabernacle, where Aaron and his sons will lay their hands on its head. [11]Then slaughter the bull in the LORD's presence at the entrance of the Tabernacle. [12]Put some of its blood on the horns of the altar with your finger, and pour out the rest at the base of the altar. [13]Take all the fat around the internal organs, the long lobe of the liver, and the two kidneys and the fat around them, and burn it all on the altar. [14]Then take the rest of the bull, including its hide, meat, and dung, and burn it outside the camp as a sin offering.

[15]"Next Aaron and his sons must lay their hands on the head of one of the rams. [16]Then slaughter the ram, and splatter its blood against all sides of the altar.

28:43 Hebrew *Tent of Meeting.* **29:4** Hebrew *Tent of Meeting;* also in 29:10, 11, 30, 32, 42, 44.

KING JAMES VERSION

17 And thou shalt cut the ram in pieces, and wash
the inwards of him, and his legs, and put *them* unto
his pieces, and unto his head.
18 And thou shalt burn the whole ram upon the altar: it *is* a burnt offering unto the LORD: it *is* a sweet
savour, an offering made by fire unto the LORD.
19 And thou shalt take the other ram; and Aaron
and his sons shall put their hands upon the head of
the ram.
20 Then shalt thou kill the ram, and take of his
blood, and put *it* upon the tip of the right ear of
Aaron, and upon the tip of the right ear of his sons,
and upon the thumb of their right hand, and upon
the great toe of their right foot, and sprinkle the
blood upon the altar round about.
21 And thou shalt take of the blood that *is* upon the
altar, and of the anointing oil, and sprinkle *it* upon
Aaron, and upon his garments, and upon his sons,
and upon the garments of his sons with him: and he
shall be hallowed, and his garments, and his sons,
and his sons' garments with him.
22 Also thou shalt take of the ram the fat and the
rump, and the fat that covereth the inwards, and the
caul *above* the liver, and the two kidneys, and the fat
that *is* upon them, and the right shoulder; for it *is* a
ram of consecration:
23 And one loaf of bread, and one cake of oiled
bread, and one wafer out of the basket of the unleavened bread that *is* before the LORD:
24 And thou shalt put all in the hands of Aaron, and
in the hands of his sons; and shalt wave them *for* a
wave offering before the LORD.
25 And thou shalt receive them of their hands, and
burn *them* upon the altar for a burnt offering, for a
sweet savour before the LORD: it *is* an offering made
by fire unto the LORD.
26 And thou shalt take the breast of the ram of
Aaron's consecration, and wave it *for* a wave offering
before the LORD: and it shall be thy part.
27 And thou shalt sanctify the breast of the wave
offering, and the shoulder of the heave offering,
which is waved, and which is heaved up, of the ram of
the consecration, *even* of *that* which *is* for Aaron,
and of *that* which is for his sons:
28 And it shall be Aaron's and his sons' by a statute
for ever from the children of Israel: for it *is* an heave
offering: and it shall be an heave offering from the
children of Israel of the sacrifice of their peace offerings, *even* their heave offering unto the LORD.
29 And the holy garments of Aaron shall be his
sons' after him, to be anointed therein, and to be
consecrated in them.
30 *And* that son that is priest in his stead shall put
them on seven days, when he cometh into the tabernacle of the congregation to minister in the holy
place.
31 And thou shalt take the ram of the consecration,
and seethe his flesh in the holy place.

NEW LIVING TRANSLATION

17 Cut the ram into pieces, and wash off the internal
organs and the legs. Set them alongside the head and
the other pieces of the body, 18 then burn the entire
animal on the altar. This is a burnt offering to the
LORD; it is a pleasing aroma, a special gift presented to
the LORD.
19 "Now take the other ram, and have Aaron and
his sons lay their hands on its head. 20 Then slaughter
it, and apply some of its blood to the right earlobes of
Aaron and his sons. Also put it on the thumbs of their
right hands and the big toes of their right feet. Splatter the rest of the blood against all sides of the altar.
21 Then take some of the blood from the altar and
some of the anointing oil, and sprinkle it on Aaron
and his sons and on their garments. In this way, they
and their garments will be set apart as holy.
22 "Since this is the ram for the ordination of
Aaron and his sons, take the fat of the ram, including
the fat of the broad tail, the fat around the internal
organs, the long lobe of the liver, and the two kidneys
and the fat around them, along with the right thigh.
23 Then take one round loaf of bread, one thin cake
mixed with olive oil, and one wafer from the basket
of bread without yeast that was placed in the LORD's
presence. 24 Put all these in the hands of Aaron and
his sons to be lifted up as a special offering to the
LORD. 25 Afterward take the various breads from
their hands, and burn them on the altar along with
the burnt offering. It is a pleasing aroma to the LORD,
a special gift for him. 26 Then take the breast of
Aaron's ordination ram, and lift it up in the LORD's
presence as a special offering to him. Then keep it as
your own portion.
27 "Set aside the portions of the ordination ram
that belong to Aaron and his sons. This includes the
breast and the thigh that were lifted up before the
LORD as a special offering. 28 In the future, whenever
the people of Israel lift up a peace offering, a portion
of it must be set aside for Aaron and his descendants. This is their permanent right, and it is a sacred offering from the Israelites to the LORD.
29 "Aaron's sacred garments must be preserved for
his descendants who succeed him, and they will
wear them when they are anointed and ordained.
30 The descendant who succeeds him as high priest
will wear these clothes for seven days as he ministers
in the Tabernacle and the Holy Place.
31 "Take the ram used in the ordination ceremony,

KING JAMES VERSION

32 And Aaron and his sons shall eat the flesh of the ram, and the bread that *is* in the basket, *by* the door of the tabernacle of the congregation.

33 And they shall eat those things wherewith the atonement was made, to consecrate *and* to sanctify them: but a stranger shall not eat *thereof*, because they *are* holy.

34 And if aught of the flesh of the consecrations, or of the bread, remain unto the morning, then thou shalt burn the remainder with fire: it shall not be eaten, because it *is* holy.

35 And thus shalt thou do unto Aaron, and to his sons, according to all *things* which I have commanded thee: seven days shalt thou consecrate them.

36 And thou shalt offer every day a bullock *for* a sin offering for atonement: and thou shalt cleanse the altar, when thou hast made an atonement for it, and thou shalt anoint it, to sanctify it.

37 Seven days thou shalt make an atonement for the altar, and sanctify it; and it shall be an altar most holy: whatsoever toucheth the altar shall be holy.

38 Now this *is that* which thou shalt offer upon the altar; two lambs of the first year day by day continually.

39 The one lamb thou shalt offer in the morning; and the other lamb thou shalt offer at even:

40 And with the one lamb a tenth deal of flour mingled with the fourth part of an hin of beaten oil; and the fourth part of an hin of wine *for* a drink offering.

41 And the other lamb thou shalt offer at even, and shalt do thereto according to the meat offering of the morning, and according to the drink offering thereof, for a sweet savour, an offering made by fire unto the LORD.

42 *This shall be* a continual burnt offering throughout your generations *at* the door of the tabernacle of the congregation before the LORD: where I will meet you, to speak there unto thee.

43 And there I will meet with the children of Israel, and *the tabernacle* shall be sanctified by my glory.

44 And I will sanctify the tabernacle of the congregation, and the altar: I will sanctify also both Aaron and his sons, to minister to me in the priest's office.

45 And I will dwell among the children of Israel, and will be their God.

46 And they shall know that I *am* the LORD their God, that brought them forth out of the land of Egypt, that I may dwell among them: I *am* the LORD their God.

30 1 And thou shalt make an altar to burn incense upon: *of* shittim wood shalt thou make it.

2 A cubit *shall be* the length thereof, and a cubit the breadth thereof; foursquare shall it be: and two cubits *shall be* the height thereof: the horns thereof *shall be* of the same.

NEW LIVING TRANSLATION

and boil its meat in a sacred place. 32 Then Aaron and
his sons will eat this meat, along with the bread in
the basket, at the Tabernacle entrance. 33 They alone
may eat the meat and bread used for their purification* in the ordination ceremony. No one else may
eat them, for these things are set apart and holy. 34 If
any of the ordination meat or bread remains until
the morning, it must be burned. It may not be eaten,
for it is holy.

35 "This is how you will ordain Aaron and his sons
to their offices, just as I have commanded you. The
ordination ceremony will go on for seven days.
36 Each day you must sacrifice a young bull as a sin
offering to purify them, making them right with the
LORD.* Afterward, cleanse the altar by purifying it*;
make it holy by anointing it with oil. 37 Purify the altar, and consecrate it every day for seven days. After
that, the altar will be absolutely holy, and whatever
touches it will become holy.

38 "These are the sacrifices you are to offer regularly on the altar. Each day, offer two lambs that are
a year old, 39 one in the morning and the other in
the evening. 40 With one of them, offer two quarts
of choice flour mixed with one quart of pure oil of
pressed olives; also, offer one quart of wine* as a liquid offering. 41 Offer the other lamb in the evening,
along with the same offerings of flour and wine as in
the morning. It will be a pleasing aroma, a special gift
presented to the LORD.

42 "These burnt offerings are to be made each day
from generation to generation. Offer them in the
LORD's presence at the Tabernacle entrance; there I
will meet with you and speak with you. 43 I will meet
the people of Israel there, in the place made holy by
my glorious presence. 44 Yes, I will consecrate the
Tabernacle and the altar, and I will consecrate Aaron
and his sons to serve me as priests. 45 Then I will live
among the people of Israel and be their God, 46 and
they will know that I am the LORD their God. I am
the one who brought them out of the land of Egypt
so that I could live among them. I am the LORD
their God.

Plans for the Incense Altar

30 "Then make another altar of acacia wood
for burning incense. 2 Make it 18 inches
square and 36 inches high,* with horns at the
corners carved from the same piece of wood as the

29:33 Or *their atonement.* **29:36a** Or *to make atonement.* **29:36b** Or *by making atonement for it;* similarly in 29:37. **29:40** Hebrew *1/10 of an ephah* [2.2 liters] *of choice flour . . . 1/4 of a hin* [1 liter] *of pure oil . . . 1/4 of a hin of wine.* **30:2** Hebrew *1 cubit* [46 centimeters] *long and 1 cubit wide, a square, and 2 cubits* [92 centimeters] *high.*

KING JAMES VERSION

3And thou shalt overlay it with pure gold, the top
thereof, and the sides thereof round about, and the
horns thereof; and thou shalt make unto it a crown of
gold round about.

4And two golden rings shalt thou make to it under
the crown of it, by the two corners thereof, upon the
two sides of it shalt thou make *it;* and they shall be
for places for the staves to bear it withal.

5And thou shalt make the staves *of* shittim wood,
and overlay them with gold.

6And thou shalt put it before the veil that *is* by the
ark of the testimony, before the mercy seat that *is*
over the testimony, where I will meet with thee.

7And Aaron shall burn thereon sweet incense
every morning: when he dresseth the lamps, he shall
burn incense upon it.

8And when Aaron lighteth the lamps at even, he
shall burn incense upon it, a perpetual incense before the LORD throughout your generations.

9Ye shall offer no strange incense thereon, nor
burnt sacrifice, nor meat offering; neither shall ye
pour drink offering thereon.

10And Aaron shall make an atonement upon the
horns of it once in a year with the blood of the sin
offering of atonements: once in the year shall he
make atonement upon it throughout your generations: it *is* most holy unto the LORD.

11And the LORD spake unto Moses, saying,

12When thou takest the sum of the children of Israel after their number, then shall they give every
man a ransom for his soul unto the LORD, when thou
numberest them; that there be no plague among
them, when *thou* numberest them.

13This they shall give, every one that passeth
among them that are numbered, half a shekel after
the shekel of the sanctuary: (a shekel *is* twenty
gerahs:) an half shekel *shall be* the offering of the
LORD.

14Every one that passeth among them that are
numbered, from twenty years old and above, shall
give an offering unto the LORD.

15The rich shall not give more, and the poor shall
not give less than half a shekel, when *they* give an
offering unto the LORD, to make an atonement for
your souls.

16And thou shalt take the atonement money of the
children of Israel, and shalt appoint it for the service
of the tabernacle of the congregation; that it may be
a memorial unto the children of Israel before the
LORD, to make an atonement for your souls.

17And the LORD spake unto Moses, saying,

18Thou shalt also make a laver *of* brass, and his
foot *also of* brass, to wash *withal:* and thou shalt put
it between the tabernacle of the congregation and
the altar, and thou shalt put water therein.

NEW LIVING TRANSLATION

altar itself. 3Overlay the top, sides, and horns of the
altar with pure gold, and run a gold molding around
the entire altar. 4Make two gold rings, and attach
them on opposite sides of the altar below the gold
molding to hold the carrying poles. 5Make the poles
of acacia wood and overlay them with gold. 6Place
the incense altar just outside the inner curtain that
shields the Ark of the Covenant,* in front of the
Ark's cover—the place of atonement—that covers
the tablets inscribed with the terms of the covenant.* I will meet with you there.

7"Every morning when Aaron maintains the
lamps, he must burn fragrant incense on the altar.
8And each evening when he lights the lamps, he
must again burn incense in the LORD's presence.
This must be done from generation to generation.
9Do not offer any unholy incense on this altar, or any
burnt offerings, grain offerings, or liquid offerings.

10"Once a year Aaron must purify* the altar by
smearing its horns with blood from the offering
made to purify the people from their sin. This will be
a regular, annual event from generation to generation, for this is the LORD's most holy altar."

Money for the Tabernacle

11Then the LORD said to Moses, 12"Whenever you
take a census of the people of Israel, each man who is
counted must pay a ransom for himself to the LORD.
Then no plague will strike the people as you count
them. 13Each person who is counted must give a
small piece of silver as a sacred offering to the LORD.
(This payment is half a shekel,* based on the sanctuary shekel, which equals twenty gerahs.) 14All who
have reached their twentieth birthday must give this
sacred offering to the LORD. 15When this offering is
given to the LORD to purify your lives, making you
right with him,* the rich must not give more than the
specified amount, and the poor must not give less.
16Receive this ransom money from the Israelites, and
use it for the care of the Tabernacle.* It will bring the
Israelites to the LORD's attention, and it will purify
your lives."

Plans for the Washbasin

17Then the LORD said to Moses, 18"Make a bronze
washbasin with a bronze stand. Place it between
the Tabernacle and the altar, and fill it with water.

30:6a Or *Ark of the Testimony;* also in 30:26. **30:6b** Hebrew *that covers the Testimony;* see note on 25:16. **30:10** Or *make atonement for;* also in 30:10b. **30:13** Or *0.2 ounces,* or *6 grams.* **30:15** Or *to make atonement for your lives;* similarly in 30:16. **30:16** Hebrew *Tent of Meeting;* also in 30:18, 20, 26, 36.

KING JAMES VERSION

19For Aaron and his sons shall wash their hands and their feet thereat:

20When they go into the tabernacle of the congregation, they shall wash with water, that they die not; or when they come near to the altar to minister, to burn offering made by fire unto the LORD:

21So they shall wash their hands and their feet, that they die not: and it shall be a statute for ever to them, *even* to him and to his seed throughout their generations.

22Moreover the LORD spake unto Moses, saying,

23Take thou also unto thee principal spices, of pure myrrh five hundred *shekels,* and of sweet cinnamon half so much, *even* two hundred and fifty *shekels,* and of sweet calamus two hundred and fifty *shekels,*

24And of cassia five hundred *shekels,* after the shekel of the sanctuary, and of oil olive an hin:

25And thou shalt make it an oil of holy ointment, an ointment compound after the art of the apothecary: it shall be an holy anointing oil.

26And thou shalt anoint the tabernacle of the congregation therewith, and the ark of the testimony,

27And the table and all his vessels, and the candlestick and his vessels, and the altar of incense,

28And the altar of burnt offering with all his vessels, and the laver and his foot.

29And thou shalt sanctify them, that they may be most holy: whatsoever toucheth them shall be holy.

30And thou shalt anoint Aaron and his sons, and consecrate them, that *they* may minister unto me in the priest's office.

31And thou shalt speak unto the children of Israel, saying, This shall be an holy anointing oil unto me throughout your generations.

32Upon man's flesh shall it not be poured, neither shall ye make *any other* like it, after the composition of it: it *is* holy, *and* it shall be holy unto you.

33Whosoever compoundeth *any* like it, or whosoever putteth *any* of it upon a stranger, shall even be cut off from his people.

34And the LORD said unto Moses, Take unto thee sweet spices, stacte, and onycha, and galbanum; *these* sweet spices with pure frankincense: of each shall there be a like *weight:*

35And thou shalt make it a perfume, a confection after the art of the apothecary, tempered together, pure *and* holy:

36And thou shalt beat *some* of it very small, and put of it before the testimony in the tabernacle of the congregation, where I will meet with thee: it shall be unto you most holy.

37And *as for* the perfume which thou shalt make, ye shall not make to yourselves according to the composition thereof: it shall be unto thee holy for the LORD.

NEW LIVING TRANSLATION

19Aaron and his sons will wash their hands and feet there. 20They must wash with water whenever they go into the Tabernacle to appear before the LORD and when they approach the altar to burn up their special gifts to the LORD—or they will die! 21They must always wash their hands and feet, or they willdie. This is a permanent law for Aaron and his descendants, to be observed from generation to generation."

The Anointing Oil

22Then the LORD said to Moses, 23"Collect choice spices—12½ pounds of pure myrrh, 6¼ pounds of fragrant cinnamon, 6¼ pounds of fragrant calamus,* 24and 12½ pounds of cassia*—as measured by the weight of the sanctuary shekel. Also get one gallon of olive oil.* 25Like a skilled incense maker, blend these ingredients to make a holy anointing oil. 26Use this sacred oil to anoint the Tabernacle, the Ark of the Covenant, 27the table and all its utensils, the lampstand and all its accessories, the incense altar, 28the altar of burnt offering and all its utensils, and the washbasin with its stand. 29Consecrate them to make them absolutely holy. After this, whatever touches them will also become holy.

30"Anoint Aaron and his sons also, consecrating them to serve me as priests. 31And say to the people of Israel, 'This holy anointing oil is reserved for me from generation to generation. 32It must never be used to anoint anyone else, and you must never make any blend like it for yourselves. It is holy, and you must treat it as holy. 33Anyone who makes a blend like it or anoints someone other than a priest will be cut off from the community.'"

The Incense

34Then the LORD said to Moses, "Gather fragrant spices—resin droplets, mollusk shell, and galbanum—and mix these fragrant spices with pure frankincense, weighed out in equal amounts. 35Using the usual techniques of the incense maker, blend the spices together and sprinkle them with salt to produce a pure and holy incense. 36Grind some of the mixture into a very fine powder and put it in front of the Ark of the Covenant,* where I will meet with you in the Tabernacle. You must treat this incense as most holy. 37Never use this formula to make this incense for yourselves. It is reserved for the LORD, and

30:23 Hebrew *500 shekels* [5.7 kilograms] *of pure myrrh, 250 shekels* [2.9 kilograms] *of fragrant cinnamon, 250 shekels of fragrant calamus.* **30:24a** Hebrew *500 shekels* [5.7 kilograms] *of cassia.* **30:24b** Hebrew *1 hin* [3.8 liters] *of olive oil.* **30:36** Hebrew *in front of the Testimony;* see note on 25:16.

KING JAMES VERSION

38 Whosoever shall make like unto that, to smell
thereto, shall even be cut off from his people.

31 1 And the LORD spake unto Moses, saying,
2 See, I have called by name Bezaleel the son
of Uri, the son of Hur, of the tribe of Judah:
3 And I have filled him with the spirit of God, in
wisdom, and in understanding, and in knowledge,
and in all manner of workmanship,
4 To devise cunning works, to work in gold, and in
silver, and in brass,
5 And in cutting of stones, to set *them,* and in carving of timber, to work in all manner of workmanship.
6 And I, behold, I have given with him Aholiab, the
son of Ahisamach, of the tribe of Dan: and in the
hearts of all that are wise hearted I have put wisdom,
that they may make all that I have commanded thee;
7 The tabernacle of the congregation, and the ark
of the testimony, and the mercy seat that *is* thereupon, and all the furniture of the tabernacle,
8 And the table and his furniture, and the pure
candlestick with all his furniture, and the altar of
incense,
9 And the altar of burnt offering with all his furniture, and the laver and his foot,
10 And the cloths of service, and the holy garments
for Aaron the priest, and the garments of his sons, to
minister in the priest's office,
11 And the anointing oil, and sweet incense for the
holy *place:* according to all that I have commanded
thee shall they do.

12 And the LORD spake unto Moses, saying,
13 Speak thou also unto the children of Israel, saying, Verily my sabbaths ye shall keep: for it *is* a sign
between me and you throughout your generations;
that *ye* may know that I *am* the LORD that doth sanctify you.
14 Ye shall keep the sabbath therefore; for it *is* holy
unto you: every one that defileth it shall surely be put
to death: for whosoever doeth *any* work therein, that
soul shall be cut off from among his people.
15 Six days may work be done; but in the seventh *is*
the sabbath of rest, holy to the LORD: whosoever
doeth *any* work in the sabbath day, he shall surely be
put to death.
16 Wherefore the children of Israel shall keep the
sabbath, to observe the sabbath throughout their
generations, *for* a perpetual covenant.
17 It *is* a sign between me and the children of Israel
for ever: for *in* six days the LORD made heaven and

NEW LIVING TRANSLATION

you must treat it as holy. 38 Anyone who makes incense like this for personal use will be cut off from
the community."

Craftsmen: Bezalel and Oholiab

31 Then the LORD said to Moses, 2 "Look, I have
specifically chosen Bezalel son of Uri, grandson of Hur, of the tribe of Judah. 3 I have filled him
with the Spirit of God, giving him great wisdom, ability, and expertise in all kinds of crafts. 4 He is a master
craftsman, expert in working with gold, silver, and
bronze. 5 He is skilled in engraving and mounting
gemstones and in carving wood. He is a master at
every craft!
6 "And I have personally appointed Oholiab son of
Ahisamach, of the tribe of Dan, to be his assistant.
Moreover, I have given special skill to all the gifted
craftsmen so they can make all the things I have
commanded you to make:

7 the Tabernacle;*
the Ark of the Covenant;*
the Ark's cover—the place of atonement;
all the furnishings of the Tabernacle;
8 the table and its utensils;
the pure gold lampstand with all its accessories;
the incense altar;
9 the altar of burnt offering with all its utensils;
the washbasin with its stand;
10 the beautifully stitched garments—the sacred
garments for Aaron the priest, and the
garments for his sons to wear as they minister
as priests;
11 the anointing oil;
the fragrant incense for the Holy Place.

The craftsmen must make everything as I have commanded you."

Instructions for the Sabbath

12 The LORD then gave these instructions to Moses:
13 "Tell the people of Israel: 'Be careful to keep my
Sabbath day, for the Sabbath is a sign of the covenant
between me and you from generation to generation.
It is given so you may know that I am the LORD, who
makes you holy. 14 You must keep the Sabbath day, for
it is a holy day for you. Anyone who desecrates it
must be put to death; anyone who works on that day
will be cut off from the community. 15 You have six
days each week for your ordinary work, but the seventh day must be a Sabbath day of complete rest, a
holy day dedicated to the LORD. Anyone who works
on the Sabbath must be put to death. 16 The people of
Israel must keep the Sabbath day by observing it
from generation to generation. This is a covenant
obligation for all time. 17 It is a permanent sign of my
covenant with the people of Israel. For in six days the

31:7a Hebrew *the Tent of Meeting.* **31:7b** Hebrew *the Ark of the Testimony.*

earth, and on the seventh day he rested, and was
refreshed.
18 And he gave unto Moses, when he had made an
end of communing with him upon mount Sinai, two
tables of testimony, tables of stone, written with the
finger of God.

32 1 And when the people saw that Moses delayed to come down out of the mount, the
people gathered themselves together unto Aaron,
and said unto him, Up, make us gods, which shall go
before us; for *as for* this Moses, the man that brought
us up out of the land of Egypt, we wot not what is become of him.
2 And Aaron said unto them, Break off the golden
earrings, which *are* in the ears of your wives, of
your sons, and of your daughters, and bring *them*
unto me.
3 And all the people brake off the golden earrings
which *were* in their ears, and brought *them* unto
Aaron.
4 And he received *them* at their hand, and fashioned it with a graving tool, after he had made it a
molten calf: and they said, These *be* thy gods, O Israel, which brought thee up out of the land of Egypt.
5 And when Aaron saw *it,* he built an altar before it;
and Aaron made proclamation, and said, Tomorrow
is a feast to the LORD.
6 And they rose up early on the morrow, and offered burnt offerings, and brought peace offerings;
and the people sat down to eat and to drink, and rose
up to play.
7 And the LORD said unto Moses, Go, get thee down;
for thy people, which thou broughtest out of the land
of Egypt, have corrupted *themselves:*
8 They have turned aside quickly out of the way
which I commanded them: they have made them a
molten calf, and have worshipped it, and have sacrificed thereunto, and said, These *be* thy gods, O Israel,
which have brought thee up out of the land of Egypt.
9 And the LORD said unto Moses, I have seen this
people, and, behold, it *is* a stiffnecked people:
10 Now therefore let me alone, that my wrath may
wax hot against them, and that I may consume them:
and I will make of thee a great nation.
11 And Moses besought the LORD his God, and said,
LORD, why doth thy wrath wax hot against thy people,
which thou hast brought forth out of the land of
Egypt with great power, and with a mighty hand?
12 Wherefore should the Egyptians speak, and say,
For mischief did he bring them out, to slay them in
the mountains, and to consume them from the face
of the earth? Turn from thy fierce wrath, and repent
of this evil against thy people.
13 Remember Abraham, Isaac, and Israel, thy servants, to whom thou swarest by thine own self, and

LORD made heaven and earth, but on the seventh day
he stopped working and was refreshed.'"
18 When the LORD finished speaking with Moses
on Mount Sinai, he gave him the two stone tablets inscribed with the terms of the covenant,* written by
the finger of God.

The Gold Calf

32 When the people saw how long it was taking Moses to come back down the mountain, they gathered around Aaron. "Come on," they
said, "make us some gods who can lead us. We don't
know what happened to this fellow Moses, who
brought us here from the land of Egypt."
2 So Aaron said, "Take the gold rings from the ears
of your wives and sons and daughters, and bring
them to me."
3 All the people took the gold rings from their ears
and brought them to Aaron. 4 Then Aaron took the
gold, melted it down, and molded it into the shape
of a calf. When the people saw it, they exclaimed,
"O Israel, these are the gods who brought you out of
the land of Egypt!"
5 Aaron saw how excited the people were, so he
built an altar in front of the calf. Then he announced,
"Tomorrow will be a festival to the LORD!"
6 The people got up early the next morning to sacrifice burnt offerings and peace offerings. After this,
they celebrated with feasting and drinking, and they
indulged in pagan revelry.
7 The LORD told Moses, "Quick! Go down the
mountain! Your people whom you brought from the
land of Egypt have corrupted themselves. 8 How
quickly they have turned away from the way I commanded them to live! They have melted down gold
and made a calf, and they have bowed down and sacrificed to it. They are saying, 'These are your gods,
O Israel, who brought you out of the land of Egypt.'"
9 Then the LORD said, "I have seen how stubborn
and rebellious these people are. 10 Now leave me
alone so my fierce anger can blaze against them, and
I will destroy them. Then I will make you, Moses, into
a great nation."
11 But Moses tried to pacify the LORD his God.
"O LORD!" he said. "Why are you so angry with your
own people whom you brought from the land of
Egypt with such great power and such a strong hand?
12 Why let the Egyptians say, 'Their God rescued
them with the evil intention of slaughtering them in
the mountains and wiping them from the face of the
earth'? Turn away from your fierce anger. Change
your mind about this terrible disaster you have
threatened against your people! 13 Remember your
servants Abraham, Isaac, and Jacob.* You bound

31:18 Hebrew *the two tablets of the Testimony;* see note on 25:16.
32:13 Hebrew *Israel.* The names "Jacob" and "Israel" are often interchanged throughout the Old Testament, referring sometimes to the individual patriarch and sometimes to the nation.

KING JAMES VERSION

saidst unto them, I will multiply your seed as the stars
of heaven, and all this land that I have spoken of will I
give unto your seed, and they shall inherit *it* for ever.
14And the LORD repented of the evil which he
thought to do unto his people.
15And Moses turned, and went down from the
mount, and the two tables of the testimony *were* in
his hand: the tables *were* written on both their sides;
on the one side and on the other *were* they written.
16And the tables *were* the work of God, and the
writing *was* the writing of God, graven upon the
tables.
17And when Joshua heard the noise of the people
as they shouted, he said unto Moses, *There is* a noise
of war in the camp.
18And he said, *It is* not the voice of *them that* shout
for mastery, neither *is it* the voice of *them that* cry
for being overcome: *but* the noise of *them that* sing
do I hear.
19And it came to pass, as soon as he came nigh
unto the camp, that he saw the calf, and the dancing:
and Moses' anger waxed hot, and he cast the tables
out of his hands, and brake them beneath the mount.
20And he took the calf which they had made, and
burnt *it* in the fire, and ground *it* to powder, and
strawed *it* upon the water, and made the children of
Israel drink *of it*.
21And Moses said unto Aaron, What did this
people unto thee, that thou hast brought so great a
sin upon them?
22And Aaron said, Let not the anger of my lord wax
hot: thou knowest the people, that they *are set* on
mischief.
23For they said unto me, Make us gods, which shall
go before us: for *as for* this Moses, the man that
brought us up out of the land of Egypt, we wot not
what is become of him.
24And I said unto them, Whosoever hath any gold,
let them break *it* off. So they gave *it* me: then I cast it
into the fire, and there came out this calf.
25And when Moses saw that the people *were* naked; (for Aaron had made them naked unto *their*
shame among their enemies:)
26Then Moses stood in the gate of the camp, and
said, Who *is* on the LORD's side? *let him come* unto
me. And all the sons of Levi gathered themselves together unto him.
27And he said unto them, Thus saith the LORD God
of Israel, Put every man his sword by his side, *and* go
in and out from gate to gate throughout the camp,
and slay every man his brother, and every man his
companion, and every man his neighbour.
28And the children of Levi did according to the
word of Moses: and there fell of the people that day
about three thousand men.
29For Moses had said, Consecrate yourselves today
to the LORD, even every man upon his son, and upon

NEW LIVING TRANSLATION

yourself with an oath to them, saying, 'I will make
your descendants as numerous as the stars of
heaven. And I will give them all of this land that I
have promised to your descendants, and they will
possess it forever.'"
14So the LORD changed his mind about the terrible
disaster he had threatened to bring on his people.
15Then Moses turned and went down the mountain. He held in his hands the two stone tablets inscribed with the terms of the covenant.* They were
inscribed on both sides, front and back. 16These tablets were God's work; the words on them were written by God himself.
17When Joshua heard the boisterous noise of the
people shouting below them, he exclaimed to Moses,
"It sounds like war in the camp!"
18But Moses replied, "No, it's not a shout of victory nor the wailing of defeat. I hear the sound of a
celebration."
19When they came near the camp, Moses saw the
calf and the dancing, and he burned with anger. He
threw the stone tablets to the ground, smashing
them at the foot of the mountain. 20He took the calf
they had made and burned it. Then he ground it into
powder, threw it into the water, and forced the
people to drink it.
21Finally, he turned to Aaron and demanded,
"What did these people do to you to make you bring
such terrible sin upon them?"
22"Don't get so upset, my lord," Aaron replied.
"You yourself know how evil these people are.
23They said to me, 'Make us gods who will lead us.
We don't know what happened to this fellow Moses,
who brought us here from the land of Egypt.' 24So I
told them, 'Whoever has gold jewelry, take it off.'
When they brought it to me, I simply threw it into the
fire—and out came this calf!"
25Moses saw that Aaron had let the people get
completely out of control, much to the amusement
of their enemies.* 26So he stood at the entrance to
the camp and shouted, "All of you who are on the
LORD's side, come here and join me." And all the
Levites gathered around him.
27Moses told them, "This is what the LORD, the
God of Israel, says: Each of you, take your swords and
go back and forth from one end of the camp to the
other. Kill everyone—even your brothers, friends,
and neighbors." 28The Levites obeyed Moses' command, and about 3,000 people died that day.
29Then Moses told the Levites, "Today you have
ordained yourselves* for the service of the LORD, for

32:15 Hebrew *the two tablets of the Testimony;* see note on 25:16.
32:25 Or *out of control, and they mocked anyone who opposed them.* The meaning of the Hebrew is unclear. **32:29** As in Greek and Latin versions; Hebrew reads *Today ordain yourselves.*

KING JAMES VERSION

his brother; that he may bestow upon you a blessing this day.

30And it came to pass on the morrow, that Moses said unto the people, Ye have sinned a great sin: and now I will go up unto the LORD; peradventure I shall make an atonement for your sin.

31And Moses returned unto the LORD, and said, Oh, this people have sinned a great sin, and have made them gods of gold.

32Yet now, if thou wilt forgive their sin—; and if not, blot me, I pray thee, out of thy book which thou hast written.

33And the LORD said unto Moses, Whosoever hath sinned against me, him will I blot out of my book.

34Therefore now go, lead the people unto *the place* of which I have spoken unto thee: behold, mine Angel shall go before thee: nevertheless in the day when I visit I will visit their sin upon them.

35And the LORD plagued the people, because they made the calf, which Aaron made.

33 1And the LORD said unto Moses, Depart, *and* go up hence, thou and the people which thou hast brought up out of the land of Egypt, unto the land which I sware unto Abraham, to Isaac, and to Jacob, saying, Unto thy seed will I give it:

2And I will send an angel before thee; and I will drive out the Canaanite, the Amorite, and the Hittite, and the Perizzite, the Hivite, and the Jebusite:

3Unto a land flowing with milk and honey: for I will not go up in the midst of thee; for thou *art* a stiffnecked people: lest I consume thee in the way.

4And when the people heard these evil tidings, they mourned: and no man did put on him his ornaments.

5For the LORD had said unto Moses, Say unto the children of Israel, Ye *are* a stiffnecked people: I will come up into the midst of thee in a moment, and consume thee: therefore now put off thy ornaments from thee, that I may know what to do unto thee.

6And the children of Israel stripped themselves of their ornaments by the mount Horeb.

7And Moses took the tabernacle, and pitched it without the camp, afar off from the camp, and called it the Tabernacle of the congregation. And it came to pass, *that* every one which sought the LORD went out unto the tabernacle of the congregation, which *was* without the camp.

8And it came to pass, when Moses went out unto the tabernacle, *that* all the people rose up, and stood every man *at* his tent door, and looked after Moses, until he was gone into the tabernacle.

9And it came to pass, as Moses entered into the tabernacle, the cloudy pillar descended, and stood *at*

NEW LIVING TRANSLATION

you obeyed him even though it meant killing your own sons and brothers. Today you have earned a blessing."

Moses Intercedes for Israel

30The next day Moses said to the people, "You have committed a terrible sin, but I will go back up to the LORD on the mountain. Perhaps I will be able to obtain forgiveness* for your sin."

31So Moses returned to the LORD and said, "Oh, what a terrible sin these people have committed. They have made gods of gold for themselves.
32But now, if you will only forgive their sin—but if not, erase my name from the record you have written!"

33But the LORD replied to Moses, "No, I will erase the name of everyone who has sinned against me.
34Now go, lead the people to the place I told you about. Look! My angel will lead the way before you. And when I come to call the people to account, I will certainly hold them responsible for their sins."

35Then the LORD sent a great plague upon the people because they had worshiped the calf Aaron had made.

33 The LORD said to Moses, "Get going, you and the people you brought up from the land of Egypt. Go up to the land I swore to give to Abraham, Isaac, and Jacob. I told them, 'I will give this land to your descendants.'
2And I will send an angel before you to drive out the Canaanites, Amorites, Hittites, Perizzites, Hivites, and Jebusites.
3Go up to this land that flows with milk and honey. But I will not travel among you, for you are a stubborn and rebellious people. If I did, I would surely destroy you along the way."

4When the people heard these stern words, they went into mourning and stopped wearing their jewelry and fine clothes.
5For the LORD had told Moses to tell them, "You are a stubborn and rebellious people. If I were to travel with you for even a moment, I would destroy you. Remove your jewelry and fine clothes while I decide what to do with you."
6So from the time they left Mount Sinai,* the Israelites wore no more jewelry or fine clothes.

7It was Moses' practice to take the Tent of Meeting* and set it up some distance from the camp. Everyone who wanted to make a request of the LORD would go to the Tent of Meeting outside the camp.

8Whenever Moses went out to the Tent of Meeting, all the people would get up and stand in the entrances of their own tents. They would all watch Moses until he disappeared inside.
9As he went into the tent, the pillar of cloud would come down and

32:30 Or *to make atonement.* **33:6** Hebrew *Horeb,* another name for Sinai. **33:7** This "Tent of Meeting" is different from the Tabernacle described in chapters 26 and 36.

KING JAMES VERSION

the door of the tabernacle, and *the* LORD talked with
Moses.
10And all the people saw the cloudy pillar stand *at*
the tabernacle door: and all the people rose up and
worshipped, every man *in* his tent door.
11And the LORD spake unto Moses face to face, as a
man speaketh unto his friend. And he turned again
into the camp: but his servant Joshua, the son of Nun,
a young man, departed not out of the tabernacle.

12And Moses said unto the LORD, See, thou sayest
unto me, Bring up this people: and thou hast not let
me know whom thou wilt send with me. Yet thou
hast said, I know thee by name, and thou hast also
found grace in my sight.
13Now therefore, I pray thee, if I have found grace
in thy sight, shew me now thy way, that I may know
thee, that I may find grace in thy sight: and consider
that this nation *is* thy people.
14And he said, My presence shall go *with thee,* and
I will give thee rest.
15And he said unto him, If thy presence go not
with me, carry us not up hence.
16For wherein shall it be known here that I and thy
people have found grace in thy sight? *is it* not in that
thou goest with us? so shall we be separated, I and
thy people, from all the people that *are* upon the face
of the earth.
17And the LORD said unto Moses, I will do this
thing also that thou hast spoken: for thou hast found
grace in my sight, and I know thee by name.
18And he said, I beseech thee, shew me thy glory.
19And he said, I will make all my goodness pass before thee, and I will proclaim the name of the LORD
before thee; and will be gracious to whom I will be
gracious, and will shew mercy on whom I will shew
mercy.
20And he said, Thou canst not see my face: for
there shall no man see me, and live.
21And the LORD said, Behold, *there is* a place by me,
and thou shalt stand upon a rock:
22And it shall come to pass, while my glory passeth
by, that I will put thee in a clift of the rock, and will
cover thee with my hand while I pass by:
23And I will take away mine hand, and thou shalt
see my back parts: but my face shall not be seen.

34 1And the LORD said unto Moses, Hew thee
two tables of stone like unto the first: and I
will write upon *these* tables the words that were in
the first tables, which thou brakest.
2And be ready in the morning, and come up in the
morning unto mount Sinai, and present thyself there
to me in the top of the mount.
3And no man shall come up with thee, neither let

NEW LIVING TRANSLATION

hover at its entrance while the LORD spoke with
Moses. 10When the people saw the cloud standing at
the entrance of the tent, they would stand and bow
down in front of their own tents. 11Inside the Tent of
Meeting, the LORD would speak to Moses face to face,
as one speaks to a friend. Afterward Moses would
return to the camp, but the young man who assisted
him, Joshua son of Nun, would remain behind in the
Tent of Meeting.

Moses Sees the LORD's Glory

12One day Moses said to the LORD, "You have been
telling me, 'Take these people up to the Promised
Land.' But you haven't told me whom you will send
with me. You have told me, 'I know you by name, and I
look favorably on you.' 13If it is true that you look favorably on me, let me know your ways so I may understand you more fully and continue to enjoy your
favor. And remember that this nation is your very
own people."
14The LORD replied, "I will personally go with you,
Moses, and I will give you rest—everything will be
fine for you."
15Then Moses said, "If you don't personally go
with us, don't make us leave this place. 16How will
anyone know that you look favorably on me—on me
and on your people—if you don't go with us? For your
presence among us sets your people and me apart
from all other people on the earth."
17The LORD replied to Moses, "I will indeed do
what you have asked, for I look favorably on you, and
I know you by name."
18Moses responded, "Then show me your glorious
presence."
19The LORD replied, "I will make all my goodness
pass before you, and I will call out my name,
Yahweh,* before you. For I will show mercy to anyone I choose, and I will show compassion to anyone I
choose. 20But you may not look directly at my face,
for no one may see me and live." 21The LORD continued, "Look, stand near me on this rock. 22As my glorious presence passes by, I will hide you in the crevice
of the rock and cover you with my hand until I have
passed by. 23Then I will remove my hand and let you
see me from behind. But my face will not be seen."

A New Copy of the Covenant

34 Then the LORD told Moses, "Chisel out two
stone tablets like the first ones. I will write
on them the same words that were on the tablets you
smashed. 2Be ready in the morning to climb up
Mount Sinai and present yourself to me on the top of
the mountain. 3No one else may come with you. In
fact, no one is to appear anywhere on the mountain.

33:19 *Yahweh* is a transliteration of the proper name *YHWH* that is sometimes rendered "Jehovah"; in this translation it is usually rendered "the LORD" (note the use of small capitals).

KING JAMES VERSION

any man be seen throughout all the mount; neither
let the flocks nor herds feed before that mount.
4And he hewed two tables of stone like unto the
first; and Moses rose up early in the morning, and
went up unto mount Sinai, as the LORD had commanded him, and took in his hand the two tables
of stone.
5And the LORD descended in the cloud, and stood
with him there, and proclaimed the name of the
LORD.
6And the LORD passed by before him, and proclaimed, The LORD, The LORD God, merciful and
gracious, longsuffering, and abundant in goodness
and truth,
7Keeping mercy for thousands, forgiving iniquity
and transgression and sin, and that will by no means
clear *the guilty;* visiting the iniquity of the fathers
upon the children, and upon the children's children,
unto the third and to the fourth *generation.*
8And Moses made haste, and bowed his head toward the earth, and worshipped.
9And he said, If now I have found grace in thy
sight, O Lord, let my Lord, I pray thee, go among us;
for it *is* a stiffnecked people; and pardon our iniquity
and our sin, and take us for thine inheritance.
10And he said, Behold, I make a covenant: before
all thy people I will do marvels, such as have not
been done in all the earth, nor in any nation: and all
the people among which thou *art* shall see the work
of the LORD: for it *is* a terrible thing that I will do
with thee.
11Observe thou that which I command thee this
day: behold, I drive out before thee the Amorite, and
the Canaanite, and the Hittite, and the Perizzite, and
the Hivite, and the Jebusite.
12Take heed to thyself, lest thou make a covenant
with the inhabitants of the land whither thou goest,
lest it be for a snare in the midst of thee:
13But ye shall destroy their altars, break their images, and cut down their groves:
14For thou shalt worship no other god: for the
LORD, whose name *is* Jealous, *is* a jealous God:
15Lest thou make a covenant with the inhabitants
of the land, and they go a whoring after their gods,
and do sacrifice unto their gods, and *one* call thee,
and thou eat of his sacrifice;
16And thou take of their daughters unto thy sons,
and their daughters go a whoring after their gods,
and make thy sons go a whoring after their gods.
17Thou shalt make thee no molten gods.

NEW LIVING TRANSLATION

Do not even let the flocks or herds graze near the
mountain."
4So Moses chiseled out two tablets of stone like
the first ones. Early in the morning he climbed
Mount Sinai as the LORD had commanded him, and
he carried the two stone tablets in his hands.
5Then the LORD came down in a cloud and stood
there with him; and he called out his own name,
Yahweh.* 6The LORD passed in front of Moses, calling out,

"Yahweh!* The LORD!
The God of compassion and mercy!
I am slow to anger
and filled with unfailing love and faithfulness.
7 I lavish unfailing love to a thousand generations.*
I forgive iniquity, rebellion, and sin.
But I do not excuse the guilty.
I lay the sins of the parents upon their children
and grandchildren;
the entire family is affected—
even children in the third and fourth
generations."

8Moses immediately threw himself to the ground
and worshiped. 9And he said, "O Lord, if it is true that
I have found favor with you, then please travel with
us. Yes, this is a stubborn and rebellious people, but
please forgive our iniquity and our sins. Claim us as
your own special possession."
10The LORD replied, "Listen, I am making a covenant with you in the presence of all your people. I will
perform miracles that have never been performed
anywhere in all the earth or in any nation. And all the
people around you will see the power of the LORD—
the awesome power I will display for you. 11But listen
carefully to everything I command you today. Then I
will go ahead of you and drive out the Amorites,
Canaanites, Hittites, Perizzites, Hivites, and Jebusites.
12"Be very careful never to make a treaty with the
people who live in the land where you are going. If
you do, you will follow their evil ways and be trapped.
13Instead, you must break down their pagan altars,
smash their sacred pillars, and cut down their Asherah poles. 14You must worship no other gods, for the
LORD, whose very name is Jealous, is a God who is
jealous about his relationship with you.
15"You must not make a treaty of any kind with the
people living in the land. They lust after their gods,
offering sacrifices to them. They will invite you to
join them in their sacrificial meals, and you will go
with them. 16Then you will accept their daughters,
who sacrifice to other gods, as wives for your sons.
And they will seduce your sons to commit adultery
against me by worshiping other gods. 17You must
not make any gods of molten metal for yourselves.

34:5 *Yahweh* is a transliteration of the proper name *YHWH* that is sometimes rendered "Jehovah"; in this translation it is usually rendered "the LORD" (note the use of small capitals). **34:6** See note on 34:5. **34:7** Hebrew *for thousands.*

KING JAMES VERSION

18 The feast of unleavened bread shalt thou keep. Seven days thou shalt eat unleavened bread, as I commanded thee, in the time of the month Abib: for in the month Abib thou camest out from Egypt.

19 All that openeth the matrix *is* mine; and every firstling among thy cattle, *whether* ox or sheep, *that is male.*

20 But the firstling of an ass thou shalt redeem with a lamb: and if thou redeem *him* not, then shalt thou break his neck. All the firstborn of thy sons thou shalt redeem. And none shall appear before me empty.

21 Six days thou shalt work, but on the seventh day thou shalt rest: in earing time and in harvest thou shalt rest.

22 And thou shalt observe the feast of weeks, of the firstfruits of wheat harvest, and the feast of ingathering at the year's end.

23 Thrice in the year shall all your menchildren appear before the Lord GOD, the God of Israel.

24 For I will cast out the nations before thee, and enlarge thy borders: neither shall any man desire thy land, when thou shalt go up to appear before the LORD thy God thrice in the year.

25 Thou shalt not offer the blood of my sacrifice with leaven; neither shall the sacrifice of the feast of the passover be left unto the morning.

26 The first of the firstfruits of thy land thou shalt bring unto the house of the LORD thy God. Thou shalt not seethe a kid in his mother's milk.

27 And the LORD said unto Moses, Write thou these words: for after the tenor of these words I have made a covenant with thee and with Israel.

28 And he was there with the LORD forty days and forty nights; he did neither eat bread, nor drink water. And he wrote upon the tables the words of the covenant, the ten commandments.

29 And it came to pass, when Moses came down from mount Sinai with the two tables of testimony in Moses' hand, when he came down from the mount, that Moses wist not that the skin of his face shone while he talked with him.

30 And when Aaron and all the children of Israel saw Moses, behold, the skin of his face shone; and they were afraid to come nigh him.

31 And Moses called unto them; and Aaron and all the rulers of the congregation returned unto him: and Moses talked with them.

NEW LIVING TRANSLATION

18 "You must celebrate the Festival of Unleavened
Bread. For seven days the bread you eat must be
made without yeast, just as I commanded you. Celebrate this festival annually at the appointed time in
early spring, in the month of Abib,* for that is the anniversary of your departure from Egypt.

19 "The firstborn of every animal belongs to me,
including the firstborn males from your herds of
cattle and your flocks of sheep and goats. 20 A firstborn donkey may be bought back from the LORD by
presenting a lamb or young goat in its place. But if
you do not buy it back, you must break its neck. However, you must buy back every firstborn son.

"No one may appear before me without an
offering.

21 "You have six days each week for your ordinary
work, but on the seventh day you must stop working,
even during the seasons of plowing and harvest.

22 "You must celebrate the Festival of Harvest*
with the first crop of the wheat harvest, and celebrate the Festival of the Final Harvest* at the end of
the harvest season. 23 Three times each year every
man in Israel must appear before the Sovereign, the
LORD, the God of Israel. 24 I will drive out the other
nations ahead of you and expand your territory, so
no one will covet and conquer your land while
you appear before the LORD your God three times
each year.

25 "You must not offer the blood of my sacrificial
offerings together with any baked goods containing
yeast. And none of the meat of the Passover sacrifice
may be kept over until the next morning.

26 "As you harvest your crops, bring the very best of
the first harvest to the house of the LORD your God.

"You must not cook a young goat in its mother's
milk."

27 Then the LORD said to Moses, "Write down all
these instructions, for they represent the terms of
the covenant I am making with you and with Israel."

28 Moses remained there on the mountain with the
LORD forty days and forty nights. In all that time
he ate no bread and drank no water. And the LORD*
wrote the terms of the covenant—the Ten Commandments*—on the stone tablets.

29 When Moses came down Mount Sinai carrying
the two stone tablets inscribed with the terms of the
covenant,* he wasn't aware that his face had become
radiant because he had spoken to the LORD. 30 So
when Aaron and the people of Israel saw the radiance
of Moses' face, they were afraid to come near him.

31 But Moses called out to them and asked Aaron
and all the leaders of the community to come over,

34:18 Hebrew *appointed time in the month of Abib.* This first month of the ancient Hebrew lunar calendar usually occurs within the months of March and April. **34:22a** Hebrew *Festival of Weeks;* compare 23:16. This was later called the Festival of Pentecost. It is celebrated today as Shavuot (or Shabuoth). **34:22b** Or *Festival of Ingathering.* This was later called the Festival of Shelters or Festival of Tabernacles (see Lev 23:33-36). It is celebrated today as Sukkot (or Succoth). **34:28a** Hebrew *he.* **34:28b** Hebrew *the ten words.* **34:29** Hebrew *the two tablets of the Testimony;* see note on 25:16.

KING JAMES VERSION

32 And afterward all the children of Israel came nigh: and he gave them in commandment all that the LORD had spoken with him in mount Sinai.

33 And *till* Moses had done speaking with them, he put a veil on his face.

34 But when Moses went in before the LORD to speak with him, he took the veil off, until he came out. And he came out, and spake unto the children of Israel *that* which he was commanded.

35 And the children of Israel saw the face of Moses, that the skin of Moses' face shone: and Moses put the veil upon his face again, until he went in to speak with him.

35 1 And Moses gathered all the congregation of the children of Israel together, and said unto them, These *are* the words which the LORD hath commanded, that *ye* should do them.

2 Six days shall work be done, but on the seventh day there shall be to you an holy day, a sabbath of rest to the LORD: whosoever doeth work therein shall be put to death.

3 Ye shall kindle no fire throughout your habitations upon the sabbath day.

4 And Moses spake unto all the congregation of the children of Israel, saying, This *is* the thing which the LORD commanded, saying,

5 Take ye from among you an offering unto the LORD: whosoever *is* of a willing heart, let him bring it, an offering of the LORD; gold, and silver, and brass,

6 And blue, and purple, and scarlet, and fine linen, and goats' *hair*,

7 And rams' skins dyed red, and badgers' skins, and shittim wood,

8 And oil for the light, and spices for anointing oil, and for the sweet incense,

9 And onyx stones, and stones to be set for the ephod, and for the breastplate.

10 And every wise hearted among you shall come, and make all that the LORD hath commanded;

11 The tabernacle, his tent, and his covering, his taches, and his boards, his bars, his pillars, and his sockets,

12 The ark, and the staves thereof, *with* the mercy seat, and the veil of the covering,

13 The table, and his staves, and all his vessels, and the shewbread,

14 The candlestick also for the light, and his furniture, and his lamps, with the oil for the light,

15 And the incense altar, and his staves, and the anointing oil, and the sweet incense, and the hanging for the door at the entering in of the tabernacle,

16 The altar of burnt offering, with his brasen grate, his staves, and all his vessels, the laver and his foot,

NEW LIVING TRANSLATION

and he talked with them. 32 Then all the people of Israel approached him, and Moses gave them all the instructions the LORD had given him on Mount Sinai. 33 When Moses finished speaking with them, he covered his face with a veil. 34 But whenever he went into the Tent of Meeting to speak with the LORD, he would remove the veil until he came out again. Then he would give the people whatever instructions the LORD had given him, 35 and the people of Israel would see the radiant glow of his face. So he would put the veil over his face until he returned to speak with the LORD.

Instructions for the Sabbath

35 Then Moses called together the whole community of Israel and told them, "These are the instructions the LORD has commanded you to follow. 2 You have six days each week for your ordinary work, but the seventh day must be a Sabbath day of complete rest, a holy day dedicated to the LORD. Anyone who works on that day must be put to death. 3 You must not even light a fire in any of your homes on the Sabbath."

Offerings for the Tabernacle

4 Then Moses said to the whole community of Israel, "This is what the LORD has commanded: 5 Take a sacred offering for the LORD. Let those with generous hearts present the following gifts to the LORD:

gold, silver, and bronze;
6 blue, purple, and scarlet thread;
fine linen and goat hair for cloth;
7 tanned ram skins and fine goatskin leather;
acacia wood;
8 olive oil for the lamps;
spices for the anointing oil and the fragrant incense;
9 onyx stones, and other gemstones to be set in the ephod and the priest's chestpiece.

10 "Come, all of you who are gifted craftsmen. Construct everything that the LORD has commanded:

11 the Tabernacle and its sacred tent, its covering, clasps, frames, crossbars, posts, and bases;
12 the Ark and its carrying poles;
the Ark's cover—the place of atonement;
the inner curtain to shield the Ark;
13 the table, its carrying poles, and all its utensils;
the Bread of the Presence;
14 for light, the lampstand, its accessories, the lamp cups, and the olive oil for lighting;
15 the incense altar and its carrying poles;
the anointing oil and fragrant incense;
the curtain for the entrance of the Tabernacle;
16 the altar of burnt offering;
the bronze grating of the altar and its carrying poles and utensils;

KING JAMES VERSION

17 The hangings of the court, his pillars, and their sockets, and the hanging for the door of the court,

18 The pins of the tabernacle, and the pins of the court, and their cords,

19 The cloths of service, to do service in the holy *place,* the holy garments for Aaron the priest, and the garments of his sons, to minister in the priest's office.

20 And all the congregation of the children of Israel departed from the presence of Moses.

21 And they came, every one whose heart stirred him up, and every one whom his spirit made willing, *and* they brought the LORD's offering to the work of the tabernacle of the congregation, and for all his service, and for the holy garments.

22 And they came, both men and women, as many as were willing hearted, *and* brought bracelets, and earrings, and rings, and tablets, all jewels of gold: and every man that offered *offered* an offering of gold unto the LORD.

23 And every man, with whom was found blue, and purple, and scarlet, and fine linen, and goats' *hair,* and red skins of rams, and badgers' skins, brought *them.*

24 Every one that did offer an offering of silver and brass brought the LORD's offering: and every man, with whom was found shittim wood for any work of the service, brought *it.*

25 And all the women that were wise hearted did spin with their hands, and brought that which they had spun, *both* of blue, and of purple, *and* of scarlet, and of fine linen.

26 And all the women whose heart stirred them up in wisdom spun goats' *hair.*

27 And the rulers brought onyx stones, and stones to be set, for the ephod, and for the breastplate;

28 And spice, and oil for the light, and for the anointing oil, and for the sweet incense.

29 The children of Israel brought a willing offering unto the LORD, every man and woman, whose heart made them willing to bring for all manner of work, which the LORD had commanded to be made by the hand of Moses.

30 And Moses said unto the children of Israel, See, the LORD hath called by name Bezaleel the son of Uri, the son of Hur, of the tribe of Judah;

31 And he hath filled him with the spirit of God, in wisdom, in understanding, and in knowledge, and in all manner of workmanship;

32 And to devise curious works, to work in gold, and in silver, and in brass,

33 And in the cutting of stones, to set *them,* and in carving of wood, to make any manner of cunning work.

34 And he hath put in his heart that he may teach, *both* he, and Aholiab, the son of Ahisamach, of the tribe of Dan.

NEW LIVING TRANSLATION

the washbasin with its stand;
17 the curtains for the walls of the courtyard;
the posts and their bases;
the curtain for the entrance to the courtyard;
18 the tent pegs of the Tabernacle and courtyard and their ropes;
19 the beautifully stitched garments for the priests to wear while ministering in the Holy Place—
the sacred garments for Aaron the priest, and the garments for his sons to wear as they minister as priests."

20 So the whole community of Israel left Moses and returned to their tents. 21 All whose hearts were stirred and whose spirits were moved came and brought their sacred offerings to the LORD. They brought all the materials needed for the Tabernacle,* for the performance of its rituals, and for the sacred garments. 22 Both men and women came, all whose hearts were willing. They brought to the LORD their offerings of gold—brooches, earrings, rings from their fingers, and necklaces. They presented gold objects of every kind as a special offering to the LORD. 23 All those who owned the following items willingly brought them: blue, purple, and scarlet thread; fine linen and goat hair for cloth; and tanned ram skins and fine goatskin leather. 24 And all who had silver and bronze objects gave them as a sacred offering to the LORD. And those who had acacia wood brought it for use in the project.

25 All the women who were skilled in sewing and spinning prepared blue, purple, and scarlet thread, and fine linen cloth. 26 All the women who were willing used their skills to spin the goat hair into yarn. 27 The leaders brought onyx stones and the special gemstones to be set in the ephod and the priest's chestpiece. 28 They also brought spices and olive oil for the light, the anointing oil, and the fragrant incense. 29 So the people of Israel—every man and woman who was eager to help in the work the LORD had given them through Moses—brought their gifts and gave them freely to the LORD.

30 Then Moses told the people of Israel, "The LORD has specifically chosen Bezalel son of Uri, grandson of Hur, of the tribe of Judah. 31 The LORD has filled Bezalel with the Spirit of God, giving him great wisdom, ability, and expertise in all kinds of crafts. 32 He is a master craftsman, expert in working with gold, silver, and bronze. 33 He is skilled in engraving and mounting gemstones and in carving wood. He is a master at every craft. 34 And the LORD has given both him and Oholiab son of Ahisamach, of the tribe of

35:21 Hebrew *Tent of Meeting.*

KING JAMES VERSION

35 Them hath he filled with wisdom of heart, to work all manner of work, of the engraver, and of the cunning workman, and of the embroiderer, in blue, and in purple, in scarlet, and in fine linen, and of the weaver, *even* of them that do any work, and of those that devise cunning work.

36 1 Then wrought Bezaleel and Aholiab, and every wise hearted man, in whom the LORD put wisdom and understanding to know how to work all manner of work for the service of the sanctuary, according to all that the LORD had commanded.

2 And Moses called Bezaleel and Aholiab, and every wise hearted man, in whose heart the LORD had put wisdom, *even* every one whose heart stirred him up to come unto the work to do it:

3 And they received of Moses all the offering, which the children of Israel had brought for the work of the service of the sanctuary, to make it *withal*. And they brought yet unto him free offerings every morning.

4 And all the wise men, that wrought all the work of the sanctuary, came every man from his work which they made;

5 And they spake unto Moses, saying, The people bring much more than enough for the service of the work, which the LORD commanded to make.

6 And Moses gave commandment, and they caused it to be proclaimed throughout the camp, saying, Let neither man nor woman make any more work for the offering of the sanctuary. So the people were restrained from bringing.

7 For the stuff they had was sufficient for all the work to make it, and too much.

8 And every wise hearted man among them that wrought the work of the tabernacle made ten curtains *of* fine twined linen, and blue, and purple, and scarlet: *with* cherubims of cunning work made he them.

9 The length of one curtain *was* twenty and eight cubits, and the breadth of one curtain four cubits: the curtains *were* all of one size.

10 And he coupled the five curtains one unto another: and *the other* five curtains he coupled one unto another.

11 And he made loops of blue on the edge of one curtain from the selvedge in the coupling: likewise he made in the uttermost side of *another* curtain, in the coupling of the second.

12 Fifty loops made he in one curtain, and fifty loops made he in the edge of the curtain which *was* in the coupling of the second: the loops held one *curtain* to another.

13 And he made fifty taches of gold, and coupled the curtains one unto another with the taches: so it became one tabernacle.

14 And he made curtains *of* goats' *hair* for the tent over the tabernacle: eleven curtains he made them.

15 The length of one curtain *was* thirty cubits, and

NEW LIVING TRANSLATION

Dan, the ability to teach their skills to others. 35 The LORD has given them special skills as engravers, designers, embroiderers in blue, purple, and scarlet thread on fine linen cloth, and weavers. They excel as craftsmen and as designers.

36 1 "The LORD has gifted Bezalel, Oholiab, and the other skilled craftsmen with wisdom and ability to perform any task involved in building the sanctuary. Let them construct and furnish the Tabernacle, just as the LORD has commanded."

2 So Moses summoned Bezalel and Oholiab and all the others who were specially gifted by the LORD and were eager to get to work. 3 Moses gave them the materials donated by the people of Israel as sacred offerings for the completion of the sanctuary. But the people continued to bring additional gifts each morning. 4 Finally the craftsmen who were working on the sanctuary left their work. 5 They went to Moses and reported, "The people have given more than enough materials to complete the job the LORD has commanded us to do!"

6 So Moses gave the command, and this message was sent throughout the camp: "Men and women, don't prepare any more gifts for the sanctuary. We have enough!" So the people stopped bringing their sacred offerings. 7 Their contributions were more than enough to complete the whole project.

Building the Tabernacle

8 The skilled craftsmen made ten curtains of finely woven linen for the Tabernacle. Then Bezalel* decorated the curtains with blue, purple, and scarlet thread and with skillfully embroidered cherubim. 9 All ten curtains were exactly the same size—42 feet long and 6 feet wide.* 10 Five of these curtains were joined together to make one long curtain, and the other five were joined to make a second long curtain. 11 He made fifty loops of blue yarn and put them along the edge of the last curtain in each set. 12 The fifty loops along the edge of one curtain matched the fifty loops along the edge of the other curtain. 13 Then he made fifty gold clasps and fastened the long curtains together with the clasps. In this way, the Tabernacle was made of one continuous piece.

14 He made eleven curtains of goat-hair cloth to serve as a tent covering for the Tabernacle. 15 These

36:8 Hebrew *he;* also in 36:16, 20, 35. See 37:1. **36:9** Hebrew *28 cubits* [12.9 meters] *long and 4 cubits* [1.8 meters] *wide.*

KING JAMES VERSION

four cubits *was* the breadth of one curtain: the eleven curtains *were* of one size.

16And he coupled five curtains by themselves, and six curtains by themselves.

17And he made fifty loops upon the uttermost edge of the curtain in the coupling, and fifty loops made he upon the edge of the curtain which coupleth the second.

18And he made fifty taches *of* brass to couple the tent together, that it might be one.

19And he made a covering for the tent *of* rams' skins dyed red, and a covering *of* badgers' skins above *that*.

20And he made boards for the tabernacle *of* shittim wood, standing up.

21The length of a board *was* ten cubits, and the breadth of a board one cubit and a half.

22One board had two tenons, equally distant one from another: thus did he make for all the boards of the tabernacle.

23And he made boards for the tabernacle; twenty boards for the south side southward:

24And forty sockets of silver he made under the twenty boards; two sockets under one board for his two tenons, and two sockets under another board for his two tenons.

25And for the other side of the tabernacle, *which is* toward the north corner, he made twenty boards,

26And their forty sockets of silver; two sockets under one board, and two sockets under another board.

27And for the sides of the tabernacle westward he made six boards.

28And two boards made he for the corners of the tabernacle in the two sides.

29And they were coupled beneath, and coupled together at the head thereof, to one ring: thus he did to both of them in both the corners.

30And there were eight boards; and their sockets *were* sixteen sockets of silver, under every board two sockets.

31And he made bars of shittim wood; five for the boards of the one side of the tabernacle,

32And five bars for the boards of the other side of the tabernacle, and five bars for the boards of the tabernacle for the sides westward.

33And he made the middle bar to shoot through the boards from the one end to the other.

34And he overlaid the boards with gold, and made their rings *of* gold *to be* places for the bars, and overlaid the bars with gold.

35And he made a veil *of* blue, and purple, and scarlet, and fine twined linen: *with* cherubims made he it of cunning work.

36And he made thereunto four pillars *of* shittim *wood*, and overlaid them with gold: their hooks *were of* gold; and he cast for them four sockets of silver.

37And he made an hanging for the tabernacle door

NEW LIVING TRANSLATION

eleven curtains were all exactly the same size—
45 feet long and 6 feet wide.* 16Bezalel joined five of
these curtains together to make one long curtain,
and the other six were joined to make a second long
curtain. 17He made fifty loops for the edge of each
large curtain. 18He also made fifty bronze clasps to
fasten the long curtains together. In this way, the tent
covering was made of one continuous piece. 19He
completed the tent covering with a layer of tanned
ram skins and a layer of fine goatskin leather.

20For the framework of the Tabernacle, Bezalel
constructed frames of acacia wood. 21Each frame
was 15 feet high and 27 inches wide,* 22with two
pegs under each frame. All the frames were identical. 23He made twenty of these frames to support the
curtains on the south side of the Tabernacle. 24He
also made forty silver bases—two bases under each
frame, with the pegs fitting securely into the bases.
25For the north side of the Tabernacle, he made another twenty frames, 26with their forty silver bases,
two bases under each frame. 27He made six frames
for the rear—the west side of the Tabernacle—
28along with two additional frames to reinforce the
rear corners of the Tabernacle. 29These corner
frames were matched at the bottom and firmly attached at the top with a single ring, forming a single
corner unit. Both of these corner units were made
the same way. 30So there were eight frames at the
rear of the Tabernacle, set in sixteen silver bases—
two bases under each frame.

31Then he made crossbars of acacia wood to link
the frames, five crossbars for the north side of the
Tabernacle 32and five for the south side. He also
made five crossbars for the rear of the Tabernacle,
which faced west. 33He made the middle crossbar to
attach halfway up the frames; it ran all the way from
one end of the Tabernacle to the other. 34He overlaid
the frames with gold and made gold rings to hold the
crossbars. Then he overlaid the crossbars with gold
as well.

35For the inside of the Tabernacle, Bezalel made a
special curtain of finely woven linen. He decorated it
with blue, purple, and scarlet thread and with skillfully embroidered cherubim. 36For the curtain, he
made four posts of acacia wood and four gold hooks.
He overlaid the posts with gold and set them in four
silver bases.

37Then he made another curtain for the entrance

36:15 Hebrew *30 cubits* [13.8 meters] *long and 4 cubits* [1.8 meters] *wide.*
36:21 Hebrew *10 cubits* [4.6 meters] *high and 1.5 cubits* [69 centimeters] *wide.*

KING JAMES VERSION

of blue, and purple, and scarlet, and fine twined
linen, of needlework;
38And the five pillars of it with their hooks: and he
overlaid their chapiters and their fillets with gold:
but their five sockets *were of* brass.

37 1And Bezaleel made the ark *of* shittim wood:
two cubits and a half *was* the length of it,
and a cubit and a half the breadth of it, and a cubit
and a half the height of it:
2And he overlaid it with pure gold within and
without, and made a crown of gold to it round about.
3And he cast for it four rings of gold, *to be set* by
the four corners of it; even two rings upon the one
side of it, and two rings upon the other side of it.
4And he made staves *of* shittim wood, and overlaid
them with gold.
5And he put the staves into the rings by the sides
of the ark, to bear the ark.
6And he made the mercy seat *of* pure gold: two cubits and a half *was* the length thereof, and one cubit
and a half the breadth thereof.
7And he made two cherubims *of* gold, beaten out
of one piece made he them, on the two ends of the
mercy seat;
8One cherub on the end on this side, and another
cherub on the *other* end on that side: out of the mercy
seat made he the cherubims on the two ends thereof.
9And the cherubims spread out *their* wings on
high, *and* covered with their wings over the mercy
seat, with their faces one to another; *even* to the
mercy seatward were the faces of the cherubims.
10And he made the table *of* shittim wood: two cubits *was* the length thereof, and a cubit the breadth
thereof, and a cubit and a half the height thereof:
11And he overlaid it with pure gold, and made
thereunto a crown of gold round about.
12Also he made thereunto a border of an handbreadth round about; and made a crown of gold for
the border thereof round about.
13And he cast for it four rings of gold, and put the
rings upon the four corners that *were* in the four feet
thereof.
14Over against the border were the rings, the
places for the staves to bear the table.
15And he made the staves *of* shittim wood, and
overlaid them with gold, to bear the table.
16And he made the vessels which *were* upon the
table, his dishes, and his spoons, and his bowls, and
his covers to cover withal, *of* pure gold.
17And he made the candlestick *of* pure gold: *of*
beaten work made he the candlestick; his shaft, and
his branch, his bowls, his knops, and his flowers,
were of the same:

NEW LIVING TRANSLATION

to the sacred tent. He made it of finely woven linen
and embroidered it with exquisite designs using
blue, purple, and scarlet thread. 38This curtain was
hung on gold hooks attached to five posts. The posts
with their decorated tops and hooks were overlaid
with gold, and the five bases were cast from bronze.

Building the Ark of the Covenant

37 Next Bezalel made the Ark of acacia wood—
a sacred chest 45 inches long, 27 inches
wide, and 27 inches high.* 2He overlaid it inside and
outside with pure gold, and he ran a molding of gold
all around it. 3He cast four gold rings and attached
them to its four feet, two rings on each side. 4Then he
made poles from acacia wood and overlaid them
with gold. 5He inserted the poles into the rings at the
sides of the Ark to carry it.
6Then he made the Ark's cover—the place of
atonement—from pure gold. It was 45 inches long
and 27 inches wide.* 7He made two cherubim from
hammered gold and placed them on the two ends of
the atonement cover. 8He molded the cherubim on
each end of the atonement cover, making it all of one
piece of gold. 9The cherubim faced each other and
looked down on the atonement cover. With their
wings spread above it, they protected it.

Building the Table

10Then Bezalel* made the table of acacia wood,
36 inches long, 18 inches wide, and 27 inches
high.* 11He overlaid it with pure gold and ran a gold
molding around the edge. 12He decorated it with a
3-inch border* all around, and he ran a gold molding along the border. 13Then he cast four gold rings
for the table and attached them at the four corners
next to the four legs. 14The rings were attached near
the border to hold the poles that were used to carry
the table. 15He made these poles from acacia wood
and overlaid them with gold. 16Then he made special containers of pure gold for the table—bowls,
pans, jars, and pitchers—to be used in pouring out
liquid offerings.

Building the Lampstand

17Then Bezalel made the lampstand of pure, hammered gold. He made the entire lampstand and its

37:1 Hebrew *2.5 cubits* [115 centimeters] *long, 1.5 cubits* [69 centimeters] *wide, and 1.5 cubits high.* **37:6** Hebrew *2.5 cubits* [115 centimeters] *long and 1.5 cubits* [69 centimeters] *wide.* **37:10a** Hebrew *he;* also in 37:17, 25. **37:10b** Hebrew *2 cubits* [92 centimeters] *long, 1 cubit* [46 centimeters] *wide, and 1.5 cubits* [69 centimeters] *high.* **37:12** Hebrew *a border of a handbreadth* [8 centimeters].

KING JAMES VERSION

18 And six branches going out of the sides thereof; three branches of the candlestick out of the one side thereof, and three branches of the candlestick out of the other side thereof:

19 Three bowls made after the fashion of almonds in one branch, a knop and a flower; and three bowls made like almonds in another branch, a knop and a flower: so throughout the six branches going out of the candlestick.

20 And in the candlestick *were* four bowls made like almonds, his knops, and his flowers:

21 And a knop under two branches of the same, and a knop under two branches of the same, and a knop under two branches of the same, according to the six branches going out of it.

22 Their knops and their branches were of the same: all of it *was* one beaten work *of* pure gold.

23 And he made his seven lamps, and his snuffers, and his snuffdishes, *of* pure gold.

24 *Of* a talent of pure gold made he it, and all the vessels thereof.

25 And he made the incense altar *of* shittim wood: the length of it *was* a cubit, and the breadth of it a cubit; *it was* foursquare; and two cubits *was* the height of it; the horns thereof were of the same.

26 And he overlaid it with pure gold, *both* the top of it, and the sides thereof round about, and the horns of it: also he made unto it a crown of gold round about.

27 And he made two rings of gold for it under the crown thereof, by the two corners of it, upon the two sides thereof, to be places for the staves to bear it withal.

28 And he made the staves *of* shittim wood, and overlaid them with gold.

29 And he made the holy anointing oil, and the pure incense of sweet spices, according to the work of the apothecary.

38 1 And he made the altar of burnt offering *of* shittim wood: five cubits *was* the length thereof, and five cubits the breadth thereof; *it was* foursquare; and three cubits the height thereof.

2 And he made the horns thereof on the four corners of it; the horns thereof were of the same: and he overlaid it with brass.

3 And he made all the vessels of the altar, the pots, and the shovels, and the basins, *and* the fleshhooks, and the firepans: all the vessels thereof made he *of* brass.

4 And he made for the altar a brasen grate of network under the compass thereof beneath unto the midst of it.

5 And he cast four rings for the four ends of the grate of brass, *to be* places for the staves.

6 And he made the staves *of* shittim wood, and overlaid them with brass.

7 And he put the staves into the rings on the sides

NEW LIVING TRANSLATION

decorations of one piece—the base, center stem, lamp cups, buds, and petals. 18 The lampstand had six branches going out from the center stem, three on each side. 19 Each of the six branches had three lamp cups shaped like almond blossoms, complete with buds and petals. 20 The center stem of the lampstand was crafted with four lamp cups shaped like almond blossoms, complete with buds and petals. 21 There was an almond bud beneath each pair of branches where the six branches extended from the center stem, all made of one piece. 22 The almond buds and branches were all of one piece with the center stem, and they were hammered from pure gold.

23 He also made seven lamps for the lampstand, lamp snuffers, and trays, all of pure gold. 24 The entire lampstand, along with its accessories, was made from seventy-five pounds* of pure gold.

Building the Incense Altar

25 Then Bezalel made the incense altar of acacia wood. It was 18 inches square and 36 inches high,* with horns at the corners carved from the same piece of wood as the altar itself. 26 He overlaid the top, sides, and horns of the altar with pure gold, and he ran a gold molding around the entire altar. 27 He made two gold rings and attached them on opposite sides of the altar below the gold molding to hold the carrying poles. 28 He made the poles of acacia wood and overlaid them with gold.

29 Then he made the sacred anointing oil and the fragrant incense, using the techniques of a skilled incense maker.

Building the Altar of Burnt Offering

38 Next Bezalel* used acacia wood to construct the square altar of burnt offering. It was 7½ feet wide, 7½ feet long, and 4½ feet high.* 2 He made horns for each of its four corners so that the horns and altar were all one piece. He overlaid the altar with bronze. 3 Then he made all the altar utensils of bronze—the ash buckets, shovels, basins, meat forks, and firepans. 4 Next he made a bronze grating and installed it halfway down the side of the altar, under the ledge. 5 He cast four rings and attached them to the corners of the bronze grating to hold the carrying poles. 6 He made the poles from acacia wood and overlaid them with bronze. 7 He inserted the poles through the rings on the sides of the

37:24 Hebrew *1 talent* [34 kilograms]. **37:25** Hebrew *1 cubit* [46 centimeters] *long and 1 cubit wide, a square, and 2 cubits* [92 centimeters] *high.* **38:1a** Hebrew *he;* also in 38:8, 9. **38:1b** Hebrew *5 cubits* [2.3 meters] *wide, 5 cubits long, a square, and 3 cubits* [1.4 meters] *high.*

KING JAMES VERSION

of the altar, to bear it withal; he made the altar hollow with boards.

8And he made the laver *of* brass, and the foot of it *of* brass, of the lookingglasses of *the women* assembling, which assembled *at* the door of the tabernacle of the congregation.

9And he made the court: on the south side southward the hangings of the court *were of* fine twined linen, an hundred cubits:
10Their pillars *were* twenty, and their brasen sockets twenty; the hooks of the pillars and their fillets *were of* silver.
11And for the north side *the hangings were* an hundred cubits, their pillars *were* twenty, and their sockets of brass twenty; the hooks of the pillars and their fillets *of* silver.
12And for the west side *were* hangings of fifty cubits, their pillars ten, and their sockets ten; the hooks of the pillars and their fillets *of* silver.
13And for the east side eastward fifty cubits.
14The hangings of the one side *of the gate were* fifteen cubits; their pillars three, and their sockets three.
15And for the other side of the court gate, on this hand and that hand, *were* hangings of fifteen cubits; their pillars three, and their sockets three.

16All the hangings of the court round about *were* of fine twined linen.

17And the sockets for the pillars *were of* brass; the hooks of the pillars and their fillets *of* silver; and the overlaying of their chapiters *of* silver; and all the pillars of the court *were* filleted with silver.

18And the hanging for the gate of the court *was* needlework, *of* blue, and purple, and scarlet, and fine twined linen: and twenty cubits *was* the length, and the height in the breadth *was* five cubits, answerable to the hangings of the court.
19And their pillars *were* four, and their sockets *of* brass four; their hooks *of* silver, and the overlaying of their chapiters and their fillets *of* silver.
20And all the pins of the tabernacle, and of the court round about, *were of* brass.

21This is the sum of the tabernacle, *even* of the tabernacle of testimony, as it was counted, according to the commandment of Moses, *for* the service of the Levites, by the hand of Ithamar, son to Aaron the priest.
22And Bezaleel the son of Uri, the son of Hur, of the tribe of Judah, made all that the LORD commanded Moses.
23And with him *was* Aholiab, son of Ahisamach, of the tribe of Dan, an engraver, and a cunning

NEW LIVING TRANSLATION

altar. The altar was hollow and was made from planks.

Building the Washbasin

8Bezalel made the bronze washbasin and its bronze stand from bronze mirrors donated by the women who served at the entrance of the Tabernacle.*

Building the Courtyard

9Then Bezalel made the courtyard, which was enclosed with curtains made of finely woven linen. On the south side the curtains were 150 feet long.*
10They were held up by twenty posts set securely in twenty bronze bases. He hung the curtains with silver hooks and rings. 11He made a similar set of curtains for the north side—150 feet of curtains held up by twenty posts set securely in bronze bases. He hung the curtains with silver hooks and rings. 12The curtains on the west end of the courtyard were 75 feet long,* hung with silver hooks and rings and supported by ten posts set into ten bases. 13The east end, the front, was also 75 feet long.

14The courtyard entrance was on the east end, flanked by two curtains. The curtain on the right side was 22½ feet long* and was supported by three posts set into three bases. 15The curtain on the left side was also 22½ feet long and was supported by three posts set into three bases. 16All the curtains used in the courtyard were made of finely woven linen. 17Each post had a bronze base, and all the hooks and rings were silver. The tops of the posts of the courtyard were overlaid with silver, and the rings to hold up the curtains were made of silver.

18He made the curtain for the entrance to the courtyard of finely woven linen, and he decorated it with beautiful embroidery in blue, purple, and scarlet thread. It was 30 feet long, and its height was 7½ feet,* just like the curtains of the courtyard walls.
19It was supported by four posts, each set securely in its own bronze base. The tops of the posts were overlaid with silver, and the hooks and rings were also made of silver.

20All the tent pegs used in the Tabernacle and courtyard were made of bronze.

Inventory of Materials

21This is an inventory of the materials used in building the Tabernacle of the Covenant.* The Levites compiled the figures, as Moses directed, and Ithamar son of Aaron the priest served as recorder. 22Bezalel son of Uri, grandson of Hur, of the tribe of Judah, made everything just as the LORD had commanded Moses. 23He was assisted by Oholiab son of Ahisamach, of the tribe of Dan, a craftsman expert at

38:8 Hebrew *Tent of Meeting;* also in 38:30. **38:9** Hebrew *100 cubits* [46 meters]; also in 38:11. **38:12** Hebrew *50 cubits* [23 meters]; also in 38:13. **38:14** Hebrew *15 cubits* [6.9 meters]; also in 38:15. **38:18** Hebrew *20 cubits* [9.2 meters] *long and 5 cubits* [2.3 meters] *high.* **38:21** Hebrew *the Tabernacle, the Tabernacle of the Testimony.*

KING JAMES VERSION

workman, and an embroiderer in blue, and in purple, and in scarlet, and fine linen.

24 All the gold that was occupied for the work in all the work of the holy *place,* even the gold of the offering, was twenty and nine talents, and seven hundred and thirty shekels, after the shekel of the sanctuary.

25 And the silver of them that were numbered of the congregation *was* an hundred talents, and a thousand seven hundred and threescore and fifteen shekels, after the shekel of the sanctuary:

26 A bekah for every man, *that is,* half a shekel, after the shekel of the sanctuary, for every one that went to be numbered, from twenty years old and upward, for six hundred thousand and three thousand and five hundred and fifty *men.*

27 And of the hundred talents of silver were cast the sockets of the sanctuary, and the sockets of the veil; an hundred sockets of the hundred talents, a talent for a socket.

28 And of the thousand seven hundred seventy and five shekels he made hooks for the pillars, and overlaid their chapiters, and filleted them.

29 And the brass of the offering *was* seventy talents, and two thousand and four hundred shekels.

30 And therewith he made the sockets to the door of the tabernacle of the congregation, and the brasen altar, and the brasen grate for it, and all the vessels of the altar,

31 And the sockets of the court round about, and the sockets of the court gate, and all the pins of the tabernacle, and all the pins of the court round about.

39 1 And of the blue, and purple, and scarlet, they made cloths of service, to do service in the holy *place,* and made the holy garments for Aaron; as the LORD commanded Moses.

2 And he made the ephod *of* gold, blue, and purple, and scarlet, and fine twined linen.

3 And they did beat the gold into thin plates, and cut *it into* wires, to work *it* in the blue, and in the purple, and in the scarlet, and in the fine linen, *with* cunning work.

4 They made shoulderpieces for it, to couple *it* together: by the two edges was it coupled together.

5 And the curious girdle of his ephod, that *was* upon it, *was* of the same, according to the work thereof; *of* gold, blue, and purple, and scarlet, and fine twined linen; as the LORD commanded Moses.

6 And they wrought onyx stones inclosed in ouches of gold, graven, as signets are graven, with the names of the children of Israel.

NEW LIVING TRANSLATION

engraving, designing, and embroidering with blue, purple, and scarlet thread on fine linen cloth.

24 The people brought special offerings of gold totaling 2,193 pounds,* as measured by the weight of the sanctuary shekel. This gold was used throughout the Tabernacle.

25 The whole community of Israel gave 7,545 pounds* of silver, as measured by the weight of the sanctuary shekel. 26 This silver came from the tax collected from each man registered in the census. (The tax is one beka, which is half a shekel,* based on the sanctuary shekel.) The tax was collected from 603,550 men who had reached their twentieth birthday. 27 The hundred bases for the frames of the sanctuary walls and for the posts supporting the inner curtain required 7,500 pounds of silver, about 75 pounds for each base.* 28 The remaining 45 pounds* of silver was used to make the hooks and rings and to overlay the tops of the posts.

29 The people also brought as special offerings 5,310 pounds* of bronze, 30 which was used for casting the bases for the posts at the entrance to the Tabernacle, and for the bronze altar with its bronze grating and all the altar utensils. 31 Bronze was also used to make the bases for the posts that supported the curtains around the courtyard, the bases for the curtain at the entrance of the courtyard, and all the tent pegs for the Tabernacle and the courtyard.

Clothing for the Priests

39 The craftsmen made beautiful sacred garments of blue, purple, and scarlet cloth—clothing for Aaron to wear while ministering in the Holy Place, just as the LORD had commanded Moses.

Making the Ephod

2 Bezalel* made the ephod of finely woven linen and embroidered it with gold and with blue, purple, and scarlet thread. 3 He made gold thread by hammering out thin sheets of gold and cutting it into fine strands. With great skill and care, he worked it into the fine linen with the blue, purple, and scarlet thread.

4 The ephod consisted of two pieces, front and back, joined at the shoulders with two shoulder-pieces. 5 The decorative sash was made of the same materials: finely woven linen embroidered with gold and with blue, purple, and scarlet thread, just as the LORD had commanded Moses. 6 They mounted the two onyx stones in settings of gold filigree. The stones were engraved with the names of the tribes

38:24 Hebrew *29 talents and 730 shekels* [994 kilograms]. Each shekel weighed about 0.4 ounces. **38:25** Hebrew *100 talents and 1,775 shekels* [3,420 kilograms]. **38:26** Or *0.2 ounces,* or *6 grams.* **38:27** Hebrew *100 talents* [3,400 kilograms] *of silver, 1 talent* [34 kilograms] *for each base.* **38:28** Hebrew *1,775 shekels* [20.2 kilograms]. **38:29** Hebrew *70 talents and 2,400 shekels* [2,407 kilograms]. **39:2** Hebrew *He;* also in 39:8, 22.

KING JAMES VERSION

7 And he put them on the shoulders of the ephod, *that they should be* stones for a memorial to the children of Israel; as the LORD commanded Moses.

8 And he made the breastplate *of* cunning work, like the work of the ephod; *of* gold, blue, and purple, and scarlet, and fine twined linen.

9 It was foursquare; they made the breastplate double: a span *was* the length thereof, and a span the breadth thereof, *being* doubled.

10 And they set in it four rows of stones: *the first* row *was* a sardius, a topaz, and a carbuncle: this *was* the first row.

11 And the second row, an emerald, a sapphire, and a diamond.

12 And the third row, a ligure, an agate, and an amethyst.

13 And the fourth row, a beryl, an onyx, and a jasper: *they were* inclosed in ouches of gold in their inclosings.

14 And the stones *were* according to the names of the children of Israel, twelve, according to their names, *like* the engravings of a signet, every one with his name, according to the twelve tribes.

15 And they made upon the breastplate chains at the ends, *of* wreathen work *of* pure gold.

16 And they made two ouches *of* gold, and two gold rings; and put the two rings in the two ends of the breastplate.

17 And they put the two wreathen chains of gold in the two rings on the ends of the breastplate.

18 And the two ends of the two wreathen chains they fastened in the two ouches, and put them on the shoulderpieces of the ephod, before it.

19 And they made two rings of gold, and put *them* on the two ends of the breastplate, upon the border of it, which *was* on the side of the ephod inward.

20 And they made two *other* golden rings, and put them on the two sides of the ephod underneath, toward the forepart of it, over against the *other* coupling thereof, above the curious girdle of the ephod.

21 And they did bind the breastplate by his rings unto the rings of the ephod with a lace of blue, that it might be above the curious girdle of the ephod, and that the breastplate might not be loosed from the ephod; as the LORD commanded Moses.

22 And he made the robe of the ephod *of* woven work, all *of* blue.

23 And *there was* an hole in the midst of the robe, as the hole of an habergeon, *with* a band round about the hole, that it should not rend.

24 And they made upon the hems of the robe pomegranates *of* blue, and purple, and scarlet, *and* twined *linen.*

25 And they made bells *of* pure gold, and put the

NEW LIVING TRANSLATION

of Israel, just as a seal is engraved. 7 He fastened
these stones on the shoulder-pieces of the ephod as
a reminder that the priest represents the people of
Israel. All this was done just as the LORD had commanded Moses.

Making the Chestpiece

8 Bezalel made the chestpiece with great skill and
care. He made it to match the ephod, using finely woven linen embroidered with gold and with blue, purple, and scarlet thread. 9 He made the chestpiece of a
single piece of cloth folded to form a pouch nine
inches* square. 10 They mounted four rows of gemstones* on it. The first row contained a red carnelian,
a pale-green peridot, and an emerald. 11 The second
row contained a turquoise, a blue lapis lazuli, and a
white moonstone. 12 The third row contained an
orange jacinth, an agate, and a purple amethyst.
13 The fourth row contained a blue-green beryl, an
onyx, and a green jasper. All these stones were set in
gold filigree. 14 Each stone represented one of the
twelve sons of Israel, and the name of that tribe was
engraved on it like a seal.

15 To attach the chestpiece to the ephod, they
made braided cords of pure gold thread. 16 They also
made two settings of gold filigree and two gold rings
and attached them to the top corners of the chestpiece. 17 They tied the two gold cords to the rings on
the chestpiece. 18 They tied the other ends of the
cords to the gold settings on the shoulder-pieces of
the ephod. 19 Then they made two more gold rings
and attached them to the inside edges of the chestpiece next to the ephod. 20 Then they made two more
gold rings and attached them to the front of the
ephod, below the shoulder-pieces, just above the
knot where the decorative sash was fastened to
the ephod. 21 They attached the bottom rings of the
chestpiece to the rings on the ephod with blue cords.
In this way, the chestpiece was held securely to the
ephod above the decorative sash. All this was done
just as the LORD had commanded Moses.

Additional Clothing for the Priests

22 Bezalel made the robe that is worn with the ephod
from a single piece of blue woven cloth, 23 with an
opening for Aaron's head in the middle of it. The
opening was reinforced with a woven collar* so it
would not tear. 24 They made pomegranates of blue,
purple, and scarlet yarn, and attached them to the
hem of the robe. 25 They also made bells of pure gold

39:9 Hebrew *1 span* [23 centimeters]. **39:10** The identification of some of these gemstones is uncertain. **39:23** The meaning of the Hebrew is uncertain.

KING JAMES VERSION

bells between the pomegranates upon the hem of
the robe, round about between the pomegranates;
26 A bell and a pomegranate, a bell and a pomegranate, round about the hem of the robe to minister
in; as the LORD commanded Moses.
27 And they made coats *of* fine linen *of* woven work
for Aaron, and for his sons,
28 And a mitre *of* fine linen, and goodly bonnets *of*
fine linen, and linen breeches *of* fine twined linen,
29 And a girdle *of* fine twined linen, and blue, and
purple, and scarlet, *of* needlework; as the LORD commanded Moses.
30 And they made the plate of the holy crown *of*
pure gold, and wrote upon it a writing, *like to* the engravings of a signet, HOLINESS TO THE LORD.
31 And they tied unto it a lace of blue, to fasten *it* on
high upon the mitre; as the LORD commanded
Moses.

32 Thus was all the work of the tabernacle of the
tent of the congregation finished: and the children
of Israel did according to all that the LORD commanded Moses, so did they.
33 And they brought the tabernacle unto Moses,
the tent, and all his furniture, his taches, his boards,
his bars, and his pillars, and his sockets,
34 And the covering of rams' skins dyed red, and
the covering of badgers' skins, and the veil of the
covering,
35 The ark of the testimony, and the staves thereof,
and the mercy seat,
36 The table, *and* all the vessels thereof, and the
shewbread,
37 The pure candlestick, *with* the lamps thereof,
even with the lamps to be set in order, and all the
vessels thereof, and the oil for light,
38 And the golden altar, and the anointing oil, and
the sweet incense, and the hanging for the tabernacle door,
39 The brasen altar, and his grate of brass, his
staves, and all his vessels, the laver and his foot,
40 The hangings of the court, his pillars, and his
sockets, and the hanging for the court gate, his cords,
and his pins, and all the vessels of the service of the
tabernacle, for the tent of the congregation,
41 The cloths of service to do service in the holy
place, and the holy garments for Aaron the priest,
and his sons' garments, to minister in the priest's
office.

NEW LIVING TRANSLATION

and placed them between the pomegranates along
the hem of the robe, 26 with bells and pomegranates
alternating all around the hem. This robe was to be
worn whenever the priest ministered before the
LORD, just as the LORD had commanded Moses.
27 They made tunics for Aaron and his sons from
fine linen cloth. 28 The turban and the special head
coverings were made of fine linen, and the undergarments were also made of finely woven linen.
29 The sashes were made of finely woven linen and
embroidered with blue, purple, and scarlet thread,
just as the LORD had commanded Moses.
30 Finally, they made the sacred medallion—the
badge of holiness—of pure gold. They engraved it
like a seal with these words: HOLY TO THE LORD.
31 They attached the medallion with a blue cord to
Aaron's turban, just as the LORD had commanded
Moses.

Moses Inspects the Work

32 And so at last the Tabernacle* was finished. The Israelites had done everything just as the LORD had
commanded Moses. 33 And they brought the entire
Tabernacle to Moses:

the sacred tent with all its furnishings, clasps,
frames, crossbars, posts, and bases;
34 the tent coverings of tanned ram skins and fine
goatskin leather;
the inner curtain to shield the Ark;
35 the Ark of the Covenant* and its carrying poles;
the Ark's cover—the place of atonement;
36 the table and all its utensils;
the Bread of the Presence;
37 the pure gold lampstand with its symmetrical
lamp cups, all its accessories, and the olive oil
for lighting;
38 the gold altar;
the anointing oil and fragrant incense;
the curtain for the entrance of the sacred tent;
39 the bronze altar;
the bronze grating and its carrying poles
and utensils;
the washbasin with its stand;
40 the curtains for the walls of the courtyard;
the posts and their bases;
the curtain for the entrance to the courtyard;
the ropes and tent pegs;
all the furnishings to be used in worship at the
Tabernacle;
41 the beautifully stitched garments for the priests
to wear while ministering in the Holy Place—
the sacred garments for Aaron the priest, and
the garments for his sons to wear as they
minister as priests.

39:32 Hebrew *the Tabernacle, the Tent of Meeting;* also in 39:40.
39:35 Or *Ark of the Testimony.*

KING JAMES VERSION

42According to all that the LORD commanded
Moses, so the children of Israel made all the work.
43And Moses did look upon all the work, and, behold, they had done it as the LORD had commanded,
even so had they done it: and Moses blessed them.

40 1And the LORD spake unto Moses, saying,
2On the first day of the first month shalt
thou set up the tabernacle of the tent of the congregation.
3And thou shalt put therein the ark of the testimony, and cover the ark with the veil.
4And thou shalt bring in the table, and set in order
the things that are to be set in order upon it; and thou
shalt bring in the candlestick, and light the lamps
thereof.
5And thou shalt set the altar of gold for the incense before the ark of the testimony, and put the
hanging of the door to the tabernacle.
6And thou shalt set the altar of the burnt offering
before the door of the tabernacle of the tent of the
congregation.
7And thou shalt set the laver between the tent of
the congregation and the altar, and shalt put water
therein.
8And thou shalt set up the court round about, and
hang up the hanging at the court gate.
9And thou shalt take the anointing oil, and anoint
the tabernacle, and all that *is* therein, and shalt hallow it, and all the vessels thereof: and it shall be holy.
10And thou shalt anoint the altar of the burnt offering, and all his vessels, and sanctify the altar: and
it shall be an altar most holy.
11And thou shalt anoint the laver and his foot, and
sanctify it.
12And thou shalt bring Aaron and his sons unto
the door of the tabernacle of the congregation, and
wash them with water.
13And thou shalt put upon Aaron the holy garments, and anoint him, and sanctify him; that he may
minister unto me in the priest's office.
14And thou shalt bring his sons, and clothe them
with coats:
15And thou shalt anoint them, as thou didst anoint
their father, that they may minister unto me in the
priest's office: for their anointing shall surely be an
everlasting priesthood throughout their generations.
16Thus did Moses: according to all that the LORD
commanded him, so did he.
17And it came to pass in the first month in the second year, on the first *day* of the month, *that* the tabernacle was reared up.
18And Moses reared up the tabernacle, and fastened his sockets, and set up the boards thereof, and
put in the bars thereof, and reared up his pillars.
19And he spread abroad the tent over the tabernacle, and put the covering of the tent above upon it; as
the LORD commanded Moses.

NEW LIVING TRANSLATION

42So the people of Israel followed all of the LORD's
instructions to Moses. 43Then Moses inspected all
their work. When he found it had been done just as
the LORD had commanded him, he blessed them.

The Tabernacle Completed

40 Then the LORD said to Moses, 2"Set up the
Tabernacle* on the first day of the new
year.* 3Place the Ark of the Covenant* inside, and install the inner curtain to enclose the Ark within the
Most Holy Place. 4Then bring in the table, and arrange the utensils on it. And bring in the lampstand,
and set up the lamps.
5"Place the gold incense altar in front of the Ark of
the Covenant. Then hang the curtain at the entrance
of the Tabernacle. 6Place the altar of burnt offering
in front of the Tabernacle entrance. 7Set the washbasin between the Tabernacle* and the altar, and fill
it with water. 8Then set up the courtyard around the
outside of the tent, and hang the curtain for the
courtyard entrance.
9"Take the anointing oil and anoint the Tabernacle and all its furnishings to consecrate them and
make them holy. 10Anoint the altar of burnt offering
and its utensils to consecrate them. Then the altar
will become absolutely holy. 11Next anoint the washbasin and its stand to consecrate them.
12"Present Aaron and his sons at the entrance of
the Tabernacle, and wash them with water. 13Dress
Aaron with the sacred garments and anoint him,
consecrating him to serve me as a priest. 14Then
present his sons and dress them in their tunics.
15Anoint them as you did their father, so they may
also serve me as priests. With their anointing,
Aaron's descendants are set apart for the priesthood
forever, from generation to generation."
16Moses proceeded to do everything just as the
LORD had commanded him. 17So the Tabernacle was
set up on the first day of the first month of the second year. 18Moses erected the Tabernacle by setting
down its bases, inserting the frames, attaching the
crossbars, and setting up the posts. 19Then he spread
the coverings over the Tabernacle framework and
put on the protective layers, just as the LORD had
commanded him.

40:2a Hebrew *the Tabernacle, the Tent of Meeting;* also in 40:6, 29. **40:2b** Hebrew *the first day of the first month.* This day of the ancient Hebrew lunar calendar occurred in March or April. **40:3** Or *Ark of the Testimony;* also in 40:5, 21. **40:7** Hebrew *Tent of Meeting;* also in 40:12, 22, 24, 26, 30, 32, 34, 35.

KING JAMES VERSION

20 And he took and put the testimony into the ark, and set the staves on the ark, and put the mercy seat above upon the ark:

21 And he brought the ark into the tabernacle, and set up the veil of the covering, and covered the ark of the testimony; as the LORD commanded Moses.

22 And he put the table in the tent of the congregation, upon the side of the tabernacle northward, without the veil.

23 And he set the bread in order upon it before the LORD; as the LORD had commanded Moses.

24 And he put the candlestick in the tent of the congregation, over against the table, on the side of the tabernacle southward.

25 And he lighted the lamps before the LORD; as the LORD commanded Moses.

26 And he put the golden altar in the tent of the congregation before the veil:

27 And he burnt sweet incense thereon; as the LORD commanded Moses.

28 And he set up the hanging *at* the door of the tabernacle.

29 And he put the altar of burnt offering *by* the door of the tabernacle of the tent of the congregation, and offered upon it the burnt offering and the meat offering; as the LORD commanded Moses.

30 And he set the laver between the tent of the congregation and the altar, and put water there, to wash *withal*.

31 And Moses and Aaron and his sons washed their hands and their feet thereat:

32 When they went into the tent of the congregation, and when they came near unto the altar, they washed; as the LORD commanded Moses.

33 And he reared up the court round about the tabernacle and the altar, and set up the hanging of the court gate. So Moses finished the work.

34 Then a cloud covered the tent of the congregation, and the glory of the LORD filled the tabernacle.

35 And Moses was not able to enter into the tent of the congregation, because the cloud abode thereon, and the glory of the LORD filled the tabernacle.

36 And when the cloud was taken up from over the tabernacle, the children of Israel went onward in all their journeys:

37 But if the cloud were not taken up, then they journeyed not till the day that it was taken up.

38 For the cloud of the LORD *was* upon the tabernacle by day, and fire was on it by night, in the sight of all the house of Israel, throughout all their journeys.

NEW LIVING TRANSLATION

20 He took the stone tablets inscribed with the terms of the covenant and placed them* inside the Ark. Then he attached the carrying poles to the Ark, and he set the Ark's cover—the place of atonement—on top of it. 21 Then he brought the Ark of the Covenant into the Tabernacle and hung the inner curtain to shield it from view, just as the LORD had commanded him.

22 Next Moses placed the table in the Tabernacle, along the north side of the Holy Place, just outside the inner curtain. 23 And he arranged the Bread of the Presence on the table before the LORD, just as the LORD had commanded him.

24 He set the lampstand in the Tabernacle across from the table on the south side of the Holy Place. 25 Then he lit the lamps in the LORD's presence, just as the LORD had commanded him. 26 He also placed the gold incense altar in the Tabernacle, in the Holy Place in front of the inner curtain. 27 On it he burned the fragrant incense, just as the LORD had commanded him.

28 He hung the curtain at the entrance of the Tabernacle, 29 and he placed the altar of burnt offering near the Tabernacle entrance. On it he offered a burnt offering and a grain offering, just as the LORD had commanded him.

30 Next Moses placed the washbasin between the Tabernacle and the altar. He filled it with water so the priests could wash themselves. 31 Moses and Aaron and Aaron's sons used water from it to wash their hands and feet. 32 Whenever they approached the altar and entered the Tabernacle, they washed themselves, just as the LORD had commanded Moses.

33 Then he hung the curtains forming the courtyard around the Tabernacle and the altar. And he set up the curtain at the entrance of the courtyard. So at last Moses finished the work.

The LORD's Glory Fills the Tabernacle

34 Then the cloud covered the Tabernacle, and the glory of the LORD filled the Tabernacle. 35 Moses could no longer enter the Tabernacle because the cloud had settled down over it, and the glory of the LORD filled the Tabernacle.

36 Now whenever the cloud lifted from the Tabernacle, the people of Israel would set out on their journey, following it. 37 But if the cloud did not rise, they remained where they were until it lifted. 38 The cloud of the LORD hovered over the Tabernacle during the day, and at night fire glowed inside the cloud so the whole family of Israel could see it. This continued throughout all their journeys.

40:20 Hebrew *He placed the Testimony;* see note on 25:16.

Leviticus

KING JAMES VERSION

1 1And the LORD called unto Moses, and spake
unto him out of the tabernacle of the congregation, saying,
2Speak unto the children of Israel, and say unto
them, If any man of you bring an offering unto the
LORD, ye shall bring your offering of the cattle, *even*
of the herd, and of the flock.
3If his offering *be* a burnt sacrifice of the herd, let
him offer a male without blemish: he shall offer it of
his own voluntary will at the door of the tabernacle
of the congregation before the LORD.
4And he shall put his hand upon the head of the
burnt offering; and it shall be accepted for him to
make atonement for him.
5And he shall kill the bullock before the LORD: and
the priests, Aaron's sons, shall bring the blood, and
sprinkle the blood round about upon the altar that *is*
by the door of the tabernacle of the congregation.
6And he shall flay the burnt offering, and cut it
into his pieces.
7And the sons of Aaron the priest shall put fire
upon the altar, and lay the wood in order upon the
fire:
8And the priests, Aaron's sons, shall lay the parts,
the head, and the fat, in order upon the wood that *is*
on the fire which *is* upon the altar:
9But his inwards and his legs shall he wash in
water: and the priest shall burn all on the altar, *to be* a
burnt sacrifice, an offering made by fire, of a sweet
savour unto the LORD.
10And if his offering *be* of the flocks, *namely,* of
the sheep, or of the goats, for a burnt sacrifice; he
shall bring it a male without blemish.
11And he shall kill it on the side of the altar northward before the LORD: and the priests, Aaron's sons,
shall sprinkle his blood round about upon the altar.
12And he shall cut it into his pieces, with his head
and his fat: and the priest shall lay them in order on
the wood that *is* on the fire which *is* upon the altar:
13But he shall wash the inwards and the legs with
water: and the priest shall bring *it* all, and burn *it*
upon the altar: it *is* a burnt sacrifice, an offering
made by fire, of a sweet savour unto the LORD.

NEW LIVING TRANSLATION

Procedures for the Burnt Offering

1 The LORD called to Moses from the Tabernacle*
and said to him, 2"Give the following instructions to the people of Israel. When you present
an animal as an offering to the LORD, you may take
it from your herd of cattle or your flock of sheep
and goats.
3"If the animal you present as a burnt offering is
from the herd, it must be a male with no defects.
Bring it to the entrance of the Tabernacle so you* may
be accepted by the LORD. 4Lay your hand on the animal's head, and the LORD will accept its death in your
place to purify you, making you right with him.*
5Then slaughter the young bull in the LORD's presence, and Aaron's sons, the priests, will present the
animal's blood by splattering it against all sides of the
altar that stands at the entrance to the Tabernacle.
6Then skin the animal and cut it into pieces. 7The
sons of Aaron the priest will build a wood fire on the
altar. 8They will arrange the pieces of the offering, including the head and fat, on the wood burning on the
altar. 9But the internal organs and the legs must first
be washed with water. Then the priest will burn the
entire sacrifice on the altar as a burnt offering. It is a
special gift, a pleasing aroma to the LORD.
10"If the animal you present as a burnt offering is
from the flock, it may be either a sheep or a goat, but
it must be a male with no defects. 11Slaughter the animal on the north side of the altar in the LORD's presence, and Aaron's sons, the priests, will splatter its
blood against all sides of the altar. 12Then cut the animal in pieces, and the priests will arrange the pieces
of the offering, including the head and fat, on the
wood burning on the altar. 13But the internal organs
and the legs must first be washed with water. Then
the priest will burn the entire sacrifice on the altar as
a burnt offering. It is a special gift, a pleasing aroma
to the LORD.

1:1 Hebrew *Tent of Meeting;* also in 1:3, 5. **1:3** Or *it.* **1:4** Or *to make atonement for you.*

KING JAMES VERSION

14And if the burnt sacrifice for his offering to the
LORD *be* of fowls, then he shall bring his offering of
turtledoves, or of young pigeons.
15And the priest shall bring it unto the altar, and
wring off his head, and burn *it* on the altar; and
the blood thereof shall be wrung out at the side of
the altar:
16And he shall pluck away his crop with his feathers, and cast it beside the altar on the east part, by the
place of the ashes:
17And he shall cleave it with the wings thereof, *but*
shall not divide *it* asunder: and the priest shall burn
it upon the altar, upon the wood that *is* upon the fire:
it *is* a burnt sacrifice, an offering made by fire, of a
sweet savour unto the LORD.

2 1And when any will offer a meat offering unto
the LORD, his offering shall be *of* fine flour; and
he shall pour oil upon it, and put frankincense
thereon:
2And he shall bring it to Aaron's sons the priests:
and he shall take thereout his handful of the flour
thereof, and of the oil thereof, with all the frankincense thereof; and the priest shall burn the memorial of it upon the altar, *to be* an offering made by fire,
of a sweet savour unto the LORD:
3And the remnant of the meat offering *shall be*
Aaron's and his sons': *it is* a thing most holy of the
offerings of the LORD made by fire.
4And if thou bring an oblation of a meat offering
baken in the oven, *it shall be* unleavened cakes of
fine flour mingled with oil, or unleavened wafers
anointed with oil.
5And if thy oblation *be* a meat offering *baken* in a
pan, it shall be *of* fine flour unleavened, mingled
with oil.
6Thou shalt part it in pieces, and pour oil thereon:
it *is* a meat offering.
7And if thy oblation *be* a meat offering *baken* in
the fryingpan, it shall be made *of* fine flour with oil.
8And thou shalt bring the meat offering that is
made of these things unto the LORD: and when it is
presented unto the priest, he shall bring it unto
the altar.
9And the priest shall take from the meat offering a
memorial thereof, and shall burn *it* upon the altar: *it*
is an offering made by fire, of a sweet savour unto
the LORD.
10And that which is left of the meat offering *shall*
be Aaron's and his sons': *it is* a thing most holy of the
offerings of the LORD made by fire.
11No meat offering, which ye shall bring unto the
LORD, shall be made with leaven: for ye shall burn no
leaven, nor any honey, in any offering of the LORD
made by fire.
12As for the oblation of the firstfruits, ye shall offer them unto the LORD: but they shall not be burnt
on the altar for a sweet savour.

NEW LIVING TRANSLATION

14"If you present a bird as a burnt offering to the
LORD, choose either a turtledove or a young pigeon.
15The priest will take the bird to the altar, wring off
its head, and burn it on the altar. But first he must
drain its blood against the side of the altar. 16The
priest must also remove the crop and the feathers*
and throw them in the ashes on the east side of the
altar. 17Then, grasping the bird by its wings, the
priest will tear the bird open, but without tearing it
apart. Then he will burn it as a burnt offering on the
wood burning on the altar. It is a special gift, a pleasing aroma to the LORD.

Procedures for the Grain Offering

2 "When you present grain as an offering to the
LORD, the offering must consist of choice flour.
You are to pour olive oil on it, sprinkle it with frankincense, 2and bring it to Aaron's sons, the priests.
The priest will scoop out a handful of the flour
moistened with oil, together with all the frankincense, and burn this representative portion on the altar. It is a special gift, a pleasing aroma to the LORD.
3The rest of the grain offering will then be given to
Aaron and his sons. This offering will be considered
a most holy part of the special gifts presented to
the LORD.
4"If your offering is a grain offering baked in an
oven, it must be made of choice flour, but without
any yeast. It may be presented in the form of thin
cakes mixed with olive oil or wafers spread with olive
oil. 5If your grain offering is cooked on a griddle, it
must be made of choice flour mixed with olive oil
but without any yeast. 6Break it in pieces and pour
olive oil on it; it is a grain offering. 7If your grain offering is prepared in a pan, it must be made of choice
flour and olive oil.
8"No matter how a grain offering for the LORD has
been prepared, bring it to the priest, who will present
it at the altar. 9The priest will take a representative
portion of the grain offering and burn it on the altar.
It is a special gift, a pleasing aroma to the LORD.
10The rest of the grain offering will then be given to
Aaron and his sons as their food. This offering will
be considered a most holy part of the special gifts
presented to the LORD.
11"Do not use yeast in preparing any of the grain
offerings you present to the LORD, because no yeast
or honey may be burned as a special gift presented to
the LORD. 12You may add yeast and honey to an offering of the first crops of your harvest, but these
must never be offered on the altar as a pleasing

1:16 Or *the crop and its contents.* The meaning of the Hebrew is uncertain.

KING JAMES VERSION

13And every oblation of thy meat offering shalt thou season with salt; neither shalt thou suffer the salt of the covenant of thy God to be lacking from thy meat offering: with all thine offerings thou shalt offer salt.

14And if thou offer a meat offering of thy firstfruits unto the LORD, thou shalt offer for the meat offering of thy firstfruits green ears of corn dried by the fire, *even* corn beaten out of full ears.

15And thou shalt put oil upon it, and lay frankincense thereon: it *is* a meat offering.

16And the priest shall burn the memorial of it, *part* of the beaten corn thereof, and *part* of the oil thereof, with all the frankincense thereof: *it is* an offering made by fire unto the LORD.

3 1And if his oblation *be* a sacrifice of peace offering, if he offer *it* of the herd; whether *it be* a male or female, he shall offer it without blemish before the LORD.

2And he shall lay his hand upon the head of his offering, and kill it *at* the door of the tabernacle of the congregation: and Aaron's sons the priests shall sprinkle the blood upon the altar round about.

3And he shall offer of the sacrifice of the peace offering an offering made by fire unto the LORD; the fat that covereth the inwards, and all the fat that *is* upon the inwards,

4And the two kidneys, and the fat that *is* on them, which *is* by the flanks, and the caul above the liver, with the kidneys, it shall he take away.

5And Aaron's sons shall burn it on the altar upon the burnt sacrifice, which *is* upon the wood that *is* on the fire: *it is* an offering made by fire, of a sweet savour unto the LORD.

6And if his offering for a sacrifice of peace offering unto the LORD *be* of the flock; male or female, he shall offer it without blemish.

7If he offer a lamb for his offering, then shall he offer it before the LORD.

8And he shall lay his hand upon the head of his offering, and kill it before the tabernacle of the congregation: and Aaron's sons shall sprinkle the blood thereof round about upon the altar.

9And he shall offer of the sacrifice of the peace offering an offering made by fire unto the LORD; the fat thereof, *and* the whole rump, it shall he take off hard by the backbone; and the fat that covereth the inwards, and all the fat that *is* upon the inwards,

10And the two kidneys, and the fat that *is* upon them, which *is* by the flanks, and the caul above the liver, with the kidneys, it shall he take away.

11And the priest shall burn it upon the altar: *it is* the food of the offering made by fire unto the LORD.

12And if his offering *be* a goat, then he shall offer it before the LORD.

13And he shall lay his hand upon the head of it, and kill it before the tabernacle of the congregation: and

NEW LIVING TRANSLATION

aroma to the LORD. 13Season all your grain offerings with salt to remind you of God's eternal covenant. Never forget to add salt to your grain offerings.

14"If you present a grain offering to the LORD from the first portion of your harvest, bring fresh grain that is coarsely ground and roasted on a fire. 15Put olive oil on this grain offering, and sprinkle it with frankincense. 16The priest will take a representative portion of the grain moistened with oil, together with all the frankincense, and burn it as a special gift presented to the LORD.

Procedures for the Peace Offering

3 "If you present an animal from the herd as a peace offering to the LORD, it may be a male or a female, but it must have no defects. 2Lay your hand on the animal's head, and slaughter it at the entrance of the Tabernacle.* Then Aaron's sons, the priests, will splatter its blood against all sides of the altar. 3The priest must present part of this peace offering as a special gift to the LORD. This includes all the fat around the internal organs, 4the two kidneys and the fat around them near the loins, and the long lobe of the liver. These must be removed with the kidneys, 5and Aaron's sons will burn them on top of the burnt offering on the wood burning on the altar. It is a special gift, a pleasing aroma to the LORD.

6"If you present an animal from the flock as a peace offering to the LORD, it may be a male or a female, but it must have no defects. 7If you present a sheep as your offering, bring it to the LORD, 8lay your hand on its head, and slaughter it in front of the Tabernacle. Aaron's sons will then splatter the sheep's blood against all sides of the altar. 9The priest must present the fat of this peace offering as a special gift to the LORD. This includes the fat of the broad tail cut off near the backbone, all the fat around the internal organs, 10the two kidneys and the fat around them near the loins, and the long lobe of the liver. These must be removed with the kidneys, 11and the priest will burn them on the altar. It is a special gift of food presented to the LORD.

12"If you present a goat as your offering, bring it to the LORD, 13lay your hand on its head, and slaughter it in front of the Tabernacle. Aaron's sons will then

3:2 Hebrew *Tent of Meeting;* also in 3:8, 13.

KING JAMES VERSION

the sons of Aaron shall sprinkle the blood thereof upon the altar round about.

14And he shall offer thereof his offering, *even* an offering made by fire unto the LORD; the fat that covereth the inwards, and all the fat that *is* upon the inwards,

15And the two kidneys, and the fat that *is* upon them, which *is* by the flanks, and the caul above the liver, with the kidneys, it shall he take away.

16And the priest shall burn them upon the altar: *it is* the food of the offering made by fire for a sweet savour: all the fat *is* the LORD'S.

17*It shall be* a perpetual statute for your generations throughout all your dwellings, that ye eat neither fat nor blood.

4 1And the LORD spake unto Moses, saying,

2Speak unto the children of Israel, saying, If a soul shall sin through ignorance against any of the commandments of the LORD *concerning things* which ought not to be done, and shall do against any of them:

3If the priest that is anointed do sin according to the sin of the people; then let him bring for his sin, which he hath sinned, a young bullock without blemish unto the LORD for a sin offering.

4And he shall bring the bullock unto the door of the tabernacle of the congregation before the LORD; and shall lay his hand upon the bullock's head, and kill the bullock before the LORD.

5And the priest that is anointed shall take of the bullock's blood, and bring it to the tabernacle of the congregation:

6And the priest shall dip his finger in the blood, and sprinkle of the blood seven times before the LORD, before the veil of the sanctuary.

7And the priest shall put *some* of the blood upon the horns of the altar of sweet incense before the LORD, which *is* in the tabernacle of the congregation; and shall pour all the blood of the bullock at the bottom of the altar of the burnt offering, which *is at* the door of the tabernacle of the congregation.

8And he shall take off from it all the fat of the bullock for the sin offering; the fat that covereth the inwards, and all the fat that *is* upon the inwards,

9And the two kidneys, and the fat that *is* upon them, which *is* by the flanks, and the caul above the liver, with the kidneys, it shall he take away,

10As it was taken off from the bullock of the sacrifice of peace offerings: and the priest shall burn them upon the altar of the burnt offering.

11And the skin of the bullock, and all his flesh, with his head, and with his legs, and his inwards, and his dung,

12Even the whole bullock shall he carry forth without the camp unto a clean place, where the ashes are poured out, and burn him on the wood with fire: where the ashes are poured out shall he be burnt.

NEW LIVING TRANSLATION

splatter the goat's blood against all sides of the altar.
14The priest must present part of this offering as a
special gift to the LORD. This includes all the fat
around the internal organs, 15the two kidneys and
the fat around them near the loins, and the long lobe
of the liver. These must be removed with the kidneys,
16and the priest will burn them on the altar. It is
a special gift of food, a pleasing aroma to the LORD.
All the fat belongs to the LORD.
17"You must never eat any fat or blood. This is a
permanent law for you, and it must be observed from
generation to generation, wherever you live."

Procedures for the Sin Offering

4 Then the LORD said to Moses, 2"Give the following instructions to the people of Israel. This is
how you are to deal with those who sin unintentionally by doing anything that violates one of the LORD's
commands.
3"If the high priest* sins, bringing guilt upon the
entire community, he must give a sin offering for the
sin he has committed. He must present to the LORD a
young bull with no defects. 4He must bring the bull
to the LORD at the entrance of the Tabernacle,* lay
his hand on the bull's head, and slaughter it before
the LORD. 5The high priest will then take some of the
bull's blood into the Tabernacle, 6dip his finger in
the blood, and sprinkle it seven times before the
LORD in front of the inner curtain of the sanctuary.
7The priest will then put some of the blood on the
horns of the altar for fragrant incense that stands in
the LORD's presence inside the Tabernacle. He will
pour out the rest of the bull's blood at the base of the
altar for burnt offerings at the entrance of the Tabernacle.
8Then the priest must remove all the fat of the
bull to be offered as a sin offering. This includes all
the fat around the internal organs, 9the two kidneys
and the fat around them near the loins, and the long
lobe of the liver. He must remove these along with
the kidneys, 10just as he does with cattle offered as a
peace offering, and burn them on the altar of burnt
offerings. 11But he must take whatever is left of the
bull—its hide, meat, head, legs, internal organs, and
dung—12and carry it away to a place outside the
camp that is ceremonially clean, the place where the
ashes are dumped. There, on the ash heap, he will
burn it on a wood fire.

4:3 Hebrew *the anointed priest;* also in 4:5, 16. 4:4 Hebrew *Tent of Meeting;* also in 4:5, 7, 14, 16, 18.

KING JAMES VERSION

13 And if the whole congregation of Israel sin
through ignorance, and the thing be hid from the
eyes of the assembly, and they have done *somewhat*
against any of the commandments of the LORD
concerning things which should not be done, and
are guilty;
14 When the sin, which they have sinned against it,
is known, then the congregation shall offer a young
bullock for the sin, and bring him before the tabernacle of the congregation.
15 And the elders of the congregation shall lay their
hands upon the head of the bullock before the LORD:
and the bullock shall be killed before the LORD.
16 And the priest that is anointed shall bring of
the bullock's blood to the tabernacle of the congregation:
17 And the priest shall dip his finger *in some* of the
blood, and sprinkle *it* seven times before the LORD,
even before the veil.
18 And he shall put *some* of the blood upon the
horns of the altar which *is* before the LORD, that *is* in
the tabernacle of the congregation, and shall pour
out all the blood at the bottom of the altar of the
burnt offering, which *is at* the door of the tabernacle
of the congregation.
19 And he shall take all his fat from him, and burn *it*
upon the altar.
20 And he shall do with the bullock as he did with
the bullock for a sin offering, so shall he do with this:
and the priest shall make an atonement for them,
and it shall be forgiven them.
21 And he shall carry forth the bullock without the
camp, and burn him as he burned the first bullock: it
is a sin offering for the congregation.
22 When a ruler hath sinned, and done *somewhat*
through ignorance *against* any of the commandments of the LORD his God *concerning things* which
should not be done, and is guilty;
23 Or if his sin, wherein he hath sinned, come to his
knowledge; he shall bring his offering, a kid of the
goats, a male without blemish:
24 And he shall lay his hand upon the head of the
goat, and kill it in the place where they kill the burnt
offering before the LORD: it *is* a sin offering.
25 And the priest shall take of the blood of the sin
offering with his finger, and put *it* upon the horns of
the altar of burnt offering, and shall pour out his
blood at the bottom of the altar of burnt offering.
26 And he shall burn all his fat upon the altar, as the
fat of the sacrifice of peace offerings: and the priest
shall make an atonement for him as concerning his
sin, and it shall be forgiven him.
27 And if any one of the common people sin
through ignorance, while he doeth *somewhat*
against any of the commandments of the LORD *con-*
cerning things which ought not to be done, and
be guilty;
28 Or if his sin, which he hath sinned, come to his

NEW LIVING TRANSLATION

13 "If the entire Israelite community sins by violating one of the LORD's commands, but the people
don't realize it, they are still guilty. 14 When they
become aware of their sin, the people must bring a
young bull as an offering for their sin and present it
before the Tabernacle. 15 The elders of the community must then lay their hands on the bull's head and
slaughter it before the LORD. 16 The high priest will
then take some of the bull's blood into the Tabernacle, 17 dip his finger in the blood, and sprinkle it
seven times before the LORD in front of the inner
curtain. 18 He will then put some of the blood on the
horns of the altar for fragrant incense that stands in
the LORD's presence inside the Tabernacle. He will
pour out the rest of the blood at the base of the altar
for burnt offerings at the entrance of the Tabernacle.
19 Then the priest must remove all the animal's fat
and burn it on the altar, 20 just as he does with the
bull offered as a sin offering for the high priest.
Through this process, the priest will purify the
people, making them right with the LORD,* and they
will be forgiven. 21 Then the priest must take what is
left of the bull and carry it outside the camp and
burn it there, just as is done with the sin offering for
the high priest. This offering is for the sin of the entire congregation of Israel.
22 "If one of Israel's leaders sins by violating one of
the commands of the LORD his God but doesn't realize it, he is still guilty. 23 When he becomes aware of
his sin, he must bring as his offering a male goat with
no defects. 24 He must lay his hand on the goat's head
and slaughter it at the place where burnt offerings
are slaughtered before the LORD. This is an offering
for his sin. 25 Then the priest will dip his finger in the
blood of the sin offering and put it on the horns of
the altar for burnt offerings. He will pour out the rest
of the blood at the base of the altar. 26 Then he must
burn all the goat's fat on the altar, just as he does with
the peace offering. Through this process, the priest
will purify the leader from his sin, making him right
with the LORD, and he will be forgiven.
27 "If any of the common people sin by violating
one of the LORD's commands, but they don't realize
it, they are still guilty. 28 When they become aware of

4:20 Or *will make atonement for the people;* similarly in 4:26, 31, 35.

KING JAMES VERSION

knowledge: then he shall bring his offering, a kid of the goats, a female without blemish, for his sin which he hath sinned.

29And he shall lay his hand upon the head of the sin offering, and slay the sin offering in the place of the burnt offering.

30And the priest shall take of the blood thereof with his finger, and put *it* upon the horns of the altar of burnt offering, and shall pour out all the blood thereof at the bottom of the altar.

31And he shall take away all the fat thereof, as the fat is taken away from off the sacrifice of peace offerings; and the priest shall burn *it* upon the altar for a sweet savour unto the LORD; and the priest shall make an atonement for him, and it shall be forgiven him.

32And if he bring a lamb for a sin offering, he shall bring it a female without blemish.

33And he shall lay his hand upon the head of the sin offering, and slay it for a sin offering in the place where they kill the burnt offering.

34And the priest shall take of the blood of the sin offering with his finger, and put *it* upon the horns of the altar of burnt offering, and shall pour out all the blood thereof at the bottom of the altar:

35And he shall take away all the fat thereof, as the fat of the lamb is taken away from the sacrifice of the peace offerings; and the priest shall burn them upon the altar, according to the offerings made by fire unto the LORD: and the priest shall make an atonement for his sin that he hath committed, and it shall be forgiven him.

5 1And if a soul sin, and hear the voice of swearing, and *is* a witness, whether he hath seen or known *of it;* if he do not utter *it,* then he shall bear his iniquity.

2Or if a soul touch any unclean thing, whether *it be* a carcase of an unclean beast, or a carcase of unclean cattle, or the carcase of unclean creeping things, and *if* it be hidden from him; he also shall be unclean, and guilty.

3Or if he touch the uncleanness of man, whatsoever uncleanness *it be* that a man shall be defiled withal, and it be hid from him; when he knoweth *of it,* then he shall be guilty.

4Or if a soul swear, pronouncing with *his* lips to do evil, or to do good, whatsoever *it be* that a man shall pronounce with an oath, and it be hid from him; when he knoweth *of it,* then he shall be guilty in one of these.

5And it shall be, when he shall be guilty in one of these *things,* that he shall confess that he hath sinned in that *thing:*

6And he shall bring his trespass offering unto the LORD for his sin which he hath sinned, a female from the flock, a lamb or a kid of the goats, for a sin offering; and the priest shall make an atonement for him concerning his sin.

NEW LIVING TRANSLATION

their sin, they must bring as an offering for their sin a female goat with no defects. 29They must lay a hand on the head of the sin offering and slaughter it at the place where burnt offerings are slaughtered. 30Then the priest will dip his finger in the blood and put it on the horns of the altar for burnt offerings. He will pour out the rest of the blood at the base of the altar. 31Then he must remove all the goat's fat, just as he does with the fat of the peace offering. He will burn the fat on the altar, and it will be a pleasing aroma to the LORD. Through this process, the priest will purify the people, making them right with the LORD, and they will be forgiven.

32"If the people bring a sheep as their sin offering, it must be a female with no defects. 33They must lay a hand on the head of the sin offering and slaughter it at the place where burnt offerings are slaughtered. 34Then the priest will dip his finger in the blood of the sin offering and put it on the horns of the altar for burnt offerings. He will pour out the rest of the blood at the base of the altar. 35Then he must remove all the sheep's fat, just as he does with the fat of a sheep presented as a peace offering. He will burn the fat on the altar on top of the special gifts presented to the LORD. Through this process, the priest will purify the people from their sin, making them right with the LORD, and they will be forgiven.

Sins Requiring a Sin Offering

5 "If you are called to testify about something you have seen or that you know about, it is sinful to refuse to testify, and you will be punished for your sin.

2"Or suppose you unknowingly touch something that is ceremonially unclean, such as the carcass of an unclean animal. When you realize what you have done, you must admit your defilement and your guilt. This is true whether it is a wild animal, a domestic animal, or an animal that scurries along the ground.

3"Or suppose you unknowingly touch something that makes a person unclean. When you realize what you have done, you must admit your guilt.

4"Or suppose you make a foolish vow of any kind, whether its purpose is for good or for bad. When you realize its foolishness, you must admit your guilt.

5"When you become aware of your guilt in any of these ways, you must confess your sin. 6Then you must bring to the LORD as the penalty for your sin a female from the flock, either a sheep or a goat. This is a sin offering with which the priest will purify you from your sin, making you right with the LORD.*

5:6 Or *will make atonement for you for your sin;* similarly in 5:10, 13, 16, 18.

KING JAMES VERSION

7And if he be not able to bring a lamb, then he
shall bring for his trespass, which he hath committed, two turtledoves, or two young pigeons, unto the
LORD; one for a sin offering, and the other for a burnt
offering.
8And he shall bring them unto the priest, who
shall offer *that* which *is* for the sin offering first, and
wring off his head from his neck, but shall not divide
it asunder:
9And he shall sprinkle of the blood of the sin offering upon the side of the altar; and the rest of the
blood shall be wrung out at the bottom of the altar: it
is a sin offering.
10And he shall offer the second *for* a burnt offering, according to the manner: and the priest shall
make an atonement for him for his sin which he hath
sinned, and it shall be forgiven him.
11But if he be not able to bring two turtledoves, or
two young pigeons, then he that sinned shall bring
for his offering the tenth part of an ephah of fine
flour for a sin offering; he shall put no oil upon it,
neither shall he put *any* frankincense thereon: for it
is a sin offering.
12Then shall he bring it to the priest, and the priest
shall take his handful of it, *even* a memorial thereof,
and burn *it* on the altar, according to the offerings
made by fire unto the LORD: it *is* a sin offering.
13And the priest shall make an atonement for him
as touching his sin that he hath sinned in one of
these, and it shall be forgiven him: and *the remnant*
shall be the priest's, as a meat offering.
14And the LORD spake unto Moses, saying,
15If a soul commit a trespass, and sin through ignorance, in the holy things of the LORD; then he shall
bring for his trespass unto the LORD a ram without
blemish out of the flocks, with thy estimation by
shekels of silver, after the shekel of the sanctuary, for
a trespass offering:
16And he shall make amends for the harm that he
hath done in the holy thing, and shall add the fifth
part thereto, and give it unto the priest: and the
priest shall make an atonement for him with the ram
of the trespass offering, and it shall be forgiven him.
17And if a soul sin, and commit any of these things
which are forbidden to be done by the commandments of the LORD; though he wist *it* not, yet is he
guilty, and shall bear his iniquity.
18And he shall bring a ram without blemish out of
the flock, with thy estimation, for a trespass offering,
unto the priest: and the priest shall make an atonement for him concerning his ignorance wherein he
erred and wist *it* not, and it shall be forgiven him.
19It *is* a trespass offering: he hath certainly trespassed against the LORD.

NEW LIVING TRANSLATION

7"But if you cannot afford to bring a sheep, you
may bring to the LORD two turtledoves or two young
pigeons as the penalty for your sin. One of the birds
will be for a sin offering, and the other for a burnt
offering. 8You must bring them to the priest, who
will present the first bird as the sin offering. He will
wring its neck but without severing its head from the
body. 9Then he will sprinkle some of the blood of the
sin offering against the sides of the altar, and the rest
of the blood will be drained out at the base of the altar. This is an offering for sin. 10The priest will then
prepare the second bird as a burnt offering, following all the procedures that have been prescribed.
Through this process the priest will purify you from
your sin, making you right with the LORD, and you
will be forgiven.
11"If you cannot afford to bring two turtledoves
or two young pigeons, you may bring two quarts* of
choice flour for your sin offering. Since it is an offering for sin, you must not moisten it with olive oil or
put any frankincense on it. 12Take the flour to the
priest, who will scoop out a handful as a representative portion. He will burn it on the altar on top of the
special gifts presented to the LORD. It is an offering
for sin. 13Through this process, the priest will purify
those who are guilty of any of these sins, making
them right with the LORD, and they will be forgiven.
The rest of the flour will belong to the priest, just as
with the grain offering."

Procedures for the Guilt Offering

14Then the LORD said to Moses, 15"If one of you commits a sin by unintentionally defiling the LORD's sacred property, you must bring a guilt offering to the
LORD. The offering must be your own ram with no
defects, or you may buy one of equal value with silver,
as measured by the weight of the sanctuary shekel.*
16You must make restitution for the sacred property
you have harmed by paying for the loss, plus an additional 20 percent. When you give the payment to the
priest, he will purify you with the ram sacrificed as a
guilt offering, making you right with the LORD, and
you will be forgiven.
17"Suppose you sin by violating one of the LORD's
commands. Even if you are unaware of what you have
done, you are guilty and will be punished for your
sin. 18For a guilt offering, you must bring to the
priest your own ram with no defects, or you may buy
one of equal value. Through this process the priest
will purify you from your unintentional sin, making
you right with the LORD, and you will be forgiven.
19This is a guilt offering, for you have been guilty of
an offense against the LORD."

5:11 Hebrew *1/10 of an ephah* [2.2 liters]. **5:15** Each shekel was about 0.4 ounces or 11 grams in weight.

KING JAMES VERSION

6 1And the LORD spake unto Moses, saying,
2If a soul sin, and commit a trespass against the LORD, and lie unto his neighbour in that which was delivered him to keep, or in fellowship, or in a thing taken away by violence, or hath deceived his neighbour;

3Or have found that which was lost, and lieth concerning it, and sweareth falsely; in any of all these that a man doeth, sinning therein:

4Then it shall be, because he hath sinned, and is guilty, that he shall restore that which he took violently away, or the thing which he hath deceitfully gotten, or that which was delivered him to keep, or the lost thing which he found,

5Or all that about which he hath sworn falsely; he shall even restore it in the principal, and shall add the fifth part more thereto, *and* give it unto him to whom it appertaineth, in the day of his trespass offering.

6And he shall bring his trespass offering unto the LORD, a ram without blemish out of the flock, with thy estimation, for a trespass offering, unto the priest:

7And the priest shall make an atonement for him before the LORD: and it shall be forgiven him for any thing of all that he hath done in trespassing therein.

8And the LORD spake unto Moses, saying,

9Command Aaron and his sons, saying, This *is* the law of the burnt offering: It *is* the burnt offering, because of the burning upon the altar all night unto the morning, and the fire of the altar shall be burning in it.

10And the priest shall put on his linen garment, and his linen breeches shall he put upon his flesh, and take up the ashes which the fire hath consumed with the burnt offering on the altar, and he shall put them beside the altar.

11And he shall put off his garments, and put on other garments, and carry forth the ashes without the camp unto a clean place.

12And the fire upon the altar shall be burning in it; it shall not be put out: and the priest shall burn wood on it every morning, and lay the burnt offering in order upon it; and he shall burn thereon the fat of the peace offerings.

13The fire shall ever be burning upon the altar; it shall never go out.

14And this *is* the law of the meat offering: the sons of Aaron shall offer it before the LORD, before the altar.

15And he shall take of it his handful, of the flour of the meat offering, and of the oil thereof, and all the frankincense which *is* upon the meat offering, and shall burn *it* upon the altar *for* a sweet savour, *even* the memorial of it, unto the LORD.

16And the remainder thereof shall Aaron and his sons eat: with unleavened bread shall it be eaten in

NEW LIVING TRANSLATION

Sins Requiring a Guilt Offering

6 1*Then the LORD said to Moses, 2"Suppose one
of you sins against your associate and is unfaithful to the LORD. Suppose you cheat in a deal
involving a security deposit, or you steal or commit
fraud, 3or you find lost property and lie about it, or
you lie while swearing to tell the truth, or you commit any other such sin. 4If you have sinned in any of
these ways, you are guilty. You must give back whatever you stole, or the money you took by extortion,
or the security deposit, or the lost property you
found, 5or anything obtained by swearing falsely.
You must make restitution by paying the full price
plus an additional 20 percent to the person you have
harmed. On the same day you must present a guilt
offering. 6As a guilt offering to the LORD, you must
bring to the priest your own ram with no defects, or
you may buy one of equal value. 7Through this process, the priest will purify you before the LORD,
making you right with him,* and you will be forgiven
for any of these sins you have committed."

Further Instructions for the Burnt Offering

8*Then the LORD said to Moses, 9"Give Aaron and his
sons the following instructions regarding the burnt
offering. The burnt offering must be left on top of the
altar until the next morning, and the fire on the altar
must be kept burning all night. 10In the morning, after
the priest on duty has put on his official linen clothing
and linen undergarments, he must clean out the ashes
of the burnt offering and put them beside the altar.
11Then he must take off these garments, change back
into his regular clothes, and carry the ashes outside
the camp to a place that is ceremonially clean.
12Meanwhile, the fire on the altar must be kept burning; it must never go out. Each morning the priest will
add fresh wood to the fire and arrange the burnt offering on it. He will then burn the fat of the peace offerings on it. 13Remember, the fire must be kept burning
on the altar at all times. It must never go out.

Further Instructions for the Grain Offering

14"These are the instructions regarding the grain offering. Aaron's sons must present this offering to the
LORD in front of the altar. 15The priest on duty will
take from the grain offering a handful of the choice
flour moistened with olive oil, together with all the
frankincense. He will burn this representative portion on the altar as a pleasing aroma to the LORD.
16Aaron and his sons may eat the rest of the flour, but
it must be baked without yeast and eaten in a sacred

6:1 Verses 6:1-7 are numbered 5:20-26 in Hebrew text. **6:7** Or *will make atonement for you before the LORD.* **6:8** Verses 6:8-30 are numbered 6:1-23 in Hebrew text.

KING JAMES VERSION

the holy place; in the court of the tabernacle of the congregation they shall eat it.

17 It shall not be baken with leaven. I have given it *unto them for* their portion of my offerings made by fire; it *is* most holy, as *is* the sin offering, and as the trespass offering.

18 All the males among the children of Aaron shall eat of it. *It shall be* a statute for ever in your generations concerning the offerings of the LORD made by fire: every one that toucheth them shall be holy.

19 And the LORD spake unto Moses, saying,

20 This *is* the offering of Aaron and of his sons, which they shall offer unto the LORD in the day when he is anointed; the tenth part of an ephah of fine flour for a meat offering perpetual, half of it in the morning, and half thereof at night.

21 In a pan it shall be made with oil; *and when it is* baken, thou shalt bring it in: *and* the baken pieces of the meat offering shalt thou offer *for* a sweet savour unto the LORD.

22 And the priest of his sons that is anointed in his stead shall offer it: *it is* a statute for ever unto the LORD; it shall be wholly burnt.

23 For every meat offering for the priest shall be wholly burnt: it shall not be eaten.

24 And the LORD spake unto Moses, saying,

25 Speak unto Aaron and to his sons, saying, This *is* the law of the sin offering: In the place where the burnt offering is killed shall the sin offering be killed before the LORD: it *is* most holy.

26 The priest that offereth it for sin shall eat it: in the holy place shall it be eaten, in the court of the tabernacle of the congregation.

27 Whatsoever shall touch the flesh thereof shall be holy: and when there is sprinkled of the blood thereof upon any garment, thou shalt wash that whereon it was sprinkled in the holy place.

28 But the earthen vessel wherein it is sodden shall be broken: and if it be sodden in a brasen pot, it shall be both scoured, and rinsed in water.

29 All the males among the priests shall eat thereof: it *is* most holy.

30 And no sin offering, whereof *any* of the blood is brought into the tabernacle of the congregation to reconcile *withal* in the holy *place*, shall be eaten: it shall be burnt in the fire.

7 1 Likewise this *is* the law of the trespass offering: it *is* most holy.

2 In the place where they kill the burnt offering shall they kill the trespass offering: and the blood thereof shall he sprinkle round about upon the altar.

3 And he shall offer of it all the fat thereof; the rump, and the fat that covereth the inwards,

NEW LIVING TRANSLATION

place within the courtyard of the Tabernacle.* 17 Remember, it must never be prepared with yeast. I have given it to the priests as their share of the special gifts presented to me. Like the sin offering and the guilt offering, it is most holy. 18 Any of Aaron's male descendants may eat from the special gifts presented to the LORD. This is their permanent right from generation to generation. Anyone or anything that touches these offerings will become holy."

Procedures for the Ordination Offering

19 Then the LORD said to Moses, 20 "On the day Aaron and his sons are anointed, they must present to the LORD a grain offering of two quarts* of choice flour, half to be offered in the morning and half to be offered in the evening. 21 It must be carefully mixed with olive oil and cooked on a griddle. Then slice* this grain offering and present it as a pleasing aroma to the LORD. 22 In each generation, the high priest* who succeeds Aaron must prepare this same offering. It belongs to the LORD and must be burned up completely. This is a permanent law. 23 All such grain offerings of a priest must be burned up entirely. None of it may be eaten."

Further Instructions for the Sin Offering

24 Then the LORD said to Moses, 25 "Give Aaron and his sons the following instructions regarding the sin offering. The animal given as an offering for sin is a most holy offering, and it must be slaughtered in the LORD's presence at the place where the burnt offerings are slaughtered. 26 The priest who offers the sacrifice as a sin offering must eat his portion in a sacred place within the courtyard of the Tabernacle. 27 Anyone or anything that touches the sacrificial meat will become holy. If any of the sacrificial blood spatters on a person's clothing, the soiled garment must be washed in a sacred place. 28 If a clay pot is used to boil the sacrificial meat, it must then be broken. If a bronze pot is used, it must be scoured and thoroughly rinsed with water. 29 Any male from a priest's family may eat from this offering; it is most holy. 30 But the offering for sin may not be eaten if its blood was brought into the Tabernacle as an offering for purification* in the Holy Place. It must be completely burned with fire.

Further Instructions for the Guilt Offering

7 "These are the instructions for the guilt offering. It is most holy. 2 The animal sacrificed as a guilt offering must be slaughtered at the place where the burnt offerings are slaughtered, and its blood must be splattered against all sides of the altar. 3 The priest will then offer all its fat on the altar, including the fat of the broad tail, the fat around the internal

6:16 Hebrew *Tent of Meeting;* also in 6:26, 30. **6:20** Hebrew *1/10 of an ephah* [2.2 liters]. **6:21** The meaning of this Hebrew term is uncertain. **6:22** Hebrew *the anointed priest.* **6:30** Or *an offering to make atonement.*

KING JAMES VERSION

4And the two kidneys, and the fat that *is* on them, which *is* by the flanks, and the caul *that is* above the liver, with the kidneys, it shall he take away:

5And the priest shall burn them upon the altar *for* an offering made by fire unto the LORD: it *is* a trespass offering.

6Every male among the priests shall eat thereof: it shall be eaten in the holy place: it *is* most holy.

7As the sin offering *is,* so *is* the trespass offering: *there is* one law for them: the priest that maketh atonement therewith shall have *it.*

8And the priest that offereth any man's burnt offering, *even* the priest shall have to himself the skin of the burnt offering which he hath offered.

9And all the meat offering that is baken in the oven, and all that is dressed in the fryingpan, and in the pan, shall be the priest's that offereth it.

10And every meat offering, mingled with oil, and dry, shall all the sons of Aaron have, one *as much* as another.

11And this *is* the law of the sacrifice of peace offerings, which he shall offer unto the LORD.

12If he offer it for a thanksgiving, then he shall offer with the sacrifice of thanksgiving unleavened cakes mingled with oil, and unleavened wafers anointed with oil, and cakes mingled with oil, of fine flour, fried.

13Besides the cakes, he shall offer *for* his offering leavened bread with the sacrifice of thanksgiving of his peace offerings.

14And of it he shall offer one out of the whole oblation *for* an heave offering unto the LORD, *and* it shall be the priest's that sprinkleth the blood of the peace offerings.

15And the flesh of the sacrifice of his peace offerings for thanksgiving shall be eaten the same day that it is offered; he shall not leave any of it until the morning.

16But if the sacrifice of his offering *be* a vow, or a voluntary offering, it shall be eaten the same day that he offereth his sacrifice: and on the morrow also the remainder of it shall be eaten:

17But the remainder of the flesh of the sacrifice on the third day shall be burnt with fire.

18And if *any* of the flesh of the sacrifice of his peace offerings be eaten at all on the third day, it shall not be accepted, neither shall it be imputed unto him that offereth it: it shall be an abomination, and the soul that eateth of it shall bear his iniquity.

19And the flesh that toucheth any unclean *thing* shall not be eaten; it shall be burnt with fire: and as for the flesh, all that be clean shall eat thereof.

20But the soul that eateth *of* the flesh of the sacrifice of peace offerings, that *pertain* unto the LORD, having his uncleanness upon him, even that soul shall be cut off from his people.

21Moreover the soul that shall touch any unclean *thing, as* the uncleanness of man, or *any* unclean

NEW LIVING TRANSLATION

organs, 4the two kidneys and the fat around them
near the loins, and the long lobe of the liver. These
are to be removed with the kidneys, 5and the priests
will burn them on the altar as a special gift presented
to the LORD. This is the guilt offering. 6Any male from
a priest's family may eat the meat. It must be eaten in
a sacred place, for it is most holy.

7"The same instructions apply to both the guilt offering and the sin offering. Both belong to the priest
who uses them to purify someone, making that person right with the LORD.* 8In the case of the burnt offering, the priest may keep the hide of the sacrificed
animal. 9Any grain offering that has been baked in an
oven, prepared in a pan, or cooked on a griddle belongs to the priest who presents it. 10All other grain
offerings, whether made of dry flour or flour moistened with olive oil, are to be shared equally among all
the priests, the descendants of Aaron.

Further Instructions for the Peace Offering

11"These are the instructions regarding the different
kinds of peace offerings that may be presented to the
LORD. 12If you present your peace offering as an expression of thanksgiving, the usual animal sacrifice
must be accompanied by various kinds of bread
made without yeast—thin cakes mixed with olive oil,
wafers spread with oil, and cakes made of choice
flour mixed with olive oil. 13This peace offering of
thanksgiving must also be accompanied by loaves of
bread made with yeast. 14One of each kind of bread
must be presented as a gift to the LORD. It will then
belong to the priest who splatters the blood of the
peace offering against the altar. 15The meat of the
peace offering of thanksgiving must be eaten on
the same day it is offered. None of it may be saved for
the next morning.

16"If you bring an offering to fulfill a vow or as a
voluntary offering, the meat must be eaten on the
same day the sacrifice is offered, but whatever is left
over may be eaten on the second day. 17Any meat left
over until the third day must be completely burned
up. 18If any of the meat from the peace offering is
eaten on the third day, the person who presented
it will not be accepted by the LORD. You will receive
no credit for offering it. By then the meat will be
contaminated; if you eat it, you will be punished for
your sin.

19"Meat that touches anything ceremonially unclean may not be eaten; it must be completely
burned up. The rest of the meat may be eaten, but
only by people who are ceremonially clean. 20If you
are ceremonially unclean and you eat meat from a
peace offering that was presented to the LORD, you
will be cut off from the community. 21If you touch
anything that is unclean (whether it is human

7:7 Or *to make atonement.*

KING JAMES VERSION

beast, or any abominable unclean *thing*, and eat of the flesh of the sacrifice of peace offerings, which *pertain* unto the LORD, even that soul shall be cut off from his people.

22And the LORD spake unto Moses, saying,
23Speak unto the children of Israel, saying, Ye shall eat no manner of fat, of ox, or of sheep, or of goat.
24And the fat of the beast that dieth of itself, and the fat of that which is torn with beasts, may be used in any other use: but ye shall in no wise eat of it.
25For whosoever eateth the fat of the beast, of which men offer an offering made by fire unto the LORD, even the soul that eateth *it* shall be cut off from his people.
26Moreover ye shall eat no manner of blood, *whether it be* of fowl or of beast, in any of your dwellings.
27Whatsoever soul *it be* that eateth any manner of blood, even that soul shall be cut off from his people.
28And the LORD spake unto Moses, saying,
29Speak unto the children of Israel, saying, He that offereth the sacrifice of his peace offerings unto the LORD shall bring his oblation unto the LORD of the sacrifice of his peace offerings.
30His own hands shall bring the offerings of the LORD made by fire, the fat with the breast, it shall he bring, that the breast may be waved *for* a wave offering before the LORD.
31And the priest shall burn the fat upon the altar: but the breast shall be Aaron's and his sons'.
32And the right shoulder shall ye give unto the priest *for* an heave offering of the sacrifices of your peace offerings.
33He among the sons of Aaron, that offereth the blood of the peace offerings, and the fat, shall have the right shoulder for *his* part.
34For the wave breast and the heave shoulder have I taken of the children of Israel from off the sacrifices of their peace offerings, and have given them unto Aaron the priest and unto his sons by a statute for ever from among the children of Israel.
35This *is the portion* of the anointing of Aaron, and of the anointing of his sons, out of the offerings of the LORD made by fire, in the day *when* he presented them to minister unto the LORD in the priest's office;
36Which the LORD commanded to be given them of the children of Israel, in the day that he anointed them, *by* a statute for ever throughout their generations.
37This *is* the law of the burnt offering, of the meat offering, and of the sin offering, and of the trespass offering, and of the consecrations, and of the sacrifice of the peace offerings;
38Which the LORD commanded Moses in mount

NEW LIVING TRANSLATION

defilement or an unclean animal or any other unclean, detestable thing) and then eat meat from a peace offering presented to the LORD, you will be cut off from the community."

The Forbidden Blood and Fat

22Then the LORD said to Moses, 23"Give the following
instructions to the people of Israel. You must never
eat fat, whether from cattle, sheep, or goats. 24The fat
of an animal found dead or torn to pieces by wild animals must never be eaten, though it may be used for
any other purpose. 25Anyone who eats fat from an
animal presented as a special gift to the LORD will be
cut off from the community. 26No matter where you
live, you must never consume the blood of any bird
or animal. 27Anyone who consumes blood will be cut
off from the community."

A Portion for the Priests

28Then the LORD said to Moses, 29"Give the following
instructions to the people of Israel. When you present a peace offering to the LORD, bring part of it as a
gift to the LORD. 30Present it to the LORD with your
own hands as a special gift to the LORD. Bring the fat of the animal, together with the breast, and lift up
the breast as a special offering to the LORD. 31Then
the priest will burn the fat on the altar, but the breast
will belong to Aaron and his descendants. 32Give the
right thigh of your peace offering to the priest as a
gift. 33The right thigh must always be given to the
priest who offers the blood and the fat of the peace
offering. 34For I have reserved the breast of the
special offering and the right thigh of the sacred offering for the priests. It is the permanent right of Aaron and his descendants to share in the peace
offerings brought by the people of Israel. 35This is
their rightful share. The special gifts presented to the LORD have been reserved for Aaron and his descendants from the time they were set apart to serve
the LORD as priests. 36On the day they were anointed,
the LORD commanded the Israelites to give these portions to the priests as their permanent share from generation to generation."

37These are the instructions for the burnt offering, the grain offering, the sin offering, and the guilt offering, as well as the ordination offering and the
peace offering. 38The LORD gave these instructions

KING JAMES VERSION

Sinai, in the day that he commanded the children of Israel to offer their oblations unto the LORD, in the wilderness of Sinai.

8 1And the LORD spake unto Moses, saying,
2Take Aaron and his sons with him, and the garments, and the anointing oil, and a bullock for the sin offering, and two rams, and a basket of unleavened bread;

3And gather thou all the congregation together unto the door of the tabernacle of the congregation.

4And Moses did as the LORD commanded him; and the assembly was gathered together unto the door of the tabernacle of the congregation.

5And Moses said unto the congregation, This *is* the thing which the LORD commanded to be done.

6And Moses brought Aaron and his sons, and washed them with water.

7And he put upon him the coat, and girded him with the girdle, and clothed him with the robe, and put the ephod upon him, and he girded him with the curious girdle of the ephod, and bound *it* unto him therewith.

8And he put the breastplate upon him: also he put in the breastplate the Urim and the Thummim.

9And he put the mitre upon his head; also upon the mitre, *even* upon his forefront, did he put the golden plate, the holy crown; as the LORD commanded Moses.

10And Moses took the anointing oil, and anointed the tabernacle and all that *was* therein, and sanctified them.

11And he sprinkled thereof upon the altar seven times, and anointed the altar and all his vessels, both the laver and his foot, to sanctify them.

12And he poured of the anointing oil upon Aaron's head, and anointed him, to sanctify him.

13And Moses brought Aaron's sons, and put coats upon them, and girded them with girdles, and put bonnets upon them; as the LORD commanded Moses.

14And he brought the bullock for the sin offering: and Aaron and his sons laid their hands upon the head of the bullock for the sin offering.

15And he slew *it;* and Moses took the blood, and put *it* upon the horns of the altar round about with his finger, and purified the altar, and poured the blood at the bottom of the altar, and sanctified it, to make reconciliation upon it.

16And he took all the fat that *was* upon the inwards, and the caul *above* the liver, and the two kidneys, and their fat, and Moses burned *it* upon the altar.

17But the bullock, and his hide, his flesh, and his dung, he burnt with fire without the camp; as the LORD commanded Moses.

18And he brought the ram for the burnt offering:

NEW LIVING TRANSLATION

to Moses on Mount Sinai when he commanded the Israelites to present their offerings to the LORD in the wilderness of Sinai.

Ordination of the Priests

8 Then the LORD said to Moses, 2"Bring Aaron
and his sons, along with their sacred garments,
the anointing oil, the bull for the sin offering, the two
rams, and the basket of bread made without yeast,
3and call the entire community of Israel together at
the entrance of the Tabernacle.*"
4So Moses followed the LORD's instructions, and
the whole community assembled at the Tabernacle
entrance. 5Moses announced to them, "This is what
the LORD has commanded us to do!" 6Then he presented Aaron and his sons and washed them with
water. 7He put the official tunic on Aaron and tied
the sash around his waist. He dressed him in the
robe, placed the ephod on him, and attached the
ephod securely with its decorative sash. 8Then
Moses placed the chestpiece on Aaron and put the
Urim and the Thummim inside it. 9He placed the
turban on Aaron's head and attached the gold medallion—the badge of holiness—to the front of the
turban, just as the LORD had commanded him.
10Then Moses took the anointing oil and anointed
the Tabernacle and everything in it, making them
holy. 11He sprinkled the oil on the altar seven times,
anointing it and all its utensils, as well as the washbasin and its stand, making them holy. 12Then he
poured some of the anointing oil on Aaron's head,
anointing him and making him holy for his work.
13Next Moses presented Aaron's sons. He clothed
them in their tunics, tied their sashes around them,
and put their special head coverings on them, just as
the LORD had commanded him.
14Then Moses presented the bull for the sin offering. Aaron and his sons laid their hands on the bull's
head, 15and Moses slaughtered it. Moses took some
of the blood, and with his finger he put it on the four
horns of the altar to purify it. He poured out the rest
of the blood at the base of the altar. Through this
process, he made the altar holy by purifying it.*
16Then Moses took all the fat around the internal organs, the long lobe of the liver, and the two kidneys
and the fat around them, and he burned it all on the
altar. 17He took the rest of the bull, including its hide,
meat, and dung, and burned it on a fire outside the
camp, just as the LORD had commanded him.
18Then Moses presented the ram for the burnt

8:3 Hebrew *Tent of Meeting;* also in 8:4, 31, 33, 35. 8:15 Or *by making atonement for it; or that offerings for purification might be made on it.*

and Aaron and his sons laid their hands upon the head of the ram.

19 And he killed *it;* and Moses sprinkled the blood upon the altar round about.

20 And he cut the ram into pieces; and Moses burnt the head, and the pieces, and the fat.

21 And he washed the inwards and the legs in water; and Moses burnt the whole ram upon the altar: it *was* a burnt sacrifice for a sweet savour, *and* an offering made by fire unto the LORD; as the LORD commanded Moses.

22 And he brought the other ram, the ram of consecration: and Aaron and his sons laid their hands upon the head of the ram.

23 And he slew *it;* and Moses took of the blood of it, and put *it* upon the tip of Aaron's right ear, and upon the thumb of his right hand, and upon the great toe of his right foot.

24 And he brought Aaron's sons, and Moses put of the blood upon the tip of their right ear, and upon the thumbs of their right hands, and upon the great toes of their right feet: and Moses sprinkled the blood upon the altar round about.

25 And he took the fat, and the rump, and all the fat that *was* upon the inwards, and the caul *above* the liver, and the two kidneys, and their fat, and the right shoulder:

26 And out of the basket of unleavened bread, that *was* before the LORD, he took one unleavened cake, and a cake of oiled bread, and one wafer, and put *them* on the fat, and upon the right shoulder:

27 And he put all upon Aaron's hands, and upon his sons' hands, and waved them *for* a wave offering before the LORD.

28 And Moses took them from off their hands, and burnt *them* on the altar upon the burnt offering: they *were* consecrations for a sweet savour: it *is* an offering made by fire unto the LORD.

29 And Moses took the breast, and waved it *for* a wave offering before the LORD: *for* of the ram of consecration it was Moses' part; as the LORD commanded Moses.

30 And Moses took of the anointing oil, and of the blood which *was* upon the altar, and sprinkled *it* upon Aaron, *and* upon his garments, and upon his sons, and upon his sons' garments with him; and sanctified Aaron, *and* his garments, and his sons, and his sons' garments with him.

31 And Moses said unto Aaron and to his sons, Boil the flesh *at* the door of the tabernacle of the congregation: and there eat it with the bread that *is* in the basket of consecrations, as I commanded, saying, Aaron and his sons shall eat it.

32 And that which remaineth of the flesh and of the bread shall ye burn with fire.

33 And ye shall not go out of the door of the tabernacle of the congregation *in* seven days, until the

offering. Aaron and his sons laid their hands on the
ram's head, 19 and Moses slaughtered it. Then Moses
took the ram's blood and splattered it against all
sides of the altar. 20 Then he cut the ram into pieces,
and he burned the head, some of its pieces, and the
fat on the altar. 21 After washing the internal organs
and the legs with water, Moses burned the entire
ram on the altar as a burnt offering. It was a pleasing
aroma, a special gift presented to the LORD, just as
the LORD had commanded him.

22 Then Moses presented the other ram, which was
the ram of ordination. Aaron and his sons laid their
hands on the ram's head, 23 and Moses slaughtered it.
Then Moses took some of its blood and applied it to
the lobe of Aaron's right ear, the thumb of his right
hand, and the big toe of his right foot. 24 Next Moses
presented Aaron's sons and applied some of the
blood to the lobes of their right ears, the thumbs of
their right hands, and the big toes of their right feet.
He then splattered the rest of the blood against all
sides of the altar.

25 Next Moses took the fat, including the fat of the
broad tail, the fat around the internal organs, the
long lobe of the liver, and the two kidneys and the fat
around them, along with the right thigh. 26 On top of
these he placed a thin cake of bread made without
yeast, a cake of bread mixed with olive oil, and a wafer spread with olive oil. All these were taken from
the basket of bread made without yeast that was
placed in the LORD's presence. 27 He put all these in
the hands of Aaron and his sons, and he lifted them
up as a special offering to the LORD. 28 Moses then
took all the offerings back from them and burned
them on the altar on top of the burnt offering. This
was the ordination offering. It was a pleasing aroma,
a special gift presented to the LORD. 29 Then Moses
took the breast and lifted it up as a special offering to
the LORD. This was Moses' portion of the ram of ordination, just as the LORD had commanded him.

30 Next Moses took some of the anointing oil and
some of the blood that was on the altar, and he
sprinkled them on Aaron and his garments and on
his sons and their garments. In this way, he made
Aaron and his sons and their garments holy.

31 Then Moses said to Aaron and his sons, "Boil the
remaining meat of the offerings at the Tabernacle
entrance, and eat it there, along with the bread that is
in the basket of offerings for the ordination, just as I
commanded when I said, 'Aaron and his sons will eat
it.' 32 Any meat or bread that is left over must then be
burned up. 33 You must not leave the Tabernacle entrance for seven days, for that is when the ordination

KING JAMES VERSION

days of your consecration be at an end: for seven
days shall he consecrate you.
34As he hath done this day, *so* the LORD hath commanded to do, to make an atonement for you.
35Therefore shall ye abide *at* the door of the tabernacle of the congregation day and night seven
days, and keep the charge of the LORD, that ye die
not: for so I am commanded.
36So Aaron and his sons did all things which the
LORD commanded by the hand of Moses.

9 1And it came to pass on the eighth day, *that*
Moses called Aaron and his sons, and the elders
of Israel;
2And he said unto Aaron, Take thee a young calf
for a sin offering, and a ram for a burnt offering,
without blemish, and offer *them* before the LORD.
3And unto the children of Israel thou shalt speak,
saying, Take ye a kid of the goats for a sin offering;
and a calf and a lamb, *both* of the first year, without
blemish, for a burnt offering;
4Also a bullock and a ram for peace offerings,
to sacrifice before the LORD; and a meat offering
mingled with oil: for today the LORD will appear
unto you.
5And they brought *that* which Moses commanded
before the tabernacle of the congregation: and all the
congregation drew near and stood before the LORD.
6And Moses said, This *is* the thing which the LORD
commanded that ye should do: and the glory of the
LORD shall appear unto you.
7And Moses said unto Aaron, Go unto the altar, and
offer thy sin offering, and thy burnt offering, and
make an atonement for thyself, and for the people:
and offer the offering of the people, and make an
atonement for them; as the LORD commanded.
8Aaron therefore went unto the altar, and slew the
calf of the sin offering, which *was* for himself.
9And the sons of Aaron brought the blood unto
him: and he dipped his finger in the blood, and put *it*
upon the horns of the altar, and poured out the blood
at the bottom of the altar:
10But the fat, and the kidneys, and the caul above
the liver of the sin offering, he burnt upon the altar;
as the LORD commanded Moses.
11And the flesh and the hide he burnt with fire
without the camp.
12And he slew the burnt offering; and Aaron's sons
presented unto him the blood, which he sprinkled
round about upon the altar.
13And they presented the burnt offering unto him,
with the pieces thereof, and the head: and he burnt
them upon the altar.
14And he did wash the inwards and the legs, and
burnt *them* upon the burnt offering on the altar.
15And he brought the people's offering, and took

NEW LIVING TRANSLATION

ceremony will be completed. 34Everything we have
done today was commanded by the LORD in order to
purify you, making you right with him.* 35Now stay
at the entrance of the Tabernacle day and night for
seven days, and do everything the LORD requires. If
you fail to do this, you will die, for this is what the
LORD has commanded." 36So Aaron and his sons
did everything the LORD had commanded through
Moses.

The Priests Begin Their Work

9 After the ordination ceremony, on the eighth
day, Moses called together Aaron and his sons
and the elders of Israel. 2He said to Aaron, "Take a
young bull for a sin offering and a ram for a burnt offering, both without defects, and present them to the
LORD. 3Then tell the Israelites, 'Take a male goat for a
sin offering, and take a calf and a lamb, both a year
old and without defects, for a burnt offering. 4Also
take a bull* and a ram for a peace offering and flour
moistened with olive oil for a grain offering. Present
all these offerings to the LORD because the LORD will
appear to you today.'"
5So the people presented all these things at the
entrance of the Tabernacle,* just as Moses had commanded. Then the whole community came forward
and stood before the LORD. 6And Moses said, "This is
what the LORD has commanded you to do so that the
glory of the LORD may appear to you."
7Then Moses said to Aaron, "Come to the altar and
sacrifice your sin offering and your burnt offering to
purify yourself and the people. Then present the offerings of the people to purify them, making them
right with the LORD,* just as he has commanded."
8So Aaron went to the altar and slaughtered the
calf as a sin offering for himself. 9His sons brought
him the blood, and he dipped his finger in it and put
it on the horns of the altar. He poured out the rest of
the blood at the base of the altar. 10Then he burned
on the altar the fat, the kidneys, and the long lobe of
the liver from the sin offering, just as the LORD had
commanded Moses. 11The meat and the hide, however, he burned outside the camp.
12Next Aaron slaughtered the animal for the burnt
offering. His sons brought him the blood, and he
splattered it against all sides of the altar. 13Then they
handed him each piece of the burnt offering, including the head, and he burned them on the altar.
14Then he washed the internal organs and the legs
and burned them on the altar along with the rest of
the burnt offering.
15Next Aaron presented the offerings of the

8:34 Or *to make atonement for you.* 9:4 Or *cow;* also in 9:18, 19.
9:5 Hebrew *Tent of Meeting;* also in 9:23. 9:7 Or *to make atonement for them.*

KING JAMES VERSION

the goat, which *was* the sin offering for the people, and slew it, and offered it for sin, as the first.

16 And he brought the burnt offering, and offered it according to the manner.

17 And he brought the meat offering, and took an handful thereof, and burnt *it* upon the altar, beside the burnt sacrifice of the morning.

18 He slew also the bullock and the ram *for* a sacrifice of peace offerings, which *was* for the people: and Aaron's sons presented unto him the blood, which he sprinkled upon the altar round about,

19 And the fat of the bullock and of the ram, the rump, and that which covereth *the inwards,* and the kidneys, and the caul *above* the liver:

20 And they put the fat upon the breasts, and he burnt the fat upon the altar:

21 And the breasts and the right shoulder Aaron waved *for* a wave offering before the LORD; as Moses commanded.

22 And Aaron lifted up his hand toward the people, and blessed them, and came down from offering of the sin offering, and the burnt offering, and peace offerings.

23 And Moses and Aaron went into the tabernacle of the congregation, and came out, and blessed the people: and the glory of the LORD appeared unto all the people.

24 And there came a fire out from before the LORD, and consumed upon the altar the burnt offering and the fat: *which* when all the people saw, they shouted, and fell on their faces.

10 1 And Nadab and Abihu, the sons of Aaron, took either of them his censer, and put fire therein, and put incense thereon, and offered strange fire before the LORD, which he commanded them not.

2 And there went out fire from the LORD, and devoured them, and they died before the LORD.

3 Then Moses said unto Aaron, This *is it* that the LORD spake, saying, I will be sanctified in them that come nigh me, and before all the people I will be glorified. And Aaron held his peace.

4 And Moses called Mishael and Elzaphan, the sons of Uzziel the uncle of Aaron, and said unto them, Come near, carry your brethren from before the sanctuary out of the camp.

5 So they went near, and carried them in their coats out of the camp; as Moses had said.

6 And Moses said unto Aaron, and unto Eleazar and unto Ithamar, his sons, Uncover not your heads,

NEW LIVING TRANSLATION

people. He slaughtered the people's goat and presented it as an offering for their sin, just as he had first done with the offering for his own sin. 16 Then he presented the burnt offering and sacrificed it in the prescribed way. 17 He also presented the grain offering, burning a handful of the flour mixture on the altar, in addition to the regular burnt offering for the morning.

18 Then Aaron slaughtered the bull and the ram for the people's peace offering. His sons brought him the blood, and he splattered it against all sides of the altar. 19 Then he took the fat of the bull and the ram—the fat of the broad tail and from around the internal organs—along with the kidneys and the long lobes of the livers. 20 He placed these fat portions on top of the breasts of these animals and burned them on the altar. 21 Aaron then lifted up the breasts and right thighs as a special offering to the LORD, just as Moses had commanded.

22 After that, Aaron raised his hands toward the people and blessed them. Then, after presenting the sin offering, the burnt offering, and the peace offering, he stepped down from the altar. 23 Then Moses and Aaron went into the Tabernacle, and when they came back out, they blessed the people again, and the glory of the LORD appeared to the whole community. 24 Fire blazed forth from the LORD's presence and consumed the burnt offering and the fat on the altar. When the people saw this, they shouted with joy and fell face down on the ground.

The Sin of Nadab and Abihu

10 Aaron's sons Nadab and Abihu put coals of fire in their incense burners and sprinkled incense over them. In this way, they disobeyed the LORD by burning before him the wrong kind of fire, different than he had commanded. 2 So fire blazed forth from the LORD's presence and burned them up, and they died there before the LORD.

3 Then Moses said to Aaron, "This is what the LORD meant when he said,

'I will display my holiness
 through those who come near me.
I will display my glory
 before all the people.'"

And Aaron was silent.

4 Then Moses called for Mishael and Elzaphan, Aaron's cousins, the sons of Aaron's uncle Uzziel. He said to them, "Come forward and carry away the bodies of your relatives from in front of the sanctuary to a place outside the camp." 5 So they came forward and picked them up by their garments and carried them out of the camp, just as Moses had commanded.

6 Then Moses said to Aaron and his sons Eleazar and Ithamar, "Do not show grief by leaving your hair

neither rend your clothes; lest ye die, and lest wrath
come upon all the people: but let your brethren, the
whole house of Israel, bewail the burning which the
LORD hath kindled.

7And ye shall not go out from the door of the tabernacle of the congregation, lest ye die: for the
anointing oil of the LORD *is* upon you. And they did
according to the word of Moses.

8And the LORD spake unto Aaron, saying,

9Do not drink wine nor strong drink, thou, nor thy
sons with thee, when ye go into the tabernacle of the
congregation, lest ye die: *it shall be* a statute for ever
throughout your generations:

10And that ye may put difference between holy
and unholy, and between unclean and clean;

11And that ye may teach the children of Israel all
the statutes which the LORD hath spoken unto them
by the hand of Moses.

12And Moses spake unto Aaron, and unto Eleazar
and unto Ithamar, his sons that were left, Take the
meat offering that remaineth of the offerings of the
LORD made by fire, and eat it without leaven beside
the altar: for it *is* most holy:

13And ye shall eat it in the holy place, because it *is*
thy due, and thy sons' due, of the sacrifices of the
LORD made by fire: for so I am commanded.

14And the wave breast and heave shoulder shall ye
eat in a clean place; thou, and thy sons, and thy
daughters with thee: for *they be* thy due, and thy
sons' due, *which* are given out of the sacrifices of
peace offerings of the children of Israel.

15The heave shoulder and the wave breast shall
they bring with the offerings made by fire of the fat,
to wave *it for* a wave offering before the LORD; and it
shall be thine, and thy sons' with thee, by a statute for
ever; as the LORD hath commanded.

16And Moses diligently sought the goat of the sin
offering, and, behold, it was burnt: and he was angry
with Eleazar and Ithamar, the sons of Aaron *which*
were left *alive*, saying,

17Wherefore have ye not eaten the sin offering in
the holy place, seeing it *is* most holy, and *God* hath
given it you to bear the iniquity of the congregation,
to make atonement for them before the LORD?

18Behold, the blood of it was not brought in within
the holy *place*: ye should indeed have eaten it in the
holy *place*, as I commanded.

19And Aaron said unto Moses, Behold, this day
have they offered their sin offering and their burnt
offering before the LORD; and such things have befallen me: and *if* I had eaten the sin offering today,
should it have been accepted in the sight of the
LORD?

20And when Moses heard *that*, he was content.

uncombed* or by tearing your clothes. If you do, you
will die, and the LORD's anger will strike the whole
community of Israel. However, the rest of the Israelites, your relatives, may mourn because of the LORD's
fiery destruction of Nadab and Abihu. 7But you must
not leave the entrance of the Tabernacle* or you will
die, for you have been anointed with the LORD's
anointing oil." So they did as Moses commanded.

Instructions for Priestly Conduct

8Then the LORD said to Aaron, 9"You and your descendants must never drink wine or any other alcoholic drink before going into the Tabernacle. If you
do, you will die. This is a permanent law for you, and
it must be observed from generation to generation.
10You must distinguish between what is sacred and
what is common, between what is ceremonially unclean and what is clean. 11And you must teach the
Israelites all the decrees that the LORD has given
them through Moses."

12Then Moses said to Aaron and his remaining
sons, Eleazar and Ithamar, "Take what is left of the
grain offering after a portion has been presented as a
special gift to the LORD, and eat it beside the altar.
Make sure it contains no yeast, for it is most holy.
13You must eat it in a sacred place, for it has been
given to you and your descendants as your portion of
the special gifts presented to the LORD. These are the
commands I have been given. 14But the breast and
thigh that were lifted up as a special offering may be
eaten in any place that is ceremonially clean. These
parts have been given to you and your descendants
as your portion of the peace offerings presented by
the people of Israel. 15You must lift up the thigh and
breast as a special offering to the LORD, along with
the fat of the special gifts. These parts will belong to
you and your descendants as your permanent right,
just as the LORD has commanded."

16Moses then asked them what had happened to
the goat of the sin offering. When he discovered it
had been burned up, he became very angry with Eleazar and Ithamar, Aaron's remaining sons. 17"Why
didn't you eat the sin offering in the sacred area?" he
demanded. "It is a holy offering! The LORD has given
it to you to remove the guilt of the community and to
purify the people, making them right with the
LORD.* 18Since the animal's blood was not brought
into the Holy Place, you should have eaten the meat
in the sacred area as I ordered you."

19Then Aaron answered Moses, "Today my sons
presented both their sin offering and their burnt
offering to the LORD. And yet this tragedy has happened to me. If I had eaten the people's sin offering
on such a tragic day as this, would the LORD have
been pleased?" 20And when Moses heard this, he was
satisfied.

10:6 Or *by uncovering your heads.* **10:7** Hebrew *Tent of Meeting;* also in 10:9. **10:17** Or *to make atonement for the people before the LORD.*

KING JAMES VERSION

11

1And the LORD spake unto Moses and to Aaron, saying unto them,

2Speak unto the children of Israel, saying, These *are* the beasts which ye shall eat among all the beasts that *are* on the earth.

3Whatsoever parteth the hoof, and is clovenfooted, *and* cheweth the cud, among the beasts, that shall ye eat.

4Nevertheless these shall ye not eat of them that chew the cud, or of them that divide the hoof: *as* the camel, because he cheweth the cud, but divideth not the hoof; he *is* unclean unto you.

5And the coney, because he cheweth the cud, but divideth not the hoof; he *is* unclean unto you.

6And the hare, because he cheweth the cud, but divideth not the hoof; he *is* unclean unto you.

7And the swine, though he divide the hoof, and be clovenfooted, yet he cheweth not the cud; he *is* unclean to you.

8Of their flesh shall ye not eat, and their carcase shall ye not touch; they *are* unclean to you.

9These shall ye eat of all that *are* in the waters: whatsoever hath fins and scales in the waters, in the seas, and in the rivers, them shall ye eat.

10And all that have not fins and scales in the seas, and in the rivers, of all that move in the waters, and of any living thing which *is* in the waters, they *shall be* an abomination unto you:

11They shall be even an abomination unto you; ye shall not eat of their flesh, but ye shall have their carcases in abomination.

12Whatsoever hath no fins nor scales in the waters, that *shall be* an abomination unto you.

13And these *are they which* ye shall have in abomination among the fowls; they shall not be eaten, they *are* an abomination: the eagle, and the ossifrage, and the osprey,

14And the vulture, and the kite after his kind;

15Every raven after his kind;

16And the owl, and the night hawk, and the cuckoo, and the hawk after his kind,

17And the little owl, and the cormorant, and the great owl,

18And the swan, and the pelican, and the gier eagle,

19And the stork, the heron after her kind, and the lapwing, and the bat.

20All fowls that creep, going upon *all* four, *shall be* an abomination unto you.

21Yet these may ye eat of every flying creeping thing that goeth upon *all* four, which have legs above their feet, to leap withal upon the earth;

22*Even* these of them ye may eat; the locust after his kind, and the bald locust after his kind, and the beetle after his kind, and the grasshopper after his kind.

23But all *other* flying creeping things, which have four feet, *shall be* an abomination unto you.

NEW LIVING TRANSLATION

Ceremonially Clean and Unclean Animals

11

Then the LORD said to Moses and Aaron, 2"Give the following instructions to the people of Israel.

"Of all the land animals, these are the ones you may use for food. 3You may eat any animal that has completely split hooves and chews the cud. 4You may not, however, eat the following animals* that have split hooves or that chew the cud, but not both. The camel chews the cud but does not have split hooves, so it is ceremonially unclean for you. 5The hyrax* chews the cud but does not have split hooves, so it is unclean. 6The hare chews the cud but does not have split hooves, so it is unclean. 7The pig has evenly split hooves but does not chew the cud, so it is unclean. 8You may not eat the meat of these animals or even touch their carcasses. They are ceremonially unclean for you.

9"Of all the marine animals, these are ones you may use for food. You may eat anything from the water if it has both fins and scales, whether taken from salt water or from streams. 10But you must never eat animals from the sea or from rivers that do not have both fins and scales. They are detestable to you. This applies both to little creatures that live in shallow water and to all creatures that live in deep water. 11They will always be detestable to you. You must never eat their meat or even touch their dead bodies. 12Any marine animal that does not have both fins and scales is detestable to you.

13"These are the birds that are detestable to you. You must never eat them: the griffon vulture, the bearded vulture, the black vulture, 14the kite, falcons of all kinds, 15ravens of all kinds, 16the eagle owl, the short-eared owl, the seagull, hawks of all kinds, 17the little owl, the cormorant, the great owl, 18the barn owl, the desert owl, the Egyptian vulture, 19the stork, herons of all kinds, the hoopoe, and the bat.

20"You must not eat winged insects that walk along the ground; they are detestable to you. 21You may, however, eat winged insects that walk along the ground and have jointed legs so they can jump. 22The insects you are permitted to eat include all kinds of locusts, bald locusts, crickets, and grasshoppers. 23All other winged insects that walk along the ground are detestable to you.

11:4 The identification of some of the animals, birds, and insects in this chapter is uncertain. **11:5** Or *coney,* or *rock badger.*

KING JAMES VERSION

24 And for these ye shall be unclean: whosoever toucheth the carcase of them shall be unclean until the even.

25 And whosoever beareth *aught* of the carcase of them shall wash his clothes, and be unclean until the even.

26 *The carcases* of every beast which divideth the hoof, and *is* not clovenfooted, nor cheweth the cud, *are* unclean unto you: every one that toucheth them shall be unclean.

27 And whatsoever goeth upon his paws, among all manner of beasts that go on *all* four, those *are* unclean unto you: whoso toucheth their carcase shall be unclean until the even.

28 And he that beareth the carcase of them shall wash his clothes, and be unclean until the even: they *are* unclean unto you.

29 These also *shall be* unclean unto you among the creeping things that creep upon the earth; the weasel, and the mouse, and the tortoise after his kind,

30 And the ferret, and the chameleon, and the lizard, and the snail, and the mole.

31 These *are* unclean to you among all that creep: whosoever doth touch them, when they be dead, shall be unclean until the even.

32 And upon whatsoever *any* of them, when they are dead, doth fall, it shall be unclean; whether *it be* any vessel of wood, or raiment, or skin, or sack, whatsoever vessel *it be,* wherein *any* work is done, it must be put into water, and it shall be unclean until the even; so it shall be cleansed.

33 And every earthen vessel, whereinto *any* of them falleth, whatsoever *is* in it shall be unclean; and ye shall break it.

34 Of all meat which may be eaten, *that* on which *such* water cometh shall be unclean: and all drink that may be drunk in every *such* vessel shall be unclean.

35 And every *thing* whereupon *any part* of their carcase falleth shall be unclean; *whether it be* oven, or ranges for pots, they shall be broken down: *for* they *are* unclean, and shall be unclean unto you.

36 Nevertheless a fountain or pit, *wherein there is* plenty of water, shall be clean: but that which toucheth their carcase shall be unclean.

37 And if *any part* of their carcase fall upon any sowing seed which is to be sown, it *shall be* clean.

38 But if *any* water be put upon the seed, and *any part* of their carcase fall thereon, it *shall be* unclean unto you.

39 And if any beast, of which ye may eat, die; he that toucheth the carcase thereof shall be unclean until the even.

40 And he that eateth of the carcase of it shall wash his clothes, and be unclean until the even: he also that beareth the carcase of it shall wash his clothes, and be unclean until the even.

41 And every creeping thing that creepeth upon the earth *shall be* an abomination; it shall not be eaten.

NEW LIVING TRANSLATION

24 "The following creatures will make you ceremonially unclean. If any of you touch their carcasses, you will be defiled until evening. 25 If you pick up their carcasses, you must wash your clothes, and you will remain defiled until evening.

26 "Any animal that has split hooves that are not evenly divided or that does not chew the cud is unclean for you. If you touch the carcass of such an animal, you will be defiled. 27 Of the animals that walk on all fours, those that have paws are unclean. If you touch the carcass of such an animal, you will be defiled until evening. 28 If you pick up its carcass, you must wash your clothes, and you will remain defiled until evening. These animals are unclean for you.

29 "Of the small animals that scurry along the ground, these are unclean for you: the mole rat, the rat, large lizards of all kinds, 30 the gecko, the monitor lizard, the common lizard, the sand lizard, and the chameleon. 31 All these small animals are unclean for you. If any of you touch the dead body of such an animal, you will be defiled until evening. 32 If such an animal dies and falls on something, that object will be unclean. This is true whether the object is made of wood, cloth, leather, or burlap. Whatever its use, you must dip it in water, and it will remain defiled until evening. After that, it will be ceremonially clean and may be used again.

33 "If such an animal falls into a clay pot, everything in the pot will be defiled, and the pot must be smashed. 34 If the water from such a container spills on any food, the food will be defiled. And any beverage in such a container will be defiled. 35 Any object on which the carcass of such an animal falls will be defiled. If it is an oven or hearth, it must be destroyed, for it is defiled, and you must treat it accordingly.

36 "However, if the carcass of such an animal falls into a spring or a cistern, the water will still be clean. But anyone who touches the carcass will be defiled. 37 If the carcass falls on seed grain to be planted in the field, the seed will still be considered clean. 38 But if the seed is wet when the carcass falls on it, the seed will be defiled.

39 "If an animal you are permitted to eat dies and you touch its carcass, you will be defiled until evening. 40 If you eat any of its meat or carry away its carcass, you must wash your clothes, and you will remain defiled until evening.

41 "All small animals that scurry along the ground

KING JAMES VERSION

42 Whatsoever goeth upon the belly, and whatsoever goeth upon *all* four, or whatsoever hath more feet among all creeping things that creep upon the earth, them ye shall not eat; for they *are* an abomination.

43 Ye shall not make yourselves abominable with any creeping thing that creepeth, neither shall ye make yourselves unclean with them, that ye should be defiled thereby.

44 For I *am* the LORD your God: ye shall therefore sanctify yourselves, and ye shall be holy; for I *am* holy: neither shall ye defile yourselves with any manner of creeping thing that creepeth upon the earth.

45 For I *am* the LORD that bringeth you up out of the land of Egypt, to be your God: ye shall therefore be holy, for I *am* holy.

46 This *is* the law of the beasts, and of the fowl, and of every living creature that moveth in the waters, and of every creature that creepeth upon the earth:

47 To make a difference between the unclean and the clean, and between the beast that may be eaten and the beast that may not be eaten.

12 1 And the LORD spake unto Moses, saying, 2 Speak unto the children of Israel, saying, If a woman have conceived seed, and born a man child: then she shall be unclean seven days; according to the days of the separation for her infirmity shall she be unclean.

3 And in the eighth day the flesh of his foreskin shall be circumcised.

4 And she shall then continue in the blood of her purifying three and thirty days; she shall touch no hallowed thing, nor come into the sanctuary, until the days of her purifying be fulfilled.

5 But if she bear a maid child, then she shall be unclean two weeks, as in her separation: and she shall continue in the blood of her purifying threescore and six days.

6 And when the days of her purifying are fulfilled, for a son, or for a daughter, she shall bring a lamb of the first year for a burnt offering, and a young pigeon, or a turtledove, for a sin offering, unto the door of the tabernacle of the congregation, unto the priest:

7 Who shall offer it before the LORD, and make an atonement for her; and she shall be cleansed from the issue of her blood. This *is* the law for her that hath born a male or a female.

8 And if she be not able to bring a lamb, then she shall bring two turtles, or two young pigeons; the one for the burnt offering, and the other for a sin offering: and the priest shall make an atonement for her, and she shall be clean.

NEW LIVING TRANSLATION

are detestable, and you must never eat them. 42 This includes all animals that slither along on their bellies, as well as those with four legs and those with many feet. All such animals that scurry along the ground are detestable, and you must never eat them. 43 Do not defile yourselves by touching them. You must not make yourselves ceremonially unclean because of them. 44 For I am the LORD your God. You must consecrate yourselves and be holy, because I am holy. So do not defile yourselves with any of these small animals that scurry along the ground. 45 For I, the LORD, am the one who brought you up from the land of Egypt, that I might be your God. Therefore, you must be holy because I am holy.

46 "These are the instructions regarding land animals, birds, marine creatures, and animals that scurry along the ground. 47 By these instructions you will know what is unclean and clean, and which animals may be eaten and which may not be eaten."

Purification after Childbirth

12 The LORD said to Moses, 2 "Give the following instructions to the people of Israel. If a woman becomes pregnant and gives birth to a son, she will be ceremonially unclean for seven days, just as she is unclean during her menstrual period. 3 On the eighth day the boy's foreskin must be circumcised. 4 After waiting thirty-three days, she will be purified from the bleeding of childbirth. During this time of purification, she must not touch anything that is set apart as holy. And she must not enter the sanctuary until her time of purification is over. 5 If a woman gives birth to a daughter, she will be ceremonially unclean for two weeks, just as she is unclean during her menstrual period. After waiting sixty-six days, she will be purified from the bleeding of childbirth.

6 "When the time of purification is completed for either a son or a daughter, the woman must bring a one-year-old lamb for a burnt offering and a young pigeon or turtledove for a purification offering. She must bring her offerings to the priest at the entrance of the Tabernacle.* 7 The priest will then present them to the LORD to purify her.* Then she will be ceremonially clean again after her bleeding at childbirth. These are the instructions for a woman after the birth of a son or a daughter.

8 "If a woman cannot afford to bring a lamb, she must bring two turtledoves or two young pigeons. One will be for the burnt offering and the other for the purification offering. The priest will sacrifice them to purify her, and she will be ceremonially clean."

12:6 Hebrew *Tent of Meeting.* **12:7** Or *to make atonement for her;* also in 12:8.

KING JAMES VERSION

13

[1]And the LORD spake unto Moses and Aaron, saying,

[2]When a man shall have in the skin of his flesh a rising, a scab, or bright spot, and it be in the skin of his flesh *like* the plague of leprosy; then he shall be brought unto Aaron the priest, or unto one of his sons the priests:

[3]And the priest shall look on the plague in the skin of the flesh: and *when* the hair in the plague is turned white, and the plague in sight *be* deeper than the skin of his flesh, it *is* a plague of leprosy: and the priest shall look on him, and pronounce him unclean.

[4]If the bright spot *be* white in the skin of his flesh, and in sight *be* not deeper than the skin, and the hair thereof be not turned white; then the priest shall shut up *him that hath* the plague seven days:

[5]And the priest shall look on him the seventh day: and, behold, *if* the plague in his sight be at a stay, *and* the plague spread not in the skin; then the priest shall shut him up seven days more:

[6]And the priest shall look on him again the seventh day: and, behold, *if* the plague *be* somewhat dark, *and* the plague spread not in the skin, the priest shall pronounce him clean: it *is but* a scab: and he shall wash his clothes, and be clean.

[7]But if the scab spread much abroad in the skin, after that he hath been seen of the priest for his cleansing, he shall be seen of the priest again:

[8]And *if* the priest see that, behold, the scab spreadeth in the skin, then the priest shall pronounce him unclean: it *is* a leprosy.

[9]When the plague of leprosy is in a man, then he shall be brought unto the priest;

[10]And the priest shall see *him*: and, behold, *if* the rising *be* white in the skin, and it have turned the hair white, and *there be* quick raw flesh in the rising;

[11]It *is* an old leprosy in the skin of his flesh, and the priest shall pronounce him unclean, and shall not shut him up: for he *is* unclean.

[12]And if a leprosy break out abroad in the skin, and the leprosy cover all the skin of *him that hath* the plague from his head even to his foot, wheresoever the priest looketh;

[13]Then the priest shall consider: and, behold, *if* the leprosy have covered all his flesh, he shall pronounce *him* clean *that hath* the plague: it is all turned white: he *is* clean.

[14]But when raw flesh appeareth in him, he shall be unclean.

[15]And the priest shall see the raw flesh, and pronounce him to be unclean: *for* the raw flesh *is* unclean: it *is* a leprosy.

[16]Or if the raw flesh turn again, and be changed unto white, he shall come unto the priest;

[17]And the priest shall see him: and, behold, *if* the plague be turned into white; then the priest shall

NEW LIVING TRANSLATION

Serious Skin Diseases

13

The LORD said to Moses and Aaron, [2]"If anyone has a swelling or a rash or discolored skin that might develop into a serious skin disease,* that person must be brought to Aaron the priest or to one of his sons.* [3]The priest will examine the affected area of the skin. If the hair in the affected area has turned white and the problem appears to be more than skin-deep, it is a serious skin disease, and the priest who examines it must pronounce the person ceremonially unclean.

[4]"But if the affected area of the skin is only a white discoloration and does not appear to be more than skin-deep, and if the hair on the spot has not turned white, the priest will quarantine the person for seven days. [5]On the seventh day the priest will make another examination. If he finds the affected area has not changed and the problem has not spread on the skin, the priest will quarantine the person for seven more days. [6]On the seventh day the priest will make another examination. If he finds the affected area has faded and has not spread, the priest will pronounce the person ceremonially clean. It was only a rash. The person's clothing must be washed, and the person will be ceremonially clean. [7]But if the rash continues to spread after the person has been examined by the priest and has been pronounced clean, the infected person must return to be examined again. [8]If the priest finds that the rash has spread, he must pronounce the person ceremonially unclean, for it is indeed a skin disease.

[9]"Anyone who develops a serious skin disease must go to the priest for an examination. [10]If the priest finds a white swelling on the skin, and some hair on the spot has turned white, and there is an open sore in the affected area, [11]it is a chronic skin disease, and the priest must pronounce the person ceremonially unclean. In such cases the person need not be quarantined, for it is obvious that the skin is defiled by the disease.

[12]"Now suppose the disease has spread all over the person's skin, covering the body from head to foot. [13]When the priest examines the infected person and finds that the disease covers the entire body, he will pronounce the person ceremonially clean. Since the skin has turned completely white, the person is clean. [14]But if any open sores appear, the infected person will be pronounced ceremonially unclean. [15]The priest must make this pronouncement as soon as he sees an open sore, since open sores indicate the presence of a skin disease. [16]However, if the open sores heal and turn white like the rest of the skin, the person must return to the priest [17]for another examination. If the affected areas have indeed turned white, the priest will then

13:2a Traditionally rendered *leprosy*. The Hebrew word used throughout this passage is used to describe various skin diseases. **13:2b** Or *one of his descendants*.

KING JAMES VERSION

pronounce *him* clean *that hath* the plague: he *is*
clean.
18 The flesh also, in which, *even* in the skin thereof,
was a boil, and is healed,
19 And in the place of the boil there be a white rising, or a bright spot, white, and somewhat reddish,
and it be shewed to the priest;
20 And if, when the priest seeth it, behold, it *be*
in sight lower than the skin, and the hair thereof be
turned white; the priest shall pronounce him unclean: it *is* a plague of leprosy broken out of the boil.
21 But if the priest look on it, and, behold, *there be*
no white hairs therein, and *if* it *be* not lower than the
skin, but *be* somewhat dark; then the priest shall
shut him up seven days:
22 And if it spread much abroad in the skin, then the
priest shall pronounce him unclean: it *is* a plague.
23 But if the bright spot stay in his place, *and*
spread not, it *is* a burning boil; and the priest shall
pronounce him clean.
24 Or if there be *any* flesh, in the skin whereof
there is a hot burning, and the quick *flesh* that
burneth have a white bright spot, somewhat reddish,
or white;
25 Then the priest shall look upon it: and, behold,
if the hair in the bright spot be turned white, and it
be in sight deeper than the skin; it *is* a leprosy broken out of the burning: wherefore the priest shall
pronounce him unclean: it *is* the plague of leprosy.
26 But if the priest look on it, and, behold, *there be*
no white hair in the bright spot, and it *be* no lower
than the *other* skin, but *be* somewhat dark; then the
priest shall shut him up seven days:
27 And the priest shall look upon him the seventh
day: *and* if it be spread much abroad in the skin, then
the priest shall pronounce him unclean: it *is* the
plague of leprosy.
28 And if the bright spot stay in his place, *and*
spread not in the skin, but it *be* somewhat dark; it *is* a
rising of the burning, and the priest shall pronounce
him clean: for it *is* an inflammation of the burning.
29 If a man or woman have a plague upon the head
or the beard;
30 Then the priest shall see the plague: and, behold,
if it *be* in sight deeper than the skin; *and there be* in it
a yellow thin hair; then the priest shall pronounce
him unclean: it *is* a dry scall, *even* a leprosy upon the
head or beard.
31 And if the priest look on the plague of the scall,
and, behold, it *be* not in sight deeper than the skin,
and *that there is* no black hair in it; then the priest
shall shut up *him that hath* the plague of the scall
seven days:
32 And in the seventh day the priest shall look on
the plague: and, behold, *if* the scall spread not, and
there be in it no yellow hair, and the scall *be* not in
sight deeper than the skin;

NEW LIVING TRANSLATION

pronounce the person ceremonially clean by declaring, 'You are clean!'
18 "If anyone has a boil on the skin that has started
to heal, 19 but a white swelling or a reddish white spot
develops in its place, that person must go to the
priest to be examined. 20 If the priest examines it and
finds it to be more than skin-deep, and if the hair in
the affected area has turned white, the priest must
pronounce the person ceremonially unclean. The
boil has become a serious skin disease. 21 But if the
priest finds no white hair on the affected area and
the problem appears to be no more than skin-deep
and has faded, the priest must quarantine the person
for seven days. 22 If during that time the affected area
spreads on the skin, the priest must pronounce the
person ceremonially unclean, because it is a serious
disease. 23 But if the area grows no larger and does
not spread, it is merely the scar from the boil, and the
priest will pronounce the person ceremonially clean.
24 "If anyone has suffered a burn on the skin and
the burned area changes color, becoming either reddish white or shiny white, 25 the priest must examine
it. If he finds that the hair in the affected area has
turned white and the problem appears to be more
than skin-deep, a skin disease has broken out in the
burn. The priest must then pronounce the person
ceremonially unclean, for it is clearly a serious skin
disease. 26 But if the priest finds no white hair on the
affected area and the problem appears to be no more
than skin-deep and has faded, the priest must quarantine the infected person for seven days. 27 On the
seventh day the priest must examine the person
again. If the affected area has spread on the skin, the
priest must pronounce that person ceremonially unclean, for it is clearly a serious skin disease. 28 But if
the affected area has not changed or spread on the
skin and has faded, it is simply a swelling from the
burn. The priest will then pronounce the person ceremonially clean, for it is only the scar from the burn.
29 "If anyone, either a man or woman, has a sore on
the head or chin, 30 the priest must examine it. If he
finds it is more than skin-deep and has fine yellow
hair on it, the priest must pronounce the person ceremonially unclean. It is a scabby sore of the head or
chin. 31 If the priest examines the scabby sore and
finds that it is only skin-deep but there is no black
hair on it, he must quarantine the person for seven
days. 32 On the seventh day the priest must examine
the sore again. If he finds that the scabby sore has
not spread, and there is no yellow hair on it, and it

KING JAMES VERSION

33 He shall be shaven, but the scall shall he not shave; and the priest shall shut up *him that hath* the scall seven days more:

34 And in the seventh day the priest shall look on the scall: and, behold, *if* the scall be not spread in the skin, nor *be* in sight deeper than the skin; then the priest shall pronounce him clean: and he shall wash his clothes, and be clean.

35 But if the scall spread much in the skin after his cleansing;

36 Then the priest shall look on him: and, behold, if the scall be spread in the skin, the priest shall not seek for yellow hair; he *is* unclean.

37 But if the scall be in his sight at a stay, and *that* there is black hair grown up therein; the scall is healed, he *is* clean: and the priest shall pronounce him clean.

38 If a man also or a woman have in the skin of their flesh bright spots, *even* white bright spots;

39 Then the priest shall look: and, behold, *if* the bright spots in the skin of their flesh *be* darkish white; it *is* a freckled spot *that* groweth in the skin; he *is* clean.

40 And the man whose hair is fallen off his head, he *is* bald; *yet is* he clean.

41 And he that hath his hair fallen off from the part of his head toward his face, he *is* forehead bald: *yet is* he clean.

42 And if there be in the bald head, or bald forehead, a white reddish sore; it *is* a leprosy sprung up in his bald head, or his bald forehead.

43 Then the priest shall look upon it: and, behold, *if* the rising of the sore *be* white reddish in his bald head, or in his bald forehead, as the leprosy appeareth in the skin of the flesh;

44 He is a leprous man, he *is* unclean: the priest shall pronounce him utterly unclean; his plague *is* in his head.

45 And the leper in whom the plague *is*, his clothes shall be rent, and his head bare, and he shall put a covering upon his upper lip, and shall cry, Unclean, unclean.

46 All the days wherein the plague *shall be* in him he shall be defiled; he *is* unclean: he shall dwell alone; without the camp *shall* his habitation *be*.

47 The garment also that the plague of leprosy is in, *whether it be* a woollen garment, or a linen garment;

48 Whether *it be* in the warp, or woof; of linen, or of woollen; whether in a skin, or in any thing made of skin;

49 And if the plague be greenish or reddish in the garment, or in the skin, either in the warp, or in the woof, or in any thing of skin; it *is* a plague of leprosy, and shall be shewed unto the priest:

50 And the priest shall look upon the plague, and shut up *it that hath* the plague seven days:

51 And he shall look on the plague on the seventh day: if the plague be spread in the garment, either in

NEW LIVING TRANSLATION

appears to be only skin-deep, 33 the person must
shave off all hair except the hair on the affected area.
Then the priest must quarantine the person for another seven days. 34 On the seventh day he will examine the sore again. If it has not spread and appears
to be no more than skin-deep, the priest will pronounce the person ceremonially clean. The person's
clothing must be washed, and the person will be ceremonially clean. 35 But if the scabby sore begins to
spread after the person is pronounced clean, 36 the
priest must do another examination. If he finds that
the sore has spread, the priest does not need to look
for yellow hair. The infected person is ceremonially
unclean. 37 But if the color of the scabby sore does
not change and black hair has grown on it, it has
healed. The priest will then pronounce the person
ceremonially clean.

38 "If anyone, either a man or woman, has shiny
white patches on the skin, 39 the priest must examine
the affected area. If he finds that the shiny patches
are only pale white, this is a harmless skin rash, and
the person is ceremonially clean.

40 "If a man loses his hair and his head becomes
bald, he is still ceremonially clean. 41 And if he loses
hair on his forehead, he simply has a bald forehead;
he is still clean. 42 However, if a reddish white sore
appears on the bald area at the top or back of his
head, this is a skin disease. 43 The priest must examine him, and if he finds swelling around the reddish
white sore anywhere on the man's head and it looks
like a skin disease, 44 the man is indeed infected with
a skin disease and is unclean. The priest must pronounce him ceremonially unclean because of the
sore on his head.

45 "Those who suffer from a serious skin disease
must tear their clothing and leave their hair uncombed.* They must cover their mouth and call out,
'Unclean! Unclean!' 46 As long as the serious disease
lasts, they will be ceremonially unclean. They must
live in isolation in their place outside the camp.

Treatment of Contaminated Clothing

47 "Now suppose mildew* contaminates some
woolen or linen clothing, 48 woolen or linen fabric,
the hide of an animal, or anything made of leather.
49 If the contaminated area in the clothing, the animal hide, the fabric, or the leather article has turned
greenish or reddish, it is contaminated with mildew
and must be shown to the priest. 50 After examining
the affected spot, the priest will put the article in
quarantine for seven days. 51 On the seventh day the
priest must inspect it again. If the contaminated area

13:45 Or *and uncover their heads.* **13:47** Traditionally rendered *leprosy.* The Hebrew term used throughout this passage is the same term used for the various skin diseases described in 13:1-46.

KING JAMES VERSION

the warp, or in the woof, or in a skin, *or* in any work
that is made of skin; the plague *is* a fretting leprosy;
it *is* unclean.

52 He shall therefore burn that garment, whether
warp or woof, in woollen or in linen, or any thing of
skin, wherein the plague is: for it *is* a fretting leprosy;
it shall be burnt in the fire.

53 And if the priest shall look, and, behold, the
plague be not spread in the garment, either in the
warp, or in the woof, or in any thing of skin;

54 Then the priest shall command that they wash
the thing wherein the plague *is,* and he shall shut it
up seven days more:

55 And the priest shall look on the plague, after that
it is washed: and, behold, *if* the plague have not
changed his colour, and the plague be not spread; it
is unclean; thou shalt burn it in the fire; it *is* fret inward, *whether* it *be* bare within or without.

56 And if the priest look, and, behold, the plague *be*
somewhat dark after the washing of it; then he shall
rend it out of the garment, or out of the skin, or out of
the warp, or out of the woof:

57 And if it appear still in the garment, either in the
warp, or in the woof, or in any thing of skin; it *is* a
spreading *plague:* thou shalt burn that wherein the
plague *is* with fire.

58 And the garment, either warp, or woof, or whatsoever thing of skin *it be,* which thou shalt wash, if
the plague be departed from them, then it shall be
washed the second time, and shall be clean.

59 This *is* the law of the plague of leprosy in a garment of woollen or linen, either in the warp, or woof,
or any thing of skins, to pronounce it clean, or to pronounce it unclean.

14 1 And the LORD spake unto Moses, saying,
2 This shall be the law of the leper in the day
of his cleansing: He shall be brought unto the priest:

3 And the priest shall go forth out of the camp; and
the priest shall look, and, behold, *if* the plague of leprosy be healed in the leper;

4 Then shall the priest command to take for him
that is to be cleansed two birds alive *and* clean, and
cedar wood, and scarlet, and hyssop:

5 And the priest shall command that one of the
birds be killed in an earthen vessel over running
water:

6 As for the living bird, he shall take it, and the cedar wood, and the scarlet, and the hyssop, and shall
dip them and the living bird in the blood of the bird
that was killed over the running water:

7 And he shall sprinkle upon him that is to be
cleansed from the leprosy seven times, and shall pronounce him clean, and shall let the living bird loose
into the open field.

8 And he that is to be cleansed shall wash his
clothes, and shave off all his hair, and wash himself

NEW LIVING TRANSLATION

has spread, the clothing or fabric or leather is clearly
contaminated by a serious mildew and is ceremonially unclean. 52 The priest must burn the item—the
clothing, the woolen or linen fabric, or piece of
leather—for it has been contaminated by a serious
mildew. It must be completely destroyed by fire.

53 "But if the priest examines it and finds that the
contaminated area has not spread in the clothing,
the fabric, or the leather, 54 the priest will order the
object to be washed and then quarantined for seven
more days. 55 Then the priest must examine the object again. If he finds that the contaminated area has
not changed color after being washed, even if it did
not spread, the object is defiled. It must be completely burned up, whether the contaminated spot*
is on the inside or outside. 56 But if the priest examines it and finds that the contaminated area has
faded after being washed, he must cut the spot from
the clothing, the fabric, or the leather. 57 If the spot
later reappears on the clothing, the fabric, or the
leather article, the mildew is clearly spreading, and
the contaminated object must be burned up. 58 But if
the spot disappears from the clothing, the fabric,
or the leather article after it has been washed, it must
be washed again; then it will be ceremonially clean.

59 "These are the instructions for dealing with mildew that contaminates woolen or linen clothing or
fabric or anything made of leather. This is how the
priest will determine whether these items are ceremonially clean or unclean."

Cleansing from Skin Diseases

14 And the LORD said to Moses, 2 "The following
instructions are for those seeking ceremonial purification from a skin disease.* Those who
have been healed must be brought to the priest,
3 who will examine them at a place outside the camp.
If the priest finds that someone has been healed of a
serious skin disease, 4 he will perform a purification
ceremony, using two live birds that are ceremonially
clean, a stick of cedar,* some scarlet yarn, and a hyssop branch. 5 The priest will order that one bird be
slaughtered over a clay pot filled with fresh water.
6 He will take the live bird, the cedar stick, the scarlet
yarn, and the hyssop branch, and dip them into the
blood of the bird that was slaughtered over the fresh
water. 7 The priest will then sprinkle the blood of the
dead bird seven times on the person being purified
of the skin disease. When the priest has purified the
person, he will release the live bird in the open field
to fly away.

8 "The persons being purified must then wash
their clothes, shave off all their hair, and bathe

13:55 The meaning of the Hebrew is uncertain. **14:2** Traditionally rendered *leprosy;* see note on 13:2a. **14:4** Or *juniper;* also in 14:6, 49, 51.

KING JAMES VERSION

in water, that he may be clean: and after that he shall come into the camp, and shall tarry abroad out of his tent seven days.

9But it shall be on the seventh day, that he shall shave all his hair off his head and his beard and his eyebrows, even all his hair he shall shave off: and he shall wash his clothes, also he shall wash his flesh in water, and he shall be clean.

10And on the eighth day he shall take two he lambs without blemish, and one ewe lamb of the first year without blemish, and three tenth deals of fine flour *for* a meat offering, mingled with oil, and one log of oil.

11And the priest that maketh *him* clean shall present the man that is to be made clean, and those things, before the LORD, *at* the door of the tabernacle of the congregation:

12And the priest shall take one he lamb, and offer him for a trespass offering, and the log of oil, and wave them *for* a wave offering before the LORD:

13And he shall slay the lamb in the place where he shall kill the sin offering and the burnt offering, in the holy place: for as the sin offering *is* the priest's, *so is* the trespass offering: it *is* most holy:

14And the priest shall take *some* of the blood of the trespass offering, and the priest shall put *it* upon the tip of the right ear of him that is to be cleansed, and upon the thumb of his right hand, and upon the great toe of his right foot:

15And the priest shall take *some* of the log of oil, and pour *it* into the palm of his own left hand:

16And the priest shall dip his right finger in the oil that *is* in his left hand, and shall sprinkle of the oil with his finger seven times before the LORD:

17And of the rest of the oil that *is* in his hand shall the priest put upon the tip of the right ear of him that is to be cleansed, and upon the thumb of his right hand, and upon the great toe of his right foot, upon the blood of the trespass offering:

18And the remnant of the oil that *is* in the priest's hand he shall pour upon the head of him that is to be cleansed: and the priest shall make an atonement for him before the LORD.

19And the priest shall offer the sin offering, and make an atonement for him that is to be cleansed from his uncleanness; and afterward he shall kill the burnt offering:

20And the priest shall offer the burnt offering and the meat offering upon the altar: and the priest shall make an atonement for him, and he shall be clean.

21And if he *be* poor, and cannot get so much; then he shall take one lamb *for* a trespass offering to be waved, to make an atonement for him, and one tenth deal of fine flour mingled with oil for a meat offering, and a log of oil;

22And two turtledoves, or two young pigeons, such as he is able to get; and the one shall be a sin offering, and the other a burnt offering.

NEW LIVING TRANSLATION

themselves in water. Then they will be ceremonially clean and may return to the camp. However, they must remain outside their tents for seven days. 9On the seventh day they must again shave all the hair from their heads, including the hair of the beard and eyebrows. They must also wash their clothes and bathe themselves in water. Then they will be ceremonially clean.

10"On the eighth day each person being purified must bring two male lambs and a one-year-old female lamb, all with no defects, along with a grain offering of six quarts* of choice flour moistened with olive oil, and a cup* of olive oil. 11Then the officiating priest will present that person for purification, along with the offerings, before the LORD at the entrance of the Tabernacle.* 12The priest will take one of the male lambs and the olive oil and present them as a guilt offering, lifting them up as a special offering before the LORD. 13He will then slaughter the male lamb in the sacred area where sin offerings and burnt offerings are slaughtered. As with the sin offering, the guilt offering belongs to the priest. It is a most holy offering. 14The priest will then take some of the blood of the guilt offering and apply it to the lobe of the right ear, the thumb of the right hand, and the big toe of the right foot of the person being purified.

15"Then the priest will pour some of the olive oil into the palm of his own left hand. 16He will dip his right finger into the oil in his palm and sprinkle some of it with his finger seven times before the LORD. 17The priest will then apply some of the oil in his palm over the blood from the guilt offering that is on the lobe of the right ear, the thumb of the right hand, and the big toe of the right foot of the person being purified. 18The priest will apply the oil remaining in his hand to the head of the person being purified. Through this process, the priest will purify* the person before the LORD.

19"Then the priest must present the sin offering to purify the person who was cured of the skin disease. After that, the priest will slaughter the burnt offering 20and offer it on the altar along with the grain offering. Through this process, the priest will purify the person who was healed, and the person will be ceremonially clean.

21"But anyone who is too poor and cannot afford these offerings may bring one male lamb for a guilt offering, to be lifted up as a special offering for purification. The person must also bring two quarts* of choice flour moistened with olive oil for the grain offering and a cup of olive oil. 22The offering must also include two turtledoves or two young pigeons, whichever the person can afford. One of the pair must be used for the sin offering and the other for a

14:10a Hebrew *3/10 of an ephah* [6.6 liters]. **14:10b** Hebrew *1 log* [0.3 liters]; also in 14:21. **14:11** Hebrew *Tent of Meeting;* also in 14:23. **14:18** Or *will make atonement for;* similarly in 14:19, 20, 21, 29, 31, 53. **14:21** Hebrew *1/10 of an ephah* [2.2 liters].

KING JAMES VERSION

23 And he shall bring them on the eighth day for his
cleansing unto the priest, unto the door of the tabernacle of the congregation, before the LORD.
24 And the priest shall take the lamb of the trespass
offering, and the log of oil, and the priest shall wave
them *for* a wave offering before the LORD:
25 And he shall kill the lamb of the trespass offering, and the priest shall take *some* of the blood of the
trespass offering, and put *it* upon the tip of the right
ear of him that is to be cleansed, and upon the
thumb of his right hand, and upon the great toe of
his right foot:
26 And the priest shall pour of the oil into the palm
of his own left hand:
27 And the priest shall sprinkle with his right finger
some of the oil that *is* in his left hand seven times
before the LORD:
28 And the priest shall put of the oil that *is* in his
hand upon the tip of the right ear of him that is to be
cleansed, and upon the thumb of his right hand, and
upon the great toe of his right foot, upon the place of
the blood of the trespass offering:
29 And the rest of the oil that *is* in the priest's hand
he shall put upon the head of him that is to be
cleansed, to make an atonement for him before the
LORD.
30 And he shall offer the one of the turtledoves, or
of the young pigeons, such as he can get;
31 *Even* such as he is able to get, the one *for* a sin offering, and the other *for* a burnt offering, with the
meat offering: and the priest shall make an atonement for him that is to be cleansed before the LORD.
32 This *is* the law *of him* in whom *is* the plague of
leprosy, whose hand is not able to get *that which*
pertaineth to his cleansing.
33 And the LORD spake unto Moses and unto Aaron,
saying,
34 When ye be come into the land of Canaan, which
I give to you for a possession, and I put the plague of
leprosy in a house of the land of your possession;
35 And he that owneth the house shall come and
tell the priest, saying, It seemeth to me *there is* as it
were a plague in the house:
36 Then the priest shall command that they empty
the house, before the priest go *into it* to see the
plague, that all that *is* in the house be not made unclean: and afterward the priest shall go in to see the
house:
37 And he shall look on the plague, and, behold, *if*
the plague *be* in the walls of the house with hollow
strakes, greenish or reddish, which in sight *are* lower
than the wall;
38 Then the priest shall go out of the house to the
door of the house, and shut up the house seven days:
39 And the priest shall come again the seventh day,
and shall look: and, behold, *if* the plague be spread in
the walls of the house;
40 Then the priest shall command that they take

NEW LIVING TRANSLATION

burnt offering. 23 On the eighth day of the purification ceremony, the person being purified must bring
the offerings to the priest in the LORD's presence
at the entrance of the Tabernacle. 24 The priest will
take the lamb for the guilt offering, along with the olive oil, and lift them up as a special offering to the
LORD. 25 Then the priest will slaughter the lamb for
the guilt offering. He will take some of its blood and
apply it to the lobe of the right ear, the thumb of the
right hand, and the big toe of the right foot of the
person being purified.
26 "The priest will also pour some of the olive oil
into the palm of his own left hand. 27 He will dip his
right finger into the oil in his palm and sprinkle
some of it seven times before the LORD. 28 The priest
will then apply some of the oil in his palm over the
blood from the guilt offering that is on the lobe of
the right ear, the thumb of the right hand, and the big
toe of the right foot of the person being purified.
29 The priest will apply the oil remaining in his hand
to the head of the person being purified. Through
this process, the priest will purify the person before
the LORD.
30 "Then the priest will offer the two turtledoves
or the two young pigeons, whichever the person can
afford. 31 One of them is for a sin offering and the
other for a burnt offering, to be presented along with
the grain offering. Through this process, the priest
will purify the person before the LORD. 32 These are
the instructions for purification for those who have
recovered from a serious skin disease but who cannot afford to bring the offerings normally required
for the ceremony of purification."

Treatment of Contaminated Houses

33 Then the LORD said to Moses and Aaron, 34 "When
you arrive in Canaan, the land I am giving you as your
own possession, I may contaminate some of the
houses in your land with mildew.* 35 The owner of
such a house must then go to the priest and say, 'It
appears that my house has some kind of mildew.'
36 Before the priest goes in to inspect the house, he
must have the house emptied so nothing inside will
be pronounced ceremonially unclean. 37 Then the
priest will go in and examine the mildew on the
walls. If he finds greenish or reddish streaks and
the contamination appears to go deeper than the
wall's surface, 38 the priest will step outside the door
and put the house in quarantine for seven days. 39 On
the seventh day the priest must return for another
inspection. If he finds that the mildew on the walls
of the house has spread, 40 the priest must order that

14:34 Traditionally rendered *leprosy;* see note on 13:47.

KING JAMES VERSION

away the stones in which the plague *is*, and they shall cast them into an unclean place without the city:

41 And he shall cause the house to be scraped within round about, and they shall pour out the dust that they scrape off without the city into an unclean place:

42 And they shall take other stones, and put *them* in the place of those stones; and he shall take other mortar, and shall plaster the house.

43 And if the plague come again, and break out in the house, after that he hath taken away the stones, and after he hath scraped the house, and after it is plastered;

44 Then the priest shall come and look, and, behold, *if* the plague be spread in the house, it *is* a fretting leprosy in the house: it *is* unclean.

45 And he shall break down the house, the stones of it, and the timber thereof, and all the mortar of the house; and he shall carry *them* forth out of the city into an unclean place.

46 Moreover he that goeth into the house all the while that it is shut up shall be unclean until the even.

47 And he that lieth in the house shall wash his clothes; and he that eateth in the house shall wash his clothes.

48 And if the priest shall come in, and look *upon it*, and, behold, the plague hath not spread in the house, after the house was plastered: then the priest shall pronounce the house clean, because the plague is healed.

49 And he shall take to cleanse the house two birds, and cedar wood, and scarlet, and hyssop:

50 And he shall kill the one of the birds in an earthen vessel over running water:

51 And he shall take the cedar wood, and the hyssop, and the scarlet, and the living bird, and dip them in the blood of the slain bird, and in the running water, and sprinkle the house seven times:

52 And he shall cleanse the house with the blood of the bird, and with the running water, and with the living bird, and with the cedar wood, and with the hyssop, and with the scarlet:

53 But he shall let go the living bird out of the city into the open fields, and make an atonement for the house: and it shall be clean.

54 This *is* the law for all manner of plague of leprosy, and scall,

55 And for the leprosy of a garment, and of a house,

56 And for a rising, and for a scab, and for a bright spot:

57 To teach when *it is* unclean, and when *it is* clean: this *is* the law of leprosy.

15 1 And the LORD spake unto Moses and to Aaron, saying,

2 Speak unto the children of Israel, and say unto them, When any man hath a running issue out of his flesh, *because of* his issue he *is* unclean.

NEW LIVING TRANSLATION

the stones from those areas be removed. The contaminated material will then be taken outside the town to an area designated as ceremonially unclean.
41 Next the inside walls of the entire house must be scraped thoroughly and the scrapings dumped in the unclean place outside the town. 42 Other stones will be brought in to replace the ones that were removed, and the walls will be replastered.

43 "But if the mildew reappears after all the stones have been replaced and the house has been scraped and replastered, 44 the priest must return and inspect the house again. If he finds that the mildew has spread, the walls are clearly contaminated with a serious mildew, and the house is defiled. 45 It must be torn down, and all its stones, timbers, and plaster must be carried out of town to the place designated as ceremonially unclean. 46 Those who enter the house during the period of quarantine will be ceremonially unclean until evening, 47 and all who sleep or eat in the house must wash their clothing.

48 "But if the priest returns for his inspection and finds that the mildew has not reappeared in the house after the fresh plastering, he will pronounce it clean because the mildew is clearly gone. 49 To purify the house the priest must take two birds, a stick of cedar, some scarlet yarn, and a hyssop branch. 50 He will slaughter one of the birds over a clay pot filled with fresh water. 51 He will take the cedar stick, the hyssop branch, the scarlet yarn, and the live bird, and dip them into the blood of the slaughtered bird and into the fresh water. Then he will sprinkle the house seven times. 52 When the priest has purified the house in exactly this way, 53 he will release the live bird in the open fields outside the town. Through this process, the priest will purify the house, and it will be ceremonially clean.

54 "These are the instructions for dealing with serious skin diseases,* including scabby sores; 55 and mildew,* whether on clothing or in a house; 56 and a swelling on the skin, a rash, or discolored skin. 57 This procedure will determine whether a person or object is ceremonially clean or unclean.

"These are the instructions regarding skin diseases and mildew."

Bodily Discharges

15 The LORD said to Moses and Aaron, 2 "Give the following instructions to the people of Israel.

14:54 Traditionally rendered *leprosy;* see note on 13:2a.
14:55 Traditionally rendered *leprosy;* see note on 13:47.

KING JAMES VERSION

3 And this shall be his uncleanness in his issue: whether his flesh run with his issue, or his flesh be stopped from his issue, it *is* his uncleanness.

4 Every bed, whereon he lieth that hath the issue, is unclean: and every thing, whereon he sitteth, shall be unclean.

5 And whosoever toucheth his bed shall wash his clothes, and bathe *himself* in water, and be unclean until the even.

6 And he that sitteth on *any* thing whereon he sat that hath the issue shall wash his clothes, and bathe *himself* in water, and be unclean until the even.

7 And he that toucheth the flesh of him that hath the issue shall wash his clothes, and bathe *himself* in water, and be unclean until the even.

8 And if he that hath the issue spit upon him that is clean; then he shall wash his clothes, and bathe *himself* in water, and be unclean until the even.

9 And what saddle soever he rideth upon that hath the issue shall be unclean.

10 And whosoever toucheth any thing that was under him shall be unclean until the even: and he that beareth *any of* those things shall wash his clothes, and bathe *himself* in water, and be unclean until the even.

11 And whomsoever he toucheth that hath the issue, and hath not rinsed his hands in water, he shall wash his clothes, and bathe *himself* in water, and be unclean until the even.

12 And the vessel of earth, that he toucheth which hath the issue, shall be broken: and every vessel of wood shall be rinsed in water.

13 And when he that hath an issue is cleansed of his issue; then he shall number to himself seven days for his cleansing, and wash his clothes, and bathe his flesh in running water, and shall be clean.

14 And on the eighth day he shall take to him two turtledoves, or two young pigeons, and come before the LORD unto the door of the tabernacle of the congregation, and give them unto the priest:

15 And the priest shall offer them, the one *for* a sin offering, and the other *for* a burnt offering; and the priest shall make an atonement for him before the LORD for his issue.

16 And if any man's seed of copulation go out from him, then he shall wash all his flesh in water, and be unclean until the even.

17 And every garment, and every skin, whereon is the seed of copulation, shall be washed with water, and be unclean until the even.

18 The woman also with whom man shall lie *with* seed of copulation, they shall *both* bathe *themselves* in water, and be unclean until the even.

19 And if a woman have an issue, *and* her issue in her flesh be blood, she shall be put apart seven days: and whosoever toucheth her shall be unclean until the even.

20 And every thing that she lieth upon in her

NEW LIVING TRANSLATION

"Any man who has a bodily discharge is ceremonially unclean. 3 This defilement is caused by his discharge, whether the discharge continues or stops. In either case the man is unclean. 4 Any bed on which the man with the discharge lies and anything on which he sits will be ceremonially unclean. 5 So if you touch the man's bed, you must wash your clothes and bathe yourself in water, and you will remain unclean until evening. 6 If you sit where the man with the discharge has sat, you must wash your clothes and bathe yourself in water, and you will remain unclean until evening. 7 If you touch the man with the discharge, you must wash your clothes and bathe yourself in water, and you will remain unclean until evening. 8 If the man spits on you, you must wash your clothes and bathe yourself in water, and you will remain unclean until evening. 9 Any saddle blanket on which the man rides will be ceremonially unclean. 10 If you touch anything that was under the man, you will be unclean until evening. You must wash your clothes and bathe yourself in water, and you will remain unclean until evening. 11 If the man touches you without first rinsing his hands, you must wash your clothes and bathe yourself in water, and you will remain unclean until evening. 12 Any clay pot the man touches must be broken, and any wooden utensil he touches must be rinsed with water.

13 "When the man with the discharge is healed, he must count off seven days for the period of purification. Then he must wash his clothes and bathe himself in fresh water, and he will be ceremonially clean. 14 On the eighth day he must get two turtledoves or two young pigeons and come before the LORD at the entrance of the Tabernacle* and give his offerings to the priest. 15 The priest will offer one bird for a sin offering and the other for a burnt offering. Through this process, the priest will purify* the man before the LORD for his discharge.

16 "Whenever a man has an emission of semen, he must bathe his entire body in water, and he will remain ceremonially unclean until the next evening.* 17 Any clothing or leather with semen on it must be washed in water, and it will remain unclean until evening. 18 After a man and a woman have sexual intercourse, they must each bathe in water, and they will remain unclean until the next evening.

19 "Whenever a woman has her menstrual period, she will be ceremonially unclean for seven days. Anyone who touches her during that time will be unclean until evening. 20 Anything on which the woman

15:14 Hebrew *Tent of Meeting;* also in 15:29. **15:15** Or *will make atonement for;* also in 15:30. **15:16** Hebrew *until evening;* also in 15:18.

KING JAMES VERSION

separation shall be unclean: every thing also that she sitteth upon shall be unclean.

21 And whosoever toucheth her bed shall wash his clothes, and bathe *himself* in water, and be unclean until the even.

22 And whosoever toucheth any thing that she sat upon shall wash his clothes, and bathe *himself* in water, and be unclean until the even.

23 And if it *be* on *her* bed, or on any thing whereon she sitteth, when he toucheth it, he shall be unclean until the even.

24 And if any man lie with her at all, and her flowers be upon him, he shall be unclean seven days; and all the bed whereon he lieth shall be unclean.

25 And if a woman have an issue of her blood many days out of the time of her separation, or if it run beyond the time of her separation; all the days of the issue of her uncleanness shall be as the days of her separation: she *shall be* unclean.

26 Every bed whereon she lieth all the days of her issue shall be unto her as the bed of her separation: and whatsoever she sitteth upon shall be unclean, as the uncleanness of her separation.

27 And whosoever toucheth those things shall be unclean, and shall wash his clothes, and bathe *himself* in water, and be unclean until the even.

28 But if she be cleansed of her issue, then she shall number to herself seven days, and after that she shall be clean.

29 And on the eighth day she shall take unto her two turtles, or two young pigeons, and bring them unto the priest, to the door of the tabernacle of the congregation.

30 And the priest shall offer the one *for* a sin offering, and the other *for* a burnt offering; and the priest shall make an atonement for her before the LORD for the issue of her uncleanness.

31 Thus shall ye separate the children of Israel from their uncleanness; that they die not in their uncleanness, when they defile my tabernacle that *is* among them.

32 This *is* the law of him that hath an issue, and *of him* whose seed goeth from him, and is defiled therewith;

33 And of her that is sick of her flowers, and of him that hath an issue, of the man, and of the woman, and of him that lieth with her that is unclean.

16 1 And the LORD spake unto Moses after the death of the two sons of Aaron, when they offered before the LORD, and died;

2 And the LORD said unto Moses, Speak unto Aaron thy brother, that he come not at all times into the holy *place* within the veil before the mercy seat, which *is* upon the ark; that he die not: for I will appear in the cloud upon the mercy seat.

3 Thus shall Aaron come into the holy *place:* with a

NEW LIVING TRANSLATION

lies or sits during the time of her period will be unclean. 21 If any of you touch her bed, you must wash your clothes and bathe yourself in water, and you will remain unclean until evening. 22 If you touch any object she has sat on, you must wash your clothes and bathe yourself in water, and you will remain unclean until evening. 23 This includes her bed or any other object she has sat on; you will be unclean until evening if you touch it. 24 If a man has sexual intercourse with her and her blood touches him, her menstrual impurity will be transmitted to him. He will remain unclean for seven days, and any bed on which he lies will be unclean.

25 "If a woman has a flow of blood for many days that is unrelated to her menstrual period, or if the blood continues beyond the normal period, she is ceremonially unclean. As during her menstrual period, the woman will be unclean as long as the discharge continues. 26 Any bed she lies on and any object she sits on during that time will be unclean, just as during her normal menstrual period. 27 If any of you touch these things, you will be ceremonially unclean. You must wash your clothes and bathe yourself in water, and you will remain unclean until evening.

28 "When the woman's bleeding stops, she must count off seven days. Then she will be ceremonially clean. 29 On the eighth day she must bring two turtledoves or two young pigeons and present them to the priest at the entrance of the Tabernacle. 30 The priest will offer one for a sin offering and the other for a burnt offering. Through this process, the priest will purify her before the LORD for the ceremonial impurity caused by her bleeding.

31 "This is how you will guard the people of Israel from ceremonial uncleanness. Otherwise they would die, for their impurity would defile my Tabernacle that stands among them. 32 These are the instructions for dealing with anyone who has a bodily discharge—a man who is unclean because of an emission of semen 33 or a woman during her menstrual period. It applies to any man or woman who has a bodily discharge, and to a man who has sexual intercourse with a woman who is ceremonially unclean."

The Day of Atonement

16 The LORD spoke to Moses after the death of Aaron's two sons, who died after they entered the LORD's presence and burned the wrong kind of fire before him. 2 The LORD said to Moses, "Warn your brother, Aaron, not to enter the Most Holy Place behind the inner curtain whenever he chooses; if he does, he will die. For the Ark's cover—the place of atonement—is there, and I myself am present in the cloud above the atonement cover.

3 "When Aaron enters the sanctuary area, he must

KING JAMES VERSION

young bullock for a sin offering, and a ram for a
burnt offering.
[4]He shall put on the holy linen coat, and he shall
have the linen breeches upon his flesh, and shall be
girded with a linen girdle, and with the linen mitre
shall he be attired: these *are* holy garments; therefore
shall he wash his flesh in water, and *so* put them on.
[5]And he shall take of the congregation of the children of Israel two kids of the goats for a sin offering,
and one ram for a burnt offering.
[6]And Aaron shall offer his bullock of the sin offering, which *is* for himself, and make an atonement for
himself, and for his house.
[7]And he shall take the two goats, and present them
before the LORD *at* the door of the tabernacle of the
congregation.
[8]And Aaron shall cast lots upon the two goats; one
lot for the LORD, and the other lot for the scapegoat.
[9]And Aaron shall bring the goat upon which the
LORD's lot fell, and offer him *for* a sin offering.
[10]But the goat, on which the lot fell to be the
scapegoat, shall be presented alive before the LORD,
to make an atonement with him, *and* to let him go
for a scapegoat into the wilderness.
[11]And Aaron shall bring the bullock of the sin offering, which *is* for himself, and shall make an atonement for himself, and for his house, and shall kill the
bullock of the sin offering which *is* for himself:
[12]And he shall take a censer full of burning coals
of fire from off the altar before the LORD, and his
hands full of sweet incense beaten small, and bring *it*
within the veil:
[13]And he shall put the incense upon the fire before the LORD, that the cloud of the incense may
cover the mercy seat that *is* upon the testimony, that
he die not:
[14]And he shall take of the blood of the bullock,
and sprinkle *it* with his finger upon the mercy seat
eastward; and before the mercy seat shall he sprinkle
of the blood with his finger seven times.
[15]Then shall he kill the goat of the sin offering,
that *is* for the people, and bring his blood within the
veil, and do with that blood as he did with the blood
of the bullock, and sprinkle it upon the mercy seat,
and before the mercy seat:
[16]And he shall make an atonement for the holy
place, because of the uncleanness of the children of
Israel, and because of their transgressions in all their
sins: and so shall he do for the tabernacle of the congregation, that remaineth among them in the midst
of their uncleanness.
[17]And there shall be no man in the tabernacle of
the congregation when he goeth in to make an
atonement in the holy *place,* until he come out, and
have made an atonement for himself, and for his
household, and for all the congregation of Israel.

NEW LIVING TRANSLATION

follow these instructions fully. He must bring a young
bull for a sin offering and a ram for a burnt offering.
[4]He must put on his linen tunic and the linen undergarments worn next to his body. He must tie the linen
sash around his waist and put the linen turban on his
head. These are sacred garments, so he must bathe
himself in water before he puts them on. [5]Aaron must
take from the community of Israel two male goats for
a sin offering and a ram for a burnt offering.
[6]"Aaron will present his own bull as a sin offering
to purify himself and his family, making them right
with the LORD.* [7]Then he must take the two male
goats and present them to the LORD at the entrance
of the Tabernacle.* [8]He is to cast sacred lots to determine which goat will be reserved as an offering to
the LORD and which will carry the sins of the people
to the wilderness of Azazel. [9]Aaron will then present
as a sin offering the goat chosen by lot for the LORD.
[10]The other goat, the scapegoat chosen by lot to be
sent away, will be kept alive, standing before the
LORD. When it is sent away to Azazel in the wilderness, the people will be purified and made right with
the LORD.*
[11]"Aaron will present his own bull as a sin offering
to purify himself and his family, making them right
with the LORD. After he has slaughtered the bull as a
sin offering, [12]he will fill an incense burner with
burning coals from the altar that stands before the
LORD. Then he will take two handfuls of fragrant
powdered incense and will carry the burner and the
incense behind the inner curtain. [13]There in the
LORD's presence he will put the incense on the burning coals so that a cloud of incense will rise over the
Ark's cover—the place of atonement—that rests on
the Ark of the Covenant.* If he follows these instructions, he will not die. [14]Then he must take some of
the blood of the bull, dip his finger in it, and sprinkle
it on the east side of the atonement cover. He must
sprinkle blood seven times with his finger in front of
the atonement cover.
[15]"Then Aaron must slaughter the first goat as a
sin offering for the people and carry its blood behind
the inner curtain. There he will sprinkle the goat's
blood over the atonement cover and in front of it, just
as he did with the bull's blood. [16]Through this process, he will purify* the Most Holy Place, and he will
do the same for the entire Tabernacle, because of the
defiling sin and rebellion of the Israelites. [17]No one
else is allowed inside the Tabernacle when Aaron enters it for the purification ceremony in the Most Holy
Place. No one may enter until he comes out again
after purifying himself, his family, and all the congregation of Israel, making them right with the LORD.

16:6 Or *to make atonement for himself and his family;* similarly in 16:11, 17b, 24, 34. **16:7** Hebrew *Tent of Meeting;* also in 16:16, 17, 20, 23, 33. **16:10** Or *wilderness, it will make atonement for the people.* **16:13** Hebrew *that is above the Testimony.* The Hebrew word for "testimony" refers to the terms of the LORD's covenant with Israel as written on stone tablets, which were kept in the Ark, and also to the covenant itself. **16:16** Or *make atonement for;* similarly in 16:17a, 18, 20, 27, 33.

KING JAMES VERSION

18 And he shall go out unto the altar that *is* before the LORD, and make an atonement for it; and shall take of the blood of the bullock, and of the blood of the goat, and put *it* upon the horns of the altar round about.

19 And he shall sprinkle of the blood upon it with his finger seven times, and cleanse it, and hallow it from the uncleanness of the children of Israel.

20 And when he hath made an end of reconciling the holy *place,* and the tabernacle of the congregation, and the altar, he shall bring the live goat:

21 And Aaron shall lay both his hands upon the head of the live goat, and confess over him all the iniquities of the children of Israel, and all their transgressions in all their sins, putting them upon the head of the goat, and shall send *him* away by the hand of a fit man into the wilderness:

22 And the goat shall bear upon him all their iniquities unto a land not inhabited: and he shall let go the goat in the wilderness.

23 And Aaron shall come into the tabernacle of the congregation, and shall put off the linen garments, which he put on when he went into the holy *place,* and shall leave them there:

24 And he shall wash his flesh with water in the holy place, and put on his garments, and come forth, and offer his burnt offering, and the burnt offering of the people, and make an atonement for himself, and for the people.

25 And the fat of the sin offering shall he burn upon the altar.

26 And he that let go the goat for the scapegoat shall wash his clothes, and bathe his flesh in water, and afterward come into the camp.

27 And the bullock *for* the sin offering, and the goat *for* the sin offering, whose blood was brought in to make atonement in the holy *place,* shall *one* carry forth without the camp; and they shall burn in the fire their skins, and their flesh, and their dung.

28 And he that burneth them shall wash his clothes, and bathe his flesh in water, and afterward he shall come into the camp.

29 And *this* shall be a statute for ever unto you: *that* in the seventh month, on the tenth *day* of the month, ye shall afflict your souls, and do no work at all, *whether it be* one of your own country, or a stranger that sojourneth among you:

30 For on that day shall *the priest* make an atonement for you, to cleanse you, *that* ye may be clean from all your sins before the LORD.

31 It *shall be* a sabbath of rest unto you, and ye shall afflict your souls, by a statute for ever.

32 And the priest, whom he shall anoint, and whom he shall consecrate to minister in the priest's office in his father's stead, shall make the atonement, and shall put on the linen clothes, *even* the holy garments:

33 And he shall make an atonement for the holy sanctuary, and he shall make an atonement for the

NEW LIVING TRANSLATION

18 "Then Aaron will come out to purify the altar that stands before the LORD. He will do this by taking some of the blood from the bull and the goat and putting it on each of the horns of the altar. 19 Then he must sprinkle the blood with his finger seven times over the altar. In this way, he will cleanse it from Israel's defilement and make it holy.

20 "When Aaron has finished purifying the Most Holy Place and the Tabernacle and the altar, he must present the live goat. 21 He will lay both of his hands on the goat's head and confess over it all the wickedness, rebellion, and sins of the people of Israel. In this way, he will transfer the people's sins to the head of the goat. Then a man specially chosen for the task will drive the goat into the wilderness. 22 As the goat goes into the wilderness, it will carry all the people's sins upon itself into a desolate land.

23 "When Aaron goes back into the Tabernacle, he must take off the linen garments he was wearing when he entered the Most Holy Place, and he must leave the garments there. 24 Then he must bathe himself with water in a sacred place, put on his regular garments, and go out to sacrifice a burnt offering for himself and a burnt offering for the people. Through this process, he will purify himself and the people, making them right with the LORD. 25 He must then burn all the fat of the sin offering on the altar.

26 "The man chosen to drive the scapegoat into the wilderness of Azazel must wash his clothes and bathe himself in water. Then he may return to the camp.

27 "The bull and the goat presented as sin offerings, whose blood Aaron takes into the Most Holy Place for the purification ceremony, will be carried outside the camp. The animals' hides, internal organs, and dung are all to be burned. 28 The man who burns them must wash his clothes and bathe himself in water before returning to the camp.

29 "On the tenth day of the appointed month in early autumn,* you must deny yourselves.* Neither native-born Israelites nor foreigners living among you may do any kind of work. This is a permanent law for you. 30 On that day offerings of purification will be made for you,* and you will be purified in the LORD's presence from all your sins. 31 It will be a Sabbath day of complete rest for you, and you must deny yourselves. This is a permanent law for you. 32 In future generations, the purification* ceremony will be performed by the priest who has been anointed and ordained to serve as high priest in place of his ancestor Aaron. He will put on the holy linen garments 33 and purify the Most Holy Place, the Tabernacle, the altar, the priests, and the entire congregation.

16:29a Hebrew *On the tenth day of the seventh month.* This day in the ancient Hebrew lunar calendar occurred in September or October. **16:29b** Or *must fast;* also in 16:31. **16:30** Or *atonement will be made for you, to purify you.* **16:32** Or *atonement.*

KING JAMES VERSION

tabernacle of the congregation, and for the altar, and
he shall make an atonement for the priests, and for
all the people of the congregation.
34And this shall be an everlasting statute unto you,
to make an atonement for the children of Israel
for all their sins once a year. And he did as the LORD
commanded Moses.

17 1And the LORD spake unto Moses, saying,
2Speak unto Aaron, and unto his sons, and
unto all the children of Israel, and say unto them;
This *is* the thing which the LORD hath commanded,
saying,
3What man soever *there be* of the house of Israel,
that killeth an ox, or lamb, or goat, in the camp, or
that killeth *it* out of the camp,
4And bringeth it not unto the door of the tabernacle of the congregation, to offer an offering unto the
LORD before the tabernacle of the LORD; blood shall
be imputed unto that man; he hath shed blood; and
that man shall be cut off from among his people:
5To the end that the children of Israel may bring
their sacrifices, which they offer in the open field,
even that they may bring them unto the LORD, unto
the door of the tabernacle of the congregation, unto
the priest, and offer them *for* peace offerings
unto the LORD.
6And the priest shall sprinkle the blood upon the
altar of the LORD *at* the door of the tabernacle of the
congregation, and burn the fat for a sweet savour
unto the LORD.
7And they shall no more offer their sacrifices unto
devils, after whom they have gone a whoring. This
shall be a statute for ever unto them throughout
their generations.
8And thou shalt say unto them, Whatsoever man
there be of the house of Israel, or of the strangers
which sojourn among you, that offereth a burnt
offering or sacrifice,
9And bringeth it not unto the door of the tabernacle of the congregation, to offer it unto the LORD; even
that man shall be cut off from among his people.
10And whatsoever man *there be* of the house of Israel, or of the strangers that sojourn among you, that
eateth any manner of blood; I will even set my face
against that soul that eateth blood, and will cut him
off from among his people.
11For the life of the flesh *is* in the blood: and I have
given it to you upon the altar to make an atonement
for your souls: for it *is* the blood *that* maketh an
atonement for the soul.
12Therefore I said unto the children of Israel, No
soul of you shall eat blood, neither shall any stranger
that sojourneth among you eat blood.
13And whatsoever man *there be* of the children of
Israel, or of the strangers that sojourn among you,
which hunteth and catcheth any beast or fowl that

NEW LIVING TRANSLATION

34This is a permanent law for you, to purify the
people of Israel from their sins, making them right
with the LORD once each year."
Moses followed all these instructions exactly as
the LORD had commanded him.

Prohibitions against Eating Blood

17 Then the LORD said to Moses, 2"Give the following instructions to Aaron and his sons
and all the people of Israel. This is what the LORD has
commanded.
3"If any native Israelite sacrifices a bull* or a lamb
or a goat anywhere inside or outside the camp 4in-
stead of bringing it to the entrance of the Tabernacle* to present it as an offering to the LORD, that
person will be as guilty as a murderer.* Such a person has shed blood and will be cut off from the community. 5The purpose of this rule is to stop the
Israelites from sacrificing animals in the open fields.
It will ensure that they bring their sacrifices to the
priest at the entrance of the Tabernacle, so he can
present them to the LORD as peace offerings. 6Then
the priest will be able to splatter the blood against
the LORD's altar at the entrance of the Tabernacle,
and he will burn the fat as a pleasing aroma to the
LORD. 7The people must no longer be unfaithful to
the LORD by offering sacrifices to the goat idols.*
This is a permanent law for them, to be observed
from generation to generation.
8"Give them this command as well. If any native
Israelite or foreigner living among you offers a burnt
offering or a sacrifice 9but does not bring it to the
entrance of the Tabernacle to offer it to the LORD,
that person will be cut off from the community.
10"And if any native Israelite or foreigner living
among you eats or drinks blood in any form, I will
turn against that person and cut him off from the
community of your people, 11for the life of the
body is in its blood. I have given you the blood on the
altar to purify you, making you right with the LORD.*
It is the blood, given in exchange for a life, that
makes purification possible. 12That is why I have
said to the people of Israel, 'You must never eat or
drink blood—neither you nor the foreigners living
among you.'
13"And if any native Israelite or foreigner living
among you goes hunting and kills an animal or bird
that is approved for eating, he must drain its blood

17:3 Or *cow.* **17:4a** Hebrew *Tent of Meeting;* also in 17:5, 6, 9.
17:4b Hebrew *will be guilty of blood.* **17:7** Or *goat demons.*
17:11 Or *to make atonement for you.*

KING JAMES VERSION

may be eaten; he shall even pour out the blood thereof, and cover it with dust.

14For *it is* the life of all flesh; the blood of it *is* for the life thereof: therefore I said unto the children of Israel, Ye shall eat the blood of no manner of flesh: for the life of all flesh *is* the blood thereof: whosoever eateth it shall be cut off.

15And every soul that eateth that which died *of itself,* or that which was torn *with beasts, whether it be* one of your own country, or a stranger, he shall both wash his clothes, and bathe *himself* in water, and be unclean until the even: then shall he be clean.

16But if he wash *them* not, nor bathe his flesh; then he shall bear his iniquity.

18 1And the LORD spake unto Moses, saying,
2Speak unto the children of Israel, and say unto them, I am the LORD your God.

3After the doings of the land of Egypt, wherein ye dwelt, shall ye not do: and after the doings of the land of Canaan, whither I bring you, shall ye not do: neither shall ye walk in their ordinances.

4Ye shall do my judgments, and keep mine ordinances, to walk therein: I *am* the LORD your God.

5Ye shall therefore keep my statutes, and my judgments: which if a man do, he shall live in them: I *am* the LORD.

6None of you shall approach to any that is near of kin to him, to uncover *their* nakedness: I *am* the LORD.

7The nakedness of thy father, or the nakedness of thy mother, shalt thou not uncover: she *is* thy mother; thou shalt not uncover her nakedness.

8The nakedness of thy father's wife shalt thou not uncover: it *is* thy father's nakedness.

9The nakedness of thy sister, the daughter of thy father, or daughter of thy mother, *whether she be* born at home, or born abroad, *even* their nakedness thou shalt not uncover.

10The nakedness of thy son's daughter, or of thy daughter's daughter, *even* their nakedness thou shalt not uncover: for theirs *is* thine own nakedness.

11The nakedness of thy father's wife's daughter, begotten of thy father, she *is* thy sister, thou shalt not uncover her nakedness.

12Thou shalt not uncover the nakedness of thy father's sister: she *is* thy father's near kinswoman.

13Thou shalt not uncover the nakedness of thy mother's sister; for she *is* thy mother's near kinswoman.

14Thou shalt not uncover the nakedness of thy father's brother, thou shalt not approach to his wife: she *is* thine aunt.

15Thou shalt not uncover the nakedness of thy daughter in law: she *is* thy son's wife; thou shalt not uncover her nakedness.

16Thou shalt not uncover the nakedness of thy brother's wife: it *is* thy brother's nakedness.

NEW LIVING TRANSLATION

and cover it with earth. 14The life of every creature is in its blood. That is why I have said to the people of Israel, 'You must never eat or drink blood, for the life of any creature is in its blood.' So whoever consumes blood will be cut off from the community.

15"And if any native-born Israelites or foreigners eat the meat of an animal that died naturally or was torn up by wild animals, they must wash their clothes and bathe themselves in water. They will remain ceremonially unclean until evening, but then they will be clean. 16But if they do not wash their clothes and bathe themselves, they will be punished for their sin."

Forbidden Sexual Practices

18 Then the LORD said to Moses, 2"Give the following instructions to the people of Israel. I am the LORD your God. 3So do not act like the people in Egypt, where you used to live, or like the people of Canaan, where I am taking you. You must not imitate their way of life. 4You must obey all my regulations and be careful to obey my decrees, for I am the LORD your God. 5If you obey my decrees and my regulations, you will find life through them. I am the LORD.

6"You must never have sexual relations with a close relative, for I am the LORD.

7"Do not violate your father by having sexual relations with your mother. She is your mother; you must not have sexual relations with her.

8"Do not have sexual relations with any of your father's wives, for this would violate your father.

9"Do not have sexual relations with your sister or half sister, whether she is your father's daughter or your mother's daughter, whether she was born into your household or someone else's.

10"Do not have sexual relations with your granddaughter, whether she is your son's daughter or your daughter's daughter, for this would violate yourself.

11"Do not have sexual relations with your stepsister, the daughter of any of your father's wives, for she is your sister.

12"Do not have sexual relations with your father's sister, for she is your father's close relative.

13"Do not have sexual relations with your mother's sister, for she is your mother's close relative.

14"Do not violate your uncle, your father's brother, by having sexual relations with his wife, for she is your aunt.

15"Do not have sexual relations with your daughter-in-law; she is your son's wife, so you must not have sexual relations with her.

16"Do not have sexual relations with your brother's wife, for this would violate your brother.

KING JAMES VERSION

17 Thou shalt not uncover the nakedness of a woman and her daughter, neither shalt thou take her son's daughter, or her daughter's daughter, to uncover her nakedness; *for* they *are* her near kinswomen: it *is* wickedness.

18 Neither shalt thou take a wife to her sister, to vex *her*, to uncover her nakedness, beside the other in her life *time*.

19 Also thou shalt not approach unto a woman to uncover her nakedness, as long as she is put apart for her uncleanness.

20 Moreover thou shalt not lie carnally with thy neighbour's wife, to defile thyself with her.

21 And thou shalt not let any of thy seed pass through *the fire* to Molech, neither shalt thou profane the name of thy God: I *am* the LORD.

22 Thou shalt not lie with mankind, as with womankind: it *is* abomination.

23 Neither shalt thou lie with any beast to defile thyself therewith: neither shall any woman stand before a beast to lie down thereto: it *is* confusion.

24 Defile not ye yourselves in any of these things: for in all these the nations are defiled which I cast out before you:

25 And the land is defiled: therefore I do visit the iniquity thereof upon it, and the land itself vomiteth out her inhabitants.

26 Ye shall therefore keep my statutes and my judgments, and shall not commit *any* of these abominations; *neither* any of your own nation, nor any stranger that sojourneth among you:

27 (For all these abominations have the men of the land done, which *were* before you, and the land is defiled;)

28 That the land spue not you out also, when ye defile it, as it spued out the nations that *were* before you.

29 For whosoever shall commit any of these abominations, even the souls that commit *them* shall be cut off from among their people.

30 Therefore shall ye keep mine ordinance, that *ye* commit not *any one* of these abominable customs, which were committed before you, and that ye defile not yourselves therein: I *am* the LORD your God.

19 1 And the LORD spake unto Moses, saying,
2 Speak unto all the congregation of the children of Israel, and say unto them, Ye shall be holy: for I the LORD your God *am* holy.

3 Ye shall fear every man his mother, and his father, and keep my sabbaths: I *am* the LORD your God.

4 Turn ye not unto idols, nor make to yourselves molten gods: I *am* the LORD your God.

5 And if ye offer a sacrifice of peace offerings unto the LORD, ye shall offer it at your own will.

6 It shall be eaten the same day ye offer it, and on the morrow: and if aught remain until the third day, it shall be burnt in the fire.

NEW LIVING TRANSLATION

17 "Do not have sexual relations with both a woman and her daughter. And do not take* her granddaughter, whether her son's daughter or her daughter's daughter, and have sexual relations with her. They are close relatives, and this would be a wicked act.

18 "While your wife is living, do not marry her sister and have sexual relations with her, for they would be rivals.

19 "Do not have sexual relations with a woman during her period of menstrual impurity.

20 "Do not defile yourself by having sexual intercourse with your neighbor's wife.

21 "Do not permit any of your children to be offered as a sacrifice to Molech, for you must not bring shame on the name of your God. I am the LORD.

22 "Do not practice homosexuality, having sex with another man as with a woman. It is a detestable sin.

23 "A man must not defile himself by having sex with an animal. And a woman must not offer herself to a male animal to have intercourse with it. This is a perverse act.

24 "Do not defile yourselves in any of these ways, for the people I am driving out before you have defiled themselves in all these ways. 25 Because the entire land has become defiled, I am punishing the people who live there. I will cause the land to vomit them out. 26 You must obey all my decrees and regulations. You must not commit any of these detestable sins. This applies both to native-born Israelites and to the foreigners living among you.

27 "All these detestable activities are practiced by the people of the land where I am taking you, and this is how the land has become defiled. 28 So do not defile the land and give it a reason to vomit you out, as it will vomit out the people who live there now. 29 Whoever commits any of these detestable sins will be cut off from the community of Israel. 30 So obey my instructions, and do not defile yourselves by committing any of these detestable practices that were committed by the people who lived in the land before you. I am the LORD your God."

Holiness in Personal Conduct

19 The LORD also said to Moses, 2 "Give the following instructions to the entire community of Israel. You must be holy because I, the LORD your God, am holy.

3 "Each of you must show great respect for your mother and father, and you must always observe my Sabbath days of rest. I am the LORD your God.

4 "Do not put your trust in idols or make metal images of gods for yourselves. I am the LORD your God.

5 "When you sacrifice a peace offering to the LORD, offer it properly so you* will be accepted by God. 6 The sacrifice must be eaten on the same day you offer it or on the next day. Whatever is left over

18:17 Or *do not marry*. **19:5** Or *it*.

KING JAMES VERSION

7 And if it be eaten at all on the third day, it *is* abominable; it shall not be accepted.

8 Therefore *every one* that eateth it shall bear his iniquity, because he hath profaned the hallowed thing of the LORD: and that soul shall be cut off from among his people.

9 And when ye reap the harvest of your land, thou shalt not wholly reap the corners of thy field, neither shalt thou gather the gleanings of thy harvest.

10 And thou shalt not glean thy vineyard, neither shalt thou gather *every* grape of thy vineyard; thou shalt leave them for the poor and stranger: I *am* the LORD your God.

11 Ye shall not steal, neither deal falsely, neither lie one to another.

12 And ye shall not swear by my name falsely, neither shalt thou profane the name of thy God: I *am* the LORD.

13 Thou shalt not defraud thy neighbour, neither rob *him:* the wages of him that is hired shall not abide with thee all night until the morning.

14 Thou shalt not curse the deaf, nor put a stumblingblock before the blind, but shalt fear thy God: I *am* the LORD.

15 Ye shall do no unrighteousness in judgment: thou shalt not respect the person of the poor, nor honour the person of the mighty: *but* in righteousness shalt thou judge thy neighbour.

16 Thou shalt not go up and down *as* a talebearer among thy people: neither shalt thou stand against the blood of thy neighbour: I *am* the LORD.

17 Thou shalt not hate thy brother in thine heart: thou shalt in any wise rebuke thy neighbour, and not suffer sin upon him.

18 Thou shalt not avenge, nor bear any grudge against the children of thy people, but thou shalt love thy neighbour as thyself: I *am* the LORD.

19 Ye shall keep my statutes. Thou shalt not let thy cattle gender with a diverse kind: thou shalt not sow thy field with mingled seed: neither shall a garment mingled of linen and woollen come upon thee.

20 And whosoever lieth carnally with a woman, that *is* a bondmaid, betrothed to an husband, and not at all redeemed, nor freedom given her; she shall be scourged; they shall not be put to death, because she was not free.

21 And he shall bring his trespass offering unto the LORD, unto the door of the tabernacle of the congregation, *even* a ram for a trespass offering.

22 And the priest shall make an atonement for him with the ram of the trespass offering before the LORD for his sin which he hath done: and the sin which he hath done shall be forgiven him.

23 And when ye shall come into the land, and shall have planted all manner of trees for food, then ye shall count the fruit thereof as uncircumcised: three years shall it be as uncircumcised unto you: it shall not be eaten of.

NEW LIVING TRANSLATION

until the third day must be completely burned up. 7 If
any of the sacrifice is eaten on the third day, it will be
contaminated, and I will not accept it. 8 Anyone who
eats it on the third day will be punished for defiling
what is holy to the LORD and will be cut off from the
community.

9 "When you harvest the crops of your land, do not
harvest the grain along the edges of your fields, and
do not pick up what the harvesters drop. 10 It is the
same with your grape crop—do not strip every last
bunch of grapes from the vines, and do not pick up
the grapes that fall to the ground. Leave them for the
poor and the foreigners living among you. I am the
LORD your God.

11 "Do not steal.

"Do not deceive or cheat one another.

12 "Do not bring shame on the name of your God
by using it to swear falsely. I am the LORD.

13 "Do not defraud or rob your neighbor.

"Do not make your hired workers wait until the
next day to receive their pay.

14 "Do not insult the deaf or cause the blind to
stumble. You must fear your God; I am the LORD.

15 "Do not twist justice in legal matters by favoring
the poor or being partial to the rich and powerful.
Always judge people fairly.

16 "Do not spread slanderous gossip among your
people.*

"Do not stand idly by when your neighbor's life is
threatened. I am the LORD.

17 "Do not nurse hatred in your heart for any of
your relatives.* Confront people directly so you will
not be held guilty for their sin.

18 "Do not seek revenge or bear a grudge against a
fellow Israelite, but love your neighbor as yourself. I
am the LORD.

19 "You must obey all my decrees.

"Do not mate two different kinds of animals. Do
not plant your field with two different kinds of seed.
Do not wear clothing woven from two different
kinds of thread.

20 "If a man has sex with a slave girl whose freedom
has never been purchased but who is committed to
become another man's wife, he must pay full compensation to her master. But since she is not a free
woman, neither the man nor the woman will be put
to death. 21 The man, however, must bring a ram as a
guilt offering and present it to the LORD at the entrance of the Tabernacle.* 22 The priest will then purify him* before the LORD with the ram of the guilt
offering, and the man's sin will be forgiven.

23 "When you enter the land and plant fruit trees,
leave the fruit unharvested for the first three years

19:16 Hebrew *Do not act as a merchant toward your own people.*
19:17 Hebrew *for your brother.* **19:21** Hebrew *Tent of Meeting.*
19:22 Or *make atonement for him.*

KING JAMES VERSION

24But in the fourth year all the fruit thereof shall be holy to praise the LORD *withal.*

25And in the fifth year shall ye eat of the fruit thereof, that it may yield unto you the increase thereof: I *am* the LORD your God.

26Ye shall not eat *any thing* with the blood: neither shall ye use enchantment, nor observe times.

27Ye shall not round the corners of your heads, neither shalt thou mar the corners of thy beard.

28Ye shall not make any cuttings in your flesh for the dead, nor print any marks upon you: I *am* the LORD.

29Do not prostitute thy daughter, to cause her to be a whore; lest the land fall to whoredom, and the land become full of wickedness.

30Ye shall keep my sabbaths, and reverence my sanctuary: I *am* the LORD.

31Regard not them that have familiar spirits, neither seek after wizards, to be defiled by them: I *am* the LORD your God.

32Thou shalt rise up before the hoary head, and honour the face of the old man, and fear thy God: I *am* the LORD.

33And if a stranger sojourn with thee in your land, ye shall not vex him.

34*But* the stranger that dwelleth with you shall be unto you as one born among you, and thou shalt love him as thyself; for ye were strangers in the land of Egypt: I *am* the LORD your God.

35Ye shall do no unrighteousness in judgment, in meteyard, in weight, or in measure.

36Just balances, just weights, a just ephah, and a just hin, shall ye have: I *am* the LORD your God, which brought you out of the land of Egypt.

37Therefore shall ye observe all my statutes, and all my judgments, and do them: I *am* the LORD.

20 1And the LORD spake unto Moses, saying, 2Again, thou shalt say to the children of Israel, Whosoever *he be* of the children of Israel, or of the strangers that sojourn in Israel, that giveth *any* of his seed unto Molech; he shall surely be put to death: the people of the land shall stone him with stones.

3And I will set my face against that man, and will cut him off from among his people; because he hath given of his seed unto Molech, to defile my sanctuary, and to profane my holy name.

4And if the people of the land do any ways hide their eyes from the man, when he giveth of his seed unto Molech, and kill him not:

5Then I will set my face against that man, and against his family, and will cut him off, and all that go a whoring after him, to commit whoredom with Molech, from among their people.

NEW LIVING TRANSLATION

and consider it forbidden.* Do not eat it. 24In the fourth year the entire crop must be consecrated to the LORD as a celebration of praise. 25Finally, in the fifth year you may eat the fruit. If you follow this pattern, your harvest will increase. I am the LORD your God.

26"Do not eat meat that has not been drained of its blood.

"Do not practice fortune-telling or witchcraft.

27"Do not trim off the hair on your temples or trim your beards.

28"Do not cut your bodies for the dead, and do not mark your skin with tattoos. I am the LORD.

29"Do not defile your daughter by making her a prostitute, or the land will be filled with prostitution and wickedness.

30"Keep my Sabbath days of rest, and show reverence toward my sanctuary. I am the LORD.

31"Do not defile yourselves by turning to mediums or to those who consult the spirits of the dead. I am the LORD your God.

32"Stand up in the presence of the elderly, and show respect for the aged. Fear your God. I am the LORD.

33"Do not take advantage of foreigners who live among you in your land. 34Treat them like native-born Israelites, and love them as you love yourself. Remember that you were once foreigners living in the land of Egypt. I am the LORD your God.

35"Do not use dishonest standards when measuring length, weight, or volume. 36Your scales and weights must be accurate. Your containers for measuring dry materials or liquids must be accurate.* I am the LORD your God who brought you out of the land of Egypt.

37"You must be careful to keep all of my decrees and regulations by putting them into practice. I am the LORD."

Punishments for Disobedience

20 The LORD said to Moses, 2"Give the people of Israel these instructions, which apply both to native Israelites and to the foreigners living in Israel.

"If any of them offer their children as a sacrifice to Molech, they must be put to death. The people of the community must stone them to death. 3I myself will turn against them and cut them off from the community, because they have defiled my sanctuary and brought shame on my holy name by offering their children to Molech. 4And if the people of the community ignore those who offer their children to Molech and refuse to execute them, 5I myself will turn against them and their families and will cut them off from the community. This will happen to all who commit spiritual prostitution by worshiping Molech.

19:23 Hebrew *consider it uncircumcised.* 19:36 Hebrew *Use an honest ephah* [a dry measure] *and an honest hin* [a liquid measure].

KING JAMES VERSION

6And the soul that turneth after such as have familiar spirits, and after wizards, to go a whoring after them, I will even set my face against that soul, and will cut him off from among his people.

7Sanctify yourselves therefore, and be ye holy: for I *am* the LORD your God.

8And ye shall keep my statutes, and do them: I *am* the LORD which sanctify you.

9For every one that curseth his father or his mother shall be surely put to death: he hath cursed his father or his mother; his blood *shall be* upon him.

10And the man that committeth adultery with *another* man's wife, *even he* that committeth adultery with his neighbour's wife, the adulterer and the adulteress shall surely be put to death.

11And the man that lieth with his father's wife hath uncovered his father's nakedness: both of them shall surely be put to death; their blood *shall be* upon them.

12And if a man lie with his daughter in law, both of them shall surely be put to death: they have wrought confusion; their blood *shall be* upon them.

13If a man also lie with mankind, as he lieth with a woman, both of them have committed an abomination: they shall surely be put to death; their blood *shall be* upon them.

14And if a man take a wife and her mother, it *is* wickedness: they shall be burnt with fire, both he and they; that there be no wickedness among you.

15And if a man lie with a beast, he shall surely be put to death: and ye shall slay the beast.

16And if a woman approach unto any beast, and lie down thereto, thou shalt kill the woman, and the beast: they shall surely be put to death; their blood *shall be* upon them.

17And if a man shall take his sister, his father's daughter, or his mother's daughter, and see her nakedness, and she see his nakedness; it *is* a wicked thing; and they shall be cut off in the sight of their people: he hath uncovered his sister's nakedness; he shall bear his iniquity.

18And if a man shall lie with a woman having her sickness, and shall uncover her nakedness; he hath discovered her fountain, and she hath uncovered the fountain of her blood: and both of them shall be cut off from among their people.

19And thou shalt not uncover the nakedness of thy mother's sister, nor of thy father's sister: for he uncovereth his near kin: they shall bear their iniquity.

20And if a man shall lie with his uncle's wife, he hath uncovered his uncle's nakedness: they shall bear their sin; they shall die childless.

21And if a man shall take his brother's wife, it *is* an unclean thing: he hath uncovered his brother's nakedness; they shall be childless.

22Ye shall therefore keep all my statutes, and all my judgments, and do them: that the land, whither I bring you to dwell therein, spue you not out.

NEW LIVING TRANSLATION

6"I will also turn against those who commit spiritual prostitution by putting their trust in mediums or in those who consult the spirits of the dead. I will cut them off from the community. 7So set yourselves apart to be holy, for I am the LORD your God. 8Keep all my decrees by putting them into practice, for I am the LORD who makes you holy.

9"Anyone who dishonors* father or mother must be put to death. Such a person is guilty of a capital offense.

10"If a man commits adultery with his neighbor's wife, both the man and the woman who have committed adultery must be put to death.

11"If a man violates his father by having sex with one of his father's wives, both the man and the woman must be put to death, for they are guilty of a capital offense.

12"If a man has sex with his daughter-in-law, both must be put to death. They have committed a perverse act and are guilty of a capital offense.

13"If a man practices homosexuality, having sex with another man as with a woman, both men have committed a detestable act. They must both be put to death, for they are guilty of a capital offense.

14"If a man marries both a woman and her mother, he has committed a wicked act. The man and both women must be burned to death to wipe out such wickedness from among you.

15"If a man has sex with an animal, he must be put to death, and the animal must be killed.

16"If a woman presents herself to a male animal to have intercourse with it, she and the animal must both be put to death. You must kill both, for they are guilty of a capital offense.

17"If a man marries his sister, the daughter of either his father or his mother, and they have sexual relations, it is a shameful disgrace. They must be publicly cut off from the community. Since the man has violated his sister, he will be punished for his sin.

18"If a man has sexual relations with a woman during her menstrual period, both of them must be cut off from the community, for together they have exposed the source of her blood flow.

19"Do not have sexual relations with your aunt, whether your mother's sister or your father's sister. This would dishonor a close relative. Both parties are guilty and will be punished for their sin.

20"If a man has sex with his uncle's wife, he has violated his uncle. Both the man and woman will be punished for their sin, and they will die childless.

21"If a man marries his brother's wife, it is an act of impurity. He has violated his brother, and the guilty couple will remain childless.

22"You must keep all my decrees and regulations by putting them into practice; otherwise the land to which I am bringing you as your new home will vomit

20:9 Greek version reads *Anyone who speaks disrespectfully of.* Compare Matt 15:4; Mark 7:10.

KING JAMES VERSION

23 And ye shall not walk in the manners of the nation, which I cast out before you: for they committed all these things, and therefore I abhorred them.

24 But I have said unto you, Ye shall inherit their land, and I will give it unto you to possess it, a land that floweth with milk and honey: I *am* the LORD your God, which have separated you from *other* people.

25 Ye shall therefore put difference between clean beasts and unclean, and between unclean fowls and clean: and ye shall not make your souls abominable by beast, or by fowl, or by any manner of living thing that creepeth on the ground, which I have separated from you as unclean.

26 And ye shall be holy unto me: for I the LORD *am* holy, and have severed you from *other* people, that ye should be mine.

27 A man also or woman that hath a familiar spirit, or that is a wizard, shall surely be put to death: they shall stone them with stones: their blood *shall be* upon them.

21

1 And the LORD said unto Moses, Speak unto the priests the sons of Aaron, and say unto them, There shall none be defiled for the dead among his people:

2 But for his kin, that is near unto him, *that is*, for his mother, and for his father, and for his son, and for his daughter, and for his brother,

3 And for his sister a virgin, that is nigh unto him, which hath had no husband; for her may he be defiled.

4 *But* he shall not defile himself, *being* a chief man among his people, to profane himself.

5 They shall not make baldness upon their head, neither shall they shave off the corner of their beard, nor make any cuttings in their flesh.

6 They shall be holy unto their God, and not profane the name of their God: for the offerings of the LORD made by fire, *and* the bread of their God, they do offer: therefore they shall be holy.

7 They shall not take a wife *that is* a whore, or profane; neither shall they take a woman put away from her husband: for he *is* holy unto his God.

8 Thou shalt sanctify him therefore; for he offereth the bread of thy God: he shall be holy unto thee: for I the LORD, which sanctify you, *am* holy.

9 And the daughter of any priest, if she profane herself by playing the whore, she profaneth her father: she shall be burnt with fire.

10 And *he that is* the high priest among his brethren, upon whose head the anointing oil was poured, and that is consecrated to put on the garments, shall not uncover his head, nor rend his clothes;

11 Neither shall he go in to any dead body, nor defile himself for his father, or for his mother;

12 Neither shall he go out of the sanctuary, nor

NEW LIVING TRANSLATION

you out. 23 Do not live according to the customs of the people I am driving out before you. It is because they do these shameful things that I detest them. 24 But I have promised you, 'You will possess their land because I will give it to you as your possession—a land flowing with milk and honey.' I am the LORD your God, who has set you apart from all other people.

25 "You must therefore make a distinction between ceremonially clean and unclean animals, and between clean and unclean birds. You must not defile yourselves by eating any unclean animal or bird or creature that scurries along the ground. I have identified them as being unclean for you. 26 You must be holy because I, the LORD, am holy. I have set you apart from all other people to be my very own.

27 "Men and women among you who act as mediums or who consult the spirits of the dead must be put to death by stoning. They are guilty of a capital offense."

Instructions for the Priests

21

The LORD said to Moses, "Give the following instructions to the priests, the descendants of Aaron.

"A priest must not make himself ceremonially unclean by touching the dead body of a relative. 2 The only exceptions are his closest relatives—his mother or father, son or daughter, brother, 3 or his virgin sister who depends on him because she has no husband. 4 But a priest must not defile himself and make himself unclean for someone who is related to him only by marriage.

5 "The priests must not shave their heads or trim their beards or cut their bodies. 6 They must be set apart as holy to their God and must never bring shame on the name of God. They must be holy, for they are the ones who present the special gifts to the LORD, gifts of food for their God.

7 "Priests may not marry a woman defiled by prostitution, and they may not marry a woman who is divorced from her husband, for the priests are set apart as holy to their God. 8 You must treat them as holy because they offer up food to your God. You must consider them holy because I, the LORD, am holy, and I make you holy.

9 "If a priest's daughter defiles herself by becoming a prostitute, she also defiles her father's holiness, and she must be burned to death.

10 "The high priest has the highest rank of all the priests. The anointing oil has been poured on his head, and he has been ordained to wear the priestly garments. He must never leave his hair uncombed* or tear his clothing. 11 He must not defile himself by going near a dead body. He may not make himself ceremonially unclean even for his father or mother. 12 He must not defile the sanctuary of his God by

21:10 Or *never uncover his head.*

KING JAMES VERSION

profane the sanctuary of his God; for the crown of the anointing oil of his God *is* upon him: I *am* the Lord.

13 And he shall take a wife in her virginity.

14 A widow, or a divorced woman, or profane, *or* an harlot, these shall he not take: but he shall take a virgin of his own people to wife.

15 Neither shall he profane his seed among his people: for I the Lord do sanctify him.

16 And the Lord spake unto Moses, saying,

17 Speak unto Aaron, saying, Whosoever *he be* of thy seed in their generations that hath *any* blemish, let him not approach to offer the bread of his God.

18 For whatsoever man *he be* that hath a blemish, he shall not approach: a blind man, or a lame, or he that hath a flat nose, or any thing superfluous,

19 Or a man that is brokenfooted, or brokenhanded,

20 Or crookbacked, or a dwarf, or that hath a blemish in his eye, or be scurvy, or scabbed, or hath his stones broken;

21 No man that hath a blemish of the seed of Aaron the priest shall come nigh to offer the offerings of the Lord made by fire: he hath a blemish; he shall not come nigh to offer the bread of his God.

22 He shall eat the bread of his God, *both* of the most holy, and of the holy.

23 Only he shall not go in unto the veil, nor come nigh unto the altar, because he hath a blemish; that he profane not my sanctuaries: for I the Lord do sanctify them.

24 And Moses told *it* unto Aaron, and to his sons, and unto all the children of Israel.

22

1 And the Lord spake unto Moses, saying, 2 Speak unto Aaron and to his sons, that they separate themselves from the holy things of the children of Israel, and that they profane not my holy name *in those things* which they hallow unto me: I *am* the Lord.

3 Say unto them, Whosoever *he be* of all your seed among your generations, that goeth unto the holy things, which the children of Israel hallow unto the Lord, having his uncleanness upon him, that soul shall be cut off from my presence: I *am* the Lord.

4 What man soever of the seed of Aaron *is* a leper, or hath a running issue; he shall not eat of the holy things, until he be clean. And whoso toucheth any thing *that is* unclean *by* the dead, or a man whose seed goeth from him;

5 Or whosoever toucheth any creeping thing, whereby he may be made unclean, or a man of whom he may take uncleanness, whatsoever uncleanness he hath;

6 The soul which hath touched any such shall be unclean until even, and shall not eat of the holy things, unless he wash his flesh with water.

7 And when the sun is down, he shall be clean, and

NEW LIVING TRANSLATION

leaving it to attend to a dead person, for he has been made holy by the anointing oil of his God. I am the Lord.

13 "The high priest may marry only a virgin. 14 He may not marry a widow, a woman who is divorced, or a woman who has defiled herself by prostitution. She must be a virgin from his own clan, 15 so that he will not dishonor his descendants among his clan, for I am the Lord who makes him holy."

16 Then the Lord said to Moses, 17 "Give the following instructions to Aaron: In all future generations, none of your descendants who has any defect will qualify to offer food to his God. 18 No one who has a defect qualifies, whether he is blind, lame, disfigured, deformed, 19 or has a broken foot or arm, 20 or is hunchbacked or dwarfed, or has a defective eye, or skin sores or scabs, or damaged testicles. 21 No descendant of Aaron who has a defect may approach the altar to present special gifts to the Lord. Since he has a defect, he may not approach the altar to offer food to his God. 22 However, he may eat from the food offered to God, including the holy offerings and the most holy offerings. 23 Yet because of his physical defect, he may not enter the room behind the inner curtain or approach the altar, for this would defile my holy places. I am the Lord who makes them holy."

24 So Moses gave these instructions to Aaron and his sons and to all the Israelites.

22

The Lord said to Moses, 2 "Tell Aaron and his sons to be very careful with the sacred gifts that the Israelites set apart for me, so they do not bring shame on my holy name. I am the Lord. 3 Give them the following instructions.

"In all future generations, if any of your descendants is ceremonially unclean when he approaches the sacred offerings that the people of Israel consecrate to the Lord, he must be cut off from my presence. I am the Lord.

4 "If any of Aaron's descendants has a skin disease* or any kind of discharge that makes him ceremonially unclean, he may not eat from the sacred offerings until he has been pronounced clean. He also becomes unclean by touching a corpse, or by having an emission of semen, 5 or by touching a small animal that is unclean, or by touching someone who is ceremonially unclean for any reason. 6 The man who is defiled in any of these ways will remain unclean until evening. He may not eat from the sacred offerings until he has bathed himself in water. 7 When the sun goes down, he will be ceremonially

22:4 Traditionally rendered *leprosy;* see note on 13:2a.

KING JAMES VERSION

shall afterward eat of the holy things; because it *is* his food.

8 That which dieth of itself, or is torn *with beasts,* he shall not eat to defile himself therewith: I *am* the LORD.

9 They shall therefore keep mine ordinance, lest they bear sin for it, and die therefore, if they profane it: I the LORD do sanctify them.

10 There shall no stranger eat *of* the holy thing: a sojourner of the priest, or an hired servant, shall not eat *of* the holy thing.

11 But if the priest buy *any* soul with his money, he shall eat of it, and he that is born in his house: they shall eat of his meat.

12 If the priest's daughter also be *married* unto a stranger, she may not eat of an offering of the holy things.

13 But if the priest's daughter be a widow, or divorced, and have no child, and is returned unto her father's house, as in her youth, she shall eat of her father's meat: but there shall no stranger eat thereof.

14 And if a man eat *of* the holy thing unwittingly, then he shall put the fifth *part* thereof unto it, and shall give *it* unto the priest with the holy thing.

15 And they shall not profane the holy things of the children of Israel, which they offer unto the LORD;

16 Or suffer them to bear the iniquity of trespass, when they eat their holy things: for I the LORD do sanctify them.

17 And the LORD spake unto Moses, saying,

18 Speak unto Aaron, and to his sons, and unto all the children of Israel, and say unto them, Whatsoever *he be* of the house of Israel, or of the strangers in Israel, that will offer his oblation for all his vows, and for all his freewill offerings, which they will offer unto the LORD for a burnt offering;

19 *Ye shall offer* at your own will a male without blemish, of the beeves, of the sheep, or of the goats.

20 *But* whatsoever hath a blemish, *that* shall ye not offer: for it shall not be acceptable for you.

21 And whosoever offereth a sacrifice of peace offerings unto the LORD to accomplish *his* vow, or a freewill offering in beeves or sheep, it shall be perfect to be accepted; there shall be no blemish therein.

22 Blind, or broken, or maimed, or having a wen, or scurvy, or scabbed, ye shall not offer these unto the LORD, nor make an offering by fire of them upon the altar unto the LORD.

23 Either a bullock or a lamb that hath any thing superfluous or lacking in his parts, that mayest thou offer *for* a freewill offering; but for a vow it shall not be accepted.

24 Ye shall not offer unto the LORD that which is bruised, or crushed, or broken, or cut; neither shall ye make *any offering thereof* in your land.

NEW LIVING TRANSLATION

clean again and may eat from the sacred offerings, for this is his food. 8 He may not eat an animal that has died a natural death or has been torn apart by wild animals, for this would defile him. I am the LORD.

9 "The priests must follow my instructions carefully. Otherwise they will be punished for their sin and will die for violating my instructions. I am the LORD who makes them holy.

10 "No one outside a priest's family may eat the sacred offerings. Even guests and hired workers in a priest's home are not allowed to eat them. 11 However, if the priest buys a slave for himself, the slave may eat from the sacred offerings. And if his slaves have children, they also may share his food. 12 If a priest's daughter marries someone outside the priestly family, she may no longer eat the sacred offerings. 13 But if she becomes a widow or is divorced and has no children to support her, and she returns to live in her father's home as in her youth, she may eat her father's food again. Otherwise, no one outside a priest's family may eat the sacred offerings.

14 "Any such person who eats the sacred offerings without realizing it must pay the priest for the amount eaten, plus an additional 20 percent. 15 The priests must not let the Israelites defile the sacred offerings brought to the LORD 16 by allowing unauthorized people to eat them. This would bring guilt upon them and require them to pay compensation. I am the LORD who makes them holy."

Worthy and Unworthy Offerings

17 And the LORD said to Moses, 18 "Give Aaron and his sons and all the Israelites these instructions, which apply both to native Israelites and to the foreigners living among you.

"If you present a gift as a burnt offering to the LORD, whether it is to fulfill a vow or is a voluntary offering, 19 you* will be accepted only if your offering is a male animal with no defects. It may be a bull, a ram, or a male goat. 20 Do not present an animal with defects, because the LORD will not accept it on your behalf.

21 "If you present a peace offering to the LORD from the herd or the flock, whether it is to fulfill a vow or is a voluntary offering, you must offer a perfect animal. It may have no defect of any kind. 22 You must not offer an animal that is blind, crippled, or injured, or that has a wart, a skin sore, or scabs. Such animals must never be offered on the altar as special gifts to the LORD. 23 If a bull* or lamb has a leg that is too long or too short, it may be offered as a voluntary offering, but it may not be offered to fulfill a vow. 24 If an animal has damaged testicles or is castrated, you may not offer it to the LORD. You must

22:19 Or *it.* **22:23** Or *cow.*

KING JAMES VERSION

25 Neither from a stranger's hand shall ye offer the
bread of your God of any of these; because their corruption *is* in them, *and* blemishes *be* in them: they
shall not be accepted for you.
26 And the LORD spake unto Moses, saying,
27 When a bullock, or a sheep, or a goat, is brought
forth, then it shall be seven days under the dam; and
from the eighth day and thenceforth it shall be accepted for an offering made by fire unto the LORD.
28 And *whether it be* cow or ewe, ye shall not kill it
and her young both in one day.
29 And when ye will offer a sacrifice of thanksgiving unto the LORD, offer *it* at your own will.
30 On the same day it shall be eaten up; ye shall
leave none of it until the morrow: I *am* the LORD.
31 Therefore shall ye keep my commandments, and
do them: I *am* the LORD.
32 Neither shall ye profane my holy name; but I will
be hallowed among the children of Israel: I *am* the
LORD which hallow you,
33 That brought you out of the land of Egypt, to be
your God: I *am* the LORD.

23 1 And the LORD spake unto Moses, saying,
2 Speak unto the children of Israel, and say
unto them, *Concerning* the feasts of the LORD, which
ye shall proclaim *to be* holy convocations, *even* these
are my feasts.
3 Six days shall work be done: but the seventh day
is the sabbath of rest, an holy convocation; ye shall do
no work *therein:* it *is* the sabbath of the LORD in all
your dwellings.
4 These *are* the feasts of the LORD, *even* holy convocations, which ye shall proclaim in their seasons.

5 In the fourteenth *day* of the first month at even
is the LORD's passover.
6 And on the fifteenth day of the same month *is* the
feast of unleavened bread unto the LORD: seven days
ye must eat unleavened bread.
7 In the first day ye shall have an holy convocation:
ye shall do no servile work therein.
8 But ye shall offer an offering made by fire unto
the LORD seven days: in the seventh day *is* an holy
convocation: ye shall do no servile work *therein.*

9 And the LORD spake unto Moses, saying,
10 Speak unto the children of Israel, and say unto
them, When ye be come into the land which I give

NEW LIVING TRANSLATION

never do this in your own land, 25 and you must not
accept such an animal from foreigners and then offer it as a sacrifice to your God. Such animals will not
be accepted on your behalf, for they are mutilated or
defective."
26 And the LORD said to Moses, 27 "When a calf or
lamb or goat is born, it must be left with its mother
for seven days. From the eighth day on, it will be acceptable as a special gift to the LORD. 28 But you must
not slaughter a mother animal and her offspring on
the same day, whether from the herd or the flock.
29 When you bring a thanksgiving offering to the
LORD, sacrifice it properly so you will be accepted.
30 Eat the entire sacrificial animal on the day it is presented. Do not leave any of it until the next morning.
I am the LORD.
31 "You must faithfully keep all my commands by
putting them into practice, for I am the LORD. 32 Do
not bring shame on my holy name, for I will display
my holiness among the people of Israel. I am the
LORD who makes you holy. 33 It was I who rescued you
from the land of Egypt, that I might be your God. I am
the LORD."

The Appointed Festivals

23 The LORD said to Moses, 2 "Give the following instructions to the people of Israel.
These are the LORD's appointed festivals, which you
are to proclaim as official days for holy assembly.
3 "You have six days each week for your ordinary
work, but the seventh day is a Sabbath day of complete rest, an official day for holy assembly. It is the
LORD's Sabbath day, and it must be observed wherever you live.
4 "In addition to the Sabbath, these are the LORD's
appointed festivals, the official days for holy assembly that are to be celebrated at their proper times
each year.

Passover and the Festival of Unleavened Bread

5 "The LORD's Passover begins at sundown on the
fourteenth day of the first month.* 6 On the next day,
the fifteenth day of the month, you must begin celebrating the Festival of Unleavened Bread. This festival to the LORD continues for seven days, and during
that time the bread you eat must be made without
yeast. 7 On the first day of the festival, all the people
must stop their ordinary work and observe an official day for holy assembly. 8 For seven days you must
present special gifts to the LORD. On the seventh day
the people must again stop all their ordinary work to
observe an official day for holy assembly."

Celebration of First Harvest

9 Then the LORD said to Moses, 10 "Give the following
instructions to the people of Israel. When you enter

23:5 This day in the ancient Hebrew lunar calendar occurred in late March, April, or early May.

KING JAMES VERSION

unto you, and shall reap the harvest thereof, then ye
shall bring a sheaf of the firstfruits of your harvest
unto the priest:
11 And he shall wave the sheaf before the LORD, to
be accepted for you: on the morrow after the sabbath the priest shall wave it.
12 And ye shall offer that day when ye wave the
sheaf an he lamb without blemish of the first year for
a burnt offering unto the LORD.
13 And the meat offering thereof *shall be* two tenth
deals of fine flour mingled with oil, an offering made
by fire unto the LORD *for* a sweet savour: and the
drink offering thereof *shall be* of wine, the fourth
part of an hin.
14 And ye shall eat neither bread, nor parched corn,
nor green ears, until the selfsame day that ye have
brought an offering unto your God: *it shall be* a statute for ever throughout your generations in all your
dwellings.
15 And ye shall count unto you from the morrow after the sabbath, from the day that ye brought the
sheaf of the wave offering; seven sabbaths shall be
complete:
16 Even unto the morrow after the seventh sabbath
shall ye number fifty days; and ye shall offer a new
meat offering unto the LORD.
17 Ye shall bring out of your habitations two wave
loaves of two tenth deals: they shall be of fine flour;
they shall be baken with leaven; *they are* the firstfruits unto the LORD.
18 And ye shall offer with the bread seven lambs
without blemish of the first year, and one young bullock, and two rams: they shall be *for* a burnt offering
unto the LORD, with their meat offering, and their
drink offerings, *even* an offering made by fire, of
sweet savour unto the LORD.
19 Then ye shall sacrifice one kid of the goats for a
sin offering, and two lambs of the first year for a sacrifice of peace offerings.
20 And the priest shall wave them with the bread of
the firstfruits *for* a wave offering before the LORD
with the two lambs: they shall be holy to the LORD for
the priest.
21 And ye shall proclaim on the selfsame day, *that* it
may be an holy convocation unto you: ye shall do no
servile work *therein: it shall be* a statute for ever in all
your dwellings throughout your generations.
22 And when ye reap the harvest of your land, thou
shalt not make clean riddance of the corners of thy
field when thou reapest, neither shalt thou gather
any gleaning of thy harvest: thou shalt leave them
unto the poor, and to the stranger: I *am* the LORD
your God.
23 And the LORD spake unto Moses, saying,
24 Speak unto the children of Israel, saying, In the
seventh month, in the first *day* of the month, shall ye

NEW LIVING TRANSLATION

the land I am giving you and you harvest its first
crops, bring the priest a bundle of grain from the
first cutting of your grain harvest. 11 On the day after
the Sabbath, the priest will lift it up before the LORD
so it may be accepted on your behalf. 12 On that same
day you must sacrifice a one-year-old male lamb with
no defects as a burnt offering to the LORD. 13 With it
you must present a grain offering consisting of four
quarts* of choice flour moistened with olive oil. It
will be a special gift, a pleasing aroma to the LORD.
You must also offer one quart* of wine as a liquid
offering. 14 Do not eat any bread or roasted grain or
fresh kernels on that day until you bring this offering
to your God. This is a permanent law for you, and it
must be observed from generation to generation
wherever you live.

The Festival of Harvest

15 "From the day after the Sabbath—the day you bring
the bundle of grain to be lifted up as a special offering—count off seven full weeks. 16 Keep counting until the day after the seventh Sabbath, fifty days later.
Then present an offering of new grain to the LORD.
17 From wherever you live, bring two loaves of bread
to be lifted up before the LORD as a special offering.
Make these loaves from four quarts of choice flour,
and bake them with yeast. They will be an offering to
the LORD from the first of your crops. 18 Along with
the bread, present seven one-year-old male lambs
with no defects, one young bull, and two rams as
burnt offerings to the LORD. These burnt offerings,
together with the grain offerings and liquid offerings, will be a special gift, a pleasing aroma to the
LORD. 19 Then you must offer one male goat as a sin
offering and two one-year-old male lambs as a peace
offering.
20 "The priest will lift up the two lambs as a special
offering to the LORD, together with the loaves representing the first of your crops. These offerings,
which are holy to the LORD, belong to the priests.
21 That same day will be proclaimed an official day
for holy assembly, a day on which you do no ordinary
work. This is a permanent law for you, and it must be
observed from generation to generation wherever
you live.*
22 "When you harvest the crops of your land, do
not harvest the grain along the edges of your fields,
and do not pick up what the harvesters drop. Leave it
for the poor and the foreigners living among you. I
am the LORD your God."

The Festival of Trumpets

23 The LORD said to Moses, 24 "Give the following instructions to the people of Israel. On the first day of

23:13a Hebrew *2/10 of an ephah* [4.4 liters]; also in 23:17. **23:13b** Hebrew *1/4 of a hin* [1 liter]. **23:21** This celebration, called the Festival of Harvest or the Festival of Weeks, was later called the Festival of Pentecost (see Acts 2:1). It is celebrated today as Shavuot (or Shabuoth).

KING JAMES VERSION

have a sabbath, a memorial of blowing of trumpets,
an holy convocation.
25 Ye shall do no servile work *therein:* but ye shall
offer an offering made by fire unto the LORD.

26 And the LORD spake unto Moses, saying,
27 Also on the tenth *day* of this seventh month
there shall be a day of atonement: it shall be an holy
convocation unto you; and ye shall afflict your souls,
and offer an offering made by fire unto the LORD.
28 And ye shall do no work in that same day: for it *is*
a day of atonement, to make an atonement for you
before the LORD your God.
29 For whatsoever soul *it be* that shall not be afflicted in that same day, he shall be cut off from
among his people.
30 And whatsoever soul *it be* that doeth any work in
that same day, the same soul will I destroy from
among his people.
31 Ye shall do no manner of work: *it shall be* a statute for ever throughout your generations in all your
dwellings.
32 It *shall be* unto you a sabbath of rest, and ye shall
afflict your souls: in the ninth *day* of the month at
even, from even unto even, shall ye celebrate your
sabbath.
33 And the LORD spake unto Moses, saying,
34 Speak unto the children of Israel, saying, The fifteenth day of this seventh month *shall be* the feast of
tabernacles *for* seven days unto the LORD.
35 On the first day *shall be* an holy convocation: ye
shall do no servile work *therein.*
36 Seven days ye shall offer an offering made by
fire unto the LORD: on the eighth day shall be an holy
convocation unto you; and ye shall offer an offering
made by fire unto the LORD: it *is* a solemn assembly;
and ye shall do no servile work *therein.*
37 These *are* the feasts of the LORD, which ye shall
proclaim *to be* holy convocations, to offer an offering made by fire unto the LORD, a burnt offering, and
a meat offering, a sacrifice, and drink offerings,
every thing upon his day:
38 Beside the sabbaths of the LORD, and beside your
gifts, and beside all your vows, and beside all your
freewill offerings, which ye give unto the LORD.

NEW LIVING TRANSLATION

the appointed month in early autumn,* you are to
observe a day of complete rest. It will be an official
day for holy assembly, a day commemorated with
loud blasts of a trumpet.
25 You must do no ordinary
work on that day. Instead, you are to present special
gifts to the LORD."

The Day of Atonement

26 Then the LORD said to Moses,
27 "Be careful to cele-
brate the Day of Atonement on the tenth day of that
same month—nine days after the Festival of Trumpets.* You must observe it as an official day for holy
assembly, a day to deny yourselves* and present special gifts to the LORD.
28 Do no work during that entire
day because it is the Day of Atonement, when offerings of purification are made for you, making you
right with* the LORD your God.
29 All who do not deny
themselves that day will be cut off from God's
people.
30 And I will destroy anyone among you who
does any work on that day.
31 You must not do any
work at all! This is a permanent law for you, and it
must be observed from generation to generation
wherever you live.
32 This will be a Sabbath day of
complete rest for you, and on that day you must deny
yourselves. This day of rest will begin at sundown on
the ninth day of the month and extend until sundown on the tenth day."

The Festival of Shelters

33 And the LORD said to Moses,
34 "Give the following
instructions to the people of Israel. Begin celebrating the Festival of Shelters* on the fifteenth day of
the appointed month—five days after the Day of
Atonement.* This festival to the LORD will last for
seven days.
35 On the first day of the festival you must
proclaim an official day for holy assembly, when you
do no ordinary work.
36 For seven days you must
present special gifts to the LORD. The eighth day is
another holy day on which you present your special
gifts to the LORD. This will be a solemn occasion, and
no ordinary work may be done that day.
37 ("These are the LORD's appointed festivals. Celebrate them each year as official days for holy assembly by presenting special gifts to the LORD—burnt
offerings, grain offerings, sacrifices, and liquid offerings—each on its proper day.
38 These festivals
must be observed in addition to the LORD's regular
Sabbath days, and the offerings are in addition to
your personal gifts, the offerings you give to fulfill
your vows, and the voluntary offerings you present to
the LORD.)

23:24 Hebrew *On the first day of the seventh month.* This day in the ancient Hebrew lunar calendar occurred in September or October. This festival is celebrated today as Rosh Hashanah, the Jewish new year. **23:27a** Hebrew *on the tenth day of the seventh month;* see 23:24 and the note there. This day in the ancient Hebrew lunar calendar occurred in September or October. It is celebrated today as Yom Kippur. **23:27b** Or *to fast;* similarly in 23:29, 32. **23:28** Or *when atonement is made for you before.* **23:34a** Or *Festival of Booths,* or *Festival of Tabernacles.* This was earlier called the Festival of the Final Harvest or Festival of Ingathering (see Exod 23:16b). It is celebrated today as Sukkot (or Succoth). **23:34b** Hebrew *on the fifteenth day of the seventh month;* see 23:27a and the note there.

KING JAMES VERSION

39 Also in the fifteenth day of the seventh month,
when ye have gathered in the fruit of the land, ye
shall keep a feast unto the LORD seven days: on the
first day *shall be* a sabbath, and on the eighth day
shall be a sabbath.

40 And ye shall take you on the first day the boughs
of goodly trees, branches of palm trees, and the
boughs of thick trees, and willows of the brook; and
ye shall rejoice before the LORD your God seven days.

41 And ye shall keep it a feast unto the LORD seven
days in the year. *It shall be* a statute for ever in your
generations: ye shall celebrate it in the seventh
month.

42 Ye shall dwell in booths seven days; all that are
Israelites born shall dwell in booths:

43 That your generations may know that I made
the children of Israel to dwell in booths, when I
brought them out of the land of Egypt: I *am* the LORD
your God.

44 And Moses declared unto the children of Israel
the feasts of the LORD.

24 1 And the LORD spake unto Moses, saying,
2 Command the children of Israel, that they
bring unto thee pure oil olive beaten for the light, to
cause the lamps to burn continually.

3 Without the veil of the testimony, in the tabernacle of the congregation, shall Aaron order it from the
evening unto the morning before the LORD continually: *it shall be* a statute for ever in your generations.

4 He shall order the lamps upon the pure candlestick before the LORD continually.

5 And thou shalt take fine flour, and bake twelve
cakes thereof: two tenth deals shall be in one cake.

6 And thou shalt set them in two rows, six on a row,
upon the pure table before the LORD.

7 And thou shalt put pure frankincense upon *each*
row, that it may be on the bread for a memorial, *even*
an offering made by fire unto the LORD.

8 Every sabbath he shall set it in order before the
LORD continually, *being taken* from the children of
Israel by an everlasting covenant.

9 And it shall be Aaron's and his sons'; and they
shall eat it in the holy place: for it *is* most holy unto
him of the offerings of the LORD made by fire by a
perpetual statute.

10 And the son of an Israelitish woman, whose father *was* an Egyptian, went out among the children
of Israel: and this son of the Israelitish *woman* and a
man of Israel strove together in the camp;

11 And the Israelitish woman's son blasphemed the
name *of the* LORD, *and cursed. And they brought him*

NEW LIVING TRANSLATION

39 "Remember that this seven-day festival to the
LORD—the Festival of Shelters—begins on the fifteenth day of the appointed month,* after you have
harvested all the produce of the land. The first day
and the eighth day of the festival will be days of complete rest. 40 On the first day gather branches from
magnificent trees*—palm fronds, boughs from leafy
trees, and willows that grow by the streams. Then celebrate with joy before the LORD your God for seven
days. 41 You must observe this festival to the LORD for
seven days every year. This is a permanent law for
you, and it must be observed in the appointed
month* from generation to generation. 42 For seven
days you must live outside in little shelters. All native-
born Israelites must live in shelters. 43 This will remind each new generation of Israelites that I made
their ancestors live in shelters when I rescued them
from the land of Egypt. I am the LORD your God."

44 So Moses gave the Israelites these instructions
regarding the annual festivals of the LORD.

Pure Oil and Holy Bread

24 The LORD said to Moses, 2 "Command the
people of Israel to bring you pure oil of
pressed olives for the light, to keep the lamps burning continually. 3 This is the lampstand that stands
in the Tabernacle, in front of the inner curtain that
shields the Ark of the Covenant.* Aaron must keep
the lamps burning in the LORD's presence all night.
This is a permanent law for you, and it must be observed from generation to generation. 4 Aaron and
the priests must tend the lamps on the pure gold
lampstand continually in the LORD's presence.

5 "You must bake twelve loaves of bread from
choice flour, using four quarts* of flour for each loaf.
6 Place the bread before the LORD on the pure gold table, and arrange the loaves in two rows, with six loaves
in each row. 7 Put some pure frankincense near each
row to serve as a representative offering, a special gift
presented to the LORD. 8 Every Sabbath day this bread
must be laid out before the LORD. The bread is to be
received from the people of Israel as a requirement of
the eternal covenant. 9 The loaves of bread will belong
to Aaron and his descendants, who must eat them in a
sacred place, for they are most holy. It is the permanent right of the priests to claim this portion of the
special gifts presented to the LORD."

An Example of Just Punishment

10 One day a man who had an Israelite mother and an
Egyptian father came out of his tent and got into a
fight with one of the Israelite men. 11 During the fight,
this son of an Israelite woman blasphemed the Name
of the LORD* with a curse. So the man was brought to

23:39 Hebrew *on the fifteenth day of the seventh month.* **23:40** Or *gather fruit from majestic trees.* **23:41** Hebrew *the seventh month.* **24:3** Hebrew *in the Tent of Meeting, outside the inner curtain of the Testimony;* see note on 16:13. **24:5** Hebrew *2/10 of an ephah* [4.4 liters]. **24:11** Hebrew *the Name;* also in 24:16b.

KING JAMES VERSION

unto Moses: (and his mother's name *was* Shelomith,
the daughter of Dibri, of the tribe of Dan:)
12 And they put him in ward, that the mind of the
LORD might be shewed them.
13 And the LORD spake unto Moses, saying,
14 Bring forth him that hath cursed without the
camp; and let all that heard *him* lay their hands upon
his head, and let all the congregation stone him.
15 And thou shalt speak unto the children of Israel,
saying, Whosoever curseth his God shall bear his sin.
16 And he that blasphemeth the name of the LORD,
he shall surely be put to death, *and* all the congregation shall certainly stone him: as well the stranger, as
he that is born in the land, when he blasphemeth the
name *of the LORD*, shall be put to death.
17 And he that killeth any man shall surely be put
to death.
18 And he that killeth a beast shall make it good;
beast for beast.
19 And if a man cause a blemish in his neighbour;
as he hath done, so shall it be done to him;
20 Breach for breach, eye for eye, tooth for tooth: as
he hath caused a blemish in a man, so shall it be done
to him *again*.
21 And he that killeth a beast, he shall restore it:
and he that killeth a man, he shall be put to death.
22 Ye shall have one manner of law, as well for the
stranger, as for one of your own country: for I *am* the
LORD your God.
23 And Moses spake to the children of Israel, that
they should bring forth him that had cursed out of
the camp, and stone him with stones. And the children of Israel did as the LORD commanded Moses.

25 1 And the LORD spake unto Moses in mount
Sinai, saying,
2 Speak unto the children of Israel, and say unto
them, When ye come into the land which I give you,
then shall the land keep a sabbath unto the LORD.
3 Six years thou shalt sow thy field, and six years
thou shalt prune thy vineyard, and gather in the fruit
thereof;
4 But in the seventh year shall be a sabbath of rest
unto the land, a sabbath for the LORD: thou shalt neither sow thy field, nor prune thy vineyard.
5 That which groweth of its own accord of thy harvest thou shalt not reap, neither gather the grapes of
thy vine undressed: *for* it is a year of rest unto the
land.
6 And the sabbath of the land shall be meat for you;
for thee, and for thy servant, and for thy maid, and for
thy hired servant, and for thy stranger that
sojourneth with thee,
7 And for thy cattle, and for the beast that *are* in thy
land, shall all the increase thereof be meat.

NEW LIVING TRANSLATION

Moses for judgment. His mother was Shelomith, the
daughter of Dibri of the tribe of Dan. 12 They kept the
man in custody until the LORD's will in the matter
should become clear to them.
13 Then the LORD said to Moses, 14 "Take the blasphemer outside the camp, and tell all those who
heard the curse to lay their hands on his head. Then
let the entire community stone him to death. 15 Say to
the people of Israel: Those who curse their God will
be punished for their sin. 16 Anyone who blasphemes
the Name of the LORD must be stoned to death by the
whole community of Israel. Any native-born Israelite
or foreigner among you who blasphemes the Name
of the LORD must be put to death.
17 "Anyone who takes another person's life must be
put to death.
18 "Anyone who kills another person's animal
must pay for it in full—a live animal for the animal
that was killed.
19 "Anyone who injures another person must be
dealt with according to the injury inflicted—20 a fracture for a fracture, an eye for an eye, a tooth for a
tooth. Whatever anyone does to injure another person must be paid back in kind.
21 "Whoever kills an animal must pay for it in full,
but whoever kills another person must be put to
death.
22 "This same standard applies both to native-
born Israelites and to the foreigners living among
you. I am the LORD your God."
23 After Moses gave all these instructions to the Israelites, they took the blasphemer outside the camp
and stoned him to death. The Israelites did just as
the LORD had commanded Moses.

The Sabbath Year

25 While Moses was on Mount Sinai, the LORD
said to him, 2 "Give the following instructions to the people of Israel. When you have entered
the land I am giving you, the land itself must observe
a Sabbath rest before the LORD every seventh year.
3 For six years you may plant your fields and prune
your vineyards and harvest your crops, 4 but during
the seventh year the land must have a Sabbath year of
complete rest. It is the LORD's Sabbath. Do not plant
your fields or prune your vineyards during that year.
5 And don't store away the crops that grow on their
own or gather the grapes from your unpruned vines.
The land must have a year of complete rest. 6 But you
may eat whatever the land produces on its own during its Sabbath. This applies to you, your male and female servants, your hired workers, and the
temporary residents who live with you. 7 Your livestock and the wild animals in your land will also be
allowed to eat what the land produces.

KING JAMES VERSION

8And thou shalt number seven sabbaths of years
unto thee, seven times seven years; and the space of
the seven sabbaths of years shall be unto thee forty
and nine years.
9Then shalt thou cause the trumpet of the jubilee
to sound on the tenth *day* of the seventh month, in
the day of atonement shall ye make the trumpet
sound throughout all your land.
10And ye shall hallow the fiftieth year, and proclaim liberty throughout *all* the land unto all the inhabitants thereof: it shall be a jubilee unto you; and
ye shall return every man unto his possession, and ye
shall return every man unto his family.
11A jubilee shall that fiftieth year be unto you: ye
shall not sow, neither reap that which groweth of
itself in it, nor gather *the grapes* in it of thy vine
undressed.
12For it *is* the jubilee; it shall be holy unto you: ye
shall eat the increase thereof out of the field.
13In the year of this jubilee ye shall return every
man unto his possession.
14And if thou sell aught unto thy neighbour, or
buyest *aught* of thy neighbour's hand, ye shall not
oppress one another:
15According to the number of years after the jubilee thou shalt buy of thy neighbour, *and* according
unto the number of years of the fruits he shall sell
unto thee:
16According to the multitude of years thou shalt
increase the price thereof, and according to the few-
ness of years thou shalt diminish the price of it: for
according to the number *of the years* of the fruits
doth he sell unto thee.
17Ye shall not therefore oppress one another; but
thou shalt fear thy God: for I *am* the LORD your God.
18Wherefore ye shall do my statutes, and keep my
judgments, and do them; and ye shall dwell in the
land in safety.
19And the land shall yield her fruit, and ye shall eat
your fill, and dwell therein in safety.
20And if ye shall say, What shall we eat the seventh
year? behold, we shall not sow, nor gather in our
increase:
21Then I will command my blessing upon you in the
sixth year, and it shall bring forth fruit for three years.
22And ye shall sow the eighth year, and eat *yet* of
old fruit until the ninth year; until her fruits come in
ye shall eat *of* the old *store*.
23The land shall not be sold for ever: for the land *is*
mine; for ye *are* strangers and sojourners with me.
24And in all the land of your possession ye shall
grant a redemption for the land.
25If thy brother be waxen poor, and hath sold
away *some* of his possession, and if any of his kin
come to redeem it, then shall he redeem that which
his brother sold.

NEW LIVING TRANSLATION

The Year of Jubilee

8"In addition, you must count off seven Sabbath
years, seven sets of seven years, adding up to forty-
nine years in all. 9Then on the Day of Atonement in
the fiftieth year,* blow the ram's horn loud and long
throughout the land. 10Set this year apart as holy, a
time to proclaim freedom throughout the land for all
who live there. It will be a jubilee year for you, when
each of you may return to the land that belonged to
your ancestors and return to your own clan. 11This
fiftieth year will be a jubilee for you. During that year
you must not plant your fields or store away any of
the crops that grow on their own, and don't gather
the grapes from your unpruned vines. 12It will be a
jubilee year for you, and you must keep it holy. But
you may eat whatever the land produces on its own.
13In the Year of Jubilee each of you may return to the
land that belonged to your ancestors.
14"When you make an agreement with your
neighbor to buy or sell property, you must not take
advantage of each other. 15When you buy land from
your neighbor, the price you pay must be based on
the number of years since the last jubilee. The seller
must set the price by taking into account the number of years remaining until the next Year of Jubilee.
16The more years until the next jubilee, the higher
the price; the fewer years, the lower the price. After
all, the person selling the land is actually selling you a
certain number of harvests. 17Show your fear of God
by not taking advantage of each other. I am the LORD
your God.
18"If you want to live securely in the land, follow
my decrees and obey my regulations. 19Then the
land will yield large crops, and you will eat your fill
and live securely in it. 20But you might ask, 'What will
we eat during the seventh year, since we are not allowed to plant or harvest crops that year?' 21Be assured that I will send my blessing for you in the sixth
year, so the land will produce a crop large enough for
three years. 22When you plant your fields in the
eighth year, you will still be eating from the large
crop of the sixth year. In fact, you will still be eating
from that large crop when the new crop is harvested
in the ninth year.

Redemption of Property

23"The land must never be sold on a permanent basis, for the land belongs to me. You are only foreigners and tenant farmers working for me.
24"With every purchase of land you must grant the
seller the right to buy it back. 25If one of your fellow
Israelites falls into poverty and is forced to sell some
family land, then a close relative should buy it back for

25:9 Hebrew *on the tenth day of the seventh month, on the Day of Atonement;* see 23:27a and the note there.

KING JAMES VERSION

26 And if the man have none to redeem it, and himself be able to redeem it;

27 Then let him count the years of the sale thereof, and restore the overplus unto the man to whom he sold it; that he may return unto his possession.

28 But if he be not able to restore *it* to him, then that which is sold shall remain in the hand of him that hath bought it until the year of jubilee: and in the jubilee it shall go out, and he shall return unto his possession.

29 And if a man sell a dwelling house in a walled city, then he may redeem it within a whole year after it is sold; *within* a full year may he redeem it.

30 And if it be not redeemed within the space of a full year, then the house that *is* in the walled city shall be established for ever to him that bought it throughout his generations: it shall not go out in the jubilee.

31 But the houses of the villages which have no wall round about them shall be counted as the fields of the country: they may be redeemed, and they shall go out in the jubilee.

32 Notwithstanding the cities of the Levites, *and* the houses of the cities of their possession, may the Levites redeem at any time.

33 And if a man purchase of the Levites, then the house that was sold, and the city of his possession, shall go out in *the year of* jubilee: for the houses of the cities of the Levites *are* their possession among the children of Israel.

34 But the field of the suburbs of their cities may not be sold; for it *is* their perpetual possession.

35 And if thy brother be waxen poor, and fallen in decay with thee; then thou shalt relieve him: *yea, though he be* a stranger, or a sojourner; that he may live with thee.

36 Take thou no usury of him, or increase: but fear thy God; that thy brother may live with thee.

37 Thou shalt not give him thy money upon usury, nor lend him thy victuals for increase.

38 I *am* the LORD your God, which brought you forth out of the land of Egypt, to give you the land of Canaan, *and* to be your God.

39 And if thy brother *that dwelleth* by thee be waxen poor, and be sold unto thee; thou shalt not compel him to serve as a bondservant:

40 *But* as an hired servant, *and* as a sojourner, he shall be with thee, *and* shall serve thee unto the year of jubilee:

41 And *then* shall he depart from thee, *both* he and his children with him, and shall return unto his own family, and unto the possession of his fathers shall he return.

42 For they *are* my servants, which I brought forth out of the land of Egypt: they shall not be sold as bondmen.

NEW LIVING TRANSLATION

him. 26 If there is no close relative to buy the land, but the person who sold it gets enough money to buy it back, 27 he then has the right to redeem it from the one who bought it. The price of the land will be discounted according to the number of years until the next Year of Jubilee. In this way the original owner can then return to the land. 28 But if the original owner cannot afford to buy back the land, it will remain with the new owner until the next Year of Jubilee. In the jubilee year, the land must be returned to the original owners so they can return to their family land.

29 "Anyone who sells a house inside a walled town has the right to buy it back for a full year after its sale. During that year, the seller retains the right to buy it back. 30 But if it is not bought back within a year, the sale of the house within the walled town cannot be reversed. It will become the permanent property of the buyer. It will not be returned to the original owner in the Year of Jubilee. 31 But a house in a village—a settlement without fortified walls—will be treated like property in the countryside. Such a house may be bought back at any time, and it must be returned to the original owner in the Year of Jubilee.

32 "The Levites always have the right to buy back a house they have sold within the towns allotted to them. 33 And any property that is sold by the Levites—all houses within the Levitical towns—must be returned in the Year of Jubilee. After all, the houses in the towns reserved for the Levites are the only property they own in all Israel. 34 The open pastureland around the Levitical towns may never be sold. It is their permanent possession.

Redemption of the Poor and Enslaved

35 "If one of your fellow Israelites falls into poverty and cannot support himself, support him as you would a foreigner or a temporary resident and allow him to live with you. 36 Do not charge interest or make a profit at his expense. Instead, show your fear of God by letting him live with you as your relative. 37 Remember, do not charge interest on money you lend him or make a profit on food you sell him. 38 I am the LORD your God, who brought you out of the land of Egypt to give you the land of Canaan and to be your God.

39 "If one of your fellow Israelites falls into poverty and is forced to sell himself to you, do not treat him as a slave. 40 Treat him instead as a hired worker or as a temporary resident who lives with you, and he will serve you only until the Year of Jubilee. 41 At that time he and his children will no longer be obligated to you, and they will return to their clans and go back to the land originally allotted to their ancestors. 42 The people of Israel are my servants, whom I brought out of the land of Egypt, so they must never be sold as

KING JAMES VERSION

43 Thou shalt not rule over him with rigour; but
shalt fear thy God.
44 Both thy bondmen, and thy bondmaids, which
thou shalt have, *shall be* of the heathen that are
round about you; of them shall ye buy bondmen and
bondmaids.
45 Moreover of the children of the strangers that
do sojourn among you, of them shall ye buy, and of
their families that *are* with you, which they begat in
your land: and they shall be your possession.
46 And ye shall take them as an inheritance for your
children after you, to inherit *them for* a possession;
they shall be your bondmen for ever: but over your
brethren the children of Israel, ye shall not rule one
over another with rigour.
47 And if a sojourner or stranger wax rich by thee,
and thy brother *that dwelleth* by him wax poor, and
sell himself unto the stranger *or* sojourner by thee,
or to the stock of the stranger's family:
48 After that he is sold he may be redeemed again;
one of his brethren may redeem him:
49 Either his uncle, or his uncle's son, may redeem
him, or *any* that is nigh of kin unto him of his family
may redeem him; or if he be able, he may redeem
himself.
50 And he shall reckon with him that bought him
from the year that he was sold to him unto the year of
jubilee: and the price of his sale shall be according
unto the number of years, according to the time of
an hired servant shall it be with him.
51 If *there be* yet many years *behind,* according
unto them he shall give again the price of his redemption out of the money that he was bought for.
52 And if there remain but few years unto the year
of jubilee, then he shall count with him, *and* according unto his years shall he give him again the price of
his redemption.
53 *And* as a yearly hired servant shall he be with
him: *and the other* shall not rule with rigour over
him in thy sight.
54 And if he be not redeemed in these *years,* then
he shall go out in the year of jubilee, *both* he, and his
children with him.
55 For unto me the children of Israel *are* servants;
they *are* my servants whom I brought forth out of the
land of Egypt: I *am* the LORD your God.

26 1 Ye shall make you no idols nor graven
image, neither rear you up a standing image, neither shall ye set up *any* image of stone in
your land, to bow down unto it: for I *am* the LORD
your God.
2 Ye shall keep my sabbaths, and reverence my
sanctuary: I *am* the LORD.
3 If ye walk in my statutes, and keep my commandments, and do them;
4 Then I will give you rain in due season, and the

NEW LIVING TRANSLATION

slaves. 43 Show your fear of God by not treating them
harshly.
44 "However, you may purchase male and female
slaves from among the nations around you. 45 You
may also purchase the children of temporary residents who live among you, including those who have
been born in your land. You may treat them as your
property, 46 passing them on to your children as a
permanent inheritance. You may treat them as
slaves, but you must never treat your fellow Israelites
this way.
47 "Suppose a foreigner or temporary resident becomes rich while living among you. If any of your fellow Israelites fall into poverty and are forced to sell
themselves to such a foreigner or to a member of his
family, 48 they still retain the right to be bought back,
even after they have been purchased. They may be
bought back by a brother, 49 an uncle, or a cousin. In
fact, anyone from the extended family may buy them
back. They may also redeem themselves if they have
prospered. 50 They will negotiate the price of their
freedom with the person who bought them. The
price will be based on the number of years from the
time they were sold until the next Year of Jubilee—
whatever it would cost to hire a worker for that
period of time. 51 If many years still remain until the
jubilee, they will repay the proper proportion of what
they received when they sold themselves. 52 If only a
few years remain until the Year of Jubilee, they will
repay a small amount for their redemption. 53 The
foreigner must treat them as workers hired on a
yearly basis. You must not allow a foreigner to treat
any of your fellow Israelites harshly. 54 If any Israelites have not been bought back by the time the Year
of Jubilee arrives, they and their children must be set
free at that time. 55 For the people of Israel belong to
me. They are my servants, whom I brought out of the
land of Egypt. I am the LORD your God.

Blessings for Obedience

26 "Do not make idols or set up carved images,
or sacred pillars, or sculptured stones in
your land so you may worship them. I am the LORD
your God. 2 You must keep my Sabbath days of rest
and show reverence for my sanctuary. I am the LORD.
3 "If you follow my decrees and are careful to obey
my commands, 4 I will send you the seasonal rains.

KING JAMES VERSION

land shall yield her increase, and the trees of the field
shall yield their fruit.

5 And your threshing shall reach unto the vintage,
and the vintage shall reach unto the sowing time:
and ye shall eat your bread to the full, and dwell in
your land safely.

6 And I will give peace in the land, and ye shall lie
down, and none shall make *you* afraid: and I will rid
evil beasts out of the land, neither shall the sword go
through your land.

7 And ye shall chase your enemies, and they shall
fall before you by the sword.

8 And five of you shall chase an hundred, and an
hundred of you shall put ten thousand to flight: and
your enemies shall fall before you by the sword.

9 For I will have respect unto you, and make you
fruitful, and multiply you, and establish my covenant
with you.

10 And ye shall eat old store, and bring forth the old
because of the new.

11 And I will set my tabernacle among you: and my
soul shall not abhor you.

12 And I will walk among you, and will be your God,
and ye shall be my people.

13 I *am* the LORD your God, which brought you
forth out of the land of Egypt, that ye should not be
their bondmen; and I have broken the bands of your
yoke, and made you go upright.

14 But if ye will not hearken unto me, and will not
do all these commandments;

15 And if ye shall despise my statutes, or if your
soul abhor my judgments, so that ye will not do all
my commandments, *but* that ye break my covenant:

16 I also will do this unto you; I will even appoint
over you terror, consumption, and the burning ague,
that shall consume the eyes, and cause sorrow of
heart: and ye shall sow your seed in vain, for your
enemies shall eat it.

17 And I will set my face against you, and ye shall
be slain before your enemies: they that hate you
shall reign over you; and ye shall flee when none
pursueth you.

18 And if ye will not yet for all this hearken unto me,
then I will punish you seven times more for your
sins.

19 And I will break the pride of your power; and I
will make your heaven as iron, and your earth as
brass:

20 And your strength shall be spent in vain: for your
land shall not yield her increase, neither shall the
trees of the land yield their fruits.

21 And if ye walk contrary unto me, and will not
hearken unto me; I will bring seven times more
plagues upon you according to your sins.

22 I will also send wild beasts among you, which
shall rob you of your children, and destroy your
cattle, and make you few in number; and your *high*
ways shall be desolate.

NEW LIVING TRANSLATION

The land will then yield its crops, and the trees of the
field will produce their fruit. 5 Your threshing season
will overlap with the grape harvest, and your grape
harvest will overlap with the season of planting
grain. You will eat your fill and live securely in your
own land.

6 "I will give you peace in the land, and you will be
able to sleep with no cause for fear. I will rid the land
of wild animals and keep your enemies out of your
land. 7 In fact, you will chase down your enemies and
slaughter them with your swords. 8 Five of you will
chase a hundred, and a hundred of you will chase
ten thousand! All your enemies will fall beneath
your sword.

9 "I will look favorably upon you, making you fertile and multiplying your people. And I will fulfill my
covenant with you. 10 You will have such a surplus of
crops that you will need to clear out the old grain to
make room for the new harvest! 11 I will live among
you, and I will not despise you. 12 I will walk among
you; I will be your God, and you will be my people. 13 I
am the LORD your God, who brought you out of the
land of Egypt so you would no longer be their slaves.
I broke the yoke of slavery from your neck so you can
walk with your heads held high.

Punishments for Disobedience

14 "However, if you do not listen to me or obey all
these commands, 15 and if you break my covenant by
rejecting my decrees, treating my regulations with
contempt, and refusing to obey my commands, 16 I
will punish you. I will bring sudden terrors upon
you—wasting diseases and burning fevers that will
cause your eyes to fail and your life to ebb away. You
will plant your crops in vain because your enemies
will eat them. 17 I will turn against you, and you will
be defeated by your enemies. Those who hate you
will rule over you, and you will run even when no one
is chasing you!

18 "And if, in spite of all this, you still disobey me, I
will punish you seven times over for your sins. 19 I
will break your proud spirit by making the skies as
unyielding as iron and the earth as hard as bronze.
20 All your work will be for nothing, for your land will
yield no crops, and your trees will bear no fruit.

21 "If even then you remain hostile toward me and
refuse to obey me, I will inflict disaster on you seven
times over for your sins. 22 I will send wild animals
that will rob you of your children and destroy your
livestock. Your numbers will dwindle, and your
roads will be deserted.

KING JAMES VERSION

[23]And if ye will not be reformed by me by these things, but will walk contrary unto me;

[24]Then will I also walk contrary unto you, and will punish you yet seven times for your sins.

[25]And I will bring a sword upon you, that shall avenge the quarrel of *my* covenant: and when ye are gathered together within your cities, I will send the pestilence among you; and ye shall be delivered into the hand of the enemy.

[26]*And* when I have broken the staff of your bread, ten women shall bake your bread in one oven, and they shall deliver *you* your bread again by weight: and ye shall eat, and not be satisfied.

[27]And if ye will not for all this hearken unto me, but walk contrary unto me;

[28]Then I will walk contrary unto you also in fury; and I, even I, will chastise you seven times for your sins.

[29]And ye shall eat the flesh of your sons, and the flesh of your daughters shall ye eat.

[30]And I will destroy your high places, and cut down your images, and cast your carcases upon the carcases of your idols, and my soul shall abhor you.

[31]And I will make your cities waste, and bring your sanctuaries unto desolation, and I will not smell the savour of your sweet odours.

[32]And I will bring the land into desolation: and your enemies which dwell therein shall be astonished at it.

[33]And I will scatter you among the heathen, and will draw out a sword after you: and your land shall be desolate, and your cities waste.

[34]Then shall the land enjoy her sabbaths, as long as it lieth desolate, and ye *be* in your enemies' land; *even* then shall the land rest, and enjoy her sabbaths.

[35]As long as it lieth desolate it shall rest; because it did not rest in your sabbaths, when ye dwelt upon it.

[36]And upon them that are left *alive* of you I will send a faintness into their hearts in the lands of their enemies; and the sound of a shaken leaf shall chase them; and they shall flee, as fleeing from a sword; and they shall fall when none pursueth.

[37]And they shall fall one upon another, as it were before a sword, when none pursueth: and ye shall have no power to stand before your enemies.

[38]And ye shall perish among the heathen, and the land of your enemies shall eat you up.

[39]And they that are left of you shall pine away in their iniquity in your enemies' lands; and also in the iniquities of their fathers shall they pine away with them.

[40]If they shall confess their iniquity, and the iniquity of their fathers, with their trespass which they trespassed against me, and that also they have walked contrary unto me;

[41]And *that* I also have walked contrary unto them, and have brought them into the land of their enemies; if then their uncircumcised hearts be

NEW LIVING TRANSLATION

[23]"And if you fail to learn the lesson and continue
your hostility toward me, [24]then I myself will be hostile toward you. I will personally strike you with calamity seven times over for your sins. [25]I will send
armies against you to carry out the curse of the covenant you have broken. When you run to your towns
for safety, I will send a plague to destroy you there,
and you will be handed over to your enemies. [26]I will
destroy your food supply, so that ten women will
need only one oven to bake bread for their families.
They will ration your food by weight, and though you
have food to eat, you will not be satisfied.

[27]"If in spite of all this you still refuse to listen and
still remain hostile toward me, [28]then I will give full
vent to my hostility. I myself will punish you seven
times over for your sins. [29]Then you will eat the flesh
of your own sons and daughters. [30]I will destroy your
pagan shrines and knock down your places of worship. I will leave your lifeless corpses piled on top
of your lifeless idols,* and I will despise you. [31]I will
make your cities desolate and destroy your places of
pagan worship. I will take no pleasure in your offerings that should be a pleasing aroma to me. [32]Yes, I
myself will devastate your land, and your enemies
who come to occupy it will be appalled at what they
see. [33]I will scatter you among the nations and bring
out my sword against you. Your land will become
desolate, and your cities will lie in ruins. [34]Then at
last the land will enjoy its neglected Sabbath years as
it lies desolate while you are in exile in the land of
your enemies. Then the land will finally rest and enjoy the Sabbaths it missed. [35]As long as the land lies
in ruins, it will enjoy the rest you never allowed it to
take every seventh year while you lived in it.

[36]"And for those of you who survive, I will demor-
alize you in the land of your enemies. You will live in
such fear that the sound of a leaf driven by the wind
will send you fleeing. You will run as though fleeing
from a sword, and you will fall even when no one
pursues you. [37]Though no one is chasing you, you
will stumble over each other as though fleeing from
a sword. You will have no power to stand up against
your enemies. [38]You will die among the foreign nations and be devoured in the land of your enemies.
[39]Those of you who survive will waste away in your
enemies' lands because of their sins and the sins of
their ancestors.

[40]"But at last my people will confess their sins and
the sins of their ancestors for betraying me and being hostile toward me. [41]When I have turned their
hostility back on them and brought them to the land

26:30 The Hebrew term (literally *round things*) probably alludes to dung.

KING JAMES VERSION

humbled, and they then accept of the punishment of their iniquity:

42 Then will I remember my covenant with Jacob, and also my covenant with Isaac, and also my covenant with Abraham will I remember; and I will remember the land.

43 The land also shall be left of them, and shall enjoy her sabbaths, while she lieth desolate without them: and they shall accept of the punishment of their iniquity: because, even because they despised my judgments, and because their soul abhorred my statutes.

44 And yet for all that, when they be in the land of their enemies, I will not cast them away, neither will I abhor them, to destroy them utterly, and to break my covenant with them: for I *am* the LORD their God.

45 But I will for their sakes remember the covenant of their ancestors, whom I brought forth out of the land of Egypt in the sight of the heathen, that I might be their God: I *am* the LORD.

46 These *are* the statutes and judgments and laws, which the LORD made between him and the children of Israel in mount Sinai by the hand of Moses.

27 1 And the LORD spake unto Moses, saying, 2 Speak unto the children of Israel, and say unto them, When a man shall make a singular vow, the persons *shall be* for the LORD by thy estimation.

3 And thy estimation shall be of the male from twenty years old even unto sixty years old, even thy estimation shall be fifty shekels of silver, after the shekel of the sanctuary.

4 And if it *be* a female, then thy estimation shall be thirty shekels.

5 And if *it be* from five years old even unto twenty years old, then thy estimation shall be of the male twenty shekels, and for the female ten shekels.

6 And if *it be* from a month old even unto five years old, then thy estimation shall be of the male five shekels of silver, and for the female thy estimation *shall be* three shekels of silver.

7 And if *it be* from sixty years old and above; if *it be* a male, then thy estimation shall be fifteen shekels, and for the female ten shekels.

8 But if he be poorer than thy estimation, then he shall present himself before the priest, and the priest shall value him; according to his ability that vowed shall the priest value him.

9 And if *it be* a beast, whereof men bring an offering unto the LORD, all that *any man* giveth of such unto the LORD shall be holy.

10 He shall not alter it, nor change it, a good for a bad, or a bad for a good: and if he shall at all change beast for beast, then it and the exchange thereof shall be holy.

11 And if *it be* any unclean beast, of which they do not offer a sacrifice unto the LORD, then he shall present the beast before the priest:

NEW LIVING TRANSLATION

of their enemies, then at last their stubborn hearts will be humbled, and they will pay for their sins. 42 Then I will remember my covenant with Jacob and my covenant with Isaac and my covenant with Abraham, and I will remember the land. 43 For the land must be abandoned to enjoy its years of Sabbath rest as it lies deserted. At last the people will pay for their sins, for they have continually rejected my regulations and despised my decrees.

44 "But despite all this, I will not utterly reject or despise them while they are in exile in the land of their enemies. I will not cancel my covenant with them by wiping them out, for I am the LORD their God. 45 For their sakes I will remember my ancient covenant with their ancestors, whom I brought out of the land of Egypt in the sight of all the nations, that I might be their God. I am the LORD."

46 These are the decrees, regulations, and instructions that the LORD gave through Moses on Mount Sinai as evidence of the relationship between himself and the Israelites.

Redemption of Gifts Offered to the LORD

27 The LORD said to Moses, 2 "Give the following instructions to the people of Israel. If anyone makes a special vow to dedicate someone to the LORD by paying the value of that person, 3 here is the scale of values to be used. A man between the ages of twenty and sixty is valued at fifty shekels* of silver, as measured by the sanctuary shekel. 4 A woman of that age is valued at thirty shekels* of silver. 5 A boy between the ages of five and twenty is valued at twenty shekels of silver; a girl of that age is valued at ten shekels* of silver. 6 A boy between the ages of one month and five years is valued at five shekels of silver; a girl of that age is valued at three shekels* of silver. 7 A man older than sixty is valued at fifteen shekels of silver; a woman of that age is valued at ten shekels* of silver. 8 If you desire to make such a vow but cannot afford to pay the required amount, take the person to the priest. He will determine the amount for you to pay based on what you can afford.

9 "If your vow involves giving an animal that is acceptable as an offering to the LORD, any gift to the LORD will be considered holy. 10 You may not exchange or substitute it for another animal—neither a good animal for a bad one nor a bad animal for a good one. But if you do exchange one animal for another, then both the original animal and its substitute will be considered holy. 11 If your vow involves an unclean animal—one that is not acceptable as an offering to the LORD—then you must bring the

27:3 Or *20 ounces* [570 grams]. **27:4** Or *12 ounces* [342 grams]. **27:5** Or *A boy . . . 8 ounces* [228 grams] *of silver; a girl . . . 4 ounces* [114 grams]. **27:6** Or *A boy . . . 2 ounces* [57 grams] *of silver; a girl . . . 1.2 ounces* [34 grams]. **27:7** Or *A man . . . 6 ounces* [171 grams] *of silver; a woman . . . 4 ounces* [114 grams].

KING JAMES VERSION

12 And the priest shall value it, whether it be good or bad: as thou valuest it, *who art* the priest, so shall it be.

13 But if he will at all redeem it, then he shall add a fifth *part* thereof unto thy estimation.

14 And when a man shall sanctify his house *to be* holy unto the LORD, then the priest shall estimate it, whether it be good or bad: as the priest shall estimate it, so shall it stand.

15 And if he that sanctified it will redeem his house, then he shall add the fifth *part* of the money of thy estimation unto it, and it shall be his.

16 And if a man shall sanctify unto the LORD *some part* of a field of his possession, then thy estimation shall be according to the seed thereof: an homer of barley seed *shall be valued* at fifty shekels of silver.

17 If he sanctify his field from the year of jubilee, according to thy estimation it shall stand.

18 But if he sanctify his field after the jubilee, then the priest shall reckon unto him the money according to the years that remain, even unto the year of the jubilee, and it shall be abated from thy estimation.

19 And if he that sanctified the field will in any wise redeem it, then he shall add the fifth *part* of the money of thy estimation unto it, and it shall be assured to him.

20 And if he will not redeem the field, or if he have sold the field to another man, it shall not be redeemed any more.

21 But the field, when it goeth out in the jubilee, shall be holy unto the LORD, as a field devoted; the possession thereof shall be the priest's.

22 And if *a man* sanctify unto the LORD a field which he hath bought, which *is* not of the fields of his possession;

23 Then the priest shall reckon unto him the worth of thy estimation, *even* unto the year of the jubilee: and he shall give thine estimation in that day, *as* a holy thing unto the LORD.

24 In the year of the jubilee the field shall return unto him of whom it was bought, *even* to him to whom the possession of the land *did belong.*

25 And all thy estimations shall be according to the shekel of the sanctuary: twenty gerahs shall be the shekel.

26 Only the firstling of the beasts, which should be the LORD's firstling, no man shall sanctify it; whether *it be* ox, or sheep: it *is* the LORD's.

27 And if *it be* of an unclean beast, then he shall redeem *it* according to thine estimation, and shall add a fifth *part* of it thereto: or if it be not redeemed, then it shall be sold according to thy estimation.

28 Notwithstanding no devoted thing, that a man shall devote unto the LORD of all that he hath, *both* of man and beast, and of the field of his possession, shall be sold or redeemed: every devoted thing *is* most holy unto the LORD.

NEW LIVING TRANSLATION

animal to the priest. 12 He will assess its value, and
his assessment will be final, whether high or low. 13 If
you want to buy back the animal, you must pay the
value set by the priest, plus 20 percent.

14 "If someone dedicates a house to the LORD, the
priest will come to assess its value. The priest's assessment will be final, whether high or low. 15 If the
person who dedicated the house wants to buy it
back, he must pay the value set by the priest, plus
20 percent. Then the house will again be his.

16 "If someone dedicates to the LORD a piece of his
family property, its value will be assessed according
to the amount of seed required to plant it—fifty
shekels of silver for a field planted with five bushels
of barley seed.* 17 If the field is dedicated to the LORD
in the Year of Jubilee, then the entire assessment will
apply. 18 But if the field is dedicated after the Year of
Jubilee, the priest will assess the land's value in proportion to the number of years left until the next
Year of Jubilee. Its assessed value is reduced each
year. 19 If the person who dedicated the field wants to
buy it back, he must pay the value set by the priest,
plus 20 percent. Then the field will again be legally
his. 20 But if he does not want to buy it back, and it is
sold to someone else, the field can no longer be
bought back. 21 When the field is released in the Year
of Jubilee, it will be holy, a field specially set apart*
for the LORD. It will become the property of the
priests.

22 "If someone dedicates to the LORD a field he has
purchased but which is not part of his family property, 23 the priest will assess its value based on the
number of years left until the next Year of Jubilee.
On that day he must give the assessed value of the
land as a sacred donation to the LORD. 24 In the Year
of Jubilee the field must be returned to the person
from whom he purchased it, the one who inherited it
as family property. 25 (All the payments must be measured by the weight of the sanctuary shekel,* which
equals twenty gerahs.)

26 "You may not dedicate a firstborn animal to the
LORD, for the firstborn of your cattle, sheep, and
goats already belong to him. 27 However, you may buy
back the firstborn of a ceremonially unclean animal
by paying the priest's assessment of its worth, plus
20 percent. If you do not buy it back, the priest will
sell it at its assessed value.

28 "However, anything specially set apart for the
LORD—whether a person, an animal, or family property—must never be sold or bought back. Anything
devoted in this way has been set apart as holy, and it

27:16 Hebrew *50 shekels* [20 ounces, or 570 grams] *of silver for a homer* 182 liters] *of barley seed.* **27:21** The Hebrew term used here refers to the complete consecration of things or people to the LORD, either by destroying them or by giving them as an offering; also in 27:28, 29. **27:25** Each shekel was about 0.4 ounces [11 grams] in weight.

KING JAMES VERSION

[29]None devoted, which shall be devoted of men,
shall be redeemed; *but* shall surely be put to death.
[30]And all the tithe of the land, *whether* of the seed
of the land, *or* of the fruit of the tree, *is* the LORD's: *it*
is holy unto the LORD.
[31]And if a man will at all redeem *aught* of his
tithes, he shall add thereto the fifth *part* thereof.
[32]And concerning the tithe of the herd, or of the
flock, *even* of whatsoever passeth under the rod, the
tenth shall be holy unto the LORD.
[33]He shall not search whether it be good or bad,
neither shall he change it: and if he change it at all,
then both it and the change thereof shall be holy; it
shall not be redeemed.
[34]These *are* the commandments, which the LORD
commanded Moses for the children of Israel in
mount Sinai.

NEW LIVING TRANSLATION

belongs to the LORD. [29]No person specially set apart
for destruction may be bought back. Such a person
must be put to death.
[30]"One-tenth of the produce of the land, whether
grain from the fields or fruit from the trees, belongs
to the LORD and must be set apart to him as holy. [31]If
you want to buy back the LORD's tenth of the grain or
fruit, you must pay its value, plus 20 percent. [32]Count
off every tenth animal from your herds and flocks
and set them apart for the LORD as holy. [33]You may
not pick and choose between good and bad animals,
and you may not substitute one for another. But if
you do exchange one animal for another, then both
the original animal and its substitute will be considered holy and cannot be bought back."
[34]These are the commands that the LORD gave
through Moses on Mount Sinai for the Israelites.

Numbers

KING JAMES VERSION

1 1And the LORD spake unto Moses in the wilderness of Sinai, in the tabernacle of the congregation, on the first *day* of the second month, in the second year after they were come out of the land of Egypt, saying,

2Take ye the sum of all the congregation of the children of Israel, after their families, by the house of their fathers, with the number of *their* names, every male by their polls;

3From twenty years old and upward, all that are able to go forth to war in Israel: thou and Aaron shall number them by their armies.

4And with you there shall be a man of every tribe; every one head of the house of his fathers.

5And these *are* the names of the men that shall stand with you: of *the tribe of* Reuben; Elizur the son of Shedeur.

6Of Simeon; Shelumiel the son of Zurishaddai.

7Of Judah; Nahshon the son of Amminadab.

8Of Issachar; Nethaneel the son of Zuar.

9Of Zebulun; Eliab the son of Helon.

10Of the children of Joseph: of Ephraim; Elishama the son of Ammihud: of Manasseh; Gamaliel the son of Pedahzur.

11Of Benjamin; Abidan the son of Gideoni.

12Of Dan; Ahiezer the son of Ammishaddai.

13Of Asher; Pagiel the son of Ocran.

14Of Gad; Eliasaph the son of Deuel.

15Of Naphtali; Ahira the son of Enan.

16These *were* the renowned of the congregation, princes of the tribes of their fathers, heads of thousands in Israel.

17And Moses and Aaron took these men which are expressed by *their* names:

18And they assembled all the congregation together on the first *day* of the second month, and they declared their pedigrees after their families, by the house of their fathers, according to the number of the names, from twenty years old and upward, by their polls.

19As the LORD commanded Moses, so he numbered them in the wilderness of Sinai.

NEW LIVING TRANSLATION

Registration of Israel's Troops

1 A year after Israel's departure from Egypt, the
LORD spoke to Moses in the Tabernacle* in the
wilderness of Sinai. On the first day of the second
month* of that year he said, 2"From the whole community of Israel, record the names of all the warriors
by their clans and families. List all the men 3twenty
years old or older who are able to go to war. You and
Aaron must register the troops, 4and you will be assisted by one family leader from each tribe.

5"These are the tribes and the names of the leaders who will assist you:

Tribe	*Leader*
Reuben	Elizur son of Shedeur
6 Simeon	Shelumiel son of Zurishaddai
7 Judah	Nahshon son of Amminadab
8 Issachar	Nethanel son of Zuar
9 Zebulun	Eliab son of Helon
10 Ephraim son of Joseph	Elishama son of Ammihud
Manasseh son of Joseph	Gamaliel son of Pedahzur
11 Benjamin	Abidan son of Gideoni
12 Dan	Ahiezer son of Ammishaddai
13 Asher	Pagiel son of Ocran
14 Gad	Eliasaph son of Deuel
15 Naphtali	Ahira son of Enan

16These are the chosen leaders of the community, the leaders of their ancestral tribes, the heads of the clans of Israel."

17So Moses and Aaron called together these chosen leaders, 18and they assembled the whole community of Israel on that very day.* All the people
were registered according to their ancestry by their
clans and families. The men of Israel who were
twenty years old or older were listed one by one,
19just as the LORD had commanded Moses. So Moses
recorded their names in the wilderness of Sinai.

1:1a Hebrew *the Tent of Meeting.* **1:1b** This day in the ancient Hebrew lunar calendar occurred in April or May. **1:18** Hebrew *on the first day of the second month;* see 1:1.

KING JAMES VERSION

20 And the children of Reuben, Israel's eldest son, by their generations, after their families, by the house of their fathers, according to the number of the names, by their polls, every male from twenty years old and upward, all that were able to go forth to war;

21 Those that were numbered of them, *even* of the tribe of Reuben, *were* forty and six thousand and five hundred.

22 Of the children of Simeon, by their generations, after their families, by the house of their fathers, those that were numbered of them, according to the number of the names, by their polls, every male from twenty years old and upward, all that were able to go forth to war;

23 Those that were numbered of them, *even* of the tribe of Simeon, *were* fifty and nine thousand and three hundred.

24 Of the children of Gad, by their generations, after their families, by the house of their fathers, according to the number of the names, from twenty years old and upward, all that were able to go forth to war;

25 Those that were numbered of them, *even* of the tribe of Gad, *were* forty and five thousand six hundred and fifty.

26 Of the children of Judah, by their generations, after their families, by the house of their fathers, according to the number of the names, from twenty years old and upward, all that were able to go forth to war;

27 Those that were numbered of them, *even* of the tribe of Judah, *were* threescore and fourteen thousand and six hundred.

28 Of the children of Issachar, by their generations, after their families, by the house of their fathers, according to the number of the names, from twenty years old and upward, all that were able to go forth to war;

29 Those that were numbered of them, *even* of the tribe of Issachar, *were* fifty and four thousand and four hundred.

30 Of the children of Zebulun, by their generations, after their families, by the house of their fathers, according to the number of the names, from twenty years old and upward, all that were able to go forth to war;

31 Those that were numbered of them, *even* of the tribe of Zebulun, *were* fifty and seven thousand and four hundred.

32 Of the children of Joseph, *namely*, of the children of Ephraim, by their generations, after their families, by the house of their fathers, according to the number of the names, from twenty years old and upward, all that were able to go forth to war;

33 Those that were numbered of them, *even* of the tribe of Ephraim, *were* forty thousand and five hundred.

NEW LIVING TRANSLATION

20-21 This is the number of men twenty years old or older who were able to go to war, as their names were listed in the records of their clans and families*:

	Tribe	*Number*
	Reuben (Jacob's* oldest son)	46,500
22-23	Simeon	59,300
24-25	Gad	45,650
26-27	Judah	74,600
28-29	Issachar	54,400
30-31	Zebulun	57,400
32-33	Ephraim son of Joseph	40,500
34-35	Manasseh son of Joseph	32,200
36-37	Benjamin	35,400
38-39	Dan	62,700
40-41	Asher	41,500
42-43	Naphtali	53,400

1:20-21a In the Hebrew text, this sentence (*This is the number of men twenty years old or older who were able to go to war, as their names were listed in the records of their clans and families*) is repeated in 1:22, 24, 26, 28, 30, 32, 34, 36, 38, 40, 42. **1:20-21b** Hebrew *Israel's*. The names "Jacob" and "Israel" are often interchanged throughout the Old Testament, referring sometimes to the individual patriarch and sometimes to the nation.

KING JAMES VERSION

34Of the children of Manasseh, by their generations, after their families, by the house of their fathers, according to the number of the names, from twenty years old and upward, all that were able to go forth to war;

35Those that were numbered of them, *even* of the tribe of Manasseh, *were* thirty and two thousand and two hundred.

36Of the children of Benjamin, by their generations, after their families, by the house of their fathers, according to the number of the names, from twenty years old and upward, all that were able to go forth to war;

37Those that were numbered of them, *even* of the tribe of Benjamin, *were* thirty and five thousand and four hundred.

38Of the children of Dan, by their generations, after their families, by the house of their fathers, according to the number of the names, from twenty years old and upward, all that were able to go forth to war;

39Those that were numbered of them, *even* of the tribe of Dan, *were* threescore and two thousand and seven hundred.

40Of the children of Asher, by their generations, after their families, by the house of their fathers, according to the number of the names, from twenty years old and upward, all that were able to go forth to war;

41Those that were numbered of them, *even* of the tribe of Asher, *were* forty and one thousand and five hundred.

42Of the children of Naphtali, throughout their generations, after their families, by the house of their fathers, according to the number of the names, from twenty years old and upward, all that were able to go forth to war;

43Those that were numbered of them, *even* of the tribe of Naphtali, *were* fifty and three thousand and four hundred.

44These *are* those that were numbered, which Moses and Aaron numbered, and the princes of Israel, *being* twelve men: each one was for the house of his fathers.

45So were all those that were numbered of the children of Israel, by the house of their fathers, from twenty years old and upward, all that were able to go forth to war in Israel;

46Even all they that were numbered were six hundred thousand and three thousand and five hundred and fifty.

47But the Levites after the tribe of their fathers were not numbered among them.

48For the LORD had spoken unto Moses, saying,

49Only thou shalt not number the tribe of Levi, neither take the sum of them among the children of Israel:

50But thou shalt appoint the Levites over the

NEW LIVING TRANSLATION

44These were the men registered by Moses and Aaron and the twelve leaders of Israel, all listed according to their ancestral descent. 45They were registered by families—all the men of Israel who were twenty years old or older and able to go to war. 46The total number was 603,550.

47But this total did not include the Levites. 48For the LORD had said to Moses, 49"Do not include the tribe of Levi in the registration; do not count them with the rest of the Israelites. 50Put the Levites in

KING JAMES VERSION

tabernacle of testimony, and over all the vessels thereof, and over all things that *belong* to it: they shall bear the tabernacle, and all the vessels thereof; and they shall minister unto it, and shall encamp round about the tabernacle.

51 And when the tabernacle setteth forward, the Levites shall take it down: and when the tabernacle is to be pitched, the Levites shall set it up: and the stranger that cometh nigh shall be put to death.

52 And the children of Israel shall pitch their tents, every man by his own camp, and every man by his own standard, throughout their hosts.

53 But the Levites shall pitch round about the tabernacle of testimony, that there be no wrath upon the congregation of the children of Israel: and the Levites shall keep the charge of the tabernacle of testimony.

54 And the children of Israel did according to all that the LORD commanded Moses, so did they.

2 1 And the LORD spake unto Moses and unto Aaron, saying,

2 Every man of the children of Israel shall pitch by his own standard, with the ensign of their father's house: far off about the tabernacle of the congregation shall they pitch.

3 And on the east side toward the rising of the sun shall they of the standard of the camp of Judah pitch throughout their armies: and Nahshon the son of Amminadab *shall be* captain of the children of Judah.

4 And his host, and those that were numbered of them, *were* threescore and fourteen thousand and six hundred.

5 And those that do pitch next unto him *shall be* the tribe of Issachar: and Nethaneel the son of Zuar *shall be* captain of the children of Issachar.

6 And his host, and those that were numbered thereof, *were* fifty and four thousand and four hundred.

7 *Then* the tribe of Zebulun: and Eliab the son of Helon *shall be* captain of the children of Zebulun.

8 And his host, and those that were numbered thereof, *were* fifty and seven thousand and four hundred.

9 All that were numbered in the camp of Judah *were* an hundred thousand and fourscore thousand and six thousand and four hundred, throughout their armies. These shall first set forth.

10 On the south side *shall be* the standard of the camp of Reuben according to their armies: and the captain of the children of Reuben *shall be* Elizur the son of Shedeur.

11 And his host, and those that were numbered thereof, *were* forty and six thousand and five hundred.

NEW LIVING TRANSLATION

charge of the Tabernacle of the Covenant,* along
with all its furnishings and equipment. They must
carry the Tabernacle and all its furnishings as you
travel, and they must take care of it and camp around
it. 51 Whenever it is time for the Tabernacle to move,
the Levites will take it down. And when it is time to
stop, they will set it up again. But any unauthorized
person who goes too near the Tabernacle must be
put to death. 52 Each tribe of Israel will camp in a designated area with its own family banner. 53 But the
Levites will camp around the Tabernacle of the Covenant to protect the community of Israel from the
LORD's anger. The Levites are responsible to stand
guard around the Tabernacle."

54 So the Israelites did everything just as the LORD had commanded Moses.

Organization for Israel's Camp

2 Then the LORD gave these instructions to
Moses and Aaron: 2 "When the Israelites set up
camp, each tribe will be assigned its own area. The
tribal divisions will camp beneath their family banners on all four sides of the Tabernacle,* but at some
distance from it.

3-4 "The divisions of Judah, Issachar, and Zebulun are to camp toward the sunrise on the east side of the Tabernacle, beneath their family banners. These are the names of the tribes, their leaders, and the numbers of their registered troops:

	Tribe	*Leader*	*Number*
	Judah	Nahshon son of Amminadab	74,600
5-6	Issachar	Nethanel son of Zuar	54,400
7-8	Zebulun	Eliab son of Helon	57,400

9 So the total of all the troops on Judah's side of the camp is 186,400. These three tribes are to lead the way whenever the Israelites travel to a new campsite.

10-11 "The divisions of Reuben, Simeon, and Gad are to camp on the south side of the Tabernacle, beneath their family banners. These are the names of the tribes, their leaders, and the numbers of their registered troops:

1:50 Or *Tabernacle of the Testimony;* also in 1:53. 2:2 Hebrew *the Tent of Meeting;* also in 2:17.

KING JAMES VERSION

[12]And those which pitch by him *shall be* the tribe
of Simeon: and the captain of the children of Simeon
shall be Shelumiel the son of Zurishaddai.
[13]And his host, and those that were numbered
of them, *were* fifty and nine thousand and three
hundred.
[14]Then the tribe of Gad: and the captain of the
sons of Gad *shall be* Eliasaph the son of Reuel.
[15]And his host, and those that were numbered of
them, *were* forty and five thousand and six hundred
and fifty.
[16]All that were numbered in the camp of Reuben
were an hundred thousand and fifty and one thousand and four hundred and fifty, throughout their armies. And they shall set forth in the second rank.
[17]Then the tabernacle of the congregation shall
set forward with the camp of the Levites in the midst
of the camp: as they encamp, so shall they set forward, every man in his place by their standards.
[18]On the west side *shall be* the standard of the
camp of Ephraim according to their armies: and the
captain of the sons of Ephraim *shall be* Elishama
the son of Ammihud.
[19]And his host, and those that were numbered of
them, *were* forty thousand and five hundred.
[20]And by him *shall be* the tribe of Manasseh: and
the captain of the children of Manasseh *shall be*
Gamaliel the son of Pedahzur.
[21]And his host, and those that were numbered
of them, *were* thirty and two thousand and two
hundred.
[22]Then the tribe of Benjamin: and the captain of
the sons of Benjamin *shall be* Abidan the son of
Gideoni.
[23]And his host, and those that were numbered
of them, *were* thirty and five thousand and four
hundred.
[24]All that were numbered of the camp of Ephraim
were an hundred thousand and eight thousand and
an hundred, throughout their armies. And they shall
go forward in the third rank.
[25]The standard of the camp of Dan *shall be* on the
north side by their armies: and the captain of the
children of Dan *shall be* Ahiezer the son of Ammishaddai.
[26]And his host, and those that were numbered of
them, *were* threescore and two thousand and seven
hundred.
[27]And those that encamp by him *shall be* the tribe
of Asher: and the captain of the children of Asher
shall be Pagiel the son of Ocran.
[28]And his host, and those that were numbered
of them, *were* forty and one thousand and five
hundred.
[29]Then the tribe of Naphtali: and the captain
of the children of Naphtali *shall be* Ahira the son
of Enan.
[30]And his host, and those that were numbered of

NEW LIVING TRANSLATION

	Tribe	*Leader*	*Number*
	Reuben	Elizur son of Shedeur	46,500
12-13	Simeon	Shelumiel son of Zurishaddai	59,300
14-15	Gad	Eliasaph son of Deuel*	45,650

[16]So the total of all the troops on Reuben's side of the
camp is 151,450. These three tribes will be second
in line whenever the Israelites travel.
[17]"Then the Tabernacle, carried by the Levites, will
set out from the middle of the camp. All the tribes are
to travel in the same order that they camp, each in
position under the appropriate family banner.
[18-19]"The divisions of Ephraim, Manasseh, and
Benjamin are to camp on the west side of the Tabernacle, beneath their family banners. These are the
names of the tribes, their leaders, and the numbers
of their registered troops:

	Tribe	*Leader*	*Number*
	Ephraim	Elishama son of Ammihud	40,500
20-21	Manasseh	Gamaliel son of Pedahzur	32,200
22-23	Benjamin	Abidan son of Gideoni	35,400

[24]So the total of all the troops on Ephraim's side of
the camp is 108,100. These three tribes will be third
in line whenever the Israelites travel.
[25-26]"The divisions of Dan, Asher, and Naphtali are
to camp on the north side of the Tabernacle, beneath
their family banners. These are the names of the
tribes, their leaders, and the numbers of their registered troops:

	Tribe	*Leader*	*Number*
	Dan	Ahiezer son of Ammishaddai	62,700
27-28	Asher	Pagiel son of Ocran	41,500
29-30	Naphtali	Ahira son of Enan	53,400

2:14-15 As in many Hebrew manuscripts, Samaritan Pentateuch, and Latin Vulgate (see also 1:14); most Hebrew manuscripts read *son of Reuel.*

KING JAMES VERSION

them, *were* fifty and three thousand and four hundred.

[31]All they that were numbered in the camp of Dan *were* an hundred thousand and fifty and seven thousand and six hundred. They shall go hindmost with their standards.

[32]These *are* those which were numbered of the children of Israel by the house of their fathers: all those that were numbered of the camps throughout their hosts *were* six hundred thousand and three thousand and five hundred and fifty.

[33]But the Levites were not numbered among the children of Israel; as the LORD commanded Moses.

[34]And the children of Israel did according to all that the LORD commanded Moses: so they pitched by their standards, and so they set forward, every one after their families, according to the house of their fathers.

3 [1]These also *are* the generations of Aaron and Moses in the day *that* the LORD spake with Moses in mount Sinai.

[2]And these *are* the names of the sons of Aaron; Nadab the firstborn, and Abihu, Eleazar, and Ithamar.

[3]These *are* the names of the sons of Aaron, the priests which were anointed, whom he consecrated to minister in the priest's office.

[4]And Nadab and Abihu died before the LORD, when they offered strange fire before the LORD, in the wilderness of Sinai, and they had no children: and Eleazar and Ithamar ministered in the priest's office in the sight of Aaron their father.

[5]And the LORD spake unto Moses, saying,

[6]Bring the tribe of Levi near, and present them before Aaron the priest, that they may minister unto him.

[7]And they shall keep his charge, and the charge of the whole congregation before the tabernacle of the congregation, to do the service of the tabernacle.

[8]And they shall keep all the instruments of the tabernacle of the congregation, and the charge of the children of Israel, to do the service of the tabernacle.

[9]And thou shalt give the Levites unto Aaron and to his sons: they *are* wholly given unto him out of the children of Israel.

[10]And thou shalt appoint Aaron and his sons, and they shall wait on their priest's office: and the stranger that cometh nigh shall be put to death.

[11]And the LORD spake unto Moses, saying,

[12]And I, behold, I have taken the Levites from among the children of Israel instead of all the firstborn that openeth the matrix among the children of Israel: therefore the Levites shall be mine;

[13]Because all the firstborn *are* mine; *for* on the day that I smote all the firstborn in the land of Egypt I hallowed unto me all the firstborn in Israel, both man and beast: mine shall they be: I *am* the LORD.

NEW LIVING TRANSLATION

[31]So the total of all the troops on Dan's side of the camp is 157,600. These three tribes will be last, marching under their banners whenever the Israelites travel."

[32]In summary, the troops of Israel listed by their families totaled 603,550. [33]But as the LORD had commanded, the Levites were not included in this registration. [34]So the people of Israel did everything as the LORD had commanded Moses. Each clan and family set up camp and marched under their banners exactly as the LORD had instructed them.

Levites Appointed for Service

3 This is the family line of Aaron and Moses as it was recorded when the LORD spoke to Moses on Mount Sinai: [2]The names of Aaron's sons were Nadab (the oldest), Abihu, Eleazar, and Ithamar. [3]These sons of Aaron were anointed and ordained to minister as priests. [4]But Nadab and Abihu died in the LORD's presence in the wilderness of Sinai when they burned before the LORD the wrong kind of fire, different than he had commanded. Since they had no sons, this left only Eleazar and Ithamar to serve as priests with their father, Aaron.

[5]Then the LORD said to Moses, [6]"Call forward the tribe of Levi, and present them to Aaron the priest to serve as his assistants. [7]They will serve Aaron and the whole community, performing their sacred duties in and around the Tabernacle.* [8]They will also maintain all the furnishings of the sacred tent,* serving in the Tabernacle on behalf of all the Israelites. [9]Assign the Levites to Aaron and his sons. They have been given from among all the people of Israel to serve as their assistants. [10]Appoint Aaron and his sons to carry out the duties of the priesthood. But any unauthorized person who goes too near the sanctuary must be put to death."

[11]And the LORD said to Moses, [12]"Look, I have chosen the Levites from among the Israelites to serve as substitutes for all the firstborn sons of the people of Israel. The Levites belong to me, [13]for all the firstborn males are mine. On the day I struck down all the firstborn sons of the Egyptians, I set apart for myself all the firstborn in Israel, both of people and of animals. They are mine; I am the LORD."

3:7 Hebrew *around the Tent of Meeting, doing service at the Tabernacle.*
3:8 Hebrew *the Tent of Meeting;* also in 3:25.

KING JAMES VERSION

14 And the LORD spake unto Moses in the wilderness of Sinai, saying,

15 Number the children of Levi after the house of their fathers, by their families: every male from a month old and upward shalt thou number them.

16 And Moses numbered them according to the word of the LORD, as he was commanded.

17 And these were the sons of Levi by their names; Gershon, and Kohath, and Merari.

18 And these *are* the names of the sons of Gershon by their families; Libni, and Shimei.

19 And the sons of Kohath by their families; Amram, and Izehar, Hebron, and Uzziel.

20 And the sons of Merari by their families; Mahli, and Mushi. These *are* the families of the Levites according to the house of their fathers.

21 Of Gershon *was* the family of the Libnites, and the family of the Shimites: these *are* the families of the Gershonites.

22 Those that were numbered of them, according to the number of all the males, from a month old and upward, *even* those that were numbered of them *were* seven thousand and five hundred.

23 The families of the Gershonites shall pitch behind the tabernacle westward.

24 And the chief of the house of the father of the Gershonites *shall be* Eliasaph the son of Lael.

25 And the charge of the sons of Gershon in the tabernacle of the congregation *shall be* the tabernacle, and the tent, the covering thereof, and the hanging for the door of the tabernacle of the congregation.

26 And the hangings of the court, and the curtain for the door of the court, which *is* by the tabernacle, and by the altar round about, and the cords of it for all the service thereof.

27 And of Kohath *was* the family of the Amramites, and the family of the Izeharites, and the family of the Hebronites, and the family of the Uzzielites: these *are* the families of the Kohathites.

28 In the number of all the males, from a month old and upward, *were* eight thousand and six hundred, keeping the charge of the sanctuary.

29 The families of the sons of Kohath shall pitch on the side of the tabernacle southward.

30 And the chief of the house of the father of the families of the Kohathites *shall be* Elizaphan the son of Uzziel.

31 And their charge *shall be* the ark, and the table, and the candlestick, and the altars, and the vessels of the sanctuary wherewith they minister, and the hanging, and all the service thereof.

32 And Eleazar the son of Aaron the priest *shall be* chief over the chief of the Levites, *and have* the oversight of them that keep the charge of the sanctuary.

33 Of Merari *was* the family of the Mahlites, and the family of the Mushites: these *are* the families of Merari.

NEW LIVING TRANSLATION

Registration of the Levites

14 The LORD spoke again to Moses in the wilderness of Sinai. He said, 15 "Record the names of the members of the tribe of Levi by their families and clans. List every male who is one month old or older." 16 So Moses listed them, just as the LORD had commanded.

17 Levi had three sons, whose names were Gershon, Kohath, and Merari.

18 The clans descended from Gershon were named after two of his descendants, Libni and Shimei.

19 The clans descended from Kohath were named after four of his descendants, Amram, Izhar, Hebron, and Uzziel.

20 The clans descended from Merari were named after two of his descendants, Mahli and Mushi.

These were the Levite clans, listed according to their family groups.

21 The descendants of Gershon were composed of the clans descended from Libni and Shimei. 22 There were 7,500 males one month old or older among these Gershonite clans. 23 They were assigned the area to the west of the Tabernacle for their camp. 24 The leader of the Gershonite clans was Eliasaph son of Lael. 25 These two clans were responsible to care for the Tabernacle, including the sacred tent with its layers of coverings, the curtain at its entrance, 26 the curtains of the courtyard that surrounded the Tabernacle and altar, the curtain at the courtyard entrance, the ropes, and all the equipment related to their use.

27 The descendants of Kohath were composed of the clans descended from Amram, Izhar, Hebron, and Uzziel. 28 There were 8,600* males one month old or older among these Kohathite clans. They were responsible for the care of the sanctuary, 29 and they were assigned the area south of the Tabernacle for their camp. 30 The leader of the Kohathite clans was Elizaphan son of Uzziel. 31 These four clans were responsible for the care of the Ark, the table, the lampstand, the altars, the various articles used in the sanctuary, the inner curtain, and all the equipment related to their use. 32 Eleazar, son of Aaron the priest, was the chief administrator over all the Levites, with special responsibility for the oversight of the sanctuary.

33 The descendants of Merari were composed of

3:28 Some Greek manuscripts read *8,300;* see total in 3:39.

KING JAMES VERSION

34 And those that were numbered of them, according to the number of all the males, from a month old and upward, *were* six thousand and two hundred.

35 And the chief of the house of the father of the families of Merari *was* Zuriel the son of Abihail: *these* shall pitch on the side of the tabernacle northward.

36 And *under* the custody and charge of the sons of Merari *shall be* the boards of the tabernacle, and the bars thereof, and the pillars thereof, and the sockets thereof, and all the vessels thereof, and all that serveth thereto,

37 And the pillars of the court round about, and their sockets, and their pins, and their cords.

38 But those that encamp before the tabernacle toward the east, *even* before the tabernacle of the congregation eastward, *shall be* Moses, and Aaron and his sons, keeping the charge of the sanctuary for the charge of the children of Israel; and the stranger that cometh nigh shall be put to death.

39 All that were numbered of the Levites, which Moses and Aaron numbered at the commandment of the LORD, throughout their families, all the males from a month old and upward, *were* twenty and two thousand.

40 And the LORD said unto Moses, Number all the firstborn of the males of the children of Israel from a month old and upward, and take the number of their names.

41 And thou shalt take the Levites for me (I *am* the LORD) instead of all the firstborn among the children of Israel; and the cattle of the Levites instead of all the firstlings among the cattle of the children of Israel.

42 And Moses numbered, as the LORD commanded him, all the firstborn among the children of Israel.

43 And all the firstborn males by the number of names, from a month old and upward, of those that were numbered of them, were twenty and two thousand two hundred and threescore and thirteen.

44 And the LORD spake unto Moses, saying,

45 Take the Levites instead of all the firstborn among the children of Israel, and the cattle of the Levites instead of their cattle; and the Levites shall be mine: I *am* the LORD.

46 And for those that are to be redeemed of the two hundred and threescore and thirteen of the firstborn of the children of Israel, which are more than the Levites;

47 Thou shalt even take five shekels apiece by the poll, after the shekel of the sanctuary shalt thou take *them:* (the shekel *is* twenty gerahs:)

48 And thou shalt give the money, wherewith the odd number of them is to be redeemed, unto Aaron and to his sons.

49 And Moses took the redemption money of them

NEW LIVING TRANSLATION

the clans descended from Mahli and Mushi. 34 There were 6,200 males one month old or older among these Merarite clans. 35 They were assigned the area north of the Tabernacle for their camp. The leader of the Merarite clans was Zuriel son of Abihail. 36 These two clans were responsible for the care of the frames supporting the Tabernacle, the crossbars, the pillars, the bases, and all the equipment related to their use. 37 They were also responsible for the posts of the courtyard and all their bases, pegs, and ropes.

38 The area in front of the Tabernacle, in the east toward the sunrise,* was reserved for the tents of Moses and of Aaron and his sons, who had the final responsibility for the sanctuary on behalf of the people of Israel. Anyone other than a priest or Levite who went too near the sanctuary was to be put to death.

39 When Moses and Aaron counted the Levite clans at the LORD's command, the total number was 22,000 males one month old or older.

Redeeming the Firstborn Sons

40 Then the LORD said to Moses, "Now count all the firstborn sons in Israel who are one month old or older, and make a list of their names. 41 The Levites must be reserved for me as substitutes for the firstborn sons of Israel; I am the LORD. And the Levites' livestock must be reserved for me as substitutes for the firstborn livestock of the whole nation of Israel."

42 So Moses counted the firstborn sons of the people of Israel, just as the LORD had commanded. 43 The number of firstborn sons who were one month old or older was 22,273.

44 Then the LORD said to Moses, 45 "Take the Levites as substitutes for the firstborn sons of the people of Israel. And take the livestock of the Levites as substitutes for the firstborn livestock of the people of Israel. The Levites belong to me; I am the LORD. 46 There are 273 more firstborn sons of Israel than there are Levites. To redeem these extra firstborn sons, 47 collect five pieces of silver* for each of them (each piece weighing the same as the sanctuary shekel, which equals twenty gerahs). 48 Give the silver to Aaron and his sons as the redemption price for the extra firstborn sons."

49 So Moses collected the silver for redeeming the

3:38 Hebrew *toward the sunrise, in front of the Tent of Meeting.*
3:47 Hebrew *5 shekels* [2 ounces or 57 grams].

that were over and above them that were redeemed
by the Levites:
50Of the firstborn of the children of Israel took he
the money; a thousand three hundred and threescore and five *shekels*, after the shekel of the
sanctuary:
51And Moses gave the money of them that were redeemed unto Aaron and to his sons, according to the
word of the LORD, as the LORD commanded Moses.

4 1And the LORD spake unto Moses and unto
Aaron, saying,
2Take the sum of the sons of Kohath from among
the sons of Levi, after their families, by the house of
their fathers,
3From thirty years old and upward even until fifty
years old, all that enter into the host, to do the work
in the tabernacle of the congregation.
4This *shall be* the service of the sons of Kohath in
the tabernacle of the congregation, *about* the most
holy things:
5And when the camp setteth forward, Aaron shall
come, and his sons, and they shall take down the covering veil, and cover the ark of testimony with it:
6And shall put thereon the covering of badgers'
skins, and shall spread over *it* a cloth wholly of blue,
and shall put in the staves thereof.
7And upon the table of shewbread they shall
spread a cloth of blue, and put thereon the dishes,
and the spoons, and the bowls, and covers to cover
withal: and the continual bread shall be thereon:
8And they shall spread upon them a cloth of scarlet, and cover the same with a covering of badgers'
skins, and shall put in the staves thereof.
9And they shall take a cloth of blue, and cover the
candlestick of the light, and his lamps, and his tongs,
and his snuffdishes, and all the oil vessels thereof,
wherewith they minister unto it:
10And they shall put it and all the vessels thereof
within a covering of badgers' skins, and shall put *it*
upon a bar.
11And upon the golden altar they shall spread a
cloth of blue, and cover it with a covering of badgers'
skins, and shall put to the staves thereof:
12And they shall take all the instruments of ministry, wherewith they minister in the sanctuary, and
put *them* in a cloth of blue, and cover them with
a covering of badgers' skins, and shall put *them* on
a bar:
13And they shall take away the ashes from the altar,
and spread a purple cloth thereon:
14And they shall put upon it all the vessels
thereof, wherewith they minister about it, *even* the
censers, the fleshhooks, and the shovels, and the
basins, all the vessels of the altar; and they shall
spread upon it a covering of badgers' skins, and put
to the staves of it.
15And when Aaron and his sons have made an end

firstborn sons of Israel who exceeded the number of
Levites. 50He collected 1,365 pieces of silver* on
behalf of these firstborn sons of Israel (each piece
weighing the same as the sanctuary shekel). 51And
Moses gave the silver for the redemption to Aaron
and his sons, just as the LORD had commanded.

Duties of the Kohathite Clan

4 Then the LORD said to Moses and Aaron, 2"Record the names of the members of the clans
and families of the Kohathite division of the tribe of
Levi. 3List all the men between the ages of thirty and
fifty who are eligible to serve in the Tabernacle.*
4"The duties of the Kohathites at the Tabernacle
will relate to the most sacred objects. 5When the
camp moves, Aaron and his sons must enter the Tabernacle first to take down the inner curtain and
cover the Ark of the Covenant* with it. 6Then they
must cover the inner curtain with fine goatskin
leather and spread over that a single piece of blue
cloth. Finally, they must put the carrying poles of the
Ark in place.
7"Next they must spread a blue cloth over the table
where the Bread of the Presence is displayed, and on
the cloth they will place the bowls, pans, jars, pitchers, and the special bread. 8They must spread a scarlet cloth over all of this, and finally a covering of fine
goatskin leather on top of the scarlet cloth. Then
they must insert the carrying poles into the table.
9"Next they must cover the lampstand with a blue
cloth, along with its lamps, lamp snuffers, trays, and
special jars of olive oil. 10Then they must cover the
lampstand and its accessories with fine goatskin
leather and place the bundle on a carrying frame.
11"Next they must spread a blue cloth over the
gold incense altar and cover this cloth with fine
goatskin leather. Then they must attach the carrying
poles to the altar. 12They must take all the remaining
furnishings of the sanctuary and wrap them in a blue
cloth, cover them with fine goatskin leather, and
place them on the carrying frame.
13"They must remove the ashes from the altar for
sacrifices and cover the altar with a purple cloth.
14All the altar utensils—the firepans, meat forks,
shovels, basins, and all the containers—must be
placed on the cloth, and a covering of fine goatskin
leather must be spread over them. Finally, they must
put the carrying poles in place. 15The camp will be

3:50 Hebrew *1,365 shekels* [34 pounds or 15.5 kilograms]. **4:3** Hebrew *the Tent of Meeting;* also in 4:4, 15, 23, 25, 28, 30, 31, 33, 35, 37, 39, 41, 43, 47. **4:5** Or *Ark of the Testimony.*

KING JAMES VERSION

of covering the sanctuary, and all the vessels of the
sanctuary, as the camp is to set forward; after that,
the sons of Kohath shall come to bear *it:* but they
shall not touch *any* holy thing, lest they die. These
things are the burden of the sons of Kohath in the
tabernacle of the congregation.
16 And to the office of Eleazar the son of Aaron the
priest *pertaineth* the oil for the light, and the sweet
incense, and the daily meat offering, and the anointing oil, *and* the oversight of all the tabernacle, and of
all that therein *is,* in the sanctuary, and in the vessels
thereof.
17 And the LORD spake unto Moses and unto Aaron,
saying,
18 Cut ye not off the tribe of the families of the
Kohathites from among the Levites:
19 But thus do unto them, that they may live, and
not die, when they approach unto the most holy
things: Aaron and his sons shall go in, and appoint
them every one to his service and to his burden:
20 But they shall not go in to see when the holy
things are covered, lest they die.

21 And the LORD spake unto Moses, saying,
22 Take also the sum of the sons of Gershon,
throughout the houses of their fathers, by their
families;
23 From thirty years old and upward until fifty
years old shalt thou number them; all that enter in to
perform the service, to do the work in the tabernacle
of the congregation.
24 This *is* the service of the families of the Gershonites, to serve, and for burdens:
25 And they shall bear the curtains of the tabernacle, and the tabernacle of the congregation, his
covering, and the covering of the badgers' skins that
is above upon it, and the hanging for the door of the
tabernacle of the congregation,
26 And the hangings of the court, and the hanging
for the door of the gate of the court, which *is* by the
tabernacle and by the altar round about, and their
cords, and all the instruments of their service, and all
that is made for them: so shall they serve.
27 At the appointment of Aaron and his sons shall
be all the service of the sons of the Gershonites, in all
their burdens, and in all their service: and ye shall appoint unto them in charge all their burdens.
28 This *is* the service of the families of the sons of
Gershon in the tabernacle of the congregation: and
their charge *shall be* under the hand of Ithamar the
son of Aaron the priest.
29 As for the sons of Merari, thou shalt number
them after their families, by the house of their
fathers;
30 From thirty years old and upward even unto fifty
years old shalt thou number them, every one that

NEW LIVING TRANSLATION

ready to move when Aaron and his sons have finished covering the sanctuary and all the sacred articles. The Kohathites will come and carry these
things to the next destination. But they must not
touch the sacred objects, or they will die. So these are
the things from the Tabernacle that the Kohathites
must carry.
16 "Eleazar son of Aaron the priest will be responsible for the oil of the lampstand, the fragrant incense, the daily grain offering, and the anointing oil.
In fact, Eleazar will be responsible for the entire Tabernacle and everything in it, including the sanctuary
and its furnishings."
17 Then the LORD said to Moses and Aaron, 18 "Do
not let the Kohathite clans be destroyed from among
the Levites! 19 This is what you must do so they will
live and not die when they approach the most sacred
objects. Aaron and his sons must always go in with
them and assign a specific duty or load to each person. 20 The Kohathites must never enter the sanctuary to look at the sacred objects for even a moment,
or they will die."

Duties of the Gershonite Clan

21 And the LORD said to Moses, 22 "Record the names
of the members of the clans and families of the
Gershonite division of the tribe of Levi. 23 List all the
men between the ages of thirty and fifty who are
eligible to serve in the Tabernacle.
24 "These Gershonite clans will be responsible for
general service and carrying loads. 25 They must
carry the curtains of the Tabernacle, the Tabernacle
itself with its coverings, the outer covering of fine
goatskin leather, and the curtain for the Tabernacle
entrance. 26 They are also to carry the curtains for the
courtyard walls that surround the Tabernacle and
altar, the curtain across the courtyard entrance, the
ropes, and all the equipment related to their use. The
Gershonites are responsible for all these items.
27 Aaron and his sons will direct the Gershonites regarding all their duties, whether it involves moving
the equipment or doing other work. They must assign the Gershonites responsibility for the loads they
are to carry. 28 So these are the duties assigned to the
Gershonite clans at the Tabernacle. They will be directly responsible to Ithamar son of Aaron the priest.

Duties of the Merarite Clan

29 "Now record the names of the members of the
clans and families of the Merarite division of the
tribe of Levi. 30 List all the men between the ages

KING JAMES VERSION

entereth into the service, to do the work of the tabernacle of the congregation.
31 And this *is* the charge of their burden, according
to all their service in the tabernacle of the congregation; the boards of the tabernacle, and the bars
thereof, and the pillars thereof, and sockets thereof,
32 And the pillars of the court round about, and
their sockets, and their pins, and their cords, with all
their instruments, and with all their service: and by
name ye shall reckon the instruments of the charge
of their burden.
33 This *is* the service of the families of the sons of
Merari, according to all their service, in the tabernacle of the congregation, under the hand of Ithamar
the son of Aaron the priest.
34 And Moses and Aaron and the chief of the congregation numbered the sons of the Kohathites after
their families, and after the house of their fathers,
35 From thirty years old and upward even unto fifty
years old, every one that entereth into the service, for
the work in the tabernacle of the congregation:
36 And those that were numbered of them by their
families were two thousand seven hundred and fifty.
37 These *were* they that were numbered of the
families of the Kohathites, all that might do service
in the tabernacle of the congregation, which Moses
and Aaron did number according to the commandment of the LORD by the hand of Moses.
38 And those that were numbered of the sons of
Gershon, throughout their families, and by the house
of their fathers,
39 From thirty years old and upward even unto fifty
years old, every one that entereth into the service, for
the work in the tabernacle of the congregation,
40 Even those that were numbered of them,
throughout their families, by the house of their fathers, were two thousand and six hundred and
thirty.
41 These *are* they that were numbered of the families of the sons of Gershon, of all that might do service in the tabernacle of the congregation, whom
Moses and Aaron did number according to the commandment of the LORD.
42 And those that were numbered of the families of
the sons of Merari, throughout their families, by the
house of their fathers,
43 From thirty years old and upward even unto fifty
years old, every one that entereth into the service, for
the work in the tabernacle of the congregation,
44 Even those that were numbered of them after
their families, were three thousand and two
hundred.
45 These *be* those that were numbered of the families of the sons of Merari, whom Moses and Aaron
numbered according to the word of the LORD by the
hand of Moses.
46 All those that were numbered of the Levites,
whom Moses and Aaron and the chief of Israel

NEW LIVING TRANSLATION

of thirty and fifty who are eligible to serve in the
Tabernacle.
31 "Their only duty at the Tabernacle will be to
carry loads. They will carry the frames of the Tabernacle, the crossbars, the posts, and the bases; 32 also
the posts for the courtyard walls with their bases,
pegs, and ropes; and all the accessories and everything else related to their use. Assign the various
loads to each man by name. 33 So these are the duties
of the Merarite clans at the Tabernacle. They are
directly responsible to Ithamar son of Aaron the
priest."

Summary of the Registration

34 So Moses, Aaron, and the other leaders of the community listed the members of the Kohathite division
by their clans and families. 35 The list included all the
men between thirty and fifty years of age who were
eligible for service in the Tabernacle, 36 and the total
number came to 2,750. 37 So this was the total of all
those from the Kohathite clans who were eligible to
serve at the Tabernacle. Moses and Aaron listed
them, just as the LORD had commanded through
Moses.
38 The Gershonite division was also listed by its
clans and families. 39 The list included all the men
between thirty and fifty years of age who were eligible for service in the Tabernacle, 40 and the total
number came to 2,630. 41 So this was the total of all
those from the Gershonite clans who were eligible to
serve at the Tabernacle. Moses and Aaron listed
them, just as the LORD had commanded.
42 The Merarite division was also listed by its clans
and families. 43 The list included all the men between thirty and fifty years of age who were eligible
for service in the Tabernacle, 44 and the total number
came to 3,200. 45 So this was the total of all those
from the Merarite clans who were eligible for service. Moses and Aaron listed them, just as the LORD
had commanded through Moses.
46 So Moses, Aaron, and the leaders of Israel listed

numbered, after their families, and after the house of their fathers,

47 From thirty years old and upward even unto fifty years old, every one that came to do the service of the ministry, and the service of the burden in the tabernacle of the congregation,

48 Even those that were numbered of them, were eight thousand and five hundred and fourscore.

49 According to the commandment of the LORD they were numbered by the hand of Moses, every one according to his service, and according to his burden: thus were they numbered of him, as the LORD commanded Moses.

5

1 And the LORD spake unto Moses, saying,

2 Command the children of Israel, that they put out of the camp every leper, and every one that hath an issue, and whosoever is defiled by the dead:

3 Both male and female shall ye put out, without the camp shall ye put them; that they defile not their camps, in the midst whereof I dwell.

4 And the children of Israel did so, and put them out without the camp: as the LORD spake unto Moses, so did the children of Israel.

5 And the LORD spake unto Moses, saying,

6 Speak unto the children of Israel, When a man or woman shall commit any sin that men commit, to do a trespass against the LORD, and that person be guilty;

7 Then they shall confess their sin which they have done: and he shall recompense his trespass with the principal thereof, and add unto it the fifth *part* thereof, and give *it* unto *him* against whom he hath trespassed.

8 But if the man have no kinsman to recompense the trespass unto, let the trespass be recompensed unto the LORD, *even* to the priest; beside the ram of the atonement, whereby an atonement shall be made for him.

9 And every offering of all the holy things of the children of Israel, which they bring unto the priest, shall be his.

10 And every man's hallowed things shall be his: whatsoever any man giveth the priest, it shall be his.

11 And the LORD spake unto Moses, saying,

12 Speak unto the children of Israel, and say unto them, If any man's wife go aside, and commit a trespass against him,

13 And a man lie with her carnally, and it be hid from the eyes of her husband, and be kept close, and she be defiled, and *there be* no witness against her, neither she be taken *with the manner;*

14 And the spirit of jealousy come upon him, and he be jealous of his wife, and she be defiled: or if the spirit of jealousy come upon him, and he be jealous of his wife, and she be not defiled:

15 Then shall the man bring his wife unto the priest, and he shall bring her offering for her, the tenth *part* of an ephah of barley meal; he shall pour

all the Levites by their clans and families. 47 All the men between thirty and fifty years of age who were eligible for service in the Tabernacle and for its transportation 48 numbered 8,580. 49 When their names were recorded, as the LORD had commanded through Moses, each man was assigned his task and told what to carry.

And so the registration was completed, just as the LORD had commanded Moses.

Purity in Israel's Camp

5 The LORD gave these instructions to Moses: 2 "Command the people of Israel to remove from the camp anyone who has a skin disease* or a discharge, or who has become ceremonially unclean by touching a dead person. 3 This command applies to men and women alike. Remove them so they will not defile the camp in which I live among them." 4 So the Israelites did as the LORD had commanded Moses and removed such people from the camp.

5 Then the LORD said to Moses, 6 "Give the following instructions to the people of Israel: If any of the people—men or women—betray the LORD by doing wrong to another person, they are guilty. 7 They must confess their sin and make full restitution for what they have done, adding an additional 20 percent and returning it to the person who was wronged. 8 But if the person who was wronged is dead, and there are no near relatives to whom restitution can be made, the payment belongs to the LORD and must be given to the priest. Those who are guilty must also bring a ram as a sacrifice, and they will be purified and made right with the LORD.* 9 All the sacred offerings that the Israelites bring to a priest will belong to him. 10 Each priest may keep all the sacred donations that he receives."

Protecting Marital Faithfulness

11 And the LORD said to Moses, 12 "Give the following instructions to the people of Israel.

"Suppose a man's wife goes astray, and she is unfaithful to her husband 13 and has sex with another man, but neither her husband nor anyone else knows about it. She has defiled herself, even though there was no witness and she was not caught in the act. 14 If her husband becomes jealous and is suspicious of his wife and needs to know whether or not she has defiled herself, 15 the husband must bring his wife to the priest. He must also bring an offering of two quarts* of barley flour to be presented on her behalf.

5:2 Traditionally rendered *leprosy.* The Hebrew word used here describes various skin diseases. 5:8 Or *bring a ram for atonement, which will make atonement for them.* 5:15 Hebrew 1/10 *of an ephah* (2.2 liters).

KING JAMES VERSION

no oil upon it, nor put frankincense thereon; for it *is*
an offering of jealousy, an offering of memorial,
bringing iniquity to remembrance.
16 And the priest shall bring her near, and set her
before the LORD:
17 And the priest shall take holy water in an
earthen vessel; and of the dust that is in the floor of
the tabernacle the priest shall take, and put *it* into
the water:
18 And the priest shall set the woman before the
LORD, and uncover the woman's head, and put the
offering of memorial in her hands, which *is* the jealousy offering: and the priest shall have in his hand
the bitter water that causeth the curse:
19 And the priest shall charge her by an oath, and
say unto the woman, If no man have lain with thee,
and if thou hast not gone aside to uncleanness *with
another* instead of thy husband, be thou free from
this bitter water that causeth the curse:
20 But if thou hast gone aside *to another* instead of
thy husband, and if thou be defiled, and some man
have lain with thee beside thine husband:
21 Then the priest shall charge the woman with an
oath of cursing, and the priest shall say unto the
woman, The LORD make thee a curse and an oath
among thy people, when the LORD doth make thy
thigh to rot, and thy belly to swell;
22 And this water that causeth the curse shall go
into thy bowels, to make *thy* belly to swell, and *thy*
thigh to rot: And the woman shall say, Amen, amen.
23 And the priest shall write these curses in a book,
and he shall blot *them* out with the bitter water:
24 And he shall cause the woman to drink the bitter
water that causeth the curse: and the water that
causeth the curse shall enter into her, *and become*
bitter.
25 Then the priest shall take the jealousy offering
out of the woman's hand, and shall wave the offering
before the LORD, and offer it upon the altar:
26 And the priest shall take an handful of the offering, *even* the memorial thereof, and burn *it* upon the
altar, and afterward shall cause the woman to drink
the water.
27 And when he hath made her to drink the water,
then it shall come to pass, *that,* if she be defiled, and
have done trespass against her husband, that the
water that causeth the curse shall enter into her, *and
become* bitter, and her belly shall swell, and her thigh
shall rot: and the woman shall be a curse among
her people.
28 And if the woman be not defiled, but be clean;
then she shall be free, and shall conceive seed.
29 This *is* the law of jealousies, when a wife goeth
aside *to another* instead of her husband, and is
defiled;
30 Or when the spirit of jealousy cometh upon him,
and he be jealous over his wife, and shall set the

NEW LIVING TRANSLATION

Do not mix it with olive oil or frankincense, for it is a
jealousy offering—an offering to prove whether or
not she is guilty.
16 "The priest will then present her to stand trial
before the LORD. 17 He must take some holy water in a
clay jar and pour into it dust he has taken from the
Tabernacle floor. 18 When the priest has presented
the woman before the LORD, he must unbind her hair
and place in her hands the offering of proof—the
jealousy offering to determine whether her husband's suspicions are justified. The priest will stand
before her, holding the jar of bitter water that brings
a curse to those who are guilty. 19 The priest will then
put the woman under oath and say to her, 'If no other
man has had sex with you, and you have not gone
astray and defiled yourself while under your husband's authority, may you be immune from the effects of this bitter water that brings on the curse.
20 But if you have gone astray by being unfaithful to
your husband, and have defiled yourself by having
sex with another man—'
21 "At this point the priest must put the woman under oath by saying, 'May the people know that the
LORD's curse is upon you when he makes you infertile, causing your womb to shrivel* and your abdomen to swell. 22 Now may this water that brings the
curse enter your body and cause your abdomen to
swell and your womb to shrivel.*' And the woman
will be required to say, 'Yes, let it be so.' 23 And the
priest will write these curses on a piece of leather
and wash them off into the bitter water. 24 He will
make the woman drink the bitter water that brings
on the curse. When the water enters her body, it will
cause bitter suffering if she is guilty.
25 "The priest will take the jealousy offering from
the woman's hand, lift it up before the LORD, and
carry it to the altar. 26 He will take a handful of the
flour as a token portion and burn it on the altar, and
he will require the woman to drink the water. 27 If she
has defiled herself by being unfaithful to her husband, the water that brings on the curse will cause
bitter suffering. Her abdomen will swell and her
womb will shrink,* and her name will become a
curse among her people. 28 But if she has not defiled
herself and is pure, then she will be unharmed and
will still be able to have children.
29 "This is the ritual law for dealing with suspicion.
If a woman goes astray and defiles herself while under her husband's authority, 30 or if a man becomes
jealous and is suspicious that his wife has been unfaithful, the husband must present his wife before

5:21 Hebrew *when he causes your thigh to waste away.* **5:22** Hebrew *and your thigh to waste away.* **5:27** Hebrew *and her thigh will waste away.*

KING JAMES VERSION

woman before the LORD, and the priest shall execute upon her all this law.

31 Then shall the man be guiltless from iniquity, and this woman shall bear her iniquity.

6 1 And the LORD spake unto Moses, saying, 2 Speak unto the children of Israel, and say unto them, When either man or woman shall separate *themselves* to vow a vow of a Nazarite, to separate *themselves* unto the LORD:

3 He shall separate *himself* from wine and strong drink, and shall drink no vinegar of wine, or vinegar of strong drink, neither shall he drink any liquor of grapes, nor eat moist grapes, or dried.

4 All the days of his separation shall he eat nothing that is made of the vine tree, from the kernels even to the husk.

5 All the days of the vow of his separation there shall no razor come upon his head: until the days be fulfilled, in the which he separateth *himself* unto the LORD, he shall be holy, *and* shall let the locks of the hair of his head grow.

6 All the days that he separateth *himself* unto the LORD he shall come at no dead body.

7 He shall not make himself unclean for his father, or for his mother, for his brother, or for his sister, when they die: because the consecration of his God *is* upon his head.

8 All the days of his separation he *is* holy unto the LORD.

9 And if any man die very suddenly by him, and he hath defiled the head of his consecration; then he shall shave his head in the day of his cleansing, on the seventh day shall he shave it.

10 And on the eighth day he shall bring two turtles, or two young pigeons, to the priest, to the door of the tabernacle of the congregation:

11 And the priest shall offer the one for a sin offering, and the other for a burnt offering, and make an atonement for him, for that he sinned by the dead, and shall hallow his head that same day.

12 And he shall consecrate unto the LORD the days of his separation, and shall bring a lamb of the first year for a trespass offering: but the days that were before shall be lost, because his separation was defiled.

13 And this *is* the law of the Nazarite, when the days of his separation are fulfilled: he shall be brought unto the door of the tabernacle of the congregation:

14 And he shall offer his offering unto the LORD, one he lamb of the first year without blemish for a burnt offering, and one ewe lamb of the first year without blemish for a sin offering, and one ram without blemish for peace offerings,

15 And a basket of unleavened bread, cakes of fine flour mingled with oil, and wafers of unleavened

NEW LIVING TRANSLATION

the LORD, and the priest will apply this entire ritual law to her. 31 The husband will be innocent of any guilt in this matter, but his wife will be held accountable for her sin."

Nazirite Laws

6 Then the LORD said to Moses, 2 "Give the following instructions to the people of Israel.

"If any of the people, either men or women, take the special vow of a Nazirite, setting themselves apart to the LORD in a special way, 3 they must give up wine and other alcoholic drinks. They must not use vinegar made from wine or from other alcoholic drinks, they must not drink fresh grape juice, and they must not eat grapes or raisins. 4 As long as they are bound by their Nazirite vow, they are not allowed to eat or drink anything that comes from a grapevine—not even the grape seeds or skins.

5 "They must never cut their hair throughout the time of their vow, for they are holy and set apart to the LORD. Until the time of their vow has been fulfilled, they must let their hair grow long. 6 And they must not go near a dead body during the entire period of their vow to the LORD. 7 Even if the dead person is their own father, mother, brother, or sister, they must not defile themselves, for the hair on their head is the symbol of their separation to God. 8 This requirement applies as long as they are set apart to the LORD.

9 "If someone falls dead beside them, the hair they have dedicated will be defiled. They must wait for seven days and then shave their heads. Then they will be cleansed from their defilement. 10 On the eighth day they must bring two turtledoves or two young pigeons to the priest at the entrance of the Tabernacle.* 11 The priest will offer one of the birds for a sin offering and the other for a burnt offering. In this way, he will purify them* from the guilt they incurred through contact with the dead body. Then they must reaffirm their commitment and let their hair begin to grow again. 12 The days of their vow that were completed before their defilement no longer count. They must rededicate themselves to the LORD as a Nazirite for the full term of their vow, and each must bring a one-year-old male lamb for a guilt offering.

13 "This is the ritual law for Nazirites. At the conclusion of their time of separation as Nazirites, they must each go to the entrance of the Tabernacle 14 and offer their sacrifices to the LORD: a one-year-old male lamb without defect for a burnt offering, a one-year-old female lamb without defect for a sin offering, a ram without defect for a peace offering, 15 a basket of bread made without yeast—cakes of choice flour mixed with olive oil and wafers spread

6:10 Hebrew *the Tent of Meeting;* also in 6:13, 18. **6:11** Or *make atonement for them.*

KING JAMES VERSION

bread anointed with oil, and their meat offering, and
their drink offerings.

[16]And the priest shall bring *them* before the
LORD, and shall offer his sin offering, and his burnt
offering:

[17]And he shall offer the ram *for* a sacrifice of
peace offerings unto the LORD, with the basket of unleavened bread: the priest shall offer also his meat
offering, and his drink offering.

[18]And the Nazarite shall shave the head of his separation *at* the door of the tabernacle of the congregation, and shall take the hair of the head of his
separation, and put *it* in the fire which *is* under the
sacrifice of the peace offerings.

[19]And the priest shall take the sodden shoulder of
the ram, and one unleavened cake out of the basket,
and one unleavened wafer, and shall put *them* upon
the hands of the Nazarite, after *the hair of* his separation is shaven:

[20]And the priest shall wave them *for* a wave offering before the LORD: this *is* holy for the priest, with
the wave breast and heave shoulder: and after that
the Nazarite may drink wine.

[21]This *is* the law of the Nazarite who hath vowed,
and of his offering unto the LORD for his separation,
beside *that* that his hand shall get: according to the
vow which he vowed, so he must do after the law of
his separation.

[22]And the LORD spake unto Moses, saying,

[23]Speak unto Aaron and unto his sons, saying, On
this wise ye shall bless the children of Israel, saying
unto them,

[24]The LORD bless thee, and keep thee:

[25]The LORD make his face shine upon thee, and be
gracious unto thee:

[26]The LORD lift up his countenance upon thee, and
give thee peace.

[27]And they shall put my name upon the children
of Israel; and I will bless them.

7 [1]And it came to pass on the day that Moses had
fully set up the tabernacle, and had anointed it,
and sanctified it, and all the instruments thereof,
both the altar and all the vessels thereof, and had
anointed them, and sanctified them;

[2]That the princes of Israel, heads of the house of
their fathers, who *were* the princes of the tribes, and
were over them that were numbered, offered:

[3]And they brought their offering before the LORD,
six covered wagons, and twelve oxen; a wagon for
two of the princes, and for each one an ox: and they
brought them before the tabernacle.

[4]And the LORD spake unto Moses, saying,

[5]Take *it* of them, that they may be to do the service
of the tabernacle of the congregation; and thou shalt

NEW LIVING TRANSLATION

with olive oil—along with their prescribed grain offerings and liquid offerings. [16]The priest will present these offerings before the LORD: first the sin
offering and the burnt offering; [17]then the ram for a
peace offering, along with the basket of bread made
without yeast. The priest must also present the
prescribed grain offering and liquid offering to
the LORD.

[18]"Then the Nazirites will shave their heads at the
entrance of the Tabernacle. They will take the hair
that had been dedicated and place it on the fire beneath the peace-offering sacrifice. [19]After the Nazirite's head has been shaved, the priest will take for
each of them the boiled shoulder of the ram, and he
will take from the basket a cake and a wafer made
without yeast. He will put them all into the Nazirite's
hands. [20]Then the priest will lift them up as a special
offering before the LORD. These are holy portions for
the priest, along with the breast of the special offering and the thigh of the sacred offering that are lifted
up before the LORD. After this ceremony the Nazirites may again drink wine.

[21]"This is the ritual law of the Nazirites, who vow
to bring these offerings to the LORD. They may also
bring additional offerings if they can afford it. And
they must be careful to do whatever they vowed
when they set themselves apart as Nazirites."

The Priestly Blessing

[22]Then the LORD said to Moses, [23]"Tell Aaron and his
sons to bless the people of Israel with this special
blessing:

[24] 'May the LORD bless you
and protect you.
[25] May the LORD smile on you
and be gracious to you.
[26] May the LORD show you his favor
and give you his peace.'

[27]Whenever Aaron and his sons bless the people of
Israel in my name, I myself will bless them."

Offerings of Dedication

7 On the day Moses set up the Tabernacle, he
anointed it and set it apart as holy. He also
anointed and set apart all its furnishings and the altar with its utensils. [2]Then the leaders of Israel—the
tribal leaders who had registered the troops—came
and brought their offerings. [3]Together they brought
six large wagons and twelve oxen. There was a
wagon for every two leaders and an ox for each
leader. They presented these to the LORD in front of
the Tabernacle.

[4]Then the LORD said to Moses, [5]"Receive their
gifts, and use these oxen and wagons for transporting the Tabernacle.* Distribute them among the

7:5 Hebrew *the Tent of Meeting;* also in 7:89.

KING JAMES VERSION

give them unto the Levites, to every man according to his service.

6And Moses took the wagons and the oxen, and gave them unto the Levites.

7Two wagons and four oxen he gave unto the sons of Gershon, according to their service:

8And four wagons and eight oxen he gave unto the sons of Merari, according unto their service, under the hand of Ithamar the son of Aaron the priest.

9But unto the sons of Kohath he gave none: because the service of the sanctuary belonging unto them *was that* they should bear upon their shoulders.

10And the princes offered for dedicating of the altar in the day that it was anointed, even the princes offered their offering before the altar.

11And the LORD said unto Moses, They shall offer their offering, each prince on his day, for the dedicating of the altar.

12And he that offered his offering the first day was Nahshon the son of Amminadab, of the tribe of Judah:

13And his offering *was* one silver charger, the weight thereof *was* an hundred and thirty *shekels,* one silver bowl of seventy shekels, after the shekel of the sanctuary; both of them *were* full of fine flour mingled with oil for a meat offering:

14One spoon of ten *shekels* of gold, full of incense:

15One young bullock, one ram, one lamb of the first year, for a burnt offering:

16One kid of the goats for a sin offering:

17And for a sacrifice of peace offerings, two oxen, five rams, five he goats, five lambs of the first year: this *was* the offering of Nahshon the son of Amminadab.

18On the second day Nethaneel the son of Zuar, prince of Issachar, did offer:

19He offered *for* his offering one silver charger, the weight whereof *was* an hundred and thirty *shekels,* one silver bowl of seventy shekels, after the shekel of the sanctuary; both of them full of fine flour mingled with oil for a meat offering:

20One spoon of gold of ten *shekels,* full of incense:

21One young bullock, one ram, one lamb of the first year, for a burnt offering:

22One kid of the goats for a sin offering:

23And for a sacrifice of peace offerings, two oxen, five rams, five he goats, five lambs of the first year: this *was* the offering of Nethaneel the son of Zuar.

24On the third day Eliab the son of Helon, prince of the children of Zebulun, *did offer:*

25His offering *was* one silver charger, the weight whereof *was* an hundred and thirty *shekels,* one silver bowl of seventy shekels, after the shekel of the sanctuary; both of them full of fine flour mingled with oil for a meat offering:

NEW LIVING TRANSLATION

Levites according to the work they have to do." 6So
Moses took the wagons and oxen and presented
them to the Levites. 7He gave two wagons and four
oxen to the Gershonite division for their work, 8and
he gave four wagons and eight oxen to the Merarite
division for their work. All their work was done under the leadership of Ithamar son of Aaron the
priest. 9But he gave none of the wagons or oxen to
the Kohathite division, since they were required to
carry the sacred objects of the Tabernacle on their
shoulders.

10The leaders also presented dedication gifts for
the altar at the time it was anointed. They each
placed their gifts before the altar. 11The LORD said to
Moses, "Let one leader bring his gift each day for the
dedication of the altar."

12On the first day Nahshon son of Amminadab,
leader of the tribe of Judah, presented his offering.

13His offering consisted of a silver platter
weighing 3¼ pounds and a silver basin weighing
1¾ pounds* (as measured by the weight of the
sanctuary shekel). These were both filled with
grain offerings of choice flour moistened with
olive oil. 14He also brought a gold container
weighing four ounces,* which was filled with
incense. 15He brought a young bull, a ram, and
a one-year-old male lamb for a burnt offering,
16and a male goat for a sin offering. 17For a peace
offering he brought two bulls, five rams, five male
goats, and five one-year-old male lambs. This
was the offering brought by Nahshon son of
Amminadab.

18On the second day Nethanel son of Zuar, leader
of the tribe of Issachar, presented his offering.

19His offering consisted of a silver platter
weighing 3¼ pounds and a silver basin weighing
1¾ pounds (as measured by the weight of the
sanctuary shekel). These were both filled with
grain offerings of choice flour moistened with
olive oil. 20He also brought a gold container
weighing four ounces, which was filled with
incense. 21He brought a young bull, a ram, and
a one-year-old male lamb for a burnt offering,
22and a male goat for a sin offering. 23For a peace
offering he brought two bulls, five rams, five male
goats, and five one-year-old male lambs. This was
the offering brought by Nethanel son of Zuar.

24On the third day Eliab son of Helon, leader of the
tribe of Zebulun, presented his offering.

25His offering consisted of a silver platter
weighing 3¼ pounds and a silver basin weighing
1¾ pounds (as measured by the weight of the
sanctuary shekel). These were both filled with

7:13 Hebrew *silver platter weighing 130 shekels* [1.5 kilograms] *and a silver basin weighing 70 shekels* [800 grams]; also in 7:19, 25, 31, 37, 43, 49, 55, 61, 67, 73, 79, 85. **7:14** Hebrew *10 shekels* [114 grams]; also in 7:20, 26, 32, 38, 44, 50, 56, 62, 68, 74, 80, 86.

KING JAMES VERSION

[26]One golden spoon of ten *shekels*, full of incense:
[27]One young bullock, one ram, one lamb of the
first year, for a burnt offering:
[28]One kid of the goats for a sin offering:
[29]And for a sacrifice of peace offerings, two oxen,
five rams, five he goats, five lambs of the first year:
this *was* the offering of Eliab the son of Helon.
[30]On the fourth day Elizur the son of Shedeur,
prince of the children of Reuben, *did offer:*
[31]His offering *was* one silver charger of the weight
of an hundred and thirty *shekels*, one silver bowl of
seventy shekels, after the shekel of the sanctuary;
both of them full of fine flour mingled with oil for a
meat offering:
[32]One golden spoon of ten *shekels*, full of incense:
[33]One young bullock, one ram, one lamb of the
first year, for a burnt offering:
[34]One kid of the goats for a sin offering:
[35]And for a sacrifice of peace offerings, two oxen,
five rams, five he goats, five lambs of the first year:
this *was* the offering of Elizur the son of Shedeur.
[36]On the fifth day Shelumiel the son of Zurishaddai, prince of the children of Simeon, *did offer:*
[37]His offering *was* one silver charger, the weight
whereof *was* an hundred and thirty *shekels*, one silver bowl of seventy shekels, after the shekel of the
sanctuary; both of them full of fine flour mingled
with oil for a meat offering:
[38]One golden spoon of ten *shekels*, full of incense:
[39]One young bullock, one ram, one lamb of the
first year, for a burnt offering:
[40]One kid of the goats for a sin offering:
[41]And for a sacrifice of peace offerings, two oxen,
five rams, five he goats, five lambs of the first year:
this *was* the offering of Shelumiel the son of Zurishaddai.
[42]On the sixth day Eliasaph the son of Deuel,
prince of the children of Gad, *offered:*
[43]His offering *was* one silver charger of the weight
of an hundred and thirty *shekels*, a silver bowl of seventy shekels, after the shekel of the sanctuary; both
of them full of fine flour mingled with oil for a meat
offering:
[44]One golden spoon of ten *shekels*, full of incense:
[45]One young bullock, one ram, one lamb of the
first year, for a burnt offering:
[46]One kid of the goats for a sin offering:
[47]And for a sacrifice of peace offerings, two oxen,
five rams, five he goats, five lambs of the first year:
this *was* the offering of Eliasaph the son of Deuel.

NEW LIVING TRANSLATION

grain offerings of choice flour moistened with
olive oil. [26]He also brought a gold container
weighing four ounces, which was filled with
incense. [27]He brought a young bull, a ram, and
a one-year-old male lamb for a burnt offering,
[28]and a male goat for a sin offering. [29]For a peace
offering he brought two bulls, five rams, five male
goats, and five one-year-old male lambs. This was
the offering brought by Eliab son of Helon.

[30]On the fourth day Elizur son of Shedeur, leader of
the tribe of Reuben, presented his offering.
[31]His offering consisted of a silver platter
weighing 3¼ pounds and a silver basin weighing
1¾ pounds (as measured by the weight of the
sanctuary shekel). These were both filled with
grain offerings of choice flour moistened with
olive oil. [32]He also brought a gold container
weighing four ounces, which was filled with
incense. [33]He brought a young bull, a ram, and a
one-year-old male lamb for a burnt offering,
[34]and a male goat for a sin offering. [35]For a peace
offering he brought two bulls, five rams, five male
goats, and five one-year-old male lambs. This was
the offering brought by Elizur son of Shedeur.

[36]On the fifth day Shelumiel son of Zurishaddai,
leader of the tribe of Simeon, presented his offering.
[37]His offering consisted of a silver platter
weighing 3¼ pounds and a silver basin weighing
1¾ pounds (as measured by the weight of the
sanctuary shekel). These were both filled with
grain offerings of choice flour moistened with
olive oil. [38]He also brought a gold container
weighing four ounces, which was filled with
incense. [39]He brought a young bull, a ram, and
a one-year-old male lamb for a burnt offering,
[40]and a male goat for a sin offering. [41]For a peace
offering he brought two bulls, five rams, five male
goats, and five one-year-old male lambs. This was
the offering brought by Shelumiel son of
Zurishaddai.

[42]On the sixth day Eliasaph son of Deuel, leader of
the tribe of Gad, presented his offering.
[43]His offering consisted of a silver platter
weighing 3¼ pounds and a silver basin weighing
1¾ pounds (as measured by the weight of the
sanctuary shekel). These were both filled with
grain offerings of choice flour moistened with
olive oil. [44]He also brought a gold container
weighing four ounces, which was filled with
incense. [45]He brought a young bull, a ram, and
a one-year-old male lamb for a burnt offering,
[46]and a male goat for a sin offering. [47]For a peace
offering he brought two bulls, five rams, five male
goats, and five one-year-old male lambs. This was
the offering brought by Eliasaph son of Deuel.

KING JAMES VERSION

48 On the seventh day Elishama the son of Ammihud, prince of the children of Ephraim, *offered:*
49 His offering *was* one silver charger, the weight
whereof *was* an hundred and thirty *shekels,* one silver bowl of seventy shekels, after the shekel of the
sanctuary; both of them full of fine flour mingled
with oil for a meat offering:
50 One golden spoon of ten *shekels,* full of incense:
51 One young bullock, one ram, one lamb of the
first year, for a burnt offering:
52 One kid of the goats for a sin offering:
53 And for a sacrifice of peace offerings, two
oxen, five rams, five he goats, five lambs of the first
year: this *was* the offering of Elishama the son of
Ammihud.
54 On the eighth day *offered* Gamaliel the son of
Pedahzur, prince of the children of Manasseh:
55 His offering *was* one silver charger of the weight
of an hundred and thirty *shekels,* one silver bowl of
seventy shekels, after the shekel of the sanctuary;
both of them full of fine flour mingled with oil for a
meat offering:
56 One golden spoon of ten *shekels,* full of incense:
57 One young bullock, one ram, one lamb of the
first year, for a burnt offering:
58 One kid of the goats for a sin offering:
59 And for a sacrifice of peace offerings, two
oxen, five rams, five he goats, five lambs of the first
year: this *was* the offering of Gamaliel the son of
Pedahzur.
60 On the ninth day Abidan the son of Gideoni,
prince of the children of Benjamin, *offered:*
61 His offering *was* one silver charger, the weight
whereof *was* an hundred and thirty *shekels,* one silver bowl of seventy shekels, after the shekel of the
sanctuary; both of them full of fine flour mingled
with oil for a meat offering:
62 One golden spoon of ten *shekels,* full of incense:
63 One young bullock, one ram, one lamb of the
first year, for a burnt offering:
64 One kid of the goats for a sin offering:
65 And for a sacrifice of peace offerings, two oxen,
five rams, five he goats, five lambs of the first year:
this *was* the offering of Abidan the son of Gideoni.
66 On the tenth day Ahiezer the son of Ammishaddai, prince of the children of Dan, *offered:*
67 His offering *was* one silver charger, the weight
whereof *was* an hundred and thirty *shekels,* one silver bowl of seventy shekels, after the shekel of the
sanctuary; both of them full of fine flour mingled
with oil for a meat offering:

NEW LIVING TRANSLATION

48 On the seventh day Elishama son of Ammihud,
leader of the tribe of Ephraim, presented his
offering.
49 His offering consisted of a silver platter
weighing 3¼ pounds and a silver basin weighing
1¾ pounds (as measured by the weight of the
sanctuary shekel). These were both filled with
grain offerings of choice flour moistened with
olive oil. 50 He also brought a gold container
weighing four ounces, which was filled with
incense. 51 He brought a young bull, a ram, and
a one-year-old male lamb for a burnt offering,
52 and a male goat for a sin offering. 53 For a peace
offering he brought two bulls, five rams, five male
goats, and five one-year-old male lambs. This
was the offering brought by Elishama son of
Ammihud.

54 On the eighth day Gamaliel son of Pedahzur, leader
of the tribe of Manasseh, presented his offering.
55 His offering consisted of a silver platter
weighing 3¼ pounds and a silver basin weighing
1¾ pounds (as measured by the weight of the
sanctuary shekel). These were both filled with
grain offerings of choice flour moistened with
olive oil. 56 He also brought a gold container
weighing four ounces, which was filled with
incense. 57 He brought a young bull, a ram, and
a one-year-old male lamb for a burnt offering,
58 and a male goat for a sin offering. 59 For a
peace offering he brought two bulls, five rams,
five male goats, and five one-year-old male lambs.
This was the offering brought by Gamaliel son
of Pedahzur.

60 On the ninth day Abidan son of Gideoni, leader of
the tribe of Benjamin, presented his offering.
61 His offering consisted of a silver platter
weighing 3¼ pounds and a silver basin weighing
1¾ pounds (as measured by the weight of the
sanctuary shekel). These were both filled with
grain offerings of choice flour moistened with
olive oil. 62 He also brought a gold container
weighing four ounces, which was filled with
incense. 63 He brought a young bull, a ram, and
a one-year-old male lamb for a burnt offering,
64 and a male goat for a sin offering. 65 For a
peace offering he brought two bulls, five rams,
five male goats, and five one-year-old male lambs.
This was the offering brought by Abidan son of
Gideoni.

66 On the tenth day Ahiezer son of Ammishaddai,
leader of the tribe of Dan, presented his offering.
67 His offering consisted of a silver platter
weighing 3¼ pounds and a silver basin weighing
1¾ pounds (as measured by the weight of the
sanctuary shekel). These were both filled with
grain offerings of choice flour moistened with

68One golden spoon of ten *shekels,* full of incense:
69One young bullock, one ram, one lamb of the first year, for a burnt offering:
70One kid of the goats for a sin offering:
71And for a sacrifice of peace offerings, two oxen, five rams, five he goats, five lambs of the first year: this *was* the offering of Ahiezer the son of Ammishaddai.

72On the eleventh day Pagiel the son of Ocran, prince of the children of Asher, *offered:*

73His offering *was* one silver charger, the weight whereof *was* an hundred and thirty *shekels,* one silver bowl of seventy shekels, after the shekel of the sanctuary; both of them full of fine flour mingled with oil for a meat offering:
74One golden spoon of ten *shekels,* full of incense:
75One young bullock, one ram, one lamb of the first year, for a burnt offering:
76One kid of the goats for a sin offering:
77And for a sacrifice of peace offerings, two oxen, five rams, five he goats, five lambs of the first year: this *was* the offering of Pagiel the son of Ocran.

78On the twelfth day Ahira the son of Enan, prince of the children of Naphtali, *offered:*

79His offering *was* one silver charger, the weight whereof *was* an hundred and thirty *shekels,* one silver bowl of seventy shekels, after the shekel of the sanctuary; both of them full of fine flour mingled with oil for a meat offering:
80One golden spoon of ten *shekels,* full of incense:
81One young bullock, one ram, one lamb of the first year, for a burnt offering:
82One kid of the goats for a sin offering:
83And for a sacrifice of peace offerings, two oxen, five rams, five he goats, five lambs of the first year: this *was* the offering of Ahira the son of Enan.
84This *was* the dedication of the altar, in the day when it was anointed, by the princes of Israel: twelve chargers of silver, twelve silver bowls, twelve spoons of gold:
85Each charger of silver *weighing* an hundred and thirty *shekels,* each bowl seventy: all the silver vessels *weighed* two thousand and four hundred *shekels,* after the shekel of the sanctuary:
86The golden spoons *were* twelve, full of incense, *weighing* ten *shekels* apiece, after the shekel of the sanctuary: all the gold of the spoons *was* an hundred and twenty *shekels.*
87All the oxen for the burnt offering *were* twelve bullocks, the rams twelve, the lambs of the first year twelve, with their meat offering: and the kids of the goats for sin offering twelve.

olive oil. 68He also brought a gold container weighing four ounces, which was filled with incense. 69He brought a young bull, a ram, and a one-year-old male lamb for a burnt offering, 70and a male goat for a sin offering. 71For a peace offering he brought two bulls, five rams, five male goats, and five one-year-old male lambs. This was the offering brought by Ahiezer son of Ammishaddai.

72On the eleventh day Pagiel son of Ocran, leader of the tribe of Asher, presented his offering.

73His offering consisted of a silver platter weighing 3¼ pounds and a silver basin weighing 1¾ pounds (as measured by the weight of the sanctuary shekel). These were both filled with grain offerings of choice flour moistened with olive oil. 74He also brought a gold container weighing four ounces, which was filled with incense. 75He brought a young bull, a ram, and a one-year-old male lamb for a burnt offering, 76and a male goat for a sin offering. 77For a peace offering he brought two bulls, five rams, five male goats, and five one-year-old male lambs. This was the offering brought by Pagiel son of Ocran.

78On the twelfth day Ahira son of Enan, leader of the tribe of Naphtali, presented his offering.

79His offering consisted of a silver platter weighing 3¼ pounds and a silver basin weighing 1¾ pounds (as measured by the weight of the sanctuary shekel). These were both filled with grain offerings of choice flour moistened with olive oil. 80He also brought a gold container weighing four ounces, which was filled with incense. 81He brought a young bull, a ram, and a one-year-old male lamb for a burnt offering, 82and a male goat for a sin offering. 83For a peace offering he brought two bulls, five rams, five male goats, and five one-year-old male lambs. This was the offering brought by Ahira son of Enan.

84So this was the dedication offering brought by the leaders of Israel at the time the altar was anointed: twelve silver platters, twelve silver basins, and twelve gold incense containers. 85Each silver platter weighed 3¼ pounds, and each silver basin weighed 1¾ pounds. The total weight of the silver was 60 pounds* (as measured by the weight of the sanctuary shekel). 86Each of the twelve gold containers that was filled with incense weighed four ounces (as measured by the weight of the sanctuary shekel). The total weight of the gold was three pounds.* 87Twelve young bulls, twelve rams, and twelve one-year-old male lambs were donated for the burnt offerings, along with their prescribed grain offerings. Twelve male goats were brought for the sin offerings.

7:85 Hebrew *2,400 shekels* [27.6 kilograms]. **7:86** Hebrew *120 shekels* [1.4 kilograms].

KING JAMES VERSION

88 And all the oxen for the sacrifice of the peace offerings *were* twenty and four bullocks, the rams sixty, the he goats sixty, the lambs of the first year sixty. This *was* the dedication of the altar, after that it was anointed.

89 And when Moses was gone into the tabernacle of the congregation to speak with him, then he heard the voice of one speaking unto him from off the mercy seat that *was* upon the ark of testimony, from between the two cherubims: and he spake unto him.

8 1 And the LORD spake unto Moses, saying,

2 Speak unto Aaron, and say unto him, When thou lightest the lamps, the seven lamps shall give light over against the candlestick.

3 And Aaron did so; he lighted the lamps thereof over against the candlestick, as the LORD commanded Moses.

4 And this work of the candlestick *was of* beaten gold, unto the shaft thereof, unto the flowers thereof, *was* beaten work: according unto the pattern which the LORD had shewed Moses, so he made the candlestick.

5 And the LORD spake unto Moses, saying,

6 Take the Levites from among the children of Israel, and cleanse them.

7 And thus shalt thou do unto them, to cleanse them: Sprinkle water of purifying upon them, and let them shave all their flesh, and let them wash their clothes, and *so* make themselves clean.

8 Then let them take a young bullock with his meat offering, *even* fine flour mingled with oil, and another young bullock shalt thou take for a sin offering.

9 And thou shalt bring the Levites before the tabernacle of the congregation: and thou shalt gather the whole assembly of the children of Israel together:

10 And thou shalt bring the Levites before the LORD: and the children of Israel shall put their hands upon the Levites:

11 And Aaron shall offer the Levites before the LORD *for* an offering of the children of Israel, that they may execute the service of the LORD.

12 And the Levites shall lay their hands upon the heads of the bullocks: and thou shalt offer the one *for* a sin offering, and the other *for* a burnt offering, unto the LORD, to make an atonement for the Levites.

13 And thou shalt set the Levites before Aaron, and before his sons, and offer them *for* an offering unto the LORD.

14 Thus shalt thou separate the Levites from among the children of Israel: and the Levites shall be mine.

15 And after that shall the Levites go in to do the service of the tabernacle of the congregation: and thou shalt cleanse them, and offer them *for* an offering.

16 For they *are* wholly given unto me from among the children of Israel; instead of such as open every womb, *even instead of* the firstborn of all the children of Israel, have I taken them unto me.

NEW LIVING TRANSLATION

88 Twenty-four bulls, sixty rams, sixty male goats, and sixty one-year-old male lambs were donated for the peace offerings. This was the dedication offering for the altar after it was anointed.

89 Whenever Moses went into the Tabernacle to speak with the LORD, he heard the voice speaking to him from between the two cherubim above the Ark's cover—the place of atonement—that rests on the Ark of the Covenant.* The LORD spoke to him from there.

Preparing the Lamps

8 The LORD said to Moses, 2 "Give Aaron the following instructions: When you set up the seven lamps in the lampstand, place them so their light shines forward in front of the lampstand." 3 So Aaron did this. He set up the seven lamps so they reflected their light forward, just as the LORD had commanded Moses. 4 The entire lampstand, from its base to its decorative blossoms, was made of beaten gold. It was built according to the exact design the LORD had shown Moses.

The Levites Dedicated

5 Then the LORD said to Moses, 6 "Now set the Levites apart from the rest of the people of Israel and make them ceremonially clean. 7 Do this by sprinkling them with the water of purification, and have them shave their entire body and wash their clothing. Then they will be ceremonially clean. 8 Have them bring a young bull and a grain offering of choice flour moistened with olive oil, along with a second young bull for a sin offering. 9 Then assemble the whole community of Israel, and present the Levites at the entrance of the Tabernacle.* 10 When you present the Levites before the LORD, the people of Israel must lay their hands on them. 11 Raising his hands, Aaron must then present the Levites to the LORD as a special offering from the people of Israel, thus dedicating them to the LORD's service.

12 "Next the Levites will lay their hands on the heads of the young bulls. Present one as a sin offering and the other as a burnt offering to the LORD, to purify the Levites and make them right with the LORD.* 13 Then have the Levites stand in front of Aaron and his sons, and raise your hands and present them as a special offering to the LORD. 14 In this way, you will set the Levites apart from the rest of the people of Israel, and the Levites will belong to me. 15 After this, they may go into the Tabernacle to do their work, because you have purified them and presented them as a special offering.

16 "Of all the people of Israel, the Levites are reserved for me. I have claimed them for myself in place of all the firstborn sons of the Israelites; I have

7:89 Or *Ark of the Testimony.* **8:9** Hebrew *the Tent of Meeting;* also in 8:15, 19, 22, 24, 26. **8:12** Or *to make atonement for the Levites.*

17 For all the firstborn of the children of Israel *are*
mine, *both* man and beast: on the day that I smote
every firstborn in the land of Egypt I sanctified them
for myself.
18 And I have taken the Levites for all the firstborn
of the children of Israel.
19 And I have given the Levites *as* a gift to Aaron
and to his sons from among the children of Israel, to
do the service of the children of Israel in the tabernacle of the congregation, and to make an atonement for the children of Israel: that there be no
plague among the children of Israel, when the children of Israel come nigh unto the sanctuary.
20 And Moses, and Aaron, and all the congregation
of the children of Israel, did to the Levites according
unto all that the LORD commanded Moses concerning the Levites, so did the children of Israel unto
them.
21 And the Levites were purified, and they washed
their clothes; and Aaron offered them *as* an offering
before the LORD; and Aaron made an atonement for
them to cleanse them.
22 And after that went the Levites in to do their service in the tabernacle of the congregation before
Aaron, and before his sons: as the LORD had commanded Moses concerning the Levites, so did they
unto them.
23 And the LORD spake unto Moses, saying,
24 This *is it* that *belongeth* unto the Levites: from
twenty and five years old and upward they shall go
in to wait upon the service of the tabernacle of the
congregation:
25 And from the age of fifty years they shall cease
waiting upon the service *thereof,* and shall serve
no more:
26 But shall minister with their brethren in the
tabernacle of the congregation, to keep the charge,
and shall do no service. Thus shalt thou do unto the
Levites touching their charge.

9 1 And the LORD spake unto Moses in the wilderness of Sinai, in the first month of the second
year after they were come out of the land of Egypt,
saying,
2 Let the children of Israel also keep the passover
at his appointed season.
3 In the fourteenth day of this month, at even, ye
shall keep it in his appointed season: according to all
the rites of it, and according to all the ceremonies
thereof, shall ye keep it.
4 And Moses spake unto the children of Israel, that
they should keep the passover.
5 And they kept the passover on the fourteenth day
of the first month at even in the wilderness of Sinai:
according to all that the LORD commanded Moses, so
did the children of Israel.
6 And there were certain men, who were defiled by
the dead body of a man, that they could not keep the

taken the Levites as their substitutes. 17 For all the
firstborn males among the people of Israel are mine,
both of people and of animals. I set them apart for
myself on the day I struck down all the firstborn sons
of the Egyptians. 18 Yes, I have claimed the Levites in
place of all the firstborn sons of Israel. 19 And of all
the Israelites, I have assigned the Levites to Aaron
and his sons. They will serve in the Tabernacle on behalf of the Israelites and make sacrifices to purify*
the people so no plague will strike them when they
approach the sanctuary."
20 So Moses, Aaron, and the whole community of
Israel dedicated the Levites, carefully following all
the LORD's instructions to Moses. 21 The Levites purified themselves from sin and washed their clothes,
and Aaron lifted them up and presented them to the
LORD as a special offering. He then offered a sacrifice to purify them and make them right with the
LORD.* 22 After that the Levites went into the Tabernacle to perform their duties, assisting Aaron and his
sons. So they carried out all the commands that the
LORD gave Moses concerning the Levites.
23 The LORD also instructed Moses, 24 "This is the
rule the Levites must follow: They must begin serving in the Tabernacle at the age of twenty-five, 25 and
they must retire at the age of fifty. 26 After retirement
they may assist their fellow Levites by serving as
guards at the Tabernacle, but they may not officiate
in the service. This is how you must assign duties to
the Levites."

The Second Passover

9 A year after Israel's departure from Egypt, the
LORD spoke to Moses in the wilderness of Sinai.
In the first month* of that year he said, 2 "Tell the Israelites to celebrate the Passover at the prescribed
time, 3 at twilight on the fourteenth day of the first
month.* Be sure to follow all my decrees and regulations concerning this celebration."
4 So Moses told the people to celebrate the Passover 5 in the wilderness of Sinai as twilight fell on the
fourteenth day of the month. And they celebrated
the festival there, just as the LORD had commanded
Moses. 6 But some of the men had been ceremonially
defiled by touching a dead body, so they could not

8:19 Or *make atonement for.* **8:21** Or *then made atonement for them to purify them.* **9:1** The first month of the ancient Hebrew lunar calendar usually occurs within the months of March and April. **9:3** This day in the ancient Hebrew lunar calendar occurred in late March, April, or early May.

KING JAMES VERSION

passover on that day: and they came before Moses and before Aaron on that day:

7 And those men said unto him, We *are* defiled by the dead body of a man: wherefore are we kept back, that we may not offer an offering of the LORD in his appointed season among the children of Israel?

8 And Moses said unto them, Stand still, and I will hear what the LORD will command concerning you.

9 And the LORD spake unto Moses, saying,

10 Speak unto the children of Israel, saying, If any man of you or of your posterity shall be unclean by reason of a dead body, or *be* in a journey afar off, yet he shall keep the passover unto the LORD.

11 The fourteenth day of the second month at even they shall keep it, *and* eat it with unleavened bread and bitter *herbs*.

12 They shall leave none of it unto the morning, nor break any bone of it: according to all the ordinances of the passover they shall keep it.

13 But the man that *is* clean, and is not in a journey, and forbeareth to keep the passover, even the same soul shall be cut off from among his people: because he brought not the offering of the LORD in his appointed season, that man shall bear his sin.

14 And if a stranger shall sojourn among you, and will keep the passover unto the LORD; according to the ordinance of the passover, and according to the manner thereof, so shall he do: ye shall have one ordinance, both for the stranger, and for him that was born in the land.

15 And on the day that the tabernacle was reared up the cloud covered the tabernacle, *namely*, the tent of the testimony: and at even there was upon the tabernacle as it were the appearance of fire, until the morning.

16 So it was alway: the cloud covered it *by day*, and the appearance of fire by night.

17 And when the cloud was taken up from the tabernacle, then after that the children of Israel journeyed: and in the place where the cloud abode, there the children of Israel pitched their tents.

18 At the commandment of the LORD the children of Israel journeyed, and at the commandment of the LORD they pitched: as long as the cloud abode upon the tabernacle they rested in their tents.

19 And when the cloud tarried long upon the tabernacle many days, then the children of Israel kept the charge of the LORD, and journeyed not.

20 And *so* it was, when the cloud was a few days upon the tabernacle; according to the commandment of the LORD they abode in their tents, and according to the commandment of the LORD they journeyed.

21 And *so* it was, when the cloud abode from even

NEW LIVING TRANSLATION

celebrate the Passover that day. They came to Moses and Aaron that day 7 and said, "We have become ceremonially unclean by touching a dead body. But why should we be prevented from presenting the LORD's offering at the proper time with the rest of the Israelites?"

8 Moses answered, "Wait here until I have received instructions for you from the LORD."

9 This was the LORD's reply to Moses. 10 "Give the following instructions to the people of Israel: If any of the people now or in future generations are ceremonially unclean at Passover time because of touching a dead body, or if they are on a journey and cannot be present at the ceremony, they may still celebrate the LORD's Passover. 11 They must offer the Passover sacrifice one month later, at twilight on the fourteenth day of the second month.* They must eat the Passover lamb at that time with bitter salad greens and bread made without yeast. 12 They must not leave any of the lamb until the next morning, and they must not break any of its bones. They must follow all the normal regulations concerning the Passover.

13 "But those who neglect to celebrate the Passover at the regular time, even though they are ceremonially clean and not away on a trip, will be cut off from the community of Israel. If they fail to present the LORD's offering at the proper time, they will suffer the consequences of their guilt. 14 And if foreigners living among you want to celebrate the Passover to the LORD, they must follow these same decrees and regulations. The same laws apply both to native-born Israelites and to the foreigners living among you."

The Fiery Cloud

15 On the day the Tabernacle was set up, the cloud covered it.* But from evening until morning the cloud over the Tabernacle looked like a pillar of fire. 16 This was the regular pattern—at night the cloud that covered the Tabernacle had the appearance of fire. 17 Whenever the cloud lifted from over the sacred tent, the people of Israel would break camp and follow it. And wherever the cloud settled, the people of Israel would set up camp. 18 In this way, they traveled and camped at the LORD's command wherever he told them to go. Then they remained in their camp as long as the cloud stayed over the Tabernacle. 19 If the cloud remained over the Tabernacle for a long time, the Israelites stayed and performed their duty to the LORD. 20 Sometimes the cloud would stay over the Tabernacle for only a few days, so the people would stay for only a few days, as the LORD commanded. Then at the LORD's command they would break camp and move on. 21 Sometimes the cloud

9:11 This day in the ancient Hebrew lunar calendar occurred in late April, May, or early June. **9:15** Hebrew *covered the Tabernacle, the Tent of the Testimony.*

KING JAMES VERSION

unto the morning, and *that* the cloud was taken up
in the morning, then they journeyed: whether *it was*
by day or by night that the cloud was taken up, they
journeyed.
22 Or *whether it were* two days, or a month, or a
year, that the cloud tarried upon the tabernacle, remaining thereon, the children of Israel abode in
their tents, and journeyed not: but when it was taken
up, they journeyed.
23 At the commandment of the LORD they rested in
the tents, and at the commandment of the LORD they
journeyed: they kept the charge of the LORD, at the
commandment of the LORD by the hand of Moses.

10 1 And the LORD spake unto Moses, saying,
2 Make thee two trumpets of silver; of a whole
piece shalt thou make them: that thou mayest use
them for the calling of the assembly, and for the journeying of the camps.
3 And when they shall blow with them, all the assembly shall assemble themselves to thee at the door
of the tabernacle of the congregation.
4 And if they blow *but* with one *trumpet,* then the
princes, *which are* heads of the thousands of Israel,
shall gather themselves unto thee.
5 When ye blow an alarm, then the camps that lie
on the east parts shall go forward.
6 When ye blow an alarm the second time, then the
camps that lie on the south side shall take their journey: they shall blow an alarm for their journeys.
7 But when the congregation is to be gathered together, ye shall blow, but ye shall not sound an alarm.
8 And the sons of Aaron, the priests, shall blow
with the trumpets; and they shall be to you for an ordinance for ever throughout your generations.
9 And if ye go to war in your land against the enemy that oppresseth you, then ye shall blow an alarm
with the trumpets; and ye shall be remembered before the LORD your God, and ye shall be saved from
your enemies.
10 Also in the day of your gladness, and in your solemn days, and in the beginnings of your months, ye
shall blow with the trumpets over your burnt offerings, and over the sacrifices of your peace offerings;
that they may be to you for a memorial before your
God: I *am* the LORD your God.
11 And it came to pass on the twentieth *day* of the
second month, in the second year, that the cloud was
taken up from off the tabernacle of the testimony.
12 And the children of Israel took their journeys
out of the wilderness of Sinai; and the cloud rested in
the wilderness of Paran.
13 And they first took their journey according to
the commandment of the LORD by the hand of
Moses.
14 In the first *place* went the standard of the camp

NEW LIVING TRANSLATION

stayed only overnight and lifted the next morning.
But day or night, when the cloud lifted, the people
broke camp and moved on. 22 Whether the cloud
stayed above the Tabernacle for two days, a month, or
a year, the people of Israel stayed in camp and did not
move on. But as soon as it lifted, they broke camp and
moved on. 23 So they camped or traveled at the LORD's
command, and they did whatever the LORD told them
through Moses.

The Silver Trumpets

10 Now the LORD said to Moses, 2 "Make two
trumpets of hammered silver for calling the
community to assemble and for signaling the breaking of camp. 3 When both trumpets are blown, everyone must gather before you at the entrance of the
Tabernacle.* 4 But if only one trumpet is blown, then
only the leaders—the heads of the clans of Israel—
must present themselves to you.
5 "When you sound the signal to move on, the
tribes camped on the east side of the Tabernacle
must break camp and move forward. 6 When you
sound the signal a second time, the tribes camped on
the south will follow. You must sound short blasts as
the signal for moving on. 7 But when you call the
people to an assembly, blow the trumpets with a different signal. 8 Only the priests, Aaron's descendants,
are allowed to blow the trumpets. This is a permanent law for you, to be observed from generation to
generation.
9 "When you arrive in your own land and go to war
against your enemies who attack you, sound the
alarm with the trumpets. Then the LORD your God
will remember you and rescue you from your enemies. 10 Blow the trumpets in times of gladness, too,
sounding them at your annual festivals and at the beginning of each month. And blow the trumpets over
your burnt offerings and peace offerings. The trumpets will remind the LORD your God of his covenant
with you. I am the LORD your God."

The Israelites Leave Sinai

11 In the second year after Israel's departure from
Egypt—on the twentieth day of the second month*—
the cloud lifted from the Tabernacle of the Covenant.* 12 So the Israelites set out from the wilderness
of Sinai and traveled on from place to place until the
cloud stopped in the wilderness of Paran.
13 When the people set out for the first time, following the instructions the LORD had given through
Moses, 14 Judah's troops led the way. They marched

10:3 Hebrew *Tent of Meeting.* **10:11a** This day in the ancient Hebrew lunar calendar occurred in late April, May, or early June. **10:11b** Or *Tabernacle of the Testimony.*

KING JAMES VERSION

of the children of Judah according to their armies: and over his host *was* Nahshon the son of Amminadab.

15 And over the host of the tribe of the children of Issachar *was* Nethaneel the son of Zuar.

16 And over the host of the tribe of the children of Zebulun *was* Eliab the son of Helon.

17 And the tabernacle was taken down; and the sons of Gershon and the sons of Merari set forward, bearing the tabernacle.

18 And the standard of the camp of Reuben set forward according to their armies: and over his host *was* Elizur the son of Shedeur.

19 And over the host of the tribe of the children of Simeon *was* Shelumiel the son of Zurishaddai.

20 And over the host of the tribe of the children of Gad *was* Eliasaph the son of Deuel.

21 And the Kohathites set forward, bearing the sanctuary: and *the other* did set up the tabernacle against they came.

22 And the standard of the camp of the children of Ephraim set forward according to their armies: and over his host *was* Elishama the son of Ammihud.

23 And over the host of the tribe of the children of Manasseh *was* Gamaliel the son of Pedahzur.

24 And over the host of the tribe of the children of Benjamin *was* Abidan the son of Gideoni.

25 And the standard of the camp of the children of Dan set forward, *which was* the rereward of all the camps throughout their hosts: and over his host *was* Ahiezer the son of Ammishaddai.

26 And over the host of the tribe of the children of Asher *was* Pagiel the son of Ocran.

27 And over the host of the tribe of the children of Naphtali *was* Ahira the son of Enan.

28 Thus *were* the journeyings of the children of Israel according to their armies, when they set forward.

29 And Moses said unto Hobab, the son of Raguel the Midianite, Moses' father in law, We are journeying unto the place of which the LORD said, I will give it you: come thou with us, and we will do thee good: for the LORD hath spoken good concerning Israel.

30 And he said unto him, I will not go; but I will depart to mine own land, and to my kindred.

31 And he said, Leave us not, I pray thee; forasmuch as thou knowest how we are to encamp in the wilderness, and thou mayest be to us instead of eyes.

32 And it shall be, if thou go with us, yea, it shall be, that what goodness the LORD shall do unto us, the same will we do unto thee.

33 And they departed from the mount of the LORD three days' journey: and the ark of the covenant of the LORD went before them in the three days' journey, to search out a resting place for them.

34 And the cloud of the LORD *was* upon them by day, when they went out of the camp.

35 And it came to pass, when the ark set forward, that Moses said, Rise up, LORD, and let thine enemies

NEW LIVING TRANSLATION

behind their banner, and their leader was Nahshon
son of Amminadab. 15 They were joined by the troops
of the tribe of Issachar, led by Nethanel son of Zuar,
16 and the troops of the tribe of Zebulun, led by Eliab
son of Helon.

17 Then the Tabernacle was taken down, and the
Gershonite and Merarite divisions of the Levites
were next in the line of march, carrying the Tabernacle with them. 18 Reuben's troops went next, marching behind their banner. Their leader was Elizur son
of Shedeur. 19 They were joined by the troops of the
tribe of Simeon, led by Shelumiel son of Zurishaddai,
20 and the troops of the tribe of Gad, led by Eliasaph
son of Deuel.

21 Next came the Kohathite division of the Levites,
carrying the sacred objects from the Tabernacle. Before they arrived at the next camp, the Tabernacle
would already be set up at its new location. 22 Ephraim's troops went next, marching behind their banner. Their leader was Elishama son of Ammihud.
23 They were joined by the troops of the tribe of
Manasseh, led by Gamaliel son of Pedahzur, 24 and
the troops of the tribe of Benjamin, led by Abidan
son of Gideoni.

25 Dan's troops went last, marching behind their
banner and serving as the rear guard for all the tribal
camps. Their leader was Ahiezer son of Ammishaddai. 26 They were joined by the troops of the tribe of
Asher, led by Pagiel son of Ocran, 27 and the troops of
the tribe of Naphtali, led by Ahira son of Enan.

28 This was the order in which the Israelites
marched, division by division.

29 One day Moses said to his brother-in-law,
Hobab son of Reuel the Midianite, "We are on our
way to the place the LORD promised us, for he said, 'I
will give it to you.' Come with us and we will treat you
well, for the LORD has promised wonderful blessings
for Israel!"

30 But Hobab replied, "No, I will not go. I must return to my own land and family."

31 "Please don't leave us," Moses pleaded. "You
know the places in the wilderness where we should
camp. Come, be our guide. 32 If you do, we'll share
with you all the blessings the LORD gives us."

33 They marched for three days after leaving the
mountain of the LORD, with the Ark of the LORD's
Covenant moving ahead of them to show them
where to stop and rest. 34 As they moved on each day,
the cloud of the LORD hovered over them. 35 And
whenever the Ark set out, Moses would shout, "Arise,

be scattered; and let them that hate thee flee before thee.

36 And when it rested, he said, Return, O LORD, unto the many thousands of Israel.

11 1 And *when* the people complained, it displeased the LORD: and the LORD heard *it;* and his anger was kindled; and the fire of the LORD burnt among them, and consumed *them that were* in the uttermost parts of the camp.

2 And the people cried unto Moses; and when Moses prayed unto the LORD, the fire was quenched.

3 And he called the name of the place Taberah: because the fire of the LORD burnt among them.

4 And the mixed multitude that *was* among them fell a lusting: and the children of Israel also wept again, and said, Who shall give us flesh to eat?

5 We remember the fish, which we did eat in Egypt freely; the cucumbers, and the melons, and the leeks, and the onions, and the garlic:

6 But now our soul *is* dried away: *there is* nothing at all, beside this manna, *before* our eyes.

7 And the manna *was* as coriander seed, and the colour thereof as the colour of bdellium.

8 *And* the people went about, and gathered *it,* and ground *it* in mills, or beat *it* in a mortar, and baked *it* in pans, and made cakes of it: and the taste of it was as the taste of fresh oil.

9 And when the dew fell upon the camp in the night, the manna fell upon it.

10 Then Moses heard the people weep throughout their families, every man in the door of his tent: and the anger of the LORD was kindled greatly; Moses also was displeased.

11 And Moses said unto the LORD, Wherefore hast thou afflicted thy servant? and wherefore have I not found favour in thy sight, that thou layest the burden of all this people upon me?

12 Have I conceived all this people? have I begotten them, that thou shouldest say unto me, Carry them in thy bosom, as a nursing father beareth the sucking child, unto the land which thou swarest unto their fathers?

13 Whence should I have flesh to give unto all this people? for they weep unto me, saying, Give us flesh, that we may eat.

14 I am not able to bear all this people alone, because *it is* too heavy for me.

15 And if thou deal thus with me, kill me, I pray thee, out of hand, if I have found favour in thy sight; and let me not see my wretchedness.

16 And the LORD said unto Moses, Gather unto me seventy men of the elders of Israel, whom thou knowest to be the elders of the people, and officers over them; and bring them unto the tabernacle of the congregation, that they may stand there with thee.

17 And I will come down and talk with thee there:

O LORD, and let your enemies be scattered! Let them flee before you!" 36 And when the Ark was set down, he would say, "Return, O LORD, to the countless thousands of Israel!"

The People Complain to Moses

11 Soon the people began to complain about their hardship, and the LORD heard everything they said. Then the LORD's anger blazed against them, and he sent a fire to rage among them, and he destroyed some of the people in the outskirts of the camp. 2 Then the people screamed to Moses for help, and when he prayed to the LORD, the fire stopped. 3 After that, the area was known as Taberah (which means "the place of burning"), because fire from the LORD had burned among them there.

4 Then the foreign rabble who were traveling with the Israelites began to crave the good things of Egypt. And the people of Israel also began to complain. "Oh, for some meat!" they exclaimed. 5 "We remember the fish we used to eat for free in Egypt. And we had all the cucumbers, melons, leeks, onions, and garlic we wanted. 6 But now our appetites are gone. All we ever see is this manna!"

7 The manna looked like small coriander seeds, and it was pale yellow like gum resin. 8 The people would go out and gather it from the ground. They made flour by grinding it with hand mills or pounding it in mortars. Then they boiled it in a pot and made it into flat cakes. These cakes tasted like pastries baked with olive oil. 9 The manna came down on the camp with the dew during the night.

10 Moses heard all the families standing in the doorways of their tents whining, and the LORD became extremely angry. Moses was also very aggravated. 11 And Moses said to the LORD, "Why are you treating me, your servant, so harshly? Have mercy on me! What did I do to deserve the burden of all these people? 12 Did I give birth to them? Did I bring them into the world? Why did you tell me to carry them in my arms like a mother carries a nursing baby? How can I carry them to the land you swore to give their ancestors? 13 Where am I supposed to get meat for all these people? They keep whining to me, saying, 'Give us meat to eat!' 14 I can't carry all these people by myself! The load is far too heavy! 15 If this is how you intend to treat me, just go ahead and kill me. Do me a favor and spare me this misery!"

Moses Chooses Seventy Leaders

16 Then the LORD said to Moses, "Gather before me seventy men who are recognized as elders and leaders of Israel. Bring them to the Tabernacle* to stand there with you. 17 I will come down and talk to you

11:16 Hebrew *the Tent of Meeting.*

KING JAMES VERSION

and I will take of the spirit which *is* upon thee, and
will put *it* upon them; and they shall bear the burden
of the people with thee, that thou bear *it* not thyself
alone.
18 And say thou unto the people, Sanctify yourselves against tomorrow, and ye shall eat flesh: for
ye have wept in the ears of the LORD, saying, Who
shall give us flesh to eat? for *it was* well with us in
Egypt: therefore the LORD will give you flesh, and ye
shall eat.
19 Ye shall not eat one day, nor two days, nor five
days, neither ten days, nor twenty days;
20 *But* even a whole month, until it come out at
your nostrils, and it be loathsome unto you: because
that ye have despised the LORD which *is* among you,
and have wept before him, saying, Why came we
forth out of Egypt?
21 And Moses said, The people, among whom I *am,*
are six hundred thousand footmen; and thou hast
said, I will give them flesh, that they may eat a whole
month.
22 Shall the flocks and the herds be slain for them,
to suffice them? or shall all the fish of the sea be
gathered together for them, to suffice them?
23 And the LORD said unto Moses, Is the LORD's
hand waxed short? thou shalt see now whether my
word shall come to pass unto thee or not.
24 And Moses went out, and told the people the
words of the LORD, and gathered the seventy men of
the elders of the people, and set them round about
the tabernacle.
25 And the LORD came down in a cloud, and spake
unto him, and took of the spirit that *was* upon him,
and gave *it* unto the seventy elders: and it came to
pass, *that,* when the spirit rested upon them, they
prophesied, and did not cease.
26 But there remained two *of the* men in the camp,
the name of the one *was* Eldad, and the name of the
other Medad: and the spirit rested upon them; and
they *were* of them that were written, but went not
out unto the tabernacle: and they prophesied in
the camp.
27 And there ran a young man, and told Moses, and
said, Eldad and Medad do prophesy in the camp.
28 And Joshua the son of Nun, the servant of Moses,
one of his young men, answered and said, My lord
Moses, forbid them.
29 And Moses said unto him, Enviest thou for my
sake? would God that all the LORD's people were
prophets, *and* that the LORD would put his spirit
upon them!
30 And Moses gat him into the camp, he and the
elders of Israel.
31 And there went forth a wind from the LORD, and
brought quails from the sea, and let *them* fall by the
camp, as it were a day's journey on this side, and as it
were a day's journey on the other side, round about

NEW LIVING TRANSLATION

there. I will take some of the Spirit that is upon you,
and I will put the Spirit upon them also. They will
bear the burden of the people along with you, so you
will not have to carry it alone.
18 "And say to the people, 'Purify yourselves, for tomorrow you will have meat to eat. You were whining,
and the LORD heard you when you cried, "Oh, for
some meat! We were better off in Egypt!" Now the
LORD will give you meat, and you will have to eat it.
19 And it won't be for just a day or two, or for five or
ten or even twenty. 20 You will eat it for a whole
month until you gag and are sick of it. For you have
rejected the LORD, who is here among you, and you
have whined to him, saying, "Why did we ever leave
Egypt?"'"
21 But Moses responded to the LORD, "There are
600,000 foot soldiers here with me, and yet you say,
'I will give them meat for a whole month!' 22 Even if
we butchered all our flocks and herds, would that
satisfy them? Even if we caught all the fish in the sea,
would that be enough?"
23 Then the LORD said to Moses, "Has my arm lost
its power? Now you will see whether or not my word
comes true!"
24 So Moses went out and reported the LORD's
words to the people. He gathered the seventy elders
and stationed them around the Tabernacle.* 25 And
the LORD came down in the cloud and spoke to
Moses. Then he gave the seventy elders the same
Spirit that was upon Moses. And when the Spirit
rested upon them, they prophesied. But this never
happened again.
26 Two men, Eldad and Medad, had stayed behind
in the camp. They were listed among the elders, but
they had not gone out to the Tabernacle. Yet the
Spirit rested upon them as well, so they prophesied
there in the camp. 27 A young man ran and reported
to Moses, "Eldad and Medad are prophesying in
the camp!"
28 Joshua son of Nun, who had been Moses' assistant since his youth, protested, "Moses, my master,
make them stop!"
29 But Moses replied, "Are you jealous for my sake?
I wish that all the LORD's people were prophets and
that the LORD would put his Spirit upon them all!"
30 Then Moses returned to the camp with the elders
of Israel.

The LORD Sends Quail

31 Now the LORD sent a wind that brought quail from
the sea and let them fall all around the camp. For
miles in every direction there were quail flying about

11:24 Hebrew *the tent;* also in 11:26.

KING JAMES VERSION

the camp, and as it were two cubits *high* upon the
face of the earth.
32 And the people stood up all that day, and all *that*
night, and all the next day, and they gathered the
quails: he that gathered least gathered ten homers:
and they spread *them* all abroad for themselves
round about the camp.
33 And while the flesh *was* yet between their teeth,
ere it was chewed, the wrath of the LORD was kindled
against the people, and the LORD smote the people
with a very great plague.
34 And he called the name of that place Kibroth-
hattaavah: because there they buried the people that
lusted.
35 *And* the people journeyed from Kibroth-
hattaavah unto Hazeroth; and abode at Hazeroth.

12 1 And Miriam and Aaron spake against Moses
because of the Ethiopian woman whom he
had married: for he had married an Ethiopian
woman.
2 And they said, Hath the LORD indeed spoken only
by Moses? hath he not spoken also by us? And the
LORD heard *it*.
3 (Now the man Moses *was* very meek, above all
the men which *were* upon the face of the earth.)
4 And the LORD spake suddenly unto Moses, and
unto Aaron, and unto Miriam, Come out ye three
unto the tabernacle of the congregation. And they
three came out.
5 And the LORD came down in the pillar of the
cloud, and stood *in* the door of the tabernacle, and
called Aaron and Miriam: and they both came forth.
6 And he said, Hear now my words: If there be a
prophet among you, *I* the LORD will make myself
known unto him in a vision, *and* will speak unto him
in a dream.
7 My servant Moses *is* not so, who *is* faithful in all
mine house.
8 With him will I speak mouth to mouth, even apparently, and not in dark speeches; and the similitude
of the LORD shall he behold: wherefore then were ye
not afraid to speak against my servant Moses?
9 And the anger of the LORD was kindled against
them; and he departed.
10 And the cloud departed from off the tabernacle;
and, behold, Miriam *became* leprous, *white* as snow:
and Aaron looked upon Miriam, and, behold, *she was*
leprous.
11 And Aaron said unto Moses, Alas, my lord, I beseech thee, lay not the sin upon us, wherein we have
done foolishly, and wherein we have sinned.
12 Let her not be as one dead, of whom the flesh is
half consumed when he cometh out of his mother's
womb.

NEW LIVING TRANSLATION

three feet above the ground.* 32 So the people went
out and caught quail all that day and throughout the
night and all the next day, too. No one gathered less
than fifty bushels*! They spread the quail all around
the camp to dry. 33 But while they were gorging themselves on the meat—while it was still in their
mouths—the anger of the LORD blazed against the
people, and he struck them with a severe plague. 34 So
that place was called Kibroth-hattaavah (which
means "graves of gluttony") because there they buried the people who had craved meat from Egypt.
35 From Kibroth-hattaavah the Israelites traveled to
Hazeroth, where they stayed for some time.

The Complaints of Miriam and Aaron

12 While they were at Hazeroth, Miriam and
Aaron criticized Moses because he had married a Cushite woman. 2 They said, "Has the LORD
spoken only through Moses? Hasn't he spoken
through us, too?" But the LORD heard them. 3 (Now
Moses was very humble—more humble than any
other person on earth.)
4 So immediately the LORD called to Moses, Aaron,
and Miriam and said, "Go out to the Tabernacle,* all
three of you!" So the three of them went to the Tabernacle. 5 Then the LORD descended in the pillar of
cloud and stood at the entrance of the Tabernacle.*
"Aaron and Miriam!" he called, and they stepped forward. 6 And the LORD said to them, "Now listen to
what I say:

"If there were prophets among you,
I, the LORD, would reveal myself in visions.
I would speak to them in dreams.
7 But not with my servant Moses.
Of all my house, he is the one I trust.
8 I speak to him face to face,
clearly, and not in riddles!
He sees the LORD as he is.
So why were you not afraid
to criticize my servant Moses?"

9 The LORD was very angry with them, and he departed. 10 As the cloud moved from above the Tabernacle, there stood Miriam, her skin as white as snow
from leprosy.* When Aaron saw what had happened
to her, 11 he cried out to Moses, "Oh, my master!
Please don't punish us for this sin we have so foolishly committed. 12 Don't let her be like a stillborn
baby, already decayed at birth."

11:31 Or *there were quail 3 feet* [2 cubits or 92 centimeters] *deep on the ground.* **11:32** Hebrew *10 homers* [1.8 kiloliters]. **12:4** Hebrew *the Tent of Meeting.* **12:5** Hebrew *the tent;* also in 12:10. **12:10** Or *with a skin disease.* The Hebrew word used here can describe various skin diseases.

KING JAMES VERSION

13 And Moses cried unto the LORD, saying, Heal her
now, O God, I beseech thee.
14 And the LORD said unto Moses, If her father had
but spit in her face, should she not be ashamed seven
days? let her be shut out from the camp seven days,
and after that let her be received in *again*.
15 And Miriam was shut out from the camp seven
days: and the people journeyed not till Miriam was
brought in *again*.
16 And afterward the people removed from Hazeroth, and pitched in the wilderness of Paran.

13 1 And the LORD spake unto Moses, saying,
2 Send thou men, that they may search the
land of Canaan, which I give unto the children of
Israel: of every tribe of their fathers shall ye send a
man, every one a ruler among them.
3 And Moses by the commandment of the LORD
sent them from the wilderness of Paran: all those
men *were* heads of the children of Israel.
4 And these *were* their names: of the tribe of Reuben, Shammua the son of Zaccur.
5 Of the tribe of Simeon, Shaphat the son of Hori.
6 Of the tribe of Judah, Caleb the son of Jephunneh.
7 Of the tribe of Issachar, Igal the son of Joseph.
8 Of the tribe of Ephraim, Oshea the son of Nun.
9 Of the tribe of Benjamin, Palti the son of Raphu.
10 Of the tribe of Zebulun, Gaddiel the son of Sodi.
11 Of the tribe of Joseph, *namely*, of the tribe of
Manasseh, Gaddi the son of Susi.
12 Of the tribe of Dan, Ammiel the son of Gemalli.
13 Of the tribe of Asher, Sethur the son of Michael.
14 Of the tribe of Naphtali, Nahbi the son of Vophsi.
15 Of the tribe of Gad, Geuel the son of Machi.
16 These *are* the names of the men which Moses
sent to spy out the land. And Moses called Oshea the
son of Nun Jehoshua.
17 And Moses sent them to spy out the land of Canaan, and said unto them, Get you up this *way* southward, and go up into the mountain:
18 And see the land, what it *is*; and the people that
dwelleth therein, whether they *be* strong or weak,
few or many;
19 And what the land *is* that they dwell in, whether
it *be* good or bad; and what cities *they be* that they
dwell in, whether in tents, or in strong holds;
20 And what the land *is*, whether it *be* fat or lean,
whether there be wood therein, or not. And be ye of
good courage, and bring of the fruit of the land. Now
the time *was* the time of the firstripe grapes.
21 So they went up, and searched the land from the
wilderness of Zin unto Rehob, as men come to
Hamath.
22 And they ascended by the south, and came unto
Hebron; where Ahiman, Sheshai, and Talmai, the

NEW LIVING TRANSLATION

13 So Moses cried out to the LORD, "O God, I beg
you, please heal her!"
14 But the LORD said to Moses, "If her father had
done nothing more than spit in her face, wouldn't
she be defiled for seven days? So keep her outside
the camp for seven days, and after that she may be
accepted back."
15 So Miriam was kept outside the camp for seven
days, and the people waited until she was brought
back before they traveled again. 16 Then they left
Hazeroth and camped in the wilderness of Paran.

Twelve Scouts Explore Canaan

13 The LORD now said to Moses, 2 "Send out men
to explore the land of Canaan, the land I am
giving to the Israelites. Send one leader from each of
the twelve ancestral tribes." 3 So Moses did as the
LORD commanded him. He sent out twelve men, all
tribal leaders of Israel, from their camp in the wilderness of Paran. 4 These were the tribes and the names
of their leaders:

Tribe	*Leader*
Reuben	Shammua son of Zaccur
5 Simeon	Shaphat son of Hori
6 Judah	Caleb son of Jephunneh
7 Issachar	Igal son of Joseph
8 Ephraim	Hoshea son of Nun
9 Benjamin	Palti son of Raphu
10 Zebulun	Gaddiel son of Sodi
11 Manasseh son of Joseph	Gaddi son of Susi
12 Dan	Ammiel son of Gemalli
13 Asher	Sethur son of Michael
14 Naphtali	Nahbi son of Vophsi
15 Gad	Geuel son of Maki

16 These are the names of the men Moses sent out to
explore the land. (Moses called Hoshea son of Nun
by the name Joshua.)
17 Moses gave the men these instructions as he
sent them out to explore the land: "Go north through
the Negev into the hill country. 18 See what the land is
like, and find out whether the people living there are
strong or weak, few or many. 19 See what kind of land
they live in. Is it good or bad? Do their towns have
walls, or are they unprotected like open camps? 20 Is
the soil fertile or poor? Are there many trees? Do
your best to bring back samples of the crops you
see." (It happened to be the season for harvesting the
first ripe grapes.)
21 So they went up and explored the land from the
wilderness of Zin as far as Rehob, near Lebo-
hamath. 22 Going north, they passed through the Negev and arrived at Hebron, where Ahiman, Sheshai,

KING JAMES VERSION

children of Anak, *were*. (Now Hebron was built seven
years before Zoan in Egypt.)
23 And they came unto the brook of Eshcol, and cut
down from thence a branch with one cluster of
grapes, and they bare it between two upon a staff; and
they brought of the pomegranates, and of the figs.
24 The place was called the brook Eshcol, because
of the cluster of grapes which the children of Israel
cut down from thence.

25 And they returned from searching of the land
after forty days.
26 And they went and came to Moses, and to Aaron,
and to all the congregation of the children of Israel,
unto the wilderness of Paran, to Kadesh; and brought
back word unto them, and unto all the congregation,
and shewed them the fruit of the land.
27 And they told him, and said, We came unto the
land whither thou sentest us, and surely it floweth
with milk and honey; and this *is* the fruit of it.
28 Nevertheless the people *be* strong that dwell in
the land, and the cities *are* walled, *and* very great:
and moreover we saw the children of Anak there.
29 The Amalekites dwell in the land of the south:
and the Hittites, and the Jebusites, and the Amorites,
dwell in the mountains: and the Canaanites dwell by
the sea, and by the coast of Jordan.
30 And Caleb stilled the people before Moses, and
said, Let us go up at once, and possess it; for we are
well able to overcome it.
31 But the men that went up with him said, We be
not able to go up against the people; for they *are*
stronger than we.
32 And they brought up an evil report of the land
which they had searched unto the children of Israel,
saying, The land, through which we have gone to
search it, *is* a land that eateth up the inhabitants
thereof; and all the people that we saw in it *are* men
of a great stature.
33 And there we saw the giants, the sons of Anak,
which come of the giants: and we were in our own
sight as grasshoppers, and so we were in their sight.

14 1 And all the congregation lifted up their voice,
and cried; and the people wept that night.
2 And all the children of Israel murmured against
Moses and against Aaron: and the whole congregation said unto them, Would God that we had died in
the land of Egypt! or would God we had died in this
wilderness!
3 And wherefore hath the LORD brought us unto
this land, to fall by the sword, that our wives and our
children should be a prey? were it not better for us to
return into Egypt?
4 And they said one to another, Let us make a captain, and let us return into Egypt.

NEW LIVING TRANSLATION

and Talmai—all descendants of Anak—lived. (The
ancient town of Hebron was founded seven years
before the Egyptian city of Zoan.) 23 When they came
to the valley of Eshcol, they cut down a branch with a
single cluster of grapes so large that it took two of
them to carry it on a pole between them! They also
brought back samples of the pomegranates and figs.
24 That place was called the valley of Eshcol (which
means "cluster"), because of the cluster of grapes the
Israelite men cut there.

The Scouting Report

25 After exploring the land for forty days, the men returned 26 to Moses, Aaron, and the whole community
of Israel at Kadesh in the wilderness of Paran. They
reported to the whole community what they had
seen and showed them the fruit they had taken from
the land. 27 This was their report to Moses: "We entered the land you sent us to explore, and it is indeed
a bountiful country—a land flowing with milk and
honey. Here is the kind of fruit it produces. 28 But the
people living there are powerful, and their towns are
large and fortified. We even saw giants there, the
descendants of Anak! 29 The Amalekites live in the
Negev, and the Hittites, Jebusites, and Amorites live
in the hill country. The Canaanites live along the
coast of the Mediterranean Sea* and along the
Jordan Valley."
30 But Caleb tried to quiet the people as they stood
before Moses. "Let's go at once to take the land," he
said. "We can certainly conquer it!"
31 But the other men who had explored the land
with him disagreed. "We can't go up against them!
They are stronger than we are!" 32 So they spread this
bad report about the land among the Israelites: "The
land we traveled through and explored will devour
anyone who goes to live there. All the people we saw
were huge. 33 We even saw giants* there, the descendants of Anak. Next to them we felt like grasshoppers, and that's what they thought, too!"

The People Rebel

14 Then the whole community began weeping
aloud, and they cried all night. 2 Their voices
rose in a great chorus of protest against Moses and
Aaron. "If only we had died in Egypt, or even here in
the wilderness!" they complained. 3 "Why is the
LORD taking us to this country only to have us die in
battle? Our wives and our little ones will be carried
off as plunder! Wouldn't it be better for us to return
to Egypt?" 4 Then they plotted among themselves,
"Let's choose a new leader and go back to Egypt!"

13:29 Hebrew *the sea.* **13:33** Hebrew *nephilim.*

KING JAMES VERSION

5 Then Moses and Aaron fell on their faces before all the assembly of the congregation of the children of Israel.

6 And Joshua the son of Nun, and Caleb the son of Jephunneh, *which were* of them that searched the land, rent their clothes:

7 And they spake unto all the company of the children of Israel, saying, The land, which we passed through to search it, *is* an exceeding good land.

8 If the LORD delight in us, then he will bring us into this land, and give it us; a land which floweth with milk and honey.

9 Only rebel not ye against the LORD, neither fear ye the people of the land; for they *are* bread for us: their defence is departed from them, and the LORD *is* with us: fear them not.

10 But all the congregation bade stone them with stones. And the glory of the LORD appeared in the tabernacle of the congregation before all the children of Israel.

11 And the LORD said unto Moses, How long will this people provoke me? and how long will it be ere they believe me, for all the signs which I have shewed among them?

12 I will smite them with the pestilence, and disinherit them, and will make of thee a greater nation and mightier than they.

13 And Moses said unto the LORD, Then the Egyptians shall hear *it*, (for thou broughtest up this people in thy might from among them;)

14 And they will tell *it* to the inhabitants of this land: *for* they have heard that thou LORD *art* among this people, that thou LORD art seen face to face, and *that* thy cloud standeth over them, and *that* thou goest before them, by day time in a pillar of a cloud, and in a pillar of fire by night.

15 Now *if* thou shalt kill *all* this people as one man, then the nations which have heard the fame of thee will speak, saying,

16 Because the LORD was not able to bring this people into the land which he sware unto them, therefore he hath slain them in the wilderness.

17 And now, I beseech thee, let the power of my Lord be great, according as thou hast spoken, saying,

18 The LORD *is* longsuffering, and of great mercy, forgiving iniquity and transgression, and by no means clearing *the guilty*, visiting the iniquity of the fathers upon the children unto the third and fourth *generation*.

19 Pardon, I beseech thee, the iniquity of this people according unto the greatness of thy mercy, and as thou hast forgiven this people, from Egypt even until now.

20 And the LORD said, I have pardoned according to thy word:

21 But *as* truly *as* I live, all the earth shall be filled with the glory of the LORD.

22 Because all those men which have seen my glory,

NEW LIVING TRANSLATION

5 Then Moses and Aaron fell face down on the
ground before the whole community of Israel. 6 Two
of the men who had explored the land, Joshua son of
Nun and Caleb son of Jephunneh, tore their clothing.
7 They said to all the people of Israel, "The land we
traveled through and explored is a wonderful land!
8 And if the LORD is pleased with us, he will bring us
safely into that land and give it to us. It is a rich land
flowing with milk and honey. 9 Do not rebel against
the LORD, and don't be afraid of the people of the
land. They are only helpless prey to us! They have no
protection, but the LORD is with us! Don't be afraid
of them!"

10 But the whole community began to talk about
stoning Joshua and Caleb. Then the glorious presence of the LORD appeared to all the Israelites at the
Tabernacle.* 11 And the LORD said to Moses, "How
long will these people treat me with contempt? Will
they never believe me, even after all the miraculous
signs I have done among them? 12 I will disown them
and destroy them with a plague. Then I will make you
into a nation greater and mightier than they are!"

Moses Intercedes for the People

13 But Moses objected. "What will the Egyptians
think when they hear about it?" he asked the LORD.
"They know full well the power you displayed in rescuing your people from Egypt. 14 Now if you destroy
them, the Egyptians will send a report to the inhabitants of this land, who have already heard that you live
among your people. They know, LORD, that you have
appeared to your people face to face and that your
pillar of cloud hovers over them. They know that you
go before them in the pillar of cloud by day and the
pillar of fire by night. 15 Now if you slaughter all these
people with a single blow, the nations that have
heard of your fame will say, 16 'The LORD was not able
to bring them into the land he swore to give them, so
he killed them in the wilderness.'

17 "Please, Lord, prove that your power is as great
as you have claimed. For you said, 18 'The LORD is slow
to anger and filled with unfailing love, forgiving
every kind of sin and rebellion. But he does not excuse the guilty. He lays the sins of the parents upon
their children; the entire family is affected—even
children in the third and fourth generations.' 19 In
keeping with your magnificent, unfailing love, please
pardon the sins of this people, just as you have forgiven them ever since they left Egypt."

20 Then the LORD said, "I will pardon them as you
have requested. 21 But as surely as I live, and as surely
as the earth is filled with the LORD's glory, 22 not one

14:10 Hebrew *the Tent of Meeting*.

and my miracles, which I did in Egypt and in the wilderness, and have tempted me now these ten times, and have not hearkened to my voice;

23 Surely they shall not see the land which I sware unto their fathers, neither shall any of them that provoked me see it:

24 But my servant Caleb, because he had another spirit with him, and hath followed me fully, him will I bring into the land whereinto he went; and his seed shall possess it.

25 (Now the Amalekites and the Canaanites dwelt in the valley.) Tomorrow turn you, and get you into the wilderness by the way of the Red sea.

26 And the LORD spake unto Moses and unto Aaron, saying,

27 How long *shall I bear with* this evil congregation, which murmur against me? I have heard the murmurings of the children of Israel, which they murmur against me.

28 Say unto them, *As truly as* I live, saith the LORD, as ye have spoken in mine ears, so will I do to you:

29 Your carcases shall fall in this wilderness; and all that were numbered of you, according to your whole number, from twenty years old and upward, which have murmured against me,

30 Doubtless ye shall not come into the land, *concerning* which I sware to make you dwell therein, save Caleb the son of Jephunneh, and Joshua the son of Nun.

31 But your little ones, which ye said should be a prey, them will I bring in, and they shall know the land which ye have despised.

32 But *as for* you, your carcases, they shall fall in this wilderness.

33 And your children shall wander in the wilderness forty years, and bear your whoredoms, until your carcases be wasted in the wilderness.

34 After the number of the days in which ye searched the land, *even* forty days, each day for a year, shall ye bear your iniquities, *even* forty years, and ye shall know my breach of promise.

35 I the LORD have said, I will surely do it unto all this evil congregation, that are gathered together against me: in this wilderness they shall be consumed, and there they shall die.

36 And the men, which Moses sent to search the land, who returned, and made all the congregation to murmur against him, by bringing up a slander upon the land,

37 Even those men that did bring up the evil report upon the land, died by the plague before the LORD.

38 But Joshua the son of Nun, and Caleb the son of Jephunneh, *which were* of the men that went to search the land, lived *still*.

of these people will ever enter that land. They have
all seen my glorious presence and the miraculous
signs I performed both in Egypt and in the wilderness, but again and again they have tested me by refusing to listen to my voice. 23 They will never even
see the land I swore to give their ancestors. None of
those who have treated me with contempt will ever
see it. 24 But my servant Caleb has a different attitude
than the others have. He has remained loyal to me, so
I will bring him into the land he explored. His descendants will possess their full share of that land.
25 Now turn around, and don't go on toward the land
where the Amalekites and Canaanites live. Tomorrow you must set out for the wilderness in the direction of the Red Sea.*"

The LORD Punishes the Israelites

26 Then the LORD said to Moses and Aaron, 27 "How
long must I put up with this wicked community and
its complaints about me? Yes, I have heard the complaints the Israelites are making against me. 28 Now
tell them this: 'As surely as I live, declares the LORD, I
will do to you the very things I heard you say. 29 You
will all drop dead in this wilderness! Because you
complained against me, every one of you who is
twenty years old or older and was included in the
registration will die. 30 You will not enter and occupy
the land I swore to give you. The only exceptions will
be Caleb son of Jephunneh and Joshua son of Nun.

31 "'You said your children would be carried off as
plunder. Well, I will bring them safely into the land,
and they will enjoy what you have despised. 32 But as
for you, you will drop dead in this wilderness. 33 And
your children will be like shepherds, wandering in
the wilderness for forty years. In this way, they will
pay for your faithlessness, until the last of you lies
dead in the wilderness.

34 "'Because your men explored the land for forty
days, you must wander in the wilderness for forty
years—a year for each day, suffering the consequences of your sins. Then you will discover what it
is like to have me for an enemy.' 35 I, the LORD, have
spoken! I will certainly do these things to every member of the community who has conspired against me.
They will be destroyed here in this wilderness, and
here they will die!"

36 The ten men Moses had sent to explore the
land—the ones who incited rebellion against the
LORD with their bad report—37 were struck dead
with a plague before the LORD. 38 Of the twelve who
had explored the land, only Joshua and Caleb remained alive.

14:25 Hebrew *sea of reeds.*

KING JAMES VERSION

39 And Moses told these sayings unto all the children of Israel: and the people mourned greatly.

40 And they rose up early in the morning, and gat them up into the top of the mountain, saying, Lo, we *be here*, and will go up unto the place which the LORD hath promised: for we have sinned.

41 And Moses said, Wherefore now do ye transgress the commandment of the LORD? but it shall not prosper.

42 Go not up, for the LORD *is* not among you; that ye be not smitten before your enemies.

43 For the Amalekites and the Canaanites *are* there before you, and ye shall fall by the sword: because ye are turned away from the LORD, therefore the LORD will not be with you.

44 But they presumed to go up unto the hill top: nevertheless the ark of the covenant of the LORD, and Moses, departed not out of the camp.

45 Then the Amalekites came down, and the Canaanites which dwelt in that hill, and smote them, and discomfited them, *even* unto Hormah.

15 1 And the LORD spake unto Moses, saying, 2 Speak unto the children of Israel, and say unto them, When ye be come into the land of your habitations, which I give unto you,

3 And will make an offering by fire unto the LORD, a burnt offering, or a sacrifice in performing a vow, or in a freewill offering, or in your solemn feasts, to make a sweet savour unto the LORD, of the herd, or of the flock:

4 Then shall he that offereth his offering unto the LORD bring a meat offering of a tenth deal of flour mingled with the fourth *part* of an hin of oil.

5 And the fourth *part* of an hin of wine for a drink offering shalt thou prepare with the burnt offering or sacrifice, for one lamb.

6 Or for a ram, thou shalt prepare *for* a meat offering two tenth deals of flour mingled with the third *part* of an hin of oil.

7 And for a drink offering thou shalt offer the third *part* of an hin of wine, *for* a sweet savour unto the LORD.

8 And when thou preparest a bullock *for* a burnt offering, or *for* a sacrifice in performing a vow, or peace offerings unto the LORD:

9 Then shall he bring with a bullock a meat offering of three tenth deals of flour mingled with half an hin of oil.

10 And thou shalt bring for a drink offering half an hin of wine, *for* an offering made by fire, of a sweet savour unto the LORD.

11 Thus shall it be done for one bullock, or for one ram, or for a lamb, or a kid.

12 According to the number that ye shall prepare, so shall ye do to every one according to their number.

13 All that are born of the country shall do these

NEW LIVING TRANSLATION

39 When Moses reported the LORD's words to all the Israelites, the people were filled with grief.
40 Then they got up early the next morning and went to the top of the range of hills. "Let's go," they said. "We realize that we have sinned, but now we are ready to enter the land the LORD has promised us."

41 But Moses said, "Why are you now disobeying the LORD's orders to return to the wilderness? It won't work. 42 Do not go up into the land now. You will only be crushed by your enemies because the LORD is not with you. 43 When you face the Amalekites and Canaanites in battle, you will be slaughtered. The LORD will abandon you because you have abandoned the LORD."

44 But the people defiantly pushed ahead toward the hill country, even though neither Moses nor the Ark of the LORD's Covenant left the camp. 45 Then the Amalekites and the Canaanites who lived in those hills came down and attacked them and chased them back as far as Hormah.

Laws concerning Offerings

15 Then the LORD told Moses, 2 "Give the following instructions to the people of Israel.

"When you finally settle in the land I am giving you, 3 you will offer special gifts as a pleasing aroma to the LORD. These gifts may take the form of a burnt offering, a sacrifice to fulfill a vow, a voluntary offering, or an offering at any of your annual festivals, and they may be taken from your herds of cattle or your flocks of sheep and goats. 4 When you present these offerings, you must also give the LORD a grain offering of two quarts* of choice flour mixed with one quart* of olive oil. 5 For each lamb offered as a burnt offering or a special sacrifice, you must also present one quart of wine as a liquid offering.

6 "If the sacrifice is a ram, give a grain offering of four quarts* of choice flour mixed with a third of a gallon* of olive oil, 7 and give a third of a gallon of wine as a liquid offering. This will be a pleasing aroma to the LORD.

8 "When you present a young bull as a burnt offering or as a sacrifice to fulfill a vow or as a peace offering to the LORD, 9 you must also give a grain offering of six quarts* of choice flour mixed with two quarts* of olive oil, 10 and give two quarts of wine as a liquid offering. This will be a special gift, a pleasing aroma to the LORD.

11 "Each sacrifice of a bull, ram, lamb, or young goat should be prepared in this way. 12 Follow these instructions with each offering you present. 13 All of

15:4a Hebrew *1/10 of an ephah* [2.2 liters]. **15:4b** Hebrew *1/4 of a hin* [1 liter]; also in 15:5. **15:6a** Hebrew *2/10 of an ephah* [4.4 liters]. **15:6b** Hebrew *1/3 of a hin* [1.3 liters]; also in 15:7. **15:9a** Hebrew *3/10 of an ephah* [6.6 liters]. **15:9b** Hebrew *1/2 of a hin* [2 liters]; also in 15:10.

KING JAMES VERSION

things after this manner, in offering an offering
made by fire, of a sweet savour unto the LORD.
14 And if a stranger sojourn with you, or whosoever
be among you in your generations, and will offer an
offering made by fire, of a sweet savour unto the
LORD; as ye do, so he shall do.
15 One ordinance *shall be both* for you of the congregation, and also for the stranger that sojourneth
with you, an ordinance for ever in your generations:
as ye *are*, so shall the stranger be before the LORD.
16 One law and one manner shall be for you, and
for the stranger that sojourneth with you.
17 And the LORD spake unto Moses, saying,
18 Speak unto the children of Israel, and say
unto them, When ye come into the land whither I
bring you,
19 Then it shall be, that, when ye eat of the bread
of the land, ye shall offer up an heave offering unto
the LORD.
20 Ye shall offer up a cake of the first of your dough
for an heave offering: as *ye do* the heave offering of
the threshingfloor, so shall ye heave it.
21 Of the first of your dough ye shall give unto the
LORD an heave offering in your generations.
22 And if ye have erred, and not observed all these
commandments, which the LORD hath spoken unto
Moses,
23 *Even* all that the LORD hath commanded you by
the hand of Moses, from the day that the LORD commanded *Moses*, and henceforward among your generations;
24 Then it shall be, if *aught* be committed by ignorance without the knowledge of the congregation,
that all the congregation shall offer one young bullock for a burnt offering, for a sweet savour unto the
LORD, with his meat offering, and his drink offering,
according to the manner, and one kid of the goats for
a sin offering.
25 And the priest shall make an atonement for all
the congregation of the children of Israel, and it
shall be forgiven them; for it *is* ignorance: and they
shall bring their offering, a sacrifice made by fire
unto the LORD, and their sin offering before the LORD,
for their ignorance:
26 And it shall be forgiven all the congregation of
the children of Israel, and the stranger that
sojourneth among them; seeing all the people *were*
in ignorance.
27 And if any soul sin through ignorance, then
he shall bring a she goat of the first year for a sin
offering.
28 And the priest shall make an atonement for the
soul that sinneth ignorantly, when he sinneth by ignorance before the LORD, to make an atonement for
him; and it shall be forgiven him.
29 Ye shall have one law for him that sinneth
through ignorance, *both for* him that is born among

NEW LIVING TRANSLATION

you native-born Israelites must follow these instructions when you offer a special gift as a pleasing
aroma to the LORD. 14 And if any foreigners visit you
or live among you and want to present a special gift
as a pleasing aroma to the LORD, they must follow
these same procedures. 15 Native-born Israelites and
foreigners are equal before the LORD and are subject
to the same decrees. This is a permanent law for you,
to be observed from generation to generation. 16 The
same instructions and regulations will apply both to
you and to the foreigners living among you."
17 Then the LORD said to Moses, 18 "Give the following instructions to the people of Israel.
"When you arrive in the land where I am taking
you, 19 and you eat the crops that grow there, you
must set some aside as a sacred offering to the LORD.
20 Present a cake from the first of the flour you grind,
and set it aside as a sacred offering, as you do with
the first grain from the threshing floor. 21 Throughout the generations to come, you are to present a sacred offering to the LORD each year from the first of
your ground flour.
22 "But suppose you unintentionally fail to carry
out all these commands that the LORD has given you
through Moses. 23 And suppose your descendants in
the future fail to do everything the LORD has commanded through Moses. 24 If the mistake was made
unintentionally, and the community was unaware of
it, the whole community must present a young bull
for a burnt offering as a pleasing aroma to the LORD.
It must be offered along with its prescribed grain offering and liquid offering and with one male goat for
a sin offering. 25 With it the priest will purify the
whole community of Israel, making them right with
the LORD,* and they will be forgiven. For it was an unintentional sin, and they have corrected it with their
offerings to the LORD—the special gift and the sin
offering. 26 The whole community of Israel will be
forgiven, including the foreigners living among you,
for all the people were involved in the sin.
27 "If one individual commits an unintentional sin,
the guilty person must bring a one-year-old female
goat for a sin offering. 28 The priest will sacrifice it to
purify* the guilty person before the LORD, and that
person will be forgiven. 29 These same instructions
apply both to native-born Israelites and to the foreigners living among you.

15:25 Or *will make atonement for the whole community of Israel.*
15:28 Or *to make atonement for.*

KING JAMES VERSION

the children of Israel, and for the stranger that sojourneth among them.

30But the soul that doeth *aught* presumptuously, *whether he be* born in the land, or a stranger, the same reproacheth the LORD; and that soul shall be cut off from among his people.

31Because he hath despised the word of the LORD, and hath broken his commandment, that soul shall utterly be cut off; his iniquity *shall be* upon him.

32And while the children of Israel were in the wilderness, they found a man that gathered sticks upon the sabbath day.

33And they that found him gathering sticks brought him unto Moses and Aaron, and unto all the congregation.

34And they put him in ward, because it was not declared what should be done to him.

35And the LORD said unto Moses, The man shall be surely put to death: all the congregation shall stone him with stones without the camp.

36And all the congregation brought him without the camp, and stoned him with stones, and he died; as the LORD commanded Moses.

37And the LORD spake unto Moses, saying,

38Speak unto the children of Israel, and bid them that they make them fringes in the borders of their garments throughout their generations, and that they put upon the fringe of the borders a ribband of blue:

39And it shall be unto you for a fringe, that ye may look upon it, and remember all the commandments of the LORD, and do them; and that ye seek not after your own heart and your own eyes, after which ye use to go a whoring:

40That ye may remember, and do all my commandments, and be holy unto your God.

41I *am* the LORD your God, which brought you out of the land of Egypt, to be your God: I *am* the LORD your God.

16 1Now Korah, the son of Izhar, the son of Kohath, the son of Levi, and Dathan and Abiram, the sons of Eliab, and On, the son of Peleth, sons of Reuben, took *men:*

2And they rose up before Moses, with certain of the children of Israel, two hundred and fifty princes of the assembly, famous in the congregation, men of renown:

3And they gathered themselves together against Moses and against Aaron, and said unto them, *Ye take* too much upon you, seeing all the congregation *are* holy, every one of them, and the LORD *is* among them: wherefore then lift ye up yourselves above the congregation of the LORD?

4And when Moses heard *it,* he fell upon his face:

5And he spake unto Korah and unto all his company, saying, Even tomorrow the LORD will shew who *are* his, and *who is* holy; and will cause *him* to come

NEW LIVING TRANSLATION

30"But those who brazenly violate the LORD's will, whether native-born Israelites or foreigners, have blasphemed the LORD, and they must be cut off from the community. 31Since they have treated the LORD's word with contempt and deliberately disobeyed his command, they must be completely cut off and suffer the punishment for their guilt."

Penalty for Breaking the Sabbath

32One day while the people of Israel were in the wilderness, they discovered a man gathering wood on the Sabbath day. 33The people who found him doing this took him before Moses, Aaron, and the rest of the community. 34They held him in custody because they did not know what to do with him. 35Then the LORD said to Moses, "The man must be put to death! The whole community must stone him outside the camp." 36So the whole community took the man outside the camp and stoned him to death, just as the LORD had commanded Moses.

Tassels on Clothing

37Then the LORD said to Moses, 38"Give the following instructions to the people of Israel: Throughout the generations to come you must make tassels for the hems of your clothing and attach them with a blue cord. 39When you see the tassels, you will remember and obey all the commands of the LORD instead of following your own desires and defiling yourselves, as you are prone to do. 40The tassels will help you remember that you must obey all my commands and be holy to your God. 41I am the LORD your God who brought you out of the land of Egypt that I might be your God. I am the LORD your God!"

Korah's Rebellion

16 One day Korah son of Izhar, a descendant of Kohath son of Levi, conspired with Dathan and Abiram, the sons of Eliab, and On son of Peleth, from the tribe of Reuben. 2They incited a rebellion against Moses, along with 250 other leaders of the community, all prominent members of the assembly. 3They united against Moses and Aaron and said, "You have gone too far! The whole community of Israel has been set apart by the LORD, and he is with all of us. What right do you have to act as though you are greater than the rest of the LORD's people?"

4When Moses heard what they were saying, he fell face down on the ground. 5Then he said to Korah and his followers, "Tomorrow morning the LORD will show us who belongs to him* and who is holy. The

16:5 Greek version reads *God has visited and knows those who are his.* Compare 2 Tim 2:19.

KING JAMES VERSION

near unto him: even *him* whom he hath chosen will
he cause to come near unto him.
6This do; Take you censers, Korah, and all his
company;
7And put fire therein, and put incense in them before the LORD tomorrow: and it shall be *that* the man
whom the LORD doth choose, he *shall be* holy: *ye
take* too much upon you, ye sons of Levi.
8And Moses said unto Korah, Hear, I pray you, ye
sons of Levi:
9*Seemeth it but* a small thing unto you, that the
God of Israel hath separated you from the congregation of Israel, to bring you near to himself to
do the service of the tabernacle of the LORD, and
to stand before the congregation to minister unto
them?
10And he hath brought thee near *to him,* and all
thy brethren the sons of Levi with thee: and seek ye
the priesthood also?
11For which cause *both* thou and all thy company
are gathered together against the LORD: and what *is*
Aaron, that ye murmur against him?
12And Moses sent to call Dathan and Abiram, the
sons of Eliab: which said, We will not come up:
13*Is it* a small thing that thou hast brought us up
out of a land that floweth with milk and honey, to
kill us in the wilderness, except thou make thyself
altogether a prince over us?
14Moreover thou hast not brought us into a land
that floweth with milk and honey, or given us inheritance of fields and vineyards: wilt thou put out the
eyes of these men? we will not come up.
15And Moses was very wroth, and said unto the
LORD, Respect not thou their offering: I have not
taken one ass from them, neither have I hurt one of
them.
16And Moses said unto Korah, Be thou and all thy
company before the LORD, thou, and they, and Aaron,
tomorrow:
17And take every man his censer, and put incense
in them, and bring ye before the LORD every man his
censer, two hundred and fifty censers; thou also, and
Aaron, each *of you* his censer.
18And they took every man his censer, and put fire
in them, and laid incense thereon, and stood in the
door of the tabernacle of the congregation with
Moses and Aaron.
19And Korah gathered all the congregation against
them unto the door of the tabernacle of the congregation: and the glory of the LORD appeared unto all
the congregation.
20And the LORD spake unto Moses and unto Aaron,
saying,
21Separate yourselves from among this congregation, that I may consume them in a moment.
22And they fell upon their faces, and said, O God,
the God of the spirits of all flesh, shall one man sin,
and wilt thou be wroth with all the congregation?

NEW LIVING TRANSLATION

LORD will allow only those whom he selects to enter
his own presence. 6Korah, you and all your followers
must prepare your incense burners. 7Light fires in
them tomorrow, and burn incense before the LORD.
Then we will see whom the LORD chooses as his holy
one. You Levites are the ones who have gone too far!"
8Then Moses spoke again to Korah: "Now listen,
you Levites! 9Does it seem insignificant to you that
the God of Israel has chosen you from among all the
community of Israel to be near him so you can serve
in the LORD's Tabernacle and stand before the people
to minister to them? 10Korah, he has already given
this special ministry to you and your fellow Levites.
Are you now demanding the priesthood as well?
11The LORD is the one you and your followers are
really revolting against! For who is Aaron that you are
complaining about him?"
12Then Moses summoned Dathan and Abiram, the
sons of Eliab, but they replied, "We refuse to come before you! 13Isn't it enough that you brought us out of
Egypt, a land flowing with milk and honey, to kill us
here in this wilderness, and that you now treat us like
your subjects? 14What's more, you haven't brought us
into another land flowing with milk and honey. You
haven't given us a new homeland with fields and vineyards. Are you trying to fool these men?* We will not
come."
15Then Moses became very angry and said to the
LORD, "Do not accept their grain offerings! I have not
taken so much as a donkey from them, and I have
never hurt a single one of them." 16And Moses said to
Korah, "You and all your followers must come here
tomorrow and present yourselves before the LORD.
Aaron will also be here. 17You and each of your
250 followers must prepare an incense burner and
put incense on it, so you can all present them before
the LORD. Aaron will also bring his incense burner."
18So each of these men prepared an incense
burner, lit the fire, and placed incense on it. Then
they all stood at the entrance of the Tabernacle* with
Moses and Aaron. 19Meanwhile, Korah had stirred up
the entire community against Moses and Aaron, and
they all gathered at the Tabernacle entrance. Then
the glorious presence of the LORD appeared to the
whole community, 20and the LORD said to Moses and
Aaron, 21"Get away from all these people so that I
may instantly destroy them!"
22But Moses and Aaron fell face down on the
ground. "O God," they pleaded, "you are the God who
gives breath to all creatures. Must you be angry with
all the people when only one man sins?"

16:14 Hebrew *Are you trying to put out the eyes of these men?*
16:18 Hebrew *the Tent of Meeting;* also in 16:19, 42, 43, 50.

KING JAMES VERSION

23 And the LORD spake unto Moses, saying,

24 Speak unto the congregation, saying, Get you up from about the tabernacle of Korah, Dathan, and Abiram.

25 And Moses rose up and went unto Dathan and Abiram; and the elders of Israel followed him.

26 And he spake unto the congregation, saying, Depart, I pray you, from the tents of these wicked men, and touch nothing of theirs, lest ye be consumed in all their sins.

27 So they gat up from the tabernacle of Korah, Dathan, and Abiram, on every side: and Dathan and Abiram came out, and stood in the door of their tents, and their wives, and their sons, and their little children.

28 And Moses said, Hereby ye shall know that the LORD hath sent me to do all these works; for *I have* not *done them* of mine own mind.

29 If these men die the common death of all men, or if they be visited after the visitation of all men; *then* the LORD hath not sent me.

30 But if the LORD make a new thing, and the earth open her mouth, and swallow them up, with all that *appertain* unto them, and they go down quick into the pit; then ye shall understand that these men have provoked the LORD.

31 And it came to pass, as he had made an end of speaking all these words, that the ground clave asunder that *was* under them:

32 And the earth opened her mouth, and swallowed them up, and their houses, and all the men that *appertained* unto Korah, and all *their* goods.

33 They, and all that *appertained* to them, went down alive into the pit, and the earth closed upon them: and they perished from among the congregation.

34 And all Israel that *were* round about them fled at the cry of them: for they said, Lest the earth swallow us up *also.*

35 And there came out a fire from the LORD, and consumed the two hundred and fifty men that offered incense.

36 And the LORD spake unto Moses, saying,

37 Speak unto Eleazar the son of Aaron the priest, that he take up the censers out of the burning, and scatter thou the fire yonder; for they are hallowed.

38 The censers of these sinners against their own souls, let them make them broad plates *for* a covering of the altar: for they offered them before the LORD, therefore they are hallowed: and they shall be a sign unto the children of Israel.

39 And Eleazar the priest took the brasen censers, wherewith they that were burnt had offered; and they were made broad *plates for* a covering of the altar:

40 *To be* a memorial unto the children of Israel, that no stranger, which *is* not of the seed of Aaron, come near to offer incense before the LORD; that he be not

NEW LIVING TRANSLATION

23 And the LORD said to Moses, 24 "Then tell all the
people to get away from the tents of Korah, Dathan,
and Abiram."

25 So Moses got up and rushed over to the tents of
Dathan and Abiram, followed by the elders of Israel.
26 "Quick!" he told the people. "Get away from the
tents of these wicked men, and don't touch anything
that belongs to them. If you do, you will be destroyed
for their sins." 27 So all the people stood back from
the tents of Korah, Dathan, and Abiram. Then
Dathan and Abiram came out and stood at the entrances of their tents, together with their wives and
children and little ones.

28 And Moses said, "This is how you will know that
the LORD has sent me to do all these things that I have
done—for I have not done them on my own. 29 If
these men die a natural death, or if nothing unusual
happens, then the LORD has not sent me. 30 But if the
LORD does something entirely new and the ground
opens its mouth and swallows them and all their belongings, and they go down alive into the grave,*
then you will know that these men have shown contempt for the LORD."

31 He had hardly finished speaking the words
when the ground suddenly split open beneath them.
32 The earth opened its mouth and swallowed the
men, along with their households and all their followers who were standing with them, and everything
they owned. 33 So they went down alive into the
grave, along with all their belongings. The earth
closed over them, and they all vanished from among
the people of Israel. 34 All the people around them
fled when they heard their screams. "The earth will
swallow us, too!" they cried. 35 Then fire blazed forth
from the LORD and burned up the 250 men who
were offering incense.

36 *And the LORD said to Moses, 37 "Tell Eleazar son
of Aaron the priest to pull all the incense burners
from the fire, for they are holy. Also tell him to scatter
the burning coals. 38 Take the incense burners of
these men who have sinned at the cost of their lives,
and hammer the metal into a thin sheet to overlay
the altar. Since these burners were used in the LORD's
presence, they have become holy. Let them serve as a
warning to the people of Israel."

39 So Eleazar the priest collected the 250 bronze
incense burners that had been used by the men who
died in the fire, and he hammered them into a thin
sheet to overlay the altar. 40 This would warn the Israelites that no unauthorized person—no one who was
not a descendant of Aaron—should ever enter the
LORD's presence to burn incense. If anyone did, the
same thing would happen to him as happened to Korah and his followers. So the LORD's instructions to
Moses were carried out.

16:30 Hebrew *into Sheol;* also in 16:33. **16:36** Verses 16:36-50 are numbered 17:1-15 in Hebrew text.

KING JAMES VERSION

as Korah, and as his company: as the LORD said to him by the hand of Moses.

41But on the morrow all the congregation of the children of Israel murmured against Moses and against Aaron, saying, Ye have killed the people of the LORD.

42And it came to pass, when the congregation was gathered against Moses and against Aaron, that they looked toward the tabernacle of the congregation: and, behold, the cloud covered it, and the glory of the LORD appeared.

43And Moses and Aaron came before the tabernacle of the congregation.

44And the LORD spake unto Moses, saying,

45Get you up from among this congregation, that I may consume them as in a moment. And they fell upon their faces.

46And Moses said unto Aaron, Take a censer, and put fire therein from off the altar, and put on incense, and go quickly unto the congregation, and make an atonement for them: for there is wrath gone out from the LORD; the plague is begun.

47And Aaron took as Moses commanded, and ran into the midst of the congregation; and, behold, the plague was begun among the people: and he put on incense, and made an atonement for the people.

48And he stood between the dead and the living; and the plague was stayed.

49Now they that died in the plague were fourteen thousand and seven hundred, beside them that died about the matter of Korah.

50And Aaron returned unto Moses unto the door of the tabernacle of the congregation: and the plague was stayed.

17 1And the LORD spake unto Moses, saying,

2Speak unto the children of Israel, and take of every one of them a rod according to the house of *their* fathers, of all their princes according to the house of their fathers twelve rods: write thou every man's name upon his rod.

3And thou shalt write Aaron's name upon the rod of Levi: for one rod *shall be* for the head of the house of their fathers.

4And thou shalt lay them up in the tabernacle of the congregation before the testimony, where I will meet with you.

5And it shall come to pass, *that* the man's rod, whom I shall choose, shall blossom: and I will make to cease from me the murmurings of the children of Israel, whereby they murmur against you.

6And Moses spake unto the children of Israel, and every one of their princes gave him a rod apiece, for each prince one, according to their fathers' houses, *even* twelve rods: and the rod of Aaron *was* among their rods.

7And Moses laid up the rods before the LORD in the tabernacle of witness.

NEW LIVING TRANSLATION

41But the very next morning the whole community of Israel began muttering again against Moses
and Aaron, saying, "You have killed the LORD's
people!" 42As the community gathered to protest
against Moses and Aaron, they turned toward the
Tabernacle and saw that the cloud had covered it,
and the glorious presence of the LORD appeared.
43Moses and Aaron came and stood in front of
the Tabernacle, 44and the LORD said to Moses, 45"Get
away from all these people so that I can instantly
destroy them!" But Moses and Aaron fell face down
on the ground.
46And Moses said to Aaron, "Quick, take an incense burner and place burning coals on it from the
altar. Lay incense on it, and carry it out among the
people to purify them and make them right with
the LORD.* The LORD's anger is blazing against
them—the plague has already begun."
47Aaron did as Moses told him and ran out among
the people. The plague had already begun to strike
down the people, but Aaron burned the incense and
purified* the people. 48He stood between the dead
and the living, and the plague stopped. 49But 14,700
people died in that plague, in addition to those who
had died in the affair involving Korah. 50Then because the plague had stopped, Aaron returned to
Moses at the entrance of the Tabernacle.

The Budding of Aaron's Staff

17 1*Then the LORD said to Moses, 2"Tell the
people of Israel to bring you twelve wooden
staffs, one from each leader of Israel's ancestral
tribes, and inscribe each leader's name on his staff.
3Inscribe Aaron's name on the staff of the tribe of
Levi, for there must be one staff for the leader of each
ancestral tribe. 4Place these staffs in the Tabernacle
in front of the Ark containing the tablets of the Covenant,* where I meet with you. 5Buds will sprout on
the staff belonging to the man I choose. Then I will
finally put an end to the people's murmuring and
complaining against you."
6So Moses gave the instructions to the people of
Israel, and each of the twelve tribal leaders, including Aaron, brought Moses a staff. 7Moses placed the
staffs in the LORD's presence in the Tabernacle of the

16:46 Or *to make atonement for them.* **16:47** Or *and made atonement for.* **17:1** Verses 17:1-13 are numbered 17:16-28 in Hebrew text. **17:4** Hebrew *in the Tent of Meeting before the Testimony.* The Hebrew word for "testimony" refers to the terms of the LORD's covenant with Israel as written on stone tablets, which were kept in the Ark, and also to the covenant itself.

KING JAMES VERSION

8And it came to pass, that on the morrow Moses went into the tabernacle of witness; and, behold, the rod of Aaron for the house of Levi was budded, and brought forth buds, and bloomed blossoms, and yielded almonds.

9And Moses brought out all the rods from before the LORD unto all the children of Israel: and they looked, and took every man his rod.

10And the LORD said unto Moses, Bring Aaron's rod again before the testimony, to be kept for a token against the rebels; and thou shalt quite take away their murmurings from me, that they die not.

11And Moses did *so*: as the LORD commanded him, so did he.

12And the children of Israel spake unto Moses, saying, Behold, we die, we perish, we all perish.

13Whosoever cometh any thing near unto the tabernacle of the LORD shall die: shall we be consumed with dying?

18 1And the LORD said unto Aaron, Thou and thy sons and thy father's house with thee shall bear the iniquity of the sanctuary: and thou and thy sons with thee shall bear the iniquity of your priesthood.

2And thy brethren also of the tribe of Levi, the tribe of thy father, bring thou with thee, that they may be joined unto thee, and minister unto thee: but thou and thy sons with thee *shall minister* before the tabernacle of witness.

3And they shall keep thy charge, and the charge of all the tabernacle: only they shall not come nigh the vessels of the sanctuary and the altar, that neither they, nor ye also, die.

4And they shall be joined unto thee, and keep the charge of the tabernacle of the congregation, for all the service of the tabernacle: and a stranger shall not come nigh unto you.

5And ye shall keep the charge of the sanctuary, and the charge of the altar: that there be no wrath any more upon the children of Israel.

6And I, behold, I have taken your brethren the Levites from among the children of Israel: to you *they are* given *as* a gift for the LORD, to do the service of the tabernacle of the congregation.

7Therefore thou and thy sons with thee shall keep your priest's office for every thing of the altar, and within the vail; and ye shall serve: I have given your priest's office *unto you as* a service of gift: and the stranger that cometh nigh shall be put to death.

8And the LORD spake unto Aaron, Behold, I also have given thee the charge of mine heave offerings of all the hallowed things of the children of Israel; unto thee have I given them by reason of the anointing, and to thy sons, by an ordinance for ever.

NEW LIVING TRANSLATION

Covenant.* 8When he went into the Tabernacle of the Covenant the next day, he found that Aaron's staff, representing the tribe of Levi, had sprouted, budded, blossomed, and produced ripe almonds!

9When Moses brought all the staffs out from the LORD's presence, he showed them to the people. Each man claimed his own staff. 10And the LORD said to Moses: "Place Aaron's staff permanently before the Ark of the Covenant* to serve as a warning to rebels. This should put an end to their complaints against me and prevent any further deaths." 11So Moses did as the LORD commanded him.

12Then the people of Israel said to Moses, "Look, we are doomed! We are dead! We are ruined! 13Everyone who even comes close to the Tabernacle of the LORD dies. Are we all doomed to die?"

Duties of Priests and Levites

18 Then the LORD said to Aaron: "You, your sons, and your relatives from the tribe of Levi will be held responsible for any offenses related to the sanctuary. But you and your sons alone will be held responsible for violations connected with the priesthood.

2"Bring your relatives of the tribe of Levi—your ancestral tribe—to assist you and your sons as you perform the sacred duties in front of the Tabernacle of the Covenant.* 3But as the Levites go about all their assigned duties at the Tabernacle, they must be careful not to go near any of the sacred objects or the altar. If they do, both you and they will die. 4The Levites must join you in fulfilling their responsibilities for the care and maintenance of the Tabernacle,* but no unauthorized person may assist you.

5"You yourselves must perform the sacred duties inside the sanctuary and at the altar. If you follow these instructions, the LORD's anger will never again blaze against the people of Israel. 6I myself have chosen your fellow Levites from among the Israelites to be your special assistants. They are a gift to you, dedicated to the LORD for service in the Tabernacle. 7But you and your sons, the priests, must personally handle all the priestly rituals associated with the altar and with everything behind the inner curtain. I am giving you the priesthood as your special privilege of service. Any unauthorized person who comes too near the sanctuary will be put to death."

Support for the Priests and Levites

8The LORD gave these further instructions to Aaron: "I myself have put you in charge of all the holy offerings that are brought to me by the people of Israel. I have given all these consecrated offerings to you and

17:7 Or *Tabernacle of the Testimony;* also in 17:8. **17:10** Hebrew *before the Testimony;* see note on 17:4. **18:2** Or *Tabernacle of the Testimony.* **18:4** Hebrew *the Tent of Meeting;* also in 18:6, 21, 22, 23, 31.

KING JAMES VERSION

9 This shall be thine of the most holy things, *reserved* from the fire: every oblation of theirs, every meat offering of theirs, and every sin offering of theirs, and every trespass offering of theirs which they shall render unto me, *shall be* most holy for thee and for thy sons.

10 In the most holy *place* shalt thou eat it; every male shall eat it: it shall be holy unto thee.

11 And this *is* thine; the heave offering of their gift, with all the wave offerings of the children of Israel: I have given them unto thee, and to thy sons and to thy daughters with thee, by a statute for ever: every one that is clean in thy house shall eat of it.

12 All the best of the oil, and all the best of the wine, and of the wheat, the firstfruits of them which they shall offer unto the LORD, them have I given thee.

13 *And* whatsoever is first ripe in the land, which they shall bring unto the LORD, shall be thine; every one that is clean in thine house shall eat *of* it.

14 Every thing devoted in Israel shall be thine.

15 Every thing that openeth the matrix in all flesh, which they bring unto the LORD, *whether it be* of men or beasts, shall be thine: nevertheless the firstborn of man shalt thou surely redeem, and the firstling of unclean beasts shalt thou redeem.

16 And those that are to be redeemed from a month old shalt thou redeem, according to thine estimation, for the money of five shekels, after the shekel of the sanctuary, which *is* twenty gerahs.

17 But the firstling of a cow, or the firstling of a sheep, or the firstling of a goat, thou shalt not redeem; they *are* holy: thou shalt sprinkle their blood upon the altar, and shalt burn their fat *for* an offering made by fire, for a sweet savour unto the LORD.

18 And the flesh of them shall be thine, as the wave breast and as the right shoulder are thine.

19 All the heave offerings of the holy things, which the children of Israel offer unto the LORD, have I given thee, and thy sons and thy daughters with thee, by a statute for ever: it *is* a covenant of salt for ever before the LORD unto thee and to thy seed with thee.

20 And the LORD spake unto Aaron, Thou shalt have no inheritance in their land, neither shalt thou have any part among them: I *am* thy part and thine inheritance among the children of Israel.

21 And, behold, I have given the children of Levi all the tenth in Israel for an inheritance, for their service which they serve, *even* the service of the tabernacle of the congregation.

22 Neither must the children of Israel henceforth come nigh the tabernacle of the congregation, lest they bear sin, and die.

23 But the Levites shall do the service of the tabernacle of the congregation, and they shall bear their iniquity: *it shall be* a statute for ever throughout your generations, that among the children of Israel they have no inheritance.

NEW LIVING TRANSLATION

your sons as your permanent share. 9 You are allotted the portion of the most holy offerings that is not burned on the fire. This portion of all the most holy offerings—including the grain offerings, sin offerings, and guilt offerings—will be most holy, and it belongs to you and your sons. 10 You must eat it as a most holy offering. All the males may eat of it, and you must treat it as most holy.

11 "All the sacred offerings and special offerings presented to me when the Israelites lift them up before the altar also belong to you. I have given them to you and to your sons and daughters as your permanent share. Any member of your family who is ceremonially clean may eat of these offerings.

12 "I also give you the harvest gifts brought by the people as offerings to the LORD—the best of the olive oil, new wine, and grain. 13 All the first crops of their land that the people present to the LORD belong to you. Any member of your family who is ceremonially clean may eat this food.

14 "Everything in Israel that is specially set apart for the LORD* also belongs to you.

15 "The firstborn of every mother, whether human or animal, that is offered to the LORD will be yours. But you must always redeem your firstborn sons and the firstborn of ceremonially unclean animals. 16 Redeem them when they are one month old. The redemption price is five pieces of silver* (as measured by the weight of the sanctuary shekel, which equals twenty gerahs).

17 "However, you may not redeem the firstborn of cattle, sheep, or goats. They are holy and have been set apart for the LORD. Sprinkle their blood on the altar, and burn their fat as a special gift, a pleasing aroma to the LORD. 18 The meat of these animals will be yours, just like the breast and right thigh that are presented by lifting them up as a special offering before the altar. 19 Yes, I am giving you all these holy offerings that the people of Israel bring to the LORD. They are for you and your sons and daughters, to be eaten as your permanent share. This is an eternal and unbreakable covenant* between the LORD and you, and it also applies to your descendants."

20 And the LORD said to Aaron, "You priests will receive no allotment of land or share of property among the people of Israel. I am your share and your allotment. 21 As for the tribe of Levi, your relatives, I will compensate them for their service in the Tabernacle. Instead of an allotment of land, I will give them the tithes from the entire land of Israel.

22 "From now on, no Israelites except priests or Levites may approach the Tabernacle. If they come too near, they will be judged guilty and will die. 23 Only the Levites may serve at the Tabernacle, and they will be held responsible for any offenses against it. This is a

18:14 The Hebrew term used here refers to the complete consecration of things or people to the LORD, either by destroying them or by giving them as an offering. **18:16** Hebrew *5 shekels* [2 ounces or 57 grams] *of silver.* **18:19** Hebrew *a covenant of salt.*

KING JAMES VERSION

24 But the tithes of the children of Israel, which they offer *as* an heave offering unto the LORD, I have given to the Levites to inherit: therefore I have said unto them, Among the children of Israel they shall have no inheritance.

25 And the LORD spake unto Moses, saying,

26 Thus speak unto the Levites, and say unto them, When ye take of the children of Israel the tithes which I have given you from them for your inheritance, then ye shall offer up an heave offering of it for the LORD, *even* a tenth *part* of the tithe.

27 And *this* your heave offering shall be reckoned unto you, as though *it were* the corn of the threshingfloor, and as the fulness of the winepress.

28 Thus ye also shall offer an heave offering unto the LORD of all your tithes, which ye receive of the children of Israel; and ye shall give thereof the LORD'S heave offering to Aaron the priest.

29 Out of all your gifts ye shall offer every heave offering of the LORD, of all the best thereof, *even* the hallowed part thereof out of it.

30 Therefore thou shalt say unto them, When ye have heaved the best thereof from it, then it shall be counted unto the Levites as the increase of the threshingfloor, and as the increase of the winepress.

31 And ye shall eat it in every place, ye and your households: for it *is* your reward for your service in the tabernacle of the congregation.

32 And ye shall bear no sin by reason of it, when ye have heaved from it the best of it: neither shall ye pollute the holy things of the children of Israel, lest ye die.

19 1 And the LORD spake unto Moses and unto Aaron, saying,

2 This *is* the ordinance of the law which the LORD hath commanded, saying, Speak unto the children of Israel, that they bring thee a red heifer without spot, wherein *is* no blemish, *and* upon which never came yoke:

3 And ye shall give her unto Eleazar the priest, that he may bring her forth without the camp, and *one* shall slay her before his face:

4 And Eleazar the priest shall take of her blood with his finger, and sprinkle of her blood directly before the tabernacle of the congregation seven times:

5 And *one* shall burn the heifer in his sight; her skin, and her flesh, and her blood, with her dung, shall he burn:

6 And the priest shall take cedar wood, and hyssop, and scarlet, and cast *it* into the midst of the burning of the heifer.

7 Then the priest shall wash his clothes, and he shall bathe his flesh in water, and afterward he shall come into the camp, and the priest shall be unclean until the even.

8 And he that burneth her shall wash his clothes in

NEW LIVING TRANSLATION

permanent law for you, to be observed from generation to generation. The Levites will receive no allotment of land among the Israelites,
24 because I have
given them the Israelites' tithes, which have been presented as sacred offerings to the LORD. This will be the Levites' share. That is why I said they would receive no allotment of land among the Israelites."

25 The LORD also told Moses,
26 "Give these instructions to the Levites: When you receive from the people of Israel the tithes I have assigned as your allotment, give a tenth of the tithes you receive—a tithe of the tithe—to the LORD as a sacred offering.
27 The LORD will consider this offering to be your harvest offering, as though it were the first grain from your own threshing floor or wine from your own winepress.
28 You must present one-tenth of the tithe received from the Israelites as a sacred offering to the LORD. This is the LORD's sacred portion, and you must present it to Aaron the priest.
29 Be sure to give to the LORD the best portions of the gifts given to you.

30 "Also, give these instructions to the Levites: When you present the best part as your offering, it will be considered as though it came from your own threshing floor or winepress.
31 You Levites and your families may eat this food anywhere you wish, for it is your compensation for serving in the Tabernacle.
32 You will not be considered guilty for accepting the LORD's tithes if you give the best portion to the priests. But be careful not to treat the holy gifts of the people of Israel as though they were common. If you do, you will die."

The Water of Purification

19 The LORD said to Moses and Aaron,
2 "Here is another legal requirement commanded by the LORD: Tell the people of Israel to bring you a red heifer, a perfect animal that has no defects and has never been yoked to a plow.
3 Give it to Eleazar the priest, and it will be taken outside the camp and slaughtered in his presence.
4 Eleazar will take some of its blood on his finger and sprinkle it seven times toward the front of the Tabernacle.*
5 As Eleazar watches, the heifer must be burned—its hide, meat, blood, and dung.
6 Eleazar the priest must then take a stick of cedar,* a hyssop branch, and some scarlet yarn and throw them into the fire where the heifer is burning.

7 "Then the priest must wash his clothes and bathe himself in water. Afterward he may return to the camp, though he will remain ceremonially unclean until evening.
8 The man who burns the animal must

19:4 Hebrew *the Tent of Meeting.* 19:6 Or *juniper.*

KING JAMES VERSION

water, and bathe his flesh in water, and shall be unclean until the even.
9 And a man *that is* clean shall gather up the ashes
of the heifer, and lay *them* up without the camp in a
clean place, and it shall be kept for the congregation
of the children of Israel for a water of separation: it *is*
a purification for sin.
10 And he that gathereth the ashes of the heifer
shall wash his clothes, and be unclean until the even:
and it shall be unto the children of Israel, and unto
the stranger that sojourneth among them, for a statute for ever.
11 He that toucheth the dead body of any man shall
be unclean seven days.
12 He shall purify himself with it on the third day,
and on the seventh day he shall be clean: but if he
purify not himself the third day, then the seventh day
he shall not be clean.
13 Whosoever toucheth the dead body of any man
that is dead, and purifieth not himself, defileth the
tabernacle of the LORD; and that soul shall be cut off
from Israel: because the water of separation was
not sprinkled upon him, he shall be unclean; his
uncleanness *is* yet upon him.
14 This *is* the law, when a man dieth in a tent: all
that come into the tent, and all that *is* in the tent,
shall be unclean seven days.
15 And every open vessel, which hath no covering
bound upon it, *is* unclean.
16 And whosoever toucheth one that is slain with a
sword in the open fields, or a dead body, or a bone of
a man, or a grave, shall be unclean seven days.
17 And for an unclean *person* they shall take of the
ashes of the burnt heifer of purification for sin, and
running water shall be put thereto in a vessel:
18 And a clean person shall take hyssop, and dip *it*
in the water, and sprinkle *it* upon the tent, and upon
all the vessels, and upon the persons that were there,
and upon him that touched a bone, or one slain, or
one dead, or a grave:
19 And the clean *person* shall sprinkle upon the unclean on the third day, and on the seventh day: and
on the seventh day he shall purify himself, and wash
his clothes, and bathe himself in water, and shall be
clean at even.
20 But the man that shall be unclean, and shall not
purify himself, that soul shall be cut off from among
the congregation, because he hath defiled the sanctuary of the LORD: the water of separation hath not
been sprinkled upon him; he *is* unclean.
21 And it shall be a perpetual statute unto them,
that he that sprinkleth the water of separation shall
wash his clothes; and he that toucheth the water of
separation shall be unclean until even.

NEW LIVING TRANSLATION

also wash his clothes and bathe himself in water, and
he, too, will remain unclean until evening. 9 Then
someone who is ceremonially clean will gather up
the ashes of the heifer and deposit them in a purified
place outside the camp. They will be kept there for
the community of Israel to use in the water for the
purification ceremony. This ceremony is performed
for the removal of sin. 10 The man who gathers up the
ashes of the heifer must also wash his clothes, and he
will remain ceremonially unclean until evening. This
is a permanent law for the people of Israel and any
foreigners who live among them.
11 "All those who touch a dead human body will be
ceremonially unclean for seven days. 12 They must
purify themselves on the third and seventh days with
the water of purification; then they will be purified.
But if they do not do this on the third and seventh
days, they will continue to be unclean even after the
seventh day. 13 All those who touch a dead body and
do not purify themselves in the proper way defile
the LORD's Tabernacle, and they will be cut off from
the community of Israel. Since the water of purification was not sprinkled on them, their defilement
continues.
14 "This is the ritual law that applies when someone dies inside a tent: All those who enter that tent
and those who were inside when the death occurred
will be ceremonially unclean for seven days. 15 Any
open container in the tent that was not covered with
a lid is also defiled. 16 And if someone in an open
field touches the corpse of someone who was killed
with a sword or who died a natural death, or if someone touches a human bone or a grave, that person
will be defiled for seven days.
17 "To remove the defilement, put some of the
ashes from the burnt purification offering in a jar,
and pour fresh water over them. 18 Then someone
who is ceremonially clean must take a hyssop branch
and dip it into the water. That person must sprinkle
the water on the tent, on all the furnishings in the
tent, and on the people who were in the tent; also on
the person who touched a human bone, or touched
someone who was killed or who died naturally, or
touched a grave. 19 On the third and seventh days the
person who is ceremonially clean must sprinkle the
water on those who are defiled. Then on the seventh
day the people being cleansed must wash their
clothes and bathe themselves, and that evening they
will be cleansed of their defilement.
20 "But those who become defiled and do not purify themselves will be cut off from the community,
for they have defiled the sanctuary of the LORD. Since
the water of purification has not been sprinkled on
them, they remain defiled. 21 This is a permanent law
for the people. Those who sprinkle the water of purification must afterward wash their clothes, and anyone who then touches the water used for purification

KING JAMES VERSION

22And whatsoever the unclean *person* toucheth shall be unclean; and the soul that toucheth *it* shall be unclean until even.

20 1Then came the children of Israel, *even* the whole congregation, into the desert of Zin in the first month: and the people abode in Kadesh; and Miriam died there, and was buried there.

2And there was no water for the congregation: and they gathered themselves together against Moses and against Aaron.

3And the people chode with Moses, and spake, saying, Would God that we had died when our brethren died before the LORD!

4And why have ye brought up the congregation of the LORD into this wilderness, that we and our cattle should die there?

5And wherefore have ye made us to come up out of Egypt, to bring us in unto this evil place? it *is* no place of seed, or of figs, or of vines, or of pomegranates; neither *is* there any water to drink.

6And Moses and Aaron went from the presence of the assembly unto the door of the tabernacle of the congregation, and they fell upon their faces: and the glory of the LORD appeared unto them.

7And the LORD spake unto Moses, saying,

8Take the rod, and gather thou the assembly together, thou, and Aaron thy brother, and speak ye unto the rock before their eyes; and it shall give forth his water, and thou shalt bring forth to them water out of the rock: so thou shalt give the congregation and their beasts drink.

9And Moses took the rod from before the LORD, as he commanded him.

10And Moses and Aaron gathered the congregation together before the rock, and he said unto them, Hear now, ye rebels; must we fetch you water out of this rock?

11And Moses lifted up his hand, and with his rod he smote the rock twice: and the water came out abundantly, and the congregation drank, and their beasts *also*.

12And the LORD spake unto Moses and Aaron, Because ye believed me not, to sanctify me in the eyes of the children of Israel, therefore ye shall not bring this congregation into the land which I have given them.

13This *is* the water of Meribah, because the children of Israel strove with the LORD, and he was sanctified in them.

14And Moses sent messengers from Kadesh unto the king of Edom, Thus saith thy brother Israel, Thou knowest all the travail that hath befallen us:

15How our fathers went down into Egypt, and we

NEW LIVING TRANSLATION

will remain defiled until evening. 22Anything and anyone that a defiled person touches will be ceremonially unclean until evening."

Moses Strikes the Rock

20 In the first month of the year,* the whole community of Israel arrived in the wilderness of Zin and camped at Kadesh. While they were there, Miriam died and was buried.

2There was no water for the people to drink at that place, so they rebelled against Moses and Aaron. 3The people blamed Moses and said, "If only we had died in the LORD's presence with our brothers! 4Why have you brought the congregation of the LORD's people into this wilderness to die, along with all our livestock? 5Why did you make us leave Egypt and bring us here to this terrible place? This land has no grain, no figs, no grapes, no pomegranates, and no water to drink!"

6Moses and Aaron turned away from the people and went to the entrance of the Tabernacle,* where they fell face down on the ground. Then the glorious presence of the LORD appeared to them, 7and the LORD said to Moses, 8"You and Aaron must take the staff and assemble the entire community. As the people watch, speak to the rock over there, and it will pour out its water. You will provide enough water from the rock to satisfy the whole community and their livestock."

9So Moses did as he was told. He took the staff from the place where it was kept before the LORD. 10Then he and Aaron summoned the people to come and gather at the rock. "Listen, you rebels!" he shouted. "Must we bring you water from this rock?" 11Then Moses raised his hand and struck the rock twice with the staff, and water gushed out. So the entire community and their livestock drank their fill.

12But the LORD said to Moses and Aaron, "Because you did not trust me enough to demonstrate my holiness to the people of Israel, you will not lead them into the land I am giving them!" 13This place was known as the waters of Meribah (which means "arguing") because there the people of Israel argued with the LORD, and there he demonstrated his holiness among them.

Edom Refuses Israel Passage

14While Moses was at Kadesh, he sent ambassadors to the king of Edom with this message:

"This is what your relatives, the people of Israel, say: You know all the hardships we have been through. 15Our ancestors went down to Egypt,

20:1 The first month of the ancient Hebrew lunar calendar usually occurs within the months of March and April. The number of years since leaving Egypt is not specified. **20:6** Hebrew *the Tent of Meeting.*

KING JAMES VERSION

have dwelt in Egypt a long time; and the Egyptians
vexed us, and our fathers:
16And when we cried unto the LORD, he heard our
voice, and sent an angel, and hath brought us forth
out of Egypt: and, behold, we *are* in Kadesh, a city in
the uttermost of thy border:
17Let us pass, I pray thee, through thy country: we
will not pass through the fields, or through the vineyards, neither will we drink *of* the water of the wells:
we will go by the king's *high* way, we will not turn to
the right hand nor to the left, until we have passed
thy borders.
18And Edom said unto him, Thou shalt not pass by
me, lest I come out against thee with the sword.
19And the children of Israel said unto him, We will
go by the high way: and if I and my cattle drink of thy
water, then I will pay for it: I will only, without *doing*
any thing *else,* go through on my feet.
20And he said, Thou shalt not go through. And
Edom came out against him with much people, and
with a strong hand.
21Thus Edom refused to give Israel passage through
his border: wherefore Israel turned away from him.

22And the children of Israel, *even* the whole congregation, journeyed from Kadesh, and came unto
mount Hor.
23And the LORD spake unto Moses and Aaron in
mount Hor, by the coast of the land of Edom, saying,
24Aaron shall be gathered unto his people: for he
shall not enter into the land which I have given unto
the children of Israel, because ye rebelled against my
word at the water of Meribah.
25Take Aaron and Eleazar his son, and bring them
up unto mount Hor:
26And strip Aaron of his garments, and put them
upon Eleazar his son: and Aaron shall be gathered
unto his people, and shall die there.
27And Moses did as the LORD commanded: and
they went up into mount Hor in the sight of all the
congregation.
28And Moses stripped Aaron of his garments, and
put them upon Eleazar his son; and Aaron died there
in the top of the mount: and Moses and Eleazar came
down from the mount.
29And when all the congregation saw that Aaron
was dead, they mourned for Aaron thirty days, *even*
all the house of Israel.

21 1And *when* king Arad the Canaanite, which
dwelt in the south, heard tell that Israel
came by the way of the spies; then he fought against
Israel, and took *some* of them prisoners.
2And Israel vowed a vow unto the LORD, and said, If
thou wilt indeed deliver this people into my hand,
then I will utterly destroy their cities.

NEW LIVING TRANSLATION

and we lived there a long time, and we and
our ancestors were brutally mistreated by the
Egyptians. 16But when we cried out to the LORD,
he heard us and sent an angel who brought us out
of Egypt. Now we are camped at Kadesh, a town
on the border of your land. 17Please let us travel
through your land. We will be careful not to go
through your fields and vineyards. We won't even
drink water from your wells. We will stay on the
king's road and never leave it until we have passed
through your territory."
18But the king of Edom said, "Stay out of my land,
or I will meet you with an army!"
19The Israelites answered, "We will stay on the
main road. If our livestock drink your water, we will
pay for it. Just let us pass through your country. That's
all we ask."
20But the king of Edom replied, "Stay out! You may
not pass through our land." With that he mobilized
his army and marched out against them with an imposing force. 21Because Edom refused to allow Israel
to pass through their country, Israel was forced to
turn around.

The Death of Aaron

22The whole community of Israel left Kadesh and arrived at Mount Hor. 23There, on the border of the
land of Edom, the LORD said to Moses and Aaron,
24"The time has come for Aaron to join his ancestors
in death. He will not enter the land I am giving the
people of Israel, because the two of you rebelled
against my instructions concerning the water at
Meribah. 25Now take Aaron and his son Eleazar up
Mount Hor. 26There you will remove Aaron's priestly
garments and put them on Eleazar, his son. Aaron
will die there and join his ancestors."
27So Moses did as the LORD commanded. The
three of them went up Mount Hor together as the
whole community watched. 28At the summit, Moses
removed the priestly garments from Aaron and put
them on Eleazar, Aaron's son. Then Aaron died there
on top of the mountain, and Moses and Eleazar went
back down. 29When the people realized that Aaron
had died, all Israel mourned for him thirty days.

Victory over the Canaanites

21 The Canaanite king of Arad, who lived in the
Negev, heard that the Israelites were approaching on the road through Atharim. So he attacked the Israelites and took some of them as
prisoners. 2Then the people of Israel made this vow
to the LORD: "If you will hand these people over to us,

KING JAMES VERSION

3And the LORD hearkened to the voice of Israel,
and delivered up the Canaanites; and they utterly destroyed them and their cities: and he called the name
of the place Hormah.

4And they journeyed from mount Hor by the way
of the Red sea, to compass the land of Edom: and the
soul of the people was much discouraged because of
the way.

5And the people spake against God, and against
Moses, Wherefore have ye brought us up out of
Egypt to die in the wilderness? for *there is* no bread,
neither *is there any* water; and our soul loatheth this
light bread.

6And the LORD sent fiery serpents among the
people, and they bit the people; and much people of
Israel died.

7Therefore the people came to Moses, and said,
We have sinned, for we have spoken against the
LORD, and against thee; pray unto the LORD, that he
take away the serpents from us. And Moses prayed
for the people.

8And the LORD said unto Moses, Make thee a fiery
serpent, and set it upon a pole: and it shall come to
pass, that every one that is bitten, when he looketh
upon it, shall live.

9And Moses made a serpent of brass, and put it
upon a pole, and it came to pass, that if a serpent had
bitten any man, when he beheld the serpent of brass,
he lived.

10And the children of Israel set forward, and
pitched in Oboth.

11And they journeyed from Oboth, and pitched at
Ije-abarim, in the wilderness which *is* before Moab,
toward the sunrising.

12From thence they removed, and pitched in the
valley of Zared.

13From thence they removed, and pitched on the
other side of Arnon, which *is* in the wilderness that
cometh out of the coasts of the Amorites: for Arnon
is the border of Moab, between Moab and the
Amorites.

14Wherefore it is said in the book of the wars of
the LORD, What he did in the Red sea, and in the
brooks of Arnon,

15And at the stream of the brooks that goeth down
to the dwelling of Ar, and lieth upon the border of
Moab.

16And from thence *they went* to Beer: that *is* the
well whereof the LORD spake unto Moses, Gather the
people together, and I will give them water.

17Then Israel sang this song, Spring up, O well;
sing ye unto it:

18The princes digged the well, the nobles of the
people digged it, by *the direction of* the lawgiver,

NEW LIVING TRANSLATION

we will completely destroy* all their towns." 3The
LORD heard the Israelites' request and gave them victory over the Canaanites. The Israelites completely
destroyed them and their towns, and the place has
been called Hormah* ever since.

The Bronze Snake

4Then the people of Israel set out from Mount Hor,
taking the road to the Red Sea* to go around the land
of Edom. But the people grew impatient with the
long journey, 5and they began to speak against God
and Moses. "Why have you brought us out of Egypt to
die here in the wilderness?" they complained.
"There is nothing to eat here and nothing to drink.
And we hate this horrible manna!"

6So the LORD sent poisonous snakes among the
people, and many were bitten and died. 7Then the
people came to Moses and cried out, "We have
sinned by speaking against the LORD and against you.
Pray that the LORD will take away the snakes." So
Moses prayed for the people.

8Then the LORD told him, "Make a replica of a poisonous snake and attach it to a pole. All who are bitten will live if they simply look at it!" 9So Moses
made a snake out of bronze and attached it to a pole.
Then anyone who was bitten by a snake could look at
the bronze snake and be healed!

Israel's Journey to Moab

10The Israelites traveled next to Oboth and camped
there. 11Then they went on to Iye-abarim, in the wilderness on the eastern border of Moab. 12From there
they traveled to the valley of Zered Brook and set up
camp. 13Then they moved out and camped on the far
side of the Arnon River, in the wilderness adjacent
to the territory of the Amorites. The Arnon is the
boundary line between the Moabites and the Amorites. 14For this reason *The Book of the Wars of the
LORD* speaks of "the town of Waheb in the area of
Suphah, and the ravines of the Arnon River, 15and the
ravines that extend as far as the settlement of Ar on
the border of Moab."

16From there the Israelites traveled to Beer,*
which is the well where the LORD said to Moses, "Assemble the people, and I will give them water."
17There the Israelites sang this song:

"Spring up, O well!
Yes, sing its praises!
18 Sing of this well,
which princes dug,

21:2 The Hebrew term used here refers to the complete consecration of things or people to the LORD, either by destroying them or by giving them as an offering; also in 21:3. **21:3** *Hormah* means "destruction." **21:4** Hebrew *sea of reeds.* **21:16** *Beer* means "well."

with their staves. And from the wilderness *they went*
to Mattanah:
19And from Mattanah to Nahaliel: and from Nahaliel to Bamoth:
20And from Bamoth *in* the valley that *is* in the
country of Moab, to the top of Pisgah, which looketh
toward Jeshimon.

21And Israel sent messengers unto Sihon king of
the Amorites, saying,
22Let me pass through thy land: we will not turn
into the fields, or into the vineyards; we will not
drink *of* the waters of the well: *but* we will go along
by the king's *high* way, until we be past thy borders.
23And Sihon would not suffer Israel to pass
through his border: but Sihon gathered all his people
together, and went out against Israel into the wilderness: and he came to Jahaz, and fought against Israel.
24And Israel smote him with the edge of the
sword, and possessed his land from Arnon unto
Jabbok, even unto the children of Ammon: for the
border of the children of Ammon *was* strong.
25And Israel took all these cities: and Israel dwelt
in all the cities of the Amorites, in Heshbon, and in
all the villages thereof.
26For Heshbon *was* the city of Sihon the king of
the Amorites, who had fought against the former
king of Moab, and taken all his land out of his hand,
even unto Arnon.
27Wherefore they that speak in proverbs say,
Come into Heshbon, let the city of Sihon be built and
prepared:
28For there is a fire gone out of Heshbon, a flame
from the city of Sihon: it hath consumed Ar of Moab,
and the lords of the high places of Arnon.
29Woe to thee, Moab! thou art undone, O people of
Chemosh: he hath given his sons that escaped, and
his daughters, into captivity unto Sihon king of the
Amorites.
30We have shot at them; Heshbon is perished even
unto Dibon, and we have laid them waste even unto
Nophah, which *reacheth* unto Medeba.
31Thus Israel dwelt in the land of the Amorites.
32And Moses sent to spy out Jaazer, and they took
the villages thereof, and drove out the Amorites that
were there.
33And they turned and went up by the way of Bashan: and Og the king of Bashan went out against
them, he, and all his people, to the battle at Edrei.

which great leaders hollowed out
with their scepters and staffs."

Then the Israelites left the wilderness and proceeded on through Mattanah, 19Nahaliel, and Bamoth. 20After that they went to the valley in Moab
where Pisgah Peak overlooks the wasteland.*

Victory over Sihon and Og

21The Israelites sent ambassadors to King Sihon of
the Amorites with this message:

22"Let us travel through your land. We will be
careful not to go through your fields and
vineyards. We won't even drink water from your
wells. We will stay on the king's road until we
have passed through your territory."

23But King Sihon refused to let them cross his
territory. Instead, he mobilized his entire army and
attacked Israel in the wilderness, engaging them in
battle at Jahaz. 24But the Israelites slaughtered them
with their swords and occupied their land from the
Arnon River to the Jabbok River. They went only as
far as the Ammonite border because the boundary of
the Ammonites was fortified.*
25So Israel captured all the towns of the Amorites
and settled in them, including the city of Heshbon
and its surrounding villages. 26Heshbon had been
the capital of King Sihon of the Amorites. He had defeated a former Moabite king and seized all his land
as far as the Arnon River. 27Therefore, the ancient
poets wrote this about him:

"Come to Heshbon and let it be rebuilt!
Let the city of Sihon be restored.
28 A fire flamed forth from Heshbon,
a blaze from the city of Sihon.
It burned the city of Ar in Moab;
it destroyed the rulers of the Arnon heights.
29 What sorrow awaits you, O people of Moab!
You are finished, O worshipers of Chemosh!
Chemosh has left his sons as refugees,
his daughters as captives of Sihon, the Amorite
king.
30 We have utterly destroyed them,
from Heshbon to Dibon.
We have completely wiped them out
as far away as Nophah and Medeba.*"

31So the people of Israel occupied the territory of
the Amorites. 32After Moses sent men to explore the
Jazer area, they captured all the towns in the region
and drove out the Amorites who lived there. 33Then
they turned and marched up the road to Bashan, but
King Og of Bashan and all his people attacked them

21:20 Or *overlooks Jeshimon.* **21:24** Or *because the terrain of the Ammonite frontier was rugged;* Hebrew reads *because the boundary of the Ammonites was strong.* **21:30** Or *until fire spread to Medeba.* The meaning of the Hebrew is uncertain.

KING JAMES VERSION

34And the LORD said unto Moses, Fear him not: for I have delivered him into thy hand, and all his people, and his land; and thou shalt do to him as thou didst unto Sihon king of the Amorites, which dwelt at Heshbon.

35So they smote him, and his sons, and all his people, until there was none left him alive: and they possessed his land.

22 1And the children of Israel set forward, and pitched in the plains of Moab on this side Jordan *by* Jericho.

2And Balak the son of Zippor saw all that Israel had done to the Amorites.

3And Moab was sore afraid of the people, because they *were* many: and Moab was distressed because of the children of Israel.

4And Moab said unto the elders of Midian, Now shall this company lick up all *that are* round about us, as the ox licketh up the grass of the field. And Balak the son of Zippor *was* king of the Moabites at that time.

5He sent messengers therefore unto Balaam the son of Beor to Pethor, which *is* by the river of the land of the children of his people, to call him, saying, Behold, there is a people come out from Egypt: behold, they cover the face of the earth, and they abide over against me:

6Come now therefore, I pray thee, curse me this people; for they *are* too mighty for me: peradventure I shall prevail, *that* we may smite them, and *that* I may drive them out of the land: for I wot that he whom thou blessest *is* blessed, and he whom thou cursest is cursed.

7And the elders of Moab and the elders of Midian departed with the rewards of divination in their hand; and they came unto Balaam, and spake unto him the words of Balak.

8And he said unto them, Lodge here this night, and I will bring you word again, as the LORD shall speak unto me: and the princes of Moab abode with Balaam.

9And God came unto Balaam, and said, What men *are* these with thee?

10And Balaam said unto God, Balak the son of Zippor, king of Moab, hath sent unto me, *saying*,

11Behold, *there is* a people come out of Egypt, which covereth the face of the earth: come now, curse me them; peradventure I shall be able to overcome them, and drive them out.

12And God said unto Balaam, Thou shalt not go with them; thou shalt not curse the people: for they *are* blessed.

13And Balaam rose up in the morning, and said unto the princes of Balak, Get you into your land: for the LORD refuseth to give me leave to go with you.

14And the princes of Moab rose up, and they went unto Balak, and said, Balaam refuseth to come with us.

NEW LIVING TRANSLATION

at Edrei. 34The LORD said to Moses, "Do not be afraid
of him, for I have handed him over to you, along with
all his people and his land. Do the same to him as
you did to King Sihon of the Amorites, who ruled in
Heshbon." 35And Israel killed King Og, his sons, and
all his subjects; not a single survivor remained. Then
Israel occupied their land.

Balak Sends for Balaam

22 Then the people of Israel traveled to the plains of Moab and camped east of the Jordan River, across from Jericho. 2Balak son of Zippor,
the Moabite king, had seen everything the Israelites
did to the Amorites. 3And when the people of Moab
saw how many Israelites there were, they were terrified. 4The king of Moab said to the elders of Midian,
"This mob will devour everything in sight, like an ox
devours grass in the field!"

So Balak, king of Moab, 5sent messengers to call
Balaam son of Beor, who was living in his native land
of Pethor* near the Euphrates River.* His message
said:

"Look, a vast horde of people has arrived from
Egypt. They cover the face of the earth and are
threatening me. 6Please come and curse these
people for me because they are too powerful
for me. Then perhaps I will be able to conquer
them and drive them from the land. I know that
blessings fall on any people you bless, and curses
fall on people you curse."

7Balak's messengers, who were elders of Moab
and Midian, set out with money to pay Balaam to
place a curse upon Israel.* They went to Balaam and
delivered Balak's message to him. 8"Stay here overnight," Balaam said. "In the morning I will tell you
whatever the LORD directs me to say." So the officials
from Moab stayed there with Balaam.

9That night God came to Balaam and asked him,
"Who are these men visiting you?"

10Balaam said to God, "Balak son of Zippor, king of
Moab, has sent me this message: 11'Look, a vast horde
of people has arrived from Egypt, and they cover the
face of the earth. Come and curse these people for
me. Then perhaps I will be able to stand up to them
and drive them from the land.'"

12But God told Balaam, "Do not go with them. You
are not to curse these people, for they have been
blessed!"

13The next morning Balaam got up and told Balak's officials, "Go on home! The LORD will not let me
go with you."

14So the Moabite officials returned to King Balak
and reported, "Balaam refused to come with us."

22:5a Or *who was at Pethor in the land of the Amavites.* **22:5b** Hebrew *the river.* **22:7** Hebrew *set out with the money of divination in their hand.*

KING JAMES VERSION

15And Balak sent yet again princes, more, and
more honourable than they.
16And they came to Balaam, and said to him, Thus
saith Balak the son of Zippor, Let nothing, I pray thee,
hinder thee from coming unto me:
17For I will promote thee unto very great honour,
and I will do whatsoever thou sayest unto me: come
therefore, I pray thee, curse me this people.
18And Balaam answered and said unto the servants of Balak, If Balak would give me his house full
of silver and gold, I cannot go beyond the word of the
LORD my God, to do less or more.
19Now therefore, I pray you, tarry ye also here this
night, that I may know what the LORD will say unto
me more.
20And God came unto Balaam at night, and said
unto him, If the men come to call thee, rise up, *and*
go with them; but yet the word which I shall say unto
thee, that shalt thou do.
21And Balaam rose up in the morning, and saddled
his ass, and went with the princes of Moab.
22And God's anger was kindled because he went:
and the angel of the LORD stood in the way for an
adversary against him. Now he was riding upon his
ass, and his two servants *were* with him.
23And the ass saw the angel of the LORD standing
in the way, and his sword drawn in his hand: and
the ass turned aside out of the way, and went into the
field: and Balaam smote the ass, to turn her into
the way.
24But the angel of the LORD stood in a path of
the vineyards, a wall *being* on this side, and a wall on
that side.
25And when the ass saw the angel of the LORD, she
thrust herself unto the wall, and crushed Balaam's
foot against the wall: and he smote her again.
26And the angel of the LORD went further, and
stood in a narrow place, where *was* no way to turn
either to the right hand or to the left.
27And when the ass saw the angel of the LORD, she
fell down under Balaam: and Balaam's anger was
kindled, and he smote the ass with a staff.
28And the LORD opened the mouth of the ass, and
she said unto Balaam, What have I done unto thee,
that thou hast smitten me these three times?
29And Balaam said unto the ass, Because thou hast
mocked me: I would there were a sword in mine
hand, for now would I kill thee.
30And the ass said unto Balaam, *Am* not I thine ass,
upon which thou hast ridden ever since *I was* thine
unto this day? was I ever wont to do so unto thee?
And he said, Nay.
31Then the LORD opened the eyes of Balaam, and
he saw the angel of the LORD standing in the way, and
his sword drawn in his hand: and he bowed down his
head, and fell flat on his face.
32And the angel of the LORD said unto him,

NEW LIVING TRANSLATION

15Then Balak tried again. This time he sent a larger
number of even more distinguished officials than
those he had sent the first time. 16They went to Balaam and delivered this message to him:

"This is what Balak son of Zippor says: Please
don't let anything stop you from coming to help
me. 17I will pay you very well and do whatever you
tell me. Just come and curse these people for me!"

18But Balaam responded to Balak's messengers,
"Even if Balak were to give me his palace filled with
silver and gold, I would be powerless to do anything
against the will of the LORD my God. 19But stay here
one more night, and I will see if the LORD has anything else to say to me."
20That night God came to Balaam and told him,
"Since these men have come for you, get up and go
with them. But do only what I tell you to do."

Balaam and His Donkey

21So the next morning Balaam got up, saddled his
donkey, and started off with the Moabite officials.
22But God was angry that Balaam was going, so he
sent the angel of the LORD to stand in the road to
block his way. As Balaam and two servants were riding along, 23Balaam's donkey saw the angel of the
LORD standing in the road with a drawn sword in his
hand. The donkey bolted off the road into a field, but
Balaam beat it and turned it back onto the road.
24Then the angel of the LORD stood at a place where
the road narrowed between two vineyard walls.
25When the donkey saw the angel of the LORD, it
tried to squeeze by and crushed Balaam's foot
against the wall. So Balaam beat the donkey again.
26Then the angel of the LORD moved farther down
the road and stood in a place too narrow for the donkey to get by at all. 27This time when the donkey saw
the angel, it lay down under Balaam. In a fit of rage
Balaam beat the animal again with his staff.
28Then the LORD gave the donkey the ability to
speak. "What have I done to you that deserves your
beating me three times?" it asked Balaam.
29"You have made me look like a fool!" Balaam
shouted. "If I had a sword with me, I would kill you!"
30"But I am the same donkey you have ridden all
your life," the donkey answered. "Have I ever done
anything like this before?"

"No," Balaam admitted.
31Then the LORD opened Balaam's eyes, and he
saw the angel of the LORD standing in the roadway
with a drawn sword in his hand. Balaam bowed his
head and fell face down on the ground before him.
32"Why did you beat your donkey those three

KING JAMES VERSION

Wherefore hast thou smitten thine ass these three
times? behold, I went out to withstand thee, because
thy way is perverse before me:
33 And the ass saw me, and turned from me these
three times: unless she had turned from me, surely
now also I had slain thee, and saved her alive.
34 And Balaam said unto the angel of the LORD, I
have sinned; for I knew not that thou stoodest in the
way against me: now therefore, if it displease thee,
I will get me back again.
35 And the angel of the LORD said unto Balaam, Go
with the men: but only the word that I shall speak
unto thee, that thou shalt speak. So Balaam went
with the princes of Balak.
36 And when Balak heard that Balaam was come, he
went out to meet him unto a city of Moab, which *is* in
the border of Arnon, which *is* in the utmost coast.
37 And Balak said unto Balaam, Did I not earnestly
send unto thee to call thee? wherefore camest thou
not unto me? am I not able indeed to promote thee
to honour?
38 And Balaam said unto Balak, Lo, I am come unto
thee: have I now any power at all to say any thing? the
word that God putteth in my mouth, that shall I
speak.
39 And Balaam went with Balak, and they came
unto Kirjath-huzoth.
40 And Balak offered oxen and sheep, and sent to
Balaam, and to the princes that *were* with him.
41 And it came to pass on the morrow, that Balak
took Balaam, and brought him up into the high
places of Baal, that thence he might see the utmost
part of the people.

23 1 And Balaam said unto Balak, Build me here
seven altars, and prepare me here seven
oxen and seven rams.
2 And Balak did as Balaam had spoken; and Balak
and Balaam offered on *every* altar a bullock and a
ram.
3 And Balaam said unto Balak, Stand by thy burnt
offering, and I will go: peradventure the LORD will
come to meet me: and whatsoever he sheweth me I
will tell thee. And he went to an high place.
4 And God met Balaam: and he said unto him, I
have prepared seven altars, and I have offered upon
every altar a bullock and a ram.
5 And the LORD put a word in Balaam's mouth, and
said, Return unto Balak, and thus thou shalt speak.
6 And he returned unto him, and, lo, he stood by his
burnt sacrifice, he, and all the princes of Moab.
7 And he took up his parable, and said, Balak the
king of Moab hath brought me from Aram, out of the
mountains of the east, *saying*, Come, curse me Jacob,
and come, defy Israel.

NEW LIVING TRANSLATION

times?" the angel of the LORD demanded. "Look, I
have come to block your way because you are stubbornly resisting me. 33 Three times the donkey saw
me and shied away; otherwise, I would certainly have
killed you by now and spared the donkey."
34 Then Balaam confessed to the angel of the LORD,
"I have sinned. I didn't realize you were standing in
the road to block my way. I will return home if you
are against my going."
35 But the angel of the LORD told Balaam, "Go with
these men, but say only what I tell you to say." So
Balaam went on with Balak's officials. 36 When King
Balak heard that Balaam was on the way, he went out
to meet him at a Moabite town on the Arnon River at
the farthest border of his land.
37 "Didn't I send you an urgent invitation? Why
didn't you come right away?" Balak asked Balaam.
"Didn't you believe me when I said I would reward
you richly?"
38 Balaam replied, "Look, now I have come, but I
have no power to say whatever I want. I will speak
only the message that God puts in my mouth." 39 Then
Balaam accompanied Balak to Kiriath-huzoth,
40 where the king sacrificed cattle and sheep. He sent
portions of the meat to Balaam and the officials who
were with him. 41 The next morning Balak took Balaam up to Bamoth-baal. From there he could see
some of the people of Israel spread out below him.

Balaam Blesses Israel

23 Then Balaam said to King Balak, "Build me
seven altars here, and prepare seven young
bulls and seven rams for me to sacrifice." 2 Balak followed his instructions, and the two of them sacrificed a young bull and a ram on each altar.
3 Then Balaam said to Balak, "Stand here by your
burnt offerings, and I will go to see if the LORD will
respond to me. Then I will tell you whatever he reveals to me." So Balaam went alone to the top of a
bare hill, 4 and God met him there. Balaam said to
him, "I have prepared seven altars and have sacrificed a young bull and a ram on each altar."
5 The LORD gave Balaam a message for King Balak.
Then he said, "Go back to Balak and give him my
message."
6 So Balaam returned and found the king standing
beside his burnt offerings with all the officials of
Moab. 7 This was the message Balaam delivered:

"Balak summoned me to come from Aram;
the king of Moab brought me from the eastern
hills.
'Come,' he said, 'curse Jacob for me!
Come and announce Israel's doom.'

KING JAMES VERSION

8 How shall I curse, whom God hath not cursed? or how shall I defy, *whom* the LORD hath not defied?

9 For from the top of the rocks I see him, and from the hills I behold him: lo, the people shall dwell alone, and shall not be reckoned among the nations.

10 Who can count the dust of Jacob, and the number of the fourth *part* of Israel? Let me die the death of the righteous, and let my last end be like his!

11 And Balak said unto Balaam, What hast thou done unto me? I took thee to curse mine enemies, and, behold, thou hast blessed *them* altogether.

12 And he answered and said, Must I not take heed to speak that which the LORD hath put in my mouth?

13 And Balak said unto him, Come, I pray thee, with me unto another place, from whence thou mayest see them: thou shalt see but the utmost part of them, and shalt not see them all: and curse me them from thence.

14 And he brought him into the field of Zophim, to the top of Pisgah, and built seven altars, and offered a bullock and a ram on *every* altar.

15 And he said unto Balak, Stand here by thy burnt offering, while I meet *the LORD yonder.*

16 And the LORD met Balaam, and put a word in his mouth, and said, Go again unto Balak, and say thus.

17 And when he came to him, behold, he stood by his burnt offering, and the princes of Moab with him. And Balak said unto him, What hath the LORD spoken?

18 And he took up his parable, and said, Rise up, Balak, and hear; hearken unto me, thou son of Zippor:

19 God *is* not a man, that he should lie; neither the son of man, that he should repent: hath he said, and shall he not do *it?* or hath he spoken, and shall he not make it good?

20 Behold, I have received *commandment* to bless: and he hath blessed; and I cannot reverse it.

21 He hath not beheld iniquity in Jacob, neither hath he seen perverseness in Israel: the LORD his God *is* with him, and the shout of a king *is* among them.

22 God brought them out of Egypt; he hath as it were the strength of an unicorn.

23 Surely *there is* no enchantment against Jacob, neither *is there* any divination against Israel: according to this time it shall be said of Jacob and of Israel, What hath God wrought!

NEW LIVING TRANSLATION

8 But how can I curse those
whom God has not cursed?
How can I condemn those
whom the LORD has not condemned?
9 I see them from the cliff tops;
I watch them from the hills.
I see a people who live by themselves,
set apart from other nations.
10 Who can count Jacob's descendants,
as numerous as dust?
Who can count even a fourth of Israel's
people?
Let me die like the righteous;
let my life end like theirs."

11 Then King Balak demanded of Balaam, "What have you done to me? I brought you to curse my enemies. Instead, you have blessed them!"

12 But Balaam replied, "I will speak only the message that the LORD puts in my mouth."

Balaam's Second Message

13 Then King Balak told him, "Come with me to another place. There you will see another part of the
nation of Israel, but not all of them. Curse at least that
many!" 14 So Balak took Balaam to the plateau of Zophim on Pisgah Peak. He built seven altars there and offered a young bull and a ram on each altar.

15 Then Balaam said to the king, "Stand here by your burnt offerings while I go over there to meet the LORD."

16 And the LORD met Balaam and gave him a message. Then he said, "Go back to Balak and give him my message."

17 So Balaam returned and found the king standing beside his burnt offerings with all the officials of Moab. "What did the LORD say?" Balak asked eagerly.

18 This was the message Balaam delivered:

"Rise up, Balak, and listen!
Hear me, son of Zippor.
19 God is not a man, so he does not lie.
He is not human, so he does not change
his mind.
Has he ever spoken and failed to act?
Has he ever promised and not carried
it through?
20 Listen, I received a command to bless;
God has blessed, and I cannot reverse it!
21 No misfortune is in his plan for Jacob;
no trouble is in store for Israel.
For the LORD their God is with them;
he has been proclaimed their king.
22 God brought them out of Egypt;
for them he is as strong as a wild ox.
23 No curse can touch Jacob;
no magic has any power against Israel.
For now it will be said of Jacob,
'What wonders God has done for Israel!'

KING JAMES VERSION

24 Behold, the people shall rise up as a great lion,
and lift up himself as a young lion: he shall not lie
down until he eat *of* the prey, and drink the blood of
the slain.
25 And Balak said unto Balaam, Neither curse them
at all, nor bless them at all.
26 But Balaam answered and said unto Balak, Told
not I thee, saying, All that the LORD speaketh, that I
must do?

27 And Balak said unto Balaam, Come, I pray thee, I
will bring thee unto another place; peradventure it
will please God that thou mayest curse me them
from thence.
28 And Balak brought Balaam unto the top of Peor,
that looketh toward Jeshimon.
29 And Balaam said unto Balak, Build me here
seven altars, and prepare me here seven bullocks and
seven rams.
30 And Balak did as Balaam had said, and offered a
bullock and a ram on *every* altar.

24 1 And when Balaam saw that it pleased the
LORD to bless Israel, he went not, as at other
times, to seek for enchantments, but he set his face
toward the wilderness.
2 And Balaam lifted up his eyes, and he saw Israel
abiding *in his tents* according to their tribes; and the
spirit of God came upon him.
3 And he took up his parable, and said, Balaam the
son of Beor hath said, and the man whose eyes are
open hath said:
4 He hath said, which heard the words of God,
which saw the vision of the Almighty, falling *into a
trance,* but having his eyes open:
5 How goodly are thy tents, O Jacob, *and* thy tabernacles, O Israel!
6 As the valleys are they spread forth, as gardens by
the river's side, as the trees of lign aloes which the
LORD hath planted, *and* as cedar trees beside the
waters.
7 He shall pour the water out of his buckets, and
his seed *shall be* in many waters, and his king shall be
higher than Agag, and his kingdom shall be exalted.
8 God brought him forth out of Egypt; he hath as it
were the strength of an unicorn: he shall eat up the
nations his enemies, and shall break their bones, and
pierce *them* through with his arrows.
9 He couched, he lay down as a lion, and as a great
lion: who shall stir him up? Blessed *is* he that
blesseth thee, and cursed *is* he that curseth thee.

NEW LIVING TRANSLATION

24 These people rise up like a lioness,
like a majestic lion rousing itself.
They refuse to rest
until they have feasted on prey,
drinking the blood of the slaughtered!"
25 Then Balak said to Balaam, "Fine, but if you
won't curse them, at least don't bless them!"
26 But Balaam replied to Balak, "Didn't I tell you
that I can do only what the LORD tells me?"

Balaam's Third Message

27 Then King Balak said to Balaam, "Come, I will take
you to one more place. Perhaps it will please God to
let you curse them from there."
28 So Balak took Balaam to the top of Mount Peor,
overlooking the wasteland.* 29 Balaam again told Balak, "Build me seven altars, and prepare seven young
bulls and seven rams for me to sacrifice." 30 So Balak
did as Balaam ordered and offered a young bull and
a ram on each altar.

24 By now Balaam realized that the LORD was
determined to bless Israel, so he did not resort to divination as before. Instead, he turned and
looked out toward the wilderness, 2 where he saw the
people of Israel camped, tribe by tribe. Then the
Spirit of God came upon him, 3 and this is the message he delivered:

"This is the message of Balaam son of Beor,
the message of the man whose eyes see
clearly,
4 the message of one who hears the words of God,
who sees a vision from the Almighty,
who bows down with eyes wide open:
5 How beautiful are your tents, O Jacob;
how lovely are your homes, O Israel!
6 They spread before me like palm groves,*
like gardens by the riverside.
They are like tall trees planted by the LORD,
like cedars beside the waters.
7 Water will flow from their buckets;
their offspring have all they need.
Their king will be greater than Agag;
their kingdom will be exalted.
8 God brought them out of Egypt;
for them he is as strong as a wild ox.
He devours all the nations that oppose him,
breaking their bones in pieces,
shooting them with arrows.
9 Like a lion, Israel crouches and lies down;
like a lioness, who dares to arouse her?
Blessed is everyone who blesses you, O Israel,
and cursed is everyone who curses you."

23:28 Or *overlooking Jeshimon.* **24:6** Or *like a majestic valley.*

KING JAMES VERSION

10And Balak's anger was kindled against Balaam,
and he smote his hands together: and Balak said
unto Balaam, I called thee to curse mine enemies,
and, behold, thou hast altogether blessed *them* these
three times.
11Therefore now flee thou to thy place: I thought
to promote thee unto great honour; but, lo, the LORD
hath kept thee back from honour.
12And Balaam said unto Balak, Spake I not also to
thy messengers which thou sentest unto me, saying,
13If Balak would give me his house full of silver
and gold, I cannot go beyond the commandment of
the LORD, to do *either* good or bad of mine own
mind; *but* what the LORD saith, that will I speak?
14And now, behold, I go unto my people: come
therefore, and I will advertise thee what this people
shall do to thy people in the latter days.
15And he took up his parable, and said, Balaam the
son of Beor hath said, and the man whose eyes are
open hath said:
16He hath said, which heard the words of God, and
knew the knowledge of the most High, *which* saw
the vision of the Almighty, falling *into a trance,* but
having his eyes open:
17I shall see him, but not now: I shall behold him,
but not nigh: there shall come a Star out of Jacob, and
a Sceptre shall rise out of Israel, and shall smite the
corners of Moab, and destroy all the children of
Sheth.
18And Edom shall be a possession, Seir also shall
be a possession for his enemies; and Israel shall do
valiantly.
19Out of Jacob shall come he that shall have
dominion, and shall destroy him that remaineth of
the city.
20And when he looked on Amalek, he took up his
parable, and said, Amalek *was* the first of the nations; but his latter end *shall be* that he perish for
ever.
21And he looked on the Kenites, and took up his
parable, and said, Strong is thy dwellingplace, and
thou puttest thy nest in a rock.
22Nevertheless the Kenite shall be wasted, until
Asshur shall carry thee away captive.
23And he took up his parable, and said, Alas, who
shall live when God doeth this!
24And ships *shall come* from the coast of Chittim,
and shall afflict Asshur, and shall afflict Eber, and he
also shall perish for ever.
25And Balaam rose up, and went and returned to
his place: and Balak also went his way.

NEW LIVING TRANSLATION

10King Balak flew into a rage against Balaam. He
angrily clapped his hands and shouted, "I called you
to curse my enemies! Instead, you have blessed them
three times. 11Now get out of here! Go back home! I
promised to reward you richly, but the LORD has kept
you from your reward."
12Balaam told Balak, "Don't you remember what I
told your messengers? I said, 13'Even if Balak were to
give me his palace filled with silver and gold, I would
be powerless to do anything against the will of the
LORD.' I told you that I could say only what the LORD
says! 14Now I am returning to my own people. But
first let me tell you what the Israelites will do to your
people in the future."

Balaam's Final Messages

15This is the message Balaam delivered:

"This is the message of Balaam son of Beor,
the message of the man whose eyes see clearly,
16 the message of one who hears the words of God,
who has knowledge from the Most High,
who sees a vision from the Almighty,
who bows down with eyes wide open:
17 I see him, but not here and now.
I perceive him, but far in the distant future.
A star will rise from Jacob;
a scepter will emerge from Israel.
It will crush the foreheads of Moab's people,
cracking the skulls of the people of Sheth.
18 Edom will be taken over,
and Seir, its enemy, will be conquered,
while Israel marches on in triumph.
19 A ruler will rise in Jacob
who will destroy the survivors of Ir."

20Then Balaam looked over toward the people of
Amalek and delivered this message:

"Amalek was the greatest of nations,
but its destiny is destruction!"

21Then he looked over toward the Kenites and delivered this message:

"Your home is secure;
your nest is set in the rocks.
22 But the Kenites will be destroyed
when Assyria* takes you captive."

23Balaam concluded his messages by saying:

"Alas, who can survive
unless God has willed it?
24 Ships will come from the coasts of Cyprus*;
they will oppress Assyria and afflict Eber,
but they, too, will be utterly destroyed."

25Then Balaam and Balak returned to their homes.

24:22 Hebrew *Asshur;* also in 24:24. **24:24** Hebrew *Kittim.*

KING JAMES VERSION

25 1 And Israel abode in Shittim, and the people began to commit whoredom with the daughters of Moab.

2 And they called the people unto the sacrifices of their gods: and the people did eat, and bowed down to their gods.

3 And Israel joined himself unto Baal-peor: and the anger of the LORD was kindled against Israel.

4 And the LORD said unto Moses, Take all the heads of the people, and hang them up before the LORD against the sun, that the fierce anger of the LORD may be turned away from Israel.

5 And Moses said unto the judges of Israel, Slay ye every one his men that were joined unto Baal-peor.

6 And, behold, one of the children of Israel came and brought unto his brethren a Midianitish woman in the sight of Moses, and in the sight of all the congregation of the children of Israel, who *were* weeping *before* the door of the tabernacle of the congregation.

7 And when Phinehas, the son of Eleazar, the son of Aaron the priest, saw *it,* he rose up from among the congregation, and took a javelin in his hand;

8 And he went after the man of Israel into the tent, and thrust both of them through, the man of Israel, and the woman through her belly. So the plague was stayed from the children of Israel.

9 And those that died in the plague were twenty and four thousand.

10 And the LORD spake unto Moses, saying,

11 Phinehas, the son of Eleazar, the son of Aaron the priest, hath turned my wrath away from the children of Israel, while he was zealous for my sake among them, that I consumed not the children of Israel in my jealousy.

12 Wherefore say, Behold, I give unto him my covenant of peace:

13 And he shall have it, and his seed after him, *even* the covenant of an everlasting priesthood; because he was zealous for his God, and made an atonement for the children of Israel.

14 Now the name of the Israelite that was slain, *even* that was slain with the Midianitish woman, *was* Zimri, the son of Salu, a prince of a chief house among the Simeonites.

15 And the name of the Midianitish woman that was slain *was* Cozbi, the daughter of Zur; he *was* head over a people, *and* of a chief house in Midian.

16 And the LORD spake unto Moses, saying,

17 Vex the Midianites, and smite them:

18 For they vex you with their wiles, wherewith they have beguiled you in the matter of Peor, and in the matter of Cozbi, the daughter of a prince of Midian, their sister, which was slain in the day of the plague for Peor's sake.

NEW LIVING TRANSLATION

Moab Seduces Israel

25 While the Israelites were camped at Acacia
Grove,* some of the men defiled them-
selves by having* sexual relations with local Moabite
women. 2 These women invited them to attend sacrifices to their gods, so the Israelites feasted with them
and worshiped the gods of Moab. 3 In this way, Israel
joined in the worship of Baal of Peor, causing the
LORD's anger to blaze against his people.
4 The LORD issued the following command to
Moses: "Seize all the ringleaders and execute them
before the LORD in broad daylight, so his fierce anger
will turn away from the people of Israel."
5 So Moses ordered Israel's judges, "Each of you
must put to death the men under your authority who
have joined in worshiping Baal of Peor."
6 Just then one of the Israelite men brought a Midianite woman into his tent, right before the eyes of
Moses and all the people, as everyone was weeping at
the entrance of the Tabernacle.* 7 When Phinehas
son of Eleazar and grandson of Aaron the priest saw
this, he jumped up and left the assembly. He took a
spear 8 and rushed after the man into his tent. Phinehas thrust the spear all the way through the man's
body and into the woman's stomach. So the plague
against the Israelites was stopped, 9 but not before
24,000 people had died.
10 Then the LORD said to Moses, 11 "Phinehas son of
Eleazar and grandson of Aaron the priest has turned
my anger away from the Israelites by being as zealous among them as I was. So I stopped destroying all
Israel as I had intended to do in my zealous anger.
12 Now tell him that I am making my special covenant
of peace with him. 13 In this covenant, I give him and
his descendants a permanent right to the priesthood, for in his zeal for me, his God, he purified the
people of Israel, making them right with me.*"
14 The Israelite man killed with the Midianite
woman was named Zimri son of Salu, the leader of
a family from the tribe of Simeon. 15 The woman's
name was Cozbi; she was the daughter of Zur, the
leader of a Midianite clan.
16 Then the LORD said to Moses, 17 "Attack the Midianites and destroy them, 18 because they assaulted
you with deceit and tricked you into worshiping Baal
of Peor, and because of Cozbi, the daughter of a Midianite leader, who was killed at the time of the plague
because of what happened at Peor."

25:1a Hebrew *Shittim.* **25:1b** As in Greek version; Hebrew reads *some of the men began having.* **25:6** Hebrew *the Tent of Meeting.* **25:13** Or *he made atonement for the people of Israel.*

KING JAMES VERSION

26 1And it came to pass after the plague, that
the LORD spake unto Moses and unto Eleazar the son of Aaron the priest, saying,
2Take the sum of all the congregation of the children of Israel, from twenty years old and upward,
throughout their fathers' house, all that are able to go
to war in Israel.
3And Moses and Eleazar the priest spake with
them in the plains of Moab by Jordan *near* Jericho,
saying,
4*Take the sum of the people,* from twenty years old
and upward; as the LORD commanded Moses and the
children of Israel, which went forth out of the land
of Egypt.

5Reuben, the eldest son of Israel: the children of
Reuben; Hanoch, *of whom cometh* the family of the
Hanochites: of Pallu, the family of the Palluites:
6Of Hezron, the family of the Hezronites: of
Carmi, the family of the Carmites.
7These *are* the families of the Reubenites: and
they that were numbered of them were forty and
three thousand and seven hundred and thirty.
8And the sons of Pallu; Eliab.
9And the sons of Eliab; Nemuel, and Dathan, and
Abiram. This *is that* Dathan and Abiram, *which were*
famous in the congregation, who strove against
Moses and against Aaron in the company of Korah,
when they strove against the LORD:
10And the earth opened her mouth, and swallowed them up together with Korah, when that company died, what time the fire devoured two hundred
and fifty men: and they became a sign.
11Notwithstanding the children of Korah died not.

12The sons of Simeon after their families: of Nemuel, the family of the Nemuelites: of Jamin, the family
of the Jaminites: of Jachin, the family of the
Jachinites:
13Of Zerah, the family of the Zarhites: of Shaul, the
family of the Shaulites.
14These *are* the families of the Simeonites, twenty
and two thousand and two hundred.

NEW LIVING TRANSLATION

The Second Registration of Israel's Troops

26 After the plague had ended, the LORD said
to Moses and to Eleazar son of Aaron the
priest, 2"From the whole community of Israel, record
the names of all the warriors by their families. List all
the men twenty years old or older who are able to
go to war."
3So there on the plains of Moab beside the Jordan
River, across from Jericho, Moses and Eleazar the
priest issued these instructions to the leaders of
Israel: 4"List all the men of Israel twenty years old
and older, just as the LORD commanded Moses."
This is the record of all the descendants of Israel
who came out of Egypt.

The Tribe of Reuben

5These were the clans descended from the sons of
Reuben, Jacob's* oldest son:
The Hanochite clan, named after their
ancestor Hanoch.
The Palluite clan, named after their
ancestor Pallu.
6 The Hezronite clan, named after their
ancestor Hezron.
The Carmite clan, named after their
ancestor Carmi.
7These were the clans of Reuben. Their registered
troops numbered 43,730.
8Pallu was the ancestor of Eliab, 9and Eliab was the
father of Nemuel, Dathan, and Abiram. This Dathan
and Abiram are the same community leaders who
conspired with Korah against Moses and Aaron, rebelling against the LORD. 10But the earth opened up
its mouth and swallowed them with Korah, and fire
devoured 250 of their followers. This served as a
warning to the entire nation of Israel. 11However, the
sons of Korah did not die that day.

The Tribe of Simeon

12These were the clans descended from the sons of
Simeon:
The Jemuelite clan, named after their ancestor
Jemuel.*
The Jaminite clan, named after their ancestor
Jamin.
The Jakinite clan, named after their ancestor
Jakin.
13 The Zoharite clan, named after their ancestor
Zohar.*
The Shaulite clan, named after their ancestor
Shaul.
14These were the clans of Simeon. Their registered
troops numbered 22,200.

26:5 Hebrew *Israel's;* see note on 1:20-21b. **26:12** As in Syriac version (see also Gen 46:10; Exod 6:15); Hebrew reads *Nemuelite . . . Nemuel.* **26:13** As in parallel texts at Gen 46:10 and Exod 6:15; Hebrew reads *Zerahite . . . Zerah.*

KING JAMES VERSION

15 The children of Gad after their families: of Zephon, the family of the Zephonites: of Haggi, the family of the Haggites: of Shuni, the family of the Shunites:

16 Of Ozni, the family of the Oznites: of Eri, the family of the Erites:

17 Of Arod, the family of the Arodites: of Areli, the family of the Arelites.

18 These *are* the families of the children of Gad according to those that were numbered of them, forty thousand and five hundred.

19 The sons of Judah *were* Er and Onan: and Er and Onan died in the land of Canaan.

20 And the sons of Judah after their families were; of Shelah, the family of the Shelanites: of Pharez, the family of the Pharzites: of Zerah, the family of the Zarhites.

21 And the sons of Pharez were; of Hezron, the family of the Hezronites: of Hamul, the family of the Hamulites.

22 These *are* the families of Judah according to those that were numbered of them, threescore and sixteen thousand and five hundred.

23 *Of* the sons of Issachar after their families: *of* Tola, the family of the Tolaites: of Pua, the family of the Punites:

24 Of Jashub, the family of the Jashubites: of Shimron, the family of the Shimronites.

25 These *are* the families of Issachar according to those that were numbered of them, threescore and four thousand and three hundred.

26 *Of* the sons of Zebulun after their families: of Sered, the family of the Sardites: of Elon, the family of the Elonites: of Jahleel, the family of the Jahleelites.

NEW LIVING TRANSLATION

The Tribe of Gad

15 These were the clans descended from the sons of Gad:

The Zephonite clan, named after their ancestor Zephon.
The Haggite clan, named after their ancestor Haggi.
The Shunite clan, named after their ancestor Shuni.
16 The Oznite clan, named after their ancestor Ozni.
The Erite clan, named after their ancestor Eri.
17 The Arodite clan, named after their ancestor Arodi.*
The Arelite clan, named after their ancestor Areli.

18 These were the clans of Gad. Their registered troops numbered 40,500.

The Tribe of Judah

19 Judah had two sons, Er and Onan, who had died in the land of Canaan. 20 These were the clans descended from Judah's surviving sons:

The Shelanite clan, named after their ancestor Shelah.
The Perezite clan, named after their ancestor Perez.
The Zerahite clan, named after their ancestor Zerah.

21 These were the subclans descended from the Perezites:

The Hezronites, named after their ancestor Hezron.
The Hamulites, named after their ancestor Hamul.

22 These were the clans of Judah. Their registered troops numbered 76,500.

The Tribe of Issachar

23 These were the clans descended from the sons of Issachar:

The Tolaite clan, named after their ancestor Tola.
The Puite clan, named after their ancestor Puah.*
24 The Jashubite clan, named after their ancestor Jashub.
The Shimronite clan, named after their ancestor Shimron.

25 These were the clans of Issachar. Their registered troops numbered 64,300.

The Tribe of Zebulun

26 These were the clans descended from the sons of Zebulun:

The Seredite clan, named after their ancestor Sered.
The Elonite clan, named after their ancestor Elon.

26:17 As in Samaritan Pentateuch and Greek and Syriac versions (see also Gen 46:16); Hebrew reads *Arod.* **26:23** As in Samaritan Pentateuch, Greek and Syriac versions, and Latin Vulgate (see also 1 Chr 7:1); Hebrew reads *The Punite clan, named after its ancestor Puvah.*

KING JAMES VERSION

27 These *are* the families of the Zebulunites according to those that were numbered of them, threescore thousand and five hundred.

28 The sons of Joseph after their families *were* Manasseh and Ephraim.
29 Of the sons of Manasseh: of Machir, the family of the Machirites: and Machir begat Gilead: of Gilead *come* the family of the Gileadites.
30 These *are* the sons of Gilead: *of* Jeezer, the family of the Jeezerites: of Helek, the family of the Helekites:
31 And *of* Asriel, the family of the Asrielites: and *of* Shechem, the family of the Shechemites:
32 And *of* Shemida, the family of the Shemidaites: and *of* Hepher, the family of the Hepherites.
33 And Zelophehad the son of Hepher had no sons, but daughters: and the names of the daughters of Zelophehad *were* Mahlah, and Noah, Hoglah, Milcah, and Tirzah.
34 These *are* the families of Manasseh, and those that were numbered of them, fifty and two thousand and seven hundred.

35 These *are* the sons of Ephraim after their families: of Shuthelah, the family of the Shuthalhites: of Becher, the family of the Bachrites: of Tahan, the family of the Tahanites.
36 And these *are* the sons of Shuthelah: of Eran, the family of the Eranites.
37 These *are* the families of the sons of Ephraim according to those that were numbered of them, thirty and two thousand and five hundred. These *are* the sons of Joseph after their families.

38 The sons of Benjamin after their families: of Bela, the family of the Belaites: of Ashbel, the family of the Ashbelites: of Ahiram, the family of the Ahiramites:

NEW LIVING TRANSLATION

The Jahleelite clan, named after their ancestor Jahleel.

27 These were the clans of Zebulun. Their registered troops numbered 60,500.

The Tribe of Manasseh

28 Two clans were descended from Joseph through Manasseh and Ephraim.

29 These were the clans descended from Manasseh:
The Makirite clan, named after their ancestor Makir.
The Gileadite clan, named after their ancestor Gilead, Makir's son.

30 These were the subclans descended from the Gileadites:
The Iezerites, named after their ancestor Iezer.
The Helekites, named after their ancestor Helek.
31 The Asrielites, named after their ancestor Asriel.
The Shechemites, named after their ancestor Shechem.
32 The Shemidaites, named after their ancestor Shemida.
The Hepherites, named after their ancestor Hepher.
33 (One of Hepher's descendants, Zelophehad, had no sons, but his daughters' names were Mahlah, Noah, Hoglah, Milcah, and Tirzah.)

34 These were the clans of Manasseh. Their registered troops numbered 52,700.

The Tribe of Ephraim

35 These were the clans descended from the sons of Ephraim:
The Shuthelahite clan, named after their ancestor Shuthelah.
The Bekerite clan, named after their ancestor Beker.
The Tahanite clan, named after their ancestor Tahan.

36 This was the subclan descended from the Shuthelahites:
The Eranites, named after their ancestor Eran.

37 These were the clans of Ephraim. Their registered troops numbered 32,500.

These clans of Manasseh and Ephraim were all descendants of Joseph.

The Tribe of Benjamin

38 These were the clans descended from the sons of Benjamin:
The Belaite clan, named after their ancestor Bela.
The Ashbelite clan, named after their ancestor Ashbel.
The Ahiramite clan, named after their ancestor Ahiram.

KING JAMES VERSION

39 Of Shupham, the family of the Shuphamites: of
Hupham, the family of the Huphamites.
40 And the sons of Bela were Ard and Naaman: *of*
Ard, the family of the Ardites: *and* of Naaman, the
family of the Naamites.
41 These *are* the sons of Benjamin after their families: and they that were numbered of them *were* forty
and five thousand and six hundred.

42 These *are* the sons of Dan after their families:
of Shuham, the family of the Shuhamites. These *are*
the families of Dan after their families.
43 All the families of the Shuhamites, according to
those that were numbered of them, *were* threescore
and four thousand and four hundred.

44 *Of* the children of Asher after their families: of
Jimna, the family of the Jimnites: of Jesui, the family
of the Jesuites: of Beriah, the family of the Beriites.
45 Of the sons of Beriah: of Heber, the family of the
Heberites: of Malchiel, the family of the Malchi-
elites.
46 And the name of the daughter of Asher *was*
Sarah.
47 These *are* the families of the sons of Asher according to those that were numbered of them; *who*
were fifty and three thousand and four hundred.

48 *Of* the sons of Naphtali after their families: of
Jahzeel, the family of the Jahzeelites: of Guni, the
family of the Gunites:
49 Of Jezer, the family of the Jezerites: of Shillem,
the family of the Shillemites.
50 These *are* the families of Naphtali according to
their families: and they that were numbered of them
were forty and five thousand and four hundred.

NEW LIVING TRANSLATION

39 The Shuphamite clan, named after their ancestor
Shupham.*
The Huphamite clan, named after their ancestor
Hupham.

40 These were the subclans descended from the Bela-
ites:
The Ardites, named after their ancestor Ard.*
The Naamites, named after their ancestor
Naaman.

41 These were the clans of Benjamin. Their registered
troops numbered 45,600.

The Tribe of Dan

42 These were the clans descended from the sons of
Dan:
The Shuhamite clan, named after their ancestor
Shuham.

43 These were the Shuhamite clans of Dan. Their registered troops numbered 64,400.

The Tribe of Asher

44 These were the clans descended from the sons of
Asher:
The Imnite clan, named after their ancestor
Imnah.
The Ishvite clan, named after their ancestor Ishvi.
The Beriite clan, named after their ancestor
Beriah.

45 These were the subclans descended from the Beri-
ites:
The Heberites, named after their ancestor Heber.
The Malkielites, named after their ancestor
Malkiel.
46 Asher also had a daughter named Serah.

47 These were the clans of Asher. Their registered
troops numbered 53,400.

The Tribe of Naphtali

48 These were the clans descended from the sons of
Naphtali:
The Jahzeelite clan, named after their ancestor
Jahzeel.
The Gunite clan, named after their ancestor Guni.
49 The Jezerite clan, named after their ancestor
Jezer.
The Shillemite clan, named after their ancestor
Shillem.

50 These were the clans of Naphtali. Their registered
troops numbered 45,400.

26:39 As in some Hebrew manuscripts, Samaritan Pentateuch, Greek and Syriac versions, and Latin Vulgate; most Hebrew manuscripts read *Shephupham.* **26:40** As in Samaritan Pentateuch, some Greek manuscripts, and Latin Vulgate; Hebrew lacks *named after their ancestor Ard.*

KING JAMES VERSION

51These *were* the numbered of the children of Israel, six hundred thousand and a thousand seven hundred and thirty.

52And the LORD spake unto Moses, saying,

53Unto these the land shall be divided for an inheritance according to the number of names.

54To many thou shalt give the more inheritance, and to few thou shalt give the less inheritance: to every one shall his inheritance be given according to those that were numbered of him.

55Notwithstanding the land shall be divided by lot: according to the names of the tribes of their fathers they shall inherit.

56According to the lot shall the possession thereof be divided between many and few.

57And these *are* they that were numbered of the Levites after their families: of Gershon, the family of the Gershonites: of Kohath, the family of the Kohathites: of Merari, the family of the Merarites.

58These *are* the families of the Levites: the family of the Libnites, the family of the Hebronites, the family of the Mahlites, the family of the Mushites, the family of the Korathites. And Kohath begat Amram.

59And the name of Amram's wife *was* Jochebed, the daughter of Levi, whom *her mother* bare to Levi in Egypt: and she bare unto Amram Aaron and Moses, and Miriam their sister.

60And unto Aaron was born Nadab, and Abihu, Eleazar, and Ithamar.

61And Nadab and Abihu died, when they offered strange fire before the LORD.

62And those that were numbered of them were twenty and three thousand, all males from a month old and upward: for they were not numbered among the children of Israel, because there was no inheritance given them among the children of Israel.

63These *are* they that were numbered by Moses and Eleazar the priest, who numbered the children of Israel in the plains of Moab by Jordan *near* Jericho.

64But among these there was not a man of them whom Moses and Aaron the priest numbered, when they numbered the children of Israel in the wilderness of Sinai.

65For the LORD had said of them, They shall surely die in the wilderness. And there was not left a man of them, save Caleb the son of Jephunneh, and Joshua the son of Nun.

27 1Then came the daughters of Zelophehad, the son of Hepher, the son of Gilead, the son of Machir, the son of Manasseh, of the families of Manasseh the son of Joseph: and these *are* the names

NEW LIVING TRANSLATION

Results of the Registration

51In summary, the registered troops of all Israel numbered 601,730.

52Then the LORD said to Moses, 53"Divide the land among the tribes, and distribute the grants of land in proportion to the tribes' populations, as indicated by the number of names on the list. 54Give the larger tribes more land and the smaller tribes less land, each group receiving a grant in proportion to the size of its population. 55But you must assign the land by lot, and give land to each ancestral tribe according to the number of names on the list. 56Each grant of land must be assigned by lot among the larger and smaller tribal groups."

The Tribe of Levi

57This is the record of the Levites who were counted according to their clans:

The Gershonite clan, named after their ancestor Gershon.
The Kohathite clan, named after their ancestor Kohath.
The Merarite clan, named after their ancestor Merari.

58The Libnites, the Hebronites, the Mahlites, the Mushites, and the Korahites were all subclans of the Levites.

Now Kohath was the ancestor of Amram, 59and Amram's wife was named Jochebed. She also was a descendant of Levi, born among the Levites in the land of Egypt. Amram and Jochebed became the parents of Aaron, Moses, and their sister, Miriam. 60To Aaron were born Nadab, Abihu, Eleazar, and Ithamar. 61But Nadab and Abihu died when they burned before the LORD the wrong kind of fire, different than he had commanded.

62The men from the Levite clans who were one month old or older numbered 23,000. But the Levites were not included in the registration of the rest of the people of Israel because they were not given an allotment of land when it was divided among the Israelites.

63So these are the results of the registration of the people of Israel as conducted by Moses and Eleazar the priest on the plains of Moab beside the Jordan River, across from Jericho. 64Not one person on this list had been among those listed in the previous registration taken by Moses and Aaron in the wilderness of Sinai. 65For the LORD had said of them, "They will all die in the wilderness." Not one of them survived except Caleb son of Jephunneh and Joshua son of Nun.

The Daughters of Zelophehad

27 One day a petition was presented by the daughters of Zelophehad—Mahlah, Noah, Hoglah, Milcah, and Tirzah. Their father, Zelophehad, was a descendant of Hepher son of Gilead, son

KING JAMES VERSION

of his daughters; Mahlah, Noah, and Hoglah, and Milcah, and Tirzah.

2And they stood before Moses, and before Eleazar the priest, and before the princes and all the congregation, *by* the door of the tabernacle of the congregation, saying,

3Our father died in the wilderness, and he was not in the company of them that gathered themselves together against the LORD in the company of Korah; but died in his own sin, and had no sons.

4Why should the name of our father be done away from among his family, because he hath no son? Give unto us *therefore* a possession among the brethren of our father.

5And Moses brought their cause before the LORD.

6And the LORD spake unto Moses, saying,

7The daughters of Zelophehad speak right: thou shalt surely give them a possession of an inheritance among their father's brethren; and thou shalt cause the inheritance of their father to pass unto them.

8And thou shalt speak unto the children of Israel, saying, If a man die, and have no son, then ye shall cause his inheritance to pass unto his daughter.

9And if he have no daughter, then ye shall give his inheritance unto his brethren.

10And if he have no brethren, then ye shall give his inheritance unto his father's brethren.

11And if his father have no brethren, then ye shall give his inheritance unto his kinsman that is next to him of his family, and he shall possess it: and it shall be unto the children of Israel a statute of judgment, as the LORD commanded Moses.

12And the LORD said unto Moses, Get thee up into this mount Abarim, and see the land which I have given unto the children of Israel.

13And when thou hast seen it, thou also shalt be gathered unto thy people, as Aaron thy brother was gathered.

14For ye rebelled against my commandment in the desert of Zin, in the strife of the congregation, to sanctify me at the water before their eyes: that *is* the water of Meribah in Kadesh in the wilderness of Zin.

15And Moses spake unto the LORD, saying,

16Let the LORD, the God of the spirits of all flesh, set a man over the congregation,

17Which may go out before them, and which may go in before them, and which may lead them out, and which may bring them in; that the congregation of the LORD be not as sheep which have no shepherd.

18And the LORD said unto Moses, Take thee Joshua the son of Nun, a man in whom *is* the spirit, and lay thine hand upon him;

19And set him before Eleazar the priest, and before all the congregation; and give him a charge in their sight.

20And thou shalt put *some* of thine honour upon him, that all the congregation of the children of Israel may be obedient.

NEW LIVING TRANSLATION

of Makir, son of Manasseh, son of Joseph. 2These women stood before Moses, Eleazar the priest, the tribal leaders, and the entire community at the entrance of the Tabernacle.* 3"Our father died in the wilderness," they said. "He was not among Korah's followers, who rebelled against the LORD; he died because of his own sin. But he had no sons. 4Why should the name of our father disappear from his clan just because he had no sons? Give us property along with the rest of our relatives."

5So Moses brought their case before the LORD. 6And the LORD replied to Moses, 7"The claim of the daughters of Zelophehad is legitimate. You must give them a grant of land along with their father's relatives. Assign them the property that would have been given to their father.

8"And give the following instructions to the people of Israel: If a man dies and has no son, then give his inheritance to his daughters. 9And if he has no daughter either, transfer his inheritance to his brothers. 10If he has no brothers, give his inheritance to his father's brothers. 11But if his father has no brothers, give his inheritance to the nearest relative in his clan. This is a legal requirement for the people of Israel, just as the LORD commanded Moses."

Joshua Chosen to Lead Israel

12One day the LORD said to Moses, "Climb one of the mountains east of the river,* and look out over the land I have given the people of Israel. 13After you have seen it, you will die like your brother, Aaron, 14for you both rebelled against my instructions in the wilderness of Zin. When the people of Israel rebelled, you failed to demonstrate my holiness to them at the waters." (These are the waters of Meribah at Kadesh* in the wilderness of Zin.)

15Then Moses said to the LORD, 16"O LORD, you are the God who gives breath to all creatures. Please appoint a new man as leader for the community. 17Give them someone who will guide them wherever they go and will lead them into battle, so the community of the LORD will not be like sheep without a shepherd."

18The LORD replied, "Take Joshua son of Nun, who has the Spirit in him, and lay your hands on him. 19Present him to Eleazar the priest before the whole community, and publicly commission him to lead the people. 20Transfer some of your authority to him so the whole community of Israel will obey him.

27:2 Hebrew *the Tent of Meeting.* **27:12** Or *the mountains of Abarim.* **27:14** Hebrew *waters of Meribah-kadesh.*

KING JAMES VERSION

21And he shall stand before Eleazar the priest, who
shall ask *counsel* for him after the judgment of Urim
before the LORD: at his word shall they go out, and at
his word they shall come in, *both* he, and all the children of Israel with him, even all the congregation.
22And Moses did as the LORD commanded him:
and he took Joshua, and set him before Eleazar the
priest, and before all the congregation:
23And he laid his hands upon him, and gave him a
charge, as the LORD commanded by the hand of
Moses.

28 1And the LORD spake unto Moses, saying,
2Command the children of Israel, and say
unto them, My offering, *and* my bread for my sacrifices made by fire, *for* a sweet savour unto me, shall
ye observe to offer unto me in their due season.
3And thou shalt say unto them, This *is* the offering
made by fire which ye shall offer unto the LORD; two
lambs of the first year without spot day by day, *for* a
continual burnt offering.
4The one lamb shalt thou offer in the morning,
and the other lamb shalt thou offer at even;
5And a tenth *part* of an ephah of flour for a meat
offering, mingled with the fourth *part* of an hin of
beaten oil.
6*It is* a continual burnt offering, which was ordained in mount Sinai for a sweet savour, a sacrifice
made by fire unto the LORD.
7And the drink offering thereof *shall be* the fourth
part of an hin for the one lamb: in the holy *place*
shalt thou cause the strong wine to be poured unto
the LORD *for* a drink offering.
8And the other lamb shalt thou offer at even: as
the meat offering of the morning, and as the drink
offering thereof, thou shalt offer *it*, a sacrifice made
by fire, of a sweet savour unto the LORD.
9And on the sabbath day two lambs of the first
year without spot, and two tenth deals of flour *for* a
meat offering, mingled with oil, and the drink offering thereof:
10*This is* the burnt offering of every sabbath, beside the continual burnt offering, and his drink
offering.
11And in the beginnings of your months ye shall
offer a burnt offering unto the LORD; two young bullocks, and one ram, seven lambs of the first year without spot;
12And three tenth deals of flour *for* a meat offering, mingled with oil, for one bullock; and two tenth
deals of flour *for* a meat offering, mingled with oil,
for one ram;
13And a several tenth deal of flour mingled with
oil *for* a meat offering unto one lamb; *for* a burnt
offering of a sweet savour, a sacrifice made by fire
unto the LORD.

NEW LIVING TRANSLATION

21When direction from the LORD is needed, Joshua
will stand before Eleazar the priest, who will use the
Urim—one of the sacred lots cast before the LORD—
to determine his will. This is how Joshua and the rest
of the community of Israel will determine everything they should do."
22So Moses did as the LORD commanded. He presented Joshua to Eleazar the priest and the whole
community. 23Moses laid his hands on him and commissioned him to lead the people, just as the LORD
had commanded through Moses.

The Daily Offerings

28 The LORD said to Moses, 2"Give these instructions to the people of Israel: The offerings you present as special gifts are a pleasing aroma
to me; they are my food. See to it that they are
brought at the appointed times and offered according to my instructions.
3"Say to the people: This is the special gift you
must present to the LORD as your daily burnt offering. You must offer two one-year-old male lambs
with no defects. 4Sacrifice one lamb in the morning
and the other in the evening. 5With each lamb you
must offer a grain offering of two quarts* of choice
flour mixed with one quart* of pure oil of pressed olives. 6This is the regular burnt offering instituted at
Mount Sinai as a special gift, a pleasing aroma to
the LORD. 7Along with it you must present the proper
liquid offering of one quart of alcoholic drink with
each lamb, poured out in the Holy Place as an offering to the LORD. 8Offer the second lamb in the
evening with the same grain offering and liquid
offering. It, too, is a special gift, a pleasing aroma to
the LORD.

The Sabbath Offerings

9"On the Sabbath day, sacrifice two one-year-old
male lambs with no defects. They must be accompanied by a grain offering of four quarts* of choice
flour moistened with olive oil, and a liquid offering.
10This is the burnt offering to be presented each Sabbath day, in addition to the regular burnt offering
and its accompanying liquid offering.

The Monthly Offerings

11"On the first day of each month, present an extra
burnt offering to the LORD of two young bulls, one
ram, and seven one-year-old male lambs, all with no
defects. 12These must be accompanied by grain offerings of choice flour moistened with olive oil—six
quarts* with each bull, four quarts with the ram,
13and two quarts with each lamb. This burnt offering
will be a special gift, a pleasing aroma to the LORD.

28:5a Hebrew ⅒ *of an ephah* [2.2 liters]; also in 28:13, 21, 29.
28:5b Hebrew ¼ *of a hin* [1 liter]; also in 28:7. **28:9** Hebrew 2/10 *of an ephah* [4.4 liters]; also in 28:12, 20, 28. **28:12** Hebrew 3/10 *of an ephah* [6.6 liters]; also in 28:20, 28.

KING JAMES VERSION

14 And their drink offerings shall be half an hin of wine unto a bullock, and the third *part* of an hin unto a ram, and a fourth *part* of an hin unto a lamb: this *is* the burnt offering of every month throughout the months of the year.

15 And one kid of the goats for a sin offering unto the LORD shall be offered, beside the continual burnt offering, and his drink offering.

16 And in the fourteenth day of the first month *is* the passover of the LORD.

17 And in the fifteenth day of this month *is* the feast: seven days shall unleavened bread be eaten.

18 In the first day *shall be* an holy convocation; ye shall do no manner of servile work *therein:*

19 But ye shall offer a sacrifice made by fire *for* a burnt offering unto the LORD; two young bullocks, and one ram, and seven lambs of the first year: they shall be unto you without blemish:

20 And their meat offering *shall be of* flour mingled with oil: three tenth deals shall ye offer for a bullock, and two tenth deals for a ram;

21 A several tenth deal shalt thou offer for every lamb, throughout the seven lambs:

22 And one goat *for* a sin offering, to make an atonement for you.

23 Ye shall offer these beside the burnt offering in the morning, which *is* for a continual burnt offering.

24 After this manner ye shall offer daily, throughout the seven days, the meat of the sacrifice made by fire, of a sweet savour unto the LORD: it shall be offered beside the continual burnt offering, and his drink offering.

25 And on the seventh day ye shall have an holy convocation; ye shall do no servile work.

26 Also in the day of the firstfruits, when ye bring a new meat offering unto the LORD, after your weeks *be out,* ye shall have an holy convocation; ye shall do no servile work:

27 But ye shall offer the burnt offering for a sweet savour unto the LORD; two young bullocks, one ram, seven lambs of the first year;

28 And their meat offering of flour mingled with oil, three tenth deals unto one bullock, two tenth deals unto one ram,

29 A several tenth deal unto one lamb, throughout the seven lambs;

30 *And* one kid of the goats, to make an atonement for you.

31 Ye shall offer *them* beside the continual burnt offering, and his meat offering, (they shall be unto you without blemish) and their drink offerings.

NEW LIVING TRANSLATION

14 You must also present a liquid offering with each sacrifice: two quarts* of wine for each bull, a third of a gallon* for the ram, and one quart* for each lamb. Present this monthly burnt offering on the first day of each month throughout the year.

15 "On the first day of each month, you must also offer one male goat for a sin offering to the LORD. This is in addition to the regular burnt offering and its accompanying liquid offering.

Offerings for the Passover

16 "On the fourteenth day of the first month,* you must celebrate the LORD's Passover. 17 On the following day—the fifteenth day of the month—a joyous, seven-day festival will begin, but no bread made with yeast may be eaten. 18 The first day of the festival will be an official day for holy assembly, and no ordinary work may be done on that day. 19 As a special gift you must present a burnt offering to the LORD—two young bulls, one ram, and seven one-year-old male lambs, all with no defects. 20 These will be accompanied by grain offerings of choice flour moistened with olive oil—six quarts with each bull, four quarts with the ram, 21 and two quarts with each of the seven lambs. 22 You must also offer a male goat as a sin offering to purify yourselves and make yourselves right with the LORD.* 23 Present these offerings in addition to your regular morning burnt offering. 24 On each of the seven days of the festival, this is how you must prepare the food offering that is presented as a special gift, a pleasing aroma to the LORD. These will be offered in addition to the regular burnt offerings and liquid offerings. 25 The seventh day of the festival will be another official day for holy assembly, and no ordinary work may be done on that day.

Offerings for the Festival of Harvest

26 "At the Festival of Harvest,* when you present the first of your new grain to the LORD, you must call an official day for holy assembly, and you may do no ordinary work on that day. 27 Present a special burnt offering on that day as a pleasing aroma to the LORD. It will consist of two young bulls, one ram, and seven one-year-old male lambs. 28 These will be accompanied by grain offerings of choice flour moistened with olive oil—six quarts with each bull, four quarts with the ram, 29 and two quarts with each of the seven lambs. 30 Also, offer one male goat to purify yourselves and make yourselves right with the LORD. 31 Prepare these special burnt offerings, along with their liquid offerings, in addition to the regular burnt offering and its accompanying grain offering. Be sure that all the animals you sacrifice have no defects.

28:14a Hebrew *½ of a hin* [2 liters]. **28:14b** Hebrew *⅓ of a hin* [1.3 liters]. **28:14c** Hebrew *¼ of a hin* [1 liter]. **28:16** This day in the ancient Hebrew lunar calendar occurred in late March, April, or early May. **28:22** Or *to make atonement for yourselves;* also in 28:30. **28:26** Hebrew *Festival of Weeks.* This was later called the Festival of Pentecost (see Acts 2:1). It is celebrated today as Shavuot (or Shabuoth).

KING JAMES VERSION

29 1And in the seventh month, on the first *day*
of the month, ye shall have an holy convocation; ye shall do no servile work: it is a day of blowing the trumpets unto you.
2And ye shall offer a burnt offering for a sweet savour unto the LORD; one young bullock, one ram, *and*
seven lambs of the first year without blemish:
3And their meat offering *shall be of* flour mingled
with oil, three tenth deals for a bullock, *and* two
tenth deals for a ram,
4And one tenth deal for one lamb, throughout the
seven lambs:
5And one kid of the goats *for* a sin offering, to
make an atonement for you:
6Beside the burnt offering of the month, and his
meat offering, and the daily burnt offering, and
his meat offering, and their drink offerings, according unto their manner, for a sweet savour, a sacrifice
made by fire unto the LORD.

7And ye shall have on the tenth *day* of this seventh
month an holy convocation; and ye shall afflict your
souls: ye shall not do any work *therein:*
8But ye shall offer a burnt offering unto the LORD
for a sweet savour; one young bullock, one ram, *and*
seven lambs of the first year; they shall be unto you
without blemish:
9And their meat offering *shall be of* flour mingled
with oil, three tenth deals to a bullock, *and* two tenth
deals to one ram,
10A several tenth deal for one lamb, throughout
the seven lambs:
11One kid of the goats *for* a sin offering; beside the
sin offering of atonement, and the continual burnt
offering, and the meat offering of it, and their drink
offerings.

12And on the fifteenth day of the seventh month
ye shall have an holy convocation; ye shall do no servile work, and ye shall keep a feast unto the LORD
seven days:
13And ye shall offer a burnt offering, a sacrifice
made by fire, of a sweet savour unto the LORD; thirteen young bullocks, two rams, *and* fourteen lambs
of the first year; they shall be without blemish:

NEW LIVING TRANSLATION

Offerings for the Festival of Trumpets

29 "Celebrate the Festival of Trumpets each
year on the first day of the appointed
month in early autumn.* You must call an official day
for holy assembly, and you may do no ordinary work.
2On that day you must present a burnt offering as a
pleasing aroma to the LORD. It will consist of one
young bull, one ram, and seven one-year-old male
lambs, all with no defects. 3These must be accompanied by grain offerings of choice flour moistened
with olive oil—six quarts* with the bull, four quarts*
with the ram, 4and two quarts* with each of the
seven lambs. 5In addition, you must sacrifice a male
goat as a sin offering to purify yourselves and make
yourselves right with the LORD.* 6These special sacrifices are in addition to your regular monthly and
daily burnt offerings, and they must be given with
their prescribed grain offerings and liquid offerings.
These offerings are given as a special gift to the LORD,
a pleasing aroma to him.

Offerings for the Day of Atonement

7"Ten days later, on the tenth day of the same
month,* you must call another holy assembly. On
that day, the Day of Atonement, the people must go
without food and must do no ordinary work. 8You
must present a burnt offering as a pleasing aroma to
the LORD. It will consist of one young bull, one ram,
and seven one-year-old male lambs, all with no defects. 9These offerings must be accompanied by the
prescribed grain offerings of choice flour moistened
with olive oil—six quarts of choice flour with the
bull, four quarts of choice flour with the ram, 10and
two quarts of choice flour with each of the seven
lambs. 11You must also sacrifice one male goat for a
sin offering. This is in addition to the sin offering of
atonement and the regular daily burnt offering with
its grain offering, and their accompanying liquid
offerings.

Offerings for the Festival of Shelters

12"Five days later, on the fifteenth day of the same
month,* you must call another holy assembly of all
the people, and you may do no ordinary work on that
day. It is the beginning of the Festival of Shelters,* a
seven-day festival to the LORD. 13On the first day of
the festival, you must present a burnt offering as a
special gift, a pleasing aroma to the LORD. It will consist of thirteen young bulls, two rams, and fourteen

29:1 Hebrew *the first day of the seventh month*. This day in the ancient Hebrew lunar calendar occurred in September or October. This festival is celebrated today as Rosh Hashanah, the Jewish new year. **29:3a** Hebrew *3/10 of an ephah* [6.6 liters]; also in 29:9, 14. **29:3b** Hebrew *2/10 of an ephah* [4.4 liters]; also in 29:9, 14. **29:4** Hebrew *1/10 of an ephah* [2.2 liters]; also in 29:10, 15. **29:5** Or *to make atonement for yourselves*. **29:7** Hebrew *On the tenth day of the seventh month;* see 29:1 and the note there. This day in the ancient Hebrew lunar calendar occurred in September or October. It is celebrated today as Yom Kippur. **29:12a** Hebrew *On the fifteenth day of the seventh month;* see 29:1, 7 and the notes there. This day in the ancient Hebrew lunar calendar occurred in late September, October, or early November. **29:12b** Or *Festival of Booths*, or *Festival of Tabernacles*. This was earlier called the Festival of the Final Harvest or Festival of Ingathering (see Exod 23:16b). It is celebrated today as Sukkot (or Succoth).

KING JAMES VERSION

14 And their meat offering *shall be of* flour mingled with oil, three tenth deals unto every bullock of the thirteen bullocks, two tenth deals to each ram of the two rams,

15 And a several tenth deal to each lamb of the fourteen lambs:

16 And one kid of the goats *for* a sin offering; beside the continual burnt offering, his meat offering, and his drink offering.

17 And on the second day *ye shall offer* twelve young bullocks, two rams, fourteen lambs of the first year without spot:

18 And their meat offering and their drink offerings for the bullocks, for the rams, and for the lambs, *shall be* according to their number, after the manner:

19 And one kid of the goats *for* a sin offering; beside the continual burnt offering, and the meat offering thereof, and their drink offerings.

20 And on the third day eleven bullocks, two rams, fourteen lambs of the first year without blemish;

21 And their meat offering and their drink offerings for the bullocks, for the rams, and for the lambs, *shall be* according to their number, after the manner:

22 And one goat *for* a sin offering; beside the continual burnt offering, and his meat offering, and his drink offering.

23 And on the fourth day ten bullocks, two rams, *and* fourteen lambs of the first year without blemish:

24 Their meat offering and their drink offerings for the bullocks, for the rams, and for the lambs, *shall be* according to their number, after the manner:

25 And one kid of the goats *for* a sin offering; beside the continual burnt offering, his meat offering, and his drink offering.

26 And on the fifth day nine bullocks, two rams, *and* fourteen lambs of the first year without spot:

27 And their meat offering and their drink offerings for the bullocks, for the rams, and for the lambs, *shall be* according to their number, after the manner:

28 And one goat *for* a sin offering; beside the continual burnt offering, and his meat offering, and his drink offering.

29 And on the sixth day eight bullocks, two rams, *and* fourteen lambs of the first year without blemish:

30 And their meat offering and their drink offerings for the bullocks, for the rams, and for the lambs, *shall be* according to their number, after the manner:

31 And one goat *for* a sin offering; beside the continual burnt offering, his meat offering, and his drink offering.

32 And on the seventh day seven bullocks, two rams, *and* fourteen lambs of the first year without blemish:

33 And their meat offering and their drink offerings for the bullocks, for the rams, and for the lambs, *shall be* according to their number, after the manner:

NEW LIVING TRANSLATION

one-year-old male lambs, all with no defects. 14 Each
of these offerings must be accompanied by a grain
offering of choice flour moistened with olive oil—six
quarts for each of the thirteen bulls, four quarts for
each of the two rams, 15 and two quarts for each of the
fourteen lambs. 16 You must also sacrifice a male goat
as a sin offering, in addition to the regular burnt
offering with its accompanying grain offering and
liquid offering.

17 "On the second day of this seven-day festival,
sacrifice twelve young bulls, two rams, and fourteen
one-year-old male lambs, all with no defects. 18 Each
of these offerings of bulls, rams, and lambs must be
accompanied by its prescribed grain offering and
liquid offering. 19 You must also sacrifice a male goat
as a sin offering, in addition to the regular burnt
offering with its accompanying grain offering and
liquid offering.

20 "On the third day of the festival, sacrifice eleven
young bulls, two rams, and fourteen one-year-old
male lambs, all with no defects. 21 Each of these offerings of bulls, rams, and lambs must be accompanied by its prescribed grain offering and liquid
offering. 22 You must also sacrifice a male goat as a
sin offering, in addition to the regular burnt offering
with its accompanying grain offering and liquid
offering.

23 "On the fourth day of the festival, sacrifice ten
young bulls, two rams, and fourteen one-year-old
male lambs, all with no defects. 24 Each of these offerings of bulls, rams, and lambs must be accompanied by its prescribed grain offering and liquid
offering. 25 You must also sacrifice a male goat as a
sin offering, in addition to the regular burnt offering
with its accompanying grain offering and liquid
offering.

26 "On the fifth day of the festival, sacrifice nine
young bulls, two rams, and fourteen one-year-old
male lambs, all with no defects. 27 Each of these offerings of bulls, rams, and lambs must be accompanied by its prescribed grain offering and liquid
offering. 28 You must also sacrifice a male goat as a
sin offering, in addition to the regular burnt offering
with its accompanying grain offering and liquid
offering.

29 "On the sixth day of the festival, sacrifice eight
young bulls, two rams, and fourteen one-year-old
male lambs, all with no defects. 30 Each of these offerings of bulls, rams, and lambs must be accompanied by its prescribed grain offering and liquid
offering. 31 You must also sacrifice a male goat as a
sin offering, in addition to the regular burnt offering
with its accompanying grain offering and liquid
offering.

32 "On the seventh day of the festival, sacrifice
seven young bulls, two rams, and fourteen one-
year-old male lambs, all with no defects. 33 Each of
these offerings of bulls, rams, and lambs must be

KING JAMES VERSION

[34]And one goat *for* a sin offering; beside the continual burnt offering, his meat offering, and his drink offering.

[35]On the eighth day ye shall have a solemn assembly: ye shall do no servile work *therein:*

[36]But ye shall offer a burnt offering, a sacrifice made by fire, of a sweet savour unto the LORD: one bullock, one ram, seven lambs of the first year without blemish:

[37]Their meat offering and their drink offerings for the bullock, for the ram, and for the lambs, *shall be* according to their number, after the manner:

[38]And one goat *for* a sin offering; beside the continual burnt offering, and his meat offering, and his drink offering.

[39]These *things* ye shall do unto the LORD in your set feasts, beside your vows, and your freewill offerings, for your burnt offerings, and for your meat offerings, and for your drink offerings, and for your peace offerings.

[40]And Moses told the children of Israel according to all that the LORD commanded Moses.

30 [1]And Moses spake unto the heads of the tribes concerning the children of Israel, saying, This *is* the thing which the LORD hath commanded.

[2]If a man vow a vow unto the LORD, or swear an oath to bind his soul with a bond; he shall not break his word, he shall do according to all that proceedeth out of his mouth.

[3]If a woman also vow a vow unto the LORD, and bind *herself* by a bond, *being* in her father's house in her youth;

[4]And her father hear her vow, and her bond wherewith she hath bound her soul, and her father shall hold his peace at her: then all her vows shall stand, and every bond wherewith she hath bound her soul shall stand.

[5]But if her father disallow her in the day that he heareth; not any of her vows, or of her bonds wherewith she hath bound her soul, shall stand: and the LORD shall forgive her, because her father disallowed her.

[6]And if she had at all an husband, when she vowed, or uttered aught out of her lips, wherewith she bound her soul;

[7]And her husband heard *it,* and held his peace at her in the day that he heard *it:* then her vows shall stand, and her bonds wherewith she bound her soul shall stand.

[8]But if her husband disallowed her on the day that he heard *it;* then he shall make her vow which she vowed, and that which she uttered with her lips, wherewith she bound her soul, of none effect: and the LORD shall forgive her.

NEW LIVING TRANSLATION

accompanied by its prescribed grain offering and liquid offering. [34]You must also sacrifice one male goat as a sin offering, in addition to the regular burnt offering with its accompanying grain offering and liquid offering.

[35]"On the eighth day of the festival, proclaim another holy day. You must do no ordinary work on that day. [36]You must present a burnt offering as a special gift, a pleasing aroma to the LORD. It will consist of one young bull, one ram, and seven one-year-old male lambs, all with no defects. [37]Each of these offerings must be accompanied by its prescribed grain offering and liquid offering. [38]You must also sacrifice one male goat as a sin offering, in addition to the regular burnt offering with its accompanying grain offering and liquid offering.

[39]"You must present these offerings to the LORD at your annual festivals. These are in addition to the sacrifices and offerings you present in connection with vows, or as voluntary offerings, burnt offerings, grain offerings, liquid offerings, or peace offerings."

[40]*So Moses gave all of these instructions to the people of Israel as the LORD had commanded him.

Laws concerning Vows

30 [1]*Then Moses summoned the leaders of the tribes of Israel and told them, "This is what the LORD has commanded: [2]A man who makes a vow to the LORD or makes a pledge under oath must never break it. He must do exactly what he said he would do.

[3]"If a young woman makes a vow to the LORD or a pledge under oath while she is still living at her father's home, [4]and her father hears of the vow or pledge and does not object to it, then all her vows and pledges will stand. [5]But if her father refuses to let her fulfill the vow or pledge on the day he hears of it, then all her vows and pledges will become invalid. The LORD will forgive her because her father would not let her fulfill them.

[6]"Now suppose a young woman makes a vow or binds herself with an impulsive pledge and later marries. [7]If her husband learns of her vow or pledge and does not object on the day he hears of it, her vows and pledges will stand. [8]But if her husband refuses to accept her vow or impulsive pledge on the day he hears of it, he nullifies her commitments, and

29:40 Verse 29:40 is numbered 30:1 in Hebrew text. **30:1** Verses 30:1-16 are numbered 30:2-17 in Hebrew text.

KING JAMES VERSION

9But every vow of a widow, and of her that is divorced, wherewith they have bound their souls, shall stand against her.

10And if she vowed in her husband's house, or bound her soul by a bond with an oath;

11And her husband heard *it,* and held his peace at her, *and* disallowed her not: then all her vows shall stand, and every bond wherewith she bound her soul shall stand.

12But if her husband hath utterly made them void on the day he heard *them; then* whatsoever proceeded out of her lips concerning her vows, or concerning the bond of her soul, shall not stand: her husband hath made them void; and the LORD shall forgive her.

13Every vow, and every binding oath to afflict the soul, her husband may establish it, or her husband may make it void.

14But if her husband altogether hold his peace at her from day to day; then he establisheth all her vows, or all her bonds, which *are* upon her: he confirmeth them, because he held his peace at her in the day that he heard *them.*

15But if he shall any ways make them void after that he hath heard *them;* then he shall bear her iniquity.

16These *are* the statutes, which the LORD commanded Moses, between a man and his wife, between the father and his daughter, *being yet* in her youth in her father's house.

31 1And the LORD spake unto Moses, saying, 2Avenge the children of Israel of the Midianites: afterward shalt thou be gathered unto thy people.

3And Moses spake unto the people, saying, Arm some of yourselves unto the war, and let them go against the Midianites, and avenge the LORD of Midian.

4Of every tribe a thousand, throughout all the tribes of Israel, shall ye send to the war.

5So there were delivered out of the thousands of Israel, a thousand of *every tribe,* twelve thousand armed for war.

6And Moses sent them to the war, a thousand of *every* tribe, them and Phinehas the son of Eleazar the priest, to the war, with the holy instruments, and the trumpets to blow in his hand.

7And they warred against the Midianites, as the LORD commanded Moses; and they slew all the males.

8And they slew the kings of Midian, beside the rest of them that were slain; *namely,* Evi, and Rekem, and Zur, and Hur, and Reba, five kings of Midian: Balaam also the son of Beor they slew with the sword.

9And the children of Israel took *all* the women of Midian captives, and their little ones, and took the spoil of all their cattle, and all their flocks, and all their goods.

NEW LIVING TRANSLATION

the LORD will forgive her. 9If, however, a woman is a widow or is divorced, she must fulfill all her vows and pledges.

10"But suppose a woman is married and living in her husband's home when she makes a vow or binds herself with a pledge. 11If her husband hears of it and does not object to it, her vow or pledge will stand. 12But if her husband refuses to accept it on the day he hears of it, her vow or pledge will be nullified, and the LORD will forgive her. 13So her husband may either confirm or nullify any vows or pledges she makes to deny herself. 14But if he does not object on the day he hears of it, then he is agreeing to all her vows and pledges. 15If he waits more than a day and then tries to nullify a vow or pledge, he will be punished for her guilt."

16These are the regulations the LORD gave Moses concerning relationships between a man and his wife, and between a father and a young daughter who still lives at home.

Conquest of the Midianites

31 Then the LORD said to Moses, 2"On behalf of the people of Israel, take revenge on the Midianites for leading them into idolatry. After that, you will die and join your ancestors."

3So Moses said to the people, "Choose some men, and arm them to fight the LORD's war of revenge against Midian. 4From each tribe of Israel, send 1,000 men into battle." 5So they chose 1,000 men from each tribe of Israel, a total of 12,000 men armed for battle. 6Then Moses sent them out, 1,000 men from each tribe, and Phinehas son of Eleazar the priest led them into battle. They carried along the holy objects of the sanctuary and the trumpets for sounding the charge. 7They attacked Midian as the LORD had commanded Moses, and they killed all the men. 8All five of the Midianite kings—Evi, Rekem, Zur, Hur, and Reba—died in the battle. They also killed Balaam son of Beor with the sword.

9Then the Israelite army captured the Midianite women and children and seized their cattle and

KING JAMES VERSION

10 And they burnt all their cities wherein they dwelt, and all their goodly castles, with fire.

11 And they took all the spoil, and all the prey, *both* of men and of beasts.

12 And they brought the captives, and the prey, and the spoil, unto Moses, and Eleazar the priest, and unto the congregation of the children of Israel, unto the camp at the plains of Moab, which are by Jordan *near* Jericho.

13 And Moses, and Eleazar the priest, and all the princes of the congregation, went forth to meet them without the camp.

14 And Moses was wroth with the officers of the host, *with* the captains over thousands, and captains over hundreds, which came from the battle.

15 And Moses said unto them, Have ye saved all the women alive?

16 Behold, these caused the children of Israel, through the counsel of Balaam, to commit trespass against the LORD in the matter of Peor, and there was a plague among the congregation of the LORD.

17 Now therefore kill every male among the little ones, and kill every woman that hath known man by lying with him.

18 But all the women children, that have not known a man by lying with him, keep alive for yourselves.

19 And do ye abide without the camp seven days: whosoever hath killed any person, and whosoever hath touched any slain, purify *both* yourselves and your captives on the third day, and on the seventh day.

20 And purify all *your* raiment, and all that is made of skins, and all work of goats' *hair,* and all things made of wood.

21 And Eleazar the priest said unto the men of war which went to the battle, This *is* the ordinance of the law which the LORD commanded Moses;

22 Only the gold, and the silver, the brass, the iron, the tin, and the lead,

23 Every thing that may abide the fire, ye shall make *it* go through the fire, and it shall be clean: nevertheless it shall be purified with the water of separation: and all that abideth not the fire ye shall make go through the water.

24 And ye shall wash your clothes on the seventh day, and ye shall be clean, and afterward ye shall come into the camp.

25 And the LORD spake unto Moses, saying,

26 Take the sum of the prey that was taken, *both* of man and of beast, thou, and Eleazar the priest, and the chief fathers of the congregation:

27 And divide the prey into two parts; between them that took the war upon them, who went out to battle, and between all the congregation:

28 And levy a tribute unto the LORD of the men of war which went out to battle: one soul of five hundred, *both* of the persons, and of the beeves, and of the asses, and of the sheep:

NEW LIVING TRANSLATION

flocks and all their wealth as plunder. 10 They burned
all the towns and villages where the Midianites had
lived. 11 After they had gathered the plunder and captives, both people and animals, 12 they brought them
all to Moses and Eleazar the priest, and to the whole
community of Israel, which was camped on the
plains of Moab beside the Jordan River, across from
Jericho. 13 Moses, Eleazar the priest, and all the leaders of the community went to meet them outside the
camp. 14 But Moses was furious with all the generals
and captains* who had returned from the battle.

15 "Why have you let all the women live?" he demanded. 16 "These are the very ones who followed
Balaam's advice and caused the people of Israel to rebel against the LORD at Mount Peor. They are the
ones who caused the plague to strike the LORD's
people. 17 So kill all the boys and all the women who
have had intercourse with a man. 18 Only the young
girls who are virgins may live; you may keep them for
yourselves. 19 And all of you who have killed anyone
or touched a dead body must stay outside the camp
for seven days. You must purify yourselves and your
captives on the third and seventh days. 20 Purify all
your clothing, too, and everything made of leather,
goat hair, or wood."

21 Then Eleazar the priest said to the men who
were in the battle, "The LORD has given Moses this legal requirement: 22 Anything made of gold, silver,
bronze, iron, tin, or lead—23 that is, all metals that do
not burn—must be passed through fire in order to be
made ceremonially pure. These metal objects must
then be further purified with the water of purification. But everything that burns must be purified by
the water alone. 24 On the seventh day you must wash
your clothes and be purified. Then you may return to
the camp."

Division of the Plunder

25 And the LORD said to Moses, 26 "You and Eleazar the
priest and the family leaders of each tribe are to
make a list of all the plunder taken in the battle, including the people and animals. 27 Then divide the
plunder into two parts, and give half to the men who
fought the battle and half to the rest of the people.
28 From the army's portion, first give the LORD his
share of the plunder—one of every 500 of the prisoners and of the cattle, donkeys, sheep, and goats.

31:14 Hebrew *the commanders of thousands, and the commanders of hundreds;* also in 31:48, 52, 54.

KING JAMES VERSION

29 Take *it* of their half, and give *it* unto Eleazar the priest, *for* an heave offering of the LORD.

30 And of the children of Israel's half, thou shalt take one portion of fifty, of the persons, of the beeves, of the asses, and of the flocks, of all manner of beasts, and give them unto the Levites, which keep the charge of the tabernacle of the LORD.

31 And Moses and Eleazar the priest did as the LORD commanded Moses.

32 And the booty, *being* the rest of the prey which the men of war had caught, was six hundred thousand and seventy thousand and five thousand sheep,

33 And threescore and twelve thousand beeves,

34 And threescore and one thousand asses,

35 And thirty and two thousand persons in all, of women that had not known man by lying with him.

36 And the half, *which was* the portion of them that went out to war, was in number three hundred thousand and seven and thirty thousand and five hundred sheep:

37 And the LORD's tribute of the sheep was six hundred and threescore and fifteen.

38 And the beeves *were* thirty and six thousand; of which the LORD's tribute *was* threescore and twelve.

39 And the asses *were* thirty thousand and five hundred; of which the LORD's tribute *was* threescore and one.

40 And the persons *were* sixteen thousand; of which the LORD's tribute *was* thirty and two persons.

41 And Moses gave the tribute, *which was* the LORD's heave offering, unto Eleazar the priest, as the LORD commanded Moses.

42 And of the children of Israel's half, which Moses divided from the men that warred,

43 (Now the half *that pertained unto* the congregation was three hundred thousand and thirty thousand *and* seven thousand and five hundred sheep,

44 And thirty and six thousand beeves,

45 And thirty thousand asses and five hundred,

46 And sixteen thousand persons;)

47 Even of the children of Israel's half, Moses took one portion of fifty, *both* of man and of beast, and gave them unto the Levites, which kept the charge of the tabernacle of the LORD; as the LORD commanded Moses.

48 And the officers which *were* over thousands of the host, the captains of thousands, and captains of hundreds, came near unto Moses:

49 And they said unto Moses, Thy servants have taken the sum of the men of war which *are* under our charge, and there lacketh not one man of us.

50 We have therefore brought an oblation for the LORD, what every man hath gotten, of jewels of gold, chains, and bracelets, rings, earrings, and tablets, to make an atonement for our souls before the LORD.

51 And Moses and Eleazar the priest took the gold of them, *even* all wrought jewels.

52 And all the gold of the offering that they offered

NEW LIVING TRANSLATION

29 Give this share of the army's half to Eleazar the
priest as an offering to the LORD. 30 From the half that
belongs to the people of Israel, take one of every fifty
of the prisoners and of the cattle, donkeys, sheep,
goats, and other animals. Give this share to the Levites, who are in charge of maintaining the LORD's
Tabernacle." 31 So Moses and Eleazar the priest did as
the LORD commanded Moses.

32 The plunder remaining from everything the
fighting men had taken totaled 675,000 sheep and
goats, 33 72,000 cattle, 34 61,000 donkeys, 35 and
32,000 virgin girls.

36 Half of the plunder was given to the fighting
men. It totaled 337,500 sheep and goats, 37 of which
675 were the LORD's share; 38 36,000 cattle, of which
72 were the LORD's share; 39 30,500 donkeys, of
which 61 were the LORD's share; 40 and 16,000 virgin
girls, of whom 32 were the LORD's share. 41 Moses
gave all the LORD's share to Eleazar the priest, just as
the LORD had directed him.

42 Half of the plunder belonged to the people of Israel, and Moses separated it from the half belonging
to the fighting men. 43 It totaled 337,500 sheep and
goats, 44 36,000 cattle, 45 30,500 donkeys, 46 and
16,000 virgin girls. 47 From the half-share given to
the people, Moses took one of every fifty prisoners
and animals and gave them to the Levites, who maintained the LORD's Tabernacle. All this was done as
the LORD had commanded Moses.

48 Then all the generals and captains came to
Moses 49 and said, "We, your servants, have accounted for all the men who went out to battle under
our command; not one of us is missing! 50 So we are
presenting the items of gold we captured as an offering to the LORD from our share of the plunder—arm-
bands, bracelets, rings, earrings, and necklaces. This
will purify our lives before the LORD and make us
right with him.*"

51 So Moses and Eleazar the priest received the
gold from all the military commanders—all kinds of
jewelry and crafted objects. 52 In all, the gold that the

31:50 Or *will make atonement for our lives before the LORD.*

up to the LORD, of the captains of thousands, and of the captains of hundreds, was sixteen thousand seven hundred and fifty shekels.

53 (*For* the men of war had taken spoil, every man for himself.)

54 And Moses and Eleazar the priest took the gold of the captains of thousands and of hundreds, and brought it into the tabernacle of the congregation, *for* a memorial for the children of Israel before the LORD.

32 1 Now the children of Reuben and the children of Gad had a very great multitude of cattle: and when they saw the land of Jazer, and the land of Gilead, that, behold, the place *was* a place for cattle;

2 The children of Gad and the children of Reuben came and spake unto Moses, and to Eleazar the priest, and unto the princes of the congregation, saying,

3 Ataroth, and Dibon, and Jazer, and Nimrah, and Heshbon, and Elealeh, and Shebam, and Nebo, and Beon,

4 *Even* the country which the LORD smote before the congregation of Israel, *is* a land for cattle, and thy servants have cattle:

5 Wherefore, said they, if we have found grace in thy sight, let this land be given unto thy servants for a possession, *and* bring us not over Jordan.

6 And Moses said unto the children of Gad and to the children of Reuben, Shall your brethren go to war, and shall ye sit here?

7 And wherefore discourage ye the heart of the children of Israel from going over into the land which the LORD hath given them?

8 Thus did your fathers, when I sent them from Kadesh-barnea to see the land.

9 For when they went up unto the valley of Eshcol, and saw the land, they discouraged the heart of the children of Israel, that they should not go into the land which the LORD had given them.

10 And the LORD's anger was kindled the same time, and he sware, saying,

11 Surely none of the men that came up out of Egypt, from twenty years old and upward, shall see the land which I sware unto Abraham, unto Isaac, and unto Jacob; because they have not wholly followed me:

12 Save Caleb the son of Jephunneh the Kenezite, and Joshua the son of Nun: for they have wholly followed the LORD.

13 And the LORD's anger was kindled against Israel, and he made them wander in the wilderness forty years, until all the generation, that had done evil in the sight of the LORD, was consumed.

14 And, behold, ye are risen up in your fathers' stead, an increase of sinful men, to augment yet the fierce anger of the LORD toward Israel.

generals and captains presented as a gift to the LORD
weighed about 420 pounds.* 53 All the fighting men
had taken some of the plunder for themselves. 54 So
Moses and Eleazar the priest accepted the gifts from
the generals and captains and brought the gold to
the Tabernacle* as a reminder to the LORD that the
people of Israel belong to him.

The Tribes East of the Jordan

32 The tribes of Reuben and Gad owned vast
numbers of livestock. So when they saw that
the lands of Jazer and Gilead were ideally suited for
their flocks and herds, 2 they came to Moses, Eleazar
the priest, and the other leaders of the community.
They said, 3 "Notice the towns of Ataroth, Dibon, Jazer, Nimrah, Heshbon, Elealeh, Sibmah,* Nebo, and
Beon. 4 The LORD has conquered this whole area for
the community of Israel, and it is ideally suited for all
our livestock. 5 If we have found favor with you,
please let us have this land as our property instead of
giving us land across the Jordan River."

6 "Do you intend to stay here while your brothers
go across and do all the fighting?" Moses asked the
men of Gad and Reuben. 7 "Why do you want to discourage the rest of the people of Israel from going
across to the land the LORD has given them? 8 Your
ancestors did the same thing when I sent them from
Kadesh-barnea to explore the land. 9 After they went
up to the valley of Eshcol and explored the land, they
discouraged the people of Israel from entering the
land the LORD was giving them. 10 Then the LORD was
very angry with them, and he vowed, 11 'Of all those I
rescued from Egypt, no one who is twenty years old
or older will ever see the land I swore to give to Abraham, Isaac, and Jacob, for they have not obeyed me
wholeheartedly. 12 The only exceptions are Caleb son
of Jephunneh the Kenizzite and Joshua son of Nun,
for they have wholeheartedly followed the LORD.'

13 "The LORD was angry with Israel and made them
wander in the wilderness for forty years until the entire generation that sinned in the LORD's sight had
died. 14 But here you are, a brood of sinners, doing exactly the same thing! You are making the LORD even

31:52 Hebrew *16,750 shekels* [191 kilograms]. 31:54 Hebrew *the Tent of Meeting.* 32:3 As in Samaritan Pentateuch and Greek version (see also 32:38); Hebrew reads *Sebam.*

KING JAMES VERSION

15 For if ye turn away from after him, he will yet
again leave them in the wilderness; and ye shall destroy all this people.
16 And they came near unto him, and said, We will
build sheepfolds here for our cattle, and cities for
our little ones:
17 But we ourselves will go ready armed before the
children of Israel, until we have brought them unto
their place: and our little ones shall dwell in the
fenced cities because of the inhabitants of the land.
18 We will not return unto our houses, until the
children of Israel have inherited every man his
inheritance.
19 For we will not inherit with them on yonder side
Jordan, or forward; because our inheritance is fallen
to us on this side Jordan eastward.
20 And Moses said unto them, If ye will do this
thing, if ye will go armed before the LORD to war,
21 And will go all of you armed over Jordan before
the LORD, until he hath driven out his enemies from
before him,
22 And the land be subdued before the LORD: then
afterward ye shall return, and be guiltless before the
LORD, and before Israel; and this land shall be your
possession before the LORD.
23 But if ye will not do so, behold, ye have sinned
against the LORD: and be sure your sin will find
you out.
24 Build you cities for your little ones, and folds for
your sheep; and do that which hath proceeded out of
your mouth.
25 And the children of Gad and the children of Reuben spake unto Moses, saying, Thy servants will do as
my lord commandeth.
26 Our little ones, our wives, our flocks, and all our
cattle, shall be there in the cities of Gilead:
27 But thy servants will pass over, every man armed
for war, before the LORD to battle, as my lord saith.
28 So concerning them Moses commanded Eleazar
the priest, and Joshua the son of Nun, and the chief
fathers of the tribes of the children of Israel:
29 And Moses said unto them, If the children of
Gad and the children of Reuben will pass with you
over Jordan, every man armed to battle, before the
LORD, and the land shall be subdued before you; then
ye shall give them the land of Gilead for a possession:
30 But if they will not pass over with you armed,
they shall have possessions among you in the land of
Canaan.
31 And the children of Gad and the children of Reuben answered, saying, As the LORD hath said unto thy
servants, so will we do.
32 We will pass over armed before the LORD into
the land of Canaan, that the possession of our inheritance on this side Jordan *may* be ours.
33 And Moses gave unto them, *even* to the children
of Gad, and to the children of Reuben, and unto half
the tribe of Manasseh the son of Joseph, the kingdom

NEW LIVING TRANSLATION

angrier with Israel.
15 If you turn away from him like
this and he abandons them again in the wilderness,
you will be responsible for destroying this entire
nation!"
16 But they approached Moses and said, "We simply want to build pens for our livestock and fortified
towns for our wives and children.
17 Then we will arm
ourselves and lead our fellow Israelites into battle
until we have brought them safely to their land.
Meanwhile, our families will stay in the fortified
towns we build here, so they will be safe from any
attacks by the local people.
18 We will not return to
our homes until all the people of Israel have received
their portions of land.
19 But we do not claim any of
the land on the other side of the Jordan. We would
rather live here on the east side and accept this as
our grant of land."
20 Then Moses said, "If you keep your word and
arm yourselves for the LORD's battles,
21 and if your
troops cross the Jordan and keep fighting until the
LORD has driven out his enemies,
22 then you may re-
turn when the LORD has conquered the land. You will
have fulfilled your duty to the LORD and to the rest of
the people of Israel. And the land on the east side of
the Jordan will be your property from the LORD.
23 But if you fail to keep your word, then you will have
sinned against the LORD, and you may be sure that
your sin will find you out.
24 Go ahead and build
towns for your families and pens for your flocks, but
do everything you have promised."
25 Then the men of Gad and Reuben replied, "We,
your servants, will follow your instructions exactly.
26 Our children, wives, flocks, and cattle will stay here
in the towns of Gilead.
27 But all who are able to bear
arms will cross over to fight for the LORD, just as you
have said."
28 So Moses gave orders to Eleazar the priest, Joshua son of Nun, and the leaders of the clans of Israel.
29 He said, "The men of Gad and Reuben who are
armed for battle must cross the Jordan with you to
fight for the LORD. If they do, give them the land of
Gilead as their property when the land is conquered.
30 But if they refuse to arm themselves and cross over
with you, then they must accept land with the rest of
you in the land of Canaan."
31 The tribes of Gad and Reuben said again, "We
are your servants, and we will do as the LORD has
commanded!
32 We will cross the Jordan into Canaan
fully armed to fight for the LORD, but our property
will be here on this side of the Jordan."
33 So Moses assigned land to the tribes of Gad,
Reuben, and half the tribe of Manasseh son of Joseph. He gave them the territory of King Sihon of the

KING JAMES VERSION

of Sihon king of the Amorites, and the kingdom of Og king of Bashan, the land, with the cities thereof in the coasts, *even* the cities of the country round about.

34 And the children of Gad built Dibon, and Ataroth, and Aroer,

35 And Atroth, Shophan, and Jaazer, and Jogbehah,

36 And Beth-nimrah, and Beth-haran, fenced cities: and folds for sheep.

37 And the children of Reuben built Heshbon, and Elealeh, and Kirjathaim,

38 And Nebo, and Baal-meon, (their names being changed,) and Shibmah: and gave other names unto the cities which they builded.

39 And the children of Machir the son of Manasseh went to Gilead, and took it, and dispossessed the Amorite which *was* in it.

40 And Moses gave Gilead unto Machir the son of Manasseh; and he dwelt therein.

41 And Jair the son of Manasseh went and took the small towns thereof, and called them Havoth-jair.

42 And Nobah went and took Kenath, and the villages thereof, and called it Nobah, after his own name.

33 1 These *are* the journeys of the children of Israel, which went forth out of the land of Egypt with their armies under the hand of Moses and Aaron.

2 And Moses wrote their goings out according to their journeys by the commandment of the LORD: and these *are* their journeys according to their goings out.

3 And they departed from Rameses in the first month, on the fifteenth day of the first month; on the morrow after the passover the children of Israel went out with an high hand in the sight of all the Egyptians.

4 For the Egyptians buried all *their* firstborn, which the LORD had smitten among them: upon their gods also the LORD executed judgments.

5 And the children of Israel removed from Rameses, and pitched in Succoth.

6 And they departed from Succoth, and pitched in Etham, which *is* in the edge of the wilderness.

7 And they removed from Etham, and turned again unto Pi-hahiroth, which *is* before Baal-zephon: and they pitched before Migdol.

8 And they departed from before Pi-hahiroth, and passed through the midst of the sea into the wilderness, and went three days' journey in the wilderness of Etham, and pitched in Marah.

9 And they removed from Marah, and came unto Elim: and in Elim *were* twelve fountains of water, and threescore and ten palm trees; and they pitched there.

10 And they removed from Elim, and encamped by the Red sea.

NEW LIVING TRANSLATION

Amorites and the land of King Og of Bashan—the whole land with its cities and surrounding lands.

34 The descendants of Gad built the towns of Dibon, Ataroth, Aroer, 35 Atroth-shophan, Jazer, Jogbehah, 36 Beth-nimrah, and Beth-haran. These were all fortified towns with pens for their flocks.

37 The descendants of Reuben built the towns of Heshbon, Elealeh, Kiriathaim, 38 Nebo, Baal-meon, and Sibmah. They changed the names of some of the towns they conquered and rebuilt.

39 Then the descendants of Makir of the tribe of Manasseh went to Gilead and conquered it, and they drove out the Amorites living there. 40 So Moses gave Gilead to the Makirites, descendants of Manasseh, and they settled there. 41 The people of Jair, another clan of the tribe of Manasseh, captured many of the towns in Gilead and changed the name of that region to the Towns of Jair.* 42 Meanwhile, a man named Nobah captured the town of Kenath and its surrounding villages, and he renamed that area Nobah after himself.

Remembering Israel's Journey

33 This is the route the Israelites followed as they marched out of Egypt under the leadership of Moses and Aaron. 2 At the LORD's direction, Moses kept a written record of their progress. These are the stages of their march, identified by the different places where they stopped along the way.

3 They set out from the city of Rameses in early spring—on the fifteenth day of the first month*—on the morning after the first Passover celebration. The people of Israel left defiantly, in full view of all the Egyptians. 4 Meanwhile, the Egyptians were burying all their firstborn sons, whom the LORD had killed the night before. The LORD had defeated the gods of Egypt that night with great acts of judgment!

5 After leaving Rameses, the Israelites set up camp at Succoth.

6 Then they left Succoth and camped at Etham on the edge of the wilderness.

7 They left Etham and turned back toward Pi-hahiroth, opposite Baal-zephon, and camped near Migdol.

8 They left Pi-hahiroth and crossed the Red Sea* into the wilderness beyond. Then they traveled for three days into the Etham wilderness and camped at Marah.

9 They left Marah and camped at Elim, where there were twelve springs of water and seventy palm trees.

10 They left Elim and camped beside the Red Sea.*

32:41 Hebrew *Havvoth-jair.* **33:3** This day in the ancient Hebrew lunar calendar occurred in late March, April, or early May. **33:8** Hebrew *the sea.* **33:10** Hebrew *sea of reeds;* also in 33:11.

KING JAMES VERSION

[11]And they removed from the Red sea, and encamped in the wilderness of Sin.
[12]And they took their journey out of the wilderness of Sin, and encamped in Dophkah.
[13]And they departed from Dophkah, and encamped in Alush.
[14]And they removed from Alush, and encamped at
Rephidim, where was no water for the people to
drink.
[15]And they departed from Rephidim, and pitched
in the wilderness of Sinai.
[16]And they removed from the desert of Sinai, and
pitched at Kibroth-hattaavah.
[17]And they departed from Kibroth-hattaavah, and
encamped at Hazeroth.
[18]And they departed from Hazeroth, and pitched
in Rithmah.
[19]And they departed from Rithmah, and pitched
at Rimmon-parez.
[20]And they departed from Rimmon-parez, and
pitched in Libnah.
[21]And they removed from Libnah, and pitched at
Rissah.
[22]And they journeyed from Rissah, and pitched in
Kehelathah.
[23]And they went from Kehelathah, and pitched
in mount Shapher.
[24]And they removed from mount Shapher, and
encamped in Haradah.
[25]And they removed from Haradah, and pitched
in Makheloth.
[26]And they removed from Makheloth, and encamped at Tahath.
[27]And they departed from Tahath, and pitched at
Tarah.
[28]And they removed from Tarah, and pitched in
Mithcah.
[29]And they went from Mithcah, and pitched in
Hashmonah.
[30]And they departed from Hashmonah, and encamped at Moseroth.
[31]And they departed from Moseroth, and pitched
in Bene-jaakan.
[32]And they removed from Bene-jaakan, and encamped at Hor-hagidgad.
[33]And they went from Hor-hagidgad, and pitched
in Jotbathah.
[34]And they removed from Jotbathah, and encamped at Ebronah.
[35]And they departed from Ebronah, and encamped at Ezion-gaber.
[36]And they removed from Ezion-gaber, and
pitched in the wilderness of Zin, which *is* Kadesh.
[37]And they removed from Kadesh, and pitched in
mount Hor, in the edge of the land of Edom.
[38]And Aaron the priest went up into mount Hor at
the commandment of the LORD, and died there, in
the fortieth year after the children of Israel were

NEW LIVING TRANSLATION

[11]They left the Red Sea and camped in the wilderness of Sin.*
[12]They left the wilderness of Sin and camped at Dophkah.
[13]They left Dophkah and camped at Alush.
[14]They left Alush and camped at Rephidim, where there was no water for the people to drink.
[15]They left Rephidim and camped in the wilderness of Sinai.
[16]They left the wilderness of Sinai and camped at Kibroth-hattaavah.
[17]They left Kibroth-hattaavah and camped at Hazeroth.
[18]They left Hazeroth and camped at Rithmah.
[19]They left Rithmah and camped at Rimmon-perez.
[20]They left Rimmon-perez and camped at Libnah.
[21]They left Libnah and camped at Rissah.
[22]They left Rissah and camped at Kehelathah.
[23]They left Kehelathah and camped at Mount Shepher.
[24]They left Mount Shepher and camped at Haradah.
[25]They left Haradah and camped at Makheloth.
[26]They left Makheloth and camped at Tahath.
[27]They left Tahath and camped at Terah.
[28]They left Terah and camped at Mithcah.
[29]They left Mithcah and camped at Hashmonah.
[30]They left Hashmonah and camped at Moseroth.
[31]They left Moseroth and camped at Bene-jaakan.
[32]They left Bene-jaakan and camped at Hor-haggidgad.
[33]They left Hor-haggidgad and camped at Jotbathah.
[34]They left Jotbathah and camped at Abronah.
[35]They left Abronah and camped at Ezion-geber.
[36]They left Ezion-geber and camped at Kadesh in the wilderness of Zin.
[37]They left Kadesh and camped at Mount Hor, at the
border of Edom. [38]While they were at the foot of
Mount Hor, Aaron the priest was directed by the
LORD to go up the mountain, and there he died.

33:11 The geographical name *Sin* is related to *Sinai* and should not be confused with the English word *sin.*

KING JAMES VERSION

come out of the land of Egypt, in the first *day* of the
fifth month.
39 And Aaron *was* an hundred and twenty and
three years old when he died in mount Hor.
40 And king Arad the Canaanite, which dwelt in the
south in the land of Canaan, heard of the coming of
the children of Israel.
41 And they departed from mount Hor, and pitched
in Zalmonah.
42 And they departed from Zalmonah, and pitched
in Punon.
43 And they departed from Punon, and pitched in
Oboth.
44 And they departed from Oboth, and pitched in
Ije-abarim, in the border of Moab.
45 And they departed from Iim, and pitched in
Dibon-gad.
46 And they removed from Dibon-gad, and encamped in Almon-diblathaim.
47 And they removed from Almon-diblathaim, and
pitched in the mountains of Abarim, before Nebo.
48 And they departed from the mountains of Abarim, and pitched in the plains of Moab by Jordan
near Jericho.
49 And they pitched by Jordan, from Beth-jesimoth
even unto Abel-shittim in the plains of Moab.
50 And the LORD spake unto Moses in the plains of
Moab by Jordan *near* Jericho, saying,
51 Speak unto the children of Israel, and say unto
them, When ye are passed over Jordan into the land
of Canaan;
52 Then ye shall drive out all the inhabitants of the
land from before you, and destroy all their pictures,
and destroy all their molten images, and quite pluck
down all their high places:
53 And ye shall dispossess *the inhabitants* of the
land, and dwell therein: for I have given you the land
to possess it.
54 And ye shall divide the land by lot for an inheritance among your families: *and* to the more ye shall
give the more inheritance, and to the fewer ye shall
give the less inheritance: every man's *inheritance*
shall be in the place where his lot falleth; according
to the tribes of your fathers ye shall inherit.
55 But if ye will not drive out the inhabitants of the
land from before you; then it shall come to pass, that
those which ye let remain of them *shall be* pricks in
your eyes, and thorns in your sides, and shall vex you
in the land wherein ye dwell.
56 Moreover it shall come to pass, *that* I shall do
unto you, as I thought to do unto them.

34 1 And the LORD spake unto Moses, saying,
2 Command the children of Israel, and say
unto them, When ye come into the land of Canaan;
(this *is* the land that shall fall unto you for an inheritance, *even* the land of Canaan with the coasts
thereof:)

NEW LIVING TRANSLATION

This happened in midsummer, on the first day of
the fifth month* of the fortieth year after Israel's
departure from Egypt. 39 Aaron was 123 years old
when he died there on Mount Hor.
40 At that time the Canaanite king of Arad, who lived
in the Negev in the land of Canaan, heard that the
people of Israel were approaching his land.
41 Meanwhile, the Israelites left Mount Hor and
camped at Zalmonah.
42 Then they left Zalmonah and camped at Punon.
43 They left Punon and camped at Oboth.
44 They left Oboth and camped at Iye-abarim on the
border of Moab.
45 They left Iye-abarim* and camped at Dibon-gad.
46 They left Dibon-gad and camped at Almon-
diblathaim.
47 They left Almon-diblathaim and camped in the
mountains east of the river,* near Mount Nebo.
48 They left the mountains east of the river and
camped on the plains of Moab beside the Jordan
River, across from Jericho. 49 Along the Jordan
River they camped from Beth-jeshimoth as far as
the meadows of Acacia* on the plains of Moab.

50 While they were camped near the Jordan River
on the plains of Moab opposite Jericho, the LORD said
to Moses, 51 "Give the following instructions to the
people of Israel: When you cross the Jordan River
into the land of Canaan, 52 you must drive out all the
people living there. You must destroy all their carved
and molten images and demolish all their pagan
shrines. 53 Take possession of the land and settle in it,
because I have given it to you to occupy. 54 You must
distribute the land among the clans by sacred lot and
in proportion to their size. A larger portion of land
will be allotted to each of the larger clans, and a
smaller portion will be allotted to each of the smaller
clans. The decision of the sacred lot is final. In this
way, the portions of land will be divided among your
ancestral tribes. 55 But if you fail to drive out the
people who live in the land, those who remain will be
like splinters in your eyes and thorns in your sides.
They will harass you in the land where you live. 56 And
I will do to you what I had planned to do to them."

Boundaries of the Land

34 Then the LORD said to Moses, 2 "Give these
instructions to the Israelites: When you
come into the land of Canaan, which I am giving you

33:38 This day in the ancient Hebrew lunar calendar occurred in July or August. 33:45 As in 33:44; Hebrew reads *Iyim,* another name for Iye-abarim. 33:47 Or *the mountains of Abarim;* also in 33:48. 33:49 Hebrew *as far as Abel-shittim.*

KING JAMES VERSION

3 Then your south quarter shall be from the wilderness of Zin along by the coast of Edom, and your south border shall be the outmost coast of the salt sea eastward:

4 And your border shall turn from the south to the ascent of Akrabbim, and pass on to Zin: and the going forth thereof shall be from the south to Kadesh-barnea, and shall go on to Hazar-addar, and pass on to Azmon:

5 And the border shall fetch a compass from Azmon unto the river of Egypt, and the goings out of it shall be at the sea.

6 And *as for* the western border, ye shall even have the great sea for a border: this shall be your west border.

7 And this shall be your north border: from the great sea ye shall point out for you mount Hor:

8 From mount Hor ye shall point out *your border* unto the entrance of Hamath; and the goings forth of the border shall be to Zedad:

9 And the border shall go on to Ziphron, and the goings out of it shall be at Hazar-enan: this shall be your north border.

10 And ye shall point out your east border from Hazar-enan to Shepham:

11 And the coast shall go down from Shepham to Riblah, on the east side of Ain; and the border shall descend, and shall reach unto the side of the sea of Chinnereth eastward:

12 And the border shall go down to Jordan, and the goings out of it shall be at the salt sea: this shall be your land with the coasts thereof round about.

13 And Moses commanded the children of Israel, saying, This *is* the land which ye shall inherit by lot, which the LORD commanded to give unto the nine tribes, and to the half tribe:

14 For the tribe of the children of Reuben according to the house of their fathers, and the tribe of the children of Gad according to the house of their fathers, have received *their inheritance;* and half the tribe of Manasseh have received their inheritance:

15 The two tribes and the half tribe have received their inheritance on this side Jordan *near* Jericho eastward, toward the sunrising.

16 And the LORD spake unto Moses, saying,

17 These *are* the names of the men which shall divide the land unto you: Eleazar the priest, and Joshua the son of Nun.

18 And ye shall take one prince of every tribe, to divide the land by inheritance.

19 And the names of the men *are* these: Of the tribe of Judah, Caleb the son of Jephunneh.

20 And of the tribe of the children of Simeon, SheuMel the son of Ammihud.

21 Of the tribe of Benjamin, Elidad the son of Chislon.

22 And the prince of the tribe of the children of Dan, Bukki the son of Jogli.

NEW LIVING TRANSLATION

as your special possession, these will be the boundaries. 3 The southern portion of your country will extend from the wilderness of Zin, along the edge of
Edom. The southern boundary will begin on the east
at the Dead Sea.* 4 It will then run south past Scorpion Pass* in the direction of Zin. Its southernmost
point will be Kadesh-barnea, from which it will go to
Hazar-addar, and on to Azmon. 5 From Azmon the
boundary will turn toward the Brook of Egypt and
end at the Mediterranean Sea.*
6 "Your western boundary will be the coastline of
the Mediterranean Sea.
7 "Your northern boundary will begin at the Mediterranean Sea and run east to Mount Hor, 8 then to
Lebo-hamath, and on through Zedad 9 and Ziphron
to Hazar-enan. This will be your northern boundary.
10 "The eastern boundary will start at Hazar-enan
and run south to Shepham, 11 then down to Riblah on
the east side of Ain. From there the boundary will
run down along the eastern edge of the Sea of Galilee,* 12 and then along the Jordan River to the Dead
Sea. These are the boundaries of your land."
13 Then Moses told the Israelites, "This territory is
the homeland you are to divide among yourselves by
sacred lot. The LORD has commanded that the land
be divided among the nine and a half remaining
tribes. 14 The families of the tribes of Reuben, Gad,
and half the tribe of Manasseh have already received
their grants of land 15 on the east side of the Jordan
River, across from Jericho toward the sunrise."

Leaders to Divide the Land

16 And the LORD said to Moses, 17 "Eleazar the priest
and Joshua son of Nun are the men designated to divide the grants of land among the people. 18 Enlist
one leader from each tribe to help them with the
task. 19 These are the tribes and the names of the
leaders:

Tribe	*Leader*
Judah	Caleb son of Jephunneh
20 Simeon	Shemuel son of Ammihud
21 Benjamin	Elidad son of Kislon
22 Dan	Bukki son of Jogli

34:3 Hebrew *Salt Sea;* also in 34:12. **34:4** Or *the ascent of Akrabbim.* **34:5** Hebrew *the sea;* also in 34:6, 7. **34:11** Hebrew *Sea of Kinnereth.*

KING JAMES VERSION

23 The prince of the children of Joseph, for the
tribe of the children of Manasseh, Hanniel the son
of Ephod.
24 And the prince of the tribe of the children of
Ephraim, Kemuel the son of Shiphtan.
25 And the prince of the tribe of the children of
Zebulun, Elizaphan the son of Parnach.
26 And the prince of the tribe of the children of
Issachar, Paltiel the son of Azzan.
27 And the prince of the tribe of the children of
Asher, Ahihud the son of Shelomi.
28 And the prince of the tribe of the children of
Naphtali, Pedahel the son of Ammihud.
29 These *are they* whom the LORD commanded
to divide the inheritance unto the children of Israel
in the land of Canaan.

35 1 And the LORD spake unto Moses in the
plains of Moab by Jordan *near* Jericho,
saying,
2 Command the children of Israel, that they give
unto the Levites of the inheritance of their possession cities to dwell in; and ye shall give *also* unto the
Levites suburbs for the cities round about them.
3 And the cities shall they have to dwell in; and the
suburbs of them shall be for their cattle, and for their
goods, and for all their beasts.
4 And the suburbs of the cities, which ye shall give
unto the Levites, *shall reach* from the wall of the city
and outward a thousand cubits round about.
5 And ye shall measure from without the city on
the east side two thousand cubits, and on the south
side two thousand cubits, and on the west side two
thousand cubits, and on the north side two thousand
cubits; and the city *shall be* in the midst: this shall be
to them the suburbs of the cities.
6 And among the cities which ye shall give unto the
Levites *there shall be* six cities for refuge, which ye
shall appoint for the manslayer, that he may flee
thither: and to them ye shall add forty and two cities.
7 *So* all the cities which ye shall give to the Levites
shall be forty and eight cities: them *shall ye give* with
their suburbs.
8 And the cities which ye shall give *shall be* of the
possession of the children of Israel: from *them that
have* many ye shall give many; but from *them that
have* few ye shall give few: every one shall give of his
cities unto the Levites according to his inheritance
which he inheriteth.

9 And the LORD spake unto Moses, saying,
10 Speak unto the children of Israel, and say unto
them, When ye be come over Jordan into the land of
Canaan;
11 Then ye shall appoint you cities to be cities of
refuge for you; that the slayer may flee thither, which
killeth any person at unawares.
12 And they shall be unto you cities for refuge from

NEW LIVING TRANSLATION

23 Manasseh son of Joseph . . . . . . Hanniel son of Ephod
24 Ephraim son of Joseph . . . . . . Kemuel son of Shiphtan
25 Zebulun . . . . Elizaphan son of Parnach
26 Issachar . . . . Paltiel son of Azzan
27 Asher . . . . Ahihud son of Shelomi
28 Naphtali . . . . Pedahel son of Ammihud

29 These are the men the LORD has appointed to
divide the grants of land in Canaan among the
Israelites."

Towns for the Levites

35 While Israel was camped beside the Jordan
on the plains of Moab across from Jericho,
the LORD said to Moses, 2 "Command the people of Israel to give to the Levites from their property certain
towns to live in, along with the surrounding pasturelands. 3 These towns will be for the Levites to live in,
and the surrounding lands will provide pasture for
their cattle, flocks, and other livestock. 4 The pastureland assigned to the Levites around these towns will
extend 1,500 feet* from the town walls in every direction. 5 Measure off 3,000 feet* outside the town
walls in every direction—east, south, west, north—
with the town at the center. This area will serve as the
larger pastureland for the towns.
6 "Six of the towns you give the Levites will be cities of refuge, where a person who has accidentally
killed someone can flee for safety. In addition, give
them forty-two other towns. 7 In all, forty-eight
towns with the surrounding pastureland will be
given to the Levites. 8 These towns will come from
the property of the people of Israel. The larger tribes
will give more towns to the Levites, while the smaller
tribes will give fewer. Each tribe will give property in
proportion to the size of its land."

Cities of Refuge

9 The LORD said to Moses, 10 "Give the following instructions to the people of Israel.
"When you cross the Jordan into the land of
Canaan, 11 designate cities of refuge to which people
can flee if they have killed someone accidentally.
12 These cities will be places of protection from a

35:4 Hebrew *1,000 cubits* [460 meters]. 35:5 Hebrew *2,000 cubits* [920 meters].

KING JAMES VERSION

the avenger; that the manslayer die not, until he
stand before the congregation in judgment.
13And of these cities which ye shall give six cities
shall ye have for refuge.
14Ye shall give three cities on this side Jordan, and
three cities shall ye give in the land of Canaan, *which*
shall be cities of refuge.
15These six cities shall be a refuge, *both* for the
children of Israel, and for the stranger, and for the sojourner among them: that every one that killeth any
person unawares may flee thither.
16And if he smite him with an instrument of iron,
so that he die, he *is* a murderer: the murderer shall
surely be put to death.
17And if he smite him with throwing a stone,
wherewith he may die, and he die, he is a murderer:
the murderer shall surely be put to death.
18Or if he smite him with an hand weapon of
wood, wherewith he may die, and he die, he is a murderer: the murderer shall surely be put to death.
19The revenger of blood himself shall slay the
murderer: when he meeteth him, he shall slay him.
20But if he thrust him of hatred, or hurl at him by
laying of wait, that he die;
21Or in enmity smite him with his hand, that he
die: he that smote *him* shall surely be put to death;
for he *is* a murderer: the revenger of blood shall slay
the murderer, when he meeteth him.
22But if he thrust him suddenly without enmity, or
have cast upon him any thing without laying of wait,
23Or with any stone, wherewith a man may die,
seeing *him* not, and cast *it* upon him, that he die, and
was not his enemy, neither sought his harm:
24Then the congregation shall judge between the
slayer and the revenger of blood according to these
judgments:
25And the congregation shall deliver the slayer out
of the hand of the revenger of blood, and the congregation shall restore him to the city of his refuge,
whither he was fled: and he shall abide in it unto the
death of the high priest, which was anointed with
the holy oil.
26But if the slayer shall at any time come without
the border of the city of his refuge, whither he was
fled;
27And the revenger of blood find him without the
borders of the city of his refuge, and the revenger of
blood kill the slayer; he shall not be guilty of blood:
28Because he should have remained in the city of
his refuge until the death of the high priest: but after
the death of the high priest the slayer shall return
into the land of his possession.
29So these *things* shall be for a statute of judgment unto you throughout your generations in all
your dwellings.
30Whoso killeth any person, the murderer shall
be put to death by the mouth of witnesses: but one

NEW LIVING TRANSLATION

dead person's relatives who want to avenge the
death. The slayer must not be put to death before being tried by the community. 13Designate six cities of
refuge for yourselves, 14three on the east side of the
Jordan River and three on the west in the land of Canaan. 15These cities are for the protection of Israelites, foreigners living among you, and traveling
merchants. Anyone who accidentally kills someone
may flee there for safety.
16"But if someone strikes and kills another person
with a piece of iron, it is murder, and the murderer
must be executed. 17Or if someone with a stone in
his hand strikes and kills another person, it is murder, and the murderer must be put to death. 18Or if
someone strikes and kills another person with a
wooden object, it is murder, and the murderer must
be put to death. 19The victim's nearest relative is responsible for putting the murderer to death. When
they meet, the avenger must put the murderer to
death. 20So if someone hates another person and
pushes him or throws a dangerous object at him and
he dies, it is murder. 21Or if someone hates another
person and hits him with a fist and he dies, it is murder. In such cases, the avenger must put the murderer to death when they meet.
22"But suppose someone pushes another person
without having shown previous hostility, or throws
something that unintentionally hits another person,
23or accidentally drops a huge stone on someone,
though they were not enemies, and the person dies.
24If this should happen, the community must follow
these regulations in making a judgment between the
slayer and the avenger, the victim's nearest relative:
25The community must protect the slayer from the
avenger and must escort the slayer back to live in the
city of refuge to which he fled. There he must remain
until the death of the high priest, who was anointed
with the sacred oil.
26"But if the slayer ever leaves the limits of the city
of refuge, 27and the avenger finds him outside the
city and kills him, it will not be considered murder.
28The slayer should have stayed inside the city of refuge until the death of the high priest. But after the
death of the high priest, the slayer may return to his
own property. 29These are legal requirements for you
to observe from generation to generation, wherever
you may live.
30"All murderers must be put to death, but only if
evidence is presented by more than one witness. No

KING JAMES VERSION

witness shall not testify against any person *to cause*
him to die.
[31]Moreover ye shall take no satisfaction for the life
of a murderer, which *is* guilty of death: but he shall
be surely put to death.
[32]And ye shall take no satisfaction for him that is
fled to the city of his refuge, that he should come
again to dwell in the land, until the death of the
priest.
[33]So ye shall not pollute the land wherein ye *are:*
for blood it defileth the land: and the land cannot be
cleansed of the blood that is shed therein, but by the
blood of him that shed it.
[34]Defile not therefore the land which ye shall inhabit, wherein I dwell: for I the LORD dwell among
the children of Israel.

36 [1]And the chief fathers of the families of the
children of Gilead, the son of Machir, the son
of Manasseh, of the families of the sons of Joseph,
came near, and spake before Moses, and before the
princes, the chief fathers of the children of Israel:
[2]And they said, The LORD commanded my lord to
give the land for an inheritance by lot to the children
of Israel: and my lord was commanded by the LORD
to give the inheritance of Zelophehad our brother
unto his daughters.
[3]And if they be married to any of the sons of the
other tribes of the children of Israel, then shall their
inheritance be taken from the inheritance of our fathers, and shall be put to the inheritance of the tribe
whereunto they are received: so shall it be taken
from the lot of our inheritance.
[4]And when the jubile of the children of Israel shall
be, then shall their inheritance be put unto the inheritance of the tribe whereunto they are received:
so shall their inheritance be taken away from the inheritance of the tribe of our fathers.
[5]And Moses commanded the children of Israel according to the word of the LORD, saying, The tribe of
the sons of Joseph hath said well.
[6]This *is* the thing which the LORD doth command
concerning the daughters of Zelophehad, saying, Let
them marry to whom they think best; only to the
family of the tribe of their father shall they marry.
[7]So shall not the inheritance of the children of
Israel remove from tribe to tribe: for every one of the
children of Israel shall keep himself to the inheritance of the tribe of his fathers.
[8]And every daughter, that possesseth an inheritance in any tribe of the children of Israel, shall be
wife unto one of the family of the tribe of her father,
that the children of Israel may enjoy every man the
inheritance of his fathers.
[9]Neither shall the inheritance remove from *one*
tribe to another tribe; but every one of the tribes of
the children of Israel shall keep himself to his own
inheritance.

NEW LIVING TRANSLATION

one may be put to death on the testimony of only one
witness. [31]Also, you must never accept a ransom payment for the life of someone judged guilty of murder
and subject to execution; murderers must always be
put to death. [32]And never accept a ransom payment
from someone who has fled to a city of refuge, allowing a slayer to return to his property before the death
of the high priest. [33]This will ensure that the land
where you live will not be polluted, for murder pol-
lutes the land. And no sacrifice except the execution
of the murderer can purify the land from murder.*
[34]You must not defile the land where you live, for I
live there myself. I am the LORD, who lives among the
people of Israel."

Women Who Inherit Property

36 Then the heads of the clans of Gilead—
descendants of Makir, son of Manasseh,
son of Joseph—came to Moses and the family leaders of Israel with a petition. [2]They said, "Sir, the
LORD instructed you to divide the land by sacred lot
among the people of Israel. You were told by the
LORD to give the grant of land owned by our brother
Zelophehad to his daughters. [3]But if they marry men
from another tribe, their grants of land will go with
them to the tribe into which they marry. In this way,
the total area of our tribal land will be reduced.
[4]Then when the Year of Jubilee comes, their portion
of land will be added to that of the new tribe, causing
it to be lost forever to our ancestral tribe."
[5]So Moses gave the Israelites this command from
the LORD: "The claim of the men of the tribe of Joseph is legitimate. [6]This is what the LORD commands
concerning the daughters of Zelophehad: Let them
marry anyone they like, as long as it is within their
own ancestral tribe. [7]None of the territorial land may
pass from tribe to tribe, for all the land given to each
tribe must remain within the tribe to which it was
first allotted. [8]The daughters throughout the tribes
of Israel who are in line to inherit property must
marry within their tribe, so that all the Israelites will
keep their ancestral property. [9]No grant of land may
pass from one tribe to another; each tribe of Israel
must keep its allotted portion of land."

35:33 Or *can make atonement for murder.*

KING JAMES VERSION

[10]Even as the LORD commanded Moses, so did the daughters of Zelophehad:

[11]For Mahlah, Tirzah, and Hoglah, and Milcah, and Noah, the daughters of Zelophehad, were married unto their father's brothers' sons:

[12]*And* they were married into the families of the sons of Manasseh the son of Joseph, and their inheritance remained in the tribe of the family of their father.

[13]These *are* the commandments and the judgments, which the LORD commanded by the hand of Moses unto the children of Israel in the plains of Moab by Jordan *near* Jericho.

NEW LIVING TRANSLATION

[10]The daughters of Zelophehad did as the LORD commanded Moses. [11]Mahlah, Tirzah, Hoglah, Milcah, and Noah all married cousins on their father's side. [12]They married into the clans of Manasseh son of Joseph. Thus, their inheritance of land remained within their ancestral tribe.

[13]These are the commands and regulations that the LORD gave to the people of Israel through Moses while they were camped on the plains of Moab beside the Jordan River across from Jericho.

Deuteronomy

KING JAMES VERSION

1 1These *be* the words which Moses spake unto all Israel on this side Jordan in the wilderness, in the plain over against the Red *sea*, between Paran, and Tophel, and Laban, and Hazeroth, and Dizahab.

2(*There are* eleven days' *journey* from Horeb by the way of mount Seir unto Kadesh-barnea.)

3And it came to pass in the fortieth year, in the eleventh month, on the first *day* of the month, *that* Moses spake unto the children of Israel, according unto all that the LORD had given him in commandment unto them;

4After he had slain Sihon the king of the Amorites, which dwelt in Heshbon, and Og the king of Bashan, which dwelt at Astaroth in Edrei:

5On this side Jordan, in the land of Moab, began Moses to declare this law, saying,

6The LORD our God spake unto us in Horeb, saying, Ye have dwelt long enough in this mount:

7Turn you, and take your journey, and go to the mount of the Amorites, and unto all *the places* nigh thereunto, in the plain, in the hills, and in the vale, and in the south, and by the sea side, to the land of the Canaanites, and unto Lebanon, unto the great river, the river Euphrates.

8Behold, I have set the land before you: go in and possess the land which the LORD sware unto your fathers, Abraham, Isaac, and Jacob, to give unto them and to their seed after them.

9And I spake unto you at that time, saying, I am not able to bear you myself alone:

10The LORD your God hath multiplied you, and, behold, ye *are* this day as the stars of heaven for multitude.

11(The LORD God of your fathers make you a thousand times so many more as ye *are*, and bless you, as he hath promised you!)

NEW LIVING TRANSLATION

Introduction to Moses' First Address

1 These are the words that Moses spoke to all the people of Israel while they were in the wilderness east of the Jordan River. They were camped in the Jordan Valley* near Suph, between Paran on one side and Tophel, Laban, Hazeroth, and Di-zahab on the other.

2Normally it takes only eleven days to travel from Mount Sinai* to Kadesh-barnea, going by way of Mount Seir. 3But forty years after the Israelites left Egypt, on the first day of the eleventh month,* Moses addressed the people of Israel, telling them everything the LORD had commanded him to say. 4This took place after he had defeated King Sihon of the Amorites, who had ruled in Heshbon, and King Og of Bashan, who had ruled in Ashtaroth and Edrei.

5While the Israelites were in the land of Moab east of the Jordan River, Moses carefully explained the LORD's instructions as follows.

The Command to Leave Sinai

6"When we were at Mount Sinai, the LORD our God said to us, 'You have stayed at this mountain long enough. 7It is time to break camp and move on. Go to the hill country of the Amorites and to all the neighboring regions—the Jordan Valley, the hill country, the western foothills,* the Negev, and the coastal plain. Go to the land of the Canaanites and to Lebanon, and all the way to the great Euphrates River. 8Look, I am giving all this land to you! Go in and occupy it, for it is the land the LORD swore to give to your ancestors Abraham, Isaac, and Jacob, and to all their descendants.'"

Moses Appoints Leaders from Each Tribe

9Moses continued, "At that time I told you, 'You are too great a burden for me to carry all by myself. 10The LORD your God has increased your population, making you as numerous as the stars! 11And may the LORD, the God of your ancestors, multiply you a thousand times more and bless you as he promised!

1:1 Hebrew *the Arabah;* also in 1:7. **1:2** Hebrew *Horeb,* another name for Sinai; also in 1:6, 19. **1:3** Hebrew *In the fortieth year, on the first day of the eleventh month.* This day in the ancient Hebrew lunar calendar occurred in January or February. **1:7** Hebrew *the Shephelah.*

KING JAMES VERSION

12 How can I myself alone bear your cumbrance, and your burden, and your strife?

13 Take you wise men, and understanding, and known among your tribes, and I will make them rulers over you.

14 And ye answered me, and said, The thing which thou hast spoken *is* good *for us* to do.

15 So I took the chief of your tribes, wise men, and known, and made them heads over you, captains over thousands, and captains over hundreds, and captains over fifties, and captains over tens, and officers among your tribes.

16 And I charged your judges at that time, saying, Hear *the causes* between your brethren, and judge righteously between *every* man and his brother, and the stranger *that is* with him.

17 Ye shall not respect persons in judgment; *but* ye shall hear the small as well as the great; ye shall not be afraid of the face of man; for the judgment *is* God's: and the cause that is too hard for you, bring *it* unto me, and I will hear it.

18 And I commanded you at that time all the things which ye should do.

19 And when we departed from Horeb, we went through all that great and terrible wilderness, which ye saw by the way of the mountain of the Amorites, as the LORD our God commanded us; and we came to Kadesh-barnea.

20 And I said unto you, Ye are come unto the mountain of the Amorites, which the LORD our God doth give unto us.

21 Behold, the LORD thy God hath set the land before thee: go up *and* possess *it,* as the LORD God of thy fathers hath said unto thee; fear not, neither be discouraged.

22 And ye came near unto me every one of you, and said, We will send men before us, and they shall search us out the land, and bring us word again by what way we must go up, and into what cities we shall come.

23 And the saying pleased me well: and I took twelve men of you, one of a tribe:

24 And they turned and went up into the mountain, and came unto the valley of Eshcol, and searched it out.

25 And they took of the fruit of the land in their hands, and brought *it* down unto us, and brought us word again, and said, *It is* a good land which the LORD our God doth give us.

26 Notwithstanding ye would not go up, but rebelled against the commandment of the LORD your God:

27 And ye murmured in your tents, and said, Because the LORD hated us, he hath brought us forth out of the land of Egypt, to deliver us into the hand of the Amorites, to destroy us.

28 Whither shall we go up? our brethren have discouraged our heart, saying, The people *is* greater and

NEW LIVING TRANSLATION

12 But you are such a heavy load to carry! How can I deal with all your problems and bickering? 13 Choose some well-respected men from each tribe who are known for their wisdom and understanding, and I will appoint them as your leaders.'

14 "Then you responded, 'Your plan is a good one.' 15 So I took the wise and respected men you had selected from your tribes and appointed them to serve as judges and officials over you. Some were responsible for a thousand people, some for a hundred, some for fifty, and some for ten.

16 "At that time I instructed the judges, 'You must hear the cases of your fellow Israelites and the foreigners living among you. Be perfectly fair in your decisions 17 and impartial in your judgments. Hear the cases of those who are poor as well as those who are rich. Don't be afraid of anyone's anger, for the decision you make is God's decision. Bring me any cases that are too difficult for you, and I will handle them.'

18 "At that time I gave you instructions about everything you were to do.

Scouts Explore the Land

19 "Then, just as the LORD our God commanded us, we left Mount Sinai and traveled through the great and terrifying wilderness, as you yourselves remember, and headed toward the hill country of the Amorites. When we arrived at Kadesh-barnea, 20 I said to you, 'You have now reached the hill country of the Amorites that the LORD our God is giving us. 21 Look! He has placed the land in front of you. Go and occupy it as the LORD, the God of your ancestors, has promised you. Don't be afraid! Don't be discouraged!'

22 "But you all came to me and said, 'First, let's send out scouts to explore the land for us. They will advise us on the best route to take and which towns we should enter.'

23 "This seemed like a good idea to me, so I chose twelve scouts, one from each of your tribes. 24 They headed for the hill country and came to the valley of Eshcol and explored it. 25 They picked some of its fruit and brought it back to us. And they reported, 'The land the LORD our God has given us is indeed a good land.'

Israel's Rebellion against the LORD

26 "But you rebelled against the command of the LORD your God and refused to go in. 27 You complained in your tents and said, 'The LORD must hate us. That's why he has brought us here from Egypt—to hand us over to the Amorites to be slaughtered. 28 Where can we go? Our brothers have demoralized us with their report. They tell us, "The people of the land are taller and more powerful than we are, and

KING JAMES VERSION

taller than we; the cities *are* great and walled up to heaven; and moreover we have seen the sons of the Anakims there.

29 Then I said unto you, Dread not, neither be afraid of them.

30 The LORD your God which goeth before you, he shall fight for you, according to all that he did for you in Egypt before your eyes;

31 And in the wilderness, where thou hast seen how that the LORD thy God bare thee, as a man doth bear his son, in all the way that ye went, until ye came into this place.

32 Yet in this thing ye did not believe the LORD your God,

33 Who went in the way before you, to search you out a place to pitch your tents *in*, in fire by night, to shew you by what way ye should go, and in a cloud by day.

34 And the LORD heard the voice of your words, and was wroth, and sware, saying,

35 Surely there shall not one of these men of this evil generation see that good land, which I sware to give unto your fathers,

36 Save Caleb the son of Jephunneh; he shall see it, and to him will I give the land that he hath trodden upon, and to his children, because he hath wholly followed the LORD.

37 Also the LORD was angry with me for your sakes, saying, Thou also shalt not go in thither.

38 *But* Joshua the son of Nun, which standeth before thee, he shall go in thither: encourage him: for he shall cause Israel to inherit it.

39 Moreover your little ones, which ye said should be a prey, and your children, which in that day had no knowledge between good and evil, they shall go in thither, and unto them will I give it, and they shall possess it.

40 But *as for* you, turn you, and take your journey into the wilderness by the way of the Red sea.

41 Then ye answered and said unto me, We have sinned against the LORD, we will go up and fight, according to all that the LORD our God commanded us. And when ye had girded on every man his weapons of war, ye were ready to go up into the hill.

42 And the LORD said unto me, Say unto them, Go not up, neither fight; for I *am* not among you; lest ye be smitten before your enemies.

43 So I spake unto you; and ye would not hear, but rebelled against the commandment of the LORD, and went presumptuously up into the hill.

44 And the Amorites, which dwelt in that mountain, came out against you, and chased you, as bees do, and destroyed you in Seir, *even* unto Hormah.

45 And ye returned and wept before the LORD; but the LORD would not hearken to your voice, nor give ear unto you.

46 So ye abode in Kadesh many days, according unto the days that ye abode *there*.

NEW LIVING TRANSLATION

their towns are large, with walls rising high into
the sky! We even saw giants there—the descendants
of Anak!'"

29 "But I said to you, 'Don't be shocked or afraid of
them! 30 The LORD your God is going ahead of you. He
will fight for you, just as you saw him do in Egypt.
31 And you saw how the LORD your God cared for you
all along the way as you traveled through the wilderness, just as a father cares for his child. Now he has
brought you to this place.'

32 "But even after all he did, you refused to trust
the LORD your God, 33 who goes before you looking
for the best places to camp, guiding you with a pillar
of fire by night and a pillar of cloud by day.

34 "When the LORD heard your complaining, he
became very angry. So he solemnly swore, 35 'Not one
of you from this wicked generation will live to see
the good land I swore to give your ancestors, 36 except Caleb son of Jephunneh. He will see this land
because he has followed the LORD completely. I will
give to him and his descendants some of the very
land he explored during his scouting mission.'

37 "And the LORD was also angry with me because
of you. He said to me, 'Moses, not even you will enter
the Promised Land! 38 Instead, your assistant, Joshua
son of Nun, will lead the people into the land. Encourage him, for he will lead Israel as they take possession of it. 39 I will give the land to your little ones—
your innocent children. You were afraid they would
be captured, but they will be the ones who occupy it.
40 As for you, turn around now and go on back
through the wilderness toward the Red Sea.*'

41 "Then you confessed, 'We have sinned against
the LORD! We will go into the land and fight for it, as
the LORD our God has commanded us.' So your men
strapped on their weapons, thinking it would be easy
to attack the hill country.

42 "But the LORD told me to tell you, 'Do not attack,
for I am not with you. If you go ahead on your own,
you will be crushed by your enemies.'

43 "This is what I told you, but you would not listen.
Instead, you again rebelled against the LORD's command and arrogantly went into the hill country to
fight. 44 But the Amorites who lived there came out
against you like a swarm of bees. They chased and
battered you all the way from Seir to Hormah.
45 Then you returned and wept before the LORD, but
he refused to listen. 46 So you stayed there at Kadesh
for a long time.

1:40 Hebrew *sea of reeds.*

KING JAMES VERSION

2 1Then we turned, and took our journey into the
wilderness by the way of the Red sea, as the
LORD spake unto me: and we compassed mount Seir
many days.
2And the LORD spake unto me, saying,
3Ye have compassed this mountain long enough:
turn you northward.
4And command thou the people, saying, Ye *are* to
pass through the coast of your brethren the children
of Esau, which dwell in Seir; and they shall be afraid
of you: take ye good heed unto yourselves therefore:
5Meddle not with them; for I will not give you of
their land, no, not so much as a foot breadth; because
I have given mount Seir unto Esau *for* a possession.
6Ye shall buy meat of them for money, that ye may
eat; and ye shall also buy water of them for money,
that ye may drink.
7For the LORD thy God hath blessed thee in all the
works of thy hand: he knoweth thy walking through
this great wilderness: these forty years the LORD thy
God *hath been* with thee; thou hast lacked nothing.
8And when we passed by from our brethren the
children of Esau, which dwelt in Seir, through the
way of the plain from Elath, and from Ezion-gaber,
we turned and passed by the way of the wilderness
of Moab.
9And the LORD said unto me, Distress not the Moabites, neither contend with them in battle: for I will not
give thee of their land *for* a possession; because I have
given Ar unto the children of Lot *for* a possession.
10The Emims dwelt therein in times past, a people
great, and many, and tall, as the Anakims;
11Which also were accounted giants, as the
Anakims; but the Moabites call them Emims.
12The Horims also dwelt in Seir beforetime; but
the children of Esau succeeded them, when they had
destroyed them from before them, and dwelt in their
stead; as Israel did unto the land of his possession,
which the LORD gave unto them.
13Now rise up, *said I,* and get you over the brook
Zered. And we went over the brook Zered.
14And the space in which we came from Kadesh-
barnea, until we were come over the brook Zered,
was thirty and eight years; until all the generation of
the men of war were wasted out from among the
host, as the LORD sware unto them.
15For indeed the hand of the LORD was against
them, to destroy them from among the host, until
they were consumed.
16So it came to pass, when all the men of war were
consumed and dead from among the people,
17That the LORD spake unto me, saying,
18Thou art to pass over through Ar, the coast of
Moab, this day:
19And *when* thou comest nigh over against the
children of Ammon, distress them not, nor meddle
with them: for I will not give thee of the land of the

NEW LIVING TRANSLATION

Remembering Israel's Wanderings

2 "Then we turned around and headed back
across the wilderness toward the Red Sea,* just
as the LORD had instructed me, and we wandered
around in the region of Mount Seir for a long time.
2"Then at last the LORD said to me, 3'You have been
wandering around in this hill country long enough;
turn to the north. 4Give these orders to the people:
"You will pass through the country belonging to your
relatives the Edomites, the descendants of Esau, who
live in Seir. The Edomites will feel threatened, so be
careful. 5Do not bother them, for I have given them
all the hill country around Mount Seir as their property, and I will not give you even one square foot of
their land. 6If you need food to eat or water to drink,
pay them for it. 7For the LORD your God has blessed
you in everything you have done. He has watched
your every step through this great wilderness. During
these forty years, the LORD your God has been with
you, and you have lacked nothing."'
8"So we bypassed the territory of our relatives,
the descendants of Esau, who live in Seir. We avoided
the road through the Arabah Valley that comes up
from Elath and Ezion-geber.
"Then as we turned north along the desert route
through Moab, 9the LORD warned us, 'Do not bother
the Moabites, the descendants of Lot, or start a war
with them. I have given them Ar as their property,
and I will not give you any of their land.'"
10(A race of giants called the Emites had once lived
in the area of Ar. They were as strong and numerous
and tall as the Anakites, another race of giants. 11Both
the Emites and the Anakites are also known as the
Rephaites, though the Moabites call them Emites.
12In earlier times the Horites had lived in Seir, but
they were driven out and displaced by the descendants of Esau, just as Israel drove out the people of
Canaan when the LORD gave Israel their land.)
13Moses continued, "Then the LORD said to us,
'Get moving. Cross the Zered Brook.' So we crossed
the brook.
14"Thirty-eight years passed from the time we
first left Kadesh-barnea until we finally crossed the
Zered Brook! By then, all the men old enough to fight
in battle had died in the wilderness, as the LORD had
vowed would happen. 15The LORD struck them
down until they had all been eliminated from the
community.
16"When all the men of fighting age had died,
17the LORD said to me, 18'Today you will cross the
border of Moab at Ar 19and enter the land of the Ammonites, the descendants of Lot. But do not bother
them or start a war with them. I have given the land
of Ammon to them as their property, and I will not
give you any of their land.'"

2:1 Hebrew *sea of reeds.*

KING JAMES VERSION

children of Ammon *any* possession; because I have
given it unto the children of Lot *for* a possession.
20(That also was accounted a land of giants: giants
dwelt therein in old time; and the Ammonites call
them Zamzummims;
21A people great, and many, and tall, as the
Anakims; but the LORD destroyed them before them;
and they succeeded them, and dwelt in their stead:
22As he did to the children of Esau, which dwelt in
Seir, when he destroyed the Horims from before
them; and they succeeded them, and dwelt in their
stead even unto this day:
23And the Avims which dwelt in Hazerim, *even* unto
Azzah, the Caphtorims, which came forth out of
Caphtor, destroyed them, and dwelt in their stead.)
24Rise ye up, take your journey, and pass over the
river Arnon: behold, I have given into thine hand
Sihon the Amorite, king of Heshbon, and his land:
begin to possess *it,* and contend with him in battle.
25This day will I begin to put the dread of thee and
the fear of thee upon the nations *that are* under the
whole heaven, who shall hear report of thee, and
shall tremble, and be in anguish because of thee.
26And I sent messengers out of the wilderness of
Kedemoth unto Sihon king of Heshbon with words
of peace, saying,
27Let me pass through thy land: I will go along by
the high way, I will neither turn unto the right hand
nor to the left.
28Thou shalt sell me meat for money, that I may
eat; and give me water for money, that I may drink:
only I will pass through on my feet;
29(As the children of Esau which dwell in Seir, and
the Moabites which dwell in Ar, did unto me;) until I
shall pass over Jordan into the land which the LORD
our God giveth us.
30But Sihon king of Heshbon would not let us pass
by him: for the LORD thy God hardened his spirit, and
made his heart obstinate, that he might deliver him
into thy hand, as *appeareth* this day.
31And the LORD said unto me, Behold, I have begun
to give Sihon and his land before thee: begin to possess, that thou mayest inherit his land.
32Then Sihon came out against us, he and all his
people, to fight at Jahaz.
33And the LORD our God delivered him before us;
and we smote him, and his sons, and all his people.
34And we took all his cities at that time, and utterly
destroyed the men, and the women, and the little
ones, of every city, we left none to remain:
35Only the cattle we took for a prey unto ourselves,
and the spoil of the cities which we took.
36From Aroer, which *is* by the brink of the river of
Arnon, and *from* the city that *is* by the river, even
unto Gilead, there was not one city too strong for us:
the LORD our God delivered all unto us:

NEW LIVING TRANSLATION

20(That area was once considered the land of the
Rephaites, who had lived there, though the Ammonites call them Zamzummites. 21They were also as
strong and numerous and tall as the Anakites. But
the LORD destroyed them so the Ammonites could
occupy their land. 22He had done the same for the
descendants of Esau who lived in Seir, for he destroyed the Horites so they could settle there in their
place. The descendants of Esau live there to this day.
23A similar thing happened when the Caphtorites
from Crete* invaded and destroyed the Avvites, who
had lived in villages in the area of Gaza.)
24Moses continued, "Then the LORD said, 'Now get
moving! Cross the Arnon Gorge. Look, I will hand
over to you Sihon the Amorite, king of Heshbon, and
I will give you his land. Attack him and begin to occupy the land. 25Beginning today I will make people
throughout the earth terrified because of you. When
they hear reports about you, they will tremble with
dread and fear.'"

Victory over Sihon of Heshbon

26Moses continued, "From the wilderness of Kedemoth I sent ambassadors to King Sihon of Heshbon
with this proposal of peace:

> 27'Let us travel through your land. We will stay
> on the main road and won't turn off into the
> fields on either side. 28Sell us food to eat and
> water to drink, and we will pay for it. All we want
> is permission to pass through your land. 29The
> descendants of Esau who live in Seir allowed
> us to go through their country, and so did the
> Moabites, who live in Ar. Let us pass through
> until we cross the Jordan into the land the LORD
> our God is giving us.'

30"But King Sihon of Heshbon refused to allow us
to pass through, because the LORD your God made
Sihon stubborn and defiant so he could help you
defeat him, as he has now done.
31"Then the LORD said to me, 'Look, I have begun
to hand King Sihon and his land over to you. Begin
now to conquer and occupy his land.'
32"Then King Sihon declared war on us and mobilized his forces at Jahaz. 33But the LORD our God
handed him over to us, and we crushed him, his sons,
and all his people. 34We conquered all his towns and
completely destroyed* everyone—men, women, and
children. Not a single person was spared. 35We took
all the livestock as plunder for ourselves, along with
anything of value from the towns we ransacked.
36"The LORD our God also helped us conquer
Aroer on the edge of the Arnon Gorge, and the town
in the gorge, and the whole area as far as Gilead. No

2:23 Hebrew *from Caphtor.* **2:34** The Hebrew term used here refers to the complete consecration of things or people to the LORD, either by destroying them or by giving them as an offering.

KING JAMES VERSION

[37]Only unto the land of the children of Ammon thou camest not, *nor* unto any place of the river Jabbok, nor unto the cities in the mountains, nor unto whatsoever the LORD our God forbad us.

3 [1]Then we turned, and went up the way to Bashan: and Og the king of Bashan came out against us, he and all his people, to battle at Edrei.

[2]And the LORD said unto me, Fear him not: for I will deliver him, and all his people, and his land, into thy hand; and thou shalt do unto him as thou didst unto Sihon king of the Amorites, which dwelt at Heshbon.

[3]So the LORD our God delivered into our hands Og also, the king of Bashan, and all his people: and we smote him until none was left to him remaining.

[4]And we took all his cities at that time, there was not a city which we took not from them, threescore cities, all the region of Argob, the kingdom of Og in Bashan.

[5]All these cities *were* fenced with high walls, gates, and bars; beside unwalled towns a great many.

[6]And we utterly destroyed them, as we did unto Sihon king of Heshbon, utterly destroying the men, women, and children, of every city.

[7]But all the cattle, and the spoil of the cities, we took for a prey to ourselves.

[8]And we took at that time out of the hand of the two kings of the Amorites the land that *was* on this side Jordan, from the river of Arnon unto mount Hermon;

[9](*Which* Hermon the Sidonians call Sirion; and the Amorites call it Shenir;)

[10]All the cities of the plain, and all Gilead, and all Bashan, unto Salchah and Edrei, cities of the kingdom of Og in Bashan.

[11]For only Og king of Bashan remained of the remnant of giants; behold, his bedstead *was* a bedstead of iron; *is* it not in Rabbath of the children of Ammon? nine cubits *was* the length thereof, and four cubits the breadth of it, after the cubit of a man.

[12]And this land, *which* we possessed at that time, from Aroer, which *is* by the river Arnon, and half mount Gilead, and the cities thereof, gave I unto the Reubenites and to the Gadites.

[13]And the rest of Gilead, and all Bashan, *being* the kingdom of Og, gave I unto the half tribe of Manasseh; all the region of Argob, with all Bashan, which was called the land of giants.

[14]Jair the son of Manasseh took all the country of Argob unto the coasts of Geshuri and Maachathi; and called them after his own name, Bashan-havoth-jair, unto this day.

NEW LIVING TRANSLATION

town had walls too strong for us. [37]However, we
avoided the land of the Ammonites all along the
Jabbok River and the towns in the hill country—all
the places the LORD our God had commanded us to
leave alone.

Victory over Og of Bashan

3 "Next we turned and headed for the land of
Bashan, where King Og and his entire army
attacked us at Edrei. [2]But the LORD told me, 'Do not
be afraid of him, for I have given you victory over Og
and his entire army, and I will give you all his land.
Treat him just as you treated King Sihon of the Amorites, who ruled in Heshbon.'

[3]"So the LORD our God handed King Og and all his
people over to us, and we killed them all. Not a single
person survived. [4]We conquered all sixty of his
towns—the entire Argob region in his kingdom of
Bashan. Not a single town escaped our conquest.
[5]These towns were all fortified with high walls and
barred gates. We also took many unwalled villages at
the same time. [6]We completely destroyed* the kingdom of Bashan, just as we had destroyed King Sihon
of Heshbon. We destroyed all the people in every
town we conquered—men, women, and children
alike. [7]But we kept all the livestock for ourselves and
took plunder from all the towns.

[8]"So we took the land of the two Amorite kings
east of the Jordan River—all the way from the Arnon
Gorge to Mount Hermon. [9](Mount Hermon is called
Sirion by the Sidonians, and the Amorites call it
Senir.) [10]We had now conquered all the cities on the
plateau and all Gilead and Bashan, as far as the towns
of Salecah and Edrei, which were part of Og's kingdom in Bashan. [11](King Og of Bashan was the last
survivor of the giant Rephaites. His bed was made of
iron and was more than thirteen feet long and six
feet wide.* It can still be seen in the Ammonite city
of Rabbah.)

Land Division East of the Jordan

[12]"When we took possession of this land, I gave to
the tribes of Reuben and Gad the territory beyond
Aroer along the Arnon Gorge, plus half of the hill
country of Gilead with its towns. [13]Then I gave the
rest of Gilead and all of Bashan—Og's former kingdom—to the half-tribe of Manasseh. (This entire
Argob region of Bashan used to be known as the land
of the Rephaites. [14]Jair, a leader from the tribe of
Manasseh, conquered the whole Argob region in Bashan, all the way to the border of the Geshurites and
Maacathites. Jair renamed this region after himself,
calling it the Towns of Jair,* as it is still known today.)

3:6 The Hebrew term used here refers to the complete consecration of things or people to the LORD, either by destroying them or by giving them as an offering; also in 3:6b. **3:11** Hebrew *9 cubits* [4.1 meters] *long and 4 cubits* [1.8 meters] *wide.* **3:14** Hebrew *Havvoth-jair.*

KING JAMES VERSION

15 And I gave Gilead unto Machir.
16 And unto the Reubenites and unto the Gadites I
gave from Gilead even unto the river Arnon half the
valley, and the border even unto the river Jabbok,
which is the border of the children of Ammon;
17 The plain also, and Jordan, and the coast *thereof,*
from Chinnereth even unto the sea of the plain, *even*
the salt sea, under Ashdoth-pisgah eastward.
18 And I commanded you at that time, saying, The
LORD your God hath given you this land to possess it:
ye shall pass over armed before your brethren the
children of Israel, all *that are* meet for the war.
19 But your wives, and your little ones, and your
cattle, (*for* I know that ye have much cattle,) shall
abide in your cities which I have given you;
20 Until the LORD have given rest unto your brethren, as well as unto you, and *until* they also possess
the land which the LORD your God hath given them
beyond Jordan: and *then* shall ye return every man
unto his possession, which I have given you.

21 And I commanded Joshua at that time, saying,
Thine eyes have seen all that the LORD your God hath
done unto these two kings: so shall the LORD do unto
all the kingdoms whither thou passest.
22 Ye shall not fear them: for the LORD your God he
shall fight for you.
23 And I besought the LORD at that time, saying,
24 O Lord GOD, thou hast begun to shew thy servant
thy greatness, and thy mighty hand: for what God *is*
there in heaven or in earth, that can do according to
thy works, and according to thy might?
25 I pray thee, let me go over, and see the good land
that *is* beyond Jordan, that goodly mountain, and
Lebanon.
26 But the LORD was wroth with me for your sakes,
and would not hear me: and the LORD said unto
me, Let it suffice thee; speak no more unto me of
this matter.
27 Get thee up into the top of Pisgah, and lift up
thine eyes westward, and northward, and southward,
and eastward, and behold *it* with thine eyes: for thou
shalt not go over this Jordan.
28 But charge Joshua, and encourage him, and
strengthen him: for he shall go over before this
people, and he shall cause them to inherit the land
which thou shalt see.
29 So we abode in the valley over against Beth-peor.

4 1 Now therefore hearken, O Israel, unto the statutes and unto the judgments, which I teach
you, for to do *them,* that ye may live, and go in and
possess the land which the LORD God of your fathers
giveth you.
2 Ye shall not add unto the word which I command
you, neither shall ye diminish *aught* from it, that ye

NEW LIVING TRANSLATION

15 I gave Gilead to the clan of Makir. 16 But I also gave
part of Gilead to the tribes of Reuben and Gad. The
area I gave them extended from the middle of the
Arnon Gorge in the south to the Jabbok River on
the Ammonite frontier. 17 They also received the
Jordan Valley, all the way from the Sea of Galilee
down to the Dead Sea,* with the Jordan River serving
as the western boundary. To the east were the slopes
of Pisgah.
18 "At that time I gave this command to the tribes
that would live east of the Jordan: 'Although the LORD
your God has given you this land as your property,
all your fighting men must cross the Jordan ahead of
your Israelite relatives, armed and ready to assist
them. 19 Your wives, children, and numerous livestock, however, may stay behind in the towns I have
given you. 20 When the LORD has given security to the
rest of the Israelites, as he has to you, and when they
occupy the land the LORD your God is giving them
across the Jordan River, then you may all return here
to the land I have given you.'

Moses Forbidden to Enter the Land

21 "At that time I gave Joshua this charge: 'You have
seen for yourself everything the LORD your God has
done to these two kings. He will do the same to all the
kingdoms on the west side of the Jordan. 22 Do not be
afraid of the nations there, for the LORD your God will
fight for you.'
23 "At that time I pleaded with the LORD and said,
24 'O Sovereign LORD, you have only begun to show
your greatness and the strength of your hand to me,
your servant. Is there any god in heaven or on earth
who can perform such great and mighty deeds as
you do? 25 Please let me cross the Jordan to see the
wonderful land on the other side, the beautiful hill
country and the Lebanon mountains.'
26 "But the LORD was angry with me because of you,
and he would not listen to me. 'That's enough!' he declared. 'Speak of it no more. 27 But go up to Pisgah
Peak, and look over the land in every direction. Take a
good look, but you may not cross the Jordan River.
28 Instead, commission Joshua and encourage and
strengthen him, for he will lead the people across the
Jordan. He will give them all the land you now see
before you as their possession.' 29 So we stayed in the
valley near Beth-peor.

Moses Urges Israel to Obey

4 "And now, Israel, listen carefully to these decrees and regulations that I am about to teach
you. Obey them so that you may live, so you may enter and occupy the land that the LORD, the God of
your ancestors, is giving you. 2 Do not add to or subtract from these commands I am giving you. Just

3:17 Hebrew *from Kinnereth to the Sea of the Arabah, the Salt Sea.*

KING JAMES VERSION

may keep the commandments of the LORD your God which I command you.

3 Your eyes have seen what the LORD did because of Baal-peor: for all the men that followed Baal-peor, the LORD thy God hath destroyed them from among you.

4 But ye that did cleave unto the LORD your God *are* alive every one of you this day.

5 Behold, I have taught you statutes and judgments, even as the LORD my God commanded me, that ye should do so in the land whither ye go to possess it.

6 Keep therefore and do *them;* for this *is* your wisdom and your understanding in the sight of the nations, which shall hear all these statutes, and say, Surely this great nation *is* a wise and understanding people.

7 For what nation *is there so* great, who *hath* God *so* nigh unto them, as the LORD our God *is* in all *things that* we call upon him *for?*

8 And what nation *is there so* great, that hath statutes and judgments *so* righteous as all this law, which I set before you this day?

9 Only take heed to thyself, and keep thy soul diligently, lest thou forget the things which thine eyes have seen, and lest they depart from thy heart all the days of thy life: but teach them thy sons, and thy sons' sons;

10 *Specially* the day that thou stoodest before the LORD thy God in Horeb, when the LORD said unto me, Gather me the people together, and I will make them hear my words, that they may learn to fear me all the days that they shall live upon the earth, and *that* they may teach their children.

11 And ye came near and stood under the mountain; and the mountain burned with fire unto the midst of heaven, with darkness, clouds, and thick darkness.

12 And the LORD spake unto you out of the midst of the fire: ye heard the voice of the words, but saw no similitude; only *ye heard* a voice.

13 And he declared unto you his covenant, which he commanded you to perform, *even* ten commandments; and he wrote them upon two tables of stone.

14 And the LORD commanded me at that time to teach you statutes and judgments, that ye might do them in the land whither ye go over to possess it.

15 Take ye therefore good heed unto yourselves; for ye saw no manner of similitude on the day *that* the LORD spake unto you in Horeb out of the midst of the fire:

16 Lest ye corrupt *yourselves,* and make you a graven image, the similitude of any figure, the likeness of male or female,

17 The likeness of any beast that *is* on the earth, the likeness of any winged fowl that flieth in the air,

18 The likeness of any thing that creepeth on the ground, the likeness of any fish that *is* in the waters beneath the earth:

NEW LIVING TRANSLATION

obey the commands of the LORD your God that I am giving you.

3 "You saw for yourself what the LORD did to you at Baal-peor. There the LORD your God destroyed everyone who had worshiped Baal, the god of Peor. 4 But all
of you who were faithful to the LORD your God are still alive today—every one of you.

5 "Look, I now teach you these decrees and regulations just as the LORD my God commanded me, so that you may obey them in the land you are about to
enter and occupy. 6 Obey them completely, and you will display your wisdom and intelligence among the surrounding nations. When they hear all these decrees, they will exclaim, 'How wise and prudent are
the people of this great nation!' 7 For what great
nation has a god as near to them as the LORD our God
is near to us whenever we call on him? 8 And what
great nation has decrees and regulations as righteous and fair as this body of instructions that I am giving you today?

9 "But watch out! Be careful never to forget what you yourself have seen. Do not let these memories escape from your mind as long as you live! And be sure to pass them on to your children and grandchildren. 10 Never forget the day when you stood be-
fore the LORD your God at Mount Sinai,* where he told me, 'Summon the people before me, and I will personally instruct them. Then they will learn to fear me as long as they live, and they will teach their children to fear me also.'

11 "You came near and stood at the foot of the mountain, while flames from the mountain shot into the sky. The mountain was shrouded in black clouds
and deep darkness. 12 And the LORD spoke to you
from the heart of the fire. You heard the sound of his words but didn't see his form; there was only a voice.
13 He proclaimed his covenant—the Ten Commandments*—which he commanded you to keep, and
which he wrote on two stone tablets. 14 It was at that
time that the LORD commanded me to teach you his decrees and regulations so you would obey them in the land you are about to enter and occupy.

A Warning against Idolatry

15 "But be very careful! You did not see the LORD's form on the day he spoke to you from the heart of
the fire at Mount Sinai. 16 So do not corrupt your-
selves by making an idol in any form—whether of a
man or a woman, 17 an animal on the ground, a bird
in the sky, 18 a small animal that scurries along the

4:10 Hebrew *Horeb,* another name for Sinai; also in 4:15. 4:13 Hebrew *the ten words.*

KING JAMES VERSION

19And lest thou lift up thine eyes unto heaven, and
when thou seest the sun, and the moon, and the
stars, *even* all the host of heaven, shouldest be driven
to worship them, and serve them, which the LORD thy
God hath divided unto all nations under the whole
heaven.
20But the LORD hath taken you, and brought you
forth out of the iron furnace, *even* out of Egypt, to be
unto him a people of inheritance, as *ye are* this day.
21Furthermore the LORD was angry with me for
your sakes, and sware that I should not go over
Jordan, and that I should not go in unto that good
land, which the LORD thy God giveth thee *for* an
inheritance:
22But I must die in this land, I must not go over Jordan: but ye shall go over, and possess that good land.
23Take heed unto yourselves, lest ye forget the
covenant of the LORD your God, which he made with
you, and make you a graven image, *or* the likeness
of any *thing,* which the LORD thy God hath forbidden thee.
24For the LORD thy God *is* a consuming fire, *even* a
jealous God.
25When thou shalt beget children, and children's
children, and ye shall have remained long in the
land, and shall corrupt *yourselves,* and make a
graven image, *or* the likeness of any *thing,* and shall
do evil in the sight of the LORD thy God, to provoke
him to anger:
26I call heaven and earth to witness against you
this day, that ye shall soon utterly perish from off the
land whereunto ye go over Jordan to possess it; ye
shall not prolong *your* days upon it, but shall utterly
be destroyed.
27And the LORD shall scatter you among the nations, and ye shall be left few in number among the
heathen, whither the LORD shall lead you.
28And there ye shall serve gods, the work of men's
hands, wood and stone, which neither see, nor hear,
nor eat, nor smell.
29But if from thence thou shalt seek the LORD thy
God, thou shalt find *him,* if thou seek him with all thy
heart and with all thy soul.
30When thou art in tribulation, and all these
things are come upon thee, *even* in the latter days, if
thou turn to the LORD thy God, and shalt be obedient
unto his voice;
31(For the LORD thy God *is* a merciful God;) he will
not forsake thee, neither destroy thee, nor forget the
covenant of thy fathers which he sware unto them.
32For ask now of the days that are past, which were
before thee, since the day that God created man
upon the earth, and *ask* from the one side of heaven
unto the other, whether there hath been *any such
thing* as this great thing *is,* or hath been heard like it?
33Did *ever* people hear the voice of God speaking
out of the midst of the fire, as thou hast heard,
and live?

NEW LIVING TRANSLATION

ground, or a fish in the deepest sea. 19And when you
look up into the sky and see the sun, moon, and
stars—all the forces of heaven—don't be seduced
into worshiping them. The LORD your God gave
them to all the peoples of the earth. 20Remember
that the LORD rescued you from the iron-smelting
furnace of Egypt in order to make you his very own
people and his special possession, which is what you
are today.
21"But the LORD was angry with me because of you.
He vowed that I would not cross the Jordan River
into the good land the LORD your God is giving you as
your special possession. 22You will cross the Jordan
to occupy the land, but I will not. Instead, I will die
here on the east side of the river. 23So be careful not
to break the covenant the LORD your God has made
with you. Do not make idols of any shape or form, for
the LORD your God has forbidden this. 24The LORD
your God is a devouring fire; he is a jealous God.
25"In the future, when you have children and
grandchildren and have lived in the land a long time,
do not corrupt yourselves by making idols of any
kind. This is evil in the sight of the LORD your God
and will arouse his anger.
26"Today I call on heaven and earth as witnesses
against you. If you break my covenant, you will
quickly disappear from the land you are crossing the
Jordan to occupy. You will live there only a short
time; then you will be utterly destroyed. 27For the
LORD will scatter you among the nations, where only
a few of you will survive. 28There, in a foreign land,
you will worship idols made from wood and stone—
gods that neither see nor hear nor eat nor smell.
29But from there you will search again for the LORD
your God. And if you search for him with all your
heart and soul, you will find him.
30"In the distant future, when you are suffering all
these things, you will finally return to the LORD your
God and listen to what he tells you. 31For the LORD
your God is a merciful God; he will not abandon you
or destroy you or forget the solemn covenant he
made with your ancestors.

There Is Only One God

32"Now search all of history, from the time God created people on the earth until now, and search from
one end of the heavens to the other. Has anything as
great as this ever been seen or heard before? 33Has
any nation ever heard the voice of God* speaking

4:33 Or *voice of a god.*

KING JAMES VERSION

34 Or hath God assayed to go *and* take him a nation from the midst of *another* nation, by temptations, by signs, and by wonders, and by war, and by a mighty hand, and by a stretched out arm, and by great terrors, according to all that the LORD your God did for you in Egypt before your eyes?

35 Unto thee it was shewed, that thou mightest know that the LORD he *is* God; *there is* none else beside him.

36 Out of heaven he made thee to hear his voice, that he might instruct thee: and upon earth he shewed thee his great fire; and thou heardest his words out of the midst of the fire.

37 And because he loved thy fathers, therefore he chose their seed after them, and brought thee out in his sight with his mighty power out of Egypt;

38 To drive out nations from before thee greater and mightier than thou *art,* to bring thee in, to give thee their land *for* an inheritance, as *it is* this day.

39 Know therefore this day, and consider *it* in thine heart, that the LORD he *is* God in heaven above, and upon the earth beneath: *there is* none else.

40 Thou shalt keep therefore his statutes, and his commandments, which I command thee this day, that it may go well with thee, and with thy children after thee, and that thou mayest prolong *thy* days upon the earth, which the LORD thy God giveth thee, for ever.

41 Then Moses severed three cities on this side Jordan toward the sun rising;

42 That the slayer might flee thither, which should kill his neighbour unawares, and hated him not in times past; and that fleeing unto one of these cities he might live:

43 *Namely,* Bezer in the wilderness, in the plain country, of the Reubenites; and Ramoth in Gilead, of the Gadites; and Golan in Bashan, of the Manassites.

44 And this *is* the law which Moses set before the children of Israel:

45 These *are* the testimonies, and the statutes, and the judgments, which Moses spake unto the children of Israel, after they came forth out of Egypt,

46 On this side Jordan, in the valley over against Beth-peor, in the land of Sihon king of the Amorites, who dwelt at Heshbon, whom Moses and the children of Israel smote, after they were come forth out of Egypt:

47 And they possessed his land, and the land of Og king of Bashan, two kings of the Amorites, which *were* on this side Jordan toward the sun rising;

48 From Aroer, which *is* by the bank of the river Arnon, even unto mount Sion, which *is* Hermon,

49 And all the plain on this side Jordan eastward, even unto the sea of the plain, under the springs of Pisgah.

NEW LIVING TRANSLATION

from fire—as you did—and survived? 34 Has any other
god dared to take a nation for himself out of another
nation by means of trials, miraculous signs, wonders,
war, a strong hand, a powerful arm, and terrifying
acts? Yet that is what the LORD your God did for you
in Egypt, right before your eyes.
35 "He showed you these things so you would know
that the LORD is God and there is no other. 36 He let
you hear his voice from heaven so he could instruct
you. He let you see his great fire here on earth so he
could speak to you from it. 37 Because he loved your
ancestors, he chose to bless their descendants, and
he personally brought you out of Egypt with a great
display of power. 38 He drove out nations far greater
than you, so he could bring you in and give you their
land as your special possession, as it is today.
39 "So remember this and keep it firmly in mind:
The LORD is God both in heaven and on earth, and
there is no other. 40 If you obey all the decrees and
commands I am giving you today, all will be well with
you and your children. I am giving you these instructions so you will enjoy a long life in the land the LORD
your God is giving you for all time."

Eastern Cities of Refuge

41 Then Moses set apart three cities of refuge east of
the Jordan River. 42 Anyone who killed another person unintentionally, without previous hostility, could
flee there to live in safety. 43 These were the cities:
Bezer on the wilderness plateau for the tribe of
Reuben; Ramoth in Gilead for the tribe of Gad; Golan
in Bashan for the tribe of Manasseh.

Introduction to Moses' Second Address

44 This is the body of instruction that Moses presented to the Israelites. 45 These are the laws, decrees, and regulations that Moses gave to the people
of Israel when they left Egypt, 46 and as they camped
in the valley near Beth-peor east of the Jordan River.
(This land was formerly occupied by the Amorites
under King Sihon, who ruled from Heshbon. But
Moses and the Israelites destroyed him and his
people when they came up from Egypt. 47 Israel took
possession of his land and that of King Og of
Bashan—the two Amorite kings east of the Jordan.
48 So Israel conquered the entire area from Aroer at
the edge of the Arnon Gorge all the way to Mount
Sirion,* also called Mount Hermon. 49 And they conquered the eastern bank of the Jordan River as far
south as the Dead Sea,* below the slopes of Pisgah.)

4:48 As in Syriac version (see also 3:9); Hebrew reads *Mount Sion.*
4:49 Hebrew *took the Arabah on the east side of the Jordan as far as the sea of the Arabah.*

KING JAMES VERSION

5 1And Moses called all Israel, and said unto
them, Hear, O Israel, the statutes and judgments which I speak in your ears this day, that ye may
learn them, and keep, and do them.
2The LORD our God made a covenant with us in
Horeb.
3The LORD made not this covenant with our fathers, but with us, *even* us, who *are* all of us here alive
this day.
4The LORD talked with you face to face in the
mount out of the midst of the fire,
5(I stood between the LORD and you at that time,
to shew you the word of the LORD: for ye were afraid
by reason of the fire, and went not up into the
mount;) saying,
6I *am* the LORD thy God, which brought thee out of
the land of Egypt, from the house of bondage.
7Thou shalt have none other gods before me.
8Thou shalt not make thee *any* graven image, *or*
any likeness *of any thing* that *is* in heaven above, or
that *is* in the earth beneath, or that *is* in the waters
beneath the earth:
9Thou shalt not bow down thyself unto them, nor
serve them: for I the LORD thy God *am* a jealous God,
visiting the iniquity of the fathers upon the children
unto the third and fourth *generation* of them that
hate me,
10And shewing mercy unto thousands of them
that love me and keep my commandments.
11Thou shalt not take the name of the LORD thy
God in vain: for the LORD will not hold *him* guiltless
that taketh his name in vain.
12Keep the sabbath day to sanctify it, as the LORD
thy God hath commanded thee.
13Six days thou shalt labour, and do all thy work:
14But the seventh day *is* the sabbath of the LORD
thy God: *in it* thou shalt not do any work, thou, nor
thy son, nor thy daughter, nor thy manservant, nor thy
maidservant, nor thine ox, nor thine ass, nor any of
thy cattle, nor thy stranger that *is* within thy gates;
that thy manservant and thy maidservant may rest as
well as thou.
15And remember that thou wast a servant in the
land of Egypt, and *that* the LORD thy God brought
thee out thence through a mighty hand and by a
stretched out arm: therefore the LORD thy God commanded thee to keep the sabbath day.
16Honour thy father and thy mother, as the LORD
thy God hath commanded thee; that thy days may be
prolonged, and that it may go well with thee, in the
land which the LORD thy God giveth thee.
17Thou shalt not kill.
18Neither shalt thou commit adultery.
19Neither shalt thou steal.
20Neither shalt thou bear false witness against thy
neighbour.

NEW LIVING TRANSLATION

Ten Commandments for the Covenant Community

5 Moses called all the people of Israel together
and said, "Listen carefully, Israel. Hear the decrees and regulations I am giving you today, so you
may learn them and obey them!
2"The LORD our God made a covenant with us at
Mount Sinai.* 3The LORD did not make this covenant
with our ancestors, but with all of us who are alive today. 4At the mountain the LORD spoke to you face to
face from the heart of the fire. 5I stood as an inter-
mediary between you and the LORD, for you were
afraid of the fire and did not want to approach the
mountain. He spoke to me, and I passed his words on
to you. This is what he said:

6"I am the LORD your God, who rescued you from
the land of Egypt, the place of your slavery.
7"You must not have any other god but me.
8"You must not make for yourself an idol of any
kind, or an image of anything in the heavens or
on the earth or in the sea. 9You must not bow
down to them or worship them, for I, the LORD
your God, am a jealous God who will not tolerate
your affection for any other gods. I lay the sins of
the parents upon their children; the entire family
is affected—even children in the third and fourth
generations of those who reject me. 10But I lavish
unfailing love for a thousand generations on
those* who love me and obey my commands.
11"You must not misuse the name of the LORD your
God. The LORD will not let you go unpunished if
you misuse his name.
12"Observe the Sabbath day by keeping it holy, as
the LORD your God has commanded you. 13You
have six days each week for your ordinary work,
14but the seventh day is a Sabbath day of rest
dedicated to the LORD your God. On that day no
one in your household may do any work. This
includes you, your sons and daughters, your male
and female servants, your oxen and donkeys and
other livestock, and any foreigners living among
you. All your male and female servants must rest
as you do. 15Remember that you were once slaves
in Egypt, but the LORD your God brought you out
with his strong hand and powerful arm. That is
why the LORD your God has commanded you to
rest on the Sabbath day.
16"Honor your father and mother, as the LORD your
God commanded you. Then you will live a long,
full life in the land the LORD your God is giving
you.
17"You must not murder.
18"You must not commit adultery.
19"You must not steal.
20"You must not testify falsely against your
neighbor.

5:2 Hebrew *Horeb*, another name for Sinai. 5:10 Hebrew *for thousands of those*.

KING JAMES VERSION

21 Neither shalt thou desire thy neighbour's wife,
neither shalt thou covet thy neighbour's house, his
field, or his manservant, or his maidservant, his ox,
or his ass, or any *thing* that *is* thy neighbour's.
22 These words the LORD spake unto all your assembly in the mount out of the midst of the fire, of
the cloud, and of the thick darkness, with a great
voice: and he added no more. And he wrote them in
two tables of stone, and delivered them unto me.
23 And it came to pass, when ye heard the voice out
of the midst of the darkness, (for the mountain did
burn with fire,) that ye came near unto me, *even* all
the heads of your tribes, and your elders;
24 And ye said, Behold, the LORD our God hath
shewed us his glory and his greatness, and we have
heard his voice out of the midst of the fire: we have
seen this day that God doth talk with man, and he
liveth.
25 Now therefore why should we die? for this great
fire will consume us: if we hear the voice of the LORD
our God any more, then we shall die.
26 For who *is there of* all flesh, that hath heard the
voice of the living God speaking out of the midst of
the fire, as we *have*, and lived?
27 Go thou near, and hear all that the LORD our God
shall say: and speak thou unto us all that the LORD
our God shall speak unto thee; and we will hear *it*,
and do *it*.
28 And the LORD heard the voice of your words,
when ye spake unto me; and the LORD said unto me, I
have heard the voice of the words of this people,
which they have spoken unto thee: they have well
said all that they have spoken.
29 O that there were such an heart in them, that
they would fear me, and keep all my commandments
always, that it might be well with them, and with
their children for ever!
30 Go say to them, Get you into your tents again.
31 But as for thee, stand thou here by me, and I will
speak unto thee all the commandments, and the
statutes, and the judgments, which thou shalt teach
them, that they may do *them* in the land which I give
them to possess it.
32 Ye shall observe to do therefore as the LORD your
God hath commanded you: ye shall not turn aside to
the right hand or to the left.
33 Ye shall walk in all the ways which the LORD your
God hath commanded you, that ye may live, and *that
it may be* well with you, and *that* ye may prolong
your days in the land which ye shall possess.

6 1 Now these *are* the commandments, the statutes, and the judgments, which the LORD your
God commanded to teach you, that ye might do *them*
in the land whither ye go to possess it:
2 That thou mightest fear the LORD thy God, to
keep all his statutes and his commandments, which I
command thee, thou, and thy son, and thy son's son,

NEW LIVING TRANSLATION

21 "You must not covet your neighbor's wife. You
must not covet your neighbor's house or land,
male or female servant, ox or donkey, or anything
else that belongs to your neighbor.

22 "The LORD spoke these words to all of you assembled there at the foot of the mountain. He spoke
with a loud voice from the heart of the fire, surrounded by clouds and deep darkness. This was all
he said at that time, and he wrote his words on two
stone tablets and gave them to me.
23 "But when you heard the voice from the heart of
the darkness, while the mountain was blazing with
fire, all your tribal leaders and elders came to me.
24 They said, 'Look, the LORD our God has shown us his
glory and greatness, and we have heard his voice from
the heart of the fire. Today we have seen that God can
speak to us humans, and yet we live! 25 But now, why
should we risk death again? If the LORD our God
speaks to us again, we will certainly die and be consumed by this awesome fire. 26 Can any living thing
hear the voice of the living God from the heart of the
fire as we did and yet survive? 27 Go yourself and listen
to what the LORD our God says. Then come and tell us
everything he tells you, and we will listen and obey.'
28 "The LORD heard the request you made to me.
And he said, 'I have heard what the people said to
you, and they are right. 29 Oh, that they would always
have hearts like this, that they might fear me and
obey all my commands! If they did, they and their descendants would prosper forever. 30 Go and tell them,
"Return to your tents." 31 But you stand here with me
so I can give you all my commands, decrees, and regulations. You must teach them to the people so they
can obey them in the land I am giving them as their
possession.'"
32 So Moses told the people, "You must be careful
to obey all the commands of the LORD your God, following his instructions in every detail. 33 Stay on the
path that the LORD your God has commanded you to
follow. Then you will live long and prosperous lives
in the land you are about to enter and occupy.

A Call for Wholehearted Commitment

6 "These are the commands, decrees, and regulations that the LORD your God commanded me
to teach you. You must obey them in the land you are
about to enter and occupy, 2 and you and your children and grandchildren must fear the LORD your God
as long as you live. If you obey all his decrees and

KING JAMES VERSION

all the days of thy life; and that thy days may be prolonged.

3Hear therefore, O Israel, and observe to do *it;* that it may be well with thee, and that ye may increase mightily, as the LORD God of thy fathers hath promised thee, in the land that floweth with milk and honey.

4Hear, O Israel: The LORD our God *is* one LORD:

5And thou shalt love the LORD thy God with all thine heart, and with all thy soul, and with all thy might.

6And these words, which I command thee this day, shall be in thine heart:

7And thou shalt teach them diligently unto thy children, and shalt talk of them when thou sittest in thine house, and when thou walkest by the way, and when thou liest down, and when thou risest up.

8And thou shalt bind them for a sign upon thine hand, and they shall be as frontlets between thine eyes.

9And thou shalt write them upon the posts of thy house, and on thy gates.

10And it shall be, when the LORD thy God shall have brought thee into the land which he sware unto thy fathers, to Abraham, to Isaac, and to Jacob, to give thee great and goodly cities, which thou buildedst not,

11And houses full of all good *things,* which thou filledst not, and wells digged, which thou diggedst not, vineyards and olive trees, which thou plantedst not; when thou shalt have eaten and be full;

12*Then* beware lest thou forget the LORD, which brought thee forth out of the land of Egypt, from the house of bondage.

13Thou shalt fear the LORD thy God, and serve him, and shalt swear by his name.

14Ye shall not go after other gods, of the gods of the people which *are* round about you;

15(For the LORD thy God *is* a jealous God among you) lest the anger of the LORD thy God be kindled against thee, and destroy thee from off the face of the earth.

16Ye shall not tempt the LORD your God, as ye tempted *him* in Massah.

17Ye shall diligently keep the commandments of the LORD your God, and his testimonies, and his statutes, which he hath commanded thee.

18And thou shalt do *that which is* right and good in the sight of the LORD: that it may be well with thee, and that thou mayest go in and possess the good land which the LORD sware unto thy fathers,

19To cast out all thine enemies from before thee, as the LORD hath spoken.

20*And* when thy son asketh thee in time to come, saying, What *mean* the testimonies, and the statutes, and the judgments, which the LORD our God hath commanded you?

21Then thou shalt say unto thy son, We were

NEW LIVING TRANSLATION

commands, you will enjoy a long life. 3Listen closely, Israel, and be careful to obey. Then all will go well with you, and you will have many children in the land flowing with milk and honey, just as the LORD, the God of your ancestors, promised you.

4"Listen, O Israel! The LORD is our God, the LORD alone.* 5And you must love the LORD your God with all your heart, all your soul, and all your strength. 6And you must commit yourselves wholeheartedly to these commands that I am giving you today. 7Repeat them again and again to your children. Talk about them when you are at home and when you are on the road, when you are going to bed and when you are getting up. 8Tie them to your hands and wear them on your forehead as reminders. 9Write them on the doorposts of your house and on your gates.

10"The LORD your God will soon bring you into the land he swore to give you when he made a vow to your ancestors Abraham, Isaac, and Jacob. It is a land with large, prosperous cities that you did not build. 11The houses will be richly stocked with goods you did not produce. You will draw water from cisterns you did not dig, and you will eat from vineyards and olive trees you did not plant. When you have eaten your fill in this land, 12be careful not to forget the LORD, who rescued you from slavery in the land of Egypt. 13You must fear the LORD your God and serve him. When you take an oath, you must use only his name.

14"You must not worship any of the gods of neighboring nations, 15for the LORD your God, who lives among you, is a jealous God. His anger will flare up against you, and he will wipe you from the face of the earth. 16You must not test the LORD your God as you did when you complained at Massah. 17You must diligently obey the commands of the LORD your God—all the laws and decrees he has given you. 18Do what is right and good in the LORD's sight, so all will go well with you. Then you will enter and occupy the good land that the LORD swore to give your ancestors. 19You will drive out all the enemies living in the land, just as the LORD said you would.

20"In the future your children will ask you, 'What is the meaning of these laws, decrees, and regulations that the LORD our God has commanded us to obey?'

21"Then you must tell them, 'We were Pharaoh's

6:4 Or *The LORD our God is one LORD;* or *The LORD our God, the LORD is one;* or *The LORD is our God, the LORD is one.*

KING JAMES VERSION

Pharaoh's bondmen in Egypt; and the LORD brought us out of Egypt with a mighty hand:

22 And the LORD shewed signs and wonders, great and sore, upon Egypt, upon Pharaoh, and upon all his household, before our eyes:

23 And he brought us out from thence, that he might bring us in, to give us the land which he sware unto our fathers.

24 And the LORD commanded us to do all these statutes, to fear the LORD our God, for our good always, that he might preserve us alive, as *it is* at this day.

25 And it shall be our righteousness, if we observe to do all these commandments before the LORD our God, as he hath commanded us.

7 1 When the LORD thy God shall bring thee into the land whither thou goest to possess it, and hath cast out many nations before thee, the Hittites, and the Girgashites, and the Amorites, and the Canaanites, and the Perizzites, and the Hivites, and the Jebusites, seven nations greater and mightier than thou;

2 And when the LORD thy God shall deliver them before thee; thou shalt smite them, *and* utterly destroy them; thou shalt make no covenant with them, nor shew mercy unto them:

3 Neither shalt thou make marriages with them; thy daughter thou shalt not give unto his son, nor his daughter shalt thou take unto thy son.

4 For they will turn away thy son from following me, that they may serve other gods: so will the anger of the LORD be kindled against you, and destroy thee suddenly.

5 But thus shall ye deal with them; ye shall destroy their altars, and break down their images, and cut down their groves, and burn their graven images with fire.

6 For thou *art* an holy people unto the LORD thy God: the LORD thy God hath chosen thee to be a special people unto himself, above all people that *are* upon the face of the earth.

7 The LORD did not set his love upon you, nor choose you, because ye were more in number than any people; for ye *were* the fewest of all people:

8 But because the LORD loved you, and because he would keep the oath which he had sworn unto your fathers, hath the LORD brought you out with a mighty hand, and redeemed you out of the house of bondmen, from the hand of Pharaoh king of Egypt.

9 Know therefore that the LORD thy God, he *is* God, the faithful God, which keepeth covenant and mercy with them that love him and keep his commandments to a thousand generations;

10 And repayeth them that hate him to their face, to destroy them: he will not be slack to him that hateth him, he will repay him to his face.

11 Thou shalt therefore keep the commandments,

NEW LIVING TRANSLATION

slaves in Egypt, but the LORD brought us out of Egypt with his strong hand. 22 The LORD did miraculous signs and wonders before our eyes, dealing terrifying blows against Egypt and Pharaoh and all his people. 23 He brought us out of Egypt so he could give us this land he had sworn to give our ancestors. 24 And the LORD our God commanded us to obey all these decrees and to fear him so he can continue to bless us and preserve our lives, as he has done to this day. 25 For we will be counted as righteous when we obey all the commands the LORD our God has given us.'

The Privilege of Holiness

7 "When the LORD your God brings you into the land you are about to enter and occupy, he will clear away many nations ahead of you: the Hittites, Girgashites, Amorites, Canaanites, Perizzites, Hivites, and Jebusites. These seven nations are greater and more numerous than you. 2 When the LORD your God hands these nations over to you and you conquer them, you must completely destroy* them. Make no treaties with them and show them no mercy. 3 You must not intermarry with them. Do not let your daughters and sons marry their sons and daughters, 4 for they will lead your children away from me to worship other gods. Then the anger of the LORD will burn against you, and he will quickly destroy you. 5 This is what you must do. You must break down their pagan altars and shatter their sacred pillars. Cut down their Asherah poles and burn their idols. 6 For you are a holy people, who belong to the LORD your God. Of all the people on earth, the LORD your God has chosen you to be his own special treasure.

7 "The LORD did not set his heart on you and choose you because you were more numerous than other nations, for you were the smallest of all nations! 8 Rather, it was simply that the LORD loves you, and he was keeping the oath he had sworn to your ancestors. That is why the LORD rescued you with such a strong hand from your slavery and from the oppressive hand of Pharaoh, king of Egypt. 9 Understand, therefore, that the LORD your God is indeed God. He is the faithful God who keeps his covenant for a thousand generations and lavishes his unfailing love on those who love him and obey his commands. 10 But he does not hesitate to punish and destroy those who reject him. 11 Therefore, you must obey all

7:2 The Hebrew term used here refers to the complete consecration of things or people to the LORD, either by destroying them or by giving them as an offering; also in 7:26.

KING JAMES VERSION

and the statutes, and the judgments, which I command thee this day, to do them.
12 Wherefore it shall come to pass, if ye hearken to
these judgments, and keep, and do them, that the
LORD thy God shall keep unto thee the covenant and
the mercy which he sware unto thy fathers:
13 And he will love thee, and bless thee, and multiply thee: he will also bless the fruit of thy womb, and
the fruit of thy land, thy corn, and thy wine, and thine
oil, the increase of thy kine, and the flocks of thy
sheep, in the land which he sware unto thy fathers to
give thee.
14 Thou shalt be blessed above all people: there
shall not be male or female barren among you, or
among your cattle.
15 And the LORD will take away from thee all sickness, and will put none of the evil diseases of Egypt,
which thou knowest, upon thee; but will lay them
upon all *them* that hate thee.
16 And thou shalt consume all the people which
the LORD thy God shall deliver thee; thine eye shall
have no pity upon them: neither shalt thou serve
their gods; for that *will be* a snare unto thee.
17 If thou shalt say in thine heart, These nations *are*
more than I; how can I dispossess them?
18 Thou shalt not be afraid of them: *but* shalt well
remember what the LORD thy God did unto Pharaoh,
and unto all Egypt;
19 The great temptations which thine eyes saw, and
the signs, and the wonders, and the mighty hand, and
the stretched out arm, whereby the LORD thy God
brought thee out: so shall the LORD thy God do unto
all the people of whom thou art afraid.
20 Moreover the LORD thy God will send the hornet
among them, until they that are left, and hide themselves from thee, be destroyed.
21 Thou shalt not be affrighted at them: for the
LORD thy God *is* among you, a mighty God and
terrible.
22 And the LORD thy God will put out those nations
before thee by little and little: thou mayest not consume them at once, lest the beasts of the field increase upon thee.
23 But the LORD thy God shall deliver them unto
thee, and shall destroy them with a mighty destruction, until they be destroyed.
24 And he shall deliver their kings into thine hand,
and thou shalt destroy their name from under
heaven: there shall no man be able to stand before
thee, until thou have destroyed them.
25 The graven images of their gods shall ye burn
with fire: thou shalt not desire the silver or gold *that*
is on them, nor take *it* unto thee, lest thou be snared
therein: for it *is* an abomination to the LORD thy God.
26 Neither shalt thou bring an abomination into
thine house, lest thou be a cursed thing like it: *but*
thou shalt utterly detest it, and thou shalt utterly abhor it; for it *is* a cursed thing.

NEW LIVING TRANSLATION

these commands, decrees, and regulations I am
giving you today.
12 "If you listen to these regulations and faithfully
obey them, the LORD your God will keep his covenant
of unfailing love with you, as he promised with an
oath to your ancestors. 13 He will love you and bless
you, and he will give you many children. He will give
fertility to your land and your animals. When you arrive in the land he swore to give your ancestors, you
will have large harvests of grain, new wine, and olive
oil, and great herds of cattle, sheep, and goats. 14 You
will be blessed above all the nations of the earth.
None of your men or women will be childless, and all
your livestock will bear young. 15 And the LORD will
protect you from all sickness. He will not let you
suffer from the terrible diseases you knew in Egypt,
but he will inflict them on all your enemies!
16 "You must destroy all the nations the LORD your
God hands over to you. Show them no mercy, and do
not worship their gods, or they will trap you.
17 Perhaps you will think to yourselves, 'How can we
ever conquer these nations that are so much more
powerful than we are?' 18 But don't be afraid of them!
Just remember what the LORD your God did to Pharaoh and to all the land of Egypt. 19 Remember the
great terrors the LORD your God sent against them.
You saw it all with your own eyes! And remember the
miraculous signs and wonders, and the strong hand
and powerful arm with which he brought you out of
Egypt. The LORD your God will use this same power
against all the people you fear. 20 And then the LORD
your God will send terror* to drive out the few survivors still hiding from you!
21 "No, do not be afraid of those nations, for the
LORD your God is among you, and he is a great and
awesome God. 22 The LORD your God will drive those
nations out ahead of you little by little. You will not
clear them away all at once, otherwise the wild animals would multiply too quickly for you. 23 But the
LORD your God will hand them over to you. He will
throw them into complete confusion until they are
destroyed. 24 He will put their kings in your power,
and you will erase their names from the face of the
earth. No one will be able to stand against you, and
you will destroy them all.
25 "You must burn their idols in fire, and you must
not covet the silver or gold that covers them. You
must not take it or it will become a trap to you, for
it is detestable to the LORD your God. 26 Do not
bring any detestable objects into your home, for
then you will be destroyed, just like them. You must
utterly detest such things, for they are set apart for
destruction.

7:20 Often rendered *the hornet*. The meaning of the Hebrew is uncertain.

KING JAMES VERSION

8 1All the commandments which I command
thee this day shall ye observe to do, that ye may
live, and multiply, and go in and possess the land
which the LORD sware unto your fathers.

2And thou shalt remember all the way which the
LORD thy God led thee these forty years in the wilderness, to humble thee, *and* to prove thee, to know
what *was* in thine heart, whether thou wouldest
keep his commandments, or no.

3And he humbled thee, and suffered thee to
hunger, and fed thee with manna, which thou
knewest not, neither did thy fathers know; that he
might make thee know that man doth not live by
bread only, but by every *word* that proceedeth out of
the mouth of the LORD doth man live.

4Thy raiment waxed not old upon thee, neither
did thy foot swell, these forty years.

5Thou shalt also consider in thine heart, that, as
a man chasteneth his son, *so* the LORD thy God
chasteneth thee.

6Therefore thou shalt keep the commandments
of the LORD thy God, to walk in his ways, and to
fear him.

7For the LORD thy God bringeth thee into a good
land, a land of brooks of water, of fountains and
depths that spring out of valleys and hills;

8A land of wheat, and barley, and vines, and fig
trees, and pomegranates; a land of oil olive, and
honey;

9A land wherein thou shalt eat bread without
scarceness, thou shalt not lack any *thing* in it; a land
whose stones *are* iron, and out of whose hills thou
mayest dig brass.

10When thou hast eaten and art full, then thou
shalt bless the LORD thy God for the good land which
he hath given thee.

11Beware that thou forget not the LORD thy God, in
not keeping his commandments, and his judgments,
and his statutes, which I command thee this day:

12Lest *when* thou hast eaten and art full, and hast
built goodly houses, and dwelt *therein;*

13And *when* thy herds and thy flocks multiply, and
thy silver and thy gold is multiplied, and all that thou
hast is multiplied;

14Then thine heart be lifted up, and thou forget
the LORD thy God, which brought thee forth out of
the land of Egypt, from the house of bondage;

15Who led thee through that great and terrible
wilderness, *wherein were* fiery serpents, and scorpions, and drought, where *there was* no water; who
brought thee forth water out of the rock of flint;

16Who fed thee in the wilderness with manna,
which thy fathers knew not, that he might humble
thee, and that he might prove thee, to do thee good at
thy latter end;

17And thou say in thine heart, My power and the
might of *mine* hand hath gotten me this wealth.

NEW LIVING TRANSLATION

A Call to Remember and Obey

8 "Be careful to obey all the commands I am giving you today. Then you will live and multiply,
and you will enter and occupy the land the LORD
swore to give your ancestors. 2Remember how the
LORD your God led you through the wilderness for
these forty years, humbling you and testing you to
prove your character, and to find out whether or not
you would obey his commands. 3Yes, he humbled
you by letting you go hungry and then feeding you
with manna, a food previously unknown to you and
your ancestors. He did it to teach you that people do
not live by bread alone; rather, we live by every word
that comes from the mouth of the LORD. 4For all
these forty years your clothes didn't wear out, and
your feet didn't blister or swell. 5Think about it: Just
as a parent disciplines a child, the LORD your God disciplines you for your own good.

6"So obey the commands of the LORD your God by
walking in his ways and fearing him. 7For the LORD
your God is bringing you into a good land of flowing
streams and pools of water, with fountains and
springs that gush out in the valleys and hills. 8It is a
land of wheat and barley; of grapevines, fig trees, and
pomegranates; of olive oil and honey. 9It is a land
where food is plentiful and nothing is lacking. It is a
land where iron is as common as stone, and copper is
abundant in the hills. 10When you have eaten your
fill, be sure to praise the LORD your God for the good
land he has given you.

11"But that is the time to be careful! Beware that in
your plenty you do not forget the LORD your God and
disobey his commands, regulations, and decrees that
I am giving you today. 12For when you have become
full and prosperous and have built fine homes to live
in, 13and when your flocks and herds have become
very large and your silver and gold have multiplied
along with everything else, be careful! 14Do not become proud at that time and forget the LORD your
God, who rescued you from slavery in the land of
Egypt. 15Do not forget that he led you through the
great and terrifying wilderness with its poisonous
snakes and scorpions, where it was so hot and dry. He
gave you water from the rock! 16He fed you with
manna in the wilderness, a food unknown to your
ancestors. He did this to humble you and test you for
your own good. 17He did all this so you would never
say to yourself, 'I have achieved this wealth with my

KING JAMES VERSION

18But thou shalt remember the LORD thy God: for
it is he that giveth thee power to get wealth, that he
may establish his covenant which he sware unto thy
fathers, as *it is* this day.
19And it shall be, if thou do at all forget the LORD
thy God, and walk after other gods, and serve them,
and worship them, I testify against you this day that
ye shall surely perish.
20As the nations which the LORD destroyeth before
your face, so shall ye perish; because ye would not be
obedient unto the voice of the LORD your God.

9 1Hear, O Israel: Thou *art* to pass over Jordan
this day, to go in to possess nations greater and
mightier than thyself, cities great and fenced up to
heaven,
2A people great and tall, the children of the
Anakims, whom thou knowest, and *of whom* thou
hast heard *say,* Who can stand before the children of
Anak!
3Understand therefore this day, that the LORD thy
God *is* he which goeth over before thee; *as* a consuming fire he shall destroy them, and he shall bring
them down before thy face: so shalt thou drive them
out, and destroy them quickly, as the LORD hath said
unto thee.
4Speak not thou in thine heart, after that the
LORD thy God hath cast them out from before thee,
saying, For my righteousness the LORD hath brought
me in to possess this land: but for the wickedness of
these nations the LORD doth drive them out from
before thee.
5Not for thy righteousness, or for the uprightness
of thine heart, dost thou go to possess their land: but
for the wickedness of these nations the LORD thy
God doth drive them out from before thee, and that
he may perform the word which the LORD sware
unto thy fathers, Abraham, Isaac, and Jacob.
6Understand therefore, that the LORD thy God
giveth thee not this good land to possess it for thy
righteousness; for thou *art* a stiffnecked people.
7Remember, *and* forget not, how thou provokedst
the LORD thy God to wrath in the wilderness: from
the day that thou didst depart out of the land of
Egypt, until ye came unto this place, ye have been rebellious against the LORD.
8Also in Horeb ye provoked the LORD to wrath,
so that the LORD was angry with you to have destroyed you.
9When I was gone up into the mount to receive
the tables of stone, *even* the tables of the covenant
which the LORD made with you, then I abode in the
mount forty days and forty nights, I neither did eat
bread nor drink water:
10And the LORD delivered unto me two tables of
stone written with the finger of God; and on them
was written according to all the words, which the

NEW LIVING TRANSLATION

own strength and energy.' 18Remember the LORD
your God. He is the one who gives you power to be
successful, in order to fulfill the covenant he confirmed to your ancestors with an oath.
19"But I assure you of this: If you ever forget the
LORD your God and follow other gods, worshiping
and bowing down to them, you will certainly be destroyed. 20Just as the LORD has destroyed other nations in your path, you also will be destroyed if you
refuse to obey the LORD your God.

Victory by God's Grace

9 "Listen, O Israel! Today you are about to cross
the Jordan River to take over the land belonging to nations much greater and more powerful than
you. They live in cities with walls that reach to the
sky! 2The people are strong and tall—descendants of
the famous Anakite giants. You've heard the saying,
'Who can stand up to the Anakites?' 3But recognize
today that the LORD your God is the one who will
cross over ahead of you like a devouring fire to destroy them. He will subdue them so that you will
quickly conquer them and drive them out, just as the
LORD has promised.
4"After the LORD your God has done this for you,
don't say in your hearts, 'The LORD has given us this
land because we are such good people!' No, it is because of the wickedness of the other nations that he
is pushing them out of your way. 5It is not because
you are so good or have such integrity that you are
about to occupy their land. The LORD your God will
drive these nations out ahead of you only because of
their wickedness, and to fulfill the oath he swore to
your ancestors Abraham, Isaac, and Jacob. 6You must
recognize that the LORD your God is not giving you
this good land because you are good, for you are
not—you are a stubborn people.

Remembering the Gold Calf

7"Remember and never forget how angry you made
the LORD your God out in the wilderness. From the
day you left Egypt until now, you have been constantly rebelling against him. 8Even at Mount Sinai*
you made the LORD so angry he was ready to destroy
you. 9This happened when I was on the mountain receiving the tablets of stone inscribed with the words
of the covenant that the LORD had made with you. I
was there for forty days and forty nights, and all that
time I ate no food and drank no water. 10The LORD
gave me the two tablets on which God had written
with his own finger all the words he had spoken to

9:8 Hebrew *Horeb,* another name for Sinai.

KING JAMES VERSION

LORD spake with you in the mount out of the midst of the fire in the day of the assembly.

11 And it came to pass at the end of forty days and forty nights, *that* the LORD gave me the two tables of stone, *even* the tables of the covenant.

12 And the LORD said unto me, Arise, get thee down quickly from hence; for thy people which thou hast brought forth out of Egypt have corrupted *themselves;* they are quickly turned aside out of the way which I commanded them; they have made them a molten image.

13 Furthermore the LORD spake unto me, saying, I have seen this people, and, behold, it *is* a stiffnecked people:

14 Let me alone, that I may destroy them, and blot out their name from under heaven: and I will make of thee a nation mightier and greater than they.

15 So I turned and came down from the mount, and the mount burned with fire: and the two tables of the covenant *were* in my two hands.

16 And I looked, and, behold, ye had sinned against the LORD your God, *and* had made you a molten calf: ye had turned aside quickly out of the way which the LORD had commanded you.

17 And I took the two tables, and cast them out of my two hands, and brake them before your eyes.

18 And I fell down before the LORD, as at the first, forty days and forty nights: I did neither eat bread, nor drink water, because of all your sins which ye sinned, in doing wickedly in the sight of the LORD, to provoke him to anger.

19 For I was afraid of the anger and hot displeasure, wherewith the LORD was wroth against you to destroy you. But the LORD hearkened unto me at that time also.

20 And the LORD was very angry with Aaron to have destroyed him: and I prayed for Aaron also the same time.

21 And I took your sin, the calf which ye had made, and burnt it with fire, and stamped it, *and* ground *it* very small, *even* until it was as small as dust: and I cast the dust thereof into the brook that descended out of the mount.

22 And at Taberah, and at Massah, and at Kibroth-hattaavah, ye provoked the LORD to wrath.

23 Likewise when the LORD sent you from Kadesh-barnea, saying, Go up and possess the land which I have given you; then ye rebelled against the commandment of the LORD your God, and ye believed him not, nor hearkened to his voice.

24 Ye have been rebellious against the LORD from the day that I knew you.

25 Thus I fell down before the LORD forty days and forty nights, as I fell down *at the first;* because the LORD had said he would destroy you.

26 I prayed therefore unto the LORD, and said, O Lord GOD, destroy not thy people and thine inheritance, which thou hast redeemed through thy

NEW LIVING TRANSLATION

you from the heart of the fire when you were assembled at the mountain.

11 "At the end of the forty days and nights, the LORD handed me the two stone tablets inscribed with the words of the covenant. 12 Then the LORD said to me, 'Get up! Go down immediately, for the people you brought out of Egypt have corrupted themselves. How quickly they have turned away from the way I commanded them to live! They have melted gold and made an idol for themselves!'

13 "The LORD also said to me, 'I have seen how stubborn and rebellious these people are. 14 Leave me alone so I may destroy them and erase their name from under heaven. Then I will make a mighty nation of your descendants, a nation larger and more powerful than they are.'

15 "So while the mountain was blazing with fire I turned and came down, holding in my hands the two stone tablets inscribed with the terms of the covenant. 16 There below me I could see that you had sinned against the LORD your God. You had melted gold and made a calf idol for yourselves. How quickly you had turned away from the path the LORD had commanded you to follow! 17 So I took the stone tablets and threw them to the ground, smashing them before your eyes.

18 "Then, as before, I threw myself down before the LORD for forty days and nights. I ate no bread and drank no water because of the great sin you had committed by doing what the LORD hated, provoking him to anger. 19 I feared that the furious anger of the LORD, which turned him against you, would drive him to destroy you. But again he listened to me. 20 The LORD was so angry with Aaron that he wanted to destroy him, too. But I prayed for Aaron, and the LORD spared him. 21 I took your sin—the calf you had made—and I melted it down in the fire and ground it into fine dust. Then I threw the dust into the stream that flows down the mountain.

22 "You also made the LORD angry at Taberah,* Massah,* and Kibroth-hattaavah.* 23 And at Kadesh-barnea the LORD sent you out with this command: 'Go up and take over the land I have given you.' But you rebelled against the command of the LORD your God and refused to put your trust in him or obey him. 24 Yes, you have been rebelling against the LORD as long as I have known you.

25 "That is why I threw myself down before the LORD for forty days and nights—for the LORD said he would destroy you. 26 I prayed to the LORD and said, 'O Sovereign LORD, do not destroy them. They are your own people. They are your special possession,

9:22a *Taberah* means "place of burning." See Num 11:1-3. **9:22b** *Massah* means "place of testing." See Exod 17:1-7. **9:22c** *Kibroth-hattaavah* means "graves of gluttony." See Num 11:31-34.

KING JAMES VERSION

greatness, which thou hast brought forth out of Egypt with a mighty hand.

27 Remember thy servants, Abraham, Isaac, and Jacob; look not unto the stubbornness of this people, nor to their wickedness, nor to their sin:

28 Lest the land whence thou broughtest us out say, Because the LORD was not able to bring them into the land which he promised them, and because he hated them, he hath brought them out to slay them in the wilderness.

29 Yet they *are* thy people and thine inheritance, which thou broughtest out by thy mighty power and by thy stretched out arm.

10 1 At that time the LORD said unto me, Hew thee two tables of stone like unto the first, and come up unto me into the mount, and make thee an ark of wood.

2 And I will write on the tables the words that were in the first tables which thou brakest, and thou shalt put them in the ark.

3 And I made an ark *of* shittim wood, and hewed two tables of stone like unto the first, and went up into the mount, having the two tables in mine hand.

4 And he wrote on the tables, according to the first writing, the ten commandments, which the LORD spake unto you in the mount out of the midst of the fire in the day of the assembly: and the LORD gave them unto me.

5 And I turned myself and came down from the mount, and put the tables in the ark which I had made; and there they be, as the LORD commanded me.

6 And the children of Israel took their journey from Beeroth of the children of Jaakan to Mosera: there Aaron died, and there he was buried; and Eleazar his son ministered in the priest's office in his stead.

7 From thence they journeyed unto Gudgodah; and from Gudgodah to Jotbath, a land of rivers of waters.

8 At that time the LORD separated the tribe of Levi, to bear the ark of the covenant of the LORD, to stand before the LORD to minister unto him, and to bless in his name, unto this day.

9 Wherefore Levi hath no part nor inheritance with his brethren; the LORD *is* his inheritance, according as the LORD thy God promised him.

10 And I stayed in the mount, according to the first time, forty days and forty nights; and the LORD hearkened unto me at that time also, *and* the LORD would not destroy thee.

11 And the LORD said unto me, Arise, take *thy* journey before the people, that they may go in and possess the land, which I sware unto their fathers to give unto them.

NEW LIVING TRANSLATION

whom you redeemed from Egypt by your mighty power and your strong hand. 27 Please overlook the stubbornness and the awful sin of these people, and remember instead your servants Abraham, Isaac, and Jacob. 28 If you destroy these people, the Egyptians will say, "The Israelites died because the LORD wasn't able to bring them to the land he had promised to give them." Or they might say, "He destroyed them because he hated them; he deliberately took them into the wilderness to slaughter them." 29 But they are your people and your special possession, whom you brought out of Egypt by your great strength and powerful arm.'

A New Copy of the Covenant

10 "At that time the LORD said to me, 'Chisel out two stone tablets like the first ones. Also make a wooden Ark—a sacred chest to store them in. Come up to me on the mountain, 2 and I will write on the tablets the same words that were on the ones you smashed. Then place the tablets in the Ark.'

3 "So I made an Ark of acacia wood and cut two stone tablets like the first two. Then I went up the mountain with the tablets in my hand. 4 Once again the LORD wrote the Ten Commandments* on the tablets and gave them to me. They were the same words the LORD had spoken to you from the heart of the fire on the day you were assembled at the foot of the mountain. 5 Then I turned and came down the mountain and placed the tablets in the Ark of the Covenant, which I had made, just as the LORD commanded me. And the tablets are still there in the Ark."

6 (The people of Israel set out from the wells of the people of Jaakan* and traveled to Moserah, where Aaron died and was buried. His son Eleazar ministered as high priest in his place. 7 Then they journeyed to Gudgodah, and from there to Jotbathah, a land with many brooks and streams. 8 At that time the LORD set apart the tribe of Levi to carry the Ark of the LORD's Covenant, and to stand before the LORD as his ministers, and to pronounce blessings in his name. These are their duties to this day. 9 That is why the Levites have no share of property or possession of land among the other Israelite tribes. The LORD himself is their special possession, as the LORD your God told them.)

10 "As for me, I stayed on the mountain in the LORD's presence for forty days and nights, as I had done the first time. And once again the LORD listened to my pleas and agreed not to destroy you. 11 Then the LORD said to me, 'Get up and resume the journey, and lead the people to the land I swore to give to their ancestors, so they may take possession of it.'

10:4 Hebrew *the ten words.* **10:6** Or *set out from Beeroth of Bene-jaakan.*

KING JAMES VERSION

12 And now, Israel, what doth the LORD thy God require of thee, but to fear the LORD thy God, to walk in all his ways, and to love him, and to serve the LORD thy God with all thy heart and with all thy soul,

13 To keep the commandments of the LORD, and his statutes, which I command thee this day for thy good?

14 Behold, the heaven and the heaven of heavens *is* the LORD's thy God, the earth *also,* with all that therein *is.*

15 Only the LORD had a delight in thy fathers to love them, and he chose their seed after them, *even* you above all people, as *it is* this day.

16 Circumcise therefore the foreskin of your heart, and be no more stiffnecked.

17 For the LORD your God *is* God of gods, and Lord of lords, a great God, a mighty, and a terrible, which regardeth not persons, nor taketh reward:

18 He doth execute the judgment of the fatherless and widow, and loveth the stranger, in giving him food and raiment.

19 Love ye therefore the stranger: for ye were strangers in the land of Egypt.

20 Thou shalt fear the LORD thy God; him shalt thou serve, and to him shalt thou cleave, and swear by his name.

21 He *is* thy praise, and he *is* thy God, that hath done for thee these great and terrible things, which thine eyes have seen.

22 Thy fathers went down into Egypt with threescore and ten persons; and now the LORD thy God hath made thee as the stars of heaven for multitude.

11 1 Therefore thou shalt love the LORD thy God, and keep his charge, and his statutes, and his judgments, and his commandments, alway.

2 And know ye this day: for *I speak* not with your children which have not known, and which have not seen the chastisement of the LORD your God, his greatness, his mighty hand, and his stretched out arm,

3 And his miracles, and his acts, which he did in the midst of Egypt unto Pharaoh the king of Egypt, and unto all his land;

4 And what he did unto the army of Egypt, unto their horses, and to their chariots; how he made the water of the Red sea to overflow them as they pursued after you, and *how* the LORD hath destroyed them unto this day;

5 And what he did unto you in the wilderness, until ye came into this place;

6 And what he did unto Dathan and Abiram, the sons of Eliab, the son of Reuben: how the earth opened her mouth, and swallowed them up, and their households, and their tents, and all the substance that *was* in their possession, in the midst of all Israel:

NEW LIVING TRANSLATION

A Call to Love and Obedience

12 "And now, Israel, what does the LORD your God require of you? He requires only that you fear the LORD
your God, and live in a way that pleases him, and love
him and serve him with all your heart and soul. 13 And
you must always obey the LORD's commands and decrees that I am giving you today for your own good.
14 "Look, the highest heavens and the earth and
everything in it all belong to the LORD your God.
15 Yet the LORD chose your ancestors as the objects of
his love. And he chose you, their descendants, above
all other nations, as is evident today. 16 Therefore,
change your hearts* and stop being stubborn.
17 "For the LORD your God is the God of gods and
Lord of lords. He is the great God, the mighty and
awesome God, who shows no partiality and cannot
be bribed. 18 He ensures that orphans and widows receive justice. He shows love to the foreigners living
among you and gives them food and clothing. 19 So
you, too, must show love to foreigners, for you yourselves were once foreigners in the land of Egypt.
20 You must fear the LORD your God and worship him
and cling to him. Your oaths must be in his name
alone. 21 He alone is your God, the only one who is
worthy of your praise, the one who has done these
mighty miracles that you have seen with your own
eyes. 22 When your ancestors went down into Egypt,
there were only seventy of them. But now the LORD
your God has made you as numerous as the stars in
the sky!

11 "You must love the LORD your God and obey all his requirements, decrees, regulations, and
commands. 2 Keep in mind that I am not talking now
to your children, who have never experienced the
discipline of the LORD your God or seen his greatness
and his strong hand and powerful arm. 3 They didn't
see the miraculous signs and wonders he performed
in Egypt against Pharaoh and all his land. 4 They
didn't see what the LORD did to the armies of Egypt
and to their horses and chariots—how he drowned
them in the Red Sea* as they were chasing you. He
destroyed them, and they have not recovered to this
very day!
5 "Your children didn't see how the LORD cared for
you in the wilderness until you arrived here. 6 They
didn't see what he did to Dathan and Abiram (the
sons of Eliab, a descendant of Reuben) when the
earth opened its mouth in the Israelite camp and
swallowed them, along with their households and
tents and every living thing that belonged to them.

10:16 Hebrew *circumcise the foreskin of your hearts.* 11:4 Hebrew *sea of reeds.*

KING JAMES VERSION

7 But your eyes have seen all the great acts of the LORD which he did.

8 Therefore shall ye keep all the commandments which I command you this day, that ye may be strong, and go in and possess the land, whither ye go to possess it;

9 And that ye may prolong *your* days in the land, which the LORD sware unto your fathers to give unto them and to their seed, a land that floweth with milk and honey.

10 For the land, whither thou goest in to possess it, *is* not as the land of Egypt, from whence ye came out, where thou sowedst thy seed, and wateredst *it* with thy foot, as a garden of herbs:

11 But the land, whither ye go to possess it, *is* a land of hills and valleys, *and* drinketh water of the rain of heaven:

12 A land which the LORD thy God careth for: the eyes of the LORD thy God *are* always upon it, from the beginning of the year even unto the end of the year.

13 And it shall come to pass, if ye shall hearken diligently unto my commandments which I command you this day, to love the LORD your God, and to serve him with all your heart and with all your soul,

14 That I will give *you* the rain of your land in his due season, the first rain and the latter rain, that thou mayest gather in thy corn, and thy wine, and thine oil.

15 And I will send grass in thy fields for thy cattle, that thou mayest eat and be full.

16 Take heed to yourselves, that your heart be not deceived, and ye turn aside, and serve other gods, and worship them;

17 And *then* the LORD's wrath be kindled against you, and he shut up the heaven, that there be no rain, and that the land yield not her fruit; and *lest* ye perish quickly from off the good land which the LORD giveth you.

18 Therefore shall ye lay up these my words in your heart and in your soul, and bind them for a sign upon your hand, that they may be as frontlets between your eyes.

19 And ye shall teach them your children, speaking of them when thou sittest in thine house, and when thou walkest by the way, when thou liest down, and when thou risest up.

20 And thou shalt write them upon the door posts of thine house, and upon thy gates:

21 That your days may be multiplied, and the days of your children, in the land which the LORD sware unto your fathers to give them, as the days of heaven upon the earth.

22 For if ye shall diligently keep all these commandments which I command you, to do them, to love the LORD your God, to walk in all his ways, and to cleave unto him;

NEW LIVING TRANSLATION

7 But you have seen the LORD perform all these mighty deeds with your own eyes!

The Blessings of Obedience

8 "Therefore, be careful to obey every command I am
giving you today, so you may have strength to go in
and take over the land you are about to enter. 9 If you
obey, you will enjoy a long life in the land the LORD
swore to give to your ancestors and to you, their descendants—a land flowing with milk and honey!
10 For the land you are about to enter and take over
is not like the land of Egypt from which you came,
where you planted your seed and made irrigation
ditches with your foot as in a vegetable garden.
11 Rather, the land you will soon take over is a land of
hills and valleys with plenty of rain—12 a land that the
LORD your God cares for. He watches over it through
each season of the year!

13 "If you carefully obey all the commands I am
giving you today, and if you love the LORD your God
and serve him with all your heart and soul, 14 then he
will send the rains in their proper seasons—the early
and late rains—so you can bring in your harvests of
grain, new wine, and olive oil. 15 He will give you lush
pastureland for your livestock, and you yourselves
will have all you want to eat.

16 "But be careful. Don't let your heart be deceived
so that you turn away from the LORD and serve and
worship other gods. 17 If you do, the LORD's anger will
burn against you. He will shut up the sky and hold
back the rain, and the ground will fail to produce its
harvests. Then you will quickly die in that good land
the LORD is giving you.

18 "So commit yourselves wholeheartedly to these
words of mine. Tie them to your hands and wear
them on your forehead as reminders. 19 Teach them
to your children. Talk about them when you are at
home and when you are on the road, when you are
going to bed and when you are getting up. 20 Write
them on the doorposts of your house and on your
gates, 21 so that as long as the sky remains above the
earth, you and your children may flourish in the land
the LORD swore to give your ancestors.

22 "Be careful to obey all these commands I am giving you. Show love to the LORD your God by walking

KING JAMES VERSION

[23]Then will the LORD drive out all these nations
from before you, and ye shall possess greater nations
and mightier than yourselves.

[24]Every place whereon the soles of your feet shall
tread shall be yours: from the wilderness and Lebanon, from the river, the river Euphrates, even unto
the uttermost sea shall your coast be.

[25]There shall no man be able to stand before you:
for the LORD your God shall lay the fear of you and
the dread of you upon all the land that ye shall tread
upon, as he hath said unto you.

[26]Behold, I set before you this day a blessing and
a curse;

[27]A blessing, if ye obey the commandments of the
LORD your God, which I command you this day:

[28]And a curse, if ye will not obey the commandments of the LORD your God, but turn aside out of
the way which I command you this day, to go after
other gods, which ye have not known.

[29]And it shall come to pass, when the LORD thy
God hath brought thee in unto the land whither
thou goest to possess it, that thou shalt put the
blessing upon mount Gerizim, and the curse upon
mount Ebal.

[30]*Are* they not on the other side Jordan, by the way
where the sun goeth down, in the land of the Canaanites, which dwell in the champaign over against
Gilgal, beside the plains of Moreh?

[31]For ye shall pass over Jordan to go in to possess
the land which the LORD your God giveth you, and
ye shall possess it, and dwell therein.

[32]And ye shall observe to do all the statutes and
judgments which I set before you this day.

12 [1]These *are* the statutes and judgments,
which ye shall observe to do in the land,
which the LORD God of thy fathers giveth thee to possess it, all the days that ye live upon the earth.

[2]Ye shall utterly destroy all the places, wherein the
nations which ye shall possess served their gods,
upon the high mountains, and upon the hills, and
under every green tree:

[3]And ye shall overthrow their altars, and break
their pillars, and burn their groves with fire; and ye
shall hew down the graven images of their gods, and
destroy the names of them out of that place.

[4]Ye shall not do so unto the LORD your God.

[5]But unto the place which the LORD your God shall
choose out of all your tribes to put his name there,
even unto his habitation shall ye seek, and thither
thou shalt come:

[6]And thither ye shall bring your burnt offerings,
and your sacrifices, and your tithes, and heave offerings of your hand, and your vows, and your freewill
offerings, and the firstlings of your herds and of
your flocks:

[7]And there ye shall eat before the LORD your God,
and ye shall rejoice in all that ye put your hand unto,

NEW LIVING TRANSLATION

in his ways and holding tightly to him. [23]Then the
LORD will drive out all the nations ahead of you,
though they are much greater and stronger than you,
and you will take over their land. [24]Wherever you set
foot, that land will be yours. Your frontiers will
stretch from the wilderness in the south to Lebanon
in the north, and from the Euphrates River in the east
to the Mediterranean Sea in the west.* [25]No one will
be able to stand against you, for the LORD your God
will cause the people to fear and dread you, as he
promised, wherever you go in the whole land.

[26]"Look, today I am giving you the choice between
a blessing and a curse! [27]You will be blessed if you
obey the commands of the LORD your God that I am
giving you today. [28]But you will be cursed if you reject the commands of the LORD your God and turn
away from him and worship gods you have not
known before.

[29]"When the LORD your God brings you into the
land and helps you take possession of it, you must
pronounce the blessing at Mount Gerizim and the
curse at Mount Ebal. [30](These two mountains are
west of the Jordan River in the land of the Canaanites
who live in the Jordan Valley,* near the town of Gilgal, not far from the oaks of Moreh.) [31]For you are
about to cross the Jordan River to take over the land
the LORD your God is giving you. When you take that
land and are living in it, [32]you must be careful to obey
all the decrees and regulations I am giving you today.

The LORD's Chosen Place for Worship

12 "These are the decrees and regulations you
must be careful to obey when you live in the
land that the LORD, the God of your ancestors, is giving you. You must obey them as long as you live.

[2]"When you drive out the nations that live there,
you must destroy all the places where they worship
their gods—high on the mountains, up on the hills,
and under every green tree. [3]Break down their altars
and smash their sacred pillars. Burn their Asherah
poles and cut down their carved idols. Completely
erase the names of their gods!

[4]"Do not worship the LORD your God in the way
these pagan peoples worship their gods. [5]Rather, you
must seek the LORD your God at the place of worship
he himself will choose from among all the tribes—
the place where his name will be honored. [6]There
you will bring your burnt offerings, your sacrifices,
your tithes, your sacred offerings, your offerings to
fulfill a vow, your voluntary offerings, and your offerings of the firstborn animals of your herds and
flocks. [7]There you and your families will feast in the
presence of the LORD your God, and you will rejoice

11:24 Hebrew *to the western sea.* **11:30** Hebrew *the Arabah.*

ye and your households, wherein the LORD thy God hath blessed thee.

8 Ye shall not do after all *the things* that we do here this day, every man whatsoever *is* right in his own eyes.

9 For ye are not as yet come to the rest and to the inheritance, which the LORD your God giveth you.

10 But *when* ye go over Jordan, and dwell in the land which the LORD your God giveth you to inherit, and *when* he giveth you rest from all your enemies round about, so that ye dwell in safety;

11 Then there shall be a place which the LORD your God shall choose to cause his name to dwell there; thither shall ye bring all that I command you; your burnt offerings, and your sacrifices, your tithes, and the heave offering of your hand, and all your choice vows which ye vow unto the LORD:

12 And ye shall rejoice before the LORD your God, ye, and your sons, and your daughters, and your menservants, and your maidservants, and the Levite that *is* within your gates; forasmuch as he hath no part nor inheritance with you.

13 Take heed to thyself that thou offer not thy burnt offerings in every place that thou seest:

14 But in the place which the LORD shall choose in one of thy tribes, there thou shalt offer thy burnt offerings, and there thou shalt do all that I command thee.

15 Notwithstanding thou mayest kill and eat flesh in all thy gates, whatsoever thy soul lusteth after, according to the blessing of the LORD thy God which he hath given thee: the unclean and the clean may eat thereof, as of the roebuck, and as of the hart.

16 Only ye shall not eat the blood; ye shall pour it upon the earth as water.

17 Thou mayest not eat within thy gates the tithe of thy corn, or of thy wine, or of thy oil, or the firstlings of thy herds or of thy flock, nor any of thy vows which thou vowest, nor thy freewill offerings, or heave offering of thine hand:

18 But thou must eat them before the LORD thy God in the place which the LORD thy God shall choose, thou, and thy son, and thy daughter, and thy manservant, and thy maidservant, and the Levite that *is* within thy gates: and thou shalt rejoice before the LORD thy God in all that thou puttest thine hands unto.

19 Take heed to thyself that thou forsake not the Levite as long as thou livest upon the earth.

20 When the LORD thy God shall enlarge thy border, as he hath promised thee, and thou shalt say, I will eat flesh, because thy soul longeth to eat flesh; thou mayest eat flesh, whatsoever thy soul lusteth after.

21 If the place which the LORD thy God hath chosen to put his name there be too far from thee, then thou shalt kill of thy herd and of thy flock, which the LORD hath given thee, as I have commanded thee, and thou shalt eat in thy gates whatsoever thy soul lusteth after.

in all you have accomplished because the LORD your God has blessed you.

8 "Your pattern of worship will change. Today all of you are doing as you please, 9 because you have not yet arrived at the place of rest, the land the LORD your God is giving you as your special possession. 10 But you will soon cross the Jordan River and live in the land the LORD your God is giving you. When he gives you rest from all your enemies and you're living safely in the land, 11 you must bring everything I command you—your burnt offerings, your sacrifices, your tithes, your sacred offerings, and your offerings to fulfill a vow—to the designated place of worship, the place the LORD your God chooses for his name to be honored.

12 "You must celebrate there in the presence of the LORD your God with your sons and daughters and all your servants. And remember to include the Levites who live in your towns, for they will receive no allotment of land among you. 13 Be careful not to sacrifice your burnt offerings just anywhere you like. 14 You may do so only at the place the LORD will choose within one of your tribal territories. There you must offer your burnt offerings and do everything I command you.

15 "But you may butcher your animals and eat their meat in any town whenever you want. You may freely eat the animals with which the LORD your God blesses you. All of you, whether ceremonially clean or unclean, may eat that meat, just as you now eat gazelle and deer. 16 But you must not consume the blood. You must pour it out on the ground like water.

17 "But you may not eat your offerings in your hometown—neither the tithe of your grain and new wine and olive oil, nor the firstborn of your flocks and herds, nor any offering to fulfill a vow, nor your voluntary offerings, nor your sacred offerings. 18 You must eat these in the presence of the LORD your God at the place he will choose. Eat them there with your children, your servants, and the Levites who live in your towns, celebrating in the presence of the LORD your God in all you do. 19 And be very careful never to neglect the Levites as long as you live in your land.

20 "When the LORD your God expands your territory as he has promised, and you have the urge to eat meat, you may freely eat meat whenever you want. 21 It might happen that the designated place of worship—the place the LORD your God chooses for his name to be honored—is a long way from your home. If so, you may butcher any of the cattle, sheep, or goats the LORD has given you, and you may freely eat the meat in your hometown, as I have commanded

KING JAMES VERSION

22Even as the roebuck and the hart is eaten, so thou shalt eat them: the unclean and the clean shall eat *of* them alike.

23Only be sure that thou eat not the blood: for the blood *is* the life; and thou mayest not eat the life with the flesh.

24Thou shalt not eat it; thou shalt pour it upon the earth as water.

25Thou shalt not eat it; that it may go well with thee, and with thy children after thee, when thou shalt do *that which is* right in the sight of the LORD.

26Only thy holy things which thou hast, and thy vows, thou shalt take, and go unto the place which the LORD shall choose.

27And thou shalt offer thy burnt offerings, the flesh and the blood, upon the altar of the LORD thy God: and the blood of thy sacrifices shall be poured out upon the altar of the LORD thy God, and thou shalt eat the flesh.

28Observe and hear all these words which I command thee, that it may go well with thee, and with thy children after thee for ever, when thou doest *that which is* good and right in the sight of the LORD thy God.

29When the LORD thy God shall cut off the nations from before thee, whither thou goest to possess them, and thou succeedest them, and dwellest in their land;

30Take heed to thyself that thou be not snared by following them, after that they be destroyed from before thee; and that thou inquire not after their gods, saying, How did these nations serve their gods? even so will I do likewise.

31Thou shalt not do so unto the LORD thy God: for every abomination to the LORD, which he hateth, have they done unto their gods; for even their sons and their daughters they have burnt in the fire to their gods.

32What thing soever I command you, observe to do it: thou shalt not add thereto, nor diminish from it.

13 1If there arise among you a prophet, or a dreamer of dreams, and giveth thee a sign or a wonder,

2And the sign or the wonder come to pass, whereof he spake unto thee, saying, Let us go after other gods, which thou hast not known, and let us serve them;

3Thou shalt not hearken unto the words of that prophet, or that dreamer of dreams: for the LORD your God proveth you, to know whether ye love the LORD your God with all your heart and with all your soul.

4Ye shall walk after the LORD your God, and fear him, and keep his commandments, and obey his voice, and ye shall serve him, and cleave unto him.

5And that prophet, or that dreamer of dreams, shall be put to death; because he hath spoken to turn

NEW LIVING TRANSLATION

you. 22Anyone, whether ceremonially clean or unclean, may eat that meat, just as you do now with gazelle and deer. 23But never consume the blood, for the blood is the life, and you must not consume the lifeblood with the meat. 24Instead, pour out the blood on the ground like water. 25Do not consume the blood, so that all may go well with you and your children after you, because you will be doing what pleases the LORD.

26"Take your sacred gifts and your offerings given to fulfill a vow to the place the LORD chooses. 27You must offer the meat and blood of your burnt offerings on the altar of the LORD your God. The blood of your other sacrifices must be poured out on the altar of the LORD your God, but you may eat the meat. 28Be careful to obey all my commands, so that all will go well with you and your children after you, because you will be doing what is good and pleasing to the LORD your God.

29"When the LORD your God goes ahead of you and destroys the nations and you drive them out and live in their land, 30do not fall into the trap of following their customs and worshiping their gods. Do not inquire about their gods, saying, 'How do these nations worship their gods? I want to follow their example.' 31You must not worship the LORD your God the way the other nations worship their gods, for they perform for their gods every detestable act that the LORD hates. They even burn their sons and daughters as sacrifices to their gods.

32*"So be careful to obey all the commands I give you. You must not add anything to them or subtract anything from them.

A Warning against Idolatry

13 1*"Suppose there are prophets among you or those who dream dreams about the future, and they promise you signs or miracles, 2and the predicted signs or miracles occur. If they then say, 'Come, let us worship other gods'—gods you have not known before—3do not listen to them. The LORD your God is testing you to see if you truly love him with all your heart and soul. 4Serve only the LORD your God and fear him alone. Obey his commands, listen to his voice, and cling to him. 5The false prophets or visionaries who try to lead you astray must be put to death, for they encourage rebellion against the

12:32 Verse 12:32 is numbered 13:1 in Hebrew text. **13:1** Verses 13:1-18 are numbered 13:2-19 in Hebrew text.

KING JAMES VERSION

you away from the LORD your God, which brought you out of the land of Egypt, and redeemed you out of the house of bondage, to thrust thee out of the way which the LORD thy God commanded thee to walk in. So shalt thou put the evil away from the midst of thee.

6 If thy brother, the son of thy mother, or thy son, or thy daughter, or the wife of thy bosom, or thy friend, which *is* as thine own soul, entice thee secretly, saying, Let us go and serve other gods, which thou hast not known, thou, nor thy fathers;

7 *Namely,* of the gods of the people which *are* round about you, nigh unto thee, or far off from thee, from the *one* end of the earth even unto the *other* end of the earth;

8 Thou shalt not consent unto him, nor hearken unto him; neither shall thine eye pity him, neither shalt thou spare, neither shalt thou conceal him:

9 But thou shalt surely kill him; thine hand shall be first upon him to put him to death, and afterwards the hand of all the people.

10 And thou shalt stone him with stones, that he die; because he hath sought to thrust thee away from the LORD thy God, which brought thee out of the land of Egypt, from the house of bondage.

11 And all Israel shall hear, and fear, and shall do no more any such wickedness as this is among you.

12 If thou shalt hear *say* in one of thy cities, which the LORD thy God hath given thee to dwell there, saying,

13 *Certain* men, the children of Belial, are gone out from among you, and have withdrawn the inhabitants of their city, saying, Let us go and serve other gods, which ye have not known;

14 Then shalt thou inquire, and make search, and ask diligently; and, behold, *if it be* truth, *and* the thing certain, *that* such abomination is wrought among you;

15 Thou shalt surely smite the inhabitants of that city with the edge of the sword, destroying it utterly, and all that *is* therein, and the cattle thereof, with the edge of the sword.

16 And thou shalt gather all the spoil of it into the midst of the street thereof, and shalt burn with fire the city, and all the spoil thereof every whit, for the LORD thy God: and it shall be an heap for ever; it shall not be built again.

17 And there shall cleave nought of the cursed thing to thine hand: that the LORD may turn from the fierceness of his anger, and shew thee mercy, and have compassion upon thee, and multiply thee, as he hath sworn unto thy fathers;

18 When thou shalt hearken to the voice of the LORD thy God, to keep all his commandments which I command thee this day, to do *that which is* right in the eyes of the LORD thy God.

NEW LIVING TRANSLATION

LORD your God, who redeemed you from slavery and
brought you out of the land of Egypt. Since they try to
lead you astray from the way the LORD your God commanded you to live, you must put them to death. In
this way you will purge the evil from among you.

6 "Suppose someone secretly entices you—even
your brother, your son or daughter, your beloved
wife, or your closest friend—and says, 'Let us go worship other gods'—gods that neither you nor your ancestors have known. 7 They might suggest that you
worship the gods of peoples who live nearby or who
come from the ends of the earth. 8 But do not give in
or listen. Have no pity, and do not spare or protect
them. 9 You must put them to death! Strike the first
blow yourself, and then all the people must join in.
10 Stone the guilty ones to death because they have
tried to draw you away from the LORD your God, who
rescued you from the land of Egypt, the place of slavery. 11 Then all Israel will hear about it and be afraid,
and no one will act so wickedly again.

12 "When you begin living in the towns the LORD
your God is giving you, you may hear 13 that scoundrels among you are leading their fellow citizens
astray by saying, 'Let us go worship other gods'—
gods you have not known before. 14 In such cases, you
must examine the facts carefully. If you find that the
report is true and such a detestable act has been
committed among you, 15 you must attack that town
and completely destroy* all its inhabitants, as well as
all the livestock. 16 Then you must pile all the plunder
in the middle of the open square and burn it. Burn
the entire town as a burnt offering to the LORD your
God. That town must remain a ruin forever; it may
never be rebuilt. 17 Keep none of the plunder that has
been set apart for destruction. Then the LORD will
turn from his fierce anger and be merciful to you. He
will have compassion on you and make you a large
nation, just as he swore to your ancestors.

18 "The LORD your God will be merciful only if you
listen to his voice and keep all his commands that I
am giving you today, doing what pleases him.

13:15 The Hebrew term used here refers to the complete consecration of things or people to the LORD, either by destroying them or by giving them as an offering; similarly in 13:17.

KING JAMES VERSION

14 1Ye *are* the children of the LORD your God: ye
shall not cut yourselves, nor make any baldness between your eyes for the dead.
2For thou *art* an holy people unto the LORD thy
God, and the LORD hath chosen thee to be a peculiar
people unto himself, above all the nations that *are*
upon the earth.
3Thou shalt not eat any abominable thing.
4These *are* the beasts which ye shall eat: the ox,
the sheep, and the goat,
5The hart, and the roebuck, and the fallow deer,
and the wild goat, and the pygarg, and the wild ox,
and the chamois.
6And every beast that parteth the hoof, and
cleaveth the cleft into two claws, *and* cheweth the
cud among the beasts, that ye shall eat.
7Nevertheless these ye shall not eat of them that
chew the cud, or of them that divide the cloven hoof;
as the camel, and the hare, and the coney: for they
chew the cud, but divide not the hoof; *therefore* they
are unclean unto you.
8And the swine, because it divideth the hoof, yet
cheweth not the cud, it *is* unclean unto you: ye shall
not eat of their flesh, nor touch their dead carcase.
9These ye shall eat of all that *are* in the waters: all
that have fins and scales shall ye eat:
10And whatsoever hath not fins and scales ye may
not eat; it *is* unclean unto you.
11*Of* all clean birds ye shall eat.
12But these *are they* of which ye shall not eat: the
eagle, and the ossifrage, and the osprey,
13And the glede, and the kite, and the vulture after
his kind,
14And every raven after his kind,
15And the owl, and the night hawk, and the
cuckow, and the hawk after his kind,
16The little owl, and the great owl, and the swan,
17And the pelican, and the gier eagle, and the
cormorant,
18And the stork, and the heron after her kind, and
the lapwing, and the bat.
19And every creeping thing that flieth *is* unclean
unto you: they shall not be eaten.
20*But of* all clean fowls ye may eat.
21Ye shall not eat *of* any thing that dieth of itself:
thou shalt give it unto the stranger that *is* in thy gates,
that he may eat it; or thou mayest sell it unto an alien:
for thou *art* an holy people unto the LORD thy God.
Thou shalt not seethe a kid in his mother's milk.
22Thou shalt truly tithe all the increase of thy seed,
that the field bringeth forth year by year.
23And thou shalt eat before the LORD thy God, in the
place which he shall choose to place his name there,
the tithe of thy corn, of thy wine, and of thine oil, and

NEW LIVING TRANSLATION

Ceremonially Clean and Unclean Animals

14 "Since you are the people of the LORD your
God, never cut yourselves or shave the hair
above your foreheads in mourning for the dead. 2You
have been set apart as holy to the LORD your God, and
he has chosen you from all the nations of the earth to
be his own special treasure.
3"You must not eat any detestable animals that are
ceremonially unclean. 4These are the animals* you
may eat: the ox, the sheep, the goat, 5the deer, the
gazelle, the roe deer, the wild goat, the addax, the
antelope, and the mountain sheep.
6"You may eat any animal that has completely
split hooves and chews the cud, 7but if the animal
doesn't have both, it may not be eaten. So you may
not eat the camel, the hare, or the hyrax.* They chew
the cud but do not have split hooves, so they are ceremonially unclean for you. 8And you may not eat the
pig. It has split hooves but does not chew the cud,
so it is ceremonially unclean for you. You may not
eat the meat of these animals or even touch their
carcasses.
9"Of all the marine animals, you may eat whatever
has both fins and scales. 10You may not, however, eat
marine animals that do not have both fins and
scales. They are ceremonially unclean for you.
11"You may eat any bird that is ceremonially clean.
12These are the birds you may not eat: the griffon
vulture, the bearded vulture, the black vulture, 13the
kite, the falcon, buzzards of all kinds, 14ravens of all
kinds, 15the eagle owl, the short-eared owl, the seagull, hawks of all kinds, 16the little owl, the great owl,
the barn owl, 17the desert owl, the Egyptian vulture,
the cormorant, 18the stork, herons of all kinds, the
hoopoe, and the bat.
19"All winged insects that walk along the ground
are ceremonially unclean for you and may not be
eaten. 20But you may eat any winged bird or insect
that is ceremonially clean.
21"You must not eat anything that has died a natural death. You may give it to a foreigner living in your
town, or you may sell it to a stranger. But do not eat it
yourselves, for you are set apart as holy to the LORD
your God.
"You must not cook a young goat in its mother's
milk.

The Giving of Tithes

22"You must set aside a tithe of your crops—one-
tenth of all the crops you harvest each year. 23Bring
this tithe to the designated place of worship—the
place the LORD your God chooses for his name to be
honored—and eat it there in his presence. This applies to your tithes of grain, new wine, olive oil, and

14:4 The identification of some of the animals and birds listed in this chapter is uncertain. **14:7** Or *coney,* or *rock badger.*

the firstlings of thy herds and of thy flocks; that thou
mayest learn to fear the LORD thy God always.
24And if the way be too long for thee, so that thou
art not able to carry it; *or* if the place be too far from
thee, which the LORD thy God shall choose to set his
name there, when the LORD thy God hath blessed thee:
25Then shalt thou turn *it* into money, and bind up
the money in thine hand, and shalt go unto the place
which the LORD thy God shall choose:
26And thou shalt bestow that money for whatsoever thy soul lusteth after, for oxen, or for sheep, or
for wine, or for strong drink, or for whatsoever thy
soul desireth: and thou shalt eat there before the
LORD thy God, and thou shalt rejoice, thou, and thine
household,
27And the Levite that *is* within thy gates; thou shalt
not forsake him; for he hath no part nor inheritance
with thee.
28At the end of three years thou shalt bring forth
all the tithe of thine increase the same year, and shalt
lay *it* up within thy gates:
29And the Levite, (because he hath no part nor
inheritance with thee,) and the stranger, and the
fatherless, and the widow, which *are* within thy gates,
shall come, and shall eat and be satisfied; that the
LORD thy God may bless thee in all the work of thine
hand which thou doest.

15 1At the end of *every* seven years thou shalt
make a release.
2And this *is* the manner of the release: Every creditor that lendeth *aught* unto his neighbour shall release *it;* he shall not exact *it* of his neighbour, or of
his brother; because it is called the LORD's release.
3Of a foreigner thou mayest exact *it again:* but
that which is thine with thy brother thine hand shall
release;
4Save when there shall be no poor among you; for
the LORD shall greatly bless thee in the land which
the LORD thy God giveth thee *for* an inheritance to
possess it:
5Only if thou carefully hearken unto the voice of
the LORD thy God, to observe to do all these commandments which I command thee this day.
6For the LORD thy God blesseth thee, as he promised thee: and thou shalt lend unto many nations, but
thou shalt not borrow; and thou shalt reign over
many nations, but they shall not reign over thee.
7If there be among you a poor man of one of thy
brethren within any of thy gates in thy land which the
LORD thy God giveth thee, thou shalt not harden thine
heart, nor shut thine hand from thy poor brother:
8But thou shalt open thine hand wide unto him,
and shalt surely lend him sufficient for his need, *in
that* which he wanteth.
9Beware that there be not a thought in thy wicked
heart, saying, The seventh year, the year of release, is
at hand; and thine eye be evil against thy poor

the firstborn males of your flocks and herds. Doing
this will teach you always to fear the LORD your God.
24"Now when the LORD your God blesses you with a
good harvest, the place of worship he chooses for his
name to be honored might be too far for you to bring
the tithe. 25If so, you may sell the tithe portion of your
crops and herds, put the money in a pouch, and go to
the place the LORD your God has chosen. 26When you
arrive, you may use the money to buy any kind of food
you want—cattle, sheep, goats, wine, or other alcoholic drink. Then feast there in the presence of the
LORD your God and celebrate with your household.
27And do not neglect the Levites in your town, for they
will receive no allotment of land among you.
28"At the end of every third year, bring the entire
tithe of that year's harvest and store it in the nearest
town. 29Give it to the Levites, who will receive no
allotment of land among you, as well as to the foreigners living among you, the orphans, and the widows
in your towns, so they can eat and be satisfied. Then
the LORD your God will bless you in all your work.

Release for Debtors

15 "At the end of every seventh year you must
cancel the debts of everyone who owes you
money. 2This is how it must be done. Everyone must
cancel the loans they have made to their fellow Israelites. They must not demand payment from their
neighbors or relatives, for the LORD's time of release
has arrived. 3This release from debt, however, applies only to your fellow Israelites—not to the foreigners living among you.
4"There should be no poor among you, for the
LORD your God will greatly bless you in the land he is
giving you as a special possession. 5You will receive
this blessing if you are careful to obey all the commands of the LORD your God that I am giving you today. 6The LORD your God will bless you as he has
promised. You will lend money to many nations but
will never need to borrow. You will rule many nations, but they will not rule over you.
7"But if there are any poor Israelites in your towns
when you arrive in the land the LORD your God is giving you, do not be hard-hearted or tightfisted toward
them. 8Instead, be generous and lend them whatever
they need. 9Do not be mean-spirited and refuse
someone a loan because the year for canceling debts
is close at hand. If you refuse to make the loan and

KING JAMES VERSION

brother, and thou givest him nought; and he cry unto
the LORD against thee, and it be sin unto thee.
10 Thou shalt surely give him, and thine heart shall
not be grieved when thou givest unto him: because
that for this thing the LORD thy God shall bless thee
in all thy works, and in all that thou puttest thine
hand unto.
11 For the poor shall never cease out of the land:
therefore I command thee, saying, Thou shalt open
thine hand wide unto thy brother, to thy poor, and to
thy needy, in thy land.
12 *And* if thy brother, an Hebrew man, or an Hebrew woman, be sold unto thee, and serve thee six
years; then in the seventh year thou shalt let him go
free from thee.
13 And when thou sendest him out free from thee,
thou shalt not let him go away empty:
14 Thou shalt furnish him liberally out of thy flock,
and out of thy floor, and out of thy winepress: *of that*
wherewith the LORD thy God hath blessed thee thou
shalt give unto him.
15 And thou shalt remember that thou wast a
bondman in the land of Egypt, and the LORD thy
God redeemed thee: therefore I command thee this
thing today.
16 And it shall be, if he say unto thee, I will not go
away from thee; because he loveth thee and thine
house, because he is well with thee;
17 Then thou shalt take an awl, and thrust *it*
through his ear unto the door, and he shall be thy
servant for ever. And also unto thy maidservant thou
shalt do likewise.
18 It shall not seem hard unto thee, when thou
sendest him away free from thee; for he hath been
worth a double hired servant *to thee*, in serving thee
six years: and the LORD thy God shall bless thee in all
that thou doest.
19 All the firstling males that come of thy herd and
of thy flock thou shalt sanctify unto the LORD thy
God: thou shalt do no work with the firstling of thy
bullock, nor shear the firstling of thy sheep.
20 Thou shalt eat *it* before the LORD thy God year by
year in the place which the LORD shall choose, thou
and thy household.
21 And if there be *any* blemish therein, *as if it be*
lame, or blind, *or have* any ill blemish, thou shalt not
sacrifice it unto the LORD thy God.
22 Thou shalt eat it within thy gates: the unclean
and the clean *person shall eat it* alike, as the roebuck,
and as the hart.
23 Only thou shalt not eat the blood thereof; thou
shalt pour it upon the ground as water.

16 1 Observe the month of Abib, and keep the
passover unto the LORD thy God: for in the

NEW LIVING TRANSLATION

the needy person cries out to the LORD, you will be
considered guilty of sin. 10 Give generously to the
poor, not grudgingly, for the LORD your God will bless
you in everything you do. 11 There will always be
some in the land who are poor. That is why I am
commanding you to share freely with the poor and
with other Israelites in need.

Release for Hebrew Slaves

12 "If a fellow Hebrew sells himself or herself to be
your servant* and serves you for six years, in the
seventh year you must set that servant free.
13 "When you release a male servant, do not send
him away empty-handed. 14 Give him a generous
farewell gift from your flock, your threshing floor,
and your winepress. Share with him some of the
bounty with which the LORD your God has blessed
you. 15 Remember that you were once slaves in the
land of Egypt and the LORD your God redeemed you!
That is why I am giving you this command.
16 "But suppose your servant says, 'I will not leave
you,' because he loves you and your family, and he
has done well with you. 17 In that case, take an awl
and push it through his earlobe into the door. After
that, he will be your servant for life. And do the same
for your female servants.
18 "You must not consider it a hardship when you
release your servants. Remember that for six years
they have given you services worth double the wages
of hired workers, and the LORD your God will bless
you in all you do.

Sacrificing Firstborn Male Animals

19 "You must set aside for the LORD your God all the
firstborn males from your flocks and herds. Do not
use the firstborn of your herds to work your fields,
and do not shear the firstborn of your flocks. 20 Instead, you and your family must eat these animals in
the presence of the LORD your God each year at the
place he chooses. 21 But if this firstborn animal has
any defect, such as lameness or blindness, or if anything else is wrong with it, you must not sacrifice it to
the LORD your God. 22 Instead, use it for food for your
family in your hometown. Anyone, whether ceremonially clean or unclean, may eat it, just as anyone may
eat a gazelle or deer. 23 But you must not consume the
blood. You must pour it out on the ground like water.

Passover and the Festival of Unleavened Bread

16 "In honor of the LORD your God, celebrate
the Passover each year in the early spring, in

15:12 Or *If a Hebrew man or woman is sold to you.*

KING JAMES VERSION

month of Abib the LORD thy God brought thee forth
out of Egypt by night.
2 Thou shalt therefore sacrifice the passover unto
the LORD thy God, of the flock and the herd, in the
place which the LORD shall choose to place his name
there.
3 Thou shalt eat no leavened bread with it; seven
days shalt thou eat unleavened bread therewith, *even*
the bread of affliction: for thou camest forth out of
the land of Egypt in haste: that thou mayest remember the day when thou camest forth out of the land of
Egypt all the days of thy life.
4 And there shall be no leavened bread seen with
thee in all thy coast seven days; neither shall there
any thing of the flesh, which thou sacrificedst the
first day at even, remain all night until the morning.
5 Thou mayest not sacrifice the passover within
any of thy gates, which the LORD thy God giveth thee:
6 But at the place which the LORD thy God shall
choose to place his name in, there thou shalt sacrifice
the passover at even, at the going down of the sun, at
the season that thou camest forth out of Egypt.
7 And thou shalt roast and eat *it* in the place which
the LORD thy God shall choose: and thou shalt turn in
the morning, and go unto thy tents.
8 Six days thou shalt eat unleavened bread: and on
the seventh day *shall be* a solemn assembly to the
LORD thy God: thou shalt do no work *therein*.

9 Seven weeks shalt thou number unto thee: begin
to number the seven weeks from *such time as* thou
beginnest *to put* the sickle to the corn.
10 And thou shalt keep the feast of weeks unto the
LORD thy God with a tribute of a freewill offering of
thine hand, which thou shalt give *unto the LORD thy*
God, according as the LORD thy God hath blessed thee:
11 And thou shalt rejoice before the LORD thy God,
thou, and thy son, and thy daughter, and thy manservant, and thy maidservant, and the Levite that *is*
within thy gates, and the stranger, and the fatherless,
and the widow, that *are* among you, in the place which
the LORD thy God hath chosen to place his name there.
12 And thou shalt remember that thou wast a
bondman in Egypt: and thou shalt observe and do
these statutes.
13 Thou shalt observe the feast of tabernacles
seven days, after that thou hast gathered in thy corn
and thy wine:
14 And thou shalt rejoice in thy feast, thou, and thy
son, and thy daughter, and thy manservant, and thy
maidservant, and the Levite, the stranger, and the
fatherless, and the widow, that *are* within thy gates.
15 Seven days shalt thou keep a solemn feast unto

NEW LIVING TRANSLATION

the month of Abib,* for that was the month in which
the LORD your God brought you out of Egypt by night.
2 Your Passover sacrifice may be from either the flock
or the herd, and it must be sacrificed to the LORD
your God at the designated place of worship—the
place he chooses for his name to be honored. 3 Eat it
with bread made without yeast. For seven days the
bread you eat must be made without yeast, as when
you escaped from Egypt in such a hurry. Eat this
bread—the bread of suffering—so that as long as you
live you will remember the day you departed from
Egypt. 4 Let no yeast be found in any house throughout your land for those seven days. And when you
sacrifice the Passover lamb on the evening of the
first day, do not let any of the meat remain until the
next morning.
5 "You may not sacrifice the Passover in just any of
the towns that the LORD your God is giving you. 6 You
must offer it only at the designated place of worship—
the place the LORD your God chooses for his name to
be honored. Sacrifice it there in the evening as the sun
goes down on the anniversary of your exodus from
Egypt. 7 Roast the lamb and eat it in the place the LORD
your God chooses. Then you may go back to your tents
the next morning. 8 For the next six days you may not
eat any bread made with yeast. On the seventh day
proclaim another holy day in honor of the LORD your
God, and no work may be done on that day.

The Festival of Harvest

9 "Count off seven weeks from when you first begin to
cut the grain at the time of harvest. 10 Then celebrate
the Festival of Harvest* to honor the LORD your God.
Bring him a voluntary offering in proportion to the
blessings you have received from him. 11 This is a time
to celebrate before the LORD your God at the designated place of worship he will choose for his name to
be honored. Celebrate with your sons and daughters,
your male and female servants, the Levites from your
towns, and the foreigners, orphans, and widows who
live among you. 12 Remember that you were once
slaves in Egypt, so be careful to obey all these decrees.

The Festival of Shelters

13 "You must observe the Festival of Shelters* for
seven days at the end of the harvest season, after the
grain has been threshed and the grapes have been
pressed. 14 This festival will be a happy time of celebrating with your sons and daughters, your male and
female servants, and the Levites, foreigners, orphans,
and widows from your towns. 15 For seven days you

16:1 Hebrew *Observe the month of Abib, and keep the Passover unto the LORD your God.* Abib, the first month of the ancient Hebrew lunar calendar, usually occurs within the months of March and April. **16:10** Hebrew *Festival of Weeks;* also in 16:16. This was later called the Festival of Pentecost (see Acts 2:1). It is celebrated today as Shavuot (or Shabuoth). **16:13** Or *Festival of Booths,* or *Festival of Tabernacles;* also in 16:16. This was earlier called the Festival of the Final Harvest or Festival of Ingathering (see Exod 23:16b). It is celebrated today as Sukkot (or Succoth).

KING JAMES VERSION

the LORD thy God in the place which the LORD shall choose: because the LORD thy God shall bless thee in all thine increase, and in all the works of thine hands, therefore thou shalt surely rejoice.

16 Three times in a year shall all thy males appear before the LORD thy God in the place which he shall choose; in the feast of unleavened bread, and in the feast of weeks, and in the feast of tabernacles: and they shall not appear before the LORD empty:

17 Every man *shall give* as he is able, according to the blessing of the LORD thy God which he hath given thee.

18 Judges and officers shalt thou make thee in all thy gates, which the LORD thy God giveth thee, throughout thy tribes: and they shall judge the people with just judgment.

19 Thou shalt not wrest judgment; thou shalt not respect persons, neither take a gift: for a gift doth blind the eyes of the wise, and pervert the words of the righteous.

20 That which is altogether just shalt thou follow, that thou mayest live, and inherit the land which the LORD thy God giveth thee.

21 Thou shalt not plant thee a grove of any trees near unto the altar of the LORD thy God, which thou shalt make thee.

22 Neither shalt thou set thee up *any* image; which the LORD thy God hateth.

17 1 Thou shalt not sacrifice unto the LORD thy God *any* bullock, or sheep, wherein is blemish, *or* any evilfavouredness: for that *is* an abomination unto the LORD thy God.

2 If there be found among you, within any of thy gates which the LORD thy God giveth thee, man or woman, that hath wrought wickedness in the sight of the LORD thy God, in transgressing his covenant,

3 And hath gone and served other gods, and worshipped them, either the sun, or moon, or any of the host of heaven, which I have not commanded;

4 And it be told thee, and thou hast heard *of it,* and inquired diligently, and, behold, *it be* true, *and* the thing certain, *that* such abomination is wrought in Israel:

5 Then shalt thou bring forth that man or that woman, which have committed that wicked thing, unto thy gates, *even* that man or that woman, and shalt stone them with stones, till they die.

6 At the mouth of two witnesses, or three witnesses, shall he that is worthy of death be put to death; *but* at the mouth of one witness he shall not be put to death.

7 The hands of the witnesses shall be first upon him to put him to death, and afterward the hands of

NEW LIVING TRANSLATION

must celebrate this festival to honor the LORD your God at the place he chooses, for it is he who blesses you with bountiful harvests and gives you success in all your work. This festival will be a time of great joy for all.

16 "Each year every man in Israel must celebrate these three festivals: the Festival of Unleavened Bread, the Festival of Harvest, and the Festival of Shelters. On each of these occasions, all men must appear before the LORD your God at the place he chooses, but they must not appear before the LORD without a gift for him. 17 All must give as they are able, according to the blessings given to them by the LORD your God.

Justice for the People

18 "Appoint judges and officials for yourselves from each of your tribes in all the towns the LORD your God is giving you. They must judge the people fairly. 19 You must never twist justice or show partiality. Never accept a bribe, for bribes blind the eyes of the wise and corrupt the decisions of the godly. 20 Let true justice prevail, so you may live and occupy the land that the LORD your God is giving you.

21 "You must never set up a wooden Asherah pole beside the altar you build for the LORD your God. 22 And never set up sacred pillars for worship, for the LORD your God hates them.

17 "Never sacrifice sick or defective cattle, sheep, or goats to the LORD your God, for he detests such gifts.

2 "When you begin living in the towns the LORD your God is giving you, a man or woman among you might do evil in the sight of the LORD your God and violate the covenant. 3 For instance, they might serve other gods or worship the sun, the moon, or any of the stars—the forces of heaven—which I have strictly forbidden. 4 When you hear about it, investigate the matter thoroughly. If it is true that this detestable thing has been done in Israel, 5 then the man or woman who has committed such an evil act must be taken to the gates of the town and stoned to death. 6 But never put a person to death on the testimony of only one witness. There must always be two or three witnesses. 7 The witnesses must throw the first

KING JAMES VERSION

all the people. So thou shalt put the evil away from among you.

8 If there arise a matter too hard for thee in judgment, between blood and blood, between plea and plea, and between stroke and stroke, *being* matters of controversy within thy gates: then shalt thou arise, and get thee up into the place which the LORD thy God shall choose;

9 And thou shalt come unto the priests the Levites, and unto the judge that shall be in those days, and inquire; and they shall shew thee the sentence of judgment:

10 And thou shalt do according to the sentence, which they of that place which the LORD shall choose shall shew thee; and thou shalt observe to do according to all that they inform thee:

11 According to the sentence of the law which they shall teach thee, and according to the judgment which they shall tell thee, thou shalt do: thou shalt not decline from the sentence which they shall shew thee, *to* the right hand, nor *to* the left.

12 And the man that will do presumptuously, and will not hearken unto the priest that standeth to minister there before the LORD thy God, or unto the judge, even that man shall die: and thou shalt put away the evil from Israel.

13 And all the people shall hear, and fear, and do no more presumptuously.

14 When thou art come unto the land which the LORD thy God giveth thee, and shalt possess it, and shalt dwell therein, and shalt say, I will set a king over me, like as all the nations that *are* about me;

15 Thou shalt in any wise set *him* king over thee, whom the LORD thy God shall choose: *one* from among thy brethren shalt thou set king over thee: thou mayest not set a stranger over thee, which *is* not thy brother.

16 But he shall not multiply horses to himself, nor cause the people to return to Egypt, to the end that he should multiply horses: forasmuch as the LORD hath said unto you, Ye shall henceforth return no more that way.

17 Neither shall he multiply wives to himself, that his heart turn not away: neither shall he greatly multiply to himself silver and gold.

18 And it shall be, when he sitteth upon the throne of his kingdom, that he shall write him a copy of this law in a book out of *that which is* before the priests the Levites:

19 And it shall be with him, and he shall read therein all the days of his life: that he may learn to fear the LORD his God, to keep all the words of this law and these statutes, to do them:

20 That his heart be not lifted up above his brethren, and that he turn not aside from the commandment, *to* the right hand, or *to* the left: to the end that he may prolong *his* days in his kingdom, he, and his children, in the midst of Israel.

NEW LIVING TRANSLATION

stones, and then all the people may join in. In this
way, you will purge the evil from among you.
8 "Suppose a case arises in a local court that is too
hard for you to decide—for instance, whether someone is guilty of murder or only of manslaughter, or a
difficult lawsuit, or a case involving different kinds
of assault. Take such legal cases to the place the
LORD your God will choose, 9 and present them to the
Levitical priests or the judge on duty at that time.
They will hear the case and declare the verdict.
10 You must carry out the verdict they announce and
the sentence they prescribe at the place the LORD
chooses. You must do exactly what they say. 11 After
they have interpreted the law and declared their
verdict, the sentence they impose must be fully executed; do not modify it in any way. 12 Anyone arrogant enough to reject the verdict of the judge or of
the priest who represents the LORD your God must
die. In this way you will purge the evil from Israel.
13 Then everyone else will hear about it and be afraid
to act so arrogantly.

Guidelines for a King

14 "You are about to enter the land the LORD your God
is giving you. When you take it over and settle there,
you may think, 'We should select a king to rule over
us like the other nations around us.' 15 If this happens, be sure to select as king the man the LORD your
God chooses. You must appoint a fellow Israelite; he
may not be a foreigner.
16 "The king must not build up a large stable of
horses for himself or send his people to Egypt to buy
horses, for the LORD has told you, 'You must never return to Egypt.' 17 The king must not take many wives
for himself, because they will turn his heart away
from the LORD. And he must not accumulate large
amounts of wealth in silver and gold for himself.
18 "When he sits on the throne as king, he must
copy for himself this body of instruction on a scroll
in the presence of the Levitical priests. 19 He must always keep that copy with him and read it daily as
long as he lives. That way he will learn to fear the
LORD his God by obeying all the terms of these instructions and decrees. 20 This regular reading will
prevent him from becoming proud and acting as if
he is above his fellow citizens. It will also prevent
him from turning away from these commands in the
smallest way. And it will ensure that he and his descendants will reign for many generations in Israel.

KING JAMES VERSION

18 1The priests the Levites, *and* all the tribe of Levi, shall have no part nor inheritance with Israel: they shall eat the offerings of the LORD made by fire, and his inheritance.

2Therefore shall they have no inheritance among their brethren: the LORD *is* their inheritance, as he hath said unto them.

3And this shall be the priest's due from the people, from them that offer a sacrifice, whether *it be* ox or sheep; and they shall give unto the priest the shoulder, and the two cheeks, and the maw.

4The firstfruit *also* of thy corn, of thy wine, and of thine oil, and the first of the fleece of thy sheep, shalt thou give him.

5For the LORD thy God hath chosen him out of all thy tribes, to stand to minister in the name of the LORD, him and his sons for ever.

6And if a Levite come from any of thy gates out of all Israel, where he sojourned, and come with all the desire of his mind unto the place which the LORD shall choose;

7Then he shall minister in the name of the LORD his God, as all his brethren the Levites *do*, which stand there before the LORD.

8They shall have like portions to eat, beside that which cometh of the sale of his patrimony.

9When thou art come into the land which the LORD thy God giveth thee, thou shalt not learn to do after the abominations of those nations.

10There shall not be found among you *any one* that maketh his son or his daughter to pass through the fire, *or* that useth divination, *or* an observer of times, or an enchanter, or a witch,

11Or a charmer, or a consulter with familiar spirits, or a wizard, or a necromancer.

12For all that do these things *are* an abomination unto the LORD: and because of these abominations the LORD thy God doth drive them out from before thee.

13Thou shalt be perfect with the LORD thy God.

14For these nations, which thou shalt possess, hearkened unto observers of times, and unto diviners: but as for thee, the LORD thy God hath not suffered thee so *to do*.

15The LORD thy God will raise up unto thee a Prophet from the midst of thee, of thy brethren, like unto me; unto him ye shall hearken;

16According to all that thou desiredst of the LORD thy God in Horeb in the day of the assembly, saying, Let me not hear again the voice of the LORD my God, neither let me see this great fire any more, that I die not.

17And the LORD said unto me, They have well *spoken that* which they have spoken.

18I will raise them up a Prophet from among their brethren, like unto thee, and will put my words in his

NEW LIVING TRANSLATION

Gifts for the Priests and Levites

18 "Remember that the Levitical priests—that
is, the whole of the tribe of Levi—will receive
no allotment of land among the other tribes in Israel.
Instead, the priests and Levites will eat from the
special gifts given to the LORD, for that is their share.
2They will have no land of their own among the Israelites. The LORD himself is their special possession,
just as he promised them.

3"These are the parts the priests may claim as
their share from the cattle, sheep, and goats that the
people bring as offerings: the shoulder, the cheeks,
and the stomach. 4You must also give to the priests
the first share of the grain, the new wine, the olive oil,
and the wool at shearing time. 5For the LORD your
God chose the tribe of Levi out of all your tribes to
minister in the LORD's name forever.

6"Suppose a Levite chooses to move from his town
in Israel, wherever he is living, to the place the LORD
chooses for worship. 7He may minister there in the
name of the LORD his God, just like all his fellow
Levites who are serving the LORD there. 8He may eat
his share of the sacrifices and offerings, even if he
also receives support from his family.

A Call to Holy Living

9"When you enter the land the LORD your God is giving you, be very careful not to imitate the detestable
customs of the nations living there. 10For example,
never sacrifice your son or daughter as a burnt offering.* And do not let your people practice fortune-
telling, or use sorcery, or interpret omens, or engage
in witchcraft, 11or cast spells, or function as mediums or psychics, or call forth the spirits of the dead.
12Anyone who does these things is detestable to the
LORD. It is because the other nations have done these
detestable things that the LORD your God will drive
them out ahead of you. 13But you must be blameless
before the LORD your God. 14The nations you are
about to displace consult sorcerers and fortune-
tellers, but the LORD your God forbids you to do such
things."

True and False Prophets

15Moses continued, "The LORD your God will raise up
for you a prophet like me from among your fellow Israelites. You must listen to him. 16For this is what you
yourselves requested of the LORD your God when you
were assembled at Mount Sinai.* You said, 'Don't let
us hear the voice of the LORD our God anymore or see
this blazing fire, for we will die.'

17"Then the LORD said to me, 'What they have said
is right. 18I will raise up a prophet like you from
among their fellow Israelites. I will put my words in

18:10 Or *never make your son or daughter pass through the fire.*
18:16 Hebrew *Horeb*, another name for Sinai.

KING JAMES VERSION

mouth; and he shall speak unto them all that I shall
command him.
19 And it shall come to pass, *that* whosoever will
not hearken unto my words which he shall speak in
my name, I will require *it* of him.
20 But the prophet, which shall presume to speak a
word in my name, which I have not commanded him
to speak, or that shall speak in the name of other
gods, even that prophet shall die.
21 And if thou say in thine heart, How shall we
know the word which the LORD hath not spoken?
22 When a prophet speaketh in the name of the
LORD, if the thing follow not, nor come to pass, that *is*
the thing which the LORD hath not spoken, *but* the
prophet hath spoken it presumptuously: thou shalt
not be afraid of him.

19 1 When the LORD thy God hath cut off the nations, whose land the LORD thy God giveth
thee, and thou succeedest them, and dwellest in their
cities, and in their houses;
2 Thou shalt separate three cities for thee in the
midst of thy land, which the LORD thy God giveth
thee to possess it.
3 Thou shalt prepare thee a way, and divide the
coasts of thy land, which the LORD thy God giveth
thee to inherit, into three parts, that every slayer may
flee thither.
4 And this *is* the case of the slayer, which shall flee
thither, that he may live: Whoso killeth his neighbour ignorantly, whom he hated not in time past;
5 As when a man goeth into the wood with his
neighbour to hew wood, and his hand fetcheth a
stroke with the ax to cut down the tree, and the head
slippeth from the helve, and lighteth upon his neighbour, that he die; he shall flee unto one of those cities, and live:
6 Lest the avenger of the blood pursue the slayer,
while his heart is hot, and overtake him, because the
way is long, and slay him; whereas he *was* not worthy
of death, inasmuch as he hated him not in time past.
7 Wherefore I command thee, saying, Thou shalt
separate three cities for thee.
8 And if the LORD thy God enlarge thy coast, as he
hath sworn unto thy fathers, and give thee all the
land which he promised to give unto thy fathers;
9 If thou shalt keep all these commandments to do
them, which I command thee this day, to love the
LORD thy God, and to walk ever in his ways; then shalt
thou add three cities more for thee, beside these
three:
10 That innocent blood be not shed in thy land,
which the LORD thy God giveth thee *for* an inheritance, and *so* blood be upon thee.
11 But if any man hate his neighbour, and lie in wait
for him, and rise up against him, and smite him mortally that he die, and fleeth into one of these cities:
12 Then the elders of his city shall send and fetch

NEW LIVING TRANSLATION

his mouth, and he will tell the people everything I
command him. 19 I will personally deal with anyone
who will not listen to the messages the prophet proclaims on my behalf. 20 But any prophet who falsely
claims to speak in my name or who speaks in the
name of another god must die.'
21 "But you may wonder, 'How will we know
whether or not a prophecy is from the LORD?' 22 If the
prophet speaks in the LORD's name but his prediction does not happen or come true, you will know
that the LORD did not give that message. That
prophet has spoken without my authority and need
not be feared.

Cities of Refuge

19 "When the LORD your God destroys the nations whose land he is giving you, you will
take over their land and settle in their towns and
homes. 2 Then you must set apart three cities of refuge in the land the LORD your God is giving you. 3 Survey the territory,* and divide the land the LORD your
God is giving you into three districts, with one of
these cities in each district. Then anyone who has
killed someone can flee to one of the cities of refuge
for safety.
4 "If someone kills another person unintentionally,
without previous hostility, the slayer may flee to any
of these cities to live in safety. 5 For example, suppose
someone goes into the forest with a neighbor to cut
wood. And suppose one of them swings an ax to chop
down a tree, and the ax head flies off the handle, killing the other person. In such cases, the slayer may
flee to one of the cities of refuge to live in safety.
6 "If the distance to the nearest city of refuge is
too far, an enraged avenger might be able to chase
down and kill the person who caused the death.
Then the slayer would die unfairly, since he had
never shown hostility toward the person who died.
7 That is why I am commanding you to set aside three
cities of refuge.
8 "And if the LORD your God enlarges your territory, as he swore to your ancestors, and gives you all
the land he promised them, 9 you must designate
three additional cities of refuge. (He will give you
this land if you are careful to obey all the commands
I have given you—if you always love the LORD your
God and walk in his ways.) 10 That way you will prevent the death of innocent people in the land the
LORD your God is giving you as your special possession. You will not be held responsible for the death
of innocent people.
11 "But suppose someone is hostile toward a neighbor and deliberately ambushes and murders him
and then flees to one of the cities of refuge. 12 In that
case, the elders of the murderer's hometown must

19:3 Or *Keep the roads in good repair.*

KING JAMES VERSION

him thence, and deliver him into the hand of the avenger of blood, that he may die.

13 Thine eye shall not pity him, but thou shalt put away *the guilt of* innocent blood from Israel, that it may go well with thee.

14 Thou shalt not remove thy neighbour's landmark, which they of old time have set in thine inheritance, which thou shalt inherit in the land that the LORD thy God giveth thee to possess it.

15 One witness shall not rise up against a man for any iniquity, or for any sin, in any sin that he sinneth: at the mouth of two witnesses, or at the mouth of three witnesses, shall the matter be established.

16 If a false witness rise up against any man to testify against him *that which is* wrong;

17 Then both the men, between whom the controversy *is,* shall stand before the LORD, before the priests and the judges, which shall be in those days;

18 And the judges shall make diligent inquisition: and, behold, *if* the witness *be* a false witness, *and* hath testified falsely against his brother;

19 Then shall ye do unto him, as he had thought to have done unto his brother: so shalt thou put the evil away from among you.

20 And those which remain shall hear, and fear, and shall henceforth commit no more any such evil among you.

21 And thine eye shall not pity; *but* life *shall go* for life, eye for eye, tooth for tooth, hand for hand, foot for foot.

20 1 When thou goest out to battle against thine enemies, and seest horses, and chariots, *and* a people more than thou, be not afraid of them: for the LORD thy God *is* with thee, which brought thee up out of the land of Egypt.

2 And it shall be, when ye are come nigh unto the battle, that the priest shall approach and speak unto the people,

3 And shall say unto them, Hear, O Israel, ye approach this day unto battle against your enemies: let not your hearts faint, fear not, and do not tremble, neither be ye terrified because of them;

4 For the LORD your God *is* he that goeth with you, to fight for you against your enemies, to save you.

5 And the officers shall speak unto the people, saying, What man *is there* that hath built a new house, and hath not dedicated it? let him go and return to his house, lest he die in the battle, and another man dedicate it.

6 And what man *is he* that hath planted a vineyard, and hath not *yet* eaten of it? let him *also* go and return unto his house, lest he die in the battle, and another man eat of it.

7 And what man *is there* that hath betrothed a wife, and hath not taken her? let him go and return unto

NEW LIVING TRANSLATION

send agents to the city of refuge to bring him back
and hand him over to the dead person's avenger to be
put to death. 13 Do not feel sorry for that murderer!
Purge from Israel the guilt of murdering innocent
people; then all will go well with you.

Concern for Justice

14 "When you arrive in the land the LORD your God is
giving you as your special possession, you must never
steal anyone's land by moving the boundary markers
your ancestors set up to mark their property.

15 "You must not convict anyone of a crime on the
testimony of only one witness. The facts of the case
must be established by the testimony of two or three
witnesses.

16 "If a malicious witness comes forward and accuses someone of a crime, 17 then both the accuser
and accused must appear before the LORD by coming
to the priests and judges in office at that time. 18 The
judges must investigate the case thoroughly. If the
accuser has brought false charges against his fellow
Israelite, 19 you must impose on the accuser the sentence he intended for the other person. In this way,
you will purge such evil from among you. 20 Then the
rest of the people will hear about it and be afraid to
do such an evil thing. 21 You must show no pity for the
guilty! Your rule should be life for life, eye for eye,
tooth for tooth, hand for hand, foot for foot.

Regulations concerning War

20 "When you go out to fight your enemies
and you face horses and chariots and an
army greater than your own, do not be afraid. The
LORD your God, who brought you out of the land of
Egypt, is with you! 2 When you prepare for battle, the
priest must come forward to speak to the troops. 3 He
will say to them, 'Listen to me, all you men of Israel!
Do not be afraid as you go out to fight your enemies
today! Do not lose heart or panic or tremble before
them. 4 For the LORD your God is going with you! He
will fight for you against your enemies, and he will
give you victory!'

5 "Then the officers of the army must address the
troops and say, 'Has anyone here just built a new
house but not yet dedicated it? If so, you may go
home! You might be killed in the battle, and someone else would dedicate your house. 6 Has anyone
here just planted a vineyard but not yet eaten any of
its fruit? If so, you may go home! You might die in
battle, and someone else would eat the first fruit.
7 Has anyone here just become engaged to a woman
but not yet married her? Well, you may go home and
get married! You might die in the battle, and someone else would marry her.'

KING JAMES VERSION

his house, lest he die in the battle, and another man take her.

8 And the officers shall speak further unto the people, and they shall say, What man *is there that is* fearful and fainthearted? let him go and return unto his house, lest his brethren's heart faint as well as his heart.

9 And it shall be, when the officers have made an end of speaking unto the people, that they shall make captains of the armies to lead the people.

10 When thou comest nigh unto a city to fight against it, then proclaim peace unto it.

11 And it shall be, if it make thee answer of peace, and open unto thee, then it shall be, *that* all the people *that is* found therein shall be tributaries unto thee, and they shall serve thee.

12 And if it will make no peace with thee, but will make war against thee, then thou shalt besiege it:

13 And when the LORD thy God hath delivered it into thine hands, thou shalt smite every male thereof with the edge of the sword:

14 But the women, and the little ones, and the cattle, and all that is in the city, *even* all the spoil thereof, shalt thou take unto thyself; and thou shalt eat the spoil of thine enemies, which the LORD thy God hath given thee.

15 Thus shalt thou do unto all the cities *which are* very far off from thee, which *are* not of the cities of these nations.

16 But of the cities of these people, which the LORD thy God doth give thee *for* an inheritance, thou shalt save alive nothing that breatheth:

17 But thou shalt utterly destroy them; *namely,* the Hittites, and the Amorites, the Canaanites, and the Perizzites, the Hivites, and the Jebusites; as the LORD thy God hath commanded thee:

18 That they teach you not to do after all their abominations, which they have done unto their gods; so should ye sin against the LORD your God.

19 When thou shalt besiege a city a long time, in making war against it to take it, thou shalt not destroy the trees thereof by forcing an ax against them: for thou mayest eat of them, and thou shalt not cut them down (for the tree of the field *is* man's *life*) to employ *them* in the siege:

20 Only the trees which thou knowest that they *be* not trees for meat, thou shalt destroy and cut them down; and thou shalt build bulwarks against the city that maketh war with thee, until it be subdued.

21 1 If *one* be found slain in the land which the LORD thy God giveth thee to possess it, lying in the field, *and* it be not known who hath slain him:

2 Then thy elders and thy judges shall come forth, and they shall measure unto the cities which *are* round about him that is slain:

NEW LIVING TRANSLATION

8 "Then the officers will also say, 'Is anyone here afraid or worried? If you are, you may go home before you frighten anyone else.' 9 When the officers have finished speaking to their troops, they will appoint the unit commanders.

10 "As you approach a town to attack it, you must first offer its people terms for peace. 11 If they accept your terms and open the gates to you, then all the people inside will serve you in forced labor. 12 But if they refuse to make peace and prepare to fight, you must attack the town. 13 When the LORD your God hands the town over to you, use your swords to kill every man in the town. 14 But you may keep for yourselves all the women, children, livestock, and other plunder. You may enjoy the plunder from your enemies that the LORD your God has given you.

15 "But these instructions apply only to distant towns, not to the towns of the nations in the land you will enter. 16 In those towns that the LORD your God is giving you as a special possession, destroy every living thing. 17 You must completely destroy* the Hittites, Amorites, Canaanites, Perizzites, Hivites, and Jebusites, just as the LORD your God has commanded you. 18 This will prevent the people of the land from teaching you to imitate their detestable customs in the worship of their gods, which would cause you to sin deeply against the LORD your God.

19 "When you are attacking a town and the war drags on, you must not cut down the trees with your axes. You may eat the fruit, but do not cut down the trees. Are the trees your enemies, that you should attack them? 20 You may only cut down trees that you know are not valuable for food. Use them to make the equipment you need to attack the enemy town until it falls.

Cleansing for Unsolved Murder

21 "When you are in the land the LORD your God is giving you, someone may be found murdered in a field, and you don't know who committed the murder. 2 In such a case, your elders and judges must measure the distance from the site of

20:17 The Hebrew term used here refers to the complete consecration of things or people to the LORD, either by destroying them or by giving them as an offering.

KING JAMES VERSION

3And it shall be, *that* the city *which is* next unto the slain man, even the elders of that city shall take an heifer, which hath not been wrought with, *and* which hath not drawn in the yoke;

4And the elders of that city shall bring down the heifer unto a rough valley, which is neither eared nor sown, and shall strike off the heifer's neck there in the valley:

5And the priests the sons of Levi shall come near; for them the LORD thy God hath chosen to minister unto him, and to bless in the name of the LORD; and by their word shall every controversy and every stroke be *tried:*

6And all the elders of that city, *that are* next unto the slain *man,* shall wash their hands over the heifer that is beheaded in the valley:

7And they shall answer and say, Our hands have not shed this blood, neither have our eyes seen *it.*

8Be merciful, O LORD, unto thy people Israel, whom thou hast redeemed, and lay not innocent blood unto thy people of Israel's charge. And the blood shall be forgiven them.

9So shalt thou put away the *guilt of* innocent blood from among you, when thou shalt do *that which is* right in the sight of the LORD.

10When thou goest forth to war against thine enemies, and the LORD thy God hath delivered them into thine hands, and thou hast taken them captive,

11And seest among the captives a beautiful woman, and hast a desire unto her, that thou wouldest have her to thy wife;

12Then thou shalt bring her home to thine house; and she shall shave her head, and pare her nails;

13And she shall put the raiment of her captivity from off her, and shall remain in thine house, and bewail her father and her mother a full month: and after that thou shalt go in unto her, and be her husband, and she shall be thy wife.

14And it shall be, if thou have no delight in her, then thou shalt let her go whither she will; but thou shalt not sell her at all for money, thou shalt not make merchandise of her, because thou hast humbled her.

15If a man have two wives, one beloved, and another hated, and they have born him children, *both* the beloved and the hated; and *if* the firstborn son be hers that was hated:

16Then it shall be, when he maketh his sons to inherit *that* which he hath, *that* he may not make the son of the beloved firstborn before the son of the hated, *which is indeed* the firstborn:

17But he shall acknowledge the son of the hated *for* the firstborn, by giving him a double portion of all that he hath: for he *is* the beginning of his strength; the right of the firstborn *is* his.

18If a man have a stubborn and rebellious son, which will not obey the voice of his father, or the

NEW LIVING TRANSLATION

the crime to the nearby towns. 3When the nearest
town has been determined, that town's elders must
select from the herd a young cow that has never been
trained or yoked to a plow. 4They must lead it down
to a valley that has not been plowed or planted and
that has a stream running through it. There in the
valley they must break the young cow's neck. 5Then
the Levitical priests must step forward, for the LORD
your God has chosen them to minister before him
and to pronounce blessings in the LORD's name. They
are to decide all legal and criminal cases.

6"The elders of the town must wash their hands
over the young cow whose neck was broken. 7Then
they must say, 'Our hands did not shed this person's
blood, nor did we see it happen. 8O LORD, forgive
your people Israel whom you have redeemed. Do not
charge your people with the guilt of murdering an
innocent person.' Then they will be absolved of the
guilt of this person's blood. 9By following these instructions, you will do what is right in the LORD's
sight and will cleanse the guilt of murder from your
community.

Marriage to a Captive Woman

10"Suppose you go out to war against your enemies
and the LORD your God hands them over to you, and
you take some of them as captives. 11And suppose
you see among the captives a beautiful woman,
and you are attracted to her and want to marry her.
12If this happens, you may take her to your home,
where she must shave her head, cut her nails, 13and
change the clothes she was wearing when she was
captured. She will stay in your home, but let her
mourn for her father and mother for a full month.
Then you may marry her, and you will be her husband and she will be your wife. 14But if you marry
her and she does not please you, you must let her go
free. You may not sell her or treat her as a slave, for
you have humiliated her.

Rights of the Firstborn

15"Suppose a man has two wives, but he loves one
and not the other, and both have given him sons. And
suppose the firstborn son is the son of the wife he
does not love. 16When the man divides his inheritance, he may not give the larger inheritance to his
younger son, the son of the wife he loves, as if he were
the firstborn son. 17He must recognize the rights of
his oldest son, the son of the wife he does not love, by
giving him a double portion. He is the first son of his
father's virility, and the rights of the firstborn belong
to him.

Dealing with a Rebellious Son

18"Suppose a man has a stubborn and rebellious son
who will not obey his father or mother, even though

KING JAMES VERSION

voice of his mother, and *that,* when they have chastened him, will not hearken unto them:
19 Then shall his father and his mother lay hold on
him, and bring him out unto the elders of his city,
and unto the gate of his place;
20 And they shall say unto the elders of his city, This
our son *is* stubborn and rebellious, he will not obey
our voice; *he is* a glutton, and a drunkard.
21 And all the men of his city shall stone him with
stones, that he die: so shalt thou put evil away from
among you; and all Israel shall hear, and fear.
22 And if a man have committed a sin worthy of
death, and he be to be put to death, and thou hang
him on a tree:
23 His body shall not remain all night upon the tree,
but thou shalt in any wise bury him that day; (for he
that is hanged *is* accursed of God;) that thy land be
not defiled, which the LORD thy God giveth thee *for*
an inheritance.

22 1 Thou shalt not see thy brother's ox or his
sheep go astray, and hide thyself from
them: thou shalt in any case bring them again unto
thy brother.
2 And if thy brother *be* not nigh unto thee, or if
thou know him not, then thou shalt bring it unto
thine own house, and it shall be with thee until thy
brother seek after it, and thou shalt restore it to
him again.
3 In like manner shalt thou do with his ass; and so
shalt thou do with his raiment; and with all lost thing
of thy brother's, which he hath lost, and thou hast
found, shalt thou do likewise: thou mayest not hide
thyself.
4 Thou shalt not see thy brother's ass or his ox fall
down by the way, and hide thyself from them: thou
shalt surely help him to lift *them* up again.
5 The woman shall not wear that which pertaineth
unto a man, neither shall a man put on a woman's
garment: for all that do so *are* abomination unto the
LORD thy God.
6 If a bird's nest chance to be before thee in the
way in any tree, or on the ground, *whether they be*
young ones, or eggs, and the dam sitting upon the
young, or upon the eggs, thou shalt not take the dam
with the young:
7 *But* thou shalt in any wise let the dam go, and take
the young to thee; that it may be well with thee, and
that thou mayest prolong *thy* days.
8 When thou buildest a new house, then thou shalt
make a battlement for thy roof, that thou bring not
blood upon thine house, if any man fall from thence.
9 Thou shalt not sow thy vineyard with divers
seeds: lest the fruit of thy seed which thou hast sown,
and the fruit of thy vineyard, be defiled.
10 Thou shalt not plow with an ox and an ass
together.

NEW LIVING TRANSLATION

they discipline him. 19 In such a case, the father and
mother must take the son to the elders as they hold
court at the town gate. 20 The parents must say to the
elders, 'This son of ours is stubborn and rebellious
and refuses to obey. He is a glutton and a drunkard.'
21 Then all the men of his town must stone him to
death. In this way, you will purge this evil from
among you, and all Israel will hear about it and be
afraid.

Various Regulations

22 "If someone has committed a crime worthy of
death and is executed and hung on a tree,* 23 the
body must not remain hanging from the tree overnight. You must bury the body that same day, for
anyone who is hung* is cursed in the sight of God.
In this way, you will prevent the defilement of the
land the LORD your God is giving you as your special
possession.

22 "If you see your neighbor's ox or sheep or
goat wandering away, don't ignore your responsibility.* Take it back to its owner. 2 If its owner
does not live nearby or you don't know who the
owner is, take it to your place and keep it until the
owner comes looking for it. Then you must return it.
3 Do the same if you find your neighbor's donkey,
clothing, or anything else your neighbor loses. Don't
ignore your responsibility.
4 "If you see that your neighbor's donkey or ox has
collapsed on the road, do not look the other way. Go
and help your neighbor get it back on its feet!
5 "A woman must not put on men's clothing, and
a man must not wear women's clothing. Anyone
who does this is detestable in the sight of the LORD
your God.
6 "If you happen to find a bird's nest in a tree or on
the ground, and there are young ones or eggs in it
with the mother sitting in the nest, do not take the
mother with the young. 7 You may take the young, but
let the mother go, so that you may prosper and enjoy
a long life.
8 "When you build a new house, you must build a
railing around the edge of its flat roof. That way you
will not be considered guilty of murder if someone
falls from the roof.
9 "You must not plant any other crop between the
rows of your vineyard. If you do, you are forbidden
to use either the grapes from the vineyard or the
other crop.
10 "You must not plow with an ox and a donkey
harnessed together.

21:22 Or *impaled on a pole;* similarly in 21:23. **21:23** Greek version reads *for everyone who is hung on a tree.* Compare Gal 3:13. **22:1** Hebrew *don't hide yourself;* similarly in 22:3.

KING JAMES VERSION

11 Thou shalt not wear a garment of divers sorts, *as* of woollen and linen together.

12 Thou shalt make thee fringes upon the four quarters of thy vesture, wherewith thou coverest *thyself.*

13 If any man take a wife, and go in unto her, and hate her,

14 And give occasions of speech against her, and bring up an evil name upon her, and say, I took this woman, and when I came to her, I found her not a maid:

15 Then shall the father of the damsel, and her mother, take and bring forth *the tokens of* the damsel's virginity unto the elders of the city in the gate:

16 And the damsel's father shall say unto the elders, I gave my daughter unto this man to wife, and he hateth her;

17 And, lo, he hath given occasions of speech *against her,* saying, I found not thy daughter a maid; and yet these *are the tokens of* my daughter's virginity. And they shall spread the cloth before the elders of the city.

18 And the elders of that city shall take that man and chastise him;

19 And they shall amerce him in an hundred *shekels* of silver, and give *them* unto the father of the damsel, because he hath brought up an evil name upon a virgin of Israel: and she shall be his wife; he may not put her away all his days.

20 But if this thing be true, *and the tokens of* virginity be not found for the damsel:

21 Then they shall bring out the damsel to the door of her father's house, and the men of her city shall stone her with stones that she die: because she hath wrought folly in Israel, to play the whore in her father's house: so shalt thou put evil away from among you.

22 If a man be found lying with a woman married to an husband, then they shall both of them die, *both* the man that lay with the woman, and the woman: so shalt thou put away evil from Israel.

23 If a damsel *that is* a virgin be betrothed unto an husband, and a man find her in the city, and lie with her;

24 Then ye shall bring them both out unto the gate of that city, and ye shall stone them with stones that they die; the damsel, because she cried not, *being* in the city; and the man, because he hath humbled his neighbour's wife: so thou shalt put away evil from among you.

25 But if a man find a betrothed damsel in the field, and the man force her, and lie with her: then the man only that lay with her shall die:

26 But unto the damsel thou shalt do nothing; *there is* in the damsel no sin *worthy* of death: for as when a

NEW LIVING TRANSLATION

11 "You must not wear clothing made of wool and linen woven together.

12 "You must put four tassels on the hem of the cloak with which you cover yourself—on the front, back, and sides.

Regulations for Sexual Purity

13 "Suppose a man marries a woman, but after sleeping with her, he turns against her 14 and publicly
accuses her of shameful conduct, saying, 'When I
married this woman, I discovered she was not a virgin.' 15 Then the woman's father and mother must
bring the proof of her virginity to the elders as they
hold court at the town gate. 16 Her father must say to
them, 'I gave my daughter to this man to be his wife,
and now he has turned against her. 17 He has accused
her of shameful conduct, saying, "I discovered that
your daughter was not a virgin." But here is the proof
of my daughter's virginity.' Then they must spread
her bed sheet before the elders. 18 The elders must
then take the man and punish him. 19 They must also
fine him 100 pieces of silver,* which he must pay to
the woman's father because he publicly accused a
virgin of Israel of shameful conduct. The woman will
then remain the man's wife, and he may never divorce her.

20 "But suppose the man's accusations are true,
and he can show that she was not a virgin. 21 The
woman must be taken to the door of her father's
home, and there the men of the town must stone her
to death, for she has committed a disgraceful crime
in Israel by being promiscuous while living in her
parents' home. In this way, you will purge this evil
from among you.

22 "If a man is discovered committing adultery, both he and the woman must die. In this way, you will purge Israel of such evil.

23 "Suppose a man meets a young woman, a virgin
who is engaged to be married, and he has sexual
intercourse with her. If this happens within a town,
24 you must take both of them to the gates of that
town and stone them to death. The woman is guilty
because she did not scream for help. The man must
die because he violated another man's wife. In this
way, you will purge this evil from among you.

25 "But if the man meets the engaged woman out
in the country, and he rapes her, then only the man
must die. 26 Do nothing to the young woman; she
has committed no crime worthy of death. She is as

22:19 Hebrew *100 shekels of silver,* about 2.5 pounds or 1.1 kilograms in weight.

KING JAMES VERSION

man riseth against his neighbour, and slayeth him,
even so *is* this matter:
27 For he found her in the field, *and* the betrothed
damsel cried, and *there was* none to save her.
28 If a man find a damsel *that is* a virgin, which is
not betrothed, and lay hold on her, and lie with her,
and they be found;
29 Then the man that lay with her shall give unto
the damsel's father fifty *shekels* of silver, and she
shall be his wife; because he hath humbled her, he
may not put her away all his days.
30 A man shall not take his father's wife, nor discover his father's skirt.

23 1 He that is wounded in the stones, or hath
his privy member cut off, shall not enter
into the congregation of the LORD.
2 A bastard shall not enter into the congregation of
the LORD; even to his tenth generation shall he not
enter into the congregation of the LORD.
3 An Ammonite or Moabite shall not enter into the
congregation of the LORD; even to their tenth generation shall they not enter into the congregation of the
LORD for ever:
4 Because they met you not with bread and with
water in the way, when ye came forth out of Egypt;
and because they hired against thee Balaam the son
of Beor of Pethor of Mesopotamia, to curse thee.
5 Nevertheless the LORD thy God would not hearken unto Balaam; but the LORD thy God turned the
curse into a blessing unto thee, because the LORD thy
God loved thee.
6 Thou shalt not seek their peace nor their prosperity all thy days for ever.
7 Thou shalt not abhor an Edomite; for he *is* thy
brother: thou shalt not abhor an Egyptian; because
thou wast a stranger in his land.
8 The children that are begotten of them shall enter into the congregation of the LORD in their third
generation.
9 When the host goeth forth against thine enemies, then keep thee from every wicked thing.
10 If there be among you any man, that is not clean
by reason of uncleanness that chanceth him by
night, then shall he go abroad out of the camp, he
shall not come within the camp:
11 But it shall be, when evening cometh on, he shall
wash *himself* with water: and when the sun is down,
he shall come into the camp *again*.
12 Thou shalt have a place also without the camp,
whither thou shalt go forth abroad:
13 And thou shalt have a paddle upon thy weapon;
and it shall be, when thou wilt ease thyself abroad,
thou shalt dig therewith, and shalt turn back and
cover that which cometh from thee:
14 For the LORD thy God walketh in the midst of thy
camp, to deliver thee, and to give up thine enemies
before thee; therefore shall thy camp be holy: that he

NEW LIVING TRANSLATION

innocent as a murder victim. 27 Since the man raped
her out in the country, it must be assumed that she
screamed, but there was no one to rescue her.
28 "Suppose a man has intercourse with a young
woman who is a virgin but is not engaged to be married. If they are discovered, 29 he must pay her father
fifty pieces of silver.* Then he must marry the young
woman because he violated her, and he may never divorce her as long as he lives.
30 *"A man must not marry his father's former wife,
for this would violate his father.

Regulations concerning Worship

23 1 *"If a man's testicles are crushed or his
penis is cut off, he may not be admitted
to the assembly of the LORD.
2 "If a person is illegitimate by birth, neither he
nor his descendants for ten generations may be admitted to the assembly of the LORD.
3 "No Ammonite or Moabite or any of their descendants for ten generations may be admitted to
the assembly of the LORD. 4 These nations did not
welcome you with food and water when you came
out of Egypt. Instead, they hired Balaam son of Beor
from Pethor in distant Aram-naharaim to curse you.
5 But the LORD your God refused to listen to Balaam.
He turned the intended curse into a blessing because the LORD your God loves you. 6 As long as you
live, you must never promote the welfare and prosperity of the Ammonites or Moabites.
7 "Do not detest the Edomites or the Egyptians, because the Edomites are your relatives and you lived
as foreigners among the Egyptians. 8 The third generation of Edomites and Egyptians may enter the assembly of the LORD.

Miscellaneous Regulations

9 "When you go to war against your enemies, be sure
to stay away from anything that is impure.
10 "Any man who becomes ceremonially defiled
because of a nocturnal emission must leave the
camp and stay away all day. 11 Toward evening he
must bathe himself, and at sunset he may return to
the camp.
12 "You must have a designated area outside the
camp where you can go to relieve yourself. 13 Each of
you must have a spade as part of your equipment.
Whenever you relieve yourself, dig a hole with the
spade and cover the excrement. 14 The camp must be
holy, for the LORD your God moves around in your
camp to protect you and to defeat your enemies. He

22:29 Hebrew *50 shekels of silver,* about 1.25 pounds or 570 grams in weight. **22:30** Verse 22:30 is numbered 23:1 in Hebrew text. **23:1** Verses 23:1-25 are numbered 23:2-26 in Hebrew text.

see no unclean thing in thee, and turn away from
thee.
15 Thou shalt not deliver unto his master the servant which is escaped from his master unto thee:
16 He shall dwell with thee, *even* among you, in that
place which he shall choose in one of thy gates,
where it liketh him best: thou shalt not oppress him.
17 There shall be no whore of the daughters of Israel, nor a sodomite of the sons of Israel.
18 Thou shalt not bring the hire of a whore, or the
price of a dog, into the house of the LORD thy God for
any vow: for even both these *are* abomination unto
the LORD thy God.
19 Thou shalt not lend upon usury to thy brother;
usury of money, usury of victuals, usury of any thing
that is lent upon usury:
20 Unto a stranger thou mayest lend upon usury;
but unto thy brother thou shalt not lend upon usury:
that the LORD thy God may bless thee in all that thou
settest thine hand to in the land whither thou goest
to possess it.
21 When thou shalt vow a vow unto the LORD thy
God, thou shalt not slack to pay it: for the LORD thy
God will surely require it of thee; and it would be sin
in thee.
22 But if thou shalt forbear to vow, it shall be no sin
in thee.
23 That which is gone out of thy lips thou shalt
keep and perform; *even* a freewill offering, according as thou hast vowed unto the LORD thy God, which
thou hast promised with thy mouth.
24 When thou comest into thy neighbour's vineyard, then thou mayest eat grapes thy fill at thine
own pleasure; but thou shalt not put *any* in thy
vessel.
25 When thou comest into the standing corn of thy
neighbour, then thou mayest pluck the ears with
thine hand; but thou shalt not move a sickle unto thy
neighbour's standing corn.

24 1 When a man hath taken a wife, and married her, and it come to pass that she find no
favour in his eyes, because he hath found some uncleanness in her: then let him write her a bill of divorcement, and give *it* in her hand, and send her out
of his house.
2 And when she is departed out of his house, she
may go and be another man's *wife*.
3 And *if* the latter husband hate her, and write her a
bill of divorcement, and giveth *it* in her hand, and
sendeth her out of his house; or if the latter husband
die, which took her *to be* his wife;
4 Her former husband, which sent her away, may
not take her again to be his wife, after that she is defiled; for that *is* abomination before the LORD: and
thou shalt not cause the land to sin, which the LORD
thy God giveth thee *for* an inheritance.
5 When a man hath taken a new wife, he shall not

must not see any shameful thing among you, or he
will turn away from you.
15 "If slaves should escape from their masters and
take refuge with you, you must not hand them over
to their masters. 16 Let them live among you in any
town they choose, and do not oppress them.
17 "No Israelite, whether man or woman, may become a temple prostitute. 18 When you are bringing
an offering to fulfill a vow, you must not bring to the
house of the LORD your God any offering from the
earnings of a prostitute, whether a man* or a woman,
for both are detestable to the LORD your God.
19 "Do not charge interest on the loans you make to
a fellow Israelite, whether you loan money, or food,
or anything else. 20 You may charge interest to foreigners, but you may not charge interest to Israelites,
so that the LORD your God may bless you in everything you do in the land you are about to enter and
occupy.
21 "When you make a vow to the LORD your God, be
prompt in fulfilling whatever you promised him. For
the LORD your God demands that you promptly fulfill
all your vows, or you will be guilty of sin. 22 However,
it is not a sin to refrain from making a vow. 23 But
once you have voluntarily made a vow, be careful to
fulfill your promise to the LORD your God.
24 "When you enter your neighbor's vineyard, you
may eat your fill of grapes, but you must not carry
any away in a basket. 25 And when you enter your
neighbor's field of grain, you may pluck the heads of
grain with your hand, but you must not harvest it
with a sickle.

24 "Suppose a man marries a woman but she
does not please him. Having discovered
something wrong with her, he writes her a letter of
divorce, hands it to her, and sends her away from his
house. 2 When she leaves his house, she is free to
marry another man. 3 But if the second husband also
turns against her and divorces her, or if he dies, 4 the
first husband may not marry her again, for she has
been defiled. That would be detestable to the LORD.
You must not bring guilt upon the land the LORD your
God is giving you as a special possession.
5 "A newly married man must not be drafted into

23:18 Hebrew *a dog*.

KING JAMES VERSION

go out to war, neither shall he be charged with any
business: *but* he shall be free at home one year, and
shall cheer up his wife which he hath taken.
6No man shall take the nether or the upper millstone to pledge: for he taketh *a man's* life to pledge.
7If a man be found stealing any of his brethren of
the children of Israel, and maketh merchandise of
him, or selleth him; then that thief shall die; and thou
shalt put evil away from among you.
8Take heed in the plague of leprosy, that thou
observe diligently, and do according to all that the
priests the Levites shall teach you: as I commanded
them, *so* ye shall observe to do.
9Remember what the LORD thy God did unto
Miriam by the way, after that ye were come forth out
of Egypt.
10When thou dost lend thy brother any thing,
thou shalt not go into his house to fetch his pledge.
11Thou shalt stand abroad, and the man to whom
thou dost lend shall bring out the pledge abroad
unto thee.
12And if the man *be* poor, thou shalt not sleep with
his pledge:
13In any case thou shalt deliver him the pledge
again when the sun goeth down, that he may sleep in
his own raiment, and bless thee: and it shall be righteousness unto thee before the LORD thy God.
14Thou shalt not oppress an hired servant *that is*
poor and needy, *whether he be* of thy brethren, or of
thy strangers that *are* in thy land within thy gates:
15At his day thou shalt give *him* his hire, neither
shall the sun go down upon it; for he *is* poor, and
setteth his heart upon it: lest he cry against thee unto
the LORD, and it be sin unto thee.
16The fathers shall not be put to death for the children, neither shall the children be put to death for
the fathers: every man shall be put to death for his
own sin.
17Thou shalt not pervert the judgment of the
stranger, *nor* of the fatherless; nor take a widow's
raiment to pledge:
18But thou shalt remember that thou wast a bondman in Egypt, and the LORD thy God redeemed thee
thence: therefore I command thee to do this thing.
19When thou cuttest down thine harvest in thy
field, and hast forgot a sheaf in the field, thou shalt
not go again to fetch it: it shall be for the stranger, for
the fatherless, and for the widow: that the LORD thy
God may bless thee in all the work of thine hands.
20When thou beatest thine olive tree, thou shalt
not go over the boughs again: it shall be for the
stranger, for the fatherless, and for the widow.
21When thou gatherest the grapes of thy vineyard,
thou shalt not glean *it* afterward: it shall be for the
stranger, for the fatherless, and for the widow.
22And thou shalt remember that thou wast a
bondman in the land of Egypt: therefore I command
thee to do this thing.

NEW LIVING TRANSLATION

the army or be given any other official responsibilities. He must be free to spend one year at home,
bringing happiness to the wife he has married.
6"It is wrong to take a set of millstones, or even
just the upper millstone, as security for a loan, for the
owner uses it to make a living.
7"If anyone kidnaps a fellow Israelite and treats
him as a slave or sells him, the kidnapper must die.
In this way, you will purge the evil from among you.
8"In all cases involving serious skin diseases,* be
careful to follow the instructions of the Levitical
priests; obey all the commands I have given them.
9Remember what the LORD your God did to Miriam
as you were coming from Egypt.
10"If you lend anything to your neighbor, do not
enter his house to pick up the item he is giving as security. 11You must wait outside while he goes in and
brings it out to you. 12If your neighbor is poor and
gives you his cloak as security for a loan, do not keep
the cloak overnight. 13Return the cloak to its owner
by sunset so he can stay warm through the night and
bless you, and the LORD your God will count you as
righteous.
14"Never take advantage of poor and destitute laborers, whether they are fellow Israelites or foreigners living in your towns. 15You must pay them their
wages each day before sunset because they are poor
and are counting on it. If you don't, they might cry
out to the LORD against you, and it would be counted
against you as sin.
16"Parents must not be put to death for the sins of
their children, nor children for the sins of their parents. Those deserving to die must be put to death for
their own crimes.
17"True justice must be given to foreigners living
among you and to orphans, and you must never accept a widow's garment as security for her debt.
18Always remember that you were slaves in Egypt
and that the LORD your God redeemed you from your
slavery. That is why I have given you this command.
19"When you are harvesting your crops and forget
to bring in a bundle of grain from your field, don't go
back to get it. Leave it for the foreigners, orphans,
and widows. Then the LORD your God will bless you
in all you do. 20When you beat the olives from your
olive trees, don't go over the boughs twice. Leave the
remaining olives for the foreigners, orphans, and
widows. 21When you gather the grapes in your vineyard, don't glean the vines after they are picked.
Leave the remaining grapes for the foreigners, orphans, and widows. 22Remember that you were
slaves in the land of Egypt. That is why I am giving
you this command.

24:8 Traditionally rendered *leprosy*. The Hebrew word used here can describe various skin diseases.

KING JAMES VERSION

25

[1]If there be a controversy between men, and they come unto judgment, that *the judges* may judge them; then they shall justify the righteous, and condemn the wicked.

[2]And it shall be, if the wicked man *be* worthy to be beaten, that the judge shall cause him to lie down, and to be beaten before his face, according to his fault, by a certain number.

[3]Forty stripes he may give him, *and* not exceed: lest, *if* he should exceed, and beat him above these with many stripes, then thy brother should seem vile unto thee.

[4]Thou shalt not muzzle the ox when he treadeth out *the corn.*

[5]If brethren dwell together, and one of them die, and have no child, the wife of the dead shall not marry without unto a stranger: her husband's brother shall go in unto her, and take her to him to wife, and perform the duty of an husband's brother unto her.

[6]And it shall be, *that* the firstborn which she beareth shall succeed in the name of his brother *which is* dead, that his name be not put out of Israel.

[7]And if the man like not to take his brother's wife, then let his brother's wife go up to the gate unto the elders, and say, My husband's brother refuseth to raise up unto his brother a name in Israel, he will not perform the duty of my husband's brother.

[8]Then the elders of his city shall call him, and speak unto him: and *if* he stand *to it,* and say, I like not to take her;

[9]Then shall his brother's wife come unto him in the presence of the elders, and loose his shoe from off his foot, and spit in his face, and shall answer and say, So shall it be done unto that man that will not build up his brother's house.

[10]And his name shall be called in Israel, The house of him that hath his shoe loosed.

[11]When men strive together one with another, and the wife of the one draweth near for to deliver her husband out of the hand of him that smiteth him, and putteth forth her hand, and taketh him by the secrets:

[12]Then thou shalt cut off her hand, thine eye shall not pity *her.*

[13]Thou shalt not have in thy bag divers weights, a great and a small.

[14]Thou shalt not have in thine house divers measures, a great and a small.

[15]*But* thou shalt have a perfect and just weight, a perfect and just measure shalt thou have: that thy days may be lengthened in the land which the LORD thy God giveth thee.

[16]For all that do such things, *and* all that do unrighteously, *are* an abomination unto the LORD thy God.

[17]Remember what Amalek did unto thee by the way, when ye were come forth out of Egypt;

[18]How he met thee by the way, and smote the hindmost of thee, *even* all *that were* feeble behind

NEW LIVING TRANSLATION

25

"Suppose two people take a dispute to court, and the judges declare that one is right and the other is wrong. [2]If the person in the wrong is sentenced to be flogged, the judge must command him to lie down and be beaten in his presence with the number of lashes appropriate to the crime. [3]But never give more than forty lashes; more than forty lashes would publicly humiliate your neighbor.

[4]"You must not muzzle an ox to keep it from eating as it treads out the grain.

[5]"If two brothers are living together on the same property and one of them dies without a son, his widow may not be married to anyone from outside the family. Instead, her husband's brother should marry her and have intercourse with her to fulfill the duties of a brother-in-law. [6]The first son she bears to him will be considered the son of the dead brother, so that his name will not be forgotten in Israel.

[7]"But if the man refuses to marry his brother's widow, she must go to the town gate and say to the elders assembled there, 'My husband's brother refuses to preserve his brother's name in Israel—he refuses to fulfill the duties of a brother-in-law by marrying me.' [8]The elders of the town will then summon him and talk with him. If he still refuses and says, 'I don't want to marry her,' [9]the widow must walk over to him in the presence of the elders, pull his sandal from his foot, and spit in his face. Then she must declare, 'This is what happens to a man who refuses to provide his brother with children.' [10]Ever afterward in Israel his family will be referred to as 'the family of the man whose sandal was pulled off'!

[11]"If two Israelite men get into a fight and the wife of one tries to rescue her husband by grabbing the testicles of the other man, [12]you must cut off her hand. Show her no pity.

[13]"You must use accurate scales when you weigh out merchandise, [14]and you must use full and honest measures. [15]Yes, always use honest weights and measures, so that you may enjoy a long life in the land the LORD your God is giving you. [16]All who cheat with dishonest weights and measures are detestable to the LORD your God.

[17]"Never forget what the Amalekites did to you as you came from Egypt. [18]They attacked you when you were exhausted and weary, and they struck down

KING JAMES VERSION

thee, when thou *wast* faint and weary; and he feared
not God.
19 Therefore it shall be, when the LORD thy God
hath given thee rest from all thine enemies round
about, in the land which the LORD thy God giveth
thee *for* an inheritance to possess it, *that* thou shalt
blot out the remembrance of Amalek from under
heaven; thou shalt not forget *it*.

26 1 And it shall be, when thou *art* come in
unto the land which the LORD thy God giveth thee *for* an inheritance, and possessest it, and
dwellest therein;
2 That thou shalt take of the first of all the fruit of
the earth, which thou shalt bring of thy land that the
LORD thy God giveth thee, and shalt put *it* in a basket,
and shalt go unto the place which the LORD thy God
shall choose to place his name there.
3 And thou shalt go unto the priest that shall be in
those days, and say unto him, I profess this day unto
the LORD thy God, that I am come unto the country
which the LORD sware unto our fathers for to give us.
4 And the priest shall take the basket out of thine
hand, and set it down before the altar of the LORD
thy God.
5 And thou shalt speak and say before the LORD thy
God, A Syrian ready to perish *was* my father, and he
went down into Egypt, and sojourned there with a
few, and became there a nation, great, mighty, and
populous:
6 And the Egyptians evil entreated us, and afflicted
us, and laid upon us hard bondage:
7 And when we cried unto the LORD God of our
fathers, the LORD heard our voice, and looked on our
affliction, and our labour, and our oppression:
8 And the LORD brought us forth out of Egypt with a
mighty hand, and with an outstretched arm, and
with great terribleness, and with signs, and with
wonders:
9 And he hath brought us into this place, and hath
given us this land, *even* a land that floweth with milk
and honey.
10 And now, behold, I have brought the firstfruits
of the land, which thou, O LORD, hast given me. And
thou shalt set it before the LORD thy God, and worship before the LORD thy God:
11 And thou shalt rejoice in every good *thing* which
the LORD thy God hath given unto thee, and unto
thine house, thou, and the Levite, and the stranger
that *is* among you.
12 When thou hast made an end of tithing all the
tithes of thine increase the third year, *which is* the
year of tithing, and hast given *it* unto the Levite,
the stranger, the fatherless, and the widow, that they
may eat within thy gates, and be filled;
13 Then thou shalt say before the LORD thy God, I
have brought away the hallowed things out of *mine*
house, and also have given them unto the Levite, and

NEW LIVING TRANSLATION

those who were straggling behind. They had no fear
of God. 19 Therefore, when the LORD your God has
given you rest from all your enemies in the land he is
giving you as a special possession, you must destroy
the Amalekites and erase their memory from under
heaven. Never forget this!

Harvest Offerings and Tithes

26 "When you enter the land the LORD your
God is giving you as a special possession
and you have conquered it and settled there, 2 put
some of the first produce from each crop you harvest into a basket and bring it to the designated
place of worship—the place the LORD your God
chooses for his name to be honored. 3 Go to the
priest in charge at that time and say to him, 'With
this gift I acknowledge to the LORD your God that I
have entered the land he swore to our ancestors he
would give us.' 4 The priest will then take the basket
from your hand and set it before the altar of the
LORD your God.
5 "You must then say in the presence of the LORD
your God, 'My ancestor Jacob was a wandering Aramean who went to live as a foreigner in Egypt. His
family arrived few in number, but in Egypt they became a large and mighty nation. 6 When the Egyptians oppressed and humiliated us by making us
their slaves, 7 we cried out to the LORD, the God of our
ancestors. He heard our cries and saw our hardship,
toil, and oppression. 8 So the LORD brought us out of
Egypt with a strong hand and powerful arm, with
overwhelming terror, and with miraculous signs and
wonders. 9 He brought us to this place and gave us
this land flowing with milk and honey! 10 And now,
O LORD, I have brought you the first portion of the
harvest you have given me from the ground.' Then
place the produce before the LORD your God, and
bow to the ground in worship before him. 11 Afterward you may go and celebrate because of all the
good things the LORD your God has given to you
and your household. Remember to include the
Levites and the foreigners living among you in the
celebration.
12 "Every third year you must offer a special tithe
of your crops. In this year of the special tithe you
must give your tithes to the Levites, foreigners, orphans, and widows, so that they will have enough to
eat in your towns. 13 Then you must declare in the
presence of the LORD your God, 'I have taken the

KING JAMES VERSION

unto the stranger, to the fatherless, and to the widow,
according to all thy commandments which thou hast
commanded me: I have not transgressed thy commandments, neither have I forgotten *them:*
14 I have not eaten thereof in my mourning, neither have I taken away *aught* thereof for *any* unclean *use,* nor given *aught* thereof for the dead: *but* I
have hearkened to the voice of the LORD my God,
and have done according to all that thou hast commanded me.
15 Look down from thy holy habitation, from
heaven, and bless thy people Israel, and the land
which thou hast given us, as thou swarest unto our
fathers, a land that floweth with milk and honey.
16 This day the LORD thy God hath commanded
thee to do these statutes and judgments: thou shalt
therefore keep and do them with all thine heart, and
with all thy soul.
17 Thou hast avouched the LORD this day to be thy
God, and to walk in his ways, and to keep his statutes,
and his commandments, and his judgments, and to
hearken unto his voice:
18 And the LORD hath avouched thee this day to be
his peculiar people, as he hath promised thee, and
that *thou* shouldest keep all his commandments;
19 And to make thee high above all nations which
he hath made, in praise, and in name, and in honour;
and that thou mayest be an holy people unto the
LORD thy God, as he hath spoken.

27 1 And Moses with the elders of Israel commanded the people, saying, Keep all the
commandments which I command you this day.
2 And it shall be on the day when ye shall pass over
Jordan unto the land which the LORD thy God giveth
thee, that thou shalt set thee up great stones, and
plaster them with plaster:
3 And thou shalt write upon them all the words of
this law, when thou art passed over, that thou mayest
go in unto the land which the LORD thy God giveth
thee, a land that floweth with milk and honey; as the
LORD God of thy fathers hath promised thee.
4 Therefore it shall be when ye be gone over Jordan, *that* ye shall set up these stones, which I command you this day, in mount Ebal, and thou shalt
plaster them with plaster.
5 And there shalt thou build an altar unto the LORD
thy God, an altar of stones: thou shalt not lift up *any*
iron *tool* upon them.
6 Thou shalt build the altar of the LORD thy God of
whole stones: and thou shalt offer burnt offerings
thereon unto the LORD thy God:
7 And thou shalt offer peace offerings, and shalt
eat there, and rejoice before the LORD thy God.
8 And thou shalt write upon the stones all the
words of this law very plainly.
9 And Moses and the priests the Levites spake unto
all Israel, saying, Take heed, and hearken, O Israel;

NEW LIVING TRANSLATION

sacred gift from my house and have given it to the
Levites, foreigners, orphans, and widows, just as you
commanded me. I have not violated or forgotten any
of your commands. 14 I have not eaten any of it while
in mourning; I have not handled it while I was ceremonially unclean; and I have not offered any of it to
the dead. I have obeyed the LORD my God and have
done everything you commanded me. 15 Now look
down from your holy dwelling place in heaven and
bless your people Israel and the land you swore to
our ancestors to give us—a land flowing with milk
and honey.'

A Call to Obey the LORD's Commands

16 "Today the LORD your God has commanded you to
obey all these decrees and regulations. So be careful
to obey them wholeheartedly. 17 You have declared
today that the LORD is your God. And you have promised to walk in his ways, and to obey his decrees,
commands, and regulations, and to do everything he
tells you. 18 The LORD has declared today that you are
his people, his own special treasure, just as he promised, and that you must obey all his commands.
19 And if you do, he will set you high above all the
other nations he has made. Then you will receive
praise, honor, and renown. You will be a nation that is
holy to the LORD your God, just as he promised."

The Altar on Mount Ebal

27 Then Moses and the leaders of Israel gave
this charge to the people: "Obey all these
commands that I am giving you today. 2 When you
cross the Jordan River and enter the land the LORD
your God is giving you, set up some large stones and
coat them with plaster. 3 Write this whole body of instruction on them when you cross the river to enter
the land the LORD your God is giving you—a land
flowing with milk and honey, just as the LORD, the
God of your ancestors, promised you. 4 When you
cross the Jordan, set up these stones at Mount Ebal
and coat them with plaster, as I am commanding
you today.
5 "Then build an altar there to the LORD your God,
using natural, uncut stones. You must not shape the
stones with an iron tool. 6 Build the altar of uncut
stones, and use it to offer burnt offerings to the LORD
your God. 7 Also sacrifice peace offerings on it, and
celebrate by feasting there before the LORD your
God. 8 You must clearly write all these instructions on
the stones coated with plaster."
9 Then Moses and the Levitical priests addressed
all Israel as follows: "O Israel, be quiet and listen!

KING JAMES VERSION

this day thou art become the people of the LORD
thy God.
10 Thou shalt therefore obey the voice of the LORD
thy God, and do his commandments and his statutes,
which I command thee this day.
11 And Moses charged the people the same day,
saying,
12 These shall stand upon mount Gerizim to bless
the people, when ye are come over Jordan; Simeon,
and Levi, and Judah, and Issachar, and Joseph, and
Benjamin:
13 And these shall stand upon mount Ebal to curse;
Reuben, Gad, and Asher, and Zebulun, Dan, and
Naphtali.
14 And the Levites shall speak, and say unto all the
men of Israel with a loud voice,
15 Cursed *be* the man that maketh *any* graven or
molten image, an abomination unto the LORD, the
work of the hands of the craftsman, and putteth *it* in
a secret *place*. And all the people shall answer and
say, Amen.
16 Cursed *be* he that setteth light by his father or
his mother. And all the people shall say, Amen.
17 Cursed *be* he that removeth his neighbour's
landmark. And all the people shall say, Amen.
18 Cursed *be* he that maketh the blind to wander
out of the way. And all the people shall say, Amen.
19 Cursed *be* he that perverteth the judgment of the
stranger, fatherless, and widow. And all the people
shall say, Amen.
20 Cursed *be* he that lieth with his father's wife;
because he uncovereth his father's skirt. And all the
people shall say, Amen.
21 Cursed *be* he that lieth with any manner of
beast. And all the people shall say, Amen.
22 Cursed *be* he that lieth with his sister, the daughter of his father, or the daughter of his mother. And
all the people shall say, Amen.
23 Cursed *be* he that lieth with his mother in law.
And all the people shall say, Amen.
24 Cursed *be* he that smiteth his neighbour secretly. And all the people shall say, Amen.
25 Cursed *be* he that taketh reward to slay an innocent person. And all the people shall say, Amen.

NEW LIVING TRANSLATION

Today you have become the people of the LORD your
God. 10 So you must obey the LORD your God by keeping all these commands and decrees that I am giving
you today."

Curses from Mount Ebal

11 That same day Moses also gave this charge to the
people: 12 "When you cross the Jordan River, the
tribes of Simeon, Levi, Judah, Issachar, Joseph, and
Benjamin must stand on Mount Gerizim to proclaim
a blessing over the people. 13 And the tribes of Reuben, Gad, Asher, Zebulun, Dan, and Naphtali must
stand on Mount Ebal to proclaim a curse.
14 "Then the Levites will shout to all the people of
Israel:

15 'Cursed is anyone who carves or casts an idol
and secretly sets it up. These idols, the work
of craftsmen, are detestable to the LORD.'
And all the people will reply, 'Amen.'

16 'Cursed is anyone who dishonors father
or mother.'
And all the people will reply, 'Amen.'

17 'Cursed is anyone who steals property from
a neighbor by moving a boundary marker.'
And all the people will reply, 'Amen.'

18 'Cursed is anyone who leads a blind person
astray on the road.'
And all the people will reply, 'Amen.'

19 'Cursed is anyone who denies justice to foreigners,
orphans, or widows.'
And all the people will reply, 'Amen.'

20 'Cursed is anyone who has sexual intercourse
with one of his father's wives, for he has violated
his father.'
And all the people will reply, 'Amen.'

21 'Cursed is anyone who has sexual intercourse
with an animal.'
And all the people will reply, 'Amen.'

22 'Cursed is anyone who has sexual intercourse
with his sister, whether she is the daughter of
his father or his mother.'
And all the people will reply, 'Amen.'

23 'Cursed is anyone who has sexual intercourse
with his mother-in-law.'
And all the people will reply, 'Amen.'

24 'Cursed is anyone who attacks a neighbor
in secret.'
And all the people will reply, 'Amen.'

25 'Cursed is anyone who accepts payment to kill
an innocent person.'
And all the people will reply, 'Amen.'

KING JAMES VERSION

[26]Cursed *be* he that confirmeth not *all* the words
of this law to do them. And all the people shall say,
Amen.

28 [1]And it shall come to pass, if thou shalt
hearken diligently unto the voice of the
LORD thy God, to observe *and* to do all his commandments which I command thee this day, that the LORD
thy God will set thee on high above all nations of
the earth:
[2]And all these blessings shall come on thee, and
overtake thee, if thou shalt hearken unto the voice of
the LORD thy God.
[3]Blessed *shalt* thou *be* in the city, and blessed *shalt*
thou *be* in the field.
[4]Blessed *shall be* the fruit of thy body, and the fruit
of thy ground, and the fruit of thy cattle, the increase
of thy kine, and the flocks of thy sheep.
[5]Blessed *shall be* thy basket and thy store.
[6]Blessed *shalt* thou *be* when thou comest in, and
blessed *shalt* thou *be* when thou goest out.
[7]The LORD shall cause thine enemies that rise up
against thee to be smitten before thy face: they shall
come out against thee one way, and flee before thee
seven ways.
[8]The LORD shall command the blessing upon thee
in thy storehouses, and in all that thou settest thine
hand unto; and he shall bless thee in the land which
the LORD thy God giveth thee.
[9]The LORD shall establish thee an holy people
unto himself, as he hath sworn unto thee, if thou
shalt keep the commandments of the LORD thy God,
and walk in his ways.
[10]And all people of the earth shall see that thou art
called by the name of the LORD; and they shall be
afraid of thee.
[11]And the LORD shall make thee plenteous in
goods, in the fruit of thy body, and in the fruit of thy
cattle, and in the fruit of thy ground, in the land
which the LORD sware unto thy fathers to give thee.
[12]The LORD shall open unto thee his good treasure, the heaven to give the rain unto thy land in his
season, and to bless all the work of thine hand: and
thou shalt lend unto many nations, and thou shalt
not borrow.
[13]And the LORD shall make thee the head, and not
the tail; and thou shalt be above only, and thou shalt
not be beneath; if that thou hearken unto the commandments of the LORD thy God, which I command
thee this day, to observe and to do *them:*
[14]And thou shalt not go aside from any of the
words which I command thee this day, *to* the right
hand, or *to* the left, to go after other gods to serve
them.
[15]But it shall come to pass, if thou wilt not hearken unto the voice of the LORD thy God, to observe to
do all his commandments and his statutes which I

NEW LIVING TRANSLATION

[26]'Cursed is anyone who does not affirm and obey
the terms of these instructions.'
And all the people will reply, 'Amen.'

Blessings for Obedience

28 "If you fully obey the LORD your God and
carefully keep all his commands that I am
giving you today, the LORD your God will set you
high above all the nations of the world. [2]You will experience all these blessings if you obey the LORD
your God:

[3] Your towns and your fields
will be blessed.
[4] Your children and your crops
will be blessed.
The offspring of your herds and flocks
will be blessed.
[5] Your fruit baskets and breadboards
will be blessed.
[6] Wherever you go and whatever you do,
you will be blessed.

[7]"The LORD will conquer your enemies when they
attack you. They will attack you from one direction,
but they will scatter from you in seven!
[8]"The LORD will guarantee a blessing on everything you do and will fill your storehouses with
grain. The LORD your God will bless you in the land
he is giving you.
[9]"If you obey the commands of the LORD your
God and walk in his ways, the LORD will establish you
as his holy people as he swore he would do. [10]Then
all the nations of the world will see that you are a
people claimed by the LORD, and they will stand in
awe of you.
[11]"The LORD will give you prosperity in the land he
swore to your ancestors to give you, blessing you
with many children, numerous livestock, and abundant crops. [12]The LORD will send rain at the proper
time from his rich treasury in the heavens and will
bless all the work you do. You will lend to many nations, but you will never need to borrow from them.
[13]If you listen to these commands of the LORD your
God that I am giving you today, and if you carefully
obey them, the LORD will make you the head and
not the tail, and you will always be on top and never
at the bottom. [14]You must not turn away from any of
the commands I am giving you today, nor follow after
other gods and worship them.

Curses for Disobedience

[15]"But if you refuse to listen to the LORD your God
and do not obey all the commands and decrees I am

command thee this day; that all these curses shall
come upon thee, and overtake thee:
16 Cursed *shalt* thou *be* in the city, and cursed *shalt*
thou *be* in the field.
17 Cursed *shall be* thy basket and thy store.
18 Cursed *shall be* the fruit of thy body, and the
fruit of thy land, the increase of thy kine, and the
flocks of thy sheep.
19 Cursed *shalt* thou *be* when thou comest in, and
cursed *shalt* thou *be* when thou goest out.
20 The LORD shall send upon thee cursing, vexation, and rebuke, in all that thou settest thine hand
unto for to do, until thou be destroyed, and until thou
perish quickly; because of the wickedness of thy doings, whereby thou hast forsaken me.
21 The LORD shall make the pestilence cleave unto
thee, until he have consumed thee from off the land,
whither thou goest to possess it.
22 The LORD shall smite thee with a consumption,
and with a fever, and with an inflammation, and with
an extreme burning, and with the sword, and with
blasting, and with mildew; and they shall pursue
thee until thou perish.
23 And thy heaven that *is* over thy head shall be
brass, and the earth that is under thee *shall be* iron.
24 The LORD shall make the rain of thy land powder
and dust: from heaven shall it come down upon thee,
until thou be destroyed.
25 The LORD shall cause thee to be smitten before
thine enemies: thou shalt go out one way against
them, and flee seven ways before them: and shalt be
removed into all the kingdoms of the earth.
26 And thy carcase shall be meat unto all fowls of
the air, and unto the beasts of the earth, and no man
shall fray *them* away.
27 The LORD will smite thee with the botch of
Egypt, and with the emerods, and with the scab, and
with the itch, whereof thou canst not be healed.
28 The LORD shall smite thee with madness, and
blindness, and astonishment of heart:
29 And thou shalt grope at noonday, as the blind
gropeth in darkness, and thou shalt not prosper in
thy ways: and thou shalt be only oppressed and
spoiled evermore, and no man shall save *thee*.
30 Thou shalt betroth a wife, and another man shall
lie with her: thou shalt build an house, and thou shalt
not dwell therein: thou shalt plant a vineyard, and
shalt not gather the grapes thereof.
31 Thine ox *shall be* slain before thine eyes, and
thou shalt not eat thereof: thine ass *shall be* violently
taken away from before thy face, and shall not be restored to thee: thy sheep *shall be* given unto thine
enemies, and thou shalt have none to rescue *them*.
32 Thy sons and thy daughters *shall be* given unto
another people, and thine eyes shall look, and fail
with longing for them all the day long: and *there*
shall be no might in thine hand.
33 The fruit of thy land, and all thy labours, shall a

giving you today, all these curses will come and
overwhelm you:

16 Your towns and your fields
will be cursed.
17 Your fruit baskets and breadboards
will be cursed.
18 Your children and your crops
will be cursed.
The offspring of your herds and flocks
will be cursed.
19 Wherever you go and whatever you do,
you will be cursed.

20 "The LORD himself will send on you curses, confusion, and frustration in everything you do, until at
last you are completely destroyed for doing evil and
abandoning me. 21 The LORD will afflict you with diseases until none of you are left in the land you are
about to enter and occupy. 22 The LORD will strike you
with wasting diseases, fever, and inflammation, with
scorching heat and drought, and with blight and mildew. These disasters will pursue you until you die.
23 The skies above will be as unyielding as bronze,
and the earth beneath will be as hard as iron. 24 The
LORD will change the rain that falls on your land into
powder, and dust will pour down from the sky until
you are destroyed.
25 "The LORD will cause you to be defeated by your
enemies. You will attack your enemies from one direction, but you will scatter from them in seven! You
will be an object of horror to all the kingdoms of the
earth. 26 Your corpses will be food for all the scaveng-
ing birds and wild animals, and no one will be there
to chase them away.
27 "The LORD will afflict you with the boils of Egypt
and with tumors, scurvy, and the itch, from which
you cannot be cured. 28 The LORD will strike you with
madness, blindness, and panic. 29 You will grope
around in broad daylight like a blind person groping
in the darkness, but you will not find your way. You
will be oppressed and robbed continually, and no
one will come to save you.
30 "You will be engaged to a woman, but another
man will sleep with her. You will build a house, but
someone else will live in it. You will plant a vineyard,
but you will never enjoy its fruit. 31 Your ox will be
butchered before your eyes, but you will not eat a
single bite of the meat. Your donkey will be taken
from you, never to be returned. Your sheep and goats
will be given to your enemies, and no one will be
there to help you. 32 You will watch as your sons and
daughters are taken away as slaves. Your heart will
break for them, but you won't be able to help them.
33 A foreign nation you have never heard about will

KING JAMES VERSION

nation which thou knowest not eat up; and thou
shalt be only oppressed and crushed alway:
34So that thou shalt be mad for the sight of thine
eyes which thou shalt see.
35The Lord shall smite thee in the knees, and in
the legs, with a sore botch that cannot be healed,
from the sole of thy foot unto the top of thy head.
36The Lord shall bring thee, and thy king which
thou shalt set over thee, unto a nation which neither
thou nor thy fathers have known; and there shalt thou
serve other gods, wood and stone.
37And thou shalt become an astonishment, a proverb, and a byword, among all nations whither the
Lord shall lead thee.
38Thou shalt carry much seed out into the field,
and shalt gather *but* little in; for the locust shall
consume it.
39Thou shalt plant vineyards, and dress *them,* but
shalt neither drink *of* the wine, nor gather *the
grapes;* for the worms shall eat them.
40Thou shalt have olive trees throughout all thy
coasts, but thou shalt not anoint *thyself* with the oil;
for thine olive shall cast *his fruit.*
41Thou shalt beget sons and daughters, but thou
shalt not enjoy them; for they shall go into captivity.
42All thy trees and fruit of thy land shall the locust
consume.
43The stranger that *is* within thee shall get up above
thee very high; and thou shalt come down very low.
44He shall lend to thee, and thou shalt not lend to
him: he shall be the head, and thou shalt be the tail.
45Moreover all these curses shall come upon thee,
and shall pursue thee, and overtake thee, till thou be
destroyed; because thou hearkenedst not unto the
voice of the Lord thy God, to keep his commandments and his statutes which he commanded thee:
46And they shall be upon thee for a sign and for a
wonder, and upon thy seed for ever.
47Because thou servedst not the Lord thy God
with joyfulness, and with gladness of heart, for the
abundance of all *things;*
48Therefore shalt thou serve thine enemies which
the Lord shall send against thee, in hunger, and in
thirst, and in nakedness, and in want of all *things:*
and he shall put a yoke of iron upon thy neck, until he
have destroyed thee.
49The Lord shall bring a nation against thee from
far, from the end of the earth, *as swift* as the eagle
flieth; a nation whose tongue thou shalt not understand;
50A nation of fierce countenance, which shall not
regard the person of the old, nor shew favour to the
young:
51And he shall eat the fruit of thy cattle, and the
fruit of thy land, until thou be destroyed: which *also*
shall not leave thee *either* corn, wine, or oil, *or* the
increase of thy kine, or flocks of thy sheep, until he
have destroyed thee.

NEW LIVING TRANSLATION

eat the crops you worked so hard to grow. You will
suffer under constant oppression and harsh treatment. 34You will go mad because of all the tragedy
you see around you. 35The Lord will cover your
knees and legs with incurable boils. In fact, you will
be covered from head to foot.
36"The Lord will exile you and your king to a nation unknown to you and your ancestors. There in
exile you will worship gods of wood and stone!
37You will become an object of horror, ridicule, and
mockery among all the nations to which the Lord
sends you.
38"You will plant much but harvest little, for locusts will eat your crops. 39You will plant vineyards
and care for them, but you will not drink the wine or
eat the grapes, for worms will destroy the vines.
40You will grow olive trees throughout your land, but
you will never use the olive oil, for the fruit will drop
before it ripens. 41You will have sons and daughters,
but you will lose them, for they will be led away into
captivity. 42Swarms of insects will destroy your trees
and crops.
43"The foreigners living among you will become
stronger and stronger, while you become weaker and
weaker. 44They will lend money to you, but you will
not lend to them. They will be the head, and you will
be the tail!
45"If you refuse to listen to the Lord your God and
to obey the commands and decrees he has given you,
all these curses will pursue and overtake you until
you are destroyed. 46These horrors will serve as a
sign and warning among you and your descendants
forever. 47If you do not serve the Lord your God with
joy and enthusiasm for the abundant benefits you
have received, 48you will serve your enemies whom
the Lord will send against you. You will be left hungry, thirsty, naked, and lacking in everything. The
Lord will put an iron yoke on your neck, oppressing
you harshly until he has destroyed you.
49"The Lord will bring a distant nation against
you from the end of the earth, and it will swoop down
on you like a vulture. It is a nation whose language
you do not understand, 50a fierce and heartless nation that shows no respect for the old and no pity for
the young. 51Its armies will devour your livestock and
crops, and you will be destroyed. They will leave you
no grain, new wine, olive oil, calves, or lambs, and you

KING JAMES VERSION

[52]And he shall besiege thee in all thy gates, until thy high and fenced walls come down, wherein thou trustedst, throughout all thy land: and he shall besiege thee in all thy gates throughout all thy land, which the LORD thy God hath given thee.

[53]And thou shalt eat the fruit of thine own body, the flesh of thy sons and of thy daughters, which the LORD thy God hath given thee, in the siege, and in the straitness, wherewith thine enemies shall distress thee:

[54]*So that* the man *that is* tender among you, and very delicate, his eye shall be evil toward his brother, and toward the wife of his bosom, and toward the remnant of his children which he shall leave:

[55]So that he will not give to any of them of the flesh of his children whom he shall eat: because he hath nothing left him in the siege, and in the straitness, wherewith thine enemies shall distress thee in all thy gates.

[56]The tender and delicate woman among you, which would not adventure to set the sole of her foot upon the ground for delicateness and tenderness, her eye shall be evil toward the husband of her bosom, and toward her son, and toward her daughter,

[57]And toward her young one that cometh out from between her feet, and toward her children which she shall bear: for she shall eat them for want of all *things* secretly in the siege and straitness, wherewith thine enemy shall distress thee in thy gates.

[58]If thou wilt not observe to do all the words of this law that are written in this book, that thou mayest fear this glorious and fearful name, THE LORD THY GOD;

[59]Then the LORD will make thy plagues wonderful, and the plagues of thy seed, *even* great plagues, and of long continuance, and sore sicknesses, and of long continuance.

[60]Moreover he will bring upon thee all the diseases of Egypt, which thou wast afraid of; and they shall cleave unto thee.

[61]Also every sickness, and every plague, which *is* not written in the book of this law, them will the LORD bring upon thee, until thou be destroyed.

[62]And ye shall be left few in number, whereas ye were as the stars of heaven for multitude; because thou wouldest not obey the voice of the LORD thy God.

[63]And it shall come to pass, *that* as the LORD rejoiced over you to do you good, and to multiply you; so the LORD will rejoice over you to destroy you, and to bring you to nought; and ye shall be plucked from off the land whither thou goest to possess it.

[64]And the LORD shall scatter thee among all people, from the one end of the earth even unto the other; and there thou shalt serve other gods, which neither thou nor thy fathers have known, *even* wood and stone.

[65]And among these nations shalt thou find no

NEW LIVING TRANSLATION

will starve to death. [52]They will attack your cities until all the fortified walls in your land—the walls you
trusted to protect you—are knocked down. They will
attack all the towns in the land the LORD your God
has given you.

[53]"The siege and terrible distress of the enemy's
attack will be so severe that you will eat the flesh of
your own sons and daughters, whom the LORD your
God has given you. [54]The most tenderhearted man
among you will have no compassion for his own
brother, his beloved wife, and his surviving children.
[55]He will refuse to share with them the flesh he is
devouring—the flesh of one of his own children—because he has nothing else to eat during the siege and
terrible distress that your enemy will inflict on all
your towns. [56]The most tender and delicate woman
among you—so delicate she would not so much as
touch the ground with her foot—will be selfish toward the husband she loves and toward her own son
or daughter. [57]She will hide from them the afterbirth
and the new baby she has borne, so that she herself
can secretly eat them. She will have nothing else to
eat during the siege and terrible distress that your
enemy will inflict on all your towns.

[58]"If you refuse to obey all the words of instruction that are written in this book, and if you do not
fear the glorious and awesome name of the LORD
your God, [59]then the LORD will overwhelm you and
your children with indescribable plagues. These
plagues will be intense and without relief, making
you miserable and unbearably sick. [60]He will afflict
you with all the diseases of Egypt that you feared so
much, and you will have no relief. [61]The LORD will
afflict you with every sickness and plague there is,
even those not mentioned in this Book of Instruction, until you are destroyed. [62]Though you become
as numerous as the stars in the sky, few of you will
be left because you would not listen to the LORD
your God.

[63]"Just as the LORD has found great pleasure in
causing you to prosper and multiply, the LORD will
find pleasure in destroying you. You will be torn
from the land you are about to enter and occupy.
[64]For the LORD will scatter you among all the nations
from one end of the earth to the other. There you will
worship foreign gods that neither you nor your ancestors have known, gods made of wood and stone!
[65]There among those nations you will find no peace

KING JAMES VERSION

ease, neither shall the sole of thy foot have rest: but the LORD shall give thee there a trembling heart, and failing of eyes, and sorrow of mind:

66 And thy life shall hang in doubt before thee; and thou shalt fear day and night, and shalt have none assurance of thy life:

67 In the morning thou shalt say, Would God it were even! and at even thou shalt say, Would God it were morning! for the fear of thine heart wherewith thou shalt fear, and for the sight of thine eyes which thou shalt see.

68 And the LORD shall bring thee into Egypt again with ships, by the way whereof I spake unto thee, Thou shalt see it no more again: and there ye shall be sold unto your enemies for bondmen and bondwomen, and no man shall buy *you*.

29 1 These *are* the words of the covenant, which the LORD commanded Moses to make with the children of Israel in the land of Moab, beside the covenant which he made with them in Horeb.

2 And Moses called unto all Israel, and said unto them, Ye have seen all that the LORD did before your eyes in the land of Egypt unto Pharaoh, and unto all his servants, and unto all his land;

3 The great temptations which thine eyes have seen, the signs, and those great miracles:

4 Yet the LORD hath not given you an heart to perceive, and eyes to see, and ears to hear, unto this day.

5 And I have led you forty years in the wilderness: your clothes are not waxen old upon you, and thy shoe is not waxen old upon thy foot.

6 Ye have not eaten bread, neither have ye drunk wine or strong drink: that ye might know that I *am* the LORD your God.

7 And when ye came unto this place, Sihon the king of Heshbon, and Og the king of Bashan, came out against us unto battle, and we smote them:

8 And we took their land, and gave it for an inheritance unto the Reubenites, and to the Gadites, and to the half tribe of Manasseh.

9 Keep therefore the words of this covenant, and do them, that ye may prosper in all that ye do.

10 Ye stand this day all of you before the LORD your God; your captains of your tribes, your elders, and your officers, *with* all the men of Israel,

11 Your little ones, your wives, and thy stranger that *is* in thy camp, from the hewer of thy wood unto the drawer of thy water:

12 That thou shouldest enter into covenant with the LORD thy God, and into his oath, which the LORD thy God maketh with thee this day:

13 That he may establish thee today for a people unto himself, and *that* he may be unto thee a God, as

NEW LIVING TRANSLATION

or place to rest. And the LORD will cause your heart
to tremble, your eyesight to fail, and your soul to despair. 66 Your life will constantly hang in the balance.
You will live night and day in fear, unsure if you will
survive. 67 In the morning you will say, 'If only it were
night!' And in the evening you will say, 'If only it were
morning!' For you will be terrified by the awful horrors you see around you. 68 Then the LORD will send
you back to Egypt in ships, to a destination I promised you would never see again. There you will offer
to sell yourselves to your enemies as slaves, but no
one will buy you."

29 1* These are the terms of the covenant the
LORD commanded Moses to make with the
Israelites while they were in the land of Moab, in ad-
dition to the covenant he had made with them at
Mount Sinai.*

Moses Reviews the Covenant

2* Moses summoned all the Israelites and said to
them, "You have seen with your own eyes everything
the LORD did in the land of Egypt to Pharaoh and to
all his servants and to his whole country—3 all the
great tests of strength, the miraculous signs, and the
amazing wonders. 4 But to this day the LORD has not
given you minds that understand, nor eyes that see,
nor ears that hear! 5 For forty years I led you through
the wilderness, yet your clothes and sandals did not
wear out. 6 You ate no bread and drank no wine or
other alcoholic drink, but he gave you food so you
would know that he is the LORD your God.

7 "When we came here, King Sihon of Heshbon
and King Og of Bashan came out to fight against us,
but we defeated them. 8 We took their land and gave
it to the tribes of Reuben and Gad and to the half-
tribe of Manasseh as their grant of land.

9 "Therefore, obey the terms of this covenant so
that you will prosper in everything you do. 10 All of
you—tribal leaders, elders, officers, all the men of Israel—are standing today in the presence of the LORD
your God. 11 Your little ones and your wives are with
you, as well as the foreigners living among you who
chop your wood and carry your water. 12 You are
standing here today to enter into the covenant of the
LORD your God. The LORD is making this covenant,
including the curses. 13 By entering into the covenant
today, he will establish you as his people and confirm

29:1a Verse 29:1 is numbered 28:69 in Hebrew text. **29:1b** Hebrew *Horeb,* another name for Sinai. **29:2** Verses 29:2-29 are numbered 29:1-28 in Hebrew text.

KING JAMES VERSION

he hath said unto thee, and as he hath sworn unto thy fathers, to Abraham, to Isaac, and to Jacob.

14 Neither with you only do I make this covenant and this oath;

15 But with *him* that standeth here with us this day before the LORD our God, and also with *him* that *is* not here with us this day:

16 (For ye know how we have dwelt in the land of Egypt; and how we came through the nations which ye passed by;

17 And ye have seen their abominations, and their idols, wood and stone, silver and gold, which *were* among them:)

18 Lest there should be among you man, or woman, or family, or tribe, whose heart turneth away this day from the LORD our God, to go *and* serve the gods of these nations; lest there should be among you a root that beareth gall and wormwood;

19 And it come to pass, when he heareth the words of this curse, that he bless himself in his heart, saying, I shall have peace, though I walk in the imagination of mine heart, to add drunkenness to thirst:

20 The LORD will not spare him, but then the anger of the LORD and his jealousy shall smoke against that man, and all the curses that are written in this book shall lie upon him, and the LORD shall blot out his name from under heaven.

21 And the LORD shall separate him unto evil out of all the tribes of Israel, according to all the curses of the covenant that are written in this book of the law:

22 So that the generation to come of your children that shall rise up after you, and the stranger that shall come from a far land, shall say, when they see the plagues of that land, and the sicknesses which the LORD hath laid upon it;

23 *And that* the whole land thereof *is* brimstone, and salt, *and* burning, *that* it is not sown, nor beareth, nor any grass groweth therein, like the overthrow of Sodom, and Gomorrah, Admah, and Zeboim, which the LORD overthrew in his anger, and in his wrath:

24 Even all nations shall say, Wherefore hath the LORD done thus unto this land? what *meaneth* the heat of this great anger?

25 Then men shall say, Because they have forsaken the covenant of the LORD God of their fathers, which he made with them when he brought them forth out of the land of Egypt:

26 For they went and served other gods, and worshipped them, gods whom they knew not, and *whom* he had not given unto them:

27 And the anger of the LORD was kindled against this land, to bring upon it all the curses that are written in this book:

28 And the LORD rooted them out of their land in anger, and in wrath, and in great indignation, and cast them into another land, as *it is* this day.

29 The secret *things belong* unto the LORD our God:

NEW LIVING TRANSLATION

that he is your God, just as he promised you and as he swore to your ancestors Abraham, Isaac, and Jacob.

14 "But you are not the only ones with whom I am making this covenant with its curses. 15 I am making this covenant both with you who stand here today in the presence of the LORD our God, and also with the future generations who are not standing here today.

16 "You remember how we lived in the land of Egypt and how we traveled through the lands of enemy nations as we left. 17 You have seen their detestable practices and their idols* made of wood, stone, silver, and gold. 18 I am making this covenant with you so that no one among you—no man, woman, clan, or tribe—will turn away from the LORD our God to worship these gods of other nations, and so that no root among you bears bitter and poisonous fruit.

19 "Those who hear the warnings of this curse should not congratulate themselves, thinking, 'I am safe, even though I am following the desires of my own stubborn heart.' This would lead to utter ruin! 20 The LORD will never pardon such people. Instead his anger and jealousy will burn against them. All the curses written in this book will come down on them, and the LORD will erase their names from under heaven. 21 The LORD will separate them from all the tribes of Israel, to pour out on them all the curses of the covenant recorded in this Book of Instruction.

22 "Then the generations to come, both your own descendants and the foreigners who come from distant lands, will see the devastation of the land and the diseases the LORD inflicts on it. 23 They will exclaim, 'The whole land is devastated by sulfur and salt. It is a wasteland with nothing planted and nothing growing, not even a blade of grass. It is like the cities of Sodom and Gomorrah, Admah and Zeboiim, which the LORD destroyed in his intense anger.'

24 "And all the surrounding nations will ask, 'Why has the LORD done this to this land? Why was he so angry?'

25 "And the answer will be, 'This happened because the people of the land abandoned the covenant that the LORD, the God of their ancestors, made with them when he brought them out of the land of Egypt. 26 Instead, they turned away to serve and worship gods they had not known before, gods that were not from the LORD. 27 That is why the LORD's anger has burned against this land, bringing down on it every curse recorded in this book. 28 In great anger and fury the LORD uprooted his people from their land and banished them to another land, where they still live today!'

29 "The LORD our God has secrets known to no one.

29:17 The Hebrew term (literally *round things*) probably alludes to dung.

KING JAMES VERSION

but those *things which are* revealed *belong* unto us and to our children for ever, that *we* may do all the words of this law.

30

1And it shall come to pass, when all these things are come upon thee, the blessing and the curse, which I have set before thee, and thou shalt call *them* to mind among all the nations, whither the LORD thy God hath driven thee,

2And shalt return unto the LORD thy God, and shalt obey his voice according to all that I command thee this day, thou and thy children, with all thine heart, and with all thy soul;

3That then the LORD thy God will turn thy captivity, and have compassion upon thee, and will return and gather thee from all the nations, whither the LORD thy God hath scattered thee.

4If *any* of thine be driven out unto the outmost *parts* of heaven, from thence will the LORD thy God gather thee, and from thence will he fetch thee:

5And the LORD thy God will bring thee into the land which thy fathers possessed, and thou shalt possess it; and he will do thee good, and multiply thee above thy fathers.

6And the LORD thy God will circumcise thine heart, and the heart of thy seed, to love the LORD thy God with all thine heart, and with all thy soul, that thou mayest live.

7And the LORD thy God will put all these curses upon thine enemies, and on them that hate thee, which persecuted thee.

8And thou shalt return and obey the voice of the LORD, and do all his commandments which I command thee this day.

9And the LORD thy God will make thee plenteous in every work of thine hand, in the fruit of thy body, and in the fruit of thy cattle, and in the fruit of thy land, for good: for the LORD will again rejoice over thee for good, as he rejoiced over thy fathers:

10If thou shalt hearken unto the voice of the LORD thy God, to keep his commandments and his statutes which are written in this book of the law, *and* if thou turn unto the LORD thy God with all thine heart, and with all thy soul.

11For this commandment which I command thee this day, it *is* not hidden from thee, neither *is* it far off.

12It *is* not in heaven, that thou shouldest say, Who shall go up for us to heaven, and bring it unto us, that we may hear it, and do it?

13Neither *is* it beyond the sea, that thou shouldest say, Who shall go over the sea for us, and bring it unto us, that we may hear it, and do it?

14But the word *is* very nigh unto thee, in thy mouth, and in thy heart, that thou mayest do it.

NEW LIVING TRANSLATION

We are not accountable for them, but we and our children are accountable forever for all that he has revealed to us, so that we may obey all the terms of these instructions.

A Call to Return to the LORD

30

"In the future, when you experience all these blessings and curses I have listed for you, and when you are living among the nations to which the LORD your God has exiled you, take to heart all these instructions. 2If at that time you and your children return to the LORD your God, and if you obey with all your heart and all your soul all the commands I have given you today, 3then the LORD your God will restore your fortunes. He will have mercy on you and gather you back from all the nations where he has scattered you. 4Even though you are banished to the ends of the earth, the LORD your God will gather you from there and bring you back again. 5The LORD your God will return you to the land that belonged to your ancestors, and you will possess that land again. Then he will make you even more prosperous and numerous than your ancestors!

6"The LORD your God will change your heart* and the hearts of all your descendants, so that you will love him with all your heart and soul and so you may live! 7The LORD your God will inflict all these curses on your enemies and on those who hate and persecute you. 8Then you will again obey the LORD and keep all his commands that I am giving you today.

9"The LORD your God will then make you successful in everything you do. He will give you many children and numerous livestock, and he will cause your fields to produce abundant harvests, for the LORD will again delight in being good to you as he was to your ancestors. 10The LORD your God will delight in you if you obey his voice and keep the commands and decrees written in this Book of Instruction, and if you turn to the LORD your God with all your heart and soul.

The Choice of Life or Death

11"This command I am giving you today is not too difficult for you to understand, and it is not beyond your reach. 12It is not kept in heaven, so distant that you must ask, 'Who will go up to heaven and bring it down so we can hear it and obey?' 13It is not kept beyond the sea, so far away that you must ask, 'Who will cross the sea to bring it to us so we can hear it and obey?' 14No, the message is very close at hand; it is on your lips and in your heart so that you can obey it.

30:6 Hebrew *circumcise your heart.*

KING JAMES VERSION

15 See, I have set before thee this day life and good, and death and evil;

16 In that I command thee this day to love the LORD thy God, to walk in his ways, and to keep his commandments and his statutes and his judgments, that thou mayest live and multiply: and the LORD thy God shall bless thee in the land whither thou goest to possess it.

17 But if thine heart turn away, so that thou wilt not hear, but shalt be drawn away, and worship other gods, and serve them;

18 I denounce unto you this day, that ye shall surely perish, *and that* ye shall not prolong *your* days upon the land, whither thou passest over Jordan to go to possess it.

19 I call heaven and earth to record this day against you, *that* I have set before you life and death, blessing and cursing: therefore choose life, that both thou and thy seed may live:

20 That thou mayest love the LORD thy God, *and* that thou mayest obey his voice, and that thou mayest cleave unto him: for he *is* thy life, and the length of thy days: that thou mayest dwell in the land which the LORD sware unto thy fathers, to Abraham, to Isaac, and to Jacob, to give them.

31 1 And Moses went and spake these words unto all Israel.

2 And he said unto them, I *am* an hundred and twenty years old this day; I can no more go out and come in: also the LORD hath said unto me, Thou shalt not go over this Jordan.

3 The LORD thy God, he will go over before thee, *and* he will destroy these nations from before thee, and thou shalt possess them: *and* Joshua, he shall go over before thee, as the LORD hath said.

4 And the LORD shall do unto them as he did to Sihon and to Og, kings of the Amorites, and unto the land of them, whom he destroyed.

5 And the LORD shall give them up before your face, that ye may do unto them according unto all the commandments which I have commanded you.

6 Be strong and of a good courage, fear not, nor be afraid of them: for the LORD thy God, he *it is* that doth go with thee; he will not fail thee, nor forsake thee.

7 And Moses called unto Joshua, and said unto him in the sight of all Israel, Be strong and of a good courage: for thou must go with this people unto the land which the LORD hath sworn unto their fathers to give them; and thou shalt cause them to inherit it.

8 And the LORD, he *it is* that doth go before thee; he will be with thee, he will not fail thee, neither forsake thee: fear not, neither be dismayed.

NEW LIVING TRANSLATION

15 "Now listen! Today I am giving you a choice between life and death, between prosperity and disaster. 16 For I command you this day to love the LORD
your God and to keep his commands, decrees, and
regulations by walking in his ways. If you do this, you
will live and multiply, and the LORD your God will
bless you and the land you are about to enter and
occupy.

17 "But if your heart turns away and you refuse to
listen, and if you are drawn away to serve and worship other gods, 18 then I warn you now that you will
certainly be destroyed. You will not live a long, good
life in the land you are crossing the Jordan to occupy.

19 "Today I have given you the choice between life
and death, between blessings and curses. Now I call
on heaven and earth to witness the choice you make.
Oh, that you would choose life, so that you and your
descendants might live! 20 You can make this choice
by loving the LORD your God, obeying him, and committing yourself firmly to him. This* is the key to
your life. And if you love and obey the LORD, you will
live long in the land the LORD swore to give your ancestors Abraham, Isaac, and Jacob."

Joshua Becomes Israel's Leader

31 When Moses had finished giving these instructions* to all the people of Israel, 2 he
said, "I am now 120 years old, and I am no longer
able to lead you. The LORD has told me, 'You will not
cross the Jordan River.' 3 But the LORD your God himself will cross over ahead of you. He will destroy the
nations living there, and you will take possession of
their land. Joshua will lead you across the river, just as
the LORD promised.

4 "The LORD will destroy the nations living in the
land, just as he destroyed Sihon and Og, the kings
of the Amorites. 5 The LORD will hand over to you
the people who live there, and you must deal with
them as I have commanded you. 6 So be strong
and courageous! Do not be afraid and do not panic
before them. For the LORD your God will personally
go ahead of you. He will neither fail you nor abandon you."

7 Then Moses called for Joshua, and as all Israel
watched, he said to him, "Be strong and courageous!
For you will lead these people into the land that the
LORD swore to their ancestors he would give them.
You are the one who will divide it among them as
their grants of land. 8 Do not be afraid or discouraged, for the LORD will personally go ahead of you.
He will be with you; he will neither fail you nor abandon you."

30:20 Or *He.* **31:1** As in Dead Sea Scrolls and Greek version; Masoretic Text reads *Moses went and spoke.*

KING JAMES VERSION

9And Moses wrote this law, and delivered it unto the priests the sons of Levi, which bare the ark of the covenant of the LORD, and unto all the elders of Israel.

10And Moses commanded them, saying, At the end of *every* seven years, in the solemnity of the year of release, in the feast of tabernacles,

11When all Israel is come to appear before the LORD thy God in the place which he shall choose, thou shalt read this law before all Israel in their hearing.

12Gather the people together, men, and women, and children, and thy stranger that *is* within thy gates, that they may hear, and that they may learn, and fear the LORD your God, and observe to do all the words of this law:

13And *that* their children, which have not known *any thing*, may hear, and learn to fear the LORD your God, as long as ye live in the land whither ye go over Jordan to possess it.

14And the LORD said unto Moses, Behold, thy days approach that thou must die: call Joshua, and present yourselves in the tabernacle of the congregation, that I may give him a charge. And Moses and Joshua went, and presented themselves in the tabernacle of the congregation.

15And the LORD appeared in the tabernacle in a pillar of a cloud: and the pillar of the cloud stood over the door of the tabernacle.

16And the LORD said unto Moses, Behold, thou shalt sleep with thy fathers; and this people will rise up, and go a whoring after the gods of the strangers of the land, whither they go *to be* among them, and will forsake me, and break my covenant which I have made with them.

17Then my anger shall be kindled against them in that day, and I will forsake them, and I will hide my face from them, and they shall be devoured, and many evils and troubles shall befall them; so that they will say in that day, Are not these evils come upon us, because our God *is* not among us?

18And I will surely hide my face in that day for all the evils which they shall have wrought, in that they are turned unto other gods.

19Now therefore write ye this song for you, and teach it the children of Israel: put it in their mouths, that this song may be a witness for me against the children of Israel.

20For when I shall have brought them into the land which I sware unto their fathers, that floweth with milk and honey; and they shall have eaten and filled themselves, and waxen fat; then will they turn unto other gods, and serve them, and provoke me, and break my covenant.

21And it shall come to pass, when many evils and troubles are befallen them, that this song shall testify against them as a witness; for it shall not be forgotten

NEW LIVING TRANSLATION

Public Reading of the Book of Instruction

9So Moses wrote this entire body of instruction in a book and gave it to the priests, who carried the Ark of the LORD's Covenant, and to the elders of Israel. 10Then Moses gave them this command: "At the end of every seventh year, the Year of Release, during the Festival of Shelters, 11you must read this Book of Instruction to all the people of Israel when they assemble before the LORD your God at the place he chooses. 12Call them all together—men, women, children, and the foreigners living in your towns—so they may hear this Book of Instruction and learn to fear the LORD your God and carefully obey all the terms of these instructions. 13Do this so that your children who have not known these instructions will hear them and will learn to fear the LORD your God. Do this as long as you live in the land you are crossing the Jordan to occupy."

Israel's Disobedience Predicted

14Then the LORD said to Moses, "The time has come for you to die. Call Joshua and present yourselves at the Tabernacle,* so that I may commission him there." So Moses and Joshua went and presented themselves at the Tabernacle. 15And the LORD appeared to them in a pillar of cloud that stood at the entrance to the sacred tent.

16The LORD said to Moses, "You are about to die and join your ancestors. After you are gone, these people will begin to worship foreign gods, the gods of the land where they are going. They will abandon me and break my covenant that I have made with them. 17Then my anger will blaze forth against them. I will abandon them, hiding my face from them, and they will be devoured. Terrible trouble will come down on them, and on that day they will say, 'These disasters have come down on us because God is no longer among us!' 18At that time I will hide my face from them on account of all the evil they commit by worshiping other gods.

19"So write down the words of this song, and teach it to the people of Israel. Help them learn it, so it may serve as a witness for me against them. 20For I will bring them into the land I swore to give their ancestors—a land flowing with milk and honey. There they will become prosperous, eat all the food they want, and become fat. But they will begin to worship other gods; they will despise me and break my covenant. 21And when great disasters come down on them, this song will stand as evidence against them, for it will never be forgotten by their descendants. I know the

31:14 Hebrew *Tent of Meeting;* also in 31:14b.

KING JAMES VERSION

out of the mouths of their seed: for I know their
imagination which they go about, even now, before
I have brought them into the land which I sware.
22 Moses therefore wrote this song the same day,
and taught it the children of Israel.
23 And he gave Joshua the son of Nun a charge, and
said, Be strong and of a good courage: for thou shalt
bring the children of Israel into the land which I
sware unto them: and I will be with thee.
24 And it came to pass, when Moses had made an
end of writing the words of this law in a book, until
they were finished,
25 That Moses commanded the Levites, which bare
the ark of the covenant of the LORD, saying,
26 Take this book of the law, and put it in the side of
the ark of the covenant of the LORD your God, that it
may be there for a witness against thee.
27 For I know thy rebellion, and thy stiff neck: behold, while I am yet alive with you this day, ye have
been rebellious against the LORD; and how much
more after my death?
28 Gather unto me all the elders of your tribes, and
your officers, that I may speak these words in their
ears, and call heaven and earth to record against
them.
29 For I know that after my death ye will utterly corrupt *yourselves*, and turn aside from the way which I
have commanded you; and evil will befall you in the
latter days; because ye will do evil in the sight of the
LORD, to provoke him to anger through the work of
your hands.
30 And Moses spake in the ears of all the congregation of Israel the words of this song, until they were
ended.

32 1 Give ear, O ye heavens, and I will speak; and
hear, O earth, the words of my mouth.
2 My doctrine shall drop as the rain, my speech
shall distil as the dew, as the small rain upon the tender herb, and as the showers upon the grass:
3 Because I will publish the name of the LORD: ascribe ye greatness unto our God.
4 *He is* the Rock, his work *is* perfect: for all his ways
are judgment: a God of truth and without iniquity,
just and right *is* he.
5 They have corrupted themselves, their spot *is* not
the spot of his children: *they are* a perverse and
crooked generation.
6 Do ye thus requite the LORD, O foolish people and
unwise? *is* not he thy father *that* hath bought thee?
hath he not made thee, and established thee?

NEW LIVING TRANSLATION

intentions of these people, even now before they
have entered the land I swore to give them."
22 So that very day Moses wrote down the words of
the song and taught it to the Israelites.
23 Then the LORD commissioned Joshua son of
Nun with these words: "Be strong and courageous,
for you must bring the people of Israel into the land I
swore to give them. I will be with you."
24 When Moses had finished writing this entire
body of instruction in a book, 25 he gave this command to the Levites who carried the Ark of the
LORD's Covenant: 26 "Take this Book of Instruction
and place it beside the Ark of the Covenant of the
LORD your God, so it may remain there as a witness
against the people of Israel. 27 For I know how rebellious and stubborn you are. Even now, while I am still
alive and am here with you, you have rebelled against
the LORD. How much more rebellious will you be
after my death!
28 "Now summon all the elders and officials of
your tribes, so that I can speak to them directly and
call heaven and earth to witness against them. 29 I
know that after my death you will become utterly
corrupt and will turn from the way I have commanded you to follow. In the days to come, disaster
will come down on you, for you will do what is evil in
the LORD's sight, making him very angry with your
actions."

The Song of Moses

30 So Moses recited this entire song publicly to the
assembly of Israel:

32 1 "Listen, O heavens, and I will speak!
Hear, O earth, the words that I say!
2 Let my teaching fall on you like rain;
let my speech settle like dew.
Let my words fall like rain on tender grass,
like gentle showers on young plants.
3 I will proclaim the name of the LORD;
how glorious is our God!
4 He is the Rock; his deeds are perfect.
Everything he does is just and fair.
He is a faithful God who does no wrong;
how just and upright he is!

5 "But they have acted corruptly toward him;
when they act so perversely,
are they really his children?*
They are a deceitful and twisted generation.
6 Is this the way you repay the LORD,
you foolish and senseless people?
Isn't he your Father who created you?
Has he not made you and established you?

32:5 The meaning of the Hebrew is uncertain.

KING JAMES VERSION

7 Remember the days of old, consider the years of many generations: ask thy father, and he will shew thee; thy elders, and they will tell thee.

8 When the Most High divided to the nations their inheritance, when he separated the sons of Adam, he set the bounds of the people according to the number of the children of Israel.

9 For the LORD's portion *is* his people; Jacob *is* the lot of his inheritance.

10 He found him in a desert land, and in the waste howling wilderness; he led him about, he instructed him, he kept him as the apple of his eye.

11 As an eagle stirreth up her nest, fluttereth over her young, spreadeth abroad her wings, taketh them, beareth them on her wings:

12 *So* the LORD alone did lead him, and *there was* no strange god with him.

13 He made him ride on the high places of the earth, that he might eat the increase of the fields; and he made him to suck honey out of the rock, and oil out of the flinty rock;

14 Butter of kine, and milk of sheep, with fat of lambs, and rams of the breed of Bashan, and goats, with the fat of kidneys of wheat; and thou didst drink the pure blood of the grape.

15 But Jeshurun waxed fat, and kicked: thou art waxen fat, thou art grown thick, thou art covered *with fatness;* then he forsook God *which* made him, and lightly esteemed the Rock of his salvation.

16 They provoked him to jealousy with strange *gods,* with abominations provoked they him to anger.

17 They sacrificed unto devils, not to God; to gods whom they knew not, to new *gods that* came newly up, whom your fathers feared not.

18 Of the Rock *that* begat thee thou art unmindful, and hast forgotten God that formed thee.

19 And when the LORD saw *it,* he abhorred *them,* because of the provoking of his sons, and of his daughters.

NEW LIVING TRANSLATION

7 Remember the days of long ago;
think about the generations past.
Ask your father, and he will inform you.
Inquire of your elders, and they will tell you.
8 When the Most High assigned lands to the nations,
when he divided up the human race,
he established the boundaries of the peoples
according to the number in his heavenly court.*
9 "For the people of Israel belong to the LORD;
Jacob is his special possession.
10 He found them in a desert land,
in an empty, howling wasteland.
He surrounded them and watched over them;
he guarded them as he would guard his own eyes.*
11 Like an eagle that rouses her chicks
and hovers over her young,
so he spread his wings to take them up
and carried them safely on his pinions.
12 The LORD alone guided them;
they followed no foreign gods.
13 He let them ride over the highlands
and feast on the crops of the fields.
He nourished them with honey from the rock
and olive oil from the stony ground.
14 He fed them yogurt from the herd
and milk from the flock,
together with the fat of lambs.
He gave them choice rams from Bashan, and goats,
together with the choicest wheat.
You drank the finest wine,
made from the juice of grapes.
15 "But Israel* soon became fat and unruly;
the people grew heavy, plump, and stuffed!
Then they abandoned the God who had made them;
they made light of the Rock of their salvation.
16 They stirred up his jealousy by worshiping foreign gods;
they provoked his fury with detestable deeds.
17 They offered sacrifices to demons, which are not God,
to gods they had not known before,
to new gods only recently arrived,
to gods their ancestors had never feared.
18 You neglected the Rock who had fathered you;
you forgot the God who had given you birth.

19 "The LORD saw this and drew back,
provoked to anger by his own sons and daughters.

32:8 As in Dead Sea Scrolls, which read *the number of the sons of God,* and Greek version, which reads *the number of the angels of God;* Masoretic Text reads *the number of the sons of Israel.* **32:10** Hebrew *as the pupil of his eye.* **32:15** Hebrew *Jeshurun,* a term of endearment for Israel.

KING JAMES VERSION

20 And he said, I will hide my face from them, I will see what their end *shall be:* for they *are* a very froward generation, children in whom *is* no faith.

21 They have moved me to jealousy with *that which is* not God; they have provoked me to anger with their vanities: and I will move them to jealousy with *those which are* not a people; I will provoke them to anger with a foolish nation.

22 For a fire is kindled in mine anger, and shall burn unto the lowest hell, and shall consume the earth with her increase, and set on fire the foundations of the mountains.

23 I will heap mischiefs upon them; I will spend mine arrows upon them.

24 *They shall be* burnt with hunger, and devoured with burning heat, and with bitter destruction: I will also send the teeth of beasts upon them, with the poison of serpents of the dust.

25 The sword without, and terror within, shall destroy both the young man and the virgin, the suckling *also* with the man of gray hairs.

26 I said, I would scatter them into corners, I would make the remembrance of them to cease from among men:

27 Were it not that I feared the wrath of the enemy, lest their adversaries should behave themselves strangely, *and* lest they should say, Our hand *is* high, and the LORD hath not done all this.

28 For they *are* a nation void of counsel, neither *is there any* understanding in them.

29 O that they were wise, *that* they understood this, *that* they would consider their latter end!

30 How should one chase a thousand, and two put ten thousand to flight, except their Rock had sold them, and the LORD had shut them up?

31 For their rock *is* not as our Rock, even our enemies themselves *being* judges.

32 For their vine *is* of the vine of Sodom, and of the fields of Gomorrah: their grapes *are* grapes of gall, their clusters *are* bitter:

33 Their wine *is* the poison of dragons, and the cruel venom of asps.

34 *Is* not this laid up in store with me, *and* sealed up among my treasures?

35 To me *belongeth* vengeance, and recompense; their foot shall slide in *due* time: for the day of their calamity *is* at hand, and the things that shall come upon them make haste.

NEW LIVING TRANSLATION

20 He said, 'I will abandon them;
then see what becomes of them.
For they are a twisted generation,
children without integrity.
21 They have roused my jealousy by worshiping
things that are not God;
they have provoked my anger with their
useless idols.
Now I will rouse their jealousy through people
who are not even a people;
I will provoke their anger through the foolish
Gentiles.
22 For my anger blazes forth like fire
and burns to the depths of the grave.*
It devours the earth and all its crops
and ignites the foundations of the mountains.
23 I will heap disasters upon them
and shoot them down with my arrows.
24 I will weaken them with famine,
burning fever, and deadly disease.
I will send the fangs of wild beasts
and poisonous snakes that glide in the dust.
25 Outside, the sword will bring death,
and inside, terror will strike
both young men and young women,
both infants and the aged.
26 I would have annihilated them,
wiping out even the memory of them.
27 But I feared the taunt of Israel's enemy,
who might misunderstand and say,
"Our own power has triumphed!
The LORD had nothing to do with this!"'

28 "But Israel is a senseless nation;
the people are foolish, without understanding.
29 Oh, that they were wise and could understand
this!
Oh, that they might know their fate!
30 How could one person chase a thousand of them,
and two people put ten thousand to flight,
unless their Rock had sold them,
unless the LORD had given them up?
31 But the rock of our enemies is not like our Rock,
as even they recognize.*
32 Their vine grows from the vine of Sodom,
from the vineyards of Gomorrah.
Their grapes are poison,
and their clusters are bitter.
33 Their wine is the venom of serpents,
the deadly poison of cobras.

34 "The LORD says, 'Am I not storing up these things,
sealing them away in my treasury?
35 I will take revenge; I will pay them back.
In due time their feet will slip.
Their day of disaster will arrive,
and their destiny will overtake them.'

32:22 Hebrew *of Sheol.* **32:31** The meaning of the Hebrew is uncertain. Greek version reads *our enemies are fools.*

KING JAMES VERSION

36 For the LORD shall judge his people, and repent himself for his servants, when he seeth that *their* power is gone, and *there is* none shut up, or left.

37 And he shall say, Where *are* their gods, *their* rock in whom they trusted,

38 Which did eat the fat of their sacrifices, *and* drank the wine of their drink offerings? let them rise up and help you, *and* be your protection.

39 See now that I, *even* I, *am* he, and *there is* no god with me: I kill, and I make alive; I wound, and I heal: neither *is there any* that can deliver out of my hand.

40 For I lift up my hand to heaven, and say, I live for ever.

41 If I whet my glittering sword, and mine hand take hold on judgment; I will render vengeance to mine enemies, and will reward them that hate me.

42 I will make mine arrows drunk with blood, and my sword shall devour flesh; *and that* with the blood of the slain and of the captives, from the beginning of revengers upon the enemy.

43 Rejoice, O ye nations, *with* his people: for he will avenge the blood of his servants, and will render vengeance to his adversaries, and will be merciful unto his land, *and* to his people.

44 And Moses came and spake all the words of this song in the ears of the people, he, and Hoshea the son of Nun.

45 And Moses made an end of speaking all these words to all Israel:

46 And he said unto them, Set your hearts unto all the words which I testify among you this day, which ye shall command your children to observe to do, all the words of this law.

47 For it *is* not a vain thing for you; because it *is* your life: and through this thing ye shall prolong *your* days in the land, whither ye go over Jordan to possess it.

48 And the LORD spake unto Moses that selfsame day, saying,

49 Get thee up into this mountain Abarim, *unto* mount Nebo, which *is* in the land of Moab, that *is* over against Jericho; and behold the land of Canaan, which I give unto the children of Israel for a possession:

NEW LIVING TRANSLATION

36 "Indeed, the LORD will give justice to his people,
and he will change his mind about*
his servants,
when he sees their strength is gone
and no one is left, slave or free.
37 Then he will ask, 'Where are their gods,
the rocks they fled to for refuge?
38 Where now are those gods,
who ate the fat of their sacrifices
and drank the wine of their offerings?
Let those gods arise and help you!
Let them provide you with shelter!
39 Look now; I myself am he!
There is no other god but me!
I am the one who kills and gives life;
I am the one who wounds and heals;
no one can be rescued from my
powerful hand!
40 Now I raise my hand to heaven
and declare, "As surely as I live,
41 when I sharpen my flashing sword
and begin to carry out justice,
I will take revenge on my enemies
and repay those who reject me.
42 I will make my arrows drunk with blood,
and my sword will devour flesh—
the blood of the slaughtered and the captives,
and the heads of the enemy leaders."'

43 "Rejoice with him, you heavens,
and let all of God's angels worship him.*
Rejoice with his people, you nations,
and let all the angels be strengthened in him.*
For he will avenge the blood of his servants;
he will take revenge against his enemies.
He will repay those who hate him*
and cleanse the land for his people."

44 So Moses came with Joshua* son of Nun and recited all the words of this song to the people.
45 When Moses had finished reciting all these
words to the people of Israel, 46 he added: "Take to
heart all the words of warning I have given you today.
Pass them on as a command to your children so they
will obey every word of these instructions. 47 These
instructions are not empty words—they are your life!
By obeying them you will enjoy a long life in the land
you will occupy when you cross the Jordan River."

Moses' Death Foretold

48 That same day the LORD said to Moses, 49 "Go to
Moab, to the mountains east of the river,* and climb
Mount Nebo, which is across from Jericho. Look out
across the land of Canaan, the land I am giving to the
people of Israel as their own special possession.

32:36 Or *will take revenge for.* **32:43a** As in Dead Sea Scrolls and Greek version; Masoretic Text lacks the first two lines. Compare Heb 1:6. **32:43b** As in Greek version; Hebrew text lacks this line. **32:43c** As in Dead Sea Scrolls and Greek version; Masoretic Text lacks this line. **32:44** Hebrew *Hoshea,* a variant name for Joshua. **32:49** Hebrew *the mountains of Abarim.*

KING JAMES VERSION

50 And die in the mount whither thou goest up,
and be gathered unto thy people; as Aaron thy
brother died in mount Hor, and was gathered unto
his people:
51 Because ye trespassed against me among the
children of Israel at the waters of Meribah-Kadesh,
in the wilderness of Zin; because ye sanctified me
not in the midst of the children of Israel.
52 Yet thou shalt see the land before *thee;* but thou
shalt not go thither unto the land which I give the
children of Israel.

33

1 And this *is* the blessing, wherewith Moses
the man of God blessed the children of Israel before his death.
2 And he said, The LORD came from Sinai, and rose
up from Seir unto them; he shined forth from mount
Paran, and he came with ten thousands of saints:
from his right hand *went* a fiery law for them.
3 Yea, he loved the people; all his saints *are* in thy
hand: and they sat down at thy feet; *every one* shall
receive of thy words.
4 Moses commanded us a law, *even* the inheritance
of the congregation of Jacob.
5 And he was king in Jeshurun, when the heads of
the people *and* the tribes of Israel were gathered
together.
6 Let Reuben live, and not die; and let *not* his men
be few.
7 And this *is the blessing* of Judah: and he said,
Hear, LORD, the voice of Judah, and bring him unto
his people: let his hands be sufficient for him; and be
thou an help *to him* from his enemies.
8 And of Levi he said, *Let* thy Thummim and thy
Urim *be* with thy holy one, whom thou didst prove
at Massah, *and with* whom thou didst strive at the
waters of Meribah;
9 Who said unto his father and to his mother, I
have not seen him; neither did he acknowledge his

NEW LIVING TRANSLATION

50 Then you will die there on the mountain. You will
join your ancestors, just as Aaron, your brother, died
on Mount Hor and joined his ancestors. 51 For both of
you betrayed me with the Israelites at the waters of
Meribah at Kadesh* in the wilderness of Zin. You
failed to demonstrate my holiness to the people of
Israel there. 52 So you will see the land from a distance, but you may not enter the land I am giving to
the people of Israel."

Moses Blesses the People

33

This is the blessing that Moses, the man of
God, gave to the people of Israel before his
death:

2 "The LORD came from Mount Sinai
and dawned upon us* from Mount Seir;
he shone forth from Mount Paran
and came from Meribah-kadesh
with flaming fire at his right hand.*
3 Indeed, he loves his people;*
all his holy ones are in his hands.
They follow in his steps
and accept his teaching.
4 Moses gave us the LORD's instruction,
the special possession of the people of Israel.*
5 The LORD became king in Israel*—
when the leaders of the people assembled,
when the tribes of Israel gathered as one."

6 Moses said this about the tribe of Reuben:*

"Let the tribe of Reuben live and not die out,
though they are few in number."

7 Moses said this about the tribe of Judah:

"O LORD, hear the cry of Judah
and bring them together as a people.
Give them strength to defend their cause;
help them against their enemies!"

8 Moses said this about the tribe of Levi:

"O LORD, you have given your Thummim and
Urim—the sacred lots—
to your faithful servants the Levites.*
You put them to the test at Massah
and struggled with them at the waters
of Meribah.
9 The Levites obeyed your word
and guarded your covenant.
They were more loyal to you
than to their own parents.

32:51 Hebrew *waters of Meribah-kadesh.* **33:2a** As in Greek and Syriac versions; Hebrew reads *upon them.* **33:2b** Or *came from myriads of holy ones, from the south, from his mountain slopes.* The meaning of the Hebrew is uncertain. **33:3** As in Greek version; Hebrew reads *Indeed, lover of the peoples.* **33:4** Hebrew *of Jacob.* The names "Jacob" and "Israel" are often interchanged throughout the Old Testament, referring sometimes to the individual patriarch and sometimes to the nation. **33:5** Hebrew *in Jeshurun,* a term of endearment for Israel. **33:6** Hebrew lacks *Moses said this about the tribe of Reuben.* **33:8** As in Greek version; Hebrew lacks *the Levites.*

KING JAMES VERSION

brethren, nor knew his own children: for they have
observed thy word, and kept thy covenant.
10 They shall teach Jacob thy judgments, and Israel
thy law: they shall put incense before thee, and whole
burnt sacrifice upon thine altar.
11 Bless, LORD, his substance, and accept the work
of his hands: smite through the loins of them that
rise against him, and of them that hate him, that they
rise not again.
12 *And* of Benjamin he said, The beloved of the
LORD shall dwell in safety by him; *and the LORD* shall
cover him all the day long, and he shall dwell between his shoulders.
13 And of Joseph he said, Blessed of the LORD *be* his
land, for the precious things of heaven, for the dew,
and for the deep that coucheth beneath,
14 And for the precious fruits *brought forth* by the
sun, and for the precious things put forth by the
moon,
15 And for the chief things of the ancient mountains, and for the precious things of the lasting hills,
16 And for the precious things of the earth and
fulness thereof, and *for* the good will of him that
dwelt in the bush: let *the blessing* come upon the
head of Joseph, and upon the top of the head of him
that was separated from his brethren.
17 His glory *is like* the firstling of his bullock, and
his horns *are like* the horns of unicorns: with them
he shall push the people together to the ends of the
earth: and they *are* the ten thousands of Ephraim,
and they *are* the thousands of Manasseh.
18 And of Zebulun he said, Rejoice, Zebulun, in thy
going out; and, Issachar, in thy tents.
19 They shall call the people unto the mountain;
there they shall offer sacrifices of righteousness: for
they shall suck *of* the abundance of the seas, and *of*
treasures hid in the sand.
20 And of Gad he said, Blessed *be* he that enlargeth
Gad; he dwelleth as a lion, and teareth the arm with
the crown of the head.
21 And he provided the first part for himself, because there, *in* a portion of the lawgiver, *was he*
seated; and he came with the heads of the people, he
executed the justice of the LORD, and his judgments
with Israel.

NEW LIVING TRANSLATION

They ignored their relatives
and did not acknowledge their own children.
10 They teach your regulations to Jacob;
they give your instructions to Israel.
They present incense before you
and offer whole burnt offerings on the altar.
11 Bless the ministry of the Levites, O LORD,
and accept all the work of their hands.
Hit their enemies where it hurts the most;
strike down their foes so they never
rise again."

12 Moses said this about the tribe of Benjamin:

"The people of Benjamin are loved by the LORD
and live in safety beside him.
He surrounds them continuously
and preserves them from every harm."

13 Moses said this about the tribes of Joseph:

"May their land be blessed by the LORD
with the precious gift of dew from the heavens
and water from beneath the earth;
14 with the rich fruit that grows in the sun,
and the rich harvest produced each month;
15 with the finest crops of the ancient mountains,
and the abundance from the everlasting hills;
16 with the best gifts of the earth and its bounty,
and the favor of the one who appeared in the
burning bush.
May these blessings rest on Joseph's head,
crowning the brow of the prince among his
brothers.
17 Joseph has the majesty of a young bull;
he has the horns of a wild ox.
He will gore distant nations,
driving them to the ends of the earth.
This is my blessing for the multitudes of Ephraim
and the thousands of Manasseh."

18 Moses said this about the tribes of Zebulun and Issachar*:

"May the people of Zebulun prosper in their
travels.
May the people of Issachar prosper at home in
their tents.
19 They summon the people to the mountain
to offer proper sacrifices there.
They benefit from the riches of the sea
and the hidden treasures in the sand."

20 Moses said this about the tribe of Gad:

"Blessed is the one who enlarges Gad's territory!
Gad is poised there like a lion
to tear off an arm or a head.
21 The people of Gad took the best land for
themselves;
a leader's share was assigned to them.

33:18 Hebrew lacks *and Issachar.*

KING JAMES VERSION

22 And of Dan he said, Dan *is* a lion's whelp: he shall leap from Bashan.

23 And of Naphtali he said, O Naphtali, satisfied with favour, and full with the blessing of the LORD: possess thou the west and the south.

24 And of Asher he said, *Let* Asher *be* blessed with children; let him be acceptable to his brethren, and let him dip his foot in oil.

25 Thy shoes *shall be* iron and brass; and as thy days, *so shall* thy strength *be*.

26 *There is* none like unto the God of Jeshurun, *who* rideth upon the heaven in thy help, and in his excellency on the sky.

27 The eternal God *is thy* refuge, and underneath *are* the everlasting arms: and he shall thrust out the enemy from before thee; and shall say, Destroy *them*.

28 Israel then shall dwell in safety alone: the fountain of Jacob *shall be* upon a land of corn and wine; also his heavens shall drop down dew.

29 Happy *art* thou, O Israel: who *is* like unto thee, O people saved by the LORD, the shield of thy help, and who *is* the sword of thy excellency! and thine enemies shall be found liars unto thee; and thou shalt tread upon their high places.

34 1 And Moses went up from the plains of Moab unto the mountain of Nebo, to the top of Pisgah, that *is* over against Jericho. And the LORD shewed him all the land of Gilead, unto Dan,

2 And all Naphtali, and the land of Ephraim, and Manasseh, and all the land of Judah, unto the utmost sea,

3 And the south, and the plain of the valley of Jericho, the city of palm trees, unto Zoar.

4 And the LORD said unto him, This *is* the land which I sware unto Abraham, unto Isaac, and unto Jacob, saying, I will give it unto thy seed: I have caused thee to see *it* with thine eyes, but thou shalt not go over thither.

5 So Moses the servant of the LORD died there in the land of Moab, according to the word of the LORD.

6 And he buried him in a valley in the land of Moab,

NEW LIVING TRANSLATION

When the leaders of the people were assembled,
they carried out the LORD's justice
and obeyed his regulations for Israel."

22 Moses said this about the tribe of Dan:

"Dan is a lion's cub,
leaping out from Bashan."

23 Moses said this about the tribe of Naphtali:

"O Naphtali, you are rich in favor
and full of the LORD's blessings;
may you possess the west and the south."

24 Moses said this about the tribe of Asher:

"May Asher be blessed above other sons;
may he be esteemed by his brothers;
may he bathe his feet in olive oil.
25 May the bolts of your gates be of iron and bronze;
may you be secure all your days."

26 "There is no one like the God of Israel.*
He rides across the heavens to help you,
across the skies in majestic splendor.
27 The eternal God is your refuge,
and his everlasting arms are under you.
He drives out the enemy before you;
he cries out, 'Destroy them!'
28 So Israel will live in safety,
prosperous Jacob in security,
in a land of grain and new wine,
while the heavens drop down dew.
29 How blessed you are, O Israel!
Who else is like you, a people saved
by the LORD?
He is your protecting shield
and your triumphant sword!
Your enemies will cringe before you,
and you will stomp on their backs!"

The Death of Moses

34 Then Moses went up to Mount Nebo from
the plains of Moab and climbed Pisgah
Peak, which is across from Jericho. And the LORD
showed him the whole land, from Gilead as far as
Dan; 2 all the land of Naphtali; the land of Ephraim
and Manasseh; all the land of Judah, extending to the
Mediterranean Sea*; 3 the Negev; the Jordan Valley
with Jericho—the city of palms—as far as Zoar. 4 Then
the LORD said to Moses, "This is the land I promised
on oath to Abraham, Isaac, and Jacob when I said, 'I
will give it to your descendants.' I have now allowed
you to see it with your own eyes, but you will not enter the land."

5 So Moses, the servant of the LORD, died there in
the land of Moab, just as the LORD had said. 6 The
LORD buried him* in a valley near Beth-peor in Moab,

33:26 Hebrew *of Jeshurun,* a term of endearment for Israel. **34:2** Hebrew *the western sea.* **34:6** Hebrew *He buried him;* Samaritan Pentateuch and some Greek manuscripts read *They buried him.*

KING JAMES VERSION

over against Beth-peor: but no man knoweth of his
sepulchre unto this day.
7And Moses *was* an hundred and twenty years old
when he died: his eye was not dim, nor his natural
force abated.
8And the children of Israel wept for Moses in the
plains of Moab thirty days: so the days of weeping
and mourning for Moses were ended.
9And Joshua the son of Nun was full of the spirit of
wisdom; for Moses had laid his hands upon him: and
the children of Israel hearkened unto him, and did as
the LORD commanded Moses.
10And there arose not a prophet since in Israel like
unto Moses, whom the LORD knew face to face,
11In all the signs and the wonders, which the LORD
sent him to do in the land of Egypt to Pharaoh, and to
all his servants, and to all his land,
12And in all that mighty hand, and in all the great
terror which Moses shewed in the sight of all Israel.

NEW LIVING TRANSLATION

but to this day no one knows the exact place. 7Moses
was 120 years old when he died, yet his eyesight was
clear, and he was as strong as ever. 8The people of Israel mourned for Moses on the plains of Moab for
thirty days, until the customary period of mourning
was over.
9Now Joshua son of Nun was full of the spirit of
wisdom, for Moses had laid his hands on him. So the
people of Israel obeyed him, doing just as the LORD
had commanded Moses.
10There has never been another prophet in Israel
like Moses, whom the LORD knew face to face. 11The
LORD sent him to perform all the miraculous signs
and wonders in the land of Egypt against Pharaoh,
and all his servants, and his entire land. 12With
mighty power, Moses performed terrifying acts in
the sight of all Israel.

Joshua

KING JAMES VERSION

1 1 Now after the death of Moses the servant of the
LORD it came to pass, that the LORD spake unto
Joshua the son of Nun, Moses' minister, saying,
2 Moses my servant is dead; now therefore arise, go
over this Jordan, thou, and all this people, unto the
land which I do give to them, *even* to the children
of Israel.
3 Every place that the sole of your foot shall tread
upon, that have I given unto you, as I said unto Moses.
4 From the wilderness and this Lebanon even unto
the great river, the river Euphrates, all the land of the
Hittites, and unto the great sea toward the going
down of the sun, shall be your coast.
5 There shall not any man be able to stand before
thee all the days of thy life: as I was with Moses, *so* I
will be with thee: I will not fail thee, nor forsake thee.
6 Be strong and of a good courage: for unto this
people shalt thou divide for an inheritance the land,
which I sware unto their fathers to give them.
7 Only be thou strong and very courageous, that
thou mayest observe to do according to all the law,
which Moses my servant commanded thee: turn not
from it *to* the right hand or *to* the left, that thou mayest prosper whithersoever thou goest.
8 This book of the law shall not depart out of thy
mouth; but thou shalt meditate therein day and night,
that thou mayest observe to do according to all that
is written therein: for then thou shalt make thy way
prosperous, and then thou shalt have good success.
9 Have not I commanded thee? Be strong and of a
good courage; be not afraid, neither be thou dismayed: for the LORD thy God *is* with thee whithersoever thou goest.
10 Then Joshua commanded the officers of the
people, saying,
11 Pass through the host, and command the
people, saying, Prepare you victuals; for within three
days ye shall pass over this Jordan, to go in to possess
the land, which the LORD your God giveth you to possess it.
12 And to the Reubenites, and to the Gadites, and to
half the tribe of Manasseh, spake Joshua, saying,
13 Remember the word which Moses the servant of

NEW LIVING TRANSLATION

The LORD's Charge to Joshua

1 After the death of Moses the LORD's servant, the
LORD spoke to Joshua son of Nun, Moses' assistant. He said, 2 "Moses my servant is dead. Therefore,
the time has come for you to lead these people, the
Israelites, across the Jordan River into the land I am
giving them. 3 I promise you what I promised Moses:
'Wherever you set foot, you will be on land I have
given you—4 from the Negev wilderness in the south
to the Lebanon mountains in the north, from the Euphrates River in the east to the Mediterranean Sea*
in the west, including all the land of the Hittites.' 5 No
one will be able to stand against you as long as you
live. For I will be with you as I was with Moses. I will
not fail you or abandon you.
6 "Be strong and courageous, for you are the one
who will lead these people to possess all the land
I swore to their ancestors I would give them. 7 Be
strong and very courageous. Be careful to obey all the
instructions Moses gave you. Do not deviate from
them, turning either to the right or to the left. Then
you will be successful in everything you do. 8 Study
this Book of Instruction continually. Meditate on it
day and night so you will be sure to obey everything
written in it. Only then will you prosper and succeed
in all you do. 9 This is my command—be strong and
courageous! Do not be afraid or discouraged. For the
LORD your God is with you wherever you go."

Joshua's Charge to the Israelites

10 Joshua then commanded the officers of Israel,
11 "Go through the camp and tell the people to get
their provisions ready. In three days you will cross the
Jordan River and take possession of the land the
LORD your God is giving you."
12 Then Joshua called together the tribes of Reuben, Gad, and the half-tribe of Manasseh. He told
them, 13 "Remember what Moses, the servant of the

1:4 Hebrew *the Great Sea.*

KING JAMES VERSION

the LORD commanded you, saying, The LORD your God hath given you rest, and hath given you this land.

14 Your wives, your little ones, and your cattle, shall remain in the land which Moses gave you on this side Jordan; but ye shall pass before your brethren armed, all the mighty men of valour, and help them;

15 Until the LORD have given your brethren rest, as *he hath given* you, and they also have possessed the land which the LORD your God giveth them: then ye shall return unto the land of your possession, and enjoy it, which Moses the LORD's servant gave you on this side Jordan toward the sunrising.

16 And they answered Joshua, saying, All that thou commandest us we will do, and whithersoever thou sendest us, we will go.

17 According as we hearkened unto Moses in all things, so will we hearken unto thee: only the LORD thy God be with thee, as he was with Moses.

18 Whosoever *he be* that doth rebel against thy commandment, and will not hearken unto thy words in all that thou commandest him, he shall be put to death: only be strong and of a good courage.

2 1 And Joshua the son of Nun sent out of Shittim two men to spy secretly, saying, Go view the land, even Jericho. And they went, and came into an harlot's house, named Rahab, and lodged there.

2 And it was told the king of Jericho, saying, Behold, there came men in hither to night of the children of Israel to search out the country.

3 And the king of Jericho sent unto Rahab, saying, Bring forth the men that are come to thee, which are entered into thine house: for they be come to search out all the country.

4 And the woman took the two men, and hid them, and said thus, There came men unto me, but I wist not whence they *were:*

5 And it came to pass *about the time* of shutting of the gate, when it was dark, that the men went out: whither the men went I wot not: pursue after them quickly; for ye shall overtake them.

6 But she had brought them up to the roof of the house, and hid them with the stalks of flax, which she had laid in order upon the roof.

7 And the men pursued after them the way to Jordan unto the fords: and as soon as they which pursued after them were gone out, they shut the gate.

8 And before they were laid down, she came up unto them upon the roof;

9 And she said unto the men, I know that the LORD hath given you the land, and that your terror is fallen upon us, and that all the inhabitants of the land faint because of you.

10 For we have heard how the LORD dried up the water of the Red sea for you, when ye came out of Egypt; and what ye did unto the two kings of the Amorites, that *were* on the other side Jordan, Sihon and Og, whom ye utterly destroyed.

NEW LIVING TRANSLATION

LORD, commanded you: 'The LORD your God is giving you a place of rest. He has given you this land.' 14 Your wives, children, and livestock may remain here in the land Moses assigned to you on the east side of the Jordan River. But your strong warriors, fully armed, must lead the other tribes across the Jordan to help them conquer their territory. Stay with them 15 until the LORD gives them rest, as he has given you rest, and until they, too, possess the land the LORD your God is giving them. Only then may you return and settle here on the east side of the Jordan River in the land that Moses, the servant of the LORD, assigned to you."

16 They answered Joshua, "We will do whatever you command us, and we will go wherever you send us. 17 We will obey you just as we obeyed Moses. And may the LORD your God be with you as he was with Moses. 18 Anyone who rebels against your orders and does not obey your words and everything you command will be put to death. So be strong and courageous!"

Rahab Protects the Spies

2 Then Joshua secretly sent out two spies from the Israelite camp at Acacia Grove.* He instructed them, "Scout out the land on the other side of the Jordan River, especially around Jericho." So the two men set out and came to the house of a prostitute named Rahab and stayed there that night.

2 But someone told the king of Jericho, "Some Israelites have come here tonight to spy out the land." 3 So the king of Jericho sent orders to Rahab: "Bring out the men who have come into your house, for they have come here to spy out the whole land."

4 Rahab had hidden the two men, but she replied, "Yes, the men were here earlier, but I didn't know where they were from. 5 They left the town at dusk, as the gates were about to close. I don't know where they went. If you hurry, you can probably catch up with them." 6 (Actually, she had taken them up to the roof and hidden them beneath bundles of flax she had laid out.) 7 So the king's men went looking for the spies along the road leading to the shallow crossings of the Jordan River. And as soon as the king's men had left, the gate of Jericho was shut.

8 Before the spies went to sleep that night, Rahab went up on the roof to talk with them. 9 "I know the LORD has given you this land," she told them. "We are all afraid of you. Everyone in the land is living in terror. 10 For we have heard how the LORD made a dry path for you through the Red Sea* when you left Egypt. And we know what you did to Sihon and Og, the two Amorite kings east of the Jordan River,

2:1 Hebrew *Shittim.* **2:10a** Hebrew *sea of reeds.*

KING JAMES VERSION

11 And as soon as we had heard *these things,* our
hearts did melt, neither did there remain any more
courage in any man, because of you: for the LORD your
God, he *is* God in heaven above, and in earth beneath.
12 Now therefore, I pray you, swear unto me by the
LORD, since I have shewed you kindness, that ye will
also shew kindness unto my father's house, and give
me a true token:

13 And *that* ye will save alive my father, and my
mother, and my brethren, and my sisters, and all that
they have, and deliver our lives from death.

14 And the men answered her, Our life for yours, if
ye utter not this our business. And it shall be, when
the LORD hath given us the land, that we will deal
kindly and truly with thee.

15 Then she let them down by a cord through the
window: for her house *was* upon the town wall, and
she dwelt upon the wall.

16 And she said unto them, Get you to the mountain, lest the pursuers meet you; and hide yourselves
there three days, until the pursuers be returned: and
afterward may ye go your way.

17 And the men said unto her, We *will be* blameless
of this thine oath which thou hast made us swear.
18 Behold, *when* we come into the land, thou shalt
bind this line of scarlet thread in the window which
thou didst let us down by: and thou shalt bring thy
father, and thy mother, and thy brethren, and all thy
father's household, home unto thee.

19 And it shall be, *that* whosoever shall go out of
the doors of thy house into the street, his blood *shall
be* upon his head, and we *will be* guiltless: and whosoever shall be with thee in the house, his blood *shall
be* on our head, if *any* hand be upon him.

20 And if thou utter this our business, then we will
be quit of thine oath which thou hast made us to
swear.

21 And she said, According unto your words, so *be*
it. And she sent them away, and they departed: and
she bound the scarlet line in the window.

22 And they went, and came unto the mountain,
and abode there three days, until the pursuers were
returned: and the pursuers sought *them* throughout
all the way, but found *them* not.
23 So the two men returned, and descended from
the mountain, and passed over, and came to Joshua
the son of Nun, and told him all *things* that befell
them:
24 And they said unto Joshua, Truly the LORD hath
delivered into our hands all the land; for even all the
inhabitants of the country do faint because of us.

3 1 And Joshua rose early in the morning; and they
removed from Shittim, and came to Jordan, he
and all the children of Israel, and lodged there before
they passed over.

NEW LIVING TRANSLATION

whose people you completely destroyed.* 11 No
wonder our hearts have melted in fear! No one has
the courage to fight after hearing such things. For
the LORD your God is the supreme God of the heavens above and the earth below.

12 "Now swear to me by the LORD that you will be
kind to me and my family since I have helped you.
Give me some guarantee that 13 when Jericho is
conquered, you will let me live, along with my father
and mother, my brothers and sisters, and all their
families."

14 "We offer our own lives as a guarantee for your
safety," the men agreed. "If you don't betray us, we
will keep our promise and be kind to you when the
LORD gives us the land."

15 Then, since Rahab's house was built into the
town wall, she let them down by a rope through the
window. 16 "Escape to the hill country," she told
them. "Hide there for three days from the men
searching for you. Then, when they have returned,
you can go on your way."

17 Before they left, the men told her, "We will be
bound by the oath we have taken only if you follow
these instructions. 18 When we come into the land,
you must leave this scarlet rope hanging from the
window through which you let us down. And all your
family members—your father, mother, brothers, and
all your relatives—must be here inside the house. 19 If
they go out into the street and are killed, it will not be
our fault. But if anyone lays a hand on people inside
this house, we will accept the responsibility for their
death. 20 If you betray us, however, we are not bound
by this oath in any way."

21 "I accept your terms," she replied. And she sent
them on their way, leaving the scarlet rope hanging
from the window.

22 The spies went up into the hill country and
stayed there three days. The men who were chasing
them searched everywhere along the road, but they
finally returned without success.

23 Then the two spies came down from the hill
country, crossed the Jordan River, and reported to
Joshua all that had happened to them. 24 "The LORD
has given us the whole land," they said, "for all the
people in the land are terrified of us."

The Israelites Cross the Jordan

3 Early the next morning Joshua and all the
Israelites left Acacia Grove* and arrived at
the banks of the Jordan River, where they camped

2:10b The Hebrew term used here refers to the complete consecration of things or people to the LORD, either by destroying them or by giving them as an offering. **3:1** Hebrew *Shittim.*

KING JAMES VERSION

2 And it came to pass after three days, that the officers went through the host;

3 And they commanded the people, saying, When ye see the ark of the covenant of the LORD your God, and the priests the Levites bearing it, then ye shall remove from your place, and go after it.

4 Yet there shall be a space between you and it, about two thousand cubits by measure: come not near unto it, that ye may know the way by which ye must go: for ye have not passed *this* way heretofore.

5 And Joshua said unto the people, Sanctify yourselves: for tomorrow the LORD will do wonders among you.

6 And Joshua spake unto the priests, saying, Take up the ark of the covenant, and pass over before the people. And they took up the ark of the covenant, and went before the people.

7 And the LORD said unto Joshua, This day will I begin to magnify thee in the sight of all Israel, that they may know that, as I was with Moses, *so* I will be with thee.

8 And thou shalt command the priests that bear the ark of the covenant, saying, When ye are come to the brink of the water of Jordan, ye shall stand still in Jordan.

9 And Joshua said unto the children of Israel, Come hither, and hear the words of the LORD your God.

10 And Joshua said, Hereby ye shall know that the living God *is* among you, and *that* he will without fail drive out from before you the Canaanites, and the Hittites, and the Hivites, and the Perizzites, and the Girgashites, and the Amorites, and the Jebusites.

11 Behold, the ark of the covenant of the LORD of all the earth passeth over before you into Jordan.

12 Now therefore take you twelve men out of the tribes of Israel, out of every tribe a man.

13 And it shall come to pass, as soon as the soles of the feet of the priests that bear the ark of the LORD, the Lord of all the earth, shall rest in the waters of Jordan, *that* the waters of Jordan shall be cut off *from* the waters that come down from above; and they shall stand upon an heap.

14 And it came to pass, when the people removed from their tents, to pass over Jordan, and the priests bearing the ark of the covenant before the people;

15 And as they that bare the ark were come unto Jordan, and the feet of the priests that bare the ark were dipped in the brim of the water, (for Jordan overfloweth all his banks all the time of harvest,)

16 That the waters which came down from above stood *and* rose up upon an heap very far from the city Adam, that *is* beside Zaretan: and those that came down toward the sea of the plain, *even* the salt sea, failed, *and* were cut off: and the people passed over right against Jericho.

17 And the priests that bare the ark of the covenant of the LORD stood firm on dry ground in the midst of Jordan, and all the Israelites passed over on dry

NEW LIVING TRANSLATION

before crossing. 2 Three days later the Israelite officers went through the camp, 3 giving these instructions to the people: "When you see the Levitical
priests carrying the Ark of the Covenant of the LORD
your God, move out from your positions and follow
them. 4 Since you have never traveled this way before,
they will guide you. Stay about a half mile* behind
them, keeping a clear distance between you and the
Ark. Make sure you don't come any closer."

5 Then Joshua told the people, "Purify yourselves,
for tomorrow the LORD will do great wonders
among you."

6 In the morning Joshua said to the priests, "Lift up
the Ark of the Covenant and lead the people across
the river." And so they started out and went ahead
of the people.

7 The LORD told Joshua, "Today I will begin to make
you a great leader in the eyes of all the Israelites.
They will know that I am with you, just as I was with
Moses. 8 Give this command to the priests who carry
the Ark of the Covenant: 'When you reach the banks
of the Jordan River, take a few steps into the river and
stop there.'"

9 So Joshua told the Israelites, "Come and listen
to what the LORD your God says. 10 Today you will
know that the living God is among you. He will surely
drive out the Canaanites, Hittites, Hivites, Perizzites,
Girgashites, Amorites, and Jebusites ahead of you.
11 Look, the Ark of the Covenant, which belongs to
the Lord of the whole earth, will lead you across the
Jordan River! 12 Now choose twelve men from the
tribes of Israel, one from each tribe. 13 The priests
will carry the Ark of the LORD, the Lord of all the
earth. As soon as their feet touch the water, the flow
of water will be cut off upstream, and the river will
stand up like a wall."

14 So the people left their camp to cross the Jordan,
and the priests who were carrying the Ark of the Covenant went ahead of them. 15 It was the harvest season, and the Jordan was overflowing its banks. But as
soon as the feet of the priests who were carrying the
Ark touched the water at the river's edge, 16 the water
above that point began backing up a great distance
away at a town called Adam, which is near Zarethan.
And the water below that point flowed on to the
Dead Sea* until the riverbed was dry. Then all the
people crossed over near the town of Jericho.

17 Meanwhile, the priests who were carrying the
Ark of the LORD's Covenant stood on dry ground in
the middle of the riverbed as the people passed by.

3:4 Hebrew *about 2,000 cubits* [920 meters]. **3:16** Hebrew *the sea of the Arabah, the Salt Sea.*

KING JAMES VERSION

ground, until all the people were passed clean over
Jordan.

4 1And it came to pass, when all the people were
clean passed over Jordan, that the LORD spake
unto Joshua, saying,
2Take you twelve men out of the people, out of
every tribe a man,
3And command ye them, saying, Take you hence
out of the midst of Jordan, out of the place where the
priests' feet stood firm, twelve stones, and ye shall
carry them over with you, and leave them in the lodging place, where ye shall lodge this night.
4Then Joshua called the twelve men, whom he
had prepared of the children of Israel, out of every
tribe a man:
5And Joshua said unto them, Pass over before the
ark of the LORD your God into the midst of Jordan,
and take you up every man of you a stone upon his
shoulder, according unto the number of the tribes of
the children of Israel:
6That this may be a sign among you, *that* when
your children ask *their fathers* in time to come, saying, What *mean* ye by these stones?
7Then ye shall answer them, That the waters of
Jordan were cut off before the ark of the covenant of
the LORD; when it passed over Jordan, the waters
of Jordan were cut off: and these stones shall be for
a memorial unto the children of Israel for ever.
8And the children of Israel did so as Joshua commanded, and took up twelve stones out of the midst
of Jordan, as the LORD spake unto Joshua, according
to the number of the tribes of the children of Israel,
and carried them over with them unto the place
where they lodged, and laid them down there.
9And Joshua set up twelve stones in the midst of
Jordan, in the place where the feet of the priests
which bare the ark of the covenant stood: and they
are there unto this day.
10For the priests which bare the ark stood in the
midst of Jordan, until every thing was finished that
the LORD commanded Joshua to speak unto the
people, according to all that Moses commanded
Joshua: and the people hasted and passed over.
11And it came to pass, when all the people were
clean passed over, that the ark of the LORD passed
over, and the priests, in the presence of the people.
12And the children of Reuben, and the children of
Gad, and half the tribe of Manasseh, passed over
armed before the children of Israel, as Moses spake
unto them:
13About forty thousand prepared for war passed
over before the LORD unto battle, to the plains of
Jericho.
14On that day the LORD magnified Joshua in the
sight of all Israel; and they feared him, as they feared
Moses, all the days of his life.

NEW LIVING TRANSLATION

They waited there until the whole nation of Israel
had crossed the Jordan on dry ground.

Memorials to the Jordan Crossing

4 When all the people had crossed the Jordan,
the LORD said to Joshua, 2"Now choose twelve
men, one from each tribe. 3Tell them, 'Take twelve
stones from the very place where the priests are
standing in the middle of the Jordan. Carry them out
and pile them up at the place where you will camp
tonight.'"
4So Joshua called together the twelve men he had
chosen—one from each of the tribes of Israel. 5He
told them, "Go into the middle of the Jordan, in front
of the Ark of the LORD your God. Each of you must
pick up one stone and carry it out on your shoulder—
twelve stones in all, one for each of the twelve tribes
of Israel. 6We will use these stones to build a memorial. In the future your children will ask you, 'What
do these stones mean?' 7Then you can tell them,
'They remind us that the Jordan River stopped flowing when the Ark of the LORD's Covenant went
across.' These stones will stand as a memorial
among the people of Israel forever."
8So the men did as Joshua had commanded them.
They took twelve stones from the middle of the Jordan River, one for each tribe, just as the LORD had
told Joshua. They carried them to the place where
they camped for the night and constructed the
memorial there.
9Joshua also set up another pile of twelve stones
in the middle of the Jordan, at the place where the
priests who carried the Ark of the Covenant were
standing. And they are there to this day.
10The priests who were carrying the Ark stood in
the middle of the river until all of the LORD's commands that Moses had given to Joshua were carried
out. Meanwhile, the people hurried across the
riverbed. 11And when everyone was safely on the
other side, the priests crossed over with the Ark of
the LORD as the people watched.
12The armed warriors from the tribes of Reuben,
Gad, and the half-tribe of Manasseh led the Israelites
across the Jordan, just as Moses had directed.
13These armed men—about 40,000 strong—were
ready for battle, and the LORD was with them as they
crossed over to the plains of Jericho.
14That day the LORD made Joshua a great leader in
the eyes of all the Israelites, and for the rest of his life
they revered him as much as they had revered
Moses.

KING JAMES VERSION

15And the LORD spake unto Joshua, saying,
16Command the priests that bear the ark of the
testimony, that they come up out of Jordan.
17Joshua therefore commanded the priests, saying, Come ye up out of Jordan.
18And it came to pass, when the priests that bare
the ark of the covenant of the LORD were come up
out of the midst of Jordan, *and* the soles of the
priests' feet were lifted up unto the dry land, that the
waters of Jordan returned unto their place, and
flowed over all his banks, as *they did* before.
19And the people came up out of Jordan on the
tenth *day* of the first month, and encamped in Gilgal,
in the east border of Jericho.
20And those twelve stones, which they took out of
Jordan, did Joshua pitch in Gilgal.
21And he spake unto the children of Israel, saying,
When your children shall ask their fathers in time to
come, saying, What *mean* these stones?
22Then ye shall let your children know, saying,
Israel came over this Jordan on dry land.
23For the LORD your God dried up the waters of
Jordan from before you, until ye were passed over, as
the LORD your God did to the Red sea, which he dried
up from before us, until we were gone over:
24That all the people of the earth might know the
hand of the LORD, that it *is* mighty: that ye might fear
the LORD your God for ever.

5 1And it came to pass, when all the kings of the
Amorites, which *were* on the side of Jordan
westward, and all the kings of the Canaanites, which
were by the sea, heard that the LORD had dried up the
waters of Jordan from before the children of Israel,
until we were passed over, that their heart melted,
neither was there spirit in them any more, because of
the children of Israel.
2At that time the LORD said unto Joshua, Make
thee sharp knives, and circumcise again the children
of Israel the second time.
3And Joshua made him sharp knives, and circumcised the children of Israel at the hill of the foreskins.
4And this *is* the cause why Joshua did circumcise:
All the people that came out of Egypt, *that were*
males, *even* all the men of war, died in the wilderness
by the way, after they came out of Egypt.
5Now all the people that came out were circumcised: but all the people *that were* born in the wilderness by the way as they came forth out of Egypt, *them*
they had not circumcised.
6For the children of Israel walked forty years in
the wilderness, till all the people *that were* men of
war, which came out of Egypt, were consumed, because they obeyed not the voice of the LORD: unto
whom the LORD sware that he would not shew them
the land, which the LORD sware unto their fathers
that he would give us, a land that floweth with milk
and honey.

NEW LIVING TRANSLATION

15The LORD had said to Joshua, 16"Command the
priests carrying the Ark of the Covenant* to come up
out of the riverbed." 17So Joshua gave the command.
18As soon as the priests carrying the Ark of the
LORD's Covenant came up out of the riverbed and
their feet were on high ground, the water of the Jordan returned and overflowed its banks as before.
19The people crossed the Jordan on the tenth day
of the first month.* Then they camped at Gilgal, just
east of Jericho. 20It was there at Gilgal that Joshua
piled up the twelve stones taken from the Jordan
River.
21Then Joshua said to the Israelites, "In the future
your children will ask, 'What do these stones mean?'
22Then you can tell them, 'This is where the Israelites
crossed the Jordan on dry ground.' 23For the LORD
your God dried up the river right before your eyes,
and he kept it dry until you were all across, just as he
did at the Red Sea* when he dried it up until we had
all crossed over. 24He did this so all the nations of the
earth might know that the LORD's hand is powerful,
and so you might fear the LORD your God forever."

5 When all the Amorite kings west of the Jordan
and all the Canaanite kings who lived along the
Mediterranean coast* heard how the LORD had dried
up the Jordan River so the people of Israel could
cross, they lost heart and were paralyzed with fear
because of them.

Israel Reestablishes Covenant Ceremonies

2At that time the LORD told Joshua, "Make flint knives
and circumcise this second generation of Israelites.*" 3So Joshua made flint knives and circumcised
the entire male population of Israel at Gibeath-
haaraloth.*
4Joshua had to circumcise them because all the
men who were old enough to fight in battle when
they left Egypt had died in the wilderness. 5Those
who left Egypt had all been circumcised, but none of
those born after the Exodus, during the years in the
wilderness, had been circumcised. 6The Israelites
had traveled in the wilderness for forty years until all
the men who were old enough to fight in battle when
they left Egypt had died. For they had disobeyed the
LORD, and the LORD vowed he would not let them enter the land he had sworn to give us—a land flowing

4:16 Hebrew *Ark of the Testimony.* **4:19** This day in the ancient Hebrew lunar calendar occurred in late March, April, or early May. **4:23** Hebrew *sea of reeds.* **5:1** Hebrew *along the sea.* **5:2** Or *circumcise the Israelites a second time.* **5:3** *Gibeath-haaraloth* means "hill of foreskins."

KING JAMES VERSION

7 And their children, *whom* he raised up in their
stead, them Joshua circumcised: for they were uncircumcised, because they had not circumcised
them by the way.
8 And it came to pass, when they had done circumcising all the people, that they abode in their places
in the camp, till they were whole.
9 And the LORD said unto Joshua, This day have
I rolled away the reproach of Egypt from off you.
Wherefore the name of the place is called Gilgal unto
this day.
10 And the children of Israel encamped in Gilgal,
and kept the passover on the fourteenth day of the
month at even in the plains of Jericho.
11 And they did eat of the old corn of the land on
the morrow after the passover, unleavened cakes,
and parched *corn* in the selfsame day.
12 And the manna ceased on the morrow after they
had eaten of the old corn of the land; neither had the
children of Israel manna any more; but they did eat
of the fruit of the land of Canaan that year.
13 And it came to pass, when Joshua was by Jericho,
that he lifted up his eyes and looked, and, behold,
there stood a man over against him with his sword
drawn in his hand: and Joshua went unto him, and
said unto him, *Art* thou for us, or for our adversaries?
14 And he said, Nay; but *as* captain of the host of
the LORD am I now come. And Joshua fell on his face
to the earth, and did worship, and said unto him,
What saith my lord unto his servant?
15 And the captain of the LORD's host said unto
Joshua, Loose thy shoe from off thy foot; for the
place whereon thou standest *is* holy. And Joshua
did so.

6 1 Now Jericho was straitly shut up because of
the children of Israel: none went out, and none
came in.
2 And the LORD said unto Joshua, See, I have given
into thine hand Jericho, and the king thereof, *and* the
mighty men of valour.
3 And ye shall compass the city, all *ye* men of war,
and go round about the city once. Thus shalt thou do
six days.
4 And seven priests shall bear before the ark seven
trumpets of rams' horns: and the seventh day ye shall
compass the city seven times, and the priests shall
blow with the trumpets.
5 And it shall come to pass, that when they make a
long *blast* with the ram's horn, *and* when ye hear the
sound of the trumpet, all the people shall shout with
a great shout; and the wall of the city shall fall down
flat, and the people shall ascend up every man
straight before him.
6 And Joshua the son of Nun called the priests, and
said unto them, Take up the ark of the covenant, and
let seven priests bear seven trumpets of rams' horns
before the ark of the LORD.

NEW LIVING TRANSLATION

with milk and honey. 7 So Joshua circumcised their
sons—those who had grown up to take their fathers'
places—for they had not been circumcised on the
way to the Promised Land. 8 After all the males had
been circumcised, they rested in the camp until they
were healed.
9 Then the LORD said to Joshua, "Today I have
rolled away the shame of your slavery in Egypt." So
that place has been called Gilgal* to this day.
10 While the Israelites were camped at Gilgal on
the plains of Jericho, they celebrated Passover on the
evening of the fourteenth day of the first month.*
11 The very next day they began to eat unleavened
bread and roasted grain harvested from the land.
12 No manna appeared on the day they first ate from
the crops of the land, and it was never seen again. So
from that time on the Israelites ate from the crops
of Canaan.

The LORD's Commander Confronts Joshua

13 When Joshua was near the town of Jericho, he
looked up and saw a man standing in front of him
with sword in hand. Joshua went up to him and demanded, "Are you friend or foe?"
14 "Neither one," he replied. "I am the commander
of the LORD's army."

At this, Joshua fell with his face to the ground in
reverence. "I am at your command," Joshua said.
"What do you want your servant to do?"
15 The commander of the LORD's army replied,
"Take off your sandals, for the place where you are
standing is holy." And Joshua did as he was told.

The Fall of Jericho

6 Now the gates of Jericho were tightly shut because the people were afraid of the Israelites.
No one was allowed to go out or in. 2 But the LORD
said to Joshua, "I have given you Jericho, its king, and
all its strong warriors. 3 You and your fighting men
should march around the town once a day for six
days. 4 Seven priests will walk ahead of the Ark, each
carrying a ram's horn. On the seventh day you are to
march around the town seven times, with the priests
blowing the horns. 5 When you hear the priests give
one long blast on the rams' horns, have all the people
shout as loud as they can. Then the walls of the town
will collapse, and the people can charge straight into
the town."
6 So Joshua called together the priests and said,
"Take up the Ark of the LORD's Covenant, and assign
seven priests to walk in front of it, each carrying a

5:9 *Gilgal* sounds like the Hebrew word *galal,* meaning "to roll." **5:10** This day in the ancient Hebrew lunar calendar occurred in late March, April, or early May.

KING JAMES VERSION

7And he said unto the people, Pass on, and compass the city, and let him that is armed pass on before the ark of the LORD.

8And it came to pass, when Joshua had spoken unto the people, that the seven priests bearing the seven trumpets of rams' horns passed on before the LORD, and blew with the trumpets: and the ark of the covenant of the LORD followed them.

9And the armed men went before the priests that blew with the trumpets, and the rereward came after the ark, *the priests* going on, and blowing with the trumpets.

10And Joshua had commanded the people, saying, Ye shall not shout, nor make any noise with your voice, neither shall *any* word proceed out of your mouth, until the day I bid you shout; then shall ye shout.

11So the ark of the LORD compassed the city, going about *it* once: and they came into the camp, and lodged in the camp.

12And Joshua rose early in the morning, and the priests took up the ark of the LORD.

13And seven priests bearing seven trumpets of rams' horns before the ark of the LORD went on continually, and blew with the trumpets: and the armed men went before them; but the rereward came after the ark of the LORD, *the priests* going on, and blowing with the trumpets.

14And the second day they compassed the city once, and returned into the camp: so they did six days.

15And it came to pass on the seventh day, that they rose early about the dawning of the day, and compassed the city after the same manner seven times: only on that day they compassed the city seven times.

16And it came to pass at the seventh time, when the priests blew with the trumpets, Joshua said unto the people, Shout; for the LORD hath given you the city.

17And the city shall be accursed, *even* it, and all that *are* therein, to the LORD: only Rahab the harlot shall live, she and all that *are* with her in the house, because she hid the messengers that we sent.

18And ye, in any wise keep *yourselves* from the accursed thing, lest ye make *yourselves* accursed, when ye take of the accursed thing, and make the camp of Israel a curse, and trouble it.

19But all the silver, and gold, and vessels of brass and iron, *are* consecrated unto the LORD: they shall come into the treasury of the LORD.

20So the people shouted when *the priests* blew with the trumpets: and it came to pass, when the people heard the sound of the trumpet, and the people shouted with a great shout, that the wall fell down flat, so that the people went up into the city, every man straight before him, and they took the city.

21And they utterly destroyed all that *was* in the city, both man and woman, young and old, and ox, and sheep, and ass, with the edge of the sword.

22But Joshua had said unto the two men that had spied out the country, Go into the harlot's house, and

NEW LIVING TRANSLATION

ram's horn." 7Then he gave orders to the people: "March around the town, and the armed men will lead the way in front of the Ark of the LORD."

8After Joshua spoke to the people, the seven priests with the rams' horns started marching in the presence of the LORD, blowing the horns as they marched. And the Ark of the LORD's Covenant followed behind them. 9Some of the armed men marched in front of the priests with the horns and some behind the Ark, with the priests continually blowing the horns. 10"Do not shout; do not even talk," Joshua commanded. "Not a single word from any of you until I tell you to shout. Then shout!" 11So the Ark of the LORD was carried around the town once that day, and then everyone returned to spend the night in the camp.

12Joshua got up early the next morning, and the priests again carried the Ark of the LORD. 13The seven priests with the rams' horns marched in front of the Ark of the LORD, blowing their horns. Again the armed men marched both in front of the priests with the horns and behind the Ark of the LORD. All this time the priests were blowing their horns. 14On the second day they again marched around the town once and returned to the camp. They followed this pattern for six days.

15On the seventh day the Israelites got up at dawn and marched around the town as they had done before. But this time they went around the town seven times. 16The seventh time around, as the priests sounded the long blast on their horns, Joshua commanded the people, "Shout! For the LORD has given you the town! 17Jericho and everything in it must be completely destroyed* as an offering to the LORD. Only Rahab the prostitute and the others in her house will be spared, for she protected our spies.

18"Do not take any of the things set apart for destruction, or you yourselves will be completely destroyed, and you will bring trouble on the camp of Israel. 19Everything made from silver, gold, bronze, or iron is sacred to the LORD and must be brought into his treasury."

20When the people heard the sound of the rams' horns, they shouted as loud as they could. Suddenly, the walls of Jericho collapsed, and the Israelites charged straight into the town and captured it. 21They completely destroyed everything in it with their swords—men and women, young and old, cattle, sheep, goats, and donkeys.

22Meanwhile, Joshua said to the two spies, "Keep

6:17 The Hebrew term used here refers to the complete consecration of things or people to the LORD, either by destroying them or by giving them as an offering; similarly in 6:18, 21.

KING JAMES VERSION

bring out thence the woman, and all that she hath, as ye sware unto her.

23 And the young men that were spies went in, and brought out Rahab, and her father, and her mother, and her brethren, and all that she had; and they brought out all her kindred, and left them without the camp of Israel.

24 And they burnt the city with fire, and all that *was* therein: only the silver, and the gold, and the vessels of brass and of iron, they put into the treasury of the house of the LORD.

25 And Joshua saved Rahab the harlot alive, and her father's household, and all that she had; and she dwelleth in Israel *even* unto this day; because she hid the messengers, which Joshua sent to spy out Jericho.

26 And Joshua adjured *them* at that time, saying, Cursed *be* the man before the LORD, that riseth up and buildeth this city Jericho: he shall lay the foundation thereof in his firstborn, and in his youngest *son* shall he set up the gates of it.

27 So the LORD was with Joshua; and his fame was *noised* throughout all the country.

7 1 But the children of Israel committed a trespass in the accursed thing: for Achan, the son of Carmi, the son of Zabdi, the son of Zerah, of the tribe of Judah, took of the accursed thing: and the anger of the LORD was kindled against the children of Israel.

2 And Joshua sent men from Jericho to Ai, which *is* beside Beth-aven, on the east side of Bethel, and spake unto them, saying, Go up and view the country. And the men went up and viewed Ai.

3 And they returned to Joshua, and said unto him, Let not all the people go up; but let about two or three thousand men go up and smite Ai; *and* make not all the people to labour thither; for they *are but* few.

4 So there went up thither of the people about three thousand men: and they fled before the men of Ai.

5 And the men of Ai smote of them about thirty and six men: for they chased them *from* before the gate *even* unto Shebarim, and smote them in the going down: wherefore the hearts of the people melted, and became as water.

6 And Joshua rent his clothes, and fell to the earth upon his face before the ark of the LORD until the eventide, he and the elders of Israel, and put dust upon their heads.

7 And Joshua said, Alas, O Lord GOD, wherefore hast thou at all brought this people over Jordan, to deliver us into the hand of the Amorites, to destroy us? would to God we had been content, and dwelt on the other side Jordan!

NEW LIVING TRANSLATION

your promise. Go to the prostitute's house and bring her out, along with all her family."

23 The men who had been spies went in and brought out Rahab, her father, mother, brothers, and all the other relatives who were with her. They moved her whole family to a safe place near the camp of Israel.

24 Then the Israelites burned the town and everything in it. Only the things made from silver, gold, bronze, or iron were kept for the treasury of the LORD's house. 25 So Joshua spared Rahab the prostitute and her relatives who were with her in the house, because she had hidden the spies Joshua sent to Jericho. And she lives among the Israelites to this day.

26 At that time Joshua invoked this curse:

"May the curse of the LORD fall on anyone
    who tries to rebuild the town of Jericho.
At the cost of his firstborn son,
    he will lay its foundation.
At the cost of his youngest son,
    he will set up its gates."

27 So the LORD was with Joshua, and his reputation spread throughout the land.

Ai Defeats the Israelites

7 But Israel violated the instructions about the things set apart for the LORD.* A man named Achan had stolen some of these dedicated things, so the LORD was very angry with the Israelites. Achan was the son of Carmi, a descendant of Zimri* son of Zerah, of the tribe of Judah.

2 Joshua sent some of his men from Jericho to spy out the town of Ai, east of Bethel, near Beth-aven. 3 When they returned, they told Joshua, "There's no need for all of us to go up there; it won't take more than two or three thousand men to attack Ai. Since there are so few of them, don't make all our people struggle to go up there."

4 So approximately 3,000 warriors were sent, but they were soundly defeated. The men of Ai 5 chased the Israelites from the town gate as far as the quarries,* and they killed about thirty-six who were retreating down the slope. The Israelites were paralyzed with fear at this turn of events, and their courage melted away.

6 Joshua and the elders of Israel tore their clothing in dismay, threw dust on their heads, and bowed face down to the ground before the Ark of the LORD until evening. 7 Then Joshua cried out, "Oh, Sovereign LORD, why did you bring us across the Jordan River if you are going to let the Amorites kill us? If only we

7:1a The Hebrew term used here refers to the complete consecration of things or people to the LORD, either by destroying them or by giving them as an offering; similarly in 7:11, 12, 13, 15. **7:1b** As in parallel text at 1 Chr 2:6; Hebrew reads *Zabdi*. Also in 7:17, 18. **7:5** Or *as far as Shebarim*.

KING JAMES VERSION

[8]O LORD, what shall I say, when Israel turneth their backs before their enemies!

[9]For the Canaanites and all the inhabitants of the land shall hear *of it,* and shall environ us round, and cut off our name from the earth: and what wilt thou do unto thy great name?

[10]And the LORD said unto Joshua, Get thee up; wherefore liest thou thus upon thy face?

[11]Israel hath sinned, and they have also transgressed my covenant which I commanded them: for they have even taken of the accursed thing, and have also stolen, and dissembled also, and they have put *it* even among their own stuff.

[12]Therefore the children of Israel could not stand before their enemies, *but* turned *their* backs before their enemies, because they were accursed: neither will I be with you any more, except ye destroy the accursed from among you.

[13]Up, sanctify the people, and say, Sanctify yourselves against tomorrow: for thus saith the LORD God of Israel, *There is* an accursed thing in the midst of thee, O Israel: thou canst not stand before thine enemies, until ye take away the accursed thing from among you.

[14]In the morning therefore ye shall be brought according to your tribes: and it shall be, *that* the tribe which the LORD taketh shall come according to the families *thereof;* and the family which the LORD shall take shall come by households; and the household which the LORD shall take shall come man by man.

[15]And it shall be, *that* he that is taken with the accursed thing shall be burnt with fire, he and all that he hath: because he hath transgressed the covenant of the LORD, and because he hath wrought folly in Israel.

[16]So Joshua rose up early in the morning, and brought Israel by their tribes; and the tribe of Judah was taken:

[17]And he brought the family of Judah; and he took the family of the Zarhites: and he brought the family of the Zarhites man by man; and Zabdi was taken:

[18]And he brought his household man by man; and Achan, the son of Carmi, the son of Zabdi, the son of Zerah, of the tribe of Judah, was taken.

[19]And Joshua said unto Achan, My son, give, I pray thee, glory to the LORD God of Israel, and make confession unto him; and tell me now what thou hast done; hide *it* not from me.

[20]And Achan answered Joshua, and said, Indeed I have sinned against the LORD God of Israel, and thus and thus have I done:

[21]When I saw among the spoils a goodly Babylonish garment, and two hundred shekels of silver, and a wedge of gold of fifty shekels weight, then I coveted them, and took them; and, behold, they *are*

NEW LIVING TRANSLATION

had been content to stay on the other side! [8]Lord, what can I say now that Israel has fled from its enemies? [9]For when the Canaanites and all the other people living in the land hear about it, they will surround us and wipe our name off the face of the earth. And then what will happen to the honor of your great name?"

[10]But the LORD said to Joshua, "Get up! Why are you lying on your face like this? [11]Israel has sinned and broken my covenant! They have stolen some of the things that I commanded must be set apart for me. And they have not only stolen them but have lied about it and hidden the things among their own belongings. [12]That is why the Israelites are running from their enemies in defeat. For now Israel itself has been set apart for destruction. I will not remain with you any longer unless you destroy the things among you that were set apart for destruction.

[13]"Get up! Command the people to purify themselves in preparation for tomorrow. For this is what the LORD, the God of Israel, says: Hidden among you, O Israel, are things set apart for the LORD. You will never defeat your enemies until you remove these things from among you.

[14]"In the morning you must present yourselves by tribes, and the LORD will point out the tribe to which the guilty man belongs. That tribe must come forward with its clans, and the LORD will point out the guilty clan. That clan will then come forward, and the LORD will point out the guilty family. Finally, each member of the guilty family must come forward one by one. [15]The one who has stolen what was set apart for destruction will himself be burned with fire, along with everything he has, for he has broken the covenant of the LORD and has done a horrible thing in Israel."

Achan's Sin

[16]Early the next morning Joshua brought the tribes of Israel before the LORD, and the tribe of Judah was singled out. [17]Then the clans of Judah came forward, and the clan of Zerah was singled out. Then the families of Zerah came forward, and the family of Zimri was singled out. [18]Every member of Zimri's family was brought forward person by person, and Achan was singled out.

[19]Then Joshua said to Achan, "My son, give glory to the LORD, the God of Israel, by telling the truth. Make your confession and tell me what you have done. Don't hide it from me."

[20]Achan replied, "It is true! I have sinned against the LORD, the God of Israel. [21]Among the plunder I saw a beautiful robe from Babylon,* 200 silver coins,* and a bar of gold weighing more than a pound.* I wanted them so much that I took them.

7:21a Hebrew *Shinar.* **7:21b** Hebrew *200 shekels of silver,* about 5 pounds or 2.3 kilograms in weight. **7:21c** Hebrew *50 shekels,* about 20 ounces or 570 grams in weight.

KING JAMES VERSION

hid in the earth in the midst of my tent, and the silver under it.

22 So Joshua sent messengers, and they ran unto the tent; and, behold, *it was* hid in his tent, and the silver under it.

23 And they took them out of the midst of the tent, and brought them unto Joshua, and unto all the children of Israel, and laid them out before the LORD.

24 And Joshua, and all Israel with him, took Achan the son of Zerah, and the silver, and the garment, and the wedge of gold, and his sons, and his daughters, and his oxen, and his asses, and his sheep, and his tent, and all that he had: and they brought them unto the valley of Achor.

25 And Joshua said, Why hast thou troubled us? the LORD shall trouble thee this day. And all Israel stoned him with stones, and burned them with fire, after they had stoned them with stones.

26 And they raised over him a great heap of stones unto this day. So the LORD turned from the fierceness of his anger. Wherefore the name of that place was called, The valley of Achor, unto this day.

8 1 And the LORD said unto Joshua, Fear not, neither be thou dismayed: take all the people of war with thee, and arise, go up to Ai: see, I have given into thy hand the king of Ai, and his people, and his city, and his land:

2 And thou shalt do to Ai and her king as thou didst unto Jericho and her king: only the spoil thereof, and the cattle thereof, shall ye take for a prey unto yourselves: lay thee an ambush for the city behind it.

3 So Joshua arose, and all the people of war, to go up against Ai: and Joshua chose out thirty thousand mighty men of valour, and sent them away by night.

4 And he commanded them, saying, Behold, ye shall lie in wait against the city, *even* behind the city: go not very far from the city, but be ye all ready:

5 And I, and all the people that *are* with me, will approach unto the city: and it shall come to pass, when they come out against us, as at the first, that we will flee before them,

6 (For they will come out after us) till we have drawn them from the city; for they will say, They flee before us, as at the first: therefore we will flee before them.

7 Then ye shall rise up from the ambush, and seize upon the city: for the LORD your God will deliver it into your hand.

8 And it shall be, when ye have taken the city, *that* ye shall set the city on fire: according to the commandment of the LORD shall ye do. See, I have commanded you.

9 Joshua therefore sent them forth: and they went to lie in ambush, and abode between Bethel and Ai, on the west side of Ai: but Joshua lodged that night among the people.

10 And Joshua rose up early in the morning, and

NEW LIVING TRANSLATION

They are hidden in the ground beneath my tent, with the silver buried deeper than the rest."

22 So Joshua sent some men to make a search. They ran to the tent and found the stolen goods hidden there, just as Achan had said, with the silver buried beneath the rest. 23 They took the things from the tent and brought them to Joshua and all the Israelites. Then they laid them on the ground in the presence of the LORD.

24 Then Joshua and all the Israelites took Achan, the silver, the robe, the bar of gold, his sons, daughters, cattle, donkeys, sheep, goats, tent, and everything he had, and they brought them to the valley of Achor. 25 Then Joshua said to Achan, "Why have you brought trouble on us? The LORD will now bring trouble on you." And all the Israelites stoned Achan and his family and burned their bodies. 26 They piled a great heap of stones over Achan, which remains to this day. That is why the place has been called the Valley of Trouble* ever since. So the LORD was no longer angry.

The Israelites Defeat Ai

8 Then the LORD said to Joshua, "Do not be afraid or discouraged. Take all your fighting men and attack Ai, for I have given you the king of Ai, his people, his town, and his land. 2 You will destroy them as you destroyed Jericho and its king. But this time you may keep the plunder and the livestock for yourselves. Set an ambush behind the town."

3 So Joshua and all the fighting men set out to attack Ai. Joshua chose 30,000 of his best warriors and sent them out at night 4 with these orders: "Hide in ambush close behind the town and be ready for action. 5 When our main army attacks, the men of Ai will come out to fight as they did before, and we will run away from them. 6 We will let them chase us until we have drawn them away from the town. For they will say, 'The Israelites are running away from us as they did before.' Then, while we are running from them, 7 you will jump up from your ambush and take possession of the town, for the LORD your God will give it to you. 8 Set the town on fire, as the LORD has commanded. You have your orders."

9 So they left and went to the place of ambush between Bethel and the west side of Ai. But Joshua remained among the people in the camp that night. 10 Early the next morning Joshua roused his men and

7:26 Hebrew *valley of Achor.*

KING JAMES VERSION

numbered the people, and went up, he and the elders
of Israel, before the people to Ai.
11 And all the people, *even the people* of war that
were with him, went up, and drew nigh, and came before the city, and pitched on the north side of Ai: now
there was a valley between them and Ai.
12 And he took about five thousand men, and set
them to lie in ambush between Bethel and Ai, on the
west side of the city.
13 And when they had set the people, *even* all the
host that *was* on the north of the city, and their liers
in wait on the west of the city, Joshua went that night
into the midst of the valley.
14 And it came to pass, when the king of Ai saw *it*,
that they hasted and rose up early, and the men of the
city went out against Israel to battle, he and all his
people, at a time appointed, before the plain; but he
wist not that *there were* liers in ambush against him
behind the city.
15 And Joshua and all Israel made as if they were
beaten before them, and fled by the way of the
wilderness.
16 And all the people that *were* in Ai were called together to pursue after them: and they pursued after
Joshua, and were drawn away from the city.
17 And there was not a man left in Ai or Bethel, that
went not out after Israel: and they left the city open,
and pursued after Israel.
18 And the LORD said unto Joshua, Stretch out the
spear that *is* in thy hand toward Ai; for I will give it
into thine hand. And Joshua stretched out the spear
that *he had* in his hand toward the city.
19 And the ambush arose quickly out of their place,
and they ran as soon as he had stretched out his
hand: and they entered into the city, and took it, and
hasted and set the city on fire.
20 And when the men of Ai looked behind them,
they saw, and, behold, the smoke of the city ascended
up to heaven, and they had no power to flee this way
or that way: and the people that fled to the wilderness turned back upon the pursuers.
21 And when Joshua and all Israel saw that the ambush had taken the city, and that the smoke of the
city ascended, then they turned again, and slew the
men of Ai.
22 And the other issued out of the city against
them; so they were in the midst of Israel, some on
this side, and some on that side: and they smote
them, so that they let none of them remain or escape.
23 And the king of Ai they took alive, and brought
him to Joshua.
24 And it came to pass, when Israel had made an
end of slaying all the inhabitants of Ai in the field, in
the wilderness wherein they chased them, and when
they were all fallen on the edge of the sword, until
they were consumed, that all the Israelites returned
unto Ai, and smote it with the edge of the sword.
25 And *so* it was, *that* all that fell that day, both of

NEW LIVING TRANSLATION

started toward Ai, accompanied by the elders of Israel. 11 All the fighting men who were with Joshua
marched in front of the town and camped on the
north side of Ai, with a valley between them and the
town. 12 That night Joshua sent 5,000 men to lie in
ambush between Bethel and Ai, on the west side of
the town. 13 So they stationed the main army north
of the town and the ambush west of the town. Joshua
himself spent that night in the valley.
14 When the king of Ai saw the Israelites across the
valley, he and all his army hurried out early in the
morning and attacked the Israelites at a place overlooking the Jordan Valley.* But he didn't realize there
was an ambush behind the town. 15 Joshua and the
Israelite army fled toward the wilderness as though
they were badly beaten. 16 Then all the men in the
town were called out to chase after them. In this way,
they were lured away from the town. 17 There was not
a man left in Ai or Bethel* who did not chase after
the Israelites, and the town was left wide open.
18 Then the LORD said to Joshua, "Point the spear in
your hand toward Ai, for I will hand the town over to
you." Joshua did as he was commanded. 19 As soon as
Joshua gave this signal, all the men in ambush
jumped up from their position and poured into the
town. They quickly captured it and set it on fire.
20 When the men of Ai looked behind them, smoke
from the town was filling the sky, and they had nowhere to go. For the Israelites who had fled in the
direction of the wilderness now turned on their pursuers. 21 When Joshua and all the other Israelites saw
that the ambush had succeeded and that smoke was
rising from the town, they turned and attacked the
men of Ai. 22 Meanwhile, the Israelites who were inside the town came out and attacked the enemy from
the rear. So the men of Ai were caught in the middle,
with Israelite fighters on both sides. Israel attacked
them, and not a single person survived or escaped.
23 Only the king of Ai was taken alive and brought
to Joshua.
24 When the Israelite army finished chasing and
killing all the men of Ai in the open fields, they went
back and finished off everyone inside. 25 So the

8:14 Hebrew *the Arabah.* **8:17** Some manuscripts lack *or Bethel.*

KING JAMES VERSION

men and women, *were* twelve thousand, *even* all the
men of Ai.
26For Joshua drew not his hand back, wherewith
he stretched out the spear, until he had utterly destroyed all the inhabitants of Ai.
27Only the cattle and the spoil of that city Israel
took for a prey unto themselves, according unto the
word of the LORD which he commanded Joshua.
28And Joshua burnt Ai, and made it an heap for
ever, *even* a desolation unto this day.
29And the king of Ai he hanged on a tree until
eventide: and as soon as the sun was down, Joshua
commanded that they should take his carcase down
from the tree, and cast it at the entering of the gate of
the city, and raise thereon a great heap of stones, *that
remaineth* unto this day.

30Then Joshua built an altar unto the LORD God of
Israel in mount Ebal,
31As Moses the servant of the LORD commanded
the children of Israel, as it is written in the book of
the law of Moses, an altar of whole stones, over
which no man hath lift up *any* iron: and they offered
thereon burnt offerings unto the LORD, and sacrificed peace offerings.
32And he wrote there upon the stones a copy of the
law of Moses, which he wrote in the presence of the
children of Israel.
33And all Israel, and their elders, and officers, and
their judges, stood on this side the ark and on that
side before the priests the Levites, which bare the ark
of the covenant of the LORD, as well the stranger, as
he that was born among them; half of them over
against mount Gerizim, and half of them over
against mount Ebal; as Moses the servant of the LORD
had commanded before, that they should bless the
people of Israel.
34And afterward he read all the words of the law,
the blessings and cursings, according to all that is
written in the book of the law.
35There was not a word of all that Moses commanded, which Joshua read not before all the congregation of Israel, with the women, and the little ones,
and the strangers that were conversant among them.

9 1And it came to pass, when all the kings which
were on this side Jordan, in the hills, and in the
valleys, and in all the coasts of the great sea over
against Lebanon, the Hittite, and the Amorite, the
Canaanite, the Perizzite, the Hivite, and the Jebusite,
heard *thereof;*
2That they gathered themselves together, to fight
with Joshua and with Israel, with one accord.
3And when the inhabitants of Gibeon heard what
Joshua had done unto Jericho and to Ai,

NEW LIVING TRANSLATION

entire population of Ai, including men and women,
was wiped out that day—12,000 in all. 26For Joshua
kept holding out his spear until everyone who had
lived in Ai was completely destroyed.* 27Only the
livestock and the treasures of the town were not destroyed, for the Israelites kept these as plunder for
themselves, as the LORD had commanded Joshua.
28So Joshua burned the town of Ai,* and it became a
permanent mound of ruins, desolate to this very day.
29Joshua impaled the king of Ai on a sharpened
pole and left him there until evening. At sunset the
Israelites took down the body, as Joshua commanded, and threw it in front of the town gate. They
piled a great heap of stones over him that can still be
seen today.

The LORD's Covenant Renewed

30Then Joshua built an altar to the LORD, the God of
Israel, on Mount Ebal. 31He followed the commands
that Moses the LORD's servant had written in the
Book of Instruction: "Make me an altar from stones
that are uncut and have not been shaped with iron
tools."* Then on the altar they presented burnt offerings and peace offerings to the LORD. 32And as the Israelites watched, Joshua copied onto the stones of
the altar* the instructions Moses had given them.
33Then all the Israelites—foreigners and native-
born alike—along with the elders, officers, and
judges, were divided into two groups. One group
stood in front of Mount Gerizim, the other in front of
Mount Ebal. Each group faced the other, and between
them stood the Levitical priests carrying the Ark of
the LORD's Covenant. This was all done according to
the commands that Moses, the servant of the LORD,
had previously given for blessing the people of Israel.
34Joshua then read to them all the blessings and
curses Moses had written in the Book of Instruction.
35Every word of every command that Moses had ever
given was read to the entire assembly of Israel, including the women and children and the foreigners
who lived among them.

The Gibeonites Deceive Israel

9 Now all the kings west of the Jordan River heard
about what had happened. These were the
kings of the Hittites, Amorites, Canaanites, Perizzites,
Hivites, and Jebusites, who lived in the hill country, in
the western foothills,* and along the coast of the
Mediterranean Sea* as far north as the Lebanon
mountains. 2These kings combined their armies to
fight as one against Joshua and the Israelites.
3But when the people of Gibeon heard what Joshua

8:26 The Hebrew term used here refers to the complete consecration of things or people to the LORD, either by destroying them or by giving them as an offering. **8:28** *Ai* means "ruin." **8:31** Exod 20:25; Deut 27:5-6. **8:32** Hebrew *onto the stones.* **9:1a** Hebrew *the Shephelah.* **9:1b** Hebrew *the Great Sea.*

KING JAMES VERSION

4They did work wilily, and went and made as if
they had been ambassadors, and took old sacks
upon their asses, and wine bottles, old, and rent, and
bound up;
5And old shoes and clouted upon their feet, and
old garments upon them; and all the bread of their
provision was dry *and* mouldy.
6And they went to Joshua unto the camp at Gilgal,
and said unto him, and to the men of Israel, We be
come from a far country: now therefore make ye a
league with us.
7And the men of Israel said unto the Hivites, Peradventure ye dwell among us; and how shall we make
a league with you?
8And they said unto Joshua, We *are* thy servants.
And Joshua said unto them, Who *are* ye? and from
whence come ye?
9And they said unto him, From a very far country
thy servants are come because of the name of the
LORD thy God: for we have heard the fame of him,
and all that he did in Egypt,
10And all that he did to the two kings of the Amorites, that *were* beyond Jordan, to Sihon king of
Heshbon, and to Og king of Bashan, which *was* at
Ashtaroth.
11Wherefore our elders and all the inhabitants of
our country spake to us, saying, Take victuals with
you for the journey, and go to meet them, and say
unto them, We *are* your servants: therefore now
make ye a league with us.
12This our bread we took hot *for* our provision out
of our houses on the day we came forth to go unto
you; but now, behold, it is dry, and it is mouldy:
13And these bottles of wine, which we filled, *were*
new; and, behold, they be rent: and these our garments and our shoes are become old by reason of the
very long journey.
14And the men took of their victuals, and asked
not *counsel* at the mouth of the LORD.
15And Joshua made peace with them, and made a
league with them, to let them live: and the princes of
the congregation sware unto them.
16And it came to pass at the end of three days after
they had made a league with them, that they heard
that they *were* their neighbours, and *that* they dwelt
among them.
17And the children of Israel journeyed, and came
unto their cities on the third day. Now their cities
were Gibeon, and Chephirah, and Beeroth, and
Kirjath-jearim.
18And the children of Israel smote them not, because the princes of the congregation had sworn
unto them by the LORD God of Israel. And all the congregation murmured against the princes.
19But all the princes said unto all the congregation,
We have sworn unto them by the LORD God of Israel:
now therefore we may not touch them.
20This we will do to them; we will even let them

NEW LIVING TRANSLATION

had done to Jericho and Ai, 4they resorted to deception to save themselves. They sent ambassadors to
Joshua, loading their donkeys with weathered saddle-
bags and old, patched wineskins. 5They put on worn-
out, patched sandals and ragged clothes. And the
bread they took with them was dry and moldy.
6When they arrived at the camp of Israel at Gilgal,
they told Joshua and the men of Israel, "We have
come from a distant land to ask you to make a peace
treaty with us."
7The Israelites replied to these Hivites, "How do
we know you don't live nearby? For if you do, we cannot make a treaty with you."
8They replied, "We are your servants."
"But who are you?" Joshua demanded. "Where do
you come from?"
9They answered, "Your servants have come from a
very distant country. We have heard of the might of
the LORD your God and of all he did in Egypt. 10We
have also heard what he did to the two Amorite kings
east of the Jordan River—King Sihon of Heshbon
and King Og of Bashan (who lived in Ashtaroth). 11So
our elders and all our people instructed us, 'Take
supplies for a long journey. Go meet with the people
of Israel and tell them, "We are your servants; please
make a treaty with us."'
12"This bread was hot from the ovens when we
left our homes. But now, as you can see, it is dry and
moldy. 13These wineskins were new when we filled
them, but now they are old and split open. And our
clothing and sandals are worn out from our very
long journey."
14So the Israelites examined their food, but they
did not consult the LORD. 15Then Joshua made a
peace treaty with them and guaranteed their safety,
and the leaders of the community ratified their
agreement with a binding oath.
16Three days after making the treaty, they learned
that these people actually lived nearby! 17The Israelites set out at once to investigate and reached their
towns in three days. The names of these towns were
Gibeon, Kephirah, Beeroth, and Kiriath-jearim. 18But
the Israelites did not attack the towns, for the Israelite leaders had made a vow to them in the name of
the LORD, the God of Israel.
The people of Israel grumbled against their leaders because of the treaty. 19But the leaders replied,
"Since we have sworn an oath in the presence of the
LORD, the God of Israel, we cannot touch them.
20This is what we must do. We must let them live, for

live, lest wrath be upon us, because of the oath which
we sware unto them.
21 And the princes said unto them, Let them live;
but let them be hewers of wood and drawers of water
unto all the congregation; as the princes had promised them.
22 And Joshua called for them, and he spake unto
them, saying, Wherefore have ye beguiled us, saying,
We *are* very far from you; when ye dwell among us?
23 Now therefore ye *are* cursed, and there shall
none of you be freed from being bondmen, and hewers of wood and drawers of water for the house of
my God.
24 And they answered Joshua, and said, Because it
was certainly told thy servants, how that the LORD thy
God commanded his servant Moses to give you all
the land, and to destroy all the inhabitants of the
land from before you, therefore we were sore afraid
of our lives because of you, and have done this thing.
25 And now, behold, we *are* in thine hand: as it
seemeth good and right unto thee to do unto us, do.
26 And so did he unto them, and delivered them
out of the hand of the children of Israel, that they
slew them not.
27 And Joshua made them that day hewers of wood
and drawers of water for the congregation, and for
the altar of the LORD, even unto this day, in the place
which he should choose.

10 1 Now it came to pass, when Adoni-zedek
king of Jerusalem had heard how Joshua had
taken Ai, and had utterly destroyed it; as he had done
to Jericho and her king, so he had done to Ai and her
king; and how the inhabitants of Gibeon had made
peace with Israel, and were among them;
2 That they feared greatly, because Gibeon *was* a
great city, as one of the royal cities, and because it
was greater than Ai, and all the men thereof *were*
mighty.
3 Wherefore Adoni-zedek king of Jerusalem sent
unto Hoham king of Hebron, and unto Piram king of
Jarmuth, and unto Japhia king of Lachish, and unto
Debir king of Eglon, saying,
4 Come up unto me, and help me, that we may
smite Gibeon: for it hath made peace with Joshua
and with the children of Israel.
5 Therefore the five kings of the Amorites, the king
of Jerusalem, the king of Hebron, the king of Jarmuth, the king of Lachish, the king of Eglon, gathered themselves together, and went up, they and all
their hosts, and encamped before Gibeon, and made
war against it.
6 And the men of Gibeon sent unto Joshua to the
camp to Gilgal, saying, Slack not thy hand from thy
servants; come up to us quickly, and save us, and help
us: for all the kings of the Amorites that dwell in the
mountains are gathered together against us.
7 So Joshua ascended from Gilgal, he, and all the

divine anger would come upon us if we broke our
oath. 21 Let them live." So they made them woodcutters and water carriers for the entire community,
as the Israelite leaders directed.
22 Joshua called together the Gibeonites and said,
"Why did you lie to us? Why did you say that you live
in a distant land when you live right here among us?
23 May you be cursed! From now on you will always be
servants who cut wood and carry water for the house
of my God."
24 They replied, "We did it because we—your servants—were clearly told that the LORD your God commanded his servant Moses to give you this entire
land and to destroy all the people living in it. So we
feared greatly for our lives because of you. That is
why we have done this. 25 Now we are at your mercy—
do to us whatever you think is right."
26 So Joshua did not allow the people of Israel to
kill them. 27 But that day he made the Gibeonites the
woodcutters and water carriers for the community
of Israel and for the altar of the LORD—wherever the
LORD would choose to build it. And that is what they
do to this day.

Israel Defeats the Southern Armies

10 Adoni-zedek, king of Jerusalem, heard that
Joshua had captured and completely destroyed* Ai and killed its king, just as he had destroyed the town of Jericho and killed its king. He
also learned that the Gibeonites had made peace
with Israel and were now their allies. 2 He and his
people became very afraid when they heard all this
because Gibeon was a large town—as large as the
royal cities and larger than Ai. And the Gibeonite
men were strong warriors.
3 So King Adoni-zedek of Jerusalem sent messengers to several other kings: Hoham of Hebron, Piram
of Jarmuth, Japhia of Lachish, and Debir of Eglon.
4 "Come and help me destroy Gibeon," he urged
them, "for they have made peace with Joshua and the
people of Israel." 5 So these five Amorite kings combined their armies for a united attack. They moved
all their troops into place and attacked Gibeon.
6 The men of Gibeon quickly sent messengers to
Joshua at his camp in Gilgal. "Don't abandon your
servants now!" they pleaded. "Come at once! Save us!
Help us! For all the Amorite kings who live in the hill
country have joined forces to attack us."
7 So Joshua and his entire army, including his best

10:1 The Hebrew term used here refers to the complete consecration of things or people to the LORD, either by destroying them or by giving them as an offering; also in 10:28, 35, 37, 39, 40.

people of war with him, and all the mighty men of
valour.

8And the LORD said unto Joshua, Fear them not: for
I have delivered them into thine hand; there shall not
a man of them stand before thee.

9Joshua therefore came unto them suddenly, *and*
went up from Gilgal all night.

10And the LORD discomfited them before Israel,
and slew them with a great slaughter at Gibeon,
and chased them along the way that goeth up to
Beth- horon, and smote them to Azekah, and unto
Makkedah.

11And it came to pass, as they fled from before Israel, *and* were in the going down to Beth-horon, that
the LORD cast down great stones from heaven upon
them unto Azekah, and they died: *they were* more
which died with hailstones than *they* whom the children of Israel slew with the sword.

12Then spake Joshua to the LORD in the day when
the LORD delivered up the Amorites before the children of Israel, and he said in the sight of Israel, Sun,
stand thou still upon Gibeon; and thou, Moon, in the
valley of Ajalon.

13And the sun stood still, and the moon stayed, until the people had avenged themselves upon their enemies. *Is* not this written in the book of Jasher? So
the sun stood still in the midst of heaven, and hasted
not to go down about a whole day.

14And there was no day like that before it or after
it, that the LORD hearkened unto the voice of a man:
for the LORD fought for Israel.

15And Joshua returned, and all Israel with him,
unto the camp to Gilgal.

16But these five kings fled, and hid themselves in a
cave at Makkedah.

17And it was told Joshua, saying, The five kings are
found hid in a cave at Makkedah.

18And Joshua said, Roll great stones upon the
mouth of the cave, and set men by it for to keep
them:

19And stay ye not, *but* pursue after your enemies,
and smite the hindmost of them; suffer them not to
enter into their cities: for the LORD your God hath delivered them into your hand.

20And it came to pass, when Joshua and the children of Israel had made an end of slaying them with
a very great slaughter, till they were consumed, that
the rest *which* remained of them entered into fenced
cities.

21And all the people returned to the camp to
Joshua at Makkedah in peace: none moved his
tongue against any of the children of Israel.

22Then said Joshua, Open the mouth of the cave,
and bring out those five kings unto me out of the
cave.

23And they did so, and brought forth those five
kings unto him out of the cave, the king of Jerusalem,

warriors, left Gilgal and set out for Gibeon. 8"Do not
be afraid of them," the LORD said to Joshua, "for I
have given you victory over them. Not a single one of
them will be able to stand up to you."

9Joshua traveled all night from Gilgal and took the
Amorite armies by surprise. 10The LORD threw them
into a panic, and the Israelites slaughtered great
numbers of them at Gibeon. Then the Israelites
chased the enemy along the road to Beth-horon, killing them all along the way to Azekah and Makkedah.
11As the Amorites retreated down the road from
Beth-horon, the LORD destroyed them with a terrible
hailstorm from heaven that continued until they
reached Azekah. The hail killed more of the enemy
than the Israelites killed with the sword.

12On the day the LORD gave the Israelites victory
over the Amorites, Joshua prayed to the LORD in front
of all the people of Israel. He said,

"Let the sun stand still over Gibeon,
and the moon over the valley of Aijalon."

13So the sun stood still and the moon stayed in place
until the nation of Israel had defeated its enemies.

Is this event not recorded in *The Book of Jashar**?
The sun stayed in the middle of the sky, and it did not
set as on a normal day.* 14There has never been a
day like this one before or since, when the LORD answered such a prayer. Surely the LORD fought for
Israel that day!

15Then Joshua and the Israelite army returned to
their camp at Gilgal.

Joshua Kills the Five Southern Kings

16During the battle the five kings escaped and hid in
a cave at Makkedah. 17When Joshua heard that they
had been found, 18he issued this command: "Cover
the opening of the cave with large rocks, and place
guards at the entrance to keep the kings inside.
19The rest of you continue chasing the enemy and
cut them down from the rear. Don't give them a
chance to get back to their towns, for the LORD your
God has given you victory over them."

20So Joshua and the Israelite army continued the
slaughter and completely crushed the enemy. They
totally wiped out the five armies except for a tiny
remnant that managed to reach their fortified towns.
21Then the Israelites returned safely to Joshua in the
camp at Makkedah. After that, no one dared to speak
even a word against Israel.

22Then Joshua said, "Remove the rocks covering
the opening of the cave, and bring the five kings
to me." 23So they brought the five kings out of the
cave—the kings of Jerusalem, Hebron, Jarmuth,

10:13a Or *The Book of the Upright.* **10:13b** Or *did not set for about a whole day.*

KING JAMES VERSION

the king of Hebron, the king of Jarmuth, the king of
Lachish, *and* the king of Eglon.
24And it came to pass, when they brought out
those kings unto Joshua, that Joshua called for all the
men of Israel, and said unto the captains of the men
of war which went with him, Come near, put your
feet upon the necks of these kings. And they came
near, and put their feet upon the necks of them.
25And Joshua said unto them, Fear not, nor be dismayed, be strong and of good courage: for thus shall
the LORD do to all your enemies against whom ye
fight.
26And afterward Joshua smote them, and slew
them, and hanged them on five trees: and they were
hanging upon the trees until the evening.
27And it came to pass at the time of the going down
of the sun, *that* Joshua commanded, and they took
them down off the trees, and cast them into the cave
wherein they had been hid, and laid great stones in
the cave's mouth, *which remain* until this very day.
28And that day Joshua took Makkedah, and smote
it with the edge of the sword, and the king thereof he
utterly destroyed, them, and all the souls that *were*
therein; he let none remain: and he did to the king of
Makkedah as he did unto the king of Jericho.
29Then Joshua passed from Makkedah, and all
Israel with him, unto Libnah, and fought against
Libnah:
30And the LORD delivered it also, and the king
thereof, into the hand of Israel; and he smote it with
the edge of the sword, and all the souls that *were*
therein; he let none remain in it; but did unto the
king thereof as he did unto the king of Jericho.
31And Joshua passed from Libnah, and all Israel
with him, unto Lachish, and encamped against it,
and fought against it:
32And the LORD delivered Lachish into the hand of
Israel, which took it on the second day, and smote it
with the edge of the sword, and all the souls that
were therein, according to all that he had done to
Libnah.
33Then Horam king of Gezer came up to help
Lachish; and Joshua smote him and his people, until
he had left him none remaining.
34And from Lachish Joshua passed unto Eglon,
and all Israel with him; and they encamped against it,
and fought against it:
35And they took it on that day, and smote it with
the edge of the sword, and all the souls that *were*
therein he utterly destroyed that day, according to all
that he had done to Lachish.
36And Joshua went up from Eglon, and all Israel
with him, unto Hebron; and they fought against it:
37And they took it, and smote it with the edge of
the sword, and the king thereof, and all the cities
thereof, and all the souls that *were* therein; he left
none remaining, according to all that he had done to

NEW LIVING TRANSLATION

Lachish, and Eglon. 24When they brought them out,
Joshua told the commanders of his army, "Come and
put your feet on the kings' necks." And they did as
they were told.
25"Don't ever be afraid or discouraged," Joshua
told his men. "Be strong and courageous, for the
LORD is going to do this to all of your enemies."
26Then Joshua killed each of the five kings and impaled them on five sharpened poles, where they
hung until evening.
27As the sun was going down, Joshua gave instructions for the bodies of the kings to be taken down
from the poles and thrown into the cave where they
had been hiding. Then they covered the opening of
the cave with a pile of large rocks, which remains to
this very day.

Israel Destroys the Southern Towns

28That same day Joshua captured and destroyed the
town of Makkedah. He killed everyone in it, including the king, leaving no survivors. He destroyed them
all, and he killed the king of Makkedah as he had
killed the king of Jericho. 29Then Joshua and the Israelites went to Libnah and attacked it. 30There, too, the
LORD gave them the town and its king. He killed
everyone in it, leaving no survivors. Then Joshua
killed the king of Libnah as he had killed the king of
Jericho.
31From Libnah, Joshua and the Israelites went to
Lachish and attacked it. 32Here again, the LORD gave
them Lachish. Joshua took it on the second day and
killed everyone in it, just as he had done at Libnah.
33During the attack on Lachish, King Horam of Gezer
arrived with his army to help defend the town. But
Joshua's men killed him and his army, leaving no
survivors.
34Then Joshua and the Israelite army went on to
Eglon and attacked it. 35They captured it that day
and killed everyone in it. He completely destroyed
everyone, just as he had done at Lachish. 36From Eglon, Joshua and the Israelite army went up to Hebron
and attacked it. 37They captured the town and killed
everyone in it, including its king, leaving no survivors. They did the same thing to all of its surrounding

KING JAMES VERSION

Eglon; but destroyed it utterly, and all the souls that
were therein.
38And Joshua returned, and all Israel with him, to
Debir; and fought against it:
39And he took it, and the king thereof, and all the
cities thereof; and they smote them with the edge of
the sword, and utterly destroyed all the souls that
were therein; he left none remaining: as he had done
to Hebron, so he did to Debir, and to the king thereof;
as he had done also to Libnah, and to her king.
40So Joshua smote all the country of the hills, and
of the south, and of the vale, and of the springs, and
all their kings: he left none remaining, but utterly destroyed all that breathed, as the LORD God of Israel
commanded.
41And Joshua smote them from Kadesh-barnea
even unto Gaza, and all the country of Goshen, even
unto Gibeon.
42And all these kings and their land did Joshua
take at one time, because the LORD God of Israel
fought for Israel.
43And Joshua returned, and all Israel with him,
unto the camp to Gilgal.

11 1And it came to pass, when Jabin king of Hazor had heard *those things*, that he sent to
Jobab king of Madon, and to the king of Shimron,
and to the king of Achshaph,
2And to the kings that *were* on the north of the
mountains, and of the plains south of Chinneroth,
and in the valley, and in the borders of Dor on the
west,
3*And to* the Canaanite on the east and on the west,
and *to* the Amorite, and the Hittite, and the Perizzite,
and the Jebusite in the mountains, and *to* the Hivite
under Hermon in the land of Mizpeh.
4And they went out, they and all their hosts with
them, much people, even as the sand that *is* upon
the sea shore in multitude, with horses and chariots
very many.
5And when all these kings were met together, they
came and pitched together at the waters of Merom,
to fight against Israel.
6And the LORD said unto Joshua, Be not afraid because of them: for tomorrow about this time will I
deliver them up all slain before Israel: thou shalt
hough their horses, and burn their chariots with fire.
7So Joshua came, and all the people of war with
him, against them by the waters of Merom suddenly;
and they fell upon them.
8And the LORD delivered them into the hand of
Israel, who smote them, and chased them unto great
Zidon, and unto Misrephoth-maim, and unto the
valley of Mizpeh eastward; and they smote them, until they left them none remaining.
9And Joshua did unto them as the LORD bade him:
he houghed their horses, and burnt their chariots
with fire.

NEW LIVING TRANSLATION

villages. And just as he had done at Eglon, he completely destroyed the entire population.
38Then Joshua and the Israelites turned back and
attacked Debir. 39He captured the town, its king, and
all of its surrounding villages. He completely destroyed everyone in it, leaving no survivors. He did to
Debir and its king just what he had done to Hebron
and to Libnah and its king.
40So Joshua conquered the whole region—the
kings and people of the hill country, the Negev, the
western foothills,* and the mountain slopes. He
completely destroyed everyone in the land, leaving
no survivors, just as the LORD, the God of Israel, had
commanded. 41Joshua slaughtered them from
Kadesh-barnea to Gaza and from the region around
the town of Goshen up to Gibeon. 42Joshua conquered all these kings and their land in a single campaign, for the LORD, the God of Israel, was fighting for
his people.
43Then Joshua and the Israelite army returned to
their camp at Gilgal.

Israel Defeats the Northern Armies

11 When King Jabin of Hazor heard what had
happened, he sent messages to the following
kings: King Jobab of Madon; the king of Shimron; the
king of Acshaph; 2all the kings of the northern hill
country; the kings in the Jordan Valley south of Galilee*; the kings in the Galilean foothills*; the kings of
Naphoth-dor on the west; 3the kings of Canaan, both
east and west; the kings of the Amorites, the Hittites,
the Perizzites, the Jebusites in the hill country, and
the Hivites in the towns on the slopes of Mount Hermon in the land of Mizpah.
4All these kings came out to fight. Their combined
armies formed a vast horde. And with all their horses
and chariots, they covered the landscape like the
sand on the seashore. 5The kings joined forces and
established their camp around the water near Merom to fight against Israel.
6Then the LORD said to Joshua, "Do not be afraid
of them. By this time tomorrow I will hand all of
them over to Israel as dead men. Then you must
cripple their horses and burn their chariots."
7So Joshua and all his fighting men traveled to the
water near Merom and attacked suddenly. 8And the
LORD gave them victory over their enemies. The Israelites chased them as far as Greater Sidon and
Misrephoth-maim, and eastward into the valley of
Mizpah, until not one enemy warrior was left alive.
9Then Joshua crippled the horses and burned all the
chariots, as the LORD had instructed.

10:40 Hebrew *the Shephelah.* 11:2a Hebrew *in the Arabah south of Kinnereth.* 11:2b Hebrew *the Shephelah;* also in 11:16.

KING JAMES VERSION

10 And Joshua at that time turned back, and took
Hazor, and smote the king thereof with the sword:
for Hazor beforetime was the head of all those
kingdoms.

11 And they smote all the souls that *were* therein
with the edge of the sword, utterly destroying *them:*
there was not any left to breathe: and he burnt Hazor
with fire.

12 And all the cities of those kings, and all the kings
of them, did Joshua take, and smote them with the
edge of the sword, *and* he utterly destroyed them,
as Moses the servant of the LORD commanded.

13 But *as for* the cities that stood still in their
strength, Israel burned none of them, save Hazor
only; *that* did Joshua burn.

14 And all the spoil of these cities, and the cattle,
the children of Israel took for a prey unto themselves; but every man they smote with the edge of the
sword, until they had destroyed them, neither left
they any to breathe.

15 As the LORD commanded Moses his servant, so
did Moses command Joshua, and so did Joshua; he
left nothing undone of all that the LORD commanded
Moses.

16 So Joshua took all that land, the hills, and all the
south country, and all the land of Goshen, and the
valley, and the plain, and the mountain of Israel, and
the valley of the same;

17 *Even* from the mount Halak, that goeth up to
Seir, even unto Baal-gad in the valley of Lebanon under mount Hermon: and all their kings he took, and
smote them, and slew them.

18 Joshua made war a long time with all those kings.

19 There was not a city that made peace with the
children of Israel, save the Hivites the inhabitants of
Gibeon: all *other* they took in battle.

20 For it was of the LORD to harden their hearts,
that they should come against Israel in battle, that he
might destroy them utterly, *and* that they might have
no favour, but that he might destroy them, as the
LORD commanded Moses.

21 And at that time came Joshua, and cut off the
Anakims from the mountains, from Hebron, from
Debir, from Anab, and from all the mountains of
Judah, and from all the mountains of Israel: Joshua
destroyed them utterly with their cities.

22 There was none of the Anakims left in the land
of the children of Israel: only in Gaza, in Gath, and in
Ashdod, there remained.

23 So Joshua took the whole land, according to all
that the LORD said unto Moses; and Joshua gave it for
an inheritance unto Israel according to their divisions by their tribes. And the land rested from war.

NEW LIVING TRANSLATION

10 Joshua then turned back and captured Hazor
and killed its king. (Hazor had at one time been the
capital of all these kingdoms.) 11 The Israelites completely destroyed* every living thing in the city, leaving no survivors. Not a single person was spared. And
then Joshua burned the city.

12 Joshua slaughtered all the other kings and their
people, completely destroying them, just as Moses,
the servant of the LORD, had commanded. 13 But the
Israelites did not burn any of the towns built on
mounds except Hazor, which Joshua burned. 14 And
the Israelites took all the plunder and livestock of
the ravaged towns for themselves. But they killed
all the people, leaving no survivors. 15 As the LORD
had commanded his servant Moses, so Moses commanded Joshua. And Joshua did as he was told, carefully obeying all the commands that the LORD had
given to Moses.

16 So Joshua conquered the entire region—the hill
country, the entire Negev, the whole area around the
town of Goshen, the western foothills, the Jordan
Valley,* the mountains of Israel, and the Galilean
foothills. 17 The Israelite territory now extended all
the way from Mount Halak, which leads up to Seir
in the south, as far north as Baal-gad at the foot of
Mount Hermon in the valley of Lebanon. Joshua
killed all the kings of those territories, 18 waging war
for a long time to accomplish this. 19 No one in this
region made peace with the Israelites except the
Hivites of Gibeon. All the others were defeated. 20 For
the LORD hardened their hearts and caused them to
fight the Israelites. So they were completely destroyed without mercy, as the LORD had commanded
Moses.

21 During this period Joshua destroyed all the descendants of Anak, who lived in the hill country of
Hebron, Debir, Anab, and the entire hill country of
Judah and Israel. He killed them all and completely
destroyed their towns. 22 None of the descendants of
Anak were left in all the land of Israel, though some
still remained in Gaza, Gath, and Ashdod.

23 So Joshua took control of the entire land, just as
the LORD had instructed Moses. He gave it to the
people of Israel as their special possession, dividing
the land among the tribes. So the land finally had
rest from war.

11:11 The Hebrew term used here refers to the complete consecration of things or people to the LORD, either by destroying them or by giving them as an offering; also in 11:12, 20, 21. **11:16** Hebrew *the Shephelah, the Arabah.*

KING JAMES VERSION

12

1 Now these *are* the kings of the land, which the children of Israel smote, and possessed their land on the other side Jordan toward the rising of the sun, from the river Arnon unto mount Hermon, and all the plain on the east:

2 Sihon king of the Amorites, who dwelt in Heshbon, *and* ruled from Aroer, which *is* upon the bank of the river Arnon, and from the middle of the river, and from half Gilead, even unto the river Jabbok, *which is* the border of the children of Ammon;

3 And from the plain to the sea of Chinneroth on the east, and unto the sea of the plain, *even* the salt sea on the east, the way to Beth-jeshimoth; and from the south, under Ashdoth-pisgah:

4 And the coast of Og king of Bashan, *which was* of the remnant of the giants, that dwelt at Ashtaroth and at Edrei,

5 And reigned in mount Hermon, and in Salcah, and in all Bashan, unto the border of the Geshurites and the Maachathites, and half Gilead, the border of Sihon king of Heshbon.

6 Them did Moses the servant of the LORD and the children of Israel smite: and Moses the servant of the LORD gave it *for* a possession unto the Reubenites, and the Gadites, and the half tribe of Manasseh.

7 And these *are* the kings of the country which Joshua and the children of Israel smote on this side Jordan on the west, from Baal-gad in the valley of Lebanon even unto the mount Halak, that goeth up to Seir; which Joshua gave unto the tribes of Israel *for* a possession according to their divisions;

8 In the mountains, and in the valleys, and in the plains, and in the springs, and in the wilderness, and in the south country; the Hittites, the Amorites, and the Canaanites, the Perizzites, the Hivites, and the Jebusites:

9 The king of Jericho, one; the king of Ai, which *is* beside Bethel, one;

10 The king of Jerusalem, one; the king of Hebron, one;

11 The king of Jarmuth, one; the king of Lachish, one;

12 The king of Eglon, one; the king of Gezer, one;

13 The king of Debir, one; the king of Geder, one;

14 The king of Hormah, one; the king of Arad, one;

NEW LIVING TRANSLATION

Kings Defeated East of the Jordan

12

These are the kings east of the Jordan River who had been killed by the Israelites and whose land was taken. Their territory extended from the Arnon Gorge to Mount Hermon and included all the land east of the Jordan Valley.*

2 King Sihon of the Amorites, who lived in Heshbon, was defeated. His kingdom included Aroer, on the edge of the Arnon Gorge, and extended from the middle of the Arnon Gorge to the Jabbok River, which serves as a border for the Ammonites. This territory included the southern half of the territory
of Gilead. 3 Sihon also controlled the Jordan Valley and regions to the east—from as far north as the Sea of Galilee to as far south as the Dead Sea,* including the road to Beth-jeshimoth and southward to the slopes of Pisgah.

4 King Og of Bashan, the last of the Rephaites, lived
at Ashtaroth and Edrei. 5 He ruled a territory stretching from Mount Hermon to Salecah in the north and to all of Bashan in the east, and westward to the borders of the kingdoms of Geshur and Maacah. This territory included the northern half of Gilead, as far as the boundary of King Sihon of Heshbon.

6 Moses, the servant of the LORD, and the Israelites had destroyed the people of King Sihon and King Og. And Moses gave their land as a possession to the tribes of Reuben, Gad, and the half-tribe of Manasseh.

Kings Defeated West of the Jordan

7 The following is a list of the kings that Joshua and the Israelite armies defeated on the west side of the Jordan, from Baal-gad in the valley of Lebanon to Mount Halak, which leads up to Seir. (Joshua gave this land to the tribes of Israel as their possession,
8 including the hill country, the western foothills,* the Jordan Valley, the mountain slopes, the Judean wilderness, and the Negev. The people who lived in this region were the Hittites, the Amorites, the Canaanites, the Perizzites, the Hivites, and the Jebusites.) These are the kings Israel defeated:

9 The king of Jericho
The king of Ai, near Bethel
10 The king of Jerusalem
The king of Hebron
11 The king of Jarmuth
The king of Lachish
12 The king of Eglon
The king of Gezer
13 The king of Debir
The king of Geder
14 The king of Hormah
The king of Arad

12:1 Hebrew *the Arabah;* also in 12:3, 8. **12:3** Hebrew *from the Sea of Kinnereth to the Sea of the Arabah, which is the Salt Sea.* **12:8** Hebrew *the Shephelah.*

KING JAMES VERSION

15 The king of Libnah, one; the king of Adullam, one;

16 The king of Makkedah, one; the king of Bethel, one;

17 The king of Tappuah, one; the king of Hepher, one;

18 The king of Aphek, one; the king of Lasharon, one;

19 The king of Madon, one; the king of Hazor, one;

20 The king of Shimron-meron, one; the king of Achshaph, one;

21 The king of Taanach, one; the king of Megiddo, one;

22 The king of Kedesh, one; the king of Jokneam of Carmel, one;

23 The king of Dor in the coast of Dor, one; the king of the nations of Gilgal, one;

24 The king of Tirzah, one: all the kings thirty and one.

13 1 Now Joshua was old *and* stricken in years; and the LORD said unto him, Thou art old *and* stricken in years, and there remaineth yet very much land to be possessed.

2 This *is* the land that yet remaineth: all the borders of the Philistines, and all Geshuri,

3 From Sihor, which *is* before Egypt, even unto the borders of Ekron northward, *which* is counted to the Canaanite: five lords of the Philistines; the Gazathites, and the Ashdothites, the Eshkalonites, the Gittites, and the Ekronites; also the Avites:

4 From the south, all the land of the Canaanites, and Mearah that *is* beside the Sidonians unto Aphek, to the borders of the Amorites:

5 And the land of the Giblites, and all Lebanon, toward the sunrising, from Baal-gad under mount Hermon unto the entering into Hamath.

6 All the inhabitants of the hill country from Lebanon unto Misrephoth-maim, *and* all the Sidonians, them will I drive out from before the children of Israel: only divide thou it by lot unto the Israelites for an inheritance, as I have commanded thee.

7 Now therefore divide this land for an inheritance unto the nine tribes, and the half tribe of Manasseh,

8 With whom the Reubenites and the Gadites have received their inheritance, which Moses gave them, beyond Jordan eastward, *even* as Moses the servant of the LORD gave them;

9 From Aroer, that *is* upon the bank of the river Arnon, and the city that *is* in the midst of the river, and all the plain of Medeba unto Dibon;

NEW LIVING TRANSLATION

15 The king of Libnah
The king of Adullam
16 The king of Makkedah
The king of Bethel
17 The king of Tappuah
The king of Hepher
18 The king of Aphek
The king of Lasharon
19 The king of Madon
The king of Hazor
20 The king of Shimron-meron
The king of Acshaph
21 The king of Taanach
The king of Megiddo
22 The king of Kedesh
The king of Jokneam in Carmel
23 The king of Dor in the town of Naphoth-dor*
The king of Goyim in Gilgal*
24 The king of Tirzah.

In all, thirty-one kings were defeated.

The Land Yet to Be Conquered

13 When Joshua was an old man, the LORD said
to him, "You are growing old, and much land
remains to be conquered. 2 This is the territory that
remains: all the regions of the Philistines and the
Geshurites, 3 and the larger territory of the Canaanites, extending from the stream of Shihor on the border of Egypt, northward to the boundary of Ekron. It
includes the territory of the five Philistine rulers of
Gaza, Ashdod, Ashkelon, Gath, and Ekron. The land
of the Avvites 4 in the south also remains to be conquered. In the north, the following area has not yet
been conquered: all the land of the Canaanites, including Mearah (which belongs to the Sidonians),
stretching northward to Aphek on the border of the
Amorites; 5 the land of the Gebalites and all of the
Lebanon mountain area to the east, from Baal-gad
below Mount Hermon to Lebo-hamath; 6 and all the
hill country from Lebanon to Misrephoth-maim, including all the land of the Sidonians.

"I myself will drive these people out of the land
ahead of the Israelites. So be sure to give this land to
Israel as a special possession, just as I have commanded you. 7 Include all this territory as Israel's
possession when you divide this land among the
nine tribes and the half-tribe of Manasseh."

The Land Divided East of the Jordan

8 Half the tribe of Manasseh and the tribes of Reuben and Gad had already received their grants of land on the east side of the Jordan, for Moses, the servant of the LORD, had previously assigned this land to them.

9 Their territory extended from Aroer on the edge
of the Arnon Gorge (including the town in the

12:23a Hebrew *Naphath-dor*, a variant spelling of Naphoth-dor.
12:23b Greek version reads *Goyim in Galilee*.

KING JAMES VERSION

10 And all the cities of Sihon king of the Amorites, which reigned in Heshbon, unto the border of the children of Ammon;

11 And Gilead, and the border of the Geshurites and Maachathites, and all mount Hermon, and all Bashan unto Salcah;

12 All the kingdom of Og in Bashan, which reigned in Ashtaroth and in Edrei, who remained of the remnant of the giants: for these did Moses smite, and cast them out.

13 Nevertheless the children of Israel expelled not the Geshurites, nor the Maachathites: but the Geshurites and the Maachathites dwell among the Israelites until this day.

14 Only unto the tribe of Levi he gave none inheritance; the sacrifices of the LORD God of Israel made by fire *are* their inheritance, as he said unto them.

15 And Moses gave unto the tribe of the children of Reuben *inheritance* according to their families.

16 And their coast was from Aroer, that *is* on the bank of the river Arnon, and the city that *is* in the midst of the river, and all the plain by Medeba;

17 Heshbon, and all her cities that *are* in the plain; Dibon, and Bamoth-baal, and Beth-baal-meon,

18 And Jahaza, and Kedemoth, and Mephaath,

19 And Kirjathaim, and Sibmah, and Zareth-shahar in the mount of the valley,

20 And Beth-peor, and Ashdoth-pisgah, and Beth-jeshimoth,

21 And all the cities of the plain, and all the kingdom of Sihon king of the Amorites, which reigned in Heshbon, whom Moses smote with the princes of Midian, Evi, and Rekem, and Zur, and Hur, and Reba, *which were* dukes of Sihon, dwelling in the country.

22 Balaam also the son of Beor, the soothsayer, did the children of Israel slay with the sword among them that were slain by them.

23 And the border of the children of Reuben was Jordan, and the border *thereof*. This *was* the inheritance of the children of Reuben after their families, the cities and the villages thereof.

24 And Moses gave *inheritance* unto the tribe of Gad, *even* unto the children of Gad according to their families.

25 And their coast was Jazer, and all the cities of Gilead, and half the land of the children of Ammon, unto Aroer that *is* before Rabbah;

26 And from Heshbon unto Ramath-mizpeh, and Betonim; and from Mahanaim unto the border of Debir;

NEW LIVING TRANSLATION

middle of the gorge) to the plain beyond Medeba,
as far as Dibon. 10 It also included all the towns of
King Sihon of the Amorites, who had reigned in
Heshbon, and extended as far as the borders of
Ammon. 11 It included Gilead, the territory of the
kingdoms of Geshur and Maacah, all of Mount
Hermon, all of Bashan as far as Salecah, 12 and
all the territory of King Og of Bashan, who had
reigned in Ashtaroth and Edrei. King Og was the
last of the Rephaites, for Moses had attacked
them and driven them out. 13 But the Israelites
failed to drive out the people of Geshur and
Maacah, so they continue to live among the
Israelites to this day.

An Allotment for the Tribe of Levi

14 Moses did not assign any allotment of land to the tribe of Levi. Instead, as the LORD had promised them, their allotment came from the offerings burned on the altar to the LORD, the God of Israel.

The Land Given to the Tribe of Reuben

15 Moses had assigned the following area to the clans of the tribe of Reuben.

16 Their territory extended from Aroer on the
edge of the Arnon Gorge (including the town in
the middle of the gorge) to the plain beyond
Medeba. 17 It included Heshbon and the other
towns on the plain—Dibon, Bamoth-baal, Beth-
baal-meon, 18 Jahaz, Kedemoth, Mephaath,
19 Kiriathaim, Sibmah, Zereth-shahar on the hill
above the valley, 20 Beth-peor, the slopes of Pisgah,
and Beth-jeshimoth.

21 The land of Reuben also included all the
towns of the plain and the entire kingdom of
Sihon. Sihon was the Amorite king who had
reigned in Heshbon and was killed by Moses along
with the leaders of Midian—Evi, Rekem, Zur, Hur,
and Reba—princes living in the region who were
allied with Sihon. 22 The Israelites had also killed
Balaam son of Beor, who used magic to tell the
future. 23 The Jordan River marked the western
boundary for the tribe of Reuben. The towns and
their surrounding villages in this area were given
as a homeland to the clans of the tribe of Reuben.

The Land Given to the Tribe of Gad

24 Moses had assigned the following area to the clans of the tribe of Gad.

25 Their territory included Jazer, all the towns
of Gilead, and half of the land of Ammon, as far
as the town of Aroer just west of* Rabbah. 26 It
extended from Heshbon to Ramath-mizpeh and
Betonim, and from Mahanaim to the territory
of Lo-debar.* 27 In the valley were Beth-haram,

13:25 Hebrew *in front of.* **13:26** Hebrew *Li-debir*, apparently a variant spelling of Lo-debar (compare 2 Sam 9:4; 17:27; Amos 6:13).

27And in the valley, Beth-aram, and Beth-nimrah,
and Succoth, and Zaphon, the rest of the kingdom of
Sihon king of Heshbon, Jordan and *his* border, *even*
unto the edge of the sea of Chinnereth on the other
side Jordan eastward.
28This *is* the inheritance of the children of Gad
after their families, the cities, and their villages.

29And Moses gave *inheritance* unto the half tribe
of Manasseh: and *this* was *the possession* of the half
tribe of the children of Manasseh by their families.
30And their coast was from Mahanaim, all Bashan,
all the kingdom of Og king of Bashan, and all the
towns of Jair, which *are* in Bashan, threescore cities:
31And half Gilead, and Ashtaroth, and Edrei, cities
of the kingdom of Og in Bashan, *were pertaining*
unto the children of Machir the son of Manasseh,
even to the one half of the children of Machir by
their families.
32These *are the countries* which Moses did distribute for inheritance in the plains of Moab, on the
other side Jordan, by Jericho, eastward.
33But unto the tribe of Levi Moses gave not *any* inheritance: the LORD God of Israel *was* their inheritance, as he said unto them.

14 1And these *are the countries* which the
children of Israel inherited in the land of
Canaan, which Eleazar the priest, and Joshua the son
of Nun, and the heads of the fathers of the tribes
of the children of Israel, distributed for inheritance
to them.
2By lot *was* their inheritance, as the LORD commanded by the hand of Moses, for the nine tribes,
and *for* the half tribe.
3For Moses had given the inheritance of two tribes
and an half tribe on the other side Jordan: but unto
the Levites he gave none inheritance among them.
4For the children of Joseph were two tribes, Manasseh and Ephraim: therefore they gave no part unto
the Levites in the land, save cities to dwell *in*, with
their suburbs for their cattle and for their substance.
5As the LORD commanded Moses, so the children
of Israel did, and they divided the land.
6Then the children of Judah came unto Joshua in
Gilgal: and Caleb the son of Jephunneh the Kenezite
said unto him, Thou knowest the thing that the LORD
said unto Moses the man of God concerning me and
thee in Kadesh-barnea.
7Forty years old *was* I when Moses the servant of
the LORD sent me from Kadesh-barnea to espy out
the land; and I brought him word again as *it was* in
mine heart.
8Nevertheless my brethren that went up with me
made the heart of the people melt: but I wholly followed the LORD my God.

Beth-nimrah, Succoth, Zaphon, and the rest of the
kingdom of King Sihon of Heshbon. The western
boundary ran along the Jordan River, extended
as far north as the tip of the Sea of Galilee,* and
then turned eastward. 28The towns and their
surrounding villages in this area were given as
a homeland to the clans of the tribe of Gad.

The Land Given to the Half-Tribe of Manasseh

29Moses had assigned the following area to the clans
of the half-tribe of Manasseh.

30Their territory extended from Mahanaim,
including all of Bashan, all the former kingdom of
King Og, and the sixty towns of Jair in Bashan. 31It
also included half of Gilead and King Og's royal
cities of Ashtaroth and Edrei. All this was given to
the clans of the descendants of Makir, who was
Manasseh's son.

32These are the allotments Moses had made while
he was on the plains of Moab, across the Jordan
River, east of Jericho. 33But Moses gave no allotment
of land to the tribe of Levi, for the LORD, the God of
Israel, had promised that he himself would be their
allotment.

The Land Divided West of the Jordan

14 The remaining tribes of Israel received land
in Canaan as allotted by Eleazar the priest,
Joshua son of Nun, and the tribal leaders. 2These
nine and a half tribes received their grants of land by
means of sacred lots, in accordance with the LORD's
command through Moses. 3Moses had already given
a grant of land to the two and a half tribes on the east
side of the Jordan River, but he had given the Levites
no such allotment. 4The descendants of Joseph had
become two separate tribes—Manasseh and Ephraim. And the Levites were given no land at all, only
towns to live in with surrounding pasturelands for
their livestock and all their possessions. 5So the land
was distributed in strict accordance with the LORD's
commands to Moses.

Caleb Requests His Land

6A delegation from the tribe of Judah, led by Caleb
son of Jephunneh the Kenizzite, came to Joshua at
Gilgal. Caleb said to Joshua, "Remember what the
LORD said to Moses, the man of God, about you and
me when we were at Kadesh-barnea. 7I was forty
years old when Moses, the servant of the LORD, sent
me from Kadesh-barnea to explore the land of Canaan. I returned and gave an honest report, 8but my
brothers who went with me frightened the people
from entering the Promised Land. For my part, I

13:27 Hebrew *Sea of Kinnereth.*

KING JAMES VERSION

9And Moses sware on that day, saying, Surely the land whereon thy feet have trodden shall be thine inheritance, and thy children's for ever, because thou hast wholly followed the LORD my God.

10And now, behold, the LORD hath kept me alive, as he said, these forty and five years, even since the LORD spake this word unto Moses, while *the children of* Israel wandered in the wilderness: and now, lo, I *am* this day fourscore and five years old.

11As yet I *am as* strong this day as *I was* in the day that Moses sent me: as my strength *was* then, even so *is* my strength now, for war, both to go out, and to come in.

12Now therefore give me this mountain, whereof the LORD spake in that day; for thou heardest in that day how the Anakims *were* there, and *that* the cities *were* great *and* fenced: if so be the LORD *will be* with me, then I shall be able to drive them out, as the LORD said.

13And Joshua blessed him, and gave unto Caleb the son of Jephunneh Hebron for an inheritance.

14Hebron therefore became the inheritance of Caleb the son of Jephunneh the Kenezite unto this day, because that he wholly followed the LORD God of Israel.

15And the name of Hebron before *was* Kirjath-arba; *which Arba was* a great man among the Anakims. And the land had rest from war.

15 1*This* then was the lot of the tribe of the children of Judah by their families; *even* to the border of Edom the wilderness of Zin southward *was* the uttermost part of the south coast.

2And their south border was from the shore of the salt sea, from the bay that looketh southward:

3And it went out to the south side to Maaleh-acrabbim, and passed along to Zin, and ascended up on the south side unto Kadesh-barnea, and passed along to Hezron, and went up to Adar, and fetched a compass to Karkaa:

4*From thence* it passed toward Azmon, and went out unto the river of Egypt; and the goings out of that coast were at the sea: this shall be your south coast.

5And the east border *was* the salt sea, *even* unto the end of Jordan. And *their* border in the north quarter *was* from the bay of the sea at the uttermost part of Jordan:

6And the border went up to Beth-hogla, and passed along by the north of Beth-arabah; and the border went up to the stone of Bohan the son of Reuben:

7And the border went up toward Debir from the valley of Achor, and so northward, looking toward Gilgal, that *is* before the going up to Adummim, which *is* on the south side of the river: and the border passed toward the waters of En-shemesh, and the goings out thereof were at En-rogel:

8And the border went up by the valley of the son of

NEW LIVING TRANSLATION

wholeheartedly followed the LORD my God. 9So that day Moses solemnly promised me, 'The land of Canaan on which you were just walking will be your grant of land and that of your descendants forever, because you wholeheartedly followed the LORD my God.'

10"Now, as you can see, the LORD has kept me alive and well as he promised for all these forty-five years since Moses made this promise—even while Israel wandered in the wilderness. Today I am eighty-five years old. 11I am as strong now as I was when Moses sent me on that journey, and I can still travel and fight as well as I could then. 12So give me the hill country that the LORD promised me. You will remember that as scouts we found the descendants of Anak living there in great, walled towns. But if the LORD is with me, I will drive them out of the land, just as the LORD said."

13So Joshua blessed Caleb son of Jephunneh and gave Hebron to him as his portion of land. 14Hebron still belongs to the descendants of Caleb son of Jephunneh the Kenizzite because he wholeheartedly followed the LORD, the God of Israel. 15(Previously Hebron had been called Kiriath-arba. It had been named after Arba, a great hero of the descendants of Anak.)

And the land had rest from war.

The Land Given to the Tribe of Judah

15 The allotment for the clans of the tribe of Judah reached southward to the border of Edom, as far south as the wilderness of Zin.

2The southern boundary began at the south bay of the Dead Sea,* 3ran south of Scorpion Pass* into the wilderness of Zin, and then went south of Kadesh-barnea to Hezron. Then it went up to Addar, where it turned toward Karka. 4From there it passed to Azmon until it finally reached the Brook of Egypt, which it followed to the Mediterranean Sea.* This was their* southern boundary.

5The eastern boundary extended along the Dead Sea to the mouth of the Jordan River.

The northern boundary began at the bay where the Jordan River empties into the Dead Sea, 6went up from there to Beth-hoglah, then proceeded north of Beth-arabah to the Stone of Bohan. (Bohan was Reuben's son.) 7From that point it went through the valley of Achor to Debir, turning north toward Gilgal, which is across from the slopes of Adummim on the south side of the valley. From there the boundary extended to the springs at En-shemesh and on to En-rogel. 8The boundary then passed through the

15:2 Hebrew *the Salt Sea;* also in 15:5. **15:3** Hebrew *Akrabbim.* **15:4a** Hebrew *the sea;* also in 15:11. **15:4b** Hebrew *your.*

KING JAMES VERSION

Hinnom unto the south side of the Jebusite; the same *is* Jerusalem: and the border went up to the top of the mountain that *lieth* before the valley of Hinnom westward, which *is* at the end of the valley of the giants northward:

9 And the border was drawn from the top of the hill unto the fountain of the water of Nephtoah, and went out to the cities of mount Ephron; and the border was drawn to Baalah, which *is* Kirjath-jearim:

10 And the border compassed from Baalah westward unto mount Seir, and passed along unto the side of mount Jearim, which *is* Chesalon, on the north side, and went down to Beth-shemesh, and passed on to Timnah:

11 And the border went out unto the side of Ekron northward: and the border was drawn to Shicron, and passed along to mount Baalah, and went out unto Jabneel; and the goings out of the border were at the sea.

12 And the west border *was* to the great sea, and the coast *thereof.* This *is* the coast of the children of Judah round about according to their families.

13 And unto Caleb the son of Jephunneh he gave a part among the children of Judah, according to the commandment of the LORD to Joshua, *even* the city of Arba the father of Anak, which *city is* Hebron.

14 And Caleb drove thence the three sons of Anak, Sheshai, and Ahiman, and Talmai, the children of Anak.

15 And he went up thence to the inhabitants of Debir: and the name of Debir before *was* Kirjath-sepher.

16 And Caleb said, He that smiteth Kirjath-sepher, and taketh it, to him will I give Achsah my daughter to wife.

17 And Othniel the son of Kenaz, the brother of Caleb, took it: and he gave him Achsah his daughter to wife.

18 And it came to pass, as she came *unto him,* that she moved him to ask of her father a field: and she lighted off *her* ass; and Caleb said unto her, What wouldest thou?

19 Who answered, Give me a blessing; for thou hast given me a south land; give me also springs of water. And he gave her the upper springs, and the nether springs.

20 This *is* the inheritance of the tribe of the children of Judah according to their families.

21 And the uttermost cities of the tribe of the children of Judah toward the coast of Edom southward were Kabzeel, and Eder, and Jagur,

22 And Kinah, and Dimonah, and Adadah,

23 And Kedesh, and Hazor, and Ithnan,

24 Ziph, and Telem, and Bealoth,

NEW LIVING TRANSLATION

valley of Ben-Hinnom, along the southern
slopes of the Jebusites, where the city of
Jerusalem is located. Then it went west to the
top of the mountain above the valley of Hinnom,
and on up to the northern end of the valley of
Rephaim. 9 From there the boundary extended
from the top of the mountain to the spring at
the waters of Nephtoah,* and from there to the
towns on Mount Ephron. Then it turned toward
Baalah (that is, Kiriath-jearim). 10 The boundary
circled west of Baalah to Mount Seir, passed
along to the town of Kesalon on the northern
slope of Mount Jearim, and went down to Beth-
shemesh and on to Timnah. 11 The boundary
then proceeded to the slope of the hill north of
Ekron, where it turned toward Shikkeron and
Mount Baalah. It passed Jabneel and ended at
the Mediterranean Sea.

12 The western boundary was the shoreline of
the Mediterranean Sea.*

These are the boundaries for the clans of the tribe of Judah.

The Land Given to Caleb

13 The LORD commanded Joshua to assign some of
Judah's territory to Caleb son of Jephunneh. So Caleb was given the town of Kiriath-arba (that is, Hebron), which had been named after Anak's ancestor.
14 Caleb drove out the three groups of Anakites—the
descendants of Sheshai, Ahiman, and Talmai, the
sons of Anak.

15 From there he went to fight against the people
living in the town of Debir (formerly called Kiriath-
sepher). 16 Caleb said, "I will give my daughter Acsah
in marriage to the one who attacks and captures
Kiriath-sepher." 17 Othniel, the son of Caleb's brother
Kenaz, was the one who conquered it, so Acsah became Othniel's wife.

18 When Acsah married Othniel, she urged him* to
ask her father for a field. As she got down off her
donkey, Caleb asked her, "What's the matter?"

19 She said, "Give me another gift. You have already
given me land in the Negev; now please give me
springs of water, too." So Caleb gave her the upper
and lower springs.

The Towns Allotted to Judah

20 This was the homeland allocated to the clans of the
tribe of Judah.

21 The towns of Judah situated along the borders
of Edom in the extreme south were Kabzeel,
Eder, Jagur, 22 Kinah, Dimonah, Adadah,
23 Kedesh, Hazor, Ithnan, 24 Ziph, Telem, Bealoth,

15:9 Or *the spring at Me-nephtoah.* 15:12 Hebrew *the Great Sea;* also in 15:47. 15:18 Some Greek manuscripts read *he urged her.*

KING JAMES VERSION

25 And Hazor, Hadattah, and Kerioth, *and* Hezron,
which *is* Hazor,
26 Amam, and Shema, and Moladah,
27 And Hazar-gaddah, and Heshmon, and Beth-
palet,
28 And Hazar-shual, and Beer-sheba, and Biz-
jothjah,
29 Baalah, and Iim, and Azem,
30 And Eltolad, and Chesil, and Hormah,
31 And Ziklag, and Madmannah, and Sansannah,
32 And Lebaoth, and Shilhim, and Ain, and Rimmon: all the cities *are* twenty and nine, with their
villages:
33 *And* in the valley, Eshtaol, and Zoreah, and
Ashnah,
34 And Zanoah, and En-gannim, Tappuah, and
Enam,
35 Jarmuth, and Adullam, Socoh, and Azekah,
36 And Sharaim, and Adithaim, and Gederah, and
Gederothaim; fourteen cities with their villages:
37 Zenan, and Hadashah, and Migdal-gad,
38 And Dilean, and Mizpeh, and Joktheel,
39 Lachish, and Bozkath, and Eglon,
40 And Cabbon, and Lahmam, and Kithlish,
41 And Gederoth, Beth-dagon, and Naamah, and
Makkedah; sixteen cities with their villages:
42 Libnah, and Ether, and Ashan,
43 And Jiphtah, and Ashnah, and Nezib,
44 And Keilah, and Achzib, and Mareshah; nine
cities with their villages:
45 Ekron, with her towns and her villages:
46 From Ekron even unto the sea, all that *lay* near
Ashdod, with their villages:
47 Ashdod with her towns and her villages, Gaza
with her towns and her villages, unto the river of
Egypt, and the great sea, and the border *thereof:*
48 And in the mountains, Shamir, and Jattir, and
Socoh,
49 And Dannah, and Kirjath-sannah, which *is*
Debir,
50 And Anab, and Eshtemoh, and Anim,
51 And Goshen, and Holon, and Giloh; eleven cities
with their villages:
52 Arab, and Dumah, and Eshean,
53 And Janum, and Beth-tappuah, and Aphekah,
54 And Humtah, and Kirjath-arba, which *is* Hebron,
and Zior; nine cities with their villages:
55 Maon, Carmel, and Ziph, and Juttah,
56 And Jezreel, and Jokdeam, and Zanoah,
57 Cain, Gibeah, and Timnah; ten cities with their
villages:
58 Halhul, Beth-zur, and Gedor,
59 And Maarath, and Beth-anoth, and Eltekon; six
cities with their villages:
60 Kirjath-baal, which *is* Kirjath-jearim, and Rabbah; two cities with their villages:
61 In the wilderness, Beth-arabah, Middin, and
Secacah,

NEW LIVING TRANSLATION

25 Hazor-hadattah, Kerioth-hezron (that is, Hazor),
26 Amam, Shema, Moladah, 27 Hazar-gaddah,
Heshmon, Beth-pelet, 28 Hazar-shual, Beersheba,
Biziothiah, 29 Baalah, Iim, Ezem, 30 Eltolad, Kesil,
Hormah, 31 Ziklag, Madmannah, Sansannah,
32 Lebaoth, Shilhim, Ain, and Rimmon—twenty-
nine towns with their surrounding villages.
33 The following towns situated in the western
foothills* were also given to Judah: Eshtaol,
Zorah, Ashnah, 34 Zanoah, En-gannim, Tappuah,
Enam, 35 Jarmuth, Adullam, Socoh, Azekah,
36 Shaaraim, Adithaim, Gederah, and
Gederothaim—fourteen towns with their
surrounding villages.
37 Also included were Zenan, Hadashah,
Migdal-gad, 38 Dilean, Mizpeh, Joktheel,
39 Lachish, Bozkath, Eglon, 40 Cabbon, Lahmam,
Kitlish, 41 Gederoth, Beth-dagon, Naamah,
and Makkedah—sixteen towns with their
surrounding villages.
42 Besides these, there were Libnah, Ether,
Ashan, 43 Iphtah, Ashnah, Nezib, 44 Keilah,
Aczib, and Mareshah—nine towns with their
surrounding villages.
45 The territory of the tribe of Judah also
included Ekron and its surrounding settlements
and villages. 46 From Ekron the boundary
extended west and included the towns near
Ashdod with their surrounding villages. 47 It also
included Ashdod with its surrounding settlements and villages and Gaza with its settlements
and villages, as far as the Brook of Egypt and
along the coast of the Mediterranean Sea.
48 Judah also received the following towns in
the hill country: Shamir, Jattir, Socoh, 49 Dannah,
Kiriath-sannah (that is, Debir), 50 Anab, Eshtemoh,
Anim, 51 Goshen, Holon, and Giloh—eleven towns
with their surrounding villages.
52 Also included were the towns of Arab,
Dumah, Eshan, 53 Janim, Beth-tappuah, Aphekah,
54 Humtah, Kiriath-arba (that is, Hebron), and
Zior—nine towns with their surrounding villages.
55 Besides these, there were Maon, Carmel,
Ziph, Juttah, 56 Jezreel, Jokdeam, Zanoah, 57 Kain,
Gibeah, and Timnah—ten towns with their
surrounding villages.
58 In addition, there were Halhul, Beth-zur,
Gedor, 59 Maarath, Beth-anoth, and Eltekon—
six towns with their surrounding villages.
60 There were also Kiriath-baal (that is, Kiriath-
jearim) and Rabbah—two towns with their
surrounding villages.
61 In the wilderness there were the towns of

15:33 Hebrew *the Shephelah.*

62 And Nibshan, and the city of Salt, and En-gedi;
six cities with their villages.
63 As for the Jebusites the inhabitants of Jerusalem,
the children of Judah could not drive them out: but
the Jebusites dwell with the children of Judah at
Jerusalem unto this day.

16 1 And the lot of the children of Joseph fell
from Jordan by Jericho, unto the water of Jericho on the east, to the wilderness that goeth up from
Jericho throughout mount Bethel.
2 And goeth out from Bethel to Luz, and passeth
along unto the borders of Archi to Ataroth,
3 And goeth down westward to the coast of Japh-
leti, unto the coast of Beth-horon the nether, and to
Gezer: and the goings out thereof are at the sea.
4 So the children of Joseph, Manasseh and Ephraim, took their inheritance.

5 And the border of the children of Ephraim according to their families was *thus:* even the border of
their inheritance on the east side was Ataroth-addar,
unto Beth-horon the upper;
6 And the border went out toward the sea to
Michmethah on the north side; and the border went
about eastward unto Taanath-shiloh, and passed by
it on the east to Janohah;
7 And it went down from Janohah to Ataroth, and
to Naarath, and came to Jericho, and went out at
Jordan.
8 The border went out from Tappuah westward
unto the river Kanah; and the goings out thereof
were at the sea. This *is* the inheritance of the tribe of
the children of Ephraim by their families.
9 And the separate cities for the children of Ephraim *were* among the inheritance of the children of
Manasseh, all the cities with their villages.
10 And they drave not out the Canaanites that dwelt
in Gezer: but the Canaanites dwell among the Ephraimites unto this day, and serve under tribute.

17 1 There was also a lot for the tribe of Manasseh; for he *was* the firstborn of Joseph; *to wit,*
for Machir the firstborn of Manasseh, the father of
Gilead: because he was a man of war, therefore he
had Gilead and Bashan.
2 There was also *a lot* for the rest of the children of
Manasseh by their families; for the children of Abiezer, and for the children of Helek, and for the children of Asriel, and for the children of Shechem, and
for the children of Hepher, and for the children of

Beth-arabah, Middin, Secacah, 62 Nibshan, the
City of Salt, and En-gedi—six towns with their
surrounding villages.

63 But the tribe of Judah could not drive out the
Jebusites, who lived in the city of Jerusalem, so the
Jebusites live there among the people of Judah to
this day.

The Land Given to Ephraim and West Manasseh

16 The allotment for the descendants of Joseph
extended from the Jordan River near
Jericho, east of the springs of Jericho, through the
wilderness and into the hill country of Bethel.
2 From Bethel (that is, Luz)* it ran over to Ataroth
in the territory of the Arkites. 3 Then it descended
westward to the territory of the Japhletites as far
as Lower Beth-horon, then to Gezer and over to
the Mediterranean Sea.*

4 This was the homeland allocated to the families of
Joseph's sons, Manasseh and Ephraim.

The Land Given to Ephraim

5 The following territory was given to the clans of the
tribe of Ephraim.

The boundary of their homeland began at
Ataroth-addar in the east. From there it
ran to Upper Beth-horon, 6 then on to the
Mediterranean Sea. From Micmethath on the
north, the boundary curved eastward past
Taanath-shiloh to the east of Janoah. 7 From
Janoah it turned southward to Ataroth and
Naarah, touched Jericho, and ended at the Jordan
River. 8 From Tappuah the boundary extended
westward, following the Kanah Ravine to the
Mediterranean Sea. This is the homeland
allocated to the clans of the tribe of Ephraim.
9 In addition, some towns with their
surrounding villages in the territory allocated
to the half-tribe of Manasseh were set aside for
the tribe of Ephraim. 10 They did not drive the
Canaanites out of Gezer, however, so the people
of Gezer live as slaves among the people of
Ephraim to this day.

The Land Given to West Manasseh

17 The next allotment of land was given to the
half-tribe of Manasseh, the descendants of
Joseph's older son. Makir, the firstborn son of Manasseh, was the father of Gilead. Because his descendants were experienced soldiers, the regions of
Gilead and Bashan on the east side of the Jordan had
already been given to them. 2 So the allotment on the
west side of the Jordan was for the remaining families within the clans of the tribe of Manasseh: Abiezer, Helek, Asriel, Shechem, Hepher, and Shemida.

16:2 As in Greek version (also see 18:13); Hebrew reads *From Bethel to Luz.*
16:3 Hebrew *the sea;* also in 16:6, 8.

KING JAMES VERSION

Shemida: these *were* the male children of Manasseh
the son of Joseph by their families.
3But Zelophehad, the son of Hepher, the son of
Gilead, the son of Machir, the son of Manasseh, had
no sons, but daughters: and these *are* the names
of his daughters, Mahlah, and Noah, Hoglah, Milcah,
and Tirzah.
4And they came near before Eleazar the priest, and
before Joshua the son of Nun, and before the princes,
saying, The LORD commanded Moses to give us an inheritance among our brethren. Therefore according
to the commandment of the LORD he gave them an inheritance among the brethren of their father.
5And there fell ten portions to Manasseh, beside
the land of Gilead and Bashan, which *were* on the
other side Jordan;
6Because the daughters of Manasseh had an inheritance among his sons: and the rest of Manasseh's
sons had the land of Gilead.
7And the coast of Manasseh was from Asher to
Michmethah, that *lieth* before Shechem; and the
border went along on the right hand unto the inhabitants of En-tappuah.
8*Now* Manasseh had the land of Tappuah: but
Tappuah on the border of Manasseh *belonged* to the
children of Ephraim;
9And the coast descended unto the river Kanah,
southward of the river: these cities of Ephraim *are*
among the cities of Manasseh: the coast of Manasseh
also *was* on the north side of the river, and the outgoings of it were at the sea:
10Southward *it was* Ephraim's, and northward *it
was* Manasseh's, and the sea is his border; and they
met together in Asher on the north, and in Issachar
on the east.
11And Manasseh had in Issachar and in Asher
Beth-shean and her towns, and Ibleam and her
towns, and the inhabitants of Dor and her towns,
and the inhabitants of En-dor and her towns, and
the inhabitants of Taanach and her towns, and the
inhabitants of Megiddo and her towns, *even* three
countries.
12Yet the children of Manasseh could not drive
out *the inhabitants of* those cities; but the Canaanites would dwell in that land.
13Yet it came to pass, when the children of Israel
were waxen strong, that they put the Canaanites to
tribute; but did not utterly drive them out.
14And the children of Joseph spake unto Joshua,
saying, Why hast thou given me *but* one lot and one
portion to inherit, seeing I *am* a great people, forasmuch as the LORD hath blessed me hitherto?

NEW LIVING TRANSLATION

These clans represent the male descendants of
Manasseh son of Joseph.
3However, Zelophehad, a descendant of Hepher
son of Gilead, son of Makir, son of Manasseh, had
no sons. He had only daughters, whose names were
Mahlah, Noah, Hoglah, Milcah, and Tirzah. 4These
women came to Eleazar the priest, Joshua son of
Nun, and the Israelite leaders and said, "The LORD
commanded Moses to give us a grant of land along
with the men of our tribe."
So Joshua gave them a grant of land along with
their uncles, as the LORD had commanded. 5As a result, Manasseh's total allocation came to ten parcels
of land, in addition to the land of Gilead and Bashan
across the Jordan River, 6because the female descendants of Manasseh received a grant of land
along with the male descendants. (The land of Gilead was given to the rest of the male descendants of
Manasseh.)

7The boundary of the tribe of Manasseh extended
from the border of Asher to Micmethath, near
Shechem. Then the boundary went south from
Micmethath to the settlement near the spring
of Tappuah. 8The land surrounding Tappuah
belonged to Manasseh, but the town of Tappuah
itself, on the border of Manasseh's territory,
belonged to the tribe of Ephraim. 9From the
spring of Tappuah, the boundary of Manasseh
followed the Kanah Ravine to the Mediterranean
Sea.* Several towns south of the ravine were
inside Manasseh's territory, but they actually
belonged to the tribe of Ephraim. 10In general,
however, the land south of the ravine belonged
to Ephraim, and the land north of the ravine
belonged to Manasseh. Manasseh's boundary ran
along the northern side of the ravine and ended at
the Mediterranean Sea. North of Manasseh was
the territory of Asher, and to the east was the
territory of Issachar.
11The following towns within the territory
of Issachar and Asher, however, were given to
Manasseh: Beth-shan,* Ibleam, Dor (that is,
Naphoth-dor),* Endor, Taanach, and Megiddo,
each with their surrounding settlements.

12But the descendants of Manasseh were unable to
occupy these towns. They could not drive out the Canaanites who continued to live there. 13Later, however, when the Israelites became strong enough, they
forced the Canaanites to work as slaves. But they did
not drive them out of the land.
14The descendants of Joseph came to Joshua and
asked, "Why have you given us only one portion of
land as our homeland when the LORD has blessed us
with so many people?"

17:9 Hebrew *the sea;* also in 17:10. **17:11a** Hebrew *Beth-shean,* a variant spelling of Beth-shan; also in 17:16. **17:11b** The meaning of the Hebrew here is uncertain.

KING JAMES VERSION

15 And Joshua answered them, If thou *be* a great
people, *then* get thee up to the wood *country,* and
cut down for thyself there in the land of the Perizzites and of the giants, if mount Ephraim be too
narrow for thee.
16 And the children of Joseph said, The hill is not
enough for us: and all the Canaanites that dwell in
the land of the valley have chariots of iron, *both they*
who *are* of Beth-shean and her towns, and *they* who
are of the valley of Jezreel.
17 And Joshua spake unto the house of Joseph,
even to Ephraim and to Manasseh, saying, Thou *art* a
great people, and hast great power: thou shalt not
have one lot *only:*
18 But the mountain shall be thine; for it *is* a wood,
and thou shalt cut it down: and the outgoings of it
shall be thine: for thou shalt drive out the Canaanites, though they have iron chariots, *and* though they
be strong.

18 1 And the whole congregation of the children
of Israel assembled together at Shiloh, and
set up the tabernacle of the congregation there. And
the land was subdued before them.
2 And there remained among the children of Israel seven tribes, which had not yet received their
inheritance.
3 And Joshua said unto the children of Israel, How
long *are* ye slack to go to possess the land, which the
LORD God of your fathers hath given you?
4 Give out from among you three men for *each*
tribe: and I will send them, and they shall rise, and go
through the land, and describe it according to the inheritance of them; and they shall come *again* to me.
5 And they shall divide it into seven parts: Judah
shall abide in their coast on the south, and the house
of Joseph shall abide in their coasts on the north.
6 Ye shall therefore describe the land *into* seven
parts, and bring *the description* hither to me, that I
may cast lots for you here before the LORD our God.
7 But the Levites have no part among you; for the
priesthood of the LORD *is* their inheritance: and Gad,
and Reuben, and half the tribe of Manasseh, have received their inheritance beyond Jordan on the east,
which Moses the servant of the LORD gave them.
8 And the men arose, and went away: and Joshua
charged them that went to describe the land, saying,
Go and walk through the land, and describe it, and
come again to me, that I may here cast lots for you before the LORD in Shiloh.
9 And the men went and passed through the land,
and described it by cities into seven parts in a book,
and came *again* to Joshua to the host at Shiloh.
10 And Joshua cast lots for them in Shiloh before
the LORD: and there Joshua divided the land unto the
children of Israel according to their divisions.

NEW LIVING TRANSLATION

15 Joshua replied, "If there are so many of you, and
if the hill country of Ephraim is not large enough for
you, clear out land for yourselves in the forest where
the Perizzites and Rephaites live."
16 The descendants of Joseph responded, "It's true
that the hill country is not large enough for us. But all
the Canaanites in the lowlands have iron chariots,
both those in Beth-shan and its surrounding settlements and those in the valley of Jezreel. They are too
strong for us."
17 Then Joshua said to the tribes of Ephraim and
Manasseh, the descendants of Joseph, "Since you are
so large and strong, you will be given more than one
portion. 18 The forests of the hill country will be
yours as well. Clear as much of the land as you wish,
and take possession of its farthest corners. And you
will drive out the Canaanites from the valleys, too,
even though they are strong and have iron chariots."

The Allotments of the Remaining Land

18 Now that the land was under Israelite control, the entire community of Israel gathered
at Shiloh and set up the Tabernacle.* 2 But there remained seven tribes who had not yet been allotted
their grants of land.
3 Then Joshua asked them, "How long are you going to wait before taking possession of the remaining
land the LORD, the God of your ancestors, has given to
you? 4 Select three men from each tribe, and I will
send them out to explore the land and map it out.
They will then return to me with a written report of
their proposed divisions of their new homeland. 5 Let
them divide the land into seven sections, excluding
Judah's territory in the south and Joseph's territory
in the north. 6 And when you record the seven divisions of the land and bring them to me, I will cast sacred lots in the presence of the LORD our God to
assign land to each tribe.
7 "The Levites, however, will not receive any allotment of land. Their role as priests of the LORD is their
allotment. And the tribes of Gad, Reuben, and the
half-tribe of Manasseh won't receive any more land,
for they have already received their grant of land,
which Moses, the servant of the LORD, gave them on
the east side of the Jordan River."
8 As the men started on their way to map out the
land, Joshua commanded them, "Go and explore the
land and write a description of it. Then return to me,
and I will assign the land to the tribes by casting sacred lots here in the presence of the LORD at Shiloh."
9 The men did as they were told and mapped the entire territory into seven sections, listing the towns in
each section. They made a written record and then
returned to Joshua in the camp at Shiloh. 10 And
there at Shiloh, Joshua cast sacred lots in the presence of the LORD to determine which tribe should
have each section.

18:1 Hebrew *Tent of Meeting.*

KING JAMES VERSION

11 And the lot of the tribe of the children of Benjamin came up according to their families: and the coast of their lot came forth between the children of Judah and the children of Joseph.

12 And their border on the north side was from Jordan; and the border went up to the side of Jericho on the north side, and went up through the mountains westward; and the goings out thereof were at the wilderness of Beth-aven.

13 And the border went over from thence toward Luz, to the side of Luz, which *is* Bethel, southward; and the border descended to Ataroth-adar, near the hill that *lieth* on the south side of the nether Beth-horon.

14 And the border was drawn *thence*, and compassed the corner of the sea southward, from the hill that *lieth* before Beth-horon southward; and the goings out thereof were at Kirjath-baal, which *is* Kirjath-jearim, a city of the children of Judah: this *was* the west quarter.

15 And the south quarter *was* from the end of Kirjath-jearim, and the border went out on the west, and went out to the well of waters of Nephtoah:

16 And the border came down to the end of the mountain that *lieth* before the valley of the son of Hinnom, *and* which *is* in the valley of the giants on the north, and descended to the valley of Hinnom, to the side of Jebusi on the south, and descended to En-rogel,

17 And was drawn from the north, and went forth to En-shemesh, and went forth toward Geliloth, which *is* over against the going up of Adummim, and descended to the stone of Bohan the son of Reuben,

18 And passed along toward the side over against Arabah northward, and went down unto Arabah:

19 And the border passed along to the side of Beth-hoglah northward: and the outgoings of the border were at the north bay of the salt sea at the south end of Jordan: this *was* the south coast.

20 And Jordan was the border of it on the east side. This *was* the inheritance of the children of Benjamin, by the coasts thereof round about, according to their families.

21 Now the cities of the tribe of the children of Benjamin according to their families were Jericho, and Beth-hoglah, and the valley of Keziz,

22 And Beth-arabah, and Zemaraim, and Bethel,

23 And Avim, and Parah, and Ophrah,

24 And Chephar-haammonai, and Ophni, and Gaba; twelve cities with their villages:

25 Gibeon, and Ramah, and Beeroth,

26 And Mizpah, and Chephirah, and Mozah,

27 And Rekem, and Irpeel, and Taralah,

28 And Zelah, Eleph, and Jebusi, which *is* Jerusalem, Gibeath, *and* Kirjath; fourteen cities with their

NEW LIVING TRANSLATION

The Land Given to Benjamin

11 The first allotment of land went to the clans of the tribe of Benjamin. It lay between the territory assigned to the tribes of Judah and Joseph.

12 The northern boundary of Benjamin's land
began at the Jordan River, went north of the slope
of Jericho, then west through the hill country and
the wilderness of Beth-aven. 13 From there the
boundary went south to Luz (that is, Bethel) and
proceeded down to Ataroth-addar on the hill that
lies south of Lower Beth-horon.

14 The boundary then made a turn and swung
south along the western edge of the hill facing
Beth-horon, ending at the village of Kiriath-baal
(that is, Kiriath-jearim), a town belonging to the
tribe of Judah. This was the western boundary.

15 The southern boundary began at the
outskirts of Kiriath-jearim. From that western
point it ran* to the spring at the waters of
Nephtoah,* 16 and down to the base of the
mountain beside the valley of Ben-Hinnom,
at the northern end of the valley of Rephaim.
From there it went down the valley of Hinnom,
crossing south of the slope where the Jebusites
lived, and continued down to En-rogel. 17 From
En-rogel the boundary proceeded in a northerly
direction and came to En-shemesh and on to
Geliloth (which is across from the slopes of
Adummim). Then it went down to the Stone of
Bohan. (Bohan was Reuben's son.) 18 From there
it passed along the north side of the slope
overlooking the Jordan Valley.* The border then
went down into the valley, 19 ran past the north
slope of Beth-hoglah, and ended at the north
bay of the Dead Sea,* which is the southern
end of the Jordan River. This was the southern
boundary.

20 The eastern boundary was the Jordan River.

These were the boundaries of the homeland allocated to the clans of the tribe of Benjamin.

The Towns Given to Benjamin

21 These were the towns given to the clans of the tribe of Benjamin.

Jericho, Beth-hoglah, Emek-keziz, 22 Beth-arabah,
Zemaraim, Bethel, 23 Avvim, Parah, Ophrah,
24 Kephar-ammoni, Ophni, and Geba—twelve
towns with their surrounding villages. 25 Also
Gibeon, Ramah, Beeroth, 26 Mizpah, Kephirah,
Mozah, 27 Rekem, Irpeel, Taralah, 28 Zela, Haeleph,
Jebus (that is, Jerusalem), Gibeah, and Kiriath*—
fourteen towns with their surrounding villages.

18:15a Or *From there it went to Mozah.* The meaning of the Hebrew is uncertain. **18:15b** Or *the spring at Me-nephtoah.* **18:18** Hebrew *overlooking the Arabah,* or *overlooking Beth-arabah.* **18:19** Hebrew *Salt Sea.* **18:28** Some Greek manuscripts read *Kiriath-jearim.*

KING JAMES VERSION

villages. This *is* the inheritance of the children of
Benjamin according to their families.

19 1 And the second lot came forth to Simeon,
even for the tribe of the children of Simeon
according to their families: and their inheritance
was within the inheritance of the children of Judah.
2 And they had in their inheritance Beer-sheba, or
Sheba, and Moladah,
3 And Hazar-shual, and Balah, and Azem,
4 And Eltolad, and Bethul, and Hormah,
5 And Ziklag, and Beth-marcaboth, and Hazar-
susah,
6 And Beth-lebaoth, and Sharuhen; thirteen cities
and their villages:
7 Ain, Remmon, and Ether, and Ashan; four cities
and their villages:
8 And all the villages that *were* round about these
cities to Baalath-beer, Ramath of the south. This *is*
the inheritance of the tribe of the children of Simeon according to their families.
9 Out of the portion of the children of Judah *was*
the inheritance of the children of Simeon: for the
part of the children of Judah was too much for them:
therefore the children of Simeon had their inheritance within the inheritance of them.
10 And the third lot came up for the children of
Zebulun according to their families: and the border
of their inheritance was unto Sarid:
11 And their border went up toward the sea, and
Maralah, and reached to Dabbasheth, and reached to
the river that *is* before Jokneam;
12 And turned from Sarid eastward toward the
sunrising unto the border of Chisloth-tabor, and
then goeth out to Daberath, and goeth up to Japhia.
13 And from thence passeth on along on the east to
Gittah-hepher, to Ittah-kazin, and goeth out to
Remmon-methoar to Neah;
14 And the border compasseth it on the north side
to Hannathon: and the outgoings thereof are in the
valley of Jiphthah-el:
15 And Kattath, and Nahallal, and Shimron, and Idalah, and Bethlehem: twelve cities with their villages.
16 This *is* the inheritance of the children of Zebulun according to their families, these cities with their
villages.

17 *And* the fourth lot came out to Issachar, for the
children of Issachar according to their families.
18 And their border was toward Jezreel, and
Chesulloth, and Shunem,
19 And Hapharaim, and Shihon, and Anaharath,
20 And Rabbith, and Kishion, and Abez,
21 And Remeth, and En-gannim, and En-haddah,
and Beth-pazzez;
22 And the coast reacheth to Tabor, and Shahaz-
imah, and Beth-shemesh; and the outgoings of their

NEW LIVING TRANSLATION

This was the homeland allocated to the clans of the
tribe of Benjamin.

The Land Given to Simeon

19 The second allotment of land went to the
clans of the tribe of Simeon. Their homeland
was surrounded by Judah's territory.

2 Simeon's homeland included Beersheba, Sheba,
Moladah, 3 Hazar-shual, Balah, Ezem, 4 Eltolad,
Bethul, Hormah, 5 Ziklag, Beth-marcaboth, Hazar-
susah, 6 Beth-lebaoth, and Sharuhen—thirteen
towns with their surrounding villages. 7 It also
included Ain, Rimmon, Ether, and Ashan—four
towns with their villages, 8 including all the
surrounding villages as far south as Baalath-beer
(also known as Ramah of the Negev).

This was the homeland allocated to the clans of the
tribe of Simeon. 9 Their allocation of land came from
part of what had been given to Judah because Judah's
territory was too large for them. So the tribe of
Simeon received an allocation within the territory
of Judah.

The Land Given to Zebulun

10 The third allotment of land went to the clans of the
tribe of Zebulun.

The boundary of Zebulun's homeland started
at Sarid. 11 From there it went west, going past
Maralah, touching Dabbesheth, and proceeding to
the brook east of Jokneam. 12 In the other direction,
the boundary went east from Sarid to the border of
Kisloth-tabor, and from there to Daberath and up
to Japhia. 13 Then it continued east to Gath-hepher,
Eth-kazin, and Rimmon and turned toward Neah.
14 The northern boundary of Zebulun passed
Hannathon and ended at the valley of Iphtah-el.
15 The towns in these areas included Kattath,
Nahalal, Shimron, Idalah, and Bethlehem—
twelve towns with their surrounding villages.

16 The homeland allocated to the clans of the tribe of
Zebulun included these towns and their surrounding villages.

The Land Given to Issachar

17 The fourth allotment of land went to the clans of
the tribe of Issachar.

18 Its boundaries included the following towns:
Jezreel, Kesulloth, Shunem, 19 Hapharaim, Shion,
Anaharath, 20 Rabbith, Kishion, Ebez, 21 Remeth,
En-gannim, En-haddah, and Beth-pazzez. 22 The
boundary also touched Tabor, Shahazumah, and

KING JAMES VERSION

border were at Jordan: sixteen cities with their
villages.
23 This *is* the inheritance of the tribe of the children of Issachar according to their families, the
cities and their villages.

24 And the fifth lot came out for the tribe of the
children of Asher according to their families.
25 And their border was Helkath, and Hali, and
Beten, and Achshaph,
26 And Alammelech, and Amad, and Misheal; and
reacheth to Carmel westward, and to Shihor-libnath;
27 And turneth toward the sunrising to Beth-
dagon, and reacheth to Zebulun, and to the valley of
Jiphthah-el toward the north side of Beth-emek, and
Neiel, and goeth out to Cabul on the left hand,
28 And Hebron, and Rehob, and Hammon, and
Kanah, *even* unto great Zidon;
29 And *then* the coast turneth to Ramah, and to the
strong city Tyre; and the coast turneth to Hosah; and
the outgoings thereof are at the sea from the coast to
Achzib:
30 Ummah also, and Aphek, and Rehob: twenty and
two cities with their villages.
31 This *is* the inheritance of the tribe of the children of Asher according to their families, these cities
with their villages.

32 The sixth lot came out to the children of Naphtali, *even* for the children of Naphtali according to
their families.
33 And their coast was from Heleph, from Allon to
Zaanannim, and Adami, Nekeb, and Jabneel, unto
Lakum; and the outgoings thereof were at Jordan:
34 And *then* the coast turneth westward to Aznoth-
tabor, and goeth out from thence to Hukkok, and
reacheth to Zebulun on the south side, and reacheth
to Asher on the west side, and to Judah upon Jordan
toward the sunrising.
35 And the fenced cities *are* Ziddim, Zer, and Hammath, Rakkath, and Chinnereth,
36 And Adamah, and Ramah, and Hazor,
37 And Kedesh, and Edrei, and En-hazor,
38 And Iron, and Migdal-el, Horem, and Beth-
anath, and Beth-shemesh; nineteen cities with their
villages.
39 This *is* the inheritance of the tribe of the children of Naphtali according to their families, the cities and their villages.
40 *And* the seventh lot came out for the tribe of the
children of Dan according to their families.
41 And the coast of their inheritance was Zorah,
and Eshtaol, and Ir-shemesh,

NEW LIVING TRANSLATION

Beth-shemesh, ending at the Jordan River—
sixteen towns with their surrounding villages.

23 The homeland allocated to the clans of the tribe of
Issachar included these towns and their surrounding
villages.

The Land Given to Asher

24 The fifth allotment of land went to the clans of the
tribe of Asher.

25 Its boundaries included these towns: Helkath,
Hali, Beten, Acshaph, 26 Allammelech, Amad, and
Mishal. The boundary on the west touched
Carmel and Shihor-libnath, 27 then it turned east
toward Beth-dagon, and ran as far as Zebulun in
the valley of Iphtah-el, going north to Beth-emek
and Neiel. It then continued north to Cabul,
28 Abdon,* Rehob, Hammon, Kanah, and as far
as Greater Sidon. 29 Then the boundary turned
toward Ramah and the fortress of Tyre, where
it turned toward Hosah and came to the
Mediterranean Sea.* The territory also included
Mehebel, Aczib, 30 Ummah, Aphek, and Rehob—
twenty-two towns with their surrounding villages.

31 The homeland allocated to the clans of the tribe of
Asher included these towns and their surrounding
villages.

The Land Given to Naphtali

32 The sixth allotment of land went to the clans of the
tribe of Naphtali.

33 Its boundary ran from Heleph, from the oak
at Zaanannim, and extended across to Adami-
nekeb, Jabneel, and as far as Lakkum, ending at
the Jordan River. 34 The western boundary ran
past Aznoth-tabor, then to Hukkok, and touched
the border of Zebulun in the south, the border
of Asher on the west, and the Jordan River* on
the east. 35 The fortified towns included in this
territory were Ziddim, Zer, Hammath, Rakkath,
Kinnereth, 36 Adamah, Ramah, Hazor, 37 Kedesh,
Edrei, En-hazor, 38 Yiron, Migdal-el, Horem, Beth-
anath, and Beth-shemesh—nineteen towns with
their surrounding villages.

39 The homeland allocated to the clans of the tribe of
Naphtali included these towns and their surrounding villages.

The Land Given to Dan

40 The seventh allotment of land went to the clans of
the tribe of Dan.

41 The land allocated as their homeland included
the following towns: Zorah, Eshtaol, Ir-shemesh,

19:28 As in some Hebrew manuscripts (see also 21:30); most Hebrew manuscripts read *Ebron.* **19:29** Hebrew *the sea.* **19:34** Hebrew *and Judah at the Jordan River.*

KING JAMES VERSION

42And Shaalabbin, and Ajalon, and Jethlah,
43And Elon, and Thimnathah, and Ekron,
44And Eltekeh, and Gibbethon, and Baalath,
45And Jehud, and Bene-berak, and Gath-rimmon,
46And Me-jarkon, and Rakkon, with the border before Japho.

47And the coast of the children of Dan went out *too little* for them: therefore the children of Dan went up to fight against Leshem, and took it, and smote it with the edge of the sword, and possessed it, and dwelt therein, and called Leshem, Dan, after the name of Dan their father.

48This *is* the inheritance of the tribe of the children of Dan according to their families, these cities with their villages.

49When they had made an end of dividing the land for inheritance by their coasts, the children of Israel gave an inheritance to Joshua the son of Nun among them:

50According to the word of the LORD they gave him the city which he asked, *even* Timnath-serah in mount Ephraim: and he built the city, and dwelt therein.

51These *are* the inheritances, which Eleazar the priest, and Joshua the son of Nun, and the heads of the fathers of the tribes of the children of Israel, divided for an inheritance by lot in Shiloh before the LORD, at the door of the tabernacle of the congregation. So they made an end of dividing the country.

20 1The LORD also spake unto Joshua, saying, 2Speak to the children of Israel, saying, Appoint out for you cities of refuge, whereof I spake unto you by the hand of Moses:

3That the slayer that killeth *any* person unawares *and* unwittingly may flee thither: and they shall be your refuge from the avenger of blood.

4And when he that doth flee unto one of those cities shall stand at the entering of the gate of the city, and shall declare his cause in the ears of the elders of that city, they shall take him into the city unto them, and give him a place, that he may dwell among them.

5And if the avenger of blood pursue after him, then they shall not deliver the slayer up into his hand; because he smote his neighbour unwittingly, and hated him not beforetime.

6And he shall dwell in that city, until he stand before the congregation for judgment, *and* until the death of the high priest that shall be in those days: then shall the slayer return, and come unto his own city, and unto his own house, unto the city from whence he fled.

7And they appointed Kedesh in Galilee in mount Naphtali, and Shechem in mount Ephraim, and Kirjath-arba, which *is* Hebron, in the mountain of Judah.

8And on the other side Jordan by Jericho eastward, they assigned Bezer in the wilderness upon the plain

NEW LIVING TRANSLATION

42Shaalabbin, Aijalon, Ithlah, 43Elon, Timnah,
Ekron, 44Eltekeh, Gibbethon, Baalath, 45Jehud,
Bene-berak, Gath-rimmon, 46Me-jarkon, Rakkon,
and the territory across from Joppa.

47But the tribe of Dan had trouble taking possession of their land,* so they attacked the town of Laish.* They captured it, slaughtered its people, and settled there. They renamed the town Dan after their ancestor.

48The homeland allocated to the clans of the tribe of Dan included these towns and their surrounding villages.

The Land Given to Joshua

49After all the land was divided among the tribes, the Israelites gave a piece of land to Joshua as his allocation. 50For the LORD had said he could have any town he wanted. He chose Timnath-serah in the hill country of Ephraim. He rebuilt the town and lived there.

51These are the territories that Eleazar the priest, Joshua son of Nun, and the tribal leaders allocated as grants of land to the tribes of Israel by casting sacred lots in the presence of the LORD at the entrance of the Tabernacle* at Shiloh. So the division of the land was completed.

The Cities of Refuge

20 The LORD said to Joshua, 2"Now tell the Israelites to designate the cities of refuge, as I instructed Moses. 3Anyone who kills another person accidentally and unintentionally can run to one of these cities; they will be places of refuge from relatives seeking revenge for the person who was killed.

4"Upon reaching one of these cities, the one who caused the death will appear before the elders at the city gate and present his case. They must allow him to enter the city and give him a place to live among them. 5If the relatives of the victim come to avenge the killing, the leaders must not release the slayer to them, for he killed the other person unintentionally and without previous hostility. 6But the slayer must stay in that city and be tried by the local assembly, which will render a judgment. And he must continue to live in that city until the death of the high priest who was in office at the time of the accident. After that, he is free to return to his own home in the town from which he fled."

7The following cities were designated as cities of refuge: Kedesh of Galilee, in the hill country of Naphtali; Shechem, in the hill country of Ephraim; and Kiriath-arba (that is, Hebron), in the hill country of Judah. 8On the east side of the Jordan River, across from Jericho, the following cities were designated:

19:47a Or *had trouble holding on to their land.* **19:47b** Hebrew *Leshem,* a variant spelling of Laish. **19:51** Hebrew *Tent of Meeting.*

KING JAMES VERSION

out of the tribe of Reuben, and Ramoth in Gilead out of the tribe of Gad, and Golan in Bashan out of the tribe of Manasseh.

9 These were the cities appointed for all the children of Israel, and for the stranger that sojourneth among them, that whosoever killeth *any* person at unawares might flee thither, and not die by the hand of the avenger of blood, until he stood before the congregation.

21 1 Then came near the heads of the fathers of the Levites unto Eleazar the priest, and unto Joshua the son of Nun, and unto the heads of the fathers of the tribes of the children of Israel;

2 And they spake unto them at Shiloh in the land of Canaan, saying, The LORD commanded by the hand of Moses to give us cities to dwell in, with the suburbs thereof for our cattle.

3 And the children of Israel gave unto the Levites out of their inheritance, at the commandment of the LORD, these cities and their suburbs.

4 And the lot came out for the families of the Kohathites: and the children of Aaron the priest, *which were* of the Levites, had by lot out of the tribe of Judah, and out of the tribe of Simeon, and out of the tribe of Benjamin, thirteen cities.

5 And the rest of the children of Kohath *had* by lot out of the families of the tribe of Ephraim, and out of the tribe of Dan, and out of the half tribe of Manasseh, ten cities.

6 And the children of Gershon *had* by lot out of the families of the tribe of Issachar, and out of the tribe of Asher, and out of the tribe of Naphtali, and out of the half tribe of Manasseh in Bashan, thirteen cities.

7 The children of Merari by their families *had* out of the tribe of Reuben, and out of the tribe of Gad, and out of the tribe of Zebulun, twelve cities.

8 And the children of Israel gave by lot unto the Levites these cities with their suburbs, as the LORD commanded by the hand of Moses.

9 And they gave out of the tribe of the children of Judah, and out of the tribe of the children of Simeon, these cities which are *here* mentioned by name,

10 Which the children of Aaron, *being* of the families of the Kohathites, *who were* of the children of Levi, had: for theirs was the first lot.

11 And they gave them the city of Arba the father of Anak, which *city is* Hebron, in the hill *country* of Judah, with the suburbs thereof round about it.

12 But the fields of the city, and the villages thereof, gave they to Caleb the son of Jephunneh for his possession.

13 Thus they gave to the children of Aaron the priest Hebron with her suburbs, *to be* a city of refuge for the slayer; and Libnah with her suburbs,

NEW LIVING TRANSLATION

Bezer, in the wilderness plain of the tribe of Reuben; Ramoth in Gilead, in the territory of the tribe of Gad; and Golan in Bashan, in the land of the tribe of Manasseh. 9 These cities were set apart for all the Israelites as well as the foreigners living among them. Anyone who accidentally killed another person could take refuge in one of these cities. In this way, they could escape being killed in revenge prior to standing trial before the local assembly.

The Towns Given to the Levites

21 Then the leaders of the tribe of Levi came to consult with Eleazar the priest, Joshua son of Nun, and the leaders of the other tribes of Israel. 2 They came to them at Shiloh in the land of Canaan and said, "The LORD commanded Moses to give us towns to live in and pasturelands for our livestock." 3 So by the command of the LORD the people of Israel gave the Levites the following towns and pasturelands out of their own grants of land.

4 The descendants of Aaron, who were members of the Kohathite clan within the tribe of Levi, were allotted thirteen towns that were originally assigned to the tribes of Judah, Simeon, and Benjamin. 5 The other families of the Kohathite clan were allotted ten towns from the tribes of Ephraim, Dan, and the half-tribe of Manasseh.

6 The clan of Gershon was allotted thirteen towns from the tribes of Issachar, Asher, Naphtali, and the half-tribe of Manasseh in Bashan.

7 The clan of Merari was allotted twelve towns from the tribes of Reuben, Gad, and Zebulun.

8 So the Israelites obeyed the LORD's command to Moses and assigned these towns and pasturelands to the Levites by casting sacred lots.

9 The Israelites gave the following towns from the tribes of Judah and Simeon 10 to the descendants of Aaron, who were members of the Kohathite clan within the tribe of Levi, since the sacred lot fell to them first: 11 Kiriath-arba (that is, Hebron), in the hill country of Judah, along with its surrounding pasturelands. (Arba was an ancestor of Anak.) 12 But the open fields beyond the town and the surrounding villages were given to Caleb son of Jephunneh as his possession.

13 The following towns with their pasturelands were given to the descendants of Aaron the priest: Hebron (a city of refuge for those who accidentally

KING JAMES VERSION

14 And Jattir with her suburbs, and Eshtemoa with
her suburbs,
15 And Holon with her suburbs, and Debir with her
suburbs,
16 And Ain with her suburbs, and Juttah with her
suburbs, *and* Beth-shemesh with her suburbs; nine
cities out of those two tribes.
17 And out of the tribe of Benjamin, Gibeon with
her suburbs, Geba with her suburbs,
18 Anathoth with her suburbs, and Almon with her
suburbs; four cities.
19 All the cities of the children of Aaron, the priests,
were thirteen cities with their suburbs.
20 And the families of the children of Kohath, the
Levites which remained of the children of Kohath,
even they had the cities of their lot out of the tribe of
Ephraim.
21 For they gave them Shechem with her suburbs
in mount Ephraim, *to be* a city of refuge for the
slayer; and Gezer with her suburbs,
22 And Kibzaim with her suburbs, and Beth-horon
with her suburbs; four cities.
23 And out of the tribe of Dan, Eltekeh with her
suburbs, Gibbethon with her suburbs,
24 Aijalon with her suburbs, Gath-rimmon with her
suburbs; four cities.
25 And out of the half tribe of Manasseh, Tanach
with her suburbs, and Gath-rimmon with her suburbs; two cities.
26 All the cities *were* ten with their suburbs for the
families of the children of Kohath that remained.
27 And unto the children of Gershon, of the families of the Levites, out of the *other* half tribe of Manasseh *they gave* Golan in Bashan with her suburbs,
to be a city of refuge for the slayer; and Be-eshterah
with her suburbs; two cities.
28 And out of the tribe of Issachar, Kishon with
her suburbs, Dabareh with her suburbs,
29 Jarmuth with her suburbs, En-gannim with her
suburbs; four cities.
30 And out of the tribe of Asher, Mishal with her
suburbs, Abdon with her suburbs,
31 Helkath with her suburbs, and Rehob with
her suburbs; four cities.
32 And out of the tribe of Naphtali, Kedesh in Galilee with her suburbs, *to be* a city of refuge for the
slayer; and Hammoth-dor with her suburbs, and Kartan with her suburbs; three cities.
33 All the cities of the Gershonites according to
their families *were* thirteen cities with their suburbs.
34 And unto the families of the children of Merari,
the rest of the Levites, out of the tribe of Zebulun,
Jokneam with her suburbs, and Kartah with her
suburbs,
35 Dimnah with her suburbs, Nahalal with her suburbs; four cities.

NEW LIVING TRANSLATION

killed someone), Libnah, 14 Jattir, Eshtemoa, 15 Holon,
Debir, 16 Ain, Juttah, and Beth-shemesh—nine towns
from these two tribes.
17 From the tribe of Benjamin the priests were
given the following towns with their pasturelands:
Gibeon, Geba, 18 Anathoth, and Almon—four towns.
19 So in all, thirteen towns with their pasturelands
were given to the priests, the descendants of Aaron.
20 The rest of the Kohathite clan from the tribe of
Levi was allotted the following towns and pasturelands from the tribe of Ephraim: 21 Shechem in the
hill country of Ephraim (a city of refuge for those
who accidentally killed someone), Gezer, 22 Kibzaim,
and Beth-horon—four towns.
23 The following towns and pasturelands were
allotted to the priests from the tribe of Dan: Eltekeh,
Gibbethon, 24 Aijalon, and Gath-rimmon—four towns.
25 The half-tribe of Manasseh allotted the following towns with their pasturelands to the priests: Taanach and Gath-rimmon—two towns. 26 So in all, ten
towns with their pasturelands were given to the rest
of the Kohathite clan.
27 The descendants of Gershon, another clan
within the tribe of Levi, received the following towns
with their pasturelands from the half-tribe of Manasseh: Golan in Bashan (a city of refuge for those
who accidentally killed someone) and Be-eshterah—
two towns.
28 From the tribe of Issachar they received the following towns with their pasturelands: Kishion,
Daberath, 29 Jarmuth, and En-gannim—four towns.
30 From the tribe of Asher they received the following towns with their pasturelands: Mishal, Abdon,
31 Helkath, and Rehob—four towns.
32 From the tribe of Naphtali they received the following towns with their pasturelands: Kedesh in
Galilee (a city of refuge for those who accidentally
killed someone), Hammoth-dor, and Kartan—three
towns. 33 So in all, thirteen towns with their pasturelands were allotted to the clan of Gershon.
34 The rest of the Levites—the Merari clan—were
given the following towns with their pasturelands
from the tribe of Zebulun: Jokneam, Kartah, 35 Dimnah, and Nahalal—four towns.

KING JAMES VERSION

36And out of the tribe of Reuben, Bezer with her suburbs, and Jahazah with her suburbs,

37Kedemoth with her suburbs, and Mephaath with her suburbs; four cities.

38And out of the tribe of Gad, Ramoth in Gilead with her suburbs, *to be* a city of refuge for the slayer; and Mahanaim with her suburbs,

39Heshbon with her suburbs, Jazer with her suburbs; four cities in all.

40So all the cities for the children of Merari by their families, which were remaining of the families of the Levites, were *by* their lot twelve cities.

41All the cities of the Levites within the possession of the children of Israel *were* forty and eight cities with their suburbs.

42These cities were every one with their suburbs round about them: thus *were* all these cities.

43And the LORD gave unto Israel all the land which he sware to give unto their fathers; and they possessed it, and dwelt therein.

44And the LORD gave them rest round about, according to all that he sware unto their fathers: and there stood not a man of all their enemies before them; the LORD delivered all their enemies into their hand.

45There failed not aught of any good thing which the LORD had spoken unto the house of Israel; all came to pass.

22 1Then Joshua called the Reubenites, and the Gadites, and the half tribe of Manasseh,

2And said unto them, Ye have kept all that Moses the servant of the LORD commanded you, and have obeyed my voice in all that I commanded you:

3Ye have not left your brethren these many days unto this day, but have kept the charge of the commandment of the LORD your God.

4And now the LORD your God hath given rest unto your brethren, as he promised them: therefore now return ye, and get you unto your tents, *and* unto the land of your possession, which Moses the servant of the LORD gave you on the other side Jordan.

5But take diligent heed to do the commandment and the law, which Moses the servant of the LORD charged you, to love the LORD your God, and to walk in all his ways, and to keep his commandments, and to cleave unto him, and to serve him with all your heart and with all your soul.

6So Joshua blessed them, and sent them away: and they went unto their tents.

7Now to the *one* half of the tribe of Manasseh Moses had given *possession* in Bashan: but unto the *other* half thereof gave Joshua among their brethren on this side Jordan westward. And when Joshua sent hem away also unto their tents, then he blessed em,

And he spake unto them, saying, Return with h riches unto your tents, and with very much

NEW LIVING TRANSLATION

36From the tribe of Reuben they received the following towns with their pasturelands: Bezer, Jahaz,* 37Kedemoth, and Mephaath—four towns.

38From the tribe of Gad they received the following towns with their pasturelands: Ramoth in Gilead (a city of refuge for those who accidentally killed someone), Mahanaim, 39Heshbon, and Jazer—four towns. 40So in all, twelve towns were allotted to the clan of Merari.

41The total number of towns and pasturelands within Israelite territory given to the Levites came to forty-eight. 42Every one of these towns had pasturelands surrounding it.

43So the LORD gave to Israel all the land he had sworn to give their ancestors, and they took possession of it and settled there. 44And the LORD gave them rest on every side, just as he had solemnly promised their ancestors. None of their enemies could stand against them, for the LORD helped them conquer all their enemies. 45Not a single one of all the good promises the LORD had given to the family of Israel was left unfulfilled; everything he had spoken came true.

The Eastern Tribes Return Home

22 Then Joshua called together the tribes of Reuben, Gad, and the half-tribe of Manasseh. 2He told them, "You have done as Moses, the servant of the LORD, commanded you, and you have obeyed every order I have given you. 3During all this time you have not deserted the other tribes. You have been careful to obey the commands of the LORD your God right up to the present day. 4And now the LORD your God has given the other tribes rest, as he promised them. So go back home to the land that Moses, the servant of the LORD, gave you as your possession on the east side of the Jordan River. 5But be very careful to obey all the commands and the instructions that Moses gave to you. Love the LORD your God, walk in all his ways, obey his commands, hold firmly to him, and serve him with all your heart and all your soul." 6So Joshua blessed them and sent them away, and they went home.

7Moses had given the land of Bashan, east of the Jordan River, to the half-tribe of Manasseh. (The other half of the tribe was given land west of the Jordan.) As Joshua sent them away and blessed them, 8he said to them, "Go back to your homes with the great wealth you have taken from your enemies—the vast herds of livestock, the silver, gold, bronze, and

21:36 Hebrew *Jahzah,* a variant spelling of Jahaz.

KING JAMES VERSION

cattle, with silver, and with gold, and with brass, and
with iron, and with very much raiment: divide the
spoil of your enemies with your brethren.
9And the children of Reuben and the children of
Gad and the half tribe of Manasseh returned, and
departed from the children of Israel out of Shiloh,
which *is* in the land of Canaan, to go unto the country
of Gilead, to the land of their possession, whereof
they were possessed, according to the word of the
LORD by the hand of Moses.
10And when they came unto the borders of Jordan,
that *are* in the land of Canaan, the children of Reuben and the children of Gad and the half tribe of
Manasseh built there an altar by Jordan, a great altar
to see to.
11And the children of Israel heard say, Behold, the
children of Reuben and the children of Gad and the
half tribe of Manasseh have built an altar over
against the land of Canaan, in the borders of Jordan,
at the passage of the children of Israel.
12And when the children of Israel heard *of it,* the
whole congregation of the children of Israel gathered themselves together at Shiloh, to go up to war
against them.
13And the children of Israel sent unto the children
of Reuben, and to the children of Gad, and to the half
tribe of Manasseh, into the land of Gilead, Phinehas
the son of Eleazar the priest,
14And with him ten princes, of each chief house a
prince throughout all the tribes of Israel; and each
one *was* an head of the house of their fathers among
the thousands of Israel.
15And they came unto the children of Reuben, and
to the children of Gad, and to the half tribe of Manasseh, unto the land of Gilead, and they spake with
them, saying,
16Thus saith the whole congregation of the LORD,
What trespass *is* this that ye have committed against
the God of Israel, to turn away this day from following the LORD, in that ye have builded you an altar, that
ye might rebel this day against the LORD?
17*Is* the iniquity of Peor too little for us, from
which we are not cleansed until this day, although
there was a plague in the congregation of the LORD,
18But that ye must turn away this day from following the LORD? and it will be, *seeing* ye rebel today
against the LORD, that tomorrow he will be wroth
with the whole congregation of Israel.
19Notwithstanding, if the land of your possession
be unclean, *then* pass ye over unto the land of the possession of the LORD, wherein the LORD's tabernacle
dwelleth, and take possession among us: but rebel not
against the LORD, nor rebel against us, in building you
an altar beside the altar of the LORD our God.
20Did not Achan the son of Zerah commit a trespass in the accursed thing, and wrath fell on all the
congregation of Israel? and that man perished not
alone in his iniquity.

NEW LIVING TRANSLATION

iron, and the large supply of clothing. Share the
plunder with your relatives."
9So the men of Reuben, Gad, and the half-tribe of
Manasseh left the rest of Israel at Shiloh in the land
of Canaan. They started the journey back to their
own land of Gilead, the territory that belonged to
them according to the LORD's command through
Moses.

The Eastern Tribes Build an Altar

10But while they were still in Canaan, and when they
came to a place called Geliloth* near the Jordan
River, the men of Reuben, Gad, and the half-tribe of
Manasseh stopped to build a large and imposing
altar.
11The rest of Israel heard that the people of Reuben, Gad, and the half-tribe of Manasseh had built
an altar at Geliloth at the edge of the land of Canaan,
on the west side of the Jordan River. 12So the whole
community of Israel gathered at Shiloh and prepared to go to war against them. 13First, however,
they sent a delegation led by Phinehas son of Eleazar, the priest, to talk with the tribes of Reuben, Gad,
and the half-tribe of Manasseh. 14In this delegation
were ten leaders of Israel, one from each of the ten
tribes, and each the head of his family within the
clans of Israel.
15When they arrived in the land of Gilead, they
said to the tribes of Reuben, Gad, and the half-tribe
of Manasseh, 16"The whole community of the LORD
demands to know why you are betraying the God of
Israel. How could you turn away from the LORD and
build an altar for yourselves in rebellion against
him? 17Was our sin at Peor not enough? To this day
we are not fully cleansed of it, even after the plague
that struck the entire community of the LORD. 18And
yet today you are turning away from following the
LORD. If you rebel against the LORD today, he will be
angry with all of us tomorrow.
19"If you need the altar because the land you possess is defiled, then join us in the LORD's land, where
the Tabernacle of the LORD is situated, and share our
land with us. But do not rebel against the LORD or
against us by building an altar other than the one
true altar of the LORD our God. 20Didn't divine anger
fall on the entire community of Israel when Achan, a
member of the clan of Zerah, sinned by stealing the
things set apart for the LORD*? He was not the only
one who died because of his sin."

22:10 Or *to the circle of stones;* similarly in 22:11. **22:20** The Hebrew term used here refers to the complete consecration of things or people to the LORD, either by destroying them or by giving them as an offering.

KING JAMES VERSION

21Then the children of Reuben and the children of
Gad and the half tribe of Manasseh answered, and
said unto the heads of the thousands of Israel,
22The LORD God of gods, the LORD God of gods, he
knoweth, and Israel he shall know; if *it be* in rebellion, or if in transgression against the LORD, (save us
not this day,)
23That we have built us an altar to turn from following the LORD, or if to offer thereon burnt offering
or meat offering, or if to offer peace offerings
thereon, let the LORD himself require *it;*
24And if we have not *rather* done it for fear of *this*
thing, saying, In time to come your children might
speak unto our children, saying, What have ye to do
with the LORD God of Israel?
25For the LORD hath made Jordan a border between
us and you, ye children of Reuben and children of
Gad; ye have no part in the LORD: so shall your children make our children cease from fearing the LORD.
26Therefore we said, Let us now prepare to build
us an altar, not for burnt offering, nor for sacrifice:
27But *that* it *may be* a witness between us, and you,
and our generations after us, that we might do the
service of the LORD before him with our burnt offerings, and with our sacrifices, and with our peace offerings; that your children may not say to our children
in time to come, Ye have no part in the LORD.
28Therefore said we, that it shall be, when they
should *so* say to us or to our generations in time to
come, that we may say *again,* Behold the pattern of
the altar of the LORD, which our fathers made, not for
burnt offerings, nor for sacrifices; but it *is* a witness
between us and you.
29God forbid that we should rebel against the
LORD, and turn this day from following the LORD, to
build an altar for burnt offerings, for meat offerings,
or for sacrifices, beside the altar of the LORD our God
that *is* before his tabernacle.
30And when Phinehas the priest, and the princes
of the congregation and heads of the thousands of
Israel which *were* with him, heard the words that the
children of Reuben and the children of Gad and the
children of Manasseh spake, it pleased them.
31And Phinehas the son of Eleazar the priest said
unto the children of Reuben, and to the children of
Gad, and to the children of Manasseh, This day we
perceive that the LORD *is* among us, because ye have
not committed this trespass against the LORD: now
ye have delivered the children of Israel out of the
hand of the LORD.
32And Phinehas the son of Eleazar the priest, and
the princes, returned from the children of Reuben,
and from the children of Gad, out of the land of
Gilead, unto the land of Canaan, to the children of
Israel, and brought them word again.
33And the thing pleased the children of Israel; and
the children of Israel blessed God, and did not intend

NEW LIVING TRANSLATION

21Then the people of Reuben, Gad, and the half-
tribe of Manasseh answered the heads of the clans of
Israel: 22"The LORD, the Mighty One, is God! The LORD,
the Mighty One, is God! He knows the truth, and may
Israel know it, too! We have not built the altar in
treacherous rebellion against the LORD. If we have
done so, do not spare our lives this day. 23If we have
built an altar for ourselves to turn away from the LORD
or to offer burnt offerings or grain offerings or peace
offerings, may the LORD himself punish us.
24"The truth is, we have built this altar because we
fear that in the future your descendants will say to
ours, 'What right do you have to worship the LORD,
the God of Israel? 25The LORD has placed the Jordan
River as a barrier between our people and you people of Reuben and Gad. You have no claim to the
LORD.' So your descendants may prevent our descendants from worshiping the LORD.
26"So we decided to build the altar, not for burnt
offerings or sacrifices, 27but as a memorial. It will remind our descendants and your descendants that
we, too, have the right to worship the LORD at his
sanctuary with our burnt offerings, sacrifices, and
peace offerings. Then your descendants will not be
able to say to ours, 'You have no claim to the LORD.'
28"If they say this, our descendants can reply, 'Look
at this copy of the LORD's altar that our ancestors
made. It is not for burnt offerings or sacrifices; it is a
reminder of the relationship both of us have with the
LORD.' 29Far be it from us to rebel against the LORD
or turn away from him by building our own altar for
burnt offerings, grain offerings, or sacrifices. Only
the altar of the LORD our God that stands in front of
the Tabernacle may be used for that purpose."
30When Phinehas the priest and the leaders of the
community—the heads of the clans of Israel—heard
this from the tribes of Reuben, Gad, and the half-
tribe of Manasseh, they were satisfied. 31Phinehas
son of Eleazar, the priest, replied to them, "Today we
know the LORD is among us because you have not
committed this treachery against the LORD as we
thought. Instead, you have rescued Israel from being
destroyed by the hand of the LORD."
32Then Phinehas son of Eleazar, the priest, and the
other leaders left the tribes of Reuben and Gad in
Gilead and returned to the land of Canaan to tell the
Israelites what had happened. 33And all the Israelites
were satisfied and praised God and spoke no more of
war against Reuben and Gad.

to go up against them in battle, to destroy the land
wherein the children of Reuben and Gad dwelt.
34 And the children of Reuben and the children of
Gad called the altar *Ed:* for it *shall be* a witness between us that the LORD *is* God.

23 1 And it came to pass a long time after that
the LORD had given rest unto Israel from all
their enemies round about, that Joshua waxed old
and stricken in age.
2 And Joshua called for all Israel, *and* for their elders, and for their heads, and for their judges, and for
their officers, and said unto them, I am old *and*
stricken in age:
3 And ye have seen all that the LORD your God hath
done unto all these nations because of you; for the
LORD your God *is* he that hath fought for you.
4 Behold, I have divided unto you by lot these nations that remain, to be an inheritance for your
tribes, from Jordan, with all the nations that I have
cut off, even unto the great sea westward.
5 And the LORD your God, he shall expel them from
before you, and drive them from out of your sight;
and ye shall possess their land, as the LORD your God
hath promised unto you.
6 Be ye therefore very courageous to keep and to do
all that is written in the book of the law of Moses,
that ye turn not aside therefrom *to* the right hand or
to the left;
7 That ye come not among these nations, these
that remain among you; neither make mention of the
name of their gods, nor cause to swear *by them,* neither serve them, nor bow yourselves unto them:
8 But cleave unto the LORD your God, as ye have
done unto this day.
9 For the LORD hath driven out from before you
great nations and strong: but *as for* you, no man hath
been able to stand before you unto this day.
10 One man of you shall chase a thousand: for the
LORD your God, he *it is* that fighteth for you, as he
hath promised you.
11 Take good heed therefore unto yourselves, that
ye love the LORD your God.
12 Else if ye do in any wise go back, and cleave unto
the remnant of these nations, *even* these that remain
among you, and shall make marriages with them,
and go in unto them, and they to you:
13 Know for a certainty that the LORD your God will
no more drive out *any of* these nations from before
you; but they shall be snares and traps unto you, and
scourges in your sides, and thorns in your eyes, until
ye perish from off this good land which the LORD
your God hath given you.
14 And, behold, this day I *am* going the way of all the
earth: and ye know in all your hearts and in all your
souls, that not one thing hath failed of all the good
things which the LORD your God spake concerning

34 The people of Reuben and Gad named the altar
"Witness,"* for they said, "It is a witness between us
and them that the LORD is our God, too."

Joshua's Final Words to Israel

23 The years passed, and the LORD had given
the people of Israel rest from all their enemies. Joshua, who was now very old, 2 called together
all the elders, leaders, judges, and officers of Israel.
He said to them, "I am now a very old man. 3 You have
seen everything the LORD your God has done for you
during my lifetime. The LORD your God has fought
for you against your enemies. 4 I have allotted to you
as your homeland all the land of the nations yet
unconquered, as well as the land of those we have
already conquered—from the Jordan River to the
Mediterranean Sea* in the west. 5 This land will be
yours, for the LORD your God will himself drive out
all the people living there now. You will take possession of their land, just as the LORD your God promised you.
6 "So be very careful to follow everything Moses
wrote in the Book of Instruction. Do not deviate
from it, turning either to the right or to the left.
7 Make sure you do not associate with the other people still remaining in the land. Do not even mention
the names of their gods, much less swear by them or
serve them or worship them. 8 Rather, cling tightly to
the LORD your God as you have done until now.
9 "For the LORD has driven out great and powerful
nations for you, and no one has yet been able to defeat you. 10 Each one of you will put to flight a thousand of the enemy, for the LORD your God fights for
you, just as he has promised. 11 So be very careful to
love the LORD your God.
12 "But if you turn away from him and cling to the
customs of the survivors of these nations remaining
among you, and if you intermarry with them, 13 then
know for certain that the LORD your God will no
longer drive them out of your land. Instead, they
will be a snare and a trap to you, a whip for your
backs and thorny brambles in your eyes, and you will
vanish from this good land the LORD your God has
given you.
14 "Soon I will die, going the way of everything on
earth. Deep in your hearts you know that every
promise of the LORD your God has come true. Not a

22:34 Some manuscripts lack this word. **23:4** Hebrew *the Great Sea.*

KING JAMES VERSION

you; all are come to pass unto you, *and* not one thing
hath failed thereof.
15 Therefore it shall come to pass, *that* as all good
things are come upon you, which the LORD your God
promised you; so shall the LORD bring upon you all
evil things, until he have destroyed you from off this
good land which the LORD your God hath given you.
16 When ye have transgressed the covenant of the
LORD your God, which he commanded you, and have
gone and served other gods, and bowed yourselves
to them; then shall the anger of the LORD be kindled
against you, and ye shall perish quickly from off the
good land which he hath given unto you.

24 1 And Joshua gathered all the tribes of Israel
to Shechem, and called for the elders of
Israel, and for their heads, and for their judges, and
for their officers; and they presented themselves before God.
2 And Joshua said unto all the people, Thus saith
the LORD God of Israel, Your fathers dwelt on the
other side of the flood in old time, *even* Terah, the father of Abraham, and the father of Nachor: and they
served other gods.
3 And I took your father Abraham from the other
side of the flood, and led him throughout all the land
of Canaan, and multiplied his seed, and gave him
Isaac.
4 And I gave unto Isaac Jacob and Esau: and I gave
unto Esau mount Seir, to possess it; but Jacob and his
children went down into Egypt.
5 I sent Moses also and Aaron, and I plagued Egypt,
according to that which I did among them: and afterward I brought you out.
6 And I brought your fathers out of Egypt: and ye
came unto the sea; and the Egyptians pursued after
your fathers with chariots and horsemen unto the
Red sea.
7 And when they cried unto the LORD, he put darkness between you and the Egyptians, and brought
the sea upon them, and covered them; and your eyes
have seen what I have done in Egypt: and ye dwelt in
the wilderness a long season.
8 And I brought you into the land of the Amorites,
which dwelt on the other side Jordan; and they
fought with you: and I gave them into your hand, that
ye might possess their land; and I destroyed them
from before you.
9 Then Balak the son of Zippor, king of Moab, arose
and warred against Israel, and sent and called Balaam the son of Beor to curse you:
10 But I would not hearken unto Balaam; therefore
he blessed you still: so I delivered you out of his hand.
11 And ye went over Jordan, and came unto Jericho:
and the men of Jericho fought against you, the Amorites, and the Perizzites, and the Canaanites, and the
Hittites, and the Girgashites, the Hivites, and the Jebusites; and I delivered them into your hand.

NEW LIVING TRANSLATION

single one has failed! 15 But as surely as the LORD your
God has given you the good things he promised, he
will also bring disaster on you if you disobey him. He
will completely destroy you from this good land
he has given you. 16 If you break the covenant of the
LORD your God by worshiping and serving other
gods, his anger will burn against you, and you will
quickly vanish from the good land he has given you."

The LORD's Covenant Renewed

24 Then Joshua summoned all the tribes of
Israel to Shechem, including their elders,
leaders, judges, and officers. So they came and presented themselves to God.
2 Joshua said to the people, "This is what the LORD,
the God of Israel, says: Long ago your ancestors, including Terah, the father of Abraham and Nahor,
lived beyond the Euphrates River,* and they worshiped other gods. 3 But I took your ancestor Abraham from the land beyond the Euphrates and led
him into the land of Canaan. I gave him many descendants through his son Isaac. 4 To Isaac I gave Jacob and Esau. To Esau I gave the mountains of Seir,
while Jacob and his children went down into Egypt.
5 "Then I sent Moses and Aaron, and I brought terrible plagues on Egypt; and afterward I brought you
out as a free people. 6 But when your ancestors arrived at the Red Sea,* the Egyptians chased after you
with chariots and charioteers. 7 When your ancestors cried out to the LORD, I put darkness between
you and the Egyptians. I brought the sea crashing
down on the Egyptians, drowning them. With your
very own eyes you saw what I did. Then you lived in
the wilderness for many years.
8 "Finally, I brought you into the land of the Amorites on the east side of the Jordan. They fought
against you, but I destroyed them before you. I gave
you victory over them, and you took possession of
their land. 9 Then Balak son of Zippor, king of Moab,
started a war against Israel. He summoned Balaam
son of Beor to curse you, 10 but I would not listen to
him. Instead, I made Balaam bless you, and so I rescued you from Balak.
11 "When you crossed the Jordan River and came
to Jericho, the men of Jericho fought against you, as
did the Amorites, the Perizzites, the Canaanites, the

24:2 Hebrew *the river;* also in 24:3, 14, 15. **24:6** Hebrew *sea of reeds.*

KING JAMES VERSION

[12]And I sent the hornet before you, which drave them out from before you, *even* the two kings of the Amorites; *but* not with thy sword, nor with thy bow.

[13]And I have given you a land for which ye did not labour, and cities which ye built not, and ye dwell in them; of the vineyards and oliveyards which ye planted not do ye eat.

[14]Now therefore fear the LORD, and serve him in sincerity and in truth: and put away the gods which your fathers served on the other side of the flood, and in Egypt; and serve ye the LORD.

[15]And if it seem evil unto you to serve the LORD, choose you this day whom ye will serve; whether the gods which your fathers served that *were* on the other side of the flood, or the gods of the Amorites, in whose land ye dwell: but as for me and my house, we will serve the LORD.

[16]And the people answered and said, God forbid that we should forsake the LORD, to serve other gods;

[17]For the LORD our God, he *it is* that brought us up and our fathers out of the land of Egypt, from the house of bondage, and which did those great signs in our sight, and preserved us in all the way wherein we went, and among all the people through whom we passed:

[18]And the LORD drave out from before us all the people, even the Amorites which dwelt in the land: *therefore* will we also serve the LORD; for he *is* our God.

[19]And Joshua said unto the people, Ye cannot serve the LORD: for he *is* an holy God; he *is* a jealous God; he will not forgive your transgressions nor your sins.

[20]If ye forsake the LORD, and serve strange gods, then he will turn and do you hurt, and consume you, after that he hath done you good.

[21]And the people said unto Joshua, Nay; but we will serve the LORD.

[22]And Joshua said unto the people, Ye *are* witnesses against yourselves that ye have chosen you the LORD, to serve him. And they said, *We are* witnesses.

[23]Now therefore put away, *said he,* the strange gods which *are* among you, and incline your heart unto the LORD God of Israel.

[24]And the people said unto Joshua, The LORD our God will we serve, and his voice will we obey.

[25]So Joshua made a covenant with the people that day, and set them a statute and an ordinance in Shechem.

[26]And Joshua wrote these words in the book of the law of God, and took a great stone, and set it up there under an oak, that *was* by the sanctuary of the LORD.

[27]And Joshua said unto all the people, Behold, this stone shall be a witness unto us; for it hath heard all the words of the LORD which he spake unto us: it shall be therefore a witness unto you, lest ye deny your God.

NEW LIVING TRANSLATION

Hittites, the Girgashites, the Hivites, and the Jebusites. But I gave you victory over them. [12]And I sent
terror* ahead of you to drive out the two kings of the
Amorites. It was not your swords or bows that
brought you victory. [13]I gave you land you had not
worked on, and I gave you towns you did not build—
the towns where you are now living. I gave you vineyards and olive groves for food, though you did not
plant them.
[14]"So fear the LORD and serve him wholeheartedly. Put away forever the idols your ancestors worshiped when they lived beyond the Euphrates River
and in Egypt. Serve the LORD alone. [15]But if you refuse to serve the LORD, then choose today whom you
will serve. Would you prefer the gods your ancestors
served beyond the Euphrates? Or will it be the gods
of the Amorites in whose land you now live? But as
for me and my family, we will serve the LORD."
[16]The people replied, "We would never abandon
the LORD and serve other gods. [17]For the LORD our
God is the one who rescued us and our ancestors
from slavery in the land of Egypt. He performed
mighty miracles before our very eyes. As we traveled
through the wilderness among our enemies, he preserved us. [18]It was the LORD who drove out the Amorites and the other nations living here in the land. So
we, too, will serve the LORD, for he alone is our God."
[19]Then Joshua warned the people, "You are not
able to serve the LORD, for he is a holy and jealous
God. He will not forgive your rebellion and your sins.
[20]If you abandon the LORD and serve other gods, he
will turn against you and destroy you, even though he
has been so good to you."
[21]But the people answered Joshua, "No, we will
serve the LORD!"
[22]"You are a witness to your own decision," Joshua
said. "You have chosen to serve the LORD."

"Yes," they replied, "we are witnesses to what we have said."

[23]"All right then," Joshua said, "destroy the idols
among you, and turn your hearts to the LORD, the God
of Israel."
[24]The people said to Joshua, "We will serve the
LORD our God. We will obey him alone."
[25]So Joshua made a covenant with the people that
day at Shechem, committing them to follow the decrees and regulations of the LORD. [26]Joshua recorded
these things in the Book of God's Instructions. As a
reminder of their agreement, he took a huge stone
and rolled it beneath the terebinth tree beside the
Tabernacle of the LORD.
[27]Joshua said to all the people, "This stone has
heard everything the LORD said to us. It will be a witness to testify against you if you go back on your
word to God."

24:12 Often rendered *the hornet*. The meaning of the Hebrew is uncertain.

KING JAMES VERSION

28So Joshua let the people depart, every man unto
his inheritance.

29And it came to pass after these things, that
Joshua the son of Nun, the servant of the LORD, died,
being an hundred and ten years old.
30And they buried him in the border of his inheritance in Timnath-serah, which *is* in mount Ephraim,
on the north side of the hill of Gaash.
31And Israel served the LORD all the days of Joshua,
and all the days of the elders that overlived Joshua,
and which had known all the works of the LORD, that
he had done for Israel.
32And the bones of Joseph, which the children of
Israel brought up out of Egypt, buried they in Shechem, in a parcel of ground which Jacob bought of
the sons of Hamor the father of Shechem for an hundred pieces of silver: and it became the inheritance
of the children of Joseph.
33And Eleazar the son of Aaron died; and they buried him in a hill *that pertained to* Phinehas his son,
which was given him in mount Ephraim.

NEW LIVING TRANSLATION

28Then Joshua sent all the people away to their
own homelands.

Leaders Buried in the Promised Land

29After this, Joshua son of Nun, the servant of the
LORD, died at the age of 110. 30They buried him in
the land he had been allocated, at Timnath-serah in
the hill country of Ephraim, north of Mount Gaash.
31The people of Israel served the LORD throughout
the lifetime of Joshua and of the elders who outlived
him—those who had personally experienced all that
the LORD had done for Israel.
32The bones of Joseph, which the Israelites had
brought along with them when they left Egypt, were
buried at Shechem, in the parcel of ground Jacob had
bought from the sons of Hamor for 100 pieces of
silver.* This land was located in the territory allotted
to the descendants of Joseph.
33Eleazar son of Aaron also died. He was buried in
the hill country of Ephraim, in the town of Gibeah,
which had been given to his son Phinehas.

24:32 Hebrew *100 kesitahs;* the value or weight of the kesitah is no longer known.

Judges

KING JAMES VERSION

1 1Now after the death of Joshua it came to pass,
that the children of Israel asked the LORD, saying, Who shall go up for us against the Canaanites
first, to fight against them?
2And the LORD said, Judah shall go up: behold, I
have delivered the land into his hand.
3And Judah said unto Simeon his brother, Come
up with me into my lot, that we may fight against the
Canaanites; and I likewise will go with thee into thy
lot. So Simeon went with him.
4And Judah went up; and the LORD delivered the
Canaanites and the Perizzites into their hand: and
they slew of them in Bezek ten thousand men.
5And they found Adoni-bezek in Bezek: and they
fought against him, and they slew the Canaanites and
the Perizzites.
6But Adoni-bezek fled; and they pursued after
him, and caught him, and cut off his thumbs and his
great toes.
7And Adoni-bezek said, Threescore and ten kings,
having their thumbs and their great toes cut off,
gathered *their meat* under my table: as I have done,
so God hath requited me. And they brought him to
Jerusalem, and there he died.
8Now the children of Judah had fought against
Jerusalem, and had taken it, and smitten it with the
edge of the sword, and set the city on fire.
9And afterward the children of Judah went down
to fight against the Canaanites, that dwelt in the
mountain, and in the south, and in the valley.
10And Judah went against the Canaanites that
dwelt in Hebron: (now the name of Hebron before
was Kirjath-arba:) and they slew Sheshai, and Ahiman, and Talmai.
11And from thence he went against the inhabitants of Debir: and the name of Debir before *was*
Kirjath-sepher:
12And Caleb said, He that smiteth Kirjath-sepher,
and taketh it, to him will I give Achsah my daughter
to wife.
13And Othniel the son of Kenaz, Caleb's younger
brother, took it: and he gave him Achsah his daughter to wife.

NEW LIVING TRANSLATION

Judah and Simeon Conquer the Land

1 After the death of Joshua, the Israelites asked
the LORD, "Which tribe should go first to attack
the Canaanites?"
2The LORD answered, "Judah, for I have given them
victory over the land."
3The men of Judah said to their relatives from the
tribe of Simeon, "Join with us to fight against the
Canaanites living in the territory allotted to us. Then
we will help you conquer your territory." So the men
of Simeon went with Judah.
4When the men of Judah attacked, the LORD gave
them victory over the Canaanites and Perizzites, and
they killed 10,000 enemy warriors at the town of Bezek. 5While at Bezek they encountered King Adoni-
bezek and fought against him, and the Canaanites
and Perizzites were defeated. 6Adoni-bezek escaped,
but the Israelites soon captured him and cut off his
thumbs and big toes.
7Adoni-bezek said, "I once had seventy kings with
their thumbs and big toes cut off, eating scraps from
under my table. Now God has paid me back for what
I did to them." They took him to Jerusalem, and he
died there.
8The men of Judah attacked Jerusalem and captured it, killing all its people and setting the city on
fire. 9Then they went down to fight the Canaanites
living in the hill country, the Negev, and the western
foothills.* 10Judah marched against the Canaanites
in Hebron (formerly called Kiriath-arba), defeating
the forces of Sheshai, Ahiman, and Talmai.
11From there they went to fight against the people
living in the town of Debir (formerly called Kiriath-
sepher). 12Caleb said, "I will give my daughter Acsah
in marriage to the one who attacks and captures
Kiriath-sepher." 13Othniel, the son of Caleb's younger brother, Kenaz, was the one who conquered it, so
Acsah became Othniel's wife.

1:9 Hebrew *the Shephelah.*

KING JAMES VERSION

14 And it came to pass, when she came *to him,* that she moved him to ask of her father a field: and she lighted from off *her* ass; and Caleb said unto her, What wilt thou?

15 And she said unto him, Give me a blessing: for thou hast given me a south land; give me also springs of water. And Caleb gave her the upper springs and the nether springs.

16 And the children of the Kenite, Moses' father in law, went up out of the city of palm trees with the children of Judah into the wilderness of Judah, which *lieth* in the south of Arad; and they went and dwelt among the people.

17 And Judah went with Simeon his brother, and they slew the Canaanites that inhabited Zephath, and utterly destroyed it. And the name of the city was called Hormah.

18 Also Judah took Gaza with the coast thereof, and Askelon with the coast thereof, and Ekron with the coast thereof.

19 And the LORD was with Judah; and he drave out *the inhabitants of* the mountain; but could not drive out the inhabitants of the valley, because they had chariots of iron.

20 And they gave Hebron unto Caleb, as Moses said: and he expelled thence the three sons of Anak.

21 And the children of Benjamin did not drive out the Jebusites that inhabited Jerusalem; but the Jebusites dwell with the children of Benjamin in Jerusalem unto this day.

22 And the house of Joseph, they also went up against Bethel: and the LORD *was* with them.

23 And the house of Joseph sent to descry Bethel. (Now the name of the city before *was* Luz.)

24 And the spies saw a man come forth out of the city, and they said unto him, Shew us, we pray thee, the entrance into the city, and we will shew thee mercy.

25 And when he shewed them the entrance into the city, they smote the city with the edge of the sword; but they let go the man and all his family.

26 And the man went into the land of the Hittites, and built a city, and called the name thereof Luz: which *is* the name thereof unto this day.

27 Neither did Manasseh drive out *the inhabitants of* Beth-shean and her towns, nor Taanach and her towns, nor the inhabitants of Dor and her towns, nor the inhabitants of Ibleam and her towns, nor the inhabitants of Megiddo and her towns: but the Canaanites would dwell in that land.

28 And it came to pass, when Israel was strong, that they put the Canaanites to tribute, and did not utterly drive them out.

29 Neither did Ephraim drive out the Canaanites that dwelt in Gezer; but the Canaanites dwelt in Gezer among them.

30 Neither did Zebulun drive out the inhabitants of Kitron, nor the inhabitants of Nahalol; but the Canaanites dwelt among them, and became tributaries.

NEW LIVING TRANSLATION

14 When Acsah married Othniel, she urged him* to ask her father for a field. As she got down off her donkey, Caleb asked her, "What's the matter?"

15 She said, "Let me have another gift. You have already given me land in the Negev; now please give me springs of water, too." So Caleb gave her the upper and lower springs.

16 When the tribe of Judah left Jericho—the city of palms—the Kenites, who were descendants of Moses' father-in-law, traveled with them into the wilderness of Judah. They settled among the people there, near the town of Arad in the Negev.

17 Then Judah joined with Simeon to fight against the Canaanites living in Zephath, and they completely destroyed* the town. So the town was named Hormah.* 18 In addition, Judah captured the towns of Gaza, Ashkelon, and Ekron, along with their surrounding territories.

Israel Fails to Conquer the Land

19 The LORD was with the people of Judah, and they took possession of the hill country. But they failed to drive out the people living in the plains, who had iron chariots. 20 The town of Hebron was given to Caleb as Moses had promised. And Caleb drove out the people living there, who were descendants of the three sons of Anak.

21 The tribe of Benjamin, however, failed to drive out the Jebusites, who were living in Jerusalem. So to this day the Jebusites live in Jerusalem among the people of Benjamin.

22 The descendants of Joseph attacked the town of Bethel, and the LORD was with them. 23 They sent men to scout out Bethel (formerly known as Luz). 24 They confronted a man coming out of the town and said to him, "Show us a way into the town, and we will have mercy on you." 25 So he showed them a way in, and they killed everyone in the town except that man and his family. 26 Later the man moved to the land of the Hittites, where he built a town. He named it Luz, which is its name to this day.

27 The tribe of Manasseh failed to drive out the people living in Beth-shan,* Taanach, Dor, Ibleam, Megiddo, and all their surrounding settlements, because the Canaanites were determined to stay in that region. 28 When the Israelites grew stronger, they forced the Canaanites to work as slaves, but they never did drive them completely out of the land.

29 The tribe of Ephraim failed to drive out the Canaanites living in Gezer, so the Canaanites continued to live there among them.

30 The tribe of Zebulun failed to drive out the residents of Kitron and Nahalol, so the Canaanites continued to live among them. But the Canaanites were forced to work as slaves for the people of Zebulun.

1:14 Greek version and Latin Vulgate read *he urged her.* **1:17a** The Hebrew term used here refers to the complete consecration of things or people to the LORD, either by destroying them or by giving them as an offering. **1:17b** *Hormah* means "destruction." **1:27** Hebrew *Beth-shean,* a variant spelling of Beth-shan.

KING JAMES VERSION

31Neither did Asher drive out the inhabitants of Accho, nor the inhabitants of Zidon, nor of Ahlab, nor of Achzib, nor of Helbah, nor of Aphik, nor of Rehob:

32But the Asherites dwelt among the Canaanites, the inhabitants of the land: for they did not drive them out.

33Neither did Naphtali drive out the inhabitants of Beth-shemesh, nor the inhabitants of Beth-anath; but he dwelt among the Canaanites, the inhabitants of the land: nevertheless the inhabitants of Beth-shemesh and of Beth-anath became tributaries unto them.

34And the Amorites forced the children of Dan into the mountain: for they would not suffer them to come down to the valley:

35But the Amorites would dwell in mount Heres in Aijalon, and in Shaalbim: yet the hand of the house of Joseph prevailed, so that they became tributaries.

36And the coast of the Amorites *was* from the going up to Akrabbim, from the rock, and upward.

2 1And an angel of the LORD came up from Gilgal to Bochim, and said, I made you to go up out of Egypt, and have brought you unto the land which I sware unto your fathers; and I said, I will never break my covenant with you.

2And ye shall make no league with the inhabitants of this land; ye shall throw down their altars: but ye have not obeyed my voice: why have ye done this?

3Wherefore I also said, I will not drive them out from before you; but they shall be *as thorns* in your sides, and their gods shall be a snare unto you.

4And it came to pass, when the angel of the LORD spake these words unto all the children of Israel, that the people lifted up their voice, and wept.

5And they called the name of that place Bochim: and they sacrificed there unto the LORD.

6And when Joshua had let the people go, the children of Israel went every man unto his inheritance to possess the land.

7And the people served the LORD all the days of Joshua, and all the days of the elders that outlived Joshua, who had seen all the great works of the LORD, that he did for Israel.

8And Joshua, the son of Nun, the servant of the LORD, died, *being* an hundred and ten years old.

9And they buried him in the border of his inheritance in Timnath-heres, in the mount of Ephraim, on the north side of the hill Gaash.

10And also all that generation were gathered unto their fathers: and there arose another generation after them, which knew not the LORD, nor yet the works which he had done for Israel.

11And the children of Israel did evil in the sight of the LORD, and served Baalim:

NEW LIVING TRANSLATION

31The tribe of Asher failed to drive out the residents of Acco, Sidon, Ahlab, Aczib, Helbah, Aphik, and Rehob. 32Instead, the people of Asher moved in among the Canaanites, who controlled the land, for they failed to drive them out.

33Likewise, the tribe of Naphtali failed to drive out the residents of Beth-shemesh and Beth-anath. Instead, they moved in among the Canaanites, who controlled the land. Nevertheless, the people of Beth-shemesh and Beth-anath were forced to work as slaves for the people of Naphtali.

34As for the tribe of Dan, the Amorites forced them back into the hill country and would not let them come down into the plains. 35The Amorites were determined to stay in Mount Heres, Aijalon, and Shaalbim, but when the descendants of Joseph became stronger, they forced the Amorites to work as slaves. 36The boundary of the Amorites ran from Scorpion Pass* to Sela and continued upward from there.

The LORD's Messenger Comes to Bokim

2 The angel of the LORD went up from Gilgal to Bokim and said to the Israelites, "I brought you out of Egypt into this land that I swore to give your ancestors, and I said I would never break my covenant with you. 2For your part, you were not to make any covenants with the people living in this land; instead, you were to destroy their altars. But you disobeyed my command. Why did you do this? 3So now I declare that I will no longer drive out the people living in your land. They will be thorns in your sides,* and their gods will be a constant temptation to you."

4When the angel of the LORD finished speaking to all the Israelites, the people wept loudly. 5So they called the place Bokim (which means "weeping"), and they offered sacrifices there to the LORD.

The Death of Joshua

6After Joshua sent the people away, each of the tribes left to take possession of the land allotted to them. 7And the Israelites served the LORD throughout the lifetime of Joshua and the leaders who outlived him—those who had seen all the great things the LORD had done for Israel.

8Joshua son of Nun, the servant of the LORD, died at the age of 110. 9They buried him in the land he had been allocated, at Timnath-serah* in the hill country of Ephraim, north of Mount Gaash.

Israel Disobeys the LORD

10After that generation died, another generation grew up who did not acknowledge the LORD or remember the mighty things he had done for Israel.

11The Israelites did evil in the LORD's sight and

1:36 Hebrew *Akrabbim.* **2:3** Hebrew *They will be in your sides;* compare Num 33:55. **2:9** As in parallel text at Josh 24:30; Hebrew reads *Timnath-heres,* a variant spelling of Timnath-serah.

KING JAMES VERSION

12 And they forsook the LORD God of their fathers, which brought them out of the land of Egypt, and followed other gods, of the gods of the people that *were* round about them, and bowed themselves unto them, and provoked the LORD to anger.

13 And they forsook the LORD, and served Baal and Ashtaroth.

14 And the anger of the LORD was hot against Israel, and he delivered them into the hands of spoilers that spoiled them, and he sold them into the hands of their enemies round about, so that they could not any longer stand before their enemies.

15 Whithersoever they went out, the hand of the LORD was against them for evil, as the LORD had said, and as the LORD had sworn unto them: and they were greatly distressed.

16 Nevertheless the LORD raised up judges, which delivered them out of the hand of those that spoiled them.

17 And yet they would not hearken unto their judges, but they went a whoring after other gods, and bowed themselves unto them: they turned quickly out of the way which their fathers walked in, obeying the commandments of the LORD; *but* they did not so.

18 And when the LORD raised them up judges, then the LORD was with the judge, and delivered them out of the hand of their enemies all the days of the judge: for it repented the LORD because of their groanings by reason of them that oppressed them and vexed them.

19 And it came to pass, when the judge was dead, *that* they returned, and corrupted *themselves* more than their fathers, in following other gods to serve them, and to bow down unto them; they ceased not from their own doings, nor from their stubborn way.

20 And the anger of the LORD was hot against Israel; and he said, Because that this people hath transgressed my covenant which I commanded their fathers, and have not hearkened unto my voice;

21 I also will not henceforth drive out any from before them of the nations which Joshua left when he died:

22 That through them I may prove Israel, whether they will keep the way of the LORD to walk therein, as their fathers did keep *it,* or not.

23 Therefore the LORD left those nations, without driving them out hastily; neither delivered he them into the hand of Joshua.

3 1 Now these *are* the nations which the LORD left, to prove Israel by them, *even* as many *of Israel* as had not known all the wars of Canaan;

2 Only that the generations of the children of Israel might know, to teach them war, at the least such as before knew nothing thereof;

3 *Namely,* five lords of the Philistines, and all the Canaanites, and the Sidonians, and the Hivites that dwelt in mount Lebanon, from mount Baal-hermon unto the entering in of Hamath.

NEW LIVING TRANSLATION

served the images of Baal. 12 They abandoned the LORD, the God of their ancestors, who had brought them out of Egypt. They went after other gods, worshiping the gods of the people around them. And they angered the LORD. 13 They abandoned the LORD to serve Baal and the images of Ashtoreth. 14 This made the LORD burn with anger against Israel, so he handed them over to raiders who stole their possessions. He turned them over to their enemies all around, and they were no longer able to resist them. 15 Every time Israel went out to battle, the LORD fought against them, causing them to be defeated, just as he had warned. And the people were in great distress.

The LORD Rescues His People

16 Then the LORD raised up judges to rescue the Israelites from their attackers. 17 Yet Israel did not listen to the judges but prostituted themselves by worshiping other gods. How quickly they turned away from the path of their ancestors, who had walked in obedience to the LORD's commands.

18 Whenever the LORD raised up a judge over Israel, he was with that judge and rescued the people from their enemies throughout the judge's lifetime. For the LORD took pity on his people, who were burdened by oppression and suffering. 19 But when the judge died, the people returned to their corrupt ways, behaving worse than those who had lived before them. They went after other gods, serving and worshiping them. And they refused to give up their evil practices and stubborn ways.

20 So the LORD burned with anger against Israel. He said, "Because these people have violated my covenant, which I made with their ancestors, and have ignored my commands, 21 I will no longer drive out the nations that Joshua left unconquered when he died. 22 I did this to test Israel—to see whether or not they would follow the ways of the LORD as their ancestors did." 23 That is why the LORD left those nations in place. He did not quickly drive them out or allow Joshua to conquer them all.

The Nations Left in Canaan

3 These are the nations that the LORD left in the land to test those Israelites who had not experienced the wars of Canaan. 2 He did this to teach warfare to generations of Israelites who had no experience in battle. 3 These are the nations: the Philistines (those living under the five Philistine rulers), all the Canaanites, the Sidonians, and the Hivites living in the mountains of Lebanon from Mount

KING JAMES VERSION

4And they were to prove Israel by them, to know
whether they would hearken unto the commandments of the LORD, which he commanded their fathers by the hand of Moses.
5And the children of Israel dwelt among the Canaanites, Hittites, and Amorites, and Perizzites, and
Hivites, and Jebusites:
6And they took their daughters to be their wives,
and gave their daughters to their sons, and served
their gods.

7And the children of Israel did evil in the sight of
the LORD, and forgat the LORD their God, and served
Baalim and the groves.
8Therefore the anger of the LORD was hot against
Israel, and he sold them into the hand of Chushan-
rishathaim king of Mesopotamia: and the children of
Israel served Chushan-rishathaim eight years.
9And when the children of Israel cried unto the
LORD, the LORD raised up a deliverer to the children
of Israel, who delivered them, *even* Othniel the son
of Kenaz, Caleb's younger brother.
10And the spirit of the LORD came upon him, and
he judged Israel, and went out to war: and the LORD
delivered Chushan-rishathaim king of Mesopotamia
into his hand; and his hand prevailed against
Chushan-rishathaim.
11And the land had rest forty years. And Othniel
the son of Kenaz died.
12And the children of Israel did evil again in the
sight of the LORD: and the LORD strengthened Eglon
the king of Moab against Israel, because they had
done evil in the sight of the LORD.
13And he gathered unto him the children of Ammon and Amalek, and went and smote Israel, and
possessed the city of palm trees.
14So the children of Israel served Eglon the king of
Moab eighteen years.
15But when the children of Israel cried unto the
LORD, the LORD raised them up a deliverer, Ehud the
son of Gera, a Benjamite, a man lefthanded: and by
him the children of Israel sent a present unto Eglon
the king of Moab.
16But Ehud made him a dagger which had two
edges, of a cubit length; and he did gird it under his
raiment upon his right thigh.
17And he brought the present unto Eglon king of
Moab: and Eglon *was* a very fat man.
18And when he had made an end to offer the present, he sent away the people that bare the present.
19But he himself turned again from the quarries
that *were* by Gilgal, and said, I have a secret errand
unto thee, O king: who said, Keep silence. And all
that stood by him went out from him.
20And Ehud came unto him; and he was sitting in
a summer parlour, which he had for himself alone.

NEW LIVING TRANSLATION

Baal-hermon to Lebo-hamath. 4These people were
left to test the Israelites—to see whether they would
obey the commands the LORD had given to their
ancestors through Moses.
5So the people of Israel lived among the Canaanites, Hittites, Amorites, Perizzites, Hivites, and Jebusites, 6and they intermarried with them. Israelite
sons married their daughters, and Israelite daughters were given in marriage to their sons. And the
Israelites served their gods.

Othniel Becomes Israel's Judge

7The Israelites did evil in the LORD's sight. They forgot about the LORD their God, and they served the
images of Baal and the Asherah poles. 8Then the
LORD burned with anger against Israel, and he
turned them over to King Cushan-rishathaim of
Aram-naharaim.* And the Israelites served Cushan-
rishathaim for eight years.
9But when the people of Israel cried out to the
LORD for help, the LORD raised up a rescuer to save
them. His name was Othniel, the son of Caleb's younger brother, Kenaz. 10The Spirit of the LORD came
upon him, and he became Israel's judge. He went to
war against King Cushan-rishathaim of Aram, and
the LORD gave Othniel victory over him. 11So there
was peace in the land for forty years. Then Othniel
son of Kenaz died.

Ehud Becomes Israel's Judge

12Once again the Israelites did evil in the LORD's
sight, and the LORD gave King Eglon of Moab control
over Israel because of their evil. 13Eglon enlisted the
Ammonites and Amalekites as allies, and then he
went out and defeated Israel, taking possession of
Jericho, the city of palms. 14And the Israelites served
Eglon of Moab for eighteen years.
15But when the people of Israel cried out to the
LORD for help, the LORD again raised up a rescuer to
save them. His name was Ehud son of Gera, a left-
handed man of the tribe of Benjamin. The Israelites
sent Ehud to deliver their tribute money to King Eglon of Moab. 16So Ehud made a double-edged dagger
that was about a foot* long, and he strapped it to his
right thigh, keeping it hidden under his clothing.
17He brought the tribute money to Eglon, who was
very fat.
18After delivering the payment, Ehud started
home with those who had helped carry the tribute.
19But when Ehud reached the stone idols near Gilgal,
he turned back. He came to Eglon and said, "I have a
secret message for you."
So the king commanded his servants, "Be quiet!"
and he sent them all out of the room.
20Ehud walked over to Eglon, who was sitting

3:8 *Aram-naharaim* means "Aram of the two rivers," thought to have been located between the Euphrates and Balih Rivers in northwestern Mesopotamia. **3:16** Hebrew *gomed,* the length of which is uncertain.

KING JAMES VERSION

And Ehud said, I have a message from God unto thee.
And he arose out of *his* seat.
21 And Ehud put forth his left hand, and took the
dagger from his right thigh, and thrust it into his
belly:
22 And the haft also went in after the blade; and the
fat closed upon the blade, so that he could not draw
the dagger out of his belly; and the dirt came out.
23 Then Ehud went forth through the porch, and
shut the doors of the parlour upon him, and locked
them.
24 When he was gone out, his servants came; and
when they saw that, behold, the doors of the parlour
were locked, they said, Surely he covereth his feet in
his summer chamber.
25 And they tarried till they were ashamed: and, behold, he opened not the doors of the parlour; therefore they took a key, and opened *them:* and, behold,
their lord *was* fallen down dead on the earth.
26 And Ehud escaped while they tarried, and
passed beyond the quarries, and escaped unto
Seirath.
27 And it came to pass, when he was come, that he
blew a trumpet in the mountain of Ephraim, and the
children of Israel went down with him from the
mount, and he before them.
28 And he said unto them, Follow after me: for the
LORD hath delivered your enemies the Moabites into
your hand. And they went down after him, and took
the fords of Jordan toward Moab, and suffered not
a man to pass over.
29 And they slew of Moab at that time about ten
thousand men, all lusty, and all men of valour; and
there escaped not a man.
30 So Moab was subdued that day under the hand
of Israel. And the land had rest fourscore years.
31 And after him was Shamgar the son of Anath,
which slew of the Philistines six hundred men with
an ox goad: and he also delivered Israel.

4 1 And the children of Israel again did evil in the
sight of the LORD, when Ehud was dead.
2 And the LORD sold them into the hand of Jabin
king of Canaan, that reigned in Hazor; the captain of
whose host *was* Sisera, which dwelt in Harosheth of
the Gentiles.
3 And the children of Israel cried unto the LORD:
for he had nine hundred chariots of iron; and twenty
years he mightily oppressed the children of Israel.
4 And Deborah, a prophetess, the wife of Lapidoth,
she judged Israel at that time.
5 And she dwelt under the palm tree of Deborah
between Ramah and Bethel in mount Ephraim: and
the children of Israel came up to her for judgment.
6 And she sent and called Barak the son of Abinoam out of Kedesh-naphtali, and said unto him, Hath
not the LORD God of Israel commanded, *saying,* Go
and draw toward mount Tabor, and take with thee

NEW LIVING TRANSLATION

alone in a cool upstairs room. And Ehud said, "I have
a message from God for you!" As King Eglon rose
from his seat, 21 Ehud reached with his left hand,
pulled out the dagger strapped to his right thigh, and
plunged it into the king's belly. 22 The dagger went so
deep that the handle disappeared beneath the king's
fat. So Ehud did not pull out the dagger, and the
king's bowels emptied.* 23 Then Ehud closed and
locked the doors of the room and escaped down the
latrine.*
24 After Ehud was gone, the king's servants returned and found the doors to the upstairs room
locked. They thought he might be using the latrine
in the room, 25 so they waited. But when the king
didn't come out after a long delay, they became concerned and got a key. And when they opened the
doors, they found their master dead on the floor.
26 While the servants were waiting, Ehud escaped,
passing the stone idols on his way to Seirah. 27 When
he arrived in the hill country of Ephraim, Ehud
sounded a call to arms. Then he led a band of Israelites down from the hills.
28 "Follow me," he said, "for the LORD has given you
victory over Moab your enemy." So they followed
him. And the Israelites took control of the shallow
crossings of the Jordan River across from Moab, pre-
venting anyone from crossing.
29 They attacked the Moabites and killed about
10,000 of their strongest and most able-bodied warriors. Not one of them escaped. 30 So Moab was conquered by Israel that day, and there was peace in the
land for eighty years.

Shamgar Becomes Israel's Judge

31 After Ehud, Shamgar son of Anath rescued Israel.
He once killed 600 Philistines with an ox goad.

Deborah Becomes Israel's Judge

4 After Ehud's death, the Israelites again did evil
in the LORD's sight. 2 So the LORD turned them
over to King Jabin of Hazor, a Canaanite king. The
commander of his army was Sisera, who lived in
Harosheth-haggoyim. 3 Sisera, who had 900 iron
chariots, ruthlessly oppressed the Israelites for
twenty years. Then the people of Israel cried out to
the LORD for help.
4 Deborah, the wife of Lappidoth, was a prophet
who was judging Israel at that time. 5 She would sit
under the Palm of Deborah, between Ramah and
Bethel in the hill country of Ephraim, and the Israelites would go to her for judgment. 6 One day she sent
for Barak son of Abinoam, who lived in Kedesh in the
land of Naphtali. She said to him, "This is what the

3:22 Or *and it came out behind.* **3:23** Or *and went out through the porch;* the meaning of the Hebrew is uncertain.

KING JAMES VERSION

ten thousand men of the children of Naphtali and
of the children of Zebulun?
7 And I will draw unto thee to the river Kishon Sisera, the captain of Jabin's army, with his chariots and
his multitude; and I will deliver him into thine hand.
8 And Barak said unto her, If thou wilt go with me,
then I will go: but if thou wilt not go with me, *then* I
will not go.
9 And she said, I will surely go with thee: notwithstanding the journey that thou takest shall not be for
thine honour; for the LORD shall sell Sisera into the
hand of a woman. And Deborah arose, and went with
Barak to Kedesh.
10 And Barak called Zebulun and Naphtali to Kedesh; and he went up with ten thousand men at his
feet: and Deborah went up with him.
11 Now Heber the Kenite, *which was* of the children of Hobab the father in law of Moses, had severed himself from the Kenites, and pitched his tent
unto the plain of Zaanaim, which *is* by Kedesh.
12 And they shewed Sisera that Barak the son of
Abinoam was gone up to mount Tabor.
13 And Sisera gathered together all his chariots,
even nine hundred chariots of iron, and all the
people that *were* with him, from Harosheth of the
Gentiles unto the river of Kishon.
14 And Deborah said unto Barak, Up; for this *is* the
day in which the LORD hath delivered Sisera into
thine hand: is not the LORD gone out before thee?
So Barak went down from mount Tabor, and ten
thousand men after him.
15 And the LORD discomfited Sisera, and all *his*
chariots, and all *his* host, with the edge of the sword
before Barak; so that Sisera lighted down off *his*
chariot, and fled away on his feet.
16 But Barak pursued after the chariots, and after
the host, unto Harosheth of the Gentiles: and all the
host of Sisera fell upon the edge of the sword; *and*
there was not a man left.
17 Howbeit Sisera fled away on his feet to the tent
of Jael the wife of Heber the Kenite: for *there was*
peace between Jabin the king of Hazor and the
house of Heber the Kenite.
18 And Jael went out to meet Sisera, and said unto
him, Turn in, my lord, turn in to me; fear not. And
when he had turned in unto her into the tent, she
covered him with a mantle.
19 And he said unto her, Give me, I pray thee, a little
water to drink; for I am thirsty. And she opened a
bottle of milk, and gave him drink, and covered him.
20 Again he said unto her, Stand in the door of the
tent, and it shall be, when any man doth come and
inquire of thee, and say, Is there any man here? that
thou shalt say, No.
21 Then Jael Heber's wife took a nail of the tent,
and took an hammer in her hand, and went softly
unto him, and smote the nail into his temples, and

NEW LIVING TRANSLATION

LORD, the God of Israel, commands you: Call out
10,000 warriors from the tribes of Naphtali and
Zebulun at Mount Tabor.
7 And I will call out Sisera,
commander of Jabin's army, along with his chariots
and warriors, to the Kishon River. There I will give
you victory over him."
8 Barak told her, "I will go, but only if you go
with me."
9 "Very well," she replied, "I will go with you. But
you will receive no honor in this venture, for the
LORD's victory over Sisera will be at the hands of a
woman." So Deborah went with Barak to Kedesh.
10 At Kedesh, Barak called together the tribes of Zebulun and Naphtali, and 10,000 warriors went up
with him. Deborah also went with him.
11 Now Heber the Kenite, a descendant of Moses'
brother-in-law* Hobab, had moved away from the
other members of his tribe and pitched his tent by
the oak of Zaanannim near Kedesh.
12 When Sisera was told that Barak son of Abinoam had gone up to Mount Tabor,
13 he called for all
900 of his iron chariots and all of his warriors, and
they marched from Harosheth-haggoyim to the
Kishon River.
14 Then Deborah said to Barak, "Get ready! This is
the day the LORD will give you victory over Sisera, for
the LORD is marching ahead of you." So Barak led his
10,000 warriors down the slopes of Mount Tabor
into battle.
15 When Barak attacked, the LORD threw
Sisera and all his chariots and warriors into a panic.
Sisera leaped down from his chariot and escaped on
foot.
16 Then Barak chased the chariots and the enemy army all the way to Harosheth-haggoyim, killing
all of Sisera's warriors. Not a single one was left alive.
17 Meanwhile, Sisera ran to the tent of Jael, the wife
of Heber the Kenite, because Heber's family was on
friendly terms with King Jabin of Hazor.
18 Jael went
out to meet Sisera and said to him, "Come into my
tent, sir. Come in. Don't be afraid." So he went into
her tent, and she covered him with a blanket.
19 "Please give me some water," he said. "I'm
thirsty." So she gave him some milk from a leather
bag and covered him again.
20 "Stand at the door of the tent," he told her. "If
anybody comes and asks you if there is anyone here,
say no."
21 But when Sisera fell asleep from exhaustion, Jael
quietly crept up to him with a hammer and tent peg

4:11 Or *father-in-law.*

KING JAMES VERSION

fastened it into the ground: for he was fast asleep and weary. So he died.

22 And, behold, as Barak pursued Sisera, Jael came out to meet him, and said unto him, Come, and I will shew thee the man whom thou seekest. And when he came into her *tent,* behold, Sisera lay dead, and the nail *was* in his temples.

23 So God subdued on that day Jabin the king of Canaan before the children of Israel.

24 And the hand of the children of Israel prospered, and prevailed against Jabin the king of Canaan, until they had destroyed Jabin king of Canaan.

5 1 Then sang Deborah and Barak the son of Abinoam on that day, saying,

2 Praise ye the LORD for the avenging of Israel, when the people willingly offered themselves.

3 Hear, O ye kings; give ear, O ye princes; I, *even* I, will sing unto the LORD; I will sing *praise* to the LORD God of Israel.

4 LORD, when thou wentest out of Seir, when thou marchedst out of the field of Edom, the earth trembled, and the heavens dropped, the clouds also dropped water.

5 The mountains melted from before the LORD, *even* that Sinai from before the LORD God of Israel.

6 In the days of Shamgar the son of Anath, in the days of Jael, the highways were unoccupied, and the travellers walked through byways.

7 *The inhabitants of* the villages ceased, they ceased in Israel, until that I Deborah arose, that I arose a mother in Israel.

8 They chose new gods; then *was* war in the gates: was there a shield or spear seen among forty thousand in Israel?

9 My heart *is* toward the governors of Israel, that offered themselves willingly among the people. Bless ye the LORD.

10 Speak, ye that ride on white asses, ye that sit in judgment, and walk by the way.

11 *They that are delivered* from the noise of archers in the places of drawing water, there shall they rehearse the righteous acts of the LORD, *even* the righteous acts *toward the inhabitants* of his villages

NEW LIVING TRANSLATION

in her hand. Then she drove the tent peg through his temple and into the ground, and so he died.

22 When Barak came looking for Sisera, Jael went out to meet him. She said, "Come, and I will show you the man you are looking for." So he followed her into the tent and found Sisera lying there dead, with the tent peg through his temple.

23 So on that day Israel saw God defeat Jabin, the Canaanite king. 24 And from that time on Israel became stronger and stronger against King Jabin until they finally destroyed him.

The Song of Deborah

5 On that day Deborah and Barak son of Abinoam sang this song:

2 "Israel's leaders took charge,
and the people gladly followed.
Praise the LORD!

3 "Listen, you kings!
Pay attention, you mighty rulers!
For I will sing to the LORD.
I will make music to the LORD, the God
of Israel.

4 "LORD, when you set out from Seir
and marched across the fields of Edom,
the earth trembled,
and the cloudy skies poured down rain.
5 The mountains quaked in the presence of
the LORD,
the God of Mount Sinai—
in the presence of the LORD,
the God of Israel.

6 "In the days of Shamgar son of Anath,
and in the days of Jael,
people avoided the main roads,
and travelers stayed on winding pathways.
7 There were few people left in the villages of
Israel*—
until Deborah arose as a mother for Israel.
8 When Israel chose new gods,
war erupted at the city gates.
Yet not a shield or spear could be seen
among forty thousand warriors in Israel!
9 My heart is with the commanders of Israel,
with those who volunteered for war.
Praise the LORD!

10 "Consider this, you who ride on fine donkeys,
you who sit on fancy saddle blankets,
and you who walk along the road.
11 Listen to the village musicians*
gathered at the watering holes.
They recount the righteous victories of the LORD
and the victories of his villagers in Israel.

5:7 The meaning of the Hebrew is uncertain. **5:11** The meaning of the Hebrew is uncertain.

KING JAMES VERSION

in Israel: then shall the people of the LORD go down
to the gates.
12 Awake, awake, Deborah: awake, awake, utter a
song: arise, Barak, and lead thy captivity captive, thou
son of Abinoam.
13 Then he made him that remaineth have dominion over the nobles among the people: the LORD
made me have dominion over the mighty.
14 Out of Ephraim *was there* a root of them against
Amalek; after thee, Benjamin, among thy people; out
of Machir came down governors, and out of Zebulun
they that handle the pen of the writer.
15 And the princes of Issachar *were* with Deborah;
even Issachar, and also Barak: he was sent on foot
into the valley. For the divisions of Reuben *there
were* great thoughts of heart.
16 Why abodest thou among the sheepfolds, to
hear the bleatings of the flocks? For the divisions of
Reuben *there were* great searchings of heart.
17 Gilead abode beyond Jordan: and why did Dan
remain in ships? Asher continued on the sea shore,
and abode in his breaches.
18 Zebulun and Naphtali *were* a people *that*
jeoparded their lives unto the death in the high
places of the field.
19 The kings came *and* fought, then fought the
kings of Canaan in Taanach by the waters of Megiddo; they took no gain of money.
20 They fought from heaven; the stars in their
courses fought against Sisera.
21 The river of Kishon swept them away, that ancient river, the river Kishon. O my soul, thou hast
trodden down strength.
22 Then were the horsehoofs broken by the means
of the pransings, the pransings of their mighty ones.
23 Curse ye Meroz, said the angel of the LORD, curse
ye bitterly the inhabitants thereof; because they
came not to the help of the LORD, to the help of the
LORD against the mighty.
24 Blessed above women shall Jael the wife of Heber the Kenite be, blessed shall she be above women
in the tent.
25 He asked water, *and* she gave *him* milk; she
brought forth butter in a lordly dish.

NEW LIVING TRANSLATION

Then the people of the LORD
marched down to the city gates.

12 "Wake up, Deborah, wake up!
Wake up, wake up, and sing a song!
Arise, Barak!
Lead your captives away, son of Abinoam!

13 "Down from Tabor marched the few against
the nobles.
The people of the LORD marched down against
mighty warriors.
14 They came down from Ephraim—
a land that once belonged to the Amalekites;
they followed you, Benjamin, with your troops.
From Makir the commanders marched down;
from Zebulun came those who carry a
commander's staff.
15 The princes of Issachar were with Deborah
and Barak.
They followed Barak, rushing into the valley.
But in the tribe of Reuben
there was great indecision.
16 Why did you sit at home among the sheepfolds—
to hear the shepherds whistle for their flocks?
Yes, in the tribe of Reuben
there was great indecision.
17 Gilead remained east of the Jordan.
And why did Dan stay home?
Asher sat unmoved at the seashore,
remaining in his harbors.
18 But Zebulun risked his life,
as did Naphtali, on the heights of the
battlefield.

19 "The kings of Canaan came and fought,
at Taanach near Megiddo's springs,
but they carried off no silver treasures.
20 The stars fought from heaven.
The stars in their orbits fought against Sisera.
21 The Kishon River swept them away—
that ancient torrent, the Kishon.
March on with courage, my soul!
22 Then the horses' hooves hammered the ground,
the galloping, galloping of Sisera's mighty
steeds.
23 'Let the people of Meroz be cursed,' said the
angel of the LORD.
'Let them be utterly cursed,
because they did not come to help the LORD—
to help the LORD against the mighty warriors.'
24 "Most blessed among women is Jael,
the wife of Heber the Kenite.
May she be blessed above all women who
live in tents.
25 Sisera asked for water,
and she gave him milk.
In a bowl fit for nobles,
she brought him yogurt.

KING JAMES VERSION

26 She put her hand to the nail, and her right hand to the workmen's hammer; and with the hammer she smote Sisera, she smote off his head, when she had pierced and stricken through his temples.

27 At her feet he bowed, he fell, he lay down: at her feet he bowed, he fell: where he bowed, there he fell down dead.

28 The mother of Sisera looked out at a window, and cried through the lattice, Why is his chariot *so* long in coming? why tarry the wheels of his chariots?

29 Her wise ladies answered her, yea, she returned answer to herself,

30 Have they not sped? have they *not* divided the prey; to every man a damsel *or* two; to Sisera a prey of divers colours, a prey of divers colours of needlework, of divers colours of needlework on both sides, *meet* for the necks of *them that take* the spoil?

31 So let all thine enemies perish, O LORD: but *let* them that love him *be* as the sun when he goeth forth in his might. And the land had rest forty years.

6 1 And the children of Israel did evil in the sight of the LORD: and the LORD delivered them into the hand of Midian seven years.

2 And the hand of Midian prevailed against Israel: *and* because of the Midianites the children of Israel made them the dens which *are* in the mountains, and caves, and strong holds.

3 And *so* it was, when Israel had sown, that the Midianites came up, and the Amalekites, and the children of the east, even they came up against them;

4 And they encamped against them, and destroyed the increase of the earth, till thou come unto Gaza, and left no sustenance for Israel, neither sheep, nor ox, nor ass.

5 For they came up with their cattle and their tents, and they came as grasshoppers for multitude; *for* both they and their camels were without number: and they entered into the land to destroy it.

6 And Israel was greatly impoverished because of the Midianites; and the children of Israel cried unto the LORD.

7 And it came to pass, when the children of Israel cried unto the LORD because of the Midianites,

8 That the LORD sent a prophet unto the children

NEW LIVING TRANSLATION

26 Then with her left hand she reached for
a tent peg,
and with her right hand for the workman's
hammer.
She struck Sisera with the hammer, crushing
his head.
With a shattering blow, she pierced his
temples.
27 He sank, he fell,
he lay still at her feet.
And where he sank,
there he died.

28 "From the window Sisera's mother looked out.
Through the window she watched for his
return, saying,
'Why is his chariot so long in coming?
Why don't we hear the sound of chariot
wheels?'
29 "Her wise women answer,
and she repeats these words to herself:
30 'They must be dividing the captured plunder—
with a woman or two for every man.
There will be colorful robes for Sisera,
and colorful, embroidered robes for me.
Yes, the plunder will include
colorful robes embroidered on both sides.'

31 "LORD, may all your enemies die like Sisera!
But may those who love you rise like the sun
in all its power!"

Then there was peace in the land for forty years.

Gideon Becomes Israel's Judge

6 The Israelites did evil in the LORD's sight. So
the LORD handed them over to the Midianites
for seven years. 2 The Midianites were so cruel that
the Israelites made hiding places for themselves
in the mountains, caves, and strongholds. 3 Whenever
the Israelites planted their crops, marauders from
Midian, Amalek, and the people of the east would
attack Israel, 4 camping in the land and destroying
crops as far away as Gaza. They left the Israelites with
nothing to eat, taking all the sheep, goats, cattle, and
donkeys. 5 These enemy hordes, coming with their
livestock and tents, were as thick as locusts; they arrived on droves of camels too numerous to count.
And they stayed until the land was stripped bare. 6 So
Israel was reduced to starvation by the Midianites.
Then the Israelites cried out to the LORD for help.

7 When they cried out to the LORD because of Midian, 8 the LORD sent a prophet to the Israelites. He

KING JAMES VERSION

of Israel, which said unto them, Thus saith the LORD
God of Israel, I brought you up from Egypt, and
brought you forth out of the house of bondage;
9And I delivered you out of the hand of the Egyptians, and out of the hand of all that oppressed you,
and drave them out from before you, and gave you
their land;
10And I said unto you, I *am* the LORD your God;
fear not the gods of the Amorites, in whose land ye
dwell: but ye have not obeyed my voice.
11And there came an angel of the LORD, and sat
under an oak which *was* in Ophrah, that *pertained*
unto Joash the Abiezrite: and his son Gideon
threshed wheat by the winepress, to hide *it* from the
Midianites.
12And the angel of the LORD appeared unto him,
and said unto him, The LORD *is* with thee, thou
mighty man of valour.
13And Gideon said unto him, Oh my Lord, if the
LORD be with us, why then is all this befallen us? and
where *be* all his miracles which our fathers told us of,
saying, Did not the LORD bring us up from Egypt? but
now the LORD hath forsaken us, and delivered us into
the hands of the Midianites.
14And the LORD looked upon him, and said, Go in
this thy might, and thou shalt save Israel from the
hand of the Midianites: have not I sent thee?
15And he said unto him, Oh my Lord, wherewith
shall I save Israel? behold, my family *is* poor in Manasseh, and I *am* the least in my father's house.
16And the LORD said unto him, Surely I will be with
thee, and thou shalt smite the Midianites as one man.
17And he said unto him, If now I have found grace
in thy sight, then shew me a sign that thou talkest
with me.
18Depart not hence, I pray thee, until I come unto
thee, and bring forth my present, and set *it* before
thee. And he said, I will tarry until thou come again.
19And Gideon went in, and made ready a kid,
and unleavened cakes of an ephah of flour: the flesh
he put in a basket, and he put the broth in a pot, and
brought *it* out unto him under the oak, and presented *it*.
20And the angel of God said unto him, Take the
flesh and the unleavened cakes, and lay *them* upon
this rock, and pour out the broth. And he did so.
21Then the angel of the LORD put forth the end of
the staff that *was* in his hand, and touched the flesh
and the unleavened cakes; and there rose up fire out
of the rock, and consumed the flesh and the unleavened cakes. Then the angel of the LORD departed
out of his sight.
22And when Gideon perceived that he *was* an angel of the LORD, Gideon said, Alas, O Lord GOD! for because I have seen an angel of the LORD face to face.
23And the LORD said unto him, Peace *be* unto thee;
fear not: thou shalt not die.
24Then Gideon built an altar there unto the LORD,

NEW LIVING TRANSLATION

said, "This is what the LORD, the God of Israel, says: I
brought you up out of slavery in Egypt. 9I rescued
you from the Egyptians and from all who oppressed
you. I drove out your enemies and gave you their
land. 10I told you, 'I am the LORD your God. You must
not worship the gods of the Amorites, in whose land
you now live.' But you have not listened to me."
11Then the angel of the LORD came and sat beneath the great tree at Ophrah, which belonged to Joash of the clan of Abiezer. Gideon son of Joash was
threshing wheat at the bottom of a winepress to hide
the grain from the Midianites. 12The angel of the
LORD appeared to him and said, "Mighty hero, the
LORD is with you!"
13"Sir," Gideon replied, "if the LORD is with us, why
has all this happened to us? And where are all the
miracles our ancestors told us about? Didn't they say,
'The LORD brought us up out of Egypt'? But now the
LORD has abandoned us and handed us over to the
Midianites."
14Then the LORD turned to him and said, "Go with
the strength you have, and rescue Israel from the
Midianites. I am sending you!"
15"But Lord," Gideon replied, "how can I rescue
Israel? My clan is the weakest in the whole tribe of
Manasseh, and I am the least in my entire family!"
16The LORD said to him, "I will be with you. And
you will destroy the Midianites as if you were fighting against one man."
17Gideon replied, "If you are truly going to help
me, show me a sign to prove that it is really the LORD
speaking to me. 18Don't go away until I come back
and bring my offering to you."
He answered, "I will stay here until you return."
19Gideon hurried home. He cooked a young goat,
and with a basket* of flour he baked some bread
without yeast. Then, carrying the meat in a basket
and the broth in a pot, he brought them out and
presented them to the angel, who was under the
great tree.
20The angel of God said to him, "Place the meat
and the unleavened bread on this rock, and pour the
broth over it." And Gideon did as he was told. 21Then
the angel of the LORD touched the meat and bread
with the tip of the staff in his hand, and fire flamed
up from the rock and consumed all he had brought.
And the angel of the LORD disappeared.
22When Gideon realized that it was the angel of
the LORD, he cried out, "Oh, Sovereign LORD, I'm
doomed! I have seen the angel of the LORD face to
face!"
23"It is all right," the LORD replied. "Do not be afraid.
You will not die." 24And Gideon built an altar to the
LORD there and named it Yahweh-Shalom (which

6:19 Hebrew *an ephah* [20 quarts or 22 liters].

KING JAMES VERSION

and called it Jehovah-shalom: unto this day it *is* yet in Ophrah of the Abiezrites.

25 And it came to pass the same night, that the LORD said unto him, Take thy father's young bullock, even the second bullock of seven years old, and throw down the altar of Baal that thy father hath, and cut down the grove that *is* by it:

26 And build an altar unto the LORD thy God upon the top of this rock, in the ordered place, and take the second bullock, and offer a burnt sacrifice with the wood of the grove which thou shalt cut down.

27 Then Gideon took ten men of his servants, and did as the LORD had said unto him: and *so* it was, because he feared his father's household, and the men of the city, that he could not do *it* by day, that he did *it* by night.

28 And when the men of the city arose early in the morning, behold, the altar of Baal was cast down, and the grove was cut down that *was* by it, and the second bullock was offered upon the altar *that was* built.

29 And they said one to another, Who hath done this thing? And when they inquired and asked, they said, Gideon the son of Joash hath done this thing.

30 Then the men of the city said unto Joash, Bring out thy son, that he may die: because he hath cast down the altar of Baal, and because he hath cut down the grove that *was* by it.

31 And Joash said unto all that stood against him, Will ye plead for Baal? will ye save him? he that will plead for him, let him be put to death whilst *it is yet* morning: if he *be* a god, let him plead for himself, because *one* hath cast down his altar.

32 Therefore on that day he called him Jerubbaal, saying, Let Baal plead against him, because he hath thrown down his altar.

33 Then all the Midianites and the Amalekites and the children of the east were gathered together, and went over, and pitched in the valley of Jezreel.

34 But the Spirit of the LORD came upon Gideon, and he blew a trumpet; and Abiezer was gathered after him.

35 And he sent messengers throughout all Manasseh; who also was gathered after him: and he sent messengers unto Asher, and unto Zebulun, and unto Naphtali; and they came up to meet them.

36 And Gideon said unto God, If thou wilt save Israel by mine hand, as thou hast said,

37 Behold, I will put a fleece of wool in the floor; *and* if the dew be on the fleece only, and *it be* dry upon all the earth *beside*, then shall I know that thou wilt save Israel by mine hand, as thou hast said.

38 And it was so: for he rose up early on the morrow, and thrust the fleece together, and wringed the dew out of the fleece, a bowl full of water.

39 And Gideon said unto God, Let not thine anger be hot against me, and I will speak but this once: let

NEW LIVING TRANSLATION

means "the LORD is peace"). The altar remains in Ophrah in the land of the clan of Abiezer to this day.

25 That night the LORD said to Gideon, "Take the second bull from your father's herd, the one that is seven years old. Pull down your father's altar to Baal, and cut down the Asherah pole standing beside it.
26 Then build an altar to the LORD your God here on this hilltop sanctuary, laying the stones carefully. Sacrifice the bull as a burnt offering on the altar, using as fuel the wood of the Asherah pole you cut down."

27 So Gideon took ten of his servants and did as the LORD had commanded. But he did it at night because he was afraid of the other members of his father's household and the people of the town.

28 Early the next morning, as the people of the town began to stir, someone discovered that the altar of Baal had been broken down and that the Asherah pole beside it had been cut down. In their place a new altar had been built, and on it were the remains of the bull that had been sacrificed.
29 The people said to each other, "Who did this?" And after asking around and making a careful search, they learned that it was Gideon, the son of Joash.

30 "Bring out your son," the men of the town demanded of Joash. "He must die for destroying the altar of Baal and for cutting down the Asherah pole."

31 But Joash shouted to the mob that confronted him, "Why are you defending Baal? Will you argue his case? Whoever pleads his case will be put to death by morning! If Baal truly is a god, let him defend himself and destroy the one who broke down his altar!"
32 From then on Gideon was called Jerubbaal, which means "Let Baal defend himself," because he broke down Baal's altar.

Gideon Asks for a Sign

33 Soon afterward the armies of Midian, Amalek, and the people of the east formed an alliance against Israel and crossed the Jordan, camping in the valley of Jezreel.
34 Then the Spirit of the LORD took possession of Gideon. He blew a ram's horn as a call to arms, and the men of the clan of Abiezer came to him.
35 He also sent messengers throughout Manasseh, Asher, Zebulun, and Naphtali, summoning their warriors, and all of them responded.

36 Then Gideon said to God, "If you are truly going to use me to rescue Israel as you promised,
37 prove it to me in this way. I will put a wool fleece on the threshing floor tonight. If the fleece is wet with dew in the morning but the ground is dry, then I will know that you are going to help me rescue Israel as you promised."
38 And that is just what happened. When Gideon got up early the next morning, he squeezed the fleece and wrung out a whole bowlful of water.

39 Then Gideon said to God, "Please don't be angry with me, but let me make one more request. Let me

KING JAMES VERSION

me prove, I pray thee, but this once with the fleece;
let it now be dry only upon the fleece, and upon all
the ground let there be dew.
40And God did so that night: for it was dry upon
the fleece only, and there was dew on all the ground.

7 1Then Jerubbaal, who *is* Gideon, and all the
people that *were* with him, rose up early, and
pitched beside the well of Harod: so that the host of
the Midianites were on the north side of them, by the
hill of Moreh, in the valley.
2And the LORD said unto Gideon, The people that
are with thee *are* too many for me to give the Midianites into their hands, lest Israel vaunt themselves
against me, saying, Mine own hand hath saved me.
3Now therefore go to, proclaim in the ears of the
people, saying, Whosoever *is* fearful and afraid, let
him return and depart early from mount Gilead. And
there returned of the people twenty and two thousand; and there remained ten thousand.
4And the LORD said unto Gideon, The people *are*
yet *too* many; bring them down unto the water, and
I will try them for thee there: and it shall be, *that*
of whom I say unto thee, This shall go with thee,
the same shall go with thee; and of whomsoever I say
unto thee, This shall not go with thee, the same shall
not go.
5So he brought down the people unto the water:
and the LORD said unto Gideon, Every one that
lappeth of the water with his tongue, as a dog lappeth, him shalt thou set by himself; likewise every
one that boweth down upon his knees to drink.
6And the number of them that lapped, *putting*
their hand to their mouth, were three hundred men:
but all the rest of the people bowed down upon their
knees to drink water.
7And the LORD said unto Gideon, By the three hundred men that lapped will I save you, and deliver the
Midianites into thine hand: and let all the *other*
people go every man unto his place.
8So the people took victuals in their hand, and
their trumpets: and he sent all *the rest of* Israel every
man unto his tent, and retained those three hundred
men: and the host of Midian was beneath him in the
valley.
9And it came to pass the same night, that the LORD
said unto him, Arise, get thee down unto the host; for
I have delivered it into thine hand.
10But if thou fear to go down, go thou with Phurah
thy servant down to the host:
11And thou shalt hear what they say; and afterward shall thine hands be strengthened to go down
unto the host. Then went he down with Phurah his
servant unto the outside of the armed men that *were*
in the host.
12And the Midianites and the Amalekites and all
the children of the east lay along in the valley like

NEW LIVING TRANSLATION

use the fleece for one more test. This time let the
fleece remain dry while the ground around it is wet
with dew." 40So that night God did as Gideon asked.
The fleece was dry in the morning, but the ground
was covered with dew.

Gideon Defeats the Midianites

7 So Jerub-baal (that is, Gideon) and his army got
up early and went as far as the spring of Harod.
The armies of Midian were camped north of them in
the valley near the hill of Moreh. 2The LORD said to
Gideon, "You have too many warriors with you. If I let
all of you fight the Midianites, the Israelites will
boast to me that they saved themselves by their own
strength. 3Therefore, tell the people, 'Whoever is
timid or afraid may leave this mountain* and go
home.'" So 22,000 of them went home, leaving only
10,000 who were willing to fight.
4But the LORD told Gideon, "There are still too
many! Bring them down to the spring, and I will test
them to determine who will go with you and who will
not." 5When Gideon took his warriors down to the
water, the LORD told him, "Divide the men into two
groups. In one group put all those who cup water in
their hands and lap it up with their tongues like
dogs. In the other group put all those who kneel
down and drink with their mouths in the stream."
6Only 300 of the men drank from their hands. All
the others got down on their knees and drank with
their mouths in the stream.
7The LORD told Gideon, "With these 300 men I will
rescue you and give you victory over the Midianites.
Send all the others home." 8So Gideon collected the
provisions and rams' horns of the other warriors and
sent them home. But he kept the 300 men with him.
The Midianite camp was in the valley just below
Gideon. 9That night the LORD said, "Get up! Go down
into the Midianite camp, for I have given you victory
over them! 10But if you are afraid to attack, go down
to the camp with your servant Purah. 11Listen to what
the Midianites are saying, and you will be greatly encouraged. Then you will be eager to attack."
So Gideon took Purah and went down to the edge
of the enemy camp. 12The armies of Midian, Amalek,
and the people of the east had settled in the valley

7:3 Hebrew *may leave Mount Gilead.* The identity of Mount Gilead is uncertain in this context. It is perhaps used here as another name for Mount Gilboa.

KING JAMES VERSION

grasshoppers for multitude; and their camels *were*
without number, as the sand by the sea side for
multitude.
13 And when Gideon was come, behold, *there was*
a man that told a dream unto his fellow, and said,
Behold, I dreamed a dream, and, lo, a cake of barley
bread tumbled into the host of Midian, and came
unto a tent, and smote it that it fell, and overturned it,
that the tent lay along.
14 And his fellow answered and said, This *is* nothing else save the sword of Gideon the son of Joash, a
man of Israel: *for* into his hand hath God delivered
Midian, and all the host.
15 And it was *so,* when Gideon heard the telling of
the dream, and the interpretation thereof, that he
worshipped, and returned into the host of Israel, and
said, Arise; for the LORD hath delivered into your
hand the host of Midian.
16 And he divided the three hundred men *into*
three companies, and he put a trumpet in every
man's hand, with empty pitchers, and lamps within
the pitchers.
17 And he said unto them, Look on me, and do likewise: and, behold, when I come to the outside of the
camp, it shall be *that,* as I do, so shall ye do.
18 When I blow with a trumpet, I and all that *are*
with me, then blow ye the trumpets also on every
side of all the camp, and say, *The sword* of the LORD,
and of Gideon.
19 So Gideon, and the hundred men that *were* with
him, came unto the outside of the camp in the beginning of the middle watch; and they had but newly set
the watch: and they blew the trumpets, and brake the
pitchers that *were* in their hands.
20 And the three companies blew the trumpets,
and brake the pitchers, and held the lamps in their
left hands, and the trumpets in their right hands to
blow *withal:* and they cried, The sword of the LORD,
and of Gideon.
21 And they stood every man in his place round
about the camp: and all the host ran, and cried,
and fled.
22 And the three hundred blew the trumpets, and
the LORD set every man's sword against his fellow,
even throughout all the host: and the host fled to
Beth-shittah in Zererath, *and* to the border of Abel-
meholah, unto Tabbath.
23 And the men of Israel gathered themselves together out of Naphtali, and out of Asher, and out of
all Manasseh, and pursued after the Midianites.
24 And Gideon sent messengers throughout all
mount Ephraim, saying, Come down against the
Midianites, and take before them the waters unto
Beth-barah and Jordan. Then all the men of Ephraim
gathered themselves together, and took the waters
unto Beth-barah and Jordan.
25 And they took two princes of the Midianites,
Oreb and Zeeb; and they slew Oreb upon the rock

NEW LIVING TRANSLATION

like a swarm of locusts. Their camels were like grains
of sand on the seashore—too many to count! 13 Gideon crept up just as a man was telling his companion
about a dream. The man said, "I had this dream, and
in my dream a loaf of barley bread came tumbling
down into the Midianite camp. It hit a tent, turned it
over, and knocked it flat!"
14 His companion answered, "Your dream can
mean only one thing—God has given Gideon son of
Joash, the Israelite, victory over Midian and all its
allies!"
15 When Gideon heard the dream and its interpretation, he bowed in worship before the LORD.* Then
he returned to the Israelite camp and shouted, "Get
up! For the LORD has given you victory over the Midianite hordes!" 16 He divided the 300 men into three
groups and gave each man a ram's horn and a clay jar
with a torch in it.
17 Then he said to them, "Keep your eyes on me.
When I come to the edge of the camp, do just as I do.
18 As soon as I and those with me blow the rams'
horns, blow your horns, too, all around the entire
camp, and shout, 'For the LORD and for Gideon!'"
19 It was just after midnight,* after the changing of
the guard, when Gideon and the 100 men with him
reached the edge of the Midianite camp. Suddenly,
they blew the rams' horns and broke their clay jars.
20 Then all three groups blew their horns and broke
their jars. They held the blazing torches in their left
hands and the horns in their right hands, and they all
shouted, "A sword for the LORD and for Gideon!"
21 Each man stood at his position around the camp
and watched as all the Midianites rushed around in
a panic, shouting as they ran to escape. 22 When the
300 Israelites blew their rams' horns, the LORD
caused the warriors in the camp to fight against each
other with their swords. Those who were not killed
fled to places as far away as Beth-shittah near Zererah
and to the border of Abel-meholah near Tabbath.
23 Then Gideon sent for the warriors of Naphtali,
Asher, and Manasseh, who joined in chasing the
army of Midian. 24 Gideon also sent messengers
throughout the hill country of Ephraim, saying,
"Come down to attack the Midianites. Cut them off
at the shallow crossings of the Jordan River at Beth-
barah."
So all the men of Ephraim did as they were told.
25 They captured Oreb and Zeeb, the two Midianite
commanders, killing Oreb at the rock of Oreb, and
Zeeb at the winepress of Zeeb. And they continued

7:15 As in Greek version; Hebrew reads *he bowed.* **7:19** Hebrew *at the beginning of the second watch.*

KING JAMES VERSION

Oreb, and Zeeb they slew at the winepress of Zeeb,
and pursued Midian, and brought the heads of Oreb
and Zeeb to Gideon on the other side Jordan.

8 1And the men of Ephraim said unto him, Why
hast thou served us thus, that thou calledst us
not, when thou wentest to fight with the Midianites?
And they did chide with him sharply.
2And he said unto them, What have I done now in
comparison of you? *Is* not the gleaning of the grapes
of Ephraim better than the vintage of Abiezer?
3God hath delivered into your hands the princes
of Midian, Oreb and Zeeb: and what was I able to do
in comparison of you? Then their anger was abated
toward him, when he had said that.
4And Gideon came to Jordan, *and* passed over, he,
and the three hundred men that *were* with him, faint,
yet pursuing *them*.
5And he said unto the men of Succoth, Give, I pray
you, loaves of bread unto the people that follow me;
for they *be* faint, and I am pursuing after Zebah and
Zalmunna, kings of Midian.
6And the princes of Succoth said, *Are* the hands of
Zebah and Zalmunna now in thine hand, that we
should give bread unto thine army?
7And Gideon said, Therefore when the LORD hath
delivered Zebah and Zalmunna into mine hand, then
I will tear your flesh with the thorns of the wilderness and with briers.
8And he went up thence to Penuel, and spake unto
them likewise: and the men of Penuel answered him
as the men of Succoth had answered *him*.
9And he spake also unto the men of Penuel, saying,
When I come again in peace, I will break down this
tower.
10Now Zebah and Zalmunna *were* in Karkor, and
their hosts with them, about fifteen thousand *men*,
all that were left of all the hosts of the children of the
east: for there fell an hundred and twenty thousand
men that drew sword.
11And Gideon went up by the way of them that
dwelt in tents on the east of Nobah and Jogbehah,
and smote the host: for the host was secure.
12And when Zebah and Zalmunna fled, he pursued after them, and took the two kings of Midian,
Zebah and Zalmunna, and discomfited all the host.
13And Gideon the son of Joash returned from
battle before the sun *was up*,
14And caught a young man of the men of Succoth,
and inquired of him: and he described unto him the
princes of Succoth, and the elders thereof, *even*
threescore and seventeen men.
15And he came unto the men of Succoth, and said,
Behold Zebah and Zalmunna with whom ye did upbraid me, saying, *Are* the hands of Zebah and Zalmunna now in thine hand, that we should give bread
unto thy men *that are* weary?

NEW LIVING TRANSLATION

to chase the Midianites. Afterward the Israelites
brought the heads of Oreb and Zeeb to Gideon, who
was by the Jordan River.

Gideon Kills Zebah and Zalmunna

8 Then the people of Ephraim asked Gideon,
"Why have you treated us this way? Why didn't
you send for us when you first went out to fight the
Midianites?" And they argued heatedly with Gideon.
2But Gideon replied, "What have I accomplished
compared to you? Aren't even the leftover grapes of
Ephraim's harvest better than the entire crop of my
little clan of Abiezer? 3God gave you victory over
Oreb and Zeeb, the commanders of the Midianite
army. What have I accomplished compared to that?"
When the men of Ephraim heard Gideon's answer,
their anger subsided.
4Gideon then crossed the Jordan River with his
300 men, and though exhausted, they continued to
chase the enemy. 5When they reached Succoth, Gideon asked the leaders of the town, "Please give my
warriors some food. They are very tired. I am chasing
Zebah and Zalmunna, the kings of Midian."
6But the officials of Succoth replied, "Catch Zebah
and Zalmunna first, and then we will feed your
army."
7So Gideon said, "After the LORD gives me victory
over Zebah and Zalmunna, I will return and tear
your flesh with the thorns and briers from the
wilderness."
8From there Gideon went up to Peniel* and again
asked for food, but he got the same answer. 9So he
said to the people of Peniel, "After I return in victory,
I will tear down this tower."
10By this time Zebah and Zalmunna were in Karkor with 15,000 warriors—all that remained of the
allied armies of the east, for 120,000 had already
been killed. 11Gideon circled around by the caravan
route east of Nobah and Jogbehah, taking the Midianite army by surprise. 12Zebah and Zalmunna, the
two Midianite kings, fled, but Gideon chased them
down and captured all their warriors.
13After this, Gideon returned from the battle by
way of Heres Pass. 14There he captured a young man
from Succoth and demanded that he write down the
names of all the seventy-seven officials and elders in
the town. 15Gideon then returned to Succoth and
said to the leaders, "Here are Zebah and Zalmunna.
When we were here before, you taunted me, saying,
'Catch Zebah and Zalmunna first, and then we will

8:8 Hebrew *Penuel*, a variant spelling of Peniel; also in 8:9, 17.

KING JAMES VERSION

16And he took the elders of the city, and thorns of the wilderness and briers, and with them he taught the men of Succoth.

17And he beat down the tower of Penuel, and slew the men of the city.

18Then said he unto Zebah and Zalmunna, What manner of men *were they* whom ye slew at Tabor? And they answered, As thou *art*, so *were* they; each one resembled the children of a king.

19And he said, They *were* my brethren, *even* the sons of my mother: *as* the LORD liveth, if ye had saved them alive, I would not slay you.

20And he said unto Jether his firstborn, Up, *and* slay them. But the youth drew not his sword: for he feared, because he *was* yet a youth.

21Then Zebah and Zalmunna said, Rise thou, and fall upon us: for as the man *is, so is* his strength. And Gideon arose, and slew Zebah and Zalmunna, and took away the ornaments that *were* on their camels' necks.

22Then the men of Israel said unto Gideon, Rule thou over us, both thou, and thy son, and thy son's son also: for thou hast delivered us from the hand of Midian.

23And Gideon said unto them, I will not rule over you, neither shall my son rule over you: the LORD shall rule over you.

24And Gideon said unto them, I would desire a request of you, that ye would give me every man the earrings of his prey. (For they had golden earrings, because they *were* Ishmaelites.)

25And they answered, We will willingly give *them*. And they spread a garment, and did cast therein every man the earrings of his prey.

26And the weight of the golden earrings that he requested was a thousand and seven hundred *shekels* of gold; beside ornaments, and collars, and purple raiment that *was* on the kings of Midian, and beside the chains that *were* about their camels' necks.

27And Gideon made an ephod thereof, and put it in his city, *even* in Ophrah: and all Israel went thither a whoring after it: which thing became a snare unto Gideon, and to his house.

28Thus was Midian subdued before the children of Israel, so that they lifted up their heads no more. And the country was in quietness forty years in the days of Gideon.

29And Jerubbaal the son of Joash went and dwelt in his own house.

30And Gideon had threescore and ten sons of his body begotten: for he had many wives.

31And his concubine that *was* in Shechem, she also bare him a son, whose name he called Abimelech.

32And Gideon the son of Joash died in a good old age, and was buried in the sepulchre of Joash his father, in Ophrah of the Abiezrites.

NEW LIVING TRANSLATION

feed your exhausted army.'" 16Then Gideon took the elders of the town and taught them a lesson, punishing them with thorns and briers from the wilderness. 17He also tore down the tower of Peniel and killed all the men in the town.

18Then Gideon asked Zebah and Zalmunna, "The men you killed at Tabor—what were they like?"

"Like you," they replied. "They all had the look of a king's son."

19"They were my brothers, the sons of my own mother!" Gideon exclaimed. "As surely as the LORD lives, I wouldn't kill you if you hadn't killed them." 20Turning to Jether, his oldest son, he said, "Kill them!" But Jether did not draw his sword, for he was only a boy and was afraid.

21Then Zebah and Zalmunna said to Gideon, "Be a man! Kill us yourself!" So Gideon killed them both and took the royal ornaments from the necks of their camels.

Gideon's Sacred Ephod

22Then the Israelites said to Gideon, "Be our ruler! You and your son and your grandson will be our rulers, for you have rescued us from Midian."

23But Gideon replied, "I will not rule over you, nor will my son. The LORD will rule over you! 24However, I do have one request—that each of you give me an earring from the plunder you collected from your fallen enemies." (The enemies, being Ishmaelites, all wore gold earrings.)

25"Gladly!" they replied. They spread out a cloak, and each one threw in a gold earring he had gathered from the plunder. 26The weight of the gold earrings was forty-three pounds,* not including the royal ornaments and pendants, the purple clothing worn by the kings of Midian, or the chains around the necks of their camels.

27Gideon made a sacred ephod from the gold and put it in Ophrah, his hometown. But soon all the Israelites prostituted themselves by worshiping it, and it became a trap for Gideon and his family.

28That is the story of how the people of Israel defeated Midian, which never recovered. Throughout the rest of Gideon's lifetime—about forty years—there was peace in the land.

29Then Gideon* son of Joash returned home. 30He had seventy sons born to him, for he had many wives. 31He also had a concubine in Shechem, who gave birth to a son, whom he named Abimelech. 32Gideon died when he was very old, and he was buried in the grave of his father, Joash, at Ophrah in the land of the clan of Abiezer.

8:26 Hebrew *1,700 shekels* [19.4 kilograms]. **8:29** Hebrew *Jerub-baal;* see 6:32.

KING JAMES VERSION

33 And it came to pass, as soon as Gideon was dead,
that the children of Israel turned again, and went a
whoring after Baalim, and made Baal-berith their god.
34 And the children of Israel remembered not the
LORD their God, who had delivered them out of the
hands of all their enemies on every side:
35 Neither shewed they kindness to the house of
Jerubbaal, *namely,* Gideon, according to all the
goodness which he had shewed unto Israel.

9 1 And Abimelech the son of Jerubbaal went to
Shechem unto his mother's brethren, and communed with them, and with all the family of the
house of his mother's father, saying,
2 Speak, I pray you, in the ears of all the men of
Shechem, Whether *is* better for you, either that all
the sons of Jerubbaal, *which are* threescore and ten
persons, reign over you, or that one reign over you?
remember also that I *am* your bone and your flesh.
3 And his mother's brethren spake of him in the
ears of all the men of Shechem all these words: and
their hearts inclined to follow Abimelech; for they
said, He *is* our brother.
4 And they gave him threescore and ten *pieces* of
silver out of the house of Baal-berith, wherewith
Abimelech hired vain and light persons, which followed him.
5 And he went unto his father's house at Ophrah,
and slew his brethren the sons of Jerubbaal, *being*
threescore and ten persons, upon one stone: notwithstanding yet Jotham the youngest son of Jerub-
baal was left; for he hid himself.
6 And all the men of Shechem gathered together,
and all the house of Millo, and went, and made
Abimelech king, by the plain of the pillar that *was* in
Shechem.
7 And when they told *it* to Jotham, he went and
stood in the top of mount Gerizim, and lifted up
his voice, and cried, and said unto them, Hearken
unto me, ye men of Shechem, that God may hearken
unto you.
8 The trees went forth *on a time* to anoint a king
over them; and they said unto the olive tree, Reign
thou over us.
9 But the olive tree said unto them, Should I leave
my fatness, wherewith by me they honour God and
man, and go to be promoted over the trees?
10 And the trees said to the fig tree, Come thou, *and*
reign over us.
11 But the fig tree said unto them, Should I forsake
my sweetness, and my good fruit, and go to be promoted over the trees?
12 Then said the trees unto the vine, Come thou,
and reign over us.

NEW LIVING TRANSLATION

33 As soon as Gideon died, the Israelites prostituted themselves by worshiping the images of Baal,
making Baal-berith their god. 34 They forgot the
LORD their God, who had rescued them from all their
enemies surrounding them. 35 Nor did they show any
loyalty to the family of Jerub-baal (that is, Gideon),
despite all the good he had done for Israel.

Abimelech Rules over Shechem

9 One day Gideon's* son Abimelech went to Shechem to visit his uncles—his mother's brothers.
He said to them and to the rest of his mother's family,
2 "Ask the leading citizens of Shechem whether they
want to be ruled by all seventy of Gideon's sons or by
one man. And remember that I am your own flesh
and blood!"
3 So Abimelech's uncles gave his message to all the
citizens of Shechem on his behalf. And after listening to this proposal, the people of Shechem decided
in favor of Abimelech because he was their relative.
4 They gave him seventy silver coins from the temple
of Baal-berith, which he used to hire some reckless
troublemakers who agreed to follow him. 5 He went
to his father's home at Ophrah, and there, on one
stone, they killed all seventy of his half brothers, the
sons of Gideon.* But the youngest brother, Jotham,
escaped and hid.
6 Then all the leading citizens of Shechem and
Beth-millo called a meeting under the oak beside the
pillar* at Shechem and made Abimelech their king.

Jotham's Parable

7 When Jotham heard about this, he climbed to the
top of Mount Gerizim and shouted,

"Listen to me, citizens of Shechem!
Listen to me if you want God to listen to you!
8 Once upon a time the trees decided to choose
a king.
First they said to the olive tree,
'Be our king!'
9 But the olive tree refused, saying,
'Should I quit producing the olive oil
that blesses both God and people,
just to wave back and forth over the trees?'
10 "Then they said to the fig tree,
'You be our king!'
11 But the fig tree also refused, saying,
'Should I quit producing my sweet fruit
just to wave back and forth over the trees?'
12 "Then they said to the grapevine,
'You be our king!'

9:1 Hebrew *Jerub-baal's* (see 6:32); also in 9:2, 24. **9:5** Hebrew *Jerub-baal* (see 6:32); also in 9:16, 19, 28, 57. **9:6** The meaning of the Hebrew is uncertain.

KING JAMES VERSION

13 And the vine said unto them, Should I leave my
wine, which cheereth God and man, and go to be promoted over the trees?
14 Then said all the trees unto the bramble, Come
thou, *and* reign over us.
15 And the bramble said unto the trees, If in truth
ye anoint me king over you, *then* come *and* put your
trust in my shadow: and if not, let fire come out of
the bramble, and devour the cedars of Lebanon.

16 Now therefore, if ye have done truly and sincerely, in that ye have made Abimelech king, and if ye
have dealt well with Jerubbaal and his house, and
have done unto him according to the deserving of
his hands;
17 (For my father fought for you, and adventured
his life far, and delivered you out of the hand of
Midian:
18 And ye are risen up against my father's house
this day, and have slain his sons, threescore and ten
persons, upon one stone, and have made Abimelech,
the son of his maidservant, king over the men of
Shechem, because he *is* your brother;)
19 If ye then have dealt truly and sincerely with
Jerubbaal and with his house this day, *then* rejoice
ye in Abimelech, and let him also rejoice in you:
20 But if not, let fire come out from Abimelech, and
devour the men of Shechem, and the house of Millo;
and let fire come out from the men of Shechem, and
from the house of Millo, and devour Abimelech.
21 And Jotham ran away, and fled, and went to Beer,
and dwelt there, for fear of Abimelech his brother.

22 When Abimelech had reigned three years over
Israel,
23 Then God sent an evil spirit between Abimelech
and the men of Shechem; and the men of Shechem
dealt treacherously with Abimelech:
24 That the cruelty *done* to the threescore and ten
sons of Jerubbaal might come, and their blood be
laid upon Abimelech their brother, which slew them;
and upon the men of Shechem, which aided him in
the killing of his brethren.
25 And the men of Shechem set liers in wait for
him in the top of the mountains, and they robbed
all that came along that way by them: and it was told
Abimelech.
26 And Gaal the son of Ebed came with his brethren, and went over to Shechem: and the men of
Shechem put their confidence in him.
27 And they went out into the fields, and gathered
their vineyards, and trode *the grapes,* and made
merry, and went into the house of their god, and did
eat and drink, and cursed Abimelech.
28 And Gaal the son of Ebed said, Who *is* Abimelech,

NEW LIVING TRANSLATION

13 But the grapevine also refused, saying,
'Should I quit producing the wine
that cheers both God and people,
just to wave back and forth over the trees?'
14 "Then all the trees finally turned to the
thornbush and said,
'Come, you be our king!'
15 And the thornbush replied to the trees,
'If you truly want to make me your king,
come and take shelter in my shade.
If not, let fire come out from me
and devour the cedars of Lebanon.'"

16 Jotham continued, "Now make sure you have
acted honorably and in good faith by making Abimelech your king, and that you have done right by Gideon and all of his descendants. Have you treated him
with the honor he deserves for all he accomplished?
17 For he fought for you and risked his life when he
rescued you from the Midianites. 18 But today you
have revolted against my father and his descendants,
killing his seventy sons on one stone. And you have
chosen his slave woman's son, Abimelech, to be your
king just because he is your relative.
19 "If you have acted honorably and in good faith
toward Gideon and his descendants today, then may
you find joy in Abimelech, and may he find joy in
you. 20 But if you have not acted in good faith, then
may fire come out from Abimelech and devour the
leading citizens of Shechem and Beth-millo; and
may fire come out from the citizens of Shechem and
Beth-millo and devour Abimelech!"
21 Then Jotham escaped and lived in Beer because
he was afraid of his brother Abimelech.

Shechem Rebels against Abimelech

22 After Abimelech had ruled over Israel for three
years, 23 God sent a spirit that stirred up trouble between Abimelech and the leading citizens of Shechem, and they revolted. 24 God was punishing
Abimelech for murdering Gideon's seventy sons, and
the citizens of Shechem for supporting him in this
treachery of murdering his brothers. 25 The citizens
of Shechem set an ambush for Abimelech on the hilltops and robbed everyone who passed that way. But
someone warned Abimelech about their plot.

26 One day Gaal son of Ebed moved to Shechem
with his brothers and gained the confidence of the
leading citizens of Shechem. 27 During the annual
harvest festival at Shechem, held in the temple of the
local god, the wine flowed freely, and everyone began
cursing Abimelech. 28 "Who is Abimelech?" Gaal
shouted. "He's not a true son of Shechem,* so why

9:28 Hebrew *Who is Shechem?*

KING JAMES VERSION

and who *is* Shechem, that we should serve him? *is* not *he* the son of Jerubbaal? and Zebul his officer? serve the men of Hamor the father of Shechem: for why should we serve him?

29 And would to God this people were under my hand! then would I remove Abimelech. And he said to Abimelech, Increase thine army, and come out.

30 And when Zebul the ruler of the city heard the words of Gaal the son of Ebed, his anger was kindled.

31 And he sent messengers unto Abimelech privily, saying, Behold, Gaal the son of Ebed and his brethren be come to Shechem; and, behold, they fortify the city against thee.

32 Now therefore up by night, thou and the people that *is* with thee, and lie in wait in the field:

33 And it shall be, *that* in the morning, as soon as the sun is up, thou shalt rise early, and set upon the city: and, behold, *when* he and the people that *is* with him come out against thee, then mayest thou do to them as thou shalt find occasion.

34 And Abimelech rose up, and all the people that *were* with him, by night, and they laid wait against Shechem in four companies.

35 And Gaal the son of Ebed went out, and stood in the entering of the gate of the city: and Abimelech rose up, and the people that *were* with him, from lying in wait.

36 And when Gaal saw the people, he said to Zebul, Behold, there come people down from the top of the mountains. And Zebul said unto him, Thou seest the shadow of the mountains as *if they were* men.

37 And Gaal spake again and said, See there come people down by the middle of the land, and another company come along by the plain of Meonenim.

38 Then said Zebul unto him, Where *is* now thy mouth, wherewith thou saidst, Who *is* Abimelech, that we should serve him? *is* not this the people that thou hast despised? go out, I pray now, and fight with them.

39 And Gaal went out before the men of Shechem, and fought with Abimelech.

40 And Abimelech chased him, and he fled before him, and many were overthrown *and* wounded, *even* unto the entering of the gate.

41 And Abimelech dwelt at Arumah: and Zebul thrust out Gaal and his brethren, that they should not dwell in Shechem.

42 And it came to pass on the morrow, that the people went out into the field; and they told Abimelech.

43 And he took the people, and divided them into three companies, and laid wait in the field, and looked, and, behold, the people *were* come forth out of the city; and he rose up against them, and smote them.

44 And Abimelech, and the company that *was* with him, rushed forward, and stood in the entering of the gate of the city: and the two *other* companies ran

NEW LIVING TRANSLATION

should we be his servants? He's merely the son of
Gideon, and this Zebul is merely his deputy. Serve
the true sons of Hamor, the founder of Shechem.
Why should we serve Abimelech? 29 If I were in
charge here, I would get rid of Abimelech. I would
say* to him, 'Get some soldiers, and come out and
fight!'"

30 But when Zebul, the leader of the city, heard
what Gaal was saying, he was furious. 31 He sent messengers to Abimelech in Arumah,* telling him, "Gaal
son of Ebed and his brothers have come to live in
Shechem, and now they are inciting the city to rebel
against you. 32 Come by night with an army and hide
out in the fields. 33 In the morning, as soon as it is
daylight, attack the city. When Gaal and those who
are with him come out against you, you can do with
them as you wish."

34 So Abimelech and all his men went by night and
split into four groups, stationing themselves around
Shechem. 35 Gaal was standing at the city gates when
Abimelech and his army came out of hiding. 36 When
Gaal saw them, he said to Zebul, "Look, there are
people coming down from the hilltops!"

Zebul replied, "It's just the shadows on the hills
that look like men."

37 But again Gaal said, "No, people are coming
down from the hills.* And another group is coming
down the road past the Diviners' Oak.*"

38 Then Zebul turned on him and asked, "Now
where is that big mouth of yours? Wasn't it you that
said, 'Who is Abimelech, and why should we be his
servants?' The men you mocked are right outside the
city! Go out and fight them!"

39 So Gaal led the leading citizens of Shechem into
battle against Abimelech. 40 But Abimelech chased
him, and many of Shechem's men were wounded
and fell along the road as they retreated to the city
gate. 41 Abimelech returned to Arumah, and Zebul
drove Gaal and his brothers out of Shechem.

42 The next day the people of Shechem went out
into the fields to battle. When Abimelech heard
about it, 43 he divided his men into three groups and
set an ambush in the fields. When Abimelech saw
the people coming out of the city, he and his men
jumped up from their hiding places and attacked
them. 44 Abimelech and his group stormed the city
gate to keep the men of Shechem from getting back

9:29 As in Greek version; Hebrew reads *And he said.* **9:31** Or *in secret;* Hebrew reads *in Tormah;* compare 9:41. **9:37a** Or *the center of the land.* **9:37b** Hebrew *Elon-meonenim.*

KING JAMES VERSION

upon all *the people* that *were* in the fields, and slew
them.
45And Abimelech fought against the city all that
day; and he took the city, and slew the people that
was therein, and beat down the city, and sowed it
with salt.
46And when all the men of the tower of Shechem
heard *that,* they entered into an hold of the house of
the god Berith.
47And it was told Abimelech, that all the men of
the tower of Shechem were gathered together.
48And Abimelech gat him up to mount Zalmon, he
and all the people that *were* with him; and Abimelech took an ax in his hand, and cut down a bough
from the trees, and took it, and laid *it* on his shoulder,
and said unto the people that *were* with him, What
ye have seen me do, make haste, *and* do as I *have*
done.
49And all the people likewise cut down every man
his bough, and followed Abimelech, and put *them* to
the hold, and set the hold on fire upon them; so that
all the men of the tower of Shechem died also, about
a thousand men and women.
50Then went Abimelech to Thebez, and encamped
against Thebez, and took it.
51But there was a strong tower within the city, and
thither fled all the men and women, and all they of
the city, and shut *it* to them, and gat them up to the
top of the tower.
52And Abimelech came unto the tower, and fought
against it, and went hard unto the door of the tower
to burn it with fire.
53And a certain woman cast a piece of a millstone
upon Abimelech's head, and all to brake his skull.
54Then he called hastily unto the young man his
armourbearer, and said unto him, Draw thy sword,
and slay me, that men say not of me, A woman slew
him. And his young man thrust him through, and
he died.
55And when the men of Israel saw that Abimelech
was dead, they departed every man unto his place.
56Thus God rendered the wickedness of Abimelech, which he did unto his father, in slaying his
seventy brethren:
57And all the evil of the men of Shechem did God
render upon their heads: and upon them came the
curse of Jotham the son of Jerubbaal.

10 1And after Abimelech there arose to defend
Israel Tola the son of Puah the son of Dodo, a
man of Issachar, and he dwelt in Shamir in mount
Ephraim.
2And he judged Israel twenty and three years, and
died, and was buried in Shamir.

NEW LIVING TRANSLATION

in, while Abimelech's other two groups cut them
down in the fields. 45The battle went on all day before Abimelech finally captured the city. He killed
the people, leveled the city, and scattered salt all over
the ground.
46When the leading citizens who lived in the
tower of Shechem heard what had happened, they
ran and hid in the temple of Baal-berith.*
47Someone reported to Abimelech that the citizens
had gathered in the temple, 48so he led his forces to
Mount Zalmon. He took an ax and chopped some
branches from a tree, then put them on his shoulder.
"Quick, do as I have done!" he told his men. 49So each
of them cut down some branches, following Abimelech's example. They piled the branches against the
walls of the temple and set them on fire. So all the
people who had lived in the tower of Shechem
died—about 1,000 men and women.
50Then Abimelech attacked the town of Thebez
and captured it. 51But there was a strong tower inside
the town, and all the men and women—the entire
population—fled to it. They barricaded themselves
in and climbed up to the roof of the tower. 52Abime-
lech followed them to attack the tower. But as he prepared to set fire to the entrance, 53a woman on the
roof dropped a millstone that landed on Abimelech's
head and crushed his skull.
54He quickly said to his young armor bearer, "Draw
your sword and kill me! Don't let it be said that a
woman killed Abimelech!" So the young man ran him
through with his sword, and he died. 55When Abimelech's men saw that he was dead, they disbanded and
returned to their homes.
56In this way, God punished Abimelech for the evil
he had done against his father by murdering his
seventy brothers. 57God also punished the men of
Shechem for all their evil. So the curse of Jotham son
of Gideon was fulfilled.

Tola Becomes Israel's Judge

10 After Abimelech died, Tola son of Puah, son
of Dodo, was the next person to rescue Israel.
He was from the tribe of Issachar but lived in the
town of Shamir in the hill country of Ephraim. 2He
judged Israel for twenty-three years. When he died,
he was buried in Shamir.

9:46 Hebrew *El-berith,* another name for Baal-berith; compare 9:4.

KING JAMES VERSION

3And after him arose Jair, a Gileadite, and judged Israel twenty and two years.

4And he had thirty sons that rode on thirty ass colts, and they had thirty cities, which are called Havoth-jair unto this day, which *are* in the land of Gilead.

5And Jair died, and was buried in Camon.

6And the children of Israel did evil again in the sight of the LORD, and served Baalim, and Ashtaroth, and the gods of Syria, and the gods of Zidon, and the gods of Moab, and the gods of the children of Ammon, and the gods of the Philistines, and forsook the LORD, and served not him.

7And the anger of the LORD was hot against Israel, and he sold them into the hands of the Philistines, and into the hands of the children of Ammon.

8And that year they vexed and oppressed the children of Israel: eighteen years, all the children of Israel that *were* on the other side Jordan in the land of the Amorites, which *is* in Gilead.

9Moreover the children of Ammon passed over Jordan to fight also against Judah, and against Benjamin, and against the house of Ephraim; so that Israel was sore distressed.

10And the children of Israel cried unto the LORD, saying, We have sinned against thee, both because we have forsaken our God, and also served Baalim.

11And the LORD said unto the children of Israel, *Did* not *I deliver you* from the Egyptians, and from the Amorites, from the children of Ammon, and from the Philistines?

12The Zidonians also, and the Amalekites, and the Maonites, did oppress you; and ye cried to me, and I delivered you out of their hand.

13Yet ye have forsaken me, and served other gods: wherefore I will deliver you no more.

14Go and cry unto the gods which ye have chosen; let them deliver you in the time of your tribulation.

15And the children of Israel said unto the LORD, We have sinned: do thou unto us whatsoever seemeth good unto thee; deliver us only, we pray thee, this day.

16And they put away the strange gods from among them, and served the LORD: and his soul was grieved for the misery of Israel.

17Then the children of Ammon were gathered together, and encamped in Gilead. And the children of Israel assembled themselves together, and encamped in Mizpeh.

18And the people *and* princes of Gilead said one to another, What man *is he* that will begin to fight against the children of Ammon? he shall be head over all the inhabitants of Gilead.

11 1Now Jephthah the Gileadite was a mighty man of valour, and he *was* the son of an harlot: and Gilead begat Jephthah.

NEW LIVING TRANSLATION

Jair Becomes Israel's Judge

3After Tola died, Jair from Gilead judged Israel for
twenty-two years. 4His thirty sons rode around on
thirty donkeys, and they owned thirty towns in the
land of Gilead, which are still called the Towns of
Jair.* 5When Jair died, he was buried in Kamon.

The Ammonites Oppress Israel

6Again the Israelites did evil in the LORD's sight. They
served the images of Baal and Ashtoreth, and the
gods of Aram, Sidon, Moab, Ammon, and Philistia.
They abandoned the LORD and no longer served him
at all. 7So the LORD burned with anger against Israel,
and he turned them over to the Philistines and the
Ammonites, 8who began to oppress them that year.
For eighteen years they oppressed all the Israelites
east of the Jordan River in the land of the Amorites
(that is, in Gilead). 9The Ammonites also crossed to
the west side of the Jordan and attacked Judah, Benjamin, and Ephraim.

The Israelites were in great distress. 10Finally, they
cried out to the LORD for help, saying, "We have
sinned against you because we have abandoned you
as our God and have served the images of Baal."

11The LORD replied, "Did I not rescue you from the
Egyptians, the Amorites, the Ammonites, the Philistines, 12the Sidonians, the Amalekites, and the Maonites? When they oppressed you, you cried out to
me for help, and I rescued you. 13Yet you have abandoned me and served other gods. So I will not rescue
you anymore. 14Go and cry out to the gods you have
chosen! Let them rescue you in your hour of distress!"

15But the Israelites pleaded with the LORD and
said, "We have sinned. Punish us as you see fit, only
rescue us today from our enemies." 16Then the Israelites put aside their foreign gods and served the
LORD. And he was grieved by their misery.

17At that time the armies of Ammon had gathered
for war and were camped in Gilead, and the people of
Israel assembled and camped at Mizpah. 18The leaders of Gilead said to each other, "Whoever attacks
the Ammonites first will become ruler over all the
people of Gilead."

Jephthah Becomes Israel's Judge

11 Now Jephthah of Gilead was a great warrior. He was the son of Gilead, but his mother was a

10:4 Hebrew *Havvoth-jair.*

KING JAMES VERSION

2And Gilead's wife bare him sons; and his wife's sons grew up, and they thrust out Jephthah, and said unto him, Thou shalt not inherit in our father's house; for thou *art* the son of a strange woman.

3Then Jephthah fled from his brethren, and dwelt in the land of Tob: and there were gathered vain men to Jephthah, and went out with him.

4And it came to pass in process of time, that the children of Ammon made war against Israel.

5And it was so, that when the children of Ammon made war against Israel, the elders of Gilead went to fetch Jephthah out of the land of Tob:

6And they said unto Jephthah, Come, and be our captain, that we may fight with the children of Ammon.

7And Jephthah said unto the elders of Gilead, Did not ye hate me, and expel me out of my father's house? and why are ye come unto me now when ye are in distress?

8And the elders of Gilead said unto Jephthah, Therefore we turn again to thee now, that thou mayest go with us, and fight against the children of Ammon, and be our head over all the inhabitants of Gilead.

9And Jephthah said unto the elders of Gilead, If ye bring me home again to fight against the children of Ammon, and the LORD deliver them before me, shall I be your head?

10And the elders of Gilead said unto Jephthah, The LORD be witness between us, if we do not so according to thy words.

11Then Jephthah went with the elders of Gilead, and the people made him head and captain over them: and Jephthah uttered all his words before the LORD in Mizpeh.

12And Jephthah sent messengers unto the king of the children of Ammon, saying, What hast thou to do with me, that thou art come against me to fight in my land?

13And the king of the children of Ammon answered unto the messengers of Jephthah, Because Israel took away my land, when they came up out of Egypt, from Arnon even unto Jabbok, and unto Jordan: now therefore restore those *lands* again peaceably.

14And Jephthah sent messengers again unto the king of the children of Ammon:

15And said unto him, Thus saith Jephthah, Israel took not away the land of Moab, nor the land of the children of Ammon:

16But when Israel came up from Egypt, and walked through the wilderness unto the Red sea, and came to Kadesh;

17Then Israel sent messengers unto the king of Edom, saying, Let me, I pray thee, pass through thy land: but the king of Edom would not hearken *thereto.* And in like manner they sent unto the king of Moab: but he would not *consent:* and Israel abode in Kadesh.

NEW LIVING TRANSLATION

prostitute. 2Gilead's wife also had several sons, and when these half brothers grew up, they chased Jephthah off the land. "You will not get any of our father's inheritance," they said, "for you are the son of a prostitute." 3So Jephthah fled from his brothers and lived in the land of Tob. Soon he had a band of worthless rebels following him.

4At about this time, the Ammonites began their war against Israel. 5When the Ammonites attacked, the elders of Gilead sent for Jephthah in the land of Tob. The elders said, 6"Come and be our commander! Help us fight the Ammonites!"

7But Jephthah said to them, "Aren't you the ones who hated me and drove me from my father's house? Why do you come to me now when you're in trouble?"

8"Because we need you," the elders replied. "If you lead us in battle against the Ammonites, we will make you ruler over all the people of Gilead."

9Jephthah said to the elders, "Let me get this straight. If I come with you and if the LORD gives me victory over the Ammonites, will you really make me ruler over all the people?"

10"The LORD is our witness," the elders replied. "We promise to do whatever you say."

11So Jephthah went with the elders of Gilead, and the people made him their ruler and commander of the army. At Mizpah, in the presence of the LORD, Jephthah repeated what he had said to the elders.

12Then Jephthah sent messengers to the king of Ammon, asking, "Why have you come out to fight against my land?"

13The king of Ammon answered Jephthah's messengers, "When the Israelites came out of Egypt, they stole my land from the Arnon River to the Jabbok River and all the way to the Jordan. Now then, give back the land peaceably."

14Jephthah sent this message back to the Ammonite king:

15"This is what Jephthah says: Israel did not steal any land from Moab or Ammon. 16When the people of Israel arrived at Kadesh on their journey from Egypt after crossing the Red Sea,* 17they sent messengers to the king of Edom asking for permission to pass through his land. But their request was denied. Then they asked the king of Moab for similar permission, but he wouldn't let them pass through either. So the people of Israel stayed in Kadesh.

11:16 Hebrew *sea of reeds.*

KING JAMES VERSION

18 Then they went along through the wilderness, and compassed the land of Edom, and the land of Moab, and came by the east side of the land of Moab, and pitched on the other side of Arnon, but came not within the border of Moab: for Arnon *was* the border of Moab.

19 And Israel sent messengers unto Sihon king of the Amorites, the king of Heshbon; and Israel said unto him, Let us pass, we pray thee, through thy land into my place.

20 But Sihon trusted not Israel to pass through his coast: but Sihon gathered all his people together, and pitched in Jahaz, and fought against Israel.

21 And the LORD God of Israel delivered Sihon and all his people into the hand of Israel, and they smote them: so Israel possessed all the land of the Amorites, the inhabitants of that country.

22 And they possessed all the coasts of the Amorites, from Arnon even unto Jabbok, and from the wilderness even unto Jordan.

23 So now the LORD God of Israel hath dispossessed the Amorites from before his people Israel, and shouldest thou possess it?

24 Wilt not thou possess that which Chemosh thy god giveth thee to possess? So whomsoever the LORD our God shall drive out from before us, them will we possess.

25 And now *art* thou any thing better than Balak the son of Zippor, king of Moab? did he ever strive against Israel, or did he ever fight against them,

26 While Israel dwelt in Heshbon and her towns, and in Aroer and her towns, and in all the cities that *be* along by the coasts of Arnon, three hundred years? why therefore did ye not recover *them* within that time?

27 Wherefore I have not sinned against thee, but thou doest me wrong to war against me: the LORD the Judge be judge this day between the children of Israel and the children of Ammon.

28 Howbeit the king of the children of Ammon hearkened not unto the words of Jephthah which he sent him.

29 Then the Spirit of the LORD came upon Jephthah, and he passed over Gilead, and Manasseh, and passed over Mizpeh of Gilead, and from Mizpeh of Gilead he passed over *unto* the children of Ammon.

30 And Jephthah vowed a vow unto the LORD, and said, If thou shalt without fail deliver the children of Ammon into mine hands,

31 Then it shall be, that whatsoever cometh forth of the doors of my house to meet me, when I return in peace from the children of Ammon, shall surely be the LORD's, and I will offer it up for a burnt offering.

32 So Jephthah passed over unto the children of Ammon to fight against them; and the LORD delivered them into his hands.

33 And he smote them from Aroer, even till thou come to Minnith, *even* twenty cities, and unto the

NEW LIVING TRANSLATION

18 "Finally, they went around Edom and Moab
through the wilderness. They traveled along
Moab's eastern border and camped on the other
side of the Arnon River. But they never once
crossed the Arnon River into Moab, for the Arnon
was the border of Moab.

19 "Then Israel sent messengers to King Sihon
of the Amorites, who ruled from Heshbon, asking
for permission to cross through his land to get
to their destination. 20 But King Sihon didn't
trust Israel to pass through his land. Instead, he
mobilized his army at Jahaz and attacked them.
21 But the LORD, the God of Israel, gave his people
victory over King Sihon. So Israel took control
of all the land of the Amorites, who lived in that
region, 22 from the Arnon River to the Jabbok
River, and from the eastern wilderness to the
Jordan.

23 "So you see, it was the LORD, the God of Israel,
who took away the land from the Amorites and
gave it to Israel. Why, then, should we give it back
to you? 24 You keep whatever your god Chemosh
gives you, and we will keep whatever the LORD
our God gives us. 25 Are you any better than Balak
son of Zippor, king of Moab? Did he try to make a
case against Israel for disputed land? Did he go to
war against them?

26 "Israel has been living here for 300 years,
inhabiting Heshbon and its surrounding
settlements, all the way to Aroer and its
settlements, and in all the towns along the Arnon
River. Why have you made no effort to recover
it before now? 27 Therefore, I have not sinned
against you. Rather, you have wronged me by
attacking me. Let the LORD, who is judge, decide
today which of us is right—Israel or Ammon."

28 But the king of Ammon paid no attention to Jephthah's message.

Jephthah's Vow

29 At that time the Spirit of the LORD came upon Jephthah, and he went throughout the land of Gilead and Manasseh, including Mizpah in Gilead, and from there he led an army against the Ammonites. 30 And
Jephthah made a vow to the LORD. He said, "If you
give me victory over the Ammonites, 31 I will give to
the LORD whatever comes out of my house to meet me when I return in triumph. I will sacrifice it as a burnt offering."

32 So Jephthah led his army against the Ammonites, and the LORD gave him victory. 33 He crushed the
Ammonites, devastating about twenty towns from

KING JAMES VERSION

plain of the vineyards, with a very great slaughter.
Thus the children of Ammon were subdued before
the children of Israel.
34 And Jephthah came to Mizpeh unto his house,
and, behold, his daughter came out to meet him with
timbrels and with dances: and she *was his* only child;
beside her he had neither son nor daughter.
35 And it came to pass, when he saw her, that he
rent his clothes, and said, Alas, my daughter! thou
hast brought me very low, and thou art one of them
that trouble me: for I have opened my mouth unto
the LORD, and I cannot go back.
36 And she said unto him, My father, *if* thou hast
opened thy mouth unto the LORD, do to me according to that which hath proceeded out of thy mouth;
forasmuch as the LORD hath taken vengeance
for thee of thine enemies, *even* of the children of
Ammon.
37 And she said unto her father, Let this thing be
done for me: let me alone two months, that I may go
up and down upon the mountains, and bewail my
virginity, I and my fellows.
38 And he said, Go. And he sent her away *for* two
months: and she went with her companions, and
bewailed her virginity upon the mountains.
39 And it came to pass at the end of two months,
that she returned unto her father, who did with her
according to his vow which he had vowed: and she
knew no man. And it was a custom in Israel,
40 *That* the daughters of Israel went yearly to lament the daughter of Jephthah the Gileadite four
days in a year.

12 1 And the men of Ephraim gathered themselves together, and went northward, and
said unto Jephthah, Wherefore passedst thou over to
fight against the children of Ammon, and didst not
call us to go with thee? we will burn thine house
upon thee with fire.
2 And Jephthah said unto them, I and my people
were at great strife with the children of Ammon; and
when I called you, ye delivered me not out of their
hands.
3 And when I saw that ye delivered *me* not, I put my
life in my hands, and passed over against the children of Ammon, and the LORD delivered them into
my hand: wherefore then are ye come up unto me
this day, to fight against me?
4 Then Jephthah gathered together all the men of
Gilead, and fought with Ephraim: and the men of Gilead smote Ephraim, because they said, Ye Gileadites
are fugitives of Ephraim among the Ephraimites,
and among the Manassites.
5 And the Gileadites took the passages of Jordan
before the Ephraimites: and it was *so* that when
those Ephraimites which were escaped said, Let me
go over; that the men of Gilead said unto him, *Art*
thou an Ephraimite? If he said, Nay;

NEW LIVING TRANSLATION

Aroer to an area near Minnith and as far away as
Abel-keramim. In this way Israel defeated the
Ammonites.
34 When Jephthah returned home to Mizpah, his
daughter came out to meet him, playing on a tambourine and dancing for joy. She was his one and
only child; he had no other sons or daughters.
35 When he saw her, he tore his clothes in anguish.
"Oh, my daughter!" he cried out. "You have completely destroyed me! You've brought disaster on me!
For I have made a vow to the LORD, and I cannot take
it back."
36 And she said, "Father, if you have made a vow to
the LORD, you must do to me what you have vowed,
for the LORD has given you a great victory over your
enemies, the Ammonites. 37 But first let me do this
one thing: Let me go up and roam in the hills and
weep with my friends for two months, because I will
die a virgin."
38 "You may go," Jephthah said. And he sent her
away for two months. She and her friends went into
the hills and wept because she would never have
children. 39 When she returned home, her father
kept the vow he had made, and she died a virgin.
So it has become a custom in Israel 40 for young
Israelite women to go away for four days each year to
lament the fate of Jephthah's daughter.

Ephraim Fights with Jephthah

12 Then the people of Ephraim mobilized an
army and crossed over the Jordan River to
Zaphon. They sent this message to Jephthah: "Why
didn't you call for us to help you fight against the Ammonites? We are going to burn down your house
with you in it!"
2 Jephthah replied, "I summoned you at the beginning of the dispute, but you refused to come! You
failed to help us in our struggle against Ammon. 3 So
when I realized you weren't coming, I risked my life
and went to battle without you, and the LORD gave
me victory over the Ammonites. So why have you
now come to fight me?"
4 The people of Ephraim responded, "You men of
Gilead are nothing more than fugitives from Ephraim and Manasseh." So Jephthah gathered all the men
of Gilead and attacked the men of Ephraim and defeated them.
5 Jephthah captured the shallow crossings of the
Jordan River, and whenever a fugitive from Ephraim
tried to go back across, the men of Gilead would
challenge him. "Are you a member of the tribe of
Ephraim?" they would ask. If the man said, "No, I'm

KING JAMES VERSION

6 Then said they unto him, Say now Shibboleth:
and he said Sibboleth: for he could not frame to pronounce *it* right. Then they took him, and slew him at
the passages of Jordan: and there fell at that time of
the Ephraimites forty and two thousand.
7 And Jephthah judged Israel six years. Then died
Jephthah the Gileadite, and was buried in *one of* the
cities of Gilead.

8 And after him Ibzan of Bethlehem judged Israel.
9 And he had thirty sons, and thirty daughters,
whom he sent abroad, and took in thirty daughters
from abroad for his sons. And he judged Israel seven
years.
10 Then died Ibzan, and was buried at Bethlehem.

11 And after him Elon, a Zebulonite, judged Israel;
and he judged Israel ten years.
12 And Elon the Zebulonite died, and was buried in
Aijalon in the country of Zebulun.

13 And after him Abdon the son of Hillel, a Pirathonite, judged Israel.
14 And he had forty sons and thirty nephews, that
rode on threescore and ten ass colts: and he judged
Israel eight years.
15 And Abdon the son of Hillel the Pirathonite
died, and was buried in Pirathon in the land of
Ephraim, in the mount of the Amalekites.

13 1 And the children of Israel did evil again in
the sight of the LORD; and the LORD delivered
them into the hand of the Philistines forty years.
2 And there was a certain man of Zorah, of the family of the Danites, whose name *was* Manoah; and his
wife *was* barren, and bare not.
3 And the angel of the LORD appeared unto the
woman, and said unto her, Behold now, thou *art* barren, and bearest not: but thou shalt conceive, and
bear a son.
4 Now therefore beware, I pray thee, and drink not
wine nor strong drink, and eat not any unclean
thing:
5 For, lo, thou shalt conceive, and bear a son; and no
razor shall come on his head: for the child shall be a
Nazarite unto God from the womb: and he shall begin to deliver Israel out of the hand of the Philistines.
6 Then the woman came and told her husband,
saying, A man of God came unto me, and his countenance *was* like the countenance of an angel of God,
very terrible: but I asked him not whence he *was,*
neither told he me his name:
7 But he said unto me, Behold, thou shalt conceive,
and bear a son; and now drink no wine nor strong
drink, neither eat any unclean *thing:* for the child

NEW LIVING TRANSLATION

not," 6 they would tell him to say "Shibboleth." If he
was from Ephraim, he would say "Sibboleth," because people from Ephraim cannot pronounce the
word correctly. Then they would take him and kill
him at the shallow crossings of the Jordan. In all,
42,000 Ephraimites were killed at that time.
7 Jephthah judged Israel for six years. When he
died, he was buried in one of the towns of Gilead.

Ibzan Becomes Israel's Judge

8 After Jephthah died, Ibzan from Bethlehem judged
Israel. 9 He had thirty sons and thirty daughters.
He sent his daughters to marry men outside his
clan, and he brought in thirty young women from
outside his clan to marry his sons. Ibzan judged
Israel for seven years. 10 When he died, he was buried at Bethlehem.

Elon Becomes Israel's Judge

11 After Ibzan died, Elon from the tribe of Zebulun
judged Israel for ten years. 12 When he died, he was
buried at Aijalon in Zebulun.

Abdon Becomes Israel's Judge

13 After Elon died, Abdon son of Hillel, from Pirathon, judged Israel. 14 He had forty sons and thirty
grandsons, who rode on seventy donkeys. He judged
Israel for eight years. 15 When he died, he was buried
at Pirathon in Ephraim, in the hill country of the
Amalekites.

The Birth of Samson

13 Again the Israelites did evil in the LORD's
sight, so the LORD handed them over to the
Philistines, who oppressed them for forty years.
2 In those days a man named Manoah from the
tribe of Dan lived in the town of Zorah. His wife was
unable to become pregnant, and they had no children. 3 The angel of the LORD appeared to Manoah's
wife and said, "Even though you have been unable to
have children, you will soon become pregnant and
give birth to a son. 4 So be careful; you must not drink
wine or any other alcoholic drink nor eat any forbidden food.* 5 You will become pregnant and give birth
to a son, and his hair must never be cut. For he will be
dedicated to God as a Nazirite from birth. He will
begin to rescue Israel from the Philistines."
6 The woman ran and told her husband, "A man of
God appeared to me! He looked like one of God's angels, terrifying to see. I didn't ask where he was from,
and he didn't tell me his name. 7 But he told me, 'You
will become pregnant and give birth to a son. You
must not drink wine or any other alcoholic drink nor

13:4 Hebrew *any unclean thing;* also in 13:7, 14.

KING JAMES VERSION

shall be a Nazarite to God from the womb to the day
of his death.
8Then Manoah intreated the LORD, and said, O my
Lord, let the man of God which thou didst send come
again unto us, and teach us what we shall do unto the
child that shall be born.
9And God hearkened to the voice of Manoah; and
the angel of God came again unto the woman as she
sat in the field: but Manoah her husband *was* not
with her.
10And the woman made haste, and ran, and
shewed her husband, and said unto him, Behold, the
man hath appeared unto me, that came unto me the
other day.
11And Manoah arose, and went after his wife, and
came to the man, and said unto him, *Art* thou the
man that spakest unto the woman? And he said, I *am*.
12And Manoah said, Now let thy words come to
pass. How shall we order the child, and *how* shall we
do unto him?
13And the angel of the LORD said unto Manoah, Of
all that I said unto the woman let her beware.
14She may not eat of any *thing* that cometh of the
vine, neither let her drink wine or strong drink, nor
eat any unclean *thing*: all that I commanded her let
her observe.
15And Manoah said unto the angel of the LORD, I
pray thee, let us detain thee, until we shall have made
ready a kid for thee.
16And the angel of the LORD said unto Manoah,
Though thou detain me, I will not eat of thy bread:
and if thou wilt offer a burnt offering, thou must offer it unto the LORD. For Manoah knew not that he
was an angel of the LORD.
17And Manoah said unto the angel of the LORD,
What *is* thy name, that when thy sayings come to
pass we may do thee honour?
18And the angel of the LORD said unto him, Why
askest thou thus after my name, seeing it *is* secret?
19So Manoah took a kid with a meat offering,
and offered *it* upon a rock unto the LORD: and *the*
angel did wonderously; and Manoah and his wife
looked on.
20For it came to pass, when the flame went up toward heaven from off the altar, that the angel of the
LORD ascended in the flame of the altar. And Manoah
and his wife looked on *it*, and fell on their faces to
the ground.
21But the angel of the LORD did no more appear to
Manoah and to his wife. Then Manoah knew that he
was an angel of the LORD.
22And Manoah said unto his wife, We shall surely
die, because we have seen God.
23But his wife said unto him, If the LORD were
pleased to kill us, he would not have received a burnt
offering and a meat offering at our hands, neither
would he have shewed us all these *things*, nor would
as at this time have told us *such things* as these.

NEW LIVING TRANSLATION

eat any forbidden food. For your son will be dedicated to God as a Nazirite from the moment of his
birth until the day of his death.'"
8Then Manoah prayed to the LORD, saying, "Lord,
please let the man of God come back to us again and
give us more instructions about this son who is to
be born."
9God answered Manoah's prayer, and the angel of
God appeared once again to his wife as she was sitting in the field. But her husband, Manoah, was not
with her. 10So she quickly ran and told her husband,
"The man who appeared to me the other day is here
again!"
11Manoah ran back with his wife and asked, "Are
you the man who spoke to my wife the other day?"
"Yes," he replied, "I am."
12So Manoah asked him, "When your words come
true, what kind of rules should govern the boy's life
and work?"
13The angel of the LORD replied, "Be sure your wife
follows the instructions I gave her. 14She must not
eat grapes or raisins, drink wine or any other alcoholic drink, or eat any forbidden food."
15Then Manoah said to the angel of the LORD,
"Please stay here until we can prepare a young goat
for you to eat."
16"I will stay," the angel of the LORD replied, "but I
will not eat anything. However, you may prepare a
burnt offering as a sacrifice to the LORD." (Manoah
didn't realize it was the angel of the LORD.)
17Then Manoah asked the angel of the LORD,
"What is your name? For when all this comes true,
we want to honor you."
18"Why do you ask my name?" the angel of the
LORD replied. "It is too wonderful for you to understand."
19Then Manoah took a young goat and a grain
offering and offered it on a rock as a sacrifice to the
LORD. And as Manoah and his wife watched, the
LORD did an amazing thing. 20As the flames from
the altar shot up toward the sky, the angel of the
LORD ascended in the fire. When Manoah and his
wife saw this, they fell with their faces to the ground.
21The angel did not appear again to Manoah and
his wife. Manoah finally realized it was the angel of
the LORD, 22and he said to his wife, "We will certainly
die, for we have seen God!"
23But his wife said, "If the LORD were going to kill
us, he wouldn't have accepted our burnt offering
and grain offering. He wouldn't have appeared to
us and told us this wonderful thing and done these
miracles."

KING JAMES VERSION

[24]And the woman bare a son, and called his name Samson: and the child grew, and the LORD blessed him.

[25]And the Spirit of the LORD began to move him at times in the camp of Dan between Zorah and Eshtaol.

14 [1]And Samson went down to Timnath, and saw a woman in Timnath of the daughters of the Philistines.

[2]And he came up, and told his father and his mother, and said, I have seen a woman in Timnath of the daughters of the Philistines: now therefore get her for me to wife.

[3]Then his father and his mother said unto him, *Is there* never a woman among the daughters of thy brethren, or among all my people, that thou goest to take a wife of the uncircumcised Philistines? And Samson said unto his father, Get her for me; for she pleaseth me well.

[4]But his father and his mother knew not that it *was* of the LORD, that he sought an occasion against the Philistines: for at that time the Philistines had dominion over Israel.

[5]Then went Samson down, and his father and his mother, to Timnath, and came to the vineyards of Timnath: and, behold, a young lion roared against him.

[6]And the Spirit of the LORD came mightily upon him, and he rent him as he would have rent a kid, and *he had* nothing in his hand: but he told not his father or his mother what he had done.

[7]And he went down, and talked with the woman; and she pleased Samson well.

[8]And after a time he returned to take her, and he turned aside to see the carcase of the lion: and, behold, *there was* a swarm of bees and honey in the carcase of the lion.

[9]And he took thereof in his hands, and went on eating, and came to his father and mother, and he gave them, and they did eat: but he told not them that he had taken the honey out of the carcase of the lion.

[10]So his father went down unto the woman: and Samson made there a feast; for so used the young men to do.

[11]And it came to pass, when they saw him, that they brought thirty companions to be with him.

[12]And Samson said unto them, I will now put forth a riddle unto you: if ye can certainly declare it me within the seven days of the feast, and find *it* out, then I will give you thirty sheets and thirty change of garments:

[13]But if ye cannot declare *it* me, then shall ye give me thirty sheets and thirty change of garments. And they said unto him, Put forth thy riddle, that we may hear it.

[14]And he said unto them, Out of the eater came forth meat, and out of the strong came forth

NEW LIVING TRANSLATION

[24]When her son was born, she named him Samson. And the LORD blessed him as he grew up. [25]And
the Spirit of the LORD began to stir him while he lived in Mahaneh-dan, which is located between the towns of Zorah and Eshtaol.

Samson's Riddle

14 One day when Samson was in Timnah, one of the Philistine women caught his eye. [2]When
he returned home, he told his father and mother, "A young Philistine woman in Timnah caught my eye. I want to marry her. Get her for me."

[3]His father and mother objected. "Isn't there even one woman in our tribe or among all the Israelites you could marry?" they asked. "Why must you go to the pagan Philistines to find a wife?"

But Samson told his father, "Get her for me! She looks good to me." [4]His father and mother didn't realize the LORD was at work in this, creating an opportunity to work against the Philistines, who ruled over Israel at that time.

[5]As Samson and his parents were going down to Timnah, a young lion suddenly attacked Samson near the vineyards of Timnah. [6]At that moment the
Spirit of the LORD came powerfully upon him, and he ripped the lion's jaws apart with his bare hands. He did it as easily as if it were a young goat. But he didn't tell his father or mother about it. [7]When Samson arrived in Timnah, he talked with the woman and was very pleased with her.

[8]Later, when he returned to Timnah for the wedding, he turned off the path to look at the carcass of the lion. And he found that a swarm of bees had made some honey in the carcass. [9]He scooped some
of the honey into his hands and ate it along the way. He also gave some to his father and mother, and they ate it. But he didn't tell them he had taken the honey from the carcass of the lion.

[10]As his father was making final arrangements for the marriage, Samson threw a party at Timnah, as was the custom for elite young men. [11]When the
bride's parents* saw him, they selected thirty young men from the town to be his companions.

[12]Samson said to them, "Let me tell you a riddle. If you solve my riddle during these seven days of the celebration, I will give you thirty fine linen robes and thirty sets of festive clothing. [13]But if you can't solve
it, then you must give me thirty fine linen robes and thirty sets of festive clothing."

"All right," they agreed, "let's hear your riddle."

[14]So he said:

"Out of the one who eats came something to eat;
out of the strong came something sweet."

14:11 Hebrew *they*.

KING JAMES VERSION

sweetness. And they could not in three days ex-
pound the riddle.
15 And it came to pass on the seventh day, that they
said unto Samson's wife, Entice thy husband, that he
may declare unto us the riddle, lest we burn thee and
thy father's house with fire: have ye called us to take
that we have? *is it* not *so?*
16 And Samson's wife wept before him, and said,
Thou dost but hate me, and lovest me not: thou hast
put forth a riddle unto the children of my people,
and hast not told *it* me. And he said unto her, Behold,
I have not told *it* my father nor my mother, and shall I
tell *it* thee?
17 And she wept before him the seven days, while
their feast lasted: and it came to pass on the seventh
day, that he told her, because she lay sore upon him:
and she told the riddle to the children of her people.
18 And the men of the city said unto him on the
seventh day before the sun went down, What *is*
sweeter than honey? and what *is* stronger than a
lion? And he said unto them, If ye had not plowed
with my heifer, ye had not found out my riddle.
19 And the Spirit of the LORD came upon him, and
he went down to Ashkelon, and slew thirty men of
them, and took their spoil, and gave change of garments unto them which expounded the riddle.
And his anger was kindled, and he went up to his father's house.
20 But Samson's wife was *given* to his companion,
whom he had used as his friend.

15 1 But it came to pass within a while after, in
the time of wheat harvest, that Samson visited his wife with a kid; and he said, I will go in to my
wife into the chamber. But her father would not suffer him to go in.
2 And her father said, I verily thought that thou
hadst utterly hated her; therefore I gave her to thy
companion: *is* not her younger sister fairer than she?
take her, I pray thee, instead of her.
3 And Samson said concerning them, Now shall I
be more blameless than the Philistines, though I do
them a displeasure.
4 And Samson went and caught three hundred
foxes, and took firebrands, and turned tail to tail, and
put a firebrand in the midst between two tails.
5 And when he had set the brands on fire, he let
them go into the standing corn of the Philistines, and
burnt up both the shocks, and also the standing corn,
with the vineyards *and* olives.
6 Then the Philistines said, Who hath done this?
And they answered, Samson, the son in law of the
Timnite, because he had taken his wife, and given
her to his companion. And the Philistines came up,
and burnt her and her father with fire.
7 And Samson said unto them, Though ye have

NEW LIVING TRANSLATION

Three days later they were still trying to figure it
out. 15 On the fourth* day they said to Samson's wife,
"Entice your husband to explain the riddle for us, or
we will burn down your father's house with you in it.
Did you invite us to this party just to make us poor?"
16 So Samson's wife came to him in tears and said,
"You don't love me; you hate me! You have given my
people a riddle, but you haven't told me the answer."
"I haven't even given the answer to my father or
mother," he replied. "Why should I tell you?" 17 So
she cried whenever she was with him and kept it up
for the rest of the celebration. At last, on the seventh
day he told her the answer because she was tormenting him with her nagging. Then she explained the
riddle to the young men.
18 So before sunset of the seventh day, the men of
the town came to Samson with their answer:

"What is sweeter than honey?
What is stronger than a lion?"

Samson replied, "If you hadn't plowed with my
heifer, you wouldn't have solved my riddle!"
19 Then the Spirit of the LORD came powerfully
upon him. He went down to the town of Ashkelon,
killed thirty men, took their belongings, and gave
their clothing to the men who had solved his riddle.
But Samson was furious about what had happened,
and he went back home to live with his father and
mother. 20 So his wife was given in marriage to the
man who had been Samson's best man at the
wedding.

Samson's Vengeance on the Philistines

15 Later on, during the wheat harvest, Samson
took a young goat as a present to his wife. He
said, "I'm going into my wife's room to sleep with
her," but her father wouldn't let him in.
2 "I truly thought you must hate her," her father explained, "so I gave her in marriage to your best man.
But look, her younger sister is even more beautiful
than she is. Marry her instead."
3 Samson said, "This time I cannot be blamed for
everything I am going to do to you Philistines."
4 Then he went out and caught 300 foxes. He tied
their tails together in pairs, and he fastened a torch
to each pair of tails. 5 Then he lit the torches and let
the foxes run through the grain fields of the Philistines. He burned all their grain to the ground, including the sheaves and the uncut grain. He also
destroyed their vineyards and olive groves.
6 "Who did this?" the Philistines demanded.
"Samson," was the reply, "because his father-in-
law from Timnah gave Samson's wife to be married
to his best man." So the Philistines went and got the
woman and her father and burned them to death.
7 "Because you did this," Samson vowed, "I won't

14:15 As in Greek version; Hebrew reads *seventh.*

done this, yet will I be avenged of you, and after that I will cease.

8And he smote them hip and thigh with a great slaughter: and he went down and dwelt in the top of the rock Etam.

9Then the Philistines went up, and pitched in Judah, and spread themselves in Lehi.

10And the men of Judah said, Why are ye come up against us? And they answered, To bind Samson are we come up, to do to him as he hath done to us.

11Then three thousand men of Judah went to the top of the rock Etam, and said to Samson, Knowest thou not that the Philistines *are* rulers over us? what *is* this *that* thou hast done unto us? And he said unto them, As they did unto me, so have I done unto them.

12And they said unto him, We are come down to bind thee, that we may deliver thee into the hand of the Philistines. And Samson said unto them, Swear unto me, that ye will not fall upon me yourselves.

13And they spake unto him, saying, No; but we will bind thee fast, and deliver thee into their hand: but surely we will not kill thee. And they bound him with two new cords, and brought him up from the rock.

14*And* when he came unto Lehi, the Philistines shouted against him: and the Spirit of the LORD came mightily upon him, and the cords that *were* upon his arms became as flax that was burnt with fire, and his bands loosed from off his hands.

15And he found a new jawbone of an ass, and put forth his hand, and took it, and slew a thousand men therewith.

16And Samson said, With the jawbone of an ass, heaps upon heaps, with the jaw of an ass have I slain a thousand men.

17And it came to pass, when he had made an end of speaking, that he cast away the jawbone out of his hand, and called that place Ramath-lehi.

18And he was sore athirst, and called on the LORD, and said, Thou hast given this great deliverance into the hand of thy servant: and now shall I die for thirst, and fall into the hand of the uncircumcised?

19But God clave an hollow place that *was* in the jaw, and there came water thereout; and when he had drunk, his spirit came again, and he revived: wherefore he called the name thereof En-hakkore, which *is* in Lehi unto this day.

20And he judged Israel in the days of the Philistines twenty years.

16 1Then went Samson to Gaza, and saw there an harlot, and went in unto her.

2*And it was told* the Gazites, saying, Samson is come hither. And they compassed *him* in, and laid wait for him all night in the gate of the city, and were

rest until I take my revenge on you!" 8So he attacked the Philistines with great fury and killed many of them. Then he went to live in a cave in the rock of Etam.

9The Philistines retaliated by setting up camp in Judah and spreading out near the town of Lehi. 10The men of Judah asked the Philistines, "Why are you attacking us?"

The Philistines replied, "We've come to capture Samson. We've come to pay him back for what he did to us."

11So 3,000 men of Judah went down to get Samson at the cave in the rock of Etam. They said to Samson, "Don't you realize the Philistines rule over us? What are you doing to us?"

But Samson replied, "I only did to them what they did to me."

12But the men of Judah told him, "We have come to tie you up and hand you over to the Philistines."

"All right," Samson said. "But promise that you won't kill me yourselves."

13"We will only tie you up and hand you over to the Philistines," they replied. "We won't kill you." So they tied him up with two new ropes and brought him up from the rock.

14As Samson arrived at Lehi, the Philistines came shouting in triumph. But the Spirit of the LORD came powerfully upon Samson, and he snapped the ropes on his arms as if they were burnt strands of flax, and they fell from his wrists. 15Then he found the jawbone of a recently killed donkey. He picked it up and killed 1,000 Philistines with it. 16Then Samson said,

"With the jawbone of a donkey,
  I've piled them in heaps!
With the jawbone of a donkey,
  I've killed a thousand men!"

17When he finished his boasting, he threw away the jawbone; and the place was named Jawbone Hill.*

18Samson was now very thirsty, and he cried out to the LORD, "You have accomplished this great victory by the strength of your servant. Must I now die of thirst and fall into the hands of these pagans?" 19So God caused water to gush out of a hollow in the ground at Lehi, and Samson was revived as he drank. Then he named that place "The Spring of the One Who Cried Out,"* and it is still in Lehi to this day.

20Samson judged Israel for twenty years during the period when the Philistines dominated the land.

Samson Carries Away Gaza's Gates

16 One day Samson went to the Philistine town of Gaza and spent the night with a prostitute. 2Word soon spread* that Samson was there, so the men of Gaza gathered together and waited all night at the town gates. They kept quiet during the night,

15:17 Hebrew *Ramath-lehi.* **15:19** Hebrew *En-hakkore.* **16:2** As in Greek and Syriac versions and Latin Vulgate; Hebrew lacks *Word soon spread.*

KING JAMES VERSION

quiet all the night, saying, In the morning, when it is
day, we shall kill him.
3 And Samson lay till midnight, and arose at midnight, and took the doors of the gate of the city, and
the two posts, and went away with them, bar and all,
and put *them* upon his shoulders, and carried them
up to the top of an hill that *is* before Hebron.

4 And it came to pass afterward, that he loved a
woman in the valley of Sorek, whose name *was*
Delilah.
5 And the lords of the Philistines came up unto her,
and said unto her, Entice him, and see wherein his
great strength *lieth,* and by what *means* we may prevail against him, that we may bind him to afflict him:
and we will give thee every one of us eleven hundred
pieces of silver.
6 And Delilah said to Samson, Tell me, I pray thee,
wherein thy great strength *lieth,* and wherewith thou
mightest be bound to afflict thee.
7 And Samson said unto her, If they bind me with
seven green withs that were never dried, then shall I
be weak, and be as another man.
8 Then the lords of the Philistines brought up to
her seven green withs which had not been dried, and
she bound him with them.
9 Now *there were* men lying in wait, abiding with
her in the chamber. And she said unto him, The Philistines *be* upon thee, Samson. And he brake the
withs, as a thread of tow is broken when it toucheth
the fire. So his strength was not known.
10 And Delilah said unto Samson, Behold, thou hast
mocked me, and told me lies: now tell me, I pray thee,
wherewith thou mightest be bound.
11 And he said unto her, If they bind me fast with
new ropes that never were occupied, then shall I be
weak, and be as another man.
12 Delilah therefore took new ropes, and bound
him therewith, and said unto him, The Philistines *be*
upon thee, Samson. And *there were* liers in wait
abiding in the chamber. And he brake them from off
his arms like a thread.
13 And Delilah said unto Samson, Hitherto thou
hast mocked me, and told me lies: tell me wherewith
thou mightest be bound. And he said unto her, If
thou weavest the seven locks of my head with the
web.
14 And she fastened *it* with the pin, and said unto
him, The Philistines *be* upon thee, Samson. And he
awaked out of his sleep, and went away with the pin
of the beam, and with the web.

NEW LIVING TRANSLATION

saying to themselves, "When the light of morning
comes, we will kill him."
3 But Samson stayed in bed only until midnight.
Then he got up, took hold of the doors of the town
gate, including the two posts, and lifted them up, bar
and all. He put them on his shoulders and carried
them all the way to the top of the hill across from
Hebron.

Samson and Delilah

4 Some time later Samson fell in love with a woman
named Delilah, who lived in the valley of Sorek. 5 The
rulers of the Philistines went to her and said, "Entice
Samson to tell you what makes him so strong and
how he can be overpowered and tied up securely.
Then each of us will give you 1,100 pieces* of silver."
6 So Delilah said to Samson, "Please tell me what
makes you so strong and what it would take to tie you
up securely."
7 Samson replied, "If I were tied up with seven new
bowstrings that have not yet been dried, I would become as weak as anyone else."
8 So the Philistine rulers brought Delilah seven
new bowstrings, and she tied Samson up with them.
9 She had hidden some men in one of the inner
rooms of her house, and she cried out, "Samson! The
Philistines have come to capture you!" But Samson
snapped the bowstrings as a piece of string snaps
when it is burned by a fire. So the secret of his
strength was not discovered.
10 Afterward Delilah said to him, "You've been
making fun of me and telling me lies! Now please tell
me how you can be tied up securely."
11 Samson replied, "If I were tied up with brand-
new ropes that had never been used, I would become
as weak as anyone else."
12 So Delilah took new ropes and tied him up with
them. The men were hiding in the inner room as before, and again Delilah cried out, "Samson! The Philistines have come to capture you!" But again Samson
snapped the ropes from his arms as if they were
thread.
13 Then Delilah said, "You've been making fun of
me and telling me lies! Now tell me how you can be
tied up securely."

Samson replied, "If you were to weave the seven
braids of my hair into the fabric on your loom and
tighten it with the loom shuttle, I would become as
weak as anyone else."

So while he slept, Delilah wove the seven braids of
his hair into the fabric. 14 Then she tightened it with
the loom shuttle.* Again she cried out, "Samson! The
Philistines have come to capture you!" But Samson
woke up, pulled back the loom shuttle, and yanked
his hair away from the loom and the fabric.

16:5 Hebrew *1,100 shekels,* about 28 pounds or 12.5 kilograms in weight.
16:13-14 As in Greek version and Latin Vulgate; Hebrew lacks *I would become as weak as anyone else. / So while he slept, Delilah wove the seven braids of his hair into the fabric. [14]Then she tightened it with the loom shuttle.*

KING JAMES VERSION

15 And she said unto him, How canst thou say, I love thee, when thine heart *is* not with me? thou hast mocked me these three times, and hast not told me wherein thy great strength *lieth*.

16 And it came to pass, when she pressed him daily with her words, and urged him, *so* that his soul was vexed unto death;

17 That he told her all his heart, and said unto her, There hath not come a razor upon mine head; for I *have been* a Nazarite unto God from my mother's womb: if I be shaven, then my strength will go from me, and I shall become weak, and be like any *other* man.

18 And when Delilah saw that he had told her all his heart, she sent and called for the lords of the Philistines, saying, Come up this once, for he hath shewed me all his heart. Then the lords of the Philistines came up unto her, and brought money in their hand.

19 And she made him sleep upon her knees; and she called for a man, and she caused him to shave off the seven locks of his head; and she began to afflict him, and his strength went from him.

20 And she said, The Philistines *be* upon thee, Samson. And he awoke out of his sleep, and said, I will go out as at other times before, and shake myself. And he wist not that the LORD was departed from him.

21 But the Philistines took him, and put out his eyes, and brought him down to Gaza, and bound him with fetters of brass; and he did grind in the prison house.

22 Howbeit the hair of his head began to grow again after he was shaven.

23 Then the lords of the Philistines gathered them together for to offer a great sacrifice unto Dagon their god, and to rejoice: for they said, Our god hath delivered Samson our enemy into our hand.

24 And when the people saw him, they praised their god: for they said, Our god hath delivered into our hands our enemy, and the destroyer of our country, which slew many of us.

25 And it came to pass, when their hearts were merry, that they said, Call for Samson, that he may make us sport. And they called for Samson out of the prison house; and he made them sport: and they set him between the pillars.

26 And Samson said unto the lad that held him by the hand, Suffer me that I may feel the pillars whereupon the house standeth, that I may lean upon them.

27 Now the house was full of men and women; and all the lords of the Philistines *were* there; and *there were* upon the roof about three thousand men and women, that beheld while Samson made sport.

28 And Samson called unto the LORD, and said, O Lord GOD, remember me, I pray thee, and strengthen me, I pray thee, only this once, O God, that I may be at once avenged of the Philistines for my two eyes.

NEW LIVING TRANSLATION

15 Then Delilah pouted, "How can you tell me, 'I love you,' when you don't share your secrets with me? You've made fun of me three times now, and you still haven't told me what makes you so strong!" 16 She tormented him with her nagging day after day until he was sick to death of it.

17 Finally, Samson shared his secret with her. "My hair has never been cut," he confessed, "for I was dedicated to God as a Nazirite from birth. If my head were shaved, my strength would leave me, and I would become as weak as anyone else."

18 Delilah realized he had finally told her the truth, so she sent for the Philistine rulers. "Come back one more time," she said, "for he has finally told me his secret." So the Philistine rulers returned with the money in their hands. 19 Delilah lulled Samson to sleep with his head in her lap, and then she called in a man to shave off the seven locks of his hair. In this way she began to bring him down,* and his strength left him.

20 Then she cried out, "Samson! The Philistines have come to capture you!"

When he woke up, he thought, "I will do as before and shake myself free." But he didn't realize the LORD had left him.

21 So the Philistines captured him and gouged out his eyes. They took him to Gaza, where he was bound with bronze chains and forced to grind grain in the prison.

22 But before long, his hair began to grow back.

Samson's Final Victory

23 The Philistine rulers held a great festival, offering sacrifices and praising their god, Dagon. They said, "Our god has given us victory over our enemy Samson!"

24 When the people saw him, they praised their god, saying, "Our god has delivered our enemy to us! The one who killed so many of us is now in our power!"

25 Half drunk by now, the people demanded, "Bring out Samson so he can amuse us!" So he was brought from the prison to amuse them, and they had him stand between the pillars supporting the roof.

26 Samson said to the young servant who was leading him by the hand, "Place my hands against the pillars that hold up the temple. I want to rest against them." 27 Now the temple was completely filled with people. All the Philistine rulers were there, and there were about 3,000 men and women on the roof who were watching as Samson amused them.

28 Then Samson prayed to the LORD, "Sovereign LORD, remember me again. O God, please strengthen me just one more time. With one blow let me pay back the Philistines for the loss of my two eyes."

16:19 Or *she began to torment him.* Greek version reads *He began to grow weak.*

KING JAMES VERSION

29 And Samson took hold of the two middle pillars upon which the house stood, and on which it was borne up, of the one with his right hand, and of the other with his left.

30 And Samson said, Let me die with the Philistines. And he bowed himself with *all his* might; and the house fell upon the lords, and upon all the people that *were* therein. So the dead which he slew at his death were more than *they* which he slew in his life.

31 Then his brethren and all the house of his father came down, and took him, and brought *him* up, and buried him between Zorah and Eshtaol in the buryingplace of Manoah his father. And he judged Israel twenty years.

17 1 And there was a man of mount Ephraim, whose name *was* Micah.

2 And he said unto his mother, The eleven hundred *shekels* of silver that were taken from thee, about which thou cursedst, and spakest of also in mine ears, behold, the silver *is* with me; I took it. And his mother said, Blessed *be thou* of the LORD, my son.

3 And when he had restored the eleven hundred *shekels* of silver to his mother, his mother said, I had wholly dedicated the silver unto the LORD from my hand for my son, to make a graven image and a molten image: now therefore I will restore it unto thee.

4 Yet he restored the money unto his mother; and his mother took two hundred *shekels* of silver, and gave them to the founder, who made thereof a graven image and a molten image: and they were in the house of Micah.

5 And the man Micah had an house of gods, and made an ephod, and teraphim, and consecrated one of his sons, who became his priest.

6 In those days *there was* no king in Israel, *but* every man did *that which was* right in his own eyes.

7 And there was a young man out of Bethlehem-judah of the family of Judah, who *was* a Levite, and he sojourned there.

8 And the man departed out of the city from Bethlehem-judah to sojourn where he could find *a place:* and he came to mount Ephraim to the house of Micah, as he journeyed.

9 And Micah said unto him, Whence comest thou? And he said unto him, I *am* a Levite of Bethlehem-judah, and I go to sojourn where I may find *a place*.

10 And Micah said unto him, Dwell with me, and be unto me a father and a priest, and I will give thee ten *shekels* of silver by the year, and a suit of apparel, and thy victuals. So the Levite went in.

11 And the Levite was content to dwell with the man; and the young man was unto him as one of his sons.

12 And Micah consecrated the Levite; and the young man became his priest, and was in the house of Micah.

13 Then said Micah, Now know I that the LORD will do me good, seeing I have a Levite to *my* priest.

NEW LIVING TRANSLATION

29 Then Samson put his hands on the two center pillars that held up the temple. Pushing against them with both hands, 30 he prayed, "Let me die with the Philistines." And the temple crashed down on the Philistine rulers and all the people. So he killed more people when he died than he had during his entire lifetime.

31 Later his brothers and other relatives went down to get his body. They took him back home and buried him between Zorah and Eshtaol, where his father, Manoah, was buried. Samson had judged Israel for twenty years.

Micah's Idols

17 There was a man named Micah, who lived in the hill country of Ephraim. 2 One day he said to his mother, "I heard you place a curse on the person who stole 1,100 pieces* of silver from you. Well, I have the money. I was the one who took it."

"The LORD bless you for admitting it," his mother replied. 3 He returned the money to her, and she said, "I now dedicate these silver coins to the LORD. In honor of my son, I will have an image carved and an idol cast."

4 So when he returned the money to his mother, she took 200 silver coins and gave them to a silversmith, who made them into an image and an idol. And these were placed in Micah's house. 5 Micah set up a shrine for the idol, and he made a sacred ephod and some household idols. Then he installed one of his sons as his personal priest.

6 In those days Israel had no king; all the people did whatever seemed right in their own eyes.

7 One day a young Levite, who had been living in Bethlehem in Judah, arrived in that area. 8 He had left Bethlehem in search of another place to live, and as he traveled, he came to the hill country of Ephraim. He happened to stop at Micah's house as he was traveling through. 9 "Where are you from?" Micah asked him.

He replied, "I am a Levite from Bethlehem in Judah, and I am looking for a place to live."

10 "Stay here with me," Micah said, "and you can be a father and priest to me. I will give you ten pieces* of silver a year, plus a change of clothes and your food." 11 The Levite agreed to this, and the young man became like one of Micah's sons.

12 So Micah installed the Levite as his personal priest, and he lived in Micah's house. 13 "I know the LORD will bless me now," Micah said, "because I have a Levite serving as my priest."

17:2 Hebrew *1,100 shekels,* about 28 pounds or 12.5 kilograms in weight.
17:10 Hebrew *10 shekels,* about 4 ounces or 114 grams in weight.

KING JAMES VERSION

18 1 In those days *there was* no king in Israel:
and in those days the tribe of the Danites
sought them an inheritance to dwell in; for unto that
day *all their* inheritance had not fallen unto them
among the tribes of Israel.
2 And the children of Dan sent of their family five
men from their coasts, men of valour, from Zorah,
and from Eshtaol, to spy out the land, and to search it;
and they said unto them, Go, search the land: who
when they came to mount Ephraim, to the house of
Micah, they lodged there.
3 When they *were* by the house of Micah, they
knew the voice of the young man the Levite: and they
turned in thither, and said unto him, Who brought
thee hither? and what makest thou in this *place?* and
what hast thou here?
4 And he said unto them, Thus and thus dealeth Micah with me, and hath hired me, and I am his priest.
5 And they said unto him, Ask counsel, we pray
thee, of God, that we may know whether our way
which we go shall be prosperous.
6 And the priest said unto them, Go in peace: before the LORD *is* your way wherein ye go.
7 Then the five men departed, and came to Laish,
and saw the people that *were* therein, how they dwelt
careless, after the manner of the Zidonians, quiet
and secure; and *there was* no magistrate in the land,
that might put *them* to shame in *any* thing; and they
were far from the Zidonians, and had no business
with *any* man.
8 And they came unto their brethren to Zorah and
Eshtaol: and their brethren said unto them, What
say ye?
9 And they said, Arise, that we may go up against
them: for we have seen the land, and, behold, it *is*
very good: and *are* ye still? be not slothful to go, *and*
to enter to possess the land.
10 When ye go, ye shall come unto a people secure,
and to a large land: for God hath given it into your
hands; a place where *there is* no want of any thing
that *is* in the earth.
11 And there went from thence of the family of the
Danites, out of Zorah and out of Eshtaol, six hundred
men appointed with weapons of war.
12 And they went up, and pitched in Kirjath-jearim,
in Judah: wherefore they called that place Mahaneh-
dan unto this day: behold, *it is* behind Kirjath-jearim.
13 And they passed thence unto mount Ephraim,
and came unto the house of Micah.
14 Then answered the five men that went to spy out
the country of Laish, and said unto their brethren, Do
ye know that there is in these houses an ephod, and
teraphim, and a graven image, and a molten image?
now therefore consider what ye have to do.
15 And they turned thitherward, and came to the
house of the young man the Levite, *even* unto the
house of Micah, and saluted him.

NEW LIVING TRANSLATION

Idolatry in the Tribe of Dan

18 Now in those days Israel had no king. And
the tribe of Dan was trying to find a place
where they could settle, for they had not yet moved
into the land assigned to them when the land was
divided among the tribes of Israel. 2 So the men of
Dan chose from their clans five capable warriors
from the towns of Zorah and Eshtaol to scout out a
land for them to settle in.
When these warriors arrived in the hill country of
Ephraim, they came to Micah's house and spent the
night there. 3 While at Micah's house, they recognized the young Levite's accent, so they went over
and asked him, "Who brought you here, and what are
you doing in this place? Why are you here?" 4 He told
them about his agreement with Micah and that he
had been hired as Micah's personal priest.
5 Then they said, "Ask God whether or not our journey will be successful."
6 "Go in peace," the priest replied. "For the LORD is
watching over your journey."
7 So the five men went on to the town of Laish,
where they noticed the people living carefree lives,
like the Sidonians; they were peaceful and secure.*
The people were also wealthy because their land was
very fertile. And they lived a great distance from
Sidon and had no allies nearby.
8 When the men returned to Zorah and Eshtaol,
their relatives asked them, "What did you find?"
9 The men replied, "Come on, let's attack them! We
have seen the land, and it is very good. What are you
waiting for? Don't hesitate to go and take possession
of it. 10 When you get there, you will find the people
living carefree lives. God has given us a spacious and
fertile land, lacking in nothing!"
11 So 600 men from the tribe of Dan, armed with
weapons of war, set out from Zorah and Eshtaol.
12 They camped at a place west of Kiriath-jearim in
Judah, which is called Mahaneh-dan* to this day.
13 Then they went on from there into the hill country
of Ephraim and came to the house of Micah.
14 The five men who had scouted out the land
around Laish explained to the others, "These buildings contain a sacred ephod, as well as some household idols, a carved image, and a cast idol. What do
you think you should do?" 15 Then the five men
turned off the road and went over to Micah's house,
where the young Levite lived, and greeted him

18:7 The meaning of the Hebrew is uncertain. **18:12** *Mahaneh-dan* means "the camp of Dan."

KING JAMES VERSION

16And the six hundred men appointed with their weapons of war, which *were* of the children of Dan, stood by the entering of the gate.

17And the five men that went to spy out the land went up, *and* came in thither, *and* took the graven image, and the ephod, and the teraphim, and the molten image: and the priest stood in the entering of the gate with the six hundred men *that were* appointed with weapons of war.

18And these went into Micah's house, and fetched the carved image, the ephod, and the teraphim, and the molten image. Then said the priest unto them, What do ye?

19And they said unto him, Hold thy peace, lay thine hand upon thy mouth, and go with us, and be to us a father and a priest: *is it* better for thee to be a priest unto the house of one man, or that thou be a priest unto a tribe and a family in Israel?

20And the priest's heart was glad, and he took the ephod, and the teraphim, and the graven image, and went in the midst of the people.

21So they turned and departed, and put the little ones and the cattle and the carriage before them.

22*And* when they were a good way from the house of Micah, the men that *were* in the houses near to Micah's house were gathered together, and overtook the children of Dan.

23And they cried unto the children of Dan. And they turned their faces, and said unto Micah, What aileth thee, that thou comest with such a company?

24And he said, Ye have taken away my gods which I made, and the priest, and ye are gone away: and what have I more? and what *is* this *that* ye say unto me, What aileth thee?

25And the children of Dan said unto him, Let not thy voice be heard among us, lest angry fellows run upon thee, and thou lose thy life, with the lives of thy household.

26And the children of Dan went their way: and when Micah saw that they *were* too strong for him, he turned and went back unto his house.

27And they took *the things* which Micah had made, and the priest which he had, and came unto Laish, unto a people *that were* at quiet and secure: and they smote them with the edge of the sword, and burnt the city with fire.

28And *there was* no deliverer, because it *was* far from Zidon, and they had no business with *any* man; and it was in the valley that *lieth* by Beth-rehob. And they built a city, and dwelt therein.

29And they called the name of the city Dan, after the name of Dan their father, who was born unto Israel: howbeit the name of the city *was* Laish at the first.

30And the children of Dan set up the graven image: and Jonathan, the son of Gershom, the son of Manasseh, he and his sons were priests to the tribe of Dan until the day of the captivity of the land.

NEW LIVING TRANSLATION

kindly. 16As the 600 armed warriors from the tribe of Dan stood at the entrance of the gate, 17the five scouts entered the shrine and removed the carved image, the sacred ephod, the household idols, and the cast idol. Meanwhile, the priest was standing at the gate with the 600 armed warriors.

18When the priest saw the men carrying all the sacred objects out of Micah's shrine, he said, "What are you doing?"

19"Be quiet and come with us," they said. "Be a father and priest to all of us. Isn't it better to be a priest for an entire tribe and clan of Israel than for the household of just one man?"

20The young priest was quite happy to go with them, so he took along the sacred ephod, the household idols, and the carved image. 21They turned and started on their way again, placing their children, livestock, and possessions in front of them.

22When the people from the tribe of Dan were quite a distance from Micah's house, the people who lived near Micah came chasing after them. 23They were shouting as they caught up with them. The men of Dan turned around and said to Micah, "What's the matter? Why have you called these men together and chased after us like this?"

24"What do you mean, 'What's the matter?'" Micah replied. "You've taken away all the gods I have made, and my priest, and I have nothing left!"

25The men of Dan said, "Watch what you say! There are some short-tempered men around here who might get angry and kill you and your family." 26So the men of Dan continued on their way. When Micah saw that there were too many of them for him to attack, he turned around and went home.

27Then, with Micah's idols and his priest, the men of Dan came to the town of Laish, whose people were peaceful and secure. They attacked with swords and burned the town to the ground. 28There was no one to rescue the people, for they lived a great distance from Sidon and had no allies nearby. This happened in the valley near Beth-rehob.

Then the people of the tribe of Dan rebuilt the town and lived there. 29They renamed the town Dan after their ancestor, Israel's son, but it had originally been called Laish.

30Then they set up the carved image, and they appointed Jonathan son of Gershom, son of Moses,* as their priest. This family continued as priests for the

18:30 As in an ancient Hebrew tradition, some Greek manuscripts, and Latin Vulgate; Masoretic Text reads *son of Manasseh.*

KING JAMES VERSION

31And they set them up Micah's graven image, which he made, all the time that the house of God was in Shiloh.

19 1And it came to pass in those days, when *there was* no king in Israel, that there was a certain Levite sojourning on the side of mount Ephraim, who took to him a concubine out of Bethlehem-judah.

2And his concubine played the whore against him, and went away from him unto her father's house to Bethlehem-judah, and was there four whole months.

3And her husband arose, and went after her, to speak friendly unto her, *and* to bring her again, having his servant with him, and a couple of asses: and she brought him into her father's house: and when the father of the damsel saw him, he rejoiced to meet him.

4And his father in law, the damsel's father, retained him; and he abode with him three days: so they did eat and drink, and lodged there.

5And it came to pass on the fourth day, when they arose early in the morning, that he rose up to depart: and the damsel's father said unto his son in law, Comfort thine heart with a morsel of bread, and afterward go your way.

6And they sat down, and did eat and drink both of them together: for the damsel's father had said unto the man, Be content, I pray thee, and tarry all night, and let thine heart be merry.

7And when the man rose up to depart, his father in law urged him: therefore he lodged there again.

8And he arose early in the morning on the fifth day to depart: and the damsel's father said, Comfort thine heart, I pray thee. And they tarried until afternoon, and they did eat both of them.

9And when the man rose up to depart, he, and his concubine, and his servant, his father in law, the damsel's father, said unto him, Behold, now the day draweth toward evening, I pray you tarry all night: behold, the day groweth to an end, lodge here, that thine heart may be merry; and tomorrow get you early on your way, that thou mayest go home.

10But the man would not tarry that night, but he rose up and departed, and came over against Jebus, which *is* Jerusalem; and *there were* with him two asses saddled, his concubine also *was* with him.

11*And* when they *were* by Jebus, the day was far spent; and the servant said unto his master, Come, I pray thee, and let us turn in into this city of the Jebusites, and lodge in it.

12And his master said unto him, We will not turn aside hither into the city of a stranger, that *is* not of the children of Israel; we will pass over to Gibeah.

13And he said unto his servant, Come, and let us draw near to one of these places to lodge all night, in Gibeah, or in Ramah.

NEW LIVING TRANSLATION

tribe of Dan until the Exile. 31So Micah's carved image was worshiped by the tribe of Dan as long as the Tabernacle of God remained at Shiloh.

The Levite and His Concubine

19 Now in those days Israel had no king. There was a man from the tribe of Levi living in a remote area of the hill country of Ephraim. One day he brought home a woman from Bethlehem in Judah to be his concubine. 2But she became angry with him* and returned to her father's home in Bethlehem.

After about four months, 3her husband set out for Bethlehem to speak personally to her and persuade her to come back. He took with him a servant and a pair of donkeys. When he arrived at* her father's house, her father saw him and welcomed him. 4Her father urged him to stay awhile, so he stayed three days, eating, drinking, and sleeping there.

5On the fourth day the man was up early, ready to leave, but the woman's father said to his son-in-law, "Have something to eat before you go." 6So the two men sat down together and had something to eat and drink. Then the woman's father said, "Please stay another night and enjoy yourself." 7The man got up to leave, but his father-in-law kept urging him to stay, so he finally gave in and stayed the night.

8On the morning of the fifth day he was up early again, ready to leave, and again the woman's father said, "Have something to eat; then you can leave later this afternoon." So they had another day of feasting. 9Later, as the man and his concubine and servant were preparing to leave, his father-in-law said, "Look, it's almost evening. Stay the night and enjoy yourself. Tomorrow you can get up early and be on your way."

10But this time the man was determined to leave. So he took his two saddled donkeys and his concubine and headed in the direction of Jebus (that is, Jerusalem). 11It was late in the day when they neared Jebus, and the man's servant said to him, "Let's stop at this Jebusite town and spend the night there."

12"No," his master said, "we can't stay in this foreign town where there are no Israelites. Instead, we will go on to Gibeah. 13Come on, let's try to get as far as Gibeah or Ramah, and we'll spend the night in one

19:2 Or *she was unfaithful to him.* **19:3** As in Greek version; Hebrew reads *When she brought him to.*

KING JAMES VERSION

14 And they passed on and went their way; and
the sun went down upon them *when they were* by
Gibeah, which *belongeth* to Benjamin.
15 And they turned aside thither, to go in *and* to
lodge in Gibeah: and when he went in, he sat him
down in a street of the city: for *there was* no man that
took them into his house to lodging.
16 And, behold, there came an old man from his
work out of the field at even, which *was* also of
mount Ephraim; and he sojourned in Gibeah: but the
men of the place *were* Benjamites.
17 And when he had lifted up his eyes, he saw a
wayfaring man in the street of the city: and the old
man said, Whither goest thou? and whence comest
thou?
18 And he said unto him, We *are* passing from
Bethlehem-judah toward the side of mount Ephraim; from thence *am* I: and I went to Bethlehem-
judah, but I *am now* going to the house of the LORD;
and there *is* no man that receiveth me to house.
19 Yet there is both straw and provender for our
asses; and there is bread and wine also for me, and
for thy handmaid, and for the young man *which is*
with thy servants: *there is* no want of any thing.
20 And the old man said, Peace *be* with thee; howsoever *let* all thy wants *lie* upon me; only lodge not in
the street.
21 So he brought him into his house, and gave provender unto the asses: and they washed their feet, and
did eat and drink.
22 *Now* as they were making their hearts merry, behold, the men of the city, certain sons of Belial, beset
the house round about, *and* beat at the door, and
spake to the master of the house, the old man, saying,
Bring forth the man that came into thine house, that
we may know him.
23 And the man, the master of the house, went out
unto them, and said unto them, Nay, my brethren,
nay, I pray you, do not *so* wickedly; seeing that this
man is come into mine house, do not this folly.
24 Behold, *here is* my daughter a maiden, and his
concubine; them I will bring out now, and humble ye
them, and do with them what seemeth good unto
you: but unto this man do not so vile a thing.
25 But the men would not hearken to him: so the
man took his concubine, and brought her forth unto
them; and they knew her, and abused her all the
night until the morning: and when the day began to
spring, they let her go.
26 Then came the woman in the dawning of the
day, and fell down at the door of the man's house
where her lord *was,* till it was light.
27 And her lord rose up in the morning, and
opened the doors of the house, and went out to go
his way: and, behold, the woman his concubine was
fallen down *at* the door of the house, and her hands
were upon the threshold.
28 And he said unto her, Up, and let us be going. But

NEW LIVING TRANSLATION

of those towns." 14 So they went on. The sun was setting as they came to Gibeah, a town in the land of
Benjamin, 15 so they stopped there to spend the
night. They rested in the town square, but no one
took them in for the night.
16 That evening an old man came home from his
work in the fields. He was from the hill country of
Ephraim, but he was living in Gibeah, where the people were from the tribe of Benjamin. 17 When he saw
the travelers sitting in the town square, he asked
them where they were from and where they were
going.
18 "We have been in Bethlehem in Judah," the man
replied. "We are on our way to a remote area in the
hill country of Ephraim, which is my home. I traveled
to Bethlehem, and now I'm returning home.* But no
one has taken us in for the night, 19 even though
we have everything we need. We have straw and feed
for our donkeys and plenty of bread and wine for
ourselves."
20 "You are welcome to stay with me," the old man
said. "I will give you anything you might need. But
whatever you do, don't spend the night in the
square." 21 So he took them home with him and fed
the donkeys. After they washed their feet, they ate
and drank together.
22 While they were enjoying themselves, a crowd
of troublemakers from the town surrounded the
house. They began beating at the door and shouting
to the old man, "Bring out the man who is staying
with you so we can have sex with him."
23 The old man stepped outside to talk to them.
"No, my brothers, don't do such an evil thing. For this
man is a guest in my house, and such a thing would
be shameful. 24 Here, take my virgin daughter and
this man's concubine. I will bring them out to you,
and you can abuse them and do whatever you like.
But don't do such a shameful thing to this man."
25 But they wouldn't listen to him. So the Levite
took hold of his concubine and pushed her out the
door. The men of the town abused her all night, taking turns raping her until morning. Finally, at dawn
they let her go. 26 At daybreak the woman returned to
the house where her husband was staying. She collapsed at the door of the house and lay there until it
was light.
27 When her husband opened the door to leave,
there lay his concubine with her hands on the
threshold. 28 He said, "Get up! Let's go!" But there was

19:18 As in Greek version (see also 19:29); Hebrew reads *now I'm going to the Tabernacle of the LORD.*

none answered. Then the man took her *up* upon an ass, and the man rose up, and gat him unto his place.

29 And when he was come into his house, he took a knife, and laid hold on his concubine, and divided her, *together* with her bones, into twelve pieces, and sent her into all the coasts of Israel.

30 And it was so, that all that saw it said, There was no such deed done nor seen from the day that the children of Israel came up out of the land of Egypt unto this day: consider of it, take advice, and speak *your minds.*

20 1 Then all the children of Israel went out, and the congregation was gathered together as one man, from Dan even to Beer-sheba, with the land of Gilead, unto the LORD in Mizpeh.

2 And the chief of all the people, *even* of all the tribes of Israel, presented themselves in the assembly of the people of God, four hundred thousand footmen that drew sword.

3 (Now the children of Benjamin heard that the children of Israel were gone up to Mizpeh.) Then said the children of Israel, Tell *us,* how was this wickedness?

4 And the Levite, the husband of the woman that was slain, answered and said, I came into Gibeah that *belongeth* to Benjamin, I and my concubine, to lodge.

5 And the men of Gibeah rose against me, and beset the house round about upon me by night, *and* thought to have slain me: and my concubine have they forced, that she is dead.

6 And I took my concubine, and cut her in pieces, and sent her throughout all the country of the inheritance of Israel: for they have committed lewdness and folly in Israel.

7 Behold, ye *are* all children of Israel; give here your advice and counsel.

8 And all the people arose as one man, saying, We will not any *of us* go to his tent, neither will we any *of us* turn into his house.

9 But now this *shall be* the thing which we will do to Gibeah; *we will go up* by lot against it;

10 And we will take ten men of an hundred throughout all the tribes of Israel, and an hundred of a thousand, and a thousand out of ten thousand, to fetch victual for the people, that they may do, when they come to Gibeah of Benjamin, according to all the folly that they have wrought in Israel.

11 So all the men of Israel were gathered against the city, knit together as one man.

12 And the tribes of Israel sent men through all the tribe of Benjamin, saying, What wickedness *is* this that is done among you?

13 Now therefore deliver *us* the men, the children of Belial, which *are* in Gibeah, that we may put them to death, and put away evil from Israel. But the children of Benjamin would not hearken to the voice of their brethren the children of Israel:

no answer.* So he put her body on his donkey and took her home.

29 When he got home, he took a knife and cut his concubine's body into twelve pieces. Then he sent one piece to each tribe throughout all the territory of Israel.

30 Everyone who saw it said, "Such a horrible crime has not been committed in all the time since Israel left Egypt. Think about it! What are we going to do? Who's going to speak up?"

Israel's War with Benjamin

20 Then all the Israelites were united as one
man, from Dan in the north to Beersheba in
the south, including those from across the Jordan in
the land of Gilead. The entire community assembled
in the presence of the LORD at Mizpah.
2 The leaders
of all the people and all the tribes of Israel—400,000
warriors armed with swords—took their positions
in the assembly of the people of God.
3 (Word soon
reached the land of Benjamin that the other tribes
had gone up to Mizpah.) The Israelites then asked
how this terrible crime had happened.
4 The Levite, the husband of the woman who had
been murdered, said, "My concubine and I came to
spend the night in Gibeah, a town that belongs to the
people of Benjamin.
5 That night some of the leading
citizens of Gibeah surrounded the house, planning
to kill me, and they raped my concubine until she
was dead.
6 So I cut her body into twelve pieces and
sent the pieces throughout the territory assigned
to Israel, for these men have committed a terrible
and shameful crime.
7 Now then, all of you—the entire community of Israel—must decide here and now
what should be done about this!"
8 And all the people rose to their feet in unison and
declared, "None of us will return home! No, not even
one of us!
9 Instead, this is what we will do to Gibeah;
we will draw lots to decide who will attack it.
10 One-tenth of the men* from each tribe will be chosen to
supply the warriors with food, and the rest of us will
take revenge on Gibeah* of Benjamin for this shameful thing they have done in Israel."
11 So all the Israelites were completely united, and they gathered
together to attack the town.
12 The Israelites sent messengers to the tribe of
Benjamin, saying, "What a terrible thing has been
done among you!
13 Give up those evil men, those
troublemakers from Gibeah, so we can execute them
and purge Israel of this evil."

19:28 Greek version adds *for she was dead.* **20:10a** Hebrew *10 men from every hundred, 100 men from every thousand, and 1,000 men from every 10,000.* **20:10b** Hebrew *Geba,* in this case a variant spelling of Gibeah; also in 20:33.

KING JAMES VERSION

14But the children of Benjamin gathered themselves together out of the cities unto Gibeah, to go out to battle against the children of Israel.

15And the children of Benjamin were numbered at that time out of the cities twenty and six thousand men that drew sword, beside the inhabitants of Gibeah, which were numbered seven hundred chosen men.

16Among all this people *there were* seven hundred chosen men lefthanded; every one could sling stones at an hair *breadth,* and not miss.

17And the men of Israel, beside Benjamin, were numbered four hundred thousand men that drew sword: all these *were* men of war.

18And the children of Israel arose, and went up to the house of God, and asked counsel of God, and said, Which of us shall go up first to the battle against the children of Benjamin? And the LORD said, Judah *shall go up* first.

19And the children of Israel rose up in the morning, and encamped against Gibeah.

20And the men of Israel went out to battle against Benjamin; and the men of Israel put themselves in array to fight against them at Gibeah.

21And the children of Benjamin came forth out of Gibeah, and destroyed down to the ground of the Israelites that day twenty and two thousand men.

22And the people the men of Israel encouraged themselves, and set their battle again in array in the place where they put themselves in array the first day.

23(And the children of Israel went up and wept before the LORD until even, and asked counsel of the LORD, saying, Shall I go up again to battle against the children of Benjamin my brother? And the LORD said, Go up against him.)

24And the children of Israel came near against the children of Benjamin the second day.

25And Benjamin went forth against them out of Gibeah the second day, and destroyed down to the ground of the children of Israel again eighteen thousand men; all these drew the sword.

26Then all the children of Israel, and all the people, went up, and came unto the house of God, and wept, and sat there before the LORD, and fasted that day until even, and offered burnt offerings and peace offerings before the LORD.

27And the children of Israel inquired of the LORD, (for the ark of the covenant of God *was* there in those days,

28And Phinehas, the son of Eleazar, the son of Aaron, stood before it in those days,) saying, Shall I yet again go out to battle against the children of Benjamin my brother, or shall I cease? And the LORD said, Go up; for tomorrow I will deliver them into thine hand.

29And Israel set liers in wait round about Gibeah.

30And the children of Israel went up against the children of Benjamin on the third day, and put themselves in array against Gibeah, as at other times.

NEW LIVING TRANSLATION

But the people of Benjamin would not listen.
14Instead, they came from their towns and gathered
at Gibeah to fight the Israelites. 15In all, 26,000 of
their warriors armed with swords arrived in Gibeah
to join the 700 elite troops who lived there. 16Among
Benjamin's elite troops, 700 were left-handed, and
each of them could sling a rock and hit a target
within a hairsbreadth without missing. 17Israel had
400,000 experienced soldiers armed with swords,
not counting Benjamin's warriors.

18Before the battle the Israelites went to Bethel
and asked God, "Which tribe should go first to attack the people of Benjamin?"

The LORD answered, "Judah is to go first."

19So the Israelites left early the next morning and
camped near Gibeah. 20Then they advanced toward
Gibeah to attack the men of Benjamin. 21But Benjamin's warriors, who were defending the town, came
out and killed 22,000 Israelites on the battlefield
that day.

22But the Israelites encouraged each other and
took their positions again at the same place they had
fought the previous day. 23For they had gone up to
Bethel and wept in the presence of the LORD until
evening. They had asked the LORD, "Should we fight
against our relatives from Benjamin again?"

And the LORD had said, "Go out and fight against
them."

24So the next day they went out again to fight
against the men of Benjamin, 25but the men of Benjamin killed another 18,000 Israelites, all of whom
were experienced with the sword.

26Then all the Israelites went up to Bethel and
wept in the presence of the LORD and fasted until
evening. They also brought burnt offerings and
peace offerings to the LORD. 27The Israelites went up
seeking direction from the LORD. (In those days the
Ark of the Covenant of God was in Bethel, 28and
Phinehas son of Eleazar and grandson of Aaron was
the priest.) The Israelites asked the LORD, "Should we
fight against our relatives from Benjamin again, or
should we stop?"

The LORD said, "Go! Tomorrow I will hand them
over to you."

29So the Israelites set an ambush all around Gibeah. 30They went out on the third day and took their

31And the children of Benjamin went out against
the people, *and* were drawn away from the city; and
they began to smite of the people, *and* kill, as at other
times, in the highways, of which one goeth up to the
house of God, and the other to Gibeah in the field,
about thirty men of Israel.
32And the children of Benjamin said, They *are*
smitten down before us, as at the first. But the children of Israel said, Let us flee, and draw them from
the city unto the highways.
33And all the men of Israel rose up out of their
place, and put themselves in array at Baal-tamar: and
the liers in wait of Israel came forth out of their
places, *even* out of the meadows of Gibeah.
34And there came against Gibeah ten thousand
chosen men out of all Israel, and the battle was sore:
but they knew not that evil *was* near them.
35And the LORD smote Benjamin before Israel: and
the children of Israel destroyed of the Benjamites
that day twenty and five thousand and an hundred
men: all these drew the sword.
36So the children of Benjamin saw that they were
smitten: for the men of Israel gave place to the
Benjamites, because they trusted unto the liers in
wait which they had set beside Gibeah.
37And the liers in wait hasted, and rushed upon
Gibeah; and the liers in wait drew *themselves* along,
and smote all the city with the edge of the sword.
38Now there was an appointed sign between the
men of Israel and the liers in wait, that they should
make a great flame with smoke rise up out of the city.
39And when the men of Israel retired in the battle,
Benjamin began to smite *and* kill of the men of Israel
about thirty persons: for they said, Surely they are
smitten down before us, as *in* the first battle.
40But when the flame began to arise up out of the
city with a pillar of smoke, the Benjamites looked
behind them, and, behold, the flame of the city ascended up to heaven.
41And when the men of Israel turned again, the
men of Benjamin were amazed: for they saw that evil
was come upon them.
42Therefore they turned *their backs* before the
men of Israel unto the way of the wilderness; but the
battle overtook them; and them which *came* out of
the cities they destroyed in the midst of them.
43*Thus* they inclosed the Benjamites round about,
and chased them, *and* trode them down with ease
over against Gibeah toward the sunrising.
44And there fell of Benjamin eighteen thousand
men; all these *were* men of valour.
45And they turned and fled toward the wilderness
unto the rock of Rimmon: and they gleaned of them
in the highways five thousand men; and pursued
hard after them unto Gidom, and slew two thousand
men of them.
46So that all which fell that day of Benjamin were

positions at the same place as before. 31When the
men of Benjamin came out to attack, they were
drawn away from the town. And as they had done
before, they began to kill the Israelites. About thirty
Israelites died in the open fields and along the roads,
one leading to Bethel and the other leading back to
Gibeah.
32Then the warriors of Benjamin shouted, "We're
defeating them as we did before!" But the Israelites
had planned in advance to run away so that the men
of Benjamin would chase them along the roads and
be drawn away from the town.
33When the main group of Israelite warriors
reached Baal-tamar, they turned and took up their
positions. Meanwhile, the Israelites hiding in ambush to the west* of Gibeah jumped up to fight.
34There were 10,000 elite Israelite troops who advanced against Gibeah. The fighting was so heavy
that Benjamin didn't realize the impending disaster.
35So the LORD helped Israel defeat Benjamin, and
that day the Israelites killed 25,100 of Benjamin's
warriors, all of whom were experienced swordsmen.
36Then the men of Benjamin saw that they were
beaten.

The Israelites had retreated from Benjamin's warriors in order to give those hiding in ambush more
room to maneuver against Gibeah. 37Then those
who were hiding rushed in from all sides and killed
everyone in the town. 38They had arranged to send
up a large cloud of smoke from the town as a signal.
39When the Israelites saw the smoke, they turned
and attacked Benjamin's warriors.

By that time Benjamin's warriors had killed about
thirty Israelites, and they shouted, "We're defeating
them as we did in the first battle!" 40But when the
warriors of Benjamin looked behind them and saw
the smoke rising into the sky from every part of the
town, 41the men of Israel turned and attacked. At this
point the men of Benjamin became terrified, because they realized disaster was close at hand. 42So
they turned around and fled before the Israelites
toward the wilderness. But they couldn't escape the
battle, and the people who came out of the nearby
towns were also killed.* 43The Israelites surrounded
the men of Benjamin and chased them relentlessly,
finally overtaking them east of Gibeah.* 44That day
18,000 of Benjamin's strongest warriors died in
battle. 45The survivors fled into the wilderness toward the rock of Rimmon, but Israel killed 5,000 of
them along the road. They continued the chase until
they had killed another 2,000 near Gidom.
46So that day the tribe of Benjamin lost 25,000

20:33 As in Greek and Syriac versions and Latin Vulgate; Hebrew reads *hiding in the open space.* **20:42** Or *battle, for the people from the nearby towns also came out and killed them.* **20:43** The meaning of the Hebrew is uncertain.

KING JAMES VERSION

twenty and five thousand men that drew the sword;
all these *were* men of valour.
47But six hundred men turned and fled to the
wilderness unto the rock Rimmon, and abode in the
rock Rimmon four months.
48And the men of Israel turned again upon the
children of Benjamin, and smote them with the edge
of the sword, as well the men of *every* city, as the
beast, and all that came to hand: also they set on fire
all the cities that they came to.

21 1Now the men of Israel had sworn in Mizpeh, saying, There shall not any of us give his
daughter unto Benjamin to wife.
2And the people came to the house of God, and
abode there till even before God, and lifted up their
voices, and wept sore;
3And said, O LORD God of Israel, why is this come
to pass in Israel, that there should be today one tribe
lacking in Israel?
4And it came to pass on the morrow, that the
people rose early, and built there an altar, and offered
burnt offerings and peace offerings.
5And the children of Israel said, Who *is there*
among all the tribes of Israel that came not up with
the congregation unto the LORD? For they had made
a great oath concerning him that came not up to
the LORD to Mizpeh, saying, He shall surely be put
to death.
6And the children of Israel repented them for Benjamin their brother, and said, There is one tribe cut
off from Israel this day.
7How shall we do for wives for them that remain,
seeing we have sworn by the LORD that we will not
give them of our daughters to wives?
8And they said, What one *is there* of the tribes of
Israel that came not up to Mizpeh to the LORD? And,
behold, there came none to the camp from Jabesh-
gilead to the assembly.
9For the people were numbered, and, behold, *there
were* none of the inhabitants of Jabesh-gilead there.
10And the congregation sent thither twelve thousand men of the valiantest, and commanded them,
saying, Go and smite the inhabitants of Jabesh-
gilead with the edge of the sword, with the women
and the children.
11And this *is* the thing that ye shall do, Ye shall utterly destroy every male, and every woman that hath
lain by man.
12And they found among the inhabitants of
Jabesh-gilead four hundred young virgins, that had
known no man by lying with any male: and they
brought them unto the camp to Shiloh, which *is* in
the land of Canaan.
13And the whole congregation sent *some* to speak
to the children of Benjamin that *were* in the rock
Rimmon, and to call peaceably unto them.
14And Benjamin came again at that time; and they

NEW LIVING TRANSLATION

strong warriors armed with swords, 47leaving only
600 men who escaped to the rock of Rimmon, where
they lived for four months. 48And the Israelites returned and slaughtered every living thing in all the
towns—the people, the livestock, and everything
they found. They also burned down all the towns
they came to.

Israel Provides Wives for Benjamin

21 The Israelites had vowed at Mizpah, "We
will never give our daughters in marriage to
a man from the tribe of Benjamin." 2Now the people
went to Bethel and sat in the presence of God until
evening, weeping loudly and bitterly. 3"O LORD, God
of Israel," they cried out, "why has this happened in
Israel? Now one of our tribes is missing from Israel!"
4Early the next morning the people built an altar
and presented their burnt offerings and peace offerings on it. 5Then they said, "Who among the tribes of
Israel did not join us at Mizpah when we held our
assembly in the presence of the LORD?" At that time
they had taken a solemn oath in the LORD's presence,
vowing that anyone who refused to come would be
put to death.
6The Israelites felt sorry for their brother Benjamin and said, "Today one of the tribes of Israel has
been cut off. 7How can we find wives for the few who
remain, since we have sworn by the LORD not to give
them our daughters in marriage?"
8So they asked, "Who among the tribes of Israel
did not join us at Mizpah when we assembled in the
presence of the LORD?" And they discovered that no
one from Jabesh-gilead had attended the assembly.
9For after they counted all the people, no one from
Jabesh-gilead was present.
10So the assembly sent 12,000 of their best warriors to Jabesh-gilead with orders to kill everyone
there, including women and children. 11"This is
what you are to do," they said. "Completely destroy*
all the males and every woman who is not a virgin."
12Among the residents of Jabesh-gilead they found
400 young virgins who had never slept with a man,
and they brought them to the camp at Shiloh in the
land of Canaan.
13The Israelite assembly sent a peace delegation
to the remaining people of Benjamin who were living
at the rock of Rimmon. 14Then the men of Benjamin
returned to their homes, and the 400 women of

21:11 The Hebrew term used here refers to the complete consecration of things or people to the LORD, either by destroying them or by giving them as an offering.

KING JAMES VERSION

gave them wives which they had saved alive of the women of Jabesh-gilead: and yet so they sufficed them not.

15 And the people repented them for Benjamin, because that the LORD had made a breach in the tribes of Israel.

16 Then the elders of the congregation said, How shall we do for wives for them that remain, seeing the women are destroyed out of Benjamin?

17 And they said, *There must be* an inheritance for them that be escaped of Benjamin, that a tribe be not destroyed out of Israel.

18 Howbeit we may not give them wives of our daughters: for the children of Israel have sworn, saying, Cursed *be* he that giveth a wife to Benjamin.

19 Then they said, Behold, *there is* a feast of the LORD in Shiloh yearly *in a place* which *is* on the north side of Bethel, on the east side of the highway that goeth up from Bethel to Shechem, and on the south of Lebonah.

20 Therefore they commanded the children of Benjamin, saying, Go and lie in wait in the vineyards;

21 And see, and, behold, if the daughters of Shiloh come out to dance in dances, then come ye out of the vineyards, and catch you every man his wife of the daughters of Shiloh, and go to the land of Benjamin.

22 And it shall be, when their fathers or their brethren come unto us to complain, that we will say unto them, Be favourable unto them for our sakes: because we reserved not to each man his wife in the war: for ye did not give unto them at this time, *that* ye should be guilty.

23 And the children of Benjamin did so, and took *them* wives, according to their number, of them that danced, whom they caught: and they went and returned unto their inheritance, and repaired the cities, and dwelt in them.

24 And the children of Israel departed thence at that time, every man to his tribe and to his family, and they went out from thence every man to his inheritance.

25 In those days *there was* no king in Israel: every man did *that which was* right in his own eyes.

NEW LIVING TRANSLATION

Jabesh-gilead who had been spared were given to them as wives. But there were not enough women for all of them.

15 The people felt sorry for Benjamin because the LORD had made this gap among the tribes of Israel. 16 So the elders of the assembly asked, "How can we find wives for the few who remain, since the women of the tribe of Benjamin are dead? 17 There must be heirs for the survivors so that an entire tribe of Israel is not wiped out. 18 But we cannot give them our own daughters in marriage because we have sworn with a solemn oath that anyone who does this will fall under God's curse."

19 Then they thought of the annual festival of the LORD held in Shiloh, south of Lebonah and north of Bethel, along the east side of the road that goes from Bethel to Shechem. 20 They told the men of Benjamin who still needed wives, "Go and hide in the vineyards. 21 When you see the young women of Shiloh come out for their dances, rush out from the vineyards, and each of you can take one of them home to the land of Benjamin to be your wife! 22 And when their fathers and brothers come to us in protest, we will tell them, 'Please be sympathetic. Let them have your daughters, for we didn't find wives for all of them when we destroyed Jabesh-gilead. And you are not guilty of breaking the vow since you did not actually give your daughters to them in marriage.'"

23 So the men of Benjamin did as they were told. Each man caught one of the women as she danced in the celebration and carried her off to be his wife. They returned to their own land, and they rebuilt their towns and lived in them.

24 Then the people of Israel departed by tribes and families, and they returned to their own homes.

25 In those days Israel had no king; all the people did whatever seemed right in their own eyes.

Ruth

KING JAMES VERSION

1 1Now it came to pass in the days when the judges ruled, that there was a famine in the land. And a certain man of Bethlehem-judah went to sojourn in the country of Moab, he, and his wife, and his two sons.

2And the name of the man *was* Elimelech, and the name of his wife Naomi, and the name of his two sons Mahlon and Chilion, Ephrathites of Bethlehem-judah. And they came into the country of Moab, and continued there.

3And Elimelech Naomi's husband died; and she was left, and her two sons.

4And they took them wives of the women of Moab; the name of the one *was* Orpah, and the name of the other Ruth: and they dwelled there about ten years.

5And Mahlon and Chilion died also both of them; and the woman was left of her two sons and her husband.

6Then she arose with her daughters in law, that she might return from the country of Moab: for she had heard in the country of Moab how that the LORD had visited his people in giving them bread.

7Wherefore she went forth out of the place where she was, and her two daughters in law with her; and they went on the way to return unto the land of Judah.

8And Naomi said unto her two daughters in law, Go, return each to her mother's house: the LORD deal kindly with you, as ye have dealt with the dead, and with me.

9The LORD grant you that ye may find rest, each *of you* in the house of her husband. Then she kissed them; and they lifted up their voice, and wept.

10And they said unto her, Surely we will return with thee unto thy people.

11And Naomi said, Turn again, my daughters: why will ye go with me? *are* there yet *any more* sons in my womb, that they may be your husbands?

12Turn again, my daughters, go *your way;* for I am too old to have an husband. If I should say, I have hope, *if* I should have an husband also to night, and should also bear sons;

13Would ye tarry for them till they were grown? would ye stay for them from having husbands? nay,

NEW LIVING TRANSLATION

Elimelech Moves His Family to Moab

1 In the days when the judges ruled in Israel, a severe famine came upon the land. So a man from
Bethlehem in Judah left his home and went to live
in the country of Moab, taking his wife and two sons
with him. 2The man's name was Elimelech, and his
wife was Naomi. Their two sons were Mahlon and
Kilion. They were Ephrathites from Bethlehem in the
land of Judah. And when they reached Moab, they
settled there.
3Then Elimelech died, and Naomi was left with her
two sons. 4The two sons married Moabite women.
One married a woman named Orpah, and the other a
woman named Ruth. But about ten years later, 5both
Mahlon and Kilion died. This left Naomi alone, without her two sons or her husband.

Naomi and Ruth Return

6Then Naomi heard in Moab that the LORD had
blessed his people in Judah by giving them good
crops again. So Naomi and her daughters-in-law got
ready to leave Moab to return to her homeland.
7With her two daughters-in-law she set out from the
place where she had been living, and they took the
road that would lead them back to Judah.
8But on the way, Naomi said to her two daughters-
in-law, "Go back to your mothers' homes. And may
the LORD reward you for your kindness to your husbands and to me. 9May the LORD bless you with the
security of another marriage." Then she kissed them
good-bye, and they all broke down and wept.
10"No," they said. "We want to go with you to your
people."
11But Naomi replied, "Why should you go on with
me? Can I still give birth to other sons who could
grow up to be your husbands? 12No, my daughters,
return to your parents' homes, for I am too old to
marry again. And even if it were possible, and I were
to get married tonight and bear sons, then what?
13Would you wait for them to grow up and refuse
to marry someone else? No, of course not, my
daughters! Things are far more bitter for me than

KING JAMES VERSION

my daughters; for it grieveth me much for your sakes
that the hand of the LORD is gone out against me.
14 And they lifted up their voice, and wept again:
and Orpah kissed her mother in law; but Ruth clave
unto her.
15 And she said, Behold, thy sister in law is gone
back unto her people, and unto her gods: return thou
after thy sister in law.
16 And Ruth said, Intreat me not to leave thee, *or* to
return from following after thee: for whither thou
goest, I will go; and where thou lodgest, I will lodge:
thy people *shall be* my people, and thy God my God:
17 Where thou diest, will I die, and there will I be
buried: the LORD do so to me, and more also, *if aught*
but death part thee and me.
18 When she saw that she was stedfastly minded to
go with her, then she left speaking unto her.
19 So they two went until they came to Bethlehem.
And it came to pass, when they were come to Bethlehem, that all the city was moved about them, and
they said, *Is* this Naomi?
20 And she said unto them, Call me not Naomi, call
me Mara: for the Almighty hath dealt very bitterly
with me.
21 I went out full, and the LORD hath brought me
home again empty: why *then* call ye me Naomi, seeing the LORD hath testified against me, and the Almighty hath afflicted me?
22 So Naomi returned, and Ruth the Moabitess, her
daughter in law, with her, which returned out of the
country of Moab: and they came to Bethlehem in the
beginning of barley harvest.

2 1 And Naomi had a kinsman of her husband's, a
mighty man of wealth, of the family of Elimelech; and his name *was* Boaz.
2 And Ruth the Moabitess said unto Naomi, Let me
now go to the field, and glean ears of corn after *him*
in whose sight I shall find grace. And she said unto
her, Go, my daughter.
3 And she went, and came, and gleaned in the field
after the reapers: and her hap was to light on a part
of the field *belonging* unto Boaz, who *was* of the kindred of Elimelech.
4 And, behold, Boaz came from Bethlehem, and
said unto the reapers, The LORD *be* with you. And
they answered him, The LORD bless thee.
5 Then said Boaz unto his servant that was set over
the reapers, Whose damsel *is* this?
6 And the servant that was set over the reapers answered and said, It *is* the Moabitish damsel that
came back with Naomi out of the country of Moab:
7 And she said, I pray you, let me glean and gather
after the reapers among the sheaves: so she came,
and hath continued even from the morning until
now, that she tarried a little in the house.

NEW LIVING TRANSLATION

for you, because the LORD himself has raised his fist
against me."
14 And again they wept together, and Orpah kissed
her mother-in-law good-bye. But Ruth clung tightly
to Naomi. 15 "Look," Naomi said to her, "your sister-
in-law has gone back to her people and to her gods.
You should do the same."
16 But Ruth replied, "Don't ask me to leave you and
turn back. Wherever you go, I will go; wherever you
live, I will live. Your people will be my people, and
your God will be my God. 17 Wherever you die, I will
die, and there I will be buried. May the LORD punish
me severely if I allow anything but death to separate
us!" 18 When Naomi saw that Ruth was determined to
go with her, she said nothing more.
19 So the two of them continued on their journey.
When they came to Bethlehem, the entire town
was excited by their arrival. "Is it really Naomi?" the
women asked.
20 "Don't call me Naomi," she responded. "Instead,
call me Mara,* for the Almighty has made life very
bitter for me. 21 I went away full, but the LORD has
brought me home empty. Why call me Naomi when
the LORD has caused me to suffer* and the Almighty
has sent such tragedy upon me?"
22 So Naomi returned from Moab, accompanied by
her daughter-in-law Ruth, the young Moabite
woman. They arrived in Bethlehem in late spring,
at the beginning of the barley harvest.

Ruth Works in Boaz's Field

2 Now there was a wealthy and influential man in
Bethlehem named Boaz, who was a relative of
Naomi's husband, Elimelech.
2 One day Ruth the Moabite said to Naomi, "Let me
go out into the harvest fields to pick up the stalks of
grain left behind by anyone who is kind enough to let
me do it."
Naomi replied, "All right, my daughter, go ahead."
3 So Ruth went out to gather grain behind the harvesters. And as it happened, she found herself working in a field that belonged to Boaz, the relative of
her father-in-law, Elimelech.
4 While she was there, Boaz arrived from Bethlehem and greeted the harvesters. "The LORD be
with you!" he said.
"The LORD bless you!" the harvesters replied.
5 Then Boaz asked his foreman, "Who is that
young woman over there? Who does she belong to?"
6 And the foreman replied, "She is the young
woman from Moab who came back with Naomi. 7 She
asked me this morning if she could gather grain behind the harvesters. She has been hard at work ever
since, except for a few minutes' rest in the shelter."

1:20 *Naomi* means "pleasant"; *Mara* means "bitter." **1:21** Or *has testified against me.*

KING JAMES VERSION

8Then said Boaz unto Ruth, Hearest thou not, my daughter? Go not to glean in another field, neither go from hence, but abide here fast by my maidens:

9*Let* thine eyes *be* on the field that they do reap, and go thou after them: have I not charged the young men that they shall not touch thee? and when thou art athirst, go unto the vessels, and drink of *that* which the young men have drawn.

10Then she fell on her face, and bowed herself to the ground, and said unto him, Why have I found grace in thine eyes, that thou shouldest take knowledge of me, seeing I *am* a stranger?

11And Boaz answered and said unto her, It hath fully been shewed me, all that thou hast done unto thy mother in law since the death of thine husband: and *how* thou hast left thy father and thy mother, and the land of thy nativity, and art come unto a people which thou knewest not heretofore.

12The LORD recompense thy work, and a full reward be given thee of the LORD God of Israel, under whose wings thou art come to trust.

13Then she said, Let me find favour in thy sight, my lord; for that thou hast comforted me, and for that thou hast spoken friendly unto thine handmaid, though I be not like unto one of thine handmaidens.

14And Boaz said unto her, At mealtime come thou hither, and eat of the bread, and dip thy morsel in the vinegar. And she sat beside the reapers: and he reached her parched *corn*, and she did eat, and was sufficed, and left.

15And when she was risen up to glean, Boaz commanded his young men, saying, Let her glean even among the sheaves, and reproach her not:

16And let fall also *some* of the handfuls of purpose for her, and leave *them*, that she may glean *them*, and rebuke her not.

17So she gleaned in the field until even, and beat out that she had gleaned: and it was about an ephah of barley.

18And she took *it* up, and went into the city: and her mother in law saw what she had gleaned: and she brought forth, and gave to her that she had reserved after she was sufficed.

19And her mother in law said unto her, Where hast thou gleaned today? and where wroughtest thou? blessed be he that did take knowledge of thee. And she shewed her mother in law with whom she had wrought, and said, The man's name with whom I wrought today *is* Boaz.

20And Naomi said unto her daughter in law, Blessed *be* he of the LORD, who hath not left off his kindness to the living and to the dead. And Naomi said unto her, The man *is* near of kin unto us, one of our next kinsmen.

21And Ruth the Moabitess said, He said unto me also, Thou shalt keep fast by my young men, until they have ended all my harvest.

22And Naomi said unto Ruth her daughter in law,

NEW LIVING TRANSLATION

8Boaz went over and said to Ruth, "Listen, my daughter. Stay right here with us when you gather grain; don't go to any other fields. Stay right behind the young women working in my field. 9See which part of the field they are harvesting, and then follow them. I have warned the young men not to treat you roughly. And when you are thirsty, help yourself to the water they have drawn from the well."

10Ruth fell at his feet and thanked him warmly. "What have I done to deserve such kindness?" she asked. "I am only a foreigner."

11"Yes, I know," Boaz replied. "But I also know about everything you have done for your mother-in-law since the death of your husband. I have heard how you left your father and mother and your own land to live here among complete strangers. 12May the LORD, the God of Israel, under whose wings you have come to take refuge, reward you fully for what you have done."

13"I hope I continue to please you, sir," she replied. "You have comforted me by speaking so kindly to me, even though I am not one of your workers."

14At mealtime Boaz called to her, "Come over here, and help yourself to some food. You can dip your bread in the sour wine." So she sat with his harvesters, and Boaz gave her some roasted grain to eat. She ate all she wanted and still had some left over.

15When Ruth went back to work again, Boaz ordered his young men, "Let her gather grain right among the sheaves without stopping her. 16And pull out some heads of barley from the bundles and drop them on purpose for her. Let her pick them up, and don't give her a hard time!"

17So Ruth gathered barley there all day, and when she beat out the grain that evening, it filled an entire basket.* 18She carried it back into town and showed it to her mother-in-law. Ruth also gave her the roasted grain that was left over from her meal.

19"Where did you gather all this grain today?" Naomi asked. "Where did you work? May the LORD bless the one who helped you!"

So Ruth told her mother-in-law about the man in whose field she had worked. She said, "The man I worked with today is named Boaz."

20"May the LORD bless him!" Naomi told her daughter-in-law. "He is showing his kindness to us as well as to your dead husband.* That man is one of our closest relatives, one of our family redeemers."

21Then Ruth* said, "What's more, Boaz even told me to come back and stay with his harvesters until the entire harvest is completed."

22"Good!" Naomi exclaimed. "Do as he said, my daughter. Stay with his young women right through

2:17 Hebrew *it was about an ephah* [20 quarts or 22 liters]. **2:20** Hebrew *to the living and to the dead.* **2:21** Hebrew *Ruth the Moabite.*

KING JAMES VERSION

It is good, my daughter, that thou go out with his maidens, that they meet thee not in any other field. 23 So she kept fast by the maidens of Boaz to glean unto the end of barley harvest and of wheat harvest; and dwelt with her mother in law.

3 1Then Naomi her mother in law said unto her, My daughter, shall I not seek rest for thee, that it may be well with thee?

2And now *is* not Boaz of our kindred, with whose maidens thou wast? Behold, he winnoweth barley to night in the threshingfloor.

3Wash thy self therefore, and anoint thee, and put thy raiment upon thee, and get thee down to the floor: *but* make not thyself known unto the man, until he shall have done eating and drinking.

4And it shall be, when he lieth down, that thou shalt mark the place where he shall lie, and thou shalt go in, and uncover his feet, and lay thee down; and he will tell thee what thou shalt do.

5And she said unto her, All that thou sayest unto me I will do.

6And she went down unto the floor, and did according to all that her mother in law bade her.

7And when Boaz had eaten and drunk, and his heart was merry, he went to lie down at the end of the heap of corn: and she came softly, and uncovered his feet, and laid her down.

8And it came to pass at midnight, that the man was afraid, and turned himself: and, behold, a woman lay at his feet.

9And he said, Who *art* thou? And she answered, I *am* Ruth thine handmaid: spread therefore thy skirt over thine handmaid; for thou *art* a near kinsman.

10And he said, Blessed *be* thou of the LORD, my daughter: *for* thou hast shewed more kindness in the latter end than at the beginning, inasmuch as thou followedst not young men, whether poor or rich.

11And now, my daughter, fear not; I will do to thee all that thou requirest: for all the city of my people doth know that thou *art* a virtuous woman.

12And now it is true that I *am thy* near kinsman: howbeit there is a kinsman nearer than I.

13Tarry this night, and it shall be in the morning, *that* if he will perform unto thee the part of a kinsman, well; let him do the kinsman's part: but if he will not do the part of a kinsman to thee, then will I do the part of a kinsman to thee, *as* the LORD liveth: lie down until the morning.

14And she lay at his feet until the morning: and she rose up before one could know another. And he said, Let it not be known that a woman came into the floor.

15Also he said, Bring the veil that *thou hast* upon thee, and hold it. And when she held it, he measured

NEW LIVING TRANSLATION

the whole harvest. You might be harassed in other fields, but you'll be safe with him." 23So Ruth worked alongside the women in Boaz's fields and gathered grain with them until the end of the barley harvest. Then she continued working with them through the wheat harvest in early summer. And all the while she lived with her mother-in-law.

Ruth at the Threshing Floor

3 One day Naomi said to Ruth, "My daughter, it's time that I found a permanent home for you, so that you will be provided for. 2Boaz is a close relative of ours, and he's been very kind by letting you gather grain with his young women. Tonight he will be winnowing barley at the threshing floor. 3Now do as I tell you—take a bath and put on perfume and dress in your nicest clothes. Then go to the threshing floor, but don't let Boaz see you until he has finished eating and drinking. 4Be sure to notice where he lies down; then go and uncover his feet and lie down there. He will tell you what to do."

5"I will do everything you say," Ruth replied. 6So she went down to the threshing floor that night and followed the instructions of her mother-in-law.

7After Boaz had finished eating and drinking and was in good spirits, he lay down at the far end of the pile of grain and went to sleep. Then Ruth came quietly, uncovered his feet, and lay down. 8Around midnight Boaz suddenly woke up and turned over. He was surprised to find a woman lying at his feet! 9"Who are you?" he asked.

"I am your servant Ruth," she replied. "Spread the corner of your covering over me, for you are my family redeemer."

10"The LORD bless you, my daughter!" Boaz exclaimed. "You are showing even more family loyalty now than you did before, for you have not gone after a younger man, whether rich or poor. 11Now don't worry about a thing, my daughter. I will do what is necessary, for everyone in town knows you are a virtuous woman. 12But while it's true that I am one of your family redeemers, there is another man who is more closely related to you than I am. 13Stay here tonight, and in the morning I will talk to him. If he is willing to redeem you, very well. Let him marry you. But if he is not willing, then as surely as the LORD lives, I will redeem you myself! Now lie down here until morning."

14So Ruth lay at Boaz's feet until the morning, but she got up before it was light enough for people to recognize each other. For Boaz had said, "No one must know that a woman was here at the threshing floor." 15Then Boaz said to her, "Bring your cloak and spread it out." He measured six scoops* of barley

3:15a Hebrew *six measures,* an unknown quantity.

KING JAMES VERSION

six *measures* of barley, and laid *it* on her: and she
went into the city.
16And when she came to her mother in law, she
said, Who *art* thou, my daughter? And she told her
all that the man had done to her.
17And she said, These six *measures* of barley gave
he me; for he said to me, Go not empty unto thy
mother in law.
18Then said she, Sit still, my daughter, until thou
know how the matter will fall: for the man will not
be in rest, until he have finished the thing this day.

4 1Then went Boaz up to the gate, and sat him
down there: and, behold, the kinsman of whom
Boaz spake came by; unto whom he said, Ho, such a
one! turn aside, sit down here. And he turned aside,
and sat down.
2And he took ten men of the elders of the city, and
said, Sit ye down here. And they sat down.
3And he said unto the kinsman, Naomi, that is
come again out of the country of Moab, selleth a parcel of land, which *was* our brother Elimelech's:
4And I thought to advertise thee, saying, Buy *it*
before the inhabitants, and before the elders of my
people. If thou wilt redeem *it*, redeem *it*: but if thou
wilt not redeem *it*, *then* tell me, that I may know: for
there is none to redeem *it* beside thee; and I *am* after
thee. And he said, I will redeem *it*.
5Then said Boaz, What day thou buyest the field
of the hand of Naomi, thou must buy *it* also of Ruth
the Moabitess, the wife of the dead, to raise up the
name of the dead upon his inheritance.
6And the kinsman said, I cannot redeem *it* for myself, lest I mar mine own inheritance: redeem thou
my right to thyself; for I cannot redeem *it*.
7Now this *was the manner* in former time in Israel
concerning redeeming and concerning changing,
for to confirm all things; a man plucked off his shoe,
and gave *it* to his neighbour: and this *was* a testimony in Israel.
8Therefore the kinsman said unto Boaz, Buy *it* for
thee. So he drew off his shoe.
9And Boaz said unto the elders, and *unto* all the
people, Ye *are* witnesses this day, that I have bought
all that *was* Elimelech's, and all that *was* Chilion's
and Mahlon's, of the hand of Naomi.
10Moreover Ruth the Moabitess, the wife of Mahlon, have I purchased to be my wife, to raise up the
name of the dead upon his inheritance, that the
name of the dead be not cut off from among his
brethren, and from the gate of his place: ye *are* witnesses this day.
11And all the people that *were* in the gate, and the
elders, said, *We are* witnesses. The LORD make the
woman that is come into thine house like Rachel and
like Leah, which two did build the house of Israel:

NEW LIVING TRANSLATION

into the cloak and placed it on her back. Then he*
returned to the town.
16When Ruth went back to her mother-in-law,
Naomi asked, "What happened, my daughter?"
Ruth told Naomi everything Boaz had done for
her, 17and she added, "He gave me these six scoops
of barley and said, 'Don't go back to your mother-in-
law empty-handed.'"
18Then Naomi said to her, "Just be patient, my
daughter, until we hear what happens. The man
won't rest until he has settled things today."

Boaz Marries Ruth

4 Boaz went to the town gate and took a seat
there. Just then the family redeemer he had
mentioned came by, so Boaz called out to him, "Come
over here and sit down, friend. I want to talk to you."
So they sat down together. 2Then Boaz called ten
leaders from the town and asked them to sit as witnesses. 3And Boaz said to the family redeemer, "You
know Naomi, who came back from Moab. She is selling the land that belonged to our relative Elimelech.
4I thought I should speak to you about it so that you
can redeem it if you wish. If you want the land, then
buy it here in the presence of these witnesses. But if
you don't want it, let me know right away, because I
am next in line to redeem it after you."
The man replied, "All right, I'll redeem it."
5Then Boaz told him, "Of course, your purchase of
the land from Naomi also requires that you marry
Ruth, the Moabite widow. That way she can have
children who will carry on her husband's name and
keep the land in the family."
6"Then I can't redeem it," the family redeemer replied, "because this might endanger my own estate.
You redeem the land; I cannot do it."
7Now in those days it was the custom in Israel for
anyone transferring a right of purchase to remove
his sandal and hand it to the other party. This publicly validated the transaction. 8So the other family
redeemer drew off his sandal as he said to Boaz, "You
buy the land."
9Then Boaz said to the elders and to the crowd
standing around, "You are witnesses that today I
have bought from Naomi all the property of Elimelech, Kilion, and Mahlon. 10And with the land I have
acquired Ruth, the Moabite widow of Mahlon, to be
my wife. This way she can have a son to carry on the
family name of her dead husband and to inherit the
family property here in his hometown. You are all
witnesses today."
11Then the elders and all the people standing in
the gate replied, "We are witnesses! May the LORD
make this woman who is coming into your home like
Rachel and Leah, from whom all the nation of Israel
descended! May you prosper in Ephrathah and be

3:15b Most Hebrew manuscripts read *he;* many Hebrew manuscripts, Syriac version, and Latin Vulgate read *she*.

KING JAMES VERSION

and do thou worthily in Ephratah, and be famous in
Bethlehem:
12 And let thy house be like the house of Pharez,
whom Tamar bare unto Judah, of the seed which the
LORD shall give thee of this young woman.

13 So Boaz took Ruth, and she was his wife: and
when he went in unto her, the LORD gave her conception, and she bare a son.
14 And the women said unto Naomi, Blessed *be* the
LORD, which hath not left thee this day without a
kinsman, that his name may be famous in Israel.
15 And he shall be unto thee a restorer of *thy* life,
and a nourisher of thine old age: for thy daughter in
law, which loveth thee, which is better to thee than
seven sons, hath borne him.
16 And Naomi took the child, and laid it in her
bosom, and became nurse unto it.
17 And the women her neighbours gave it a name,
saying, There is a son born to Naomi; and they called
his name Obed: he *is* the father of Jesse, the father of
David.
18 Now these *are* the generations of Pharez: Pharez
begat Hezron,
19 And Hezron begat Ram, and Ram begat Amminadab,
20 And Amminadab begat Nahshon, and Nahshon
begat Salmon,
21 And Salmon begat Boaz, and Boaz begat Obed,
22 And Obed begat Jesse, and Jesse begat David.

NEW LIVING TRANSLATION

famous in Bethlehem. 12 And may the LORD give you
descendants by this young woman who will be like
those of our ancestor Perez, the son of Tamar and
Judah."

The Descendants of Boaz

13 So Boaz took Ruth into his home, and she became
his wife. When he slept with her, the LORD enabled
her to become pregnant, and she gave birth to a son.
14 Then the women of the town said to Naomi, "Praise
the LORD, who has now provided a redeemer for your
family! May this child be famous in Israel. 15 May he
restore your youth and care for you in your old age.
For he is the son of your daughter-in-law who loves
you and has been better to you than seven sons!"
16 Naomi took the baby and cuddled him to her
breast. And she cared for him as if he were her own.
17 The neighbor women said, "Now at last Naomi has
a son again!" And they named him Obed. He became
the father of Jesse and the grandfather of David.
18 This is the genealogical record of their ancestor
Perez:

Perez was the father of Hezron.
19 Hezron was the father of Ram.
Ram was the father of Amminadab.
20 Amminadab was the father of Nahshon.
Nahshon was the father of Salmon.*
21 Salmon was the father of Boaz.
Boaz was the father of Obed.
22 Obed was the father of Jesse.
Jesse was the father of David.

4:20 As in some Greek manuscripts (see also 4:21); Hebrew reads *Salma*.

1 Samuel

KING JAMES VERSION

1 [1]Now there was a certain man of Ramathaim-
zophim, of mount Ephraim, and his name *was*
Elkanah, the son of Jeroham, the son of Elihu, the son
of Tohu, the son of Zuph, an Ephrathite:
2And he had two wives; the name of the one *was*
Hannah, and the name of the other Peninnah: and
Peninnah had children, but Hannah had no children.
3And this man went up out of his city yearly to
worship and to sacrifice unto the LORD of hosts in
Shiloh. And the two sons of Eli, Hophni and Phinehas, the priests of the LORD, *were* there.
4And when the time was that Elkanah offered, he
gave to Peninnah his wife, and to all her sons and her
daughters, portions:
5But unto Hannah he gave a worthy portion; for he
loved Hannah: but the LORD had shut up her womb.
6And her adversary also provoked her sore, for
to make her fret, because the LORD had shut up
her womb.
7And *as* he did so year by year, when she went up
to the house of the LORD, so she provoked her; therefore she wept, and did not eat.
8Then said Elkanah her husband to her, Hannah,
why weepest thou? and why eatest thou not? and
why is thy heart grieved? *am* not I better to thee than
ten sons?
9So Hannah rose up after they had eaten in Shiloh,
and after they had drunk. Now Eli the priest sat upon
a seat by a post of the temple of the LORD.
10And she *was* in bitterness of soul, and prayed
unto the LORD, and wept sore.
11And she vowed a vow, and said, O LORD of hosts, if
thou wilt indeed look on the affliction of thine
handmaid, and remember me, and not forget thine
handmaid, but wilt give unto thine handmaid a man
child, then I will give him unto the LORD all the
days of his life, and there shall no razor come upon
his head.
12And it came to pass, as she continued praying
before the LORD, that Eli marked her mouth.
13Now Hannah, she spake in her heart; only her
lips moved, but her voice was not heard: therefore Eli
thought she had been drunken.

NEW LIVING TRANSLATION

Elkanah and His Family

1 There was a man named Elkanah who lived in
Ramah in the region of Zuph* in the hill country
of Ephraim. He was the son of Jeroham, son of Elihu,
son of Tohu, son of Zuph, of Ephraim. 2Elkanah had
two wives, Hannah and Peninnah. Peninnah had children, but Hannah did not.
3Each year Elkanah would travel to Shiloh to worship and sacrifice to the LORD of Heaven's Armies at
the Tabernacle. The priests of the LORD at that time
were the two sons of Eli—Hophni and Phinehas. 4On
the days Elkanah presented his sacrifice, he would
give portions of the meat to Peninnah and each of
her children. 5And though he loved Hannah, he
would give her only one choice portion* because the
LORD had given her no children. 6So Peninnah would
taunt Hannah and make fun of her because the LORD
had kept her from having children. 7Year after year it
was the same—Peninnah would taunt Hannah
as they went to the Tabernacle.* Each time, Hannah
would be reduced to tears and would not even eat.
8"Why are you crying, Hannah?" Elkanah would
ask. "Why aren't you eating? Why be downhearted
just because you have no children? You have me—
isn't that better than having ten sons?"

Hannah's Prayer for a Son

9Once after a sacrificial meal at Shiloh, Hannah got
up and went to pray. Eli the priest was sitting at his
customary place beside the entrance of the Tabernacle.* 10Hannah was in deep anguish, crying bitterly as she prayed to the LORD. 11And she made this
vow: "O LORD of Heaven's Armies, if you will look
upon my sorrow and answer my prayer and give me a
son, then I will give him back to you. He will be yours
for his entire lifetime, and as a sign that he has been
dedicated to the LORD, his hair will never be cut.*"
12As she was praying to the LORD, Eli watched her.
13Seeing her lips moving but hearing no sound, he

1:1 As in Greek version; Hebrew reads *in Ramathaim-zophim;* compare 1:19. **1:5** Or *And because he loved Hannah, he would give her a choice portion.* The meaning of the Hebrew is uncertain. **1:7** Hebrew *the house of the LORD;* also in 1:24. **1:9** Hebrew *the Temple of the LORD.* **1:11** Some manuscripts add *He will drink neither wine nor intoxicants.*

KING JAMES VERSION

14And Eli said unto her, How long wilt thou be drunken? put away thy wine from thee.

15And Hannah answered and said, No, my lord, I *am* a woman of a sorrowful spirit: I have drunk neither wine nor strong drink, but have poured out my soul before the LORD.

16Count not thine handmaid for a daughter of Belial: for out of the abundance of my complaint and grief have I spoken hitherto.

17Then Eli answered and said, Go in peace: and the God of Israel grant *thee* thy petition that thou hast asked of him.

18And she said, Let thine handmaid find grace in thy sight. So the woman went her way, and did eat, and her countenance was no more *sad.*

19And they rose up in the morning early, and worshipped before the LORD, and returned, and came to their house to Ramah: and Elkanah knew Hannah his wife; and the LORD remembered her.

20Wherefore it came to pass, when the time was come about after Hannah had conceived, that she bare a son, and called his name Samuel, *saying,* Because I have asked him of the LORD.

21And the man Elkanah, and all his house, went up to offer unto the LORD the yearly sacrifice, and his vow.

22But Hannah went not up; for she said unto her husband, *I will not go up* until the child be weaned, and *then* I will bring him, that he may appear before the LORD, and there abide for ever.

23And Elkanah her husband said unto her, Do what seemeth thee good; tarry until thou have weaned him; only the LORD establish his word. So the woman abode, and gave her son suck until she weaned him.

24And when she had weaned him, she took him up with her, with three bullocks, and one ephah of flour, and a bottle of wine, and brought him unto the house of the LORD in Shiloh: and the child *was* young.

25And they slew a bullock, and brought the child to Eli.

26And she said, Oh my lord, *as* thy soul liveth, my lord, I *am* the woman that stood by thee here, praying unto the LORD.

27For this child I prayed; and the LORD hath given me my petition which I asked of him:

28Therefore also I have lent him to the LORD; as long as he liveth he shall be lent to the LORD. And he worshipped the LORD there.

2 1And Hannah prayed, and said, My heart rejoiceth in the LORD, mine horn is exalted in the

NEW LIVING TRANSLATION

thought she had been drinking. 14"Must you come
here drunk?" he demanded. "Throw away your wine!"
15"Oh no, sir!" she replied. "I haven't been drinking wine or anything stronger. But I am very discouraged, and I was pouring out my heart to the LORD.
16Don't think I am a wicked woman! For I have been
praying out of great anguish and sorrow."
17"In that case," Eli said, "go in peace! May the God
of Israel grant the request you have asked of him."
18"Oh, thank you, sir!" she exclaimed. Then she
went back and began to eat again, and she was no
longer sad.

Samuel's Birth and Dedication

19The entire family got up early the next morning
and went to worship the LORD once more. Then they
returned home to Ramah. When Elkanah slept with
Hannah, the LORD remembered her plea, 20and in
due time she gave birth to a son. She named him
Samuel,* for she said, "I asked the LORD for him."

21The next year Elkanah and his family went on
their annual trip to offer a sacrifice to the LORD.
22But Hannah did not go. She told her husband,
"Wait until the boy is weaned. Then I will take him to
the Tabernacle and leave him there with the LORD
permanently.*"
23"Whatever you think is best," Elkanah agreed.
"Stay here for now, and may the LORD help you keep
your promise." So she stayed home and nursed the
boy until he was weaned.
24When the child was weaned, Hannah took him
to the Tabernacle in Shiloh. They brought along a
three-year-old bull* for the sacrifice and a basket* of
flour and some wine. 25After sacrificing the bull,
they brought the boy to Eli. 26"Sir, do you remember
me?" Hannah asked. "I am the woman who stood
here several years ago praying to the LORD. 27I asked
the LORD to give me this boy, and he has granted my
request. 28Now I am giving him to the LORD, and he
will belong to the LORD his whole life." And they*
worshiped the LORD there.

Hannah's Prayer of Praise

2 Then Hannah prayed:

"My heart rejoices in the LORD!
The LORD has made me strong.*

1:20 *Samuel* sounds like the Hebrew term for "asked of God" or "heard by God." **1:22** Some manuscripts add *I will offer him as a Nazirite for all time.* **1:24a** As in Dead Sea Scrolls, Greek and Syriac versions; Masoretic Text reads *three bulls.* **1:24b** Hebrew *and an ephah* [20 quarts or 22 liters]. **1:28** Hebrew *he.* **2:1** Hebrew *has exalted my horn.*

KING JAMES VERSION

LORD: my mouth is enlarged over mine enemies; because I rejoice in thy salvation.

2 *There is* none holy as the LORD: for *there is* none beside thee: neither *is there* any rock like our God.

3 Talk no more so exceeding proudly; let *not* arrogancy come out of your mouth: for the LORD *is* a God of knowledge, and by him actions are weighed.

4 The bows of the mighty men *are* broken, and they that stumbled are girded with strength.

5 *They that were* full have hired out themselves for bread; and *they that were* hungry ceased: so that the barren hath born seven; and she that hath many children is waxed feeble.

6 The LORD killeth, and maketh alive: he bringeth down to the grave, and bringeth up.

7 The LORD maketh poor, and maketh rich: he bringeth low, and lifteth up.

8 He raiseth up the poor out of the dust, *and* lifteth up the beggar from the dunghill, to set *them* among princes, and to make them inherit the throne of glory: for the pillars of the earth *are* the LORD's, and he hath set the world upon them.

9 He will keep the feet of his saints, and the wicked shall be silent in darkness; for by strength shall no man prevail.

10 The adversaries of the LORD shall be broken to pieces; out of heaven shall he thunder upon them: the LORD shall judge the ends of the earth; and he shall give strength unto his king, and exalt the horn of his anointed.

11 And Elkanah went to Ramah to his house. And the child did minister unto the LORD before Eli the priest.

12 Now the sons of Eli *were* sons of Belial; they knew not the LORD.

13 And the priests' custom with the people *was, that,* when any man offered sacrifice, the priest's servant came, while the flesh was in seething, with a fleshhook of three teeth in his hand;

14 And he struck *it* into the pan, or kettle, or caldron, or pot; all that the fleshhook brought up the priest took for himself. So they did in Shiloh, unto all the Israelites that came thither.

15 Also before they burnt the fat, the priest's servant came, and said to the man that sacrificed, Give flesh to roast for the priest; for he will not have sodden flesh of thee, but raw.

NEW LIVING TRANSLATION

Now I have an answer for my enemies;
 I rejoice because you rescued me.
2 No one is holy like the LORD!
 There is no one besides you;
 there is no Rock like our God.

3 "Stop acting so proud and haughty!
 Don't speak with such arrogance!
For the LORD is a God who knows what
 you have done;
 he will judge your actions.
4 The bow of the mighty is now broken,
 and those who stumbled are now strong.
5 Those who were well fed are now starving,
 and those who were starving are now full.
The childless woman now has seven children,
 and the woman with many children wastes
 away.
6 The LORD gives both death and life;
 he brings some down to the grave* but
 raises others up.
7 The LORD makes some poor and others rich;
 he brings some down and lifts others up.
8 He lifts the poor from the dust
 and the needy from the garbage dump.
He sets them among princes,
 placing them in seats of honor.
For all the earth is the LORD's,
 and he has set the world in order.
9 "He will protect his faithful ones,
 but the wicked will disappear in darkness.
No one will succeed by strength alone.
10 Those who fight against the LORD will be
 shattered.
He thunders against them from heaven;
 the LORD judges throughout the earth.
He gives power to his king;
 he increases the strength* of his anointed one."

11 Then Elkanah returned home to Ramah without Samuel. And the boy served the LORD by assisting Eli the priest.

Eli's Wicked Sons

12 Now the sons of Eli were scoundrels who had no respect for the LORD 13 or for their duties as priests.
Whenever anyone offered a sacrifice, Eli's sons
would send over a servant with a three-pronged fork.
While the meat of the sacrificed animal was still
boiling, 14 the servant would stick the fork into the
pot and demand that whatever it brought up be given
to Eli's sons. All the Israelites who came to worship at
Shiloh were treated this way. 15 Sometimes the servant would come even before the animal's fat had
been burned on the altar. He would demand raw
meat before it had been boiled so that it could be
used for roasting.

2:6 Hebrew *to Sheol.* **2:10** Hebrew *he exalts the horn.*

KING JAMES VERSION

16And *if* any man said unto him, Let them not fail to burn the fat presently, and *then* take *as much* as thy soul desireth; then he would answer him, *Nay;* but thou shalt give *it me* now: and if not, I will take *it* by force.

17Wherefore the sin of the young men was very great before the LORD: for men abhorred the offering of the LORD.

18But Samuel ministered before the LORD, *being* a child, girded with a linen ephod.

19Moreover his mother made him a little coat, and brought *it* to him from year to year, when she came up with her husband to offer the yearly sacrifice.

20And Eli blessed Elkanah and his wife, and said, The LORD give thee seed of this woman for the loan which is lent to the LORD. And they went unto their own home.

21And the LORD visited Hannah, so that she conceived, and bare three sons and two daughters. And the child Samuel grew before the LORD.

22Now Eli was very old, and heard all that his sons did unto all Israel; and how they lay with the women that assembled *at* the door of the tabernacle of the congregation.

23And he said unto them, Why do ye such things? for I hear of your evil dealings by all this people.

24Nay, my sons; for *it is* no good report that I hear: ye make the LORD's people to transgress.

25If one man sin against another, the judge shall judge him: but if a man sin against the LORD, who shall intreat for him? Notwithstanding they hearkened not unto the voice of their father, because the LORD would slay them.

26And the child Samuel grew on, and was in favour both with the LORD, and also with men.

27And there came a man of God unto Eli, and said unto him, Thus saith the LORD, Did I plainly appear unto the house of thy father, when they were in Egypt in Pharaoh's house?

28And did I choose him out of all the tribes of Israel *to be* my priest, to offer upon mine altar, to burn incense, to wear an ephod before me? and did I give unto the house of thy father all the offerings made by fire of the children of Israel?

29Wherefore kick ye at my sacrifice and at mine offering, which I have commanded *in my* habitation; and honourest thy sons above me, to make yourselves fat with the chiefest of all the offerings of Israel my people?

30Wherefore the LORD God of Israel saith, I said indeed *that* thy house, and the house of thy father, should walk before me for ever: but now the LORD saith, Be it far from me; for them that honour me I will honour, and they that despise me shall be lightly esteemed.

31Behold, the days come, that I will cut off thine arm, and the arm of thy father's house, that there shall not be an old man in thine house.

NEW LIVING TRANSLATION

16The man offering the sacrifice might reply, "Take as much as you want, but the fat must be burned first." Then the servant would demand, "No, give it to me now, or I'll take it by force." 17So the sin of these young men was very serious in the LORD's sight, for they treated the LORD's offerings with contempt.

18But Samuel, though he was only a boy, served the LORD. He wore a linen garment like that of a priest.* 19Each year his mother made a small coat for him and brought it to him when she came with her husband for the sacrifice. 20Before they returned home, Eli would bless Elkanah and his wife and say, "May the LORD give you other children to take the place of this one she gave to the LORD.*" 21And the LORD gave Hannah three sons and two daughters. Meanwhile, Samuel grew up in the presence of the LORD.

22Now Eli was very old, but he was aware of what his sons were doing to the people of Israel. He knew, for instance, that his sons were seducing the young women who assisted at the entrance of the Tabernacle.* 23Eli said to them, "I have been hearing reports from all the people about the wicked things you are doing. Why do you keep sinning? 24You must stop, my sons! The reports I hear among the LORD's people are not good. 25If someone sins against another person, God* can mediate for the guilty party. But if someone sins against the LORD, who can intercede?" But Eli's sons wouldn't listen to their father, for the LORD was already planning to put them to death.

26Meanwhile, the boy Samuel grew taller and grew in favor with the LORD and with the people.

A Warning for Eli's Family

27One day a man of God came to Eli and gave him this message from the LORD: "I revealed myself* to your ancestors when the people of Israel were slaves in Egypt. 28I chose your ancestor Aaron* from among all the tribes of Israel to be my priest, to offer sacrifices on my altar, to burn incense, and to wear the priestly vest* as he served me. And I assigned the sacrificial offerings to you priests. 29So why do you scorn my sacrifices and offerings? Why do you give your sons more honor than you give me—for you and they have become fat from the best offerings of my people Israel!

30"Therefore, the LORD, the God of Israel, says: I promised that your branch of the tribe of Levi* would always be my priests. But I will honor those who honor me, and I will despise those who think lightly of me. 31The time is coming when I will put an end to your family, so it will no longer serve as my priests. All the members of your family will die before their

2:18 Hebrew *He wore a linen ephod.* **2:20** As in Dead Sea Scrolls and Greek version; Masoretic Text reads *this one he requested of the LORD.* **2:22** Hebrew *Tent of Meeting.* Some manuscripts lack this entire sentence. **2:25** Or *the judges.* **2:27** As in Greek and Syriac versions; Hebrew reads *Did I reveal myself.* **2:28a** Hebrew *your father.* **2:28b** Hebrew *an ephod.* **2:30** Hebrew *that your house and your father's house.*

KING JAMES VERSION

32And thou shalt see an enemy *in my* habitation, in all *the wealth* which *God* shall give Israel: and there shall not be an old man in thine house for ever.

33And the man of thine, *whom* I shall not cut off from mine altar, *shall be* to consume thine eyes, and to grieve thine heart: and all the increase of thine house shall die in the flower of their age.

34And this *shall be* a sign unto thee, that shall come upon thy two sons, on Hophni and Phinehas; in one day they shall die both of them.

35And I will raise me up a faithful priest, *that* shall do according to *that* which *is* in mine heart and in my mind: and I will build him a sure house; and he shall walk before mine anointed for ever.

36And it shall come to pass, *that* every one that is left in thine house shall come *and* crouch to him for a piece of silver and a morsel of bread, and shall say, Put me, I pray thee, into one of the priests' offices, that I may eat a piece of bread.

3 1And the child Samuel ministered unto the LORD before Eli. And the word of the LORD was precious in those days; *there was* no open vision.

2And it came to pass at that time, when Eli *was* laid down in his place, and his eyes began to wax dim, *that* he could not see;

3And ere the lamp of God went out in the temple of the LORD, where the ark of God *was,* and Samuel was laid down *to sleep;*

4That the LORD called Samuel: and he answered, Here *am* I.

5And he ran unto Eli, and said, Here *am* I; for thou calledst me. And he said, I called not; lie down again. And he went and lay down.

6And the LORD called yet again, Samuel. And Samuel arose and went to Eli, and said, Here *am* I; for thou didst call me. And he answered, I called not, my son; lie down again.

7Now Samuel did not yet know the LORD, neither was the word of the LORD yet revealed unto him.

8And the LORD called Samuel again the third time. And he arose and went to Eli, and said, Here *am* I; for thou didst call me. And Eli perceived that the LORD had called the child.

9Therefore Eli said unto Samuel, Go, lie down: and it shall be, if he call thee, that thou shalt say, Speak, LORD; for thy servant heareth. So Samuel went and lay down in his place.

10And the LORD came, and stood, and called as at other times, Samuel, Samuel. Then Samuel answered, Speak; for thy servant heareth.

11And the LORD said to Samuel, Behold, I will do a thing in Israel, at which both the ears of every one that heareth it shall tingle.

12In that day I will perform against Eli all *things* which I have spoken concerning his house: when I begin, I will also make an end.

13For I have told him that I will judge his house for

NEW LIVING TRANSLATION

time. None will reach old age. 32You will watch with envy as I pour out prosperity on the people of Israel. But no members of your family will ever live out their days. 33Those who survive will live in sadness and grief, and their children will die a violent death.* 34And to prove that what I have said will come true, I will cause your two sons, Hophni and Phinehas, to die on the same day!

35"Then I will raise up a faithful priest who will serve me and do what I desire. I will establish his family, and they will be priests to my anointed kings forever. 36Then all of your surviving family will bow before him, begging for money and food. 'Please,' they will say, 'give us jobs among the priests so we will have enough to eat.'"

The LORD Speaks to Samuel

3 Meanwhile, the boy Samuel served the LORD by assisting Eli. Now in those days messages from the LORD were very rare, and visions were quite uncommon.

2One night Eli, who was almost blind by now, had gone to bed. 3The lamp of God had not yet gone out, and Samuel was sleeping in the Tabernacle* near the Ark of God. 4Suddenly the LORD called out, "Samuel!"

"Yes?" Samuel replied. "What is it?" 5He got up and ran to Eli. "Here I am. Did you call me?"

"I didn't call you," Eli replied. "Go back to bed." So he did.

6Then the LORD called out again, "Samuel!"

Again Samuel got up and went to Eli. "Here I am. Did you call me?"

"I didn't call you, my son," Eli said. "Go back to bed."

7Samuel did not yet know the LORD because he had never had a message from the LORD before. 8So the LORD called a third time, and once more Samuel got up and went to Eli. "Here I am. Did you call me?"

Then Eli realized it was the LORD who was calling the boy. 9So he said to Samuel, "Go and lie down again, and if someone calls again, say, 'Speak, LORD, your servant is listening.'" So Samuel went back to bed.

10And the LORD came and called as before, "Samuel! Samuel!"

And Samuel replied, "Speak, your servant is listening."

11Then the LORD said to Samuel, "I am about to do a shocking thing in Israel. 12I am going to carry out all my threats against Eli and his family, from beginning to end. 13I have warned him that judgment is coming

2:33 As in Dead Sea Scrolls, which read *die by the sword;* Masoretic Text reads *die like mortals.* 3:3 Hebrew *the Temple of the LORD.*

KING JAMES VERSION

ever for the iniquity which he knoweth; because his sons made themselves vile, and he restrained them not.

14And therefore I have sworn unto the house of Eli, that the iniquity of Eli's house shall not be purged with sacrifice nor offering for ever.

15And Samuel lay until the morning, and opened the doors of the house of the LORD. And Samuel feared to shew Eli the vision.

16Then Eli called Samuel, and said, Samuel, my son. And he answered, Here *am* I.

17And he said, What *is* the thing that *the* LORD *hath said unto thee? I pray thee hide it* not from me: God do so to thee, and more also, if thou hide *any* thing from me of all the things that he said unto thee.

18And Samuel told him every whit, and hid nothing from him. And he said, It *is* the LORD: let him do what seemeth him good.

19And Samuel grew, and the LORD was with him, and did let none of his words fall to the ground.

20And all Israel from Dan even to Beer-sheba knew that Samuel *was* established *to be* a prophet of the LORD.

21And the LORD appeared again in Shiloh: for the LORD revealed himself to Samuel in Shiloh by the word of the LORD.

4 1And the word of Samuel came to all Israel. Now Israel went out against the Philistines to battle, and pitched beside Ebenezer: and the Philistines pitched in Aphek.

2And the Philistines put themselves in array against Israel: and when they joined battle, Israel was smitten before the Philistines: and they slew of the army in the field about four thousand men.

3And when the people were come into the camp, the elders of Israel said, Wherefore hath the LORD smitten us today before the Philistines? Let us fetch the ark of the covenant of the LORD out of Shiloh unto us, that, when it cometh among us, it may save us out of the hand of our enemies.

4So the people sent to Shiloh, that they might bring from thence the ark of the covenant of the LORD of hosts, which dwelleth *between* the cherubims: and the two sons of Eli, Hophni and Phinehas, *were* there with the ark of the covenant of God.

5And when the ark of the covenant of the LORD came into the camp, all Israel shouted with a great shout, so that the earth rang again.

6And when the Philistines heard the noise of the shout, they said, What *meaneth* the noise of this great shout in the camp of the Hebrews? And they understood that the ark of the LORD was come into the camp.

7And the Philistines were afraid, for they said, God is come into the camp. And they said, Woe unto us! for there hath not been such a thing heretofore.

8Woe unto us! who shall deliver us out of the hand

NEW LIVING TRANSLATION

upon his family forever, because his sons are blaspheming God* and he hasn't disciplined them. 14So I have vowed that the sins of Eli and his sons will never be forgiven by sacrifices or offerings."

Samuel Speaks for the LORD

15Samuel stayed in bed until morning, then got up and opened the doors of the Tabernacle* as usual. He was afraid to tell Eli what the LORD had said to him. 16But Eli called out to him, "Samuel, my son."

"Here I am," Samuel replied.

17"What did the LORD say to you? Tell me everything. And may God strike you and even kill you if you hide anything from me!" 18So Samuel told Eli everything; he didn't hold anything back. "It is the LORD's will," Eli replied. "Let him do what he thinks best."

19As Samuel grew up, the LORD was with him, and everything Samuel said proved to be reliable. 20And all Israel, from Dan in the north to Beersheba in the south, knew that Samuel was confirmed as a prophet of the LORD. 21The LORD continued to appear at Shiloh and gave messages to Samuel there at the Tabernacle. 4:1And Samuel's words went out to all the people of Israel.

The Philistines Capture the Ark

4 At that time Israel was at war with the Philistines. The Israelite army was camped near Ebenezer, and the Philistines were at Aphek. 2The Philistines attacked and defeated the army of Israel, killing 4,000 men. 3After the battle was over, the troops retreated to their camp, and the elders of Israel asked, "Why did the LORD allow us to be defeated by the Philistines?" Then they said, "Let's bring the Ark of the Covenant of the LORD from Shiloh. If we carry it into battle with us, it* will save us from our enemies."

4So they sent men to Shiloh to bring the Ark of the Covenant of the LORD of Heaven's Armies, who is enthroned between the cherubim. Hophni and Phinehas, the sons of Eli, were also there with the Ark of the Covenant of God. 5When all the Israelites saw the Ark of the Covenant of the LORD coming into the camp, their shout of joy was so loud it made the ground shake!

6"What's going on?" the Philistines asked. "What's all the shouting about in the Hebrew camp?" When they were told it was because the Ark of the LORD had arrived, 7they panicked. "The gods have* come into their camp!" they cried. "This is a disaster! We have never had to face anything like this before! 8Help! Who can save us from these mighty gods of

3:13 As in Greek version; Hebrew reads *his sons have made themselves contemptible.* **3:15** Hebrew *the house of the LORD.* **4:3** Or *he.* **4:7** Or *A god has.*

KING JAMES VERSION

of these mighty Gods? these *are* the Gods that smote
the Egyptians with all the plagues in the wilderness.
9 Be strong, and quit yourselves like men, O ye
Philistines, that ye be not servants unto the Hebrews,
as they have been to you: quit yourselves like men,
and fight.
10 And the Philistines fought, and Israel was smitten, and they fled every man into his tent: and there
was a very great slaughter; for there fell of Israel
thirty thousand footmen.
11 And the ark of God was taken; and the two sons
of Eli, Hophni and Phinehas, were slain.

12 And there ran a man of Benjamin out of the
army, and came to Shiloh the same day with his
clothes rent, and with earth upon his head.
13 And when he came, lo, Eli sat upon a seat by the
wayside watching: for his heart trembled for the ark
of God. And when the man came into the city, and
told *it,* all the city cried out.
14 And when Eli heard the noise of the crying, he
said, What *meaneth* the noise of this tumult? And
the man came in hastily, and told Eli.
15 Now Eli was ninety and eight years old; and his
eyes were dim, that he could not see.
16 And the man said unto Eli, I *am* he that came out
of the army, and I fled today out of the army. And he
said, What is there done, my son?
17 And the messenger answered and said, Israel is
fled before the Philistines, and there hath been also a
great slaughter among the people, and thy two sons
also, Hophni and Phinehas, are dead, and the ark of
God is taken.
18 And it came to pass, when he made mention of
the ark of God, that he fell from off the seat backward by the side of the gate, and his neck brake, and
he died: for he was an old man, and heavy. And he
had judged Israel forty years.
19 And his daughter in law, Phinehas' wife, was with
child, *near* to be delivered: and when she heard the
tidings that the ark of God was taken, and that her father in law and her husband were dead, she bowed
herself and travailed; for her pains came upon her.
20 And about the time of her death the women that
stood by her said unto her, Fear not; for thou hast
borne a son. But she answered not, neither did she
regard *it.*
21 And she named the child Ichabod, saying, The
glory is departed from Israel: because the ark of God
was taken, and because of her father in law and her
husband.
22 And she said, The glory is departed from Israel:
for the ark of God is taken.

5 1 And the Philistines took the ark of God, and
brought it from Ebenezer unto Ashdod.
2 When the Philistines took the ark of God, they

NEW LIVING TRANSLATION

Israel? They are the same gods who destroyed the
Egyptians with plagues when Israel was in the wilderness. 9 Fight as never before, Philistines! If you don't,
we will become the Hebrews' slaves just as they have
been ours! Stand up like men and fight!"
10 So the Philistines fought desperately, and Israel
was defeated again. The slaughter was great; 30,000
Israelite soldiers died that day. The survivors turned
and fled to their tents. 11 The Ark of God was captured, and Hophni and Phinehas, the two sons of Eli,
were killed.

The Death of Eli

12 A man from the tribe of Benjamin ran from the battlefield and arrived at Shiloh later that same day. He
had torn his clothes and put dust on his head to show
his grief. 13 Eli was waiting beside the road to hear the
news of the battle, for his heart trembled for the
safety of the Ark of God. When the messenger arrived and told what had happened, an outcry resounded throughout the town.
14 "What is all the noise about?" Eli asked.
The messenger rushed over to Eli, 15 who was
ninety-eight years old and blind. 16 He said to Eli, "I
have just come from the battlefield—I was there this
very day."
"What happened, my son?" Eli demanded.
17 "Israel has been defeated by the Philistines," the
messenger replied. "The people have been slaughtered, and your two sons, Hophni and Phinehas, were
also killed. And the Ark of God has been captured."
18 When the messenger mentioned what had happened to the Ark of God, Eli fell backward from his
seat beside the gate. He broke his neck and died, for
he was old and overweight. He had been Israel's
judge for forty years.
19 Eli's daughter-in-law, the wife of Phinehas, was
pregnant and near her time of delivery. When she
heard that the Ark of God had been captured and
that her father-in-law and husband were dead, she
went into labor and gave birth. 20 She died in childbirth, but before she passed away the midwives tried
to encourage her. "Don't be afraid," they said. "You
have a baby boy!" But she did not answer or pay attention to them.
21 She named the child Ichabod (which means
"Where is the glory?"), for she said, "Israel's glory is
gone." She named him this because the Ark of God
had been captured and because her father-in-law
and husband were dead. 22 Then she said, "The glory
has departed from Israel, for the Ark of God has been
captured."

The Ark in Philistia

5 After the Philistines captured the Ark of God,
they took it from the battleground at Ebenezer
to the town of Ashdod. 2 They carried the Ark of God

brought it into the house of Dagon, and set it by Dagon.

3 And when they of Ashdod arose early on the morrow, behold, Dagon *was* fallen upon his face to the earth before the ark of the LORD. And they took Dagon, and set him in his place again.

4 And when they arose early on the morrow morning, behold, Dagon *was* fallen upon his face to the ground before the ark of the LORD; and the head of Dagon and both the palms of his hands *were* cut off upon the threshold; only *the stump of* Dagon was left to him.

5 Therefore neither the priests of Dagon, nor any that come into Dagon's house, tread on the threshold of Dagon in Ashdod unto this day.

6 But the hand of the LORD was heavy upon them of Ashdod, and he destroyed them, and smote them with emerods, *even* Ashdod and the coasts thereof.

7 And when the men of Ashdod saw that *it was* so, they said, The ark of the God of Israel shall not abide with us: for his hand is sore upon us, and upon Dagon our god.

8 They sent therefore and gathered all the lords of the Philistines unto them, and said, What shall we do with the ark of the God of Israel? And they answered, Let the ark of the God of Israel be carried about unto Gath. And they carried the ark of the God of Israel about *thither.*

9 And it was *so,* that, after they had carried it about, the hand of the LORD was against the city with a very great destruction: and he smote the men of the city, both small and great, and they had emerods in their secret parts.

10 Therefore they sent the ark of God to Ekron. And it came to pass, as the ark of God came to Ekron, that the Ekronites cried out, saying, They have brought about the ark of the God of Israel to us, to slay us and our people.

11 So they sent and gathered together all the lords of the Philistines, and said, Send away the ark of the God of Israel, and let it go again to his own place, that it slay us not, and our people: for there was a deadly destruction throughout all the city; the hand of God was very heavy there.

12 And the men that died not were smitten with the emerods: and the cry of the city went up to heaven.

6 1 And the ark of the LORD was in the country of the Philistines seven months.

2 And the Philistines called for the priests and the diviners, saying, What shall we do to the ark of the LORD? tell us wherewith we shall send it to his place.

3 And they said, If ye send away the ark of the God of Israel, send it not empty; but in any wise return him a trespass offering: then ye shall be healed, and it shall be known to you why his hand is not removed from you.

into the temple of Dagon and placed it beside an idol of Dagon. 3 But when the citizens of Ashdod went to see it the next morning, Dagon had fallen with his face to the ground in front of the Ark of the LORD! So they took Dagon and put him in his place again. 4 But the next morning the same thing happened—Dagon had fallen face down before the Ark of the LORD again. This time his head and hands had broken off and were lying in the doorway. Only the trunk of his body was left intact. 5 That is why to this day neither the priests of Dagon nor anyone who enters the temple of Dagon in Ashdod will step on its threshold.

6 Then the LORD's heavy hand struck the people of Ashdod and the nearby villages with a plague of tumors.* 7 When the people realized what was happening, they cried out, "We can't keep the Ark of the God of Israel here any longer! He is against us! We will all be destroyed along with Dagon, our god." 8 So they called together the rulers of the Philistine towns and asked, "What should we do with the Ark of the God of Israel?"

The rulers discussed it and replied, "Move it to the town of Gath." So they moved the Ark of the God of Israel to Gath. 9 But when the Ark arrived at Gath, the LORD's heavy hand fell on its men, young and old; he struck them with a plague of tumors, and there was a great panic.

10 So they sent the Ark of God to the town of Ekron, but when the people of Ekron saw it coming they cried out, "They are bringing the Ark of the God of Israel here to kill us, too!" 11 The people summoned the Philistine rulers again and begged them, "Please send the Ark of the God of Israel back to its own country, or it* will kill us all." For the deadly plague from God had already begun, and great fear was sweeping across the town. 12 Those who didn't die were afflicted with tumors; and the cry from the town rose to heaven.

The Philistines Return the Ark

6 The Ark of the LORD remained in Philistine territory seven months in all. 2 Then the Philistines called in their priests and diviners and asked them, "What should we do about the Ark of the LORD? Tell us how to return it to its own country."

3 "Send the Ark of the God of Israel back with a gift," they were told. "Send a guilt offering so the plague will stop. Then, if you are healed, you will know it was his hand that caused the plague."

5:6 Greek version and Latin Vulgate read *tumors; and rats appeared in their land, and death and destruction were throughout the city.* **5:11** Or *he.*

KING JAMES VERSION

4 Then said they, What *shall be* the trespass offering which we shall return to him? They answered, Five golden emerods, and five golden mice, *according to* the number of the lords of the Philistines: for one plague *was* on you all, and on your lords.

5 Wherefore ye shall make images of your emerods, and images of your mice that mar the land; and ye shall give glory unto the God of Israel: peradventure he will lighten his hand from off you, and from off your gods, and from off your land.

6 Wherefore then do ye harden your hearts, as the Egyptians and Pharaoh hardened their hearts? when he had wrought wonderfully among them, did they not let the people go, and they departed?

7 Now therefore make a new cart, and take two milch kine, on which there hath come no yoke, and tie the kine to the cart, and bring their calves home from them:

8 And take the ark of the LORD, and lay it upon the cart; and put the jewels of gold, which ye return him *for* a trespass offering, in a coffer by the side thereof; and send it away, that it may go.

9 And see, if it goeth up by the way of his own coast to Beth-shemesh, *then* he hath done us this great evil: but if not, then we shall know that *it is* not his hand *that* smote us: it *was* a chance *that* happened to us.

10 And the men did so; and took two milch kine, and tied them to the cart, and shut up their calves at home:

11 And they laid the ark of the LORD upon the cart, and the coffer with the mice of gold and the images of their emerods.

12 And the kine took the straight way to the way of Beth-shemesh, *and* went along the highway, lowing as they went, and turned not aside *to* the right hand or *to* the left; and the lords of the Philistines went after them unto the border of Beth-shemesh.

13 And *they of* Beth-shemesh *were* reaping their wheat harvest in the valley: and they lifted up their eyes, and saw the ark, and rejoiced to see *it*.

14 And the cart came into the field of Joshua, a Beth-shemite, and stood there, where *there was* a great stone: and they clave the wood of the cart, and offered the kine a burnt offering unto the LORD.

15 And the Levites took down the ark of the LORD, and the coffer that *was* with it, wherein the jewels of gold *were*, and put *them* on the great stone: and the men of Beth-shemesh offered burnt offerings and sacrificed sacrifices the same day unto the LORD.

16 And when the five lords of the Philistines had seen *it*, they returned to Ekron the same day.

17 And these *are* the golden emerods which the Philistines returned *for* a trespass offering unto the LORD; for Ashdod one, for Gaza one, for Askelon one, for Gath one, for Ekron one;

18 And the golden mice, *according to* the number of all the cities of the Philistines *belonging* to the

NEW LIVING TRANSLATION

4 "What sort of guilt offering should we send?" they asked.

And they were told, "Since the plague has struck both you and your five rulers, make five gold tumors and five gold rats, just like those that have ravaged your land. 5 Make these things to show honor to the God of Israel. Perhaps then he will stop afflicting you, your gods, and your land. 6 Don't be stubborn and rebellious as Pharaoh and the Egyptians were. By the time God was finished with them, they were eager to let Israel go.

7 "Now build a new cart, and find two cows that have just given birth to calves. Make sure the cows have never been yoked to a cart. Hitch the cows to the cart, but shut their calves away from them in a pen. 8 Put the Ark of the LORD on the cart, and beside it place a chest containing the gold rats and gold tumors you are sending as a guilt offering. Then let the cows go wherever they want. 9 If they cross the border of our land and go to Beth-shemesh, we will know it was the LORD who brought this great disaster upon us. If they don't, we will know it was not his hand that caused the plague. It came simply by chance."

10 So these instructions were carried out. Two cows were hitched to the cart, and their newborn calves were shut up in a pen. 11 Then the Ark of the LORD and the chest containing the gold rats and gold tumors were placed on the cart. 12 And sure enough, without veering off in other directions, the cows went straight along the road toward Beth-shemesh, lowing as they went. The Philistine rulers followed them as far as the border of Beth-shemesh.

13 The people of Beth-shemesh were harvesting wheat in the valley, and when they saw the Ark, they were overjoyed! 14 The cart came into the field of a man named Joshua and stopped beside a large rock. So the people broke up the wood of the cart for a fire and killed the cows and sacrificed them to the LORD as a burnt offering. 15 Several men of the tribe of Levi lifted the Ark of the LORD and the chest containing the gold rats and gold tumors from the cart and placed them on the large rock. Many sacrifices and burnt offerings were offered to the LORD that day by the people of Beth-shemesh. 16 The five Philistine rulers watched all this and then returned to Ekron that same day.

17 The five gold tumors sent by the Philistines as a guilt offering to the LORD were gifts from the rulers of Ashdod, Gaza, Ashkelon, Gath, and Ekron. 18 The five gold rats represented the five Philistine towns

KING JAMES VERSION

five lords, *both* of fenced cities, and of country villages, even unto the great *stone of* Abel, whereon
they set down the ark of the LORD: *which stone remaineth* unto this day in the field of Joshua, the
Beth-shemite.

[19]And he smote the men of Beth-shemesh, because they had looked into the ark of the LORD, even
he smote of the people fifty thousand and threescore
and ten men: and the people lamented, because the
LORD had smitten *many* of the people with a great
slaughter.
[20]And the men of Beth-shemesh said, Who is able
to stand before this holy LORD God? and to whom
shall he go up from us?
[21]And they sent messengers to the inhabitants of
Kirjath-jearim, saying, The Philistines have brought
again the ark of the LORD; come ye down, *and* fetch
it up to you.

7 [1]And the men of Kirjath-jearim came, and
fetched up the ark of the LORD, and brought it
into the house of Abinadab in the hill, and sanctified
Eleazar his son to keep the ark of the LORD.
[2]And it came to pass, while the ark abode in
Kirjath-jearim, that the time was long; for it was
twenty years: and all the house of Israel lamented
after the LORD.

[3]And Samuel spake unto all the house of Israel,
saying, If ye do return unto the LORD with all your
hearts, *then* put away the strange gods and Ashtaroth
from among you, and prepare your hearts unto the
LORD, and serve him only: and he will deliver you out
of the hand of the Philistines.
[4]Then the children of Israel did put away Baalim
and Ashtaroth, and served the LORD only.
[5]And Samuel said, Gather all Israel to Mizpeh, and
I will pray for you unto the LORD.
[6]And they gathered together to Mizpeh, and drew
water, and poured *it* out before the LORD, and fasted
on that day, and said there, We have sinned against
the LORD. And Samuel judged the children of Israel
in Mizpeh.
[7]And when the Philistines heard that the children
of Israel were gathered together to Mizpeh, the lords
of the Philistines went up against Israel. And when
the children of Israel heard *it*, they were afraid of the
Philistines.
[8]And the children of Israel said to Samuel, Cease
not to cry unto the LORD our God for us, that he will
save us out of the hand of the Philistines.
[9]And Samuel took a sucking lamb, and offered *it*
for a burnt offering wholly unto the LORD: and Samuel cried unto the LORD for Israel; and the LORD heard
him.
[10]And as Samuel was offering up the burnt offer-

NEW LIVING TRANSLATION

and their surrounding villages, which were controlled by the five rulers. The large rock at Beth-
shemesh, where they set the Ark of the LORD, still
stands in the field of Joshua as a witness to what
happened there.

The Ark Moved to Kiriath-Jearim

[19]But the LORD killed seventy men* from Beth-
shemesh because they looked into the Ark of the
LORD. And the people mourned greatly because of
what the LORD had done. [20]"Who is able to stand in
the presence of the LORD, this holy God?" they cried
out. "Where can we send the Ark from here?"
[21]So they sent messengers to the people at
Kiriath-jearim and told them, "The Philistines have
returned the Ark of the LORD. Come here and get it!"

7 So the men of Kiriath-jearim came to get the
Ark of the LORD. They took it to the hillside
home of Abinadab and ordained Eleazar, his son,
to be in charge of it. [2]The Ark remained in Kiriath-
jearim for a long time—twenty years in all. During
that time all Israel mourned because it seemed the
LORD had abandoned them.

Samuel Leads Israel to Victory

[3]Then Samuel said to all the people of Israel, "If you
are really serious about wanting to return to the
LORD, get rid of your foreign gods and your images of
Ashtoreth. Determine to obey only the LORD; then
he will rescue you from the Philistines." [4]So the Israelites got rid of their images of Baal and Ashtoreth
and worshiped only the LORD.
[5]Then Samuel told them, "Gather all of Israel to
Mizpah, and I will pray to the LORD for you." [6]So they
gathered at Mizpah and, in a great ceremony, drew
water from a well and poured it out before the LORD.
They also went without food all day and confessed
that they had sinned against the LORD. (It was at Mizpah that Samuel became Israel's judge.)
[7]When the Philistine rulers heard that Israel had
gathered at Mizpah, they mobilized their army and
advanced. The Israelites were badly frightened when
they learned that the Philistines were approaching.
[8]"Don't stop pleading with the LORD our God to save
us from the Philistines!" they begged Samuel. [9]So
Samuel took a young lamb and offered it to the LORD
as a whole burnt offering. He pleaded with the LORD
to help Israel, and the LORD answered him.
[10]Just as Samuel was sacrificing the burnt offering,

6:19 As in a few Hebrew manuscripts; most Hebrew manuscripts read *70 men, 50,000 men.* Perhaps the text should be understood to read *the LORD killed 70 men and 50 oxen.*

KING JAMES VERSION

ing, the Philistines drew near to battle against Israel:
but the LORD thundered with a great thunder on that
day upon the Philistines, and discomfited them; and
they were smitten before Israel.
11 And the men of Israel went out of Mizpeh, and
pursued the Philistines, and smote them, until *they*
came under Beth-car.
12 Then Samuel took a stone, and set *it* between
Mizpeh and Shen, and called the name of it Ebenezer, saying, Hitherto hath the LORD helped us.
13 So the Philistines were subdued, and they came
no more into the coast of Israel: and the hand of
the LORD was against the Philistines all the days
of Samuel.
14 And the cities which the Philistines had taken
from Israel were restored to Israel, from Ekron even
unto Gath; and the coasts thereof did Israel deliver
out of the hands of the Philistines. And there was
peace between Israel and the Amorites.
15 And Samuel judged Israel all the days of his life.
16 And he went from year to year in circuit to
Bethel, and Gilgal, and Mizpeh, and judged Israel in
all those places.
17 And his return *was* to Ramah; for there *was* his
house; and there he judged Israel; and there he built
an altar unto the LORD.

8 1 And it came to pass, when Samuel was old, that
he made his sons judges over Israel.
2 Now the name of his firstborn was Joel; and the
name of his second, Abiah: *they were* judges in Beer-
sheba.
3 And his sons walked not in his ways, but turned
aside after lucre, and took bribes, and perverted
judgment.
4 Then all the elders of Israel gathered themselves
together, and came to Samuel unto Ramah,
5 And said unto him, Behold, thou art old, and thy
sons walk not in thy ways: now make us a king to
judge us like all the nations.
6 But the thing displeased Samuel, when they said,
Give us a king to judge us. And Samuel prayed unto
the LORD.
7 And the LORD said unto Samuel, Hearken unto
the voice of the people in all that they say unto thee:
for they have not rejected thee, but they have rejected me, that I should not reign over them.
8 According to all the works which they have done
since the day that I brought them up out of Egypt
even unto this day, wherewith they have forsaken me,
and served other gods, so do they also unto thee.
9 Now therefore hearken unto their voice: howbeit
yet protest solemnly unto them, and shew them the
manner of the king that shall reign over them.

NEW LIVING TRANSLATION

the Philistines arrived to attack Israel. But the LORD
spoke with a mighty voice of thunder from heaven
that day, and the Philistines were thrown into such
confusion that the Israelites defeated them. 11 The
men of Israel chased them from Mizpah to a place
below Beth-car, slaughtering them all along the way.
12 Samuel then took a large stone and placed it
between the towns of Mizpah and Jeshanah.* He
named it Ebenezer (which means "the stone of
help"), for he said, "Up to this point the LORD has
helped us!"
13 So the Philistines were subdued and didn't invade Israel again for some time. And throughout
Samuel's lifetime, the LORD's powerful hand was
raised against the Philistines. 14 The Israelite villages
near Ekron and Gath that the Philistines had captured were restored to Israel, along with the rest of
the territory that the Philistines had taken. And
there was peace between Israel and the Amorites in
those days.
15 Samuel continued as Israel's judge for the rest of
his life. 16 Each year he traveled around, setting up his
court first at Bethel, then at Gilgal, and then at
Mizpah. He judged the people of Israel at each of
these places. 17 Then he would return to his home
at Ramah, and he would hear cases there, too. And
Samuel built an altar to the LORD at Ramah.

Israel Requests a King

8 As Samuel grew old, he appointed his sons to
be judges over Israel. 2 Joel and Abijah, his oldest sons, held court in Beersheba. 3 But they were not
like their father, for they were greedy for money. They
accepted bribes and perverted justice.
4 Finally, all the elders of Israel met at Ramah to
discuss the matter with Samuel. 5 "Look," they told
him, "you are now old, and your sons are not like you.
Give us a king to judge us like all the other nations
have."
6 Samuel was displeased with their request and
went to the LORD for guidance. 7 "Do everything they
say to you," the LORD replied, "for it is me they are rejecting, not you. They don't want me to be their king
any longer. 8 Ever since I brought them from Egypt
they have continually abandoned me and followed
other gods. And now they are giving you the same
treatment. 9 Do as they ask, but solemnly warn them
about the way a king will reign over them."

7:12 As in Greek and Syriac versions; Hebrew reads *Shen.*

KING JAMES VERSION

10 And Samuel told all the words of the LORD unto
the people that asked of him a king.
11 And he said, This will be the manner of the king
that shall reign over you: He will take your sons, and
appoint *them* for himself, for his chariots, and *to be*
his horsemen; and *some* shall run before his chariots.
12 And he will appoint him captains over thousands, and captains over fifties; and *will set them*
to ear his ground, and to reap his harvest, and to
make his instruments of war, and instruments of
his chariots.
13 And he will take your daughters *to be* confec-
tionaries, and *to be* cooks, and *to be* bakers.
14 And he will take your fields, and your vineyards,
and your oliveyards, *even* the best *of them,* and give
them to his servants.
15 And he will take the tenth of your seed, and of
your vineyards, and give to his officers, and to his
servants.
16 And he will take your menservants, and your
maidservants, and your goodliest young men, and
your asses, and put *them* to his work.
17 He will take the tenth of your sheep: and ye shall
be his servants.
18 And ye shall cry out in that day because of your
king which ye shall have chosen you; and the LORD
will not hear you in that day.
19 Nevertheless the people refused to obey the
voice of Samuel; and they said, Nay; but we will have a
king over us;
20 That we also may be like all the nations; and that
our king may judge us, and go out before us, and
fight our battles.
21 And Samuel heard all the words of the people,
and he rehearsed them in the ears of the LORD.
22 And the LORD said to Samuel, Hearken unto
their voice, and make them a king. And Samuel said
unto the men of Israel, Go ye every man unto his city.

9 1 Now there was a man of Benjamin, whose
name *was* Kish, the son of Abiel, the son of
Zeror, the son of Bechorath, the son of Aphiah, a
Benjamite, a mighty man of power.
2 And he had a son, whose name *was* Saul, a choice
young man, and a goodly: and *there was* not among
the children of Israel a goodlier person than he: from
his shoulders and upward *he was* higher than any of
the people.
3 And the asses of Kish Saul's father were lost. And
Kish said to Saul his son, Take now one of the servants with thee, and arise, go seek the asses.
4 And he passed through mount Ephraim, and
passed through the land of Shalisha, but they found
them not: then they passed through the land of
Shalim, and *there they were* not: and he passed
through the land of the Benjamites, but they found
them not.

NEW LIVING TRANSLATION

Samuel Warns against a Kingdom

10 So Samuel passed on the LORD's warning to the
people who were asking him for a king. 11 "This is
how a king will reign over you," Samuel said. "The
king will draft your sons and assign them to his chariots and his charioteers, making them run before his
chariots. 12 Some will be generals and captains in his
army,* some will be forced to plow in his fields and
harvest his crops, and some will make his weapons
and chariot equipment. 13 The king will take your
daughters from you and force them to cook and bake
and make perfumes for him. 14 He will take away the
best of your fields and vineyards and olive groves and
give them to his own officials. 15 He will take a tenth
of your grain and your grape harvest and distribute it
among his officers and attendants. 16 He will take
your male and female slaves and demand the finest
of your cattle* and donkeys for his own use. 17 He will
demand a tenth of your flocks, and you will be his
slaves. 18 When that day comes, you will beg for relief
from this king you are demanding, but then the LORD
will not help you."
19 But the people refused to listen to Samuel's
warning. "Even so, we still want a king," they said.
20 "We want to be like the nations around us. Our
king will judge us and lead us into battle."
21 So Samuel repeated to the LORD what the people
had said, 22 and the LORD replied, "Do as they say, and
give them a king." Then Samuel agreed and sent the
people home.

Saul Meets Samuel

9 There was a wealthy, influential man named
Kish from the tribe of Benjamin. He was the
son of Abiel, son of Zeror, son of Becorath, son of
Aphiah, of the tribe of Benjamin. 2 His son Saul was
the most handsome man in Israel—head and shoulders taller than anyone else in the land.
3 One day Kish's donkeys strayed away, and he told
Saul, "Take a servant with you, and go look for the
donkeys." 4 So Saul took one of the servants and
traveled through the hill country of Ephraim, the
land of Shalishah, the Shaalim area, and the entire
land of Benjamin, but they couldn't find the donkeys
anywhere.

8:12 Hebrew *commanders of thousands and commanders of fifties.*
8:16 As in Greek version; Hebrew reads *young men.*

KING JAMES VERSION

5 *And* when they were come to the land of Zuph, Saul said to his servant that *was* with him, Come, and let us return; lest my father leave *caring* for the asses, and take thought for us.

6 And he said unto him, Behold now, *there is* in this city a man of God, and *he is* an honourable man; all that he saith cometh surely to pass: now let us go thither; peradventure he can shew us our way that we should go.

7 Then said Saul to his servant, But, behold, *if* we go, what shall we bring the man? for the bread is spent in our vessels, and *there is* not a present to bring to the man of God: what have we?

8 And the servant answered Saul again, and said, Behold, I have here at hand the fourth part of a shekel of silver: *that* will I give to the man of God, to tell us our way.

9 (Beforetime in Israel, when a man went to inquire of God, thus he spake, Come, and let us go to the seer: for *he that is* now *called* a Prophet was beforetime called a Seer.)

10 Then said Saul to his servant, Well said; come, let us go. So they went unto the city where the man of God *was*.

11 *And* as they went up the hill to the city, they found young maidens going out to draw water, and said unto them, Is the seer here?

12 And they answered them, and said, He is; behold, *he is* before you: make haste now, for he came today to the city; for *there is* a sacrifice of the people today in the high place:

13 As soon as ye be come into the city, ye shall straightway find him, before he go up to the high place to eat: for the people will not eat until he come, because he doth bless the sacrifice; *and* afterwards they eat that be bidden. Now therefore get you up; for about this time ye shall find him.

14 And they went up into the city: *and* when they were come into the city, behold, Samuel came out against them, for to go up to the high place.

15 Now the LORD had told Samuel in his ear a day before Saul came, saying,

16 Tomorrow about this time I will send thee a man out of the land of Benjamin, and thou shalt anoint him *to be* captain over my people Israel, that he may save my people out of the hand of the Philistines: for I have looked upon my people, because their cry is come unto me.

17 And when Samuel saw Saul, the LORD said unto him, Behold the man whom I spake to thee of! this same shall reign over my people.

18 Then Saul drew near to Samuel in the gate, and said, Tell me, I pray thee, where the seer's house *is*.

19 And Samuel answered Saul, and said, I *am* the seer: go up before me unto the high place; for ye shall eat with me today, and tomorrow I will let thee go, and will tell thee all that *is* in thine heart.

20 And as for thine asses that were lost three days

NEW LIVING TRANSLATION

5 Finally, they entered the region of Zuph, and Saul said to his servant, "Let's go home. By now my father will be more worried about us than about the donkeys!"

6 But the servant said, "I've just thought of something! There is a man of God who lives here in this town. He is held in high honor by all the people because everything he says comes true. Let's go find him. Perhaps he can tell us which way to go."

7 "But we don't have anything to offer him," Saul replied. "Even our food is gone, and we don't have a thing to give him."

8 "Well," the servant said, "I have one small silver piece.* We can at least offer it to the man of God and see what happens!" 9 (In those days if people wanted a message from God, they would say, "Let's go and ask the seer," for prophets used to be called seers.)

10 "All right," Saul agreed, "let's try it!" So they started into the town where the man of God lived.

11 As they were climbing the hill to the town, they met some young women coming out to draw water. So Saul and his servant asked, "Is the seer here today?"

12 "Yes," they replied. "Stay right on this road. He is at the town gates. He has just arrived to take part in a public sacrifice up at the place of worship. 13 Hurry and catch him before he goes up there to eat. The guests won't begin eating until he arrives to bless the food."

14 So they entered the town, and as they passed through the gates, Samuel was coming out toward them to go up to the place of worship.

15 Now the LORD had told Samuel the previous day, 16 "About this time tomorrow I will send you a man from the land of Benjamin. Anoint him to be the leader of my people, Israel. He will rescue them from the Philistines, for I have looked down on my people in mercy and have heard their cry."

17 When Samuel saw Saul, the LORD said, "That's the man I told you about! He will rule my people."

18 Just then Saul approached Samuel at the gateway and asked, "Can you please tell me where the seer's house is?"

19 "I am the seer!" Samuel replied. "Go up to the place of worship ahead of me. We will eat there together, and in the morning I'll tell you what you want to know and send you on your way. 20 And don't worry about those donkeys that were lost three days

9:8 Hebrew *¼ shekel of silver,* about 0.1 ounces or 3 grams in weight.

KING JAMES VERSION

ago, set not thy mind on them; for they are found.
And on whom *is* all the desire of Israel? *Is it* not on
thee, and on all thy father's house?
21 And Saul answered and said, *Am* not I a Benjamite, of the smallest of the tribes of Israel? and my
family the least of all the families of the tribe of Benjamin? wherefore then speakest thou so to me?
22 And Samuel took Saul and his servant, and
brought them into the parlour, and made them sit in
the chiefest place among them that were bidden,
which *were* about thirty persons.
23 And Samuel said unto the cook, Bring the portion which I gave thee, of which I said unto thee, Set
it by thee.
24 And the cook took up the shoulder, and *that*
which *was* upon it, and set *it* before Saul. And *Samuel* said, Behold that which is left! set *it* before thee,
and eat: for unto this time hath it been kept for thee
since I said, I have invited the people. So Saul did eat
with Samuel that day.
25 And when they were come down from the high
place into the city, *Samuel* communed with Saul
upon the top of the house.
26 And they arose early: and it came to pass about
the spring of the day, that Samuel called Saul to the
top of the house, saying, Up, that I may send thee
away. And Saul arose, and they went out both of
them, he and Samuel, abroad.
27 *And* as they were going down to the end of the
city, Samuel said to Saul, Bid the servant pass on before us, (and he passed on,) but stand thou still a
while, that I may shew thee the word of God.

10 1 Then Samuel took a vial of oil, and poured *it*
upon his head, and kissed him, and said, *Is it*
not because the LORD hath anointed thee *to be* captain over his inheritance?
2 When thou art departed from me today, then
thou shalt find two men by Rachel's sepulchre in the
border of Benjamin at Zelzah; and they will say unto
thee, The asses which thou wentest to seek are
found: and, lo, thy father hath left the care of the
asses, and sorroweth for you, saying, What shall I do
for my son?
3 Then shalt thou go on forward from thence, and
thou shalt come to the plain of Tabor, and there shall
meet thee three men going up to God to Bethel, one
carrying three kids, and another carrying three loaves
of bread, and another carrying a bottle of wine:
4 And they will salute thee, and give thee two *loaves*
of bread; which thou shalt receive of their hands.
5 After that thou shalt come to the hill of God,
where *is* the garrison of the Philistines: and it shall
come to pass, when thou art come thither to the city,
that thou shalt meet a company of prophets coming
down from the high place with a psaltery, and a tabret, and a pipe, and a harp, before them; and they
shall prophesy:

NEW LIVING TRANSLATION

ago, for they have been found. And I am here to tell
you that you and your family are the focus of all
Israel's hopes."
21 Saul replied, "But I'm only from the tribe of Benjamin, the smallest tribe in Israel, and my family is
the least important of all the families of that tribe!
Why are you talking like this to me?"
22 Then Samuel brought Saul and his servant into
the hall and placed them at the head of the table,
honoring them above the thirty special guests.
23 Samuel then instructed the cook to bring Saul the
finest cut of meat, the piece that had been set aside
for the guest of honor. 24 So the cook brought in the
meat and placed it before Saul. "Go ahead and eat it,"
Samuel said. "I was saving it for you even before I invited these others!" So Saul ate with Samuel that day.
25 When they came down from the place of worship and returned to town, Samuel took Saul up to the
roof of the house and prepared a bed for him there.*
26 At daybreak the next morning, Samuel called to
Saul, "Get up! It's time you were on your way." So Saul
got ready, and he and Samuel left the house together.
27 When they reached the edge of town, Samuel told
Saul to send his servant on ahead. After the servant
was gone, Samuel said, "Stay here, for I have received a
special message for you from God."

Samuel Anoints Saul as King

10 Then Samuel took a flask of olive oil and
poured it over Saul's head. He kissed Saul
and said, "I am doing this because the LORD has appointed you to be the ruler over Israel, his special
possession.* 2 When you leave me today, you will see
two men beside Rachel's tomb at Zelzah, on the border of Benjamin. They will tell you that the donkeys
have been found and that your father has stopped
worrying about them and is now worried about you.
He is asking, 'Have you seen my son?'
3 "When you get to the oak of Tabor, you will see
three men coming toward you who are on their way
to worship God at Bethel. One will be bringing three
young goats, another will have three loaves of bread,
and the third will be carrying a wineskin full of wine.
4 They will greet you and offer you two of the loaves,
which you are to accept.
5 "When you arrive at Gibeah of God,* where the
garrison of the Philistines is located, you will meet a
band of prophets coming down from the place of
worship. They will be playing a harp, a tambourine,

9:25 As in Greek version; Hebrew reads *and talked with him there.*
10:1 Greek version reads *over Israel. And you will rule over the LORD's people and save them from their enemies around them. This will be the sign to you that the LORD has appointed you to be leader over his special possession.* **10:5** Hebrew *Gibeath-elohim.*

KING JAMES VERSION

6And the Spirit of the LORD will come upon thee,
and thou shalt prophesy with them, and shalt be
turned into another man.
7And let it be, when these signs are come unto
thee, *that* thou do as occasion serve thee; for God *is*
with thee.
8And thou shalt go down before me to Gilgal; and,
behold, I will come down unto thee, to offer burnt
offerings, *and* to sacrifice sacrifices of peace offerings: seven days shalt thou tarry, till I come to thee,
and shew thee what thou shalt do.
9And it was *so,* that when he had turned his back
to go from Samuel, God gave him another heart: and
all those signs came to pass that day.
10And when they came thither to the hill, behold, a
company of prophets met him; and the Spirit of God
came upon him, and he prophesied among them.
11And it came to pass, when all that knew him
beforetime saw that, behold, he prophesied among
the prophets, then the people said one to another,
What *is* this *that* is come unto the son of Kish? *Is*
Saul also among the prophets?
12And one of the same place answered and said,
But who *is* their father? Therefore it became a proverb, *Is* Saul also among the prophets?
13And when he had made an end of prophesying,
he came to the high place.
14And Saul's uncle said unto him and to his servant, Whither went ye? And he said, To seek the
asses: and when we saw that *they were* no where,
we came to Samuel.
15And Saul's uncle said, Tell me, I pray thee, what
Samuel said unto you.
16And Saul said unto his uncle, He told us plainly
that the asses were found. But of the matter of the
kingdom, whereof Samuel spake, he told him not.
17And Samuel called the people together unto the
LORD to Mizpeh;
18And said unto the children of Israel, Thus saith
the LORD God of Israel, I brought up Israel out of
Egypt, and delivered you out of the hand of the Egyptians, and out of the hand of all kingdoms, *and* of
them that oppressed you:
19And ye have this day rejected your God, who
himself saved you out of all your adversities and your
tribulations; and ye have said unto him, *Nay,* but set
a king over us. Now therefore present yourselves before the LORD by your tribes, and by your thousands.
20And when Samuel had caused all the tribes of Israel to come near, the tribe of Benjamin was taken.
21When he had caused the tribe of Benjamin to
come near by their families, the family of Matri was
taken, and Saul the son of Kish was taken: and when
they sought him, he could not be found.
22Therefore they inquired of the LORD further, if
the man should yet come thither. And the LORD answered, Behold, he hath hid himself among the stuff.
23And they ran and fetched him thence: and when

NEW LIVING TRANSLATION

a flute, and a lyre, and they will be prophesying. 6At
that time the Spirit of the LORD will come powerfully
upon you, and you will prophesy with them. You will
be changed into a different person. 7After these
signs take place, do what must be done, for God is
with you. 8Then go down to Gilgal ahead of me. I will
join you there to sacrifice burnt offerings and peace
offerings. You must wait for seven days until I arrive
and give you further instructions."

Samuel's Signs Are Fulfilled

9As Saul turned and started to leave, God gave him a
new heart, and all Samuel's signs were fulfilled that
day. 10When Saul and his servant arrived at Gibeah,
they saw a group of prophets coming toward them.
Then the Spirit of God came powerfully upon Saul,
and he, too, began to prophesy. 11When those who
knew Saul heard about it, they exclaimed, "What? Is
even Saul a prophet? How did the son of Kish become a prophet?"
12And one of those standing there said, "Can anyone become a prophet, no matter who his father
is?"* So that is the origin of the saying "Is even Saul
a prophet?"
13When Saul had finished prophesying, he went
up to the place of worship. 14"Where have you
been?" Saul's uncle asked him and his servant.
"We were looking for the donkeys," Saul replied,
"but we couldn't find them. So we went to Samuel to
ask him where they were."
15"Oh? And what did he say?" his uncle asked.
16"He told us that the donkeys had already been
found," Saul replied. But Saul didn't tell his uncle
what Samuel said about the kingdom.

Saul Is Acclaimed King

17Later Samuel called all the people of Israel to meet
before the LORD at Mizpah. 18And he said, "This is
what the LORD, the God of Israel, has declared: I
brought you from Egypt and rescued you from the
Egyptians and from all of the nations that were oppressing you. 19But though I have rescued you from
your misery and distress, you have rejected your God
today and have said, 'No, we want a king instead!'
Now, therefore, present yourselves before the LORD
by tribes and clans."
20So Samuel brought all the tribes of Israel before
the LORD, and the tribe of Benjamin was chosen by
lot. 21Then he brought each family of the tribe of
Benjamin before the LORD, and the family of the Ma-
trites was chosen. And finally Saul son of Kish was
chosen from among them. But when they looked for
him, he had disappeared! 22So they asked the LORD,
"Where is he?"
And the LORD replied, "He is hiding among the
baggage." 23So they found him and brought him out,
and he stood head and shoulders above anyone else.

10:12 Hebrew *said, "Who is their father?"*

KING JAMES VERSION

he stood among the people, he was higher than any
of the people from his shoulders and upward.
24And Samuel said to all the people, See ye him
whom the LORD hath chosen, that *there is* none like
him among all the people? And all the people
shouted, and said, God save the king.
25Then Samuel told the people the manner of the
kingdom, and wrote *it* in a book, and laid *it* up before
the LORD. And Samuel sent all the people away, every
man to his house.
26And Saul also went home to Gibeah; and there
went with him a band of men, whose hearts God had
touched.
27But the children of Belial said, How shall this
man save us? And they despised him, and brought
him no presents. But he held his peace.

11 1Then Nahash the Ammonite came up, and
encamped against Jabesh-gilead: and all the
men of Jabesh said unto Nahash, Make a covenant
with us, and we will serve thee.
2And Nahash the Ammonite answered them, On
this *condition* will I make *a covenant* with you, that I
may thrust out all your right eyes, and lay it *for* a
reproach upon all Israel.
3And the elders of Jabesh said unto him, Give us
seven days' respite, that we may send messengers
unto all the coasts of Israel: and then, if *there be* no
man to save us, we will come out to thee.
4Then came the messengers to Gibeah of Saul,
and told the tidings in the ears of the people: and all
the people lifted up their voices, and wept.
5And, behold, Saul came after the herd out of the
field; and Saul said, What *aileth* the people that they
weep? And they told him the tidings of the men of
Jabesh.
6And the Spirit of God came upon Saul when he
heard those tidings, and his anger was kindled
greatly.
7And he took a yoke of oxen, and hewed them in
pieces, and sent *them* throughout all the coasts of Israel by the hands of messengers, saying, Whosoever
cometh not forth after Saul and after Samuel, so
shall it be done unto his oxen. And the fear of the
LORD fell on the people, and they came out with
one consent.
8And when he numbered them in Bezek, the children of Israel were three hundred thousand, and the
men of Judah thirty thousand.

NEW LIVING TRANSLATION

24Then Samuel said to all the people, "This is the
man the LORD has chosen as your king. No one in all
Israel is like him!"
And all the people shouted, "Long live the king!"
25Then Samuel told the people what the rights
and duties of a king were. He wrote them down on a
scroll and placed it before the LORD. Then Samuel
sent the people home again.
26When Saul returned to his home at Gibeah, a
group of men whose hearts God had touched went
with him. 27But there were some scoundrels who
complained, "How can this man save us?" And they
scorned him and refused to bring him gifts. But Saul
ignored them.
[Nahash, king of the Ammonites, had been grievously oppressing the people of Gad and Reuben who
lived east of the Jordan River. He gouged out the
right eye of each of the Israelites living there, and he
didn't allow anyone to come and rescue them. In
fact, of all the Israelites east of the Jordan, there
wasn't a single one whose right eye Nahash had not
gouged out. But there were 7,000 men who had
escaped from the Ammonites, and they had settled
in Jabesh-gilead.]*

Saul Defeats the Ammonites

11 About a month later,* King Nahash of Ammon led his army against the Israelite town
of Jabesh-gilead. But all the citizens of Jabesh asked
for peace. "Make a treaty with us, and we will be your
servants," they pleaded.
2"All right," Nahash said, "but only on one condition. I will gouge out the right eye of every one of you
as a disgrace to all Israel!"
3"Give us seven days to send messengers throughout Israel!" replied the elders of Jabesh. "If no one
comes to save us, we will agree to your terms."
4When the messengers came to Gibeah of Saul
and told the people about their plight, everyone
broke into tears. 5Saul had been plowing a field with
his oxen, and when he returned to town, he asked,
"What's the matter? Why is everyone crying?" So
they told him about the message from Jabesh.
6Then the Spirit of God came powerfully upon
Saul, and he became very angry. 7He took two oxen
and cut them into pieces and sent the messengers
to carry them throughout Israel with this message:
"This is what will happen to the oxen of anyone who
refuses to follow Saul and Samuel into battle!" And
the LORD made the people afraid of Saul's anger, and
all of them came out together as one. 8When Saul
mobilized them at Bezek, he found that there were
300,000 men from Israel and 30,000* men from
Judah.

10:27 This paragraph, which is not included in the Masoretic Text, is found in Dead Sea Scroll 4QSam^a^. **11:1** As in Greek version; Hebrew lacks *About a month later.* **11:8** Dead Sea Scrolls and Greek version read *70,000.*

KING JAMES VERSION

9 And they said unto the messengers that came,
Thus shall ye say unto the men of Jabesh-gilead, Tomorrow, by *that time* the sun be hot, ye shall have
help. And the messengers came and shewed *it* to the
men of Jabesh; and they were glad.
10 Therefore the men of Jabesh said, Tomorrow we
will come out unto you, and ye shall do with us all
that seemeth good unto you.
11 And it was *so* on the morrow, that Saul put the
people in three companies; and they came into the
midst of the host in the morning watch, and slew
the Ammonites until the heat of the day: and it came
to pass, that they which remained were scattered, so
that two of them were not left together.
12 And the people said unto Samuel, Who *is* he that
said, Shall Saul reign over us? bring the men, that we
may put them to death.
13 And Saul said, There shall not a man be put to
death this day: for today the LORD hath wrought
salvation in Israel.
14 Then said Samuel to the people, Come, and let
us go to Gilgal, and renew the kingdom there.
15 And all the people went to Gilgal; and there they
made Saul king before the LORD in Gilgal; and there
they sacrificed sacrifices of peace offerings before
the LORD; and there Saul and all the men of Israel
rejoiced greatly.

12 1 And Samuel said unto all Israel, Behold, I
have hearkened unto your voice in all that ye
said unto me, and have made a king over you.
2 And now, behold, the king walketh before you:
and I am old and grayheaded; and, behold, my sons
are with you: and I have walked before you from my
childhood unto this day.
3 Behold, here I *am*: witness against me before the
LORD, and before his anointed: whose ox have I
taken? or whose ass have I taken? or whom have I
defrauded? whom have I oppressed? or of whose
hand have I received *any* bribe to blind mine eyes
therewith? and I will restore it you.
4 And they said, Thou hast not defrauded us, nor
oppressed us, neither hast thou taken aught of any
man's hand.
5 And he said unto them, The LORD *is* witness
against you, and his anointed *is* witness this day, that
ye have not found aught in my hand. And they answered, *He is* witness.
6 And Samuel said unto the people, *It is* the LORD
that advanced Moses and Aaron, and that brought
your fathers up out of the land of Egypt.
7 Now therefore stand still, that I may reason with
you before the LORD of all the righteous acts of the
LORD, which he did to you and to your fathers.
8 When Jacob was come into Egypt, and your fathers cried unto the LORD, then the LORD sent Moses
and Aaron, which brought forth your fathers out of
Egypt, and made them dwell in this place.

NEW LIVING TRANSLATION

9 So Saul sent the messengers back to Jabesh-
gilead to say, "We will rescue you by noontime tomorrow!" There was great joy throughout the town
when that message arrived!
10 The men of Jabesh then told their enemies, "Tomorrow we will come out to you, and you can do to
us whatever you wish." 11 But before dawn the next
morning, Saul arrived, having divided his army into
three detachments. He launched a surprise attack
against the Ammonites and slaughtered them the
whole morning. The remnant of their army was
so badly scattered that no two of them were left
together.
12 Then the people exclaimed to Samuel, "Now
where are those men who said, 'Why should Saul
rule over us?' Bring them here, and we will kill them!"
13 But Saul replied, "No one will be executed today,
for today the LORD has rescued Israel!"
14 Then Samuel said to the people, "Come, let us all
go to Gilgal to renew the kingdom." 15 So they all
went to Gilgal, and in a solemn ceremony before the
LORD they made Saul king. Then they offered peace
offerings to the LORD, and Saul and all the Israelites
were filled with joy.

Samuel's Farewell Address

12 Then Samuel addressed all Israel: "I have
done as you asked and given you a king.
2 Your king is now your leader. I stand here before
you—an old, gray-haired man—and my sons serve
you. I have served as your leader from the time I was
a boy to this very day. 3 Now testify against me in
the presence of the LORD and before his anointed
one. Whose ox or donkey have I stolen? Have I ever
cheated any of you? Have I ever oppressed you? Have
I ever taken a bribe and perverted justice? Tell me
and I will make right whatever I have done wrong."
4 "No," they replied, "you have never cheated or oppressed us, and you have never taken even a single
bribe."
5 "The LORD and his anointed one are my witnesses today," Samuel declared, "that my hands are
clean."
"Yes, he is a witness," they replied.
6 "It was the LORD who appointed Moses and
Aaron," Samuel continued. "He brought your ancestors out of the land of Egypt. 7 Now stand here quietly
before the LORD as I remind you of all the great
things the LORD has done for you and your ancestors.
8 "When the Israelites were* in Egypt and cried
out to the LORD, he sent Moses and Aaron to rescue
them from Egypt and to bring them into this land.

12:8 Hebrew *When Jacob was.* The names "Jacob" and "Israel" are often interchanged throughout the Old Testament, referring sometimes to the individual patriarch and sometimes to the nation.

KING JAMES VERSION

9And when they forgat the LORD their God, he sold them into the hand of Sisera, captain of the host of Hazor, and into the hand of the Philistines, and into the hand of the king of Moab, and they fought against them.

10And they cried unto the LORD, and said, We have sinned, because we have forsaken the LORD, and have served Baalim and Ashtaroth: but now deliver us out of the hand of our enemies, and we will serve thee.

11And the LORD sent Jerubbaal, and Bedan, and Jephthah, and Samuel, and delivered you out of the hand of your enemies on every side, and ye dwelled safe.

12And when ye saw that Nahash the king of the children of Ammon came against you, ye said unto me, Nay; but a king shall reign over us: when the LORD your God *was* your king.

13Now therefore behold the king whom ye have chosen, *and* whom ye have desired! and, behold, the LORD hath set a king over you.

14If ye will fear the LORD, and serve him, and obey his voice, and not rebel against the commandment of the LORD, then shall both ye and also the king that reigneth over you continue following the LORD your God:

15But if ye will not obey the voice of the LORD, but rebel against the commandment of the LORD, then shall the hand of the LORD be against you, as *it was* against your fathers.

16Now therefore stand and see this great thing, which the LORD will do before your eyes.

17*Is it* not wheat harvest today? I will call unto the LORD, and he shall send thunder and rain; that ye may perceive and see that your wickedness *is* great, which ye have done in the sight of the LORD, in asking you a king.

18So Samuel called unto the LORD; and the LORD sent thunder and rain that day: and all the people greatly feared the LORD and Samuel.

19And all the people said unto Samuel, Pray for thy servants unto the LORD thy God, that we die not: for we have added unto all our sins *this* evil, to ask us a king.

20And Samuel said unto the people, Fear not: ye have done all this wickedness: yet turn not aside from following the LORD, but serve the LORD with all your heart;

21And turn ye not aside: for *then should ye go* after vain *things,* which cannot profit nor deliver; for they *are* vain.

22For the LORD will not forsake his people for his great name's sake: because it hath pleased the LORD to make you his people.

23Moreover as for me, God forbid that I should sin against the LORD in ceasing to pray for you: but I will teach you the good and the right way:

24Only fear the LORD, and serve him in truth with all your heart; for consider how great *things* he hath done for you.

NEW LIVING TRANSLATION

9But the people soon forgot about the LORD their
God, so he handed them over to Sisera, the commander of Hazor's army, and also to the Philistines
and to the king of Moab, who fought against them.
10"Then they cried to the LORD again and confessed, 'We have sinned by turning away from the
LORD and worshiping the images of Baal and Ashtoreth. But we will worship you and you alone if you
will rescue us from our enemies.' 11Then the LORD
sent Gideon,* Bedan,* Jephthah, and Samuel* to save
you, and you lived in safety.
12"But when you were afraid of Nahash, the king
of Ammon, you came to me and said that you wanted
a king to reign over you, even though the LORD your
God was already your king. 13All right, here is the
king you have chosen. You asked for him, and the
LORD has granted your request.
14"Now if you fear and worship the LORD and listen
to his voice, and if you do not rebel against the LORD's
commands, then both you and your king will show
that you recognize the LORD as your God. 15But if you
rebel against the LORD's commands and refuse to listen to him, then his hand will be as heavy upon you as
it was upon your ancestors.
16"Now stand here and see the great thing the
LORD is about to do. 17You know that it does not rain
at this time of the year during the wheat harvest. I
will ask the LORD to send thunder and rain today.
Then you will realize how wicked you have been in
asking the LORD for a king!"
18So Samuel called to the LORD, and the LORD sent
thunder and rain that day. And all the people were
terrified of the LORD and of Samuel. 19"Pray to the
LORD your God for us, or we will die!" they all said to
Samuel. "For now we have added to our sins by asking for a king."
20"Don't be afraid," Samuel reassured them. "You
have certainly done wrong, but make sure now that
you worship the LORD with all your heart, and don't
turn your back on him. 21Don't go back to worshiping worthless idols that cannot help or rescue you—
they are totally useless! 22The LORD will not abandon
his people, because that would dishonor his great
name. For it has pleased the LORD to make you his
very own people.
23"As for me, I will certainly not sin against the
LORD by ending my prayers for you. And I will continue to teach you what is good and right. 24But be
sure to fear the LORD and faithfully serve him. Think
of all the wonderful things he has done for you.

12:11a Hebrew *Jerub-baal,* another name for Gideon; see Judg 6:32. **12:11b** Greek and Syriac versions read *Barak.* **12:11c** Greek and Syriac versions read *Samson.*

KING JAMES VERSION

25 But if ye shall still do wickedly, ye shall be consumed, both ye and your king.

13

1 Saul reigned one year; and when he had reigned two years over Israel,

2 Saul chose him three thousand *men* of Israel; *whereof* two thousand were with Saul in Michmash and in mount Bethel, and a thousand were with Jonathan in Gibeah of Benjamin: and the rest of the people he sent every man to his tent.

3 And Jonathan smote the garrison of the Philistines that *was* in Geba, and the Philistines heard *of it*. And Saul blew the trumpet throughout all the land, saying, Let the Hebrews hear.

4 And all Israel heard say *that* Saul had smitten a garrison of the Philistines, and *that* Israel also was had in abomination with the Philistines. And the people were called together after Saul to Gilgal.

5 And the Philistines gathered themselves together to fight with Israel, thirty thousand chariots, and six thousand horsemen, and people as the sand which *is* on the sea shore in multitude: and they came up, and pitched in Michmash, eastward from Beth-aven.

6 When the men of Israel saw that they were in a strait, (for the people were distressed,) then the people did hide themselves in caves, and in thickets, and in rocks, and in high places, and in pits.

7 And *some of* the Hebrews went over Jordan to the land of Gad and Gilead. As for Saul, he *was* yet in Gilgal, and all the people followed him trembling.

8 And he tarried seven days, according to the set time that Samuel *had appointed*: but Samuel came not to Gilgal; and the people were scattered from him.

9 And Saul said, Bring hither a burnt offering to me, and peace offerings. And he offered the burnt offering.

10 And it came to pass, that as soon as he had made an end of offering the burnt offering, behold, Samuel came; and Saul went out to meet him, that he might salute him.

11 And Samuel said, What hast thou done? And Saul said, Because I saw that the people were scattered from me, and *that* thou camest not within the days appointed, and *that* the Philistines gathered themselves together at Michmash;

12 Therefore said I, The Philistines will come down now upon me to Gilgal, and I have not made supplication unto the LORD: I forced myself therefore, and offered a burnt offering.

13 And Samuel said to Saul, Thou hast done foolishly: thou hast not kept the commandment of the LORD thy God, which he commanded thee: for now would the LORD have established thy kingdom upon Israel for ever.

NEW LIVING TRANSLATION

25 But if you continue to sin, you and your king will
be swept away."

Continued War with Philistia

13

Saul was thirty* years old when he became
king, and he reigned for forty-two years.*
2 Saul selected 3,000 special troops from the army
of Israel and sent the rest of the men home. He took
2,000 of the chosen men with him to Micmash
and the hill country of Bethel. The other 1,000 went
with Saul's son Jonathan to Gibeah in the land of
Benjamin.
3 Soon after this, Jonathan attacked and defeated
the garrison of Philistines at Geba. The news spread
quickly among the Philistines. So Saul blew the ram's
horn throughout the land, saying, "Hebrews, hear
this! Rise up in revolt!" 4 All Israel heard the news that
Saul had destroyed the Philistine garrison at Geba
and that the Philistines now hated the Israelites
more than ever. So the entire Israelite army was summoned to join Saul at Gilgal.
5 The Philistines mustered a mighty army of
3,000* chariots, 6,000 charioteers, and as many
warriors as the grains of sand on the seashore! They
camped at Micmash east of Beth-aven. 6 The men of
Israel saw what a tight spot they were in; and because
they were hard pressed by the enemy, they tried to
hide in caves, thickets, rocks, holes, and cisterns.
7 Some of them crossed the Jordan River and escaped
into the land of Gad and Gilead.

Saul's Disobedience and Samuel's Rebuke

Meanwhile, Saul stayed at Gilgal, and his men were
trembling with fear. 8 Saul waited there seven days for
Samuel, as Samuel had instructed him earlier, but
Samuel still didn't come. Saul realized that his troops
were rapidly slipping away. 9 So he demanded, "Bring
me the burnt offering and the peace offerings!" And
Saul sacrificed the burnt offering himself.
10 Just as Saul was finishing with the burnt offering, Samuel arrived. Saul went out to meet and
welcome him, 11 but Samuel said, "What is this you
have done?"

Saul replied, "I saw my men scattering from me,
and you didn't arrive when you said you would, and
the Philistines are at Micmash ready for battle. 12 So I
said, 'The Philistines are ready to march against us at
Gilgal, and I haven't even asked for the LORD's help!'
So I felt compelled to offer the burnt offering myself
before you came."
13 "How foolish!" Samuel exclaimed. "You have
not kept the command the LORD your God gave you.
Had you kept it, the LORD would have established

13:1a As in a few Greek manuscripts; the number is missing in the Hebrew.
13:1b Hebrew *reigned . . . and two*; the number is incomplete in the Hebrew. Compare Acts 13:21. 13:5 As in Greek and Syriac versions; Hebrew reads *30,000*.

KING JAMES VERSION

14But now thy kingdom shall not continue: the
LORD hath sought him a man after his own heart, and
the LORD hath commanded him *to be* captain over
his people, because thou hast not kept *that* which
the LORD commanded thee.

15And Samuel arose, and gat him up from Gilgal
unto Gibeah of Benjamin. And Saul numbered the
people *that were* present with him, about six hundred men.
16And Saul, and Jonathan his son, and the people
that were present with them, abode in Gibeah of Benjamin: but the Philistines encamped in Michmash.
17And the spoilers came out of the camp of the
Philistines in three companies: one company turned
unto the way *that leadeth to* Ophrah, unto the land
of Shual:
18And another company turned the way *to* Beth-
horon: and another company turned *to* the way of
the border that looketh to the valley of Zeboim toward the wilderness.
19Now there was no smith found throughout all
the land of Israel: for the Philistines said, Lest the
Hebrews make *them* swords or spears:
20But all the Israelites went down to the Philistines, to sharpen every man his share, and his coulter,
and his ax, and his mattock.
21Yet they had a file for the mattocks, and for the
coulters, and for the forks, and for the axes, and to
sharpen the goads.
22So it came to pass in the day of battle, that there
was neither sword nor spear found in the hand of
any of the people that *were* with Saul and Jonathan:
but with Saul and with Jonathan his son was there
found.
23And the garrison of the Philistines went out to
the passage of Michmash.

14 1Now it came to pass upon a day, that Jonathan the son of Saul said unto the young man
that bare his armour, Come, and let us go over to the
Philistines' garrison, that *is* on the other side. But he
told not his father.
2And Saul tarried in the uttermost part of Gibeah
under a pomegranate tree which *is* in Migron: and
the people that *were* with him *were* about six hundred men;
3And Ahiah, the son of Ahitub, Ichabod's brother,
the son of Phinehas, the son of Eli, the LORD's priest
in Shiloh, wearing an ephod. And the people knew
not that Jonathan was gone.
4And between the passages, by which Jonathan
sought to go over unto the Philistines' garrison, *there
was* a sharp rock on the one side, and a sharp rock on
the other side: and the name of the one *was* Bozez,
and the name of the other Seneh.
5The forefront of the one *was* situate northward

NEW LIVING TRANSLATION

your kingdom over Israel forever. 14But now your
kingdom must end, for the LORD has sought out a
man after his own heart. The LORD has already appointed him to be the leader of his people, because
you have not kept the LORD's command."

Israel's Military Disadvantage

15Samuel then left Gilgal and went on his way, but
the rest of the troops went with Saul to meet the
army. They went up from Gilgal to Gibeah in the land
of Benjamin.* When Saul counted the men who
were still with him, he found only 600 were left!
16Saul and Jonathan and the troops with them were
staying at Geba in the land of Benjamin. The Philistines set up their camp at Micmash. 17Three raiding
parties soon left the camp of the Philistines. One
went north toward Ophrah in the land of Shual,
18another went west to Beth-horon, and the third
moved toward the border above the valley of Zeboim near the wilderness.
19There were no blacksmiths in the land of Israel
in those days. The Philistines wouldn't allow them
for fear they would make swords and spears for the
Hebrews. 20So whenever the Israelites needed to
sharpen their plowshares, picks, axes, or sickles,*
they had to take them to a Philistine blacksmith.
21(The charges were as follows: a quarter of an ounce
of silver* for sharpening a plowshare or a pick, and
an eighth of an ounce* for sharpening an ax, a sickle,
or an ox goad.) 22So on the day of the battle none of
the people of Israel had a sword or spear, except for
Saul and Jonathan.
23The pass at Micmash had meanwhile been
secured by a contingent of the Philistine army.

Jonathan's Daring Plan

14 One day Jonathan said to his armor bearer,
"Come on, let's go over to where the Philistines have their outpost." But Jonathan did not tell
his father what he was doing.
2Meanwhile, Saul and his 600 men were camped
on the outskirts of Gibeah, around the pomegranate
tree* at Migron. 3Among Saul's men was Ahijah the
priest, who was wearing the ephod, the priestly vest.
Ahijah was the son of Ichabod's brother Ahitub, son
of Phinehas, son of Eli, the priest of the LORD who
had served at Shiloh.
No one realized that Jonathan had left the Israelite
camp. 4To reach the Philistine outpost, Jonathan had
to go down between two rocky cliffs that were called
Bozez and Seneh. 5The cliff on the north was in front

13:15 As in Greek version; Hebrew reads *Samuel then left Gilgal and went to Gibeah in the land of Benjamin.* **13:20** As in Greek version; Hebrew reads *or plowshares.* **13:21a** Hebrew *1 pim* [8 grams]. **13:21b** Hebrew *⅓ of a shekel* [4 grams]. **14:2** Or *around the rock of Rimmon;* compare Judg 20:45, 47; 21:13.

over against Michmash, and the other southward
over against Gibeah.
6And Jonathan said to the young man that bare his
armour, Come, and let us go over unto the garrison of
these uncircumcised: it may be that the LORD will
work for us: for *there is* no restraint to the LORD to
save by many or by few.
7And his armourbearer said unto him, Do all that
is in thine heart: turn thee; behold, I *am* with thee
according to thy heart.
8Then said Jonathan, Behold, we will pass over
unto *these* men, and we will discover ourselves unto
them.
9If they say thus unto us, Tarry until we come to
you; then we will stand still in our place, and will not
go up unto them.
10But if they say thus, Come up unto us; then we
will go up: for the LORD hath delivered them into our
hand: and this *shall be* a sign unto us.
11And both of them discovered themselves unto
the garrison of the Philistines: and the Philistines
said, Behold, the Hebrews come forth out of the
holes where they had hid themselves.
12And the men of the garrison answered Jonathan
and his armourbearer, and said, Come up to us, and
we will shew you a thing. And Jonathan said unto his
armourbearer, Come up after me: for the LORD hath
delivered them into the hand of Israel.
13And Jonathan climbed up upon his hands and
upon his feet, and his armourbearer after him: and
they fell before Jonathan; and his armourbearer slew
after him.
14And that first slaughter, which Jonathan and his
armourbearer made, was about twenty men, within
as it were an half acre of land, *which* a yoke *of oxen
might plow.*
15And there was trembling in the host, in the field,
and among all the people: the garrison, and the spoilers, they also trembled, and the earth quaked: so it
was a very great trembling.
16And the watchmen of Saul in Gibeah of Benjamin looked; and, behold, the multitude melted away,
and they went on beating down *one another.*
17Then said Saul unto the people that *were* with
him, Number now, and see who is gone from us. And
when they had numbered, behold, Jonathan and his
armourbearer *were* not *there.*
18And Saul said unto Ahiah, Bring hither the ark of
God. For the ark of God was at that time with the children of Israel.
19And it came to pass, while Saul talked unto the
priest, that the noise that *was* in the host of the Philistines went on and increased: and Saul said unto
the priest, Withdraw thine hand.
20And Saul and all the people that *were* with him
assembled themselves, and they came to the battle:
and, behold, every man's sword was against his fellow, *and there was* a very great discomfiture.

of Micmash, and the one on the south was in front of
Geba. 6"Let's go across to the outpost of those pagans," Jonathan said to his armor bearer. "Perhaps
the LORD will help us, for nothing can hinder the
LORD. He can win a battle whether he has many warriors or only a few!"
7"Do what you think is best," the armor bearer
replied. "I'm with you completely, whatever you
decide."
8"All right then," Jonathan told him. "We will cross
over and let them see us. 9If they say to us, 'Stay
where you are or we'll kill you,' then we will stop and
not go up to them. 10But if they say, 'Come on up and
fight,' then we will go up. That will be the LORD's sign
that he will help us defeat them."
11When the Philistines saw them coming, they
shouted, "Look! The Hebrews are crawling out of
their holes!" 12Then the men from the outpost
shouted to Jonathan, "Come on up here, and we'll
teach you a lesson!"
"Come on, climb right behind me," Jonathan said
to his armor bearer, "for the LORD will help us defeat
them!"
13So they climbed up using both hands and feet,
and the Philistines fell before Jonathan, and his armor bearer killed those who came behind them.
14They killed some twenty men in all, and their
bodies were scattered over about half an acre.*
15Suddenly, panic broke out in the Philistine army,
both in the camp and in the field, including even the
outposts and raiding parties. And just then an earthquake struck, and everyone was terrified.

Israel Defeats the Philistines

16Saul's lookouts in Gibeah of Benjamin saw a
strange sight—the vast army of Philistines began to
melt away in every direction. 17"Call the roll and find
out who's missing," Saul ordered. And when they
checked, they found that Jonathan and his armor
bearer were gone.
18Then Saul shouted to Ahijah, "Bring the ephod
here!" For at that time Ahijah was wearing the ephod
in front of the Israelites.* 19But while Saul was talking to the priest, the confusion in the Philistine camp
grew louder and louder. So Saul said to the priest,
"Never mind; let's get going!"*
20Then Saul and all his men rushed out to the
battle and found the Philistines killing each other.

14:14 Hebrew *half a yoke;* a "yoke" was the amount of land plowed by a pair of yoked oxen in one day. **14:18** As in some Greek manuscripts; Hebrew reads *"Bring the Ark of God." For at that time the Ark of God was with the Israelites.* **14:19** Hebrew *Withdraw your hand.*

KING JAMES VERSION

21 Moreover the Hebrews *that* were with the Philistines before that time, which went up with them
into the camp *from the country* round about, even
they also *turned* to be with the Israelites that *were*
with Saul and Jonathan.
22 Likewise all the men of Israel which had hid
themselves in mount Ephraim, *when* they heard that
the Philistines fled, even they also followed hard
after them in the battle.
23 So the LORD saved Israel that day: and the battle
passed over unto Beth-aven.
24 And the men of Israel were distressed that day:
for Saul had adjured the people, saying, Cursed *be*
the man that eateth *any* food until evening, that I
may be avenged on mine enemies. So none of the
people tasted *any* food.
25 And all *they of* the land came to a wood; and
there was honey upon the ground.
26 And when the people were come into the wood,
behold, the honey dropped; but no man put his hand
to his mouth: for the people feared the oath.
27 But Jonathan heard not when his father charged
the people with the oath: wherefore he put forth the
end of the rod that *was* in his hand, and dipped it in
an honeycomb, and put his hand to his mouth; and
his eyes were enlightened.
28 Then answered one of the people, and said, Thy
father straitly charged the people with an oath, saying, Cursed *be* the man that eateth *any* food this day.
And the people were faint.
29 Then said Jonathan, My father hath troubled the
land: see, I pray you, how mine eyes have been enlightened, because I tasted a little of this honey.
30 How much more, if haply the people had eaten
freely today of the spoil of their enemies which they
found? for had there not been now a much greater
slaughter among the Philistines?
31 And they smote the Philistines that day from
Michmash to Aijalon: and the people were very faint.
32 And the people flew upon the spoil, and took
sheep, and oxen, and calves, and slew *them* on the
ground: and the people did eat *them* with the blood.
33 Then they told Saul, saying, Behold, the people
sin against the LORD, in that they eat with the blood.
And he said, Ye have transgressed: roll a great stone
unto me this day.
34 And Saul said, Disperse yourselves among the
people, and say unto them, Bring me hither every
man his ox, and every man his sheep, and slay *them*
here, and eat; and sin not against the LORD in eating
with the blood. And all the people brought every
man his ox with him that night, and slew *them* there.
35 And Saul built an altar unto the LORD: the same
was the first altar that he built unto the LORD.
36 And Saul said, Let us go down after the Philistines by night, and spoil them until the morning
light, and let us not leave a man of them. And they

NEW LIVING TRANSLATION

There was terrible confusion everywhere. 21 Even the
Hebrews who had previously gone over to the Philistine army revolted and joined in with Saul, Jonathan,
and the rest of the Israelites. 22 Likewise, the men of
Israel who were hiding in the hill country of Ephraim
joined the chase when they saw the Philistines running away. 23 So the LORD saved Israel that day, and
the battle continued to rage even beyond Beth-aven.

Saul's Foolish Oath

24 Now the men of Israel were pressed to exhaustion
that day, because Saul had placed them under an
oath, saying, "Let a curse fall on anyone who eats before evening—before I have full revenge on my enemies." So no one ate anything all day, 25 even though
they had all found honeycomb on the ground in the
forest. 26 They didn't dare touch the honey because
they all feared the oath they had taken.
27 But Jonathan had not heard his father's command, and he dipped the end of his stick into a piece
of honeycomb and ate the honey. After he had eaten
it, he felt refreshed.* 28 But one of the men saw him
and said, "Your father made the army take a strict
oath that anyone who eats food today will be cursed.
That is why everyone is weary and faint."
29 "My father has made trouble for us all!" Jonathan exclaimed. "A command like that only hurts us.
See how refreshed I am now that I have eaten this
little bit of honey. 30 If the men had been allowed to
eat freely from the food they found among our enemies, think how many more Philistines we could
have killed!"
31 They chased and killed the Philistines all day
from Micmash to Aijalon, growing more and more
faint. 32 That evening they rushed for the battle
plunder and butchered the sheep, goats, cattle, and
calves, but they ate them without draining the
blood. 33 Someone reported to Saul, "Look, the men
are sinning against the LORD by eating meat that still
has blood in it."
"That is very wrong," Saul said. "Find a large stone
and roll it over here. 34 Then go out among the troops
and tell them, 'Bring the cattle, sheep, and goats here
to me. Kill them here, and drain the blood before you
eat them. Do not sin against the LORD by eating meat
with the blood still in it.'"
So that night all the troops brought their animals
and slaughtered them there. 35 Then Saul built an altar to the LORD; it was the first of the altars he built
to the LORD.
36 Then Saul said, "Let's chase the Philistines all
night and plunder them until sunrise. Let's destroy
every last one of them."
His men replied, "We'll do whatever you think is
best."

14:27 Or *his eyes brightened;* similarly in 14:29.

KING JAMES VERSION

said, Do whatsoever seemeth good unto thee. Then
said the priest, Let us draw near hither unto God.
37 And Saul asked counsel of God, Shall I go down
after the Philistines? wilt thou deliver them into the
hand of Israel? But he answered him not that day.
38 And Saul said, Draw ye near hither, all the chief
of the people: and know and see wherein this sin
hath been this day.
39 For, *as* the LORD liveth, which saveth Israel,
though it be in Jonathan my son, he shall surely die.
But *there was* not a man among all the people *that*
answered him.
40 Then said he unto all Israel, Be ye on one side,
and I and Jonathan my son will be on the other side.
And the people said unto Saul, Do what seemeth
good unto thee.
41 Therefore Saul said unto the LORD God of Israel,
Give a perfect *lot*. And Saul and Jonathan were taken:
but the people escaped.
42 And Saul said, Cast *lots* between me and Jonathan my son. And Jonathan was taken.
43 Then Saul said to Jonathan, Tell me what thou
hast done. And Jonathan told him, and said, I did but
taste a little honey with the end of the rod that *was* in
mine hand, *and*, lo, I must die.
44 And Saul answered, God do so and more also: for
thou shalt surely die, Jonathan.
45 And the people said unto Saul, Shall Jonathan
die, who hath wrought this great salvation in Israel?
God forbid: *as* the LORD liveth, there shall not one
hair of his head fall to the ground; for he hath
wrought with God this day. So the people rescued
Jonathan, that he died not.
46 Then Saul went up from following the Philistines: and the Philistines went to their own place.

47 So Saul took the kingdom over Israel, and fought
against all his enemies on every side, against Moab,
and against the children of Ammon, and against
Edom, and against the kings of Zobah, and against
the Philistines: and whithersoever he turned himself, he vexed *them*.
48 And he gathered an host, and smote the Amalekites, and delivered Israel out of the hands of them
that spoiled them.
49 Now the sons of Saul were Jonathan, and Ishui,
and Melchi-shua: and the names of his two daughters *were these;* the name of the firstborn Merab,
and the name of the younger Michal:
50 And the name of Saul's wife *was* Ahinoam, the
daughter of Ahimaaz: and the name of the captain of
his host *was* Abner, the son of Ner, Saul's uncle.

NEW LIVING TRANSLATION

But the priest said, "Let's ask God first."
37 So Saul asked God, "Should we go after the Philistines? Will you help us defeat them?" But God
made no reply that day.
38 Then Saul said to the leaders, "Something's
wrong! I want all my army commanders to come
here. We must find out what sin was committed
today. 39 I vow by the name of the LORD who rescued
Israel that the sinner will surely die, even if it is my
own son Jonathan!" But no one would tell him what
the trouble was.
40 Then Saul said, "Jonathan and I will stand over
here, and all of you stand over there."
And the people responded to Saul, "Whatever you
think is best."
41 Then Saul prayed, "O LORD, God of Israel, please
show us who is guilty and who is innocent.*" Then
they cast sacred lots, and Jonathan and Saul were
chosen as the guilty ones, and the people were declared innocent.
42 Then Saul said, "Now cast lots again and choose
between me and Jonathan." And Jonathan was
shown to be the guilty one.
43 "Tell me what you have done," Saul demanded
of Jonathan.
"I tasted a little honey," Jonathan admitted. "It was
only a little bit on the end of my stick. Does that deserve death?"
44 "Yes, Jonathan," Saul said, "you must die! May
God strike me and even kill me if you do not die
for this."
45 But the people broke in and said to Saul, "Jonathan has won this great victory for Israel. Should he
die? Far from it! As surely as the LORD lives, not one
hair on his head will be touched, for God helped him
do a great deed today." So the people rescued Jonathan, and he was not put to death.
46 Then Saul called back the army from chasing
the Philistines, and the Philistines returned home.

Saul's Military Successes

47 Now when Saul had secured his grasp on Israel's
throne, he fought against his enemies in every direction—against Moab, Ammon, Edom, the kings of
Zobah, and the Philistines. And wherever he turned,
he was victorious.* 48 He performed great deeds and
conquered the Amalekites, saving Israel from all
those who had plundered them.
49 Saul's sons included Jonathan, Ishbosheth,*
and Malkishua. He also had two daughters: Merab,
who was older, and Michal. 50 Saul's wife was Ahinoam, the daughter of Ahimaaz. The commander of
Saul's army was Abner, the son of Saul's uncle Ner.

14:41 Greek version adds *If the fault is with me or my son Jonathan, respond with Urim; but if the men of Israel are at fault, respond with Thummim.* **14:47** As in Greek version; Hebrew reads *he acted wickedly.* **14:49** Hebrew *Ishvi*, a variant name for Ishbosheth; also known as Esh-baal.

KING JAMES VERSION

[51]And Kish *was* the father of Saul; and Ner the father of Abner *was* the son of Abiel.

[52]And there was sore war against the Philistines all the days of Saul: and when Saul saw any strong man, or any valiant man, he took him unto him.

15 [1]Samuel also said unto Saul, The LORD sent me to anoint thee *to be* king over his people, over Israel: now therefore hearken thou unto the voice of the words of the LORD.

[2]Thus saith the LORD of hosts, I remember *that* which Amalek did to Israel, how he laid *wait* for him in the way, when he came up from Egypt.

[3]Now go and smite Amalek, and utterly destroy all that they have, and spare them not; but slay both man and woman, infant and suckling, ox and sheep, camel and ass.

[4]And Saul gathered the people together, and numbered them in Telaim, two hundred thousand footmen, and ten thousand men of Judah.

[5]And Saul came to a city of Amalek, and laid wait in the valley.

[6]And Saul said unto the Kenites, Go, depart, get you down from among the Amalekites, lest I destroy you with them: for ye shewed kindness to all the children of Israel, when they came up out of Egypt. So the Kenites departed from among the Amalekites.

[7]And Saul smote the Amalekites from Havilah *until* thou comest to Shur, that *is* over against Egypt.

[8]And he took Agag the king of the Amalekites alive, and utterly destroyed all the people with the edge of the sword.

[9]But Saul and the people spared Agag, and the best of the sheep, and of the oxen, and of the fatlings, and the lambs, and all *that was* good, and would not utterly destroy them: but every thing *that was* vile and refuse, that they destroyed utterly.

[10]Then came the word of the LORD unto Samuel, saying,

[11]It repenteth me that I have set up Saul *to be* king: for he is turned back from following me, and hath not performed my commandments. And it grieved Samuel; and he cried unto the LORD all night.

[12]And when Samuel rose early to meet Saul in the morning, it was told Samuel, saying, Saul came to Carmel, and, behold, he set him up a place, and is gone about, and passed on, and gone down to Gilgal.

[13]And Samuel came to Saul: and Saul said unto him, Blessed *be* thou of the LORD: I have performed the commandment of the LORD.

[14]And Samuel said, What *meaneth* then this bleating of the sheep in mine ears, and the lowing of the oxen which I hear?

[15]And Saul said, They have brought them from the Amalekites: for the people spared the best of the

NEW LIVING TRANSLATION

[51]Saul's father, Kish, and Abner's father, Ner, were both sons of Abiel.

[52]The Israelites fought constantly with the Philistines throughout Saul's lifetime. So whenever Saul observed a young man who was brave and strong, he drafted him into his army.

Saul Destroys the Amalekites

15 One day Samuel said to Saul, "It was the LORD who told me to anoint you as king of his people, Israel. Now listen to this message from the LORD!
[2]This is what the LORD of Heaven's Armies has declared: I have decided to settle accounts with the nation of Amalek for opposing Israel when they came
from Egypt. [3]Now go and completely destroy* the entire Amalekite nation—men, women, children, babies, cattle, sheep, goats, camels, and donkeys."

[4]So Saul mobilized his army at Telaim. There were 200,000 soldiers from Israel and 10,000 men from
Judah. [5]Then Saul and his army went to a town of the
Amalekites and lay in wait in the valley. [6]Saul sent
this warning to the Kenites: "Move away from where the Amalekites live, or you will die with them. For you showed kindness to all the people of Israel when they came up from Egypt." So the Kenites packed up and left.

[7]Then Saul slaughtered the Amalekites from Havilah all the way to Shur, east of Egypt. [8]He captured
Agag, the Amalekite king, but completely destroyed
everyone else. [9]Saul and his men spared Agag's life
and kept the best of the sheep and goats, the cattle, the fat calves, and the lambs—everything, in fact, that appealed to them. They destroyed only what was worthless or of poor quality.

The LORD Rejects Saul

[10]Then the LORD said to Samuel, [11]"I am sorry that I
ever made Saul king, for he has not been loyal to me and has refused to obey my command." Samuel was so deeply moved when he heard this that he cried out to the LORD all night.

[12]Early the next morning Samuel went to find Saul. Someone told him, "Saul went to the town of Carmel to set up a monument to himself; then he went on to Gilgal."

[13]When Samuel finally found him, Saul greeted him cheerfully. "May the LORD bless you," he said. "I have carried out the LORD's command!"

[14]"Then what is all the bleating of sheep and goats and the lowing of cattle I hear?" Samuel demanded.

[15]"It's true that the army spared the best of the sheep, goats, and cattle," Saul admitted. "But they are

15:3 The Hebrew term used here refers to the complete consecration of things or people to the LORD, either by destroying them or by giving them as an offering; also in 15:8, 9, 15, 18, 20, 21.

KING JAMES VERSION

sheep and of the oxen, to sacrifice unto the LORD thy God; and the rest we have utterly destroyed.

16 Then Samuel said unto Saul, Stay, and I will tell thee what the LORD hath said to me this night. And he said unto him, Say on.

17 And Samuel said, When thou *wast* little in thine own sight, *wast* thou not *made* the head of the tribes of Israel, and the LORD anointed thee king over Israel? 18 And the LORD sent thee on a journey, and said, Go and utterly destroy the sinners the Amalekites, and fight against them until they be consumed. 19 Wherefore then didst thou not obey the voice of the LORD, but didst fly upon the spoil, and didst evil in the sight of the LORD?

20 And Saul said unto Samuel, Yea, I have obeyed the voice of the LORD, and have gone the way which the LORD sent me, and have brought Agag the king of Amalek, and have utterly destroyed the Amalekites. 21 But the people took of the spoil, sheep and oxen, the chief of the things which should have been utterly destroyed, to sacrifice unto the LORD thy God in Gilgal.

22 And Samuel said, Hath the LORD *as great* delight in burnt offerings and sacrifices, as in obeying the voice of the LORD? Behold, to obey *is* better than sacrifice, *and* to hearken than the fat of rams. 23 For rebellion *is as* the sin of witchcraft, and stubbornness *is as* iniquity and idolatry. Because thou hast rejected the word of the LORD, he hath also rejected thee from *being* king.

24 And Saul said unto Samuel, I have sinned: for I have transgressed the commandment of the LORD, and thy words: because I feared the people, and obeyed their voice. 25 Now therefore, I pray thee, pardon my sin, and turn again with me, that I may worship the LORD. 26 And Samuel said unto Saul, I will not return with thee: for thou hast rejected the word of the LORD, and the LORD hath rejected thee from being king over Israel. 27 And as Samuel turned about to go away, he laid hold upon the skirt of his mantle, and it rent. 28 And Samuel said unto him, The LORD hath rent the kingdom of Israel from thee this day, and hath given it to a neighbour of thine, *that is* better than thou. 29 And also the Strength of Israel will not lie nor repent: for he *is* not a man, that he should repent. 30 Then he said, I have sinned: *yet* honour me now, I pray thee, before the elders of my people, and before Israel, and turn again with me, that I may worship the LORD thy God. 31 So Samuel turned again after Saul; and Saul worshipped the LORD.

NEW LIVING TRANSLATION

going to sacrifice them to the LORD your God. We have destroyed everything else."

16 Then Samuel said to Saul, "Stop! Listen to what the LORD told me last night!"

"What did he tell you?" Saul asked.

17 And Samuel told him, "Although you may think little of yourself, are you not the leader of the tribes of Israel? The LORD has anointed you king of Israel. 18 And the LORD sent you on a mission and told you, 'Go and completely destroy the sinners, the Amalekites, until they are all dead.' 19 Why haven't you obeyed the LORD? Why did you rush for the plunder and do what was evil in the LORD's sight?"

20 "But I did obey the LORD," Saul insisted. "I carried out the mission he gave me. I brought back King Agag, but I destroyed everyone else. 21 Then my troops brought in the best of the sheep, goats, cattle, and plunder to sacrifice to the LORD your God in Gilgal."

22 But Samuel replied,

"What is more pleasing to the LORD:
your burnt offerings and sacrifices
or your obedience to his voice?
Listen! Obedience is better than sacrifice,
and submission is better than offering the fat of rams.
23 Rebellion is as sinful as witchcraft,
and stubbornness as bad as worshiping idols.
So because you have rejected the command of the LORD,
he has rejected you as king."

Saul Pleads for Forgiveness

24 Then Saul admitted to Samuel, "Yes, I have sinned. I have disobeyed your instructions and the LORD's command, for I was afraid of the people and did what they demanded. 25 But now, please forgive my sin and come back with me so that I may worship the LORD."

26 But Samuel replied, "I will not go back with you! Since you have rejected the LORD's command, he has rejected you as king of Israel."

27 As Samuel turned to go, Saul tried to hold him back and tore the hem of his robe. 28 And Samuel said to him, "The LORD has torn the kingdom of Israel from you today and has given it to someone else—one who is better than you. 29 And he who is the Glory of Israel will not lie, nor will he change his mind, for he is not human that he should change his mind!"

30 Then Saul pleaded again, "I know I have sinned. But please, at least honor me before the elders of my people and before Israel by coming back with me so that I may worship the LORD your God." 31 So Samuel finally agreed and went back with him, and Saul worshiped the LORD.

KING JAMES VERSION

32 Then said Samuel, Bring ye hither to me Agag the king of the Amalekites. And Agag came unto him delicately. And Agag said, Surely the bitterness of death is past.

33 And Samuel said, As thy sword hath made women childless, so shall thy mother be childless among women. And Samuel hewed Agag in pieces before the LORD in Gilgal.

34 Then Samuel went to Ramah; and Saul went up to his house to Gibeah of Saul.

35 And Samuel came no more to see Saul until the day of his death: nevertheless Samuel mourned for Saul: and the LORD repented that he had made Saul king over Israel.

16 1 And the LORD said unto Samuel, How long wilt thou mourn for Saul, seeing I have rejected him from reigning over Israel? fill thine horn with oil, and go, I will send thee to Jesse the Bethlehemite: for I have provided me a king among his sons.

2 And Samuel said, How can I go? if Saul hear *it,* he will kill me. And the LORD said, Take an heifer with thee, and say, I am come to sacrifice to the LORD.

3 And call Jesse to the sacrifice, and I will shew thee what thou shalt do: and thou shalt anoint unto me *him* whom I name unto thee.

4 And Samuel did that which the LORD spake, and came to Bethlehem. And the elders of the town trembled at his coming, and said, Comest thou peaceably?

5 And he said, Peaceably: I am come to sacrifice unto the LORD: sanctify yourselves, and come with me to the sacrifice. And he sanctified Jesse and his sons, and called them to the sacrifice.

6 And it came to pass, when they were come, that he looked on Eliab, and said, Surely the LORD's anointed *is* before him.

7 But the LORD said unto Samuel, Look not on his countenance, or on the height of his stature; because I have refused him: for *the LORD seeth* not as man seeth; for man looketh on the outward appearance, but the LORD looketh on the heart.

8 Then Jesse called Abinadab, and made him pass before Samuel. And he said, Neither hath the LORD chosen this.

9 Then Jesse made Shammah to pass by. And he said, Neither hath the LORD chosen this.

10 Again, Jesse made seven of his sons to pass before Samuel. And Samuel said unto Jesse, The LORD hath not chosen these.

11 And Samuel said unto Jesse, Are here all *thy* children? And he said, There remaineth yet the youngest, and, behold, he keepeth the sheep. And Samuel

NEW LIVING TRANSLATION

Samuel Executes King Agag

32 Then Samuel said, "Bring King Agag to me." Agag
arrived full of hope, for he thought, "Surely the worst
is over, and I have been spared!"* 33 But Samuel said,
"As your sword has killed the sons of many mothers,
now your mother will be childless." And Samuel cut
Agag to pieces before the LORD at Gilgal.
34 Then Samuel went home to Ramah, and Saul
returned to his house at Gibeah of Saul. 35 Samuel
never went to meet with Saul again, but he mourned
constantly for him. And the LORD was sorry he had
ever made Saul king of Israel.

Samuel Anoints David as King

16 Now the LORD said to Samuel, "You have
mourned long enough for Saul. I have rejected him as king of Israel, so fill your flask with
olive oil and go to Bethlehem. Find a man named
Jesse who lives there, for I have selected one of his
sons to be my king."
2 But Samuel asked, "How can I do that? If Saul
hears about it, he will kill me."
"Take a heifer with you," the LORD replied, "and
say that you have come to make a sacrifice to the
LORD. 3 Invite Jesse to the sacrifice, and I will show
you which of his sons to anoint for me."
4 So Samuel did as the LORD instructed. When he
arrived at Bethlehem, the elders of the town came
trembling to meet him. "What's wrong?" they asked.
"Do you come in peace?"
5 "Yes," Samuel replied. "I have come to sacrifice
to the LORD. Purify yourselves and come with me to
the sacrifice." Then Samuel performed the purification rite for Jesse and his sons and invited them to
the sacrifice, too.
6 When they arrived, Samuel took one look at Eliab
and thought, "Surely this is the LORD's anointed!"
7 But the LORD said to Samuel, "Don't judge by his
appearance or height, for I have rejected him. The
LORD doesn't see things the way you see them. People
judge by outward appearance, but the LORD looks at
the heart."
8 Then Jesse told his son Abinadab to step forward
and walk in front of Samuel. But Samuel said, "This
is not the one the LORD has chosen." 9 Next Jesse
summoned Shimea,* but Samuel said, "Neither is
this the one the LORD has chosen." 10 In the same way
all seven of Jesse's sons were presented to Samuel.
But Samuel said to Jesse, "The LORD has not chosen
any of these." 11 Then Samuel asked, "Are these all the
sons you have?"
"There is still the youngest," Jesse replied. "But
he's out in the fields watching the sheep and goats."

15:32 Dead Sea Scrolls and Greek version read *Agag arrived hesitantly, for he thought, "Surely this is the bitterness of death."* **16:9** Hebrew *Shammah,* a variant spelling of Shimea; compare 1 Chr 2:13; 20:7.

KING JAMES VERSION

said unto Jesse, Send and fetch him: for we will not
sit down till he come hither.
12And he sent, and brought him in. Now he *was*
ruddy, *and* withal of a beautiful countenance, and
goodly to look to. And the LORD said, Arise, anoint
him: for this *is* he.
13Then Samuel took the horn of oil, and anointed
him in the midst of his brethren: and the Spirit of the
LORD came upon David from that day forward. So
Samuel rose up, and went to Ramah.

14But the spirit of the LORD departed from Saul,
and an evil spirit from the LORD troubled him.
15And Saul's servants said unto him, Behold now,
an evil spirit from God troubleth thee.
16Let our lord now command thy servants, *which*
are before thee, to seek out a man, *who is* a cunning
player on an harp: and it shall come to pass, when the
evil spirit from God is upon thee, that he shall play
with his hand, and thou shalt be well.
17And Saul said unto his servants, Provide me now
a man that can play well, and bring *him* to me.
18Then answered one of the servants, and said, Behold, I have seen a son of Jesse the Bethlehemite,
that is cunning in playing, and a mighty valiant man,
and a man of war, and prudent in matters, and a
comely person, and the LORD *is* with him.
19Wherefore Saul sent messengers unto Jesse,
and said, Send me David thy son, which *is* with the
sheep.
20And Jesse took an ass *laden* with bread, and a
bottle of wine, and a kid, and sent *them* by David his
son unto Saul.
21And David came to Saul, and stood before him:
and he loved him greatly; and he became his armourbearer.
22And Saul sent to Jesse, saying, Let David, I pray
thee, stand before me; for he hath found favour in
my sight.
23And it came to pass, when the *evil* spirit from
God was upon Saul, that David took an harp, and
played with his hand: so Saul was refreshed, and was
well, and the evil spirit departed from him.

17 1Now the Philistines gathered together their
armies to battle, and were gathered together
at Shochoh, which *belongeth* to Judah, and pitched
between Shochoh and Azekah, in Ephes-dammin.
2And Saul and the men of Israel were gathered together, and pitched by the valley of Elah, and set the
battle in array against the Philistines.
3And the Philistines stood on a mountain on the
one side, and Israel stood on a mountain on the other
side: and *there was* a valley between them.
4And there went out a champion out of the camp
of the Philistines, named Goliath, of Gath, whose
height *was* six cubits and a span.

NEW LIVING TRANSLATION

"Send for him at once," Samuel said. "We will not
sit down to eat until he arrives."
12So Jesse sent for him. He was dark and handsome, with beautiful eyes.
And the LORD said, "This is the one; anoint him."
13So as David stood there among his brothers,
Samuel took the flask of olive oil he had brought and
anointed David with the oil. And the Spirit of the
LORD came powerfully upon David from that day on.
Then Samuel returned to Ramah.

David Serves in Saul's Court
14Now the Spirit of the LORD had left Saul, and the
LORD sent a tormenting spirit* that filled him with
depression and fear.
15Some of Saul's servants said to him, "A tormenting spirit from God is troubling you. 16Let us find a
good musician to play the harp whenever the tormenting spirit troubles you. He will play soothing
music, and you will soon be well again."
17"All right," Saul said. "Find me someone who
plays well, and bring him here."
18One of the servants said to Saul, "One of Jesse's
sons from Bethlehem is a talented harp player. Not
only that—he is a brave warrior, a man of war, and has
good judgment. He is also a fine-looking young man,
and the LORD is with him."
19So Saul sent messengers to Jesse to say, "Send
me your son David, the shepherd." 20Jesse responded by sending David to Saul, along with a
young goat, a donkey loaded with bread, and a wineskin full of wine.
21So David went to Saul and began serving him.
Saul loved David very much, and David became his
armor bearer.
22Then Saul sent word to Jesse asking, "Please let
David remain in my service, for I am very pleased
with him."
23And whenever the tormenting spirit from God
troubled Saul, David would play the harp. Then Saul
would feel better, and the tormenting spirit would
go away.

Goliath Challenges the Israelites
17 The Philistines now mustered their army for
battle and camped between Socoh in Judah
and Azekah at Ephes-dammim. 2Saul countered by
gathering his Israelite troops near the valley of Elah.
3So the Philistines and Israelites faced each other on
opposite hills, with the valley between them.
4Then Goliath, a Philistine champion from Gath,
came out of the Philistine ranks to face the forces of

16:14 Or *an evil spirit;* also in 16:15, 16, 23.

KING JAMES VERSION

5 And *he had* an helmet of brass upon his head, and he *was* armed with a coat of mail; and the weight of the coat *was* five thousand shekels of brass.

6 And *he had* greaves of brass upon his legs, and a target of brass between his shoulders.

7 And the staff of his spear *was* like a weaver's beam; and his spear's head *weighed* six hundred shekels of iron: and one bearing a shield went before him.

8 And he stood and cried unto the armies of Israel, and said unto them, Why are ye come out to set *your* battle in array? *am* not I a Philistine, and ye servants to Saul? choose you a man for you, and let him come down to me.

9 If he be able to fight with me, and to kill me, then will we be your servants: but if I prevail against him, and kill him, then shall ye be our servants, and serve us.

10 And the Philistine said, I defy the armies of Israel this day; give me a man, that we may fight together.

11 When Saul and all Israel heard those words of the Philistine, they were dismayed, and greatly afraid.

12 Now David *was* the son of that Ephrathite of Bethlehem-judah, whose name *was* Jesse; and he had eight sons: and the man went among men *for* an old man in the days of Saul.

13 And the three eldest sons of Jesse went *and* followed Saul to the battle: and the names of his three sons that went to the battle *were* Eliab the firstborn, and next unto him Abinadab, and the third Shammah.

14 And David *was* the youngest: and the three eldest followed Saul.

15 But David went and returned from Saul to feed his father's sheep at Bethlehem.

16 And the Philistine drew near morning and evening, and presented himself forty days.

17 And Jesse said unto David his son, Take now for thy brethren an ephah of this parched *corn,* and these ten loaves, and run to the camp to thy brethren;

18 And carry these ten cheeses unto the captain of *their* thousand, and look how thy brethren fare, and take their pledge.

19 Now Saul, and they, and all the men of Israel, *were* in the valley of Elah, fighting with the Philistines.

20 And David rose up early in the morning, and left the sheep with a keeper, and took, and went, as Jesse had commanded him; and he came to the trench, as the host was going forth to the fight, and shouted for the battle.

21 For Israel and the Philistines had put the battle in array, army against army.

22 And David left his carriage in the hand of the keeper of the carriage, and ran into the army, and came and saluted his brethren.

23 And as he talked with them, behold, there came up the champion, the Philistine of Gath, Goliath by name, out of the armies of the Philistines, and spake according to the same words: and David heard *them*.

NEW LIVING TRANSLATION

Israel. He was over nine feet* tall!
5 He wore a bronze helmet, and his bronze coat of mail weighed 125 pounds.*
6 He also wore bronze leg armor, and he carried a bronze javelin on his shoulder.
7 The shaft of his spear was as heavy and thick as a weaver's beam, tipped with an iron spearhead that weighed 15 pounds.* His armor bearer walked ahead of him carrying a shield.

8 Goliath stood and shouted a taunt across to the Israelites. "Why are you all coming out to fight?" he called. "I am the Philistine champion, but you are only the servants of Saul. Choose one man to come down here and fight me!
9 If he kills me, then we will be your slaves. But if I kill him, you will be our slaves!
10 I defy the armies of Israel today! Send me a man who will fight me!"
11 When Saul and the Israelites heard this, they were terrified and deeply shaken.

Jesse Sends David to Saul's Camp

12 Now David was the son of a man named Jesse, an Ephrathite from Bethlehem in the land of Judah. Jesse was an old man at that time, and he had eight sons.
13 Jesse's three oldest sons—Eliab, Abinadab, and Shimea*—had already joined Saul's army to fight the Philistines.
14 David was the youngest son. David's three oldest brothers stayed with Saul's army,
15 but David went back and forth so he could help his father with the sheep in Bethlehem.

16 For forty days, every morning and evening, the Philistine champion strutted in front of the Israelite army.

17 One day Jesse said to David, "Take this basket* of roasted grain and these ten loaves of bread, and carry them quickly to your brothers.
18 And give these ten cuts of cheese to their captain. See how your brothers are getting along, and bring back a report on how they are doing.*"
19 David's brothers were with Saul and the Israelite army at the valley of Elah, fighting against the Philistines.

20 So David left the sheep with another shepherd and set out early the next morning with the gifts, as Jesse had directed him. He arrived at the camp just as the Israelite army was leaving for the battlefield with shouts and battle cries.
21 Soon the Israelite and Philistine forces stood facing each other, army against army.
22 David left his things with the keeper of supplies and hurried out to the ranks to greet his brothers.
23 As he was talking with them, Goliath, the Philistine champion from Gath, came out from the Philistine ranks. Then David heard him shout his usual taunt to the army of Israel.

17:4 Hebrew *6 cubits and 1 span* [which totals about 9.75 feet or 3 meters]; Dead Sea Scrolls and Greek version read *4 cubits and 1 span* [which totals about 6.75 feet or 2 meters]. **17:5** Hebrew *5,000 shekels* [57 kilograms]. **17:7** Hebrew *600 shekels* [6.8 kilograms]. **17:13** Hebrew *Shammah,* a variant spelling of Shimea; compare 1 Chr 2:13; 20:7. **17:17** Hebrew *ephah* [20 quarts or 22 liters]. **17:18** Hebrew *and take their pledge.*

KING JAMES VERSION

24 And all the men of Israel, when they saw the man, fled from him, and were sore afraid.

25 And the men of Israel said, Have ye seen this man that is come up? surely to defy Israel is he come up: and it shall be, *that* the man who killeth him, the king will enrich him with great riches, and will give him his daughter, and make his father's house free in Israel.

26 And David spake to the men that stood by him, saying, What shall be done to the man that killeth this Philistine, and taketh away the reproach from Israel? for who *is* this uncircumcised Philistine, that he should defy the armies of the living God?

27 And the people answered him after this manner, saying, So shall it be done to the man that killeth him.

28 And Eliab his eldest brother heard when he spake unto the men; and Eliab's anger was kindled against David, and he said, Why camest thou down hither? and with whom hast thou left those few sheep in the wilderness? I know thy pride, and the naughtiness of thine heart; for thou art come down that thou mightest see the battle.

29 And David said, What have I now done? *Is there* not a cause?

30 And he turned from him toward another, and spake after the same manner: and the people answered him again after the former manner.

31 And when the words were heard which David spake, they rehearsed *them* before Saul: and he sent for him.

32 And David said to Saul, Let no man's heart fail because of him; thy servant will go and fight with this Philistine.

33 And Saul said to David, Thou art not able to go against this Philistine to fight with him: for thou *art but* a youth, and he a man of war from his youth.

34 And David said unto Saul, Thy servant kept his father's sheep, and there came a lion, and a bear, and took a lamb out of the flock:

35 And I went out after him, and smote him, and delivered *it* out of his mouth: and when he arose against me, I caught *him* by his beard, and smote him, and slew him.

36 Thy servant slew both the lion and the bear: and this uncircumcised Philistine shall be as one of them, seeing he hath defied the armies of the living God.

37 David said moreover, The LORD that delivered me out of the paw of the lion, and out of the paw of the bear, he will deliver me out of the hand of this Philistine. And Saul said unto David, Go, and the LORD be with thee.

38 And Saul armed David with his armour, and he put an helmet of brass upon his head; also he armed him with a coat of mail.

39 And David girded his sword upon his armour, and he assayed to go; for he had not proved *it*. And David said unto Saul, I cannot go with these; for I have not proved *them*. And David put them off him.

NEW LIVING TRANSLATION

24 As soon as the Israelite army saw him, they
began to run away in fright. 25 "Have you seen the
giant?" the men asked. "He comes out each day to
defy Israel. The king has offered a huge reward to
anyone who kills him. He will give that man one of
his daughters for a wife, and the man's entire family
will be exempted from paying taxes!"
26 David asked the soldiers standing nearby,
"What will a man get for killing this Philistine and
ending his defiance of Israel? Who is this pagan Philistine anyway, that he is allowed to defy the armies
of the living God?"
27 And these men gave David the same reply. They
said, "Yes, that is the reward for killing him."
28 But when David's oldest brother, Eliab, heard
David talking to the men, he was angry. "What are
you doing around here anyway?" he demanded.
"What about those few sheep you're supposed to be
taking care of? I know about your pride and deceit.
You just want to see the battle!"
29 "What have I done now?" David replied. "I was
only asking a question!" 30 He walked over to some
others and asked them the same thing and received
the same answer. 31 Then David's question was reported to King Saul, and the king sent for him.

David Kills Goliath

32 "Don't worry about this Philistine," David told Saul.
"I'll go fight him!"
33 "Don't be ridiculous!" Saul replied. "There's no
way you can fight this Philistine and possibly win!
You're only a boy, and he's been a man of war since
his youth."
34 But David persisted. "I have been taking care of
my father's sheep and goats," he said. "When a lion
or a bear comes to steal a lamb from the flock, 35 I go
after it with a club and rescue the lamb from its
mouth. If the animal turns on me, I catch it by the jaw
and club it to death. 36 I have done this to both lions
and bears, and I'll do it to this pagan Philistine, too,
for he has defied the armies of the living God! 37 The
LORD who rescued me from the claws of the lion and
the bear will rescue me from this Philistine!"

Saul finally consented. "All right, go ahead," he
said. "And may the LORD be with you!"

38 Then Saul gave David his own armor—a bronze
helmet and a coat of mail. 39 David put it on, strapped
the sword over it, and took a step or two to see what it
was like, for he had never worn such things before.

"I can't go in these," he protested to Saul. "I'm not

KING JAMES VERSION

40 And he took his staff in his hand, and chose him
five smooth stones out of the brook, and put them in
a shepherd's bag which he had, even in a scrip; and
his sling *was* in his hand: and he drew near to the
Philistine.
41 And the Philistine came on and drew near unto
David; and the man that bare the shield *went* before him.
42 And when the Philistine looked about, and saw
David, he disdained him: for he was *but* a youth, and
ruddy, and of a fair countenance.
43 And the Philistine said unto David, *Am* I a dog,
that thou comest to me with staves? And the Philistine cursed David by his gods.
44 And the Philistine said to David, Come to me,
and I will give thy flesh unto the fowls of the air, and
to the beasts of the field.
45 Then said David to the Philistine, Thou comest
to me with a sword, and with a spear, and with a
shield: but I come to thee in the name of the LORD of
hosts, the God of the armies of Israel, whom thou
hast defied.
46 This day will the LORD deliver thee into mine
hand; and I will smite thee, and take thine head from
thee; and I will give the carcases of the host of the
Philistines this day unto the fowls of the air, and to
the wild beasts of the earth; that all the earth may
know that there is a God in Israel.
47 And all this assembly shall know that the LORD
saveth not with sword and spear: for the battle *is* the
LORD's, and he will give you into our hands.
48 And it came to pass, when the Philistine arose,
and came and drew nigh to meet David, that David
hasted, and ran toward the army to meet the Philistine.
49 And David put his hand in his bag, and took
thence a stone, and slang *it*, and smote the Philistine
in his forehead, that the stone sunk into his forehead;
and he fell upon his face to the earth.
50 So David prevailed over the Philistine with a
sling and with a stone, and smote the Philistine, and
slew him; but *there was* no sword in the hand of
David.
51 Therefore David ran, and stood upon the Philistine, and took his sword, and drew it out of the
sheath thereof, and slew him, and cut off his head
therewith. And when the Philistines saw their champion was dead, they fled.
52 And the men of Israel and of Judah arose, and
shouted, and pursued the Philistines, until thou
come to the valley, and to the gates of Ekron. And the
wounded of the Philistines fell down by the way to
Shaaraim, even unto Gath, and unto Ekron.
53 And the children of Israel returned from chasing after the Philistines, and they spoiled their tents.
54 And David took the head of the Philistine, and

NEW LIVING TRANSLATION

used to them." So David took them off again. 40 He
picked up five smooth stones from a stream and put
them into his shepherd's bag. Then, armed only with
his shepherd's staff and sling, he started across the
valley to fight the Philistine.
41 Goliath walked out toward David with his shield
bearer ahead of him, 42 sneering in contempt at this
ruddy-faced boy. 43 "Am I a dog," he roared at David,
"that you come at me with a stick?" And he cursed
David by the names of his gods. 44 "Come over here,
and I'll give your flesh to the birds and wild animals!"
Goliath yelled.
45 David replied to the Philistine, "You come to me
with sword, spear, and javelin, but I come to you in
the name of the LORD of Heaven's Armies—the God
of the armies of Israel, whom you have defied. 46 Today the LORD will conquer you, and I will kill you and
cut off your head. And then I will give the dead bodies of your men to the birds and wild animals, and
the whole world will know that there is a God in Israel! 47 And everyone assembled here will know that
the LORD rescues his people, but not with sword and
spear. This is the LORD's battle, and he will give you
to us!"
48 As Goliath moved closer to attack, David quickly
ran out to meet him. 49 Reaching into his shepherd's
bag and taking out a stone, he hurled it with his sling
and hit the Philistine in the forehead. The stone sank
in, and Goliath stumbled and fell face down on the
ground.
50 So David triumphed over the Philistine with
only a sling and a stone, for he had no sword. 51 Then
David ran over and pulled Goliath's sword from its
sheath. David used it to kill him and cut off his head.

Israel Routs the Philistines

When the Philistines saw that their champion was
dead, they turned and ran. 52 Then the men of Israel
and Judah gave a great shout of triumph and rushed
after the Philistines, chasing them as far as Gath*
and the gates of Ekron. The bodies of the dead and
wounded Philistines were strewn all along the road
from Shaaraim, as far as Gath and Ekron. 53 Then the
Israelite army returned and plundered the deserted
Philistine camp. 54 (David took the Philistine's head

17:52 As in some Greek manuscripts; Hebrew reads *a valley*.

KING JAMES VERSION

brought it to Jerusalem; but he put his armour in his tent.

55And when Saul saw David go forth against the Philistine, he said unto Abner, the captain of the host, Abner, whose son *is* this youth? And Abner said, *As* thy soul liveth, O king, I cannot tell.

56And the king said, Inquire thou whose son the stripling *is*.

57And as David returned from the slaughter of the Philistine, Abner took him, and brought him before Saul with the head of the Philistine in his hand.

58And Saul said to him, Whose son *art* thou, *thou* young man? And David answered, I *am* the son of thy servant Jesse the Bethlehemite.

18 1And it came to pass, when he had made an end of speaking unto Saul, that the soul of Jonathan was knit with the soul of David, and Jonathan loved him as his own soul.

2And Saul took him that day, and would let him go no more home to his father's house.

3Then Jonathan and David made a covenant, because he loved him as his own soul.

4And Jonathan stripped himself of the robe that *was* upon him, and gave it to David, and his garments, even to his sword, and to his bow, and to his girdle.

5And David went out whithersoever Saul sent him, *and* behaved himself wisely: and Saul set him over the men of war, and he was accepted in the sight of all the people, and also in the sight of Saul's servants.

6And it came to pass as they came, when David was returned from the slaughter of the Philistine, that the women came out of all cities of Israel, singing and dancing, to meet king Saul, with tabrets, with joy, and with instruments of musick.

7And the women answered *one another* as they played, and said, Saul hath slain his thousands, and David his ten thousands.

8And Saul was very wroth, and the saying displeased him; and he said, They have ascribed unto David ten thousands, and to me they have ascribed *but* thousands: and *what* can he have more but the kingdom?

9And Saul eyed David from that day and forward.

10And it came to pass on the morrow, that the evil spirit from God came upon Saul, and he prophesied in the midst of the house: and David played with his hand, as at other times: and *there was* a javelin in Saul's hand.

11And Saul cast the javelin; for he said, I will smite David even to the wall *with it*. And David avoided out of his presence twice.

12And Saul was afraid of David, because the LORD was with him, and was departed from Saul.

13Therefore Saul removed him from him, and made him his captain over a thousand; and he went out and came in before the people.

NEW LIVING TRANSLATION

to Jerusalem, but he stored the man's armor in his own tent.)

55As Saul watched David go out to fight the Philistine, he asked Abner, the commander of his army, "Abner, whose son is this young man?"

"I really don't know," Abner declared.

56"Well, find out who he is!" the king told him.

57As soon as David returned from killing Goliath, Abner brought him to Saul with the Philistine's head still in his hand. 58"Tell me about your father, young man," Saul said.

And David replied, "His name is Jesse, and we live in Bethlehem."

Saul Becomes Jealous of David

18 After David had finished talking with Saul, he met Jonathan, the king's son. There was an immediate bond between them, for Jonathan loved David. 2From that day on Saul kept David with him and wouldn't let him return home. 3And Jonathan made a solemn pact with David, because he loved him as he loved himself. 4Jonathan sealed the pact by taking off his robe and giving it to David, together with his tunic, sword, bow, and belt.

5Whatever Saul asked David to do, David did it successfully. So Saul made him a commander over the men of war, an appointment that was welcomed by the people and Saul's officers alike.

6When the victorious Israelite army was returning home after David had killed the Philistine, women from all the towns of Israel came out to meet King Saul. They sang and danced for joy with tambourines and cymbals.* 7This was their song:

"Saul has killed his thousands,
and David his ten thousands!"

8This made Saul very angry. "What's this?" he said. "They credit David with ten thousands and me with only thousands. Next they'll be making him their king!" 9So from that time on Saul kept a jealous eye on David.

10The very next day a tormenting spirit* from God overwhelmed Saul, and he began to rave in his house like a madman. David was playing the harp, as he did each day. But Saul had a spear in his hand, 11and he suddenly hurled it at David, intending to pin him to the wall. But David escaped him twice.

12Saul was then afraid of David, for the LORD was with David and had turned away from Saul. 13Finally, Saul sent him away and appointed him commander over 1,000 men, and David faithfully led his troops into battle.

18:6 The type of instrument represented by the word *cymbals* is uncertain.
18:10 Or *an evil spirit*.

KING JAMES VERSION

14And David behaved himself wisely in all his ways; and the LORD *was* with him.

15Wherefore when Saul saw that he behaved himself very wisely, he was afraid of him.

16But all Israel and Judah loved David, because he went out and came in before them.

17And Saul said to David, Behold my elder daughter Merab, her will I give thee to wife: only be thou valiant for me, and fight the LORD's battles. For Saul said, Let not mine hand be upon him, but let the hand of the Philistines be upon him.

18And David said unto Saul, Who *am* I? and what *is* my life, *or* my father's family in Israel, that I should be son in law to the king?

19But it came to pass at the time when Merab Saul's daughter should have been given to David, that she was given unto Adriel the Meholathite to wife.

20And Michal Saul's daughter loved David: and they told Saul, and the thing pleased him.

21And Saul said, I will give him her, that she may be a snare to him, and that the hand of the Philistines may be against him. Wherefore Saul said to David, Thou shalt this day be my son in law in *the one of* the twain.

22And Saul commanded his servants, *saying*, Commune with David secretly, and say, Behold, the king hath delight in thee, and all his servants love thee: now therefore be the king's son in law.

23And Saul's servants spake those words in the ears of David. And David said, Seemeth it to you *a* light *thing* to be a king's son in law, seeing that I *am* a poor man, and lightly esteemed?

24And the servants of Saul told him, saying, On this manner spake David.

25And Saul said, Thus shall ye say to David, The king desireth not any dowry, but an hundred foreskins of the Philistines, to be avenged of the king's enemies. But Saul thought to make David fall by the hand of the Philistines.

26And when his servants told David these words, it pleased David well to be the king's son in law: and the days were not expired.

27Wherefore David arose and went, he and his men, and slew of the Philistines two hundred men; and David brought their foreskins, and they gave them in full tale to the king, that he might be the king's son in law. And Saul gave him Michal his daughter to wife.

28And Saul saw and knew that the LORD *was* with David, and *that* Michal Saul's daughter loved him.

29And Saul was yet the more afraid of David; and Saul became David's enemy continually.

30Then the princes of the Philistines went forth: and it came to pass, after they went forth, *that* David behaved himself more wisely than all the servants of Saul; so that his name was much set by.

NEW LIVING TRANSLATION

14David continued to succeed in everything he
did, for the LORD was with him. 15When Saul recognized this, he became even more afraid of him. 16But
all Israel and Judah loved David because he was so
successful at leading his troops into battle.

David Marries Saul's Daughter

17One day Saul said to David, "I am ready to give you
my older daughter, Merab, as your wife. But first you
must prove yourself to be a real warrior by fighting
the LORD's battles." For Saul thought, "I'll send him
out against the Philistines and let them kill him
rather than doing it myself."

18"Who am I, and what is my family in Israel that I
should be the king's son-in-law?" David exclaimed.
"My father's family is nothing!" 19So* when the time
came for Saul to give his daughter Merab in marriage
to David, he gave her instead to Adriel, a man from
Meholah.

20In the meantime, Saul's daughter Michal had
fallen in love with David, and Saul was delighted
when he heard about it. 21"Here's another chance to
see him killed by the Philistines!" Saul said to himself. But to David he said, "Today you have a second
chance to become my son-in-law!"

22Then Saul told his men to say to David, "The
king really likes you, and so do we. Why don't you accept the king's offer and become his son-in-law?"

23When Saul's men said these things to David, he
replied, "How can a poor man from a humble family
afford the bride price for the daughter of a king?"

24When Saul's men reported this back to the king,
25he told them, "Tell David that all I want for the
bride price is 100 Philistine foreskins! Vengeance on
my enemies is all I really want." But what Saul had in
mind was that David would be killed in the fight.

26David was delighted to accept the offer. Before
the time limit expired, 27he and his men went out
and killed 200 Philistines. Then David fulfilled the
king's requirement by presenting all their foreskins
to him. So Saul gave his daughter Michal to David to
be his wife.

28When Saul realized that the LORD was with David and how much his daughter Michal loved him,
29Saul became even more afraid of him, and he remained David's enemy for the rest of his life.

30Every time the commanders of the Philistines
attacked, David was more successful against them
than all the rest of Saul's officers. So David's name
became very famous.

18:19 Or *But.*

KING JAMES VERSION

19 1And Saul spake to Jonathan his son, and to
all his servants, that they should kill David.
2But Jonathan Saul's son delighted much in David:
and Jonathan told David, saying, Saul my father
seeketh to kill thee: now therefore, I pray thee, take
heed to thyself until the morning, and abide in a secret *place,* and hide thyself:
3And I will go out and stand beside my father in
the field where thou *art,* and I will commune with
my father of thee; and what I see, that I will tell thee.
4And Jonathan spake good of David unto Saul his
father, and said unto him, Let not the king sin against
his servant, against David; because he hath not
sinned against thee, and because his works *have
been* to thee-ward very good:
5For he did put his life in his hand, and slew the
Philistine, and the LORD wrought a great salvation for
all Israel: thou sawest *it,* and didst rejoice: wherefore
then wilt thou sin against innocent blood, to slay David without a cause?
6And Saul hearkened unto the voice of Jonathan:
and Saul sware, *As* the LORD liveth, he shall not be
slain.
7And Jonathan called David, and Jonathan shewed
him all those things. And Jonathan brought David to
Saul, and he was in his presence, as in times past.
8And there was war again: and David went out, and
fought with the Philistines, and slew them with a
great slaughter; and they fled from him.
9And the evil spirit from the LORD was upon Saul,
as he sat in his house with his javelin in his hand: and
David played with *his* hand.
10And Saul sought to smite David even to the wall
with the javelin; but he slipped away out of Saul's
presence, and he smote the javelin into the wall: and
David fled, and escaped that night.
11Saul also sent messengers unto David's house, to
watch him, and to slay him in the morning: and
Michal David's wife told him, saying, If thou save not
thy life to night, tomorrow thou shalt be slain.
12So Michal let David down through a window:
and he went, and fled, and escaped.
13And Michal took an image, and laid *it* in the bed,
and put a pillow of goats' *hair* for his bolster, and
covered *it* with a cloth.
14And when Saul sent messengers to take David,
she said, He *is* sick.
15And Saul sent the messengers *again* to see
David, saying, Bring him up to me in the bed, that I
may slay him.
16And when the messengers were come in, behold, *there was* an image in the bed, with a pillow of
goats' *hair* for his bolster.
17And Saul said unto Michal, Why hast thou deceived me so, and sent away mine enemy, that he is
escaped? And Michal answered Saul, He said unto
me, Let me go; why should I kill thee?

NEW LIVING TRANSLATION

Saul Tries to Kill David

19 Saul now urged his servants and his son Jonathan to assassinate David. But Jonathan, because of his strong affection for David, 2told him
what his father was planning. "Tomorrow morning,"
he warned him, "you must find a hiding place out in
the fields. 3I'll ask my father to go out there with me,
and I'll talk to him about you. Then I'll tell you everything I can find out."
4The next morning Jonathan spoke with his father
about David, saying many good things about him.
"The king must not sin against his servant David,"
Jonathan said. "He's never done anything to harm
you. He has always helped you in any way he could.
5Have you forgotten about the time he risked his life
to kill the Philistine giant and how the LORD brought
a great victory to all Israel as a result? You were certainly happy about it then. Why should you murder
an innocent man like David? There is no reason for
it at all!"
6So Saul listened to Jonathan and vowed, "As surely
as the LORD lives, David will not be killed."
7Afterward Jonathan called David and told him
what had happened. Then he brought David to Saul,
and David served in the court as before.
8War broke out again after that, and David led his
troops against the Philistines. He attacked them with
such fury that they all ran away.
9But one day when Saul was sitting at home, with
spear in hand, the tormenting spirit* from the LORD
suddenly came upon him again. As David played his
harp, 10Saul hurled his spear at David. But David
dodged out of the way, and leaving the spear stuck in
the wall, he fled and escaped into the night.

Michal Saves David's Life

11Then Saul sent troops to watch David's house. They
were told to kill David when he came out the next
morning. But Michal, David's wife, warned him, "If
you don't escape tonight, you will be dead by morning." 12So she helped him climb out through a window, and he fled and escaped. 13Then she took an
idol* and put it in his bed, covered it with blankets,
and put a cushion of goat's hair at its head.
14When the troops came to arrest David, she told
them he was sick and couldn't get out of bed.
15But Saul sent the troops back to get David. He
ordered, "Bring him to me in his bed so I can kill
him!" 16But when they came to carry David out, they
discovered that it was only an idol in the bed with a
cushion of goat's hair at its head.
17"Why have you betrayed me like this and let my
enemy escape?" Saul demanded of Michal.
"I had to," Michal replied. "He threatened to kill
me if I didn't help him."

19:9 Or *evil spirit.* **19:13** Hebrew *teraphim;* also in 19:16.

KING JAMES VERSION

18 So David fled, and escaped, and came to Samuel to Ramah, and told him all that Saul had done to him. And he and Samuel went and dwelt in Naioth.

19 And it was told Saul, saying, Behold, David *is* at Naioth in Ramah.

20 And Saul sent messengers to take David: and when they saw the company of the prophets prophesying, and Samuel standing *as* appointed over them, the Spirit of God was upon the messengers of Saul, and they also prophesied.

21 And when it was told Saul, he sent other messengers, and they prophesied likewise. And Saul sent messengers again the third time, and they prophesied also.

22 Then went he also to Ramah, and came to a great well that *is* in Sechu: and he asked and said, Where *are* Samuel and David? And *one* said, Behold, *they be at* Naioth in Ramah.

23 And he went thither to Naioth in Ramah: and the Spirit of God was upon him also, and he went on, and prophesied, until he came to Naioth in Ramah.

24 And he stripped off his clothes also, and prophesied before Samuel in like manner, and lay down naked all that day and all that night. Wherefore they say, *Is* Saul also among the prophets?

20 1 And David fled from Naioth in Ramah, and came and said before Jonathan, What have I done? what *is* mine iniquity? and what *is* my sin before thy father, that he seeketh my life?

2 And he said unto him, God forbid; thou shalt not die: behold, my father will do nothing either great or small, but that he will shew it me: and why should my father hide this thing from me? it *is* not *so*.

3 And David sware moreover, and said, Thy father certainly knoweth that I have found grace in thine eyes; and he saith, Let not Jonathan know this, lest he be grieved: but truly *as* the LORD liveth, and *as* thy soul liveth, *there is* but a step between me and death.

4 Then said Jonathan unto David, Whatsoever thy soul desireth, I will even do *it* for thee.

5 And David said unto Jonathan, Behold, tomorrow *is* the new moon, and I should not fail to sit with the king at meat: but let me go, that I may hide myself in the field unto the third *day* at even.

6 If thy father at all miss me, then say, David earnestly asked *leave* of me that he might run to Bethlehem his city: for *there is* a yearly sacrifice there for all the family.

7 If he say thus, *It is* well; thy servant shall have peace: but if he be very wroth, *then* be sure that evil is determined by him.

8 Therefore thou shalt deal kindly with thy servant; for thou hast brought thy servant into a covenant of the LORD with thee: notwithstanding, if there be in me iniquity, slay me thyself; for why shouldest thou bring me to thy father?

9 And Jonathan said, Far be it from thee: for if I

NEW LIVING TRANSLATION

18 So David escaped and went to Ramah to see Samuel, and he told him all that Saul had done to him. Then Samuel took David with him to live at Naioth. 19 When the report reached Saul that David was at Naioth in Ramah, 20 he sent troops to capture him. But when they arrived and saw Samuel leading a group of prophets who were prophesying, the Spirit of God came upon Saul's men, and they also began to prophesy. 21 When Saul heard what had happened, he sent other troops, but they, too, prophesied! The same thing happened a third time. 22 Finally, Saul himself went to Ramah and arrived at the great well in Secu. "Where are Samuel and David?" he demanded.

"They are at Naioth in Ramah," someone told him.

23 But on the way to Naioth in Ramah the Spirit of God came even upon Saul, and he, too, began to prophesy all the way to Naioth! 24 He tore off his clothes and lay naked on the ground all day and all night, prophesying in the presence of Samuel. The people who were watching exclaimed, "What? Is even Saul a prophet?"

Jonathan Helps David

20 David now fled from Naioth in Ramah and found Jonathan. "What have I done?" he exclaimed. "What is my crime? How have I offended your father that he is so determined to kill me?"

2 "That's not true!" Jonathan protested. "You're not going to die. He always tells me everything he's going to do, even the little things. I know my father wouldn't hide something like this from me. It just isn't so!"

3 Then David took an oath before Jonathan and said, "Your father knows perfectly well about our friendship, so he has said to himself, 'I won't tell Jonathan—why should I hurt him?' But I swear to you that I am only a step away from death! I swear it by the LORD and by your own soul!"

4 "Tell me what I can do to help you," Jonathan exclaimed.

5 David replied, "Tomorrow we celebrate the new moon festival. I've always eaten with the king on this occasion, but tomorrow I'll hide in the field and stay there until the evening of the third day. 6 If your father asks where I am, tell him I asked permission to go home to Bethlehem for an annual family sacrifice. 7 If he says, 'Fine!' you will know all is well. But if he is angry and loses his temper, you will know he is determined to kill me. 8 Show me this loyalty as my sworn friend—for we made a solemn pact before the LORD—or kill me yourself if I have sinned against your father. But please don't betray me to him!"

9 "Never!" Jonathan exclaimed. "You know that if I

KING JAMES VERSION

knew certainly that evil were determined by my father to come upon thee, then would not I tell it thee?
10 Then said David to Jonathan, Who shall tell me?
or what *if* thy father answer thee roughly?
11 And Jonathan said unto David, Come, and let us
go out into the field. And they went out both of them
into the field.
12 And Jonathan said unto David, O LORD God of Israel, when I have sounded my father about tomorrow
any time, *or* the third *day,* and, behold, *if there be*
good toward David, and I then send not unto thee,
and shew it thee;
13 The LORD do so and much more to Jonathan: but
if it please my father *to do* thee evil, then I will shew
it thee, and send thee away, that thou mayest go in
peace: and the LORD be with thee, as he hath been
with my father.
14 And thou shalt not only while yet I live shew me
the kindness of the LORD, that I die not:
15 But *also* thou shalt not cut off thy kindness from
my house for ever: no, not when the LORD hath cut
off the enemies of David every one from the face of
the earth.
16 So Jonathan made *a covenant* with the house of
David, *saying,* Let the LORD even require *it* at the
hand of David's enemies.
17 And Jonathan caused David to swear again, because he loved him: for he loved him as he loved his
own soul.
18 Then Jonathan said to David, Tomorrow *is* the
new moon: and thou shalt be missed, because thy
seat will be empty.
19 And *when* thou hast stayed three days, *then* thou
shalt go down quickly, and come to the place where
thou didst hide thyself when the business was *in*
hand, and shalt remain by the stone Ezel.
20 And I will shoot three arrows on the side *thereof,*
as though I shot at a mark.
21 And, behold, I will send a lad, *saying,* Go, find
out the arrows. If I expressly say unto the lad, Behold,
the arrows *are* on this side of thee, take them; then
come thou: for *there is* peace to thee, and no hurt; *as*
the LORD liveth.
22 But if I say thus unto the young man, Behold, the
arrows *are* beyond thee; go thy way: for the LORD
hath sent thee away.
23 And *as touching* the matter which thou and I
have spoken of, behold, the LORD *be* between thee
and me for ever.
24 So David hid himself in the field: and when the
new moon was come, the king sat him down to eat
meat.
25 And the king sat upon his seat, as at other times,
even upon a seat by the wall: and Jonathan arose, and
Abner sat by Saul's side, and David's place was empty.
26 Nevertheless Saul spake not any thing that day:
for he thought, Something hath befallen him, he *is*
not clean; surely he *is* not clean.

NEW LIVING TRANSLATION

had the slightest notion my father was planning to
kill you, I would tell you at once."
10 Then David asked, "How will I know whether or
not your father is angry?"
11 "Come out to the field with me," Jonathan replied. And they went out there together. 12 Then Jonathan told David, "I promise by the LORD, the God of
Israel, that by this time tomorrow, or the next day at
the latest, I will talk to my father and let you know at
once how he feels about you. If he speaks favorably
about you, I will let you know. 13 But if he is angry and
wants you killed, may the LORD strike me and even
kill me if I don't warn you so you can escape and live.
May the LORD be with you as he used to be with my
father. 14 And may you treat me with the faithful love
of the LORD as long as I live. But if I die, 15 treat my
family with this faithful love, even when the LORD
destroys all your enemies from the face of the earth."
16 So Jonathan made a solemn pact with David,*
saying, "May the LORD destroy all your enemies!"
17 And Jonathan made David reaffirm his vow of
friendship again, for Jonathan loved David as he
loved himself.
18 Then Jonathan said, "Tomorrow we celebrate
the new moon festival. You will be missed when your
place at the table is empty. 19 The day after tomorrow, toward evening, go to the place where you hid
before, and wait there by the stone pile.* 20 I will
come out and shoot three arrows to the side of the
stone pile as though I were shooting at a target.
21 Then I will send a boy to bring the arrows back. If
you hear me tell him, 'They're on this side,' then you
will know, as surely as the LORD lives, that all is well,
and there is no trouble. 22 But if I tell him, 'Go farther—the arrows are still ahead of you,' then it will
mean that you must leave immediately, for the LORD
is sending you away. 23 And may the LORD make us
keep our promises to each other, for he has witnessed them."
24 So David hid himself in the field, and when the
new moon festival began, the king sat down to eat.
25 He sat at his usual place against the wall, with Jonathan sitting opposite him* and Abner beside him.
But David's place was empty. 26 Saul didn't say anything about it that day, for he said to himself, "Something must have made David ceremonially unclean."

20:16 Hebrew *with the house of David.* **20:19** Hebrew *the stone Ezel.* The meaning of the Hebrew is uncertain. **20:25** As in Greek version; Hebrew reads *with Jonathan standing.*

KING JAMES VERSION

27And it came to pass on the morrow, *which was*
the second *day* of the month, that David's place was
empty: and Saul said unto Jonathan his son, Wherefore cometh not the son of Jesse to meat, neither yesterday, nor today?
28And Jonathan answered Saul, David earnestly
asked *leave* of me *to go* to Bethlehem:
29And he said, Let me go, I pray thee; for our family
hath a sacrifice in the city; and my brother, he hath
commanded me *to be there:* and now, if I have found
favour in thine eyes, let me get away, I pray thee, and
see my brethren. Therefore he cometh not unto the
king's table.
30Then Saul's anger was kindled against Jonathan,
and he said unto him, Thou son of the perverse
rebellious *woman,* do not I know that thou hast
chosen the son of Jesse to thine own confusion, and
unto the confusion of thy mother's nakedness?
31For as long as the son of Jesse liveth upon the
ground, thou shalt not be established, nor thy kingdom. Wherefore now send and fetch him unto me,
for he shall surely die.
32And Jonathan answered Saul his father, and said
unto him, Wherefore shall he be slain? what hath
he done?
33And Saul cast a javelin at him to smite him:
whereby Jonathan knew that it was determined of
his father to slay David.
34So Jonathan arose from the table in fierce anger,
and did eat no meat the second day of the month: for
he was grieved for David, because his father had
done him shame.
35And it came to pass in the morning, that Jonathan went out into the field at the time appointed
with David, and a little lad with him.
36And he said unto his lad, Run, find out now the
arrows which I shoot. *And* as the lad ran, he shot an
arrow beyond him.
37And when the lad was come to the place of the
arrow which Jonathan had shot, Jonathan cried after
the lad, and said, *Is* not the arrow beyond thee?
38And Jonathan cried after the lad, Make speed,
haste, stay not. And Jonathan's lad gathered up the
arrows, and came to his master.
39But the lad knew not any thing: only Jonathan
and David knew the matter.
40And Jonathan gave his artillery unto his lad, and
said unto him, Go, carry *them* to the city.
41*And* as soon as the lad was gone, David arose out
of *a place* toward the south, and fell on his face to the
ground, and bowed himself three times: and they
kissed one another, and wept one with another, until
David exceeded.
42And Jonathan said to David, Go in peace, forasmuch as we have sworn both of us in the name of the
LORD, saying, The LORD be between me and thee, and
between my seed and thy seed for ever. And he arose
and departed: and Jonathan went into the city.

NEW LIVING TRANSLATION

27But when David's place was empty again the next
day, Saul asked Jonathan, "Why hasn't the son of Jesse
been here for the meal either yesterday or today?"
28Jonathan replied, "David earnestly asked me if
he could go to Bethlehem. 29He said, 'Please let me
go, for we are having a family sacrifice. My brother
demanded that I be there. So please let me get away
to see my brothers.' That's why he isn't here at the
king's table."
30Saul boiled with rage at Jonathan. "You stupid
son of a whore!"* he swore at him. "Do you think I
don't know that you want him to be king in your
place, shaming yourself and your mother? 31As long
as that son of Jesse is alive, you'll never be king. Now
go and get him so I can kill him!"
32"But why should he be put to death?" Jonathan
asked his father. "What has he done?" 33Then Saul
hurled his spear at Jonathan, intending to kill him.
So at last Jonathan realized that his father was really
determined to kill David.
34Jonathan left the table in fierce anger and refused to eat on that second day of the festival, for
he was crushed by his father's shameful behavior
toward David.
35The next morning, as agreed, Jonathan went out
into the field and took a young boy with him to
gather his arrows. 36"Start running," he told the boy,
"so you can find the arrows as I shoot them." So the
boy ran, and Jonathan shot an arrow beyond him.
37When the boy had almost reached the arrow, Jonathan shouted, "The arrow is still ahead of you.
38Hurry, hurry, don't wait." So the boy quickly gathered up the arrows and ran back to his master. 39He,
of course, suspected nothing; only Jonathan and
David understood the signal. 40Then Jonathan gave
his bow and arrows to the boy and told him to take
them back to town.
41As soon as the boy was gone, David came out
from where he had been hiding near the stone pile.*
Then David bowed three times to Jonathan with his
face to the ground. Both of them were in tears as they
embraced each other and said good-bye, especially
David.
42At last Jonathan said to David, "Go in peace, for
we have sworn loyalty to each other in the LORD's
name. The LORD is the witness of a bond between us
and our children forever." Then David left, and Jonathan returned to the town.*

20:30 Hebrew *You son of a perverse and rebellious woman.* **20:41** As in Greek version; Hebrew reads *near the south edge.* **20:42** This sentence is numbered 21:1 in Hebrew text.

KING JAMES VERSION

21 1 Then came David to Nob to Ahimelech the
priest: and Ahimelech was afraid at the
meeting of David, and said unto him, Why *art* thou
alone, and no man with thee?

2 And David said unto Ahimelech the priest, The
king hath commanded me a business, and hath said
unto me, Let no man know any thing of the business
whereabout I send thee, and what I have commanded thee: and I have appointed *my* servants to
such and such a place.

3 Now therefore what is under thine hand? give
me five *loaves of* bread in mine hand, or what there
is present.

4 And the priest answered David, and said, *There is*
no common bread under mine hand, but there is hallowed bread; if the young men have kept themselves
at least from women.

5 And David answered the priest, and said unto
him, Of a truth women *have been* kept from us about
these three days, since I came out, and the vessels of
the young men are holy, and *the bread is* in a manner
common, yea, though it were sanctified this day in
the vessel.

6 So the priest gave him hallowed *bread:* for there
was no bread there but the shewbread, that was
taken from before the LORD, to put hot bread in the
day when it was taken away.

7 Now a certain man of the servants of Saul *was*
there that day, detained before the LORD; and his
name *was* Doeg, an Edomite, the chiefest of the
herdmen that *belonged* to Saul.

8 And David said unto Ahimelech, And is there not
here under thine hand spear or sword? for I have neither brought my sword nor my weapons with me,
because the king's business required haste.

9 And the priest said, The sword of Goliath the Philistine, whom thou slewest in the valley of Elah, behold, it *is here* wrapped in a cloth behind the ephod:
if thou wilt take that, take *it:* for *there is* no other
save that here. And David said, *There is* none like
that; give it me.

10 And David arose, and fled that day for fear of
Saul, and went to Achish the king of Gath.

11 And the servants of Achish said unto him, *Is* not
this David the king of the land? did they not sing one
to another of him in dances, saying, Saul hath slain
his thousands, and David his ten thousands?

12 And David laid up these words in his heart, and
was sore afraid of Achish the king of Gath.

13 And he changed his behaviour before them, and
feigned himself mad in their hands, and scrabbled
on the doors of the gate, and let his spittle fall down
upon his beard.

14 Then said Achish unto his servants, Lo, ye see
the man is mad: wherefore *then* have ye brought him
to me?

15 Have I need of mad men, that ye have brought

NEW LIVING TRANSLATION

David Runs from Saul

21 1 *David went to the town of Nob to see
Ahimelech the priest. Ahimelech trembled
when he saw him. "Why are you alone?" he asked.
"Why is no one with you?"

2 "The king has sent me on a private matter," David
said. "He told me not to tell anyone why I am here.
I have told my men where to meet me later. 3 Now,
what is there to eat? Give me five loaves of bread or
anything else you have."

4 "We don't have any regular bread," the priest
replied. "But there is the holy bread, which you can
have if your young men have not slept with any
women recently."

5 "Don't worry," David replied. "I never allow my
men to be with women when they are on a campaign.
And since they stay clean even on ordinary trips,
how much more on this one!"

6 Since there was no other food available, the priest
gave him the holy bread—the Bread of the Presence
that was placed before the LORD in the Tabernacle. It
had just been replaced that day with fresh bread.

7 Now Doeg the Edomite, Saul's chief herdsman,
was there that day, having been detained before the
LORD.*

8 David asked Ahimelech, "Do you have a spear
or sword? The king's business was so urgent that I
didn't even have time to grab a weapon!"

9 "I only have the sword of Goliath the Philistine,
whom you killed in the valley of Elah," the priest
replied. "It is wrapped in a cloth behind the ephod.
Take that if you want it, for there is nothing else
here."

"There is nothing like it!" David replied. "Give it
to me!"

10 So David escaped from Saul and went to King
Achish of Gath. 11 But the officers of Achish were unhappy about his being there. "Isn't this David, the
king of the land?" they asked. "Isn't he the one the
people honor with dances, singing,

'Saul has killed his thousands,
and David his ten thousands'?"

12 David heard these comments and was very
afraid of what King Achish of Gath might do to him.
13 So he pretended to be insane, scratching on doors
and drooling down his beard.

14 Finally, King Achish said to his men, "Must you
bring me a madman? 15 We already have enough of

21:1 Verses 21:1-15 are numbered 21:2-16 in Hebrew text. **21:7** The meaning of the Hebrew is uncertain.

KING JAMES VERSION

this *fellow* to play the mad man in my presence? shall
this *fellow* come into my house?

22 1David therefore departed thence, and escaped to the cave Adullam: and when his
brethren and all his father's house heard *it*, they went
down thither to him.
2And every one *that was* in distress, and every one
that *was* in debt, and every one *that was* discontented, gathered themselves unto him; and he became a captain over them: and there were with him
about four hundred men.
3And David went thence to Mizpeh of Moab: and
he said unto the king of Moab, Let my father and my
mother, I pray thee, come forth, *and be* with you, till
I know what God will do for me.
4And he brought them before the king of Moab:
and they dwelt with him all the while that David was
in the hold.
5And the prophet Gad said unto David, Abide not
in the hold; depart, and get thee into the land of
Judah. Then David departed, and came into the forest of Hareth.
6When Saul heard that David was discovered, and
the men that *were* with him, (now Saul abode in Gibeah under a tree in Ramah, having his spear in his
hand, and all his servants *were* standing about him;)
7Then Saul said unto his servants that stood
about him, Hear now, ye Benjamites; will the son of
Jesse give every one of you fields and vineyards, *and*
make you all captains of thousands, and captains of
hundreds;
8That all of you have conspired against me, and
there is none that sheweth me that my son hath
made a league with the son of Jesse, and *there is* none
of you that is sorry for me, or sheweth unto me that
my son hath stirred up my servant against me, to lie
in wait, as at this day?
9Then answered Doeg the Edomite, which was set
over the servants of Saul, and said, I saw the son of
Jesse coming to Nob, to Ahimelech the son of Ahitub.
10And he inquired of the LORD for him, and gave
him victuals, and gave him the sword of Goliath the
Philistine.
11Then the king sent to call Ahimelech the priest,
the son of Ahitub, and all his father's house, the
priests that *were* in Nob: and they came all of them
to the king.
12And Saul said, Hear now, thou son of Ahitub.
And he answered, Here I *am*, my lord.
13And Saul said unto him, Why have ye conspired
against me, thou and the son of Jesse, in that thou
hast given him bread, and a sword, and hast inquired
of God for him, that he should rise against me, to lie
in wait, as at this day?
14Then Ahimelech answered the king, and said,

NEW LIVING TRANSLATION

them around here! Why should I let someone like
this be my guest?"

David at the Cave of Adullam

22 So David left Gath and escaped to the cave
of Adullam. Soon his brothers and all his
other relatives joined him there. 2Then others began
coming—men who were in trouble or in debt or who
were just discontented—until David was the captain
of about 400 men.
3Later David went to Mizpeh in Moab, where he
asked the king, "Please allow my father and mother
to live here with you until I know what God is going
to do for me." 4So David's parents stayed in Moab
with the king during the entire time David was living
in his stronghold.
5One day the prophet Gad told David, "Leave the
stronghold and return to the land of Judah." So David
went to the forest of Hereth.
6The news of his arrival in Judah soon reached
Saul. At the time, the king was sitting beneath the
tamarisk tree on the hill at Gibeah, holding his spear
and surrounded by his officers.
7"Listen here, you men of Benjamin!" Saul shouted
to his officers when he heard the news. "Has that son
of Jesse promised every one of you fields and vineyards? Has he promised to make you all generals and
captains in his army?* 8Is that why you have conspired against me? For not one of you told me when
my own son made a solemn pact with the son of
Jesse. You're not even sorry for me. Think of it! My
own son—encouraging him to kill me, as he is trying
to do this very day!"
9Then Doeg the Edomite, who was standing there
with Saul's men, spoke up. "When I was at Nob," he
said, "I saw the son of Jesse talking to the priest,
Ahimelech son of Ahitub. 10Ahimelech consulted
the LORD for him. Then he gave him food and the
sword of Goliath the Philistine."

The Slaughter of the Priests

11King Saul immediately sent for Ahimelech and all
his family, who served as priests at Nob. 12When
they arrived, Saul shouted at him, "Listen to me, you
son of Ahitub!"
"What is it, my king?" Ahimelech asked.
13"Why have you and the son of Jesse conspired
against me?" Saul demanded. "Why did you give him
food and a sword? Why have you consulted God for
him? Why have you encouraged him to kill me, as he
is trying to do this very day?"
14"But sir," Ahimelech replied, "is anyone among

22:7 Hebrew *commanders of thousands and commanders of hundreds?*

KING JAMES VERSION

And who *is so* faithful among all thy servants as David, which is the king's son in law, and goeth at thy bidding, and is honourable in thine house?

15 Did I then begin to inquire of God for him? be it far from me: let not the king impute *any* thing unto his servant, *nor* to all the house of my father: for thy servant knew nothing of all this, less or more.

16 And the king said, Thou shalt surely die, Ahimelech, thou, and all thy father's house.

17 And the king said unto the footmen that stood about him, Turn, and slay the priests of the LORD; because their hand also *is* with David, and because they knew when he fled, and did not shew it to me. But the servants of the king would not put forth their hand to fall upon the priests of the LORD.

18 And the king said to Doeg, Turn thou, and fall upon the priests. And Doeg the Edomite turned, and he fell upon the priests, and slew on that day fourscore and five persons that did wear a linen ephod.

19 And Nob, the city of the priests, smote he with the edge of the sword, both men and women, children and sucklings, and oxen, and asses, and sheep, with the edge of the sword.

20 And one of the sons of Ahimelech the son of Ahitub, named Abiathar, escaped, and fled after David.

21 And Abiathar shewed David that Saul had slain the LORD's priests.

22 And David said unto Abiathar, I knew *it* that day, when Doeg the Edomite *was* there, that he would surely tell Saul: I have occasioned *the death* of all the persons of thy father's house.

23 Abide thou with me, fear not: for he that seeketh my life seeketh thy life: but with me thou *shalt be* in safeguard.

23 1 Then they told David, saying, Behold, the Philistines fight against Keilah, and they rob the threshingfloors.

2 Therefore David inquired of the LORD, saying, Shall I go and smite these Philistines? And the LORD said unto David, Go, and smite the Philistines, and save Keilah.

3 And David's men said unto him, Behold, we be afraid here in Judah: how much more then if we come to Keilah against the armies of the Philistines?

4 Then David inquired of the LORD yet again. And the LORD answered him and said, Arise, go down to Keilah: for I will deliver the Philistines into thine hand.

5 So David and his men went to Keilah, and fought with the Philistines, and brought away their cattle, and smote them with a great slaughter. So David saved the inhabitants of Keilah.

6 And it came to pass, when Abiathar the son of Ahimelech fled to David to Keilah, *that* he came down *with* an ephod in his hand.

7 And it was told Saul that David was come to

NEW LIVING TRANSLATION

all your servants as faithful as David, your son-in-law? Why, he is the captain of your bodyguard and a highly honored member of your household! 15 This was certainly not the first time I had consulted God for him! May the king not accuse me and my family in this matter, for I knew nothing at all of any plot against you."

16 "You will surely die, Ahimelech, along with your entire family!" the king shouted. 17 And he ordered his bodyguards, "Kill these priests of the LORD, for they are allies and conspirators with David! They knew he was running away from me, but they didn't tell me!" But Saul's men refused to kill the LORD's priests.

18 Then the king said to Doeg, "You do it." So Doeg the Edomite turned on them and killed them that day, eighty-five priests in all, still wearing their priestly garments. 19 Then he went to Nob, the town of the priests, and killed the priests' families—men and women, children and babies—and all the cattle, donkeys, sheep, and goats.

20 Only Abiathar, one of the sons of Ahimelech, escaped and fled to David. 21 When he told David that Saul had killed the priests of the LORD, 22 David exclaimed, "I knew it! When I saw Doeg the Edomite there that day, I knew he was sure to tell Saul. Now I have caused the death of all your father's family. 23 Stay here with me, and don't be afraid. I will protect you with my own life, for the same person wants to kill us both."

David Protects the Town of Keilah

23 One day news came to David that the Philistines were at Keilah stealing grain from the threshing floors. 2 David asked the LORD, "Should I go and attack them?"

"Yes, go and save Keilah," the LORD told him.

3 But David's men said, "We're afraid even here in Judah. We certainly don't want to go to Keilah to fight the whole Philistine army!"

4 So David asked the LORD again, and again the LORD replied, "Go down to Keilah, for I will help you conquer the Philistines."

5 So David and his men went to Keilah. They slaughtered the Philistines and took all their livestock and rescued the people of Keilah. 6 Now when Abiathar son of Ahimelech fled to David at Keilah, he brought the ephod with him.

7 Saul soon learned that David was at Keilah.

KING JAMES VERSION

Keilah. And Saul said, God hath delivered him into
mine hand; for he is shut in, by entering into a town
that hath gates and bars.
8And Saul called all the people together to war, to
go down to Keilah, to besiege David and his men.
9And David knew that Saul secretly practised mischief against him; and he said to Abiathar the priest,
Bring hither the ephod.
10Then said David, O LORD God of Israel, thy servant hath certainly heard that Saul seeketh to come
to Keilah, to destroy the city for my sake.
11Will the men of Keilah deliver me up into his
hand? will Saul come down, as thy servant hath
heard? O LORD God of Israel, I beseech thee, tell thy
servant. And the LORD said, He will come down.
12Then said David, Will the men of Keilah deliver
me and my men into the hand of Saul? And the LORD
said, They will deliver *thee* up.
13Then David and his men, *which were* about six
hundred, arose and departed out of Keilah, and went
whithersoever they could go. And it was told Saul
that David was escaped from Keilah; and he forbare
to go forth.
14And David abode in the wilderness in strong
holds, and remained in a mountain in the wilderness
of Ziph. And Saul sought him every day, but God delivered him not into his hand.
15And David saw that Saul was come out to seek
his life: and David *was* in the wilderness of Ziph in a
wood.
16And Jonathan Saul's son arose, and went to David into the wood, and strengthened his hand in God.
17And he said unto him, Fear not: for the hand of
Saul my father shall not find thee; and thou shalt be
king over Israel, and I shall be next unto thee; and
that also Saul my father knoweth.
18And they two made a covenant before the LORD:
and David abode in the wood, and Jonathan went to
his house.
19Then came up the Ziphites to Saul to Gibeah,
saying, Doth not David hide himself with us in strong
holds in the wood, in the hill of Hachilah, which *is* on
the south of Jeshimon?
20Now therefore, O king, come down according to
all the desire of thy soul to come down; and our part
shall be to deliver him into the king's hand.
21And Saul said, Blessed *be* ye of the LORD; for ye
have compassion on me.
22Go, I pray you, prepare yet, and know and see his
place where his haunt is, *and* who hath seen him
there: for it is told me *that* he dealeth very subtilly.
23See therefore, and take knowledge of all the
lurking places where he hideth himself, and come ye
again to me with the certainty, and I will go with you:
and it shall come to pass, if he be in the land, that
I will search him out throughout all the thousands
of Judah.
24And they arose, and went to Ziph before Saul:

NEW LIVING TRANSLATION

"Good!" he exclaimed. "We've got him now! God has
handed him over to me, for he has trapped himself in
a walled town!" 8So Saul mobilized his entire army to
march to Keilah and besiege David and his men.
9But David learned of Saul's plan and told Abiathar the priest to bring the ephod and ask the LORD
what he should do. 10Then David prayed, "O LORD,
God of Israel, I have heard that Saul is planning to
come and destroy Keilah because I am here. 11Will
the leaders of Keilah betray me to him?* And will
Saul actually come as I have heard? O LORD, God of
Israel, please tell me."
And the LORD said, "He will come."
12Again David asked, "Will the leaders of Keilah
betray me and my men to Saul?"
And the LORD replied, "Yes, they will betray you."

David Hides in the Wilderness

13So David and his men—about 600 of them now—
left Keilah and began roaming the countryside.
Word soon reached Saul that David had escaped, so
he didn't go to Keilah after all. 14David now stayed in
the strongholds of the wilderness and in the hill
country of Ziph. Saul hunted him day after day, but
God didn't let Saul find him.
15One day near Horesh, David received the news
that Saul was on the way to Ziph to search for him
and kill him. 16Jonathan went to find David and
encouraged him to stay strong in his faith in God.
17"Don't be afraid," Jonathan reassured him. "My father will never find you! You are going to be the king
of Israel, and I will be next to you, as my father, Saul,
is well aware." 18So the two of them renewed their
solemn pact before the LORD. Then Jonathan returned home, while David stayed at Horesh.
19But now the men of Ziph went to Saul in Gibeah
and betrayed David to him. "We know where David is
hiding," they said. "He is in the strongholds of
Horesh on the hill of Hakilah, which is in the southern part of Jeshimon. 20Come down whenever you're
ready, O king, and we will catch him and hand him
over to you!"
21"The LORD bless you," Saul said. "At last someone
is concerned about me! 22Go and check again to be
sure of where he is staying and who has seen him
there, for I know that he is very crafty. 23Discover his
hiding places, and come back when you are sure.
Then I'll go with you. And if he is in the area at all, I'll
track him down, even if I have to search every hiding
place in Judah!" 24So the men of Ziph returned home
ahead of Saul.

23:11 Some manuscripts lack the first sentence of 23:11.

KING JAMES VERSION

but David and his men *were* in the wilderness of
Maon, in the plain on the south of Jeshimon.
25Saul also and his men went to seek *him.* And
they told David: wherefore he came down into a rock,
and abode in the wilderness of Maon. And when Saul
heard *that,* he pursued after David in the wilderness
of Maon.
26And Saul went on this side of the mountain, and
David and his men on that side of the mountain: and
David made haste to get away for fear of Saul; for Saul
and his men compassed David and his men round
about to take them.
27But there came a messenger unto Saul, saying,
Haste thee, and come; for the Philistines have invaded the land.
28Wherefore Saul returned from pursuing after
David, and went against the Philistines: therefore
they called that place Sela-hammahlekoth.
29And David went up from thence, and dwelt in
strong holds at En-gedi.

24 1And it came to pass, when Saul was returned from following the Philistines, that
it was told him, saying, Behold, David *is* in the wilderness of En-gedi.
2Then Saul took three thousand chosen men out
of all Israel, and went to seek David and his men
upon the rocks of the wild goats.
3And he came to the sheepcotes by the way, where
was a cave; and Saul went in to cover his feet: and
David and his men remained in the sides of the cave.
4And the men of David said unto him, Behold the
day of which the LORD said unto thee, Behold, I will
deliver thine enemy into thine hand, that thou
mayest do to him as it shall seem good unto thee.
Then David arose, and cut off the skirt of Saul's robe
privily.
5And it came to pass afterward, that David's heart
smote him, because he had cut off Saul's skirt.
6And he said unto his men, The LORD forbid that
I should do this thing unto my master, the LORD's
anointed, to stretch forth mine hand against him,
seeing he *is* the anointed of the LORD.
7So David stayed his servants with these words,
and suffered them not to rise against Saul. But Saul
rose up out of the cave, and went on *his* way.
8David also arose afterward, and went out of the
cave, and cried after Saul, saying, My lord the king.
And when Saul looked behind him, David stooped
with his face to the earth, and bowed himself.
9And David said to Saul, Wherefore hearest thou
men's words, saying, Behold, David seeketh thy hurt?
10Behold, this day thine eyes have seen how that
the LORD had delivered thee today into mine hand in
the cave: and *some* bade *me* kill thee: but *mine eye*
spared thee; and I said, I will not put forth mine hand
against my lord; for he *is* the LORD's anointed.
11Moreover, my father, see, yea, see the skirt of thy

NEW LIVING TRANSLATION

Meanwhile, David and his men had moved into
the wilderness of Maon in the Arabah Valley south of
Jeshimon. 25When David heard that Saul and his
men were searching for him, he went even farther
into the wilderness to the great rock, and he remained there in the wilderness of Maon. But Saul
kept after him in the wilderness.
26Saul and David were now on opposite sides of a
mountain. Just as Saul and his men began to close in
on David and his men, 27an urgent message reached
Saul that the Philistines were raiding Israel again.
28So Saul quit chasing David and returned to fight
the Philistines. Ever since that time, the place where
David was camped has been called the Rock of Escape.* 29*David then went to live in the strongholds
of En-gedi.

David Spares Saul's Life

24 1*After Saul returned from fighting the Philistines, he was told that David had gone
into the wilderness of En-gedi. 2So Saul chose 3,000
elite troops from all Israel and went to search for
David and his men near the rocks of the wild goats.
3At the place where the road passes some sheepfolds, Saul went into a cave to relieve himself. But as
it happened, David and his men were hiding farther
back in that very cave!
4"Now's your opportunity!" David's men whispered to him. "Today the LORD is telling you, 'I will
certainly put your enemy into your power, to do with
as you wish.'" So David crept forward and cut off a
piece of the hem of Saul's robe.
5But then David's conscience began bothering
him because he had cut Saul's robe. 6"The LORD
knows I shouldn't have done that to my lord the
king," he said to his men. "The LORD forbid that I
should do this to my lord the king and attack the
LORD's anointed one, for the LORD himself has chosen him." 7So David restrained his men and did not
let them kill Saul.
After Saul had left the cave and gone on his way,
8David came out and shouted after him, "My lord the
king!" And when Saul looked around, David bowed
low before him.
9Then he shouted to Saul, "Why do you listen to
the people who say I am trying to harm you? 10This
very day you can see with your own eyes it isn't true.
For the LORD placed you at my mercy back there in
the cave. Some of my men told me to kill you, but I
spared you. For I said, 'I will never harm the king—
he is the LORD's anointed one.' 11Look, my father, at

23:28 Hebrew *Sela-hammahlekoth.* **23:29** Verse 23:29 is numbered 24:1 in Hebrew text. **24:1** Verses 24:1-22 are numbered 24:2-23 in Hebrew text.

KING JAMES VERSION

robe in my hand: for in that I cut off the skirt of thy
robe, and killed thee not, know thou and see that
there is neither evil nor transgression in mine hand,
and I have not sinned against thee; yet thou huntest
my soul to take it.
12 The LORD judge between me and thee, and the
LORD avenge me of thee: but mine hand shall not be
upon thee.
13 As saith the proverb of the ancients, Wickedness proceedeth from the wicked: but mine hand
shall not be upon thee.
14 After whom is the king of Israel come out? after
whom dost thou pursue? after a dead dog, after
a flea.
15 The LORD therefore be judge, and judge between
me and thee, and see, and plead my cause, and deliver me out of thine hand.
16 And it came to pass, when David had made an
end of speaking these words unto Saul, that Saul
said, *Is* this thy voice, my son David? And Saul lifted
up his voice, and wept.
17 And he said to David, Thou *art* more righteous
than I: for thou hast rewarded me good, whereas I
have rewarded thee evil.
18 And thou hast shewed this day how that thou
hast dealt well with me: forasmuch as when the
LORD had delivered me into thine hand, thou killedst
me not.
19 For if a man find his enemy, will he let him go
well away? wherefore the LORD reward thee good for
that thou hast done unto me this day.
20 And now, behold, I know well that thou shalt
surely be king, and that the kingdom of Israel shall
be established in thine hand.
21 Swear now therefore unto me by the LORD, that
thou wilt not cut off my seed after me, and that thou
wilt not destroy my name out of my father's house.
22 And David sware unto Saul. And Saul went
home; but David and his men gat them up unto
the hold.

25 1 And Samuel died; and all the Israelites
were gathered together, and lamented him,
and buried him in his house at Ramah. And David
arose, and went down to the wilderness of Paran.

2 And *there was* a man in Maon, whose possessions
were in Carmel; and the man *was* very great, and he
had three thousand sheep, and a thousand goats: and
he was shearing his sheep in Carmel.
3 Now the name of the man *was* Nabal; and the
name of his wife Abigail: and *she was* a woman of
good understanding, and of a beautiful countenance: but the man *was* churlish and evil in his
doings; and he *was* of the house of Caleb.
4 And David heard in the wilderness that Nabal did
shear his sheep.

NEW LIVING TRANSLATION

what I have in my hand. It is a piece of the hem of
your robe! I cut it off, but I didn't kill you. This proves
that I am not trying to harm you and that I have not
sinned against you, even though you have been hunting for me to kill me.
12 "May the LORD judge between us. Perhaps the
LORD will punish you for what you are trying to do to
me, but I will never harm you. 13 As that old proverb
says, 'From evil people come evil deeds.' So you can
be sure I will never harm you. 14 Who is the king of
Israel trying to catch anyway? Should he spend his
time chasing one who is as worthless as a dead dog or
a single flea? 15 May the LORD therefore judge which
of us is right and punish the guilty one. He is my advocate, and he will rescue me from your power!"
16 When David had finished speaking, Saul called
back, "Is that really you, my son David?" Then he began to cry. 17 And he said to David, "You are a better
man than I am, for you have repaid me good for evil.
18 Yes, you have been amazingly kind to me today, for
when the LORD put me in a place where you could
have killed me, you didn't do it. 19 Who else would let
his enemy get away when he had him in his power?
May the LORD reward you well for the kindness you
have shown me today. 20 And now I realize that you
are surely going to be king, and that the kingdom of
Israel will flourish under your rule. 21 Now swear to
me by the LORD that when that happens you will not
kill my family and destroy my line of descendants!"
22 So David promised this to Saul with an oath.
Then Saul went home, but David and his men went
back to their stronghold.

The Death of Samuel

25 Now Samuel died, and all Israel gathered for
his funeral. They buried him at his house in
Ramah.

Nabal Angers David

Then David moved down to the wilderness of
Maon.* 2 There was a wealthy man from Maon who
owned property near the town of Carmel. He had
3,000 sheep and 1,000 goats, and it was sheep-
shearing time. 3 This man's name was Nabal, and his
wife, Abigail, was a sensible and beautiful woman.
But Nabal, a descendant of Caleb, was crude and
mean in all his dealings.
4 When David heard that Nabal was shearing his

25:1 As in Greek version (see also 25:2); Hebrew reads *Paran*.

KING JAMES VERSION

5And David sent out ten young men, and David said unto the young men, Get you up to Carmel, and go to Nabal, and greet him in my name:

6And thus shall ye say to him that liveth *in prosperity,* Peace *be* both to thee, and peace *be* to thine house, and peace *be* unto all that thou hast.

7And now I have heard that thou hast shearers: now thy shepherds which were with us, we hurt them not, neither was there aught missing unto them, all the while they were in Carmel.

8Ask thy young men, and they will shew thee. Wherefore let the young men find favour in thine eyes: for we come in a good day: give, I pray thee, whatsoever cometh to thine hand unto thy servants, and to thy son David.

9And when David's young men came, they spake to Nabal according to all those words in the name of David, and ceased.

10And Nabal answered David's servants, and said, Who *is* David? and who *is* the son of Jesse? there be many servants now a days that break away every man from his master.

11Shall I then take my bread, and my water, and my flesh that I have killed for my shearers, and give *it* unto men, whom I know not whence they *be?*

12So David's young men turned their way, and went again, and came and told him all those sayings.

13And David said unto his men, Gird ye on every man his sword. And they girded on every man his sword; and David also girded on his sword: and there went up after David about four hundred men; and two hundred abode by the stuff.

14But one of the young men told Abigail, Nabal's wife, saying, Behold, David sent messengers out of the wilderness to salute our master; and he railed on them.

15But the men *were* very good unto us, and we were not hurt, neither missed we any thing, as long as we were conversant with them, when we were in the fields:

16They were a wall unto us both by night and day, all the while we were with them keeping the sheep.

17Now therefore know and consider what thou wilt do; for evil is determined against our master, and against all his household: for he *is such* a son of Belial, that *a man* cannot speak to him.

18Then Abigail made haste, and took two hundred loaves, and two bottles of wine, and five sheep ready dressed, and five measures of parched *corn,* and an hundred clusters of raisins, and two hundred cakes of figs, and laid *them* on asses.

19And she said unto her servants, Go on before me; behold, I come after you. But she told not her husband Nabal.

20And it was *so, as* she rode on the ass, that she came down by the covert of the hill, and, behold, David and his men came down against her; and she met them.

NEW LIVING TRANSLATION

sheep, 5he sent ten of his young men to Carmel with
this message for Nabal: 6"Peace and prosperity to
you, your family, and everything you own! 7I am told
that it is sheep-shearing time. While your shepherds
stayed among us near Carmel, we never harmed
them, and nothing was ever stolen from them. 8Ask
your own men, and they will tell you this is true. So
would you be kind to us, since we have come at a
time of celebration? Please share any provisions you
might have on hand with us and with your friend David." 9David's young men gave this message to Nabal
in David's name, and they waited for a reply.

10"Who is this fellow David?" Nabal sneered to
the young men. "Who does this son of Jesse think he
is? There are lots of servants these days who run
away from their masters. 11Should I take my bread
and my water and my meat that I've slaughtered for
my shearers and give it to a band of outlaws who
come from who knows where?"

12So David's young men returned and told him
what Nabal had said. 13"Get your swords!" was David's reply as he strapped on his own. Then 400 men
started off with David, and 200 remained behind to
guard their equipment.

14Meanwhile, one of Nabal's servants went to Abigail and told her, "David sent messengers from the
wilderness to greet our master, but he screamed insults at them. 15These men have been very good to
us, and we never suffered any harm from them.
Nothing was stolen from us the whole time they
were with us. 16In fact, day and night they were like a
wall of protection to us and the sheep. 17You need to
know this and figure out what to do, for there is
going to be trouble for our master and his whole
family. He's so ill-tempered that no one can even talk
to him!"

18Abigail wasted no time. She quickly gathered
200 loaves of bread, two wineskins full of wine, five
sheep that had been slaughtered, nearly a bushel* of
roasted grain, 100 clusters of raisins, and 200 fig
cakes. She packed them on donkeys 19and said to her
servants, "Go on ahead. I will follow you shortly." But
she didn't tell her husband Nabal what she was
doing.

20As she was riding her donkey into a mountain
ravine, she saw David and his men coming toward

25:18 Hebrew *5 seahs* [30 liters].

KING JAMES VERSION

21Now David had said, Surely in vain have I kept all
that this *fellow* hath in the wilderness, so that nothing was missed of all that *pertained* unto him: and
he hath requited me evil for good.
22So and more also do God unto the enemies of
David, if I leave of all that *pertain* to him by the
morning light any that pisseth against the wall.

23And when Abigail saw David, she hasted, and
lighted off the ass, and fell before David on her face,
and bowed herself to the ground,
24And fell at his feet, and said, Upon me, my lord,
upon me *let this* iniquity *be:* and let thine handmaid,
I pray thee, speak in thine audience, and hear the
words of thine handmaid.
25Let not my lord, I pray thee, regard this man of
Belial, *even* Nabal: for as his name *is,* so *is* he; Nabal
is his name, and folly *is* with him: but I thine handmaid saw not the young men of my lord, whom thou
didst send.
26Now therefore, my lord, *as* the LORD liveth, and
as thy soul liveth, seeing the LORD hath withholden
thee from coming to *shed* blood, and from avenging
thyself with thine own hand, now let thine enemies,
and they that seek evil to my lord, be as Nabal.
27And now this blessing which thine handmaid
hath brought unto my lord, let it even be given unto
the young men that follow my lord.
28I pray thee, forgive the trespass of thine handmaid: for the LORD will certainly make my lord a sure
house; because my lord fighteth the battles of the
LORD, and evil hath not been found in thee *all* thy
days.
29Yet a man is risen to pursue thee, and to seek thy
soul: but the soul of my lord shall be bound in the
bundle of life with the LORD thy God; and the souls
of thine enemies, them shall he sling out, *as out* of
the middle of a sling.
30And it shall come to pass, when the LORD shall
have done to my lord according to all the good that
he hath spoken concerning thee, and shall have
appointed thee ruler over Israel;
31That this shall be no grief unto thee, nor offence
of heart unto my lord, either that thou hast shed
blood causeless, or that my lord hath avenged himself: but when the LORD shall have dealt well with my
lord, then remember thine handmaid.
32And David said to Abigail, Blessed *be* the LORD
God of Israel, which sent thee this day to meet me:
33And blessed *be* thy advice, and blessed *be* thou,
which hast kept me this day from coming to *shed*
blood, and from avenging myself with mine own
hand.
34For in very deed, *as* the LORD God of Israel liveth,
which hath kept me back from hurting thee, except
thou hadst hasted and come to meet me, surely there
had not been left unto Nabal by the morning light
any that pisseth against the wall.

NEW LIVING TRANSLATION

her. 21David had just been saying, "A lot of good it did
to help this fellow. We protected his flocks in the
wilderness, and nothing he owned was lost or stolen.
But he has repaid me evil for good. 22May God strike
me and kill me* if even one man of his household is
still alive tomorrow morning!"

Abigail Intercedes for Nabal

23When Abigail saw David, she quickly got off her
donkey and bowed low before him. 24She fell at his
feet and said, "I accept all blame in this matter, my
lord. Please listen to what I have to say. 25I know
Nabal is a wicked and ill-tempered man; please
don't pay any attention to him. He is a fool, just as his
name suggests.* But I never even saw the young men
you sent.
26"Now, my lord, as surely as the LORD lives and
you yourself live, since the LORD has kept you from
murdering and taking vengeance into your own
hands, let all your enemies and those who try to
harm you be as cursed as Nabal is. 27And here is a
present that I, your servant, have brought to you and
your young men. 28Please forgive me if I have offended you in any way. The LORD will surely reward
you with a lasting dynasty, for you are fighting the
LORD's battles. And you have not done wrong
throughout your entire life.
29"Even when you are chased by those who seek to
kill you, your life is safe in the care of the LORD your
God, secure in his treasure pouch! But the lives of
your enemies will disappear like stones shot from a
sling! 30When the LORD has done all he promised
and has made you leader of Israel, 31don't let this be a
blemish on your record. Then your conscience won't
have to bear the staggering burden of needless
bloodshed and vengeance. And when the LORD has
done these great things for you, please remember
me, your servant!"
32David replied to Abigail, "Praise the LORD, the
God of Israel, who has sent you to meet me today!
33Thank God for your good sense! Bless you for keeping me from murder and from carrying out vengeance with my own hands. 34For I swear by the
LORD, the God of Israel, who has kept me from hurting you, that if you had not hurried out to meet me,
not one of Nabal's men would still be alive tomorrow

25:22 As in Greek version; Hebrew reads *May God strike and kill the enemies of David.* **25:25** The name *Nabal* means "fool."

KING JAMES VERSION

35 So David received of her hand *that* which she
had brought him, and said unto her, Go up in peace
to thine house; see, I have hearkened to thy voice,
and have accepted thy person.
36 And Abigail came to Nabal; and, behold, he held
a feast in his house, like the feast of a king; and
Nabal's heart *was* merry within him, for he *was* very
drunken: wherefore she told him nothing, less or
more, until the morning light.
37 But it came to pass in the morning, when the
wine was gone out of Nabal, and his wife had told
him these things, that his heart died within him, and
he became *as* a stone.
38 And it came to pass about ten days *after*, that the
LORD smote Nabal, that he died.
39 And when David heard that Nabal was dead, he
said, Blessed *be* the LORD, that hath pleaded the
cause of my reproach from the hand of Nabal, and
hath kept his servant from evil: for the LORD hath returned the wickedness of Nabal upon his own head.
And David sent and communed with Abigail, to take
her to him to wife.
40 And when the servants of David were come to
Abigail to Carmel, they spake unto her, saying, David
sent us unto thee, to take thee to him to wife.
41 And she arose, and bowed herself on *her* face to
the earth, and said, Behold, *let* thine handmaid *be* a
servant to wash the feet of the servants of my lord.
42 And Abigail hasted, and arose, and rode upon an
ass, with five damsels of hers that went after her; and
she went after the messengers of David, and became
his wife.
43 David also took Ahinoam of Jezreel; and they
were also both of them his wives.
44 But Saul had given Michal his daughter, David's
wife, to Phalti the son of Laish, which *was* of Gallim.

26 1 And the Ziphites came unto Saul to Gibeah, saying, Doth not David hide himself in
the hill of Hachilah, *which is* before Jeshimon?
2 Then Saul arose, and went down to the wilderness of Ziph, having three thousand chosen men of
Israel with him, to seek David in the wilderness
of Ziph.
3 And Saul pitched in the hill of Hachilah, which *is*
before Jeshimon, by the way. But David abode in the
wilderness, and he saw that Saul came after him into
the wilderness.
4 David therefore sent out spies, and understood
that Saul was come in very deed.
5 And David arose, and came to the place where
Saul had pitched: and David beheld the place where
Saul lay, and Abner the son of Ner, the captain of his
host: and Saul lay in the trench, and the people
pitched round about him.
6 Then answered David and said to Ahimelech the
Hittite, and to Abishai the son of Zeruiah, brother to

NEW LIVING TRANSLATION

morning." 35 Then David accepted her present and
told her, "Return home in peace. I have heard what
you said. We will not kill your husband."
36 When Abigail arrived home, she found that
Nabal was throwing a big party and was celebrating
like a king. He was very drunk, so she didn't tell him
anything about her meeting with David until dawn
the next day. 37 In the morning when Nabal was sober, his wife told him what had happened. As a result
he had a stroke,* and he lay paralyzed on his bed like
a stone. 38 About ten days later, the LORD struck him,
and he died.

David Marries Abigail

39 When David heard that Nabal was dead, he said,
"Praise the LORD, who has avenged the insult I received from Nabal and has kept me from doing it myself. Nabal has received the punishment for his sin."
Then David sent messengers to Abigail to ask her to
become his wife.
40 When the messengers arrived at Carmel, they
told Abigail, "David has sent us to take you back to
marry him."
41 She bowed low to the ground and responded, "I,
your servant, would be happy to marry David. I would
even be willing to become a slave, washing the feet of
his servants!" 42 Quickly getting ready, she took along
five of her servant girls as attendants, mounted her
donkey, and went with David's messengers. And so
she became his wife. 43 David also married Ahinoam
from Jezreel, making both of them his wives. 44 Saul,
meanwhile, had given his daughter Michal, David's
wife, to a man from Gallim named Palti son of Laish.

David Spares Saul Again

26 Now some men from Ziph came to Saul at
Gibeah to tell him, "David is hiding on the
hill of Hakilah, which overlooks Jeshimon."
2 So Saul took 3,000 of Israel's elite troops and
went to hunt him down in the wilderness of Ziph.
3 Saul camped along the road beside the hill of Hakilah, near Jeshimon, where David was hiding. When
David learned that Saul had come after him into the
wilderness, 4 he sent out spies to verify the report of
Saul's arrival.
5 David slipped over to Saul's camp one night to
look around. Saul and Abner son of Ner, the commander of his army, were sleeping inside a ring
formed by the slumbering warriors. 6 "Who will
volunteer to go in there with me?" David asked

25:37 Hebrew *his heart failed him.*

KING JAMES VERSION

Joab, saying, Who will go down with me to Saul to the
camp? And Abishai said, I will go down with thee.
7So David and Abishai came to the people by
night: and, behold, Saul lay sleeping within the
trench, and his spear stuck in the ground at his bolster: but Abner and the people lay round about him.
8Then said Abishai to David, God hath delivered
thine enemy into thine hand this day: now therefore
let me smite him, I pray thee, with the spear even to
the earth at once, and I will not *smite* him the second
time.
9And David said to Abishai, Destroy him not: for
who can stretch forth his hand against the LORD's
anointed, and be guiltless?
10David said furthermore, *As* the LORD liveth, the
LORD shall smite him; or his day shall come to die; or
he shall descend into battle, and perish.
11The LORD forbid that I should stretch forth mine
hand against the LORD's anointed: but, I pray thee,
take thou now the spear that *is* at his bolster, and the
cruse of water, and let us go.
12So David took the spear and the cruse of water
from Saul's bolster; and they gat them away, and no
man saw *it*, nor knew *it*, neither awaked: for they
were all asleep; because a deep sleep from the LORD
was fallen upon them.
13Then David went over to the other side, and
stood on the top of an hill afar off; a great space *being* between them:
14And David cried to the people, and to Abner the
son of Ner, saying, Answerest thou not, Abner? Then
Abner answered and said, Who *art* thou *that* criest
to the king?
15And David said to Abner, *Art* not thou a *valiant*
man? and who *is* like to thee in Israel? wherefore
then hast thou not kept thy lord the king? for there
came one of the people in to destroy the king thy
lord.
16This thing *is* not good that thou hast done. *As*
the LORD liveth, ye *are* worthy to die, because ye have
not kept your master, the LORD's anointed. And now
see where the king's spear *is*, and the cruse of water
that *was* at his bolster.
17And Saul knew David's voice, and said, *Is* this thy
voice, my son David? And David said, *It is* my voice,
my lord, O king.
18And he said, Wherefore doth my lord thus pursue after his servant? for what have I done? or what
evil *is* in mine hand?
19Now therefore, I pray thee, let my lord the king
hear the words of his servant. If the LORD have
stirred thee up against me, let him accept an offering: but if *they be* the children of men, cursed *be* they
before the LORD; for they have driven me out this day
from abiding in the inheritance of the LORD, saying,
Go, serve other gods.
20Now therefore, let not my blood fall to the earth
before the face of the LORD: for the king of Israel is

NEW LIVING TRANSLATION

Ahimelech the Hittite and Abishai son of Zeruiah,
Joab's brother.
"I'll go with you," Abishai replied. 7So David and
Abishai went right into Saul's camp and found him
asleep, with his spear stuck in the ground beside his
head. Abner and the soldiers were lying asleep
around him.
8"God has surely handed your enemy over to you
this time!" Abishai whispered to David. "Let me pin
him to the ground with one thrust of the spear; I
won't need to strike twice!"
9"No!" David said. "Don't kill him. For who can remain innocent after attacking the LORD's anointed
one? 10Surely the LORD will strike Saul down someday, or he will die of old age or in battle. 11The LORD
forbid that I should kill the one he has anointed! But
take his spear and that jug of water beside his head,
and then let's get out of here!"
12So David took the spear and jug of water that
were near Saul's head. Then he and Abishai got away
without anyone seeing them or even waking up, because the LORD had put Saul's men into a deep sleep.
13David climbed the hill opposite the camp until
he was at a safe distance. 14Then he shouted down to
the soldiers and to Abner son of Ner, "Wake up,
Abner!"
"Who is it?" Abner demanded.
15"Well, Abner, you're a great man, aren't you?"
David taunted. "Where in all Israel is there anyone as
mighty? So why haven't you guarded your master the
king when someone came to kill him? 16This isn't
good at all! I swear by the LORD that you and your
men deserve to die, because you failed to protect
your master, the LORD's anointed! Look around!
Where are the king's spear and the jug of water that
were beside his head?"
17Saul recognized David's voice and called out, "Is
that you, my son David?"
And David replied, "Yes, my lord the king. 18Why
are you chasing me? What have I done? What is my
crime? 19But now let my lord the king listen to his
servant. If the LORD has stirred you up against me,
then let him accept my offering. But if this is simply a
human scheme, then may those involved be cursed
by the LORD. For they have driven me from my home,
so I can no longer live among the LORD's people, and
they have said, 'Go, worship pagan gods.' 20Must I die
on foreign soil, far from the presence of the LORD?

KING JAMES VERSION

come out to seek a flea, as when one doth hunt a partridge in the mountains.

21 Then said Saul, I have sinned: return, my son David: for I will no more do thee harm, because my soul was precious in thine eyes this day: behold, I have played the fool, and have erred exceedingly.

22 And David answered and said, Behold the king's spear! and let one of the young men come over and fetch it.

23 The LORD render to every man his righteousness and his faithfulness: for the LORD delivered thee into *my* hand today, but I would not stretch forth mine hand against the LORD's anointed.

24 And, behold, as thy life was much set by this day in mine eyes, so let my life be much set by in the eyes of the LORD, and let him deliver me out of all tribulation.

25 Then Saul said to David, Blessed *be* thou, my son David: thou shalt both do great *things,* and also shalt still prevail. So David went on his way, and Saul returned to his place.

27 1 And David said in his heart, I shall now perish one day by the hand of Saul: *there is* nothing better for me than that I should speedily escape into the land of the Philistines; and Saul shall despair of me, to seek me any more in any coast of Israel: so shall I escape out of his hand.

2 And David arose, and he passed over with the six hundred men that *were* with him unto Achish, the son of Maoch, king of Gath.

3 And David dwelt with Achish at Gath, he and his men, every man with his household, *even* David with his two wives, Ahinoam the Jezreelitess, and Abigail the Carmelitess, Nabal's wife.

4 And it was told Saul that David was fled to Gath: and he sought no more again for him.

5 And David said unto Achish, If I have now found grace in thine eyes, let them give me a place in some town in the country, that I may dwell there: for why should thy servant dwell in the royal city with thee?

6 Then Achish gave him Ziklag that day: wherefore Ziklag pertaineth unto the kings of Judah unto this day.

7 And the time that David dwelt in the country of the Philistines was a full year and four months.

8 And David and his men went up, and invaded the Geshurites, and the Gezrites, and the Amalekites: for those *nations were* of old the inhabitants of the land, as thou goest to Shur, even unto the land of Egypt.

9 And David smote the land, and left neither man nor woman alive, and took away the sheep, and the oxen, and the asses, and the camels, and the apparel, and returned, and came to Achish.

10 And Achish said, Whither have ye made a road today? And David said, Against the south of Judah, and against the south of the Jerahmeelites, and against the south of the Kenites.

NEW LIVING TRANSLATION

Why has the king of Israel come out to search for a single flea? Why does he hunt me down like a partridge on the mountains?"

21 Then Saul confessed, "I have sinned. Come back home, my son, and I will no longer try to harm you, for you valued my life today. I have been a fool and very, very wrong."

22 "Here is your spear, O king," David replied. "Let one of your young men come over and get it. 23 The LORD gives his own reward for doing good and for being loyal, and I refused to kill you even when the LORD placed you in my power, for you are the LORD's anointed one. 24 Now may the LORD value my life, even as I have valued yours today. May he rescue me from all my troubles."

25 And Saul said to David, "Blessings on you, my son David. You will do many heroic deeds, and you will surely succeed." Then David went away, and Saul returned home.

David among the Philistines

27 But David kept thinking to himself, "Someday Saul is going to get me. The best thing I can do is escape to the Philistines. Then Saul will stop hunting for me in Israelite territory, and I will finally be safe."

2 So David took his 600 men and went over and joined Achish son of Maoch, the king of Gath. 3 David and his men and their families settled there with Achish at Gath. David brought his two wives along with him—Ahinoam from Jezreel and Abigail, Nabal's widow from Carmel. 4 Word soon reached Saul that David had fled to Gath, so he stopped hunting for him.

5 One day David said to Achish, "If it is all right with you, we would rather live in one of the country towns instead of here in the royal city."

6 So Achish gave him the town of Ziklag (which still belongs to the kings of Judah to this day), 7 and they lived there among the Philistines for a year and four months.

8 David and his men spent their time raiding the Geshurites, the Girzites, and the Amalekites—people who had lived near Shur, toward the land of Egypt, since ancient times. 9 David did not leave one person alive in the villages he attacked. He took the sheep, goats, cattle, donkeys, camels, and clothing before returning home to see King Achish.

10 "Where did you make your raid today?" Achish would ask.

And David would reply, "Against the south of Judah, the Jerahmeelites, and the Kenites."

KING JAMES VERSION

11And David saved neither man nor woman alive,
to bring *tidings* to Gath, saying, Lest they should tell
on us, saying, So did David, and so *will be* his manner all the while he dwelleth in the country of the
Philistines.
12And Achish believed David, saying, He hath
made his people Israel utterly to abhor him; therefore he shall be my servant for ever.

28 1And it came to pass in those days, that the
Philistines gathered their armies together
for warfare, to fight with Israel. And Achish said unto
David, Know thou assuredly, that thou shalt go out
with me to battle, thou and thy men.
2And David said to Achish, Surely thou shalt know
what thy servant can do. And Achish said to David,
Therefore will I make thee keeper of mine head for
ever.
3Now Samuel was dead, and all Israel had lamented him, and buried him in Ramah, even in his
own city. And Saul had put away those that had
familiar spirits, and the wizards, out of the land.
4And the Philistines gathered themselves together, and came and pitched in Shunem: and Saul
gathered all Israel together, and they pitched in
Gilboa.
5And when Saul saw the host of the Philistines, he
was afraid, and his heart greatly trembled.
6And when Saul inquired of the LORD, the LORD
answered him not, neither by dreams, nor by Urim,
nor by prophets.
7Then said Saul unto his servants, Seek me a
woman that hath a familiar spirit, that I may go to
her, and inquire of her. And his servants said to him,
Behold, *there is* a woman that hath a familiar spirit at
En-dor.
8And Saul disguised himself, and put on other raiment, and he went, and two men with him, and they
came to the woman by night: and he said, I pray thee,
divine unto me by the familiar spirit, and bring me
him up, whom I shall name unto thee.
9And the woman said unto him, Behold, thou
knowest what Saul hath done, how he hath cut off
those that have familiar spirits, and the wizards, out
of the land: wherefore then layest thou a snare for my
life, to cause me to die?
10And Saul sware to her by the LORD, saying, *As* the
LORD liveth, there shall no punishment happen to
thee for this thing.
11Then said the woman, Whom shall I bring up
unto thee? And he said, Bring me up Samuel.
12And when the woman saw Samuel, she cried
with a loud voice: and the woman spake to Saul, saying, Why hast thou deceived me? for thou *art* Saul.
13And the king said unto her, Be not afraid: for
what sawest thou? And the woman said unto Saul, I
saw gods ascending out of the earth.
14And he said unto her, What form *is* he of? And

NEW LIVING TRANSLATION

11No one was left alive to come to Gath and tell
where he had really been. This happened again and
again while he was living among the Philistines.
12Achish believed David and thought to himself, "By
now the people of Israel must hate him bitterly. Now
he will have to stay here and serve me forever!"

Saul Consults a Medium

28 About that time the Philistines mustered
their armies for another war with Israel.
King Achish told David, "You and your men will be
expected to join me in battle."
2"Very well!" David agreed. "Now you will see for
yourself what we can do."
Then Achish told David, "I will make you my personal bodyguard for life."
3Meanwhile, Samuel had died, and all Israel had
mourned for him. He was buried in Ramah, his
hometown. And Saul had banned from the land of
Israel all mediums and those who consult the spirits
of the dead.
4The Philistines set up their camp at Shunem, and
Saul gathered all the army of Israel and camped at
Gilboa. 5When Saul saw the vast Philistine army, he
became frantic with fear. 6He asked the LORD what
he should do, but the LORD refused to answer him, either by dreams or by sacred lots* or by the prophets.
7Saul then said to his advisers, "Find a woman who is
a medium, so I can go and ask her what to do."
His advisers replied, "There is a medium at
Endor."
8So Saul disguised himself by wearing ordinary
clothing instead of his royal robes. Then he went to
the woman's home at night, accompanied by two of
his men.
"I have to talk to a man who has died," he said.
"Will you call up his spirit for me?"
9"Are you trying to get me killed?" the woman demanded. "You know that Saul has outlawed all the
mediums and all who consult the spirits of the dead.
Why are you setting a trap for me?"
10But Saul took an oath in the name of the LORD
and promised, "As surely as the LORD lives, nothing
bad will happen to you for doing this."
11Finally, the woman said, "Well, whose spirit do
you want me to call up?"
"Call up Samuel," Saul replied.
12When the woman saw Samuel, she screamed,
"You've deceived me! You are Saul!"
13"Don't be afraid!" the king told her. "What do
you see?"
"I see a god* coming up out of the earth," she said.
14"What does he look like?" Saul asked.

28:6 Hebrew *by Urim.* **28:13** Or *gods.*

KING JAMES VERSION

she said, An old man cometh up; and he *is* covered with a mantle. And Saul perceived that it *was* Samuel, and he stooped with *his* face to the ground, and bowed himself.

15 And Samuel said to Saul, Why hast thou disquieted me, to bring me up? And Saul answered, I am sore distressed; for the Philistines make war against me, and God is departed from me, and answereth me no more, neither by prophets, nor by dreams: therefore I have called thee, that thou mayest make known unto me what I shall do.

16 Then said Samuel, Wherefore then dost thou ask of me, seeing the LORD is departed from thee, and is become thine enemy?

17 And the LORD hath done to him, as he spake by me: for the LORD hath rent the kingdom out of thine hand, and given it to thy neighbour, *even* to David:

18 Because thou obeyedst not the voice of the LORD, nor executedst his fierce wrath upon Amalek, therefore hath the LORD done this thing unto thee this day.

19 Moreover the LORD will also deliver Israel with thee into the hand of the Philistines: and tomorrow *shalt* thou and thy sons *be* with me: the LORD also shall deliver the host of Israel into the hand of the Philistines.

20 Then Saul fell straightway all along on the earth, and was sore afraid, because of the words of Samuel: and there was no strength in him; for he had eaten no bread all the day, nor all the night.

21 And the woman came unto Saul, and saw that he was sore troubled, and said unto him, Behold, thine handmaid hath obeyed thy voice, and I have put my life in my hand, and have hearkened unto thy words which thou spakest unto me.

22 Now therefore, I pray thee, hearken thou also unto the voice of thine handmaid, and let me set a morsel of bread before thee; and eat, that thou mayest have strength, when thou goest on thy way.

23 But he refused, and said, I will not eat. But his servants, together with the woman, compelled him; and he hearkened unto their voice. So he arose from the earth, and sat upon the bed.

24 And the woman had a fat calf in the house; and she hasted, and killed it, and took flour, and kneaded *it*, and did bake unleavened bread thereof:

25 And she brought *it* before Saul, and before his servants; and they did eat. Then they rose up, and went away that night.

29 1 Now the Philistines gathered together all their armies to Aphek: and the Israelites pitched by a fountain which *is* in Jezreel.

2 And the lords of the Philistines passed on by hundreds, and by thousands: but David and his men passed on in the rereward with Achish.

3 Then said the princes of the Philistines, What *do* these Hebrews *here?* And Achish said unto the princes of the Philistines, *Is* not this David, the

NEW LIVING TRANSLATION

"He is an old man wrapped in a robe," she replied.
Saul realized it was Samuel, and he fell to the ground
before him.

15 "Why have you disturbed me by calling me
back?" Samuel asked Saul.

"Because I am in deep trouble," Saul replied. "The
Philistines are at war with me, and God has left me
and won't reply by prophets or dreams. So I have
called for you to tell me what to do."

16 But Samuel replied, "Why ask me, since the
LORD has left you and has become your enemy?
17 The LORD has done just as he said he would. He has
torn the kingdom from you and given it to your rival,
David. 18 The LORD has done this to you today because you refused to carry out his fierce anger
against the Amalekites. 19 What's more, the LORD will
hand you and the army of Israel over to the Philistines tomorrow, and you and your sons will be here
with me. The LORD will bring down the entire army
of Israel in defeat."

20 Saul fell full length on the ground, paralyzed
with fright because of Samuel's words. He was also
faint with hunger, for he had eaten nothing all day
and all night.

21 When the woman saw how distraught he was,
she said, "Sir, I obeyed your command at the risk of
my life. 22 Now do what I say, and let me give you a
little something to eat so you can regain your
strength for the trip back."

23 But Saul refused to eat anything. Then his advisers joined the woman in urging him to eat, so he
finally yielded and got up from the ground and sat on
the couch.

24 The woman had been fattening a calf, so she
hurried out and killed it. She took some flour,
kneaded it into dough and baked unleavened bread.
25 She brought the meal to Saul and his advisers, and
they ate it. Then they went out into the night.

The Philistines Reject David

29 The entire Philistine army now mobilized
at Aphek, and the Israelites camped at the
spring in Jezreel. 2 As the Philistine rulers were leading out their troops in groups of hundreds and thousands, David and his men marched at the rear with
King Achish. 3 But the Philistine commanders demanded, "What are these Hebrews doing here?"

And Achish told them, "This is David, the servant
of King Saul of Israel. He's been with me for years,

KING JAMES VERSION

servant of Saul the king of Israel, which hath been with me these days, or these years, and I have found no fault in him since he fell *unto me* unto this day?

4And the princes of the Philistines were wroth with him; and the princes of the Philistines said unto him, Make this fellow return, that he may go again to his place which thou hast appointed him, and let him not go down with us to battle, lest in the battle he be an adversary to us: for wherewith should he reconcile himself unto his master? *should it* not *be* with the heads of these men?

5*Is* not this David, of whom they sang one to another in dances, saying, Saul slew his thousands, and David his ten thousands?

6Then Achish called David, and said unto him, Surely, *as* the LORD liveth, thou hast been upright, and thy going out and thy coming in with me in the host *is* good in my sight: for I have not found evil in thee since the day of thy coming unto me unto this day: nevertheless the lords favour thee not.

7Wherefore now return, and go in peace, that thou displease not the lords of the Philistines.

8And David said unto Achish, But what have I done? and what hast thou found in thy servant so long as I have been with thee unto this day, that I may not go fight against the enemies of my lord the king?

9And Achish answered and said to David, I know that thou *art* good in my sight, as an angel of God: notwithstanding the princes of the Philistines have said, He shall not go up with us to the battle.

10Wherefore now rise up early in the morning with thy master's servants that are come with thee: and as soon as ye be up early in the morning, and have light, depart.

11So David and his men rose up early to depart in the morning, to return into the land of the Philistines. And the Philistines went up to Jezreel.

30 1And it came to pass, when David and his men were come to Ziklag on the third day, that the Amalekites had invaded the south, and Ziklag, and smitten Ziklag, and burned it with fire;

2And had taken the women captives, that *were* therein: they slew not any, either great or small, but carried *them* away, and went on their way.

3So David and his men came to the city, and, behold, *it was* burned with fire; and their wives, and their sons, and their daughters, were taken captives.

4Then David and the people that *were* with him lifted up their voice and wept, until they had no more power to weep.

5And David's two wives were taken captives, Ahinoam the Jezreelitess, and Abigail the wife of Nabal the Carmelite.

6And David was greatly distressed; for the people spake of stoning him, because the soul of all the people was grieved, every man for his sons and for his

NEW LIVING TRANSLATION

and I've never found a single fault in him from the day he arrived until today."

4But the Philistine commanders were angry. "Send him back to the town you've given him!" they demanded. "He can't go into the battle with us. What if he turns against us in battle and becomes our adversary? Is there any better way for him to reconcile himself with his master than by handing our heads over to him? 5Isn't this the same David about whom the women of Israel sing in their dances,

'Saul has killed his thousands,
and David his ten thousands'?"

6So Achish finally summoned David and said to him, "I swear by the LORD that you have been a trustworthy ally. I think you should go with me into battle, for I've never found a single flaw in you from the day you arrived until today. But the other Philistine rulers won't hear of it. 7Please don't upset them, but go back quietly."

8"What have I done to deserve this treatment?" David demanded. "What have you ever found in your servant, that I can't go and fight the enemies of my lord the king?"

9But Achish insisted, "As far as I'm concerned, you're as perfect as an angel of God. But the Philistine commanders are afraid to have you with them in the battle. 10Now get up early in the morning, and leave with your men as soon as it gets light."

11So David and his men headed back into the land of the Philistines, while the Philistine army went on to Jezreel.

David Destroys the Amalekites

30 Three days later, when David and his men arrived home at their town of Ziklag, they found that the Amalekites had made a raid into the Negev and Ziklag; they had crushed Ziklag and burned it to the ground. 2They had carried off the women and children and everyone else but without killing anyone.

3When David and his men saw the ruins and realized what had happened to their families, 4they wept until they could weep no more. 5David's two wives, Ahinoam from Jezreel and Abigail, the widow of Nabal from Carmel, were among those captured. 6David was now in great danger because all his men were very bitter about losing their sons and daughters,

KING JAMES VERSION

daughters: but David encouraged himself in the LORD
his God.
7And David said to Abiathar the priest, Ahimelech's son, I pray thee, bring me hither the ephod.
And Abiathar brought thither the ephod to David.
8And David inquired at the LORD, saying, Shall I
pursue after this troop? shall I overtake them? And
he answered him, Pursue: for thou shalt surely overtake *them*, and without fail recover *all*.
9So David went, he and the six hundred men that
were with him, and came to the brook Besor, where
those that were left behind stayed.
10But David pursued, he and four hundred men:
for two hundred abode behind, which were so faint
that they could not go over the brook Besor.
11And they found an Egyptian in the field, and
brought him to David, and gave him bread, and he
did eat; and they made him drink water;
12And they gave him a piece of a cake of figs, and
two clusters of raisins: and when he had eaten, his
spirit came again to him: for he had eaten no bread,
nor drunk *any* water, three days and three nights.
13And David said unto him, To whom *belongest*
thou? and whence *art* thou? And he said, I *am* a
young man of Egypt, servant to an Amalekite; and my
master left me, because three days agone I fell sick.
14We made an invasion *upon* the south of the
Cherethites, and upon *the coast* which *belongeth* to
Judah, and upon the south of Caleb; and we burned
Ziklag with fire.
15And David said to him, Canst thou bring me
down to this company? And he said, Swear unto me
by God, that thou wilt neither kill me, nor deliver
me into the hands of my master, and I will bring thee
down to this company.
16And when he had brought him down, behold,
they were spread abroad upon all the earth, eating
and drinking, and dancing, because of all the great
spoil that they had taken out of the land of the Philistines, and out of the land of Judah.
17And David smote them from the twilight even
unto the evening of the next day: and there escaped
not a man of them, save four hundred young men,
which rode upon camels, and fled.
18And David recovered all that the Amalekites had
carried away: and David rescued his two wives.
19And there was nothing lacking to them, neither
small nor great, neither sons nor daughters, neither
spoil, nor any *thing* that they had taken to them: David recovered all.
20And David took all the flocks and the herds,
which they drave before those *other* cattle, and said,
This *is* David's spoil.
21And David came to the two hundred men,
which were so faint that they could not follow David, whom they had made also to abide at the brook
Besor: and they went forth to meet David, and to

NEW LIVING TRANSLATION

and they began to talk of stoning him. But David
found strength in the LORD his God.
7Then he said to Abiathar the priest, "Bring me the
ephod!" So Abiathar brought it. 8Then David asked
the LORD, "Should I chase after this band of raiders?
Will I catch them?"
And the LORD told him, "Yes, go after them. You
will surely recover everything that was taken from
you!"
9So David and his 600 men set out, and they came
to the brook Besor. 10But 200 of the men were too
exhausted to cross the brook, so David continued the
pursuit with 400 men.
11Along the way they found an Egyptian man in a
field and brought him to David. They gave him some
bread to eat and water to drink. 12They also gave him
part of a fig cake and two clusters of raisins, for he
hadn't had anything to eat or drink for three days and
nights. Before long his strength returned.
13"To whom do you belong, and where do you
come from?" David asked him.
"I am an Egyptian—the slave of an Amalekite," he
replied. "My master abandoned me three days ago
because I was sick. 14We were on our way back from
raiding the Kerethites in the Negev, the territory of
Judah, and the land of Caleb, and we had just burned
Ziklag."
15"Will you lead me to this band of raiders?"
David asked.
The young man replied, "If you take an oath in
God's name that you will not kill me or give me back
to my master, then I will guide you to them."
16So he led David to them, and they found the Amalekites spread out across the fields, eating and
drinking and dancing with joy because of the vast
amount of plunder they had taken from the Philistines and the land of Judah. 17David and his men
rushed in among them and slaughtered them
throughout that night and the entire next day until
evening. None of the Amalekites escaped except
400 young men who fled on camels. 18David got
back everything the Amalekites had taken, and he
rescued his two wives. 19Nothing was missing: small
or great, son or daughter, nor anything else that had
been taken. David brought everything back. 20He
also recovered all the flocks and herds, and his men
drove them ahead of the other livestock. "This plunder belongs to David!" they said.
21Then David returned to the brook Besor and met
up with the 200 men who had been left behind because they were too exhausted to go with him. They

KING JAMES VERSION

meet the people that *were* with him: and when
David came near to the people, he saluted them.
22 Then answered all the wicked men and *men* of
Belial, of those that went with David, and said, Because they went not with us, we will not give them
aught of the spoil that we have recovered, save to
every man his wife and his children, that they may
lead *them* away, and depart.
23 Then said David, Ye shall not do so, my brethren,
with that which the LORD hath given us, who hath
preserved us, and delivered the company that came
against us into our hand.
24 For who will hearken unto you in this matter?
but as his part *is* that goeth down to the battle, so
shall his part *be* that tarrieth by the stuff: they shall
part alike.
25 And it was *so* from that day forward, that he
made it a statute and an ordinance for Israel unto
this day.
26 And when David came to Ziklag, he sent of the
spoil unto the elders of Judah, *even* to his friends,
saying, Behold a present for you of the spoil of the
enemies of the LORD;
27 To *them* which *were* in Bethel, and to *them*
which *were* in south Ramoth, and to *them* which
were in Jattir,
28 And to *them* which *were* in Aroer, and to *them*
which *were* in Siphmoth, and to *them* which *were*
in Eshtemoa,
29 And to *them* which *were* in Rachal, and to *them*
which *were* in the cities of the Jerahmeelites, and to
them which *were* in the cities of the Kenites,
30 And to *them* which *were* in Hormah, and to
them which *were* in Chor-ashan, and to *them* which
were in Athach,
31 And to *them* which *were* in Hebron, and to all
the places where David himself and his men were
wont to haunt.

31 1 Now the Philistines fought against Israel:
and the men of Israel fled from before the
Philistines, and fell down slain in mount Gilboa.
2 And the Philistines followed hard upon Saul and
upon his sons; and the Philistines slew Jonathan, and
Abinadab, and Melchi-shua, Saul's sons.
3 And the battle went sore against Saul, and the
archers hit him; and he was sore wounded of the
archers.
4 Then said Saul unto his armourbearer, Draw thy
sword, and thrust me through therewith; lest these
uncircumcised come and thrust me through, and
abuse me. But his armourbearer would not; for he
was sore afraid. Therefore Saul took a sword, and fell
upon it.
5 And when his armourbearer saw that Saul was
dead, he fell likewise upon his sword, and died
with him.

NEW LIVING TRANSLATION

went out to meet David and his men, and David
greeted them joyfully. 22 But some evil troublemakers
among David's men said, "They didn't go with us, so
they can't have any of the plunder we recovered. Give
them their wives and children, and tell them to
be one."
23 But David said, "No, my brothers! Don't be selfish
with what the LORD has given us. He has kept us safe
and helped us defeat the band of raiders that attacked us. 24 Who will listen when you talk like this?
We share and share alike—those who go to battle and
those who guard the equipment." 25 From then on
David made this a decree and regulation for Israel,
and it is still followed today.
26 When he arrived at Ziklag, David sent part of the
plunder to the elders of Judah, who were his friends.
"Here is a present for you, taken from the LORD's
enemies," he said.
27 The gifts were sent to the people of the following towns David had visited: Bethel, Ramoth-negev,
Jattir, 28 Aroer, Siphmoth, Eshtemoa, 29 Racal,* the
towns of the Jerahmeelites, the towns of the Kenites,
30 Hormah, Bor-ashan, Athach, 31 Hebron, and all the
other places David and his men had visited.

The Death of Saul

31 Now the Philistines attacked Israel, and the
men of Israel fled before them. Many were
slaughtered on the slopes of Mount Gilboa. 2 The Philistines closed in on Saul and his sons, and they killed
three of his sons—Jonathan, Abinadab, and Malkishua. 3 The fighting grew very fierce around Saul, and
the Philistine archers caught up with him and
wounded him severely.
4 Saul groaned to his armor bearer, "Take your
sword and kill me before these pagan Philistines
come to run me through and taunt and torture me."
But his armor bearer was afraid and would not do
it. So Saul took his own sword and fell on it. 5 When
his armor bearer realized that Saul was dead, he fell

30:29 Greek version reads *Carmel.*

KING JAMES VERSION

6So Saul died, and his three sons, and his armourbearer, and all his men, that same day together.
7And when the men of Israel that *were* on the
other side of the valley, and *they* that *were* on the
other side Jordan, saw that the men of Israel fled, and
that Saul and his sons were dead, they forsook the
cities, and fled; and the Philistines came and dwelt
in them.
8And it came to pass on the morrow, when the Philistines came to strip the slain, that they found Saul
and his three sons fallen in mount Gilboa.
9And they cut off his head, and stripped off his armour, and sent into the land of the Philistines round
about, to publish *it in* the house of their idols, and
among the people.
10And they put his armour in the house of Ashtaroth: and they fastened his body to the wall of Beth-
shan.
11And when the inhabitants of Jabesh-gilead
heard of that which the Philistines had done to Saul;
12All the valiant men arose, and went all night, and
took the body of Saul and the bodies of his sons from
the wall of Beth-shan, and came to Jabesh, and burnt
them there.
13And they took their bones, and buried *them* under a tree at Jabesh, and fasted seven days.

NEW LIVING TRANSLATION

on his own sword and died beside the king. 6So Saul,
his three sons, his armor bearer, and his troops all
died together that same day.
7When the Israelites on the other side of the Jezreel Valley and beyond the Jordan saw that the Israelite army had fled and that Saul and his sons were
dead, they abandoned their towns and fled. So the
Philistines moved in and occupied their towns.
8The next day, when the Philistines went out to
strip the dead, they found the bodies of Saul and
his three sons on Mount Gilboa. 9So they cut off
Saul's head and stripped off his armor. Then they
proclaimed the good news of Saul's death in their
pagan temple and to the people throughout the land
of Philistia. 10They placed his armor in the temple of
the Ashtoreths, and they fastened his body to the
wall of the city of Beth-shan.
11But when the people of Jabesh-gilead heard
what the Philistines had done to Saul, 12all their
mighty warriors traveled through the night to Beth-
shan and took the bodies of Saul and his sons down
from the wall. They brought them to Jabesh, where
they burned the bodies. 13Then they took their
bones and buried them beneath the tamarisk tree at
Jabesh, and they fasted for seven days.

2 Samuel

KING JAMES VERSION

1 1 Now it came to pass after the death of Saul, when David was returned from the slaughter of the Amalekites, and David had abode two days in Ziklag;

2 It came even to pass on the third day, that, behold, a man came out of the camp from Saul with his clothes rent, and earth upon his head: and *so* it was, when he came to David, that he fell to the earth, and did obeisance.

3 And David said unto him, From whence comest thou? And he said unto him, Out of the camp of Israel am I escaped.

4 And David said unto him, How went the matter? I pray thee, tell me. And he answered, That the people are fled from the battle, and many of the people also are fallen and dead; and Saul and Jonathan his son are dead also.

5 And David said unto the young man that told him, How knowest thou that Saul and Jonathan his son be dead?

6 And the young man that told him said, As I happened by chance upon mount Gilboa, behold, Saul leaned upon his spear; and, lo, the chariots and horsemen followed hard after him.

7 And when he looked behind him, he saw me, and called unto me. And I answered, Here *am* I.

8 And he said unto me, Who *art* thou? And I answered him, I *am* an Amalekite.

9 He said unto me again, Stand, I pray thee, upon me, and slay me: for anguish is come upon me, because my life *is* yet whole in me.

10 So I stood upon him, and slew him, because I was sure that he could not live after that he was fallen: and I took the crown that *was* upon his head, and the bracelet that *was* on his arm, and have brought them hither unto my lord.

11 Then David took hold on his clothes, and rent them; and likewise all the men that *were* with him:

12 And they mourned, and wept, and fasted until even, for Saul, and for Jonathan his son, and for the people of the LORD, and for the house of Israel; because they were fallen by the sword.

13 And David said unto the young man that told

NEW LIVING TRANSLATION

David Learns of Saul's Death

1 After the death of Saul, David returned from his
victory over the Amalekites and spent two days
in Ziklag. 2 On the third day a man arrived from Saul's
army camp. He had torn his clothes and put dirt on
his head to show that he was in mourning. He fell to
the ground before David in deep respect.
3 "Where have you come from?" David asked.
"I escaped from the Israelite camp," the man
replied.
4 "What happened?" David demanded. "Tell me
how the battle went."
The man replied, "Our entire army fled from the
battle. Many of the men are dead, and Saul and his
son Jonathan are also dead."
5 "How do you know Saul and Jonathan are dead?"
David demanded of the young man.
6 The man answered, "I happened to be on Mount
Gilboa, and there was Saul leaning on his spear with
the enemy chariots and charioteers closing in on
him. 7 When he turned and saw me, he cried out for
me to come to him. 'How can I help?' I asked him.
8 "He responded, 'Who are you?'
"'I am an Amalekite,' I told him.
9 "Then he begged me, 'Come over here and put
me out of my misery, for I am in terrible pain and
want to die.'
10 "So I killed him," the Amalekite told David, "for I
knew he couldn't live. Then I took his crown and his
armband, and I have brought them here to you, my
lord."
11 David and his men tore their clothes in sorrow
when they heard the news. 12 They mourned and
wept and fasted all day for Saul and his son Jonathan,
and for the LORD's army and the nation of Israel,
because they had died by the sword that day.
13 Then David said to the young man who had
brought the news, "Where are you from?"

KING JAMES VERSION

him, Whence *art* thou? And he answered, I *am* the
son of a stranger, an Amalekite.
14 And David said unto him, How wast thou not
afraid to stretch forth thine hand to destroy the
LORD's anointed?
15 And David called one of the young men, and
said, Go near, *and* fall upon him. And he smote him
that he died.
16 And David said unto him, Thy blood *be* upon thy
head; for thy mouth hath testified against thee, saying, I have slain the LORD's anointed.
17 And David lamented with this lamentation over
Saul and over Jonathan his son:
18 (Also he bade them teach the children of Judah
the use of the bow: behold, *it is* written in the book
of Jasher.)
19 The beauty of Israel is slain upon thy high
places: how are the mighty fallen!
20 Tell *it* not in Gath, publish *it* not in the streets of
Askelon; lest the daughters of the Philistines rejoice,
lest the daughters of the uncircumcised triumph.
21 Ye mountains of Gilboa, *let there be* no dew, neither *let there be* rain, upon you, nor fields of offerings: for there the shield of the mighty is vilely cast
away, the shield of Saul, *as though he had* not *been*
anointed with oil.
22 From the blood of the slain, from the fat of the
mighty, the bow of Jonathan turned not back, and the
sword of Saul returned not empty.
23 Saul and Jonathan *were* lovely and pleasant in
their lives, and in their death they were not divided:
they were swifter than eagles, they were stronger
than lions.
24 Ye daughters of Israel, weep over Saul, who
clothed you in scarlet, with *other* delights, who put
on ornaments of gold upon your apparel.
25 How are the mighty fallen in the midst of the
battle! O Jonathan, *thou wast* slain in thine high
places.
26 I am distressed for thee, my brother Jonathan:
very pleasant hast thou been unto me: thy love to me
was wonderful, passing the love of women.
27 How are the mighty fallen, and the weapons of
war perished!

2 1 And it came to pass after this, that David
inquired of the LORD, saying, Shall I go up into
any of the cities of Judah? And the LORD said unto

NEW LIVING TRANSLATION

And he replied, "I am a foreigner, an Amalekite,
who lives in your land."
14 "Why were you not afraid to kill the LORD's
anointed one?" David asked.
15 Then David said to one of his men, "Kill him!"
So the man thrust his sword into the Amalekite
and killed him. 16 "You have condemned yourself,"
David said, "for you yourself confessed that you
killed the LORD's anointed one."

David's Song for Saul and Jonathan

17 Then David composed a funeral song for Saul and
Jonathan, 18 and he commanded that it be taught to
the people of Judah. It is known as the Song of the
Bow, and it is recorded in *The Book of Jashar.**

19 Your pride and joy, O Israel, lies dead on the hills!
Oh, how the mighty heroes have fallen!
20 Don't announce the news in Gath,
don't proclaim it in the streets of Ashkelon,
or the daughters of the Philistines will rejoice
and the pagans will laugh in triumph.

21 O mountains of Gilboa,
let there be no dew or rain upon you,
nor fruitful fields producing offerings
of grain.*
For there the shield of the mighty heroes
was defiled;
the shield of Saul will no longer be anointed
with oil.
22 The bow of Jonathan was powerful,
and the sword of Saul did its mighty work.
They shed the blood of their enemies
and pierced the bodies of mighty heroes.

23 How beloved and gracious were Saul and
Jonathan!
They were together in life and in death.
They were swifter than eagles,
stronger than lions.
24 O women of Israel, weep for Saul,
for he dressed you in luxurious scarlet clothing,
in garments decorated with gold.

25 Oh, how the mighty heroes have fallen in battle!
Jonathan lies dead on the hills.
26 How I weep for you, my brother Jonathan!
Oh, how much I loved you!
And your love for me was deep,
deeper than the love of women!
27 Oh, how the mighty heroes have fallen!
Stripped of their weapons, they lie dead.

David Anointed King of Judah

2 After this, David asked the LORD, "Should I
move back to one of the towns of Judah?"
"Yes," the LORD replied.

1:18 Or *The Book of the Upright.* **1:21** The meaning of the Hebrew is uncertain.

KING JAMES VERSION

him, Go up. And David said, Whither shall I go up?
And he said, Unto Hebron.
2So David went up thither, and his two wives also,
Ahinoam the Jezreelitess, and Abigail Nabal's wife
the Carmelite.
3And his men that *were* with him did David bring
up, every man with his household: and they dwelt in
the cities of Hebron.
4And the men of Judah came, and there they
anointed David king over the house of Judah. And
they told David, saying, *That* the men of Jabesh-
gilead *were they* that buried Saul.
5And David sent messengers unto the men of
Jabesh-gilead, and said unto them, Blessed *be* ye of
the LORD, that ye have shewed this kindness unto
your lord, *even* unto Saul, and have buried him.
6And now the LORD shew kindness and truth unto
you: and I also will requite you this kindness, because ye have done this thing.
7Therefore now let your hands be strengthened,
and be ye valiant: for your master Saul is dead, and
also the house of Judah have anointed me king over
them.
8But Abner the son of Ner, captain of Saul's host,
took Ish-bosheth the son of Saul, and brought him
over to Mahanaim;
9And made him king over Gilead, and over the
Ashurites, and over Jezreel, and over Ephraim, and
over Benjamin, and over all Israel.
10Ish-bosheth Saul's son *was* forty years old when
he began to reign over Israel, and reigned two years.
But the house of Judah followed David.
11And the time that David was king in Hebron over
the house of Judah was seven years and six months.

12And Abner the son of Ner, and the servants of
Ish-bosheth the son of Saul, went out from Mahanaim to Gibeon.
13And Joab the son of Zeruiah, and the servants of
David, went out, and met together by the pool of Gibeon: and they sat down, the one on the one side of the
pool, and the other on the other side of the pool.
14And Abner said to Joab, Let the young men now
arise, and play before us. And Joab said, Let them
arise.
15Then there arose and went over by number
twelve of Benjamin, which *pertained* to Ish-bosheth
the son of Saul, and twelve of the servants of David.
16And they caught every one his fellow by the
head, and *thrust* his sword in his fellow's side; so
they fell down together: wherefore that place was
called Helkath-hazzurim, which *is* in Gibeon.
17And there was a very sore battle that day; and
Abner was beaten, and the men of Israel, before the
servants of David.
18And there were three sons of Zeruiah there, Joab,
and Abishai, and Asahel: and Asahel *was as* light of
foot as a wild roe.

NEW LIVING TRANSLATION

Then David asked, "Which town should I go to?"
"To Hebron," the LORD answered.
2David's two wives were Ahinoam from Jezreel
and Abigail, the widow of Nabal from Carmel. So
David and his wives 3and his men and their families
all moved to Judah, and they settled in the villages
near Hebron. 4Then the men of Judah came to David
and anointed him king over the people of Judah.
When David heard that the men of Jabesh-gilead
had buried Saul, 5he sent them this message: "May
the LORD bless you for being so loyal to your master
Saul and giving him a decent burial. 6May the LORD
be loyal to you in return and reward you with his unfailing love! And I, too, will reward you for what you
have done. 7Now that Saul is dead, I ask you to be my
strong and loyal subjects like the people of Judah,
who have anointed me as their new king."

Ishbosheth Proclaimed King of Israel

8But Abner son of Ner, the commander of Saul's
army, had already gone to Mahanaim with Saul's son
Ishbosheth.* 9There he proclaimed Ishbosheth king
over Gilead, Jezreel, Ephraim, Benjamin, the land of
the Ashurites, and all the rest of Israel.
10Ishbosheth, Saul's son, was forty years old when
he became king, and he ruled from Mahanaim for
two years. Meanwhile, the people of Judah remained
loyal to David. 11David made Hebron his capital, and
he ruled as king of Judah for seven and a half years.

War between Israel and Judah

12One day Abner led Ishbosheth's troops from Mahanaim to Gibeon. 13About the same time, Joab son of
Zeruiah led David's troops out and met them at the
pool of Gibeon. The two groups sat down there,
facing each other from opposite sides of the pool.
14Then Abner suggested to Joab, "Let's have a few
of our warriors fight hand to hand here in front
of us."
"All right," Joab agreed. 15So twelve men were chosen to fight from each side—twelve men of Benjamin
representing Ishbosheth son of Saul, and twelve representing David. 16Each one grabbed his opponent
by the hair and thrust his sword into the other's side
so that all of them died. So this place at Gibeon has
been known ever since as the Field of Swords.*
17A fierce battle followed that day, and Abner and
the men of Israel were defeated by the forces of
David.

The Death of Asahel

18Joab, Abishai, and Asahel—the three sons of Zeruiah—were among David's forces that day. Asahel

2:8 *Ishbosheth* is another name for Esh-baal. **2:16** Hebrew *Helkath-hazzurim.*

19And Asahel pursued after Abner; and in going he
turned not to the right hand nor to the left from
following Abner.
20Then Abner looked behind him, and said, *Art*
thou Asahel? And he answered, I *am*.
21And Abner said to him, Turn thee aside to thy
right hand or to thy left, and lay thee hold on one of
the young men, and take thee his armour. But Asahel
would not turn aside from following of him.
22And Abner said again to Asahel, Turn thee aside
from following me: wherefore should I smite thee
to the ground? how then should I hold up my face to
Joab thy brother?
23Howbeit he refused to turn aside: wherefore
Abner with the hinder end of the spear smote him
under the fifth *rib*, that the spear came out behind
him; and he fell down there, and died in the same
place: and it came to pass, *that* as many as came to
the place where Asahel fell down and died stood still.
24Joab also and Abishai pursued after Abner: and
the sun went down when they were come to the hill
of Ammah, that *lieth* before Giah by the way of the
wilderness of Gibeon.
25And the children of Benjamin gathered themselves together after Abner, and became one troop,
and stood on the top of an hill.
26Then Abner called to Joab, and said, Shall the
sword devour for ever? knowest thou not that it will
be bitterness in the latter end? how long shall it be
then, ere thou bid the people return from following
their brethren?
27And Joab said, *As* God liveth, unless thou hadst
spoken, surely then in the morning the people had
gone up every one from following his brother.
28So Joab blew a trumpet, and all the people stood
still, and pursued after Israel no more, neither fought
they any more.
29And Abner and his men walked all that night
through the plain, and passed over Jordan, and went
through all Bithron, and they came to Mahanaim.
30And Joab returned from following Abner: and
when he had gathered all the people together, there
lacked of David's servants nineteen men and Asahel.
31But the servants of David had smitten of Benjamin, and of Abner's men, *so that* three hundred and
threescore men died.
32And they took up Asahel, and buried him in the
sepulchre of his father, which *was in* Bethlehem.
And Joab and his men went all night, and they came
to Hebron at break of day.

3 1Now there was long war between the house of
Saul and the house of David: but David waxed
stronger and stronger, and the house of Saul waxed
weaker and weaker.

could run like a gazelle, 19and he began chasing
Abner. He pursued him relentlessly, not stopping for
anything. 20When Abner looked back and saw him
coming, he called out, "Is that you, Asahel?"
"Yes, it is," he replied.
21"Go fight someone else!" Abner warned. "Take
on one of the younger men, and strip him of his
weapons." But Asahel kept right on chasing Abner.
22Again Abner shouted to him, "Get away from
here! I don't want to kill you. How could I ever face
your brother Joab again?"
23But Asahel refused to turn back, so Abner
thrust the butt end of his spear through Asahel's
stomach, and the spear came out through his back.
He stumbled to the ground and died there. And
everyone who came by that spot stopped and stood
still when they saw Asahel lying there.
24When Joab and Abishai found out what had
happened, they set out after Abner. The sun was just
going down as they arrived at the hill of Ammah near
Giah, along the road to the wilderness of Gibeon.
25Abner's troops from the tribe of Benjamin regrouped there at the top of the hill to take a stand.
26Abner shouted down to Joab, "Must we always be
killing each other? Don't you realize that bitterness
is the only result? When will you call off your men
from chasing their Israelite brothers?"
27Then Joab said, "God only knows what would
have happened if you hadn't spoken, for we would
have chased you all night if necessary." 28So Joab
blew the ram's horn, and his men stopped chasing
the troops of Israel.
29All that night Abner and his men retreated
through the Jordan Valley.* They crossed the Jordan
River, traveling all through the morning,* and didn't
stop until they arrived at Mahanaim.
30Meanwhile, Joab and his men also returned
home. When Joab counted his casualties, he discovered that only 19 men were missing in addition to
Asahel. 31But 360 of Abner's men had been killed, all
from the tribe of Benjamin. 32Joab and his men took
Asahel's body to Bethlehem and buried him there
in his father's tomb. Then they traveled all night and
reached Hebron at daybreak.

3 That was the beginning of a long war between
those who were loyal to Saul and those loyal to
David. As time passed David became stronger and
stronger, while Saul's dynasty became weaker and
weaker.

2:29a Hebrew *the Arabah*. **2:29b** Or *continued on through the Bithron*.
The meaning of the Hebrew is uncertain.

KING JAMES VERSION

2And unto David were sons born in Hebron: and his firstborn was Amnon, of Ahinoam the Jezreelitess;

3And his second, Chileab, of Abigail the wife of Nabal the Carmelite; and the third, Absalom the son of Maacah the daughter of Talmai king of Geshur;

4And the fourth, Adonijah the son of Haggith; and the fifth, Shephatiah the son of Abital;

5And the sixth, Ithream, by Eglah David's wife. These were born to David in Hebron.

6And it came to pass, while there was war between the house of Saul and the house of David, that Abner made himself strong for the house of Saul.

7And Saul had a concubine, whose name *was* Rizpah, the daughter of Aiah: and *Ish-bosheth* said to Abner, Wherefore hast thou gone in unto my father's concubine?

8Then was Abner very wroth for the words of Ish-bosheth, and said, *Am* I a dog's head, which against Judah do shew kindness this day unto the house of Saul thy father, to his brethren, and to his friends, and have not delivered thee into the hand of David, that thou chargest me today with a fault concerning this woman?

9So do God to Abner, and more also, except, as the LORD hath sworn to David, even so I do to him;

10To translate the kingdom from the house of Saul, and to set up the throne of David over Israel and over Judah, from Dan even to Beer-sheba.

11And he could not answer Abner a word again, because he feared him.

12And Abner sent messengers to David on his behalf, saying, Whose *is* the land? saying *also,* Make thy league with me, and, behold, my hand *shall be* with thee, to bring about all Israel unto thee.

13And he said, Well; I will make a league with thee: but one thing I require of thee, that is, Thou shalt not see my face, except thou first bring Michal Saul's daughter, when thou comest to see my face.

14And David sent messengers to Ish-bosheth Saul's son, saying, Deliver *me* my wife Michal, which I espoused to me for an hundred foreskins of the Philistines.

15And Ish-bosheth sent, and took her from *her* husband, *even* from Phaltiel the son of Laish.

16And her husband went with her along weeping behind her to Bahurim. Then said Abner unto him, Go, return. And he returned.

NEW LIVING TRANSLATION

David's Sons Born in Hebron

2These are the sons who were born to David in Hebron:

The oldest was Amnon, whose mother was Ahinoam from Jezreel.
3 The second was Daniel,* whose mother was Abigail, the widow of Nabal from Carmel.
The third was Absalom, whose mother was Maacah, the daughter of Talmai, king of Geshur.
4 The fourth was Adonijah, whose mother was Haggith.
The fifth was Shephatiah, whose mother was Abital.
5 The sixth was Ithream, whose mother was Eglah, David's wife.

These sons were all born to David in Hebron.

Abner Joins Forces with David

6As the war between the house of Saul and the house
of David went on, Abner became a powerful leader
among those loyal to Saul. 7One day Ishbosheth,*
Saul's son, accused Abner of sleeping with one of his
father's concubines, a woman named Rizpah, daughter of Aiah.

8Abner was furious. "Am I some Judean dog to be
kicked around like this?" he shouted. "After all I have
done for your father, Saul, and his family and friends
by not handing you over to David, is this my reward—
that you find fault with me about this woman? 9May
God strike me and even kill me if I don't do everything I can to help David get what the LORD has
promised him! 10I'm going to take Saul's kingdom
and give it to David. I will establish the throne of
David over Israel as well as Judah, all the way from
Dan in the north to Beersheba in the south." 11Ishbosheth didn't dare say another word because he was
afraid of what Abner might do.

12Then Abner sent messengers to David, saying, "Doesn't the entire land belong to you? Make a solemn pact with me, and I will help turn over all of Israel to you."

13"All right," David replied, "but I will not negotiate with you unless you bring back my wife Michal, Saul's daughter, when you come."

14David then sent this message to Ishbosheth, Saul's son: "Give me back my wife Michal, for I bought her with the lives* of 100 Philistines."

15So Ishbosheth took Michal away from her husband, Palti* son of Laish. 16Palti followed along behind her as far as Bahurim, weeping as he went. Then
Abner told him, "Go back home!" So Palti returned.

3:3 As in parallel text at 1 Chr 3:1 (see also Greek version, which reads *Daluia,* and Dead Sea Scrolls, which read *Dan[iel]*); Hebrew reads *Kileab.* **3:7** *Ishbosheth* is another name for Esh-baal. **3:14** Hebrew *the foreskins.* **3:15** As in 1 Sam 25:44; Hebrew reads *Paltiel,* a variant spelling of Palti.

KING JAMES VERSION

17 And Abner had communication with the elders
of Israel, saying, Ye sought for David in times past *to
be* king over you:
18 Now then do *it:* for the LORD hath spoken of
David, saying, By the hand of my servant David I will
save my people Israel out of the hand of the Philistines, and out of the hand of all their enemies.
19 And Abner also spake in the ears of Benjamin:
and Abner went also to speak in the ears of David in
Hebron all that seemed good to Israel, and that
seemed good to the whole house of Benjamin.
20 So Abner came to David to Hebron, and twenty
men with him. And David made Abner and the men
that *were* with him a feast.
21 And Abner said unto David, I will arise and go,
and will gather all Israel unto my lord the king, that
they may make a league with thee, and that thou
mayest reign over all that thine heart desireth. And
David sent Abner away; and he went in peace.
22 And, behold, the servants of David and Joab came
from *pursuing* a troop, and brought in a great spoil
with them: but Abner *was* not with David in Hebron;
for he had sent him away, and he was gone in peace.
23 When Joab and all the host that *was* with him
were come, they told Joab, saying, Abner the son of
Ner came to the king, and he hath sent him away, and
he is gone in peace.
24 Then Joab came to the king, and said, What hast
thou done? behold, Abner came unto thee; why *is* it
that thou hast sent him away, and he is quite gone?
25 Thou knowest Abner the son of Ner, that he
came to deceive thee, and to know thy going out and
thy coming in, and to know all that thou doest.
26 And when Joab was come out from David, he
sent messengers after Abner, which brought him
again from the well of Sirah: but David knew *it* not.
27 And when Abner was returned to Hebron, Joab
took him aside in the gate to speak with him quietly,
and smote him there under the fifth *rib,* that he died,
for the blood of Asahel his brother.
28 And afterward when David heard *it,* he said, I
and my kingdom *are* guiltless before the LORD for
ever from the blood of Abner the son of Ner:
29 Let it rest on the head of Joab, and on all his
father's house; and let there not fail from the house
of Joab one that hath an issue, or that is a leper, or
that leaneth on a staff, or that falleth on the sword, or
that lacketh bread.
30 So Joab and Abishai his brother slew Abner, because he had slain their brother Asahel at Gibeon in
the battle.
31 And David said to Joab, and to all the people that
were with him, Rend your clothes, and gird you with
sackcloth, and mourn before Abner. And king David
himself followed the bier.
32 And they buried Abner in Hebron: and the king
lifted up his voice, and wept at the grave of Abner;
and all the people wept.

NEW LIVING TRANSLATION

17 Meanwhile, Abner had consulted with the elders
of Israel. "For some time now," he told them, "you
have wanted to make David your king. 18 Now is the
time! For the LORD has said, 'I have chosen David to
save my people Israel from the hands of the Philistines and from all their other enemies.'" 19 Abner also
spoke with the men of Benjamin. Then he went to
Hebron to tell David that all the people of Israel and
Benjamin had agreed to support him.
20 When Abner and twenty of his men came to
Hebron, David entertained them with a great feast.
21 Then Abner said to David, "Let me go and call an
assembly of all Israel to support my lord the king.
They will make a covenant with you to make you
their king, and you will rule over everything your
heart desires." So David sent Abner safely on his way.

Joab Murders Abner

22 But just after David had sent Abner away in safety,
Joab and some of David's troops returned from a
raid, bringing much plunder with them. 23 When
Joab arrived, he was told that Abner had just been
there visiting the king and had been sent away in
safety.
24 Joab rushed to the king and demanded, "What
have you done? What do you mean by letting Abner
get away? 25 You know perfectly well that he came
to spy on you and find out everything you're doing!"
26 Joab then left David and sent messengers to
catch up with Abner, asking him to return. They
found him at the well of Sirah and brought him back,
though David knew nothing about it. 27 When Abner
arrived back at Hebron, Joab took him aside at the
gateway as if to speak with him privately. But then
he stabbed Abner in the stomach and killed him in
revenge for killing his brother Asahel.
28 When David heard about it, he declared, "I vow
by the LORD that I and my kingdom are forever innocent of this crime against Abner son of Ner. 29 Joab
and his family are the guilty ones. May the family of
Joab be cursed in every generation with a man who
has open sores or leprosy* or who walks on crutches*
or dies by the sword or begs for food!"
30 So Joab and his brother Abishai killed Abner because Abner had killed their brother Asahel at the
battle of Gibeon.

David Mourns Abner's Death

31 Then David said to Joab and all those who were
with him, "Tear your clothes and put on burlap.
Mourn for Abner." And King David himself walked
behind the procession to the grave. 32 They buried
Abner in Hebron, and the king and all the people

3:29a Or *or a contagious skin disease.* The Hebrew word used here can describe various skin diseases. **3:29b** Or *who is effeminate;* Hebrew reads *who handles a spindle.*

KING JAMES VERSION

33 And the king lamented over Abner, and said,
Died Abner as a fool dieth?
34 Thy hands *were* not bound, nor thy feet put into
fetters: as a man falleth before wicked men, *so* fellest
thou. And all the people wept again over him.
35 And when all the people came to cause David to
eat meat while it was yet day, David sware, saying, So
do God to me, and more also, if I taste bread, or aught
else, till the sun be down.
36 And all the people took notice *of it*, and it
pleased them: as whatsoever the king did pleased
all the people.
37 For all the people and all Israel understood that
day that it was not of the king to slay Abner the son
of Ner.
38 And the king said unto his servants, Know ye not
that there is a prince and a great man fallen this day
in Israel?
39 And I *am* this day weak, though anointed king;
and these men the sons of Zeruiah *be* too hard for
me: the LORD shall reward the doer of evil according
to his wickedness.

4 1 And when Saul's son heard that Abner was
dead in Hebron, his hands were feeble, and all
the Israelites were troubled.
2 And Saul's son had two men *that were* captains of
bands: the name of the one *was* Baanah, and the
name of the other Rechab, the sons of Rimmon a
Beerothite, of the children of Benjamin: (for Beeroth
also was reckoned to Benjamin.
3 And the Beerothites fled to Gittaim, and were
sojourners there until this day.)
4 And Jonathan, Saul's son, had a son *that was* lame
of *his* feet. He was five years old when the tidings
came of Saul and Jonathan out of Jezreel, and his
nurse took him up, and fled: and it came to pass, as
she made haste to flee, that he fell, and became lame.
And his name *was* Mephibosheth.
5 And the sons of Rimmon the Beerothite, Rechab
and Baanah, went, and came about the heat of the
day to the house of Ish-bosheth, who lay on a bed
at noon.
6 And they came thither into the midst of the
house, *as though* they would have fetched wheat; and
they smote him under the fifth *rib:* and Rechab and
Baanah his brother escaped.
7 For when they came into the house, he lay on his
bed in his bedchamber, and they smote him, and
slew him, and beheaded him, and took his head, and
gat them away through the plain all night.
8 And they brought the head of Ish-bosheth unto
David to Hebron, and said to the king, Behold the
head of Ish-bosheth the son of Saul thine enemy,

NEW LIVING TRANSLATION

wept at his graveside. 33 Then the king sang this
funeral song for Abner:

"Should Abner have died as fools die?
34 Your hands were not bound;
your feet were not chained.
No, you were murdered—
the victim of a wicked plot."

All the people wept again for Abner. 35 David had
refused to eat anything on the day of the funeral, and
now everyone begged him to eat. But David had
made a vow, saying, "May God strike me and even kill
me if I eat anything before sundown."
36 This pleased the people very much. In fact,
everything the king did pleased them! 37 So everyone
in Judah and all Israel understood that David was not
responsible for Abner's murder.
38 Then King David said to his officials, "Don't you
realize that a great commander has fallen today in
Israel? 39 And even though I am the anointed king,
these two sons of Zeruiah—Joab and Abishai—are
too strong for me to control. So may the LORD repay
these evil men for their evil deeds."

The Murder of Ishbosheth

4 When Ishbosheth,* Saul's son, heard about
Abner's death at Hebron, he lost all courage,
and all Israel became paralyzed with fear. 2 Now
there were two brothers, Baanah and Recab, who
were captains of Ishbosheth's raiding parties. They
were sons of Rimmon, a member of the tribe of Benjamin who lived in Beeroth. The town of Beeroth is
now part of Benjamin's territory 3 because the original people of Beeroth fled to Gittaim, where they still
live as foreigners.
4 (Saul's son Jonathan had a son named Mephibosheth,* who was crippled as a child. He was five
years old when the report came from Jezreel that
Saul and Jonathan had been killed in battle. When
the child's nurse heard the news, she picked him up
and fled. But as she hurried away, she dropped him,
and he became crippled.)
5 One day Recab and Baanah, the sons of Rimmon
from Beeroth, went to Ishbosheth's house around
noon as he was taking his midday rest. 6 The doorkeeper, who had been sifting wheat, became drowsy
and fell asleep. So Recab and Baanah slipped past
her.* 7 They went into the house and found Ishbosheth sleeping on his bed. They struck and killed
him and cut off his head. Then, taking his head with
them, they fled across the Jordan Valley* through the
night. 8 When they arrived at Hebron, they presented
Ishbosheth's head to David. "Look!" they exclaimed
to the king. "Here is the head of Ishbosheth, the son
of your enemy Saul who tried to kill you. Today the

4:1 *Ishbosheth* is another name for Esh-baal. 4:4 *Mephibosheth* is another name for Merib-baal. 4:6 As in Greek version; Hebrew reads *So they went into the house pretending to fetch wheat, but they stabbed him in the stomach. Then Recab and Baanah escaped.* 4:7 Hebrew *the Arabah.*

KING JAMES VERSION

which sought thy life; and the LORD hath avenged my lord the king this day of Saul, and of his seed.

9And David answered Rechab and Baanah his brother, the sons of Rimmon the Beerothite, and said unto them, *As* the LORD liveth, who hath redeemed my soul out of all adversity,

10When one told me, saying, Behold, Saul is dead, thinking to have brought good tidings, I took hold of him, and slew him in Ziklag, who *thought* that I would have given him a reward for his tidings:

11How much more, when wicked men have slain a righteous person in his own house upon his bed? shall I not therefore now require his blood of your hand, and take you away from the earth?

12And David commanded his young men, and they slew them, and cut off their hands and their feet, and hanged *them* up over the pool in Hebron. But they took the head of Ish-bosheth, and buried *it* in the sepulchre of Abner in Hebron.

5 1Then came all the tribes of Israel to David unto Hebron, and spake, saying, Behold, we *are* thy bone and thy flesh.

2Also in time past, when Saul was king over us, thou wast he that leddest out and broughtest in Israel: and the LORD said to thee, Thou shalt feed my people Israel, and thou shalt be a captain over Israel.

3So all the elders of Israel came to the king to Hebron; and king David made a league with them in Hebron before the LORD: and they anointed David king over Israel.

4David *was* thirty years old when he began to reign, *and* he reigned forty years.

5In Hebron he reigned over Judah seven years and six months: and in Jerusalem he reigned thirty and three years over all Israel and Judah.

6And the king and his men went to Jerusalem unto the Jebusites, the inhabitants of the land: which spake unto David, saying, Except thou take away the blind and the lame, thou shalt not come in hither: thinking, David cannot come in hither.

7Nevertheless David took the strong hold of Zion: the same *is* the city of David.

8And David said on that day, Whosoever getteth up to the gutter, and smiteth the Jebusites, and the lame and the blind, *that are* hated of David's soul, *he shall be chief and captain.* Wherefore they said, The blind and the lame shall not come into the house.

9So David dwelt in the fort, and called it the city of David. And David built round about from Millo and inward.

10And David went on, and grew great, and the LORD God of hosts *was* with him.

NEW LIVING TRANSLATION

LORD has given my lord the king revenge on Saul and his entire family!"

9But David said to Recab and Baanah, "The LORD, who saves me from all my enemies, is my witness. 10Someone once told me, 'Saul is dead,' thinking he was bringing me good news. But I seized him and killed him at Ziklag. That's the reward I gave him for his news! 11How much more should I reward evil men who have killed an innocent man in his own house and on his own bed? Shouldn't I hold you responsible for his blood and rid the earth of you?"

12So David ordered his young men to kill them, and they did. They cut off their hands and feet and hung their bodies beside the pool in Hebron. Then they took Ishbosheth's head and buried it in Abner's tomb in Hebron.

David Becomes King of All Israel

5 Then all the tribes of Israel went to David at Hebron and told him, "We are your own flesh and blood. 2In the past,* when Saul was our king, you were the one who really led the forces of Israel. And the LORD told you, 'You will be the shepherd of my people Israel. You will be Israel's leader.'"

3So there at Hebron, King David made a covenant before the LORD with all the elders of Israel. And they anointed him king of Israel.

4David was thirty years old when he began to reign, and he reigned forty years in all. 5He had reigned over Judah from Hebron for seven years and six months, and from Jerusalem he reigned over all Israel and Judah for thirty-three years.

David Captures Jerusalem

6David then led his men to Jerusalem to fight against the Jebusites, the original inhabitants of the land who were living there. The Jebusites taunted David, saying, "You'll never get in here! Even the blind and lame could keep you out!" For the Jebusites thought they were safe. 7But David captured the fortress of Zion, which is now called the City of David.

8On the day of the attack, David said to his troops, "I hate those 'lame' and 'blind' Jebusites.* Whoever attacks them should strike by going into the city through the water tunnel.*" That is the origin of the saying, "The blind and the lame may not enter the house."*

9So David made the fortress his home, and he called it the City of David. He extended the city, starting at the supporting terraces* and working inward. 10And David became more and more powerful, because the LORD God of Heaven's Armies was with him.

5:2 Or *For some time.* **5:8a** Or *Those 'lame' and 'blind' Jebusites hate me.* **5:8b** Or *with scaling hooks.* The meaning of the Hebrew is uncertain. **5:8c** The meaning of this saying is uncertain. **5:9** Hebrew *the millo.* The meaning of the Hebrew is uncertain.

KING JAMES VERSION

11 And Hiram king of Tyre sent messengers to David, and cedar trees, and carpenters, and masons: and they built David an house.

12 And David perceived that the LORD had established him king over Israel, and that he had exalted his kingdom for his people Israel's sake.

13 And David took *him* more concubines and wives out of Jerusalem, after he was come from Hebron: and there were yet sons and daughters born to David.

14 And these *be* the names of those that were born unto him in Jerusalem; Shammuah, and Shobab, and Nathan, and Solomon,

15 Ibhar also, and Elishua, and Nepheg, and Japhia,

16 And Elishama, and Eliada, and Eliphalet.

17 But when the Philistines heard that they had anointed David king over Israel, all the Philistines came up to seek David; and David heard *of it,* and went down to the hold.

18 The Philistines also came and spread themselves in the valley of Rephaim.

19 And David inquired of the LORD, saying, Shall I go up to the Philistines? wilt thou deliver them into mine hand? And the LORD said unto David, Go up: for I will doubtless deliver the Philistines into thine hand.

20 And David came to Baal-perazim, and David smote them there, and said, The LORD hath broken forth upon mine enemies before me, as the breach of waters. Therefore he called the name of that place Baal-perazim.

21 And there they left their images, and David and his men burned them.

22 And the Philistines came up yet again, and spread themselves in the valley of Rephaim.

23 And when David inquired of the LORD, he said, Thou shalt not go up; *but* fetch a compass behind them, and come upon them over against the mulberry trees.

24 And let it be, when thou hearest the sound of a going in the tops of the mulberry trees, that then thou shalt bestir thyself: for then shall the LORD go out before thee, to smite the host of the Philistines.

25 And David did so, as the LORD had commanded him; and smote the Philistines from Geba until thou come to Gazer.

6

1 Again, David gathered together all *the* chosen *men* of Israel, thirty thousand.

2 And David arose, and went with all the people that *were* with him from Baale of Judah, to bring up from thence the ark of God, whose name is called by the name of the LORD of hosts that dwelleth *between* the cherubims.

3 And they set the ark of God upon a new cart, and brought it out of the house of Abinadab that *was* in Gibeah: and Uzzah and Ahio, the sons of Abinadab, drave the new cart.

NEW LIVING TRANSLATION

11 Then King Hiram of Tyre sent messengers to David, along with cedar timber and carpenters and stonemasons, and they built David a palace. 12 And David realized that the LORD had confirmed him as king over Israel and had blessed his kingdom for the sake of his people Israel.

13 After moving from Hebron to Jerusalem, David married more concubines and wives, and they had more sons and daughters. 14 These are the names of David's sons who were born in Jerusalem: Shammua, Shobab, Nathan, Solomon, 15 Ibhar, Elishua, Nepheg, Japhia, 16 Elishama, Eliada, and Eliphelet.

David Conquers the Philistines

17 When the Philistines heard that David had been anointed king of Israel, they mobilized all their forces to capture him. But David was told they were coming, so he went into the stronghold. 18 The Philistines arrived and spread out across the valley of Rephaim. 19 So David asked the LORD, "Should I go out to fight the Philistines? Will you hand them over to me?"

The LORD replied to David, "Yes, go ahead. I will certainly hand them over to you."

20 So David went to Baal-perazim and defeated the Philistines there. "The LORD did it!" David exclaimed. "He burst through my enemies like a raging flood!" So he named that place Baal-perazim (which means "the Lord who bursts through"). 21 The Philistines had abandoned their idols there, so David and his men confiscated them.

22 But after a while the Philistines returned and again spread out across the valley of Rephaim. 23 And again David asked the LORD what to do. "Do not attack them straight on," the LORD replied. "Instead, circle around behind and attack them near the poplar* trees. 24 When you hear a sound like marching feet in the tops of the poplar trees, be on the alert! That will be the signal that the LORD is moving ahead of you to strike down the Philistine army." 25 So David did what the LORD commanded, and he struck down the Philistines all the way from Gibeon* to Gezer.

Moving the Ark to Jerusalem

6

Then David again gathered all the elite troops in Israel, 30,000 in all. 2 He led them to Baalah of Judah* to bring back the Ark of God, which bears the name of the LORD of Heaven's Armies,* who is enthroned between the cherubim. 3 They placed the Ark of God on a new cart and brought it from Abinadab's house, which was on a hill. Uzzah and Ahio, Abinadab's sons, were guiding the cart as it left the

5:23 Or *aspen,* or *balsam;* also in 5:24. The exact identification of this tree is uncertain. **5:25** As in Greek version (see also 1 Chr 14:16); Hebrew reads *Geba.* **6:2a** *Baalah of Judah* is another name for Kiriath-jearim; compare 1 Chr 13:6. **6:2b** Or *the Ark of God where the Name is proclaimed—the name of the LORD of Heaven's Armies.*

KING JAMES VERSION

4And they brought it out of the house of Abinadab which *was* at Gibeah, accompanying the ark of God: and Ahio went before the ark.

5And David and all the house of Israel played before the LORD on all manner of *instruments made of* fir wood, even on harps, and on psalteries, and on timbrels, and on cornets, and on cymbals.

6And when they came to Nachon's threshingfloor, Uzzah put forth *his hand* to the ark of God, and took hold of it; for the oxen shook *it*.

7And the anger of the LORD was kindled against Uzzah; and God smote him there for *his* error; and there he died by the ark of God.

8And David was displeased, because the LORD had made a breach upon Uzzah: and he called the name of the place Perez-uzzah to this day.

9And David was afraid of the LORD that day, and said, How shall the ark of the LORD come to me?

10So David would not remove the ark of the LORD unto him into the city of David: but David carried it aside into the house of Obed-edom the Gittite.

11And the ark of the LORD continued in the house of Obed-edom the Gittite three months: and the LORD blessed Obed-edom, and all his household.

12And it was told king David, saying, The LORD hath blessed the house of Obed-edom, and all that *pertaineth* unto him, because of the ark of God. So David went and brought up the ark of God from the house of Obed-edom into the city of David with gladness.

13And it was *so,* that when they that bare the ark of the LORD had gone six paces, he sacrificed oxen and fatlings.

14And David danced before the LORD with all *his* might; and David *was* girded with a linen ephod.

15So David and all the house of Israel brought up the ark of the LORD with shouting, and with the sound of the trumpet.

16And as the ark of the LORD came into the city of David, Michal Saul's daughter looked through a window, and saw king David leaping and dancing before the LORD; and she despised him in her heart.

17And they brought in the ark of the LORD, and set it in his place, in the midst of the tabernacle that David had pitched for it: and David offered burnt offerings and peace offerings before the LORD.

18And as soon as David had made an end of offering burnt offerings and peace offerings, he blessed the people in the name of the LORD of hosts.

19And he dealt among all the people, *even* among the whole multitude of Israel, as well to the women as men, to every one a cake of bread, and a good piece *of flesh,* and a flagon *of wine.* So all the people departed every one to his house.

20Then David returned to bless his household. And Michal the daughter of Saul came out to meet David, and said, How glorious was the king of Israel today, who uncovered himself today in the eyes of

NEW LIVING TRANSLATION

house, 4carrying the Ark of God. Ahio walked in front of the Ark. 5David and all the people of Israel were celebrating before the LORD, singing songs* and playing all kinds of musical instruments—lyres, harps, tambourines, castanets, and cymbals.

6But when they arrived at the threshing floor of Nacon, the oxen stumbled, and Uzzah reached out his hand and steadied the Ark of God. 7Then the LORD's anger was aroused against Uzzah, and God struck him dead because of this.* So Uzzah died right there beside the Ark of God.

8David was angry because the LORD's anger had burst out against Uzzah. He named that place Perez-uzzah (which means "to burst out against Uzzah"), as it is still called today.

9David was now afraid of the LORD, and he asked, "How can I ever bring the Ark of the LORD back into my care?" 10So David decided not to move the Ark of the LORD into the City of David. Instead, he took it to the house of Obed-edom of Gath. 11The Ark of the LORD remained there in Obed-edom's house for three months, and the LORD blessed Obed-edom and his entire household.

12Then King David was told, "The LORD has blessed Obed-edom's household and everything he has because of the Ark of God." So David went there and brought the Ark of God from the house of Obed-edom to the City of David with a great celebration. 13After the men who were carrying the Ark of the LORD had gone six steps, David sacrificed a bull and a fattened calf. 14And David danced before the LORD with all his might, wearing a priestly garment.* 15So David and all the people of Israel brought up the Ark of the LORD with shouts of joy and the blowing of rams' horns.

Michal's Contempt for David

16But as the Ark of the LORD entered the City of David, Michal, the daughter of Saul, looked down from her window. When she saw King David leaping and dancing before the LORD, she was filled with contempt for him.

17They brought the Ark of the LORD and set it in its place inside the special tent David had prepared for it. And David sacrificed burnt offerings and peace offerings to the LORD. 18When he had finished his sacrifices, David blessed the people in the name of the LORD of Heaven's Armies. 19Then he gave to every Israelite man and woman in the crowd a loaf of bread, a cake of dates,* and a cake of raisins. Then all the people returned to their homes.

20When David returned home to bless his own family, Michal, the daughter of Saul, came out to meet him. She said in disgust, "How distinguished

6:5 As in Dead Seas Scrolls and Greek version (see also 1 Chr 13:8); Masoretic Text reads *before the LORD with all manner of cypress wood.* **6:7** As in Dead Sea Scrolls; Masoretic Text reads *because of his irreverence.* **6:14** Hebrew *a linen ephod.* **6:19** Or *a portion of meat.* The meaning of the Hebrew is uncertain.

KING JAMES VERSION

the handmaids of his servants, as one of the vain
fellows shamelessly uncovereth himself!
21 And David said unto Michal, *It was* before the
LORD, which chose me before thy father, and before
all his house, to appoint me ruler over the people of
the LORD, over Israel: therefore will I play before
the LORD.
22 And I will yet be more vile than thus, and will be
base in mine own sight: and of the maidservants
which thou hast spoken of, of them shall I be had in
honour.
23 Therefore Michal the daughter of Saul had no
child unto the day of her death.

7 1 And it came to pass, when the king sat in his
house, and the LORD had given him rest round
about from all his enemies;
2 That the king said unto Nathan the prophet, See
now, I dwell in an house of cedar, but the ark of God
dwelleth within curtains.
3 And Nathan said to the king, Go, do all that *is* in
thine heart; for the LORD *is* with thee.
4 And it came to pass that night, that the word of
the LORD came unto Nathan, saying,
5 Go and tell my servant David, Thus saith the LORD,
Shalt thou build me an house for me to dwell in?
6 Whereas I have not dwelt in *any* house since the
time that I brought up the children of Israel out of
Egypt, even to this day, but have walked in a tent and
in a tabernacle.
7 In all *the places* wherein I have walked with all
the children of Israel spake I a word with any of the
tribes of Israel, whom I commanded to feed my
people Israel, saying, Why build ye not me an house
of cedar?
8 Now therefore so shalt thou say unto my servant
David, Thus saith the LORD of hosts, I took thee from
the sheepcote, from following the sheep, to be ruler
over my people, over Israel:
9 And I was with thee whithersoever thou wentest,
and have cut off all thine enemies out of thy sight,
and have made thee a great name, like unto the name
of the great *men* that *are* in the earth.
10 Moreover I will appoint a place for my people
Israel, and will plant them, that they may dwell in a
place of their own, and move no more; neither shall
the children of wickedness afflict them any more,
as beforetime,
11 And as since the time that I commanded judges
to be over my people Israel, and have caused thee to
rest from all thine enemies. Also the LORD telleth
thee that he will make thee an house.
12 And when thy days be fulfilled, and thou shalt
sleep with thy fathers, I will set up thy seed after
thee, which shall proceed out of thy bowels, and I
will establish his kingdom.

NEW LIVING TRANSLATION

the king of Israel looked today, shamelessly exposing
himself to the servant girls like any vulgar person
might do!"
21 David retorted to Michal, "I was dancing before
the LORD, who chose me above your father and all his
family! He appointed me as the leader of Israel, the
people of the LORD, so I celebrate before the LORD.
22 Yes, and I am willing to look even more foolish
than this, even to be humiliated in my own eyes! But
those servant girls you mentioned will indeed think I
am distinguished!" 23 So Michal, the daughter of
Saul, remained childless throughout her entire life.

The LORD's Covenant Promise to David

7 When King David was settled in his palace and
the LORD had given him rest from all the surrounding enemies, 2 the king summoned Nathan the
prophet. "Look," David said, "I am living in a beautiful cedar palace,* but the Ark of God is out there in
a tent!"
3 Nathan replied to the king, "Go ahead and do
whatever you have in mind, for the LORD is with you."
4 But that same night the LORD said to Nathan,

5 "Go and tell my servant David, 'This is what the
LORD has declared: Are you the one to build a
house for me to live in? 6 I have never lived in a
house, from the day I brought the Israelites out
of Egypt until this very day. I have always moved
from one place to another with a tent and a
Tabernacle as my dwelling. 7 Yet no matter
where I have gone with the Israelites, I have
never once complained to Israel's tribal leaders,
the shepherds of my people Israel. I have never
asked them, "Why haven't you built me a
beautiful cedar house?"'
8 "Now go and say to my servant David, 'This is
what the LORD of Heaven's Armies has declared:
I took you from tending sheep in the pasture and
selected you to be the leader of my people Israel.
9 I have been with you wherever you have gone,
and I have destroyed all your enemies before your
eyes. Now I will make your name as famous as
anyone who has ever lived on the earth! 10 And I
will provide a homeland for my people Israel,
planting them in a secure place where they will
never be disturbed. Evil nations won't oppress
them as they've done in the past, 11 starting from
the time I appointed judges to rule my people
Israel. And I will give you rest from all your
enemies.
"'Furthermore, the LORD declares that he will
make a house for you—a dynasty of kings! 12 For
when you die and are buried with your ancestors,
I will raise up one of your descendants, your own
offspring, and I will make his kingdom strong.

7:2 Hebrew *a house of cedar.*

KING JAMES VERSION

13He shall build an house for my name, and I will
stablish the throne of his kingdom for ever.
14I will be his father, and he shall be my son. If he
commit iniquity, I will chasten him with the rod of
men, and with the stripes of the children of men:
15But my mercy shall not depart away from him,
as I took *it* from Saul, whom I put away before thee.
16And thine house and thy kingdom shall be established for ever before thee: thy throne shall be
established for ever.
17According to all these words, and according to
all this vision, so did Nathan speak unto David.

18Then went king David in, and sat before the
LORD, and he said, Who *am* I, O Lord GOD? and what
is my house, that thou hast brought me hitherto?
19And this was yet a small thing in thy sight, O Lord
GOD; but thou hast spoken also of thy servant's house
for a great while to come. And *is* this the manner of
man, O Lord GOD?
20And what can David say more unto thee? for
thou, Lord GOD, knowest thy servant.
21For thy word's sake, and according to thine own
heart, hast thou done all these great things, to make
thy servant know *them*.
22Wherefore thou art great, O LORD God: for *there*
is none like thee, neither *is there any* God beside
thee, according to all that we have heard with our
ears.
23And what one nation in the earth *is* like thy
people, *even* like Israel, whom God went to redeem
for a people to himself, and to make him a name, and
to do for you great things and terrible, for thy land,
before thy people, which thou redeemedst to thee
from Egypt, *from* the nations and their gods?
24For thou hast confirmed to thyself thy people
Israel *to be* a people unto thee for ever: and thou,
LORD, art become their God.
25And now, O LORD God, the word that thou hast
spoken concerning thy servant, and concerning his
house, establish *it* for ever, and do as thou hast said.
26And let thy name be magnified for ever, saying,
The LORD of hosts *is* the God over Israel: and let the
house of thy servant David be established before
thee.
27For thou, O LORD of hosts, God of Israel, hast
revealed to thy servant, saying, I will build thee an
house: therefore hath thy servant found in his heart
to pray this prayer unto thee.
28And now, O Lord GOD, thou *art* that God, and thy
words be true, and thou hast promised this goodness
unto thy servant:
29Therefore now let it please thee to bless the
house of thy servant, that it may continue for ever

NEW LIVING TRANSLATION

13He is the one who will build a house—a
temple—for my name. And I will secure his royal
throne forever. 14I will be his father, and he will
be my son. If he sins, I will correct and discipline
him with the rod, like any father would do. 15But
my favor will not be taken from him as I took it
from Saul, whom I removed from your sight.
16Your house and your kingdom will continue
before me* for all time, and your throne will be
secure forever.'"

17So Nathan went back to David and told him everything the LORD had said in this vision.

David's Prayer of Thanks

18Then King David went in and sat before the LORD
and prayed,

"Who am I, O Sovereign LORD, and what is my
family, that you have brought me this far? 19And
now, Sovereign LORD, in addition to everything
else, you speak of giving your servant a lasting
dynasty! Do you deal with everyone this way,
O Sovereign LORD?*
20"What more can I say to you? You know
what your servant is really like, Sovereign LORD.
21Because of your promise and according to your
will, you have done all these great things and have
made them known to your servant.
22"How great you are, O Sovereign LORD! There
is no one like you. We have never even heard of
another God like you! 23What other nation on
earth is like your people Israel? What other nation,
O God, have you redeemed from slavery to be your
own people? You made a great name for yourself
when you redeemed your people from Egypt. You
performed awesome miracles and drove out the
nations and gods that stood in their way.* 24You
made Israel your very own people forever, and you,
O LORD, became their God.
25"And now, O LORD God, I am your servant;
do as you have promised concerning me and
my family. Confirm it as a promise that will last
forever. 26And may your name be honored forever
so that everyone will say, 'The LORD of Heaven's
Armies is God over Israel!' And may the house of
your servant David continue before you forever.
27"O LORD of Heaven's Armies, God of Israel, I
have been bold enough to pray this prayer to you
because you have revealed all this to your servant,
saying, 'I will build a house for you—a dynasty of
kings!' 28For you are God, O Sovereign LORD. Your
words are truth, and you have promised these
good things to your servant. 29And now, may it
please you to bless the house of your servant,

7:16 As in Greek version and some Hebrew manuscripts; Masoretic Text reads *before you.* **7:19** Or *This is your instruction for all humanity, O Sovereign* LORD. **7:23** As in Greek version (see also 1 Chr 17:21); Hebrew reads *You made a great name for yourself and performed awesome miracles for your land. You did this in the sight of your people, whom you redeemed from Egypt, from nations and their gods.*

KING JAMES VERSION

before thee: for thou, O Lord GOD, hast spoken *it:*
and with thy blessing let the house of thy servant be
blessed for ever.

8 1 And after this it came to pass, that David
smote the Philistines, and subdued them: and
David took Metheg-ammah out of the hand of the
Philistines.
2 And he smote Moab, and measured them with a
line, casting them down to the ground; even with two
lines measured he to put to death, and with one full
line to keep alive. And *so* the Moabites became
David's servants, *and* brought gifts.
3 David smote also Hadadezer, the son of Rehob,
king of Zobah, as he went to recover his border at the
river Euphrates.
4 And David took from him a thousand *chariots,*
and seven hundred horsemen, and twenty thousand
footmen: and David houghed all the chariot *horses,*
but reserved of them *for* an hundred chariots.
5 And when the Syrians of Damascus came to succour Hadadezer king of Zobah, David slew of the
Syrians two and twenty thousand men.
6 Then David put garrisons in Syria of Damascus:
and the Syrians became servants to David, *and*
brought gifts. And the LORD preserved David whithersoever he went.
7 And David took the shields of gold that were on
the servants of Hadadezer, and brought them to
Jerusalem.
8 And from Betah, and from Berothai, cities of
Hadadezer, king David took exceeding much brass.
9 When Toi king of Hamath heard that David had
smitten all the host of Hadadezer,
10 Then Toi sent Joram his son unto king David, to
salute him, and to bless him, because he had fought
against Hadadezer, and smitten him: for Hadadezer
had wars with Toi. And *Joram* brought with him vessels of silver, and vessels of gold, and vessels of brass:
11 Which also king David did dedicate unto the
LORD, with the silver and gold that he had dedicated
of all nations which he subdued;
12 Of Syria, and of Moab, and of the children of
Ammon, and of the Philistines, and of Amalek, and
of the spoil of Hadadezer, son of Rehob, king of
Zobah.
13 And David gat *him* a name when he returned
from smiting of the Syrians in the valley of salt, *being*
eighteen thousand *men.*
14 And he put garrisons in Edom; throughout all
Edom put he garrisons, and all they of Edom became
David's servants. And the LORD preserved David
whithersoever he went.
15 And David reigned over all Israel; and David executed judgment and justice unto all his people.

NEW LIVING TRANSLATION

so that it may continue forever before you. For
you have spoken, and when you grant a blessing
to your servant, O Sovereign LORD, it is an eternal
blessing!"

David's Military Victories

8 After this, David defeated and subdued the Philistines by conquering Gath, their largest
town.* 2 David also conquered the land of Moab. He
made the people lie down on the ground in a row, and
he measured them off in groups with a length of
rope. He measured off two groups to be executed for
every one group to be spared. The Moabites who
were spared became David's subjects and paid him
tribute money.
3 David also destroyed the forces of Hadadezer son
of Rehob, king of Zobah, when Hadadezer marched
out to strengthen his control along the Euphrates
River. 4 David captured 1,000 chariots, 7,000 charioteers,* and 20,000 foot soldiers. He crippled all the
chariot horses except enough for 100 chariots.
5 When Arameans from Damascus arrived to help
King Hadadezer, David killed 22,000 of them. 6 Then
he placed several army garrisons in Damascus, the
Aramean capital, and the Arameans became David's
subjects and paid him tribute money. So the LORD
made David victorious wherever he went.
7 David brought the gold shields of Hadadezer's
officers to Jerusalem, 8 along with a large amount
of bronze from Hadadezer's towns of Tebah* and
Berothai.
9 When King Toi of Hamath heard that David had
destroyed the entire army of Hadadezer, 10 he sent
his son Joram to congratulate King David for his successful campaign. Hadadezer and Toi had been enemies and were often at war. Joram presented David
with many gifts of silver, gold, and bronze.
11 King David dedicated all these gifts to the LORD,
as he did with the silver and gold from the other
nations he had defeated—12 from Edom,* Moab, Ammon, Philistia, and Amalek—and from Hadadezer
son of Rehob, king of Zobah.
13 So David became even more famous when he
returned from destroying 18,000 Edomites* in the
Valley of Salt. 14 He placed army garrisons throughout Edom, and all the Edomites became David's
subjects. In fact, the LORD made David victorious
wherever he went.
15 So David reigned over all Israel and did what was

8:1 Hebrew *by conquering Metheg-ammah,* a name that means "the bridle," possibly referring to the size of the town or the tribute money taken from it. Compare 1 Chr 18:1. **8:4** As in Dead Sea Scrolls and Greek version (see also 1 Chr 18:4); Masoretic Text reads *captured 1,700 charioteers.* **8:8** As in some Greek manuscripts (see also 1 Chr 18:8); Hebrew reads *Betah.* **8:12** As in a few Hebrew manuscripts and Greek and Syriac versions (see also 8:14; 1 Chr 18:11); most Hebrew manuscripts read *Aram.* **8:13** As in a few Hebrew manuscripts and Greek and Syriac versions (see also 8:14; 1 Chr 18:12); most Hebrew manuscripts read *Arameans.*

KING JAMES VERSION

16And Joab the son of Zeruiah *was* over the host; and Jehoshaphat the son of Ahilud *was* recorder;

17And Zadok the son of Ahitub, and Ahimelech the son of Abiathar, *were* the priests; and Seraiah *was* the scribe;

18And Benaiah the son of Jehoiada *was over* both the Cherethites and the Pelethites; and David's sons were chief rulers.

9 1And David said, Is there yet any that is left of the house of Saul, that I may shew him kindness for Jonathan's sake?

2And *there was* of the house of Saul a servant whose name *was* Ziba. And when they had called him unto David, the king said unto him, *Art* thou Ziba? And he said, Thy servant *is he*.

3And the king said, *Is* there not yet any of the house of Saul, that I may shew the kindness of God unto him? And Ziba said unto the king, Jonathan hath yet a son, *which is* lame on *his* feet.

4And the king said unto him, Where *is* he? And Ziba said unto the king, Behold, he *is* in the house of Machir, the son of Ammiel, in Lo-debar.

5Then king David sent, and fetched him out of the house of Machir, the son of Ammiel, from Lo-debar.

6Now when Mephibosheth, the son of Jonathan, the son of Saul, was come unto David, he fell on his face, and did reverence. And David said, Mephibosheth. And he answered, Behold thy servant!

7And David said unto him, Fear not: for I will surely shew thee kindness for Jonathan thy father's sake, and will restore thee all the land of Saul thy father; and thou shalt eat bread at my table continually.

8And he bowed himself, and said, What *is* thy servant, that thou shouldest look upon such a dead dog as I *am?*

9Then the king called to Ziba, Saul's servant, and said unto him, I have given unto thy master's son all that pertained to Saul and to all his house.

10Thou therefore, and thy sons, and thy servants, shall till the land for him, and thou shalt bring in *the fruits,* that thy master's son may have food to eat: but Mephibosheth thy master's son shall eat bread alway at my table. Now Ziba had fifteen sons and twenty servants.

11Then said Ziba unto the king, According to all that my lord the king hath commanded his servant, so shall thy servant do. As for Mephibosheth, *said the king,* he shall eat at my table, as one of the king's sons.

12And Mephibosheth had a young son, whose name *was* Micha. And all that dwelt in the house of Ziba *were* servants unto Mephibosheth.

13So Mephibosheth dwelt in Jerusalem: for he did eat continually at the king's table; and was lame on both his feet.

NEW LIVING TRANSLATION

just and right for all his people. 16Joab son of Zeruiah was commander of the army. Jehoshaphat son of Ahilud was the royal historian. 17Zadok son of Ahitub and Ahimelech son of Abiathar were the priests. Seraiah was the court secretary. 18Benaiah son of Jehoiada was captain of the king's bodyguard.* And David's sons served as priestly leaders.*

David's Kindness to Mephibosheth

9 One day David asked, "Is anyone in Saul's family still alive—anyone to whom I can show kindness for Jonathan's sake?" 2He summoned a man named Ziba, who had been one of Saul's servants. "Are you Ziba?" the king asked.

"Yes sir, I am," Ziba replied.

3The king then asked him, "Is anyone still alive from Saul's family? If so, I want to show God's kindness to them."

Ziba replied, "Yes, one of Jonathan's sons is still alive. He is crippled in both feet."

4"Where is he?" the king asked.

"In Lo-debar," Ziba told him, "at the home of Makir son of Ammiel."

5So David sent for him and brought him from Makir's home. 6His name was Mephibosheth*; he was Jonathan's son and Saul's grandson. When he came to David, he bowed low to the ground in deep respect. David said, "Greetings, Mephibosheth."

Mephibosheth replied, "I am your servant."

7"Don't be afraid!" David said. "I intend to show kindness to you because of my promise to your father, Jonathan. I will give you all the property that once belonged to your grandfather Saul, and you will eat here with me at the king's table!"

8Mephibosheth bowed respectfully and exclaimed, "Who is your servant, that you should show such kindness to a dead dog like me?"

9Then the king summoned Saul's servant Ziba and said, "I have given your master's grandson everything that belonged to Saul and his family. 10You and your sons and servants are to farm the land for him to produce food for your master's household.* But Mephibosheth, your master's grandson, will eat here at my table." (Ziba had fifteen sons and twenty servants.)

11Ziba replied, "Yes, my lord the king; I am your servant, and I will do all that you have commanded." And from that time on, Mephibosheth ate regularly at David's table,* like one of the king's own sons.

12Mephibosheth had a young son named Mica. From then on, all the members of Ziba's household were Mephibosheth's servants. 13And Mephibosheth, who was crippled in both feet, lived in Jerusalem and ate regularly at the king's table.

8:18a Hebrew *of the Kerethites and Pelethites.* **8:18b** Hebrew *David's sons were priests;* compare parallel text at 1 Chr 18:17. **9:6** *Mephibosheth* is another name for Merib-baal. **9:10** As in Greek version; Hebrew reads *your master's grandson.* **9:11** As in Greek version; Hebrew reads *my table.*

KING JAMES VERSION

10 1 And it came to pass after this, that the king
of the children of Ammon died, and Hanun
his son reigned in his stead.
2 Then said David, I will shew kindness unto
Hanun the son of Nahash, as his father shewed kindness unto me. And David sent to comfort him by the
hand of his servants for his father. And David's servants came into the land of the children of Ammon.
3 And the princes of the children of Ammon said
unto Hanun their lord, Thinkest thou that David
doth honour thy father, that he hath sent comforters
unto thee? hath not David *rather* sent his servants
unto thee, to search the city, and to spy it out, and to
overthrow it?
4 Wherefore Hanun took David's servants, and
shaved off the one half of their beards, and cut off
their garments in the middle, *even* to their buttocks,
and sent them away.
5 When they told *it* unto David, he sent to meet
them, because the men were greatly ashamed: and
the king said, Tarry at Jericho until your beards be
grown, and *then* return.
6 And when the children of Ammon saw that they
stank before David, the children of Ammon sent
and hired the Syrians of Beth-rehob, and the Syrians of Zoba, twenty thousand footmen, and of king
Maacah a thousand men, and of Ish-tob twelve
thousand men.
7 And when David heard of *it,* he sent Joab, and all
the host of the mighty men.
8 And the children of Ammon came out, and put
the battle in array at the entering in of the gate: and
the Syrians of Zoba, and of Rehob, and Ish-tob, and
Maacah, *were* by themselves in the field.
9 When Joab saw that the front of the battle was
against him before and behind, he chose of all the
choice *men* of Israel, and put *them* in array against
the Syrians:
10 And the rest of the people he delivered into the
hand of Abishai his brother, that he might put *them*
in array against the children of Ammon.
11 And he said, If the Syrians be too strong for me,
then thou shalt help me: but if the children of
Ammon be too strong for thee, then I will come and
help thee.
12 Be of good courage, and let us play the men for
our people, and for the cities of our God: and the
LORD do that which seemeth him good.
13 And Joab drew nigh, and the people that *were*
with him, unto the battle against the Syrians: and
they fled before him.
14 And when the children of Ammon saw that the
Syrians were fled, then fled they also before Abishai,
and entered into the city. So Joab returned from the
children of Ammon, and came to Jerusalem.
15 And when the Syrians saw that they were smitten before Israel, they gathered themselves together.

NEW LIVING TRANSLATION

David Defeats the Ammonites

10 Some time after this, King Nahash* of the
Ammonites died, and his son Hanun became
king. 2 David said, "I am going to show loyalty to
Hanun just as his father, Nahash, was always loyal to
me." So David sent ambassadors to express sympathy to Hanun about his father's death.
But when David's ambassadors arrived in the land
of Ammon, 3 the Ammonite commanders said to
Hanun, their master, "Do you really think these men
are coming here to honor your father? No! David has
sent them to spy out the city so they can come in and
conquer it!" 4 So Hanun seized David's ambassadors
and shaved off half of each man's beard, cut off their
robes at the buttocks, and sent them back to David
in shame.
5 When David heard what had happened, he sent
messengers to tell the men, "Stay at Jericho until
your beards grow out, and then come back." For they
felt deep shame because of their appearance.
6 When the people of Ammon realized how seriously they had angered David, they sent and hired
20,000 Aramean foot soldiers from the lands of
Beth-rehob and Zobah, 1,000 from the king of Maacah, and 12,000 from the land of Tob. 7 When David
heard about this, he sent Joab and all his warriors
to fight them. 8 The Ammonite troops came out and
drew up their battle lines at the entrance of the city
gate, while the Arameans from Zobah and Rehob
and the men from Tob and Maacah positioned
themselves to fight in the open fields.
9 When Joab saw that he would have to fight on
both the front and the rear, he chose some of Israel's
elite troops and placed them under his personal
command to fight the Arameans in the fields. 10 He
left the rest of the army under the command of his
brother Abishai, who was to attack the Ammonites.
11 "If the Arameans are too strong for me, then come
over and help me," Joab told his brother. "And if the
Ammonites are too strong for you, I will come and
help you. 12 Be courageous! Let us fight bravely for
our people and the cities of our God. May the LORD's
will be done."
13 When Joab and his troops attacked, the Arameans began to run away. 14 And when the Ammonites
saw the Arameans running, they ran from Abishai
and retreated into the city. After the battle was over,
Joab returned to Jerusalem.
15 The Arameans now realized that they were

10:1 As in parallel text at 1 Chr 19:1; Hebrew reads *the king.*

KING JAMES VERSION

16 And Hadarezer sent, and brought out the Syrians that *were* beyond the river: and they came to
Helam; and Shobach the captain of the host of
Hadarezer *went* before them.
17 And when it was told David, he gathered all Israel together, and passed over Jordan, and came to Helam. And the Syrians set themselves in array against
David, and fought with him.
18 And the Syrians fled before Israel; and David
slew *the men of* seven hundred chariots of the Syrians, and forty thousand horsemen, and smote Shobach the captain of their host, who died there.
19 And when all the kings *that were* servants to
Hadarezer saw that they were smitten before Israel,
they made peace with Israel, and served them. So
the Syrians feared to help the children of Ammon
any more.

11 1 And it came to pass, after the year was expired, at the time when kings go forth *to
battle,* that David sent Joab, and his servants with
him, and all Israel; and they destroyed the children of
Ammon, and besieged Rabbah. But David tarried still
at Jerusalem.
2 And it came to pass in an eveningtide, that David
arose from off his bed, and walked upon the roof of
the king's house: and from the roof he saw a woman
washing herself; and the woman *was* very beautiful
to look upon.
3 And David sent and inquired after the woman.
And *one* said, *Is* not this Bath-sheba, the daughter of
Eliam, the wife of Uriah the Hittite?
4 And David sent messengers, and took her; and
she came in unto him, and he lay with her; for she
was purified from her uncleanness: and she returned unto her house.
5 And the woman conceived, and sent and told
David, and said, I *am* with child.
6 And David sent to Joab, *saying,* Send me Uriah
the Hittite. And Joab sent Uriah to David.
7 And when Uriah was come unto him, David demanded *of him* how Joab did, and how the people
did, and how the war prospered.
8 And David said to Uriah, Go down to thy house,
and wash thy feet. And Uriah departed out of the
king's house, and there followed him a mess *of meat*
from the king.
9 But Uriah slept at the door of the king's house
with all the servants of his lord, and went not down
to his house.
10 And when they had told David, saying, Uriah
went not down unto his house, David said unto
Uriah, Camest thou not from *thy* journey? why *then*
didst thou not go down unto thine house?
11 And Uriah said unto David, The ark, and Israel,
and Judah, abide in tents; and my lord Joab, and the

NEW LIVING TRANSLATION

no match for Israel. So when they regrouped, 16 they
were joined by additional Aramean troops summoned by Hadadezer from the other side of the
Euphrates River.* These troops arrived at Helam
under the command of Shobach, the commander
of Hadadezer's forces.
17 When David heard what was happening, he
mobilized all Israel, crossed the Jordan River, and
led the army to Helam. The Arameans positioned
themselves in battle formation and fought against
David. 18 But again the Arameans fled from the Israelites. This time David's forces killed 700 charioteers
and 40,000 foot soldiers,* including Shobach, the
commander of their army. 19 When all the kings allied
with Hadadezer saw that they had been defeated by
Israel, they surrendered to Israel and became their
subjects. After that, the Arameans were afraid to help
the Ammonites.

David and Bathsheba

11 In the spring of the year,* when kings normally go out to war, David sent Joab and the
Israelite army to fight the Ammonites. They destroyed the Ammonite army and laid siege to the
city of Rabbah. However, David stayed behind in
Jerusalem.
2 Late one afternoon, after his midday rest, David
got out of bed and was walking on the roof of the
palace. As he looked out over the city, he noticed a
woman of unusual beauty taking a bath. 3 He sent
someone to find out who she was, and he was told,
"She is Bathsheba, the daughter of Eliam and the
wife of Uriah the Hittite." 4 Then David sent messengers to get her; and when she came to the palace, he
slept with her. She had just completed the purification rites after having her menstrual period. Then
she returned home. 5 Later, when Bathsheba discovered that she was pregnant, she sent David a message, saying, "I'm pregnant."
6 Then David sent word to Joab: "Send me Uriah
the Hittite." So Joab sent him to David. 7 When Uriah
arrived, David asked him how Joab and the army
were getting along and how the war was progressing.
8 Then he told Uriah, "Go on home and relax.*" David
even sent a gift to Uriah after he had left the palace.
9 But Uriah didn't go home. He slept that night at the
palace entrance with the king's palace guard.
10 When David heard that Uriah had not gone
home, he summoned him and asked, "What's the
matter? Why didn't you go home last night after being away for so long?"
11 Uriah replied, "The Ark and the armies of Israel
and Judah are living in tents,* and Joab and my master's men are camping in the open fields. How could

10:16 Hebrew *the river.* **10:18** As in some Greek manuscripts (see also 1 Chr 19:18); Hebrew reads *charioteers.* **11:1** Hebrew *At the turn of the year.* The first day of the year in the ancient Hebrew lunar calendar occurred in March or April. **11:8** Hebrew *and wash your feet,* an expression that may also have a connotation of ritualistic washing. **11:11** Or *at Succoth.*

KING JAMES VERSION

servants of my lord, are encamped in the open fields;
shall I then go into mine house, to eat and to drink,
and to lie with my wife? *as* thou livest, and *as* thy soul
liveth, I will not do this thing.
12And David said to Uriah, Tarry here today also,
and tomorrow I will let thee depart. So Uriah abode
in Jerusalem that day, and the morrow.
13And when David had called him, he did eat and
drink before him; and he made him drunk: and at
even he went out to lie on his bed with the servants
of his lord, but went not down to his house.
14And it came to pass in the morning, that David
wrote a letter to Joab, and sent *it* by the hand of Uriah.
15And he wrote in the letter, saying, Set ye Uriah in
the forefront of the hottest battle, and retire ye from
him, that he may be smitten, and die.
16And it came to pass, when Joab observed the city,
that he assigned Uriah unto a place where he knew
that valiant men *were*.
17And the men of the city went out, and fought
with Joab: and there fell *some* of the people of the
servants of David; and Uriah the Hittite died also.
18Then Joab sent and told David all the things concerning the war;
19And charged the messenger, saying, When thou
hast made an end of telling the matters of the war
unto the king,
20And if so be that the king's wrath arise, and he
say unto thee, Wherefore approached ye so nigh
unto the city when ye did fight? knew ye not that
they would shoot from the wall?
21Who smote Abimelech the son of Jerubbesheth? did not a woman cast a piece of a millstone
upon him from the wall, that he died in Thebez? why
went ye nigh the wall? then say thou, Thy servant
Uriah the Hittite is dead also.
22So the messenger went, and came and shewed
David all that Joab had sent him for.
23And the messenger said unto David, Surely the
men prevailed against us, and came out unto us into
the field, and we were upon them even unto the entering of the gate.
24And the shooters shot from off the wall upon thy
servants; and *some* of the king's servants be dead,
and thy servant Uriah the Hittite is dead also.
25Then David said unto the messenger, Thus shalt
thou say unto Joab, Let not this thing displease thee,
for the sword devoureth one as well as another: make
thy battle more strong against the city, and overthrow it: and encourage thou him.
26And when the wife of Uriah heard that Uriah her
husband was dead, she mourned for her husband.
27And when the mourning was past, David sent
and fetched her to his house, and she became his
wife, and bare him a son. But the thing that David had
done displeased the LORD.

NEW LIVING TRANSLATION

I go home to wine and dine and sleep with my wife?
I swear that I would never do such a thing."
12"Well, stay here today," David told him, "and tomorrow you may return to the army." So Uriah stayed
in Jerusalem that day and the next.
13Then David
invited him to dinner and got him drunk. But even
then he couldn't get Uriah to go home to his wife.
Again he slept at the palace entrance with the king's
palace guard.

David Arranges for Uriah's Death

14So the next morning David wrote a letter to Joab
and gave it to Uriah to deliver.
15The letter instructed
Joab, "Station Uriah on the front lines where the
battle is fiercest. Then pull back so that he will be
killed."
16So Joab assigned Uriah to a spot close to the
city wall where he knew the enemy's strongest men
were fighting.
17And when the enemy soldiers came
out of the city to fight, Uriah the Hittite was killed
along with several other Israelite soldiers.
18Then Joab sent a battle report to David.
19He told
his messenger, "Report all the news of the battle to
the king.
20But he might get angry and ask, 'Why did
the troops go so close to the city? Didn't they know
there would be shooting from the walls?
21Wasn't
Abimelech son of Gideon* killed at Thebez by a
woman who threw a millstone down on him from
the wall? Why would you get so close to the wall?'
Then tell him, 'Uriah the Hittite was killed, too.'"
22So the messenger went to Jerusalem and gave a
complete report to David.
23"The enemy came out
against us in the open fields," he said. "And as we
chased them back to the city gate,
24the archers on
the wall shot arrows at us. Some of the king's men
were killed, including Uriah the Hittite."
25"Well, tell Joab not to be discouraged," David
said. "The sword devours this one today and that
one tomorrow! Fight harder next time, and conquer
the city!"
26When Uriah's wife heard that her husband was
dead, she mourned for him.
27When the period of
mourning was over, David sent for her and brought
her to the palace, and she became one of his wives.
Then she gave birth to a son. But the LORD was displeased with what David had done.

11:21 Hebrew *son of Jerub-besheth*. Jerub-besheth is a variation on the name Jerub-baal, which is another name for Gideon; see Judg 6:32.

KING JAMES VERSION

12 1And the LORD sent Nathan unto David. And
he came unto him, and said unto him, There
were two men in one city; the one rich, and the other
poor.
2The rich *man* had exceeding many flocks and
herds:
3But the poor *man* had nothing, save one little
ewe lamb, which he had bought and nourished up:
and it grew up together with him, and with his children; it did eat of his own meat, and drank of his own
cup, and lay in his bosom, and was unto him as
a daughter.
4And there came a traveller unto the rich man, and
he spared to take of his own flock and of his own
herd, to dress for the wayfaring man that was come
unto him; but took the poor man's lamb, and dressed
it for the man that was come to him.
5And David's anger was greatly kindled against the
man; and he said to Nathan, *As* the LORD liveth, the
man that hath done this *thing* shall surely die:
6And he shall restore the lamb fourfold, because
he did this thing, and because he had no pity.
7And Nathan said to David, Thou *art* the man.
Thus saith the LORD God of Israel, I anointed thee
king over Israel, and I delivered thee out of the hand
of Saul;
8And I gave thee thy master's house, and thy master's wives into thy bosom, and gave thee the house
of Israel and of Judah; and if *that had been* too little,
I would moreover have given unto thee such and
such things.
9Wherefore hast thou despised the commandment of the LORD, to do evil in his sight? thou hast
killed Uriah the Hittite with the sword, and hast
taken his wife *to be* thy wife, and hast slain him with
the sword of the children of Ammon.
10Now therefore the sword shall never depart
from thine house; because thou hast despised me,
and hast taken the wife of Uriah the Hittite to be
thy wife.
11Thus saith the LORD, Behold, I will raise up evil
against thee out of thine own house, and I will take
thy wives before thine eyes, and give *them* unto thy
neighbour, and he shall lie with thy wives in the sight
of this sun.
12For thou didst *it* secretly: but I will do this thing
before all Israel, and before the sun.
13And David said unto Nathan, I have sinned
against the LORD. And Nathan said unto David, The
LORD also hath put away thy sin; thou shalt not die.
14Howbeit, because by this deed thou hast given
great occasion to the enemies of the LORD to blaspheme, the child also *that is* born unto thee shall
surely die.
15And Nathan departed unto his house. And the
LORD struck the child that Uriah's wife bare unto
David, and it was very sick.

NEW LIVING TRANSLATION

Nathan Rebukes David

12 So the LORD sent Nathan the prophet to tell
David this story: "There were two men in a
certain town. One was rich, and one was poor. 2The
rich man owned a great many sheep and cattle. 3The
poor man owned nothing but one little lamb he had
bought. He raised that little lamb, and it grew up with
his children. It ate from the man's own plate and
drank from his cup. He cuddled it in his arms like a
baby daughter. 4One day a guest arrived at the home
of the rich man. But instead of killing an animal from
his own flock or herd, he took the poor man's lamb
and killed it and prepared it for his guest."
5David was furious. "As surely as the LORD lives,"
he vowed, "any man who would do such a thing deserves to die! 6He must repay four lambs to the poor
man for the one he stole and for having no pity."
7Then Nathan said to David, "You are that man!
The LORD, the God of Israel, says: I anointed you king
of Israel and saved you from the power of Saul. 8I
gave you your master's house and his wives and the
kingdoms of Israel and Judah. And if that had not
been enough, I would have given you much, much
more. 9Why, then, have you despised the word of the
LORD and done this horrible deed? For you have
murdered Uriah the Hittite with the sword of the
Ammonites and stolen his wife. 10From this time on,
your family will live by the sword because you have
despised me by taking Uriah's wife to be your own.
11"This is what the LORD says: Because of what you
have done, I will cause your own household to rebel
against you. I will give your wives to another man before your very eyes, and he will go to bed with them
in public view. 12You did it secretly, but I will make
this happen to you openly in the sight of all Israel."

David Confesses His Guilt

13Then David confessed to Nathan, "I have sinned
against the LORD."
Nathan replied, "Yes, but the LORD has forgiven
you, and you won't die for this sin. 14Nevertheless,
because you have shown utter contempt for the
LORD* by doing this, your child will die."
15After Nathan returned to his home, the LORD
sent a deadly illness to the child of David and Uriah's

12:14 As in Dead Sea Scrolls; Masoretic Text reads *the LORD's enemies.*

KING JAMES VERSION

16David therefore besought God for the child; and David fasted, and went in, and lay all night upon the earth.

17And the elders of his house arose, *and went* to him, to raise him up from the earth: but he would not, neither did he eat bread with them.

18And it came to pass on the seventh day, that the child died. And the servants of David feared to tell him that the child was dead: for they said, Behold, while the child was yet alive, we spake unto him, and he would not hearken unto our voice: how will he then vex himself, if we tell him that the child is dead?

19But when David saw that his servants whispered, David perceived that the child was dead: therefore David said unto his servants, Is the child dead? And they said, He is dead.

20Then David arose from the earth, and washed, and anointed *himself,* and changed his apparel, and came into the house of the LORD, and worshipped: then he came to his own house; and when he required, they set bread before him, and he did eat.

21Then said his servants unto him, What thing *is* this that thou hast done? thou didst fast and weep for the child, *while it was* alive; but when the child was dead, thou didst rise and eat bread.

22And he said, While the child was yet alive, I fasted and wept: for I said, Who can tell *whether* God will be gracious to me, that the child may live?

23But now he is dead, wherefore should I fast? can I bring him back again? I shall go to him, but he shall not return to me.

24And David comforted Bath-sheba his wife, and went in unto her, and lay with her: and she bare a son, and he called his name Solomon: and the LORD loved him.

25And he sent by the hand of Nathan the prophet; and he called his name Jedidiah, because of the LORD.

26And Joab fought against Rabbah of the children of Ammon, and took the royal city.

27And Joab sent messengers to David, and said, I have fought against Rabbah, and have taken the city of waters.

28Now therefore gather the rest of the people together, and encamp against the city, and take it: lest I take the city, and it be called after my name.

29And David gathered all the people together, and went to Rabbah, and fought against it, and took it.

30And he took their king's crown from off his head, the weight whereof *was* a talent of gold with the precious stones: and it was *set* on David's head. And he brought forth the spoil of the city in great abundance.

31And he brought forth the people that *were* therein, and put *them* under saws, and under harrows of iron, and under axes of iron, and made them pass through the brickkiln: and thus did he unto all

NEW LIVING TRANSLATION

wife. 16David begged God to spare the child. He went without food and lay all night on the bare ground. 17The elders of his household pleaded with him to get up and eat with them, but he refused.

18Then on the seventh day the child died. David's advisers were afraid to tell him. "He wouldn't listen to reason while the child was ill," they said. "What drastic thing will he do when we tell him the child is dead?"

19When David saw them whispering, he realized what had happened. "Is the child dead?" he asked.

"Yes," they replied, "he is dead."

20Then David got up from the ground, washed himself, put on lotions,* and changed his clothes. He went to the Tabernacle and worshiped the LORD. After that, he returned to the palace and was served food and ate.

21His advisers were amazed. "We don't understand you," they told him. "While the child was still living, you wept and refused to eat. But now that the child is dead, you have stopped your mourning and are eating again."

22David replied, "I fasted and wept while the child was alive, for I said, 'Perhaps the LORD will be gracious to me and let the child live.' 23But why should I fast when he is dead? Can I bring him back again? I will go to him one day, but he cannot return to me."

24Then David comforted Bathsheba, his wife, and slept with her. She became pregnant and gave birth to a son, and David* named him Solomon. The LORD loved the child 25and sent word through Nathan the prophet that they should name him Jedidiah (which means "beloved of the LORD"), as the LORD had commanded.*

David Captures Rabbah

26Meanwhile, Joab was fighting against Rabbah, the capital of Ammon, and he captured the royal fortifications.* 27Joab sent messengers to tell David, "I have fought against Rabbah and captured its water supply.* 28Now bring the rest of the army and capture the city. Otherwise, I will capture it and get credit for the victory."

29So David gathered the rest of the army and went to Rabbah, and he fought against it and captured it. 30David removed the crown from the king's head,* and it was placed on his own head. The crown was made of gold and set with gems, and it weighed seventy-five pounds.* David took a vast amount of plunder from the city. 31He also made slaves of the people of Rabbah and forced them to labor with* saws, iron picks, and iron axes, and to work in the

12:20 Hebrew *anointed himself.* **12:24** Hebrew *he;* an alternate Hebrew reading and some Hebrew manuscripts read *she.* **12:25** As in Greek version; Hebrew reads *because of the LORD.* **12:26** Or *the royal city.* **12:27** Or *captured the city of water.* **12:30a** Or *from the head of Milcom* (as in Greek version). Milcom, also called Molech, was the god of the Ammonites. **12:30b** Hebrew *1 talent* [34 kilograms]. **12:31a** Or *He also brought out the people of Rabbah and put them under.*

KING JAMES VERSION

the cities of the children of Ammon. So David and all the people returned unto Jerusalem.

13

1And it came to pass after this, that Absalom the son of David had a fair sister, whose name *was* Tamar; and Amnon the son of David loved her.

2And Amnon was so vexed, that he fell sick for his sister Tamar; for she *was* a virgin; and Amnon thought it hard for him to do any thing to her.

3But Amnon had a friend, whose name *was* Jonadab, the son of Shimeah David's brother: and Jonadab *was* a very subtil man.

4And he said unto him, Why *art* thou, *being* the king's son, lean from day to day? wilt thou not tell me? And Amnon said unto him, I love Tamar, my brother Absalom's sister.

5And Jonadab said unto him, Lay thee down on thy bed, and make thyself sick: and when thy father cometh to see thee, say unto him, I pray thee, let my sister Tamar come, and give me meat, and dress the meat in my sight, that I may see *it,* and eat *it* at her hand.

6So Amnon lay down, and made himself sick: and when the king was come to see him, Amnon said unto the king, I pray thee, let Tamar my sister come, and make me a couple of cakes in my sight, that I may eat at her hand.

7Then David sent home to Tamar, saying, Go now to thy brother Amnon's house, and dress him meat.

8So Tamar went to her brother Amnon's house; and he was laid down. And she took flour, and kneaded *it,* and made cakes in his sight, and did bake the cakes.

9And she took a pan, and poured *them* out before him; but he refused to eat. And Amnon said, Have out all men from me. And they went out every man from him.

10And Amnon said unto Tamar, Bring the meat into the chamber, that I may eat of thine hand. And Tamar took the cakes which she had made, and brought *them* into the chamber to Amnon her brother.

11And when she had brought *them* unto him to eat, he took hold of her, and said unto her, Come lie with me, my sister.

12And she answered him, Nay, my brother, do not force me; for no such thing ought to be done in Israel: do not thou this folly.

13And I, whither shall I cause my shame to go? and as for thee, thou shalt be as one of the fools in Israel. Now therefore, I pray thee, speak unto the king; for he will not withhold me from thee.

14Howbeit he would not hearken unto her voice: but, being stronger than she, forced her, and lay with her.

15Then Amnon hated her exceedingly; so that the hatred wherewith he hated her *was* greater than the

NEW LIVING TRANSLATION

brick kilns.* That is how he dealt with the people of all the Ammonite towns. Then David and all the army returned to Jerusalem.

The Rape of Tamar

13

Now David's son Absalom had a beautiful sister named Tamar. And Amnon, her half brother, fell desperately in love with her. 2Amnon became so obsessed with Tamar that he became ill. She was a virgin, and Amnon thought he could never have her.

3But Amnon had a very crafty friend—his cousin Jonadab. He was the son of David's brother Shimea.* 4One day Jonadab said to Amnon, "What's the trouble? Why should the son of a king look so dejected morning after morning?"

So Amnon told him, "I am in love with Tamar, my brother Absalom's sister."

5"Well," Jonadab said, "I'll tell you what to do. Go back to bed and pretend you are ill. When your father comes to see you, ask him to let Tamar come and prepare some food for you. Tell him you'll feel better if she prepares it as you watch and feeds you with her own hands."

6So Amnon lay down and pretended to be sick. And when the king came to see him, Amnon asked him, "Please let my sister Tamar come and cook my favorite dish* as I watch. Then I can eat it from her own hands." 7So David agreed and sent Tamar to Amnon's house to prepare some food for him.

8When Tamar arrived at Amnon's house, she went to the place where he was lying down so he could watch her mix some dough. Then she baked his favorite dish for him. 9But when she set the serving tray before him, he refused to eat. "Everyone get out of here," Amnon told his servants. So they all left.

10Then he said to Tamar, "Now bring the food into my bedroom and feed it to me here." So Tamar took his favorite dish to him. 11But as she was feeding him, he grabbed her and demanded, "Come to bed with me, my darling sister."

12"No, my brother!" she cried. "Don't be foolish! Don't do this to me! Such wicked things aren't done in Israel. 13Where could I go in my shame? And you would be called one of the greatest fools in Israel. Please, just speak to the king about it, and he will let you marry me."

14But Amnon wouldn't listen to her, and since he was stronger than she was, he raped her. 15Then suddenly Amnon's love turned to hate, and he hated her

12:31b Or *and he made them pass through the brick kilns.* **13:3** Hebrew *Shimeah* (also in 13:32), a variant spelling of Shimea; compare 1 Chr 2:13. **13:6** Or *a couple of cakes;* also in 13:8, 10.

KING JAMES VERSION

love wherewith he had loved her. And Amnon said
unto her, Arise, be gone.
16And she said unto him, *There is* no cause: this
evil in sending me away *is* greater than the other
that thou didst unto me. But he would not hearken
unto her.
17Then he called his servant that ministered unto
him, and said, Put now this *woman* out from me, and
bolt the door after her.
18And *she had* a garment of divers colours upon
her: for with such robes were the king's daughters
that were virgins apparelled. Then his servant
brought her out, and bolted the door after her.
19And Tamar put ashes on her head, and rent her
garment of divers colours that *was* on her, and laid
her hand on her head, and went on crying.
20And Absalom her brother said unto her, Hath
Amnon thy brother been with thee? but hold now
thy peace, my sister: he *is* thy brother; regard not this
thing. So Tamar remained desolate in her brother
Absalom's house.
21But when king David heard of all these things, he
was very wroth.
22And Absalom spake unto his brother Amnon
neither good nor bad: for Absalom hated Amnon,
because he had forced his sister Tamar.
23And it came to pass after two full years, that Absalom had sheepshearers in Baal-hazor, which *is*
beside Ephraim: and Absalom invited all the king's
sons.
24And Absalom came to the king, and said, Behold
now, thy servant hath sheepshearers; let the king, I
beseech thee, and his servants go with thy servant.
25And the king said to Absalom, Nay, my son, let
us not all now go, lest we be chargeable unto thee.
And he pressed him: howbeit he would not go, but
blessed him.
26Then said Absalom, If not, I pray thee, let my
brother Amnon go with us. And the king said unto
him, Why should he go with thee?
27But Absalom pressed him, that he let Amnon
and all the king's sons go with him.
28Now Absalom had commanded his servants,
saying, Mark ye now when Amnon's heart is merry
with wine, and when I say unto you, Smite Amnon;
then kill him, fear not: have not I commanded you?
be courageous, and be valiant.
29And the servants of Absalom did unto Amnon as
Absalom had commanded. Then all the king's sons
arose, and every man gat him up upon his mule,
and fled.
30And it came to pass, while they were in the
way, that tidings came to David, saying, Absalom
hath slain all the king's sons, and there is not one of
them left.
31Then the king arose, and tare his garments, and
lay on the earth; and all his servants stood by with
their clothes rent.

NEW LIVING TRANSLATION

even more than he had loved her. "Get out of here!"
he snarled at her.
16"No, no!" Tamar cried. "Sending me away now is
worse than what you've already done to me."
But Amnon wouldn't listen to her. 17He shouted
for his servant and demanded, "Throw this woman
out, and lock the door behind her!"
18So the servant put her out and locked the door
behind her. She was wearing a long, beautiful robe,*
as was the custom in those days for the king's virgin
daughters. 19But now Tamar tore her robe and put
ashes on her head. And then, with her face in her
hands, she went away crying.
20Her brother Absalom saw her and asked, "Is it
true that Amnon has been with you? Well, my sister,
keep quiet for now, since he's your brother. Don't you
worry about it." So Tamar lived as a desolate woman
in her brother Absalom's house.
21When King David heard what had happened, he
was very angry.* 22And though Absalom never spoke
to Amnon about this, he hated Amnon deeply because of what he had done to his sister.

Absalom's Revenge on Amnon

23Two years later, when Absalom's sheep were being
sheared at Baal-hazor near Ephraim, Absalom invited all the king's sons to come to a feast. 24He went
to the king and said, "My sheep-shearers are now at
work. Would the king and his servants please come
to celebrate the occasion with me?"
25The king replied, "No, my son. If we all came, we
would be too much of a burden on you." Absalom
pressed him, but the king would not come, though
he gave Absalom his blessing.
26"Well, then," Absalom said, "if you can't come,
how about sending my brother Amnon with us?"
"Why Amnon?" the king asked. 27But Absalom
kept on pressing the king until he finally agreed to
let all his sons attend, including Amnon. So Absalom
prepared a feast fit for a king.*
28Absalom told his men, "Wait until Amnon gets
drunk; then at my signal, kill him! Don't be afraid. I'm
the one who has given the command. Take courage
and do it!" 29So at Absalom's signal they murdered
Amnon. Then the other sons of the king jumped on
their mules and fled.
30As they were on the way back to Jerusalem, this
report reached David: "Absalom has killed all the
king's sons; not one is left alive!" 31The king got up,
tore his robe, and threw himself on the ground. His
advisers also tore their clothes in horror and sorrow.

13:18 Or *a robe with sleeves*, or *an ornamented robe*. The meaning of the Hebrew is uncertain. **13:21** Dead Sea Scrolls and Greek version add *But he did not punish his son Amnon, because he loved him, for he was his firstborn.* **13:27** As in Greek and Latin versions (compare also Dead Sea Scrolls); the Hebrew text lacks this sentence.

KING JAMES VERSION

32And Jonadab, the son of Shimeah David's
brother, answered and said, Let not my lord suppose
that they have slain all the young men the king's
sons; for Amnon only is dead: for by the appointment of Absalom this hath been determined from
the day that he forced his sister Tamar.
33Now therefore let not my lord the king take the
thing to his heart, to think that all the king's sons are
dead: for Amnon only is dead.
34But Absalom fled. And the young man that kept
the watch lifted up his eyes, and looked, and, behold,
there came much people by the way of the hill side
behind him.
35And Jonadab said unto the king, Behold, the
king's sons come: as thy servant said, so it is.
36And it came to pass, as soon as he had made an
end of speaking, that, behold, the king's sons came,
and lifted up their voice and wept: and the king also
and all his servants wept very sore.
37But Absalom fled, and went to Talmai, the son of
Ammihud, king of Geshur. And *David* mourned for
his son every day.
38So Absalom fled, and went to Geshur, and was
there three years.
39And *the soul of* king David longed to go forth
unto Absalom: for he was comforted concerning
Amnon, seeing he was dead.

14 1Now Joab the son of Zeruiah perceived that
the king's heart *was* toward Absalom.
2And Joab sent to Tekoah, and fetched thence a
wise woman, and said unto her, I pray thee, feign thyself to be a mourner, and put on now mourning
apparel, and anoint not thyself with oil, but be as a
woman that had a long time mourned for the dead:
3And come to the king, and speak on this manner
unto him. So Joab put the words in her mouth.
4And when the woman of Tekoah spake to the
king, she fell on her face to the ground, and did obeisance, and said, Help, O king.
5And the king said unto her, What aileth thee?
And she answered, I *am* indeed a widow woman, and
mine husband is dead.
6And thy handmaid had two sons, and they two
strove together in the field, and *there was* none to
part them, but the one smote the other, and slew him.
7And, behold, the whole family is risen against
thine handmaid, and they said, Deliver him that
smote his brother, that we may kill him, for the life of
his brother whom he slew; and we will destroy the
heir also: and so they shall quench my coal which is
left, and shall not leave to my husband *neither* name
nor remainder upon the earth.
8And the king said unto the woman, Go to thine
house, and I will give charge concerning thee.
9And the woman of Tekoah said unto the king, My
lord, O king, the iniquity *be* on me, and on my father's
house: and the king and his throne *be* guiltless.

NEW LIVING TRANSLATION

32But just then Jonadab, the son of David's brother
Shimea, arrived and said, "No, don't believe that all
the king's sons have been killed! It was only Amnon!
Absalom has been plotting this ever since Amnon
raped his sister Tamar. 33No, my lord the king, your
sons aren't all dead! It was only Amnon." 34Mean-
while Absalom escaped.
Then the watchman on the Jerusalem wall saw a
great crowd coming down the hill on the road from
the west. He ran to tell the king, "I see a crowd of
people coming from the Horonaim road along the
side of the hill."*
35"Look!" Jonadab told the king. "There they are
now! The king's sons are coming, just as I said."
36They soon arrived, weeping and sobbing, and
the king and all his servants wept bitterly with them.
37And David mourned many days for his son Amnon.
Absalom fled to his grandfather, Talmai son of
Ammihud, the king of Geshur. 38He stayed there in
Geshur for three years. 39And King David,* now reconciled to Amnon's death, longed to be reunited with
his son Absalom.*

Joab Arranges for Absalom's Return

14 Joab realized how much the king longed to
see Absalom. 2So he sent for a woman from
Tekoa who had a reputation for great wisdom. He said
to her, "Pretend you are in mourning; wear mourning
clothes and don't put on lotions.* Act like a woman
who has been mourning for the dead for a long
time. 3Then go to the king and tell him the story I am
about to tell you." Then Joab told her what to say.
4When the woman from Tekoa approached the
king, she bowed with her face to the ground in deep
respect and cried out, "O king! Help me!"
5"What's the trouble?" the king asked.
"Alas, I am a widow!" she replied. "My husband is
dead. 6My two sons had a fight out in the field. And
since no one was there to stop it, one of them was
killed. 7Now the rest of the family is demanding, 'Let
us have your son. We will execute him for murdering
his brother. He doesn't deserve to inherit his family's
property.' They want to extinguish the only coal I
have left, and my husband's name and family will
disappear from the face of the earth."
8"Leave it to me," the king told her. "Go home, and
I'll see to it that no one touches him."
9"Oh, thank you, my lord the king," the woman
from Tekoa replied. "If you are criticized for helping
me, let the blame fall on me and on my father's
house, and let the king and his throne be innocent."

13:34 As in Greek version; Hebrew lacks this sentence. **13:39a** Dead Sea Scrolls and Greek version read *And the spirit of the king.* **13:39b** Or *no longer felt a need to go out after Absalom.* **14:2** Hebrew *don't anoint yourself with oil.*

KING JAMES VERSION

10And the king said, Whosoever saith *aught* unto
thee, bring him to me, and he shall not touch thee
any more.
11Then said she, I pray thee, let the king remember
the Lord thy God, that thou wouldest not suffer the
revengers of blood to destroy any more, lest they destroy my son. And he said, *As* the Lord liveth, there
shall not one hair of thy son fall to the earth.
12Then the woman said, Let thine handmaid, I
pray thee, speak *one* word unto my lord the king.
And he said, Say on.
13And the woman said, Wherefore then hast thou
thought such a thing against the people of God? for
the king doth speak this thing as one which is faulty,
in that the king doth not fetch home again his
banished.
14For we must needs die, and *are* as water spilled
on the ground, which cannot be gathered up again;
neither doth God respect *any* person: yet doth he
devise means, that his banished be not expelled
from him.
15Now therefore that I am come to speak of this
thing unto my lord the king, *it is* because the people
have made me afraid: and thy handmaid said, I will
now speak unto the king; it may be that the king will
perform the request of his handmaid.
16For the king will hear, to deliver his handmaid
out of the hand of the man *that would* destroy me
and my son together out of the inheritance of God.
17Then thine handmaid said, The word of my lord
the king shall now be comfortable: for as an angel of
God, so *is* my lord the king to discern good and bad:
therefore the Lord thy God will be with thee.
18Then the king answered and said unto the
woman, Hide not from me, I pray thee, the thing that
I shall ask thee. And the woman said, Let my lord the
king now speak.
19And the king said, *Is not* the hand of Joab with
thee in all this? And the woman answered and said,
As thy soul liveth, my lord the king, none can turn to
the right hand or to the left from aught that my lord
the king hath spoken: for thy servant Joab, he bade
me, and he put all these words in the mouth of thine
handmaid:
20To fetch about this form of speech hath thy
servant Joab done this thing: and my lord *is* wise,
according to the wisdom of an angel of God, to know
all *things* that *are* in the earth.
21And the king said unto Joab, Behold now, I have
done this thing: go therefore, bring the young man
Absalom again.
22And Joab fell to the ground on his face, and
bowed himself, and thanked the king: and Joab said,
Today thy servant knoweth that I have found grace in
thy sight, my lord, O king, in that the king hath fulfilled the request of his servant.
23So Joab arose and went to Geshur, and brought
Absalom to Jerusalem.

NEW LIVING TRANSLATION

10"If anyone objects," the king said, "bring him to
me. I can assure you he will never complain again!"
11Then she said, "Please swear to me by the Lord
your God that you won't let anyone take vengeance
against my son. I want no more bloodshed."
"As surely as the Lord lives," he replied, "not a hair
on your son's head will be disturbed!"
12"Please allow me to ask one more thing of my
lord the king," she said.
"Go ahead and speak," he responded.
13She replied, "Why don't you do as much for the
people of God as you have promised to do for me?
You have convicted yourself in making this decision,
because you have refused to bring home your own
banished son. 14All of us must die eventually. Our
lives are like water spilled out on the ground, which
cannot be gathered up again. But God does not just
sweep life away; instead, he devises ways to bring us
back when we have been separated from him.
15"I have come to plead with my lord the king because people have threatened me. I said to myself,
'Perhaps the king will listen to me 16and rescue us
from those who would cut us off from the inheritance* God has given us. 17Yes, my lord the king will
give us peace of mind again.' I know that you are like
an angel of God in discerning good from evil. May
the Lord your God be with you."
18"I must know one thing," the king replied, "and
tell me the truth."
"Yes, my lord the king," she responded.
19"Did Joab put you up to this?"
And the woman replied, "My lord the king, how
can I deny it? Nobody can hide anything from you.
Yes, Joab sent me and told me what to say. 20He did it
to place the matter before you in a different light. But
you are as wise as an angel of God, and you understand everything that happens among us!"
21So the king sent for Joab and told him, "All right,
go and bring back the young man Absalom."
22Joab bowed with his face to the ground in deep
respect and said, "At last I know that I have gained
your approval, my lord the king, for you have granted
me this request!"
23Then Joab went to Geshur and brought Absalom

14:16 Or *the property;* or *the people.*

KING JAMES VERSION

[24]And the king said, Let him turn to his own house, and let him not see my face. So Absalom returned to his own house, and saw not the king's face.

[25]But in all Israel there was none to be so much praised as Absalom for his beauty: from the sole of his foot even to the crown of his head there was no blemish in him.

[26]And when he polled his head, (for it was at every year's end that he polled *it:* because *the hair* was heavy on him, therefore he polled it:) he weighed the hair of his head at two hundred shekels after the king's weight.

[27]And unto Absalom there were born three sons, and one daughter, whose name *was* Tamar: she was a woman of a fair countenance.

[28]So Absalom dwelt two full years in Jerusalem, and saw not the king's face.

[29]Therefore Absalom sent for Joab, to have sent him to the king; but he would not come to him: and when he sent again the second time, he would not come.

[30]Therefore he said unto his servants, See, Joab's field is near mine, and he hath barley there; go and set it on fire. And Absalom's servants set the field on fire.

[31]Then Joab arose, and came to Absalom unto *his* house, and said unto him, Wherefore have thy servants set my field on fire?

[32]And Absalom answered Joab, Behold, I sent unto thee, saying, Come hither, that I may send thee to the king, to say, Wherefore am I come from Geshur? *it had been* good for me *to have been* there still: now therefore let me see the king's face; and if there be *any* iniquity in me, let him kill me.

[33]So Joab came to the king, and told him: and when he had called for Absalom, he came to the king, and bowed himself on his face to the ground before the king: and the king kissed Absalom.

15 [1]And it came to pass after this, that Absalom prepared him chariots and horses, and fifty men to run before him.

[2]And Absalom rose up early, and stood beside the way of the gate: and it was *so,* that when any man that had a controversy came to the king for judgment, then Absalom called unto him, and said, Of what city *art* thou? And he said, Thy servant *is* of one of the tribes of Israel.

[3]And Absalom said unto him, See, thy matters *are* good and right; but *there is* no man *deputed* of the king to hear thee.

[4]Absalom said moreover, Oh that I were made judge in the land, that every man which hath any suit or cause might come unto me, and I would do him justice!

NEW LIVING TRANSLATION

back to Jerusalem. [24]But the king gave this order: "Absalom may go to his own house, but he must never come into my presence." So Absalom did not see the king.

Absalom Reconciled to David

[25]Now Absalom was praised as the most handsome man in all Israel. He was flawless from head to foot.
[26]He cut his hair only once a year, and then only because it was so heavy. When he weighed it out, it came to five pounds!* [27]He had three sons and one daughter. His daughter's name was Tamar, and she was very beautiful.

[28]Absalom lived in Jerusalem for two years, but he never got to see the king. [29]Then Absalom sent for Joab to ask him to intercede for him, but Joab refused to come. Absalom sent for him a second time, but again Joab refused to come. [30]So Absalom said to his servants, "Go and set fire to Joab's barley field, the field next to mine." So they set his field on fire, as Absalom had commanded.

[31]Then Joab came to Absalom at his house and demanded, "Why did your servants set my field on fire?"

[32]And Absalom replied, "Because I wanted you to ask the king why he brought me back from Geshur if he didn't intend to see me. I might as well have stayed there. Let me see the king; if he finds me guilty of anything, then let him kill me."

[33]So Joab told the king what Absalom had said. Then at last David summoned Absalom, who came and bowed low before the king, and the king kissed him.

Absalom's Rebellion

15 After this, Absalom bought a chariot and horses, and he hired fifty bodyguards to run ahead of him. [2]He got up early every morning and went out to the gate of the city. When people brought a case to the king for judgment, Absalom would ask where in Israel they were from, and they would tell him their tribe. [3]Then Absalom would say, "You've really got a strong case here! It's too bad the king doesn't have anyone to hear it. [4]I wish I were the judge. Then everyone could bring their cases to me for judgment, and I would give them justice!"

14:26 Hebrew *200 shekels* [2.3 kilograms] *by the royal standard.*

KING JAMES VERSION

5 And it was *so,* that when any man came nigh *to him* to do him obeisance, he put forth his hand, and took him, and kissed him.

6 And on this manner did Absalom to all Israel that came to the king for judgment: so Absalom stole the hearts of the men of Israel.

7 And it came to pass after forty years, that Absalom said unto the king, I pray thee, let me go and pay my vow, which I have vowed unto the LORD, in Hebron.

8 For thy servant vowed a vow while I abode at Geshur in Syria, saying, If the LORD shall bring me again indeed to Jerusalem, then I will serve the LORD.

9 And the king said unto him, Go in peace. So he arose, and went to Hebron.

10 But Absalom sent spies throughout all the tribes of Israel, saying, As soon as ye hear the sound of the trumpet, then ye shall say, Absalom reigneth in Hebron.

11 And with Absalom went two hundred men out of Jerusalem, *that were* called; and they went in their simplicity, and they knew not any thing.

12 And Absalom sent for Ahithophel the Gilonite, David's counsellor, from his city, *even* from Giloh, while he offered sacrifices. And the conspiracy was strong; for the people increased continually with Absalom.

13 And there came a messenger to David, saying, The hearts of the men of Israel are after Absalom.

14 And David said unto all his servants that *were* with him at Jerusalem, Arise, and let us flee; for we shall not *else* escape from Absalom: make speed to depart, lest he overtake us suddenly, and bring evil upon us, and smite the city with the edge of the sword.

15 And the king's servants said unto the king, Behold, thy servants *are ready to do* whatsoever my lord the king shall appoint.

16 And the king went forth, and all his household after him. And the king left ten women, *which were* concubines, to keep the house.

17 And the king went forth, and all the people after him, and tarried in a place that was far off.

18 And all his servants passed on beside him; and all the Cherethites, and all the Pelethites, and all the Gittites, six hundred men which came after him from Gath, passed on before the king.

19 Then said the king to Ittai the Gittite, Wherefore goest thou also with us? return to thy place, and abide with the king: for thou *art* a stranger, and also an exile.

20 Whereas thou camest *but* yesterday, should I this day make thee go up and down with us? seeing I go whither I may, return thou, and take back thy brethren: mercy and truth *be* with thee.

21 And Ittai answered the king, and said, *As* the LORD liveth, and *as* my lord the king liveth, surely in what place my lord the king shall be, whether in death or life, even there also will thy servant be.

NEW LIVING TRANSLATION

5 When people tried to bow before him, Absalom wouldn't let them. Instead, he took them by the hand and kissed them. 6 Absalom did this with everyone who came to the king for judgment, and so he stole the hearts of all the people of Israel.

7 After four years,* Absalom said to the king, "Let me go to Hebron to offer a sacrifice to the LORD and fulfill a vow I made to him. 8 For while your servant was at Geshur in Aram, I promised to sacrifice to the LORD in Hebron* if he would bring me back to Jerusalem."

9 "All right," the king told him. "Go and fulfill your vow."

So Absalom went to Hebron. 10 But while he was there, he sent secret messengers to all the tribes of Israel to stir up a rebellion against the king. "As soon as you hear the ram's horn," his message read, "you are to say, 'Absalom has been crowned king in Hebron.'" 11 He took 200 men from Jerusalem with him as guests, but they knew nothing of his intentions. 12 While Absalom was offering the sacrifices, he sent for Ahithophel, one of David's counselors who lived in Giloh. Soon many others also joined Absalom, and the conspiracy gained momentum.

David Escapes from Jerusalem

13 A messenger soon arrived in Jerusalem to tell David, "All Israel has joined Absalom in a conspiracy against you!"

14 "Then we must flee at once, or it will be too late!" David urged his men. "Hurry! If we get out of the city before Absalom arrives, both we and the city of Jerusalem will be spared from disaster."

15 "We are with you," his advisers replied. "Do what you think is best."

16 So the king and all his household set out at once. He left no one behind except ten of his concubines to look after the palace. 17 The king and all his people set out on foot, pausing at the last house 18 to let all the king's men move past to lead the way. There were 600 men from Gath who had come with David, along with the king's bodyguard.*

19 Then the king turned and said to Ittai, a leader of the men from Gath, "Why are you coming with us? Go on back to King Absalom, for you are a guest in Israel, a foreigner in exile. 20 You arrived only recently, and should I force you today to wander with us? I don't even know where we will go. Go on back and take your kinsmen with you, and may the LORD show you his unfailing love and faithfulness.*"

21 But Ittai said to the king, "I vow by the LORD and by your own life that I will go wherever my lord the king goes, no matter what happens—whether it means life or death."

15:7 As in Greek and Syriac versions; Hebrew reads *forty years.* **15:8** As in some Greek manuscripts; Hebrew lacks *in Hebron.* **15:18** Hebrew *the Kerethites and Pelethites.* **15:20** As in Greek version; Hebrew reads *and may unfailing love and faithfulness go with you.*

KING JAMES VERSION

22 And David said to Ittai, Go and pass over. And
Ittai the Gittite passed over, and all his men, and all
the little ones that *were* with him.
23 And all the country wept with a loud voice, and
all the people passed over: the king also himself
passed over the brook Kidron, and all the people
passed over, toward the way of the wilderness.
24 And lo Zadok also, and all the Levites *were* with
him, bearing the ark of the covenant of God: and they
set down the ark of God; and Abiathar went up, until
all the people had done passing out of the city.
25 And the king said unto Zadok, Carry back the ark
of God into the city: if I shall find favour in the eyes of
the LORD, he will bring me again, and shew me *both*
it, and his habitation:
26 But if he thus say, I have no delight in thee; behold, *here am* I, let him do to me as seemeth good
unto him.
27 The king said also unto Zadok the priest, *Art not*
thou a seer? return into the city in peace, and your
two sons with you, Ahimaaz thy son, and Jonathan
the son of Abiathar.
28 See, I will tarry in the plain of the wilderness,
until there come word from you to certify me.
29 Zadok therefore and Abiathar carried the ark of
God again to Jerusalem: and they tarried there.
30 And David went up by the ascent of *mount*
Olivet, and wept as he went up, and had his head covered, and he went barefoot: and all the people that
was with him covered every man his head, and they
went up, weeping as they went up.
31 And *one* told David, saying, Ahithophel *is* among
the conspirators with Absalom. And David said,
O LORD, I pray thee, turn the counsel of Ahithophel
into foolishness.
32 And it came to pass, that *when* David was come
to the top *of the mount,* where he worshipped God,
behold, Hushai the Archite came to meet him with
his coat rent, and earth upon his head:
33 Unto whom David said, If thou passest on with
me, then thou shalt be a burden unto me:
34 But if thou return to the city, and say unto Absalom, I will be thy servant, O king; *as* I *have been* thy
father's servant hitherto, so *will* I now also *be* thy servant: then mayest thou for me defeat the counsel of
Ahithophel.
35 And *hast thou* not there with thee Zadok and
Abiathar the priests? therefore it shall be, *that* what
thing soever thou shalt hear out of the king's house,
thou shalt tell *it* to Zadok and Abiathar the priests.
36 Behold, *they have* there with them their two
sons, Ahimaaz Zadok's *son,* and Jonathan Abiathar's
son; and by them ye shall send unto me every thing
that ye can hear.
37 So Hushai David's friend came into the city, and
Absalom came into Jerusalem.

NEW LIVING TRANSLATION

22 David replied, "All right, come with us." So Ittai
and all his men and their families went along.
23 Everyone cried loudly as the king and his followers passed by. They crossed the Kidron Valley and
then went out toward the wilderness.
24 Zadok and all the Levites also came along, carrying the Ark of the Covenant of God. They set down
the Ark of God, and Abiathar offered sacrifices* until
everyone had passed out of the city.
25 Then the king instructed Zadok to take the Ark
of God back into the city. "If the LORD sees fit," David
said, "he will bring me back to see the Ark and the
Tabernacle* again. 26 But if he is through with me,
then let him do what seems best to him."
27 The king also told Zadok the priest, "Look,* here
is my plan. You and Abiathar* should return quietly
to the city with your son Ahimaaz and Abiathar's son
Jonathan. 28 I will stop at the shallows of the Jordan
River* and wait there for a report from you." 29 So
Zadok and Abiathar took the Ark of God back to the
city and stayed there.
30 David walked up the road to the Mount of Olives,
weeping as he went. His head was covered and his
feet were bare as a sign of mourning. And the people
who were with him covered their heads and wept as
they climbed the hill. 31 When someone told David
that his adviser Ahithophel was now backing Absalom, David prayed, "O LORD, let Ahithophel give Absalom foolish advice!"
32 When David reached the summit of the Mount
of Olives where people worshiped God, Hushai the
Arkite was waiting there for him. Hushai had torn his
clothing and put dirt on his head as a sign of mourning. 33 But David told him, "If you go with me, you will
only be a burden. 34 Return to Jerusalem and tell Absalom, 'I will now be your adviser, O king, just as I was
your father's adviser in the past.' Then you can frustrate and counter Ahithophel's advice. 35 Zadok and
Abiathar, the priests, will be there. Tell them about
the plans being made in the king's palace, 36 and they
will send their sons Ahimaaz and Jonathan to tell me
what is going on."
37 So David's friend Hushai returned to Jerusalem,
getting there just as Absalom arrived.

15:24 Or *Abiathar went up.* **15:25** Hebrew *and his dwelling place.* **15:27a** As in Greek version; Hebrew reads *Are you a seer?* or *Do you see?* **15:27b** Hebrew lacks *and Abiathar;* compare 15:29. **15:28** Hebrew *at the crossing points of the wilderness.*

KING JAMES VERSION

16

1 And when David was a little past the top *of the hill,* behold, Ziba the servant of Mephibosheth met him, with a couple of asses saddled, and upon them two hundred *loaves* of bread, and an hundred bunches of raisins, and an hundred of summer fruits, and a bottle of wine.

2 And the king said unto Ziba, What meanest thou by these? And Ziba said, The asses *be* for the king's household to ride on; and the bread and summer fruit for the young men to eat; and the wine, that such as be faint in the wilderness may drink.

3 And the king said, And where *is* thy master's son? And Ziba said unto the king, Behold, he abideth at Jerusalem: for he said, To day shall the house of Israel restore me the kingdom of my father.

4 Then said the king to Ziba, Behold, thine *are* all that *pertained* unto Mephibosheth. And Ziba said, I humbly beseech thee *that* I may find grace in thy sight, my lord, O king.

5 And when king David came to Bahurim, behold, thence came out a man of the family of the house of Saul, whose name *was* Shimei, the son of Gera: he came forth, and cursed still as he came.

6 And he cast stones at David, and at all the servants of king David: and all the people and all the mighty men *were* on his right hand and on his left.

7 And thus said Shimei when he cursed, Come out, come out, thou bloody man, and thou man of Belial:

8 The LORD hath returned upon thee all the blood of the house of Saul, in whose stead thou hast reigned; and the LORD hath delivered the kingdom into the hand of Absalom thy son: and, behold, thou *art taken* in thy mischief, because thou *art* a bloody man.

9 Then said Abishai the son of Zeruiah unto the king, Why should this dead dog curse my lord the king? let me go over, I pray thee, and take off his head.

10 And the king said, What have I to do with you, ye sons of Zeruiah? so let him curse, because the LORD hath said unto him, Curse David. Who shall then say, Wherefore hast thou done so?

11 And David said to Abishai, and to all his servants, Behold, my son, which came forth of my bowels, seeketh my life: how much more now *may this* Benjamite *do it?* let him alone, and let him curse; for the LORD hath bidden him.

12 It may be that the LORD will look on mine affliction, and that the LORD will requite me good for his cursing this day.

13 And as David and his men went by the way, Shimei went along on the hill's side over against him, and cursed as he went, and threw stones at him, and cast dust.

NEW LIVING TRANSLATION

David and Ziba

16

When David had gone a little beyond the summit of the Mount of Olives, Ziba, the servant of Mephibosheth,* was waiting there for him. He had two donkeys loaded with 200 loaves of bread, 100 clusters of raisins, 100 bunches of summer fruit, and a wineskin full of wine.

2 "What are these for?" the king asked Ziba.

Ziba replied, "The donkeys are for the king's people to ride on, and the bread and summer fruit are for the young men to eat. The wine is for those who become exhausted in the wilderness."

3 "And where is Mephibosheth, Saul's grandson?" the king asked him.

"He stayed in Jerusalem," Ziba replied. "He said, 'Today I will get back the kingdom of my grandfather Saul.'"

4 "In that case," the king told Ziba, "I give you everything Mephibosheth owns."

"I bow before you," Ziba replied. "May I always be pleasing to you, my lord the king."

Shimei Curses David

5 As King David came to Bahurim, a man came out of the village cursing them. It was Shimei son of Gera, from the same clan as Saul's family. 6 He threw stones at the king and the king's officers and all the mighty warriors who surrounded him. 7 "Get out of here, you murderer, you scoundrel!" he shouted at David. 8 "The LORD is paying you back for all the bloodshed in Saul's clan. You stole his throne, and now the LORD has given it to your son Absalom. At last you will taste some of your own medicine, for you are a murderer!"

9 "Why should this dead dog curse my lord the king?" Abishai son of Zeruiah demanded. "Let me go over and cut off his head!"

10 "No!" the king said. "Who asked your opinion, you sons of Zeruiah! If the LORD has told him to curse me, who are you to stop him?"

11 Then David said to Abishai and to all his servants, "My own son is trying to kill me. Doesn't this relative of Saul* have even more reason to do so? Leave him alone and let him curse, for the LORD has told him to do it. 12 And perhaps the LORD will see that I am being wronged and will bless me because of these curses today." 13 So David and his men continued down the road, and Shimei kept pace with them on a nearby hillside, cursing as he went and throwing stones at David and tossing dust into the air.

16:1 *Mephibosheth* is another name for Merib-baal. **16:11** Hebrew *this Benjaminite.*

KING JAMES VERSION

14 And the king, and all the people that *were* with him, came weary, and refreshed themselves there.

15 And Absalom, and all the people the men of Israel, came to Jerusalem, and Ahithophel with him.

16 And it came to pass, when Hushai the Archite, David's friend, was come unto Absalom, that Hushai said unto Absalom, God save the king, God save the king.

17 And Absalom said to Hushai, *Is* this thy kindness to thy friend? why wentest thou not with thy friend?

18 And Hushai said unto Absalom, Nay; but whom the LORD, and this people, and all the men of Israel, choose, his will I be, and with him will I abide.

19 And again, whom should I serve? *should I* not *serve* in the presence of his son? as I have served in thy father's presence, so will I be in thy presence.

20 Then said Absalom to Ahithophel, Give counsel among you what we shall do.

21 And Ahithophel said unto Absalom, Go in unto thy father's concubines, which he hath left to keep the house; and all Israel shall hear that thou art abhorred of thy father: then shall the hands of all that *are* with thee be strong.

22 So they spread Absalom a tent upon the top of the house; and Absalom went in unto his father's concubines in the sight of all Israel.

23 And the counsel of Ahithophel, which he counselled in those days, *was* as if a man had inquired at the oracle of God: so *was* all the counsel of Ahithophel both with David and with Absalom.

17 1 Moreover Ahithophel said unto Absalom, Let me now choose out twelve thousand men, and I will arise and pursue after David this night:

2 And I will come upon him while he *is* weary and weak handed, and will make him afraid: and all the people that *are* with him shall flee; and I will smite the king only:

3 And I will bring back all the people unto thee: the man whom thou seekest *is* as if all returned: *so* all the people shall be in peace.

4 And the saying pleased Absalom well, and all the elders of Israel.

5 Then said Absalom, Call now Hushai the Archite also, and let us hear likewise what he saith.

6 And when Hushai was come to Absalom, Absalom spake unto him, saying, Ahithophel hath spoken after this manner: shall we do *after* his saying? if not; speak thou.

7 And Hushai said unto Absalom, The counsel that Ahithophel hath given *is* not good at this time.

8 For, said Hushai, thou knowest thy father and his men, that they *be* mighty men, and they *be* chafed in their minds, as a bear robbed of her whelps in the

NEW LIVING TRANSLATION

14 The king and all who were with him grew weary along the way, so they rested when they reached the Jordan River.*

Ahithophel Advises Absalom

15 Meanwhile, Absalom and all the army of Israel arrived at Jerusalem, accompanied by Ahithophel. 16 When David's friend Hushai the Arkite arrived, he went immediately to see Absalom. "Long live the king!" he exclaimed. "Long live the king!"

17 "Is this the way you treat your friend David?" Absalom asked him. "Why aren't you with him?"

18 "I'm here because I belong to the man who is chosen by the LORD and by all the men of Israel," Hushai replied. 19 "And anyway, why shouldn't I serve you? Just as I was your father's adviser, now I will be your adviser!"

20 Then Absalom turned to Ahithophel and asked him, "What should I do next?"

21 Ahithophel told him, "Go and sleep with your father's concubines, for he has left them here to look after the palace. Then all Israel will know that you have insulted your father beyond hope of reconciliation, and they will throw their support to you." 22 So they set up a tent on the palace roof where everyone could see it, and Absalom went in and had sex with his father's concubines.

23 Absalom followed Ahithophel's advice, just as David had done. For every word Ahithophel spoke seemed as wise as though it had come directly from the mouth of God.

17 Now Ahithophel urged Absalom, "Let me choose 12,000 men to start out after David tonight. 2 I will catch up with him while he is weary and discouraged. He and his troops will panic, and everyone will run away. Then I will kill only the king, 3 and I will bring all the people back to you as a bride returns to her husband. After all, it is only one man's life that you seek.* Then you will be at peace with all the people." 4 This plan seemed good to Absalom and to all the elders of Israel.

Hushai Counters Ahithophel's Advice

5 But then Absalom said, "Bring in Hushai the Arkite. Let's see what he thinks about this." 6 When Hushai arrived, Absalom told him what Ahithophel had said. Then he asked, "What is your opinion? Should we follow Ahithophel's advice? If not, what do you suggest?"

7 "Well," Hushai replied to Absalom, "this time Ahithophel has made a mistake. 8 You know your father and his men; they are mighty warriors. Right now they are as enraged as a mother bear who has

16:14 As in Greek version (see also 17:16); Hebrew reads *when they reached their destination.* **17:3** As in Greek version; Hebrew reads *like the return of all is the man whom you seek.*

KING JAMES VERSION

field: and thy father *is* a man of war, and will not
lodge with the people.
9 Behold, he is hid now in some pit, or in some
other place: and it will come to pass, when some of
them be overthrown at the first, that whosoever
heareth it will say, There is a slaughter among the
people that follow Absalom.
10 And he also *that is* valiant, whose heart *is* as the
heart of a lion, shall utterly melt: for all Israel
knoweth that thy father *is* a mighty man, and *they*
which *be* with him *are* valiant men.
11 Therefore I counsel that all Israel be generally
gathered unto thee, from Dan even to Beer-sheba, as
the sand that *is* by the sea for multitude; and that
thou go to battle in thine own person.
12 So shall we come upon him in some place where
he shall be found, and we will light upon him as the
dew falleth on the ground: and of him and of all the
men that *are* with him there shall not be left so much
as one.
13 Moreover, if he be gotten into a city, then shall all
Israel bring ropes to that city, and we will draw it into
the river, until there be not one small stone found
there.
14 And Absalom and all the men of Israel said, The
counsel of Hushai the Archite *is* better than the
counsel of Ahithophel. For the LORD had appointed
to defeat the good counsel of Ahithophel, to the intent that the LORD might bring evil upon Absalom.

15 Then said Hushai unto Zadok and to Abiathar
the priests, Thus and thus did Ahithophel counsel
Absalom and the elders of Israel; and thus and thus
have I counselled.
16 Now therefore send quickly, and tell David,
saying, Lodge not this night in the plains of the
wilderness, but speedily pass over; lest the king be
swallowed up, and all the people that *are* with him.
17 Now Jonathan and Ahimaaz stayed by En-rogel;
for they might not be seen to come into the city: and
a wench went and told them; and they went and told
king David.
18 Nevertheless a lad saw them, and told Absalom:
but they went both of them away quickly, and came
to a man's house in Bahurim, which had a well in his
court; whither they went down.
19 And the woman took and spread a covering over
the well's mouth, and spread ground corn thereon;
and the thing was not known.
20 And when Absalom's servants came to the
woman to the house, they said, Where *is* Ahimaaz
and Jonathan? And the woman said unto them, They
be gone over the brook of water. And when they had
sought and could not find *them,* they returned to
Jerusalem.
21 And it came to pass, after they were departed,
that they came up out of the well, and went and told

NEW LIVING TRANSLATION

been robbed of her cubs. And remember that your
father is an experienced man of war. He won't be
spending the night among the troops. 9 He has probably already hidden in some pit or cave. And when he
comes out and attacks and a few of your men fall,
there will be panic among your troops, and the word
will spread that Absalom's men are being slaughtered. 10 Then even the bravest soldiers, though they
have the heart of a lion, will be paralyzed with fear.
For all Israel knows what a mighty warrior your father is and how courageous his men are.
11 "I recommend that you mobilize the entire army
of Israel, bringing them from as far away as Dan in
the north and Beersheba in the south. That way you
will have an army as numerous as the sand on the
seashore. And I advise that you personally lead the
troops. 12 When we find David, we'll fall on him like
dew that falls on the ground. Then neither he nor
any of his men will be left alive. 13 And if David were
to escape into some town, you will have all Israel
there at your command. Then we can take ropes and
drag the walls of the town into the nearest valley until every stone is torn down."
14 Then Absalom and all the men of Israel said,
"Hushai's advice is better than Ahithophel's." For the
LORD had determined to defeat the counsel of Ahithophel, which really was the better plan, so that he
could bring disaster on Absalom!

Hushai Warns David to Escape

15 Hushai told Zadok and Abiathar, the priests, what
Ahithophel had said to Absalom and the elders of Israel and what he himself had advised instead.
16 "Quick!" he told them. "Find David and urge him
not to stay at the shallows of the Jordan River* tonight. He must go across at once into the wilderness
beyond. Otherwise he will die and his entire army
with him."
17 Jonathan and Ahimaaz had been staying at En-
rogel so as not to be seen entering and leaving the
city. Arrangements had been made for a servant girl
to bring them the message they were to take to King
David. 18 But a boy spotted them at En-rogel, and he
told Absalom about it. So they quickly escaped to
Bahurim, where a man hid them down inside a well
in his courtyard. 19 The man's wife put a cloth over
the top of the well and scattered grain on it to dry in
the sun; so no one suspected they were there.
20 When Absalom's men arrived, they asked her,
"Have you seen Ahimaaz and Jonathan?"
The woman replied, "They were here, but they
crossed over the brook." Absalom's men looked for
them without success and returned to Jerusalem.
21 Then the two men crawled out of the well and
hurried on to King David. "Quick!" they told him,
"cross the Jordan tonight!" And they told him how

17:16 Hebrew *at the crossing points of the wilderness.*

KING JAMES VERSION

king David, and said unto David, Arise, and pass
quickly over the water: for thus hath Ahithophel
counselled against you.
22 Then David arose, and all the people that *were*
with him, and they passed over Jordan: by the morning light there lacked not one of them that was not
gone over Jordan.
23 And when Ahithophel saw that his counsel was
not followed, he saddled *his* ass, and arose, and gat
him home to his house, to his city, and put his household in order, and hanged himself, and died, and was
buried in the sepulchre of his father.
24 Then David came to Mahanaim. And Absalom
passed over Jordan, he and all the men of Israel
with him.
25 And Absalom made Amasa captain of the host
instead of Joab: which Amasa *was* a man's son,
whose name *was* Ithra an Israelite, that went in to
Abigail the daughter of Nahash, sister to Zeruiah
Joab's mother.
26 So Israel and Absalom pitched in the land of
Gilead.
27 And it came to pass, when David was come to
Mahanaim, that Shobi the son of Nahash of Rabbah
of the children of Ammon, and Machir the son of
Ammiel of Lo-debar, and Barzillai the Gileadite of
Rogelim,
28 Brought beds, and basins, and earthen vessels,
and wheat, and barley, and flour, and parched *corn,*
and beans, and lentiles, and parched *pulse,*
29 And honey, and butter, and sheep, and cheese of
kine, for David, and for the people that *were* with
him, to eat: for they said, The people *is* hungry, and
weary, and thirsty, in the wilderness.

18 1 And David numbered the people that *were*
with him, and set captains of thousands and
captains of hundreds over them.
2 And David sent forth a third part of the people
under the hand of Joab, and a third part under the
hand of Abishai the son of Zeruiah, Joab's brother,
and a third part under the hand of Ittai the Gittite.
And the king said unto the people, I will surely go
forth with you myself also.
3 But the people answered, Thou shalt not go forth:
for if we flee away, they will not care for us; neither if
half of us die, will they care for us: but now *thou art*
worth ten thousand of us: therefore now *it is* better
that thou succour us out of the city.
4 And the king said unto them, What seemeth you
best I will do. And the king stood by the gate side,
and all the people came out by hundreds and by
thousands.
5 And the king commanded Joab and Abishai and
Ittai, saying, *Deal* gently for my sake with the young
man, *even* with Absalom. And all the people heard

NEW LIVING TRANSLATION

Ahithophel had advised that he be captured and
killed. 22 So David and all the people with him went
across the Jordan River during the night, and they
were all on the other bank before dawn.
23 When Ahithophel realized that his advice had
not been followed, he saddled his donkey, went to his
hometown, set his affairs in order, and hanged himself. He died there and was buried in the family
tomb.
24 David soon arrived at Mahanaim. By now, Absalom had mobilized the entire army of Israel and was
leading his troops across the Jordan River. 25 Absalom had appointed Amasa as commander of his
army, replacing Joab, who had been commander under David. (Amasa was Joab's cousin. His father was
Jether,* an Ishmaelite.* His mother, Abigail daughter
of Nahash, was the sister of Joab's mother, Zeruiah.)
26 Absalom and the Israelite army set up camp in the
land of Gilead.
27 When David arrived at Mahanaim, he was
warmly greeted by Shobi son of Nahash, who came
from Rabbah of the Ammonites, and by Makir son of
Ammiel from Lo-debar, and by Barzillai of Gilead
from Rogelim. 28 They brought sleeping mats, cooking pots, serving bowls, wheat and barley, flour and
roasted grain, beans, lentils, 29 honey, butter, sheep,
goats, and cheese for David and those who were with
him. For they said, "You must all be very hungry and
tired and thirsty after your long march through the
wilderness."

Absalom's Defeat and Death

18 David now mustered the men who were with
him and appointed generals and captains* to
lead them. 2 He sent the troops out in three groups,
placing one group under Joab, one under Joab's
brother Abishai son of Zeruiah, and one under Ittai,
the man from Gath. The king told his troops, "I am
going out with you."
3 But his men objected strongly. "You must not go,"
they urged. "If we have to turn and run—and even
if half of us die—it will make no difference to Absalom's troops; they will be looking only for you. You
are worth 10,000 of us,* and it is better that you stay
here in the town and send help if we need it."
4 "If you think that's the best plan, I'll do it," the
king answered. So he stood alongside the gate of the
town as all the troops marched out in groups of hundreds and of thousands.
5 And the king gave this command to Joab, Abishai, and Ittai: "For my sake, deal gently with young

17:25a Hebrew *Ithra,* a variant spelling of Jether. **17:25b** As in some Greek manuscripts (see also 1 Chr 2:17); Hebrew reads *an Israelite.* **18:1** Hebrew *appointed commanders of thousands and commanders of hundreds.*
18:3 As in two Hebrew manuscripts and some Greek and Latin manuscripts; most Hebrew manuscripts read *Now there are 10,000 like us.*

KING JAMES VERSION

when the king gave all the captains charge concerning Absalom.
[6]So the people went out into the field against Israel: and the battle was in the wood of Ephraim;
[7]Where the people of Israel were slain before the
servants of David, and there was there a great slaughter that day of twenty thousand *men*.
[8]For the battle was there scattered over the face of
all the country: and the wood devoured more people
that day than the sword devoured.
[9]And Absalom met the servants of David. And Absalom rode upon a mule, and the mule went under
the thick boughs of a great oak, and his head caught
hold of the oak, and he was taken up between the
heaven and the earth; and the mule that *was* under
him went away.
[10]And a certain man saw *it*, and told Joab, and said,
Behold, I saw Absalom hanged in an oak.
[11]And Joab said unto the man that told him, And,
behold, thou sawest *him*, and why didst thou not
smite him there to the ground? And I would have
given thee ten *shekels* of silver, and a girdle.
[12]And the man said unto Joab, Though I should receive a thousand *shekels* of silver in mine hand, *yet*
would I not put forth mine hand against the king's
son: for in our hearing the king charged thee and
Abishai and Ittai, saying, Beware that none *touch* the
young man Absalom.
[13]Otherwise I should have wrought falsehood
against mine own life: for there is no matter hid from
the king, and thou thyself wouldest have set thyself
against *me*.
[14]Then said Joab, I may not tarry thus with thee.
And he took three darts in his hand, and thrust them
through the heart of Absalom, while he *was* yet alive
in the midst of the oak.
[15]And ten young men that bare Joab's armour
compassed about and smote Absalom, and slew him.
[16]And Joab blew the trumpet, and the people returned from pursuing after Israel: for Joab held back
the people.
[17]And they took Absalom, and cast him into a great
pit in the wood, and laid a very great heap of stones
upon him: and all Israel fled every one to his tent.
[18]Now Absalom in his lifetime had taken and
reared up for himself a pillar, which *is* in the king's
dale: for he said, I have no son to keep my name in remembrance: and he called the pillar after his own
name: and it is called unto this day, Absalom's place.
[19]Then said Ahimaaz the son of Zadok, Let me
now run, and bear the king tidings, how that the
LORD hath avenged him of his enemies.
[20]And Joab said unto him, Thou shalt not bear tidings this day, but thou shalt bear tidings another day:
but this day thou shalt bear no tidings, because the
king's son is dead.

NEW LIVING TRANSLATION

Absalom." And all the troops heard the king give
this order to his commanders.
[6]So the battle began in the forest of Ephraim, [7]and
the Israelite troops were beaten back by David's
men. There was a great slaughter that day, and
20,000 men laid down their lives. [8]The battle raged
all across the countryside, and more men died because of the forest than were killed by the sword.
[9]During the battle, Absalom happened to come
upon some of David's men. He tried to escape on his
mule, but as he rode beneath the thick branches of a
great tree, his hair* got caught in the tree. His mule
kept going and left him dangling in the air. [10]One of
David's men saw what had happened and told Joab, "I
saw Absalom dangling from a great tree."
[11]"What?" Joab demanded. "You saw him there
and didn't kill him? I would have rewarded you with
ten pieces of silver* and a hero's belt!"
[12]"I would not kill the king's son for even a thousand pieces of silver,*" the man replied to Joab. "We
all heard the king say to you and Abishai and Ittai,
'For my sake, please spare young Absalom.' [13]And if
I had betrayed the king by killing his son—and the
king would certainly find out who did it—you yourself would be the first to abandon me."
[14]"Enough of this nonsense," Joab said. Then he
took three daggers and plunged them into Absalom's
heart as he dangled, still alive, in the great tree. [15]Ten
of Joab's young armor bearers then surrounded
Absalom and killed him.
[16]Then Joab blew the ram's horn, and his men
returned from chasing the army of Israel. [17]They
threw Absalom's body into a deep pit in the forest
and piled a great heap of stones over it. And all Israel
fled to their homes.
[18]During his lifetime, Absalom had built a monument to himself in the King's Valley, for he said, "I
have no son to carry on my name." He named the
monument after himself, and it is known as Absalom's Monument to this day.

David Mourns Absalom's Death

[19]Then Zadok's son Ahimaaz said, "Let me run to the
king with the good news that the LORD has rescued
him from his enemies."
[20]"No," Joab told him, "it wouldn't be good news to
the king that his son is dead. You can be my messenger another time, but not today."

18:9 Hebrew *his head.* **18:11** Hebrew *10 shekels of silver,* about 4 ounces or 114 grams in weight. **18:12** Hebrew *1,000 shekels,* about 25 pounds or 11.4 kilograms in weight.

KING JAMES VERSION

21 Then said Joab to Cushi, Go tell the king what thou hast seen. And Cushi bowed himself unto Joab, and ran.

22 Then said Ahimaaz the son of Zadok yet again to Joab, But howsoever, let me, I pray thee, also run after Cushi. And Joab said, Wherefore wilt thou run, my son, seeing that thou hast no tidings ready?

23 But howsoever, *said he,* let me run. And he said unto him, Run. Then Ahimaaz ran by the way of the plain, and overran Cushi.

24 And David sat between the two gates: and the watchman went up to the roof over the gate unto the wall, and lifted up his eyes, and looked, and behold a man running alone.

25 And the watchman cried, and told the king. And the king said, If he *be* alone, *there is* tidings in his mouth. And he came apace, and drew near.

26 And the watchman saw another man running: and the watchman called unto the porter, and said, Behold *another* man running alone. And the king said, He also bringeth tidings.

27 And the watchman said, Me thinketh the running of the foremost is like the running of Ahimaaz the son of Zadok. And the king said, He *is* a good man, and cometh with good tidings.

28 And Ahimaaz called, and said unto the king, All is well. And he fell down to the earth upon his face before the king, and said, Blessed *be* the LORD thy God, which hath delivered up the men that lifted up their hand against my lord the king.

29 And the king said, Is the young man Absalom safe? And Ahimaaz answered, When Joab sent the king's servant, and *me* thy servant, I saw a great tumult, but I knew not what *it was.*

30 And the king said *unto him,* Turn aside, *and* stand here. And he turned aside, and stood still.

31 And, behold, Cushi came; and Cushi said, Tidings, my lord the king: for the LORD hath avenged thee this day of all them that rose up against thee.

32 And the king said unto Cushi, Is the young man Absalom safe? And Cushi answered, The enemies of my lord the king, and all that rise against thee to do *thee* hurt, be as *that* young man *is.*

33 And the king was much moved, and went up to the chamber over the gate, and wept: and as he went, thus he said, O my son Absalom, my son, my son Absalom! would God I had died for thee, O Absalom, my son, my son!

19 1 And it was told Joab, Behold, the king weepeth and mourneth for Absalom.

2 And the victory that day was *turned* into mourning unto all the people: for the people heard say that day how the king was grieved for his son.

NEW LIVING TRANSLATION

21 Then Joab said to a man from Ethiopia,* "Go tell the king what you have seen." The man bowed and ran off.

22 But Ahimaaz continued to plead with Joab, "Whatever happens, please let me go, too."

"Why should you go, my son?" Joab replied. "There will be no reward for your news."

23 "Yes, but let me go anyway," he begged.

Joab finally said, "All right, go ahead." So Ahimaaz took the less demanding route by way of the plain and ran to Mahanaim ahead of the Ethiopian.

24 While David was sitting between the inner and outer gates of the town, the watchman climbed to the roof of the gateway by the wall. As he looked, he saw a lone man running toward them. 25 He shouted the news down to David, and the king replied, "If he is alone, he has news."

As the messenger came closer, 26 the watchman saw another man running toward them. He shouted down, "Here comes another one!"

The king replied, "He also will have news."

27 "The first man runs like Ahimaaz son of Zadok," the watchman said.

"He is a good man and comes with good news," the king replied.

28 Then Ahimaaz cried out to the king, "Everything is all right!" He bowed before the king with his face to the ground and said, "Praise to the LORD your God, who has handed over the rebels who dared to stand against my lord the king."

29 "What about young Absalom?" the king demanded. "Is he all right?"

Ahimaaz replied, "When Joab told me to come, there was a lot of commotion. But I didn't know what was happening."

30 "Wait here," the king told him. So Ahimaaz stepped aside.

31 Then the man from Ethiopia arrived and said, "I have good news for my lord the king. Today the LORD has rescued you from all those who rebelled against you."

32 "What about young Absalom?" the king demanded. "Is he all right?"

And the Ethiopian replied, "May all of your enemies, my lord the king, both now and in the future, share the fate of that young man!"

33 *The king was overcome with emotion. He went up to the room over the gateway and burst into tears. And as he went, he cried, "O my son Absalom! My son, my son Absalom! If only I had died instead of you! O Absalom, my son, my son."

Joab Rebukes the King

19 1 *Word soon reached Joab that the king was weeping and mourning for Absalom. 2 As all the people heard of the king's deep grief for his son,

18:21 Hebrew *from Cush;* similarly in 18:23, 31, 32. **18:33** Verse 18:33 is numbered 19:1 in Hebrew text. **19:1** Verses 19:1-43 are numbered 19:2-44 in Hebrew text.

KING JAMES VERSION

3 And the people gat them by stealth that day into the city, as people being ashamed steal away when they flee in battle.

4 But the king covered his face, and the king cried with a loud voice, O my son Absalom, O Absalom, my son, my son!

5 And Joab came into the house to the king, and said, Thou hast shamed this day the faces of all thy servants, which this day have saved thy life, and the lives of thy sons and of thy daughters, and the lives of thy wives, and the lives of thy concubines;

6 In that thou lovest thine enemies, and hatest thy friends. For thou hast declared this day, that thou regardest neither princes nor servants: for this day I perceive, that if Absalom had lived, and all we had died this day, then it had pleased thee well.

7 Now therefore arise, go forth, and speak comfortably unto thy servants: for I swear by the LORD, if thou go not forth, there will not tarry one with thee this night: and that will be worse unto thee than all the evil that befell thee from thy youth until now.

8 Then the king arose, and sat in the gate. And they told unto all the people, saying, Behold, the king doth sit in the gate. And all the people came before the king: for Israel had fled every man to his tent.

9 And all the people were at strife throughout all the tribes of Israel, saying, The king saved us out of the hand of our enemies, and he delivered us out of the hand of the Philistines; and now he is fled out of the land for Absalom.

10 And Absalom, whom we anointed over us, is dead in battle. Now therefore why speak ye not a word of bringing the king back?

11 And king David sent to Zadok and to Abiathar the priests, saying, Speak unto the elders of Judah, saying, Why are ye the last to bring the king back to his house? seeing the speech of all Israel is come to the king, *even* to his house.

12 Ye *are* my brethren, ye *are* my bones and my flesh: wherefore then are ye the last to bring back the king?

13 And say ye to Amasa, *Art* thou not of my bone, and of my flesh? God do so to me, and more also, if thou be not captain of the host before me continually in the room of Joab.

14 And he bowed the heart of all the men of Judah, even as *the heart of* one man; so that they sent *this word* unto the king, Return thou, and all thy servants.

15 So the king returned, and came to Jordan. And Judah came to Gilgal, to go to meet the king, to conduct the king over Jordan.

16 And Shimei the son of Gera, a Benjamite, which *was* of Bahurim, hasted and came down with the men of Judah to meet king David.

17 And *there were* a thousand men of Benjamin with him, and Ziba the servant of the house of Saul, and his fifteen sons and his twenty servants with him; and they went over Jordan before the king.

NEW LIVING TRANSLATION

the joy of that day's victory was turned into deep sadness. 3 They crept back into the town that day as
though they were ashamed and had deserted in
battle. 4 The king covered his face with his hands and
kept on crying, "O my son Absalom! O Absalom, my
son, my son!"

5 Then Joab went to the king's room and said to
him, "We saved your life today and the lives of your
sons, your daughters, and your wives and concubines. Yet you act like this, making us feel ashamed
of ourselves. 6 You seem to love those who hate you
and hate those who love you. You have made it clear
today that your commanders and troops mean nothing to you. It seems that if Absalom had lived and all
of us had died, you would be pleased. 7 Now go out
there and congratulate your troops, for I swear by the
LORD that if you don't go out, not a single one of them
will remain here tonight. Then you will be worse off
than ever before."

8 So the king went out and took his seat at the town
gate, and as the news spread throughout the town
that he was there, everyone went to him.

Meanwhile, the Israelites who had supported Absalom fled to their homes. 9 And throughout all the
tribes of Israel there was much discussion and argument going on. The people were saying, "The king
rescued us from our enemies and saved us from the
Philistines, but Absalom chased him out of the country. 10 Now Absalom, whom we anointed to rule over
us, is dead. Why not ask David to come back and be
our king again?"

11 Then King David sent Zadok and Abiathar, the
priests, to say to the elders of Judah, "Why are you
the last ones to welcome back the king into his
palace? For I have heard that all Israel is ready. 12 You
are my relatives, my own tribe, my own flesh and
blood! So why are you the last ones to welcome back
the king?" 13 And David told them to tell Amasa,
"Since you are my own flesh and blood, like Joab, may
God strike me and even kill me if I do not appoint
you as commander of my army in his place."

14 Then Amasa* convinced all the men of Judah,
and they responded unanimously. They sent word to
the king, "Return to us, and bring back all who are
with you."

David's Return to Jerusalem

15 So the king started back to Jerusalem. And when
he arrived at the Jordan River, the people of Judah
came to Gilgal to meet him and escort him across the
river. 16 Shimei son of Gera, the man from Bahurim in
Benjamin, hurried across with the men of Judah to
welcome King David. 17 A thousand other men from
the tribe of Benjamin were with him, including Ziba,
the chief servant of the house of Saul, and Ziba's fifteen sons and twenty servants. They rushed down to

19:14 Or *David;* Hebrew reads *he.*

KING JAMES VERSION

18 And there went over a ferry boat to carry over the king's household, and to do what he thought good. And Shimei the son of Gera fell down before the king, as he was come over Jordan;

19 And said unto the king, Let not my lord impute iniquity unto me, neither do thou remember that which thy servant did perversely the day that my lord the king went out of Jerusalem, that the king should take it to his heart.

20 For thy servant doth know that I have sinned: therefore, behold, I am come the first this day of all the house of Joseph to go down to meet my lord the king.

21 But Abishai the son of Zeruiah answered and said, Shall not Shimei be put to death for this, because he cursed the LORD's anointed?

22 And David said, What have I to do with you, ye sons of Zeruiah, that ye should this day be adversaries unto me? shall there any man be put to death this day in Israel? for do not I know that I *am* this day king over Israel?

23 Therefore the king said unto Shimei, Thou shalt not die. And the king sware unto him.

24 And Mephibosheth the son of Saul came down to meet the king, and had neither dressed his feet, nor trimmed his beard, nor washed his clothes, from the day the king departed until the day he came *again* in peace.

25 And it came to pass, when he was come to Jerusalem to meet the king, that the king said unto him, Wherefore wentest not thou with me, Mephibosheth?

26 And he answered, My lord, O king, my servant deceived me: for thy servant said, I will saddle me an ass, that I may ride thereon, and go to the king; because thy servant *is* lame.

27 And he hath slandered thy servant unto my lord the king; but my lord the king *is* as an angel of God: do therefore *what is* good in thine eyes.

28 For all *of* my father's house were but dead men before my lord the king: yet didst thou set thy servant among them that did eat at thine own table. What right therefore have I yet to cry any more unto the king?

29 And the king said unto him, Why speakest thou any more of thy matters? I have said, Thou and Ziba divide the land.

30 And Mephibosheth said unto the king, Yea, let him take all, forasmuch as my lord the king is come again in peace unto his own house.

31 And Barzillai the Gileadite came down from Rogelim, and went over Jordan with the king, to conduct him over Jordan.

32 Now Barzillai was a very aged man, *even* fourscore years old: and he had provided the king of sustenance while he lay at Mahanaim; for he *was* a very great man.

NEW LIVING TRANSLATION

the Jordan to meet the king. 18 They crossed the shallows of the Jordan to bring the king's household across the river, helping him in every way they could.

David's Mercy to Shimei

As the king was about to cross the river, Shimei fell down before him. 19 "My lord the king, please forgive me," he pleaded. "Forget the terrible thing your servant did when you left Jerusalem. May the king put it out of his mind. 20 I know how much I sinned. That is why I have come here today, the very first person in all Israel* to greet my lord the king."

21 Then Abishai son of Zeruiah said, "Shimei should die, for he cursed the LORD's anointed king!"

22 "Who asked your opinion, you sons of Zeruiah!" David exclaimed. "Why have you become my adversary* today? This is not a day for execution but for celebration! Today I am once again the king of Israel!" 23 Then, turning to Shimei, David vowed, "Your life will be spared."

David's Kindness to Mephibosheth

24 Now Mephibosheth,* Saul's grandson, came down from Jerusalem to meet the king. He had not cared for his feet, trimmed his beard, or washed his clothes since the day the king left Jerusalem. 25 "Why didn't you come with me, Mephibosheth?" the king asked him.

26 Mephibosheth replied, "My lord the king, my servant Ziba deceived me. I told him, 'Saddle my donkey* so I can go with the king.' For as you know I am crippled. 27 Ziba has slandered me by saying that I refused to come. But I know that my lord the king is like an angel of God, so do what you think is best. 28 All my relatives and I could expect only death from you, my lord, but instead you have honored me by allowing me to eat at your own table! What more can I ask?"

29 "You've said enough," David replied. "I've decided that you and Ziba will divide your land equally between you."

30 "Give him all of it," Mephibosheth said. "I am content just to have you safely back again, my lord the king!"

David's Kindness to Barzillai

31 Barzillai of Gilead had come down from Rogelim to escort the king across the Jordan. 32 He was very old, about eighty, and very wealthy. He was the one who had provided food for the king during his stay in

19:20 Hebrew *in the house of Joseph.* **19:22** Or *my prosecutor.* **19:24** *Mephibosheth* is another name for Merib-baal. **19:26** As in Greek, Syriac, and Latin versions; Hebrew reads *I will saddle a donkey for myself.*

KING JAMES VERSION

33And the king said unto Barzillai, Come thou over
with me, and I will feed thee with me in Jerusalem.
34And Barzillai said unto the king, How long have
I to live, that I should go up with the king unto Jerusalem?
35I *am* this day fourscore years old: *and* can I discern between good and evil? can thy servant taste
what I eat or what I drink? can I hear any more the
voice of singing men and singing women? wherefore
then should thy servant be yet a burden unto my lord
the king?
36Thy servant will go a little way over Jordan with
the king: and why should the king recompense it me
with such a reward?
37Let thy servant, I pray thee, turn back again, that I
may die in mine own city, *and be buried* by the grave
of my father and of my mother. But behold thy servant Chimham; let him go over with my lord the king;
and do to him what shall seem good unto thee.
38And the king answered, Chimham shall go over
with me, and I will do to him that which shall seem
good unto thee: and whatsoever thou shalt require of
me, *that* will I do for thee.
39And all the people went over Jordan. And when
the king was come over, the king kissed Barzillai, and
blessed him; and he returned unto his own place.
40Then the king went on to Gilgal, and Chimham
went on with him: and all the people of Judah conducted the king, and also half the people of Israel.
41And, behold, all the men of Israel came to the
king, and said unto the king, Why have our brethren
the men of Judah stolen thee away, and have brought
the king, and his household, and all David's men with
him, over Jordan?
42And all the men of Judah answered the men of
Israel, Because the king *is* near of kin to us: wherefore then be ye angry for this matter? have we eaten
at all of the king's *cost?* or hath he given us any gift?
43And the men of Israel answered the men of
Judah, and said, We have ten parts in the king, and
we have also more *right* in David than ye: why then
did ye despise us, that our advice should not be first
had in bringing back our king? And the words of the
men of Judah were fiercer than the words of the men
of Israel.

20 1And there happened to be there a man of
Belial, whose name *was* Sheba, the son of
Bichri, a Benjamite: and he blew a trumpet, and
said, We have no part in David, neither have we inheritance in the son of Jesse: every man to his tents,
O Israel.
2So every man of Israel went up from after David,
and followed Sheba the son of Bichri: but the men of

NEW LIVING TRANSLATION

Mahanaim. 33"Come across with me and live in Jerusalem," the king said to Barzillai. "I will take care of
you there."
34"No," he replied, "I am far too old to go with the
king to Jerusalem. 35I am eighty years old today, and
I can no longer enjoy anything. Food and wine are no
longer tasty, and I cannot hear the singers as they
sing. I would only be a burden to my lord the king.
36Just to go across the Jordan River with the king is
all the honor I need! 37Then let me return again to
die in my own town, where my father and mother are
buried. But here is your servant, my son Kimham. Let
him go with my lord the king and receive whatever
you want to give him."
38"Good," the king agreed. "Kimham will go with
me, and I will help him in any way you would like.
And I will do for you anything you want." 39So all the
people crossed the Jordan with the king. After David
had blessed Barzillai and kissed him, Barzillai returned to his own home.
40The king then crossed over to Gilgal, taking
Kimham with him. All the troops of Judah and half
the troops of Israel escorted the king on his way.

An Argument over the King

41But all the men of Israel complained to the king,
"The men of Judah stole the king and didn't give us
the honor of helping take you, your household, and
all your men across the Jordan."
42The men of Judah replied, "The king is one of
our own kinsmen. Why should this make you angry?
We haven't eaten any of the king's food or received
any special favors!"
43"But there are ten tribes in Israel," the others
replied. "So we have ten times as much right to the
king as you do. What right do you have to treat us
with such contempt? Weren't we the first to speak of
bringing him back to be our king again?" The argument continued back and forth, and the men of Judah spoke even more harshly than the men of Israel.

The Revolt of Sheba

20 There happened to be a troublemaker
there named Sheba son of Bicri, a man
from the tribe of Benjamin. Sheba blew a ram's horn
and began to chant:

"Down with the dynasty of David!
We have no interest in the son of Jesse.
Come on, you men of Israel,
back to your homes!"

2So all the men of Israel deserted David and
followed Sheba son of Bicri. But the men of Judah

KING JAMES VERSION

Judah clave unto their king, from Jordan even to
Jerusalem.
3And David came to his house at Jerusalem; and
the king took the ten women *his* concubines, whom
he had left to keep the house, and put them in ward,
and fed them, but went not in unto them. So they
were shut up unto the day of their death, living in
widowhood.
4Then said the king to Amasa, Assemble me the
men of Judah within three days, and be thou here
present.
5So Amasa went to assemble *the men of* Judah: but
he tarried longer than the set time which he had
appointed him.
6And David said to Abishai, Now shall Sheba the
son of Bichri do us more harm than *did* Absalom:
take thou thy lord's servants, and pursue after him,
lest he get him fenced cities, and escape us.
7And there went out after him Joab's men, and the
Cherethites, and the Pelethites, and all the mighty
men: and they went out of Jerusalem, to pursue after
Sheba the son of Bichri.
8When they *were* at the great stone which *is* in
Gibeon, Amasa went before them. And Joab's garment that he had put on was girded unto him, and
upon it a girdle *with* a sword fastened upon his loins
in the sheath thereof; and as he went forth it fell out.
9And Joab said to Amasa, *Art* thou in health, my
brother? And Joab took Amasa by the beard with the
right hand to kiss him.
10But Amasa took no heed to the sword that *was* in
Joab's hand: so he smote him therewith in the fifth
rib, and shed out his bowels to the ground, and
struck him not again; and he died. So Joab and Abishai his brother pursued after Sheba the son of Bichri.
11And one of Joab's men stood by him, and said,
He that favoureth Joab, and he that *is* for David, *let*
him go after Joab.
12And Amasa wallowed in blood in the midst of
the highway. And when the man saw that all the
people stood still, he removed Amasa out of the highway into the field, and cast a cloth upon him, when
he saw that every one that came by him stood still.
13When he was removed out of the highway, all
the people went on after Joab, to pursue after Sheba
the son of Bichri.
14And he went through all the tribes of Israel unto
Abel, and to Beth-maachah, and all the Berites: and
they were gathered together, and went also after him.
15And they came and besieged him in Abel of
Beth-maachah, and they cast up a bank against the
city, and it stood in the trench: and all the people that
were with Joab battered the wall, to throw it down.
16Then cried a wise woman out of the city, Hear,
hear; say, I pray you, unto Joab, Come near hither, that
I may speak with thee.
17And when he was come near unto her, the
woman said, *Art* thou Joab? And he answered, I *am*

NEW LIVING TRANSLATION

stayed with their king and escorted him from the
Jordan River to Jerusalem.
3When David came to his palace in Jerusalem, he
took the ten concubines he had left to look after the
palace and placed them in seclusion. Their needs
were provided for, but he no longer slept with them.
So each of them lived like a widow until she died.
4Then the king told Amasa, "Mobilize the army
of Judah within three days, and report back at that
time." 5So Amasa went out to notify Judah, but it
took him longer than the time he had been given.
6Then David said to Abishai, "Sheba son of Bicri is
going to hurt us more than Absalom did. Quick, take
my troops and chase after him before he gets into a
fortified town where we can't reach him."
7So Abishai and Joab,* together with the king's
bodyguard* and all the mighty warriors, set out from
Jerusalem to go after Sheba. 8As they arrived at the
great stone in Gibeon, Amasa met them. Joab was
wearing his military tunic with a dagger strapped to
his belt. As he stepped forward to greet Amasa, he
slipped the dagger from its sheath.*
9"How are you, my cousin?" Joab said and took
him by the beard with his right hand as though to
kiss him. 10Amasa didn't notice the dagger in his left
hand, and Joab stabbed him in the stomach with it so
that his insides gushed out onto the ground. Joab did
not need to strike again, and Amasa soon died. Joab
and his brother Abishai left him lying there and continued after Sheba.
11One of Joab's young men shouted to Amasa's
troops, "If you are for Joab and David, come and follow Joab." 12But Amasa lay in his blood in the middle
of the road, and Joab's man saw that everyone was
stopping to stare at him. So he pulled him off the
road into a field and threw a cloak over him. 13With
Amasa's body out of the way, everyone went on with
Joab to capture Sheba son of Bicri.
14Meanwhile, Sheba traveled through all the tribes
of Israel and eventually came to the town of Abel-
beth-maacah. All the members of his own clan, the
Bicrites,* assembled for battle and followed him
into the town. 15When Joab's forces arrived, they
attacked Abel-beth-maacah. They built a siege ramp
against the town's fortifications and began battering
down the wall. 16But a wise woman in the town
called out to Joab, "Listen to me, Joab. Come over
here so I can talk to you." 17As he approached, the
woman asked, "Are you Joab?"

"I am," he replied.

So she said, "Listen carefully to your servant."

20:7a Hebrew *So Joab's men.* **20:7b** Hebrew *the Kerethites and Pelethites;* also in 20:23. **20:8** Hebrew *As he stepped forward, it fell out.* **20:14** As in Greek and Latin versions; Hebrew reads *All the Berites.*

KING JAMES VERSION

he. Then she said unto him, Hear the words of thine
handmaid. And he answered, I do hear.
18 Then she spake, saying, They were wont to speak
in old time, saying, They shall surely ask *counsel* at
Abel: and so they ended *the matter*.
19 I *am one of them that are* peaceable *and* faithful
in Israel: thou seekest to destroy a city and a mother
in Israel: why wilt thou swallow up the inheritance
of the LORD?
20 And Joab answered and said, Far be it, far be it
from me, that I should swallow up or destroy.
21 The matter *is* not so: but a man of mount Ephraim, Sheba the son of Bichri by name, hath lifted up
his hand against the king, *even* against David: deliver
him only, and I will depart from the city. And the
woman said unto Joab, Behold, his head shall be
thrown to thee over the wall.
22 Then the woman went unto all the people in her
wisdom. And they cut off the head of Sheba the son
of Bichri, and cast *it* out to Joab. And he blew a trumpet, and they retired from the city, every man to his
tent. And Joab returned to Jerusalem unto the king.
23 Now Joab *was* over all the host of Israel: and Benaiah the son of Jehoiada *was* over the Cherethites
and over the Pelethites:
24 And Adoram *was* over the tribute: and Jehoshaphat the son of Ahilud *was* recorder:
25 And Sheva *was* scribe: and Zadok and Abiathar
were the priests:
26 And Ira also the Jairite was a chief ruler about
David.

21 1 Then there was a famine in the days of
David three years, year after year; and David
inquired of the LORD. And the LORD answered, *It is*
for Saul, and for *his* bloody house, because he slew
the Gibeonites.
2 And the king called the Gibeonites, and said unto
them; (now the Gibeonites *were* not of the children
of Israel, but of the remnant of the Amorites; and the
children of Israel had sworn unto them: and Saul
sought to slay them in his zeal to the children of Israel and Judah.)
3 Wherefore David said unto the Gibeonites, What
shall I do for you? and wherewith shall I make the
atonement, that ye may bless the inheritance of the
LORD?
4 And the Gibeonites said unto him, We will have
no silver nor gold of Saul, nor of his house; neither
for us shalt thou kill any man in Israel. And he said,
What ye shall say, *that* will I do for you.
5 And they answered the king, The man that consumed us, and that devised against us *that* we should
be destroyed from remaining in any of the coasts of
Israel,
6 Let seven men of his sons be delivered unto us,
and we will hang them up unto the LORD in Gibeah of

NEW LIVING TRANSLATION

"I'm listening," he said.
18 Then she continued, "There used to be a saying,
'If you want to settle an argument, ask advice at the
town of Abel.' 19 I am one who is peace loving and
faithful in Israel. But you are destroying an important town in Israel.* Why do you want to devour
what belongs to the LORD?"
20 And Joab replied, "Believe me, I don't want to devour or destroy your town! 21 That's not my purpose.
All I want is a man named Sheba son of Bicri from
the hill country of Ephraim, who has revolted against
King David. If you hand over this one man to me, I
will leave the town in peace."
"All right," the woman replied, "we will throw his
head over the wall to you." 22 Then the woman went
to all the people with her wise advice, and they cut
off Sheba's head and threw it out to Joab. So he blew
the ram's horn and called his troops back from the
attack. They all returned to their homes, and Joab
returned to the king at Jerusalem.
23 Now Joab was the commander of the army of
Israel. Benaiah son of Jehoiada was captain of the
king's bodyguard. 24 Adoniram* was in charge of the
labor force. Jehoshaphat son of Ahilud was the royal
historian. 25 Sheva was the court secretary. Zadok
and Abiathar were the priests. 26 And Ira, a descendant of Jair, was David's personal priest.

David Avenges the Gibeonites

21 There was a famine during David's reign that
lasted for three years, so David asked the
LORD about it. And the LORD said, "The famine has
come because Saul and his family are guilty of murdering the Gibeonites."
2 So the king summoned the Gibeonites. They
were not part of Israel but were all that was left of the
nation of the Amorites. The people of Israel had
sworn not to kill them, but Saul, in his zeal for Israel
and Judah, had tried to wipe them out. 3 David asked
them, "What can I do for you? How can I make
amends so that you will bless the LORD's people
again?"
4 "Well, money can't settle this matter between us
and the family of Saul," the Gibeonites replied. "Neither can we demand the life of anyone in Israel."
"What can I do then?" David asked. "Just tell me
and I will do it for you."
5 Then they replied, "It was Saul who planned to
destroy us, to keep us from having any place at all in
the territory of Israel. 6 So let seven of Saul's sons be
handed over to us, and we will execute them before
the LORD at Gibeon, on the mountain of the LORD.*"

20:19 Hebrew *a town that is a mother in Israel.* **20:24** As in Greek version (see also 1 Kgs 4:6; 5:14); Hebrew reads *Adoram.* **21:6** As in Greek version (see also 21:9); Hebrew reads *at Gibeah of Saul, the chosen of the LORD.*

KING JAMES VERSION

Saul, *whom* the LORD did choose. And the king said, I will give *them.*

7But the king spared Mephibosheth, the son of Jonathan the son of Saul, because of the LORD's oath that *was* between them, between David and Jonathan the son of Saul.

8But the king took the two sons of Rizpah the daughter of Aiah, whom she bare unto Saul, Armoni and Mephibosheth; and the five sons of Michal the daughter of Saul, whom she brought up for Adriel the son of Barzillai the Meholathite:

9And he delivered them into the hands of the Gibeonites, and they hanged them in the hill before the LORD: and they fell *all* seven together, and were put to death in the days of harvest, in the first *days,* in the beginning of barley harvest.

10And Rizpah the daughter of Aiah took sackcloth, and spread it for her upon the rock, from the beginning of harvest until water dropped upon them out of heaven, and suffered neither the birds of the air to rest on them by day, nor the beasts of the field by night.

11And it was told David what Rizpah the daughter of Aiah, the concubine of Saul, had done.

12And David went and took the bones of Saul and the bones of Jonathan his son from the men of Jabesh-gilead, which had stolen them from the street of Beth-shan, where the Philistines had hanged them, when the Philistines had slain Saul in Gilboa:

13And he brought up from thence the bones of Saul and the bones of Jonathan his son; and they gathered the bones of them that were hanged.

14And the bones of Saul and Jonathan his son buried they in the country of Benjamin in Zelah, in the sepulchre of Kish his father: and they performed all that the king commanded. And after that God was intreated for the land.

15Moreover the Philistines had yet war again with Israel; and David went down, and his servants with him, and fought against the Philistines: and David waxed faint.

16And Ishbi-benob, which *was* of the sons of the giant, the weight of whose spear *weighed* three hundred *shekels* of brass in weight, he being girded with a new *sword,* thought to have slain David.

17But Abishai the son of Zeruiah succoured him, and smote the Philistine, and killed him. Then the men of David sware unto him, saying, Thou shalt go no more out with us to battle, that thou quench not the light of Israel.

18And it came to pass after this, that there was again a battle with the Philistines at Gob: then Sibbechai the Hushathite slew Saph, which *was* of the sons of the giant.

19And there was again a battle in Gob with the Philistines, where Elhanan the son of Jaare-oregim, a

NEW LIVING TRANSLATION

"All right," the king said, "I will do it." 7The king spared Jonathan's son Mephibosheth,* who was Saul's grandson, because of the oath David and Jonathan had sworn before the LORD. 8But he gave them Saul's two sons Armoni and Mephibosheth, whose mother was Rizpah daughter of Aiah. He also gave them the five sons of Saul's daughter Merab,* the wife of Adriel son of Barzillai from Meholah. 9The men of Gibeon executed them on the mountain before the LORD. So all seven of them died together at the beginning of the barley harvest.

10Then Rizpah daughter of Aiah, the mother of two of the men, spread burlap on a rock and stayed there the entire harvest season. She prevented the scavenger birds from tearing at their bodies during the day and stopped wild animals from eating them at night. 11When David learned what Rizpah, Saul's concubine, had done, 12he went to the people of Jabesh-gilead and retrieved the bones of Saul and his son Jonathan. (When the Philistines had killed Saul and Jonathan on Mount Gilboa, the people of Jabesh-gilead stole their bodies from the public square of Beth-shan, where the Philistines had hung them.) 13So David obtained the bones of Saul and Jonathan, as well as the bones of the men the Gibeonites had executed.

14Then the king ordered that they bury the bones in the tomb of Kish, Saul's father, at the town of Zela in the land of Benjamin. After that, God ended the famine in the land.

Battles against Philistine Giants

15Once again the Philistines were at war with Israel. And when David and his men were in the thick of battle, David became weak and exhausted. 16Ishbi-benob was a descendant of the giants*; his bronze spearhead weighed more than seven pounds,* and he was armed with a new sword. He had cornered David and was about to kill him. 17But Abishai son of Zeruiah came to David's rescue and killed the Philistine. Then David's men declared, "You are not going out to battle with us again! Why risk snuffing out the light of Israel?"

18After this, there was another battle against the Philistines at Gob. As they fought, Sibbecai from Hushah killed Saph, another descendant of the giants.

19During another battle at Gob, Elhanan son of Jair* from Bethlehem killed the brother of Goliath

21:7 *Mephibosheth* is another name for Merib-baal. **21:8** As in a few Hebrew and Greek manuscripts and Syriac version (see also 1 Sam 18:19); most Hebrew manuscripts read *Michal.* **21:16a** Or *a descendant of the Rapha;* also in 21:18, 20, 22. **21:16b** Hebrew *300 shekels* [3.4 kilograms]. **21:19a** As in parallel text at 1 Chr 20:5; Hebrew reads *son of Jaare-oregim.*

KING JAMES VERSION

Bethlehemite, slew *the brother of* Goliath the Gittite,
the staff of whose spear *was* like a weaver's beam.
20 And there was yet a battle in Gath, where was a
man of *great* stature, that had on every hand six
fingers, and on every foot six toes, four and twenty in
number; and he also was born to the giant.
21 And when he defied Israel, Jonathan the son of
Shimeah the brother of David slew him.
22 These four were born to the giant in Gath, and
fell by the hand of David, and by the hand of his
servants.

22

1 And David spake unto the LORD the words
of this song in the day *that* the LORD had
delivered him out of the hand of all his enemies, and
out of the hand of Saul:
2 And he said, The LORD *is* my rock, and my fortress, and my deliverer;
3 The God of my rock; in him will I trust: *he is* my
shield, and the horn of my salvation, my high tower,
and my refuge, my saviour; thou savest me from
violence.
4 I will call on the LORD, *who is* worthy to be
praised: so shall I be saved from mine enemies.
5 When the waves of death compassed me, the
floods of ungodly men made me afraid;
6 The sorrows of hell compassed me about; the
snares of death prevented me;
7 In my distress I called upon the LORD, and cried
to my God: and he did hear my voice out of his temple, and my cry *did enter* into his ears.
8 Then the earth shook and trembled; the foundations of heaven moved and shook, because he was
wroth.
9 There went up a smoke out of his nostrils, and
fire out of his mouth devoured: coals were kindled
by it.
10 He bowed the heavens also, and came down; and
darkness *was* under his feet.
11 And he rode upon a cherub, and did fly: and he
was seen upon the wings of the wind.
12 And he made darkness pavilions round about
him, dark waters, *and* thick clouds of the skies.
13 Through the brightness before him were coals
of fire kindled.
14 The LORD thundered from heaven, and the most
High uttered his voice.
15 And he sent out arrows, and scattered them;
lightning, and discomfited them.
16 And the channels of the sea appeared, the foundations of the world were discovered, at the rebuking
of the LORD, at the blast of the breath of his nostrils.

NEW LIVING TRANSLATION

of Gath.* The handle of his spear was as thick as a
weaver's beam!
20 In another battle with the Philistines at Gath,
they encountered a huge man with six fingers on
each hand and six toes on each foot, twenty-four in
all, who was also a descendant of the giants. 21 But
when he defied and taunted Israel, he was killed by
Jonathan, the son of David's brother Shimea.*
22 These four Philistines were descendants of the
giants of Gath, but David and his warriors killed them.

David's Song of Praise

22

David sang this song to the LORD on the day
the LORD rescued him from all his enemies
and from Saul. 2 He sang:

"The LORD is my rock, my fortress, and my savior;
3 my God is my rock, in whom I find protection.
He is my shield, the power that saves me,
and my place of safety.
He is my refuge, my savior,
the one who saves me from violence.
4 I called on the LORD, who is worthy of praise,
and he saved me from my enemies.

5 "The waves of death overwhelmed me;
floods of destruction swept over me.
6 The grave* wrapped its ropes around me;
death laid a trap in my path.
7 But in my distress I cried out to the LORD;
yes, I cried to my God for help.
He heard me from his sanctuary;
my cry reached his ears.

8 "Then the earth quaked and trembled.
The foundations of the heavens shook;
they quaked because of his anger.
9 Smoke poured from his nostrils;
fierce flames leaped from his mouth.
Glowing coals blazed forth from him.
10 He opened the heavens and came down;
dark storm clouds were beneath his feet.
11 Mounted on a mighty angelic being,* he flew,
soaring* on the wings of the wind.
12 He shrouded himself in darkness,
veiling his approach with dense rain clouds.
13 A great brightness shone around him,
and burning coals* blazed forth.
14 The LORD thundered from heaven;
the voice of the Most High resounded.
15 He shot arrows and scattered his enemies;
his lightning flashed, and they were confused.
16 Then at the command of the LORD,
at the blast of his breath,
the bottom of the sea could be seen,
and the foundations of the earth were laid bare.

21:19b As in parallel text at 1 Chr 20:5; Hebrew reads *killed Goliath of Gath.* **21:21** As in parallel text at 1 Chr 20:7; Hebrew reads *Shimei,* a variant spelling of Shimea. **22:6** Hebrew *Sheol.* **22:11a** Hebrew *a cherub.* **22:11b** As in some Hebrew manuscripts (see also Ps 18:10); other Hebrew manuscripts read *appearing.* **22:13** Or *and lightning bolts.*

KING JAMES VERSION

17 He sent from above, he took me; he drew me out of many waters;

18 He delivered me from my strong enemy, *and* from them that hated me: for they were too strong for me.

19 They prevented me in the day of my calamity: but the LORD was my stay.

20 He brought me forth also into a large place: he delivered me, because he delighted in me.

21 The LORD rewarded me according to my righteousness: according to the cleanness of my hands hath he recompensed me.

22 For I have kept the ways of the LORD, and have not wickedly departed from my God.

23 For all his judgments *were* before me: and *as for* his statutes, I did not depart from them.

24 I was also upright before him, and have kept myself from mine iniquity.

25 Therefore the LORD hath recompensed me according to my righteousness; according to my cleanness in his eye sight.

26 With the merciful thou wilt shew thyself merciful, *and* with the upright man thou wilt shew thyself upright.

27 With the pure thou wilt shew thyself pure; and with the froward thou wilt shew thyself unsavoury.

28 And the afflicted people thou wilt save: but thine eyes *are* upon the haughty, *that* thou mayest bring *them* down.

29 For thou *art* my lamp, O LORD: and the LORD will lighten my darkness.

30 For by thee I have run through a troop: by my God have I leaped over a wall.

31 *As for* God, his way *is* perfect; the word of the LORD *is* tried: he *is* a buckler to all them that trust in him.

32 For who *is* God, save the LORD? and who *is* a rock, save our God?

33 God *is* my strength *and* power: And he maketh my way perfect.

34 He maketh my feet like hinds' *feet:* and setteth me upon my high places.

35 He teacheth my hands to war; so that a bow of steel is broken by mine arms.

36 Thou hast also given me the shield of thy salvation: and thy gentleness hath made me great.

37 Thou hast enlarged my steps under me; so that my feet did not slip.

38 I have pursued mine enemies, and destroyed them; and turned not again until I had consumed them.

39 And I have consumed them, and wounded them, that they could not arise: yea, they are fallen under my feet.

40 For thou hast girded me with strength to battle: them that rose up against me hast thou subdued under me.

NEW LIVING TRANSLATION

17 "He reached down from heaven and rescued me;
he drew me out of deep waters.
18 He rescued me from my powerful enemies,
from those who hated me and were too
strong for me.
19 They attacked me at a moment when I was
in distress,
but the LORD supported me.
20 He led me to a place of safety;
he rescued me because he delights in me.
21 The LORD rewarded me for doing right;
he restored me because of my innocence.
22 For I have kept the ways of the LORD;
I have not turned from my God to follow evil.
23 I have followed all his regulations;
I have never abandoned his decrees.
24 I am blameless before God;
I have kept myself from sin.
25 The LORD rewarded me for doing right.
He has seen my innocence.

26 "To the faithful you show yourself faithful;
to those with integrity you show integrity.
27 To the pure you show yourself pure,
but to the wicked you show yourself hostile.
28 You rescue the humble,
but your eyes watch the proud and
humiliate them.
29 O LORD, you are my lamp.
The LORD lights up my darkness.
30 In your strength I can crush an army;
with my God I can scale any wall.

31 "God's way is perfect.
All the LORD's promises prove true.
He is a shield for all who look to him for
protection.
32 For who is God except the LORD?
Who but our God is a solid rock?
33 God is my strong fortress,
and he makes my way perfect.
34 He makes me as surefooted as a deer,
enabling me to stand on mountain heights.
35 He trains my hands for battle;
he strengthens my arm to draw a bronze bow.
36 You have given me your shield of victory;
your help* has made me great.
37 You have made a wide path for my feet
to keep them from slipping.

38 "I chased my enemies and destroyed them;
I did not stop until they were conquered.
39 I consumed them;
I struck them down so they did not get up;
they fell beneath my feet.
40 You have armed me with strength for the battle;
you have subdued my enemies under my feet.

22:36 As in Dead Sea Scrolls (see also Ps 18:35); Masoretic Text reads *your answering.*

KING JAMES VERSION

41 Thou hast also given me the necks of mine enemies, that I might destroy them that hate me.
42 They looked, but *there was* none to save; *even*
unto the LORD, but he answered them not.
43 Then did I beat them as small as the dust of the
earth, I did stamp them as the mire of the street, *and*
did spread them abroad.
44 Thou also hast delivered me from the strivings
of my people, thou hast kept me *to be* head of the
heathen: a people *which* I knew not shall serve me.
45 Strangers shall submit themselves unto me: as
soon as they hear, they shall be obedient unto me.
46 Strangers shall fade away, and they shall be
afraid out of their close places.
47 The LORD liveth; and blessed *be* my rock; and
exalted be the God of the rock of my salvation.
48 It *is* God that avengeth me, and that bringeth
down the people under me,
49 And that bringeth me forth from mine enemies:
thou also hast lifted me up on high above them that
rose up against me: thou hast delivered me from the
violent man.
50 Therefore I will give thanks unto thee, O LORD,
among the heathen, and I will sing praises unto thy
name.
51 *He is* the tower of salvation for his king: and
sheweth mercy to his anointed, unto David, and to
his seed for evermore.

23 1 Now these *be* the last words of David.
David the son of Jesse said, and the man
who was raised up on high, the anointed of the God
of Jacob, and the sweet psalmist of Israel, said,
2 The Spirit of the LORD spake by me, and his word
was in my tongue.
3 The God of Israel said, the Rock of Israel spake to
me, He that ruleth over men *must be* just, ruling in
the fear of God.
4 And *he shall be* as the light of the morning, *when*
the sun riseth, *even* a morning without clouds; *as* the
tender grass *springing* out of the earth by clear shining after rain.
5 Although my house *be* not so with God; yet he
hath made with me an everlasting covenant, ordered
in all *things*, and sure: for *this is* all my salvation, and
all *my* desire, although he make *it* not to grow.

NEW LIVING TRANSLATION

41 You placed my foot on their necks.
I have destroyed all who hated me.
42 They looked for help, but no one came
to their rescue.
They even cried to the LORD, but he
refused to answer.
43 I ground them as fine as the dust of the earth;
I trampled them* in the gutter like dirt.
44 "You gave me victory over my accusers.
You preserved me as the ruler over nations;
people I don't even know now serve me.
45 Foreign nations cringe before me;
as soon as they hear of me, they submit.
46 They all lose their courage
and come trembling* from their strongholds.

47 "The LORD lives! Praise to my Rock!
May God, the Rock of my salvation, be exalted!
48 He is the God who pays back those who harm me;
he brings down the nations under me
49 and delivers me from my enemies.
You hold me safe beyond the reach of
my enemies;
you save me from violent opponents.
50 For this, O LORD, I will praise you among
the nations;
I will sing praises to your name.
51 You give great victories to your king;
you show unfailing love to your anointed,
to David and all his descendants forever."

David's Last Words

23 These are the last words of David:
"David, the son of Jesse, speaks—
David, the man who was raised up so high,
David, the man anointed by the God of Jacob,
David, the sweet psalmist of Israel.*

2 "The Spirit of the LORD speaks through me;
his words are upon my tongue.
3 The God of Israel spoke.
The Rock of Israel said to me:
'The one who rules righteously,
who rules in the fear of God,
4 is like the light of morning at sunrise,
like a morning without clouds,
like the gleaming of the sun
on new grass after rain.'

5 "Is it not my family God has chosen?
Yes, he has made an everlasting covenant
with me.
His agreement is arranged and guaranteed
in every detail.
He will ensure my safety and success.

22:43 As in Dead Sea Scrolls (see also Ps 18:42); Masoretic Text reads *I crushed and trampled them.* **22:46** As in parallel text at Ps 18:45; Hebrew reads *come girding themselves.* **23:1** Or *the favorite subject of the songs of Israel;* or *the favorite of the Strong One of Israel.*

KING JAMES VERSION

6 But *the sons* of Belial *shall be* all of them as thorns thrust away, because they cannot be taken with hands:

7 But the man *that* shall touch them must be fenced with iron and the staff of a spear; and they shall be utterly burned with fire in the *same* place.

8 These *be* the names of the mighty men whom David had: The Tachmonite that sat in the seat, chief among the captains; the same *was* Adino the Eznite: *he lift up his spear* against eight hundred, whom he slew at one time.

9 And after him *was* Eleazar the son of Dodo the Ahohite, *one* of the three mighty men with David, when they defied the Philistines *that* were there gathered together to battle, and the men of Israel were gone away:

10 He arose, and smote the Philistines until his hand was weary, and his hand clave unto the sword: and the LORD wrought a great victory that day; and the people returned after him only to spoil.

11 And after him *was* Shammah the son of Agee the Hararite. And the Philistines were gathered together into a troop, where was a piece of ground full of lentiles: and the people fled from the Philistines.

12 But he stood in the midst of the ground, and defended it, and slew the Philistines: and the LORD wrought a great victory.

13 And three of the thirty chief went down, and came to David in the harvest time unto the cave of Adullam: and the troop of the Philistines pitched in the valley of Rephaim.

14 And David *was* then in an hold, and the garrison of the Philistines *was* then *in* Bethlehem.

15 And David longed, and said, Oh that one would give me drink of the water of the well of Bethlehem, which *is* by the gate!

16 And the three mighty men brake through the host of the Philistines, and drew water out of the well of Bethlehem, that *was* by the gate, and took *it,* and brought *it* to David: nevertheless he would not drink thereof, but poured it out unto the LORD.

17 And he said, Be it far from me, O LORD, that I should do this: *is not this* the blood of the men that went in jeopardy of their lives? therefore he would not drink it. These things did these three mighty men.

18 And Abishai, the brother of Joab, the son of Zeruiah, was chief among three. And he lifted up his spear against three hundred, *and* slew *them,* and had the name among three.

19 Was he not most honourable of three? therefore he was their captain: howbeit he attained not unto the *first* three.

NEW LIVING TRANSLATION

6 But the godless are like thorns to be thrown away,
for they tear the hand that touches them.
7 One must use iron tools to chop them down;
they will be totally consumed by fire."

David's Mightiest Warriors

8 These are the names of David's mightiest warriors.
The first was Jashobeam the Hacmonite,* who was
leader of the Three*—the three mightiest warriors
among David's men. He once used his spear to kill
800 enemy warriors in a single battle.*

9 Next in rank among the Three was Eleazar son of
Dodai, a descendant of Ahoah. Once Eleazar and
David stood together against the Philistines when
the entire Israelite army had fled. 10 He killed Philistines until his hand was too tired to lift his sword,
and the LORD gave him a great victory that day. The
rest of the army did not return until it was time to
collect the plunder!

11 Next in rank was Shammah son of Agee from
Harar. One time the Philistines gathered at Lehi and
attacked the Israelites in a field full of lentils. The Israelite army fled, 12 but Shammah* held his ground
in the middle of the field and beat back the Philistines. So the LORD brought about a great victory.

13 Once during the harvest, when David was at the
cave of Adullam, the Philistine army was camped in
the valley of Rephaim. The Three (who were among
the Thirty—an elite group among David's fighting
men) went down to meet him there. 14 David was staying in the stronghold at the time, and a Philistine
detachment had occupied the town of Bethlehem.

15 David remarked longingly to his men, "Oh, how I
would love some of that good water from the well by
the gate in Bethlehem." 16 So the Three broke through
the Philistine lines, drew some water from the well
by the gate in Bethlehem, and brought it back to
David. But he refused to drink it. Instead, he poured
it out as an offering to the LORD. 17 "The LORD forbid
that I should drink this!" he exclaimed. "This water is
as precious as the blood of these men* who risked
their lives to bring it to me." So David did not drink it.
These are examples of the exploits of the Three.

David's Thirty Mighty Men

18 Abishai son of Zeruiah, the brother of Joab, was the
leader of the Thirty.* He once used his spear to kill
300 enemy warriors in a single battle. It was by such
feats that he became as famous as the Three.
19 Abishai was the most famous of the Thirty* and
was their commander, though he was not one of
the Three.

23:8a As in parallel text at 1 Chr 11:11; Hebrew reads *Josheb-basshebeth the Tahkemonite.* **23:8b** As in Greek and Latin versions (see also 1 Chr 11:11); the meaning of the Hebrew is uncertain. **23:8c** As in some Greek manuscripts (see also 1 Chr 11:11); the meaning of the Hebrew is uncertain, though it might be rendered *the Three. It was Adino the Eznite who killed 800 men at one time.* **23:12** Hebrew *he.* **23:17** Hebrew *Shall I drink the blood of these men?* **23:18** As in a few Hebrew manuscripts and Syriac version; most Hebrew manuscripts read *the Three.* **23:19** As in Syriac version; Hebrew reads *the Three.*

KING JAMES VERSION

20And Benaiah the son of Jehoiada, the son of a
valiant man, of Kabzeel, who had done many acts, he
slew two lionlike men of Moab: he went down also
and slew a lion in the midst of a pit in time of snow:
21And he slew an Egyptian, a goodly man: and the
Egyptian had a spear in his hand; but he went down
to him with a staff, and plucked the spear out of the
Egyptian's hand, and slew him with his own spear.
22These *things* did Benaiah the son of Jehoiada,
and had the name among three mighty men.
23He was more honourable than the thirty, but he
attained not to the *first* three. And David set him
over his guard.
24Asahel the brother of Joab *was* one of the thirty;
Elhanan the son of Dodo of Bethlehem,
25Shammah the Harodite, Elika the Harodite,
26Helez the Paltite, Ira the son of Ikkesh the
Tekoite,
27Abiezer the Anethothite, Mebunnai the Hushathite,
28Zalmon the Ahohite, Maharai the Netophathite,
29Heleb the son of Baanah, a Netophathite, Ittai
the son of Ribai out of Gibeah of the children of
Benjamin,
30Benaiah the Pirathonite, Hiddai of the brooks of
Gaash,
31Abi-albon the Arbathite, Azmaveth the Bar-
humite,
32Eliahba the Shaalbonite, of the sons of Jashen,
Jonathan,
33Shammah the Hararite, Ahiam the son of Sharar
the Hararite,
34Eliphelet the son of Ahasbai, the son of the Maachathite, Eliam the son of Ahithophel the Gilonite,
35Hezrai the Carmelite, Paarai the Arbite,
36Igal the son of Nathan of Zobah, Bani the Gadite,
37Zelek the Ammonite, Nahari the Beerothite,
armourbearer to Joab the son of Zeruiah,
38Ira an Ithrite, Gareb an Ithrite,
39Uriah the Hittite: thirty and seven in all.

NEW LIVING TRANSLATION

20There was also Benaiah son of Jehoiada, a valiant
warrior* from Kabzeel. He did many heroic deeds,
which included killing two champions* of Moab.
Another time, on a snowy day, he chased a lion down
into a pit and killed it. 21Once, armed only with a
club, he killed a great Egyptian warrior who was
armed with a spear. Benaiah wrenched the spear
from the Egyptian's hand and killed him with it.
22Deeds like these made Benaiah as famous as the
Three mightiest warriors. 23He was more honored
than the other members of the Thirty, though he was
not one of the Three. And David made him captain of
his bodyguard.
24Other members of the Thirty included:

Asahel, Joab's brother;
Elhanan son of Dodo from Bethlehem;
25 Shammah from Harod;
Elika from Harod;
26 Helez from Pelon*;
Ira son of Ikkesh from Tekoa;
27 Abiezer from Anathoth;
Sibbecai* from Hushah;
28 Zalmon from Ahoah;
Maharai from Netophah;
29 Heled* son of Baanah from Netophah;
Ithai* son of Ribai from Gibeah (in the
land of Benjamin);
30 Benaiah from Pirathon;
Hurai* from Nahale-gaash*;
31 Abi-albon from Arabah;
Azmaveth from Bahurim;
32 Eliahba from Shaalbon;
the sons of Jashen;
Jonathan 33son of Shagee* from Harar;
Ahiam son of Sharar from Harar;
34 Eliphelet son of Ahasbai from Maacah;
Eliam son of Ahithophel from Giloh;
35 Hezro from Carmel;
Paarai from Arba;
36 Igal son of Nathan from Zobah;
Bani from Gad;
37 Zelek from Ammon;
Naharai from Beeroth, Joab's armor bearer;
38 Ira from Jattir;
Gareb from Jattir;
39 Uriah the Hittite.

There were thirty-seven in all.

23:20a Or *son of Jehoiada, son of Ish-hai.* **23:20b** Hebrew *two of Ariel.* **23:26** As in parallel text at 1 Chr 11:27 (see also 1 Chr 27:10); Hebrew reads *from Palti.* **23:27** As in some Greek manuscripts (see also 1 Chr 11:29); Hebrew reads *Mebunnai.* **23:29a** As in some Hebrew manuscripts (see also 1 Chr 11:30); most Hebrew manuscripts read *Heleb.* **23:29b** As in parallel text at 1 Chr 11:31; Hebrew reads *Ittai.* **23:30a** As in some Greek manuscripts (see also 1 Chr 11:32); Hebrew reads *Hiddai.* **23:30b** Or *from the ravines of Gaash.* **23:33** As in parallel text at 1 Chr 11:34; Hebrew reads *Jonathan, Shammah;* some Greek manuscripts read *Jonathan son of Shammah.*

KING JAMES VERSION

24 1And again the anger of the LORD was
kindled against Israel, and he moved David
against them to say, Go, number Israel and Judah.
2For the king said to Joab the captain of the host,
which *was* with him, Go now through all the tribes of
Israel, from Dan even to Beer-sheba, and number ye
the people, that I may know the number of the people.
3And Joab said unto the king, Now the LORD thy
God add unto the people, how many soever they be,
an hundredfold, and that the eyes of my lord the king
may see *it:* but why doth my lord the king delight in
this thing?
4Notwithstanding the king's word prevailed
against Joab, and against the captains of the host. And
Joab and the captains of the host went out from the
presence of the king, to number the people of Israel.
5And they passed over Jordan, and pitched in Aroer, on the right side of the city that *lieth* in the midst
of the river of Gad, and toward Jazer:
6Then they came to Gilead, and to the land of
Tahtim-hodshi; and they came to Dan-jaan, and
about to Zidon,
7And came to the strong hold of Tyre, and to all the
cities of the Hivites, and of the Canaanites: and they
went out to the south of Judah, *even* to Beer-sheba.
8So when they had gone through all the land, they
came to Jerusalem at the end of nine months and
twenty days.
9And Joab gave up the sum of the number of the
people unto the king: and there were in Israel eight
hundred thousand valiant men that drew the sword;
and the men of Judah *were* five hundred thousand
men.
10And David's heart smote him after that he had
numbered the people. And David said unto the LORD,
I have sinned greatly in that I have done: and now, I
beseech thee, O LORD, take away the iniquity of thy
servant; for I have done very foolishly.
11For when David was up in the morning, the word
of the LORD came unto the prophet Gad, David's seer,
saying,
12Go and say unto David, Thus saith the LORD, I
offer thee three *things;* choose thee one of them,
that I may *do it* unto thee.
13So Gad came to David, and told him, and said
unto him, Shall seven years of famine come unto
thee in thy land? or wilt thou flee three months before thine enemies, while they pursue thee? or that
there be three days' pestilence in thy land? now advise, and see what answer I shall return to him that
sent me.
14And David said unto Gad, I am in a great strait: let
us fall now into the hand of the LORD; for his mercies
are great: and let me not fall into the hand of man.
15So the LORD sent a pestilence upon Israel from
the morning even to the time appointed: and there

NEW LIVING TRANSLATION

David Takes a Census

24 Once again the anger of the LORD burned
against Israel, and he caused David to harm
them by taking a census. "Go and count the people of
Israel and Judah," the LORD told him.
2So the king said to Joab and the commanders* of
the army, "Take a census of all the tribes of Israel—
from Dan in the north to Beersheba in the south—so
I may know how many people there are."
3But Joab replied to the king, "May the LORD your
God let you live to see a hundred times as many people as there are now! But why, my lord the king, do
you want to do this?"
4But the king insisted that they take the census, so
Joab and the commanders of the army went out to
count the people of Israel. 5First they crossed the Jordan and camped at Aroer, south of the town in the
valley, in the direction of Gad. Then they went on to
Jazer, 6then to Gilead in the land of Tahtim-hodshi*
and to Dan-jaan and around to Sidon. 7Then they
came to the fortress of Tyre, and all the towns of the
Hivites and Canaanites. Finally, they went south to
Judah* as far as Beersheba.
8Having gone through the entire land for nine
months and twenty days, they returned to Jerusalem.
9Joab reported the number of people to the king.
There were 800,000 capable warriors in Israel who
could handle a sword, and 500,000 in Judah.

Judgment for David's Sin

10But after he had taken the census, David's conscience began to bother him. And he said to the LORD,
"I have sinned greatly by taking this census. Please
forgive my guilt, LORD, for doing this foolish thing."
11The next morning the word of the LORD came to
the prophet Gad, who was David's seer. This was the
message: 12"Go and say to David, 'This is what the
LORD says: I will give you three choices. Choose one
of these punishments, and I will inflict it on you.'"
13So Gad came to David and asked him, "Will you
choose three* years of famine throughout your land,
three months of fleeing from your enemies, or three
days of severe plague throughout your land? Think
this over and decide what answer I should give the
LORD who sent me."
14"I'm in a desperate situation!" David replied to
Gad. "But let us fall into the hands of the LORD, for his
mercy is great. Do not let me fall into human hands."
15So the LORD sent a plague upon Israel that morning, and it lasted for three days.* A total of 70,000

24:2 As in Greek version (see also 24:4 and 1 Chr 21:2); Hebrew reads *Joab the commander.* **24:6** Greek version reads *to Gilead and to Kadesh in the land of the Hittites.* **24:7** Or *they went to the Negev of Judah.* **24:13** As in Greek version (see also 1 Chr 21:12); Hebrew reads *seven.* **24:15** Hebrew *for the designated time.*

KING JAMES VERSION

died of the people from Dan even to Beer-sheba
seventy thousand men.
16 And when the angel stretched out his hand upon
Jerusalem to destroy it, the LORD repented him of the
evil, and said to the angel that destroyed the people,
It is enough: stay now thine hand. And the angel of
the LORD was by the threshingplace of Araunah the
Jebusite.
17 And David spake unto the LORD when he saw the
angel that smote the people, and said, Lo, I have
sinned, and I have done wickedly: but these sheep,
what have they done? let thine hand, I pray thee, be
against me, and against my father's house.
18 And Gad came that day to David, and said unto
him, Go up, rear an altar unto the LORD in the
threshingfloor of Araunah the Jebusite.
19 And David, according to the saying of Gad, went
up as the LORD commanded.
20 And Araunah looked, and saw the king and his
servants coming on toward him: and Araunah went
out, and bowed himself before the king on his face
upon the ground.
21 And Araunah said, Wherefore is my lord the
king come to his servant? And David said, To buy
the threshingfloor of thee, to build an altar unto the
LORD, that the plague may be stayed from the people.
22 And Araunah said unto David, Let my lord the
king take and offer up what *seemeth* good unto him:
behold, *here be* oxen for burnt sacrifice, and threshing instruments and *other* instruments of the oxen
for wood.
23 All these *things* did Araunah, *as* a king, give unto
the king. And Araunah said unto the king, The LORD
thy God accept thee.
24 And the king said unto Araunah, Nay; but I will
surely buy *it* of thee at a price: neither will I offer
burnt offerings unto the LORD my God of that which
doth cost me nothing. So David bought the threshingfloor and the oxen for fifty shekels of silver.
25 And David built there an altar unto the LORD, and
offered burnt offerings and peace offerings. So the
LORD was intreated for the land, and the plague was
stayed from Israel.

NEW LIVING TRANSLATION

people died throughout the nation, from Dan in the
north to Beersheba in the south. 16 But as the angel
was preparing to destroy Jerusalem, the LORD relented and said to the death angel, "Stop! That is
enough!" At that moment the angel of the LORD was
by the threshing floor of Araunah the Jebusite.
17 When David saw the angel, he said to the LORD,
"I am the one who has sinned and done wrong! But
these people are as innocent as sheep—what have
they done? Let your anger fall against me and my
family."

David Builds an Altar

18 That day Gad came to David and said to him, "Go up
and build an altar to the LORD on the threshing floor
of Araunah the Jebusite."
19 So David went up to do what the LORD had commanded him. 20 When Araunah saw the king and his
men coming toward him, he came and bowed before
the king with his face to the ground. 21 "Why have
you come, my lord the king?" Araunah asked.
David replied, "I have come to buy your threshing
floor and to build an altar to the LORD there, so that
he will stop the plague."
22 "Take it, my lord the king, and use it as you
wish," Araunah said to David. "Here are oxen for the
burnt offering, and you can use the threshing boards
and ox yokes for wood to build a fire on the altar. 23 I
will give it all to you, Your Majesty, and may the LORD
your God accept your sacrifice."
24 But the king replied to Araunah, "No, I insist on
buying it, for I will not present burnt offerings to the
LORD my God that have cost me nothing." So David
paid him fifty pieces of silver* for the threshing
floor and the oxen.
25 David built an altar there to the LORD and sacrificed burnt offerings and peace offerings. And the
LORD answered his prayer for the land, and the
plague on Israel was stopped.

24:24 Hebrew *50 shekels of silver,* about 20 ounces or 570 grams in weight.

1 Kings

KING JAMES VERSION

1 1Now king David was old *and* stricken in years;
and they covered him with clothes, but he gat
no heat.
2Wherefore his servants said unto him, Let there
be sought for my lord the king a young virgin: and let
her stand before the king, and let her cherish him,
and let her lie in thy bosom, that my lord the king
may get heat.
3So they sought for a fair damsel throughout all
the coasts of Israel, and found Abishag a Shunammite, and brought her to the king.
4And the damsel *was* very fair, and cherished the
king, and ministered to him: but the king knew
her not.
5Then Adonijah the son of Haggith exalted himself, saying, I will be king: and he prepared him chariots and horsemen, and fifty men to run before him.
6And his father had not displeased him at any
time in saying, Why hast thou done so? and he also
was a very goodly *man;* and *his mother* bare him
after Absalom.
7And he conferred with Joab the son of Zeruiah,
and with Abiathar the priest: and they following
Adonijah helped *him.*
8But Zadok the priest, and Benaiah the son of
Jehoiada, and Nathan the prophet, and Shimei, and
Rei, and the mighty men which *belonged* to David,
were not with Adonijah.
9And Adonijah slew sheep and oxen and fat cattle
by the stone of Zoheleth, which *is* by En-rogel, and
called all his brethren the king's sons, and all the men
of Judah the king's servants:
10But Nathan the prophet, and Benaiah, and the
mighty men, and Solomon his brother, he called not.
11Wherefore Nathan spake unto Bath-sheba the
mother of Solomon, saying, Hast thou not heard that
Adonijah the son of Haggith doth reign, and David
our lord knoweth *it* not?
12Now therefore come, let me, I pray thee, give
thee counsel, that thou mayest save thine own life,
and the life of thy son Solomon.
13Go and get thee in unto king David, and say unto
him, Didst not thou, my lord, O king, swear unto

NEW LIVING TRANSLATION

David in His Old Age

1 King David was now very old, and no matter
how many blankets covered him, he could not
keep warm. 2So his advisers told him, "Let us find a
young virgin to wait on you and look after you, my
lord. She will lie in your arms and keep you warm."
3So they searched throughout the land of Israel
for a beautiful girl, and they found Abishag from
Shunem and brought her to the king. 4The girl was
very beautiful, and she looked after the king and
took care of him. But the king had no sexual relations
with her.

Adonijah Claims the Throne

5About that time David's son Adonijah, whose
mother was Haggith, began boasting, "I will make
myself king." So he provided himself with chariots
and charioteers and recruited fifty men to run in
front of him. 6Now his father, King David, had never
disciplined him at any time, even by asking, "Why
are you doing that?" Adonijah had been born next
after Absalom, and he was very handsome.
7Adonijah took Joab son of Zeruiah and Abiathar
the priest into his confidence, and they agreed to
help him become king. 8But Zadok the priest, Benaiah son of Jehoiada, Nathan the prophet, Shimei, Rei,
and David's personal bodyguard refused to support
Adonijah.
9Adonijah went to the Stone of Zoheleth* near the
spring of En-rogel, where he sacrificed sheep, cattle,
and fattened calves. He invited all his brothers—the
other sons of King David—and all the royal officials
of Judah. 10But he did not invite Nathan the prophet
or Benaiah or the king's bodyguard or his brother
Solomon.
11Then Nathan went to Bathsheba, Solomon's
mother, and asked her, "Haven't you heard that
Haggith's son, Adonijah, has made himself king, and
our lord David doesn't even know about it? 12If you
want to save your own life and the life of your son Solomon, follow my advice. 13Go at once to King David

1:9 Or *to the Serpent's Stone;* Greek version supports reading *Zoheleth* as a proper name.

thine handmaid, saying, Assuredly Solomon thy son
shall reign after me, and he shall sit upon my throne?
why then doth Adonijah reign?
14 Behold, while thou yet talkest there with the king,
I also will come in after thee, and confirm thy words.
15 And Bath-sheba went in unto the king into the
chamber: and the king was very old; and Abishag the
Shunammite ministered unto the king.
16 And Bath-sheba bowed, and did obeisance unto
the king. And the king said, What wouldest thou?
17 And she said unto him, My lord, thou swarest by
the LORD thy God unto thine handmaid, *saying,* Assuredly Solomon thy son shall reign after me, and he
shall sit upon my throne.
18 And now, behold, Adonijah reigneth; and now,
my lord the king, thou knowest *it* not:
19 And he hath slain oxen and fat cattle and sheep
in abundance, and hath called all the sons of the
king, and Abiathar the priest, and Joab the captain of
the host: but Solomon thy servant hath he not called.
20 And thou, my lord, O king, the eyes of all Israel
are upon thee, that thou shouldest tell them who
shall sit on the throne of my lord the king after him.
21 Otherwise it shall come to pass, when my lord
the king shall sleep with his fathers, that I and my
son Solomon shall be counted offenders.
22 And, lo, while she yet talked with the king, Nathan the prophet also came in.
23 And they told the king, saying, Behold Nathan
the prophet. And when he was come in before the
king, he bowed himself before the king with his face
to the ground.
24 And Nathan said, My lord, O king, hast thou said,
Adonijah shall reign after me, and he shall sit upon
my throne?
25 For he is gone down this day, and hath slain oxen
and fat cattle and sheep in abundance, and hath
called all the king's sons, and the captains of the host,
and Abiathar the priest; and, behold, they eat and
drink before him, and say, God save king Adonijah.
26 But me, *even* me thy servant, and Zadok the
priest, and Benaiah the son of Jehoiada, and thy servant Solomon, hath he not called.
27 Is this thing done by my lord the king, and thou
hast not shewed *it* unto thy servant, who should sit
on the throne of my lord the king after him?
28 Then king David answered and said, Call me
Bath-sheba. And she came into the king's presence,
and stood before the king.
29 And the king sware, and said, *As* the LORD liveth,
that hath redeemed my soul out of all distress,
30 Even as I sware unto thee by the LORD God of
Israel, saying, Assuredly Solomon thy son shall reign
after me, and he shall sit upon my throne in my stead;
even so will I certainly do this day.
31 Then Bath-sheba bowed with *her* face to the
earth, and did reverence to the king, and said, Let my
lord king David live for ever.

and say to him, 'My lord the king, didn't you make a
vow and say to me, "Your son Solomon will surely be
the next king and will sit on my throne"? Why then
has Adonijah become king?' 14 And while you are still
talking with him, I will come and confirm everything
you have said."
15 So Bathsheba went into the king's bedroom. (He
was very old now, and Abishag was taking care of
him.) 16 Bathsheba bowed down before the king.
"What can I do for you?" he asked her.
17 She replied, "My lord, you made a vow before the
LORD your God when you said to me, 'Your son Solomon will surely be the next king and will sit on my
throne.' 18 But instead, Adonijah has made himself
king, and my lord the king does not even know about
it. 19 He has sacrificed many cattle, fattened calves,
and sheep, and he has invited all the king's sons to
attend the celebration. He also invited Abiathar the
priest and Joab, the commander of the army. But he
did not invite your servant Solomon. 20 And now, my
lord the king, all Israel is waiting for you to announce
who will become king after you. 21 If you do not act,
my son Solomon and I will be treated as criminals
as soon as my lord the king has died."
22 While she was still speaking with the king, Nathan the prophet arrived. 23 The king's officials told
him, "Nathan the prophet is here to see you."
Nathan went in and bowed before the king with
his face to the ground. 24 Nathan asked, "My lord the
king, have you decided that Adonijah will be the next
king and that he will sit on your throne? 25 Today he
has sacrificed many cattle, fattened calves, and
sheep, and he has invited all the king's sons to attend
the celebration. He also invited the commanders of
the army and Abiathar the priest. They are feasting
and drinking with him and shouting, 'Long live King
Adonijah!' 26 But he did not invite me or Zadok the
priest or Benaiah or your servant Solomon. 27 Has my
lord the king really done this without letting any of
his officials know who should be the next king?"

David Makes Solomon King

28 King David responded, "Call Bathsheba!" So she
came back in and stood before the king. 29 And the
king repeated his vow: "As surely as the LORD lives,
who has rescued me from every danger, 30 your son
Solomon will be the next king and will sit on my
throne this very day, just as I vowed to you before the
LORD, the God of Israel."
31 Then Bathsheba bowed down with her face to
the ground before the king and exclaimed, "May my
lord King David live forever!"

KING JAMES VERSION

32 And king David said, Call me Zadok the priest, and Nathan the prophet, and Benaiah the son of Jehoiada. And they came before the king.

33 The king also said unto them, Take with you the servants of your lord, and cause Solomon my son to ride upon mine own mule, and bring him down to Gihon:

34 And let Zadok the priest and Nathan the prophet anoint him there king over Israel: and blow ye with the trumpet, and say, God save king Solomon.

35 Then ye shall come up after him, that he may come and sit upon my throne; for he shall be king in my stead: and I have appointed him to be ruler over Israel and over Judah.

36 And Benaiah the son of Jehoiada answered the king, and said, Amen: the LORD God of my lord the king say so *too.*

37 As the LORD hath been with my lord the king, even so be he with Solomon, and make his throne greater than the throne of my lord king David.

38 So Zadok the priest, and Nathan the prophet, and Benaiah the son of Jehoiada, and the Cherethites, and the Pelethites, went down, and caused Solomon to ride upon king David's mule, and brought him to Gihon.

39 And Zadok the priest took an horn of oil out of the tabernacle, and anointed Solomon. And they blew the trumpet; and all the people said, God save king Solomon.

40 And all the people came up after him, and the people piped with pipes, and rejoiced with great joy, so that the earth rent with the sound of them.

41 And Adonijah and all the guests that *were* with him heard *it* as they had made an end of eating. And when Joab heard the sound of the trumpet, he said, Wherefore *is this* noise of the city being in an uproar?

42 And while he yet spake, behold, Jonathan the son of Abiathar the priest came: and Adonijah said unto him, Come in; for thou *art* a valiant man, and bringest good tidings.

43 And Jonathan answered and said to Adonijah, Verily our lord king David hath made Solomon king.

44 And the king hath sent with him Zadok the priest, and Nathan the prophet, and Benaiah the son of Jehoiada, and the Cherethites, and the Pelethites, and they have caused him to ride upon the king's mule:

45 And Zadok the priest and Nathan the prophet have anointed him king in Gihon: and they are come up from thence rejoicing, so that the city rang again. This *is* the noise that ye have heard.

46 And also Solomon sitteth on the throne of the kingdom.

47 And moreover the king's servants came to bless our lord king David, saying, God make the name of Solomon better than thy name, and make his throne greater than thy throne. And the king bowed himself upon the bed.

NEW LIVING TRANSLATION

32 Then King David ordered, "Call Zadok the priest, Nathan the prophet, and Benaiah son of Jehoiada." When they came into the king's presence, 33 the king said to them, "Take Solomon and my officials down to Gihon Spring. Solomon is to ride on my own mule. 34 There Zadok the priest and Nathan the prophet are to anoint him king over Israel. Blow the ram's horn and shout, 'Long live King Solomon!' 35 Then escort him back here, and he will sit on my throne. He will succeed me as king, for I have appointed him to be ruler over Israel and Judah."

36 "Amen!" Benaiah son of Jehoiada replied. "May the LORD, the God of my lord the king, decree that it happen. 37 And may the LORD be with Solomon as he has been with you, my lord the king, and may he make Solomon's reign even greater than yours!"

38 So Zadok the priest, Nathan the prophet, Benaiah son of Jehoiada, and the king's bodyguard* took Solomon down to Gihon Spring, with Solomon riding on King David's own mule. 39 There Zadok the priest took the flask of olive oil from the sacred tent and anointed Solomon with the oil. Then they sounded the ram's horn and all the people shouted, "Long live King Solomon!" 40 And all the people followed Solomon into Jerusalem, playing flutes and shouting for joy. The celebration was so joyous and noisy that the earth shook with the sound.

41 Adonijah and his guests heard the celebrating and shouting just as they were finishing their banquet. When Joab heard the sound of the ram's horn, he asked, "What's going on? Why is the city in such an uproar?"

42 And while he was still speaking, Jonathan son of Abiathar the priest arrived. "Come in," Adonijah said to him, "for you are a good man. You must have good news."

43 "Not at all!" Jonathan replied. "Our lord King David has just declared Solomon king! 44 The king sent him down to Gihon Spring with Zadok the priest, Nathan the prophet, and Benaiah son of Jehoiada, protected by the king's bodyguard. They had him ride on the king's own mule, 45 and Zadok and Nathan have anointed him at Gihon Spring as the new king. They have just returned, and the whole city is celebrating and rejoicing. That's what all the noise is about. 46 What's more, Solomon is now sitting on the royal throne as king. 47 And all the royal officials have gone to King David and congratulated him, saying, 'May your God make Solomon's fame even greater than your own, and may Solomon's reign be even greater than yours!' Then the king bowed his head in worship

1:38 Hebrew *the Kerethites and Pelethites;* also in 1:44.

KING JAMES VERSION

[48]And also thus said the king, Blessed *be* the LORD God of Israel, which hath given *one* to sit on my throne this day, mine eyes even seeing *it*.

[49]And all the guests that *were* with Adonijah were afraid, and rose up, and went every man his way.

[50]And Adonijah feared because of Solomon, and arose, and went, and caught hold on the horns of the altar.

[51]And it was told Solomon, saying, Behold, Adonijah feareth king Solomon: for, lo, he hath caught hold on the horns of the altar, saying, Let king Solomon swear unto me today that he will not slay his servant with the sword.

[52]And Solomon said, If he will shew himself a worthy man, there shall not an hair of him fall to the earth: but if wickedness shall be found in him, he shall die.

[53]So king Solomon sent, and they brought him down from the altar. And he came and bowed himself to king Solomon: and Solomon said unto him, Go to thine house.

2 [1]Now the days of David drew nigh that he should die; and he charged Solomon his son, saying,

[2]I go the way of all the earth: be thou strong therefore, and shew thyself a man;

[3]And keep the charge of the LORD thy God, to walk in his ways, to keep his statutes, and his commandments, and his judgments, and his testimonies, as it is written in the law of Moses, that thou mayest prosper in all that thou doest, and whithersoever thou turnest thyself:

[4]That the LORD may continue his word which he spake concerning me, saying, If thy children take heed to their way, to walk before me in truth with all their heart and with all their soul, there shall not fail thee (said he) a man on the throne of Israel.

[5]Moreover thou knowest also what Joab the son of Zeruiah did to me, *and* what he did to the two captains of the hosts of Israel, unto Abner the son of Ner, and unto Amasa the son of Jether, whom he slew, and shed the blood of war in peace, and put the blood of war upon his girdle that *was* about his loins, and in his shoes that *were* on his feet.

[6]Do therefore according to thy wisdom, and let not his hoar head go down to the grave in peace.

[7]But shew kindness unto the sons of Barzillai the Gileadite, and let them be of those that eat at thy table: for so they came to me when I fled because of Absalom thy brother.

[8]And, behold, *thou hast* with thee Shimei the son of Gera, a Benjamite of Bahurim, which cursed me with a grievous curse in the day when I went to Mahanaim: but he came down to meet me at Jordan, and I sware to him by the LORD, saying, I will not put thee to death with the sword.

[9]Now therefore hold him not guiltless: for thou

NEW LIVING TRANSLATION

as he lay in his bed, [48]and he said, 'Praise the LORD, the God of Israel, who today has chosen a successor to sit on my throne while I am still alive to see it.'"

[49]Then all of Adonijah's guests jumped up in panic from the banquet table and quickly scattered. [50]Adonijah was afraid of Solomon, so he rushed to the sacred tent and grabbed on to the horns of the altar. [51]Word soon reached Solomon that Adonijah had seized the horns of the altar in fear, and that he was pleading, "Let King Solomon swear today that he will not kill me!"

[52]Solomon replied, "If he proves himself to be loyal, not a hair on his head will be touched. But if he makes trouble, he will die." [53]So King Solomon summoned Adonijah, and they brought him down from the altar. He came and bowed respectfully before King Solomon, who dismissed him, saying, "Go on home."

David's Final Instructions to Solomon

2 As the time of King David's death approached, he gave this charge to his son Solomon:

[2]"I am going where everyone on earth must someday go. Take courage and be a man. [3]Observe the requirements of the LORD your God, and follow all his ways. Keep the decrees, commands, regulations, and laws written in the Law of Moses so that you will be successful in all you do and wherever you go. [4]If you do this, then the LORD will keep the promise he made to me. He told me, 'If your descendants live as they should and follow me faithfully with all their heart and soul, one of them will always sit on the throne of Israel.'

[5]"And there is something else. You know what Joab son of Zeruiah did to me when he murdered my two army commanders, Abner son of Ner and Amasa son of Jether. He pretended that it was an act of war, but it was done in a time of peace,* staining his belt and sandals with innocent blood.* [6]Do with him what you think best, but don't let him grow old and go to his grave in peace.*

[7]"Be kind to the sons of Barzillai of Gilead. Make them permanent guests at your table, for they took care of me when I fled from your brother Absalom.

[8]"And remember Shimei son of Gera, the man from Bahurim in Benjamin. He cursed me with a terrible curse as I was fleeing to Mahanaim. When he came down to meet me at the Jordan River, I swore by the LORD that I would not kill him. [9]But that oath does

2:5a Or *He murdered them during a time of peace as revenge for deaths they had caused in time of war.* **2:5b** As in some Greek and Old Latin manuscripts; Hebrew reads *with the blood of war.* **2:6** Hebrew *don't let his white head go down to Sheol in peace.*

KING JAMES VERSION

art a wise man, and knowest what thou oughtest to do unto him; but his hoar head bring thou down to the grave with blood.

10 So David slept with his fathers, and was buried in the city of David.

11 And the days that David reigned over Israel *were* forty years: seven years reigned he in Hebron, and thirty and three years reigned he in Jerusalem.

12 Then sat Solomon upon the throne of David his father; and his kingdom was established greatly.

13 And Adonijah the son of Haggith came to Bath-sheba the mother of Solomon. And she said, Comest thou peaceably? And he said, Peaceably.

14 He said moreover, I have somewhat to say unto thee. And she said, Say on.

15 And he said, Thou knowest that the kingdom was mine, and *that* all Israel set their faces on me, that I should reign: howbeit the kingdom is turned about, and is become my brother's: for it was his from the LORD.

16 And now I ask one petition of thee, deny me not. And she said unto him, Say on.

17 And he said, Speak, I pray thee, unto Solomon the king, (for he will not say thee nay,) that he give me Abishag the Shunammite to wife.

18 And Bath-sheba said, Well; I will speak for thee unto the king.

19 Bath-sheba therefore went unto king Solomon, to speak unto him for Adonijah. And the king rose up to meet her, and bowed himself unto her, and sat down on his throne, and caused a seat to be set for the king's mother; and she sat on his right hand.

20 Then she said, I desire one small petition of thee; *I pray thee,* say me not nay. And the king said unto her, Ask on, my mother: for I will not say thee nay.

21 And she said, Let Abishag the Shunammite be given to Adonijah thy brother to wife.

22 And king Solomon answered and said unto his mother, And why dost thou ask Abishag the Shunammite for Adonijah? ask for him the kingdom also; for he *is* mine elder brother; even for him, and for Abiathar the priest, and for Joab the son of Zeruiah.

23 Then king Solomon sware by the LORD, saying, God do so to me, and more also, if Adonijah have not spoken this word against his own life.

24 Now therefore, *as* the LORD liveth, which hath established me, and set me on the throne of David my father, and who hath made me an house, as he promised, Adonijah shall be put to death this day.

25 And king Solomon sent by the hand of Benaiah the son of Jehoiada; and he fell upon him that he died.

26 And unto Abiathar the priest said the king, Get thee to Anathoth, unto thine own fields; for thou *art* worthy of death: but I will not at this time put thee to death, because thou barest the ark of the Lord GOD

NEW LIVING TRANSLATION

not make him innocent. You are a wise man, and you will know how to arrange a bloody death for him.*"

10 Then David died and was buried with his ancestors in the City of David. 11 David had reigned over Israel for forty years, seven of them in Hebron and thirty-three in Jerusalem. 12 Solomon became king and sat on the throne of David his father, and his kingdom was firmly established.

Solomon Establishes His Rule

13 One day Adonijah, whose mother was Haggith, came to see Bathsheba, Solomon's mother. "Have you come with peaceful intentions?" she asked him.

"Yes," he said, "I come in peace. 14 In fact, I have a favor to ask of you."

"What is it?" she asked.

15 He replied, "As you know, the kingdom was rightfully mine; all Israel wanted me to be the next king. But the tables were turned, and the kingdom went to my brother instead; for that is the way the LORD wanted it. 16 So now I have just one favor to ask of you. Please don't turn me down."

"What is it?" she asked.

17 He replied, "Speak to King Solomon on my behalf, for I know he will do anything you request. Ask him to let me marry Abishag, the girl from Shunem."

18 "All right," Bathsheba replied. "I will speak to the king for you."

19 So Bathsheba went to King Solomon to speak on Adonijah's behalf. The king rose from his throne to meet her, and he bowed down before her. When he sat down on his throne again, the king ordered that a throne be brought for his mother, and she sat at his right hand.

20 "I have one small request to make of you," she said. "I hope you won't turn me down."

"What is it, my mother?" he asked. "You know I won't refuse you."

21 "Then let your brother Adonijah marry Abishag, the girl from Shunem," she replied.

22 "How can you possibly ask me to give Abishag to Adonijah?" King Solomon demanded. "You might as well ask me to give him the kingdom! You know that he is my older brother, and that he has Abiathar the priest and Joab son of Zeruiah on his side."

23 Then King Solomon made a vow before the LORD: "May God strike me and even kill me if Adonijah has not sealed his fate with this request. 24 The LORD has confirmed me and placed me on the throne of my father, David; he has established my dynasty as he promised. So as surely as the LORD lives, Adonijah will die this very day!" 25 So King Solomon ordered Benaiah son of Jehoiada to execute him, and Adonijah was put to death.

26 Then the king said to Abiathar the priest, "Go back to your home in Anathoth. You deserve to die,

2:9 Hebrew *how to bring his white head down to Sheol in blood.*

KING JAMES VERSION

before David my father, and because thou hast been
afflicted in all wherein my father was afflicted.
27 So Solomon thrust out Abiathar from being
priest unto the LORD; that he might fulfil the word of
the LORD, which he spake concerning the house of
Eli in Shiloh.
28 Then tidings came to Joab: for Joab had turned
after Adonijah, though he turned not after Absalom.
And Joab fled unto the tabernacle of the LORD, and
caught hold on the horns of the altar.
29 And it was told king Solomon that Joab was fled
unto the tabernacle of the LORD; and, behold, *he is*
by the altar. Then Solomon sent Benaiah the son of
Jehoiada, saying, Go, fall upon him.
30 And Benaiah came to the tabernacle of the LORD,
and said unto him, Thus saith the king, Come forth.
And he said, Nay; but I will die here. And Benaiah
brought the king word again, saying, Thus said Joab,
and thus he answered me.
31 And the king said unto him, Do as he hath said,
and fall upon him, and bury him; that thou mayest
take away the innocent blood, which Joab shed, from
me, and from the house of my father.
32 And the LORD shall return his blood upon his
own head, who fell upon two men more righteous
and better than he, and slew them with the sword,
my father David not knowing *thereof, to wit,* Abner
the son of Ner, captain of the host of Israel, and Amasa the son of Jether, captain of the host of Judah.
33 Their blood shall therefore return upon the
head of Joab, and upon the head of his seed for ever:
but upon David, and upon his seed, and upon his
house, and upon his throne, shall there be peace for
ever from the LORD.
34 So Benaiah the son of Jehoiada went up, and fell
upon him, and slew him: and he was buried in his
own house in the wilderness.
35 And the king put Benaiah the son of Jehoiada in
his room over the host: and Zadok the priest did the
king put in the room of Abiathar.
36 And the king sent and called for Shimei, and said
unto him, Build thee an house in Jerusalem, and
dwell there, and go not forth thence any whither.
37 For it shall be, *that* on the day thou goest out,
and passest over the brook Kidron, thou shalt know
for certain that thou shalt surely die: thy blood shall
be upon thine own head.
38 And Shimei said unto the king, The saying *is*
good: as my lord the king hath said, so will thy servant do. And Shimei dwelt in Jerusalem many days.
39 And it came to pass at the end of three years, that
two of the servants of Shimei ran away unto Achish
son of Maachah king of Gath. And they told Shimei,
saying, Behold, thy servants *be* in Gath.
40 And Shimei arose, and saddled his ass, and went
to Gath to Achish to seek his servants: and Shimei
went, and brought his servants from Gath.

NEW LIVING TRANSLATION

but I will not kill you now, because you carried the
Ark of the Sovereign LORD for David my father and
you shared all his hardships." 27 So Solomon deposed
Abiathar from his position as priest of the LORD,
thereby fulfilling the prophecy the LORD had given
at Shiloh concerning the descendants of Eli.
28 Joab had not joined Absalom's earlier rebellion,
but he had joined Adonijah's rebellion. So when Joab
heard about Adonijah's death, he ran to the sacred
tent of the LORD and grabbed on to the horns of the
altar. 29 When this was reported to King Solomon, he
sent Benaiah son of Jehoiada to execute him.
30 Benaiah went to the sacred tent of the LORD and
said to Joab, "The king orders you to come out!"
But Joab answered, "No, I will die here."
So Benaiah returned to the king and told him what
Joab had said.
31 "Do as he said," the king replied. "Kill him there
beside the altar and bury him. This will remove the
guilt of Joab's senseless murders from me and from
my father's family. 32 The LORD will repay him* for
the murders of two men who were more righteous
and better than he. For my father knew nothing
about the deaths of Abner son of Ner, commander of
the army of Israel, and of Amasa son of Jether, commander of the army of Judah. 33 May their blood be
on Joab and his descendants forever, and may the
LORD grant peace forever to David, his descendants,
his dynasty, and his throne."
34 So Benaiah son of Jehoiada returned to the sacred tent and killed Joab, and he was buried at his
home in the wilderness. 35 Then the king appointed
Benaiah to command the army in place of Joab,
and he installed Zadok the priest to take the place of
Abiathar.
36 The king then sent for Shimei and told him,
"Build a house here in Jerusalem and live there. But
don't step outside the city to go anywhere else. 37 On
the day you so much as cross the Kidron Valley,
you will surely die; and your blood will be on your
own head."
38 Shimei replied, "Your sentence is fair; I will do
whatever my lord the king commands." So Shimei
lived in Jerusalem for a long time.
39 But three years later two of Shimei's slaves ran
away to King Achish son of Maacah of Gath. When
Shimei learned where they were, 40 he saddled his
donkey and went to Gath to search for them. When
he found them, he brought them back to Jerusalem.

2:32 Hebrew *will return his blood on his own head.*

KING JAMES VERSION

41 And it was told Solomon that Shimei had gone from Jerusalem to Gath, and was come again.

42 And the king sent and called for Shimei, and said unto him, Did I not make thee to swear by the LORD, and protested unto thee, saying, Know for a certain, on the day thou goest out, and walkest abroad any whither, that thou shalt surely die? and thou saidst unto me, The word *that* I have heard *is* good.

43 Why then hast thou not kept the oath of the LORD, and the commandment that I have charged thee with?

44 The king said moreover to Shimei, Thou knowest all the wickedness which thine heart is privy to, that thou didst to David my father: therefore the LORD shall return thy wickedness upon thine own head;

45 And king Solomon *shall be* blessed, and the throne of David shall be established before the LORD for ever.

46 So the king commanded Benaiah the son of Jehoiada; which went out, and fell upon him, that he died. And the kingdom was established in the hand of Solomon.

3 1 And Solomon made affinity with Pharaoh king of Egypt, and took Pharaoh's daughter, and brought her into the city of David, until he had made an end of building his own house, and the house of the LORD, and the wall of Jerusalem round about.

2 Only the people sacrificed in high places, because there was no house built unto the name of the LORD, until those days.

3 And Solomon loved the LORD, walking in the statutes of David his father: only he sacrificed and burnt incense in high places.

4 And the king went to Gibeon to sacrifice there; for that *was* the great high place: a thousand burnt offerings did Solomon offer upon that altar.

5 In Gibeon the LORD appeared to Solomon in a dream by night: and God said, Ask what I shall give thee.

6 And Solomon said, Thou hast shewed unto thy servant David my father great mercy, according as he walked before thee in truth, and in righteousness, and in uprightness of heart with thee; and thou hast kept for him this great kindness, that thou hast given him a son to sit on his throne, as *it is* this day.

7 And now, O LORD my God, thou hast made thy servant king instead of David my father: and I *am but* a little child: I know not *how* to go out or come in.

8 And thy servant *is* in the midst of thy people which thou hast chosen, a great people, that cannot be numbered nor counted for multitude.

9 Give therefore thy servant an understanding heart to judge thy people, that I may discern between good and bad: for who is able to judge this thy so great a people?

NEW LIVING TRANSLATION

41 Solomon heard that Shimei had left Jerusalem and had gone to Gath and returned. 42 So the king sent for Shimei and demanded, "Didn't I make you swear by the LORD and warn you not to go anywhere else or you would surely die? And you replied, 'The sentence is fair; I will do as you say.' 43 Then why haven't you kept your oath to the LORD and obeyed my command?"

44 The king also said to Shimei, "You certainly remember all the wicked things you did to my father, David. May the LORD now bring that evil on your own head. 45 But may I, King Solomon, receive the LORD's blessings, and may one of David's descendants always sit on this throne in the presence of the LORD." 46 Then, at the king's command, Benaiah son of Jehoiada took Shimei outside and killed him.

So the kingdom was now firmly in Solomon's grip.

Solomon Asks for Wisdom

3 Solomon made an alliance with Pharaoh, the king of Egypt, and married one of his daughters. He brought her to live in the City of David until he could finish building his palace and the Temple of the LORD and the wall around the city. 2 At that time the people of Israel sacrificed their offerings at local places of worship, for a temple honoring the name of the LORD had not yet been built.

3 Solomon loved the LORD and followed all the decrees of his father, David, except that Solomon, too, offered sacrifices and burned incense at the local places of worship. 4 The most important of these places of worship was at Gibeon, so the king went there and sacrificed 1,000 burnt offerings. 5 That night the LORD appeared to Solomon in a dream, and God said, "What do you want? Ask, and I will give it to you!"

6 Solomon replied, "You showed faithful love to your servant my father, David, because he was honest and true and faithful to you. And you have continued your faithful love to him today by giving him a son to sit on his throne.

7 "Now, O LORD my God, you have made me king instead of my father, David, but I am like a little child who doesn't know his way around. 8 And here I am in the midst of your own chosen people, a nation so great and numerous they cannot be counted! 9 Give me an understanding heart so that I can govern your people well and know the difference between right and wrong. For who by himself is able to govern this great people of yours?"

KING JAMES VERSION

10And the speech pleased the Lord, that Solomon had asked this thing.

11And God said unto him, Because thou hast asked this thing, and hast not asked for thyself long life; neither hast asked riches for thyself, nor hast asked the life of thine enemies; but hast asked for thyself understanding to discern judgment;

12Behold, I have done according to thy words: lo, I have given thee a wise and an understanding heart; so that there was none like thee before thee, neither after thee shall any arise like unto thee.

13And I have also given thee that which thou hast not asked, both riches, and honour: so that there shall not be any among the kings like unto thee all thy days.

14And if thou wilt walk in my ways, to keep my statutes and my commandments, as thy father David did walk, then I will lengthen thy days.

15And Solomon awoke; and, behold, *it was* a dream. And he came to Jerusalem, and stood before the ark of the covenant of the LORD, and offered up burnt offerings, and offered peace offerings, and made a feast to all his servants.

16Then came there two women, *that were* harlots, unto the king, and stood before him.

17And the one woman said, O my lord, I and this woman dwell in one house; and I was delivered of a child with her in the house.

18And it came to pass the third day after that I was delivered, that this woman was delivered also: and we *were* together; *there was* no stranger with us in the house, save we two in the house.

19And this woman's child died in the night; because she overlaid it.

20And she arose at midnight, and took my son from beside me, while thine handmaid slept, and laid it in her bosom, and laid her dead child in my bosom.

21And when I rose in the morning to give my child suck, behold, it was dead: but when I had considered it in the morning, behold, it was not my son, which I did bear.

22And the other woman said, Nay; but the living *is* my son, and the dead *is* thy son. And this said, No; but the dead *is* thy son, and the living *is* my son. Thus they spake before the king.

23Then said the king, The one saith, This *is* my son that liveth, and thy son *is* the dead: and the other saith, Nay; but thy son *is* the dead, and my son *is* the living.

24And the king said, Bring me a sword. And they brought a sword before the king.

25And the king said, Divide the living child in two, and give half to the one, and half to the other.

26Then spake the woman whose the living child *was* unto the king, for her bowels yearned upon her son, and she said, O my lord, give her the living child, and in no wise slay it. But the other said, Let it be neither mine nor thine, *but* divide *it*.

NEW LIVING TRANSLATION

10The Lord was pleased that Solomon had asked
for wisdom. 11So God replied, "Because you have
asked for wisdom in governing my people with justice and have not asked for a long life or wealth or the
death of your enemies—12I will give you what you
asked for! I will give you a wise and understanding heart such as no one else has had or ever will have!
13And I will also give you what you did not ask for—
riches and fame! No other king in all the world will
be compared to you for the rest of your life! 14And
if you follow me and obey my decrees and my commands as your father, David, did, I will give you a long life."

15Then Solomon woke up and realized it had been a dream. He returned to Jerusalem and stood before the Ark of the Lord's Covenant, where he sacrificed burnt offerings and peace offerings. Then he invited all his officials to a great banquet.

Solomon Judges Wisely

16Some time later two prostitutes came to the king
to have an argument settled. 17"Please, my lord," one
of them began, "this woman and I live in the same house. I gave birth to a baby while she was with me in
the house. 18Three days later this woman also had a
baby. We were alone; there were only two of us in the house.

19"But her baby died during the night when she
rolled over on it. 20Then she got up in the night and
took my son from beside me while I was asleep. She laid her dead child in my arms and took mine to
sleep beside her. 21And in the morning when I tried
to nurse my son, he was dead! But when I looked more closely in the morning light, I saw that it wasn't my son at all."

22Then the other woman interrupted, "It certainly was your son, and the living child is mine."

"No," the first woman said, "the living child is mine, and the dead one is yours." And so they argued back and forth before the king.

23Then the king said, "Let's get the facts straight.
Both of you claim the living child is yours, and each says that the dead one belongs to the other. 24All
right, bring me a sword." So a sword was brought to the king.

25Then he said, "Cut the living child in two, and give half to one woman and half to the other!"

26Then the woman who was the real mother of the living child, and who loved him very much, cried out, "Oh no, my lord! Give her the child—please do not kill him!"

But the other woman said, "All right, he will be neither yours nor mine; divide him between us!"

KING JAMES VERSION

27 Then the king answered and said, Give her the
living child, and in no wise slay it: she *is* the mother
thereof.
28 And all Israel heard of the judgment which the
king had judged; and they feared the king: for they
saw that the wisdom of God *was* in him, to do
judgment.

4 1 So king Solomon was king over all Israel.
2 And these *were* the princes which he had;
Azariah the son of Zadok the priest,
3 Elihoreph and Ahiah, the sons of Shisha, scribes;
Jehoshaphat the son of Ahilud, the recorder.
4 And Benaiah the son of Jehoiada *was* over the
host: and Zadok and Abiathar *were* the priests:
5 And Azariah the son of Nathan *was* over the officers; and Zabud the son of Nathan *was* principal
officer, *and* the king's friend:
6 And Ahishar *was* over the household: and Adoniram the son of Abda *was* over the tribute.
7 And Solomon had twelve officers over all Israel,
which provided victuals for the king and his household: each man his month in a year made provision.
8 And these *are* their names: The son of Hur, in
mount Ephraim:
9 The son of Dekar, in Makaz, and in Shaalbim, and
Beth-shemesh, and Elon-beth-hanan:
10 The son of Hesed, in Aruboth; to him *pertained*
Sochoh, and all the land of Hepher:
11 The son of Abinadab, in all the region of Dor;
which had Taphath the daughter of Solomon to wife:
12 Baana the son of Ahilud; *to him pertained*
Taanach and Megiddo, and all Beth-shean, which *is*
by Zartanah beneath Jezreel, from Beth-shean to
Abel-meholah, *even* unto *the place that is* beyond
Jokneam:
13 The son of Geber, in Ramoth-gilead; to him *pertained* the towns of Jair the son of Manasseh, which
are in Gilead; to him *also pertained* the region of
Argob, which *is* in Bashan, threescore great cities
with walls and brasen bars:
14 Ahinadab the son of Iddo *had* Mahanaim:
15 Ahimaaz *was* in Naphtali; he also took Basmath
the daughter of Solomon to wife:
16 Baanah the son of Hushai *was* in Asher and in
Aloth:
17 Jehoshaphat the son of Paruah, in Issachar:
18 Shimei the son of Elah, in Benjamin:

NEW LIVING TRANSLATION

27 Then the king said, "Do not kill the child, but
give him to the woman who wants him to live, for she
is his mother!"
28 When all Israel heard the king's decision, the
people were in awe of the king, for they saw the wisdom God had given him for rendering justice.

Solomon's Officials and Governors

4 King Solomon now ruled over all Israel, 2 and
these were his high officials:

Azariah son of Zadok was the priest.
3 Elihoreph and Ahijah, the sons of Shisha,
were court secretaries.
Jehoshaphat son of Ahilud was the royal
historian.
4 Benaiah son of Jehoiada was commander
of the army.
Zadok and Abiathar were priests.
5 Azariah son of Nathan was in charge of the
district governors.
Zabud son of Nathan, a priest, was a trusted
adviser to the king.
6 Ahishar was manager of the palace property.
Adoniram son of Abda was in charge of the
labor force.

7 Solomon also had twelve district governors who
were over all Israel. They were responsible for providing food for the king's household. Each of them
arranged provisions for one month of the year.
8 These are the names of the twelve governors:

Ben-hur, in the hill country of Ephraim.
9 Ben-deker, in Makaz, Shaalbim, Beth-shemesh,
and Elon-bethhanan.
10 Ben-hesed, in Arubboth, including Socoh and all
the land of Hepher.
11 Ben-abinadab, in all of Naphoth-dor.* (He was
married to Taphath, one of Solomon's
daughters.)
12 Baana son of Ahilud, in Taanach and Megiddo, all
of Beth-shan* near Zarethan below Jezreel, and
all the territory from Beth-shan to Abel-
meholah and over to Jokmeam.
13 Ben-geber, in Ramoth-gilead, including the Towns
of Jair (named for Jair of the tribe of
Manasseh*) in Gilead, and in the Argob region
of Bashan, including sixty large fortified towns
with bronze bars on their gates.
14 Ahinadab son of Iddo, in Mahanaim.
15 Ahimaaz, in Naphtali. (He was married to
Basemath, another of Solomon's daughters.)
16 Baana son of Hushai, in Asher and in Aloth.
17 Jehoshaphat son of Paruah, in Issachar.
18 Shimei son of Ela, in Benjamin.

4:11 Hebrew *Naphath-dor,* a variant spelling of Naphoth-dor.
4:12 Hebrew *Beth-shean,* a variant spelling of Beth-shan; also in 4:12b.
4:13 Hebrew *Jair son of Manasseh;* compare 1 Chr 2:22.

KING JAMES VERSION

19 Geber the son of Uri *was* in the country of Gilead, *in* the country of Sihon king of the Amorites, and of Og king of Bashan; and *he was* the only officer which *was* in the land.

20 Judah and Israel *were* many, as the sand which *is* by the sea in multitude, eating and drinking, and making merry.

21 And Solomon reigned over all kingdoms from the river unto the land of the Philistines, and unto the border of Egypt: they brought presents, and served Solomon all the days of his life.

22 And Solomon's provision for one day was thirty measures of fine flour, and threescore measures of meal,

23 Ten fat oxen, and twenty oxen out of the pastures, and an hundred sheep, beside harts, and roebucks, and fallowdeer, and fatted fowl.

24 For he had dominion over all *the region* on this side the river, from Tiphsah even to Azzah, over all the kings on this side the river: and he had peace on all sides round about him.

25 And Judah and Israel dwelt safely, every man under his vine and under his fig tree, from Dan even to Beer-sheba, all the days of Solomon.

26 And Solomon had forty thousand stalls of horses for his chariots, and twelve thousand horsemen.

27 And those officers provided victual for king Solomon, and for all that came unto king Solomon's table, every man in his month: they lacked nothing.

28 Barley also and straw for the horses and dromedaries brought they unto the place where *the officers* were, every man according to his charge.

29 And God gave Solomon wisdom and understanding exceeding much, and largeness of heart, even as the sand that *is* on the sea shore.

30 And Solomon's wisdom excelled the wisdom of all the children of the east country, and all the wisdom of Egypt.

31 For he was wiser than all men; than Ethan the Ezrahite, and Heman, and Chalcol, and Darda, the sons of Mahol: and his fame was in all nations round about.

32 And he spake three thousand proverbs: and his songs were a thousand and five.

33 And he spake of trees, from the cedar tree that *is* in Lebanon even unto the hyssop that springeth out of the wall: he spake also of beasts, and of fowl, and of creeping things, and of fishes.

34 And there came of all people to hear the wisdom of Solomon, from all kings of the earth, which had heard of his wisdom.

NEW LIVING TRANSLATION

19 Geber son of Uri, in the land of Gilead,* including
the territories of King Sihon of the Amorites
and King Og of Bashan.
There was also one governor over the land
of Judah.*

Solomon's Prosperity and Wisdom

20 The people of Judah and Israel were as numerous as the sand on the seashore. They were very contented, with plenty to eat and drink. 21 *Solomon ruled over all the kingdoms from the Euphrates River* in the north to the land of the Philistines and the border of Egypt in the south. The conquered peoples of those lands sent tribute money to Solomon and continued to serve him throughout his lifetime.

22 The daily food requirements for Solomon's palace were 150 bushels of choice flour and 300 bushels of meal*; 23 also 10 oxen from the fattening pens, 20 pasture-fed cattle, 100 sheep or goats, as well as deer, gazelles, roe deer, and choice poultry.*

24 Solomon's dominion extended over all the kingdoms west of the Euphrates River, from Tiphsah to Gaza. And there was peace on all his borders. 25 During the lifetime of Solomon, all of Judah and Israel lived in peace and safety. And from Dan in the north to Beersheba in the south, each family had its own home and garden.*

26 Solomon had 4,000* stalls for his chariot horses, and he had 12,000 horses.*

27 The district governors faithfully provided food for King Solomon and his court; each made sure nothing was lacking during the month assigned to him. 28 They also brought the necessary barley and straw for the royal horses in the stables.

29 God gave Solomon very great wisdom and understanding, and knowledge as vast as the sands of the seashore. 30 In fact, his wisdom exceeded that of all the wise men of the East and the wise men of Egypt. 31 He was wiser than anyone else, including Ethan the Ezrahite and the sons of Mahol—Heman, Calcol, and Darda. His fame spread throughout all the surrounding nations. 32 He composed some 3,000 proverbs and wrote 1,005 songs. 33 He could speak with authority about all kinds of plants, from the great cedar of Lebanon to the tiny hyssop that grows from cracks in a wall. He could also speak about animals, birds, small creatures, and fish. 34 And kings from every nation sent their ambassadors to listen to the wisdom of Solomon.

4:19a Greek version reads *of Gad;* compare 4:13. **4:19b** As in some Greek manuscripts; Hebrew lacks *of Judah.* The meaning of the Hebrew is uncertain. **4:21a** Verses 4:21-34 are numbered 5:1-14 in Hebrew text. **4:21b** Hebrew *the river;* also in 4:24. **4:22** Hebrew *30 cors* [5.5 kiloliters] *of choice flour and 60 cors* [11 kiloliters] *of meal.* **4:23** Or *and fattened geese.* **4:25** Hebrew *each family lived under its own grapevine and under its own fig tree.* **4:26a** As in some Greek manuscripts (see also 2 Chr 9:25); Hebrew reads *40,000.* **4:26b** Or *12,000 charioteers.*

KING JAMES VERSION

5 1And Hiram king of Tyre sent his servants unto
Solomon; for he had heard that they had
anointed him king in the room of his father: for
Hiram was ever a lover of David.
2And Solomon sent to Hiram, saying,
3Thou knowest how that David my father could
not build an house unto the name of the LORD his God
for the wars which were about him on every side,
until the LORD put them under the soles of his feet.
4But now the LORD my God hath given me rest on
every side, *so that there is* neither adversary nor evil
occurrent.
5And, behold, I purpose to build an house unto the
name of the LORD my God, as the LORD spake unto
David my father, saying, Thy son, whom I will set
upon thy throne in thy room, he shall build an house
unto my name.
6Now therefore command thou that they hew me
cedar trees out of Lebanon; and my servants shall be
with thy servants: and unto thee will I give hire for
thy servants according to all that thou shalt appoint:
for thou knowest that *there is* not among us any that
can skill to hew timber like unto the Sidonians.
7And it came to pass, when Hiram heard the words
of Solomon, that he rejoiced greatly, and said,
Blessed *be* the LORD this day, which hath given unto
David a wise son over this great people.
8And Hiram sent to Solomon, saying, I have considered the things which thou sentest to me for: *and*
I will do all thy desire concerning timber of cedar,
and concerning timber of fir.
9My servants shall bring *them* down from Lebanon unto the sea: and I will convey them by sea in
floats unto the place that thou shalt appoint me, and
will cause them to be discharged there, and thou
shalt receive *them:* and thou shalt accomplish my
desire, in giving food for my household.
10So Hiram gave Solomon cedar trees and fir trees
according to all his desire.
11And Solomon gave Hiram twenty thousand measures of wheat *for* food to his household, and twenty
measures of pure oil: thus gave Solomon to Hiram
year by year.
12And the LORD gave Solomon wisdom, as he
promised him: and there was peace between Hiram
and Solomon; and they two made a league together.
13And king Solomon raised a levy out of all Israel;
and the levy was thirty thousand men.
14And he sent them to Lebanon, ten thousand a
month by courses: a month they were in Lebanon, *and*
two months at home: and Adoniram *was* over the levy.
15And Solomon had threescore and ten thousand
that bare burdens, and fourscore thousand hewers in
the mountains;
16Beside the chief of Solomon's officers which *were*
over the work, three thousand and three hundred,
which ruled over the people that wrought in the work.

NEW LIVING TRANSLATION

Preparations for Building the Temple

5 1*King Hiram of Tyre had always been a loyal
friend of David. When Hiram learned that
David's son Solomon was the new king of Israel, he
sent ambassadors to congratulate him.
2Then Solomon sent this message back to Hiram:

3"You know that my father, David, was not able to
build a Temple to honor the name of the LORD his
God because of the many wars waged against him
by surrounding nations. He could not build until
the LORD gave him victory over all his enemies.
4But now the LORD my God has given me peace
on every side; I have no enemies, and all is well.
5So I am planning to build a Temple to honor
the name of the LORD my God, just as he had
instructed my father, David. For the LORD told
him, 'Your son, whom I will place on your throne,
will build the Temple to honor my name.'
6"Therefore, please command that cedars
from Lebanon be cut for me. Let my men work
alongside yours, and I will pay your men whatever
wages you ask. As you know, there is no one
among us who can cut timber like you
Sidonians!"

7When Hiram received Solomon's message, he
was very pleased and said, "Praise the LORD today for
giving David a wise son to be king of the great nation
of Israel." 8Then he sent this reply to Solomon:

"I have received your message, and I will supply
all the cedar and cypress timber you need. 9My
servants will bring the logs from the Lebanon
mountains to the Mediterranean Sea* and make
them into rafts and float them along the coast to
whatever place you choose. Then we will break
the rafts apart so you can carry the logs away.
You can pay me by supplying me with food for
my household."

10So Hiram supplied as much cedar and cypress
timber as Solomon desired. 11In return, Solomon
sent him an annual payment of 100,000 bushels*
of wheat for his household and 110,000 gallons* of
pure olive oil. 12So the LORD gave wisdom to Solomon, just as he had promised. And Hiram and
Solomon made a formal alliance of peace.
13Then King Solomon conscripted a labor force
of 30,000 men from all Israel. 14He sent them to
Lebanon in shifts, 10,000 every month, so that each
man would be one month in Lebanon and two
months at home. Adoniram was in charge of this
labor force. 15Solomon also had 70,000 common
laborers, 80,000 quarry workers in the hill country,
16and 3,600* foremen to supervise the work.

5:1 Verses 5:1-18 are numbered 5:15-32 in Hebrew text. **5:9** Hebrew *the sea.* **5:11a** Hebrew *20,000 cors* [3,640 kiloliters]. **5:11b** As in Greek version, which reads *20,000 baths* [420 kiloliters] (see also 2 Chr 2:10); Hebrew reads *20 cors,* about 800 gallons or 3.6 kiloliters in volume.
5:16 As in some Greek manuscripts (see also 2 Chr 2:2, 18); Hebrew reads *3,300.*

KING JAMES VERSION

17And the king commanded, and they brought great stones, costly stones, *and* hewed stones, to lay the foundation of the house.

18And Solomon's builders and Hiram's builders did hew *them,* and the stonesquarers: so they prepared timber and stones to build the house.

6 1And it came to pass in the four hundred and eightieth year after the children of Israel were come out of the land of Egypt, in the fourth year of Solomon's reign over Israel, in the month Zif, which *is* the second month, that he began to build the house of the LORD.

2And the house which king Solomon built for the LORD, the length thereof *was* threescore cubits, and the breadth thereof twenty *cubits,* and the height thereof thirty cubits.

3And the porch before the temple of the house, twenty cubits *was* the length thereof, according to the breadth of the house; *and* ten cubits *was* the breadth thereof before the house.

4And for the house he made windows of narrow lights.

5And against the wall of the house he built chambers round about, *against* the walls of the house round about, *both* of the temple and of the oracle: and he made chambers round about:

6The nethermost chamber *was* five cubits broad, and the middle *was* six cubits broad, and the third *was* seven cubits broad: for without *in the wall* of the house he made narrowed rests round about, that *the beams* should not be fastened in the walls of the house.

7And the house, when it was in building, was built of stone made ready before it was brought thither: so that there was neither hammer nor ax *nor* any tool of iron heard in the house, while it was in building.

8The door for the middle chamber *was* in the right side of the house: and they went up with winding stairs into the middle *chamber,* and out of the middle into the third.

9So he built the house, and finished it; and covered the house with beams and boards of cedar.

10And *then* he built chambers against all the house, five cubits high: and they rested on the house *with* timber of cedar.

11And the word of the LORD came to Solomon, saying,

12*Concerning* this house which thou art in building, if thou wilt walk in my statutes, and execute my judgments, and keep all my commandments to walk in them; then will I perform my word with thee, which I spake unto David thy father:

13And I will dwell among the children of Israel, and will not forsake my people Israel.

NEW LIVING TRANSLATION

17At the king's command, they quarried large blocks of high-quality stone and shaped them to make the foundation of the Temple. 18Men from the city of Gebal helped Solomon's and Hiram's builders prepare the timber and stone for the Temple.

Solomon Builds the Temple

6 It was in midspring, in the month of Ziv,* during the fourth year of Solomon's reign, that he began to construct the Temple of the LORD. This was 480 years after the people of Israel were rescued from their slavery in the land of Egypt.

2The Temple that King Solomon built for the LORD was 90 feet long, 30 feet wide, and 45 feet high.* 3The entry room at the front of the Temple was 30 feet* wide, running across the entire width of the Temple. It projected outward 15 feet* from the front of the Temple. 4Solomon also made narrow recessed windows throughout the Temple.

5He built a complex of rooms against the outer walls of the Temple, all the way around the sides and rear of the building. 6The complex was three stories high, the bottom floor being 7½ feet wide, the second floor 9 feet wide, and the top floor 10½ feet wide.* The rooms were connected to the walls of the Temple by beams resting on ledges built out from the wall. So the beams were not inserted into the walls themselves.

7The stones used in the construction of the Temple were finished at the quarry, so there was no sound of hammer, ax, or any other iron tool at the building site.

8The entrance to the bottom floor* was on the south side of the Temple. There were winding stairs going up to the second floor, and another flight of stairs between the second and third floors. 9After completing the Temple structure, Solomon put in a ceiling made of cedar beams and planks. 10As already stated, he built a complex of rooms on three sides of the building, attached to the Temple walls by cedar timbers. Each story of the complex was 7½ feet* high.

11Then the LORD gave this message to Solomon: 12"Concerning this Temple you are building, if you keep all my decrees and regulations and obey all my commands, I will fulfill through you the promise I made to your father, David. 13I will live among the Israelites and will never abandon my people Israel."

6:1 Hebrew *It was in the month of Ziv, which is the second month.* This month of the ancient Hebrew lunar calendar usually occurs within the months of April and May. **6:2** Hebrew *60 cubits* [27.6 meters] *long, 20 cubits* [9.2 meters] *wide, and 30 cubits* [13.8 meters] *high.* **6:3a** Hebrew *20 cubits* [9.2 meters]; also in 6:16, 20. **6:3b** Hebrew *10 cubits* [4.6 meters]. **6:6** Hebrew *the bottom floor being 5 cubits* [2.3 meters] *wide, the second floor 6 cubits* [2.8 meters] *wide, and the top floor 7 cubits* [3.2 meters] *wide.* **6:8** As in Greek version; Hebrew reads *middle floor.* **6:10** Hebrew *5 cubits* [2.3 meters].

KING JAMES VERSION

14So Solomon built the house, and finished it.
15And he built the walls of the house within with
boards of cedar, both the floor of the house, and the
walls of the ceiling: *and* he covered *them* on the inside with wood, and covered the floor of the house
with planks of fir.
16And he built twenty cubits on the sides of the
house, both the floor and the walls with boards of
cedar: he even built *them* for it within, *even* for the
oracle, *even* for the most holy *place*.
17And the house, that *is*, the temple before it, was
forty cubits *long*.
18And the cedar of the house within *was* carved
with knops and open flowers: all *was* cedar; there
was no stone seen.
19And the oracle he prepared in the house within,
to set there the ark of the covenant of the LORD.
20And the oracle in the forepart *was* twenty
cubits in length, and twenty cubits in breadth, and
twenty cubits in the height thereof: and he overlaid
it with pure gold; and *so* covered the altar *which was
of* cedar.
21So Solomon overlaid the house within with pure
gold: and he made a partition by the chains of gold
before the oracle; and he overlaid it with gold.
22And the whole house he overlaid with gold, until
he had finished all the house: also the whole altar
that *was* by the oracle he overlaid with gold.
23And within the oracle he made two cherubims
of olive tree, *each* ten cubits high.
24And five cubits *was* the one wing of the cherub,
and five cubits the other wing of the cherub: from
the uttermost part of the one wing unto the uttermost part of the other *were* ten cubits.
25And the other cherub *was* ten cubits: both the
cherubims *were* of one measure and one size.
26The height of the one cherub *was* ten cubits,
and so *was it* of the other cherub.
27And he set the cherubims within the inner
house: and they stretched forth the wings of the
cherubims, so that the wing of the one touched the
one wall, and the wing of the other cherub touched
the other wall; and their wings touched one another
in the midst of the house.
28And he overlaid the cherubims with gold.
29And he carved all the walls of the house round
about with carved figures of cherubims and palm
trees and open flowers, within and without.
30And the floor of the house he overlaid with gold,
within and without.
31And for the entering of the oracle he made
doors *of* olive tree: the lintel *and* side posts *were* a
fifth part *of the wall*.
32The two doors also *were of* olive tree; and he
carved upon them carvings of cherubims and palm
trees and open flowers, and overlaid *them* with gold,

NEW LIVING TRANSLATION

The Temple's Interior

14So Solomon finished building the Temple. 15The
entire inside, from floor to ceiling, was paneled with
wood. He paneled the walls and ceilings with cedar,
and he used planks of cypress for the floors. 16He
partitioned off an inner sanctuary—the Most Holy
Place—at the far end of the Temple. It was 30 feet
deep and was paneled with cedar from floor to ceiling. 17The main room of the Temple, outside the
Most Holy Place, was 60 feet* long. 18Cedar paneling
completely covered the stone walls throughout the
Temple, and the paneling was decorated with carvings of gourds and open flowers.
19He prepared the inner sanctuary at the far end
of the Temple, where the Ark of the LORD's Covenant
would be placed. 20This inner sanctuary was 30 feet
long, 30 feet wide, and 30 feet high. He overlaid the
inside with solid gold. He also overlaid the altar
made of cedar.* 21Then Solomon overlaid the rest of
the Temple's interior with solid gold, and he made
gold chains to protect the entrance* to the Most
Holy Place. 22So he finished overlaying the entire
Temple with gold, including the altar that belonged
to the Most Holy Place.
23He made two cherubim of wild olive* wood,
each 15 feet* tall, and placed them in the inner sanctuary. 24The wingspan of each of the cherubim was
15 feet, each wing being 7½ feet* long. 25The two
cherubim were identical in shape and size; 26each
was 15 feet tall. 27He placed them side by side in
the inner sanctuary of the Temple. Their outspread
wings reached from wall to wall, while their inner
wings touched at the center of the room. 28He overlaid the two cherubim with gold.
29He decorated all the walls of the inner sanctuary
and the main room with carvings of cherubim, palm
trees, and open flowers. 30He overlaid the floor in
both rooms with gold.
31For the entrance to the inner sanctuary, he made
double doors of wild olive wood with five-sided
doorposts.* 32These double doors were decorated
with carvings of cherubim, palm trees, and open

6:17 Hebrew *40 cubits* [18.4 meters]. **6:20** Or *overlaid the altar with cedar.* The meaning of the Hebrew is uncertain. **6:21** Or *to draw curtains across.* The meaning of the Hebrew is uncertain. **6:23a** Or *pine;* Hebrew reads *oil tree;* also in 6:31, 33. **6:23b** Hebrew *10 cubits* [4.6 meters]; also in 6:24, 25. **6:24** Hebrew *5 cubits* [2.3 meters]. **6:31** The meaning of the Hebrew is uncertain.

KING JAMES VERSION

and spread gold upon the cherubims, and upon the
palm trees.
33So also made he for the door of the temple posts
of olive tree, a fourth part *of the wall.*
34And the two doors *were of* fir tree: the two leaves
of the one door *were* folding, and the two leaves of
the other door *were* folding.
35And he carved *thereon* cherubims and palm
trees and open flowers: and covered *them* with gold
fitted upon the carved work.
36And he built the inner court with three rows of
hewed stone, and a row of cedar beams.
37In the fourth year was the foundation of the
house of the LORD laid, in the month Zif:
38And in the eleventh year, in the month Bul,
which *is* the eighth month, was the house finished
throughout all the parts thereof, and according to all
the fashion of it. So was he seven years in building it.

7 1But Solomon was building his own house thirteen years, and he finished all his house.
2He built also the house of the forest of Lebanon;
the length thereof *was* an hundred cubits, and the
breadth thereof fifty cubits, and the height thereof
thirty cubits, upon four rows of cedar pillars, with
cedar beams upon the pillars.
3And *it was* covered with cedar above upon the
beams, that *lay* on forty five pillars, fifteen *in* a row.
4And *there were* windows *in* three rows, and light
was against light *in* three ranks.
5And all the doors and posts *were* square, with the
windows: and light *was* against light *in* three ranks.
6And he made a porch of pillars; the length thereof
was fifty cubits, and the breadth thereof thirty
cubits: and the porch *was* before them: and the *other*
pillars and the thick beam *were* before them.
7Then he made a porch for the throne where he
might judge, *even* the porch of judgment: and *it was*
covered with cedar from one side of the floor to the
other.
8And his house where he dwelt *had* another court
within the porch, *which* was of the like work. Solomon made also an house for Pharaoh's daughter,
whom he had taken *to wife,* like unto this porch.
9All these *were of* costly stones, according to the
measures of hewed stones, sawed with saws, within
and without, even from the foundation unto the cop-
ing, and *so* on the outside toward the great court.
10And the foundation *was of* costly stones, even
great stones, stones of ten cubits, and stones of eight
cubits.
11And above *were* costly stones, after the measures of hewed stones, and cedars.

NEW LIVING TRANSLATION

flowers. The doors, including the decorations of
cherubim and palm trees, were overlaid with gold.
33Then he made four-sided doorposts of wild
olive wood for the entrance to the Temple. 34There
were two folding doors of cypress wood, and each
door was hinged to fold back upon itself. 35These
doors were decorated with carvings of cherubim,
palm trees, and open flowers—all overlaid evenly
with gold.
36The walls of the inner courtyard were built so
that there was one layer of cedar beams between
every three layers of finished stone.
37The foundation of the LORD's Temple was laid in
midspring, in the month of Ziv,* during the fourth
year of Solomon's reign. 38The entire building was
completed in every detail by midautumn, in the
month of Bul,* during the eleventh year of his reign.
So it took seven years to build the Temple.

Solomon Builds His Palace

7 Solomon also built a palace for himself, and
it took him thirteen years to complete the
construction.
2One of Solomon's buildings was called the Palace
of the Forest of Lebanon. It was 150 feet long, 75 feet
wide, and 45 feet high.* There were four rows of
cedar pillars, and great cedar beams rested on the
pillars. 3The hall had a cedar roof. Above the beams
on the pillars were forty-five side rooms,* arranged
in three tiers of fifteen each. 4On each end of the
long hall were three rows of windows facing each
other. 5All the doorways and doorposts* had rectan-
gular frames and were arranged in sets of three, facing each other.
6Solomon also built the Hall of Pillars, which was
75 feet long and 45 feet wide.* There was a porch in
front, along with a canopy supported by pillars.
7Solomon also built the throne room, known as
the Hall of Justice, where he sat to hear legal matters.
It was paneled with cedar from floor to ceiling.*
8Solomon's living quarters surrounded a courtyard
behind this hall, and they were constructed the same
way. He also built similar living quarters for Pharaoh's daughter, whom he had married.
9From foundation to eaves, all these buildings
were built from huge blocks of high-quality stone,
cut with saws and trimmed to exact measure on all
sides. 10Some of the huge foundation stones were
15 feet long, and some were 12 feet* long. 11The
blocks of high-quality stone used in the walls were
also cut to measure, and cedar beams were also used.

6:37 Hebrew *was laid in the month of Ziv.* This month of the ancient Hebrew lunar calendar usually occurs within the months of April and May. **6:38** Hebrew *by the month of Bul, which is the eighth month.* This month of the ancient Hebrew lunar calendar usually occurs within the months of October and November. **7:2** Hebrew *100 cubits* [46 meters] *long, 50 cubits* [23 meters] *wide, and 30 cubits* [13.5 meters] *high.* **7:3** Or *45 rafters,* or *45 beams,* or *45 pillars.* The architectural details in 7:2-6 can be interpreted in many different ways. **7:5** Greek version reads *windows.* **7:6** Hebrew *50 cubits* [23 meters] *long and 30 cubits* [13.8 meters] *wide.* **7:7** As in Syriac version and Latin Vulgate; Hebrew reads *from floor to floor.* **7:10** Hebrew *10 cubits* [4.6 meters] . . . *8 cubits* [3.7 meters].

KING JAMES VERSION

12 And the great court round about *was* with three rows of hewed stones, and a row of cedar beams, both for the inner court of the house of the LORD, and for the porch of the house.

13 And king Solomon sent and fetched Hiram out of Tyre.

14 He *was* a widow's son of the tribe of Naphtali, and his father *was* a man of Tyre, a worker in brass: and he was filled with wisdom, and understanding, and cunning to work all works in brass. And he came to king Solomon, and wrought all his work.

15 For he cast two pillars of brass, of eighteen cubits high apiece: and a line of twelve cubits did compass either of them about.

16 And he made two chapiters *of* molten brass, to set upon the tops of the pillars: the height of the one chapiter *was* five cubits, and the height of the other chapiter *was* five cubits:

17 *And* nets of checker work, and wreaths of chain work, for the chapiters which *were* upon the top of the pillars; seven for the one chapiter, and seven for the other chapiter.

18 And he made the pillars, and two rows round about upon the one network, to cover the chapiters that *were* upon the top, with pomegranates: and so did he for the other chapiter.

19 And the chapiters that *were* upon the top of the pillars *were* of lily work in the porch, four cubits.

20 And the chapiters upon the two pillars *had pomegranates* also above, over against the belly which *was* by the network: and the pomegranates *were* two hundred in rows round about upon the other chapiter.

21 And he set up the pillars in the porch of the temple: and he set up the right pillar, and called the name thereof Jachin: and he set up the left pillar, and called the name thereof Boaz.

22 And upon the top of the pillars *was* lily work: so was the work of the pillars finished.

23 And he made a molten sea, ten cubits from the one brim to the other: *it was* round all about, and his height *was* five cubits: and a line of thirty cubits did compass it round about.

24 And under the brim of it round about *there were* knops compassing it, ten in a cubit, compassing the sea round about: the knops *were* cast in two rows, when it was cast.

25 It stood upon twelve oxen, three looking toward the north, and three looking toward the west, and three looking toward the south, and three looking toward the east: and the sea *was set* above upon them, and all their hinder parts *were* inward.

26 And it *was* an hand breadth thick, and the brim thereof was wrought like the brim of a cup, with flowers of lilies: it contained two thousand baths.

NEW LIVING TRANSLATION

12 The walls of the great courtyard were built so that
there was one layer of cedar beams between every
three layers of finished stone, just like the walls of
the inner courtyard of the LORD's Temple with its
entry room.

Furnishings for the Temple

13 King Solomon then asked for a man named Huram* to come from Tyre. 14 He was half Israelite, since
his mother was a widow from the tribe of Naphtali,
and his father had been a craftsman in bronze from
Tyre. Huram was extremely skillful and talented in
any work in bronze, and he came to do all the metal
work for King Solomon.

15 Huram cast two bronze pillars, each 27 feet tall
and 18 feet in circumference.* 16 For the tops of the
pillars he cast bronze capitals, each 7½ feet* tall.
17 Each capital was decorated with seven sets of
latticework and interwoven chains. 18 He also encircled the latticework with two rows of pomegranates to decorate the capitals over the pillars. 19 The
capitals on the columns inside the entry room were
shaped like water lilies, and they were six feet* tall.
20 The capitals on the two pillars had 200 pomegranates in two rows around them, beside the rounded
surface next to the latticework. 21 Huram set the pillars at the entrance of the Temple, one toward the
south and one toward the north. He named the one
on the south Jakin, and the one on the north Boaz.*
22 The capitals on the pillars were shaped like water
lilies. And so the work on the pillars was finished.

23 Then Huram cast a great round basin, 15 feet
across from rim to rim, called the Sea. It was 7½ feet
deep and about 45 feet in circumference.* 24 It was
encircled just below its rim by two rows of decorative gourds. There were about six gourds per foot*
all the way around, and they were cast as part of
the basin.

25 The Sea was placed on a base of twelve bronze
oxen,* all facing outward. Three faced north, three
faced west, three faced south, and three faced east,
and the Sea rested on them. 26 The walls of the Sea
were about three inches* thick, and its rim flared out
like a cup and resembled a water lily blossom. It
could hold about 11,000 gallons* of water.

7:13 Hebrew *Hiram* (also in 7:40, 45); compare 2 Chr 2:13. This is not the same person mentioned in 5:1. **7:15** Hebrew *18 cubits* [8.3 meters] *tall and 12 cubits* [5.5 meters] *in circumference.* **7:16** Hebrew *5 cubits* [2.3 meters]. **7:19** Hebrew *4 cubits* [1.8 meters]; also in 7:38. **7:21** *Jakin* probably means "he establishes"; *Boaz* probably means "in him is strength." **7:23** Hebrew *10 cubits* [4.6 meters] *across. . . . 5 cubits* [2.3 meters] *deep and 30 cubits* [13.8 meters] *in circumference.* **7:24** Or *20 gourds per meter;* Hebrew reads *10 per cubit.* **7:25** Hebrew *12 oxen;* compare 2 Kgs 16:17, which specifies *bronze oxen.* **7:26a** Hebrew *a handbreadth* [8 centimeters]. **7:26b** Hebrew *2,000 baths* [42 kiloliters].

KING JAMES VERSION

27 And he made ten bases of brass; four cubits *was*
the length of one base, and four cubits the breadth
thereof, and three cubits the height of it.
28 And the work of the bases *was* on this *manner*:
they had borders, and the borders *were* between
the ledges:
29 And on the borders that *were* between the ledges
were lions, oxen, and cherubims: and upon the ledges
there was a base above: and beneath the lions and
oxen *were* certain additions made of thin work.
30 And every base had four brasen wheels, and
plates of brass: and the four corners thereof had
undersetters: under the laver *were* undersetters
molten, at the side of every addition.
31 And the mouth of it within the chapiter and
above *was* a cubit: but the mouth thereof *was* round
after the work of the base, a cubit and an half: and
also upon the mouth of it *were* gravings with their
borders, foursquare, not round.
32 And under the borders *were* four wheels; and the
axletrees of the wheels *were joined* to the base: and
the height of a wheel *was* a cubit and half a cubit.
33 And the work of the wheels *was* like the work of
a chariot wheel: their axletrees, and their naves, and
their felloes, and their spokes, *were* all molten.
34 And *there were* four undersetters to the four
corners of one base: *and* the undersetters *were* of
the very base itself.
35 And in the top of the base *was there* a round
compass of half a cubit high: and on the top of the
base the ledges thereof and the borders thereof *were*
of the same.
36 For on the plates of the ledges thereof, and on
the borders thereof, he graved cherubims, lions, and
palm trees, according to the proportion of every one,
and additions round about.
37 After this *manner* he made the ten bases: all of
them had one casting, one measure, *and* one size.
38 Then made he ten lavers of brass: one laver contained forty baths: *and* every laver was four cubits:
and upon every one of the ten bases one laver.
39 And he put five bases on the right side of the
house, and five on the left side of the house: and he
set the sea on the right side of the house eastward
over against the south.
40 And Hiram made the lavers, and the shovels, and
the basins. So Hiram made an end of doing all the
work that he made king Solomon for the house of
the LORD:
41 The two pillars, and the *two* bowls of the
chapiters that *were* on the top of the two pillars; and
the two networks, to cover the two bowls of the
chapiters which *were* upon the top of the pillars;
42 And four hundred pomegranates for the two
networks, *even* two rows of pomegranates for one
network, to cover the two bowls of the chapiters that
were upon the pillars;

NEW LIVING TRANSLATION

27 Huram also made ten bronze water carts, each
6 feet long, 6 feet wide, and 4½ feet tall.* 28 They
were constructed with side panels braced with
crossbars. 29 Both the panels and the crossbars were
decorated with carved lions, oxen, and cherubim.
Above and below the lions and oxen were wreath
decorations. 30 Each of these carts had four bronze
wheels and bronze axles. There were supporting
posts for the bronze basins at the corners of the
carts; these supports were decorated on each side
with carvings of wreaths. 31 The top of each cart had
a rounded frame for the basin. It projected 1½ feet*
above the cart's top like a round pedestal, and its
opening was 2¼ feet* across; it was decorated on the
outside with carvings of wreaths. The panels of the
carts were square, not round. 32 Under the panels
were four wheels that were connected to axles that
had been cast as one unit with the cart. The wheels
were 2¼ feet in diameter 33 and were similar to chariot wheels. The axles, spokes, rims, and hubs were all
cast from molten bronze.
34 There were handles at each of the four corners
of the carts, and these, too, were cast as one unit
with the cart. 35 Around the top of each cart was a rim
nine inches wide.* The corner supports and side
panels were cast as one unit with the cart. 36 Carvings
of cherubim, lions, and palm trees decorated the
panels and corner supports wherever there was
room, and there were wreaths all around. 37 All ten
water carts were the same size and were made alike,
for each was cast from the same mold.
38 Huram also made ten smaller bronze basins,
one for each cart. Each basin was six feet across and
could hold 220 gallons* of water. 39 He set five water
carts on the south side of the Temple and five on the
north side. The great bronze basin called the Sea was
placed near the southeast corner of the Temple. 40 He
also made the necessary washbasins, shovels, and
bowls.

So at last Huram completed everything King Solomon had assigned him to make for the Temple of
the LORD:

41 the two pillars;
the two bowl-shaped capitals on top of the pillars;
the two networks of interwoven chains that
decorated the capitals;
42 the 400 pomegranates that hung from the chains
on the capitals (two rows of pomegranates for
each of the chain networks that decorated the
capitals on top of the pillars);

7:27 Hebrew *4 cubits* [1.8 meters] *long, 4 cubits wide, and 3 cubits* [1.4 meters] *high.* **7:31a** Hebrew *a cubit* [46 centimeters]. **7:31b** Hebrew *1½ cubits* [69 centimeters]; also in 7:32. **7:35** Hebrew *half a cubit wide* [23 centimeters]. **7:38** Hebrew *40 baths* [840 liters].

KING JAMES VERSION

43 And the ten bases, and ten lavers on the bases;
44 And one sea, and twelve oxen under the sea;
45 And the pots, and the shovels, and the basins:
and all these vessels, which Hiram made to king
Solomon for the house of the LORD, *were of* bright
brass.
46 In the plain of Jordan did the king cast them, in
the clay ground between Succoth and Zarthan.
47 And Solomon left all the vessels *unweighed,*
because they were exceeding many: neither was the
weight of the brass found out.
48 And Solomon made all the vessels that *pertained*
unto the house of the LORD: the altar of gold, and the
table of gold, whereupon the shewbread *was,*
49 And the candlesticks of pure gold, five on the
right *side,* and five on the left, before the oracle, with
the flowers, and the lamps, and the tongs *of* gold,
50 And the bowls, and the snuffers, and the basins,
and the spoons, and the censers *of* pure gold; and the
hinges *of* gold, *both* for the doors of the inner house,
the most holy *place, and* for the doors of the house,
to wit, of the temple.
51 So was ended all the work that king Solomon
made for the house of the LORD. And Solomon
brought in the things which David his father had
dedicated; *even* the silver, and the gold, and the
vessels, did he put among the treasures of the house
of the LORD.

8 1 Then Solomon assembled the elders of Israel,
and all the heads of the tribes, the chief of the
fathers of the children of Israel, unto king Solomon
in Jerusalem, that they might bring up the ark of the
covenant of the LORD out of the city of David, which
is Zion.
2 And all the men of Israel assembled themselves
unto king Solomon at the feast in the month Ethanim, which *is* the seventh month.
3 And all the elders of Israel came, and the priests
took up the ark.
4 And they brought up the ark of the LORD, and
the tabernacle of the congregation, and all the holy
vessels that *were* in the tabernacle, even those did
the priests and the Levites bring up.
5 And king Solomon, and all the congregation of
Israel, that were assembled unto him, *were* with him
before the ark, sacrificing sheep and oxen, that could
not be told nor numbered for multitude.
6 And the priests brought in the ark of the covenant of the LORD unto his place, into the oracle of
the house, to the most holy *place, even* under the
wings of the cherubims.
7 For the cherubims spread forth *their* two wings

NEW LIVING TRANSLATION

43 the ten water carts holding the ten basins;
44 the Sea and the twelve oxen under it;
45 the ash buckets, the shovels, and the bowls.
Huram made all these things of burnished bronze
for the Temple of the LORD, just as King Solomon had
directed. 46 The king had them cast in clay molds in
the Jordan Valley between Succoth and Zarethan.
47 Solomon did not weigh all these things because
there were so many; the weight of the bronze could
not be measured.
48 Solomon also made all the furnishings of the
Temple of the LORD:

the gold altar;
the gold table for the Bread of the Presence;
49 the lampstands of solid gold, five on the south
and five on the north, in front of the Most
Holy Place;
the flower decorations, lamps, and tongs—
all of gold;
50 the small bowls, lamp snuffers, bowls, dishes,
and incense burners—all of solid gold;
the doors for the entrances to the Most Holy
Place and the main room of the Temple,
with their fronts overlaid with gold.

51 So King Solomon finished all his work on the
Temple of the LORD. Then he brought all the gifts
his father, David, had dedicated—the silver, the gold,
and the various articles—and he stored them in the
treasuries of the LORD's Temple.

The Ark Brought to the Temple

8 Solomon then summoned to Jerusalem the elders of Israel and all the heads of the tribes—
the leaders of the ancestral families of the Israelites.
They were to bring the Ark of the LORD's Covenant to
the Temple from its location in the City of David, also
known as Zion. 2 So all the men of Israel assembled
before King Solomon at the annual Festival of Shelters, which is held in early autumn in the month of
Ethanim.*
3 When all the elders of Israel arrived, the priests
picked up the Ark. 4 The priests and Levites brought
up the Ark of the LORD along with the special tent*
and all the sacred items that had been in it. 5 There,
before the Ark, King Solomon and the entire community of Israel sacrificed so many sheep, goats, and
cattle that no one could keep count!
6 Then the priests carried the Ark of the LORD's
Covenant into the inner sanctuary of the Temple—
the Most Holy Place—and placed it beneath the
wings of the cherubim. 7 The cherubim spread their

8:2 Hebrew *at the festival in the month Ethanim, which is the seventh month.* The Festival of Shelters began on the fifteenth day of the seventh month of the ancient Hebrew lunar calendar. This day occurred in late September, October, or early November. **8:4** Hebrew *the Tent of Meeting;* i.e., the tent mentioned in 2 Sam 6:17 and 1 Chr 16:1.

KING JAMES VERSION

over the place of the ark, and the cherubims covered the ark and the staves thereof above.

8 And they drew out the staves, that the ends of the staves were seen out in the holy *place* before the oracle, and they were not seen without: and there they are unto this day.

9 *There was* nothing in the ark save the two tables of stone, which Moses put there at Horeb, when the LORD made *a covenant* with the children of Israel, when they came out of the land of Egypt.

10 And it came to pass, when the priests were come out of the holy *place,* that the cloud filled the house of the LORD,

11 So that the priests could not stand to minister because of the cloud: for the glory of the LORD had filled the house of the LORD.

12 Then spake Solomon, The LORD said that he would dwell in the thick darkness.

13 I have surely built thee an house to dwell in, a settled place for thee to abide in for ever.

14 And the king turned his face about, and blessed all the congregation of Israel: (and all the congregation of Israel stood;)

15 And he said, Blessed *be* the LORD God of Israel, which spake with his mouth unto David my father, and hath with his hand fulfilled *it,* saying,

16 Since the day that I brought forth my people Israel out of Egypt, I chose no city out of all the tribes of Israel to build an house, that my name might be therein; but I chose David to be over my people Israel.

17 And it was in the heart of David my father to build an house for the name of the LORD God of Israel.

18 And the LORD said unto David my father, Whereas it was in thine heart to build an house unto my name, thou didst well that it was in thine heart.

19 Nevertheless thou shalt not build the house; but thy son that shall come forth out of thy loins, he shall build the house unto my name.

20 And the LORD hath performed his word that he spake, and I am risen up in the room of David my father, and sit on the throne of Israel, as the LORD promised, and have built an house for the name of the LORD God of Israel.

21 And I have set there a place for the ark, wherein *is* the covenant of the LORD, which he made with our fathers, when he brought them out of the land of Egypt.

22 And Solomon stood before the altar of the LORD in the presence of all the congregation of Israel, and spread forth his hands toward heaven:

23 And he said, LORD God of Israel, *there is* no God like thee, in heaven above, or on earth beneath, who

NEW LIVING TRANSLATION

wings over the Ark, forming a canopy over the Ark
and its carrying poles. 8 These poles were so long that
their ends could be seen from the Temple's main
room—the Holy Place—but not from the outside.
They are still there to this day. 9 Nothing was in the
Ark except the two stone tablets that Moses had
placed in it at Mount Sinai,* where the LORD made a
covenant with the people of Israel when they left the
land of Egypt.

10 When the priests came out of the Holy Place,
a thick cloud filled the Temple of the LORD. 11 The
priests could not continue their service because of
the cloud, for the glorious presence of the LORD
filled the Temple.

Solomon Praises the LORD

12 Then Solomon prayed, "O LORD, you have said that
you would live in a thick cloud of darkness. 13 Now I
have built a glorious Temple for you, a place where
you can live forever!*"

14 Then the king turned around to the entire community of Israel standing before him and gave this
blessing: 15 "Praise the LORD, the God of Israel, who
has kept the promise he made to my father, David.
For he told my father, 16 'From the day I brought my
people Israel out of Egypt, I have never chosen a city
among any of the tribes of Israel as the place where a
Temple should be built to honor my name. But I have
chosen David to be king over my people Israel.'"

17 Then Solomon said, "My father, David, wanted
to build this Temple to honor the name of the LORD,
the God of Israel. 18 But the LORD told him, 'You
wanted to build the Temple to honor my name. Your
intention is good, 19 but you are not the one to do
it. One of your own sons will build the Temple to
honor me.'

20 "And now the LORD has fulfilled the promise he
made, for I have become king in my father's place,
and I now sit on the throne of Israel, just as the LORD
promised. I have built this Temple to honor the
name of the LORD, the God of Israel. 21 And I have prepared a place there for the Ark, which contains the
covenant that the LORD made with our ancestors
when he brought them out of Egypt."

Solomon's Prayer of Dedication

22 Then Solomon stood before the altar of the LORD in
front of the entire community of Israel. He lifted his
hands toward heaven, 23 and he prayed,

"O LORD, God of Israel, there is no God like you
in all of heaven above or on the earth below. You

8:9 Hebrew *at Horeb,* another name for Sinai. **8:13** Some Greek texts add the line *Is this not written in the Book of Jashar?*

KING JAMES VERSION

keepest covenant and mercy with thy servants that
walk before thee with all their heart:
24 Who hast kept with thy servant David my father
that thou promisedst him: thou spakest also with thy
mouth, and hast fulfilled *it* with thine hand, as *it is*
this day.
25 Therefore now, LORD God of Israel, keep with thy
servant David my father that thou promisedst him,
saying, There shall not fail thee a man in my sight to
sit on the throne of Israel; so that thy children take
heed to their way, that they walk before me as thou
hast walked before me.
26 And now, O God of Israel, let thy word, I pray
thee, be verified, which thou spakest unto thy servant David my father.
27 But will God indeed dwell on the earth? behold,
the heaven and heaven of heavens cannot contain
thee; how much less this house that I have builded?
28 Yet have thou respect unto the prayer of thy servant, and to his supplication, O LORD my God, to
hearken unto the cry and to the prayer, which thy
servant prayeth before thee today:
29 That thine eyes may be open toward this house
night and day, *even* toward the place of which thou
hast said, My name shall be there: that thou mayest
hearken unto the prayer which thy servant shall
make toward this place.
30 And hearken thou to the supplication of thy servant, and of thy people Israel, when they shall pray
toward this place: and hear thou in heaven thy dwelling place: and when thou hearest, forgive.
31 If any man trespass against his neighbour, and
an oath be laid upon him to cause him to swear, and
the oath come before thine altar in this house:
32 Then hear thou in heaven, and do, and judge thy
servants, condemning the wicked, to bring his way
upon his head; and justifying the righteous, to give
him according to his righteousness.
33 When thy people Israel be smitten down before
the enemy, because they have sinned against thee, and
shall turn again to thee, and confess thy name, and
pray, and make supplication unto thee in this house:
34 Then hear thou in heaven, and forgive the sin of
thy people Israel, and bring them again unto the land
which thou gavest unto their fathers.
35 When heaven is shut up, and there is no rain, because they have sinned against thee; if they pray toward this place, and confess thy name, and turn from
their sin, when thou afflictest them:
36 Then hear thou in heaven, and forgive the sin of
thy servants, and of thy people Israel, that thou teach
them the good way wherein they should walk, and
give rain upon thy land, which thou hast given to thy
people for an inheritance.
37 If there be in the land famine, if there be pestilence, blasting, mildew, locust, *or* if there be caterpiller;
if their enemy besiege them in the land of their cities;
whatsoever plague, whatsoever sickness *there be;*

NEW LIVING TRANSLATION

keep your covenant and show unfailing love to all
who walk before you in wholehearted devotion.
24 You have kept your promise to your servant
David, my father. You made that promise with
your own mouth, and with your own hands you
have fulfilled it today.
25 "And now, O LORD, God of Israel, carry out
the additional promise you made to your servant
David, my father. For you said to him, 'If your
descendants guard their behavior and faithfully
follow me as you have done, one of them will
always sit on the throne of Israel.' 26 Now, O God
of Israel, fulfill this promise to your servant
David, my father.
27 "But will God really live on earth? Why,
even the highest heavens cannot contain you.
How much less this Temple I have built!
28 Nevertheless, listen to my prayer and my plea,
O LORD my God. Hear the cry and the prayer that
your servant is making to you today. 29 May you
watch over this Temple night and day, this place
where you have said, 'My name will be there.' May
you always hear the prayers I make toward this
place. 30 May you hear the humble and earnest
requests from me and your people Israel when
we pray toward this place. Yes, hear us from
heaven where you live, and when you hear,
forgive.
31 "If someone wrongs another person and is
required to take an oath of innocence in front
of your altar in this Temple, 32 then hear from
heaven and judge between your servants—the
accuser and the accused. Punish the guilty as
they deserve. Acquit the innocent because of
their innocence.
33 "If your people Israel are defeated by their
enemies because they have sinned against you,
and if they turn to you and acknowledge your
name and pray to you here in this Temple,
34 then hear from heaven and forgive the sin of
your people Israel and return them to this land
you gave their ancestors.
35 "If the skies are shut up and there is no rain
because your people have sinned against you, and
if they pray toward this Temple and acknowledge
your name and turn from their sins because you
have punished them, 36 then hear from heaven
and forgive the sins of your servants, your people
Israel. Teach them to follow the right path, and
send rain on your land that you have given to your
people as their special possession.
37 "If there is a famine in the land or a
plague or crop disease or attacks of locusts or
caterpillars, or if your people's enemies are in the
land besieging their towns—whatever disaster or

KING JAMES VERSION

38 What prayer and supplication soever be *made*
by any man, *or* by all thy people Israel, which shall
know every man the plague of his own heart, and
spread forth his hands toward this house:
39 Then hear thou in heaven thy dwelling place,
and forgive, and do, and give to every man according
to his ways, whose heart thou knowest; (for thou,
even thou only, knowest the hearts of all the children
of men;)
40 That they may fear thee all the days that they live
in the land which thou gavest unto our fathers.
41 Moreover concerning a stranger, that *is* not of
thy people Israel, but cometh out of a far country for
thy name's sake;
42 (For they shall hear of thy great name, and of thy
strong hand, and of thy stretched out arm;) when he
shall come and pray toward this house;
43 Hear thou in heaven thy dwelling place, and do
according to all that the stranger calleth to thee for:
that all people of the earth may know thy name, to
fear thee, as *do* thy people Israel; and that they may
know that this house, which I have builded, is called
by thy name.
44 If thy people go out to battle against their enemy,
whithersoever thou shalt send them, and shall pray
unto the LORD toward the city which thou hast chosen,
and *toward* the house that I have built for thy name:
45 Then hear thou in heaven their prayer and their
supplication, and maintain their cause.
46 If they sin against thee, (for *there is* no man that
sinneth not,) and thou be angry with them, and deliver them to the enemy, so that they carry them away
captives unto the land of the enemy, far or near;
47 *Yet* if they shall bethink themselves in the land
whither they were carried captives, and repent, and
make supplication unto thee in the land of them that
carried them captives, saying, We have sinned, and
have done perversely, we have committed wickedness;
48 And *so* return unto thee with all their heart, and
with all their soul, in the land of their enemies, which
led them away captive, and pray unto thee toward
their land, which thou gavest unto their fathers, the
city which thou hast chosen, and the house which I
have built for thy name:
49 Then hear thou their prayer and their supplication in heaven thy dwelling place, and maintain their
cause,
50 And forgive thy people that have sinned against
thee, and all their transgressions wherein they have
transgressed against thee, and give them compassion before them who carried them captive, that they
may have compassion on them:
51 For they *be* thy people, and thine inheritance,
which thou broughtest forth out of Egypt, from the
midst of the furnace of iron:
52 That thine eyes may be open unto the supplication of thy servant, and unto the supplication of thy

NEW LIVING TRANSLATION

disease there is—38 and if your people Israel pray
about their troubles, raising their hands toward
this Temple, 39 then hear from heaven where you
live, and forgive. Give your people what their
actions deserve, for you alone know each human
heart. 40 Then they will fear you as long as they
live in the land you gave to our ancestors.
41 "In the future, foreigners who do not belong
to your people Israel will hear of you. They will
come from distant lands because of your name,
42 for they will hear of your great name and your
strong hand and your powerful arm. And when
they pray toward this Temple, 43 then hear from
heaven where you live, and grant what they ask
of you. In this way, all the people of the earth
will come to know and fear you, just as your own
people Israel do. They, too, will know that this
Temple I have built honors your name.
44 "If your people go out where you send them
to fight their enemies, and if they pray to the
LORD by turning toward this city you have chosen
and toward this Temple I have built to honor your
name, 45 then hear their prayers from heaven and
uphold their cause.
46 "If they sin against you—and who has never
sinned?—you might become angry with them
and let their enemies conquer them and take
them captive to their land far away or near.
47 But in that land of exile, they might turn to
you in repentance and pray, 'We have sinned,
done evil, and acted wickedly.' 48 If they turn to
you with their whole heart and soul in the land
of their enemies and pray toward the land you
gave to their ancestors—toward this city you
have chosen, and toward this Temple I have built
to honor your name—49 then hear their prayers
and their petition from heaven where you live,
and uphold their cause. 50 Forgive your people
who have sinned against you. Forgive all the
offenses they have committed against you. Make
their captors merciful to them, 51 for they are
your people—your special possession—whom
you brought out of the iron-smelting furnace
of Egypt.
52 "May your eyes be open to my requests and
to the requests of your people Israel. May you

KING JAMES VERSION

people Israel, to hearken unto them in all that they call for unto thee.

53 For thou didst separate them from among all the people of the earth, *to be* thine inheritance, as thou spakest by the hand of Moses thy servant, when thou broughtest our fathers out of Egypt, O Lord GOD.

54 And it was *so*, that when Solomon had made an end of praying all this prayer and supplication unto the LORD, he arose from before the altar of the LORD, from kneeling on his knees with his hands spread up to heaven.

55 And he stood, and blessed all the congregation of Israel with a loud voice, saying,

56 Blessed *be* the LORD, that hath given rest unto his people Israel, according to all that he promised: there hath not failed one word of all his good promise, which he promised by the hand of Moses his servant.

57 The LORD our God be with us, as he was with our fathers: let him not leave us, nor forsake us:

58 That he may incline our hearts unto him, to walk in all his ways, and to keep his commandments, and his statutes, and his judgments, which he commanded our fathers.

59 And let these my words, wherewith I have made supplication before the LORD, be nigh unto the LORD our God day and night, that he maintain the cause of his servant, and the cause of his people Israel at all times, as the matter shall require:

60 That all the people of the earth may know that the LORD *is* God, *and that there is* none else.

61 Let your heart therefore be perfect with the LORD our God, to walk in his statutes, and to keep his commandments, as at this day.

62 And the king, and all Israel with him, offered sacrifice before the LORD.

63 And Solomon offered a sacrifice of peace offerings, which he offered unto the LORD, two and twenty thousand oxen, and an hundred and twenty thousand sheep. So the king and all the children of Israel dedicated the house of the LORD.

64 The same day did the king hallow the middle of the court that *was* before the house of the LORD for there he offered burnt offerings, and meat offerings, and the fat of the peace offerings: because the brasen altar that *was* before the LORD *was* too little to receive the burnt offerings, and meat offerings, and the fat of the peace offerings.

65 And at that time Solomon held a feast, and all Israel with him, a great congregation, from the entering in of Hamath unto the river of Egypt, before the LORD our God, seven days and seven days, *even* fourteen days.

66 On the eighth day he sent the people away: and they blessed the king, and went unto their tents joyful and glad of heart for all the goodness that the

NEW LIVING TRANSLATION

hear and answer them whenever they cry out to you. 53 For when you brought our ancestors out of Egypt, O Sovereign LORD, you told your servant Moses that you had set Israel apart from all the nations of the earth to be your own special possession."

The Dedication of the Temple

54 When Solomon finished making these prayers and petitions to the LORD, he stood up in front of the altar of the LORD, where he had been kneeling with his hands raised toward heaven. 55 He stood and in a loud voice blessed the entire congregation of Israel:

56 "Praise the LORD who has given rest to his people Israel, just as he promised. Not one word has failed of all the wonderful promises he gave through his servant Moses. 57 May the LORD our God be with us as he was with our ancestors; may he never leave us or abandon us. 58 May he give us the desire to do his will in everything and to obey all the commands, decrees, and regulations that he gave our ancestors. 59 And may these words that I have prayed in the presence of the LORD be before him constantly, day and night, so that the LORD our God may give justice to me and to his people Israel, according to each day's needs. 60 Then people all over the earth will know that the LORD alone is God and there is no other. 61 And may you be completely faithful to the LORD our God. May you always obey his decrees and commands, just as you are doing today."

62 Then the king and all Israel with him offered sacrifices to the LORD. 63 Solomon offered to the LORD a peace offering of 22,000 cattle and 120,000 sheep and goats. And so the king and all the people of Israel dedicated the Temple of the LORD.

64 That same day the king consecrated the central area of the courtyard in front of the LORD's Temple. He offered burnt offerings, grain offerings, and the fat of peace offerings there, because the bronze altar in the LORD's presence was too small to hold all the burnt offerings, grain offerings, and the fat of the peace offerings.

65 Then Solomon and all Israel celebrated the Festival of Shelters* in the presence of the LORD our God. A large congregation had gathered from as far away as Lebo-hamath in the north and the Brook of Egypt in the south. The celebration went on for fourteen days in all—seven days for the dedication of the altar and seven days for the Festival of Shelters.* 66 After the festival was over,* Solomon sent the people home. They blessed the king and went to their homes joyful and glad because the LORD had

8:65a Hebrew *the festival;* see note on 8:2. **8:65b** Hebrew *seven days and seven days, fourteen days;* compare parallel text at 2 Chr 7:8-10. **8:66** Hebrew *On the eighth day,* probably referring to the day following the seven-day Festival of Shelters; compare parallel text at 2 Chr 7:9-10.

KING JAMES VERSION

LORD had done for David his servant, and for Israel his people.

9

1And it came to pass, when Solomon had finished the building of the house of the LORD, and the king's house, and all Solomon's desire which he was pleased to do,

2That the LORD appeared to Solomon the second time, as he had appeared unto him at Gibeon.

3And the LORD said unto him, I have heard thy prayer and thy supplication, that thou hast made before me: I have hallowed this house, which thou hast built, to put my name there for ever; and mine eyes and mine heart shall be there perpetually.

4And if thou wilt walk before me, as David thy father walked, in integrity of heart, and in uprightness, to do according to all that I have commanded thee, *and* wilt keep my statutes and my judgments:

5Then I will establish the throne of thy kingdom upon Israel for ever, as I promised to David thy father, saying, There shall not fail thee a man upon the throne of Israel.

6*But* if ye shall at all turn from following me, ye or your children, and will not keep my commandments *and* my statutes which I have set before you, but go and serve other gods, and worship them:

7Then will I cut off Israel out of the land which I have given them; and this house, which I have hallowed for my name, will I cast out of my sight; and Israel shall be a proverb and a byword among all people:

8And at this house, *which* is high, every one that passeth by it shall be astonished, and shall hiss; and they shall say, Why hath the LORD done thus unto this land, and to this house?

9And they shall answer, Because they forsook the LORD their God, who brought forth their fathers out of the land of Egypt, and have taken hold upon other gods, and have worshipped them, and served them: therefore hath the LORD brought upon them all this evil.

10And it came to pass at the end of twenty years, when Solomon had built the two houses, the house of the LORD, and the king's house,

11(*Now* Hiram the king of Tyre had furnished Solomon with cedar trees and fir trees, and with gold, according to all his desire,) that then king Solomon gave Hiram twenty cities in the land of Galilee.

12And Hiram came out from Tyre to see the cities which Solomon had given him; and they pleased him not.

13And he said, What cities *are* these which thou hast given me, my brother? And he called them the land of Cabul unto this day.

14And Hiram sent to the king sixscore talents of gold.

NEW LIVING TRANSLATION

been good to his servant David and to his people Israel.

The LORD's Response to Solomon

9

So Solomon finished building the Temple of the LORD, as well as the royal palace. He completed everything he had planned to do. 2Then the LORD appeared to Solomon a second time, as he had done before at Gibeon. 3The LORD said to him,

"I have heard your prayer and your petition. I have set this Temple apart to be holy—this place you have built where my name will be honored forever. I will always watch over it, for it is dear to my heart.

4"As for you, if you will follow me with integrity and godliness, as David your father did, obeying all my commands, decrees, and regulations, 5then I will establish the throne of your dynasty over Israel forever. For I made this promise to your father, David: 'One of your descendants will always sit on the throne of Israel.'

6"But if you or your descendants abandon me and disobey the commands and decrees I have given you, and if you serve and worship other gods, 7then I will uproot Israel from this land that I have given them. I will reject this Temple that I have made holy to honor my name. I will make Israel an object of mockery and ridicule among the nations. 8And though this Temple is impressive now, all who pass by will be appalled and will shake their heads in amazement. They will ask, 'Why did the LORD do such terrible things to this land and to this Temple?'

9"And the answer will be, 'Because his people abandoned the LORD their God, who brought their ancestors out of Egypt, and they worshiped other gods instead and bowed down to them. That is why the LORD has brought all these disasters on them.'"

Solomon's Agreement with Hiram

10It took Solomon twenty years to build the LORD's Temple and his own royal palace. At the end of that time, 11he gave twenty towns in the land of Galilee to King Hiram of Tyre. (Hiram had previously provided all the cedar and cypress timber and gold that Solomon had requested.) 12But when Hiram came from Tyre to see the towns Solomon had given him, he was not at all pleased with them. 13"What kind of towns are these, my brother?" he asked. So Hiram called that area Cabul (which means "worthless"), as it is still known today. 14Nevertheless, Hiram paid* Solomon 9,000 pounds* of gold.

9:14a Or *For Hiram had paid.* **9:14b** Hebrew *120 talents* [4,000 kilograms].

KING JAMES VERSION

15And this *is* the reason of the levy which king Solomon raised; for to build the house of the LORD, and his own house, and Millo, and the wall of Jerusalem, and Hazor, and Megiddo, and Gezer.

16*For* Pharaoh king of Egypt had gone up, and taken Gezer, and burnt it with fire, and slain the Canaanites that dwelt in the city, and given it *for* a present unto his daughter, Solomon's wife.

17And Solomon built Gezer, and Beth-horon the nether,

18And Baalath, and Tadmor in the wilderness, in the land,

19And all the cities of store that Solomon had, and cities for his chariots, and cities for his horsemen, and that which Solomon desired to build in Jerusaem, and in Lebanon, and in all the land of his dominion.

20*And* all the people *that were* left of the Amorites, Hittites, Perizzites, Hivites, and Jebusites, which *were* not of the children of Israel,

21Their children that were left after them in the land, whom the children of Israel also were not able utterly to destroy, upon those did Solomon levy a tribute of bondservice unto this day.

22But of the children of Israel did Solomon make no bondmen: but they *were* men of war, and his servants, and his princes, and his captains, and rulers of his chariots, and his horsemen.

23These *were* the chief of the officers that *were* over Solomon's work, five hundred and fifty, which bare rule over the people that wrought in the work.

24But Pharaoh's daughter came up out of the city of David unto her house which *Solomon* had built for her: then did he build Millo.

25And three times in a year did Solomon offer burnt offerings and peace offerings upon the altar which he built unto the LORD, and he burnt incense upon the altar that *was* before the LORD. So he finished the house.

26And king Solomon made a navy of ships in Ezion-geber, which *is* beside Eloth, on the shore of the Red sea, in the land of Edom.

27And Hiram sent in the navy his servants, shipmen that had knowledge of the sea, with the servants of Solomon.

28And they came to Ophir, and fetched from thence gold, four hundred and twenty talents, and brought *it* to king Solomon.

10 1And when the queen of Sheba heard of the fame of Solomon concerning the name of the LORD, she came to prove him with hard questions.

NEW LIVING TRANSLATION

Solomon's Many Achievements

15This is the account of the forced labor that King Solomon conscripted to build the LORD's Temple, the royal palace, the supporting terraces,* the wall of Jerusalem, and the cities of Hazor, Megiddo, and Gezer. 16(Pharaoh, the king of Egypt, had attacked and captured Gezer, killing the Canaanite population and burning it down. He gave the city to his daughter as a wedding gift when she married Solomon. 17So Solomon rebuilt the city of Gezer.) He also built up the towns of Lower Beth-horon, 18Baalath, and Tamar* in the wilderness within his land. 19He built towns as supply centers and constructed towns where his chariots and horses* could be stationed. He built everything he desired in Jerusalem and Lebanon and throughout his entire realm.

20There were still some people living in the land who were not Israelites, including Amorites, Hittites, Perizzites, Hivites, and Jebusites. 21These were descendants of the nations whom the people of Israel had not completely destroyed.* So Solomon conscripted them for his labor force, and they serve in the labor force to this day. 22But Solomon did not conscript any of the Israelites for forced labor. Instead, he assigned them to serve as fighting men, government officials, officers and captains in his army, commanders of his chariots, and charioteers. 23Solomon appointed 550 of them to supervise the people working on his various projects.

24Solomon moved his wife, Pharaoh's daughter, from the City of David to the new palace he had built for her. Then he constructed the supporting terraces.

25Three times each year Solomon presented burnt offerings and peace offerings on the altar he had built for the LORD. He also burned incense to the LORD. And so he finished the work of building the Temple.

26King Solomon also built a fleet of ships at Ezion-geber, a port near Elath* in the land of Edom, along the shore of the Red Sea.* 27Hiram sent experienced crews of sailors to sail the ships with Solomon's men. 28They sailed to Ophir and brought back to Solomon some sixteen tons* of gold.

Visit of the Queen of Sheba

10 When the queen of Sheba heard of Solomon's fame, which brought honor to the name of the LORD,* she came to test him with hard

9:15 Hebrew *the millo;* also in 9:24. The meaning of the Hebrew is uncertain. **9:18** An alternate reading in the Masoretic Text reads *Tadmor.* **9:19** Or *and charioteers.* **9:21** The Hebrew term used here refers to the complete consecration of things or people to the LORD, either by destroying them or by giving them as an offering. **9:26a** As in Greek version (see also 2 Kgs 14:22; 16:6); Hebrew reads *Eloth,* a variant spelling of Elath. **9:26b** Hebrew *sea of reeds.* **9:28** Hebrew *420 talents* [14 metric tons]. **10:1** Or *which was due to the name of the LORD.* The meaning of the Hebrew is uncertain.

KING JAMES VERSION

[2]And she came to Jerusalem with a very great train, with camels that bare spices, and very much gold, and precious stones: and when she was come to Solomon, she communed with him of all that was in her heart.

[3]And Solomon told her all her questions: there was not *any* thing hid from the king, which he told her not.

[4]And when the queen of Sheba had seen all Solomon's wisdom, and the house that he had built,

[5]And the meat of his table, and the sitting of his servants, and the attendance of his ministers, and their apparel, and his cupbearers, and his ascent by which he went up unto the house of the LORD; there was no more spirit in her.

[6]And she said to the king, It was a true report that I heard in mine own land of thy acts and of thy wisdom.

[7]Howbeit I believed not the words, until I came, and mine eyes had seen *it:* and, behold, the half was not told me: thy wisdom and prosperity exceedeth the fame which I heard.

[8]Happy *are* thy men, happy *are* these thy servants, which stand continually before thee, *and* that hear thy wisdom.

[9]Blessed be the LORD thy God, which delighted in thee, to set thee on the throne of Israel: because the LORD loved Israel for ever, therefore made he thee king, to do judgment and justice.

[10]And she gave the king an hundred and twenty talents of gold, and of spices very great store, and precious stones: there came no more such abundance of spices as these which the queen of Sheba gave to king Solomon.

[11]And the navy also of Hiram, that brought gold from Ophir, brought in from Ophir great plenty of almug trees, and precious stones.

[12]And the king made of the almug trees pillars for the house of the LORD, and for the king's house, harps also and psalteries for singers: there came no such almug trees, nor were seen unto this day.

[13]And king Solomon gave unto the queen of Sheba all her desire, whatsoever she asked, beside *that* which Solomon gave her of his royal bounty. So she turned and went to her own country, she and her servants.

[14]Now the weight of gold that came to Solomon in one year was six hundred threescore and six talents of gold,

[15]Beside *that he had* of the merchantmen, and of the traffick of the spice merchants, and of all the kings of Arabia, and of the governors of the country.

[16]And king Solomon made two hundred targets *of* beaten gold: six hundred *shekels* of gold went to one target.

[17]And *he made* three hundred shields *of* beaten gold; three pound of gold went to one shield: and the king put them in the house of the forest of Lebanon.

NEW LIVING TRANSLATION

questions. [2]She arrived in Jerusalem with a large group of attendants and a great caravan of camels loaded with spices, large quantities of gold, and precious jewels. When she met with Solomon, she talked with him about everything she had on her mind. [3]Solomon had answers for all her questions; nothing was too hard for the king to explain to her. [4]When the queen of Sheba realized how very wise Solomon was, and when she saw the palace he had built, [5]she was overwhelmed. She was also amazed at the food on his tables, the organization of his officials and their splendid clothing, the cup-bearers, and the burnt offerings Solomon made at the Temple of the LORD.

[6]She exclaimed to the king, "Everything I heard in my country about your achievements* and wisdom is true! [7]I didn't believe what was said until I arrived here and saw it with my own eyes. In fact, I had not heard the half of it! Your wisdom and prosperity are far beyond what I was told. [8]How happy your people* must be! What a privilege for your officials to stand here day after day, listening to your wisdom! [9]Praise the LORD your God, who delights in you and has placed you on the throne of Israel. Because of the LORD's eternal love for Israel, he has made you king so you can rule with justice and righteousness."

[10]Then she gave the king a gift of 9,000 pounds* of gold, great quantities of spices, and precious jewels. Never again were so many spices brought in as those the queen of Sheba gave to King Solomon.

[11](In addition, Hiram's ships brought gold from Ophir, and they also brought rich cargoes of red sandalwood* and precious jewels. [12]The king used the sandalwood to make railings for the Temple of the LORD and the royal palace, and to construct lyres and harps for the musicians. Never before or since has there been such a supply of sandalwood.)

[13]King Solomon gave the queen of Sheba whatever she asked for, besides all the customary gifts he had so generously given. Then she and all her attendants returned to their own land.

Solomon's Wealth and Splendor

[14]Each year Solomon received about 25 tons* of gold. [15]This did not include the additional revenue he received from merchants and traders, all the kings of Arabia, and the governors of the land.

[16]King Solomon made 200 large shields of hammered gold, each weighing more than fifteen pounds.* [17]He also made 300 smaller shields of hammered gold, each weighing nearly four pounds.* The king placed these shields in the Palace of the Forest of Lebanon.

10:6 Hebrew *your words.* **10:8** Greek and Syriac versions and Latin Vulgate read *your wives.* **10:10** Hebrew *120 talents* [4,000 kilograms]. **10:11** Hebrew *almug wood;* also in 10:12. **10:14** Hebrew *666 talents* [23 metric tons]. **10:16** Hebrew *600 [shekels]* of gold [6.8 kilograms]. **10:17** Hebrew *3 minas* [1.8 kilograms].

KING JAMES VERSION

18Moreover the king made a great throne of ivory,
and overlaid it with the best gold.
19The throne had six steps, and the top of the
throne *was* round behind: and *there were* stays on
either side on the place of the seat, and two lions
stood beside the stays.
20And twelve lions stood there on the one side and
on the other upon the six steps: there was not the like
made in any kingdom.
21And all king Solomon's drinking vessels *were of*
gold, and all the vessels of the house of the forest of
Lebanon *were of* pure gold; none *were of* silver: it
was nothing accounted of in the days of Solomon.
22For the king had at sea a navy of Tarshish with
the navy of Hiram: once in three years came the navy
of Tarshish, bringing gold, and silver, ivory, and apes,
and peacocks.
23So king Solomon exceeded all the kings of the
earth for riches and for wisdom.
24And all the earth sought to Solomon, to hear his
wisdom, which God had put in his heart.
25And they brought every man his present, vessels
of silver, and vessels of gold, and garments, and armour, and spices, horses, and mules, a rate year by
year.
26And Solomon gathered together chariots and
horsemen: and he had a thousand and four hundred
chariots, and twelve thousand horsemen, whom he
bestowed in the cities for chariots, and with the king
at Jerusalem.
27And the king made silver *to be* in Jerusalem as
stones, and cedars made he *to be* as the sycamore
trees that *are* in the vale, for abundance.
28And Solomon had horses brought out of Egypt,
and linen yarn: the king's merchants received the
linen yarn at a price.
29And a chariot came up and went out of Egypt for
six hundred *shekels* of silver, and an horse for an
hundred and fifty: and so for all the kings of the Hittites, and for the kings of Syria, did they bring *them*
out by their means.

11 1But king Solomon loved many strange wom-
en, together with the daughter of Pharaoh,
women of the Moabites, Ammonites, Edomites,
Zidonians, *and* Hittites;
2Of the nations *concerning* which the LORD said
unto the children of Israel, Ye shall not go in to them,
neither shall they come in unto you: *for* surely they
will turn away your heart after their gods: Solomon
clave unto these in love.
3And he had seven hundred wives, princesses, and
three hundred concubines: and his wives turned
away his heart.
4For it came to pass, when Solomon was old, *that*
his wives turned away his heart after other gods: and
his heart was not perfect with the LORD his God, as
was the heart of David his father.

NEW LIVING TRANSLATION

18Then the king made a huge throne, decorated
with ivory and overlaid with fine gold. 19The throne
had six steps and a rounded back. There were armrests on both sides of the seat, and the figure of a lion
stood on each side of the throne. 20There were also
twelve other lions, one standing on each end of the
six steps. No other throne in all the world could be
compared with it!
21All of King Solomon's drinking cups were solid
gold, as were all the utensils in the Palace of the Forest of Lebanon. They were not made of silver, for
silver was considered worthless in Solomon's day!
22The king had a fleet of trading ships* that sailed
with Hiram's fleet. Once every three years the ships
returned, loaded with gold, silver, ivory, apes, and
peacocks.*
23So King Solomon became richer and wiser than
any other king on earth. 24People from every nation
came to consult him and to hear the wisdom God
had given him. 25Year after year everyone who visited brought him gifts of silver and gold, clothing,
weapons, spices, horses, and mules.
26Solomon built up a huge force of chariots and
horses.* He had 1,400 chariots and 12,000 horses.
He stationed some of them in the chariot cities and
some near him in Jerusalem. 27The king made silver
as plentiful in Jerusalem as stone. And valuable cedar timber was as common as the sycamore-fig trees
that grow in the foothills of Judah.* 28Solomon's
horses were imported from Egypt* and from Cilicia*; the king's traders acquired them from Cilicia at
the standard price. 29At that time chariots from
Egypt could be purchased for 600 pieces of silver,*
and horses for 150 pieces of silver.* They were then
exported to the kings of the Hittites and the kings
of Aram.

Solomon's Many Wives

11 Now King Solomon loved many foreign wom-
en. Besides Pharaoh's daughter, he married
women from Moab, Ammon, Edom, Sidon, and from
among the Hittites. 2The LORD had clearly instructed
the people of Israel, 'You must not marry them, because they will turn your hearts to their gods.' Yet Solomon insisted on loving them anyway. 3He had
700 wives of royal birth and 300 concubines. And
in fact, they did turn his heart away from the LORD.
4In Solomon's old age, they turned his heart to
worship other gods instead of being completely
faithful to the LORD his God, as his father, David, had

10:22a Hebrew *fleet of ships of Tarshish.* **10:22b** Or *and baboons.*
10:26 Or *charioteers;* also in 10:26b. **10:27** Hebrew *the Shephelah.*
10:28a Possibly *Muzur,* a district near Cilicia; also in 10:29.
10:28b Hebrew *Kue,* probably another name for Cilicia. **10:29a** Hebrew *600 [shekels] of silver,* about 15 pounds or 6.8 kilograms in weight.
10:29b Hebrew *150 [shekels],* about 3.8 pounds or 1.7 kilograms in weight.

KING JAMES VERSION

5 For Solomon went after Ashtoreth the goddess of the Zidonians, and after Milcom the abomination of the Ammonites.

6 And Solomon did evil in the sight of the LORD, and went not fully after the LORD, as *did* David his father.

7 Then did Solomon build an high place for Chemosh, the abomination of Moab, in the hill that *is* before Jerusalem, and for Molech, the abomination of the children of Ammon.

8 And likewise did he for all his strange wives, which burnt incense and sacrificed unto their gods.

9 And the LORD was angry with Solomon, because his heart was turned from the LORD God of Israel, which had appeared unto him twice,

10 And had commanded him concerning this thing, that he should not go after other gods: but he kept not that which the LORD commanded.

11 Wherefore the LORD said unto Solomon, Forasmuch as this is done of thee, and thou hast not kept my covenant and my statutes, which I have commanded thee, I will surely rend the kingdom from thee, and will give it to thy servant.

12 Notwithstanding in thy days I will not do it for David thy father's sake: *but* I will rend it out of the hand of thy son.

13 Howbeit I will not rend away all the kingdom; *but* will give one tribe to thy son for David my servant's sake, and for Jerusalem's sake which I have chosen.

14 And the LORD stirred up an adversary unto Solomon, Hadad the Edomite: he *was* of the king's seed in Edom.

15 For it came to pass, when David was in Edom, and Joab the captain of the host was gone up to bury the slain, after he had smitten every male in Edom;

16 (For six months did Joab remain there with all Israel, until he had cut off every male in Edom:)

17 That Hadad fled, he and certain Edomites of his father's servants with him, to go into Egypt; Hadad *being* yet a little child.

18 And they arose out of Midian, and came to Paran: and they took men with them out of Paran, and they came to Egypt, unto Pharaoh king of Egypt; which gave him an house, and appointed him victuals, and gave him land.

19 And Hadad found great favour in the sight of Pharaoh, so that he gave him to wife the sister of his own wife, the sister of Tahpenes the queen.

20 And the sister of Tahpenes bare him Genubath his son, whom Tahpenes weaned in Pharaoh's house: and Genubath was in Pharaoh's household among the sons of Pharaoh.

21 And when Hadad heard in Egypt that David slept with his fathers, and that Joab the captain of the host was dead, Hadad said to Pharaoh, Let me depart, that I may go to mine own country.

NEW LIVING TRANSLATION

been. 5 Solomon worshiped Ashtoreth, the goddess
of the Sidonians, and Molech,* the detestable god of
the Ammonites. 6 In this way, Solomon did what was
evil in the LORD's sight; he refused to follow the LORD
completely, as his father, David, had done.
7 On the Mount of Olives, east of Jerusalem,* he
even built a pagan shrine for Chemosh, the detestable god of Moab, and another for Molech, the detestable god of the Ammonites. 8 Solomon built such
shrines for all his foreign wives to use for burning
incense and sacrificing to their gods.
9 The LORD was very angry with Solomon, for his
heart had turned away from the LORD, the God of
Israel, who had appeared to him twice. 10 He had
warned Solomon specifically about worshiping
other gods, but Solomon did not listen to the LORD's
command. 11 So now the LORD said to him, "Since you
have not kept my covenant and have disobeyed my
decrees, I will surely tear the kingdom away from you
and give it to one of your servants. 12 But for the sake
of your father, David, I will not do this while you are
still alive. I will take the kingdom away from your
son. 13 And even so, I will not take away the entire
kingdom; I will let him be king of one tribe, for the
sake of my servant David and for the sake of Jerusalem, my chosen city."

Solomon's Adversaries

14 Then the LORD raised up Hadad the Edomite, a
member of Edom's royal family, to be Solomon's adversary. 15 Years before, David had defeated Edom.
Joab, his army commander, had stayed to bury some
of the Israelite soldiers who had died in battle. While
there, they killed every male in Edom. 16 Joab and the
army of Israel had stayed there for six months, killing
them.
17 But Hadad and a few of his father's royal officials
escaped and headed for Egypt. (Hadad was just a boy
at the time.) 18 They set out from Midian and went to
Paran, where others joined them. Then they traveled
to Egypt and went to Pharaoh, who gave them a home,
food, and some land. 19 Pharaoh grew very fond of Hadad, and he gave him his wife's sister in marriage—
the sister of Queen Tahpenes. 20 She bore him a son
named Genubath. Tahpenes raised him* in Pharaoh's
palace among Pharaoh's own sons.
21 When the news reached Hadad in Egypt that
David and his commander Joab were both dead, he
said to Pharaoh, "Let me return to my own country."

11:5 Hebrew *Milcom,* a variant spelling of Molech; also in 11:33. **11:7** Hebrew *On the mountain east of Jerusalem.* **11:20** As in Greek version; Hebrew reads *weaned him.*

KING JAMES VERSION

22 Then Pharaoh said unto him, But what hast thou
lacked with me, that, behold, thou seekest to go to
thine own country? And he answered, Nothing:
howbeit let me go in any wise.

23 And God stirred him up *another* adversary, Rezon the son of Eliadah, which fled from his lord
Hadadezer king of Zobah:

24 And he gathered men unto him, and became
captain over a band, when David slew them *of Zobah:*
and they went to Damascus, and dwelt therein, and
reigned in Damascus.

25 And he was an adversary to Israel all the days of
Solomon, beside the mischief that Hadad *did:* and
he abhorred Israel, and reigned over Syria.

26 And Jeroboam the son of Nebat, an Ephrathite of
Zereda, Solomon's servant, whose mother's name
was Zeruah, a widow woman, even he lifted up *his*
hand against the king.

27 And this *was* the cause that he lifted up *his* hand
against the king: Solomon built Millo, *and* repaired
the breaches of the city of David his father.

28 And the man Jeroboam *was* a mighty man of valour: and Solomon seeing the young man that he was
industrious, he made him ruler over all the charge of
the house of Joseph.

29 And it came to pass at that time when Jeroboam
went out of Jerusalem, that the prophet Ahijah the
Shilonite found him in the way; and he had clad himself with a new garment; and they two *were* alone in
the field:

30 And Ahijah caught the new garment that *was* on
him, and rent it *in* twelve pieces:

31 And he said to Jeroboam, Take thee ten pieces:
for thus saith the LORD, the God of Israel, Behold, I
will rend the kingdom out of the hand of Solomon,
and will give ten tribes to thee:

32 (But he shall have one tribe for my servant
David's sake, and for Jerusalem's sake, the city which
I have chosen out of all the tribes of Israel:)

33 Because that they have forsaken me, and have
worshipped Ashtoreth the goddess of the Zidonians,
Chemosh the god of the Moabites, and Milcom the
god of the children of Ammon, and have not walked
in my ways, to do *that which is* right in mine eyes,
and *to keep* my statutes and my judgments, as *did*
David his father.

34 Howbeit I will not take the whole kingdom out of
his hand: but I will make him prince all the days of his
life for David my servant's sake, whom I chose, because he kept my commandments and my statutes:

35 But I will take the kingdom out of his son's hand,
and will give it unto thee, *even* ten tribes.

36 And unto his son will I give one tribe, that David
my servant may have a light alway before me in Jerusalem, the city which I have chosen me to put my
name there.

NEW LIVING TRANSLATION

22 "Why?" Pharaoh asked him. "What do you lack
here that makes you want to go home?"

"Nothing," he replied. "But even so, please let me
return home."

23 God also raised up Rezon son of Eliada as Solomon's adversary. Rezon had fled from his master,
King Hadadezer of Zobah, 24 and had become the
leader of a gang of rebels. After David conquered
Hadadezer, Rezon and his men fled to Damascus,
where he became king. 25 Rezon was Israel's bitter
adversary for the rest of Solomon's reign, and he
made trouble, just as Hadad did. Rezon hated Israel
intensely and continued to reign in Aram.

Jeroboam Rebels against Solomon

26 Another rebel leader was Jeroboam son of Nebat,
one of Solomon's own officials. He came from the
town of Zeredah in Ephraim, and his mother was
Zeruah, a widow.

27 This is the story behind his rebellion. Solomon
was rebuilding the supporting terraces* and repairing the walls of the city of his father, David. 28 Jeroboam was a very capable young man, and when
Solomon saw how industrious he was, he put him in
charge of the labor force from the tribes of Ephraim
and Manasseh, the descendants of Joseph.

29 One day as Jeroboam was leaving Jerusalem, the
prophet Ahijah from Shiloh met him along the way.
Ahijah was wearing a new cloak. The two of them
were alone in a field, 30 and Ahijah took hold of the
new cloak he was wearing and tore it into twelve
pieces. 31 Then he said to Jeroboam, "Take ten of
these pieces, for this is what the LORD, the God of Israel, says: 'I am about to tear the kingdom from the
hand of Solomon, and I will give ten of the tribes to
you! 32 But I will leave him one tribe for the sake of my
servant David and for the sake of Jerusalem, which I
have chosen out of all the tribes of Israel. 33 For Solomon has* abandoned me and worshiped Ashtoreth, the goddess of the Sidonians; Chemosh, the god
of Moab; and Molech, the god of the Ammonites. He
has not followed my ways and done what is pleasing
in my sight. He has not obeyed my decrees and regulations as David his father did.

34 "'But I will not take the entire kingdom from Solomon at this time. For the sake of my servant David,
the one whom I chose and who obeyed my commands and decrees, I will keep Solomon as leader for
the rest of his life. 35 But I will take the kingdom away
from his son and give ten of the tribes to you. 36 His
son will have one tribe so that the descendants of
David my servant will continue to reign, shining like
a lamp in Jerusalem, the city I have chosen to be the

11:27 Hebrew *the millo.* The meaning of the Hebrew is uncertain.
11:33 As in Greek, Syriac, and Latin Vulgate; Hebrew reads *For they have.*

KING JAMES VERSION

37And I will take thee, and thou shalt reign according to all that thy soul desireth, and shalt be king over Israel.

38And it shall be, if thou wilt hearken unto all that I command thee, and wilt walk in my ways, and do *that is* right in my sight, to keep my statutes and my commandments, as David my servant did; that I will be with thee, and build thee a sure house, as I built for David, and will give Israel unto thee.

39And I will for this afflict the seed of David, but not for ever.

40Solomon sought therefore to kill Jeroboam. And Jeroboam arose, and fled into Egypt, unto Shishak king of Egypt, and was in Egypt until the death of Solomon.

41And the rest of the acts of Solomon, and all that he did, and his wisdom, *are* they not written in the book of the acts of Solomon?

42And the time that Solomon reigned in Jerusalem over all Israel *was* forty years.

43And Solomon slept with his fathers, and was buried in the city of David his father: and Rehoboam his son reigned in his stead.

12 1And Rehoboam went to Shechem: for all Israel were come to Shechem to make him king.

2And it came to pass, when Jeroboam the son of Nebat, who was yet in Egypt, heard *of it,* (for he was fled from the presence of king Solomon, and Jeroboam dwelt in Egypt;)

3That they sent and called him. And Jeroboam and all the congregation of Israel came, and spake unto Rehoboam, saying,

4Thy father made our yoke grievous: now therefore make thou the grievous service of thy father, and his heavy yoke which he put upon us, lighter, and we will serve thee.

5And he said unto them, Depart yet *for* three days, then come again to me. And the people departed.

6And king Rehoboam consulted with the old men, that stood before Solomon his father while he yet lived, and said, How do ye advise that I may answer this people?

7And they spake unto him, saying, If thou wilt be a servant unto this people this day, and wilt serve them, and answer them, and speak good words to them, then they will be thy servants for ever.

8But he forsook the counsel of the old men, which they had given him, and consulted with the young men that were grown up with him, *and* which stood before him:

9And he said unto them, What counsel give ye that we may answer this people, who have spoken to me, saying, Make the yoke which thy father did put upon us lighter?

NEW LIVING TRANSLATION

place for my name. 37And I will place you on the throne of Israel, and you will rule over all that your heart desires. 38If you listen to what I tell you and follow my ways and do whatever I consider to be right, and if you obey my decrees and commands, as my servant David did, then I will always be with you. I will establish an enduring dynasty for you as I did for David, and I will give Israel to you. 39Because of Solomon's sin I will punish the descendants of David—though not forever.'"

40Solomon tried to kill Jeroboam, but he fled to King Shishak of Egypt and stayed there until Solomon died.

Summary of Solomon's Reign

41The rest of the events in Solomon's reign, including all his deeds and his wisdom, are recorded in *The Book of the Acts of Solomon.* 42Solomon ruled in Jerusalem over all Israel for forty years. 43When he died, he was buried in the City of David, named for his father. Then his son Rehoboam became the next king.

The Northern Tribes Revolt

12 Rehoboam went to Shechem, where all Israel had gathered to make him king. 2When Jeroboam son of Nebat heard of this, he returned from Egypt,* for he had fled to Egypt to escape from King Solomon. 3The leaders of Israel summoned him, and Jeroboam and the whole assembly of Israel went to speak with Rehoboam. 4"Your father was a hard master," they said. "Lighten the harsh labor demands and heavy taxes that your father imposed on us. Then we will be your loyal subjects."

5Rehoboam replied, "Give me three days to think this over. Then come back for my answer." So the people went away.

6Then King Rehoboam discussed the matter with the older men who had counseled his father, Solomon. "What is your advice?" he asked. "How should I answer these people?"

7The older counselors replied, "If you are willing to be a servant to these people today and give them a favorable answer, they will always be your loyal subjects."

8But Rehoboam rejected the advice of the older men and instead asked the opinion of the young men who had grown up with him and were now his advisers. 9"What is your advice?" he asked them. "How should I answer these people who want me to lighten the burdens imposed by my father?"

12:2 As in Greek version and Latin Vulgate (see also 2 Chr 10:2); Hebrew reads *he lived in Egypt.*

KING JAMES VERSION

10And the young men that were grown up with him spake unto him, saying, Thus shalt thou speak unto this people that spake unto thee, saying, Thy father made our yoke heavy, but make thou *it* lighter unto us; thus shalt thou say unto them, My little *finger* shall be thicker than my father's loins.

11And now whereas my father did lade you with a heavy yoke, I will add to your yoke: my father hath chastised you with whips, but I will chastise you with scorpions.

12So Jeroboam and all the people came to Rehoboam the third day, as the king had appointed, saying, Come to me again the third day.

13And the king answered the people roughly, and forsook the old men's counsel that they gave him;

14And spake to them after the counsel of the young men, saying, My father made your yoke heavy, and I will add to your yoke: my father *also* chastised you with whips, but I will chastise you with scorpions.

15Wherefore the king hearkened not unto the people; for the cause was from the LORD, that he might perform his saying, which the LORD spake by Ahijah the Shilonite unto Jeroboam the son of Nebat.

16So when all Israel saw that the king hearkened not unto them, the people answered the king, saying, What portion have we in David? neither *have we* inheritance in the son of Jesse: to your tents, O Israel: now see to thine own house, David. So Israel departed unto their tents.

17But *as for* the children of Israel which dwelt in the cities of Judah, Rehoboam reigned over them.

18Then king Rehoboam sent Adoram, who *was* over the tribute; and all Israel stoned him with stones, that he died. Therefore king Rehoboam made speed to get him up to his chariot, to flee to Jerusalem.

19So Israel rebelled against the house of David unto this day.

20And it came to pass, when all Israel heard that Jeroboam was come again, that they sent and called him unto the congregation, and made him king over all Israel: there was none that followed the house of David, but the tribe of Judah only.

21And when Rehoboam was come to Jerusalem, he assembled all the house of Judah, with the tribe of Benjamin, an hundred and fourscore thousand chosen men, which were warriors, to fight against the house of Israel, to bring the kingdom again to Rehoboam the son of Solomon.

22But the word of God came unto Shemaiah the man of God, saying,

23Speak unto Rehoboam, the son of Solomon, king of Judah, and unto all the house of Judah and Benjamin, and to the remnant of the people, saying,

24Thus saith the LORD, Ye shall not go up, nor fight against your brethren the children of Israel: return every man to his house; for this thing is from me. They

NEW LIVING TRANSLATION

10The young men replied, "This is what you should tell those complainers who want a lighter burden: 'My little finger is thicker than my father's waist! 11Yes, my father laid heavy burdens on you, but I'm going to make them even heavier! My father beat you with whips, but I will beat you with scorpions!'"

12Three days later Jeroboam and all the people returned to hear Rehoboam's decision, just as the king had ordered. 13But Rehoboam spoke harshly to the people, for he rejected the advice of the older counselors 14and followed the counsel of his younger advisers. He told the people, "My father laid heavy burdens on you, but I'm going to make them even heavier! My father beat you with whips, but I will beat you with scorpions!"

15So the king paid no attention to the people. This turn of events was the will of the LORD, for it fulfilled the LORD's message to Jeroboam son of Nebat through the prophet Ahijah from Shiloh.

16When all Israel realized that the king had refused to listen to them, they responded,

"Down with the dynasty of David!
  We have no interest in the son of Jesse.
Back to your homes, O Israel!
  Look out for your own house, O David!"

So the people of Israel returned home. 17But Rehoboam continued to rule over the Israelites who lived in the towns of Judah.

18King Rehoboam sent Adoniram,* who was in charge of the labor force, to restore order, but the people of Israel stoned him to death. When this news reached King Rehoboam, he quickly jumped into his chariot and fled to Jerusalem. 19And to this day the northern tribes of Israel have refused to be ruled by a descendant of David.

20When the people of Israel learned of Jeroboam's return from Egypt, they called an assembly and made him king over all Israel. So only the tribe of Judah remained loyal to the family of David.

Shemaiah's Prophecy

21When Rehoboam arrived at Jerusalem, he mobilized the men of Judah and the tribe of Benjamin—180,000 select troops—to fight against the men of Israel and to restore the kingdom to himself.

22But God said to Shemaiah, the man of God, 23"Say to Rehoboam son of Solomon, king of Judah, and to all the people of Judah and Benjamin, and to the rest of the people, 24'This is what the LORD says: Do not fight against your relatives, the Israelites. Go back home, for what has happened is my doing!'" So

12:18 As in some Greek manuscripts and Syriac version (see also 4:6; 5:14); Hebrew reads *Adoram*.

KING JAMES VERSION

hearkened therefore to the word of the LORD, and returned to depart, according to the word of the LORD.

25 Then Jeroboam built Shechem in mount Ephraim, and dwelt therein; and went out from thence, and
built Penuel.
26 And Jeroboam said in his heart, Now shall the
kingdom return to the house of David:
27 If this people go up to do sacrifice in the house
of the LORD at Jerusalem, then shall the heart of this
people turn again unto their lord, *even* unto Rehoboam king of Judah, and they shall kill me, and go again
to Rehoboam king of Judah.
28 Whereupon the king took counsel, and made
two calves *of* gold, and said unto them, It is too much
for you to go up to Jerusalem: behold thy gods, O Israel, which brought thee up out of the land of Egypt.
29 And he set the one in Bethel, and the other put
he in Dan.
30 And this thing became a sin: for the people went
to worship before the one, *even* unto Dan.
31 And he made an house of high places, and made
priests of the lowest of the people, which were not of
the sons of Levi.
32 And Jeroboam ordained a feast in the eighth
month, on the fifteenth day of the month, like unto
the feast that *is* in Judah, and he offered upon the
altar. So did he in Bethel, sacrificing unto the calves
that he had made: and he placed in Bethel the priests
of the high places which he had made.
33 So he offered upon the altar which he had made
in Bethel the fifteenth day of the eighth month, *even*
in the month which he had devised of his own heart;
and ordained a feast unto the children of Israel: and
he offered upon the altar, and burnt incense.

13 1 And, behold, there came a man of God out
of Judah by the word of the LORD unto Bethel: and Jeroboam stood by the altar to burn incense.
2 And he cried against the altar in the word of the
LORD, and said, O altar, altar, thus saith the LORD; Behold, a child shall be born unto the house of David,
Josiah by name; and upon thee shall he offer the
priests of the high places that burn incense upon
thee, and men's bones shall be burnt upon thee.
3 And he gave a sign the same day, saying, This *is*
the sign which the LORD hath spoken; Behold, the altar shall be rent, and the ashes that *are* upon it shall
be poured out.
4 And it came to pass, when king Jeroboam heard
the saying of the man of God, which had cried
against the altar in Bethel, that he put forth his hand
from the altar, saying, Lay hold on him. And his hand,
which he put forth against him, dried up, so that he
could not pull it in again to him.
5 The altar also was rent, and the ashes poured out

NEW LIVING TRANSLATION

they obeyed the message of the LORD and went
home, as the LORD had commanded.

Jeroboam Makes Gold Calves

25 Jeroboam then built up the city of Shechem in the
hill country of Ephraim, and it became his capital.
Later he went and built up the town of Peniel.*
26 Jeroboam thought to himself, "Unless I am careful, the kingdom will return to the dynasty of David.
27 When these people go to Jerusalem to offer sacrifices at the Temple of the LORD, they will again give
their allegiance to King Rehoboam of Judah. They
will kill me and make him their king instead."
28 So on the advice of his counselors, the king
made two gold calves. He said to the people,* "It is
too much trouble for you to worship in Jerusalem.
Look, Israel, these are the gods who brought you out
of Egypt!"
29 He placed these calf idols in Bethel and in Dan—
at either end of his kingdom. 30 But this became a
great sin, for the people worshiped the idols, traveling as far north as Dan to worship the one there.
31 Jeroboam also erected buildings at the pagan
shrines and ordained priests from the common people—those who were not from the priestly tribe of
Levi. 32 And Jeroboam instituted a religious festival in
Bethel, held on the fifteenth day of the eighth
month,* in imitation of the annual Festival of Shelters in Judah. There at Bethel he himself offered sacrifices to the calves he had made, and he appointed
priests for the pagan shrines he had made. 33 So on
the fifteenth day of the eighth month, a day that he
himself had designated, Jeroboam offered sacrifices
on the altar at Bethel. He instituted a religious festival for Israel, and he went up to the altar to burn
incense.

A Prophet Denounces Jeroboam

13 At the LORD's command, a man of God from
Judah went to Bethel, arriving there just as
Jeroboam was approaching the altar to burn incense.
2 Then at the LORD's command, he shouted, "O altar,
altar! This is what the LORD says: A child named Josiah will be born into the dynasty of David. On you he
will sacrifice the priests from the pagan shrines who
come here to burn incense, and human bones will be
burned on you." 3 That same day the man of God gave
a sign to prove his message. He said, "The LORD has
promised to give this sign: This altar will split apart,
and its ashes will be poured out on the ground."
4 When King Jeroboam heard the man of God
speaking against the altar at Bethel, he pointed at
him and shouted, "Seize that man!" But instantly the
king's hand became paralyzed in that position, and
he couldn't pull it back. 5 At the same time a wide

12:25 Hebrew *Penuel,* a variant spelling of Peniel. **12:28** Hebrew *to them.* **12:32** This day of the ancient Hebrew lunar calendar occurred in late October or early November, exactly one month after the annual Festival of Shelters in Judah (see Lev 23:34).

KING JAMES VERSION

from the altar, according to the sign which the man
of God had given by the word of the LORD.
6 And the king answered and said unto the man of
God, Intreat now the face of the LORD thy God, and
pray for me, that my hand may be restored me again.
And the man of God besought the LORD, and the
king's hand was restored him again, and became as *it*
was before.
7 And the king said unto the man of God, Come
home with me, and refresh thyself, and I will give
thee a reward.
8 And the man of God said unto the king, If thou
wilt give me half thine house, I will not go in with
thee, neither will I eat bread nor drink water in this
place:
9 For so was it charged me by the word of the LORD,
saying, Eat no bread, nor drink water, nor turn again
by the same way that thou camest.
10 So he went another way, and returned not by the
way that he came to Bethel.
11 Now there dwelt an old prophet in Bethel; and
his sons came and told him all the works that the
man of God had done that day in Bethel: the words
which he had spoken unto the king, them they told
also to their father.
12 And their father said unto them, What way went
he? For his sons had seen what way the man of God
went, which came from Judah.
13 And he said unto his sons, Saddle me the ass. So
they saddled him the ass: and he rode thereon,
14 And went after the man of God, and found him
sitting under an oak: and he said unto him, *Art* thou
the man of God that camest from Judah? And he
said, I *am*.
15 Then he said unto him, Come home with me,
and eat bread.
16 And he said, I may not return with thee, nor go in
with thee: neither will I eat bread nor drink water
with thee in this place:
17 For it was said to me by the word of the LORD,
Thou shalt eat no bread nor drink water there, nor
turn again to go by the way that thou camest.
18 He said unto him, I *am* a prophet also as thou
art; and an angel spake unto me by the word of the
LORD, saying, Bring him back with thee into thine
house, that he may eat bread and drink water. *But* he
lied unto him.
19 So he went back with him, and did eat bread in
his house, and drank water.
20 And it came to pass, as they sat at the table, that
the word of the LORD came unto the prophet that
brought him back:
21 And he cried unto the man of God that came
from Judah, saying, Thus saith the LORD, Forasmuch
as thou hast disobeyed the mouth of the LORD, and
hast not kept the commandment which the LORD thy
God commanded thee,
22 But camest back, and hast eaten bread and

NEW LIVING TRANSLATION

crack appeared in the altar, and the ashes poured out,
just as the man of God had predicted in his message
from the LORD.
6 The king cried out to the man of God, "Please ask
the LORD your God to restore my hand again!" So the
man of God prayed to the LORD, and the king's hand
was restored and he could move it again.
7 Then the king said to the man of God, "Come to
the palace with me and have something to eat, and I
will give you a gift."
8 But the man of God said to the king, "Even if you
gave me half of everything you own, I would not
go with you. I would not eat or drink anything in
this place. 9 For the LORD gave me this command:
'You must not eat or drink anything while you are
there, and do not return to Judah by the same way
you came.'" 10 So he left Bethel and went home another way.
11 As it happened, there was an old prophet living
in Bethel, and his sons* came home and told him
what the man of God had done in Bethel that day.
They also told their father what the man had said to
the king. 12 The old prophet asked them, "Which way
did he go?" So they showed their father* which road
the man of God had taken. 13 "Quick, saddle the donkey," the old man said. So they saddled the donkey
for him, and he mounted it.
14 Then he rode after the man of God and found
him sitting under a great tree. The old prophet asked
him, "Are you the man of God who came from
Judah?"
"Yes, I am," he replied.
15 Then he said to the man of God, "Come home
with me and eat some food."
16 "No, I cannot," he replied. "I am not allowed to
eat or drink anything here in this place. 17 For the
LORD gave me this command: 'You must not eat or
drink anything while you are there, and do not return
to Judah by the same way you came.'"
18 But the old prophet answered, "I am a prophet,
too, just as you are. And an angel gave me this command from the LORD: 'Bring him home with you so
he can have something to eat and drink.'" But the old
man was lying to him. 19 So they went back together,
and the man of God ate and drank at the prophet's
home.
20 Then while they were sitting at the table, a command from the LORD came to the old prophet. 21 He
cried out to the man of God from Judah, "This is
what the LORD says: You have defied the word of the
LORD and have disobeyed the command the LORD
your God gave you. 22 You came back to this place

13:11 As in Greek version; Hebrew reads *son.* **13:12** As in Greek version; Hebrew reads *They had seen.*

KING JAMES VERSION

drunk water in the place, of the which *the* LORD
did say to thee, Eat no bread, and drink no water;
thy carcase shall not come unto the sepulchre of thy
fathers.
23 And it came to pass, after he had eaten bread,
and after he had drunk, that he saddled for him the
ass, *to wit,* for the prophet whom he had brought
back.
24 And when he was gone, a lion met him by the
way, and slew him: and his carcase was cast in the
way, and the ass stood by it, the lion also stood by
the carcase.
25 And, behold, men passed by, and saw the carcase
cast in the way, and the lion standing by the carcase:
and they came and told *it* in the city where the old
prophet dwelt.
26 And when the prophet that brought him back
from the way heard *thereof,* he said, It *is* the man of
God, who was disobedient unto the word of the LORD:
therefore the LORD hath delivered him unto the lion,
which hath torn him, and slain him, according to the
word of the LORD, which he spake unto him.
27 And he spake to his sons, saying, Saddle me the
ass. And they saddled *him.*
28 And he went and found his carcase cast in the
way, and the ass and the lion standing by the carcase:
the lion had not eaten the carcase, nor torn the ass.
29 And the prophet took up the carcase of the man
of God, and laid it upon the ass, and brought it back:
and the old prophet came to the city, to mourn and to
bury him.
30 And he laid his carcase in his own grave; and
they mourned over him, *saying,* Alas, my brother!
31 And it came to pass, after he had buried him,
that he spake to his sons, saying, When I am dead,
then bury me in the sepulchre wherein the man of
God *is* buried; lay my bones beside his bones:
32 For the saying which he cried by the word of the
LORD against the altar in Bethel, and against all the
houses of the high places which *are* in the cities of
Samaria, shall surely come to pass.
33 After this thing Jeroboam returned not from his
evil way, but made again of the lowest of the people
priests of the high places: whosoever would, he consecrated him, and he became *one* of the priests of
the high places.
34 And this thing became sin unto the house of
Jeroboam, even to cut *it* off, and to destroy *it* from
off the face of the earth.

14 1 At that time Abijah the son of Jeroboam fell
sick.
2 And Jeroboam said to his wife, Arise, I pray thee,
and disguise thyself, that thou be not known to be
the wife of Jeroboam; and get thee to Shiloh: behold,
there *is* Ahijah the prophet, which told me that *I*
should be king over this people.

NEW LIVING TRANSLATION

and ate and drank where he told you not to eat or
drink. Because of this, your body will not be buried
in the grave of your ancestors."
23 After the man of God had finished eating and
drinking, the old prophet saddled his own donkey
for him, 24 and the man of God started off again. But
as he was traveling along, a lion came out and killed
him. His body lay there on the road, with the donkey
and the lion standing beside it. 25 People who passed
by saw the body lying in the road and the lion standing beside it, and they went and reported it in Bethel,
where the old prophet lived.
26 When the prophet heard the report, he said, "It
is the man of God who disobeyed the LORD's command. The LORD has fulfilled his word by causing the
lion to attack and kill him."
27 Then the prophet said to his sons, "Saddle a
donkey for me." So they saddled a donkey, 28 and he
went out and found the body lying in the road. The
donkey and lion were still standing there beside it,
for the lion had not eaten the body nor attacked the
donkey. 29 So the prophet laid the body of the man of
God on the donkey and took it back to the town to
mourn over him and bury him. 30 He laid the body in
his own grave, crying out in grief, "Oh, my brother!"
31 Afterward the prophet said to his sons, "When
I die, bury me in the grave where the man of God
is buried. Lay my bones beside his bones. 32 For the
message the LORD told him to proclaim against
the altar in Bethel and against the pagan shrines in
the towns of Samaria will certainly come true."
33 But even after this, Jeroboam did not turn from
his evil ways. He continued to choose priests from
the common people. He appointed anyone who
wanted to become a priest for the pagan shrines.
34 This became a great sin and resulted in the utter
destruction of Jeroboam's dynasty from the face of
the earth.

Ahijah's Prophecy against Jeroboam

14 At that time Jeroboam's son Abijah became
very sick. 2 So Jeroboam told his wife, "Disguise yourself so that no one will recognize you as my
wife. Then go to the prophet Ahijah at Shiloh—the

KING JAMES VERSION

3And take with thee ten loaves, and cracknels, and
a cruse of honey, and go to him: he shall tell thee
what shall become of the child.
4And Jeroboam's wife did so, and arose, and went
to Shiloh, and came to the house of Ahijah. But Ahijah could not see; for his eyes were set by reason of
his age.
5And the LORD said unto Ahijah, Behold, the wife
of Jeroboam cometh to ask a thing of thee for her
son; for he *is* sick: thus and thus shalt thou say unto
her: for it shall be, when she cometh in, that she shall
feign herself *to be* another *woman*.
6And it was *so*, when Ahijah heard the sound of
her feet, as she came in at the door, that he said,
Come in, thou wife of Jeroboam; why feignest thou
thyself *to be* another? for I *am* sent to thee *with*
heavy *tidings*.
7Go, tell Jeroboam, Thus saith the LORD God of Israel, Forasmuch as I exalted thee from among the
people, and made thee prince over my people Israel,
8And rent the kingdom away from the house of
David, and gave it thee: and *yet* thou hast not been as
my servant David, who kept my commandments, and
who followed me with all his heart, to do *that* only
which was right in mine eyes;
9But hast done evil above all that were before thee:
for thou hast gone and made thee other gods, and
molten images, to provoke me to anger, and hast cast
me behind thy back:
10Therefore, behold, I will bring evil upon the
house of Jeroboam, and will cut off from Jeroboam
him that pisseth against the wall, *and* him that is
shut up and left in Israel, and will take away the remnant of the house of Jeroboam, as a man taketh away
dung, till it be all gone.
11Him that dieth of Jeroboam in the city shall the
dogs eat; and him that dieth in the field shall the
fowls of the air eat: for the LORD hath spoken *it*.
12Arise thou therefore, get thee to thine own
house: *and* when thy feet enter into the city, the child
shall die.
13And all Israel shall mourn for him, and bury him:
for he only of Jeroboam shall come to the grave, because in him there is found *some* good thing toward
the LORD God of Israel in the house of Jeroboam.
14Moreover the LORD shall raise him up a king
over Israel, who shall cut off the house of Jeroboam
that day: but what? even now.
15For the LORD shall smite Israel, as a reed is
shaken in the water, and he shall root up Israel out of
this good land, which he gave to their fathers, and
shall scatter them beyond the river, because they
have made their groves, provoking the LORD to anger.
16And he shall give Israel up because of the sins of
Jeroboam, who did sin, and who made Israel to sin.
17And Jeroboam's wife arose, and departed, and
came to Tirzah: *and* when she came to the threshold
of the door, the child died;

NEW LIVING TRANSLATION

man who told me I would become king. 3Take him a
gift of ten loaves of bread, some cakes, and a jar of
honey, and ask him what will happen to the boy."
4So Jeroboam's wife went to Ahijah's home at Shiloh. He was an old man now and could no longer see.
5But the LORD had told Ahijah, "Jeroboam's wife will
come here, pretending to be someone else. She will
ask you about her son, for he is very sick. Give her the
answer I give you."
6So when Ahijah heard her footsteps at the door,
he called out, "Come in, wife of Jeroboam! Why are
you pretending to be someone else?" Then he told
her, "I have bad news for you. 7Give your husband,
Jeroboam, this message from the LORD, the God of Israel: 'I promoted you from the ranks of the common
people and made you ruler over my people Israel. 8I
ripped the kingdom away from the family of David
and gave it to you. But you have not been like my servant David, who obeyed my commands and followed
me with all his heart and always did whatever I
wanted. 9You have done more evil than all who lived
before you. You have made other gods for yourself
and have made me furious with your gold calves.
And since you have turned your back on me, 10I will
bring disaster on your dynasty and will destroy every
one of your male descendants, slave and free alike,
anywhere in Israel. I will burn up your royal dynasty
as one burns up trash until it is all gone. 11The members of Jeroboam's family who die in the city will be
eaten by dogs, and those who die in the field will be
eaten by vultures. I, the LORD, have spoken.'"
12Then Ahijah said to Jeroboam's wife, "Go on
home, and when you enter the city, the child will die.
13All Israel will mourn for him and bury him. He is
the only member of your family who will have a
proper burial, for this child is the only good thing
that the LORD, the God of Israel, sees in the entire
family of Jeroboam.
14"In addition, the LORD will raise up a king over
Israel who will destroy the family of Jeroboam. This
will happen today, even now! 15Then the LORD will
shake Israel like a reed whipped about in a stream.
He will uproot the people of Israel from this good
land that he gave their ancestors and will scatter
them beyond the Euphrates River,* for they have angered the LORD with the Asherah poles they have set
up for worship. 16He will abandon Israel because Jeroboam sinned and made Israel sin along with him."
17So Jeroboam's wife returned to Tirzah, and the
child died just as she walked through the door of her

14:15 Hebrew *the river.*

KING JAMES VERSION

18 And they buried him; and all Israel mourned for
him, according to the word of the LORD, which he
spake by the hand of his servant Ahijah the prophet.
19 And the rest of the acts of Jeroboam, how he
warred, and how he reigned, behold, they *are* written
in the book of the chronicles of the kings of Israel.
20 And the days which Jeroboam reigned *were* two
and twenty years: and he slept with his fathers, and
Nadab his son reigned in his stead.

21 And Rehoboam the son of Solomon reigned in
Judah. Rehoboam *was* forty and one years old when
he began to reign, and he reigned seventeen years in
Jerusalem, the city which the LORD did choose out of
all the tribes of Israel, to put his name there. And his
mother's name *was* Naamah an Ammonitess.
22 And Judah did evil in the sight of the LORD, and
they provoked him to jealousy with their sins which
they had committed, above all that their fathers
had done.
23 For they also built them high places, and images,
and groves, on every high hill, and under every green
tree.
24 And there were also sodomites in the land: *and*
they did according to all the abominations of the
nations which the LORD cast out before the children
of Israel.
25 And it came to pass in the fifth year of king Rehoboam, *that* Shishak king of Egypt came up against
Jerusalem:
26 And he took away the treasures of the house of
the LORD, and the treasures of the king's house; he
even took away all: and he took away all the shields of
gold which Solomon had made.
27 And king Rehoboam made in their stead brasen
shields, and committed *them* unto the hands of the
chief of the guard, which kept the door of the king's
house.
28 And it was *so,* when the king went into the house
of the LORD, that the guard bare them, and brought
them back into the guard chamber.
29 Now the rest of the acts of Rehoboam, and all
that he did, *are* they not written in the book of the
chronicles of the kings of Judah?
30 And there was war between Rehoboam and Jeroboam all *their* days.
31 And Rehoboam slept with his fathers, and was
buried with his fathers in the city of David. And his
mother's name *was* Naamah an Ammonitess. And
Abijam his son reigned in his stead.

15 1 Now in the eighteenth year of king Jeroboam the son of Nebat reigned Abijam over
Judah.
2 Three years reigned he in Jerusalem. And his
mother's name *was* Maachah, the daughter of
Abishalom.
3 And he walked in all the sins of his father, which he

NEW LIVING TRANSLATION

home. 18 And all Israel buried him and mourned for
him, as the LORD had promised through the prophet
Ahijah.
19 The rest of the events in Jeroboam's reign, including all his wars and how he ruled, are recorded
in *The Book of the History of the Kings of Israel.* 20 Jeroboam reigned in Israel twenty-two years. When Jeroboam died, his son Nadab became the next king.

Rehoboam Rules in Judah

21 Meanwhile, Rehoboam son of Solomon was king in
Judah. He was forty-one years old when he became
king, and he reigned seventeen years in Jerusalem,
the city the LORD had chosen from among all the
tribes of Israel as the place to honor his name. Rehoboam's mother was Naamah, an Ammonite woman.
22 During Rehoboam's reign, the people of Judah
did what was evil in the LORD's sight, provoking his
anger with their sin, for it was even worse than that
of their ancestors. 23 For they also built for themselves pagan shrines and set up sacred pillars and
Asherah poles on every high hill and under every
green tree. 24 There were even male and female
shrine prostitutes throughout the land. The people
imitated the detestable practices of the pagan nations the LORD had driven from the land ahead of the
Israelites.
25 In the fifth year of King Rehoboam's reign,
King Shishak of Egypt came up and attacked Jerusalem. 26 He ransacked the treasuries of the LORD's
Temple and the royal palace; he stole everything, including all the gold shields Solomon had made.
27 King Rehoboam later replaced them with bronze
shields as substitutes, and he entrusted them to the
care of the commanders of the guard who protected
the entrance to the royal palace. 28 Whenever the
king went to the Temple of the LORD, the guards
would also take the shields and then return them to
the guardroom.
29 The rest of the events in Rehoboam's reign and
everything he did are recorded in *The Book of the
History of the Kings of Judah.* 30 There was constant
war between Rehoboam and Jeroboam. 31 When
Rehoboam died, he was buried among his ancestors
in the City of David. His mother was Naamah, an
Ammonite woman. Then his son Abijam* became
the next king.

Abijam Rules in Judah

15 Abijam* began to rule over Judah in the eighteenth year of Jeroboam's reign in Israel. 2 He
reigned in Jerusalem three years. His mother was
Maacah, the daughter of Absalom.*
3 He committed the same sins as his father before

14:31 Also known as *Abijah.* **15:1** Also known as *Abijah.* **15:2** Hebrew *Abishalom* (also in 15:10), a variant spelling of Absalom; compare 2 Chr 11:20.

KING JAMES VERSION

had done before him: and his heart was not perfect with the LORD his God, as the heart of David his father.

4 Nevertheless for David's sake did the LORD his God give him a lamp in Jerusalem, to set up his son after him, and to establish Jerusalem:

5 Because David did *that which was* right in the eyes of the LORD, and turned not aside from any *thing* that he commanded him all the days of his life, save only in the matter of Uriah the Hittite.

6 And there was war between Rehoboam and Jeroboam all the days of his life.

7 Now the rest of the acts of Abijam, and all that he did, *are* they not written in the book of the chronicles of the kings of Judah? And there was war between Abijam and Jeroboam.

8 And Abijam slept with his fathers; and they buried him in the city of David: and Asa his son reigned in his stead.

9 And in the twentieth year of Jeroboam king of Israel reigned Asa over Judah.

10 And forty and one years reigned he in Jerusalem. And his mother's name *was* Maachah, the daughter of Abishalom.

11 And Asa did *that which was* right in the eyes of the LORD, as *did* David his father.

12 And he took away the sodomites out of the land, and removed all the idols that his fathers had made.

13 And also Maachah his mother, even her he removed from *being* queen, because she had made an idol in a grove; and Asa destroyed her idol, and burnt *it* by the brook Kidron.

14 But the high places were not removed: nevertheless Asa's heart was perfect with the LORD all his days.

15 And he brought in the things which his father had dedicated, and the things which himself had dedicated, into the house of the LORD, silver, and gold, and vessels.

16 And there was war between Asa and Baasha king of Israel all their days.

17 And Baasha king of Israel went up against Judah, and built Ramah, that he might not suffer any to go out or come in to Asa king of Judah.

18 Then Asa took all the silver and the gold *that were* left in the treasures of the house of the LORD, and the treasures of the king's house, and delivered them into the hand of his servants: and king Asa sent them to Ben-hadad, the son of Tabrimon, the son of Hezion, king of Syria, that dwelt at Damascus, saying,

19 *There is* a league between me and thee, *and* between my father and thy father: behold, I have sent unto thee a present of silver and gold; come and break thy league with Baasha king of Israel, that he may depart from me.

20 So Ben-hadad hearkened unto king Asa, and sent the captains of the hosts which he had against the cities of Israel, and smote Ijon, and Dan, and

NEW LIVING TRANSLATION

him, and he was not faithful to the LORD his God, as his ancestor David had been. 4 But for David's sake, the LORD his God allowed his descendants to continue ruling, shining like a lamp, and he gave Abijam a son to rule after him in Jerusalem. 5 For David had done what was pleasing in the LORD's sight and had obeyed the LORD's commands throughout his life, except in the affair concerning Uriah the Hittite.

6 There was war between Abijam and Jeroboam* throughout Abijam's reign. 7 The rest of the events in Abijam's reign and everything he did are recorded in *The Book of the History of the Kings of Judah.* There was constant war between Abijam and Jeroboam. 8 When Abijam died, he was buried in the City of David. Then his son Asa became the next king.

Asa Rules in Judah

9 Asa began to rule over Judah in the twentieth year of Jeroboam's reign in Israel. 10 He reigned in Jerusalem forty-one years. His grandmother* was Maacah, the daughter of Absalom.

11 Asa did what was pleasing in the LORD's sight, as his ancestor David had done. 12 He banished the male and female shrine prostitutes from the land and got rid of all the idols* his ancestors had made. 13 He even deposed his grandmother Maacah from her position as queen mother because she had made an obscene Asherah pole. He cut down her obscene pole and burned it in the Kidron Valley. 14 Although the pagan shrines were not removed, Asa's heart remained completely faithful to the LORD throughout his life. 15 He brought into the Temple of the LORD the silver and gold and the various items that he and his father had dedicated.

16 There was constant war between King Asa of Judah and King Baasha of Israel. 17 King Baasha of Israel invaded Judah and fortified Ramah in order to prevent anyone from entering or leaving King Asa's territory in Judah.

18 Asa responded by removing all the silver and gold that was left in the treasuries of the Temple of the LORD and the royal palace. He sent it with some of his officials to Ben-hadad son of Tabrimmon, son of Hezion, the king of Aram, who was ruling in Damascus, along with this message:

> 19 "Let there be a treaty* between you and me like the one between your father and my father. See, I am sending you a gift of silver and gold. Break your treaty with King Baasha of Israel so that he will leave me alone."

20 Ben-hadad agreed to King Asa's request and sent the commanders of his army to attack the towns of

15:6 As in a few Hebrew and Greek manuscripts; most Hebrew manuscripts read *between Rehoboam and Jeroboam.* **15:10** Or *The queen mother;* Hebrew reads *His mother* (also in 15:13); compare 15:2. **15:12** The Hebrew term (literally *round things*) probably alludes to dung. **15:19** As in Greek version; Hebrew reads *There is a treaty.*

KING JAMES VERSION

Abel-beth-maachah, and all Cinneroth, with all the
land of Naphtali.
21 And it came to pass, when Baasha heard *thereof,*
that he left off building of Ramah, and dwelt in Tirzah.
22 Then king Asa made a proclamation throughout
all Judah; none *was* exempted: and they took away
the stones of Ramah, and the timber thereof, wherewith Baasha had builded; and king Asa built with
them Geba of Benjamin, and Mizpah.
23 The rest of all the acts of Asa, and all his might,
and all that he did, and the cities which he built, *are*
they not written in the book of the chronicles of the
kings of Judah? Nevertheless in the time of his old
age he was diseased in his feet.
24 And Asa slept with his fathers, and was buried
with his fathers in the city of David his father: and
Jehoshaphat his son reigned in his stead.

25 And Nadab the son of Jeroboam began to reign
over Israel in the second year of Asa king of Judah,
and reigned over Israel two years.
26 And he did evil in the sight of the LORD, and
walked in the way of his father, and in his sin wherewith he made Israel to sin.
27 And Baasha the son of Ahijah, of the house of
Issachar, conspired against him; and Baasha smote
him at Gibbethon, which *belonged* to the Philistines;
for Nadab and all Israel laid siege to Gibbethon.
28 Even in the third year of Asa king of Judah did
Baasha slay him, and reigned in his stead.
29 And it came to pass, when he reigned, *that* he
smote all the house of Jeroboam; he left not to Jeroboam any that breathed, until he had destroyed him,
according unto the saying of the LORD, which he
spake by his servant Ahijah the Shilonite:
30 Because of the sins of Jeroboam which he
sinned, and which he made Israel sin, by his provocation wherewith he provoked the LORD God of Israel
to anger.
31 Now the rest of the acts of Nadab, and all that he
did, *are* they not written in the book of the chronicles of the kings of Israel?
32 And there was war between Asa and Baasha king
of Israel all their days.
33 In the third year of Asa king of Judah began Baasha the son of Ahijah to reign over all Israel in Tirzah,
twenty and four years.
34 And he did evil in the sight of the LORD, and
walked in the way of Jeroboam, and in his sin wherewith he made Israel to sin.

16 1 Then the word of the LORD came to Jehu the
son of Hanani against Baasha, saying,
2 Forasmuch as I exalted thee out of the dust, and
made thee prince over my people Israel; and thou
hast walked in the way of Jeroboam, and hast made

NEW LIVING TRANSLATION

Israel. They conquered the towns of Ijon, Dan, Abel-
beth-maacah, and all Kinnereth, and all the land of
Naphtali. 21 As soon as Baasha of Israel heard what
was happening, he abandoned his project of fortifying Ramah and withdrew to Tirzah. 22 Then King
Asa sent an order throughout Judah, requiring that
everyone, without exception, help to carry away the
building stones and timbers that Baasha had been
using to fortify Ramah. Asa used these materials to
fortify the town of Geba in Benjamin and the town
of Mizpah.
23 The rest of the events in Asa's reign—the extent
of his power, everything he did, and the names of the
cities he built—are recorded in *The Book of the History of the Kings of Judah.* In his old age his feet became diseased. 24 When Asa died, he was buried with
his ancestors in the City of David.
Then Jehoshaphat, Asa's son, became the next king.

Nadab Rules in Israel

25 Nadab son of Jeroboam began to rule over Israel in
the second year of King Asa's reign in Judah. He
reigned in Israel two years. 26 But he did what was evil
in the LORD's sight and followed the example of his
father, continuing the sins that Jeroboam had led
Israel to commit.
27 Then Baasha son of Ahijah, from the tribe of Issachar, plotted against Nadab and assassinated him
while he and the Israelite army were laying siege to
the Philistine town of Gibbethon. 28 Baasha killed
Nadab in the third year of King Asa's reign in Judah,
and he became the next king of Israel.
29 He immediately slaughtered all the descendants
of King Jeroboam, so that not one of the royal family
was left, just as the LORD had promised concerning
Jeroboam by the prophet Ahijah from Shiloh. 30 This
was done because Jeroboam had provoked the anger
of the LORD, the God of Israel, by the sins he had committed and the sins he had led Israel to commit.
31 The rest of the events in Nadab's reign and
everything he did are recorded in *The Book of the
History of the Kings of Israel.*

Baasha Rules in Israel

32 There was constant war between King Asa of Judah
and King Baasha of Israel. 33 Baasha son of Ahijah began to rule over all Israel in the third year of King
Asa's reign in Judah. Baasha reigned in Tirzah
twenty-four years. 34 But he did what was evil in the
LORD's sight and followed the example of Jeroboam,
continuing the sins that Jeroboam had led Israel to
commit.

16 This message from the LORD was delivered
to King Baasha by the prophet Jehu son of
Hanani: 2 "I lifted you out of the dust to make you

KING JAMES VERSION

my people Israel to sin, to provoke me to anger with their sins;

3 Behold, I will take away the posterity of Baasha, and the posterity of his house; and will make thy house like the house of Jeroboam the son of Nebat.

4 Him that dieth of Baasha in the city shall the dogs eat; and him that dieth of his in the fields shall the fowls of the air eat.

5 Now the rest of the acts of Baasha, and what he did, and his might, *are* they not written in the book of the chronicles of the kings of Israel?

6 So Baasha slept with his fathers, and was buried in Tirzah: and Elah his son reigned in his stead.

7 And also by the hand of the prophet Jehu the son of Hanani came the word of the LORD against Baasha, and against his house, even for all the evil that he did in the sight of the LORD, in provoking him to anger with the work of his hands, in being like the house of Jeroboam; and because he killed him.

8 In the twenty and sixth year of Asa king of Judah began Elah the son of Baasha to reign over Israel in Tirzah, two years.

9 And his servant Zimri, captain of half *his* chariots, conspired against him, as he was in Tirzah, drinking himself drunk in the house of Arza steward of *his* house in Tirzah.

10 And Zimri went in and smote him, and killed him, in the twenty and seventh year of Asa king of Judah, and reigned in his stead.

11 And it came to pass, when he began to reign, as soon as he sat on his throne, *that* he slew all the house of Baasha: he left him not one that pisseth against a wall, neither of his kinsfolks, nor of his friends.

12 Thus did Zimri destroy all the house of Baasha, according to the word of the LORD, which he spake against Baasha by Jehu the prophet,

13 For all the sins of Baasha, and the sins of Elah his son, by which they sinned, and by which they made Israel to sin, in provoking the LORD God of Israel to anger with their vanities.

14 Now the rest of the acts of Elah, and all that he did, *are* they not written in the book of the chronicles of the kings of Israel?

15 In the twenty and seventh year of Asa king of Judah did Zimri reign seven days in Tirzah. And the people *were* encamped against Gibbethon, which *belonged* to the Philistines.

16 And the people *that were* encamped heard say, Zimri hath conspired, and hath also slain the king: wherefore all Israel made Omri, the captain of the host, king over Israel that day in the camp.

17 And Omri went up from Gibbethon, and all Israel with him, and they besieged Tirzah.

18 And it came to pass, when Zimri saw that the city was taken, that he went into the palace of the king's

NEW LIVING TRANSLATION

ruler of my people Israel, but you have followed the evil example of Jeroboam. You have provoked my anger by causing my people Israel to sin. 3 So now I will destroy you and your family, just as I destroyed the descendants of Jeroboam son of Nebat. 4 The members of Baasha's family who die in the city will be eaten by dogs, and those who die in the field will be eaten by vultures."

5 The rest of the events in Baasha's reign and the extent of his power are recorded in *The Book of the History of the Kings of Israel.* 6 When Baasha died, he was buried in Tirzah. Then his son Elah became the next king.

7 The message from the LORD against Baasha and his family came through the prophet Jehu son of Hanani. It was delivered because Baasha had done what was evil in the LORD's sight (just as the family of Jeroboam had done), and also because Baasha had destroyed the family of Jeroboam. The LORD's anger was provoked by Baasha's sins.

Elah Rules in Israel

8 Elah son of Baasha began to rule over Israel in the twenty-sixth year of King Asa's reign in Judah. He reigned in the city of Tirzah for two years.

9 Then Zimri, who commanded half of the royal chariots, made plans to kill him. One day in Tirzah, Elah was getting drunk at the home of Arza, the supervisor of the palace. 10 Zimri walked in and struck him down and killed him. This happened in the twenty-seventh year of King Asa's reign in Judah. Then Zimri became the next king.

11 Zimri immediately killed the entire royal family of Baasha, leaving him not even a single male child. He even destroyed distant relatives and friends. 12 So Zimri destroyed the dynasty of Baasha as the LORD had promised through the prophet Jehu. 13 This happened because of all the sins Baasha and his son Elah had committed, and because of the sins they led Israel to commit. They provoked the anger of the LORD, the God of Israel, with their worthless idols.

14 The rest of the events in Elah's reign and everything he did are recorded in *The Book of the History of the Kings of Israel.*

Zimri Rules in Israel

15 Zimri began to rule over Israel in the twenty-seventh year of King Asa's reign in Judah, but his reign in Tirzah lasted only seven days. The army of Israel was then attacking the Philistine town of Gibbethon. 16 When they heard that Zimri had committed treason and had assassinated the king, that very day they chose Omri, commander of the army, as the new king of Israel. 17 So Omri led the entire army of Israel up from Gibbethon to attack Tirzah, Israel's capital. 18 When Zimri saw that the city had been

KING JAMES VERSION

house, and burnt the king's house over him with fire, and died,

19 For his sins which he sinned in doing evil in the sight of the LORD, in walking in the way of Jeroboam, and in his sin which he did, to make Israel to sin.

20 Now the rest of the acts of Zimri, and his treason that he wrought, *are* they not written in the book of the chronicles of the kings of Israel?

21 Then were the people of Israel divided into two parts: half of the people followed Tibni the son of Ginath, to make him king; and half followed Omri.

22 But the people that followed Omri prevailed against the people that followed Tibni the son of Ginath: so Tibni died, and Omri reigned.

23 In the thirty and first year of Asa king of Judah began Omri to reign over Israel, twelve years: six years reigned he in Tirzah.

24 And he bought the hill Samaria of Shemer for two talents of silver, and built on the hill, and called the name of the city which he built, after the name of Shemer, owner of the hill, Samaria.

25 But Omri wrought evil in the eyes of the LORD, and did worse than all that *were* before him.

26 For he walked in all the way of Jeroboam the son of Nebat, and in his sin wherewith he made Israel to sin, to provoke the LORD God of Israel to anger with their vanities.

27 Now the rest of the acts of Omri which he did, and his might that he shewed, *are* they not written in the book of the chronicles of the kings of Israel?

28 So Omri slept with his fathers, and was buried in Samaria: and Ahab his son reigned in his stead.

29 And in the thirty and eighth year of Asa king of Judah began Ahab the son of Omri to reign over Israel: and Ahab the son of Omri reigned over Israel in Samaria twenty and two years.

30 And Ahab the son of Omri did evil in the sight of the LORD above all that *were* before him.

31 And it came to pass, as if it had been a light thing for him to walk in the sins of Jeroboam the son of Nebat, that he took to wife Jezebel the daughter of Ethbaal king of the Zidonians, and went and served Baal, and worshipped him.

32 And he reared up an altar for Baal in the house of Baal, which he had built in Samaria.

33 And Ahab made a grove; and Ahab did more to provoke the LORD God of Israel to anger than all the kings of Israel that were before him.

34 In his days did Hiel the Bethelite build Jericho: he laid the foundation thereof in Abiram his firstborn, and set up the gates thereof in his youngest *son* Segub, according to the word of the LORD, which he spake by Joshua the son of Nun.

NEW LIVING TRANSLATION

taken, he went into the citadel of the palace and burned it down over himself and died in the flames. 19 For he, too, had done what was evil in the LORD's sight. He followed the example of Jeroboam in all the sins he had committed and led Israel to commit.

20 The rest of the events in Zimri's reign and his conspiracy are recorded in *The Book of the History of the Kings of Israel.*

Omri Rules in Israel

21 But now the people of Israel were split into two factions. Half the people tried to make Tibni son of Ginath their king, while the other half supported Omri. 22 But Omri's supporters defeated the supporters of Tibni. So Tibni was killed, and Omri became the next king.

23 Omri began to rule over Israel in the thirty-first year of King Asa's reign in Judah. He reigned twelve years in all, six of them in Tirzah. 24 Then Omri bought the hill now known as Samaria from its owner, Shemer, for 150 pounds of silver.* He built a city on it and called the city Samaria in honor of Shemer.

25 But Omri did what was evil in the LORD's sight, even more than any of the kings before him. 26 He followed the example of Jeroboam son of Nebat in all the sins he had committed and led Israel to commit. The people provoked the anger of the LORD, the God of Israel, with their worthless idols.

27 The rest of the events in Omri's reign, the extent of his power, and everything he did are recorded in *The Book of the History of the Kings of Israel.* 28 When Omri died, he was buried in Samaria. Then his son Ahab became the next king.

Ahab Rules in Israel

29 Ahab son of Omri began to rule over Israel in the thirty-eighth year of King Asa's reign in Judah. He reigned in Samaria twenty-two years. 30 But Ahab son of Omri did what was evil in the LORD's sight, even more than any of the kings before him. 31 And as though it were not enough to follow the example of Jeroboam, he married Jezebel, the daughter of King Ethbaal of the Sidonians, and he began to bow down in worship of Baal. 32 First Ahab built a temple and an altar for Baal in Samaria. 33 Then he set up an Asherah pole. He did more to provoke the anger of the LORD, the God of Israel, than any of the other kings of Israel before him.

34 It was during his reign that Hiel, a man from Bethel, rebuilt Jericho. When he laid its foundations, it cost him the life of his oldest son, Abiram. And when he completed it and set up its gates, it cost him the life of his youngest son, Segub.* This all happened according to the message from the LORD concerning Jericho spoken by Joshua son of Nun.

16:24 Hebrew *for 2 talents* [68 kilograms] *of silver.* **16:34** An ancient Hebrew scribal tradition reads *He killed his oldest son when he laid its foundations, and he killed his youngest son when he set up its gates.*

KING JAMES VERSION

17 1 And Elijah the Tishbite, *who was* of the inhabitants of Gilead, said unto Ahab, *As* the LORD God of Israel liveth, before whom I stand, there shall not be dew nor rain these years, but according to my word.

2 And the word of the LORD came unto him, saying,

3 Get thee hence, and turn thee eastward, and hide thyself by the brook Cherith, that *is* before Jordan.

4 And it shall be, *that* thou shalt drink of the brook; and I have commanded the ravens to feed thee there.

5 So he went and did according unto the word of the LORD: for he went and dwelt by the brook Cherith, that *is* before Jordan.

6 And the ravens brought him bread and flesh in the morning, and bread and flesh in the evening; and he drank of the brook.

7 And it came to pass after a while, that the brook dried up, because there had been no rain in the land.

8 And the word of the LORD came unto him, saying,

9 Arise, get thee to Zarephath, which *belongeth* to Zidon, and dwell there: behold, I have commanded a widow woman there to sustain thee.

10 So he arose and went to Zarephath. And when he came to the gate of the city, behold, the widow woman *was* there gathering of sticks: and he called to her, and said, Fetch me, I pray thee, a little water in a vessel, that I may drink.

11 And as she was going to fetch *it*, he called to her, and said, Bring me, I pray thee, a morsel of bread in thine hand.

12 And she said, *As* the LORD thy God liveth, I have not a cake, but an handful of meal in a barrel, and a little oil in a cruse: and, behold, I *am* gathering two sticks, that I may go in and dress it for me and my son, that we may eat it, and die.

13 And Elijah said unto her, Fear not; go *and* do as thou hast said: but make me thereof a little cake first, and bring *it* unto me, and after make for thee and for thy son.

14 For thus saith the LORD God of Israel, The barrel of meal shall not waste, neither shall the cruse of oil fail, until the day *that* the LORD sendeth rain upon the earth.

15 And she went and did according to the saying of Elijah: and she, and he, and her house, did eat *many* days.

16 *And* the barrel of meal wasted not, neither did the cruse of oil fail, according to the word of the LORD, which he spake by Elijah.

17 And it came to pass after these things, *that* the son of the woman, the mistress of the house, fell sick; and his sickness was so sore, that there was no breath left in him.

18 And she said unto Elijah, What have I to do with thee, O thou man of God? art thou come unto me to call my sin to remembrance, and to slay my son?

19 And he said unto her, Give me thy son. And he

NEW LIVING TRANSLATION

Elijah Fed by Ravens

17 Now Elijah, who was from Tishbe in Gilead, told King Ahab, "As surely as the LORD, the God of Israel, lives—the God I serve—there will be no dew or rain during the next few years until I give the word!"

2 Then the LORD said to Elijah, 3 "Go to the east and hide by Kerith Brook, near where it enters the Jordan River. 4 Drink from the brook and eat what the ravens bring you, for I have commanded them to bring you food."

5 So Elijah did as the LORD told him and camped beside Kerith Brook, east of the Jordan. 6 The ravens brought him bread and meat each morning and evening, and he drank from the brook. 7 But after a while the brook dried up, for there was no rainfall anywhere in the land.

The Widow at Zarephath

8 Then the LORD said to Elijah, 9 "Go and live in the village of Zarephath, near the city of Sidon. I have instructed a widow there to feed you."

10 So he went to Zarephath. As he arrived at the gates of the village, he saw a widow gathering sticks, and he asked her, "Would you please bring me a little water in a cup?" 11 As she was going to get it, he called to her, "Bring me a bite of bread, too."

12 But she said, "I swear by the LORD your God that I don't have a single piece of bread in the house. And I have only a handful of flour left in the jar and a little cooking oil in the bottom of the jug. I was just gathering a few sticks to cook this last meal, and then my son and I will die."

13 But Elijah said to her, "Don't be afraid! Go ahead and do just what you've said, but make a little bread for me first. Then use what's left to prepare a meal for yourself and your son. 14 For this is what the LORD, the God of Israel, says: There will always be flour and olive oil left in your containers until the time when the LORD sends rain and the crops grow again!"

15 So she did as Elijah said, and she and Elijah and her family continued to eat for many days. 16 There was always enough flour and olive oil left in the containers, just as the LORD had promised through Elijah.

17 Some time later the woman's son became sick. He grew worse and worse, and finally he died. 18 Then she said to Elijah, "O man of God, what have you done to me? Have you come here to point out my sins and kill my son?"

19 But Elijah replied, "Give me your son." And he

took him out of her bosom, and carried him up into a
loft, where he abode, and laid him upon his own bed.
20 And he cried unto the LORD, and said, O LORD my
God, hast thou also brought evil upon the widow
with whom I sojourn, by slaying her son?
21 And he stretched himself upon the child three
times, and cried unto the LORD, and said, O LORD
my God, I pray thee, let this child's soul come into
him again.
22 And the LORD heard the voice of Elijah; and the
soul of the child came into him again, and he revived.
23 And Elijah took the child, and brought him down
out of the chamber into the house, and delivered him
unto his mother: and Elijah said, See, thy son liveth.
24 And the woman said to Elijah, Now by this I
know that thou *art* a man of God, *and* that the word
of the LORD in thy mouth *is* truth.

18 1 And it came to pass *after* many days, that
the word of the LORD came to Elijah in the
third year, saying, Go, shew thyself unto Ahab; and I
will send rain upon the earth.
2 And Elijah went to shew himself unto Ahab. And
there was a sore famine in Samaria.
3 And Ahab called Obadiah, which *was* the governor
of *his* house. (Now Obadiah feared the LORD greatly:
4 For it was *so*, when Jezebel cut off the prophets of
the LORD, that Obadiah took an hundred prophets,
and hid them by fifty in a cave, and fed them with
bread and water.)
5 And Ahab said unto Obadiah, Go into the land,
unto all fountains of water, and unto all brooks: peradventure we may find grass to save the horses and
mules alive, that we lose not all the beasts.
6 So they divided the land between them to pass
throughout it: Ahab went one way by himself, and
Obadiah went another way by himself.
7 And as Obadiah was in the way, behold, Elijah met
him: and he knew him, and fell on his face, and said,
Art thou that my lord Elijah?
8 And he answered him, I *am*: go, tell thy lord, Behold, Elijah *is here*.
9 And he said, What have I sinned, that thou
wouldest deliver thy servant into the hand of Ahab,
to slay me?
10 *As* the LORD thy God liveth, there is no nation or
kingdom, whither my lord hath not sent to seek thee:
and when they said, *He is* not *there;* he took an oath
of the kingdom and nation, that they found thee not.
11 And now thou sayest, Go, tell thy lord, Behold,
Elijah *is here*.
12 And it shall come to pass, *as soon as* I am gone
from thee, that the Spirit of the LORD shall carry thee
whither I know not; and *so* when I come and tell
Ahab, and he cannot find thee, he shall slay me: but I
thy servant fear the LORD from my youth.
13 Was it not told my lord what I did when Jezebel
slew the prophets of the LORD, how I hid an hundred

took the child's body from her arms, carried him up
the stairs to the room where he was staying, and laid
the body on his bed. 20 Then Elijah cried out to the
LORD, "O LORD my God, why have you brought tragedy to this widow who has opened her home to me,
causing her son to die?"
21 And he stretched himself out over the child
three times and cried out to the LORD, "O LORD my
God, please let this child's life return to him." 22 The
LORD heard Elijah's prayer, and the life of the child
returned, and he revived! 23 Then Elijah brought him
down from the upper room and gave him to his
mother. "Look!" he said. "Your son is alive!"
24 Then the woman told Elijah, "Now I know for
sure that you are a man of God, and that the LORD
truly speaks through you."

The Contest on Mount Carmel

18 Later on, in the third year of the drought, the
LORD said to Elijah, "Go and present yourself
to King Ahab. Tell him that I will soon send rain!" 2 So
Elijah went to appear before Ahab.
Meanwhile, the famine had become very severe in
Samaria. 3 So Ahab summoned Obadiah, who was in
charge of the palace. (Obadiah was a devoted follower of the LORD. 4 Once when Jezebel had tried to
kill all the LORD's prophets, Obadiah had hidden
100 of them in two caves. He put fifty prophets in
each cave and supplied them with food and water.)
5 Ahab said to Obadiah, "We must check every spring
and valley in the land to see if we can find enough
grass to save at least some of my horses and mules."
6 So they divided the land between them. Ahab went
one way by himself, and Obadiah went another way
by himself.
7 As Obadiah was walking along, he suddenly saw
Elijah coming toward him. Obadiah recognized him
at once and bowed low to the ground before him. "Is
it really you, my lord Elijah?" he asked.
8 "Yes, it is," Elijah replied. "Now go and tell your
master, 'Elijah is here.'"
9 "Oh, sir," Obadiah protested, "what harm have I
done to you that you are sending me to my death at
the hands of Ahab? 10 For I swear by the LORD your
God that the king has searched every nation and
kingdom on earth from end to end to find you. And
each time he was told, 'Elijah isn't here,' King Ahab
forced the king of that nation to swear to the truth of
his claim. 11 And now you say, 'Go and tell your master, "Elijah is here."' 12 But as soon as I leave you, the
Spirit of the LORD will carry you away to who knows
where. When Ahab comes and cannot find you, he
will kill me. Yet I have been a true servant of the LORD
all my life. 13 Has no one told you, my lord, about the

KING JAMES VERSION

men of the LORD's prophets by fifty in a cave, and fed
them with bread and water?

14And now thou sayest, Go, tell thy lord, Behold,
Elijah *is here:* and he shall slay me.

15And Elijah said, *As* the LORD of hosts liveth,
before whom I stand, I will surely shew myself unto
him today.

16So Obadiah went to meet Ahab, and told him:
and Ahab went to meet Elijah.

17And it came to pass, when Ahab saw Elijah, that
Ahab said unto him, *Art* thou he that troubleth
Israel?

18And he answered, I have not troubled Israel; but
thou, and thy father's house, in that ye have forsaken
the commandments of the LORD, and thou hast followed Baalim.

19Now therefore send, *and* gather to me all Israel
unto mount Carmel, and the prophets of Baal four
hundred and fifty, and the prophets of the groves
four hundred, which eat at Jezebel's table.

20So Ahab sent unto all the children of Israel, and
gathered the prophets together unto mount Carmel.

21And Elijah came unto all the people, and said,
How long halt ye between two opinions? if the LORD
be God, follow him: but if Baal, *then* follow him. And
the people answered him not a word.

22Then said Elijah unto the people, I, *even* I only,
remain a prophet of the LORD; but Baal's prophets *are*
four hundred and fifty men.

23Let them therefore give us two bullocks; and let
them choose one bullock for themselves, and cut it
in pieces, and lay *it* on wood, and put no fire *under:*
and I will dress the other bullock, and lay *it* on wood,
and put no fire *under:*

24And call ye on the name of your gods, and I will
call on the name of the LORD: and the God that
answereth by fire, let him be God. And all the people
answered and said, It is well spoken.

25And Elijah said unto the prophets of Baal,
Choose you one bullock for yourselves, and dress *it*
first; for ye *are* many; and call on the name of your
gods, but put no fire *under.*

26And they took the bullock which was given
them, and they dressed *it,* and called on the name of
Baal from morning even until noon, saying, O Baal,
hear us. But *there was* no voice, nor any that answered. And they leaped upon the altar which was
made.

27And it came to pass at noon, that Elijah mocked
them, and said, Cry aloud: for he *is* a god; either he is
talking, or he is pursuing, or he is in a journey, *or* peradventure he sleepeth, and must be awaked.

28And they cried aloud, and cut themselves after
their manner with knives and lancets, till the blood
gushed out upon them.

29And it came to pass, when midday was past, and
they prophesied until the *time* of the offering of the

NEW LIVING TRANSLATION

time when Jezebel was trying to kill the LORD's
prophets? I hid 100 of them in two caves and supplied them with food and water. 14And now you say,
'Go and tell your master, "Elijah is here."' Sir, if I do
that, Ahab will certainly kill me."

15But Elijah said, "I swear by the LORD Almighty, in
whose presence I stand, that I will present myself to
Ahab this very day."

16So Obadiah went to tell Ahab that Elijah had
come, and Ahab went out to meet Elijah. 17When
Ahab saw him, he exclaimed, "So, is it really you, you
troublemaker of Israel?"

18"I have made no trouble for Israel," Elijah replied. "You and your family are the troublemakers,
for you have refused to obey the commands of the
LORD and have worshiped the images of Baal instead. 19Now summon all Israel to join me at Mount
Carmel, along with the 450 prophets of Baal and the
400 prophets of Asherah who are supported by Jezebel.*"

20So Ahab summoned all the people of Israel and
the prophets to Mount Carmel. 21Then Elijah stood
in front of them and said, "How much longer will you
waver, hobbling between two opinions? If the LORD
is God, follow him! But if Baal is God, then follow
him!" But the people were completely silent.

22Then Elijah said to them, "I am the only prophet
of the LORD who is left, but Baal has 450 prophets.
23Now bring two bulls. The prophets of Baal may
choose whichever one they wish and cut it into
pieces and lay it on the wood of their altar, but without setting fire to it. I will prepare the other bull and
lay it on the wood on the altar, but not set fire to it.
24Then call on the name of your god, and I will call
on the name of the LORD. The god who answers by
setting fire to the wood is the true God!" And all the
people agreed.

25Then Elijah said to the prophets of Baal, "You go
first, for there are many of you. Choose one of the
bulls, and prepare it and call on the name of your
god. But do not set fire to the wood."

26So they prepared one of the bulls and placed it
on the altar. Then they called on the name of Baal
from morning until noontime, shouting, "O Baal, answer us!" But there was no reply of any kind. Then
they danced, hobbling around the altar they had
made.

27About noontime Elijah began mocking them.
"You'll have to shout louder," he scoffed, "for surely
he is a god! Perhaps he is daydreaming, or is relieving
himself.* Or maybe he is away on a trip, or is asleep
and needs to be wakened!"

28So they shouted louder, and following their normal custom, they cut themselves with knives and
swords until the blood gushed out. 29They raved all

18:19 Hebrew *who eat at Jezebel's table.* **18:27** Or *is busy somewhere else,* or *is engaged in business.*

KING JAMES VERSION

evening sacrifice, that *there was* neither voice, nor any to answer, nor any that regarded.

30 And Elijah said unto all the people, Come near unto me. And all the people came near unto him. And he repaired the altar of the LORD *that was* broken down.

31 And Elijah took twelve stones, according to the number of the tribes of the sons of Jacob, unto whom the word of the LORD came, saying, Israel shall be thy name:

32 And with the stones he built an altar in the name of the LORD: and he made a trench about the altar, as great as would contain two measures of seed.

33 And he put the wood in order, and cut the bullock in pieces, and laid *him* on the wood, and said, Fill four barrels with water, and pour *it* on the burnt sacrifice, and on the wood.

34 And he said, Do *it* the second time. And they did *it* the second time. And he said, Do *it* the third time. And they did *it* the third time.

35 And the water ran round about the altar; and he filled the trench also with water.

36 And it came to pass at *the time of* the offering of the *evening* sacrifice, that Elijah the prophet came near, and said, LORD God of Abraham, Isaac, and of Israel, let it be known this day that thou *art* God in Israel, and *that* I *am* thy servant, and *that* I have done all these things at thy word.

37 Hear me, O LORD, hear me, that this people may know that thou *art* the LORD God, and *that* thou hast turned their heart back again.

38 Then the fire of the LORD fell, and consumed the burnt sacrifice, and the wood, and the stones, and the dust, and licked up the water that *was* in the trench.

39 And when all the people saw *it*, they fell on their faces: and they said, The LORD, he *is* the God; the LORD, he *is* the God.

40 And Elijah said unto them, Take the prophets of Baal; let not one of them escape. And they took them: and Elijah brought them down to the brook Kishon, and slew them there.

41 And Elijah said unto Ahab, Get thee up, eat and drink; for *there is* a sound of abundance of rain.

42 So Ahab went up to eat and to drink. And Elijah went up to the top of Carmel; and he cast himself down upon the earth, and put his face between his knees,

43 And said to his servant, Go up now, look toward the sea. And he went up, and looked, and said, *There is* nothing. And he said, Go again seven times.

44 And it came to pass at the seventh time, that he said, Behold, there ariseth a little cloud out of the sea,

NEW LIVING TRANSLATION

afternoon until the time of the evening sacrifice, but still there was no sound, no reply, no response.

30 Then Elijah called to the people, "Come over here!" They all crowded around him as he repaired the altar of the LORD that had been torn down. 31 He took twelve stones, one to represent each of the tribes of Israel,* 32 and he used the stones to rebuild the altar in the name of the LORD. Then he dug a trench around the altar large enough to hold about three gallons.* 33 He piled wood on the altar, cut the bull into pieces, and laid the pieces on the wood.

Then he said, "Fill four large jars with water, and pour the water over the offering and the wood."

34 After they had done this, he said, "Do the same thing again!" And when they were finished, he said, "Now do it a third time!" So they did as he said, 35 and the water ran around the altar and even filled the trench.

36 At the usual time for offering the evening sacrifice, Elijah the prophet walked up to the altar and prayed, "O LORD, God of Abraham, Isaac, and Jacob,* prove today that you are God in Israel and that I am your servant. Prove that I have done all this at your command. 37 O LORD, answer me! Answer me so these people will know that you, O LORD, are God and that you have brought them back to yourself."

38 Immediately the fire of the LORD flashed down from heaven and burned up the young bull, the wood, the stones, and the dust. It even licked up all the water in the trench! 39 And when all the people saw it, they fell face down on the ground and cried out, "The LORD—he is God! Yes, the LORD is God!"

40 Then Elijah commanded, "Seize all the prophets of Baal. Don't let a single one escape!" So the people seized them all, and Elijah took them down to the Kishon Valley and killed them there.

Elijah Prays for Rain

41 Then Elijah said to Ahab, "Go get something to eat and drink, for I hear a mighty rainstorm coming!"

42 So Ahab went to eat and drink. But Elijah climbed to the top of Mount Carmel and bowed low to the ground and prayed with his face between his knees.

43 Then he said to his servant, "Go and look out toward the sea."

The servant went and looked, then returned to Elijah and said, "I didn't see anything."

Seven times Elijah told him to go and look. 44 Finally the seventh time, his servant told him, "I saw a little cloud about the size of a man's hand rising from the sea."

18:31 Hebrew *each of the tribes of the sons of Jacob to whom the LORD had said, "Your name will be Israel."* **18:32** Hebrew *2 seahs* [12 liters] *of seed.* **18:36** Hebrew *and Israel.* The names "Jacob" and "Israel" are often interchanged throughout the Old Testament, referring sometimes to the individual patriarch and sometimes to the nation.

KING JAMES VERSION

like a man's hand. And he said, Go up, say unto Ahab,
Prepare *thy chariot,* and get thee down, that the rain
stop thee not.
45 And it came to pass in the mean while, that the
heaven was black with clouds and wind, and there
was a great rain. And Ahab rode, and went to Jezreel.
46 And the hand of the LORD was on Elijah; and he
girded up his loins, and ran before Ahab to the entrance of Jezreel.

19 1 And Ahab told Jezebel all that Elijah had
done, and withal how he had slain all the
prophets with the sword.
2 Then Jezebel sent a messenger unto Elijah, saying, So let the gods do *to me,* and more also, if I make
not thy life as the life of one of them by tomorrow
about this time.
3 And when he saw *that,* he arose, and went for his
life, and came to Beer-sheba, which *belongeth* to
Judah, and left his servant there.
4 But he himself went a day's journey into the wilderness, and came and sat down under a juniper
tree: and he requested for himself that he might die;
and said, It is enough; now, O LORD, take away my life;
for I *am* not better than my fathers.
5 And as he lay and slept under a juniper tree, behold, then an angel touched him, and said unto him,
Arise *and* eat.
6 And he looked, and, behold, *there was* a cake
baken on the coals, and a cruse of water at his head.
And he did eat and drink, and laid him down again.
7 And the angel of the LORD came again the second
time, and touched him, and said, Arise *and* eat; because the journey *is* too great for thee.
8 And he arose, and did eat and drink, and went in
the strength of that meat forty days and forty nights
unto Horeb the mount of God.
9 And he came thither unto a cave, and lodged
there; and, behold, the word of the LORD *came* to
him, and he said unto him, What doest thou here,
Elijah?
10 And he said, I have been very jealous for the
LORD God of hosts: for the children of Israel have forsaken thy covenant, thrown down thine altars, and
slain thy prophets with the sword; and I, *even* I only,
am left; and they seek my life, to take it away.
11 And he said, Go forth, and stand upon the mount
before the LORD. And, behold, the LORD passed by,
and a great and strong wind rent the mountains, and
brake in pieces the rocks before the LORD; *but* the
LORD *was* not in the wind: and after the wind an
earthquake; *but* the LORD *was* not in the earthquake:
12 And after the earthquake a fire; *but* the LORD *was*
not in the fire: and after the fire a still small voice.

NEW LIVING TRANSLATION

Then Elijah shouted, "Hurry to Ahab and tell him,
'Climb into your chariot and go back home. If you
don't hurry, the rain will stop you!'"
45 And soon the sky was black with clouds. A heavy
wind brought a terrific rainstorm, and Ahab left
quickly for Jezreel. 46 Then the LORD gave special
strength to Elijah. He tucked his cloak into his belt*
and ran ahead of Ahab's chariot all the way to the entrance of Jezreel.

Elijah Flees to Sinai

19 When Ahab got home, he told Jezebel everything Elijah had done, including the way he
had killed all the prophets of Baal. 2 So Jezebel sent
this message to Elijah: "May the gods strike me and
even kill me if by this time tomorrow I have not killed
you just as you killed them."
3 Elijah was afraid and fled for his life. He went to
Beersheba, a town in Judah, and he left his servant
there. 4 Then he went on alone into the wilderness,
traveling all day. He sat down under a solitary broom
tree and prayed that he might die. "I have had
enough, LORD," he said. "Take my life, for I am no
better than my ancestors who have already died."
5 Then he lay down and slept under the broom
tree. But as he was sleeping, an angel touched him
and told him, "Get up and eat!" 6 He looked around
and there beside his head was some bread baked on
hot stones and a jar of water! So he ate and drank and
lay down again.
7 Then the angel of the LORD came again and
touched him and said, "Get up and eat some more, or
the journey ahead will be too much for you."
8 So he got up and ate and drank, and the food gave
him enough strength to travel forty days and forty
nights to Mount Sinai,* the mountain of God. 9 There
he came to a cave, where he spent the night.

The LORD Speaks to Elijah

But the LORD said to him, "What are you doing here,
Elijah?"
10 Elijah replied, "I have zealously served the LORD
God Almighty. But the people of Israel have broken
their covenant with you, torn down your altars, and
killed every one of your prophets. I am the only one
left, and now they are trying to kill me, too."
11 "Go out and stand before me on the mountain,"
the LORD told him. And as Elijah stood there, the
LORD passed by, and a mighty windstorm hit the
mountain. It was such a terrible blast that the rocks
were torn loose, but the LORD was not in the wind.
After the wind there was an earthquake, but the
LORD was not in the earthquake. 12 And after the
earthquake there was a fire, but the LORD was not in
the fire. And after the fire there was the sound of a

18:46 Hebrew *He bound up his loins.* **19:8** Hebrew *to Horeb,* another name for Sinai.

KING JAMES VERSION

13And it was *so,* when Elijah heard *it* that he wrapped his face in his mantle, and went out, and stood in the entering in of the cave. And, behold, *there came* a voice unto him, and said, What doest thou here, Elijah?

14And he said, I have been very jealous for the LORD God of hosts: because the children of Israel have forsaken thy covenant, thrown down thine altars, and slain thy prophets with the sword; and I, *even* I only, am left; and they seek my life, to take it away.

15And the LORD said unto him, Go, return on thy way to the wilderness of Damascus: and when thou comest, anoint Hazael *to be* king over Syria:

16And Jehu the son of Nimshi shalt thou anoint *to be* king over Israel: and Elisha the son of Shaphat of Abel-meholah shalt thou anoint *to be* prophet in thy room.

17And it shall come to pass, *that* him that escapeth the sword of Hazael shall Jehu slay: and him that escapeth from the sword of Jehu shall Elisha slay.

18Yet I have left *me* seven thousand in Israel, all the knees which have not bowed unto Baal, and every mouth which hath not kissed him.

19So he departed thence, and found Elisha the son of Shaphat, who *was* plowing *with* twelve yoke *of oxen* before him, and he with the twelfth: and Elijah passed by him, and cast his mantle upon him.

20And he left the oxen, and ran after Elijah, and said, Let me, I pray thee, kiss my father and my mother, and *then* I will follow thee. And he said unto him, Go back again: for what have I done to thee?

21And he returned back from him, and took a yoke of oxen, and slew them, and boiled their flesh with the instruments of the oxen, and gave unto the people, and they did eat. Then he arose, and went after Elijah, and ministered unto him.

20 1And Ben-hadad the king of Syria gathered all his host together: and *there were* thirty and two kings with him, and horses, and chariots: and he went up and besieged Samaria, and warred against it.

2And he sent messengers to Ahab king of Israel into the city, and said unto him, Thus saith Ben-hadad,

3Thy silver and thy gold *is* mine; thy wives also and thy children, *even* the goodliest, *are* mine.

4And the king of Israel answered and said, My lord, O king, according to thy saying, I *am* thine, and all that I have.

5And the messengers came again, and said, Thus speaketh Ben-hadad, saying, Although I have sent unto thee, saying, Thou shalt deliver me thy silver, and thy gold, and thy wives, and thy children;

NEW LIVING TRANSLATION

gentle whisper. 13When Elijah heard it, he wrapped his face in his cloak and went out and stood at the entrance of the cave.

And a voice said, "What are you doing here, Elijah?"

14He replied again, "I have zealously served the LORD God Almighty. But the people of Israel have broken their covenant with you, torn down your altars, and killed every one of your prophets. I am the only one left, and now they are trying to kill me, too."

15Then the LORD told him, "Go back the same way you came, and travel to the wilderness of Damascus. When you arrive there, anoint Hazael to be king of Aram. 16Then anoint Jehu grandson of Nimshi* to be king of Israel, and anoint Elisha son of Shaphat from the town of Abel-meholah to replace you as my prophet. 17Anyone who escapes from Hazael will be killed by Jehu, and those who escape Jehu will be killed by Elisha! 18Yet I will preserve 7,000 others in Israel who have never bowed down to Baal or kissed him!"

The Call of Elisha

19So Elijah went and found Elisha son of Shaphat plowing a field. There were twelve teams of oxen in the field, and Elisha was plowing with the twelfth team. Elijah went over to him and threw his cloak across his shoulders and then walked away. 20Elisha left the oxen standing there, ran after Elijah, and said to him, "First let me go and kiss my father and mother good-bye, and then I will go with you!"

Elijah replied, "Go on back, but think about what I have done to you."

21So Elisha returned to his oxen and slaughtered them. He used the wood from the plow to build a fire to roast their flesh. He passed around the meat to the townspeople, and they all ate. Then he went with Elijah as his assistant.

Ben-Hadad Attacks Samaria

20 About that time King Ben-hadad of Aram mobilized his army, supported by the chariots and horses of thirty-two allied kings. They went to besiege Samaria, the capital of Israel, and launched attacks against it. 2Ben-hadad sent messengers into the city to relay this message to King Ahab of Israel: "This is what Ben-hadad says: 3'Your silver and gold are mine, and so are your wives and the best of your children!'"

4"All right, my lord the king," Israel's king replied. "All that I have is yours!"

5Soon Ben-hadad's messengers returned again and said, "This is what Ben-hadad says: 'I have already demanded that you give me your silver, gold,

19:16 Hebrew *descendant of Nimshi;* compare 2 Kgs 9:2, 14.

KING JAMES VERSION

6 Yet I will send my servants unto thee tomorrow
about this time, and they shall search thine house,
and the houses of thy servants; and it shall be, *that*
whatsoever is pleasant in thine eyes, they shall put *it*
in their hand, and take *it* away.
7 Then the king of Israel called all the elders of the
land, and said, Mark, I pray you, and see how this
man seeketh mischief: for he sent unto me for my
wives, and for my children, and for my silver, and for
my gold; and I denied him not.
8 And all the elders and all the people said unto
him, Hearken not *unto him,* nor consent.
9 Wherefore he said unto the messengers of Ben-
hadad, Tell my lord the king, All that thou didst send
for to thy servant at the first I will do: but this thing
I may not do. And the messengers departed, and
brought him word again.
10 And Ben-hadad sent unto him, and said, The
gods do so unto me, and more also, if the dust of
Samaria shall suffice for handfuls for all the people
that follow me.
11 And the king of Israel answered and said, Tell
him, Let not him that girdeth on *his harness* boast
himself as he that putteth it off.
12 And it came to pass, when *Ben-hadad* heard this
message, as he *was* drinking, he and the kings in the
pavilions, that he said unto his servants, Set *yourselves in array.* And they set *themselves in array*
against the city.
13 And, behold, there came a prophet unto Ahab
king of Israel, saying, Thus saith the LORD, Hast thou
seen all this great multitude? behold, I will deliver it
into thine hand this day; and thou shalt know that I
am the LORD.
14 And Ahab said, By whom? And he said, Thus
saith the LORD, *Even* by the young men of the princes
of the provinces. Then he said, Who shall order the
battle? And he answered, Thou.
15 Then he numbered the young men of the
princes of the provinces, and they were two hundred
and thirty two: and after them he numbered all the
people, *even* all the children of Israel, *being* seven
thousand.
16 And they went out at noon. But Ben-hadad *was*
drinking himself drunk in the pavilions, he and the
kings, the thirty and two kings that helped him.
17 And the young men of the princes of the provinces went out first; and Ben-hadad sent out, and
they told him, saying, There are men come out of
Samaria.
18 And he said, Whether they be come out for
peace, take them alive; or whether they be come out
for war, take them alive.
19 So these young men of the princes of the provinces came out of the city, and the army which followed them.
20 And they slew every one his man: and the Syrians
fled; and Israel pursued them: and Ben-hadad the

NEW LIVING TRANSLATION

wives, and children. 6 But about this time tomorrow
I will send my officials to search your palace and the
homes of your people. They will take away everything you consider valuable!'"
7 Then Ahab summoned all the elders of the land
and said to them, "Look how this man is stirring up
trouble! I already agreed with his demand that I give
him my wives and children and silver and gold."
8 "Don't give in to any more demands," all the
elders and the people advised.
9 So Ahab told the messengers from Ben-hadad,
"Say this to my lord the king: 'I will give you everything you asked for the first time, but I cannot accept
this last demand of yours.' " So the messengers returned to Ben-hadad with that response.
10 Then Ben-hadad sent this message to Ahab:
"May the gods strike me and even kill me if there remains enough dust from Samaria to provide even a
handful for each of my soldiers."
11 The king of Israel sent back this answer: "A warrior putting on his sword for battle should not boast
like a warrior who has already won."
12 Ahab's reply reached Ben-hadad and the other
kings as they were drinking in their tents.* "Prepare
to attack!" Ben-hadad commanded his officers. So
they prepared to attack the city.

Ahab's Victory over Ben-Hadad

13 Then a certain prophet came to see King Ahab of
Israel and told him, "This is what the LORD says: Do
you see all these enemy forces? Today I will hand
them all over to you. Then you will know that I am
the LORD."
14 Ahab asked, "How will he do it?"
And the prophet replied, "This is what the LORD
says: The troops of the provincial commanders will
do it."
"Should we attack first?" Ahab asked.
"Yes," the prophet answered.
15 So Ahab mustered the troops of the 232 provincial commanders. Then he called out the rest of the
army of Israel, some 7,000 men. 16 About noontime,
as Ben-hadad and the thirty-two allied kings were
still in their tents drinking themselves into a stupor,
17 the troops of the provincial commanders marched
out of the city as the first contingent.
As they approached, Ben-hadad's scouts reported
to him, "Some troops are coming from Samaria."
18 "Take them alive," Ben-hadad commanded,
"whether they have come for peace or for war."
19 But Ahab's provincial commanders and the entire army had now come out to fight. 20 Each Israelite
soldier killed his Aramean opponent, and suddenly

20:12 Or *in Succoth;* also in 20:16.

KING JAMES VERSION

king of Syria escaped on an horse with the horsemen.
21 And the king of Israel went out, and smote the
horses and chariots, and slew the Syrians with a great
slaughter.
22 And the prophet came to the king of Israel, and
said unto him, Go, strengthen thyself, and mark, and
see what thou doest: for at the return of the year the
king of Syria will come up against thee.
23 And the servants of the king of Syria said unto
him, Their gods *are* gods of the hills; therefore they
were stronger than we; but let us fight against them
in the plain, and surely we shall be stronger than
they.
24 And do this thing, Take the kings away, every
man out of his place, and put captains in their rooms:
25 And number thee an army, like the army that
thou hast lost, horse for horse, and chariot for chariot: and we will fight against them in the plain, *and*
surely we shall be stronger than they. And he hearkened unto their voice, and did so.
26 And it came to pass at the return of the year, that
Ben-hadad numbered the Syrians, and went up to
Aphek, to fight against Israel.
27 And the children of Israel were numbered, and
were all present, and went against them: and the children of Israel pitched before them like two little
flocks of kids; but the Syrians filled the country.
28 And there came a man of God, and spake unto
the king of Israel, and said, Thus saith the LORD, Because the Syrians have said, The LORD *is* God of the
hills, but he *is* not God of the valleys, therefore will I
deliver all this great multitude into thine hand, and
ye shall know that I *am* the LORD.
29 And they pitched one over against the other seven
days. And *so* it was, that in the seventh day the battle
was joined: and the children of Israel slew of the Syrians an hundred thousand footmen in one day.
30 But the rest fled to Aphek, into the city; and
there a wall fell upon twenty and seven thousand of
the men *that were* left. And Ben-hadad fled, and
came into the city, into an inner chamber.
31 And his servants said unto him, Behold now, we
have heard that the kings of the house of Israel *are*
merciful kings: let us, I pray thee, put sackcloth on
our loins, and ropes upon our heads, and go out to
the king of Israel: peradventure he will save thy life.
32 So they girded sackcloth on their loins, and *put*
ropes on their heads, and came to the king of Israel,
and said, Thy servant Ben-hadad saith, I pray thee, let
me live. And he said, *Is* he yet alive? he *is* my brother.
33 Now the men did diligently observe whether
any thing would come from him, and did hastily
catch *it:* and they said, Thy brother Ben-hadad. Then
he said, Go ye, bring him. Then Ben-hadad came
forth to him; and he caused him to come up into the
chariot.

NEW LIVING TRANSLATION

the entire Aramean army panicked and fled. The
Israelites chased them, but King Ben-hadad and a
few of his charioteers escaped on horses. 21 However,
the king of Israel destroyed the other horses and
chariots and slaughtered the Arameans.
22 Afterward the prophet said to King Ahab, "Get
ready for another attack. Begin making plans now,
for the king of Aram will come back next spring.*"

Ben-Hadad's Second Attack

23 After their defeat, Ben-hadad's officers said to him,
"The Israelite gods are gods of the hills; that is why
they won. But we can beat them easily on the plains.
24 Only this time replace the kings with field commanders! 25 Recruit another army like the one you
lost. Give us the same number of horses, chariots,
and men, and we will fight against them on the
plains. There's no doubt that we will beat them." So
King Ben-hadad did as they suggested.
26 The following spring he called up the Aramean
army and marched out against Israel, this time at
Aphek. 27 Israel then mustered its army, set up supply
lines, and marched out for battle. But the Israelite
army looked like two little flocks of goats in comparison to the vast Aramean forces that filled the
countryside!
28 Then the man of God went to the king of Israel
and said, "This is what the LORD says: The Arameans
have said, 'The LORD is a god of the hills and not of
the plains.' So I will defeat this vast army for you.
Then you will know that I am the LORD."
29 The two armies camped opposite each other for
seven days, and on the seventh day the battle began.
The Israelites killed 100,000 Aramean foot soldiers
in one day. 30 The rest fled into the town of Aphek,
but the wall fell on them and killed another 27,000.
Ben-hadad fled into the town and hid in a secret
room.
31 Ben-hadad's officers said to him, "Sir, we have
heard that the kings of Israel are merciful. So let's
humble ourselves by wearing burlap around our
waists and putting ropes on our heads, and surrender to the king of Israel. Then perhaps he will let
you live."
32 So they put on burlap and ropes, and they went
to the king of Israel and begged, "Your servant Ben-
hadad says, 'Please let me live!'"
The king of Israel responded, "Is he still alive? He
is my brother!"
33 The men took this as a good sign and quickly
picked up on his words. "Yes," they said, "your
brother Ben-hadad!"
"Go and get him," the king of Israel told them. And
when Ben-hadad arrived, Ahab invited him up into
his chariot.

20:22 Hebrew *at the turn of the year;* similarly in 20:26. The first day of the year in the ancient Hebrew lunar calendar occurred in March or April.

KING JAMES VERSION

34 And *Ben-hadad* said unto him, The cities, which my father took from thy father, I will restore; and thou shalt make streets for thee in Damascus, as my father made in Samaria. Then *said Ahab,* I will send thee away with this covenant. So he made a covenant with him, and sent him away.

35 And a certain man of the sons of the prophets said unto his neighbour in the word of the LORD, Smite me, I pray thee. And the man refused to smite him.

36 Then said he unto him, Because thou hast not obeyed the voice of the LORD, behold, as soon as thou art departed from me, a lion shall slay thee. And as soon as he was departed from him, a lion found him, and slew him.

37 Then he found another man, and said, Smite me, I pray thee. And the man smote him, so that in smiting he wounded *him.*

38 So the prophet departed, and waited for the king by the way, and disguised himself with ashes upon his face.

39 And as the king passed by, he cried unto the king: and he said, Thy servant went out into the midst of the battle; and, behold, a man turned aside, and brought a man unto me, and said, Keep this man: if by any means he be missing, then shall thy life be for his life, or else thou shalt pay a talent of silver.

40 And as thy servant was busy here and there, he was gone. And the king of Israel said unto him, So *shall* thy judgment *be;* thyself hast decided *it.*

41 And he hasted, and took the ashes away from his face; and the king of Israel discerned him that he *was* of the prophets.

42 And he said unto him, Thus saith the LORD, Because thou hast let go out of *thy* hand a man whom I appointed to utter destruction, therefore thy life shall go for his life, and thy people for his people.

43 And the king of Israel went to his house heavy and displeased, and came to Samaria.

21 1 And it came to pass after these things, *that* Naboth the Jezreelite had a vineyard, which *was* in Jezreel, hard by the palace of Ahab king of Samaria.

2 And Ahab spake unto Naboth, saying, Give me thy vineyard, that I may have it for a garden of herbs, because it *is* near unto my house: and I will give thee for it a better vineyard than it; *or,* if it seem good to thee, I will give thee the worth of it in money.

3 And Naboth said to Ahab, The LORD forbid it me, that I should give the inheritance of my fathers unto thee.

4 And Ahab came into his house heavy and displeased because of the word which Naboth the Jezreelite had spoken to him: for he had said, I will not give thee the inheritance of my fathers. And he

NEW LIVING TRANSLATION

34 Ben-hadad told him, "I will give back the towns my father took from your father, and you may establish places of trade in Damascus, as my father did in Samaria."

Then Ahab said, "I will release you under these conditions." So they made a new treaty, and Ben-hadad was set free.

A Prophet Condemns Ahab

35 Meanwhile, the LORD instructed one of the group of prophets to say to another man, "Hit me!" But the man refused to hit the prophet. 36 Then the prophet told him, "Because you have not obeyed the voice of the LORD, a lion will kill you as soon as you leave me." And when he had gone, a lion did attack and kill him.

37 Then the prophet turned to another man and said, "Hit me!" So he struck the prophet and wounded him.

38 The prophet placed a bandage over his eyes to disguise himself and then waited beside the road for the king. 39 As the king passed by, the prophet called out to him, "Sir, I was in the thick of battle, and suddenly a man brought me a prisoner. He said, 'Guard this man; if for any reason he gets away, you will either die or pay a fine of seventy-five pounds* of silver!' 40 But while I was busy doing something else, the prisoner disappeared!"

"Well, it's your own fault," the king replied. "You have brought the judgment on yourself."

41 Then the prophet quickly pulled the bandage from his eyes, and the king of Israel recognized him as one of the prophets. 42 The prophet said to him, "This is what the LORD says: Because you have spared the man I said must be destroyed,* now you must die in his place, and your people will die instead of his people." 43 So the king of Israel went home to Samaria angry and sullen.

Naboth's Vineyard

21 Now there was a man named Naboth, from Jezreel, who owned a vineyard in Jezreel beside the palace of King Ahab of Samaria. 2 One day Ahab said to Naboth, "Since your vineyard is so convenient to my palace, I would like to buy it to use as a vegetable garden. I will give you a better vineyard in exchange, or if you prefer, I will pay you for it."

3 But Naboth replied, "The LORD forbid that I should give you the inheritance that was passed down by my ancestors."

4 So Ahab went home angry and sullen because of

20:39 Hebrew *1 talent* [34 kilograms]. **20:42** The Hebrew term used here refers to the complete consecration of things or people to the LORD, either by destroying them or by giving them as an offering.

KING JAMES VERSION

laid him down upon his bed, and turned away his
face, and would eat no bread.
5But Jezebel his wife came to him, and said unto
him, Why is thy spirit so sad, that thou eatest no bread?
6And he said unto her, Because I spake unto Naboth the Jezreelite, and said unto him, Give me thy
vineyard for money; or else, if it please thee, I will
give thee *another* vineyard for it: and he answered,
I will not give thee my vineyard.
7And Jezebel his wife said unto him, Dost thou
now govern the kingdom of Israel? arise, *and* eat
bread, and let thine heart be merry: I will give thee
the vineyard of Naboth the Jezreelite.
8So she wrote letters in Ahab's name, and sealed
them with his seal, and sent the letters unto the elders and to the nobles that *were* in his city, dwelling
with Naboth.
9And she wrote in the letters, saying, Proclaim a
fast, and set Naboth on high among the people:
10And set two men, sons of Belial, before him, to
bear witness against him, saying, Thou didst blaspheme God and the king. And *then* carry him out,
and stone him, that he may die.
11And the men of his city, *even* the elders and the
nobles who were the inhabitants in his city, did as
Jezebel had sent unto them, *and* as it *was* written in
the letters which she had sent unto them.
12They proclaimed a fast, and set Naboth on high
among the people.
13And there came in two men, children of Belial,
and sat before him: and the men of Belial witnessed
against him, *even* against Naboth, in the presence of
the people, saying, Naboth did blaspheme God and
the king. Then they carried him forth out of the city,
and stoned him with stones, that he died.
14Then they sent to Jezebel, saying, Naboth is
stoned, and is dead.
15And it came to pass, when Jezebel heard that
Naboth was stoned, and was dead, that Jezebel said
to Ahab, Arise, take possession of the vineyard of
Naboth the Jezreelite, which he refused to give thee
for money: for Naboth is not alive, but dead.
16And it came to pass, when Ahab heard that
Naboth was dead, that Ahab rose up to go down to
the vineyard of Naboth the Jezreelite, to take possession of it.
17And the word of the LORD came to Elijah the
Tishbite, saying,
18Arise, go down to meet Ahab king of Israel,
which *is* in Samaria: behold, *he is* in the vineyard of
Naboth, whither he is gone down to possess it.
19And thou shalt speak unto him, saying, Thus
saith the LORD, Hast thou killed, and also taken possession? And thou shalt speak unto him, saying, Thus
saith the LORD, In the place where dogs licked the
blood of Naboth shall dogs lick thy blood, even thine.
20And Ahab said to Elijah, hast thou found me,
O mine enemy? And he answered, I have found *thee;*

NEW LIVING TRANSLATION

Naboth's answer. The king went to bed with his face
to the wall and refused to eat!
5"What's the matter?" his wife Jezebel asked him.
"What's made you so upset that you're not eating?"
6"I asked Naboth to sell me his vineyard or trade it,
but he refused!" Ahab told her.
7"Are you the king of Israel or not?" Jezebel demanded. "Get up and eat something, and don't worry
about it. I'll get you Naboth's vineyard!"
8So she wrote letters in Ahab's name, sealed them
with his seal, and sent them to the elders and other
leaders of the town where Naboth lived. 9In her letters she commanded: "Call the citizens together for
fasting and prayer, and give Naboth a place of honor.
10And then seat two scoundrels across from him who
will accuse him of cursing God and the king. Then
take him out and stone him to death."
11So the elders and other town leaders followed
the instructions Jezebel had written in the letters.
12They called for a fast and put Naboth at a prominent place before the people. 13Then the two scoundrels came and sat down across from him. And they
accused Naboth before all the people, saying, "He
cursed God and the king." So he was dragged outside
the town and stoned to death. 14The town leaders
then sent word to Jezebel, "Naboth has been stoned
to death."
15When Jezebel heard the news, she said to Ahab,
"You know the vineyard Naboth wouldn't sell you?
Well, you can have it now! He's dead!" 16So Ahab
immediately went down to the vineyard of Naboth to
claim it.
17But the LORD said to Elijah,* 18"Go down to meet
King Ahab of Israel, who rules in Samaria. He will be
at Naboth's vineyard in Jezreel, claiming it for himself. 19Give him this message: 'This is what the LORD
says: Wasn't it enough that you killed Naboth? Must
you rob him, too? Because you have done this, dogs
will lick your blood at the very place where they
licked the blood of Naboth!'"
20"So, my enemy, you have found me!" Ahab exclaimed to Elijah.

21:17 Hebrew *Elijah the Tishbite;* also in 21:28.

KING JAMES VERSION

because thou hast sold thyself to work evil in the
sight of the LORD.
21 Behold, I will bring evil upon thee, and will take
away thy posterity, and will cut off from Ahab him
that pisseth against the wall, and him that is shut up
and left in Israel,
22 And will make thine house like the house of
Jeroboam the son of Nebat, and like the house of
Baasha the son of Ahijah, for the provocation wherewith thou hast provoked *me* to anger, and made Israel to sin.
23 And of Jezebel also spake the LORD, saying, The
dogs shall eat Jezebel by the wall of Jezreel.
24 Him that dieth of Ahab in the city the dogs shall
eat; and him that dieth in the field shall the fowls of
the air eat.
25 But there was none like unto Ahab, which did
sell himself to work wickedness in the sight of the
LORD, whom Jezebel his wife stirred up.
26 And he did very abominably in following idols,
according to all *things* as did the Amorites, whom
the LORD cast out before the children of Israel.
27 And it came to pass, when Ahab heard those
words, that he rent his clothes, and put sackcloth
upon his flesh, and fasted, and lay in sackcloth, and
went softly.
28 And the word of the LORD came to Elijah the
Tishbite, saying,
29 Seest thou how Ahab humbleth himself before
me? because he humbleth himself before me, I will
not bring the evil in his days: *but* in his son's days will
I bring the evil upon his house.

22 1 And they continued three years without
war between Syria and Israel.
2 And it came to pass in the third year, that
Jehoshaphat the king of Judah came down to the
king of Israel.
3 And the king of Israel said unto his servants,
Know ye that Ramoth in Gilead *is* ours, and we *be*
still, *and* take it not out of the hand of the king of
Syria?
4 And he said unto Jehoshaphat, Wilt thou go with
me to battle to Ramoth-gilead? And Jehoshaphat
said to the king of Israel, I *am* as thou *art*, my people
as thy people, my horses as thy horses.
5 And Jehoshaphat said unto the king of Israel,
Inquire, I pray thee, at the word of the LORD today.
6 Then the king of Israel gathered the prophets together, about four hundred men, and said unto them,
Shall I go against Ramoth-gilead to battle, or shall I
forbear? And they said, Go up; for the Lord shall deliver *it* into the hand of the king.
7 And Jehoshaphat said, *Is there* not here a prophet
of the LORD besides, that we might inquire of him?

NEW LIVING TRANSLATION

"Yes," Elijah answered, "I have come because you
have sold yourself to what is evil in the LORD's sight.
21 So now the LORD says, 'I will bring disaster on you
and consume you. I will destroy every one of your
male descendants, slave and free alike, anywhere in
Israel! 22 I am going to destroy your family as I did the
family of Jeroboam son of Nebat and the family of
Baasha son of Ahijah, for you have made me very
angry and have led Israel into sin.'
23 "And regarding Jezebel, the LORD says, 'Dogs will
eat Jezebel's body at the plot of land in Jezreel.*'
24 "The members of Ahab's family who die in the
city will be eaten by dogs, and those who die in the
field will be eaten by vultures."
25 (No one else so completely sold himself to what
was evil in the LORD's sight as Ahab did under the influence of his wife Jezebel. 26 His worst outrage was
worshiping idols* just as the Amorites had done—
the people whom the LORD had driven out from the
land ahead of the Israelites.)
27 But when Ahab heard this message, he tore his
clothing, dressed in burlap, and fasted. He even slept
in burlap and went about in deep mourning.
28 Then another message from the LORD came to
Elijah: 29 "Do you see how Ahab has humbled himself
before me? Because he has done this, I will not do
what I promised during his lifetime. It will happen to
his sons; I will destroy his dynasty."

Jehoshaphat and Ahab

22 For three years there was no war between
Aram and Israel. 2 Then during the third
year, King Jehoshaphat of Judah went to visit King
Ahab of Israel. 3 During the visit, the king of Israel
said to his officials, "Do you realize that the town of
Ramoth-gilead belongs to us? And yet we've done
nothing to recapture it from the king of Aram!"
4 Then he turned to Jehoshaphat and asked, "Will
you join me in battle to recover Ramoth-gilead?"
Jehoshaphat replied to the king of Israel, "Why,
of course! You and I are as one. My troops are your
troops, and my horses are your horses." 5 Then Jehoshaphat added, "But first let's find out what the
LORD says."
6 So the king of Israel summoned the prophets,
about 400 of them, and asked them, "Should I go to
war against Ramoth-gilead, or should I hold back?"
They all replied, "Yes, go right ahead! The Lord
will give the king victory."
7 But Jehoshaphat asked, "Is there not also a
prophet of the LORD here? We should ask him the
same question."

21:23 As in several Hebrew manuscripts, Syriac, and Latin Vulgate (see also 2 Kgs 9:26, 36); most Hebrew manuscripts read *at the city wall.* **21:26** The Hebrew term (literally *round things*) probably alludes to dung.

KING JAMES VERSION

8 And the king of Israel said unto Jehoshaphat, *There is* yet one man, Micaiah the son of Imlah, by whom we may inquire of the LORD: but I hate him; for he doth not prophesy good concerning me, but evil. And Jehoshaphat said, Let not the king say so.

9 Then the king of Israel called an officer, and said, Hasten *hither* Micaiah the son of Imlah.

10 And the king of Israel and Jehoshaphat the king of Judah sat each on his throne, having put on their robes, in a void place in the entrance of the gate of Samaria; and all the prophets prophesied before them.

11 And Zedekiah the son of Chenaanah made him horns of iron: and he said, Thus saith the LORD, With these shalt thou push the Syrians, until thou have consumed them.

12 And all the prophets prophesied so, saying, Go up to Ramoth-gilead, and prosper: for the LORD shall deliver *it* into the king's hand.

13 And the messenger that was gone to call Micaiah spake unto him, saying, Behold now, the words of the prophets *declare* good unto the king with one mouth: let thy word, I pray thee, be like the word of one of them, and speak *that which is* good.

14 And Micaiah said, *As* the LORD liveth, what the LORD saith unto me, that will I speak.

15 So he came to the king. And the king said unto him, Micaiah, shall we go against Ramoth-gilead to battle, or shall we forbear? And he answered him, Go, and prosper: for the LORD shall deliver *it* into the hand of the king.

16 And the king said unto him, How many times shall I adjure thee that thou tell me nothing but *that which is* true in the name of the LORD?

17 And he said, I saw all Israel scattered upon the hills, as sheep that have not a shepherd: and the LORD said, These have no master: let them return every man to his house in peace.

18 And the king of Israel said unto Jehoshaphat, Did I not tell thee that he would prophesy no good concerning me, but evil?

19 And he said, Hear thou therefore the word of the LORD: I saw the LORD sitting on his throne, and all the host of heaven standing by him on his right hand and on his left.

20 And the LORD said, Who shall persuade Ahab, that he may go up and fall at Ramoth-gilead? And one said on this manner, and another said on that manner.

21 And there came forth a spirit, and stood before the LORD, and said, I will persuade him.

22 And the LORD said unto him, Wherewith? And he said, I will go forth, and I will be a lying spirit in the mouth of all his prophets. And he said, Thou shalt persuade *him*, and prevail also: go forth, and do so.

23 Now therefore, behold, the LORD hath put a lying

NEW LIVING TRANSLATION

8 The king of Israel replied to Jehoshaphat, "There is one more man who could consult the LORD for us, but I hate him. He never prophesies anything but trouble for me! His name is Micaiah son of Imlah."

Jehoshaphat replied, "That's not the way a king should talk! Let's hear what he has to say."

9 So the king of Israel called one of his officials and said, "Quick! Bring Micaiah son of Imlah."

Micaiah Prophesies against Ahab

10 King Ahab of Israel and King Jehoshaphat of Judah, dressed in their royal robes, were sitting on thrones at the threshing floor near the gate of Samaria. All of Ahab's prophets were prophesying there in front of them. 11 One of them, Zedekiah son of Kenaanah, made some iron horns and proclaimed, "This is what the LORD says: With these horns you will gore the Arameans to death!"

12 All the other prophets agreed. "Yes," they said, "go up to Ramoth-gilead and be victorious, for the LORD will give the king victory!"

13 Meanwhile, the messenger who went to get Micaiah said to him, "Look, all the prophets are promising victory for the king. Be sure that you agree with them and promise success."

14 But Micaiah replied, "As surely as the LORD lives, I will say only what the LORD tells me to say."

15 When Micaiah arrived before the king, Ahab asked him, "Micaiah, should we go to war against Ramoth-gilead, or should we hold back?"

Micaiah replied sarcastically, "Yes, go up and be victorious, for the LORD will give the king victory!"

16 But the king replied sharply, "How many times must I demand that you speak only the truth to me when you speak for the LORD?"

17 Then Micaiah told him, "In a vision I saw all Israel scattered on the mountains, like sheep without a shepherd. And the LORD said, 'Their master has been killed.* Send them home in peace.'"

18 "Didn't I tell you?" the king of Israel exclaimed to Jehoshaphat. "He never prophesies anything but trouble for me."

19 Then Micaiah continued, "Listen to what the LORD says! I saw the LORD sitting on his throne with all the armies of heaven around him, on his right and on his left. 20 And the LORD said, 'Who can entice Ahab to go into battle against Ramoth-gilead so he can be killed?'

"There were many suggestions, 21 and finally a spirit approached the LORD and said, 'I can do it!'

22 "'How will you do this?' the LORD asked.

"And the spirit replied, 'I will go out and inspire all of Ahab's prophets to speak lies.'

"'You will succeed,' said the LORD. 'Go ahead and do it.'

23 "So you see, the LORD has put a lying spirit in the

22:17 Hebrew *These people have no master.*

KING JAMES VERSION

spirit in the mouth of all these thy prophets, and the LORD hath spoken evil concerning thee.

24But Zedekiah the son of Chenaanah went near, and smote Micaiah on the cheek, and said, Which way went the spirit of the LORD from me to speak unto thee?

25And Micaiah said, Behold, thou shalt see in that day, when thou shalt go into an inner chamber to hide thyself.

26And the king of Israel said, Take Micaiah, and carry him back unto Amon the governor of the city, and to Joash the king's son;

27And say, Thus saith the king, Put this *fellow* in the prison, and feed him with bread of affliction and with water of affliction, until I come in peace.

28And Micaiah said, If thou return at all in peace, the LORD hath not spoken by me. And he said, Hearken, O people, every one of you.

29So the king of Israel and Jehoshaphat the king of Judah went up to Ramoth-gilead.

30And the king of Israel said unto Jehoshaphat, I will disguise myself, and enter into the battle; but put thou on thy robes. And the king of Israel disguised himself, and went into the battle.

31But the king of Syria commanded his thirty and two captains that had rule over his chariots, saying, Fight neither with small nor great, save only with the king of Israel.

32And it came to pass, when the captains of the chariots saw Jehoshaphat, that they said, Surely it *is* the king of Israel. And they turned aside to fight against him: and Jehoshaphat cried out.

33And it came to pass, when the captains of the chariots perceived that it *was* not the king of Israel, that they turned back from pursuing him.

34And a *certain* man drew a bow at a venture, and smote the king of Israel between the joints of the harness: wherefore he said unto the driver of his chariot, Turn thine hand, and carry me out of the host; for I am wounded.

35And the battle increased that day: and the king was stayed up in his chariot against the Syrians, and died at even: and the blood ran out of the wound into the midst of the chariot.

36And there went a proclamation throughout the host about the going down of the sun, saying, Every man to his city, and every man to his own country.

37So the king died, and was brought to Samaria; and they buried the king in Samaria.

38And *one* washed the chariot in the pool of Samaria; and the dogs licked up his blood; and they washed his armour; according unto the word of the LORD which he spake.

39Now the rest of the acts of Ahab, and all that he did, and the ivory house which he made, and all the

NEW LIVING TRANSLATION

mouths of all your prophets. For the LORD has pronounced your doom."

24Then Zedekiah son of Kenaanah walked up to Micaiah and slapped him across the face. "Since when did the Spirit of the LORD leave me to speak to you?" he demanded.

25And Micaiah replied, "You will find out soon enough when you are trying to hide in some secret room!"

26"Arrest him!" the king of Israel ordered. "Take him back to Amon, the governor of the city, and to my son Joash. 27Give them this order from the king: 'Put this man in prison, and feed him nothing but bread and water until I return safely from the battle!'"

28But Micaiah replied, "If you return safely, it will mean that the LORD has not spoken through me!" Then he added to those standing around, "Everyone mark my words!"

The Death of Ahab

29So King Ahab of Israel and King Jehoshaphat of Judah led their armies against Ramoth-gilead. 30The king of Israel said to Jehoshaphat, "As we go into battle, I will disguise myself so no one will recognize me, but you wear your royal robes." So the king of Israel disguised himself, and they went into battle.

31Meanwhile, the king of Aram had issued these orders to his thirty-two chariot commanders: "Attack only the king of Israel. Don't bother with anyone else!" 32So when the Aramean chariot commanders saw Jehoshaphat in his royal robes, they went after him. "There is the king of Israel!" they shouted. But when Jehoshaphat called out, 33the chariot commanders realized he was not the king of Israel, and they stopped chasing him.

34An Aramean soldier, however, randomly shot an arrow at the Israelite troops and hit the king of Israel between the joints of his armor. "Turn the horses* and get me out of here!" Ahab groaned to the driver of his chariot. "I'm badly wounded!"

35The battle raged all that day, and the king remained propped up in his chariot facing the Arameans. The blood from his wound ran down to the floor of his chariot, and as evening arrived he died. 36Just as the sun was setting, the cry ran through his troops: "We're done for! Run for your lives!"

37So the king died, and his body was taken to Samaria and buried there. 38Then his chariot was washed beside the pool of Samaria, and dogs came and licked his blood at the place where the prostitutes bathed,* just as the LORD had promised.

39The rest of the events in Ahab's reign and everything he did, including the story of the ivory palace

22:34 Hebrew *Turn your hand.* **22:38** Or *his blood, and the prostitutes bathed [in it]; or his blood, and they washed his armor.*

KING JAMES VERSION

cities that he built, *are* they not written in the book
of the chronicles of the kings of Israel?
40So Ahab slept with his fathers; and Ahaziah his
son reigned in his stead.

41And Jehoshaphat the son of Asa began to reign
over Judah in the fourth year of Ahab king of Israel.
42Jehoshaphat *was* thirty and five years old when
he began to reign; and he reigned twenty and five
years in Jerusalem. And his mother's name *was* Azubah the daughter of Shilhi.
43And he walked in all the ways of Asa his father;
he turned not aside from it, doing *that which was*
right in the eyes of the LORD: nevertheless the high
places were not taken away; *for* the people offered
and burnt incense yet in the high places.
44And Jehoshaphat made peace with the king of
Israel.
45Now the rest of the acts of Jehoshaphat, and his
might that he shewed, and how he warred, *are* they
not written in the book of the chronicles of the kings
of Judah?
46And the remnant of the sodomites, which remained in the days of his father Asa, he took out of
the land.
47*There was* then no king in Edom: a deputy *was*
king.
48Jehoshaphat made ships of Tharshish to go to
Ophir for gold: but they went not; for the ships were
broken at Ezion-geber.
49Then said Ahaziah the son of Ahab unto
Jehoshaphat, Let my servants go with thy servants in
the ships. But Jehoshaphat would not.
50And Jehoshaphat slept with his fathers, and was
buried with his fathers in the city of David his father:
and Jehoram his son reigned in his stead.
51Ahaziah the son of Ahab began to reign over Israel in Samaria the seventeenth year of Jehoshaphat
king of Judah, and reigned two years over Israel.
52And he did evil in the sight of the LORD, and
walked in the way of his father, and in the way of his
mother, and in the way of Jeroboam the son of Nebat,
who made Israel to sin:
53For he served Baal, and worshipped him, and
provoked to anger the LORD God of Israel, according
to all that his father had done.

NEW LIVING TRANSLATION

and the towns he built, are recorded in *The Book of
the History of the Kings of Israel.* 40So Ahab died, and
his son Ahaziah became the next king.

Jehoshaphat Rules in Judah

41Jehoshaphat son of Asa began to rule over Judah in
the fourth year of King Ahab's reign in Israel. 42Je-
hoshaphat was thirty-five years old when he became
king, and he reigned in Jerusalem twenty-five years.
His mother was Azubah, the daughter of Shilhi.
43Jehoshaphat was a good king, following the example of his father, Asa. He did what was pleasing in
the LORD's sight. *During his reign, however, he failed
to remove all the pagan shrines, and the people still
offered sacrifices and burned incense there. 44Je-
hoshaphat also made peace with the king of Israel.
45The rest of the events in Jehoshaphat's reign, the
extent of his power, and the wars he waged are recorded in *The Book of the History of the Kings of
Judah.* 46He banished from the land the rest of the
male and female shrine prostitutes, who still continued their practices from the days of his father, Asa.
47(There was no king in Edom at that time, only a
deputy.)
48Jehoshaphat also built a fleet of trading ships*
to sail to Ophir for gold. But the ships never set sail,
for they met with disaster in their home port of
Ezion- geber. 49At one time Ahaziah son of Ahab
had proposed to Jehoshaphat, "Let my men sail with
your men in the ships." But Jehoshaphat refused the
request.
50When Jehoshaphat died, he was buried with his
ancestors in the City of David. Then his son Jehoram
became the next king.

Ahaziah Rules in Israel

51Ahaziah son of Ahab began to rule over Israel in
the seventeenth year of King Jehoshaphat's reign in
Judah. He reigned in Samaria two years. 52But he did
what was evil in the LORD's sight, following the
example of his father and mother and the example
of Jeroboam son of Nebat, who had led Israel to sin.
53He served Baal and worshiped him, provoking the
anger of the LORD, the God of Israel, just as his father
had done.

22:43 Verses 22:43b-53 are numbered 22:44-54 in Hebrew text.
22:48 Hebrew *fleet of ships of Tarshish.*

2 Kings

KING JAMES VERSION

1 1Then Moab rebelled against Israel after the
death of Ahab.
2And Ahaziah fell down through a lattice in his
upper chamber that *was* in Samaria, and was sick:
and he sent messengers, and said unto them, Go, inquire of Baal-zebub the god of Ekron whether I shall
recover of this disease.
3But the angel of the LORD said to Elijah the
Tishbite, Arise, go up to meet the messengers of the
king of Samaria, and say unto them, *Is it* not because
there is not a God in Israel, *that* ye go to inquire of
Baal-zebub the god of Ekron?
4Now therefore thus saith the LORD, Thou shalt
not come down from that bed on which thou art
gone up, but shalt surely die. And Elijah departed.
5And when the messengers turned back unto him,
he said unto them, Why are ye now turned back?
6And they said unto him, There came a man up to
meet us, and said unto us, Go, turn again unto the king
that sent you, and say unto him, Thus saith the LORD,
Is it not because *there is* not a God in Israel, *that* thou
sendest to inquire of Baal-zebub the god of Ekron?
therefore thou shalt not come down from that bed on
which thou art gone up, but shalt surely die.
7And he said unto them, What manner of man
was he which came up to meet you, and told you
these words?
8And they answered him, *He was* an hairy man,
and girt with a girdle of leather about his loins. And
he said, It *is* Elijah the Tishbite.
9Then the king sent unto him a captain of fifty
with his fifty. And he went up to him: and, behold, he
sat on the top of an hill. And he spake unto him, Thou
man of God, the king hath said, Come down.
10And Elijah answered and said to the captain of
fifty, If I *be* a man of God, then let fire come down
from heaven, and consume thee and thy fifty. And
there came down fire from heaven, and consumed
him and his fifty.
11Again also he sent unto him another captain of
fifty with his fifty. And he answered and said unto
him, O man of God, thus hath the king said, Come
down quickly.

NEW LIVING TRANSLATION

Elijah Confronts King Ahaziah

1 After King Ahab's death, the land of Moab rebelled against Israel.
2One day Israel's new king, Ahaziah, fell through
the latticework of an upper room at his palace in Samaria and was seriously injured. So he sent messengers to the temple of Baal-zebub, the god of Ekron, to
ask whether he would recover.
3But the angel of the LORD told Elijah, who was
from Tishbe, "Go and confront the messengers of the
king of Samaria and ask them, 'Is there no God in
Israel? Why are you going to Baal-zebub, the god of
Ekron, to ask whether the king will recover? 4Now,
therefore, this is what the LORD says: You will never
leave the bed you are lying on; you will surely die.'" So
Elijah went to deliver the message.
5When the messengers returned to the king, he
asked them, "Why have you returned so soon?"
6They replied, "A man came up to us and told us to
go back to the king and give him this message. 'This
is what the LORD says: Is there no God in Israel? Why
are you sending men to Baal-zebub, the god of Ekron,
to ask whether you will recover? Therefore, because
you have done this, you will never leave the bed you
are lying on; you will surely die.'"
7"What sort of man was he?" the king demanded.
"What did he look like?"
8They replied, "He was a hairy man,* and he wore a
leather belt around his waist."
"Elijah from Tishbe!" the king exclaimed.
9Then he sent an army captain with fifty soldiers
to arrest him. They found him sitting on top of a hill.
The captain said to him, "Man of God, the king has
commanded you to come down with us."
10But Elijah replied to the captain, "If I am a man of
God, let fire come down from heaven and destroy
you and your fifty men!" Then fire fell from heaven
and killed them all.
11So the king sent another captain with fifty men.
The captain said to him, "Man of God, the king demands that you come down at once."

1:8 Or *He was wearing clothing made of hair.*

KING JAMES VERSION

12 And Elijah answered and said unto them, If I *be* a man of God, let fire come down from heaven, and consume thee and thy fifty. And the fire of God came down from heaven, and consumed him and his fifty.

13 And he sent again a captain of the third fifty with his fifty. And the third captain of fifty went up, and came and fell on his knees before Elijah, and besought him, and said unto him, O man of God, I pray thee, let my life, and the life of these fifty thy servants, be precious in thy sight.

14 Behold, there came fire down from heaven, and burnt up the two captains of the former fifties with their fifties: therefore let my life now be precious in thy sight.

15 And the angel of the LORD said unto Elijah, Go down with him: be not afraid of him. And he arose, and went down with him unto the king.

16 And he said unto him, Thus saith the LORD, Forasmuch as thou hast sent messengers to inquire of Baal-zebub the god of Ekron, *is it* not because *there is* no God in Israel to inquire of his word? therefore thou shalt not come down off that bed on which thou art gone up, but shalt surely die.

17 So he died according to the word of the LORD which Elijah had spoken. And Jehoram reigned in his stead in the second year of Jehoram the son of Jehoshaphat king of Judah; because he had no son.

18 Now the rest of the acts of Ahaziah which he did, *are* they not written in the book of the chronicles of the kings of Israel?

2 1 And it came to pass, when the LORD would take up Elijah into heaven by a whirlwind, that Elijah went with Elisha from Gilgal.

2 And Elijah said unto Elisha, Tarry here, I pray thee; for the LORD hath sent me to Bethel. And Elisha said *unto him, As* the LORD liveth, and *as* thy soul liveth, I will not leave thee. So they went down to Bethel.

3 And the sons of the prophets that *were* at Bethel came forth to Elisha, and said unto him, Knowest thou that the LORD will take away thy master from thy head today? And he said, Yea, I know *it;* hold ye your peace.

4 And Elijah said unto him, Elisha, tarry here, I pray thee; for the LORD hath sent me to Jericho. And he said, *As* the LORD liveth, and *as* thy soul liveth, I will not leave thee. So they came to Jericho.

5 And the sons of the prophets that *were* at Jericho came to Elisha, and said unto him, Knowest thou that the LORD will take away thy master from thy head today? And he answered, Yea, I know *it;* hold ye your peace.

6 And Elijah said unto him, Tarry, I pray thee, here; for the LORD hath sent me to Jordan. And he said, *As*

NEW LIVING TRANSLATION

12 Elijah replied, "If I am a man of God, let fire come down from heaven and destroy you and your fifty men!" And again the fire of God fell from heaven and killed them all.

13 Once more the king sent a third captain with fifty men. But this time the captain went up the hill and fell to his knees before Elijah. He pleaded with him, "O man of God, please spare my life and the lives of these, your fifty servants. 14 See how the fire from heaven came down and destroyed the first two groups. But now please spare my life!"

15 Then the angel of the LORD said to Elijah, "Go down with him, and don't be afraid of him." So Elijah got up and went with him to the king.

16 And Elijah said to the king, "This is what the LORD says: Why did you send messengers to Baal-zebub, the god of Ekron, to ask whether you will recover? Is there no God in Israel to answer your question? Therefore, because you have done this, you will never leave the bed you are lying on; you will surely die."

17 So Ahaziah died, just as the LORD had promised through Elijah. Since Ahaziah did not have a son to succeed him, his brother Joram* became the next king. This took place in the second year of the reign of Jehoram son of Jehoshaphat, king of Judah.

18 The rest of the events in Ahaziah's reign are recorded in *The Book of the History of the Kings of Israel.*

Elijah Taken into Heaven

2 When the LORD was about to take Elijah up to heaven in a whirlwind, Elijah and Elisha were traveling from Gilgal. 2 And Elijah said to Elisha, "Stay here, for the LORD has told me to go to Bethel."

But Elisha replied, "As surely as the LORD lives and you yourself live, I will never leave you!" So they went down together to Bethel.

3 The group of prophets from Bethel came to Elisha and asked him, "Did you know that the LORD is going to take your master away from you today?"

"Of course I know," Elisha answered. "But be quiet about it."

4 Then Elijah said to Elisha, "Stay here, for the LORD has told me to go to Jericho."

But Elisha replied again, "As surely as the LORD lives and you yourself live, I will never leave you." So they went on together to Jericho.

5 Then the group of prophets from Jericho came to Elisha and asked him, "Did you know that the LORD is going to take your master away from you today?"

"Of course I know," Elisha answered. "But be quiet about it."

6 Then Elijah said to Elisha, "Stay here, for the LORD has told me to go to the Jordan River."

But again Elisha replied, "As surely as the LORD

1:17 Hebrew *Jehoram,* a variant spelling of Joram.

KING JAMES VERSION

the LORD liveth, and *as* thy soul liveth, I will not leave
thee. And they two went on.
7 And fifty men of the sons of the prophets went, and
stood to view afar off: and they two stood by Jordan.
8 And Elijah took his mantle, and wrapped *it* together, and smote the waters, and they were divided
hither and thither, so that they two went over on dry
ground.
9 And it came to pass, when they were gone over, that
Elijah said unto Elisha, Ask what I shall do for thee, before I be taken away from thee. And Elisha said, I pray
thee, let a double portion of thy spirit be upon me.
10 And he said, Thou hast asked a hard thing: *nevertheless,* if thou see me *when I am* taken from thee,
it shall be so unto thee; but if not, it shall not be *so.*
11 And it came to pass, as they still went on, and
talked, that, behold, *there appeared* a chariot of fire,
and horses of fire, and parted them both asunder;
and Elijah went up by a whirlwind into heaven.
12 And Elisha saw *it,* and he cried, My father, my father, the chariot of Israel, and the horsemen thereof.
And he saw him no more: and he took hold of his
own clothes, and rent them in two pieces.
13 He took up also the mantle of Elijah that fell
from him, and went back, and stood by the bank of
Jordan;
14 And he took the mantle of Elijah that fell from
him, and smote the waters, and said, Where *is* the
LORD God of Elijah? and when he also had smitten
the waters, they parted hither and thither: and Elisha
went over.
15 And when the sons of the prophets which *were*
to view at Jericho saw him, they said, The spirit of Elijah doth rest on Elisha. And they came to meet him,
and bowed themselves to the ground before him.
16 And they said unto him, Behold now, there be
with thy servants fifty strong men; let them go, we
pray thee, and seek thy master: lest peradventure the
spirit of the LORD hath taken him up, and cast him
upon some mountain, or into some valley. And he
said, Ye shall not send.
17 And when they urged him till he was ashamed,
he said, Send. They sent therefore fifty men; and they
sought three days, but found him not.
18 And when they came again to him, (for he tarried at Jericho,) he said unto them, Did I not say unto
you, Go not?
19 And the men of the city said unto Elisha, Behold,
I pray thee, the situation of this city *is* pleasant, as my
lord seeth: but the water *is* naught, and the ground
barren.
20 And he said, Bring me a new cruse, and put salt
therein. And they brought *it* to him.
21 And he went forth unto the spring of the waters,
and cast the salt in there, and said, Thus saith the
LORD, I have healed these waters; there shall not be
from thence any more death or barren *land.*

NEW LIVING TRANSLATION

lives and you yourself live, I will never leave you." So
they went on together.
7 Fifty men from the group of prophets also went
and watched from a distance as Elijah and Elisha
stopped beside the Jordan River. 8 Then Elijah folded
his cloak together and struck the water with it. The
river divided, and the two of them went across on dry
ground!
9 When they came to the other side, Elijah said
to Elisha, "Tell me what I can do for you before I am
taken away."
And Elisha replied, "Please let me inherit a double
share of your spirit and become your successor."
10 "You have asked a difficult thing," Elijah replied.
"If you see me when I am taken from you, then you
will get your request. But if not, then you won't."
11 As they were walking along and talking, suddenly
a chariot of fire appeared, drawn by horses of fire. It
drove between the two men, separating them, and Elijah was carried by a whirlwind into heaven. 12 Elisha
saw it and cried out, "My father! My father! I see the
chariots and charioteers of Israel!" And as they dis-
apeared from sight, Elisha tore his clothes in distress.
13 Elisha picked up Elijah's cloak, which had fallen
when he was taken up. Then Elisha returned to the
bank of the Jordan River. 14 He struck the water with
Elijah's cloak and cried out, "Where is the LORD, the
God of Elijah?" Then the river divided, and Elisha
went across.
15 When the group of prophets from Jericho saw
from a distance what happened, they exclaimed,
"Elijah's spirit rests upon Elisha!" And they went to
meet him and bowed to the ground before him.
16 "Sir," they said, "just say the word and fifty of our
strongest men will search the wilderness for your
master. Perhaps the Spirit of the LORD has left him on
some mountain or in some valley."
"No," Elisha said, "don't send them." 17 But they
kept urging him until they shamed him into agreeing, and he finally said, "All right, send them." So fifty
men searched for three days but did not find Elijah.
18 Elisha was still at Jericho when they returned.
"Didn't I tell you not to go?" he asked.

Elisha's First Miracles

19 One day the leaders of the town of Jericho visited
Elisha. "We have a problem, my lord," they told him.
"This town is located in pleasant surroundings, as
you can see. But the water is bad, and the land is
unproductive."
20 Elisha said, "Bring me a new bowl with salt in it."
So they brought it to him. 21 Then he went out to the
spring that supplied the town with water and threw
the salt into it. And he said, "This is what the LORD
says: I have purified this water. It will no longer cause

KING JAMES VERSION

22 So the waters were healed unto this day, according to the saying of Elisha which he spake.
23 And he went up from thence unto Bethel: and as
he was going up by the way, there came forth little
children out of the city, and mocked him, and said
unto him, Go up, thou bald head; go up, thou bald
head.
24 And he turned back, and looked on them, and
cursed them in the name of the LORD. And there
came forth two she bears out of the wood, and tare
forty and two children of them.
25 And he went from thence to mount Carmel, and
from thence he returned to Samaria.

3 1 Now Jehoram the son of Ahab began to reign
over Israel in Samaria the eighteenth year of
Jehoshaphat king of Judah, and reigned twelve years.
2 And he wrought evil in the sight of the LORD; but
not like his father, and like his mother: for he put
away the image of Baal that his father had made.
3 Nevertheless he cleaved unto the sins of Jeroboam the son of Nebat, which made Israel to sin; he
departed not therefrom.
4 And Mesha king of Moab was a sheepmaster, and
rendered unto the king of Israel an hundred thousand lambs, and an hundred thousand rams, with
the wool.
5 But it came to pass, when Ahab was dead, that the
king of Moab rebelled against the king of Israel.
6 And king Jehoram went out of Samaria the same
time, and numbered all Israel.
7 And he went and sent to Jehoshaphat the king of
Judah, saying, The king of Moab hath rebelled against
me: wilt thou go with me against Moab to battle? And
he said, I will go up: I *am* as thou *art*, my people as thy
people, *and* my horses as thy horses.
8 And he said, Which way shall we go up? And he
answered, The way through the wilderness of Edom.
9 So the king of Israel went, and the king of Judah,
and the king of Edom: and they fetched a compass of
seven days' journey: and there was no water for the
host, and for the cattle that followed them.
10 And the king of Israel said, Alas! that the LORD
hath called these three kings together, to deliver
them into the hand of Moab!
11 But Jehoshaphat said, *Is there* not here a prophet
of the LORD, that we may inquire of the LORD by him?
And one of the king of Israel's servants answered and
said, Here *is* Elisha the son of Shaphat, which poured
water on the hands of Elijah.
12 And Jehoshaphat said, The word of the LORD is
with him. So the king of Israel and Jehoshaphat and
the king of Edom went down to him.
13 And Elisha said unto the king of Israel, What

NEW LIVING TRANSLATION

death or infertility.*" 22 And the water has remained
pure ever since, just as Elisha said.
23 Elisha left Jericho and went up to Bethel. As he
was walking along the road, a group of boys from the
town began mocking and making fun of him. "Go
away, baldy!" they chanted. "Go away, baldy!" 24 Elisha
turned around and looked at them, and he cursed
them in the name of the LORD. Then two bears came
out of the woods and mauled forty-two of them.
25 From there Elisha went to Mount Carmel and finally returned to Samaria.

War between Israel and Moab

3 Ahab's son Joram* began to rule over Israel in
the eighteenth year of King Jehoshaphat's reign
in Judah. He reigned in Samaria twelve years. 2 He did
what was evil in the LORD's sight, but not to the same
extent as his father and mother. He at least tore down
the sacred pillar of Baal that his father had set up.
3 Nevertheless, he continued in the sins that Jeroboam son of Nebat had committed and led the people
of Israel to commit.
4 King Mesha of Moab was a sheep breeder. He
used to pay the king of Israel an annual tribute of
100,000 lambs and the wool of 100,000 rams. 5 But
after Ahab's death, the king of Moab rebelled against
the king of Israel. 6 So King Joram promptly mustered
the army of Israel and marched from Samaria. 7 On
the way, he sent this message to King Jehoshaphat of
Judah: "The king of Moab has rebelled against me.
Will you join me in battle against him?"
And Jehoshaphat replied, "Why, of course! You
and I are as one. My troops are your troops, and my
horses are your horses." 8 Then Jehoshaphat asked,
"What route will we take?"
"We will attack from the wilderness of Edom,"
Joram replied.
9 The king of Edom and his troops joined them,
and all three armies traveled along a roundabout
route through the wilderness for seven days. But
there was no water for the men or their animals.
10 "What should we do?" the king of Israel cried
out. "The LORD has brought the three of us here to let
the king of Moab defeat us."
11 But King Jehoshaphat of Judah asked, "Is there
no prophet of the LORD with us? If there is, we can
ask the LORD what to do through him."
One of King Joram's officers replied, "Elisha son of
Shaphat is here. He used to be Elijah's personal assistant.*"
12 Jehoshaphat said, "Yes, the LORD speaks through
him." So the kings of Israel, Judah, and Edom went to
consult with Elisha.
13 "Why are you coming to me?"* Elisha asked the

2:21 Or *or make the land unproductive;* Hebrew reads *or barrenness.*
3:1 Hebrew *Jehoram,* a variant spelling of Joram; also in 3:6. **3:11** Hebrew *He used to pour water on the hands of Elijah.* **3:13** Hebrew *What is there in common between you and me?*

have I to do with thee? get thee to the prophets of thy father, and to the prophets of thy mother. And the king of Israel said unto him, Nay: for the LORD hath called these three kings together, to deliver them into the hand of Moab.

14 And Elisha said, *As* the LORD of hosts liveth, before whom I stand, surely, were it not that I regard the presence of Jehoshaphat the king of Judah, I would not look toward thee, nor see thee.

15 But now bring me a minstrel. And it came to pass, when the minstrel played, that the hand of the LORD came upon him.

16 And he said, Thus saith the LORD, Make this valley full of ditches.

17 For thus saith the LORD, Ye shall not see wind, neither shall ye see rain; yet that valley shall be filled with water, that ye may drink, both ye, and your cattle, and your beasts.

18 And this is *but* a light thing in the sight of the LORD: he will deliver the Moabites also into your hand.

19 And ye shall smite every fenced city, and every choice city, and shall fell every good tree, and stop all wells of water, and mar every good piece of land with stones.

20 And it came to pass in the morning, when the meat offering was offered, that, behold, there came water by the way of Edom, and the country was filled with water.

21 And when all the Moabites heard that the kings were come up to fight against them, they gathered all that were able to put on armour, and upward, and stood in the border.

22 And they rose up early in the morning, and the sun shone upon the water, and the Moabites saw the water on the other side *as* red as blood:

23 And they said, This *is* blood: the kings are surely slain, and they have smitten one another: now therefore, Moab, to the spoil.

24 And when they came to the camp of Israel, the Israelites rose up and smote the Moabites, so that they fled before them: but they went forward smiting the Moabites, even in *their* country.

25 And they beat down the cities, and on every good piece of land cast every man his stone, and filled it; and they stopped all the wells of water, and felled all the good trees: only in Kir-haraseth left they the stones thereof; howbeit the slingers went about *it*, and smote it.

26 And when the king of Moab saw that the battle was too sore for him, he took with him seven hundred men that drew swords, to break through *even* unto the king of Edom: but they could not.

27 Then he took his eldest son that should have reigned in his stead, and offered him *for* a burnt offering upon the wall. And there was great indignation against Israel: and they departed from him, and returned to *their own* land.

king of Israel. "Go to the pagan prophets of your father and mother!"

But King Joram of Israel said, "No! For it was the LORD who called us three kings here—only to be defeated by the king of Moab!"

14 Elisha replied, "As surely as the LORD Almighty lives, whom I serve, I wouldn't even bother with you except for my respect for King Jehoshaphat of Judah. 15 Now bring me someone who can play the harp."

While the harp was being played, the power* of the LORD came upon Elisha, 16 and he said, "This is what the LORD says: This dry valley will be filled with pools of water! 17 You will see neither wind nor rain, says the LORD, but this valley will be filled with water. You will have plenty for yourselves and your cattle and other animals. 18 But this is only a simple thing for the LORD, for he will make you victorious over the army of Moab! 19 You will conquer the best of their towns, even the fortified ones. You will cut down all their good trees, stop up all their springs, and ruin all their good land with stones."

20 The next day at about the time when the morning sacrifice was offered, water suddenly appeared! It was flowing from the direction of Edom, and soon there was water everywhere.

21 Meanwhile, when the people of Moab heard about the three armies marching against them, they mobilized every man who was old enough to strap on a sword, and they stationed themselves along their border. 22 But when they got up the next morning, the sun was shining across the water, making it appear red to the Moabites—like blood. 23 "It's blood!" the Moabites exclaimed. "The three armies must have attacked and killed each other! Let's go, men of Moab, and collect the plunder!"

24 But when the Moabites arrived at the Israelite camp, the army of Israel rushed out and attacked them until they turned and ran. The army of Israel chased them into the land of Moab, destroying everything as they went.* 25 They destroyed the towns, covered their good land with stones, stopped up all the springs, and cut down all the good trees. Finally, only Kir-hareseth and its stone walls were left, but men with slings surrounded and attacked it.

26 When the king of Moab saw that he was losing the battle, he led 700 of his swordsmen in a desperate attempt to break through the enemy lines near the king of Edom, but they failed. 27 Then the king of Moab took his oldest son, who would have been the next king, and sacrificed him as a burnt offering on the wall. So there was great anger against Israel,* and the Israelites withdrew and returned to their own land.

3:15 Hebrew *the hand.* **3:24** The meaning of the Hebrew is uncertain. **3:27** Or *So Israel's anger was great.* The meaning of the Hebrew is uncertain.

4 1Now there cried a certain woman of the wives
of the sons of the prophets unto Elisha, saying,
Thy servant my husband is dead; and thou knowest
that thy servant did fear the LORD: and the creditor is
come to take unto him my two sons to be bondmen.
2And Elisha said unto her, What shall I do for thee?
tell me, what hast thou in the house? And she said,
Thine handmaid hath not any thing in the house,
save a pot of oil.
3Then he said, Go, borrow thee vessels abroad of
all thy neighbours, *even* empty vessels; borrow not
a few.
4And when thou art come in, thou shalt shut the
door upon thee and upon thy sons, and shalt pour
out into all those vessels, and thou shalt set aside that
which is full.
5So she went from him, and shut the door upon
her and upon her sons, who brought *the vessels* to
her; and she poured out.
6And it came to pass, when the vessels were full,
that she said unto her son, Bring me yet a vessel. And
he said unto her, *There is* not a vessel more. And the
oil stayed.
7Then she came and told the man of God. And he
said, Go, sell the oil, and pay thy debt, and live thou
and thy children of the rest.
8And it fell on a day, that Elisha passed to Shunem,
where *was* a great woman; and she constrained him
to eat bread. And *so* it was, *that* as oft as he passed by,
he turned in thither to eat bread.
9And she said unto her husband, Behold now, I
perceive that this *is* an holy man of God, which
passeth by us continually.
10Let us make a little chamber, I pray thee, on the
wall; and let us set for him there a bed, and a table,
and a stool, and a candlestick: and it shall be, when
he cometh to us, that he shall turn in thither.
11And it fell on a day, that he came thither, and he
turned into the chamber, and lay there.
12And he said to Gehazi his servant, Call this
Shunammite. And when he had called her, she stood
before him.
13And he said unto him, Say now unto her, Behold,
thou hast been careful for us with all this care; what
is to be done for thee? wouldest thou be spoken for
to the king, or to the captain of the host? And she
answered, I dwell among mine own people.
14And he said, What then *is* to be done for her?
And Gehazi answered, Verily she hath no child, and
her husband is old.
15And he said, Call her. And when he had called
her, she stood in the door.
16And he said, About this season, according to the
time of life, thou shalt embrace a son. And she said,
Nay, my lord, *thou* man of God, do not lie unto thine
handmaid.

Elisha Helps a Poor Widow

4 One day the widow of a member of the group of
prophets came to Elisha and cried out, "My husband who served you is dead, and you know how he
feared the LORD. But now a creditor has come, threatening to take my two sons as slaves."
2"What can I do to help you?" Elisha asked. "Tell
me, what do you have in the house?"
"Nothing at all, except a flask of olive oil," she
replied.
3And Elisha said, "Borrow as many empty jars as
you can from your friends and neighbors. 4Then go
into your house with your sons and shut the door behind you. Pour olive oil from your flask into the jars,
setting each one aside when it is filled."
5So she did as she was told. Her sons kept bringing jars to her, and she filled one after another. 6Soon
every container was full to the brim!
"Bring me another jar," she said to one of her sons.
"There aren't any more!" he told her. And then the
olive oil stopped flowing.
7When she told the man of God what had happened, he said to her, "Now sell the olive oil and pay
your debts, and you and your sons can live on what is
left over."

Elisha and the Woman from Shunem

8One day Elisha went to the town of Shunem. A
wealthy woman lived there, and she urged him to
come to her home for a meal. After that, whenever he
passed that way, he would stop there for something
to eat.
9She said to her husband, "I am sure this man
who stops in from time to time is a holy man of
God. 10Let's build a small room for him on the roof
and furnish it with a bed, a table, a chair, and a
lamp. Then he will have a place to stay whenever he
comes by."
11One day Elisha returned to Shunem, and he went
up to this upper room to rest. 12He said to his servant
Gehazi, "Tell the woman from Shunem I want to
speak to her." When she appeared, 13Elisha said to
Gehazi, "Tell her, 'We appreciate the kind concern
you have shown us. What can we do for you? Can we
put in a good word for you to the king or to the commander of the army?'"
"No," she replied, "my family takes good care
of me."
14Later Elisha asked Gehazi, "What can we do
for her?"
Gehazi replied, "She doesn't have a son, and her
husband is an old man."
15"Call her back again," Elisha told him. When the
woman returned, Elisha said to her as she stood in
the doorway, 16"Next year at this time you will be
holding a son in your arms!"
"No, my lord!" she cried. "O man of God, don't deceive me and get my hopes up like that."

KING JAMES VERSION

17 And the woman conceived, and bare a son at that
season that Elisha had said unto her, according to the
time of life.
18 And when the child was grown, it fell on a day,
that he went out to his father to the reapers.
19 And he said unto his father, My head, my head.
And he said to a lad, Carry him to his mother.
20 And when he had taken him, and brought him
to his mother, he sat on her knees till noon, and *then*
died.
21 And she went up, and laid him on the bed of
the man of God, and shut *the door* upon him, and
went out.
22 And she called unto her husband, and said, Send
me, I pray thee, one of the young men, and one of the
asses, that I may run to the man of God, and come
again.
23 And he said, Wherefore wilt thou go to him today? *it is* neither new moon, nor sabbath. And she
said, *It shall be* well.
24 Then she saddled an ass, and said to her servant,
Drive, and go forward; slack not *thy* riding for me,
except I bid thee.
25 So she went and came unto the man of God to
mount Carmel. And it came to pass, when the man of
God saw her afar off, that he said to Gehazi his servant, Behold, *yonder is* that Shunammite:
26 Run now, I pray thee, to meet her, and say unto
her, *Is it* well with thee? *is it* well with thy husband? *is
it* well with the child? And she answered, *It is* well.
27 And when she came to the man of God to the
hill, she caught him by the feet: but Gehazi came
near to thrust her away. And the man of God said, Let
her alone; for her soul *is* vexed within her: and the
LORD hath hid *it* from me, and hath not told me.
28 Then she said, Did I desire a son of my lord? did I
not say, Do not deceive me?
29 Then he said to Gehazi, Gird up thy loins, and
take my staff in thine hand, and go thy way: if thou
meet any man, salute him not; and if any salute thee,
answer him not again: and lay my staff upon the face
of the child.
30 And the mother of the child said, *As* the LORD
liveth, and *as* thy soul liveth, I will not leave thee. And
he arose, and followed her.
31 And Gehazi passed on before them, and laid the
staff upon the face of the child; but *there was* neither
voice, nor hearing. Wherefore he went again to meet
him, and told him, saying, The child is not awaked.
32 And when Elisha was come into the house, behold, the child was dead, *and* laid upon his bed.
33 He went in therefore, and shut the door upon
them twain, and prayed unto the LORD.
34 And he went up, and lay upon the child, and put
his mouth upon his mouth, and his eyes upon his
eyes, and his hands upon his hands: and he stretched
himself upon the child; and the flesh of the child
waxed warm.

NEW LIVING TRANSLATION

17 But sure enough, the woman soon became pregnant. And at that time the following year she had a
son, just as Elisha had said.
18 One day when her child was older, he went out to
help his father, who was working with the harvesters.
19 Suddenly he cried out, "My head hurts! My head
hurts!"
His father said to one of the servants, "Carry him
home to his mother."
20 So the servant took him home, and his mother
held him on her lap. But around noontime he died.
21 She carried him up and laid him on the bed of the
man of God, then shut the door and left him there.
22 She sent a message to her husband: "Send one of
the servants and a donkey so that I can hurry to the
man of God and come right back."
23 "Why go today?" he asked. "It is neither a new
moon festival nor a Sabbath."
But she said, "It will be all right."
24 So she saddled the donkey and said to the servant, "Hurry! Don't slow down unless I tell you to."
25 As she approached the man of God at Mount
Carmel, Elisha saw her in the distance. He said to Gehazi, "Look, the woman from Shunem is coming.
26 Run out to meet her and ask her, 'Is everything all
right with you, your husband, and your child?'"
"Yes," the woman told Gehazi, "everything is fine."
27 But when she came to the man of God at the
mountain, she fell to the ground before him and
caught hold of his feet. Gehazi began to push her
away, but the man of God said, "Leave her alone. She
is deeply troubled, but the LORD has not told me
what it is."
28 Then she said, "Did I ask you for a son, my lord?
And didn't I say, 'Don't deceive me and get my
hopes up'?"
29 Then Elisha said to Gehazi, "Get ready to travel*;
take my staff and go! Don't talk to anyone along the
way. Go quickly and lay the staff on the child's face."
30 But the boy's mother said, "As surely as the LORD
lives and you yourself live, I won't go home unless
you go with me." So Elisha returned with her.
31 Gehazi hurried on ahead and laid the staff on
the child's face, but nothing happened. There was no
sign of life. He returned to meet Elisha and told him,
"The child is still dead."
32 When Elisha arrived, the child was indeed dead,
lying there on the prophet's bed. 33 He went in alone
and shut the door behind him and prayed to the
LORD. 34 Then he lay down on the child's body, placing his mouth on the child's mouth, his eyes on the
child's eyes, and his hands on the child's hands. And
as he stretched out on him, the child's body began to

4:29 Hebrew *Bind up your loins.*

KING JAMES VERSION

35 Then he returned, and walked in the house to
and fro; and went up, and stretched himself upon
him: and the child sneezed seven times, and the
child opened his eyes.
36 And he called Gehazi, and said, Call this Shunammite. So he called her. And when she was come in
unto him, he said, Take up thy son.
37 Then she went in, and fell at his feet, and bowed
herself to the ground, and took up her son, and
went out.

38 And Elisha came again to Gilgal: and *there was* a
dearth in the land; and the sons of the prophets *were*
sitting before him: and he said unto his servant, Set
on the great pot, and seethe pottage for the sons of
the prophets.
39 And one went out into the field to gather herbs,
and found a wild vine, and gathered thereof wild
gourds his lap full, and came and shred *them* into the
pot of pottage: for they knew *them* not.
40 So they poured out for the men to eat. And it
came to pass, as they were eating of the pottage, that
they cried out, and said, O *thou* man of God, *there is*
death in the pot. And they could not eat *thereof.*
41 But he said, Then bring meal. And he cast *it* into
the pot; and he said, Pour out for the people, that they
may eat. And there was no harm in the pot.
42 And there came a man from Baal-shalisha, and
brought the man of God bread of the firstfruits,
twenty loaves of barley, and full ears of corn in the
husk thereof. And he said, Give unto the people, that
they may eat.
43 And his servitor said, What, should I set this before an hundred men? He said again, Give the people,
that they may eat: for thus saith the LORD, They shall
eat, and shall leave *thereof.*
44 So he set *it* before them, and they did eat, and
left *thereof,* according to the word of the LORD.

5 1 Now Naaman, captain of the host of the king
of Syria, was a great man with his master, and
honourable, because by him the LORD had given deliverance unto Syria: he was also a mighty man in
valour, *but he was* a leper.
2 And the Syrians had gone out by companies, and
had brought away captive out of the land of Israel a
little maid; and she waited on Naaman's wife.
3 And she said unto her mistress, Would God my
lord *were* with the prophet that *is* in Samaria! for he
would recover him of his leprosy.
4 And *one* went in, and told his lord, saying, Thus
and thus said the maid that *is* of the land of Israel.
5 And the king of Syria said, Go to, go, and I will
send a letter unto the king of Israel. And he departed,
and took with him ten talents of silver, and six thousand *pieces* of gold, and ten changes of raiment.

NEW LIVING TRANSLATION

grow warm again! 35 Elisha got up, walked back and
forth across the room once, and then stretched himself out again on the child. This time the boy sneezed
seven times and opened his eyes!
36 Then Elisha summoned Gehazi. "Call the child's
mother!" he said. And when she came in, Elisha said,
"Here, take your son!" 37 She fell at his feet and bowed
before him, overwhelmed with gratitude. Then she
took her son in her arms and carried him downstairs.

Miracles during a Famine

38 Elisha now returned to Gilgal, and there was a famine in the land. One day as the group of prophets was
seated before him, he said to his servant, "Put a large
pot on the fire, and make some stew for the rest of
the group."
39 One of the young men went out into the field to
gather herbs and came back with a pocketful of wild
gourds. He shredded them and put them into the pot
without realizing they were poisonous. 40 Some of
the stew was served to the men. But after they had
eaten a bite or two they cried out, "Man of God,
there's poison in this stew!" So they would not eat it.
41 Elisha said, "Bring me some flour." Then he
threw it into the pot and said, "Now it's all right;
go ahead and eat." And then it did not harm them.
42 One day a man from Baal-shalishah brought the
man of God a sack of fresh grain and twenty loaves of
barley bread made from the first grain of his harvest.
Elisha said, "Give it to the people so they can eat."
43 "What?" his servant exclaimed. "Feed a hundred people with only this?"
But Elisha repeated, "Give it to the people so they
can eat, for this is what the LORD says: Everyone will
eat, and there will even be some left over!" 44 And
when they gave it to the people, there was plenty for
all and some left over, just as the LORD had promised.

The Healing of Naaman

5 The king of Aram had great admiration for
Naaman, the commander of his army, because
through him the LORD had given Aram great victories. But though Naaman was a mighty warrior, he
suffered from leprosy.*
2 At this time Aramean raiders had invaded the
land of Israel, and among their captives was a young
girl who had been given to Naaman's wife as a maid.
3 One day the girl said to her mistress, "I wish my
master would go to see the prophet in Samaria. He
would heal him of his leprosy."
4 So Naaman told the king what the young girl
from Israel had said. 5 "Go and visit the prophet," the
king of Aram told him. "I will send a letter of introduction for you to take to the king of Israel." So Naaman started out, carrying as gifts 750 pounds of
silver, 150 pounds of gold,* and ten sets of clothing.

5:1 Or *from a contagious skin disease.* The Hebrew word used here and throughout this passage can describe various skin diseases. **5:5** Hebrew *10 talents* [340 kilograms] *of silver, 6,000 shekels* [68 kilograms] *of gold.*

KING JAMES VERSION

6 And he brought the letter to the king of Israel,
saying, Now when this letter is come unto thee, behold, I have *therewith* sent Naaman my servant to
thee, that thou mayest recover him of his leprosy.
7 And it came to pass, when the king of Israel had
read the letter, that he rent his clothes, and said, *Am* I
God, to kill and to make alive, that this man doth
send unto me to recover a man of his leprosy? wherefore consider, I pray you, and see how he seeketh a
quarrel against me.
8 And it was *so,* when Elisha the man of God had
heard that the king of Israel had rent his clothes, that
he sent to the king, saying, Wherefore hast thou rent
thy clothes? let him come now to me, and he shall
know that there is a prophet in Israel.
9 So Naaman came with his horses and with his
chariot, and stood at the door of the house of Elisha.
10 And Elisha sent a messenger unto him, saying,
Go and wash in Jordan seven times, and thy flesh
shall come again to thee, and thou shalt be clean.
11 But Naaman was wroth, and went away, and said,
Behold, I thought, He will surely come out to me, and
stand, and call on the name of the LORD his God, and
strike his hand over the place, and recover the leper.
12 *Are* not Abana and Pharpar, rivers of Damascus,
better than all the waters of Israel? may I not wash
in them, and be clean? So he turned and went away
in a rage.
13 And his servants came near, and spake unto him,
and said, My father, *if* the prophet had bid thee *do
some* great thing, wouldest thou not have done *it?*
how much rather then, when he saith to thee, Wash,
and be clean?
14 Then went he down, and dipped himself seven
times in Jordan, according to the saying of the man
of God: and his flesh came again like unto the flesh
of a little child, and he was clean.
15 And he returned to the man of God, he and all
his company, and came, and stood before him: and
he said, Behold, now I know that *there is* no God in all
the earth, but in Israel: now therefore, I pray thee,
take a blessing of thy servant.
16 But he said, *As* the LORD liveth, before whom I
stand, I will receive none. And he urged him to take
it; but he refused.
17 And Naaman said, Shall there not then, I pray
thee, be given to thy servant two mules' burden of
earth? for thy servant will henceforth offer neither
burnt offering nor sacrifice unto other gods, but
unto the LORD.
18 In this thing the LORD pardon thy servant, *that*
when my master goeth into the house of Rimmon to
worship there, and he leaneth on my hand, and I bow
myself in the house of Rimmon: when I bow down
myself in the house of Rimmon, the LORD pardon thy
servant in this thing.
19 And he said unto him, Go in peace. So he departed from him a little way.

NEW LIVING TRANSLATION

6 The letter to the king of Israel said: "With this letter
I present my servant Naaman. I want you to heal him
of his leprosy."
7 When the king of Israel read the letter, he tore his
clothes in dismay and said, "This man sends me a
leper to heal! Am I God, that I can give life and take it
away? I can see that he's just trying to pick a fight
with me."
8 But when Elisha, the man of God, heard that the
king of Israel had torn his clothes in dismay, he sent
this message to him: "Why are you so upset? Send
Naaman to me, and he will learn that there is a true
prophet here in Israel."
9 So Naaman went with his horses and chariots
and waited at the door of Elisha's house. 10 But Elisha
sent a messenger out to him with this message: "Go
and wash yourself seven times in the Jordan River.
Then your skin will be restored, and you will be
healed of your leprosy."
11 But Naaman became angry and stalked away. "I
thought he would certainly come out to meet me!"
he said. "I expected him to wave his hand over the
leprosy and call on the name of the LORD his God and
heal me! 12 Aren't the rivers of Damascus, the Abana
and the Pharpar, better than any of the rivers of Israel? Why shouldn't I wash in them and be healed?"
So Naaman turned and went away in a rage.
13 But his officers tried to reason with him and
said, "Sir,* if the prophet had told you to do something very difficult, wouldn't you have done it? So
you should certainly obey him when he says simply,
'Go and wash and be cured!' " 14 So Naaman went
down to the Jordan River and dipped himself seven
times, as the man of God had instructed him. And his
skin became as healthy as the skin of a young child's,
and he was healed!
15 Then Naaman and his entire party went back to
find the man of God. They stood before him, and Naaman said, "Now I know that there is no God in all the
world except in Israel. So please accept a gift from
your servant."
16 But Elisha replied, "As surely as the LORD lives,
whom I serve, I will not accept any gifts." And though
Naaman urged him to take the gift, Elisha refused.
17 Then Naaman said, "All right, but please allow
me to load two of my mules with earth from this
place, and I will take it back home with me. From
now on I will never again offer burnt offerings or
sacrifices to any other god except the LORD. 18 However, may the LORD pardon me in this one thing:
When my master the king goes into the temple of
the god Rimmon to worship there and leans on my
arm, may the LORD pardon me when I bow, too."
19 "Go in peace," Elisha said. So Naaman started
home again.

5:13 Hebrew *My father.*

20 But Gehazi, the servant of Elisha the man of God,
said, Behold, my master hath spared Naaman this
Syrian, in not receiving at his hands that which he
brought: but, *as* the LORD liveth, I will run after him,
and take somewhat of him.
21 So Gehazi followed after Naaman. And when
Naaman saw *him* running after him, he lighted down
from the chariot to meet him, and said, *Is* all well?
22 And he said, All *is* well. My master hath sent me,
saying, Behold, even now there be come to me from
mount Ephraim two young men of the sons of the
prophets: give them, I pray thee, a talent of silver, and
two changes of garments.
23 And Naaman said, Be content, take two talents.
And he urged him, and bound two talents of silver in
two bags, with two changes of garments, and laid
them upon two of his servants; and they bare *them*
before him.
24 And when he came to the tower, he took *them*
from their hand, and bestowed *them* in the house:
and he let the men go, and they departed.
25 But he went in, and stood before his master. And
Elisha said unto him, Whence *comest thou,* Gehazi?
And he said, Thy servant went no whither.
26 And he said unto him, Went not mine heart *with
thee,* when the man turned again from his chariot to
meet thee? *Is it* a time to receive money, and to receive garments, and oliveyards, and vineyards, and
sheep, and oxen, and menservants, and maidservants?
27 The leprosy therefore of Naaman shall cleave
unto thee, and unto thy seed for ever. And he went
out from his presence a leper *as white* as snow.

6 1 And the sons of the prophets said unto Elisha,
Behold now, the place where we dwell with thee
is too strait for us.
2 Let us go, we pray thee, unto Jordan, and take
thence every man a beam, and let us make us a place
there, where we may dwell. And he answered, Go ye.
3 And one said, Be content, I pray thee, and go with
thy servants. And he answered, I will go.
4 So he went with them. And when they came to
Jordan, they cut down wood.
5 But as one was felling a beam, the ax head fell
into the water: and he cried, and said, Alas, master!
for it was borrowed.
6 And the man of God said, Where fell it? And he
shewed him the place. And he cut down a stick, and
cast *it* in thither; and the iron did swim.
7 Therefore said he, Take *it* up to thee. And he put
out his hand, and took it.

The Greed of Gehazi

20 But Gehazi, the servant of Elisha, the man of God,
said to himself, "My master should not have let this
Aramean get away without accepting any of his gifts.
As surely as the LORD lives, I will chase after him and
get something from him." 21 So Gehazi set off after
Naaman.
When Naaman saw Gehazi running after him, he
climbed down from his chariot and went to meet
him. "Is everything all right?" Naaman asked.
22 "Yes," Gehazi said, "but my master has sent me
to tell you that two young prophets from the hill
country of Ephraim have just arrived. He would like
75 pounds* of silver and two sets of clothing to give
to them."
23 "By all means, take twice as much* silver," Naaman insisted. He gave him two sets of clothing, tied
up the money in two bags, and sent two of his servants to carry the gifts for Gehazi. 24 But when they
arrived at the citadel,* Gehazi took the gifts from the
servants and sent the men back. Then he went and
hid the gifts inside the house.
25 When he went in to his master, Elisha asked
him, "Where have you been, Gehazi?"
"I haven't been anywhere," he replied.
26 But Elisha asked him, "Don't you realize that I
was there in spirit when Naaman stepped down
from his chariot to meet you? Is this the time to receive money and clothing, olive groves and vineyards, sheep and cattle, and male and female
servants? 27 Because you have done this, you and your
descendants will suffer from Naaman's leprosy forever." When Gehazi left the room, he was covered
with leprosy; his skin was white as snow.

The Floating Ax Head

6 One day the group of prophets came to Elisha
and told him, "As you can see, this place where
we meet with you is too small. 2 Let's go down to the
Jordan River, where there are plenty of logs. There we
can build a new place for us to meet."
"All right," he told them, "go ahead."
3 "Please come with us," someone suggested.
"I will," he said. 4 So he went with them.
When they arrived at the Jordan, they began cutting down trees. 5 But as one of them was cutting a
tree, his ax head fell into the river. "Oh, sir!" he cried.
"It was a borrowed ax!"
6 "Where did it fall?" the man of God asked. When
he showed him the place, Elisha cut a stick and threw
it into the water at that spot. Then the ax head
floated to the surface. 7 "Grab it," Elisha said. And the
man reached out and grabbed it.

5:22 Hebrew *1 talent* [34 kilograms]. **5:23** Hebrew *take 2 talents* [68 kilograms]. **5:24** Hebrew *the Ophel.*

KING JAMES VERSION

8 Then the king of Syria warred against Israel, and
took counsel with his servants, saying, In such and
such a place *shall be* my camp.
9 And the man of God sent unto the king of Israel,
saying, Beware that thou pass not such a place; for
thither the Syrians are come down.
10 And the king of Israel sent to the place which the
man of God told him and warned him of, and saved
himself there, not once nor twice.
11 Therefore the heart of the king of Syria was sore
troubled for this thing; and he called his servants,
and said unto them, Will ye not shew me which of us
is for the king of Israel?
12 And one of his servants said, None, my lord,
O king: but Elisha, the prophet that *is* in Israel, telleth
the king of Israel the words that thou speakest in thy
bedchamber.
13 And he said, Go and spy where he *is,* that I may
send and fetch him. And it was told him, saying,
Behold, *he is* in Dothan.
14 Therefore sent he thither horses, and chariots,
and a great host: and they came by night, and compassed the city about.
15 And when the servant of the man of God was
risen early, and gone forth, behold, an host compassed
the city both with horses and chariots. And his servant
said unto him, Alas, my master! how shall we do?
16 And he answered, Fear not: for they that *be* with
us *are* more than they that *be* with them.
17 And Elisha prayed, and said, LORD, I pray thee,
open his eyes, that he may see. And the LORD opened
the eyes of the young man; and he saw: and, behold,
the mountain *was* full of horses and chariots of fire
round about Elisha.
18 And when they came down to him, Elisha prayed
unto the LORD, and said, Smite this people, I pray
thee, with blindness. And he smote them with blindness according to the word of Elisha.
19 And Elisha said unto them, This *is* not the way,
neither *is* this the city: follow me, and I will bring you
to the man whom ye seek. But he led them to Samaria.
20 And it came to pass, when they were come into
Samaria, that Elisha said, LORD, open the eyes of
these *men,* that they may see. And the LORD opened
their eyes, and they saw; and, behold, *they were* in
the midst of Samaria.
21 And the king of Israel said unto Elisha, when he
saw them, My father, shall I smite *them?* shall I smite
them?
22 And he answered, Thou shalt not smite *them:*
wouldest thou smite those whom thou hast taken
captive with thy sword and with thy bow? set bread
and water before them, that they may eat and drink,
and go to their master.
23 And he prepared great provision for them: and
when they had eaten and drunk, he sent them away,

NEW LIVING TRANSLATION

Elisha Traps the Arameans

8 When the king of Aram was at war with Israel, he
would confer with his officers and say, "We will mobilize our forces at such and such a place."
9 But immediately Elisha, the man of God, would
warn the king of Israel, "Do not go near that place, for
the Arameans are planning to mobilize their troops
there." 10 So the king of Israel would send word to the
place indicated by the man of God. Time and again
Elisha warned the king, so that he would be on the
alert there.
11 The king of Aram became very upset over this.
He called his officers together and demanded,
"Which of you is the traitor? Who has been inform-
ing the king of Israel of my plans?"
12 "It's not us, my lord the king," one of the officers
replied. "Elisha, the prophet in Israel, tells the king of
Israel even the words you speak in the privacy of
your bedroom!"
13 "Go and find out where he is," the king commanded, "so I can send troops to seize him."
And the report came back: "Elisha is at Dothan."
14 So one night the king of Aram sent a great army
with many chariots and horses to surround the city.
15 When the servant of the man of God got up early
the next morning and went outside, there were
troops, horses, and chariots everywhere. "Oh, sir,
what will we do now?" the young man cried to Elisha.
16 "Don't be afraid!" Elisha told him. "For there are
more on our side than on theirs!" 17 Then Elisha
prayed, "O LORD, open his eyes and let him see!" The
LORD opened the young man's eyes, and when he
looked up, he saw that the hillside around Elisha was
filled with horses and chariots of fire.
18 As the Aramean army advanced toward him, Elisha prayed, "O LORD, please make them blind." So the
LORD struck them with blindness as Elisha had asked.
19 Then Elisha went out and told them, "You have
come the wrong way! This isn't the right city! Follow
me, and I will take you to the man you are looking
for." And he led them to the city of Samaria.
20 As soon as they had entered Samaria, Elisha
prayed, "O LORD, now open their eyes and let them
see." So the LORD opened their eyes, and they discovered that they were in the middle of Samaria.
21 When the king of Israel saw them, he shouted to
Elisha, "My father, should I kill them? Should I kill
them?"
22 "Of course not!" Elisha replied. "Do we kill prisoners of war? Give them food and drink and send
them home again to their master."
23 So the king made a great feast for them and then

KING JAMES VERSION

and they went to their master. So the bands of Syria came no more into the land of Israel.

24 And it came to pass after this, that Ben-hadad king of Syria gathered all his host, and went up, and besieged Samaria.

25 And there was a great famine in Samaria: and, behold, they besieged it, until an ass's head was *sold* for fourscore *pieces* of silver, and the fourth part of a cab of dove's dung for five *pieces* of silver.

26 And as the king of Israel was passing by upon the wall, there cried a woman unto him, saying, Help, my lord, O king.

27 And he said, If the LORD do not help thee, whence shall I help thee? out of the barnfloor, or out of the winepress?

28 And the king said unto her, What aileth thee? And she answered, This woman said unto me, Give thy son, that we may eat him today, and we will eat my son tomorrow.

29 So we boiled my son, and did eat him: and I said unto her on the next day, Give thy son, that we may eat him: and she hath hid her son.

30 And it came to pass, when the king heard the words of the woman, that he rent his clothes; and he passed by upon the wall, and the people looked, and, behold, *he had* sackcloth within upon his flesh.

31 Then he said, God do so and more also to me, if the head of Elisha the son of Shaphat shall stand on him this day.

32 But Elisha sat in his house, and the elders sat with him; and *the king* sent a man from before him: but ere the messenger came to him, he said to the elders, See ye how this son of a murderer hath sent to take away mine head? look, when the messenger cometh, shut the door, and hold him fast at the door: *is* not the sound of his master's feet behind him?

33 And while he yet talked with them, behold, the messenger came down unto him: and he said, Behold, this evil *is* of the LORD; what should I wait for the LORD any longer?

7 1 Then Elisha said, Hear ye the word of the LORD; Thus saith the LORD, Tomorrow about this time *shall* a measure of fine flour *be sold* for a shekel, and two measures of barley for a shekel, in the gate of Samaria.

2 Then a lord on whose hand the king leaned answered the man of God, and said, Behold, *if* the LORD would make windows in heaven, might this thing be?

NEW LIVING TRANSLATION

sent them home to their master. After that, the Aramean raiders stayed away from the land of Israel.

Ben-Hadad Besieges Samaria

24 Some time later, however, King Ben-hadad of Aram
mustered his entire army and besieged Samaria. 25 As
a result, there was a great famine in the city. The siege lasted so long that a donkey's head sold for eighty pieces of silver, and a cup of dove's dung sold for five pieces* of silver.

26 One day as the king of Israel was walking along the wall of the city, a woman called to him, "Please help me, my lord the king!"

27 He answered, "If the LORD doesn't help you, what can I do? I have neither food from the threshing
floor nor wine from the press to give you." 28 But then
the king asked, "What is the matter?"

She replied, "This woman said to me: 'Come on, let's eat your son today, then we will eat my son tomorrow.' 29 So we cooked my son and ate him. Then
the next day I said to her, 'Kill your son so we can eat him,' but she has hidden her son."

30 When the king heard this, he tore his clothes in despair. And as the king walked along the wall, the people could see that he was wearing burlap under
his robe next to his skin. 31 "May God strike me and
even kill me if I don't separate Elisha's head from his shoulders this very day," the king vowed.

32 Elisha was sitting in his house with the elders of Israel when the king sent a messenger to summon him. But before the messenger arrived, Elisha said to the elders, "A murderer has sent a man to cut off my head. When he arrives, shut the door and keep him out. We will soon hear his master's steps following him."

33 While Elisha was still saying this, the messenger arrived. And the king* said, "All this misery is from the LORD! Why should I wait for the LORD any longer?"

7 Elisha replied, "Listen to this message from the LORD! This is what the LORD says: By this time tomorrow in the markets of Samaria, five quarts of choice flour will cost only one piece of silver,* and ten quarts of barley grain will cost only one piece of silver.*"

2 The officer assisting the king said to the man of God, "That couldn't happen even if the LORD opened the windows of heaven!"

6:25 Hebrew *sold for 80 shekels* [2 pounds, or 0.9 kilograms] *of silver, and ¼ of a cab* [0.3 liters] *of dove's dung sold for 5 shekels* [2 ounces, or 57 grams]. *Dove's dung* may be a variety of wild vegetable. **6:33** Hebrew *he.* **7:1a** Hebrew *1 seah* [6 liters] *of choice flour will cost 1 shekel* [0.4 ounces, or 11 grams]; also in 7:16, 18. **7:1b** Hebrew *2 seahs* [12 liters] *of barley grain will cost 1 shekel* [0.4 ounces, or 11 grams]; also in 7:16, 18.

KING JAMES VERSION

And he said, Behold, thou shalt see *it* with thine eyes, but shalt not eat thereof.

3And there were four leprous men at the entering in of the gate: and they said one to another, Why sit we here until we die? 4If we say, We will enter into the city, then the famine *is* in the city, and we shall die there: and if we sit still here, we die also. Now therefore come, and let us fall unto the host of the Syrians: if they save us alive, we shall live; and if they kill us, we shall but die.

5And they rose up in the twilight, to go unto the camp of the Syrians: and when they were come to the uttermost part of the camp of Syria, behold, *there was* no man there.

6For the Lord had made the host of the Syrians to hear a noise of chariots, and a noise of horses, *even* the noise of a great host: and they said one to another, Lo, the king of Israel hath hired against us the kings of the Hittites, and the kings of the Egyptians, to come upon us.

7Wherefore they arose and fled in the twilight, and left their tents, and their horses, and their asses, even the camp as it *was*, and fled for their life. 8And when these lepers came to the uttermost part of the camp, they went into one tent, and did eat and drink, and carried thence silver, and gold, and raiment, and went and hid *it*; and came again, and entered into another tent, and carried thence *also*, and went and hid *it*.

9Then they said one to another, We do not well: this day *is* a day of good tidings, and we hold our peace: if we tarry till the morning light, some mischief will come upon us: now therefore come, that we may go and tell the king's household. 10So they came and called unto the porter of the city: and they told them, saying, We came to the camp of the Syrians, and, behold, *there was* no man there, neither voice of man, but horses tied, and asses tied, and the tents as they *were*.

11And he called the porters; and they told *it* to the king's house within. 12And the king arose in the night, and said unto his servants, I will now shew you what the Syrians have done to us. They know that we *be* hungry; therefore are they gone out of the camp to hide themselves in the field, saying, When they come out of the city, we shall catch them alive, and get into the city. 13And one of his servants answered and said, Let *some* take, I pray thee, five of the horses that remain, which are left in the city, (behold, they *are* as all the multitude of Israel that are left in it: behold, *I say*, they *are* even as all the multitude of the Israelites that are consumed:) and let us send and see.

14They took therefore two chariot horses; and the king sent after the host of the Syrians, saying, Go and see.

NEW LIVING TRANSLATION

But Elisha replied, "You will see it happen with your own eyes, but you won't be able to eat any of it!"

Lepers Visit the Enemy Camp

3Now there were four men with leprosy* sitting at the entrance of the city gates. "Why should we sit here waiting to die?" they asked each other. 4"We will starve if we stay here, but with the famine in the city, we will starve if we go back there. So we might as well go out and surrender to the Aramean army. If they let us live, so much the better. But if they kill us, we would have died anyway."

5So at twilight they set out for the camp of the Arameans. But when they came to the edge of the camp, no one was there! 6For the Lord had caused the Aramean army to hear the clatter of speeding chariots and the galloping of horses and the sounds of a great army approaching. "The king of Israel has hired the Hittites and Egyptians* to attack us!" they cried to one another. 7So they panicked and ran into the night, abandoning their tents, horses, donkeys, and everything else, as they fled for their lives.

8When the lepers arrived at the edge of the camp, they went into one tent after another, eating and drinking wine; and they carried off silver and gold and clothing and hid it. 9Finally, they said to each other, "This is not right. This is a day of good news, and we aren't sharing it with anyone! If we wait until morning, some calamity will certainly fall upon us. Come on, let's go back and tell the people at the palace."

10So they went back to the city and told the gatekeepers what had happened. "We went out to the Aramean camp," they said, "and no one was there! The horses and donkeys were tethered and the tents were all in order, but there wasn't a single person around!" 11Then the gatekeepers shouted the news to the people in the palace.

Israel Plunders the Camp

12The king got out of bed in the middle of the night and told his officers, "I know what has happened. The Arameans know we are starving, so they have left their camp and have hidden in the fields. They are expecting us to leave the city, and then they will take us alive and capture the city."

13One of his officers replied, "We had better send out scouts to check into this. Let them take five of the remaining horses. If something happens to them, it will be no worse than if they stay here and die with the rest of us."

14So two chariots with horses were prepared, and the king sent scouts to see what had happened to the

7:3 Or *with a contagious skin disease.* The Hebrew word used here and throughout this passage can describe various skin diseases. 7:6 Possibly *and the people of Muzur,* a district near Cilicia.

KING JAMES VERSION

15And they went after them unto Jordan: and, lo,
all the way *was* full of garments and vessels, which
the Syrians had cast away in their haste. And the
messengers returned, and told the king.

16And the people went out, and spoiled the tents
of the Syrians. So a measure of fine flour was *sold* for
a shekel, and two measures of barley for a shekel,
according to the word of the LORD.

17And the king appointed the lord on whose hand
he leaned to have the charge of the gate: and the
people trode upon him in the gate, and he died, as
the man of God had said, who spake when the king
came down to him.

18And it came to pass as the man of God had spoken to the king, saying, Two measures of barley for a
shekel, and a measure of fine flour for a shekel, shall
be tomorrow about this time in the gate of Samaria:

19And that lord answered the man of God, and
said, Now, behold, *if* the LORD should make windows
in heaven, might such a thing be? And he said, Behold, thou shalt see it with thine eyes, but shalt not
eat thereof.

20And so it fell out unto him: for the people trode
upon him in the gate, and he died.

8 1Then spake Elisha unto the woman, whose
son he had restored to life, saying, Arise, and go
thou and thine household, and sojourn wheresoever
thou canst sojourn: for the LORD hath called for a
famine; and it shall also come upon the land seven
years.

2And the woman arose, and did after the saying of
the man of God: and she went with her household,
and sojourned in the land of the Philistines seven
years.

3And it came to pass at the seven years' end, that
the woman returned out of the land of the Philistines: and she went forth to cry unto the king for her
house and for her land.

4And the king talked with Gehazi the servant of
the man of God, saying, Tell me, I pray thee, all the
great things that Elisha hath done.

5And it came to pass, as he was telling the king
how he had restored a dead body to life, that, behold,
the woman, whose son he had restored to life, cried
to the king for her house and for her land. And Gehazi said, My lord, O king, this *is* the woman, and this *is*
her son, whom Elisha restored to life.

6And when the king asked the woman, she told
him. So the king appointed unto her a certain officer,
saying, Restore all that *was* hers, and all the fruits of
the field since the day that she left the land, even
until now.

7And Elisha came to Damascus; and Ben-hadad
the king of Syria was sick; and it was told him, saying,
The man of God is come hither.

NEW LIVING TRANSLATION

Aramean army. 15They went all the way to the Jordan
River, following a trail of clothing and equipment
that the Arameans had thrown away in their mad
rush to escape. The scouts returned and told the
king about it. 16Then the people of Samaria rushed
out and plundered the Aramean camp. So it was true
that five quarts of choice flour were sold that day for
one piece of silver, and ten quarts of barley grain
were sold for one piece of silver, just as the LORD had
promised. 17The king appointed his officer to control the traffic at the gate, but he was knocked down
and trampled to death as the people rushed out.

So everything happened exactly as the man of God
had predicted when the king came to his house.
18The man of God had said to the king, "By this time
tomorrow in the markets of Samaria, five quarts of
choice flour will cost one piece of silver, and ten
quarts of barley grain will cost one piece of silver."

19The king's officer had replied, "That couldn't
happen even if the LORD opened the windows of
heaven!" And the man of God had said, "You will
see it happen with your own eyes, but you won't be
able to eat any of it!" 20And so it was, for the people
trampled him to death at the gate!

The Woman from Shunem Returns Home

8 Elisha had told the woman whose son he had
brought back to life, "Take your family and
move to some other place, for the LORD has called for
a famine on Israel that will last for seven years." 2So
the woman did as the man of God instructed. She
took her family and settled in the land of the Philistines for seven years.

3After the famine ended she returned from the
land of the Philistines, and she went to see the king
about getting back her house and land. 4As she came
in, the king was talking with Gehazi, the servant of
the man of God. The king had just said, "Tell me
some stories about the great things Elisha has done."
5And Gehazi was telling the king about the time
Elisha had brought a boy back to life. At that very
moment, the mother of the boy walked in to make
her appeal to the king about her house and land.

"Look, my lord the king!" Gehazi exclaimed. "Here
is the woman now, and this is her son—the very one
Elisha brought back to life!"

6"Is this true?" the king asked her. And she told
him the story. So he directed one of his officials to
see that everything she had lost was restored to her,
including the value of any crops that had been harvested during her absence.

Hazael Murders Ben-Hadad

7Elisha went to Damascus, the capital of Aram, where
King Ben-hadad lay sick. When someone told the

KING JAMES VERSION

8And the king said unto Hazael, Take a present in thine hand, and go, meet the man of God, and inquire of the LORD by him, saying, Shall I recover of this disease?

9So Hazael went to meet him, and took a present with him, even of every good thing of Damascus, forty camels' burden, and came and stood before him, and said, Thy son Ben-hadad king of Syria hath sent me to thee, saying, Shall I recover of this disease?

10And Elisha said unto him, Go, say unto him, Thou mayest certainly recover: howbeit the LORD hath shewed me that he shall surely die.

11And he settled his countenance stedfastly, until he was ashamed: and the man of God wept.

12And Hazael said, Why weepeth my lord? And he answered, Because I know the evil that thou wilt do unto the children of Israel: their strong holds wilt thou set on fire, and their young men wilt thou slay with the sword, and wilt dash their children, and rip up their women with child.

13And Hazael said, But what, *is* thy servant a dog, that he should do this great thing? And Elisha answered, The LORD hath shewed me that thou *shalt be* king over Syria.

14So he departed from Elisha, and came to his master; who said to him, What said Elisha to thee? And he answered, He told me *that* thou shouldest surely recover.

15And it came to pass on the morrow, that he took a thick cloth, and dipped *it* in water, and spread *it* on his face, so that he died: and Hazael reigned in his stead.

16And in the fifth year of Joram the son of Ahab king of Israel, Jehoshaphat *being* then king of Judah, Jehoram the son of Jehoshaphat king of Judah began to reign.

17Thirty and two years old was he when he began to reign; and he reigned eight years in Jerusalem.

18And he walked in the way of the kings of Israel, as did the house of Ahab: for the daughter of Ahab was his wife: and he did evil in the sight of the LORD.

19Yet the LORD would not destroy Judah for David his servant's sake, as he promised him to give him alway a light, *and* to his children.

20In his days Edom revolted from under the hand of Judah, and made a king over themselves.

21So Joram went over to Zair, and all the chariots with him: and he rose by night, and smote the Edomites which compassed him about, and the captains of the chariots: and the people fled into their tents.

22Yet Edom revolted from under the hand of Judah unto this day. Then Libnah revolted at the same time.

NEW LIVING TRANSLATION

king that the man of God had come, 8the king said to Hazael, "Take a gift to the man of God. Then tell him to ask the LORD, 'Will I recover from this illness?'"

9So Hazael loaded down forty camels with the finest products of Damascus as a gift for Elisha. He went to him and said, "Your servant Ben-hadad, the king of Aram, has sent me to ask, 'Will I recover from this illness?'"

10And Elisha replied, "Go and tell him, 'You will surely recover.' But actually the LORD has shown me that he will surely die!" 11Elisha stared at Hazael* with a fixed gaze until Hazael became uneasy.* Then the man of God started weeping.

12"What's the matter, my lord?" Hazael asked him.

Elisha replied, "I know the terrible things you will do to the people of Israel. You will burn their fortified cities, kill their young men with the sword, dash their little children to the ground, and rip open their pregnant women!"

13Hazael responded, "How could a nobody like me* ever accomplish such great things?"

Elisha answered, "The LORD has shown me that you are going to be the king of Aram."

14When Hazael left Elisha and went back, the king asked him, "What did Elisha tell you?"

And Hazael replied, "He told me that you will surely recover."

15But the next day Hazael took a blanket, soaked it in water, and held it over the king's face until he died. Then Hazael became the next king of Aram.

Jehoram Rules in Judah

16Jehoram son of King Jehoshaphat of Judah began to rule over Judah in the fifth year of the reign of Joram son of Ahab, king of Israel. 17Jehoram was thirty-two years old when he became king, and he reigned in Jerusalem eight years. 18But Jehoram followed the example of the kings of Israel and was as wicked as King Ahab, for he had married one of Ahab's daughters. So Jehoram did what was evil in the LORD's sight. 19But the LORD did not want to destroy Judah, for he had made a covenant with David and promised that his descendants would continue to rule, shining like a lamp forever.

20During Jehoram's reign, the Edomites revolted against Judah and crowned their own king. 21So Jehoram* went with all his chariots to attack the town of Zair.* The Edomites surrounded him and his chariot commanders, but he went out at night and attacked them* under cover of darkness. But Jehoram's army deserted him and fled to their homes. 22So Edom has been independent from Judah to this day. The town of Libnah also revolted about that same time.

8:11a Hebrew *He stared at him.* **8:11b** The meaning of the Hebrew is uncertain. **8:13** Hebrew *a dog.* **8:21a** Hebrew *Joram,* a variant spelling of Jehoram; also in 8:23, 24. **8:21b** Greek version reads *Seir.* **8:21c** Or *he went out and escaped.* The meaning of the Hebrew is uncertain.

KING JAMES VERSION

23And the rest of the acts of Joram, and all that he
did, *are* they not written in the book of the chronicles of the kings of Judah?
24And Joram slept with his fathers, and was buried
with his fathers in the city of David: and Ahaziah his
son reigned in his stead.

25In the twelfth year of Joram the son of Ahab king
of Israel did Ahaziah the son of Jehoram king of
Judah begin to reign.
26Two and twenty years old *was* Ahaziah when he
began to reign; and he reigned one year in Jerusalem.
And his mother's name *was* Athaliah, the daughter of
Omri king of Israel.
27And he walked in the way of the house of Ahab,
and did evil in the sight of the LORD, as *did* the house of
Ahab: for he *was* the son in law of the house of Ahab.
28And he went with Joram the son of Ahab to the
war against Hazael king of Syria in Ramoth-gilead;
and the Syrians wounded Joram.
29And king Joram went back to be healed in Jezreel of the wounds which the Syrians had given him
at Ramah, when he fought against Hazael king of
Syria. And Ahaziah the son of Jehoram king of Judah
went down to see Joram the son of Ahab in Jezreel,
because he was sick.

9 1And Elisha the prophet called one of the children of the prophets, and said unto him, Gird
up thy loins, and take this box of oil in thine hand,
and go to Ramoth-gilead:
2And when thou comest thither, look out there
Jehu the son of Jehoshaphat the son of Nimshi, and
go in, and make him arise up from among his brethren, and carry him to an inner chamber;
3Then take the box of oil, and pour *it* on his head,
and say, Thus saith the LORD, I have anointed thee
king over Israel. Then open the door, and flee, and
tarry not.
4So the young man, *even* the young man the
prophet, went to Ramoth-gilead.
5And when he came, behold, the captains of the
host *were* sitting; and he said, I have an errand to
thee, O captain. And Jehu said, Unto which of all us?
And he said, To thee, O captain.
6And he arose, and went into the house; and he
poured the oil on his head, and said unto him, Thus
saith the LORD God of Israel, I have anointed thee
king over the people of the LORD, *even* over Israel.
7And thou shalt smite the house of Ahab thy master, that I may avenge the blood of my servants the
prophets, and the blood of all the servants of the
LORD, at the hand of Jezebel.
8For the whole house of Ahab shall perish: and I
will cut off from Ahab him that pisseth against the
wall, and him that is shut up and left in Israel:
9And I will make the house of Ahab like the house

NEW LIVING TRANSLATION

23The rest of the events in Jehoram's reign and
everything he did are recorded in *The Book of the
History of the Kings of Judah*. 24When Jehoram died,
he was buried with his ancestors in the City of David.
Then his son Ahaziah became the next king.

Ahaziah Rules in Judah

25Ahaziah son of Jehoram began to rule over Judah in
the twelfth year of the reign of Joram son of Ahab,
king of Israel.
26Ahaziah was twenty-two years old when he became king, and he reigned in Jerusalem one year. His
mother was Athaliah, a granddaughter of King Omri
of Israel. 27Ahaziah followed the evil example of
King Ahab's family. He did what was evil in the
LORD's sight, just as Ahab's family had done, for he
was related by marriage to the family of Ahab.
28Ahaziah joined Joram son of Ahab, the king of
Israel, in his war against King Hazael of Aram at
Ramoth-gilead. When the Arameans wounded King
Joram in the battle, 29he returned to Jezreel to recover from the wounds he had received at Ramoth.*
Because Joram was wounded, King Ahaziah of Judah
went to Jezreel to visit him.

Jehu Anointed King of Israel

9 Meanwhile, Elisha the prophet had summoned
a member of the group of prophets. "Get ready
to travel,"* he told him, "and take this flask of olive
oil with you. Go to Ramoth-gilead, 2and find Jehu son
of Jehoshaphat, son of Nimshi. Call him into a private
room away from his friends, 3and pour the oil over
his head. Say to him, 'This is what the LORD says: I
anoint you to be the king over Israel.' Then open the
door and run for your life!"
4So the young prophet did as he was told and went
to Ramoth-gilead. 5When he arrived there, he found
Jehu sitting around with the other army officers. "I
have a message for you, Commander," he said.
"For which one of us?" Jehu asked.
"For you, Commander," he replied.
6So Jehu left the others and went into the house.
Then the young prophet poured the oil over Jehu's
head and said, "This is what the LORD, the God of Israel, says: I anoint you king over the LORD's people,
Israel. 7You are to destroy the family of Ahab, your
master. In this way, I will avenge the murder of my
prophets and all the LORD's servants who were killed
by Jezebel. 8The entire family of Ahab must be wiped
out. I will destroy every one of his male descendants,
slave and free alike, anywhere in Israel. 9I will destroy

8:29 Hebrew *Ramah*, a variant spelling of Ramoth. **9:1** Hebrew *Bind up your loins.*

KING JAMES VERSION

of Jeroboam the son of Nebat, and like the house of
Baasha the son of Ahijah:
10 And the dogs shall eat Jezebel in the portion of
Jezreel, and *there shall be* none to bury *her.* And he
opened the door, and fled.
11 Then Jehu came forth to the servants of his lord:
and *one* said unto him, *Is* all well? wherefore came
this mad *fellow* to thee? And he said unto them, Ye
know the man, and his communication.
12 And they said, *It is* false; tell us now. And he said,
Thus and thus spake he to me, saying, Thus saith the
LORD, I have anointed thee king over Israel.
13 Then they hasted, and took every man his garment, and put *it* under him on the top of the stairs,
and blew with trumpets, saying, Jehu is king.
14 So Jehu the son of Jehoshaphat the son of Nimshi conspired against Joram. (Now Joram had kept
Ramoth-gilead, he and all Israel, because of Hazael
king of Syria.
15 But king Joram was returned to be healed in Jezreel of the wounds which the Syrians had given him,
when he fought with Hazael king of Syria.) And Jehu
said, If it be your minds, *then* let none go forth *nor*
escape out of the city to go to tell *it* in Jezreel.
16 So Jehu rode in a chariot, and went to Jezreel; for
Joram lay there. And Ahaziah king of Judah was
come down to see Joram.
17 And there stood a watchman on the tower in
Jezreel, and he spied the company of Jehu as he
came, and said, I see a company. And Joram said,
Take an horseman, and send to meet them, and let
him say, *Is it* peace?
18 So there went one on horseback to meet him,
and said, Thus saith the king, *Is it* peace? And Jehu
said, What hast thou to do with peace? turn thee behind me. And the watchman told, saying, The messenger came to them, but he cometh not again.
19 Then he sent out a second on horseback, which
came to them, and said, Thus saith the king, *Is it*
peace? And Jehu answered, What hast thou to do
with peace? turn thee behind me.
20 And the watchman told, saying, He came even
unto them, and cometh not again: and the driving *is*
like the driving of Jehu the son of Nimshi; for he
driveth furiously.
21 And Joram said, Make ready. And his chariot was
made ready. And Joram king of Israel and Ahaziah
king of Judah went out, each in his chariot, and they
went out against Jehu, and met him in the portion of
Naboth the Jezreelite.
22 And it came to pass, when Joram saw Jehu, that

NEW LIVING TRANSLATION

the family of Ahab as I destroyed the families of Jeroboam son of Nebat and of Baasha son of Ahijah.
10 Dogs will eat Ahab's wife Jezebel at the plot of land
in Jezreel, and no one will bury her." Then the young
prophet opened the door and ran.
11 Jehu went back to his fellow officers, and one of
them asked him, "What did that madman want? Is
everything all right?"
"You know how a man like that babbles on," Jehu
replied.
12 "You're hiding something," they said. "Tell us."
So Jehu told them, "He said to me, 'This is what the
LORD says: I have anointed you to be king over Israel.'"
13 Then they quickly spread out their cloaks on the
bare steps and blew the ram's horn, shouting, "Jehu
is king!"

Jehu Kills Joram and Ahaziah

14 So Jehu son of Jehoshaphat, son of Nimshi, led a
conspiracy against King Joram. (Now Joram had been
with the army at Ramoth-gilead, defending Israel
against the forces of King Hazael of Aram. 15 But King
Joram* was wounded in the fighting and returned to
Jezreel to recover from his wounds.) So Jehu told the
men with him, "If you want me to be king, don't let
anyone leave town and go to Jezreel to report what
we have done."
16 Then Jehu got into a chariot and rode to Jezreel
to find King Joram, who was lying there wounded.
King Ahaziah of Judah was there, too, for he had
gone to visit him. 17 The watchman on the tower of
Jezreel saw Jehu and his company approaching, so
he shouted to Joram, "I see a company of troops
coming!"
"Send out a rider to ask if they are coming in
peace," King Joram ordered.
18 So a horseman went out to meet Jehu and said,
"The king wants to know if you are coming in peace."
Jehu replied, "What do you know about peace?
Fall in behind me!"
The watchman called out to the king, "The messenger has met them, but he's not returning."
19 So the king sent out a second horseman. He
rode up to them and said, "The king wants to know if
you come in peace."
Again Jehu answered, "What do you know about
peace? Fall in behind me!"
20 The watchman exclaimed, "The messenger has
met them, but he isn't returning either! It must be
Jehu son of Nimshi, for he's driving like a madman."
21 "Quick! Get my chariot ready!" King Joram commanded.
Then King Joram of Israel and King Ahaziah of
Judah rode out in their chariots to meet Jehu. They
met him at the plot of land that had belonged to
Naboth of Jezreel. 22 King Joram demanded, "Do you
come in peace, Jehu?"

9:15 Hebrew *Jehoram,* a variant spelling of Joram; also in 9:17, 21, 22, 23, 24.

KING JAMES VERSION

he said, *Is it* peace, Jehu? And he answered, What
peace, so long as the whoredoms of thy mother Jezebel and her witchcrafts *are so* many?
23 And Joram turned his hands, and fled, and said
to Ahaziah, *There is* treachery, O Ahaziah.
24 And Jehu drew a bow with his full strength, and
smote Jehoram between his arms, and the arrow went
out at his heart, and he sunk down in his chariot.
25 Then said *Jehu* to Bidkar his captain, Take up,
and cast him in the portion of the field of Naboth the
Jezreelite: for remember how that, when I and thou
rode together after Ahab his father, the LORD laid
this burden upon him;
26 Surely I have seen yesterday the blood of Naboth, and the blood of his sons, saith the LORD; and I
will requite thee in this plat, saith the LORD. Now
therefore take *and* cast him into the plat *of ground,*
according to the word of the LORD.
27 But when Ahaziah the king of Judah saw *this,* he
fled by the way of the garden house. And Jehu followed after him, and said, Smite him also in the chariot. *And they did so* at the going up to Gur, which *is* by
Ibleam. And he fled to Megiddo, and died there.
28 And his servants carried him in a chariot to Jerusalem, and buried him in his sepulchre with his
fathers in the city of David.
29 And in the eleventh year of Joram the son of
Ahab began Ahaziah to reign over Judah.

30 And when Jehu was come to Jezreel, Jezebel
heard *of it;* and she painted her face, and tired her
head, and looked out at a window.
31 And as Jehu entered in at the gate, she said, *Had*
Zimri peace, who slew his master?
32 And he lifted up his face to the window, and said,
Who *is* on my side? who? And there looked out to
him two *or* three eunuchs.
33 And he said, Throw her down. So they threw her
down: and *some* of her blood was sprinkled on the
wall, and on the horses: and he trode her under foot.
34 And when he was come in, he did eat and drink,
and said, Go, see now this cursed *woman,* and bury
her: for she *is* a king's daughter.
35 And they went to bury her: but they found no
more of her than the skull, and the feet, and the
palms of *her* hands.
36 Wherefore they came again, and told him. And
he said, This *is* the word of the LORD, which he spake
by his servant Elijah the Tishbite, saying, In the portion of Jezreel shall dogs eat the flesh of Jezebel:
37 And the carcase of Jezebel shall be as dung upon
the face of the field in the portion of Jezreel; *so* that
they shall not say, This *is* Jezebel.

NEW LIVING TRANSLATION

Jehu replied, "How can there be peace as long as
the idolatry and witchcraft of your mother, Jezebel,
are all around us?"
23 Then King Joram turned the horses around*
and fled, shouting to King Ahaziah, "Treason, Ahaziah!" 24 But Jehu drew his bow and shot Joram between the shoulders. The arrow pierced his heart,
and he sank down dead in his chariot.
25 Jehu said to Bidkar, his officer, "Throw him into
the plot of land that belonged to Naboth of Jezreel.
Do you remember when you and I were riding along
behind his father, Ahab? The LORD pronounced this
message against him: 26 'I solemnly swear that I will
repay him here on this plot of land, says the LORD, for
the murder of Naboth and his sons that I saw yesterday.' So throw him out on Naboth's property, just as
the LORD said."
27 When King Ahaziah of Judah saw what was happening, he fled along the road to Beth-haggan. Jehu
rode after him, shouting, "Shoot him, too!" So they
shot Ahaziah in his chariot at the Ascent of Gur, near
Ibleam. He was able to go on as far as Megiddo, but
he died there. 28 His servants took him by chariot to
Jerusalem, where they buried him with his ancestors
in the City of David. 29 Ahaziah had become king over
Judah in the eleventh year of the reign of Joram son
of Ahab.

The Death of Jezebel

30 When Jezebel, the queen mother, heard that Jehu
had come to Jezreel, she painted her eyelids and
fixed her hair and sat at a window. 31 When Jehu
entered the gate of the palace, she shouted at him,
"Have you come in peace, you murderer? You're just
like Zimri, who murdered his master!"*
32 Jehu looked up and saw her at the window and
shouted, "Who is on my side?" And two or three eunuchs looked out at him. 33 "Throw her down!" Jehu
yelled. So they threw her out the window, and her
blood spattered against the wall and on the horses.
And Jehu trampled her body under his horses'
hooves.
34 Then Jehu went into the palace and ate and
drank. Afterward he said, "Someone go and bury this
cursed woman, for she is the daughter of a king."
35 But when they went out to bury her, they found
only her skull, her feet, and her hands.
36 When they returned and told Jehu, he stated,
"This fulfills the message from the LORD, which he
spoke through his servant Elijah from Tishbe: 'At the
plot of land in Jezreel, dogs will eat Jezebel's body.
37 Her remains will be scattered like dung on the plot
of land in Jezreel, so that no one will be able to recognize her.'"

9:23 Hebrew *turned his hands.* **9:31** See 1 Kgs 16:9-10, where Zimri killed his master, King Elah.

KING JAMES VERSION

10 1 And Ahab had seventy sons in Samaria. And
Jehu wrote letters, and sent to Samaria, unto
the rulers of Jezreel, to the elders, and to them that
brought up Ahab's *children,* saying,
2 Now as soon as this letter cometh to you, seeing
your master's sons *are* with you, and *there are* with
you chariots and horses, a fenced city also, and
armour;
3 Look even out the best and meetest of your master's
sons, and set *him* on his father's throne, and
fight for your master's house.
4 But they were exceedingly afraid, and said, Behold,
two kings stood not before him: how then shall
we stand?
5 And he that *was* over the house, and he that *was*
over the city, the elders also, and the bringers up *of*
the children, sent to Jehu, saying, We *are* thy servants,
and will do all that thou shalt bid us; we will
not make any king: do thou *that which is* good in
thine eyes.
6 Then he wrote a letter the second time to them,
saying, If ye *be* mine, and *if* ye will hearken unto my
voice, take ye the heads of the men your master's
sons, and come to me to Jezreel by tomorrow this
time. Now the king's sons, *being* seventy persons,
were with the great men of the city, which brought
them up.
7 And it came to pass, when the letter came to
them, that they took the king's sons, and slew seventy
persons, and put their heads in baskets, and sent him
them to Jezreel.
8 And there came a messenger, and told him, saying,
They have brought the heads of the king's sons.
And he said, Lay ye them in two heaps at the entering
in of the gate until the morning.
9 And it came to pass in the morning, that he went
out, and stood, and said to all the people, Ye *be* righteous:
behold, I conspired against my master, and
slew him: but who slew all these?
10 Know now that there shall fall unto the earth
nothing of the word of the LORD, which the LORD
spake concerning the house of Ahab: for the LORD
hath done *that* which he spake by his servant Elijah.
11 So Jehu slew all that remained of the house of
Ahab in Jezreel, and all his great men, and his
kinsfolks, and his priests, until he left him none
remaining.
12 And he arose and departed, and came to Samaria.
And as he *was* at the shearing house in the way,
13 Jehu met with the brethren of Ahaziah king of
Judah, and said, Who *are* ye? And they answered, We
are the brethren of Ahaziah; and we go down to salute
the children of the king and the children of the
queen.
14 And he said, Take them alive. And they took them
alive, and slew them at the pit of the shearing house,
even two and forty men; neither left he any of them.

NEW LIVING TRANSLATION

Jehu Kills Ahab's Family

10 Ahab had seventy sons living in the city of
Samaria. So Jehu wrote letters and sent them
to Samaria, to the elders and officials of the city,* and
to the guardians of King Ahab's sons. He said, 2 "The
king's sons are with you, and you have at your disposal
chariots, horses, a fortified city, and weapons.
As soon as you receive this letter, 3 select the best
qualified of your master's sons to be your king, and
prepare to fight for Ahab's dynasty."
4 But they were paralyzed with fear and said,
"We've seen that two kings couldn't stand against
this man! What can we do?"
5 So the palace and city administrators, together
with the elders and the guardians of the king's sons,
sent this message to Jehu: "We are your servants and
will do anything you tell us. We will not make anyone
king; do whatever you think is best."
6 Jehu responded with a second letter: "If you are
on my side and are going to obey me, bring the heads
of your master's sons to me at Jezreel by this time tomorrow."
Now the seventy sons of the king were being
cared for by the leaders of Samaria, where they
had been raised since childhood. 7 When the letter
arrived, the leaders killed all seventy of the king's
sons. They placed their heads in baskets and presented
them to Jehu at Jezreel.
8 A messenger went to Jehu and said, "They have
brought the heads of the king's sons."
So Jehu ordered, "Pile them in two heaps at the entrance
of the city gate, and leave them there until
morning."
9 In the morning he went out and spoke to the
crowd that had gathered around them. "You are not
to blame," he told them. "I am the one who conspired
against my master and killed him. But who
killed all these? 10 You can be sure that the message
of the LORD that was spoken concerning Ahab's family
will not fail. The LORD declared through his servant
Elijah that this would happen." 11 Then Jehu
killed all who were left of Ahab's relatives living in
Jezreel and all his important officials, his personal
friends, and his priests. So Ahab was left without a
single survivor.
12 Then Jehu set out for Samaria. Along the way,
while he was at Beth-eked of the Shepherds, 13 he
met some relatives of King Ahaziah of Judah. "Who
are you?" he asked them.
And they replied, "We are relatives of King Ahaziah.
We are going to visit the sons of King Ahab and
the sons of the queen mother."
14 "Take them alive!" Jehu shouted to his men. And
they captured all forty-two of them and killed them
at the well of Beth-eked. None of them escaped.

10:1 As in some Greek manuscripts and Latin Vulgate (see also 10:6); Hebrew reads *of Jezreel.*

KING JAMES VERSION

15And when he was departed thence, he lighted on
Jehonadab the son of Rechab *coming* to meet him:
and he saluted him, and said to him, Is thine heart
right, as my heart *is* with thy heart? And Jehonadab
answered, It is. If it be, give *me* thine hand. And he
gave *him* his hand; and he took him up to him into
the chariot.
16And he said, Come with me, and see my zeal for
the LORD. So they made him ride in his chariot.
17And when he came to Samaria, he slew all that
remained unto Ahab in Samaria, till he had destroyed him, according to the saying of the LORD,
which he spake to Elijah.

18And Jehu gathered all the people together, and
said unto them, Ahab served Baal a little; *but* Jehu
shall serve him much.
19Now therefore call unto me all the prophets of
Baal, all his servants, and all his priests; let none be
wanting: for I have a great sacrifice *to do* to Baal;
whosoever shall be wanting, he shall not live. But
Jehu did *it* in subtilty, to the intent that he might
destroy the worshippers of Baal.
20And Jehu said, Proclaim a solemn assembly for
Baal. And they proclaimed *it*.
21And Jehu sent through all Israel: and all the worshippers of Baal came, so that there was not a man
left that came not. And they came into the house of
Baal; and the house of Baal was full from one end to
another.
22And he said unto him that *was* over the vestry,
Bring forth vestments for all the worshippers of Baal.
And he brought them forth vestments.
23And Jehu went, and Jehonadab the son of
Rechab, into the house of Baal, and said unto the
worshippers of Baal, Search, and look that there be
here with you none of the servants of the LORD, but
the worshippers of Baal only.
24And when they went in to offer sacrifices and
burnt offerings, Jehu appointed fourscore men without, and said, *If* any of the men whom I have brought
into your hands escape, *he that letteth him go*, his
life *shall be* for the life of him.
25And it came to pass, as soon as he had made an
end of offering the burnt offering, that Jehu said to
the guard and to the captains, Go in, *and* slay them;
let none come forth. And they smote them with the
edge of the sword; and the guard and the captains
cast *them* out, and went to the city of the house of
Baal.
26And they brought forth the images out of the
house of Baal, and burned them.
27And they brake down the image of Baal, and
brake down the house of Baal, and made it a draught
house unto this day.
28Thus Jehu destroyed Baal out of Israel.

NEW LIVING TRANSLATION

15When Jehu left there, he met Jehonadab son of
Recab, who was coming to meet him. After they had
greeted each other, Jehu said to him, "Are you as loyal
to me as I am to you?"
"Yes, I am," Jehonadab replied.
"If you are," Jehu said, "then give me your hand."
So Jehonadab put out his hand, and Jehu helped him
into the chariot. 16Then Jehu said, "Now come with
me, and see how devoted I am to the LORD." So Jehonadab rode along with him.
17When Jehu arrived in Samaria, he killed everyone who was left there from Ahab's family, just as the
LORD had promised through Elijah.

Jehu Kills the Priests of Baal

18Then Jehu called a meeting of all the people of the
city and said to them, "Ahab's worship of Baal was
nothing compared to the way I will worship him!
19Therefore, summon all the prophets and worshipers of Baal, and call together all his priests. See to it
that every one of them comes, for I am going to offer
a great sacrifice to Baal. Anyone who fails to come
will be put to death." But Jehu's cunning plan was to
destroy all the worshipers of Baal.
20Then Jehu ordered, "Prepare a solemn assembly
to worship Baal!" So they did. 21He sent messengers
throughout all Israel summoning those who worshiped Baal. They all came—not a single one remained behind—and they filled the temple of Baal
from one end to the other. 22And Jehu instructed the
keeper of the wardrobe, "Be sure that every wor-
shiper of Baal wears one of these robes." So robes
were given to them.
23Then Jehu went into the temple of Baal with Jehonadab son of Recab. Jehu said to the worshipers
of Baal, "Make sure no one who worships the LORD is
here—only those who worship Baal." 24So they were
all inside the temple to offer sacrifices and burnt
offerings. Now Jehu had stationed eighty of his
men outside the building and had warned them, "If
you let anyone escape, you will pay for it with your
own life."
25As soon as Jehu had finished sacrificing the
burnt offering, he commanded his guards and officers, "Go in and kill all of them. Don't let a single one
escape!" So they killed them all with their swords,
and the guards and officers dragged their bodies
outside.* Then Jehu's men went into the innermost
fortress* of the temple of Baal. 26They dragged out
the sacred pillar* used in the worship of Baal and
burned it. 27They smashed the sacred pillar and
wrecked the temple of Baal, converting it into a
public toilet, as it remains to this day.
28In this way, Jehu destroyed every trace of Baal

10:25a Or *they left their bodies lying there;* or *they threw them out into the outermost court.* **10:25b** Hebrew *city.* **10:26** As in Greek and Syriac versions and Latin Vulgate; Hebrew reads *sacred pillars.*

KING JAMES VERSION

29 Howbeit *from* the sins of Jeroboam the son of Nebat, who made Israel to sin, Jehu departed not from after them, *to wit*, the golden calves that *were* in Bethel, and that *were* in Dan.

30 And the LORD said unto Jehu, Because thou hast done well in executing *that which is* right in mine eyes, *and* hast done unto the house of Ahab according to all that *was* in mine heart, thy children of the fourth *generation* shall sit on the throne of Israel.

31 But Jehu took no heed to walk in the law of the LORD God of Israel with all his heart: for he departed not from the sins of Jeroboam, which made Israel to sin.

32 In those days the LORD began to cut Israel short: and Hazael smote them in all the coasts of Israel;

33 From Jordan eastward, all the land of Gilead, the Gadites, and the Reubenites, and the Manassites, from Aroer, which *is* by the river Arnon, even Gilead and Bashan.

34 Now the rest of the acts of Jehu, and all that he did, and all his might, *are* they not written in the book of the chronicles of the kings of Israel?

35 And Jehu slept with his fathers: and they buried him in Samaria. And Jehoahaz his son reigned in his stead.

36 And the time that Jehu reigned over Israel in Samaria *was* twenty and eight years.

11 1 And when Athaliah the mother of Ahaziah saw that her son was dead, she arose and destroyed all the seed royal.

2 But Jehosheba, the daughter of king Joram, sister of Ahaziah, took Joash the son of Ahaziah, and stole him from among the king's sons *which were* slain; and they hid him, *even* him and his nurse, in the bedchamber from Athaliah, so that he was not slain.

3 And he was with her hid in the house of the LORD six years. And Athaliah did reign over the land.

4 And the seventh year Jehoiada sent and fetched the rulers over hundreds, with the captains and the guard, and brought them to him into the house of the LORD, and made a covenant with them, and took an oath of them in the house of the LORD, and shewed them the king's son.

5 And he commanded them, saying, This *is* the thing that ye shall do; A third part of you that enter in on the sabbath shall even be keepers of the watch of the king's house;

6 And a third part *shall be* at the gate of Sur; and a third part at the gate behind the guard: so shall ye keep the watch of the house, that it be not broken down.

7 And two parts of all you that go forth on the sabbath, even they shall keep the watch of the house of the LORD about the king.

NEW LIVING TRANSLATION

worship from Israel. 29 He did not, however, destroy the gold calves at Bethel and Dan, with which Jeroboam son of Nebat had caused Israel to sin.

30 Nonetheless the LORD said to Jehu, "You have done well in following my instructions to destroy the family of Ahab. Therefore, your descendants will be kings of Israel down to the fourth generation." 31 But Jehu did not obey the Law of the LORD, the God of Israel, with all his heart. He refused to turn from the sins that Jeroboam had led Israel to commit.

The Death of Jehu

32 At about that time the LORD began to cut down the size of Israel's territory. King Hazael conquered several sections of the country 33 east of the Jordan River, including all of Gilead, Gad, Reuben, and Manasseh. He conquered the area from the town of Aroer by the Arnon Gorge to as far north as Gilead and Bashan.

34 The rest of the events in Jehu's reign—everything he did and all his achievements—are recorded in *The Book of the History of the Kings of Israel.*

35 When Jehu died, he was buried in Samaria. Then his son Jehoahaz became the next king. 36 In all, Jehu reigned over Israel from Samaria for twenty-eight years.

Queen Athaliah Rules in Judah

11 When Athaliah, the mother of King Ahaziah of Judah, learned that her son was dead, she began to destroy the rest of the royal family. 2 But Ahaziah's sister Jehosheba, the daughter of King Jehoram,* took Ahaziah's infant son, Joash, and stole him away from among the rest of the king's children, who were about to be killed. She put Joash and his nurse in a bedroom to hide him from Athaliah, so the child was not murdered. 3 Joash remained hidden in the Temple of the LORD for six years while Athaliah ruled over the land.

Revolt against Athaliah

4 In the seventh year of Athaliah's reign, Jehoiada the priest summoned the commanders, the Carite mercenaries, and the palace guards to come to the Temple of the LORD. He made a solemn pact with them and made them swear an oath of loyalty there in the LORD's Temple; then he showed them the king's son.

5 Jehoiada told them, "This is what you must do. A third of you who are on duty on the Sabbath are to guard the royal palace itself. 6 Another third of you are to stand guard at the Sur Gate. And the final third must stand guard behind the palace guard. These three groups will all guard the palace. 7 The other two units who are off duty on the Sabbath must stand

11:2 Hebrew *Joram*, a variant spelling of Jehoram.

KING JAMES VERSION

8 And ye shall compass the king round about, every man with his weapons in his hand: and he that cometh within the ranges, let him be slain: and be ye with the king as he goeth out and as he cometh in.

9 And the captains over the hundreds did according to all *things* that Jehoiada the priest commanded: and they took every man his men that were to come in on the sabbath, with them that should go out on the sabbath, and came to Jehoiada the priest.

10 And to the captains over hundreds did the priest give king David's spears and shields, that *were* in the temple of the LORD.

11 And the guard stood, every man with his weapons in his hand, round about the king, from the right corner of the temple to the left corner of the temple, *along* by the altar and the temple.

12 And he brought forth the king's son, and put the crown upon him, and *gave him* the testimony; and they made him king, and anointed him; and they clapped their hands, and said, God save the king.

13 And when Athaliah heard the noise of the guard *and* of the people, she came to the people into the temple of the LORD.

14 And when she looked, behold, the king stood by a pillar, as the manner *was,* and the princes and the trumpeters by the king, and all the people of the land rejoiced, and blew with trumpets: and Athaliah rent her clothes, and cried, Treason, Treason.

15 But Jehoiada the priest commanded the captains of the hundreds, the officers of the host, and said unto them, Have her forth without the ranges: and him that followeth her kill with the sword. For the priest had said, Let her not be slain in the house of the LORD.

16 And they laid hands on her; and she went by the way by the which the horses came into the king's house: and there was she slain.

17 And Jehoiada made a covenant between the LORD and the king and the people, that they should be the LORD's people; between the king also and the people.

18 And all the people of the land went into the house of Baal, and brake it down; his altars and his images brake they in pieces thoroughly, and slew Mattan the priest of Baal before the altars. And the priest appointed officers over the house of the LORD.

19 And he took the rulers over hundreds, and the captains, and the guard, and all the people of the land; and they brought down the king from the house of the LORD, and came by the way of the gate of the guard to the king's house. And he sat on the throne of the kings.

20 And all the people of the land rejoiced, and the

NEW LIVING TRANSLATION

guard for the king at the LORD's Temple. 8 Form a bodyguard around the king and keep your weapons in hand. Kill anyone who tries to break through. Stay with the king wherever he goes."

9 So the commanders did everything as Jehoiada the priest ordered. The commanders took charge of the men reporting for duty that Sabbath, as well as those who were going off duty. They brought them all to Jehoiada the priest, 10 and he supplied them with the spears and small shields that had once belonged to King David and were stored in the Temple of the LORD. 11 The palace guards stationed themselves around the king, with their weapons ready. They formed a line from the south side of the Temple around to the north side and all around the altar.

12 Then Jehoiada brought out Joash, the king's son, placed the crown on his head, and presented him with a copy of God's laws.* They anointed him and proclaimed him king, and everyone clapped their hands and shouted, "Long live the king!"

The Death of Athaliah

13 When Athaliah heard all the noise made by the palace guards and the people, she hurried to the LORD's Temple to see what was happening. 14 When she arrived, she saw the newly crowned king standing in his place of authority by the pillar, as was the custom at times of coronation. The commanders and trumpeters were surrounding him, and people from all over the land were rejoicing and blowing trumpets. When Athaliah saw all this, she tore her clothes in despair and shouted, "Treason! Treason!"

15 Then Jehoiada the priest ordered the commanders who were in charge of the troops, "Take her to the soldiers in front of the Temple,* and kill anyone who tries to rescue her." For the priest had said, "She must not be killed in the Temple of the LORD." 16 So they seized her and led her out to the gate where horses enter the palace grounds, and she was killed there.

Jehoiada's Religious Reforms

17 Then Jehoiada made a covenant between the LORD and the king and the people that they would be the LORD's people. He also made a covenant between the king and the people. 18 And all the people of the land went over to the temple of Baal and tore it down. They demolished the altars and smashed the idols to pieces, and they killed Mattan the priest of Baal in front of the altars.

Jehoiada the priest stationed guards at the Temple of the LORD. 19 Then the commanders, the Carite mercenaries, the palace guards, and all the people of the land escorted the king from the Temple of the LORD. They went through the gate of the guards and into the palace, and the king took his seat on the royal throne. 20 So all the people of the land rejoiced,

11:12 Or *a copy of the covenant.* **11:15** Or *Bring her out from between the ranks;* or *Take her out of the Temple precincts.* The meaning of the Hebrew is uncertain.

KING JAMES VERSION

city was in quiet: and they slew Athaliah with the
sword *beside* the king's house.
21 Seven years old *was* Jehoash when he began to
reign.

12 1 In the seventh year of Jehu Jehoash began
to reign; and forty years reigned he in Jerusalem. And his mother's name *was* Zibiah of Beer-
sheba.
2 And Jehoash did *that which was* right in the sight
of the LORD all his days wherein Jehoiada the priest
instructed him.
3 But the high places were not taken away: the
people still sacrificed and burnt incense in the high
places.
4 And Jehoash said to the priests, All the money of
the dedicated things that is brought into the house
of the LORD, *even* the money of every one that
passeth *the account,* the money that every man is set
at, *and* all the money that cometh into any man's
heart to bring into the house of the LORD,
5 Let the priests take *it* to them, every man of his
acquaintance: and let them repair the breaches of
the house, wheresoever any breach shall be found.
6 But it was *so, that* in the three and twentieth year
of king Jehoash the priests had not repaired the
breaches of the house.
7 Then king Jehoash called for Jehoiada the priest,
and the *other* priests, and said unto them, Why repair ye not the breaches of the house? now therefore
receive no *more* money of your acquaintance, but
deliver it for the breaches of the house.
8 And the priests consented to receive no *more*
money of the people, neither to repair the breaches
of the house.
9 But Jehoiada the priest took a chest, and bored a
hole in the lid of it, and set it beside the altar, on the
right side as one cometh into the house of the LORD:
and the priests that kept the door put therein all the
money *that was* brought into the house of the LORD.
10 And it was *so,* when they saw that *there was* much
money in the chest, that the king's scribe and the high
priest came up, and they put up in bags, and told the
money that was found in the house of the LORD.
11 And they gave the money, being told, into the
hands of them that did the work, that had the oversight of the house of the LORD: and they laid it out to
the carpenters and builders, that wrought upon the
house of the LORD,
12 And to masons, and hewers of stone, and to buy
timber and hewed stone to repair the breaches of the
house of the LORD, and for all that was laid out for the
house to repair *it.*
13 Howbeit there were not made for the house of
the LORD bowls of silver, snuffers, basins, trumpets,
any vessels of gold, or vessels of silver, of the money
that was brought into the house of the LORD:

NEW LIVING TRANSLATION

and the city was peaceful because Athaliah had been
killed at the king's palace.
21 *Joash* was seven years old when he became
king.

Joash Repairs the Temple

12 1 *Joash* began to rule over Judah in the seventh year of King Jehu's reign in Israel. He
reigned in Jerusalem forty years. His mother was Zibiah from Beersheba. 2 All his life Joash did what was
pleasing in the LORD's sight because Jehoiada the
priest instructed him. 3 Yet even so, he did not destroy the pagan shrines, and the people still offered
sacrifices and burned incense there.
4 One day King Joash said to the priests, "Collect all
the money brought as a sacred offering to the LORD's
Temple, whether it is a regular assessment, a payment of vows, or a voluntary gift. 5 Let the priests take
some of that money to pay for whatever repairs are
needed at the Temple."
6 But by the twenty-third year of Joash's reign, the
priests still had not repaired the Temple. 7 So King
Joash called for Jehoiada and the other priests and
asked them, "Why haven't you repaired the Temple?
Don't use any more money for your own needs. From
now on, it must all be spent on Temple repairs." 8 So
the priests agreed not to accept any more money
from the people, and they also agreed to let others
take responsibility for repairing the Temple.
9 Then Jehoiada the priest bored a hole in the lid of
a large chest and set it on the right-hand side of the
altar at the entrance of the Temple of the LORD. The
priests guarding the entrance put all of the people's
contributions into the chest. 10 Whenever the chest
became full, the court secretary and the high priest
counted the money that had been brought to the
LORD's Temple and put it into bags. 11 Then they gave
the money to the construction supervisors, who
used it to pay the people working on the LORD's Temple—the carpenters, the builders, 12 the masons, and
the stonecutters. They also used the money to buy
the timber and the finished stone needed for repairing the LORD's Temple, and they paid any other expenses related to the Temple's restoration.
13 The money brought to the Temple was not used
for making silver bowls, lamp snuffers, basins, trumpets, or other articles of gold or silver for the Temple

11:21a Verse 11:21 is numbered 12:1 in Hebrew text. **11:21b** Hebrew *Jehoash,* a variant spelling of Joash. **12:1a** Verses 12:1-21 are numbered 12:2-22 in Hebrew text. **12:1b** Hebrew *Jehoash,* a variant spelling of Joash; also in 12:2, 4, 6, 7, 18.

KING JAMES VERSION

14But they gave that to the workmen, and repaired therewith the house of the LORD.

15Moreover they reckoned not with the men, into whose hand they delivered the money to be bestowed on workmen: for they dealt faithfully.

16The trespass money and sin money was not brought into the house of the LORD: it was the priests'.

17Then Hazael king of Syria went up, and fought against Gath, and took it: and Hazael set his face to go up to Jerusalem.

18And Jehoash king of Judah took all the hallowed things that Jehoshaphat, and Jehoram, and Ahaziah, his fathers, kings of Judah, had dedicated, and his own hallowed things, and all the gold *that was* found in the treasures of the house of the LORD, and in the king's house, and sent *it* to Hazael king of Syria: and he went away from Jerusalem.

19And the rest of the acts of Joash, and all that he did, *are* they not written in the book of the chronicles of the kings of Judah?

20And his servants arose, and made a conspiracy, and slew Joash in the house of Millo, which goeth down to Silla.

21For Jozachar the son of Shimeath, and Jehozabad the son of Shomer, his servants, smote him, and he died; and they buried him with his fathers in the city of David: and Amaziah his son reigned in his stead.

13 1In the three and twentieth year of Joash the son of Ahaziah king of Judah Jehoahaz the son of Jehu began to reign over Israel in Samaria, *and reigned* seventeen years.

2And he did *that which was* evil in the sight of the LORD, and followed the sins of Jeroboam the son of Nebat, which made Israel to sin; he departed not therefrom.

3And the anger of the LORD was kindled against Israel, and he delivered them into the hand of Hazael king of Syria, and into the hand of Ben-hadad the son of Hazael, all *their* days.

4And Jehoahaz besought the LORD, and the LORD hearkened unto him: for he saw the oppression of Israel, because the king of Syria oppressed them.

5(And the LORD gave Israel a saviour, so that they went out from under the hand of the Syrians: and the children of Israel dwelt in their tents, as beforetime.

6Nevertheless they departed not from the sins of the house of Jeroboam, who made Israel sin, *but* walked therein: and there remained the grove also in Samaria.)

7Neither did he leave of the people to Jehoahaz but fifty horsemen, and ten chariots, and ten thousand footmen; for the king of Syria had destroyed them, and had made them like the dust by threshing.

NEW LIVING TRANSLATION

of the LORD. 14It was paid to the workmen, who used it for the Temple repairs. 15No accounting of this money was required from the construction supervisors, because they were honest and trustworthy men. 16However, the money that was contributed for guilt offerings and sin offerings was not brought into the LORD's Temple. It was given to the priests for their own use.

The End of Joash's Reign

17About this time King Hazael of Aram went to war against Gath and captured it. Then he turned to attack Jerusalem. 18King Joash collected all the sacred objects that Jehoshaphat, Jehoram, and Ahaziah, the previous kings of Judah, had dedicated, along with what he himself had dedicated. He sent them all to Hazael, along with all the gold in the treasuries of the LORD's Temple and the royal palace. So Hazael called off his attack on Jerusalem.

19The rest of the events in Joash's reign and everything he did are recorded in *The Book of the History of the Kings of Judah*.

20Joash's officers plotted against him and assassinated him at Beth-millo on the road to Silla. 21The assassins were Jozacar* son of Shimeath and Jehozabad son of Shomer—both trusted advisers. Joash was buried with his ancestors in the City of David. Then his son Amaziah became the next king.

Jehoahaz Rules in Israel

13 Jehoahaz son of Jehu began to rule over Israel in the twenty-third year of King Joash's reign in Judah. He reigned in Samaria seventeen years. 2But he did what was evil in the LORD's sight. He followed the example of Jeroboam son of Nebat, continuing the sins that Jeroboam had led Israel to commit. 3So the LORD was very angry with Israel, and he allowed King Hazael of Aram and his son Ben-hadad to defeat them repeatedly.

4Then Jehoahaz prayed for the LORD's help, and the LORD heard his prayer, for he could see how severely the king of Aram was oppressing Israel. 5So the LORD provided someone to rescue the Israelites from the tyranny of the Arameans. Then Israel lived in safety again as they had in former days.

6But they continued to sin, following the evil example of Jeroboam. They also allowed the Asherah pole in Samaria to remain standing. 7Finally, Jehoahaz's army was reduced to 50 charioteers, 10 chariots, and 10,000 foot soldiers. The king of Aram had killed the others, trampling them like dust under his feet.

12:21 As in Greek and Syriac versions; Hebrew reads *Jozabad*.

KING JAMES VERSION

8 Now the rest of the acts of Jehoahaz, and all that
he did, and his might, *are* they not written in the
book of the chronicles of the kings of Israel?
9 And Jehoahaz slept with his fathers; and they
buried him in Samaria: and Joash his son reigned
in his stead.

10 In the thirty and seventh year of Joash king of
Judah began Jehoash the son of Jehoahaz to reign
over Israel in Samaria, *and reigned* sixteen years.
11 And he did *that which was* evil in the sight of
the LORD; he departed not from all the sins of Jeroboam the son of Nebat, who made Israel sin: *but* he
walked therein.
12 And the rest of the acts of Joash, and all that he
did, and his might wherewith he fought against Amaziah king of Judah, *are* they not written in the book
of the chronicles of the kings of Israel?
13 And Joash slept with his fathers; and Jeroboam
sat upon his throne: and Joash was buried in Samaria
with the kings of Israel.

14 Now Elisha was fallen sick of his sickness
whereof he died. And Joash the king of Israel came
down unto him, and wept over his face, and said,
O my father, my father, the chariot of Israel, and the
horsemen thereof.
15 And Elisha said unto him, Take bow and arrows.
And he took unto him bow and arrows.
16 And he said to the king of Israel, Put thine hand
upon the bow. And he put his hand *upon it:* and Elisha put his hands upon the king's hands.
17 And he said, Open the window eastward. And he
opened *it.* Then Elisha said, Shoot. And he shot. And
he said, The arrow of the LORD's deliverance, and the
arrow of deliverance from Syria: for thou shalt smite
the Syrians in Aphek, till thou have consumed *them.*
18 And he said, Take the arrows. And he took *them.*
And he said unto the king of Israel, Smite upon the
ground. And he smote thrice, and stayed.
19 And the man of God was wroth with him, and
said, Thou shouldest have smitten five or six times;
then hadst thou smitten Syria till thou hadst consumed *it:* whereas now thou shalt smite Syria *but*
thrice.
20 And Elisha died, and they buried him. And the
bands of the Moabites invaded the land at the coming in of the year.
21 And it came to pass, as they were burying a man,
that, behold, they spied a band *of men;* and they cast
the man into the sepulchre of Elisha: and when the
man was let down, and touched the bones of Elisha,
he revived, and stood up on his feet.
22 But Hazael king of Syria oppressed Israel all the
days of Jehoahaz.
23 And the LORD was gracious unto them, and had
compassion on them, and had respect unto them,
because of his covenant with Abraham, Isaac, and

NEW LIVING TRANSLATION

8 The rest of the events in Jehoahaz's reign—everything he did and the extent of his power—are recorded in *The Book of the History of the Kings of*
Israel. 9 When Jehoahaz died, he was buried in Samaria. Then his son Jehoash* became the next king.

Jehoash Rules in Israel

10 Jehoash son of Jehoahaz began to rule over Israel
in the thirty-seventh year of King Joash's reign in
Judah. He reigned in Samaria sixteen years. 11 But he
did what was evil in the LORD's sight. He refused to
turn from the sins that Jeroboam son of Nebat had
led Israel to commit.
12 The rest of the events in Jehoash's reign and
everything he did, including the extent of his power
and his war with King Amaziah of Judah, are recorded in *The Book of the History of the Kings of Is-*
rael. 13 When Jehoash died, he was buried in Samaria
with the kings of Israel. Then his son Jeroboam II
became the next king.

Elisha's Final Prophecy

14 When Elisha was in his last illness, King Jehoash of
Israel visited him and wept over him. "My father! My
father! I see the chariots and charioteers of Israel!"
he cried.
15 Elisha told him, "Get a bow and some arrows."
And the king did as he was told. 16 Elisha told him,
"Put your hand on the bow," and Elisha laid his own
hands on the king's hands.
17 Then he commanded, "Open that eastern window," and he opened it. Then he said, "Shoot!" So he
shot an arrow. Elisha proclaimed, "This is the LORD's
arrow, an arrow of victory over Aram, for you will
completely conquer the Arameans at Aphek."
18 Then he said, "Now pick up the other arrows and
strike them against the ground." So the king picked
them up and struck the ground three times. 19 But the
man of God was angry with him. "You should have
struck the ground five or six times!" he exclaimed.
"Then you would have beaten Aram until it was
entirely destroyed. Now you will be victorious only
three times."
20 Then Elisha died and was buried.
Groups of Moabite raiders used to invade the land
each spring. 21 Once when some Israelites were burying a man, they spied a band of these raiders. So they
hastily threw the corpse into the tomb of Elisha and
fled. But as soon as the body touched Elisha's bones,
the dead man revived and jumped to his feet!
22 King Hazael of Aram had oppressed Israel during
the entire reign of King Jehoahaz. 23 But the LORD
was gracious and merciful to the people of Israel, and
they were not totally destroyed. He pitied them because of his covenant with Abraham, Isaac, and Jacob.

13:9 Hebrew *Joash,* a variant spelling of Jehoash; also in 13:10, 12, 13, 14, 25.

KING JAMES VERSION

Jacob, and would not destroy them, neither cast he
them from his presence as yet.
24So Hazael king of Syria died; and Ben-hadad his
son reigned in his stead.
25And Jehoash the son of Jehoahaz took again out
of the hand of Ben-hadad the son of Hazael the cities, which he had taken out of the hand of Jehoahaz
his father by war. Three times did Joash beat him,
and recovered the cities of Israel.

14 1In the second year of Joash son of Jehoahaz
king of Israel reigned Amaziah the son of Joash king of Judah.
2He was twenty and five years old when he began
to reign, and reigned twenty and nine years in Jerusalem. And his mother's name *was* Jehoaddan of
Jerusalem.
3And he did *that which was* right in the sight of
the LORD, yet not like David his father: he did according to all things as Joash his father did.
4Howbeit the high places were not taken away: as
yet the people did sacrifice and burnt incense on the
high places.
5And it came to pass, as soon as the kingdom was
confirmed in his hand, that he slew his servants
which had slain the king his father.
6But the children of the murderers he slew not: according unto that which is written in the book of the
law of Moses, wherein the LORD commanded, saying,
The fathers shall not be put to death for the children,
nor the children be put to death for the fathers; but
every man shall be put to death for his own sin.
7He slew of Edom in the valley of salt ten thousand, and took Selah by war, and called the name of it
Joktheel unto this day.
8Then Amaziah sent messengers to Jehoash, the
son of Jehoahaz son of Jehu, king of Israel, saying,
Come, let us look one another in the face.
9And Jehoash the king of Israel sent to Amaziah
king of Judah, saying, The thistle that *was* in Lebanon
sent to the cedar that *was* in Lebanon, saying, Give thy
daughter to my son to wife: and there passed by a wild
beast that *was* in Lebanon, and trode down the thistle.
10Thou hast indeed smitten Edom, and thine heart
hath lifted thee up: glory *of this,* and tarry at home:
for why shouldest thou meddle to *thy* hurt, that thou
shouldest fall, *even* thou, and Judah with thee?
11But Amaziah would not hear. Therefore Jehoash
king of Israel went up; and he and Amaziah king
of Judah looked one another in the face at Beth-
shemesh, which *belongeth* to Judah.
12And Judah was put to the worse before Israel;
and they fled every man to their tents.
13And Jehoash king of Israel took Amaziah king of
Judah, the son of Jehoash the son of Ahaziah, at Beth-
shemesh, and came to Jerusalem, and brake down
the wall of Jerusalem from the gate of Ephraim unto
the corner gate, four hundred cubits.

NEW LIVING TRANSLATION

And to this day he still has not completely destroyed
them or banished them from his presence.
24King Hazael of Aram died, and his son Ben-
hadad became the next king. 25Then Jehoash son of
Jehoahaz recaptured from Ben-hadad son of Hazael
the towns that had been taken from Jehoash's father,
Jehoahaz. Jehoash defeated Ben-hadad on three occasions, and he recovered the Israelite towns.

Amaziah Rules in Judah

14 Amaziah son of Joash began to rule over Judah in the second year of the reign of King
Jehoash* of Israel. 2Amaziah was twenty-five years
old when he became king, and he reigned in Jerusalem twenty-nine years. His mother was Jehoaddin
from Jerusalem. 3Amaziah did what was pleasing in
the LORD's sight, but not like his ancestor David. Instead, he followed the example of his father, Joash.
4Amaziah did not destroy the pagan shrines, and the
people still offered sacrifices and burned incense
there.
5When Amaziah was well established as king, he
executed the officials who had assassinated his father. 6However, he did not kill the children of the assassins, for he obeyed the command of the LORD as
written by Moses in the Book of the Law: "Parents
must not be put to death for the sins of their children, nor children for the sins of their parents. Those
deserving to die must be put to death for their own
crimes."*
7Amaziah also killed 10,000 Edomites in the Valley of Salt. He also conquered Sela and changed its
name to Joktheel, as it is called to this day.
8One day Amaziah sent messengers with this challenge to Israel's king Jehoash, the son of Jehoahaz and
grandson of Jehu: "Come and meet me in battle!"*
9But King Jehoash of Israel replied to King Amaziah of Judah with this story: "Out in the Lebanon
mountains, a thistle sent a message to a mighty cedar
tree: 'Give your daughter in marriage to my son.' But
just then a wild animal of Lebanon came by and
stepped on the thistle, crushing it!
10"You have indeed defeated Edom, and you are
very proud of it. But be content with your victory and
stay at home! Why stir up trouble that will only bring
disaster on you and the people of Judah?"
11But Amaziah refused to listen, so King Jehoash
of Israel mobilized his army against King Amaziah of
Judah. The two armies drew up their battle lines at
Beth-shemesh in Judah. 12Judah was routed by the
army of Israel, and its army scattered and fled for
home. 13King Jehoash of Israel captured Judah's
king, Amaziah son of Joash and grandson of Ahaziah,
at Beth-shemesh. Then he marched to Jerusalem,
where he demolished 600 feet* of Jerusalem's wall,

14:1 Hebrew *Joash,* a variant spelling of Jehoash; also in 14:13, 23, 27.
14:6 Deut 24:16. **14:8** Hebrew *Come, let us look one another in the face.*
14:13 Hebrew *400 cubits* [180 meters].

KING JAMES VERSION

14 And he took all the gold and silver, and all the vessels that were found in the house of the LORD, and in the treasures of the king's house, and hostages, and returned to Samaria.

15 Now the rest of the acts of Jehoash which he did, and his might, and how he fought with Amaziah king of Judah, *are* they not written in the book of the chronicles of the kings of Israel?

16 And Jehoash slept with his fathers, and was buried in Samaria with the kings of Israel; and Jeroboam his son reigned in his stead.

17 And Amaziah the son of Joash king of Judah lived after the death of Jehoash son of Jehoahaz king of Israel fifteen years.

18 And the rest of the acts of Amaziah, *are* they not written in the book of the chronicles of the kings of Judah?

19 Now they made a conspiracy against him in Jerusalem: and he fled to Lachish; but they sent after him to Lachish, and slew him there.

20 And they brought him on horses: and he was buried at Jerusalem with his fathers in the city of David.

21 And all the people of Judah took Azariah, which *was* sixteen years old, and made him king instead of his father Amaziah.

22 He built Elath, and restored it to Judah, after that the king slept with his fathers.

23 In the fifteenth year of Amaziah the son of Joash king of Judah Jeroboam the son of Joash king of Israel began to reign in Samaria, *and reigned* forty and one years.

24 And he did *that which was* evil in the sight of the LORD: he departed not from all the sins of Jeroboam the son of Nebat, who made Israel to sin.

25 He restored the coast of Israel from the entering of Hamath unto the sea of the plain, according to the word of the LORD God of Israel, which he spake by the hand of his servant Jonah, the son of Amittai, the prophet, which *was* of Gathhepher.

26 For the LORD saw the affliction of Israel, *that it was* very bitter: for *there was* not any shut up, nor any left, nor any helper for Israel.

27 And the LORD said not that he would blot out the name of Israel from under heaven: but he saved them by the hand of Jeroboam the son of Joash.

28 Now the rest of the acts of Jeroboam, and all that he did, and his might, how he warred, and how he recovered Damascus, and Hamath, *which belonged* to Judah, for Israel, are they not written in the book of the chronicles of the kings of Israel?

29 And Jeroboam slept with his fathers, *even* with the kings of Israel; and Zachariah his son reigned in his stead.

NEW LIVING TRANSLATION

from the Ephraim Gate to the Corner Gate.
14 He carried off all the gold and silver and all the articles
from the Temple of the LORD. He also seized the treasures from the royal palace, along with hostages, and then returned to Samaria.
15 The rest of the events in Jehoash's reign and everything he did, including the extent of his power and his war with King Amaziah of Judah, are recorded in *The Book of the History of the Kings of Israel.*
16 When Jehoash died, he was buried in Samaria
with the kings of Israel. And his son Jeroboam II became the next king.
17 King Amaziah of Judah lived for fifteen years
after the death of King Jehoash of Israel.
18 The rest
of the events in Amaziah's reign are recorded in *The Book of the History of the Kings of Judah.*
19 There was a conspiracy against Amaziah's life in
Jerusalem, and he fled to Lachish. But his enemies
sent assassins after him, and they killed him there.
20 They brought his body back to Jerusalem on a
horse, and he was buried with his ancestors in the
City of David.
21 All the people of Judah had crowned Amaziah's
sixteen-year-old son, Uzziah,* as king in place of his
father, Amaziah.
22 After his father's death, Uzziah
rebuilt the town of Elath and restored it to Judah.

Jeroboam II Rules in Israel

23 Jeroboam II, the son of Jehoash, began to rule over
Israel in the fifteenth year of King Amaziah's reign in
Judah. Jeroboam reigned in Samaria forty-one years.
24 He did what was evil in the LORD's sight. He refused
to turn from the sins that Jeroboam son of Nebat had
led Israel to commit.
25 Jeroboam II recovered the
territories of Israel between Lebo-hamath and the
Dead Sea,* just as the LORD, the God of Israel, had
promised through Jonah son of Amittai, the prophet
from Gath-hepher.
26 For the LORD saw the bitter suffering of everyone in Israel, and that there was no one in Israel,
slave or free, to help them.
27 And because the LORD
had not said he would blot out the name of Israel
completely, he used Jeroboam II, the son of Jehoash,
to save them.
28 The rest of the events in the reign of Jeroboam II
and everything he did—including the extent of his
power, his wars, and how he recovered for Israel both
Damascus and Hamath, which had belonged to Judah*—are recorded in *The Book of the History of the Kings of Israel.*
29 When Jeroboam II died, he was
buried in Samaria* with the kings of Israel. Then his
son Zechariah became the next king.

14:21 Hebrew *Azariah,* a variant spelling of Uzziah. **14:25** Hebrew *the sea of the Arabah.* **14:28** Or *to Yaudi.* The meaning of the Hebrew is uncertain. **14:29** As in some Greek manuscripts; Hebrew lacks *he was buried in Samaria.*

KING JAMES VERSION

15

1In the twenty and seventh year of Jeroboam king of Israel began Azariah son of Amaziah king of Judah to reign.

2Sixteen years old was he when he began to reign, and he reigned two and fifty years in Jerusalem. And his mother's name *was* Jecholiah of Jerusalem.

3And he did *that which was* right in the sight of the LORD, according to all that his father Amaziah had done;

4Save that the high places were not removed: the people sacrificed and burnt incense still on the high places.

5And the LORD smote the king, so that he was a leper unto the day of his death, and dwelt in a several house. And Jotham the king's son *was* over the house, judging the people of the land.

6And the rest of the acts of Azariah, and all that he did, *are* they not written in the book of the chronicles of the kings of Judah?

7So Azariah slept with his fathers; and they buried him with his fathers in the city of David: and Jotham his son reigned in his stead.

8In the thirty and eighth year of Azariah king of Judah did Zachariah the son of Jeroboam reign over Israel in Samaria six months.

9And he did *that which was* evil in the sight of the LORD, as his fathers had done: he departed not from the sins of Jeroboam the son of Nebat, who made Israel to sin.

10And Shallum the son of Jabesh conspired against him, and smote him before the people, and slew him, and reigned in his stead.

11And the rest of the acts of Zachariah, behold, they *are* written in the book of the chronicles of the kings of Israel.

12This *was* the word of the LORD which he spake unto Jehu, saying, Thy sons shall sit on the throne of Israel unto the fourth *generation.* And so it came to pass.

13Shallum the son of Jabesh began to reign in the nine and thirtieth year of Uzziah king of Judah; and he reigned a full month in Samaria.

14For Menahem the son of Gadi went up from Tirzah, and came to Samaria, and smote Shallum the son of Jabesh in Samaria, and slew him, and reigned in his stead.

15And the rest of the acts of Shallum, and his conspiracy which he made, behold, they *are* written in the book of the chronicles of the kings of Israel.

16Then Menahem smote Tiphsah, and all that *were* therein, and the coasts thereof from Tirzah: because they opened not *to him,* therefore he smote *it; and* all the women therein that were with child he ripped up.

NEW LIVING TRANSLATION

Uzziah Rules in Judah

15

Uzziah* son of Amaziah began to rule over Judah in the twenty-seventh year of the reign of King Jeroboam II of Israel. 2He was sixteen years old when he became king, and he reigned in Jerusalem fifty-two years. His mother was Jecoliah from Jerusalem.

3He did what was pleasing in the LORD's sight, just as his father, Amaziah, had done. 4But he did not destroy the pagan shrines, and the people still offered sacrifices and burned incense there. 5The LORD struck the king with leprosy,* which lasted until the day he died. He lived in isolation in a separate house. The king's son Jotham was put in charge of the royal palace, and he governed the people of the land.

6The rest of the events in Uzziah's reign and everything he did are recorded in *The Book of the History of the Kings of Judah.* 7When Uzziah died, he was buried with his ancestors in the City of David. And his son Jotham became the next king.

Zechariah Rules in Israel

8Zechariah son of Jeroboam II began to rule over Israel in the thirty-eighth year of King Uzziah's reign in Judah. He reigned in Samaria six months. 9Zechariah did what was evil in the LORD's sight, as his ancestors had done. He refused to turn from the sins that Jeroboam son of Nebat had led Israel to commit. 10Then Shallum son of Jabesh conspired against Zechariah, assassinated him in public,* and became the next king.

11The rest of the events in Zechariah's reign are recorded in *The Book of the History of the Kings of Israel.* 12So the LORD's message to Jehu came true: "Your descendants will be kings of Israel down to the fourth generation."

Shallum Rules in Israel

13Shallum son of Jabesh began to rule over Israel in the thirty-ninth year of King Uzziah's reign in Judah. Shallum reigned in Samaria only one month. 14Then Menahem son of Gadi went to Samaria from Tirzah and assassinated him, and he became the next king.

15The rest of the events in Shallum's reign, including his conspiracy, are recorded in *The Book of the History of the Kings of Israel.*

Menahem Rules in Israel

16At that time Menahem destroyed the town of Tappuah* and all the surrounding countryside as far as Tirzah, because its citizens refused to surrender the town. He killed the entire population and ripped open the pregnant women.

15:1 Hebrew *Azariah,* a variant spelling of Uzziah; also in 15:6, 7, 8, 17, 23, 27. **15:5** Or *with a contagious skin disease.* The Hebrew word used here and throughout this passage can describe various skin diseases. **15:10** Or *at Ibleam.* **15:16** As in some Greek manuscripts; other Greek manuscripts read *at Ibleam.* Hebrew reads *Tiphsah.*

KING JAMES VERSION

17 In the nine and thirtieth year of Azariah king of Judah began Menahem the son of Gadi to reign over Israel, *and reigned* ten years in Samaria.

18 And he did *that which was* evil in the sight of the LORD: he departed not all his days from the sins of Jeroboam the son of Nebat, who made Israel to sin.

19 *And* Pul the king of Assyria came against the land: and Menahem gave Pul a thousand talents of silver, that his hand might be with him to confirm the kingdom in his hand.

20 And Menahem exacted the money of Israel, *even* of all the mighty men of wealth, of each man fifty shekels of silver, to give to the king of Assyria. So the king of Assyria turned back, and stayed not there in the land.

21 And the rest of the acts of Menahem, and all that he did, *are* they not written in the book of the chronicles of the kings of Israel?

22 And Menahem slept with his fathers; and Pekahiah his son reigned in his stead.

23 In the fiftieth year of Azariah king of Judah Pekahiah the son of Menahem began to reign over Israel in Samaria, *and reigned* two years.

24 And he did *that which was* evil in the sight of the LORD: he departed not from the sins of Jeroboam the son of Nebat, who made Israel to sin.

25 But Pekah the son of Remaliah, a captain of his, conspired against him, and smote him in Samaria, in the palace of the king's house, with Argob and Arieh, and with him fifty men of the Gileadites: and he killed him, and reigned in his room.

26 And the rest of the acts of Pekahiah, and all that he did, behold, they *are* written in the book of the chronicles of the kings of Israel.

27 In the two and fiftieth year of Azariah king of Judah Pekah the son of Remaliah began to reign over Israel in Samaria, *and reigned* twenty years.

28 And he did *that which was* evil in the sight of the LORD: he departed not from the sins of Jeroboam the son of Nebat, who made Israel to sin.

29 In the days of Pekah king of Israel came Tiglath-pileser king of Assyria, and took Ijon, and Abel-beth-maachah, and Janoah, and Kedesh, and Hazor, and Gilead, and Galilee, all the land of Naphtali, and carried them captive to Assyria.

30 And Hoshea the son of Elah made a conspiracy against Pekah the son of Remaliah, and smote him, and slew him, and reigned in his stead, in the twentieth year of Jotham the son of Uzziah.

31 And the rest of the acts of Pekah, and all that he did, behold, they *are* written in the book of the chronicles of the kings of Israel.

NEW LIVING TRANSLATION

17 Menahem son of Gadi began to rule over Israel in the thirty-ninth year of King Uzziah's reign in Judah. He reigned in Samaria ten years. 18 But Menahem did what was evil in the LORD's sight. During his entire reign, he refused to turn from the sins that Jeroboam son of Nebat had led Israel to commit.

19 Then King Tiglath-pileser* of Assyria invaded the land. But Menahem paid him thirty-seven tons* of silver to gain his support in tightening his grip on royal power. 20 Menahem extorted the money from the rich of Israel, demanding that each of them pay fifty pieces* of silver to the king of Assyria. So the king of Assyria turned from attacking Israel and did not stay in the land.

21 The rest of the events in Menahem's reign and everything he did are recorded in *The Book of the History of the Kings of Israel.* 22 When Menahem died, his son Pekahiah became the next king.

Pekahiah Rules in Israel

23 Pekahiah son of Menahem began to rule over Israel in the fiftieth year of King Uzziah's reign in Judah. He reigned in Samaria two years. 24 But Pekahiah did what was evil in the LORD's sight. He refused to turn from the sins that Jeroboam son of Nebat had led Israel to commit.

25 Then Pekah son of Remaliah, the commander of Pekahiah's army, conspired against him. With fifty men from Gilead, Pekah assassinated the king, along with Argob and Arieh, in the citadel of the palace at Samaria. And Pekah reigned in his place.

26 The rest of the events in Pekahiah's reign and everything he did are recorded in *The Book of the History of the Kings of Israel.*

Pekah Rules in Israel

27 Pekah son of Remaliah began to rule over Israel in the fifty-second year of King Uzziah's reign in Judah. He reigned in Samaria twenty years. 28 But Pekah did what was evil in the LORD's sight. He refused to turn from the sins that Jeroboam son of Nebat had led Israel to commit.

29 During Pekah's reign, King Tiglath-pileser of Assyria attacked Israel again, and he captured the towns of Ijon, Abel-beth-maacah, Janoah, Kedesh, and Hazor. He also conquered the regions of Gilead, Galilee, and all of Naphtali, and he took the people to Assyria as captives. 30 Then Hoshea son of Elah conspired against Pekah and assassinated him. He began to rule over Israel in the twentieth year of Jotham son of Uzziah.

31 The rest of the events in Pekah's reign and everything he did are recorded in *The Book of the History of the Kings of Israel.*

15:19a Hebrew *Pul,* another name for Tiglath-pileser. **15:19b** Hebrew *1,000 talents* [34 metric tons]. **15:20** Hebrew *50 shekels* [20 ounces, or 570 grams].

KING JAMES VERSION

32In the second year of Pekah the son of Remaliah
king of Israel began Jotham the son of Uzziah king
of Judah to reign.
33Five and twenty years old was he when he began
to reign, and he reigned sixteen years in Jerusalem.
And his mother's name *was* Jerusha, the daughter of
Zadok.
34And he did *that which was* right in the sight
of the LORD: he did according to all that his father
Uzziah had done.
35Howbeit the high places were not removed: the
people sacrificed and burned incense still in the
high places. He built the higher gate of the house of
the LORD.
36Now the rest of the acts of Jotham, and all that he
did, *are* they not written in the book of the chronicles of the kings of Judah?
37In those days the LORD began to send against
Judah Rezin the king of Syria, and Pekah the son of
Remaliah.
38And Jotham slept with his fathers, and was buried with his fathers in the city of David his father:
and Ahaz his son reigned in his stead.

16 1In the seventeenth year of Pekah the son of
Remaliah Ahaz the son of Jotham king of
Judah began to reign.
2Twenty years old *was* Ahaz when he began to
reign, and reigned sixteen years in Jerusalem, and
did not *that which was* right in the sight of the LORD
his God, like David his father.
3But he walked in the way of the kings of Israel,
yea, and made his son to pass through the fire, according to the abominations of the heathen, whom
the LORD cast out from before the children of Israel.
4And he sacrificed and burnt incense in the high
places, and on the hills, and under every green tree.
5Then Rezin king of Syria and Pekah son of Remaliah king of Israel came up to Jerusalem to war: and
they besieged Ahaz, but could not overcome *him*.
6At that time Rezin king of Syria recovered Elath
to Syria, and drave the Jews from Elath: and the Syrians came to Elath, and dwelt there unto this day.
7So Ahaz sent messengers to Tiglath-pileser king
of Assyria, saying, I *am* thy servant and thy son: come
up, and save me out of the hand of the king of Syria,
and out of the hand of the king of Israel, which rise
up against me.
8And Ahaz took the silver and gold that was found
in the house of the LORD, and in the treasures of the
king's house, and sent *it for* a present to the king of
Assyria.
9And the king of Assyria hearkened unto him: for
the king of Assyria went up against Damascus, and
took it, and carried *the people of* it captive to Kir, and
slew Rezin.

NEW LIVING TRANSLATION

Jotham Rules in Judah

32Jotham son of Uzziah began to rule over Judah in
the second year of King Pekah's reign in Israel. 33He
was twenty-five years old when he became king, and
he reigned in Jerusalem sixteen years. His mother
was Jerusha, the daughter of Zadok.
34Jotham did what was pleasing in the LORD's
sight. He did everything his father, Uzziah, had done.
35But he did not destroy the pagan shrines, and the
people still offered sacrifices and burned incense
there. He rebuilt the upper gate of the Temple of the
LORD.
36The rest of the events in Jotham's reign and
everything he did are recorded in *The Book of the
History of the Kings of Judah*. 37In those days the
LORD began to send King Rezin of Aram and King
Pekah of Israel to attack Judah. 38When Jotham died,
he was buried with his ancestors in the City of David.
And his son Ahaz became the next king.

Ahaz Rules in Judah

16 Ahaz son of Jotham began to rule over Judah
in the seventeenth year of King Pekah's reign
in Israel. 2Ahaz was twenty years old when he became king, and he reigned in Jerusalem sixteen
years. He did not do what was pleasing in the sight of
the LORD his God, as his ancestor David had done.
3Instead, he followed the example of the kings of Israel, even sacrificing his own son in the fire.* In this
way, he followed the detestable practices of the pagan nations the LORD had driven from the land ahead
of the Israelites. 4He offered sacrifices and burned
incense at the pagan shrines and on the hills and
under every green tree.
5Then King Rezin of Aram and King Pekah of Israel came up to attack Jerusalem. They besieged Ahaz
but could not conquer him. 6At that time the king of
Edom* recovered the town of Elath for Edom.* He
drove out the people of Judah and sent Edomites* to
live there, as they do to this day.
7King Ahaz sent messengers to King Tiglath-pileser of Assyria with this message: "I am your servant and your vassal.* Come up and rescue me from
the attacking armies of Aram and Israel." 8Then
Ahaz took the silver and gold from the Temple of the
LORD and the palace treasury and sent it as a payment to the Assyrian king. 9So the king of Assyria attacked the Aramean capital of Damascus and led its
population away as captives, resettling them in Kir.
He also killed King Rezin.

16:3 Or *even making his son pass through the fire.* **16:6a** As in Latin Vulgate; Hebrew reads *Rezin king of Aram.* **16:6b** As in Latin Vulgate; Hebrew reads *Aram.* **16:6c** As in Greek version, Latin Vulgate, and an alternate reading of the Masoretic Text; the other alternate reads *Arameans.* **16:7** Hebrew *your son.*

KING JAMES VERSION

10 And king Ahaz went to Damascus to meet Tiglath-pileser king of Assyria, and saw an altar that *was* at Damascus: and king Ahaz sent to Urijah the priest the fashion of the altar, and the pattern of it, according to all the workmanship thereof.

11 And Urijah the priest built an altar according to all that king Ahaz had sent from Damascus: so Urijah the priest made *it* against king Ahaz came from Damascus.

12 And when the king was come from Damascus, the king saw the altar: and the king approached to the altar, and offered thereon.

13 And he burnt his burnt offering and his meat offering, and poured his drink offering, and sprinkled the blood of his peace offerings, upon the altar.

14 And he brought also the brasen altar, which *was* before the LORD, from the forefront of the house, from between the altar and the house of the LORD, and put it on the north side of the altar.

15 And king Ahaz commanded Urijah the priest, saying, Upon the great altar burn the morning burnt offering, and the evening meat offering, and the king's burnt sacrifice, and his meat offering, with the burnt offering of all the people of the land, and their meat offering, and their drink offerings; and sprinkle upon it all the blood of the burnt offering, and all the blood of the sacrifice: and the brasen altar shall be for me to inquire *by*.

16 Thus did Urijah the priest, according to all that king Ahaz commanded.

17 And king Ahaz cut off the borders of the bases, and removed the laver from off them; and took down the sea from off the brasen oxen that *were* under it, and put it upon a pavement of stones.

18 And the covert for the sabbath that they had built in the house, and the king's entry without, turned he from the house of the LORD for the king of Assyria.

19 Now the rest of the acts of Ahaz which he did, *are* they not written in the book of the chronicles of the kings of Judah?

20 And Ahaz slept with his fathers, and was buried with his fathers in the city of David: and Hezekiah his son reigned in his stead.

17 1 In the twelfth year of Ahaz king of Judah began Hoshea the son of Elah to reign in Samaria over Israel nine years.

2 And he did *that which was* evil in the sight of the LORD, but not as the kings of Israel that were before him.

3 Against him came up Shalmaneser king of Assyria; and Hoshea became his servant, and gave him presents.

4 And the king of Assyria found conspiracy in Hoshea: for he had sent messengers to So king of Egypt,

NEW LIVING TRANSLATION

10 King Ahaz then went to Damascus to meet with
King Tiglath-pileser of Assyria. While he was there,
he took special note of the altar. Then he sent a
model of the altar to Uriah the priest, along with its
design in full detail. 11 Uriah followed the king's instructions and built an altar just like it, and it was
ready before the king returned from Damascus.
12 When the king returned, he inspected the altar
and made offerings on it. 13 He presented a burnt offering and a grain offering, he poured out a liquid offering, and he sprinkled the blood of peace offerings
on the altar.

14 Then King Ahaz removed the old bronze altar
from its place in front of the LORD's Temple, between
the entrance and the new altar, and placed it on the
north side of the new altar. 15 He told Uriah the
priest, "Use the new altar* for the morning sacrifices
of burnt offering, the evening grain offering, the
king's burnt offering and grain offering, and the
burnt offerings of all the people, as well as their grain
offerings and liquid offerings. Sprinkle the blood
from all the burnt offerings and sacrifices on the
new altar. The bronze altar will be for my personal
use only." 16 Uriah the priest did just as King Ahaz
commanded him.

17 Then the king removed the side panels and basins from the portable water carts. He also removed
the great bronze basin called the Sea from the backs
of the bronze oxen and placed it on the stone pavement. 18 In deference to the king of Assyria, he also
removed the canopy that had been constructed inside the palace for use on the Sabbath day,* as well as
the king's outer entrance to the Temple of the LORD.

19 The rest of the events in Ahaz's reign and everything he did are recorded in *The Book of the History
of the Kings of Judah*. 20 When Ahaz died, he was buried with his ancestors in the City of David. Then his
son Hezekiah became the next king.

Hoshea Rules in Israel

17 Hoshea son of Elah began to rule over Israel
in the twelfth year of King Ahaz's reign in Judah. He reigned in Samaria nine years. 2 He did what
was evil in the LORD's sight, but not to the same extent as the kings of Israel who ruled before him.

3 King Shalmaneser of Assyria attacked King Hoshea, so Hoshea was forced to pay heavy tribute to Assyria. 4 But Hoshea stopped paying the annual tribute
and conspired against the king of Assyria by asking
King So of Egypt* to help him shake free of Assyria's

16:15 Hebrew *the great altar.* **16:18** The meaning of the Hebrew is uncertain. **17:4** Or *by asking the king of Egypt at Sais.*

KING JAMES VERSION

and brought no present to the king of Assyria, as *he*
had done year by year: therefore the king of Assyria
shut him up, and bound him in prison.

5 Then the king of Assyria came up throughout all
the land, and went up to Samaria, and besieged it
three years.

6 In the ninth year of Hoshea the king of Assyria
took Samaria, and carried Israel away into Assyria,
and placed them in Halah and in Habor *by* the river
of Gozan, and in the cities of the Medes.

7 For *so* it was, that the children of Israel had sinned
against the LORD their God, which had brought them
up out of the land of Egypt, from under the hand of
Pharaoh king of Egypt, and had feared other gods,

8 And walked in the statutes of the heathen, whom
the LORD cast out from before the children of Israel,
and of the kings of Israel, which they had made.

9 And the children of Israel did secretly *those*
things that *were* not right against the LORD their God,
and they built them high places in all their cities,
from the tower of the watchmen to the fenced city.

10 And they set them up images and groves in every
high hill, and under every green tree:

11 And there they burnt incense in all the high
places, as *did* the heathen whom the LORD carried
away before them; and wrought wicked things to
provoke the LORD to anger:

12 For they served idols, whereof the LORD had said
unto them, Ye shall not do this thing.

13 Yet the LORD testified against Israel, and against
Judah, by all the prophets, *and by* all the seers, saying, Turn ye from your evil ways, and keep my commandments *and* my statutes, according to all the law
which I commanded your fathers, and which I sent
to you by my servants the prophets.

14 Notwithstanding they would not hear, but hardened their necks, like to the neck of their fathers,
that did not believe in the LORD their God.

15 And they rejected his statutes, and his covenant
that he made with their fathers, and his testimonies
which he testified against them; and they followed
vanity, and became vain, and went after the heathen
that *were* round about them, *concerning* whom the
LORD had charged them, that they should not do
like them.

16 And they left all the commandments of the LORD
their God, and made them molten images, *even* two
calves, and made a grove, and worshipped all the
host of heaven, and served Baal.

17 And they caused their sons and their daughters
to pass through the fire, and used divination and enchantments, and sold themselves to do evil in the
sight of the LORD, to provoke him to anger.

18 Therefore the LORD was very angry with Israel,
and removed them out of his sight: there was none
left but the tribe of Judah only.

NEW LIVING TRANSLATION

power. When the king of Assyria discovered this
treachery, he seized Hoshea and put him in prison.

Samaria Falls to Assyria

5 Then the king of Assyria invaded the entire land,
and for three years he besieged the city of Samaria.
6 Finally, in the ninth year of King Hoshea's reign,
Samaria fell, and the people of Israel were exiled to
Assyria. They were settled in colonies in Halah, along
the banks of the Habor River in Gozan, and in the
cities of the Medes.

7 This disaster came upon the people of Israel because they worshiped other gods. They sinned
against the LORD their God, who had brought them
safely out of Egypt and had rescued them from the
power of Pharaoh, the king of Egypt. 8 They had followed the practices of the pagan nations the LORD
had driven from the land ahead of them, as well
as the practices the kings of Israel had introduced.
9 The people of Israel had also secretly done many
things that were not pleasing to the LORD their God.
They built pagan shrines for themselves in all their
towns, from the smallest outpost to the largest
walled city. 10 They set up sacred pillars and Asherah
poles at the top of every hill and under every green
tree. 11 They offered sacrifices on all the hilltops,
just like the nations the LORD had driven from the
land ahead of them. So the people of Israel had done
many evil things, arousing the LORD's anger. 12 Yes,
they worshiped idols,* despite the LORD's specific
and repeated warnings.

13 Again and again the LORD had sent his prophets
and seers to warn both Israel and Judah: "Turn from
all your evil ways. Obey my commands and decrees—
the entire law that I commanded your ancestors to
obey, and that I gave you through my servants the
prophets."

14 But the Israelites would not listen. They were as
stubborn as their ancestors who had refused to believe in the LORD their God. 15 They rejected his
decrees and the covenant he had made with their ancestors, and they despised all his warnings. They
worshiped worthless idols, so they became worthless themselves. They followed the example of the
nations around them, disobeying the LORD's command not to imitate them.

16 They rejected all the commands of the LORD
their God and made two calves from metal. They set
up an Asherah pole and worshiped Baal and all the
forces of heaven. 17 They even sacrificed their own
sons and daughters in the fire.* They consulted fortune-tellers and practiced sorcery and sold themselves to evil, arousing the LORD's anger.

18 Because the LORD was very angry with Israel, he
swept them away from his presence. Only the tribe

17:12 The Hebrew term (literally *round things*) probably alludes to dung.
17:17 Or *They even made their sons and daughters pass through the fire.*

KING JAMES VERSION

19 Also Judah kept not the commandments of the
LORD their God, but walked in the statutes of Israel
which they made.
20 And the LORD rejected all the seed of Israel, and
afflicted them, and delivered them into the hand of
spoilers, until he had cast them out of his sight.
21 For he rent Israel from the house of David; and
they made Jeroboam the son of Nebat king: and
Jeroboam drave Israel from following the LORD, and
made them sin a great sin.
22 For the children of Israel walked in all the sins
of Jeroboam which he did; they departed not from
them;
23 Until the LORD removed Israel out of his sight, as
he had said by all his servants the prophets. So was
Israel carried away out of their own land to Assyria
unto this day.

24 And the king of Assyria brought *men* from Babylon, and from Cuthah, and from Ava, and from Hamath, and from Sepharvaim, and placed *them* in the
cities of Samaria instead of the children of Israel:
and they possessed Samaria, and dwelt in the cities
thereof.
25 And *so* it was at the beginning of their dwelling
there, *that* they feared not the LORD: therefore the
LORD sent lions among them, which slew *some* of
them.
26 Wherefore they spake to the king of Assyria, saying, The nations which thou hast removed, and
placed in the cities of Samaria, know not the manner
of the God of the land: therefore he hath sent lions
among them, and, behold, they slay them, because
they know not the manner of the God of the land.
27 Then the king of Assyria commanded, saying,
Carry thither one of the priests whom ye brought
from thence; and let them go and dwell there, and let
him teach them the manner of the God of the land.
28 Then one of the priests whom they had carried
away from Samaria came and dwelt in Bethel, and
taught them how they should fear the LORD.
29 Howbeit every nation made gods of their own,
and put *them* in the houses of the high places which
the Samaritans had made, every nation in their cities
wherein they dwelt.
30 And the men of Babylon made Succoth-benoth,
and the men of Cuth made Nergal, and the men of
Hamath made Ashima,
31 And the Avites made Nibhaz and Tartak, and the
Sepharvites burnt their children in fire to Adrammelech and Anammelech, the gods of Sepharvaim.
32 So they feared the LORD, and made unto themselves of the lowest of them priests of the high
places, which sacrificed for them in the houses of
the high places.
33 They feared the LORD, and served their own

NEW LIVING TRANSLATION

of Judah remained in the land. 19 But even the people
of Judah refused to obey the commands of the LORD
their God, for they followed the evil practices that Israel had introduced. 20 The LORD rejected all the descendants of Israel. He punished them by handing
them over to their attackers until he had banished
Israel from his presence.
21 For when the LORD* tore Israel away from the
kingdom of David, they chose Jeroboam son of Nebat as their king. But Jeroboam drew Israel away
from following the LORD and made them commit a
great sin. 22 And the people of Israel persisted in all
the evil ways of Jeroboam. They did not turn from
these sins 23 until the LORD finally swept them away
from his presence, just as all his prophets had
warned. So Israel was exiled from their land to Assyria, where they remain to this day.

Foreigners Settle in Israel

24 The king of Assyria transported groups of people
from Babylon, Cuthah, Avva, Hamath, and Sepharvaim and resettled them in the towns of Samaria, replacing the people of Israel. They took possession of
Samaria and lived in its towns. 25 But since these foreign settlers did not worship the LORD when they
first arrived, the LORD sent lions among them, which
killed some of them.
26 So a message was sent to the king of Assyria: "The
people you have sent to live in the towns of Samaria do
not know the religious customs of the God of the land.
He has sent lions among them to destroy them because they have not worshiped him correctly."
27 The king of Assyria then commanded, "Send
one of the exiled priests back to Samaria. Let him
live there and teach the new residents the religious
customs of the God of the land." 28 So one of the
priests who had been exiled from Samaria returned
to Bethel and taught the new residents how to worship the LORD.
29 But these various groups of foreigners also continued to worship their own gods. In town after town
where they lived, they placed their idols at the pagan
shrines that the people of Samaria had built. 30 Those
from Babylon worshiped idols of their god Succoth-
benoth. Those from Cuthah worshiped their god
Nergal. And those from Hamath worshiped Ashima.
31 The Avvites worshiped their gods Nibhaz and
Tartak. And the people from Sepharvaim even
burned their own children as sacrifices to their gods
Adrammelech and Anammelech.
32 These new residents worshiped the LORD, but
they also appointed from among themselves all sorts
of people as priests to offer sacrifices at their places
of worship. 33 And though they worshiped the LORD,

17:21 Hebrew *he;* compare 1 Kgs 11:31-32.

KING JAMES VERSION

gods, after the manner of the nations whom they
carried away from thence.
34 Unto this day they do after the former manners:
they fear not the LORD, neither do they after their
statutes, or after their ordinances, or after the law
and commandment which the LORD commanded
the children of Jacob, whom he named Israel;
35 With whom the LORD had made a covenant, and
charged them, saying, Ye shall not fear other gods,
nor bow yourselves to them, nor serve them, nor sacrifice to them:
36 But the LORD, who brought you up out of the
land of Egypt with great power and a stretched out
arm, him shall ye fear, and him shall ye worship, and
to him shall ye do sacrifice.
37 And the statutes, and the ordinances, and the
law, and the commandment, which he wrote for you,
ye shall observe to do for evermore; and ye shall not
fear other gods.
38 And the covenant that I have made with you ye
shall not forget; neither shall ye fear other gods.
39 But the LORD your God ye shall fear; and he shall
deliver you out of the hand of all your enemies.
40 Howbeit they did not hearken, but they did after
their former manner.
41 So these nations feared the LORD, and served
their graven images, both their children, and their
children's children: as did their fathers, so do they
unto this day.

18 1 Now it came to pass in the third year of Hoshea son of Elah king of Israel, *that* Hezekiah
the son of Ahaz king of Judah began to reign.
2 Twenty and five years old was he when he began
to reign; and he reigned twenty and nine years in Jerusalem. His mother's name also *was* Abi, the daughter of Zachariah.
3 And he did *that which was* right in the sight of
the LORD, according to all that David his father did.
4 He removed the high places, and brake the images, and cut down the groves, and brake in pieces
the brasen serpent that Moses had made: for unto
those days the children of Israel did burn incense to
it: and he called it Nehushtan.
5 He trusted in the LORD God of Israel; so that after
him was none like him among all the kings of Judah,
nor *any* that were before him.
6 For he clave to the LORD, *and* departed not from
following him, but kept his commandments, which
the LORD commanded Moses.
7 And the LORD was with him; *and* he prospered
whithersoever he went forth: and he rebelled against
the king of Assyria, and served him not.
8 He smote the Philistines, *even* unto Gaza, and the
borders thereof, from the tower of the watchmen to
the fenced city.
9 And it came to pass in the fourth year of king
Hezekiah, which *was* the seventh year of Hoshea son

NEW LIVING TRANSLATION

they continued to follow their own gods according
to the religious customs of the nations from which
they came. 34 And this is still going on today. They
continue to follow their former practices instead of
truly worshiping the LORD and obeying the decrees,
regulations, instructions, and commands he gave
the descendants of Jacob, whose name he changed
to Israel.
35 For the LORD had made a covenant with the descendants of Jacob and commanded them: "Do not
worship any other gods or bow before them or serve
them or offer sacrifices to them. 36 But worship only
the LORD, who brought you out of Egypt with great
strength and a powerful arm. Bow down to him
alone, and offer sacrifices only to him. 37 Be careful at
all times to obey the decrees, regulations, instructions, and commands that he wrote for you. You
must not worship other gods. 38 Do not forget the
covenant I made with you, and do not worship other
gods. 39 You must worship only the LORD your God.
He is the one who will rescue you from all your
enemies."
40 But the people would not listen and continued
to follow their former practices. 41 So while these
new residents worshiped the LORD, they also worshiped their idols. And to this day their descendants
do the same.

Hezekiah Rules in Judah

18 Hezekiah son of Ahaz began to rule over Judah in the third year of King Hoshea's reign
in Israel. 2 He was twenty-five years old when he became king, and he reigned in Jerusalem twenty-nine
years. His mother was Abijah,* the daughter of Zechariah. 3 He did what was pleasing in the LORD's sight,
just as his ancestor David had done. 4 He removed the
pagan shrines, smashed the sacred pillars, and cut
down the Asherah poles. He broke up the bronze serpent that Moses had made, because the people of Israel had been offering sacrifices to it. The bronze
serpent was called Nehushtan.*
5 Hezekiah trusted in the LORD, the God of Israel.
There was no one like him among all the kings of
Judah, either before or after his time. 6 He remained
faithful to the LORD in everything, and he carefully
obeyed all the commands the LORD had given Moses.
7 So the LORD was with him, and Hezekiah was successful in everything he did. He revolted against the
king of Assyria and refused to pay him tribute. 8 He
also conquered the Philistines as far distant as Gaza
and its territory, from their smallest outpost to their
largest walled city.
9 During the fourth year of Hezekiah's reign, which
was the seventh year of King Hoshea's reign in Israel,

18:2 As in parallel text at 2 Chr 29:1; Hebrew reads *Abi*, a variant spelling of Abijah. **18:4** *Nehushtan* sounds like the Hebrew terms that mean "snake," "bronze," and "unclean thing."

KING JAMES VERSION

of Elah king of Israel, *that* Shalmaneser king of Assyria came up against Samaria, and besieged it.
10And at the end of three years they took it: *even* in
the sixth year of Hezekiah, that *is* the ninth year of
Hoshea king of Israel, Samaria was taken.
11And the king of Assyria did carry away Israel
unto Assyria, and put them in Halah and in Habor *by*
the river of Gozan, and in the cities of the Medes:
12Because they obeyed not the voice of the LORD
their God, but transgressed his covenant, *and* all that
Moses the servant of the LORD commanded, and
would not hear *them*, nor do *them*.

13Now in the fourteenth year of king Hezekiah did
Sennacherib king of Assyria come up against all the
fenced cities of Judah, and took them.
14And Hezekiah king of Judah sent to the king of
Assyria to Lachish, saying, I have offended; return
from me: that which thou puttest on me will I bear.
And the king of Assyria appointed unto Hezekiah
king of Judah three hundred talents of silver and
thirty talents of gold.
15And Hezekiah gave *him* all the silver that was
found in the house of the LORD, and in the treasures
of the king's house.
16At that time did Hezekiah cut off *the gold from*
the doors of the temple of the LORD, and *from* the pillars which Hezekiah king of Judah had overlaid, and
gave it to the king of Assyria.
17And the king of Assyria sent Tartan and Rab-
saris and Rab-shakeh from Lachish to king Hezekiah
with a great host against Jerusalem. And they went
up and came to Jerusalem. And when they were
come up, they came and stood by the conduit of the
upper pool, which *is* in the highway of the fuller's
field.
18And when they had called to the king, there
came out to them Eliakim the son of Hilkiah, which
was over the household, and Shebna the scribe, and
Joah the son of Asaph the recorder.
19And Rab-shakeh said unto them, Speak ye now
to Hezekiah, Thus saith the great king, the king of
Assyria, What confidence *is* this wherein thou
trustest?
20Thou sayest, (but *they are but* vain words,) *I have*
counsel and strength for the war. Now on whom dost
thou trust, that thou rebellest against me?
21Now, behold, thou trustest upon the staff of this
bruised reed, *even* upon Egypt, on which if a man
lean, it will go into his hand, and pierce it: so *is* Pharaoh king of Egypt unto all that trust on him.
22But if ye say unto me, We trust in the LORD our

NEW LIVING TRANSLATION

King Shalmaneser of Assyria attacked the city of
Samaria and began a siege against it. 10Three years
later, during the sixth year of King Hezekiah's reign
and the ninth year of King Hoshea's reign in Israel,
Samaria fell. 11At that time the king of Assyria exiled
the Israelites to Assyria and placed them in colonies
in Halah, along the banks of the Habor River in
Gozan, and in the cities of the Medes. 12For they refused to listen to the LORD their God and obey him.
Instead, they violated his covenant—all the laws that
Moses the LORD's servant had commanded them
to obey.

Assyria Invades Judah

13In the fourteenth year of King Hezekiah's reign,*
King Sennacherib of Assyria came to attack the fortified towns of Judah and conquered them. 14King
Hezekiah sent this message to the king of Assyria at
Lachish: "I have done wrong. I will pay whatever tribute money you demand if you will only withdraw."
The king of Assyria then demanded a settlement of
more than eleven tons of silver and one ton of gold.*
15To gather this amount, King Hezekiah used all the
silver stored in the Temple of the LORD and in the palace treasury. 16Hezekiah even stripped the gold from
the doors of the LORD's Temple and from the
doorposts he had overlaid with gold, and he gave it all
to the Assyrian king.
17Nevertheless, the king of Assyria sent his commander in chief, his field commander, and his chief
of staff* from Lachish with a huge army to confront
King Hezekiah in Jerusalem. The Assyrians took up
a position beside the aqueduct that feeds water into
the upper pool, near the road leading to the field
where cloth is washed.* 18They summoned King
Hezekiah, but the king sent these officials to meet
with them: Eliakim son of Hilkiah, the palace administrator; Shebna the court secretary; and Joah son of
Asaph, the royal historian.

Sennacherib Threatens Jerusalem

19Then the Assyrian king's chief of staff told them to
give this message to Hezekiah:

"This is what the great king of Assyria says: What
are you trusting in that makes you so confident?
20Do you think that mere words can substitute for
military skill and strength? Who are you counting
on, that you have rebelled against me? 21On
Egypt? If you lean on Egypt, it will be like a reed
that splinters beneath your weight and pierces
your hand. Pharaoh, the king of Egypt, is
completely unreliable!
22"But perhaps you will say to me, 'We are
trusting in the LORD our God!' But isn't he the one

18:13 The fourteenth year of Hezekiah's reign was 701 B.C. **18:14** Hebrew *300 talents* [10 metric tons] *of silver and 30 talents* [1 metric ton] *of gold.* **18:17a** Or *the rabshakeh;* also in 18:19, 26, 27, 28, 37. **18:17b** Or *bleached.*

KING JAMES VERSION

God: *is* not that he, whose high places and whose altars Hezekiah hath taken away, and hath said to Judah and Jerusalem, Ye shall worship before this altar in Jerusalem?

23 Now therefore, I pray thee, give pledges to my lord the king of Assyria, and I will deliver thee two thousand horses, if thou be able on thy part to set riders upon them.

24 How then wilt thou turn away the face of one captain of the least of my master's servants, and put thy trust on Egypt for chariots and for horsemen?

25 Am I now come up without the LORD against this place to destroy it? The LORD said to me, Go up against this land, and destroy it.

26 Then said Eliakim the son of Hilkiah, and Shebna, and Joah, unto Rab-shakeh, Speak, I pray thee, to thy servants in the Syrian language; for we understand *it:* and talk not with us in the Jews' language in the ears of the people that *are* on the wall.

27 But Rab-shakeh said unto them, Hath my master sent me to thy master, and to thee, to speak these words? *hath he* not *sent me* to the men which sit on the wall, that they may eat their own dung, and drink their own piss with you?

28 Then Rab-shakeh stood and cried with a loud voice in the Jews' language, and spake, saying, Hear the word of the great king, the king of Assyria:

29 Thus saith the king, Let not Hezekiah deceive you: for he shall not be able to deliver you out of his hand:

30 Neither let Hezekiah make you trust in the LORD, saying, The LORD will surely deliver us, and this city shall not be delivered into the hand of the king of Assyria.

31 Hearken not to Hezekiah: for thus saith the king of Assyria, Make *an agreement* with me by a present, and come out to me, and *then* eat ye every man of his own vine, and every one of his fig tree, and drink ye every one the waters of his cistern:

32 Until I come and take you away to a land like your own land, a land of corn and wine, a land of bread and vineyards, a land of oil olive and of honey, that ye may live, and not die: and hearken not unto Hezekiah, when he persuadeth you, saying, The LORD will deliver us.

33 Hath any of the gods of the nations delivered at all his land out of the hand of the king of Assyria?

34 Where *are* the gods of Hamath, and of Arpad? where *are* the gods of Sepharvaim, Hena, and Ivah? have they delivered Samaria out of mine hand?

35 Who *are* they among all the gods of the countries, that have delivered their country out of mine hand, that the LORD should deliver Jerusalem out of mine hand?

36 But the people held their peace, and answered him not a word: for the king's commandment was, saying, Answer him not.

37 Then came Eliakim the son of Hilkiah, which

NEW LIVING TRANSLATION

who was insulted by Hezekiah? Didn't Hezekiah tear down his shrines and altars and make everyone in Judah and Jerusalem worship only at the altar here in Jerusalem?

23 "I'll tell you what! Strike a bargain with my master, the king of Assyria. I will give you 2,000 horses if you can find that many men to ride on them! 24 With your tiny army, how can you think of challenging even the weakest contingent of my master's troops, even with the help of Egypt's chariots and charioteers? 25 What's more, do you think we have invaded your land without the LORD's direction? The LORD himself told us, 'Attack this land and destroy it!'"

26 Then Eliakim son of Hilkiah, Shebna, and Joah said to the Assyrian chief of staff, "Please speak to us in Aramaic, for we understand it well. Don't speak in Hebrew,* for the people on the wall will hear."

27 But Sennacherib's chief of staff replied, "Do you think my master sent this message only to you and your master? He wants all the people to hear it, for when we put this city under siege, they will suffer along with you. They will be so hungry and thirsty that they will eat their own dung and drink their own urine."

28 Then the chief of staff stood and shouted in Hebrew to the people on the wall, "Listen to this message from the great king of Assyria! 29 This is what the king says: Don't let Hezekiah deceive you. He will never be able to rescue you from my power. 30 Don't let him fool you into trusting in the LORD by saying, 'The LORD will surely rescue us. This city will never fall into the hands of the Assyrian king!'

31 "Don't listen to Hezekiah! These are the terms the king of Assyria is offering: Make peace with me—open the gates and come out. Then each of you can continue eating from your own grapevine and fig tree and drinking from your own well. 32 Then I will arrange to take you to another land like this one—a land of grain and new wine, bread and vineyards, olive groves and honey. Choose life instead of death!

"Don't listen to Hezekiah when he tries to mislead you by saying, 'The LORD will rescue us!' 33 Have the gods of any other nations ever saved their people from the king of Assyria? 34 What happened to the gods of Hamath and Arpad? And what about the gods of Sepharvaim, Hena, and Ivvah? Did any god rescue Samaria from my power? 35 What god of any nation has ever been able to save its people from my power? So what makes you think that the LORD can rescue Jerusalem from me?"

36 But the people were silent and did not utter a word because Hezekiah had commanded them, "Do not answer him."

37 Then Eliakim son of Hilkiah, the palace administrator; Shebna the court secretary; and Joah son of

18:26 Hebrew *in the dialect of Judah;* also in 18:28.

KING JAMES VERSION

was over the household, and Shebna the scribe, and
Joah the son of Asaph the recorder, to Hezekiah
with *their* clothes rent, and told him the words of
Rab-shakeh.

19 1And it came to pass, when king Hezekiah
heard *it*, that he rent his clothes, and covered
himself with sackcloth, and went into the house of
the LORD.
2And he sent Eliakim, which *was* over the household, and Shebna the scribe, and the elders of the
priests, covered with sackcloth, to Isaiah the prophet
the son of Amoz.
3And they said unto him, Thus saith Hezekiah,
This day *is* a day of trouble, and of rebuke, and blasphemy: for the children are come to the birth, and
there is not strength to bring forth.
4It may be the LORD thy God will hear all the words
of Rab-shakeh, whom the king of Assyria his master
hath sent to reproach the living God; and will reprove
the words which the LORD thy God hath heard:
wherefore lift up *thy* prayer for the remnant that
are left.
5So the servants of king Hezekiah came to Isaiah.
6And Isaiah said unto them, Thus shall ye say to
your master, Thus saith the LORD, Be not afraid of the
words which thou hast heard, with which the servants of the king of Assyria have blasphemed me.
7Behold, I will send a blast upon him, and he shall
hear a rumour, and shall return to his own land; and
I will cause him to fall by the sword in his own land.
8So Rab-shakeh returned, and found the king of
Assyria warring against Libnah: for he had heard that
he was departed from Lachish.
9And when he heard say of Tirhakah king of Ethiopia, Behold, he is come out to fight against thee: he
sent messengers again unto Hezekiah, saying,
10Thus shall ye speak to Hezekiah king of Judah,
saying, Let not thy God in whom thou trustest deceive thee, saying, Jerusalem shall not be delivered
into the hand of the king of Assyria.
11Behold, thou hast heard what the kings of Assyria have done to all lands, by destroying them utterly:
and shalt thou be delivered?
12Have the gods of the nations delivered them
which my fathers have destroyed; *as* Gozan, and
Haran, and Rezeph, and the children of Eden which
were in Thelasar?
13Where *is* the king of Hamath, and the king of Arpad, and the king of the city of Sepharvaim, of Hena,
and Ivah?
14And Hezekiah received the letter of the hand of
the messengers, and read it: and Hezekiah went up
into the house of the LORD, and spread it before the
LORD.
15And Hezekiah prayed before the LORD, and said,
O LORD God of Israel, which dwellest *between* the

NEW LIVING TRANSLATION

Asaph, the royal historian, went back to Hezekiah.
They tore their clothes in despair, and they went in to
see the king and told him what the Assyrian chief of
staff had said.

Hezekiah Seeks the LORD's Help

19 When King Hezekiah heard their report, he
tore his clothes and put on burlap and went
into the Temple of the LORD. 2And he sent Eliakim
the palace administrator, Shebna the court secretary, and the leading priests, all dressed in burlap, to
the prophet Isaiah son of Amoz. 3They told him,
"This is what King Hezekiah says: Today is a day of
trouble, insults, and disgrace. It is like when a child
is ready to be born, but the mother has no strength
to deliver the baby. 4But perhaps the LORD your God
has heard the Assyrian chief of staff,* sent by the
king to defy the living God, and will punish him for
his words. Oh, pray for those of us who are left!"
5After King Hezekiah's officials delivered the
king's message to Isaiah, 6the prophet replied, "Say
to your master, 'This is what the LORD says: Do not be
disturbed by this blasphemous speech against me
from the Assyrian king's messengers. 7Listen! I myself will move against him,* and the king will receive
a message that he is needed at home. So he will return to his land, where I will have him killed with a
sword.'"
8Meanwhile, the Assyrian chief of staff left Jerusalem and went to consult the king of Assyria, who had
left Lachish and was attacking Libnah.
9Soon afterward King Sennacherib received word
that King Tirhakah of Ethiopia* was leading an army
to fight against him. Before leaving to meet the attack, he sent messengers back to Hezekiah in Jerusalem with this message:

10"This message is for King Hezekiah of Judah.
Don't let your God, in whom you trust, deceive
you with promises that Jerusalem will not be
captured by the king of Assyria. 11You know
perfectly well what the kings of Assyria have done
wherever they have gone. They have completely
destroyed everyone who stood in their way! Why
should you be any different? 12Have the gods of
other nations rescued them—such nations as
Gozan, Haran, Rezeph, and the people of Eden
who were in Tel-assar? My predecessors
destroyed them all! 13What happened to the
king of Hamath and the king of Arpad? What
happened to the kings of Sepharvaim, Hena,
and Ivvah?"

14After Hezekiah received the letter from the messengers and read it, he went up to the LORD's Temple
and spread it out before the LORD. 15And Hezekiah
prayed this prayer before the LORD: "O LORD, God of

19:4 Or *the rabshakeh;* also in 19:8. **19:7** Hebrew *I will put a spirit in him.* **19:9** Hebrew *of Cush.*

KING JAMES VERSION

cherubims, thou art the God, *even* thou alone, of all
the kingdoms of the earth; thou hast made heaven
and earth.
16 LORD, bow down thine ear, and hear: open, LORD,
thine eyes, and see: and hear the words of Sennacherib, which hath sent him to reproach the living God.
17 Of a truth, LORD, the kings of Assyria have destroyed the nations and their lands,
18 And have cast their gods into the fire: for they
were no gods, but the work of men's hands, wood and
stone: therefore they have destroyed them.
19 Now therefore, O LORD our God, I beseech thee,
save thou us out of his hand, that all the kingdoms of
the earth may know that thou *art* the LORD God, *even*
thou only.

20 Then Isaiah the son of Amoz sent to Hezekiah,
saying, Thus saith the LORD God of Israel, *That* which
thou hast prayed to me against Sennacherib king of
Assyria I have heard.
21 This *is* the word that the LORD hath spoken concerning him; The virgin the daughter of Zion hath
despised thee, *and* laughed thee to scorn; the daughter of Jerusalem hath shaken her head at thee.
22 Whom hast thou reproached and blasphemed?
and against whom hast thou exalted *thy* voice, and
lifted up thine eyes on high? *even* against the Holy
One of Israel.
23 By thy messengers thou hast reproached the
Lord, and hast said, With the multitude of my chariots I am come up to the height of the mountains, to
the sides of Lebanon, and will cut down the tall cedar
trees thereof, *and* the choice fir trees thereof: and I
will enter into the lodgings of his borders, *and into*
the forest of his Carmel.
24 I have digged and drunk strange waters, and
with the sole of my feet have I dried up all the rivers
of besieged places.
25 Hast thou not heard long ago *how* I have done it,
and of ancient times that I have formed it? now have
I brought it to pass, that thou shouldest be to lay
waste fenced cities *into* ruinous heaps.
26 Therefore their inhabitants were of small power,
they were dismayed and confounded; they were *as*
the grass of the field, and *as* the green herb, *as* the
grass on the house tops, and *as corn* blasted before it
be grown up.

NEW LIVING TRANSLATION

Israel, you are enthroned between the mighty cherubim! You alone are God of all the kingdoms of the
earth. You alone created the heavens and the earth.
16 Bend down, O LORD, and listen! Open your eyes,
O LORD, and see! Listen to Sennacherib's words of
defiance against the living God.
17 "It is true, LORD, that the kings of Assyria have
destroyed all these nations. 18 And they have thrown
the gods of these nations into the fire and burned
them. But of course the Assyrians could destroy
them! They were not gods at all—only idols of wood
and stone shaped by human hands. 19 Now, O LORD
our God, rescue us from his power; then all the kingdoms of the earth will know that you alone, O LORD,
are God."

Isaiah Predicts Judah's Deliverance

20 Then Isaiah son of Amoz sent this message to
Hezekiah: "This is what the LORD, the God of Israel,
says: I have heard your prayer about King Sennacherib of Assyria. 21 And the LORD has spoken this word
against him:

"The virgin daughter of Zion
despises you and laughs at you.
The daughter of Jerusalem
shakes her head in derision as you flee.

22 "Whom have you been defying and ridiculing?
Against whom did you raise your voice?
At whom did you look with such haughty eyes?
It was the Holy One of Israel!
23 By your messengers you have defied the Lord.
You have said, 'With my many chariots
I have conquered the highest mountains—
yes, the remotest peaks of Lebanon.
I have cut down its tallest cedars
and its finest cypress trees.
I have reached its farthest corners
and explored its deepest forests.
24 I have dug wells in many foreign lands
and refreshed myself with their water.
With the sole of my foot
I stopped up all the rivers of Egypt!'

25 "But have you not heard?
I decided this long ago.
Long ago I planned it,
and now I am making it happen.
I planned for you to crush fortified cities
into heaps of rubble.
26 That is why their people have so little power
and are so frightened and confused.
They are as weak as grass,
as easily trampled as tender green shoots.
They are like grass sprouting on a housetop,
scorched before it can grow lush and tall.

KING JAMES VERSION

27 But I know thy abode, and thy going out, and thy
coming in, and thy rage against me.
28 Because thy rage against me and thy tumult is
come up into mine ears, therefore I will put my hook
in thy nose, and my bridle in thy lips, and I will turn
thee back by the way by which thou camest.
29 And this *shall be* a sign unto thee, Ye shall eat
this year such things as grow of themselves, and in
the second year that which springeth of the same;
and in the third year sow ye, and reap, and plant vineyards, and eat the fruits thereof.
30 And the remnant that is escaped of the house of
Judah shall yet again take root downward, and bear
fruit upward.
31 For out of Jerusalem shall go forth a remnant,
and they that escape out of mount Zion: the zeal of
the LORD *of hosts* shall do this.
32 Therefore thus saith the LORD concerning the
king of Assyria, He shall not come into this city, nor
shoot an arrow there, nor come before it with shield,
nor cast a bank against it.
33 By the way that he came, by the same shall he return, and shall not come into this city, saith the LORD.
34 For I will defend this city, to save it, for mine own
sake, and for my servant David's sake.
35 And it came to pass that night, that the angel of
the LORD went out, and smote in the camp of the Assyrians an hundred fourscore and five thousand: and
when they arose early in the morning, behold, they
were all dead corpses.
36 So Sennacherib king of Assyria departed, and
went and returned, and dwelt at Nineveh.
37 And it came to pass, as he was worshipping in

NEW LIVING TRANSLATION

27 "But I know you well—
where you stay
and when you come and go.
I know the way you have raged against me.
28 And because of your raging against me
and your arrogance, which I have heard
for myself,
I will put my hook in your nose
and my bit in your mouth.
I will make you return
by the same road on which you came."

29 Then Isaiah said to Hezekiah, "Here is the proof
that what I say is true:

"This year you will eat only what grows
up by itself,
and next year you will eat what springs
up from that.
But in the third year you will plant crops and
harvest them;
you will tend vineyards and eat their fruit.
30 And you who are left in Judah,
who have escaped the ravages of the siege,
will put roots down in your own soil
and will grow up and flourish.
31 For a remnant of my people will spread out
from Jerusalem,
a group of survivors from Mount Zion.
The passionate commitment of the LORD of
Heaven's Armies*
will make this happen!

32 "And this is what the LORD says about the king
of Assyria:

"His armies will not enter Jerusalem.
They will not even shoot an arrow at it.
They will not march outside its gates with
their shields
nor build banks of earth against its walls.
33 The king will return to his own country
by the same road on which he came.
He will not enter this city,
says the LORD.
34 For my own honor and for the sake of my
servant David,
I will defend this city and protect it."

35 That night the angel of the LORD went out to
the Assyrian camp and killed 185,000 Assyrian
soldiers. When the surviving Assyrians* woke up
the next morning, they found corpses everywhere. 36 Then King Sennacherib of Assyria broke
camp and returned to his own land. He went
home to his capital of Nineveh and stayed there.
37 One day while he was worshiping in the

19:31 As in Greek and Syriac versions, Latin Vulgate, and an alternate reading of the Masoretic Text (see also Isa 37:32); the other alternate reads *the LORD*.
19:35 Hebrew *When they*.

KING JAMES VERSION

the house of Nisroch his god, that Adrammelech and Sharezer his sons smote him with the sword: and they escaped into the land of Armenia. And Esarhaddon his son reigned in his stead.

20 1In those days was Hezekiah sick unto death. And the prophet Isaiah the son of Amoz came to him, and said unto him, Thus saith the LORD, Set thine house in order; for thou shalt die, and not live.

2Then he turned his face to the wall, and prayed unto the LORD, saying,

3I beseech thee, O LORD, remember now how I have walked before thee in truth and with a perfect heart, and have done *that which is* good in thy sight. And Hezekiah wept sore.

4And it came to pass, afore Isaiah was gone out into the middle court, that the word of the LORD came to him, saying,

5Turn again, and tell Hezekiah the captain of my people, Thus saith the LORD, the God of David thy father, I have heard thy prayer, I have seen thy tears: behold, I will heal thee: on the third day thou shalt go up unto the house of the LORD.

6And I will add unto thy days fifteen years; and I will deliver thee and this city out of the hand of the king of Assyria; and I will defend this city for mine own sake, and for my servant David's sake.

7And Isaiah said, Take a lump of figs. And they took and laid *it* on the boil, and he recovered.

8And Hezekiah said unto Isaiah, What *shall be* the sign that the LORD will heal me, and that I shall go up into the house of the LORD the third day?

9And Isaiah said, This sign shalt thou have of the LORD, that the LORD will do the thing that he hath spoken: shall the shadow go forward ten degrees, or go back ten degrees?

10And Hezekiah answered, It is a light thing for the shadow to go down ten degrees: nay, but let the shadow return backward ten degrees.

11And Isaiah the prophet cried unto the LORD: and he brought the shadow ten degrees backward, by which it had gone down in the dial of Ahaz.

12At that time Berodach-baladan, the son of Baladan, king of Babylon, sent letters and a present unto Hezekiah: for he had heard that Hezekiah had been sick.

13And Hezekiah hearkened unto them, and shewed them all the house of his precious things, the silver, and the gold, and the spices, and the precious ointment, and *all* the house of his armour, and all that was found in his treasures: there was nothing in his house, nor in all his dominion, that Hezekiah shewed them not.

NEW LIVING TRANSLATION

temple of his god Nisroch, his sons* Adrammelech and Sharezer killed him with their swords. They then escaped to the land of Ararat, and another son, Esarhaddon, became the next king of Assyria.

Hezekiah's Sickness and Recovery

20 About that time Hezekiah became deathly ill, and the prophet Isaiah son of Amoz went to visit him. He gave the king this message: "This is what the LORD says: Set your affairs in order, for you are going to die. You will not recover from this illness."

2When Hezekiah heard this, he turned his face to the wall and prayed to the LORD, 3"Remember, O LORD, how I have always been faithful to you and have served you single-mindedly, always doing what pleases you." Then he broke down and wept bitterly.

4But before Isaiah had left the middle courtyard,* this message came to him from the LORD: 5"Go back to Hezekiah, the leader of my people. Tell him, 'This is what the LORD, the God of your ancestor David, says: I have heard your prayer and seen your tears. I will heal you, and three days from now you will get out of bed and go to the Temple of the LORD. 6I will add fifteen years to your life, and I will rescue you and this city from the king of Assyria. I will defend this city for my own honor and for the sake of my servant David.'"

7Then Isaiah said, "Make an ointment from figs." So Hezekiah's servants spread the ointment over the boil, and Hezekiah recovered!

8Meanwhile, Hezekiah had said to Isaiah, "What sign will the LORD give to prove that he will heal me and that I will go to the Temple of the LORD three days from now?"

9Isaiah replied, "This is the sign from the LORD to prove that he will do as he promised. Would you like the shadow on the sundial to go forward ten steps or backward ten steps?*"

10"The shadow always moves forward," Hezekiah replied, "so that would be easy. Make it go ten steps backward instead." 11So Isaiah the prophet asked the LORD to do this, and he caused the shadow to move ten steps backward on the sundial* of Ahaz!

Envoys from Babylon

12Soon after this, Merodach-baladan son of Baladan, king of Babylon, sent Hezekiah his best wishes and a gift, for he had heard that Hezekiah had been very sick. 13Hezekiah received the Babylonian envoys and showed them everything in his treasure-houses—the silver, the gold, the spices, and the aromatic oils. He also took them to see his armory and showed them everything in his royal treasuries! There was nothing in his palace or kingdom that Hezekiah did not show them.

19:37 As in Greek version and an alternate reading of the Masoretic Text (see also Isa 37:38); the other alternate reading lacks *his sons.* **20:4** As in Greek version and an alternate reading in the Masoretic Text; the other alternate reads *the middle of the city.* **20:9** Or *The shadow on the sundial has gone forward ten steps; do you want it to go backward ten steps?* **20:11** Hebrew *the steps.*

KING JAMES VERSION

14 Then came Isaiah the prophet unto king Hezekiah, and said unto him, What said these men? and from whence came they unto thee? And Hezekiah said, They are come from a far country, *even* from Babylon.

15 And he said, What have they seen in thine house? And Hezekiah answered, All *the things* that *are* in mine house have they seen: there is nothing among my treasures that I have not shewed them.

16 And Isaiah said unto Hezekiah, Hear the word of the LORD.

17 Behold, the days come, that all that *is* in thine house, and that which thy fathers have laid up in store unto this day, shall be carried into Babylon: nothing shall be left, saith the LORD.

18 And of thy sons that shall issue from thee, which thou shalt beget, shall they take away; and they shall be eunuchs in the palace of the king of Babylon.

19 Then said Hezekiah unto Isaiah, Good *is* the word of the LORD which thou hast spoken. And he said, *Is it* not *good*, if peace and truth be in my days?

20 And the rest of the acts of Hezekiah, and all his might, and how he made a pool, and a conduit, and brought water into the city, *are* they not written in the book of the chronicles of the kings of Judah?

21 And Hezekiah slept with his fathers: and Manasseh his son reigned in his stead.

21 1 Manasseh *was* twelve years old when he began to reign, and reigned fifty and five years in Jerusalem. And his mother's name *was* Hephzi-bah.

2 And he did *that which was* evil in the sight of the LORD, after the abominations of the heathen, whom the LORD cast out before the children of Israel.

3 For he built up again the high places which Hezekiah his father had destroyed; and he reared up altars for Baal, and made a grove, as did Ahab king of Israel; and worshipped all the host of heaven, and served them.

4 And he built altars in the house of the LORD, of which the LORD said, In Jerusalem will I put my name.

5 And he built altars for all the host of heaven in the two courts of the house of the LORD.

6 And he made his son pass through the fire, and observed times, and used enchantments, and dealt with familiar spirits and wizards: he wrought much wickedness in the sight of the LORD, to provoke *him* to anger.

7 And he set a graven image of the grove that he had made in the house, of which the LORD said to David, and to Solomon his son, In this house, and in Jerusalem, which I have chosen out of all tribes of Israel, will I put my name for ever:

8 Neither will I make the feet of Israel move any more out of the land which I gave their fathers; only

NEW LIVING TRANSLATION

14 Then Isaiah the prophet went to King Hezekiah
and asked him, "What did those men want? Where
were they from?"
Hezekiah replied, "They came from the distant
land of Babylon."
15 "What did they see in your palace?" Isaiah
asked.
"They saw everything," Hezekiah replied. "I showed
them everything I own—all my royal treasuries."
16 Then Isaiah said to Hezekiah, "Listen to this
message from the LORD: 17 The time is coming when
everything in your palace—all the treasures stored
up by your ancestors until now—will be carried off to
Babylon. Nothing will be left, says the LORD. 18 Some
of your very own sons will be taken away into exile.
They will become eunuchs who will serve in the palace of Babylon's king."
19 Then Hezekiah said to Isaiah, "This message
you have given me from the LORD is good." For the
king was thinking, "At least there will be peace and
security during my lifetime."
20 The rest of the events in Hezekiah's reign, including the extent of his power and how he built a
pool and dug a tunnel* to bring water into the city,
are recorded in *The Book of the History of the Kings
of Judah*. 21 Hezekiah died, and his son Manasseh became the next king.

Manasseh Rules in Judah

21 Manasseh was twelve years old when he became king, and he reigned in Jerusalem
fifty-five years. His mother was Hephzibah. 2 He did
what was evil in the LORD's sight, following the detestable practices of the pagan nations that the LORD
had driven from the land ahead of the Israelites. 3 He
rebuilt the pagan shrines his father, Hezekiah, had
destroyed. He constructed altars for Baal and set up
an Asherah pole, just as King Ahab of Israel had done.
He also bowed before all the powers of the heavens
and worshiped them.
4 He built pagan altars in the Temple of the LORD,
the place where the LORD had said, "My name will remain in Jerusalem forever." 5 He built these altars for
all the powers of the heavens in both courtyards of
the LORD's Temple. 6 Manasseh also sacrificed his
own son in the fire.* He practiced sorcery and divination, and he consulted with mediums and psychics. He did much that was evil in the LORD's sight,
arousing his anger.
7 Manasseh even made a carved image of Asherah
and set it up in the Temple, the very place where the
LORD had told David and his son Solomon: "My name
will be honored forever in this Temple and in Jerusalem—the city I have chosen from among all the tribes
of Israel. 8 If the Israelites will be careful to obey my

20:20 Hebrew *watercourse*. **21:6** Or *also made his son pass through the fire*.

KING JAMES VERSION

if they will observe to do according to all that I have
commanded them, and according to all the law that
my servant Moses commanded them.
9 But they hearkened not: and Manasseh seduced
them to do more evil than did the nations whom the
LORD destroyed before the children of Israel.
10 And the LORD spake by his servants the prophets, saying,
11 Because Manasseh king of Judah hath done
these abominations, *and* hath done wickedly above
all that the Amorites did, which *were* before him, and
hath made Judah also to sin with his idols:
12 Therefore thus saith the LORD God of Israel, Behold, I *am* bringing *such* evil upon Jerusalem and
Judah, that whosoever heareth of it, both his ears
shall tingle.
13 And I will stretch over Jerusalem the line of Samaria, and the plummet of the house of Ahab: and I
will wipe Jerusalem as *a man* wipeth a dish, wiping
it, and turning *it* upside down.
14 And I will forsake the remnant of mine inheritance, and deliver them into the hand of their enemies; and they shall become a prey and a spoil to all
their enemies;
15 Because they have done *that which was* evil in
my sight, and have provoked me to anger, since the
day their fathers came forth out of Egypt, even unto
this day.
16 Moreover Manasseh shed innocent blood very
much, till he had filled Jerusalem from one end to
another; beside his sin wherewith he made Judah to
sin, in doing *that which was* evil in the sight of the
LORD.
17 Now the rest of the acts of Manasseh, and all that
he did, and his sin that he sinned, *are* they not written
in the book of the chronicles of the kings of Judah?
18 And Manasseh slept with his fathers, and was
buried in the garden of his own house, in the garden
of Uzza: and Amon his son reigned in his stead.
19 Amon *was* twenty and two years old when he began to reign, and he reigned two years in Jerusalem.
And his mother's name *was* Meshullemeth, the
daughter of Haruz of Jotbah.
20 And he did *that which was* evil in the sight of
the LORD, as his father Manasseh did.
21 And he walked in all the way that his father
walked in, and served the idols that his father served,
and worshipped them:
22 And he forsook the LORD God of his fathers, and
walked not in the way of the LORD.
23 And the servants of Amon conspired against
him, and slew the king in his own house.
24 And the people of the land slew all them that
had conspired against king Amon; and the people of
the land made Josiah his son king in his stead.
25 Now the rest of the acts of Amon which he did,
are they not written in the book of the chronicles of
the kings of Judah?

NEW LIVING TRANSLATION

commands—all the laws my servant Moses gave
them—I will not send them into exile from this land
that I gave their ancestors." 9 But the people refused
to listen, and Manasseh led them to do even more
evil than the pagan nations that the LORD had destroyed when the people of Israel entered the land.
10 Then the LORD said through his servants the
prophets: 11 "King Manasseh of Judah has done many
detestable things. He is even more wicked than the
Amorites, who lived in this land before Israel. He has
caused the people of Judah to sin with his idols.*
12 So this is what the LORD, the God of Israel, says: I
will bring such disaster on Jerusalem and Judah that
the ears of those who hear about it will tingle with
horror. 13 I will judge Jerusalem by the same standard
I used for Samaria and the same measure* I used for
the family of Ahab. I will wipe away the people of
Jerusalem as one wipes a dish and turns it upside
down. 14 Then I will reject even the remnant of my
own people who are left, and I will hand them over as
plunder for their enemies. 15 For they have done
great evil in my sight and have angered me ever since
their ancestors came out of Egypt."
16 Manasseh also murdered many innocent people
until Jerusalem was filled from one end to the other
with innocent blood. This was in addition to the sin
that he caused the people of Judah to commit, leading them to do evil in the LORD's sight.
17 The rest of the events in Manasseh's reign and
everything he did, including the sins he committed,
are recorded in *The Book of the History of the Kings
of Judah*. 18 When Manasseh died, he was buried in
the palace garden, the garden of Uzza. Then his son
Amon became the next king.

Amon Rules in Judah

19 Amon was twenty-two years old when he became
king, and he reigned in Jerusalem two years. His
mother was Meshullemeth, the daughter of Haruz
from Jotbah. 20 He did what was evil in the LORD's
sight, just as his father, Manasseh, had done. 21 He followed the example of his father, worshiping the
same idols his father had worshiped. 22 He abandoned the LORD, the God of his ancestors, and he
refused to follow the LORD's ways.
23 Then Amon's own officials conspired against
him and assassinated him in his palace. 24 But the
people of the land killed all those who had conspired
against King Amon, and they made his son Josiah the
next king.
25 The rest of the events in Amon's reign and what
he did are recorded in *The Book of the History of the*

21:11 The Hebrew term (literally *round things*) probably alludes to dung; also in 21:21. **21:13** Hebrew *the same plumb line I used for Samaria and the same plumb bob.*

KING JAMES VERSION

26And he was buried in his sepulchre in the garden of Uzza: and Josiah his son reigned in his stead.

22 1Josiah *was* eight years old when he began
to reign, and he reigned thirty and one
years in Jerusalem. And his mother's name *was* Jedidah, the daughter of Adaiah of Boscath.
2And he did *that which was* right in the sight of the
LORD, and walked in all the way of David his father, and
turned not aside to the right hand or to the left.
3And it came to pass in the eighteenth year of king
Josiah, *that* the king sent Shaphan the son of Azaliah,
the son of Meshullam, the scribe, to the house of the
LORD, saying,
4Go up to Hilkiah the high priest, that he may sum
the silver which is brought into the house of the
LORD, which the keepers of the door have gathered of
the people:
5And let them deliver it into the hand of the doers
of the work, that have the oversight of the house of
the LORD: and let them give it to the doers of the
work which *is* in the house of the LORD, to repair the
breaches of the house,
6Unto carpenters, and builders, and masons, and
to buy timber and hewn stone to repair the house.
7Howbeit there was no reckoning made with them
of the money that was delivered into their hand, because they dealt faithfully.
8And Hilkiah the high priest said unto Shaphan
the scribe, I have found the book of the law in the
house of the LORD. And Hilkiah gave the book to
Shaphan, and he read it.
9And Shaphan the scribe came to the king, and
brought the king word again, and said, Thy servants
have gathered the money that was found in the
house, and have delivered it into the hand of them
that do the work, that have the oversight of the house
of the LORD.
10And Shaphan the scribe shewed the king, saying, Hilkiah the priest hath delivered me a book. And
Shaphan read it before the king.
11And it came to pass, when the king had heard the
words of the book of the law, that he rent his clothes.
12And the king commanded Hilkiah the priest,
and Ahikam the son of Shaphan, and Achbor the son
of Michaiah, and Shaphan the scribe, and Asahiah a
servant of the king's, saying,
13Go ye, inquire of the LORD for me, and for the people, and for all Judah, concerning the words of this
book that is found: for great *is* the wrath of the LORD
that is kindled against us, because our fathers have
not hearkened unto the words of this book, to do according unto all that which is written concerning us.
14So Hilkiah the priest, and Ahikam, and Achbor,
and Shaphan, and Asahiah, went unto Huldah the
prophetess, the wife of Shallum the son of Tikvah,

NEW LIVING TRANSLATION

Kings of Judah. 26He was buried in his tomb in the
garden of Uzza. Then his son Josiah became the next
king.

Josiah Rules in Judah

22 Josiah was eight years old when he became
king, and he reigned in Jerusalem thirty-
one years. His mother was Jedidah, the daughter of
Adaiah from Bozkath. 2He did what was pleasing in
the LORD's sight and followed the example of his ancestor David. He did not turn away from doing what
was right.
3In the eighteenth year of his reign, King Josiah
sent Shaphan son of Azaliah and grandson of Meshullam, the court secretary, to the Temple of the
LORD. He told him, 4"Go to Hilkiah the high priest
and have him count the money the gatekeepers have
collected from the people at the LORD's Temple.
5Entrust this money to the men assigned to supervise the Temple's restoration. Then they can use it to
pay workers to repair the Temple of the LORD. 6They
will need to hire carpenters, builders, and masons.
Also have them buy the timber and the finished
stone needed to repair the Temple. 7But don't require the construction supervisors to keep account
of the money they receive, for they are honest and
trustworthy men."

Hilkiah Discovers God's Law

8Hilkiah the high priest said to Shaphan the court
secretary, "I have found the Book of the Law in the
LORD's Temple!" Then Hilkiah gave the scroll to Shaphan, and he read it.
9Shaphan went to the king and reported, "Your officials have turned over the money collected at the
Temple of the LORD to the workers and supervisors
at the Temple." 10Shaphan also told the king, "Hilkiah the priest has given me a scroll." So Shaphan read
it to the king.
11When the king heard what was written in the
Book of the Law, he tore his clothes in despair.
12Then he gave these orders to Hilkiah the priest,
Ahikam son of Shaphan, Acbor son of Micaiah, Shaphan the court secretary, and Asaiah the king's personal adviser: 13"Go to the Temple and speak to the
LORD for me and for the people and for all Judah. Inquire about the words written in this scroll that has
been found. For the LORD's great anger is burning
against us because our ancestors have not obeyed
the words in this scroll. We have not been doing
everything it says we must do."
14So Hilkiah the priest, Ahikam, Acbor, Shaphan,
and Asaiah went to the New Quarter* of Jerusalem to

22:14 Or *the Second Quarter,* a newer section of Jerusalem. Hebrew reads *the Mishneh.*

KING JAMES VERSION

the son of Harhas, keeper of the wardrobe; (now she
dwelt in Jerusalem in the college;) and they communed with her.
15And she said unto them, Thus saith the LORD
God of Israel, Tell the man that sent you to me.
16Thus saith the LORD, Behold, I will bring evil
upon this place, and upon the inhabitants thereof,
even all the words of the book which the king of
Judah hath read:
17Because they have forsaken me, and have burned
incense unto other gods, that they might provoke me
to anger with all the works of their hands; therefore
my wrath shall be kindled against this place, and shall
not be quenched.
18But to the king of Judah which sent you to inquire of the LORD, thus shall ye say to him, Thus saith
the LORD God of Israel, *As touching* the words which
thou hast heard;
19Because thine heart was tender, and thou hast
humbled thyself before the LORD, when thou heardest
what I spake against this place, and against the inhabitants thereof, that they should become a desolation
and a curse, and hast rent thy clothes, and wept before
me; I also have heard *thee,* saith the LORD.
20Behold therefore, I will gather thee unto thy fathers, and thou shalt be gathered into thy grave in
peace; and thine eyes shall not see all the evil which I
will bring upon this place. And they brought the king
word again.

23 1And the king sent, and they gathered unto
him all the elders of Judah and of Jerusalem.
2And the king went up into the house of the LORD,
and all the men of Judah and all the inhabitants of Jerusalem with him, and the priests, and the prophets,
and all the people, both small and great: and he read
in their ears all the words of the book of the covenant which was found in the house of the LORD.
3And the king stood by a pillar, and made a covenant before the LORD, to walk after the LORD, and to
keep his commandments and his testimonies and his
statutes with all *their* heart and all *their* soul, to perform the words of this covenant that were written in
this book. And all the people stood to the covenant.
4And the king commanded Hilkiah the high
priest, and the priests of the second order, and the
keepers of the door, to bring forth out of the temple
of the LORD all the vessels that were made for Baal,
and for the grove, and for all the host of heaven: and
he burned them without Jerusalem in the fields of
Kidron, and carried the ashes of them unto Bethel.
5And he put down the idolatrous priests, whom
the kings of Judah had ordained to burn incense in
the high places in the cities of Judah, and in the
places round about Jerusalem; them also that burned
incense unto Baal, to the sun, and to the moon, and to
the planets, and to all the host of heaven.

NEW LIVING TRANSLATION

consult with the prophet Huldah. She was the wife of
Shallum son of Tikvah, son of Harhas, the keeper of
the Temple wardrobe.
15She said to them, "The LORD, the God of Israel,
has spoken! Go back and tell the man who sent you,
16'This is what the LORD says: I am going to bring
disaster on this city* and its people. All the words
written in the scroll that the king of Judah has read
will come true. 17For my people have abandoned me
and offered sacrifices to pagan gods, and I am very
angry with them for everything they have done. My
anger will burn against this place, and it will not be
quenched.'
18"But go to the king of Judah who sent you to seek
the LORD and tell him: 'This is what the LORD, the
God of Israel, says concerning the message you have
just heard: 19You were sorry and humbled yourself
before the LORD when you heard what I said against
this city and its people—that this land would be
cursed and become desolate. You tore your clothing
in despair and wept before me in repentance. And I
have indeed heard you, says the LORD. 20So I will not
send the promised disaster until after you have died
and been buried in peace. You will not see the disaster I am going to bring on this city.'"
So they took her message back to the king.

Josiah's Religious Reforms

23 Then the king summoned all the elders of
Judah and Jerusalem. 2And the king went up
to the Temple of the LORD with all the people of Judah
and Jerusalem, along with the priests and the prophets—all the people from the least to the greatest.
There the king read to them the entire Book of the
Covenant that had been found in the LORD's Temple.
3The king took his place of authority beside the pillar
and renewed the covenant in the LORD's presence.
He pledged to obey the LORD by keeping all his
commands, laws, and decrees with all his heart and
soul. In this way, he confirmed all the terms of the
covenant that were written in the scroll, and all the
people pledged themselves to the covenant.
4Then the king instructed Hilkiah the high priest
and the priests of the second rank and the Temple
gatekeepers to remove from the LORD's Temple all
the articles that were used to worship Baal, Asherah,
and all the powers of the heavens. The king had all
these things burned outside Jerusalem on the terraces of the Kidron Valley, and he carried the ashes
away to Bethel. 5He did away with the idolatrous
priests, who had been appointed by the previous
kings of Judah, for they had offered sacrifices at
the pagan shrines throughout Judah and even in the
vicinity of Jerusalem. They had also offered sacrifices
to Baal, and to the sun, the moon, the constellations,

22:16 Hebrew *this place;* also in 22:19, 20.

KING JAMES VERSION

6 And he brought out the grove from the house of
the LORD, without Jerusalem, unto the brook Kidron,
and burned it at the brook Kidron, and stamped *it*
small to powder, and cast the powder thereof upon
the graves of the children of the people.
7 And he brake down the houses of the sodomites,
that *were* by the house of the LORD, where the
women wove hangings for the grove.
8 And he brought all the priests out of the cities of
Judah, and defiled the high places where the priests
had burned incense, from Geba to Beer-sheba, and
brake down the high places of the gates that *were* in
the entering in of the gate of Joshua the governor of
the city, which *were* on a man's left hand at the gate
of the city.
9 Nevertheless the priests of the high places came
not up to the altar of the LORD in Jerusalem, but
they did eat of the unleavened bread among their
brethren.
10 And he defiled Topheth, which *is* in the valley
of the children of Hinnom, that no man might make
his son or his daughter to pass through the fire to
Molech.
11 And he took away the horses that the kings of
Judah had given to the sun, at the entering in of the
house of the LORD, by the chamber of Nathan-
melech the chamberlain, which *was* in the suburbs,
and burned the chariots of the sun with fire.
12 And the altars that *were* on the top of the upper
chamber of Ahaz, which the kings of Judah had
made, and the altars which Manasseh had made in
the two courts of the house of the LORD, did the king
beat down, and brake *them* down from thence, and
cast the dust of them into the brook Kidron.
13 And the high places that *were* before Jerusalem,
which *were* on the right hand of the mount of corruption, which Solomon the king of Israel had
builded for Ashtoreth the abomination of the Zidonians, and for Chemosh the abomination of the
Moabites, and for Milcom the abomination of the
children of Ammon, did the king defile.
14 And he brake in pieces the images, and cut down
the groves, and filled their places with the bones of
men.
15 Moreover the altar that *was* at Bethel, *and* the
high place which Jeroboam the son of Nebat, who
made Israel to sin, had made, both that altar and the
high place he brake down, and burned the high
place, *and* stamped *it* small to powder, and burned
the grove.
16 And as Josiah turned himself, he spied the
sepulchres that *were* there in the mount, and sent,
and took the bones out of the sepulchres, and burned
them upon the altar, and polluted it, according to the
word of the LORD which the man of God proclaimed,
who proclaimed these words.

NEW LIVING TRANSLATION

and to all the powers of the heavens. 6 The king
removed the Asherah pole from the LORD's Temple
and took it outside Jerusalem to the Kidron Valley,
where he burned it. Then he ground the ashes of the
pole to dust and threw the dust over the graves of
the people. 7 He also tore down the living quarters
of the male and female shrine prostitutes that were
inside the Temple of the LORD, where the women
wove coverings for the Asherah pole.
8 Josiah brought to Jerusalem all the priests who
were living in other towns of Judah. He also defiled the
pagan shrines, where they had offered sacrifices—all
the way from Geba to Beersheba. He destroyed the
shrines at the entrance to the gate of Joshua, the governor of Jerusalem. This gate was located to the left of
the city gate as one enters the city. 9 The priests who
had served at the pagan shrines were not allowed* to
serve at the LORD's altar in Jerusalem, but they were allowed to eat unleavened bread with the other priests.
10 Then the king defiled the altar of Topheth in the
valley of Ben-Hinnom, so no one could ever again use
it to sacrifice a son or daughter in the fire* as an offering to Molech. 11 He removed from the entrance of
the LORD's Temple the horse statues that the former
kings of Judah had dedicated to the sun. They were
near the quarters of Nathan-melech the eunuch, an
officer of the court.* The king also burned the chariots dedicated to the sun.
12 Josiah tore down the altars that the kings of Judah
had built on the palace roof above the upper room of
Ahaz. The king destroyed the altars that Manasseh had
built in the two courtyards of the LORD's Temple. He
smashed them to bits* and scattered the pieces in the
Kidron Valley. 13 The king also desecrated the pagan
shrines east of Jerusalem, to the south of the Mount of
Corruption, where King Solomon of Israel had built
shrines for Ashtoreth, the detestable goddess of the
Sidonians; and for Chemosh, the detestable god of
the Moabites; and for Molech,* the vile god of the
Ammonites. 14 He smashed the sacred pillars and cut
down the Asherah poles. Then he desecrated these
places by scattering human bones over them.
15 The king also tore down the altar at Bethel—the
pagan shrine that Jeroboam son of Nebat had made
when he caused Israel to sin. He burned down the
shrine and ground it to dust, and he burned the Asherah pole. 16 Then Josiah turned around and noticed
several tombs in the side of the hill. He ordered that
the bones be brought out, and he burned them on the
altar at Bethel to desecrate it. (This happened just as
the LORD had promised through the man of God
when Jeroboam stood beside the altar at the festival.)
Then Josiah turned and looked up at the tomb of
the man of God* who had predicted these things.

23:9 Hebrew *did not come up.* **23:10** Or *to make a son or daughter pass through the fire.* **23:11** The meaning of the Hebrew is uncertain. **23:12** Or *He quickly removed them.* **23:13** Hebrew *Milcom,* a variant spelling of Molech. **23:16** As in Greek version; Hebrew lacks *when Jeroboam stood beside the altar at the festival. Then Josiah turned and looked up at the tomb of the man of God.*

KING JAMES VERSION

17 Then he said, What title *is* that that I see? And
the men of the city told him, *It is* the sepulchre of the
man of God, which came from Judah, and proclaimed these things that thou hast done against the
altar of Bethel.

18 And he said, Let him alone; let no man move his
bones. So they let his bones alone, with the bones of
the prophet that came out of Samaria.

19 And all the houses also of the high places that
were in the cities of Samaria, which the kings of Israel had made to provoke *the* LORD to anger, Josiah took
away, and did to them according to all the acts that
he had done in Bethel.

20 And he slew all the priests of the high places that
were there upon the altars, and burned men's bones
upon them, and returned to Jerusalem.

21 And the king commanded all the people, saying,
Keep the passover unto the LORD your God, as *it is*
written in the book of this covenant.

22 Surely there was not holden such a passover
from the days of the judges that judged Israel, nor in
all the days of the kings of Israel, nor of the kings of
Judah;

23 But in the eighteenth year of king Josiah,
wherein this passover was holden to the LORD in
Jerusalem.

24 Moreover the *workers with* familiar spirits, and
the wizards, and the images, and the idols, and all the
abominations that were spied in the land of Judah
and in Jerusalem, did Josiah put away, that he might
perform the words of the law which were written in
the book that Hilkiah the priest found in the house
of the LORD.

25 And like unto him was there no king before him,
that turned to the LORD with all his heart, and with all
his soul, and with all his might, according to all the law
of Moses; neither after him arose there *any* like him.

26 Notwithstanding the LORD turned not from the
fierceness of his great wrath, wherewith his anger
was kindled against Judah, because of all the provocations that Manasseh had provoked him withal.

27 And the LORD said, I will remove Judah also out
of my sight, as I have removed Israel, and will cast off
this city Jerusalem which I have chosen, and the
house of which I said, My name shall be there.

28 Now the rest of the acts of Josiah, and all that he
did, *are* they not written in the book of the chronicles of the kings of Judah?

29 In his days Pharaoh-nechoh king of Egypt went
up against the king of Assyria to the river Euphrates:
and king Josiah went against him; and he slew him at
Megiddo, when he had seen him.

30 And his servants carried him in a chariot dead
from Megiddo, and brought him to Jerusalem, and
buried him in his own sepulchre. And the people of
the land took Jehoahaz the son of Josiah, and anointed
him, and made him king in his father's stead.

NEW LIVING TRANSLATION

17 "What is that monument over there?" Josiah asked.
And the people of the town told him, "It is the
tomb of the man of God who came from Judah and
predicted the very things that you have just done to
the altar at Bethel!"

18 Josiah replied, "Leave it alone. Don't disturb his
bones." So they did not burn his bones or those of
the old prophet from Samaria.

19 Then Josiah demolished all the buildings at the
pagan shrines in the towns of Samaria, just as he had
done at Bethel. They had been built by the various
kings of Israel and had made the LORD* very angry.
20 He executed the priests of the pagan shrines on their
own altars, and he burned human bones on the altars
to desecrate them. Finally, he returned to Jerusalem.

Josiah Celebrates Passover

21 King Josiah then issued this order to all the people:
"You must celebrate the Passover to the LORD your
God, as required in this Book of the Covenant."
22 There had not been a Passover celebration like that
since the time when the judges ruled in Israel, nor
throughout all the years of the kings of Israel and
Judah. 23 This Passover was celebrated to the LORD
in Jerusalem in the eighteenth year of King Josiah's
reign.

24 Josiah also got rid of the mediums and psychics,
the household gods, the idols,* and every other kind
of detestable practice, both in Jerusalem and
throughout the land of Judah. He did this in obedience to the laws written in the scroll that Hilkiah the
priest had found in the LORD's Temple. 25 Never before had there been a king like Josiah, who turned to
the LORD with all his heart and soul and strength,
obeying all the laws of Moses. And there has never
been a king like him since.

26 Even so, the LORD was very angry with Judah because of all the wicked things Manasseh had done to
provoke him. 27 For the LORD said, "I will also banish
Judah from my presence just as I have banished Israel. And I will reject my chosen city of Jerusalem and
the Temple where my name was to be honored."

28 The rest of the events in Josiah's reign and all his
deeds are recorded in *The Book of the History of the
Kings of Judah*.

29 While Josiah was king, Pharaoh Neco, king of
Egypt, went to the Euphrates River to help the king
of Assyria. King Josiah and his army marched out to
fight him,* but King Neco* killed him when they
met at Megiddo. 30 Josiah's officers took his body
back in a chariot from Megiddo to Jerusalem and
buried him in his own tomb. Then the people of the
land anointed Josiah's son Jehoahaz and made him
the next king.

23:19 As in Greek and Syriac versions and Latin Vulgate; Hebrew lacks *the LORD*. **23:24** The Hebrew term (literally *round things*) probably alludes to dung. **23:29a** Or *Josiah went out to meet him*. **23:29b** Hebrew *he*.

KING JAMES VERSION

31 Jehoahaz *was* twenty and three years old when
he began to reign; and he reigned three months in
Jerusalem. And his mother's name *was* Hamutal, the
daughter of Jeremiah of Libnah.
32 And he did *that which was* evil in the sight of
the LORD, according to all that his fathers had done.
33 And Pharaoh-nechoh put him in bands at Riblah
in the land of Hamath, that he might not reign in
Jerusalem; and put the land to a tribute of an hundred talents of silver, and a talent of gold.

34 And Pharaoh-nechoh made Eliakim the son of
Josiah king in the room of Josiah his father, and
turned his name to Jehoiakim, and took Jehoahaz
away: and he came to Egypt, and died there.
35 And Jehoiakim gave the silver and the gold to
Pharaoh; but he taxed the land to give the money according to the commandment of Pharaoh: he exacted the silver and the gold of the people of the
land, of every one according to his taxation, to give *it*
unto Pharaoh-nechoh.
36 Jehoiakim *was* twenty and five years old when
he began to reign; and he reigned eleven years in Jerusalem. And his mother's name *was* Zebudah, the
daughter of Pedaiah of Rumah.
37 And he did *that which was* evil in the sight of
the LORD, according to all that his fathers had done.

24 1 In his days Nebuchadnezzar king of Babylon came up, and Jehoiakim became his
servant three years: then he turned and rebelled
against him.
2 And the LORD sent against him bands of the
Chaldees, and bands of the Syrians, and bands of the
Moabites, and bands of the children of Ammon, and
sent them against Judah to destroy it, according to
the word of the LORD, which he spake by his servants
the prophets.
3 Surely at the commandment of the LORD came
this upon Judah, to remove *them* out of his sight, for
the sins of Manasseh, according to all that he did;
4 And also for the innocent blood that he shed: for
he filled Jerusalem with innocent blood; which the
LORD would not pardon.
5 Now the rest of the acts of Jehoiakim, and all that
he did, *are* they not written in the book of the chronicles of the kings of Judah?
6 So Jehoiakim slept with his fathers: and Jehoiachin his son reigned in his stead.
7 And the king of Egypt came not again any more
out of his land: for the king of Babylon had taken
from the river of Egypt unto the river Euphrates all
that pertained to the king of Egypt.
8 Jehoiachin *was* eighteen years old when he began to reign, and he reigned in Jerusalem three
months. And his mother's name *was* Nehushta, the
daughter of Elnathan of Jerusalem.

NEW LIVING TRANSLATION

Jehoahaz Rules in Judah

31 Jehoahaz was twenty-three years old when he
became king, and he reigned in Jerusalem three
months. His mother was Hamutal, the daughter of
Jeremiah from Libnah. 32 He did what was evil in the
LORD's sight, just as his ancestors had done.
33 Pharaoh Neco put Jehoahaz in prison at Riblah
in the land of Hamath to prevent him from ruling* in
Jerusalem. He also demanded that Judah pay 7,500
pounds of silver and 75 pounds of gold* as tribute.

Jehoiakim Rules in Judah

34 Pharaoh Neco then installed Eliakim, another of
Josiah's sons, to reign in place of his father, and he
changed Eliakim's name to Jehoiakim. Jehoahaz was
taken to Egypt as a prisoner, where he died.
35 In order to get the silver and gold demanded as
tribute by Pharaoh Neco, Jehoiakim collected a tax
from the people of Judah, requiring them to pay in
proportion to their wealth.
36 Jehoiakim was twenty-five years old when he became king, and he reigned in Jerusalem eleven years.
His mother was Zebidah, the daughter of Pedaiah
from Rumah. 37 He did what was evil in the LORD's
sight, just as his ancestors had done.

24 During Jehoiakim's reign, King Nebuchadnezzar of Babylon invaded the land of Judah. Jehoiakim surrendered and paid him tribute for
three years but then rebelled. 2 Then the LORD sent
bands of Babylonian,* Aramean, Moabite, and Ammonite raiders against Judah to destroy it, just as the
LORD had promised through his prophets. 3 These
disasters happened to Judah because of the LORD's
command. He had decided to banish Judah from his
presence because of the many sins of Manasseh,
4 who had filled Jerusalem with innocent blood. The
LORD would not forgive this.
5 The rest of the events in Jehoiakim's reign and all
his deeds are recorded in *The Book of the History of
the Kings of Judah.* 6 When Jehoiakim died, his son
Jehoiachin became the next king.
7 The king of Egypt did not venture out of his country after that, for the king of Babylon captured the entire area formerly claimed by Egypt—from the Brook
of Egypt to the Euphrates River.

Jehoiachin Rules in Judah

8 Jehoiachin was eighteen years old when he became
king, and he reigned in Jerusalem three months. His

23:33a The meaning of the Hebrew is uncertain. **23:33b** Hebrew *100 talents* [3,400 kilograms] *of silver and 1 talent* [34 kilograms] *of gold.*
24:2 Or *Chaldean.*

KING JAMES VERSION

9And he did *that which was* evil in the sight of the LORD, according to all that his father had done.

10At that time the servants of Nebuchadnezzar king of Babylon came up against Jerusalem, and the city was besieged.

11And Nebuchadnezzar king of Babylon came against the city, and his servants did besiege it.

12And Jehoiachin the king of Judah went out to the king of Babylon, he, and his mother, and his servants, and his princes, and his officers: and the king of Babylon took him in the eighth year of his reign.

13And he carried out thence all the treasures of the house of the LORD, and the treasures of the king's house, and cut in pieces all the vessels of gold which Solomon king of Israel had made in the temple of the LORD, as the LORD had said.

14And he carried away all Jerusalem, and all the princes, and all the mighty men of valour, *even* ten thousand captives, and all the craftsmen and smiths: none remained, save the poorest sort of the people of the land.

15And he carried away Jehoiachin to Babylon, and the king's mother, and the king's wives, and his officers, and the mighty of the land, *those* carried he into captivity from Jerusalem to Babylon.

16And all the men of might, *even* seven thousand, and craftsmen and smiths a thousand, all *that were* strong *and* apt for war, even them the king of Babylon brought captive to Babylon.

17And the king of Babylon made Mattaniah his father's brother king in his stead, and changed his name to Zedekiah.

18Zedekiah *was* twenty and one years old when he began to reign, and he reigned eleven years in Jerusalem. And his mother's name *was* Hamutal, the daughter of Jeremiah of Libnah.

19And he did *that which was* evil in the sight of the LORD, according to all that Jehoiakim had done.

20For through the anger of the LORD it came to pass in Jerusalem and Judah, until he had cast them out from his presence, that Zedekiah rebelled against the king of Babylon.

25 1And it came to pass in the ninth year of his reign, in the tenth month, in the tenth *day* of the month, *that* Nebuchadnezzar king of Babylon came, he, and all his host, against Jerusalem, and pitched against it: and they built forts against it round about.

2And the city was besieged unto the eleventh year of king Zedekiah.

3And on the ninth *day* of the *fourth* month the

NEW LIVING TRANSLATION

mother was Nehushta, the daughter of Elnathan from Jerusalem. 9Jehoiachin did what was evil in the LORD's sight, just as his father had done.

10During Jehoiachin's reign, the officers of King Nebuchadnezzar of Babylon came up against Jerusalem and besieged it. 11Nebuchadnezzar himself arrived at the city during the siege. 12Then King Jehoiachin, along with the queen mother, his advisers, his commanders, and his officials, surrendered to the Babylonians.

In the eighth year of Nebuchadnezzar's reign, he took Jehoiachin prisoner. 13As the LORD had said beforehand, Nebuchadnezzar carried away all the treasures from the LORD's Temple and the royal palace. He stripped away* all the gold objects that King Solomon of Israel had placed in the Temple. 14King Nebuchadnezzar took all of Jerusalem captive, including all the commanders and the best of the soldiers, craftsmen, and artisans—10,000 in all. Only the poorest people were left in the land.

15Nebuchadnezzar led King Jehoiachin away as a captive to Babylon, along with the queen mother, his wives and officials, and all Jerusalem's elite. 16He also exiled 7,000 of the best troops and 1,000 craftsmen and artisans, all of whom were strong and fit for war. 17Then the king of Babylon installed Mattaniah, Jehoiachin's* uncle, as the next king, and he changed Mattaniah's name to Zedekiah.

Zedekiah Rules in Judah

18Zedekiah was twenty-one years old when he became king, and he reigned in Jerusalem eleven years. His mother was Hamutal, the daughter of Jeremiah from Libnah. 19But Zedekiah did what was evil in the LORD's sight, just as Jehoiakim had done. 20These things happened because of the LORD's anger against the people of Jerusalem and Judah, until he finally banished them from his presence and sent them into exile.

The Fall of Jerusalem

Zedekiah rebelled against the king of Babylon.

25 So on January 15,* during the ninth year of Zedekiah's reign, King Nebuchadnezzar of Babylon led his entire army against Jerusalem. They surrounded the city and built siege ramps against its walls. 2Jerusalem was kept under siege until the eleventh year of King Zedekiah's reign.

3By July 18 in the eleventh year of Zedekiah's

24:13 Or *He cut apart.* **24:17** Hebrew *his.* **25:1** Hebrew *on the tenth day of the tenth month,* of the ancient Hebrew lunar calendar. A number of events in 2 Kings can be cross-checked with dates in surviving Babylonian records and related accurately to our modern calendar. This day was January 15, 588 B.C.

KING JAMES VERSION

famine prevailed in the city, and there was no bread for the people of the land.

4And the city was broken up, and all the men of war *fled* by night by the way of the gate between two walls, which *is* by the king's garden: (now the Chaldees *were* against the city round about:) and *the king* went the way toward the plain.

5And the army of the Chaldees pursued after the king, and overtook him in the plains of Jericho: and all his army were scattered from him.

6So they took the king, and brought him up to the king of Babylon to Riblah; and they gave judgment upon him.

7And they slew the sons of Zedekiah before his eyes, and put out the eyes of Zedekiah, and bound him with fetters of brass, and carried him to Babylon.

8And in the fifth month, on the seventh *day* of the month, which *is* the nineteenth year of king Nebuchadnezzar king of Babylon, came Nebuzar-adan, captain of the guard, a servant of the king of Babylon, unto Jerusalem:

9And he burnt the house of the LORD, and the king's house, and all the houses of Jerusalem, and every great *man's* house burnt he with fire.

10And all the army of the Chaldees, that *were with* the captain of the guard, brake down the walls of Jerusalem round about.

11Now the rest of the people *that were* left in the city, and the fugitives that fell away to the king of Babylon, with the remnant of the multitude, did Nebuzar-adan the captain of the guard carry away.

12But the captain of the guard left of the poor of the land *to be* vinedressers and husbandmen.

13And the pillars of brass that *were* in the house of the LORD, and the bases, and the brasen sea that *was* in the house of the LORD, did the Chaldees break in pieces, and carried the brass of them to Babylon.

14And the pots, and the shovels, and the snuffers, and the spoons, and all the vessels of brass wherewith they ministered, took they away.

15And the firepans, and the bowls, *and* such things as *were* of gold, *in* gold, and of silver, *in* silver, the captain of the guard took away.

16The two pillars, one sea, and the bases which Solomon had made for the house of the LORD; the brass of all these vessels was without weight.

17The height of the one pillar *was* eighteen cubits, and the chapiter upon it *was* brass: and the height of the chapiter three cubits; and the wreathen work, and pomegranates upon the chapiter round about, all of brass: and like unto these had the second pillar with wreathen work.

18And the captain of the guard took Seraiah the

NEW LIVING TRANSLATION

reign,* the famine in the city had become very severe, and the last of the food was entirely gone.
4Then a section of the city wall was broken down,
and all the soldiers fled. Since the city was surrounded by the Babylonians,* they waited for nightfall. Then they slipped through the gate between the two walls behind the king's garden and headed toward the Jordan Valley.*
5But the Babylonian* troops chased the king and
caught him on the plains of Jericho, for his men
had all deserted him and scattered. 6They took him
to the king of Babylon at Riblah, where they pronounced judgment upon Zedekiah. 7They made
Zedekiah watch as they slaughtered his sons. Then
they gouged out Zedekiah's eyes, bound him in
bronze chains, and led him away to Babylon.

The Temple Destroyed

8On August 14 of that year,* which was the nineteenth year of King Nebuchadnezzar's reign, Nebuzaradan, the captain of the guard and an official of
the Babylonian king, arrived in Jerusalem. 9He
burned down the Temple of the LORD, the royal palace, and all the houses of Jerusalem. He destroyed all
the important buildings* in the city. 10Then he supervised the entire Babylonian army as they tore
down the walls of Jerusalem on every side. 11Nebuzaradan, the captain of the guard, then took as exiles
the rest of the people who remained in the city, the
defectors who had declared their allegiance to the
king of Babylon, and the rest of the population. 12But
the captain of the guard allowed some of the poorest
people to stay behind in Judah to care for the vineyards and fields.
13The Babylonians broke up the bronze pillars in
front of the LORD's Temple, the bronze water carts,
and the great bronze basin called the Sea, and they
carried all the bronze away to Babylon. 14They also
took all the ash buckets, shovels, lamp snuffers,
dishes, and all the other bronze articles used for
making sacrifices at the Temple. 15Nebuzaradan, the
captain of the guard, also took the incense burners
and basins, and all the other articles made of pure
gold or silver.
16The weight of the bronze from the two pillars, the
Sea, and the water carts was too great to be measured.
These things had been made for the LORD's Temple in
the days of King Solomon. 17Each of the pillars was
27 feet* tall. The bronze capital on top of each pillar
was 7½ feet* high and was decorated with a network
of bronze pomegranates all the way around.
18Nebuzaradan, the captain of the guard, took

25:3 Hebrew *By the ninth day of the [fourth] month* [in the eleventh year of Zedekiah's reign] (compare Jer 52:6 and the note there). This day was July 18, 586 B.C.; also see note on 25:1. **25:4a** Or *the Chaldeans;* also in 25:13, 25, 26. **25:4b** Hebrew *the Arabah.* **25:5** Or *Chaldean*; also in 25:10, 24. **25:8** Hebrew *On the seventh day of the fifth month,* of the ancient Hebrew lunar calendar. This day was August 14, 586 B.C.; also see note on 25:1. **25:9** Or *destroyed the houses of all the important people.* **25:17a** Hebrew *18 cubits* [8.1 meters].

KING JAMES VERSION

chief priest, and Zephaniah the second priest, and the three keepers of the door:

19 And out of the city he took an officer that was set over the men of war, and five men of them that were in the king's presence, which were found in the city, and the principal scribe of the host, which mustered the people of the land, and threescore men of the people of the land *that were* found in the city:

20 And Nebuzar-adan captain of the guard took these, and brought them to the king of Babylon to Riblah:

21 And the king of Babylon smote them, and slew them at Riblah in the land of Hamath. So Judah was carried away out of their land.

22 And *as for* the people that remained in the land of Judah, whom Nebuchadnezzar king of Babylon had left, even over them he made Gedaliah the son of Ahikam, the son of Shaphan, ruler.

23 And when all the captains of the armies, they and their men, heard that the king of Babylon had made Gedaliah governor, there came to Gedaliah to Mizpah, even Ishmael the son of Nethaniah, and Johanan the son of Careah, and Seraiah the son of Tanhumeth the Netophathite, and Jaazaniah the son of a Maachathite, they and their men.

24 And Gedaliah sware to them, and to their men, and said unto them, Fear not to be the servants of the Chaldees: dwell in the land, and serve the king of Babylon; and it shall be well with you.

25 But it came to pass in the seventh month, that Ishmael the son of Nethaniah, the son of Elishama, of the seed royal, came, and ten men with him, and smote Gedaliah, that he died, and the Jews and the Chaldees that were with him at Mizpah.

26 And all the people, both small and great, and the captains of the armies, arose, and came to Egypt: for they were afraid of the Chaldees.

27 And it came to pass in the seven and thirtieth year of the captivity of Jehoiachin king of Judah, in the twelfth month, on the seven and twentieth *day* of the month, *that* Evil-merodach king of Babylon in the year that he began to reign did lift up the head of Jehoiachin king of Judah out of prison;

28 And he spake kindly to him, and set his throne above the throne of the kings that *were* with him in Babylon;

29 And changed his prison garments: and he did eat bread continually before him all the days of his life.

30 And his allowance *was* a continual allowance given him of the king, a daily rate for every day, all the days of his life.

NEW LIVING TRANSLATION

with him as prisoners Seraiah the high priest, Zephaniah the priest of the second rank, and the three
chief gatekeepers. 19 And from among the people
still hiding in the city, he took an officer who had
been in charge of the Judean army; five of the king's
personal advisers; the army commander's chief secretary, who was in charge of recruitment; and sixty
other citizens. 20 Nebuzaradan, the captain of the
guard, took them all to the king of Babylon at Riblah.
21 And there at Riblah, in the land of Hamath, the king
of Babylon had them all put to death. So the people
of Judah were sent into exile from their land.

Gedaliah Governs in Judah

22 Then King Nebuchadnezzar appointed Gedaliah
son of Ahikam and grandson of Shaphan as governor
over the people he had left in Judah. 23 When all the
army commanders and their men learned that the
king of Babylon had appointed Gedaliah as governor,
they went to see him at Mizpah. These included
Ishmael son of Nethaniah, Johanan son of Kareah,
Seraiah son of Tanhumeth the Netophathite, and
Jezaniah* son of the Maacathite, and all their men.

24 Gedaliah vowed to them that the Babylonian
officials meant them no harm. "Don't be afraid of
them. Live in the land and serve the king of Babylon,
and all will go well for you," he promised.

25 But in midautumn of that year,* Ishmael son of
Nethaniah and grandson of Elishama, who was of the
royal family, went to Mizpah with ten men and killed
Gedaliah. He also killed all the Judeans and Babylonians who were with Gedaliah at Mizpah.

26 Then all the people of Judah, from the least to
the greatest, as well as the army commanders, fled in
panic to Egypt, for they were afraid of what the Babylonians would do to them.

Hope for Israel's Royal Line

27 In the thirty-seventh year of the exile of King Jehoiachin of Judah, Evil-merodach ascended to the Babylonian throne. He was kind to* Jehoiachin and
released him from prison on April 2 of that year.*
28 He spoke kindly to Jehoiachin and gave him a
higher place than all the other exiled kings in Babylon. 29 He supplied Jehoiachin with new clothes to
replace his prison garb and allowed him to dine in
the king's presence for the rest of his life. 30 So the
Babylonian king gave him a regular food allowance
as long as he lived.

25:17b As in parallel texts at 1 Kgs 7:16, 2 Chr 3:15, and Jer 52:22, all of which read *5 cubits* [2.3 meters]; Hebrew reads *3 cubits*, which is 4.5 feet or 1.4 meters. **25:23** As in parallel text at Jer 40:8; Hebrew reads *Jaazaniah*, a variant spelling of Jezaniah. **25:25** Hebrew *in the seventh month*, of the ancient Hebrew lunar calendar. This month occurred within the months of October and November 586 B.C.; also see note on 25:1. **25:27a** Hebrew *He raised the head of.* **25:27b** Hebrew *on the twenty-seventh day of the twelfth month*, of the ancient Hebrew lunar calendar. This day was April 2, 561 B.C.; also see note on 25:1.

1 Chronicles

KING JAMES VERSION

1 1 Adam, Sheth, Enosh,
2 Kenan, Mahalaleel, Jered,
3 Henoch, Methuselah, Lamech,
4 Noah, Shem, Ham, and Japheth.

5 The sons of Japheth; Gomer, and Magog, and
Madai, and Javan, and Tubal, and Meshech, and Tiras.
6 And the sons of Gomer; Ashchenaz, and Riphath,
and Togarmah.
7 And the sons of Javan; Elishah, and Tarshish,
Kittim, and Dodanim.

8 The sons of Ham; Cush, and Mizraim, Put, and
Canaan.
9 And the sons of Cush; Seba, and Havilah, and
Sabta, and Raamah, and Sabtecha. And the sons of
Raamah; Sheba, and Dedan.
10 And Cush begat Nimrod: he began to be mighty
upon the earth.
11 And Mizraim begat Ludim, and Anamim, and
Lehabim, and Naphtuhim,
12 And Pathrusim, and Casluhim, (of whom came
the Philistines,) and Caphthorim.
13 And Canaan begat Zidon his firstborn, and Heth,
14 The Jebusite also, and the Amorite, and the
Girgashite,
15 And the Hivite, and the Arkite, and the Sinite,
16 And the Arvadite, and the Zemarite, and the
Hamathite.

17 The sons of Shem; Elam, and Asshur, and Arphaxad, and Lud, and Aram, and Uz, and Hul, and
Gether, and Meshech.

NEW LIVING TRANSLATION

From Adam to Noah's Sons

1 The descendants of Adam were Seth, Enosh,
2 Kenan, Mahalalel, Jared, 3 Enoch, Methuselah,
Lamech, 4 and Noah.
The sons of Noah were* Shem, Ham, and Japheth.

Descendants of Japheth

5 The descendants of Japheth were Gomer, Magog,
Madai, Javan, Tubal, Meshech, and Tiras.
6 The descendants of Gomer were Ashkenaz,
Riphath,* and Togarmah.
7 The descendants of Javan were Elishah, Tarshish,
Kittim, and Rodanim.

Descendants of Ham

8 The descendants of Ham were Cush, Mizraim,*
Put, and Canaan.
9 The descendants of Cush were Seba, Havilah,
Sabtah, Raamah, and Sabteca. The descendants
of Raamah were Sheba and Dedan. 10 Cush was
also the ancestor of Nimrod, who was the first
heroic warrior on earth.
11 Mizraim was the ancestor of the Ludites,
Anamites, Lehabites, Naphtuhites, 12 Pathrusites,
Casluhites, and the Caphtorites, from whom the
Philistines came.*
13 Canaan's oldest son was Sidon, the ancestor of
the Sidonians. Canaan was also the ancestor of
the Hittites,* 14 Jebusites, Amorites, Girgashites,
15 Hivites, Arkites, Sinites, 16 Arvadites, Zemarites,
and Hamathites.

Descendants of Shem

17 The descendants of Shem were Elam, Asshur,
Arphaxad, Lud, and Aram.
The descendants of Aram were* Uz, Hul, Gether,
and Mash.*

1:4 As in Greek version (see also Gen 5:3-32); Hebrew lacks *The sons of Noah were.* **1:6** As in some Hebrew manuscripts and Greek version (see also Gen 10:3); most Hebrew manuscripts read *Diphath.* **1:8** Or *Egypt;* also in 1:11. **1:12** Hebrew *Casluhites, from whom the Philistines came, Caphtorites.* See Jer 47:4; Amos 9:7. **1:13** Hebrew *ancestor of Heth.* **1:17a** As in one Hebrew manuscript and some Greek manuscripts (see also Gen 10:23); most Hebrew manuscripts lack *The descendants of Aram were.* **1:17b** As in parallel text at Gen 10:23; Hebrew reads *and Meshech.*

KING JAMES VERSION

18 And Arphaxad begat Shelah, and Shelah begat
Eber.
19 And unto Eber were born two sons: the name of
the one *was* Peleg; because in his days the earth was
divided: and his brother's name *was* Joktan.
20 And Joktan begat Almodad, and Sheleph, and
Hazarmaveth, and Jerah,
21 Hadoram also, and Uzal, and Diklah,
22 And Ebal, and Abimael, and Sheba,
23 And Ophir, and Havilah, and Jobab. All these
were the sons of Joktan.
24 Shem, Arphaxad, Shelah,
25 Eber, Peleg, Reu,
26 Serug, Nahor, Terah,
27 Abram; the same *is* Abraham.

28 The sons of Abraham; Isaac, and Ishmael.
29 These *are* their generations: The firstborn of
Ishmael, Nebaioth; then Kedar, and Adbeel, and
Mibsam,
30 Mishma, and Dumah, Massa, Hadad, and Tema,
31 Jetur, Naphish, and Kedemah. These are the
sons of Ishmael.
32 Now the sons of Keturah, Abraham's concubine:
she bare Zimran, and Jokshan, and Medan, and Midian, and Ishbak, and Shuah. And the sons of Jokshan;
Sheba, and Dedan.
33 And the sons of Midian; Ephah, and Epher, and
Henoch, and Abida, and Eldaah. All these *are* the
sons of Keturah.

34 And Abraham begat Isaac. The sons of Isaac;
Esau and Israel.

35 The sons of Esau; Eliphaz, Reuel, and Jeush, and
Jaalam, and Korah.
36 The sons of Eliphaz; Teman, and Omar, Zephi,
and Gatam, Kenaz, and Timna, and Amalek.
37 The sons of Reuel; Nahath, Zerah, Shammah,
and Mizzah.

38 And the sons of Seir; Lotan, and Shobal, and Zibeon, and Anah, and Dishon, and Ezar, and Dishan.
39 And the sons of Lotan; Hori, and Homam: and
Timna *was* Lotan's sister.

NEW LIVING TRANSLATION

18 Arphaxad was the father of Shelah.
Shelah was the father of Eber.
19 Eber had two sons. The first was named Peleg
(which means "division"), for during his lifetime
the people of the world were divided into
different language groups. His brother's name
was Joktan.
20 Joktan was the ancestor of Almodad, Sheleph,
Hazarmaveth, Jerah, 21 Hadoram, Uzal, Diklah,
22 Obal,* Abimael, Sheba, 23 Ophir, Havilah, and
Jobab. All these were descendants of Joktan.
24 So this is the family line descended from Shem:
Arphaxad, Shelah,* 25 Eber, Peleg, Reu, 26 Serug,
Nahor, Terah, 27 and Abram, later known as
Abraham.

Descendants of Abraham

28 The sons of Abraham were Isaac and Ishmael.
29 These are their genealogical records:
The sons of Ishmael were Nebaioth (the oldest),
Kedar, Adbeel, Mibsam, 30 Mishma, Dumah,
Massa, Hadad, Tema, 31 Jetur, Naphish, and
Kedemah. These were the sons of Ishmael.

32 The sons of Keturah, Abraham's concubine, were
Zimran, Jokshan, Medan, Midian, Ishbak, and
Shuah.
The sons of Jokshan were Sheba and Dedan.
33 The sons of Midian were Ephah, Epher, Hanoch,
Abida, and Eldaah.
All these were descendants of Abraham through his
concubine Keturah.

Descendants of Isaac

34 Abraham was the father of Isaac. The sons of
Isaac were Esau and Israel.*

Descendants of Esau

35 The descendants of Esau were Eliphaz, Reuel,
Jeush, Jalam, and Korah.
36 The descendants of Eliphaz were Teman, Omar,
Zepho,* Gatam, Kenaz, and Amalek, who was
born to Timna.*
37 The descendants of Reuel were Nahath, Zerah,
Shammah, and Mizzah.

Original Peoples of Edom

38 The descendants of Seir were Lotan, Shobal,
Zibeon, Anah, Dishon, Ezer, and Dishan.
39 The descendants of Lotan were Hori and
Hemam.* Lotan's sister was named Timna.

1:22 As in some Hebrew manuscripts and Syriac version (see also Gen 10:28); most Hebrew manuscripts read *Ebal.* **1:24** Some Greek manuscripts read *Arphaxad, Cainan, Shelah.* See notes on Gen 10:24; 11:12-13. **1:34** *Israel* is the name that God gave to Jacob. **1:36a** As in many Hebrew manuscripts and a few Greek manuscripts (see also Gen 36:11); most Hebrew manuscripts read *Zephi.* **1:36b** As in some Greek manuscripts (see also Gen 36:12); Hebrew reads *Kenaz, Timna, and Amalek.* **1:39** As in parallel text at Gen 36:22; Hebrew reads *and Homam.*

KING JAMES VERSION

40 The sons of Shobal; Alian, and Manahath, and
Ebal, Shephi, and Onam. And the sons of Zibeon;
Aiah, and Anah.
41 The sons of Anah; Dishon. And the sons of Dishon; Amram, and Esh-ban, and Ithran, and Cheran.
42 The sons of Ezer; Bilhan, and Zavan, *and* Jakan.
The sons of Dishan; Uz, and Aran.

43 Now these *are* the kings that reigned in the land
of Edom before *any* king reigned over the children
of Israel; Bela the son of Beor: and the name of his
city *was* Dinhabah.
44 And when Bela was dead, Jobab the son of Zerah
of Bozrah reigned in his stead.
45 And when Jobab was dead, Husham of the land
of the Temanites reigned in his stead.
46 And when Husham was dead, Hadad the son
of Bedad, which smote Midian in the field of Moab,
reigned in his stead: and the name of his city *was* Avith.
47 And when Hadad was dead, Samlah of Masrekah
reigned in his stead.
48 And when Samlah was dead, Shaul of Rehoboth
by the river reigned in his stead.
49 And when Shaul was dead, Baal-hanan the son
of Achbor reigned in his stead.
50 And when Baal-hanan was dead, Hadad reigned
in his stead: and the name of his city *was* Pai; and his
wife's name *was* Mehetabel, the daughter of Matred,
the daughter of Mezahab.
51 Hadad died also. And the dukes of Edom were
duke Timnah, duke Aliah, duke Jetheth,
52 Duke Aholibamah, duke Elah, duke Pinon,
53 Duke Kenaz, duke Teman, duke Mibzar,
54 Duke Magdiel, duke Iram. These *are* the dukes
of Edom.

2 1 These *are* the sons of Israel; Reuben, Simeon,
Levi, and Judah, Issachar, and Zebulun,
2 Dan, Joseph, and Benjamin, Naphtali, Gad, and
Asher.
3 The sons of Judah; Er, and Onan, and Shelah:
which three were born unto him of the daughter of
Shua the Canaanitess. And Er, the firstborn of Judah,
was evil in the sight of the LORD; and he slew him.
4 And Tamar his daughter in law bare him Pharez
and Zerah. All the sons of Judah *were* five.

NEW LIVING TRANSLATION

40 The descendants of Shobal were Alvan,*
Manahath, Ebal, Shepho,* and Onam.
The descendants of Zibeon were Aiah and Anah.
41 The son of Anah was Dishon.
The descendants of Dishon were Hemdan,*
Eshban, Ithran, and Keran.
42 The descendants of Ezer were Bilhan, Zaavan,
and Akan.*
The descendants of Dishan* were Uz and Aran.

Rulers of Edom

43 These are the kings who ruled in the land of Edom
before any king ruled over the Israelites*:

Bela son of Beor, who ruled from his city of Dinhabah.
44 When Bela died, Jobab son of Zerah from Bozrah
became king in his place.
45 When Jobab died, Husham from the land of the
Temanites became king in his place.
46 When Husham died, Hadad son of Bedad became
king in his place and ruled from the city of Avith.
He was the one who destroyed the Midianite
army in the land of Moab.
47 When Hadad died, Samlah from the city
of Masrekah became king in his place.
48 When Samlah died, Shaul from the city of
Rehoboth-on-the-River became king in his place.
49 When Shaul died, Baal-hanan son of Acbor
became king in his place.
50 When Baal-hanan died, Hadad became king in his
place and ruled from the city of Pau.* His wife
was Mehetabel, the daughter of Matred and
granddaughter of Me-zahab. 51 Then Hadad died.

The clan leaders of Edom were Timna, Alvah,*
Jetheth, 52 Oholibamah, Elah, Pinon, 53 Kenaz,
Teman, Mibzar, 54 Magdiel, and Iram. These
are the clan leaders of Edom.

Descendants of Israel

2 The sons of Israel* were Reuben, Simeon,
Levi, Judah, Issachar, Zebulun, 2 Dan, Joseph,
Benjamin, Naphtali, Gad, and Asher.

Descendants of Judah

3 Judah had three sons from Bathshua, a Canaanite
woman. Their names were Er, Onan, and Shelah.
But the LORD saw that the oldest son, Er, was a
wicked man, so he killed him. 4 Later Judah had
twin sons from Tamar, his widowed daughter-in-
law. Their names were Perez and Zerah. So Judah
had five sons in all.

1:40a As in many Hebrew manuscripts and a few Greek manuscripts (see also Gen 36:23); most Hebrew manuscripts read *Alian.* **1:40b** As in some Hebrew manuscripts (see also Gen 36:23); most Hebrew manuscripts read *Shephi.* **1:41** As in many Hebrew manuscripts and some Greek manuscripts (see also Gen 36:26); most Hebrew manuscripts read *Hamran.* **1:42a** As in many Hebrew and Greek manuscripts (see also Gen 36:27); most Hebrew manuscripts read *Jaakan.* **1:42b** Hebrew *Dishon;* compare 1:38 and parallel text at Gen 36:28. **1:43** Or *before an Israelite king ruled over them.* **1:50** As in many Hebrew manuscripts, some Greek manuscripts, Syriac version, and Latin Vulgate (see also Gen 36:39); most Hebrew manuscripts read *Pai.* **1:51** As in parallel text at Gen 36:40; Hebrew reads *Aliah.* **2:1** *Israel* is the name that God gave to Jacob.

KING JAMES VERSION

5 The sons of Pharez; Hezron, and Hamul.

6 And the sons of Zerah; Zimri, and Ethan, and Heman, and Calcol, and Dara: five of them in all.

7 And the sons of Carmi; Achar, the troubler of Israel, who transgressed in the thing accursed.

8 And the sons of Ethan; Azariah.

9 The sons also of Hezron, that were born unto him; Jerahmeel, and Ram, and Chelubai.

10 And Ram begat Amminadab; and Amminadab begat Nahshon, prince of the children of Judah;

11 And Nahshon begat Salma, and Salma begat Boaz,

12 And Boaz begat Obed, and Obed begat Jesse.

13 And Jesse begat his firstborn Eliab, and Abinadab the second, and Shimma the third,

14 Nethaneel the fourth, Raddai the fifth,

15 Ozem the sixth, David the seventh:

16 Whose sisters *were* Zeruiah, and Abigail. And the sons of Zeruiah; Abishai, and Joab, and Asahel, three.

17 And Abigail bare Amasa: and the father of Amasa *was* Jether the Ishmeelite.

18 And Caleb the son of Hezron begat *children* of Azubah *his* wife, and of Jerioth: her sons *are* these; Jesher, and Shobab, and Ardon.

19 And when Azubah was dead, Caleb took unto him Ephrath, which bare him Hur.

20 And Hur begat Uri, and Uri begat Bezaleel.

21 And afterward Hezron went in to the daughter of Machir the father of Gilead, whom he married when he *was* threescore years old; and she bare him Segub.

22 And Segub begat Jair, who had three and twenty cities in the land of Gilead.

23 And he took Geshur, and Aram, with the towns of Jair, from them, with Kenath, and the towns thereof, *even* threescore cities. All these *belonged to* the sons of Machir, the father of Gilead.

24 And after that Hezron was dead in Calebephratah, then Abiah Hezron's wife bare him Ashur the father of Tekoa.

25 And the sons of Jerahmeel the firstborn of Hezron were, Ram the firstborn, and Bunah, and Oren, and Ozem, *and* Ahijah.

26 Jerahmeel had also another wife, whose name *was* Atarah; she *was* the mother of Onam.

NEW LIVING TRANSLATION

5 The sons of Perez were Hezron and Hamul.
6 The sons of Zerah were Zimri, Ethan, Heman,
Calcol, and Darda*—five in all.
7 The son of Carmi (a descendant of Zimri) was
Achan,* who brought disaster on Israel by taking
plunder that had been set apart for the LORD.*
8 The son of Ethan was Azariah.

From Judah's Grandson Hezron to David

9 The sons of Hezron were Jerahmeel, Ram, and
Caleb.*
10 Ram was the father of Amminadab.
Amminadab was the father of Nahshon, a leader
of Judah.
11 Nahshon was the father of Salmon.*
Salmon was the father of Boaz.
12 Boaz was the father of Obed.
Obed was the father of Jesse.
13 Jesse's first son was Eliab, his second was
Abinadab, his third was Shimea, 14 his fourth
was Nethanel, his fifth was Raddai, 15 his sixth
was Ozem, and his seventh was David.
16 Their sisters were named Zeruiah and Abigail.
Zeruiah had three sons named Abishai, Joab, and
Asahel. 17 Abigail married a man named Jether,
an Ishmaelite, and they had a son named Amasa.

Other Descendants of Hezron

18 Hezron's son Caleb had sons from his wife
Azubah and from Jerioth.* Her sons were named
Jesher, Shobab, and Ardon. 19 After Azubah died,
Caleb married Ephrathah,* and they had a son
named Hur. 20 Hur was the father of Uri. Uri was
the father of Bezalel.
21 When Hezron was sixty years old, he married
Gilead's sister, the daughter of Makir. They had
a son named Segub. 22 Segub was the father of
Jair, who ruled twenty-three towns in the land
of Gilead. 23 (But Geshur and Aram captured the
Towns of Jair* and also took Kenath and its sixty
surrounding villages.) All these were descendants
of Makir, the father of Gilead.
24 Soon after Hezron died in the town of Caleb-
ephrathah, his wife Abijah gave birth to a son
named Ashhur (the father of* Tekoa).

Descendants of Hezron's Son Jerahmeel

25 The sons of Jerahmeel, the oldest son of Hezron,
were Ram (the firstborn), Bunah, Oren, Ozem,
and Ahijah. 26 Jerahmeel had a second wife
named Atarah. She was the mother of Onam.

2:6 As in many Hebrew manuscripts, some Greek manuscripts, and Syriac version (see also 1 Kgs 4:31); Hebrew reads *Dara*. **2:7a** Hebrew *Achar;* compare Josh 7:1. *Achar* means "disaster." **2:7b** The Hebrew term used here refers to the complete consecration of things or people to the LORD, either by destroying them or by giving them as an offering. **2:9** Hebrew *Kelubai,* a variant spelling of Caleb; compare 2:18. **2:11** As in Greek version (see also Ruth 4:21); Hebrew reads *Salma*. **2:18** Or *Caleb had a daughter named Jerioth from his wife, Azubah.* The meaning of the Hebrew is uncertain. **2:19** Hebrew *Ephrath,* a variant spelling of Ephrathah; compare 2:50 and 4:4. **2:23** Or *captured Havvoth-jair.* **2:24** Or *the founder of;* also in 2:42, 45, 49.

KING JAMES VERSION

27 And the sons of Ram the firstborn of Jerahmeel
were, Maaz, and Jamin, and Eker.
28 And the sons of Onam were, Shammai, and Jada.
And the sons of Shammai; Nadab, and Abishur.
29 And the name of the wife of Abishur *was* Abihail, and she bare him Ahban, and Molid.
30 And the sons of Nadab; Seled, and Appaim: but
Seled died without children.
31 And the sons of Appaim; Ishi. And the sons of
Ishi; Sheshan. And the children of Sheshan; Ahlai.
32 And the sons of Jada the brother of Shammai; Jether, and Jonathan: and Jether died without children.
33 And the sons of Jonathan; Peleth, and Zaza.
These were the sons of Jerahmeel.
34 Now Sheshan had no sons, but daughters. And
Sheshan had a servant, an Egyptian, whose name *was*
Jarha.
35 And Sheshan gave his daughter to Jarha his servant to wife; and she bare him Attai.
36 And Attai begat Nathan, and Nathan begat Zabad,
37 And Zabad begat Ephlal, and Ephlal begat Obed,
38 And Obed begat Jehu, and Jehu begat Azariah,
39 And Azariah begat Helez, and Helez begat
Eleasah,
40 And Eleasah begat Sisamai, and Sisamai begat
Shallum,
41 And Shallum begat Jekamiah, and Jekamiah
begat Elishama.

42 Now the sons of Caleb the brother of Jerahmeel
were, Mesha his firstborn, which was the father
of Ziph; and the sons of Mareshah the father of
Hebron.
43 And the sons of Hebron; Korah, and Tappuah,
and Rekem, and Shema.
44 And Shema begat Raham, the father of Jorkoam:
and Rekem begat Shammai.
45 And the son of Shammai *was* Maon: and Maon
was the father of Beth-zur.
46 And Ephah, Caleb's concubine, bare Haran, and
Moza, and Gazez: and Haran begat Gazez.
47 And the sons of Jahdai; Regem, and Jotham, and
Gesham, and Pelet, and Ephah, and Shaaph.
48 Maachah, Caleb's concubine, bare Sheber, and
Tirhanah.
49 She bare also Shaaph the father of Madmannah,
Sheva the father of Machbenah, and the father of
Gibea: and the daughter of Caleb *was* Achsa.
50 These were the sons of Caleb the son of Hur, the

NEW LIVING TRANSLATION

27 The sons of Ram, the oldest son of Jerahmeel,
were Maaz, Jamin, and Eker.
28 The sons of Onam were Shammai and Jada.
The sons of Shammai were Nadab and Abishur.
29 The sons of Abishur and his wife Abihail were
Ahban and Molid.
30 The sons of Nadab were Seled and Appaim. Seled
died without children, 31 but Appaim had a son
named Ishi. The son of Ishi was Sheshan.
Sheshan had a descendant named Ahlai.
32 The sons of Jada, Shammai's brother, were Jether
and Jonathan. Jether died without children, 33 but
Jonathan had two sons named Peleth and Zaza.
These were all descendants of Jerahmeel.
34 Sheshan had no sons, though he did have
daughters. He also had an Egyptian servant
named Jarha. 35 Sheshan gave one of his
daughters to be the wife of Jarha, and they had
a son named Attai.
36 Attai was the father of Nathan.
Nathan was the father of Zabad.
37 Zabad was the father of Ephlal.
Ephlal was the father of Obed.
38 Obed was the father of Jehu.
Jehu was the father of Azariah.
39 Azariah was the father of Helez.
Helez was the father of Eleasah.
40 Eleasah was the father of Sismai.
Sismai was the father of Shallum.
41 Shallum was the father of Jekamiah.
Jekamiah was the father of Elishama.

Descendants of Hezron's Son Caleb

42 The descendants of Caleb, the brother of
Jerahmeel, included Mesha (the firstborn), who
became the father of Ziph. Caleb's descendants
also included the sons of Mareshah, the father
of Hebron.*
43 The sons of Hebron were Korah, Tappuah,
Rekem, and Shema. 44 Shema was the father
of Raham. Raham was the father of Jorkeam.
Rekem was the father of Shammai. 45 The son
of Shammai was Maon. Maon was the father
of Beth-zur.
46 Caleb's concubine Ephah gave birth to Haran,
Moza, and Gazez. Haran was the father of Gazez.
47 The sons of Jahdai were Regem, Jotham, Geshan,
Pelet, Ephah, and Shaaph.
48 Another of Caleb's concubines, Maacah, gave
birth to Sheber and Tirhanah. 49 She also gave
birth to Shaaph (the father of Madmannah)
and Sheva (the father of Macbenah and Gibea).
Caleb also had a daughter named Acsah.
50 These were all descendants of Caleb.

2:42 Or *who founded Hebron.* The meaning of the Hebrew is uncertain.

KING JAMES VERSION

firstborn of Ephratah; Shobal the father of Kirjath-
jearim,
51 Salma the father of Bethlehem, Hareph the father of Beth-gader.
52 And Shobal the father of Kirjath-jearim had
sons; Haroeh, *and* half of the Manahethites.
53 And the families of Kirjath-jearim; the Ithrites,
and the Puhites, and the Shumathites, and the Mishraites; of them came the Zareathites, and the Esh-
taulites.
54 The sons of Salma; Bethlehem, and the Netophathites, Ataroth, the house of Joab, and half of the
Manahethites, the Zorites.
55 And the families of the scribes which dwelt at
Jabez; the Tirathites, the Shimeathites, *and* Suchath-
ites. These *are* the Kenites that came of Hemath, the
father of the house of Rechab.

3 1 Now these were the sons of David, which were
born unto him in Hebron; the firstborn Amnon, of Ahinoam the Jezreelitess; the second Daniel,
of Abigail the Carmelitess:
2 The third, Absalom the son of Maachah the
daughter of Talmai king of Geshur: the fourth,
Adonijah the son of Haggith:
3 The fifth, Shephatiah of Abital: the sixth, Ithream
by Eglah his wife.
4 *These* six were born unto him in Hebron; and
there he reigned seven years and six months: and in
Jerusalem he reigned thirty and three years.
5 And these were born unto him in Jerusalem;
Shimea, and Shobab, and Nathan, and Solomon, four,
of Bath-shua the daughter of Ammiel:
6 Ibhar also, and Elishama, and Eliphelet,
7 And Nogah, and Nepheg, and Japhia,
8 And Elishama, and Eliada, and Eliphelet, nine.
9 *These were* all the sons of David, beside the sons
of the concubines, and Tamar their sister.

10 And Solomon's son *was* Rehoboam, Abia his son,
Asa his son, Jehoshaphat his son,
11 Joram his son, Ahaziah his son, Joash his son,
12 Amaziah his son, Azariah his son, Jotham his
son,
13 Ahaz his son, Hezekiah his son, Manasseh his
son,
14 Amon his son, Josiah his son.

NEW LIVING TRANSLATION

Descendants of Caleb's Son Hur

The sons of Hur, the oldest son of Caleb's wife
Ephrathah, were Shobal (the founder of Kiriath-
jearim), 51 Salma (the founder of Bethlehem),
and Hareph (the founder of Beth-gader).
52 The descendants of Shobal (the founder
of Kiriath-jearim) were Haroeh, half the
Manahathites, 53 and the families of Kiriath-
jearim—the Ithrites, Puthites, Shumathites,
and Mishraites, from whom came the people
of Zorah and Eshtaol.
54 The descendants of Salma were the people of
Bethlehem, the Netophathites, Atroth-beth-joab,
the other half of the Manahathites, the Zorites,
55 and the families of scribes living at Jabez—the
Tirathites, Shimeathites, and Sucathites. All these
were Kenites who descended from Hammath, the
father of the family of Recab.*

Descendants of David

3 These are the sons of David who were born in
Hebron:

The oldest was Amnon, whose mother was
Ahinoam from Jezreel.
The second was Daniel, whose mother was
Abigail from Carmel.
2 The third was Absalom, whose mother was
Maacah, the daughter of Talmai, king of Geshur.
The fourth was Adonijah, whose mother was
Haggith.
3 The fifth was Shephatiah, whose mother was
Abital.
The sixth was Ithream, whose mother was Eglah,
David's wife.
4 These six sons were born to David in Hebron, where
he reigned seven and a half years.

Then David reigned another thirty-three years in
Jerusalem. 5 The sons born to David in Jerusalem
included Shammua,* Shobab, Nathan, and Solomon.
Their mother was Bathsheba,* the daughter of Ammiel. 6 David also had nine other sons: Ibhar, Elishua,*
Elpelet,* 7 Nogah, Nepheg, Japhia, 8 Elishama, Eliada,
and Eliphelet.
9 These were the sons of David, not including his
sons born to his concubines. Their sister was named
Tamar.

Descendants of Solomon

10 The descendants of Solomon were Rehoboam,
Abijah, Asa, Jehoshaphat, 11 Jehoram,* Ahaziah,
Joash, 12 Amaziah, Uzziah,* Jotham, 13 Ahaz,
Hezekiah, Manasseh, 14 Amon, and Josiah.

2:55 Or *the founder of Beth-recab.* **3:5a** As in Syriac version (see also 14:4; 2 Sam 5:14); Hebrew reads *Shimea.* **3:5b** Hebrew *Bathshua,* a variant spelling of Bathsheba. **3:6a** As in some Hebrew and Greek manuscripts (see also 14:5-7 and 2 Sam 5:15); most Hebrew manuscripts read *Elishama.* **3:6b** Hebrew *Eliphelet;* compare parallel text at 14:5-7. **3:11** Hebrew *Joram,* a variant spelling of Jehoram. **3:12** Hebrew *Azariah,* a variant spelling of Uzziah.

KING JAMES VERSION

15 And the sons of Josiah *were*, the firstborn Johanan, the second Jehoiakim, the third Zedekiah, the
fourth Shallum.
16 And the sons of Jehoiakim: Jeconiah his son,
Zedekiah his son.

17 And the sons of Jeconiah; Assir, Salathiel his son,
18 Malchiram also, and Pedaiah, and Shenazar,
Jecamiah, Hoshama, and Nedabiah.
19 And the sons of Pedaiah *were*, Zerubbabel, and
Shimei: and the sons of Zerubbabel; Meshullam,
and Hananiah, and Shelomith their sister:
20 And Hashubah, and Ohel, and Berechiah, and
Hasadiah, Jushab-hesed, five.
21 And the sons of Hananiah; Pelatiah, and Jesaiah:
the sons of Rephaiah, the sons of Arnan, the sons of
Obadiah, the sons of Shechaniah.
22 And the sons of Shechaniah; Shemaiah: and the
sons of Shemaiah; Hattush, and Igeal, and Bariah,
and Neariah, and Shaphat, six.
23 And the sons of Neariah; Elioenai, and Hezekiah,
and Azrikam, three.
24 And the sons of Elioenai *were*, Hodaiah, and
Eliashib, and Pelaiah, and Akkub, and Johanan, and
Dalaiah, and Anani, seven.

4 1 The sons of Judah; Pharez, Hezron, and Carmi,
and Hur, and Shobal.
2 And Reaiah the son of Shobal begat Jahath; and
Jahath begat Ahumai, and Lahad. These *are* the families of the Zorathites.
3 And these *were of* the father of Etam; Jezreel, and
Ishma, and Idbash: and the name of their sister *was*
Hazelelponi:
4 And Penuel the father of Gedor, and Ezer the father of Hushah. These *are* the sons of Hur, the firstborn of Ephratah, the father of Bethlehem.
5 And Ashur the father of Tekoa had two wives,
Helah and Naarah.
6 And Naarah bare him Ahuzam, and Hepher, and
Temeni, and Haahashtari. These *were* the sons of
Naarah.
7 And the sons of Helah *were*, Zereth, and Jezoar,
and Ethnan.
8 And Coz begat Anub, and Zobebah, and the families of Aharhel the son of Harum.
9 And Jabez was more honourable than his brethren: and his mother called his name Jabez, saying,
Because I bare him with sorrow.
10 And Jabez called on the God of Israel, saying, Oh
that thou wouldest bless me indeed, and enlarge my
coast, and that thine hand might be with me, and
that thou wouldest keep *me* from evil, that it may not

NEW LIVING TRANSLATION

15 The sons of Josiah were Johanan (the oldest),
Jehoiakim (the second), Zedekiah (the third),
and Jehoahaz* (the fourth).
16 The successors of Jehoiakim were his son
Jehoiachin and his brother Zedekiah.*

Descendants of Jehoiachin

17 The sons of Jehoiachin,* who was taken prisoner
by the Babylonians, were Shealtiel, 18 Malkiram,
Pedaiah, Shenazzar, Jekamiah, Hoshama, and
Nedabiah.
19 The sons of Pedaiah were Zerubbabel and Shimei.
The sons of Zerubbabel were Meshullam and
Hananiah. (Their sister was Shelomith.) 20 His
five other sons were Hashubah, Ohel, Berekiah,
Hasadiah, and Jushab-hesed.
21 The sons of Hananiah were Pelatiah and Jeshaiah.
Jeshaiah's son was Rephaiah. Rephaiah's son was
Arnan. Arnan's son was Obadiah. Obadiah's son
was Shecaniah.
22 The descendants of Shecaniah were Shemaiah
and his sons, Hattush, Igal, Bariah, Neariah, and
Shaphat—six in all.
23 The sons of Neariah were Elioenai, Hizkiah, and
Azrikam—three in all.
24 The sons of Elioenai were Hodaviah, Eliashib,
Pelaiah, Akkub, Johanan, Delaiah, and Anani—
seven in all.

Other Descendants of Judah

4 The descendants of Judah were Perez, Hezron,
Carmi, Hur, and Shobal.
2 Shobal's son Reaiah was the father of Jahath.
Jahath was the father of Ahumai and Lahad.
These were the families of the Zorathites.
3 The descendants of* Etam were Jezreel, Ishma,
Idbash, their sister Hazzelelponi, 4 Penuel (the
father of* Gedor), and Ezer (the father of Hushah).
These were the descendants of Hur (the firstborn
of Ephrathah), the ancestor of Bethlehem.
5 Ashhur (the father of Tekoa) had two wives,
named Helah and Naarah. 6 Naarah gave birth
to Ahuzzam, Hepher, Temeni, and Haahashtari.
7 Helah gave birth to Zereth, Izhar,* Ethnan, 8 and
Koz, who became the ancestor of Anub, Zobebah,
and all the families of Aharhel son of Harum.
9 There was a man named Jabez who was more
honorable than any of his brothers. His mother
named him Jabez* because his birth had been
so painful. 10 He was the one who prayed to the
God of Israel, "Oh, that you would bless me and
expand my territory! Please be with me in all that

3:15 Hebrew *Shallum*, another name for Jehoahaz. **3:16** Hebrew *The sons of Jehoiakim were his son Jeconiah* [a variant spelling of Jehoiachin] *and his son Zedekiah*. **3:17** Hebrew *Jeconiah*, a variant spelling of Jehoiachin. **4:3** As in Greek version; Hebrew reads *father of*. The meaning of the Hebrew is uncertain. **4:4** Or *the founder of*; also in 4:5, 12, 14, 17, 18, and perhaps other instances where the text reads *the father of*. **4:7** As in an alternate reading in the Masoretic Text (see also Latin Vulgate); the other alternate and the Greek version read *Zohar*. **4:9** *Jabez* sounds like a Hebrew word meaning "distress" or "pain."

KING JAMES VERSION

grieve me! And God granted him that which he
requested.
11 And Chelub the brother of Shuah begat Mehir,
which *was* the father of Eshton.
12 And Eshton begat Beth-rapha, and Paseah, and
Tehinnah the father of Ir-nahash. These *are* the men
of Recah.
13 And the sons of Kenaz; Othniel, and Seraiah: and
the sons of Othniel; Hathath.
14 And Meonothai begat Ophrah: and Seraiah
begat Joab, the father of the valley of Charashim; for
they were craftsmen.
15 And the sons of Caleb the son of Jephunneh; Iru,
Elah, and Naam: and the sons of Elah, even Kenaz.
16 And the sons of Jehaleleel; Ziph, and Ziphah,
Tiria, and Asareel.
17 And the sons of Ezra *were,* Jether, and Mered,
and Epher, and Jalon: and she bare Miriam, and
Shammai, and Ishbah the father of Eshtemoa.
18 And his wife Jehudijah bare Jered the father of
Gedor, and Heber the father of Socho, and Jekuthiel
the father of Zanoah. And these *are* the sons of Bithi-
ah the daughter of Pharaoh, which Mered took.
19 And the sons of *his* wife Hodiah the sister of Naham, the father of Keilah the Garmite, and Eshtemoa
the Maachathite.
20 And the sons of Shimon *were,* Amnon, and Rinnah, Ben-hanan, and Tilon. And the sons of Ishi
were, Zoheth, and Ben-zoheth.

21 The sons of Shelah the son of Judah *were,* Er the
father of Lecah, and Laadah the father of Mareshah,
and the families of the house of them that wrought
fine linen, of the house of Ashbea,
22 And Jokim, and the men of Chozeba, and Joash,
and Saraph, who had the dominion in Moab, and
Jashubi-lehem. And *these are* ancient things.
23 These *were* the potters, and those that dwelt
among plants and hedges: there they dwelt with the
king for his work.

24 The sons of Simeon *were,* Nemuel, and Jamin,
Jarib, Zerah, *and* Shaul:
25 Shallum his son, Mibsam his son, Mishma his
son.
26 And the sons of Mishma; Hamuel his son,
Zacchur his son, Shimei his son.
27 And Shimei had sixteen sons and six daughters;
but his brethren had not many children, neither did
all their family multiply, like to the children of Judah.

NEW LIVING TRANSLATION

I do, and keep me from all trouble and pain!"
And God granted him his request.
11 Kelub (the brother of Shuhah) was the father
of Mehir. Mehir was the father of Eshton.
12 Eshton was the father of Beth-rapha, Paseah,
and Tehinnah. Tehinnah was the father of Ir-
nahash. These were the descendants of Recah.
13 The sons of Kenaz were Othniel and Seraiah.
Othniel's sons were Hathath and Meonothai.*
14 Meonothai was the father of Ophrah. Seraiah
was the father of Joab, the founder of the Valley
of Craftsmen,* so called because they were
craftsmen.
15 The sons of Caleb son of Jephunneh were Iru,
Elah, and Naam. The son of Elah was Kenaz.
16 The sons of Jehallelel were Ziph, Ziphah, Tiria,
and Asarel.
17 The sons of Ezrah were Jether, Mered, Epher, and
Jalon. One of Mered's wives became* the mother
of Miriam, Shammai, and Ishbah (the father of
Eshtemoa). 18 He married a woman from Judah,
who became the mother of Jered (the father of
Gedor), Heber (the father of Soco), and Jekuthiel
(the father of Zanoah). Mered also married Bithia,
a daughter of Pharaoh, and she bore him children.
19 Hodiah's wife was the sister of Naham. One of
her sons was the father of Keilah the Garmite,
and another was the father of Eshtemoa the
Maacathite.
20 The sons of Shimon were Amnon, Rinnah,
Ben-hanan, and Tilon.
The descendants of Ishi were Zoheth and Ben-zoheth.

Descendants of Judah's Son Shelah

21 Shelah was one of Judah's sons. The descendants
of Shelah were Er (the father of Lecah); Laadah
(the father of Mareshah); the families of linen
workers at Beth-ashbea; 22 Jokim; the men of
Cozeba; and Joash and Saraph, who ruled over
Moab and Jashubi-lehem. These names all come
from ancient records. 23 They were the pottery
makers who lived in Netaim and Gederah.
They lived there and worked for the king.

Descendants of Simeon

24 The sons of Simeon were Jemuel,* Jamin, Jarib,
Zohar,* and Shaul.
25 The descendants of Shaul were Shallum, Mibsam,
and Mishma.
26 The descendants of Mishma were Hammuel,
Zaccur, and Shimei.
27 Shimei had sixteen sons and six daughters, but
none of his brothers had large families. So Simeon's
tribe never grew as large as the tribe of Judah.

4:13 As in some Greek manuscripts and Latin Vulgate; Hebrew lacks *and Meonothai.* **4:14** Or *Joab, the father of Ge-harashim.* **4:17** Or *Jether's wife became;* Hebrew reads *She became.* **4:24a** As in Syriac version (see also Gen 46:10; Exod 6:15); Hebrew reads *Nemuel.* **4:24b** As in parallel texts at Gen 46:10 and Exod 6:15; Hebrew reads *Zerah.*

KING JAMES VERSION

28And they dwelt at Beer-sheba, and Moladah, and
Hazar-shual,
29And at Bilhah, and at Ezem, and at Tolad,
30And at Bethuel, and at Hormah, and at Ziklag,
31And at Beth-marcaboth, and Hazar-susim, and at
Beth-birei, and at Shaaraim. These *were* their cities
unto the reign of David.
32And their villages *were,* Etam, and Ain, Rimmon,
and Tochen, and Ashan, five cities:
33And all their villages that *were* round about the
same cities, unto Baal. These *were* their habitations,
and their genealogy.
34And Meshobab, and Jamlech, and Joshah, the
son of Amaziah,
35And Joel, and Jehu the son of Josibiah, the son of
Seraiah, the son of Asiel,
36And Elioenai, and Jaakobah, and Jeshohaiah,
and Asaiah, and Adiel, and Jesimiel, and Benaiah,
37And Ziza the son of Shiphi, the son of Allon, the
son of Jedaiah, the son of Shimri, the son of Shemaiah;
38These mentioned by *their* names *were* princes
in their families: and the house of their fathers increased greatly.
39And they went to the entrance of Gedor, *even*
unto the east side of the valley, to seek pasture for
their flocks.
40And they found fat pasture and good, and the
land *was* wide, and quiet, and peaceable; for *they* of
Ham had dwelt there of old.
41And these written by name came in the days of
Hezekiah king of Judah, and smote their tents, and
the habitations that were found there, and destroyed
them utterly unto this day, and dwelt in their rooms:
because *there was* pasture there for their flocks.
42And *some* of them, *even* of the sons of Simeon,
five hundred men, went to mount Seir, having for
their captains Pelatiah, and Neariah, and Rephaiah,
and Uzziel, the sons of Ishi.
43And they smote the rest of the Amalekites that
were escaped, and dwelt there unto this day.

5 1Now the sons of Reuben the firstborn of Israel,
(for he *was* the firstborn; but, forasmuch as he
defiled his father's bed, his birthright was given unto
the sons of Joseph the son of Israel: and the genealogy is not to be reckoned after the birthright.
2For Judah prevailed above his brethren, and of
him *came* the chief ruler; but the birthright *was*
Joseph's:)
3The sons, *I say,* of Reuben the firstborn of Israel
were, Hanoch, and Pallu, Hezron, and Carmi.
4The sons of Joel; Shemaiah his son, Gog his son,
Shimei his son,
5Micah his son, Reaia his son, Baal his son,
6Beerah his son, whom Tilgath-pilneser king of

NEW LIVING TRANSLATION

28They lived in Beersheba, Moladah, Hazar-shual,
29Bilhah, Ezem, Tolad, 30Bethuel, Hormah, Ziklag,
31Beth-marcaboth, Hazar-susim, Beth-biri, and
Shaaraim. These towns were under their control
until the time of King David. 32Their descendants
also lived in Etam, Ain, Rimmon, Token, and
Ashan—five towns 33and their surrounding
villages as far away as Baalath.* This was their
territory, and these names are listed in their
genealogical records.
34Other descendants of Simeon included
Meshobab, Jamlech, Joshah son of Amaziah,
35Joel, Jehu son of Joshibiah, son of Seraiah,
son of Asiel, 36Elioenai, Jaakobah, Jeshohaiah,
Asaiah, Adiel, Jesimiel, Benaiah, 37and Ziza son
of Shiphi, son of Allon, son of Jedaiah, son of
Shimri, son of Shemaiah.

38These were the names of some of the leaders of
Simeon's wealthy clans. Their families grew, 39and
they traveled to the region of Gerar,* in the east part
of the valley, seeking pastureland for their flocks.
40They found lush pastures there, and the land was
quiet and peaceful.
Some of Ham's descendants had been living in
that region. 41But during the reign of King Hezekiah
of Judah, these leaders of Simeon invaded the region
and completely destroyed* the homes of the descendants of Ham and of the Meunites. No trace of them
remains today. They killed everyone who lived there
and took the land for themselves, because they
wanted its good pastureland for their flocks. 42Five
hundred of these invaders from the tribe of Simeon
went to Mount Seir, led by Pelatiah, Neariah, Rephaiah, and Uzziel—all sons of Ishi. 43They destroyed
the few Amalekites who had survived, and they have
lived there ever since.

Descendants of Reuben

5 The oldest son of Israel* was Reuben. But since
he dishonored his father by sleeping with one
of his father's concubines, his birthright was given to
the sons of his brother Joseph. For this reason, Reuben is not listed in the genealogical records as the
firstborn son. 2The descendants of Judah became
the most powerful tribe and provided a ruler for the
nation,* but the birthright belonged to Joseph.
3The sons of Reuben, the oldest son of Israel, were
Hanoch, Pallu, Hezron, and Carmi.
4The descendants of Joel were Shemaiah, Gog,
Shimei, 5Micah, Reaiah, Baal, 6and Beerah. Beerah
was the leader of the Reubenites when they were

4:33 As in some Greek manuscripts (see also Josh 19:8); Hebrew reads *Baal.* **4:39** As in Greek version; Hebrew reads *Gedor.* **4:41** The Hebrew term used here refers to the complete consecration of things or people to the LORD, either by destroying them or by giving them as an offering. **5:1** *Israel* is the name that God gave to Jacob. **5:2** Or *and from Judah came a prince.*

KING JAMES VERSION

Assyria carried away *captive:* he *was* prince of the Reubenites.

7 And his brethren by their families, when the genealogy of their generations was reckoned, *were* the chief, Jeiel, and Zechariah,

8 And Bela the son of Azaz, the son of Shema, the son of Joel, who dwelt in Aroer, even unto Nebo and Baal-meon:

9 And eastward he inhabited unto the entering in of the wilderness from the river Euphrates: because their cattle were multiplied in the land of Gilead.

10 And in the days of Saul they made war with the Hagarites, who fell by their hand: and they dwelt in their tents throughout all the east *land* of Gilead.

11 And the children of Gad dwelt over against them, in the land of Bashan unto Salcah:

12 Joel the chief, and Shapham the next, and Jaanai, and Shaphat in Bashan.

13 And their brethren of the house of their fathers *were,* Michael, and Meshullam, and Sheba, and Jorai, and Jachan, and Zia, and Heber, seven.

14 These *are* the children of Abihail the son of Huri, the son of Jaroah, the son of Gilead, the son of Michael, the son of Jeshishai, the son of Jahdo, the son of Buz;

15 Ahi the son of Abdiel, the son of Guni, chief of the house of their fathers.

16 And they dwelt in Gilead in Bashan, and in her towns, and in all the suburbs of Sharon, upon their borders.

17 All these were reckoned by genealogies in the days of Jotham king of Judah, and in the days of Jeroboam king of Israel.

18 The sons of Reuben, and the Gadites, and half the tribe of Manasseh, of valiant men, men able to bear buckler and sword, and to shoot with bow, and skilful in war, *were* four and forty thousand seven hundred and threescore, that went out to the war.

19 And they made war with the Hagarites, with Jetur, and Nephish, and Nodab.

20 And they were helped against them, and the Hagarites were delivered into their hand, and all that *were* with them: for they cried to God in the battle, and he was intreated of them; because they put their trust in him.

21 And they took away their cattle; of their camels fifty thousand, and of sheep two hundred and fifty thousand, and of asses two thousand, and of men an hundred thousand.

22 For there fell down many slain, because the war *was* of God. And they dwelt in their steads until the captivity.

23 And the children of the half tribe of Manasseh dwelt in the land: they increased from Bashan unto Baal-hermon and Senir, and unto mount Hermon.

NEW LIVING TRANSLATION

taken into captivity by King Tiglath-pileser* of Assyria.

7 Beerah's* relatives are listed in their genealogical records by their clans: Jeiel (the leader), Zechariah,

8 and Bela son of Azaz, son of Shema, son of Joel.

The Reubenites lived in the area that stretches from Aroer to Nebo and Baal-meon. 9 And since they had so many livestock in the land of Gilead, they spread east toward the edge of the desert that stretches to the Euphrates River.

10 During the reign of Saul, the Reubenites defeated the Hagrites in battle. Then they moved into the Hagrite settlements all along the eastern edge of Gilead.

Descendants of Gad

11 Next to the Reubenites, the descendants of Gad lived in the land of Bashan as far east as Salecah.

12 Joel was the leader in the land of Bashan, and Shapham was second-in-command, followed by Janai and Shaphat.

13 Their relatives, the leaders of seven other clans, were Michael, Meshullam, Sheba, Jorai, Jacan, Zia, and Eber. 14 These were all descendants of Abihail son of Huri, son of Jaroah, son of Gilead, son of Michael, son of Jeshishai, son of Jahdo, son of Buz. 15 Ahi son of Abdiel, son of Guni, was the leader of their clans.

16 The Gadite lived in the land of Gilead, in Bashan and its villages, and throughout all the pasturelands of Sharon. 17 All of these were listed in the genealogical records during the days of King Jotham of Judah and King Jeroboam of Israel.

The Tribes East of the Jordan

18 There were 44,760 capable warriors in the armies of Reuben, Gad, and the half-tribe of Manasseh. They were all skilled in combat and armed with shields, swords, and bows. 19 They waged war against the Hagrites, the Jeturites, the Naphishites, and the Nodabites. 20 They cried out to God during the battle, and he answered their prayer because they trusted in him. So the Hagrites and all their allies were defeated. 21 The plunder taken from the Hagrites included 50,000 camels, 250,000 sheep and goats, 2,000 donkeys, and 100,000 captives. 22 Many of the Hagrites were killed in the battle because God was fighting against them. The people of Reuben, Gad, and Manasseh lived in their land until they were taken into exile.

23 The half-tribe of Manasseh was very large and spread through the land from Bashan to Baal-hermon,

5:6 Hebrew *Tilgath-pilneser,* a variant spelling of Tiglath-pileser; also in 5:26.
5:7 Hebrew *His.*

KING JAMES VERSION

24 And these *were* the heads of the house of their fathers, even Epher, and Ishi, and Eliel, and Azriel, and Jeremiah, and Hodaviah, and Jahdiel, mighty men of valour, famous men, *and* heads of the house of their fathers.

25 And they transgressed against the God of their fathers, and went a whoring after the gods of the people of the land, whom God destroyed before them.

26 And the God of Israel stirred up the spirit of Pul king of Assyria, and the spirit of Tilgath-pilneser king of Assyria, and he carried them away, even the Reubenites, and the Gadites, and the half tribe of Manasseh, and brought them unto Halah, and Habor, and Hara, and to the river Gozan, unto this day.

6 1 The sons of Levi; Gershon, Kohath, and Merari. 2 And the sons of Kohath; Amram, Izhar, and Hebron, and Uzziel.

3 And the children of Amram; Aaron, and Moses, and Miriam. The sons also of Aaron; Nadab, and Abihu, Eleazar, and Ithamar.

4 Eleazar begat Phinehas, Phinehas begat Abishua,

5 And Abishua begat Bukki, and Bukki begat Uzzi,

6 And Uzzi begat Zerahiah, and Zerahiah begat Meraioth,

7 Meraioth begat Amariah, and Amariah begat Ahitub,

8 And Ahitub begat Zadok, and Zadok begat Ahimaaz,

9 And Ahimaaz begat Azariah, and Azariah begat Johanan,

10 And Johanan begat Azariah, (he *it is* that executed the priest's office in the temple that Solomon built in Jerusalem:)

11 And Azariah begat Amariah, and Amariah begat Ahitub,

12 And Ahitub begat Zadok, and Zadok begat Shallum,

13 And Shallum begat Hilkiah, and Hilkiah begat Azariah,

14 And Azariah begat Seraiah, and Seraiah begat Jehozadak,

15 And Jehozadak went *into captivity,* when the LORD carried away Judah and Jerusalem by the hand of Nebuchadnezzar.

16 The sons of Levi; Gershom, Kohath, and Merari.

17 And these *be* the names of the sons of Gershom; Libni, and Shimei.

NEW LIVING TRANSLATION

Senir, and Mount Hermon. 24 These were the leaders of their clans: Epher,* Ishi, Eliel, Azriel, Jeremiah, Hodaviah, and Jahdiel. These men had a great reputation as mighty warriors and leaders of their clans.

25 But these tribes were unfaithful to the God of their ancestors. They worshiped the gods of the nations that God had destroyed. 26 So the God of Israel caused King Pul of Assyria (also known as Tiglath-pileser) to invade the land and take away the people of Reuben, Gad, and the half-tribe of Manasseh as captives. The Assyrians exiled them to Halah, Habor, Hara, and the Gozan River, where they remain to this day.

The Priestly Line

6 1* The sons of Levi were Gershon, Kohath, and Merari.

2 The descendants of Kohath included Amram, Izhar, Hebron, and Uzziel.

3 The children of Amram were Aaron, Moses, and Miriam.

The sons of Aaron were Nadab, Abihu, Eleazar, and Ithamar.

4 Eleazar was the father of Phinehas.
Phinehas was the father of Abishua.
5 Abishua was the father of Bukki.
Bukki was the father of Uzzi.
6 Uzzi was the father of Zerahiah.
Zerahiah was the father of Meraioth.
7 Meraioth was the father of Amariah.
Amariah was the father of Ahitub.
8 Ahitub was the father of Zadok.
Zadok was the father of Ahimaaz.
9 Ahimaaz was the father of Azariah.
Azariah was the father of Johanan.
10 Johanan was the father of Azariah, the high priest at the Temple* built by Solomon in Jerusalem.
11 Azariah was the father of Amariah.
Amariah was the father of Ahitub.
12 Ahitub was the father of Zadok.
Zadok was the father of Shallum.
13 Shallum was the father of Hilkiah.
Hilkiah was the father of Azariah.
14 Azariah was the father of Seraiah.
Seraiah was the father of Jehozadak, 15 who went into exile when the LORD sent the people of Judah and Jerusalem into captivity under Nebuchadnezzar.

The Levite Clans

16* The sons of Levi were Gershon,* Kohath, and Merari.

17 The descendants of Gershon included Libni and Shimei.

5:24 As in Greek version and Latin Vulgate; Hebrew reads *and Epher.* **6:1** Verses 6:1-15 are numbered 5:27-41 in Hebrew text. **6:10** Hebrew *the house.* **6:16a** Verses 6:16-81 are numbered 6:1-66 in Hebrew text. **6:16b** Hebrew *Gershom,* a variant spelling of Gershon (see 6:1); also in 6:17, 20, 43, 62, 71.

KING JAMES VERSION

18 And the sons of Kohath *were*, Amram, and Izhar, and Hebron, and Uzziel.

19 The sons of Merari; Mahli, and Mushi. And these *are* the families of the Levites according to their fathers.

20 Of Gershom; Libni his son, Jahath his son, Zimmah his son,

21 Joah his son, Iddo his son, Zerah his son, Jeaterai his son.

22 The sons of Kohath; Amminadab his son, Korah his son, Assir his son,

23 Elkanah his son, and Ebiasaph his son, and Assir his son,

24 Tahath his son, Uriel his son, Uzziah his son, and Shaul his son.

25 And the sons of Elkanah; Amasai, and Ahimoth.

26 *As for* Elkanah: the sons of Elkanah; Zophai his son, and Nahath his son,

27 Eliab his son, Jeroham his son, Elkanah his son.

28 And the sons of Samuel; the firstborn Vashni, and Abiah.

29 The sons of Merari; Mahli, Libni his son, Shimei his son, Uzza his son,

30 Shimea his son, Haggiah his son, Asaiah his son.

31 And these *are they* whom David set over the service of song in the house of the LORD, after that the ark had rest.

32 And they ministered before the dwelling place of the tabernacle of the congregation with singing, until Solomon had built the house of the LORD in Jerusalem: and *then* they waited on their office according to their order.

33 And these *are* they that waited with their children. Of the sons of the Kohathites: Heman a singer, the son of Joel, the son of Shemuel,

34 The son of Elkanah, the son of Jeroham, the son of Eliel, the son of Toah,

35 The son of Zuph, the son of Elkanah, the son of Mahath, the son of Amasai,

36 The son of Elkanah, the son of Joel, the son of Azariah, the son of Zephaniah,

37 The son of Tahath, the son of Assir, the son of Ebiasaph, the son of Korah,

38 The son of Izhar, the son of Kohath, the son of Levi, the son of Israel.

39 And his brother Asaph, who stood on his right hand, *even* Asaph the son of Berachiah, the son of Shimea,

40 The son of Michael, the son of Baaseiah, the son of Malchiah,

41 The son of Ethni, the son of Zerah, the son of Adaiah,

42 The son of Ethan, the son of Zimmah, the son of Shimei,

43 The son of Jahath, the son of Gershom, the son of Levi.

44 And their brethren the sons of Merari *stood* on

NEW LIVING TRANSLATION

18 The descendants of Kohath included Amram,
Izhar, Hebron, and Uzziel.
19 The descendants of Merari included Mahli and
Mushi.

The following were the Levite clans, listed according to their ancestral descent:

20 The descendants of Gershon included Libni,
Jahath, Zimmah, 21 Joah, Iddo, Zerah, and
Jeatherai.
22 The descendants of Kohath included
Amminadab, Korah, Assir, 23 Elkanah, Abiasaph,*
Assir, 24 Tahath, Uriel, Uzziah, and Shaul.
25 The descendants of Elkanah included Amasai,
Ahimoth, 26 Elkanah, Zophai, Nahath, 27 Eliab,
Jeroham, Elkanah, and Samuel.*
28 The sons of Samuel were Joel* (the older) and
Abijah (the second).
29 The descendants of Merari included Mahli, Libni,
Shimei, Uzzah, 30 Shimea, Haggiah, and Asaiah.

The Temple Musicians

31 David assigned the following men to lead the music
at the house of the LORD after the Ark was placed
there. 32 They ministered with music at the Tabernacle* until Solomon built the Temple of the LORD in
Jerusalem. They carried out their work, following all
the regulations handed down to them. 33 These are
the men who served, along with their sons:

Heman the musician was from the clan of Kohath.
His genealogy was traced back through Joel,
Samuel, 34 Elkanah, Jeroham, Eliel, Toah, 35 Zuph,
Elkanah, Mahath, Amasai, 36 Elkanah, Joel,
Azariah, Zephaniah, 37 Tahath, Assir, Abiasaph,
Korah, 38 Izhar, Kohath, Levi, and Israel.*
39 Heman's first assistant was Asaph from the clan
of Gershon.* Asaph's genealogy was traced back
through Berekiah, Shimea, 40 Michael, Baaseiah,
Malkijah, 41 Ethni, Zerah, Adaiah, 42 Ethan,
Zimmah, Shimei, 43 Jahath, Gershon, and Levi.
44 Heman's second assistant was Ethan from the

6:23 Hebrew *Ebiasaph*, a variant spelling of Abiasaph (also in 6:37); compare parallel text at Exod 6:24. **6:27** As in some Greek manuscripts (see also 6:33-34); Hebrew lacks *and Samuel*. **6:28** As in some Greek manuscripts and the Syriac version (see also 6:33 and 1 Sam 8:2); Hebrew lacks *Joel*. **6:32** Hebrew *the Tabernacle, the Tent of Meeting*. **6:38** *Israel* is the name that God gave to Jacob. **6:39** Hebrew lacks *from the clan of Gershon*; see 6:43.

the left hand: Ethan the son of Kishi, the son of Abdi, the son of Malluch,

45 The son of Hashabiah, the son of Amaziah, the son of Hilkiah,

46 The son of Amzi, the son of Bani, the son of Shamer,

47 The son of Mahli, the son of Mushi, the son of Merari, the son of Levi.

48 Their brethren also the Levites *were* appointed unto all manner of service of the tabernacle of the house of God.

49 But Aaron and his sons offered upon the altar of the burnt offering, and on the altar of incense, *and were appointed* for all the work of the *place* most holy, and to make an atonement for Israel, according to all that Moses the servant of God had commanded.

50 And these *are* the sons of Aaron; Eleazar his son, Phinehas his son, Abishua his son,

51 Bukki his son, Uzzi his son, Zerahiah his son,

52 Meraioth his son, Amariah his son, Ahitub his son,

53 Zadok his son, Ahimaaz his son.

54 Now these *are* their dwelling places throughout their castles in their coasts, of the sons of Aaron, of the families of the Kohathites: for theirs was the lot.

55 And they gave them Hebron in the land of Judah, and the suburbs thereof round about it.

56 But the fields of the city, and the villages thereof, they gave to Caleb the son of Jephunneh.

57 And to the sons of Aaron they gave the cities of Judah, *namely,* Hebron, *the city* of refuge, and Libnah with her suburbs, and Jattir, and Eshtemoa, with their suburbs,

58 And Hilen with her suburbs, Debir with her suburbs,

59 And Ashan with her suburbs, and Beth-shemesh with her suburbs:

60 And out of the tribe of Benjamin; Geba with her suburbs, and Alemeth with her suburbs, and Anathoth with her suburbs. All their cities throughout their families *were* thirteen cities.

61 And unto the sons of Kohath, *which were* left of the family of that tribe, *were cities given* out of the half tribe, *namely, out of* the half *tribe* of Manasseh, by lot, ten cities.

62 And to the sons of Gershom throughout their families out of the tribe of Issachar, and out of the tribe of Asher, and out of the tribe of Naphtali, and out of the tribe of Manasseh in Bashan, thirteen cities.

63 Unto the sons of Merari *were given* by lot, throughout their families, out of the tribe of Reuben, and out of the tribe of Gad, and out of the tribe of Zebulun, twelve cities.

64 And the children of Israel gave to the Levites *these* cities with their suburbs.

65 And they gave by lot out of the tribe of the

clan of Merari. Ethan's genealogy was traced back
through Kishi, Abdi, Malluch, 45 Hashabiah,
Amaziah, Hilkiah, 46 Amzi, Bani, Shemer, 47 Mahli,
Mushi, Merari, and Levi.

48 Their fellow Levites were appointed to various other tasks in the Tabernacle, the house of God.

Aaron's Descendants

49 Only Aaron and his descendants served as priests. They presented the offerings on the altar of burnt offering and the altar of incense, and they performed all the other duties related to the Most Holy Place. They made atonement for Israel by doing everything that Moses, the servant of God, had commanded them.

50 The descendants of Aaron were Eleazar, Phinehas,
Abishua, 51 Bukki, Uzzi, Zerahiah, 52 Meraioth,
Amariah, Ahitub, 53 Zadok, and Ahimaaz.

Territory for the Levites

54 This is a record of the towns and territory assigned
by means of sacred lots to the descendants of Aaron,
who were from the clan of Kohath. 55 This territory
included Hebron and its surrounding pasturelands
in Judah, 56 but the fields and outlying areas belonging to the city were given to Caleb son of Jephunneh.
57 So the descendants of Aaron were given the following towns, each with its pasturelands: Hebron (a city
of refuge),* Libnah, Jattir, Eshtemoa, 58 Holon,* Debir,
59 Ain,* Juttah,* and Beth-shemesh. 60 And from the
territory of Benjamin they were given Gibeon,* Geba,
Alemeth, and Anathoth, each with its pasturelands.
So thirteen towns were given to the descendants of
Aaron. 61 The remaining descendants of Kohath received ten towns from the territory of the half-tribe
of Manasseh by means of sacred lots.

62 The descendants of Gershon received by sacred
lots thirteen towns from the territories of Issachar,
Asher, Naphtali, and from the Bashan area of Manasseh, east of the Jordan.

63 The descendants of Merari received by sacred
lots twelve towns from the territories of Reuben,
Gad, and Zebulun.

64 So the people of Israel assigned all these towns
and pasturelands to the Levites. 65 The towns in the

6:57 As in parallel text at Josh 21:13; Hebrew reads *were given the cities of refuge: Hebron, and the following towns, each with its pasturelands.* **6:58** As in parallel text at Josh 21:15; Masoretic Text reads *Hilez;* other manuscripts read *Hilen.* **6:59a** As in parallel text at Josh 21:16; Hebrew reads *Ashan.* **6:59b** As in Syriac version (see also Josh 21:16); Hebrew lacks *Juttah.* **6:60** As in parallel text at Josh 21:17; Hebrew lacks *Gibeon.*

KING JAMES VERSION

children of Judah, and out of the tribe of the children of Simeon, and out of the tribe of the children
of Benjamin, these cities, which are called by *their*
names.
66And *the residue* of the families of the sons of
Kohath had cities of their coasts out of the tribe of
Ephraim.
67And they gave unto them, *of* the cities of refuge,
Shechem in mount Ephraim with her suburbs; *they*
gave also Gezer with her suburbs,
68And Jokmeam with her suburbs, and Beth-horon
with her suburbs,
69And Aijalon with her suburbs, and Gath-rimmon
with her suburbs:
70And out of the half tribe of Manasseh; Aner with
her suburbs, and Bileam with her suburbs, for the
family of the remnant of the sons of Kohath.
71Unto the sons of Gershom *were given* out of the
family of the half tribe of Manasseh, Golan in Bashan
with her suburbs, and Ashtaroth with her suburbs:
72And out of the tribe of Issachar; Kedesh with her
suburbs, Daberath with her suburbs,
73And Ramoth with her suburbs, and Anem with
her suburbs:
74And out of the tribe of Asher; Mashal with her
suburbs, and Abdon with her suburbs,
75And Hukok with her suburbs, and Rehob with
her suburbs:
76And out of the tribe of Naphtali; Kedesh in Galilee with her suburbs, and Hammon with her suburbs,
and Kirjathaim with her suburbs.
77Unto the rest of the children of Merari *were*
given out of the tribe of Zebulun, Rimmon with her
suburbs, Tabor with her suburbs:
78And on the other side Jordan by Jericho, on the
east side of Jordan, *were given them* out of the tribe
of Reuben, Bezer in the wilderness with her suburbs,
and Jahzah with her suburbs,
79Kedemoth also with her suburbs, and Mephaath
with her suburbs:
80And out of the tribe of Gad; Ramoth in Gilead
with her suburbs, and Mahanaim with her suburbs,
81And Heshbon with her suburbs, and Jazer with
her suburbs.

7 1Now the sons of Issachar *were*, Tola, and Puah,
Jashub, and Shimrom, four.
2And the sons of Tola; Uzzi, and Rephaiah, and Jeriel, and Jahmai, and Jibsam, and Shemuel, heads of
their father's house, *to wit*, of Tola: *they were* valiant
men of might in their generations; whose number
was in the days of David two and twenty thousand
and six hundred.
3And the sons of Uzzi; Izrahiah: and the sons of Izrahiah; Michael, and Obadiah, and Joel, Ishiah, five:
all of them chief men.

NEW LIVING TRANSLATION

territories of Judah, Simeon, and Benjamin, mentioned above, were assigned to them by means of
sacred lots.
66The descendants of Kohath were given the following towns from the territory of Ephraim, each
with its pasturelands: 67Shechem (a city of refuge in
the hill country of Ephraim),* Gezer, 68Jokmeam,
Beth-horon, 69Aijalon, and Gath-rimmon. 70The remaining descendants of Kohath were assigned the
towns of Aner and Bileam from the territory of the
half-tribe of Manasseh, each with its pasturelands.
71The descendants of Gershon received the
towns of Golan (in Bashan) and Ashtaroth from the
territory of the half-tribe of Manasseh, each with
its pasturelands. 72From the territory of Issachar,
they were given Kedesh, Daberath, 73Ramoth, and
Anem, each with its pasturelands. 74From the territory of Asher, they received Mashal, Abdon, 75Hukok,
and Rehob, each with its pasturelands. 76From
the territory of Naphtali, they were given Kedesh in
Galilee, Hammon, and Kiriathaim, each with its
pasturelands.
77The remaining descendants of Merari received
the towns of Jokneam, Kartah,* Rimmon,* and Tabor
from the territory of Zebulun, each with its pasturelands. 78From the territory of Reuben, east of the Jordan River opposite Jericho, they received Bezer (a
desert town), Jahaz,* 79Kedemoth, and Mephaath,
each with its pasturelands. 80And from the territory
of Gad, they received Ramoth in Gilead, Mahanaim,
81Heshbon, and Jazer, each with its pasturelands.

Descendants of Issachar

7 The four sons of Issachar were Tola, Puah,
Jashub, and Shimron.
2The sons of Tola were Uzzi, Rephaiah, Jeriel,
Jahmai, Ibsam, and Shemuel. Each of them was
the leader of an ancestral clan. At the time of
King David, the total number of mighty warriors
listed in the records of these clans was 22,600.
3The son of Uzzi was Izrahiah. The sons of Izrahiah
were Michael, Obadiah, Joel, and Isshiah. These

6:66-67 As in parallel text at Josh 21:21. Hebrew text reads *were given the cities of refuge: Shechem in the hill country of Ephraim, and the following towns, each with its pasturelands.* **6:77a** As in Greek version (see also Josh 21:34); Hebrew lacks *Jokneam, Kartah.* **6:77b** As in Greek version (see also Josh 19:13); Hebrew reads *Rimmono.* **6:78** Hebrew *Jahzah,* a variant spelling of Jahaz.

KING JAMES VERSION

4And with them, by their generations, after the
house of their fathers, *were* bands of soldiers for war,
six and thirty thousand *men:* for they had many
wives and sons.
5And their brethren among all the families of Issachar *were* valiant men of might, reckoned in all by
their genealogies fourscore and seven thousand.

6*The sons* of Benjamin; Bela, and Becher, and Jediael, three.
7And the sons of Bela; Ezbon, and Uzzi, and Uzziel,
and Jerimoth, and Iri, five; heads of the house of
their fathers, mighty men of valour; and were reckoned by their genealogies twenty and two thousand
and thirty and four.
8And the sons of Becher; Zemira, and Joash, and
Eliezer, and Elioenai, and Omri, and Jerimoth, and
Abiah, and Anathoth, and Alameth. All these *are* the
sons of Becher.
9And the number of them, after their genealogy
by their generations, heads of the house of their fathers, mighty men of valour, *was* twenty thousand
and two hundred.
10The sons also of Jediael; Bilhan: and the sons of
Bilhan; Jeush, and Benjamin, and Ehud, and Chenaanah, and Zethan, and Tharshish, and Ahishahar.
11All these the sons of Jediael, by the heads of their
fathers, mighty men of valour, *were* seventeen thousand and two hundred *soldiers,* fit to go out for war
and battle.
12Shuppim also, and Huppim, the children of Ir,
and Hushim, the sons of Aher.

13The sons of Naphtali; Jahziel, and Guni, and
Jezer, and Shallum, the sons of Bilhah.

14The sons of Manasseh; Ashriel, whom she bare:
(*but* his concubine the Aramitess bare Machir the
father of Gilead:
15And Machir took to wife *the sister* of Huppim
and Shuppim, whose sister's name *was* Maachah;)
and the name of the second *was* Zelophehad: and
Zelophehad had daughters.
16And Maachah the wife of Machir bare a son,
and she called his name Peresh; and the name of his
brother *was* Sheresh; and his sons *were* Ulam and
Rakem.
17And the sons of Ulam; Bedan. These *were* the
sons of Gilead, the son of Machir, the son of Manasseh.
18And his sister Hammoleketh bare Ishod, and
Abiezer, and Mahalah.
19And the sons of Shemidah were, Ahian, and Shechem, and Likhi, and Aniam.

NEW LIVING TRANSLATION

five became the leaders of clans. 4All of them had
many wives and many sons, so the total number
of men available for military service among their
descendants was 36,000.
5The total number of mighty warriors from all the
clans of the tribe of Issachar was 87,000. All of them
were listed in their genealogical records.

Descendants of Benjamin

6Three of Benjamin's sons were Bela, Beker, and
Jediael.
7The five sons of Bela were Ezbon, Uzzi, Uzziel,
Jerimoth, and Iri. Each of them was the leader
of an ancestral clan. The total number of mighty
warriors from these clans was 22,034, as listed
in their genealogical records.
8The sons of Beker were Zemirah, Joash, Eliezer,
Elioenai, Omri, Jeremoth, Abijah, Anathoth, and
Alemeth. 9Each of them was the leader of an
ancestral clan. The total number of mighty
warriors and leaders from these clans was
20,200, as listed in their genealogical records.
10The son of Jediael was Bilhan. The sons of Bilhan
were Jeush, Benjamin, Ehud, Kenaanah, Zethan,
Tarshish, and Ahishahar. 11Each of them was the
leader of an ancestral clan. From these clans the
total number of mighty warriors ready for war
was 17,200.
12The sons of Ir were Shuppim and Huppim.
Hushim was the son of Aher.

Descendants of Naphtali

13The sons of Naphtali were Jahzeel,* Guni, Jezer,
and Shillem.* They were all descendants of
Jacob's concubine Bilhah.

Descendants of Manasseh

14The descendants of Manasseh through his
Aramean concubine included Asriel. She also
bore Makir, the father of Gilead. 15Makir found
wives for* Huppim and Shuppim. Makir had a
sister named Maacah. One of his descendants
was Zelophehad, who had only daughters.
16Makir's wife, Maacah, gave birth to a son whom
she named Peresh. His brother's name was
Sheresh. The sons of Peresh were Ulam and
Rakem. 17The son of Ulam was Bedan. All these
were considered Gileadites, descendants of
Makir son of Manasseh.
18Makir's sister Hammoleketh gave birth to Ishhod,
Abiezer, and Mahlah.
19The sons of Shemida were Ahian, Shechem, Likhi,
and Aniam.

7:13a As in parallel text at Gen 46:24; Hebrew reads *Jahziel,* a variant spelling of Jahzeel. **7:13b** As in some Hebrew and Greek manuscripts (see also Gen 46:24; Num 26:49); most Hebrew manuscripts read *Shallum.* **7:15** Or *Makir took a wife from.* The meaning of the Hebrew is uncertain.

KING JAMES VERSION

20 And the sons of Ephraim; Shuthelah, and Bered his son, and Tahath his son, and Eladah his son, and Tahath his son,

21 And Zabad his son, and Shuthelah his son, and Ezer, and Elead, whom the men of Gath *that were* born in *that* land slew, because they came down to take away their cattle.

22 And Ephraim their father mourned many days, and his brethren came to comfort him.

23 And when he went in to his wife, she conceived, and bare a son, and he called his name Beriah, because it went evil with his house.

24 (And his daughter *was* Sherah, who built Beth-horon the nether, and the upper, and Uzzen-sherah.)

25 And Rephah *was* his son, also Resheph, and Telah his son, and Tahan his son,

26 Laadan his son, Ammihud his son, Elishama his son,

27 Non his son, Jehoshuah his son.

28 And their possessions and habitations *were,* Bethel and the towns thereof, and eastward Naaran, and westward Gezer, with the towns thereof; Shechem also and the towns thereof, unto Gaza and the towns thereof:

29 And by the borders of the children of Manasseh, Beth-shean and her towns, Taanach and her towns, Megiddo and her towns, Dor and her towns. In these dwelt the children of Joseph the son of Israel.

30 The sons of Asher; Imnah, and Isuah, and Ishuai, and Beriah, and Serah their sister.

31 And the sons of Beriah; Heber, and Malchiel, who *is* the father of Birzavith.

32 And Heber begat Japhlet, and Shomer, and Hotham, and Shua their sister.

33 And the sons of Japhlet; Pasach, and Bimhal, and Ashvath. These *are* the children of Japhlet.

34 And the sons of Shamer; Ahi, and Rohgah, Jehubbah, and Aram.

35 And the sons of his brother Helem; Zophah, and Imna, and Shelesh, and Amal.

36 The sons of Zophah; Suah, and Harnepher, and Shual, and Beri, and Imrah,

37 Bezer, and Hod, and Shamma, and Shilshah, and Ithran, and Beera.

38 And the sons of Jether; Jephunneh, and Pispah, and Ara.

39 And the sons of Ulla; Arah, and Haniel, and Rezia.

40 All these *were* the children of Asher, heads of *their* father's house, choice *and* mighty men of valour, chief of the princes. And the number throughout the genealogy of them that were apt to the war *and* to battle *was* twenty and six thousand men.

NEW LIVING TRANSLATION

Descendants of Ephraim

20 The descendants of Ephraim were Shuthelah,
Bered, Tahath, Eleadah, Tahath, 21 Zabad,
Shuthelah, Ezer, and Elead. These two were killed
trying to steal livestock from the local farmers
near Gath. 22 Their father, Ephraim, mourned
for them a long time, and his relatives came to
comfort him. 23 Afterward Ephraim slept with his
wife, and she became pregnant and gave birth to
a son. Ephraim named him Beriah* because of
the tragedy his family had suffered. 24 He had a
daughter named Sheerah. She built the towns
of Lower and Upper Beth-horon and Uzzen-sheerah.

25 The descendants of Ephraim included Rephah,
Resheph, Telah, Tahan, 26 Ladan, Ammihud,
Elishama, 27 Nun, and Joshua.

28 The descendants of Ephraim lived in the territory that included Bethel and its surrounding towns to the south, Naaran to the east, Gezer and its villages to the west, and Shechem and its surrounding villages to the north as far as Ayyah and its towns.
29 Along the border of Manasseh were the towns of Beth-shan,* Taanach, Megiddo, Dor, and their surrounding villages. The descendants of Joseph son of Israel* lived in these towns.

Descendants of Asher

30 The sons of Asher were Imnah, Ishvah, Ishvi, and Beriah. They had a sister named Serah.

31 The sons of Beriah were Heber and Malkiel (the father of Birzaith).

32 The sons of Heber were Japhlet, Shomer, and Hotham. They had a sister named Shua.

33 The sons of Japhlet were Pasach, Bimhal, and Ashvath.

34 The sons of Shomer were Ahi,* Rohgah, Hubbah, and Aram.

35 The sons of his brother Helem* were Zophah, Imna, Shelesh, and Amal.

36 The sons of Zophah were Suah, Harnepher, Shual,
Beri, Imrah, 37 Bezer, Hod, Shamma, Shilshah,
Ithran,* and Beera.

38 The sons of Jether were Jephunneh, Pispah, and Ara.

39 The sons of Ulla were Arah, Hanniel, and Rizia.

40 Each of these descendants of Asher was the head of an ancestral clan. They were all select men—mighty warriors and outstanding leaders. The total number of men available for military service was 26,000, as listed in their genealogical records.

7:23 *Beriah* sounds like a Hebrew term meaning "tragedy" or "misfortune." **7:29a** Hebrew *Beth-shean,* a variant spelling of Beth-shan. **7:29b** *Israel* is the name that God gave to Jacob. **7:34** Or *The sons of Shomer, his brother, were.* **7:35** Possibly another name for *Hotham;* compare 7:32. **7:37** Possibly another name for *Jether;* compare 7:38.

KING JAMES VERSION

8 1Now Benjamin begat Bela his firstborn, Ashbel
the second, and Aharah the third,
2Nohah the fourth, and Rapha the fifth.
3And the sons of Bela were, Addar, and Gera, and
Abihud,
4And Abishua, and Naaman, and Ahoah,
5And Gera, and Shephuphan, and Huram.
6And these *are* the sons of Ehud: these are the
heads of the fathers of the inhabitants of Geba, and
they removed them to Manahath:
7And Naaman, and Ahiah, and Gera, he removed
them, and begat Uzza, and Ahihud.
8And Shaharaim begat *children* in the country of
Moab, after he had sent them away; Hushim and Baara *were* his wives.
9And he begat of Hodesh his wife, Jobab, and Zibia,
and Mesha, and Malcham,
10And Jeuz, and Shachia, and Mirma. These *were*
his sons, heads of the fathers.
11And of Hushim he begat Abitub, and Elpaal.
12The sons of Elpaal; Eber, and Misham, and
Shamed, who built Ono, and Lod, with the towns
thereof:
13Beriah also, and Shema, who *were* heads of the
fathers of the inhabitants of Aijalon, who drove away
the inhabitants of Gath:
14And Ahio, Shashak, and Jeremoth,
15And Zebadiah, and Arad, and Ader,
16And Michael, and Ispah, and Joha, the sons of
Beriah;
17And Zebadiah, and Meshullam, and Hezeki, and
Heber,
18Ishmerai also, and Jezliah, and Jobab, the sons
of Elpaal;
19And Jakim, and Zichri, and Zabdi,
20And Elienai, and Zilthai, and Eliel,
21And Adaiah, and Beraiah, and Shimrath, the sons
of Shimhi;
22And Ishpan, and Heber, and Eliel,
23And Abdon, and Zichri, and Hanan,
24And Hananiah, and Elam, and Antothijah,
25And Iphedeiah, and Penuel, the sons of Shashak;
26And Shamsherai, and Shehariah, and Athaliah,
27And Jaresiah, and Eliah, and Zichri, the sons of
Jeroham.
28These *were* heads of the fathers, by their generations, chief *men*. These dwelt in Jerusalem.
29And at Gibeon dwelt the father of Gibeon; whose
wife's name *was* Maachah:
30And his firstborn son Abdon, and Zur, and Kish,
and Baal, and Nadab,
31And Gedor, and Ahio, and Zacher.
32And Mikloth begat Shimeah. And these also

NEW LIVING TRANSLATION

Descendants of Benjamin

8 Benjamin's first son was Bela, the second was
Ashbel, the third was Aharah, 2the fourth was
Nohah, and the fifth was Rapha.
3The sons of Bela were Addar, Gera, Abihud,*
4Abishua, Naaman, Ahoah, 5Gera, Shephuphan,
and Huram.
6The sons of Ehud, leaders of the clans living at
Geba, were exiled to Manahath. 7Ehud's sons
were Naaman, Ahijah, and Gera. Gera, who led
them into exile, was the father of Uzza and
Ahihud.*
8After Shaharaim divorced his wives Hushim and
Baara, he had children in the land of Moab. 9His
wife Hodesh gave birth to Jobab, Zibia, Mesha,
Malcam, 10Jeuz, Sakia, and Mirmah. These sons
all became the leaders of clans.
11Shaharaim's wife Hushim had already given birth
to Abitub and Elpaal. 12The sons of Elpaal were
Eber, Misham, Shemed (who built the towns of
Ono and Lod and their nearby villages), 13Beriah,
and Shema. They were the leaders of the clans
living in Aijalon, and they drove out the
inhabitants of Gath.
14Ahio, Shashak, Jeremoth, 15Zebadiah, Arad, Eder,
16Michael, Ishpah, and Joha were the sons of
Beriah.
17Zebadiah, Meshullam, Hizki, Heber, 18Ishmerai,
Izliah, and Jobab were the sons of Elpaal.
19Jakim, Zicri, Zabdi, 20Elienai, Zillethai, Eliel,
21Adaiah, Beraiah, and Shimrath were the sons
of Shimei.
22Ishpan, Eber, Eliel, 23Abdon, Zicri, Hanan,
24Hananiah, Elam, Anthothijah, 25Iphdeiah,
and Penuel were the sons of Shashak.
26Shamsherai, Shehariah, Athaliah, 27Jaareshiah,
Elijah, and Zicri were the sons of Jeroham.
28These were the leaders of the ancestral clans; they
were listed in their genealogical records, and they all
lived in Jerusalem.

The Family of Saul

29Jeiel* (the father of* Gibeon) lived in the town of
Gibeon. His wife's name was Maacah, 30and his
oldest son was named Abdon. Jeiel's other sons
were Zur, Kish, Baal, Ner,* Nadab, 31Gedor, Ahio,
Zechariah,* 32and Mikloth, who was the father

8:3 Possibly *Gera the father of Ehud;* compare 8:6. **8:7** Or *Gera, that is Heglam, was the father of Uzza and Ahihud.* **8:29a** As in some Greek manuscripts (see also 9:35); Hebrew lacks *Jeiel.* **8:29b** Or *the founder of.* **8:30** As in some Greek manuscripts (see also 9:36); Hebrew lacks *Ner.* **8:31** As in parallel text at 9:37; Hebrew reads *Zeker,* a variant spelling of Zechariah.

KING JAMES VERSION

dwelt with their brethren in Jerusalem, over against
them.
33 And Ner begat Kish, and Kish begat Saul, and
Saul begat Jonathan, and Malchi-shua, and Abinadab, and Esh-baal.
34 And the son of Jonathan *was* Merib-baal; and
Merib-baal begat Micah.
35 And the sons of Micah *were*, Pithon, and Melech,
and Tarea, and Ahaz.
36 And Ahaz begat Jehoadah; and Jehoadah begat
Alemeth, and Azmaveth, and Zimri; and Zimri begat
Moza,
37 And Moza begat Binea: Rapha *was* his son,
Eleasah his son, Azel his son:
38 And Azel had six sons, whose names *are* these,
Azrikam, Bocheru, and Ishmael, and Sheariah, and
Obadiah, and Hanan. All these *were* the sons of
Azel.
39 And the sons of Eshek his brother *were*, Ulam
his firstborn, Jehush the second, and Eliphelet the
third.
40 And the sons of Ulam were mighty men of valour, archers, and had many sons, and sons' sons,
an hundred and fifty. All these *are* of the sons of
Benjamin.

9

1 So all Israel were reckoned by genealogies;
and, behold, they *were* written in the book of
the kings of Israel and Judah, *who* were carried away
to Babylon for their transgression.

2 Now the first inhabitants that *dwelt* in their
possessions in their cities *were*, the Israelites, the
priests, Levites, and the Nethinims.
3 And in Jerusalem dwelt of the children of Judah,
and of the children of Benjamin, and of the children
of Ephraim, and Manasseh;
4 Uthai the son of Ammihud, the son of Omri, the
son of Imri, the son of Bani, of the children of Pharez
the son of Judah.
5 And of the Shilonites; Asaiah the firstborn, and
his sons.
6 And of the sons of Zerah; Jeuel, and their brethren, six hundred and ninety.
7 And of the sons of Benjamin; Sallu the son of Meshullam, the son of Hodaviah, the son of Hasenuah,
8 And Ibneiah the son of Jeroham, and Elah the
son of Uzzi, the son of Michri, and Meshullam
the son of Shephatiah, the son of Reuel, the son of
Ibnijah;

NEW LIVING TRANSLATION

of Shimeam.* All these families lived near each
other in Jerusalem.
33 Ner was the father of Kish.
Kish was the father of Saul.
Saul was the father of Jonathan, Malkishua,
Abinadab, and Esh-baal.
34 Jonathan was the father of Merib-baal.
Merib-baal was the father of Micah.
35 Micah was the father of Pithon, Melech, Tahrea,*
and Ahaz.
36 Ahaz was the father of Jadah.*
Jadah was the father of Alemeth, Azmaveth, and
Zimri.
Zimri was the father of Moza.
37 Moza was the father of Binea.
Binea was the father of Rephaiah.*
Rephaiah was the father of Eleasah.
Eleasah was the father of Azel.
38 Azel had six sons: Azrikam, Bokeru, Ishmael,
Sheariah, Obadiah, and Hanan. These were the
sons of Azel.
39 Azel's brother Eshek had three sons: the first was
Ulam, the second was Jeush, and the third was
Eliphelet. 40 Ulam's sons were all mighty warriors
and expert archers. They had many sons and
grandsons—150 in all.

All these were descendants of Benjamin.

9

So all Israel was listed in the genealogical records in *The Book of the Kings of Israel.*

The Returning Exiles

The people of Judah were exiled to Babylon because
they were unfaithful to the LORD. 2 The first of the
exiles to return to their property in their former
towns were priests, Levites, Temple servants, and
other Israelites. 3 Some of the people from the tribes
of Judah, Benjamin, Ephraim, and Manasseh came
and settled in Jerusalem.

4 One family that returned was that of Uthai son of
Ammihud, son of Omri, son of Imri, son of Bani,
a descendant of Perez son of Judah.
5 Others returned from the Shilonite clan, including
Asaiah (the oldest) and his sons.
6 From the Zerahite clan, Jeuel returned with his
relatives.
In all, 690 families from the tribe of Judah returned.
7 From the tribe of Benjamin came Sallu son of
Meshullam, son of Hodaviah, son of Hassenuah;
8 Ibneiah son of Jeroham; Elah son of Uzzi, son of
Micri; and Meshullam son of Shephatiah, son of
Reuel, son of Ibnijah.

8:32 As in parallel text at 9:38; Hebrew reads *Shimeah,* a variant spelling of Shimeam. **8:35** As in parallel text at 9:41; Hebrew reads *Tarea,* a variant spelling of Tahrea. **8:36** As in parallel text at 9:42; Hebrew reads *Jehoaddah,* a variant spelling of Jadah. **8:37** As in parallel text at 9:43; Hebrew reads *Raphah,* a variant spelling of Rephaiah.

KING JAMES VERSION

9 And their brethren, according to their generations, nine hundred and fifty and six. All these men *were* chief of the fathers in the house of their fathers.

10 And of the priests; Jedaiah, and Jehoiarib, and Jachin,

11 And Azariah the son of Hilkiah, the son of Meshullam, the son of Zadok, the son of Meraioth, the son of Ahitub, the ruler of the house of God;

12 And Adaiah the son of Jeroham, the son of Pashur, the son of Malchijah, and Maasiai the son of Adiel, the son of Jahzerah, the son of Meshullam, the son of Meshillemith, the son of Immer;

13 And their brethren, heads of the house of their fathers, a thousand and seven hundred and threescore; very able men for the work of the service of the house of God.

14 And of the Levites; Shemaiah the son of Hasshub, the son of Azrikam, the son of Hashabiah, of the sons of Merari;

15 And Bakbakkar, Heresh, and Galal, and Mattaniah the son of Micah, the son of Zichri, the son of Asaph;

16 And Obadiah the son of Shemaiah, the son of Galal, the son of Jeduthun, and Berechiah the son of Asa, the son of Elkanah, that dwelt in the villages of the Netophathites.

17 And the porters *were*, Shallum, and Akkub, and Talmon, and Ahiman, and their brethren: Shallum *was* the chief;

18 Who hitherto *waited* in the king's gate eastward: they *were* porters in the companies of the children of Levi.

19 And Shallum the son of Kore, the son of Ebiasaph, the son of Korah, and his brethren, of the house of his father, the Korahites, *were* over the work of the service, keepers of the gates of the tabernacle: and their fathers, *being* over the host of the LORD, *were* keepers of the entry.

20 And Phinehas the son of Eleazar was the ruler over them in time past, *and* the LORD *was* with him.

21 *And* Zechariah the son of Meshelemiah *was* porter of the door of the tabernacle of the congregation.

22 All these *which were* chosen to be porters in the gates *were* two hundred and twelve. These were reckoned by their genealogy in their villages, whom David and Samuel the seer did ordain in their set office.

23 So they and their children *had* the oversight of the gates of the house of the LORD, *namely*, the house of the tabernacle, by wards.

24 In four quarters were the porters, toward the east, west, north, and south.

25 And their brethren, *which were* in their villages, *were* to come after seven days from time to time with them.

NEW LIVING TRANSLATION

9 These men were all leaders of clans, and they were listed in their genealogical records. In all, 956 families from the tribe of Benjamin returned.

The Returning Priests

10 Among the priests who returned were Jedaiah,
Jehoiarib, Jakin, 11 Azariah son of Hilkiah, son of
Meshullam, son of Zadok, son of Meraioth, son
of Ahitub. Azariah was the chief officer of the
house of God.
12 Other returning priests were Adaiah son of
Jeroham, son of Pashhur, son of Malkijah, and
Maasai son of Adiel, son of Jahzerah, son of
Meshullam, son of Meshillemith, son of Immer.
13 In all, 1,760 priests returned. They were heads of clans and very able men. They were responsible for ministering at the house of God.

The Returning Levites

14 The Levites who returned were Shemaiah son of
Hasshub, son of Azrikam, son of Hashabiah, a
descendant of Merari; 15 Bakbakkar; Heresh;
Galal; Mattaniah son of Mica, son of Zicri, son of
Asaph; 16 Obadiah son of Shemaiah, son of Galal,
son of Jeduthun; and Berekiah son of Asa, son
of Elkanah, who lived in the area of Netophah.
17 The gatekeepers who returned were Shallum,
Akkub, Talmon, Ahiman, and their relatives.
Shallum was the chief gatekeeper. 18 Prior to
this time, they were responsible for the King's
Gate on the east side. These men served as
gatekeepers for the camps of the Levites.
19 Shallum was the son of Kore, a descendant
of Abiasaph,* from the clan of Korah. He and
his relatives, the Korahites, were responsible for
guarding the entrance to the sanctuary, just as
their ancestors had guarded the Tabernacle in
the camp of the LORD.
20 Phinehas son of Eleazar had been in charge
of the gatekeepers in earlier times, and the LORD
had been with him. 21 And later Zechariah son of
Meshelemiah was responsible for guarding the
entrance to the Tabernacle.*

22 In all, there were 212 gatekeepers in those days,
and they were listed according to the genealogies
in their villages. David and Samuel the seer had appointed their ancestors because they were reliable
men. 23 These gatekeepers and their descendants, by
their divisions, were responsible for guarding the entrance to the house of the LORD when that house was
a tent. 24 The gatekeepers were stationed on all four
sides—east, west, north, and south. 25 Their relatives
in the villages came regularly to share their duties for
seven-day periods.

9:19 Hebrew *Ebiasaph*, a variant spelling of Abiasaph; compare Exod 6:24.
9:21 Hebrew *Tent of Meeting*.

KING JAMES VERSION

26 For these Levites, the four chief porters, were in
their set office, and were over the chambers and
treasuries of the house of God.
27 And they lodged round about the house of God,
because the charge *was* upon them, and the opening
thereof every morning *pertained* to them.
28 And *certain* of them had the charge of the ministering vessels, that they should bring them in and
out by tale.
29 *Some* of them also *were* appointed to oversee
the vessels and all the instruments of the sanctuary,
and the fine flour, and the wine, and the oil, and the
frankincense, and the spices.
30 And *some* of the sons of the priests made the
ointment of the spices.
31 And Mattithiah, *one* of the Levites, who *was* the
firstborn of Shallum the Korahite, had the set office
over the things that were made in the pans.
32 And *other* of their brethren, of the sons of the
Kohathites, *were* over the shewbread, to prepare *it*
every sabbath.
33 And these *are* the singers, chief of the fathers of
the Levites, *who remaining* in the chambers *were*
free: for they were employed in *that* work day and
night.
34 These chief fathers of the Levites *were* chief
throughout their generations; these dwelt at Jerusalem.
35 And in Gibeon dwelt the father of Gibeon, Jehiel,
whose wife's name *was* Maachah:
36 And his firstborn son Abdon, then Zur, and Kish,
and Baal, and Ner, and Nadab,
37 And Gedor, and Ahio, and Zechariah, and
Mikloth.
38 And Mikloth begat Shimeam. And they also
dwelt with their brethren at Jerusalem, over against
their brethren.
39 And Ner begat Kish; and Kish begat Saul; and
Saul begat Jonathan, and Malchi-shua, and Abinadab, and Esh-baal.
40 And the son of Jonathan *was* Merib-baal: and
Merib-baal begat Micah.
41 And the sons of Micah *were*, Pithon, and Melech,
and Tahrea, *and Ahaz*.
42 And Ahaz begat Jarah; and Jarah begat Alemeth,
and Azmaveth, and Zimri; and Zimri begat Moza;
43 And Moza begat Binea; and Rephaiah his son,
Eleasah his son, Azel his son.
44 And Azel had six sons, whose names *are* these,
Azrikam, Bocheru, and Ishmael, and Sheariah, and
Obadiah, and Hanan: these *were* the sons of Azel.

NEW LIVING TRANSLATION

26 The four chief gatekeepers, all Levites, were
trusted officials, for they were responsible for the
rooms and treasuries at the house of God. 27 They
would spend the night around the house of God,
since it was their duty to guard it and to open the
gates every morning.
28 Some of the gatekeepers were assigned to care
for the various articles used in worship. They
checked them in and out to avoid any loss. 29 Others
were responsible for the furnishings, the items in the
sanctuary, and the supplies, such as choice flour,
wine, olive oil, frankincense, and spices. 30 But it was
the priests who blended the spices. 31 Mattithiah, a
Levite and the oldest son of Shallum the Korahite,
was entrusted with baking the bread used in the offerings. 32 And some members of the clan of Kohath
were in charge of preparing the bread to be set on the
table each Sabbath day.
33 The musicians, all prominent Levites, lived at
the Temple. They were exempt from other responsibilities since they were on duty at all hours. 34 All
these men lived in Jerusalem. They were the heads of
Levite families and were listed as prominent leaders
in their genealogical records.

King Saul's Family Tree

35 Jeiel (the father of* Gibeon) lived in the town of
Gibeon. His wife's name was Maacah, 36 and his
oldest son was named Abdon. Jeiel's other sons
were Zur, Kish, Baal, Ner, Nadab, 37 Gedor, Ahio,
Zechariah, and Mikloth. 38 Mikloth was the father
of Shimeam. All these families lived near each
other in Jerusalem.

39 Ner was the father of Kish.
Kish was the father of Saul.
Saul was the father of Jonathan, Malkishua,
Abinadab, and Esh-baal.
40 Jonathan was the father of Merib-baal.
Merib-baal was the father of Micah.
41 The sons of Micah were Pithon, Melech, Tahrea,
and Ahaz.*
42 Ahaz was the father of Jadah.*
Jadah was the father of Alemeth, Azmaveth, and
Zimri.
Zimri was the father of Moza.
43 Moza was the father of Binea.
Binea's son was Rephaiah.
Rephaiah's son was Eleasah.
Eleasah's son was Azel.
44 Azel had six sons, whose names were Azrikam,
Bokeru, Ishmael, Sheariah, Obadiah, and Hanan.
These were the sons of Azel.

9:35 Or *the founder of.* **9:41** As in Syriac version and Latin Vulgate (see also 8:35); Hebrew lacks *and Ahaz.* **9:42** As in some Hebrew manuscripts and Greek version (see also 8:36); Hebrew reads *Jarah.*

KING JAMES VERSION

10

1 Now the Philistines fought against Israel; and the men of Israel fled from before the Philistines, and fell down slain in mount Gilboa.

2 And the Philistines followed hard after Saul, and after his sons; and the Philistines slew Jonathan, and Abinadab, and Malchi-shua, the sons of Saul.

3 And the battle went sore against Saul, and the archers hit him, and he was wounded of the archers.

4 Then said Saul to his armourbearer, Draw thy sword, and thrust me through therewith; lest these uncircumcised come and abuse me. But his armourbearer would not; for he was sore afraid. So Saul took a sword, and fell upon it.

5 And when his armourbearer saw that Saul was dead, he fell likewise on the sword, and died.

6 So Saul died, and his three sons, and all his house died together.

7 And when all the men of Israel that *were* in the valley saw that they fled, and that Saul and his sons were dead, then they forsook their cities, and fled: and the Philistines came and dwelt in them.

8 And it came to pass on the morrow, when the Philistines came to strip the slain, that they found Saul and his sons fallen in mount Gilboa.

9 And when they had stripped him, they took his head, and his armour, and sent into the land of the Philistines round about, to carry tidings unto their idols, and to the people.

10 And they put his armour in the house of their gods, and fastened his head in the temple of Dagon.

11 And when all Jabesh-gilead heard all that the Philistines had done to Saul,

12 They arose, all the valiant men, and took away the body of Saul, and the bodies of his sons, and brought them to Jabesh, and buried their bones under the oak in Jabesh, and fasted seven days.

13 So Saul died for his transgression which he committed against the LORD, *even* against the word of the LORD, which he kept not, and also for asking *counsel* of *one that had* a familiar spirit, to inquire *of it;*

14 And inquired not of the LORD: therefore he slew him, and turned the kingdom unto David the son of Jesse.

11

1 Then all Israel gathered themselves to David unto Hebron, saying, Behold, we *are* thy bone and thy flesh.

2 And moreover in time past, even when Saul was king, thou *wast* he that leddest out and broughtest in Israel: and the LORD thy God said unto thee, Thou shalt feed my people Israel, and thou shalt be ruler over my people Israel.

3 Therefore came all the elders of Israel to the king to Hebron; and David made a covenant with them in Hebron before the LORD; and they anointed David king over Israel, according to the word of the LORD by Samuel.

NEW LIVING TRANSLATION

The Death of King Saul

10

Now the Philistines attacked Israel, and the men of Israel fled before them. Many were slaughtered on the slopes of Mount Gilboa. 2 The Philistines closed in on Saul and his sons, and they killed three of his sons—Jonathan, Abinadab, and Malkishua. 3 The fighting grew very fierce around Saul, and the Philistine archers caught up with him and wounded him.

4 Saul groaned to his armor bearer, "Take your sword and kill me before these pagan Philistines come to taunt and torture me."

But his armor bearer was afraid and would not do it. So Saul took his own sword and fell on it. 5 When his armor bearer realized that Saul was dead, he fell on his own sword and died. 6 So Saul and his three sons died there together, bringing his dynasty to an end.

7 When all the Israelites in the Jezreel Valley saw that their army had fled and that Saul and his sons were dead, they abandoned their towns and fled. So the Philistines moved in and occupied their towns.

8 The next day, when the Philistines went out to strip the dead, they found the bodies of Saul and his sons on Mount Gilboa. 9 So they stripped off Saul's armor and cut off his head. Then they proclaimed the good news of Saul's death before their idols and to the people throughout the land of Philistia. 10 They placed his armor in the temple of their gods, and they fastened his head to the temple of Dagon.

11 But when everyone in Jabesh-gilead heard about everything the Philistines had done to Saul, 12 all their mighty warriors brought the bodies of Saul and his sons back to Jabesh. Then they buried their bones beneath the great tree at Jabesh, and they fasted for seven days.

13 So Saul died because he was unfaithful to the LORD. He failed to obey the LORD's command, and he even consulted a medium 14 instead of asking the LORD for guidance. So the LORD killed him and turned the kingdom over to David son of Jesse.

David Becomes King of All Israel

11

Then all Israel gathered before David at Hebron and told him, "We are your own flesh and blood. 2 In the past,* even when Saul was king, you were the one who really led the forces of Israel. And the LORD your God told you, 'You will be the shepherd of my people Israel. You will be the leader of my people Israel.'"

3 So there at Hebron, David made a covenant before the LORD with all the elders of Israel. And they anointed him king of Israel, just as the LORD had promised through Samuel.

11:2 Or *For some time.*

KING JAMES VERSION

4 And David and all Israel went to Jerusalem, which
is Jebus; where the Jebusites *were,* the inhabitants of
the land.
5 And the inhabitants of Jebus said to David, Thou
shalt not come hither. Nevertheless David took the
castle of Zion, which *is* the city of David.
6 And David said, Whosoever smiteth the Jebusites
first shall be chief and captain. So Joab the son of
Zeruiah went first up, and was chief.
7 And David dwelt in the castle; therefore they
called it the city of David.
8 And he built the city round about, even from
Millo round about: and Joab repaired the rest of
the city.
9 So David waxed greater and greater: for the LORD
of hosts *was* with him.

10 These also *are* the chief of the mighty men
whom David had, who strengthened themselves with
him in his kingdom, *and* with all Israel, to make him
king, according to the word of the LORD concerning
Israel.
11 And this *is* the number of the mighty men whom
David had; Jashobeam, an Hachmonite, the chief of
the captains: he lifted up his spear against three hundred slain *by him* at one time.
12 And after him *was* Eleazar the son of Dodo, the
Ahohite, who *was one* of the three mighties.
13 He was with David at Pas-dammim, and there
the Philistines were gathered together to battle,
where was a parcel of ground full of barley; and the
people fled from before the Philistines.
14 And they set themselves in the midst of *that*
parcel, and delivered it, and slew the Philistines; and
the LORD saved *them* by a great deliverance.
15 Now three of the thirty captains went down to
the rock to David, into the cave of Adullam; and the
host of the Philistines encamped in the valley of
Rephaim.
16 And David *was* then in the hold, and the Philistines' garrison *was* then at Bethlehem.
17 And David longed, and said, Oh that one would
give me drink of the water of the well of Bethlehem,
that *is* at the gate!
18 And the three brake through the host of the Philistines, and drew water out of the well of Bethlehem,
that *was* by the gate, and took *it,* and brought *it* to
David: but David would not drink *of* it, but poured it
out to the LORD,
19 And said, My God forbid it me, that I should do
this thing: shall I drink the blood of these men that
have put their lives in jeopardy? for with *the jeopardy of* their lives they brought it. Therefore he
would not drink it. These things did these three
mightiest.

NEW LIVING TRANSLATION

David Captures Jerusalem

4 Then David and all Israel went to Jerusalem (or
Jebus, as it used to be called), where the Jebusites,
the original inhabitants of the land, were living. 5 The
people of Jebus taunted David, saying, "You'll never
get in here!" But David captured the fortress of Zion,
which is now called the City of David.
6 David had said to his troops, "Whoever is first to
attack the Jebusites will become the commander of
my armies!" And Joab, the son of David's sister Zeruiah, was first to attack, so he became the commander
of David's armies.
7 David made the fortress his home, and that is why
it is called the City of David. 8 He extended the city
from the supporting terraces* to the surrounding
area, while Joab rebuilt the rest of Jerusalem. 9 And
David became more and more powerful, because the
LORD of Heaven's Armies was with him.

David's Mightiest Warriors

10 These are the leaders of David's mighty warriors.
Together with all Israel, they decided to make David
their king, just as the LORD had promised concerning
Israel.
11 Here is the record of David's mightiest warriors:
The first was Jashobeam the Hacmonite, who was
leader of the Three—the mightiest warriors among
David's men.* He once used his spear to kill 300
enemy warriors in a single battle.
12 Next in rank among the Three was Eleazar son of
Dodai,* a descendant of Ahoah. 13 He was with David
in the battle against the Philistines at Pas-dammim.
The battle took place in a field full of barley, and the
Israelite army fled. 14 But Eleazar and David* held
their ground in the middle of the field and beat back
the Philistines. So the LORD saved them by giving
them a great victory.
15 Once when David was at the rock near the cave
of Adullam, the Philistine army was camped in the
valley of Rephaim. The Three (who were among the
Thirty—an elite group among David's fighting men)
went down to meet him there. 16 David was staying in
the stronghold at the time, and a Philistine detachment had occupied the town of Bethlehem.
17 David remarked longingly to his men, "Oh, how I
would love some of that good water from the well by
the gate in Bethlehem." 18 So the Three broke through
the Philistine lines, drew some water from the well
by the gate in Bethlehem, and brought it back to David. But David refused to drink it. Instead, he poured
it out as an offering to the LORD. 19 "God forbid that
I should drink this!" he exclaimed. "This water is as
precious as the blood of these men* who risked their
lives to bring it to me." So David did not drink it.
These are examples of the exploits of the Three.

11:8 Hebrew *the millo.* The meaning of the Hebrew is uncertain. **11:11** As in some Greek manuscripts (see also 2 Sam 23:8); Hebrew reads *leader of the Thirty,* or *leader of the captains.* **11:12** As in parallel text at 2 Sam 23:9 (see also 1 Chr 27:4); Hebrew reads *Dodo,* a variant spelling of Dodai. **11:14** Hebrew *they.* **11:19** Hebrew *Shall I drink the lifeblood of these men?*

KING JAMES VERSION

20 And Abishai the brother of Joab, he was chief of
the three: for lifting up his spear against three hundred, he slew *them*, and had a name among the three.
21 Of the three, he was more honourable than the
two; for he was their captain: howbeit he attained
not to the *first* three.
22 Benaiah the son of Jehoiada, the son of a valiant
man of Kabzeel, who had done many acts; he slew
two lionlike men of Moab: also he went down and
slew a lion in a pit in a snowy day.
23 And he slew an Egyptian, a man of *great* stature,
five cubits high; and in the Egyptian's hand *was* a
spear like a weaver's beam; and he went down to him
with a staff, and plucked the spear out of the Egyptian's hand, and slew him with his own spear.
24 These *things* did Benaiah the son of Jehoiada,
and had the name among the three mighties.
25 Behold, he was honourable among the thirty,
but attained not to the *first* three: and David set him
over his guard.
26 Also the valiant men of the armies *were*, Asahel
the brother of Joab, Elhanan the son of Dodo of
Bethlehem,
27 Shammoth the Harorite, Helez the Pelonite,
28 Ira the son of Ikkesh the Tekoite, Abiezer the
Antothite,
29 Sibbecai the Hushathite, Ilai the Ahohite,
30 Maharai the Netophathite, Heled the son of Baanah the Netophathite,
31 Ithai the son of Ribai of Gibeah, *that pertained*
to the children of Benjamin, Benaiah the Pirathonite,
32 Hurai of the brooks of Gaash, Abiel the Arbathite,
33 Azmaveth the Baharumite, Eliahba the Shaalbonite,
34 The sons of Hashem the Gizonite, Jonathan the
son of Shage the Hararite,
35 Ahiam the son of Sacar the Hararite, Eliphal the
son of Ur,
36 Hepher the Mecherathite, Ahijah the Pelonite,
37 Hezro the Carmelite, Naarai the son of Ezbai,
38 Joel the brother of Nathan, Mibhar the son of
Haggeri,
39 Zelek the Ammonite, Naharai the Berothite, the
armourbearer of Joab the son of Zeruiah,

NEW LIVING TRANSLATION

David's Thirty Mighty Men

20 Abishai, the brother of Joab, was the leader of the
Thirty.* He once used his spear to kill 300 enemy
warriors in a single battle. It was by such feats that
he became as famous as the Three. 21 Abishai was the
most famous of the Thirty and was their commander,
though he was not one of the Three.
22 There was also Benaiah son of Jehoiada, a valiant
warrior from Kabzeel. He did many heroic deeds,
which included killing two champions* of Moab.
Another time, on a snowy day, he chased a lion down
into a pit and killed it. 23 Once, armed only with a
club, he killed an Egyptian warrior who was 7½ feet*
tall and whose spear was as thick as a weaver's beam.
Benaiah wrenched the spear from the Egyptian's
hand and killed him with it. 24 Deeds like these made
Benaiah as famous as the three mightiest warriors.
25 He was more honored than the other members of
the Thirty, though he was not one of the Three. And
David made him captain of his bodyguard.
26 David's mighty warriors also included:

Asahel, Joab's brother;
Elhanan son of Dodo from Bethlehem;
27 Shammah from Harod;*
Helez from Pelon;
28 Ira son of Ikkesh from Tekoa;
Abiezer from Anathoth;
29 Sibbecai from Hushah;
Zalmon* from Ahoah;
30 Maharai from Netophah;
Heled son of Baanah from Netophah;
31 Ithai son of Ribai from Gibeah (in the land of Benjamin);
Benaiah from Pirathon;
32 Hurai from near Nahale-gaash*;
Abi-albon* from Arabah;
33 Azmaveth from Bahurim*;
Eliahba from Shaalbon;
34 the sons of Jashen* from Gizon;
Jonathan son of Shagee from Harar;
35 Ahiam son of Sharar* from Harar;
Eliphal son of Ur;
36 Hepher from Mekerah;
Ahijah from Pelon;
37 Hezro from Carmel;
Paarai* son of Ezbai;
38 Joel, the brother of Nathan;
Mibhar son of Hagri;
39 Zelek from Ammon;
Naharai from Beeroth, Joab's armor bearer;

11:20 As in Syriac version; Hebrew reads *the Three;* also in 11:21. **11:22** Or *two sons of Ariel.* **11:23** Hebrew *5 cubits* [2.3 meters]. **11:27** As in parallel text at 2 Sam 23:25; Hebrew reads *Shammoth from Haror.* **11:29** As in parallel text at 2 Sam 23:28; Hebrew reads *Ilai.* **11:32a** Or *from the ravines of Gaash.* **11:32b** As in parallel text at 2 Sam 23:31; Hebrew reads *Abiel.* **11:33** As in parallel text at 2 Sam 23:31; Hebrew reads *Baharum.* **11:34** As in parallel text at 2 Sam 23:32; Hebrew reads *sons of Hashem.* **11:35** As in parallel text at 2 Sam 23:33; Hebrew reads *son of Sacar.* **11:37** As in parallel text at 2 Sam 23:35; Hebrew reads *Naarai.*

KING JAMES VERSION

40 Ira the Ithrite, Gareb the Ithrite,
41 Uriah the Hittite, Zabad the son of Ahlai,
42 Adina the son of Shiza the Reubenite, a captain
of the Reubenites, and thirty with him,
43 Hanan the son of Maachah, and Joshaphat the
Mithnite,
44 Uzzia the Ashterathite, Shama and Jehiel the
sons of Hothan the Aroerite,
45 Jediael the son of Shimri, and Joha his brother,
the Tizite,
46 Eliel the Mahavite, and Jeribai, and Joshaviah,
the sons of Elnaam, and Ithmah the Moabite,
47 Eliel, and Obed, and Jasiel the Mesobaite.

12 1 Now these *are* they that came to David to
Ziklag, while he yet kept himself close because of Saul the son of Kish: and they *were* among
the mighty men, helpers of the war.
2 *They were* armed with bows, and could use both
the right hand and the left in *hurling* stones and
shooting arrows out of a bow, *even* of Saul's brethren
of Benjamin.
3 The chief *was* Ahiezer, then Joash, the sons of Shemaah the Gibeathite; and Jeziel, and Pelet, the sons of
Azmaveth; and Berachah, and Jehu the Antothite,
4 And Ismaiah the Gibeonite, a mighty man among
the thirty, and over the thirty; and Jeremiah, and Jahaziel, and Johanan, and Josabad the Gederathite,
5 Eluzai, and Jerimoth, and Bealiah, and Shemariah, and Shephatiah the Haruphite,
6 Elkanah, and Jesiah, and Azareel, and Joezer, and
Jashobeam, the Korhites,
7 And Joelah, and Zebadiah, the sons of Jeroham of
Gedor.
8 And of the Gadites there separated themselves
unto David into the hold to the wilderness men of
might, *and* men of war *fit* for the battle, that could
handle shield and buckler, whose faces *were like* the
faces of lions, and *were* as swift as the roes upon the
mountains;
9 Ezer the first, Obadiah the second, Eliab the third,
10 Mishmannah the fourth, Jeremiah the fifth,
11 Attai the sixth, Eliel the seventh,

NEW LIVING TRANSLATION

40 Ira from Jattir;
Gareb from Jattir;
41 Uriah the Hittite;
Zabad son of Ahlai;
42 Adina son of Shiza, the Reubenite leader
who had thirty men with him;
43 Hanan son of Maacah;
Joshaphat from Mithna;
44 Uzzia from Ashtaroth;
Shama and Jeiel, the sons of Hotham, from Aroer;
45 Jediael son of Shimri;
Joha, his brother, from Tiz;
46 Eliel from Mahavah;
Jeribai and Joshaviah, the sons of Elnaam;
Ithmah from Moab;
47 Eliel and Obed;
Jaasiel from Zobah.*

Warriors Join David's Army

12 The following men joined David at Ziklag
while he was hiding from Saul son of Kish.
They were among the warriors who fought beside
David in battle. 2 All of them were expert archers, and
they could shoot arrows or sling stones with their left
hand as well as their right. They were all relatives of
Saul from the tribe of Benjamin. 3 Their leader was
Ahiezer son of Shemaah from Gibeah; his brother
Joash was second-in-command. These were the
other warriors:

Jeziel and Pelet, sons of Azmaveth;
Beracah;
Jehu from Anathoth;
4 Ishmaiah from Gibeon, a famous warrior and
leader among the Thirty;
*Jeremiah, Jahaziel, Johanan, and Jozabad
from Gederah;
5 Eluzai, Jerimoth, Bealiah, Shemariah, and
Shephatiah from Haruph;
6 Elkanah, Isshiah, Azarel, Joezer, and Jashobeam,
who were Korahites;
7 Joelah and Zebadiah, sons of Jeroham from
Gedor.

8 Some brave and experienced warriors from the
tribe of Gad also defected to David while he was at
the stronghold in the wilderness. They were expert
with both shield and spear, as fierce as lions and as
swift as deer on the mountains.

9 Ezer was their leader.
Obadiah was second.
Eliab was third.
10 Mishmannah was fourth.
Jeremiah was fifth.
11 Attai was sixth.
Eliel was seventh.

11:47 Or *the Mezobaite.* **12:4** Verses 12:4b-40 are numbered 12:5-41 in Hebrew text.

KING JAMES VERSION

12 Johanan the eighth, Elzabad the ninth,

13 Jeremiah the tenth, Machbanai the eleventh.

14 These *were* of the sons of Gad, captains of the host: one of the least *was* over an hundred, and the greatest over a thousand.

15 These *are* they that went over Jordan in the first month, when it had overflown all his banks; and they put to flight all *them* of the valleys, *both* toward the east, and toward the west.

16 And there came of the children of Benjamin and Judah to the hold unto David.

17 And David went out to meet them, and answered and said unto them, If ye be come peaceably unto me to help me, mine heart shall be knit unto you: but if *ye be come* to betray me to mine enemies, seeing *there is* no wrong in mine hands, the God of our fathers look *thereon,* and rebuke *it*.

18 Then the spirit came upon Amasai, *who was* chief of the captains, *and he said,* Thine *are we,* David, and on thy side, thou son of Jesse: peace, peace *be* unto thee, and peace *be* to thine helpers; for thy God helpeth thee. Then David received them, and made them captains of the band.

19 And there fell *some* of Manasseh to David, when he came with the Philistines against Saul to battle: but they helped them not: for the lords of the Philistines upon advisement sent him away, saying, He will fall to his master Saul to *the jeopardy of* our heads.

20 As he went to Ziklag, there fell to him of Manasseh, Adnah, and Jozabad, and Jediael, and Michael, and Jozabad, and Elihu, and Zilthai, captains of the thousands that *were* of Manasseh.

21 And they helped David against the band *of the rovers:* for they *were* all mighty men of valour, and were captains in the host.

22 For at *that* time day by day there came to David to help him, until *it was* a great host, like the host of God.

23 And these *are* the numbers of the bands *that were* ready armed to the war, *and* came to David to Hebron, to turn the kingdom of Saul to him, according to the word of the LORD.

24 The children of Judah that bare shield and spear *were* six thousand and eight hundred, ready armed to the war.

25 Of the children of Simeon, mighty men of valour for the war, seven thousand and one hundred.

26 Of the children of Levi four thousand and six hundred.

27 And Jehoiada *was* the leader of the Aaronites, and with him *were* three thousand and seven hundred;

28 And Zadok, a young man mighty of valour, and of his father's house twenty and two captains.

NEW LIVING TRANSLATION

12 Johanan was eighth.
Elzabad was ninth.
13 Jeremiah was tenth.
Macbannai was eleventh.

14 These warriors from Gad were army commanders. The weakest among them could take on a hundred regular troops, and the strongest could take on a thousand! 15 These were the men who crossed the Jordan River during its seasonal flooding at the beginning of the year and drove out all the people living in the lowlands on both the east and west banks.

16 Others from Benjamin and Judah came to David at the stronghold. 17 David went out to meet them and said, "If you have come in peace to help me, we are friends. But if you have come to betray me to my enemies when I am innocent, then may the God of our ancestors see it and punish you."

18 Then the Spirit came upon Amasai, the leader of the Thirty, and he said,

"We are yours, David!
 We are on your side, son of Jesse.
Peace and prosperity be with you,
 and success to all who help you,
 for your God is the one who helps you."

So David let them join him, and he made them officers over his troops.

19 Some men from Manasseh defected from the Israelite army and joined David when he set out with the Philistines to fight against Saul. But as it turned out, the Philistine rulers refused to let David and his men go with them. After much discussion, they sent them back, for they said, "It will cost us our heads if David switches loyalties to Saul and turns against us."

20 Here is a list of the men from Manasseh who defected to David as he was returning to Ziklag: Adnah, Jozabad, Jediael, Michael, Jozabad, Elihu, and Zillethai. Each commanded 1,000 troops from the tribe of Manasseh. 21 They helped David chase down bands of raiders, for they were all brave and able warriors who became commanders in his army. 22 Day after day more men joined David until he had a great army, like the army of God.

23 These are the numbers of armed warriors who joined David at Hebron. They were all eager to see David become king instead of Saul, just as the LORD had promised.

24 From the tribe of Judah, there were 6,800
 warriors armed with shields and spears.
25 From the tribe of Simeon, there were 7,100
 brave warriors.
26 From the tribe of Levi, there were 4,600 warriors.
 27 This included Jehoiada, leader of the family
 of Aaron, who had 3,700 under his command.
 28 This also included Zadok, a brave young
 warrior, with 22 members of his family who
 were all officers.

KING JAMES VERSION

29 And of the children of Benjamin, the kindred of
Saul, three thousand: for hitherto the greatest part of
them had kept the ward of the house of Saul.
30 And of the children of Ephraim twenty thousand and eight hundred, mighty men of valour, famous throughout the house of their fathers.
31 And of the half tribe of Manasseh eighteen
thousand, which were expressed by name, to come
and make David king.
32 And of the children of Issachar, *which were*
men that had understanding of the times, to know
what Israel ought to do; the heads of them *were*
two hundred; and all their brethren *were* at their
commandment.
33 Of Zebulun, such as went forth to battle, expert
in war, with all instruments of war, fifty thousand,
which could keep rank: *they were* not of double
heart.
34 And of Naphtali a thousand captains, and with
them with shield and spear thirty and seven thousand.
35 And of the Danites expert in war twenty and
eight thousand and six hundred.
36 And of Asher, such as went forth to battle, expert
in war, forty thousand.
37 And on the other side of Jordan, of the Reubenites, and the Gadites, and of the half tribe of Manasseh, with all manner of instruments of war for the
battle, an hundred and twenty thousand.
38 All these men of war, that could keep rank, came
with a perfect heart to Hebron, to make David king
over all Israel: and all the rest also of Israel *were* of
one heart to make David king.
39 And there they were with David three days, eating and drinking: for their brethren had prepared for
them.
40 Moreover they that were nigh them, *even* unto
Issachar and Zebulun and Naphtali, brought bread
on asses, and on camels, and on mules, and on oxen,
and meat, meal, cakes of figs, and bunches of raisins,
and wine, and oil, and oxen, and sheep abundantly:
for *there was* joy in Israel.

13 1 And David consulted with the captains of
thousands and hundreds, *and* with every
leader.
2 And David said unto all the congregation of Israel, If *it seem* good unto you, and *that it be* of the LORD
our God, let us send abroad unto our brethren every
where, *that are* left in all the land of Israel, and with
them *also* to the priests and Levites *which are* in
their cities *and* suburbs, that they may gather themselves unto us:
3 And let us bring again the ark of our God to us: for
we inquired not at it in the days of Saul.
4 And all the congregation said that they would do
so: for the thing was right in the eyes of all the people.
5 So David gathered all Israel together, from Shihor

NEW LIVING TRANSLATION

29 From the tribe of Benjamin, Saul's relatives, there
were 3,000 warriors. Most of the men from
Benjamin had remained loyal to Saul until this
time.
30 From the tribe of Ephraim, there were 20,800
brave warriors, each highly respected in his own
clan.
31 From the half-tribe of Manasseh west of the
Jordan, 18,000 men were designated by name
to help David become king.
32 From the tribe of Issachar, there were 200 leaders
of the tribe with their relatives. All these men
understood the signs of the times and knew the
best course for Israel to take.
33 From the tribe of Zebulun, there were 50,000
skilled warriors. They were fully armed and
prepared for battle and completely loyal to David.
34 From the tribe of Naphtali, there were 1,000
officers and 37,000 warriors armed with shields
and spears.
35 From the tribe of Dan, there were 28,600
warriors, all prepared for battle.
36 From the tribe of Asher, there were 40,000
trained warriors, all prepared for battle.
37 From the east side of the Jordan River—where
the tribes of Reuben and Gad and the half-tribe
of Manasseh lived—there were 120,000 troops
armed with every kind of weapon.

38 All these men came in battle array to Hebron
with the single purpose of making David the king
over all Israel. In fact, everyone in Israel agreed that
David should be their king. 39 They feasted and drank
with David for three days, for preparations had been
made by their relatives for their arrival. 40 And people
from as far away as Issachar, Zebulun, and Naphtali
brought food on donkeys, camels, mules, and oxen.
Vast supplies of flour, fig cakes, clusters of raisins,
wine, olive oil, cattle, sheep, and goats were brought
to the celebration. There was great joy throughout
the land of Israel.

David Attempts to Move the Ark

13 David consulted with all his officials, including the generals and captains of his army.*
2 Then he addressed the entire assembly of Israel
as follows: "If you approve and if it is the will of the
LORD our God, let us send messages to all the Israelites throughout the land, including the priests and
Levites in their towns and pasturelands. Let us invite
them to come and join us. 3 It is time to bring back
the Ark of our God, for we neglected it during the
reign of Saul."
4 The whole assembly agreed to this, for the people
could see it was the right thing to do. 5 So David summoned all Israel, from the Shihor Brook of Egypt in

13:1 Hebrew *the commanders of thousands and of hundreds.*

KING JAMES VERSION

of Egypt even unto the entering of Hemath, to bring the ark of God from Kirjath-jearim.

6 And David went up, and all Israel, to Baalah, *that is,* to Kirjath-jearim, which *belonged* to Judah, to bring up thence the ark of God the LORD, that dwelleth *between* the cherubims, whose name is called *on it.*

7 And they carried the ark of God in a new cart out of the house of Abinadab: and Uzza and Ahio drave the cart.

8 And David and all Israel played before God with all *their* might, and with singing, and with harps, and with psalteries, and with timbrels, and with cymbals, and with trumpets.

9 And when they came unto the threshingfloor of Chidon, Uzza put forth his hand to hold the ark; for the oxen stumbled.

10 And the anger of the LORD was kindled against Uzza, and he smote him, because he put his hand to the ark: and there he died before God.

11 And David was displeased, because the LORD had made a breach upon Uzza: wherefore that place is called Perez-uzza to this day.

12 And David was afraid of God that day, saying, How shall I bring the ark of God *home* to me?

13 So David brought not the ark *home* to himself to the city of David, but carried it aside into the house of Obed-edom the Gittite.

14 And the ark of God remained with the family of Obed-edom in his house three months. And the LORD blessed the house of Obed-edom, and all that he had.

14 1 Now Hiram king of Tyre sent messengers to David, and timber of cedars, with masons and carpenters, to build him an house.

2 And David perceived that the LORD had confirmed him king over Israel, for his kingdom was lifted up on high, because of his people Israel.

3 And David took more wives at Jerusalem: and David begat more sons and daughters.

4 Now these *are* the names of *his* children which he had in Jerusalem; Shammua, and Shobab, Nathan, and Solomon,

5 And Ibhar, and Elishua, and Elpalet,

6 And Nogah, and Nepheg, and Japhia,

7 And Elishama, and Beeliada, and Eliphalet.

8 And when the Philistines heard that David was anointed king over all Israel, all the Philistines went up to seek David. And David heard *of it,* and went out against them.

9 And the Philistines came and spread themselves in the valley of Rephaim.

10 And David inquired of God, saying, Shall I go up against the Philistines? and wilt thou deliver them into mine hand? And the LORD said unto him, Go up; for I will deliver them into thine hand.

NEW LIVING TRANSLATION

the south all the way to the town of Lebo-hamath
in the north, to join in bringing the Ark of God from
Kiriath-jearim. 6 Then David and all Israel went to
Baalah of Judah (also called Kiriath-jearim) to bring
back the Ark of God, which bears the name* of
the LORD who is enthroned between the cherubim.
7 They placed the Ark of God on a new cart and
brought it from Abinadab's house. Uzzah and Ahio
were guiding the cart. 8 David and all Israel were celebrating before God with all their might, singing
songs and playing all kinds of musical instruments—
lyres, harps, tambourines, cymbals, and trumpets.
9 But when they arrived at the threshing floor of
Nacon,* the oxen stumbled, and Uzzah reached out
his hand to steady the Ark. 10 Then the LORD's anger
was aroused against Uzzah, and he struck him dead
because he had laid his hand on the Ark. So Uzzah
died there in the presence of God.
11 David was angry because the LORD's anger had
burst out against Uzzah. He named that place Perez-
uzzah (which means "to burst out against Uzzah"),
as it is still called today.
12 David was now afraid of God, and he asked,
"How can I ever bring the Ark of God back into my
care?" 13 So David did not move the Ark into the City
of David. Instead, he took it to the house of Obed-
edom of Gath. 14 The Ark of God remained there in
Obed-edom's house for three months, and the LORD
blessed the household of Obed-edom and everything he owned.

David's Palace and Family

14 Then King Hiram of Tyre sent messengers to
David, along with cedar timber, and stonemasons and carpenters to build him a palace. 2 And
David realized that the LORD had confirmed him as
king over Israel and had greatly blessed his kingdom
for the sake of his people Israel.
3 Then David married more wives in Jerusalem,
and they had more sons and daughters. 4 These are
the names of David's sons who were born in Jerusalem: Shammua, Shobab, Nathan, Solomon, 5 Ibhar,
Elishua, Elpelet, 6 Nogah, Nepheg, Japhia, 7 Elishama,
Eliada,* and Eliphelet.

David Conquers the Philistines

8 When the Philistines heard that David had been
anointed king over all Israel, they mobilized all their
forces to capture him. But David was told they were
coming, so he marched out to meet them. 9 The Philistines arrived and made a raid in the valley of Rephaim. 10 So David asked God, "Should I go out to fight
the Philistines? Will you hand them over to me?"
The LORD replied, "Yes, go ahead. I will hand them
over to you."

13:6 Or *the Ark of God, where the Name is proclaimed—the name.* **13:9** As in parallel text at 2 Sam 6:6; Hebrew reads *Kidon.* **14:7** Hebrew *Beeliada,* a variant spelling of Eliada; compare 3:8 and parallel text at 2 Sam 5:16.

KING JAMES VERSION

11 So they came up to Baal-perazim; and David
smote them there. Then David said, God hath broken
in upon mine enemies by mine hand like the breaking forth of waters: therefore they called the name of
that place Baal-perazim.
12 And when they had left their gods there, David
gave a commandment, and they were burned with
fire.
13 And the Philistines yet again spread themselves
abroad in the valley.
14 Therefore David inquired again of God; and God
said unto him, Go not up after them; turn away from
them, and come upon them over against the mulberry trees.
15 And it shall be, when thou shalt hear a sound
of going in the tops of the mulberry trees, *that* then
thou shalt go out to battle: for God is gone forth before thee to smite the host of the Philistines.
16 David therefore did as God commanded him:
and they smote the host of the Philistines from Gibeon even to Gazer.
17 And the fame of David went out into all lands;
and the LORD brought the fear of him upon all nations.

15 1 And *David* made him houses in the city
of David, and prepared a place for the ark of
God, and pitched for it a tent.
2 Then David said, None ought to carry the ark of
God but the Levites: for them hath the LORD chosen
to carry the ark of God, and to minister unto him
for ever.
3 And David gathered all Israel together to Jerusalem, to bring up the ark of the LORD unto his place,
which he had prepared for it.
4 And David assembled the children of Aaron, and
the Levites:
5 Of the sons of Kohath; Uriel the chief, and his
brethren an hundred and twenty:
6 Of the sons of Merari; Asaiah the chief, and his
brethren two hundred and twenty:
7 Of the sons of Gershom; Joel the chief, and his
brethren an hundred and thirty:
8 Of the sons of Elizaphan; Shemaiah the chief,
and his brethren two hundred:
9 Of the sons of Hebron; Eliel the chief, and his
brethren fourscore:
10 Of the sons of Uzziel; Amminadab the chief,
and his brethren an hundred and twelve.
11 And David called for Zadok and Abiathar the
priests, and for the Levites, for Uriel, Asaiah, and Joel,
Shemaiah, and Eliel, and Amminadab,
12 And said unto them, Ye *are* the chief of the fathers of the Levites: sanctify yourselves, *both* ye and
your brethren, that ye may bring up the ark of the
LORD God of Israel unto *the place that* I have prepared for it.

NEW LIVING TRANSLATION

11 So David and his troops went up to Baal-perazim
and defeated the Philistines there. "God did it!" David exclaimed. "He used me to burst through my enemies like a raging flood!" So they named that place
Baal-perazim (which means "the Lord who bursts
through"). 12 The Philistines had abandoned their
gods there, so David gave orders to burn them.
13 But after a while the Philistines returned and
raided the valley again. 14 And once again David
asked God what to do. "Do not attack them straight
on," God replied. "Instead, circle around behind and
attack them near the poplar* trees. 15 When you hear
a sound like marching feet in the tops of the poplar
trees, go out and attack! That will be the signal that
God is moving ahead of you to strike down the Philistine army." 16 So David did what God commanded,
and they struck down the Philistine army all the way
from Gibeon to Gezer.
17 So David's fame spread everywhere, and the
LORD caused all the nations to fear David.

Preparing to Move the Ark

15 David now built several buildings for himself
in the City of David. He also prepared a place
for the Ark of God and set up a special tent for it.
2 Then he commanded, "No one except the Levites
may carry the Ark of God. The LORD has chosen them
to carry the Ark of the LORD and to serve him forever."
3 Then David summoned all Israel to Jerusalem to
bring the Ark of the LORD to the place he had prepared for it. 4 This is the number of the descendants
of Aaron (the priests) and the Levites who were
called together:

5 From the clan of Kohath, 120, with Uriel as their
leader.
6 From the clan of Merari, 220, with Asaiah as their
leader.
7 From the clan of Gershon,* 130, with Joel as their
leader.
8 From the descendants of Elizaphan, 200, with
Shemaiah as their leader.
9 From the descendants of Hebron, 80, with Eliel as
their leader.
10 From the descendants of Uzziel, 112, with
Amminadab as their leader.

11 Then David summoned the priests, Zadok and
Abiathar, and these Levite leaders: Uriel, Asaiah, Joel,
Shemaiah, Eliel, and Amminadab. 12 He said to them,
"You are the leaders of the Levite families. You must
purify yourselves and all your fellow Levites, so you
can bring the Ark of the LORD, the God of Israel, to

14:14 Or *aspen*, or *balsam;* also in 14:15. The exact identification of this tree is uncertain. **15:7** Hebrew *Gershom*, a variant spelling of Gershon.

KING JAMES VERSION

13 For because ye *did it* not at the first, the LORD our God made a breach upon us, for that we sought him not after the due order.

14 So the priests and the Levites sanctified themselves to bring up the ark of the LORD God of Israel.

15 And the children of the Levites bare the ark of God upon their shoulders with the staves thereon, as Moses commanded according to the word of the LORD.

16 And David spake to the chief of the Levites to appoint their brethren *to be* the singers with instruments of musick, psalteries and harps and cymbals, sounding, by lifting up the voice with joy.

17 So the Levites appointed Heman the son of Joel; and of his brethren, Asaph the son of Berechiah; and of the sons of Merari their brethren, Ethan the son of Kushaiah;

18 And with them their brethren of the second *degree,* Zechariah, Ben, and Jaaziel, and Shemiramoth, and Jehiel, and Unni, Eliab, and Benaiah, and Maaseiah, and Mattithiah, and Elipheleh, and Mikneiah, and Obed-edom, and Jeiel, the porters.

19 So the singers, Heman, Asaph, and Ethan, *were appointed* to sound with cymbals of brass;

20 And Zechariah, and Aziel, and Shemiramoth, and Jehiel, and Unni, and Eliab, and Maaseiah, and Benaiah, with psalteries on Alamoth;

21 And Mattithiah, and Elipheleh, and Mikneiah, and Obed-edom, and Jeiel, and Azaziah, with harps on the Sheminith to excel.

22 And Chenaniah, chief of the Levites, *was* for song: he instructed about the song, because he *was* skilful.

23 And Berechiah and Elkanah *were* doorkeepers for the ark.

24 And Shebaniah, and Jehoshaphat, and Nethaneel, and Amasai, and Zechariah, and Benaiah, and Eliezer, the priests, did blow with the trumpets before the ark of God: and Obed-edom and Jehiah *were* doorkeepers for the ark.

25 So David, and the elders of Israel, and the captains over thousands, went to bring up the ark of the covenant of the LORD out of the house of Obed-edom with joy.

26 And it came to pass, when God helped the Levites that bare the ark of the covenant of the LORD, that they offered seven bullocks and seven rams.

27 And David *was* clothed with a robe of fine linen, and all the Levites that bare the ark, and the singers, and Chenaniah the master of the song with the singers: David also *had* upon him an ephod of linen.

28 Thus all Israel brought up the ark of the covenant of the LORD with shouting, and with sound of the cornet, and with trumpets, and with cymbals, making a noise with psalteries and harps.

NEW LIVING TRANSLATION

the place I have prepared for it. 13 Because you Levites did not carry the Ark the first time, the anger of the LORD our God burst out against us. We failed to ask God how to move it properly." 14 So the priests and the Levites purified themselves in order to bring the Ark of the LORD, the God of Israel, to Jerusalem. 15 Then the Levites carried the Ark of God on their shoulders with its carrying poles, just as the LORD had instructed Moses.

16 David also ordered the Levite leaders to appoint a choir of Levites who were singers and musicians to sing joyful songs to the accompaniment of harps, lyres, and cymbals. 17 So the Levites appointed Heman son of Joel along with his fellow Levites: Asaph son of Berekiah, and Ethan son of Kushaiah from the clan of Merari. 18 The following men were chosen as their assistants: Zechariah, Jaaziel,* Shemiramoth, Jehiel, Unni, Eliab, Benaiah, Maaseiah, Mattithiah, Eliphelehu, Mikneiah, and the gatekeepers—Obed-edom and Jeiel.

19 The musicians Heman, Asaph, and Ethan were chosen to sound the bronze cymbals. 20 Zechariah, Aziel, Shemiramoth, Jehiel, Unni, Eliab, Maaseiah, and Benaiah were chosen to play the harps.* 21 Mattithiah, Eliphelehu, Mikneiah, Obed-edom, Jeiel, and Azaziah were chosen to play the lyres.* 22 Kenaniah, the head Levite, was chosen as the choir leader because of his skill.

23 Berekiah and Elkanah were chosen to guard* the Ark. 24 Shebaniah, Joshaphat, Nethanel, Amasai, Zechariah, Benaiah, and Eliezer—all of whom were priests—were chosen to blow the trumpets as they marched in front of the Ark of God. Obed-edom and Jehiah were chosen to guard the Ark.

Moving the Ark to Jerusalem

25 Then David and the elders of Israel and the generals of the army* went to the house of Obed-edom to bring the Ark of the LORD's Covenant up to Jerusalem with a great celebration. 26 And because God was clearly helping the Levites as they carried the Ark of the LORD's Covenant, they sacrificed seven bulls and seven rams.

27 David was dressed in a robe of fine linen, as were all the Levites who carried the Ark, and also the singers, and Kenaniah the choir leader. David was also wearing a priestly garment.* 28 So all Israel brought up the Ark of the LORD's Covenant with shouts of joy, the blowing of rams' horns and trumpets, the crashing of cymbals, and loud playing on harps and lyres.

15:18 As in several Hebrew manuscripts and Greek version (see also parallel lists in 15:20; 16:5); Masoretic Text reads *Zechariah ben Jaaziel.* **15:20** Hebrew adds *according to Alamoth,* which is probably a musical term. The meaning of the Hebrew is uncertain. **15:21** Hebrew adds *according to the Sheminith,* which is probably a musical term. The meaning of the Hebrew is uncertain. **15:23** Hebrew *chosen as gatekeepers for;* also in 15:24. **15:25** Hebrew *the commanders of thousands.* **15:27** Hebrew *a linen ephod.*

29 And it came to pass, *as* the ark of the covenant of
the LORD came to the city of David, that Michal the
daughter of Saul looking out at a window saw king
David dancing and playing: and she despised him in
her heart.

16 1 So they brought the ark of God, and set it in
the midst of the tent that David had pitched
for it: and they offered burnt sacrifices and peace
offerings before God.
2 And when David had made an end of offering the
burnt offerings and the peace offerings, he blessed
the people in the name of the LORD.
3 And he dealt to every one of Israel, both man and
woman, to every one a loaf of bread, and a good piece
of flesh, and a flagon *of wine*.
4 And he appointed *certain* of the Levites to minister before the ark of the LORD, and to record, and to
thank and praise the LORD God of Israel:
5 Asaph the chief, and next to him Zechariah, Jeiel,
and Shemiramoth, and Jehiel, and Mattithiah, and
Eliab, and Benaiah, and Obed-edom: and Jeiel with
psalteries and with harps; but Asaph made a sound
with cymbals;
6 Benaiah also and Jahaziel the priests with trumpets continually before the ark of the covenant of
God.
7 Then on that day David delivered first *this psalm*
to thank the LORD into the hand of Asaph and his
brethren.
8 Give thanks unto the LORD, call upon his name,
make known his deeds among the people.
9 Sing unto him, sing psalms unto him, talk ye of all
his wondrous works.
10 Glory ye in his holy name: let the heart of them
rejoice that seek the LORD.
11 Seek the LORD and his strength, seek his face
continually.
12 Remember his marvellous works that he hath
done, his wonders, and the judgments of his mouth;
13 O ye seed of Israel his servant, ye children of
Jacob, his chosen ones.
14 He *is* the LORD our God; his judgments *are* in all
the earth.
15 Be ye mindful always of his covenant; the word
which he commanded to a thousand generations;
16 *Even of the covenant* which he made with Abraham, and of his oath unto Isaac;
17 And hath confirmed the same to Jacob for a law,
and to Israel *for* an everlasting covenant,
18 Saying, Unto thee will I give the land of Canaan,
the lot of your inheritance;

29 But as the Ark of the LORD's Covenant entered
the City of David, Michal, the daughter of Saul,
looked down from her window. When she saw King
David skipping about and laughing with joy, she was
filled with contempt for him.

16 They brought the Ark of God and placed it inside the special tent David had prepared for
it. And they presented burnt offerings and peace
offerings to God. 2 When he had finished his sacrifices, David blessed the people in the name of the
LORD. 3 Then he gave to every man and woman in all
Israel a loaf of bread, a cake of dates,* and a cake of
raisins.
4 David appointed the following Levites to lead the
people in worship before the Ark of the LORD—to invoke his blessings, to give thanks, and to praise the
LORD, the God of Israel. 5 Asaph, the leader of this
group, sounded the cymbals. Second to him was
Zechariah, followed by Jeiel, Shemiramoth, Jehiel,
Mattithiah, Eliab, Benaiah, Obed-edom, and Jeiel.
They played the harps and lyres. 6 The priests, Benaiah and Jahaziel, played the trumpets regularly before the Ark of God's Covenant.

David's Song of Praise

7 On that day David gave to Asaph and his fellow Levites this song of thanksgiving to the LORD:

8 Give thanks to the LORD and proclaim his
greatness.
Let the whole world know what he has done.
9 Sing to him; yes, sing his praises.
Tell everyone about his wonderful deeds.
10 Exult in his holy name;
rejoice, you who worship the LORD.
11 Search for the LORD and for his strength;
continually seek him.
12 Remember the wonders he has performed,
his miracles, and the rulings he has given,
13 you children of his servant Israel,
you descendants of Jacob, his chosen ones.

14 He is the LORD our God.
His justice is seen throughout the land.
15 Remember his covenant forever—
the commitment he made to a thousand
generations.
16 This is the covenant he made with Abraham
and the oath he swore to Isaac.
17 He confirmed it to Jacob as a decree,
and to the people of Israel as a never-ending
covenant:
18 "I will give you the land of Canaan
as your special possession."

16:3 Or *a portion of meat.* The meaning of the Hebrew is uncertain.

KING JAMES VERSION

19 When ye were but few, even a few, and strangers in it.

20 And *when* they went from nation to nation, and from *one* kingdom to another people;

21 He suffered no man to do them wrong: yea, he reproved kings for their sakes,

22 *Saying,* Touch not mine anointed, and do my prophets no harm.

23 Sing unto the LORD, all the earth; shew forth from day to day his salvation.

24 Declare his glory among the heathen; his marvellous works among all nations.

25 For great *is* the LORD, and greatly to be praised: he also *is* to be feared above all gods.

26 For all the gods of the people *are* idols: but the LORD made the heavens.

27 Glory and honour *are* in his presence; strength and gladness *are* in his place.

28 Give unto the LORD, ye kindreds of the people, give unto the LORD glory and strength.

29 Give unto the LORD the glory *due* unto his name: bring an offering, and come before him: worship the LORD in the beauty of holiness.

30 Fear before him, all the earth: the world also shall be stable, that it be not moved.

31 Let the heavens be glad, and let the earth rejoice: and let *men* say among the nations, The LORD reigneth.

32 Let the sea roar, and the fulness thereof: let the fields rejoice, and all that *is* therein.

33 Then shall the trees of the wood sing out at the presence of the LORD, because he cometh to judge the earth.

34 O give thanks unto the LORD; for *he is* good; for his mercy *endureth* for ever.

35 And say ye, Save us, O God of our salvation, and gather us together, and deliver us from the heathen, that we may give thanks to thy holy name, *and* glory in thy praise.

36 Blessed *be* the LORD God of Israel for ever and ever. And all the people said, Amen, and praised the LORD.

37 So he left there before the ark of the covenant of the LORD Asaph and his brethren, to minister before the ark continually, as every day's work required:

38 And Obed-edom with their brethren, threescore and eight; Obed-edom also the son of Jeduthun and Hosah *to be* porters:

39 And Zadok the priest, and his brethren the priests, before the tabernacle of the LORD in the high place that *was* at Gibeon,

NEW LIVING TRANSLATION

19 He said this when you were few in number,
a tiny group of strangers in Canaan.
20 They wandered from nation to nation,
from one kingdom to another.
21 Yet he did not let anyone oppress them.
He warned kings on their behalf:
22 "Do not touch my chosen people,
and do not hurt my prophets."

23 Let the whole earth sing to the LORD!
Each day proclaim the good news that he saves.
24 Publish his glorious deeds among the nations.
Tell everyone about the amazing things he does.
25 Great is the LORD! He is most worthy of praise!
He is to be feared above all gods.
26 The gods of other nations are mere idols,
but the LORD made the heavens!
27 Honor and majesty surround him;
strength and joy fill his dwelling.

28 O nations of the world, recognize the LORD,
recognize that the LORD is glorious and strong.
29 Give to the LORD the glory he deserves!
Bring your offering and come into his presence.
Worship the LORD in all his holy splendor.
30 Let all the earth tremble before him.
The world stands firm and cannot be shaken.

31 Let the heavens be glad, and the earth rejoice!
Tell all the nations, "The LORD reigns!"
32 Let the sea and everything in it shout his praise!
Let the fields and their crops burst out with joy!
33 Let the trees of the forest rustle with praise,
for the LORD is coming to judge the earth.

34 Give thanks to the LORD, for he is good!
His faithful love endures forever.
35 Cry out, "Save us, O God of our salvation!
Gather and rescue us from among the nations,
so we can thank your holy name
and rejoice and praise you."

36 Praise the LORD, the God of Israel,
who lives from everlasting to everlasting!

And all the people shouted "Amen!" and praised the LORD.

Worship at Jerusalem and Gibeon

37 David arranged for Asaph and his fellow Levites to serve regularly before the Ark of the LORD's Covenant, doing whatever needed to be done each day.
38 This group included Obed-edom (son of Jeduthun), Hosah, and sixty-eight other Levites as gatekeepers.

39 Meanwhile, David stationed Zadok the priest and his fellow priests at the Tabernacle of the LORD at the place of worship in Gibeon, where they continued to

KING JAMES VERSION

40 To offer burnt offerings unto the LORD upon the altar of the burnt offering continually morning and evening, and *to do* according to all that is written in the law of the LORD, which he commanded Israel;

41 And with them Heman and Jeduthun, and the rest that were chosen, who were expressed by name, to give thanks to the LORD, because his mercy *endureth* for ever;

42 And with them Heman and Jeduthun with trumpets and cymbals for those that should make a sound, and with musical instruments of God. And the sons of Jeduthun *were* porters.

43 And all the people departed every man to his house: and David returned to bless his house.

17 1 Now it came to pass, as David sat in his house, that David said to Nathan the prophet, Lo, I dwell in an house of cedars, but the ark of the covenant of the LORD *remaineth* under curtains.

2 Then Nathan said unto David, Do all that *is* in thine heart; for God *is* with thee.

3 And it came to pass the same night, that the word of God came to Nathan, saying,

4 Go and tell David my servant, Thus saith the LORD, Thou shalt not build me an house to dwell in:

5 For I have not dwelt in an house since the day that I brought up Israel unto this day; but have gone from tent to tent, and from *one* tabernacle *to another.*

6 Wheresoever I have walked with all Israel, spake I a word to any of the judges of Israel, whom I commanded to feed my people, saying, Why have ye not built me an house of cedars?

7 Now therefore thus shalt thou say unto my servant David, Thus saith the LORD of hosts, I took thee from the sheepcote, *even* from following the sheep, that thou shouldest be ruler over my people Israel:

8 And I have been with thee whithersoever thou hast walked, and have cut off all thine enemies from before thee, and have made thee a name like the name of the great men that *are* in the earth.

9 Also I will ordain a place for my people Israel, and will plant them, and they shall dwell in their place, and shall be moved no more; neither shall the children of wickedness waste them any more, as at the beginning,

10 And since the time that I commanded judges *to be* over my people Israel. Moreover I will subdue all thine enemies. Furthermore I tell thee that the LORD will build thee an house.

11 And it shall come to pass, when thy days be expired that thou must go *to be* with thy fathers, that I will raise up thy seed after thee, which shall be of thy sons; and I will establish his kingdom.

12 He shall build me an house, and I will stablish his throne for ever.

NEW LIVING TRANSLATION

minister before the LORD. 40 They sacrificed the regular burnt offerings to the LORD each morning and evening on the altar set aside for that purpose, obeying everything written in the Law of the LORD, as he had commanded Israel. 41 David also appointed Heman, Jeduthun, and the others chosen by name to give thanks to the LORD, for "his faithful love endures forever." 42 They used their trumpets, cymbals, and other instruments to accompany their songs of praise to God.* And the sons of Jeduthun were appointed as gatekeepers.

43 Then all the people returned to their homes, and David turned and went home to bless his own family.

The LORD's Covenant Promise to David

17 When David was settled in his palace, he summoned Nathan the prophet. "Look," David said, "I am living in a beautiful cedar palace,* but the Ark of the LORD's Covenant is out there under a tent!"

2 Nathan replied to David, "Do whatever you have in mind, for God is with you."

3 But that same night God said to Nathan,

4 "Go and tell my servant David, 'This is what the
LORD has declared: You are not the one to build
a house for me to live in. 5 I have never lived in a
house, from the day I brought the Israelites out
of Egypt until this very day. My home has always
been a tent, moving from one place to another in
a Tabernacle. 6 Yet no matter where I have gone
with the Israelites, I have never once complained
to Israel's leaders,* the shepherds of my people.
I have never asked them, "Why haven't you built
me a beautiful cedar house?"'

7 "Now go and say to my servant David, 'This is
what the LORD of Heaven's Armies has declared:
I took you from tending sheep in the pasture and
selected you to be the leader of my people Israel.
8 I have been with you wherever you have gone,
and I have destroyed all your enemies before your
eyes. Now I will make your name as famous as
anyone who has ever lived on the earth! 9 And I
will provide a homeland for my people Israel,
planting them in a secure place where they will
never be disturbed. Evil nations won't oppress
them as they've done in the past, 10 starting from
the time I appointed judges to rule my people
Israel. And I will defeat all your enemies.

"'Furthermore, I declare that the LORD will
build a house for you—a dynasty of kings! 11 For
when you die and join your ancestors, I will raise
up one of your descendants, one of your sons,
and I will make his kingdom strong. 12 He is the
one who will build a house—a temple—for me.

16:42 Or *to accompany the sacred music;* or *to accompany singing to God.*
17:1 Hebrew *a house of cedar.* **17:6** As in Greek version (see also 2 Sam 7:7); Hebrew reads *judges.*

KING JAMES VERSION

[13]I will be his father, and he shall be my son: and I
will not take my mercy away from him, as I took *it*
from *him* that was before thee:
[14]But I will settle him in mine house and in my
kingdom for ever: and his throne shall be established for evermore.
[15]According to all these words, and according to
all this vision, so did Nathan speak unto David.

[16]And David the king came and sat before the
LORD, and said, Who *am* I, O LORD God, and what *is*
mine house, that thou hast brought me hitherto?
[17]And *yet* this was a small thing in thine eyes,
O God; for thou hast *also* spoken of thy servant's
house for a great while to come, and hast regarded
me according to the estate of a man of high degree,
O LORD God.
[18]What can David *speak* more to thee for the honour of thy servant? for thou knowest thy servant.
[19]O LORD, for thy servant's sake, and according to
thine own heart, hast thou done all this greatness, in
making known all *these* great things.
[20]O LORD, *there is* none like thee, neither *is there*
any God beside thee, according to all that we have
heard with our ears.
[21]And what one nation in the earth *is* like thy people Israel, whom God went to redeem *to be* his own
people, to make thee a name of greatness and terribleness, by driving out nations from before thy people, whom thou hast redeemed out of Egypt?
[22]For thy people Israel didst thou make thine own
people for ever; and thou, LORD, becamest their God.
[23]Therefore now, LORD, let the thing that thou hast
spoken concerning thy servant and concerning his
house be established for ever, and do as thou hast
said.
[24]Let it even be established, that thy name may be
magnified for ever, saying, The LORD of hosts *is* the
God of Israel, *even* a God to Israel: and *let* the house
of David thy servant *be* established before thee.
[25]For thou, O my God, hast told thy servant that
thou wilt build him an house: therefore thy servant
hath found *in his heart* to pray before thee.
[26]And now, LORD, thou art God, and hast promised
this goodness unto thy servant:
[27]Now therefore let it please thee to bless the
house of thy servant, that it may be before thee for
ever: for thou blessest, O LORD, and *it shall be* blessed
for ever.

NEW LIVING TRANSLATION

And I will secure his throne forever. [13]I will be his
father, and he will be my son. I will never take my
favor from him as I took it from the one who
ruled before you. [14]I will confirm him as king
over my house and my kingdom for all time, and
his throne will be secure forever.'"

[15]So Nathan went back to David and told him everything the LORD had said in this vision.

David's Prayer of Thanks
[16]Then King David went in and sat before the LORD
and prayed,

"Who am I, O LORD God, and what is my family,
that you have brought me this far? [17]And now,
O God, in addition to everything else, you speak
of giving your servant a lasting dynasty! You
speak as though I were someone very great,*
O LORD God!

[18]"What more can I say to you about the
way you have honored me? You know what
your servant is really like. [19]For the sake of your
servant, O LORD, and according to your will, you
have done all these great things and have made
them known.

[20]"O LORD, there is no one like you. We have
never even heard of another God like you! [21]What
other nation on earth is like your people Israel?
What other nation, O God, have you redeemed
from slavery to be your own people? You made a
great name for yourself when you redeemed your
people from Egypt. You performed awesome
miracles and drove out the nations that stood
in their way. [22]You chose Israel to be your very
own people forever, and you, O LORD, became
their God.

[23]"And now, O LORD, I am your servant; do
as you have promised concerning me and my
family. May it be a promise that will last forever.
[24]And may your name be established and
honored forever so that everyone will say, 'The
LORD of Heaven's Armies, the God of Israel, is
Israel's God!' And may the house of your servant
David continue before you forever.

[25]"O my God, I have been bold enough to pray
to you because you have revealed to your servant
that you will build a house for him—a dynasty of
kings! [26]For you are God, O LORD. And you have
promised these good things to your servant.
[27]And now, it has pleased you to bless the house
of your servant, so that it will continue forever
before you. For when you grant a blessing,
O LORD, it is an eternal blessing!"

17:17 The meaning of the Hebrew is uncertain.

KING JAMES VERSION

18 [1]Now after this it came to pass, that David smote the Philistines, and subdued them, and took Gath and her towns out of the hand of the Philistines.

[2]And he smote Moab; and the Moabites became David's servants, *and* brought gifts.

[3]And David smote Hadarezer king of Zobah unto Hamath, as he went to stablish his dominion by the river Euphrates.

[4]And David took from him a thousand chariots, and seven thousand horsemen, and twenty thousand footmen: David also houghed all the chariot *horses,* but reserved of them an hundred chariots.

[5]And when the Syrians of Damascus came to help Hadarezer king of Zobah, David slew of the Syrians two and twenty thousand men.

[6]Then David put *garrisons* in Syria-damascus; and the Syrians became David's servants, *and* brought gifts. Thus the LORD preserved David whithersoever he went.

[7]And David took the shields of gold that were on the servants of Hadarezer, and brought them to Jerusalem.

[8]Likewise from Tibhath, and from Chun, cities of Hadarezer, brought David very much brass, wherewith Solomon made the brasen sea, and the pillars, and the vessels of brass.

[9]Now when Tou king of Hamath heard how David had smitten all the host of Hadarezer king of Zobah;

[10]He sent Hadoram his son to king David, to inquire of his welfare, and to congratulate him, because he had fought against Hadarezer, and smitten him; (for Hadarezer had war with Tou;) and *with him* all manner of vessels of gold and silver and brass.

[11]Them also king David dedicated unto the LORD, with the silver and the gold that he brought from all *these* nations; from Edom, and from Moab, and from the children of Ammon, and from the Philistines, and from Amalek.

[12]Moreover Abishai the son of Zeruiah slew of the Edomites in the valley of salt eighteen thousand.

[13]And he put garrisons in Edom; and all the Edomites became David's servants. Thus the LORD preserved David whithersoever he went.

[14]So David reigned over all Israel, and executed judgment and justice among all his people.

[15]And Joab the son of Zeruiah *was* over the host; and Jehoshaphat the son of Ahilud, recorder.

[16]And Zadok the son of Ahitub, and Abimelech the son of Abiathar, *were* the priests; and Shavsha was scribe;

[17]And Benaiah the son of Jehoiada *was* over the Cherethites and the Pelethites; and the sons of David *were* chief about the king.

NEW LIVING TRANSLATION

David's Military Victories

18 After this, David defeated and subdued the Philistines by conquering Gath and its surrounding towns. [2]David also conquered the land of Moab, and the Moabites who were spared became David's subjects and paid him tribute money.

[3]David also destroyed the forces of Hadadezer, king of Zobah, as far as Hamath,* when Hadadezer marched out to strengthen his control along the Euphrates River. [4]David captured 1,000 chariots, 7,000 charioteers, and 20,000 foot soldiers. He crippled all the chariot horses except enough for 100 chariots.

[5]When Arameans from Damascus arrived to help King Hadadezer, David killed 22,000 of them. [6]Then he placed several army garrisons* in Damascus, the Aramean capital, and the Arameans became David's subjects and paid him tribute money. So the LORD made David victorious wherever he went.

[7]David brought the gold shields of Hadadezer's officers to Jerusalem, [8]along with a large amount of bronze from Hadadezer's towns of Tebah* and Cun. Later Solomon melted the bronze and molded it into the great bronze basin called the Sea, the pillars, and the various bronze articles used at the Temple.

[9]When King Toi* of Hamath heard that David had destroyed the entire army of King Hadadezer of Zobah, [10]he sent his son Joram* to congratulate King David for his successful campaign. Hadadezer and Toi had been enemies and were often at war. Joram presented David with many gifts of gold, silver, and bronze.

[11]King David dedicated all these gifts to the LORD, along with the silver and gold he had taken from the other nations—from Edom, Moab, Ammon, Philistia, and Amalek.

[12]Abishai son of Zeruiah destroyed 18,000 Edomites in the Valley of Salt. [13]He placed army garrisons in Edom, and all the Edomites became David's subjects. In fact, the LORD made David victorious wherever he went.

[14]So David reigned over all Israel and did what was just and right for all his people. [15]Joab son of Zeruiah was commander of the army. Jehoshaphat son of Ahilud was the royal historian. [16]Zadok son of Ahitub and Ahimelech* son of Abiathar were the priests. Seraiah* was the court secretary. [17]Benaiah son of Jehoiada was captain of the king's bodyguard.* And David's sons served as the king's chief assistants.

18:3 The meaning of the Hebrew is uncertain. **18:6** As in Greek version and Latin Vulgate (see also 2 Sam 8:6); Hebrew lacks *several army garrisons.* **18:8** Hebrew reads *Tibhath,* a variant spelling of Tebah; compare parallel text at 2 Sam 8:8. **18:9** As in parallel text at 2 Sam 8:9; Hebrew reads *Tou;* also in 18:10. **18:10** As in parallel text at 2 Sam 8:10; Hebrew reads *Hadoram,* a variant spelling of Joram. **18:16a** As in some Hebrew manuscripts, Syriac version, and Latin Vulgate (see also 2 Sam 8:17); most Hebrew manuscripts read *Abimelech.* **18:16b** As in parallel text at 2 Sam 8:17; Hebrew reads *Shavsha.* **18:17** Hebrew *of the Kerethites and Pelethites.*

KING JAMES VERSION

19 1Now it came to pass after this, that Nahash
the king of the children of Ammon died, and
his son reigned in his stead.
2And David said, I will shew kindness unto Hanun
the son of Nahash, because his father shewed kindness to me. And David sent messengers to comfort
him concerning his father. So the servants of David
came into the land of the children of Ammon to
Hanun, to comfort him.
3But the princes of the children of Ammon said
to Hanun, Thinkest thou that David doth honour thy
father, that he hath sent comforters unto thee? are
not his servants come unto thee for to search, and to
overthrow, and to spy out the land?
4Wherefore Hanun took David's servants, and
shaved them, and cut off their garments in the midst
hard by their buttocks, and sent them away.
5Then there went *certain,* and told David how the
men were served. And he sent to meet them: for the
men were greatly ashamed. And the king said, Tarry at
Jericho until your beards be grown, and *then* return.
6And when the children of Ammon saw that they
had made themselves odious to David, Hanun and the
children of Ammon sent a thousand talents of silver
to hire them chariots and horsemen out of Mesopotamia, and out of Syria-maachah, and out of Zobah.
7So they hired thirty and two thousand chariots,
and the king of Maachah and his people; who came
and pitched before Medeba. And the children of Ammon gathered themselves together from their cities,
and came to battle.
8And when David heard *of it,* he sent Joab, and all
the host of the mighty men.
9And the children of Ammon came out, and put the
battle in array before the gate of the city: and the
kings that were come *were* by themselves in the field.
10Now when Joab saw that the battle was set
against him before and behind, he chose out of all
the choice of Israel, and put *them* in array against the
Syrians.
11And the rest of the people he delivered unto the
hand of Abishai his brother, and they set *themselves*
in array against the children of Ammon.
12And he said, If the Syrians be too strong for me,
then thou shalt help me: but if the children of Ammon be too strong for thee, then I will help thee.
13Be of good courage, and let us behave ourselves
valiantly for our people, and for the cities of our God:
and let the LORD do *that which is* good in his sight.
14So Joab and the people that *were* with him drew
nigh before the Syrians unto the battle; and they fled
before him.
15And when the children of Ammon saw that the
Syrians were fled, they likewise fled before Abishai
his brother, and entered into the city. Then Joab
came to Jerusalem.
16And when the Syrians saw that they were put to

NEW LIVING TRANSLATION

David Defeats the Ammonites

19 Some time after this, King Nahash of the
Ammonites died, and his son Hanun* be-
came king. 2David said, "I am going to show loyalty to
Hanun because his father, Nahash, was always loyal
to me." So David sent messengers to express sympathy to Hanun about his father's death.
But when David's ambassadors arrived in the land
of Ammon, 3the Ammonite commanders said to Hanun, "Do you really think these men are coming here
to honor your father? No! David has sent them to spy
out the land so they can come in and conquer it!" 4So
Hanun seized David's ambassadors and shaved
them, cut off their robes at the buttocks, and sent
them back to David in shame.
5When David heard what had happened to the
men, he sent messengers to tell them, "Stay at Jericho
until your beards grow out, and then come back." For
they felt deep shame because of their appearance.
6When the people of Ammon realized how seriously they had angered David, Hanun and the Ammonites sent 75,000 pounds* of silver to hire
chariots and charioteers from Aram-naharaim,
Aram-maacah, and Zobah. 7They also hired 32,000
chariots and secured the support of the king of Maacah and his army. These forces camped at Medeba,
where they were joined by the Ammonite troops that
Hanun had recruited from his own towns. 8When
David heard about this, he sent Joab and all his warriors to fight them. 9The Ammonite troops came out
and drew up their battle lines at the entrance of the
city, while the other kings positioned themselves to
fight in the open fields.
10When Joab saw that he would have to fight on
both the front and the rear, he chose some of Israel's
elite troops and placed them under his personal command to fight the Arameans in the fields. 11He left the
rest of the army under the command of his brother
Abishai, who was to attack the Ammonites. 12"If the
Arameans are too strong for me, then come over and
help me," Joab told his brother. "And if the Ammonites
are too strong for you, I will help you. 13Be courageous!
Let us fight bravely for our people and the cities of our
God. May the LORD's will be done."
14When Joab and his troops attacked, the Arameans began to run away. 15And when the Ammonites
saw the Arameans running, they also ran from
Abishai and retreated into the city. Then Joab returned to Jerusalem.
16The Arameans now realized that they were no

19:1 As in parallel text at 2 Sam 10:1; Hebrew lacks *Hanun.* **19:6** Hebrew *1,000 talents* [34,000 kilograms].

KING JAMES VERSION

the worse before Israel, they sent messengers, and drew forth the Syrians that *were* beyond the river: and Shophach the captain of the host of Hadarezer *went* before them.

17 And it was told David; and he gathered all Israel, and passed over Jordan, and came upon them, and set *the battle* in array against them. So when David had put the battle in array against the Syrians, they fought with him.

18 But the Syrians fled before Israel; and David slew of the Syrians seven thousand *men which fought in* chariots, and forty thousand footmen, and killed Shophach the captain of the host.

19 And when the servants of Hadarezer saw that they were put to the worse before Israel, they made peace with David, and became his servants: neither would the Syrians help the children of Ammon any more.

20 1 And it came to pass, that after the year was expired, at the time that kings go out *to battle,* Joab led forth the power of the army, and wasted the country of the children of Ammon, and came and besieged Rabbah. But David tarried at Jerusalem. And Joab smote Rabbah, and destroyed it.

2 And David took the crown of their king from off his head, and found it to weigh a talent of gold, and *there were* precious stones in it; and it was set upon David's head: and he brought also exceeding much spoil out of the city.

3 And he brought out the people that *were* in it, and cut *them* with saws, and with harrows of iron, and with axes. Even so dealt David with all the cities of the children of Ammon. And David and all the people returned to Jerusalem.

4 And it came to pass after this, that there arose war at Gezer with the Philistines; at which time Sibbechai the Hushathite slew Sippai, *that was* of the children of the giant: and they were subdued.

5 And there was war again with the Philistines; and Elhanan the son of Jair slew Lahmi the brother of Goliath the Gittite, whose spear staff *was* like a weaver's beam.

6 And yet again there was war at Gath, where was a man of *great* stature, whose fingers and toes *were* four and twenty, six *on each hand,* and six *on each foot:* and he also was the son of the giant.

7 But when he defied Israel, Jonathan the son of Shimea David's brother slew him.

NEW LIVING TRANSLATION

match for Israel, so they sent messengers and summoned additional Aramean troops from the other side of the Euphrates River.* These troops were under the command of Shobach,* the commander of Hadadezer's forces.

17 When David heard what was happening, he mobilized all Israel, crossed the Jordan River, and positioned his troops in battle formation. Then David engaged the Arameans in battle, and they fought against him. 18 But again the Arameans fled from the Israelites. This time David's forces killed 7,000 charioteers and 40,000 foot soldiers, including Shobach, the commander of their army. 19 When Hadadezer's allies saw that they had been defeated by Israel, they surrendered to David and became his subjects. After that, the Arameans were no longer willing to help the Ammonites.

David Captures Rabbah

20 In the spring of the year,* when kings normally go out to war, Joab led the Israelite army in successful attacks against the land of the Ammonites. In the process he laid siege to the city of Rabbah. However, David stayed behind in Jerusalem.

2 When David arrived at Rabbah, he removed the crown from the king's head,* and it was placed on his own head. The crown was made of gold and set with gems, and he found that it weighed seventy-five pounds.* David took a vast amount of plunder from the city. 3 He also made slaves of the people of Rabbah and forced them to labor with saws, iron picks, and iron axes.* That is how David dealt with the people of all the Ammonite towns. Then David and all the army returned to Jerusalem.

Battles against Philistine Giants

4 After this, war broke out with the Philistines at Gezer. As they fought, Sibbecai from Hushah killed Saph,* a descendant of the giants,* and so the Philistines were subdued.

5 During another battle with the Philistines, Elhanan son of Jair killed Lahmi, the brother of Goliath of Gath. The handle of Lahmi's spear was as thick as a weaver's beam!

6 In another battle with the Philistines at Gath, they encountered a huge man with six fingers on each hand and six toes on each foot, twenty-four in all, who was also a descendant of the giants. 7 But when he defied and taunted Israel, he was killed by Jonathan, the son of David's brother Shimea.

19:16a Hebrew *the river.* **19:16b** As in parallel text at 2 Sam 10:16; Hebrew reads *Shophach;* also in 19:18. **20:1** Hebrew *At the turn of the year.* The first day of the year in the ancient Hebrew lunar calendar occurred in March or April. **20:2a** Or *from the head of Milcom* (as in Greek version and Latin Vulgate). Milcom, also called Molech, was the god of the Ammonites. **20:2b** Hebrew *1 talent* [34 kilograms]. **20:3** As in parallel text at 2 Sam 12:31; Hebrew reads *and cut them with saws, iron picks, and saws.* **20:4a** As in parallel text at 2 Sam 21:18; Hebrew reads *Sippai.* **20:4b** Hebrew *descendant of the Rephaites;* also in 20:6, 8.

KING JAMES VERSION

8These were born unto the giant in Gath; and they
fell by the hand of David, and by the hand of his
servants.

21

1And Satan stood up against Israel, and provoked David to number Israel.
2And David said to Joab and to the rulers of the
people, Go, number Israel from Beer-sheba even to
Dan; and bring the number of them to me, that I may
know *it*.
3And Joab answered, The LORD make his people an
hundred times so many more as they *be:* but, my lord
the king, *are* they not all my lord's servants? why
then doth my lord require this thing? why will he be a
cause of trespass to Israel?
4Nevertheless the king's word prevailed against
Joab. Wherefore Joab departed, and went throughout all Israel, and came to Jerusalem.
5And Joab gave the sum of the number of the
people unto David. And all *they of* Israel were a thousand thousand and an hundred thousand men that
drew sword: and Judah *was* four hundred threescore
and ten thousand men that drew sword.
6But Levi and Benjamin counted he not among
them: for the king's word was abominable to Joab.

7And God was displeased with this thing; therefore he smote Israel.
8And David said unto God, I have sinned greatly,
because I have done this thing: but now, I beseech
thee, do away the iniquity of thy servant; for I have
done very foolishly.
9And the LORD spake unto Gad, David's seer, saying,
10Go and tell David, saying, Thus saith the LORD,
I offer thee three *things:* choose thee one of them,
that I may do *it* unto thee.
11So Gad came to David, and said unto him, Thus
saith the LORD, Choose thee
12Either three years' famine; or three months to be
destroyed before thy foes, while that the sword of
thine enemies overtaketh *thee;* or else three days the
sword of the LORD, even the pestilence, in the land,
and the angel of the LORD destroying throughout all
the coasts of Israel. Now therefore advise thyself
what word I shall bring again to him that sent me.
13And David said unto Gad, I am in a great strait:
let me fall now into the hand of the LORD; for very
great *are* his mercies: but let me not fall into the
hand of man.
14So the LORD sent pestilence upon Israel: and
there fell of Israel seventy thousand men.
15And God sent an angel unto Jerusalem to destroy
it: and as he was destroying, the LORD beheld, and he
repented him of the evil, and said to the angel that
destroyed, It is enough, stay now thine hand. And the
angel of the LORD stood by the threshingfloor of
Ornan the Jebusite.
16And David lifted up his eyes, and saw the angel

NEW LIVING TRANSLATION

8These Philistines were descendants of the giants
of Gath, but David and his warriors killed them.

David Takes a Census

21

Satan rose up against Israel and caused
David to take a census of the people of Israel. 2So David said to Joab and the commanders of
the army, "Take a census of all the people of Israel—
from Beersheba in the south to Dan in the north—
and bring me a report so I may know how many
there are."
3But Joab replied, "May the LORD increase the
number of his people a hundred times over! But why,
my lord the king, do you want to do this? Are they not
all your servants? Why must you cause Israel to sin?"
4But the king insisted that they take the census, so
Joab traveled throughout all Israel to count the people. Then he returned to Jerusalem 5and reported the
number of people to David. There were 1,100,000
warriors in all Israel who could handle a sword,
and 470,000 in Judah. 6But Joab did not include the
tribes of Levi and Benjamin in the census because he
was so distressed at what the king had made him do.

Judgment for David's Sin

7God was very displeased with the census, and he
punished Israel for it. 8Then David said to God, "I
have sinned greatly by taking this census. Please forgive my guilt for doing this foolish thing."
9Then the LORD spoke to Gad, David's seer. This
was the message: 10"Go and say to David, 'This is
what the LORD says: I will give you three choices.
Choose one of these punishments, and I will inflict it
on you.'"
11So Gad came to David and said, "These are the
choices the LORD has given you. 12You may choose
three years of famine, three months of destruction
by the sword of your enemies, or three days of severe
plague as the angel of the LORD brings devastation
throughout the land of Israel. Decide what answer I
should give the LORD who sent me."
13"I'm in a desperate situation!" David replied to
Gad. "But let me fall into the hands of the LORD, for
his mercy is very great. Do not let me fall into human
hands."
14So the LORD sent a plague upon Israel, and
70,000 people died as a result. 15And God sent an
angel to destroy Jerusalem. But just as the angel was
preparing to destroy it, the LORD relented and said to
the death angel, "Stop! That is enough!" At that moment the angel of the LORD was standing by the
threshing floor of Araunah* the Jebusite.
16David looked up and saw the angel of the LORD

21:15 As in parallel text at 2 Sam 24:16; Hebrew reads *Ornan*, another name for Araunah; also in 21:18-28.

KING JAMES VERSION

of the LORD stand between the earth and the heaven, having a drawn sword in his hand stretched out over Jerusalem. Then David and the elders *of Israel, who were* clothed in sackcloth, fell upon their faces.

17And David said unto God, *Is it* not I *that* commanded the people to be numbered? even I it is that have sinned and done evil indeed; but *as for* these sheep, what have they done? let thine hand, I pray thee, O LORD my God, be on me, and on my father's house; but not on thy people, that they should be plagued.

18Then the angel of the LORD commanded Gad to say to David, that David should go up, and set up an altar unto the LORD in the threshingfloor of Ornan the Jebusite.

19And David went up at the saying of Gad, which he spake in the name of the LORD.

20And Ornan turned back, and saw the angel; and his four sons with him hid themselves. Now Ornan was threshing wheat.

21And as David came to Ornan, Ornan looked and saw David, and went out of the threshingfloor, and bowed himself to David with *his* face to the ground.

22Then David said to Ornan, Grant me the place of *this* threshingfloor, that I may build an altar therein unto the LORD: thou shalt grant it me for the full price: that the plague may be stayed from the people.

23And Ornan said unto David, Take *it* to thee, and let my lord the king do *that which is* good in his eyes: lo, I give *thee* the oxen *also* for burnt offerings, and the threshing instruments for wood, and the wheat for the meat offering; I give it all.

24And king David said to Ornan, Nay; but I will verily buy it for the full price: for I will not take *that* which *is* thine for the LORD, nor offer burnt offerings without cost.

25So David gave to Ornan for the place six hundred shekels of gold by weight.

26And David built there an altar unto the LORD, and offered burnt offerings and peace offerings, and called upon the LORD; and he answered him from heaven by fire upon the altar of burnt offering.

27And the LORD commanded the angel; and he put up his sword again into the sheath thereof.

28At that time when David saw that the LORD had answered him in the threshingfloor of Ornan the Jebusite, then he sacrificed there.

29For the tabernacle of the LORD, which Moses made in the wilderness, and the altar of the burnt offering, *were* at that season in the high place at Gibeon.

30But David could not go before it to inquire of God: for he was afraid because of the sword of the angel of the LORD.

NEW LIVING TRANSLATION

standing between heaven and earth with his sword
drawn, reaching out over Jerusalem. So David and
the leaders of Israel put on burlap to show their deep
distress and fell face down on the ground. 17And
David said to God, "I am the one who called for the
census! I am the one who has sinned and done
wrong! But these people are as innocent as sheep—
what have they done? O LORD my God, let your anger
fall against me and my family, but do not destroy
your people."

David Builds an Altar

18Then the angel of the LORD told Gad to instruct David to go up and build an altar to the LORD on the
threshing floor of Araunah the Jebusite. 19So David
went up to do what the LORD had commanded him
through Gad. 20Araunah, who was busy threshing
wheat at the time, turned and saw the angel there.
His four sons, who were with him, ran away and hid.
21When Araunah saw David approaching, he left his
threshing floor and bowed before David with his face
to the ground.

22David said to Araunah, "Let me buy this threshing floor from you at its full price. Then I will build
an altar to the LORD there, so that he will stop the
plague."

23"Take it, my lord the king, and use it as you wish,"
Araunah said to David. "I will give the oxen for the
burnt offerings, and the threshing boards for wood to
build a fire on the altar, and the wheat for the grain
offering. I will give it all to you."

24But King David replied to Araunah, "No, I insist
on buying it for the full price. I will not take what is
yours and give it to the LORD. I will not present burnt
offerings that have cost me nothing!" 25So David
gave Araunah 600 pieces of gold* in payment for the
threshing floor.

26David built an altar there to the LORD and sacrificed burnt offerings and peace offerings. And when
David prayed, the LORD answered him by sending fire
from heaven to burn up the offering on the altar.
27Then the LORD spoke to the angel, who put the
sword back into its sheath.

28When David saw that the LORD had answered his
prayer, he offered sacrifices there at Araunah's
threshing floor. 29At that time the Tabernacle of the
LORD and the altar of burnt offering that Moses had
made in the wilderness were located at the place of
worship in Gibeon. 30But David was not able to go
there to inquire of God, because he was terrified by
the drawn sword of the angel of the LORD.

21:25 Hebrew *600 shekels of gold,* about 15 pounds or 6.8 kilograms in weight.

KING JAMES VERSION

22 1Then David said, This *is* the house of the
LORD God, and this *is* the altar of the burnt
offering for Israel.
2And David commanded to gather together the
strangers that *were* in the land of Israel; and he set
masons to hew wrought stones to build the house
of God.
3And David prepared iron in abundance for the
nails for the doors of the gates, and for the joinings;
and brass in abundance without weight;
4Also cedar trees in abundance: for the Zidonians
and they of Tyre brought much cedar wood to David.
5And David said, Solomon my son *is* young and
tender, and the house *that is* to be builded for the
LORD *must be* exceeding magnifical, of fame and of
glory throughout all countries: I will *therefore* now
make preparation for it. So David prepared abundantly before his death.
6Then he called for Solomon his son, and charged
him to build an house for the LORD God of Israel.
7And David said to Solomon, My son, as for me, it
was in my mind to build an house unto the name of
the LORD my God:
8But the word of the LORD came to me, saying,
Thou hast shed blood abundantly, and hast made
great wars: thou shalt not build an house unto my
name, because thou hast shed much blood upon the
earth in my sight.
9Behold, a son shall be born to thee, who shall be a
man of rest; and I will give him rest from all his enemies round about: for his name shall be Solomon,
and I will give peace and quietness unto Israel in
his days.
10He shall build an house for my name; and he
shall be my son, and I *will be* his father; and I will establish the throne of his kingdom over Israel for
ever.
11Now, my son, the LORD be with thee; and prosper
thou, and build the house of the LORD thy God, as he
hath said of thee.
12Only the LORD give thee wisdom and understanding, and give thee charge concerning Israel,
that thou mayest keep the law of the LORD thy God.
13Then shalt thou prosper, if thou takest heed to
fulfil the statutes and judgments which the LORD
charged Moses with concerning Israel: be strong,
and of good courage; dread not, nor be dismayed.
14Now, behold, in my trouble I have prepared for
the house of the LORD an hundred thousand talents
of gold, and a thousand thousand talents of silver;
and of brass and iron without weight; for it is in
abundance: timber also and stone have I prepared;
and thou mayest add thereto.
15Moreover *there are* workmen with thee in abundance, hewers and workers of stone and timber, and
all manner of cunning men for every manner of work.

NEW LIVING TRANSLATION

22 Then David said, "This will be the location
for the Temple of the LORD God and the
place of the altar for Israel's burnt offerings!"

Preparations for the Temple

2So David gave orders to call together the foreigners
living in Israel, and he assigned them the task of preparing finished stone for building the Temple of
God. 3David provided large amounts of iron for the
nails that would be needed for the doors in the gates
and for the clamps, and he gave more bronze than
could be weighed. 4He also provided innumerable
cedar logs, for the men of Tyre and Sidon had
brought vast amounts of cedar to David.
5David said, "My son Solomon is still young and inexperienced. And since the Temple to be built for
the LORD must be a magnificent structure, famous
and glorious throughout the world, I will begin making preparations for it now." So David collected vast
amounts of building materials before his death.
6Then David sent for his son Solomon and instructed him to build a Temple for the LORD, the
God of Israel. 7"My son, I wanted to build a Temple to
honor the name of the LORD my God," David told
him. 8"But the LORD said to me, 'You have killed
many men in the battles you have fought. And since
you have shed so much blood in my sight, you will
not be the one to build a Temple to honor my name.
9But you will have a son who will be a man of peace. I
will give him peace with his enemies in all the surrounding lands. His name will be Solomon,* and I
will give peace and quiet to Israel during his reign.
10He is the one who will build a Temple to honor my
name. He will be my son, and I will be his father. And
I will secure the throne of his kingdom over Israel
forever.'
11"Now, my son, may the LORD be with you and give
you success as you follow his directions in building
the Temple of the LORD your God. 12And may the
LORD give you wisdom and understanding, that you
may obey the Law of the LORD your God as you rule
over Israel. 13For you will be successful if you carefully obey the decrees and regulations that the LORD
gave to Israel through Moses. Be strong and courageous; do not be afraid or lose heart!
14"I have worked hard to provide materials for
building the Temple of the LORD—nearly 4,000 tons
of gold, 40,000 tons of silver,* and so much iron and
bronze that it cannot be weighed. I have also gathered timber and stone for the walls, though you
may need to add more. 15You have a large number of
skilled stonemasons and carpenters and craftsmen

22:9 *Solomon* sounds like and is probably derived from the Hebrew word for "peace." **22:14** Hebrew *100,000 talents* [3,400 metric tons] *of gold, 1,000,000 talents* [34,000 metric tons] *of silver.*

KING JAMES VERSION

16 Of the gold, the silver, and the brass, and the
iron, *there is* no number. Arise *therefore,* and be
doing, and the LORD be with thee.
17 David also commanded all the princes of Israel
to help Solomon his son, *saying,*
18 *Is* not the LORD your God with you? and hath he
not given you rest on every side? for he hath given
the inhabitants of the land into mine hand; and the
land is subdued before the LORD, and before his
people.
19 Now set your heart and your soul to seek the
LORD your God; arise therefore, and build ye the sanctuary of the LORD God, to bring the ark of the covenant of the LORD, and the holy vessels of God, into
the house that is to be built to the name of the LORD.

23 1 So when David was old and full of days, he
made Solomon his son king over Israel.
2 And he gathered together all the princes of Israel,
with the priests and the Levites.
3 Now the Levites were numbered from the age of
thirty years and upward: and their number by their
polls, man by man, was thirty and eight thousand.
4 Of which, twenty and four thousand *were* to set
forward the work of the house of the LORD; and six
thousand *were* officers and judges:
5 Moreover four thousand *were* porters; and four
thousand praised the LORD with the instruments
which I made, *said David,* to praise *therewith.*
6 And David divided them into courses among the
sons of Levi, *namely,* Gershon, Kohath, and Merari.

7 Of the Gershonites *were,* Laadan, and Shimei.
8 The sons of Laadan; the chief *was* Jehiel, and
Zetham, and Joel, three.
9 The sons of Shimei; Shelomith, and Haziel, and
Haran, three. These *were* the chief of the fathers of
Laadan.
10 And the sons of Shimei *were,* Jahath, Zina, and Jeush, and Beriah. These four *were* the sons of Shimei.
11 And Jahath was the chief, and Zizah the second:
but Jeush and Beriah had not many sons; therefore
they were in one reckoning, according to *their* father's house.

12 The sons of Kohath; Amram, Izhar, Hebron, and
Uzziel, four.
13 The sons of Amram; Aaron and Moses: and
Aaron was separated, that he should sanctify the
most holy things, he and his sons for ever, to burn incense before the LORD, to minister unto him, and to
bless in his name for ever.
14 Now *concerning* Moses the man of God, his sons
were named of the tribe of Levi.
15 The sons of Moses *were,* Gershom, and Eliezer.

NEW LIVING TRANSLATION

of every kind. 16 You have expert goldsmiths and
silversmiths and workers of bronze and iron. Now
begin the work, and may the LORD be with you!"
17 Then David ordered all the leaders of Israel to
assist Solomon in this project. 18 "The LORD your God
is with you," he declared. "He has given you peace
with the surrounding nations. He has handed them
over to me, and they are now subject to the LORD and
his people. 19 Now seek the LORD your God with all
your heart and soul. Build the sanctuary of the LORD
God so that you can bring the Ark of the LORD's Covenant and the holy vessels of God into the Temple
built to honor the LORD's name."

Duties of the Levites

23 When David was an old man, he appointed
his son Solomon to be king over Israel.
2 David summoned all the leaders of Israel, together
with the priests and Levites. 3 All the Levites who
were thirty years old or older were counted, and the
total came to 38,000. 4 Then David said, "From all
the Levites, 24,000 will supervise the work at the
Temple of the LORD. Another 6,000 will serve as officials and judges. 5 Another 4,000 will work as gatekeepers, and 4,000 will praise the LORD with the
musical instruments I have made." 6 Then David divided the Levites into divisions named after the
clans descended from the three sons of Levi—Gershon, Kohath, and Merari.

The Gershonites

7 The Gershonite family units were defined by their
lines of descent from Libni* and Shimei, the sons
of Gershon. 8 Three of the descendants of Libni
were Jehiel (the family leader), Zetham, and Joel.
9 These were the leaders of the family of Libni.
Three of the descendants of Shimei were
Shelomoth, Haziel, and Haran. 10 Four other
descendants of Shimei were Jahath, Ziza,* Jeush,
and Beriah. 11 Jahath was the family leader, and
Ziza was next. Jeush and Beriah were counted as
a single family because neither had many sons.

The Kohathites

12 Four of the descendants of Kohath were Amram,
Izhar, Hebron, and Uzziel.
13 The sons of Amram were Aaron and Moses. Aaron
and his descendants were set apart to dedicate
the most holy things, to offer sacrifices in the
LORD's presence, to serve the LORD, and to
pronounce blessings in his name forever.
14 As for Moses, the man of God, his sons were
included with the tribe of Levi. 15 The sons of

23:7 Hebrew *Ladan* (also in 23:8, 9), a variant spelling of Libni; compare 6:17.
23:10 As in Greek version and Latin Vulgate (see also 23:11); Hebrew reads *Zina.*

KING JAMES VERSION

16 Of the sons of Gershom, Shebuel *was* the chief.
17 And the sons of Eliezer *were*, Rehabiah the
chief. And Eliezer had none other sons; but the sons
of Rehabiah were very many.
18 Of the sons of Izhar; Shelomith the chief.
19 Of the sons of Hebron; Jeriah the first, Amariah
the second, Jahaziel the third, and Jekameam the
fourth.
20 Of the sons of Uzziel; Micah the first, and Jesiah
the second.

21 The sons of Merari; Mahli, and Mushi. The sons
of Mahli; Eleazar, and Kish.
22 And Eleazar died, and had no sons, but daughters: and their brethren the sons of Kish took them.
23 The sons of Mushi; Mahli, and Eder, and Jeremoth, three.
24 These *were* the sons of Levi after the house of
their fathers; *even* the chief of the fathers, as they
were counted by number of names by their polls,
that did the work for the service of the house of the
LORD, from the age of twenty years and upward.
25 For David said, The LORD God of Israel hath
given rest unto his people, that they may dwell in
Jerusalem for ever:
26 And also unto the Levites; they shall no *more*
carry the tabernacle, nor any vessels of it for the service thereof.
27 For by the last words of David the Levites *were*
numbered from twenty years old and above:
28 Because their office *was* to wait on the sons of
Aaron for the service of the house of the LORD, in the
courts, and in the chambers, and in the purifying
of all holy things, and the work of the service of the
house of God;
29 Both for the shewbread, and for the fine flour
for meat offering, and for the unleavened cakes, and
for *that which is baked in* the pan, and for that which
is fried, and for all manner of measure and size;
30 And to stand every morning to thank and praise
the LORD, and likewise at even;
31 And to offer all burnt sacrifices unto the LORD in
the sabbaths, in the new moons, and on the set
feasts, by number, according to the order commanded unto them, continually before the LORD:
32 And that they should keep the charge of the tabernacle of the congregation, and the charge of the
holy *place*, and the charge of the sons of Aaron their
brethren, in the service of the house of the LORD.

NEW LIVING TRANSLATION

Moses were Gershom and Eliezer. 16 The
descendants of Gershom included Shebuel,
the family leader. 17 Eliezer had only one son,
Rehabiah, the family leader. Rehabiah had
numerous descendants.
18 The descendants of Izhar included Shelomith,
the family leader.
19 The descendants of Hebron included Jeriah (the
family leader), Amariah (the second), Jahaziel
(the third), and Jekameam (the fourth).
20 The descendants of Uzziel included Micah
(the family leader) and Isshiah (the second).

The Merarites

21 The descendants of Merari included Mahli and
Mushi.
The sons of Mahli were Eleazar and Kish. 22 Eleazar
died with no sons, only daughters. His daughters
married their cousins, the sons of Kish.
23 Three of the descendants of Mushi were Mahli,
Eder, and Jerimoth.

24 These were the descendants of Levi by clans, the
leaders of their family groups, registered carefully by
name. Each had to be twenty years old or older to
qualify for service in the house of the LORD. 25 For David said, "The LORD, the God of Israel, has given us
peace, and he will always live in Jerusalem. 26 Now the
Levites will no longer need to carry the Tabernacle
and its furnishings from place to place." 27 In accordance with David's final instructions, all the Levites
twenty years old or older were registered for service.
28 The work of the Levites was to assist the priests,
the descendants of Aaron, as they served at the
house of the LORD. They also took care of the courtyards and side rooms, helped perform the ceremonies of purification, and served in many other ways
in the house of God. 29 They were in charge of the sacred bread that was set out on the table, the choice
flour for the grain offerings, the wafers made without yeast, the cakes cooked in olive oil, and the other
mixed breads. They were also responsible to check
all the weights and measures. 30 And each morning
and evening they stood before the LORD to sing songs
of thanks and praise to him. 31 They assisted with the
burnt offerings that were presented to the LORD on
Sabbath days, at new moon celebrations, and at all
the appointed festivals. The required number of Levites served in the LORD's presence at all times, following all the procedures they had been given.
32 And so, under the supervision of the priests, the
Levites watched over the Tabernacle and the Temple* and faithfully carried out their duties of service
at the house of the LORD.

23:32 Hebrew *the Tent of Meeting and the sanctuary.*

KING JAMES VERSION

24 1Now *these are* the divisions of the sons of
Aaron. The sons of Aaron; Nadab, and Abihu, Eleazar, and Ithamar.
2But Nadab and Abihu died before their father,
and had no children: therefore Eleazar and Ithamar
executed the priest's office.
3And David distributed them, both Zadok of the
sons of Eleazar, and Ahimelech of the sons of Ithamar, according to their offices in their service.
4And there were more chief men found of the sons
of Eleazar than of the sons of Ithamar; and *thus* were
they divided. Among the sons of Eleazar *there were*
sixteen chief men of the house of *their* fathers, and
eight among the sons of Ithamar according to the
house of their fathers.
5Thus were they divided by lot, one sort with another; for the governors of the sanctuary, and governors *of the house* of God, were of the sons of Eleazar,
and of the sons of Ithamar.
6And Shemaiah the son of Nethaneel the scribe,
one of the Levites, wrote them before the king, and
the princes, and Zadok the priest, and Ahimelech the
son of Abiathar, and *before* the chief of the fathers of
the priests and Levites: one principal household being taken for Eleazar, and *one* taken for Ithamar.
7Now the first lot came forth to Jehoiarib, the second to Jedaiah,
8The third to Harim, the fourth to Seorim,
9The fifth to Malchijah, the sixth to Mijamin,
10The seventh to Hakkoz, the eighth to Abijah,
11The ninth to Jeshuah, the tenth to Shecaniah,
12The eleventh to Eliashib, the twelfth to Jakim,
13The thirteenth to Huppah, the fourteenth to
Jeshebeab,
14The fifteenth to Bilgah, the sixteenth to Immer,
15The seventeenth to Hezir, the eighteenth to
Aphses,
16The nineteenth to Pethahiah, the twentieth to
Jehezekel,
17The one and twentieth to Jachin, the two and
twentieth to Gamul,
18The three and twentieth to Delaiah, the four
and twentieth to Maaziah.
19These *were* the orderings of them in their service to come into the house of the LORD, according to
their manner, under Aaron their father, as the LORD
God of Israel had commanded him.

NEW LIVING TRANSLATION

Duties of the Priests

24 This is how Aaron's descendants, the
priests, were divided into groups for service. The sons of Aaron were Nadab, Abihu, Eleazar,
and Ithamar. 2But Nadab and Abihu died before their
father, and they had no sons. So only Eleazar and Ithamar were left to carry on as priests.
3With the help of Zadok, who was a descendant of
Eleazar, and of Ahimelech, who was a descendant
of Ithamar, David divided Aaron's descendants into
groups according to their various duties. 4Eleazar's
descendants were divided into sixteen groups and
Ithamar's into eight, for there were more family leaders among the descendants of Eleazar.
5All tasks were assigned to the various groups by
means of sacred lots so that no preference would be
shown, for there were many qualified officials serving God in the sanctuary from among the descendants of both Eleazar and Ithamar. 6Shemaiah son
of Nethanel, a Levite, acted as secretary and wrote
down the names and assignments in the presence of
the king, the officials, Zadok the priest, Ahimelech
son of Abiathar, and the family leaders of the priests
and Levites. The descendants of Eleazar and Ithamar
took turns casting lots.

7 The first lot fell to Jehoiarib.
The second lot fell to Jedaiah.
8 The third lot fell to Harim.
The fourth lot fell to Seorim.
9 The fifth lot fell to Malkijah.
The sixth lot fell to Mijamin.
10 The seventh lot fell to Hakkoz.
The eighth lot fell to Abijah.
11 The ninth lot fell to Jeshua.
The tenth lot fell to Shecaniah.
12 The eleventh lot fell to Eliashib.
The twelfth lot fell to Jakim.
13 The thirteenth lot fell to Huppah.
The fourteenth lot fell to Jeshebeab.
14 The fifteenth lot fell to Bilgah.
The sixteenth lot fell to Immer.
15 The seventeenth lot fell to Hezir.
The eighteenth lot fell to Happizzez.
16 The nineteenth lot fell to Pethahiah.
The twentieth lot fell to Jehezkel.
17 The twenty-first lot fell to Jakin.
The twenty-second lot fell to Gamul.
18 The twenty-third lot fell to Delaiah.
The twenty-fourth lot fell to Maaziah.

19Each group carried out its appointed duties in
the house of the LORD according to the procedures
established by their ancestor Aaron in obedience to
the commands of the LORD, the God of Israel.

KING JAMES VERSION

[20]And the rest of the sons of Levi *were these:* Of
the sons of Amram; Shubael: of the sons of Shubael;
Jehdeiah.
[21]Concerning Rehabiah: of the sons of Rehabiah,
the first *was* Isshiah.
[22]Of the Izharites; Shelomoth: of the sons of Shelomoth; Jahath.
[23]And the sons *of Hebron;* Jeriah *the first,* Amariah
the second, Jahaziel the third, Jekameam the fourth.
[24]*Of* the sons of Uzziel; Michah: of the sons of
Michah; Shamir.
[25]The brother of Michah *was* Isshiah: of the sons
of Isshiah; Zechariah.
[26]The sons of Merari *were* Mahli and Mushi: the
sons of Jaaziah; Beno.
[27]The sons of Merari by Jaaziah; Beno, and Shoham, and Zaccur, and Ibri.
[28]Of Mahli *came* Eleazar, who had no sons.
[29]Concerning Kish: the son of Kish *was* Jerahmeel.
[30]The sons also of Mushi; Mahli, and Eder, and
Jerimoth. These *were* the sons of the Levites after
the house of their fathers.
[31]These likewise cast lots over against their brethren the sons of Aaron in the presence of David the
king, and Zadok, and Ahimelech, and the chief of the
fathers of the priests and Levites, even the principal
fathers over against their younger brethren.

25 [1]Moreover David and the captains of the
host separated to the service of the sons of
Asaph, and of Heman, and of Jeduthun, who should
prophesy with harps, with psalteries, and with cymbals: and the number of the workmen according to
their service was:
[2]Of the sons of Asaph; Zaccur, and Joseph, and
Nethaniah, and Asarelah, the sons of Asaph under
the hands of Asaph, which prophesied according to
the order of the king.

NEW LIVING TRANSLATION

Family Leaders among the Levites

[20]These were the other family leaders descended
from Levi:

From the descendants of Amram, the leader was Shebuel.*
From the descendants of Shebuel, the leader was Jehdeiah.
[21] From the descendants of Rehabiah, the leader was Isshiah.
[22] From the descendants of Izhar, the leader was Shelomith.*
From the descendants of Shelomith, the leader was Jahath.
[23] From the descendants of Hebron, Jeriah was the leader,* Amariah was second, Jahaziel was third, and Jekameam was fourth.
[24] From the descendants of Uzziel, the leader was Micah.
From the descendants of Micah, the leader was Shamir,
[25] along with Isshiah, the brother of Micah.
From the descendants of Isshiah, the leader was Zechariah.
[26] From the descendants of Merari, the leaders were Mahli and Mushi.
From the descendants of Jaaziah, the leader was Beno.
[27] From the descendants of Merari through Jaaziah, the leaders were Beno, Shoham, Zaccur, and Ibri.
[28] From the descendants of Mahli, the leader was Eleazar, though he had no sons.
[29] From the descendants of Kish, the leader was Jerahmeel.
[30] From the descendants of Mushi, the leaders were Mahli, Eder, and Jerimoth.

These were the descendants of Levi in their various families.
[31]Like the descendants of Aaron, they
were assigned to their duties by means of sacred lots,
without regard to age or rank. Lots were drawn in the
presence of King David, Zadok, Ahimelech, and the
family leaders of the priests and the Levites.

Duties of the Musicians

25 David and the army commanders then appointed men from the families of Asaph, Heman, and Jeduthun to proclaim God's messages to the accompaniment of lyres, harps, and cymbals. Here is a list of their names and their work:

[2]From the sons of Asaph, there were Zaccur, Joseph, Nethaniah, and Asarelah. They worked under the direction of their father, Asaph, who proclaimed God's messages by the king's orders.

24:20 Hebrew *Shubael* (also in 24:20b), a variant spelling of Shebuel; compare 23:16 and 26:24. **24:22** Hebrew *Shelomoth* (also in 24:22b), a variant spelling of Shelomith; compare 23:18. **24:23** Hebrew *From the descendants of Jeriah;* compare 23:19.

KING JAMES VERSION

3 Of Jeduthun: the sons of Jeduthun; Gedaliah,
and Zeri, and Jeshaiah, Hashabiah, and Mattithiah,
six, under the hands of their father Jeduthun, who
prophesied with a harp, to give thanks and to praise
the LORD.
4 Of Heman: the sons of Heman; Bukkiah, Mattaniah, Uzziel, Shebuel, and Jerimoth, Hananiah, Hanani,
Eliathah, Giddalti, and Romamti-ezer, Joshbekashah,
Mallothi, Hothir, *and* Mahazioth:
5 All these *were* the sons of Heman the king's seer
in the words of God, to lift up the horn. And God gave
to Heman fourteen sons and three daughters.
6 All these *were* under the hands of their father for
song *in* the house of the LORD, with cymbals, psalteries, and harps, for the service of the house of God, according to the king's order to Asaph, Jeduthun, and
Heman.
7 So the number of them, with their brethren that
were instructed in the songs of the LORD, *even* all that
were cunning, was two hundred fourscore and eight.
8 And they cast lots, ward against *ward*, as well the
small as the great, the teacher as the scholar.
9 Now the first lot came forth for Asaph to Joseph:
the second to Gedaliah, who with his brethren and
sons *were* twelve:
10 The third to Zaccur, *he*, his sons, and his brethren, *were* twelve:
11 The fourth to Izri, *he*, his sons, and his brethren,
were twelve:
12 The fifth to Nethaniah, *he*, his sons, and his
brethren, *were* twelve:
13 The sixth to Bukkiah, *he*, his sons, and his brethren, *were* twelve:
14 The seventh to Jesharelah, *he*, his sons, and his
brethren, *were* twelve:
15 The eighth to Jeshaiah, *he*, his sons, and his
brethren, *were* twelve:
16 The ninth to Mattaniah, *he*, his sons, and his
brethren, *were* twelve:
17 The tenth to Shimei, *he*, his sons, and his brethren, *were* twelve:
18 The eleventh to Azareel, *he*, his sons, and his
brethren, *were* twelve:
19 The twelfth to Hashabiah, *he*, his sons, and his
brethren, *were* twelve:
20 The thirteenth to Shubael, *he*, his sons, and his
brethren, *were* twelve:

NEW LIVING TRANSLATION

3 From the sons of Jeduthun, there were Gedaliah,
Zeri, Jeshaiah, Shimei,* Hashabiah, and
Mattithiah, six in all. They worked under
the direction of their father, Jeduthun,
who proclaimed God's messages to the
accompaniment of the lyre, offering thanks
and praise to the LORD.
4 From the sons of Heman, there were Bukkiah,
Mattaniah, Uzziel, Shubael,* Jerimoth, Hananiah,
Hanani, Eliathah, Giddalti, Romamti-ezer,
Joshbekashah, Mallothi, Hothir, and Mahazioth.
5 All these were the sons of Heman, the king's
seer, for God had honored him with fourteen
sons and three daughters.

6 All these men were under the direction of their
fathers as they made music at the house of the LORD.
Their responsibilities included the playing of cymbals, harps, and lyres at the house of God. Asaph,
Jeduthun, and Heman reported directly to the king.
7 They and their families were all trained in making
music before the LORD, and each of them—288 in
all—was an accomplished musician. 8 The musicians
were appointed to their term of service by means of
sacred lots, without regard to whether they were
young or old, teacher or student.

9 The first lot fell to Joseph of the Asaph clan and
twelve of his sons and relatives.*
The second lot fell to Gedaliah and twelve of his
sons and relatives.
10 The third lot fell to Zaccur and twelve of his sons
and relatives.
11 The fourth lot fell to Zeri* and twelve of his sons
and relatives.
12 The fifth lot fell to Nethaniah and twelve of his
sons and relatives.
13 The sixth lot fell to Bukkiah and twelve of his
sons and relatives.
14 The seventh lot fell to Asarelah* and twelve of his
sons and relatives.
15 The eighth lot fell to Jeshaiah and twelve of his
sons and relatives.
16 The ninth lot fell to Mattaniah and twelve of his
sons and relatives.
17 The tenth lot fell to Shimei and twelve of his sons
and relatives.
18 The eleventh lot fell to Uzziel* and twelve of his
sons and relatives.
19 The twelfth lot fell to Hashabiah and twelve of his
sons and relatives.
20 The thirteenth lot fell to Shubael and twelve of
his sons and relatives.

25:3 As in one Hebrew manuscript and some Greek manuscripts (see also 25:17); most Hebrew manuscripts lack *Shimei.* **25:4** Hebrew *Shebuel,* a variant spelling of Shubael; compare 25:20. **25:9** As in Greek version; Hebrew lacks *and twelve of his sons and relatives.* **25:11** Hebrew *Izri,* a variant spelling of Zeri; compare 25:3. **25:14** Hebrew *Jesarelah,* a variant spelling of Asarelah; compare 25:2. **25:18** Hebrew *Azarel,* a variant spelling of Uzziel; compare 25:4.

KING JAMES VERSION

21 The fourteenth to Mattithiah, *he,* his sons, and his brethren, *were* twelve:

22 The fifteenth to Jeremoth, *he,* his sons, and his brethren, *were* twelve:

23 The sixteenth to Hananiah, *he,* his sons, and his brethren, *were* twelve:

24 The seventeenth to Joshbekashah, *he,* his sons, and his brethren, *were* twelve:

25 The eighteenth to Hanani, *he,* his sons, and his brethren, *were* twelve:

26 The nineteenth to Mallothi, *he,* his sons, and his brethren, *were* twelve:

27 The twentieth to Eliathah, *he,* his sons, and his brethren, *were* twelve:

28 The one and twentieth to Hothir, *he,* his sons, and his brethren, *were* twelve:

29 The two and twentieth to Giddalti, *he,* his sons, and his brethren, *were* twelve:

30 The three and twentieth to Mahazioth, *he,* his sons, and his brethren, *were* twelve:

31 The four and twentieth to Romamti-ezer, *he,* his sons, and his brethren, *were* twelve.

26 1 Concerning the divisions of the porters: Of the Korhites *was* Meshelemiah the son of Kore, of the sons of Asaph.

2 And the sons of Meshelemiah *were,* Zechariah the firstborn, Jediael the second, Zebadiah the third, Jathniel the fourth,

3 Elam the fifth, Jehohanan the sixth, Elioenai the seventh.

4 Moreover the sons of Obed-edom *were,* Shemaiah the firstborn, Jehozabad the second, Joah the third, and Sacar the fourth, and Nethaneel the fifth,

5 Ammiel the sixth, Issachar the seventh, Peulthai the eighth: for God blessed him.

6 Also unto Shemaiah his son were sons born, that ruled throughout the house of their father: for they *were* mighty men of valour.

7 The sons of Shemaiah; Othni, and Rephael, and Obed, Elzabad, whose brethren *were* strong men, Elihu, and Semachiah.

8 All these of the sons of Obed-edom: they and their sons and their brethren, able men for strength for the service, *were* threescore and two of Obed-edom.

9 And Meshelemiah had sons and brethren, strong men, eighteen.

10 Also Hosah, of the children of Merari, had sons; Simri the chief, (for *though* he was not the firstborn, yet his father made him the chief;)

11 Hilkiah the second, Tebaliah the third, Zechariah the fourth: all the sons and brethren of Hosah *were* thirteen.

NEW LIVING TRANSLATION

21 The fourteenth lot fell to Mattithiah and twelve of his sons and relatives.

22 The fifteenth lot fell to Jerimoth* and twelve of his sons and relatives.

23 The sixteenth lot fell to Hananiah and twelve of his sons and relatives.

24 The seventeenth lot fell to Joshbekashah* and twelve of his sons and relatives.

25 The eighteenth lot fell to Hanani and twelve of his sons and relatives.

26 The nineteenth lot fell to Mallothi and twelve of his sons and relatives.

27 The twentieth lot fell to Eliathah and twelve of his sons and relatives.

28 The twenty-first lot fell to Hothir and twelve of his sons and relatives.

29 The twenty-second lot fell to Giddalti and twelve of his sons and relatives.

30 The twenty-third lot fell to Mahazioth and twelve of his sons and relatives.

31 The twenty-fourth lot fell to Romamti-ezer and twelve of his sons and relatives.

Duties of the Gatekeepers

26 These are the divisions of the gatekeepers:
From the Korahites, there was Meshelemiah son of
Kore, of the family of Abiasaph.* 2 The sons of
Meshelemiah were Zechariah (the oldest), Jediael
(the second), Zebadiah (the third), Jathniel (the
fourth), 3 Elam (the fifth), Jehohanan (the sixth),
and Eliehoenai (the seventh).

4 The sons of Obed-edom, also gatekeepers, were
Shemaiah (the oldest), Jehozabad (the second),
Joah (the third), Sacar (the fourth), Nethanel (the
fifth), 5 Ammiel (the sixth), Issachar (the seventh),
and Peullethai (the eighth). God had richly
blessed Obed-edom.

6 Obed-edom's son Shemaiah had sons with
great ability who earned positions of great
authority in the clan. 7 Their names were Othni,
Rephael, Obed, and Elzabad. Their relatives,
Elihu and Semakiah, were also very capable men.

8 All of these descendants of Obed-edom, including their sons and grandsons—sixty-two of them in all—were very capable men, well qualified for their work.

9 Meshelemiah's eighteen sons and relatives were also very capable men.

10 Hosah, of the Merari clan, appointed Shimri as
the leader among his sons, though he was not
the oldest. 11 His other sons included Hilkiah (the
second), Tebaliah (the third), and Zechariah (the
fourth). Hosah's sons and relatives, who served
as gatekeepers, numbered thirteen in all.

25:22 Hebrew *Jeremoth,* a variant spelling of Jerimoth; compare 25:4. **25:24** Hebrew *Joshbekasha,* a variant spelling of Joshbekashah; compare 25:4. **26:1** As in Greek version (see also Exod 6:24); Hebrew reads *Asaph.*

KING JAMES VERSION

12 Among these *were* the divisions of the porters,
even among the chief men, *having* wards one
against another, to minister in the house of the LORD.

13 And they cast lots, as well the small as the great,
according to the house of their fathers, for every
gate.

14 And the lot eastward fell to Shelemiah. Then for
Zechariah his son, a wise counsellor, they cast lots;
and his lot came out northward.

15 To Obed-edom southward; and to his sons the
house of Asuppim.

16 To Shuppim and Hosah *the lot came forth* westward, with the gate Shallecheth, by the causeway of
the going up, ward against ward.

17 Eastward *were* six Levites, northward four a
day, southward four a day, and toward Asuppim two
and two.

18 At Parbar westward, four at the causeway, *and*
two at Parbar.

19 These *are* the divisions of the porters among the
sons of Kore, and among the sons of Merari.

20 And of the Levites, Ahijah *was* over the treasures
of the house of God, and over the treasures of the
dedicated things.

21 *As concerning* the sons of Laadan; the sons of
the Gershonite Laadan, chief fathers, *even* of Laadan
the Gershonite, *were* Jehieli.

22 The sons of Jehieli; Zetham, and Joel his brother,
which were over the treasures of the house of the
LORD.

23 Of the Amramites, *and* the Izharites, the Hebronites, *and* the Uzzielites:

24 And Shebuel the son of Gershom, the son of
Moses, *was* ruler of the treasures.

25 And his brethren by Eliezer; Rehabiah his son,
and Jeshaiah his son, and Joram his son, and Zichri
his son, and Shelomith his son.

26 Which Shelomith and his brethren *were* over all
the treasures of the dedicated things, which David
the king, and the chief fathers, the captains over
thousands and hundreds, and the captains of the
host, had dedicated.

27 Out of the spoils won in battles did they dedicate to maintain the house of the LORD.

28 And all that Samuel the seer, and Saul the son of
Kish, and Abner the son of Ner, and Joab the son of
Zeruiah, had dedicated; *and* whosoever had dedicated *any thing, it was* under the hand of Shelomith,
and of his brethren.

29 Of the Izharites, Chenaniah and his sons *were*
for the outward business over Israel, for officers
and judges.

NEW LIVING TRANSLATION

12 These divisions of the gatekeepers were named
for their family leaders, and like the other Levites,
they served at the house of the LORD. 13 They were assigned by families for guard duty at the various gates,
without regard to age or training, for it was all decided by means of sacred lots.

14 The responsibility for the east gate went to
Meshelemiah* and his group. The north gate was
assigned to his son Zechariah, a man of unusual wisdom. 15 The south gate went to Obed-edom, and his
sons were put in charge of the storehouse. 16 Shuppim
and Hosah were assigned the west gate and the gateway leading up to the Temple.* Guard duties were divided evenly. 17 Six Levites were assigned each day to
the east gate, four to the north gate, four to the south
gate, and two pairs at the storehouse. 18 Six were assigned each day to the west gate, four to the gateway
leading up to the Temple, and two to the courtyard.*

19 These were the divisions of the gatekeepers
from the clans of Korah and Merari.

Treasurers and Other Officials

20 Other Levites, led by Ahijah, were in charge of the
treasuries of the house of God and the treasuries of
the gifts dedicated to the LORD. 21 From the family of
Libni* in the clan of Gershon, Jehiel* was the leader.
22 The sons of Jehiel, Zetham and his brother Joel,
were in charge of the treasuries of the house of the
LORD.

23 These are the leaders that descended from Amram, Izhar, Hebron, and Uzziel:

24 From the clan of Amram, Shebuel was a descendant
of Gershom son of Moses. He was the chief officer
of the treasuries. 25 His relatives through Eliezer
were Rehabiah, Jeshaiah, Joram, Zicri, and
Shelomoth.

26 Shelomoth and his relatives were in charge
of the treasuries containing the gifts that King
David, the family leaders, and the generals and
captains* and other officers of the army had
dedicated to the LORD. 27 These men dedicated
some of the plunder they had gained in battle to
maintain the house of the LORD. 28 Shelomoth*
and his relatives also cared for the gifts dedicated
to the LORD by Samuel the seer, Saul son of Kish,
Abner son of Ner, and Joab son of Zeruiah. All
the other dedicated gifts were in their care, too.
29 From the clan of Izhar came Kenaniah. He and his
sons were given administrative responsibilities*
over Israel as officials and judges.

26:14 Hebrew *Shelemiah,* a variant spelling of Meshelemiah; compare 26:2. **26:16** Or *the gate of Shalleketh on the upper road* (also in 26:18). The meaning of the Hebrew is uncertain. **26:18** Or *the colonnade.* The meaning of the Hebrew is uncertain. **26:21a** Hebrew *Ladan,* a variant spelling of Libni; compare 6:17. **26:21b** Hebrew *Jehieli* (also in 26:22), a variant spelling of Jehiel; compare 23:8. **26:26** Hebrew *the commanders of thousands and of hundreds.* **26:28** Hebrew *Shelomith,* a variant spelling of Shelomoth. **26:29** Or *were given outside work;* or *were given work away from the Temple area.*

KING JAMES VERSION

30 *And* of the Hebronites, Hashabiah and his brethren, men of valour, a thousand and seven hundred, *were* officers among them of Israel on this side Jordan westward in all the business of the LORD, and in the service of the king.

31 Among the Hebronites *was* Jerijah the chief, *even* among the Hebronites, according to the generations of his fathers. In the fortieth year of the reign of David they were sought for, and there were found among them mighty men of valour at Jazer of Gilead.

32 And his brethren, men of valour, *were* two thousand and seven hundred chief fathers, whom king David made rulers over the Reubenites, the Gadites, and the half tribe of Manasseh, for every matter pertaining to God, and affairs of the king.

27 1 Now the children of Israel after their number, *to wit,* the chief fathers and captains of thousands and hundreds, and their officers that served the king in any matter of the courses, which came in and went out month by month throughout all the months of the year, of every course *were* twenty and four thousand.

2 Over the first course for the first month *was* Jashobeam the son of Zabdiel: and in his course *were* twenty and four thousand.

3 Of the children of Perez *was* the chief of all the captains of the host for the first month.

4 And over the course of the second month *was* Dodai an Ahohite, and of his course *was* Mikloth also the ruler: in his course likewise *were* twenty and four thousand.

5 The third captain of the host for the third month *was* Benaiah the son of Jehoiada, a chief priest: and in his course *were* twenty and four thousand.

6 This *is that* Benaiah, *who was* mighty *among* the thirty, and above the thirty: and in his course *was* Ammizabad his son.

7 The fourth *captain* for the fourth month *was* Asahel the brother of Joab, and Zebadiah his son after him: and in his course *were* twenty and four thousand.

8 The fifth captain for the fifth month *was* Shamhuth the Izrahite: and in his course *were* twenty and four thousand.

9 The sixth *captain* for the sixth month *was* Ira the son of Ikkesh the Tekoite: and in his course *were* twenty and four thousand.

10 The seventh *captain* for the seventh month *was* Helez the Pelonite, of the children of Ephraim: and in his course *were* twenty and four thousand.

NEW LIVING TRANSLATION

30 From the clan of Hebron came Hashabiah. He and his relatives—1,700 capable men—were put in charge of the Israelite lands west of the Jordan River. They were responsible for all matters related to the things of the LORD and the service of the king in that area.

31 Also from the clan of Hebron came Jeriah,* who was the leader of the Hebronites according to the genealogical records. (In the fortieth year of David's reign, a search was made in the records, and capable men from the clan of Hebron were found at Jazer in the land of Gilead.) 32 There were 2,700 capable men among the relatives of Jeriah. King David sent them to the east side of the Jordan River and put them in charge of the tribes of Reuben and Gad and the half-tribe of Manasseh. They were responsible for all matters related to God and to the king.

Military Commanders and Divisions

27 This is the list of Israelite generals and captains,* and their officers, who served the king by supervising the army divisions that were on duty each month of the year. Each division served for one month and had 24,000 troops.

2 Jashobeam son of Zabdiel was commander of the first division of 24,000 troops, which was on duty during the first month. 3 He was a descendant of Perez and was in charge of all the army officers for the first month.

4 Dodai, a descendant of Ahoah, was commander of the second division of 24,000 troops, which was on duty during the second month. Mikloth was his chief officer.

5 Benaiah son of Jehoiada the priest was commander of the third division of 24,000 troops, which was on duty during the third month. 6 This was the Benaiah who commanded David's elite military group known as the Thirty. His son Ammizabad was his chief officer.

7 Asahel, the brother of Joab, was commander of the fourth division of 24,000 troops, which was on duty during the fourth month. Asahel was succeeded by his son Zebadiah.

8 Shammah* the Izrahite was commander of the fifth division of 24,000 troops, which was on duty during the fifth month.

9 Ira son of Ikkesh from Tekoa was commander of the sixth division of 24,000 troops, which was on duty during the sixth month.

10 Helez, a descendant of Ephraim from Pelon, was commander of the seventh division of 24,000 troops, which was on duty during the seventh month.

26:31 Hebrew *Jerijah,* a variant spelling of Jeriah; compare 23:19.
27:1 Hebrew *commanders of thousands and of hundreds.* **27:8** Hebrew *Shamhuth,* a variant spelling of Shammah; compare 11:27 and 2 Sam 23:25.

KING JAMES VERSION

11The eighth *captain* for the eighth month *was* Sibbecai the Hushathite, of the Zarhites: and in his course *were* twenty and four thousand.

12The ninth *captain* for the ninth month *was* Abiezer the Anetothite, of the Benjamites: and in his course *were* twenty and four thousand.

13The tenth *captain* for the tenth month *was* Maharai the Netophathite, of the Zarhites: and in his course *were* twenty and four thousand.

14The eleventh *captain* for the eleventh month *was* Benaiah the Pirathonite, of the children of Ephraim: and in his course *were* twenty and four thousand.

15The twelfth *captain* for the twelfth month *was* Heldai the Netophathite, of Othniel: and in his course *were* twenty and four thousand.

16Furthermore over the tribes of Israel: the ruler of the Reubenites *was* Eliezer the son of Zichri: of the Simeonites, Shephatiah the son of Maachah:

17Of the Levites, Hashabiah the son of Kemuel: of the Aaronites, Zadok:

18Of Judah, Elihu, *one* of the brethren of David: of Issachar, Omri the son of Michael:

19Of Zebulun, Ishmaiah the son of Obadiah: of Naphtali, Jerimoth the son of Azriel:

20Of the children of Ephraim, Hoshea the son of Azaziah: of the half tribe of Manasseh, Joel the son of Pedaiah:

21Of the half *tribe* of Manasseh in Gilead, Iddo the son of Zechariah: of Benjamin, Jaasiel the son of Abner:

22Of Dan, Azareel the son of Jeroham. These *were* the princes of the tribes of Israel.

23But David took not the number of them from twenty years old and under: because the LORD had said he would increase Israel like to the stars of the heavens.

24Joab the son of Zeruiah began to number, but he finished not, because there fell wrath for it against Israel; neither was the number put in the account of the chronicles of king David.

25And over the king's treasures *was* Azmaveth the son of Adiel: and over the storehouses in the fields, in the cities, and in the villages, and in the castles, *was* Jehonathan the son of Uzziah:

NEW LIVING TRANSLATION

11Sibbecai, a descendant of Zerah from Hushah, was commander of the eighth division of 24,000 troops, which was on duty during the eighth month.

12Abiezer from Anathoth in the territory of Benjamin was commander of the ninth division of 24,000 troops, which was on duty during the ninth month.

13Maharai, a descendant of Zerah from Netophah, was commander of the tenth division of 24,000 troops, which was on duty during the tenth month.

14Benaiah from Pirathon in Ephraim was commander of the eleventh division of 24,000 troops, which was on duty during the eleventh month.

15Heled,* a descendant of Othniel from Netophah, was commander of the twelfth division of 24,000 troops, which was on duty during the twelfth month.

Leaders of the Tribes

16The following were the tribes of Israel and their leaders:

Tribe	*Leader*
Reuben	Eliezer son of Zicri
Simeon	Shephatiah son of Maacah
17 Levi	Hashabiah son of Kemuel
Aaron (the priests)	Zadok
18 Judah	Elihu (a brother of David)
Issachar	Omri son of Michael
19 Zebulun	Ishmaiah son of Obadiah
Naphtali	Jeremoth son of Azriel
20 Ephraim	Hoshea son of Azaziah
Manasseh (west)	Joel son of Pedaiah
21 Manasseh in Gilead (east)	Iddo son of Zechariah
Benjamin	Jaasiel son of Abner
22 Dan	Azarel son of Jeroham

These were the leaders of the tribes of Israel.

23When David took his census, he did not count those who were younger than twenty years of age, because the LORD had promised to make the Israelites as numerous as the stars in heaven. 24Joab son of Zeruiah began the census but never finished it because* the anger of God fell on Israel. The total number was never recorded in King David's official records.

Officials of David's Kingdom

25Azmaveth son of Adiel was in charge of the palace treasuries.

Jonathan son of Uzziah was in charge of the regional treasuries throughout the towns, villages, and fortresses of Israel.

27:15 Hebrew *Heldai,* a variant spelling of Heled; compare 11:30 and 2 Sam 23:29. **27:24** Or *never finished it, and yet.*

KING JAMES VERSION

26 And over them that did the work of the field for
tillage of the ground *was* Ezri the son of Chelub:
27 And over the vineyards *was* Shimei the Ramath-
ite: over the increase of the vineyards for the wine
cellars *was* Zabdi the Shiphmite:
28 And over the olive trees and the sycamore trees
that *were* in the low plains *was* Baal-hanan the
Gederite: and over the cellars of oil *was* Joash:
29 And over the herds that fed in Sharon *was*
Shitrai the Sharonite: and over the herds *that were*
in the valleys *was* Shaphat the son of Adlai:
30 Over the camels also *was* Obil the Ishmaelite:
and over the asses *was* Jehdeiah the Meronothite:
31 And over the flocks *was* Jaziz the Hagerite. All
these *were* the rulers of the substance which *was*
king David's.
32 Also Jonathan David's uncle was a counsellor,
a wise man, and a scribe: and Jehiel the son of
Hachmoni *was* with the king's sons:
33 And Ahithophel *was* the king's counsellor: and
Hushai the Archite *was* the king's companion:
34 And after Ahithophel *was* Jehoiada the son of
Benaiah, and Abiathar: and the general of the king's
army *was* Joab.

28 1 And David assembled all the princes of Israel, the princes of the tribes, and the captains of the companies that ministered to the king
by course, and the captains over the thousands, and
captains over the hundreds, and the stewards over all
the substance and possession of the king, and of his
sons, with the officers, and with the mighty men, and
with all the valiant men, unto Jerusalem.
2 Then David the king stood up upon his feet, and
said, Hear me, my brethren, and my people: *As for
me,* I *had* in mine heart to build an house of rest for
the ark of the covenant of the LORD, and for the
footstool of our God, and had made ready for the
building:
3 But God said unto me, Thou shalt not build an
house for my name, because thou *hast been* a man
of war, and hast shed blood.
4 Howbeit the LORD God of Israel chose me before
all the house of my father to be king over Israel for
ever: for he hath chosen Judah *to be* the ruler; and of
the house of Judah, the house of my father; and
among the sons of my father he liked me to make *me*
king over all Israel:
5 And of all my sons, (for the LORD hath given me
many sons,) he hath chosen Solomon my son to sit
upon the throne of the kingdom of the LORD over
Israel.

NEW LIVING TRANSLATION

26 Ezri son of Kelub was in charge of the field
workers who farmed the king's lands.
27 Shimei from Ramah was in charge of the king's
vineyards.
Zabdi from Shepham was responsible for the
grapes and the supplies of wine.
28 Baal-hanan from Geder was in charge of the king's
olive groves and sycamore-fig trees in the
foothills of Judah.*
Joash was responsible for the supplies of olive oil.
29 Shitrai from Sharon was in charge of the cattle
on the Sharon Plain.
Shaphat son of Adlai was responsible for the cattle
in the valleys.
30 Obil the Ishmaelite was in charge of the camels.
Jehdeiah from Meronoth was in charge of the
donkeys.
31 Jaziz the Hagrite was in charge of the king's flocks
of sheep and goats.
All these officials were overseers of King David's
property.

32 Jonathan, David's uncle, was a wise counselor to
the king, a man of great insight, and a scribe. Jehiel
the Hacmonite was responsible for teaching the
king's sons. 33 Ahithophel was the royal adviser. Hushai the Arkite was the king's friend. 34 Ahithophel
was succeeded by Jehoiada son of Benaiah and by
Abiathar. Joab was commander of the king's army.

David's Instructions to Solomon

28 David summoned all the officials of Israel
to Jerusalem—the leaders of the tribes, the
commanders of the army divisions, the other generals and captains,* the overseers of the royal property
and livestock, the palace officials, the mighty men,
and all the other brave warriors in the kingdom. 2 David rose to his feet and said: "My brothers and my
people! It was my desire to build a temple where the
Ark of the LORD's Covenant, God's footstool, could
rest permanently. I made the necessary preparations
for building it, 3 but God said to me, 'You must not
build a temple to honor my name, for you are a warrior and have shed much blood.'
4 "Yet the LORD, the God of Israel, has chosen me
from among all my father's family to be king over Israel forever. For he has chosen the tribe of Judah to
rule, and from among the families of Judah he chose
my father's family. And from among my father's sons
the LORD was pleased to make me king over all Israel. 5 And from among my sons—for the LORD has
given me many—he chose Solomon to succeed me
on the throne of Israel and to rule over the LORD's

27:28 Hebrew *the Shephelah.* **28:1** Hebrew *the commanders of thousands and commanders of hundreds.*

KING JAMES VERSION

6 And he said unto me, Solomon thy son, he shall build my house and my courts: for I have chosen him *to be* my son, and I will be his father.

7 Moreover I will establish his kingdom for ever, if he be constant to do my commandments and my judgments, as at this day.

8 Now therefore in the sight of all Israel the congregation of the LORD, and in the audience of our God, keep and seek for all the commandments of the LORD your God: that ye may possess this good land, and leave *it* for an inheritance for your children after you for ever.

9 And thou, Solomon my son, know thou the God of thy father, and serve him with a perfect heart and with a willing mind: for the LORD searcheth all hearts, and understandeth all the imaginations of the thoughts: if thou seek him, he will be found of thee; but if thou forsake him, he will cast thee off for ever.

10 Take heed now; for the LORD hath chosen thee to build an house for the sanctuary: be strong, and do *it*.

11 Then David gave to Solomon his son the pattern of the porch, and of the houses thereof, and of the treasuries thereof, and of the upper chambers thereof, and of the inner parlours thereof, and of the place of the mercy seat,

12 And the pattern of all that he had by the spirit, of the courts of the house of the LORD, and of all the chambers round about, of the treasuries of the house of God, and of the treasuries of the dedicated things:

13 Also for the courses of the priests and the Levites, and for all the work of the service of the house of the LORD, and for all the vessels of service in the house of the LORD.

14 *He gave* of gold by weight for *things* of gold, for all instruments of all manner of service; *silver also* for all instruments of silver by weight, for all instruments of every kind of service:

15 Even the weight for the candlesticks of gold, and for their lamps of gold, by weight for every candlestick, and for the lamps thereof: and for the candlesticks of silver by weight, *both* for the candlestick, and *also* for the lamps thereof, according to the use of every candlestick.

16 And by weight *he gave* gold for the tables of shewbread, for every table; and *likewise* silver for the tables of silver:

17 Also pure gold for the fleshhooks, and the bowls, and the cups: and for the golden basins *he gave gold* by weight for every basin; and *likewise silver* by weight for every basin of silver:

18 And for the altar of incense refined gold by weight; and gold for the pattern of the chariot of the cherubims, that spread out *their wings*, and covered the ark of the covenant of the LORD.

19 All *this, said David*, the LORD made me understand in writing by *his* hand upon me, *even* all the works of this pattern.

NEW LIVING TRANSLATION

kingdom. 6 He said to me, 'Your son Solomon will
build my Temple and its courtyards, for I have chosen him as my son, and I will be his father. 7 And if he
continues to obey my commands and regulations as
he does now, I will make his kingdom last forever.'
8 "So now, with God as our witness, and in the sight
of all Israel—the LORD's assembly—I give you this
charge. Be careful to obey all the commands of the
LORD your God, so that you may continue to possess
this good land and leave it to your children as a permanent inheritance.
9 "And Solomon, my son, learn to know the God of
your ancestors intimately. Worship and serve him
with your whole heart and a willing mind. For the
LORD sees every heart and knows every plan and
thought. If you seek him, you will find him. But if
you forsake him, he will reject you forever. 10 So take
this seriously. The LORD has chosen you to build a
Temple as his sanctuary. Be strong, and do the work."
11 Then David gave Solomon the plans for the
Temple and its surroundings, including the entry
room, the storerooms, the upstairs rooms, the inner
rooms, and the inner sanctuary—which was the
place of atonement. 12 David also gave Solomon all
the plans he had in mind* for the courtyards of the
LORD's Temple, the outside rooms, the treasuries,
and the rooms for the gifts dedicated to the LORD.
13 The king also gave Solomon the instructions concerning the work of the various divisions of priests
and Levites in the Temple of the LORD. And he gave
specifications for the items in the Temple that were
to be used for worship.
14 David gave instructions regarding how much
gold and silver should be used to make the items
needed for service. 15 He told Solomon the amount of
gold needed for the gold lampstands and lamps, and
the amount of silver for the silver lampstands and
lamps, depending on how each would be used. 16 He
designated the amount of gold for the table on
which the Bread of the Presence would be placed
and the amount of silver for other tables.
17 David also designated the amount of gold for the
solid gold meat hooks used to handle the sacrificial
meat and for the basins, pitchers, and dishes, as well
as the amount of silver for every dish. 18 He designated the amount of refined gold for the altar of incense. Finally, he gave him a plan for the LORD's
"chariot"—the gold cherubim* whose wings were
stretched out over the Ark of the LORD's Covenant.
19 "Every part of this plan," David told Solomon, "was
given to me in writing from the hand of the LORD.*"

28:12 Or *the plans of the spirit that was with him.* **28:18** Hebrew *for the gold cherub chariot.* **28:19** Or *was written under the direction of the LORD.*

KING JAMES VERSION

20 And David said to Solomon his son, Be strong and of good courage, and do *it:* fear not, nor be dismayed: for the LORD God, *even* my God, *will be* with thee; he will not fail thee, nor forsake thee, until thou hast finished all the work for the service of the house of the LORD.

21 And, behold, the courses of the priests and the Levites, *even they shall be with thee* for all the service of the house of God: and *there shall be* with thee for all manner of workmanship every willing skilful man, for any manner of service: also the princes and all the people *will be* wholly at thy commandment.

29 1 Furthermore David the king said unto all the congregation, Solomon my son, whom alone God hath chosen, *is yet* young and tender, and the work *is* great: for the palace *is* not for man, but for the LORD God.

2 Now I have prepared with all my might for the house of my God the gold for *things to be made* of gold, and the silver for *things* of silver, and the brass for *things* of brass, the iron for *things* of iron, and wood for *things* of wood; onyx stones, and *stones* to be set, glistering stones, and of divers colours, and all manner of precious stones, and marble stones in abundance.

3 Moreover, because I have set my affection to the house of my God, I have of mine own proper good, of gold and silver, *which* I have given to the house of my God, over and above all that I have prepared for the holy house,

4 *Even* three thousand talents of gold, of the gold of Ophir, and seven thousand talents of refined silver, to overlay the walls of the houses *withal:*

5 The gold for *things* of gold, and the silver for *things* of silver, and for all manner of work *to be made* by the hands of artificers. And who *then* is willing to consecrate his service this day unto the LORD?

6 Then the chief of the fathers and princes of the tribes of Israel, and the captains of thousands and of hundreds, with the rulers of the king's work, offered willingly,

7 And gave for the service of the house of God of gold five thousand talents and ten thousand drams, and of silver ten thousand talents, and of brass eighteen thousand talents, and one hundred thousand talents of iron.

8 And they with whom *precious* stones were found gave *them* to the treasure of the house of the LORD, by the hand of Jehiel the Gershonite.

9 Then the people rejoiced, for that they offered willingly, because with perfect heart they offered willingly to the LORD: and David the king also rejoiced with great joy.

NEW LIVING TRANSLATION

20 Then David continued, "Be strong and courageous, and do the work. Don't be afraid or discouraged, for the LORD God, my God, is with you. He will not fail you or forsake you. He will see to it that all the work related to the Temple of the LORD is finished correctly. 21 The various divisions of priests and Levites will serve in the Temple of God. Others with skills of every kind will volunteer, and the officials and the entire nation are at your command."

Gifts for Building the Temple

29 Then King David turned to the entire assembly and said, "My son Solomon, whom God has clearly chosen as the next king of Israel, is still young and inexperienced. The work ahead of him is enormous, for the Temple he will build is not for mere mortals—it is for the LORD God himself! 2 Using every resource at my command, I have gathered as much as I could for building the Temple of my God. Now there is enough gold, silver, bronze, iron, and wood, as well as great quantities of onyx, other precious stones, costly jewels, and all kinds of fine stone and marble.

3 "And now, because of my devotion to the Temple of my God, I am giving all of my own private treasures of gold and silver to help in the construction. This is in addition to the building materials I have already collected for his holy Temple. 4 I am donating more than 112 tons of gold* from Ophir and 262 tons of refined silver* to be used for overlaying the walls of the buildings 5 and for the other gold and silver work to be done by the craftsmen. Now then, who will follow my example and give offerings to the LORD today?"

6 Then the family leaders, the leaders of the tribes of Israel, the generals and captains of the army,* and the king's administrative officers all gave willingly. 7 For the construction of the Temple of God, they gave about 188 tons of gold,* 10,000 gold coins,* 375 tons of silver,* 675 tons of bronze,* and 3,750 tons of iron.* 8 They also contributed numerous precious stones, which were deposited in the treasury of the house of the LORD under the care of Jehiel, a descendant of Gershon. 9 The people rejoiced over the offerings, for they had given freely and wholeheartedly to the LORD, and King David was filled with joy.

29:4a Hebrew *3,000 talents* [102 metric tons] *of gold.* **29:4b** Hebrew *7,000 talents* [238 metric tons] *of silver.* **29:6** Hebrew *the commanders of thousands and commanders of hundreds.* **29:7a** Hebrew *5000 talents* [170 metric tons] *of gold.* **29:7b** Hebrew *10,000 darics* [a Persian coin] *of gold,* about 185 pounds or 84 kilograms in weight. **29:7c** Hebrew *10,000 talents* [340 metric tons] *of silver.* **29:7d** Hebrew *18,000 talents* [612 metric tons] *of bronze.* **29:7e** Hebrew *100,000 talents* [3,400 metric tons] *of iron.*

10 Wherefore David blessed the LORD before all the congregation: and David said, Blessed *be* thou, LORD God of Israel our father, for ever and ever.

11 Thine, O LORD, *is* the greatness, and the power, and the glory, and the victory, and the majesty: for all *that is* in the heaven and in the earth *is thine;* thine *is* the kingdom, O LORD, and thou art exalted as head above all.

12 Both riches and honour *come* of thee, and thou reignest over all; and in thine hand *is* power and might; and in thine hand *it is* to make great, and to give strength unto all.

13 Now therefore, our God, we thank thee, and praise thy glorious name.

14 But who *am* I, and what *is* my people, that we should be able to offer so willingly after this sort? for all things *come* of thee, and of thine own have we given thee.

15 For we *are* strangers before thee, and sojourners, as *were* all our fathers: our days on the earth *are* as a shadow, and *there is* none abiding.

16 O LORD our God, all this store that we have prepared to build thee an house for thine holy name *cometh* of thine hand, and *is* all thine own.

17 I know also, my God, that thou triest the heart, and hast pleasure in uprightness. As for me, in the uprightness of mine heart I have willingly offered all these things: and now have I seen with joy thy people, which are present here, to offer willingly unto thee.

18 O LORD God of Abraham, Isaac, and of Israel, our fathers, keep this for ever in the imagination of the thoughts of the heart of thy people, and prepare their heart unto thee:

19 And give unto Solomon my son a perfect heart, to keep thy commandments, thy testimonies, and thy statutes, and to do all *these things,* and to build the palace, *for* the which I have made provision.

20 And David said to all the congregation, Now bless the LORD your God. And all the congregation blessed the LORD God of their fathers, and bowed down their heads, and worshipped the LORD, and the king.

21 And they sacrificed sacrifices unto the LORD, and offered burnt offerings unto the LORD, on the morrow after that day, *even* a thousand bullocks, a thousand rams, *and* a thousand lambs, with their drink offerings, and sacrifices in abundance for all Israel:

22 And did eat and drink before the LORD on that day with great gladness. And they made Solomon the son of David king the second time, and anointed *him* unto the LORD *to be* the chief governor, and Zadok *to be* priest.

23 Then Solomon sat on the throne of the LORD as king instead of David his father, and prospered; and all Israel obeyed him.

David's Prayer of Praise

10 Then David praised the LORD in the presence of the whole assembly:

"O LORD, the God of our ancestor Israel,* may you
be praised forever and ever! 11 Yours, O LORD, is
the greatness, the power, the glory, the victory,
and the majesty. Everything in the heavens and on
earth is yours, O LORD, and this is your kingdom.
We adore you as the one who is over all things.
12 Wealth and honor come from you alone, for you
rule over everything. Power and might are in your
hand, and at your discretion people are made
great and given strength.

13 "O our God, we thank you and praise your
glorious name! 14 But who am I, and who are my
people, that we could give anything to you?
Everything we have has come from you, and we
give you only what you first gave us! 15 We are
here for only a moment, visitors and strangers
in the land as our ancestors were before us. Our
days on earth are like a passing shadow, gone so
soon without a trace.

16 "O LORD our God, even this material we have
gathered to build a Temple to honor your holy
name comes from you! It all belongs to you!
17 I know, my God, that you examine our hearts
and rejoice when you find integrity there. You
know I have done all this with good motives,
and I have watched your people offer their gifts
willingly and joyously.

18 "O LORD, the God of our ancestors Abraham,
Isaac, and Israel, make your people always want
to obey you. See to it that their love for you never
changes. 19 Give my son Solomon the
wholehearted desire to obey all your commands,
laws, and decrees, and to do everything necessary
to build this Temple, for which I have made these
preparations."

20 Then David said to the whole assembly, "Give praise to the LORD your God!" And the entire assembly praised the LORD, the God of their ancestors, and they bowed low and knelt before the LORD and the king.

Solomon Named as King

21 The next day they brought 1,000 bulls, 1,000 rams, and 1,000 male lambs as burnt offerings to the LORD. They also brought liquid offerings and many other sacrifices on behalf of all Israel. 22 They feasted and drank in the LORD's presence with great joy that day.

And again they crowned David's son Solomon as their new king. They anointed him before the LORD as their leader, and they anointed Zadok as priest. 23 So Solomon took the throne of the LORD in place of his father, David, and he succeeded in everything,

29:10 *Israel* is the name that God gave to Jacob.

KING JAMES VERSION

24And all the princes, and the mighty men, and all
the sons likewise of king David, submitted themselves unto Solomon the king.
25And the LORD magnified Solomon exceedingly
in the sight of all Israel, and bestowed upon him *such*
royal majesty as had not been on any king before him
in Israel.

26Thus David the son of Jesse reigned over all Israel.
27And the time that he reigned over Israel *was*
forty years; seven years reigned he in Hebron, and
thirty and three *years* reigned he in Jerusalem.
28And he died in a good old age, full of days, riches,
and honour: and Solomon his son reigned in his
stead.
29Now the acts of David the king, first and last, behold, they *are* written in the book of Samuel the seer,
and in the book of Nathan the prophet, and in the
book of Gad the seer,
30With all his reign and his might, and the times
that went over him, and over Israel, and over all the
kingdoms of the countries.

NEW LIVING TRANSLATION

and all Israel obeyed him. 24All the officials, the
warriors, and the sons of King David pledged their
loyalty to King Solomon. 25And the LORD exalted Solomon in the sight of all Israel, and he gave Solomon
greater royal splendor than any king in Israel before
him.

Summary of David's Reign

26So David son of Jesse reigned over all Israel. 27He
reigned over Israel for forty years, seven of them in
Hebron and thirty-three in Jerusalem. 28He died at a
ripe old age, having enjoyed long life, wealth, and
honor. Then his son Solomon ruled in his place.
29All the events of King David's reign, from beginning to end, are written in *The Record of Samuel
the Seer*, *The Record of Nathan the Prophet*, and *The
Record of Gad the Seer*. 30These accounts include the
mighty deeds of his reign and everything that happened to him and to Israel and to all the surrounding
kingdoms.

2 Chronicles

KING JAMES VERSION

1 1 And Solomon the son of David was strengthened in his kingdom, and the LORD his God *was*
with him, and magnified him exceedingly.
2 Then Solomon spake unto all Israel, to the captains of thousands and of hundreds, and to the
judges, and to every governor in all Israel, the chief of
the fathers.
3 So Solomon, and all the congregation with him,
went to the high place that *was* at Gibeon; for there
was the tabernacle of the congregation of God,
which Moses the servant of the LORD had made in
the wilderness.
4 But the ark of God had David brought up from
Kirjath-jearim to *the place which* David had prepared
for it: for he had pitched a tent for it at Jerusalem.
5 Moreover the brasen altar, that Bezaleel the son
of Uri, the son of Hur, had made, he put before the
tabernacle of the LORD: and Solomon and the congregation sought unto it.
6 And Solomon went up thither to the brasen altar
before the LORD, which *was* at the tabernacle of the
congregation, and offered a thousand burnt offerings upon it.
7 In that night did God appear unto Solomon, and
said unto him, Ask what I shall give thee.
8 And Solomon said unto God, Thou hast shewed
great mercy unto David my father, and hast made me
to reign in his stead.
9 Now, O LORD God, let thy promise unto David my
father be established: for thou hast made me king
over a people like the dust of the earth in multitude.
10 Give me now wisdom and knowledge, that I may
go out and come in before this people: for who can
judge this thy people, *that is so* great?
11 And God said to Solomon, Because this was in
thine heart, and thou hast not asked riches, wealth,
or honour, nor the life of thine enemies, neither yet
hast asked long life; but hast asked wisdom and
knowledge for thyself, that thou mayest judge my
people, over whom I have made thee king:
12 Wisdom and knowledge *is* granted unto thee;
and I will give thee riches, and wealth, and honour,
such as none of the kings have had that *have been*

NEW LIVING TRANSLATION

Solomon Asks for Wisdom

1 Solomon son of David took firm control of his
kingdom, for the LORD his God was with him
and made him very powerful.
2 Solomon called together all the leaders of Israel—the generals and captains of the army,* the
judges, and all the political and clan leaders. 3 Then
he led the entire assembly to the place of worship in
Gibeon, for God's Tabernacle* was located there.
(This was the Tabernacle that Moses, the LORD's servant, had made in the wilderness.)
4 David had already moved the Ark of God from
Kiriath-jearim to the tent he had prepared for it in
Jerusalem. 5 But the bronze altar made by Bezalel son
of Uri and grandson of Hur was there* at Gibeon
in front of the Tabernacle of the LORD. So Solomon
and the people gathered in front of it to consult the
LORD.* 6 There in front of the Tabernacle, Solomon
went up to the bronze altar in the LORD's presence
and sacrificed 1,000 burnt offerings on it.
7 That night God appeared to Solomon and said,
"What do you want? Ask, and I will give it to you!"
8 Solomon replied to God, "You showed faithful
love to David, my father, and now you have made me
king in his place. 9 O LORD God, please continue to
keep your promise to David my father, for you have
made me king over a people as numerous as the dust
of the earth! 10 Give me the wisdom and knowledge
to lead them properly,* for who could possibly govern this great people of yours?"
11 God said to Solomon, "Because your greatest desire is to help your people, and you did not ask for
wealth, riches, fame, or even the death of your enemies or a long life, but rather you asked for wisdom
and knowledge to properly govern my people—12 I
will certainly give you the wisdom and knowledge
you requested. But I will also give you wealth, riches,

1:2 Hebrew *the commanders of thousands and of hundreds.* **1:3** Hebrew *Tent of Meeting;* also in 1:6, 13. **1:5a** As in Greek version and Latin Vulgate, and some Hebrew manuscripts. Masoretic Text reads *he placed.* **1:5b** Hebrew *to consult him.* **1:10** Hebrew *to go out and come in before this people.*

KING JAMES VERSION

before thee, neither shall there any after thee have
the like.
13 Then Solomon came *from his journey* to the
high place that *was* at Gibeon to Jerusalem, from before the tabernacle of the congregation, and reigned
over Israel.
14 And Solomon gathered chariots and horsemen:
and he had a thousand and four hundred chariots,
and twelve thousand horsemen, which he placed in
the chariot cities, and with the king at Jerusalem.
15 And the king made silver and gold at Jerusalem
as plenteous as stones, and cedar trees made he as the
sycamore trees that *are* in the vale for abundance.
16 And Solomon had horses brought out of Egypt,
and linen yarn: the king's merchants received the
linen yarn at a price.
17 And they fetched up, and brought forth out of
Egypt a chariot for six hundred *shekels* of silver, and
an horse for an hundred and fifty: and so brought
they out *horses* for all the kings of the Hittites, and
for the kings of Syria, by their means.

2 1 And Solomon determined to build an house
for the name of the LORD, and an house for his
kingdom.
2 And Solomon told out threescore and ten thousand men to bear burdens, and fourscore thousand
to hew in the mountain, and three thousand and six
hundred to oversee them.
3 And Solomon sent to Huram the king of Tyre, saying, As thou didst deal with David my father, and
didst send him cedars to build him an house to dwell
therein, *even so deal with me*.
4 Behold, I build an house to the name of the LORD
my God, to dedicate *it* to him, *and* to burn before him
sweet incense, and for the continual shewbread, and
for the burnt offerings morning and evening, on the
sabbaths, and on the new moons, and on the solemn
feasts of the LORD our God. This *is an ordinance* for
ever to Israel.
5 And the house which I build *is* great: for great *is*
our God above all gods.
6 But who is able to build him an house, seeing the
heaven and heaven of heavens cannot contain him?
who *am* I then, that I should build him an house, save
only to burn sacrifice before him?
7 Send me now therefore a man cunning to work in
gold, and in silver, and in brass, and in iron, and in
purple, and crimson, and blue, and that can skill to
grave with the cunning men that *are* with me in
Judah and in Jerusalem, whom David my father did
provide.

NEW LIVING TRANSLATION

and fame such as no other king has had before you or
will ever have in the future!"
13 Then Solomon returned to Jerusalem from the
Tabernacle at the place of worship in Gibeon, and he
reigned over Israel.
14 Solomon built up a huge force of chariots and
horses.* He had 1,400 chariots and 12,000 horses.
He stationed some of them in the chariot cities and
some near him in Jerusalem. 15 The king made silver
and gold as plentiful in Jerusalem as stone. And valuable cedar timber was as common as the sycamore-
fig trees that grow in the foothills of Judah.* 16 Solomon's horses were imported from Egypt* and from
Cilicia*; the king's traders acquired them from Cilicia at the standard price. 17 At that time chariots from
Egypt could be purchased for 600 pieces of silver,*
and horses for 150 pieces of silver.* They were then
exported to the kings of the Hittites and the kings
of Aram.

Preparations for Building the Temple

2 1*Solomon decided to build a Temple to honor
the name of the LORD, and also a royal palace for
himself. 2*He enlisted a force of 70,000 laborers,
80,000 men to quarry stone in the hill country, and
3,600 foremen.
3 Solomon also sent this message to King Hiram*
at Tyre:

"Send me cedar logs as you did for my father,
David, when he was building his palace. 4 I am
about to build a Temple to honor the name of
the LORD my God. It will be a place set apart to
burn fragrant incense before him, to display the
special sacrificial bread, and to sacrifice burnt
offerings each morning and evening, on the
Sabbaths, at new moon celebrations, and at the
other appointed festivals of the LORD our God. He
has commanded Israel to do these things forever.
5 "This must be a magnificent Temple because
our God is greater than all other gods. 6 But who
can really build him a worthy home? Not even the
highest heavens can contain him! So who am I to
consider building a Temple for him, except as a
place to burn sacrifices to him?
7 "So send me a master craftsman who can
work with gold, silver, bronze, and iron, as well
as with purple, scarlet, and blue cloth. He must
be a skilled engraver who can work with the
craftsmen of Judah and Jerusalem who were
selected by my father, David.

1:14 Or *charioteers;* also in 1:14b. **1:15** Hebrew *the Shephelah.* **1:16a** Possibly *Muzur,* a district near Cilicia; also in 1:17. **1:16b** Hebrew *Kue,* probably another name for Cilicia. **1:17a** Hebrew *600 [shekels] of silver,* about 15 pounds or 6.8 kilograms in weight. **1:17b** Hebrew *150 [shekels],* about 3.8 pounds or 1.7 kilograms in weight. **2:1** Verse 2:1 is numbered 1:18 in Hebrew text. **2:2** Verses 2:2-18 are numbered 2:1-17 in Hebrew text. **2:3** Hebrew *Huram,* a variant spelling of Hiram; also in 2:11.

KING JAMES VERSION

[8]Send me also cedar trees, fir trees, and algum trees, out of Lebanon: for I know that thy servants can skill to cut timber in Lebanon; and, behold, my servants *shall be* with thy servants,

[9]Even to prepare me timber in abundance: for the house which I am about to build *shall be* wonderful great.

[10]And, behold, I will give to thy servants, the hewers that cut timber, twenty thousand measures of beaten wheat, and twenty thousand measures of barley, and twenty thousand baths of wine, and twenty thousand baths of oil.

[11]Then Huram the king of Tyre answered in writing, which he sent to Solomon, Because the LORD hath loved his people, he hath made thee king over them.

[12]Huram said moreover, Blessed *be* the LORD God of Israel, that made heaven and earth, who hath given to David the king a wise son, endued with prudence and understanding, that might build an house for the LORD, and an house for his kingdom.

[13]And now I have sent a cunning man, endued with understanding, of Huram my father's,

[14]The son of a woman of the daughters of Dan, and his father *was* a man of Tyre, skilful to work in gold, and in silver, in brass, in iron, in stone, and in timber, in purple, in blue, and in fine linen, and in crimson; also to grave any manner of graving, and to find out every device which shall be put to him, with thy cunning men, and with the cunning men of my lord David thy father.

[15]Now therefore the wheat, and the barley, the oil, and the wine, which my lord hath spoken of, let him send unto his servants:

[16]And we will cut wood out of Lebanon, as much as thou shalt need: and we will bring it to thee in flotes by sea to Joppa; and thou shalt carry it up to Jerusalem.

[17]And Solomon numbered all the strangers that *were* in the land of Israel, after the numbering wherewith David his father had numbered them; and they were found an hundred and fifty thousand and three thousand and six hundred.

[18]And he set threescore and ten thousand of them *to be* bearers of burdens, and fourscore thousand *to be* hewers in the mountain, and three thousand and six hundred overseers to set the people a work.

3 [1]Then Solomon began to build the house of the LORD at Jerusalem in mount Moriah, where *the LORD* appeared unto David his father, in the place that David had prepared in the threshingfloor of Ornan the Jebusite.

NEW LIVING TRANSLATION

[8]"Also send me cedar, cypress, and red sandalwood* logs from Lebanon, for I know that your men are without equal at cutting timber in Lebanon. I will send my men to help them. [9]An immense amount of timber will be needed, for the Temple I am going to build will be very large and magnificent. [10]In payment for your woodcutters, I will send 100,000 bushels of crushed wheat, 100,000 bushels of barley,* 110,000 gallons of wine, and 110,000 gallons of olive oil.*"

[11]King Hiram sent this letter of reply to Solomon:

"It is because the LORD loves his people that he has made you their king! [12]Praise the LORD, the God of Israel, who made the heavens and the earth! He has given King David a wise son, gifted with skill and understanding, who will build a Temple for the LORD and a royal palace for himself.

[13]"I am sending you a master craftsman named Huram-abi, who is extremely talented. [14]His mother is from the tribe of Dan in Israel, and his father is from Tyre. He is skillful at making things from gold, silver, bronze, and iron, and he also works with stone and wood. He can work with purple, blue, and scarlet cloth and fine linen. He is also an engraver and can follow any design given to him. He will work with your craftsmen and those appointed by my lord David, your father.

[15]"Send along the wheat, barley, olive oil, and wine that my lord has mentioned. [16]We will cut whatever timber you need from the Lebanon mountains and will float the logs in rafts down the coast of the Mediterranean Sea* to Joppa. From there you can transport the logs up to Jerusalem."

[17]Solomon took a census of all foreigners in the land of Israel, like the census his father had taken, and he counted 153,600. [18]He assigned 70,000 of them as common laborers, 80,000 as quarry workers in the hill country, and 3,600 as foremen.

Solomon Builds the Temple

3 So Solomon began to build the Temple of the LORD in Jerusalem on Mount Moriah, where the LORD had appeared to David, his father. The Temple was built on the threshing floor of Araunah* the Jebusite, the site that David had selected.

2:8 Or *juniper;* Hebrew reads *algum,* perhaps a variant spelling of *almug;* compare 9:10-11 and parallel text at 1 Kgs 10:11-12. **2:10a** Hebrew *20,000 cors* [3,640 kiloliters] *of crushed wheat, 20,000 cors of barley.* **2:10b** Hebrew *20,000 baths* [420 kiloliters] *of wine, and 20,000 baths of olive oil.* **2:16** Hebrew *the sea.* **3:1** Hebrew reads *Ornan,* a variant spelling of Araunah; compare 2 Sam 24:16.

KING JAMES VERSION

2And he began to build in the second *day* of the
second month, in the fourth year of his reign.
3Now these *are the things wherein* Solomon was
instructed for the building of the house of God. The
length by cubits after the first measure *was* threescore cubits, and the breadth twenty cubits.
4And the porch that *was* in the front *of the house*,
the length *of it was* according to the breadth of the
house, twenty cubits, and the height *was* an hundred
and twenty: and he overlaid it within with pure gold.
5And the greater house he cieled with fir tree, which
he overlaid with fine gold, and set thereon palm trees
and chains.
6And he garnished the house with precious stones
for beauty: and the gold *was* gold of Parvaim.
7He overlaid also the house, the beams, the posts,
and the walls thereof, and the doors thereof, with
gold; and graved cherubims on the walls.
8And he made the most holy house, the length
whereof *was* according to the breadth of the house,
twenty cubits, and the breadth thereof twenty cubits:
and he overlaid it with fine gold, *amounting* to six
hundred talents.
9And the weight of the nails *was* fifty shekels of
gold. And he overlaid the upper chambers with gold.
10And in the most holy house he made two cherubims of image work, and overlaid them with gold.
11And the wings of the cherubims *were* twenty cubits long: one wing *of the one cherub was* five cubits,
reaching to the wall of the house: and the other wing
was likewise five cubits, reaching to the wing of the
other cherub.
12And *one* wing of the other cherub *was* five cubits, reaching to the wall of the house: and the other
wing *was* five cubits *also*, joining to the wing of the
other cherub.
13The wings of these cherubims spread themselves forth twenty cubits: and they stood on their
feet, and their faces *were* inward.
14And he made the veil *of* blue, and purple, and
crimson, and fine linen, and wrought cherubims
thereon.
15Also he made before the house two pillars of
thirty and five cubits high, and the chapiter that *was*
on the top of each of them *was* five cubits.
16And he made chains, *as* in the oracle, and put
them on the heads of the pillars; and made an hundred pomegranates, and put *them* on the chains.
17And he reared up the pillars before the temple,
one on the right hand, and the other on the left; and
called the name of that on the right hand Jachin, and
the name of that on the left Boaz.

NEW LIVING TRANSLATION

2The construction began in midspring,* during the
fourth year of Solomon's reign.
3These are the dimensions Solomon used for the
foundation of the Temple of God (using the old standard of measurement).* It was 90 feet long and
30 feet wide.* 4The entry room at the front of the
Temple was 30 feet* wide, running across the entire
width of the Temple, and 30 feet* high. He overlaid
the inside with pure gold.
5He paneled the main room of the Temple with cypress wood, overlaid it with fine gold, and decorated
it with carvings of palm trees and chains. 6He decorated the walls of the Temple with beautiful jewels
and with gold from the land of Parvaim. 7He overlaid
the beams, thresholds, walls, and doors throughout
the Temple with gold, and he carved figures of cherubim on the walls.
8He made the Most Holy Place 30 feet wide, corresponding to the width of the Temple, and 30 feet
deep. He overlaid its interior with 23 tons* of fine
gold. 9The gold nails that were used weighed
20 ounces* each. He also overlaid the walls of the
upper rooms with gold.
10He made two figures shaped like cherubim,
overlaid them with gold, and placed them in the Most
Holy Place. 11The total wingspan of the two cherubim standing side by side was 30 feet. One wing
of the first figure was 7½ feet* long, and it touched
the Temple wall. The other wing, also 7½ feet long,
touched one of the wings of the second figure. 12In
the same way, the second figure had one wing 7½ feet
long that touched the opposite wall. The other wing,
also 7½ feet long, touched the wing of the first figure.
13So the wingspan of the two cherubim side by side
was 30 feet. They stood on their feet and faced out
toward the main room of the Temple.
14Across the entrance of the Most Holy Place he
hung a curtain made of fine linen, decorated with
blue, purple, and scarlet thread and embroidered
with figures of cherubim.
15For the front of the Temple, he made two pillars
that were 27 feet* tall, each topped by a capital
extending upward another 7½ feet. 16He made a
network of interwoven chains and used them to decorate the tops of the pillars. He also made 100 decorative pomegranates and attached them to the
chains. 17Then he set up the two pillars at the entrance of the Temple, one to the south of the entrance and the other to the north. He named the one
on the south Jakin, and the one on the north Boaz.*

3:2 Hebrew *on the second day of the second month.* This day of the ancient Hebrew lunar calendar occurred in April or May. **3:3a** The "old standard of measurement" was a cubit equal to 18 inches [46 centimeters]. The new standard was a cubit of approximately 21 inches [53 centimeters]. **3:3b** Hebrew *60 cubits* [27.6 meters] *long and 20 cubits* [9.2 meters] *wide.* **3:4a** Hebrew *20 cubits* [9.2 meters]; also in 3:8, 11, 13. **3:4b** As in some Greek and Syriac manuscripts, which read *20 cubits* [9.2 meters]; Hebrew reads *120 [cubits],* which is 180 feet or 55 meters. **3:8** Hebrew *600 talents* [20.4 metric tons]. **3:9** Hebrew *50 shekels* [570 grams]. **3:11** Hebrew *5 cubits* [2.3 meters]; also in 3:11b, 12, 15. **3:15** As in Syriac version (see also 1 Kgs 7:15; 2 Kgs 25:17; Jer 52:21), which reads *18 cubits* [8.3 meters]; Hebrew reads *35 cubits,* which is 52.5 feet or 16.5 meters. **3:17** *Jakin* probably means "he establishes"; *Boaz* probably means "in him is strength."

KING JAMES VERSION

4 1 Moreover he made an altar of brass, twenty cubits the length thereof, and twenty cubits the breadth thereof, and ten cubits the height thereof.

2 Also he made a molten sea of ten cubits from brim to brim, round in compass, and five cubits the height thereof; and a line of thirty cubits did compass it round about.

3 And under it *was* the similitude of oxen, which did compass it round about: ten in a cubit, compassing the sea round about. Two rows of oxen *were* cast, when it was cast.

4 It stood upon twelve oxen, three looking toward the north, and three looking toward the west, and three looking toward the south, and three looking toward the east: and the sea *was set* above upon them, and all their hinder parts *were* inward.

5 And the thickness of it *was* an handbreadth, and the brim of it like the work of the brim of a cup, with flowers of lilies; *and* it received and held three thousand baths.

6 He made also ten lavers, and put five on the right hand, and five on the left, to wash in them: such things as they offered for the burnt offering they washed in them; but the sea *was* for the priests to wash in.

7 And he made ten candlesticks of gold according to their form, and set *them* in the temple, five on the right hand, and five on the left.

8 He made also ten tables, and placed *them* in the temple, five on the right side, and five on the left. And he made an hundred basins of gold.

9 Furthermore he made the court of the priests, and the great court, and doors for the court, and overlaid the doors of them with brass.

10 And he set the sea on the right side of the east end, over against the south.

11 And Huram made the pots, and the shovels, and the basins. And Huram finished the work that he was to make for king Solomon for the house of God;

12 *To wit,* the two pillars, and the pommels, and the chapiters *which were* on the top of the two pillars, and the two wreaths to cover the two pommels of the chapiters which *were* on the top of the pillars;

13 And four hundred pomegranates on the two wreaths; two rows of pomegranates on each wreath, to cover the two pommels of the chapiters which *were* upon the pillars.

14 He made also bases, and lavers made he upon the bases;

15 One sea, and twelve oxen under it.

16 The pots also, and the shovels, and the fleshhooks, and all their instruments, did Huram his father make to king Solomon for the house of the LORD of bright brass.

17 In the plain of Jordan did the king cast them, in the clay ground between Succoth and Zeredathah.

NEW LIVING TRANSLATION

Furnishings for the Temple

4 Solomon* also made a bronze altar 30 feet long, 30 feet wide, and 15 feet high.* 2 Then he cast a great round basin, 15 feet across from rim to rim, called the Sea. It was 7½ feet deep and about 45 feet in circumference.* 3 It was encircled just below its rim by two rows of figures that resembled oxen. There were about six oxen per foot* all the way around, and they were cast as part of the basin.

4 The Sea was placed on a base of twelve bronze oxen, all facing outward. Three faced north, three faced west, three faced south, and three faced east, and the Sea rested on them. 5 The walls of the Sea were about three inches* thick, and its rim flared out like a cup and resembled a water lily blossom. It could hold about 16,500 gallons* of water.

6 He also made ten smaller basins for washing the utensils for the burnt offerings. He set five on the south side and five on the north. But the priests washed themselves in the Sea.

7 He then cast ten gold lampstands according to the specifications that had been given, and he put them in the Temple. Five were placed against the south wall, and five were placed against the north wall.

8 He also built ten tables and placed them in the Temple, five along the south wall and five along the north wall. Then he molded 100 gold basins.

9 He then built a courtyard for the priests, and also the large outer courtyard. He made doors for the courtyard entrances and overlaid them with bronze. 10 The great bronze basin called the Sea was placed near the southeast corner of the Temple.

11 Huram-abi also made the necessary washbasins, shovels, and bowls.

So at last Huram-abi completed everything King Solomon had assigned him to make for the Temple of God:

12 the two pillars;
the two bowl-shaped capitals on top of the pillars;
the two networks of interwoven chains that decorated the capitals;
13 the 400 pomegranates that hung from the chains on the capitals (two rows of pomegranates for each of the chain networks that decorated the capitals on top of the pillars);
14 the water carts holding the basins;
15 the Sea and the twelve oxen under it;
16 the ash buckets, the shovels, the meat hooks, and all the related articles.

Huram-abi made all these things of burnished bronze for the Temple of the LORD, just as King Solomon had directed. 17 The king had them cast in clay molds in the Jordan Valley between Succoth and

4:1a Or *Huram-abi;* Hebrew reads *He.* **4:1b** Hebrew *20 cubits* [9.2 meters] *long, 20 cubits wide, and 10 cubits* [4.6 meters] *high.* **4:2** Hebrew *10 cubits* [4.6 meters] *across . . . 5 cubits* [2.3 meters] *deep and 30 cubits* [13.8 meters] *in circumference.* **4:3** Or *20 oxen per meter;* Hebrew reads *10 per cubit.* **4:5a** Hebrew *a handbreadth* [8 centimeters]. **4:5b** Hebrew *3,000 baths* [63 kiloliters].

KING JAMES VERSION

18 Thus Solomon made all these vessels in great abundance: for the weight of the brass could not be found out.

19 And Solomon made all the vessels that *were for* the house of God, the golden altar also, and the tables whereon the shewbread *was set;*

20 Moreover the candlesticks with their lamps, that they should burn after the manner before the oracle, of pure gold;

21 And the flowers, and the lamps, and the tongs, *made he of* gold, *and* that perfect gold;

22 And the snuffers, and the basins, and the spoons, and the censers, *of* pure gold: and the entry of the house, the inner doors thereof for the most holy *place,* and the doors of the house of the temple, *were of* gold.

5 1 Thus all the work that Solomon made for the house of the LORD was finished: and Solomon brought in *all* the things that David his father had dedicated; and the silver, and the gold, and all the instruments, put he among the treasures of the house of God.

2 Then Solomon assembled the elders of Israel, and all the heads of the tribes, the chief of the fathers of the children of Israel, unto Jerusalem, to bring up the ark of the covenant of the LORD out of the city of David, which *is* Zion.

3 Wherefore all the men of Israel assembled themselves unto the king in the feast which *was* in the seventh month.

4 And all the elders of Israel came; and the Levites took up the ark.

5 And they brought up the ark, and the tabernacle of the congregation, and all the holy vessels that *were* in the tabernacle, these did the priests *and* the Levites bring up.

6 Also king Solomon, and all the congregation of Israel that were assembled unto him before the ark, sacrificed sheep and oxen, which could not be told nor numbered for multitude.

7 And the priests brought in the ark of the covenant of the LORD unto his place, to the oracle of the house, into the most holy *place, even* under the wings of the cherubims:

8 For the cherubims spread forth *their* wings over the place of the ark, and the cherubims covered the ark and the staves thereof above.

9 And they drew out the staves *of the ark,* that the ends of the staves were seen from the ark before the oracle; but they were not seen without. And there it is unto this day.

10 *There was* nothing in the ark save the two tables which Moses put *therein* at Horeb, when the LORD made *a covenant* with the children of Israel, when they came out of Egypt.

NEW LIVING TRANSLATION

Zarethan.* 18 Solomon used such great quantities of bronze that its weight could not be determined.

19 Solomon also made all the furnishings for the Temple of God:

the gold altar;
the tables for the Bread of the Presence;
20 the lampstands and their lamps of solid gold,
to burn in front of the Most Holy Place as prescribed;
21 the flower decorations, lamps, and tongs—
all of the purest gold;
22 the lamp snuffers, bowls, dishes, and incense burners—all of solid gold;
the doors for the entrances to the Most Holy Place and the main room of the Temple, overlaid with gold.

5 So Solomon finished all his work on the Temple of the LORD. Then he brought all the gifts his father, David, had dedicated—the silver, the gold, and the various articles—and he stored them in the treasuries of the Temple of God.

The Ark Brought to the Temple

2 Solomon then summoned to Jerusalem the elders of Israel and all the heads of tribes—the leaders of the ancestral families of Israel. They were to bring the Ark of the LORD's Covenant to the Temple from its location in the City of David, also known as Zion. 3 So all the men of Israel assembled before the king at the annual Festival of Shelters, which is held in early autumn.*

4 When all the elders of Israel arrived, the Levites picked up the Ark. 5 The priests and Levites brought up the Ark along with the special tent* and all the sacred items that had been in it. 6 There, before the Ark, King Solomon and the entire community of Israel sacrificed so many sheep, goats, and cattle that no one could keep count!

7 Then the priests carried the Ark of the LORD's Covenant into the inner sanctuary of the Temple—the Most Holy Place—and placed it beneath the wings of the cherubim. 8 The cherubim spread their wings over the Ark, forming a canopy over the Ark and its carrying poles. 9 These poles were so long that their ends could be seen from the Temple's main room—the Holy Place*—but not from the outside. They are still there to this day. 10 Nothing was in the Ark except the two stone tablets that Moses had placed in it at Mount Sinai,* where the LORD made a covenant with the people of Israel when they left Egypt.

4:17 As in parallel text at 1 Kgs 7:46; Hebrew reads *Zeredah.* **5:3** Hebrew *at the festival that is in the seventh month.* The Festival of Shelters began on the fifteenth day of the seventh month of the ancient Hebrew lunar calendar. This day occurred in late September, October, or early November. **5:5** Hebrew *the Tent of Meeting;* i.e., the tent mentioned in 2 Sam 6:17 and 1 Chr 16:1. **5:9** As in some Hebrew manuscripts and Greek version (see also 1 Kgs 8:8); Masoretic Text reads *from the Ark in front of the Most Holy Place.* **5:10** Hebrew *Horeb,* another name for Sinai.

KING JAMES VERSION

11 And it came to pass, when the priests were come out of the holy *place:* (for all the priests *that were* present were sanctified, *and* did not *then* wait by course:

12 Also the Levites *which were* the singers, all of them of Asaph, of Heman, of Jeduthun, with their sons and their brethren, *being* arrayed in white linen, having cymbals and psalteries and harps, stood at the east end of the altar, and with them an hundred and twenty priests sounding with trumpets:)

13 It came even to pass, as the trumpeters and singers *were* as one, to make one sound to be heard in praising and thanking the LORD; and when they lifted up *their* voice with the trumpets and cymbals and instruments of musick, and praised the LORD, *saying,* For *he is* good; for his mercy *endureth* for ever: that *then* the house was filled with a cloud, *even* the house of the LORD;

14 So that the priests could not stand to minister by reason of the cloud: for the glory of the LORD had filled the house of God.

6 1 Then said Solomon, The LORD hath said that he would dwell in the thick darkness.

2 But I have built an house of habitation for thee, and a place for thy dwelling for ever.

3 And the king turned his face, and blessed the whole congregation of Israel: and all the congregation of Israel stood.

4 And he said, Blessed *be* the LORD God of Israel, who hath with his hands fulfilled *that* which he spake with his mouth to my father David, saying,

5 Since the day that I brought forth my people out of the land of Egypt I chose no city among all the tribes of Israel to build an house in, that my name might be there; neither chose I any man to be a ruler over my people Israel:

6 But I have chosen Jerusalem, that my name might be there; and have chosen David to be over my people Israel.

7 Now it was in the heart of David my father to build an house for the name of the LORD God of Israel.

8 But the LORD said to David my father, Forasmuch as it was in thine heart to build an house for my name, thou didst well in that it was in thine heart:

9 Notwithstanding thou shalt not build the house; but thy son which shall come forth out of thy loins, he shall build the house for my name.

10 The LORD therefore hath performed his word that he hath spoken: for I am risen up in the room of David my father, and am set on the throne of Israel, as the LORD promised, and have built the house for the name of the LORD God of Israel.

11 And in it have I put the ark, wherein *is* the covenant of the LORD, that he made with the children of Israel.

12 And he stood before the altar of the LORD in the presence of all the congregation of Israel, and spread forth his hands:

NEW LIVING TRANSLATION

11 Then the priests left the Holy Place. All the priests who were present had purified themselves, whether or not they were on duty that day. 12 And the Levites who were musicians—Asaph, Heman, Jeduthun, and all their sons and brothers—were dressed in fine linen robes and stood at the east side of the altar playing cymbals, lyres, and harps. They were joined by 120 priests who were playing trumpets. 13 The trumpeters and singers performed together in unison to praise and give thanks to the LORD. Accompanied by trumpets, cymbals, and other instruments, they raised their voices and praised the LORD with these words:

"He is good!
His faithful love endures forever!"

At that moment a thick cloud filled the Temple of the LORD. 14 The priests could not continue their service because of the cloud, for the glorious presence of the LORD filled the Temple of God.

Solomon Praises the LORD

6 Then Solomon prayed, "O LORD, you have said that you would live in a thick cloud of darkness. 2 Now I have built a glorious Temple for you, a place where you can live forever!"

3 Then the king turned around to the entire community of Israel standing before him and gave this blessing: 4 "Praise the LORD, the God of Israel, who has kept the promise he made to my father, David. For he told my father, 5 'From the day I brought my people out of the land of Egypt, I have never chosen a city among any of the tribes of Israel as the place where a Temple should be built to honor my name. Nor have I chosen a king to lead my people Israel. 6 But now I have chosen Jerusalem as the place for my name to be honored, and I have chosen David to be king over my people Israel.'"

7 Then Solomon said, "My father, David, wanted to build this Temple to honor the name of the LORD, the God of Israel. 8 But the LORD told him, 'You wanted to build the Temple to honor my name. Your intention is good, 9 but you are not the one to do it. One of your own sons will build the Temple to honor me.'

10 "And now the LORD has fulfilled the promise he made, for I have become king in my father's place, and now I sit on the throne of Israel, just as the LORD promised. I have built this Temple to honor the name of the LORD, the God of Israel. 11 There I have placed the Ark, which contains the covenant that the LORD made with the people of Israel."

Solomon's Prayer of Dedication

12 Then Solomon stood before the altar of the LORD in front of the entire community of Israel, and he

KING JAMES VERSION

13 For Solomon had made a brasen scaffold, of five cubits long, and five cubits broad, and three cubits high, and had set it in the midst of the court: and upon it he stood, and kneeled down upon his knees before all the congregation of Israel, and spread forth his hands toward heaven,

14 And said, O LORD God of Israel, *there is* no God like thee in the heaven, nor in the earth; which keepest covenant, and *shewest* mercy unto thy servants, that walk before thee with all their hearts:

15 Thou which hast kept with thy servant David my father that which thou hast promised him; and spakest with thy mouth, and hast fulfilled *it* with thine hand, as *it is* this day.

16 Now therefore, O LORD God of Israel, keep with thy servant David my father that which thou hast promised him, saying, There shall not fail thee a man in my sight to sit upon the throne of Israel; yet so that thy children take heed to their way to walk in my law, as thou hast walked before me.

17 Now then, O LORD God of Israel, let thy word be verified, which thou hast spoken unto thy servant David.

18 But will God in very deed dwell with men on the earth? behold, heaven and the heaven of heavens cannot contain thee; how much less this house which I have built!

19 Have respect therefore to the prayer of thy servant, and to his supplication, O LORD my God, to hearken unto the cry and the prayer which thy servant prayeth before thee:

20 That thine eyes may be open upon this house day and night, upon the place whereof thou hast said that thou wouldest put thy name there; to hearken unto the prayer which thy servant prayeth toward this place.

21 Hearken therefore unto the supplications of thy servant, and of thy people Israel, which they shall make toward this place: hear thou from thy dwelling place, *even* from heaven; and when thou hearest, forgive.

22 If a man sin against his neighbour, and an oath be laid upon him to make him swear, and the oath come before thine altar in this house;

23 Then hear thou from heaven, and do, and judge thy servants, by requiting the wicked, by recompensing his way upon his own head; and by justifying the righteous, by giving him according to his righteousness.

24 And if thy people Israel be put to the worse before the enemy, because they have sinned against thee; and shall return and confess thy name, and pray and make supplication before thee in this house;

25 Then hear thou from the heavens, and forgive the sin of thy people Israel, and bring them again unto the land which thou gavest to them and to their fathers.

NEW LIVING TRANSLATION

lifted his hands in prayer. 13 Now Solomon had made a bronze platform 7½ feet long, 7½ feet wide, and 4½ feet high* and had placed it at the center of the Temple's outer courtyard. He stood on the platform, and then he knelt in front of the entire community of Israel and lifted his hands toward heaven. 14 He prayed,

"O LORD, God of Israel, there is no God like you in
all of heaven and earth. You keep your covenant
and show unfailing love to all who walk before
you in wholehearted devotion. 15 You have kept
your promise to your servant David, my father.
You made that promise with your own mouth,
and with your own hands you have fulfilled
it today.

16 "And now, O LORD, God of Israel, carry out
the additional promise you made to your servant
David, my father. For you said to him, 'If your
descendants guard their behavior and faithfully
follow my Law as you have done, one of them will
always sit on the throne of Israel.' 17 Now, O LORD,
God of Israel, fulfill this promise to your servant
David.

18 "But will God really live on earth among
people? Why, even the highest heavens cannot
contain you. How much less this Temple I have
built! 19 Nevertheless, listen to my prayer and my
plea, O LORD my God. Hear the cry and the prayer
that your servant is making to you. 20 May you
watch over this Temple day and night, this place
where you have said you would put your name.
May you always hear the prayers I make toward
this place. 21 May you hear the humble and
earnest requests from me and your people Israel
when we pray toward this place. Yes, hear us
from heaven where you live, and when you hear,
forgive.

22 "If someone wrongs another person and is
required to take an oath of innocence in front
of your altar at this Temple, 23 then hear from
heaven and judge between your servants—the
accuser and the accused. Pay back the guilty as
they deserve. Acquit the innocent because of
their innocence.

24 "If your people Israel are defeated by their
enemies because they have sinned against you,
and if they turn back and acknowledge your
name and pray to you here in this Temple,
25 then hear from heaven and forgive the sin of
your people Israel and return them to this land
you gave to them and to their ancestors.

6:13 Hebrew *5 cubits* [2.3 meters] *long, 5 cubits wide, and 3 cubits* [1.4 meters] *high.*

KING JAMES VERSION

26 When the heaven is shut up, and there is no rain, because they have sinned against thee; *yet* if they pray toward this place, and confess thy name, and turn from their sin, when thou dost afflict them;

27 Then hear thou from heaven, and forgive the sin of thy servants, and of thy people Israel, when thou hast taught them the good way, wherein they should walk; and send rain upon thy land, which thou hast given unto thy people for an inheritance.

28 If there be dearth in the land, if there be pestilence, if there be blasting, or mildew, locusts, or caterpillers; if their enemies besiege them in the cities of their land; whatsoever sore or whatsoever sickness *there be:*

29 *Then* what prayer *or* what supplication soever shall be made of any man, or of all thy people Israel, when every one shall know his own sore and his own grief, and shall spread forth his hands in this house:

30 Then hear thou from heaven thy dwelling place, and forgive, and render unto every man according unto all his ways, whose heart thou knowest; (for thou only knowest the hearts of the children of men:)

31 That they may fear thee, to walk in thy ways, so long as they live in the land which thou gavest unto our fathers.

32 Moreover concerning the stranger, which is not of thy people Israel, but is come from a far country for thy great name's sake, and thy mighty hand, and thy stretched out arm; if they come and pray in this house;

33 Then hear thou from the heavens, *even* from thy dwelling place, and do according to all that the stranger calleth to thee for; that all people of the earth may know thy name, and fear thee, as *doth* thy people Israel, and may know that this house which I have built is called by thy name.

34 If thy people go out to war against their enemies by the way that thou shalt send them, and they pray unto thee toward this city which thou hast chosen, and the house which I have built for thy name;

35 Then hear thou from the heavens their prayer and their supplication, and maintain their cause.

36 If they sin against thee, (for *there is* no man which sinneth not,) and thou be angry with them, and deliver them over before *their* enemies, and they carry them away captives unto a land far off or near;

37 Yet *if* they bethink themselves in the land whither they are carried captive, and turn and pray unto thee in the land of their captivity, saying, We have sinned, we have done amiss, and have dealt wickedly;

38 If they return to thee with all their heart and with all their soul in the land of their captivity, whither they have carried them captives, and pray toward their land, which thou gavest unto their fathers, and *toward* the city which thou hast chosen, and toward the house which I have built for thy name:

39 Then hear thou from the heavens, *even* from thy

NEW LIVING TRANSLATION

26 "If the skies are shut up and there is no rain because your people have sinned against you, and if they pray toward this Temple and acknowledge your name and turn from their sins because you have punished them, 27 then hear from heaven and forgive the sins of your servants, your people Israel. Teach them to follow the right path, and send rain on your land that you have given to your people as their special possession.

28 "If there is a famine in the land or a plague or crop disease or attacks of locusts or caterpillars, or if your people's enemies are in the land besieging their towns—whatever disaster or disease there is— 29 and if your people Israel pray about their troubles or sorrow, raising their hands toward this Temple, 30 then hear from heaven where you live, and forgive. Give your people what their actions deserve, for you alone know each human heart. 31 Then they will fear you and walk in your ways as long as they live in the land you gave to our ancestors.

32 "In the future, foreigners who do not belong to your people Israel will hear of you. They will come from distant lands when they hear of your great name and your strong hand and your powerful arm. And when they pray toward this Temple, 33 then hear from heaven where you live, and grant what they ask of you. In this way, all the people of the earth will come to know and fear you, just as your own people Israel do. They, too, will know that this Temple I have built honors your name.

34 "If your people go out where you send them to fight their enemies, and if they pray to you by turning toward this city you have chosen and toward this Temple I have built to honor your name, 35 then hear their prayers from heaven and uphold their cause.

36 "If they sin against you—and who has never sinned?—you might become angry with them and let their enemies conquer them and take them captive to a foreign land far away or near. 37 But in that land of exile, they might turn to you in repentance and pray, 'We have sinned, done evil, and acted wickedly.' 38 If they turn to you with their whole heart and soul in the land of their captivity and pray toward the land you gave to their ancestors—toward this city you have chosen, and toward this Temple I have built to honor your name— 39 then hear their prayers and

KING JAMES VERSION

dwelling place, their prayer and their supplications,
and maintain their cause, and forgive thy people
which have sinned against thee.
40 Now, my God, let, I beseech thee, thine eyes be
open, and *let* thine ears *be* attent unto the prayer *that*
is made in this place.
41 Now therefore arise, O LORD God, into thy resting place, thou, and the ark of thy strength: let thy
priests, O LORD God, be clothed with salvation, and
let thy saints rejoice in goodness.
42 O LORD God, turn not away the face of thine
anointed: remember the mercies of David thy servant.

7 1 Now when Solomon had made an end of praying, the fire came down from heaven, and consumed the burnt offering and the sacrifices; and the
glory of the LORD filled the house.
2 And the priests could not enter into the house of
the LORD, because the glory of the LORD had filled the
LORD's house.
3 And when all the children of Israel saw how the
fire came down, and the glory of the LORD upon the
house, they bowed themselves with their faces to
the ground upon the pavement, and worshipped,
and praised the LORD, *saying,* For *he is* good; for his
mercy *endureth* for ever.
4 Then the king and all the people offered sacrifices before the LORD.
5 And king Solomon offered a sacrifice of twenty
and two thousand oxen, and an hundred and twenty
thousand sheep: so the king and all the people dedicated the house of God.
6 And the priests waited on their offices: the Levites also with instruments of musick of the LORD,
which David the king had made to praise the LORD,
because his mercy *endureth* for ever, when David
praised by their ministry; and the priests sounded
trumpets before them, and all Israel stood.
7 Moreover Solomon hallowed the middle of the
court that *was* before the house of the LORD: for
there he offered burnt offerings, and the fat of the
peace offerings, because the brasen altar which Solomon had made was not able to receive the burnt offerings, and the meat offerings, and the fat.
8 Also at the same time Solomon kept the feast
seven days, and all Israel with him, a very great congregation, from the entering in of Hamath unto the
river of Egypt.
9 And in the eighth day they made a solemn assembly: for they kept the dedication of the altar seven
days, and the feast seven days.

NEW LIVING TRANSLATION

their petitions from heaven where you live, and
uphold their cause. Forgive your people who have
sinned against you.
40 "O my God, may your eyes be open and your
ears attentive to all the prayers made to you in
this place.

41 "And now arise, O LORD God, and enter your
resting place,
along with the Ark, the symbol of your power.
May your priests, O LORD God, be clothed with
salvation;
may your loyal servants rejoice in your
goodness.
42 O LORD God, do not reject the king you have
anointed.
Remember your unfailing love for your
servant David."

The Dedication of the Temple

7 When Solomon finished praying, fire flashed
down from heaven and burned up the burnt
offerings and sacrifices, and the glorious presence
of the LORD filled the Temple. 2 The priests could not
enter the Temple of the LORD because the glorious
presence of the LORD filled it. 3 When all the people
of Israel saw the fire coming down and the glorious
presence of the LORD filling the Temple, they fell
face down on the ground and worshiped and praised
the LORD, saying,

"He is good!
His faithful love endures forever!"

4 Then the king and all the people offered sacrifices to the LORD. 5 King Solomon offered a sacrifice
of 22,000 cattle and 120,000 sheep and goats. And
so the king and all the people dedicated the Temple
of God. 6 The priests took their assigned positions,
and so did the Levites who were singing, "His faithful
love endures forever!" They accompanied the singing with music from the instruments King David had
made for praising the LORD. Across from the Levites,
the priests blew the trumpets, while all Israel stood.
7 Solomon then consecrated the central area of the
courtyard in front of the LORD's Temple. He offered
burnt offerings and the fat of peace offerings there,
because the bronze altar he had built could not hold
all the burnt offerings, grain offerings, and sacrificial fat.
8 For the next seven days Solomon and all Israel
celebrated the Festival of Shelters.* A large congregation had gathered from as far away as Lebo-
hamath in the north and the Brook of Egypt in the
south. 9 On the eighth day they had a closing ceremony, for they had celebrated the dedication of the
altar for seven days and the Festival of Shelters for

7:8 Hebrew *the festival* (also in 7:9); see note on 5:3.

KING JAMES VERSION

10 And on the three and twentieth day of the seventh month he sent the people away into their tents, glad and merry in heart for the goodness that the LORD had shewed unto David, and to Solomon, and to Israel his people.

11 Thus Solomon finished the house of the LORD, and the king's house: and all that came into Solomon's heart to make in the house of the LORD, and in his own house, he prosperously effected.

12 And the LORD appeared to Solomon by night, and said unto him, I have heard thy prayer, and have chosen this place to myself for an house of sacrifice.

13 If I shut up heaven that there be no rain, or if I command the locusts to devour the land, or if I send pestilence among my people;

14 If my people, which are called by my name, shall humble themselves, and pray, and seek my face, and turn from their wicked ways; then will I hear from heaven, and will forgive their sin, and will heal their land.

15 Now mine eyes shall be open, and mine ears attent unto the prayer *that is made* in this place.

16 For now have I chosen and sanctified this house, that my name may be there for ever: and mine eyes and mine heart shall be there perpetually.

17 And as for thee, if thou wilt walk before me, as David thy father walked, and do according to all that I have commanded thee, and shalt observe my statutes and my judgments;

18 Then will I stablish the throne of thy kingdom, according as I have covenanted with David thy father, saying, There shall not fail thee a man *to be* ruler in Israel.

19 But if ye turn away, and forsake my statutes and my commandments, which I have set before you, and shall go and serve other gods, and worship them;

20 Then will I pluck them up by the roots out of my land which I have given them; and this house, which I have sanctified for my name, will I cast out of my sight, and will make it *to be* a proverb and a byword among all nations.

21 And this house, which is high, shall be an astonishment to every one that passeth by it; so that he shall say, Why hath the LORD done thus unto this land, and unto this house?

22 And it shall be answered, Because they forsook the LORD God of their fathers, which brought them forth out of the land of Egypt, and laid hold on other gods, and worshipped them, and served them: therefore hath he brought all this evil upon them.

8 1 And it came to pass at the end of twenty years, wherein Solomon had built the house of the LORD, and his own house,

2 That the cities which Huram had restored to

NEW LIVING TRANSLATION

seven days. 10 Then at the end of the celebration,* Solomon sent the people home. They were all joyful and glad because the LORD had been so good to David and to Solomon and to his people Israel.

The LORD's Response to Solomon

11 So Solomon finished the Temple of the LORD, as well as the royal palace. He completed everything he had planned to do in the construction of the Temple and the palace. 12 Then one night the LORD appeared to Solomon and said,

"I have heard your prayer and have chosen this Temple as the place for making sacrifices. 13 At times I might shut up the heavens so that no rain falls, or command grasshoppers to devour your crops, or send plagues among you. 14 Then if my people who are called by my name will humble themselves and pray and seek my face and turn from their wicked ways, I will hear from heaven and will forgive their sins and restore their land. 15 My eyes will be open and my ears attentive to every prayer made in this place. 16 For I have chosen this Temple and set it apart to be holy—a place where my name will be honored forever. I will always watch over it, for it is dear to my heart.

17 "As for you, if you faithfully follow me as David your father did, obeying all my commands, decrees, and regulations, 18 then I will establish the throne of your dynasty. For I made this covenant with your father, David, when I said, 'One of your descendants will always rule over Israel.'

19 "But if you or your descendants abandon me and disobey the decrees and commands I have given you, and if you serve and worship other gods, 20 then I will uproot the people from this land that I have given them. I will reject this Temple that I have made holy to honor my name. I will make it an object of mockery and ridicule among the nations. 21 And though this Temple is impressive now, all who pass by will be appalled. They will ask, 'Why did the LORD do such terrible things to this land and to this Temple?'

22 "And the answer will be, 'Because his people abandoned the LORD, the God of their ancestors, who brought them out of Egypt, and they worshiped other gods instead and bowed down to them. That is why he has brought all these disasters on them.'"

Solomon's Many Achievements

8 It took Solomon twenty years to build the LORD's Temple and his own royal palace. At the end of that time, 2 Solomon turned his attention to

7:10 Hebrew *Then on the twenty-third day of the seventh month.* This day of the ancient Hebrew lunar calendar occurred in October or early November.

KING JAMES VERSION

Solomon, Solomon built them, and caused the children of Israel to dwell there.

3And Solomon went to Hamath-zobah, and prevailed against it.

4And he built Tadmor in the wilderness, and all the store cities, which he built in Hamath.

5Also he built Beth-horon the upper, and Beth-horon the nether, fenced cities, with walls, gates, and bars;

6And Baalath, and all the store cities that Solomon had, and all the chariot cities, and the cities of the horsemen, and all that Solomon desired to build in Jerusalem, and in Lebanon, and throughout all the land of his dominion.

7*As for* all the people *that were* left of the Hittites, and the Amorites, and the Perizzites, and the Hivites, and the Jebusites, which *were* not of Israel,

8*But* of their children, who were left after them in the land, whom the children of Israel consumed not, them did Solomon make to pay tribute until this day.

9But of the children of Israel did Solomon make no servants for his work; but they *were* men of war, and chief of his captains, and captains of his chariots and horsemen.

10And these *were* the chief of king Solomon's officers, *even* two hundred and fifty, that bare rule over the people.

11And Solomon brought up the daughter of Pharaoh out of the city of David unto the house that he had built for her: for he said, My wife shall not dwell in the house of David king of Israel, because *the places are* holy, whereunto the ark of the LORD hath come.

12Then Solomon offered burnt offerings unto the LORD on the altar of the LORD, which he had built before the porch,

13Even after a certain rate every day, offering according to the commandment of Moses, on the sabbaths, and on the new moons, and on the solemn feasts, three times in the year, *even* in the feast of unleavened bread, and in the feast of weeks, and in the feast of tabernacles.

14And he appointed, according to the order of David his father, the courses of the priests to their service, and the Levites to their charges, to praise and minister before the priests, as the duty of every day required: the porters also by their courses at every gate: for so had David the man of God commanded.

15And they departed not from the commandment of the king unto the priests and Levites concerning any matter, or concerning the treasures.

16Now all the work of Solomon was prepared unto the day of the foundation of the house of the LORD, and until it was finished. *So* the house of the LORD was perfected.

17Then went Solomon to Ezion-geber, and to Eloth, at the sea side in the land of Edom.

18And Huram sent him by the hands of his servants

NEW LIVING TRANSLATION

rebuilding the towns that King Hiram* had given him, and he settled Israelites in them.

3Solomon also fought against the town of Hamath-zobah and conquered it. 4He rebuilt Tadmor in the wilderness and built towns in the region of Hamath as supply centers. 5He fortified the towns of Upper Beth-horon and Lower Beth-horon, rebuilding their walls and installing barred gates. 6He also rebuilt Baalath and other supply centers and constructed towns where his chariots and horses* could be stationed. He built everything he desired in Jerusalem and Lebanon and throughout his entire realm.

7There were still some people living in the land who were not Israelites, including the Hittites, Amorites, Perizzites, Hivites, and Jebusites. 8These were descendants of the nations whom the people of Israel had not destroyed. So Solomon conscripted them for his labor force, and they serve in the labor force to this day. 9But Solomon did not conscript any of the Israelites for his labor force. Instead, he assigned them to serve as fighting men, officers in his army, commanders of his chariots, and charioteers. 10King Solomon appointed 250 of them to supervise the people.

11Solomon moved his wife, Pharaoh's daughter, from the City of David to the new palace he had built for her. He said, "My wife must not live in King David's palace, for the Ark of the LORD has been there, and it is holy ground."

12Then Solomon presented burnt offerings to the LORD on the altar he had built for him in front of the entry room of the Temple. 13He offered the sacrifices for the Sabbaths, the new moon festivals, and the three annual festivals—the Passover celebration, the Festival of Harvest,* and the Festival of Shelters—as Moses had commanded.

14In assigning the priests to their duties, Solomon followed the regulations of his father, David. He also assigned the Levites to lead the people in praise and to assist the priests in their daily duties. And he assigned the gatekeepers to their gates by their divisions, following the commands of David, the man of God. 15Solomon did not deviate in any way from David's commands concerning the priests and Levites and the treasuries.

16So Solomon made sure that all the work related to building the Temple of the LORD was carried out, from the day its foundation was laid to the day of its completion.

17Later Solomon went to Ezion-geber and Elath,* ports along the shore of the Red Sea* in the land of Edom. 18Hiram sent him ships commanded by his

8:2 Hebrew *Huram,* a variant spelling of Hiram; also in 8:18. **8:6** Or *and charioteers.* **8:13** Or *Festival of Weeks.* **8:17a** As in Greek version (see also 2 Kgs 14:22; 16:6); Hebrew reads *Eloth,* a variant spelling of Elath. **8:17b** As in parallel text at 1 Kgs 9:26; Hebrew reads *the sea.*

KING JAMES VERSION

ships, and servants that had knowledge of the sea; and they went with the servants of Solomon to Ophir, and took thence four hundred and fifty talents of gold, and brought *them* to king Solomon.

9 1And when the queen of Sheba heard of the fame of Solomon, she came to prove Solomon with hard questions at Jerusalem, with a very great company, and camels that bare spices, and gold in abundance, and precious stones: and when she was come to Solomon, she communed with him of all that was in her heart.

2And Solomon told her all her questions: and there was nothing hid from Solomon which he told her not.

3And when the queen of Sheba had seen the wisdom of Solomon, and the house that he had built,

4And the meat of his table, and the sitting of his servants, and the attendance of his ministers, and their apparel; his cupbearers also, and their apparel; and his ascent by which he went up into the house of the LORD; there was no more spirit in her.

5And she said to the king, *It was* a true report which I heard in mine own land of thine acts, and of thy wisdom:

6Howbeit I believed not their words, until I came, and mine eyes had seen *it:* and, behold, the one half of the greatness of thy wisdom was not told me: *for* thou exceedest the fame that I heard.

7Happy *are* thy men, and happy *are* these thy servants, which stand continually before thee, and hear thy wisdom.

8Blessed be the LORD thy God, which delighted in thee to set thee on his throne, *to be* king for the LORD thy God: because thy God loved Israel, to establish them for ever, therefore made he thee king over them, to do judgment and justice.

9And she gave the king an hundred and twenty talents of gold, and of spices great abundance, and precious stones: neither was there any such spice as the queen of Sheba gave king Solomon.

10And the servants also of Huram, and the servants of Solomon, which brought gold from Ophir, brought algum trees and precious stones.

11And the king made *of* the algum trees terraces to the house of the LORD, and to the king's palace, and harps and psalteries for singers: and there were none such seen before in the land of Judah.

12And king Solomon gave to the queen of Sheba all her desire, whatsoever she asked, beside *that* which she had brought unto the king. So she turned, and went away to her own land, she and her servants.

13Now the weight of gold that came to Solomon in one year was six hundred and threescore and six talents of gold;

14Beside *that which* chapmen and merchants

NEW LIVING TRANSLATION

own officers and manned by experienced crews of sailors. These ships sailed to Ophir with Solomon's men and brought back to Solomon almost seventeen tons* of gold.

Visit of the Queen of Sheba

9 When the queen of Sheba heard of Solomon's fame, she came to Jerusalem to test him with hard questions. She arrived with a large group of attendants and a great caravan of camels loaded with spices, large quantities of gold, and precious jewels. When she met with Solomon, she talked with him about everything she had on her mind. 2Solomon had answers for all her questions; nothing was too hard for him to explain to her. 3When the queen of Sheba realized how wise Solomon was, and when she saw the palace he had built, 4she was overwhelmed. She was also amazed at the food on his tables, the organization of his officials and their splendid clothing, the cup-bearers and their robes, and the burnt offerings Solomon made at the Temple of the LORD.

5She exclaimed to the king, "Everything I heard in my country about your achievements* and wisdom is true! 6I didn't believe what was said until I arrived here and saw it with my own eyes. In fact, I had not heard the half of your great wisdom! It is far beyond what I was told. 7How happy your people must be! What a privilege for your officials to stand here day after day, listening to your wisdom! 8Praise the LORD your God, who delights in you and has placed you on the throne as king to rule for him. Because God loves Israel and desires this kingdom to last forever, he has made you king over them so you can rule with justice and righteousness."

9Then she gave the king a gift of 9,000 pounds* of gold, great quantities of spices, and precious jewels. Never before had there been spices as fine as those the queen of Sheba gave to King Solomon.

10(In addition, the crews of Hiram and Solomon brought gold from Ophir, and they also brought red sandalwood* and precious jewels. 11The king used the sandalwood to make steps* for the Temple of the LORD and the royal palace, and to construct lyres and harps for the musicians. Never before had such beautiful things been seen in Judah.)

12King Solomon gave the queen of Sheba whatever she asked for—gifts of greater value than the gifts she had given him. Then she and all her attendants returned to their own land.

Solomon's Wealth and Splendor

13Each year Solomon received about 25 tons* of gold. 14This did not include the additional revenue

8:18 Hebrew *450 talents* [15.3 metric tons]. **9:5** Hebrew *your words.* **9:9** Hebrew *120 talents* [4,000 kilograms]. **9:10** Hebrew *algum wood* (also in 9:11); perhaps a variant spelling of *almug.* Compare parallel text at 1 Kgs 10:11-12. **9:11** Or *gateways.* The meaning of the Hebrew is uncertain. **9:13** Hebrew *666 talents* [23 metric tons].

KING JAMES VERSION

brought. And all the kings of Arabia and governors of the country brought gold and silver to Solomon.

15And king Solomon made two hundred targets *of* beaten gold: six hundred *shekels* of beaten gold went to one target.

16And three hundred shields *made he of* beaten gold: three hundred *shekels* of gold went to one shield. And the king put them in the house of the forest of Lebanon.

17Moreover the king made a great throne of ivory, and overlaid it with pure gold.

18And *there were* six steps to the throne, with a footstool of gold, *which were* fastened to the throne, and stays on each side of the sitting place, and two lions standing by the stays:

19And twelve lions stood there on the one side and on the other upon the six steps. There was not the like made in any kingdom.

20And all the drinking vessels of king Solomon *were of* gold, and all the vessels of the house of the forest of Lebanon *were of* pure gold: none *were of* silver; it was *not* any thing accounted of in the days of Solomon.

21For the king's ships went to Tarshish with the servants of Huram: every three years once came the ships of Tarshish bringing gold, and silver, ivory, and apes, and peacocks.

22And king Solomon passed all the kings of the earth in riches and wisdom.

23And all the kings of the earth sought the presence of Solomon, to hear his wisdom, that God had put in his heart.

24And they brought every man his present, vessels of silver, and vessels of gold, and raiment, harness, and spices, horses, and mules, a rate year by year.

25And Solomon had four thousand stalls for horses and chariots, and twelve thousand horsemen; whom he bestowed in the chariot cities, and with the king at Jerusalem.

26And he reigned over all the kings from the river even unto the land of the Philistines, and to the border of Egypt.

27And the king made silver in Jerusalem as stones, and cedar trees made he as the sycamore trees that *are* in the low plains in abundance.

28And they brought unto Solomon horses out of Egypt, and out of all lands.

29Now the rest of the acts of Solomon, first and last, *are* they not written in the book of Nathan the prophet, and in the prophecy of Ahijah the Shilonite, and in the visions of Iddo the seer against Jeroboam the son of Nebat?

30And Solomon reigned in Jerusalem over all Israel forty years.

31And Solomon slept with his fathers, and he was buried in the city of David his father: and Rehoboam his son reigned in his stead.

NEW LIVING TRANSLATION

he received from merchants and traders. All the kings of Arabia and the governors of the provinces also brought gold and silver to Solomon.

15King Solomon made 200 large shields of hammered gold, each weighing more than 15 pounds.* 16He also made 300 smaller shields of hammered gold, each weighing more than 7½ pounds.* The king placed these shields in the Palace of the Forest of Lebanon.

17Then the king made a huge throne, decorated with ivory and overlaid with pure gold. 18The throne had six steps, with a footstool of gold. There were armrests on both sides of the seat, and the figure of a lion stood on each side of the throne. 19There were also twelve other lions, one standing on each end of the six steps. No other throne in all the world could be compared with it!

20All of King Solomon's drinking cups were solid gold, as were all the utensils in the Palace of the Forest of Lebanon. They were not made of silver, for silver was considered worthless in Solomon's day!

21The king had a fleet of trading ships* manned by the sailors sent by Hiram.* Once every three years the ships returned, loaded with gold, silver, ivory, apes, and peacocks.*

22So King Solomon became richer and wiser than any other king on earth. 23Kings from every nation came to consult him and to hear the wisdom God had given him. 24Year after year everyone who visited brought him gifts of silver and gold, clothing, weapons, spices, horses, and mules.

25Solomon had 4,000 stalls for his horses and chariots, and he had 12,000 horses.* He stationed some of them in the chariot cities, and some near him in Jerusalem. 26He ruled over all the kings from the Euphrates River* in the north to the land of the Philistines and the border of Egypt in the south. 27The king made silver as plentiful in Jerusalem as stone. And valuable cedar timber was as common as the sycamore-fig trees that grow in the foothills of Judah.* 28Solomon's horses were imported from Egypt* and many other countries.

Summary of Solomon's Reign

29The rest of the events of Solomon's reign, from beginning to end, are recorded in *The Record of Nathan the Prophet*, and *The Prophecy of Ahijah from Shiloh*, and also in *The Visions of Iddo the Seer*, concerning Jeroboam son of Nebat. 30Solomon ruled in Jerusalem over all Israel for forty years. 31When he died, he was buried in the City of David, named for his father. Then his son Rehoboam became the next king.

9:15 Hebrew *600 [shekels] of hammered gold* [6.8 kilograms]. **9:16** Hebrew *300 [shekels] of gold* [3.4 kilograms]. **9:21a** Hebrew *fleet of ships that could sail to Tarshish.* **9:21b** Hebrew *Huram*, a variant spelling of Hiram. **9:21c** Or *and baboons.* **9:25** Or *12,000 charioteers.* **9:26** Hebrew *the river.* **9:27** Hebrew *the Shephelah.* **9:28** Possibly *Muzur*, a district near Cilicia.

KING JAMES VERSION

10 1 And Rehoboam went to Shechem: for to
Shechem were all Israel come to make him
king.
2 And it came to pass, when Jeroboam the son of
Nebat, who *was* in Egypt, whither he had fled from
the presence of Solomon the king, heard *it,* that
Jeroboam returned out of Egypt.
3 And they sent and called him. So Jeroboam and
all Israel came and spake to Rehoboam, saying,
4 Thy father made our yoke grievous: now therefore ease thou somewhat the grievous servitude of
thy father, and his heavy yoke that he put upon us,
and we will serve thee.
5 And he said unto them, Come again unto me after
three days. And the people departed.
6 And king Rehoboam took counsel with the old
men that had stood before Solomon his father while
he yet lived, saying, What counsel give ye *me* to return answer to this people?
7 And they spake unto him, saying, If thou be kind
to this people, and please them, and speak good
words to them, they will be thy servants for ever.
8 But he forsook the counsel which the old men
gave him, and took counsel with the young men that
were brought up with him, that stood before him.
9 And he said unto them, What advice give ye that
we may return answer to this people, which have
spoken to me, saying, Ease somewhat the yoke that
thy father did put upon us?
10 And the young men that were brought up with
him spake unto him, saying, Thus shalt thou answer
the people that spake unto thee, saying, Thy father
made our yoke heavy, but make thou *it* somewhat
lighter for us; thus shalt thou say unto them, My little
finger shall be thicker than my father's loins.
11 For whereas my father put a heavy yoke upon you,
I will put more to your yoke: my father chastised you
with whips, but I *will chastise you* with scorpions.
12 So Jeroboam and all the people came to Rehoboam on the third day, as the king bade, saying, Come
again to me on the third day.
13 And the king answered them roughly; and king
Rehoboam forsook the counsel of the old men,
14 And answered them after the advice of the
young men, saying, My father made your yoke heavy,
but I will add thereto: my father chastised you with
whips, but I *will chastise you* with scorpions.
15 So the king hearkened not unto the people: for
the cause was of God, that the LORD might perform
his word, which he spake by the hand of Ahijah the
Shilonite to Jeroboam the son of Nebat.
16 And when all Israel *saw* that the king would not
hearken unto them, the people answered the king,
saying, What portion have we in David? and *we have*
none inheritance in the son of Jesse: every man to
your tents, O Israel: *and* now, David, see to thine own
house. So all Israel went to their tents.

NEW LIVING TRANSLATION

The Northern Tribes Revolt

10 Rehoboam went to Shechem, where all Israel
had gathered to make him king. 2 When Jeroboam son of Nebat heard of this, he returned from
Egypt, for he had fled to Egypt to escape from King
Solomon. 3 The leaders of Israel summoned him, and
Jeroboam and all Israel went to speak with Rehoboam. 4 "Your father was a hard master," they said.
"Lighten the harsh labor demands and heavy taxes
that your father imposed on us. Then we will be your
loyal subjects."
5 Rehoboam replied, "Come back in three days for
my answer." So the people went away.
6 Then King Rehoboam discussed the matter with
the older men who had counseled his father, Solomon. "What is your advice?" he asked. "How
should I answer these people?"
7 The older counselors replied, "If you are good to
these people and do your best to please them and
give them a favorable answer, they will always be
your loyal subjects."
8 But Rehoboam rejected the advice of the older
men and instead asked the opinion of the young men
who had grown up with him and were now his advisers. 9 "What is your advice?" he asked them. "How
should I answer these people who want me to
lighten the burdens imposed by my father?"
10 The young men replied, "This is what you
should tell those complainers who want a lighter
burden: 'My little finger is thicker than my father's
waist! 11 Yes, my father laid heavy burdens on you, but
I'm going to make them even heavier! My father beat
you with whips, but I will beat you with scorpions!'"
12 Three days later Jeroboam and all the people returned to hear Rehoboam's decision, just as the king
had ordered. 13 But Rehoboam spoke harshly to
them, for he rejected the advice of the older counselors 14 and followed the counsel of his younger advisers. He told the people, "My father laid* heavy
burdens on you, but I'm going to make them even
heavier! My father beat you with whips, but I will
beat you with scorpions!"
15 So the king paid no attention to the people. This
turn of events was the will of God, for it fulfilled the
LORD's message to Jeroboam son of Nebat through
the prophet Ahijah from Shiloh.
16 When all Israel realized* that the king had refused to listen to them, they responded,

"Down with the dynasty of David!
We have no interest in the son of Jesse.
Back to your homes, O Israel!
Look out for your own house, O David!"

10:14 As in Greek version and many Hebrew manuscripts (see also 1 Kgs 12:14); Masoretic Text reads *I will lay.* **10:16** As in Syriac version, Latin Vulgate, and many Hebrew manuscripts (see also 1 Kgs 12:16); Masoretic Text lacks *realized.*

KING JAMES VERSION

17But *as for* the children of Israel that dwelt in the cities of Judah, Rehoboam reigned over them.

18Then king Rehoboam sent Hadoram that *was* over the tribute; and the children of Israel stoned him with stones, that he died. But king Rehoboam made speed to get him up to *his* chariot, to flee to Jerusalem.

19And Israel rebelled against the house of David unto this day.

11 1And when Rehoboam was come to Jerusalem, he gathered of the house of Judah and Benjamin an hundred and fourscore thousand chosen *men,* which were warriors, to fight against Israel, that he might bring the kingdom again to Rehoboam.

2But the word of the LORD came to Shemaiah the man of God, saying,

3Speak unto Rehoboam the son of Solomon, king of Judah, and to all Israel in Judah and Benjamin, saying,

4Thus saith the LORD, Ye shall not go up, nor fight against your brethren: return every man to his house: for this thing is done of me. And they obeyed the words of the LORD, and returned from going against Jeroboam.

5And Rehoboam dwelt in Jerusalem, and built cities for defence in Judah.

6He built even Bethlehem, and Etam, and Tekoa,

7And Beth-zur, and Shoco, and Adullam,

8And Gath, and Mareshah, and Ziph,

9And Adoraim, and Lachish, and Azekah,

10And Zorah, and Aijalon, and Hebron, which *are* in Judah and in Benjamin fenced cities.

11And he fortified the strong holds, and put captains in them, and store of victual, and of oil and wine.

12And in every several city *he put* shields and spears, and made them exceeding strong, having Judah and Benjamin on his side.

13And the priests and the Levites that *were* in all Israel resorted to him out of all their coasts.

14For the Levites left their suburbs and their possession, and came to Judah and Jerusalem: for Jeroboam and his sons had cast them off from executing the priest's office unto the LORD:

15And he ordained him priests for the high places, and for the devils, and for the calves which he had made.

16And after them out of all the tribes of Israel such as set their hearts to seek the LORD God of Israel came to Jerusalem, to sacrifice unto the LORD God of their fathers.

17So they strengthened the kingdom of Judah, and made Rehoboam the son of Solomon strong, three years: for three years they walked in the way of David and Solomon.

NEW LIVING TRANSLATION

So all the people of Israel returned home. 17But Rehoboam continued to rule over the Israelites who lived in the towns of Judah.

18King Rehoboam sent Adoniram,* who was in charge of the labor force, to restore order, but the people of Israel stoned him to death. When this news reached King Rehoboam, he quickly jumped into his chariot and fled to Jerusalem. 19And to this day the northern tribes of Israel have refused to be ruled by a descendant of David.

Shemaiah's Prophecy

11 When Rehoboam arrived at Jerusalem, he mobilized the men of Judah and Benjamin—180,000 select troops—to fight against Israel and to restore the kingdom to himself.

2But the LORD said to Shemaiah, the man of God, 3"Say to Rehoboam son of Solomon, king of Judah, and to all the Israelites in Judah and Benjamin: 4'This is what the LORD says: Do not fight against your relatives. Go back home, for what has happened is my doing!'" So they obeyed the message of the LORD and did not fight against Jeroboam.

Rehoboam Fortifies Judah

5Rehoboam remained in Jerusalem and fortified various towns for the defense of Judah. 6He built up Bethlehem, Etam, Tekoa, 7Beth-zur, Soco, Adullam, 8Gath, Mareshah, Ziph, 9Adoraim, Lachish, Azekah, 10Zorah, Aijalon, and Hebron. These became the fortified towns of Judah and Benjamin. 11Rehoboam strengthened their defenses and stationed commanders in them, and he stored supplies of food, olive oil, and wine. 12He also put shields and spears in these towns as a further safety measure. So only Judah and Benjamin remained under his control.

13But all the priests and Levites living among the northern tribes of Israel sided with Rehoboam. 14The Levites even abandoned their pasturelands and property and moved to Judah and Jerusalem, because Jeroboam and his sons would not allow them to serve the LORD as priests. 15Jeroboam appointed his own priests to serve at the pagan shrines, where they worshiped the goat and calf idols he had made. 16From all the tribes of Israel, those who sincerely wanted to worship the LORD, the God of Israel, followed the Levites to Jerusalem, where they could offer sacrifices to the LORD, the God of their ancestors. 17This strengthened the kingdom of Judah, and for three years they supported Rehoboam son of Solomon, for during those years they faithfully followed in the footsteps of David and Solomon.

10:18 Hebrew *Hadoram,* a variant spelling of Adoniram; compare 1 Kgs 4:6; 5:14; 12:18.

KING JAMES VERSION

18 And Rehoboam took him Mahalath the daughter of Jerimoth the son of David to wife, *and* Abihail
the daughter of Eliab the son of Jesse;
19 Which bare him children; Jeush, and Shemariah, and Zaham.
20 And after her he took Maachah the daughter of
Absalom; which bare him Abijah, and Attai, and Ziza,
and Shelomith.
21 And Rehoboam loved Maachah the daughter of
Absalom above all his wives and his concubines: (for
he took eighteen wives, and threescore concubines;
and begat twenty and eight sons, and threescore
daughters.)
22 And Rehoboam made Abijah the son of Maa-
chah the chief, *to be* ruler among his brethren: for *he*
thought to make him king.
23 And he dealt wisely, and dispersed of all his children throughout all the countries of Judah and Benjamin, unto every fenced city: and he gave them
victual in abundance. And he desired many wives.

12 1 And it came to pass, when Rehoboam had
established the kingdom, and had strengthened himself, he forsook the law of the LORD, and all
Israel with him.
2 And it came to pass, *that* in the fifth year of king
Rehoboam Shishak king of Egypt came up against
Jerusalem, because they had transgressed against
the LORD,
3 With twelve hundred chariots, and threescore
thousand horsemen: and the people *were* without
number that came with him out of Egypt; the Lubims, the Sukkiims, and the Ethiopians.
4 And he took the fenced cities which *pertained* to
Judah, and came to Jerusalem.
5 Then came Shemaiah the prophet to Rehoboam,
and *to* the princes of Judah, that were gathered
together to Jerusalem because of Shishak, and said
unto them, Thus saith the LORD, Ye have forsaken
me, and therefore have I also left you in the hand of
Shishak.
6 Whereupon the princes of Israel and the king
humbled themselves; and they said, The LORD *is*
righteous.
7 And when the LORD saw that they humbled themselves, the word of the LORD came to Shemaiah, saying, They have humbled themselves; *therefore* I will
not destroy them, but I will grant them some deliverance; and my wrath shall not be poured out upon Jerusalem by the hand of Shishak.
8 Nevertheless they shall be his servants; that they
may know my service, and the service of the kingdoms of the countries.
9 So Shishak king of Egypt came up against Jerusalem, and took away the treasures of the house of the
LORD, and the treasures of the king's house; he took

NEW LIVING TRANSLATION

Rehoboam's Family

18 Rehoboam married his cousin Mahalath, the
daughter of David's son Jerimoth and of Abihail, the
daughter of Eliab son of Jesse. 19 Mahalath had three
sons—Jeush, Shemariah, and Zaham.
20 Later Rehoboam married another cousin, Maacah, the daughter of Absalom. Maacah gave birth to
Abijah, Attai, Ziza, and Shelomith. 21 Rehoboam
loved Maacah more than any of his other wives and
concubines. In all, he had eighteen wives and sixty
concubines, and they gave birth to twenty-eight sons
and sixty daughters.
22 Rehoboam appointed Maacah's son Abijah as
leader among the princes, making it clear that he
would be the next king. 23 Rehoboam also wisely gave
responsibilities to his other sons and stationed some
of them in the fortified towns throughout the land of
Judah and Benjamin. He provided them with generous provisions, and he found many wives for them.

Egypt Invades Judah

12 But when Rehoboam was firmly established
and strong, he abandoned the Law of the
LORD, and all Israel followed him in this sin. 2 Because
they were unfaithful to the LORD, King Shishak of
Egypt came up and attacked Jerusalem in the fifth
year of King Rehoboam's reign. 3 He came with 1,200
chariots, 60,000 horses,* and a countless army of
foot soldiers, including Libyans, Sukkites, and Ethiopians.* 4 Shishak conquered Judah's fortified towns
and then advanced to attack Jerusalem.
5 The prophet Shemaiah then met with Rehoboam
and Judah's leaders, who had all fled to Jerusalem because of Shishak. Shemaiah told them, "This is what
the LORD says: You have abandoned me, so I am abandoning you to Shishak."
6 Then the leaders of Israel and the king humbled
themselves and said, "The LORD is right in doing this
to us!"
7 When the LORD saw their change of heart, he
gave this message to Shemaiah: "Since the people
have humbled themselves, I will not completely destroy them and will soon give them some relief. I will
not use Shishak to pour out my anger on Jerusalem.
8 But they will become his subjects, so they will know
the difference between serving me and serving
earthly rulers."
9 So King Shishak of Egypt came up and attacked
Jerusalem. He ransacked the treasures of the LORD's

12:3a Or *charioteers,* or *horsemen.* **12:3b** Hebrew *and Cushites.*

KING JAMES VERSION

all: he carried away also the shields of gold which
Solomon had made.
10 Instead of which king Rehoboam made shields
of brass, and committed *them* to the hands of the
chief of the guard, that kept the entrance of the
king's house.
11 And when the king entered into the house of
the LORD, the guard came and fetched them, and
brought them again into the guard chamber.
12 And when he humbled himself, the wrath of the
LORD turned from him, that he would not destroy
him altogether: and also in Judah things went well.

13 So king Rehoboam strengthened himself in Jerusalem, and reigned: for Rehoboam *was* one and
forty years old when he began to reign, and he
reigned seventeen years in Jerusalem, the city which
the LORD had chosen out of all the tribes of Israel, to
put his name there. And his mother's name *was* Naamah an Ammonitess.
14 And he did evil, because he prepared not his
heart to seek the LORD.
15 Now the acts of Rehoboam, first and last, *are*
they not written in the book of Shemaiah the
prophet, and of Iddo the seer concerning genealogies? And *there were* wars between Rehoboam and
Jeroboam continually.
16 And Rehoboam slept with his fathers, and was
buried in the city of David: and Abijah his son
reigned in his stead.

13 1 Now in the eighteenth year of king Jeroboam
began Abijah to reign over Judah.
2 He reigned three years in Jerusalem. His mother's
name also *was* Michaiah the daughter of Uriel of Gibeah. And there was war between Abijah and Jeroboam.
3 And Abijah set the battle in array with an army of
valiant men of war, *even* four hundred thousand chosen men: Jeroboam also set the battle in array against
him with eight hundred thousand chosen men, *being* mighty men of valour.
4 And Abijah stood up upon mount Zemaraim,
which *is* in mount Ephraim, and said, Hear me, thou
Jeroboam, and all Israel;
5 Ought ye not to know that the LORD God of Israel
gave the kingdom over Israel to David for ever, *even*
to him and to his sons by a covenant of salt?
6 Yet Jeroboam the son of Nebat, the servant of Solomon the son of David, is risen up, and hath rebelled
against his lord.
7 And there are gathered unto him vain men, the
children of Belial, and have strengthened themselves against Rehoboam the son of Solomon, when
Rehoboam was young and tenderhearted, and could
not withstand them.
8 And now ye think to withstand the kingdom of

NEW LIVING TRANSLATION

Temple and the royal palace; he stole everything,
including all the gold shields Solomon had made.
10 King Rehoboam later replaced them with bronze
shields as substitutes, and he entrusted them to the
care of the commanders of the guard who protected
the entrance to the royal palace. 11 Whenever the
king went to the Temple of the LORD, the guards
would also take the shields and then return them to
the guardroom. 12 Because Rehoboam humbled himself, the LORD's anger was turned away, and he did
not destroy him completely. There were still some
good things in the land of Judah.

Summary of Rehoboam's Reign

13 King Rehoboam firmly established himself in Jerusalem and continued to rule. He was forty-one years
old when he became king, and he reigned seventeen
years in Jerusalem, the city the LORD had chosen
from among all the tribes of Israel as the place to
honor his name. Rehoboam's mother was Naamah,
a woman from Ammon. 14 But he was an evil king,
for he did not seek the LORD with all his heart.
15 The rest of the events of Rehoboam's reign,
from beginning to end, are recorded in *The Record
of Shemaiah the Prophet* and *The Record of Iddo the
Seer,* which are part of the genealogical record. Rehoboam and Jeroboam were continually at war with
each other. 16 When Rehoboam died, he was buried
in the City of David. Then his son Abijah became the
next king.

Abijah's War with Jeroboam

13 Abijah began to rule over Judah in the eighteenth year of Jeroboam's reign in Israel. 2 He
reigned in Jerusalem three years. His mother was
Maacah,* the daughter of Uriel from Gibeah.
Then war broke out between Abijah and Jeroboam. 3 Judah, led by King Abijah, fielded 400,000
select warriors, while Jeroboam mustered 800,000
select troops from Israel.
4 When the army of Judah arrived in the hill country of Ephraim, Abijah stood on Mount Zemaraim
and shouted to Jeroboam and all Israel: "Listen to
me! 5 Don't you realize that the LORD, the God of Israel, made a lasting covenant* with David, giving him
and his descendants the throne of Israel forever?
6 Yet Jeroboam son of Nebat, a mere servant of David's son Solomon, rebelled against his master.
7 Then a whole gang of scoundrels joined him, defying Solomon's son Rehoboam when he was young
and inexperienced and could not stand up to them.
8 "Do you really think you can stand against the

13:2 As in most Greek manuscripts and Syriac version (see also 2 Chr 11:20-21; 1 Kgs 15:2); Hebrew reads *Micaiah,* a variant spelling of Maacah. **13:5** Hebrew *a covenant of salt.*

KING JAMES VERSION

the LORD in the hand of the sons of David; and ye *be*
a great multitude, and *there are* with you golden
calves, which Jeroboam made you for gods.
9 Have ye not cast out the priests of the LORD, the
sons of Aaron, and the Levites, and have made you
priests after the manner of the nations of *other*
lands? so that whosoever cometh to consecrate himself with a young bullock and seven rams, *the same*
may be a priest of *them that are* no gods.
10 But as for us, the LORD *is* our God, and we have
not forsaken him; and the priests, which minister
unto the LORD, *are* the sons of Aaron, and the Levites
wait upon *their* business:
11 And they burn unto the LORD every morning and
every evening burnt sacrifices and sweet incense: the
shewbread also *set they in order* upon the pure table;
and the candlestick of gold with the lamps thereof,
to burn every evening: for we keep the charge of the
LORD our God; but ye have forsaken him.
12 And, behold, God himself *is* with us for *our*
captain, and his priests with sounding trumpets to
cry alarm against you. O children of Israel, fight ye
not against the LORD God of your fathers; for ye shall
not prosper.
13 But Jeroboam caused an ambushment to come
about behind them: so they were before Judah, and
the ambushment *was* behind them.
14 And when Judah looked back, behold, the battle
was before and behind: and they cried unto the
LORD, and the priests sounded with the trumpets.
15 Then the men of Judah gave a shout: and as
the men of Judah shouted, it came to pass, that God
smote Jeroboam and all Israel before Abijah and
Judah.
16 And the children of Israel fled before Judah: and
God delivered them into their hand.
17 And Abijah and his people slew them with a
great slaughter: so there fell down slain of Israel five
hundred thousand chosen men.
18 Thus the children of Israel were brought under
at that time, and the children of Judah prevailed,
because they relied upon the LORD God of their
fathers.
19 And Abijah pursued after Jeroboam, and took
cities from him, Bethel with the towns thereof, and
Jeshanah with the towns thereof, and Ephrain with
the towns thereof.
20 Neither did Jeroboam recover strength again
in the days of Abijah: and the LORD struck him, and
he died.
21 But Abijah waxed mighty, and married fourteen
wives, and begat twenty and two sons, and sixteen
daughters.
22 And the rest of the acts of Abijah, and his ways,
and his sayings, *are* written in the story of the
prophet Iddo.

NEW LIVING TRANSLATION

kingdom of the LORD that is led by the descendants
of David? You may have a vast army, and you have
those gold calves that Jeroboam made as your gods.
9 But you have chased away the priests of the LORD
(the descendants of Aaron) and the Levites, and you
have appointed your own priests, just like the pagan
nations. You let anyone become a priest these days!
Whoever comes to be dedicated with a young bull
and seven rams can become a priest of these so-
called gods of yours!
10 "But as for us, the LORD is our God, and we have
not abandoned him. Only the descendants of Aaron
serve the LORD as priests, and the Levites alone may
help them in their work. 11 They present burnt offerings and fragrant incense to the LORD every morning
and evening. They place the Bread of the Presence on
the holy table, and they light the gold lampstand
every evening. We are following the instructions of
the LORD our God, but you have abandoned him. 12 So
you see, God is with us. He is our leader. His priests
blow their trumpets and lead us into battle against
you. O people of Israel, do not fight against the LORD,
the God of your ancestors, for you will not succeed!"
13 Meanwhile, Jeroboam had secretly sent part of
his army around behind the men of Judah to ambush
them. 14 When Judah realized that they were being
attacked from the front and the rear, they cried out to
the LORD for help. Then the priests blew the trumpets, 15 and the men of Judah began to shout. At the
sound of their battle cry, God defeated Jeroboam and
all Israel and routed them before Abijah and the
army of Judah.
16 The Israelite army fled from Judah, and God
handed them over to Judah in defeat. 17 Abijah and
his army inflicted heavy losses on them; 500,000 of
Israel's select troops were killed that day. 18 So Judah
defeated Israel on that occasion because they
trusted in the LORD, the God of their ancestors.
19 Abijah and his army pursued Jeroboam's troops
and captured some of his towns, including Bethel,
Jeshanah, and Ephron, along with their surrounding
villages.
20 So Jeroboam of Israel never regained his power
during Abijah's lifetime, and finally the LORD struck
him down and he died. 21 Meanwhile, Abijah of Judah grew more and more powerful. He married
fourteen wives and had twenty-two sons and sixteen
daughters.
22 The rest of the events of Abijah's reign, including his words and deeds, are recorded in *The Commentary of Iddo the Prophet*.

KING JAMES VERSION

14 [1]So Abijah slept with his fathers, and they buried him in the city of David: and Asa his son reigned in his stead. In his days the land was quiet ten years.

[2]And Asa did *that which was* good and right in the eyes of the LORD his God:

[3]For he took away the altars of the strange *gods*, and the high places, and brake down the images, and cut down the groves:

[4]And commanded Judah to seek the LORD God of their fathers, and to do the law and the commandment.

[5]Also he took away out of all the cities of Judah the high places and the images: and the kingdom was quiet before him.

[6]And he built fenced cities in Judah: for the land had rest, and he had no war in those years; because the LORD had given him rest.

[7]Therefore he said unto Judah, Let us build these cities, and make about *them* walls, and towers, gates, and bars, *while* the land *is* yet before us; because we have sought the LORD our God, we have sought *him*, and he hath given us rest on every side. So they built and prospered.

[8]And Asa had an army *of men* that bare targets and spears, out of Judah three hundred thousand; and out of Benjamin, that bare shields and drew bows, two hundred and fourscore thousand: all these *were* mighty men of valour.

[9]And there came out against them Zerah the Ethiopian with an host of a thousand thousand, and three hundred chariots; and came unto Mareshah.

[10]Then Asa went out against him, and they set the battle in array in the valley of Zephathah at Mareshah.

[11]And Asa cried unto the LORD his God, and said, LORD, *it is* nothing with thee to help, whether with many, or with them that have no power: help us, O LORD our God; for we rest on thee, and in thy name we go against this multitude. O LORD, thou *art* our God; let not man prevail against thee.

[12]So the LORD smote the Ethiopians before Asa, and before Judah; and the Ethiopians fled.

[13]And Asa and the people that *were* with him pursued them unto Gerar: and the Ethiopians were overthrown, that they could not recover themselves; for they were destroyed before the LORD, and before his host; and they carried away very much spoil.

[14]And they smote all the cities round about Gerar; for the fear of the LORD came upon them: and they spoiled all the cities; for there was exceeding much spoil in them.

[15]They smote also the tents of cattle, and carried away sheep and camels in abundance, and returned to Jerusalem.

NEW LIVING TRANSLATION

Early Years of Asa's Reign

14 [1]*When Abijah died, he was buried in the City of David. Then his son Asa became the next king. There was peace in the land for ten years. [2]*Asa did what was pleasing and good in the sight of the LORD his God. [3]He removed the foreign altars and the pagan shrines. He smashed the sacred pillars and cut down the Asherah poles. [4]He commanded the people of Judah to seek the LORD, the God of their ancestors, and to obey his law and his commands. [5]Asa also removed the pagan shrines, as well as the incense altars from every one of Judah's towns. So Asa's kingdom enjoyed a period of peace. [6]During those peaceful years, he was able to build up the fortified towns throughout Judah. No one tried to make war against him at this time, for the LORD was giving him rest from his enemies.

[7]Asa told the people of Judah, "Let us build towns and fortify them with walls, towers, gates, and bars. The land is still ours because we sought the LORD our God, and he has given us peace on every side." So they went ahead with these projects and brought them to completion.

[8]King Asa had an army of 300,000 warriors from the tribe of Judah, armed with large shields and spears. He also had an army of 280,000 warriors from the tribe of Benjamin, armed with small shields and bows. Both armies were composed of well-trained fighting men.

[9]Once an Ethiopian* named Zerah attacked Judah with an army of 1,000,000 men* and 300 chariots. They advanced to the town of Mareshah, [10]so Asa deployed his armies for battle in the valley north of Mareshah.* [11]Then Asa cried out to the LORD his God, "O LORD, no one but you can help the powerless against the mighty! Help us, O LORD our God, for we trust in you alone. It is in your name that we have come against this vast horde. O LORD, you are our God; do not let mere men prevail against you!"

[12]So the LORD defeated the Ethiopians* in the presence of Asa and the army of Judah, and the enemy fled. [13]Asa and his army pursued them as far as Gerar, and so many Ethiopians fell that they were unable to rally. They were destroyed by the LORD and his army, and the army of Judah carried off a vast amount of plunder.

[14]While they were at Gerar, they attacked all the towns in that area, and terror from the LORD came upon the people there. As a result, a vast amount of plunder was taken from these towns, too. [15]They also attacked the camps of herdsmen and captured many sheep, goats, and camels before finally returning to Jerusalem.

14:1 Verse 14:1 is numbered 13:23 in the Hebrew text. **14:2** Verses 4:2-15 are numbered 14:1-14 in Hebrew text. **14:9a** Hebrew *a Cushite.* **14:9b** Or *an army of thousands and thousands;* Hebrew reads *an army of a thousand thousands.* **14:10** Or *in the Zephathah Valley near Mareshah.* **14:12** Hebrew *Cushites;* also in 14:13.

KING JAMES VERSION

15 1And the Spirit of God came upon Azariah the
son of Oded:
2And he went out to meet Asa, and said unto him,
Hear ye me, Asa, and all Judah and Benjamin; The
LORD *is* with you, while ye be with him; and if ye seek
him, he will be found of you; but if ye forsake him, he
will forsake you.
3Now for a long season Israel *hath been* without
the true God, and without a teaching priest, and
without law.
4But when they in their trouble did turn unto the
LORD God of Israel, and sought him, he was found of
them.
5And in those times *there was* no peace to him
that went out, nor to him that came in, but great vex-
ations *were* upon all the inhabitants of the countries.
6And nation was destroyed of nation, and city of
city: for God did vex them with all adversity.
7Be ye strong therefore, and let not your hands be
weak: for your work shall be rewarded.
8And when Asa heard these words, and the prophecy of Oded the prophet, he took courage, and put
away the abominable idols out of all the land of Judah and Benjamin, and out of the cities which he had
taken from mount Ephraim, and renewed the altar of
the LORD, that *was* before the porch of the LORD.
9And he gathered all Judah and Benjamin, and the
strangers with them out of Ephraim and Manasseh,
and out of Simeon: for they fell to him out of Israel
in abundance, when they saw that the LORD his God
was with him.
10So they gathered themselves together at Jerusalem in the third month, in the fifteenth year of the
reign of Asa.
11And they offered unto the LORD the same time,
of the spoil *which* they had brought, seven hundred
oxen and seven thousand sheep.
12And they entered into a covenant to seek the
LORD God of their fathers with all their heart and
with all their soul;
13That whosoever would not seek the LORD God of
Israel should be put to death, whether small or great,
whether man or woman.
14And they sware unto the LORD with a loud voice,
and with shouting, and with trumpets, and with
cornets.
15And all Judah rejoiced at the oath: for they had
sworn with all their heart, and sought him with their
whole desire; and he was found of them: and the
LORD gave them rest round about.
16And also *concerning* Maachah the mother of Asa
the king, he removed her from *being* queen, because
she had made an idol in a grove: and Asa cut down her
idol, and stamped *it*, and burnt *it* at the brook Kidron.
17But the high places were not taken away out of
Israel: nevertheless the heart of Asa was perfect all
his days.

NEW LIVING TRANSLATION

Asa's Religious Reforms

15 Then the Spirit of God came upon Azariah
son of Oded, 2and he went out to meet King
Asa as he was returning from the battle. "Listen to
me, Asa!" he shouted. "Listen, all you people of Judah
and Benjamin! The LORD will stay with you as long as
you stay with him! Whenever you seek him, you will
find him. But if you abandon him, he will abandon
you. 3For a long time Israel was without the true God,
without a priest to teach them, and without the Law
to instruct them. 4But whenever they were in trouble
and turned to the LORD, the God of Israel, and sought
him out, they found him.
5"During those dark times, it was not safe to travel.
Problems troubled the people of every land. 6Nation
fought against nation, and city against city, for God
was troubling them with every kind of problem. 7But
as for you, be strong and courageous, for your work
will be rewarded."
8When Asa heard this message from Azariah the
prophet,* he took courage and removed all the detestable idols from the land of Judah and Benjamin
and in the towns he had captured in the hill country
of Ephraim. And he repaired the altar of the LORD,
which stood in front of the entry room of the LORD's
Temple.
9Then Asa called together all the people of Judah
and Benjamin, along with the people of Ephraim,
Manasseh, and Simeon who had settled among
them. For many from Israel had moved to Judah during Asa's reign when they saw that the LORD his God
was with him. 10The people gathered at Jerusalem in
late spring,* during the fifteenth year of Asa's reign.
11On that day they sacrificed to the LORD 700
cattle and 7,000 sheep and goats from the plunder
they had taken in the battle. 12Then they entered into
a covenant to seek the LORD, the God of their ancestors, with all their heart and soul. 13They agreed that
anyone who refused to seek the LORD, the God of Israel, would be put to death—whether young or old,
man or woman. 14They shouted out their oath of loyalty to the LORD with trumpets blaring and rams'
horns sounding. 15All in Judah were happy about this
covenant, for they had entered into it with all their
heart. They earnestly sought after God, and they
found him. And the LORD gave them rest from their
enemies on every side.
16King Asa even deposed his grandmother* Maacah from her position as queen mother because she
had made an obscene Asherah pole. He cut down her
obscene pole, broke it up, and burned it in the Kidron
Valley. 17Although the pagan shrines were not removed from Israel, Asa's heart remained completely

15:8 As in Syriac version and Latin Vulgate (see also 15:1); Hebrew reads *from Oded the prophet.* 15:10 Hebrew *in the third month.* This month of the ancient Hebrew lunar calendar usually occurs within the months of May and June. 15:16 Hebrew *his mother.*

KING JAMES VERSION

18And he brought into the house of God the things
that his father had dedicated, and that he himself
had dedicated, silver, and gold, and vessels.

19And there was no *more* war unto the five and
thirtieth year of the reign of Asa.

16 1In the six and thirtieth year of the reign of
Asa Baasha king of Israel came up against
Judah, and built Ramah, to the intent that he might
let none go out or come in to Asa king of Judah.

2Then Asa brought out silver and gold out of the
treasures of the house of the LORD and of the king's
house, and sent to Ben-hadad king of Syria, that
dwelt at Damascus, saying,

3*There is* a league between me and thee, as *there
was* between my father and thy father: behold, I have
sent thee silver and gold; go, break thy league with
Baasha king of Israel, that he may depart from me.

4And Ben-hadad hearkened unto king Asa, and
sent the captains of his armies against the cities of
Israel; and they smote Ijon, and Dan, and Abel-maim,
and all the store cities of Naphtali.

5And it came to pass, when Baasha heard *it*, that
he left off building of Ramah, and let his work cease.

6Then Asa the king took all Judah; and they carried away the stones of Ramah, and the timber
thereof, wherewith Baasha was building; and he built
therewith Geba and Mizpah.

7And at that time Hanani the seer came to Asa
king of Judah, and said unto him, Because thou hast
relied on the king of Syria, and not relied on the LORD
thy God, therefore is the host of the king of Syria escaped out of thine hand.

8Were not the Ethiopians and the Lubims a huge
host, with very many chariots and horsemen? yet, because thou didst rely on the LORD, he delivered them
into thine hand.

9For the eyes of the LORD run to and fro throughout the whole earth, to shew himself strong in the
behalf of *them* whose heart *is* perfect toward him.
Herein thou hast done foolishly: therefore from
henceforth thou shalt have wars.

10Then Asa was wroth with the seer, and put him
in a prison house; for *he was* in a rage with him because of this *thing*. And Asa oppressed *some* of the
people the same time.

11And, behold, the acts of Asa, first and last, lo,
they *are* written in the book of the kings of Judah
and Israel.

12And Asa in the thirty and ninth year of his reign
was diseased in his feet, until his disease *was*
exceeding *great:* yet in his disease he sought not to
the LORD, but to the physicians.

NEW LIVING TRANSLATION

faithful throughout his life. 18He brought into the
Temple of God the silver and gold and the various
items that he and his father had dedicated.

19So there was no more war until the thirty-fifth
year of Asa's reign.

Final Years of Asa's Reign

16 In the thirty-sixth year of Asa's reign, King
Baasha of Israel invaded Judah and fortified
Ramah in order to prevent anyone from entering or
leaving King Asa's territory in Judah.

2Asa responded by removing the silver and gold
from the treasuries of the Temple of the LORD and
the royal palace. He sent it to King Ben-hadad of
Aram, who was ruling in Damascus, along with this
message:

> 3"Let there be a treaty* between you and me like
> the one between your father and my father. See,
> I am sending you silver and gold. Break your
> treaty with King Baasha of Israel so that he will
> leave me alone."

4Ben-hadad agreed to King Asa's request and sent
the commanders of his army to attack the towns of
Israel. They conquered the towns of Ijon, Dan, Abel-beth-maacah,* and all the store cities in Naphtali. 5As
soon as Baasha of Israel heard what was happening,
he abandoned his project of fortifying Ramah and
stopped all work on it. 6Then King Asa called out all
the men of Judah to carry away the building stones
and timbers that Baasha had been using to fortify Ramah. Asa used these materials to fortify the towns of
Geba and Mizpah.

7At that time Hanani the seer came to King Asa
and told him, "Because you have put your trust in the
king of Aram instead of in the LORD your God, you
missed your chance to destroy the army of the king
of Aram. 8Don't you remember what happened to the
Ethiopians* and Libyans and their vast army, with all
of their chariots and charioteers?* At that time you
relied on the LORD, and he handed them over to you.
9The eyes of the LORD search the whole earth in order to strengthen those whose hearts are fully committed to him. What a fool you have been! From now
on you will be at war."

10Asa became so angry with Hanani for saying this
that he threw him into prison and put him in stocks.
At that time Asa also began to oppress some of his
people.

Summary of Asa's Reign

11The rest of the events of Asa's reign, from beginning to end, are recorded in *The Book of the Kings
of Judah and Israel.* 12In the thirty-ninth year of his
reign, Asa developed a serious foot disease. Yet even
with the severity of his disease, he did not seek the

16:3 As in Greek version; Hebrew reads *There is a treaty.* **16:4** As in parallel text at 1 Kgs 15:20; Hebrew reads *Abel-maim,* another name for Abel-beth-maacah. **16:8a** Hebrew *Cushites.* **16:8b** Or *and horsemen?*

KING JAMES VERSION

13 And Asa slept with his fathers, and died in the one and fortieth year of his reign.

14 And they buried him in his own sepulchres, which he had made for himself in the city of David, and laid him in the bed which was filled with sweet odours and divers kinds *of spices* prepared by the apothecaries' art: and they made a very great burning for him.

17 1 And Jehoshaphat his son reigned in his stead, and strengthened himself against Israel.

2 And he placed forces in all the fenced cities of Judah, and set garrisons in the land of Judah, and in the cities of Ephraim, which Asa his father had taken.

3 And the LORD was with Jehoshaphat, because he walked in the first ways of his father David, and sought not unto Baalim;

4 But sought to the *LORD* God of his father, and walked in his commandments, and not after the doings of Israel.

5 Therefore the LORD stablished the kingdom in his hand; and all Judah brought to Jehoshaphat presents; and he had riches and honour in abundance.

6 And his heart was lifted up in the ways of the LORD: moreover he took away the high places and groves out of Judah.

7 Also in the third year of his reign he sent to his princes, *even* to Ben-hail, and to Obadiah, and to Zechariah, and to Nethaneel, and to Michaiah, to teach in the cities of Judah.

8 And with them *he sent* Levites, *even* Shemaiah, and Nethaniah, and Zebadiah, and Asahel, and Shemiramoth, and Jehonathan, and Adonijah, and Tobijah, and Tob-adonijah, Levites; and with them Elishama and Jehoram, priests.

9 And they taught in Judah, and *had* the book of the law of the LORD with them, and went about throughout all the cities of Judah, and taught the people.

10 And the fear of the LORD fell upon all the kingdoms of the lands that *were* round about Judah, so that they made no war against Jehoshaphat.

11 Also *some* of the Philistines brought Jehoshaphat presents, and tribute silver; and the Arabians brought him flocks, seven thousand and seven hundred rams, and seven thousand and seven hundred he goats.

12 And Jehoshaphat waxed great exceedingly; and he built in Judah castles, and cities of store.

13 And he had much business in the cities of Judah: and the men of war, mighty men of valour, *were* in Jerusalem.

14 And these *are* the numbers of them according to the house of their fathers: Of Judah, the captains of thousands; Adnah the chief, and with him mighty men of valour three hundred thousand.

15 And next to him *was* Jehohanan the captain, and with him two hundred and fourscore thousand.

NEW LIVING TRANSLATION

LORD's help but turned only to his physicians. 13 So he died in the forty-first year of his reign. 14 He was buried in the tomb he had carved out for himself in the City of David. He was laid on a bed perfumed with sweet spices and fragrant ointments, and the people built a huge funeral fire in his honor.

Jehoshaphat Rules in Judah

17 Then Jehoshaphat, Asa's son, became the next king. He strengthened Judah to stand against any attack from Israel. 2 He stationed troops in all the fortified towns of Judah, and he assigned additional garrisons to the land of Judah and to the towns of Ephraim that his father, Asa, had captured.

3 The LORD was with Jehoshaphat because he followed the example of his father's early years* and did not worship the images of Baal. 4 He sought his father's God and obeyed his commands instead of following the evil practices of the kingdom of Israel. 5 So the LORD established Jehoshaphat's control over the kingdom of Judah. All the people of Judah brought gifts to Jehoshaphat, so he became very wealthy and highly esteemed. 6 He was deeply committed to* the ways of the LORD. He removed the pagan shrines and Asherah poles from Judah.

7 In the third year of his reign Jehoshaphat sent his officials to teach in all the towns of Judah. These officials included Ben-hail, Obadiah, Zechariah, Nethanel, and Micaiah. 8 He sent Levites along with them, including Shemaiah, Nethaniah, Zebadiah, Asahel, Shemiramoth, Jehonathan, Adonijah, Tobijah, and Tob-adonijah. He also sent out the priests Elishama and Jehoram. 9 They took copies of the Book of the Law of the LORD and traveled around through all the towns of Judah, teaching the people.

10 Then the fear of the LORD fell over all the surrounding kingdoms so that none of them wanted to declare war on Jehoshaphat. 11 Some of the Philistines brought him gifts and silver as tribute, and the Arabs brought 7,700 rams and 7,700 male goats.

12 So Jehoshaphat became more and more powerful and built fortresses and storage cities throughout Judah. 13 He stored numerous supplies in Judah's towns and stationed an army of seasoned troops at Jerusalem. 14 His army was enrolled according to ancestral clans.

From Judah there were 300,000 troops organized
in units of 1,000, under the command of Adnah.
15 Next in command was Jehohanan, who

17:3 Some Hebrew manuscripts read *the example of his father, David.*
17:6 Hebrew *His heart was courageous in.*

KING JAMES VERSION

16 And next him *was* Amasiah the son of Zichri, who willingly offered himself unto the LORD; and with him two hundred thousand mighty men of valour.

17 And of Benjamin; Eliada a mighty man of valour, and with him armed men with bow and shield two hundred thousand.

18 And next him *was* Jehozabad, and with him an hundred and fourscore thousand ready prepared for the war.

19 These waited on the king, beside *those* whom the king put in the fenced cities throughout all Judah.

18 1 Now Jehoshaphat had riches and honour in abundance, and joined affinity with Ahab.

2 And after *certain* years he went down to Ahab to Samaria. And Ahab killed sheep and oxen for him in abundance, and for the people that *he had* with him, and persuaded him to go up *with him* to Ramoth-gilead.

3 And Ahab king of Israel said unto Jehoshaphat king of Judah, Wilt thou go with me to Ramoth-gilead? And he answered him, I *am* as thou *art,* and my people as thy people; and *we will be* with thee in the war.

4 And Jehoshaphat said unto the king of Israel, Inquire, I pray thee, at the word of the LORD today.

5 Therefore the king of Israel gathered together of prophets four hundred men, and said unto them, Shall we go to Ramoth-gilead to battle, or shall I forbear? And they said, Go up; for God will deliver *it* into the king's hand.

6 But Jehoshaphat said, *Is there* not here a prophet of the LORD besides, that we might inquire of him?

7 And the king of Israel said unto Jehoshaphat, *There is* yet one man, by whom we may inquire of the LORD: but I hate him; for he never prophesied good unto me, but always evil: the same *is* Micaiah the son of Imla. And Jehoshaphat said, Let not the king say so.

8 And the king of Israel called for one *of his* officers, and said, Fetch quickly Micaiah the son of Imla.

9 And the king of Israel and Jehoshaphat king of Judah sat either of them on his throne, clothed in *their* robes, and they sat in a void place at the entering in of the gate of Samaria; and all the prophets prophesied before them.

10 And Zedekiah the son of Chenaanah had made him horns of iron, and said, Thus saith the LORD, With these thou shalt push Syria until they be consumed.

11 And all the prophets prophesied so, saying, Go up to Ramoth-gilead, and prosper: for the LORD shall deliver *it* into the hand of the king.

NEW LIVING TRANSLATION

commanded 280,000 troops. 16 Next was Amasiah son of Zicri, who volunteered for the LORD's service, with 200,000 troops under his command.

17 From Benjamin there were 200,000 troops equipped with bows and shields. They were under the command of Eliada, a veteran soldier.

18 Next in command was Jehozabad, who commanded 180,000 armed men.

19 These were the troops stationed in Jerusalem to serve the king, besides those Jehoshaphat stationed in the fortified towns throughout Judah.

Jehoshaphat and Ahab

18 Jehoshaphat enjoyed great riches and high esteem, and he made an alliance with Ahab of Israel by having his son marry Ahab's daughter. 2 A few years later he went to Samaria to visit Ahab, who prepared a great banquet for him and his officials. They butchered great numbers of sheep, goats, and cattle for the feast. Then Ahab enticed Jehoshaphat to join forces with him to recover Ramoth-gilead.

3 "Will you go with me to Ramoth-gilead?" King Ahab of Israel asked King Jehoshaphat of Judah.

Jehoshaphat replied, "Why, of course! You and I are as one, and my troops are your troops. We will certainly join you in battle." 4 Then Jehoshaphat added, "But first let's find out what the LORD says."

5 So the king of Israel summoned the prophets, 400 of them, and asked them, "Should we go to war against Ramoth-gilead, or should I hold back?"

They all replied, "Yes, go right ahead! God will give the king victory."

6 But Jehoshaphat asked, "Is there not also a prophet of the LORD here? We should ask him the same question."

7 The king of Israel replied to Jehoshaphat, "There is one more man who could consult the LORD for us, but I hate him. He never prophesies anything but trouble for me! His name is Micaiah son of Imlah."

Jehoshaphat replied, "That's not the way a king should talk! Let's hear what he has to say."

8 So the king of Israel called one of his officials and said, "Quick! Bring Micaiah son of Imlah."

Micaiah Prophesies against Ahab

9 King Ahab of Israel and King Jehoshaphat of Judah, dressed in their royal robes, were sitting on thrones at the threshing floor near the gate of Samaria. All of Ahab's prophets were prophesying there in front of them. 10 One of them, Zedekiah son of Kenaanah, made some iron horns and proclaimed, "This is what the LORD says: With these horns you will gore the Arameans to death!"

11 All the other prophets agreed. "Yes," they said, "go up to Ramoth-gilead and be victorious, for the LORD will give the king victory!"

KING JAMES VERSION

12And the messenger that went to call Micaiah spake to him, saying, Behold, the words of the prophets *declare* good to the king with one assent; let thy word therefore, I pray thee, be like one of theirs, and speak thou good.
13And Micaiah said, *As* the LORD liveth, even what my God saith, that will I speak.
14And when he was come to the king, the king said unto him, Micaiah, shall we go to Ramoth-gilead to battle, or shall I forbear? And he said, Go ye up, and prosper, and they shall be delivered into your hand.
15And the king said to him, How many times shall I adjure thee that thou say nothing but the truth to me in the name of the LORD?
16Then he said, I did see all Israel scattered upon the mountains, as sheep that have no shepherd: and the LORD said, These have no master; let them return *therefore* every man to his house in peace.
17And the king of Israel said to Jehoshaphat, Did I not tell thee *that* he would not prophesy good unto me, but evil?
18Again he said, Therefore hear the word of the LORD; I saw the LORD sitting upon his throne, and all the host of heaven standing on his right hand and *on* his left.
19And the LORD said, Who shall entice Ahab king of Israel, that he may go up and fall at Ramoth-gilead? And one spake saying after this manner, and another saying after that manner.
20Then there came out a spirit, and stood before the LORD, and said, I will entice him. And the LORD said unto him, Wherewith?
21And he said, I will go out, and be a lying spirit in the mouth of all his prophets. And *the LORD* said, Thou shalt entice *him*, and thou shalt also prevail: go out, and do *even* so.
22Now therefore, behold, the LORD hath put a lying spirit in the mouth of these thy prophets, and the LORD hath spoken evil against thee.
23Then Zedekiah the son of Chenaanah came near, and smote Micaiah upon the cheek, and said, Which way went the Spirit of the LORD from me to speak unto thee?
24And Micaiah said, Behold, thou shalt see on that day when thou shalt go into an inner chamber to hide thyself.
25Then the king of Israel said, Take ye Micaiah, and carry him back to Amon the governor of the city, and to Joash the king's son;
26And say, Thus saith the king, Put this *fellow* in the prison, and feed him with bread of affliction and with water of affliction, until I return in peace.
27And Micaiah said, If thou certainly return in peace, *then* hath not the LORD spoken by me. And he said, Hearken, all ye people.
28So the king of Israel and Jehoshaphat the king of Judah went up to Ramoth-gilead.
29And the king of Israel said unto Jehoshaphat, I

NEW LIVING TRANSLATION

12Meanwhile, the messenger who went to get Micaiah said to him, "Look, all the prophets are promising victory for the king. Be sure that you agree with them and promise success."
13But Micaiah replied, "As surely as the LORD lives, I will say only what my God says."
14When Micaiah arrived before the king, Ahab asked him, "Micaiah, should we go to war against Ramoth-gilead, or should I hold back?"
Micaiah replied sarcastically, "Yes, go up and be victorious, for you will have victory over them!"
15But the king replied sharply, "How many times must I demand that you speak only the truth to me when you speak for the LORD?"
16Then Micaiah told him, "In a vision I saw all Israel scattered on the mountains, like sheep without a shepherd. And the LORD said, 'Their master has been killed.* Send them home in peace.'"
17"Didn't I tell you?" the king of Israel exclaimed to Jehoshaphat. "He never prophesies anything but trouble for me."
18Then Micaiah continued, "Listen to what the LORD says! I saw the LORD sitting on his throne with all the armies of heaven around him, on his right and
on his left. 19And the LORD said, 'Who can entice
King Ahab of Israel to go into battle against Ramoth-gilead so he can be killed?'
"There were many suggestions, 20and finally a
spirit approached the LORD and said, 'I can do it!'
"'How will you do this?' the LORD asked.
21"And the spirit replied, 'I will go out and inspire all of Ahab's prophets to speak lies.'
"'You will succeed,' said the LORD. 'Go ahead and do it.'
22"So you see, the LORD has put a lying spirit in the mouths of your prophets. For the LORD has pronounced your doom."
23Then Zedekiah son of Kenaanah walked up to Micaiah and slapped him across the face. "Since when did the Spirit of the LORD leave me to speak to you?" he demanded.
24And Micaiah replied, "You will find out soon enough when you are trying to hide in some secret room!"
25"Arrest him!" the king of Israel ordered. "Take him back to Amon, the governor of the city, and to my
son Joash. 26Give them this order from the king: 'Put
this man in prison, and feed him nothing but bread and water until I return safely from the battle!'"
27But Micaiah replied, "If you return safely, it will mean that the LORD has not spoken through me!" Then he added to those standing around, "Everyone mark my words!"

The Death of Ahab

28So King Ahab of Israel and King Jehoshaphat of Judah led their armies against Ramoth-gilead. 29The

18:16 Hebrew *These people have no master.*

KING JAMES VERSION

will disguise myself, and will go to the battle; but put thou on thy robes. So the king of Israel disguised himself; and they went to the battle.

30 Now the king of Syria had commanded the captains of the chariots that *were* with him, saying, Fight ye not with small or great, save only with the king of Israel.

31 And it came to pass, when the captains of the chariots saw Jehoshaphat, that they said, It *is* the king of Israel. Therefore they compassed about him to fight: but Jehoshaphat cried out, and the LORD helped him; and God moved them *to depart* from him.

32 For it came to pass, that, when the captains of the chariots perceived that it was not the king of Israel, they turned back again from pursuing him.

33 And a *certain* man drew a bow at a venture, and smote the king of Israel between the joints of the harness: therefore he said to his chariot man, Turn thine hand, that thou mayest carry me out of the host; for I am wounded.

34 And the battle increased that day: howbeit the king of Israel stayed *himself* up in *his* chariot against the Syrians until the even: and about the time of the sun going down he died.

19 1 And Jehoshaphat the king of Judah returned to his house in peace to Jerusalem.

2 And Jehu the son of Hanani the seer went out to meet him, and said to king Jehoshaphat, Shouldest thou help the ungodly, and love them that hate the LORD? therefore *is* wrath upon thee from before the LORD.

3 Nevertheless there are good things found in thee, in that thou hast taken away the groves out of the land, and hast prepared thine heart to seek God.

4 And Jehoshaphat dwelt at Jerusalem: and he went out again through the people from Beer-sheba to mount Ephraim, and brought them back unto the LORD God of their fathers.

5 And he set judges in the land throughout all the fenced cities of Judah, city by city,

6 And said to the judges, Take heed what ye do: for ye judge not for man, but for the LORD, who *is* with you in the judgment.

7 Wherefore now let the fear of the LORD be upon you; take heed and do *it:* for *there is* no iniquity with the LORD our God, nor respect of persons, nor taking of gifts.

8 Moreover in Jerusalem did Jehoshaphat set of the Levites, and *of* the priests, and of the chief of the fathers of Israel, for the judgment of the LORD, and for controversies, when they returned to Jerusalem.

9 And he charged them, saying, Thus shall ye do in the fear of the LORD, faithfully, and with a perfect heart.

10 And what cause soever shall come to you of your brethren that dwell in their cities, between blood and blood, between law and commandment, statutes

NEW LIVING TRANSLATION

king of Israel said to Jehoshaphat, "As we go into battle, I will disguise myself so no one will recognize me, but you wear your royal robes." So the king of Israel disguised himself, and they went into battle.

30 Meanwhile, the king of Aram had issued these orders to his chariot commanders: "Attack only the king of Israel! Don't bother with anyone else." 31 So when the Aramean chariot commanders saw Jehoshaphat in his royal robes, they went after him. "There is the king of Israel!" they shouted. But Jehoshaphat called out, and the LORD saved him. God helped him by turning the attackers away from him. 32 As soon as the chariot commanders realized he was not the king of Israel, they stopped chasing him.

33 An Aramean soldier, however, randomly shot an arrow at the Israelite troops and hit the king of Israel between the joints of his armor. "Turn the horses* and get me out of here!" Ahab groaned to the driver of the chariot. "I'm badly wounded!"

34 The battle raged all that day, and the king of Israel propped himself up in his chariot facing the Arameans. In the evening, just as the sun was setting, he died.

Jehoshaphat Appoints Judges

19 When King Jehoshaphat of Judah arrived safely home in Jerusalem, 2 Jehu son of Hanani the seer went out to meet him. "Why should you help the wicked and love those who hate the LORD?" he asked the king. "Because of what you have done, the LORD is very angry with you. 3 Even so, there is some good in you, for you have removed the Asherah poles throughout the land, and you have committed yourself to seeking God."

4 Jehoshaphat lived in Jerusalem, but he went out among the people, traveling from Beersheba to the hill country of Ephraim, encouraging the people to return to the LORD, the God of their ancestors. 5 He appointed judges throughout the nation in all the fortified towns, 6 and he said to them, "Always think carefully before pronouncing judgment. Remember that you do not judge to please people but to please the LORD. He will be with you when you render the verdict in each case. 7 Fear the LORD and judge with integrity, for the LORD our God does not tolerate perverted justice, partiality, or the taking of bribes."

8 In Jerusalem, Jehoshaphat appointed some of the Levites and priests and clan leaders in Israel to serve as judges for cases involving the LORD's regulations and for civil disputes. 9 These were his instructions to them: "You must always act in the fear of the LORD, with faithfulness and an undivided heart. 10 Whenever a case comes to you from fellow citizens in an outlying town, whether a murder case or some other violation of God's laws, commands,

18:33 Hebrew *Turn your hand.*

KING JAMES VERSION

and judgments, ye shall even warn them that they trespass not against the LORD, and *so* wrath come upon you, and upon your brethren: this do, and ye shall not trespass.

11 And, behold, Amariah the chief priest *is* over you in all matters of the LORD; and Zebadiah the son of Ishmael, the ruler of the house of Judah, for all the king's matters: also the Levites *shall be* officers before you. Deal courageously, and the LORD shall be with the good.

20 1 It came to pass after this also, *that* the children of Moab, and the children of Ammon, and with them *other* beside the Ammonites, came against Jehoshaphat to battle.

2 Then there came some that told Jehoshaphat, saying, There cometh a great multitude against thee from beyond the sea on this side Syria; and, behold, they *be* in Hazazon-tamar, which *is* En-gedi.

3 And Jehoshaphat feared, and set himself to seek the LORD, and proclaimed a fast throughout all Judah.

4 And Judah gathered themselves together, to ask *help* of the LORD: even out of all the cities of Judah they came to seek the LORD.

5 And Jehoshaphat stood in the congregation of Judah and Jerusalem, in the house of the LORD, before the new court,

6 And said, O LORD God of our fathers, *art* not thou God in heaven? and rulest *not* thou over all the kingdoms of the heathen? and in thine hand *is there not* power and might, so that none is able to withstand thee?

7 *Art* not thou our God, *who* didst drive out the inhabitants of this land before thy people Israel, and gavest it to the seed of Abraham thy friend for ever?

8 And they dwelt therein, and have built thee a sanctuary therein for thy name, saying,

9 If, *when* evil cometh upon us, *as* the sword, judgment, or pestilence, or famine, we stand before this house, and in thy presence, (for thy name *is* in this house,) and cry unto thee in our affliction, then thou wilt hear and help.

10 And now, behold, the children of Ammon and Moab and mount Seir, whom thou wouldest not let Israel invade, when they came out of the land of Egypt, but they turned from them, and destroyed them not;

11 Behold, *I say, how* they reward us, to come to cast us out of thy possession, which thou hast given us to inherit.

12 O our God, wilt thou not judge them? for we have no might against this great company that cometh against us; neither know we what to do: but our eyes *are* upon thee.

13 And all Judah stood before the LORD, with their little ones, their wives, and their children.

NEW LIVING TRANSLATION

decrees, or regulations, you must warn them not to sin against the LORD, so that he will not be angry with you and them. Do this and you will not be guilty.

11 "Amariah the high priest will have final say in all cases involving the LORD. Zebadiah son of Ishmael, a leader from the tribe of Judah, will have final say in all civil cases. The Levites will assist you in making sure that justice is served. Take courage as you fulfill your duties, and may the LORD be with those who do what is right."

War with Surrounding Nations

20 After this, the armies of the Moabites, Ammonites, and some of the Meunites* declared war on Jehoshaphat. 2 Messengers came and told Jehoshaphat, "A vast army from Edom* is marching against you from beyond the Dead Sea.* They are already at Hazazon-tamar." (This was another name for En-gedi.)

3 Jehoshaphat was terrified by this news and begged the LORD for guidance. He also ordered everyone in Judah to begin fasting. 4 So people from all the towns of Judah came to Jerusalem to seek the LORD's help.

5 Jehoshaphat stood before the community of Judah and Jerusalem in front of the new courtyard at the Temple of the LORD. 6 He prayed, "O LORD, God of our ancestors, you alone are the God who is in heaven. You are ruler of all the kingdoms of the earth. You are powerful and mighty; no one can stand against you! 7 O our God, did you not drive out those who lived in this land when your people Israel arrived? And did you not give this land forever to the descendants of your friend Abraham? 8 Your people settled here and built this Temple to honor your name. 9 They said, 'Whenever we are faced with any calamity such as war,* plague, or famine, we can come to stand in your presence before this Temple where your name is honored. We can cry out to you to save us, and you will hear us and rescue us.'

10 "And now see what the armies of Ammon, Moab, and Mount Seir are doing. You would not let our ancestors invade those nations when Israel left Egypt, so they went around them and did not destroy them. 11 Now see how they reward us! For they have come to throw us out of your land, which you gave us as an inheritance. 12 O our God, won't you stop them? We are powerless against this mighty army that is about to attack us. We do not know what to do, but we are looking to you for help."

13 As all the men of Judah stood before the LORD

20:1 As in some Greek manuscripts (see also 26:7); Hebrew repeats *Ammonites*. **20:2a** As in one Hebrew manuscript; most Hebrew manuscripts and ancient versions read *Aram*. **20:2b** Hebrew *the sea*. **20:9** Or *sword of judgment;* or *sword, judgment*.

KING JAMES VERSION

14 Then upon Jahaziel the son of Zechariah, the
son of Benaiah, the son of Jeiel, the son of Mattaniah,
a Levite of the sons of Asaph, came the Spirit of the
LORD in the midst of the congregation;
15 And he said, Hearken ye, all Judah, and ye inhabitants of Jerusalem, and thou king Jehoshaphat, Thus
saith the LORD unto you, Be not afraid nor dismayed
by reason of this great multitude; for the battle *is* not
yours, but God's.
16 Tomorrow go ye down against them: behold, they
come up by the cliff of Ziz; and ye shall find them at
the end of the brook, before the wilderness of Jeruel.
17 Ye shall not *need* to fight in this *battle:* set yourselves, stand ye *still,* and see the salvation of the LORD
with you, O Judah and Jerusalem: fear not, nor be dismayed; tomorrow go out against them: for the LORD
will be with you.
18 And Jehoshaphat bowed his head with *his* face to
the ground: and all Judah and the inhabitants of Jerusalem fell before the LORD, worshipping the LORD.
19 And the Levites, of the children of the Kohathites,
and of the children of the Korhites, stood up to praise
the LORD God of Israel with a loud voice on high.
20 And they rose early in the morning, and went
forth into the wilderness of Tekoa: and as they went
forth, Jehoshaphat stood and said, Hear me, O Judah,
and ye inhabitants of Jerusalem; Believe in the LORD
your God, so shall ye be established; believe his
prophets, so shall ye prosper.
21 And when he had consulted with the people, he
appointed singers unto the LORD, and that should
praise the beauty of holiness, as they went out before
the army, and to say, Praise the LORD; for his mercy
endureth for ever.
22 And when they began to sing and to praise, the
LORD set ambushments against the children of Ammon, Moab, and mount Seir, which were come
against Judah; and they were smitten.
23 For the children of Ammon and Moab stood up
against the inhabitants of mount Seir, utterly to slay
and destroy *them:* and when they had made an end
of the inhabitants of Seir, every one helped to destroy another.
24 And when Judah came toward the watch tower
in the wilderness, they looked unto the multitude,
and, behold, they *were* dead bodies fallen to the
earth, and none escaped.
25 And when Jehoshaphat and his people came to
take away the spoil of them, they found among them
in abundance both riches with the dead bodies, and
precious jewels, which they stripped off for themselves, more than they could carry away: and they were
three days in gathering of the spoil, it was so much.
26 And on the fourth day they assembled themselves in the valley of Berachah; for there they blessed
the LORD: therefore the name of the same place was
called, The valley of Berachah, unto this day.

NEW LIVING TRANSLATION

with their little ones, wives, and children,
14 the Spirit of the LORD came upon one of the men standing
there. His name was Jahaziel son of Zechariah, son of
Benaiah, son of Jeiel, son of Mattaniah, a Levite who
was a descendant of Asaph.
15 He said, "Listen, all you people of Judah and Jerusalem! Listen, King Jehoshaphat! This is what the
LORD says: Do not be afraid! Don't be discouraged
by this mighty army, for the battle is not yours, but
God's.
16 Tomorrow, march out against them. You
will find them coming up through the ascent of Ziz
at the end of the valley that opens into the wilderness of Jeruel.
17 But you will not even need to fight.
Take your positions; then stand still and watch the
LORD's victory. He is with you, O people of Judah and
Jerusalem. Do not be afraid or discouraged. Go out
against them tomorrow, for the LORD is with you!"
18 Then King Jehoshaphat bowed low with his face
to the ground. And all the people of Judah and Jerusalem did the same, worshiping the LORD.
19 Then
the Levites from the clans of Kohath and Korah
stood to praise the LORD, the God of Israel, with a
very loud shout.
20 Early the next morning the army of Judah went
out into the wilderness of Tekoa. On the way Jehoshaphat stopped and said, "Listen to me, all you people
of Judah and Jerusalem! Believe in the LORD your
God, and you will be able to stand firm. Believe in his
prophets, and you will succeed."
21 After consulting the people, the king appointed
singers to walk ahead of the army, singing to the
LORD and praising him for his holy splendor. This is
what they sang:

"Give thanks to the LORD;
his faithful love endures forever!"

22 At the very moment they began to sing and give
praise, the LORD caused the armies of Ammon, Moab,
and Mount Seir to start fighting among themselves.
23 The armies of Moab and Ammon turned against
their allies from Mount Seir and killed every one of
them. After they had destroyed the army of Seir, they
began attacking each other.
24 So when the army of
Judah arrived at the lookout point in the wilderness,
all they saw were dead bodies lying on the ground as
far as they could see. Not a single one of the enemy
had escaped.
25 King Jehoshaphat and his men went out to
gather the plunder. They found vast amounts of
equipment, clothing,* and other valuables—more
than they could carry. There was so much plunder
that it took them three days just to collect it all!
26 On
the fourth day they gathered in the Valley of Blessing,* which got its name that day because the people
praised and thanked the LORD there. It is still called
the Valley of Blessing today.

20:25 As in some Hebrew manuscripts and Latin Vulgate; most Hebrew manuscripts read *corpses.* **20:26** Hebrew *valley of Beracah.*

KING JAMES VERSION

27 Then they returned, every man of Judah and Jerusalem, and Jehoshaphat in the forefront of them, to go again to Jerusalem with joy; for the LORD had made them to rejoice over their enemies.

28 And they came to Jerusalem with psalteries and harps and trumpets unto the house of the LORD.

29 And the fear of God was on all the kingdoms of *those* countries, when they had heard that the LORD fought against the enemies of Israel.

30 So the realm of Jehoshaphat was quiet: for his God gave him rest round about.

31 And Jehoshaphat reigned over Judah: *he was* thirty and five years old when he began to reign, and he reigned twenty and five years in Jerusalem. And his mother's name *was* Azubah the daughter of Shilhi.

32 And he walked in the way of Asa his father, and departed not from it, doing *that which was* right in the sight of the LORD.

33 Howbeit the high places were not taken away: for as yet the people had not prepared their hearts unto the God of their fathers.

34 Now the rest of the acts of Jehoshaphat, first and last, behold, they *are* written in the book of Jehu the son of Hanani, who *is* mentioned in the book of the kings of Israel.

35 And after this did Jehoshaphat king of Judah join himself with Ahaziah king of Israel, who did very wickedly:

36 And he joined himself with him to make ships to go to Tarshish: and they made the ships in Ezion-gaber.

37 Then Eliezer the son of Dodavah of Mareshah prophesied against Jehoshaphat, saying, Because thou hast joined thyself with Ahaziah, the LORD hath broken thy works. And the ships were broken, that they were not able to go to Tarshish.

21 1 Now Jehoshaphat slept with his fathers, and was buried with his fathers in the city of David. And Jehoram his son reigned in his stead.

2 And he had brethren the sons of Jehoshaphat, Azariah, and Jehiel, and Zechariah, and Azariah, and Michael, and Shephatiah: all these *were* the sons of Jehoshaphat king of Israel.

3 And their father gave them great gifts of silver, and of gold, and of precious things, with fenced cities in Judah: but the kingdom gave he to Jehoram; because he *was* the firstborn.

4 Now when Jehoram was risen up to the kingdom of his father, he strengthened himself, and slew all his brethren with the sword, and *divers* also of the princes of Israel.

5 Jehoram *was* thirty and two years old when he began to reign, and he reigned eight years in Jerusalem.

NEW LIVING TRANSLATION

27 Then all the men returned to Jerusalem, with Jehoshaphat leading them, overjoyed that the LORD had given them victory over their enemies. 28 They marched into Jerusalem to the music of harps, lyres, and trumpets, and they proceeded to the Temple of the LORD.

29 When all the surrounding kingdoms heard that the LORD himself had fought against the enemies of Israel, the fear of God came over them. 30 So Jehoshaphat's kingdom was at peace, for his God had given him rest on every side.

Summary of Jehoshaphat's Reign

31 So Jehoshaphat ruled over the land of Judah. He was thirty-five years old when he became king, and he reigned in Jerusalem twenty-five years. His mother was Azubah, the daughter of Shilhi.

32 Jehoshaphat was a good king, following the ways of his father, Asa. He did what was pleasing in the LORD's sight. 33 During his reign, however, he failed to remove all the pagan shrines, and the people never fully committed themselves to follow the God of their ancestors.

34 The rest of the events of Jehoshaphat's reign, from beginning to end, are recorded in *The Record of Jehu Son of Hanani,* which is included in *The Book of the Kings of Israel.*

35 Some time later King Jehoshaphat of Judah made an alliance with King Ahaziah of Israel, who was very wicked.* 36 Together they built a fleet of trading ships* at the port of Ezion-geber. 37 Then Eliezer son of Dodavahu from Mareshah prophesied against Jehoshaphat. He said, "Because you have allied yourself with King Ahaziah, the LORD will destroy your work." So the ships met with disaster and never put out to sea.*

Jehoram Rules in Judah

21 When Jehoshaphat died, he was buried with his ancestors in the City of David. Then his son Jehoram became the next king.

2 Jehoram's brothers—the other sons of Jehoshaphat—were Azariah, Jehiel, Zechariah, Azariahu, Michael, and Shephatiah; all these were the sons of Jehoshaphat king of Judah.* 3 Their father had given each of them valuable gifts of silver, gold, and costly items, and also some of Judah's fortified towns. However, he designated Jehoram as the next king because he was the oldest. 4 But when Jehoram had become solidly established as king, he killed all his brothers and some of the other leaders of Judah.

5 Jehoram was thirty-two years old when he became king, and he reigned in Jerusalem eight years.

20:35 Or *who made him do what was wicked.* **20:36** Hebrew *fleet of ships that could go to Tarshish.* **20:37** Hebrew *never set sail for Tarshish.* **21:2** Masoretic Text reads *of Israel;* also in 21:4. The author of Chronicles sees Judah as representative of the true Israel. (Some Hebrew manuscripts, Greek and Syriac versions, and Latin Vulgate read *of Judah.*)

KING JAMES VERSION

6 And he walked in the way of the kings of Israel,
like as did the house of Ahab: for he had the daughter of Ahab to wife: and he wrought *that which was*
evil in the eyes of the LORD.
7 Howbeit the LORD would not destroy the house of
David, because of the covenant that he had made
with David, and as he promised to give a light to him
and to his sons for ever.
8 In his days the Edomites revolted from under the
dominion of Judah, and made themselves a king.
9 Then Jehoram went forth with his princes, and
all his chariots with him: and he rose up by night,
and smote the Edomites which compassed him in,
and the captains of the chariots.
10 So the Edomites revolted from under the hand
of Judah unto this day. The same time *also* did
Libnah revolt from under his hand; because he had
forsaken the LORD God of his fathers.
11 Moreover he made high places in the mountains
of Judah, and caused the inhabitants of Jerusalem to
commit fornication, and compelled Judah *thereto*.
12 And there came a writing to him from Elijah the
prophet, saying, Thus saith the LORD God of David
thy father, Because thou hast not walked in the ways
of Jehoshaphat thy father, nor in the ways of Asa king
of Judah,
13 But hast walked in the way of the kings of Israel,
and hast made Judah and the inhabitants of Jerusalem to go a whoring, like to the whoredoms of the
house of Ahab, and also hast slain thy brethren of thy
father's house, *which were* better than thyself:
14 Behold, with a great plague will the LORD smite
thy people, and thy children, and thy wives, and all
thy goods:
15 And thou *shalt have* great sickness by disease of
thy bowels, until thy bowels fall out by reason of the
sickness day by day.
16 Moreover the LORD stirred up against Jehoram
the spirit of the Philistines, and of the Arabians, that
were near the Ethiopians:
17 And they came up into Judah, and brake into it,
and carried away all the substance that was found in
the king's house, and his sons also, and his wives; so
that there was never a son left him, save Jehoahaz,
the youngest of his sons.
18 And after all this the LORD smote him in his
bowels with an incurable disease.
19 And it came to pass, that in process of time, after
the end of two years, his bowels fell out by reason of
his sickness: so he died of sore diseases. And his
people made no burning for him, like the burning of
his fathers.
20 Thirty and two years old was he when he began
to reign, and he reigned in Jerusalem eight years, and
departed without being desired. Howbeit they buried him in the city of David, but not in the sepulchres
of the kings.

NEW LIVING TRANSLATION

6 But Jehoram followed the example of the kings of
Israel and was as wicked as King Ahab, for he had
married one of Ahab's daughters. So Jehoram did
what was evil in the LORD's sight. 7 But the LORD did
not want to destroy David's dynasty, for he had made
a covenant with David and promised that his descendants would continue to rule, shining like a
lamp forever.
8 During Jehoram's reign, the Edomites revolted
against Judah and crowned their own king. 9 So Jehoram went out with his full army and all his chariots.
The Edomites surrounded him and his chariot
commanders, but he went out at night and attacked
them* under cover of darkness. 10 Even so, Edom has
been independent from Judah to this day. The town
of Libnah also revolted about that same time. All this
happened because Jehoram had abandoned the
LORD, the God of his ancestors. 11 He had built pagan
shrines in the hill country of Judah and had led the
people of Jerusalem and Judah to give themselves to
pagan gods and to go astray.
12 Then Elijah the prophet wrote Jehoram this letter:

"This is what the LORD, the God of your ancestor
David, says: You have not followed the good
example of your father, Jehoshaphat, or your
grandfather King Asa of Judah. 13 Instead, you
have been as evil as the kings of Israel. You have
led the people of Jerusalem and Judah to worship
idols, just as King Ahab did in Israel. And you
have even killed your own brothers, men who
were better than you. 14 So now the LORD is about
to strike you, your people, your children, your
wives, and all that is yours with a heavy blow.
15 You yourself will suffer with a severe intestinal
disease that will get worse each day until your
bowels come out."

16 Then the LORD stirred up the Philistines and the
Arabs, who lived near the Ethiopians,* to attack Jehoram. 17 They marched against Judah, broke down its
defenses, and carried away everything of value in the
royal palace, including the king's sons and his wives.
Only his youngest son, Ahaziah,* was spared.
18 After all this, the LORD struck Jehoram with the
severe intestinal disease. 19 The disease grew worse
and worse, and at the end of two years it caused his
bowels to come out, and he died in agony. His people
did not build a great funeral fire to honor him as they
had done for his ancestors.
20 Jehoram was thirty-two years old when he became king, and he reigned in Jerusalem eight years.
No one was sorry when he died. They buried him in
the City of David, but not in the royal cemetery.

21:9 Or *he went out and escaped.* The meaning of the Hebrew is uncertain. **21:16** Hebrew *the Cushites.* **21:17** Hebrew *Jehoahaz,* a variant spelling of Ahaziah; compare 22:1.

KING JAMES VERSION

22

1And the inhabitants of Jerusalem made Ahaziah his youngest son king in his stead: for the band of men that came with the Arabians to the camp had slain all the eldest. So Ahaziah the son of Jehoram king of Judah reigned.

2Forty and two years old *was* Ahaziah when he began to reign, and he reigned one year in Jerusalem. His mother's name also *was* Athaliah the daughter of Omri.

3He also walked in the ways of the house of Ahab: for his mother was his counsellor to do wickedly.

4Wherefore he did evil in the sight of the LORD like the house of Ahab: for they were his counsellors after the death of his father to his destruction.

5He walked also after their counsel, and went with Jehoram the son of Ahab king of Israel to war against Hazael king of Syria at Ramoth-gilead: and the Syrians smote Joram.

6And he returned to be healed in Jezreel because of the wounds which were given him at Ramah, when he fought with Hazael king of Syria. And Azariah the son of Jehoram king of Judah went down to see Jehoram the son of Ahab at Jezreel, because he was sick.

7And the destruction of Ahaziah was of God by coming to Joram: for when he was come, he went out with Jehoram against Jehu the son of Nimshi, whom the LORD had anointed to cut off the house of Ahab.

8And it came to pass, that, when Jehu was executing judgment upon the house of Ahab, and found the princes of Judah, and the sons of the brethren of Ahaziah, that ministered to Ahaziah, he slew them.

9And he sought Ahaziah: and they caught him, (for he was hid in Samaria,) and brought him to Jehu: and when they had slain him, they buried him: Because, said they, he *is* the son of Jehoshaphat, who sought the LORD with all his heart. So the house of Ahaziah had no power to keep still the kingdom.

10But when Athaliah the mother of Ahaziah saw that her son was dead, she arose and destroyed all the seed royal of the house of Judah.

11But Jehoshabeath, the daughter of the king, took Joash the son of Ahaziah, and stole him from among the king's sons that were slain, and put him and his nurse in a bedchamber. So Jehoshabeath, the daughter of king Jehoram, the wife of Jehoiada the priest, (for she was the sister of Ahaziah,) hid him from Athaliah, so that she slew him not.

12And he was with them hid in the house of God six years: and Athaliah reigned over the land.

NEW LIVING TRANSLATION

Ahaziah Rules in Judah

22

Then the people of Jerusalem made Ahaziah, Jehoram's youngest son, their next king, since the marauding bands who came with the Arabs* had killed all the older sons. So Ahaziah son of Jehoram reigned as king of Judah.

2Ahaziah was twenty-two* years old when he became king, and he reigned in Jerusalem one year. His mother was Athaliah, a granddaughter of King Omri. 3Ahaziah also followed the evil example of King Ahab's family, for his mother encouraged him in doing wrong. 4He did what was evil in the LORD's sight, just as Ahab's family had done. They even became his advisers after the death of his father, and they led him to ruin.

5Following their evil advice, Ahaziah joined King Joram,* the son of King Ahab of Israel, in his war against King Hazael of Aram at Ramoth-gilead. When the Arameans wounded Joram in the battle, 6he returned to Jezreel to recover from the wounds he had received at Ramoth.* Because Joram was wounded, King Ahaziah* of Judah went to Jezreel to visit him.

7But God had decided that this visit would be Ahaziah's downfall. While he was there, Ahaziah went out with Joram to meet Jehu grandson of Nimshi,* whom the LORD had appointed to destroy the dynasty of Ahab.

8While Jehu was executing judgment against the family of Ahab, he happened to meet some of Judah's officials and Ahaziah's relatives* who were traveling with Ahaziah. So Jehu killed them all. 9Then Jehu's men searched for Ahaziah, and they found him hiding in the city of Samaria. They brought him to Jehu, who killed him. Ahaziah was given a decent burial because the people said, "He was the grandson of Jehoshaphat—a man who sought the LORD with all his heart." But none of the surviving members of Ahaziah's family was capable of ruling the kingdom.

Queen Athaliah Rules in Judah

10When Athaliah, the mother of King Ahaziah of Judah, learned that her son was dead, she began to destroy the rest of Judah's royal family. 11But Ahaziah's sister Jehosheba,* the daughter of King Jehoram, took Ahaziah's infant son, Joash, and stole him away from among the rest of the king's children, who were about to be killed. She put Joash and his nurse in a bedroom. In this way, Jehosheba, wife of Jehoiada the priest and sister of Ahaziah, hid the child so that Athaliah could not murder him. 12Joash remained hidden in the Temple of God for six years while Athaliah ruled over the land.

22:1 Or *marauding bands of Arabs.* **22:2** As in some Greek manuscripts and Syriac version (see also 2 Kgs 8:26); Hebrew reads *forty-two.* **22:5** Hebrew *Jehoram,* a variant spelling of Joram; also in 22:6, 7. **22:6a** Hebrew *Ramah,* a variant spelling of Ramoth. **22:6b** As in some Hebrew manuscripts, Greek and Syriac versions, and Latin Vulgate (see also 2 Kgs 8:29); most Hebrew manuscripts read *Azariah.* **22:7** Hebrew *descendant of Nimshi;* compare 2 Kgs 9:2, 14. **22:8** As in Greek version (see also 2 Kgs 10:13); Hebrew reads *and sons of the brothers of Ahaziah.* **22:11** As in parallel text at 2 Kgs 11:2; Hebrew lacks *Ahaziah's sister* and reads *Jehoshabeath* [a variant spelling of Jehosheba].

KING JAMES VERSION

23 1And in the seventh year Jehoiada strengthened himself, and took the captains of hundreds, Azariah the son of Jeroham, and Ishmael the son of Jehohanan, and Azariah the son of Obed, and Maaseiah the son of Adaiah, and Elishaphat the son of Zichri, into covenant with him.

2And they went about in Judah, and gathered the Levites out of all the cities of Judah, and the chief of the fathers of Israel, and they came to Jerusalem.

3And all the congregation made a covenant with the king in the house of God. And he said unto them, Behold, the king's son shall reign, as the LORD hath said of the sons of David.

4This *is* the thing that ye shall do; A third part of you entering on the sabbath, of the priests and of the Levites, *shall be* porters of the doors;

5And a third part *shall be* at the king's house; and a third part at the gate of the foundation: and all the people *shall be* in the courts of the house of the LORD.

6But let none come into the house of the LORD, save the priests, and they that minister of the Levites; they shall go in, for they *are* holy: but all the people shall keep the watch of the LORD.

7And the Levites shall compass the king round about, every man with his weapons in his hand; and whosoever *else* cometh into the house, he shall be put to death: but be ye with the king when he cometh in, and when he goeth out.

8So the Levites and all Judah did according to all things that Jehoiada the priest had commanded, and took every man his men that were to come in on the sabbath, with them that were to go *out* on the sabbath: for Jehoiada the priest dismissed not the courses.

9Moreover Jehoiada the priest delivered to the captains of hundreds spears, and bucklers, and shields, that *had been* king David's, which *were* in the house of God.

10And he set all the people, every man having his weapon in his hand, from the right side of the temple to the left side of the temple, along by the altar and the temple, by the king round about.

11Then they brought out the king's son, and put upon him the crown, and *gave him* the testimony, and made him king. And Jehoiada and his sons anointed him, and said, God save the king.

12Now when Athaliah heard the noise of the people running and praising the king, she came to the people into the house of the LORD:

13And she looked, and, behold, the king stood at his pillar at the entering in, and the princes and the trumpets by the king: and all the people of the land rejoiced, and sounded with trumpets, also the singers

NEW LIVING TRANSLATION

Revolt against Athaliah

23 In the seventh year of Athaliah's reign, Jehoiada the priest decided to act. He summoned his courage and made a pact with five army commanders: Azariah son of Jeroham, Ishmael son of Jehohanan, Azariah son of Obed, Maaseiah son of Adaiah, and Elishaphat son of Zicri. 2These men traveled secretly throughout Judah and summoned the Levites and clan leaders in all the towns to come to Jerusalem. 3They all gathered at the Temple of God, where they made a solemn pact with Joash, the young king.

Jehoiada said to them, "Here is the king's son! The time has come for him to reign! The LORD has promised that a descendant of David will be our king. 4This is what you must do. When you priests and Levites come on duty on the Sabbath, a third of you will serve as gatekeepers. 5Another third will go over to the royal palace, and the final third will be at the Foundation Gate. Everyone else should stay in the courtyards of the LORD's Temple. 6Remember, only the priests and Levites on duty may enter the Temple of the LORD, for they are set apart as holy. The rest of the people must obey the LORD's instructions and stay outside. 7You Levites, form a bodyguard around the king and keep your weapons in hand. Kill anyone who tries to enter the Temple. Stay with the king wherever he goes."

8So the Levites and all the people of Judah did everything as Jehoiada the priest ordered. The commanders took charge of the men reporting for duty that Sabbath, as well as those who were going off duty. Jehoiada the priest did not let anyone go home after their shift ended. 9Then Jehoiada supplied the commanders with the spears and the large and small shields that had once belonged to King David and were stored in the Temple of God. 10He stationed all the people around the king, with their weapons ready. They formed a line from the south side of the Temple around to the north side and all around the altar.

11Then Jehoiada and his sons brought out Joash, the king's son, placed the crown on his head, and presented him with a copy of God's laws.* They anointed him and proclaimed him king, and everyone shouted, "Long live the king!"

The Death of Athaliah

12When Athaliah heard the noise of the people running and the shouts of praise to the king, she hurried to the LORD's Temple to see what was happening. 13When she arrived, she saw the newly crowned king standing in his place of authority by the pillar at the Temple entrance. The commanders and trumpeters were surrounding him, and people from all over the land were rejoicing and blowing trumpets. Singers with musical instruments were leading the people in

23:11 Or *a copy of the covenant.*

with instruments of musick, and such as taught to
sing praise. Then Athaliah rent her clothes, and said,
Treason, Treason.
14 Then Jehoiada the priest brought out the captains of hundreds that were set over the host, and
said unto them, Have her forth of the ranges: and
whoso followeth her, let him be slain with the sword.
For the priest said, Slay her not in the house of the
LORD.
15 So they laid hands on her; and when she was
come to the entering of the horse gate by the king's
house, they slew her there.

16 And Jehoiada made a covenant between him,
and between all the people, and between the king,
that they should be the LORD's people.
17 Then all the people went to the house of Baal,
and brake it down, and brake his altars and his
images in pieces, and slew Mattan the priest of Baal
before the altars.
18 Also Jehoiada appointed the offices of the house
of the LORD by the hand of the priests the Levites,
whom David had distributed in the house of the
LORD, to offer the burnt offerings of the LORD, as *it is*
written in the law of Moses, with rejoicing and with
singing, *as it was ordained* by David.
19 And he set the porters at the gates of the house
of the LORD, that none *which was* unclean in any
thing should enter in.
20 And he took the captains of hundreds, and the
nobles, and the governors of the people, and all the
people of the land, and brought down the king from
the house of the LORD: and they came through the
high gate into the king's house, and set the king upon
the throne of the kingdom.
21 And all the people of the land rejoiced: and the
city was quiet, after that they had slain Athaliah with
the sword.

24 1 Joash *was* seven years old when he began
to reign, and he reigned forty years in Jerusalem. His mother's name also *was* Zibiah of Beer-
sheba.
2 And Joash did *that which was* right in the sight of
the LORD all the days of Jehoiada the priest.
3 And Jehoiada took for him two wives; and he
begat sons and daughters.
4 And it came to pass after this, *that* Joash was
minded to repair the house of the LORD.
5 And he gathered together the priests and the
Levites, and said to them, Go out unto the cities of
Judah, and gather of all Israel money to repair the
house of your God from year to year, and see that
ye hasten the matter. Howbeit the Levites hastened
it not.
6 And the king called for Jehoiada the chief, and
said unto him, Why hast thou not required of the Levites to bring in out of Judah and out of Jerusalem the

a great celebration. When Athaliah saw all this, she
tore her clothes in despair and shouted, "Treason!
Treason!"
14 Then Jehoiada the priest ordered the commanders who were in charge of the troops, "Take her
to the soldiers in front of the Temple,* and kill anyone who tries to rescue her." For the priest had said,
"She must not be killed in the Temple of the LORD."
15 So they seized her and led her out to the entrance
of the Horse Gate on the palace grounds, and they
killed her there.

Jehoiada's Religious Reforms

16 Then Jehoiada made a covenant between himself
and the king and the people that they would be the
LORD's people. 17 And all the people went over to the
temple of Baal and tore it down. They demolished
the altars and smashed the idols, and they killed Mattan the priest of Baal in front of the altars.
18 Jehoiada now put the priests and Levites in
charge of the Temple of the LORD, following all the
directions given by David. He also commanded them
to present burnt offerings to the LORD, as prescribed
by the Law of Moses, and to sing and rejoice as David
had instructed. 19 He also stationed gatekeepers at
the gates of the LORD's Temple to keep out those who
for any reason were ceremonially unclean.
20 Then the commanders, nobles, rulers, and all
the people of the land escorted the king from the
Temple of the LORD. They went through the upper
gate and into the palace, and they seated the king on
the royal throne. 21 So all the people of the land rejoiced, and the city was peaceful because Athaliah
had been killed.

Joash Repairs the Temple

24 Joash was seven years old when he became
king, and he reigned in Jerusalem forty
years. His mother was Zibiah from Beersheba. 2 Joash
did what was pleasing in the LORD's sight throughout
the lifetime of Jehoiada the priest. 3 Jehoiada chose
two wives for Joash, and he had sons and daughters.
4 At one point Joash decided to repair and restore
the Temple of the LORD. 5 He summoned the priests
and Levites and gave them these instructions: "Go to
all the towns of Judah and collect the required annual offerings, so that we can repair the Temple of
your God. Do not delay!" But the Levites did not act
immediately.
6 So the king called for Jehoiada the high priest
and asked him, "Why haven't you demanded that
the Levites go out and collect the Temple taxes from
the towns of Judah and from Jerusalem? Moses, the

23:14 Or *Bring her out from between the ranks;* or *Take her out of the Temple precincts.* The meaning of the Hebrew is uncertain.

KING JAMES VERSION

collection, *according to the commandment* of Moses the servant of the LORD, and of the congregation of Israel, for the tabernacle of witness?

7 For the sons of Athaliah, that wicked woman, had broken up the house of God; and also all the dedicated things of the house of the LORD did they bestow upon Baalim.

8 And at the king's commandment they made a chest, and set it without at the gate of the house of the LORD.

9 And they made a proclamation through Judah and Jerusalem, to bring in to the LORD the collection *that* Moses the servant of God *laid* upon Israel in the wilderness.

10 And all the princes and all the people rejoiced, and brought in, and cast into the chest, until they had made an end.

11 Now it came to pass, that at what time the chest was brought unto the king's office by the hand of the Levites, and when they saw that *there was* much money, the king's scribe and the high priest's officer came and emptied the chest, and took it, and carried it to his place again. Thus they did day by day, and gathered money in abundance.

12 And the king and Jehoiada gave it to such as did the work of the service of the house of the LORD, and hired masons and carpenters to repair the house of the LORD, and also such as wrought iron and brass to mend the house of the LORD.

13 So the workmen wrought, and the work was perfected by them, and they set the house of God in his state, and strengthened it.

14 And when they had finished *it,* they brought the rest of the money before the king and Jehoiada, whereof were made vessels for the house of the LORD, *even* vessels to minister, and to offer *withal,* and spoons, and vessels of gold and silver. And they offered burnt offerings in the house of the LORD continually all the days of Jehoiada.

15 But Jehoiada waxed old, and was full of days when he died; an hundred and thirty years old *was he* when he died.

16 And they buried him in the city of David among the kings, because he had done good in Israel, both toward God, and toward his house.

17 Now after the death of Jehoiada came the princes of Judah, and made obeisance to the king. Then the king hearkened unto them.

18 And they left the house of the LORD God of their fathers, and served groves and idols: and wrath came upon Judah and Jerusalem for this their trespass.

19 Yet he sent prophets to them, to bring them again unto the LORD; and they testified against them: but they would not give ear.

20 And the Spirit of God came upon Zechariah the son of Jehoiada the priest, which stood above the

NEW LIVING TRANSLATION

servant of the LORD, levied this tax on the community of Israel in order to maintain the Tabernacle of the Covenant.*"

7 Over the years the followers of wicked Athaliah had broken into the Temple of God, and they had used all the dedicated things from the Temple of the LORD to worship the images of Baal.

8 So now the king ordered a chest to be made and set outside the gate leading to the Temple of the LORD. 9 Then a proclamation was sent throughout Judah and Jerusalem, telling the people to bring to the LORD the tax that Moses, the servant of God, had required of the Israelites in the wilderness. 10 This pleased all the leaders and the people, and they gladly brought their money and filled the chest with it.

11 Whenever the chest became full, the Levites would carry it to the king's officials. Then the court secretary and an officer of the high priest would come and empty the chest and take it back to the Temple again. This went on day after day, and a large amount of money was collected. 12 The king and Jehoiada gave the money to the construction supervisors, who hired masons and carpenters to restore the Temple of the LORD. They also hired metalworkers, who made articles of iron and bronze for the LORD's Temple.

13 The men in charge of the renovation worked hard and made steady progress. They restored the Temple of God according to its original design and strengthened it. 14 When all the repairs were finished, they brought the remaining money to the king and Jehoiada. It was used to make various articles for the Temple of the LORD—articles for worship services and for burnt offerings, including ladles and other articles made of gold and silver. And the burnt offerings were sacrificed continually in the Temple of the LORD during the lifetime of Jehoiada the priest.

15 Jehoiada lived to a very old age, finally dying at 130. 16 He was buried among the kings in the City of David, because he had done so much good in Israel for God and his Temple.

Jehoiada's Reforms Reversed

17 But after Jehoiada's death, the leaders of Judah came and bowed before King Joash and persuaded him to listen to their advice. 18 They decided to abandon the Temple of the LORD, the God of their ancestors, and they worshiped Asherah poles and idols instead! Because of this sin, divine anger fell on Judah and Jerusalem. 19 Yet the LORD sent prophets to bring them back to him. The prophets warned them, but still the people would not listen.

20 Then the Spirit of God came upon Zechariah son of Jehoiada the priest. He stood before the people

24:6 Hebrew *Tent of the Testimony.*

KING JAMES VERSION

people, and said unto them, Thus saith God, Why transgress ye the commandments of the LORD, that ye cannot prosper? because ye have forsaken the LORD, he hath also forsaken you.

21 And they conspired against him, and stoned him with stones at the commandment of the king in the court of the house of the LORD.

22 Thus Joash the king remembered not the kindness which Jehoiada his father had done to him, but slew his son. And when he died, he said, The LORD look upon *it*, and require *it*.

23 And it came to pass at the end of the year, *that* the host of Syria came up against him: and they came to Judah and Jerusalem, and destroyed all the princes of the people from among the people, and sent all the spoil of them unto the king of Damascus.

24 For the army of the Syrians came with a small company of men, and the LORD delivered a very great host into their hand, because they had forsaken the LORD God of their fathers. So they executed judgment against Joash.

25 And when they were departed from him, (for they left him in great diseases,) his own servants conspired against him for the blood of the sons of Jehoiada the priest, and slew him on his bed, and he died: and they buried him in the city of David, but they buried him not in the sepulchres of the kings.

26 And these are they that conspired against him; Zabad the son of Shimeath an Ammonitess, and Jehozabad the son of Shimrith a Moabitess.

27 Now *concerning* his sons, and the greatness of the burdens *laid* upon him, and the repairing of the house of God, behold, they *are* written in the story of the book of the kings. And Amaziah his son reigned in his stead.

25 1 Amaziah *was* twenty and five years old *when* he began to reign, and he reigned twenty and nine years in Jerusalem. And his mother's name *was* Jehoaddan of Jerusalem.

2 And he did *that which was* right in the sight of the LORD, but not with a perfect heart.

3 Now it came to pass, when the kingdom was established to him, that he slew his servants that had killed the king his father.

4 But he slew not their children, but *did* as *it is* written in the law in the book of Moses, where the LORD commanded, saying, The fathers shall not die for the children, neither shall the children die for the fathers, but every man shall die for his own sin.

5 Moreover Amaziah gathered Judah together, and made them captains over thousands, and captains over hundreds, according to the houses of *their* fathers, throughout all Judah and Benjamin: and he numbered them from twenty years old and above,

NEW LIVING TRANSLATION

and said, "This is what God says: Why do you disobey
the LORD's commands and keep yourselves from
prospering? You have abandoned the LORD, and now
he has abandoned you!"
21 Then the leaders plotted to kill Zechariah, and
King Joash ordered that they stone him to death in
the courtyard of the LORD's Temple.
22 That was how
King Joash repaid Jehoiada for his loyalty—by killing
his son. Zechariah's last words as he died were, "May
the LORD see what they are doing and avenge my
death!"

The End of Joash's Reign

23 In the spring of the year* the Aramean army
marched against Joash. They invaded Judah and Jerusalem and killed all the leaders of the nation. Then
they sent all the plunder back to their king in Damascus.
24 Although the Arameans attacked with only a
small army, the LORD helped them conquer the much
larger army of Judah. The people of Judah had abandoned the LORD, the God of their ancestors, so judgment was carried out against Joash.
25 The Arameans withdrew, leaving Joash severely
wounded. But his own officials plotted to kill him for
murdering the son* of Jehoiada the priest. They assassinated him as he lay in bed. Then he was buried
in the City of David, but not in the royal cemetery.
26 The assassins were Jozacar,* the son of an Ammonite woman named Shimeath, and Jehozabad, the son
of a Moabite woman named Shomer.*
27 The account of the sons of Joash, the prophecies
about him, and the record of his restoration of the
Temple of God are written in *The Commentary on
the Book of the Kings*. His son Amaziah became the
next king.

Amaziah Rules in Judah

25 Amaziah was twenty-five years old when he
became king, and he reigned in Jerusalem
twenty-nine years. His mother was Jehoaddin* from
Jerusalem.
2 Amaziah did what was pleasing in the
LORD's sight, but not wholeheartedly.
3 When Amaziah was well established as king, he
executed the officials who had assassinated his
father.
4 However, he did not kill the children of the
assassins, for he obeyed the command of the LORD as
written by Moses in the Book of the Law: "Parents
must not be put to death for the sins of their children, nor children for the sins of their parents. Those
deserving to die must be put to death for their own
crimes."*
5 Then Amaziah organized the army, assigning

24:23 Hebrew *At the turn of the year.* The first day of the year in the ancient Hebrew lunar calendar occurred in March or April. **24:25** As in Greek version and Latin Vulgate; Hebrew reads *sons.* **24:26a** As in parallel text at 2 Kgs 12:21; Hebrew reads *Zabad.* **24:26b** As in parallel text at 2 Kgs 12:21; Hebrew reads *Shimrith,* a variant spelling of Shomer. **25:1** As in parallel text at 2 Kgs 14:2; Hebrew reads *Jehoaddan,* a variant spelling of Jehoaddin. **25:4** Deut 24:16.

KING JAMES VERSION

and found them three hundred thousand choice
men, able to go forth to war, that could handle spear
and shield.
6 He hired also an hundred thousand mighty men
of valour out of Israel for an hundred talents of silver.
7 But there came a man of God to him, saying,
O king, let not the army of Israel go with thee; for the
LORD *is* not with Israel, *to wit, with* all the children
of Ephraim.
8 But if thou wilt go, do *it,* be strong for the battle:
God shall make thee fall before the enemy: for God
hath power to help, and to cast down.
9 And Amaziah said to the man of God, But what
shall we do for the hundred talents which I have
given to the army of Israel? And the man of God
answered, The LORD is able to give thee much more
than this.
10 Then Amaziah separated them, *to wit,* the army
that was come to him out of Ephraim, to go home
again: wherefore their anger was greatly kindled
against Judah, and they returned home in great anger.
11 And Amaziah strengthened himself, and led
forth his people, and went to the valley of salt, and
smote of the children of Seir ten thousand.
12 And *other* ten thousand *left* alive did the children
of Judah carry away captive, and brought them unto
the top of the rock, and cast them down from the top
of the rock, that they all were broken in pieces.
13 But the soldiers of the army which Amaziah sent
back, that they should not go with him to battle, fell
upon the cities of Judah, from Samaria even unto
Beth-horon, and smote three thousand of them, and
took much spoil.
14 Now it came to pass, after that Amaziah was
come from the slaughter of the Edomites, that he
brought the gods of the children of Seir, and set them
up *to be* his gods, and bowed down himself before
them, and burned incense unto them.
15 Wherefore the anger of the LORD was kindled
against Amaziah, and he sent unto him a prophet,
which said unto him, Why hast thou sought after the
gods of the people, which could not deliver their
own people out of thine hand?
16 And it came to pass, as he talked with him, that
the king said unto him, Art thou made of the king's
counsel? forbear; why shouldest thou be smitten?
Then the prophet forbare, and said, I know that God
hath determined to destroy thee, because thou hast
done this, and hast not hearkened unto my counsel.
17 Then Amaziah king of Judah took advice, and
sent to Joash, the son of Jehoahaz, the son of Jehu,
king of Israel, saying, Come, let us see one another in
the face.
18 And Joash king of Israel sent to Amaziah king of
Judah, saying, The thistle that *was* in Lebanon sent to
the cedar that *was* in Lebanon, saying, Give thy daughter to my son to wife: and there passed by a wild beast
that *was* in Lebanon, and trode down the thistle.

NEW LIVING TRANSLATION

generals and captains* for all Judah and Benjamin.
He took a census and found that he had an army of
300,000 select troops, twenty years old and older, all
trained in the use of spear and shield. 6 He also paid
about 7,500 pounds* of silver to hire 100,000 experienced fighting men from Israel.
7 But a man of God came to him and said, "Your
Majesty, do not hire troops from Israel, for the LORD
is not with Israel. He will not help those people of
Ephraim! 8 If you let them go with your troops into
battle, you will be defeated by the enemy no matter
how well you fight. God will overthrow you, for he
has the power to help you or to trip you up."
9 Amaziah asked the man of God, "But what about
all that silver I paid to hire the army of Israel?"
The man of God replied, "The LORD is able to give
you much more than this!" 10 So Amaziah discharged
the hired troops and sent them back to Ephraim.
This made them very angry with Judah, and they returned home in a great rage.
11 Then Amaziah summoned his courage and
led his army to the Valley of Salt, where they killed
10,000 Edomite troops from Seir. 12 They captured
another 10,000 and took them to the top of a cliff
and threw them off, dashing them to pieces on the
rocks below.
13 Meanwhile, the hired troops that Amaziah had
sent home raided several of the towns of Judah between Samaria and Beth-horon. They killed 3,000
people and carried off great quantities of plunder.
14 When King Amaziah returned from slaughtering the Edomites, he brought with him idols taken
from the people of Seir. He set them up as his own
gods, bowed down in front of them, and offered
sacrifices to them! 15 This made the LORD very angry,
and he sent a prophet to ask, "Why do you turn
to gods who could not even save their own people
from you?"
16 But the king interrupted him and said, "Since
when have I made you the king's counselor? Be quiet
now before I have you killed!"
So the prophet stopped with this warning: "I
know that God has determined to destroy you because you have done this and have refused to accept
my counsel."
17 After consulting with his advisers, King Amaziah of Judah sent this challenge to Israel's king Jehoash,* the son of Jehoahaz and grandson of Jehu:
"Come and meet me in battle!"*
18 But King Jehoash of Israel replied to King Amaziah of Judah with this story: "Out in the Lebanon
mountains, a thistle sent a message to a mighty cedar
tree: 'Give your daughter in marriage to my son.' But
just then a wild animal of Lebanon came by and
stepped on the thistle, crushing it!

25:5 Hebrew *commanders of thousands and commanders of hundreds.* **25:6** Hebrew *100 talents* [3,400 kilograms]. **25:17a** Hebrew *Joash,* a variant spelling of Jehoash; also in 25:18, 21, 23, 25. **25:17b** Hebrew *Come let us look one another in the face.*

KING JAMES VERSION

19 Thou sayest, Lo, thou hast smitten the Edomites;
and thine heart lifteth thee up to boast: abide now at
home; why shouldest thou meddle to *thine* hurt, that
thou shouldest fall, *even* thou, and Judah with thee?
20 But Amaziah would not hear; for it *came* of God,
that he might deliver them into the hand *of their enemies,* because they sought after the gods of Edom.
21 So Joash the king of Israel went up; and they saw
one another in the face, *both* he and Amaziah king of
Judah, at Beth-shemesh, which *belongeth* to Judah.
22 And Judah was put to the worse before Israel,
and they fled every man to his tent.
23 And Joash the king of Israel took Amaziah king
of Judah, the son of Joash, the son of Jehoahaz, at
Beth-shemesh, and brought him to Jerusalem, and
brake down the wall of Jerusalem from the gate of
Ephraim to the corner gate, four hundred cubits.
24 And *he took* all the gold and the silver, and all the
vessels that were found in the house of God with
Obed-edom, and the treasures of the king's house,
the hostages also, and returned to Samaria.
25 And Amaziah the son of Joash king of Judah
lived after the death of Joash son of Jehoahaz king of
Israel fifteen years.
26 Now the rest of the acts of Amaziah, first and
last, behold, *are* they not written in the book of the
kings of Judah and Israel?
27 Now after the time that Amaziah did turn away
from following the LORD they made a conspiracy
against him in Jerusalem; and he fled to Lachish: but
they sent to Lachish after him, and slew him there.
28 And they brought him upon horses, and buried
him with his fathers in the city of Judah.

26 1 Then all the people of Judah took Uzziah,
who *was* sixteen years old, and made him
king in the room of his father Amaziah.
2 He built Eloth, and restored it to Judah, after that
the king slept with his fathers.
3 Sixteen years old *was* Uzziah when he began to
reign, and he reigned fifty and two years in Jerusalem.
His mother's name also *was* Jecoliah of Jerusalem.
4 And he did *that which was* right in the sight of the
LORD, according to all that his father Amaziah did.
5 And he sought God in the days of Zechariah, who
had understanding in the visions of God: and as long
as he sought the LORD, God made him to prosper.
6 And he went forth and warred against the Philistines, and brake down the wall of Gath, and the wall
of Jabneh, and the wall of Ashdod, and built cities
about Ashdod, and among the Philistines.
7 And God helped him against the Philistines, and
against the Arabians that dwelt in Gur-baal, and the
Mehunims.
8 And the Ammonites gave gifts to Uzziah: and his

NEW LIVING TRANSLATION

19 "You are saying, 'I have defeated Edom,' and you
are very proud of it. But my advice is to stay at home.
Why stir up trouble that will only bring disaster on
you and the people of Judah?"
20 But Amaziah refused to listen, for God was determined to destroy him for turning to the gods of
Edom. 21 So King Jehoash of Israel mobilized his
army against King Amaziah of Judah. The two armies drew up their battle lines at Beth-shemesh in
Judah. 22 Judah was routed by the army of Israel, and
its army scattered and fled for home. 23 King Jehoash
of Israel captured Judah's king, Amaziah son of
Joash and grandson of Ahaziah, at Beth-shemesh.
Then he brought him to Jerusalem, where he demolished 600 feet* of Jerusalem's wall, from the Ephraim Gate to the Corner Gate. 24 He carried off all the
gold and silver and all the articles from the Temple
of God that had been in the care of Obed-edom. He
also seized the treasures of the royal palace, along
with hostages, and then returned to Samaria.
25 King Amaziah of Judah lived on for fifteen years
after the death of King Jehoash of Israel. 26 The rest
of the events in Amaziah's reign, from beginning to
end, are recorded in *The Book of the Kings of Judah
and Israel.*
27 After Amaziah turned away from the LORD,
there was a conspiracy against his life in Jerusalem,
and he fled to Lachish. But his enemies sent assassins after him, and they killed him there. 28 They
brought his body back on a horse, and he was buried
with his ancestors in the City of David.*

Uzziah Rules in Judah

26 All the people of Judah had crowned Amaziah's sixteen-year-old son, Uzziah, as king
in place of his father. 2 After his father's death, Uzziah
rebuilt the town of Elath* and restored it to Judah.
3 Uzziah was sixteen years old when he became
king, and he reigned in Jerusalem fifty-two years. His
mother was Jecoliah from Jerusalem. 4 He did what
was pleasing in the LORD's sight, just as his father,
Amaziah, had done. 5 Uzziah sought God during the
days of Zechariah, who taught him to fear God.* And
as long as the king sought guidance from the LORD,
God gave him success.
6 Uzziah declared war on the Philistines and broke
down the walls of Gath, Jabneh, and Ashdod. Then he
built new towns in the Ashdod area and in other parts
of Philistia. 7 God helped him in his wars against the
Philistines, his battles with the Arabs of Gur,* and his
wars with the Meunites. 8 The Meunites* paid annual

25:23 Hebrew *400 cubits* [180 meters]. **25:28** As in some Hebrew manuscripts and other ancient versions (see also 2 Kgs 14:20); most Hebrew manuscripts read *the city of Judah.* **26:2** As in Greek version (see also 2 Kgs 14:22; 16:6); Hebrew reads *Eloth,* a variant spelling of Elath. **26:5** As in Syriac and Greek versions; Hebrew reads *who instructed him in divine visions.* **26:7** As in Greek version; Hebrew reads *Gur-baal.* **26:8** As in Greek version; Hebrew reads *Ammonites.* Compare 26:7.

KING JAMES VERSION

name spread abroad *even* to the entering in of Egypt;
for he strengthened *himself* exceedingly.
9 Moreover Uzziah built towers in Jerusalem at the
corner gate, and at the valley gate, and at the turning
of the wall, and fortified them.
10 Also he built towers in the desert, and digged
many wells: for he had much cattle, both in the low
country, and in the plains: husbandmen *also*, and
vine dressers in the mountains, and in Carmel: for he
loved husbandry.
11 Moreover Uzziah had an host of fighting men,
that went out to war by bands, according to the number of their account by the hand of Jeiel the scribe
and Maaseiah the ruler, under the hand of Hananiah,
one of the king's captains.
12 The whole number of the chief of the fathers of
the mighty men of valour *were* two thousand and six
hundred.
13 And under their hand *was* an army, three hundred thousand and seven thousand and five hundred, that made war with mighty power, to help the
king against the enemy.
14 And Uzziah prepared for them throughout all
the host shields, and spears, and helmets, and
habergeons, and bows, and slings *to cast* stones.
15 And he made in Jerusalem engines, invented by
cunning men, to be on the towers and upon the bulwarks, to shoot arrows and great stones withal. And
his name spread far abroad; for he was marvellously
helped, till he was strong.
16 But when he was strong, his heart was lifted up
to *his* destruction: for he transgressed against the
LORD his God, and went into the temple of the LORD
to burn incense upon the altar of incense.
17 And Azariah the priest went in after him, and
with him fourscore priests of the LORD, *that were* valiant men:
18 And they withstood Uzziah the king, and said
unto him, *It appertaineth* not unto thee, Uzziah, to
burn incense unto the LORD, but to the priests the
sons of Aaron, that are consecrated to burn incense:
go out of the sanctuary; for thou hast trespassed; neither *shall it be* for thine honour from the LORD God.
19 Then Uzziah was wroth, and *had* a censer in his
hand to burn incense: and while he was wroth with
the priests, the leprosy even rose up in his forehead
before the priests in the house of the LORD, from beside the incense altar.
20 And Azariah the chief priest, and all the priests,
looked upon him, and, behold, he *was* leprous in his
forehead, and they thrust him out from thence; yea,
himself hasted also to go out, because the LORD had
smitten him.
21 And Uzziah the king was a leper unto the day of
his death, and dwelt in a several house, *being* a leper;
for he was cut off from the house of the LORD: and
Jotham his son *was* over the king's house, judging
the people of the land.

NEW LIVING TRANSLATION

tribute to him, and his fame spread even to Egypt, for
he had become very powerful.
9 Uzziah built fortified towers in Jerusalem at the
Corner Gate, at the Valley Gate, and at the angle in the
wall. 10 He also constructed forts in the wilderness
and dug many water cisterns, because he kept great
herds of livestock in the foothills of Judah* and on
the plains. He was also a man who loved the soil. He
had many workers who cared for his farms and vineyards, both on the hillsides and in the fertile valleys.
11 Uzziah had an army of well-trained warriors,
ready to march into battle, unit by unit. This army
had been mustered and organized by Jeiel, the secretary of the army, and his assistant, Maaseiah. They
were under the direction of Hananiah, one of the
king's officials. 12 These regiments of mighty warriors were commanded by 2,600 clan leaders. 13 The
army consisted of 307,500 men, all elite troops.
They were prepared to assist the king against any
enemy.
14 Uzziah provided the entire army with shields,
spears, helmets, coats of mail, bows, and sling
stones. 15 And he built structures on the walls of
Jerusalem, designed by experts to protect those
who shot arrows and hurled large stones* from the
towers and the corners of the wall. His fame spread
far and wide, for the LORD gave him marvelous help,
and he became very powerful.

Uzziah's Sin and Punishment

16 But when he had become powerful, he also became
proud, which led to his downfall. He sinned against
the LORD his God by entering the sanctuary of the
LORD's Temple and personally burning incense on
the incense altar. 17 Azariah the high priest went in
after him with eighty other priests of the LORD, all
brave men. 18 They confronted King Uzziah and said,
"It is not for you, Uzziah, to burn incense to the LORD.
That is the work of the priests alone, the descendants
of Aaron who are set apart for this work. Get out of
the sanctuary, for you have sinned. The LORD God will
not honor you for this!"
19 Uzziah, who was holding an incense burner, became furious. But as he was standing there raging
at the priests before the incense altar in the LORD's
Temple, leprosy* suddenly broke out on his forehead. 20 When Azariah the high priest and all the
other priests saw the leprosy, they rushed him out.
And the king himself was eager to get out because
the LORD had struck him. 21 So King Uzziah had
leprosy until the day he died. He lived in isolation
in a separate house, for he was excluded from the
Temple of the LORD. His son Jotham was put in
charge of the royal palace, and he governed the
people of the land.

26:10 Hebrew *the Shephelah*. **26:15** Or *to shoot arrows and hurl large stones*. **26:19** Or *a contagious skin disease*. The Hebrew word used here and throughout this passage can describe various skin diseases.

KING JAMES VERSION

22 Now the rest of the acts of Uzziah, first and last, did Isaiah the prophet, the son of Amoz, write. 23 So Uzziah slept with his fathers, and they buried him with his fathers in the field of the burial which *belonged* to the kings; for they said, He *is* a leper: and Jotham his son reigned in his stead.

27 1 Jotham *was* twenty and five years old when he began to reign, and he reigned sixteen years in Jerusalem. His mother's name also *was* Jerushah, the daughter of Zadok.

2 And he did *that which was* right in the sight of the LORD, according to all that his father Uzziah did: howbeit he entered not into the temple of the LORD. And the people did yet corruptly.

3 He built the high gate of the house of the LORD, and on the wall of Ophel he built much.

4 Moreover he built cities in the mountains of Judah, and in the forests he built castles and towers.

5 He fought also with the king of the Ammonites, and prevailed against them. And the children of Ammon gave him the same year an hundred talents of silver, and ten thousand measures of wheat, and ten thousand of barley. So much did the children of Ammon pay unto him, both the second year, and the third.

6 So Jotham became mighty, because he prepared his ways before the LORD his God.

7 Now the rest of the acts of Jotham, and all his wars, and his ways, lo, they *are* written in the book of the kings of Israel and Judah.

8 He was five and twenty years old when he began to reign, and reigned sixteen years in Jerusalem.

9 And Jotham slept with his fathers, and they buried him in the city of David: and Ahaz his son reigned in his stead.

28 1 Ahaz *was* twenty years old when he began to reign, and he reigned sixteen years in Jerusalem: but he did not *that which was* right in the sight of the LORD, like David his father:

2 For he walked in the ways of the kings of Israel, and made also molten images for Baalim.

3 Moreover he burnt incense in the valley of the son of Hinnom, and burnt his children in the fire, after the abominations of the heathen whom the LORD had cast out before the children of Israel.

4 He sacrificed also and burnt incense in the high places, and on the hills, and under every green tree.

5 Wherefore the LORD his God delivered him into the hand of the king of Syria; and they smote him, and carried away a great multitude of them captives, and brought *them* to Damascus. And he was also delivered into the hand of the king of Israel, who smote him with a great slaughter.

6 For Pekah the son of Remaliah slew in Judah an hundred and twenty thousand in one day, *which*

NEW LIVING TRANSLATION

22 The rest of the events of Uzziah's reign, from beginning to end, are recorded by the prophet Isaiah son of Amoz. 23 When Uzziah died, he was buried with his ancestors; his grave was in a nearby burial field belonging to the kings, for the people said, "He had leprosy." And his son Jotham became the next king.

Jotham Rules in Judah

27 Jotham was twenty-five years old when he became king, and he reigned in Jerusalem sixteen years. His mother was Jerusha, the daughter of Zadok.

2 Jotham did what was pleasing in the LORD's sight. He did everything his father, Uzziah, had done, except that Jotham did not sin by entering the Temple of the LORD. But the people continued in their corrupt ways.

3 Jotham rebuilt the upper gate of the Temple of the LORD. He also did extensive rebuilding on the wall at the hill of Ophel. 4 He built towns in the hill country of Judah and constructed fortresses and towers in the wooded areas. 5 Jotham went to war against the Ammonites and conquered them. Over the next three years he received from them an annual tribute of 7,500 pounds* of silver, 50,000 bushels of wheat, and 50,000 bushels of barley.*

6 King Jotham became powerful because he was careful to live in obedience to the LORD his God.

7 The rest of the events of Jotham's reign, including all his wars and other activities, are recorded in *The Book of the Kings of Israel and Judah.* 8 He was twenty-five years old when he became king, and he reigned in Jerusalem sixteen years. 9 When Jotham died, he was buried in the City of David. And his son Ahaz became the next king.

Ahaz Rules in Judah

28 Ahaz was twenty years old when he became king, and he reigned in Jerusalem sixteen years. He did not do what was pleasing in the sight of the LORD, as his ancestor David had done. 2 Instead, he followed the example of the kings of Israel. He cast metal images for the worship of Baal. 3 He offered sacrifices in the valley of Ben-Hinnom, even sacrificing his own sons in the fire.* In this way, he followed the detestable practices of the pagan nations the LORD had driven from the land ahead of the Israelites. 4 He offered sacrifices and burned incense at the pagan shrines and on the hills and under every green tree.

5 Because of all this, the LORD his God allowed the king of Aram to defeat Ahaz and to exile large numbers of his people to Damascus. The armies of the king of Israel also defeated Ahaz and inflicted many casualties on his army. 6 In a single day Pekah son of

27:5a Hebrew *100 talents* [3,400 kilograms]. **27:5b** Hebrew *10,000 cors* [1,820 kiloliters] *of wheat, and 10,000 cors of barley.* **28:3** Or *even making his sons pass through the fire.*

were all valiant men; because they had forsaken the LORD God of their fathers.

7 And Zichri, a mighty man of Ephraim, slew Maaseiah the king's son, and Azrikam the governor of the house, and Elkanah *that was* next to the king.

8 And the children of Israel carried away captive of their brethren two hundred thousand, women, sons, and daughters, and took also away much spoil from them, and brought the spoil to Samaria.

9 But a prophet of the LORD was there, whose name *was* Oded: and he went out before the host that came to Samaria, and said unto them, Behold, because the LORD God of your fathers was wroth with Judah, he hath delivered them into your hand, and ye have slain them in a rage *that* reacheth up unto heaven.

10 And now ye purpose to keep under the children of Judah and Jerusalem for bondmen and bondwomen unto you: *but are there* not with you, even with you, sins against the LORD your God?

11 Now hear me therefore, and deliver the captives again, which ye have taken captive of your brethren: for the fierce wrath of the LORD *is* upon you.

12 Then certain of the heads of the children of Ephraim, Azariah the son of Johanan, Berechiah the son of Meshillemoth, and Jehizkiah the son of Shallum, and Amasa the son of Hadlai, stood up against them that came from the war,

13 And said unto them, Ye shall not bring in the captives hither: for whereas we have offended against the LORD *already,* ye intend to add *more* to our sins and to our trespass: for our trespass is great, and *there is* fierce wrath against Israel.

14 So the armed men left the captives and the spoil before the princes and all the congregation.

15 And the men which were expressed by name rose up, and took the captives, and with the spoil clothed all that were naked among them, and arrayed them, and shod them, and gave them to eat and to drink, and anointed them, and carried all the feeble of them upon asses, and brought them to Jericho, the city of palm trees, to their brethren: then they returned to Samaria.

16 At that time did king Ahaz send unto the kings of Assyria to help him.

17 For again the Edomites had come and smitten Judah, and carried away captives.

18 The Philistines also had invaded the cities of the low country, and of the south of Judah, and had taken Beth-shemesh, and Ajalon, and Gederoth, and Shocho with the villages thereof, and Timnah with the villages thereof, Gimzo also and the villages thereof: and they dwelt there.

19 For the LORD brought Judah low because of Ahaz king of Israel; for he made Judah naked, and transgressed sore against the LORD.

Remaliah, Israel's king, killed 120,000 of Judah's troops, all of them experienced warriors, because they had abandoned the LORD, the God of their ancestors. 7 Then Zicri, a warrior from Ephraim, killed Maaseiah, the king's son; Azrikam, the king's palace commander; and Elkanah, the king's second-in-command. 8 The armies of Israel captured 200,000 women and children from Judah and seized tremendous amounts of plunder, which they took back to Samaria.

9 But a prophet of the LORD named Oded was there in Samaria when the army of Israel returned home. He went out to meet them and said, "The LORD, the God of your ancestors, was angry with Judah and let you defeat them. But you have gone too far, killing them without mercy, and all heaven is disturbed. 10 And now you are planning to make slaves of these people from Judah and Jerusalem. What about your own sins against the LORD your God? 11 Listen to me and return these prisoners you have taken, for they are your own relatives. Watch out, because now the LORD's fierce anger has been turned against you!"

12 Then some of the leaders of Israel*—Azariah son of Jehohanan, Berekiah son of Meshillemoth, Jehizkiah son of Shallum, and Amasa son of Hadlai—agreed with this and confronted the men returning from battle. 13 "You must not bring the prisoners here!" they declared. "We cannot afford to add to our sins and guilt. Our guilt is already great, and the LORD's fierce anger is already turned against Israel."

14 So the warriors released the prisoners and handed over the plunder in the sight of the leaders and all the people. 15 Then the four men just mentioned by name came forward and distributed clothes from the plunder to the prisoners who were naked. They provided clothing and sandals to wear, gave them enough food and drink, and dressed their wounds with olive oil. They put those who were weak on donkeys and took all the prisoners back to their own people in Jericho, the city of palms. Then they returned to Samaria.

Ahaz Closes the Temple

16 At that time King Ahaz of Judah asked the king of Assyria for help. 17 The armies of Edom had again invaded Judah and taken captives. 18 And the Philistines had raided towns located in the foothills of Judah* and in the Negev of Judah. They had already captured and occupied Beth-shemesh, Aijalon, Gederoth, Soco with its villages, Timnah with its villages, and Gimzo with its villages. 19 The LORD was humbling Judah because of King Ahaz of Judah,* for he had encouraged his people to sin and had been utterly unfaithful to the LORD.

28:12 Hebrew *Ephraim,* referring to the northern kingdom of Israel. **28:18** Hebrew *the Shephelah.* **28:19** Masoretic Text reads *of Israel;* also in 28:23, 27. The author of Chronicles sees Judah as representative of the true Israel. (Some Hebrew manuscripts and Greek version read *of Judah.*)

KING JAMES VERSION

20 And Tilgath-pilneser king of Assyria came unto him, and distressed him, but strengthened him not.

21 For Ahaz took away a portion *out* of the house of the LORD, and *out* of the house of the king, and of the princes, and gave *it* unto the king of Assyria: but he helped him not.

22 And in the time of his distress did he trespass yet more against the LORD: this *is that* king Ahaz.

23 For he sacrificed unto the gods of Damascus, which smote him: and he said, Because the gods of the kings of Syria help them, *therefore* will I sacrifice to them, that they may help me. But they were the ruin of him, and of all Israel.

24 And Ahaz gathered together the vessels of the house of God, and cut in pieces the vessels of the house of God, and shut up the doors of the house of the LORD, and he made him altars in every corner of Jerusalem.

25 And in every several city of Judah he made high places to burn incense unto other gods, and provoked to anger the LORD God of his fathers.

26 Now the rest of his acts and of all his ways, first and last, behold, they *are* written in the book of the kings of Judah and Israel.

27 And Ahaz slept with his fathers, and they buried him in the city, *even* in Jerusalem: but they brought him not into the sepulchres of the kings of Israel: and Hezekiah his son reigned in his stead.

29 1 Hezekiah began to reign *when he was* five and twenty years old, and he reigned nine and twenty years in Jerusalem. And his mother's name *was* Abijah, the daughter of Zechariah.

2 And he did *that which was* right in the sight of the LORD, according to all that David his father had done.

3 He in the first year of his reign, in the first month, opened the doors of the house of the LORD, and repaired them.

4 And he brought in the priests and the Levites, and gathered them together into the east street,

5 And said unto them, Hear me, ye Levites, sanctify now yourselves, and sanctify the house of the LORD God of your fathers, and carry forth the filthiness out of the holy *place*.

6 For our fathers have trespassed, and done *that which was* evil in the eyes of the LORD our God, and have forsaken him, and have turned away their faces from the habitation of the LORD, and turned *their* backs.

7 Also they have shut up the doors of the porch, and put out the lamps, and have not burned incense nor offered burnt offerings in the holy *place* unto the God of Israel.

8 Wherefore the wrath of the LORD was upon Judah and Jerusalem, and he hath delivered them to

NEW LIVING TRANSLATION

20 So when King Tiglath-pileser* of Assyria arrived, he attacked Ahaz instead of helping him. 21 Ahaz took valuable items from the LORD's Temple, the royal palace, and from the homes of his officials and gave them to the king of Assyria as tribute. But this did not help him.

22 Even during this time of trouble, King Ahaz continued to reject the LORD. 23 He offered sacrifices to the gods of Damascus who had defeated him, for he said, "Since these gods helped the kings of Aram, they will help me, too, if I sacrifice to them." But instead, they led to his ruin and the ruin of all Judah.

24 The king took the various articles from the Temple of God and broke them into pieces. He shut the doors of the LORD's Temple so that no one could worship there, and he set up altars to pagan gods in every corner of Jerusalem. 25 He made pagan shrines in all the towns of Judah for offering sacrifices to other gods. In this way, he aroused the anger of the LORD, the God of his ancestors.

26 The rest of the events of Ahaz's reign and everything he did, from beginning to end, are recorded in *The Book of the Kings of Judah and Israel.* 27 When Ahaz died, he was buried in Jerusalem but not in the royal cemetery of the kings of Judah. Then his son Hezekiah became the next king.

Hezekiah Rules in Judah

29 Hezekiah was twenty-five years old when he became the king of Judah, and he reigned in Jerusalem twenty-nine years. His mother was Abijah, the daughter of Zechariah. 2 He did what was pleasing in the LORD's sight, just as his ancestor David had done.

Hezekiah Reopens the Temple

3 In the very first month of the first year of his reign, Hezekiah reopened the doors of the Temple of the LORD and repaired them. 4 He summoned the priests and Levites to meet him at the courtyard east of the Temple. 5 He said to them, "Listen to me, you Levites! Purify yourselves, and purify the Temple of the LORD, the God of your ancestors. Remove all the defiled things from the sanctuary. 6 Our ancestors were unfaithful and did what was evil in the sight of the LORD our God. They abandoned the LORD and his dwelling place; they turned their backs on him. 7 They also shut the doors to the Temple's entry room, and they snuffed out the lamps. They stopped burning incense and presenting burnt offerings at the sanctuary of the God of Israel.

8 "That is why the LORD's anger has fallen upon Judah and Jerusalem. He has made them an object of dread, horror, and ridicule, as you can see with your

28:20 Hebrew *Tilgath-pilneser,* a variant spelling of Tiglath-pileser.

KING JAMES VERSION

trouble, to astonishment, and to hissing, as ye see
with your eyes.
9For, lo, our fathers have fallen by the sword, and
our sons and our daughters and our wives *are* in captivity for this.
10Now *it is* in mine heart to make a covenant with
the LORD God of Israel, that his fierce wrath may turn
away from us.
11My sons, be not now negligent: for the LORD hath
chosen you to stand before him, to serve him, and
that ye should minister unto him, and burn incense.
12Then the Levites arose, Mahath the son of Amasai, and Joel the son of Azariah, of the sons of the
Kohathites: and of the sons of Merari, Kish the son of
Abdi, and Azariah the son of Jehalelel: and of the
Gershonites; Joah the son of Zimmah, and Eden the
son of Joah:
13And of the sons of Elizaphan; Shimri, and Jeiel:
and of the sons of Asaph; Zechariah, and Mattaniah:
14And of the sons of Heman; Jehiel, and Shimei:
and of the sons of Jeduthun; Shemaiah, and Uzziel.
15And they gathered their brethren, and sanctified
themselves, and came, according to the commandment of the king, by the words of the LORD, to
cleanse the house of the LORD.
16And the priests went into the inner part of the
house of the LORD, to cleanse *it*, and brought out all
the uncleanness that they found in the temple of the
LORD into the court of the house of the LORD. And the
Levites took *it*, to carry *it* out abroad into the brook
Kidron.
17Now they began on the first *day* of the first
month to sanctify, and on the eighth day of the
month came they to the porch of the LORD: so they
sanctified the house of the LORD in eight days; and
in the sixteenth day of the first month they made
an end.

18Then they went in to Hezekiah the king, and
said, We have cleansed all the house of the LORD, and
the altar of burnt offering, with all the vessels
thereof, and the shewbread table, with all the vessels
thereof.
19Moreover all the vessels, which king Ahaz in his
reign did cast away in his transgression, have we prepared and sanctified, and, behold, they *are* before
the altar of the LORD.
20Then Hezekiah the king rose early, and gathered
the rulers of the city, and went up to the house of
the LORD.
21And they brought seven bullocks, and seven
rams, and seven lambs, and seven he goats, for a sin
offering for the kingdom, and for the sanctuary, and
for Judah. And he commanded the priests the sons
of Aaron to offer *them* on the altar of the LORD.

NEW LIVING TRANSLATION

own eyes. 9Because of this, our fathers have been
killed in battle, and our sons and daughters and
wives have been captured. 10But now I will make a
covenant with the LORD, the God of Israel, so that his
fierce anger will turn away from us. 11My sons, do not
neglect your duties any longer! The LORD has chosen
you to stand in his presence, to minister to him, and
to lead the people in worship and present offerings
to him."
12Then these Levites got right to work:

From the clan of Kohath: Mahath son of Amasai
and Joel son of Azariah.
From the clan of Merari: Kish son of Abdi and
Azariah son of Jehallelel.
From the clan of Gershon: Joah son of Zimmah
and Eden son of Joah.
13 From the family of Elizaphan: Shimri and Jeiel.
From the family of Asaph: Zechariah and
Mattaniah.
14 From the family of Heman: Jehiel and Shimei.
From the family of Jeduthun: Shemaiah and
Uzziel.

15These men called together their fellow Levites,
and they all purified themselves. Then they began to
cleanse the Temple of the LORD, just as the king had
commanded. They were careful to follow all the
LORD's instructions in their work. 16The priests went
into the sanctuary of the Temple of the LORD to
cleanse it, and they took out to the Temple courtyard
all the defiled things they found. From there the
Levites carted it all out to the Kidron Valley.
17They began the work in early spring, on the first
day of the new year,* and in eight days they had
reached the entry room of the LORD's Temple. Then
they purified the Temple of the LORD itself, which
took another eight days. So the entire task was completed in sixteen days.

The Temple Rededication

18Then the Levites went to King Hezekiah and gave
him this report: "We have cleansed the entire Temple
of the LORD, the altar of burnt offering with all its
utensils, and the table of the Bread of the Presence
with all its utensils. 19We have also recovered all the
items discarded by King Ahaz when he was unfaithful and closed the Temple. They are now in front of
the altar of the LORD, purified and ready for use."
20Early the next morning King Hezekiah gathered
the city officials and went to the Temple of the LORD.
21They brought seven bulls, seven rams, and seven
male lambs as a burnt offering, together with seven
male goats as a sin offering for the kingdom, for the
Temple, and for Judah. The king commanded the
priests, who were descendants of Aaron, to sacrifice
the animals on the altar of the LORD.

29:17 Hebrew *on the first day of the first month.* This day in the ancient Hebrew lunar calendar occurred in March or early April, 715 B.C.

KING JAMES VERSION

22 So they killed the bullocks, and the priests received the blood, and sprinkled *it* on the altar: likewise, when they had killed the rams, they sprinkled the blood upon the altar: they killed also the lambs, and they sprinkled the blood upon the altar.

23 And they brought forth the he goats *for* the sin offering before the king and the congregation; and they laid their hands upon them:

24 And the priests killed them, and they made reconciliation with their blood upon the altar, to make an atonement for all Israel: for the king commanded *that* the burnt offering and the sin offering *should be made* for all Israel.

25 And he set the Levites in the house of the LORD with cymbals, with psalteries, and with harps, according to the commandment of David, and of Gad the king's seer, and Nathan the prophet: for *so was* the commandment of the LORD by his prophets.

26 And the Levites stood with the instruments of David, and the priests with the trumpets.

27 And Hezekiah commanded to offer the burnt offering upon the altar. And when the burnt offering began, the song of the LORD began *also* with the trumpets, and with the instruments *ordained* by David king of Israel.

28 And all the congregation worshipped, and the singers sang, and the trumpeters sounded: *and* all *this continued* until the burnt offering was finished.

29 And when they had made an end of offering, the king and all that were present with him bowed themselves, and worshipped.

30 Moreover Hezekiah the king and the princes commanded the Levites to sing praise unto the LORD with the words of David, and of Asaph the seer. And they sang praises with gladness, and they bowed their heads and worshipped.

31 Then Hezekiah answered and said, Now ye have consecrated yourselves unto the LORD, come near and bring sacrifices and thank offerings into the house of the LORD. And the congregation brought in sacrifices and thank offerings; and as many as were of a free heart burnt offerings.

32 And the number of the burnt offerings, which the congregation brought, was threescore and ten bullocks, an hundred rams, *and* two hundred lambs: all these *were* for a burnt offering to the LORD.

33 And the consecrated things *were* six hundred oxen and three thousand sheep.

34 But the priests were too few, so that they could not flay all the burnt offerings: wherefore their brethren the Levites did help them, till the work was ended, and until the *other* priests had sanctified themselves: for the Levites *were* more upright in heart to sanctify themselves than the priests.

35 And also the burnt offerings *were* in abundance, with the fat of the peace offerings, and the drink offerings for *every* burnt offering. So the service of the house of the LORD was set in order.

NEW LIVING TRANSLATION

22 So they killed the bulls, and the priests took the blood and sprinkled it on the altar. Next they killed the rams and sprinkled their blood on the altar. And finally, they did the same with the male lambs. 23 The male goats for the sin offering were then brought before the king and the assembly of people, who laid their hands on them. 24 The priests then killed the goats as a sin offering and sprinkled their blood on the altar to make atonement for the sins of all Israel. The king had specifically commanded that this burnt offering and sin offering should be made for all Israel.

25 King Hezekiah then stationed the Levites at the Temple of the LORD with cymbals, lyres, and harps. He obeyed all the commands that the LORD had given to King David through Gad, the king's seer, and the prophet Nathan. 26 The Levites then took their positions around the Temple with the instruments of David, and the priests took their positions with the trumpets.

27 Then Hezekiah ordered that the burnt offering be placed on the altar. As the burnt offering was presented, songs of praise to the LORD were begun, accompanied by the trumpets and other instruments of David, the former king of Israel. 28 The entire assembly worshiped the LORD as the singers sang and the trumpets blew, until all the burnt offerings were finished. 29 Then the king and everyone with him bowed down in worship. 30 King Hezekiah and the officials ordered the Levites to praise the LORD with the psalms written by David and by Asaph the seer. So they offered joyous praise and bowed down in worship.

31 Then Hezekiah declared, "Now that you have consecrated yourselves to the LORD, bring your sacrifices and thanksgiving offerings to the Temple of the LORD." So the people brought their sacrifices and thanksgiving offerings, and all whose hearts were willing brought burnt offerings, too. 32 The people brought to the LORD 70 bulls, 100 rams, and 200 male lambs for burnt offerings. 33 They also brought 600 cattle and 3,000 sheep and goats as sacred offerings.

34 But there were too few priests to prepare all the burnt offerings. So their relatives the Levites helped them until the work was finished and more priests had been purified, for the Levites had been more conscientious about purifying themselves than the priests had been. 35 There was an abundance of burnt offerings, along with the usual liquid offerings, and a great deal of fat from the many peace offerings.

So the Temple of the LORD was restored to service.

36And Hezekiah rejoiced, and all the people, that God had prepared the people: for the thing was *done* suddenly.

30 1And Hezekiah sent to all Israel and Judah, and wrote letters also to Ephraim and Manasseh, that they should come to the house of the LORD at Jerusalem, to keep the passover unto the LORD God of Israel.

2For the king had taken counsel, and his princes, and all the congregation in Jerusalem, to keep the passover in the second month.

3For they could not keep it at that time, because the priests had not sanctified themselves sufficiently, neither had the people gathered themselves together to Jerusalem.

4And the thing pleased the king and all the congregation.

5So they established a decree to make proclamation throughout all Israel, from Beer-sheba even to Dan, that they should come to keep the passover unto the LORD God of Israel at Jerusalem: for they had not done *it* of a long *time in such sort* as it was written.

6So the posts went with the letters from the king and his princes throughout all Israel and Judah, and according to the commandment of the king, saying, Ye children of Israel, turn again unto the LORD God of Abraham, Isaac, and Israel, and he will return to the remnant of you, that are escaped out of the hand of the kings of Assyria.

7And be not ye like your fathers, and like your brethren, which trespassed against the LORD God of their fathers, *who* therefore gave them up to desolation, as ye see.

8Now be ye not stiffnecked, as your fathers *were, but* yield yourselves unto the LORD, and enter into his sanctuary, which he hath sanctified for ever: and serve the LORD your God, that the fierceness of his wrath may turn away from you.

9For if ye turn again unto the LORD, your brethren and your children *shall find* compassion before them that lead them captive, so that they shall come again into this land: for the LORD your God *is* gracious and merciful, and will not turn away *his* face from you, if ye return unto him.

10So the posts passed from city to city through the country of Ephraim and Manasseh even unto Zebulun: but they laughed them to scorn, and mocked them.

11Nevertheless divers of Asher and Manasseh and of Zebulun humbled themselves, and came to Jerusalem.

12Also in Judah the hand of God was to give them one heart to do the commandment of the king and of the princes, by the word of the LORD.

13And there assembled at Jerusalem much people

36And Hezekiah and all the people rejoiced because of what God had done for the people, for everything had been accomplished so quickly.

Preparations for Passover

30 King Hezekiah now sent word to all Israel and Judah, and he wrote letters of invitation to the people of Ephraim and Manasseh. He asked everyone to come to the Temple of the LORD at Jerusalem to celebrate the Passover of the LORD, the God of Israel. 2The king, his officials, and all the community of Jerusalem decided to celebrate Passover a month later than usual.* 3They were unable to celebrate it at the prescribed time because not enough priests could be purified by then, and the people had not yet assembled at Jerusalem.

4This plan for keeping the Passover seemed right to the king and all the people. 5So they sent a proclamation throughout all Israel, from Beersheba in the south to Dan in the north, inviting everyone to come to Jerusalem to celebrate the Passover of the LORD, the God of Israel. The people had not been celebrating it in great numbers as required in the Law.

6At the king's command, runners were sent throughout Israel and Judah. They carried letters that said:

> "O people of Israel, return to the LORD, the God of Abraham, Isaac, and Israel,* so that he will return to the few of us who have survived the conquest of the Assyrian kings. 7Do not be like your ancestors and relatives who abandoned the LORD, the God of their ancestors, and became an object of derision, as you yourselves can see. 8Do not be stubborn, as they were, but submit yourselves to the LORD. Come to his Temple, which he has set apart as holy forever. Worship the LORD your God so that his fierce anger will turn away from you.
>
> 9"For if you return to the LORD, your relatives and your children will be treated mercifully by their captors, and they will be able to return to this land. For the LORD your God is gracious and merciful. If you return to him, he will not continue to turn his face from you."

Celebration of Passover

10The runners went from town to town throughout Ephraim and Manasseh and as far as the territory of Zebulun. But most of the people just laughed at the runners and made fun of them. 11However, some people from Asher, Manasseh, and Zebulun humbled themselves and went to Jerusalem.

12At the same time, God's hand was on the people in the land of Judah, giving them all one heart to obey the orders of the king and his officials, who were

30:2 Hebrew *in the second month.* Passover was normally observed in the first month (of the ancient Hebrew lunar calendar). **30:6** *Israel* is the name that God gave to Jacob.

KING JAMES VERSION

to keep the feast of unleavened bread in the second month, a very great congregation.

14And they arose and took away the altars that *were* in Jerusalem, and all the altars for incense took they away, and cast *them* into the brook Kidron.

15Then they killed the passover on the fourteenth *day* of the second month: and the priests and the Levites were ashamed, and sanctified themselves, and brought in the burnt offerings into the house of the LORD.

16And they stood in their place after their manner, according to the law of Moses the man of God: the priests sprinkled the blood, *which they received* of the hand of the Levites.

17For *there were* many in the congregation that were not sanctified: therefore the Levites had the charge of the killing of the passovers for every one *that was* not clean, to sanctify *them* unto the LORD.

18For a multitude of the people, *even* many of Ephraim, and Manasseh, Issachar, and Zebulun, had not cleansed themselves, yet did they eat the passover otherwise than it was written. But Hezekiah prayed for them, saying, The good LORD pardon every one

19*That* prepareth his heart to seek God, the LORD God of his fathers, though *he be* not *cleansed* according to the purification of the sanctuary.

20And the LORD hearkened to Hezekiah, and healed the people.

21And the children of Israel that were present at Jerusalem kept the feast of unleavened bread seven days with great gladness: and the Levites and the priests praised the LORD day by day, *singing* with loud instruments unto the LORD.

22And Hezekiah spake comfortably unto all the Levites that taught the good knowledge of the LORD: and they did eat throughout the feast seven days, offering peace offerings, and making confession to the LORD God of their fathers.

23And the whole assembly took counsel to keep other seven days: and they kept *other* seven days with gladness.

24For Hezekiah king of Judah did give to the congregation a thousand bullocks and seven thousand sheep; and the princes gave to the congregation a thousand bullocks and ten thousand sheep: and a great number of priests sanctified themselves.

25And all the congregation of Judah, with the priests and the Levites, and all the congregation that came out of Israel, and the strangers that came out of the land of Israel, and that dwelt in Judah, rejoiced.

26So there was great joy in Jerusalem: for since the time of Solomon the son of David king of Israel *there was* not the like in Jerusalem.

27Then the priests the Levites arose and blessed the people: and their voice was heard, and their prayer came *up* to his holy dwelling place, *even* unto heaven.

NEW LIVING TRANSLATION

following the word of the LORD.
13So a huge crowd
assembled at Jerusalem in midspring* to celebrate
the Festival of Unleavened Bread.
14They set to work
and removed the pagan altars from Jerusalem. They
took away all the incense altars and threw them into
the Kidron Valley.

15On the fourteenth day of the second month, one
month later than usual,* the people slaughtered the
Passover lamb. This shamed the priests and Levites,
so they purified themselves and brought burnt offerings to the Temple of the LORD.
16Then they took
their places at the Temple as prescribed in the Law
of Moses, the man of God. The Levites brought the
sacrificial blood to the priests, who then sprinkled
it on the altar.

17Since many of the people had not purified
themselves, the Levites had to slaughter their Passover lamb for them, to set them apart for the LORD.
18Most of those who came from Ephraim, Manasseh,
Issachar, and Zebulun had not purified themselves.
But King Hezekiah prayed for them, and they were
allowed to eat the Passover meal anyway, even
though this was contrary to the requirements of the
Law. For Hezekiah said, "May the LORD, who is good,
pardon those
19who decide to follow the LORD, the
God of their ancestors, even though they are not
properly cleansed for the ceremony."
20And the LORD
listened to Hezekiah's prayer and healed the people.

21So the people of Israel who were present in Jerusalem joyously celebrated the Festival of Unleavened
Bread for seven days. Each day the Levites and
priests sang to the LORD, accompanied by loud instruments.*
22Hezekiah encouraged all the Levites
regarding the skill they displayed as they served the
LORD. The celebration continued for seven days.
Peace offerings were sacrificed, and the people gave
thanks to the LORD, the God of their ancestors.

23The entire assembly then decided to continue
the festival another seven days, so they celebrated
joyfully for another week.
24King Hezekiah gave the
people 1,000 bulls and 7,000 sheep and goats for offerings, and the officials donated 1,000 bulls and
10,000 sheep and goats. Meanwhile, many more
priests purified themselves.

25The entire assembly of Judah rejoiced, including
the priests, the Levites, all who came from the land of
Israel, the foreigners who came to the festival, and all
those who lived in Judah.
26There was great joy in the
city, for Jerusalem had not seen a celebration like
this one since the days of Solomon, King David's son.
27Then the priests and Levites stood and blessed the
people, and God heard their prayer from his holy
dwelling in heaven.

30:13 Hebrew *in the second month.* The second month of the ancient Hebrew lunar calendar usually occurs within the months of April and May.
30:15 Hebrew *On the fourteenth day of the second month.* Passover normally began on the fourteenth day of the first month (see Lev 23:5).
30:21 Or *sang to the LORD with all their strength.*

KING JAMES VERSION

31 1Now when all this was finished, all Israel
that were present went out to the cities of
Judah, and brake the images in pieces, and cut down
the groves, and threw down the high places and the
altars out of all Judah and Benjamin, in Ephraim also
and Manasseh, until they had utterly destroyed them
all. Then all the children of Israel returned, every
man to his possession, into their own cities.
2And Hezekiah appointed the courses of the
priests and the Levites after their courses, every man
according to his service, the priests and Levites for
burnt offerings and for peace offerings, to minister,
and to give thanks, and to praise in the gates of the
tents of the LORD.
3*He appointed* also the king's portion of his substance for the burnt offerings, *to wit,* for the morning
and evening burnt offerings, and the burnt offerings
for the sabbaths, and for the new moons, and for the
set feasts, as *it is* written in the law of the LORD.
4Moreover he commanded the people that dwelt
in Jerusalem to give the portion of the priests and the
Levites, that they might be encouraged in the law of
the LORD.
5And as soon as the commandment came abroad,
the children of Israel brought in abundance the
firstfruits of corn, wine, and oil, and honey, and of all
the increase of the field; and the tithe of all *things*
brought they in abundantly.
6And *concerning* the children of Israel and Judah,
that dwelt in the cities of Judah, they also brought
in the tithe of oxen and sheep, and the tithe of holy
things which were consecrated unto the LORD their
God, and laid *them* by heaps.
7In the third month they began to lay the foundation of the heaps, and finished *them* in the seventh
month.
8And when Hezekiah and the princes came and
saw the heaps, they blessed the LORD, and his people
Israel.
9Then Hezekiah questioned with the priests and
the Levites concerning the heaps.
10And Azariah the chief priest of the house of Zadok answered him, and said, Since *the people* began
to bring the offerings into the house of the LORD, we
have had enough to eat, and have left plenty: for the
LORD hath blessed his people; and that which is left
is this great store.
11Then Hezekiah commanded to prepare chambers in the house of the LORD; and they prepared
them,
12And brought in the offerings and the tithes and
the dedicated *things* faithfully: over which Cononiah
the Levite *was* ruler, and Shimei his brother *was* the
next.
13And Jehiel, and Azaziah, and Nahath, and Asahel,
and Jerimoth, and Jozabad, and Eliel, and Ismachiah,
and Mahath, and Benaiah, *were* overseers under the

NEW LIVING TRANSLATION

Hezekiah's Religious Reforms

31 When the festival ended, the Israelites who
attended went to all the towns of Judah, Benjamin, Ephraim, and Manasseh, and they smashed all
the sacred pillars, cut down the Asherah poles, and
removed the pagan shrines and altars. After this, the
Israelites returned to their own towns and homes.
2Hezekiah then organized the priests and Levites
into divisions to offer the burnt offerings and peace
offerings, and to worship and give thanks and praise
to the LORD at the gates of the Temple. 3The king also
made a personal contribution of animals for the
daily morning and evening burnt offerings, the
weekly Sabbath festivals, the monthly new moon
festivals, and the annual festivals as prescribed in the
Law of the LORD. 4In addition, he required the people
in Jerusalem to bring a portion of their goods to the
priests and Levites, so they could devote themselves
fully to the Law of the LORD.
5When the people of Israel heard these requirements, they responded generously by bringing the
first share of their grain, new wine, olive oil, honey,
and all the produce of their fields. They brought a
large quantity—a tithe of all they produced. 6The
people who had moved to Judah from Israel, and the
people of Judah themselves, brought in the tithes of
their cattle, sheep, and goats and a tithe of the things
that had been dedicated to the LORD their God, and
they piled them up in great heaps. 7They began piling them up in late spring, and the heaps continued
to grow until early autumn.* 8When Hezekiah and
his officials came and saw these huge piles, they
thanked the LORD and his people Israel!
9"Where did all this come from?" Hezekiah asked
the priests and Levites.
10And Azariah the high priest, from the family of
Zadok, replied, "Since the people began bringing
their gifts to the LORD's Temple, we have had enough
to eat and plenty to spare. The LORD has blessed his
people, and all this is left over."
11Hezekiah ordered that storerooms be prepared
in the Temple of the LORD. When this was done,
12the people faithfully brought all the tithes and
gifts to the Temple. Conaniah the Levite was put in
charge, assisted by his brother Shimei. 13The supervisors under them were Jehiel, Azaziah, Nahath, Asahel, Jerimoth, Jozabad, Eliel, Ismakiah, Mahath, and

31:7 Hebrew *in the third month . . . until the seventh month.* The third month of the ancient Hebrew lunar calendar usually occurs within the months of May and June; the seventh month usually occurs within September and October.

KING JAMES VERSION

hand of Cononiah and Shimei his brother, at the
commandment of Hezekiah the king, and Azariah
the ruler of the house of God.
14And Kore the son of Imnah the Levite, the porter
toward the east, *was* over the freewill offerings of
God, to distribute the oblations of the LORD, and the
most holy things.
15And next him *were* Eden, and Miniamin, and
Jeshua, and Shemaiah, Amariah, and Shecaniah, in
the cities of the priests, in *their* set office, to give to
their brethren by courses, as well to the great as to
the small:
16Beside their genealogy of males, from three
years old and upward, *even* unto every one that entereth into the house of the LORD, his daily portion
for their service in their charges according to their
courses;
17Both to the genealogy of the priests by the house
of their fathers, and the Levites from twenty years
old and upward, in their charges by their courses;
18And to the genealogy of all their little ones, their
wives, and their sons, and their daughters, through
all the congregation: for in their set office they sanctified themselves in holiness:
19Also of the sons of Aaron the priests, *which were*
in the fields of the suburbs of their cities, in every
several city, the men that were expressed by name, to
give portions to all the males among the priests, and
to all that were reckoned by genealogies among the
Levites.
20And thus did Hezekiah throughout all Judah,
and wrought *that which was* good and right and
truth before the LORD his God.
21And in every work that he began in the service of
the house of God, and in the law, and in the commandments, to seek his God, he did *it* with all his
heart, and prospered.

32 1After these things, and the establishment
thereof, Sennacherib king of Assyria came,
and entered into Judah, and encamped against the
fenced cities, and thought to win them for himself.
2And when Hezekiah saw that Sennacherib was
come, and that he was purposed to fight against
Jerusalem,
3He took counsel with his princes and his mighty
men to stop the waters of the fountains which *were*
without the city: and they did help him.
4So there was gathered much people together,
who stopped all the fountains, and the brook that ran
through the midst of the land, saying, Why should
the kings of Assyria come, and find much water?
5Also he strengthened himself, and built up all
the wall that was broken, and raised *it* up to the
towers, and another wall without, and repaired
Millo *in* the city of David, and made darts and
shields in abundance.

NEW LIVING TRANSLATION

Benaiah. These appointments were made by King
Hezekiah and Azariah, the chief official in the
Temple of God.
14Kore son of Imnah the Levite, who was the gatekeeper at the East Gate, was put in charge of distrib-
uting the voluntary offerings given to God, the gifts,
and the things that had been dedicated to the LORD.
15His faithful assistants were Eden, Miniamin, Jeshua, Shemaiah, Amariah, and Shecaniah. They distributed the gifts among the families of priests in their
towns by their divisions, dividing the gifts fairly
among old and young alike. 16They distributed the
gifts to all males three years old or older, regardless
of their place in the genealogical records. The distribution went to all who would come to the LORD's
Temple to perform their daily duties according to
their divisions. 17They distributed gifts to the priests
who were listed by their families in the genealogical
records, and to the Levites twenty years old or older
who were listed according to their jobs and their
divisions. 18Food allotments were also given to the
families of all those listed in the genealogical records, including their little babies, wives, sons, and
daughters. For they had all been faithful in purifying
themselves.
19As for the priests, the descendants of Aaron,
who were living in the open villages around the
towns, men were appointed by name to distribute
portions to every male among the priests and to all
the Levites listed in the genealogical records.
20In this way, King Hezekiah handled the distribution throughout all Judah, doing what was pleasing
and good in the sight of the LORD his God. 21In all
that he did in the service of the Temple of God and in
his efforts to follow God's laws and commands, Hezekiah sought his God wholeheartedly. As a result, he
was very successful.

Assyria Invades Judah

32 After Hezekiah had faithfully carried out
this work, King Sennacherib of Assyria invaded Judah. He laid siege to the fortified towns, giving orders for his army to break through their walls.
2When Hezekiah realized that Sennacherib also intended to attack Jerusalem, 3he consulted with his
officials and military advisers, and they decided to
stop the flow of the springs outside the city. 4They
organized a huge work crew to stop the flow of the
springs, cutting off the brook that ran through the
fields. For they said, "Why should the kings of Assyria come here and find plenty of water?"
5Then Hezekiah worked hard at repairing all the
broken sections of the wall, erecting towers, and
constructing a second wall outside the first. He also
reinforced the supporting terraces* in the City of
David and manufactured large numbers of weapons

32:5 Hebrew *the millo*. The meaning of the Hebrew is uncertain.

KING JAMES VERSION

6 And he set captains of war over the people, and gathered them together to him in the street of the gate of the city, and spake comfortably to them, saying,

7 Be strong and courageous, be not afraid nor dismayed for the king of Assyria, nor for all the multitude that *is* with him: for *there be* more with us than with him:

8 With him *is* an arm of flesh; but with us *is* the LORD our God to help us, and to fight our battles. And the people rested themselves upon the words of Hezekiah king of Judah.

9 After this did Sennacherib king of Assyria send his servants to Jerusalem, (but he *himself laid siege* against Lachish, and all his power with him,) unto Hezekiah king of Judah, and unto all Judah that *were* at Jerusalem, saying,

10 Thus saith Sennacherib king of Assyria, Whereon do ye trust, that ye abide in the siege in Jerusalem?

11 Doth not Hezekiah persuade you to give over yourselves to die by famine and by thirst, saying, The LORD our God shall deliver us out of the hand of the king of Assyria?

12 Hath not the same Hezekiah taken away his high places and his altars, and commanded Judah and Jerusalem, saying, Ye shall worship before one altar, and burn incense upon it?

13 Know ye not what I and my fathers have done unto all the people of *other* lands? were the gods of the nations of those lands any ways able to deliver their lands out of mine hand?

14 Who *was there* among all the gods of those nations that my fathers utterly destroyed, that could deliver his people out of mine hand, that your God should be able to deliver you out of mine hand?

15 Now therefore let not Hezekiah deceive you, nor persuade you on this manner, neither yet believe him: for no god of any nation or kingdom was able to deliver his people out of mine hand, and out of the hand of my fathers: how much less shall your God deliver you out of mine hand?

16 And his servants spake yet *more* against the LORD God, and against his servant Hezekiah.

17 He wrote also letters to rail on the LORD God of Israel, and to speak against him, saying, As the gods of the nations of *other* lands have not delivered their people out of mine hand, so shall not the God of Hezekiah deliver his people out of mine hand.

18 Then they cried with a loud voice in the Jews' speech unto the people of Jerusalem that *were* on the wall, to affright them, and to trouble them; that they might take the city.

19 And they spake against the God of Jerusalem, as against the gods of the people of the earth, *which were* the work of the hands of man.

20 And for this *cause* Hezekiah the king, and the prophet Isaiah the son of Amoz, prayed and cried to heaven.

NEW LIVING TRANSLATION

and shields. 6 He appointed military officers over the people and assembled them before him in the square at the city gate. Then Hezekiah encouraged them by saying: 7 "Be strong and courageous! Don't be afraid or discouraged because of the king of Assyria or his mighty army, for there is a power far greater on our side! 8 He may have a great army, but they are merely men. We have the LORD our God to help us and to fight our battles for us!" Hezekiah's words greatly encouraged the people.

Sennacherib Threatens Jerusalem

9 While King Sennacherib of Assyria was still besieging the town of Lachish, he sent his officers to Jerusalem with this message for Hezekiah and all the people in the city:

10 "This is what King Sennacherib of Assyria says:
What are you trusting in that makes you think
you can survive my siege of Jerusalem?
11 Hezekiah has said, 'The LORD our God will
rescue us from the king of Assyria.' Surely
Hezekiah is misleading you, sentencing you to
death by famine and thirst! 12 Don't you realize
that Hezekiah is the very person who destroyed
all the LORD's shrines and altars? He commanded
Judah and Jerusalem to worship only at the altar
at the Temple and to offer sacrifices on it alone.

13 "Surely you must realize what I and the other
kings of Assyria before me have done to all the
people of the earth! Were any of the gods of those
nations able to rescue their people from my
power? 14 Which of their gods was able to rescue
its people from the destructive power of my
predecessors? What makes you think your God
can rescue you from me? 15 Don't let Hezekiah
deceive you! Don't let him fool you like this! I say
it again—no god of any nation or kingdom has
ever yet been able to rescue his people from me
or my ancestors. How much less will your God
rescue you from my power!"

16 And Sennacherib's officers further mocked the LORD God and his servant Hezekiah, heaping insult upon insult. 17 The king also sent letters scorning the LORD, the God of Israel. He wrote, "Just as the gods of all the other nations failed to rescue their people from my power, so the God of Hezekiah will also fail." 18 The Assyrian officials who brought the letters shouted this in Hebrew* to the people gathered on the walls of the city, trying to terrify them so it would be easier to capture the city. 19 These officers talked about the God of Jerusalem as though he were one of the pagan gods, made by human hands.

20 Then King Hezekiah and the prophet Isaiah son

32:18 Hebrew *in the dialect of Judah.*

KING JAMES VERSION

21 And the LORD sent an angel, which cut off all the
mighty men of valour, and the leaders and captains
in the camp of the king of Assyria. So he returned
with shame of face to his own land. And when he was
come into the house of his god, they that came forth
of his own bowels slew him there with the sword.
22 Thus the LORD saved Hezekiah and the inhabitants of Jerusalem from the hand of Sennacherib the
king of Assyria, and from the hand of all *other*, and
guided them on every side.
23 And many brought gifts unto the LORD to Jerusalem, and presents to Hezekiah king of Judah: so that
he was magnified in the sight of all nations from
thenceforth.

24 In those days Hezekiah was sick to the death,
and prayed unto the LORD: and he spake unto him,
and he gave him a sign.
25 But Hezekiah rendered not again according to
the benefit *done* unto him; for his heart was lifted
up: therefore there was wrath upon him, and upon
Judah and Jerusalem.
26 Notwithstanding Hezekiah humbled himself
for the pride of his heart, *both* he and the inhabitants
of Jerusalem, so that the wrath of the LORD came not
upon them in the days of Hezekiah.
27 And Hezekiah had exceeding much riches and
honour: and he made himself treasuries for silver,
and for gold, and for precious stones, and for spices,
and for shields, and for all manner of pleasant
jewels;
28 Storehouses also for the increase of corn, and
wine, and oil; and stalls for all manner of beasts, and
cotes for flocks.
29 Moreover he provided him cities, and possessions of flocks and herds in abundance: for God had
given him substance very much.
30 This same Hezekiah also stopped the upper
watercourse of Gihon, and brought it straight down
to the west side of the city of David. And Hezekiah
prospered in all his works.
31 Howbeit in *the business of* the ambassadors of
the princes of Babylon, who sent unto him to inquire
of the wonder that was *done* in the land, God left
him, to try him, that he might know all *that was* in
his heart.
32 Now the rest of the acts of Hezekiah, and his
goodness, behold, they *are* written in the vision of
Isaiah the prophet, the son of Amoz, *and* in the book
of the kings of Judah and Israel.
33 And Hezekiah slept with his fathers, and they
buried him in the chiefest of the sepulchres of the
sons of David: and all Judah and the inhabitants of
Jerusalem did him honour at his death. And Manasseh his son reigned in his stead.

NEW LIVING TRANSLATION

of Amoz cried out in prayer to God in heaven. 21 And
the LORD sent an angel who destroyed the Assyrian
army with all its commanders and officers. So Sennacherib was forced to return home in disgrace to
his own land. And when he entered the temple of his
god, some of his own sons killed him there with a
sword.
22 That is how the LORD rescued Hezekiah and the
people of Jerusalem from King Sennacherib of Assyria and from all the others who threatened them.
So there was peace throughout the land. 23 From then
on King Hezekiah became highly respected among
all the surrounding nations, and many gifts for the
LORD arrived at Jerusalem, with valuable presents for
King Hezekiah, too.

Hezekiah's Sickness and Recovery

24 About that time Hezekiah became deathly ill. He
prayed to the LORD, who healed him and gave him a
miraculous sign. 25 But Hezekiah did not respond
appropriately to the kindness shown him, and he became proud. So the LORD's anger came against him
and against Judah and Jerusalem. 26 Then Hezekiah
humbled himself and repented of his pride, as did
the people of Jerusalem. So the LORD's anger did not
fall on them during Hezekiah's lifetime.
27 Hezekiah was very wealthy and highly honored.
He built special treasury buildings for his silver, gold,
precious stones, and spices, and for his shields and
other valuable items. 28 He also constructed many
storehouses for his grain, new wine, and olive oil; and
he made many stalls for his cattle and pens for his
flocks of sheep and goats. 29 He built many towns
and acquired vast flocks and herds, for God had
given him great wealth. 30 He blocked up the upper
spring of Gihon and brought the water down
through a tunnel to the west side of the City of David.
And so he succeeded in everything he did.
31 However, when ambassadors arrived from Babylon to ask about the remarkable events that had
taken place in the land, God withdrew from Hezekiah in order to test him and to see what was really in
his heart.

Summary of Hezekiah's Reign

32 The rest of the events in Hezekiah's reign and his
acts of devotion are recorded in *The Vision of the
Prophet Isaiah Son of Amoz,* which is included in *The
Book of the Kings of Judah and Israel.* 33 When Hezekiah died, he was buried in the upper area of the
royal cemetery, and all Judah and Jerusalem honored
him at his death. And his son Manasseh became the
next king.

KING JAMES VERSION

33

1Manasseh *was* twelve years old when he began to reign, and he reigned fifty and five years in Jerusalem:

2But did *that which was* evil in the sight of the LORD, like unto the abominations of the heathen, whom the LORD had cast out before the children of Israel.

3For he built again the high places which Hezekiah his father had broken down, and he reared up altars for Baalim, and made groves, and worshipped all the host of heaven, and served them.

4Also he built altars in the house of the LORD, whereof the LORD had said, In Jerusalem shall my name be for ever.

5And he built altars for all the host of heaven in the two courts of the house of the LORD.

6And he caused his children to pass through the fire in the valley of the son of Hinnom: also he observed times, and used enchantments, and used witchcraft, and dealt with a familiar spirit, and with wizards: he wrought much evil in the sight of the LORD, to provoke him to anger.

7And he set a carved image, the idol which he had made, in the house of God, of which God had said to David and to Solomon his son, In this house, and in Jerusalem, which I have chosen before all the tribes of Israel, will I put my name for ever:

8Neither will I any more remove the foot of Israel from out of the land which I have appointed for your fathers; so that they will take heed to do all that I have commanded them, according to the whole law and the statutes and the ordinances by the hand of Moses.

9So Manasseh made Judah and the inhabitants of Jerusalem to err, *and* to do worse than the heathen, whom the LORD had destroyed before the children of Israel.

10And the LORD spake to Manasseh, and to his people: but they would not hearken.

11Wherefore the LORD brought upon them the captains of the host of the king of Assyria, which took Manasseh among the thorns, and bound him with fetters, and carried him to Babylon.

12And when he was in affliction, he besought the LORD his God, and humbled himself greatly before the God of his fathers,

13And prayed unto him: and he was intreated of him, and heard his supplication, and brought him again to Jerusalem into his kingdom. Then Manasseh knew that the LORD he *was* God.

14Now after this he built a wall without the city of David, on the west side of Gihon, in the valley, even to the entering in at the fish gate, and compassed about Ophel, and raised it up a very great height, and put captains of war in all the fenced cities of Judah.

15And he took away the strange gods, and the idol out of the house of the LORD, and all the altars that he

NEW LIVING TRANSLATION

Manasseh Rules in Judah

33

Manasseh was twelve years old when he became king, and he reigned in Jerusalem fifty-five years. 2He did what was evil in the LORD's sight, following the detestable practices of the pagan nations that the LORD had driven from the land ahead of the Israelites. 3He rebuilt the pagan shrines his father, Hezekiah, had broken down. He constructed altars for the images of Baal and set up Asherah poles. He also bowed before all the powers of the heavens and worshiped them.

4He built pagan altars in the Temple of the LORD, the place where the LORD had said, "My name will remain in Jerusalem forever." 5He built these altars for all the powers of the heavens in both courtyards of the LORD's Temple. 6Manasseh also sacrificed his own sons in the fire* in the valley of Ben-Hinnom. He practiced sorcery, divination, and witchcraft, and he consulted with mediums and psychics. He did much that was evil in the LORD's sight, arousing his anger.

7Manasseh even took a carved idol he had made and set it up in God's Temple, the very place where God had told David and his son Solomon: "My name will be honored forever in this Temple and in Jerusalem—the city I have chosen from among all the tribes of Israel. 8If the Israelites will be careful to obey my commands—all the laws, decrees, and regulations given through Moses—I will not send them into exile from this land that I set aside for your ancestors." 9But Manasseh led the people of Judah and Jerusalem to do even more evil than the pagan nations that the LORD had destroyed when the people of Israel entered the land.

10The LORD spoke to Manasseh and his people, but they ignored all his warnings. 11So the LORD sent the commanders of the Assyrian armies, and they took Manasseh prisoner. They put a ring through his nose, bound him in bronze chains, and led him away to Babylon. 12But while in deep distress, Manasseh sought the LORD his God and sincerely humbled himself before the God of his ancestors. 13And when he prayed, the LORD listened to him and was moved by his request. So the LORD brought Manasseh back to Jerusalem and to his kingdom. Then Manasseh finally realized that the LORD alone is God!

14After this Manasseh rebuilt the outer wall of the City of David, from west of the Gihon Spring in the Kidron Valley to the Fish Gate, and continuing around the hill of Ophel. He built the wall very high. And he stationed his military officers in all of the fortified towns of Judah. 15Manasseh also removed the foreign gods and the idol from the LORD's Temple. He tore down all the altars he had built on the hill

33:6 Or *also made his sons pass through the fire.*

KING JAMES VERSION

had built in the mount of the house of the LORD, and
in Jerusalem, and cast *them* out of the city.
16 And he repaired the altar of the LORD, and sacrificed thereon peace offerings and thank offerings,
and commanded Judah to serve the LORD God of
Israel.
17 Nevertheless the people did sacrifice still in the
high places, *yet* unto the LORD their God only.
18 Now the rest of the acts of Manasseh, and his
prayer unto his God, and the words of the seers that
spake to him in the name of the LORD God of Israel,
behold, they *are written* in the book of the kings of
Israel.
19 His prayer also, and *how God* was intreated of
him, and all his sins, and his trespass, and the places
wherein he built high places, and set up groves and
graven images, before he was humbled: behold, they
are written among the sayings of the seers.
20 So Manasseh slept with his fathers, and they
buried him in his own house: and Amon his son
reigned in his stead.
21 Amon *was* two and twenty years old when he
began to reign, and reigned two years in Jerusalem.
22 But he did *that which was* evil in the sight of the
LORD, as did Manasseh his father: for Amon sacrificed unto all the carved images which Manasseh his
father had made, and served them;
23 And humbled not himself before the LORD, as
Manasseh his father had humbled himself; but
Amon trespassed more and more.
24 And his servants conspired against him, and
slew him in his own house.
25 But the people of the land slew all them that had
conspired against king Amon; and the people of the
land made Josiah his son king in his stead.

34 1 Josiah *was* eight years old when he began
to reign, and he reigned in Jerusalem one
and thirty years.
2 And he did *that which was* right in the sight of
the LORD, and walked in the ways of David his father,
and declined *neither* to the right hand, nor to the
left.
3 For in the eighth year of his reign, while he was
yet young, he began to seek after the God of David his
father: and in the twelfth year he began to purge
Judah and Jerusalem from the high places, and
the groves, and the carved images, and the molten
images.
4 And they brake down the altars of Baalim in his
presence; and the images, that *were* on high above
them, he cut down; and the groves, and the carved
images, and the molten images, he brake in pieces,
and made dust *of them*, and strowed *it* upon the
graves of them that had sacrificed unto them.
5 And he burnt the bones of the priests upon their
altars, and cleansed Judah and Jerusalem.

NEW LIVING TRANSLATION

where the Temple stood and all the altars that were in
Jerusalem, and he dumped them outside the city.
16 Then he restored the altar of the LORD and sacrificed peace offerings and thanksgiving offerings on
it. He also encouraged the people of Judah to worship
the LORD, the God of Israel. 17 However, the people still
sacrificed at the pagan shrines, though only to the
LORD their God.
18 The rest of the events of Manasseh's reign, his
prayer to God, and the words the seers spoke to him
in the name of the LORD, the God of Israel, are recorded in *The Book of the Kings of Israel*. 19 Manasseh's prayer, the account of the way God answered
him, and an account of all his sins and unfaithfulness are recorded in *The Record of the Seers*.* It includes a list of the locations where he built pagan
shrines and set up Asherah poles and idols before he
humbled himself and repented. 20 When Manasseh
died, he was buried in his palace. Then his son Amon
became the next king.

Amon Rules in Judah

21 Amon was twenty-two years old when he became
king, and he reigned in Jerusalem two years. 22 He did
what was evil in the LORD's sight, just as his father,
Manasseh, had done. He worshiped and sacrificed to
all the idols his father had made. 23 But unlike his
father, he did not humble himself before the LORD.
Instead, Amon sinned even more.
24 Then Amon's own officials conspired against
him and assassinated him in his palace. 25 But the
people of the land killed all those who had conspired
against King Amon, and they made his son Josiah the
next king.

Josiah Rules in Judah

34 Josiah was eight years old when he became
king, and he reigned in Jerusalem thirty-
one years. 2 He did what was pleasing in the LORD's
sight and followed the example of his ancestor David. He did not turn away from doing what was right.
3 During the eighth year of his reign, while he was
still young, Josiah began to seek the God of his ancestor David. Then in the twelfth year he began to purify
Judah and Jerusalem, destroying all the pagan
shrines, the Asherah poles, and the carved idols and
cast images. 4 He ordered that the altars of Baal be
demolished and that the incense altars which stood
above them be broken down. He also made sure that
the Asherah poles, the carved idols, and the cast images were smashed and scattered over the graves of
those who had sacrificed to them. 5 He burned the
bones of the pagan priests on their own altars, and so
he purified Judah and Jerusalem.

33:19 Or *The Record of Hozai*.

6 And *so did he* in the cities of Manasseh, and
Ephraim, and Simeon, even unto Naphtali, with their
mattocks round about.
7 And when he had broken down the altars and the
groves, and had beaten the graven images into powder, and cut down all the idols throughout all the
land of Israel, he returned to Jerusalem.
8 Now in the eighteenth year of his reign, when he
had purged the land, and the house, he sent Shaphan
the son of Azaliah, and Maaseiah the governor of the
city, and Joah the son of Joahaz the recorder, to repair
the house of the LORD his God.
9 And when they came to Hilkiah the high priest,
they delivered the money that was brought into the
house of God, which the Levites that kept the doors
had gathered of the hand of Manasseh and Ephraim,
and of all the remnant of Israel, and of all Judah and
Benjamin; and they returned to Jerusalem.
10 And they put *it* in the hand of the workmen that
had the oversight of the house of the LORD, and they
gave it to the workmen that wrought in the house of
the LORD, to repair and amend the house:
11 Even to the artificers and builders gave they *it*,
to buy hewn stone, and timber for couplings, and
to floor the houses which the kings of Judah had
destroyed.
12 And the men did the work faithfully: and the
overseers of them *were* Jahath and Obadiah, the Levites, of the sons of Merari; and Zechariah and
Meshullam, of the sons of the Kohathites, to set *it*
forward; and *other of* the Levites, all that could skill
of instruments of musick.
13 Also *they were* over the bearers of burdens, and
were overseers of all that wrought the work in any
manner of service: and of the Levites *there were*
scribes, and officers, and porters.
14 And when they brought out the money that was
brought into the house of the LORD, Hilkiah the priest
found a book of the law of the LORD *given* by Moses.
15 And Hilkiah answered and said to Shaphan the
scribe, I have found the book of the law in the house of
the LORD. And Hilkiah delivered the book to Shaphan.
16 And Shaphan carried the book to the king, and
brought the king word back again, saying, All that
was committed to thy servants, they do *it*.
17 And they have gathered together the money that
was found in the house of the LORD, and have delivered it into the hand of the overseers, and to the
hand of the workmen.
18 Then Shaphan the scribe told the king, saying,
Hilkiah the priest hath given me a book. And Shaphan read it before the king.
19 And it came to pass, when the king had heard
the words of the law, that he rent his clothes.
20 And the king commanded Hilkiah, and Ahikam
the son of Shaphan, and Abdon the son of Micah, and
Shaphan the scribe, and Asaiah a servant of the
king's, saying,

6 He did the same thing in the towns of Manasseh,
Ephraim, and Simeon, even as far as Naphtali, and in
the regions* all around them.
7 He destroyed the pa-
gan altars and the Asherah poles, and he crushed the
idols into dust. He cut down all the incense altars
throughout the land of Israel. Finally, he returned to
Jerusalem.
8 In the eighteenth year of his reign, after he had
purified the land and the Temple, Josiah appointed
Shaphan son of Azaliah, Maaseiah the governor of
Jerusalem, and Joah son of Joahaz, the royal historian, to repair the Temple of the LORD his God.
9 They
gave Hilkiah the high priest the money that had been
collected by the Levites who served as gatekeepers at
the Temple of God. The gifts were brought by people
from Manasseh, Ephraim, and from all the remnant
of Israel, as well as from all Judah, Benjamin, and the
people of Jerusalem.
10 He entrusted the money to the men assigned to
supervise the restoration of the LORD's Temple. Then
they paid the workers who did the repairs and renovation of the Temple.
11 They hired carpenters and
builders, who purchased finished stone for the walls
and timber for the rafters and beams. They restored
what earlier kings of Judah had allowed to fall into
ruin.
12 The workers served faithfully under the leadership of Jahath and Obadiah, Levites of the Merarite
clan, and Zechariah and Meshullam, Levites of the
Kohathite clan. Other Levites, all of whom were
skilled musicians,
13 were put in charge of the labor-
ers of the various trades. Still others assisted as secretaries, officials, and gatekeepers.

Hilkiah Discovers God's Law

14 While they were bringing out the money collected
at the LORD's Temple, Hilkiah the priest found the
Book of the Law of the LORD that was written by
Moses.
15 Hilkiah said to Shaphan the court secretary,
"I have found the Book of the Law in the LORD's Temple!" Then Hilkiah gave the scroll to Shaphan.
16 Shaphan took the scroll to the king and reported, "Your officials are doing everything they
were assigned to do.
17 The money that was collected
at the Temple of the LORD has been turned over to
the supervisors and workmen."
18 Shaphan also told
the king, "Hilkiah the priest has given me a scroll."
So Shaphan read it to the king.
19 When the king heard what was written in the
Law, he tore his clothes in despair.
20 Then he gave
these orders to Hilkiah, Ahikam son of Shaphan,
Acbor son of Micaiah,* Shaphan the court secretary,

34:6 As in Syriac version. Hebrew reads *in their temples*, or *in their ruins.* The meaning of the Hebrew is uncertain. **34:20** As in parallel text at 2 Kgs 22:12; Hebrew reads *Abdon son of Micah.*

KING JAMES VERSION

21 Go, inquire of the LORD for me, and for them that are left in Israel and in Judah, concerning the words of the book that is found: for great *is* the wrath of the LORD that is poured out upon us, because our fathers have not kept the word of the LORD, to do after all that is written in this book.

22 And Hilkiah, and *they* that the king *had appointed,* went to Huldah the prophetess, the wife of Shallum the son of Tikvath, the son of Hasrah, keeper of the wardrobe; (now she dwelt in Jerusalem in the college:) and they spake to her to that *effect.*

23 And she answered them, Thus saith the LORD God of Israel, Tell ye the man that sent you to me,

24 Thus saith the LORD, Behold, I will bring evil upon this place, and upon the inhabitants thereof, *even* all the curses that are written in the book which they have read before the king of Judah:

25 Because they have forsaken me, and have burned incense unto other gods, that they might provoke me to anger with all the works of their hands; therefore my wrath shall be poured out upon this place, and shall not be quenched.

26 And as for the king of Judah, who sent you to inquire of the LORD, so shall ye say unto him, Thus saith the LORD God of Israel *concerning* the words which thou hast heard;

27 Because thine heart was tender, and thou didst humble thyself before God, when thou heardest his words against this place, and against the inhabitants thereof, and humbledst thyself before me, and didst rend thy clothes, and weep before me; I have even heard *thee* also, saith the LORD.

28 Behold, I will gather thee to thy fathers, and thou shalt be gathered to thy grave in peace, neither shall thine eyes see all the evil that I will bring upon this place, and upon the inhabitants of the same. So they brought the king word again.

29 Then the king sent and gathered together all the elders of Judah and Jerusalem.

30 And the king went up into the house of the LORD, and all the men of Judah, and the inhabitants of Jerusalem, and the priests, and the Levites, and all the people, great and small: and he read in their ears all the words of the book of the covenant that was found in the house of the LORD.

31 And the king stood in his place, and made a covenant before the LORD, to walk after the LORD, and to keep his commandments, and his testimonies, and his statutes, with all his heart, and with all his soul, to perform the words of the covenant which are written in this book.

32 And he caused all that were present in Jerusalem and Benjamin to stand *to it.* And the inhabitants of Jerusalem did according to the covenant of God, the God of their fathers.

33 And Josiah took away all the abominations out of all the countries that *pertained* to the children of

NEW LIVING TRANSLATION

and Asaiah the king's personal adviser: 21 "Go to the Temple and speak to the LORD for me and for all the remnant of Israel and Judah. Inquire about the words written in the scroll that has been found. For the LORD's great anger has been poured out on us because our ancestors have not obeyed the word of the LORD. We have not been doing everything this scroll says we must do."

22 So Hilkiah and the other men went to the New Quarter* of Jerusalem to consult with the prophet Huldah. She was the wife of Shallum son of Tikvah, son of Harhas,* the keeper of the Temple wardrobe.

23 She said to them, "The LORD, the God of Israel, has spoken! Go back and tell the man who sent you, 24 'This is what the LORD says: I am going to bring disaster on this city* and its people. All the curses written in the scroll that was read to the king of Judah will come true. 25 For my people have abandoned me and offered sacrifices to pagan gods, and I am very angry with them for everything they have done. My anger will be poured out on this place, and it will not be quenched.'

26 "But go to the king of Judah who sent you to seek the LORD and tell him: 'This is what the LORD, the God of Israel, says concerning the message you have just heard: 27 You were sorry and humbled yourself before God when you heard his words against this city and its people. You humbled yourself and tore your clothing in despair and wept before me in repentance. And I have indeed heard you, says the LORD. 28 So I will not send the promised disaster until after you have died and been buried in peace. You yourself will not see the disaster I am going to bring on this city and its people.'"

So they took her message back to the king.

Josiah's Religious Reforms

29 Then the king summoned all the elders of Judah and Jerusalem. 30 And the king went up to the Temple of the LORD with all the people of Judah and Jerusalem, along with the priests and the Levites—all the people from the greatest to the least. There the king read to them the entire Book of the Covenant that had been found in the LORD's Temple. 31 The king took his place of authority beside the pillar and renewed the covenant in the LORD's presence. He pledged to obey the LORD by keeping all his commands, laws, and decrees with all his heart and soul. He promised to obey all the terms of the covenant that were written in the scroll. 32 And he required everyone in Jerusalem and the people of Benjamin to make a similar pledge. The people of Jerusalem did so, renewing their covenant with God, the God of their ancestors.

33 So Josiah removed all detestable idols from the

34:22a Or *the Second Quarter,* a newer section of Jerusalem. Hebrew reads *the Mishneh.* **34:22b** As in parallel text at 2 Kgs 22:14; Hebrew reads *son of Tokhath, son of Hasrah.* **34:24** Hebrew *this place;* also in 34:27, 28.

KING JAMES VERSION

Israel, and made all that were present in Israel to serve, *even* to serve the LORD their God. *And* all his days they departed not from following the LORD, the God of their fathers.

35 1 Moreover Josiah kept a passover unto the LORD in Jerusalem: and they killed the passover on the fourteenth *day* of the first month.

2 And he set the priests in their charges, and encouraged them to the service of the house of the LORD,

3 And said unto the Levites that taught all Israel, which were holy unto the LORD, Put the holy ark in the house which Solomon the son of David king of Israel did build; *it shall* not *be* a burden upon *your* shoulders: serve now the LORD your God, and his people Israel,

4 And prepare *yourselves* by the houses of your fathers, after your courses, according to the writing of David king of Israel, and according to the writing of Solomon his son.

5 And stand in the holy *place* according to the divisions of the families of the fathers of your brethren the people, and *after* the division of the families of the Levites.

6 So kill the passover, and sanctify yourselves, and prepare your brethren, that *they* may do according to the word of the LORD by the hand of Moses.

7 And Josiah gave to the people, of the flock, lambs and kids, all for the passover offerings, for all that were present, to the number of thirty thousand, and three thousand bullocks: these *were* of the king's substance.

8 And his princes gave willingly unto the people, to the priests, and to the Levites: Hilkiah and Zechariah and Jehiel, rulers of the house of God, gave unto the priests for the passover offerings two thousand and six hundred *small cattle,* and three hundred oxen.

9 Conaniah also, and Shemaiah and Nethaneel, his brethren, and Hashabiah and Jeiel and Jozabad, chief of the Levites, gave unto the Levites for passover offerings five thousand *small cattle,* and five hundred oxen.

10 So the service was prepared, and the priests stood in their place, and the Levites in their courses, according to the king's commandment.

11 And they killed the passover, and the priests sprinkled *the blood* from their hands, and the Levites flayed *them.*

12 And they removed the burnt offerings, that they might give according to the divisions of the families of the people, to offer unto the LORD, as *it is* written in the book of Moses. And so *did they* with the oxen.

13 And they roasted the passover with fire according to the ordinance: but the *other* holy *offerings* sod they in pots, and in caldrons, and in pans, and divided *them* speedily among all the people.

NEW LIVING TRANSLATION

entire land of Israel and required everyone to worship the LORD their God. And throughout the rest of his lifetime, they did not turn away from the LORD, the God of their ancestors.

Josiah Celebrates Passover

35 Then Josiah announced that the Passover of the LORD would be celebrated in Jerusalem, and so the Passover lamb was slaughtered on the fourteenth day of the first month.* 2 Josiah also assigned the priests to their duties and encouraged them in their work at the Temple of the LORD. 3 He issued this order to the Levites, who were to teach all Israel and who had been set apart to serve the LORD: "Put the holy Ark in the Temple that was built by Solomon son of David, the king of Israel. You no longer need to carry it back and forth on your shoulders. Now spend your time serving the LORD your God and his people Israel. 4 Report for duty according to the family divisions of your ancestors, following the directions of King David of Israel and the directions of his son Solomon.

5 "Then stand in the sanctuary at the place appointed for your family division and help the families assigned to you as they bring their offerings to the Temple. 6 Slaughter the Passover lambs, purify yourselves, and prepare to help those who come. Follow all the directions that the LORD gave through Moses."

7 Then Josiah provided 30,000 lambs and young goats for the people's Passover offerings, along with 3,000 cattle, all from the king's own flocks and herds. 8 The king's officials also made willing contributions to the people, priests, and Levites. Hilkiah, Zechariah, and Jehiel, the administrators of God's Temple, gave the priests 2,600 lambs and young goats and 300 cattle as Passover offerings. 9 The Levite leaders—Conaniah and his brothers Shemaiah and Nethanel, as well as Hashabiah, Jeiel, and Jozabad—gave 5,000 lambs and young goats and 500 cattle to the Levites for their Passover offerings.

10 When everything was ready for the Passover celebration, the priests and the Levites took their places, organized by their divisions, as the king had commanded. 11 The Levites then slaughtered the Passover lambs and presented the blood to the priests, who sprinkled the blood on the altar while the Levites prepared the animals. 12 They divided the burnt offerings among the people by their family groups, so they could offer them to the LORD as prescribed in the Book of Moses. They did the same with the cattle. 13 Then they roasted the Passover lambs as prescribed; and they boiled the holy offerings in pots, kettles, and pans, and brought them out quickly so the people could eat them.

35:1 This day in the ancient Hebrew lunar calendar was April 5, 622 B.C.

KING JAMES VERSION

14 And afterward they made ready for themselves, and for the priests: because the priests the sons of Aaron *were busied* in offering of burnt offerings and the fat until night; therefore the Levites prepared for themselves, and for the priests the sons of Aaron.

15 And the singers the sons of Asaph *were* in their place, according to the commandment of David, and Asaph, and Heman, and Jeduthun the king's seer; and the porters *waited* at every gate; they might not depart from their service; for their brethren the Levites prepared for them.

16 So all the service of the LORD was prepared the same day, to keep the passover, and to offer burnt offerings upon the altar of the LORD, according to the commandment of king Josiah.

17 And the children of Israel that were present kept the passover at that time, and the feast of unleavened bread seven days.

18 And there was no passover like to that kept in Israel from the days of Samuel the prophet; neither did all the kings of Israel keep such a passover as Josiah kept, and the priests, and the Levites, and all Judah and Israel that were present, and the inhabitants of Jerusalem.

19 In the eighteenth year of the reign of Josiah was this passover kept.

20 After all this, when Josiah had prepared the temple, Necho king of Egypt came up to fight against Charchemish by Euphrates: and Josiah went out against him.

21 But he sent ambassadors to him, saying, What have I to do with thee, thou king of Judah? *I come* not against thee this day, but against the house wherewith I have war: for God commanded me to make haste: forbear thee from *meddling with* God, who *is* with me, that he destroy thee not.

22 Nevertheless Josiah would not turn his face from him, but disguised himself, that he might fight with him, and hearkened not unto the words of Necho from the mouth of God, and came to fight in the valley of Megiddo.

23 And the archers shot at king Josiah; and the king said to his servants, Have me away; for I am sore wounded.

24 His servants therefore took him out of that chariot, and put him in the second chariot that he had; and they brought him to Jerusalem, and he died, and was buried in *one of* the sepulchres of his fathers. And all Judah and Jerusalem mourned for Josiah.

25 And Jeremiah lamented for Josiah: and all the singing men and the singing women spake of Josiah in their lamentations to this day, and made them an ordinance in Israel: and, behold, they *are* written in the lamentations.

26 Now the rest of the acts of Josiah, and his goodness, according to *that which was* written in the law of the LORD,

NEW LIVING TRANSLATION

14 Afterward the Levites prepared Passover offerings for themselves and for the priests—the descendants of Aaron—because the priests had been busy from morning till night offering the burnt offerings and the fat portions. The Levites took responsibility for all these preparations.

15 The musicians, descendants of Asaph, were in their assigned places, following the commands that had been given by David, Asaph, Heman, and Jeduthun, the king's seer. The gatekeepers guarded the gates and did not need to leave their posts of duty, for their Passover offerings were prepared for them by their fellow Levites.

16 The entire ceremony for the LORD's Passover was completed that day. All the burnt offerings were sacrificed on the altar of the LORD, as King Josiah had commanded. 17 All the Israelites present in Jerusalem celebrated Passover and the Festival of Unleavened Bread for seven days. 18 Never since the time of the prophet Samuel had there been such a Passover. None of the kings of Israel had ever kept a Passover as Josiah did, involving all the priests and Levites, all the people of Jerusalem, and people from all over Judah and Israel. 19 This Passover celebration took place in the eighteenth year of Josiah's reign.

Josiah Dies in Battle

20 After Josiah had finished restoring the Temple, King Neco of Egypt led his army up from Egypt to do battle at Carchemish on the Euphrates River, and Josiah and his army marched out to fight him.* 21 But King Neco sent messengers to Josiah with this message:

> "What do you want with me, king of Judah? I have
> no quarrel with you today! I am on my way to
> fight another nation, and God has told me to
> hurry! Do not interfere with God, who is with me,
> or he will destroy you."

22 But Josiah refused to listen to Neco, to whom God had indeed spoken, and he would not turn back. Instead, he disguised himself and led his army into battle on the plain of Megiddo. 23 But the enemy archers hit King Josiah with their arrows and wounded him. He cried out to his men, "Take me from the battle, for I am badly wounded!"

24 So they lifted Josiah out of his chariot and placed him in another chariot. Then they brought him back to Jerusalem, where he died. He was buried there in the royal cemetery. And all Judah and Jerusalem mourned for him. 25 The prophet Jeremiah composed funeral songs for Josiah, and to this day choirs still sing these sad songs about his death. These songs of sorrow have become a tradition and are recorded in *The Book of Laments*.

26 The rest of the events of Josiah's reign and his acts of devotion (carried out according to what was

35:20 Or *Josiah went out to meet him.*

KING JAMES VERSION

27And his deeds, first and last, behold, they *are*
written in the book of the kings of Israel and Judah.

36 1Then the people of the land took Jehoahaz
the son of Josiah, and made him king in his
father's stead in Jerusalem.
2Jehoahaz *was* twenty and three years old when
he began to reign, and he reigned three months in
Jerusalem.
3And the king of Egypt put him down at Jerusalem,
and condemned the land in an hundred talents of
silver and a talent of gold.
4And the king of Egypt made Eliakim his brother
king over Judah and Jerusalem, and turned his name
to Jehoiakim. And Necho took Jehoahaz his brother,
and carried him to Egypt.
5Jehoiakim *was* twenty and five years old when he
began to reign, and he reigned eleven years in Jerusalem: and he did *that which was* evil in the sight of
the LORD his God.
6Against him came up Nebuchadnezzar king of
Babylon, and bound him in fetters, to carry him to
Babylon.
7Nebuchadnezzar also carried of the vessels of
the house of the LORD to Babylon, and put them in
his temple at Babylon.
8Now the rest of the acts of Jehoiakim, and his
abominations which he did, and that which was
found in him, behold, they *are* written in the book of
the kings of Israel and Judah: and Jehoiachin his son
reigned in his stead.
9Jehoiachin *was* eight years old when he began to
reign, and he reigned three months and ten days in
Jerusalem: and he did *that which was* evil in the
sight of the LORD.
10And when the year was expired, king Nebuchadnezzar sent, and brought him to Babylon, with the
goodly vessels of the house of the LORD, and made
Zedekiah his brother king over Judah and Jerusalem.
11Zedekiah *was* one and twenty years old when
he began to reign, and reigned eleven years in Jerusalem.
12And he did *that which was* evil in the sight of
the LORD his God, *and* humbled not himself before
Jeremiah the prophet *speaking* from the mouth of
the LORD.
13And he also rebelled against king Nebuchadnezzar, who had made him swear by God: but he stiffened

NEW LIVING TRANSLATION

written in the Law of the LORD), 27from beginning to
end—all are recorded in *The Book of the Kings of
Israel and Judah.*

Jehoahaz Rules in Judah

36 Then the people of the land took Josiah's
son Jehoahaz and made him the next king in
Jerusalem.
2Jehoahaz* was twenty-three years old when he became king, and he reigned in Jerusalem three months.
3Then he was deposed by the king of Egypt, who
demanded that Judah pay 7,500 pounds of silver and
75 pounds of gold* as tribute.

Jehoiakim Rules in Judah

4The king of Egypt then installed Eliakim, the
brother of Jehoahaz, as the next king of Judah and Jerusalem, and he changed Eliakim's name to Jehoiakim. Then Neco took Jehoahaz to Egypt as a prisoner.
5Jehoiakim was twenty-five years old when he became king, and he reigned in Jerusalem eleven years.
He did what was evil in the sight of the LORD his God.
6Then King Nebuchadnezzar of Babylon came to
Jerusalem and captured it, and he bound Jehoiakim
in bronze chains and led him away to Babylon. 7Neb-
uchadnezzar also took some of the treasures from
the Temple of the LORD, and he placed them in his
palace* in Babylon.
8The rest of the events in Jehoiakim's reign, including all the evil things he did and everything
found against him, are recorded in *The Book of the
Kings of Israel and Judah.* Then his son Jehoiachin
became the next king.

Jehoiachin Rules in Judah

9Jehoiachin was eighteen* years old when he became king, and he reigned in Jerusalem three
months and ten days. Jehoiachin did what was evil in
the LORD's sight.
10In the spring of the year* King Nebuchadnezzar
took Jehoiachin to Babylon. Many treasures from
the Temple of the LORD were also taken to Babylon
at that time. And Nebuchadnezzar installed Jehoiachin's uncle,* Zedekiah, as the next king in Judah and
Jerusalem.

Zedekiah Rules in Judah

11Zedekiah was twenty-one years old when he became
king, and he reigned in Jerusalem eleven years. 12He
did what was evil in the sight of the LORD his God, and
he refused to humble himself when the prophet Jeremiah spoke to him directly from the LORD. 13He also
rebelled against King Nebuchadnezzar, even though

36:2 Hebrew *Joahaz,* a variant spelling of Jehoahaz; also in 36:4.
36:3 Hebrew *100 talents* [3,400 kilograms] *of silver and 1 talent* [34 kilograms] *of gold.* **36:7** Or *temple.* **36:9** As in one Hebrew manuscript, some Greek manuscripts, and Syriac version (see also 2 Kgs 24:8); most Hebrew manuscripts read *eight.* **36:10a** Hebrew *At the turn of the year.* The first day of this year in the ancient Hebrew lunar calendar was April 13, 597 B.C. **36:10b** As in parallel text at 2 Kgs 24:17; Hebrew reads *brother,* or *relative.*

KING JAMES VERSION

his neck, and hardened his heart from turning unto
the LORD God of Israel.
14 Moreover all the chief of the priests, and the
people, transgressed very much after all the abominations of the heathen; and polluted the house of the
LORD which he had hallowed in Jerusalem.
15 And the LORD God of their fathers sent to them
by his messengers, rising up betimes, and sending;
because he had compassion on his people, and on
his dwelling place:
16 But they mocked the messengers of God, and
despised his words, and misused his prophets, until
the wrath of the LORD arose against his people, till
there was no remedy.

17 Therefore he brought upon them the king of the
Chaldees, who slew their young men with the sword
in the house of their sanctuary, and had no compassion upon young man or maiden, old man, or him
that stooped for age: he gave *them* all into his hand.
18 And all the vessels of the house of God, great and
small, and the treasures of the house of the LORD, and
the treasures of the king, and of his princes; all *these*
he brought to Babylon.
19 And they burnt the house of God, and brake
down the wall of Jerusalem, and burnt all the palaces
thereof with fire, and destroyed all the goodly vessels
thereof.
20 And them that had escaped from the sword carried he away to Babylon; where they were servants to
him and his sons until the reign of the kingdom of
Persia:
21 To fulfil the word of the LORD by the mouth of
Jeremiah, until the land had enjoyed her sabbaths:
for as long as she lay desolate she kept sabbath, to
fulfil threescore and ten years.

22 Now in the first year of Cyrus king of Persia, that
the word of the LORD *spoken* by the mouth of Jeremiah might be accomplished, the LORD stirred up the
spirit of Cyrus king of Persia, that he made a proclamation throughout all his kingdom, and *put it* also in
writing, saying,
23 Thus saith Cyrus king of Persia, All the kingdoms of the earth hath the LORD God of heaven given
me; and he hath charged me to build him an house in
Jerusalem, which *is* in Judah. Who *is there* among
you of all his people? The LORD his God *be* with him,
and let him go up.

NEW LIVING TRANSLATION

he had taken an oath of loyalty in God's name. Zedekiah was a hard and stubborn man, refusing to turn to
the LORD, the God of Israel.
14 Likewise, all the leaders of the priests and the
people became more and more unfaithful. They followed all the pagan practices of the surrounding
nations, desecrating the Temple of the LORD that had
been consecrated in Jerusalem.
15 The LORD, the God of their ancestors, repeatedly
sent his prophets to warn them, for he had compassion on his people and his Temple. 16 But the people
mocked these messengers of God and despised their
words. They scoffed at the prophets until the LORD's
anger could no longer be restrained and nothing
could be done.

The Fall of Jerusalem

17 So the LORD brought the king of Babylon against
them. The Babylonians* killed Judah's young men,
even chasing after them into the Temple. They had
no pity on the people, killing both young men and
young women, the old and the infirm. God handed
all of them over to Nebuchadnezzar. 18 The king took
home to Babylon all the articles, large and small,
used in the Temple of God, and the treasures from
both the LORD's Temple and from the palace of the
king and his officials. 19 Then his army burned the
Temple of God, tore down the walls of Jerusalem,
burned all the palaces, and completely destroyed
everything of value.* 20 The few who survived were
taken as exiles to Babylon, and they became servants
to the king and his sons until the kingdom of Persia
came to power.
21 So the message of the LORD spoken through
Jeremiah was fulfilled. The land finally enjoyed its
Sabbath rest, lying desolate until the seventy years
were fulfilled, just as the prophet had said.

Cyrus Allows the Exiles to Return

22 In the first year of King Cyrus of Persia,* the LORD
fulfilled the prophecy he had given through Jeremiah.* He stirred the heart of Cyrus to put this proclamation in writing and to send it throughout his
kingdom:
23 "This is what King Cyrus of Persia says:

"The LORD, the God of heaven, has given me all
the kingdoms of the earth. He has appointed me
to build him a Temple at Jerusalem, which is in
Judah. Any of you who are the LORD's people may
go there for this task. And may the LORD your God
be with you!"

36:17 Or *Chaldeans.* **36:19** Or *destroyed all the valuable articles from the Temple.* **36:22a** The first year of Cyrus's reign over Babylon was 538 B.C. **36:22b** See Jer 25:11-12; 29:10.

Ezra

KING JAMES VERSION

1 1Now in the first year of Cyrus king of Persia,
that the word of the LORD by the mouth of Jeremiah might be fulfilled, the LORD stirred up the spirit
of Cyrus king of Persia, that he made a proclamation
throughout all his kingdom, and *put it* also in writing, saying,
2Thus saith Cyrus king of Persia, The LORD God of
heaven hath given me all the kingdoms of the earth;
and he hath charged me to build him an house at
Jerusalem, which *is* in Judah.
3Who *is there* among you of all his people? his
God be with him, and let him go up to Jerusalem,
which *is* in Judah, and build the house of the LORD
God of Israel, (he *is* the God,) which *is* in Jerusalem.
4And whosoever remaineth in any place where he
sojourneth, let the men of his place help him with
silver, and with gold, and with goods, and with
beasts, beside the freewill offering for the house of
God that *is* in Jerusalem.
5Then rose up the chief of the fathers of Judah
and Benjamin, and the priests, and the Levites, with
all *them* whose spirit God had raised, to go up to
build the house of the LORD which *is* in Jerusalem.
6And all they that *were* about them strengthened
their hands with vessels of silver, with gold, with
goods, and with beasts, and with precious things,
beside all *that* was willingly offered.
7Also Cyrus the king brought forth the vessels of
the house of the LORD, which Nebuchadnezzar had
brought forth out of Jerusalem, and had put them in
the house of his gods;
8Even those did Cyrus king of Persia bring forth by
the hand of Mithredath the treasurer, and numbered
them unto Sheshbazzar, the prince of Judah.
9And this *is* the number of them: thirty chargers of
gold, a thousand chargers of silver, nine and twenty
knives,
10Thirty basins of gold, silver basins of a second
sort four hundred and ten, *and* other vessels a
thousand.

NEW LIVING TRANSLATION

Cyrus Allows the Exiles to Return

1 In the first year of King Cyrus of Persia,* the
LORD fulfilled the prophecy he had given
through Jeremiah.* He stirred the heart of Cyrus to
put this proclamation in writing and to send it
throughout his kingdom:

2"This is what King Cyrus of Persia says:

"The LORD, the God of heaven, has given me all
the kingdoms of the earth. He has appointed me
to build him a Temple at Jerusalem, which is in
Judah. 3Any of you who are his people may go to
Jerusalem in Judah to rebuild this Temple of the
LORD, the God of Israel, who lives in Jerusalem.
And may your God be with you! 4Wherever this
Jewish remnant is found, let their neighbors
contribute toward their expenses by giving them
silver and gold, supplies for the journey, and
livestock, as well as a voluntary offering for the
Temple of God in Jerusalem."

5Then God stirred the hearts of the priests and Levites and the leaders of the tribes of Judah and Benjamin to go to Jerusalem to rebuild the Temple of the
LORD. 6And all their neighbors assisted by giving
them articles of silver and gold, supplies for the journey, and livestock. They gave them many valuable
gifts in addition to all the voluntary offerings.
7King Cyrus himself brought out the articles that
King Nebuchadnezzar had taken from the LORD's
Temple in Jerusalem and had placed in the temple of
his own gods. 8Cyrus directed Mithredath, the treasurer of Persia, to count these items and present them
to Sheshbazzar, the leader of the exiles returning to
Judah.* 9This is a list of the items that were returned:

	gold basins	30
	silver basins	1,000
	silver incense burners*	29
10	gold bowls	30
	silver bowls	410
	other items	1,000

1:1a The first year of Cyrus's reign over Babylon was 538 B.C. **1:1b** See Jer 25:11-12; 29:10. **1:8** Hebrew *Sheshbazzar, the prince of Judah.* **1:9** The meaning of this Hebrew word is uncertain.

KING JAMES VERSION

11 All the vessels of gold and of silver *were* five
thousand and four hundred. All *these* did Sheshbazzar bring up with *them of* the captivity that were
brought up from Babylon unto Jerusalem.

2 1 Now these *are* the children of the province
that went up out of the captivity, of those which
had been carried away, whom Nebuchadnezzar the
king of Babylon had carried away unto Babylon, and
came again unto Jerusalem and Judah, every one
unto his city;
2 Which came with Zerubbabel: Jeshua, Nehemiah, Seraiah, Reelaiah, Mordecai, Bilshan, Mizpar,
Bigvai, Rehum, Baanah. The number of the men of
the people of Israel:
3 The children of Parosh, two thousand an hundred seventy and two.
4 The children of Shephatiah, three hundred seventy and two.
5 The children of Arah, seven hundred seventy and
five.
6 The children of Pahath-moab, of the children
of Jeshua *and* Joab, two thousand eight hundred
and twelve.
7 The children of Elam, a thousand two hundred
fifty and four.
8 The children of Zattu, nine hundred forty and
five.
9 The children of Zaccai, seven hundred and
threescore.
10 The children of Bani, six hundred forty and two.
11 The children of Bebai, six hundred twenty and
three.
12 The children of Azgad, a thousand two hundred
twenty and two.
13 The children of Adonikam, six hundred sixty
and six.
14 The children of Bigvai, two thousand fifty and
six.
15 The children of Adin, four hundred fifty and
four.
16 The children of Ater of Hezekiah, ninety and
eight.
17 The children of Bezai, three hundred twenty and
three.
18 The children of Jorah, an hundred and twelve.
19 The children of Hashum, two hundred twenty
and three.
20 The children of Gibbar, ninety and five.
21 The children of Bethlehem, an hundred twenty
and three.
22 The men of Netophah, fifty and six.
23 The men of Anathoth, an hundred twenty and
eight.
24 The children of Azmaveth, forty and two.
25 The children of Kirjath-arim, Chephirah, and
Beeroth, seven hundred and forty and three.

NEW LIVING TRANSLATION

11 In all, there were 5,400 articles of gold and silver.
Sheshbazzar brought all of these along when the
exiles went from Babylon to Jerusalem.

Exiles Who Returned with Zerubbabel

2 Here is the list of the Jewish exiles of the provinces who returned from their captivity. King
Nebuchadnezzar had deported them to Babylon, but
now they returned to Jerusalem and the other towns
in Judah where they originally lived. 2 Their leaders
were Zerubbabel, Jeshua, Nehemiah, Seraiah, Reelaiah, Mordecai, Bilshan, Mispar, Bigvai, Rehum, and
Baanah.

This is the number of the men of Israel who returned
from exile:

3 The family of Parosh 2,172
4 The family of Shephatiah 372
5 The family of Arah 775
6 The family of Pahath-moab (descendants
of Jeshua and Joab) 2,812
7 The family of Elam 1,254
8 The family of Zattu 945
9 The family of Zaccai 760
10 The family of Bani 642
11 The family of Bebai 623
12 The family of Azgad 1,222
13 The family of Adonikam 666
14 The family of Bigvai 2,056
15 The family of Adin 454
16 The family of Ater (descendants of Hezekiah) . . . 98
17 The family of Bezai 323
18 The family of Jorah 112
19 The family of Hashum 223
20 The family of Gibbar 95
21 The people of Bethlehem 123
22 The people of Netophah 56
23 The people of Anathoth 128
24 The people of Beth-azmaveth* 42
25 The people of Kiriath-jearim,* Kephirah,
and Beeroth 743

2:24 As in parallel text at Neh 7:28; Hebrew reads *Azmaveth*. **2:25** As in some Hebrew manuscripts and Greek version (see also Neh 7:29); Hebrew reads *Kiriath-arim*.

KING JAMES VERSION

[26]The children of Ramah and Gaba, six hundred
twenty and one.
[27]The men of Michmas, an hundred twenty and
two.
[28]The men of Bethel and Ai, two hundred twenty
and three.
[29]The children of Nebo, fifty and two.
[30]The children of Magbish, an hundred fifty
and six.
[31]The children of the other Elam, a thousand two
hundred fifty and four.
[32]The children of Harim, three hundred and
twenty.
[33]The children of Lod, Hadid, and Ono, seven hundred twenty and five.
[34]The children of Jericho, three hundred forty and
five.
[35]The children of Senaah, three thousand and six
hundred and thirty.
[36]The priests: the children of Jedaiah, of the house
of Jeshua, nine hundred seventy and three.
[37]The children of Immer, a thousand fifty and two.
[38]The children of Pashur, a thousand two hundred
forty and seven.
[39]The children of Harim, a thousand and seventeen.
[40]The Levites: the children of Jeshua and Kadmiel,
of the children of Hodaviah, seventy and four.
[41]The singers: the children of Asaph, an hundred
twenty and eight.
[42]The children of the porters: the children of
Shallum, the children of Ater, the children of Talmon, the children of Akkub, the children of Hatita,
the children of Shobai, *in* all an hundred thirty and
nine.
[43]The Nethinims: the children of Ziha, the children of Hasupha, the children of Tabbaoth,
[44]The children of Keros, the children of Siaha, the
children of Padon,
[45]The children of Lebanah, the children of Hagabah, the children of Akkub,
[46]The children of Hagab, the children of Shalmai,
the children of Hanan,
[47]The children of Giddel, the children of Gahar,
the children of Reaiah,
[48]The children of Rezin, the children of Nekoda,
the children of Gazzam,
[49]The children of Uzza, the children of Paseah, the
children of Besai,
[50]The children of Asnah, the children of Mehu-
nim, the children of Nephusim,
[51]The children of Bakbuk, the children of Hakupha, the children of Harhur,
[52]The children of Bazluth, the children of Mehida,
the children of Harsha,
[53]The children of Barkos, the children of Sisera,
the children of Thamah,
[54]The children of Neziah, the children of Hatipha.

NEW LIVING TRANSLATION

[26] The people of Ramah and Geba 621
[27] The people of Micmash 122
[28] The people of Bethel and Ai 223
[29] The citizens of Nebo 52
[30] The citizens of Magbish 156
[31] The citizens of West Elam* 1,254
[32] The citizens of Harim 320
[33] The citizens of Lod, Hadid, and Ono 725
[34] The citizens of Jericho 345
[35] The citizens of Senaah 3,630

[36]These are the priests who returned from exile:
The family of Jedaiah (through the line
of Jeshua) 973
[37] The family of Immer 1,052
[38] The family of Pashhur 1,247
[39] The family of Harim 1,017

[40]These are the Levites who returned from exile:
The families of Jeshua and Kadmiel (descendants
of Hodaviah) 74
[41] The singers of the family of Asaph 128
[42] The gatekeepers of the families of Shallum, Ater,
Talmon, Akkub, Hatita, and Shobai 139

[43]The descendants of the following Temple servants
returned from exile:
Ziha, Hasupha, Tabbaoth,
[44] Keros, Siaha, Padon,
[45] Lebanah, Hagabah, Akkub,
[46] Hagab, Shalmai,* Hanan,
[47] Giddel, Gahar, Reaiah,
[48] Rezin, Nekoda, Gazzam,
[49] Uzza, Paseah, Besai,
[50] Asnah, Meunim, Nephusim,
[51] Bakbuk, Hakupha, Harhur,
[52] Bazluth, Mehida, Harsha,
[53] Barkos, Sisera, Temah,
[54] Neziah, and Hatipha.

2:31 Or *of the other Elam.* **2:46** As in an alternate reading of the Masoretic Text (see also Neh 7:48); the other alternate reads *Shamlai.*

KING JAMES VERSION

55 The children of Solomon's servants: the children of Sotai, the children of Sophereth, the children of Peruda,
56 The children of Jaalah, the children of Darkon, the children of Giddel,
57 The children of Shephatiah, the children of Hattil, the children of Pochereth of Zebaim, the children of Ami.
58 All the Nethinims, and the children of Solomon's servants, *were* three hundred ninety and two.
59 And these *were* they which went up from Tel-melah, Tel-harsa, Cherub, Addan, *and* Immer: but they could not shew their father's house, and their seed, whether they *were* of Israel:
60 The children of Delaiah, the children of Tobiah, the children of Nekoda, six hundred fifty and two.
61 And of the children of the priests: the children of Habaiah, the children of Koz, the children of Barzillai; which took a wife of the daughters of Barzillai the Gileadite, and was called after their name:
62 These sought their register *among* those that were reckoned by genealogy, but they were not found: therefore were they, as polluted, put from the priesthood.
63 And the Tirshatha said unto them, that they should not eat of the most holy things, till there stood up a priest with Urim and with Thummim.
64 The whole congregation together *was* forty and two thousand three hundred *and* threescore,
65 Beside their servants and their maids, of whom *there were* seven thousand three hundred thirty and seven: and *there were* among them two hundred singing men and singing women.
66 Their horses *were* seven hundred thirty and six; their mules, two hundred forty and five;
67 Their camels, four hundred thirty and five; *their* asses, six thousand seven hundred and twenty.
68 And *some* of the chief of the fathers, when they came to the house of the LORD which *is* at Jerusalem, offered freely for the house of God to set it up in his place:
69 They gave after their ability unto the treasure of the work threescore and one thousand drams of gold, and five thousand pound of silver, and one hundred priests' garments.
70 So the priests, and the Levites, and *some* of the people, and the singers, and the porters, and the Nethinims, dwelt in their cities, and all Israel in their cities.

3 1 And when the seventh month was come, and the children of Israel *were* in the cities, the people gathered themselves together as one man to Jerusalem.
2 Then stood up Jeshua the son of Jozadak, and his brethren the priests, and Zerubbabel the son of

NEW LIVING TRANSLATION

55 The descendants of these servants of King Solomon returned from exile:
Sotai, Hassophereth, Peruda,
56 Jaalah, Darkon, Giddel,
57 Shephatiah, Hattil, Pokereth-hazzebaim, and Ami.
58 In all, the Temple servants and the descendants of Solomon's servants numbered 392.

59 Another group returned at this time from the towns of Tel-melah, Tel-harsha, Kerub, Addan, and Immer. However, they could not prove that they or their families were descendants of Israel.
60 This group included the families of Delaiah, Tobiah, and Nekoda—a total of 652 people.
61 Three families of priests—Hobaiah, Hakkoz, and Barzillai—also returned. (This Barzillai had married a woman who was a descendant of Barzillai of Gilead, and he had taken her family name.)
62 They searched for their names in the genealogical records, but they were not found, so they were disqualified from serving as priests.
63 The governor told them not to eat the priests' share of food from the sacrifices until a priest could consult the LORD about the matter by using the Urim and Thummim—the sacred lots.
64 So a total of 42,360 people returned to Judah,
65 in addition to 7,337 servants and 200 singers, both men and women.
66 They took with them 736 horses, 245 mules,
67 435 camels, and 6,720 donkeys.
68 When they arrived at the Temple of the LORD in Jerusalem, some of the family leaders made voluntary offerings toward the rebuilding of God's Temple on its original site,
69 and each leader gave as much as he could. The total of their gifts came to 61,000 gold coins,* 6,250 pounds* of silver, and 100 robes for the priests.
70 So the priests, the Levites, the singers, the gatekeepers, the Temple servants, and some of the common people settled in villages near Jerusalem. The rest of the people returned to their own towns throughout Israel.

The Altar Is Rebuilt

3 In early autumn,* when the Israelites had settled in their towns, all the people assembled in Jerusalem with a unified purpose.
2 Then Jeshua son of Jehozadak* joined his fellow priests and Zerubbabel

2:69a Hebrew *61,000 darics of gold,* about 1,100 pounds or 500 kilograms in weight. **2:69b** Hebrew *5,000 minas* [3,000 kilograms]. **3:1** Hebrew *In the seventh month.* The year is not specified, so it may have been during Cyrus's first year (538 B.C.) or second year (537 B.C.). The seventh month of the ancient Hebrew lunar calendar occurred within the months of September/October 538 B.C. and October/November 537 B.C. **3:2** Hebrew *Jozadak,* a variant spelling of Jehozadak; also in 3:8.

KING JAMES VERSION

Shealtiel, and his brethren, and builded the altar of the God of Israel, to offer burnt offerings thereon, as *it is* written in the law of Moses the man of God.

3And they set the altar upon his bases; for fear *was* upon them because of the people of those countries: and they offered burnt offerings thereon unto the LORD, *even* burnt offerings morning and evening.

4They kept also the feast of tabernacles, as *it is* written, and *offered* the daily burnt offerings by number, according to the custom, as the duty of every day required;

5And afterward *offered* the continual burnt offering, both of the new moons, and of all the set feasts of the LORD that were consecrated, and of every one that willingly offered a freewill offering unto the LORD.

6From the first day of the seventh month began they to offer burnt offerings unto the LORD. But the foundation of the temple of the LORD was not *yet* laid.

7They gave money also unto the masons, and to the carpenters; and meat, and drink, and oil, unto them of Zidon, and to them of Tyre, to bring cedar trees from Lebanon to the sea of Joppa, according to the grant that they had of Cyrus king of Persia.

8Now in the second year of their coming unto the house of God at Jerusalem, in the second month, began Zerubbabel the son of Shealtiel, and Jeshua the son of Jozadak, and the remnant of their brethren the priests and the Levites, and all they that were come out of the captivity unto Jerusalem; and appointed the Levites, from twenty years old and upward, to set forward the work of the house of the LORD.

9Then stood Jeshua *with* his sons and his brethren, Kadmiel and his sons, the sons of Judah, together, to set forward the workmen in the house of God: the sons of Henadad, *with* their sons and their brethren the Levites.

10And when the builders laid the foundation of the temple of the LORD, they set the priests in their apparel with trumpets, and the Levites the sons of Asaph with cymbals, to praise the LORD, after the ordinance of David king of Israel.

11And they sang together by course in praising and giving thanks unto the LORD; because *he is* good, for his mercy *endureth* for ever toward Israel. And all the people shouted with a great shout, when they praised the LORD, because the foundation of the house of the LORD was laid.

NEW LIVING TRANSLATION

son of Shealtiel with his family in rebuilding the altar of the God of Israel. They wanted to sacrifice burnt offerings on it, as instructed in the Law of Moses, the man of God. 3Even though the people were afraid of the local residents, they rebuilt the altar at its old site. Then they began to sacrifice burnt offerings on the altar to the LORD each morning and evening.

4They celebrated the Festival of Shelters as prescribed in the Law, sacrificing the number of burnt offerings specified for each day of the festival. 5They also offered the regular burnt offerings and the offerings required for the new moon celebrations and the annual festivals as prescribed by the LORD. The people also gave voluntary offerings to the LORD. 6Fifteen days before the Festival of Shelters began,* the priests had begun to sacrifice burnt offerings to the LORD. This was even before they had started to lay the foundation of the LORD's Temple.

The People Begin to Rebuild the Temple

7Then the people hired masons and carpenters and bought cedar logs from the people of Tyre and Sidon, paying them with food, wine, and olive oil. The logs were brought down from the Lebanon mountains and floated along the coast of the Mediterranean Sea* to Joppa, for King Cyrus had given permission for this.

8The construction of the Temple of God began in midspring,* during the second year after they arrived in Jerusalem. The work force was made up of everyone who had returned from exile, including Zerubbabel son of Shealtiel, Jeshua son of Jehozadak and his fellow priests, and all the Levites. The Levites who were twenty years old or older were put in charge of rebuilding the LORD's Temple. 9The workers at the Temple of God were supervised by Jeshua with his sons and relatives, and Kadmiel and his sons, all descendants of Hodaviah.* They were helped in this task by the Levites of the family of Henadad.

10When the builders completed the foundation of the LORD's Temple, the priests put on their robes and took their places to blow their trumpets. And the Levites, descendants of Asaph, clashed their cymbals to praise the LORD, just as King David had prescribed. 11With praise and thanks, they sang this song to the LORD:

"He is so good!
His faithful love for Israel endures forever!"

Then all the people gave a great shout, praising the LORD because the foundation of the LORD's Temple had been laid.

3:6 Hebrew *On the first day of the seventh month.* This day in the ancient Hebrew lunar calendar occurred in September or October. The Festival of Shelters began on the fifteenth day of the seventh month. **3:7** Hebrew *the sea.* **3:8** Hebrew *in the second month.* This month in the ancient Hebrew lunar calendar occurred within the months of April and May 536 B.C. **3:9** Hebrew *sons of Judah* (i.e., *bene Yehudah*). *Bene* might also be read here as the proper name Binnui; *Yehudah* is probably another name for Hodaviah. Compare 2:40; Neh 7:43; 1 Esdras 5:58.

KING JAMES VERSION

12 But many of the priests and Levites and chief of the fathers, *who were* ancient men, that had seen the first house, when the foundation of this house was laid before their eyes, wept with a loud voice; and many shouted aloud for joy:

13 So that the people could not discern the noise of the shout of joy from the noise of the weeping of the people: for the people shouted with a loud shout, and the noise was heard afar off.

4 1 Now when the adversaries of Judah and Benjamin heard that the children of the captivity builded the temple unto the LORD God of Israel;

2 Then they came to Zerubbabel, and to the chief of the fathers, and said unto them, Let us build with you: for we seek your God, as ye *do;* and we do sacrifice unto him since the days of Esar-haddon king of Assur, which brought us up hither.

3 But Zerubbabel, and Jeshua, and the rest of the chief of the fathers of Israel, said unto them, Ye have nothing to do with us to build an house unto our God; but we ourselves together will build unto the LORD God of Israel, as king Cyrus the king of Persia hath commanded us.

4 Then the people of the land weakened the hands of the people of Judah, and troubled them in building,

5 And hired counsellors against them, to frustrate their purpose, all the days of Cyrus king of Persia, even until the reign of Darius king of Persia.

6 And in the reign of Ahasuerus, in the beginning of his reign, wrote they *unto him* an accusation against the inhabitants of Judah and Jerusalem.

7 And in the days of Artaxerxes wrote Bishlam, Mithredath, Tabeel, and the rest of their companions, unto Artaxerxes king of Persia; and the writing of the letter *was* written in the Syrian tongue, and interpreted in the Syrian tongue.

8 Rehum the chancellor and Shimshai the scribe wrote a letter against Jerusalem to Artaxerxes the king in this sort:

9 Then *wrote* Rehum the chancellor, and Shimshai the scribe, and the rest of their companions; the Dinaites, the Apharsathchites, the Tarpelites, the Apharsites, the Archevites, the Babylonians, the Susanchites, the Dehavites, *and* the Elamites,

10 And the rest of the nations whom the great and noble Asnapper brought over, and set in the cities of Samaria, and the rest *that are* on this side the river, and at such a time.

11 This *is* the copy of the letter that they sent unto him, *even* unto Artaxerxes the king; Thy servants the men on this side the river, and at such a time.

12 Be it known unto the king, that the Jews which came up from thee to us are come unto Jerusalem, building the rebellious and the bad city, and have set up the walls *thereof,* and joined the foundations.

NEW LIVING TRANSLATION

12 But many of the older priests, Levites, and other leaders who had seen the first Temple wept aloud when they saw the new Temple's foundation. The others, however, were shouting for joy. 13 The joyful shouting and weeping mingled together in a loud noise that could be heard far in the distance.

Enemies Oppose the Rebuilding

4 The enemies of Judah and Benjamin heard that the exiles were rebuilding a Temple to the LORD, the God of Israel. 2 So they approached Zerubbabel and the other leaders and said, "Let us build with you, for we worship your God just as you do. We have sacrificed to him ever since King Esarhaddon of Assyria brought us here."

3 But Zerubbabel, Jeshua, and the other leaders of Israel replied, "You may have no part in this work. We alone will build the Temple for the LORD, the God of Israel, just as King Cyrus of Persia commanded us."

4 Then the local residents tried to discourage and frighten the people of Judah to keep them from their work. 5 They bribed agents to work against them and to frustrate their plans. This went on during the entire reign of King Cyrus of Persia and lasted until King Darius of Persia took the throne.*

Later Opposition under Xerxes and Artaxerxes

6 Years later when Xerxes* began his reign, the enemies of Judah wrote a letter of accusation against the people of Judah and Jerusalem.

7 Even later, during the reign of King Artaxerxes of Persia,* the enemies of Judah, led by Bishlam, Mithredath, and Tabeel, sent a letter to Artaxerxes in the Aramaic language, and it was translated for the king.

8 *Rehum the governor and Shimshai the court secretary wrote the letter, telling King Artaxerxes about the situation in Jerusalem. 9 They greeted the king for all their colleagues—the judges and local leaders, the people of Tarpel, the Persians, the Babylonians, and the people of Erech and Susa (that is, Elam). 10 They also sent greetings from the rest of the people whom the great and noble Ashurbanipal* had deported and relocated in Samaria and throughout the neighboring lands of the province west of the Euphrates River.* 11 This is a copy of their letter:

"To King Artaxerxes, from your loyal subjects in the province west of the Euphrates River.

12 "The king should know that the Jews who came here to Jerusalem from Babylon are rebuilding this rebellious and evil city. They have already laid the foundation and will soon finish

4:5 Darius reigned 521–486 B.C. **4:6** Hebrew *Ahasuerus,* another name for Xerxes. He reigned 486–465 B.C. **4:7** Artaxerxes reigned 465–424 B.C. **4:8** The original text of 4:8–6:18 is in Aramaic. **4:10a** Aramaic *Osnappar,* another name for Ashurbanipal. **4:10b** Aramaic *the province beyond the river;* also in 4:11, 16, 17, 20.

KING JAMES VERSION

13 Be it known now unto the king, that, if this city
be builded, and the walls set up *again, then* will they
not pay toll, tribute, and custom, and *so* thou shalt
endamage the revenue of the kings.

14 Now because we have maintenance from *the*
king's palace, and it was not meet for us to see the
king's dishonour, therefore have we sent and certified the king;

15 That search may be made in the book of the records of thy fathers: so shalt thou find in the book of
the records, and know that this city *is* a rebellious
city, and hurtful unto kings and provinces, and that
they have moved sedition within the same of old
time: for which cause was this city destroyed.

16 We certify the king that, if this city be builded
again, and the walls thereof set up, by this means
thou shalt have no portion on this side the river.

17 *Then* sent the king an answer unto Rehum the
chancellor, and *to* Shimshai the scribe, and *to* the
rest of their companions that dwell in Samaria,
and *unto* the rest beyond the river, Peace, and at such
a time.

18 The letter which ye sent unto us hath been
plainly read before me.

19 And I commanded, and search hath been made,
and it is found that this city of old time hath made insurrection against kings, and *that* rebellion and sedition have been made therein.

20 There have been mighty kings also over Jerusalem, which have ruled over all *countries* beyond the
river; and toll, tribute, and custom, was paid unto
them.

21 Give ye now commandment to cause these men
to cease, and that this city be not builded, until *an-*
other commandment shall be given from me.

22 Take heed now that ye fail not to do this: why
should damage grow to the hurt of the kings?

23 Now when the copy of king Artaxerxes' letter
was read before Rehum, and Shimshai the scribe,
and their companions, they went up in haste to Jerusalem unto the Jews, and made them to cease by
force and power.

24 Then ceased the work of the house of God
which *is* at Jerusalem. So it ceased unto the second
year of the reign of Darius king of Persia.

5 1 Then the prophets, Haggai the prophet, and
Zechariah the son of Iddo, prophesied unto the
Jews that *were* in Judah and Jerusalem in the name of
the God of Israel, *even* unto them.

2 Then rose up Zerubbabel the son of Shealtiel,
and Jeshua the son of Jozadak, and began to build the
house of God which *is* at Jerusalem: and with them
were the prophets of God helping them.

3 At the same time came to them Tatnai, governor

NEW LIVING TRANSLATION

its walls. 13 And the king should know that if this
city is rebuilt and its walls are completed, it will
be much to your disadvantage, for the Jews will
then refuse to pay their tribute, customs, and
tolls to you.

14 "Since we are your loyal subjects* and do
not want to see the king dishonored in this
way, we have sent the king this information.
15 We suggest that a search be made in your
ancestors' records, where you will discover
what a rebellious city this has been in the past.
In fact, it was destroyed because of its long and
troublesome history of revolt against the kings
and countries who controlled it. 16 We declare
to the king that if this city is rebuilt and its
walls are completed, the province west of the
Euphrates River will be lost to you."

17 Then King Artaxerxes sent this reply:

"To Rehum the governor, Shimshai the court
secretary, and their colleagues living in Samaria
and throughout the province west of the
Euphrates River. Greetings.

18 "The letter you sent has been translated and
read to me. 19 I ordered a search of the records
and have found that Jerusalem has indeed been
a hotbed of insurrection against many kings.
In fact, rebellion and revolt are normal there!
20 Powerful kings have ruled over Jerusalem and
the entire province west of the Euphrates River,
receiving tribute, customs, and tolls. 21 Therefore,
issue orders to have these men stop their work.
That city must not be rebuilt except at my
express command. 22 Be diligent, and don't
neglect this matter, for we must not permit the
situation to harm the king's interests."

23 When this letter from King Artaxerxes was read
to Rehum, Shimshai, and their colleagues, they hurried to Jerusalem. Then, with a show of strength, they
forced the Jews to stop building.

The Rebuilding Resumes

24 So the work on the Temple of God in Jerusalem had
stopped, and it remained at a standstill until the second year of the reign of King Darius of Persia.*

5 At that time the prophets Haggai and Zechariah
son of Iddo prophesied to the Jews in Judah and
Jerusalem. They prophesied in the name of the God
of Israel who was over them. 2 Zerubbabel son of Shealtiel and Jeshua son of Jehozadak* responded by
starting again to rebuild the Temple of God in Jerusalem. And the prophets of God were with them and
helped them.

3 But Tattenai, governor of the province west of the

4:14 Aramaic *Since we eat the salt of the palace.* **4:24** The second year of Darius's reign was 520 B.C. The narrative started in 4:1-5 is resumed at verse 24. **5:2** Aramaic *Jozadak,* a variant spelling of Jehozadak.

KING JAMES VERSION

on this side the river, and Shethar-boznai, and their
companions, and said thus unto them, Who hath
commanded you to build this house, and to make up
this wall?
4 Then said we unto them after this manner, What
are the names of the men that make this building?
5 But the eye of their God was upon the elders of
the Jews, that they could not cause them to cease, till
the matter came to Darius: and then they returned
answer by letter concerning this *matter.*

6 The copy of the letter that Tatnai, governor on
this side the river, and Shethar-boznai, and his companions the Apharsachites, which *were* on this side
the river, sent unto Darius the king:
7 They sent a letter unto him, wherein was written
thus; Unto Darius the king, all peace.
8 Be it known unto the king, that we went into the
province of Judea, to the house of the great God,
which is builded with great stones, and timber is laid
in the walls, and this work goeth fast on, and
prospereth in their hands.
9 Then asked we those elders, *and* said unto them
thus, Who commanded you to build this house, and
to make up these walls?
10 We asked their names also, to certify thee, that
we might write the names of the men that *were* the
chief of them.
11 And thus they returned us answer, saying, We
are the servants of the God of heaven and earth, and
build the house that was builded these many years
ago, which a great king of Israel builded and set up.
12 But after that our fathers had provoked the God
of heaven unto wrath, he gave them into the hand of
Nebuchadnezzar the king of Babylon, the Chaldean,
who destroyed this house, and carried the people
away into Babylon.
13 But in the first year of Cyrus the king of Babylon
the same king Cyrus made a decree to build this
house of God.
14 And the vessels also of gold and silver of the
house of God, which Nebuchadnezzar took out of
the temple that *was* in Jerusalem, and brought them
into the temple of Babylon, those did Cyrus the king
take out of the temple of Babylon, and they were
delivered unto *one,* whose name *was* Sheshbazzar,
whom he had made governor;
15 And said unto him, Take these vessels, go, carry
them into the temple that *is* in Jerusalem, and let the
house of God be builded in his place.
16 Then came the same Sheshbazzar, *and* laid the
foundation of the house of God which *is* in Jerusalem: and since that time even until now hath it been
in building, and *yet* it is not finished.
17 Now therefore, if *it seem* good to the king, let
there be search made in the king's treasure house,
which *is* there at Babylon, whether it be *so,* that a decree was made of Cyrus the king to build this house

NEW LIVING TRANSLATION

Euphrates River,* and Shethar-bozenai and their
colleagues soon arrived in Jerusalem and asked,
"Who gave you permission to rebuild this Temple
and restore this structure?" 4 They also asked for the
names of all the men working on the Temple. 5 But
because their God was watching over them, the leaders of the Jews were not prevented from building
until a report was sent to Darius and he returned his
decision.

Tattenai's Letter to King Darius

6 This is a copy of the letter that Tattenai the governor, Shethar-bozenai, and the other officials of the
province west of the Euphrates River sent to King
Darius:

7 "To King Darius. Greetings.
8 "The king should know that we went to the
construction site of the Temple of the great God
in the province of Judah. It is being rebuilt with
specially prepared stones, and timber is being
laid in its walls. The work is going forward with
great energy and success.
9 "We asked the leaders, 'Who gave you
permission to rebuild this Temple and restore
this structure?' 10 And we demanded their names
so that we could tell you who the leaders were.
11 "This was their answer: 'We are the servants
of the God of heaven and earth, and we are
rebuilding the Temple that was built here many
years ago by a great king of Israel. 12 But because
our ancestors angered the God of heaven, he
abandoned them to King Nebuchadnezzar of
Babylon,* who destroyed this Temple and exiled
the people to Babylonia. 13 However, King Cyrus
of Babylon,* during the first year of his reign,
issued a decree that the Temple of God should be
rebuilt. 14 King Cyrus returned the gold and silver
cups that Nebuchadnezzar had taken from the
Temple of God in Jerusalem and had placed in
the temple of Babylon. These cups were taken
from that temple and presented to a man named
Sheshbazzar, whom King Cyrus appointed as
governor of Judah. 15 The king instructed him to
return the cups to their place in Jerusalem and to
rebuild the Temple of God there on its original
site. 16 So this Sheshbazzar came and laid the
foundations of the Temple of God in Jerusalem.
The people have been working on it ever since,
though it is not yet completed.'
17 "Therefore, if it pleases the king, we request
that a search be made in the royal archives of
Babylon to discover whether King Cyrus ever
issued a decree to rebuild God's Temple in

5:3 Aramaic *the province beyond the river;* also in 5:6. **5:12** Aramaic *Nebuchadnezzar the Chaldean.* **5:13** King Cyrus of Persia is here identified as the king of Babylon because Persia had conquered the Babylonian Empire.

KING JAMES VERSION

of God at Jerusalem, and let the king send his pleasure to us concerning this matter.

6 1Then Darius the king made a decree, and search
was made in the house of the rolls, where the
treasures were laid up in Babylon.
2And there was found at Achmetha, in the palace
that *is* in the province of the Medes, a roll, and
therein *was* a record thus written:
3In the first year of Cyrus the king *the same* Cyrus
the king made a decree *concerning* the house of God
at Jerusalem, Let the house be builded, the place
where they offered sacrifices, and let the foundations thereof be strongly laid; the height thereof
threescore cubits, *and* the breadth thereof threescore cubits;
4*With* three rows of great stones, and a row of new
timber: and let the expenses be given out of the
king's house:
5And also let the golden and silver vessels of the
house of God, which Nebuchadnezzar took forth out
of the temple which *is* at Jerusalem, and brought
unto Babylon, be restored, and brought again unto
the temple which *is* at Jerusalem, *every one* to his
place, and place *them* in the house of God.
6Now *therefore,* Tatnai, governor beyond the river,
Shethar-boznai, and your companions the Apharsachites, which *are* beyond the river, be ye far from
thence:
7Let the work of this house of God alone; let the
governor of the Jews and the elders of the Jews build
this house of God in his place.
8Moreover I make a decree what ye shall do to the
elders of these Jews for the building of this house of
God: that of the king's goods, *even* of the tribute
beyond the river, forthwith expenses be given unto
these men, that they be not hindered.
9And that which they have need of, both young
bullocks, and rams, and lambs, for the burnt offerings of the God of heaven, wheat, salt, wine, and oil,
according to the appointment of the priests which
are at Jerusalem, let it be given them day by day without fail:
10That they may offer sacrifices of sweet savours
unto the God of heaven, and pray for the life of the
king, and of his sons.
11Also I have made a decree, that whosoever shall
alter this word, let timber be pulled down from his
house, and being set up, let him be hanged thereon;
and let his house be made a dunghill for this.

NEW LIVING TRANSLATION

Jerusalem. And then let the king send us his
decision in this matter."

Darius Approves the Rebuilding

6 So King Darius issued orders that a search be
made in the Babylonian archives, which were
stored in the treasury. 2But it was at the fortress at
Ecbatana in the province of Media that a scroll was
found. This is what it said:

"Memorandum:
3"In the first year of King Cyrus's reign, a
decree was sent out concerning the Temple of
God at Jerusalem.
"Let the Temple be rebuilt on the site where
Jews used to offer their sacrifices, using the
original foundations. Its height will be ninety
feet, and its width will be ninety feet.* 4Every
three layers of specially prepared stones will be
topped by a layer of timber. All expenses will be
paid by the royal treasury. 5Furthermore, the gold
and silver cups, which were taken to Babylon by
Nebuchadnezzar from the Temple of God in
Jerusalem, must be returned to Jerusalem and
put back where they belong. Let them be taken
back to the Temple of God."

6So King Darius sent this message:

"Now therefore, Tattenai, governor of the
province west of the Euphrates River,* and
Shethar-bozenai, and your colleagues and other
officials west of the Euphrates River—stay away
from there! 7Do not disturb the construction of
the Temple of God. Let it be rebuilt on its original
site, and do not hinder the governor of Judah and
the elders of the Jews in their work.
8"Moreover, I hereby decree that you are to
help these elders of the Jews as they rebuild
this Temple of God. You must pay the full
construction costs, without delay, from my taxes
collected in the province west of the Euphrates
River so that the work will not be interrupted.
9"Give the priests in Jerusalem whatever is
needed in the way of young bulls, rams, and male
lambs for the burnt offerings presented to the
God of heaven. And without fail, provide them
with as much wheat, salt, wine, and olive oil as
they need each day. 10Then they will be able to
offer acceptable sacrifices to the God of heaven
and pray for the welfare of the king and his sons.
11"Those who violate this decree in any way
will have a beam pulled from their house. Then
they will be tied to it and flogged, and their house

6:3 Aramaic *Its height will be 60 cubits* [27.6 meters], *and its width will be 60 cubits.* It is commonly held that this verse should be emended to read: "Its height will be 30 cubits [45 feet, or 13.8 meters], its length will be 60 cubits [90 feet, or 27.6 meters], and its width will be 20 cubits [30 feet, or 9.2 meters]"; compare 1 Kgs 6:2. The emendation regarding the width is supported by the Syriac version. **6:6** Aramaic *the province beyond the river;* also in 6:6b, 8, 13.

KING JAMES VERSION

12 And the God that hath caused his name to dwell there destroy all kings and people, that shall put to their hand to alter *and* to destroy this house of God which *is* at Jerusalem. I Darius have made a decree; let it be done with speed.

13 Then Tatnai, governor on this side the river, Shethar-boznai, and their companions, according to that which Darius the king had sent, so they did speedily.

14 And the elders of the Jews builded, and they prospered through the prophesying of Haggai the prophet and Zechariah the son of Iddo. And they builded, and finished *it,* according to the commandment of the God of Israel, and according to the commandment of Cyrus, and Darius, and Artaxerxes king of Persia.

15 And this house was finished on the third day of the month Adar, which was in the sixth year of the reign of Darius the king.

16 And the children of Israel, the priests, and the Levites, and the rest of the children of the captivity, kept the dedication of this house of God with joy,

17 And offered at the dedication of this house of God an hundred bullocks, two hundred rams, four hundred lambs; and for a sin offering for all Israel, twelve he goats, according to the number of the tribes of Israel.

18 And they set the priests in their divisions, and the Levites in their courses, for the service of God, which *is* at Jerusalem; as it is written in the book of Moses.

19 And the children of the captivity kept the passover upon the fourteenth *day* of the first month.

20 For the priests and the Levites were purified together, all of them *were* pure, and killed the passover for all the children of the captivity, and for their brethren the priests, and for themselves.

21 And the children of Israel, which were come again out of captivity, and all such as had separated themselves unto them from the filthiness of the heathen of the land, to seek the LORD God of Israel, did eat,

22 And kept the feast of unleavened bread seven days with joy: for the LORD had made them joyful, and turned the heart of the king of Assyria unto them, to strengthen their hands in the work of the house of God, the God of Israel.

NEW LIVING TRANSLATION

will be reduced to a pile of rubble.*
12 May the God who has chosen the city of Jerusalem as the place to honor his name destroy any king or nation that violates this command and destroys this Temple.

"I, Darius, have issued this decree. Let it be obeyed with all diligence."

The Temple's Dedication

13 Tattenai, governor of the province west of the Euphrates River, and Shethar-bozenai and their colleagues complied at once with the command of King
Darius.
14 So the Jewish elders continued their work,
and they were greatly encouraged by the preaching
of the prophets Haggai and Zechariah son of Iddo.
The Temple was finally finished, as had been commanded by the God of Israel and decreed by Cyrus,
Darius, and Artaxerxes, the kings of Persia.
15 The
Temple was completed on March 12,* during the
sixth year of King Darius's reign.

16 The Temple of God was then dedicated with
great joy by the people of Israel, the priests, the Levites, and the rest of the people who had returned
from exile.
17 During the dedication ceremony for
the Temple of God, 100 young bulls, 200 rams, and
400 male lambs were sacrificed. And 12 male goats
were presented as a sin offering for the twelve tribes
of Israel.
18 Then the priests and Levites were divided
into their various divisions to serve at the Temple
of God in Jerusalem, as prescribed in the Book of
Moses.

Celebration of Passover

19 On April 21* the returned exiles celebrated Passover.
20 The priests and Levites had purified themselves and were ceremonially clean. So they
slaughtered the Passover lamb for all the returned
exiles, for their fellow priests, and for themselves.
21 The Passover meal was eaten by the people of Israel
who had returned from exile and by the others in the
land who had turned from their immoral customs to
worship the LORD, the God of Israel.
22 Then they cel-
ebrated the Festival of Unleavened Bread for seven
days. There was great joy throughout the land because the LORD had caused the king of Assyria* to be
favorable to them, so that he helped them to rebuild
the Temple of God, the God of Israel.

6:11 Aramaic *a dunghill.* **6:15** Aramaic *on the third day of the month Adar,* of the ancient Hebrew lunar calendar. A number of events in Ezra can be cross-checked with dates in surviving Persian records and related accurately to our modern calendar. This day was March 12, 515 B.C. **6:19** Hebrew *On the fourteenth day of the first month,* of the ancient Hebrew lunar calendar. This day was April 21, 515 B.C.; also see note on 6:15. **6:22** King Darius of Persia is here identified as the king of Assyria because Persia had conquered the Babylonian Empire, which included the earlier Assyrian Empire.

KING JAMES VERSION

7 1 Now after these things, in the reign of Artaxerxes king of Persia, Ezra the son of Seraiah, the son of Azariah, the son of Hilkiah,

2 The son of Shallum, the son of Zadok, the son of Ahitub,

3 The son of Amariah, the son of Azariah, the son of Meraioth,

4 The son of Zerahiah, the son of Uzzi, the son of Bukki,

5 The son of Abishua, the son of Phinehas, the son of Eleazar, the son of Aaron the chief priest:

6 This Ezra went up from Babylon; and he *was* a ready scribe in the law of Moses, which the LORD God of Israel had given: and the king granted him all his request, according to the hand of the LORD his God upon him.

7 And there went up *some* of the children of Israel, and of the priests, and the Levites, and the singers, and the porters, and the Nethinims, unto Jerusalem, in the seventh year of Artaxerxes the king.

8 And he came to Jerusalem in the fifth month, which *was* in the seventh year of the king.

9 For upon the first *day* of the first month began he to go up from Babylon, and on the first *day* of the fifth month came he to Jerusalem, according to the good hand of his God upon him.

10 For Ezra had prepared his heart to seek the law of the LORD, and to do *it*, and to teach in Israel statutes and judgments.

11 Now this *is* the copy of the letter that the king Artaxerxes gave unto Ezra the priest, the scribe, *even* a scribe of the words of the commandments of the LORD, and of his statutes to Israel.

12 Artaxerxes, king of kings, unto Ezra the priest, a scribe of the law of the God of heaven, perfect *peace*, and at such a time.

13 I make a decree, that all they of the people of Israel, and *of* his priests and Levites, in my realm, which are minded of their own freewill to go up to Jerusalem, go with thee.

14 Forasmuch as thou art sent of the king, and of his seven counsellors, to inquire concerning Judah and Jerusalem, according to the law of thy God which *is* in thine hand;

15 And to carry the silver and gold, which the king and his counsellors have freely offered unto the God of Israel, whose habitation *is* in Jerusalem,

16 And all the silver and gold that thou canst find in all the province of Babylon, with the freewill offering of the people, and of the priests, offering willingly for the house of their God which *is* in Jerusalem:

NEW LIVING TRANSLATION

Ezra Arrives in Jerusalem

7 Many years later, during the reign of King Artaxerxes of Persia,* there was a man named Ezra.
He was the son* of Seraiah, son of Azariah, son of
Hilkiah, 2 son of Shallum, son of Zadok, son of Ahitub,
3 son of Amariah, son of Azariah, son* of Meraioth,
4 son of Zerahiah, son of Uzzi, son of Bukki, 5 son of
Abishua, son of Phinehas, son of Eleazar, son of
Aaron the high priest.* 6 This Ezra was a scribe who
was well versed in the Law of Moses, which the LORD,
the God of Israel, had given to the people of Israel. He
came up to Jerusalem from Babylon, and the king
gave him everything he asked for, because the gracious hand of the LORD his God was on him. 7 Some of
the people of Israel, as well as some of the priests,
Levites, singers, gatekeepers, and Temple servants,
traveled up to Jerusalem with him in the seventh year
of King Artaxerxes' reign.

8 Ezra arrived in Jerusalem in August* of that year.
9 He had arranged to leave Babylon on April 8, the
first day of the new year,* and he arrived at Jerusalem
on August 4,* for the gracious hand of his God was
on him. 10 This was because Ezra had determined to
study and obey the Law of the LORD and to teach
those decrees and regulations to the people of Israel.

Artaxerxes' Letter to Ezra

11 King Artaxerxes had given a copy of the following
letter to Ezra, the priest and scribe who studied and
taught the commands and decrees of the LORD to
Israel:

> 12 *"From Artaxerxes, the king of kings, to Ezra the priest, the teacher of the law of the God of heaven. Greetings.
>
> 13 "I decree that any of the people of Israel in my kingdom, including the priests and Levites, may volunteer to return to Jerusalem with you.
> 14 I and my council of seven hereby instruct you to conduct an inquiry into the situation in Judah and Jerusalem, based on your God's law, which is in your hand. 15 We also commission you to take with you silver and gold, which we are freely presenting as an offering to the God of Israel who lives in Jerusalem.
>
> 16 "Furthermore, you are to take any silver and gold that you may obtain from the province of Babylon, as well as the voluntary offerings of the people and the priests that are presented for the

7:1a Artaxerxes reigned 465–424 B.C. **7:1b** Or *descendant;* see 1 Chr 6:14. **7:3** Or *descendant;* see 1 Chr 6:6-10. **7:5** Or *the first priest.* **7:8** Hebrew *in the fifth month.* This month in the ancient Hebrew lunar calendar occurred within the months of August and September 458 B.C. **7:9a** Hebrew *on the first day of the first month,* of the ancient Hebrew lunar calendar. This day was April 8, 458 B.C.; also see note on 6:15. **7:9b** Hebrew *on the first day of the fifth month,* of the ancient Hebrew lunar calendar. This day was August 4, 458 B.C.; also see note on 6:15. **7:12** The original text of 7:12-26 is in Aramaic.

KING JAMES VERSION

17 That thou mayest buy speedily with this money bullocks, rams, lambs, with their meat offerings and their drink offerings, and offer them upon the altar of the house of your God which *is* in Jerusalem.

18 And whatsoever shall seem good to thee, and to thy brethren, to do with the rest of the silver and the gold, that do after the will of your God.

19 The vessels also that are given thee for the service of the house of thy God, *those* deliver thou before the God of Jerusalem.

20 And whatsoever more shall be needful for the house of thy God, which thou shalt have occasion to bestow, bestow *it* out of the king's treasure house.

21 And I, *even* I Artaxerxes the king, do make a decree to all the treasurers which *are* beyond the river, that whatsoever Ezra the priest, the scribe of the law of the God of heaven, shall require of you, it be done speedily,

22 Unto an hundred talents of silver, and to an hundred measures of wheat, and to an hundred baths of wine, and to an hundred baths of oil, and salt without prescribing *how much*.

23 Whatsoever is commanded by the God of heaven, let it be diligently done for the house of the God of heaven: for why should there be wrath against the realm of the king and his sons?

24 Also we certify you, that touching any of the priests and Levites, singers, porters, Nethinims, or ministers of this house of God, it shall not be lawful to impose toll, tribute, or custom, upon them.

25 And thou, Ezra, after the wisdom of thy God, that *is* in thine hand, set magistrates and judges, which may judge all the people that *are* beyond the river, all such as know the laws of thy God; and teach ye them that know *them* not.

26 And whosoever will not do the law of thy God, and the law of the king, let judgment be executed speedily upon him, whether *it be* unto death, or to banishment, or to confiscation of goods, or to imprisonment.

27 Blessed *be* the LORD God of our fathers, which hath put *such a thing* as this in the king's heart, to beautify the house of the LORD which *is* in Jerusalem:

28 And hath extended mercy unto me before the king, and his counsellors, and before all the king's mighty princes. And I was strengthened as the hand of the LORD my God *was* upon me, and I gathered together out of Israel chief men to go up with me.

8

1 These *are* now the chief of their fathers, and *this is* the genealogy of them that went up with me from Babylon, in the reign of Artaxerxes the king.

NEW LIVING TRANSLATION

Temple of their God in Jerusalem. 17 These donations are to be used specifically for the purchase of bulls, rams, male lambs, and the appropriate grain offerings and liquid offerings, all of which will be offered on the altar of the Temple of your God in Jerusalem. 18 Any silver and gold that is left over may be used in whatever way you and your colleagues feel is the will of your God.

19 "But as for the cups we are entrusting to you for the service of the Temple of your God, deliver them all to the God of Jerusalem. 20 If you need anything else for your God's Temple or for any similar needs, you may take it from the royal treasury.

21 "I, Artaxerxes the king, hereby send this decree to all the treasurers in the province west of the Euphrates River*: 'You are to give Ezra, the priest and teacher of the law of the God of heaven, whatever he requests of you. 22 You are to give him up to 7,500 pounds* of silver, 500 bushels* of wheat, 550 gallons of wine, 550 gallons of olive oil,* and an unlimited supply of salt. 23 Be careful to provide whatever the God of heaven demands for his Temple, for why should we risk bringing God's anger against the realm of the king and his sons? 24 I also decree that no priest, Levite, singer, gatekeeper, Temple servant, or other worker in this Temple of God will be required to pay tribute, customs, or tolls of any kind.'

25 "And you, Ezra, are to use the wisdom your God has given you to appoint magistrates and judges who know your God's laws to govern all the people in the province west of the Euphrates River. Teach the law to anyone who does not know it. 26 Anyone who refuses to obey the law of your God and the law of the king will be punished immediately, either by death, banishment, confiscation of goods, or imprisonment."

Ezra Praises the LORD

27 Praise the LORD, the God of our ancestors, who made the king want to beautify the Temple of the LORD in Jerusalem! 28 And praise him for demonstrating such unfailing love to me by honoring me before the king, his council, and all his mighty nobles! I felt encouraged because the gracious hand of the LORD my God was on me. And I gathered some of the leaders of Israel to return with me to Jerusalem.

Exiles Who Returned with Ezra

8

Here is a list of the family leaders and the genealogies of those who came with me from Babylon during the reign of King Artaxerxes:

7:21 Aramaic *the province beyond the river;* also in 7:25. **7:22a** Aramaic *100 talents* [3,400 kilograms]. **7:22b** Aramaic *100 cors* [18.2 kiloliters]. **7:22c** Aramaic *100 baths* [2.1 kiloliters] *of wine, 100 baths of olive oil.*

KING JAMES VERSION

2 Of the sons of Phinehas; Gershom: of the sons of
Ithamar; Daniel: of the sons of David; Hattush.
3 Of the sons of Shechaniah, of the sons of Pha-
rosh; Zechariah: and with him were reckoned by
genealogy of the males an hundred and fifty.
4 Of the sons of Pahath-moab; Elihoenai the son of
Zerahiah, and with him two hundred males.
5 Of the sons of Shechaniah; the son of Jahaziel,
and with him three hundred males.
6 Of the sons also of Adin; Ebed the son of Jonathan, and with him fifty males.
7 And of the sons of Elam; Jeshaiah the son of Athaliah, and with him seventy males.
8 And of the sons of Shephatiah; Zebadiah the son
of Michael, and with him fourscore males.
9 Of the sons of Joab; Obadiah the son of Jehiel,
and with him two hundred and eighteen males.
10 And of the sons of Shelomith; the son of Josiphiah, and with him an hundred and threescore males.
11 And of the sons of Bebai; Zechariah the son of
Bebai, and with him twenty and eight males.
12 And of the sons of Azgad; Johanan the son of
Hakkatan, and with him an hundred and ten males.
13 And of the last sons of Adonikam, whose names
are these, Eliphelet, Jeiel, and Shemaiah, and with
them threescore males.
14 Of the sons also of Bigvai; Uthai, and Zabbud,
and with them seventy males.

15 And I gathered them together to the river that
runneth to Ahava; and there abode we in tents three
days: and I viewed the people, and the priests, and
found there none of the sons of Levi.
16 Then sent I for Eliezer, for Ariel, for Shemaiah,
and for Elnathan, and for Jarib, and for Elnathan, and
for Nathan, and for Zechariah, and for Meshullam,
chief men; also for Joiarib, and for Elnathan, men of
understanding.
17 And I sent them with commandment unto Iddo
the chief at the place Casiphia, and I told them what
they should say unto Iddo, *and* to his brethren the
Nethinims, at the place Casiphia, that they should
bring unto us ministers for the house of our God.
18 And by the good hand of our God upon us they
brought us a man of understanding, of the sons of
Mahli, the son of Levi, the son of Israel; and Sherebiah, with his sons and his brethren, eighteen;
19 And Hashabiah, and with him Jeshaiah of the
sons of Merari, his brethren and their sons, twenty;
20 Also of the Nethinims, whom David and the
princes had appointed for the service of the Levites,
two hundred and twenty Nethinims: all of them were
expressed by name.
21 Then I proclaimed a fast there, at the river of
Ahava, that we might afflict ourselves before our

NEW LIVING TRANSLATION

2 From the family of Phinehas: Gershom.
From the family of Ithamar: Daniel.
From the family of David: Hattush, 3 a descendant
of Shecaniah.
From the family of Parosh: Zechariah and
150 other men were registered.
4 From the family of Pahath-moab: Eliehoenai son
of Zerahiah and 200 other men.
5 From the family of Zattu*: Shecaniah son of
Jahaziel and 300 other men.
6 From the family of Adin: Ebed son of Jonathan
and 50 other men.
7 From the family of Elam: Jeshaiah son of Athaliah
and 70 other men.
8 From the family of Shephatiah: Zebadiah son of
Michael and 80 other men.
9 From the family of Joab: Obadiah son of Jehiel
and 218 other men.
10 From the family of Bani*: Shelomith son of
Josiphiah and 160 other men.
11 From the family of Bebai: Zechariah son of Bebai
and 28 other men.
12 From the family of Azgad: Johanan son of
Hakkatan and 110 other men.
13 From the family of Adonikam, who came later*:
Eliphelet, Jeuel, Shemaiah, and 60 other men.
14 From the family of Bigvai: Uthai, Zaccur,* and
70 other men.

Ezra's Journey to Jerusalem

15 I assembled the exiles at the Ahava Canal, and we
camped there for three days while I went over the lists
of the people and the priests who had arrived. I found
that not one Levite had volunteered to come along.
16 So I sent for Eliezer, Ariel, Shemaiah, Elnathan, Jarib,
Elnathan, Nathan, Zechariah, and Meshullam, who
were leaders of the people. I also sent for Joiarib and
Elnathan, who were men of discernment. 17 I sent
them to Iddo, the leader of the Levites at Casiphia, to
ask him and his relatives and the Temple servants to
send us ministers for the Temple of God at Jerusalem.
18 Since the gracious hand of our God was on us,
they sent us a man named Sherebiah, along with
eighteen of his sons and brothers. He was a very as-
tute man and a descendant of Mahli, who was a descendant of Levi son of Israel.* 19 They also sent
Hashabiah, together with Jeshaiah from the descendants of Merari, and twenty of his sons and brothers,
20 and 220 Temple servants. The Temple servants
were assistants to the Levites—a group of Temple
workers first instituted by King David and his officials. They were all listed by name.
21 And there by the Ahava Canal, I gave orders for
all of us to fast and humble ourselves before our

8:5 As in some Greek manuscripts (see also 1 Esdras 8:32); Hebrew lacks *Zattu.* **8:10** As in some Greek manuscripts (see also 1 Esdras 8:36); Hebrew lacks *Bani.* **8:13** Or *who were the last of his family.* **8:14** As in Greek and Syriac versions and an alternate reading of the Masoretic Text; the other alternate reads *Zabbud.* **8:18** *Israel* is the name that God gave to Jacob.

God, to seek of him a right way for us, and for our little ones, and for all our substance.

22 For I was ashamed to require of the king a band of soldiers and horsemen to help us against the enemy in the way: because we had spoken unto the king, saying, The hand of our God *is* upon all them for good that seek him; but his power and his wrath *is* against all them that forsake him.

23 So we fasted and besought our God for this: and he was intreated of us.

24 Then I separated twelve of the chief of the priests, Sherebiah, Hashabiah, and ten of their brethren with them,

25 And weighed unto them the silver, and the gold, and the vessels, *even* the offering of the house of our God, which the king, and his counsellors, and his lords, and all Israel *there* present, had offered:

26 I even weighed unto their hand six hundred and fifty talents of silver, and silver vessels an hundred talents, *and* of gold an hundred talents;

27 Also twenty basins of gold, of a thousand drams; and two vessels of fine copper, precious as gold.

28 And I said unto them, Ye *are* holy unto the LORD; the vessels *are* holy also; and the silver and the gold *are* a freewill offering unto the LORD God of your fathers.

29 Watch ye, and keep *them*, until ye weigh *them* before the chief of the priests and the Levites, and chief of the fathers of Israel, at Jerusalem, in the chambers of the house of the LORD.

30 So took the priests and the Levites the weight of the silver, and the gold, and the vessels, to bring *them* to Jerusalem unto the house of our God.

31 Then we departed from the river of Ahava on the twelfth *day* of the first month, to go unto Jerusalem: and the hand of our God was upon us, and he delivered us from the hand of the enemy, and of such as lay in wait by the way.

32 And we came to Jerusalem, and abode there three days.

33 Now on the fourth day was the silver and the gold and the vessels weighed in the house of our God by the hand of Meremoth the son of Uriah the priest; and with him *was* Eleazar the son of Phinehas; and with them *was* Jozabad the son of Jeshua, and Noadiah the son of Binnui, Levites;

34 By number *and* by weight of every one: and all the weight was written at that time.

35 *Also* the children of those that had been carried away, which were come out of the captivity, offered burnt offerings unto the God of Israel, twelve bullocks for all Israel, ninety and six rams, seventy and seven lambs, twelve he goats *for* a sin offering: all *this* *was* a burnt offering unto the LORD.

God. We prayed that he would give us a safe journey
and protect us, our children, and our goods as we
traveled. 22 For I was ashamed to ask the king for soldiers and horsemen* to accompany us and protect
us from enemies along the way. After all, we had told
the king, "Our God's hand of protection is on all who
worship him, but his fierce anger rages against those
who abandon him." 23 So we fasted and earnestly
prayed that our God would take care of us, and he
heard our prayer.

24 I appointed twelve leaders of the priests—Sherebiah, Hashabiah, and ten other priests—25 to be in
charge of transporting the silver, the gold, the gold
bowls, and the other items that the king, his council,
his officials, and all the people of Israel had presented for the Temple of God. 26 I weighed the treasure as I gave it to them and found the totals to be as
follows:

24 tons* of silver,
7,500 pounds* of silver articles,
7,500 pounds of gold,
27 20 gold bowls, equal in value to 1,000 gold coins,*
2 fine articles of polished bronze, as precious as gold.

28 And I said to these priests, "You and these treasures have been set apart as holy to the LORD. This silver and gold is a voluntary offering to the LORD, the
God of our ancestors. 29 Guard these treasures well
until you present them to the leading priests, the Levites, and the leaders of Israel, who will weigh them
at the storerooms of the LORD's Temple in Jerusalem." 30 So the priests and the Levites accepted the
task of transporting these treasures of silver and gold
to the Temple of our God in Jerusalem.

31 We broke camp at the Ahava Canal on April 19*
and started off to Jerusalem. And the gracious hand
of our God protected us and saved us from enemies
and bandits along the way. 32 So we arrived safely in
Jerusalem, where we rested for three days.

33 On the fourth day after our arrival, the silver,
gold, and other valuables were weighed at the Temple
of our God and entrusted to Meremoth son of Uriah
the priest and to Eleazar son of Phinehas, along with
Jozabad son of Jeshua and Noadiah son of Binnui—
both of whom were Levites. 34 Everything was accounted for by number and weight, and the total
weight was officially recorded.

35 Then the exiles who had come out of captivity
sacrificed burnt offerings to the God of Israel. They
presented twelve bulls for all the people of Israel, as
well as ninety-six rams and seventy-seven male
lambs. They also offered twelve male goats as a sin
offering. All this was given as a burnt offering to the

8:22 Or *charioteers.* **8:26a** Hebrew *650 talents* [22 metric tons]. **8:26b** Hebrew *100 talents* [3,400 kilograms]; also in 8:26c. **8:27** Hebrew *1,000 darics,* about 19 pounds or 8.6 kilograms in weight. **8:31** Hebrew *on the twelfth day of the first month,* of the ancient Hebrew lunar calendar. This day was April 19, 458 B.C.; also see note on 6:15.

KING JAMES VERSION

36 And they delivered the king's commissions unto the king's lieutenants, and to the governors on this side the river: and they furthered the people, and the house of God.

9 1 Now when these things were done, the princes came to me, saying, The people of Israel, and the priests, and the Levites, have not separated themselves from the people of the lands, *doing* according to their abominations, *even* of the Canaanites, the Hittites, the Perizzites, the Jebusites, the Ammonites, the Moabites, the Egyptians, and the Amorites.

2 For they have taken of their daughters for themselves, and for their sons: so that the holy seed have mingled themselves with the people of *those* lands: yea, the hand of the princes and rulers hath been chief in this trespass.

3 And when I heard this thing, I rent my garment and my mantle, and plucked off the hair of my head and of my beard, and sat down astonied.

4 Then were assembled unto me every one that trembled at the words of the God of Israel, because of the transgression of those that had been carried away; and I sat astonied until the evening sacrifice.

5 And at the evening sacrifice I arose up from my heaviness; and having rent my garment and my mantle, I fell upon my knees, and spread out my hands unto the LORD my God,

6 And said, O my God, I am ashamed and blush to lift up my face to thee, my God: for our iniquities are increased over *our* head, and our trespass is grown up unto the heavens.

7 Since the days of our fathers *have* we *been* in a great trespass unto this day; and for our iniquities have we, our kings, *and* our priests, been delivered into the hand of the kings of the lands, to the sword, to captivity, and to a spoil, and to confusion of face, as *it is* this day.

8 And now for a little space grace hath been *shewed* from the LORD our God, to leave us a remnant to escape, and to give us a nail in his holy place, that our God may lighten our eyes, and give us a little reviving in our bondage.

9 For we *were* bondmen; yet our God hath not forsaken us in our bondage, but hath extended mercy unto us in the sight of the kings of Persia, to give us a reviving, to set up the house of our God, and to repair the desolations thereof, and to give us a wall in Judah and in Jerusalem.

10 And now, O our God, what shall we say after this? for we have forsaken thy commandments,

11 Which thou hast commanded by thy servants the prophets, saying, The land, unto which ye go to possess it, is an unclean land with the filthiness of the people of the lands, with their abominations, which have filled it from one end to another with their uncleanness.

NEW LIVING TRANSLATION

LORD. 36 The king's decrees were delivered to his highest officers and the governors of the province west of the Euphrates River,* who then cooperated by supporting the people and the Temple of God.

Ezra's Prayer concerning Intermarriage

9 When these things had been done, the Jewish leaders came to me and said, "Many of the people of Israel, and even some of the priests and Levites, have not kept themselves separate from the other peoples living in the land. They have taken up the detestable practices of the Canaanites, Hittites, Perizzites, Jebusites, Ammonites, Moabites, Egyptians, and Amorites. 2 For the men of Israel have married women from these people and have taken them as wives for their sons. So the holy race has become polluted by these mixed marriages. Worse yet, the leaders and officials have led the way in this outrage."

3 When I heard this, I tore my cloak and my shirt, pulled hair from my head and beard, and sat down utterly shocked. 4 Then all who trembled at the words of the God of Israel came and sat with me because of this outrage committed by the returned exiles. And I sat there utterly appalled until the time of the evening sacrifice.

5 At the time of the sacrifice, I stood up from where I had sat in mourning with my clothes torn. I fell to my knees and lifted my hands to the LORD my God. 6 I prayed,

"O my God, I am utterly ashamed; I blush to lift up my face to you. For our sins are piled higher than our heads, and our guilt has reached to the heavens. 7 From the days of our ancestors until now, we have been steeped in sin. That is why we and our kings and our priests have been at the mercy of the pagan kings of the land. We have been killed, captured, robbed, and disgraced, just as we are today.

8 "But now we have been given a brief moment of grace, for the LORD our God has allowed a few of us to survive as a remnant. He has given us security in this holy place. Our God has brightened our eyes and granted us some relief from our slavery. 9 For we were slaves, but in his unfailing love our God did not abandon us in our slavery. Instead, he caused the kings of Persia to treat us favorably. He revived us so we could rebuild the Temple of our God and repair its ruins. He has given us a protective wall in Judah and Jerusalem.

10 "And now, O our God, what can we say after all of this? For once again we have abandoned your commands! 11 Your servants the prophets warned us when they said, 'The land you are entering to possess is totally defiled by the detestable practices of the people living there. From one end to the other, the land is filled with

8:36 Hebrew *the province beyond the river.*

KING JAMES VERSION

12Now therefore give not your daughters unto their sons, neither take their daughters unto your sons, nor seek their peace or their wealth for ever: that ye may be strong, and eat the good of the land, and leave *it* for an inheritance to your children for ever.

13And after all that is come upon us for our evil deeds, and for our great trespass, seeing that thou our God hast punished us less than our iniquities *deserve,* and hast given us *such* deliverance as this; 14Should we again break thy commandments, and join in affinity with the people of these abominations? wouldest not thou be angry with us till thou hadst consumed *us,* so that *there should be* no remnant nor escaping? 15O LORD God of Israel, thou *art* righteous: for we remain yet escaped, as *it is* this day: behold, we *are* before thee in our trespasses: for we cannot stand before thee because of this.

10 1Now when Ezra had prayed, and when he had confessed, weeping and casting himself down before the house of God, there assembled unto him out of Israel a very great congregation of men and women and children: for the people wept very sore.

2And Shechaniah the son of Jehiel, *one* of the sons of Elam, answered and said unto Ezra, We have trespassed against our God, and have taken strange wives of the people of the land: yet now there is hope in Israel concerning this thing.

3Now therefore let us make a covenant with our God to put away all the wives, and such as are born of them, according to the counsel of my lord, and of those that tremble at the commandment of our God; and let it be done according to the law.

4Arise; for *this* matter *belongeth* unto thee: we also *will be* with thee: be of good courage, and do *it.*

5Then arose Ezra, and made the chief priests, the Levites, and all Israel, to swear that they should do according to this word. And they sware.

6Then Ezra rose up from before the house of God, and went into the chamber of Johanan the son of Eliashib: and *when* he came thither, he did eat no bread, nor drink water: for he mourned because of the transgression of them that had been carried away.

7And they made proclamation throughout Judah and Jerusalem unto all the children of the captivity, that they should gather themselves together unto Jerusalem;

8And that whosoever would not come within three days, according to the counsel of the princes and the elders, all his substance should be forfeited, and himself separated from the congregation of those that had been carried away.

NEW LIVING TRANSLATION

corruption. 12Don't let your daughters marry their sons! Don't take their daughters as wives for your sons. Don't ever promote the peace and prosperity of those nations. If you follow these instructions, you will be strong and will enjoy the good things the land produces, and you will leave this prosperity to your children forever.'

13"Now we are being punished because of our wickedness and our great guilt. But we have actually been punished far less than we deserve, for you, our God, have allowed some of us to survive as a remnant. 14But even so, we are again breaking your commands and intermarrying with people who do these detestable things. Won't your anger be enough to destroy us, so that even this little remnant no longer survives? 15O LORD, God of Israel, you are just. We come before you in our guilt as nothing but an escaped remnant, though in such a condition none of us can stand in your presence."

The People Confess Their Sin

10 While Ezra prayed and made this confession, weeping and lying face down on the ground in front of the Temple of God, a very large crowd of people from Israel—men, women, and children—gathered and wept bitterly with him. 2Then Shecaniah son of Jehiel, a descendant of Elam, said to Ezra, "We have been unfaithful to our God, for we have married these pagan women of the land. But in spite of this there is hope for Israel. 3Let us now make a covenant with our God to divorce our pagan wives and to send them away with their children. We will follow the advice given by you and by the others who respect the commands of our God. Let it be done according to the Law of God. 4Get up, for it is your duty to tell us how to proceed in setting things straight. We are behind you, so be strong and take action."

5So Ezra stood up and demanded that the leaders of the priests and the Levites and all the people of Israel swear that they would do as Shecaniah had said. And they all swore a solemn oath. 6Then Ezra left the front of the Temple of God and went to the room of Jehohanan son of Eliashib. He spent the night* there without eating or drinking anything. He was still in mourning because of the unfaithfulness of the returned exiles.

7Then a proclamation was made throughout Judah and Jerusalem that all the exiles should come to Jerusalem. 8Those who failed to come within three days would, if the leaders and elders so decided, forfeit all their property and be expelled from the assembly of the exiles.

10:6 As in parallel text at 1 Esdras 9:2; Hebrew reads *He went.*

KING JAMES VERSION

9Then all the men of Judah and Benjamin gathered themselves together unto Jerusalem within three days. It *was* the ninth month, on the twentieth *day* of the month; and all the people sat in the street of the house of God, trembling because of *this* matter, and for the great rain.

10And Ezra the priest stood up, and said unto them, Ye have transgressed, and have taken strange wives, to increase the trespass of Israel.

11Now therefore make confession unto the LORD God of your fathers, and do his pleasure: and separate yourselves from the people of the land, and from the strange wives.

12Then all the congregation answered and said with a loud voice, As thou hast said, so must we do.

13But the people *are* many, and *it is* a time of much rain, and we are not able to stand without, neither *is this* a work of one day or two: for we are many that have transgressed in this thing.

14Let now our rulers of all the congregation stand, and let all them which have taken strange wives in our cities come at appointed times, and with them the elders of every city, and the judges thereof, until the fierce wrath of our God for this matter be turned from us.

15Only Jonathan the son of Asahel and Jahaziah the son of Tikvah were employed about this *matter*: and Meshullam and Shabbethai the Levite helped them.

16And the children of the captivity did so. And Ezra the priest, *with* certain chief of the fathers, after the house of their fathers, and all of them by *their* names, were separated, and sat down in the first day of the tenth month to examine the matter.

17And they made an end with all the men that had taken strange wives by the first day of the first month.

18And among the sons of the priests there were found that had taken strange wives: *namely*, of the sons of Jeshua the son of Jozadak, and his brethren; Maaseiah, and Eliezer, and Jarib, and Gedaliah.

19And they gave their hands that they would put away their wives; and *being* guilty, *they offered* a ram of the flock for their trespass.

20And of the sons of Immer; Hanani, and Zebadiah.

21And of the sons of Harim; Maaseiah, and Elijah, and Shemaiah, and Jehiel, and Uzziah.

22And of the sons of Pashur; Elioenai, Maaseiah, Ishmael, Nethaneel, Jozabad, and Elasah.

23Also of the Levites; Jozabad, and Shimei, and Kelaiah, (the same *is* Kelita,) Pethahiah, Judah, and Eliezer.

24Of the singers also; Eliashib: and of the porters; Shallum, and Telem, and Uri.

NEW LIVING TRANSLATION

9Within three days, all the people of Judah and
Benjamin had gathered in Jerusalem. This took place
on December 19,* and all the people were sitting in
the square before the Temple of God. They were
trembling both because of the seriousness of the
matter and because it was raining. 10Then Ezra the
priest stood and said to them: "You have committed a
terrible sin. By marrying pagan women, you have increased Israel's guilt. 11So now confess your sin to the
LORD, the God of your ancestors, and do what he demands. Separate yourselves from the people of the
land and from these pagan women."

12Then the whole assembly raised their voices and
answered, "Yes, you are right; we must do as you say!"
13Then they added, "This isn't something that can be
done in a day or two, for many of us are involved in
this extremely sinful affair. And this is the rainy season, so we cannot stay out here much longer. 14Let
our leaders act on behalf of us all. Let everyone who
has a pagan wife come at a scheduled time, accompanied by the leaders and judges of his city, so that the
fierce anger of our God concerning this affair may be
turned away from us."

15Only Jonathan son of Asahel and Jahzeiah son of
Tikvah opposed this course of action, and they were
supported by Meshullam and Shabbethai the Levite.

16So this was the plan they followed. Ezra selected
leaders to represent their families, designating each
of the representatives by name. On December 29,*
the leaders sat down to investigate the matter. 17By
March 27, the first day of the new year,* they had
finished dealing with all the men who had married
pagan wives.

Those Guilty of Intermarriage

18These are the priests who had married pagan wives:
From the family of Jeshua son of Jehozadak* and his
brothers: Maaseiah, Eliezer, Jarib, and Gedaliah.
19They vowed to divorce their wives, and they
each acknowledged their guilt by offering a ram
as a guilt offering.

20From the family of Immer: Hanani and Zebadiah.

21From the family of Harim: Maaseiah, Elijah,
Shemaiah, Jehiel, and Uzziah.

22From the family of Pashhur: Elioenai, Maaseiah,
Ishmael, Nethanel, Jozabad, and Elasah.

23These are the Levites who were guilty: Jozabad,
Shimei, Kelaiah (also called Kelita), Pethahiah,
Judah, and Eliezer.

24This is the singer who was guilty: Eliashib.

10:9 Hebrew *on the twentieth day of the ninth month*, of the ancient Hebrew lunar calendar. This day was December 19, 458 B.C.; also see note on 6:15.
10:16 Hebrew *On the first day of the tenth month*, of the ancient Hebrew lunar calendar. This day was December 29, 458 B.C.; also see note on 6:15.
10:17 Hebrew *By the first day of the first month*, of the ancient Hebrew lunar calendar. This day was March 27, 457 B.C.; also see note on 6:15.
10:18 Hebrew *Jozadak*, a variant spelling of Jehozadak.

KING JAMES VERSION

25 Moreover of Israel: of the sons of Parosh; Ramiah, and Jeziah, and Malchiah, and Miamin, and Eleazar, and Malchijah, and Benaiah.
26 And of the sons of Elam; Mattaniah, Zechariah,
and Jehiel, and Abdi, and Jeremoth, and Eliah.
27 And of the sons of Zattu; Elioenai, Eliashib,
Mattaniah, and Jeremoth, and Zabad, and Aziza.
28 Of the sons also of Bebai; Jehohanan, Hananiah,
Zabbai, *and* Athlai.
29 And of the sons of Bani; Meshullam, Malluch,
and Adaiah, Jashub, and Sheal, and Ramoth.
30 And of the sons of Pahath-moab; Adna, and
Chelal, Benaiah, Maaseiah, Mattaniah, Bezaleel, and
Binnui, and Manasseh.
31 And *of* the sons of Harim; Eliezer, Ishijah,
Malchiah, Shemaiah, Shimeon,
32 Benjamin, Malluch, *and* Shemariah.
33 Of the sons of Hashum; Mattenai, Mattathah,
Zabad, Eliphelet, Jeremai, Manasseh, *and* Shimei.
34 Of the sons of Bani; Maadai, Amram, and Uel,
35 Benaiah, Bedeiah, Chelluh,
36 Vaniah, Meremoth, Eliashib,
37 Mattaniah, Mattenai, and Jaasau,
38 And Bani, and Binnui, Shimei,
39 And Shelemiah, and Nathan, and Adaiah,
40 Machnadebai, Shashai, Sharai,
41 Azareel, and Shelemiah, Shemariah,
42 Shallum, Amariah, *and* Joseph.
43 Of the sons of Nebo; Jeiel, Mattithiah, Zabad,
Zebina, Jadau, and Joel, Benaiah.
44 All these had taken strange wives: and *some* of
them had wives by whom they had children.

NEW LIVING TRANSLATION

These are the gatekeepers who were guilty: Shallum,
Telem, and Uri.

25 These are the other people of Israel who were
guilty:
From the family of Parosh: Ramiah, Izziah,
Malkijah, Mijamin, Eleazar, Hashabiah,* and
Benaiah.
26 From the family of Elam: Mattaniah, Zechariah,
Jehiel, Abdi, Jeremoth, and Elijah.
27 From the family of Zattu: Elioenai, Eliashib,
Mattaniah, Jeremoth, Zabad, and Aziza.
28 From the family of Bebai: Jehohanan, Hananiah,
Zabbai, and Athlai.
29 From the family of Bani: Meshullam, Malluch,
Adaiah, Jashub, Sheal, and Jeremoth.
30 From the family of Pahath-moab: Adna, Kelal,
Benaiah, Maaseiah, Mattaniah, Bezalel, Binnui,
and Manasseh.
31 From the family of Harim: Eliezer, Ishijah,
Malkijah, Shemaiah, Shimeon, 32 Benjamin,
Malluch, and Shemariah.
33 From the family of Hashum: Mattenai, Mattattah,
Zabad, Eliphelet, Jeremai, Manasseh, and Shimei.
34 From the family of Bani: Maadai, Amram, Uel,
35 Benaiah, Bedeiah, Keluhi, 36 Vaniah, Meremoth,
Eliashib, 37 Mattaniah, Mattenai, and Jaasu.
38 From the family of Binnui*: Shimei, 39 Shelemiah,
Nathan, Adaiah, 40 Macnadebai, Shashai, Sharai,
41 Azarel, Shelemiah, Shemariah, 42 Shallum,
Amariah, and Joseph.
43 From the family of Nebo: Jeiel, Mattithiah, Zabad,
Zebina, Jaddai, Joel, and Benaiah.

44 Each of these men had a pagan wife, and some
even had children by these wives.*

10:25 As in parallel text at 1 Esdras 9:26; Hebrew reads *Malkijah*.
10:37-38 As in Greek version; Hebrew reads *Jaasu, 38Bani, Binnui*.
10:44 Or *and they sent them away with their children*. The meaning of the Hebrew is uncertain.

Nehemiah

KING JAMES VERSION

1 1 The words of Nehemiah the son of Hachaliah.

And it came to pass in the month Chisleu, in the
twentieth year, as I was in Shushan the palace,
2 That Hanani, one of my brethren, came, he and
certain men of Judah; and I asked them concerning
the Jews that had escaped, which were left of the captivity, and concerning Jerusalem.
3 And they said unto me, The remnant that are left
of the captivity there in the province *are* in great
affliction and reproach: the wall of Jerusalem also
is broken down, and the gates thereof are burned
with fire.
4 And it came to pass, when I heard these words,
that I sat down and wept, and mourned *certain* days,
and fasted, and prayed before the God of heaven,
5 And said, I beseech thee, O LORD God of heaven,
the great and terrible God, that keepeth covenant
and mercy for them that love him and observe his
commandments:
6 Let thine ear now be attentive, and thine eyes
open, that thou mayest hear the prayer of thy servant,
which I pray before thee now, day and night, for the
children of Israel thy servants, and confess the sins
of the children of Israel, which we have sinned
against thee: both I and my father's house have
sinned.
7 We have dealt very corruptly against thee, and
have not kept the commandments, nor the statutes,
nor the judgments, which thou commandedst thy
servant Moses.
8 Remember, I beseech thee, the word that thou
commandedst thy servant Moses, saying, *If* ye transgress, I will scatter you abroad among the nations:
9 But *if* ye turn unto me, and keep my commandments, and do them; though there were of you cast
out unto the uttermost part of the heaven, *yet* will I
gather them from thence, and will bring them unto
the place that I have chosen to set my name there.
10 Now these *are* thy servants and thy people,
whom thou hast redeemed by thy great power, and
by thy strong hand.

NEW LIVING TRANSLATION

1 These are the memoirs of Nehemiah son of
Hacaliah.

Nehemiah's Concern for Jerusalem

In late autumn, in the month of Kislev, in the twentieth year of King Artaxerxes' reign,* I was at the fortress of Susa. 2 Hanani, one of my brothers, came to
visit me with some other men who had just arrived
from Judah. I asked them about the Jews who had
returned there from captivity and about how things
were going in Jerusalem.
3 They said to me, "Things are not going well for
those who returned to the province of Judah. They
are in great trouble and disgrace. The wall of Jerusalem has been torn down, and the gates have been
destroyed by fire."
4 When I heard this, I sat down and wept. In fact,
for days I mourned, fasted, and prayed to the God
of heaven. 5 Then I said,

"O LORD, God of heaven, the great and awesome
God who keeps his covenant of unfailing love
with those who love him and obey his commands,
6 listen to my prayer! Look down and see me
praying night and day for your people Israel.
I confess that we have sinned against you. Yes,
even my own family and I have sinned! 7 We have
sinned terribly by not obeying the commands,
decrees, and regulations that you gave us through
your servant Moses.

8 "Please remember what you told your servant
Moses: 'If you are unfaithful to me, I will scatter
you among the nations. 9 But if you return to me
and obey my commands and live by them, then
even if you are exiled to the ends of the earth,
I will bring you back to the place I have chosen
for my name to be honored.'

10 "The people you rescued by your great
power and strong hand are your servants.

1:1 Hebrew *In the month of Kislev of the twentieth year.* A number of dates in the book of Nehemiah can be cross-checked with dates in surviving Persian records and related accurately to our modern calendar. This month of the ancient Hebrew lunar calendar occurred within the months of November and December 446 B.C. The *twentieth year* probably refers to the reign of King Artaxerxes I; compare 2:1; 5:14.

KING JAMES VERSION

11 O Lord, I beseech thee, let now thine ear be attentive to the prayer of thy servant, and to the prayer of thy servants, who desire to fear thy name: and prosper, I pray thee, thy servant this day, and grant him mercy in the sight of this man. For I was the king's cupbearer.

2 1 And it came to pass in the month Nisan, in the twentieth year of Artaxerxes the king, *that* wine *was* before him: and I took up the wine, and gave *it* unto the king. Now I had not been *beforetime* sad in his presence.

2 Wherefore the king said unto me, Why *is* thy countenance sad, seeing thou *art* not sick? this *is* nothing *else* but sorrow of heart. Then I was very sore afraid,

3 And said unto the king, Let the king live for ever: why should not my countenance be sad, when the city, the place of my fathers' sepulchres, *lieth* waste, and the gates thereof are consumed with fire?

4 Then the king said unto me, For what dost thou make request? So I prayed to the God of heaven.

5 And I said unto the king, If it please the king, and if thy servant have found favour in thy sight, that thou wouldest send me unto Judah, unto the city of my fathers' sepulchres, that I may build it.

6 And the king said unto me, (the queen also sitting by him,) For how long shall thy journey be? and when wilt thou return? So it pleased the king to send me; and I set him a time.

7 Moreover I said unto the king, If it please the king, let letters be given me to the governors beyond the river, that they may convey me over till I come into Judah;

8 And a letter unto Asaph the keeper of the king's forest, that he may give me timber to make beams for the gates of the palace which *appertained* to the house, and for the wall of the city, and for the house that I shall enter into. And the king granted me, according to the good hand of my God upon me.

9 Then I came to the governors beyond the river, and gave them the king's letters. Now the king had sent captains of the army and horsemen with me.

10 When Sanballat the Horonite, and Tobiah the servant, the Ammonite, heard *of it,* it grieved them exceedingly that there was come a man to seek the welfare of the children of Israel.

11 So I came to Jerusalem, and was there three days.

12 And I arose in the night, I and some few men with me; neither told I *any* man what my God had put in my heart to do at Jerusalem: neither *was there any* beast with me, save the beast that I rode upon.

13 And I went out by night by the gate of the valley, even before the dragon well, and to the dung port, and viewed the walls of Jerusalem, which were

NEW LIVING TRANSLATION

11 O Lord, please hear my prayer! Listen to the
prayers of those of us who delight in honoring
you. Please grant me success today by making
the king favorable to me.* Put it into his heart
to be kind to me."

In those days I was the king's cup-bearer.

Nehemiah Goes to Jerusalem

2 Early the following spring, in the month of Nisan,* during the twentieth year of King Artaxerxes' reign, I was serving the king his wine. I had never before appeared sad in his presence. 2 So the king asked me, "Why are you looking so sad? You don't look sick to me. You must be deeply troubled."

Then I was terrified, 3 but I replied, "Long live the king! How can I not be sad? For the city where my ancestors are buried is in ruins, and the gates have been destroyed by fire."

4 The king asked, "Well, how can I help you?"

With a prayer to the God of heaven, 5 I replied, "If it please the king, and if you are pleased with me, your servant, send me to Judah to rebuild the city where my ancestors are buried."

6 The king, with the queen sitting beside him, asked, "How long will you be gone? When will you return?" After I told him how long I would be gone, the king agreed to my request.

7 I also said to the king, "If it please the king, let me have letters addressed to the governors of the province west of the Euphrates River,* instructing them to let me travel safely through their territories on my way to Judah. 8 And please give me a letter addressed to Asaph, the manager of the king's forest, instructing him to give me timber. I will need it to make beams for the gates of the Temple fortress, for the city walls, and for a house for myself." And the king granted these requests, because the gracious hand of God was on me.

9 When I came to the governors of the province west of the Euphrates River, I delivered the king's letters to them. The king, I should add, had sent along army officers and horsemen* to protect me. 10 But when Sanballat the Horonite and Tobiah the Ammonite official heard of my arrival, they were very displeased that someone had come to help the people of Israel.

Nehemiah Inspects Jerusalem's Wall

11 So I arrived in Jerusalem. Three days later, 12 I slipped out during the night, taking only a few others with me. I had not told anyone about the plans God had put in my heart for Jerusalem. We took no pack animals with us except the donkey I was riding. 13 After dark I went out through the Valley Gate, past

1:11 Hebrew *today in the sight of this man.* **2:1** Hebrew *In the month of Nisan.* This month of the ancient Hebrew lunar calendar occurred within the months of April and May 445 B.C. **2:7** Hebrew *the province beyond the river;* also in 2:9. **2:9** Or *charioteers.*

KING JAMES VERSION

broken down, and the gates thereof were consumed
with fire.
14 Then I went on to the gate of the fountain, and to
the king's pool: but *there was* no place for the beast
that was under me to pass.
15 Then went I up in the night by the brook, and
viewed the wall, and turned back, and entered by the
gate of the valley, and *so* returned.
16 And the rulers knew not whither I went, or what
I did; neither had I as yet told *it* to the Jews, nor to the
priests, nor to the nobles, nor to the rulers, nor to the
rest that did the work.
17 Then said I unto them, Ye see the distress that
we *are* in, how Jerusalem *lieth* waste, and the gates
thereof are burned with fire: come, and let us build
up the wall of Jerusalem, that we be no more a
reproach.
18 Then I told them of the hand of my God which
was good upon me; as also the king's words that he
had spoken unto me. And they said, Let us rise up
and build. So they strengthened their hands for *this*
good *work*.
19 But when Sanballat the Horonite, and Tobiah
the servant, the Ammonite, and Geshem the Arabian,
heard *it*, they laughed us to scorn, and despised us,
and said, What *is* this thing that ye do? will ye rebel
against the king?
20 Then answered I them, and said unto them, The
God of heaven, he will prosper us; therefore we his
servants will arise and build: but ye have no portion,
nor right, nor memorial, in Jerusalem.

3 1 Then Eliashib the high priest rose up with his
brethren the priests, and they builded the
sheep gate; they sanctified it, and set up the doors of
it; even unto the tower of Meah they sanctified it,
unto the tower of Hananeel.
2 And next unto him builded the men of Jericho.
And next to them builded Zaccur the son of Imri.
3 But the fish gate did the sons of Hassenaah build,
who *also* laid the beams thereof, and set up the doors
thereof, the locks thereof, and the bars thereof.
4 And next unto them repaired Meremoth the son
of Urijah, the son of Koz. And next unto them repaired Meshullam the son of Berechiah, the son of
Meshezabeel. And next unto them repaired Zadok
the son of Baana.
5 And next unto them the Tekoites repaired; but
their nobles put not their necks to the work of their
Lord.
6 Moreover the old gate repaired Jehoiada the son
of Paseah, and Meshullam the son of Besodeiah; they
laid the beams thereof, and set up the doors thereof,
and the locks thereof, and the bars thereof.
7 And next unto them repaired Melatiah the Gibeonite, and Jadon the Meronothite, the men of Gibeon, and of Mizpah, unto the throne of the governor
on this side the river.

NEW LIVING TRANSLATION

the Jackal's Well,* and over to the Dung Gate to inspect the broken walls and burned gates. 14 Then I
went to the Fountain Gate and to the King's Pool, but
my donkey couldn't get through the rubble. 15 So,
though it was still dark, I went up the Kidron Valley*
instead, inspecting the wall before I turned back and
entered again at the Valley Gate.
16 The city officials did not know I had been out
there or what I was doing, for I had not yet said anything to anyone about my plans. I had not yet spoken
to the Jewish leaders—the priests, the nobles, the
officials, or anyone else in the administration. 17 But
now I said to them, "You know very well what trouble
we are in. Jerusalem lies in ruins, and its gates have
been destroyed by fire. Let us rebuild the wall of Jerusalem and end this disgrace!" 18 Then I told them
about how the gracious hand of God had been on me,
and about my conversation with the king.

They replied at once, "Yes, let's rebuild the wall!"
So they began the good work.
19 But when Sanballat, Tobiah, and Geshem the
Arab heard of our plan, they scoffed contemptuously. "What are you doing? Are you rebelling
against the king?" they asked.
20 I replied, "The God of heaven will help us succeed. We, his servants, will start rebuilding this wall.
But you have no share, legal right, or historic claim in
Jerusalem."

Rebuilding the Wall of Jerusalem

3 Then Eliashib the high priest and the other
priests started to rebuild at the Sheep Gate.
They dedicated it and set up its doors, building the
wall as far as the Tower of the Hundred, which they
dedicated, and the Tower of Hananel. 2 People from
the town of Jericho worked next to them, and beyond
them was Zaccur son of Imri.
3 The Fish Gate was built by the sons of Hassenaah.
They laid the beams, set up its doors, and installed its
bolts and bars. 4 Meremoth son of Uriah and grandson of Hakkoz repaired the next section of wall. Beside him were Meshullam son of Berekiah and
grandson of Meshezabel, and then Zadok son of
Baana. 5 Next were the people from Tekoa, though
their leaders refused to work with the construction
supervisors.
6 The Old City Gate* was repaired by Joiada son of
Paseah and Meshullam son of Besodeiah. They laid
the beams, set up its doors, and installed its bolts
and bars. 7 Next to them were Melatiah from Gibeon,
Jadon from Meronoth, people from Gibeon, and
people from Mizpah, the headquarters of the governor of the province west of the Euphrates River.*

2:13 Or *Serpent's Well.* **2:15** Hebrew *the valley.* **3:6** Or *The Mishneh Gate,* or *The Jeshanah Gate.* **3:7** Hebrew *the province beyond the river.*

KING JAMES VERSION

8 Next unto him repaired Uzziel the son of Harhaiah, of the goldsmiths. Next unto him also repaired
Hananiah the son of *one of* the apothecaries, and
they fortified Jerusalem unto the broad wall.
9 And next unto them repaired Rephaiah the son of
Hur, the ruler of the half part of Jerusalem.
10 And next unto them repaired Jedaiah the son
of Harumaph, even over against his house. And next
unto him repaired Hattush the son of Hashabniah.
11 Malchijah the son of Harim, and Hashub the son
of Pahath-moab, repaired the other piece, and the
tower of the furnaces.
12 And next unto him repaired Shallum the son of
Halohesh, the ruler of the half part of Jerusalem, he
and his daughters.
13 The valley gate repaired Hanun, and the inhabitants of Zanoah; they built it, and set up the doors
thereof, the locks thereof, and the bars thereof, and a
thousand cubits on the wall unto the dung gate.
14 But the dung gate repaired Malchiah the son of
Rechab, the ruler of part of Beth-haccerem; he built
it, and set up the doors thereof, the locks thereof, and
the bars thereof.
15 But the gate of the fountain repaired Shallun
the son of Col-hozeh, the ruler of part of Mizpah; he
built it, and covered it, and set up the doors thereof,
the locks thereof, and the bars thereof, and the wall
of the pool of Siloah by the king's garden, and unto
the stairs that go down from the city of David.
16 After him repaired Nehemiah the son of Azbuk,
the ruler of the half part of Beth-zur, unto *the place*
over against the sepulchres of David, and to the pool
that was made, and unto the house of the mighty.
17 After him repaired the Levites, Rehum the son of
Bani. Next unto him repaired Hashabiah, the ruler of
the half part of Keilah, in his part.
18 After him repaired their brethren, Bavai the son
of Henadad, the ruler of the half part of Keilah.
19 And next to him repaired Ezer the son of Jeshua,
the ruler of Mizpah, another piece over against the
going up to the armoury at the turning *of the wall.*
20 After him Baruch the son of Zabbai earnestly repaired the other piece, from the turning *of the wall*
unto the door of the house of Eliashib the high
priest.
21 After him repaired Meremoth the son of Urijah
the son of Koz another piece, from the door of the
house of Eliashib even to the end of the house of
Eliashib.
22 And after him repaired the priests, the men of
the plain.
23 After him repaired Benjamin and Hashub over

NEW LIVING TRANSLATION

8 Next was Uzziel son of Harhaiah, a goldsmith by
trade, who also worked on the wall. Beyond him was
Hananiah, a manufacturer of perfumes. They left
out a section of Jerusalem as they built the Broad
Wall.*
9 Rephaiah son of Hur, the leader of half the district of Jerusalem, was next to them on the wall.
10 Next Jedaiah son of Harumaph repaired the wall
across from his own house, and next to him was
Hattush son of Hashabneiah. 11 Then came Malkijah
son of Harim and Hasshub son of Pahath-moab, who
repaired another section of the wall and the Tower of
the Ovens. 12 Shallum son of Hallohesh and his
daughters repaired the next section. He was the
leader of the other half of the district of Jerusalem.
13 The Valley Gate was repaired by the people from
Zanoah, led by Hanun. They set up its doors and installed its bolts and bars. They also repaired the
1,500 feet* of wall to the Dung Gate.
14 The Dung Gate was repaired by Malkijah son of
Recab, the leader of the Beth-hakkerem district. He
rebuilt it, set up its doors, and installed its bolts
and bars.
15 The Fountain Gate was repaired by Shallum*
son of Col-hozeh, the leader of the Mizpah district.
He rebuilt it, roofed it, set up its doors, and installed
its bolts and bars. Then he repaired the wall of the
pool of Siloam* near the king's garden, and he rebuilt the wall as far as the stairs that descend from
the City of David. 16 Next to him was Nehemiah son of
Azbuk, the leader of half the district of Beth-zur. He
rebuilt the wall from a place across from the tombs
of David's family as far as the water reservoir and the
House of the Warriors.
17 Next to him, repairs were made by a group of Levites working under the supervision of Rehum son of
Bani. Then came Hashabiah, the leader of half the
district of Keilah, who supervised the building of the
wall on behalf of his own district. 18 Next down the
line were his countrymen led by Binnui* son of Henadad, the leader of the other half of the district of
Keilah.
19 Next to them, Ezer son of Jeshua, the leader of
Mizpah, repaired another section of wall across from
the ascent to the armory near the angle in the wall.
20 Next to him was Baruch son of Zabbai, who zealously repaired an additional section from the angle to
the door of the house of Eliashib the high priest.
21 Meremoth son of Uriah and grandson of Hakkoz rebuilt another section of the wall extending from the
door of Eliashib's house to the end of the house.
22 The next repairs were made by the priests from
the surrounding region. 23 After them, Benjamin and
Hasshub repaired the section across from their

3:8 Or *They fortified Jerusalem up to the Broad Wall.* **3:13** Hebrew *1,000 cubits* [450 meters]. **3:15a** As in Syriac version; Hebrew reads *Shallun.* **3:15b** Hebrew *pool of Shelah,* another name for the pool of Siloam. **3:18** As in a few Hebrew manuscripts, some Greek manuscripts, and Syriac version (see also 3:24; 10:9); most Hebrew manuscripts read *Bavvai.*

KING JAMES VERSION

against their house. After him repaired Azariah the
son of Maaseiah the son of Ananiah by his house.
24 After him repaired Binnui the son of Henadad
another piece, from the house of Azariah unto the
turning *of the wall,* even unto the corner.
25 Palal the son of Uzai, over against the turning
of the wall, and the tower which lieth out from the
king's high house, that *was* by the court of the
prison. After him Pedaiah the son of Parosh.
26 Moreover the Nethinims dwelt in Ophel, unto
the place over against the water gate toward the east,
and the tower that lieth out.
27 After them the Tekoites repaired another piece,
over against the great tower that lieth out, even unto
the wall of Ophel.
28 From above the horse gate repaired the priests,
every one over against his house.
29 After them repaired Zadok the son of Immer
over against his house. After him repaired also
Shemaiah the son of Shechaniah, the keeper of the
east gate.
30 After him repaired Hananiah the son of Shelemiah, and Hanun the sixth son of Zalaph, another
piece. After him repaired Meshullam the son of
Berechiah over against his chamber.
31 After him repaired Malchiah the goldsmith's
son unto the place of the Nethinims, and of the merchants, over against the gate Miphkad, and to the
going up of the corner.
32 And between the going up of the corner unto
the sheep gate repaired the goldsmiths and the
merchants.

4 1 But it came to pass, that when Sanballat heard
that we builded the wall, he was wroth, and
took great indignation, and mocked the Jews.
2 And he spake before his brethren and the army of
Samaria, and said, What do these feeble Jews? will
they fortify themselves? will they sacrifice? will they
make an end in a day? will they revive the stones out
of the heaps of the rubbish which are burned?
3 Now Tobiah the Ammonite *was* by him, and he
said, Even that which they build, if a fox go up, he
shall even break down their stone wall.
4 Hear, O our God; for we are despised: and turn
their reproach upon their own head, and give them
for a prey in the land of captivity:
5 And cover not their iniquity, and let not their sin
be blotted out from before thee: for they have provoked *thee* to anger before the builders.
6 So built we the wall; and all the wall was joined
together unto the half thereof: for the people had a
mind to work.
7 But it came to pass, *that* when Sanballat, and Tobiah, and the Arabians, and the Ammonites, and the
Ashdodites, heard that the walls of Jerusalem were

NEW LIVING TRANSLATION

house, and Azariah son of Maaseiah and grandson of
Ananiah repaired the section across from his house.
24 Next was Binnui son of Henadad, who rebuilt another section of the wall from Azariah's house to the
angle and the corner. 25 Palal son of Uzai carried on
the work from a point opposite the angle and the
tower that projects up from the king's upper house
beside the court of the guard. Next to him were Pedaiah son of Parosh, 26 with the Temple servants living on the hill of Ophel, who repaired the wall as far
as a point across from the Water Gate to the east and
the projecting tower. 27 Then came the people of Tekoa, who repaired another section across from the
great projecting tower and over to the wall of Ophel.
28 Above the Horse Gate, the priests repaired the
wall. Each one repaired the section immediately
across from his own house. 29 Next Zadok son of
Immer also rebuilt the wall across from his own
house, and beyond him was Shemaiah son of Shecaniah, the gatekeeper of the East Gate. 30 Next Hananiah son of Shelemiah and Hanun, the sixth son of
Zalaph, repaired another section, while Meshullam
son of Berekiah rebuilt the wall across from where
he lived. 31 Malkijah, one of the goldsmiths, repaired
the wall as far as the housing for the Temple servants
and merchants, across from the Inspection Gate.
Then he continued as far as the upper room at the
corner. 32 The other goldsmiths and merchants repaired the wall from that corner to the Sheep Gate.

Enemies Oppose the Rebuilding

4 1 *Sanballat was very angry when he learned
that we were rebuilding the wall. He flew into a
rage and mocked the Jews, 2 saying in front of his
friends and the Samarian army officers, "What does
this bunch of poor, feeble Jews think they're doing?
Do they think they can build the wall in a single day
by just offering a few sacrifices?* Do they actually
think they can make something of stones from a rubbish heap—and charred ones at that?"
3 Tobiah the Ammonite, who was standing beside
him, remarked, "That stone wall would collapse if
even a fox walked along the top of it!"
4 Then I prayed, "Hear us, our God, for we are being
mocked. May their scoffing fall back on their own
heads, and may they themselves become captives in
a foreign land! 5 Do not ignore their guilt. Do not blot
out their sins, for they have provoked you to anger
here in front of* the builders."
6 At last the wall was completed to half its height
around the entire city, for the people had worked
with enthusiasm.
7 *But when Sanballat and Tobiah and the Arabs,

4:1 Verses 4:1-6 are numbered 3:33-38 in Hebrew text. **4:2** The meaning of the Hebrew is uncertain. **4:5** Or *for they have thrown insults in the face of.* **4:7** Verses 4:7-23 are numbered 4:1-17 in Hebrew text.

KING JAMES VERSION

made up, *and* that the breaches began to be stopped,
then they were very wroth,
8And conspired all of them together to come *and*
to fight against Jerusalem, and to hinder it.
9Nevertheless we made our prayer unto our God,
and set a watch against them day and night, because
of them.
10And Judah said, The strength of the bearers of
burdens is decayed, and *there is* much rubbish; so
that we are not able to build the wall.
11And our adversaries said, They shall not know,
neither see, till we come in the midst among them,
and slay them, and cause the work to cease.
12And it came to pass, that when the Jews which
dwelt by them came, they said unto us ten times,
From all places whence ye shall return unto us *they
will be upon you.*
13Therefore set I in the lower places behind the
wall, *and* on the higher places, I even set the people
after their families with their swords, their spears,
and their bows.
14And I looked, and rose up, and said unto the nobles, and to the rulers, and to the rest of the people,
Be not ye afraid of them: remember the LORD, *which
is* great and terrible, and fight for your brethren, your
sons, and your daughters, your wives, and your
houses.
15And it came to pass, when our enemies heard
that it was known unto us, and God had brought
their counsel to nought, that we returned all of us to
the wall, every one unto his work.
16And it came to pass from that time forth, *that*
the half of my servants wrought in the work, and the
other half of them held both the spears, the shields,
and the bows, and the habergeons; and the rulers
were behind all the house of Judah.
17They which builded on the wall, and they that
bare burdens, with those that laded, *every one* with
one of his hands wrought in the work, and with the
other *hand* held a weapon.
18For the builders, every one had his sword girded
by his side, and *so* builded. And he that sounded the
trumpet *was* by me.
19And I said unto the nobles, and to the rulers, and
to the rest of the people, The work *is* great and large,
and we are separated upon the wall, one far from
another.
20In what place *therefore* ye hear the sound of the
trumpet, resort ye thither unto us: our God shall fight
for us.
21So we laboured in the work: and half of them
held the spears from the rising of the morning till
the stars appeared.
22Likewise at the same time said I unto the people,
Let every one with his servant lodge within Jerusalem, that in the night they may be a guard to us, and
labour on the day.
23So neither I, nor my brethren, nor my servants,

NEW LIVING TRANSLATION

Ammonites, and Ashdodites heard that the work
was going ahead and that the gaps in the wall of Jerusalem were being repaired, they were furious. 8They
all made plans to come and fight against Jerusalem
and throw us into confusion. 9But we prayed to our
God and guarded the city day and night to protect
ourselves.
10Then the people of Judah began to complain,
"The workers are getting tired, and there is so much
rubble to be moved. We will never be able to build
the wall by ourselves."
11Meanwhile, our enemies were saying, "Before
they know what's happening, we will swoop down on
them and kill them and end their work."
12The Jews who lived near the enemy came and
told us again and again, "They will come from all directions and attack us!"* 13So I placed armed guards
behind the lowest parts of the wall in the exposed
areas. I stationed the people to stand guard by families, armed with swords, spears, and bows.
14Then as I looked over the situation, I called together the nobles and the rest of the people and said
to them, "Don't be afraid of the enemy! Remember
the Lord, who is great and glorious, and fight for your
brothers, your sons, your daughters, your wives, and
your homes!"
15When our enemies heard that we knew of their
plans and that God had frustrated them, we all returned to our work on the wall. 16But from then on,
only half my men worked while the other half stood
guard with spears, shields, bows, and coats of mail.
The leaders stationed themselves behind the people
of Judah 17who were building the wall. The laborers
carried on their work with one hand supporting
their load and one hand holding a weapon. 18All the
builders had a sword belted to their side. The trum-
peter stayed with me to sound the alarm.
19Then I explained to the nobles and officials and
all the people, "The work is very spread out, and we
are widely separated from each other along the wall.
20When you hear the blast of the trumpet, rush
to wherever it is sounding. Then our God will fight
for us!"
21We worked early and late, from sunrise to sunset.
And half the men were always on guard. 22I also told
everyone living outside the walls to stay in Jerusalem.
That way they and their servants could help with
guard duty at night and work during the day. 23During
this time, none of us—not I, nor my relatives, nor my

4:12 The meaning of the Hebrew is uncertain.

KING JAMES VERSION

nor the men of the guard which followed me, none of
us put off our clothes, *saving that* every one put
them off for washing.

5 1And there was a great cry of the people and of
their wives against their brethren the Jews.
2For there were that said, We, our sons, and our
daughters, *are* many: therefore we take up corn *for
them,* that we may eat, and live.
3*Some* also there were that said, We have mortgaged our lands, vineyards, and houses, that we
might buy corn, because of the dearth.
4There were also that said, We have borrowed
money for the king's tribute, *and that upon* our lands
and vineyards.
5Yet now our flesh *is* as the flesh of our brethren,
our children as their children: and, lo, we bring into
bondage our sons and our daughters to be servants,
and *some* of our daughters are brought unto bondage *already:* neither *is it* in our power *to redeem
them;* for other men have our lands and vineyards.
6And I was very angry when I heard their cry and
these words.
7Then I consulted with myself, and I rebuked the
nobles, and the rulers, and said unto them, Ye exact
usury, every one of his brother. And I set a great
assembly against them.
8And I said unto them, We after our ability have redeemed our brethren the Jews, which were sold unto
the heathen; and will ye even sell your brethren? or
shall they be sold unto us? Then held they their
peace, and found nothing *to answer.*
9Also I said, It *is* not good that ye do: ought ye not
to walk in the fear of our God because of the reproach of the heathen our enemies?
10I likewise, *and* my brethren, and my servants,
might exact of them money and corn: I pray you, let
us leave off this usury.
11Restore, I pray you, to them, even this day, their
lands, their vineyards, their oliveyards, and their
houses, also the hundredth *part* of the money, and of
the corn, the wine, and the oil, that ye exact of them.
12Then said they, We will restore *them,* and will require nothing of them; so will we do as thou sayest.
Then I called the priests, and took an oath of them,
that they should do according to this promise.
13Also I shook my lap, and said, So God shake out
every man from his house, and from his labour, that
performeth not this promise, even thus be he shaken
out, and emptied. And all the congregation said,
Amen, and praised the LORD. And the people did
according to this promise.
14Moreover from the time that I was appointed to
be their governor in the land of Judah, from the
twentieth year even unto the two and thirtieth year
of Artaxerxes the king, *that is,* twelve years, I and my
brethren have not eaten the bread of the governor.

NEW LIVING TRANSLATION

servants, nor the guards who were with me—ever
took off our clothes. We carried our weapons with us
at all times, even when we went for water.*

Nehemiah Defends the Oppressed

5 About this time some of the men and their
wives raised a cry of protest against their fellow
Jews. 2They were saying, "We have such large families. We need more food to survive."
3Others said, "We have mortgaged our fields, vineyards, and homes to get food during the famine."
4And others said, "We have had to borrow money
on our fields and vineyards to pay our taxes. 5We belong to the same family as those who are wealthy, and
our children are just like theirs. Yet we must sell our
children into slavery just to get enough money to live.
We have already sold some of our daughters, and we
are helpless to do anything about it, for our fields and
vineyards are already mortgaged to others."
6When I heard their complaints, I was very angry.
7After thinking it over, I spoke out against these
nobles and officials. I told them, "You are hurting
your own relatives by charging interest when they
borrow money!" Then I called a public meeting to
deal with the problem.
8At the meeting I said to them, "We are doing all
we can to redeem our Jewish relatives who have had
to sell themselves to pagan foreigners, but you are
selling them back into slavery again. How often must
we redeem them?" And they had nothing to say in
their defense.
9Then I pressed further, "What you are doing is
not right! Should you not walk in the fear of our God
in order to avoid being mocked by enemy nations?
10I myself, as well as my brothers and my workers,
have been lending the people money and grain, but
now let us stop this business of charging interest.
11You must restore their fields, vineyards, olive
groves, and homes to them this very day. And repay
the interest you charged when you lent them money,
grain, new wine, and olive oil."
12They replied, "We will give back everything and
demand nothing more from the people. We will do as
you say." Then I called the priests and made the nobles
and officials swear to do what they had promised.
13I shook out the folds of my robe and said, "If you
fail to keep your promise, may God shake you like
this from your homes and from your property!"
The whole assembly responded, "Amen," and they
praised the LORD. And the people did as they had
promised.
14For the entire twelve years that I was governor of
Judah—from the twentieth year to the thirty-second
year of the reign of King Artaxerxes*—neither I nor
my officials drew on our official food allowance.

4:23 Or *Each carried his weapon in his right hand.* Hebrew reads *Each his weapon the water.* The meaning of the Hebrew is uncertain. **5:14** That is, 445–433 B.C.

KING JAMES VERSION

15 But the former governors that *had been* before
me were chargeable unto the people, and had taken
of them bread and wine, beside forty shekels of
silver; yea, even their servants bare rule over the
people: but so did not I, because of the fear of God.
16 Yea, also I continued in the work of this wall, neither bought we any land: and all my servants *were*
gathered thither unto the work.
17 Moreover *there were* at my table an hundred
and fifty of the Jews and rulers, beside those that
came unto us from among the heathen that *are*
about us.
18 Now *that* which was prepared *for me* daily *was*
one ox *and* six choice sheep; also fowls were prepared for me, and once in ten days store of all sorts of
wine: yet for all this required not I the bread of the
governor, because the bondage was heavy upon this
people.
19 Think upon me, my God, for good, *according* to
all that I have done for this people.

6 1 Now it came to pass, when Sanballat, and Tobiah, and Geshem the Arabian, and the rest of our
enemies, heard that I had builded the wall, and *that*
there was no breach left therein; (though at that time
I had not set up the doors upon the gates;)
2 That Sanballat and Geshem sent unto me, saying,
Come, let us meet together in *some one of* the villages in the plain of Ono. But they thought to do me
mischief.
3 And I sent messengers unto them, saying, I *am*
doing a great work, so that I cannot come down: why
should the work cease, whilst I leave it, and come
down to you?
4 Yet they sent unto me four times after this sort;
and I answered them after the same manner.
5 Then sent Sanballat his servant unto me in like
manner the fifth time with an open letter in his
hand;
6 Wherein *was* written, It is reported among the
heathen, and Gashmu saith *it, that* thou and the Jews
think to rebel: for which cause thou buildest the wall,
that thou mayest be their king, according to these
words.
7 And thou hast also appointed prophets to preach
of thee at Jerusalem, saying, *There is* a king in Judah:
and now shall it be reported to the king according
to these words. Come now therefore, and let us take
counsel together.
8 Then I sent unto him, saying, There are no such
things done as thou sayest, but thou feignest them
out of thine own heart.
9 For they all made us afraid, saying, Their hands
shall be weakened from the work, that it be not done.
Now therefore, *O God,* strengthen my hands.
10 Afterward I came unto the house of Shemaiah
the son of Delaiah the son of Mehetabeel, who *was*
shut up; and he said, Let us meet together in the

NEW LIVING TRANSLATION

15 The former governors, in contrast, had laid heavy
burdens on the people, demanding a daily ration of
food and wine, besides forty pieces* of silver. Even
their assistants took advantage of the people. But because I feared God, I did not act that way.
16 I also devoted myself to working on the wall and
refused to acquire any land. And I required all my
servants to spend time working on the wall. 17 I asked
for nothing, even though I regularly fed 150 Jewish
officials at my table, besides all the visitors from
other lands! 18 The provisions I paid for each day included one ox, six choice sheep or goats, and a large
number of poultry. And every ten days we needed
a large supply of all kinds of wine. Yet I refused to
claim the governor's food allowance because the
people already carried a heavy burden.

19 Remember, O my God, all that I have done for
these people, and bless me for it.

Continued Opposition to Rebuilding

6 Sanballat, Tobiah, Geshem the Arab, and the
rest of our enemies found out that I had finished rebuilding the wall and that no gaps remained—though we had not yet set up the doors in
the gates. 2 So Sanballat and Geshem sent a message
asking me to meet them at one of the villages* in the
plain of Ono.
But I realized they were plotting to harm me, 3 so I
replied by sending this message to them: "I am engaged in a great work, so I can't come. Why should
I stop working to come and meet with you?"
4 Four times they sent the same message, and each
time I gave the same reply. 5 The fifth time, Sanballat's servant came with an open letter in his hand,
6 and this is what it said:

"There is a rumor among the surrounding
nations, and Geshem* tells me it is true, that
you and the Jews are planning to rebel and that
is why you are building the wall. According to his
reports, you plan to be their king. 7 He also reports
that you have appointed prophets in Jerusalem
to proclaim about you, 'Look! There is a king in
Judah!'
"You can be very sure that this report will get
back to the king, so I suggest that you come and
talk it over with me."

8 I replied, "There is no truth in any part of your
story. You are making up the whole thing."
9 They were just trying to intimidate us, imagining
that they could discourage us and stop the work. So I
continued the work with even greater determination.*
10 Later I went to visit Shemaiah son of Delaiah and
grandson of Mehetabel, who was confined to his

5:15 Hebrew *40 shekels* [1 pound, or 456 grams]. **6:2** As in Greek version; Hebrew reads *at Kephirim.* **6:6** Hebrew *Gashmu,* a variant spelling of Geshem. **6:9** As in Greek version; Hebrew reads *But now to strengthen my hands.*

KING JAMES VERSION

house of God, within the temple, and let us shut the
doors of the temple: for they will come to slay thee;
yea, in the night will they come to slay thee.
11 And I said, Should such a man as I flee? and who
is there, that, *being* as I *am,* would go into the temple
to save his life? I will not go in.
12 And, lo, I perceived that God had not sent him;
but that he pronounced this prophecy against me:
for Tobiah and Sanballat had hired him.
13 Therefore *was* he hired, that I should be afraid,
and do so, and sin, and *that* they might have *matter*
for an evil report, that they might reproach me.
14 My God, think thou upon Tobiah and Sanballat
according to these their works, and on the prophetess Noadiah, and the rest of the prophets, that would
have put me in fear.

15 So the wall was finished in the twenty and fifth
day of *the month* Elul, in fifty and two days.
16 And it came to pass, that when all our enemies
heard *thereof,* and all the heathen that *were* about us
saw *these things,* they were much cast down in their
own eyes: for they perceived that this work was
wrought of our God.
17 Moreover in those days the nobles of Judah sent
many letters unto Tobiah, and *the letters* of Tobiah
came unto them.
18 For *there were* many in Judah sworn unto him,
because he *was* the son in law of Shechaniah the son
of Arah; and his son Johanan had taken the daughter
of Meshullam the son of Berechiah.
19 Also they reported his good deeds before me,
and uttered my words to him. *And* Tobiah sent letters to put me in fear.

7 1 Now it came to pass, when the wall was built,
and I had set up the doors, and the porters and
the singers and the Levites were appointed,
2 That I gave my brother Hanani, and Hananiah the
ruler of the palace, charge over Jerusalem: for he *was*
a faithful man, and feared God above many.
3 And I said unto them, Let not the gates of Jerusalem be opened until the sun be hot; and while they
stand by, let them shut the doors, and bar *them:* and
appoint watches of the inhabitants of Jerusalem,
every one in his watch, and every one *to be* over
against his house.

4 Now the city *was* large and great: but the people
were few therein, and the houses *were* not builded.
5 And my God put into mine heart to gather together the nobles, and the rulers, and the people, that
they might be reckoned by genealogy. And I found a

NEW LIVING TRANSLATION

home. He said, "Let us meet together inside the Temple of God and bolt the doors shut. Your enemies are
coming to kill you tonight."
11 But I replied, "Should someone in my position
run from danger? Should someone in my position
enter the Temple to save his life? No, I won't do it!" 12 I
realized that God had not spoken to him, but that he
had uttered this prophecy against me because Tobiah and Sanballat had hired him. 13 They were hoping
to intimidate me and make me sin. Then they would
be able to accuse and discredit me.

14 Remember, O my God, all the evil things that
Tobiah and Sanballat have done. And remember
Noadiah the prophet and all the prophets like her
who have tried to intimidate me.

The Builders Complete the Wall

15 So on October 2* the wall was finished—just fifty-
two days after we had begun. 16 When our enemies
and the surrounding nations heard about it, they
were frightened and humiliated. They realized this
work had been done with the help of our God.
17 During those fifty-two days, many letters went
back and forth between Tobiah and the nobles of
Judah. 18 For many in Judah had sworn allegiance to
him because his father-in-law was Shecaniah son
of Arah, and his son Jehohanan was married to the
daughter of Meshullam son of Berekiah. 19 They kept
telling me about Tobiah's good deeds, and then they
told him everything I said. And Tobiah kept sending
threatening letters to intimidate me.

7 After the wall was finished and I had set up the
doors in the gates, the gatekeepers, singers, and
Levites were appointed. 2 I gave the responsibility of
governing Jerusalem to my brother Hanani, along
with Hananiah, the commander of the fortress, for he
was a faithful man who feared God more than most.
3 I said to them, "Do not leave the gates open during
the hottest part of the day.* And even while the gatekeepers are on duty, have them shut and bar the
doors. Appoint the residents of Jerusalem to act as
guards, everyone on a regular watch. Some will serve
at sentry posts and some in front of their own
homes."

Nehemiah Registers the People

4 At that time the city was large and spacious, but the
population was small, and none of the houses had
been rebuilt. 5 So my God gave me the idea to call
together all the nobles and leaders of the city, along
with the ordinary citizens, for registration. I had

6:15 Hebrew *on the twenty-fifth day of the month Elul,* of the ancient Hebrew lunar calendar. This day was October 2, 445 B.C.; also see note on 1:1. **7:3** Or *Keep the gates of Jerusalem closed until the sun is hot.*

register of the genealogy of them which came up at
the first, and found written therein,
6 These *are* the children of the province, that went
up out of the captivity, of those that had been carried
away, whom Nebuchadnezzar the king of Babylon
had carried away, and came again to Jerusalem and
to Judah, every one unto his city;
7 Who came with Zerubbabel, Jeshua, Nehemiah,
Azariah, Raamiah, Nahamani, Mordecai, Bilshan,
Mispereth, Bigvai, Nehum, Baanah. The number, *I*
say, of the men of the people of Israel *was this;*
8 The children of Parosh, two thousand an hundred
seventy and two.
9 The children of Shephatiah, three hundred seventy and two.
10 The children of Arah, six hundred fifty and two.
11 The children of Pahath-moab, of the children of
Jeshua and Joab, two thousand and eight hundred
and eighteen.
12 The children of Elam, a thousand two hundred
fifty and four.
13 The children of Zattu, eight hundred forty
and five.
14 The children of Zaccai, seven hundred and
threescore.
15 The children of Binnui, six hundred forty and
eight.
16 The children of Bebai, six hundred twenty
and eight.
17 The children of Azgad, two thousand three hundred twenty and two.
18 The children of Adonikam, six hundred threescore and seven.
19 The children of Bigvai, two thousand threescore
and seven.
20 The children of Adin, six hundred fifty and five.
21 The children of Ater of Hezekiah, ninety and
eight.
22 The children of Hashum, three hundred twenty
and eight.
23 The children of Bezai, three hundred twenty and
four.
24 The children of Hariph, an hundred and twelve.
25 The children of Gibeon, ninety and five.
26 The men of Bethlehem and Netophah, an hundred fourscore and eight.
27 The men of Anathoth, an hundred twenty and
eight.
28 The men of Beth-azmaveth, forty and two.
29 The men of Kirjath-jearim, Chephirah, and
Beeroth, seven hundred forty and three.
30 The men of Ramah and Gaba, six hundred
twenty and one.
31 The men of Michmas, an hundred and twenty
and two.
32 The men of Bethel and Ai, an hundred twenty
and three.
33 The men of the other Nebo, fifty and two.

found the genealogical record of those who had first
returned to Judah. This is what was written there:
6 Here is the list of the Jewish exiles of the
provinces who returned from their captivity.
King Nebuchadnezzar had deported them to
Babylon, but now they returned to Jerusalem and
the other towns in Judah where they originally
lived. 7 Their leaders were Zerubbabel, Jeshua,
Nehemiah, Seraiah,* Reelaiah,* Nahamani,
Mordecai, Bilshan, Mispar,* Bigvai, Rehum,*
and Baanah.

This is the number of the men of Israel who
returned from exile:

8 The family of Parosh	2,172
9 The family of Shephatiah	372
10 The family of Arah	652
11 The family of Pahath-moab (descendants of Jeshua and Joab)	2,818
12 The family of Elam	1,254
13 The family of Zattu	845
14 The family of Zaccai	760
15 The family of Bani*	648
16 The family of Bebai	628
17 The family of Azgad	2,322
18 The family of Adonikam	667
19 The family of Bigvai	2,067
20 The family of Adin	655
21 The family of Ater (descendants of Hezekiah)	98
22 The family of Hashum	328
23 The family of Bezai	324
24 The family of Jorah*	112
25 The family of Gibbar*	95
26 The people of Bethlehem and Netophah	188
27 The people of Anathoth	128
28 The people of Beth-azmaveth	42
29 The people of Kiriath-jearim, Kephirah, and Beeroth	743
30 The people of Ramah and Geba	621
31 The people of Micmash	122
32 The people of Bethel and Ai	123
33 The people of West Nebo*	52

7:7a As in parallel text at Ezra 2:2; Hebrew reads *Azariah.* **7:7b** As in parallel text at Ezra 2:2; Hebrew reads *Raamiah.* **7:7c** As in parallel text at Ezra 2:2; Hebrew reads *Mispereth.* **7:7d** As in parallel text at Ezra 2:2; Hebrew reads *Nehum.* **7:15** As in parallel text at Ezra 2:10; Hebrew reads *Binnui.* **7:24** As in parallel text at Ezra 2:18; Hebrew reads *Hariph.* **7:25** As in parallel text at Ezra 2:20; Hebrew reads *Gibeon.* **7:33** Or *of the other Nebo.*

KING JAMES VERSION

34 The children of the other Elam, a thousand two hundred fifty and four.

35 The children of Harim, three hundred and twenty.

36 The children of Jericho, three hundred forty and five.

37 The children of Lod, Hadid, and Ono, seven hundred twenty and one.

38 The children of Senaah, three thousand nine hundred and thirty.

39 The priests: the children of Jedaiah, of the house of Jeshua, nine hundred seventy and three.

40 The children of Immer, a thousand fifty and two.

41 The children of Pashur, a thousand two hundred forty and seven.

42 The children of Harim, a thousand and seventeen.

43 The Levites: the children of Jeshua, of Kadmiel, *and* of the children of Hodevah, seventy and four.

44 The singers: the children of Asaph, an hundred forty and eight.

45 The porters: the children of Shallum, the children of Ater, the children of Talmon, the children of Akkub, the children of Hatita, the children of Shobai, an hundred thirty and eight.

46 The Nethinims: the children of Ziha, the children of Hashupha, the children of Tabbaoth,

47 The children of Keros, the children of Sia, the children of Padon,

48 The children of Lebana, the children of Hagaba, the children of Shalmai,

49 The children of Hanan, the children of Giddel, the children of Gahar,

50 The children of Reaiah, the children of Rezin, the children of Nekoda,

51 The children of Gazzam, the children of Uzza, the children of Phaseah,

52 The children of Besai, the children of Meunim, the children of Nephishesim,

53 The children of Bakbuk, the children of Hakupha, the children of Harhur,

54 The children of Bazlith, the children of Mehida, the children of Harsha,

55 The children of Barkos, the children of Sisera, the children of Tamah,

56 The children of Neziah, the children of Hatipha.

57 The children of Solomon's servants: the children of Sotai, the children of Sophereth, the children of Perida,

58 The children of Jaala, the children of Darkon, the children of Giddel,

59 The children of Shephatiah, the children of Hattil, the children of Pochereth of Zebaim, the children of Amon.

60 All the Nethinims, and the children of Solomon's servants, *were* three hundred ninety and two.

61 And these *were* they which went up *also* from Tel-melah, Tel-haresha, Cherub, Addon, and Immer:

NEW LIVING TRANSLATION

34 The citizens of West Elam* · · · · · · · 1,254
35 The citizens of Harim · · · · · · · 320
36 The citizens of Jericho · · · · · · · 345
37 The citizens of Lod, Hadid, and Ono · · · 721
38 The citizens of Senaah · · · · · · · 3,930

39 These are the priests who returned from exile:
The family of Jedaiah
(through the line of Jeshua) · · · · · · · 973
40 The family of Immer · · · · · · · 1,052
41 The family of Pashhur · · · · · · · 1,247
42 The family of Harim · · · · · · · 1,017

43 These are the Levites who returned from exile:
The families of Jeshua and Kadmiel (descendants of Hodaviah*) · · · · · · · 74
44 The singers of the family of Asaph · · · · 148
45 The gatekeepers of the families of Shallum,
Ater, Talmon, Akkub, Hatita, and Shobai · · · 138

46 The descendants of the following Temple servants returned from exile:
Ziha, Hasupha, Tabbaoth,
47 Keros, Siaha,* Padon,
48 Lebanah, Hagabah, Shalmai,
49 Hanan, Giddel, Gahar,
50 Reaiah, Rezin, Nekoda,
51 Gazzam, Uzza, Paseah,
52 Besai, Meunim, Nephusim,*
53 Bakbuk, Hakupha, Harhur,
54 Bazluth,* Mehida, Harsha,
55 Barkos, Sisera, Temah,
56 Neziah, and Hatipha.

57 The descendants of these servants of King Solomon returned from exile:
Sotai, Hassophereth, Peruda,*
58 Jaalah,* Darkon, Giddel,
59 Shephatiah, Hattil, Pokereth-hazzebaim, and Ami.*

60 In all, the Temple servants and the descendants of Solomon's servants numbered 392.

61 Another group returned at this time from the towns of Tel-melah, Tel-harsha, Kerub, Addan,*

7:34 Or *of the other Elam.* **7:43** As in parallel text at Ezra 2:40; Hebrew reads *Hodevah.* **7:47** As in parallel text at Ezra 2:44; Hebrew reads *Sia.* **7:52** As in parallel text at Ezra 2:50; Hebrew reads *Nephushesim.* **7:54** As in parallel text at Ezra 2:52; Hebrew reads *Bazlith.* **7:57** As in parallel text at Ezra 2:55; Hebrew reads *Sotai, Sophereth, Perida.* **7:58** As in parallel text at Ezra 2:56; Hebrew reads *Jaala.* **7:59** As in parallel text at Ezra 2:57; Hebrew reads *Amon.* **7:61** As in parallel text at Ezra 2:59; Hebrew reads *Addon.*

KING JAMES VERSION

but they could not shew their father's house, nor their seed, whether they *were* of Israel.

62 The children of Delaiah, the children of Tobiah, the children of Nekoda, six hundred forty and two.

63 And of the priests: the children of Habaiah, the children of Koz, the children of Barzillai, which took *one* of the daughters of Barzillai the Gileadite to wife, and was called after their name.

64 These sought their register *among* those that were reckoned by genealogy, but it was not found: therefore were they, as polluted, put from the priesthood.

65 And the Tirshatha said unto them, that they should not eat of the most holy things, till there stood *up* a priest with Urim and Thummim.

66 The whole congregation together *was* forty and two thousand three hundred and threescore,

67 Beside their manservants and their maidservants, of whom *there were* seven thousand three hundred thirty and seven: and they had two hundred forty and five singing men and singing women.

68 Their horses, seven hundred thirty and six: their mules, two hundred forty and five:

69 *Their* camels, four hundred thirty and five: six thousand seven hundred and twenty asses.

70 And some of the chief of the fathers gave unto the work. The Tirshatha gave to the treasure a thousand drams of gold, fifty basins, five hundred and thirty priests' garments.

71 And *some* of the chief of the fathers gave to the treasure of the work twenty thousand drams of gold, and two thousand and two hundred pound of silver.

72 And *that* which the rest of the people gave *was* twenty thousand drams of gold, and two thousand pound of silver, and threescore and seven priests' garments.

73 So the priests, and the Levites, and the porters, and the singers, and *some* of the people, and the Nethinims, and all Israel, dwelt in their cities; and when the seventh month came, the children of Israel *were* in their cities.

8 1 And all the people gathered themselves together as one man into the street that *was* before the water gate; and they spake unto Ezra the scribe to bring the book of the law of Moses, which the LORD had commanded to Israel.

2 And Ezra the priest brought the law before the congregation both of men and women, and all that could hear with understanding, upon the first day of the seventh month.

NEW LIVING TRANSLATION

and Immer. However, they could not prove that they or their families were descendants of Israel. 62 This group included the families of Delaiah, Tobiah, and Nekoda—a total of 642 people.

63 Three families of priests—Hobaiah, Hakkoz, and Barzillai—also returned. (This Barzillai had married a woman who was a descendant of Barzillai of Gilead, and he had taken her family name.) 64 They searched for their names in the genealogical records, but they were not found, so they were disqualified from serving as priests. 65 The governor told them not to eat the priests' share of food from the sacrifices until a priest could consult the LORD about the matter by using the Urim and Thummim—the sacred lots.

66 So a total of 42,360 people returned to Judah, 67 in addition to 7,337 servants and 245 singers, both men and women. 68 They took with them 736 horses, 245 mules,* 69 435 camels, and 6,720 donkeys.

70 Some of the family leaders gave gifts for the work. The governor gave to the treasury 1,000 gold coins,* 50 gold basins, and 530 robes for the priests. 71 The other leaders gave to the treasury a total of 20,000 gold coins* and some 2,750 pounds* of silver for the work. 72 The rest of the people gave 20,000 gold coins, about 2,500 pounds* of silver, and 67 robes for the priests.

73 So the priests, the Levites, the gatekeepers, the singers, the Temple servants, and some of the common people settled near Jerusalem. The rest of the people returned to their own towns throughout Israel.

Ezra Reads the Law

8 In October,* when the Israelites had settled in their towns, 8:1 all the people assembled with a unified purpose at the square just inside the Water Gate. They asked Ezra the scribe to bring out the Book of the Law of Moses, which the LORD had given for Israel to obey.

2 So on October 8* Ezra the priest brought the Book of the Law before the assembly, which included the men and women and all the children old

7:68 As in some Hebrew manuscripts (see also Ezra 2:66); most Hebrew manuscripts lack this verse. Verses 7:69-73 are numbered 7:68-72 in Hebrew text. **7:70** Hebrew *1,000 darics of gold*, about 19 pounds or 8.6 kilograms in weight. **7:71a** Hebrew *20,000 darics of gold*, about 375 pounds or 170 kilograms in weight; also in 7:72. **7:71b** Hebrew *2,200 minas* [1,300 kilograms]. **7:72** Hebrew *2,000 minas* [1,200 kilograms]. **7:73** Hebrew *in the seventh month*. This month of the ancient Hebrew lunar calendar occurred within the months of October and November 445 B.C. **8:2** Hebrew *on the first day of the seventh month*, of the ancient Hebrew lunar calendar. This day was October 8, 445 B.C.; also see note on 1:1.

KING JAMES VERSION

3And he read therein before the street that *was* before the water gate from the morning until midday, before the men and the women, and those that could understand; and the ears of all the people *were attentive* unto the book of the law.

4And Ezra the scribe stood upon a pulpit of wood, which they had made for the purpose; and beside him stood Mattithiah, and Shema, and Anaiah, and Urijah, and Hilkiah, and Maaseiah, on his right hand; and on his left hand, Pedaiah, and Mishael, and Malchiah, and Hashum, and Hashbadana, Zechariah, *and* Meshullam.

5And Ezra opened the book in the sight of all the people; (for he was above all the people;) and when he opened it, all the people stood up:

6And Ezra blessed the LORD, the great God. And all the people answered, Amen, Amen, with lifting up their hands: and they bowed their heads, and worshipped the LORD with *their* faces to the ground.

7Also Jeshua, and Bani, and Sherebiah, Jamin, Akkub, Shabbethai, Hodijah, Maaseiah, Kelita, Azariah, Jozabad, Hanan, Pelaiah, and the Levites, caused the people to understand the law: and the people *stood* in their place.

8So they read in the book in the law of God distinctly, and gave the sense, and caused *them* to understand the reading.

9And Nehemiah, which *is* the Tirshatha, and Ezra the priest the scribe, and the Levites that taught the people, said unto all the people, This day *is* holy unto the LORD your God; mourn not, nor weep. For all the people wept, when they heard the words of the law.

10Then he said unto them, Go your way, eat the fat, and drink the sweet, and send portions unto them for whom nothing is prepared: for *this* day *is* holy unto our LORD: neither be ye sorry; for the joy of the LORD is your strength.

11So the Levites stilled all the people, saying, Hold your peace, for the day *is* holy; neither be ye grieved.

12And all the people went their way to eat, and to drink, and to send portions, and to make great mirth, because they had understood the words that were declared unto them.

13And on the second day were gathered together the chief of the fathers of all the people, the priests, and the Levites, unto Ezra the scribe, even to understand the words of the law.

14And they found written in the law which the LORD had commanded by Moses, that the children of Israel should dwell in booths in the feast of the seventh month:

15And that they should publish and proclaim in all their cities, and in Jerusalem, saying, Go forth unto the mount, and fetch olive branches, and pine branches, and myrtle branches, and palm branches, and branches of thick trees, to make booths, as *it is* written.

NEW LIVING TRANSLATION

enough to understand. 3He faced the square just inside the Water Gate from early morning until noon and read aloud to everyone who could understand. All the people listened closely to the Book of the Law.

4Ezra the scribe stood on a high wooden platform that had been made for the occasion. To his right stood Mattithiah, Shema, Anaiah, Uriah, Hilkiah, and Maaseiah. To his left stood Pedaiah, Mishael, Malkijah, Hashum, Hashbaddanah, Zechariah, and Meshullam. 5Ezra stood on the platform in full view of all the people. When they saw him open the book, they all rose to their feet.

6Then Ezra praised the LORD, the great God, and all the people chanted, "Amen! Amen!" as they lifted their hands. Then they bowed down and worshiped the LORD with their faces to the ground.

7The Levites—Jeshua, Bani, Sherebiah, Jamin, Akkub, Shabbethai, Hodiah, Maaseiah, Kelita, Azariah, Jozabad, Hanan, and Pelaiah—then instructed the people in the Law while everyone remained in their places. 8They read from the Book of the Law of God and clearly explained the meaning of what was being read, helping the people understand each passage.

9Then Nehemiah the governor, Ezra the priest and scribe, and the Levites who were interpreting for the people said to them, "Don't mourn or weep on such a day as this! For today is a sacred day before the LORD your God." For the people had all been weeping as they listened to the words of the Law.

10And Nehemiah* continued, "Go and celebrate with a feast of rich foods and sweet drinks, and share gifts of food with people who have nothing prepared. This is a sacred day before our Lord. Don't be dejected and sad, for the joy of the LORD is your strength!"

11And the Levites, too, quieted the people, telling them, "Hush! Don't weep! For this is a sacred day." 12So the people went away to eat and drink at a festive meal, to share gifts of food, and to celebrate with great joy because they had heard God's words and understood them.

The Festival of Shelters

13On October 9* the family leaders of all the people, together with the priests and Levites, met with Ezra the scribe to go over the Law in greater detail. 14As they studied the Law, they discovered that the LORD had commanded through Moses that the Israelites should live in shelters during the festival to be held that month.* 15He had said that a proclamation should be made throughout their towns and in Jerusalem, telling the people to go to the hills to get branches from olive, wild olive,* myrtle, palm, and other leafy trees. They were to use these branches to

8:10 Hebrew *he.* **8:13** Hebrew *On the second day,* of the seventh month of the ancient Hebrew lunar calendar. This day was October 9, 445 B.C.; also see notes on 1:1 and 8:2. **8:14** Hebrew *in the seventh month.* This month of the ancient Hebrew lunar calendar usually occurs within the months of September and October. See Lev 23:39-43. **8:15** Or *pine;* Hebrew reads *oil tree.*

16 So the people went forth, and brought *them*, and
made themselves booths, every one upon the roof of
his house, and in their courts, and in the courts of the
house of God, and in the street of the water gate, and
in the street of the gate of Ephraim.
17 And all the congregation of them that were
come again out of the captivity made booths, and sat
under the booths: for since the days of Jeshua the
son of Nun unto that day had not the children of Israel done so. And there was very great gladness.
18 Also day by day, from the first day unto the last
day, he read in the book of the law of God. And they
kept the feast seven days; and on the eighth day *was* a
solemn assembly, according unto the manner.

9 1 Now in the twenty and fourth day of this month
the children of Israel were assembled with fasting, and with sackclothes, and earth upon them.
2 And the seed of Israel separated themselves from
all strangers, and stood and confessed their sins, and
the iniquities of their fathers.
3 And they stood up in their place, and read in the
book of the law of the LORD their God *one* fourth part
of the day; and *another* fourth part they confessed,
and worshipped the LORD their God.
4 Then stood up upon the stairs, of the Levites,
Jeshua, and Bani, Kadmiel, Shebaniah, Bunni, Sherebiah, Bani, *and* Chenani, and cried with a loud voice
unto the LORD their God.
5 Then the Levites, Jeshua, and Kadmiel, Bani,
Hashabniah, Sherebiah, Hodijah, Shebaniah, *and*
Pethahiah, said, Stand up *and* bless the LORD your
God for ever and ever: and blessed be thy glorious
name, which is exalted above all blessing and praise.
6 Thou, *even* thou, *art* LORD alone; thou hast made
heaven, the heaven of heavens, with all their host, the
earth, and all *things* that *are* therein, the seas, and all
that *is* therein, and thou preservest them all; and the
host of heaven worshippeth thee.
7 Thou *art* the LORD the God, who didst choose
Abram, and broughtest him forth out of Ur of the
Chaldees, and gavest him the name of Abraham;
8 And foundest his heart faithful before thee, and
madest a covenant with him to give the land of the
Canaanites, the Hittites, the Amorites, and the Perizzites, and the Jebusites, and the Girgashites, to give
it, I say, to his seed, and hast performed thy words;
for thou *art* righteous:
9 And didst see the affliction of our fathers in
Egypt, and heardest their cry by the Red sea;
10 And shewedst signs and wonders upon Pharaoh,

make shelters in which they would live during the
festival, as prescribed in the Law.
16 So the people went out and cut branches and
used them to build shelters on the roofs of their
houses, in their courtyards, in the courtyards of
God's Temple, or in the squares just inside the Water
Gate and the Ephraim Gate. 17 So everyone who had
returned from captivity lived in these shelters during the festival, and they were all filled with great joy!
The Israelites had not celebrated like this since the
days of Joshua* son of Nun.
18 Ezra read from the Book of the Law of God on
each of the seven days of the festival. Then on the
eighth day they held a solemn assembly, as was required by law.

The People Confess Their Sins

9 On October 31* the people assembled again,
and this time they fasted and dressed in burlap
and sprinkled dust on their heads. 2 Those of Israelite descent separated themselves from all foreigners
as they confessed their own sins and the sins of their
ancestors. 3 They remained standing in place for
three hours* while the Book of the Law of the LORD
their God was read aloud to them. Then for three
more hours they confessed their sins and worshiped
the LORD their God. 4 The Levites—Jeshua, Bani, Kadmiel, Shebaniah, Bunni, Sherebiah, Bani, and Kena-
ni—stood on the stairway of the Levites and cried out
to the LORD their God with loud voices.
5 Then the leaders of the Levites—Jeshua, Kadmiel,
Bani, Hashabneiah, Sherebiah, Hodiah, Shebaniah,
and Pethahiah—called out to the people: "Stand up
and praise the LORD your God, for he lives from everlasting to everlasting!" Then they prayed:

"May your glorious name be praised! May it be
exalted above all blessing and praise!
6 "You alone are the LORD. You made the skies
and the heavens and all the stars. You made the
earth and the seas and everything in them. You
preserve them all, and the angels of heaven
worship you.
7 "You are the LORD God, who chose Abram
and brought him from Ur of the Chaldeans and
renamed him Abraham. 8 When he had proved
himself faithful, you made a covenant with him
to give him and his descendants the land of
the Canaanites, Hittites, Amorites, Perizzites,
Jebusites, and Girgashites. And you have done
what you promised, for you are always true to
your word.
9 "You saw the misery of our ancestors in
Egypt, and you heard their cries from beside the
Red Sea.* 10 You displayed miraculous signs and

8:17 Hebrew *Jeshua*, a variant spelling of Joshua. 9:1 Hebrew *On the twenty-fourth day of that same month*, the seventh month of the ancient Hebrew lunar calendar. This day was October 31, 445 B.C.; also see notes on 1:1 and 8:2. 9:3 Hebrew *for a quarter of a day.* 9:9 Hebrew *sea of reeds.*

KING JAMES VERSION

and on all his servants, and on all the people of his
land: for thou knewest that they dealt proudly
against them. So didst thou get thee a name, as *it is*
this day.
11 And thou didst divide the sea before them, so
that they went through the midst of the sea on the
dry land; and their persecutors thou threwest into
the deeps, as a stone into the mighty waters.
12 Moreover thou leddest them in the day by a
cloudy pillar; and in the night by a pillar of fire, to
give them light in the way wherein they should go.
13 Thou camest down also upon mount Sinai, and
spakest with them from heaven, and gavest them
right judgments, and true laws, good statutes and
commandments:
14 And madest known unto them thy holy sabbath,
and commandedst them precepts, statutes, and laws,
by the hand of Moses thy servant:
15 And gavest them bread from heaven for their
hunger, and broughtest forth water for them out of
the rock for their thirst, and promisedst them that
they should go in to possess the land which thou
hadst sworn to give them.
16 But they and our fathers dealt proudly, and
hardened their necks, and hearkened not to thy
commandments,
17 And refused to obey, neither were mindful of thy
wonders that thou didst among them; but hardened
their necks, and in their rebellion appointed
a captain to return to their bondage: but thou *art* a
God ready to pardon, gracious and merciful, slow to
anger, and of great kindness, and forsookest them
not.
18 Yea, when they had made them a molten calf,
and said, This *is* thy God that brought thee up out of
Egypt, and had wrought great provocations;
19 Yet thou in thy manifold mercies forsookest
them not in the wilderness: the pillar of the cloud
departed not from them by day, to lead them in the
way; neither the pillar of fire by night, to shew them
light, and the way wherein they should go.
20 Thou gavest also thy good spirit to instruct
them, and withheldest not thy manna from their
mouth, and gavest them water for their thirst.
21 Yea, forty years didst thou sustain them in the
wilderness, *so that* they lacked nothing; their clothes
waxed not old, and their feet swelled not.
22 Moreover thou gavest them kingdoms and nations, and didst divide them into corners: so they
possessed the land of Sihon, and the land of the king
of Heshbon, and the land of Og king of Bashan.
23 Their children also multipliedst thou as the
stars of heaven, and broughtest them into the land,
concerning which thou hadst promised to their fathers, that they should go in to possess *it*.
24 So the children went in and possessed the land,
and thou subduedst before them the inhabitants of
the land, the Canaanites, and gavest them into their

NEW LIVING TRANSLATION

wonders against Pharaoh, his officials, and all
his people, for you knew how arrogantly they
were treating our ancestors. You have a glorious
reputation that has never been forgotten. 11 You
divided the sea for your people so they could
walk through on dry land! And then you hurled
their enemies into the depths of the sea. They
sank like stones beneath the mighty waters.
12 You led our ancestors by a pillar of cloud
during the day and a pillar of fire at night so
that they could find their way.
13 "You came down at Mount Sinai and spoke
to them from heaven. You gave them regulations
and instructions that were just, and decrees and
commands that were good. 14 You instructed
them concerning your holy Sabbath. And you
commanded them, through Moses your servant,
to obey all your commands, decrees, and
instructions.
15 "You gave them bread from heaven when
they were hungry and water from the rock when
they were thirsty. You commanded them to go
and take possession of the land you had sworn
to give them.
16 "But our ancestors were proud and stubborn,
and they paid no attention to your commands.
17 They refused to obey and did not remember
the miracles you had done for them. Instead, they
became stubborn and appointed a leader to take
them back to their slavery in Egypt! But you are a
God of forgiveness, gracious and merciful, slow to
become angry, and rich in unfailing love. You did
not abandon them, 18 even when they made an
idol shaped like a calf and said, 'This is your god
who brought you out of Egypt!' They committed
terrible blasphemies.
19 "But in your great mercy you did not
abandon them to die in the wilderness. The pillar
of cloud still led them forward by day, and the
pillar of fire showed them the way through the
night. 20 You sent your good Spirit to instruct
them, and you did not stop giving them manna
from heaven or water for their thirst. 21 For forty
years you sustained them in the wilderness, and
they lacked nothing. Their clothes did not wear
out, and their feet did not swell!
22 "Then you helped our ancestors conquer
kingdoms and nations, and you placed your
people in every corner of the land.* They took
over the land of King Sihon of Heshbon and the
land of King Og of Bashan. 23 You made their
descendants as numerous as the stars in the
sky and brought them into the land you had
promised to their ancestors.
24 "They went in and took possession of the
land. You subdued whole nations before them.
Even the Canaanites, who inhabited the land,

9:22 The meaning of the Hebrew is uncertain.

KING JAMES VERSION

hands, with their kings, and the people of the land,
that they might do with them as they would.
25 And they took strong cities, and a fat land, and
possessed houses full of all goods, wells digged, vineyards, and oliveyards, and fruit trees in abundance:
so they did eat, and were filled, and became fat, and
delighted themselves in thy great goodness.
26 Nevertheless they were disobedient, and rebelled
against thee, and cast thy law behind their backs, and
slew thy prophets which testified against them to turn
them to thee, and they wrought great provocations.
27 Therefore thou deliveredst them into the hand
of their enemies, who vexed them: and in the time
of their trouble, when they cried unto thee, thou
heardest *them* from heaven; and according to thy
manifold mercies thou gavest them saviours, who
saved them out of the hand of their enemies.
28 But after they had rest, they did evil again before
thee: therefore leftest thou them in the hand of their
enemies, so that they had the dominion over them:
yet when they returned, and cried unto thee, thou
heardest *them* from heaven; and many times didst
thou deliver them according to thy mercies;
29 And testifiedst against them, that thou mightest
bring them again unto thy law: yet they dealt proudly,
and hearkened not unto thy commandments, but
sinned against thy judgments, (which if a man do, he
shall live in them;) and withdrew the shoulder, and
hardened their neck, and would not hear.
30 Yet many years didst thou forbear them, and
testifiedst against them by thy spirit in thy prophets:
yet would they not give ear: therefore gavest thou
them into the hand of the people of the lands.
31 Nevertheless for thy great mercies' sake thou
didst not utterly consume them, nor forsake them;
for thou *art* a gracious and merciful God.
32 Now therefore, our God, the great, the mighty,
and the terrible God, who keepest covenant and
mercy, let not all the trouble seem little before thee,
that hath come upon us, on our kings, on our princes,
and on our priests, and on our prophets, and on our
fathers, and on all thy people, since the time of the
kings of Assyria unto this day.
33 Howbeit thou *art* just in all that is brought
upon us; for thou hast done right, but we have done
wickedly:
34 Neither have our kings, our princes, our priests,
nor our fathers, kept thy law, nor hearkened unto thy
commandments and thy testimonies, wherewith
thou didst testify against them.
35 For they have not served thee in their kingdom,
and in thy great goodness that thou gavest them, and
in the large and fat land which thou gavest before
them, neither turned they from their wicked works.
36 Behold, we *are* servants this day, and *for* the land
that thou gavest unto our fathers to eat the fruit
thereof and the good thereof, behold, we *are* servants in it:

NEW LIVING TRANSLATION

were powerless! Your people could deal with
these nations and their kings as they pleased.
25 Our ancestors captured fortified cities and
fertile land. They took over houses full of good
things, with cisterns already dug and vineyards
and olive groves and fruit trees in abundance.
So they ate until they were full and grew fat
and enjoyed themselves in all your blessings.
26 "But despite all this, they were disobedient
and rebelled against you. They turned their
backs on your Law, they killed your prophets
who warned them to return to you, and they
committed terrible blasphemies. 27 So you
handed them over to their enemies, who made
them suffer. But in their time of trouble they
cried to you, and you heard them from heaven.
In your great mercy, you sent them liberators
who rescued them from their enemies.
28 "But as soon as they were at peace, your
people again committed evil in your sight, and
once more you let their enemies conquer them.
Yet whenever your people turned and cried to
you again for help, you listened once more from
heaven. In your wonderful mercy, you rescued
them many times!
29 "You warned them to return to your Law, but
they became proud and obstinate and disobeyed
your commands. They did not follow your
regulations, by which people will find life if only
they obey. They stubbornly turned their backs on
you and refused to listen. 30 In your love, you were
patient with them for many years. You sent your
Spirit, who warned them through the prophets.
But still they wouldn't listen! So once again you
allowed the peoples of the land to conquer them.
31 But in your great mercy, you did not destroy
them completely or abandon them forever.
What a gracious and merciful God you are!
32 "And now, our God, the great and mighty
and awesome God, who keeps his covenant of
unfailing love, do not let all the hardships we have
suffered seem insignificant to you. Great trouble
has come upon us and upon our kings and leaders
and priests and prophets and ancestors—all of
your people—from the days when the kings of
Assyria first triumphed over us until now. 33 Every
time you punished us you were being just. We
have sinned greatly, and you gave us only what
we deserved. 34 Our kings, leaders, priests, and
ancestors did not obey your Law or listen to the
warnings in your commands and laws. 35 Even
while they had their own kingdom, they did not
serve you, though you showered your goodness
on them. You gave them a large, fertile land, but
they refused to turn from their wickedness.
36 "So now today we are slaves in the land
of plenty that you gave our ancestors for their
enjoyment! We are slaves here in this good land.

KING JAMES VERSION

37 And it yieldeth much increase unto the kings
whom thou hast set over us because of our sins: also
they have dominion over our bodies, and over our
cattle, at their pleasure, and we *are* in great distress.

38 And because of all this we make a sure *covenant*,
and write *it;* and our princes, Levites, *and* priests,
seal *unto it*.

10 1 Now those that sealed *were*, Nehemiah, the
Tirshatha, the son of Hachaliah, and Zidkijah,
2 Seraiah, Azariah, Jeremiah,
3 Pashur, Amariah, Malchijah,
4 Hattush, Shebaniah, Malluch,
5 Harim, Meremoth, Obadiah,
6 Daniel, Ginnethon, Baruch,
7 Meshullam, Abijah, Mijamin,
8 Maaziah, Bilgai, Shemaiah: these *were* the
priests.
9 And the Levites: both Jeshua the son of Azaniah,
Binnui of the sons of Henadad, Kadmiel;
10 And their brethren, Shebaniah, Hodijah, Kelita,
Pelaiah, Hanan,
11 Micha, Rehob, Hashabiah,
12 Zaccur, Sherebiah, Shebaniah,
13 Hodijah, Bani, Beninu.
14 The chief of the people; Parosh, Pahath-moab,
Elam, Zatthu, Bani,
15 Bunni, Azgad, Bebai,
16 Adonijah, Bigvai, Adin,
17 Ater, Hizkijah, Azzur,
18 Hodijah, Hashum, Bezai,
19 Hariph, Anathoth, Nebai,
20 Magpiash, Meshullam, Hezir,
21 Meshezabeel, Zadok, Jaddua,
22 Pelatiah, Hanan, Anaiah,
23 Hoshea, Hananiah, Hashub,
24 Hallohesh, Pileha, Shobek,
25 Rehum, Hashabnah, Maaseiah,
26 And Ahijah, Hanan, Anan,
27 Malluch, Harim, Baanah.
28 And the rest of the people, the priests, the Levites, the porters, the singers, the Nethinims, and all
they that had separated themselves from the people
of the lands unto the law of God, their wives, their
sons, and their daughters, every one having knowledge, and having understanding;
29 They clave to their brethren, their nobles, and
entered into a curse, and into an oath, to walk in God's
law, which was given by Moses the servant of God, and
to observe and do all the commandments of the LORD
our Lord, and his judgments and his statutes;

NEW LIVING TRANSLATION

37 The lush produce of this land piles up in the
hands of the kings whom you have set over us
because of our sins. They have power over us and
our livestock. We serve them at their pleasure,
and we are in great misery."

The People Agree to Obey

38 *The people responded, "In view of all this,* we are
making a solemn promise and putting it in writing.
On this sealed document are the names of our leaders and Levites and priests."

10 1 *The document was ratified and sealed
with the following names:

The governor:
Nehemiah son of Hacaliah, and also Zedekiah.
2 The following priests:
Seraiah, Azariah, Jeremiah, 3 Pashhur, Amariah,
Malkijah, 4 Hattush, Shebaniah, Malluch, 5 Harim,
Meremoth, Obadiah, 6 Daniel, Ginnethon, Baruch,
7 Meshullam, Abijah, Mijamin, 8 Maaziah, Bilgai,
and Shemaiah. These were the priests.
9 The following Levites:
Jeshua son of Azaniah, Binnui from the family
of Henadad, Kadmiel, 10 and their fellow Levites:
Shebaniah, Hodiah, Kelita, Pelaiah, Hanan,
11 Mica, Rehob, Hashabiah, 12 Zaccur, Sherebiah,
Shebaniah, 13 Hodiah, Bani, and Beninu.
14 The following leaders:
Parosh, Pahath-moab, Elam, Zattu, Bani, 15 Bunni,
Azgad, Bebai, 16 Adonijah, Bigvai, Adin, 17 Ater,
Hezekiah, Azzur, 18 Hodiah, Hashum, Bezai,
19 Hariph, Anathoth, Nebai, 20 Magpiash,
Meshullam, Hezir, 21 Meshezabel, Zadok, Jaddua,
22 Pelatiah, Hanan, Anaiah, 23 Hoshea, Hananiah,
Hasshub, 24 Hallohesh, Pilha, Shobek, 25 Rehum,
Hashabnah, Maaseiah, 26 Ahiah, Hanan, Anan,
27 Malluch, Harim, and Baanah.

The Vow of the People

28 Then the rest of the people—the priests, Levites,
gatekeepers, singers, Temple servants, and all who
had separated themselves from the pagan people of
the land in order to obey the Law of God, together
with their wives, sons, daughters, and all who were
old enough to understand—29 joined their leaders
and bound themselves with an oath. They swore a
curse on themselves if they failed to obey the Law of
God as issued by his servant Moses. They solemnly
promised to carefully follow all the commands, regulations, and decrees of the LORD our Lord:

9:38a Verse 9:38 is numbered 10:1 in Hebrew text. **9:38b** Or *In spite of all this.* **10:1** Verses 10:1-39 are numbered 10:2-40 in Hebrew text.

KING JAMES VERSION

30 And that we would not give our daughters unto
the people of the land, nor take their daughters for
our sons:
31 And *if* the people of the land bring ware or any
victuals on the sabbath day to sell, *that* we would not
buy it of them on the sabbath, or on the holy day: and
that we would leave the seventh year, and the exac-
tion of every debt.
32 Also we made ordinances for us, to charge ourselves yearly with the third part of a shekel for the
service of the house of our God;
33 For the shewbread, and for the continual meat
offering, and for the continual burnt offering, of the
sabbaths, of the new moons, for the set feasts, and
for the holy *things*, and for the sin offerings to make
an atonement for Israel, and *for* all the work of the
house of our God.
34 And we cast the lots among the priests, the Levites, and the people, for the wood offering, to bring
it into the house of our God, after the houses of our
fathers, at times appointed year by year, to burn
upon the altar of the LORD our God, as *it is* written in
the law:
35 And to bring the firstfruits of our ground, and
the firstfruits of all fruit of all trees, year by year, unto
the house of the LORD:
36 Also the firstborn of our sons, and of our cattle,
as *it is* written in the law, and the firstlings of our
herds and of our flocks, to bring to the house of our
God, unto the priests that minister in the house of
our God:
37 And *that* we should bring the firstfruits of our
dough, and our offerings, and the fruit of all manner
of trees, of wine and of oil, unto the priests, to the
chambers of the house of our God; and the tithes of
our ground unto the Levites, that the same Levites
might have the tithes in all the cities of our tillage.
38 And the priest the son of Aaron shall be with the
Levites, when the Levites take tithes: and the Levites
shall bring up the tithe of the tithes unto the house
of our God, to the chambers, into the treasure house.
39 For the children of Israel and the children of
Levi shall bring the offering of the corn, of the new
wine, and the oil, unto the chambers, where *are* the
vessels of the sanctuary, and the priests that minister,
and the porters, and the singers: and we will not forsake the house of our God.

11 1 And the rulers of the people dwelt at Jerusalem: the rest of the people also cast lots, to

NEW LIVING TRANSLATION

30 "We promise not to let our daughters marry the
pagan people of the land, and not to let our sons
marry their daughters.
31 "We also promise that if the people of the
land should bring any merchandise or grain to
be sold on the Sabbath or on any other holy day,
we will refuse to buy it. Every seventh year we
will let our land rest, and we will cancel all debts
owed to us.
32 "In addition, we promise to obey the
command to pay the annual Temple tax of one-
eighth of an ounce of silver* for the care of the
Temple of our God. 33 This will provide for the
Bread of the Presence; for the regular grain
offerings and burnt offerings; for the offerings
on the Sabbaths, the new moon celebrations,
and the annual festivals; for the holy offerings;
and for the sin offerings to make atonement for
Israel. It will provide for everything necessary
for the work of the Temple of our God.
34 "We have cast sacred lots to determine
when—at regular times each year—the families
of the priests, Levites, and the common people
should bring wood to God's Temple to be burned
on the altar of the LORD our God, as is written in
the Law.
35 "We promise to bring the first part of every
harvest to the LORD's Temple year after year—
whether it be a crop from the soil or from our
fruit trees. 36 We agree to give God our oldest
sons and the firstborn of all our herds and flocks,
as prescribed in the Law. We will present them
to the priests who minister in the Temple of
our God. 37 We will store the produce in the
storerooms of the Temple of our God. We will
bring the best of our flour and other grain
offerings, the best of our fruit, and the best of
our new wine and olive oil. And we promise to
bring to the Levites a tenth of everything our
land produces, for it is the Levites who collect
the tithes in all our rural towns.
38 "A priest—a descendant of Aaron—will be
with the Levites as they receive these tithes. And
a tenth of all that is collected as tithes will be
delivered by the Levites to the Temple of our God
and placed in the storerooms. 39 The people and
the Levites must bring these offerings of grain,
new wine, and olive oil to the storerooms and
place them in the sacred containers near the
ministering priests, the gatekeepers, and the
singers.
"We promise together not to neglect the
Temple of our God."

The People Occupy Jerusalem

11 The leaders of the people were living in Jerusalem, the holy city. A tenth of the people

10:32 Hebrew *tax of ⅓ of a shekel* [4 grams].

KING JAMES VERSION

bring one of ten to dwell in Jerusalem the holy city,
and nine parts *to dwell* in *other* cities.

2And the people blessed all the men, that willingly
offered themselves to dwell at Jerusalem.

3Now these *are* the chief of the province that
dwelt in Jerusalem: but in the cities of Judah dwelt
every one in his possession in their cities, *to wit,* Israel, the priests, and the Levites, and the Nethinims,
and the children of Solomon's servants.

4And at Jerusalem dwelt *certain* of the children of
Judah, and of the children of Benjamin. Of the children of Judah; Athaiah the son of Uzziah, the son of
Zechariah, the son of Amariah, the son of Shephatiah, the son of Mahalaleel, of the children of Perez;

5And Maaseiah the son of Baruch, the son of Col-
hozeh, the son of Hazaiah, the son of Adaiah, the son
of Joiarib, the son of Zechariah, the son of Shiloni.

6All the sons of Perez that dwelt at Jerusalem *were*
four hundred threescore and eight valiant men.

7And these *are* the sons of Benjamin; Sallu the son
of Meshullam, the son of Joed, the son of Pedaiah, the
son of Kolaiah, the son of Maaseiah, the son of Ithiel,
the son of Jesaiah.

8And after him Gabbai, Sallai, nine hundred
twenty and eight.

9And Joel the son of Zichri *was* their overseer: and
Judah the son of Senuah *was* second over the city.

10Of the priests: Jedaiah the son of Joiarib, Jachin.

11Seraiah the son of Hilkiah, the son of Meshullam, the son of Zadok, the son of Meraioth, the son of
Ahitub, *was* the ruler of the house of God.

12And their brethren that did the work of the
house *were* eight hundred twenty and two: and
Adaiah the son of Jeroham, the son of Pelaliah, the
son of Amzi, the son of Zechariah, the son of Pashur,
the son of Malchiah,

13And his brethren, chief of the fathers, two hundred forty and two: and Amashai the son of Azareel,
the son of Ahasai, the son of Meshillemoth, the son
of Immer,

14And their brethren, mighty men of valour, an
hundred twenty and eight: and their overseer *was*
Zabdiel, the son of *one of* the great men.

15Also of the Levites: Shemaiah the son of Hashub,
the son of Azrikam, the son of Hashabiah, the son of
Bunni;

16And Shabbethai and Jozabad, of the chief of the
Levites, *had* the oversight of the outward business of
the house of God.

17And Mattaniah the son of Micha, the son of Zabdi, the son of Asaph, *was* the principal to begin the
thanksgiving in prayer: and Bakbukiah the second
among his brethren, and Abda the son of Shammua,
the son of Galal, the son of Jeduthun.

18All the Levites in the holy city *were* two hundred
fourscore and four.

19Moreover the porters, Akkub, Talmon, and their

NEW LIVING TRANSLATION

from the other towns of Judah and Benjamin were
chosen by sacred lots to live there, too, while the rest
stayed where they were. 2And the people commended everyone who volunteered to resettle in
Jerusalem.

3Here is a list of the names of the provincial officials who came to live in Jerusalem. (Most of the
people, priests, Levites, Temple servants, and descendants of Solomon's servants continued to live in
their own homes in the various towns of Judah, 4but
some of the people from Judah and Benjamin resettled in Jerusalem.)

From the tribe of Judah:
Athaiah son of Uzziah, son of Zechariah, son of
Amariah, son of Shephatiah, son of Mahalalel, of
the family of Perez. 5Also Maaseiah son of Baruch,
son of Col-hozeh, son of Hazaiah, son of Adaiah,
son of Joiarib, son of Zechariah, of the family of
Shelah.* 6There were 468 descendants of Perez
who lived in Jerusalem—all outstanding men.

7From the tribe of Benjamin:
Sallu son of Meshullam, son of Joed, son of
Pedaiah, son of Kolaiah, son of Maaseiah, son of
Ithiel, son of Jeshaiah. 8After him were Gabbai
and Sallai and a total of 928 relatives. 9Their
chief officer was Joel son of Zicri, who was
assisted by Judah son of Hassenuah, second-in-
command over the city.

10From the priests:
Jedaiah son of Joiarib; Jakin; 11and Seraiah son
of Hilkiah, son of Meshullam, son of Zadok, son
of Meraioth, son of Ahitub, the supervisor of the
Temple of God. 12Also 822 of their associates,
who worked at the Temple. Also Adaiah son
of Jeroham, son of Pelaliah, son of Amzi, son
of Zechariah, son of Pashhur, son of Malkijah,
13along with 242 of his associates, who were
heads of their families. Also Amashsai son of
Azarel, son of Ahzai, son of Meshillemoth,
son of Immer, 14and 128 of his* outstanding
associates. Their chief officer was Zabdiel son
of Haggedolim.

15From the Levites:
Shemaiah son of Hasshub, son of Azrikam, son of
Hashabiah, son of Bunni. 16Also Shabbethai and
Jozabad, who were in charge of the work outside
the Temple of God. 17Also Mattaniah son of Mica,
son of Zabdi, a descendant of Asaph, who led in
thanksgiving and prayer. Also Bakbukiah, who
was Mattaniah's assistant, and Abda son of
Shammua, son of Galal, son of Jeduthun. 18In
all, there were 284 Levites in the holy city.

19From the gatekeepers:

11:5 Hebrew *son of the Shilonite.* **11:14** As in Greek version; Hebrew reads *their.*

KING JAMES VERSION

brethren that kept the gates, *were* an hundred seventy and two.
20And the residue of Israel, of the priests, *and* the
Levites, *were* in all the cities of Judah, every one in
his inheritance.
21But the Nethinims dwelt in Ophel: and Ziha and
Gispa *were* over the Nethinims.
22The overseer also of the Levites at Jerusalem
was Uzzi the son of Bani, the son of Hashabiah, the
son of Mattaniah, the son of Micha. Of the sons of
Asaph, the singers *were* over the business of the
house of God.
23For *it was* the king's commandment concerning
them, that a certain portion should be for the singers, due for every day.
24And Pethahiah the son of Meshezabeel, of the
children of Zerah the son of Judah, *was* at the king's
hand in all matters concerning the people.
25And for the villages, with their fields, *some* of the
children of Judah dwelt at Kirjath-arba, and *in* the
villages thereof, and at Dibon, and *in* the villages
thereof, and at Jekabzeel, and *in* the villages thereof,
26And at Jeshua, and at Moladah, and at Beth-
phelet,
27And at Hazar-shual, and at Beer-sheba, and *in*
the villages thereof,
28And at Ziklag, and at Mekonah, and in the villages thereof,
29And at En-rimmon, and at Zareah, and at Jarmuth,
30Zanoah, Adullam, and *in* their villages, at Lachish, and the fields thereof, at Azekah, and *in* the
villages thereof. And they dwelt from Beer-sheba
unto the valley of Hinnom.
31The children also of Benjamin from Geba *dwelt* at
Michmash, and Aija, and Bethel, and *in* their villages,
32*And* at Anathoth, Nob, Ananiah,
33Hazor, Ramah, Gittaim,
34Hadid, Zeboim, Neballat,
35Lod, and Ono, the valley of craftsmen.
36And of the Levites *were* divisions *in* Judah, *and*
in Benjamin.

12 1Now these *are* the priests and the Levites
that went up with Zerubbabel the son of
Shealtiel, and Jeshua: Seraiah, Jeremiah, Ezra,
2Amariah, Malluch, Hattush,
3Shechaniah, Rehum, Meremoth,
4Iddo, Ginnetho, Abijah,
5Miamin, Maadiah, Bilgah,
6Shemaiah, and Joiarib, Jedaiah,
7Sallu, Amok, Hilkiah, Jedaiah. These *were* the
chief of the priests and of their brethren in the days
of Jeshua.

NEW LIVING TRANSLATION

Akkub, Talmon, and 172 of their associates, who
guarded the gates.

20The other priests, Levites, and the rest of the Israelites lived wherever their family inheritance was
located in any of the towns of Judah. 21The Temple
servants, however, whose leaders were Ziha and
Gishpa, all lived on the hill of Ophel.
22The chief officer of the Levites in Jerusalem was
Uzzi son of Bani, son of Hashabiah, son of Mattaniah,
son of Mica, a descendant of Asaph, whose family
served as singers at God's Temple. 23Their daily
responsibilities were carried out according to the
terms of a royal command.
24Pethahiah son of Meshezabel, a descendant of
Zerah son of Judah, was the royal adviser in all matters of public administration.
25As for the surrounding villages with their open
fields, some of the people of Judah lived in Kiriath-
arba with its settlements, Dibon with its settlements,
and Jekabzeel with its villages. 26They also lived in
Jeshua, Moladah, Beth-pelet, 27Hazar-shual, Beer-
sheba with its settlements, 28Ziklag, and Meconah
with its settlements. 29They also lived in En-rimmon,
Zorah, Jarmuth, 30Zanoah, and Adullam with their
surrounding villages. They also lived in Lachish with
its nearby fields and Azekah with its surrounding villages. So the people of Judah were living all the way
from Beersheba in the south to the valley of Hinnom.
31Some of the people of Benjamin lived at Geba,
Micmash, Aija, and Bethel with its settlements.
32They also lived in Anathoth, Nob, Ananiah, 33Ha-
zor, Ramah, Gittaim, 34Hadid, Zeboim, Neballat,
35Lod, Ono, and the Valley of Craftsmen.* 36Some of
the Levites who lived in Judah were sent to live with
the tribe of Benjamin.

A History of the Priests and Levites

12 Here is the list of the priests and Levites who
returned with Zerubbabel son of Shealtiel
and Jeshua the high priest:

Seraiah, Jeremiah, Ezra,
2 Amariah, Malluch, Hattush,
3 Shecaniah, Harim,* Meremoth,
4 Iddo, Ginnethon,* Abijah,
5 Miniamin, Moadiah,* Bilgah,
6 Shemaiah, Joiarib, Jedaiah,
7 Sallu, Amok, Hilkiah, and Jedaiah.

These were the leaders of the priests and their associates in the days of Jeshua.

11:35 Or *and Ge-harashim.* **12:3** Hebrew *Rehum;* compare 7:42; 12:15; Ezra 2:39. **12:4** As in some Hebrew manuscripts and Latin Vulgate (see also 12:16); most Hebrew manuscripts read *Ginnethoi.* **12:5** Hebrew *Mijamin, Maadiah;* compare 12:17.

KING JAMES VERSION

8 Moreover the Levites: Jeshua, Binnui, Kadmiel,
Sherebiah, Judah, *and* Mattaniah, *which was* over
the thanksgiving, he and his brethren.
9 Also Bakbukiah and Unni, their brethren, *were*
over against them in the watches.
10 And Jeshua begat Joiakim, Joiakim also begat
Eliashib, and Eliashib begat Joiada,
11 And Joiada begat Jonathan, and Jonathan begat
Jaddua.
12 And in the days of Joiakim were priests, the chief
of the fathers: of Seraiah, Meraiah; of Jeremiah,
Hananiah;
13 Of Ezra, Meshullam; of Amariah, Jehohanan;
14 Of Melicu, Jonathan; of Shebaniah, Joseph;
15 Of Harim, Adna; of Meraioth, Helkai;
16 Of Iddo, Zechariah; of Ginnethon, Meshullam;
17 Of Abijah, Zichri; of Miniamin, of Moadiah, Piltai;
18 Of Bilgah, Shammua; of Shemaiah, Jehonathan;
19 And of Joiarib, Mattenai; of Jedaiah, Uzzi;
20 Of Sallai, Kallai; of Amok, Eber;
21 Of Hilkiah, Hashabiah; of Jedaiah, Nethaneel.
22 The Levites in the days of Eliashib, Joiada, and
Johanan, and Jaddua, *were* recorded chief of the
fathers: also the priests, to the reign of Darius the
Persian.
23 The sons of Levi, the chief of the fathers, *were*
written in the book of the chronicles, even until the
days of Johanan the son of Eliashib.
24 And the chief of the Levites: Hashabiah, Sherebiah, and Jeshua the son of Kadmiel, with their
brethren over against them, to praise *and* to give
thanks, according to the commandment of David the
man of God, ward over against ward.
25 Mattaniah, and Bakbukiah, Obadiah, Meshullam, Talmon, Akkub, *were* porters keeping the ward
at the thresholds of the gates.

NEW LIVING TRANSLATION

8 The Levites who returned with them were Jeshua,
Binnui, Kadmiel, Sherebiah, Judah, and Mattaniah,
who with his associates was in charge of the songs
of thanksgiving. 9 Their associates, Bakbukiah and
Unni, stood opposite them during the service.

10 Jeshua the high priest was the father of Joiakim.
Joiakim was the father of Eliashib.
Eliashib was the father of Joiada.
11 Joiada was the father of Johanan.*
Johanan was the father of Jaddua.

12 Now when Joiakim was high priest, the family leaders of the priests were as follows:

Meraiah was leader of the family of Seraiah.
Hananiah was leader of the family of Jeremiah.
13 Meshullam was leader of the family of Ezra.
Jehohanan was leader of the family of Amariah.
14 Jonathan was leader of the family of Malluch.*
Joseph was leader of the family of Shecaniah.*
15 Adna was leader of the family of Harim.
Helkai was leader of the family of Meremoth.*
16 Zechariah was leader of the family of Iddo.
Meshullam was leader of the family of
Ginnethon.
17 Zicri was leader of the family of Abijah.
There was also a* leader of the family of
Miniamin.
Piltai was leader of the family of Moadiah.
18 Shammua was leader of the family of Bilgah.
Jehonathan was leader of the family of Shemaiah.
19 Mattenai was leader of the family of Joiarib.
Uzzi was leader of the family of Jedaiah.
20 Kallai was leader of the family of Sallu.*
Eber was leader of the family of Amok.
21 Hashabiah was leader of the family of Hilkiah.
Nethanel was leader of the family of Jedaiah.

22 A record of the Levite families was kept during
the years when Eliashib, Joiada, Johanan, and Jaddua
served as high priest. Another record of the priests
was kept during the reign of Darius the Persian.* 23 A
record of the heads of the Levite families was kept in
The Book of History down to the days of Johanan, the
grandson* of Eliashib.
24 These were the family leaders of the Levites:
Hashabiah, Sherebiah, Jeshua, Binnui,* Kadmiel, and
other associates, who stood opposite them during
the ceremonies of praise and thanksgiving, one section responding to the other, as commanded by David, the man of God. 25 This included Mattaniah,
Bakbukiah, and Obadiah.

12:11 Hebrew *Jonathan;* compare 12:22. **12:14a** As in Greek version (see also 10:4; 12:2); Hebrew reads *Malluchi.* **12:14b** As in many Hebrew manuscripts, some Greek manuscripts, and Syriac version (see also 12:3); most Hebrew manuscripts read *Shebaniah.* **12:15** As in some Greek manuscripts (see also 12:3); Hebrew reads *Meraioth.* **12:17** Hebrew lacks the name of this family leader. **12:20** Hebrew *Sallai;* compare 12:7. **12:22** *Darius the Persian* is probably Darius II, who reigned 423–404 B.C., or possibly Darius III, who reigned 336–331 B.C. **12:23** Hebrew *descendant;* compare 12:10-11. **12:24** Hebrew *son of* (i.e., *ben*), which should probably be read here as the proper name Binnui; compare Ezra 3:9 and the note there.

KING JAMES VERSION

26 These *were* in the days of Joiakim the son of Jeshua, the son of Jozadak, and in the days of Nehemiah the governor, and of Ezra the priest, the scribe.

27 And at the dedication of the wall of Jerusalem they sought the Levites out of all their places, to bring them to Jerusalem, to keep the dedication with gladness, both with thanksgivings, and with singing, *with* cymbals, psalteries, and with harps.

28 And the sons of the singers gathered themselves together, both out of the plain country round about Jerusalem, and from the villages of Netophathi;

29 Also from the house of Gilgal, and out of the fields of Geba and Azmaveth: for the singers had builded them villages round about Jerusalem.

30 And the priests and the Levites purified themselves, and purified the people, and the gates, and the wall.

31 Then I brought up the princes of Judah upon the wall, and appointed two great *companies of them that gave* thanks, *whereof one* went on the right hand upon the wall toward the dung gate:

32 And after them went Hoshaiah, and half of the princes of Judah,

33 And Azariah, Ezra, and Meshullam,

34 Judah, and Benjamin, and Shemaiah, and Jeremiah,

35 And *certain* of the priests' sons with trumpets; *namely,* Zechariah the son of Jonathan, the son of Shemaiah, the son of Mattaniah, the son of Michaiah, the son of Zaccur, the son of Asaph:

36 And his brethren, Shemaiah, and Azarael, Milalai, Gilalai, Maai, Nethaneel, and Judah, Hanani, with the musical instruments of David the man of God, and Ezra the scribe before them.

37 And at the fountain gate, which was over against them, they went up by the stairs of the city of David, at the going up of the wall, above the house of David, even unto the water gate eastward.

38 And the other *company of them that gave* thanks went over against *them,* and I after them, and the half of the people upon the wall, from beyond the tower of the furnaces even unto the broad wall;

39 And from above the gate of Ephraim, and above the old gate, and above the fish gate, and the tower of Hananeel, and the tower of Meah, even unto the sheep gate: and they stood still in the prison gate.

40 So stood the two *companies of them that gave* thanks in the house of God, and I, and the half of the rulers with me:

41 And the priests; Eliakim, Maaseiah, Miniamin, Michaiah, Elioenai, Zechariah, *and* Hananiah, with trumpets;

42 And Maaseiah, and Shemaiah, and Eleazar, and Uzzi, and Jehohanan, and Malchijah, and Elam, and

NEW LIVING TRANSLATION

Meshullam, Talmon, and Akkub were the gatekeepers in charge of the storerooms at the gates.
26 These all served in the days of Joiakim son of Jeshua, son of Jehozadak,* and in the days of Nehemiah the governor and of Ezra the priest and scribe.

Dedication of Jerusalem's Wall

27 For the dedication of the new wall of Jerusalem, the Levites throughout the land were asked to come to Jerusalem to assist in the ceremonies. They were to take part in the joyous occasion with their songs of thanksgiving and with the music of cymbals, harps,
and lyres. 28 The singers were brought together from the region around Jerusalem and from the villages
of the Netophathites. 29 They also came from Bethgilgal and the rural areas near Geba and Azmaveth, for the singers had built their own settlements
around Jerusalem. 30 The priests and Levites first purified themselves; then they purified the people, the gates, and the wall.

31 I led the leaders of Judah to the top of the wall and organized two large choirs to give thanks. One of the choirs proceeded southward* along the top of
the wall to the Dung Gate. 32 Hoshaiah and half the
leaders of Judah followed them, 33 along with Azariah, Ezra, Meshullam, 34 Judah, Benjamin, Shemaiah,
and Jeremiah. 35 Then came some priests who played trumpets, including Zechariah son of Jonathan, son of Shemaiah, son of Mattaniah, son of Micaiah, son
of Zaccur, a descendant of Asaph. 36 And Zechariah's colleagues were Shemaiah, Azarel, Milalai, Gilalai, Maai, Nethanel, Judah, and Hanani. They used the musical instruments prescribed by David, the man
of God. Ezra the scribe led this procession. 37 At the Fountain Gate they went straight up the steps on the ascent of the city wall toward the City of David. They passed the house of David and then proceeded to the Water Gate on the east.

38 The second choir giving thanks went northward* around the other way to meet them. I followed them, together with the other half of the people, along the top of the wall past the Tower of the Ovens
to the Broad Wall, 39 then past the Ephraim Gate to the Old City Gate,* past the Fish Gate and the Tower of Hananel, and on to the Tower of the Hundred. Then we continued on to the Sheep Gate and stopped at the Guard Gate.

40 The two choirs that were giving thanks then proceeded to the Temple of God, where they took their places. So did I, together with the group of leaders
who were with me. 41 We went together with the trumpet-playing priests—Eliakim, Maaseiah, Miniamin, Micaiah, Elioenai, Zechariah, and Hananiah—
42 and the singers—Maaseiah, Shemaiah, Eleazar, Uzzi, Jehohanan, Malkijah, Elam, and Ezer. They

12:26 Hebrew *Jozadak,* a variant spelling of Jehozadak. **12:31** Hebrew *to the right.* **12:38** Hebrew *to the left.* **12:39** Or *the Mishneh Gate,* or *the Jeshanah Gate.*

KING JAMES VERSION

Ezer. And the singers sang loud, with Jezrahiah *their*
overseer.
43 Also that day they offered great sacrifices, and
rejoiced: for God had made them rejoice with great
joy: the wives also and the children rejoiced: so that
the joy of Jerusalem was heard even afar off.
44 And at that time were some appointed over the
chambers for the treasures, for the offerings, for the
firstfruits, and for the tithes, to gather into them out
of the fields of the cities the portions of the law for
the priests and Levites: for Judah rejoiced for the
priests and for the Levites that waited.
45 And both the singers and the porters kept the
ward of their God, and the ward of the purification,
according to the commandment of David, *and* of
Solomon his son.
46 For in the days of David and Asaph of old *there*
were chief of the singers, and songs of praise and
thanksgiving unto God.
47 And all Israel in the days of Zerubbabel, and in
the days of Nehemiah, gave the portions of the singers and the porters, every day his portion: and they
sanctified *holy things* unto the Levites; and the Levites sanctified *them* unto the children of Aaron.

13 1 On that day they read in the book of Moses in
the audience of the people; and therein was
found written, that the Ammonite and the Moabite
should not come into the congregation of God for
ever;
2 Because they met not the children of Israel with
bread and with water, but hired Balaam against them,
that he should curse them: howbeit our God turned
the curse into a blessing.
3 Now it came to pass, when they had heard the
law, that they separated from Israel all the mixed
multitude.
4 And before this, Eliashib the priest, having the
oversight of the chamber of the house of our God,
was allied unto Tobiah:
5 And he had prepared for him a great chamber,
where aforetime they laid the meat offerings, the
frankincense, and the vessels, and the tithes of
the corn, the new wine, and the oil, which was commanded *to be given* to the Levites, and the singers,
and the porters; and the offerings of the priests.
6 But in all this *time* was not I at Jerusalem: for in
the two and thirtieth year of Artaxerxes king of Babylon came I unto the king, and after certain days
obtained I leave of the king:
7 And I came to Jerusalem, and understood of the
evil that Eliashib did for Tobiah, in preparing him a
chamber in the courts of the house of God.

NEW LIVING TRANSLATION

played and sang loudly under the direction of Jezrahiah the choir director.
43 Many sacrifices were offered on that joyous day,
for God had given the people cause for great joy. The
women and children also participated in the celebration, and the joy of the people of Jerusalem could
be heard far away.

Provisions for Temple Worship

44 On that day men were appointed to be in charge of
the storerooms for the offerings, the first part of the
harvest, and the tithes. They were responsible to collect from the fields outside the towns the portions
required by the Law for the priests and Levites. For all
the people of Judah took joy in the priests and Levites
and their work. 45 They performed the service of
their God and the service of purification, as commanded by David and his son Solomon, and so did
the singers and the gatekeepers. 46 The custom of
having choir directors to lead the choirs in hymns of
praise and thanksgiving to God began long ago in the
days of David and Asaph. 47 So now, in the days of
Zerubbabel and of Nehemiah, all Israel brought a
daily supply of food for the singers, the gatekeepers,
and the Levites. The Levites, in turn, gave a portion of
what they received to the priests, the descendants
of Aaron.

Nehemiah's Various Reforms

13 On that same day, as the Book of Moses was
being read to the people, the passage was
found that said no Ammonite or Moabite should ever
be permitted to enter the assembly of God.* 2 For
they had not provided the Israelites with food and
water in the wilderness. Instead, they hired Balaam
to curse them, though our God turned the curse into
a blessing. 3 When this passage of the Law was read,
all those of foreign descent were immediately excluded from the assembly.
4 Before this had happened, Eliashib the priest, who
had been appointed as supervisor of the storerooms
of the Temple of our God and who was also a relative
of Tobiah, 5 had converted a large storage room and
placed it at Tobiah's disposal. The room had previously been used for storing the grain offerings, the
frankincense, various articles for the Temple, and the
tithes of grain, new wine, and olive oil (which were
prescribed for the Levites, the singers, and the gatekeepers), as well as the offerings for the priests.
6 I was not in Jerusalem at that time, for I had returned to King Artaxerxes of Babylon in the thirty-
second year of his reign,* though I later asked his
permission to return. 7 When I arrived back in Jerusalem, I learned about Eliashib's evil deed in providing Tobiah with a room in the courtyards of the

13:1 See Deut 23:3-6. **13:6** King Artaxerxes of Persia is here identified as the king of Babylon because Persia had conquered the Babylonian Empire. The thirty-second year of Artaxerxes was 433 B.C.

KING JAMES VERSION

8 And it grieved me sore: therefore I cast forth all the household stuff of Tobiah out of the chamber.

9 Then I commanded, and they cleansed the chambers: and thither brought I again the vessels of the house of God, with the meat offering and the frankincense.

10 And I perceived that the portions of the Levites had not been given *them:* for the Levites and the singers, that did the work, were fled every one to his field.

11 Then contended I with the rulers, and said, Why is the house of God forsaken? And I gathered them together, and set them in their place.

12 Then brought all Judah the tithe of the corn and the new wine and the oil unto the treasuries.

13 And I made treasurers over the treasuries, Shelemiah the priest, and Zadok the scribe, and of the Levites, Pedaiah: and next to them *was* Hanan the son of Zaccur, the son of Mattaniah: for they were counted faithful, and their office *was* to distribute unto their brethren.

14 Remember me, O my God, concerning this, and wipe not out my good deeds that I have done for the house of my God, and for the offices thereof.

15 In those days saw I in Judah *some* treading wine presses on the sabbath, and bringing in sheaves, and lading asses; as also wine, grapes, and figs, and all *manner of* burdens, which they brought into Jerusalem on the sabbath day: and I testified *against them* in the day wherein they sold victuals.

16 There dwelt men of Tyre also therein, which brought fish, and all manner of ware, and sold on the sabbath unto the children of Judah, and in Jerusalem.

17 Then I contended with the nobles of Judah, and said unto them, What evil thing *is* this that ye do, and profane the sabbath day?

18 Did not your fathers thus, and did not our God bring all this evil upon us, and upon this city? yet ye bring more wrath upon Israel by profaning the sabbath.

19 And it came to pass, that when the gates of Jerusalem began to be dark before the sabbath, I commanded that the gates should be shut, and charged that they should not be opened till after the sabbath: and *some* of my servants set I at the gates, *that* there should no burden be brought in on the sabbath day.

20 So the merchants and sellers of all kind of ware lodged without Jerusalem once or twice.

21 Then I testified against them, and said unto them, Why lodge ye about the wall? if ye do *so* again, I will lay hands on you. From that time forth came they no *more* on the sabbath.

22 And I commanded the Levites that they should cleanse themselves, and *that* they should come *and*

NEW LIVING TRANSLATION

Temple of God. 8 I became very upset and threw all
of Tobiah's belongings out of the room. 9 Then I demanded that the rooms be purified, and I brought
back the articles for God's Temple, the grain offerings, and the frankincense.
10 I also discovered that the Levites had not been
given their prescribed portions of food, so they and
the singers who were to conduct the worship services had all returned to work their fields. 11 I immediately confronted the leaders and demanded, "Why
has the Temple of God been neglected?" Then I
called all the Levites back again and restored them to
their proper duties. 12 And once more all the people
of Judah began bringing their tithes of grain, new
wine, and olive oil to the Temple storerooms.
13 I assigned supervisors for the storerooms: Shelemiah the priest, Zadok the scribe, and Pedaiah, one
of the Levites. And I appointed Hanan son of Zaccur
and grandson of Mattaniah as their assistant. These
men had an excellent reputation, and it was their job
to make honest distributions to their fellow Levites.

14 Remember this good deed, O my God, and do
not forget all that I have faithfully done for the
Temple of my God and its services.

15 In those days I saw men of Judah treading out
their winepresses on the Sabbath. They were also
bringing in grain, loading it on donkeys, and bringing
their wine, grapes, figs, and all sorts of produce to
Jerusalem to sell on the Sabbath. So I rebuked them
for selling their produce on that day. 16 Some men
from Tyre, who lived in Jerusalem, were bringing in
fish and all kinds of merchandise. They were selling
it on the Sabbath to the people of Judah—and in Jerusalem at that!
17 So I confronted the nobles of Judah. "Why are
you profaning the Sabbath in this evil way?" I asked.
18 "Wasn't it just this sort of thing that your ancestors
did that caused our God to bring all this trouble
upon us and our city? Now you are bringing even
more wrath upon Israel by permitting the Sabbath to
be desecrated in this way!"
19 Then I commanded that the gates of Jerusalem
should be shut as darkness fell every Friday evening,*
not to be opened until the Sabbath ended. I sent
some of my own servants to guard the gates so that no
merchandise could be brought in on the Sabbath
day. 20 The merchants and tradesmen with a variety of
wares camped outside Jerusalem once or twice. 21 But
I spoke sharply to them and said, "What are you doing out here, camping around the wall? If you do this
again, I will arrest you!" And that was the last time
they came on the Sabbath. 22 Then I commanded the
Levites to purify themselves and to guard the gates in
order to preserve the holiness of the Sabbath.

13:19 Hebrew *on the day before the Sabbath.*

KING JAMES VERSION

keep the gates, to sanctify the sabbath day. Remember me, O my God, *concerning* this also, and spare me according to the greatness of thy mercy.

23 In those days also saw I Jews *that* had married wives of Ashdod, of Ammon, *and* of Moab:

24 And their children spake half in the speech of Ashdod, and could not speak in the Jews' language, but according to the language of each people.

25 And I contended with them, and cursed them, and smote certain of them, and plucked off their hair, and made them swear by God, *saying,* Ye shall not give your daughters unto their sons, nor take their daughters unto your sons, or for yourselves.

26 Did not Solomon king of Israel sin by these things? yet among many nations was there no king like him, who was beloved of his God, and God made him king over all Israel: nevertheless even him did outlandish women cause to sin.

27 Shall we then hearken unto you to do all this great evil, to transgress against our God in marrying strange wives?

28 And *one* of the sons of Joiada, the son of Eliashib the high priest, *was* son in law to Sanballat the Horonite: therefore I chased him from me.

29 Remember them, O my God, because they have defiled the priesthood, and the covenant of the priesthood, and of the Levites.

30 Thus cleansed I them from all strangers, and appointed the wards of the priests and the Levites, every one in his business;

31 And for the wood offering, at times appointed, and for the firstfruits. Remember me, O my God, for good.

NEW LIVING TRANSLATION

Remember this good deed also, O my God! Have compassion on me according to your great and unfailing love.

23 About the same time I realized that some of the
men of Judah had married women from Ashdod,
Ammon, and Moab. 24 Furthermore, half their children spoke the language of Ashdod or of some other
people and could not speak the language of Judah at
all. 25 So I confronted them and called down curses
on them. I beat some of them and pulled out their
hair. I made them swear in the name of God that they
would not let their children intermarry with the pagan people of the land.

26 "Wasn't this exactly what led King Solomon of
Israel into sin?" I demanded. "There was no king
from any nation who could compare to him, and God
loved him and made him king over all Israel. But
even he was led into sin by his foreign wives. 27 How
could you even think of committing this sinful deed
and acting unfaithfully toward God by marrying foreign women?"

28 One of the sons of Joiada son of Eliashib the high priest had married a daughter of Sanballat the Horonite, so I banished him from my presence.

29 Remember them, O my God, for they have defiled the priesthood and the solemn vows of the priests and Levites.

30 So I purged out everything foreign and assigned
tasks to the priests and Levites, making certain that
each knew his work. 31 I also made sure that the supply of wood for the altar and the first portions of the
harvest were brought at the proper times.

Remember this in my favor, O my God.

Esther

KING JAMES VERSION

1 1 Now it came to pass in the days of Ahasuerus, (this *is* Ahasuerus which reigned, from India even unto Ethiopia, *over* an hundred and seven and twenty provinces:)

2 *That* in those days, when the king Ahasuerus sat on the throne of his kingdom, which *was* in Shushan the palace,

3 In the third year of his reign, he made a feast unto all his princes and his servants; the power of Persia and Media, the nobles and princes of the provinces, *being* before him:

4 When he shewed the riches of his glorious kingdom and the honour of his excellent majesty many days, *even* an hundred and fourscore days.

5 And when these days were expired, the king made a feast unto all the people that were present in Shushan the palace, both unto great and small, seven days, in the court of the garden of the king's palace;

6 *Where were* white, green, and blue, *hangings*, fastened with cords of fine linen and purple to silver rings and pillars of marble: the beds *were of* gold and silver, upon a pavement of red, and blue, and white, and black, marble.

7 And they gave *them* drink in vessels of gold, (the vessels being diverse one from another,) and royal wine in abundance, according to the state of the king.

8 And the drinking *was* according to the law; none did compel: for so the king had appointed to all the officers of his house, that they should do according to every man's pleasure.

9 Also Vashti the queen made a feast for the women *in* the royal house which *belonged* to king Ahasuerus.

10 On the seventh day, when the heart of the king was merry with wine, he commanded Mehuman, Biztha, Harbona, Bigtha, and Abagtha, Zethar, and Carcas, the seven chamberlains that served in the presence of Ahasuerus the king,

11 To bring Vashti the queen before the king with the crown royal, to shew the people and the princes her beauty: for she *was* fair to look on.

12 But the queen Vashti refused to come at the

NEW LIVING TRANSLATION

The King's Banquet

1 These events happened in the days of King Xerxes,* who reigned over 127 provinces stretching from India to Ethiopia.* 2 At that time Xerxes ruled his empire from his royal throne at the fortress of Susa. 3 In the third year of his reign, he gave a banquet for all his nobles and officials. He invited all the military officers of Persia and Media as well as the princes and nobles of the provinces. 4 The celebration lasted 180 days—a tremendous display of the opulent wealth of his empire and the pomp and splendor of his majesty.

5 When it was all over, the king gave a banquet for all the people, from the greatest to the least, who were in the fortress of Susa. It lasted for seven days and was held in the courtyard of the palace garden. 6 The courtyard was beautifully decorated with white cotton curtains and blue hangings, which were fastened with white linen cords and purple ribbons to silver rings embedded in marble pillars. Gold and silver couches stood on a mosaic pavement of porphyry, marble, mother-of-pearl, and other costly stones.

7 Drinks were served in gold goblets of many designs, and there was an abundance of royal wine, reflecting the king's generosity. 8 By edict of the king, no limits were placed on the drinking, for the king had instructed all his palace officials to serve each man as much as he wanted.

9 At the same time, Queen Vashti gave a banquet for the women in the royal palace of King Xerxes.

Queen Vashti Deposed

10 On the seventh day of the feast, when King Xerxes was in high spirits because of the wine, he told the seven eunuchs who attended him—Mehuman, Biztha, Harbona, Bigtha, Abagtha, Zethar, and Carcas— 11 to bring Queen Vashti to him with the royal crown on her head. He wanted the nobles and all the other men to gaze on her beauty, for she was a very beautiful woman. 12 But when they conveyed the king's

1:1a Hebrew *Ahasuerus,* another name for Xerxes; also throughout the book of Esther. Xerxes reigned 486–465 B.C. **1:1b** Hebrew *to Cush.*

KING JAMES VERSION

king's commandment by *his* chamberlains: therefore was the king very wroth, and his anger burned in him.

13 Then the king said to the wise men, which knew the times, (for so *was* the king's manner toward all that knew law and judgment:

14 And the next unto him *was* Carshena, Shethar, Admatha, Tarshish, Meres, Marsena, *and* Memucan, the seven princes of Persia and Media, which saw the king's face, *and* which sat the first in the kingdom;)

15 What shall we do unto the queen Vashti according to law, because she hath not performed the commandment of the king Ahasuerus by the chamberlains?

16 And Memucan answered before the king and the princes, Vashti the queen hath not done wrong to the king only, but also to all the princes, and to all the people that *are* in all the provinces of the king Ahasuerus.

17 For *this* deed of the queen shall come abroad unto all women, so that they shall despise their husbands in their eyes, when it shall be reported, The king Ahasuerus commanded Vashti the queen to be brought in before him, but she came not.

18 *Likewise* shall the ladies of Persia and Media say this day unto all the king's princes, which have heard of the deed of the queen. Thus *shall there arise* too much contempt and wrath.

19 If it please the king, let there go a royal commandment from him, and let it be written among the laws of the Persians and the Medes, that it be not altered, That Vashti come no more before king Ahasuerus; and let the king give her royal estate unto another that is better than she.

20 And when the king's decree which he shall make shall be published throughout all his empire, (for it is great,) all the wives shall give to their husbands honour, both to great and small.

21 And the saying pleased the king and the princes; and the king did according to the word of Memucan:

22 For he sent letters into all the king's provinces, into every province according to the writing thereof, and to every people after their language, that every man should bear rule in his own house, and that *it* should be published according to the language of every people.

2 1 After these things, when the wrath of king Ahasuerus was appeased, he remembered Vashti, and what she had done, and what was decreed against her.

2 Then said the king's servants that ministered unto him, Let there be fair young virgins sought for the king:

3 And let the king appoint officers in all the provinces of his kingdom, that they may gather together all the fair young virgins unto Shushan the palace, to the house of the women, unto the custody of Hege the king's chamberlain, keeper of the women; and let their things for purification be given *them*:

NEW LIVING TRANSLATION

order to Queen Vashti, she refused to come. This made the king furious, and he burned with anger.

13 He immediately consulted with his wise advisers, who knew all the Persian laws and customs, for he always asked their advice. 14 The names of these men were Carshena, Shethar, Admatha, Tarshish, Meres, Marsena, and Memucan—seven nobles of Persia and Media. They met with the king regularly and held the highest positions in the empire.

15 "What must be done to Queen Vashti?" the king demanded. "What penalty does the law provide for a queen who refuses to obey the king's orders, properly sent through his eunuchs?"

16 Memucan answered the king and his nobles, "Queen Vashti has wronged not only the king but also every noble and citizen throughout your empire. 17 Women everywhere will begin to despise their husbands when they learn that Queen Vashti has refused to appear before the king. 18 Before this day is out, the wives of all the king's nobles throughout Persia and Media will hear what the queen did and will start treating their husbands the same way. There will be no end to their contempt and anger.

19 "So if it please the king, we suggest that you issue a written decree, a law of the Persians and Medes that cannot be revoked. It should order that Queen Vashti be forever banished from the presence of King Xerxes, and that the king should choose another queen more worthy than she. 20 When this decree is published throughout the king's vast empire, husbands everywhere, whatever their rank, will receive proper respect from their wives!"

21 The king and his nobles thought this made good sense, so he followed Memucan's counsel. 22 He sent letters to all parts of the empire, to each province in its own script and language, proclaiming that every man should be the ruler of his own home and should say whatever he pleases.*

Esther Becomes Queen

2 But after Xerxes' anger had subsided, he began thinking about Vashti and what she had done and the decree he had made. 2 So his personal attendants suggested, "Let us search the empire to find beautiful young virgins for the king. 3 Let the king appoint agents in each province to bring these beautiful young women into the royal harem at the fortress of Susa. Hegai, the king's eunuch in charge of the harem, will see that they are all given beauty treatments.

1:22 Or *and should speak in the language of his own people.*

KING JAMES VERSION

4 And let the maiden which pleaseth the king be
queen instead of Vashti. And the thing pleased the
king; and he did so.
5 *Now* in Shushan the palace there was a certain
Jew, whose name *was* Mordecai, the son of Jair, the
son of Shimei, the son of Kish, a Benjamite;
6 Who had been carried away from Jerusalem with
the captivity which had been carried away with Jeconiah king of Judah, whom Nebuchadnezzar the king
of Babylon had carried away.
7 And he brought up Hadassah, that *is,* Esther, his
uncle's daughter: for she had neither father nor
mother, and the maid *was* fair and beautiful; whom
Mordecai, when her father and mother were dead,
took for his own daughter.
8 So it came to pass, when the king's commandment and his decree was heard, and when many
maidens were gathered together unto Shushan the
palace, to the custody of Hegai, that Esther was
brought also unto the king's house, to the custody of
Hegai, keeper of the women.
9 And the maiden pleased him, and she obtained
kindness of him; and he speedily gave her her things
for purification, with such things as belonged to her,
and seven maidens, *which were* meet to be given
her, out of the king's house: and he preferred her and
her maids unto the best *place* of the house of the
women.
10 Esther had not shewed her people nor her kindred: for Mordecai had charged her that she should
not shew *it.*
11 And Mordecai walked every day before the court
of the women's house, to know how Esther did, and
what should become of her.
12 Now when every maid's turn was come to go in
to king Ahasuerus, after that she had been twelve
months, according to the manner of the women, (for
so were the days of their purifications accomplished,
to wit, six months with oil of myrrh, and six months
with sweet odours, and with *other* things for the
purifying of the women;)
13 Then thus came *every* maiden unto the king;
whatsoever she desired was given her to go with her
out of the house of the women unto the king's house.
14 In the evening she went, and on the morrow she
returned into the second house of the women, to the
custody of Shaashgaz, the king's chamberlain, which
kept the concubines: she came in unto the king no
more, except the king delighted in her, and that she
were called by name.
15 Now when the turn of Esther, the daughter of
Abihail the uncle of Mordecai, who had taken her for
his daughter, was come to go in unto the king, she required nothing but what Hegai the king's chamberlain, the keeper of the women, appointed. And
Esther obtained favour in the sight of all them that
looked upon her.
16 So Esther was taken unto king Ahasuerus into

NEW LIVING TRANSLATION

4 After that, the young woman who most pleases the
king will be made queen instead of Vashti." This advice was very appealing to the king, so he put the plan
into effect.
5 At that time there was a Jewish man in the fortress of Susa whose name was Mordecai son of Jair.
He was from the tribe of Benjamin and was a descendant of Kish and Shimei.
6 His family* had been
among those who, with King Jehoiachin* of Judah,
had been exiled from Jerusalem to Babylon by King
Nebuchadnezzar.
7 This man had a very beautiful
and lovely young cousin, Hadassah, who was also
called Esther. When her father and mother died,
Mordecai adopted her into his family and raised her
as his own daughter.
8 As a result of the king's decree, Esther, along with
many other young women, was brought to the king's
harem at the fortress of Susa and placed in Hegai's
care.
9 Hegai was very impressed with Esther and
treated her kindly. He quickly ordered a special
menu for her and provided her with beauty treatments. He also assigned her seven maids specially
chosen from the king's palace, and he moved her and
her maids into the best place in the harem.
10 Esther had not told anyone of her nationality
and family background, because Mordecai had directed her not to do so.
11 Every day Mordecai would
take a walk near the courtyard of the harem to find
out about Esther and what was happening to her.
12 Before each young woman was taken to the
king's bed, she was given the prescribed twelve
months of beauty treatments—six months with oil of
myrrh, followed by six months with special perfumes and ointments.
13 When it was time for her to
go to the king's palace, she was given her choice of
whatever clothing or jewelry she wanted to take
from the harem.
14 That evening she was taken to the
king's private rooms, and the next morning she was
brought to the second harem,* where the king's
wives lived. There she would be under the care of
Shaashgaz, the king's eunuch in charge of the concubines. She would never go to the king again unless
he had especially enjoyed her and requested her
by name.
15 Esther was the daughter of Abihail, who was
Mordecai's uncle. (Mordecai had adopted his younger cousin Esther.) When it was Esther's turn to go
to the king, she accepted the advice of Hegai, the eunuch in charge of the harem. She asked for nothing
except what he suggested, and she was admired by
everyone who saw her.
16 Esther was taken to King Xerxes at the royal palace in early winter* of the seventh year of his reign.

2:6a Hebrew *He.* **2:6b** Hebrew *Jeconiah,* a variant spelling of Jehoiachin. **2:14** Or *to another part of the harem.* **2:16** Hebrew *in the tenth month, the month of Tebeth.* A number of dates in the book of Esther can be cross-checked with dates in surviving Persian records and related accurately to our modern calendar. This month of the ancient Hebrew lunar calendar occurred within the months of December 479 B.C. and January 478 B.C.

KING JAMES VERSION

his house royal in the tenth month, which *is* the
month Tebeth, in the seventh year of his reign.
17 And the king loved Esther above all the women,
and she obtained grace and favour in his sight more
than all the virgins; so that he set the royal crown upon
her head, and made her queen instead of Vashti.
18 Then the king made a great feast unto all his
princes and his servants, *even* Esther's feast; and he
made a release to the provinces, and gave gifts, according to the state of the king.
19 And when the virgins were gathered together
the second time, then Mordecai sat in the king's gate.
20 Esther had not *yet* shewed her kindred nor her
people; as Mordecai had charged her: for Esther did
the commandment of Mordecai, like as when she
was brought up with him.
21 In those days, while Mordecai sat in the king's
gate, two of the king's chamberlains, Bigthan and
Teresh, of those which kept the door, were wroth,
and sought to lay hand on the king Ahasuerus.
22 And the thing was known to Mordecai, who told
it unto Esther the queen; and Esther certified the
king *thereof* in Mordecai's name.
23 And when inquisition was made of the matter, it
was found out; therefore they were both hanged on a
tree: and it was written in the book of the chronicles
before the king.

3 1 After these things did king Ahasuerus promote Haman the son of Hammedatha the
Agagite, and advanced him, and set his seat above all
the princes that *were* with him.
2 And all the king's servants, that *were* in the king's
gate, bowed, and reverenced Haman: for the king had
so commanded concerning him. But Mordecai
bowed not, nor did *him* reverence.
3 Then the king's servants, which *were* in the king's
gate, said unto Mordecai, Why transgressest thou the
king's commandment?
4 Now it came to pass, when they spake daily unto
him, and he hearkened not unto them, that they told
Haman, to see whether Mordecai's matters would
stand: for he had told them that he *was* a Jew.
5 And when Haman saw that Mordecai bowed not,
nor did him reverence, then was Haman full of
wrath.
6 And he thought scorn to lay hands on Mordecai
alone; for they had shewed him the people of Mordecai: wherefore Haman sought to destroy all the Jews
that *were* throughout the whole kingdom of Ahasuerus, *even* the people of Mordecai.
7 In the first month, that *is*, the month Nisan, in the
twelfth year of king Ahasuerus, they cast Pur, that *is*,
the lot, before Haman from day to day, and from

NEW LIVING TRANSLATION

17 And the king loved Esther more than any of the
other young women. He was so delighted with her
that he set the royal crown on her head and declared
her queen instead of Vashti. 18 To celebrate the occasion, he gave a great banquet in Esther's honor for all
his nobles and officials, declaring a public holiday for
the provinces and giving generous gifts to everyone.
19 Even after all the young women had been transferred to the second harem* and Mordecai had become a palace official,* 20 Esther continued to keep
her family background and nationality a secret. She
was still following Mordecai's directions, just as she
did when she lived in his home.

Mordecai's Loyalty to the King

21 One day as Mordecai was on duty at the king's gate,
two of the king's eunuchs, Bigthana* and Teresh—who
were guards at the door of the king's private quarters—became angry at King Xerxes and plotted to assassinate him. 22 But Mordecai heard about the plot
and gave the information to Queen Esther. She then
told the king about it and gave Mordecai credit for the
report. 23 When an investigation was made and Mordecai's story was found to be true, the two men were
impaled on a sharpened pole. This was all recorded in
The Book of the History of King Xerxes' Reign.

Haman's Plot against the Jews

3 Some time later King Xerxes promoted Haman
son of Hammedatha the Agagite over all the
other nobles, making him the most powerful official
in the empire. 2 All the king's officials would bow
down before Haman to show him respect whenever
he passed by, for so the king had commanded. But
Mordecai refused to bow down or show him respect.
3 Then the palace officials at the king's gate asked
Mordecai, "Why are you disobeying the king's command?" 4 They spoke to him day after day, but still he
refused to comply with the order. So they spoke to
Haman about this to see if he would tolerate Mordecai's conduct, since Mordecai had told them he was
a Jew.
5 When Haman saw that Mordecai would not bow
down or show him respect, he was filled with rage.
6 He had learned of Mordecai's nationality, so he decided it was not enough to lay hands on Mordecai
alone. Instead, he looked for a way to destroy all the
Jews throughout the entire empire of Xerxes.
7 So in the month of April,* during the twelfth year
of King Xerxes' reign, lots were cast in Haman's presence (the lots were called *purim*) to determine the

2:19a The meaning of the Hebrew is uncertain. **2:19b** Hebrew *and Mordecai was sitting in the gate of the king.* **2:21** Hebrew *Bigthan;* compare 6:2. **3:7a** Hebrew *in the first month, the month of Nisan.* This month of the ancient Hebrew lunar calendar occurred within the months of April and May 474 B.C.; also see note on 2:16.

KING JAMES VERSION

month to month, *to* the twelfth *month,* that *is,* the
month Adar.
8And Haman said unto king Ahasuerus, There is a
certain people scattered abroad and dispersed
among the people in all the provinces of thy kingdom; and their laws *are* diverse from all people; neither keep they the king's laws: therefore it *is* not for
the king's profit to suffer them.
9If it please the king, let it be written that they may
be destroyed: and I will pay ten thousand talents of
silver to the hands of those that have the charge of
the business, to bring *it* into the king's treasuries.
10And the king took his ring from his hand, and
gave it unto Haman the son of Hammedatha the Agagite, the Jews' enemy.
11And the king said unto Haman, The silver *is*
given to thee, the people also, to do with them as it
seemeth good to thee.
12Then were the king's scribes called on the thirteenth day of the first month, and there was written
according to all that Haman had commanded unto
the king's lieutenants, and to the governors that *were*
over every province, and to the rulers of every people
of every province according to the writing thereof,
and *to* every people after their language; in the name
of king Ahasuerus was it written, and sealed with the
king's ring.
13And the letters were sent by posts into all the
king's provinces, to destroy, to kill, and to cause to
perish, all Jews, both young and old, little children
and women, in one day, *even* upon the thirteenth *day*
of the twelfth month, which is the month Adar, and
to take the spoil of them for a prey.
14The copy of the writing for a commandment to
be given in every province was published unto all
people, that they should be ready against that day.
15The posts went out, being hastened by the king's
commandment, and the decree was given in Shushan the palace. And the king and Haman sat down
to drink; but the city Shushan was perplexed.

4 1When Mordecai perceived all that was done,
Mordecai rent his clothes, and put on sackcloth
with ashes, and went out into the midst of the city,
and cried with a loud and a bitter cry;
2And came even before the king's gate: for none
might enter into the king's gate clothed with sackcloth.
3And in every province, whithersoever the king's
commandment and his decree came, *there was* great
mourning among the Jews, and fasting, and weeping,
and wailing; and many lay in sackcloth and ashes.
4So Esther's maids and her chamberlains came
and told *it* her. Then was the queen exceedingly
grieved; and she sent raiment to clothe Mordecai,

NEW LIVING TRANSLATION

best day and month to take action. And the day selected was March 7, nearly a year later.*
8Then Haman approached King Xerxes and said,
"There is a certain race of people scattered through
all the provinces of your empire who keep themselves separate from everyone else. Their laws are
different from those of any other people, and they
refuse to obey the laws of the king. So it is not in the
king's interest to let them live. 9If it please the king,
issue a decree that they be destroyed, and I will give
10,000 large sacks* of silver to the government administrators to be deposited in the royal treasury."
10The king agreed, confirming his decision by removing his signet ring from his finger and giving it
to Haman son of Hammedatha the Agagite, the enemy of the Jews. 11The king said, "The money and
the people are both yours to do with as you see fit."
12So on April 17* the king's secretaries were summoned, and a decree was written exactly as Haman
dictated. It was sent to the king's highest officers, the
governors of the respective provinces, and the nobles of each province in their own scripts and languages. The decree was written in the name of King
Xerxes and sealed with the king's signet ring. 13Dis-
patches were sent by swift messengers into all the
provinces of the empire, giving the order that all
Jews—young and old, including women and children—must be killed, slaughtered, and annihilated
on a single day. This was scheduled to happen on
March 7 of the next year.* The property of the Jews
would be given to those who killed them.
14A copy of this decree was to be issued as law in
every province and proclaimed to all peoples, so that
they would be ready to do their duty on the appointed day. 15At the king's command, the decree
went out by swift messengers, and it was also proclaimed in the fortress of Susa. Then the king and
Haman sat down to drink, but the city of Susa fell
into confusion.

Mordecai Requests Esther's Help

4 When Mordecai learned about all that had been
done, he tore his clothes, put on burlap and
ashes, and went out into the city, crying with a loud
and bitter wail. 2He went as far as the gate of the palace, for no one was allowed to enter the palace gate
while wearing clothes of mourning. 3And as news of
the king's decree reached all the provinces, there was
great mourning among the Jews. They fasted, wept,
and wailed, and many people lay in burlap and ashes.
4When Queen Esther's maids and eunuchs came

3:7b As in 3:13, which reads *the thirteenth day of the twelfth month, the month of Adar;* Hebrew reads *in the twelfth month,* of the ancient Hebrew lunar calendar. The date selected was March 7, 473 B.C.; also see note on 2:16.
3:9 Hebrew *10,000 talents,* about 375 tons or 340 metric tons in weight.
3:12 Hebrew *On the thirteenth day of the first month,* of the ancient Hebrew lunar calendar. This day was April 17, 474 B.C.; also see note on 2:16.
3:13 Hebrew *on the thirteenth day of the twelfth month, the month of Adar,* of the ancient Hebrew lunar calendar. The date selected was March 7, 473 B.C.; also see note on 2:16.

KING JAMES VERSION

and to take away his sackcloth from him: but he received *it* not.
5 Then called Esther for Hatach, *one* of the king's
chamberlains, whom he had appointed to attend
upon her, and gave him a commandment to Mordecai, to know what it *was*, and why it *was*.
6 So Hatach went forth to Mordecai unto the street
of the city, which *was* before the king's gate.
7 And Mordecai told him of all that had happened
unto him, and of the sum of the money that Haman
had promised to pay to the king's treasuries for the
Jews, to destroy them.
8 Also he gave him the copy of the writing of the
decree that was given at Shushan to destroy them, to
shew *it* unto Esther, and to declare *it* unto her, and
to charge her that she should go in unto the king, to
make supplication unto him, and to make request
before him for her people.
9 And Hatach came and told Esther the words of
Mordecai.
10 Again Esther spake unto Hatach, and gave him
commandment unto Mordecai;
11 All the king's servants, and the people of the
king's provinces, do know, that whosoever, whether
man or woman, shall come unto the king into the inner court, who is not called, *there is* one law of his to
put *him* to death, except such to whom the king shall
hold out the golden sceptre, that he may live: but I
have not been called to come in unto the king these
thirty days.
12 And they told to Mordecai Esther's words.
13 Then Mordecai commanded to answer Esther,
Think not with thyself that thou shalt escape in the
king's house, more than all the Jews.
14 For if thou altogether holdest thy peace at this
time, *then* shall there enlargement and deliverance
arise to the Jews from another place; but thou and
thy father's house shall be destroyed: and who
knoweth whether thou art come to the kingdom for
such a time as this?
15 Then Esther bade *them* return Mordecai *this*
answer,
16 Go, gather together all the Jews that are present
in Shushan, and fast ye for me, and neither eat nor
drink three days, night or day: I also and my maidens
will fast likewise; and so will I go in unto the king,
which *is* not according to the law: and if I perish, I
perish.
17 So Mordecai went his way, and did according to
all that Esther had commanded him.

5 1 Now it came to pass on the third day, that Esther put on *her* royal *apparel*, and stood in the
inner court of the king's house, over against the
king's house: and the king sat upon his royal throne
in the royal house, over against the gate of the house.
2 And it was so, when the king saw Esther the
queen standing in the court, *that* she obtained

NEW LIVING TRANSLATION

and told her about Mordecai, she was deeply distressed. She sent clothing to him to replace the burlap, but he refused it. 5 Then Esther sent for Hathach,
one of the king's eunuchs who had been appointed
as her attendant. She ordered him to go to Mordecai
and find out what was troubling him and why he was
in mourning. 6 So Hathach went out to Mordecai in
the square in front of the palace gate.
7 Mordecai told him the whole story, including the
exact amount of money Haman had promised to pay
into the royal treasury for the destruction of the
Jews. 8 Mordecai gave Hathach a copy of the decree
issued in Susa that called for the death of all Jews. He
asked Hathach to show it to Esther and explain the
situation to her. He also asked Hathach to direct her
to go to the king to beg for mercy and plead for her
people. 9 So Hathach returned to Esther with Mordecai's message.
10 Then Esther told Hathach to go back and relay
this message to Mordecai: 11 "All the king's officials
and even the people in the provinces know that anyone who appears before the king in his inner court
without being invited is doomed to die unless the
king holds out his gold scepter. And the king has not
called for me to come to him for thirty days." 12 So
Hathach* gave Esther's message to Mordecai.
13 Mordecai sent this reply to Esther: "Don't think
for a moment that because you're in the palace you
will escape when all other Jews are killed. 14 If you
keep quiet at a time like this, deliverance and relief
for the Jews will arise from some other place, but you
and your relatives will die. Who knows if perhaps
you were made queen for just such a time as this?"
15 Then Esther sent this reply to Mordecai: 16 "Go
and gather together all the Jews of Susa and fast for
me. Do not eat or drink for three days, night or day.
My maids and I will do the same. And then, though it
is against the law, I will go in to see the king. If I must
die, I must die." 17 So Mordecai went away and did
everything as Esther had ordered him.

Esther's Request to the King

5 On the third day of the fast, Esther put on her
royal robes and entered the inner court of the
palace, just across from the king's hall. The king was
sitting on his royal throne, facing the entrance.
2 When he saw Queen Esther standing there in the

4:12 As in Greek version; Hebrew reads *they*.

KING JAMES VERSION

favour in his sight: and the king held out to Esther
the golden sceptre that *was* in his hand. So Esther
drew near, and touched the top of the sceptre.

3 Then said the king unto her, What wilt thou,
queen Esther? and what *is* thy request? it shall be
even given thee to the half of the kingdom.

4 And Esther answered, If *it seem* good unto the
king, let the king and Haman come this day unto the
banquet that I have prepared for him.

5 Then the king said, Cause Haman to make haste,
that he may do as Esther hath said. So the king
and Haman came to the banquet that Esther had
prepared.

6 And the king said unto Esther at the banquet of
wine, What *is* thy petition? and it shall be granted
thee: and what *is* thy request? even to the half of the
kingdom it shall be performed.

7 Then answered Esther, and said, My petition and
my request *is;*

8 If I have found favour in the sight of the king, and
if it please the king to grant my petition, and to perform my request, let the king and Haman come to
the banquet that I shall prepare for them, and I will
do tomorrow as the king hath said.

9 Then went Haman forth that day joyful and with
a glad heart: but when Haman saw Mordecai in the
king's gate, that he stood not up, nor moved for him,
he was full of indignation against Mordecai.

10 Nevertheless Haman refrained himself: and
when he came home, he sent and called for his
friends, and Zeresh his wife.

11 And Haman told them of the glory of his riches,
and the multitude of his children, and all *the things*
wherein the king had promoted him, and how he
had advanced him above the princes and servants of
the king.

12 Haman said moreover, Yea, Esther the queen did
let no man come in with the king unto the banquet
that she had prepared but myself; and tomorrow am
I invited unto her also with the king.

13 Yet all this availeth me nothing, so long as I see
Mordecai the Jew sitting at the king's gate.

14 Then said Zeresh his wife and all his friends unto
him, Let a gallows be made of fifty cubits high, and tomorrow speak thou unto the king that Mordecai may
be hanged thereon: then go thou in merrily with the
king unto the banquet. And the thing pleased Haman;
and he caused the gallows to be made.

6 1 On that night could not the king sleep, and he
commanded to bring the book of records of the
chronicles; and they were read before the king.

2 And it was found written, that Mordecai had
told of Bigthana and Teresh, two of the king's

NEW LIVING TRANSLATION

inner court, he welcomed her and held out the gold
scepter to her. So Esther approached and touched
the end of the scepter.

3 Then the king asked her, "What do you want,
Queen Esther? What is your request? I will give it to
you, even if it is half the kingdom!"

4 And Esther replied, "If it please the king, let the
king and Haman come today to a banquet I have
prepared for the king."

5 The king turned to his attendants and said, "Tell
Haman to come quickly to a banquet, as Esther has
requested." So the king and Haman went to Esther's
banquet.

6 And while they were drinking wine, the king said
to Esther, "Now tell me what you really want. What is
your request? I will give it to you, even if it is half the
kingdom!"

7 Esther replied, "This is my request and deepest
wish. 8 If I have found favor with the king, and if it
pleases the king to grant my request and do what I
ask, please come with Haman tomorrow to the banquet I will prepare for you. Then I will explain what
this is all about."

Haman's Plan to Kill Mordecai

9 Haman was a happy man as he left the banquet! But
when he saw Mordecai sitting at the palace gate, not
standing up or trembling nervously before him,
Haman became furious. 10 However, he restrained
himself and went on home.

Then Haman gathered together his friends and Zeresh, his wife, 11 and boasted to them about his great
wealth and his many children. He bragged about the
honors the king had given him and how he had been
promoted over all the other nobles and officials.

12 Then Haman added, "And that's not all! Queen
Esther invited only me and the king himself to the
banquet she prepared for us. And she has invited me
to dine with her and the king again tomorrow!"
13 Then he added, "But this is all worth nothing as
long as I see Mordecai the Jew just sitting there at the
palace gate."

14 So Haman's wife, Zeresh, and all his friends suggested, "Set up a sharpened pole that stands seventy-
five feet* tall, and in the morning ask the king to impale Mordecai on it. When this is done, you can go
on your merry way to the banquet with the king."
This pleased Haman, and he ordered the pole set up.

The King Honors Mordecai

6 That night the king had trouble sleeping, so he
ordered an attendant to bring the book of the
history of his reign so it could be read to him. 2 In
those records he discovered an account of how Mordecai had exposed the plot of Bigthana and Teresh,
two of the eunuchs who guarded the door to the

5:14 Hebrew *50 cubits* [22.5 meters].

chamberlains, the keepers of the door, who sought to
lay hand on the king Ahasuerus.
[3]And the king said, What honour and dignity hath
been done to Mordecai for this? Then said the king's
servants that ministered unto him, There is nothing
done for him.
[4]And the king said, Who *is* in the court? Now
Haman was come into the outward court of the
king's house, to speak unto the king to hang Mordecai on the gallows that he had prepared for him.
[5]And the king's servants said unto him, Behold,
Haman standeth in the court. And the king said, Let
him come in.
[6]So Haman came in. And the king said unto him,
What shall be done unto the man whom the king
delighteth to honour? Now Haman thought in his
heart, To whom would the king delight to do honour
more than to myself?
[7]And Haman answered the king, For the man
whom the king delighteth to honour,
[8]Let the royal apparel be brought which the king
useth to wear, and the horse that the king rideth
upon, and the crown royal which is set upon his
head:
[9]And let this apparel and horse be delivered to the
hand of one of the king's most noble princes, that
they may array the man *withal* whom the king
delighteth to honour, and bring him on horseback
through the street of the city, and proclaim before
him, Thus shall it be done to the man whom the king
delighteth to honour.
[10]Then the king said to Haman, Make haste, *and*
take the apparel and the horse, as thou hast said, and
do even so to Mordecai the Jew, that sitteth at the
king's gate: let nothing fail of all that thou hast
spoken.
[11]Then took Haman the apparel and the horse,
and arrayed Mordecai, and brought him on horseback through the street of the city, and proclaimed
before him, Thus shall it be done unto the man
whom the king delighteth to honour.
[12]And Mordecai came again to the king's gate. But
Haman hasted to his house mourning, and having
his head covered.
[13]And Haman told Zeresh his wife and all his
friends every *thing* that had befallen him. Then said
his wise men and Zeresh his wife unto him, If Mordecai *be* of the seed of the Jews, before whom thou hast
begun to fall, thou shalt not prevail against him, but
shalt surely fall before him.
[14]And while they *were* yet talking with him, came
the king's chamberlains, and hasted to bring Haman
unto the banquet that Esther had prepared.

7 [1]So the king and Haman came to banquet with
Esther the queen.
[2]And the king said again unto Esther on the second day at the banquet of wine, What *is* thy petition,

king's private quarters. They had plotted to assassinate King Xerxes.
[3]"What reward or recognition did we ever give
Mordecai for this?" the king asked.
His attendants replied, "Nothing has been done
for him."
[4]"Who is that in the outer court?" the king inquired. As it happened, Haman had just arrived in
the outer court of the palace to ask the king to impale
Mordecai on the pole he had prepared.
[5]So the attendants replied to the king, "Haman is
out in the court."
"Bring him in," the king ordered. [6]So Haman came
in, and the king said, "What should I do to honor a
man who truly pleases me?"
Haman thought to himself, "Whom would the
king wish to honor more than me?" [7]So he replied,
"If the king wishes to honor someone, [8]he should
bring out one of the king's own royal robes, as well as
a horse that the king himself has ridden—one with a
royal emblem on its head. [9]Let the robes and the
horse be handed over to one of the king's most noble
officials. And let him see that the man whom the
king wishes to honor is dressed in the king's robes
and led through the city square on the king's horse.
Have the official shout as they go, 'This is what the
king does for someone he wishes to honor!'"
[10]"Excellent!" the king said to Haman. "Quick!
Take the robes and my horse, and do just as you have
said for Mordecai the Jew, who sits at the gate of the
palace. Leave out nothing you have suggested!"
[11]So Haman took the robes and put them on Mordecai, placed him on the king's own horse, and led
him through the city square, shouting, "This is what
the king does for someone he wishes to honor!"
[12]Afterward Mordecai returned to the palace gate,
but Haman hurried home dejected and completely
humiliated.
[13]When Haman told his wife, Zeresh, and all his
friends what had happened, his wise advisers and
his wife said, "Since Mordecai—this man who has
humiliated you—is of Jewish birth, you will never
succeed in your plans against him. It will be fatal to
continue opposing him."
[14]While they were still talking, the king's eunuchs
arrived and quickly took Haman to the banquet
Esher had prepared.

The King Executes Haman

7 So the king and Haman went to Queen Esther's
banquet. [2]On this second occasion, while they
were drinking wine, the king again said to Esther,

KING JAMES VERSION

queen Esther? and it shall be granted thee: and what *is* thy request? and it shall be performed, *even* to the half of the kingdom.

[3]Then Esther the queen answered and said, If I have found favour in thy sight, O king, and if it please the king, let my life be given me at my petition, and my people at my request:

[4]For we are sold, I and my people, to be destroyed, to be slain, and to perish. But if we had been sold for bondmen and bondwomen, I had held my tongue, although the enemy could not countervail the king's damage.

[5]Then the king Ahasuerus answered and said unto Esther the queen, Who is he, and where is he, that durst presume in his heart to do so?

[6]And Esther said, The adversary and enemy *is* this wicked Haman. Then Haman was afraid before the king and the queen.

[7]And the king arising from the banquet of wine in his wrath *went* into the palace garden: and Haman stood up to make request for his life to Esther the queen; for he saw that there was evil determined against him by the king.

[8]Then the king returned out of the palace garden into the place of the banquet of wine; and Haman was fallen upon the bed whereon Esther *was*. Then said the king, Will he force the queen also before me in the house? As the word went out of the king's mouth, they covered Haman's face.

[9]And Harbonah, one of the chamberlains, said before the king, Behold also, the gallows fifty cubits high, which Haman had made for Mordecai, who had spoken good for the king, standeth in the house of Haman. Then the king said, Hang him thereon.

[10]So they hanged Haman on the gallows that he had prepared for Mordecai. Then was the king's wrath pacified.

8 [1]On that day did the king Ahasuerus give the house of Haman the Jews' enemy unto Esther the queen. And Mordecai came before the king; for Esther had told what he *was* unto her.

[2]And the king took off his ring, which he had taken from Haman, and gave it unto Mordecai. And Esther set Mordecai over the house of Haman.

[3]And Esther spake yet again before the king, and fell down at his feet, and besought him with tears to put away the mischief of Haman the Agagite, and his device that he had devised against the Jews.

[4]Then the king held out the golden sceptre toward Esther. So Esther arose, and stood before the king,

[5]And said, If it please the king, and if I have found favour in his sight, and the thing *seem* right before the king, and I *be* pleasing in his eyes, let it be written to reverse the letters devised by Haman the son of Hammedatha the Agagite, which he wrote to destroy the Jews which *are* in all the king's provinces:

[6]For how can I endure to see the evil that shall

NEW LIVING TRANSLATION

"Tell me what you want, Queen Esther. What is your request? I will give it to you, even if it is half the kingdom!"

[3]Queen Esther replied, "If I have found favor with the king, and if it pleases the king to grant my request, I ask that my life and the lives of my people
will be spared. [4]For my people and I have been sold to those who would kill, slaughter, and annihilate us. If we had merely been sold as slaves, I could remain quiet, for that would be too trivial a matter to warrant disturbing the king."

[5]"Who would do such a thing?" King Xerxes demanded. "Who would be so presumptuous as to touch you?"

[6]Esther replied, "This wicked Haman is our adversary and our enemy." Haman grew pale with fright
before the king and queen. [7]Then the king jumped to his feet in a rage and went out into the palace garden.

Haman, however, stayed behind to plead for his life with Queen Esther, for he knew that the king in-
tended to kill him. [8]In despair he fell on the couch where Queen Esther was reclining, just as the king was returning from the palace garden.

The king exclaimed, "Will he even assault the queen right here in the palace, before my very eyes?" And as soon as the king spoke, his attendants covered Haman's face, signaling his doom.

[9]Then Harbona, one of the king's eunuchs, said, "Haman has set up a sharpened pole that stands seventy-five feet* tall in his own courtyard. He intended to use it to impale Mordecai, the man who saved the king from assassination."

"Then impale Haman on it!" the king ordered.
[10]So they impaled Haman on the pole he had set up for Mordecai, and the king's anger subsided.

A Decree to Help the Jews

8 On that same day King Xerxes gave the property of Haman, the enemy of the Jews, to Queen Esther. Then Mordecai was brought before the king, for Esther had told the king how they were related.
[2]The king took off his signet ring—which he had taken back from Haman—and gave it to Mordecai. And Esther appointed Mordecai to be in charge of Haman's property.

[3]Then Esther went again before the king, falling down at his feet and begging him with tears to stop the evil plot devised by Haman the Agagite against
the Jews. [4]Again the king held out the gold scepter to Esther. So she rose and stood before him.

[5]Esther said, "If it please the king, and if I have found favor with him, and if he thinks it is right, and if I am pleasing to him, let there be a decree that reverses the orders of Haman son of Hammedatha the Agagite, who ordered that Jews throughout all the
king's provinces should be destroyed. [6]For how can I

7:9 Hebrew *50 cubits* [22.5 meters].

KING JAMES VERSION

come unto my people? or how can I endure to see the
destruction of my kindred?

7 Then the king Ahasuerus said unto Esther the
queen and to Mordecai the Jew, Behold, I have given
Esther the house of Haman, and him they have
hanged upon the gallows, because he laid his hand
upon the Jews.

8 Write ye also for the Jews, as it liketh you, in the
king's name, and seal *it* with the king's ring: for the
writing which is written in the king's name, and
sealed with the king's ring, may no man reverse.

9 Then were the king's scribes called at that time in
the third month, that *is,* the month Sivan, on the
three and twentieth *day* thereof; and it was written
according to all that Mordecai commanded unto the
Jews, and to the lieutenants, and the deputies and
rulers of the provinces which *are* from India unto
Ethiopia, an hundred twenty and seven provinces,
unto every province according to the writing thereof,
and unto every people after their language, and to
the Jews according to their writing, and according to
their language.

10 And he wrote in the king Ahasuerus' name, and
sealed *it* with the king's ring, and sent letters by
posts on horseback, *and* riders on mules, camels,
and young dromedaries:

11 Wherein the king granted the Jews which *were*
in every city to gather themselves together, and to
stand for their life, to destroy, to slay, and to cause to
perish, all the power of the people and province that
would assault them, *both* little ones and women, and
to take the spoil of them for a prey,

12 Upon one day in all the provinces of king Ahasuerus, *namely,* upon the thirteenth *day* of the twelfth
month, which *is* the month Adar.

13 The copy of the writing for a commandment to
be given in every province *was* published unto all
people, and that the Jews should be ready against
that day to avenge themselves on their enemies.

14 *So* the posts that rode upon mules *and* camels
went out, being hastened and pressed on by the
king's commandment. And the decree was given at
Shushan the palace.

15 And Mordecai went out from the presence of
the king in royal apparel of blue and white, and with
a great crown of gold, and with a garment of fine
linen and purple: and the city of Shushan rejoiced
and was glad.

16 The Jews had light, and gladness, and joy, and
honour.

17 And in every province, and in every city,
whithersoever the king's commandment and his decree came, the Jews had joy and gladness, a feast and
a good day. And many of the people of the land became Jews; for the fear of the Jews fell upon them.

NEW LIVING TRANSLATION

endure to see my people and my family slaughtered
and destroyed?"

7 Then King Xerxes said to Queen Esther and Mordecai the Jew, "I have given Esther the property of
Haman, and he has been impaled on a pole because
he tried to destroy the Jews.
8 Now go ahead and send
a message to the Jews in the king's name, telling
them whatever you want, and seal it with the king's
signet ring. But remember that whatever has already
been written in the king's name and sealed with his
signet ring can never be revoked."

9 So on June 25* the king's secretaries were summoned, and a decree was written exactly as Mordecai dictated. It was sent to the Jews and to the
highest officers, the governors, and the nobles of all
the 127 provinces stretching from India to Ethiopia.* The decree was written in the scripts and languages of all the peoples of the empire, including
that of the Jews.
10 The decree was written in the
name of King Xerxes and sealed with the king's signet ring. Mordecai sent the dispatches by swift messengers, who rode fast horses especially bred for the
king's service.

11 The king's decree gave the Jews in every city
authority to unite to defend their lives. They were
allowed to kill, slaughter, and annihilate anyone of
any nationality or province who might attack them
or their children and wives, and to take the property
of their enemies.
12 The day chosen for this event
throughout all the provinces of King Xerxes was
March 7 of the next year.*

13 A copy of this decree was to be issued as law in
every province and proclaimed to all peoples, so that
the Jews would be ready to take revenge on their
enemies on the appointed day.
14 So urged on by the
king's command, the messengers rode out swiftly on
fast horses bred for the king's service. The same decree was also proclaimed in the fortress of Susa.

15 Then Mordecai left the king's presence, wearing
the royal robe of blue and white, the great crown of
gold, and an outer cloak of fine linen and purple.
And the people of Susa celebrated the new decree.
16 The Jews were filled with joy and gladness and
were honored everywhere.
17 In every province and
city, wherever the king's decree arrived, the Jews rejoiced and had a great celebration and declared a
public festival and holiday. And many of the people
of the land became Jews themselves, for they feared
what the Jews might do to them.

8:9a Hebrew *on the twenty-third day of the third month, the month of Sivan,* of the ancient Hebrew lunar calendar. This day was June 25, 474 B.C.; also see note on 2:16. **8:9b** Hebrew *to Cush.* **8:12** Hebrew *the thirteenth day of the twelfth month, the month of Adar,* of the ancient Hebrew lunar calendar. The date selected was March 7, 473 B.C.; also see note on 2:16.

KING JAMES VERSION

9 1 Now in the twelfth month, that *is,* the month Adar, on the thirteenth day of the same, when the king's commandment and his decree drew near to be put in execution, in the day that the enemies of the Jews hoped to have power over them, (though it was turned to the contrary, that the Jews had rule over them that hated them;)

2 The Jews gathered themselves together in their cities throughout all the provinces of the king Ahasuerus, to lay hand on such as sought their hurt: and no man could withstand them; for the fear of them fell upon all people.

3 And all the rulers of the provinces, and the lieutenants, and the deputies, and officers of the king, helped the Jews; because the fear of Mordecai fell upon them.

4 For Mordecai *was* great in the king's house, and his fame went out throughout all the provinces: for this man Mordecai waxed greater and greater.

5 Thus the Jews smote all their enemies with the stroke of the sword, and slaughter, and destruction, and did what they would unto those that hated them.

6 And in Shushan the palace the Jews slew and destroyed five hundred men.

7 And Parshandatha, and Dalphon, and Aspatha,

8 And Poratha, and Adalia, and Aridatha,

9 And Parmashta, and Arisai, and Aridai, and Vajezatha,

10 The ten sons of Haman the son of Hammedatha, the enemy of the Jews, slew they; but on the spoil laid they not their hand.

11 On that day the number of those that were slain in Shushan the palace was brought before the king.

12 And the king said unto Esther the queen, The Jews have slain and destroyed five hundred men in Shushan the palace, and the ten sons of Haman; what have they done in the rest of the king's provinces? now what *is* thy petition? and it shall be granted thee: or what *is* thy request further? and it shall be done.

13 Then said Esther, If it please the king, let it be granted to the Jews which *are* in Shushan to do tomorrow also according unto this day's decree, and let Haman's ten sons be hanged upon the gallows.

14 And the king commanded it so to be done: and the decree was given at Shushan; and they hanged Haman's ten sons.

15 For the Jews that *were* in Shushan gathered themselves together on the fourteenth day also of the month Adar, and slew three hundred men at Shushan; but on the prey they laid not their hand.

16 But the other Jews that *were* in the king's provinces gathered themselves together, and stood for their lives, and had rest from their enemies, and slew of their foes seventy and five thousand, but they laid not their hands on the prey,

17 On the thirteenth day of the month Adar; and on

NEW LIVING TRANSLATION

The Victory of the Jews

9 So on March 7* the two decrees of the king
were put into effect. On that day, the enemies of
the Jews had hoped to overpower them, but quite the
opposite happened. It was the Jews who overpowered their enemies. 2 The Jews gathered in their cities
throughout all the king's provinces to attack anyone
who tried to harm them. But no one could make a
stand against them, for everyone was afraid of them.
3 And all the nobles of the provinces, the highest officers, the governors, and the royal officials helped the
Jews for fear of Mordecai. 4 For Mordecai had been
promoted in the king's palace, and his fame spread
throughout all the provinces as he became more and
more powerful.

5 So the Jews went ahead on the appointed day and
struck down their enemies with the sword. They
killed and annihilated their enemies and did as they
pleased with those who hated them. 6 In the fortress
of Susa itself, the Jews killed 500 men. 7 They also
killed Parshandatha, Dalphon, Aspatha, 8 Poratha,
Adalia, Aridatha, 9 Parmashta, Arisai, Aridai, and Vai-
zatha—10 the ten sons of Haman son of Hammedatha, the enemy of the Jews. But they did not take any
plunder.

11 That very day, when the king was informed of
the number of people killed in the fortress of Susa,
12 he called for Queen Esther. He said, "The Jews have
killed 500 men in the fortress of Susa alone, as well
as Haman's ten sons. If they have done that here,
what has happened in the rest of the provinces? But
now, what more do you want? It will be granted to
you; tell me and I will do it."

13 Esther responded, "If it please the king, give the
Jews in Susa permission to do again tomorrow as
they have done today, and let the bodies of Haman's
ten sons be impaled on a pole."

14 So the king agreed, and the decree was announced in Susa. And they impaled the bodies of
Haman's ten sons. 15 Then the Jews at Susa gathered
together on March 8* and killed 300 more men, and
again they took no plunder.

16 Meanwhile, the other Jews throughout the king's
provinces had gathered together to defend their lives.
They gained relief from all their enemies, killing
75,000 of those who hated them. But they did not
take any plunder. 17 This was done throughout the
provinces on March 7, and on March 8 they rested,*

9:1 Hebrew *on the thirteenth day of the twelfth month, the month of Adar,* of the ancient Hebrew lunar calendar. This day was March 7, 473 B.C.; also see note on 2:16. **9:15** Hebrew *the fourteenth day of the month of Adar,* of the Hebrew lunar calendar. This day was March 8, 473 B.C.; also see note on 2:16. **9:17** Hebrew *on the thirteenth day of the month of Adar, and on the fourteenth day they rested.* These days were March 7 and 8, 473 B.C.; also see note on 2:16.

KING JAMES VERSION

the fourteenth day of the same rested they, and made it a day of feasting and gladness.

18But the Jews that *were* at Shushan assembled together on the thirteenth *day* thereof, and on the fourteenth thereof; and on the fifteenth *day* of the same they rested, and made it a day of feasting and gladness.

19Therefore the Jews of the villages, that dwelt in the unwalled towns, made the fourteenth day of the month Adar *a day of* gladness and feasting, and a good day, and of sending portions one to another.

20And Mordecai wrote these things, and sent letters unto all the Jews that *were* in all the provinces of the king Ahasuerus, *both* nigh and far,

21To stablish *this* among them, that they should keep the fourteenth day of the month Adar, and the fifteenth day of the same, yearly,

22As the days wherein the Jews rested from their enemies, and the month which was turned unto them from sorrow to joy, and from mourning into a good day: that they should make them days of feasting and joy, and of sending portions one to another, and gifts to the poor.

23And the Jews undertook to do as they had begun, and as Mordecai had written unto them;

24Because Haman the son of Hammedatha, the Agagite, the enemy of all the Jews, had devised against the Jews to destroy them, and had cast Pur, that *is*, the lot, to consume them, and to destroy them;

25But when *Esther* came before the king, he commanded by letters that his wicked device, which he devised against the Jews, should return upon his own head, and that he and his sons should be hanged on the gallows.

26Wherefore they called these days Purim after the name of Pur. Therefore for all the words of this letter, and *of that* which they had seen concerning this matter, and which had come unto them,

27The Jews ordained, and took upon them, and upon their seed, and upon all such as joined themselves unto them, so as it should not fail, that they would keep these two days according to their writing, and according to their *appointed* time every year;

28And *that* these days *should be* remembered and kept throughout every generation, every family, every province, and every city; and *that* these days of Purim should not fail from among the Jews, nor the memorial of them perish from their seed.

29Then Esther the queen, the daughter of Abihail, and Mordecai the Jew, wrote with all authority, to confirm this second letter of Purim.

30And he sent the letters unto all the Jews, to the hundred twenty and seven provinces of the kingdom of Ahasuerus, *with* words of peace and truth,

31To confirm these days of Purim in their times *appointed*, according as Mordecai the Jew and Esther the queen had enjoined them, and as they had

NEW LIVING TRANSLATION

celebrating their victory with a day of feasting and
gladness. 18(The Jews at Susa killed their enemies on
March 7 and again on March 8, then rested on
March 9,* making that their day of feasting and gladness.) 19So to this day, rural Jews living in remote villages celebrate an annual festival and holiday on the
appointed day in late winter,* when they rejoice and
send gifts of food to each other.

The Festival of Purim

20Mordecai recorded these events and sent letters to
the Jews near and far, throughout all the provinces
of King Xerxes, 21calling on them to celebrate an
annual festival on these two days.* 22He told them to
celebrate these days with feasting and gladness and
by giving gifts of food to each other and presents to
the poor. This would commemorate a time when the
Jews gained relief from their enemies, when their
sorrow was turned into gladness and their mourning
into joy.

23So the Jews accepted Mordecai's proposal and
adopted this annual custom. 24Haman son of Hammedatha the Agagite, the enemy of the Jews, had
plotted to crush and destroy them on the date determined by casting lots (the lots were called *purim*).
25But when Esther came before the king, he issued
a decree causing Haman's evil plot to backfire, and
Haman and his sons were impaled on a sharpened
pole. 26That is why this celebration is called Purim,
because it is the ancient word for casting lots.

So because of Mordecai's letter and because of
what they had experienced, 27the Jews throughout
the realm agreed to inaugurate this tradition and to
pass it on to their descendants and to all who became Jews. They declared they would never fail to
celebrate these two prescribed days at the appointed
time each year. 28These days would be remembered
and kept from generation to generation and celebrated by every family throughout the provinces and
cities of the empire. This Festival of Purim would
never cease to be celebrated among the Jews, nor
would the memory of what happened ever die out
among their descendants.

29Then Queen Esther, the daughter of Abihail,
along with Mordecai the Jew, wrote another letter
putting the queen's full authority behind Mordecai's
letter to establish the Festival of Purim. 30Letters
wishing peace and security were sent to the Jews
throughout the 127 provinces of the empire of
Xerxes. 31These letters established the Festival of
Purim—an annual celebration of these days at the appointed time, decreed by both Mordecai the Jew and
Queen Esther. (The people decided to observe this

9:18 Hebrew *killed their enemies on the thirteenth day and the fourteenth day, and then rested on the fifteenth day,* of the Hebrew month of Adar. **9:19** Hebrew *on the fourteenth day of the month of Adar.* This day of the Hebrew lunar calendar occurs in February or March. **9:21** Hebrew *on the fourteenth and fifteenth days of Adar,* of the Hebrew lunar calendar.

KING JAMES VERSION

decreed for themselves and for their seed, the matters of the fastings and their cry.

32And the decree of Esther confirmed these matters of Purim; and it was written in the book.

10 1And the king Ahasuerus laid a tribute upon the land, and *upon* the isles of the sea.

2And all the acts of his power and of his might, and the declaration of the greatness of Mordecai, whereunto the king advanced him, *are* they not written in the book of the chronicles of the kings of Media and Persia?

3For Mordecai the Jew *was* next unto king Ahasuerus, and great among the Jews, and accepted of the multitude of his brethren, seeking the wealth of his people, and speaking peace to all his seed.

NEW LIVING TRANSLATION

festival, just as they had decided for themselves and their descendants to establish the times of fasting and mourning.) 32So the command of Esther confirmed the practices of Purim, and it was all written down in the records.

The Greatness of Xerxes and Mordecai

10 King Xerxes imposed a tribute throughout his empire, even to the distant coastlands. 2His great achievements and the full account of the greatness of Mordecai, whom the king had promoted, are recorded in *The Book of the History of the Kings of Media and Persia*. 3Mordecai the Jew became the prime minister, with authority next to that of King Xerxes himself. He was very great among the Jews, who held him in high esteem, because he continued to work for the good of his people and to speak up for the welfare of all their descendants.

Job

KING JAMES VERSION

1 1 There was a man in the land of Uz, whose name
was Job; and that man was perfect and upright,
and one that feared God, and eschewed evil.
2 And there were born unto him seven sons and
three daughters.
3 His substance also was seven thousand sheep,
and three thousand camels, and five hundred yoke of
oxen, and five hundred she asses, and a very great
household; so that this man was the greatest of all
the men of the east.
4 And his sons went and feasted *in their* houses,
every one his day; and sent and called for their three
sisters to eat and to drink with them.
5 And it was so, when the days of *their* feasting
were gone about, that Job sent and sanctified them,
and rose up early in the morning, and offered burnt
offerings *according* to the number of them all: for
Job said, It may be that my sons have sinned, and
cursed God in their hearts. Thus did Job continually.
6 Now there was a day when the sons of God came
to present themselves before the LORD, and Satan
came also among them.
7 And the LORD said unto Satan, Whence comest
thou? Then Satan answered the LORD, and said, From
going to and fro in the earth, and from walking up
and down in it.
8 And the LORD said unto Satan, Hast thou considered my servant Job, that *there is* none like him in the
earth, a perfect and an upright man, one that feareth
God, and escheweth evil?
9 Then Satan answered the LORD, and said, Doth
Job fear God for nought?
10 Hast not thou made an hedge about him, and
about his house, and about all that he hath on every
side? thou hast blessed the work of his hands, and
his substance is increased in the land.
11 But put forth thine hand now, and touch all that
he hath, and he will curse thee to thy face.
12 And the LORD said unto Satan, Behold, all that he
hath *is* in thy power; only upon himself put not forth
thine hand. So Satan went forth from the presence of
the LORD.

NEW LIVING TRANSLATION

Prologue

1 There once was a man named Job who lived
in the land of Uz. He was blameless—a man of
complete integrity. He feared God and stayed away
from evil. 2 He had seven sons and three daughters.
3 He owned 7,000 sheep, 3,000 camels, 500 teams of
oxen, and 500 female donkeys. He also had many
servants. He was, in fact, the richest person in that
entire area.
4 Job's sons would take turns preparing feasts in
their homes, and they would also invite their three
sisters to celebrate with them. 5 When these celebrations ended—sometimes after several days—Job
would purify his children. He would get up early in
the morning and offer a burnt offering for each of
them. For Job said to himself, "Perhaps my children
have sinned and have cursed God in their hearts."
This was Job's regular practice.

Job's First Test

6 One day the members of the heavenly court* came
to present themselves before the LORD, and the Accuser, Satan,* came with them. 7 "Where have you
come from?" the LORD asked Satan.
Satan answered the LORD, "I have been patrolling
the earth, watching everything that's going on."
8 Then the LORD asked Satan, "Have you noticed
my servant Job? He is the finest man in all the earth.
He is blameless—a man of complete integrity. He
fears God and stays away from evil."
9 Satan replied to the LORD, "Yes, but Job has good
reason to fear God. 10 You have always put a wall of
protection around him and his home and his property. You have made him prosper in everything he
does. Look how rich he is! 11 But reach out and take
away everything he has, and he will surely curse you
to your face!"
12 "All right, you may test him," the LORD said to
Satan. "Do whatever you want with everything he
possesses, but don't harm him physically." So Satan
left the LORD's presence.

1:6a Hebrew *the sons of God.* **1:6b** Hebrew *and the satan;* similarly throughout this chapter.

KING JAMES VERSION

13 And there was a day when his sons and his
daughters *were* eating and drinking wine in their
eldest brother's house:
14 And there came a messenger unto Job, and said,
The oxen were plowing, and the asses feeding beside
them:
15 And the Sabeans fell *upon them,* and took them
away; yea, they have slain the servants with the edge
of the sword; and I only am escaped alone to tell thee.
16 While he *was* yet speaking, there came also another, and said, The fire of God is fallen from heaven,
and hath burned up the sheep, and the servants, and
consumed them; and I only am escaped alone to
tell thee.
17 While he *was* yet speaking, there came also
another, and said, The Chaldeans made out three
bands, and fell upon the camels, and have carried
them away, yea, and slain the servants with the edge
of the sword; and I only am escaped alone to tell thee.
18 While he *was* yet speaking, there came also another, and said, Thy sons and thy daughters *were* eating and drinking wine in their eldest brother's house:
19 And, behold, there came a great wind from the
wilderness, and smote the four corners of the house,
and it fell upon the young men, and they are dead;
and I only am escaped alone to tell thee.
20 Then Job arose, and rent his mantle, and shaved
his head, and fell down upon the ground, and worshipped,
21 And said, Naked came I out of my mother's
womb, and naked shall I return thither: the LORD
gave, and the LORD hath taken away; blessed be the
name of the LORD.
22 In all this Job sinned not, nor charged God
foolishly.

2 1 Again there was a day when the sons of God
came to present themselves before the LORD,
and Satan came also among them to present himself
before the LORD.
2 And the LORD said unto Satan, From whence
comest thou? And Satan answered the LORD, and
said, From going to and fro in the earth, and from
walking up and down in it.
3 And the LORD said unto Satan, Hast thou considered my servant Job, that *there is* none like him in the
earth, a perfect and an upright man, one that feareth
God, and escheweth evil? and still he holdeth fast his
integrity, although thou movedst me against him, to
destroy him without cause.
4 And Satan answered the LORD, and said, Skin for
skin, yea, all that a man hath will he give for his life.
5 But put forth thine hand now, and touch his bone
and his flesh, and he will curse thee to thy face.
6 And the LORD said unto Satan, Behold, he *is* in
thine hand; but save his life.
7 So went Satan forth from the presence of the

NEW LIVING TRANSLATION

13 One day when Job's sons and daughters were
feasting at the oldest brother's house, 14 a messenger
arrived at Job's home with this news: "Your oxen
were plowing, with the donkeys feeding beside
them, 15 when the Sabeans raided us. They stole all
the animals and killed all the farmhands. I am the
only one who escaped to tell you."
16 While he was still speaking, another messenger
arrived with this news: "The fire of God has fallen
from heaven and burned up your sheep and all
the shepherds. I am the only one who escaped to
tell you."
17 While he was still speaking, a third messenger
arrived with this news: "Three bands of Chaldean
raiders have stolen your camels and killed your servants. I am the only one who escaped to tell you."
18 While he was still speaking, another messenger
arrived with this news: "Your sons and daughters
were feasting in their oldest brother's home. 19 Suddenly, a powerful wind swept in from the wilderness
and hit the house on all sides. The house collapsed,
and all your children are dead. I am the only one who
escaped to tell you."
20 Job stood up and tore his robe in grief. Then he
shaved his head and fell to the ground to worship.
21 He said,

"I came naked from my mother's womb,
and I will be naked when I leave.
The LORD gave me what I had,
and the LORD has taken it away.
Praise the name of the LORD!"

22 In all of this, Job did not sin by blaming God.

Job's Second Test

2 One day the members of the heavenly court*
came again to present themselves before the
LORD, and the Accuser, Satan,* came with them.
2 "Where have you come from?" the LORD asked
Satan.
Satan answered the LORD, "I have been patrolling
the earth, watching everything that's going on."
3 Then the LORD asked Satan, "Have you noticed
my servant Job? He is the finest man in all the earth.
He is blameless—a man of complete integrity. He
fears God and stays away from evil. And he has maintained his integrity, even though you urged me to
harm him without cause."
4 Satan replied to the LORD, "Skin for skin! A man
will give up everything he has to save his life. 5 But
reach out and take away his health, and he will surely
curse you to your face!"
6 "All right, do with him as you please," the LORD
said to Satan. "But spare his life." 7 So Satan left the

2:1a Hebrew *the sons of God.* **2:1b** Hebrew *and the satan;* similarly throughout this chapter.

KING JAMES VERSION

LORD, and smote Job with sore boils from the sole of his foot unto his crown.

8 And he took him a potsherd to scrape himself withal; and he sat down among the ashes.

9 Then said his wife unto him, Dost thou still retain thine integrity? curse God, and die.

10 But he said unto her, Thou speakest as one of the foolish women speaketh. What? shall we receive good at the hand of God, and shall we not receive evil? In all this did not Job sin with his lips.

11 Now when Job's three friends heard of all this evil that was come upon him, they came every one from his own place; Eliphaz the Temanite, and Bildad the Shuhite, and Zophar the Naamathite: for they had made an appointment together to come to mourn with him and to comfort him.

12 And when they lifted up their eyes afar off, and knew him not, they lifted up their voice, and wept; and they rent every one his mantle, and sprinkled dust upon their heads toward heaven.

13 So they sat down with him upon the ground seven days and seven nights, and none spake a word unto him: for they saw that *his* grief was very great.

3 1 After this opened Job his mouth, and cursed his day.

2 And Job spake, and said,

3 Let the day perish wherein I was born, and the night *in which* it was said, There is a man child conceived.

4 Let that day be darkness; let not God regard it from above, neither let the light shine upon it.

5 Let darkness and the shadow of death stain it; let a cloud dwell upon it; let the blackness of the day terrify it.

6 As *for* that night, let darkness seize upon it; let it not be joined unto the days of the year, let it not come into the number of the months.

7 Lo, let that night be solitary, let no joyful voice come therein.

8 Let them curse it that curse the day, who are ready to raise up their mourning.

9 Let the stars of the twilight thereof be dark; let it look for light, but *have* none; neither let it see the dawning of the day:

10 Because it shut not up the doors of my *mother's* womb, nor hid sorrow from mine eyes.

11 Why died I not from the womb? *why* did I *not* give up the ghost when I came out of the belly?

NEW LIVING TRANSLATION

LORD's presence, and he struck Job with terrible boils from head to foot.

8 Job scraped his skin with a piece of broken pottery as he sat among the ashes. 9 His wife said to him, "Are you still trying to maintain your integrity? Curse God and die."

10 But Job replied, "You talk like a foolish woman. Should we accept only good things from the hand of God and never anything bad?" So in all this, Job said nothing wrong.

Job's Three Friends Share His Anguish

11 When three of Job's friends heard of the tragedy he had suffered, they got together and traveled from their homes to comfort and console him. Their names were Eliphaz the Temanite, Bildad the Shuhite, and Zophar the Naamathite. 12 When they saw Job from a distance, they scarcely recognized him. Wailing loudly, they tore their robes and threw dust into the air over their heads to show their grief. 13 Then they sat on the ground with him for seven days and nights. No one said a word to Job, for they saw that his suffering was too great for words.

Job's First Speech

3 At last Job spoke, and he cursed the day of his birth. 2 He said:

3 "Let the day of my birth be erased,
and the night I was conceived.
4 Let that day be turned to darkness.
Let it be lost even to God on high,
and let no light shine on it.
5 Let the darkness and utter gloom claim that
day for its own.
Let a black cloud overshadow it,
and let the darkness terrify it.
6 Let that night be blotted off the calendar,
never again to be counted among the days
of the year,
never again to appear among the months.
7 Let that night be childless.
Let it have no joy.
8 Let those who are experts at cursing—
whose cursing could rouse Leviathan*—
curse that day.
9 Let its morning stars remain dark.
Let it hope for light, but in vain;
may it never see the morning light.
10 Curse that day for failing to shut my mother's
womb,
for letting me be born to see all this trouble.

11 "Why wasn't I born dead?
Why didn't I die as I came from the womb?

3:8 The identification of Leviathan is disputed, ranging from an earthly creature to a mythical sea monster in ancient literature.

KING JAMES VERSION

12 Why did the knees prevent me? or why the
breasts that I should suck?
13 For now should I have lain still and been quiet,
I should have slept: then had I been at rest,
14 With kings and counsellors of the earth, which
built desolate places for themselves;
15 Or with princes that had gold, who filled their
houses with silver:
16 Or as an hidden untimely birth I had not been;
as infants *which* never saw light.
17 There the wicked cease *from* troubling; and
there the weary be at rest.
18 *There* the prisoners rest together; they hear not
the voice of the oppressor.
19 The small and great are there; and the servant *is*
free from his master.
20 Wherefore is light given to him that is in misery,
and life unto the bitter *in* soul;
21 Which long for death, but it *cometh* not; and dig
for it more than for hid treasures;
22 Which rejoice exceedingly, *and* are glad, when
they can find the grave?
23 *Why is light given* to a man whose way is hid,
and whom God hath hedged in?
24 For my sighing cometh before I eat, and my roar-
ings are poured out like the waters.
25 For the thing which I greatly feared is come upon
me, and that which I was afraid of is come unto me.
26 I was not in safety, neither had I rest, neither was
I quiet; yet trouble came.

4

1 Then Eliphaz the Temanite answered and
said,
2 *If* we assay to commune with thee, wilt thou
be grieved? but who can withhold himself from
speaking?
3 Behold, thou hast instructed many, and thou hast
strengthened the weak hands.
4 Thy words have upholden him that was falling,
and thou hast strengthened the feeble knees.
5 But now it is come upon thee, and thou faintest; it
toucheth thee, and thou art troubled.
6 *Is* not *this* thy fear, thy confidence, thy hope, and
the uprightness of thy ways?
7 Remember, I pray thee, who *ever* perished, being
innocent? or where were the righteous cut off?
8 Even as I have seen, they that plow iniquity, and
sow wickedness, reap the same.
9 By the blast of God they perish, and by the breath
of his nostrils are they consumed.
10 The roaring of the lion, and the voice of the fierce
lion, and the teeth of the young lions, are broken.

NEW LIVING TRANSLATION

12 Why was I laid on my mother's lap?
Why did she nurse me at her breasts?
13 Had I died at birth, I would now be at peace.
I would be asleep and at rest.
14 I would rest with the world's kings and prime
ministers,
whose great buildings now lie in ruins.
15 I would rest with princes, rich in gold,
whose palaces were filled with silver.
16 Why wasn't I buried like a stillborn child,
like a baby who never lives to see the light?
17 For in death the wicked cause no trouble,
and the weary are at rest.
18 Even captives are at ease in death,
with no guards to curse them.
19 Rich and poor are both there,
and the slave is free from his master.

20 "Oh, why give light to those in misery,
and life to those who are bitter?
21 They long for death, and it won't come.
They search for death more eagerly than for
hidden treasure.
22 They're filled with joy when they finally die,
and rejoice when they find the grave.
23 Why is life given to those with no future,
those God has surrounded with difficulties?
24 I cannot eat for sighing;
my groans pour out like water.
25 What I always feared has happened to me.
What I dreaded has come true.
26 I have no peace, no quietness.
I have no rest; only trouble comes."

Eliphaz's First Response to Job

4

Then Eliphaz the Temanite replied to Job:

2 "Will you be patient and let me say a word?
For who could keep from speaking out?

3 "In the past you have encouraged many people;
you have strengthened those who were weak.
4 Your words have supported those who were
falling;
you encouraged those with shaky knees.
5 But now when trouble strikes, you lose heart.
You are terrified when it touches you.
6 Doesn't your reverence for God give you
confidence?
Doesn't your life of integrity give you hope?

7 "Stop and think! Do the innocent die?
When have the upright been destroyed?
8 My experience shows that those who plant
trouble
and cultivate evil will harvest the same.
9 A breath from God destroys them.
They vanish in a blast of his anger.
10 The lion roars and the wildcat snarls,
but the teeth of strong lions will be broken.

KING JAMES VERSION

11The old lion perisheth for lack of prey, and the stout lion's whelps are scattered abroad.

12Now a thing was secretly brought to me, and mine ear received a little thereof.

13In thoughts from the visions of the night, when deep sleep falleth on men,

14Fear came upon me, and trembling, which made all my bones to shake.

15Then a spirit passed before my face; the hair of my flesh stood up:

16It stood still, but I could not discern the form thereof: an image *was* before mine eyes, *there was* silence, and I heard a voice, *saying*,

17Shall mortal man be more just than God? shall a man be more pure than his maker?

18Behold, he put no trust in his servants; and his angels he charged with folly:

19How much less *in* them that dwell in houses of clay, whose foundation *is* in the dust, *which* are crushed before the moth?

20They are destroyed from morning to evening: they perish for ever without any regarding *it*.

21Doth not their excellency *which is* in them go away? they die, even without wisdom.

5 1Call now, if there be any that will answer thee; and to which of the saints wilt thou turn?

2For wrath killeth the foolish man, and envy slayeth the silly one.

3I have seen the foolish taking root: but suddenly I cursed his habitation.

4His children are far from safety, and they are crushed in the gate, neither *is there* any to deliver *them*.

5Whose harvest the hungry eateth up, and taketh it even out of the thorns, and the robber swalloweth up their substance.

6Although affliction cometh not forth of the dust, neither doth trouble spring out of the ground;

7Yet man is born unto trouble, as the sparks fly upward.

8I would seek unto God, and unto God would I commit my cause:

9Which doeth great things and unsearchable; marvellous things without number:

10Who giveth rain upon the earth, and sendeth waters upon the fields:

NEW LIVING TRANSLATION

11 The fierce lion will starve for lack of prey,
and the cubs of the lioness will be scattered.

12 "This truth was given to me in secret,
as though whispered in my ear.
13 It came to me in a disturbing vision at night,
when people are in a deep sleep.
14 Fear gripped me,
and my bones trembled.
15 A spirit* swept past my face,
and my hair stood on end.*
16 The spirit stopped, but I couldn't see its shape.
There was a form before my eyes.
In the silence I heard a voice say,
17 'Can a mortal be innocent before God?
Can anyone be pure before the Creator?'

18 "If God does not trust his own angels
and has charged his messengers with foolishness,
19 how much less will he trust people made of clay!
They are made of dust, crushed as easily as a moth.
20 They are alive in the morning but dead by evening,
gone forever without a trace.
21 Their tent-cords are pulled and the tent collapses,
and they die in ignorance.

Eliphaz's Response Continues

5 1"Cry for help, but will anyone answer you?
Which of the angels* will help you?
2 Surely resentment destroys the fool,
and jealousy kills the simple.
3 I have seen that fools may be successful for the moment,
but then comes sudden disaster.
4 Their children are abandoned far from help;
they are crushed in court with no one to defend them.
5 The hungry devour their harvest,
even when it is guarded by brambles.*
The thirsty pant after their wealth.
6 But evil does not spring from the soil,
and trouble does not sprout from the earth.
7 People are born for trouble
as readily as sparks fly up from a fire.

8 "If I were you, I would go to God
and present my case to him.
9 He does great things too marvelous to understand.
He performs countless miracles.
10 He gives rain for the earth
and water for the fields.

4:15a Or *wind;* also in 4:16. **4:15b** Or *its wind sent shivers up my spine.* **5:1** Hebrew *the holy ones.* **5:5** The meaning of the Hebrew for this phrase is uncertain.

KING JAMES VERSION

11 To set up on high those that be low; that those which mourn may be exalted to safety.

12 He disappointeth the devices of the crafty, so that their hands cannot perform *their* enterprise.

13 He taketh the wise in their own craftiness: and the counsel of the froward is carried headlong.

14 They meet with darkness in the daytime, and grope in the noonday as in the night.

15 But he saveth the poor from the sword, from their mouth, and from the hand of the mighty.

16 So the poor hath hope, and iniquity stoppeth her mouth.

17 Behold, happy *is* the man whom God correcteth: therefore despise not thou the chastening of the Almighty:

18 For he maketh sore, and bindeth up: he woundeth, and his hands make whole.

19 He shall deliver thee in six troubles: yea, in seven there shall no evil touch thee.

20 In famine he shall redeem thee from death: and in war from the power of the sword.

21 Thou shalt be hid from the scourge of the tongue: neither shalt thou be afraid of destruction when it cometh.

22 At destruction and famine thou shalt laugh: neither shalt thou be afraid of the beasts of the earth.

23 For thou shalt be in league with the stones of the field: and the beasts of the field shall be at peace with thee.

24 And thou shalt know that thy tabernacle *shall be* in peace; and thou shalt visit thy habitation, and shalt not sin.

25 Thou shalt know also that thy seed *shall be* great, and thine offspring as the grass of the earth.

26 Thou shalt come to *thy* grave in a full age, like as a shock of corn cometh in his season.

27 Lo this, we have searched it, so it *is;* hear it, and know thou *it* for thy good.

6 1 But Job answered and said,

2 Oh that my grief were throughly weighed, and my calamity laid in the balances together!

3 For now it would be heavier than the sand of the sea: therefore my words are swallowed up.

4 For the arrows of the Almighty *are* within me, the poison whereof drinketh up my spirit: the terrors of God do set themselves in array against me.

5 Doth the wild ass bray when he hath grass? or loweth the ox over his fodder?

NEW LIVING TRANSLATION

11 He gives prosperity to the poor
and protects those who suffer.
12 He frustrates the plans of schemers
so the work of their hands will not succeed.
13 He traps the wise in their own cleverness
so their cunning schemes are thwarted.
14 They find it is dark in the daytime,
and they grope at noon as if it were night.
15 He rescues the poor from the cutting words
of the strong,
and rescues them from the clutches of the
powerful.
16 And so at last the poor have hope,
and the snapping jaws of the wicked are shut.

17 "But consider the joy of those corrected by God!
Do not despise the discipline of the Almighty
when you sin.
18 For though he wounds, he also bandages.
He strikes, but his hands also heal.
19 From six disasters he will rescue you;
even in the seventh, he will keep you from evil.
20 He will save you from death in time of famine,
from the power of the sword in time of war.
21 You will be safe from slander
and have no fear when destruction comes.
22 You will laugh at destruction and famine;
wild animals will not terrify you.
23 You will be at peace with the stones of the field,
and its wild animals will be at peace with you.
24 You will know that your home is safe.
When you survey your possessions, nothing
will be missing.
25 You will have many children;
your descendants will be as plentiful as grass!
26 You will go to the grave at a ripe old age,
like a sheaf of grain harvested at the proper
time!

27 "We have studied life and found all this
to be true.
Listen to my counsel, and apply it to yourself."

Job's Second Speech: A Response to Eliphaz

6 Then Job spoke again:

2 "If my misery could be weighed
and my troubles be put on the scales,
3 they would outweigh all the sands of the sea.
That is why I spoke impulsively.
4 For the Almighty has struck me down with
his arrows.
Their poison infects my spirit.
God's terrors are lined up against me.
5 Don't I have a right to complain?
Don't wild donkeys bray when they find
no grass,
and oxen bellow when they have no food?

KING JAMES VERSION

6 Can that which is unsavoury be eaten without
salt? or is there *any* taste in the white of an egg?
7 The things *that* my soul refused to touch *are* as
my sorrowful meat.
8 Oh that I might have my request; and that God
would grant *me* the thing that I long for!
9 Even that it would please God to destroy me; that
he would let loose his hand, and cut me off!
10 Then should I yet have comfort; yea, I would
harden myself in sorrow: let him not spare; for I have
not concealed the words of the Holy One.
11 What *is* my strength, that I should hope? and
what *is* mine end, that I should prolong my life?
12 *Is* my strength the strength of stones? or *is* my
flesh of brass?
13 *Is* not my help in me? and is wisdom driven quite
from me?
14 To him that is afflicted pity *should be shewed*
from his friend; but he forsaketh the fear of the
Almighty.
15 My brethren have dealt deceitfully as a brook,
and as the stream of brooks they pass away;
16 Which are blackish by reason of the ice, *and*
wherein the snow is hid:
17 What time they wax warm, they vanish: when it
is hot, they are consumed out of their place.
18 The paths of their way are turned aside; they go
to nothing, and perish.
19 The troops of Tema looked, the companies of
Sheba waited for them.
20 They were confounded because they had hoped;
they came thither, and were ashamed.
21 For now ye are nothing; ye see *my* casting down,
and are afraid.
22 Did I say, Bring unto me? or, Give a reward for me
of your substance?
23 Or, Deliver me from the enemy's hand? or, Redeem me from the hand of the mighty?
24 Teach me, and I will hold my tongue: and cause
me to understand wherein I have erred.
25 How forcible are right words! but what doth
your arguing reprove?
26 Do ye imagine to reprove words, and the
speeches of one that is desperate, *which are* as wind?
27 Yea, ye overwhelm the fatherless, and ye dig *a pit*
for your friend.
28 Now therefore be content, look upon me; for *it is*
evident unto you if I lie.
29 Return, I pray you, let it not be iniquity; yea, return again, my righteousness *is* in it.
30 Is there iniquity in my tongue? cannot my taste
discern perverse things?

NEW LIVING TRANSLATION

6 Don't people complain about unsalted food?
Does anyone want the tasteless white of
an egg?*
7 My appetite disappears when I look at it;
I gag at the thought of eating it!

8 "Oh, that I might have my request,
that God would grant my desire.
9 I wish he would crush me.
I wish he would reach out his hand and kill me.
10 At least I can take comfort in this:
Despite the pain,
I have not denied the words of the Holy One.
11 But I don't have the strength to endure.
I have nothing to live for.
12 Do I have the strength of a stone?
Is my body made of bronze?
13 No, I am utterly helpless,
without any chance of success.

14 "One should be kind to a fainting friend,
but you accuse me without any fear of the
Almighty.*
15 My brothers, you have proved as unreliable
as a seasonal brook
that overflows its banks in the spring
16 when it is swollen with ice and melting snow.
17 But when the hot weather arrives, the water
disappears.
The brook vanishes in the heat.
18 The caravans turn aside to be refreshed,
but there is nothing to drink, so they die.
19 The caravans from Tema search for this water;
the travelers from Sheba hope to find it.
20 They count on it but are disappointed.
When they arrive, their hopes are dashed.
21 You, too, have given no help.
You have seen my calamity, and you are afraid.
22 But why? Have I ever asked you for a gift?
Have I begged for anything of yours for myself?
23 Have I asked you to rescue me from my enemies,
or to save me from ruthless people?
24 Teach me, and I will keep quiet.
Show me what I have done wrong.
25 Honest words can be painful,
but what do your criticisms amount to?
26 Do you think your words are convincing
when you disregard my cry of desperation?
27 You would even send an orphan into slavery*
or sell a friend.
28 Look at me!
Would I lie to your face?
29 Stop assuming my guilt,
for I have done no wrong.
30 Do you think I am lying?
Don't I know the difference between right
and wrong?

6:6 Or *the tasteless juice of the mallow plant?* **6:14** Or *friend, / or he might lose his fear of the Almighty.* **6:27** Hebrew *even gamble over an orphan.*

KING JAMES VERSION

7

1 *Is there* not an appointed time to man upon
earth? *are not* his days also like the days of an
hireling?
2 As a servant earnestly desireth the shadow, and as
an hireling looketh for *the reward of* his work:
3 So am I made to possess months of vanity, and
wearisome nights are appointed to me.
4 When I lie down, I say, When shall I arise, and the
night be gone? and I am full of tossings to and fro
unto the dawning of the day.
5 My flesh is clothed with worms and clods of dust;
my skin is broken, and become loathsome.
6 My days are swifter than a weaver's shuttle, and
are spent without hope.
7 O remember that my life *is* wind: mine eye shall
no more see good.
8 The eye of him that hath seen me shall see me no
more: thine eyes *are* upon me, and I *am* not.
9 *As* the cloud is consumed and vanisheth away:
so he that goeth down to the grave shall come up no
more.
10 He shall return no more to his house, neither
shall his place know him any more.
11 Therefore I will not refrain my mouth; I will
speak in the anguish of my spirit; I will complain in
the bitterness of my soul.
12 *Am* I a sea, or a whale, that thou settest a watch
over me?
13 When I say, My bed shall comfort me, my couch
shall ease my complaint;
14 Then thou scarest me with dreams, and
terrifiest me through visions:
15 So that my soul chooseth strangling, *and* death
rather than my life.
16 I loathe *it;* I would not live alway: let me alone;
for my days *are* vanity.
17 What *is* man, that thou shouldest magnify him?
and that thou shouldest set thine heart upon him?
18 And *that* thou shouldest visit him every morning, *and* try him every moment?
19 How long wilt thou not depart from me, nor let
me alone till I swallow down my spittle?
20 I have sinned; what shall I do unto thee, O thou
preserver of men? why hast thou set me as a mark
against thee, so that I am a burden to myself?
21 And why dost thou not pardon my transgression, and take away mine iniquity? for now shall I
sleep in the dust; and thou shalt seek me in the
morning, but I *shall* not *be.*

8

1 Then answered Bildad the Shuhite, and said,
2 How long wilt thou speak these *things?* and
how long shall the words of thy mouth *be like* a
strong wind?

NEW LIVING TRANSLATION

7

1 "Is not all human life a struggle?
Our lives are like that of a hired hand,
2 like a worker who longs for the shade,
like a servant waiting to be paid.
3 I, too, have been assigned months of futility,
long and weary nights of misery.
4 Lying in bed, I think, 'When will it be morning?'
But the night drags on, and I toss till dawn.
5 My body is covered with maggots and scabs.
My skin breaks open, oozing with pus.

Job Cries Out to God

6 "My days fly faster than a weaver's shuttle.
They end without hope.
7 O God, remember that my life is but a breath,
and I will never again feel happiness.
8 You see me now, but not for long.
You will look for me, but I will be gone.
9 Just as a cloud dissipates and vanishes,
those who die* will not come back.
10 They are gone forever from their home—
never to be seen again.

11 "I cannot keep from speaking.
I must express my anguish.
My bitter soul must complain.
12 Am I a sea monster or a dragon
that you must place me under guard?
13 I think, 'My bed will comfort me,
and sleep will ease my misery,'
14 but then you shatter me with dreams
and terrify me with visions.
15 I would rather be strangled—
rather die than suffer like this.
16 I hate my life and don't want to go on living.
Oh, leave me alone for my few remaining days.

17 "What are people, that you should make
so much of us,
that you should think of us so often?
18 For you examine us every morning
and test us every moment.
19 Why won't you leave me alone,
at least long enough for me to swallow!
20 If I have sinned, what have I done to you,
O watcher of all humanity?
Why make me your target?
Am I a burden to you?
21 Why not just forgive my sin
and take away my guilt?
For soon I will lie down in the dust and die.
When you look for me, I will be gone."

Bildad's First Response to Job

8

1 Then Bildad the Shuhite replied to Job:

2 "How long will you go on like this?
You sound like a blustering wind.

7:9 Hebrew *who go down to Sheol.*

KING JAMES VERSION

3 Doth God pervert judgment? or doth the Almighty pervert justice?
4 If thy children have sinned against him, and he have cast them away for their transgression;
5 If thou wouldest seek unto God betimes, and make thy supplication to the Almighty;
6 If thou *wert* pure and upright; surely now he would awake for thee, and make the habitation of thy righteousness prosperous.
7 Though thy beginning was small, yet thy latter end should greatly increase.
8 For inquire, I pray thee, of the former age, and prepare thyself to the search of their fathers:
9 (For we *are but of* yesterday, and know nothing, because our days upon earth *are* a shadow:)
10 Shall not they teach thee, *and* tell thee, and utter words out of their heart?
11 Can the rush grow up without mire? can the flag grow without water?
12 Whilst it *is* yet in his greenness, *and* not cut down, it withereth before any *other* herb.
13 So *are* the paths of all that forget God; and the hypocrite's hope shall perish:
14 Whose hope shall be cut off, and whose trust *shall be* a spider's web.
15 He shall lean upon his house, but it shall not stand: he shall hold it fast, but it shall not endure.
16 He *is* green before the sun, and his branch shooteth forth in his garden.
17 His roots are wrapped about the heap, *and* seeth the place of stones.
18 If he destroy him from his place, then *it* shall deny him, *saying*, I have not seen thee.
19 Behold, this *is* the joy of his way, and out of the earth shall others grow.
20 Behold, God will not cast away a perfect *man*, neither will he help the evil doers:
21 Till he fill thy mouth with laughing, and thy lips with rejoicing.
22 They that hate thee shall be clothed with shame; and the dwelling place of the wicked shall come to nought.

9 1 Then Job answered and said,
2 I know *it is* so of a truth: but how should man be just with God?
3 If he will contend with him, he cannot answer him one of a thousand.

NEW LIVING TRANSLATION

3 Does God twist justice?
Does the Almighty twist what is right?
4 Your children must have sinned against him,
so their punishment was well deserved.
5 But if you pray to God
and seek the favor of the Almighty,
6 and if you are pure and live with integrity,
he will surely rise up and restore your happy home.
7 And though you started with little,
you will end with much.

8 "Just ask the previous generation.
Pay attention to the experience of our ancestors.
9 For we were born but yesterday and know nothing.
Our days on earth are as fleeting as a shadow.
10 But those who came before us will teach you.
They will teach you the wisdom of old.

11 "Can papyrus reeds grow tall without a marsh?
Can marsh grass flourish without water?
12 While they are still flowering, not ready to be cut,
they begin to wither more quickly than grass.
13 The same happens to all who forget God.
The hopes of the godless evaporate.
14 Their confidence hangs by a thread.
They are leaning on a spider's web.
15 They cling to their home for security, but it won't last.
They try to hold it tight, but it will not endure.
16 The godless seem like a lush plant growing in the sunshine,
its branches spreading across the garden.
17 Its roots grow down through a pile of stones;
it takes hold on a bed of rocks.
18 But when it is uprooted,
it's as though it never existed!
19 That's the end of its life,
and others spring up from the earth to replace it.

20 "But look, God will not reject a person of integrity,
nor will he lend a hand to the wicked.
21 He will once again fill your mouth with laughter
and your lips with shouts of joy.
22 Those who hate you will be clothed with shame,
and the home of the wicked will be destroyed."

Job's Third Speech: A Response to Bildad

9 Then Job spoke again:

2 "Yes, I know all this is true in principle.
But how can a person be declared innocent in God's sight?
3 If someone wanted to take God to court,*
would it be possible to answer him even once in a thousand times?

9:3 Or *If God wanted to take someone to court.*

KING JAMES VERSION

4 *He is* wise in heart, and mighty in strength: who hath hardened *himself* against him, and hath prospered?

5 Which removeth the mountains, and they know not: which overturneth them in his anger.

6 Which shaketh the earth out of her place, and the pillars thereof tremble.

7 Which commandeth the sun, and it riseth not; and sealeth up the stars.

8 Which alone spreadeth out the heavens, and treadeth upon the waves of the sea.

9 Which maketh Arcturus, Orion, and Pleiades, and the chambers of the south.

10 Which doeth great things past finding out; yea, and wonders without number.

11 Lo, he goeth by me, and I see *him* not: he passeth on also, but I perceive him not.

12 Behold, he taketh away, who can hinder him? who will say unto him, What doest thou?

13 *If* God will not withdraw his anger, the proud helpers do stoop under him.

14 How much less shall I answer him, *and* choose out my words *to reason* with him?

15 Whom, though I were righteous, *yet* would I not answer, *but* I would make supplication to my judge.

16 If I had called, and he had answered me; *yet* would I not believe that he had hearkened unto my voice.

17 For he breaketh me with a tempest, and multiplieth my wounds without cause.

18 He will not suffer me to take my breath, but filleth me with bitterness.

19 If *I speak* of strength, lo, *he is* strong: and if of judgment, who shall set me a time *to plead?*

20 If I justify myself, mine own mouth shall condemn me: *if I say,* I *am* perfect, it shall also prove me perverse.

21 *Though* I *were* perfect, *yet* would I not know my soul: I would despise my life.

22 This *is* one *thing,* therefore I said *it,* He destroyeth the perfect and the wicked.

23 If the scourge slay suddenly, he will laugh at the trial of the innocent.

24 The earth is given into the hand of the wicked: he covereth the faces of the judges thereof; if not, where, *and* who *is* he?

25 Now my days are swifter than a post: they flee away, they see no good.

NEW LIVING TRANSLATION

4 For God is so wise and so mighty.
Who has ever challenged him successfully?
5 "Without warning, he moves the mountains,
overturning them in his anger.
6 He shakes the earth from its place,
and its foundations tremble.
7 If he commands it, the sun won't rise
and the stars won't shine.
8 He alone has spread out the heavens
and marches on the waves of the sea.
9 He made all the stars—the Bear and Orion,
the Pleiades and the constellations of the southern sky.
10 He does great things too marvelous to understand.
He performs countless miracles.

11 "Yet when he comes near, I cannot see him.
When he moves by, I do not see him go.
12 If he snatches someone in death, who can stop him?
Who dares to ask, 'What are you doing?'
13 And God does not restrain his anger.
Even the monsters of the sea* are crushed beneath his feet.

14 "So who am I, that I should try to answer God
or even reason with him?
15 Even if I were right, I would have no defense.
I could only plead for mercy.
16 And even if I summoned him and he responded,
I'm not sure he would listen to me.
17 For he attacks me with a storm
and repeatedly wounds me without cause.
18 He will not let me catch my breath,
but fills me instead with bitter sorrows.
19 If it's a question of strength, he's the strong one.
If it's a matter of justice, who dares to summon him to court?
20 Though I am innocent, my own mouth would pronounce me guilty.
Though I am blameless, it* would prove me wicked.

21 "I am innocent,
but it makes no difference to me—
I despise my life.
22 Innocent or wicked, it is all the same to God.
That's why I say, 'He destroys both the blameless and the wicked.'
23 When a plague* sweeps through,
he laughs at the death of the innocent.
24 The whole earth is in the hands of the wicked,
and God blinds the eyes of the judges.
If he's not the one who does it, who is?

25 "My life passes more swiftly than a runner.
It flees away without a glimpse of happiness.

9:13 Hebrew *the helpers of Rahab,* the name of a mythical sea monster that represents chaos in ancient literature. **9:20** Or *he.* **9:23** Or *disaster.*

KING JAMES VERSION

26 They are passed away as the swift ships: as the eagle *that* hasteth to the prey.

27 If I say, I will forget my complaint, I will leave off my heaviness, and comfort *myself*:

28 I am afraid of all my sorrows, I know that thou wilt not hold me innocent.

29 *If* I be wicked, why then labour I in vain?

30 If I wash myself with snow water, and make my hands never so clean;

31 Yet shalt thou plunge me in the ditch, and mine own clothes shall abhor me.

32 For *he is* not a man, as I *am, that* I should answer him, *and* we should come together in judgment.

33 Neither is there any daysman betwixt us, *that* might lay his hand upon us both.

34 Let him take his rod away from me, and let not his fear terrify me:

35 *Then* would I speak, and not fear him; but *it is* not so with me.

10 1 My soul is weary of my life; I will leave my complaint upon myself; I will speak in the bitterness of my soul.

2 I will say unto God, Do not condemn me; shew me wherefore thou contendest with me.

3 *Is it* good unto thee that thou shouldest oppress, that thou shouldest despise the work of thine hands, and shine upon the counsel of the wicked?

4 Hast thou eyes of flesh? or seest thou as man seeth?

5 *Are* thy days as the days of man? *are* thy years as man's days,

6 That thou inquirest after mine iniquity, and searchest after my sin?

7 Thou knowest that I am not wicked; and *there is* none that can deliver out of thine hand.

8 Thine hands have made me and fashioned me together round about; yet thou dost destroy me.

9 Remember, I beseech thee, that thou hast made me as the clay; and wilt thou bring me into dust again?

10 Hast thou not poured me out as milk, and curdled me like cheese?

11 Thou hast clothed me with skin and flesh, and hast fenced me with bones and sinews.

12 Thou hast granted me life and favour, and thy visitation hath preserved my spirit.

13 And these *things* hast thou hid in thine heart: I know that this *is* with thee.

NEW LIVING TRANSLATION

26 It disappears like a swift papyrus boat,
like an eagle swooping down on its prey.
27 If I decided to forget my complaints,
to put away my sad face and be cheerful,
28 I would still dread all the pain,
for I know you will not find me innocent,
O God.
29 Whatever happens, I will be found guilty.
So what's the use of trying?
30 Even if I were to wash myself with soap
and clean my hands with lye,
31 you would plunge me into a muddy ditch,
and my own filthy clothing would hate me.

32 "God is not a mortal like me,
so I cannot argue with him or take him to trial.
33 If only there were a mediator between us,
someone who could bring us together.
34 The mediator could make God stop beating me,
and I would no longer live in terror of his
punishment.
35 Then I could speak to him without fear,
but I cannot do that in my own strength.

Job Frames His Plea to God

10 1 "I am disgusted with my life.
Let me complain freely.
My bitter soul must complain.
2 I will say to God, 'Don't simply condemn me—
tell me the charge you are bringing against me.
3 What do you gain by oppressing me?
Why do you reject me, the work of your own
hands,
while smiling on the schemes of the wicked?
4 Are your eyes like those of a human?
Do you see things only as people see them?
5 Is your lifetime only as long as ours?
Is your life so short
6 that you must quickly probe for my guilt
and search for my sin?
7 Although you know I am not guilty,
no one can rescue me from your hands.

8 "'You formed me with your hands; you made me,
yet now you completely destroy me.
9 Remember that you made me from dust—
will you turn me back to dust so soon?
10 You guided my conception
and formed me in the womb.*
11 You clothed me with skin and flesh,
and you knit my bones and sinews together.
12 You gave me life and showed me your unfailing
love.
My life was preserved by your care.

13 "'Yet your real motive—
your true intent—

10:10 Hebrew *You poured me out like milk / and curdled me like cheese.*

14 If I sin, then thou markest me, and thou wilt not acquit me from mine iniquity.

15 If I be wicked, woe unto me; and *if* I be righteous, *yet* will I not lift up my head. *I am* full of confusion; therefore see thou mine affliction;

16 For it increaseth. Thou huntest me as a fierce lion: and again thou shewest thyself marvellous upon me.

17 Thou renewest thy witnesses against me, and increasest thine indignation upon me; changes and war *are* against me.

18 Wherefore then hast thou brought me forth out of the womb? Oh that I had given up the ghost, and no eye had seen me!

19 I should have been as though I had not been; I should have been carried from the womb to the grave.

20 *Are* not my days few? cease *then, and* let me alone, that I may take comfort a little,

21 Before I go *whence* I shall not return, *even* to the land of darkness and the shadow of death;

22 A land of darkness, as darkness *itself; and* of the shadow of death, without any order, and *where* the light *is* as darkness.

11 1 Then answered Zophar the Naamathite, and said,

2 Should not the multitude of words be answered? and should a man full of talk be justified?

3 Should thy lies make men hold their peace? and when thou mockest, shall no man make thee ashamed?

4 For thou hast said, My doctrine *is* pure, and I am clean in thine eyes.

5 But oh that God would speak, and open his lips against thee;

6 And that he would shew thee the secrets of wisdom, that *they are* double to that which is! Know therefore that God exacteth of thee *less* than thine iniquity *deserveth.*

7 Canst thou by searching find out God? canst thou find out the Almighty unto perfection?

8 *It is* as high as heaven; what canst thou do? deeper than hell; what canst thou know?

9 The measure thereof *is* longer than the earth, and broader than the sea.

10 If he cut off, and shut up, or gather together, then who can hinder him?

11 For he knoweth vain men: he seeth wickedness also; will he not then consider *it?*

14 was to watch me, and if I sinned,
you would not forgive my guilt.
15 If I am guilty, too bad for me;
and even if I'm innocent, I can't hold my head high,
because I am filled with shame and misery.
16 And if I hold my head high, you hunt me like a lion
and display your awesome power against me.
17 Again and again you witness against me.
You pour out your growing anger on me
and bring fresh armies against me.

18 "'Why, then, did you deliver me from my mother's womb?
Why didn't you let me die at birth?
19 It would be as though I had never existed,
going directly from the womb to the grave.
20 I have only a few days left, so leave me alone,
that I may have a moment of comfort
21 before I leave—never to return—
for the land of darkness and utter gloom.
22 It is a land as dark as midnight,
a land of gloom and confusion,
where even the light is dark as midnight.'"

Zophar's First Response to Job

11 Then Zophar the Naamathite replied to Job:

2 "Shouldn't someone answer this torrent of words?
Is a person proved innocent just by a lot of talking?
3 Should I remain silent while you babble on?
When you mock God, shouldn't someone make you ashamed?
4 You claim, 'My beliefs are pure,'
and 'I am clean in the sight of God.'
5 If only God would speak;
if only he would tell you what he thinks!
6 If only he would tell you the secrets of wisdom,
for true wisdom is not a simple matter.
Listen! God is doubtless punishing you
far less than you deserve!
7 "Can you solve the mysteries of God?
Can you discover everything about the Almighty?
8 Such knowledge is higher than the heavens—
and who are you?
It is deeper than the underworld*—
what do you know?
9 It is broader than the earth
and wider than the sea.
10 If God comes and puts a person in prison
or calls the court to order, who can stop him?
11 For he knows those who are false,
and he takes note of all their sins.

11:8 Hebrew *than Sheol.*

KING JAMES VERSION

12 For vain man would be wise, though man be born *like* a wild ass's colt.

13 If thou prepare thine heart, and stretch out thine hands toward him;

14 If iniquity *be* in thine hand, put it far away, and let not wickedness dwell in thy tabernacles.

15 For then shalt thou lift up thy face without spot; yea, thou shalt be stedfast, and shalt not fear:

16 Because thou shalt forget *thy* misery, *and* remember *it* as waters *that* pass away:

17 And *thine* age shall be clearer than the noonday; thou shalt shine forth, thou shalt be as the morning.

18 And thou shalt be secure, because there is hope; yea, thou shalt dig *about thee, and* thou shalt take thy rest in safety.

19 Also thou shalt lie down, and none shall make *thee* afraid; yea, many shall make suit unto thee.

20 But the eyes of the wicked shall fail, and they shall not escape, and their hope *shall be as* the giving up of the ghost.

12 1 And Job answered and said,

2 No doubt but ye *are* the people, and wisdom shall die with you.

3 But I have understanding as well as you; I *am* not inferior to you: yea, who knoweth not such things as these?

4 I am *as* one mocked of his neighbour, who calleth upon God, and he answereth him: the just upright *man is* laughed to scorn.

5 He that is ready to slip with *his* feet *is as* a lamp despised in the thought of him that is at ease.

6 The tabernacles of robbers prosper, and they that provoke God are secure; into whose hand God bringeth *abundantly*.

7 But ask now the beasts, and they shall teach thee; and the fowls of the air, and they shall tell thee:

8 Or speak to the earth, and it shall teach thee: and the fishes of the sea shall declare unto thee.

9 Who knoweth not in all these that the hand of the LORD hath wrought this?

10 In whose hand *is* the soul of every living thing, and the breath of all mankind.

11 Doth not the ear try words? and the mouth taste his meat?

12 With the ancient *is* wisdom; and in length of days understanding.

13 With him *is* wisdom and strength, he hath counsel and understanding.

NEW LIVING TRANSLATION

12 An empty-headed person won't become wise
any more than a wild donkey can bear a
human child.*

13 "If only you would prepare your heart
and lift up your hands to him in prayer!

14 Get rid of your sins,
and leave all iniquity behind you.

15 Then your face will brighten with innocence.
You will be strong and free of fear.

16 You will forget your misery;
it will be like water flowing away.

17 Your life will be brighter than the noonday.
Even darkness will be as bright as morning.

18 Having hope will give you courage.
You will be protected and will rest in safety.

19 You will lie down unafraid,
and many will look to you for help.

20 But the wicked will be blinded.
They will have no escape.
Their only hope is death."

Job's Fourth Speech: A Response to Zophar

12 Then Job spoke again:

2 "You people really know everything,
don't you?
And when you die, wisdom will die with you!

3 Well, I know a few things myself—
and you're no better than I am.
Who doesn't know these things you've
been saying?

4 Yet my friends laugh at me,
for I call on God and expect an answer.
I am a just and blameless man,
yet they laugh at me.

5 People who are at ease mock those in trouble.
They give a push to people who are stumbling.

6 But robbers are left in peace,
and those who provoke God live in safety—
though God keeps them in his power.

7 "Just ask the animals, and they will teach you.
Ask the birds of the sky, and they will tell you.

8 Speak to the earth, and it will instruct you.
Let the fish in the sea speak to you.

9 For they all know
that my disaster* has come from the hand
of the LORD.

10 For the life of every living thing is in his hand,
and the breath of every human being.

11 The ear tests the words it hears
just as the mouth distinguishes between foods.

12 Wisdom belongs to the aged,
and understanding to the old.

13 "But true wisdom and power are found in God;
counsel and understanding are his.

11:12 *Or than a wild male donkey can bear a tame colt.* **12:9** Hebrew *that this.*

KING JAMES VERSION

14 Behold, he breaketh down, and it cannot be built again: he shutteth up a man, and there can be no opening.

15 Behold, he withholdeth the waters, and they dry up: also he sendeth them out, and they overturn the earth.

16 With him *is* strength and wisdom: the deceived and the deceiver *are* his.

17 He leadeth counsellors away spoiled, and maketh the judges fools.

18 He looseth the bond of kings, and girdeth their loins with a girdle.

19 He leadeth princes away spoiled, and overthroweth the mighty.

20 He removeth away the speech of the trusty, and taketh away the understanding of the aged.

21 He poureth contempt upon princes, and weakeneth the strength of the mighty.

22 He discovereth deep things out of darkness, and bringeth out to light the shadow of death.

23 He increaseth the nations, and destroyeth them: he enlargeth the nations, and straiteneth them *again*.

24 He taketh away the heart of the chief of the people of the earth, and causeth them to wander in a wilderness *where there is* no way.

25 They grope in the dark without light, and he maketh them to stagger like *a* drunken *man*.

13 1 Lo, mine eye hath seen all *this*, mine ear hath heard and understood it.

2 What ye know, *the same* do I know also: I *am* not inferior unto you.

3 Surely I would speak to the Almighty, and I desire to reason with God.

4 But ye *are* forgers of lies, ye *are* all physicians of no value.

5 O that ye would altogether hold your peace! and it should be your wisdom.

6 Hear now my reasoning, and hearken to the pleadings of my lips.

7 Will ye speak wickedly for God? and talk deceitfully for him?

8 Will ye accept his person? will ye contend for God?

9 Is it good that he should search you out? or as one man mocketh another, do ye *so* mock him?

10 He will surely reprove you, if ye do secretly accept persons.

11 Shall not his excellency make you afraid? and his dread fall upon you?

NEW LIVING TRANSLATION

14 What he destroys cannot be rebuilt.
When he puts someone in prison, there is no escape.
15 If he holds back the rain, the earth becomes a desert.
If he releases the waters, they flood the earth.
16 Yes, strength and wisdom are his;
deceivers and deceived are both in his power.
17 He leads counselors away, stripped of good judgment;
wise judges become fools.
18 He removes the royal robe of kings.
They are led away with ropes around their waist.
19 He leads priests away, stripped of status;
he overthrows those with long years in power.
20 He silences the trusted adviser
and removes the insight of the elders.
21 He pours disgrace upon princes
and disarms the strong.

22 "He uncovers mysteries hidden in darkness;
he brings light to the deepest gloom.
23 He builds up nations, and he destroys them.
He expands nations, and he abandons them.
24 He strips kings of understanding
and leaves them wandering in a pathless wasteland.
25 They grope in the darkness without a light.
He makes them stagger like drunkards.

Job Wants to Argue His Case with God

13 1 "Look, I have seen all this with my own eyes
and heard it with my own ears, and now I understand.
2 I know as much as you do.
You are no better than I am.
3 As for me, I would speak directly to the Almighty.
I want to argue my case with God himself.
4 As for you, you smear me with lies.
As physicians, you are worthless quacks.
5 If only you could be silent!
That's the wisest thing you could do.
6 Listen to my charge;
pay attention to my arguments.
7 "Are you defending God with lies?
Do you make your dishonest arguments for his sake?
8 Will you slant your testimony in his favor?
Will you argue God's case for him?
9 What will happen when he finds out what you are doing?
Can you fool him as easily as you fool people?
10 No, you will be in trouble with him
if you secretly slant your testimony in his favor.
11 Doesn't his majesty terrify you?
Doesn't your fear of him overwhelm you?

KING JAMES VERSION

12 Your remembrances *are* like unto ashes, your bodies to bodies of clay.

13 Hold your peace, let me alone, that I may speak, and let come on me what *will*.

14 Wherefore do I take my flesh in my teeth, and put my life in mine hand?

15 Though he slay me, yet will I trust in him: but I will maintain mine own ways before him.

16 He also *shall be* my salvation: for an hypocrite shall not come before him.

17 Hear diligently my speech, and my declaration with your ears.

18 Behold now, I have ordered *my* cause; I know that I shall be justified.

19 Who *is* he *that* will plead with me? for now, if I hold my tongue, I shall give up the ghost.

20 Only do not two *things* unto me: then will I not hide myself from thee.

21 Withdraw thine hand far from me: and let not thy dread make me afraid.

22 Then call thou, and I will answer: or let me speak, and answer thou me.

23 How many *are* mine iniquities and sins? make me to know my transgression and my sin.

24 Wherefore hidest thou thy face, and holdest me for thine enemy?

25 Wilt thou break a leaf driven to and fro? and wilt thou pursue the dry stubble?

26 For thou writest bitter things against me, and makest me to possess the iniquities of my youth.

27 Thou puttest my feet also in the stocks, and lookest narrowly unto all my paths; thou settest a print upon the heels of my feet.

28 And he, as a rotten thing, consumeth, as a garment that is moth eaten.

14 1 Man *that is* born of a woman *is* of few days, and full of trouble.

2 He cometh forth like a flower, and is cut down: he fleeth also as a shadow, and continueth not.

3 And dost thou open thine eyes upon such an one, and bringest me into judgment with thee?

4 Who can bring a clean *thing* out of an unclean? not one.

5 Seeing his days *are* determined, the number of his months *are* with thee, thou hast appointed his bounds that he cannot pass;

6 Turn from him, that he may rest, till he shall accomplish, as an hireling, his day.

NEW LIVING TRANSLATION

12 Your platitudes are as valuable as ashes.
Your defense is as fragile as a clay pot.

13 "Be silent now and leave me alone.
Let me speak, and I will face the consequences.
14 Yes, I will take my life in my hands
and say what I really think.
15 God might kill me, but I have no other hope.*
I am going to argue my case with him.
16 But this is what will save me—I am not godless.
If I were, I could not stand before him.

17 "Listen closely to what I am about to say.
Hear me out.
18 I have prepared my case;
I will be proved innocent.
19 Who can argue with me over this?
And if you prove me wrong, I will remain silent and die.

Job Asks How He Has Sinned

20 "O God, grant me these two things,
and then I will be able to face you.
21 Remove your heavy hand from me,
and don't terrify me with your awesome presence.
22 Now summon me, and I will answer!
Or let me speak to you, and you reply.
23 Tell me, what have I done wrong?
Show me my rebellion and my sin.
24 Why do you turn away from me?
Why do you treat me as your enemy?
25 Would you terrify a leaf blown by the wind?
Would you chase dry straw?

26 "You write bitter accusations against me
and bring up all the sins of my youth.
27 You put my feet in stocks.
You examine all my paths.
You trace all my footprints.
28 I waste away like rotting wood,
like a moth-eaten coat.

14 1 "How frail is humanity!
How short is life, how full of trouble!
2 We blossom like a flower and then wither.
Like a passing shadow, we quickly disappear.
3 Must you keep an eye on such a frail creature
and demand an accounting from me?
4 Who can bring purity out of an impure person?
No one!
5 You have decided the length of our lives.
You know how many months we will live,
and we are not given a minute longer.
6 So leave us alone and let us rest!
We are like hired hands, so let us finish our work in peace.

13:15 An alternate reading in the Masoretic Text reads ***God might kill me, but I hope in him.***

7 For there is hope of a tree, if it be cut down, that it
will sprout again, and that the tender branch thereof
will not cease.
8 Though the root thereof wax old in the earth, and
the stock thereof die in the ground;
9 *Yet* through the scent of water it will bud, and
bring forth boughs like a plant.
10 But man dieth, and wasteth away: yea, man giveth up the ghost, and where *is* he?
11 *As* the waters fail from the sea, and the flood
decayeth and drieth up:
12 So man lieth down, and riseth not: till the heavens *be* no more, they shall not awake, nor be raised
out of their sleep.
13 O that thou wouldest hide me in the grave, that
thou wouldest keep me secret, until thy wrath be
past, that thou wouldest appoint me a set time, and
remember me!
14 If a man die, shall he live *again?* all the days of
my appointed time will I wait, till my change come.
15 Thou shalt call, and I will answer thee: thou wilt
have a desire to the work of thine hands.
16 For now thou numberest my steps: dost thou not
watch over my sin?
17 My transgression *is* sealed up in a bag, and thou
sewest up mine iniquity.
18 And surely the mountain falling cometh to
nought, and the rock is removed out of his place.
19 The waters wear the stones: thou washest away
the things which grow *out* of the dust of the earth;
and thou destroyest the hope of man.
20 Thou prevailest for ever against him, and he
passeth: thou changest his countenance, and
sendest him away.
21 His sons come to honour, and he knoweth *it* not;
and they are brought low, but he perceiveth *it* not of
them.
22 But his flesh upon him shall have pain, and his
soul within him shall mourn.

15 1 Then answered Eliphaz the Temanite, and
said,
2 Should a wise man utter vain knowledge, and fill
his belly with the east wind?
3 Should he reason with unprofitable talk? or with
speeches wherewith he can do no good?
4 Yea, thou castest off fear, and restrainest prayer
before God.
5 For thy mouth uttereth thine iniquity, and thou
choosest the tongue of the crafty.

7 "Even a tree has more hope!
If it is cut down, it will sprout again
and grow new branches.
8 Though its roots have grown old in the earth
and its stump decays,
9 at the scent of water it will bud
and sprout again like a new seedling.

10 "But when people die, their strength is gone.
They breathe their last, and then where are they?
11 As water evaporates from a lake
and a river disappears in drought,
12 people are laid to rest and do not rise again.
Until the heavens are no more, they will not
wake up
nor be roused from their sleep.

13 "I wish you would hide me in the grave*
and forget me there until your anger
has passed.
But mark your calendar to think of me again!
14 Can the dead live again?
If so, this would give me hope through all my
years of struggle,
and I would eagerly await the release of death.
15 You would call and I would answer,
and you would yearn for me, your handiwork.
16 For then you would guard my steps,
instead of watching for my sins.
17 My sins would be sealed in a pouch,
and you would cover my guilt.

18 "But instead, as mountains fall and crumble
and as rocks fall from a cliff,
19 as water wears away the stones
and floods wash away the soil,
so you destroy people's hope.
20 You always overpower them, and they
pass from the scene.
You disfigure them in death and send
them away.
21 They never know if their children grow up
in honor
or sink to insignificance.
22 They suffer painfully;
their life is full of trouble."

Eliphaz's Second Response to Job

15 Then Eliphaz the Temanite replied:
2 "A wise man wouldn't answer with such
empty talk!
You are nothing but a windbag.
3 The wise don't engage in empty chatter.
What good are such words?
4 Have you no fear of God,
no reverence for him?
5 Your sins are telling your mouth what to say.
Your words are based on clever deception.

14:13 Hebrew *in Sheol.*

KING JAMES VERSION

6 Thine own mouth condemneth thee, and not I: yea, thine own lips testify against thee.

7 *Art* thou the first man *that* was born? or wast thou made before the hills?

8 Hast thou heard the secret of God? and dost thou restrain wisdom to thyself?

9 What knowest thou, that we know not? *what* understandest thou, which *is* not in us?

10 With us *are* both the grayheaded and very aged men, much elder than thy father.

11 *Are* the consolations of God small with thee? is there any secret thing with thee?

12 Why doth thine heart carry thee away? and what do thy eyes wink at,

13 That thou turnest thy spirit against God, and lettest *such* words go out of thy mouth?

14 What *is* man, that he should be clean? and *he which is* born of a woman, that he should be righteous?

15 Behold, he putteth no trust in his saints; yea, the heavens are not clean in his sight.

16 How much more abominable and filthy *is* man, which drinketh iniquity like water?

17 I will shew thee, hear me; and that *which* I have seen I will declare;

18 Which wise men have told from their fathers, and have not hid *it:*

19 Unto whom alone the earth was given, and no stranger passed among them.

20 The wicked man travaileth with pain all *his* days, and the number of years is hidden to the oppressor.

21 A dreadful sound *is* in his ears: in prosperity the destroyer shall come upon him.

22 He believeth not that he shall return out of darkness, and he is waited for of the sword.

23 He wandereth abroad for bread, *saying,* Where *is it?* he knoweth that the day of darkness is ready at his hand.

24 Trouble and anguish shall make him afraid; they shall prevail against him, as a king ready to the battle.

25 For he stretcheth out his hand against God, and strengtheneth himself against the Almighty.

26 He runneth upon him, *even* on *his* neck, upon the thick bosses of his bucklers:

27 Because he covereth his face with his fatness, and maketh collops of fat on *his* flanks.

28 And he dwelleth in desolate cities, *and* in houses which no man inhabiteth, which are ready to become heaps.

NEW LIVING TRANSLATION

6 Your own mouth condemns you, not I.
Your own lips testify against you.

7 "Were you the first person ever born?
Were you born before the hills were made?
8 Were you listening at God's secret council?
Do you have a monopoly on wisdom?
9 What do you know that we don't?
What do you understand that we do not?
10 On our side are aged, gray-haired men
much older than your father!

11 "Is God's comfort too little for you?
Is his gentle word not enough?
12 What has taken away your reason?
What has weakened your vision,*
13 that you turn against God
and say all these evil things?
14 Can any mortal be pure?
Can anyone born of a woman be just?
15 Look, God does not even trust the angels.*
Even the heavens are not absolutely pure
in his sight.
16 How much less pure is a corrupt and sinful
person
with a thirst for wickedness!

17 "If you will listen, I will show you.
I will answer you from my own experience.
18 And it is confirmed by the reports of wise men
who have heard the same thing from their
fathers—
19 from those to whom the land was given
long before any foreigners arrived.
20 "The wicked writhe in pain throughout their lives.
Years of trouble are stored up for the ruthless.
21 The sound of terror rings in their ears,
and even on good days they fear the attack
of the destroyer.
22 They dare not go out into the darkness
for fear they will be murdered.
23 They wander around, saying, 'Where can
I find bread?'*
They know their day of destruction is near.
24 That dark day terrifies them.
They live in distress and anguish,
like a king preparing for battle.
25 For they shake their fists at God,
defying the Almighty.
26 Holding their strong shields,
they defiantly charge against him.

27 "These wicked people are heavy and prosperous;
their waists bulge with fat.
28 But their cities will be ruined.
They will live in abandoned houses
that are ready to tumble down.

15:12 Or *Why do your eyes flash with anger;* Hebrew reads ***Why do your eyes blink.*** **15:15** Hebrew *the holy ones.* **15:23** Greek version reads ***He is appointed to be food for a vulture.***

KING JAMES VERSION

29 He shall not be rich, neither shall his substance
continue, neither shall he prolong the perfection
thereof upon the earth.
30 He shall not depart out of darkness; the flame
shall dry up his branches, and by the breath of his
mouth shall he go away.
31 Let not him that is deceived trust in vanity: for
vanity shall be his recompense.
32 It shall be accomplished before his time, and his
branch shall not be green.
33 He shall shake off his unripe grape as the vine,
and shall cast off his flower as the olive.
34 For the congregation of hypocrites *shall be*
desolate, and fire shall consume the tabernacles of
bribery.
35 They conceive mischief, and bring forth vanity,
and their belly prepareth deceit.

16 1 Then Job answered and said,
2 I have heard many such things: miserable
comforters *are* ye all.
3 Shall vain words have an end? or what embold-
eneth thee that thou answerest?
4 I also could speak as ye *do:* if your soul were in
my soul's stead, I could heap up words against you,
and shake mine head at you.
5 *But* I would strengthen you with my mouth, and
the moving of my lips should asswage *your grief.*
6 Though I speak, my grief is not asswaged: and
though I forbear, what am I eased?
7 But now he hath made me weary: thou hast made
desolate all my company.
8 And thou hast filled me with wrinkles, *which* is a
witness *against me:* and my leanness rising up in me
beareth witness to my face.
9 He teareth *me* in his wrath, who hateth me: he
gnasheth upon me with his teeth; mine enemy
sharpeneth his eyes upon me.
10 They have gaped upon me with their mouth;
they have smitten me upon the cheek reproachfully;
they have gathered themselves together against me.
11 God hath delivered me to the ungodly, and
turned me over into the hands of the wicked.
12 I was at ease, but he hath broken me asunder: he
hath also taken *me* by my neck, and shaken me to
pieces, and set me up for his mark.

NEW LIVING TRANSLATION

29 Their riches will not last,
and their wealth will not endure.
Their possessions will no longer spread
across the horizon.

30 "They will not escape the darkness.
The burning sun will wither their shoots,
and the breath of God will destroy them.
31 Let them no longer fool themselves by trusting
in empty riches,
for emptiness will be their only reward.
32 Like trees, they will be cut down in the prime
of life;
their branches will never again be green.
33 They will be like a vine whose grapes are
harvested too early,
like an olive tree that loses its blossoms
before the fruit can form.
34 For the godless are barren.
Their homes, enriched through bribery,
will burn.
35 They conceive trouble and give birth to evil.
Their womb produces deceit."

Job's Fifth Speech: A Response to Eliphaz

16 Then Job spoke again:
2 "I have heard all this before.
What miserable comforters you are!
3 Won't you ever stop blowing hot air?
What makes you keep on talking?
4 I could say the same things if you were
in my place.
I could spout off criticism and shake
my head at you.
5 But if it were me, I would encourage you.
I would try to take away your grief.
6 Instead, I suffer if I defend myself,
and I suffer no less if I refuse to speak.

7 "O God, you have ground me down
and devastated my family.
8 As if to prove I have sinned, you've reduced
me to skin and bones.
My gaunt flesh testifies against me.
9 God hates me and angrily tears me apart.
He snaps his teeth at me
and pierces me with his eyes.
10 People jeer and laugh at me.
They slap my cheek in contempt.
A mob gathers against me.
11 God has handed me over to sinners.
He has tossed me into the hands of
the wicked.

12 "I was living quietly until he shattered me.
He took me by the neck and broke me
in pieces.
Then he set me up as his target,

KING JAMES VERSION

13 His archers compass me round about, he cleaveth my reins asunder, and doth not spare; he poureth
out my gall upon the ground.
14 He breaketh me with breach upon breach, he
runneth upon me like a giant.
15 I have sewed sackcloth upon my skin, and defiled my horn in the dust.
16 My face is foul with weeping, and on my eyelids
is the shadow of death;
17 Not for *any* injustice in mine hands: also my
prayer *is* pure.
18 O earth, cover not thou my blood, and let my cry
have no place.
19 Also now, behold, my witness *is* in heaven, and
my record *is* on high.
20 My friends scorn me: *but* mine eye poureth out
tears unto God.
21 O that one might plead for a man with God, as
a man *pleadeth* for his neighbour!
22 When a few years are come, then I shall go the
way *whence* I shall not return.

17 1 My breath is corrupt, my days are extinct, the
graves *are ready* for me.
2 *Are there* not mockers with me? and doth not
mine eye continue in their provocation?
3 Lay down now, put me in a surety with thee; who
is he *that* will strike hands with me?
4 For thou hast hid their heart from understanding: therefore shalt thou not exalt *them*.
5 He that speaketh flattery to *his* friends, even the
eyes of his children shall fail.
6 He hath made me also a byword of the people;
and aforetime I was as a tabret.
7 Mine eye also is dim by reason of sorrow, and all
my members *are* as a shadow.
8 Upright *men* shall be astonied at this, and the innocent shall stir up himself against the hypocrite.
9 The righteous also shall hold on his way, and he
that hath clean hands shall be stronger and stronger.
10 But as for you all, do ye return, and come now:
for I cannot find *one* wise *man* among you.
11 My days are past, my purposes are broken off,
even the thoughts of my heart.
12 They change the night into day: the light *is* short
because of darkness.

NEW LIVING TRANSLATION

13 and now his archers surround me.
His arrows pierce me without mercy.
The ground is wet with my blood.*
14 Again and again he smashes against me,
charging at me like a warrior.
15 I wear burlap to show my grief.
My pride lies in the dust.
16 My eyes are red with weeping;
dark shadows circle my eyes.
17 Yet I have done no wrong,
and my prayer is pure.

18 "O earth, do not conceal my blood.
Let it cry out on my behalf.
19 Even now my witness is in heaven.
My advocate is there on high.
20 My friends scorn me,
but I pour out my tears to God.
21 I need someone to mediate between God and me,
as a person mediates between friends.
22 For soon I must go down that road
from which I will never return.

Job Continues to Defend His Innocence

17 1 "My spirit is crushed,
and my life is nearly snuffed out.
The grave is ready to receive me.
2 I am surrounded by mockers.
I watch how bitterly they taunt me.

3 "You must defend my innocence, O God,
since no one else will stand up for me.
4 You have closed their minds to understanding,
but do not let them triumph.
5 They betray their friends for their own
advantage,
so let their children faint with hunger.

6 "God has made a mockery of me among
the people;
they spit in my face.
7 My eyes are swollen with weeping,
and I am but a shadow of my former self.
8 The virtuous are horrified when they see me.
The innocent rise up against the ungodly.
9 The righteous keep moving forward,
and those with clean hands become stronger
and stronger.

10 "As for all of you, come back with a better
argument,
though I still won't find a wise man
among you.
11 My days are over.
My hopes have disappeared.
My heart's desires are broken.
12 These men say that night is day;
they claim that the darkness is light.

16:13 Hebrew *my gall.*

KING JAMES VERSION

13 If I wait, the grave *is* mine house: I have made my
bed in the darkness.
14 I have said to corruption, Thou *art* my father: to
the worm, *Thou art* my mother, and my sister.
15 And where *is* now my hope? as for my hope, who
shall see it?
16 They shall go down to the bars of the pit, when
our rest together *is* in the dust.

18 1 Then answered Bildad the Shuhite, and said,
2 How long *will it be ere* ye make an end of
words? mark, and afterwards we will speak.
3 Wherefore are we counted as beasts, *and* reputed vile in your sight?
4 He teareth himself in his anger: shall the earth
be forsaken for thee? and shall the rock be removed
out of his place?
5 Yea, the light of the wicked shall be put out, and
the spark of his fire shall not shine.
6 The light shall be dark in his tabernacle, and his
candle shall be put out with him.
7 The steps of his strength shall be straitened, and
his own counsel shall cast him down.
8 For he is cast into a net by his own feet, and he
walketh upon a snare.
9 The gin shall take *him* by the heel, *and* the robber shall prevail against him.
10 The snare *is* laid for him in the ground, and a
trap for him in the way.
11 Terrors shall make him afraid on every side, and
shall drive him to his feet.
12 His strength shall be hungerbitten, and destruction *shall be* ready at his side.
13 It shall devour the strength of his skin: *even* the
firstborn of death shall devour his strength.
14 His confidence shall be rooted out of his tabernacle, and it shall bring him to the king of terrors.
15 It shall dwell in his tabernacle, because *it is*
none of his: brimstone shall be scattered upon his
habitation.
16 His roots shall be dried up beneath, and above
shall his branch be cut off.
17 His remembrance shall perish from the earth,
and he shall have no name in the street.
18 He shall be driven from light into darkness, and
chased out of the world.
19 He shall neither have son nor nephew among his
people, nor any remaining in his dwellings.
20 They that come after *him* shall be astonied at his
day, as they that went before were affrighted.

NEW LIVING TRANSLATION

13 What if I go to the grave*
and make my bed in darkness?
14 What if I call the grave my father,
and the maggot my mother or my sister?
15 Where then is my hope?
Can anyone find it?
16 No, my hope will go down with me to the grave.
We will rest together in the dust!"

Bildad's Second Response to Job

18 Then Bildad the Shuhite replied:

2 "How long before you stop talking?
Speak sense if you want us to answer!
3 Do you think we are mere animals?
Do you think we are stupid?
4 You may tear out your hair in anger,
but will that destroy the earth?
Will it make the rocks tremble?

5 "Surely the light of the wicked will be
snuffed out.
The sparks of their fire will not glow.
6 The light in their tent will grow dark.
The lamp hanging above them will
be quenched.
7 The confident stride of the wicked will
be shortened.
Their own schemes will be their downfall.
8 The wicked walk into a net.
They fall into a pit.
9 A trap grabs them by the heel.
A snare holds them tight.
10 A noose lies hidden on the ground.
A rope is stretched across their path.

11 "Terrors surround the wicked
and trouble them at every step.
12 Hunger depletes their strength,
and calamity waits for them to stumble.
13 Disease eats their skin;
death devours their limbs.
14 They are torn from the security of their homes
and are brought down to the king of terrors.
15 The homes of the wicked will burn down;
burning sulfur rains on their houses.
16 Their roots will dry up,
and their branches will wither.
17 All memory of their existence will fade from
the earth;
no one will remember their names.
18 They will be thrust from light into darkness,
driven from the world.
19 They will have neither children nor
grandchildren,
nor any survivor in the place where they lived.
20 People in the west are appalled at their fate;
people in the east are horrified.

17:13 Hebrew *to Sheol;* also in 17:16.

KING JAMES VERSION

21 Surely such *are* the dwellings of the wicked, and this *is* the place *of him that* knoweth not God.

19 1 Then Job answered and said,

2 How long will ye vex my soul, and break me in pieces with words?

3 These ten times have ye reproached me: ye are not ashamed *that* ye make yourselves strange to me.

4 And be it indeed *that* I have erred, mine error remaineth with myself.

5 If indeed ye will magnify *yourselves* against me, and plead against me my reproach:

6 Know now that God hath overthrown me, and hath compassed me with his net.

7 Behold, I cry out of wrong, but I am not heard: I cry aloud, but *there is* no judgment.

8 He hath fenced up my way that I cannot pass, and he hath set darkness in my paths.

9 He hath stripped me of my glory, and taken the crown *from* my head.

10 He hath destroyed me on every side, and I am gone: and mine hope hath he removed like a tree.

11 He hath also kindled his wrath against me, and he counteth me unto him as *one of* his enemies.

12 His troops come together, and raise up their way against me, and encamp round about my tabernacle.

13 He hath put my brethren far from me, and mine acquaintance are verily estranged from me.

14 My kinsfolk have failed, and my familiar friends have forgotten me.

15 They that dwell in mine house, and my maids, count me for a stranger: I am an alien in their sight.

16 I called my servant, and he gave *me* no answer; I intreated him with my mouth.

17 My breath is strange to my wife, though I intreated for the children's *sake* of mine own body.

18 Yea, young children despised me; I arose, and they spake against me.

19 All my inward friends abhorred me: and they whom I loved are turned against me.

20 My bone cleaveth to my skin and to my flesh, and I am escaped with the skin of my teeth.

21 Have pity upon me, have pity upon me, O ye my friends; for the hand of God hath touched me.

22 Why do ye persecute me as God, and are not satisfied with my flesh?

23 Oh that my words were now written! oh that they were printed in a book!

NEW LIVING TRANSLATION

21 They will say, 'This was the home of a wicked
person,
the place of one who rejected God.'"

Job's Sixth Speech: A Response to Bildad

19 Then Job spoke again:
2 "How long will you torture me?
How long will you try to crush me with
your words?
3 You have already insulted me ten times.
You should be ashamed of treating me so badly.
4 Even if I have sinned,
that is my concern, not yours.
5 You think you're better than I am,
using my humiliation as evidence of my sin.
6 But it is God who has wronged me,
capturing me in his net.*

7 "I cry out, 'Help!' but no one answers me.
I protest, but there is no justice.
8 God has blocked my way so I cannot move.
He has plunged my path into darkness.
9 He has stripped me of my honor
and removed the crown from my head.
10 He has demolished me on every side, and
I am finished.
He has uprooted my hope like a fallen tree.
11 His fury burns against me;
he counts me as an enemy.
12 His troops advance.
They build up roads to attack me.
They camp all around my tent.

13 "My relatives stay far away,
and my friends have turned against me.
14 My family is gone,
and my close friends have forgotten me.
15 My servants and maids consider me a stranger.
I am like a foreigner to them.
16 When I call my servant, he doesn't come;
I have to plead with him!
17 My breath is repulsive to my wife.
I am rejected by my own family.
18 Even young children despise me.
When I stand to speak, they turn their
backs on me.
19 My close friends detest me.
Those I loved have turned against me.
20 I have been reduced to skin and bones
and have escaped death by the skin of my teeth.

21 "Have mercy on me, my friends, have mercy,
for the hand of God has struck me.
22 Must you also persecute me, like God does?
Haven't you chewed me up enough?

23 "Oh, that my words could be recorded.
Oh, that they could be inscribed on a monument,

19:6 Or *for I am like a city under siege.*

KING JAMES VERSION

24 That they were graven with an iron pen and lead
in the rock for ever!
25 For I know *that* my redeemer liveth, and *that* he
shall stand at the latter *day* upon the earth:
26 And *though* after my skin *worms* destroy this
body, yet in my flesh shall I see God:
27 Whom I shall see for myself, and mine eyes shall
behold, and not another; *though* my reins be consumed within me.
28 But ye should say, Why persecute we him, seeing
the root of the matter is found in me?
29 Be ye afraid of the sword: for wrath *bringeth* the
punishments of the sword, that ye may know *there is*
a judgment.

20 1 Then answered Zophar the Naamathite,
and said,
2 Therefore do my thoughts cause me to answer,
and for *this* I make haste.
3 I have heard the check of my reproach, and the
spirit of my understanding causeth me to answer.
4 Knowest thou *not* this of old, since man was
placed upon earth,
5 That the triumphing of the wicked *is* short, and
the joy of the hypocrite *but* for a moment?
6 Though his excellency mount up to the heavens,
and his head reach unto the clouds;
7 *Yet* he shall perish for ever like his own dung: they
which have seen him shall say, Where *is* he?
8 He shall fly away as a dream, and shall not be
found: yea, he shall be chased away as a vision of the
night.
9 The eye also *which* saw him shall *see him* no
more; neither shall his place any more behold him.
10 His children shall seek to please the poor, and
his hands shall restore their goods.
11 His bones are full *of the sin* of his youth, which
shall lie down with him in the dust.
12 Though wickedness be sweet in his mouth,
though he hide it under his tongue;
13 *Though* he spare it, and forsake it not; but keep it
still within his mouth:
14 *Yet* his meat in his bowels is turned, *it is* the gall
of asps within him.
15 He hath swallowed down riches, and he shall
vomit them up again: God shall cast them out of his
belly.
16 He shall suck the poison of asps: the viper's
tongue shall slay him.

NEW LIVING TRANSLATION

24 carved with an iron chisel and filled with lead,
engraved forever in the rock.

25 "But as for me, I know that my Redeemer lives,
and he will stand upon the earth at last.
26 And after my body has decayed,
yet in my body I will see God!*
27 I will see him for myself.
Yes, I will see him with my own eyes.
I am overwhelmed at the thought!
28 "How dare you go on persecuting me,
saying, 'It's his own fault'?
29 You should fear punishment yourselves,
for your attitude deserves punishment.
Then you will know that there is indeed
a judgment."

Zophar's Second Response to Job

20 Then Zophar the Naamathite replied:
2 "I must reply
because I am greatly disturbed.
3 I've had to endure your insults,
but now my spirit prompts me to reply.

4 "Don't you realize that from the beginning
of time,
ever since people were first placed on
the earth,
5 the triumph of the wicked has been short lived
and the joy of the godless has been only
temporary?
6 Though the pride of the godless reaches
to the heavens
and their heads touch the clouds,
7 yet they will vanish forever,
thrown away like their own dung.
Those who knew them will ask,
'Where are they?'
8 They will fade like a dream and not be found.
They will vanish like a vision in the night.
9 Those who once saw them will see them no more.
Their families will never see them again.
10 Their children will beg from the poor,
for they must give back their stolen riches.
11 Though they are young,
their bones will lie in the dust.

12 "They enjoyed the sweet taste of wickedness,
letting it melt under their tongue.
13 They savored it,
holding it long in their mouths.
14 But suddenly the food in their bellies turns sour,
a poisonous venom in their stomach.
15 They will vomit the wealth they swallowed.
God won't let them keep it down.
16 They will suck the poison of cobras.
The viper will kill them.

19:26 Or *without my body I will see God!* The meaning of the Hebrew is uncertain.

KING JAMES VERSION

17 He shall not see the rivers, the floods, the brooks of honey and butter.

18 That which he laboured for shall he restore, and shall not swallow *it* down: according to *his* substance *shall* the restitution *be,* and he shall not rejoice *therein.*

19 Because he hath oppressed *and* hath forsaken the poor; *because* he hath violently taken away an house which he builded not;

20 Surely he shall not feel quietness in his belly, he shall not save of that which he desired.

21 There shall none of his meat be left; therefore shall no man look for his goods.

22 In the fulness of his sufficiency he shall be in straits: every hand of the wicked shall come upon him.

23 *When* he is about to fill his belly, *God* shall cast the fury of his wrath upon him, and shall rain *it* upon him while he is eating.

24 He shall flee from the iron weapon, *and* the bow of steel shall strike him through.

25 It is drawn, and cometh out of the body; yea, the glittering sword cometh out of his gall: terrors *are* upon him.

26 All darkness *shall be* hid in his secret places: a fire not blown shall consume him; it shall go ill with him that is left in his tabernacle.

27 The heaven shall reveal his iniquity; and the earth shall rise up against him.

28 The increase of his house shall depart, *and his goods* shall flow away in the day of his wrath.

29 This *is* the portion of a wicked man from God, and the heritage appointed unto him by God.

21 1 But Job answered and said,

2 Hear diligently my speech, and let this be your consolations.

3 Suffer me that I may speak; and after that I have spoken, mock on.

4 As for me, *is* my complaint to man? and if *it were so,* why should not my spirit be troubled?

5 Mark me, and be astonished, and lay *your* hand upon *your* mouth.

6 Even when I remember I am afraid, and trembling taketh hold on my flesh.

7 Wherefore do the wicked live, become old, yea, are mighty in power?

8 Their seed is established in their sight with them, and their offspring before their eyes.

9 Their houses *are* safe from fear, neither *is* the rod of God upon them.

10 Their bull gendereth, and faileth not; their cow calveth, and casteth not her calf.

NEW LIVING TRANSLATION

17 They will never again enjoy streams of olive oil
or rivers of milk and honey.
18 They will give back everything they worked for.
Their wealth will bring them no joy.
19 For they oppressed the poor and left them
destitute.
They foreclosed on their homes.
20 They were always greedy and never satisfied.
Nothing remains of all the things they
dreamed about.
21 Nothing is left after they finish gorging
themselves.
Therefore, their prosperity will not endure.

22 "In the midst of plenty, they will run into trouble
and be overcome by misery.
23 May God give them a bellyful of trouble.
May God rain down his anger upon them.
24 When they try to escape an iron weapon,
a bronze-tipped arrow will pierce them.
25 The arrow is pulled from their back,
and the arrowhead glistens with blood.*
The terrors of death are upon them.
26 Their treasures will be thrown into deepest
darkness.
A wildfire will devour their goods,
consuming all they have left.
27 The heavens will reveal their guilt,
and the earth will testify against them.
28 A flood will sweep away their house.
God's anger will descend on them in torrents.
29 This is the reward that God gives the wicked.
It is the inheritance decreed by God."

Job's Seventh Speech: A Response to Zophar

21 Then Job spoke again:
2 "Listen closely to what I am saying.
That's one consolation you can give me.
3 Bear with me, and let me speak.
After I have spoken, you may resume
mocking me.

4 "My complaint is with God, not with people.
I have good reason to be so impatient.
5 Look at me and be stunned.
Put your hand over your mouth in shock.
6 When I think about what I am saying, I shudder.
My body trembles.

7 "Why do the wicked prosper,
growing old and powerful?
8 They live to see their children grow up and
settle down,
and they enjoy their grandchildren.
9 Their homes are safe from every fear,
and God does not punish them.
10 Their bulls never fail to breed.
Their cows bear calves and never miscarry.

20:25 Hebrew *with gall.*

KING JAMES VERSION

[11]They send forth their little ones like a flock, and
their children dance.
[12]They take the timbrel and harp, and rejoice at
the sound of the organ.
[13]They spend their days in wealth, and in a moment go down to the grave.
[14]Therefore they say unto God, Depart from us; for
we desire not the knowledge of thy ways.
[15]What *is* the Almighty, that we should serve him?
and what profit should we have, if we pray unto him?
[16]Lo, their good *is* not in their hand: the counsel of
the wicked is far from me.
[17]How oft is the candle of the wicked put out! and
how oft cometh their destruction upon them! *God*
distributeth sorrows in his anger.
[18]They are as stubble before the wind, and as chaff
that the storm carrieth away.
[19]God layeth up his iniquity for his children: he
rewardeth him, and he shall know *it*.
[20]His eyes shall see his destruction, and he shall
drink of the wrath of the Almighty.
[21]For what pleasure *hath* he in his house after
him, when the number of his months is cut off in
the midst?
[22]Shall *any* teach God knowledge? seeing he judgeth those that are high.
[23]One dieth in his full strength, being wholly at
ease and quiet.
[24]His breasts are full of milk, and his bones are
moistened with marrow.
[25]And another dieth in the bitterness of his soul,
and never eateth with pleasure.
[26]They shall lie down alike in the dust, and the
worms shall cover them.
[27]Behold, I know your thoughts, and the devices
which ye wrongfully imagine against me.
[28]For ye say, Where *is* the house of the prince? and
where *are* the dwelling places of the wicked?
[29]Have ye not asked them that go by the way? and
do ye not know their tokens,
[30]That the wicked is reserved to the day of destruction? they shall be brought forth to the day of
wrath.
[31]Who shall declare his way to his face? and who
shall repay him *what* he hath done?
[32]Yet shall he be brought to the grave, and shall
remain in the tomb.

NEW LIVING TRANSLATION

[11] They let their children frisk about like lambs.
Their little ones skip and dance.
[12] They sing with tambourine and harp.
They celebrate to the sound of the flute.
[13] They spend their days in prosperity,
then go down to the grave* in peace.
[14] And yet they say to God, 'Go away.
We want no part of you and your ways.
[15] Who is the Almighty, and why should we
obey him?
What good will it do us to pray?'
[16] (They think their prosperity is of their own doing,
but I will have nothing to do with that kind of
thinking.)
[17] "Yet the light of the wicked never seems to be
extinguished.
Do they ever have trouble?
Does God distribute sorrows to them in anger?
[18] Are they driven before the wind like straw?
Are they carried away by the storm like chaff?
Not at all!
[19] "'Well,' you say, 'at least God will punish their
children!'
But I say he should punish the ones who sin,
so that they understand his judgment.
[20] Let them see their destruction with their
own eyes.
Let them drink deeply of the anger of the
Almighty.
[21] For they will not care what happens to
their family
after they are dead.
[22] "But who can teach a lesson to God,
since he judges even the most powerful?
[23] One person dies in prosperity,
completely comfortable and secure,
[24] the picture of good health,
vigorous and fit.
[25] Another person dies in bitter poverty,
never having tasted the good life.
[26] But both are buried in the same dust,
both eaten by the same maggots.
[27] "Look, I know what you're thinking.
I know the schemes you plot against me.
[28] You will tell me of rich and wicked people
whose houses have vanished because
of their sins.
[29] But ask those who have been around,
and they will tell you the truth.
[30] Evil people are spared in times of calamity
and are allowed to escape disaster.
[31] No one criticizes them openly
or pays them back for what they have done.
[32] When they are carried to the grave,
an honor guard keeps watch at their tomb.

21:13 Hebrew *to Sheol.*

KING JAMES VERSION

33 The clods of the valley shall be sweet unto him,
and every man shall draw after him, as *there are* innumerable before him.
34 How then comfort ye me in vain, seeing in your
answers there remaineth falsehood?

22

1 Then Eliphaz the Temanite answered and
said,
2 Can a man be profitable unto God, as he that is
wise may be profitable unto himself?
3 *Is it* any pleasure to the Almighty, that thou art
righteous? or *is it* gain *to him,* that thou makest thy
ways perfect?
4 Will he reprove thee for fear of thee? will he enter with thee into judgment?
5 *Is* not thy wickedness great? and thine iniquities
infinite?
6 For thou hast taken a pledge from thy brother for
nought, and stripped the naked of their clothing.
7 Thou hast not given water to the weary to drink,
and thou hast withholden bread from the hungry.
8 But *as for* the mighty man, he had the earth; and
the honourable man dwelt in it.
9 Thou hast sent widows away empty, and the arms
of the fatherless have been broken.
10 Therefore snares *are* round about thee, and sudden fear troubleth thee;
11 Or darkness, *that* thou canst not see; and abundance of waters cover thee.
12 *Is* not God in the height of heaven? and behold
the height of the stars, how high they are!
13 And thou sayest, How doth God know? can he
judge through the dark cloud?
14 Thick clouds *are* a covering to him, that he seeth
not; and he walketh in the circuit of heaven.
15 Hast thou marked the old way which wicked
men have trodden?
16 Which were cut down out of time, whose foundation was overflown with a flood:
17 Which said unto God, Depart from us: and what
can the Almighty do for them?
18 Yet he filled their houses with good *things:* but
the counsel of the wicked is far from me.
19 The righteous see *it,* and are glad: and the innocent laugh them to scorn.

NEW LIVING TRANSLATION

33 A great funeral procession goes to the cemetery.
Many pay their respects as the body is laid to rest,
and the earth gives sweet repose.
34 "How can your empty clichés comfort me?
All your explanations are lies!"

Eliphaz's Third Response to Job

22

Then Eliphaz the Temanite replied:
2 "Can a person do anything to help God?
Can even a wise person be helpful to him?
3 Is it any advantage to the Almighty if you are righteous?
Would it be any gain to him if you were perfect?
4 Is it because you're so pious that he accuses you
and brings judgment against you?
5 No, it's because of your wickedness!
There's no limit to your sins.
6 "For example, you must have lent money to your friend
and demanded clothing as security.
Yes, you stripped him to the bone.
7 You must have refused water for the thirsty
and food for the hungry.
8 You probably think the land belongs to the powerful
and only the privileged have a right to it!
9 You must have sent widows away empty-handed
and crushed the hopes of orphans.
10 That is why you are surrounded by traps
and tremble from sudden fears.
11 That is why you cannot see in the darkness,
and waves of water cover you.
12 "God is so great—higher than the heavens,
higher than the farthest stars.
13 But you reply, 'That's why God can't see what I am doing!
How can he judge through the thick darkness?
14 For thick clouds swirl about him, and he cannot see us.
He is way up there, walking on the vault of heaven.'
15 "Will you continue on the old paths
where evil people have walked?
16 They were snatched away in the prime of life,
the foundations of their lives washed away.
17 For they said to God, 'Leave us alone!
What can the Almighty do to us?'
18 Yet he was the one who filled their homes with good things,
so I will have nothing to do with that kind of thinking.
19 "The righteous will be happy to see the wicked destroyed,
and the innocent will laugh in contempt.

KING JAMES VERSION

20 Whereas our substance is not cut down, but the
remnant of them the fire consumeth.
21 Acquaint now thyself with him, and be at peace:
thereby good shall come unto thee.
22 Receive, I pray thee, the law from his mouth, and
lay up his words in thine heart.
23 If thou return to the Almighty, thou shalt be
built up, thou shalt put away iniquity far from thy
tabernacles.
24 Then shalt thou lay up gold as dust, and the *gold*
of Ophir as the stones of the brooks.
25 Yea, the Almighty shall be thy defence, and thou
shalt have plenty of silver.
26 For then shalt thou have thy delight in the Almighty, and shalt lift up thy face unto God.
27 Thou shalt make thy prayer unto him, and he
shall hear thee, and thou shalt pay thy vows.
28 Thou shalt also decree a thing, and it shall be established unto thee: and the light shall shine upon
thy ways.
29 When *men* are cast down, then thou shalt say,
There is lifting up; and he shall save the humble person.
30 He shall deliver the island of the innocent: and it
is delivered by the pureness of thine hands.

23 1 Then Job answered and said,
2 Even today *is* my complaint bitter: my
stroke is heavier than my groaning.
3 Oh that I knew where I might find him! *that* I
might come *even* to his seat!
4 I would order *my* cause before him, and fill my
mouth with arguments.
5 I would know the words *which* he would answer
me, and understand what he would say unto me.
6 Will he plead against me with *his* great power?
No; but he would put *strength* in me.
7 There the righteous might dispute with him; so
should I be delivered for ever from my judge.
8 Behold, I go forward, but he *is* not *there;* and
backward, but I cannot perceive him:
9 On the left hand, where he doth work, but I cannot behold *him:* he hideth himself on the right hand,
that I cannot see *him:*
10 But he knoweth the way that I take: *when* he
hath tried me, I shall come forth as gold.
11 My foot hath held his steps, his way have I kept,
and not declined.
12 Neither have I gone back from the commandment of his lips; I have esteemed the words of his
mouth more than my necessary *food.*
13 But he *is* in one *mind,* and who can turn him?
and *what* his soul desireth, even *that* he doeth.

NEW LIVING TRANSLATION

20 They will say, 'See how our enemies have
been destroyed.
The last of them have been consumed
in the fire.'
21 "Submit to God, and you will have peace;
then things will go well for you.
22 Listen to his instructions,
and store them in your heart.
23 If you return to the Almighty, you will be
restored—
so clean up your life.
24 If you give up your lust for money
and throw your precious gold into the river,
25 the Almighty himself will be your treasure.
He will be your precious silver!
26 "Then you will take delight in the Almighty
and look up to God.
27 You will pray to him, and he will hear you,
and you will fulfill your vows to him.
28 You will succeed in whatever you choose to do,
and light will shine on the road ahead of you.
29 If people are in trouble and you say, 'Help them,'
God will save them.
30 Even sinners will be rescued;
they will be rescued because your hands
are pure."

Job's Eighth Speech: A Response to Eliphaz

23 Then Job spoke again:
2 "My complaint today is still a bitter one,
and I try hard not to groan aloud.
3 If only I knew where to find God,
I would go to his court.
4 I would lay out my case
and present my arguments.
5 Then I would listen to his reply
and understand what he says to me.
6 Would he use his great power to argue with me?
No, he would give me a fair hearing.
7 Honest people can reason with him,
so I would be forever acquitted by my judge.
8 I go east, but he is not there.
I go west, but I cannot find him.
9 I do not see him in the north, for he is hidden.
I look to the south, but he is concealed.

10 "But he knows where I am going.
And when he tests me, I will come out as pure
as gold.
11 For I have stayed on God's paths;
I have followed his ways and not turned aside.
12 I have not departed from his commands,
but have treasured his words more than
daily food.
13 But once he has made his decision, who can
change his mind?
Whatever he wants to do, he does.

KING JAMES VERSION

14 For he performeth *the thing that is* appointed for me: and many such *things are* with him.

15 Therefore am I troubled at his presence: when I consider, I am afraid of him.

16 For God maketh my heart soft, and the Almighty troubleth me:

17 Because I was not cut off before the darkness, *neither* hath he covered the darkness from my face.

24 1 Why, seeing times are not hidden from the Almighty, do they that know him not see his days?

2 *Some* remove the landmarks; they violently take away flocks, and feed *thereof*.

3 They drive away the ass of the fatherless, they take the widow's ox for a pledge.

4 They turn the needy out of the way: the poor of the earth hide themselves together.

5 Behold, *as* wild asses in the desert, go they forth to their work; rising betimes for a prey: the wilderness *yieldeth* food for them *and* for *their* children.

6 They reap *every one* his corn in the field: and they gather the vintage of the wicked.

7 They cause the naked to lodge without clothing, that *they have* no covering in the cold.

8 They are wet with the showers of the mountains, and embrace the rock for want of a shelter.

9 They pluck the fatherless from the breast, and take a pledge of the poor.

10 They cause *him* to go naked without clothing, and they take away the sheaf *from* the hungry;

11 *Which* make oil within their walls, *and* tread *their* winepresses, and suffer thirst.

12 Men groan from out of the city, and the soul of the wounded crieth out: yet God layeth not folly *to them*.

13 They are of those that rebel against the light; they know not the ways thereof, nor abide in the paths thereof.

14 The murderer rising with the light killeth the poor and needy, and in the night is as a thief.

15 The eye also of the adulterer waiteth for the twilight, saying, No eye shall see me: and disguiseth *his* face.

NEW LIVING TRANSLATION

14 So he will do to me whatever he has planned.
He controls my destiny.
15 No wonder I am so terrified in his presence.
When I think of it, terror grips me.
16 God has made me sick at heart;
the Almighty has terrified me.
17 Darkness is all around me;
thick, impenetrable darkness is everywhere.

Job Asks Why the Wicked Are Not Punished

24 1 "Why doesn't the Almighty bring the
wicked to judgment?
Why must the godly wait for him in vain?
2 Evil people steal land by moving the boundary
markers.
They steal livestock and put them in their
own pastures.
3 They take the orphan's donkey
and demand the widow's ox as security
for a loan.
4 The poor are pushed off the path;
the needy must hide together for safety.
5 Like wild donkeys in the wilderness,
the poor must spend all their time looking
for food,
searching even in the desert for food for
their children.
6 They harvest a field they do not own,
and they glean in the vineyards of the wicked.
7 All night they lie naked in the cold,
without clothing or covering.
8 They are soaked by mountain showers,
and they huddle against the rocks for want
of a home.

9 "The wicked snatch a widow's child from
her breast,
taking the baby as security for a loan.
10 The poor must go about naked, without
any clothing.
They harvest food for others while they
themselves are starving.
11 They press out olive oil without being allowed
to taste it,
and they tread in the winepress as they suffer
from thirst.
12 The groans of the dying rise from the city,
and the wounded cry for help,
yet God ignores their moaning.

13 "Wicked people rebel against the light.
They refuse to acknowledge its ways
or stay in its paths.
14 The murderer rises in the early dawn
to kill the poor and needy;
at night he is a thief.
15 The adulterer waits for the twilight,
saying, 'No one will see me then.'
He hides his face so no one will know him.

KING JAMES VERSION

[16]In the dark they dig through houses, *which* they
had marked for themselves in the daytime: they
know not the light.
[17]For the morning *is* to them even as the shadow
of death: if *one* know *them, they are in* the terrors of
the shadow of death.
[18]He *is* swift as the waters; their portion is cursed
in the earth: he beholdeth not the way of the vineyards.
[19]Drought and heat consume the snow waters: *so
doth* the grave *those which* have sinned.
[20]The womb shall forget him; the worm shall feed
sweetly on him; he shall be no more remembered;
and wickedness shall be broken as a tree.
[21]He evil entreateth the barren *that* beareth not:
and doeth not good to the widow.
[22]He draweth also the mighty with his power: he
riseth up, and no *man* is sure of life.
[23]*Though* it be given him *to be* in safety, whereon
he resteth; yet his eyes *are* upon their ways.
[24]They are exalted for a little while, but are gone
and brought low; they are taken out of the way as all
other, and cut off as the tops of the ears of corn.
[25]And if *it be* not *so* now, who will make me a liar,
and make my speech nothing worth?

25 [1]Then answered Bildad the Shuhite, and
said,
[2]Dominion and fear *are* with him, he maketh
peace in his high places.
[3]Is there any number of his armies? and upon
whom doth not his light arise?
[4]How then can man be justified with God? or how
can he be clean *that is* born of a woman?
[5]Behold even to the moon, and it shineth not; yea,
the stars are not pure in his sight.
[6]How much less man, *that is* a worm? and the son
of man, *which is* a worm?

26 [1]But Job answered and said,
[2]How hast thou helped *him that is* without
power? *how* savest thou the arm *that hath* no
strength?
[3]How hast thou counselled *him that hath* no wisdom? and *how* hast thou plentifully declared the
thing as it is?
[4]To whom hast thou uttered words? and whose
spirit came from thee?
[5]Dead *things* are formed from under the waters,
and the inhabitants thereof.

NEW LIVING TRANSLATION

[16] Thieves break into houses at night
and sleep in the daytime.
They are not acquainted with the light.
[17] The black night is their morning.
They ally themselves with the terrors of
the darkness.

[18] "But they disappear like foam down a river.
Everything they own is cursed,
and they are afraid to enter their own
vineyards.
[19] The grave* consumes sinners
just as drought and heat consume snow.
[20] Their own mothers will forget them.
Maggots will find them sweet to eat.
No one will remember them.
Wicked people are broken like a tre
in the storm.
[21] They cheat the woman who has no son to help her.
They refuse to help the needy widow.

[22] "God, in his power, drags away the rich.
They may rise high, but they have no assurance
of life.
[23] They may be allowed to live in security,
but God is always watching them.
[24] And though they are great now,
in a moment they will be gone like all others,
cut off like heads of grain.
[25] Can anyone claim otherwise?
Who can prove me wrong?"

Bildad's Third Response to Job

25 Then Bildad the Shuhite replied:
[2]"God is powerful and dreadful.
He enforces peace in the heavens.
[3] Who is able to count his heavenly army?
Doesn't his light shine on all the earth?
[4] How can a mortal be innocent before God?
Can anyone born of a woman be pure?
[5] God is more glorious than the moon;
he shines brighter than the stars.
[6] In comparison, people are maggots;
we mortals are mere worms."

Job's Ninth Speech: A Response to Bildad

26 Then Job spoke again:
[2]"How you have helped the powerless!
How you have saved the weak!
[3] How you have enlightened my stupidity!
What wise advice you have offered!
[4] Where have you gotten all these wise sayings?
Whose spirit speaks through you?

[5] "The dead tremble—
those who live beneath the waters.

24:19 Hebrew *Sheol.*

KING JAMES VERSION

6 Hell *is* naked before him, and destruction hath no covering.

7 He stretcheth out the north over the empty place, *and* hangeth the earth upon nothing.

8 He bindeth up the waters in his thick clouds; and the cloud is not rent under them.

9 He holdeth back the face of his throne, *and* spreadeth his cloud upon it.

10 He hath compassed the waters with bounds, until the day and night come to an end.

11 The pillars of heaven tremble and are astonished at his reproof.

12 He divideth the sea with his power, and by his understanding he smiteth through the proud.

13 By his spirit he hath garnished the heavens; his hand hath formed the crooked serpent.

14 Lo, these *are* parts of his ways: but how little a portion is heard of him? but the thunder of his power who can understand?

27 1 Moreover Job continued his parable, and said,

2 *As* God liveth, *who* hath taken away my judgment; and the Almighty, *who* hath vexed my soul;

3 All the while my breath *is* in me, and the spirit of God *is* in my nostrils;

4 My lips shall not speak wickedness, nor my tongue utter deceit.

5 God forbid that I should justify you: till I die I will not remove mine integrity from me.

6 My righteousness I hold fast, and will not let it go: my heart shall not reproach *me* so long as I live.

7 Let mine enemy be as the wicked, and he that riseth up against me as the unrighteous.

8 For what *is* the hope of the hypocrite, though he hath gained, when God taketh away his soul?

9 Will God hear his cry when trouble cometh upon him?

10 Will he delight himself in the Almighty? will he always call upon God?

11 I will teach you by the hand of God: *that* which *is* with the Almighty will I not conceal.

12 Behold, all ye yourselves have seen *it;* why then are ye thus altogether vain?

13 This *is* the portion of a wicked man with God, and the heritage of oppressors, *which* they shall receive of the Almighty.

NEW LIVING TRANSLATION

6 The underworld* is naked in God's presence.
The place of destruction* is uncovered.
7 God stretches the northern sky over empty space
and hangs the earth on nothing.
8 He wraps the rain in his thick clouds,
and the clouds don't burst with the weight.
9 He covers the face of the moon,*
shrouding it with his clouds.
10 He created the horizon when he separated
the waters;
he set the boundary between day and night.
11 The foundations of heaven tremble;
they shudder at his rebuke.
12 By his power the sea grew calm.
By his skill he crushed the great sea
monster.*
13 His Spirit made the heavens beautiful,
and his power pierced the gliding serpent.
14 These are just the beginning of all that he does,
merely a whisper of his power.
Who, then, can comprehend the thunder
of his power?"

Job's Final Speech

27 Job continued speaking:

2 "I vow by the living God, who has taken
away my rights,
by the Almighty who has embittered my soul—
3 As long as I live,
while I have breath from God,
4 my lips will speak no evil,
and my tongue will speak no lies.
5 I will never concede that you are right;
I will defend my integrity until I die.
6 I will maintain my innocence without
wavering.
My conscience is clear for as long as I live.
7 "May my enemy be punished like the wicked,
my adversary like those who do evil.
8 For what hope do the godless have when God
cuts them off
and takes away their life?
9 Will God listen to their cry
when trouble comes upon them?
10 Can they take delight in the Almighty?
Can they call to God at any time?
11 I will teach you about God's power.
I will not conceal anything concerning
the Almighty.
12 But you have seen all this,
yet you say all these useless things to me.
13 "This is what the wicked will receive from God;
this is their inheritance from the Almighty.

26:6a Hebrew *Sheol.* **26:6b** Hebrew *Abaddon.* **26:9** Or *covers his throne.* **26:12** Hebrew *Rahab,* the name of a mythical sea monster that represents chaos in ancient literature.

KING JAMES VERSION

14 If his children be multiplied, *it is* for the sword:
and his offspring shall not be satisfied with bread.
15 Those that remain of him shall be buried in
death: and his widows shall not weep.
16 Though he heap up silver as the dust, and prepare raiment as the clay;
17 He may prepare *it*, but the just shall put *it* on,
and the innocent shall divide the silver.
18 He buildeth his house as a moth, and as a booth
that the keeper maketh.
19 The rich man shall lie down, but he shall not be
gathered: he openeth his eyes, and he *is* not.
20 Terrors take hold on him as waters, a tempest
stealeth him away in the night.
21 The east wind carrieth him away, and he departeth: and as a storm hurleth him out of his place.
22 For *God* shall cast upon him, and not spare: he
would fain flee out of his hand.
23 *Men* shall clap their hands at him, and shall hiss
him out of his place.

28 1 Surely there is a vein for the silver, and a
place for gold *where* they fine *it*.
2 Iron is taken out of the earth, and brass *is* molten
out of the stone.
3 He setteth an end to darkness, and searcheth out
all perfection: the stones of darkness, and the
shadow of death.
4 The flood breaketh out from the inhabitant; *even*
the waters forgotten of the foot: they are dried up,
they are gone away from men.
5 *As for* the earth, out of it cometh bread: and under it is turned up as it were fire.
6 The stones of it *are* the place of sapphires: and it
hath dust of gold.
7 *There is* a path which no fowl knoweth, and which
the vulture's eye hath not seen:
8 The lion's whelps have not trodden it, nor the
fierce lion passed by it.
9 He putteth forth his hand upon the rock; he
overturneth the mountains by the roots.
10 He cutteth out rivers among the rocks; and his
eye seeth every precious thing.
11 He bindeth the floods from overflowing; and
the thing that is hid bringeth he forth to light.
12 But where shall wisdom be found? and where *is*
the place of understanding?
13 Man knoweth not the price thereof; neither is it
found in the land of the living.

NEW LIVING TRANSLATION

14 They may have many children,
but the children will die in war or starve
to death.
15 Those who survive will die of a plague,
and not even their widows will mourn them.

16 "Evil people may have piles of money
and may store away mounds of clothing.
17 But the righteous will wear that clothing,
and the innocent will divide that money.
18 The wicked build houses as fragile as a
spider's web,*
as flimsy as a shelter made of branches.
19 The wicked go to bed rich
but wake to find that all their wealth is gone.
20 Terror overwhelms them like a flood,
and they are blown away in the storms
of the night.
21 The east wind carries them away, and they
are gone.
It sweeps them away.
22 It whirls down on them without mercy.
They struggle to flee from its power.
23 But everyone jeers at them
and mocks them.

Job Speaks of Wisdom and Understanding

28 1 "People know where to mine silver
and how to refine gold.
2 They know where to dig iron from the earth
and how to smelt copper from rock.
3 They know how to shine light in the darkness
and explore the farthest regions of the earth
as they search in the dark for ore.
4 They sink a mine shaft into the earth
far from where anyone lives.
They descend on ropes, swinging back
and forth.
5 Food is grown on the earth above,
but down below, the earth is melted as by fire.
6 Here the rocks contain precious lapis lazuli,
and the dust contains gold.
7 These are treasures no bird of prey can see,
no falcon's eye observe.
8 No wild animal has walked upon these treasures;
no lion has ever set his paw there.
9 People know how to tear apart flinty rocks
and overturn the roots of mountains.
10 They cut tunnels in the rocks
and uncover precious stones.
11 They dam up the trickling streams
and bring to light the hidden treasures.

12 "But do people know where to find wisdom?
Where can they find understanding?
13 No one knows where to find it,
for it is not found among the living.

27:18 As in Greek and Syriac versions (see also 8:14); Hebrew reads *a moth.*

KING JAMES VERSION

14 The depth saith, It *is* not in me: and the sea saith,
It is not with me.
15 It cannot be gotten for gold, neither shall silver
be weighed *for* the price thereof.
16 It cannot be valued with the gold of Ophir, with
the precious onyx, or the sapphire.
17 The gold and the crystal cannot equal it: and the
exchange of it *shall not be for* jewels of fine gold.
18 No mention shall be made of coral, or of pearls:
for the price of wisdom *is* above rubies.
19 The topaz of Ethiopia shall not equal it, neither
shall it be valued with pure gold.
20 Whence then cometh wisdom? and where *is* the
place of understanding?
21 Seeing it is hid from the eyes of all living, and
kept close from the fowls of the air.
22 Destruction and death say, We have heard the
fame thereof with our ears.
23 God understandeth the way thereof, and he
knoweth the place thereof.
24 For he looketh to the ends of the earth, *and*
seeth under the whole heaven;
25 To make the weight for the winds; and he
weigheth the waters by measure.
26 When he made a decree for the rain, and a way
for the lightning of the thunder:
27 Then did he see it, and declare it; he prepared it,
yea, and searched it out.
28 And unto man he said, Behold, the fear of the
Lord, that *is* wisdom; and to depart from evil *is*
understanding.

29 1 Moreover Job continued his parable, and
said,
2 Oh that I were as *in* months past, as *in* the days
when God preserved me;
3 When his candle shined upon my head, *and*
when by his light I walked *through* darkness;
4 As I was in the days of my youth, when the secret
of God *was* upon my tabernacle;
5 When the Almighty *was* yet with me, *when* my
children *were* about me;
6 When I washed my steps with butter, and the
rock poured me out rivers of oil;
7 When I went out to the gate through the city,
when I prepared my seat in the street!
8 The young men saw me, and hid themselves: and
the aged arose, *and* stood up.
9 The princes refrained talking, and laid *their*
hand on their mouth.

NEW LIVING TRANSLATION

14 'It is not here,' says the ocean.
'Nor is it here,' says the sea.
15 It cannot be bought with gold.
It cannot be purchased with silver.
16 It's worth more than all the gold of Ophir,
greater than precious onyx or lapis lazuli.
17 Wisdom is more valuable than gold and crystal.
It cannot be purchased with jewels mounted
in fine gold.
18 Coral and jasper are worthless in trying to get it.
The price of wisdom is far above rubies.
19 Precious peridot from Ethiopia* cannot be
exchanged for it.
It's worth more than the purest gold.

20 "But do people know where to find wisdom?
Where can they find understanding?
21 It is hidden from the eyes of all humanity.
Even the sharp-eyed birds in the sky cannot
discover it.
22 Destruction* and Death say,
'We've heard only rumors of where wisdom
can be found.'

23 "God alone understands the way to wisdom;
he knows where it can be found,
24 for he looks throughout the whole earth
and sees everything under the heavens.
25 He decided how hard the winds should blow
and how much rain should fall.
26 He made the laws for the rain
and laid out a path for the lightning.
27 Then he saw wisdom and evaluated it.
He set it in place and examined it thoroughly.
28 And this is what he says to all humanity:
'The fear of the Lord is true wisdom;
to forsake evil is real understanding.'"

Job Speaks of His Former Blessings

29 Job continued speaking:
2 "I long for the years gone by
when God took care of me,
3 when he lit up the way before me
and I walked safely through the darkness.
4 When I was in my prime,
God's friendship was felt in my home.
5 The Almighty was still with me,
and my children were around me.
6 My cows produced milk in abundance,
and my groves poured out streams of olive oil.

7 "Those were the days when I went to the city gate
and took my place among the honored leaders.
8 The young stepped aside when they saw me,
and even the aged rose in respect at my
coming.
9 The princes stood in silence
and put their hands over their mouths.

28:19 Hebrew *from Cush*. **28:22** Hebrew *Abaddon*.

KING JAMES VERSION

[10]The nobles held their peace, and their tongue
cleaved to the roof of their mouth.
[11]When the ear heard *me*, then it blessed me; and
when the eye saw *me*, it gave witness to me:
[12]Because I delivered the poor that cried, and the
fatherless, and *him that had* none to help him.
[13]The blessing of him that was ready to perish
came upon me: and I caused the widow's heart to
sing for joy.
[14]I put on righteousness, and it clothed me: my
judgment *was* as a robe and a diadem.
[15]I was eyes to the blind, and feet *was* I to the
lame.
[16]I *was* a father to the poor: and the cause *which* I
knew not I searched out.
[17]And I brake the jaws of the wicked, and plucked
the spoil out of his teeth.
[18]Then I said, I shall die in my nest, and I shall
multiply *my* days as the sand.
[19]My root *was* spread out by the waters, and the
dew lay all night upon my branch.
[20]My glory *was* fresh in me, and my bow was renewed in my hand.
[21]Unto me *men* gave ear, and waited, and kept
silence at my counsel.
[22]After my words they spake not again; and my
speech dropped upon them.
[23]And they waited for me as for the rain; and they
opened their mouth wide *as* for the latter rain.
[24]*If* I laughed on them, they believed *it* not; and
the light of my countenance they cast not down.
[25]I chose out their way, and sat chief, and dwelt
as a king in the army, as one *that* comforteth the
mourners.

30 [1]But now *they that are* younger than I have
me in derision, whose fathers I would have
disdained to have set with the dogs of my flock.
[2]Yea, whereto *might* the strength of their hands
profit me, in whom old age was perished?
[3]For want and famine *they were* solitary; fleeing
into the wilderness in former time desolate and
waste.
[4]Who cut up mallows by the bushes, and juniper
roots *for* their meat.
[5]They were driven forth from among *men*, (they
cried after them as *after* a thief;)

NEW LIVING TRANSLATION

[10] The highest officials of the city stood quietly,
holding their tongues in respect.
[11] "All who heard me praised me.
All who saw me spoke well of me.
[12] For I assisted the poor in their need
and the orphans who required help.
[13] I helped those without hope, and they
blessed me.
And I caused the widows' hearts to sing for joy.
[14] Everything I did was honest.
Righteousness covered me like a robe,
and I wore justice like a turban.
[15] I served as eyes for the blind
and feet for the lame.
[16] I was a father to the poor
and assisted strangers who needed help.
[17] I broke the jaws of godless oppressors
and plucked their victims from their teeth.

[18] "I thought, 'Surely I will die surrounded by
my family
after a long, good life.*
[19] For I am like a tree whose roots reach the water,
whose branches are refreshed with the dew.
[20] New honors are constantly bestowed on me,
and my strength is continually renewed.'

[21] "Everyone listened to my advice.
They were silent as they waited for me
to speak.
[22] And after I spoke, they had nothing to add,
for my counsel satisfied them.
[23] They longed for me to speak as people long
for rain.
They drank my words like a refreshing
spring rain.
[24] When they were discouraged, I smiled at them.
My look of approval was precious to them.
[25] Like a chief, I told them what to do.
I lived like a king among his troops
and comforted those who mourned.

Job Speaks of His Anguish

30 [1]"But now I am mocked by people younger
than I,
by young men whose fathers are not worthy
to run with my sheepdogs.
[2] A lot of good they are to me—
those worn-out wretches!
[3] They are gaunt with hunger
and flee to the deserts,
to desolate and gloomy wastelands.
[4] They pluck wild greens from among the bushes
and eat from the roots of broom trees.
[5] They are driven from human society,
and people shout at them as if they
were thieves.

29:18 Hebrew *after I have counted my days like sand.*

KING JAMES VERSION

6 To dwell in the cliffs of the valleys, *in* caves of the earth, and *in* the rocks.

7 Among the bushes they brayed; under the nettles they were gathered together.

8 *They were* children of fools, yea, children of base men: they were viler than the earth.

9 And now am I their song, yea, I am their byword.

10 They abhor me, they flee far from me, and spare not to spit in my face.

11 Because he hath loosed my cord, and afflicted me, they have also let loose the bridle before me.

12 Upon *my* right *hand* rise the youth; they push away my feet, and they raise up against me the ways of their destruction.

13 They mar my path, they set forward my calamity, they have no helper.

14 They came *upon me* as a wide breaking in *of waters:* in the desolation they rolled themselves *upon me.*

15 Terrors are turned upon me: they pursue my soul as the wind: and my welfare passeth away as a cloud.

16 And now my soul is poured out upon me; the days of affliction have taken hold upon me.

17 My bones are pierced in me in the night season: and my sinews take no rest.

18 By the great force *of my disease* is my garment changed: it bindeth me about as the collar of my coat.

19 He hath cast me into the mire, and I am become like dust and ashes.

20 I cry unto thee, and thou dost not hear me: I stand up, and thou regardest me *not.*

21 Thou art become cruel to me: with thy strong hand thou opposest thyself against me.

22 Thou liftest me up to the wind; thou causest me to ride *upon it,* and dissolvest my substance.

23 For I know *that* thou wilt bring me *to* death, and *to* the house appointed for all living.

24 Howbeit he will not stretch out *his* hand to the grave, though they cry in his destruction.

25 Did not I weep for him that was in trouble? was *not* my soul grieved for the poor?

26 When I looked for good, then evil came *unto me:* and when I waited for light, there came darkness.

27 My bowels boiled, and rested not: the days of affliction prevented me.

28 I went mourning without the sun: I stood up, *and* I cried in the congregation.

29 I am a brother to dragons, and a companion to owls.

30 My skin is black upon me, and my bones are burned with heat.

NEW LIVING TRANSLATION

6 So now they live in frightening ravines,
in caves and among the rocks.
7 They sound like animals howling among
the bushes,
huddled together beneath the nettles.
8 They are nameless fools,
outcasts from society.

9 "And now they mock me with vulgar songs!
They taunt me!
10 They despise me and won't come near me,
except to spit in my face.
11 For God has cut my bowstring.
He has humbled me,
so they have thrown off all restraint.
12 These outcasts oppose me to my face.
They send me sprawling
and lay traps in my path.
13 They block my road
and do everything they can to destroy me.
They know I have no one to help me.
14 They come at me from all directions.
They jump on me when I am down.
15 I live in terror now.
My honor has blown away in the wind,
and my prosperity has vanished like a cloud.

16 "And now my life seeps away.
Depression haunts my days.
17 At night my bones are filled with pain,
which gnaws at me relentlessly.
18 With a strong hand, God grabs my shirt.
He grips me by the collar of my coat.
19 He has thrown me into the mud.
I'm nothing more than dust and ashes.

20 "I cry to you, O God, but you don't answer.
I stand before you, but you don't even look.
21 You have become cruel toward me.
You use your power to persecute me.
22 You throw me into the whirlwind
and destroy me in the storm.
23 And I know you are sending me to my death—
the destination of all who live.

24 "Surely no one would turn against the needy
when they cry for help in their trouble.
25 Did I not weep for those in trouble?
Was I not deeply grieved for the needy?
26 So I looked for good, but evil came instead.
I waited for the light, but darkness fell.
27 My heart is troubled and restless.
Days of suffering torment me.
28 I walk in gloom, without sunlight.
I stand in the public square and cry for help.
29 Instead, I am considered a brother to jackals
and a companion to owls.
30 My skin has turned dark,
and my bones burn with fever.

KING JAMES VERSION

31 My harp also is *turned* to mourning, and my
organ into the voice of them that weep.

31

1 I made a covenant with mine eyes; why then
should I think upon a maid?
2 For what portion of God *is there* from above? and
what inheritance of the Almighty from on high?
3 *Is* not destruction to the wicked? and a strange
punishment to the workers of iniquity?
4 Doth not he see my ways, and count all my steps?
5 If I have walked with vanity, or if my foot hath
hasted to deceit;
6 Let me be weighed in an even balance that God
may know mine integrity.
7 If my step hath turned out of the way, and mine
heart walked after mine eyes, and if any blot hath
cleaved to mine hands;
8 *Then* let me sow, and let another eat; yea, let my
offspring be rooted out.
9 If mine heart have been deceived by a woman, or
if I have laid wait at my neighbour's door;
10 *Then* let my wife grind unto another, and let
others bow down upon her.
11 For this *is* an heinous crime; yea, it *is* an iniquity
to be punished by the judges.
12 For it *is* a fire *that* consumeth to destruction,
and would root out all mine increase.
13 If I did despise the cause of my manservant or of
my maidservant, when they contended with me;
14 What then shall I do when God riseth up? and
when he visiteth, what shall I answer him?
15 Did not he that made me in the womb make
him? and did not one fashion us in the womb?
16 If I have withheld the poor from *their* desire, or
have caused the eyes of the widow to fail;
17 Or have eaten my morsel myself alone, and the
fatherless hath not eaten thereof;
18 (For from my youth he was brought up with me,
as *with* a father, and I have guided her from my
mother's womb;)
19 If I have seen any perish for want of clothing, or
any poor without covering;
20 If his loins have not blessed me, and *if* he were
not warmed with the fleece of my sheep;
21 If I have lifted up my hand against the fatherless,
when I saw my help in the gate:

NEW LIVING TRANSLATION

31 My harp plays sad music,
and my flute accompanies those who weep.

Job's Final Protest of Innocence

31

1 "I made a covenant with my eyes
not to look with lust at a young woman.
2 For what has God above chosen for us?
What is our inheritance from the Almighty
on high?
3 Isn't it calamity for the wicked
and misfortune for those who do evil?
4 Doesn't he see everything I do
and every step I take?

5 "Have I lied to anyone
or deceived anyone?
6 Let God weigh me on the scales of justice,
for he knows my integrity.
7 If I have strayed from his pathway,
or if my heart has lusted for what my eyes
have seen,
or if I am guilty of any other sin,
8 then let someone else eat the crops I have
planted.
Let all that I have planted be uprooted.

9 "If my heart has been seduced by a woman,
or if I have lusted for my neighbor's wife,
10 then let my wife belong to* another man;
let other men sleep with her.
11 For lust is a shameful sin,
a crime that should be punished.
12 It is a fire that burns all the way to hell.*
It would wipe out everything I own.

13 "If I have been unfair to my male or female
servants
when they brought their complaints to me,
14 how could I face God?
What could I say when he questioned me?
15 For God created both me and my servants.
He created us both in the womb.

16 "Have I refused to help the poor,
or crushed the hopes of widows?
17 Have I been stingy with my food
and refused to share it with orphans?
18 No, from childhood I have cared for orphans
like a father,
and all my life I have cared for widows.
19 Whenever I saw the homeless without clothes
and the needy with nothing to wear,
20 did they not praise me
for providing wool clothing to keep
them warm?

21 "If I raised my hand against an orphan,
knowing the judges would take my side,

31:10 Hebrew *grind for.* **31:12** Hebrew *to Abaddon.*

KING JAMES VERSION

22 *Then* let mine arm fall from my shoulder blade, and mine arm be broken from the bone.

23 For destruction *from* God *was* a terror to me, and by reason of his highness I could not endure.

24 If I have made gold my hope, or have said to the fine gold, *Thou art* my confidence;

25 If I rejoiced because my wealth *was* great, and because mine hand had gotten much;

26 If I beheld the sun when it shined, or the moon walking *in* brightness;

27 And my heart hath been secretly enticed, or my mouth hath kissed my hand:

28 This also *were* an iniquity *to be punished by* the judge: for I should have denied the God *that is* above.

29 If I rejoiced at the destruction of him that hated me, or lifted up myself when evil found him:

30 Neither have I suffered my mouth to sin by wishing a curse to his soul.

31 If the men of my tabernacle said not, Oh that we had of his flesh! we cannot be satisfied.

32 The stranger did not lodge in the street: *but* I opened my doors to the traveller.

33 If I covered my transgressions as Adam, by hiding mine iniquity in my bosom:

34 Did I fear a great multitude, or did the contempt of families terrify me, that I kept silence, *and* went not out of the door?

35 Oh that one would hear me! behold, my desire *is, that* the Almighty would answer me, and *that* mine adversary had written a book.

36 Surely I would take it upon my shoulder, *and* bind it *as* a crown to me.

37 I would declare unto him the number of my steps; as a prince would I go near unto him.

38 If my land cry against me, or that the furrows likewise thereof complain;

39 If I have eaten the fruits thereof without money, or have caused the owners thereof to lose their life:

40 Let thistles grow instead of wheat, and cockle instead of barley. The words of Job are ended.

32 1 So these three men ceased to answer Job, because he *was* righteous in his own eyes.

NEW LIVING TRANSLATION

22 then let my shoulder be wrenched out of place!
Let my arm be torn from its socket!
23 That would be better than facing God's judgment.
For if the majesty of God opposes me, what hope is there?

24 "Have I put my trust in money
or felt secure because of my gold?
25 Have I gloated about my wealth
and all that I own?
26 "Have I looked at the sun shining in the skies,
or the moon walking down its silver pathway,
27 and been secretly enticed in my heart
to throw kisses at them in worship?
28 If so, I should be punished by the judges,
for it would mean I had denied the God of heaven.

29 "Have I ever rejoiced when disaster struck my enemies,
or become excited when harm came their way?
30 No, I have never sinned by cursing anyone
or by asking for revenge.

31 "My servants have never said,
'He let others go hungry.'
32 I have never turned away a stranger
but have opened my doors to everyone.

33 "Have I tried to hide my sins like other people do,
concealing my guilt in my heart?
34 Have I feared the crowd
or the contempt of the masses,
so that I kept quiet and stayed indoors?

35 "If only someone would listen to me!
Look, I will sign my name to my defense.
Let the Almighty answer me.
Let my accuser write out the charges against me.
36 I would face the accusation proudly.
I would wear it like a crown.
37 For I would tell him exactly what I have done.
I would come before him like a prince.

38 "If my land accuses me
and all its furrows cry out together,
39 or if I have stolen its crops
or murdered its owners,
40 then let thistles grow on that land instead of wheat,
and weeds instead of barley."

Job's words are ended.

Elihu Responds to Job's Friends

32 Job's three friends refused to reply further to him because he kept insisting on his innocence.

KING JAMES VERSION

2 Then was kindled the wrath of Elihu the son of Barachel the Buzite, of the kindred of Ram: against Job was his wrath kindled, because he justified himself rather than God.

3 Also against his three friends was his wrath kindled, because they had found no answer, and *yet* had condemned Job.

4 Now Elihu had waited till Job had spoken, because they *were* elder than he.

5 When Elihu saw that *there was* no answer in the mouth of *these* three men, then his wrath was kindled.

6 And Elihu the son of Barachel the Buzite answered and said, I *am* young, and ye *are* very old; wherefore I was afraid, and durst not shew you mine opinion.

7 I said, Days should speak, and multitude of years should teach wisdom.

8 But *there is* a spirit in man: and the inspiration of the Almighty giveth them understanding.

9 Great men are not *always* wise: neither do the aged understand judgment.

10 Therefore I said, Hearken to me; I also will shew mine opinion.

11 Behold, I waited for your words; I gave ear to your reasons, whilst ye searched out what to say.

12 Yea, I attended unto you, and, behold, *there was* none of you that convinced Job, *or* that answered his words:

13 Lest ye should say, We have found out wisdom: God thrusteth him down, not man.

14 Now he hath not directed *his* words against me: neither will I answer him with your speeches.

15 They were amazed, they answered no more: they left off speaking.

16 When I had waited, (for they spake not, but stood still, *and* answered no more;)

17 *I said,* I will answer also my part, I also will shew mine opinion.

18 For I am full of matter, the spirit within me constraineth me.

19 Behold, my belly *is* as wine *which* hath no vent; it is ready to burst like new bottles.

20 I will speak, that I may be refreshed: I will open my lips and answer.

21 Let me not, I pray you, accept any man's person, neither let me give flattering titles unto man.

22 For I know not to give flattering titles; *in so doing* my maker would soon take me away.

33 1 Wherefore, Job, I pray thee, hear my speeches, and hearken to all my words.

2 Behold, now I have opened my mouth, my tongue hath spoken in my mouth.

NEW LIVING TRANSLATION

2 Then Elihu son of Barakel the Buzite, of the clan
of Ram, became angry. He was angry because Job refused to admit that he had sinned and that God was
right in punishing him. 3 He was also angry with Job's
three friends, for they made God* appear to be
wrong by their inability to answer Job's arguments.
4 Elihu had waited for the others to speak to Job because they were older than he. 5 But when he saw that
they had no further reply, he spoke out angrily. 6 Elihu son of Barakel the Buzite said,

"I am young and you are old,
so I held back from telling you what I think.
7 I thought, 'Those who are older should speak,
for wisdom comes with age.'
8 But there is a spirit* within people,
the breath of the Almighty within them,
that makes them intelligent.
9 Sometimes the elders are not wise.
Sometimes the aged do not understand justice.
10 So listen to me,
and let me tell you what I think.

11 "I have waited all this time,
listening very carefully to your arguments,
listening to you grope for words.
12 I have listened,
but not one of you has refuted Job
or answered his arguments.
13 And don't tell me, 'He is too wise for us.
Only God can convince him.'
14 If Job had been arguing with me,
I would not answer with your kind of logic!
15 You sit there baffled,
with nothing more to say.
16 Should I continue to wait, now that you
are silent?
Must I also remain silent?
17 No, I will say my piece.
I will speak my mind.
18 For I am full of pent-up words,
and the spirit within me urges me on.
19 I am like a cask of wine without a vent,
like a new wineskin ready to burst!
20 I must speak to find relief,
so let me give my answers.
21 I won't play favorites
or try to flatter anyone.
22 For if I tried flattery,
my Creator would soon destroy me.

Elihu Presents His Case against Job

33 1 "Listen to my words, Job;
pay attention to what I have to say.
2 Now that I have begun to speak,
let me continue.

32:3 As in ancient Hebrew scribal tradition; the Masoretic Text reads *Job.* **32:8** Or *Spirit;* also in 32:18.

KING JAMES VERSION

3 My words *shall be of* the uprightness of my heart:
and my lips shall utter knowledge clearly.
4 The spirit of God hath made me, and the breath
of the Almighty hath given me life.
5 If thou canst answer me, set *thy words* in order
before me, stand up.
6 Behold, I *am* according to thy wish in God's stead:
I also am formed out of the clay.
7 Behold, my terror shall not make thee afraid, neither shall my hand be heavy upon thee.
8 Surely thou hast spoken in mine hearing, and I
have heard the voice of *thy* words, *saying*,
9 I am clean without transgression, I *am* innocent;
neither *is there* iniquity in me.
10 Behold, he findeth occasions against me, he
counteth me for his enemy,
11 He putteth my feet in the stocks, he marketh all
my paths.
12 Behold, *in* this thou art not just: I will answer
thee, that God is greater than man.
13 Why dost thou strive against him? for he giveth
not account of any of his matters.
14 For God speaketh once, yea twice, *yet man*
perceiveth it not.
15 In a dream, in a vision of the night, when deep
sleep falleth upon men, in slumberings upon the
bed;
16 Then he openeth the ears of men, and sealeth
their instruction,
17 That he may withdraw man *from his* purpose,
and hide pride from man.
18 He keepeth back his soul from the pit, and his
life from perishing by the sword.
19 He is chastened also with pain upon his bed, and
the multitude of his bones with strong *pain:*
20 So that his life abhorreth bread, and his soul
dainty meat.
21 His flesh is consumed away, that it cannot be
seen; and his bones *that* were not seen stick out.
22 Yea, his soul draweth near unto the grave, and
his life to the destroyers.
23 If there be a messenger with him, an interpreter,
one among a thousand, to shew unto man his uprightness:
24 Then he is gracious unto him, and saith, Deliver
him from going down to the pit: I have found a ransom.
25 His flesh shall be fresher than a child's: he shall
return to the days of his youth:
26 He shall pray unto God, and he will be favourable
unto him: and he shall see his face with joy: for he
will render unto man his righteousness.

NEW LIVING TRANSLATION

3 I speak with all sincerity;
I speak the truth.
4 For the Spirit of God has made me,
and the breath of the Almighty gives me life.
5 Answer me, if you can;
make your case and take your stand.
6 Look, you and I both belong to God.
I, too, was formed from clay.
7 So you don't need to be afraid of me.
I won't come down hard on you.
8 "You have spoken in my hearing,
and I have heard your very words.
9 You said, 'I am pure; I am without sin;
I am innocent; I have no guilt.
10 God is picking a quarrel with me,
and he considers me his enemy.
11 He puts my feet in the stocks
and watches my every move.'
12 "But you are wrong, and I will show you why.
For God is greater than any human being.
13 So why are you bringing a charge against him?
Why say he does not respond to people's
complaints?
14 For God speaks again and again,
though people do not recognize it.
15 He speaks in dreams, in visions of the night,
when deep sleep falls on people
as they lie in their beds.
16 He whispers in their ears
and terrifies them with warnings.
17 He makes them turn from doing wrong;
he keeps them from pride.
18 He protects them from the grave,
from crossing over the river of death.
19 "Or God disciplines people with pain on their
sickbeds,
with ceaseless aching in their bones.
20 They lose their appetite
for even the most delicious food.
21 Their flesh wastes away,
and their bones stick out.
22 They are at death's door;
the angels of death wait for them.
23 "But if an angel from heaven appears—
a special messenger to intercede for a person
and declare that he is upright—
24 he will be gracious and say,
'Rescue him from the grave,
for I have found a ransom for his life.'
25 Then his body will become as healthy as a child's,
firm and youthful again.
26 When he prays to God,
he will be accepted.
And God will receive him with joy
and restore him to good standing.

KING JAMES VERSION

27 He looketh upon men, and *if any* say, I have
sinned, and perverted *that which was* right, and it
profited me not;
28 He will deliver his soul from going into the pit,
and his life shall see the light.
29 Lo, all these *things* worketh God oftentimes with
man,
30 To bring back his soul from the pit, to be enlightened with the light of the living.
31 Mark well, O Job, hearken unto me: hold thy
peace, and I will speak.
32 If thou hast any thing to say, answer me: speak,
for I desire to justify thee.
33 If not, hearken unto me: hold thy peace, and I
shall teach thee wisdom.

34 1 Furthermore Elihu answered and said,
2 Hear my words, O ye wise *men;* and give
ear unto me, ye that have knowledge.
3 For the ear trieth words, as the mouth tasteth
meat.
4 Let us choose to us judgment: let us know among
ourselves what *is* good.
5 For Job hath said, I am righteous: and God hath
taken away my judgment.
6 Should I lie against my right? my wound *is* incurable without transgression.
7 What man *is* like Job, *who* drinketh up scorning
like water?
8 Which goeth in company with the workers of
iniquity, and walketh with wicked men.
9 For he hath said, It profiteth a man nothing that
he should delight himself with God.
10 Therefore hearken unto me, ye men of understanding: far be it from God, *that he should do* wickedness; and *from* the Almighty, *that he should
commit* iniquity.
11 For the work of a man shall he render unto him,
and cause every man to find according to *his* ways.
12 Yea, surely God will not do wickedly, neither will
the Almighty pervert judgment.
13 Who hath given him a charge over the earth?
or who hath disposed the whole world?
14 If he set his heart upon man, *if* he gather unto
himself his spirit and his breath;
15 All flesh shall perish together, and man shall
turn again unto dust.
16 If now *thou hast* understanding, hear this: hearken to the voice of my words.
17 Shall even he that hateth right govern? and wilt
thou condemn him that is most just?

NEW LIVING TRANSLATION

27 He will declare to his friends,
'I sinned and twisted the truth,
but it was not worth it.*
28 God rescued me from the grave,
and now my life is filled with light.'
29 "Yes, God does these things
again and again for people.
30 He rescues them from the grave
so they may enjoy the light of life.
31 Mark this well, Job. Listen to me,
for I have more to say.
32 But if you have anything to say, go ahead.
Speak, for I am anxious to see you justified.
33 But if not, then listen to me.
Keep silent and I will teach you wisdom!"

Elihu Accuses Job of Arrogance

34 Then Elihu said:
2 "Listen to me, you wise men.
Pay attention, you who have knowledge.
3 Job said, 'The ear tests the words it hears
just as the mouth distinguishes between
foods.'
4 So let us discern for ourselves what is right;
let us learn together what is good.
5 For Job also said, 'I am innocent,
but God has taken away my rights.
6 I am innocent, but they call me a liar.
My suffering is incurable, though I have
not sinned.'
7 "Tell me, has there ever been a man like Job,
with his thirst for irreverent talk?
8 He chooses evil people as companions.
He spends his time with wicked men.
9 He has even said, 'Why waste time
trying to please God?'
10 "Listen to me, you who have understanding.
Everyone knows that God doesn't sin!
The Almighty can do no wrong.
11 He repays people according to their deeds.
He treats people as they deserve.
12 Truly, God will not do wrong.
The Almighty will not twist justice.
13 Did someone else put the world in his care?
Who set the whole world in place?
14 If God were to take back his spirit
and withdraw his breath,
15 all life would cease,
and humanity would turn again to dust.
16 "Now listen to me if you are wise.
Pay attention to what I say.
17 Could God govern if he hated justice?
Are you going to condemn the almighty judge?

33:27 Greek version reads *but he* [God] *did not punish me as my sin deserved.*

KING JAMES VERSION

18 *Is it fit* to say to a king, *Thou art* wicked? *and* to
princes, *Ye are* ungodly?
19 *How much less to him* that accepteth not the
persons of princes, nor regardeth the rich more than
the poor? for they all *are* the work of his hands.
20 In a moment shall they die, and the people shall
be troubled at midnight, and pass away: and the
mighty shall be taken away without hand.
21 For his eyes *are* upon the ways of man, and he
seeth all his goings.
22 *There is* no darkness, nor shadow of death,
where the workers of iniquity may hide themselves.
23 For he will not lay upon man more *than right;*
that he should enter into judgment with God.
24 He shall break in pieces mighty men without
number, and set others in their stead.
25 Therefore he knoweth their works, and he
overturneth *them* in the night, so that they are
destroyed.
26 He striketh them as wicked men in the open
sight of others;
27 Because they turned back from him, and would
not consider any of his ways:
28 So that they cause the cry of the poor to come
unto him, and he heareth the cry of the afflicted.
29 When he giveth quietness, who then can make
trouble? and when he hideth *his* face, who then can
behold him? whether *it be done* against a nation, or
against a man only:
30 That the hypocrite reign not, lest the people be
ensnared.
31 Surely it is meet to be said unto God, I have
borne *chastisement,* I will not offend *any more:*
32 *That which* I see not teach thou me: if I have
done iniquity, I will do no more.
33 *Should it be* according to thy mind? he will recompense it, whether thou refuse, or whether thou
choose; and not I: therefore speak what thou
knowest.
34 Let men of understanding tell me, and let a wise
man hearken unto me.
35 Job hath spoken without knowledge, and his
words *were* without wisdom.
36 My desire *is that* Job may be tried unto the end
because of *his* answers for wicked men.
37 For he addeth rebellion unto his sin, he clappeth
his hands among us, and multiplieth his words
against God.

35 1 Elihu spake moreover, and said,
2 Thinkest thou this to be right, *that* thou
saidst, My righteousness *is* more than God's?

NEW LIVING TRANSLATION

18 For he says to kings, 'You are wicked,'
and to nobles, 'You are unjust.'
19 He doesn't care how great a person may be,
and he pays no more attention to the rich
than to the poor.
He made them all.
20 In a moment they die.
In the middle of the night they pass away;
the mighty are removed without human hand.

21 "For God watches how people live;
he sees everything they do.
22 No darkness is thick enough
to hide the wicked from his eyes.
23 We don't set the time
when we will come before God in judgment.
24 He brings the mighty to ruin without asking
anyone,
and he sets up others in their place.
25 He knows what they do,
and in the night he overturns and destroys
them.
26 He strikes them down because they are wicked,
doing it openly for all to see.
27 For they turned away from following him.
They have no respect for any of his ways.
28 They cause the poor to cry out, catching
God's attention.
He hears the cries of the needy.
29 But if he chooses to remain quiet,
who can criticize him?
When he hides his face, no one can find him,
whether an individual or a nation.
30 He prevents the godless from ruling
so they cannot be a snare to the people.

31 "Why don't people say to God, 'I have sinned,
but I will sin no more'?
32 Or 'I don't know what evil I have done—tell me.
If I have done wrong, I will stop at once'?
33 "Must God tailor his justice to your demands?
But you have rejected him!
The choice is yours, not mine.
Go ahead, share your wisdom with us.
34 After all, bright people will tell me,
and wise people will hear me say,
35 'Job speaks out of ignorance;
his words lack insight.'
36 Job, you deserve the maximum penalty
for the wicked way you have talked.
37 For you have added rebellion to your sin;
you show no respect,
and you speak many angry words against God."

Elihu Reminds Job of God's Justice

35 Then Elihu said:
2 "Do you think it is right for you to claim,
'I am righteous before God'?

KING JAMES VERSION

3 For thou saidst, What advantage will it be unto thee? *and,* What profit shall I have, *if I be cleansed* from my sin?

4 I will answer thee, and thy companions with thee.

5 Look unto the heavens, and see; and behold the clouds *which* are higher than thou.

6 If thou sinnest, what doest thou against him? or *if* thy transgressions be multiplied, what doest thou unto him?

7 If thou be righteous, what givest thou him? or what receiveth he of thine hand?

8 Thy wickedness *may hurt* a man as thou *art;* and thy righteousness *may profit* the son of man.

9 By reason of the multitude of oppressions they make *the oppressed* to cry: they cry out by reason of the arm of the mighty.

10 But none saith, Where *is* God my maker, who giveth songs in the night;

11 Who teacheth us more than the beasts of the earth, and maketh us wiser than the fowls of heaven?

12 There they cry, but none giveth answer, because of the pride of evil men.

13 Surely God will not hear vanity, neither will the Almighty regard it.

14 Although thou sayest thou shalt not see him, *yet* judgment *is* before him; therefore trust thou in him.

15 But now, because *it is* not *so,* he hath visited in his anger; yet he knoweth *it* not in great extremity:

16 Therefore doth Job open his mouth in vain; he multiplieth words without knowledge.

36

1 Elihu also proceeded, and said,

2 Suffer me a little, and I will shew thee that *I have* yet to speak on God's behalf.

3 I will fetch my knowledge from afar, and will ascribe righteousness to my Maker.

4 For truly my words *shall* not *be* false: he that is perfect in knowledge *is* with thee.

5 Behold, God *is* mighty, and despiseth not *any: he is* mighty in strength *and* wisdom.

6 He preserveth not the life of the wicked: but giveth right to the poor.

7 He withdraweth not his eyes from the righteous: but with kings *are they* on the throne; yea, he doth establish them for ever, and they are exalted.

8 And if *they be* bound in fetters, *and* be holden in cords of affliction;

NEW LIVING TRANSLATION

3 For you also ask, 'What's in it for me?
What's the use of living a righteous life?'
4 "I will answer you
and all your friends, too.
5 Look up into the sky,
and see the clouds high above you.
6 If you sin, how does that affect God?
Even if you sin again and again,
what effect will it have on him?
7 If you are good, is this some great gift to him?
What could you possibly give him?
8 No, your sins affect only people like yourself,
and your good deeds also affect only humans.

9 "People cry out when they are oppressed.
They groan beneath the power of the mighty.
10 Yet they don't ask, 'Where is God my Creator,
the one who gives songs in the night?
11 Where is the one who makes us smarter than
the animals
and wiser than the birds of the sky?'
12 And when they cry out, God does not answer
because of their pride.
13 But it is wrong to say God doesn't listen,
to say the Almighty isn't concerned.
14 You say you can't see him,
but he will bring justice if you will only wait.*
15 You say he does not respond to sinners
with anger
and is not greatly concerned about
wickedness.*
16 But you are talking nonsense, Job.
You have spoken like a fool."

36

Elihu continued speaking:

2 "Let me go on, and I will show you the
truth.
For I have not finished defending God!
3 I will present profound arguments
for the righteousness of my Creator.
4 I am telling you nothing but the truth,
for I am a man of great knowledge.

5 "God is mighty, but he does not despise anyone!
He is mighty in both power and
understanding.
6 He does not let the wicked live
but gives justice to the afflicted.
7 He never takes his eyes off the innocent,
but he sets them on thrones with kings
and exalts them forever.
8 If they are bound in chains
and caught up in a web of trouble,

35:13-14 These verses can also be translated as follows: [13]*Indeed, God doesn't listen to their empty plea; / the Almighty is not concerned. /* [14]*How much less will he listen when you say you don't see him, / and that your case is before him and you're waiting for justice.* **35:15** As in Greek and Latin versions; the meaning of this Hebrew word is uncertain.

KING JAMES VERSION

9 Then he sheweth them their work, and their
transgressions that they have exceeded.
10 He openeth also their ear to discipline, and commandeth that they return from iniquity.
11 If they obey and serve *him*, they shall spend
their days in prosperity, and their years in pleasures.
12 But if they obey not, they shall perish by the
sword, and they shall die without knowledge.
13 But the hypocrites in heart heap up wrath: they
cry not when he bindeth them.
14 They die in youth, and their life *is* among the
unclean.
15 He delivereth the poor in his affliction, and
openeth their ears in oppression.
16 Even so would he have removed thee out of the
strait *into* a broad place, where *there is* no straitness;
and that which should be set on thy table *should be*
full of fatness.
17 But thou hast fulfilled the judgment of the
wicked: judgment and justice take hold *on thee*.
18 Because *there is* wrath, *beware* lest he take thee
away with *his* stroke: then a great ransom cannot deliver thee.
19 Will he esteem thy riches? *no*, not gold, nor all
the forces of strength.
20 Desire not the night, when people are cut off in
their place.
21 Take heed, regard not iniquity: for this hast thou
chosen rather than affliction.

22 Behold, God exalteth by his power: who
teacheth like him?
23 Who hath enjoined him his way? or who can say,
Thou hast wrought iniquity?
24 Remember that thou magnify his work, which
men behold.
25 Every man may see it; man may behold *it*
afar off.
26 Behold, God *is* great, and we know *him* not, neither can the number of his years be searched out.
27 For he maketh small the drops of water: they
pour down rain according to the vapour thereof:
28 Which the clouds do drop *and* distil upon man
abundantly.
29 Also can *any* understand the spreadings of the
clouds, *or* the noise of his tabernacle?

NEW LIVING TRANSLATION

9 he shows them the reason.
He shows them their sins of pride.
10 He gets their attention
and commands that they turn from evil.
11 "If they listen and obey God,
they will be blessed with prosperity
throughout their lives.
All their years will be pleasant.
12 But if they refuse to listen to him,
they will be killed by the sword*
and die from lack of understanding.
13 For the godless are full of resentment.
Even when he punishes them,
they refuse to cry out to him for help.
14 They die when they are young,
after wasting their lives in immoral living.
15 But by means of their suffering, he rescues
those who suffer.
For he gets their attention through adversity.
16 "God is leading you away from danger, Job,
to a place free from distress.
He is setting your table with the best food.
17 But you are obsessed with whether the godless
will be judged.
Don't worry, judgment and justice will be
upheld.
18 But watch out, or you may be seduced by wealth.*
Don't let yourself be bribed into sin.
19 Could all your wealth*
or all your mighty efforts
keep you from distress?
20 Do not long for the cover of night,
for that is when people will be destroyed.*
21 Be on guard! Turn back from evil,
for God sent this suffering
to keep you from a life of evil.

Elihu Reminds Job of God's Power

22 "Look, God is all-powerful.
Who is a teacher like him?
23 No one can tell him what to do,
or say to him, 'You have done wrong.'
24 Instead, glorify his mighty works,
singing songs of praise.
25 Everyone has seen these things,
though only from a distance.
26 "Look, God is greater than we can understand.
His years cannot be counted.
27 He draws up the water vapor
and then distills it into rain.
28 The rain pours down from the clouds,
and everyone benefits.
29 Who can understand the spreading of the clouds
and the thunder that rolls forth from heaven?

36:12 Or *they will cross the river* [of death]. **36:18** Or *But don't let your anger lead you to mockery.* **36:19** Or *Could all your cries for help.* **36:16-20** The meaning of the Hebrew in this passage is uncertain.

KING JAMES VERSION

30 Behold, he spreadeth his light upon it, and
covereth the bottom of the sea.
31 For by them judgeth he the people; he giveth
meat in abundance.
32 With clouds he covereth the light; and commandeth it *not to shine* by *the cloud* that cometh
betwixt.
33 The noise thereof sheweth concerning it, the
cattle also concerning the vapour.

37 1 At this also my heart trembleth, and is
moved out of his place.
2 Hear attentively the noise of his voice, and the
sound *that* goeth out of his mouth.
3 He directeth it under the whole heaven, and his
lightning unto the ends of the earth.
4 After it a voice roareth: he thundereth with the
voice of his excellency; and he will not stay them
when his voice is heard.
5 God thundereth marvellously with his voice;
great things doeth he, which we cannot comprehend.
6 For he saith to the snow, Be thou *on* the earth;
likewise to the small rain, and to the great rain of his
strength.
7 He sealeth up the hand of every man; that all men
may know his work.
8 Then the beasts go into dens, and remain in their
places.
9 Out of the south cometh the whirlwind: and cold
out of the north.
10 By the breath of God frost is given: and the
breadth of the waters is straitened.
11 Also by watering he wearieth the thick cloud: he
scattereth his bright cloud:
12 And it is turned round about by his counsels:
that they may do whatsoever he commandeth them
upon the face of the world in the earth.
13 He causeth it to come, whether for correction, or
for his land, or for mercy.
14 Hearken unto this, O Job: stand still, and consider the wondrous works of God.
15 Dost thou know when God disposed them,
and caused the light of his cloud to shine?
16 Dost thou know the balancings of the clouds,
the wondrous works of him which is perfect in
knowledge?
17 How thy garments *are* warm, when he quieteth
the earth by the south *wind*?
18 Hast thou with him spread out the sky, *which is*
strong, *and* as a molten looking glass?

NEW LIVING TRANSLATION

30 See how he spreads the lightning around him
and how it lights up the depths of the sea.
31 By these mighty acts he nourishes* the people,
giving them food in abundance.
32 He fills his hands with lightning bolts
and hurls each at its target.
33 The thunder announces his presence;
the storm announces his indignant anger.*

37 1 "My heart pounds as I think of this.
It trembles within me.
2 Listen carefully to the thunder of God's voice
as it rolls from his mouth.
3 It rolls across the heavens,
and his lightning flashes in every direction.
4 Then comes the roaring of the thunder—
the tremendous voice of his majesty.
He does not restrain it when he speaks.
5 God's voice is glorious in the thunder.
We can't even imagine the greatness
of his power.

6 "He directs the snow to fall on the earth
and tells the rain to pour down.
7 Then everyone stops working
so they can watch his power.
8 The wild animals take cover
and stay inside their dens.
9 The stormy wind comes from its chamber,
and the driving winds bring the cold.
10 God's breath sends the ice,
freezing wide expanses of water.
11 He loads the clouds with moisture,
and they flash with his lightning.
12 The clouds churn about at his direction.
They do whatever he commands throughout
the earth.
13 He makes these things happen either to
punish people
or to show his unfailing love.

14 "Pay attention to this, Job.
Stop and consider the wonderful miracles
of God!
15 Do you know how God controls the storm
and causes the lightning to flash from
his clouds?
16 Do you understand how he moves the clouds
with wonderful perfection and skill?
17 When you are sweltering in your clothes
and the south wind dies down and everything
is still,
18 he makes the skies reflect the heat like
a bronze mirror.
Can you do that?

36:31 Or *he governs.* **36:33** Or *even the cattle know when a storm is coming.* The meaning of the Hebrew is uncertain.

KING JAMES VERSION

19 Teach us what we shall say unto him; *for* we cannot order *our speech* by reason of darkness.
20 Shall it be told him that I speak? if a man speak,
surely he shall be swallowed up.
21 And now *men* see not the bright light which *is*
in the clouds: but the wind passeth, and cleanseth
them.
22 Fair weather cometh out of the north: with God
is terrible majesty.
23 *Touching* the Almighty, we cannot find him out:
he is excellent in power, and in judgment, and in
plenty of justice: he will not afflict.
24 Men do therefore fear him: he respecteth not
any *that are* wise of heart.

38 1 Then the LORD answered Job out of the
whirlwind, and said,
2 Who *is* this that darkeneth counsel by words
without knowledge?
3 Gird up now thy loins like a man; for I will demand of thee, and answer thou me.
4 Where wast thou when I laid the foundations of
the earth? declare, if thou hast understanding.
5 Who hath laid the measures thereof, if thou
knowest? or who hath stretched the line upon it?
6 Whereupon are the foundations thereof fastened? or who laid the corner stone thereof;
7 When the morning stars sang together, and all
the sons of God shouted for joy?
8 Or *who* shut up the sea with doors, when it brake
forth, *as if* it had issued out of the womb?
9 When I made the cloud the garment thereof, and
thick darkness a swaddlingband for it,
10 And brake up for it my decreed *place*, and set
bars and doors,
11 And said, Hitherto shalt thou come, but no further: and here shall thy proud waves be stayed?
12 Hast thou commanded the morning since thy
days; *and* caused the dayspring to know his place;
13 That it might take hold of the ends of the earth,
that the wicked might be shaken out of it?
14 It is turned as clay *to* the seal; and they stand as a
garment.

NEW LIVING TRANSLATION

19 "So teach the rest of us what to say to God.
We are too ignorant to make our own
arguments.
20 Should God be notified that I want to speak?
Can people even speak when they are
confused?*
21 We cannot look at the sun,
for it shines brightly in the sky
when the wind clears away the clouds.
22 So also, golden splendor comes from the
mountain of God.*
He is clothed in dazzling splendor.
23 We cannot imagine the power of the Almighty;
but even though he is just and righteous,
he does not destroy us.
24 No wonder people everywhere fear him.
All who are wise show him reverence."

The LORD Challenges Job

38 Then the LORD answered Job from the
whirlwind:

2 "Who is this that questions my wisdom
with such ignorant words?
3 Brace yourself like a man,
because I have some questions for you,
and you must answer them.

4 "Where were you when I laid the foundations
of the earth?
Tell me, if you know so much.
5 Who determined its dimensions
and stretched out the surveying line?
6 What supports its foundations,
and who laid its cornerstone
7 as the morning stars sang together
and all the angels* shouted for joy?

8 "Who kept the sea inside its boundaries
as it burst from the womb,
9 and as I clothed it with clouds
and wrapped it in thick darkness?
10 For I locked it behind barred gates,
limiting its shores.
11 I said, 'This far and no farther will you come.
Here your proud waves must stop!'

12 "Have you ever commanded the morning
to appear
and caused the dawn to rise in the east?
13 Have you made daylight spread to the ends
of the earth,
to bring an end to the night's wickedness?
14 As the light approaches,
the earth takes shape like clay pressed
beneath a seal;
it is robed in brilliant colors.*

37:20 Or *speak without being swallowed up?* 37:22 Or *from the north;* or *from the abode.* 38:7 Hebrew *the sons of God.* 38:14 Or *its features stand out like folds in a robe.*

KING JAMES VERSION

15 And from the wicked their light is withholden,
and the high arm shall be broken.
16 Hast thou entered into the springs of the sea? or
hast thou walked in the search of the depth?
17 Have the gates of death been opened unto thee?
or hast thou seen the doors of the shadow of death?
18 Hast thou perceived the breadth of the earth?
declare if thou knowest it all.
19 Where *is* the way *where* light dwelleth? and *as*
for darkness, where *is* the place thereof,
20 That thou shouldest take it to the bound thereof,
and that thou shouldest know the paths *to* the house
thereof?
21 Knowest thou *it,* because thou wast then born?
or *because* the number of thy days *is* great?
22 Hast thou entered into the treasures of the
snow? or hast thou seen the treasures of the hail,
23 Which I have reserved against the time of
trouble, against the day of battle and war?
24 By what way is the light parted, *which* scattereth
the east wind upon the earth?
25 Who hath divided a watercourse for the overflowing of waters, or a way for the lightning of
thunder;
26 To cause it to rain on the earth, *where* no man *is;*
on the wilderness, wherein *there is* no man;
27 To satisfy the desolate and waste *ground;* and
to cause the bud of the tender herb to spring forth?
28 Hath the rain a father? or who hath begotten the
drops of dew?
29 Out of whose womb came the ice? and the hoary
frost of heaven, who hath gendered it?
30 The waters are hid as *with* a stone, and the face
of the deep is frozen.
31 Canst thou bind the sweet influences of Pleiades, or loose the bands of Orion?
32 Canst thou bring forth Mazzaroth in his season?
or canst thou guide Arcturus with his sons?
33 Knowest thou the ordinances of heaven? canst
thou set the dominion thereof in the earth?
34 Canst thou lift up thy voice to the clouds, that
abundance of waters may cover thee?
35 Canst thou send lightnings, that they may go,
and say unto thee, Here we *are?*
36 Who hath put wisdom in the inward parts? or
who hath given understanding to the heart?
37 Who can number the clouds in wisdom? or who
can stay the bottles of heaven,
38 When the dust groweth into hardness, and the
clods cleave fast together?

NEW LIVING TRANSLATION

15 The light disturbs the wicked
and stops the arm that is raised in violence.
16 "Have you explored the springs from which
the seas come?
Have you explored their depths?
17 Do you know where the gates of death are
located?
Have you seen the gates of utter gloom?
18 Do you realize the extent of the earth?
Tell me about it if you know!
19 "Where does light come from,
and where does darkness go?
20 Can you take each to its home?
Do you know how to get there?
21 But of course you know all this!
For you were born before it was all created,
and you are so very experienced!
22 "Have you visited the storehouses of the snow
or seen the storehouses of hail?
23 (I have reserved them as weapons for the time
of trouble,
for the day of battle and war.)
24 Where is the path to the source of light?
Where is the home of the east wind?
25 "Who created a channel for the torrents of rain?
Who laid out the path for the lightning?
26 Who makes the rain fall on barren land,
in a desert where no one lives?
27 Who sends rain to satisfy the parched ground
and make the tender grass spring up?
28 "Does the rain have a father?
Who gives birth to the dew?
29 Who is the mother of the ice?
Who gives birth to the frost from the heavens?
30 For the water turns to ice as hard as rock,
and the surface of the water freezes.
31 "Can you direct the movement of the stars—
binding the cluster of the Pleiades
or loosening the cords of Orion?
32 Can you direct the sequence of the seasons
or guide the Bear with her cubs across the
heavens?
33 Do you know the laws of the universe?
Can you use them to regulate the earth?
34 "Can you shout to the clouds
and make it rain?
35 Can you make lightning appear
and cause it to strike as you direct?
36 Who gives intuition to the heart
and instinct to the mind?
37 Who is wise enough to count all the clouds?
Who can tilt the water jars of heaven
38 when the parched ground is dry
and the soil has hardened into clods?

KING JAMES VERSION

39 Wilt thou hunt the prey for the lion? or fill the
appetite of the young lions,
40 When they couch in *their* dens, *and* abide in the
covert to lie in wait?
41 Who provideth for the raven his food? when his
young ones cry unto God, they wander for lack of
meat.

39 1 Knowest thou the time when the wild goats
of the rock bring forth? *or* canst thou mark
when the hinds do calve?
2 Canst thou number the months *that* they fulfil?
or knowest thou the time when they bring forth?
3 They bow themselves, they bring forth their
young ones, they cast out their sorrows.
4 Their young ones are in good liking, they grow up
with corn; they go forth, and return not unto them.
5 Who hath sent out the wild ass free? or who hath
loosed the bands of the wild ass?
6 Whose house I have made the wilderness, and
the barren land his dwellings.
7 He scorneth the multitude of the city, neither
regardeth he the crying of the driver.
8 The range of the mountains *is* his pasture, and he
searcheth after every green thing.
9 Will the unicorn be willing to serve thee, or abide
by thy crib?
10 Canst thou bind the unicorn with his band in the
furrow? or will he harrow the valleys after thee?
11 Wilt thou trust him, because his strength *is*
great? or wilt thou leave thy labour to him?
12 Wilt thou believe him, that he will bring home
thy seed, and gather *it into* thy barn?
13 *Gavest thou* the goodly wings unto the peacocks? or wings and feathers unto the ostrich?
14 Which leaveth her eggs in the earth, and
warmeth them in dust,
15 And forgetteth that the foot may crush them, or
that the wild beast may break them.
16 She is hardened against her young ones, as
though *they were* not hers: her labour is in vain without fear;
17 Because God hath deprived her of wisdom, neither hath he imparted to her understanding.
18 What time she lifteth up herself on high, she
scorneth the horse and his rider.
19 Hast thou given the horse strength? hast thou
clothed his neck with thunder?
20 Canst thou make him afraid as a grasshopper?
the glory of his nostrils *is* terrible.
21 He paweth in the valley, and rejoiceth in *his*
strength: he goeth on to meet the armed men.

NEW LIVING TRANSLATION

39 "Can you stalk prey for a lioness
and satisfy the young lions' appetites
40 as they lie in their dens
or crouch in the thicket?
41 Who provides food for the ravens
when their young cry out to God
and wander about in hunger?

The LORD's Challenge Continues

39 1 "Do you know when the wild goats
give birth?
Have you watched as deer are born in the wild?
2 Do you know how many months they carry
their young?
Are you aware of the time of their delivery?
3 They crouch down to give birth to their young
and deliver their offspring.
4 Their young grow up in the open fields,
then leave home and never return.

5 "Who gives the wild donkey its freedom?
Who untied its ropes?
6 I have placed it in the wilderness;
its home is the wasteland.
7 It hates the noise of the city
and has no driver to shout at it.
8 The mountains are its pastureland,
where it searches for every blade of grass.

9 "Will the wild ox consent to being tamed?
Will it spend the night in your stall?
10 Can you hitch a wild ox to a plow?
Will it plow a field for you?
11 Given its strength, can you trust it?
Can you leave and trust the ox to do
your work?
12 Can you rely on it to bring home your grain
and deliver it to your threshing floor?

13 "The ostrich flaps her wings grandly,
but they are no match for the feathers
of the stork.
14 She lays her eggs on top of the earth,
letting them be warmed in the dust.
15 She doesn't worry that a foot might crush them
or a wild animal might destroy them.
16 She is harsh toward her young,
as if they were not her own.
She doesn't care if they die.
17 For God has deprived her of wisdom.
He has given her no understanding.
18 But whenever she jumps up to run,
she passes the swiftest horse with its rider.

19 "Have you given the horse its strength
or clothed its neck with a flowing mane?
20 Did you give it the ability to leap like a locust?
Its majestic snorting is terrifying!
21 It paws the earth and rejoices in its strength
when it charges out to battle.

KING JAMES VERSION

22 He mocketh at fear, and is not affrighted; neither turneth he back from the sword.
23 The quiver rattleth against him, the glittering
spear and the shield.
24 He swalloweth the ground with fierceness and
rage: neither believeth he that *it is* the sound of the
trumpet.
25 He saith among the trumpets, Ha, ha; and he
smelleth the battle afar off, the thunder of the captains, and the shouting.
26 Doth the hawk fly by thy wisdom, *and* stretch
her wings toward the south?
27 Doth the eagle mount up at thy command, and
make her nest on high?
28 She dwelleth and abideth on the rock, upon the
crag of the rock, and the strong place.
29 From thence she seeketh the prey, *and* her eyes
behold afar off.
30 Her young ones also suck up blood: and where
the slain *are*, there *is* she.

40

1 Moreover the LORD answered Job, and
said,
2 Shall he that contendeth with the Almighty instruct *him?* he that reproveth God, let him answer it.

3 Then Job answered the LORD, and said,
4 Behold, I am vile; what shall I answer thee? I will
lay mine hand upon my mouth.
5 Once have I spoken; but I will not answer: yea,
twice; but I will proceed no further.

6 Then answered the LORD unto Job out of the
whirlwind, and said,
7 Gird up thy loins now like a man: I will demand of
thee, and declare thou unto me.
8 Wilt thou also disannul my judgment? wilt thou
condemn me, that thou mayest be righteous?
9 Hast thou an arm like God? or canst thou thunder
with a voice like him?
10 Deck thyself now *with* majesty and excellency;
and array thyself with glory and beauty.
11 Cast abroad the rage of thy wrath: and behold
every one *that is* proud, and abase him.
12 Look on every one *that is* proud, *and* bring him
low; and tread down the wicked in their place.
13 Hide them in the dust together; *and* bind their
faces in secret.
14 Then will I also confess unto thee that thine own
right hand can save thee.

NEW LIVING TRANSLATION

22 It laughs at fear and is unafraid.
It does not run from the sword.
23 The arrows rattle against it,
and the spear and javelin flash.
24 It paws the ground fiercely
and rushes forward into battle when the ram's
horn blows.
25 It snorts at the sound of the horn.
It senses the battle in the distance.
It quivers at the captain's commands and the
noise of battle.

26 "Is it your wisdom that makes the hawk soar
and spread its wings toward the south?
27 Is it at your command that the eagle rises
to the heights to make its nest?
28 It lives on the cliffs,
making its home on a distant, rocky crag.
29 From there it hunts its prey,
keeping watch with piercing eyes.
30 Its young gulp down blood.
Where there's a carcass, there you'll find it."

40

Then the LORD said to Job,

2 "Do you still want to argue with
the Almighty?
You are God's critic, but do you have
the answers?"

Job Responds to the LORD

3 Then Job replied to the LORD,

4 "I am nothing—how could I ever find
the answers?
I will cover my mouth with my hand.
5 I have said too much already.
I have nothing more to say."

The LORD Challenges Job Again

6 Then the LORD answered Job from the whirlwind:

7 "Brace yourself like a man,
because I have some questions for you,
and you must answer them.

8 "Will you discredit my justice
and condemn me just to prove you are right?
9 Are you as strong as God?
Can you thunder with a voice like his?
10 All right, put on your glory and splendor,
your honor and majesty.
11 Give vent to your anger.
Let it overflow against the proud.
12 Humiliate the proud with a glance;
walk on the wicked where they stand.
13 Bury them in the dust.
Imprison them in the world of the dead.
14 Then even I would praise you,
for your own strength would save you.

KING JAMES VERSION

15 Behold now behemoth, which I made with thee;
he eateth grass as an ox.
16 Lo now, his strength *is* in his loins, and his force
is in the navel of his belly.
17 He moveth his tail like a cedar: the sinews of his
stones are wrapped together.
18 His bones *are as* strong pieces of brass; his
bones *are* like bars of iron.
19 He *is* the chief of the ways of God: he that made
him can make his sword to approach *unto him.*
20 Surely the mountains bring him forth food,
where all the beasts of the field play.
21 He lieth under the shady trees, in the covert of
the reed, and fens.
22 The shady trees cover him *with* their shadow;
the willows of the brook compass him about.
23 Behold, he drinketh up a river, *and* hasteth not:
he trusteth that he can draw up Jordan into his
mouth.
24 He taketh it with his eyes: *his* nose pierceth
through snares.

41 1 Canst thou draw out leviathan with an
hook? or his tongue with a cord *which* thou
lettest down?
2 Canst thou put an hook into his nose? or bore his
jaw through with a thorn?
3 Will he make many supplications unto thee? will
he speak soft *words* unto thee?
4 Will he make a covenant with thee? wilt thou
take him for a servant for ever?
5 Wilt thou play with him as *with* a bird? or wilt
thou bind him for thy maidens?
6 Shall the companions make a banquet of him?
shall they part him among the merchants?
7 Canst thou fill his skin with barbed irons? or his
head with fish spears?
8 Lay thine hand upon him, remember the battle,
do no more.
9 Behold, the hope of him is in vain: shall not *one*
be cast down even at the sight of him?
10 None *is so* fierce that dare stir him up: who then
is able to stand before me?
11 Who hath prevented me, that I should repay
him? whatsoever is under the whole heaven is mine.
12 I will not conceal his parts, nor his power, nor his
comely proportion.

NEW LIVING TRANSLATION

15 "Take a look at Behemoth,*
which I made, just as I made you.
It eats grass like an ox.
16 See its powerful loins
and the muscles of its belly.
17 Its tail is as strong as a cedar.
The sinews of its thighs are knit tightly
together.
18 Its bones are tubes of bronze.
Its limbs are bars of iron.
19 It is a prime example of God's handiwork,
and only its Creator can threaten it.
20 The mountains offer it their best food,
where all the wild animals play.
21 It lies under the lotus plants,*
hidden by the reeds in the marsh.
22 The lotus plants give it shade
among the willows beside the stream.
23 It is not disturbed by the raging river,
not concerned when the swelling Jordan
rushes around it.
24 No one can catch it off guard
or put a ring in its nose and lead it away.

The LORD*'s Challenge Continues*

41 1 *"Can you catch Leviathan* with a hook
or put a noose around its jaw?
2 Can you tie it with a rope through the nose
or pierce its jaw with a spike?
3 Will it beg you for mercy
or implore you for pity?
4 Will it agree to work for you,
to be your slave for life?
5 Can you make it a pet like a bird,
or give it to your little girls to play with?
6 Will merchants try to buy it
to sell it in their shops?
7 Will its hide be hurt by spears
or its head by a harpoon?
8 If you lay a hand on it,
you will certainly remember the battle
that follows.
You won't try that again!
9* No, it is useless to try to capture it.
The hunter who attempts it will be
knocked down.
10 And since no one dares to disturb it,
who then can stand up to me?
11 Who has given me anything that I need
to pay back?
Everything under heaven is mine.
12 "I want to emphasize Leviathan's limbs
and its enormous strength and graceful form.

40:15 The identification of Behemoth is disputed, ranging from an earthly creature to a mythical sea monster in ancient literature. **40:21** Or *bramble bushes;* also in 40:22. **41:1a** Verses 41:1-8 are numbered 40:25-32 in Hebrew text. **41:1b** The identification of Leviathan is disputed, ranging from an earthly creature to a mythical sea monster in ancient literature. **41:9** Verses 41:9-34 are numbered 41:1-26 in Hebrew text.

KING JAMES VERSION

13 Who can discover the face of his garment? *or* who can come *to him* with his double bridle?

14 Who can open the doors of his face? his teeth *are* terrible round about.

15 *His* scales *are his* pride, shut up together *as with* a close seal.

16 One is so near to another, that no air can come between them.

17 They are joined one to another, they stick together, that they cannot be sundered.

18 By his neesings a light doth shine, and his eyes *are* like the eyelids of the morning.

19 Out of his mouth go burning lamps, *and* sparks of fire leap out.

20 Out of his nostrils goeth smoke, as *out* of a seething pot or caldron.

21 His breath kindleth coals, and a flame goeth out of his mouth.

22 In his neck remaineth strength, and sorrow is turned into joy before him.

23 The flakes of his flesh are joined together: they are firm in themselves; they cannot be moved.

24 His heart is as firm as a stone; yea, as hard as a piece of the nether *millstone*.

25 When he raiseth up himself, the mighty are afraid: by reason of breakings they purify themselves.

26 The sword of him that layeth at him cannot hold: the spear, the dart, nor the habergeon.

27 He esteemeth iron as straw, *and* brass as rotten wood.

28 The arrow cannot make him flee: slingstones are turned with him into stubble.

29 Darts are counted as stubble: he laugheth at the shaking of a spear.

30 Sharp stones *are* under him: he spreadeth sharp pointed things upon the mire.

31 He maketh the deep to boil like a pot: he maketh the sea like a pot of ointment.

32 He maketh a path to shine after him; *one* would think the deep *to be* hoary.

33 Upon earth there is not his like, who is made without fear.

34 He beholdeth all high *things:* he *is* a king over all the children of pride.

42 1 Then Job answered the LORD, and said,

2 I know that thou canst do every *thing,* and *that* no thought can be withholden from thee.

3 Who *is* he that hideth counsel without knowledge?

NEW LIVING TRANSLATION

13 Who can strip off its hide,
and who can penetrate its double layer
of armor?*
14 Who could pry open its jaws?
For its teeth are terrible!
15 Its scales are like rows of shields
tightly sealed together.
16 They are so close together
that no air can get between them.
17 Each scale sticks tight to the next.
They interlock and cannot be penetrated.

18 "When it sneezes, it flashes light!
Its eyes are like the red of dawn.
19 Lightning leaps from its mouth;
flames of fire flash out.
20 Smoke streams from its nostrils
like steam from a pot heated over
burning rushes.
21 Its breath would kindle coals,
for flames shoot from its mouth.
22 "The tremendous strength in Leviathan's neck
strikes terror wherever it goes.
23 Its flesh is hard and firm
and cannot be penetrated.
24 Its heart is hard as rock,
hard as a millstone.
25 When it rises, the mighty are afraid,
gripped by terror.
26 No sword can stop it,
no spear, dart, or javelin.
27 Iron is nothing but straw to that creature,
and bronze is like rotten wood.
28 Arrows cannot make it flee.
Stones shot from a sling are like bits of grass.
29 Clubs are like a blade of grass,
and it laughs at the swish of javelins.
30 Its belly is covered with scales as sharp as glass.
It plows up the ground as it drags through
the mud.

31 "Leviathan makes the water boil with its
commotion.
It stirs the depths like a pot of ointment.
32 The water glistens in its wake,
making the sea look white.
33 Nothing on earth is its equal,
no other creature so fearless.
34 Of all the creatures, it is the proudest.
It is the king of beasts."

Job Responds to the LORD

42 Then Job replied to the LORD:
2 "I know that you can do anything,
and no one can stop you.
3 You asked, 'Who is this that questions my
wisdom with such ignorance?'

41:13 As in Greek version; Hebrew reads *its bridle?*

KING JAMES VERSION

therefore have I uttered that I understood not; things too wonderful for me, which I knew not.

4 Hear, I beseech thee, and I will speak: I will demand of thee, and declare thou unto me.

5 I have heard of thee by the hearing of the ear: but now mine eye seeth thee.

6 Wherefore I abhor *myself,* and repent in dust and ashes.

7 And it was *so,* that after the LORD had spoken these words unto Job, the LORD said to Eliphaz the Temanite, My wrath is kindled against thee, and against thy two friends: for ye have not spoken of me *the thing that is* right, as my servant Job *hath.*

8 Therefore take unto you now seven bullocks and seven rams, and go to my servant Job, and offer up for yourselves a burnt offering; and my servant Job shall pray for you: for him will I accept: lest I deal with you *after your* folly, in that ye have not spoken of me *the thing which is* right, like my servant Job.

9 So Eliphaz the Temanite and Bildad the Shuhite *and* Zophar the Naamathite went, and did according as the LORD commanded them: the LORD also accepted Job.

10 And the LORD turned the captivity of Job, when he prayed for his friends: also the LORD gave Job twice as much as he had before.

11 Then came there unto him all his brethren, and all his sisters, and all they that had been of his acquaintance before, and did eat bread with him in his house: and they bemoaned him, and comforted him over all the evil that the LORD had brought upon him: every man also gave him a piece of money, and every one an earring of gold.

12 So the LORD blessed the latter end of Job more than his beginning: for he had fourteen thousand sheep, and six thousand camels, and a thousand yoke of oxen, and a thousand she asses.

13 He had also seven sons and three daughters.

14 And he called the name of the first, Jemima; and the name of the second, Kezia; and the name of the third, Keren-happuch.

15 And in all the land were no women found *so* fair as the daughters of Job: and their father gave them inheritance among their brethren.

16 After this lived Job an hundred and forty years, and saw his sons, and his sons' sons, *even* four generations.

17 So Job died, *being* old and full of days.

NEW LIVING TRANSLATION

It is I—and I was talking about things
I knew nothing about,
things far too wonderful for me.
4 You said, 'Listen and I will speak!
I have some questions for you,
and you must answer them.'
5 I had only heard about you before,
but now I have seen you with my own eyes.
6 I take back everything I said,
and I sit in dust and ashes to show my
repentance."

Conclusion: The LORD Blesses Job

7 After the LORD had finished speaking to Job, he said to Eliphaz the Temanite: "I am angry with you and your two friends, for you have not spoken accurately about me, as my servant Job has. 8 So take seven bulls and seven rams and go to my servant Job and offer a burnt offering for yourselves. My servant Job will pray for you, and I will accept his prayer on your behalf. I will not treat you as you deserve, for you have not spoken accurately about me, as my servant Job has." 9 So Eliphaz the Temanite, Bildad the Shuhite, and Zophar the Naamathite did as the LORD commanded them, and the LORD accepted Job's prayer.

10 When Job prayed for his friends, the LORD restored his fortunes. In fact, the LORD gave him twice as much as before! 11 Then all his brothers, sisters, and former friends came and feasted with him in his home. And they consoled him and comforted him because of all the trials the LORD had brought against him. And each of them brought him a gift of money* and a gold ring.

12 So the LORD blessed Job in the second half of his life even more than in the beginning. For now he had 14,000 sheep, 6,000 camels, 1,000 teams of oxen, and 1,000 female donkeys. 13 He also gave Job seven more sons and three more daughters. 14 He named his first daughter Jemimah, the second Keziah, and the third Keren-happuch. 15 In all the land no women were as lovely as the daughters of Job. And their father put them into his will along with their brothers.

16 Job lived 140 years after that, living to see four generations of his children and grandchildren. 17 Then he died, an old man who had lived a long, full life.

42:11 Hebrew *a kesitah;* the value or weight of the kesitah is no longer known.

Psalms

KING JAMES VERSION

1 1 Blessed *is* the man that walketh not in the counsel of the ungodly, nor standeth in the way of sinners, nor sitteth in the seat of the scornful.

2 But his delight *is* in the law of the LORD; and in his law doth he meditate day and night.

3 And he shall be like a tree planted by the rivers of water, that bringeth forth his fruit in his season; his leaf also shall not wither; and whatsoever he doeth shall prosper.

4 The ungodly *are* not so: but *are* like the chaff which the wind driveth away.

5 Therefore the ungodly shall not stand in the judgment, nor sinners in the congregation of the righteous.

6 For the LORD knoweth the way of the righteous: but the way of the ungodly shall perish.

2 1 Why do the heathen rage, and the people imagine a vain thing?

2 The kings of the earth set themselves, and the rulers take counsel together, against the LORD, and against his anointed, *saying,*

3 Let us break their bands asunder, and cast away their cords from us.

4 He that sitteth in the heavens shall laugh: the LORD shall have them in derision.

5 Then shall he speak unto them in his wrath, and vex them in his sore displeasure.

6 Yet have I set my king upon my holy hill of Zion.

7 I will declare the decree: the LORD hath said unto me, Thou *art* my Son; this day have I begotten thee.

NEW LIVING TRANSLATION

BOOK ONE (Psalms 1–41)

1 1 Oh, the joys of those who do not
follow the advice of the wicked,
or stand around with sinners,
or join in with mockers.
2 But they delight in the law of the LORD,
meditating on it day and night.
3 They are like trees planted along the riverbank,
bearing fruit each season.
Their leaves never wither,
and they prosper in all they do.
4 But not the wicked!
They are like worthless chaff, scattered
by the wind.
5 They will be condemned at the time of judgment.
Sinners will have no place among the godly.
6 For the LORD watches over the path of the godly,
but the path of the wicked leads to
destruction.

2 1 Why are the nations so angry?
Why do they waste their time with
futile plans?
2 The kings of the earth prepare for battle;
the rulers plot together
against the LORD
and against his anointed one.
3 "Let us break their chains," they cry,
"and free ourselves from slavery to God."

4 But the one who rules in heaven laughs.
The Lord scoffs at them.
5 Then in anger he rebukes them,
terrifying them with his fierce fury.
6 For the Lord declares, "I have placed my chosen
king on the throne
in Jerusalem,* on my holy mountain."

7 The king proclaims the LORD's decree:
"The LORD said to me, 'You are my son.*
Today I have become your Father.*

2:6 Hebrew *on Zion.* **2:7a** Or *Son;* also in 2:12. **2:7b** Or *Today I reveal you as my son.*

KING JAMES VERSION

8 Ask of me, and I shall give *thee* the heathen *for*
thine inheritance, and the uttermost parts of the
earth *for* thy possession.
9 Thou shalt break them with a rod of iron; thou
shalt dash them in pieces like a potter's vessel.
10 Be wise now therefore, O ye kings: be instructed,
ye judges of the earth.
11 Serve the LORD with fear, and rejoice with
trembling.
12 Kiss the Son, lest he be angry, and ye perish *from*
the way, when his wrath is kindled but a little.
Blessed *are* all they that put their trust in him.

3 *A Psalm of David, when he fled from Absalom his son*

1 LORD, how are they increased that trouble me!
many *are* they that rise up against me.
2 Many *there be* which say of my soul, *There is* no
help for him in God. Selah.
3 But thou, O LORD, *art* a shield for me; my glory,
and the lifter up of mine head.
4 I cried unto the LORD with my voice, and he heard
me out of his holy hill. Selah.
5 I laid me down and slept; I awaked; for the LORD
sustained me.
6 I will not be afraid of ten thousands of people,
that have set *themselves* against me round about.
7 Arise, O LORD; save me, O my God: for thou hast
smitten all mine enemies *upon* the cheek bone; thou
hast broken the teeth of the ungodly.
8 Salvation *belongeth* unto the LORD: thy blessing
is upon thy people. Selah.

4 *To the chief Musician on Neginoth, A Psalm of David*

1 Hear me when I call, O God of my righteousness:
thou hast enlarged me *when I was* in distress; have
mercy upon me, and hear my prayer.
2 O ye sons of men, how long *will ye turn* my glory
into shame? *how long* will ye love vanity, *and* seek
after leasing? Selah.

NEW LIVING TRANSLATION

8 Only ask, and I will give you the nations as your
inheritance,
the whole earth as your possession.
9 You will break* them with an iron rod
and smash them like clay pots.'"

10 Now then, you kings, act wisely!
Be warned, you rulers of the earth!
11 Serve the LORD with reverent fear,
and rejoice with trembling.
12 Submit to God's royal son,* or he will
become angry,
and you will be destroyed in the midst of all
your activities—
for his anger flares up in an instant.
But what joy for all who take refuge in him!

3 *A psalm of David, regarding the time David fled from his son Absalom.*

1 O LORD, I have so many enemies;
so many are against me.
2 So many are saying,
"God will never rescue him!" *Interlude**
3 But you, O LORD, are a shield around me;
you are my glory, the one who holds my
head high.
4 I cried out to the LORD,
and he answered me from his holy mountain.
Interlude

5 I lay down and slept,
yet I woke up in safety,
for the LORD was watching over me.
6 I am not afraid of ten thousand enemies
who surround me on every side.
7 Arise, O LORD!
Rescue me, my God!
Slap all my enemies in the face!
Shatter the teeth of the wicked!
8 Victory comes from you, O LORD.
May you bless your people. *Interlude*

4 *For the choir director: A psalm of David, to be accompanied by stringed instruments.*

1 Answer me when I call to you,
O God who declares me innocent.
Free me from my troubles.
Have mercy on me and hear my prayer.

2 How long will you people ruin my reputation?
How long will you make groundless
accusations?
How long will you continue your lies?
Interlude

2:9 Greek version reads *rule*. Compare Rev 2:27. **2:12** The meaning of the Hebrew is uncertain. **3:2** Hebrew *Selah*. The meaning of this word is uncertain, though it is probably a musical or literary term. It is rendered *Interlude* throughout the Psalms.

KING JAMES VERSION

3 But know that the LORD hath set apart him that is godly for himself: the LORD will hear when I call unto him.

4 Stand in awe, and sin not: commune with your own heart upon your bed, and be still. Selah.

5 Offer the sacrifices of righteousness, and put your trust in the LORD.

6 *There be* many that say, Who will shew us *any* good? LORD, lift thou up the light of thy countenance upon us.

7 Thou hast put gladness in my heart, more than in the time *that* their corn and their wine increased.

8 I will both lay me down in peace, and sleep: for thou, LORD, only makest me dwell in safety.

5 *To the chief Musician upon Nehiloth, A Psalm of David*

1 Give ear to my words, O LORD, consider my meditation.

2 Hearken unto the voice of my cry, my King, and my God: for unto thee will I pray.

3 My voice shalt thou hear in the morning, O LORD; in the morning will I direct *my prayer* unto thee, and will look up.

4 For thou *art* not a God that hath pleasure in wickedness: neither shall evil dwell with thee.

5 The foolish shall not stand in thy sight: thou hatest all workers of iniquity.

6 Thou shalt destroy them that speak leasing: the LORD will abhor the bloody and deceitful man.

7 But as for me, I will come *into* thy house in the multitude of thy mercy: *and* in thy fear will I worship toward thy holy temple.

8 Lead me, O LORD, in thy righteousness because of mine enemies; make thy way straight before my face.

9 For *there is* no faithfulness in their mouth; their inward part *is* very wickedness; their throat *is* an open sepulchre; they flatter with their tongue.

10 Destroy thou them, O God; let them fall by their own counsels; cast them out in the multitude of their transgressions; for they have rebelled against thee.

11 But let all those that put their trust in thee rejoice: let them ever shout for joy, because thou defendest them: let them also that love thy name be joyful in thee.

NEW LIVING TRANSLATION

3 You can be sure of this:
The LORD set apart the godly for himself.
The LORD will answer when I call to him.
4 Don't sin by letting anger control you.
Think about it overnight and remain silent.
Interlude
5 Offer sacrifices in the right spirit,
and trust the LORD.
6 Many people say, "Who will show us better times?"
Let your face smile on us, LORD.
7 You have given me greater joy
than those who have abundant harvests of grain and new wine.
8 In peace I will lie down and sleep,
for you alone, O LORD, will keep me safe.

5 *For the choir director: A psalm of David, to be accompanied by the flute.*

1 O LORD, hear me as I pray;
pay attention to my groaning.
2 Listen to my cry for help, my King and my God,
for I pray to no one but you.
3 Listen to my voice in the morning, LORD.
Each morning I bring my requests to you
and wait expectantly.

4 O God, you take no pleasure in wickedness;
you cannot tolerate the sins of the wicked.
5 Therefore, the proud may not stand in your presence,
for you hate all who do evil.
6 You will destroy those who tell lies.
The LORD detests murderers and deceivers.
7 Because of your unfailing love, I can enter your house;
I will worship at your Temple with deepest awe.
8 Lead me in the right path, O LORD,
or my enemies will conquer me.
Make your way plain for me to follow.
9 My enemies cannot speak a truthful word.
Their deepest desire is to destroy others.
Their talk is foul, like the stench from an open grave.
Their tongues are filled with flattery.*
10 O God, declare them guilty.
Let them be caught in their own traps.
Drive them away because of their many sins,
for they have rebelled against you.
11 But let all who take refuge in you rejoice;
let them sing joyful praises forever.
Spread your protection over them,
that all who love your name may be filled with joy.

5:9 Greek version reads *with lies.* Compare Rom 3:13.

KING JAMES VERSION

12 For thou, LORD, wilt bless the righteous; with favour wilt thou compass him as *with* a shield.

6

To the chief Musician on Neginoth upon Sheminith, A Psalm of David

1 O LORD, rebuke me not in thine anger, neither chasten me in thy hot displeasure.

2 Have mercy upon me, O LORD; for I *am* weak: O LORD, heal me; for my bones are vexed.

3 My soul is also sore vexed: but thou, O LORD, how long?

4 Return, O LORD, deliver my soul: oh save me for thy mercies' sake.

5 For in death *there is* no remembrance of thee: in the grave who shall give thee thanks?

6 I am weary with my groaning; all the night make I my bed to swim; I water my couch with my tears.

7 Mine eye is consumed because of grief; it waxeth old because of all mine enemies.

8 Depart from me, all ye workers of iniquity; for the LORD hath heard the voice of my weeping.

9 The LORD hath heard my supplication; the LORD will receive my prayer.

10 Let all mine enemies be ashamed and sore vexed: let them return *and* be ashamed suddenly.

7

Shiggaion of David, which he sang unto the LORD, concerning the words of Cush the Benjamite

1 O LORD my God, in thee do I put my trust: save me from all them that persecute me, and deliver me:

2 Lest he tear my soul like a lion, rending *it* in pieces, while *there is* none to deliver.

3 O LORD my God, if I have done this; if there be iniquity in my hands;

4 If I have rewarded evil unto him that was at peace with me; (yea, I have delivered him that without cause is mine enemy:)

5 Let the enemy persecute my soul, and take *it;* yea, let him tread down my life upon the earth, and lay mine honour in the dust. Selah.

6 Arise, O LORD, in thine anger, lift up thyself because of the rage of mine enemies: and awake for me *to* the judgment *that* thou hast commanded.

7 So shall the congregation of the people compass thee about: for their sakes therefore return thou on high.

8 The LORD shall judge the people: judge me, O LORD, according to my righteousness, and according to mine integrity *that is* in me.

9 Oh let the wickedness of the wicked come to an end; but establish the just: for the righteous God trieth the hearts and reins.

NEW LIVING TRANSLATION

12 For you bless the godly, O LORD;
you surround them with your shield of love.

6

*For the choir director: A psalm of David, to be accompanied by an eight-stringed instrument.**

1 O LORD, don't rebuke me in your anger
or discipline me in your rage.
2 Have compassion on me, LORD, for I am weak.
Heal me, LORD, for my bones are in agony.
3 I am sick at heart.
How long, O LORD, until you restore me?
4 Return, O LORD, and rescue me.
Save me because of your unfailing love.
5 For the dead do not remember you.
Who can praise you from the grave?*

6 I am worn out from sobbing.
All night I flood my bed with weeping,
drenching it with my tears.
7 My vision is blurred by grief;
my eyes are worn out because of all
my enemies.

8 Go away, all you who do evil,
for the LORD has heard my weeping.
9 The LORD has heard my plea;
the LORD will answer my prayer.
10 May all my enemies be disgraced and terrified.
May they suddenly turn back in shame.

7

A psalm of David, which he sang to the LORD concerning Cush of the tribe of Benjamin.

1 I come to you for protection, O LORD my God.
Save me from my persecutors—rescue me!
2 If you don't, they will maul me like a lion,
tearing me to pieces with no one to rescue me.
3 O LORD my God, if I have done wrong
or am guilty of injustice,
4 if I have betrayed a friend
or plundered my enemy without cause,
5 then let my enemies capture me.
Let them trample me into the ground
and drag my honor in the dust. *Interlude*

6 Arise, O LORD, in anger!
Stand up against the fury of my enemies!
Wake up, my God, and bring justice!
7 Gather the nations before you.
Rule over them from on high.
8 The LORD judges the nations.
Declare me righteous, O LORD,
for I am innocent, O Most High!
9 End the evil of those who are wicked,
and defend the righteous.
For you look deep within the mind and heart,
O righteous God.

6:TITLE Hebrew *with stringed instruments; according to the sheminith.*
6:5 Hebrew *from Sheol?*

KING JAMES VERSION

10 My defence *is* of God, which saveth the upright
in heart.
11 God judgeth the righteous, and God is angry
with the wicked every day.
12 If he turn not, he will whet his sword; he hath
bent his bow, and made it ready.
13 He hath also prepared for him the instruments
of death; he ordaineth his arrows against the persecutors.
14 Behold, he travaileth with iniquity, and hath
conceived mischief, and brought forth falsehood.
15 He made a pit, and digged it, and is fallen into
the ditch *which* he made.
16 His mischief shall return upon his own head,
and his violent dealing shall come down upon his
own pate.
17 I will praise the LORD according to his righteousness: and will sing praise to the name of the
LORD most high.

8 *To the chief Musician upon Gittith, A Psalm of David*

1 O LORD our Lord, how excellent *is* thy name in all
the earth! who hast set thy glory above the heavens.
2 Out of the mouth of babes and sucklings hast
thou ordained strength because of thine enemies,
that thou mightest still the enemy and the avenger.
3 When I consider thy heavens, the work of thy
fingers, the moon and the stars, which thou hast
ordained;
4 What is man, that thou art mindful of him? and
the son of man, that thou visitest him?
5 For thou hast made him a little lower than the angels, and hast crowned him with glory and honour.
6 Thou madest him to have dominion over the
works of thy hands; thou hast put all *things* under
his feet:
7 All sheep and oxen, yea, and the beasts of the
field;
8 The fowl of the air, and the fish of the sea, *and
whatsoever* passeth through the paths of the seas.
9 O LORD our Lord, how excellent *is* thy name in all
the earth!

9 *To the chief Musician upon Muth-labben, A Psalm of David*

1 I will praise *thee,* O LORD, with my whole heart;
I will shew forth all thy marvellous works.

NEW LIVING TRANSLATION

10 God is my shield,
saving those whose hearts are true and right.
11 God is an honest judge.
He is angry with the wicked every day.

12 If a person does not repent,
God* will sharpen his sword;
he will bend and string his bow.
13 He will prepare his deadly weapons
and shoot his flaming arrows.
14 The wicked conceive evil;
they are pregnant with trouble
and give birth to lies.
15 They dig a deep pit to trap others,
then fall into it themselves.
16 The trouble they make for others backfires
on them.
The violence they plan falls on their own heads.
17 I will thank the LORD because he is just;
I will sing praise to the name of the LORD
Most High.

8 *For the choir director: A psalm of David, to be accompanied by a stringed instrument.**

1 O LORD, our Lord, your majestic name fills
the earth!
Your glory is higher than the heavens.
2 You have taught children and infants
to tell of your strength,*
silencing your enemies
and all who oppose you.
3 When I look at the night sky and see the work
of your fingers—
the moon and the stars you set in place—
4 what are mere mortals that you should think
about them,
human beings that you should care for them?*
5 Yet you made them only a little lower than God*
and crowned them* with glory and honor.
6 You gave them charge of everything you made,
putting all things under their authority—
7 the flocks and the herds
and all the wild animals,
8 the birds in the sky, the fish in the sea,
and everything that swims the ocean currents.
9 O LORD, our Lord, your majestic name fills
the earth!

9 *For the choir director: A psalm of David, to be sung to the tune "Death of the Son."*

1 I will praise you, LORD, with all my heart;
I will tell of all the marvelous things you
have done.

7:12 Hebrew *he.* **8:TITLE** Hebrew *according to the gittith.* **8:2** Greek version reads *to give you praise.* Compare Matt 21:16. **8:4** Hebrew *what is man that you should think of him, / the son of man that you should care for him?* **8:5a** Or *Yet you made them only a little lower than the angels;* Hebrew reads *Yet you made him* [i.e., man] *a little lower than Elohim.* **8:5b** Hebrew *him* [i.e., man]; similarly in 8:6.

KING JAMES VERSION

[2]I will be glad and rejoice in thee: I will sing praise
to thy name, O thou most High.
[3]When mine enemies are turned back, they shall
fall and perish at thy presence.
[4]For thou hast maintained my right and my cause;
thou satest in the throne judging right.
[5]Thou hast rebuked the heathen, thou hast destroyed the wicked, thou hast put out their name for
ever and ever.
[6]O thou enemy, destructions are come to a perpetual end: and thou hast destroyed cities; their memorial is perished with them.
[7]But the LORD shall endure for ever: he hath prepared his throne for judgment.
[8]And he shall judge the world in righteousness,
he shall minister judgment to the people in uprightness.
[9]The LORD also will be a refuge for the oppressed,
a refuge in times of trouble.
[10]And they that know thy name will put their trust
in thee: for thou, LORD, hast not forsaken them that
seek thee.
[11]Sing praises to the LORD, which dwelleth in Zion:
declare among the people his doings.
[12]When he maketh inquisition for blood, he
remembereth them: he forgetteth not the cry of the
humble.
[13]Have mercy upon me, O LORD; consider my
trouble *which I suffer* of them that hate me, thou
that liftest me up from the gates of death:
[14]That I may shew forth all thy praise in the gates
of the daughter of Zion: I will rejoice in thy salvation.
[15]The heathen are sunk down in the pit *that* they
made: in the net which they hid is their own foot
taken.
[16]The LORD is known *by* the judgment *which* he
executeth: the wicked is snared in the work of his
own hands. Higgaion. Selah.
[17]The wicked shall be turned into hell, *and* all the
nations that forget God.
[18]For the needy shall not alway be forgotten: the
expectation of the poor shall *not* perish for ever.
[19]Arise, O LORD; let not man prevail: let the heathen be judged in thy sight.
[20]Put them in fear, O LORD: *that* the nations may
know themselves *to be but* men. Selah.

NEW LIVING TRANSLATION

[2] I will be filled with joy because of you.
I will sing praises to your name, O Most High.

[3] My enemies retreated;
they staggered and died when you appeared.
[4] For you have judged in my favor;
from your throne you have judged
with fairness.
[5] You have rebuked the nations and destroyed
the wicked;
you have erased their names forever.
[6] The enemy is finished, in endless ruins;
the cities you uprooted are now forgotten.

[7] But the LORD reigns forever,
executing judgment from his throne.
[8] He will judge the world with justice
and rule the nations with fairness.
[9] The LORD is a shelter for the oppressed,
a refuge in times of trouble.
[10] Those who know your name trust in you,
for you, O LORD, do not abandon those who
search for you.

[11] Sing praises to the LORD who reigns
in Jerusalem.*
Tell the world about his unforgettable deeds.
[12] For he who avenges murder cares for the
helpless.
He does not ignore the cries of those
who suffer.
[13] LORD, have mercy on me.
See how my enemies torment me.
Snatch me back from the jaws of death.
[14] Save me so I can praise you publicly at
Jerusalem's gates,
so I can rejoice that you have rescued me.

[15] The nations have fallen into the pit they
dug for others.
Their own feet have been caught in the
trap they set.
[16] The LORD is known for his justice.
The wicked are trapped by their own deeds.
*Quiet Interlude**

[17] The wicked will go down to the grave.*
This is the fate of all the nations who
ignore God.
[18] But the needy will not be ignored forever;
the hopes of the poor will not always
be crushed.

[19] Arise, O LORD!
Do not let mere mortals defy you!
Judge the nations!
[20] Make them tremble in fear, O LORD.
Let the nations know they are merely human.
Interlude

9:11 Hebrew *Zion;* also in 9:14. **9:16** Hebrew *Higgaion Selah.* The meaning of this phrase is uncertain. **9:17** Hebrew *to Sheol.*

KING JAMES VERSION

10

1 Why standest thou afar off, O LORD? *why*
hidest thou *thyself* in times of trouble?
2 The wicked in *his* pride doth persecute the poor:
let them be taken in the devices that they have
imagined.
3 For the wicked boasteth of his heart's desire, and
blesseth the covetous, *whom* the LORD abhorreth.
4 The wicked, through the pride of his countenance, will not seek *after God:* God *is* not in all his
thoughts.
5 His ways are always grievous; thy judgments *are*
far above out of his sight: *as for* all his enemies, he
puffeth at them.
6 He hath said in his heart, I shall not be moved: for
I shall never *be* in adversity.
7 His mouth is full of cursing and deceit and fraud:
under his tongue *is* mischief and vanity.
8 He sitteth in the lurking places of the villages: in
the secret places doth he murder the innocent: his
eyes are privily set against the poor.
9 He lieth in wait secretly as a lion in his den: he
lieth in wait to catch the poor: he doth catch the
poor, when he draweth him into his net.
10 He croucheth, *and* humbleth himself, that the
poor may fall by his strong ones.
11 He hath said in his heart, God hath forgotten: he
hideth his face; he will never see *it*.
12 Arise, O LORD; O God, lift up thine hand: forget
not the humble.
13 Wherefore doth the wicked contemn God? he
hath said in his heart, Thou wilt not require *it*.
14 Thou hast seen *it;* for thou beholdest mischief
and spite, to requite *it* with thy hand: the poor
committeth himself unto thee; thou art the helper of
the fatherless.
15 Break thou the arm of the wicked and the evil
man: seek out his wickedness *till* thou find none.
16 The LORD *is* King for ever and ever: the heathen
are perished out of his land.
17 LORD, thou hast heard the desire of the humble:
thou wilt prepare their heart, thou wilt cause thine
ear to hear:
18 To judge the fatherless and the oppressed, that
the man of the earth may no more oppress.

11

To the chief Musician, A Psalm *of David*

1 In the LORD put I my trust: how say ye to my soul,
Flee *as* a bird to your mountain?

NEW LIVING TRANSLATION

10

1 O LORD, why do you stand so far away?
Why do you hide when I am in trouble?
2 The wicked arrogantly hunt down the poor.
Let them be caught in the evil they plan
for others.
3 For they brag about their evil desires;
they praise the greedy and curse the LORD.

4 The wicked are too proud to seek God.
They seem to think that God is dead.
5 Yet they succeed in everything they do.
They do not see your punishment
awaiting them.
They sneer at all their enemies.
6 They think, "Nothing bad will ever happen to us!
We will be free of trouble forever!"

7 Their mouths are full of cursing, lies, and threats.*
Trouble and evil are on the tips of their tongues.
8 They lurk in ambush in the villages,
waiting to murder innocent people.
They are always searching for helpless victims.
9 Like lions crouched in hiding,
they wait to pounce on the helpless.
Like hunters they capture the helpless
and drag them away in nets.
10 Their helpless victims are crushed;
they fall beneath the strength of the wicked.
11 The wicked think, "God isn't watching us!
He has closed his eyes and won't even see
what we do!"

12 Arise, O LORD!
Punish the wicked, O God!
Do not ignore the helpless!
13 Why do the wicked get away with despising God?
They think, "God will never call us to account."
14 But you see the trouble and grief they cause.
You take note of it and punish them.
The helpless put their trust in you.
You defend the orphans.

15 Break the arms of these wicked, evil people!
Go after them until the last one is destroyed.
16 The LORD is king forever and ever!
The godless nations will vanish from the land.
17 LORD, you know the hopes of the helpless.
Surely you will hear their cries and
comfort them.
18 You will bring justice to the orphans and the
oppressed,
so mere people can no longer terrify them.

11

For the choir director: A psalm of David.

1 I trust in the LORD for protection.
So why do you say to me,
"Fly like a bird to the mountains for safety!

10:7 Greek version reads *cursing and bitterness*. Compare Rom 3:14.

KING JAMES VERSION

2 For, lo, the wicked bend *their* bow, they make ready their arrow upon the string, that they may privily shoot at the upright in heart.

3 If the foundations be destroyed, what can the righteous do?

4 The LORD *is* in his holy temple, the LORD's throne *is* in heaven: his eyes behold, his eyelids try, the children of men.

5 The LORD trieth the righteous: but the wicked and him that loveth violence his soul hateth.

6 Upon the wicked he shall rain snares, fire and brimstone, and an horrible tempest: *this shall be* the portion of their cup.

7 For the righteous LORD loveth righteousness; his countenance doth behold the upright.

12 *To the chief Musician upon Sheminith, A Psalm of David*

1 Help, LORD; for the godly man ceaseth; for the faithful fail from among the children of men.

2 They speak vanity every one with his neighbour: *with* flattering lips *and* with a double heart do they speak.

3 The LORD shall cut off all flattering lips, *and* the tongue that speaketh proud things:

4 Who have said, With our tongue will we prevail; our lips *are* our own: who *is* LORD over us?

5 For the oppression of the poor, for the sighing of the needy, now will I arise, saith the LORD; I will set *him* in safety *from him that* puffeth at him.

6 The words of the LORD *are* pure words: *as* silver tried in a furnace of earth, purified seven times.

7 Thou shalt keep them, O LORD, thou shalt preserve them from this generation for ever.

8 The wicked walk on every side, when the vilest men are exalted.

13 *To the chief Musician, A Psalm of David*

1 How long wilt thou forget me, O LORD? for ever? how long wilt thou hide thy face from me?

2 How long shall I take counsel in my soul, *having* sorrow in my heart daily? how long shall mine enemy be exalted over me?

NEW LIVING TRANSLATION

2 The wicked are stringing their bows
and fitting their arrows on the bowstrings.
They shoot from the shadows
at those whose hearts are right.
3 The foundations of law and order have collapsed.
What can the righteous do?"

4 But the LORD is in his holy Temple;
the LORD still rules from heaven.
He watches everyone closely,
examining every person on earth.
5 The LORD examines both the righteous and
the wicked.
He hates those who love violence.
6 He will rain down blazing coals and burning
sulfur on the wicked,
punishing them with scorching winds.
7 For the righteous LORD loves justice.
The virtuous will see his face.

12 *For the choir director: A psalm of David, to be accompanied by an eight-stringed instrument.**

1 Help, O LORD, for the godly are fast disappearing!
The faithful have vanished from the earth!
2 Neighbors lie to each other,
speaking with flattering lips and
deceitful hearts.
3 May the LORD cut off their flattering lips
and silence their boastful tongues.
4 They say, "We will lie to our hearts' content.
Our lips are our own—who can stop us?"

5 The LORD replies, "I have seen violence done
to the helpless,
and I have heard the groans of the poor.
Now I will rise up to rescue them,
as they have longed for me to do."
6 The LORD's promises are pure,
like silver refined in a furnace,
purified seven times over.
7 Therefore, LORD, we know you will protect
the oppressed,
preserving them forever from this lying
generation,
8 even though the wicked strut about,
and evil is praised throughout the land.

13 *For the choir director: A psalm of David.*

1 O LORD, how long will you forget me? Forever?
How long will you look the other way?
2 How long must I struggle with anguish
in my soul,
with sorrow in my heart every day?
How long will my enemy have the upper hand?

12:TITLE Hebrew *according to the sheminith.*

KING JAMES VERSION

3 Consider *and* hear me, O LORD my God: lighten mine eyes, lest I sleep the *sleep of* death;

4 Lest mine enemy say, I have prevailed against him; *and* those that trouble me rejoice when I am moved.

5 But I have trusted in thy mercy; my heart shall rejoice in thy salvation.

6 I will sing unto the LORD, because he hath dealt bountifully with me.

14 *To the chief Musician, A Psalm of David*

1 The fool hath said in his heart, *There is* no God. They are corrupt, they have done abominable works, *there is* none that doeth good.

2 The LORD looked down from heaven upon the children of men, to see if there were any that did understand, *and* seek God.

3 They are all gone aside, they are *all* together become filthy: *there is* none that doeth good, no, not one.

4 Have all the workers of iniquity no knowledge? who eat up my people *as* they eat bread, and call not upon the LORD.

5 There were they in great fear: for God *is* in the generation of the righteous.

6 Ye have shamed the counsel of the poor, because the LORD *is* his refuge.

7 Oh that the salvation of Israel *were come* out of Zion! when the LORD bringeth back the captivity of his people, Jacob shall rejoice, *and* Israel shall be glad.

15 *A Psalm of David*

1 LORD, who shall abide in thy tabernacle? who shall dwell in thy holy hill?

2 He that walketh uprightly, and worketh righteousness, and speaketh the truth in his heart.

3 *He that* backbiteth not with his tongue, nor doeth evil to his neighbour, nor taketh up a reproach against his neighbour.

4 In whose eyes a vile person is contemned; but he honoureth them that fear the LORD. *He that* sweareth to *his own* hurt, and changeth not.

5 *He that* putteth not out his money to usury, nor taketh reward against the innocent. He that doeth these *things* shall never be moved.

NEW LIVING TRANSLATION

3 Turn and answer me, O LORD my God!
Restore the sparkle to my eyes, or I will die.
4 Don't let my enemies gloat, saying, "We have defeated him!"
Don't let them rejoice at my downfall.
5 But I trust in your unfailing love.
I will rejoice because you have rescued me.
6 I will sing to the LORD
because he is good to me.

14 *For the choir director: A psalm of David.*

1 Only fools say in their hearts,
"There is no God."
They are corrupt, and their actions are evil;
not one of them does good!

2 The LORD looks down from heaven
on the entire human race;
he looks to see if anyone is truly wise,
if anyone seeks God.
3 But no, all have turned away;
all have become corrupt.*
No one does good,
not a single one!

4 Will those who do evil never learn?
They eat up my people like bread
and wouldn't think of praying to the LORD.
5 Terror will grip them,
for God is with those who obey him.
6 The wicked frustrate the plans of the oppressed,
but the LORD will protect his people.

7 Who will come from Mount Zion to rescue Israel?
When the LORD restores his people,
Jacob will shout with joy, and Israel will rejoice.

15 *A psalm of David.*

1 Who may worship in your sanctuary, LORD?
Who may enter your presence on your holy hill?
2 Those who lead blameless lives and do what is right,
speaking the truth from sincere hearts.
3 Those who refuse to gossip
or harm their neighbors
or speak evil of their friends.
4 Those who despise flagrant sinners,
and honor the faithful followers of the LORD,
and keep their promises even when it hurts.
5 Those who lend money without charging interest,
and who cannot be bribed to lie about the innocent.
Such people will stand firm forever.

14:3 Greek version reads *have become useless.* Compare Rom 3:12.

KING JAMES VERSION

16 *Michtam of David*

1 Preserve me, O God: for in thee do I put my trust.
2 *O my soul,* thou hast said unto the LORD, Thou *art*
my LORD: my goodness *extendeth* not to thee;
3 *But* to the saints that *are* in the earth, and *to* the
excellent, in whom *is* all my delight.
4 Their sorrows shall be multiplied *that* hasten
affer another *god:* their drink offerings of blood will
I not offer, nor take up their names into my lips.
5 The LORD *is* the portion of mine inheritance and
of my cup: thou maintainest my lot.
6 The lines are fallen unto me in pleasant *places;*
yea, I have a goodly heritage.
7 I will bless the LORD, who hath given me counsel:
my reins also instruct me in the night seasons.
8 I have set the LORD always before me: because *he*
is at my right hand, I shall not be moved.
9 Therefore my heart is glad, and my glory
rejoiceth: my flesh also shall rest in hope.
10 For thou wilt not leave my soul in hell; neither
wilt thou suffer thine Holy One to see corruption.
11 Thou wilt shew me the path of life: in thy presence *is* fulness of joy; at thy right hand *there are* pleasures for evermore.

17 *A prayer of David*

1 Hear the right, O LORD, attend unto my cry, give
ear unto my prayer, *that goeth* not out of feigned
lips.
2 Let my sentence come forth from thy presence;
let thine eyes behold the things that are equal.
3 Thou hast proved mine heart; thou hast visited
me in the night; thou hast tried me, *and* shalt find
nothing; I am purposed *that* my mouth shall not
transgress.
4 Concerning the works of men, by the word of thy
lips I have kept *me from* the paths of the destroyer.
5 Hold up my goings in thy paths, *that* my footsteps slip not.
6 I have called upon thee, for thou wilt hear me,
O God: incline thine ear unto me, *and hear* my
speech.

NEW LIVING TRANSLATION

16 *A psalm* of David.*

1 Keep me safe, O God,
for I have come to you for refuge.

2 I said to the LORD, "You are my Master!
Every good thing I have comes from you."
3 The godly people in the land
are my true heroes!
I take pleasure in them!
4 Troubles multiply for those who chase after
other gods.
I will not take part in their sacrifices of blood
or even speak the names of their gods.

5 LORD, you alone are my inheritance, my cup
of blessing.
You guard all that is mine.
6 The land you have given me is a pleasant land.
What a wonderful inheritance!
7 I will bless the LORD who guides me;
even at night my heart instructs me.
8 I know the LORD is always with me.
I will not be shaken, for he is right beside me.

9 No wonder my heart is glad, and I rejoice.*
My body rests in safety.
10 For you will not leave my soul among the dead*
or allow your holy one* to rot in the grave.
11 You will show me the way of life,
granting me the joy of your presence
and the pleasures of living with you forever.*

17 *A prayer of David.*

1 O LORD, hear my plea for justice.
Listen to my cry for help.
Pay attention to my prayer,
for it comes from honest lips.
2 Declare me innocent,
for you see those who do right.
3 You have tested my thoughts and examined
my heart in the night.
You have scrutinized me and found
nothing wrong.
I am determined not to sin in what I say.
4 I have followed your commands,
which keep me from following cruel and
evil people.
5 My steps have stayed on your path;
I have not wavered from following you.
6 I am praying to you because I know you will
answer, O God.
Bend down and listen as I pray.

16:TITLE Hebrew *miktam.* This may be a literary or musical term. **16:9** Greek version reads *and my tongue shouts his praises.* Compare Acts 2:26. **16:10a** Hebrew *in Sheol.* **16:10b** Or *your Holy One.* **16:11** Greek version reads *You have shown me the way of life, / and you will fill me with the joy of your presence.* Compare Acts 2:28.

7Shew thy marvellous lovingkindness, O thou that
savest by thy right hand them which put their trust
in thee from those that rise up *against them.*
8Keep me as the apple of the eye, hide me under
the shadow of thy wings,
9From the wicked that oppress me, *from* my
deadly enemies, *who* compass me about.
10They are inclosed in their own fat: with their
mouth they speak proudly.
11They have now compassed us in our steps: they
have set their eyes bowing down to the earth;
12Like as a lion *that* is greedy of his prey, and as it
were a young lion lurking in secret places.
13Arise, O LORD, disappoint him, cast him down:
deliver my soul from the wicked, *which is* thy sword:
14From men *which are* thy hand, O LORD, from
men of the world, *which have* their portion in *this*
life, and whose belly thou fillest with thy hid *trea-*
sure: they are full of children, and leave the rest of
their *substance* to their babes.
15As for me, I will behold thy face in righteousness: I shall be satisfied, when I awake, with thy
likeness.

18 *To the chief Musician,* A Psalm *of David, the servant of the LORD, who spake unto the LORD the words of this song in the day* that *the LORD delivered him from the hand of all his enemies, and from the hand of Saul: And he said,*

1I will love thee, O LORD, my strength.
2The LORD *is* my rock, and my fortress, and my deliverer; my God, my strength, in whom I will trust; my
buckler, and the horn of my salvation, *and* my high
tower.
3I will call upon the LORD, *who is worthy* to be
praised: so shall I be saved from mine enemies.
4The sorrows of death compassed me, and the
floods of ungodly men made me afraid.
5The sorrows of hell compassed me about: the
snares of death prevented me.
6In my distress I called upon the LORD, and cried
unto my God: he heard my voice out of his temple,
and my cry came before him, *even* into his ears.
7Then the earth shook and trembled; the foundations also of the hills moved and were shaken, because he was wroth.
8There went up a smoke out of his nostrils, and
fire out of his mouth devoured: coals were kindled
by it.

7 Show me your unfailing love in wonderful ways.
By your mighty power you rescue
those who seek refuge from their enemies.
8 Guard me as you would guard your own eyes.*
Hide me in the shadow of your wings.
9 Protect me from wicked people who attack me,
from murderous enemies who surround me.
10 They are without pity.
Listen to their boasting!
11 They track me down and surround me,
watching for the chance to throw me to
the ground.
12 They are like hungry lions, eager to tear me apart—
like young lions hiding in ambush.

13 Arise, O LORD!
Stand against them, and bring them to
their knees!
Rescue me from the wicked with your sword!
14 By the power of your hand, O LORD,
destroy those who look to this world for
their reward.
But satisfy the hunger of your treasured ones.
May their children have plenty,
leaving an inheritance for their descendants.
15 Because I am righteous, I will see you.
When I awake, I will see you face to face and
be satisfied.

18 *For the choir director: A psalm of David, the servant of the LORD. He sang this song to the LORD on the day the LORD rescued him from all his enemies and from Saul. He sang:*

1 I love you, LORD;
you are my strength.
2 The LORD is my rock, my fortress, and my savior;
my God is my rock, in whom I find protection.
He is my shield, the power that saves me,
and my place of safety.
3 I called on the LORD, who is worthy of praise,
and he saved me from my enemies.

4 The ropes of death entangled me;
floods of destruction swept over me.
5 The grave* wrapped its ropes around me;
death laid a trap in my path.
6 But in my distress I cried out to the LORD;
yes, I prayed to my God for help.
He heard me from his sanctuary;
my cry to him reached his ears.
7 Then the earth quaked and trembled.
The foundations of the mountains shook;
they quaked because of his anger.
8 Smoke poured from his nostrils;
fierce flames leaped from his mouth.
Glowing coals blazed forth from him.

17:8 Hebrew *as the pupil of your eye.* **18:5** Hebrew *Sheol.*

KING JAMES VERSION

9 He bowed the heavens also, and came down: and
darkness *was* under his feet.
10 And he rode upon a cherub, and did fly: yea, he
did fly upon the wings of the wind.
11 He made darkness his secret place; his pavilion
round about him *were* dark waters *and* thick clouds
of the skies.
12 At the brightness *that was* before him his thick
clouds passed, hail *stones* and coals of fire.
13 The LORD also thundered in the heavens, and
the Highest gave his voice; hail *stones* and coals of
fire.
14 Yea, he sent out his arrows, and scattered them;
and he shot out lightnings, and discomfited them.
15 Then the channels of waters were seen, and the
foundations of the world were discovered at thy rebuke, O LORD, at the blast of the breath of thy nostrils.
16 He sent from above, he took me, he drew me out
of many waters.
17 He delivered me from my strong enemy, and
from them which hated me: for they were too strong
for me.
18 They prevented me in the day of my calamity:
but the LORD was my stay.
19 He brought me forth also into a large place; he
delivered me, because he delighted in me.
20 The LORD rewarded me according to my righteousness; according to the cleanness of my hands
hath he recompensed me.
21 For I have kept the ways of the LORD, and have
not wickedly departed from my God.
22 For all his judgments *were* before me, and I did
not put away his statutes from me.
23 I was also upright before him, and I kept myself
from mine iniquity.
24 Therefore hath the LORD recompensed me according to my righteousness, according to the cleanness of my hands in his eyesight.
25 With the merciful thou wilt shew thyself merciful; with an upright man thou wilt shew thyself
upright;
26 With the pure thou wilt shew thyself pure; and
with the froward thou wilt shew thyself froward.
27 For thou wilt save the afflicted people; but wilt
bring down high looks.
28 For thou wilt light my candle: the LORD my God
will enlighten my darkness.
29 For by thee I have run through a troop; and by
my God have I leaped over a wall.
30 *As for* God, his way *is* perfect: the word of the
LORD is tried: he *is* a buckler to all those that trust
in him.
31 For who *is* God save the LORD? or who *is* a rock
save our God?

NEW LIVING TRANSLATION

9 He opened the heavens and came down;
dark storm clouds were beneath his feet.
10 Mounted on a mighty angelic being,* he flew,
soaring on the wings of the wind.
11 He shrouded himself in darkness,
veiling his approach with dark rain clouds.
12 Thick clouds shielded the brightness around him
and rained down hail and burning coals.*
13 The LORD thundered from heaven;
the voice of the Most High resounded
amid the hail and burning coals.
14 He shot his arrows and scattered his enemies;
his lightning flashed, and they were greatly
confused.
15 Then at your command, O LORD,
at the blast of your breath,
the bottom of the sea could be seen,
and the foundations of the earth were laid bare.

16 He reached down from heaven and rescued me;
he drew me out of deep waters.
17 He rescued me from my powerful enemies,
from those who hated me and were too
strong for me.
18 They attacked me at a moment when I was
in distress,
but the LORD supported me.
19 He led me to a place of safety;
he rescued me because he delights in me.
20 The LORD rewarded me for doing right;
he restored me because of my innocence.
21 For I have kept the ways of the LORD;
I have not turned from my God to follow evil.
22 I have followed all his regulations;
I have never abandoned his decrees.
23 I am blameless before God;
I have kept myself from sin.
24 The LORD rewarded me for doing right.
He has seen my innocence.

25 To the faithful you show yourself faithful;
to those with integrity you show integrity.
26 To the pure you show yourself pure,
but to the wicked you show yourself hostile.
27 You rescue the humble,
but you humiliate the proud.
28 You light a lamp for me.
The LORD, my God, lights up my darkness.
29 In your strength I can crush an army;
with my God I can scale any wall.
30 God's way is perfect.
All the LORD's promises prove true.
He is a shield for all who look to him
for protection.
31 For who is God except the LORD?
Who but our God is a solid rock?

18:10 Hebrew *a cherub.* **18:12** Or *and lightning bolts;* also in 18:13.

32 *It is* God that girdeth me with strength, and maketh my way perfect.

33 He maketh my feet like hinds' *feet,* and setteth me upon my high places.

34 He teacheth my hands to war, so that a bow of steel is broken by mine arms.

35 Thou hast also given me the shield of thy salvation: and thy right hand hath holden me up, and thy gentleness hath made me great.

36 Thou hast enlarged my steps under me, that my feet did not slip.

37 I have pursued mine enemies, and overtaken them: neither did I turn again till they were consumed.

38 I have wounded them that they were not able to rise: they are fallen under my feet.

39 For thou hast girded me with strength unto the battle: thou hast subdued under me those that rose up against me.

40 Thou hast also given me the necks of mine enemies; that I might destroy them that hate me.

41 They cried, but *there was* none to save *them: even* unto the LORD, but he answered them not.

42 Then did I beat them small as the dust before the wind: I did cast them out as the dirt in the streets.

43 Thou hast delivered me from the strivings of the people; *and* thou hast made me the head of the heathen: a people *whom* I have not known shall serve me.

44 As soon as they hear of me, they shall obey me: the strangers shall submit themselves unto me.

45 The strangers shall fade away, and be afraid out of their close places.

46 The LORD liveth; and blessed *be* my rock; and let the God of my salvation be exalted.

47 *It is* God that avengeth me, and subdueth the people under me.

48 He delivereth me from mine enemies: yea, thou liftest me up above those that rise up against me: thou hast delivered me from the violent man.

49 Therefore will I give thanks unto thee, O LORD, among the heathen, and sing praises unto thy name.

50 Great deliverance giveth he to his king; and sheweth mercy to his anointed, to David, and to his seed for evermore.

19 *To the chief Musician, A Psalm of David*

1 The heavens declare the glory of God; and the firmament sheweth his handiwork.

2 Day unto day uttereth speech, and night unto night sheweth knowledge.

3 *There is* no speech nor language, *where* their voice is not heard.

32 God arms me with strength,
and he makes my way perfect.
33 He makes me as surefooted as a deer,
enabling me to stand on mountain heights.
34 He trains my hands for battle;
he strengthens my arm to draw a bronze bow.
35 You have given me your shield of victory.
Your right hand supports me;
your help has made me great.
36 You have made a wide path for my feet
to keep them from slipping.
37 I chased my enemies and caught them;
I did not stop until they were conquered.
38 I struck them down so they could not get up;
they fell beneath my feet.
39 You have armed me with strength for the battle;
you have subdued my enemies under my feet.
40 You placed my foot on their necks.
I have destroyed all who hated me.
41 They called for help, but no one came to
their rescue.
They even cried to the LORD, but he refused
to answer.
42 I ground them as fine as dust in the wind.
I swept them into the gutter like dirt.
43 You gave me victory over my accusers.
You appointed me ruler over nations;
people I don't even know now serve me.
44 As soon as they hear of me, they submit;
foreign nations cringe before me.
45 They all lose their courage
and come trembling from their strongholds.

46 The LORD lives! Praise to my Rock!
May the God of my salvation be exalted!
47 He is the God who pays back those who harm me;
he subdues the nations under me
48 and rescues me from my enemies.
You hold me safe beyond the reach of
my enemies;
you save me from violent opponents.
49 For this, O LORD, I will praise you among
the nations;
I will sing praises to your name.
50 You give great victories to your king;
you show unfailing love to your anointed,
to David and all his descendants forever.

19 *For the choir director: A psalm of David.*

1 The heavens proclaim the glory of God.
The skies display his craftsmanship.
2 Day after day they continue to speak;
night after night they make him known.
3 They speak without a sound or word;
their voice is never heard.*

19:3 Or *There is no speech or language where their voice is not heard.*

KING JAMES VERSION

4 Their line is gone out through all the earth, and their words to the end of the world. In them hath he set a tabernacle for the sun,

5 Which *is* as a bridegroom coming out of his chamber, *and* rejoiceth as a strong man to run a race.

6 His going forth *is* from the end of the heaven, and his circuit unto the ends of it: and there is nothing hid from the heat thereof.

7 The law of the LORD *is* perfect, converting the soul: the testimony of the LORD *is* sure, making wise the simple.

8 The statutes of the LORD *are* right, rejoicing the heart: the commandment of the LORD *is* pure, enlightening the eyes.

9 The fear of the LORD *is* clean, enduring for ever: the judgments of the LORD *are* true *and* righteous altogether.

10 More to be desired *are they* than gold, yea, than much fine gold: sweeter also than honey and the honeycomb.

11 Moreover by them is thy servant warned: *and* in keeping of them *there is* great reward.

12 Who can understand *his* errors? cleanse thou me from secret *faults*.

13 Keep back thy servant also from presumptuous *sins;* let them not have dominion over me: then shall I be upright, and I shall be innocent from the great transgression.

14 Let the words of my mouth, and the meditation of my heart, be acceptable in thy sight, O LORD, my strength, and my redeemer.

20 *To the chief Musician, A Psalm of David*

1 The LORD hear thee in the day of trouble; the name of the God of Jacob defend thee;

2 Send thee help from the sanctuary, and strengthen thee out of Zion;

3 Remember all thy offerings, and accept thy burnt sacrifice; Selah.

4 Grant thee according to thine own heart, and fulfil all thy counsel.

5 We will rejoice in thy salvation, and in the name

NEW LIVING TRANSLATION

4 Yet their message has gone throughout the earth,
and their words to all the world.

God has made a home in the heavens for the sun.
5 It bursts forth like a radiant bridegroom after
his wedding.
It rejoices like a great athlete eager to run
the race.
6 The sun rises at one end of the heavens
and follows its course to the other end.
Nothing can hide from its heat.

7 The instructions of the LORD are perfect,
reviving the soul.
The decrees of the LORD are trustworthy,
making wise the simple.
8 The commandments of the LORD are right,
bringing joy to the heart.
The commands of the LORD are clear,
giving insight for living.
9 Reverence for the LORD is pure,
lasting forever.
The laws of the LORD are true;
each one is fair.
10 They are more desirable than gold,
even the finest gold.
They are sweeter than honey,
even honey dripping from the comb.
11 They are a warning to your servant,
a great reward for those who obey them.

12 How can I know all the sins lurking in my heart?
Cleanse me from these hidden faults.
13 Keep your servant from deliberate sins!
Don't let them control me.
Then I will be free of guilt
and innocent of great sin.

14 May the words of my mouth
and the meditation of my heart
be pleasing to you,
O LORD, my rock and my redeemer.

20 *For the choir director: A psalm of David.*

1 In times of trouble, may the LORD answer
your cry.
May the name of the God of Jacob keep
you safe from all harm.
2 May he send you help from his sanctuary
and strengthen you from Jerusalem.*
3 May he remember all your gifts
and look favorably on your burnt offerings.
Interlude

4 May he grant your heart's desires
and make all your plans succeed.
5 May we shout for joy when we hear of
your victory

20:2 Hebrew *Zion*.

KING JAMES VERSION

of our God we will set up *our* banners: the LORD fulfil
all thy petitions.
6Now know I that the LORD saveth his anointed; he
will hear him from his holy heaven with the saving
strength of his right hand.
7Some *trust* in chariots, and some in horses: but
we will remember the name of the LORD our God.
8They are brought down and fallen: but we are
risen, and stand upright.
9Save, LORD: let the king hear us when we call.

21 *To the chief Musician, A Psalm of David*

1The king shall joy in thy strength, O LORD; and in
thy salvation how greatly shall he rejoice!
2Thou hast given him his heart's desire, and hast
not withholden the request of his lips. Selah.
3For thou preventest him with the blessings of
goodness: thou settest a crown of pure gold on his
head.
4He asked life of thee, *and* thou gavest *it* him, *even*
length of days for ever and ever.
5His glory *is* great in thy salvation: honour and
majesty hast thou laid upon him.
6For thou hast made him most blessed for ever:
thou hast made him exceeding glad with thy countenance.
7For the king trusteth in the LORD, and through
the mercy of the most High he shall not be moved.
8Thine hand shall find out all thine enemies: thy
right hand shall find out those that hate thee.
9Thou shalt make them as a fiery oven in the time
of thine anger: the LORD shall swallow them up in his
wrath, and the fire shall devour them.
10Their fruit shalt thou destroy from the earth,
and their seed from among the children of men.
11For they intended evil against thee: they imagined a mischievous device, *which* they are not able *to*
perform.
12Therefore shalt thou make them turn their back,
when thou shalt make ready *thine arrows* upon thy
strings against the face of them.
13Be thou exalted, LORD, in thine own strength: *so*
will we sing and praise thy power.

NEW LIVING TRANSLATION

and raise a victory banner in the name
of our God.
May the LORD answer all your prayers.

6 Now I know that the LORD rescues his
anointed king.
He will answer him from his holy heaven
and rescue him by his great power.
7 Some nations boast of their chariots and horses,
but we boast in the name of the LORD our God.
8 Those nations will fall down and collapse,
but we will rise up and stand firm.
9 Give victory to our king, O LORD!
Answer our cry for help.

21 *For the choir director: A psalm of David.*

1 How the king rejoices in your strength, O LORD!
He shouts with joy because you give him
victory.
2 For you have given him his heart's desire;
you have withheld nothing he requested.
Interlude
3 You welcomed him back with success and
prosperity.
You placed a crown of finest gold on his head.
4 He asked you to preserve his life,
and you granted his request.
The days of his life stretch on forever.
5 Your victory brings him great honor,
and you have clothed him with splendor
and majesty.
6 You have endowed him with eternal blessings
and given him the joy of your presence.
7 For the king trusts in the LORD.
The unfailing love of the Most High will keep
him from stumbling.

8 You will capture all your enemies.
Your strong right hand will seize all who
hate you.
9 You will throw them in a flaming furnace
when you appear.
The LORD will consume them in his anger;
fire will devour them.
10 You will wipe their children from the face
of the earth;
they will never have descendants.
11 Although they plot against you,
their evil schemes will never succeed.
12 For they will turn and run
when they see your arrows aimed at them.
13 Rise up, O LORD, in all your power.
With music and singing we celebrate your
mighty acts.

KING JAMES VERSION

22

To the chief Musician upon Aijeleth Shahar, A Psalm of David

1My God, my God, why hast thou forsaken me?
why art thou so far from helping me, *and from* the
words of my roaring?
2O my God, I cry in the daytime, but thou hearest
not; and in the night season, and am not silent.
3But thou *art* holy, *O thou* that inhabitest the
praises of Israel.
4Our fathers trusted in thee: they trusted, and
thou didst deliver them.
5They cried unto thee, and were delivered: they
trusted in thee, and were not confounded.
6But I *am* a worm, and no man; a reproach of men,
and despised of the people.
7All they that see me laugh me to scorn: they shoot
out the lip, they shake the head, *saying*,
8He trusted on the LORD *that* he would deliver
him: let him deliver him, seeing he delighted in him.
9But thou *art* he that took me out of the womb:
thou didst make me hope *when I was* upon my
mother's breasts.
10I was cast upon thee from the womb: thou *art*
my God from my mother's belly.
11Be not far from me; for trouble *is* near; for *there*
is none to help.
12Many bulls have compassed me: strong *bulls* of
Bashan have beset me round.
13They gaped upon me *with* their mouths, *as* a
ravening and a roaring lion.
14I am poured out like water, and all my bones are
out of joint: my heart is like wax; it is melted in the
midst of my bowels.
15My strength is dried up like a potsherd; and my
tongue cleaveth to my jaws; and thou hast brought
me into the dust of death.
16For dogs have compassed me: the assembly of
the wicked have inclosed me: they pierced my hands
and my feet.
17I may tell all my bones: they look *and* stare
upon me.
18They part my garments among them, and cast
lots upon my vesture.
19But be not thou far from me, O LORD: O my
strength, haste thee to help me.

NEW LIVING TRANSLATION

22

For the choir director: A psalm of David, to be sung to the tune "Doe of the Dawn."

1 My God, my God, why have you abandoned me?
Why are you so far away when I groan
for help?
2 Every day I call to you, my God, but you do
not answer.
Every night you hear my voice, but I find
no relief.

3 Yet you are holy,
enthroned on the praises of Israel.
4 Our ancestors trusted in you,
and you rescued them.
5 They cried out to you and were saved.
They trusted in you and were never disgraced.

6 But I am a worm and not a man.
I am scorned and despised by all!
7 Everyone who sees me mocks me.
They sneer and shake their heads, saying,
8 "Is this the one who relies on the LORD?
Then let the LORD save him!
If the LORD loves him so much,
let the LORD rescue him!"

9 Yet you brought me safely from my
mother's womb
and led me to trust you at my mother's breast.
10 I was thrust into your arms at my birth.
You have been my God from the moment
I was born.

11 Do not stay so far from me,
for trouble is near,
and no one else can help me.
12 My enemies surround me like a herd of bulls;
fierce bulls of Bashan have hemmed me in!
13 Like lions they open their jaws against me,
roaring and tearing into their prey.
14 My life is poured out like water,
and all my bones are out of joint.
My heart is like wax,
melting within me.
15 My strength has dried up like sunbaked clay.
My tongue sticks to the roof of my mouth.
You have laid me in the dust and left me
for dead.
16 My enemies surround me like a pack of dogs;
an evil gang closes in on me.
They have pierced my hands and feet.
17 I can count all my bones.
My enemies stare at me and gloat.
18 They divide my garments among themselves
and throw dice* for my clothing.

19 O LORD, do not stay far away!
You are my strength; come quickly to my aid!

22:18 Hebrew *cast lots.*

KING JAMES VERSION

20 Deliver my soul from the sword; my darling from the power of the dog.

21 Save me from the lion's mouth: for thou hast heard me from the horns of the unicorns.

22 I will declare thy name unto my brethren: in the midst of the congregation will I praise thee.

23 Ye that fear the LORD, praise him; all ye the seed of Jacob, glorify him; and fear him, all ye the seed of Israel.

24 For he hath not despised nor abhorred the affliction of the afflicted; neither hath he hid his face from him; but when he cried unto him, he heard.

25 My praise *shall be* of thee in the great congregation: I will pay my vows before them that fear him.

26 The meek shall eat and be satisfied: they shall praise the LORD that seek him: your heart shall live for ever.

27 All the ends of the world shall remember and turn unto the LORD: and all the kindreds of the nations shall worship before thee.

28 For the kingdom *is* the LORD's: and he *is* the governor among the nations.

29 All *they that be* fat upon earth shall eat and worship: all they that go down to the dust shall bow before him: and none can keep alive his own soul.

30 A seed shall serve him; it shall be accounted to the LORD for a generation.

31 They shall come, and shall declare his righteousness unto a people that shall be born, that he hath done *this*.

23 *A Psalm of David*

1 The LORD *is* my shepherd; I shall not want.

2 He maketh me to lie down in green pastures: he leadeth me beside the still waters.

3 He restoreth my soul: he leadeth me in the paths of righteousness for his name's sake.

4 Yea, though I walk through the valley of the shadow of death, I will fear no evil: for thou *art* with me; thy rod and thy staff they comfort me.

5 Thou preparest a table before me in the presence

NEW LIVING TRANSLATION

20 Save me from the sword;
spare my precious life from these dogs.
21 Snatch me from the lion's jaws
and from the horns of these wild oxen.

22 I will proclaim your name to my brothers
and sisters.*
I will praise you among your assembled
people.
23 Praise the LORD, all you who fear him!
Honor him, all you descendants of Jacob!
Show him reverence, all you descendants
of Israel!
24 For he has not ignored or belittled the suffering
of the needy.
He has not turned his back on them,
but has listened to their cries for help.
25 I will praise you in the great assembly.
I will fulfill my vows in the presence of those
who worship you.
26 The poor will eat and be satisfied.
All who seek the LORD will praise him.
Their hearts will rejoice with everlasting joy.
27 The whole earth will acknowledge the LORD
and return to him.
All the families of the nations will bow down
before him.
28 For royal power belongs to the LORD.
He rules all the nations.
29 Let the rich of the earth feast and worship.
Bow before him, all who are mortal,
all whose lives will end as dust.
30 Our children will also serve him.
Future generations will hear about the
wonders of the Lord.
31 His righteous acts will be told to those not
yet born.
They will hear about everything he has done.

23 *A psalm of David.*

1 The LORD is my shepherd;
I have all that I need.
2 He lets me rest in green meadows;
he leads me beside peaceful streams.
3 He renews my strength.
He guides me along right paths,
bringing honor to his name.
4 Even when I walk
through the darkest valley,*
I will not be afraid,
for you are close beside me.
Your rod and your staff
protect and comfort me.
5 You prepare a feast for me
in the presence of my enemies.

22:22 Hebrew *my brothers.* **23:4** Or *the dark valley of death.*

KING JAMES VERSION

of mine enemies: thou anointest my head with oil;
my cup runneth over.
6 Surely goodness and mercy shall follow me all the
days of my life: and I will dwell in the house of the
LORD for ever.

24 *A Psalm of David*

1 The earth *is* the LORD's, and the fulness thereof;
the world, and they that dwell therein.
2 For he hath founded it upon the seas, and established it upon the floods.
3 Who shall ascend into the hill of the LORD? or
who shall stand in his holy place?
4 He that hath clean hands, and a pure heart; who
hath not lifted up his soul unto vanity, nor sworn
deceitfully.
5 He shall receive the blessing from the LORD, and
righteousness from the God of his salvation.
6 This *is* the generation of them that seek him, that
seek thy face, O Jacob. Selah.
7 Lift up your heads, O ye gates; and be ye lift up, ye
everlasting doors; and the King of glory shall come in.
8 Who *is* this King of glory? The LORD strong and
mighty, the LORD mighty in battle.
9 Lift up your heads, O ye gates; even lift *them*
up, ye everlasting doors; and the King of glory shall
come in.
10 Who is this King of glory? The LORD of hosts,
he *is* the King of glory. Selah.

25 A Psalm *of David*

1 Unto thee, O LORD, do I lift up my soul.
2 O my God, I trust in thee: let me not be ashamed,
let not mine enemies triumph over me.
3 Yea, let none that wait on thee be ashamed: let
them be ashamed which transgress without cause.
4 Shew me thy ways, O LORD; teach me thy paths.
5 Lead me in thy truth, and teach me: for thou *art*
the God of my salvation; on thee do I wait all the day.

NEW LIVING TRANSLATION

You honor me by anointing my head with oil.
My cup overflows with blessings.
6 Surely your goodness and unfailing love will
pursue me
all the days of my life,
and I will live in the house of the LORD
forever.

24 *A psalm of David.*

1 The earth is the LORD's, and everything in it.
The world and all its people belong to him.
2 For he laid the earth's foundation on the seas
and built it on the ocean depths.
3 Who may climb the mountain of the LORD?
Who may stand in his holy place?
4 Only those whose hands and hearts are pure,
who do not worship idols
and never tell lies.
5 They will receive the LORD's blessing
and have a right relationship with God
their savior.
6 Such people may seek you
and worship in your presence, O God of Jacob.
Interlude

7 Open up, ancient gates!
Open up, ancient doors,
and let the King of glory enter.
8 Who is the King of glory?
The LORD, strong and mighty;
the LORD, invincible in battle.
9 Open up, ancient gates!
Open up, ancient doors,
and let the King of glory enter.
10 Who is the King of glory?
The LORD of Heaven's Armies—
he is the King of glory. *Interlude*

25* *A psalm of David.*

1 O LORD, I give my life to you.
2 I trust in you, my God!
Do not let me be disgraced,
or let my enemies rejoice in my defeat.
3 No one who trusts in you will ever be disgraced,
but disgrace comes to those who try to
deceive others.

4 Show me the right path, O LORD;
point out the road for me to follow.
5 Lead me by your truth and teach me,
for you are the God who saves me.
All day long I put my hope in you.

25 This psalm is a Hebrew acrostic poem; each verse begins with a successive letter of the Hebrew alphabet.

KING JAMES VERSION

6 Remember, O LORD, thy tender mercies and thy
lovingkindnesses; for they *have been* ever of old.
7 Remember not the sins of my youth, nor my
transgressions: according to thy mercy remember
thou me for thy goodness' sake, O LORD.
8 Good and upright *is* the LORD: therefore will he
teach sinners in the way.
9 The meek will he guide in judgment: and the
meek will he teach his way.
10 All the paths of the LORD *are* mercy and truth
unto such as keep his covenant and his testimonies.
11 For thy name's sake, O LORD, pardon mine iniquity; for it *is* great.
12 What man *is* he that feareth the LORD? him shall
he teach in the way *that* he shall choose.
13 His soul shall dwell at ease; and his seed shall inherit the earth.
14 The secret of the LORD *is* with them that fear
him; and he will shew them his covenant.
15 Mine eyes *are* ever toward the LORD; for he shall
pluck my feet out of the net.
16 Turn thee unto me, and have mercy upon me; for
I *am* desolate and afflicted.
17 The troubles of my heart are enlarged: *O* bring
thou me out of my distresses.
18 Look upon mine affliction and my pain; and
forgive all my sins.
19 Consider mine enemies; for they are many; and
they hate me with cruel hatred.
20 O keep my soul, and deliver me: let me not be
ashamed; for I put my trust in thee.
21 Let integrity and uprightness preserve me; for I
wait on thee.
22 Redeem Israel, O God, out of all his troubles.

26 A Psalm *of David*

1 Judge me, O LORD; for I have walked in mine integrity: I have trusted also in the LORD; *therefore* I
shall not slide.
2 Examine me, O LORD, and prove me; try my reins
and my heart.
3 For thy lovingkindness *is* before mine eyes: and I
have walked in thy truth.
4 I have not sat with vain persons, neither will I go
in with dissemblers.

NEW LIVING TRANSLATION

6 Remember, O LORD, your compassion and
unfailing love,
which you have shown from long ages past.
7 Do not remember the rebellious sins of
my youth.
Remember me in the light of your
unfailing love,
for you are merciful, O LORD.
8 The LORD is good and does what is right;
he shows the proper path to those who
go astray.
9 He leads the humble in doing right,
teaching them his way.
10 The LORD leads with unfailing love and
faithfulness
all who keep his covenant and obey
his demands.

11 For the honor of your name, O LORD,
forgive my many, many sins.
12 Who are those who fear the LORD?
He will show them the path they
should choose.
13 They will live in prosperity,
and their children will inherit the land.
14 The LORD is a friend to those who fear him.
He teaches them his covenant.
15 My eyes are always on the LORD,
for he rescues me from the traps of my enemies.
16 Turn to me and have mercy,
for I am alone and in deep distress.
17 My problems go from bad to worse.
Oh, save me from them all!
18 Feel my pain and see my trouble.
Forgive all my sins.
19 See how many enemies I have
and how viciously they hate me!
20 Protect me! Rescue my life from them!
Do not let me be disgraced, for in you
I take refuge.
21 May integrity and honesty protect me,
for I put my hope in you.

22 O God, ransom Israel
from all its troubles.

26 *A psalm of David.*

1 Declare me innocent, O LORD,
for I have acted with integrity;
I have trusted in the LORD without wavering.
2 Put me on trial, LORD, and cross-examine me.
Test my motives and my heart.
3 For I am always aware of your unfailing love,
and I have lived according to your truth.
4 I do not spend time with liars
or go along with hypocrites.

KING JAMES VERSION

5 I have hated the congregation of evildoers; and
will not sit with the wicked.
6 I will wash mine hands in innocency: so will I
compass thine altar, O LORD:
7 That I may publish with the voice of thanksgiving, and tell of all thy wondrous works.
8 LORD, I have loved the habitation of thy house,
and the place where thine honour dwelleth.
9 Gather not my soul with sinners, nor my life with
bloody men:
10 In whose hands *is* mischief, and their right hand
is full of bribes.
11 But as for me, I will walk in mine integrity: redeem me, and be merciful unto me.
12 My foot standeth in an even place: in the congregations will I bless the LORD.

27 A Psalm *of David*

1 The LORD *is* my light and my salvation; whom
shall I fear? the LORD *is* the strength of my life; of
whom shall I be afraid?
2 When the wicked, *even* mine enemies and my
foes, came upon me to eat up my flesh, they stumbled
and fell.
3 Though an host should encamp against me, my
heart shall not fear: though war should rise against
me, in this *will* I *be* confident.
4 One *thing* have I desired of the LORD, that will I
seek after; that I may dwell in the house of the LORD
all the days of my life, to behold the beauty of the
LORD, and to inquire in his temple.
5 For in the time of trouble he shall hide me in his
pavilion: in the secret of his tabernacle shall he hide
me; he shall set me up upon a rock.
6 And now shall mine head be lifted up above mine
enemies round about me: therefore will I offer in his
tabernacle sacrifices of joy; I will sing, yea, I will sing
praises unto the LORD.
7 Hear, O LORD, *when* I cry with my voice: have
mercy also upon me, and answer me.
8 *When thou saidst,* Seek ye my face; my heart said
unto thee, Thy face, LORD, will I seek.
9 Hide not thy face *far* from me; put not thy servant
away in anger: thou hast been my help; leave me not,
neither forsake me, O God of my salvation.

NEW LIVING TRANSLATION

5 I hate the gatherings of those who do evil,
and I refuse to join in with the wicked.
6 I wash my hands to declare my innocence.
I come to your altar, O LORD,
7 singing a song of thanksgiving
and telling of all your wonders.
8 I love your sanctuary, LORD,
the place where your glorious presence dwells.

9 Don't let me suffer the fate of sinners.
Don't condemn me along with murderers.
10 Their hands are dirty with evil schemes,
and they constantly take bribes.
11 But I am not like that; I live with integrity.
So redeem me and show me mercy.
12 Now I stand on solid ground,
and I will publicly praise the LORD.

27 *A psalm of David.*

1 The LORD is my light and my salvation—
so why should I be afraid?
The LORD is my fortress, protecting me
from danger,
so why should I tremble?
2 When evil people come to devour me,
when my enemies and foes attack me,
they will stumble and fall.
3 Though a mighty army surrounds me,
my heart will not be afraid.
Even if I am attacked,
I will remain confident.

4 The one thing I ask of the LORD—
the thing I seek most—
is to live in the house of the LORD all the
days of my life,
delighting in the LORD's perfections
and meditating in his Temple.
5 For he will conceal me there when troubles come;
he will hide me in his sanctuary.
He will place me out of reach on a high rock.
6 Then I will hold my head high
above my enemies who surround me.
At his sanctuary I will offer sacrifices with
shouts of joy,
singing and praising the LORD with music.

7 Hear me as I pray, O LORD.
Be merciful and answer me!
8 My heart has heard you say, "Come and talk
with me."
And my heart responds, "LORD, I am coming."
9 Do not turn your back on me.
Do not reject your servant in anger.
You have always been my helper.
Don't leave me now; don't abandon me,
O God of my salvation!

KING JAMES VERSION

10 When my father and my mother forsake me, then the LORD will take me up.

11 Teach me thy way, O LORD, and lead me in a plain path, because of mine enemies.

12 Deliver me not over unto the will of mine enemies: for false witnesses are risen up against me, and such as breathe out cruelty.

13 *I had fainted,* unless I had believed to see the goodness of the LORD in the land of the living.

14 Wait on the LORD: be of good courage, and he shall strengthen thine heart: wait, I say, on the LORD.

28 A Psalm *of David*

1 Unto thee will I cry, O LORD my rock; be not silent to me: lest, *if* thou be silent to me, I become like them that go down into the pit.

2 Hear the voice of my supplications, when I cry unto thee, when I lift up my hands toward thy holy oracle.

3 Draw me not away with the wicked, and with the workers of iniquity, which speak peace to their neighbours, but mischief *is* in their hearts.

4 Give them according to their deeds, and according to the wickedness of their endeavours: give them after the work of their hands; render to them their desert.

5 Because they regard not the works of the LORD, nor the operation of his hands, he shall destroy them, and not build them up.

6 Blessed *be* the LORD, because he hath heard the voice of my supplications.

7 The LORD *is* my strength and my shield; my heart trusted in him, and I am helped: therefore my heart greatly rejoiceth; and with my song will I praise him.

8 The LORD *is* their strength, and he *is* the saving strength of his anointed.

9 Save thy people, and bless thine inheritance: feed them also, and lift them up for ever.

NEW LIVING TRANSLATION

10 Even if my father and mother abandon me,
the LORD will hold me close.

11 Teach me how to live, O LORD.
Lead me along the right path,
for my enemies are waiting for me.
12 Do not let me fall into their hands.
For they accuse me of things I've never done;
with every breath they threaten me with violence.
13 Yet I am confident I will see the LORD's goodness
while I am here in the land of the living.

14 Wait patiently for the LORD.
Be brave and courageous.
Yes, wait patiently for the LORD.

28 *A psalm of David.*

1 I pray to you, O LORD, my rock.
Do not turn a deaf ear to me.
For if you are silent,
I might as well give up and die.
2 Listen to my prayer for mercy
as I cry out to you for help,
as I lift my hands toward your holy sanctuary.

3 Do not drag me away with the wicked—
with those who do evil—
those who speak friendly words to their neighbors
while planning evil in their hearts.
4 Give them the punishment they so richly deserve!
Measure it out in proportion to their wickedness.
Pay them back for all their evil deeds!
Give them a taste of what they have done to others.
5 They care nothing for what the LORD has done
or for what his hands have made.
So he will tear them down,
and they will never be rebuilt!
6 Praise the LORD!
For he has heard my cry for mercy.
7 The LORD is my strength and shield.
I trust him with all my heart.
He helps me, and my heart is filled with joy.
I burst out in songs of thanksgiving.

8 The LORD gives his people strength.
He is a safe fortress for his anointed king.
9 Save your people!
Bless Israel, your special possession.*
Lead them like a shepherd,
and carry them in your arms forever.

28:9 Hebrew *Bless your inheritance.*

KING JAMES VERSION

29
A Psalm of David

1 Give unto the LORD, O ye mighty, give unto the
LORD glory and strength.
2 Give unto the LORD the glory due unto his name;
worship the LORD in the beauty of holiness.
3 The voice of the LORD *is* upon the waters: the God
of glory thundereth: the LORD *is* upon many waters.
4 The voice of the LORD *is* powerful; the voice of
the LORD *is* full of majesty.
5 The voice of the LORD breaketh the cedars; yea,
the LORD breaketh the cedars of Lebanon.
6 He maketh them also to skip like a calf; Lebanon
and Sirion like a young unicorn.
7 The voice of the LORD divideth the flames of fire.
8 The voice of the LORD shaketh the wilderness; the
LORD shaketh the wilderness of Kadesh.
9 The voice of the LORD maketh the hinds to calve,
and discovereth the forests: and in his temple doth
every one speak of *his* glory.
10 The LORD sitteth upon the flood; yea, the LORD
sitteth King for ever.
11 The LORD will give strength unto his people; the
LORD will bless his people with peace.

30
A Psalm and Song at the dedication of the house of David

1 I will extol thee, O LORD; for thou hast lifted me
up, and hast not made my foes to rejoice over me.
2 O LORD my God, I cried unto thee, and thou hast
healed me.
3 O LORD, thou hast brought up my soul from the
grave: thou hast kept me alive, that I should not go
down to the pit.
4 Sing unto the LORD, O ye saints of his, and give
thanks at the remembrance of his holiness.
5 For his anger *endureth but* a moment; in his favour *is* life: weeping may endure for a night, but joy
cometh in the morning.
6 And in my prosperity I said, I shall never be
moved.
7 LORD, by thy favour thou hast made my mountain
to stand strong: thou didst hide thy face, *and* I was
troubled.

NEW LIVING TRANSLATION

29
A psalm of David.

1 Honor the LORD, you heavenly beings*;
honor the LORD for his glory and strength.
2 Honor the LORD for the glory of his name.
Worship the LORD in the splendor of
his holiness.

3 The voice of the LORD echoes above the sea.
The God of glory thunders.
The LORD thunders over the mighty sea.
4 The voice of the LORD is powerful;
the voice of the LORD is majestic.
5 The voice of the LORD splits the mighty cedars;
the LORD shatters the cedars of Lebanon.
6 He makes Lebanon's mountains skip like a calf;
he makes Mount Hermon* leap like a young
wild ox.
7 The voice of the LORD strikes
with bolts of lightning.
8 The voice of the LORD makes the barren
wilderness quake;
the LORD shakes the wilderness of Kadesh.
9 The voice of the LORD twists mighty oaks*
and strips the forests bare.
In his Temple everyone shouts, "Glory!"

10 The LORD rules over the floodwaters.
The LORD reigns as king forever.
11 The LORD gives his people strength.
The LORD blesses them with peace.

30
A psalm of David. A song for the dedication of the Temple.

1 I will exalt you, LORD, for you rescued me.
You refused to let my enemies triumph
over me.
2 O LORD my God, I cried to you for help,
and you restored my health.
3 You brought me up from the grave,* O LORD.
You kept me from falling into the pit of death.

4 Sing to the LORD, all you godly ones!
Praise his holy name.
5 For his anger lasts only a moment,
but his favor lasts a lifetime!
Weeping may last through the night,
but joy comes with the morning.

6 When I was prosperous, I said,
"Nothing can stop me now!"
7 Your favor, O LORD, made me as secure
as a mountain.
Then you turned away from me, and
I was shattered.

29:1 Hebrew *you sons of God.* **29:6** Hebrew *Sirion,* another name for Mount Hermon. **29:9** Or *causes the deer to writhe in labor.* **30:3** Hebrew *from Sheol.*

KING JAMES VERSION

8 I cried to thee, O LORD; and unto the LORD I made
supplication.
9 What profit *is there* in my blood, when I go down
to the pit? Shall the dust praise thee? shall it declare
thy truth?
10 Hear, O LORD, and have mercy upon me: LORD, be
thou my helper.
11 Thou hast turned for me my mourning into
dancing: thou hast put off my sackcloth, and girded
me with gladness;
12 To the end that *my* glory may sing praise to thee,
and not be silent. O LORD my God, I will give thanks
unto thee for ever.

31 *To the chief Musician, A Psalm of David*

1 In thee, O LORD, do I put my trust; let me never be
ashamed: deliver me in thy righteousness.
2 Bow down thine ear to me; deliver me speedily:
be thou my strong rock, for an house of defence to
save me.
3 For thou *art* my rock and my fortress; therefore
for thy name's sake lead me, and guide me.
4 Pull me out of the net that they have laid privily
for me: for thou *art* my strength.
5 Into thine hand I commit my spirit: thou hast redeemed me, O LORD God of truth.
6 I have hated them that regard lying vanities: but
I trust in the LORD.
7 I will be glad and rejoice in thy mercy: for thou
hast considered my trouble; thou hast known my
soul in adversities;
8 And hast not shut me up into the hand of the
enemy: thou hast set my feet in a large room.
9 Have mercy upon me, O LORD, for I am in trouble:
mine eye is consumed with grief, *yea,* my soul and
my belly.
10 For my life is spent with grief, and my years with
sighing: my strength faileth because of mine iniquity, and my bones are consumed.
11 I was a reproach among all mine enemies, but
especially among my neighbours, and a fear to mine
acquaintance: they that did see me without fled
from me.
12 I am forgotten as a dead man out of mind: I am
like a broken vessel.
13 For I have heard the slander of many: fear *was*
on every side: while they took counsel together
against me, they devised to take away my life.

NEW LIVING TRANSLATION

8 I cried out to you, O LORD.
I begged the Lord for mercy, saying,
9 "What will you gain if I die,
if I sink into the grave?
Can my dust praise you?
Can it tell of your faithfulness?
10 Hear me, LORD, and have mercy on me.
Help me, O LORD."
11 You have turned my mourning into joyful
dancing.
You have taken away my clothes of mourning
and clothed me with joy,
12 that I might sing praises to you and not be silent.
O LORD my God, I will give you thanks forever!

31 *For the choir director: A psalm of David.*

1 O LORD, I have come to you for protection;
don't let me be disgraced.
Save me, for you do what is right.
2 Turn your ear to listen to me;
rescue me quickly.
Be my rock of protection,
a fortress where I will be safe.
3 You are my rock and my fortress.
For the honor of your name, lead me out
of this danger.
4 Pull me from the trap my enemies set for me,
for I find protection in you alone.
5 I entrust my spirit into your hand.
Rescue me, LORD, for you are a faithful God.

6 I hate those who worship worthless idols.
I trust in the LORD.
7 I will be glad and rejoice in your unfailing love,
for you have seen my troubles,
and you care about the anguish of my soul.
8 You have not handed me over to my enemies
but have set me in a safe place.

9 Have mercy on me, LORD, for I am in distress.
Tears blur my eyes.
My body and soul are withering away.
10 I am dying from grief;
my years are shortened by sadness.
Sin has drained my strength;
I am wasting away from within.
11 I am scorned by all my enemies
and despised by my neighbors—
even my friends are afraid to come near me.
When they see me on the street,
they run the other way.
12 I am ignored as if I were dead,
as if I were a broken pot.
13 I have heard the many rumors about me,
and I am surrounded by terror.
My enemies conspire against me,
plotting to take my life.

KING JAMES VERSION

14 But I trusted in thee, O LORD: I said, Thou *art*
my God.
15 My times *are* in thy hand: deliver me from the
hand of mine enemies, and from them that persecute me.
16 Make thy face to shine upon thy servant: save me
for thy mercies' sake.
17 Let me not be ashamed, O LORD; for I have called
upon thee: let the wicked be ashamed, *and* let them
be silent in the grave.
18 Let the lying lips be put to silence; which speak
grievous things proudly and contemptuously against
the righteous.
19 *Oh* how great *is* thy goodness, which thou hast
laid up for them that fear thee; *which* thou hast
wrought for them that trust in thee before the sons
of men!
20 Thou shalt hide them in the secret of thy presence from the pride of man: thou shalt keep them secretly in a pavilion from the strife of tongues.
21 Blessed *be* the LORD: for he hath shewed me his
marvellous kindness in a strong city.
22 For I said in my haste, I am cut off from before
thine eyes: nevertheless thou heardest the voice of
my supplications when I cried unto thee.
23 O love the LORD, all ye his saints: *for* the LORD
preserveth the faithful, and plentifully rewardeth
the proud doer.
24 Be of good courage, and he shall strengthen your
heart, all ye that hope in the LORD.

32 A Psalm *of David, Maschil*

1 Blessed *is he whose* transgression *is* forgiven,
whose sin *is* covered.
2 Blessed *is* the man unto whom the LORD imputeth
not iniquity, and in whose spirit *there is* no guile.
3 When I kept silence, my bones waxed old
through my roaring all the day long.
4 For day and night thy hand was heavy upon me:
my moisture is turned into the drought of summer.
Selah.
5 I acknowledged my sin unto thee, and mine iniquity have I not hid. I said, I will confess my transgressions unto the LORD; and thou forgavest the iniquity
of my sin. Selah.
6 For this shall every one that is godly pray unto
thee in a time when thou mayest be found: surely in

NEW LIVING TRANSLATION

14 But I am trusting you, O LORD,
saying, "You are my God!"
15 My future is in your hands.
Rescue me from those who hunt
me down relentlessly.
16 Let your favor shine on your servant.
In your unfailing love, rescue me.
17 Don't let me be disgraced, O LORD,
for I call out to you for help.
Let the wicked be disgraced;
let them lie silent in the grave.*
18 Silence their lying lips—
those proud and arrogant lips that
accuse the godly.

19 How great is the goodness
you have stored up for those who fear you.
You lavish it on those who come to you for
protection,
blessing them before the watching world.
20 You hide them in the shelter of your presence,
safe from those who conspire against them.
You shelter them in your presence,
far from accusing tongues.

21 Praise the LORD,
for he has shown me the wonders of
his unfailing love.
He kept me safe when my city was
under attack.
22 In panic I cried out,
"I am cut off from the LORD!"
But you heard my cry for mercy
and answered my call for help.

23 Love the LORD, all you godly ones!
For the LORD protects those who are
loyal to him,
but he harshly punishes the arrogant.
24 So be strong and courageous,
all you who put your hope in the LORD!

32 *A psalm* of David.*

1 Oh, what joy for those
whose disobedience is forgiven,
whose sin is put out of sight!
2 Yes, what joy for those
whose record the LORD has cleared of guilt,*
whose lives are lived in complete honesty!
3 When I refused to confess my sin,
my body wasted away,
and I groaned all day long.
4 Day and night your hand of discipline was
heavy on me.
My strength evaporated like water in the
summer heat. *Interlude*

31:17 Hebrew *in Sheol.* 32:TITLE Hebrew *maskil.* This may be a literary or musical term. 32:2 Greek version reads *of sin.* Compare Rom 4:7.

KING JAMES VERSION

the floods of great waters they shall not come nigh
unto him.
7 Thou *art* my hiding place; thou shalt preserve me
from trouble; thou shalt compass me about with
songs of deliverance. Selah.
8 I will instruct thee and teach thee in the way
which thou shalt go: I will guide thee with mine eye.
9 Be ye not as the horse, *or* as the mule, *which* have
no understanding: whose mouth must be held in
with bit and bridle, lest they come near unto thee.
10 Many sorrows *shall be* to the wicked: but he that
trusteth in the LORD, mercy shall compass him about.
11 Be glad in the LORD, and rejoice, ye righteous:
and shout for joy, all *ye that are* upright in heart.

33 1 Rejoice in the LORD, O ye righteous: *for*
praise is comely for the upright.
2 Praise the LORD with harp: sing unto him with the
psaltery *and* an instrument of ten strings.
3 Sing unto him a new song; play skilfully with a
loud noise.
4 For the word of the LORD *is* right; and all his
works *are done* in truth.
5 He loveth righteousness and judgment: the earth
is full of the goodness of the LORD.
6 By the word of the LORD were the heavens made;
and all the host of them by the breath of his mouth.
7 He gathereth the waters of the sea together as an
heap: he layeth up the depth in storehouses.
8 Let all the earth fear the LORD: let all the inhabitants of the world stand in awe of him.
9 For he spake, and it was *done;* he commanded,
and it stood fast.
10 The LORD bringeth the counsel of the heathen
to nought: he maketh the devices of the people of
none effect.
11 The counsel of the LORD standeth for ever, the
thoughts of his heart to all generations.
12 Blessed *is* the nation whose God *is* the LORD;
and the people *whom* he hath chosen for his own
inheritance.

NEW LIVING TRANSLATION

5 Finally, I confessed all my sins to you
and stopped trying to hide my guilt.
I said to myself, "I will confess my rebellion
to the LORD."
And you forgave me! All my guilt is gone.
Interlude

6 Therefore, let all the godly pray to you while there
is still time,
that they may not drown in the floodwaters
of judgment.
7 For you are my hiding place;
you protect me from trouble.
You surround me with songs of victory.
Interlude

8 The LORD says, "I will guide you along the best
pathway for your life.
I will advise you and watch over you.
9 Do not be like a senseless horse or mule
that needs a bit and bridle to keep it
under control."

10 Many sorrows come to the wicked,
but unfailing love surrounds those who trust
the LORD.
11 So rejoice in the LORD and be glad, all you who
obey him!
Shout for joy, all you whose hearts are pure!

33 1 Let the godly sing for joy to the LORD;
it is fitting for the pure to praise him.
2 Praise the LORD with melodies on the lyre;
make music for him on the ten-stringed harp.
3 Sing a new song of praise to him;
play skillfully on the harp, and sing with joy.
4 For the word of the LORD holds true,
and we can trust everything he does.
5 He loves whatever is just and good;
the unfailing love of the LORD fills the earth.

6 The LORD merely spoke,
and the heavens were created.
He breathed the word,
and all the stars were born.
7 He assigned the sea its boundaries
and locked the oceans in vast reservoirs.
8 Let the whole world fear the LORD,
and let everyone stand in awe of him.
9 For when he spoke, the world began!
It appeared at his command.

10 The LORD frustrates the plans of the nations
and thwarts all their schemes.
11 But the LORD's plans stand firm forever;
his intentions can never be shaken.

12 What joy for the nation whose God is the LORD,
whose people he has chosen as his inheritance.

KING JAMES VERSION

13 The LORD looketh from heaven; he beholdeth all the sons of men.

14 From the place of his habitation he looketh upon all the inhabitants of the earth.

15 He fashioneth their hearts alike; he considereth all their works.

16 There is no king saved by the multitude of an host: a mighty man is not delivered by much strength.

17 An horse *is* a vain thing for safety: neither shall he deliver *any* by his great strength.

18 Behold, the eye of the LORD *is* upon them that fear him, upon them that hope in his mercy;

19 To deliver their soul from death, and to keep them alive in famine.

20 Our soul waiteth for the LORD: he *is* our help and our shield.

21 For our heart shall rejoice in him, because we have trusted in his holy name.

22 Let thy mercy, O LORD, be upon us, according as we hope in thee.

34

A Psalm *of David, when he changed his behaviour before Abimelech; who drove him away, and he departed.*

1 I will bless the LORD at all times: his praise *shall* continually *be* in my mouth.

2 My soul shall make her boast in the LORD: the humble shall hear *thereof*, and be glad.

3 O magnify the LORD with me, and let us exalt his name together.

4 I sought the LORD, and he heard me, and delivered me from all my fears.

5 They looked unto him, and were lightened: and their faces were not ashamed.

6 This poor man cried, and the LORD heard *him*, and saved him out of all his troubles.

7 The angel of the LORD encampeth round about them that fear him, and delivereth them.

8 O taste and see that the LORD *is* good: blessed *is* the man *that* trusteth in him.

9 O fear the LORD, ye his saints: for *there is* no want to them that fear him.

10 The young lions do lack, and suffer hunger: but they that seek the LORD shall not want any good *thing*.

11 Come, ye children, hearken unto me: I will teach you the fear of the LORD.

12 What man *is he that* desireth life, *and* loveth *many* days, that he may see good?

13 Keep thy tongue from evil, and thy lips from speaking guile.

NEW LIVING TRANSLATION

13 The LORD looks down from heaven
and sees the whole human race.
14 From his throne he observes
all who live on the earth.
15 He made their hearts,
so he understands everything they do.
16 The best-equipped army cannot save a king,
nor is great strength enough to save a warrior.
17 Don't count on your warhorse to give you victory—
for all its strength, it cannot save you.

18 But the LORD watches over those who fear him,
those who rely on his unfailing love.
19 He rescues them from death
and keeps them alive in times of famine.

20 We put our hope in the LORD.
He is our help and our shield.
21 In him our hearts rejoice,
for we trust in his holy name.
22 Let your unfailing love surround us, LORD,
for our hope is in you alone.

34*

A psalm of David, regarding the time he pretended to be insane in front of Abimelech, who sent him away.

1 I will praise the LORD at all times.
I will constantly speak his praises.
2 I will boast only in the LORD;
let all who are helpless take heart.
3 Come, let us tell of the LORD's greatness;
let us exalt his name together.

4 I prayed to the LORD, and he answered me.
He freed me from all my fears.
5 Those who look to him for help will be radiant with joy;
no shadow of shame will darken their faces.
6 In my desperation I prayed, and the LORD listened;
he saved me from all my troubles.
7 For the angel of the LORD is a guard;
he surrounds and defends all who fear him.

8 Taste and see that the LORD is good.
Oh, the joys of those who take refuge in him!
9 Fear the LORD, you his godly people,
for those who fear him will have all they need.
10 Even strong young lions sometimes go hungry,
but those who trust in the LORD will lack no good thing.

11 Come, my children, and listen to me,
and I will teach you to fear the LORD.
12 Does anyone want to live a life
that is long and prosperous?
13 Then keep your tongue from speaking evil
and your lips from telling lies!

34 This psalm is a Hebrew acrostic poem; each verse begins with a successive letter of the Hebrew alphabet.

14 Depart from evil, and do good; seek peace, and pursue it.

15 The eyes of the LORD *are* upon the righteous, and his ears *are open* unto their cry.

16 The face of the LORD *is* against them that do evil, to cut off the remembrance of them from the earth.

17 *The righteous* cry, and the LORD heareth, and delivereth them out of all their troubles.

18 The LORD *is* nigh unto them that are of a broken heart; and saveth such as be of a contrite spirit.

19 Many *are* the afflictions of the righteous: but the LORD delivereth him out of them all.

20 He keepeth all his bones: not one of them is broken.

21 Evil shall slay the wicked: and they that hate the righteous shall be desolate.

22 The LORD redeemeth the soul of his servants: and none of them that trust in him shall be desolate.

35 A Psalm *of David*

1 Plead *my cause,* O LORD, with them that strive with me: fight against them that fight against me.

2 Take hold of shield and buckler, and stand up for mine help.

3 Draw out also the spear, and stop *the way* against them that persecute me: say unto my soul, I *am* thy salvation.

4 Let them be confounded and put to shame that seek after my soul: let them be turned back and brought to confusion that devise my hurt.

5 Let them be as chaff before the wind: and let the angel of the LORD chase *them.*

6 Let their way be dark and slippery: and let the angel of the LORD persecute them.

7 For without cause have they hid for me their net *in* a pit, *which* without cause they have digged for my soul.

8 Let destruction come upon him at unawares; and let his net that he hath hid catch himself: into that very destruction let him fall.

9 And my soul shall be joyful in the LORD: it shall rejoice in his salvation.

10 All my bones shall say, LORD, who *is* like unto thee, which deliverest the poor from him that is too strong for him, yea, the poor and the needy from him that spoileth him?

14 Turn away from evil and do good.
Search for peace, and work to maintain it.

15 The eyes of the LORD watch over those
who do right;
his ears are open to their cries for help.
16 But the LORD turns his face against those
who do evil;
he will erase their memory from the earth.
17 The LORD hears his people when they call to
him for help.
He rescues them from all their troubles.
18 The LORD is close to the brokenhearted;
he rescues those whose spirits are crushed.

19 The righteous person faces many troubles,
but the LORD comes to the rescue each time.
20 For the LORD protects the bones of the righteous;
not one of them is broken!

21 Calamity will surely overtake the wicked,
and those who hate the righteous will
be punished.
22 But the LORD will redeem those who serve him.
No one who takes refuge in him will be
condemned.

35 *A psalm of David.*

1 O LORD, oppose those who oppose me.
Fight those who fight against me.
2 Put on your armor, and take up your shield.
Prepare for battle, and come to my aid.
3 Lift up your spear and javelin
against those who pursue me.
Let me hear you say,
"I will give you victory!"
4 Bring shame and disgrace on those trying
to kill me;
turn them back and humiliate those who
want to harm me.
5 Blow them away like chaff in the wind—
a wind sent by the angel of the LORD.
6 Make their path dark and slippery,
with the angel of the LORD pursuing them.
7 I did them no wrong, but they laid a trap for me.
I did them no wrong, but they dug a pit to
catch me.
8 So let sudden ruin come upon them!
Let them be caught in the trap they set for me!
Let them be destroyed in the pit they dug for me.

9 Then I will rejoice in the LORD.
I will be glad because he rescues me.
10 With every bone in my body I will praise him:
"LORD, who can compare with you?
Who else rescues the helpless from the strong?
Who else protects the helpless and poor from
those who rob them?"

KING JAMES VERSION

11 False witnesses did rise up; they laid to my
charge *things* that I knew not.
12 They rewarded me evil for good *to* the spoiling
of my soul.
13 But as for me, when they were sick, my clothing
was sackcloth: I humbled my soul with fasting; and
my prayer returned into mine own bosom.
14 I behaved myself as though *he had been* my
friend *or* brother: I bowed down heavily, as one that
mourneth *for his* mother.
15 But in mine adversity they rejoiced, and gathered themselves together: *yea,* the abjects gathered
themselves together against me, and I knew *it* not;
they did tear *me,* and ceased not:
16 With hypocritical mockers in feasts, they
gnashed upon me with their teeth.
17 LORD, how long wilt thou look on? rescue my
soul from their destructions, my darling from the
lions.
18 I will give thee thanks in the great congregation:
I will praise thee among much people.
19 Let not them that are mine enemies wrongfully
rejoice over me: *neither* let them wink with the eye
that hate me without a cause.
20 For they speak not peace: but they devise deceitful matters against *them that are* quiet in the land.
21 Yea, they opened their mouth wide against me,
and said, Aha, aha, our eye hath seen *it.*
22 *This* thou hast seen, O LORD: keep not silence:
O Lord, be not far from me.
23 Stir up thyself, and awake to my judgment, *even*
unto my cause, my God and my LORD.
24 Judge me, O LORD my God, according to thy righteousness; and let them not rejoice over me.
25 Let them not say in their hearts, Ah, so would we
have it: let them not say, We have swallowed him up.
26 Let them be ashamed and brought to confusion
together that rejoice at mine hurt: let them be
clothed with shame and dishonour that magnify
themselves against me.
27 Let them shout for joy, and be glad, that favour
my righteous cause: yea, let them say continually, Let
the LORD be magnified, which hath pleasure in the
prosperity of his servant.
28 And my tongue shall speak of thy righteousness
and of thy praise all the day long.

NEW LIVING TRANSLATION

11 Malicious witnesses testify against me.
They accuse me of crimes I know
nothing about.
12 They repay me evil for good.
I am sick with despair.
13 Yet when they were ill, I grieved for them.
I denied myself by fasting for them,
but my prayers returned unanswered.
14 I was sad, as though they were my friends
or family,
as if I were grieving for my own mother.
15 But they are glad now that I am in trouble;
they gleefully join together against me.
I am attacked by people I don't even know;
they slander me constantly.
16 They mock me and call me names;
they snarl at me.

17 How long, O Lord, will you look on and
do nothing?
Rescue me from their fierce attacks.
Protect my life from these lions!
18 Then I will thank you in front of the great
assembly.
I will praise you before all the people.
19 Don't let my treacherous enemies rejoice over
my defeat.
Don't let those who hate me without cause
gloat over my sorrow.
20 They don't talk of peace;
they plot against innocent people who mind
their own business.
21 They shout, "Aha! Aha!
With our own eyes we saw him do it!"

22 O LORD, you know all about this.
Do not stay silent.
Do not abandon me now, O Lord.
23 Wake up! Rise to my defense!
Take up my case, my God and my Lord.
24 Declare me not guilty, O LORD my God, for you
give justice.
Don't let my enemies laugh about me in
my troubles.
25 Don't let them say, "Look, we got what we wanted!
Now we will eat him alive!"
26 May those who rejoice at my troubles
be humiliated and disgraced.
May those who triumph over me
be covered with shame and dishonor.
27 But give great joy to those who came to my
defense.
Let them continually say, "Great is the LORD,
who delights in blessing his servant with
peace!"
28 Then I will proclaim your justice,
and I will praise you all day long.

KING JAMES VERSION

36 *To the chief Musician, A Psalm of David the servant of the LORD*

1 The transgression of the wicked saith within my heart, *that there is* no fear of God before his eyes.

2 For he flattereth himself in his own eyes, until his iniquity be found to be hateful.

3 The words of his mouth *are* iniquity and deceit: he hath left off to be wise, *and* to do good.

4 He deviseth mischief upon his bed; he setteth himself in a way *that is* not good; he abhorreth not evil.

5 Thy mercy, O LORD, *is* in the heavens; *and* thy faithfulness *reacheth* unto the clouds.

6 Thy righteousness *is* like the great mountains; thy judgments *are* a great deep: O LORD, thou preservest man and beast.

7 How excellent *is* thy lovingkindness, O God! therefore the children of men put their trust under the shadow of thy wings.

8 They shall be abundantly satisfied with the fatness of thy house; and thou shalt make them drink of the river of thy pleasures.

9 For with thee *is* the fountain of life: in thy light shall we see light.

10 O continue thy lovingkindness unto them that know thee; and thy righteousness to the upright in heart.

11 Let not the foot of pride come against me, and let not the hand of the wicked remove me.

12 There are the workers of iniquity fallen: they are cast down, and shall not be able to rise.

37 A Psalm *of David*

1 Fret not thyself because of evildoers, neither be thou envious against the workers of iniquity.

2 For they shall soon be cut down like the grass, and wither as the green herb.

3 Trust in the LORD, and do good; *so* shalt thou dwell in the land, and verily thou shalt be fed.

4 Delight thyself also in the LORD; and he shall give thee the desires of thine heart.

5 Commit thy way unto the LORD; trust also in him; and he shall bring *it* to pass.

6 And he shall bring forth thy righteousness as the light, and thy judgment as the noonday.

7 Rest in the LORD, and wait patiently for him: fret not thyself because of him who prospereth in his way, because of the man who bringeth wicked devices to pass.

NEW LIVING TRANSLATION

36 *For the choir director: A psalm of David, the servant of the LORD.*

1 Sin whispers to the wicked, deep within their
hearts.
They have no fear of God at all.
2 In their blind conceit,
they cannot see how wicked they really are.
3 Everything they say is crooked and deceitful.
They refuse to act wisely or do good.
4 They lie awake at night, hatching sinful plots.
Their actions are never good.
They make no attempt to turn from evil.

5 Your unfailing love, O LORD, is as vast as the
heavens;
your faithfulness reaches beyond the clouds.
6 Your righteousness is like the mighty mountains,
your justice like the ocean depths.
You care for people and animals alike, O LORD.
7 How precious is your unfailing love, O God!
All humanity finds shelter
in the shadow of your wings.
8 You feed them from the abundance of your
own house,
letting them drink from your river of delights.
9 For you are the fountain of life,
the light by which we see.

10 Pour out your unfailing love on those who love you;
give justice to those with honest hearts.
11 Don't let the proud trample me
or the wicked push me around.
12 Look! Those who do evil have fallen!
They are thrown down, never to rise again.

37* *A psalm of David.*

1 Don't worry about the wicked
or envy those who do wrong.
2 For like grass, they soon fade away.
Like spring flowers, they soon wither.

3 Trust in the LORD and do good.
Then you will live safely in the land and prosper.
4 Take delight in the LORD,
and he will give you your heart's desires.
5 Commit everything you do to the LORD.
Trust him, and he will help you.
6 He will make your innocence radiate like
the dawn,
and the justice of your cause will shine
like the noonday sun.

7 Be still in the presence of the LORD,
and wait patiently for him to act.
Don't worry about evil people who prosper
or fret about their wicked schemes.

37 This psalm is a Hebrew acrostic poem; each stanza begins with a successive letter of the Hebrew alphabet.

KING JAMES VERSION

8 Cease from anger, and forsake wrath: fret not thyself in any wise to do evil.
9 For evildoers shall be cut off: but those that wait
upon the LORD, they shall inherit the earth.
10 For yet a little while, and the wicked *shall* not *be:*
yea, thou shalt diligently consider his place, and it
shall not *be*.
11 But the meek shall inherit the earth; and shall
delight themselves in the abundance of peace.
12 The wicked plotteth against the just, and
gnasheth upon him with his teeth.
13 The Lord shall laugh at him: for he seeth that his
day is coming.
14 The wicked have drawn out the sword, and have
bent their bow, to cast down the poor and needy, *and*
to slay such as be of upright conversation.
15 Their sword shall enter into their own heart,
and their bows shall be broken.
16 A little that a righteous man hath *is* better than
the riches of many wicked.
17 For the arms of the wicked shall be broken: but
the LORD upholdeth the righteous.
18 The LORD knoweth the days of the upright: and
their inheritance shall be for ever.
19 They shall not be ashamed in the evil time: and
in the days of famine they shall be satisfied.
20 But the wicked shall perish, and the enemies of
the LORD *shall be* as the fat of lambs: they shall consume; into smoke shall they consume away.
21 The wicked borroweth, and payeth not again:
but the righteous sheweth mercy, and giveth.
22 For *such as be* blessed of him shall inherit the
earth; and *they that be* cursed of him shall be cut off.
23 The steps of a *good* man are ordered by the
LORD: and he delighteth in his way.
24 Though he fall, he shall not be utterly cast down:
for the LORD upholdeth *him with* his hand.
25 I have been young, and *now* am old; yet have I
not seen the righteous forsaken, nor his seed begging bread.
26 *He is* ever merciful, and lendeth; and his seed *is*
blessed.
27 Depart from evil, and do good; and dwell for
evermore.
28 For the LORD loveth judgment, and forsaketh not
his saints; they are preserved for ever: but the seed of
the wicked shall be cut off.

NEW LIVING TRANSLATION

8 Stop being angry!
Turn from your rage!
Do not lose your temper—
it only leads to harm.
9 For the wicked will be destroyed,
but those who trust in the LORD will possess
the land.
10 Soon the wicked will disappear.
Though you look for them, they will be gone.
11 The lowly will possess the land
and will live in peace and prosperity.
12 The wicked plot against the godly;
they snarl at them in defiance.
13 But the Lord just laughs,
for he sees their day of judgment coming.

14 The wicked draw their swords
and string their bows
to kill the poor and the oppressed,
to slaughter those who do right.
15 But their swords will stab their own hearts,
and their bows will be broken.
16 It is better to be godly and have little
than to be evil and rich.
17 For the strength of the wicked will be shattered,
but the LORD takes care of the godly.

18 Day by day the LORD takes care of the innocent,
and they will receive an inheritance that
lasts forever.
19 They will not be disgraced in hard times;
even in famine they will have more than enough.

20 But the wicked will die.
The LORD's enemies are like flowers in a field—
they will disappear like smoke.

21 The wicked borrow and never repay,
but the godly are generous givers.
22 Those the LORD blesses will possess the land,
but those he curses will die.

23 The LORD directs the steps of the godly.
He delights in every detail of their lives.
24 Though they stumble, they will never fall,
for the LORD holds them by the hand.
25 Once I was young, and now I am old.
Yet I have never seen the godly abandoned
or their children begging for bread.
26 The godly always give generous loans to others,
and their children are a blessing.
27 Turn from evil and do good,
and you will live in the land forever.
28 For the LORD loves justice,
and he will never abandon the godly.

He will keep them safe forever,
but the children of the wicked will die.

KING JAMES VERSION

29 The righteous shall inherit the land, and dwell
therein for ever.
30 The mouth of the righteous speaketh wisdom,
and his tongue talketh of judgment.
31 The law of his God *is* in his heart; none of his
steps shall slide.
32 The wicked watcheth the righteous, and
seeketh to slay him.
33 The LORD will not leave him in his hand, nor
condemn him when he is judged.
34 Wait on the LORD, and keep his way, and he shall
exalt thee to inherit the land: when the wicked are
cut off, thou shalt see *it*.
35 I have seen the wicked in great power, and
spreading himself like a green bay tree.
36 Yet he passed away, and, lo, he *was* not: yea, I
sought him, but he could not be found.
37 Mark the perfect *man*, and behold the upright:
for the end of *that* man *is* peace.
38 But the transgressors shall be destroyed together: the end of the wicked shall be cut off.
39 But the salvation of the righteous *is* of the LORD:
he is their strength in the time of trouble.
40 And the LORD shall help them, and deliver them:
he shall deliver them from the wicked, and save
them, because they trust in him.

38 *A Psalm of David, to bring to remembrance*

1 O LORD, rebuke me not in thy wrath: neither chasten me in thy hot displeasure.
2 For thine arrows stick fast in me, and thy hand
presseth me sore.
3 *There is* no soundness in my flesh because of
thine anger; neither *is there any* rest in my bones
because of my sin.
4 For mine iniquities are gone over mine head: as
an heavy burden they are too heavy for me.
5 My wounds stink *and* are corrupt because of my
foolishness.
6 I am troubled; I am bowed down greatly; I go
mourning all the day long.
7 For my loins are filled with a loathsome *disease:*
and *there is* no soundness in my flesh.
8 I am feeble and sore broken: I have roared by
reason of the disquietness of my heart.
9 Lord, all my desire *is* before thee; and my groaning is not hid from thee.

NEW LIVING TRANSLATION

29 The godly will possess the land
and will live there forever.
30 The godly offer good counsel;
they teach right from wrong.
31 They have made God's law their own,
so they will never slip from his path.
32 The wicked wait in ambush for the godly,
looking for an excuse to kill them.
33 But the LORD will not let the wicked succeed
or let the godly be condemned when they
are put on trial.

34 Put your hope in the LORD.
Travel steadily along his path.
He will honor you by giving you the land.
You will see the wicked destroyed.
35 I have seen wicked and ruthless people
flourishing like a tree in its native soil.
36 But when I looked again, they were gone!
Though I searched for them, I could not
find them!
37 Look at those who are honest and good,
for a wonderful future awaits those who
love peace.
38 But the rebellious will be destroyed;
they have no future.

39 The LORD rescues the godly;
he is their fortress in times of trouble.
40 The LORD helps them,
rescuing them from the wicked.
He saves them,
and they find shelter in him.

38 *A psalm of David, asking God to remember him.*

1 O LORD, don't rebuke me in your anger
or discipline me in your rage!
2 Your arrows have struck deep,
and your blows are crushing me.
3 Because of your anger, my whole body is sick;
my health is broken because of my sins.
4 My guilt overwhelms me—
it is a burden too heavy to bear.
5 My wounds fester and stink
because of my foolish sins.
6 I am bent over and racked with pain.
All day long I walk around filled with grief.
7 A raging fever burns within me,
and my health is broken.
8 I am exhausted and completely crushed.
My groans come from an anguished heart.
9 You know what I long for, Lord;
you hear my every sigh.

10 My heart panteth, my strength faileth me: as for
the light of mine eyes, it also is gone from me.
11 My lovers and my friends stand aloof from my
sore; and my kinsmen stand afar off.
12 They also that seek after my life lay snares *for*
me: and they that seek my hurt speak mischievous
things, and imagine deceits all the day long.
13 But I, as a deaf *man*, heard not; and *I was* as a
dumb man *that* openeth not his mouth.
14 Thus I was as a man that heareth not, and in
whose mouth *are* no reproofs.
15 For in thee, O LORD, do I hope: thou wilt hear,
O Lord my God.
16 For I said, *Hear me*, lest *otherwise* they should
rejoice over me: when my foot slippeth, they magnify
themselves against me.
17 For I *am* ready to halt, and my sorrow *is* continually before me.
18 For I will declare mine iniquity; I will be sorry for
my sin.
19 But mine enemies *are* lively, *and* they are strong:
and they that hate me wrongfully are multiplied.
20 They also that render evil for good are mine adversaries; because I follow *the thing that* good *is*.
21 Forsake me not, O LORD: O my God, be not far
from me.
22 Make haste to help me, O Lord my salvation.

39 *To the chief Musician, even to Jeduthun, A Psalm of David*

1 I said, I will take heed to my ways, that I sin not
with my tongue: I will keep my mouth with a bridle,
while the wicked is before me.
2 I was dumb with silence, I held my peace, *even*
from good; and my sorrow was stirred.
3 My heart was hot within me, while I was musing
the fire burned: *then* spake I with my tongue,
4 LORD, make me to know mine end, and the measure of my days, what it *is; that* I may know how frail
I *am*.
5 Behold, thou hast made my days *as* an handbreadth; and mine age *is* as nothing before thee: verily every man at his best state *is* altogether vanity.
Selah.
6 Surely every man walketh in a vain shew: surely
they are disquieted in vain: he heapeth up *riches*, and
knoweth not who shall gather them.

10 My heart beats wildly, my strength fails,
and I am going blind.
11 My loved ones and friends stay away, fearing
my disease.
Even my own family stands at a distance.
12 Meanwhile, my enemies lay traps to kill me.
Those who wish me harm make plans
to ruin me.
All day long they plan their treachery.

13 But I am deaf to all their threats.
I am silent before them as one who
cannot speak.
14 I choose to hear nothing,
and I make no reply.
15 For I am waiting for you, O LORD.
You must answer for me, O Lord my God.
16 I prayed, "Don't let my enemies gloat over me
or rejoice at my downfall."

17 I am on the verge of collapse,
facing constant pain.
18 But I confess my sins;
I am deeply sorry for what I have done.
19 I have many aggressive enemies;
they hate me without reason.
20 They repay me evil for good
and oppose me for pursuing good.
21 Do not abandon me, O LORD.
Do not stand at a distance, my God.
22 Come quickly to help me,
O Lord my savior.

39 *For Jeduthun, the choir director: A psalm of David.*

1 I said to myself, "I will watch what I do
and not sin in what I say.
I will hold my tongue
when the ungodly are around me."
2 But as I stood there in silence—
not even speaking of good things—
the turmoil within me grew worse.
3 The more I thought about it,
the hotter I got,
igniting a fire of words:
4 "LORD, remind me how brief my time
on earth will be.
Remind me that my days are numbered—
how fleeting my life is.
5 You have made my life no longer than the width
of my hand.
My entire lifetime is just a moment to you;
at best, each of us is but a breath." *Interlude*

6 We are merely moving shadows,
and all our busy rushing ends in nothing.
We heap up wealth,
not knowing who will spend it.

KING JAMES VERSION

7And now, Lord, what wait I for? my hope *is* in
thee.
8Deliver me from all my transgressions: make me
not the reproach of the foolish.
9I was dumb, I opened not my mouth; because
thou didst *it*.
10Remove thy stroke away from me: I am consumed by the blow of thine hand.
11When thou with rebukes dost correct man for
iniquity, thou makest his beauty to consume away
like a moth: surely every man *is* vanity. Selah.
12Hear my prayer, O LORD, and give ear unto my
cry; hold not thy peace at my tears: for I *am* a
stranger with thee, *and* a sojourner, as all my fathers
were.
13O spare me, that I may recover strength, before I
go hence, and be no more.

40 *To the chief Musician, A Psalm of David*

1I waited patiently for the LORD; and he inclined
unto me, and heard my cry.
2He brought me up also out of an horrible pit, out
of the miry clay, and set my feet upon a rock, *and* established my goings.
3And he hath put a new song in my mouth, *even*
praise unto our God: many shall see *it*, and fear, and
shall trust in the LORD.
4Blessed *is* that man that maketh the LORD his
trust, and respecteth not the proud, nor such as turn
aside to lies.
5Many, O LORD my God, *are* thy wonderful works
which thou hast done, and thy thoughts *which are* to
us-ward: they cannot be reckoned up in order unto
thee: *if* I would declare and speak *of them*, they are
more than can be numbered.
6Sacrifice and offering thou didst not desire; mine
ears hast thou opened: burnt offering and sin offering hast thou not required.
7Then said I, Lo, I come: in the volume of the book
it is written of me,
8I delight to do thy will, O my God: yea, thy law *is*
within my heart.
9I have preached righteousness in the great congregation: lo, I have not refrained my lips, O LORD,
thou knowest.

NEW LIVING TRANSLATION

7 And so, Lord, where do I put my hope?
My only hope is in you.
8 Rescue me from my rebellion.
Do not let fools mock me.
9 I am silent before you; I won't say a word,
for my punishment is from you.
10 But please stop striking me!
I am exhausted by the blows from your hand.
11 When you discipline us for our sins,
you consume like a moth what is precious
to us.
Each of us is but a breath. *Interlude*

12 Hear my prayer, O LORD!
Listen to my cries for help!
Don't ignore my tears.
For I am your guest—
a traveler passing through,
as my ancestors were before me.
13 Leave me alone so I can smile again
before I am gone and exist no more.

40 *For the choir director: A psalm of David.*

1 I waited patiently for the LORD to help me,
and he turned to me and heard my cry.
2 He lifted me out of the pit of despair,
out of the mud and the mire.
He set my feet on solid ground
and steadied me as I walked along.
3 He has given me a new song to sing,
a hymn of praise to our God.
Many will see what he has done and be amazed.
They will put their trust in the LORD.

4 Oh, the joys of those who trust the LORD,
who have no confidence in the proud
or in those who worship idols.
5 O LORD my God, you have performed many
wonders for us.
Your plans for us are too numerous to list.
You have no equal.
If I tried to recite all your wonderful deeds,
I would never come to the end of them.
6 You take no delight in sacrifices or offerings.
Now that you have made me listen, I finally
understand*—
you don't require burnt offerings or sin
offerings.
7 Then I said, "Look, I have come.
As is written about me in the Scriptures:
8 I take joy in doing your will, my God,
for your instructions are written on my heart."
9 I have told all your people about your justice.
I have not been afraid to speak out,
as you, O LORD, well know.

40:6 Greek text reads *You have given me a body*. Compare Heb 10:5.

KING JAMES VERSION

10 I have not hid thy righteousness within my heart; I have declared thy faithfulness and thy salvation: I have not concealed thy lovingkindness and thy truth from the great congregation.

11 Withhold not thou thy tender mercies from me, O LORD: let thy lovingkindness and thy truth continually preserve me.

12 For innumerable evils have compassed me about: mine iniquities have taken hold upon me, so that I am not able to look up; they are more than the hairs of mine head: therefore my heart faileth me.

13 Be pleased, O LORD, to deliver me: O LORD, make haste to help me.

14 Let them be ashamed and confounded together that seek after my soul to destroy it; let them be driven backward and put to shame that wish me evil.

15 Let them be desolate for a reward of their shame that say unto me, Aha, aha.

16 Let all those that seek thee rejoice and be glad in thee: let such as love thy salvation say continually, The LORD be magnified.

17 But I *am* poor and needy; *yet* the Lord thinketh upon me: thou *art* my help and my deliverer; make no tarrying, O my God.

41 *To the chief Musician, A Psalm of David*

1 Blessed *is* he that considereth the poor: the LORD will deliver him in time of trouble.

2 The LORD will preserve him, and keep him alive; *and* he shall be blessed upon the earth: and thou wilt not deliver him unto the will of his enemies.

3 The LORD will strengthen him upon the bed of languishing: thou wilt make all his bed in his sickness.

4 I said, LORD, be merciful unto me: heal my soul; for I have sinned against thee.

5 Mine enemies speak evil of me, When shall he die, and his name perish?

6 And if he come to see *me,* he speaketh vanity: his heart gathereth iniquity to itself; *when* he goeth abroad, he telleth *it.*

7 All that hate me whisper together against me: against me do they devise my hurt.

NEW LIVING TRANSLATION

10 I have not kept the good news of your justice
hidden in my heart;
I have talked about your faithfulness and
saving power.
I have told everyone in the great assembly
of your unfailing love and faithfulness.

11 LORD, don't hold back your tender mercies
from me.
Let your unfailing love and faithfulness
always protect me.
12 For troubles surround me—
too many to count!
My sins pile up so high
I can't see my way out.
They outnumber the hairs on my head.
I have lost all courage.

13 Please, LORD, rescue me!
Come quickly, LORD, and help me.
14 May those who try to destroy me
be humiliated and put to shame.
May those who take delight in my trouble
be turned back in disgrace.
15 Let them be horrified by their shame,
for they said, "Aha! We've got him now!"

16 But may all who search for you
be filled with joy and gladness in you.
May those who love your salvation
repeatedly shout, "The LORD is great!"
17 As for me, since I am poor and needy,
let the Lord keep me in his thoughts.
You are my helper and my savior.
O my God, do not delay.

41 *For the choir director: A psalm of David.*

1 Oh, the joys of those who are kind to the poor!
The LORD rescues them when they are
in trouble.
2 The LORD protects them
and keeps them alive.
He gives them prosperity in the land
and rescues them from their enemies.
3 The LORD nurses them when they are sick
and restores them to health.

4 "O LORD," I prayed, "have mercy on me.
Heal me, for I have sinned against you."
5 But my enemies say nothing but evil about me.
"How soon will he die and be forgotten?"
they ask.
6 They visit me as if they were my friends,
but all the while they gather gossip,
and when they leave, they spread it
everywhere.
7 All who hate me whisper about me,
imagining the worst.

KING JAMES VERSION

8 An evil disease, *say they,* cleaveth fast unto him:
and *now* that he lieth he shall rise up no more.
9 Yea, mine own familiar friend, in whom I trusted,
which did eat of my bread, hath lifted up *his* heel
against me.
10 But thou, O LORD, be merciful unto me, and raise
me up, that I may requite them.
11 By this I know that thou favourest me, because
mine enemy doth not triumph over me.
12 And as for me, thou upholdest me in mine integrity, and settest me before thy face for ever.
13 Blessed *be* the LORD God of Israel from everlasting, and to everlasting. Amen, and Amen.

42 *To the chief Musician, Maschil, for the sons of Korah*

1 As the hart panteth after the water brooks, so
panteth my soul after thee, O God.
2 My soul thirsteth for God, for the living God:
when shall I come and appear before God?
3 My tears have been my meat day and night, while
they continually say unto me, Where *is* thy God?
4 When I remember these *things,* I pour out my
soul in me: for I had gone with the multitude, I went
with them to the house of God, with the voice of joy
and praise, with a multitude that kept holyday.
5 Why art thou cast down, O my soul? and *why* art
thou disquieted in me? hope thou in God: for I shall
yet praise him *for* the help of his countenance.
6 O my God, my soul is cast down within me: therefore will I remember thee from the land of Jordan,
and of the Hermonites, from the hill Mizar.
7 Deep calleth unto deep at the noise of thy water-
spouts: all thy waves and thy billows are gone
over me.
8 *Yet* the LORD will command his lovingkindness in
the daytime, and in the night his song *shall be* with
me, *and* my prayer unto the God of my life.
9 I will say unto God my rock, Why hast thou
forgotten me? why go I mourning because of the
oppression of the enemy?

NEW LIVING TRANSLATION

8 "He has some fatal disease," they say.
"He will never get out of that bed!"
9 Even my best friend, the one I trusted completely,
the one who shared my food, has turned
against me.
10 LORD, have mercy on me.
Make me well again, so I can pay them back!
11 I know you are pleased with me,
for you have not let my enemies triumph
over me.
12 You have preserved my life because I am
innocent;
you have brought me into your presence forever.

13 Praise the LORD, the God of Israel,
who lives from everlasting to everlasting.
Amen and amen!

BOOK TWO (Psalms 42–72)

42 *For the choir director: A psalm* of the descendants of Korah.*

1 As the deer longs for streams of water,
so I long for you, O God.
2 I thirst for God, the living God.
When can I go and stand before him?
3 Day and night I have only tears for food,
while my enemies continually taunt me, saying,
"Where is this God of yours?"

4 My heart is breaking
as I remember how it used to be:
I walked among the crowds of worshipers,
leading a great procession to the house of God,
singing for joy and giving thanks
amid the sound of a great celebration!

5 Why am I discouraged?
Why is my heart so sad?
I will put my hope in God!
I will praise him again—
my Savior and 6 my God!
Now I am deeply discouraged,
but I will remember you—
even from distant Mount Hermon, the source
of the Jordan,
from the land of Mount Mizar.
7 I hear the tumult of the raging seas
as your waves and surging tides sweep over me.
8 But each day the LORD pours his unfailing love
upon me,
and through each night I sing his songs,
praying to God who gives me life.

9 "O God my rock," I cry,
"Why have you forgotten me?
Why must I wander around in grief,
oppressed by my enemies?"

42:TITLE Hebrew *maskil.* This may be a literary or musical term.

KING JAMES VERSION

10 *As* with a sword in my bones, mine enemies reproach me; while they say daily unto me, Where *is*
thy God?
11 Why art thou cast down, O my soul? and why art
thou disquieted within me? hope thou in God: for I
shall yet praise him, *who is* the health of my countenance, and my God.

43

1 Judge me, O God, and plead my cause
against an ungodly nation: O deliver me
from the deceitful and unjust man.
2 For thou *art* the God of my strength: why dost
thou cast me off? why go I mourning because of the
oppression of the enemy?
3 O send out thy light and thy truth: let them lead
me; let them bring me unto thy holy hill, and to thy
tabernacles.
4 Then will I go unto the altar of God, unto God my
exceeding joy: yea, upon the harp will I praise thee,
O God my God.
5 Why art thou cast down, O my soul? and why art
thou disquieted within me? hope in God: for I shall
yet praise him, *who is* the health of my countenance,
and my God.

44

To the chief Musician for the sons of Korah, Maschil

1 We have heard with our ears, O God, our fathers
have told us, *what* work thou didst in their days, in
the times of old.
2 *How* thou didst drive out the heathen with thy
hand, and plantedst them; *how* thou didst afflict the
people, and cast them out.
3 For they got not the land in possession by their
own sword, neither did their own arm save them: but
thy right hand, and thine arm, and the light of thy
countenance, because thou hadst a favour unto
them.
4 Thou art my King, O God: command deliver-
ances for Jacob.
5 Through thee will we push down our enemies:
through thy name will we tread them under that rise
up against us.
6 For I will not trust in my bow, neither shall my
sword save me.

NEW LIVING TRANSLATION

10 Their taunts break my bones.
They scoff, "Where is this God of yours?"
11 Why am I discouraged?
Why is my heart so sad?
I will put my hope in God!
I will praise him again—
my Savior and my God!

43

1 Declare me innocent, O God!
Defend me against these ungodly people.
Rescue me from these unjust liars.
2 For you are God, my only safe haven.
Why have you tossed me aside?
Why must I wander around in grief,
oppressed by my enemies?
3 Send out your light and your truth;
let them guide me.
Let them lead me to your holy mountain,
to the place where you live.
4 There I will go to the altar of God,
to God—the source of all my joy.
I will praise you with my harp,
O God, my God!

5 Why am I discouraged?
Why is my heart so sad?
I will put my hope in God!
I will praise him again—
my Savior and my God!

44

For the choir director: A psalm of the descendants of Korah.*

1 O God, we have heard it with our own ears—
our ancestors have told us
of all you did in their day,
in days long ago:
2 You drove out the pagan nations by your power
and gave all the land to our ancestors.
You crushed their enemies
and set our ancestors free.
3 They did not conquer the land with their swords;
it was not their own strong arm that gave
them victory.
It was your right hand and strong arm
and the blinding light from your face that
helped them,
for you loved them.

4 You are my King and my God.
You command victories for Israel.*
5 Only by your power can we push back
our enemies;
only in your name can we trample our foes.
6 I do not trust in my bow;
I do not count on my sword to save me.

44:TITLE Hebrew *maskil.* This may be a literary or musical term.
44:4 Hebrew *for Jacob.* The names "Jacob" and "Israel" are often interchanged throughout the Old Testament, referring sometimes to the individual patriarch and sometimes to the nation.

KING JAMES VERSION

[7]But thou hast saved us from our enemies, and hast put them to shame that hated us.

[8]In God we boast all the day long, and praise thy name for ever. Selah.

[9]But thou hast cast off, and put us to shame; and goest not forth with our armies.

[10]Thou makest us to turn back from the enemy: and they which hate us spoil for themselves.

[11]Thou hast given us like sheep *appointed* for meat; and hast scattered us among the heathen.

[12]Thou sellest thy people for nought, and dost not increase *thy wealth* by their price.

[13]Thou makest us a reproach to our neighbours, a scorn and a derision to them that are round about us.

[14]Thou makest us a byword among the heathen, a shaking of the head among the people.

[15]My confusion *is* continually before me, and the shame of my face hath covered me,

[16]For the voice of him that reproacheth and blasphemeth; by reason of the enemy and avenger.

[17]All this is come upon us; yet have we not forgotten thee, neither have we dealt falsely in thy covenant.

[18]Our heart is not turned back, neither have our steps declined from thy way;

[19]Though thou hast sore broken us in the place of dragons, and covered us with the shadow of death.

[20]If we have forgotten the name of our God, or stretched out our hands to a strange god;

[21]Shall not God search this out? for he knoweth the secrets of the heart.

[22]Yea, for thy sake are we killed all the day long; we are counted as sheep for the slaughter.

[23]Awake, why sleepest thou, O Lord? arise, cast *us* not off for ever.

[24]Wherefore hidest thou thy face, *and* forgettest our affliction and our oppression?

[25]For our soul is bowed down to the dust: our belly cleaveth unto the earth.

[26]Arise for our help, and redeem us for thy mercies' sake.

45

To the chief Musician upon Shoshannim, for the sons of Korah, Maschil, A Song of loves

[1]My heart is inditing a good matter: I speak of the things which I have made touching the king: my tongue *is* the pen of a ready writer.

[2]Thou art fairer than the children of men: grace is poured into thy lips: therefore God hath blessed thee for ever.

NEW LIVING TRANSLATION

[7] You are the one who gives us victory over
our enemies;
you disgrace those who hate us.
[8] O God, we give glory to you all day long
and constantly praise your name. *Interlude*
[9] But now you have tossed us aside in dishonor.
You no longer lead our armies to battle.
[10] You make us retreat from our enemies
and allow those who hate us to plunder our land.
[11] You have butchered us like sheep
and scattered us among the nations.
[12] You sold your precious people for a pittance,
making nothing on the sale.
[13] You let our neighbors mock us.
We are an object of scorn and derision to those around us.
[14] You have made us the butt of their jokes;
they shake their heads at us in scorn.
[15] We can't escape the constant humiliation;
shame is written across our faces.
[16] All we hear are the taunts of our mockers.
All we see are our vengeful enemies.
[17] All this has happened though we have not
forgotten you.
We have not violated your covenant.
[18] Our hearts have not deserted you.
We have not strayed from your path.
[19] Yet you have crushed us in the jackal's
desert home.
You have covered us with darkness and death.
[20] If we had forgotten the name of our God
or spread our hands in prayer to foreign gods,
[21] God would surely have known it,
for he knows the secrets of every heart.
[22] But for your sake we are killed every day;
we are being slaughtered like sheep.
[23] Wake up, O Lord! Why do you sleep?
Get up! Do not reject us forever.
[24] Why do you look the other way?
Why do you ignore our suffering and
oppression?
[25] We collapse in the dust,
lying face down in the dirt.
[26] Rise up! Help us!
Ransom us because of your unfailing love.

45

For the choir director: A love song to be sung to the tune "Lilies." A psalm of the descendants of Korah.*

[1] Beautiful words stir my heart.
I will recite a lovely poem about the king,
for my tongue is like the pen of a skillful poet.
[2] You are the most handsome of all.
Gracious words stream from your lips.
God himself has blessed you forever.

45:TITLE Hebrew *maskil.* This may be a literary or musical term.

KING JAMES VERSION

3 Gird thy sword upon *thy* thigh, O *most* mighty, with thy glory and thy majesty.

4 And in thy majesty ride prosperously because of truth and meekness *and* righteousness; and thy right hand shall teach thee terrible things.

5 Thine arrows *are* sharp in the heart of the king's enemies; *whereby* the people fall under thee.

6 Thy throne, O God, *is* for ever and ever: the sceptre of thy kingdom *is* a right sceptre.

7 Thou lovest righteousness, and hatest wickedness: therefore God, thy God, hath anointed thee with the oil of gladness above thy fellows.

8 All thy garments *smell* of myrrh, and aloes, *and* cassia, out of the ivory palaces, whereby they have made thee glad.

9 Kings' daughters *were* among thy honourable women: upon thy right hand did stand the queen in gold of Ophir.

10 Hearken, O daughter, and consider, and incline thine ear; forget also thine own people, and thy father's house;

11 So shall the king greatly desire thy beauty: for he *is* thy Lord; and worship thou him.

12 And the daughter of Tyre *shall be there* with a gift; *even* the rich among the people shall intreat thy favour.

13 The king's daughter *is* all glorious within: her clothing *is* of wrought gold.

14 She shall be brought unto the king in raiment of needlework: the virgins her companions that follow her shall be brought unto thee.

15 With gladness and rejoicing shall they be brought: they shall enter into the king's palace.

16 Instead of thy fathers shall be thy children, whom thou mayest make princes in all the earth.

17 I will make thy name to be remembered in all generations: therefore shall the people praise thee for ever and ever.

46

To the chief Musician for the sons of Korah, A Song upon Alamoth

1 God *is* our refuge and strength, a very present help in trouble.

2 Therefore will not we fear, though the earth be removed, and though the mountains be carried into the midst of the sea;

3 *Though* the waters thereof roar *and* be troubled, *though* the mountains shake with the swelling thereof. Selah.

4 *There is* a river, the streams whereof shall make glad the city of God, the holy *place* of the tabernacles of the most High.

5 God *is* in the midst of her; she shall not be moved: God shall help her, *and that* right early.

NEW LIVING TRANSLATION

3 Put on your sword, O mighty warrior!
You are so glorious, so majestic!
4 In your majesty, ride out to victory,
defending truth, humility, and justice.
Go forth to perform awe-inspiring deeds!
5 Your arrows are sharp, piercing your
enemies' hearts.
The nations fall beneath your feet.
6 Your throne, O God,* endures forever and ever.
You rule with a scepter of justice.
7 You love justice and hate evil.
Therefore God, your God, has anointed you,
pouring out the oil of joy on you more than
on anyone else.
8 Myrrh, aloes, and cassia perfume your robes.
In ivory palaces the music of strings
entertains you.
9 Kings' daughters are among your noble women.
At your right side stands the queen,
wearing jewelry of finest gold from Ophir!
10 Listen to me, O royal daughter; take to heart what
I say.
Forget your people and your family far away.
11 For your royal husband delights in your beauty;
honor him, for he is your lord.
12 The princess of Tyre* will shower you with gifts.
The wealthy will beg your favor.
13 The bride, a princess, looks glorious
in her golden gown.
14 In her beautiful robes, she is led to the king,
accompanied by her bridesmaids.
15 What a joyful and enthusiastic procession
as they enter the king's palace!
16 Your sons will become kings like their father.
You will make them rulers over many lands.
17 I will bring honor to your name in every
generation.
Therefore, the nations will praise you
forever and ever.

46

*For the choir director: A song of the descendants of Korah, to be sung by soprano voices.**

1 God is our refuge and strength,
always ready to help in times of trouble.
2 So we will not fear when earthquakes come
and the mountains crumble into the sea.
3 Let the oceans roar and foam.
Let the mountains tremble as the waters surge!
Interlude
4 A river brings joy to the city of our God,
the sacred home of the Most High.
5 God dwells in that city; it cannot be destroyed.
From the very break of day, God will protect it.

45:6 Or *Your divine throne.* **45:12** Hebrew *The daughter of Tyre.* **46:TITLE** Hebrew *according to alamoth.*

KING JAMES VERSION

6 The heathen raged, the kingdoms were moved:
he uttered his voice, the earth melted.
7 The LORD of hosts *is* with us; the God of Jacob *is*
our refuge. Selah.
8 Come, behold the works of the LORD, what desolations he hath made in the earth.
9 He maketh wars to cease unto the end of the
earth; he breaketh the bow, and cutteth the spear in
sunder; he burneth the chariot in the fire.
10 Be still, and know that I *am* God: I will be exalted
among the heathen, I will be exalted in the earth.
11 The LORD of hosts *is* with us; the God of Jacob *is*
our refuge. Selah.

47 *To the chief Musician, A Psalm for the sons of Korah*

1 O clap your hands, all ye people; shout unto God
with the voice of triumph.
2 For the LORD most high *is* terrible; *he is* a great
King over all the earth.
3 He shall subdue the people under us, and the nations under our feet.
4 He shall choose our inheritance for us, the excellency of Jacob whom he loved. Selah.
5 God is gone up with a shout, the LORD with the
sound of a trumpet.
6 Sing praises to God, sing praises: sing praises
unto our King, sing praises.
7 For God *is* the King of all the earth: sing ye praises
with understanding.
8 God reigneth over the heathen: God sitteth upon
the throne of his holiness.
9 The princes of the people are gathered together,
even the people of the God of Abraham: for the
shields of the earth *belong* unto God: he is greatly
exalted.

48 *A Song and Psalm for the sons of Korah*

1 Great *is* the LORD, and greatly to be praised in the
city of our God, *in* the mountain of his holiness.
2 Beautiful for situation, the joy of the whole earth,
is mount Zion, *on* the sides of the north, the city of
the great King.
3 God is known in her palaces for a refuge.

NEW LIVING TRANSLATION

6 The nations are in chaos,
and their kingdoms crumble!
God's voice thunders,
and the earth melts!
7 The LORD of Heaven's Armies is here among us;
the God of Israel* is our fortress. *Interlude*
8 Come, see the glorious works of the LORD:
See how he brings destruction upon the world.
9 He causes wars to end throughout the earth.
He breaks the bow and snaps the spear;
he burns the shields with fire.
10 "Be still, and know that I am God!
I will be honored by every nation.
I will be honored throughout the world."
11 The LORD of Heaven's Armies is here among us;
the God of Israel is our fortress. *Interlude*

47 *For the choir director: A psalm of the descendants of Korah.*

1 Come, everyone! Clap your hands!
Shout to God with joyful praise!
2 For the LORD Most High is awesome.
He is the great King of all the earth.
3 He subdues the nations before us,
putting our enemies beneath our feet.
4 He chose the Promised Land as our inheritance,
the proud possession of Jacob's descendants,
whom he loves. *Interlude*
5 God has ascended with a mighty shout.
The LORD has ascended with trumpets blaring.
6 Sing praises to God, sing praises;
sing praises to our King, sing praises!
7 For God is the King over all the earth.
Praise him with a psalm.*
8 God reigns above the nations,
sitting on his holy throne.
9 The rulers of the world have gathered together
with the people of the God of Abraham.
For all the kings of the earth belong to God.
He is highly honored everywhere.

48 *A song. A psalm of the descendants of Korah.*

1 How great is the LORD,
how deserving of praise,
in the city of our God,
which sits on his holy mountain!
2 It is high and magnificent;
the whole earth rejoices to see it!
Mount Zion, the holy mountain,*
is the city of the great King!
3 God himself is in Jerusalem's towers,
revealing himself as its defender.

46:7 Hebrew *of Jacob;* also in 46:11. See note on 44:4. **47:7** Hebrew *maskil.* This may be a literary or musical term. **48:2** Or *Mount Zion, in the far north;* Hebrew reads *Mount Zion, the heights of Zaphon.*

KING JAMES VERSION

4 For, lo, the kings were assembled, they passed by
together.
5 They saw *it, and* so they marvelled; they were
troubled, *and* hasted away.
6 Fear took hold upon them there, *and* pain, as of a
woman in travail.
7 Thou breakest the ships of Tarshish with an east
wind.
8 As we have heard, so have we seen in the city of
the LORD of hosts, in the city of our God: God will establish it for ever. Selah.
9 We have thought of thy lovingkindness, O God, in
the midst of thy temple.
10 According to thy name, O God, so *is* thy praise
unto the ends of the earth: thy right hand is full of
righteousness.
11 Let mount Zion rejoice, let the daughters of
Judah be glad, because of thy judgments.
12 Walk about Zion, and go round about her: tell
the towers thereof.
13 Mark ye well her bulwarks, consider her palaces;
that ye may tell *it* to the generation following.
14 For this God *is* our God for ever and ever: he will
be our guide *even* unto death.

49 *To the chief Musician, A Psalm for the sons of Korah*

1 Hear this, all *ye* people; give ear, all *ye* inhabitants
of the world:
2 Both low and high, rich and poor, together.
3 My mouth shall speak of wisdom; and the meditation of my heart *shall be* of understanding.
4 I will incline mine ear to a parable: I will open my
dark saying upon the harp.
5 Wherefore should I fear in the days of evil, *when*
the iniquity of my heels shall compass me about?
6 They that trust in their wealth, and boast themselves in the multitude of their riches;
7 None *of them* can by any means redeem his
brother, nor give to God a ransom for him:
8 (For the redemption of their soul *is* precious, and
it ceaseth for ever:)
9 That he should still live for ever, *and* not see
corruption.

NEW LIVING TRANSLATION

4 The kings of the earth joined forces
and advanced against the city.
5 But when they saw it, they were stunned;
they were terrified and ran away.
6 They were gripped with terror
and writhed in pain like a woman in labor.
7 You destroyed them like the mighty ships
of Tarshish
shattered by a powerful east wind.
8 We had heard of the city's glory,
but now we have seen it ourselves—
the city of the LORD of Heaven's Armies.
It is the city of our God;
he will make it safe forever. *Interlude*

9 O God, we meditate on your unfailing love
as we worship in your Temple.
10 As your name deserves, O God,
you will be praised to the ends of the earth.
Your strong right hand is filled with victory.
11 Let the people on Mount Zion rejoice.
Let all the towns of Judah be glad
because of your justice.
12 Go, inspect the city of Jerusalem.*
Walk around and count the many towers.
13 Take note of the fortified walls,
and tour all the citadels,
that you may describe them
to future generations.
14 For that is what God is like.
He is our God forever and ever,
and he will guide us until we die.

49 *For the choir director: A psalm of the descendants of Korah.*

1 Listen to this, all you people!
Pay attention, everyone in the world!
2 High and low,
rich and poor—listen!
3 For my words are wise,
and my thoughts are filled with insight.
4 I listen carefully to many proverbs
and solve riddles with inspiration from a harp.

5 Why should I fear when trouble comes,
when enemies surround me?
6 They trust in their wealth
and boast of great riches.
7 Yet they cannot redeem themselves from death*
by paying a ransom to God.
8 Redemption does not come so easily,
for no one can ever pay enough
9 to live forever
and never see the grave.

48:12 Hebrew *Zion.* **49:7** Or *no one can redeem the life of another.*

KING JAMES VERSION

10 For he seeth *that* wise men die, likewise the fool and the brutish person perish, and leave their wealth to others.

11 Their inward thought *is, that* their houses *shall continue* for ever, *and* their dwelling places to all generations; they call *their* lands after their own names.

12 Nevertheless man *being* in honour abideth not: he is like the beasts *that* perish.

13 This their way *is* their folly: yet their posterity approve their sayings. Selah.

14 Like sheep they are laid in the grave; death shall feed on them; and the upright shall have dominion over them in the morning; and their beauty shall consume in the grave from their dwelling.

15 But God will redeem my soul from the power of the grave: for he shall receive me. Selah.

16 Be not thou afraid when one is made rich, when the glory of his house is increased;

17 For when he dieth he shall carry nothing away: his glory shall not descend after him.

18 Though while he lived he blessed his soul: and *men* will praise thee, when thou doest well to thyself.

19 He shall go to the generation of his fathers; they shall never see light.

20 Man *that is* in honour, and understandeth not, is like the beasts *that* perish.

50 *A Psalm of Asaph*

1 The mighty God, *even* the LORD, hath spoken, and called the earth from the rising of the sun unto the going down thereof.

2 Out of Zion, the perfection of beauty, God hath shined.

3 Our God shall come, and shall not keep silence: a fire shall devour before him, and it shall be very tempestuous round about him.

4 He shall call to the heavens from above, and to the earth, that he may judge his people.

5 Gather my saints together unto me; those that have made a covenant with me by sacrifice.

6 And the heavens shall declare his righteousness: for God *is* judge himself. Selah.

7 Hear, O my people, and I will speak; O Israel, and I will testify against thee: I *am* God, *even* thy God.

NEW LIVING TRANSLATION

10 Those who are wise must finally die,
just like the foolish and senseless,
leaving all their wealth behind.
11 The grave is their eternal home,
where they will stay forever.
They may name their estates after themselves,
12 but their fame will not last.
They will die, just like animals.
13 This is the fate of fools,
though they are remembered as being wise.*
Interlude

14 Like sheep, they are led to the grave,*
where death will be their shepherd.
In the morning the godly will rule over them.
Their bodies will rot in the grave,
far from their grand estates.
15 But as for me, God will redeem my life.
He will snatch me from the power of the grave.
Interlude

16 So don't be dismayed when the wicked grow rich
and their homes become ever more splendid.
17 For when they die, they take nothing with them.
Their wealth will not follow them into
the grave.
18 In this life they consider themselves fortunate
and are applauded for their success.
19 But they will die like all before them
and never again see the light of day.
20 People who boast of their wealth don't
understand;
they will die, just like animals.

50 *A psalm of Asaph.*

1 The LORD, the Mighty One, is God,
and he has spoken;
he has summoned all humanity
from where the sun rises to where it sets.
2 From Mount Zion, the perfection of beauty,
God shines in glorious radiance.
3 Our God approaches,
and he is not silent.
Fire devours everything in his way,
and a great storm rages around him.
4 He calls on the heavens above and earth below
to witness the judgment of his people.
5 "Bring my faithful people to me—
those who made a covenant with me by
giving sacrifices."
6 Then let the heavens proclaim his justice,
for God himself will be the judge. *Interlude*
7 "O my people, listen as I speak.
Here are my charges against you, O Israel:
I am God, your God!

49:13 The meaning of the Hebrew is uncertain. **49:14** Hebrew *Sheol;* also in 49:14b, 15.

KING JAMES VERSION

8 I will not reprove thee for thy sacrifices or thy
burnt offerings, *to have been* continually before me.
9 I will take no bullock out of thy house, *nor* he
goats out of thy folds.
10 For every beast of the forest *is* mine, *and* the
cattle upon a thousand hills.
11 I know all the fowls of the mountains: and the
wild beasts of the field *are* mine.
12 If I were hungry, I would not tell thee: for the
world *is* mine, and the fulness thereof.
13 Will I eat the flesh of bulls, or drink the blood of
goats?
14 Offer unto God thanksgiving; and pay thy vows
unto the most High:
15 And call upon me in the day of trouble: I will deliver thee, and thou shalt glorify me.
16 But unto the wicked God saith, What hast thou
to do to declare my statutes, or *that* thou shouldest
take my covenant in thy mouth?
17 Seeing thou hatest instruction, and castest my
words behind thee.
18 When thou sawest a thief, then thou consentedst
with him, and hast been partaker with adulterers.
19 Thou givest thy mouth to evil, and thy tongue
frameth deceit.
20 Thou sittest *and* speakest against thy brother;
thou slanderest thine own mother's son.
21 These *things* hast thou done, and I kept silence;
thou thoughtest that I was altogether *such an one* as
thyself: *but* I will reprove thee, and set *them* in order
before thine eyes.
22 Now consider this, ye that forget God, lest I tear
you in pieces, and *there be* none to deliver.
23 Whoso offereth praise glorifieth me: and to him
that ordereth *his* conversation *aright* will I shew the
salvation of God.

51

To the chief Musician, A Psalm of David, when Nathan the prophet came unto him, after he had gone in to Bath-sheba.

1 Have mercy upon me, O God, according to thy
lovingkindness: according unto the multitude of thy
tender mercies blot out my transgressions.
2 Wash me throughly from mine iniquity, and
cleanse me from my sin.
3 For I acknowledge my transgressions: and my sin
is ever before me.
4 Against thee, thee only, have I sinned, and done
this evil in thy sight: that thou mightest be justified
when thou speakest, *and* be clear when thou judgest.

NEW LIVING TRANSLATION

8 I have no complaint about your sacrifices
or the burnt offerings you constantly offer.
9 But I do not need the bulls from your barns
or the goats from your pens.
10 For all the animals of the forest are mine,
and I own the cattle on a thousand hills.
11 I know every bird on the mountains,
and all the animals of the field are mine.
12 If I were hungry, I would not tell you,
for all the world is mine and everything in it.
13 Do I eat the meat of bulls?
Do I drink the blood of goats?
14 Make thankfulness your sacrifice to God,
and keep the vows you made to the Most High.
15 Then call on me when you are in trouble,
and I will rescue you,
and you will give me glory."
16 But God says to the wicked:
"Why bother reciting my decrees
and pretending to obey my covenant?
17 For you refuse my discipline
and treat my words like trash.
18 When you see thieves, you approve of them,
and you spend your time with adulterers.
19 Your mouth is filled with wickedness,
and your tongue is full of lies.
20 You sit around and slander your brother—
your own mother's son.
21 While you did all this, I remained silent,
and you thought I didn't care.
But now I will rebuke you,
listing all my charges against you.
22 Repent, all of you who forget me,
or I will tear you apart,
and no one will help you.
23 But giving thanks is a sacrifice that truly
honors me.
If you keep to my path,
I will reveal to you the salvation of God."

51

For the choir director: A psalm of David, regarding the time Nathan the prophet came to him after David had committed adultery with Bathsheba.

1 Have mercy on me, O God,
because of your unfailing love.
Because of your great compassion,
blot out the stain of my sins.
2 Wash me clean from my guilt.
Purify me from my sin.
3 For I recognize my rebellion;
it haunts me day and night.
4 Against you, and you alone, have I sinned;
I have done what is evil in your sight.
You will be proved right in what you say,
and your judgment against me is just.*

51:4 Greek version reads *and you will win your case in court.* Compare Rom 3:4.

KING JAMES VERSION

5 Behold, I was shapen in iniquity, and in sin did
my mother conceive me.
6 Behold, thou desirest truth in the inward parts:
and in the hidden *part* thou shalt make me to know
wisdom.
7 Purge me with hyssop, and I shall be clean: wash
me, and I shall be whiter than snow.
8 Make me to hear joy and gladness; *that* the bones
which thou hast broken may rejoice.
9 Hide thy face from my sins, and blot out all mine
iniquities.
10 Create in me a clean heart, O God; and renew a
right spirit within me.
11 Cast me not away from thy presence; and take
not thy holy spirit from me.
12 Restore unto me the joy of thy salvation; and uphold me *with thy* free spirit.
13 *Then* will I teach transgressors thy ways; and sinners shall be converted unto thee.
14 Deliver me from bloodguiltiness, O God, thou
God of my salvation: *and* my tongue shall sing aloud
of thy righteousness.
15 O Lord, open thou my lips; and my mouth shall
shew forth thy praise.
16 For thou desirest not sacrifice; else would I give
it: thou delightest not in burnt offering.
17 The sacrifices of God *are* a broken spirit: a
broken and a contrite heart, O God, thou wilt not
despise.
18 Do good in thy good pleasure unto Zion: build
thou the walls of Jerusalem.
19 Then shalt thou be pleased with the sacrifices
of righteousness, with burnt offering and whole
burnt offering: then shall they offer bullocks upon
thine altar.

52

To the chief Musician, Maschil, A Psalm *of David, when Doeg the Edomite came and told Saul, and said unto him, David is come to the house of Ahimelech.*

1 Why boastest thou thyself in mischief, O mighty
man? the goodness of God *endureth* continually.
2 Thy tongue deviseth mischiefs; like a sharp razor,
working deceitfully.
3 Thou lovest evil more than good; *and* lying rather
than to speak righteousness. Selah.
4 Thou lovest all devouring words, O *thou* deceitful tongue.

NEW LIVING TRANSLATION

5 For I was born a sinner—
yes, from the moment my mother
conceived me.
6 But you desire honesty from the womb,*
teaching me wisdom even there.

7 Purify me from my sins,* and I will be clean;
wash me, and I will be whiter than snow.
8 Oh, give me back my joy again;
you have broken me—
now let me rejoice.
9 Don't keep looking at my sins.
Remove the stain of my guilt.
10 Create in me a clean heart, O God.
Renew a loyal spirit within me.
11 Do not banish me from your presence,
and don't take your Holy Spirit* from me.

12 Restore to me the joy of your salvation,
and make me willing to obey you.
13 Then I will teach your ways to rebels,
and they will return to you.
14 Forgive me for shedding blood, O God who saves;
then I will joyfully sing of your forgiveness.
15 Unseal my lips, O Lord,
that my mouth may praise you.

16 You do not desire a sacrifice, or I would
offer one.
You do not want a burnt offering.
17 The sacrifice you desire is a broken spirit.
You will not reject a broken and repentant
heart, O God.
18 Look with favor on Zion and help her;
rebuild the walls of Jerusalem.
19 Then you will be pleased with sacrifices offered
in the right spirit—
with burnt offerings and whole burnt
offerings.
Then bulls will again be sacrificed on
your altar.

52

For the choir director: A psalm of David, regarding the time Doeg the Edomite said to Saul, "David has gone to see Ahimelech."*

1 Why do you boast about your crimes, great
warrior?
Don't you realize God's justice continues
forever?
2 All day long you plot destruction.
Your tongue cuts like a sharp razor;
you're an expert at telling lies.
3 You love evil more than good
and lies more than truth. *Interlude*

4 You love to destroy others with your words,
you liar!

51:6 Or *from the heart;* Hebrew reads *in the inward parts.* **51:7** Hebrew *Purify me with the hyssop branch.* **51:11** Or *your spirit of holiness.*
52:TITLE Hebrew *maskil.* This may be a literary or musical term.

KING JAMES VERSION

5 God shall likewise destroy thee for ever, he shall
take thee away, and pluck thee out of *thy* dwelling
place, and root thee out of the land of the living.
Selah.
6 The righteous also shall see, and fear, and shall
laugh at him:
7 Lo, *this is* the man *that* made not God his
strength; but trusted in the abundance of his riches,
and strengthened himself in his wickedness.
8 But I *am* like a green olive tree in the house of
God: I trust in the mercy of God for ever and ever.
9 I will praise thee for ever, because thou hast done
it: and I will wait on thy name; for *it is* good before
thy saints.

53 *To the chief Musician upon Mahalath Maschil,* A Psalm *of David*

1 The fool hath said in his heart, *There is* no God.
Corrupt are they, and have done abominable iniquity:
there is none that doeth good.
2 God looked down from heaven upon the children
of men, to see if there were *any* that did understand,
that did seek God.
3 Every one of them is gone back: they are altogether become filthy; *there is* none that doeth good,
no, not one.
4 Have the workers of iniquity no knowledge? who
eat up my people *as* they eat bread: they have not
called upon God.
5 There were they in great fear, *where* no fear was:
for God hath scattered the bones of him that
encampeth *against* thee: thou hast put *them* to
shame, because God hath despised them.
6 Oh that the salvation of Israel *were come* out of
Zion! When God bringeth back the captivity of his
people, Jacob shall rejoice, *and* Israel shall be glad.

54 *To the chief Musician on Neginoth, Maschil,* A Psalm *of David, when the Ziphims came and said to Saul, Doth not David hide himself with us?*

1 Save me, O God, by thy name, and judge me by thy
strength.

NEW LIVING TRANSLATION

5 But God will strike you down once and for all.
He will pull you from your home
and uproot you from the land of the living.
Interlude

6 The righteous will see it and be amazed.
They will laugh and say,
7 "Look what happens to mighty warriors
who do not trust in God.
They trust their wealth instead
and grow more and more bold in their
wickedness."
8 But I am like an olive tree, thriving in the
house of God.
I will always trust in God's unfailing love.
9 I will praise you forever, O God,
for what you have done.
I will trust in your good name
in the presence of your faithful people.

53 *For the choir director: A meditation; a psalm* of David.*

1 Only fools say in their hearts,
"There is no God."
They are corrupt, and their actions are evil;
not one of them does good!
2 God looks down from heaven
on the entire human race;
he looks to see if anyone is truly wise,
if anyone seeks God.
3 But no, all have turned away;
all have become corrupt.*
No one does good,
not a single one!
4 Will those who do evil never learn?
They eat up my people like bread
and wouldn't think of praying to God.
5 Terror will grip them,
terror like they have never known before.
God will scatter the bones of your enemies.
You will put them to shame, for God has
rejected them.
6 Who will come from Mount Zion to rescue
Israel?
When God restores his people,
Jacob will shout with joy, and Israel will rejoice.

54 *For the choir director: A psalm* of David, regarding the time the Ziphites came and said to Saul, "We know where David is hiding." To be accompanied by stringed instruments.*

1 Come with great power, O God, and rescue me!
Defend me with your might.

53:TITLE Hebrew *According to mahalath; a maskil.* These may be literary or musical terms. 53:3 Greek version reads *have become useless.* Compare Rom 3:12. 54:TITLE Hebrew *maskil.* This may be a literary or musical term.

KING JAMES VERSION

2 Hear my prayer, O God; give ear to the words of my mouth.

3 For strangers are risen up against me, and oppressors seek after my soul: they have not set God before them. Selah.

4 Behold, God *is* mine helper: the Lord *is* with them that uphold my soul.

5 He shall reward evil unto mine enemies: cut them off in thy truth.

6 I will freely sacrifice unto thee: I will praise thy name, O LORD; for *it is* good.

7 For he hath delivered me out of all trouble: and mine eye hath seen *his desire* upon mine enemies.

55

To the chief Musician on Neginoth, Maschil, A Psalm of David

1 Give ear to my prayer, O God; and hide not thyself from my supplication.

2 Attend unto me, and hear me: I mourn in my complaint, and make a noise;

3 Because of the voice of the enemy, because of the oppression of the wicked: for they cast iniquity upon me, and in wrath they hate me.

4 My heart is sore pained within me: and the terrors of death are fallen upon me.

5 Fearfulness and trembling are come upon me, and horror hath overwhelmed me.

6 And I said, Oh that I had wings like a dove! *for then* would I fly away, and be at rest.

7 Lo, *then* would I wander far off, *and* remain in the wilderness. Selah.

8 I would hasten my escape from the windy storm *and* tempest.

9 Destroy, O Lord, *and* divide their tongues: for I have seen violence and strife in the city.

10 Day and night they go about it upon the walls thereof: mischief also and sorrow *are* in the midst of it.

11 Wickedness *is* in the midst thereof: deceit and guile depart not from her streets.

12 For *it was* not an enemy *that* reproached me; then I could have borne *it:* neither *was it* he that hated me *that* did magnify *himself* against me; then I would have hid myself from him:

13 But *it was* thou, a man mine equal, my guide, and mine acquaintance.

14 We took sweet counsel together, *and* walked unto the house of God in company.

NEW LIVING TRANSLATION

2 Listen to my prayer, O God.
Pay attention to my plea.
3 For strangers are attacking me;
violent people are trying to kill me.
They care nothing for God. *Interlude*
4 But God is my helper.
The Lord keeps me alive!
5 May the evil plans of my enemies be turned against them.
Do as you promised and put an end to them.
6 I will sacrifice a voluntary offering to you;
I will praise your name, O LORD,
for it is good.
7 For you have rescued me from my troubles
and helped me to triumph over my enemies.

55

For the choir director: A psalm of David, to be accompanied by stringed instruments.*

1 Listen to my prayer, O God.
Do not ignore my cry for help!
2 Please listen and answer me,
for I am overwhelmed by my troubles.
3 My enemies shout at me,
making loud and wicked threats.
They bring trouble on me
and angrily hunt me down.

4 My heart pounds in my chest.
The terror of death assaults me.
5 Fear and trembling overwhelm me,
and I can't stop shaking.
6 Oh, that I had wings like a dove;
then I would fly away and rest!
7 I would fly far away
to the quiet of the wilderness. *Interlude*
8 How quickly I would escape—
far from this wild storm of hatred.

9 Confuse them, Lord, and frustrate their plans,
for I see violence and conflict in the city.
10 Its walls are patrolled day and night against invaders,
but the real danger is wickedness within the city.
11 Everything is falling apart;
threats and cheating are rampant in the streets.

12 It is not an enemy who taunts me—
I could bear that.
It is not my foes who so arrogantly insult me—
I could have hidden from them.
13 Instead, it is you—my equal,
my companion and close friend.
14 What good fellowship we once enjoyed
as we walked together to the house of God.

55:TITLE Hebrew *maskil.* This may be a literary or musical term.

KING JAMES VERSION

15Let death seize upon them, *and* let them go
down quick into hell: for wickedness *is* in their
dwellings, *and* among them.
16As for me, I will call upon God; and the LORD
shall save me.
17Evening, and morning, and at noon, will I pray,
and cry aloud: and he shall hear my voice.
18He hath delivered my soul in peace from the
battle *that was* against me: for there were many
with me.
19God shall hear, and afflict them, even he that
abideth of old. Selah. Because they have no changes,
therefore they fear not God.
20He hath put forth his hands against such as be at
peace with him: he hath broken his covenant.
21*The words* of his mouth were smoother than
butter, but war *was* in his heart: his words were
softer than oil, yet *were* they drawn swords.
22Cast thy burden upon the LORD, and he shall sustain thee: he shall never suffer the righteous to be
moved.
23But thou, O God, shalt bring them down into the
pit of destruction: bloody and deceitful men shall
not live out half their days; but I will trust in thee.

56

To the chief Musician upon Jonath-elem-rechokim, Michtam of David, when the Philistines took him in Gath.

1Be merciful unto me, O God: for man would swallow me up; he fighting daily oppresseth me.
2Mine enemies would daily swallow *me* up: for *they*
be many that fight against me, O thou most High.
3What time I am afraid, I will trust in thee.
4In God I will praise his word, in God I have put my
trust; I will not fear what flesh can do unto me.
5Every day they wrest my words: all their thoughts
are against me for evil.
6They gather themselves together, they hide
themselves, they mark my steps, when they wait for
my soul.
7Shall they escape by iniquity? in *thine* anger cast
down the people, O God.
8Thou tellest my wanderings: put thou my tears
into thy bottle: *are they* not in thy book?
9When I cry *unto thee,* then shall mine enemies
turn back: this I know; for God *is* for me.

NEW LIVING TRANSLATION

15 Let death stalk my enemies;
let the grave* swallow them alive,
for evil makes its home within them.

16 But I will call on God,
and the LORD will rescue me.
17 Morning, noon, and night
I cry out in my distress,
and the LORD hears my voice.
18 He ransoms me and keeps me safe
from the battle waged against me,
though many still oppose me.
19 God, who has ruled forever,
will hear me and humble them. *Interlude*
For my enemies refuse to change their ways;
they do not fear God.

20 As for my companion, he betrayed his friends;
he broke his promises.
21 His words are as smooth as butter,
but in his heart is war.
His words are as soothing as lotion,
but underneath are daggers!

22 Give your burdens to the LORD,
and he will take care of you.
He will not permit the godly to slip and fall.

23 But you, O God, will send the wicked
down to the pit of destruction.
Murderers and liars will die young,
but I am trusting you to save me.

56

For the choir director: A psalm of David, regarding the time the Philistines seized him in Gath. To be sung to the tune "Dove on Distant Oaks."*

1 O God, have mercy on me,
for people are hounding me.
My foes attack me all day long.
2 I am constantly hounded by those who slander me,
and many are boldly attacking me.
3 But when I am afraid,
I will put my trust in you.
4 I praise God for what he has promised.
I trust in God, so why should I be afraid?
What can mere mortals do to me?

5 They are always twisting what I say;
they spend their days plotting to harm me.
6 They come together to spy on me—
watching my every step, eager to kill me.
7 Don't let them get away with their wickedness;
in your anger, O God, bring them down.

8 You keep track of all my sorrows.*
You have collected all my tears in your bottle.
You have recorded each one in your book.

9 My enemies will retreat when I call to you for help.
This I know: God is on my side!

55:15 Hebrew *let Sheol.* **56:TITLE** Hebrew *miktam.* This may be a literary or musical term. **56:8** Or *my wanderings.*

KING JAMES VERSION

10 In God will I praise *his* word: in the LORD will I praise *his* word.

11 In God have I put my trust: I will not be afraid what man can do unto me.

12 Thy vows *are* upon me, O God: I will render praises unto thee.

13 For thou hast delivered my soul from death: *wilt* not *thou deliver* my feet from falling, that I may walk before God in the light of the living?

57

To the chief Musician, Al-taschith, Michtam of David, when he fled from Saul in the cave.

1 Be merciful unto me, O God, be merciful unto me: for my soul trusteth in thee: yea, in the shadow of thy wings will I make my refuge, until *these* calamities be overpast.

2 I will cry unto God most high; unto God that performeth *all things* for me.

3 He shall send from heaven, and save me *from* the reproach of him that would swallow me up. Selah. God shall send forth his mercy and his truth.

4 My soul *is* among lions: *and* I lie *even among* them that are set on fire, *even* the sons of men, whose teeth *are* spears and arrows, and their tongue a sharp sword.

5 Be thou exalted, O God, above the heavens; *let* thy glory *be* above all the earth.

6 They have prepared a net for my steps; my soul is bowed down: they have digged a pit before me, into the midst whereof they are fallen *themselves*. Selah.

7 My heart is fixed, O God, my heart is fixed: I will sing and give praise.

8 Awake up, my glory; awake, psaltery and harp: I *myself* will awake early.

9 I will praise thee, O Lord, among the people: I will sing unto thee among the nations.

10 For thy mercy *is* great unto the heavens, and thy truth unto the clouds.

11 Be thou exalted, O God, above the heavens: *let* thy glory *be* above all the earth.

58

To the chief Musician, Al-taschith, Michtam of David

1 Do ye indeed speak righteousness, O congregation? do ye judge uprightly, O ye sons of men?

NEW LIVING TRANSLATION

10 I praise God for what he has promised;
yes, I praise the LORD for what he has promised.
11 I trust in God, so why should I be afraid?
What can mere mortals do to me?

12 I will fulfill my vows to you, O God,
and will offer a sacrifice of thanks for your help.
13 For you have rescued me from death;
you have kept my feet from slipping.
So now I can walk in your presence, O God,
in your life-giving light.

57

For the choir director: A psalm of David, regarding the time he fled from Saul and went into the cave. To be sung to the tune "Do Not Destroy!"*

1 Have mercy on me, O God, have mercy!
I look to you for protection.
I will hide beneath the shadow of your wings
until the danger passes by.
2 I cry out to God Most High,*
to God who will fulfill his purpose for me.
3 He will send help from heaven to rescue me,
disgracing those who hound me. *Interlude*
My God will send forth his unfailing love and
faithfulness.

4 I am surrounded by fierce lions
who greedily devour human prey—
whose teeth pierce like spears and arrows,
and whose tongues cut like swords.

5 Be exalted, O God, above the highest heavens!
May your glory shine over all the earth.
6 My enemies have set a trap for me.
I am weary from distress.
They have dug a deep pit in my path,
but they themselves have fallen into it.
Interlude

7 My heart is confident in you, O God;
my heart is confident.
No wonder I can sing your praises!
8 Wake up, my heart!
Wake up, O lyre and harp!
I will wake the dawn with my song.
9 I will thank you, Lord, among all the people.
I will sing your praises among the nations.
10 For your unfailing love is as high as the heavens.
Your faithfulness reaches to the clouds.
11 Be exalted, O God, above the highest heavens.
May your glory shine over all the earth.

58

For the choir director: A psalm of David, to be sung to the tune "Do Not Destroy!"*

1 Justice—do you rulers* know the meaning
of the word?
Do you judge the people fairly?

57:TITLE Hebrew *miktam.* This may be a literary or musical term. **57:2** Hebrew *Elohim-Elyon.* **58:TITLE** Hebrew *miktam.* This may be a literary or musical term. **58:1** Or *you gods.*

2 Yea, in heart ye work wickedness; ye weigh the violence of your hands in the earth.

3 The wicked are estranged from the womb: they go astray as soon as they be born, speaking lies.

4 Their poison *is* like the poison of a serpent: *they are* like the deaf adder *that* stoppeth her ear;

5 Which will not hearken to the voice of charmers, charming never so wisely.

6 Break their teeth, O God, in their mouth: break out the great teeth of the young lions, O LORD.

7 Let them melt away as waters *which* run continually: *when* he bendeth *his bow to shoot* his arrows, let them be as cut in pieces.

8 As a snail *which* melteth, let *every one of them* pass away: *like* the untimely birth of a woman, *that* they may not see the sun.

9 Before your pots can feel the thorns, he shall take them away as with a whirlwind, both living, and in *his* wrath.

10 The righteous shall rejoice when he seeth the vengeance: he shall wash his feet in the blood of the wicked.

11 So that a man shall say, Verily *there is* a reward for the righteous: verily he is a God that judgeth in the earth.

59

To the chief Musician, Al-taschith, Michtam of David; when Saul sent, and they watched the house to kill him.

1 Deliver me from mine enemies, O my God: defend me from them that rise up against me.

2 Deliver me from the workers of iniquity, and save me from bloody men.

3 For, lo, they lie in wait for my soul: the mighty are gathered against me; not *for* my transgression, nor *for* my sin, O LORD.

4 They run and prepare themselves without *my* fault: awake to help me, and behold.

5 Thou therefore, O LORD God of hosts, the God of Israel, awake to visit all the heathen: be not merciful to any wicked transgressors. Selah.

6 They return at evening: they make a noise like a dog, and go round about the city.

7 Behold, they belch out with their mouth: swords *are* in their lips: for who, *say they*, doth hear?

2 No! You plot injustice in your hearts.
You spread violence throughout the land.
3 These wicked people are born sinners;
even from birth they have lied and gone their own way.
4 They spit venom like deadly snakes;
they are like cobras that refuse to listen,
5 ignoring the tunes of the snake charmers,
no matter how skillfully they play.

6 Break off their fangs, O God!
Smash the jaws of these lions, O LORD!
7 May they disappear like water into thirsty ground.
Make their weapons useless in their hands.*
8 May they be like snails that dissolve into slime,
like a stillborn child who will never see the sun.
9 God will sweep them away, both young and old,
faster than a pot heats over burning thorns.

10 The godly will rejoice when they see injustice avenged.
They will wash their feet in the blood of the wicked.
11 Then at last everyone will say,
"There truly is a reward for those who live for God;
surely there is a God who judges justly here on earth."

59

For the choir director: A psalm of David, regarding the time Saul sent soldiers to watch David's house in order to kill him. To be sung to the tune "Do Not Destroy!"*

1 Rescue me from my enemies, O God.
Protect me from those who have come to destroy me.
2 Rescue me from these criminals;
save me from these murderers.
3 They have set an ambush for me.
Fierce enemies are out there waiting, LORD,
though I have not sinned or offended them.
4 I have done nothing wrong,
yet they prepare to attack me.
Wake up! See what is happening and help me!
5 O LORD God of Heaven's Armies, the God of Israel,
wake up and punish those hostile nations.
Show no mercy to wicked traitors. *Interlude*

6 They come out at night,
snarling like vicious dogs
as they prowl the streets.
7 Listen to the filth that comes from their mouths;
their words cut like swords.
"After all, who can hear us?" they sneer.

58:7 Or *Let them be trodden down and wither like grass.* The meaning of the Hebrew is uncertain. **59:TITLE** Hebrew *miktam.* This may be a literary or musical term.

8But thou, O LORD, shalt laugh at them; thou shalt
have all the heathen in derision.
9*Because of* his strength will I wait upon thee: for
God *is* my defence.
10The God of my mercy shall prevent me: God
shall let me see *my desire* upon mine enemies.
11Slay them not, lest my people forget: scatter
them by thy power; and bring them down, O Lord
our shield.
12*For* the sin of their mouth *and* the words of their
lips let them even be taken in their pride: and for
cursing and lying *which* they speak.
13Consume *them* in wrath, consume *them,* that
they *may* not *be:* and let them know that God ruleth
in Jacob unto the ends of the earth. Selah.
14And at evening let them return; *and* let them
make a noise like a dog, and go round about the city.
15Let them wander up and down for meat, and
grudge if they be not satisfied.
16But I will sing of thy power; yea, I will sing aloud
of thy mercy in the morning: for thou hast been my
defence and refuge in the day of my trouble.
17Unto thee, O my strength, will I sing: for God *is*
my defence, *and* the God of my mercy.

60 *To the chief Musician upon Shushan-eduth, Michtam of David, to teach; when he strove with Aram-naharaim and with Aram-zobah, when Joab returned, and smote of Edom in the valley of salt twelve thousand.*

1O God, thou hast cast us off, thou hast scattered
us, thou hast been displeased; O turn thyself to us
again.
2Thou hast made the earth to tremble; thou hast
broken it: heal the breaches thereof; for it shaketh.
3Thou hast shewed thy people hard things: thou
hast made us to drink the wine of astonishment.
4Thou hast given a banner to them that fear thee,
that it may be displayed because of the truth. Selah.
5That thy beloved may be delivered; save *with* thy
right hand, and hear me.
6God hath spoken in his holiness; I will rejoice, I

8 But LORD, you laugh at them.
You scoff at all the hostile nations.
9 You are my strength; I wait for you to rescue me,
for you, O God, are my fortress.
10 In his unfailing love, my God will stand with me.
He will let me look down in triumph on all
my enemies.

11 Don't kill them, for my people soon forget
such lessons;
stagger them with your power, and bring
them to their knees,
O Lord our shield.
12 Because of the sinful things they say,
because of the evil that is on their lips,
let them be captured by their pride,
their curses, and their lies.
13 Destroy them in your anger!
Wipe them out completely!
Then the whole world will know
that God reigns in Israel.* *Interlude*

14 My enemies come out at night,
snarling like vicious dogs
as they prowl the streets.
15 They scavenge for food
but go to sleep unsatisfied.*

16 But as for me, I will sing about your power.
Each morning I will sing with joy about your
unfailing love.
For you have been my refuge,
a place of safety when I am in distress.
17 O my Strength, to you I sing praises,
for you, O God, are my refuge,
the God who shows me unfailing love.

60 *For the choir director: A psalm* of David useful for teaching, regarding the time David fought Aram-naharaim and Aram-zobah, and Joab returned and killed 12,000 Edomites in the Valley of Salt. To be sung to the tune "Lily of the Testimony."*

1 You have rejected us, O God, and broken
our defenses.
You have been angry with us; now restore
us to your favor.
2 You have shaken our land and split it open.
Seal the cracks, for the land trembles.
3 You have been very hard on us,
making us drink wine that sent us reeling.
4 But you have raised a banner for those who
fear you—
a rallying point in the face of attack. *Interlude*

5 Now rescue your beloved people.
Answer and save us by your power.
6 God has promised this by his holiness*:

59:13 Hebrew *in Jacob.* See note on 44:4. **59:15** Or *and growl if they don't get enough.* **60:TITLE** Hebrew *miktam.* This may be a literary or musical term. **60:6** Or *in his sanctuary.*

KING JAMES VERSION

will divide Shechem, and mete out the valley of
Succoth.
7 Gilead *is* mine, and Manasseh *is* mine; Ephraim
also *is* the strength of mine head; Judah *is* my
lawgiver;
8 Moab *is* my washpot; over Edom will I cast out my
shoe: Philistia, triumph thou because of me.
9 Who will bring me *into* the strong city? who will
lead me into Edom?
10 *Wilt* not thou, O God, *which* hadst cast us off?
and *thou,* O God, *which* didst not go out with our
armies?
11 Give us help from trouble: for vain *is* the help of
man.
12 Through God we shall do valiantly: for he *it is*
that shall tread down our enemies.

61 *To the chief Musician upon Neginah, A Psalm of David*

1 Hear my cry, O God; attend unto my prayer.
2 From the end of the earth will I cry unto thee,
when my heart is overwhelmed: lead me to the rock
that is higher than I.
3 For thou hast been a shelter for me, *and* a strong
tower from the enemy.
4 I will abide in thy tabernacle for ever: I will trust
in the covert of thy wings. Selah.
5 For thou, O God, hast heard my vows: thou hast
given *me* the heritage of those that fear thy name.
6 Thou wilt prolong the king's life: *and* his years as
many generations.
7 He shall abide before God for ever: O prepare
mercy and truth, *which* may preserve him.
8 So will I sing praise unto thy name for ever, that I
may daily perform my vows.

62 *To the chief Musician, to Jeduthun, A Psalm of David*

1 Truly my soul waiteth upon God: from him *com-*
eth my salvation.
2 He only *is* my rock and my salvation; *he is* my defence; I shall not be greatly moved.
3 How long will ye imagine mischief against a
man? ye shall be slain all of you: as a bowing wall
shall ye be, and as a tottering fence.
4 They only consult to cast *him* down from his excellency: they delight in lies: they bless with their
mouth, but they curse inwardly. Selah.

NEW LIVING TRANSLATION

"I will divide up Shechem with joy.
I will measure out the valley of Succoth.
7 Gilead is mine,
and Manasseh, too.
Ephraim, my helmet, will produce my warriors,
and Judah, my scepter, will produce my kings.
8 But Moab, my washbasin, will become my servant,
and I will wipe my feet on Edom
and shout in triumph over Philistia."
9 Who will bring me into the fortified city?
Who will bring me victory over Edom?
10 Have you rejected us, O God?
Will you no longer march with our armies?
11 Oh, please help us against our enemies,
for all human help is useless.
12 With God's help we will do mighty things,
for he will trample down our foes.

61 *For the choir director: A psalm of David, to be accompanied by stringed instruments.*

1 O God, listen to my cry!
Hear my prayer!
2 From the ends of the earth,
I cry to you for help
when my heart is overwhelmed.
Lead me to the towering rock of safety,
3 for you are my safe refuge,
a fortress where my enemies cannot reach me.
4 Let me live forever in your sanctuary,
safe beneath the shelter of your wings!
Interlude

5 For you have heard my vows, O God.
You have given me an inheritance reserved for
those who fear your name.
6 Add many years to the life of the king!
May his years span the generations!
7 May he reign under God's protection forever.
May your unfailing love and faithfulness watch
over him.
8 Then I will sing praises to your name forever
as I fulfill my vows each day.

62 *For Jeduthun, the choir director: A psalm of David.*

1 I wait quietly before God,
for my victory comes from him.
2 He alone is my rock and my salvation,
my fortress where I will never be shaken.
3 So many enemies against one man—
all of them trying to kill me.
To them I'm just a broken-down wall
or a tottering fence.
4 They plan to topple me from my high position.
They delight in telling lies about me.
They praise me to my face
but curse me in their hearts. *Interlude*

KING JAMES VERSION

5 My soul, wait thou only upon God; for my expectation *is* from him.

6 He only *is* my rock and my salvation: *he is* my defence; I shall not be moved.

7 In God *is* my salvation and my glory: the rock of my strength, *and* my refuge, *is* in God.

8 Trust in him at all times; *ye* people, pour out your heart before him: God *is* a refuge for us. Selah.

9 Surely men of low degree *are* vanity, *and* men of high degree *are* a lie: to be laid in the balance, they *are* altogether *lighter* than vanity.

10 Trust not in oppression, and become not vain in robbery: if riches increase, set not your heart *upon them.*

11 God hath spoken once; twice have I heard this; that power *belongeth* unto God.

12 Also unto thee, O Lord, *belongeth* mercy: for thou renderest to every man according to his work.

63

A Psalm of David, when he was in the wilderness of Judah.

1 O God, thou *art* my God; early will I seek thee: my soul thirsteth for thee, my flesh longeth for thee in a dry and thirsty land, where no water is;

2 To see thy power and thy glory, so *as* I have seen thee in the sanctuary.

3 Because thy lovingkindness *is* better than life, my lips shall praise thee.

4 Thus will I bless thee while I live: I will lift up my hands in thy name.

5 My soul shall be satisfied as *with* marrow and fatness; and my mouth shall praise *thee* with joyful lips:

6 When I remember thee upon my bed, *and* meditate on thee in the *night* watches.

7 Because thou hast been my help, therefore in the shadow of thy wings will I rejoice.

8 My soul followeth hard after thee: thy right hand upholdeth me.

9 But those *that* seek my soul, to destroy *it,* shall go into the lower parts of the earth.

10 They shall fall by the sword: they shall be a portion for foxes.

11 But the king shall rejoice in God; every one that sweareth by him shall glory: but the mouth of them that speak lies shall be stopped.

NEW LIVING TRANSLATION

5 Let all that I am wait quietly before God,
for my hope is in him.
6 He alone is my rock and my salvation,
my fortress where I will not be shaken.
7 My victory and honor come from God alone.
He is my refuge, a rock where no enemy can reach me.
8 O my people, trust in him at all times.
Pour out your heart to him,
for God is our refuge. *Interlude*

9 Common people are as worthless as a puff of wind,
and the powerful are not what they appear to be.
If you weigh them on the scales,
together they are lighter than a breath of air.

10 Don't make your living by extortion
or put your hope in stealing.
And if your wealth increases,
don't make it the center of your life.

11 God has spoken plainly,
and I have heard it many times:
Power, O God, belongs to you;
12 unfailing love, O Lord, is yours.
Surely you repay all people
according to what they have done.

63

A psalm of David, regarding a time when David was in the wilderness of Judah.

1 O God, you are my God;
I earnestly search for you.
My soul thirsts for you;
my whole body longs for you
in this parched and weary land
where there is no water.
2 I have seen you in your sanctuary
and gazed upon your power and glory.
3 Your unfailing love is better than life itself;
how I praise you!
4 I will praise you as long as I live,
lifting up my hands to you in prayer.
5 You satisfy me more than the richest feast.
I will praise you with songs of joy.

6 I lie awake thinking of you,
meditating on you through the night.
7 Because you are my helper,
I sing for joy in the shadow of your wings.
8 I cling to you;
your strong right hand holds me securely.

9 But those plotting to destroy me will come to ruin.
They will go down into the depths of the earth.
10 They will die by the sword
and become the food of jackals.
11 But the king will rejoice in God.
All who trust in him will praise him,
while liars will be silenced.

KING JAMES VERSION

64 *To the chief Musician, A Psalm of David*

1 Hear my voice, O God, in my prayer: preserve my
life from fear of the enemy.
2 Hide me from the secret counsel of the wicked;
from the insurrection of the workers of iniquity:
3 Who whet their tongue like a sword, *and* bend
their bows to shoot their arrows, *even* bitter words:
4 That they may shoot in secret at the perfect: suddenly do they shoot at him, and fear not.
5 They encourage themselves *in* an evil matter:
they commune of laying snares privily; they say, Who
shall see them?
6 They search out iniquities; they accomplish a
diligent search: both the inward *thought* of every
one *of them,* and the heart, *is* deep.
7 But God shall shoot at them *with* an arrow; suddenly shall they be wounded.
8 So they shall make their own tongue to fall upon
themselves: all that see them shall flee away.
9 And all men shall fear, and shall declare the work
of God; for they shall wisely consider of his doing.
10 The righteous shall be glad in the LORD, and shall
trust in him; and all the upright in heart shall glory.

65 *To the chief Musician, A Psalm* and *Song of David*

1 Praise waiteth for thee, O God, in Sion: and unto
thee shall the vow be performed.
2 O thou that hearest prayer, unto thee shall all
flesh come.
3 Iniquities prevail against me: *as for* our transgressions, thou shalt purge them away.
4 Blessed *is the man whom* thou choosest, and
causest to approach *unto thee, that* he may dwell in
thy courts: we shall be satisfied with the goodness of
thy house, *even* of thy holy temple.
5 *By* terrible things in righteousness wilt thou answer us, O God of our salvation; *who art* the confidence of all the ends of the earth, and of them that
are afar off *upon* the sea:
6 Which by his strength setteth fast the mountains; *being* girded with power:
7 Which stilleth the noise of the seas, the noise of
their waves, and the tumult of the people.
8 They also that dwell in the uttermost parts are
afraid at thy tokens: thou makest the outgoings of
the morning and evening to rejoice.

NEW LIVING TRANSLATION

64 *For the choir director: A psalm of David.*

1 O God, listen to my complaint.
Protect my life from my enemies' threats.
2 Hide me from the plots of this evil mob,
from this gang of wrongdoers.
3 They sharpen their tongues like swords
and aim their bitter words like arrows.
4 They shoot from ambush at the innocent,
attacking suddenly and fearlessly.
5 They encourage each other to do evil
and plan how to set their traps in secret.
"Who will ever notice?" they ask.
6 As they plot their crimes, they say,
"We have devised the perfect plan!"
Yes, the human heart and mind are cunning.
7 But God himself will shoot them with his arrows,
suddenly striking them down.
8 Their own tongues will ruin them,
and all who see them will shake their heads
in scorn.
9 Then everyone will be afraid;
they will proclaim the mighty acts of God
and realize all the amazing things he does.
10 The godly will rejoice in the LORD
and find shelter in him.
And those who do what is right
will praise him.

65 *For the choir director: A song. A psalm of David.*

1 What mighty praise, O God,
belongs to you in Zion.
We will fulfill our vows to you,
2 for you answer our prayers.
All of us must come to you.
3 Though we are overwhelmed by our sins,
you forgive them all.
4 What joy for those you choose to bring near,
those who live in your holy courts.
What festivities await us
inside your holy Temple.
5 You faithfully answer our prayers with
awesome deeds,
O God our savior.
You are the hope of everyone on earth,
even those who sail on distant seas.
6 You formed the mountains by your power
and armed yourself with mighty strength.
7 You quieted the raging oceans
with their pounding waves
and silenced the shouting of the nations.
8 Those who live at the ends of the earth
stand in awe of your wonders.
From where the sun rises to where it sets,
you inspire shouts of joy.

KING JAMES VERSION

[9]Thou visitest the earth, and waterest it: thou
greatly enrichest it with the river of God, *which* is
full of water: thou preparest them corn, when thou
hast so provided for it.
[10]Thou waterest the ridges thereof abundantly:
thou settlest the furrows thereof: thou makest it soft
with showers: thou blessest the springing thereof.
[11]Thou crownest the year with thy goodness; and
thy paths drop fatness.
[12]They drop *upon* the pastures of the wilderness:
and the little hills rejoice on every side.
[13]The pastures are clothed with flocks; the valleys
also are covered over with corn; they shout for joy,
they also sing.

66 *To the chief Musician, A Song* or *Psalm*

[1]Make a joyful noise unto God, all ye lands:
[2]Sing forth the honour of his name: make his
praise glorious.
[3]Say unto God, How terrible *art thou in* thy works!
through the greatness of thy power shall thine enemies submit themselves unto thee.
[4]All the earth shall worship thee, and shall sing
unto thee; they shall sing *to* thy name. Selah.
[5]Come and see the works of God: *he is* terrible *in*
his doing toward the children of men.
[6]He turned the sea into dry *land:* they went
through the flood on foot: there did we rejoice in
him.
[7]He ruleth by his power for ever; his eyes behold
the nations: let not the rebellious exalt themselves.
Selah.
[8]O bless our God, ye people, and make the voice of
his praise to be heard:
[9]Which holdeth our soul in life, and suffereth not
our feet to be moved.
[10]For thou, O God, hast proved us: thou hast tried
us, as silver is tried.
[11]Thou broughtest us into the net; thou laidst affliction upon our loins.
[12]Thou hast caused men to ride over our heads;
we went through fire and through water: but thou
broughtest us out into a wealthy *place*.
[13]I will go into thy house with burnt offerings: I
will pay thee my vows,
[14]Which my lips have uttered, and my mouth hath
spoken, when I was in trouble.

NEW LIVING TRANSLATION

[9] You take care of the earth and water it,
making it rich and fertile.
The river of God has plenty of water;
it provides a bountiful harvest of grain,
for you have ordered it so.
[10] You drench the plowed ground with rain,
melting the clods and leveling the ridges.
You soften the earth with showers
and bless its abundant crops.
[11] You crown the year with a bountiful harvest;
even the hard pathways overflow with
abundance.
[12] The grasslands of the wilderness become
a lush pasture,
and the hillsides blossom with joy.
[13] The meadows are clothed with flocks of sheep,
and the valleys are carpeted with grain.
They all shout and sing for joy!

66 *For the choir director: A song. A psalm.*

[1] Shout joyful praises to God, all the earth!
[2] Sing about the glory of his name!
Tell the world how glorious he is.
[3] Say to God, "How awesome are your deeds!
Your enemies cringe before your mighty power.
[4] Everything on earth will worship you;
they will sing your praises,
shouting your name in glorious songs."
Interlude
[5] Come and see what our God has done,
what awesome miracles he performs
for people!
[6] He made a dry path through the Red Sea,*
and his people went across on foot.
There we rejoiced in him.
[7] For by his great power he rules forever.
He watches every movement of the nations;
let no rebel rise in defiance. *Interlude*
[8] Let the whole world bless our God
and loudly sing his praises.
[9] Our lives are in his hands,
and he keeps our feet from stumbling.
[10] You have tested us, O God;
you have purified us like silver.
[11] You captured us in your net
and laid the burden of slavery on our backs.
[12] Then you put a leader over us.*
We went through fire and flood,
but you brought us to a place of great
abundance.

[13] Now I come to your Temple with burnt offerings
to fulfill the vows I made to you—
[14] yes, the sacred vows that I made
when I was in deep trouble.

66:6 Hebrew *the sea.* **66:12** Or *You made people ride over our heads.*

KING JAMES VERSION

15 I will offer unto thee burnt sacrifices of fatlings,
with the incense of rams; I will offer bullocks with
goats. Selah.
16 Come *and* hear, all ye that fear God, and I will
declare what he hath done for my soul.
17 I cried unto him with my mouth, and he was
extolled with my tongue.
18 If I regard iniquity in my heart, the Lord will not
hear *me:*
19 *But* verily God hath heard *me;* he hath attended
to the voice of my prayer.
20 Blessed *be* God, which hath not turned away my
prayer, nor his mercy from me.

67 *To the chief Musician on Neginoth, A Psalm* or *Song*

1 God be merciful unto us, and bless us; *and* cause
his face to shine upon us; Selah.
2 That thy way may be known upon earth, thy
saving health among all nations.
3 Let the people praise thee, O God; let all the
people praise thee.
4 O let the nations be glad and sing for joy: for thou
shalt judge the people righteously, and govern the
nations upon earth. Selah.
5 Let the people praise thee, O God; let all the
people praise thee.
6 *Then* shall the earth yield her increase; *and* God,
even our own God, shall bless us.
7 God shall bless us; and all the ends of the earth
shall fear him.

68 *To the chief Musician, A Psalm* or *Song of David*

1 Let God arise, let his enemies be scattered: let
them also that hate him flee before him.
2 As smoke is driven away, *so* drive *them* away: as
wax melteth before the fire, *so* let the wicked perish
at the presence of God.
3 But let the righteous be glad; let them rejoice before God: yea, let them exceedingly rejoice.
4 Sing unto God, sing praises to his name: extol
him that rideth upon the heavens by his name JAH,
and rejoice before him.
5 A father of the fatherless, and a judge of the widows, *is* God in his holy habitation.
6 God setteth the solitary in families: he bringeth
out those which are bound with chains: but the rebellious dwell in a dry *land.*

NEW LIVING TRANSLATION

15 That is why I am sacrificing burnt offerings
to you—
the best of my rams as a pleasing aroma,
and a sacrifice of bulls and male goats. *Interlude*

16 Come and listen, all you who fear God,
and I will tell you what he did for me.
17 For I cried out to him for help,
praising him as I spoke.
18 If I had not confessed the sin in my heart,
the Lord would not have listened.
19 But God did listen!
He paid attention to my prayer.
20 Praise God, who did not ignore my prayer
or withdraw his unfailing love from me.

67 *For the choir director: A song. A psalm, to be accompanied by stringed instruments.*

1 May God be merciful and bless us.
May his face smile with favor on us. *Interlude*

2 May your ways be known throughout the earth,
your saving power among people everywhere.
3 May the nations praise you, O God.
Yes, may all the nations praise you.
4 Let the whole world sing for joy,
because you govern the nations with justice
and guide the people of the whole world.
Interlude

5 May the nations praise you, O God.
Yes, may all the nations praise you.
6 Then the earth will yield its harvests,
and God, our God, will richly bless us.
7 Yes, God will bless us,
and people all over the world will fear him.

68 *For the choir director: A song. A psalm of David.*

1 Rise up, O God, and scatter your enemies.
Let those who hate God run for their lives.
2 Blow them away like smoke.
Melt them like wax in a fire.
Let the wicked perish in the presence of God.
3 But let the godly rejoice.
Let them be glad in God's presence.
Let them be filled with joy.
4 Sing praises to God and to his name!
Sing loud praises to him who rides the clouds.
His name is the LORD—
rejoice in his presence!

5 Father to the fatherless, defender of widows—
this is God, whose dwelling is holy.
6 God places the lonely in families;
he sets the prisoners free and gives them joy.
But he makes the rebellious live in a sun-
scorched land.

KING JAMES VERSION

7 O God, when thou wentest forth before thy people, when thou didst march through the wilderness;
Selah:
8 The earth shook, the heavens also dropped at the
presence of God: *even* Sinai itself *was moved* at the
presence of God, the God of Israel.
9 Thou, O God, didst send a plentiful rain, whereby
thou didst confirm thine inheritance, when it was
weary.
10 Thy congregation hath dwelt therein: thou,
O God, hast prepared of thy goodness for the poor.
11 The Lord gave the word: great *was* the company
of those that published *it*.
12 Kings of armies did flee apace: and she that tarried at home divided the spoil.
13 Though ye have lien among the pots, *yet shall ye
be as* the wings of a dove covered with silver, and her
feathers with yellow gold.
14 When the Almighty scattered kings in it, it was
white as snow in Salmon.
15 The hill of God *is as* the hill of Bashan; an high
hill *as* the hill of Bashan.
16 Why leap ye, ye high hills? *this is* the hill *which*
God desireth to dwell in; yea, the LORD will dwell *in it*
for ever.
17 The chariots of God *are* twenty thousand, *even*
thousands of angels: the Lord *is* among them, *as in*
Sinai, in the holy *place*.
18 Thou hast ascended on high, thou hast led captivity captive: thou hast received gifts for men; yea,
for the rebellious also, that the LORD God might dwell
among them.
19 Blessed *be* the Lord, *who* daily loadeth us *with
benefits, even* the God of our salvation. Selah.
20 *He that is* our God *is* the God of salvation; and
unto GOD the Lord *belong* the issues from death.
21 But God shall wound the head of his enemies,
and the hairy scalp of such an one as goeth on still in
his trespasses.
22 The Lord said, I will bring again from Bashan, I
will bring *my people* again from the depths of the
sea:
23 That thy foot may be dipped in the blood of
thine enemies, *and* the tongue of thy dogs in the
same.
24 They have seen thy goings, O God; *even* the
goings of my God, my King, in the sanctuary.

NEW LIVING TRANSLATION

7 O God, when you led your people out from Egypt,
when you marched through the dry
wasteland, *Interlude*
8 the earth trembled, and the heavens poured
down rain
before you, the God of Sinai,
before God, the God of Israel.
9 You sent abundant rain, O God,
to refresh the weary land.
10 There your people finally settled,
and with a bountiful harvest, O God,
you provided for your needy people.

11 The Lord gives the word,
and a great army* brings the good news.
12 Enemy kings and their armies flee,
while the women of Israel divide the plunder.
13 Even those who lived among the sheepfolds
found treasures—
doves with wings of silver
and feathers of gold.
14 The Almighty scattered the enemy kings
like a blowing snowstorm on Mount Zalmon.

15 The mountains of Bashan are majestic,
with many peaks stretching high into the sky.
16 Why do you look with envy, O rugged mountains,
at Mount Zion, where God has chosen to live,
where the LORD himself will live forever?

17 Surrounded by unnumbered thousands
of chariots,
the Lord came from Mount Sinai into
his sanctuary.
18 When you ascended to the heights,
you led a crowd of captives.
You received gifts from the people,
even from those who rebelled against you.
Now the LORD God will live among us there.
19 Praise the Lord; praise God our savior!
For each day he carries us in his arms.
Interlude
20 Our God is a God who saves!
The Sovereign LORD rescues us from death.
21 But God will smash the heads of his enemies,
crushing the skulls of those who love their
guilty ways.
22 The Lord says, "I will bring my enemies down
from Bashan;
I will bring them up from the depths of the sea.
23 You, my people, will wash your feet in
their blood,
and even your dogs will get their share!"

24 Your procession has come into view, O God—
the procession of my God and King as he goes
into the sanctuary.

68:11 Or *a host of women.*

25 The singers went before, the players on instruments *followed* after; among *them were* the damsels playing with timbrels.

26 Bless ye God in the congregations, *even* the Lord, from the fountain of Israel.

27 There *is* little Benjamin *with* their ruler, the princes of Judah *and* their council, the princes of Zebulun, *and* the princes of Naphtali.

28 Thy God hath commanded thy strength: strengthen, O God, that which thou hast wrought for us.

29 Because of thy temple at Jerusalem shall kings bring presents unto thee.

30 Rebuke the company of spearmen, the multitude of the bulls, with the calves of the people, *till every one* submit himself with pieces of silver: scatter thou the people *that* delight in war.

31 Princes shall come out of Egypt; Ethiopia shall soon stretch out her hands unto God.

32 Sing unto God, ye kingdoms of the earth; O sing praises unto the Lord; Selah:

33 To him that rideth upon the heavens of heavens, *which were* of old; lo, he doth send out his voice, *and that* a mighty voice.

34 Ascribe ye strength unto God: his excellency *is* over Israel, and his strength *is* in the clouds.

35 O God, *thou art* terrible out of thy holy places: the God of Israel *is* he that giveth strength and power unto *his* people. Blessed *be* God.

69 *To the chief Musician upon Shoshannim,* A Psalm *of David*

1 Save me, O God; for the waters are come in unto *my* soul.

2 I sink in deep mire, where *there is* no standing: I am come into deep waters, where the floods overflow me.

3 I am weary of my crying: my throat is dried: mine eyes fail while I wait for my God.

4 They that hate me without a cause are more than the hairs of mine head: they that would destroy me, *being* mine enemies wrongfully, are mighty: then I restored *that* which I took not away.

5 O God, thou knowest my foolishness; and my sins are not hid from thee.

6 Let not them that wait on thee, O Lord GOD of

25 Singers are in front, musicians behind;
between them are young women playing
tambourines.
26 Praise God, all you people of Israel;
praise the LORD, the source of Israel's life.
27 Look, the little tribe of Benjamin leads the way.
Then comes a great throng of rulers
from Judah
and all the rulers of Zebulun and Naphtali.

28 Summon your might, O God.
Display your power, O God, as you have
in the past.
29 The kings of the earth are bringing tribute
to your Temple in Jerusalem.
30 Rebuke these enemy nations—
these wild animals lurking in the reeds,
this herd of bulls among the weaker calves.
Make them bring bars of silver in humble tribute.
Scatter the nations that delight in war.
31 Let Egypt come with gifts of precious metals*;
let Ethiopia* bow in submission to God.
32 Sing to God, you kingdoms of the earth.
Sing praises to the Lord. *Interlude*
33 Sing to the one who rides across the ancient
heavens,
his mighty voice thundering from the sky.
34 Tell everyone about God's power.
His majesty shines down on Israel;
his strength is mighty in the heavens.
35 God is awesome in his sanctuary.
The God of Israel gives power and strength
to his people.

Praise be to God!

69 *For the choir director: A psalm of David, to be sung to the tune "Lilies."*

1 Save me, O God,
for the floodwaters are up to my neck.
2 Deeper and deeper I sink into the mire;
I can't find a foothold.
I am in deep water,
and the floods overwhelm me.
3 I am exhausted from crying for help;
my throat is parched.
My eyes are swollen with weeping,
waiting for my God to help me.
4 Those who hate me without cause
outnumber the hairs on my head.
Many enemies try to destroy me with lies,
demanding that I give back what I didn't steal.

5 O God, you know how foolish I am;
my sins cannot be hidden from you.
6 Don't let those who trust in you be ashamed
because of me,
O Sovereign LORD of Heaven's Armies.

68:31a Or *of rich cloth.* **68:31b** Hebrew *Cush.*

hosts, be ashamed for my sake: let not those that seek
thee be confounded for my sake, O God of Israel.
7 Because for thy sake I have borne reproach;
shame hath covered my face.
8 I am become a stranger unto my brethren, and an
alien unto my mother's children.
9 For the zeal of thine house hath eaten me up; and
the reproaches of them that reproached thee are
fallen upon me.
10 When I wept, *and chastened* my soul with fasting, that was to my reproach.
11 I made sackcloth also my garment; and I became
a proverb to them.
12 They that sit in the gate speak against me; and I
was the song of the drunkards.
13 But as for me, my prayer *is* unto thee, O LORD, *in*
an acceptable time: O God, in the multitude of thy
mercy hear me, in the truth of thy salvation.
14 Deliver me out of the mire, and let me not sink:
let me be delivered from them that hate me, and out
of the deep waters.
15 Let not the waterflood overflow me, neither let
the deep swallow me up, and let not the pit shut her
mouth upon me.
16 Hear me, O LORD; for thy lovingkindness *is* good:
turn unto me according to the multitude of thy tender mercies.
17 And hide not thy face from thy servant; for I am
in trouble: hear me speedily.
18 Draw nigh unto my soul, *and* redeem it: deliver
me because of mine enemies.
19 Thou hast known my reproach, and my shame,
and my dishonour: mine adversaries *are* all before
thee.
20 Reproach hath broken my heart; and I am full
of heaviness: and I looked *for some* to take pity, but
there was none; and for comforters, but I found
none.
21 They gave me also gall for my meat; and in my
thirst they gave me vinegar to drink.
22 Let their table become a snare before them: and
that which should have been for *their* welfare, *let it*
become a trap.
23 Let their eyes be darkened, that they see not; and
make their loins continually to shake.
24 Pour out thine indignation upon them, and let
thy wrathful anger take hold of them.
25 Let their habitation be desolate; *and* let none
dwell in their tents.

Don't let me cause them to be humiliated,
O God of Israel.
7 For I endure insults for your sake;
humiliation is written all over my face.
8 Even my own brothers pretend they don't
know me;
they treat me like a stranger.
9 Passion for your house has consumed me,
and the insults of those who insult you have
fallen on me.
10 When I weep and fast,
they scoff at me.
11 When I dress in burlap to show sorrow,
they make fun of me.
12 I am the favorite topic of town gossip,
and all the drunks sing about me.

13 But I keep praying to you, LORD,
hoping this time you will show me favor.
In your unfailing love, O God,
answer my prayer with your sure salvation.
14 Rescue me from the mud;
don't let me sink any deeper!
Save me from those who hate me,
and pull me from these deep waters.
15 Don't let the floods overwhelm me,
or the deep waters swallow me,
or the pit of death devour me.

16 Answer my prayers, O LORD,
for your unfailing love is wonderful.
Take care of me,
for your mercy is so plentiful.
17 Don't hide from your servant;
answer me quickly, for I am in deep trouble!
18 Come and redeem me;
free me from my enemies.
19 You know of my shame, scorn, and disgrace.
You see all that my enemies are doing.
20 Their insults have broken my heart,
and I am in despair.
If only one person would show some pity;
if only one would turn and comfort me.
21 But instead, they give me poison* for food;
they offer me sour wine for my thirst.

22 Let the bountiful table set before them
become a snare
and their prosperity become a trap.*
23 Let their eyes go blind so they cannot see,
and make their bodies shake continually.*
24 Pour out your fury on them;
consume them with your burning anger.
25 Let their homes become desolate
and their tents be deserted.

69:21 Or *gall.* **69:22** Greek version reads *Let their bountiful table set before them become a snare, / a trap that makes them think all is well. / Let their blessings cause them to stumble, / and let them get what they deserve.* Compare Rom 11:9. **69:23** Greek version reads *and let their backs be bent forever.* Compare Rom 11:10.

KING JAMES VERSION

26 For they persecute *him* whom thou hast smitten; and they talk to the grief of those whom thou
hast wounded.
27 Add iniquity unto their iniquity: and let them
not come into thy righteousness.
28 Let them be blotted out of the book of the living,
and not be written with the righteous.
29 But I *am* poor and sorrowful: let thy salvation,
O God, set me up on high.
30 I will praise the name of God with a song, and
will magnify him with thanksgiving.
31 *This* also shall please the LORD better than an ox
or bullock that hath horns and hoofs.
32 The humble shall see *this, and* be glad: and your
heart shall live that seek God.
33 For the LORD heareth the poor, and despiseth
not his prisoners.
34 Let the heaven and earth praise him, the seas,
and every thing that moveth therein.
35 For God will save Zion, and will build the cities of
Judah: that they may dwell there, and have it in possession.
36 The seed also of his servants shall inherit it: and
they that love his name shall dwell therein.

70

To the chief Musician, A Psalm *of David, to bring to remembrance*

1 *Make haste,* O God, to deliver me; make haste to
help me, O LORD.
2 Let them be ashamed and confounded that seek
after my soul: let them be turned backward, and put
to confusion, that desire my hurt.
3 Let them be turned back for a reward of their
shame that say, Aha, aha.
4 Let all those that seek thee rejoice and be glad in
thee: and let such as love thy salvation say continually, Let God be magnified.
5 But I *am* poor and needy: make haste unto me,
O God: thou *art* my help and my deliverer; O LORD,
make no tarrying.

71

1 In thee, O LORD, do I put my trust: let me
never be put to confusion.
2 Deliver me in thy righteousness, and cause me to
escape: incline thine ear unto me, and save me.

NEW LIVING TRANSLATION

26 To the one you have punished, they add insult
to injury;
they add to the pain of those you have hurt.
27 Pile their sins up high,
and don't let them go free.
28 Erase their names from the Book of Life;
don't let them be counted among the
righteous.

29 I am suffering and in pain.
Rescue me, O God, by your saving power.
30 Then I will praise God's name with singing,
and I will honor him with thanksgiving.
31 For this will please the LORD more than
sacrificing cattle,
more than presenting a bull with its horns
and hooves.
32 The humble will see their God at work and be glad.
Let all who seek God's help be encouraged.
33 For the LORD hears the cries of the needy;
he does not despise his imprisoned people.
34 Praise him, O heaven and earth,
the seas and all that move in them.
35 For God will save Jerusalem*
and rebuild the towns of Judah.
His people will live there
and settle in their own land.
36 The descendants of those who obey him will
inherit the land,
and those who love him will live there in safety.

70

For the choir director: A psalm of David, asking God to remember him.

1 Please, God, rescue me!
Come quickly, LORD, and help me.
2 May those who try to kill me
be humiliated and put to shame.
May those who take delight in my trouble
be turned back in disgrace.
3 Let them be horrified by their shame,
for they said, "Aha! We've got him now!"
4 But may all who search for you
be filled with joy and gladness in you.
May those who love your salvation
repeatedly shout, "God is great!"
5 But as for me, I am poor and needy;
please hurry to my aid, O God.
You are my helper and my savior;
O LORD, do not delay.

71

1 O LORD, I have come to you for protection;
don't let me be disgraced.
2 Save me and rescue me,
for you do what is right.
Turn your ear to listen to me,
and set me free.

69:35 Hebrew *Zion.*

KING JAMES VERSION

[3]Be thou my strong habitation, whereunto I may
continually resort: thou hast given commandment to
save me; for thou *art* my rock and my fortress.
[4]Deliver me, O my God, out of the hand of the
wicked, out of the hand of the unrighteous and cruel
man.
[5]For thou *art* my hope, O Lord God: *thou art* my
trust from my youth.
[6]By thee have I been holden up from the womb:
thou art he that took me out of my mother's bowels:
my praise *shall be* continually of thee.
[7]I am as a wonder unto many; but thou *art* my
strong refuge.
[8]Let my mouth be filled *with* thy praise *and with*
thy honour all the day.
[9]Cast me not off in the time of old age; forsake me
not when my strength faileth.
[10]For mine enemies speak against me; and they
that lay wait for my soul take counsel together,
[11]Saying, God hath forsaken him: persecute and
take him; for *there is* none to deliver *him*.
[12]O God, be not far from me: O my God, make
haste for my help.
[13]Let them be confounded *and* consumed that are
adversaries to my soul; let them be covered *with* reproach and dishonour that seek my hurt.
[14]But I will hope continually, and will yet praise
thee more and more.
[15]My mouth shall shew forth thy righteousness
and thy salvation all the day; for I know not the numbers *thereof.*
[16]I will go in the strength of the Lord God: I will
make mention of thy righteousness, *even* of thine
only.
[17]O God, thou hast taught me from my youth: and
hitherto have I declared thy wondrous works.
[18]Now also when I am old and greyheaded, O God,
forsake me not; until I have shewed thy strength unto
this generation, *and* thy power to every one *that* is to
come.
[19]Thy righteousness also, O God, *is* very high, who
hast done great things: O God, who *is* like unto thee!
[20]*Thou,* which hast shewed me great and sore
troubles, shalt quicken me again, and shalt bring me
up again from the depths of the earth.

NEW LIVING TRANSLATION

[3] Be my rock of safety
where I can always hide.
Give the order to save me,
for you are my rock and my fortress.
[4] My God, rescue me from the power of
the wicked,
from the clutches of cruel oppressors.
[5] O Lord, you alone are my hope.
I've trusted you, O Lord, from childhood.
[6] Yes, you have been with me from birth;
from my mother's womb you have cared
for me.
No wonder I am always praising you!

[7] My life is an example to many,
because you have been my strength and
protection.
[8] That is why I can never stop praising you;
I declare your glory all day long.
[9] And now, in my old age, don't set me aside.
Don't abandon me when my strength is failing.
[10] For my enemies are whispering against me.
They are plotting together to kill me.
[11] They say, "God has abandoned him.
Let's go and get him,
for no one will help him now."

[12] O God, don't stay away.
My God, please hurry to help me.
[13] Bring disgrace and destruction on my accusers.
Humiliate and shame those who want to
harm me.
[14] But I will keep on hoping for your help;
I will praise you more and more.
[15] I will tell everyone about your righteousness.
All day long I will proclaim your saving power,
though I am not skilled with words.*
[16] I will praise your mighty deeds, O Sovereign Lord.
I will tell everyone that you alone are just.

[17] O God, you have taught me from my earliest
childhood,
and I constantly tell others about the
wonderful things you do.
[18] Now that I am old and gray,
do not abandon me, O God.
Let me proclaim your power to this new
generation,
your mighty miracles to all who come after me.

[19] Your righteousness, O God, reaches to the
highest heavens.
You have done such wonderful things.
Who can compare with you, O God?
[20] You have allowed me to suffer much hardship,
but you will restore me to life again
and lift me up from the depths of the earth.

71:15 Or *though I cannot count it.*

KING JAMES VERSION

21 Thou shalt increase my greatness, and comfort
me on every side.
22 I will also praise thee with the psaltery, *even* thy
truth, O my God: unto thee will I sing with the harp,
O thou Holy One of Israel.
23 My lips shall greatly rejoice when I sing unto
thee; and my soul, which thou hast redeemed.
24 My tongue also shall talk of thy righteousness all
the day long: for they are confounded, for they are
brought unto shame, that seek my hurt.

72 A Psalm *for Solomon*

1 Give the king thy judgments, O God, and thy righteousness unto the king's son.
2 He shall judge thy people with righteousness,
and thy poor with judgment.
3 The mountains shall bring peace to the people,
and the little hills, by righteousness.
4 He shall judge the poor of the people, he shall
save the children of the needy, and shall break in
pieces the oppressor.
5 They shall fear thee as long as the sun and moon
endure, throughout all generations.
6 He shall come down like rain upon the mown
grass: as showers *that* water the earth.
7 In his days shall the righteous flourish; and
abundance of peace so long as the moon endureth.
8 He shall have dominion also from sea to sea, and
from the river unto the ends of the earth.
9 They that dwell in the wilderness shall bow before him; and his enemies shall lick the dust.
10 The kings of Tarshish and of the isles shall bring
presents: the kings of Sheba and Seba shall offer
gifts.
11 Yea, all kings shall fall down before him: all nations shall serve him.
12 For he shall deliver the needy when he crieth;
the poor also, and *him* that hath no helper.
13 He shall spare the poor and needy, and shall save
the souls of the needy.
14 He shall redeem their soul from deceit and violence: and precious shall their blood be in his sight.

NEW LIVING TRANSLATION

21 You will restore me to even greater honor
and comfort me once again.

22 Then I will praise you with music on the harp,
because you are faithful to your promises,
O my God.
I will sing praises to you with a lyre,
O Holy One of Israel.
23 I will shout for joy and sing your praises,
for you have ransomed me.
24 I will tell about your righteous deeds
all day long,
for everyone who tried to hurt me
has been shamed and humiliated.

72 *A psalm of Solomon.*

1 Give your love of justice to the king, O God,
and righteousness to the king's son.
2 Help him judge your people in the right way;
let the poor always be treated fairly.
3 May the mountains yield prosperity for all,
and may the hills be fruitful.
4 Help him to defend the poor,
to rescue the children of the needy,
and to crush their oppressors.
5 May they fear you* as long as the sun shines,
as long as the moon remains in the sky.
Yes, forever!
6 May the king's rule be refreshing like spring rain
on freshly cut grass,
like the showers that water the earth.
7 May all the godly flourish during his reign.
May there be abundant prosperity until the
moon is no more.
8 May he reign from sea to sea,
and from the Euphrates River* to the ends
of the earth.
9 Desert nomads will bow before him;
his enemies will fall before him in the dust.
10 The western kings of Tarshish and other
distant lands
will bring him tribute.
The eastern kings of Sheba and Seba
will bring him gifts.
11 All kings will bow before him,
and all nations will serve him.

12 He will rescue the poor when they cry to him;
he will help the oppressed, who have no one
to defend them.
13 He feels pity for the weak and the needy,
and he will rescue them.
14 He will redeem them from oppression and
violence,
for their lives are precious to him.

72:5 Greek version reads *May they endure.* 72:8 Hebrew *the river.*

KING JAMES VERSION

15 And he shall live, and to him shall be given of the gold of Sheba: prayer also shall be made for him continually; *and* daily shall he be praised.

16 There shall be an handful of corn in the earth upon the top of the mountains; the fruit thereof shall shake like Lebanon: and *they* of the city shall flourish like grass of the earth.

17 His name shall endure for ever: his name shall be continued as long as the sun: and *men* shall be blessed in him: all nations shall call him blessed.

18 Blessed *be* the LORD God, the God of Israel, who only doeth wondrous things.

19 And blessed *be* his glorious name for ever: and let the whole earth be filled *with* his glory; Amen, and Amen.

20 The prayers of David the son of Jesse are ended.

73 *A Psalm of Asaph*

1 Truly God *is* good to Israel, *even* to such as are of a clean heart.

2 But as for me, my feet were almost gone; my steps had well nigh slipped.

3 For I was envious at the foolish, *when* I saw the prosperity of the wicked.

4 For *there are* no bands in their death: but their strength *is* firm.

5 They *are* not in trouble *as other* men; neither are they plagued like *other* men.

6 Therefore pride compasseth them about as a chain; violence covereth them *as* a garment.

7 Their eyes stand out with fatness: they have more than heart could wish.

8 They are corrupt, and speak wickedly *concerning* oppression: they speak loftily.

9 They set their mouth against the heavens, and their tongue walketh through the earth.

10 Therefore his people return hither: and waters of a full *cup* are wrung out to them.

11 And they say, How doth God know? and is there knowledge in the most High?

12 Behold, these *are* the ungodly, who prosper in the world; they increase *in* riches.

13 Verily I have cleansed my heart *in* vain, and washed my hands in innocency.

14 For all the day long have I been plagued, and chastened every morning.

NEW LIVING TRANSLATION

15 Long live the king!
May the gold of Sheba be given to him.
May the people always pray for him
and bless him all day long.
16 May there be abundant grain throughout the land,
flourishing even on the hilltops.
May the fruit trees flourish like the trees
of Lebanon,
and may the people thrive like grass in a field.
17 May the king's name endure forever;
may it continue as long as the sun shines.
May all nations be blessed through him
and bring him praise.

18 Praise the LORD God, the God of Israel,
who alone does such wonderful things.
19 Praise his glorious name forever!
Let the whole earth be filled with his glory.
Amen and amen!
20 (This ends the prayers of David son of Jesse.)

BOOK THREE (Psalms 73–89)

73 *A psalm of Asaph.*

1 Truly God is good to Israel,
to those whose hearts are pure.
2 But as for me, I almost lost my footing.
My feet were slipping, and I was almost gone.
3 For I envied the proud
when I saw them prosper despite their
wickedness.
4 They seem to live such painless lives;
their bodies are so healthy and strong.
5 They don't have troubles like other people;
they're not plagued with problems like
everyone else.
6 They wear pride like a jeweled necklace
and clothe themselves with cruelty.
7 These fat cats have everything
their hearts could ever wish for!
8 They scoff and speak only evil;
in their pride they seek to crush others.
9 They boast against the very heavens,
and their words strut throughout the earth.
10 And so the people are dismayed and confused,
drinking in all their words.
11 "What does God know?" they ask.
"Does the Most High even know what's
happening?"
12 Look at these wicked people—
enjoying a life of ease while their riches
multiply.

13 Did I keep my heart pure for nothing?
Did I keep myself innocent for no reason?
14 I get nothing but trouble all day long;
every morning brings me pain.

KING JAMES VERSION

15 If I say, I will speak thus; behold, I should offend *against* the generation of thy children.

16 When I thought to know this, it *was* too painful for me;

17 Until I went into the sanctuary of God; *then* understood I their end.

18 Surely thou didst set them in slippery places: thou castedst them down into destruction.

19 How are they *brought* into desolation, as in a moment! they are utterly consumed with terrors.

20 As a dream when *one* awaketh; *so*, O Lord, when thou awakest, thou shalt despise their image.

21 Thus my heart was grieved, and I was pricked in my reins.

22 So foolish *was* I, and ignorant: I was *as* a beast before thee.

23 Nevertheless I *am* continually with thee: thou hast holden *me* by my right hand.

24 Thou shalt guide me with thy counsel, and afterward receive me *to* glory.

25 Whom have I in heaven *but thee?* and *there is* none upon earth *that* I desire beside thee.

26 My flesh and my heart faileth: *but* God *is* the strength of my heart, and my portion for ever.

27 For, lo, they that are far from thee shall perish: thou hast destroyed all them that go a whoring from thee.

28 But *it is* good for me to draw near to God: I have put my trust in the Lord GOD, that I may declare all thy works.

74

Maschil of Asaph

1 O God, why hast thou cast *us* off for ever? *why* doth thine anger smoke against the sheep of thy pasture?

2 Remember thy congregation, *which* thou hast purchased of old; the rod of thine inheritance, *which* thou hast redeemed; this mount Zion, wherein thou hast dwelt.

3 Lift up thy feet unto the perpetual desolations; *even* all *that* the enemy hath done wickedly in the sanctuary.

4 Thine enemies roar in the midst of thy congregations; they set up their ensigns *for* signs.

NEW LIVING TRANSLATION

15 If I had really spoken this way to others,
I would have been a traitor to your people.
16 So I tried to understand why the wicked prosper.
But what a difficult task it is!
17 Then I went into your sanctuary, O God,
and I finally understood the destiny of the wicked.
18 Truly, you put them on a slippery path
and send them sliding over the cliff to destruction.
19 In an instant they are destroyed,
completely swept away by terrors.
20 When you arise, O Lord,
you will laugh at their silly ideas
as a person laughs at dreams in the morning.

21 Then I realized that my heart was bitter,
and I was all torn up inside.
22 I was so foolish and ignorant—
I must have seemed like a senseless animal to you.
23 Yet I still belong to you;
you hold my right hand.
24 You guide me with your counsel,
leading me to a glorious destiny.
25 Whom have I in heaven but you?
I desire you more than anything on earth.
26 My health may fail, and my spirit may grow weak,
but God remains the strength of my heart;
he is mine forever.

27 Those who desert him will perish,
for you destroy those who abandon you.
28 But as for me, how good it is to be near God!
I have made the Sovereign LORD my shelter,
and I will tell everyone about the wonderful things you do.

74

A psalm of Asaph.*

1 O God, why have you rejected us so long?
Why is your anger so intense against the sheep of your own pasture?
2 Remember that we are the people you chose long ago,
the tribe you redeemed as your own special possession!
And remember Jerusalem,* your home here on earth.
3 Walk through the awful ruins of the city;
see how the enemy has destroyed your sanctuary.
4 There your enemies shouted their victorious battle cries;
there they set up their battle standards.

74:TITLE Hebrew *maskil.* This may be a literary or musical term.
74:2 Hebrew *Mount Zion.*

KING JAMES VERSION

5 *A man* was famous according as he had lifted up
axes upon the thick trees.
6 But now they break down the carved work
thereof at once with axes and hammers.
7 They have cast fire into thy sanctuary, they have
defiled *by casting down* the dwelling place of thy
name to the ground.
8 They said in their hearts, Let us destroy them
together: they have burned up all the synagogues of
God in the land.
9 We see not our signs: *there is* no more any prophet: neither *is there* among us any that knoweth how
long.
10 O God, how long shall the adversary reproach?
shall the enemy blaspheme thy name for ever?
11 Why withdrawest thou thy hand, even thy right
hand? pluck *it* out of thy bosom.
12 For God *is* my King of old, working salvation in
the midst of the earth.
13 Thou didst divide the sea by thy strength: thou
brakest the heads of the dragons in the waters.
14 Thou brakest the heads of leviathan in pieces,
and gavest him *to be* meat to the people inhabiting
the wilderness.
15 Thou didst cleave the fountain and the flood:
thou driedst up mighty rivers.
16 The day *is* thine, the night also *is* thine: thou hast
prepared the light and the sun.
17 Thou hast set all the borders of the earth: thou
hast made summer and winter.
18 Remember this, *that* the enemy hath reproached,
O LORD, and *that* the foolish people have blasphemed
thy name.
19 O deliver not the soul of thy turtledove unto the
multitude *of the wicked:* forget not the congregation
of thy poor for ever.
20 Have respect unto the covenant: for the dark
places of the earth are full of the habitations of
cruelty.
21 O let not the oppressed return ashamed: let the
poor and needy praise thy name.
22 Arise, O God, plead thine own cause: remember
how the foolish man reproacheth thee daily.
23 Forget not the voice of thine enemies: the tumult of those that rise up against thee increaseth
continually.

75

To the chief Musician, Al-taschith, A Psalm or *Song of Asaph*

1 Unto thee, O God, do we give thanks, *unto thee* do
we give thanks: for *that* thy name is near thy wondrous works declare.
2 When I shall receive the congregation I will
judge uprightly.

NEW LIVING TRANSLATION

5 They swung their axes
like woodcutters in a forest.
6 With axes and picks,
they smashed the carved paneling.
7 They burned your sanctuary to the ground.
They defiled the place that bears your name.
8 Then they thought, "Let's destroy everything!"
So they burned down all the places where God
was worshiped.

9 We no longer see your miraculous signs.
All the prophets are gone,
and no one can tell us when it will end.
10 How long, O God, will you allow our enemies to
insult you?
Will you let them dishonor your name forever?
11 Why do you hold back your strong right hand?
Unleash your powerful fist and destroy them.

12 You, O God, are my king from ages past,
bringing salvation to the earth.
13 You split the sea by your strength
and smashed the heads of the sea monsters.
14 You crushed the heads of Leviathan*
and let the desert animals eat him.
15 You caused the springs and streams to gush forth,
and you dried up rivers that never run dry.
16 Both day and night belong to you;
you made the starlight* and the sun.
17 You set the boundaries of the earth,
and you made both summer and winter.

18 See how these enemies insult you, LORD.
A foolish nation has dishonored your name.
19 Don't let these wild beasts destroy your
turtledoves.
Don't forget your suffering people forever.

20 Remember your covenant promises,
for the land is full of darkness and violence!
21 Don't let the downtrodden be humiliated again.
Instead, let the poor and needy praise
your name.

22 Arise, O God, and defend your cause.
Remember how these fools insult you
all day long.
23 Don't overlook what your enemies have said
or their growing uproar.

75

For the choir director: A psalm of Asaph. A song to be sung to the tune "Do Not Destroy!"

1 We thank you, O God!
We give thanks because you are near.
People everywhere tell of your wonderful deeds.

2 God says, "At the time I have planned,
I will bring justice against the wicked.

74:14 The identification of Leviathan is disputed, ranging from an earthly creature to a mythical sea monster in ancient literature. **74:16** Or *moon;* Hebrew reads *light.*

KING JAMES VERSION

[3]The earth and all the inhabitants thereof are dissolved: I bear up the pillars of it. Selah.
[4]I said unto the fools, Deal not foolishly: and to the
wicked, Lift not up the horn:
[5]Lift not up your horn on high: speak *not with* a
stiff neck.
[6]For promotion *cometh* neither from the east, nor
from the west, nor from the south.
[7]But God *is* the judge: he putteth down one, and
setteth up another.
[8]For in the hand of the LORD *there is* a cup, and the
wine is red; it is full of mixture; and he poureth out of
the same: but the dregs thereof, all the wicked of the
earth shall wring *them* out, *and* drink *them*.
[9]But I will declare for ever; I will sing praises to the
God of Jacob.
[10]All the horns of the wicked also will I cut off; *but*
the horns of the righteous shall be exalted.

76 *To the chief Musician on Neginoth, A Psalm* or *Song of Asaph*

[1]In Judah *is* God known: his name *is* great in Israel.
[2]In Salem also is his tabernacle, and his dwelling
place in Zion.
[3]There brake he the arrows of the bow, the shield,
and the sword, and the battle. Selah.
[4]Thou *art* more glorious *and* excellent than the
mountains of prey.
[5]The stouthearted are spoiled, they have slept
their sleep: and none of the men of might have found
their hands.
[6]At thy rebuke, O God of Jacob, both the chariot
and horse are cast into a dead sleep.
[7]Thou, *even* thou, *art* to be feared: and who may
stand in thy sight when once thou art angry?
[8]Thou didst cause judgment to be heard from
heaven; the earth feared, and was still,
[9]When God arose to judgment, to save all the
meek of the earth. Selah.
[10]Surely the wrath of man shall praise thee: the
remainder of wrath shalt thou restrain.
[11]Vow, and pay unto the LORD your God: let all that
be round about him bring presents unto him that
ought to be feared.

NEW LIVING TRANSLATION

[3] When the earth quakes and its people live
in turmoil,
I am the one who keeps its foundations firm.
Interlude

[4] "I warned the proud, 'Stop your boasting!'
I told the wicked, 'Don't raise your fists!
[5] Don't raise your fists in defiance at the heavens
or speak with such arrogance.'"
[6] For no one on earth—from east or west,
or even from the wilderness—
should raise a defiant fist.*
[7] It is God alone who judges;
he decides who will rise and who will fall.
[8] For the LORD holds a cup in his hand
that is full of foaming wine mixed with spices.
He pours out the wine in judgment,
and all the wicked must drink it,
draining it to the dregs.

[9] But as for me, I will always proclaim what God
has done;
I will sing praises to the God of Jacob.
[10] For God says, "I will break the strength of the
wicked,
but I will increase the power of the godly."

76 *For the choir director: A psalm of Asaph. A song to be accompanied by stringed instruments.*

[1] God is honored in Judah;
his name is great in Israel.
[2] Jerusalem* is where he lives;
Mount Zion is his home.
[3] There he has broken the fiery arrows of the enemy,
the shields and swords and weapons of war.
Interlude

[4] You are glorious and more majestic
than the everlasting mountains.*
[5] Our boldest enemies have been plundered.
They lie before us in the sleep of death.
No warrior could lift a hand against us.
[6] At the blast of your breath, O God of Jacob,
their horses and chariots lay still.

[7] No wonder you are greatly feared!
Who can stand before you when your anger
explodes?
[8] From heaven you sentenced your enemies;
the earth trembled and stood silent before you.
[9] You stand up to judge those who do evil, O God,
and to rescue the oppressed of the earth.
Interlude
[10] Human defiance only enhances your glory,
for you use it as a weapon.*
[11] Make vows to the LORD your God, and keep them.
Let everyone bring tribute to the Awesome One.

75:6 Hebrew *should lift.* **76:2** Hebrew *Salem,* another name for Jerusalem. **76:4** As in Greek version; Hebrew reads *than mountains filled with beasts of prey.* **76:10** The meaning of the Hebrew is uncertain.

KING JAMES VERSION

12 He shall cut off the spirit of princes: *he is* terrible to the kings of the earth.

77

To the chief Musician, to Jeduthun, A Psalm of Asaph

1 I cried unto God with my voice, *even* unto God with my voice; and he gave ear unto me.

2 In the day of my trouble I sought the Lord: my sore ran in the night, and ceased not: my soul refused to be comforted.

3 I remembered God, and was troubled: I complained, and my spirit was overwhelmed. Selah.

4 Thou holdest mine eyes waking: I am so troubled that I cannot speak.

5 I have considered the days of old, the years of ancient times.

6 I call to remembrance my song in the night: I commune with mine own heart: and my spirit made diligent search.

7 Will the Lord cast off for ever? and will he be favourable no more?

8 Is his mercy clean gone for ever? doth *his* promise fail for evermore?

9 Hath God forgotten to be gracious? hath he in anger shut up his tender mercies? Selah.

10 And I said, This *is* my infirmity: *but I will remember* the years of the right hand of the most High.

11 I will remember the works of the LORD: surely I will remember thy wonders of old.

12 I will meditate also of all thy work, and talk of thy doings.

13 Thy way, O God, *is* in the sanctuary: who *is so* great a God as *our* God?

14 Thou *art* the God that doest wonders: thou hast declared thy strength among the people.

15 Thou hast with *thine* arm redeemed thy people, the sons of Jacob and Joseph. Selah.

16 The waters saw thee, O God, the waters saw thee; they were afraid: the depths also were troubled.

17 The clouds poured out water: the skies sent out a sound: thine arrows also went abroad.

18 The voice of thy thunder *was* in the heaven: the lightnings lightened the world: the earth trembled and shook.

19 Thy way *is* in the sea, and thy path in the great waters, and thy footsteps are not known.

NEW LIVING TRANSLATION

12 For he breaks the pride of princes,
and the kings of the earth fear him.

77

For Jeduthun, the choir director: A psalm of Asaph.

1 I cry out to God; yes, I shout.
Oh, that God would listen to me!
2 When I was in deep trouble,
I searched for the Lord.
All night long I prayed, with hands lifted toward heaven,
but my soul was not comforted.
3 I think of God, and I moan,
overwhelmed with longing for his help. *Interlude*

4 You don't let me sleep.
I am too distressed even to pray!
5 I think of the good old days,
long since ended,
6 when my nights were filled with joyful songs.
I search my soul and ponder the difference now.
7 Has the Lord rejected me forever?
Will he never again be kind to me?
8 Is his unfailing love gone forever?
Have his promises permanently failed?
9 Has God forgotten to be gracious?
Has he slammed the door on his compassion? *Interlude*

10 And I said, "This is my fate;
the Most High has turned his hand against me."
11 But then I recall all you have done, O LORD;
I remember your wonderful deeds of long ago.
12 They are constantly in my thoughts.
I cannot stop thinking about your mighty works.

13 O God, your ways are holy.
Is there any god as mighty as you?
14 You are the God of great wonders!
You demonstrate your awesome power among the nations.
15 By your strong arm, you redeemed your people,
the descendants of Jacob and Joseph. *Interlude*

16 When the Red Sea* saw you, O God,
its waters looked and trembled!
The sea quaked to its very depths.
17 The clouds poured down rain;
the thunder rumbled in the sky.
Your arrows of lightning flashed.
18 Your thunder roared from the whirlwind;
the lightning lit up the world!
The earth trembled and shook.
19 Your road led through the sea,
your pathway through the mighty waters—
a pathway no one knew was there!

77:16 Hebrew *the waters.*

KING JAMES VERSION

20 Thou leddest thy people like a flock by the hand
of Moses and Aaron.

78 *Maschil of Asaph*

1 Give ear, O my people, *to* my law: incline your ears
to the words of my mouth.
2 I will open my mouth in a parable: I will utter
dark sayings of old:
3 Which we have heard and known, and our fathers have told us.
4 We will not hide *them* from their children,
shewing to the generation to come the praises of the
LORD, and his strength, and his wonderful works that
he hath done.
5 For he established a testimony in Jacob, and appointed a law in Israel, which he commanded our
fathers, that they should make them known to their
children:
6 That the generation to come might know *them,*
even the children *which* should be born; *who* should
arise and declare *them* to their children:
7 That they might set their hope in God, and not
forget the works of God, but keep his commandments:
8 And might not be as their fathers, a stubborn
and rebellious generation; a generation *that* set not
their heart aright, and whose spirit was not stedfast
with God.
9 The children of Ephraim, *being* armed, *and* carrying bows, turned back in the day of battle.
10 They kept not the covenant of God, and refused
to walk in his law;
11 And forgat his works, and his wonders that he
had shewed them.
12 Marvellous things did he in the sight of their fathers, in the land of Egypt, *in* the field of Zoan.
13 He divided the sea, and caused them to pass
through; and he made the waters to stand as an heap.
14 In the daytime also he led them with a cloud,
and all the night with a light of fire.
15 He clave the rocks in the wilderness, and gave
them drink as *out of* the great depths.
16 He brought streams also out of the rock, and
caused waters to run down like rivers.
17 And they sinned yet more against him by provoking the most High in the wilderness.
18 And they tempted God in their heart by asking
meat for their lust.
19 Yea, they spake against God; they said, Can God
furnish a table in the wilderness?
20 Behold, he smote the rock, that the waters
gushed out, and the streams overflowed; can he give
bread also? can he provide flesh for his people?

NEW LIVING TRANSLATION

20 You led your people along that road like
a flock of sheep,
with Moses and Aaron as their shepherds.

78 *A psalm* of Asaph.*

1 O my people, listen to my instructions.
Open your ears to what I am saying,
2 for I will speak to you in a parable.
I will teach you hidden lessons from our past—
3 stories we have heard and known,
stories our ancestors handed down to us.
4 We will not hide these truths from our children;
we will tell the next generation
about the glorious deeds of the LORD,
about his power and his mighty wonders.
5 For he issued his laws to Jacob;
he gave his instructions to Israel.
He commanded our ancestors
to teach them to their children,
6 so the next generation might know them—
even the children not yet born—
and they in turn will teach their own children.
7 So each generation should set its hope anew
on God,
not forgetting his glorious miracles
and obeying his commands.
8 Then they will not be like their ancestors—
stubborn, rebellious, and unfaithful,
refusing to give their hearts to God.

9 The warriors of Ephraim, though armed
with bows,
turned their backs and fled on the day of battle.
10 They did not keep God's covenant
and refused to live by his instructions.
11 They forgot what he had done—
the great wonders he had shown them,
12 the miracles he did for their ancestors
on the plain of Zoan in the land of Egypt.
13 For he divided the sea and led them through,
making the water stand up like walls!
14 In the daytime he led them by a cloud,
and all night by a pillar of fire.
15 He split open the rocks in the wilderness
to give them water, as from a gushing spring.
16 He made streams pour from the rock,
making the waters flow down like a river!

17 Yet they kept on sinning against him,
rebelling against the Most High in the desert.
18 They stubbornly tested God in their hearts,
demanding the foods they craved.
19 They even spoke against God himself, saying,
"God can't give us food in the wilderness.
20 Yes, he can strike a rock so water gushes out,
but he can't give his people bread and meat."

78:TITLE Hebrew *maskil.* This may be a literary or musical term.

KING JAMES VERSION

21 Therefore the LORD heard *this,* and was wroth:
so a fire was kindled against Jacob, and anger also
came up against Israel;
22 Because they believed not in God, and trusted
not in his salvation:
23 Though he had commanded the clouds from
above, and opened the doors of heaven,
24 And had rained down manna upon them to eat,
and had given them of the corn of heaven.
25 Man did eat angels' food: he sent them meat to
the full.
26 He caused an east wind to blow in the heaven:
and by his power he brought in the south wind.
27 He rained flesh also upon them as dust, and
feathered fowls like as the sand of the sea:
28 And he let *it* fall in the midst of their camp,
round about their habitations.
29 So they did eat, and were well filled: for he gave
them their own desire;
30 They were not estranged from their lust. But
while their meat *was* yet in their mouths,
31 The wrath of God came upon them, and slew the
fattest of them, and smote down the chosen *men* of
Israel.
32 For all this they sinned still, and believed not for
his wondrous works.
33 Therefore their days did he consume in vanity,
and their years in trouble.
34 When he slew them, then they sought him: and
they returned and inquired early after God.
35 And they remembered that God *was* their rock,
and the high God their redeemer.
36 Nevertheless they did flatter him with their
mouth, and they lied unto him with their tongues.
37 For their heart was not right with him, neither
were they stedfast in his covenant.
38 But he, *being* full of compassion, forgave *their*
iniquity, and destroyed *them* not: yea, many a time
turned he his anger away, and did not stir up all his
wrath.
39 For he remembered that they *were but* flesh;
a wind that passeth away, and cometh not again.
40 How oft did they provoke him in the wilderness,
and grieve him in the desert!
41 Yea, they turned back and tempted God, and
limited the Holy One of Israel.
42 They remembered not his hand, *nor* the day
when he delivered them from the enemy.
43 How he had wrought his signs in Egypt, and his
wonders in the field of Zoan:
44 And had turned their rivers into blood; and their
floods, that they could not drink.

NEW LIVING TRANSLATION

21 When the LORD heard them, he was furious.
 The fire of his wrath burned against Jacob.
 Yes, his anger rose against Israel,
22 for they did not believe God
 or trust him to care for them.
23 But he commanded the skies to open;
 he opened the doors of heaven.
24 He rained down manna for them to eat;
 he gave them bread from heaven.
25 They ate the food of angels!
 God gave them all they could hold.
26 He released the east wind in the heavens
 and guided the south wind by his mighty power.
27 He rained down meat as thick as dust—
 birds as plentiful as the sand on the seashore!
28 He caused the birds to fall within their camp
 and all around their tents.
29 The people ate their fill.
 He gave them what they craved.
30 But before they satisfied their craving,
 while the meat was yet in their mouths,
31 the anger of God rose against them,
 and he killed their strongest men.
 He struck down the finest of Israel's young men.
32 But in spite of this, the people kept sinning.
 Despite his wonders, they refused to trust him.
33 So he ended their lives in failure,
 their years in terror.
34 When God began killing them,
 they finally sought him.
 They repented and took God seriously.
35 Then they remembered that God was their rock,
 that God Most High* was their redeemer.
36 But all they gave him was lip service;
 they lied to him with their tongues.
37 Their hearts were not loyal to him.
 They did not keep his covenant.
38 Yet he was merciful and forgave their sins
 and did not destroy them all.
Many times he held back his anger
 and did not unleash his fury!
39 For he remembered that they were merely mortal,
 gone like a breath of wind that never returns.
40 Oh, how often they rebelled against him in
 the wilderness
 and grieved his heart in that dry wasteland.
41 Again and again they tested God's patience
 and provoked the Holy One of Israel.
42 They did not remember his power
 and how he rescued them from their enemies.
43 They did not remember his miraculous signs
 in Egypt,
 his wonders on the plain of Zoan.
44 For he turned their rivers into blood,
 so no one could drink from the streams.

78:35 Hebrew *El-Elyon.*

KING JAMES VERSION

45 He sent divers sorts of flies among them, which
devoured them; and frogs, which destroyed them.
46 He gave also their increase unto the caterpiller,
and their labour unto the locust.
47 He destroyed their vines with hail, and their
sycamore trees with frost.
48 He gave up their cattle also to the hail, and their
flocks to hot thunderbolts.
49 He cast upon them the fierceness of his anger,
wrath, and indignation, and trouble, by sending evil
angels *among them.*
50 He made a way to his anger; he spared not their
soul from death, but gave their life over to the pestilence;
51 And smote all the firstborn in Egypt; the chief of
their strength in the tabernacles of Ham:
52 But made his own people to go forth like sheep,
and guided them in the wilderness like a flock.
53 And he led them on safely, so that they feared
not: but the sea overwhelmed their enemies.
54 And he brought them to the border of his sanctuary, *even to* this mountain, *which* his right hand
had purchased.
55 He cast out the heathen also before them, and
divided them an inheritance by line, and made the
tribes of Israel to dwell in their tents.
56 Yet they tempted and provoked the most high
God, and kept not his testimonies:
57 But turned back, and dealt unfaithfully like their
fathers: they were turned aside like a deceitful bow.
58 For they provoked him to anger with their high
places, and moved him to jealousy with their graven
images.
59 When God heard *this,* he was wroth, and greatly
abhorred Israel:
60 So that he forsook the tabernacle of Shiloh, the
tent *which* he placed among men;
61 And delivered his strength into captivity, and his
glory into the enemy's hand.
62 He gave his people over also unto the sword; and
was wroth with his inheritance.
63 The fire consumed their young men; and their
maidens were not given to marriage.
64 Their priests fell by the sword; and their widows
made no lamentation.
65 Then the LORD awaked as one out of sleep, *and*
like a mighty man that shouteth by reason of wine.

NEW LIVING TRANSLATION

45 He sent vast swarms of flies to consume them
and hordes of frogs to ruin them.
46 He gave their crops to caterpillars;
their harvest was consumed by locusts.
47 He destroyed their grapevines with hail
and shattered their sycamore-figs with sleet.
48 He abandoned their cattle to the hail,
their livestock to bolts of lightning.
49 He loosed on them his fierce anger—
all his fury, rage, and hostility.
He dispatched against them
a band of destroying angels.
50 He turned his anger against them;
he did not spare the Egyptians' lives
but ravaged them with the plague.
51 He killed the oldest son in each Egyptian family,
the flower of youth throughout the land
of Egypt.*
52 But he led his own people like a flock of sheep,
guiding them safely through the wilderness.
53 He kept them safe so they were not afraid;
but the sea covered their enemies.
54 He brought them to the border of his holy land,
to this land of hills he had won for them.
55 He drove out the nations before them;
he gave them their inheritance by lot.
He settled the tribes of Israel into their homes.

56 But they kept testing and rebelling against
God Most High.
They did not obey his laws.
57 They turned back and were as faithless as
their parents.
They were as undependable as a crooked bow.
58 They angered God by building shrines to
other gods;
they made him jealous with their idols.
59 When God heard them, he was very angry,
and he completely rejected Israel.
60 Then he abandoned his dwelling at Shiloh,
the Tabernacle where he had lived among
the people.
61 He allowed the Ark of his might to be captured;
he surrendered his glory into enemy hands.
62 He gave his people over to be butchered by
the sword,
because he was so angry with his own people—
his special possession.
63 Their young men were killed by fire;
their young women died before singing their
wedding songs.
64 Their priests were slaughtered,
and their widows could not mourn
their deaths.

65 Then the Lord rose up as though waking
from sleep,
like a warrior aroused from a drunken stupor.

78:51 Hebrew *in the tents of Ham.*

KING JAMES VERSION

66And he smote his enemies in the hinder parts:
he put them to a perpetual reproach.
67Moreover he refused the tabernacle of Joseph,
and chose not the tribe of Ephraim:
68But chose the tribe of Judah, the mount Zion
which he loved.
69And he built his sanctuary like high *palaces*, like
the earth which he hath established for ever.
70He chose David also his servant, and took him
from the sheepfolds:
71From following the ewes great with young he
brought him to feed Jacob his people, and Israel his
inheritance.
72So he fed them according to the integrity of his
heart; and guided them by the skilfulness of his
hands.

79 *A Psalm of Asaph*

1O God, the heathen are come into thine inheritance; thy holy temple have they defiled; they have
laid Jerusalem on heaps.
2The dead bodies of thy servants have they given
to be meat unto the fowls of the heaven, the flesh of
thy saints unto the beasts of the earth.
3Their blood have they shed like water round
about Jerusalem; and *there was* none to bury *them*.
4We are become a reproach to our neighbours, a
scorn and derision to them that are round about us.
5How long, LORD? wilt thou be angry for ever?
shall thy jealousy burn like fire?
6Pour out thy wrath upon the heathen that have
not known thee, and upon the kingdoms that have
not called upon thy name.
7For they have devoured Jacob, and laid waste his
dwelling place.
8O remember not against us former iniquities: let
thy tender mercies speedily prevent us: for we are
brought very low.
9Help us, O God of our salvation, for the glory of
thy name: and deliver us, and purge away our sins, for
thy name's sake.
10Wherefore should the heathen say, Where *is*
their God? let him be known among the heathen in
our sight *by* the revenging of the blood of thy servants *which is* shed.
11Let the sighing of the prisoner come before thee;
according to the greatness of thy power preserve
thou those that are appointed to die;

NEW LIVING TRANSLATION

66 He routed his enemies
and sent them to eternal shame.
67 But he rejected Joseph's descendants;
he did not choose the tribe of Ephraim.
68 He chose instead the tribe of Judah,
and Mount Zion, which he loved.
69 There he built his sanctuary as high as the heavens,
as solid and enduring as the earth.
70 He chose his servant David,
calling him from the sheep pens.
71 He took David from tending the ewes and lambs
and made him the shepherd of Jacob's
descendants—
God's own people, Israel.
72 He cared for them with a true heart
and led them with skillful hands.

79 *A psalm of Asaph.*

1 O God, pagan nations have conquered your land,
your special possession.
They have defiled your holy Temple
and made Jerusalem a heap of ruins.
2 They have left the bodies of your servants
as food for the birds of heaven.
The flesh of your godly ones
has become food for the wild animals.
3 Blood has flowed like water all around Jerusalem;
no one is left to bury the dead.
4 We are mocked by our neighbors,
an object of scorn and derision to those
around us.
5 O LORD, how long will you be angry with us?
Forever?
How long will your jealousy burn like fire?
6 Pour out your wrath on the nations that refuse to
acknowledge you—
on kingdoms that do not call upon your name.
7 For they have devoured your people Israel,*
making the land a desolate wilderness.
8 Do not hold us guilty for the sins of our ancestors!
Let your compassion quickly meet our needs,
for we are on the brink of despair.
9 Help us, O God of our salvation!
Help us for the glory of your name.
Save us and forgive our sins
for the honor of your name.
10 Why should pagan nations be allowed to scoff,
asking, "Where is their God?"
Show us your vengeance against the nations,
for they have spilled the blood of
your servants.
11 Listen to the moaning of the prisoners.
Demonstrate your great power by saving those
condemned to die.

79:7 Hebrew *devoured Jacob.* See note on 44:4.

KING JAMES VERSION

12 And render unto our neighbours sevenfold into
their bosom their reproach, wherewith they have
reproached thee, O Lord.
13 So we thy people and sheep of thy pasture will
give thee thanks for ever: we will shew forth thy
praise to all generations.

80 *To the chief Musician upon Shoshannim-Eduth, A Psalm of Asaph*

1 Give ear, O Shepherd of Israel, thou that leadest
Joseph like a flock; thou that dwellest *between* the
cherubims, shine forth.
2 Before Ephraim and Benjamin and Manasseh stir
up thy strength, and come *and* save us.
3 Turn us again, O God, and cause thy face to shine;
and we shall be saved.
4 O LORD God of hosts, how long wilt thou be angry
against the prayer of thy people?
5 Thou feedest them with the bread of tears; and
givest them tears to drink in great measure.
6 Thou makest us a strife unto our neighbours: and
our enemies laugh among themselves.
7 Turn us again, O God of hosts, and cause thy face
to shine; and we shall be saved.
8 Thou hast brought a vine out of Egypt: thou hast
cast out the heathen, and planted it.
9 Thou preparedst *room* before it, and didst cause
it to take deep root, and it filled the land.
10 The hills were covered with the shadow of it, and
the boughs thereof *were like* the goodly cedars.
11 She sent out her boughs unto the sea, and her
branches unto the river.
12 Why hast thou *then* broken down her hedges, so
that all they which pass by the way do pluck her?
13 The boar out of the wood doth waste it, and the
wild beast of the field doth devour it.
14 Return, we beseech thee, O God of hosts: look
down from heaven, and behold, and visit this vine;
15 And the vineyard which thy right hand hath
planted, and the branch *that* thou madest strong for
thyself.
16 *It is* burned with fire, *it is* cut down: they perish
at the rebuke of thy countenance.
17 Let thy hand be upon the man of thy right hand,
upon the son of man *whom* thou madest strong for
thyself.

NEW LIVING TRANSLATION

12 O Lord, pay back our neighbors seven times
for the scorn they have hurled at you.
13 Then we your people, the sheep of your pasture,
will thank you forever and ever,
praising your greatness from generation
to generation.

80 *For the choir director: A psalm of Asaph, to be sung to the tune "Lilies of the Covenant."*

1 Please listen, O Shepherd of Israel,
you who lead Joseph's descendants like a flock.
O God, enthroned above the cherubim,
display your radiant glory
2 to Ephraim, Benjamin, and Manasseh.
Show us your mighty power.
Come to rescue us!

3 Turn us again to yourself, O God.
Make your face shine down upon us.
Only then will we be saved.
4 O LORD God of Heaven's Armies,
how long will you be angry with our prayers?
5 You have fed us with sorrow
and made us drink tears by the bucketful.
6 You have made us the scorn* of neighboring
nations.
Our enemies treat us as a joke.

7 Turn us again to yourself, O God of
Heaven's Armies.
Make your face shine down upon us.
Only then will we be saved.
8 You brought us from Egypt like a grapevine;
you drove away the pagan nations and
transplanted us into your land.
9 You cleared the ground for us,
and we took root and filled the land.
10 Our shade covered the mountains;
our branches covered the mighty cedars.
11 We spread our branches west to the
Mediterranean Sea;
our shoots spread east to the Euphrates River.*
12 But now, why have you broken down our walls
so that all who pass by may steal our fruit?
13 The wild boar from the forest devours it,
and the wild animals feed on it.

14 Come back, we beg you, O God of Heaven's Armies.
Look down from heaven and see our plight.
Take care of this grapevine
15 that you yourself have planted,
this son you have raised for yourself.
16 For we are chopped up and burned by
our enemies.
May they perish at the sight of your frown.
17 Strengthen the man you love,
the son of your choice.

80:6 As in Syriac version; Hebrew reads *the strife.* **80:11** Hebrew *west to the sea, . . . east to the river.*

KING JAMES VERSION

18 So will not we go back from thee: quicken us,
and we will call upon thy name.
19 Turn us again, O LORD God of hosts, cause thy
face to shine; and we shall be saved.

81 *To the chief Musician upon Gittith,* A Psalm *of Asaph*

1 Sing aloud unto God our strength: make a joyful
noise unto the God of Jacob.
2 Take a psalm, and bring hither the timbrel, the
pleasant harp with the psaltery.
3 Blow up the trumpet in the new moon, in the
time appointed, on our solemn feast day.
4 For this *was* a statute for Israel, *and* a law of the
God of Jacob.
5 This he ordained in Joseph *for* a testimony, when
he went out through the land of Egypt: *where* I heard
a language *that* I understood not.
6 I removed his shoulder from the burden: his
hands were delivered from the pots.
7 Thou calledst in trouble, and I delivered thee;
I answered thee in the secret place of thunder: I
proved thee at the waters of Meribah. Selah.
8 Hear, O my people, and I will testify unto thee:
O Israel, if thou wilt hearken unto me;
9 There shall no strange god be in thee; neither
shalt thou worship any strange god.
10 I *am* the LORD thy God, which brought thee out
of the land of Egypt: open thy mouth wide, and I will
fill it.
11 But my people would not hearken to my voice;
and Israel would none of me.
12 So I gave them up unto their own hearts' lust:
and they walked in their own counsels.
13 Oh that my people had hearkened unto me, *and*
Israel had walked in my ways!
14 I should soon have subdued their enemies, and
turned my hand against their adversaries.
15 The haters of the LORD should have submitted
themselves unto him: but their time should have endured for ever.
16 He should have fed them also with the finest of
the wheat: and with honey out of the rock should I
have satisfied thee.

NEW LIVING TRANSLATION

18 Then we will never abandon you again.
Revive us so we can call on your name
once more.
19 Turn us again to yourself, O LORD God of
Heaven's Armies.
Make your face shine down upon us.
Only then will we be saved.

81 *For the choir director: A psalm of Asaph, to be accompanied by a stringed instrument.**

1 Sing praises to God, our strength.
Sing to the God of Jacob.
2 Sing! Beat the tambourine.
Play the sweet lyre and the harp.
3 Blow the ram's horn at new moon,
and again at full moon to call a festival!
4 For this is required by the decrees of Israel;
it is a regulation of the God of Jacob.
5 He made it a law for Israel*
when he attacked Egypt to set us free.

I heard an unknown voice say,
6 "Now I will take the load from your shoulders;
I will free your hands from their heavy tasks.
7 You cried to me in trouble, and I saved you;
I answered out of the thundercloud
and tested your faith when there was
no water at Meribah. *Interlude*

8 "Listen to me, O my people, while I give you
stern warnings.
O Israel, if you would only listen to me!
9 You must never have a foreign god;
you must not bow down before a false god.
10 For it was I, the LORD your God,
who rescued you from the land of Egypt.
Open your mouth wide, and I will fill it with
good things.

11 "But no, my people wouldn't listen.
Israel did not want me around.
12 So I let them follow their own stubborn desires,
living according to their own ideas.
13 Oh, that my people would listen to me!
Oh, that Israel would follow me, walking
in my paths!
14 How quickly I would then subdue their enemies!
How soon my hands would be upon their foes!
15 Those who hate the LORD would cringe
before him;
they would be doomed forever.
16 But I would feed you with the finest wheat.
I would satisfy you with wild honey from
the rock."

81:TITLE Hebrew *according to the gittith.* **81:5** Hebrew *for Joseph.*

KING JAMES VERSION

82 *A Psalm of Asaph*

1 God standeth in the congregation of the mighty;
he judgeth among the gods.
2 How long will ye judge unjustly, and accept the
persons of the wicked? Selah.
3 Defend the poor and fatherless: do justice to the
afflicted and needy.
4 Deliver the poor and needy: rid *them* out of the
hand of the wicked.
5 They know not, neither will they understand;
they walk on in darkness: all the foundations of the
earth are out of course.
6 I have said, Ye *are* gods; and all of you *are* children
of the most High.
7 But ye shall die like men, and fall like one of the
princes.
8 Arise, O God, judge the earth: for thou shalt inherit all nations.

83 *A Song* or *Psalm of Asaph*

1 Keep not thou silence, O God: hold not thy peace,
and be not still, O God.
2 For, lo, thine enemies make a tumult: and they
that hate thee have lifted up the head.
3 They have taken crafty counsel against thy
people, and consulted against thy hidden ones.
4 They have said, Come, and let us cut them off
from *being* a nation; that the name of Israel may be
no more in remembrance.
5 For they have consulted together with one consent: they are confederate against thee:
6 The tabernacles of Edom, and the Ishmaelites;
of Moab, and the Hagarenes;
7 Gebal, and Ammon, and Amalek; the Philistines
with the inhabitants of Tyre;
8 Assur also is joined with them: they have holpen
the children of Lot. Selah.
9 Do unto them as *unto* the Midianites; as *to* Sisera,
as *to* Jabin, at the brook of Kison:
10 *Which* perished at En-dor: they became *as* dung
for the earth.
11 Make their nobles like Oreb, and like Zeeb: yea,
all their princes as Zebah, and as Zalmunna:
12 Who said, Let us take to ourselves the houses of
God in possession.

NEW LIVING TRANSLATION

82 *A psalm of Asaph.*

1 God presides over heaven's court;
he pronounces judgment on the
heavenly beings:
2 "How long will you hand down unjust decisions
by favoring the wicked? *Interlude*

3 "Give justice to the poor and the orphan;
uphold the rights of the oppressed and
the destitute.
4 Rescue the poor and helpless;
deliver them from the grasp of evil people.
5 But these oppressors know nothing;
they are so ignorant!
They wander about in darkness,
while the whole world is shaken to the core.
6 I say, 'You are gods;
you are all children of the Most High.
7 But you will die like mere mortals
and fall like every other ruler.'"

8 Rise up, O God, and judge the earth,
for all the nations belong to you.

83 *A song. A psalm of Asaph.*

1 O God, do not be silent!
Do not be deaf.
Do not be quiet, O God.
2 Don't you hear the uproar of your enemies?
Don't you see that your arrogant enemies
are rising up?
3 They devise crafty schemes against your people;
they conspire against your precious ones.
4 "Come," they say, "let us wipe out Israel as a nation.
We will destroy the very memory of its
existence."
5 Yes, this was their unanimous decision.
They signed a treaty as allies against you—
6 these Edomites and Ishmaelites;
Moabites and Hagrites;
7 Gebalites, Ammonites, and Amalekites;
and people from Philistia and Tyre.
8 Assyria has joined them, too,
and is allied with the descendants of Lot.
Interlude

9 Do to them as you did to the Midianites
and as you did to Sisera and Jabin at the
Kishon River.
10 They were destroyed at Endor,
and their decaying corpses fertilized the soil.
11 Let their mighty nobles die as Oreb and Zeeb did.
Let all their princes die like Zebah and
Zalmunna,
12 for they said, "Let us seize for our own use
these pasturelands of God!"

KING JAMES VERSION

13 O my God, make them like a wheel; as the stubble before the wind.
14 As the fire burneth a wood, and as the flame
setteth the mountains on fire;
15 So persecute them with thy tempest, and make
them afraid with thy storm.
16 Fill their faces with shame; that they may seek
thy name, O LORD.
17 Let them be confounded and troubled for ever;
yea, let them be put to shame, and perish:
18 That *men* may know that thou, whose name
alone *is* JEHOVAH, *art* the most high over all the
earth.

84

To the chief Musician upon Gittith, A Psalm for the sons of Korah

1 How amiable *are* thy tabernacles, O LORD of
hosts!
2 My soul longeth, yea, even fainteth for the courts
of the LORD: my heart and my flesh crieth out for the
living God.
3 Yea, the sparrow hath found an house, and the
swallow a nest for herself, where she may lay her
young, *even* thine altars, O LORD of hosts, my King,
and my God.
4 Blessed *are* they that dwell in thy house: they will
be still praising thee. Selah.
5 Blessed *is* the man whose strength *is* in thee; in
whose heart *are* the ways *of them.*
6 *Who* passing through the valley of Baca make it a
well; the rain also filleth the pools.
7 They go from strength to strength, *every one of*
them in Zion appeareth before God.
8 O LORD God of hosts, hear my prayer: give ear,
O God of Jacob. Selah.
9 Behold, O God our shield, and look upon the face
of thine anointed.
10 For a day in thy courts *is* better than a thousand.
I had rather be a doorkeeper in the house of my God,
than to dwell in the tents of wickedness.

NEW LIVING TRANSLATION

13 O my God, scatter them like tumbleweed,
like chaff before the wind!
14 As a fire burns a forest
and as a flame sets mountains ablaze,
15 chase them with your fierce storm;
terrify them with your tempest.
16 Utterly disgrace them
until they submit to your name, O LORD.
17 Let them be ashamed and terrified forever.
Let them die in disgrace.
18 Then they will learn that you alone are called
the LORD,
that you alone are the Most High,
supreme over all the earth.

84

*For the choir director: A psalm of the descendants of Korah, to be accompanied by a stringed instrument.**

1 How lovely is your dwelling place,
O LORD of Heaven's Armies.
2 I long, yes, I faint with longing
to enter the courts of the LORD.
With my whole being, body and soul,
I will shout joyfully to the living God.
3 Even the sparrow finds a home,
and the swallow builds her nest and raises
her young
at a place near your altar,
O LORD of Heaven's Armies, my King and
my God!
4 What joy for those who can live in your house,
always singing your praises. *Interlude*
5 What joy for those whose strength comes from
the LORD,
who have set their minds on a pilgrimage
to Jerusalem.
6 When they walk through the Valley of Weeping,*
it will become a place of refreshing springs.
The autumn rains will clothe it with blessings.
7 They will continue to grow stronger,
and each of them will appear before God
in Jerusalem.*
8 O LORD God of Heaven's Armies, hear my prayer.
Listen, O God of Jacob. *Interlude*
9 O God, look with favor upon the king, our shield!
Show favor to the one you have anointed.
10 A single day in your courts
is better than a thousand anywhere else!
I would rather be a gatekeeper in the house
of my God
than live the good life in the homes of
the wicked.

84:TITLE Hebrew *according to the gittith.* **84:6** Or *Valley of Poplars;* Hebrew reads *valley of Baca.* **84:7** Hebrew *Zion.*

KING JAMES VERSION

11 For the LORD God *is* a sun and shield: the LORD will give grace and glory: no good *thing* will he withhold from them that walk uprightly.

12 O LORD of hosts, blessed *is* the man that trusteth in thee.

85 *To the chief Musician, A Psalm for the sons of Korah*

1 LORD, thou hast been favourable unto thy land: thou hast brought back the captivity of Jacob.

2 Thou hast forgiven the iniquity of thy people, thou hast covered all their sin. Selah.

3 Thou hast taken away all thy wrath: thou hast turned *thyself* from the fierceness of thine anger.

4 Turn us, O God of our salvation, and cause thine anger toward us to cease.

5 Wilt thou be angry with us for ever? wilt thou draw out thine anger to all generations?

6 Wilt thou not revive us again: that thy people may rejoice in thee?

7 Shew us thy mercy, O LORD, and grant us thy salvation.

8 I will hear what God the LORD will speak: for he will speak peace unto his people, and to his saints: but let them not turn again to folly.

9 Surely his salvation *is* nigh them that fear him; that glory may dwell in our land.

10 Mercy and truth are met together; righteousness and peace have kissed *each other.*

11 Truth shall spring out of the earth; and righteousness shall look down from heaven.

12 Yea, the LORD shall give *that which is* good; and our land shall yield her increase.

13 Righteousness shall go before him; and shall set *us* in the way of his steps.

86 *A Prayer of David*

1 Bow down thine ear, O LORD, hear me: for I *am* poor and needy.

2 Preserve my soul; for I *am* holy: O thou my God, save thy servant that trusteth in thee.

3 Be merciful unto me, O Lord: for I cry unto thee daily.

4 Rejoice the soul of thy servant: for unto thee, O Lord, do I lift up my soul.

5 For thou, Lord, *art* good, and ready to forgive; and plenteous in mercy unto all them that call upon thee.

6 Give ear, O LORD, unto my prayer; and attend to the voice of my supplications.

7 In the day of my trouble I will call upon thee: for thou wilt answer me.

NEW LIVING TRANSLATION

11 For the LORD God is our sun and our shield.
He gives us grace and glory.
The LORD will withhold no good thing
from those who do what is right.
12 O LORD of Heaven's Armies,
what joy for those who trust in you.

85 *For the choir director: A psalm of the descendants of Korah.*

1 LORD, you poured out blessings on your land!
You restored the fortunes of Israel.*
2 You forgave the guilt of your people—
yes, you covered all their sins. *Interlude*
3 You held back your fury.
You kept back your blazing anger.

4 Now restore us again, O God of our salvation.
Put aside your anger against us once more.
5 Will you be angry with us always?
Will you prolong your wrath to all generations?
6 Won't you revive us again,
so your people can rejoice in you?
7 Show us your unfailing love, O LORD,
and grant us your salvation.

8 I listen carefully to what God the LORD is saying,
for he speaks peace to his faithful people.
But let them not return to their foolish ways.
9 Surely his salvation is near to those who fear him,
so our land will be filled with his glory.

10 Unfailing love and truth have met together.
Righteousness and peace have kissed!
11 Truth springs up from the earth,
and righteousness smiles down from heaven.
12 Yes, the LORD pours down his blessings.
Our land will yield its bountiful harvest.
13 Righteousness goes as a herald before him,
preparing the way for his steps.

86 *A prayer of David.*

1 Bend down, O LORD, and hear my prayer;
answer me, for I need your help.
2 Protect me, for I am devoted to you.
Save me, for I serve you and trust you.
You are my God.
3 Be merciful to me, O Lord,
for I am calling on you constantly.
4 Give me happiness, O Lord,
for I give myself to you.
5 O Lord, you are so good, so ready to forgive,
so full of unfailing love for all who ask
for your help.
6 Listen closely to my prayer, O LORD;
hear my urgent cry.
7 I will call to you whenever I'm in trouble,
and you will answer me.

85:1 Hebrew *of Jacob.* See note on 44:4.

KING JAMES VERSION

8 Among the gods *there is* none like unto thee,
O Lord; neither *are there any works* like unto thy
works.
9 All nations whom thou hast made shall come and
worship before thee, O Lord; and shall glorify thy
name.
10 For thou *art* great, and doest wondrous things:
thou *art* God alone.
11 Teach me thy way, O LORD; I will walk in thy
truth: unite my heart to fear thy name.
12 I will praise thee, O Lord my God, with all my
heart: and I will glorify thy name for evermore.
13 For great *is* thy mercy toward me: and thou hast
delivered my soul from the lowest hell.
14 O God, the proud are risen against me, and the
assemblies of violent *men* have sought after my soul;
and have not set thee before them.
15 But thou, O Lord, *art* a God full of compassion,
and gracious, longsuffering, and plenteous in mercy
and truth.
16 O turn unto me, and have mercy upon me; give
thy strength unto thy servant, and save the son of
thine handmaid.
17 Shew me a token for good; that they which hate
me may see *it*, and be ashamed: because thou, LORD,
hast holpen me, and comforted me.

87 *A Psalm or Song for the sons of Korah*

1 His foundation *is* in the holy mountains.
2 The LORD loveth the gates of Zion more than all
the dwellings of Jacob.
3 Glorious things are spoken of thee, O city of God.
Selah.
4 I will make mention of Rahab and Babylon to
them that know me: behold Philistia, and Tyre, with
Ethiopia; this *man* was born there.
5 And of Zion it shall be said, This and that man
was born in her: and the highest himself shall establish her.
6 The LORD shall count, when he writeth up the
people, *that* this *man* was born there. Selah.
7 As well the singers as the players on instruments
shall be there: all my springs *are* in thee.

NEW LIVING TRANSLATION

8 No pagan god is like you, O Lord.
None can do what you do!
9 All the nations you made
will come and bow before you, Lord;
they will praise your holy name.
10 For you are great and perform wonderful deeds.
You alone are God.

11 Teach me your ways, O LORD,
that I may live according to your truth!
Grant me purity of heart,
so that I may honor you.
12 With all my heart I will praise you, O Lord my God.
I will give glory to your name forever,
13 for your love for me is very great.
You have rescued me from the depths of death.*
14 O God, insolent people rise up against me;
a violent gang is trying to kill me.
You mean nothing to them.
15 But you, O Lord,
are a God of compassion and mercy,
slow to get angry
and filled with unfailing love and faithfulness.
16 Look down and have mercy on me.
Give your strength to your servant;
save me, the son of your servant.
17 Send me a sign of your favor.
Then those who hate me will be put to shame,
for you, O LORD, help and comfort me.

87 *A song. A psalm of the descendants of Korah.*

1 On the holy mountain
stands the city founded by the LORD.
2 He loves the city of Jerusalem
more than any other city in Israel.*
3 O city of God,
what glorious things are said of you! *Interlude*

4 I will count Egypt* and Babylon among those
who know me—
also Philistia and Tyre, and even distant
Ethiopia.*
They have all become citizens of Jerusalem!
5 Regarding Jerusalem* it will be said,
"Everyone enjoys the rights of citizenship
there."
And the Most High will personally bless this city.
6 When the LORD registers the nations, he will say,
"They have all become citizens of Jerusalem."
Interlude

7 The people will play flutes* and sing,
"The source of my life springs from
Jerusalem!"

86:13 Hebrew *of Sheol.* **87:2** Hebrew *He loves the gates of Zion more than all the dwellings of Jacob.* See note on 44:4. **87:4a** Hebrew *Rahab*, the name of a mythical sea monster that represents chaos in ancient literature. The name is used here as a poetic name for Egypt. **87:4b** Hebrew *Cush.* **87:5** Hebrew *Zion.* **87:7** Or *will dance.*

KING JAMES VERSION

88

A Song or *Psalm for the sons of Korah, to the chief Musician upon Mahalath Leannoth, Maschil of Heman the Ezrahite.*

1 O LORD God of my salvation, I have cried day *and*
night before thee:
2 Let my prayer come before thee: incline thine ear
unto my cry;
3 For my soul is full of troubles: and my life
draweth nigh unto the grave.
4 I am counted with them that go down into the
pit: I am as a man *that hath* no strength:
5 Free among the dead, like the slain that lie in the
grave, whom thou rememberest no more: and they
are cut off from thy hand.
6 Thou hast laid me in the lowest pit, in darkness,
in the deeps.
7 Thy wrath lieth hard upon me, and thou hast afflicted *me* with all thy waves. Selah.
8 Thou hast put away mine acquaintance far from
me; thou hast made me an abomination unto them: *I*
am shut up, and I cannot come forth.
9 Mine eye mourneth by reason of affliction: LORD,
I have called daily upon thee, I have stretched out my
hands unto thee.
10 Wilt thou shew wonders to the dead? shall the
dead arise *and* praise thee? Selah.
11 Shall thy lovingkindness be declared in the
grave? *or* thy faithfulness in destruction?
12 Shall thy wonders be known in the dark? and thy
righteousness in the land of forgetfulness?
13 But unto thee have I cried, O LORD; and in the
morning shall my prayer prevent thee.
14 LORD, why castest thou off my soul? *why* hidest
thou thy face from me?
15 I *am* afflicted and ready to die from *my* youth
up: *while* I suffer thy terrors I am distracted.
16 Thy fierce wrath goeth over me; thy terrors have
cut me off.
17 They came round about me daily like water; they
compassed me about together.
18 Lover and friend hast thou put far from me, *and*
mine acquaintance into darkness.

NEW LIVING TRANSLATION

88

For the choir director: A psalm of the descendants of Korah. A song to be sung to the tune "The Suffering of Affliction." A psalm of Heman the Ezrahite.*

1 O LORD, God of my salvation,
I cry out to you by day.
I come to you at night.
2 Now hear my prayer;
listen to my cry.
3 For my life is full of troubles,
and death* draws near.
4 I am as good as dead,
like a strong man with no strength left.
5 They have left me among the dead,
and I lie like a corpse in a grave.
I am forgotten,
cut off from your care.
6 You have thrown me into the lowest pit,
into the darkest depths.
7 Your anger weighs me down;
with wave after wave you have engulfed me.
Interlude

8 You have driven my friends away
by making me repulsive to them.
I am in a trap with no way of escape.
9 My eyes are blinded by my tears.
Each day I beg for your help, O LORD;
I lift my hands to you for mercy.
10 Are your wonderful deeds of any use to the dead?
Do the dead rise up and praise you?
Interlude

11 Can those in the grave declare your
unfailing love?
Can they proclaim your faithfulness in the
place of destruction?*
12 Can the darkness speak of your wonderful deeds?
Can anyone in the land of forgetfulness talk
about your righteousness?
13 O LORD, I cry out to you.
I will keep on pleading day by day.
14 O LORD, why do you reject me?
Why do you turn your face from me?
15 I have been sick and close to death since
my youth.
I stand helpless and desperate before your
terrors.
16 Your fierce anger has overwhelmed me.
Your terrors have paralyzed me.
17 They swirl around me like floodwaters
all day long.
They have engulfed me completely.
18 You have taken away my companions and
loved ones.
Darkness is my closest friend.

88:TITLE Hebrew *maskil.* This may be a literary or musical term.
88:3 Hebrew *Sheol.* **88:11** Hebrew *in Abaddon?*

KING JAMES VERSION

89 *Maschil of Ethan the Ezrahite*

1 I will sing of the mercies of the LORD for ever:
with my mouth will I make known thy faithfulness to
all generations.
2 For I have said, Mercy shall be built up for ever: thy
faithfulness shalt thou establish in the very heavens.
3 I have made a covenant with my chosen, I have
sworn unto David my servant,
4 Thy seed will I establish for ever, and build up thy
throne to all generations. Selah.
5 And the heavens shall praise thy wonders,
O LORD: thy faithfulness also in the congregation of
the saints.
6 For who in the heaven can be compared unto the
LORD? *who* among the sons of the mighty can be
likened unto the LORD?
7 God is greatly to be feared in the assembly of the
saints, and to be had in reverence of all *them that are*
about him.
8 O LORD God of hosts, who *is* a strong LORD like
unto thee? or to thy faithfulness round about thee?
9 Thou rulest the raging of the sea: when the waves
thereof arise, thou stillest them.
10 Thou hast broken Rahab in pieces, as one that
is slain; thou hast scattered thine enemies with thy
strong arm.
11 The heavens *are* thine, the earth also *is* thine:
as for the world and the fulness thereof, thou hast
founded them.
12 The north and the south thou hast created
them: Tabor and Hermon shall rejoice in thy name.
13 Thou hast a mighty arm: strong is thy hand, *and*
high is thy right hand.
14 Justice and judgment *are* the habitation of thy
throne: mercy and truth shall go before thy face.
15 Blessed *is* the people that know the joyful
sound: they shall walk, O LORD, in the light of thy
countenance.
16 In thy name shall they rejoice all the day: and in
thy righteousness shall they be exalted.

NEW LIVING TRANSLATION

89 *A psalm* of Ethan the Ezrahite.*

1 I will sing of the LORD's unfailing love forever!
Young and old will hear of your faithfulness.
2 Your unfailing love will last forever.
Your faithfulness is as enduring as
the heavens.
3 The LORD said, "I have made a covenant
with David, my chosen servant.
I have sworn this oath to him:
4 'I will establish your descendants as kings
forever;
they will sit on your throne from now until
eternity.'" *Interlude*
5 All heaven will praise your great wonders, LORD;
myriads of angels will praise you for your
faithfulness.
6 For who in all of heaven can compare with
the LORD?
What mightiest angel is anything like
the LORD?
7 The highest angelic powers stand in awe of God.
He is far more awesome than all who surround
his throne.
8 O LORD God of Heaven's Armies!
Where is there anyone as mighty as you,
O LORD?
You are entirely faithful.
9 You rule the oceans.
You subdue their storm-tossed waves.
10 You crushed the great sea monster.*
You scattered your enemies with your
mighty arm.
11 The heavens are yours, and the earth is yours;
everything in the world is yours—you created
it all.
12 You created north and south.
Mount Tabor and Mount Hermon praise
your name.
13 Powerful is your arm!
Strong is your hand!
Your right hand is lifted high in glorious
strength.
14 Righteousness and justice are the foundation
of your throne.
Unfailing love and truth walk before you
as attendants.
15 Happy are those who hear the joyful call to
worship,
for they will walk in the light of your presence,
LORD.
16 They rejoice all day long in your wonderful
reputation.
They exult in your righteousness.

89:TITLE Hebrew *maskil*. This may be a literary or musical term.
8910 Hebrew *Rahab*, the name of a mythical sea monster that represents chaos in ancient literature.

KING JAMES VERSION

17 For thou *art* the glory of their strength: and in
thy favour our horn shall be exalted.
18 For the LORD *is* our defence; and the Holy One of
Israel *is* our king.
19 Then thou spakest in vision to thy holy one, and
saidst, I have laid help upon *one that is* mighty; I have
exalted *one* chosen out of the people.
20 I have found David my servant; with my holy oil
have I anointed him:
21 With whom my hand shall be established: mine
arm also shall strengthen him.
22 The enemy shall not exact upon him; nor the
son of wickedness afflict him.
23 And I will beat down his foes before his face, and
plague them that hate him.
24 But my faithfulness and my mercy *shall be* with
him: and in my name shall his horn be exalted.
25 I will set his hand also in the sea, and his right
hand in the rivers.
26 He shall cry unto me, Thou *art* my father, my
God, and the rock of my salvation.
27 Also I will make him *my* firstborn, higher than
the kings of the earth.
28 My mercy will I keep for him for evermore, and
my covenant shall stand fast with him.
29 His seed also will I make *to endure* for ever, and
his throne as the days of heaven.
30 If his children forsake my law, and walk not in
my judgments;
31 If they break my statutes, and keep not my commandments;
32 Then will I visit their transgression with the rod,
and their iniquity with stripes.
33 Nevertheless my lovingkindness will I not utterly take from him, nor suffer my faithfulness to
fail.
34 My covenant will I not break, nor alter the thing
that is gone out of my lips.
35 Once have I sworn by my holiness that I will not
lie unto David.
36 His seed shall endure for ever, and his throne as
the sun before me.
37 It shall be established for ever as the moon, and
as a faithful witness in heaven. Selah.
38 But thou hast cast off and abhorred, thou hast
been wroth with thine anointed.
39 Thou hast made void the covenant of thy servant: thou hast profaned his crown *by casting it* to
the ground.
40 Thou hast broken down all his hedges; thou hast
brought his strong holds to ruin.
41 All that pass by the way spoil him: he is a reproach to his neighbours.
42 Thou hast set up the right hand of his adversaries; thou hast made all his enemies to rejoice.

NEW LIVING TRANSLATION

17 You are their glorious strength.
It pleases you to make us strong.
18 Yes, our protection comes from the LORD,
and he, the Holy One of Israel, has given
us our king.

19 Long ago you spoke in a vision to your
faithful people.
You said, "I have raised up a warrior.
I have selected him from the common
people to be king.
20 I have found my servant David.
I have anointed him with my holy oil.
21 I will steady him with my hand;
with my powerful arm I will make him strong.
22 His enemies will not defeat him,
nor will the wicked overpower him.
23 I will beat down his adversaries before him
and destroy those who hate him.
24 My faithfulness and unfailing love will be with him,
and by my authority he will grow in power.
25 I will extend his rule over the sea,
his dominion over the rivers.
26 And he will call out to me, 'You are my Father,
my God, and the Rock of my salvation.'
27 I will make him my firstborn son,
the mightiest king on earth.
28 I will love him and be kind to him forever;
my covenant with him will never end.
29 I will preserve an heir for him;
his throne will be as endless as the days
of heaven.
30 But if his descendants forsake my instructions
and fail to obey my regulations,
31 if they do not obey my decrees
and fail to keep my commands,
32 then I will punish their sin with the rod,
and their disobedience with beating.
33 But I will never stop loving him
nor fail to keep my promise to him.
34 No, I will not break my covenant;
I will not take back a single word I said.
35 I have sworn an oath to David,
and in my holiness I cannot lie:
36 His dynasty will go on forever;
his kingdom will endure as the sun.
37 It will be as eternal as the moon,
my faithful witness in the sky!" *Interlude*

38 But now you have rejected him and cast him off.
You are angry with your anointed king.
39 You have renounced your covenant with him;
you have thrown his crown in the dust.
40 You have broken down the walls protecting him
and ruined every fort defending him.
41 Everyone who comes along has robbed him,
and he has become a joke to his neighbors.
42 You have strengthened his enemies
and made them all rejoice.

43 Thou hast also turned the edge of his sword, and hast not made him to stand in the battle.

44 Thou hast made his glory to cease, and cast his throne down to the ground.

45 The days of his youth hast thou shortened: thou hast covered him with shame. Selah.

46 How long, LORD? wilt thou hide thyself for ever? shall thy wrath burn like fire?

47 Remember how short my time is: wherefore hast thou made all men in vain?

48 What man *is he that* liveth, and shall not see death? shall he deliver his soul from the hand of the grave? Selah.

49 Lord, where *are* thy former lovingkindnesses, *which* thou swarest unto David in thy truth?

50 Remember, Lord, the reproach of thy servants; *how* I do bear in my bosom *the reproach of* all the mighty people;

51 Wherewith thine enemies have reproached, O LORD; wherewith they have reproached the footsteps of thine anointed.

52 Blessed *be* the LORD for evermore. Amen, and Amen.

90

A Prayer of Moses the man of God

1 Lord, thou hast been our dwelling place in all generations.

2 Before the mountains were brought forth, or ever thou hadst formed the earth and the world, even from everlasting to everlasting, thou *art* God.

3 Thou turnest man to destruction; and sayest, Return, ye children of men.

4 For a thousand years in thy sight *are but* as yesterday when it is past, and *as* a watch in the night.

5 Thou carriest them away as with a flood; they are *as* a sleep: in the morning *they are* like grass *which* groweth up.

6 In the morning it flourisheth, and groweth up; in the evening it is cut down, and withereth.

7 For we are consumed by thine anger, and by thy wrath are we troubled.

8 Thou hast set our iniquities before thee, our secret *sins* in the light of thy countenance.

9 For all our days are passed away in thy wrath: we spend our years as a tale *that is told*.

10 The days of our years *are* threescore years and ten; and if by reason of strength *they be* fourscore years, yet *is* their strength labour and sorrow; for it is soon cut off, and we fly away.

43 You have made his sword useless
and refused to help him in battle.
44 You have ended his splendor
and overturned his throne.
45 You have made him old before his time
and publicly disgraced him. *Interlude*

46 O LORD, how long will this go on?
Will you hide yourself forever?
How long will your anger burn like fire?
47 Remember how short my life is,
how empty and futile this human existence!
48 No one can live forever; all will die.
No one can escape the power of the grave.*
Interlude

49 Lord, where is your unfailing love?
You promised it to David with a faithful pledge.
50 Consider, Lord, how your servants are disgraced!
I carry in my heart the insults of so
many people.
51 Your enemies have mocked me, O LORD;
they mock your anointed king wherever
he goes.

52 Praise the LORD forever!
Amen and amen!

BOOK FOUR (Psalms 90–106)

90

A prayer of Moses, the man of God.

1 Lord, through all the generations
you have been our home!
2 Before the mountains were born,
before you gave birth to the earth and the world,
from beginning to end, you are God.

3 You turn people back to dust, saying,
"Return to dust, you mortals!"
4 For you, a thousand years are as a passing day,
as brief as a few night hours.
5 You sweep people away like dreams that disappear.
They are like grass that springs up in the
morning.
6 In the morning it blooms and flourishes,
but by evening it is dry and withered.
7 We wither beneath your anger;
we are overwhelmed by your fury.
8 You spread out our sins before you—
our secret sins—and you see them all.
9 We live our lives beneath your wrath,
ending our years with a groan.
10 Seventy years are given to us!
Some even live to eighty.
But even the best years are filled with pain
and trouble;
soon they disappear, and we fly away.

89:48 Hebrew *of Sheol.*

KING JAMES VERSION

11 Who knoweth the power of thine anger? even
according to thy fear, *so is* thy wrath.
12 So teach *us* to number our days, that we may apply *our* hearts unto wisdom.
13 Return, O LORD, how long? and let it repent thee
concerning thy servants.
14 O satisfy us early with thy mercy; that we may
rejoice and be glad all our days.
15 Make us glad according to the days *wherein*
thou hast afflicted us, *and* the years *wherein* we have
seen evil.
16 Let thy work appear unto thy servants, and thy
glory unto their children.
17 And let the beauty of the LORD our God be upon
us: and establish thou the work of our hands upon
us; yea, the work of our hands establish thou it.

91

1 He that dwelleth in the secret place of the
most High shall abide under the shadow of
the Almighty.
2 I will say of the LORD, *He is* my refuge and my fortress: my God; in him will I trust.
3 Surely he shall deliver thee from the snare of the
fowler, *and* from the noisome pestilence.
4 He shall cover thee with his feathers, and under
his wings shalt thou trust: his truth *shall be thy*
shield and buckler.
5 Thou shalt not be afraid for the terror by night;
nor for the arrow *that* flieth by day;
6 *Nor* for the pestilence *that* walketh in darkness;
nor for the destruction *that* wasteth at noonday.
7 A thousand shall fall at thy side, and ten thousand
at thy right hand; *but* it shall not come nigh thee.
8 Only with thine eyes shalt thou behold and see
the reward of the wicked.
9 Because thou hast made the LORD, *which is* my
refuge, *even* the most High, thy habitation;
10 There shall no evil befall thee, neither shall any
plague come nigh thy dwelling.
11 For he shall give his angels charge over thee, to
keep thee in all thy ways.
12 They shall bear thee up in *their* hands, lest thou
dash thy foot against a stone.
13 Thou shalt tread upon the lion and adder: the
young lion and the dragon shalt thou trample under
feet.
14 Because he hath set his love upon me, therefore
will I deliver him: I will set him on high, because he
hath known my name.
15 He shall call upon me, and I will answer him: I
will be with him in trouble; I will deliver him, and
honour him.

NEW LIVING TRANSLATION

11 Who can comprehend the power of your anger?
Your wrath is as awesome as the fear you deserve.
12 Teach us to realize the brevity of life,
so that we may grow in wisdom.
13 O LORD, come back to us!
How long will you delay?
Take pity on your servants!
14 Satisfy us each morning with your unfailing love,
so we may sing for joy to the end of our lives.
15 Give us gladness in proportion to our former misery!
Replace the evil years with good.
16 Let us, your servants, see you work again;
let our children see your glory.
17 And may the Lord our God show us his approval
and make our efforts successful.
Yes, make our efforts successful!

91

1 Those who live in the shelter of the Most High
will find rest in the shadow of the Almighty.
2 This I declare about the LORD:
He alone is my refuge, my place of safety;
he is my God, and I trust him.
3 For he will rescue you from every trap
and protect you from deadly disease.
4 He will cover you with his feathers.
He will shelter you with his wings.
His faithful promises are your armor and protection.
5 Do not be afraid of the terrors of the night,
nor the arrow that flies in the day.
6 Do not dread the disease that stalks in darkness,
nor the disaster that strikes at midday.
7 Though a thousand fall at your side,
though ten thousand are dying around you,
these evils will not touch you.
8 Just open your eyes,
and see how the wicked are punished.
9 If you make the LORD your refuge,
if you make the Most High your shelter,
10 no evil will conquer you;
no plague will come near your home.
11 For he will order his angels
to protect you wherever you go.
12 They will hold you up with their hands
so you won't even hurt your foot on a stone.
13 You will trample upon lions and cobras;
you will crush fierce lions and serpents under your feet!
14 The LORD says, "I will rescue those who love me.
I will protect those who trust in my name.
15 When they call on me, I will answer;
I will be with them in trouble.
I will rescue and honor them.

KING JAMES VERSION

16 With long life will I satisfy him, and shew him
my salvation.

92 *A Psalm* or *Song for the sabbath day*

1 *It is a* good *thing* to give thanks unto the LORD,
and to sing praises unto thy name, O most High:
2 To shew forth thy lovingkindness in the morning, and thy faithfulness every night,
3 Upon an instrument of ten strings, and upon the
psaltery; upon the harp with a solemn sound.
4 For thou, LORD, hast made me glad through thy
work: I will triumph in the works of thy hands.
5 O LORD, how great are thy works! *and* thy
thoughts are very deep.
6 A brutish man knoweth not; neither doth a fool
understand this.
7 When the wicked spring as the grass, and when
all the workers of iniquity do flourish; *it is* that they
shall be destroyed for ever:
8 But thou, LORD, *art most* high for evermore.
9 For, lo, thine enemies, O LORD, for, lo, thine enemies shall perish; all the workers of iniquity shall be
scattered.
10 But my horn shalt thou exalt like *the horn of* an
unicorn: I shall be anointed with fresh oil.
11 Mine eye also shall see *my desire* on mine enemies, *and* mine ears shall hear *my desire* of the
wicked that rise up against me.
12 The righteous shall flourish like the palm tree:
he shall grow like a cedar in Lebanon.
13 Those that be planted in the house of the LORD
shall flourish in the courts of our God.
14 They shall still bring forth fruit in old age; they
shall be fat and flourishing;
15 To shew that the LORD *is* upright: *he is* my rock,
and *there is* no unrighteousness in him.

93

1 The LORD reigneth, he is clothed with
majesty; the LORD is clothed with strength,
wherewith he hath girded himself: the world also is
stablished, that it cannot be moved.
2 Thy throne *is* established of old: thou *art* from
everlasting.
3 The floods have lifted up, O LORD, the floods have
lifted up their voice; the floods lift up their waves.
4 The LORD on high *is* mightier than the noise of
many waters, *yea, than* the mighty waves of the sea.
5 Thy testimonies are very sure: holiness becometh
thine house, O LORD, for ever.

NEW LIVING TRANSLATION

16 I will reward them with a long life
and give them my salvation."

92 *A psalm. A song to be sung on the Sabbath Day.*

1 It is good to give thanks to the LORD,
to sing praises to the Most High.
2 It is good to proclaim your unfailing love
in the morning,
your faithfulness in the evening,
3 accompanied by the ten-stringed harp
and the melody of the lyre.

4 You thrill me, LORD, with all you have done for me!
I sing for joy because of what you have done.
5 O LORD, what great works you do!
And how deep are your thoughts.
6 Only a simpleton would not know,
and only a fool would not understand this:
7 Though the wicked sprout like weeds
and evildoers flourish,
they will be destroyed forever.

8 But you, O LORD, will be exalted forever.
9 Your enemies, LORD, will surely perish;
all evildoers will be scattered.
10 But you have made me as strong as a wild ox.
You have anointed me with the finest oil.
11 My eyes have seen the downfall of my enemies;
my ears have heard the defeat of my wicked
opponents.
12 But the godly will flourish like palm trees
and grow strong like the cedars of Lebanon.
13 For they are transplanted to the LORD's own house.
They flourish in the courts of our God.
14 Even in old age they will still produce fruit;
they will remain vital and green.
15 They will declare, "The LORD is just!
He is my rock!
There is no evil in him!"

93

1 The LORD is king! He is robed in majesty.
Indeed, the LORD is robed in majesty
and armed with strength.
The world stands firm
and cannot be shaken.

2 Your throne, O LORD, has stood from time
immemorial.
You yourself are from the everlasting past.
3 The floods have risen up, O LORD.
The floods have roared like thunder;
the floods have lifted their pounding waves.
4 But mightier than the violent raging of the seas,
mightier than the breakers on the shore—
the LORD above is mightier than these!
5 Your royal laws cannot be changed.
Your reign, O LORD, is holy forever and ever.

KING JAMES VERSION

94 1 O LORD God, to whom vengeance belongeth; O God, to whom vengeance belongeth, shew thyself.
2 Lift up thyself, thou judge of the earth: render a
reward to the proud.
3 LORD, how long shall the wicked, how long shall
the wicked triumph?
4 *How long* shall they utter *and* speak hard things?
and all the workers of iniquity boast themselves?
5 They break in pieces thy people, O LORD, and afflict thine heritage.
6 They slay the widow and the stranger, and murder the fatherless.
7 Yet they say, The LORD shall not see, neither shall
the God of Jacob regard *it*.
8 Understand, ye brutish among the people: and *ye*
fools, when will ye be wise?
9 He that planted the ear, shall he not hear? he that
formed the eye, shall he not see?
10 He that chastiseth the heathen, shall not he correct? he that teacheth man knowledge, *shall not he
know?*
11 The LORD knoweth the thoughts of man, that
they *are* vanity.
12 Blessed *is* the man whom thou chastenest,
O LORD, and teachest him out of thy law;
13 That thou mayest give him rest from the days of
adversity, until the pit be digged for the wicked.
14 For the LORD will not cast off his people, neither
will he forsake his inheritance.
15 But judgment shall return unto righteousness:
and all the upright in heart shall follow it.
16 Who will rise up for me against the evildoers?
or who will stand up for me against the workers of
iniquity?
17 Unless the LORD *had been* my help, my soul had
almost dwelt in silence.
18 When I said, My foot slippeth; thy mercy,
O LORD, held me up.
19 In the multitude of my thoughts within me thy
comforts delight my soul.
20 Shall the throne of iniquity have fellowship with
thee, which frameth mischief by a law?
21 They gather themselves together against the
soul of the righteous, and condemn the innocent
blood.
22 But the LORD is my defence; and my God *is* the
rock of my refuge.
23 And he shall bring upon them their own iniquity,
and shall cut them off in their own wickedness; *yea*,
the LORD our God shall cut them off.

NEW LIVING TRANSLATION

94 1 O LORD, the God of vengeance,
O God of vengeance, let your glorious
justice shine forth!
2 Arise, O judge of the earth.
Give the proud what they deserve.
3 How long, O LORD?
How long will the wicked be allowed to gloat?
4 How long will they speak with arrogance?
How long will these evil people boast?
5 They crush your people, LORD,
hurting those you claim as your own.
6 They kill widows and foreigners
and murder orphans.
7 "The LORD isn't looking," they say,
"and besides, the God of Israel* doesn't care."

8 Think again, you fools!
When will you finally catch on?
9 Is he deaf—the one who made your ears?
Is he blind—the one who formed your eyes?
10 He punishes the nations—won't he also
punish you?
He knows everything—doesn't he also know
what you are doing?
11 The LORD knows people's thoughts;
he knows they are worthless!

12 Joyful are those you discipline, LORD,
those you teach with your instructions.
13 You give them relief from troubled times
until a pit is dug to capture the wicked.
14 The LORD will not reject his people;
he will not abandon his special possession.
15 Judgment will again be founded on justice,
and those with virtuous hearts will pursue it.

16 Who will protect me from the wicked?
Who will stand up for me against evildoers?
17 Unless the LORD had helped me,
I would soon have settled in the silence
of the grave.
18 I cried out, "I am slipping!"
but your unfailing love, O LORD, supported me.
19 When doubts filled my mind,
your comfort gave me renewed hope and cheer.

20 Can unjust leaders claim that God is on
their side—
leaders whose decrees permit injustice?
21 They gang up against the righteous
and condemn the innocent to death.
22 But the LORD is my fortress;
my God is the mighty rock where I hide.
23 God will turn the sins of evil people back
on them.
He will destroy them for their sins.
The LORD our God will destroy them.

94:7 Hebrew *of Jacob.* See note on 44:4.

KING JAMES VERSION

95
1 O come, let us sing unto the LORD: let us
make a joyful noise to the rock of our salvation.
2 Let us come before his presence with thanksgiving, and make a joyful noise unto him with
psalms.
3 For the LORD *is* a great God, and a great King
above all gods.
4 In his hand *are* the deep places of the earth: the
strength of the hills *is* his also.
5 The sea *is* his, and he made it: and his hands
formed the dry *land*.
6 O come, let us worship and bow down: let us
kneel before the LORD our maker.
7 For he *is* our God; and we *are* the people of his
pasture, and the sheep of his hand. Today if ye will
hear his voice,
8 Harden not your heart, as in the provocation, *and*
as *in* the day of temptation in the wilderness:
9 When your fathers tempted me, proved me, and
saw my work.
10 Forty years long was I grieved with *this* generation, and said, It *is* a people that do err in their heart,
and they have not known my ways:
11 Unto whom I sware in my wrath that they should
not enter into my rest.

96
1 O sing unto the LORD a new song: sing unto
the LORD, all the earth.
2 Sing unto the LORD, bless his name; shew forth
his salvation from day to day.
3 Declare his glory among the heathen, his wonders among all people.
4 For the LORD *is* great, and greatly to be praised: he
is to be feared above all gods.
5 For all the gods of the nations *are* idols: but the
LORD made the heavens.
6 Honour and majesty *are* before him: strength and
beauty *are* in his sanctuary.
7 Give unto the LORD, O ye kindreds of the people,
give unto the LORD glory and strength.
8 Give unto the LORD the glory *due unto* his name:
bring an offering, and come into his courts.
9 O worship the LORD in the beauty of holiness:
fear before him, all the earth.
10 Say among the heathen *that* the LORD reigneth:
the world also shall be established that it shall not be
moved: he shall judge the people righteously.
11 Let the heavens rejoice, and let the earth be glad;
let the sea roar, and the fulness thereof.

NEW LIVING TRANSLATION

95
1 Come, let us sing to the LORD!
Let us shout joyfully to the Rock of
our salvation.
2 Let us come to him with thanksgiving.
Let us sing psalms of praise to him.
3 For the LORD is a great God,
a great King above all gods.
4 He holds in his hands the depths of the earth
and the mightiest mountains.
5 The sea belongs to him, for he made it.
His hands formed the dry land, too.

6 Come, let us worship and bow down.
Let us kneel before the LORD our maker,
7 for he is our God.
We are the people he watches over,
the flock under his care.

If only you would listen to his voice today!
8 The LORD says, "Don't harden your hearts
as Israel did at Meribah,
as they did at Massah in the wilderness.
9 For there your ancestors tested and tried my
patience,
even though they saw everything I did.
10 For forty years I was angry with them, and I said,
'They are a people whose hearts turn away
from me.
They refuse to do what I tell them.'
11 So in my anger I took an oath:
'They will never enter my place of rest.'"

96
1 Sing a new song to the LORD!
Let the whole earth sing to the LORD!
2 Sing to the LORD; praise his name.
Each day proclaim the good news that
he saves.
3 Publish his glorious deeds among the nations.
Tell everyone about the amazing things
he does.
4 Great is the LORD! He is most worthy of praise!
He is to be feared above all gods.
5 The gods of other nations are mere idols,
but the LORD made the heavens!
6 Honor and majesty surround him;
strength and beauty fill his sanctuary.
7 O nations of the world, recognize the LORD;
recognize that the LORD is glorious and strong.
8 Give to the LORD the glory he deserves!
Bring your offering and come into his courts.
9 Worship the LORD in all his holy splendor.
Let all the earth tremble before him.
10 Tell all the nations, "The LORD reigns!"
The world stands firm and cannot be shaken.
He will judge all peoples fairly.

11 Let the heavens be glad, and the earth rejoice!
Let the sea and everything in it shout
his praise!

KING JAMES VERSION

12 Let the field be joyful, and all that *is* therein:
then shall all the trees of the wood rejoice
13 Before the LORD: for he cometh, for he cometh to
judge the earth: he shall judge the world with righteousness, and the people with his truth.

97

1 The LORD reigneth; let the earth rejoice; let
the multitude of isles be glad *thereof.*
2 Clouds and darkness *are* round about him: righteousness and judgment *are* the habitation of his
throne.
3 A fire goeth before him, and burneth up his enemies round about.
4 His lightnings enlightened the world: the earth
saw, and trembled.
5 The hills melted like wax at the presence of the
LORD, at the presence of the Lord of the whole earth.
6 The heavens declare his righteousness, and all
the people see his glory.
7 Confounded be all they that serve graven images,
that boast themselves of idols: worship him, all *ye*
gods.
8 Zion heard, and was glad; and the daughters of
Judah rejoiced because of thy judgments, O LORD.
9 For thou, LORD, *art* high above all the earth: thou
art exalted far above all gods.
10 Ye that love the LORD, hate evil: he preserveth the
souls of his saints; he delivereth them out of the
hand of the wicked.
11 Light is sown for the righteous, and gladness for
the upright in heart.
12 Rejoice in the LORD, ye righteous; and give
thanks at the remembrance of his holiness.

98

A Psalm

1 O sing unto the LORD a new song; for he hath
done marvellous things: his right hand, and his holy
arm, hath gotten him the victory.
2 The LORD hath made known his salvation: his
righteousness hath he openly shewed in the sight of
the heathen.
3 He hath remembered his mercy and his truth toward the house of Israel: all the ends of the earth
have seen the salvation of our God.
4 Make a joyful noise unto the LORD, all the earth:
make a loud noise, and rejoice, and sing praise.
5 Sing unto the LORD with the harp; with the harp,
and the voice of a psalm.

NEW LIVING TRANSLATION

12 Let the fields and their crops burst out with joy!
Let the trees of the forest rustle with praise
13 before the LORD, for he is coming!
He is coming to judge the earth.
He will judge the world with justice,
and the nations with his truth.

97

1 The LORD is king!
Let the earth rejoice!
Let the farthest coastlands be glad.
2 Dark clouds surround him.
Righteousness and justice are the foundation
of his throne.
3 Fire spreads ahead of him
and burns up all his foes.
4 His lightning flashes out across the world.
The earth sees and trembles.
5 The mountains melt like wax before the LORD,
before the Lord of all the earth.
6 The heavens proclaim his righteousness;
every nation sees his glory.
7 Those who worship idols are disgraced—
all who brag about their worthless gods—
for every god must bow to him.
8 Jerusalem* has heard and rejoiced,
and all the towns of Judah are glad
because of your justice, O LORD!
9 For you, O LORD, are supreme over all the earth;
you are exalted far above all gods.

10 You who love the LORD, hate evil!
He protects the lives of his godly people
and rescues them from the power of
the wicked.
11 Light shines on the godly,
and joy on those whose hearts are right.
12 May all who are godly rejoice in the LORD
and praise his holy name!

98

A psalm.

1 Sing a new song to the LORD,
for he has done wonderful deeds.
His right hand has won a mighty victory;
his holy arm has shown his saving power!
2 The LORD has announced his victory
and has revealed his righteousness to
every nation!
3 He has remembered his promise to love and
be faithful to Israel.
The ends of the earth have seen the victory
of our God.
4 Shout to the LORD, all the earth;
break out in praise and sing for joy!
5 Sing your praise to the LORD with the harp,
with the harp and melodious song,

97:8 Hebrew *Zion.*

KING JAMES VERSION

6 With trumpets and sound of cornet make a joyful noise before the LORD, the King.
7 Let the sea roar, and the fulness thereof; the world, and they that dwell therein.
8 Let the floods clap *their* hands: let the hills be joyful together
9 Before the LORD; for he cometh to judge the earth: with righteousness shall he judge the world, and the people with equity.

99

1 The LORD reigneth; let the people tremble: he sitteth *between* the cherubims; let the earth be moved.
2 The LORD *is* great in Zion; and he *is* high above all the people.
3 Let them praise thy great and terrible name; *for* it *is* holy.
4 The king's strength also loveth judgment; thou dost establish equity, thou executest judgment and righteousness in Jacob.
5 Exalt ye the LORD our God, and worship at his footstool; *for* he *is* holy.
6 Moses and Aaron among his priests, and Samuel among them that call upon his name; they called upon the LORD, and he answered them.
7 He spake unto them in the cloudy pillar: they kept his testimonies, and the ordinance *that* he gave them.
8 Thou answeredst them, O LORD our God: thou wast a God that forgavest them, though thou tookest vengeance of their inventions.
9 Exalt the LORD our God, and worship at his holy hill; for the LORD our God *is* holy.

100 *A Psalm of praise*

1 Make a joyful noise unto the LORD, all ye lands.
2 Serve the LORD with gladness: come before his presence with singing.
3 Know ye that the LORD he *is* God: *it is* he *that* hath made us, and not we ourselves; *we are* his people, and the sheep of his pasture.
4 Enter into his gates with thanksgiving, *and* into his courts with praise: be thankful unto him, *and* bless his name.
5 For the LORD *is* good; his mercy *is* everlasting; and his truth *endureth* to all generations.

NEW LIVING TRANSLATION

6 with trumpets and the sound of the ram's horn.
Make a joyful symphony before the LORD,
the King!
7 Let the sea and everything in it shout his praise!
Let the earth and all living things join in.
8 Let the rivers clap their hands in glee!
Let the hills sing out their songs of joy
9 before the LORD.
For the LORD is coming to judge the earth.
He will judge the world with justice,
and the nations with fairness.

99

1 The LORD is king!
Let the nations tremble!
He sits on his throne between the cherubim.
Let the whole earth quake!
2 The LORD sits in majesty in Jerusalem,*
exalted above all the nations.
3 Let them praise your great and awesome name.
Your name is holy!
4 Mighty King, lover of justice,
you have established fairness.
You have acted with justice
and righteousness throughout Israel.*
5 Exalt the LORD our God!
Bow low before his feet, for he is holy!

6 Moses and Aaron were among his priests;
Samuel also called on his name.
They cried to the LORD for help,
and he answered them.
7 He spoke to Israel from the pillar of cloud,
and they followed the laws and decrees
he gave them.
8 O LORD our God, you answered them.
You were a forgiving God to them,
but you punished them when they went wrong.
9 Exalt the LORD our God,
and worship at his holy mountain in Jerusalem,
for the LORD our God is holy!

100 *A psalm of thanksgiving.*

1 Shout with joy to the LORD, all the earth!
2 Worship the LORD with gladness.
Come before him, singing with joy.
3 Acknowledge that the LORD is God!
He made us, and we are his.*
We are his people, the sheep of his pasture.
4 Enter his gates with thanksgiving;
go into his courts with praise.
Give thanks to him and praise his name.
5 For the LORD is good.
His unfailing love continues forever,
and his faithfulness continues to each
generation.

99:2 Hebrew *Zion.* **99:4** Hebrew *Jacob.* See note on 44:4. **100:3** As in an alternate reading in the Masoretic Text; the other alternate and some ancient versions read *and not we ourselves.*

KING JAMES VERSION

101 *A Psalm of David*

1 I will sing of mercy and judgment: unto thee, O LORD, will I sing.

2 I will behave myself wisely in a perfect way. O when wilt thou come unto me? I will walk within my house with a perfect heart.

3 I will set no wicked thing before mine eyes: I hate the work of them that turn aside; *it* shall not cleave to me.

4 A froward heart shall depart from me: I will not know a wicked *person*.

5 Whoso privily slandereth his neighbour, him will I cut off: him that hath an high look and a proud heart will not I suffer.

6 Mine eyes *shall be* upon the faithful of the land, that they may dwell with me: he that walketh in a perfect way, he shall serve me.

7 He that worketh deceit shall not dwell within my house: he that telleth lies shall not tarry in my sight.

8 I will early destroy all the wicked of the land; that I may cut off all wicked doers from the city of the LORD.

102 *A Prayer of the afflicted, when he is overwhelmed, and poureth out his complaint before the LORD.*

1 Hear my prayer, O LORD, and let my cry come unto thee.

2 Hide not thy face from me in the day *when* I am in trouble; incline thine ear unto me: in the day *when* I call answer me speedily.

3 For my days are consumed like smoke, and my bones are burned as an hearth.

4 My heart is smitten, and withered like grass; so that I forget to eat my bread.

5 By reason of the voice of my groaning my bones cleave to my skin.

6 I am like a pelican of the wilderness: I am like an owl of the desert.

7 I watch, and am as a sparrow alone upon the house top.

8 Mine enemies reproach me all the day; *and* they that are mad against me are sworn against me.

9 For I have eaten ashes like bread, and mingled my drink with weeping,

10 Because of thine indignation and thy wrath: for thou hast lifted me up, and cast me down.

11 My days *are* like a shadow that declineth; and I am withered like grass.

12 But thou, O LORD, shalt endure for ever; and thy remembrance unto all generations.

NEW LIVING TRANSLATION

101 *A psalm of David.*

1 I will sing of your love and justice, LORD.
I will praise you with songs.
2 I will be careful to live a blameless life—
when will you come to help me?
I will lead a life of integrity
in my own home.
3 I will refuse to look at
anything vile and vulgar.
I hate all who deal crookedly;
I will have nothing to do with them.
4 I will reject perverse ideas
and stay away from every evil.
5 I will not tolerate people who slander
their neighbors.
I will not endure conceit and pride.
6 I will search for faithful people
to be my companions.
Only those who are above reproach
will be allowed to serve me.
7 I will not allow deceivers to serve in my house,
and liars will not stay in my presence.
8 My daily task will be to ferret out the wicked
and free the city of the LORD from their grip.

102 *A prayer of one overwhelmed with trouble, pouring out problems before the LORD.*

1 LORD, hear my prayer!
Listen to my plea!
2 Don't turn away from me
in my time of distress.
Bend down to listen,
and answer me quickly when I call to you.
3 For my days disappear like smoke,
and my bones burn like red-hot coals.
4 My heart is sick, withered like grass,
and I have lost my appetite.
5 Because of my groaning,
I am reduced to skin and bones.
6 I am like an owl in the desert,
like a little owl in a far-off wilderness.
7 I lie awake,
lonely as a solitary bird on the roof.
8 My enemies taunt me day after day.
They mock and curse me.
9 I eat ashes for food.
My tears run down into my drink
10 because of your anger and wrath.
For you have picked me up and thrown me out.
11 My life passes as swiftly as the evening shadows.
I am withering away like grass.

12 But you, O LORD, will sit on your throne forever.
Your fame will endure to every generation.

KING JAMES VERSION

13 Thou shalt arise, *and* have mercy upon Zion: for
the time to favour her, yea, the set time, is come.
14 For thy servants take pleasure in her stones, and
favour the dust thereof.
15 So the heathen shall fear the name of the LORD,
and all the kings of the earth thy glory.
16 When the LORD shall build up Zion, he shall appear in his glory.
17 He will regard the prayer of the destitute, and
not despise their prayer.
18 This shall be written for the generation to come:
and the people which shall be created shall praise
the LORD.
19 For he hath looked down from the height of his
sanctuary; from heaven did the LORD behold the
earth;
20 To hear the groaning of the prisoner; to loose
those that are appointed to death;
21 To declare the name of the LORD in Zion, and his
praise in Jerusalem;
22 When the people are gathered together, and the
kingdoms, to serve the LORD.
23 He weakened my strength in the way; he shortened my days.
24 I said, O my God, take me not away in the midst
of my days: thy years *are* throughout all generations.
25 Of old hast thou laid the foundation of the earth:
and the heavens *are* the work of thy hands.
26 They shall perish, but thou shalt endure: yea,
all of them shall wax old like a garment; as a vesture
shalt thou change them, and they shall be changed:
27 But thou *art* the same, and thy years shall have
no end.
28 The children of thy servants shall continue, and
their seed shall be established before thee.

103 A Psalm *of David*

1 Bless the LORD, O my soul: and all that is within
me, *bless* his holy name.
2 Bless the LORD, O my soul, and forget not all his
benefits:
3 Who forgiveth all thine iniquities; who healeth
all thy diseases;
4 Who redeemeth thy life from destruction; who
crowneth thee with lovingkindness and tender mercies;
5 Who satisfieth thy mouth with good *things; so
that* thy youth is renewed like the eagle's.

NEW LIVING TRANSLATION

13 You will arise and have mercy on Jerusalem*—
and now is the time to pity her,
now is the time you promised to help.
14 For your people love every stone in her walls
and cherish even the dust in her streets.
15 Then the nations will tremble before the LORD.
The kings of the earth will tremble before
his glory.
16 For the LORD will rebuild Jerusalem.
He will appear in his glory.
17 He will listen to the prayers of the destitute.
He will not reject their pleas.
18 Let this be recorded for future generations,
so that a people not yet born will praise
the LORD.
19 Tell them the LORD looked down
from his heavenly sanctuary.
He looked down to earth from heaven
20 to hear the groans of the prisoners,
to release those condemned to die.
21 And so the LORD's fame will be celebrated
in Zion,
his praises in Jerusalem,
22 when multitudes gather together
and kingdoms come to worship the LORD.
23 He broke my strength in midlife,
cutting short my days.
24 But I cried to him, "O my God, who lives forever,
don't take my life while I am so young!
25 Long ago you laid the foundation of the earth
and made the heavens with your hands.
26 They will perish, but you remain forever;
they will wear out like old clothing.
You will change them like a garment
and discard them.
27 But you are always the same;
you will live forever.
28 The children of your people
will live in security.
Their children's children
will thrive in your presence."

103 *A psalm of David.*

1 Let all that I am praise the LORD;
with my whole heart, I will praise his holy name.
2 Let all that I am praise the LORD;
may I never forget the good things he does
for me.
3 He forgives all my sins
and heals all my diseases.
4 He redeems me from death
and crowns me with love and tender mercies.
5 He fills my life with good things.
My youth is renewed like the eagle's!

102:13 Hebrew *Zion;* also in 102:16.

KING JAMES VERSION

6 The LORD executeth righteousness and judgment
for all that are oppressed.
7 He made known his ways unto Moses, his acts
unto the children of Israel.
8 The LORD *is* merciful and gracious, slow to anger,
and plenteous in mercy.
9 He will not always chide: neither will he keep *his*
anger for ever.
10 He hath not dealt with us after our sins; nor rewarded us according to our iniquities.
11 For as the heaven is high above the earth, *so*
great is his mercy toward them that fear him.
12 As far as the east is from the west, *so* far hath he
removed our transgressions from us.
13 Like as a father pitieth *his* children, *so* the LORD
pitieth them that fear him.
14 For he knoweth our frame; he remembereth that
we *are* dust.
15 *As for* man, his days *are* as grass: as a flower of
the field, so he flourisheth.
16 For the wind passeth over it, and it is gone; and
the place thereof shall know it no more.
17 But the mercy of the LORD *is* from everlasting to
everlasting upon them that fear him, and his righteousness unto children's children;
18 To such as keep his covenant, and to those that
remember his commandments to do them.
19 The LORD hath prepared his throne in the heavens; and his kingdom ruleth over all.
20 Bless the LORD, ye his angels, that excel in
strength, that do his commandments, hearkening
unto the voice of his word.
21 Bless ye the LORD, all *ye* his hosts; *ye* ministers of
his, that do his pleasure.
22 Bless the LORD, all his works in all places of his
dominion: bless the LORD, O my soul.

104

1 Bless the LORD, O my soul. O LORD my
God, thou art very great; thou art clothed
with honour and majesty.
2 Who coverest *thyself* with light as *with* a garment: who stretchest out the heavens like a curtain:
3 Who layeth the beams of his chambers in the
waters: who maketh the clouds his chariot: who
walketh upon the wings of the wind:
4 Who maketh his angels spirits; his ministers a
flaming fire:
5 *Who* laid the foundations of the earth, *that* it
should not be removed for ever.

NEW LIVING TRANSLATION

6 The LORD gives righteousness
and justice to all who are treated unfairly.
7 He revealed his character to Moses
and his deeds to the people of Israel.
8 The LORD is compassionate and merciful,
slow to get angry and filled with unfailing love.
9 He will not constantly accuse us,
nor remain angry forever.
10 He does not punish us for all our sins;
he does not deal harshly with us, as we deserve.
11 For his unfailing love toward those who fear him
is as great as the height of the heavens above
the earth.
12 He has removed our sins as far from us
as the east is from the west.
13 The LORD is like a father to his children,
tender and compassionate to those who
fear him.
14 For he knows how weak we are;
he remembers we are only dust.
15 Our days on earth are like grass;
like wildflowers, we bloom and die.
16 The wind blows, and we are gone—
as though we had never been here.
17 But the love of the LORD remains forever
with those who fear him.
His salvation extends to the children's children
18 of those who are faithful to his covenant,
of those who obey his commandments!
19 The LORD has made the heavens his throne;
from there he rules over everything.

20 Praise the LORD, you angels,
you mighty ones who carry out his plans,
listening for each of his commands.
21 Yes, praise the LORD, you armies of angels
who serve him and do his will!
22 Praise the LORD, everything he has created,
everything in all his kingdom.

Let all that I am praise the LORD.

104

1 Let all that I am praise the LORD.

O LORD my God, how great you are!
You are robed with honor and majesty.
2 You are dressed in a robe of light.
You stretch out the starry curtain of the heavens;
3 you lay out the rafters of your home in the rain
clouds.
You make the clouds your chariot;
you ride upon the wings of the wind.
4 The winds are your messengers;
flames of fire are your servants.*

5 You placed the world on its foundation
so it would never be moved.

104:4 Greek version reads *He sends his angels like the winds, / his servants like flames of fire.* Compare Heb 1:7.

KING JAMES VERSION

6 Thou coveredst it with the deep as *with* a garment: the waters stood above the mountains.
7 At thy rebuke they fled; at the voice of thy thunder they hasted away.
8 They go up by the mountains; they go down by the valleys unto the place which thou hast founded for them.
9 Thou hast set a bound that they may not pass over; that they turn not again to cover the earth.
10 He sendeth the springs into the valleys, *which* run among the hills.
11 They give drink to every beast of the field: the wild asses quench their thirst.
12 By them shall the fowls of the heaven have their habitation, *which* sing among the branches.
13 He watereth the hills from his chambers: the earth is satisfied with the fruit of thy works.
14 He causeth the grass to grow for the cattle, and herb for the service of man: that he may bring forth food out of the earth;
15 And wine *that* maketh glad the heart of man, *and* oil to make *his* face to shine, and bread *which* strengtheneth man's heart.
16 The trees of the LORD are full *of sap;* the cedars of Lebanon, which he hath planted;
17 Where the birds make their nests: *as for* the stork, the fir trees *are* her house.
18 The high hills *are* a refuge for the wild goats; *and* the rocks for the conies.
19 He appointed the moon for seasons: the sun knoweth his going down.
20 Thou makest darkness, and it is night: wherein all the beasts of the forest do creep *forth*.
21 The young lions roar after their prey, and seek their meat from God.
22 The sun ariseth, they gather themselves together, and lay them down in their dens.
23 Man goeth forth unto his work and to his labour until the evening.
24 O LORD, how manifold are thy works! in wisdom hast thou made them all: the earth is full of thy riches.
25 *So is* this great and wide sea, wherein *are* things creeping innumerable, both small and great beasts.
26 There go the ships: *there is* that leviathan, *whom* thou hast made to play therein.
27 These wait all upon thee; that thou mayest give *them* their meat in due season.
28 *That* thou givest them they gather: thou openest thine hand, they are filled with good.

NEW LIVING TRANSLATION

6 You clothed the earth with floods of water,
water that covered even the mountains.
7 At your command, the water fled;
at the sound of your thunder, it hurried away.
8 Mountains rose and valleys sank
to the levels you decreed.
9 Then you set a firm boundary for the seas,
so they would never again cover the earth.

10 You make springs pour water into the ravines,
so streams gush down from the mountains.
11 They provide water for all the animals,
and the wild donkeys quench their thirst.
12 The birds nest beside the streams
and sing among the branches of the trees.
13 You send rain on the mountains from your heavenly home,
and you fill the earth with the fruit of your labor.
14 You cause grass to grow for the livestock
and plants for people to use.
You allow them to produce food from the earth—
15 wine to make them glad,
olive oil to soothe their skin,
and bread to give them strength.
16 The trees of the LORD are well cared for—
the cedars of Lebanon that he planted.
17 There the birds make their nests,
and the storks make their homes in the cypresses.
18 High in the mountains live the wild goats,
and the rocks form a refuge for the hyraxes.*
19 You made the moon to mark the seasons,
and the sun knows when to set.
20 You send the darkness, and it becomes night,
when all the forest animals prowl about.
21 Then the young lions roar for their prey,
stalking the food provided by God.
22 At dawn they slink back
into their dens to rest.
23 Then people go off to their work,
where they labor until evening.

24 O LORD, what a variety of things you have made!
In wisdom you have made them all.
The earth is full of your creatures.
25 Here is the ocean, vast and wide,
teeming with life of every kind,
both large and small.
26 See the ships sailing along,
and Leviathan,* which you made to play in the sea.

27 They all depend on you
to give them food as they need it.
28 When you supply it, they gather it.
You open your hand to feed them,
and they are richly satisfied.

104:18 Or *coneys*, or *rock badgers*. **104:26** The identification of Leviathan is disputed, ranging from an earthly creature to a mythical sea monster in ancient literature.

KING JAMES VERSION

29 Thou hidest thy face, they are troubled: thou
takest away their breath, they die, and return to their
dust.
30 Thou sendest forth thy spirit, they are created:
and thou renewest the face of the earth.
31 The glory of the LORD shall endure for ever: the
LORD shall rejoice in his works.
32 He looketh on the earth, and it trembleth: he
toucheth the hills, and they smoke.
33 I will sing unto the LORD as long as I live: I will
sing praise to my God while I have my being.
34 My meditation of him shall be sweet: I will be
glad in the LORD.
35 Let the sinners be consumed out of the earth,
and let the wicked be no more. Bless thou the LORD,
O my soul. Praise ye the LORD.

105

1 O give thanks unto the LORD; call upon
his name: make known his deeds among
the people.
2 Sing unto him, sing psalms unto him: talk ye of all
his wondrous works.
3 Glory ye in his holy name: let the heart of them
rejoice that seek the LORD.
4 Seek the LORD, and his strength: seek his face
evermore.
5 Remember his marvellous works that he hath
done; his wonders, and the judgments of his mouth;
6 O ye seed of Abraham his servant, ye children of
Jacob his chosen.
7 He *is* the LORD our God: his judgments *are* in all
the earth.
8 He hath remembered his covenant for ever, the
word *which* he commanded to a thousand generations.
9 Which *covenant* he made with Abraham, and his
oath unto Isaac;
10 And confirmed the same unto Jacob for a law,
and to Israel *for* an everlasting covenant:
11 Saying, Unto thee will I give the land of Canaan,
the lot of your inheritance:
12 When they were *but* a few men in number; yea,
very few, and strangers in it.
13 When they went from one nation to another,
from *one* kingdom to another people;
14 He suffered no man to do them wrong: yea, he
reproved kings for their sakes;
15 *Saying*, Touch not mine anointed, and do my
prophets no harm.
16 Moreover he called for a famine upon the land:
he brake the whole staff of bread.

NEW LIVING TRANSLATION

29 But if you turn away from them, they panic.
When you take away their breath,
they die and turn again to dust.
30 When you give them your breath,* life is created,
and you renew the face of the earth.
31 May the glory of the LORD continue forever!
The LORD takes pleasure in all he has made!
32 The earth trembles at his glance;
the mountains smoke at his touch.
33 I will sing to the LORD as long as I live.
I will praise my God to my last breath!
34 May all my thoughts be pleasing to him,
for I rejoice in the LORD.
35 Let all sinners vanish from the face of the earth;
let the wicked disappear forever.

Let all that I am praise the LORD.

Praise the LORD!

105

1 Give thanks to the LORD and proclaim
his greatness.
Let the whole world know what he has done.
2 Sing to him; yes, sing his praises.
Tell everyone about his wonderful deeds.
3 Exult in his holy name;
rejoice, you who worship the LORD.
4 Search for the LORD and for his strength;
continually seek him.
5 Remember the wonders he has performed,
his miracles, and the rulings he has given,
6 you children of his servant Abraham,
you descendants of Jacob, his chosen ones.
7 He is the LORD our God.
His justice is seen throughout the land.
8 He always stands by his covenant—
the commitment he made to a thousand
generations.
9 This is the covenant he made with Abraham
and the oath he swore to Isaac.
10 He confirmed it to Jacob as a decree,
and to the people of Israel as a never-ending
covenant:
11 "I will give you the land of Canaan
as your special possession."
12 He said this when they were few in number,
a tiny group of strangers in Canaan.
13 They wandered from nation to nation,
from one kingdom to another.
14 Yet he did not let anyone oppress them.
He warned kings on their behalf:
15 "Do not touch my chosen people,
and do not hurt my prophets."
16 He called for a famine on the land of Canaan,
cutting off its food supply.

104:30 Or *When you send your Spirit.*

KING JAMES VERSION

17 He sent a man before them, *even* Joseph, *who* was sold for a servant:

18 Whose feet they hurt with fetters: he was laid in iron:

19 Until the time that his word came: the word of the LORD tried him.

20 The king sent and loosed him; *even* the ruler of the people, and let him go free.

21 He made him lord of his house, and ruler of all his substance:

22 To bind his princes at his pleasure; and teach his senators wisdom.

23 Israel also came into Egypt; and Jacob sojourned in the land of Ham.

24 And he increased his people greatly; and made them stronger than their enemies.

25 He turned their heart to hate his people, to deal subtilly with his servants.

26 He sent Moses his servant; *and* Aaron whom he had chosen.

27 They shewed his signs among them, and wonders in the land of Ham.

28 He sent darkness, and made it dark; and they rebelled not against his word.

29 He turned their waters into blood, and slew their fish.

30 Their land brought forth frogs in abundance, in the chambers of their kings.

31 He spake, and there came divers sorts of flies, *and* lice in all their coasts.

32 He gave them hail for rain, *and* flaming fire in their land.

33 He smote their vines also and their fig trees; and brake the trees of their coasts.

34 He spake, and the locusts came, and caterpillers, and that without number,

35 And did eat up all the herbs in their land, and devoured the fruit of their ground.

36 He smote also all the firstborn in their land, the chief of all their strength.

37 He brought them forth also with silver and gold: and *there was* not one feeble *person* among their tribes.

38 Egypt was glad when they departed: for the fear of them fell upon them.

NEW LIVING TRANSLATION

17 Then he sent someone to Egypt ahead of them—
Joseph, who was sold as a slave.
18 They bruised his feet with fetters
and placed his neck in an iron collar.
19 Until the time came to fulfill his dreams,*
the LORD tested Joseph's character.
20 Then Pharaoh sent for him and set him free;
the ruler of the nation opened his prison door.
21 Joseph was put in charge of all the king's
household;
he became ruler over all the king's
possessions.
22 He could instruct the king's aides as he pleased
and teach the king's advisers.

23 Then Israel arrived in Egypt;
Jacob lived as a foreigner in the land of Ham.
24 And the LORD multiplied the people of Israel
until they became too mighty for their
enemies.
25 Then he turned the Egyptians against the
Israelites,
and they plotted against the LORD's servants.
26 But the LORD sent his servant Moses,
along with Aaron, whom he had chosen.
27 They performed miraculous signs among the
Egyptians,
and wonders in the land of Ham.
28 The LORD blanketed Egypt in darkness,
for they had defied his commands to let his
people go.
29 He turned their water into blood,
poisoning all the fish.
30 Then frogs overran the land
and even invaded the king's bedrooms.
31 When the LORD spoke, flies descended
on the Egyptians,
and gnats swarmed across Egypt.
32 He sent them hail instead of rain,
and lightning flashed over the land.
33 He ruined their grapevines and fig trees
and shattered all the trees.
34 He spoke, and hordes of locusts came—
young locusts beyond number.
35 They ate up everything green in the land,
destroying all the crops in their fields.
36 Then he killed the oldest son in each
Egyptian home,
the pride and joy of each family.

37 The LORD brought his people out of Egypt,
loaded with silver and gold;
and not one among the tribes of Israel
even stumbled.
38 Egypt was glad when they were gone,
for they feared them greatly.

105:19 Hebrew *his word.*

KING JAMES VERSION

39 He spread a cloud for a covering; and fire to give
light in the night.
40 *The people* asked, and he brought quails, and
satisfied them with the bread of heaven.
41 He opened the rock, and the waters gushed out;
they ran in the dry places *like* a river.
42 For he remembered his holy promise, *and* Abraham his servant.
43 And he brought forth his people with joy, *and*
his chosen with gladness:
44 And gave them the lands of the heathen: and
they inherited the labour of the people;
45 That they might observe his statutes, and keep
his laws. Praise ye the LORD.

106 1 Praise ye the LORD. O give thanks unto
the LORD; for *he is* good: for his mercy *en-*
dureth for ever.
2 Who can utter the mighty acts of the LORD? *who*
can shew forth all his praise?
3 Blessed *are* they that keep judgment, *and* he that
doeth righteousness at all times.
4 Remember me, O LORD, with the favour *that thou*
bearest unto thy people: O visit me with thy salvation;
5 That I may see the good of thy chosen, that I may
rejoice in the gladness of thy nation, that I may glory
with thine inheritance.
6 We have sinned with our fathers, we have committed iniquity, we have done wickedly.
7 Our fathers understood not thy wonders in
Egypt; they remembered not the multitude of thy
mercies; but provoked *him* at the sea, *even* at the
Red sea.
8 Nevertheless he saved them for his name's sake,
that he might make his mighty power to be known.
9 He rebuked the Red sea also, and it was dried up:
so he led them through the depths, as through the
wilderness.
10 And he saved them from the hand of him that
hated *them,* and redeemed them from the hand of
the enemy.

NEW LIVING TRANSLATION

39 The LORD spread a cloud above them as
a covering
and gave them a great fire to light the
darkness.
40 They asked for meat, and he sent them quail;
he satisfied their hunger with manna—bread
from heaven.
41 He split open a rock, and water gushed out
to form a river through the dry wasteland.
42 For he remembered his sacred promise
to his servant Abraham.
43 So he brought his people out of Egypt with joy,
his chosen ones with rejoicing.
44 He gave his people the lands of pagan nations,
and they harvested crops that others
had planted.
45 All this happened so they would follow
his decrees
and obey his instructions.

Praise the LORD!

106 1 Praise the LORD!
Give thanks to the LORD, for he is good!
His faithful love endures forever.
2 Who can list the glorious miracles of the LORD?
Who can ever praise him enough?
3 There is joy for those who deal justly with others
and always do what is right.

4 Remember me, LORD, when you show favor
to your people;
come near and rescue me.
5 Let me share in the prosperity of your
chosen ones.
Let me rejoice in the joy of your people;
let me praise you with those who are
your heritage.

6 Like our ancestors, we have sinned.
We have done wrong! We have acted wickedly!
7 Our ancestors in Egypt
were not impressed by the LORD's
miraculous deeds.
They soon forgot his many acts of kindness
to them.
Instead, they rebelled against him at the
Red Sea.*
8 Even so, he saved them—
to defend the honor of his name
and to demonstrate his mighty power.
9 He commanded the Red Sea* to dry up.
He led Israel across the sea as if it were
a desert.
10 So he rescued them from their enemies
and redeemed them from their foes.

106:7 Hebrew *at the sea, the sea of reeds.* **106:9** Hebrew *sea of reeds;* also in 106:22.

KING JAMES VERSION

11 And the waters covered their enemies: there was not one of them left.

12 Then believed they his words; they sang his praise.

13 They soon forgat his works; they waited not for his counsel:

14 But lusted exceedingly in the wilderness, and tempted God in the desert.

15 And he gave them their request; but sent leanness into their soul.

16 They envied Moses also in the camp, *and* Aaron the saint of the LORD.

17 The earth opened and swallowed up Dathan, and covered the company of Abiram.

18 And a fire was kindled in their company; the flame burned up the wicked.

19 They made a calf in Horeb, and worshipped the molten image.

20 Thus they changed their glory into the similitude of an ox that eateth grass.

21 They forgat God their saviour, which had done great things in Egypt;

22 Wondrous works in the land of Ham, *and* terrible things by the Red sea.

23 Therefore he said that he would destroy them, had not Moses his chosen stood before him in the breach, to turn away his wrath, lest he should destroy *them*.

24 Yea, they despised the pleasant land, they believed not his word:

25 But murmured in their tents, *and* hearkened not unto the voice of the LORD.

26 Therefore he lifted up his hand against them, to overthrow them in the wilderness:

27 To overthrow their seed also among the nations, and to scatter them in the lands.

28 They joined themselves also unto Baal-peor, and ate the sacrifices of the dead.

29 Thus they provoked *him* to anger with their inventions: and the plague brake in upon them.

30 Then stood up Phinehas, and executed judgment: and *so* the plague was stayed.

31 And that was counted unto him for righteousness unto all generations for evermore.

32 They angered *him* also at the waters of strife, so that it went ill with Moses for their sakes:

33 Because they provoked his spirit, so that he spake unadvisedly with his lips.

NEW LIVING TRANSLATION

11 Then the water returned and covered
their enemies;
not one of them survived.
12 Then his people believed his promises.
Then they sang his praise.

13 Yet how quickly they forgot what he had done!
They wouldn't wait for his counsel!
14 In the wilderness their desires ran wild,
testing God's patience in that dry wasteland.
15 So he gave them what they asked for,
but he sent a plague along with it.
16 The people in the camp were jealous of Moses
and envious of Aaron, the LORD's holy priest.
17 Because of this, the earth opened up;
it swallowed Dathan
and buried Abiram and the other rebels.
18 Fire fell upon their followers;
a flame consumed the wicked.

19 The people made a calf at Mount Sinai*;
they bowed before an image made of gold.
20 They traded their glorious God
for a statue of a grass-eating bull.
21 They forgot God, their savior,
who had done such great things in Egypt—
22 such wonderful things in the land of Ham,
such awesome deeds at the Red Sea.
23 So he declared he would destroy them.
But Moses, his chosen one, stepped between
the LORD and the people.
He begged him to turn from his anger and
not destroy them.

24 The people refused to enter the pleasant land,
for they wouldn't believe his promise to
care for them.
25 Instead, they grumbled in their tents
and refused to obey the LORD.
26 Therefore, he solemnly swore
that he would kill them in the wilderness,
27 that he would scatter their descendants among
the nations,
exiling them to distant lands.

28 Then our ancestors joined in the worship
of Baal at Peor;
they even ate sacrifices offered to the dead!
29 They angered the LORD with all these things,
so a plague broke out among them.
30 But Phinehas had the courage to intervene,
and the plague was stopped.
31 So he has been regarded as a righteous man
ever since that time.

32 At Meribah, too, they angered the LORD,
causing Moses serious trouble.
33 They made Moses angry,*
and he spoke foolishly.

106:19 Hebrew *at Horeb,* another name for Sinai. **106:33** Hebrew *They embittered his spirit.*

KING JAMES VERSION

34 They did not destroy the nations, concerning whom the LORD commanded them:

35 But were mingled among the heathen, and learned their works.

36 And they served their idols: which were a snare unto them.

37 Yea, they sacrificed their sons and their daughters unto devils,

38 And shed innocent blood, *even* the blood of their sons and of their daughters, whom they sacrificed unto the idols of Canaan: and the land was polluted with blood.

39 Thus were they defiled with their own works, and went a whoring with their own inventions.

40 Therefore was the wrath of the LORD kindled against his people, insomuch that he abhorred his own inheritance.

41 And he gave them into the hand of the heathen; and they that hated them ruled over them.

42 Their enemies also oppressed them, and they were brought into subjection under their hand.

43 Many times did he deliver them; but they provoked *him* with their counsel, and were brought low for their iniquity.

44 Nevertheless he regarded their affliction, when he heard their cry:

45 And he remembered for them his covenant, and repented according to the multitude of his mercies.

46 He made them also to be pitied of all those that carried them captives.

47 Save us, O LORD our God, and gather us from among the heathen, to give thanks unto thy holy name, *and* to triumph in thy praise.

48 Blessed *be* the LORD God of Israel from everlasting to everlasting: and let all the people say, Amen. Praise ye the LORD.

107

1 O give thanks unto the LORD, for *he is* good: for his mercy *endureth* for ever.

2 Let the redeemed of the LORD say *so,* whom he hath redeemed from the hand of the enemy;

3 And gathered them out of the lands, from the east, and from the west, from the north, and from the south.

4 They wandered in the wilderness in a solitary way; they found no city to dwell in.

5 Hungry and thirsty, their soul fainted in them.

6 Then they cried unto the LORD in their trouble, *and* he delivered them out of their distresses.

NEW LIVING TRANSLATION

34 Israel failed to destroy the nations in the land,
as the LORD had commanded them.
35 Instead, they mingled among the pagans
and adopted their evil customs.
36 They worshiped their idols,
which led to their downfall.
37 They even sacrificed their sons
and their daughters to the demons.
38 They shed innocent blood,
the blood of their sons and daughters.
By sacrificing them to the idols of Canaan,
they polluted the land with murder.
39 They defiled themselves by their evil deeds,
and their love of idols was adultery in the LORD's sight.

40 That is why the LORD's anger burned against his people,
and he abhorred his own special possession.
41 He handed them over to pagan nations,
and they were ruled by those who hated them.
42 Their enemies crushed them
and brought them under their cruel power.
43 Again and again he rescued them,
but they chose to rebel against him,
and they were finally destroyed by their sin.
44 Even so, he pitied them in their distress
and listened to their cries.
45 He remembered his covenant with them
and relented because of his unfailing love.
46 He even caused their captors
to treat them with kindness.

47 Save us, O LORD our God!
Gather us back from among the nations,
so we can thank your holy name
and rejoice and praise you.

48 Praise the LORD, the God of Israel,
who lives from everlasting to everlasting!
Let all the people say, "Amen!"
Praise the LORD!

BOOK FIVE (Psalms 107–150)

107

1 Give thanks to the LORD, for he is good!
His faithful love endures forever.
2 Has the LORD redeemed you? Then speak out!
Tell others he has redeemed you from your enemies.
3 For he has gathered the exiles from many lands,
from east and west,
from north and south.

4 Some wandered in the wilderness,
lost and homeless.
5 Hungry and thirsty,
they nearly died.
6 "LORD, help!" they cried in their trouble,
and he rescued them from their distress.

KING JAMES VERSION

7 And he led them forth by the right way, that they
might go to a city of habitation.
8 Oh that *men* would praise the LORD *for* his goodness, and *for* his wonderful works to the children of
men!
9 For he satisfieth the longing soul, and filleth the
hungry soul with goodness.
10 Such as sit in darkness and in the shadow of
death, *being* bound in affliction and iron;
11 Because they rebelled against the words of God,
and contemned the counsel of the most High:
12 Therefore he brought down their heart with labour; they fell down, and *there was* none to help.
13 Then they cried unto the LORD in their trouble,
and he saved them out of their distresses.
14 He brought them out of darkness and the
shadow of death, and brake their bands in sunder.
15 Oh that *men* would praise the LORD *for* his goodness, and *for* his wonderful works to the children
of men!
16 For he hath broken the gates of brass, and cut
the bars of iron in sunder.
17 Fools because of their transgression, and because of their iniquities, are afflicted.
18 Their soul abhorreth all manner of meat; and
they draw near unto the gates of death.
19 Then they cry unto the LORD in their trouble,
and he saveth them out of their distresses.
20 He sent his word, and healed them, and delivered *them* from their destructions.
21 Oh that *men* would praise the LORD *for* his goodness, and *for* his wonderful works to the children
of men!
22 And let them sacrifice the sacrifices of thanksgiving, and declare his works with rejoicing.
23 They that go down to the sea in ships, that do
business in great waters;
24 These see the works of the LORD, and his wonders in the deep.
25 For he commandeth, and raiseth the stormy
wind, which lifteth up the waves thereof.
26 They mount up to the heaven, they go down
again to the depths: their soul is melted because of
trouble.
27 They reel to and fro, and stagger like a drunken
man, and are at their wit's end.
28 Then they cry unto the LORD in their trouble, and
he bringeth them out of their distresses.
29 He maketh the storm a calm, so that the waves
thereof are still.
30 Then are they glad because they be quiet; so he
bringeth them unto their desired haven.
31 Oh that *men* would praise the LORD *for* his goodness, and *for* his wonderful works to the children
of men!

NEW LIVING TRANSLATION

7 He led them straight to safety,
to a city where they could live.
8 Let them praise the LORD for his great love
and for the wonderful things he has done
for them.
9 For he satisfies the thirsty
and fills the hungry with good things.

10 Some sat in darkness and deepest gloom,
imprisoned in iron chains of misery.
11 They rebelled against the words of God,
scorning the counsel of the Most High.
12 That is why he broke them with hard labor;
they fell, and no one was there to help them.
13 "LORD, help!" they cried in their trouble,
and he saved them from their distress.
14 He led them from the darkness and
deepest gloom;
he snapped their chains.
15 Let them praise the LORD for his great love
and for the wonderful things he has done
for them.
16 For he broke down their prison gates of bronze;
he cut apart their bars of iron.

17 Some were fools; they rebelled
and suffered for their sins.
18 They couldn't stand the thought of food,
and they were knocking on death's door.
19 "LORD, help!" they cried in their trouble,
and he saved them from their distress.
20 He sent out his word and healed them,
snatching them from the door of death.
21 Let them praise the LORD for his great love
and for the wonderful things he has done
for them.
22 Let them offer sacrifices of thanksgiving
and sing joyfully about his glorious acts.

23 Some went off to sea in ships,
plying the trade routes of the world.
24 They, too, observed the LORD's power in action,
his impressive works on the deepest seas.
25 He spoke, and the winds rose,
stirring up the waves.
26 Their ships were tossed to the heavens
and plunged again to the depths;
the sailors cringed in terror.
27 They reeled and staggered like drunkards
and were at their wits' end.
28 "LORD, help!" they cried in their trouble,
and he saved them from their distress.
29 He calmed the storm to a whisper
and stilled the waves.
30 What a blessing was that stillness
as he brought them safely into harbor!
31 Let them praise the LORD for his great love
and for the wonderful things he has done
for them.

KING JAMES VERSION

32 Let them exalt him also in the congregation of
the people, and praise him in the assembly of the
elders.
33 He turneth rivers into a wilderness, and the
watersprings into dry ground;
34 A fruitful land into barrenness, for the wickedness of them that dwell therein.
35 He turneth the wilderness into a standing water,
and dry ground into watersprings.
36 And there he maketh the hungry to dwell, that
they may prepare a city for habitation;
37 And sow the fields, and plant vineyards, which
may yield fruits of increase.
38 He blesseth them also, so that they are multiplied greatly; and suffereth not their cattle to decrease.
39 Again, they are minished and brought low
through oppression, affliction, and sorrow.
40 He poureth contempt upon princes, and
causeth them to wander in the wilderness, *where
there is* no way.
41 Yet setteth he the poor on high from affliction,
and maketh *him* families like a flock.
42 The righteous shall see *it,* and rejoice: and all
iniquity shall stop her mouth.
43 Whoso *is* wise, and will observe these *things,*
even they shall understand the lovingkindness of the
LORD.

108 *A Song* or *Psalm of David*

1 O God, my heart is fixed; I will sing and give
praise, even with my glory.
2 Awake, psaltery and harp: I *myself* will awake
early.
3 I will praise thee, O LORD, among the people: and I
will sing praises unto thee among the nations.
4 For thy mercy *is* great above the heavens: and thy
truth *reacheth* unto the clouds.
5 Be thou exalted, O God, above the heavens: and
thy glory above all the earth;
6 That thy beloved may be delivered: save *with* thy
right hand, and answer me.
7 God hath spoken in his holiness; I will rejoice, I
will divide Shechem, and mete out the valley of
Succoth.
8 Gilead *is* mine; Manasseh *is* mine; Ephraim also *is*
the strength of mine head; Judah *is* my lawgiver;

NEW LIVING TRANSLATION

32 Let them exalt him publicly before the
congregation
and before the leaders of the nation.

33 He changes rivers into deserts,
and springs of water into dry, thirsty land.
34 He turns the fruitful land into salty wastelands,
because of the wickedness of those who
live there.
35 But he also turns deserts into pools of water,
the dry land into springs of water.
36 He brings the hungry to settle there
and to build their cities.
37 They sow their fields, plant their vineyards,
and harvest their bumper crops.
38 How he blesses them!
They raise large families there,
and their herds of livestock increase.

39 When they decrease in number and become
impoverished
through oppression, trouble, and sorrow,
40 the LORD pours contempt on their princes,
causing them to wander in trackless
wastelands.
41 But he rescues the poor from trouble
and increases their families like flocks
of sheep.
42 The godly will see these things and be glad,
while the wicked are struck silent.
43 Those who are wise will take all this to heart;
they will see in our history the faithful love
of the LORD.

108 *A song. A psalm of David.*

1 My heart is confident in you, O God;
no wonder I can sing your praises with
all my heart!
2 Wake up, lyre and harp!
I will wake the dawn with my song.
3 I will thank you, LORD, among all the people.
I will sing your praises among the nations.
4 For your unfailing love is higher than
the heavens.
Your faithfulness reaches to the clouds.
5 Be exalted, O God, above the highest heavens.
May your glory shine over all the earth.

6 Now rescue your beloved people.
Answer and save us by your power.
7 God has promised this by his holiness*:
"I will divide up Shechem with joy.
I will measure out the valley of Succoth.
8 Gilead is mine,
and Manasseh, too.
Ephraim, my helmet, will produce my warriors,
and Judah, my scepter, will produce my kings.

108:7 Or *in his sanctuary.*

9 Moab *is* my washpot; over Edom will I cast out my
shoe; over Philistia will I triumph.
10 Who will bring me into the strong city? who will
lead me into Edom?
11 *Wilt* not *thou*, O God, *who* hast cast us off? and
wilt not thou, O God, go forth with our hosts?
12 Give us help from trouble: for vain *is* the help
of man.
13 Through God we shall do valiantly: for he *it is*
that shall tread down our enemies.

109 *To the chief Musician, A Psalm of David*

1 Hold not thy peace, O God of my praise;
2 For the mouth of the wicked and the mouth of
the deceitful are opened against me: they have spoken against me with a lying tongue.
3 They compassed me about also with words of hatred; and fought against me without a cause.
4 For my love they are my adversaries: but I *give*
myself unto prayer.
5 And they have rewarded me evil for good, and
hatred for my love.
6 Set thou a wicked man over him: and let Satan
stand at his right hand.
7 When he shall be judged, let him be condemned:
and let his prayer become sin.
8 Let his days be few; *and* let another take his
office.
9 Let his children be fatherless, and his wife a
widow.
10 Let his children be continually vagabonds, and
beg: let them seek *their bread* also out of their desolate places.
11 Let the extortioner catch all that he hath; and let
the strangers spoil his labour.
12 Let there be none to extend mercy unto him:
neither let there be any to favour his fatherless
children.
13 Let his posterity be cut off; *and* in the generation following let their name be blotted out.
14 Let the iniquity of his fathers be remembered
with the LORD; and let not the sin of his mother be
blotted out.
15 Let them be before the LORD continually, that he
may cut off the memory of them from the earth.
16 Because that he remembered not to shew mercy,
but persecuted the poor and needy man, that he
might even slay the broken in heart.
17 As he loved cursing, so let it come unto him: as
he delighted not in blessing, so let it be far from him.

9 But Moab, my washbasin, will become my servant,
and I will wipe my feet on Edom
and shout in triumph over Philistia."
10 Who will bring me into the fortified city?
Who will bring me victory over Edom?
11 Have you rejected us, O God?
Will you no longer march with our armies?
12 Oh, please help us against our enemies,
for all human help is useless.
13 With God's help we will do mighty things,
for he will trample down our foes.

109 *For the choir director: A psalm of David.*

1 O God, whom I praise,
don't stand silent and aloof
2 while the wicked slander me
and tell lies about me.
3 They surround me with hateful words
and fight against me for no reason.
4 I love them, but they try to destroy me with
accusations
even as I am praying for them!
5 They repay evil for good,
and hatred for my love.
6 They say,* "Get an evil person to turn against him.
Send an accuser to bring him to trial.
7 When his case comes up for judgment,
let him be pronounced guilty.
Count his prayers as sins.
8 Let his years be few;
let someone else take his position.
9 May his children become fatherless,
and his wife a widow.
10 May his children wander as beggars
and be driven from their ruined homes.
11 May creditors seize his entire estate,
and strangers take all he has earned.
12 Let no one be kind to him;
let no one pity his fatherless children.
13 May all his offspring die.
May his family name be blotted out in a single
generation.
14 May the LORD never forget the sins of his fathers;
may his mother's sins never be erased from
the record.
15 May the LORD always remember these sins,
and may his name disappear from human
memory.
16 For he refused all kindness to others;
he persecuted the poor and needy,
and he hounded the brokenhearted to death.
17 He loved to curse others;
now you curse him.
He never blessed others;
now don't you bless him.

109:6 Hebrew lacks *They say*.

KING JAMES VERSION

18 As he clothed himself with cursing like as with his garment, so let it come into his bowels like water, and like oil into his bones.

19 Let it be unto him as the garment *which* covereth him, and for a girdle wherewith he is girded continually.

20 *Let* this *be* the reward of mine adversaries from the LORD, and of them that speak evil against my soul.

21 But do thou for me, O GOD the Lord, for thy name's sake: because thy mercy *is* good, deliver thou me.

22 For I *am* poor and needy, and my heart is wounded within me.

23 I am gone like the shadow when it declineth: I am tossed up and down as the locust.

24 My knees are weak through fasting; and my flesh faileth of fatness.

25 I became also a reproach unto them: *when* they looked upon me they shaked their heads.

26 Help me, O LORD my God: O save me according to thy mercy:

27 That they may know that this *is* thy hand; *that* thou, LORD, hast done it.

28 Let them curse, but bless thou: when they arise, let them be ashamed; but let thy servant rejoice.

29 Let mine adversaries be clothed with shame, and let them cover themselves with their own confusion, as with a mantle.

30 I will greatly praise the LORD with my mouth; yea, I will praise him among the multitude.

31 For he shall stand at the right hand of the poor, to save *him* from those that condemn his soul.

110 *A Psalm of David*

1 The LORD said unto my Lord, Sit thou at my right hand, until I make thine enemies thy footstool.

2 The LORD shall send the rod of thy strength out of Zion: rule thou in the midst of thine enemies.

3 Thy people *shall be* willing in the day of thy power, in the beauties of holiness from the womb of the morning: thou hast the dew of thy youth.

4 The LORD hath sworn, and will not repent, Thou *art* a priest for ever after the order of Melchizedek.

NEW LIVING TRANSLATION

18 Cursing is as natural to him as his clothing,
or the water he drinks,
or the rich food he eats.
19 Now may his curses return and cling to him
like clothing;
may they be tied around him like a belt."
20 May those curses become the LORD's punishment
for my accusers who speak evil of me.
21 But deal well with me, O Sovereign LORD,
for the sake of your own reputation!
Rescue me
because you are so faithful and good.
22 For I am poor and needy,
and my heart is full of pain.
23 I am fading like a shadow at dusk;
I am brushed off like a locust.
24 My knees are weak from fasting,
and I am skin and bones.
25 I am a joke to people everywhere;
when they see me, they shake their heads
in scorn.
26 Help me, O LORD my God!
Save me because of your unfailing love.
27 Let them see that this is your doing,
that you yourself have done it, LORD.
28 Then let them curse me if they like,
but you will bless me!
When they attack me, they will be disgraced!
But I, your servant, will go right on rejoicing!
29 May my accusers be clothed with disgrace;
may their humiliation cover them like a cloak.
30 But I will give repeated thanks to the LORD,
praising him to everyone.
31 For he stands beside the needy,
ready to save them from those who
condemn them.

110 *A psalm of David.*

1 The LORD said to my Lord,
"Sit in the place of honor at my right hand
until I humble your enemies,
making them a footstool under your feet."
2 The LORD will extend your powerful kingdom
from Jerusalem*;
you will rule over your enemies.
3 When you go to war,
your people will serve you willingly.
You are arrayed in holy garments,
and your strength will be renewed each day
like the morning dew.
4 The LORD has taken an oath and will not break
his vow:
"You are a priest forever in the order of
Melchizedek."

110:2 Hebrew *Zion.*

KING JAMES VERSION

[5]The LORD at thy right hand shall strike through
kings in the day of his wrath.
[6]He shall judge among the heathen, he shall fill
the places with the dead bodies; he shall wound the
heads over many countries.
[7]He shall drink of the brook in the way: therefore
shall he lift up the head.

111

[1]Praise ye the LORD. I will praise the LORD
with *my* whole heart, in the assembly of the
upright, and *in* the congregation.
[2]The works of the LORD *are* great, sought out of all
them that have pleasure therein.
[3]His work *is* honourable and glorious: and his
righteousness endureth for ever.
[4]He hath made his wonderful works to be remembered: the LORD *is* gracious and full of compassion.
[5]He hath given meat unto them that fear him: he
will ever be mindful of his covenant.
[6]He hath shewed his people the power of his
works, that he may give them the heritage of the
heathen.
[7]The works of his hands *are* verity and judgment;
all his commandments *are* sure.
[8]They stand fast for ever and ever, *and are* done in
truth and uprightness.
[9]He sent redemption unto his people: he hath
commanded his covenant for ever: holy and rever-
end *is* his name.
[10]The fear of the LORD *is* the beginning of wisdom:
a good understanding have all they that do *his commandments:* his praise endureth for ever.

112

[1]Praise ye the LORD. Blessed *is* the man
that feareth the LORD, *that* delighteth
greatly in his commandments.
[2]His seed shall be mighty upon earth: the generation of the upright shall be blessed.
[3]Wealth and riches *shall be* in his house: and his
righteousness endureth for ever.
[4]Unto the upright there ariseth light in the
darkness: *he is* gracious, and full of compassion, and
righteous.
[5]A good man sheweth favour, and lendeth: he will
guide his affairs with discretion.
[6]Surely he shall not be moved for ever: the righteous shall be in everlasting remembrance.

NEW LIVING TRANSLATION

[5] The Lord stands at your right hand to
protect you.
He will strike down many kings when
his anger erupts.
[6] He will punish the nations
and fill their lands with corpses;
he will shatter heads over the whole earth.
[7] But he himself will be refreshed from brooks
along the way.
He will be victorious.

111*

[1]Praise the LORD!

I will thank the LORD with all my heart
as I meet with his godly people.
[2] How amazing are the deeds of the LORD!
All who delight in him should ponder them.
[3] Everything he does reveals his glory and majesty.
His righteousness never fails.
[4] He causes us to remember his wonderful works.
How gracious and merciful is our LORD!
[5] He gives food to those who fear him;
he always remembers his covenant.
[6] He has shown his great power to his people
by giving them the lands of other nations.
[7] All he does is just and good,
and all his commandments are trustworthy.
[8] They are forever true,
to be obeyed faithfully and with integrity.
[9] He has paid a full ransom for his people.
He has guaranteed his covenant with
them forever.
What a holy, awe-inspiring name he has!
[10] Fear of the LORD is the foundation of true wisdom.
All who obey his commandments will grow
in wisdom.

Praise him forever!

112*

[1]Praise the LORD!

How joyful are those who fear the LORD
and delight in obeying his commands.
[2] Their children will be successful everywhere;
an entire generation of godly people will be
blessed.
[3] They themselves will be wealthy,
and their good deeds will last forever.
[4] Light shines in the darkness for the godly.
They are generous, compassionate, and
righteous.
[5] Good comes to those who lend money generously
and conduct their business fairly.
[6] Such people will not be overcome by evil.
Those who are righteous will be long
remembered.

111 This psalm is a Hebrew acrostic poem; after the introductory note of praise, each line begins with a successive letter of the Hebrew alphabet.
112 This psalm is a Hebrew acrostic poem; after the introductory note of praise, each line begins with a successive letter of the Hebrew alphabet.

KING JAMES VERSION

7He shall not be afraid of evil tidings: his heart is
fixed, trusting in the LORD.
8His heart *is* established, he shall not be afraid,
until he see *his desire* upon his enemies.
9He hath dispersed, he hath given to the poor; his
righteousness endureth for ever; his horn shall be
exalted with honour.
10The wicked shall see *it,* and be grieved; he shall
gnash with his teeth, and melt away: the desire of the
wicked shall perish.

113

1Praise ye the LORD. Praise, O ye servants of
the LORD, praise the name of the LORD.
2Blessed be the name of the LORD from this time
forth and for evermore.
3From the rising of the sun unto the going down of
the same the LORD's name *is* to be praised.
4The LORD *is* high above all nations, *and* his glory
above the heavens.
5Who *is* like unto the LORD our God, who dwelleth
on high,
6Who humbleth *himself* to behold *the things that*
are in heaven, and in the earth!
7He raiseth up the poor out of the dust, *and* lifteth
the needy out of the dunghill;
8That he may set *him* with princes, *even* with the
princes of his people.
9He maketh the barren woman to keep house, *and*
to be a joyful mother of children. Praise ye the LORD.

114

1When Israel went out of Egypt, the house
of Jacob from a people of strange language;
2Judah was his sanctuary, *and* Israel his dominion.
3The sea saw *it,* and fled: Jordan was driven back.
4The mountains skipped like rams, *and* the little
hills like lambs.
5What *ailed* thee, O thou sea, that thou fleddest?
thou Jordan, *that* thou wast driven back?
6Ye mountains, *that* ye skipped like rams; *and* ye
little hills, like lambs?
7Tremble, thou earth, at the presence of the LORD,
at the presence of the God of Jacob;
8Which turned the rock *into* a standing water, the
flint into a fountain of waters.

NEW LIVING TRANSLATION

7 They do not fear bad news;
they confidently trust the LORD to care
for them.
8 They are confident and fearless
and can face their foes triumphantly.
9 They share freely and give generously to
those in need.
Their good deeds will be remembered forever.
They will have influence and honor.
10 The wicked will see this and be infuriated.
They will grind their teeth in anger;
they will slink away, their hopes thwarted.

113

1 Praise the LORD!
Yes, give praise, O servants of the LORD.
Praise the name of the LORD!
2 Blessed be the name of the LORD
now and forever.
3 Everywhere—from east to west—
praise the name of the LORD.
4 For the LORD is high above the nations;
his glory is higher than the heavens.
5 Who can be compared with the LORD our God,
who is enthroned on high?
6 He stoops to look down
on heaven and on earth.
7 He lifts the poor from the dust
and the needy from the garbage dump.
8 He sets them among princes,
even the princes of his own people!
9 He gives the childless woman a family,
making her a happy mother.
Praise the LORD!

114

1 When the Israelites escaped from
Egypt—
when the family of Jacob left that foreign land—
2 the land of Judah became God's sanctuary,
and Israel became his kingdom.

3 The Red Sea* saw them coming and hurried out
of their way!
The water of the Jordan River turned away.
4 The mountains skipped like rams,
the hills like lambs!
5 What's wrong, Red Sea, that made you hurry
out of their way?
What happened, Jordan River, that you
turned away?
6 Why, mountains, did you skip like rams?
Why, hills, like lambs?

7 Tremble, O earth, at the presence of the Lord,
at the presence of the God of Jacob.
8 He turned the rock into a pool of water;
yes, a spring of water flowed from solid rock.

114:3 Hebrew *the sea;* also in 114:5.

KING JAMES VERSION

115 1Not unto us, O LORD, not unto us, but unto
thy name give glory, for thy mercy, *and* for
thy truth's sake.
2Wherefore should the heathen say, Where *is* now
their God?
3But our God *is* in the heavens: he hath done whatsoever he hath pleased.
4Their idols *are* silver and gold, the work of men's
hands.
5They have mouths, but they speak not: eyes have
they, but they see not:
6They have ears, but they hear not: noses have
they, but they smell not:
7They have hands, but they handle not: feet have
they, but they walk not: neither speak they through
their throat.
8They that make them are like unto them; *so is*
every one that trusteth in them.
9O Israel, trust thou in the LORD: he *is* their help
and their shield.
10O house of Aaron, trust in the LORD: he *is* their
help and their shield.
11Ye that fear the LORD, trust in the LORD: he *is*
their help and their shield.
12The LORD hath been mindful of us: he will bless
us; he will bless the house of Israel; he will bless the
house of Aaron.
13He will bless them that fear the LORD, *both* small
and great.
14The LORD shall increase you more and more, you
and your children.
15Ye *are* blessed of the LORD which made heaven
and earth.
16The heaven, *even* the heavens, *are* the LORD'S:
but the earth hath he given to the children of men.
17The dead praise not the LORD, neither any that
go down into silence.
18But we will bless the LORD from this time forth
and for evermore. Praise the LORD.

116 1I love the LORD, because he hath heard my
voice *and* my supplications.
2Because he hath inclined his ear unto me, therefore will I call upon *him* as long as I live.
3The sorrows of death compassed me, and the
pains of hell gat hold upon me: I found trouble and
sorrow.
4Then called I upon the name of the LORD; O LORD,
I beseech thee, deliver my soul.
5Gracious *is* the LORD, and righteous; yea, our God
is merciful.

NEW LIVING TRANSLATION

115 1 Not to us, O LORD, not to us,
but to your name goes all the glory
for your unfailing love and faithfulness.
2 Why let the nations say,
"Where is their God?"
3 Our God is in the heavens,
and he does as he wishes.
4 Their idols are merely things of silver and gold,
shaped by human hands.
5 They have mouths but cannot speak,
and eyes but cannot see.
6 They have ears but cannot hear,
and noses but cannot smell.
7 They have hands but cannot feel,
and feet but cannot walk,
and throats but cannot make a sound.
8 And those who make idols are just like them,
as are all who trust in them.

9 O Israel, trust the LORD!
He is your helper and your shield.
10 O priests, descendants of Aaron, trust the LORD!
He is your helper and your shield.
11 All you who fear the LORD, trust the LORD!
He is your helper and your shield.
12 The LORD remembers us and will bless us.
He will bless the people of Israel
and bless the priests, the descendants
of Aaron.
13 He will bless those who fear the LORD,
both great and lowly.

14 May the LORD richly bless
both you and your children.
15 May you be blessed by the LORD,
who made heaven and earth.
16 The heavens belong to the LORD,
but he has given the earth to all humanity.
17 The dead cannot sing praises to the LORD,
for they have gone into the silence of
the grave.
18 But we can praise the LORD
both now and forever!

Praise the LORD!

116 1 I love the LORD because he hears
my voice
and my prayer for mercy.
2 Because he bends down to listen,
I will pray as long as I have breath!
3 Death wrapped its ropes around me;
the terrors of the grave* overtook me.
I saw only trouble and sorrow.
4 Then I called on the name of the LORD:
"Please, LORD, save me!"
5 How kind the LORD is! How good he is!
So merciful, this God of ours!

116:3 Hebrew *of Sheol.*

KING JAMES VERSION

6 The LORD preserveth the simple: I was brought
low, and he helped me.
7 Return unto thy rest, O my soul; for the LORD hath
dealt bountifully with thee.
8 For thou hast delivered my soul from death, mine
eyes from tears, *and* my feet from falling.
9 I will walk before the LORD in the land of the
living.
10 I believed, therefore have I spoken: I was greatly
afflicted:
11 I said in my haste, All men *are* liars.
12 What shall I render unto the LORD *for* all his
benefits toward me?
13 I will take the cup of salvation, and call upon the
name of the LORD.
14 I will pay my vows unto the LORD now in the
presence of all his people.
15 Precious in the sight of the LORD *is* the death of
his saints.
16 O LORD, truly I *am* thy servant; I *am* thy servant,
and the son of thine handmaid: thou hast loosed my
bonds.
17 I will offer to thee the sacrifice of thanksgiving,
and will call upon the name of the LORD.
18 I will pay my vows unto the LORD now in the
presence of all his people,
19 In the courts of the LORD's house, in the midst of
thee, O Jerusalem. Praise ye the LORD.

117

1 O Praise the LORD, all ye nations: praise
him, all ye people.
2 For his merciful kindness is great toward us: and
the truth of the LORD *endureth* for ever. Praise ye the
LORD.

118

1 O give thanks unto the LORD; for *he is*
good: because his mercy *endureth* for ever.
2 Let Israel now say, that his mercy *endureth* for
ever.
3 Let the house of Aaron now say, that his mercy
endureth for ever.
4 Let them now that fear the LORD say, that his
mercy *endureth* for ever.
5 I called upon the LORD in distress: the LORD
answered me, *and set me* in a large place.
6 The LORD *is* on my side; I will not fear: what can
man do unto me?
7 The LORD taketh my part with them that help
me: therefore shall I see *my desire* upon them that
hate me.
8 *It is* better to trust in the LORD than to put confidence in man.

NEW LIVING TRANSLATION

6 The LORD protects those of childlike faith;
I was facing death, and he saved me.
7 Let my soul be at rest again,
for the LORD has been good to me.
8 He has saved me from death,
my eyes from tears,
my feet from stumbling.
9 And so I walk in the LORD's presence
as I live here on earth!
10 I believed in you, so I said,
"I am deeply troubled, LORD."
11 In my anxiety I cried out to you,
"These people are all liars!"
12 What can I offer the LORD
for all he has done for me?
13 I will lift up the cup of salvation
and praise the LORD's name for saving me.
14 I will keep my promises to the LORD
in the presence of all his people.
15 The LORD cares deeply
when his loved ones die.
16 O LORD, I am your servant;
yes, I am your servant, born into your household;
you have freed me from my chains.
17 I will offer you a sacrifice of thanksgiving
and call on the name of the LORD.
18 I will fulfill my vows to the LORD
in the presence of all his people—
19 in the house of the LORD
in the heart of Jerusalem.

Praise the LORD!

117

1 Praise the LORD, all you nations.
Praise him, all you people of
the earth.
2 For he loves us with unfailing love;
the LORD's faithfulness endures forever.

Praise the LORD!

118

1 Give thanks to the LORD, for he is good!
His faithful love endures forever.

2 Let all Israel repeat:
"His faithful love endures forever."
3 Let Aaron's descendants, the priests, repeat:
"His faithful love endures forever."
4 Let all who fear the LORD repeat:
"His faithful love endures forever."
5 In my distress I prayed to the LORD,
and the LORD answered me and set me free.
6 The LORD is for me, so I will have no fear.
What can mere people do to me?
7 Yes, the LORD is for me; he will help me.
I will look in triumph at those who hate me.
8 It is better to take refuge in the LORD
than to trust in people.

KING JAMES VERSION

9 *It is* better to trust in the LORD than to put confidence in princes.
10 All nations compassed me about: but in the
name of the LORD will I destroy them.
11 They compassed me about; yea, they compassed
me about: but in the name of the LORD I will destroy
them.
12 They compassed me about like bees; they are
quenched as the fire of thorns: for in the name of the
LORD I will destroy them.
13 Thou hast thrust sore at me that I might fall: but
the LORD helped me.
14 The LORD *is* my strength and song, and is become my salvation.
15 The voice of rejoicing and salvation *is* in the tabernacles of the righteous: the right hand of the LORD
doeth valiantly.
16 The right hand of the LORD is exalted: the right
hand of the LORD doeth valiantly.
17 I shall not die, but live, and declare the works of
the LORD.
18 The LORD hath chastened me sore: but he hath
not given me over unto death.
19 Open to me the gates of righteousness: I will go
into them, *and* I will praise the LORD:
20 This gate of the LORD, into which the righteous
shall enter.
21 I will praise thee: for thou hast heard me, and art
become my salvation.
22 The stone *which* the builders refused is become
the head *stone* of the corner.
23 This is the LORD's doing; it *is* marvellous in our
eyes.
24 This *is* the day *which* the LORD hath made; we
will rejoice and be glad in it.
25 Save now, I beseech thee, O LORD: O LORD, I beseech thee, send now prosperity.
26 Blessed *be* he that cometh in the name of the
LORD: we have blessed you out of the house of the
LORD.
27 God *is* the LORD, which hath shewed us light:
bind the sacrifice with cords, *even* unto the horns of
the altar.
28 Thou *art* my God, and I will praise thee: *thou art*
my God, I will exalt thee.
29 O give thanks unto the LORD; for *he is* good: for
his mercy *endureth* for ever.

NEW LIVING TRANSLATION

9 It is better to take refuge in the LORD
than to trust in princes.
10 Though hostile nations surrounded me,
I destroyed them all with the authority
of the LORD.
11 Yes, they surrounded and attacked me,
but I destroyed them all with the authority
of the LORD.
12 They swarmed around me like bees;
they blazed against me like a crackling fire.
But I destroyed them all with the authority
of the LORD.
13 My enemies did their best to kill me,
but the LORD rescued me.
14 The LORD is my strength and my song;
he has given me victory.
15 Songs of joy and victory are sung in the camp
of the godly.
The strong right arm of the LORD has done
glorious things!
16 The strong right arm of the LORD is raised
in triumph.
The strong right arm of the LORD has done
glorious things!
17 I will not die; instead, I will live
to tell what the LORD has done.
18 The LORD has punished me severely,
but he did not let me die.

19 Open for me the gates where the righteous enter,
and I will go in and thank the LORD.
20 These gates lead to the presence of the LORD,
and the godly enter there.
21 I thank you for answering my prayer
and giving me victory!

22 The stone that the builders rejected
has now become the cornerstone.
23 This is the LORD's doing,
and it is wonderful to see.
24 This is the day the LORD has made.
We will rejoice and be glad in it.
25 Please, LORD, please save us.
Please, LORD, please give us success.
26 Bless the one who comes in the name
of the LORD.
We bless you from the house of the LORD.
27 The LORD is God, shining upon us.
Take the sacrifice and bind it with cords
on the altar.
28 You are my God, and I will praise you!
You are my God, and I will exalt you!

29 Give thanks to the LORD, for he is good!
His faithful love endures forever.

KING JAMES VERSION

119

ALEPH

[1]Blessed *are* the undefiled in the way, who walk in
the law of the LORD.
[2]Blessed *are* they that keep his testimonies, *and*
that seek him with the whole heart.
[3]They also do no iniquity: they walk in his ways.
[4]Thou hast commanded *us* to keep thy precepts
diligently.
[5]O that my ways were directed to keep thy statutes!
[6]Then shall I not be ashamed, when I have respect
unto all thy commandments.
[7]I will praise thee with uprightness of heart, when
I shall have learned thy righteous judgments.
[8]I will keep thy statutes: O forsake me not utterly.

BETH

[9]Wherewithal shall a young man cleanse his way?
by taking heed *thereto* according to thy word.
[10]With my whole heart have I sought thee: O let
me not wander from thy commandments.
[11]Thy word have I hid in mine heart, that I might
not sin against thee.
[12]Blessed *art* thou, O LORD: teach me thy statutes.
[13]With my lips have I declared all the judgments
of thy mouth.
[14]I have rejoiced in the way of thy testimonies, as
much as in all riches.
[15]I will meditate in thy precepts, and have respect
unto thy ways.
[16]I will delight myself in thy statutes: I will not forget thy word.

GIMEL

[17]Deal bountifully with thy servant, *that* I may live,
and keep thy word.
[18]Open thou mine eyes, that I may behold wondrous things out of thy law.
[19]I *am* a stranger in the earth: hide not thy commandments from me.
[20]My soul breaketh for the longing *that it hath*
unto thy judgments at all times.
[21]Thou hast rebuked the proud *that are* cursed,
which do err from thy commandments.
[22]Remove from me reproach and contempt; for I
have kept thy testimonies.
[23]Princes also did sit *and* speak against me: *but*
thy servant did meditate in thy statutes.
[24]Thy testimonies also *are* my delight *and* my
counsellors.

NEW LIVING TRANSLATION

119*

Aleph

1 Joyful are people of integrity,
who follow the instructions of the LORD.
2 Joyful are those who obey his laws
and search for him with all their hearts.
3 They do not compromise with evil,
and they walk only in his paths.
4 You have charged us
to keep your commandments carefully.
5 Oh, that my actions would consistently
reflect your decrees!
6 Then I will not be ashamed
when I compare my life with your commands.
7 As I learn your righteous regulations,
I will thank you by living as I should!
8 I will obey your decrees.
Please don't give up on me!

Beth

9 How can a young person stay pure?
By obeying your word.
10 I have tried hard to find you—
don't let me wander from your commands.
11 I have hidden your word in my heart,
that I might not sin against you.
12 I praise you, O LORD;
teach me your decrees.
13 I have recited aloud
all the regulations you have given us.
14 I have rejoiced in your laws
as much as in riches.
15 I will study your commandments
and reflect on your ways.
16 I will delight in your decrees
and not forget your word.

Gimel

17 Be good to your servant,
that I may live and obey your word.
18 Open my eyes to see
the wonderful truths in your instructions.
19 I am only a foreigner in the land.
Don't hide your commands from me!
20 I am always overwhelmed
with a desire for your regulations.
21 You rebuke the arrogant;
those who wander from your commands
are cursed.
22 Don't let them scorn and insult me,
for I have obeyed your laws.
23 Even princes sit and speak against me,
but I will meditate on your decrees.
24 Your laws please me;
they give me wise advice.

119 This psalm is a Hebrew acrostic poem; there are twenty-two stanzas, one for each successive letter of the Hebrew alphabet. Each of the eight verses within each stanza begins with the Hebrew letter named in its heading.

KING JAMES VERSION

DALETH

25 My soul cleaveth unto the dust: quicken thou me
according to thy word.
26 I have declared my ways, and thou heardest me:
teach me thy statutes.
27 Make me to understand the way of thy precepts:
so shall I talk of thy wondrous works.
28 My soul melteth for heaviness: strengthen thou
me according unto thy word.
29 Remove from me the way of lying: and grant me
thy law graciously.
30 I have chosen the way of truth: thy judgments
have I laid *before me*.
31 I have stuck unto thy testimonies: O LORD, put
me not to shame.
32 I will run the way of thy commandments, when
thou shalt enlarge my heart.

HE

33 Teach me, O LORD, the way of thy statutes; and
I shall keep it *unto* the end.
34 Give me understanding, and I shall keep thy law;
yea, I shall observe it with *my* whole heart.
35 Make me to go in the path of thy commandments; for therein do I delight.
36 Incline my heart unto thy testimonies, and not
to covetousness.
37 Turn away mine eyes from beholding vanity;
and quicken thou me in thy way.
38 Stablish thy word unto thy servant, who *is devoted* to thy fear.
39 Turn away my reproach which I fear: for thy
judgments *are* good.
40 Behold, I have longed after thy precepts: quicken
me in thy righteousness.

VAU

41 Let thy mercies come also unto me, O LORD, *even*
thy salvation, according to thy word.
42 So shall I have wherewith to answer him that
reproacheth me: for I trust in thy word.
43 And take not the word of truth utterly out of my
mouth; for I have hoped in thy judgments.
44 So shall I keep thy law continually for ever and
ever.
45 And I will walk at liberty: for I seek thy precepts.
46 I will speak of thy testimonies also before kings,
and will not be ashamed.
47 And I will delight myself in thy commandments,
which I have loved.
48 My hands also will I lift up unto thy commandments, which I have loved; and I will meditate in thy
statutes.

NEW LIVING TRANSLATION

Daleth

25 I lie in the dust;
revive me by your word.
26 I told you my plans, and you answered.
Now teach me your decrees.
27 Help me understand the meaning of your
commandments,
and I will meditate on your wonderful deeds.
28 I weep with sorrow;
encourage me by your word.
29 Keep me from lying to myself;
give me the privilege of knowing your
instructions.
30 I have chosen to be faithful;
I have determined to live by your regulations.
31 I cling to your laws.
LORD, don't let me be put to shame!
32 I will pursue your commands,
for you expand my understanding.

He

33 Teach me your decrees, O LORD;
I will keep them to the end.
34 Give me understanding and I will obey your
instructions;
I will put them into practice with all my heart.
35 Make me walk along the path of your commands,
for that is where my happiness is found.
36 Give me an eagerness for your laws
rather than a love for money!
37 Turn my eyes from worthless things,
and give me life through your word.*
38 Reassure me of your promise,
made to those who fear you.
39 Help me abandon my shameful ways;
for your regulations are good.
40 I long to obey your commandments!
Renew my life with your goodness.

Waw

41 LORD, give me your unfailing love,
the salvation that you promised me.
42 Then I can answer those who taunt me,
for I trust in your word.
43 Do not snatch your word of truth from me,
for your regulations are my only hope.
44 I will keep on obeying your instructions
forever and ever.
45 I will walk in freedom,
for I have devoted myself to your
commandments.
46 I will speak to kings about your laws,
and I will not be ashamed.
47 How I delight in your commands!
How I love them!
48 I honor and love your commands.
I meditate on your decrees.

119:37 Some manuscripts read *in your ways*.

KING JAMES VERSION

ZAIN

49 Remember the word unto thy servant, upon which thou hast caused me to hope.

50 This *is* my comfort in my affliction: for thy word hath quickened me.

51 The proud have had me greatly in derision: *yet* have I not declined from thy law.

52 I remembered thy judgments of old, O LORD; and have comforted myself.

53 Horror hath taken hold upon me because of the wicked that forsake thy law.

54 Thy statutes have been my songs in the house of my pilgrimage.

55 I have remembered thy name, O LORD, in the night, and have kept thy law.

56 This I had, because I kept thy precepts.

CHETH

57 *Thou art* my portion, O LORD: I have said that I would keep thy words.

58 I intreated thy favour with *my* whole heart: be merciful unto me according to thy word.

59 I thought on my ways, and turned my feet unto thy testimonies.

60 I made haste, and delayed not to keep thy commandments.

61 The bands of the wicked have robbed me: *but* I have not forgotten thy law.

62 At midnight I will rise to give thanks unto thee because of thy righteous judgments.

63 I *am* a companion of all *them* that fear thee, and of them that keep thy precepts.

64 The earth, O LORD, is full of thy mercy: teach me thy statutes.

TETH

65 Thou hast dealt well with thy servant, O LORD, according unto thy word.

66 Teach me good judgment and knowledge: for I have believed thy commandments.

67 Before I was afflicted I went astray: but now have I kept thy word.

68 Thou *art* good, and doest good; teach me thy statutes.

69 The proud have forged a lie against me: *but* I will keep thy precepts with *my* whole heart.

70 Their heart is as fat as grease; *but* I delight in thy law.

71 *It is* good for me that I have been afflicted; that I might learn thy statutes.

72 The law of thy mouth *is* better unto me than thousands of gold and silver.

NEW LIVING TRANSLATION

Zayin

49 Remember your promise to me;
it is my only hope.
50 Your promise revives me;
it comforts me in all my troubles.
51 The proud hold me in utter contempt,
but I do not turn away from your instructions.
52 I meditate on your age-old regulations;
O LORD, they comfort me.
53 I become furious with the wicked,
because they reject your instructions.
54 Your decrees have been the theme of my songs
wherever I have lived.
55 I reflect at night on who you are, O LORD;
therefore, I obey your instructions.
56 This is how I spend my life:
obeying your commandments.

Heth

57 LORD, you are mine!
I promise to obey your words!
58 With all my heart I want your blessings.
Be merciful as you promised.
59 I pondered the direction of my life,
and I turned to follow your laws.
60 I will hurry, without delay,
to obey your commands.
61 Evil people try to drag me into sin,
but I am firmly anchored to your
instructions.
62 I rise at midnight to thank you
for your just regulations.
63 I am a friend to anyone who fears you—
anyone who obeys your commandments.
64 O LORD, your unfailing love fills the earth;
teach me your decrees.

Teth

65 You have done many good things for me, LORD,
just as you promised.
66 I believe in your commands;
now teach me good judgment and knowledge.
67 I used to wander off until you disciplined me;
but now I closely follow your word.
68 You are good and do only good;
teach me your decrees.
69 Arrogant people smear me with lies,
but in truth I obey your commandments
with all my heart.
70 Their hearts are dull and stupid,
but I delight in your instructions.
71 My suffering was good for me,
for it taught me to pay attention to
your decrees.
72 Your instructions are more valuable to me
than millions in gold and silver.

JOD

73 Thy hands have made me and fashioned me: give me understanding, that I may learn thy commandments.

74 They that fear thee will be glad when they see me; because I have hoped in thy word.

75 I know, O LORD, that thy judgments *are* right, and *that* thou in faithfulness hast afflicted me.

76 Let, I pray thee, thy merciful kindness be for my comfort, according to thy word unto thy servant.

77 Let thy tender mercies come unto me, that I may live: for thy law *is* my delight.

78 Let the proud be ashamed; for they dealt perversely with me without a cause: *but* I will meditate in thy precepts.

79 Let those that fear thee turn unto me, and those that have known thy testimonies.

80 Let my heart be sound in thy statutes; that I be not ashamed.

CAPH

81 My soul fainteth for thy salvation: *but* I hope in thy word.

82 Mine eyes fail for thy word, saying, When wilt thou comfort me?

83 For I am become like a bottle in the smoke; *yet* do I not forget thy statutes.

84 How many *are* the days of thy servant? when wilt thou execute judgment on them that persecute me?

85 The proud have digged pits for me, which *are* not after thy law.

86 All thy commandments *are* faithful: they persecute me wrongfully; help thou me.

87 They had almost consumed me upon earth; but I forsook not thy precepts.

88 Quicken me after thy lovingkindness; so shall I keep the testimony of thy mouth.

LAMED

89 For ever, O LORD, thy word is settled in heaven.

90 Thy faithfulness *is* unto all generations: thou hast established the earth, and it abideth.

91 They continue this day according to thine ordinances: for all *are* thy servants.

92 Unless thy law *had been* my delights, I should then have perished in mine affliction.

93 I will never forget thy precepts: for with them thou hast quickened me.

94 I *am* thine, save me; for I have sought thy precepts.

Yodh

73 You made me; you created me.
Now give me the sense to follow your
commands.
74 May all who fear you find in me a cause for joy,
for I have put my hope in your word.
75 I know, O LORD, that your regulations are fair;
you disciplined me because I needed it.
76 Now let your unfailing love comfort me,
just as you promised me, your servant.
77 Surround me with your tender mercies
so I may live,
for your instructions are my delight.
78 Bring disgrace upon the arrogant people
who lied about me;
meanwhile, I will concentrate on your
commandments.
79 Let me be united with all who fear you,
with those who know your laws.
80 May I be blameless in keeping your decrees;
then I will never be ashamed.

Kaph

81 I am worn out waiting for your rescue,
but I have put my hope in your word.
82 My eyes are straining to see your promises
come true.
When will you comfort me?
83 I am shriveled like a wineskin in the smoke,
but I have not forgotten to obey your decrees.
84 How long must I wait?
When will you punish those who persecute me?
85 These arrogant people who hate your
instructions
have dug deep pits to trap me.
86 All your commands are trustworthy.
Protect me from those who hunt me down
without cause.
87 They almost finished me off,
but I refused to abandon your
commandments.
88 In your unfailing love, spare my life;
then I can continue to obey your laws.

Lamedh

89 Your eternal word, O LORD,
stands firm in heaven.
90 Your faithfulness extends to every generation,
as enduring as the earth you created.
91 Your regulations remain true to this day,
for everything serves your plans.
92 If your instructions hadn't sustained me with joy,
I would have died in my misery.
93 I will never forget your commandments,
for by them you give me life.
94 I am yours; rescue me!
For I have worked hard at obeying your
commandments.

KING JAMES VERSION

95 The wicked have waited for me to destroy me: *but* I will consider thy testimonies.

96 I have seen an end of all perfection: *but* thy commandment *is* exceeding broad.

MEM

97 O how love I thy law! it *is* my meditation all the day.

98 Thou through thy commandments hast made me wiser than mine enemies: for they *are* ever with me.

99 I have more understanding than all my teachers: for thy testimonies *are* my meditation.

100 I understand more than the ancients, because I keep thy precepts.

101 I have refrained my feet from every evil way, that I might keep thy word.

102 I have not departed from thy judgments: for thou hast taught me.

103 How sweet are thy words unto my taste! *yea, sweeter* than honey to my mouth!

104 Through thy precepts I get understanding: therefore I hate every false way.

NUN

105 Thy word *is* a lamp unto my feet, and a light unto my path.

106 I have sworn, and I will perform *it,* that I will keep thy righteous judgments.

107 I am afflicted very much: quicken me, O LORD, according unto thy word.

108 Accept, I beseech thee, the freewill offerings of my mouth, O LORD, and teach me thy judgments.

109 My soul *is* continually in my hand: yet do I not forget thy law.

110 The wicked have laid a snare for me: yet I erred not from thy precepts.

111 Thy testimonies have I taken as an heritage for ever: for they *are* the rejoicing of my heart.

112 I have inclined mine heart to perform thy statutes alway, *even unto* the end.

SAMECH

113 I hate *vain* thoughts: but thy law do I love.

114 Thou *art* my hiding place and my shield: I hope in thy word.

115 Depart from me, ye evildoers: for I will keep the commandments of my God.

116 Uphold me according unto thy word, that I may live: and let me not be ashamed of my hope.

117 Hold thou me up, and I shall be safe: and I will have respect unto thy statutes continually.

118 Thou hast trodden down all them that err from thy statutes: for their deceit *is* falsehood.

119 Thou puttest away all the wicked of the earth *like* dross: therefore I love thy testimonies.

NEW LIVING TRANSLATION

95 Though the wicked hide along the way to kill me,
I will quietly keep my mind on your laws.
96 Even perfection has its limits,
but your commands have no limit.

Mem

97 Oh, how I love your instructions!
I think about them all day long.
98 Your commands make me wiser than
my enemies,
for they are my constant guide.
99 Yes, I have more insight than my teachers,
for I am always thinking of your laws.
100 I am even wiser than my elders,
for I have kept your commandments.
101 I have refused to walk on any evil path,
so that I may remain obedient to your word.
102 I haven't turned away from your regulations,
for you have taught me well.
103 How sweet your words taste to me;
they are sweeter than honey.
104 Your commandments give me understanding;
no wonder I hate every false way of life.

Nun

105 Your word is a lamp to guide my feet
and a light for my path.
106 I've promised it once, and I'll promise it again:
I will obey your righteous regulations.
107 I have suffered much, O LORD;
restore my life again as you promised.
108 LORD, accept my offering of praise,
and teach me your regulations.
109 My life constantly hangs in the balance,
but I will not stop obeying your instructions.
110 The wicked have set their traps for me,
but I will not turn from your commandments.
111 Your laws are my treasure;
they are my heart's delight.
112 I am determined to keep your decrees
to the very end.

Samekh

113 I hate those with divided loyalties,
but I love your instructions.
114 You are my refuge and my shield;
your word is my source of hope.
115 Get out of my life, you evil-minded people,
for I intend to obey the commands of my God.
116 LORD, sustain me as you promised, that I may live!
Do not let my hope be crushed.
117 Sustain me, and I will be rescued;
then I will meditate continually on your decrees.
118 But you have rejected all who stray from
your decrees.
They are only fooling themselves.
119 You skim off the wicked of the earth like scum;
no wonder I love to obey your laws!

120 My flesh trembleth for fear of thee; and I am
afraid of thy judgments.

AIN

121 I have done judgment and justice: leave me not
to mine oppressors.
122 Be surety for thy servant for good: let not the
proud oppress me.
123 Mine eyes fail for thy salvation, and for the
word of thy righteousness.
124 Deal with thy servant according unto thy mercy,
and teach me thy statutes.
125 I *am* thy servant; give me understanding, that I
may know thy testimonies.
126 *It is* time for *thee,* LORD, to work: *for* they have
made void thy law.
127 Therefore I love thy commandments above
gold; yea, above fine gold.
128 Therefore I esteem all *thy* precepts *concerning*
all *things to be* right; *and* I hate every false way.

PE

129 Thy testimonies *are* wonderful: therefore doth
my soul keep them.
130 The entrance of thy words giveth light; it giveth
understanding unto the simple.
131 I opened my mouth, and panted: for I longed
for thy commandments.
132 Look thou upon me, and be merciful unto me,
as thou usest to do unto those that love thy name.
133 Order my steps in thy word: and let not any iniquity have dominion over me.
134 Deliver me from the oppression of man: so will
I keep thy precepts.
135 Make thy face to shine upon thy servant; and
teach me thy statutes.
136 Rivers of waters run down mine eyes, because
they keep not thy law.

TZADDI

137 Righteous *art* thou, O LORD, and upright *are* thy
judgments.
138 Thy testimonies *that* thou hast commanded
are righteous and very faithful.
139 My zeal hath consumed me, because mine enemies have forgotten thy words.
140 Thy word *is* very pure: therefore thy servant
loveth it.
141 I *am* small and despised: *yet* do not I forget thy
precepts.
142 Thy righteousness *is* an everlasting righteousness, and thy law *is* the truth.
143 Trouble and anguish have taken hold on me:
yet thy commandments *are* my delights.
144 The righteousness of thy testimonies *is* everlasting: give me understanding, and I shall live.

120 I tremble in fear of you;
I stand in awe of your regulations.

Ayin

121 Don't leave me to the mercy of my enemies,
for I have done what is just and right.
122 Please guarantee a blessing for me.
Don't let the arrogant oppress me!
123 My eyes strain to see your rescue,
to see the truth of your promise fulfilled.
124 I am your servant; deal with me in unfailing love,
and teach me your decrees.
125 Give discernment to me, your servant;
then I will understand your laws.
126 LORD, it is time for you to act,
for these evil people have violated your
instructions.
127 Truly, I love your commands
more than gold, even the finest gold.
128 Each of your commandments is right.
That is why I hate every false way.

Pe

129 Your laws are wonderful.
No wonder I obey them!
130 The teaching of your word gives light,
so even the simple can understand.
131 I pant with expectation,
longing for your commands.
132 Come and show me your mercy,
as you do for all who love your name.
133 Guide my steps by your word,
so I will not be overcome by evil.
134 Ransom me from the oppression of evil people;
then I can obey your commandments.
135 Look upon me with love;
teach me your decrees.
136 Rivers of tears gush from my eyes
because people disobey your instructions.

Tsadhe

137 O LORD, you are righteous,
and your regulations are fair.
138 Your laws are perfect
and completely trustworthy.
139 I am overwhelmed with indignation,
for my enemies have disregarded your words.
140 Your promises have been thoroughly tested;
that is why I love them so much.
141 I am insignificant and despised,
but I don't forget your commandments.
142 Your justice is eternal,
and your instructions are perfectly true.
143 As pressure and stress bear down on me,
I find joy in your commands.
144 Your laws are always right;
help me to understand them so I may live.

KING JAMES VERSION

KOPH

145 I cried with *my* whole heart; hear me, O LORD: I
will keep thy statutes.
146 I cried unto thee; save me, and I shall keep thy
testimonies.
147 I prevented the dawning of the morning, and
cried: I hoped in thy word.
148 Mine eyes prevent the *night* watches, that I
might meditate in thy word.
149 Hear my voice according unto thy lovingkindness: O LORD, quicken me according to thy
judgment.
150 They draw nigh that follow after mischief: they
are far from thy law.
151 Thou *art* near, O LORD; and all thy commandments *are* truth.
152 Concerning thy testimonies, I have known of
old that thou hast founded them for ever.

RESH

153 Consider mine affliction, and deliver me: for I
do not forget thy law.
154 Plead my cause, and deliver me: quicken me according to thy word.
155 Salvation *is* far from the wicked: for they seek
not thy statutes.
156 Great *are* thy tender mercies, O LORD: quicken
me according to thy judgments.
157 Many *are* my persecutors and mine enemies;
yet do I not decline from thy testimonies.
158 I beheld the transgressors, and was grieved;
because they kept not thy word.
159 Consider how I love thy precepts: quicken me,
O LORD, according to thy lovingkindness.
160 Thy word *is* true *from* the beginning: and every
one of thy righteous judgments *endureth* for ever.

SCHIN

161 Princes have persecuted me without a cause:
but my heart standeth in awe of thy word.
162 I rejoice at thy word, as one that findeth great
spoil.
163 I hate and abhor lying: *but* thy law do I love.
164 Seven times a day do I praise thee because of
thy righteous judgments.
165 Great peace have they which love thy law: and
nothing shall offend them.
166 LORD, I have hoped for thy salvation, and done
thy commandments.
167 My soul hath kept thy testimonies; and I love
them exceedingly.
168 I have kept thy precepts and thy testimonies:
for all my ways *are* before thee.

NEW LIVING TRANSLATION

Qoph

145 I pray with all my heart; answer me, LORD!
I will obey your decrees.
146 I cry out to you; rescue me,
that I may obey your laws.
147 I rise early, before the sun is up;
I cry out for help and put my hope in
your words.
148 I stay awake through the night,
thinking about your promise.
149 In your faithful love, O LORD, hear my cry;
let me be revived by following your
regulations.
150 Lawless people are coming to attack me;
they live far from your instructions.
151 But you are near, O LORD,
and all your commands are true.
152 I have known from my earliest days
that your laws will last forever.

Resh

153 Look upon my suffering and rescue me,
for I have not forgotten your instructions.
154 Argue my case; take my side!
Protect my life as you promised.
155 The wicked are far from rescue,
for they do not bother with your decrees.
156 LORD, how great is your mercy;
let me be revived by following your
regulations.
157 Many persecute and trouble me,
yet I have not swerved from your laws.
158 Seeing these traitors makes me sick at heart,
because they care nothing for your word.
159 See how I love your commandments, LORD.
Give back my life because of your
unfailing love.
160 The very essence of your words is truth;
all your just regulations will stand forever.

Shin

161 Powerful people harass me without cause,
but my heart trembles only at your word.
162 I rejoice in your word
like one who discovers a great treasure.
163 I hate and abhor all falsehood,
but I love your instructions.
164 I will praise you seven times a day
because all your regulations are just.
165 Those who love your instructions have
great peace
and do not stumble.
166 I long for your rescue, LORD,
so I have obeyed your commands.
167 I have obeyed your laws,
for I love them very much.
168 Yes, I obey your commandments and laws
because you know everything I do.

TAU

169 Let my cry come near before thee, O LORD: give me understanding according to thy word.

170 Let my supplication come before thee: deliver me according to thy word.

171 My lips shall utter praise, when thou hast taught me thy statutes.

172 My tongue shall speak of thy word: for all thy commandments *are* righteousness.

173 Let thine hand help me; for I have chosen thy precepts.

174 I have longed for thy salvation, O LORD; and thy law *is* my delight.

175 Let my soul live, and it shall praise thee; and let thy judgments help me.

176 I have gone astray like a lost sheep; seek thy servant; for I do not forget thy commandments.

120 *A Song of degrees*

1 In my distress I cried unto the LORD, and he heard me.

2 Deliver my soul, O LORD, from lying lips, *and* from a deceitful tongue.

3 What shall be given unto thee? or what shall be done unto thee, thou false tongue?

4 Sharp arrows of the mighty, with coals of juniper.

5 Woe is me, that I sojourn in Mesech, *that* I dwell in the tents of Kedar!

6 My soul hath long dwelt with him that hateth peace.

7 I *am for* peace: but when I speak, they *are* for war.

121 *A Song of degrees*

1 I will lift up mine eyes unto the hills, from whence cometh my help.

2 My help *cometh* from the LORD, which made heaven and earth.

3 He will not suffer thy foot to be moved: he that keepeth thee will not slumber.

4 Behold, he that keepeth Israel shall neither slumber nor sleep.

5 The LORD *is* thy keeper: the LORD *is* thy shade upon thy right hand.

6 The sun shall not smite thee by day, nor the moon by night.

7 The LORD shall preserve thee from all evil: he shall preserve thy soul.

Taw

169 O LORD, listen to my cry;
give me the discerning mind you promised.
170 Listen to my prayer;
rescue me as you promised.
171 Let praise flow from my lips,
for you have taught me your decrees.
172 Let my tongue sing about your word,
for all your commands are right.
173 Give me a helping hand,
for I have chosen to follow your commandments.
174 O LORD, I have longed for your rescue,
and your instructions are my delight.
175 Let me live so I can praise you,
and may your regulations help me.
176 I have wandered away like a lost sheep;
come and find me,
for I have not forgotten your commands.

120 *A song for pilgrims ascending to Jerusalem.*

1 I took my troubles to the LORD;
I cried out to him, and he answered my prayer.
2 Rescue me, O LORD, from liars
and from all deceitful people.
3 O deceptive tongue, what will God do to you?
How will he increase your punishment?
4 You will be pierced with sharp arrows
and burned with glowing coals.

5 How I suffer in far-off Meshech.
It pains me to live in distant Kedar.
6 I am tired of living
among people who hate peace.
7 I search for peace;
but when I speak of peace, they want war!

121 *A song for pilgrims ascending to Jerusalem.*

1 I look up to the mountains—
does my help come from there?
2 My help comes from the LORD,
who made heaven and earth!

3 He will not let you stumble;
the one who watches over you will not slumber.
4 Indeed, he who watches over Israel
never slumbers or sleeps.
5 The LORD himself watches over you!
The LORD stands beside you as your protective shade.
6 The sun will not harm you by day,
nor the moon at night.
7 The LORD keeps you from all harm
and watches over your life.

KING JAMES VERSION

8 The LORD shall preserve thy going out and thy
coming in from this time forth, and even for evermore.

122 *A Song of degrees of David*

1 I was glad when they said unto me, Let us go into
the house of the LORD.
2 Our feet shall stand within thy gates, O Jerusalem.
3 Jerusalem is builded as a city that is compact
together:
4 Whither the tribes go up, the tribes of the LORD,
unto the testimony of Israel, to give thanks unto the
name of the LORD.
5 For there are set thrones of judgment, the thrones
of the house of David.
6 Pray for the peace of Jerusalem: they shall prosper that love thee.
7 Peace be within thy walls, *and* prosperity within
thy palaces.
8 For my brethren and companions' sakes, I will
now say, Peace *be* within thee.
9 Because of the house of the LORD our God I will
seek thy good.

123 *A Song of degrees*

1 Unto thee lift I up mine eyes, O thou that dwellest
in the heavens.
2 Behold, as the eyes of servants *look* unto the hand
of their masters, *and* as the eyes of a maiden unto the
hand of her mistress; so our eyes *wait* upon the LORD
our God, until that he have mercy upon us.
3 Have mercy upon us, O LORD, have mercy upon
us: for we are exceedingly filled with contempt.
4 Our soul is exceedingly filled with the scorning
of those that are at ease, *and* with the contempt of
the proud.

124 *A Song of degrees of David*

1 If *it had not been* the LORD who was on our side,
now may Israel say;
2 If *it had not been* the LORD who was on our side,
when men rose up against us:
3 Then they had swallowed us up quick, when their
wrath was kindled against us:
4 Then the waters had overwhelmed us, the stream
had gone over our soul:
5 Then the proud waters had gone over our soul.

NEW LIVING TRANSLATION

8 The LORD keeps watch over you as you come
and go,
both now and forever.

122 *A song for pilgrims ascending to Jerusalem. A psalm of David.*

1 I was glad when they said to me,
"Let us go to the house of the LORD."
2 And now here we are,
standing inside your gates, O Jerusalem.
3 Jerusalem is a well-built city;
its seamless walls cannot be breached.
4 All the tribes of Israel—the LORD's people—
make their pilgrimage here.
They come to give thanks to the name
of the LORD,
as the law requires of Israel.
5 Here stand the thrones where judgment is given,
the thrones of the dynasty of David.

6 Pray for peace in Jerusalem.
May all who love this city prosper.
7 O Jerusalem, may there be peace within
your walls
and prosperity in your palaces.
8 For the sake of my family and friends, I will say,
"May you have peace."
9 For the sake of the house of the LORD our God,
I will seek what is best for you, O Jerusalem.

123 *A song for pilgrims ascending to Jerusalem.*

1 I lift my eyes to you,
O God, enthroned in heaven.
2 We keep looking to the LORD our God for
his mercy,
just as servants keep their eyes on their master,
as a slave girl watches her mistress for the
slightest signal.
3 Have mercy on us, LORD, have mercy,
for we have had our fill of contempt.
4 We have had more than our fill of the scoffing
of the proud
and the contempt of the arrogant.

124 *A song for pilgrims ascending to Jerusalem. A psalm of David.*

1 What if the LORD had not been on our side?
Let all Israel repeat:
2 What if the LORD had not been on our side
when people attacked us?
3 They would have swallowed us alive
in their burning anger.
4 The waters would have engulfed us;
a torrent would have overwhelmed us.
5 Yes, the raging waters of their fury
would have overwhelmed our very lives.

KING JAMES VERSION

6 Blessed *be* the LORD, who hath not given us *as* a
prey to their teeth.
7 Our soul is escaped as a bird out of the snare of
the fowlers: the snare is broken, and we are escaped.
8 Our help *is* in the name of the LORD, who made
heaven and earth.

125 *A Song of degrees*

1 They that trust in the LORD *shall be* as mount
Zion, *which* cannot be removed, *but* abideth for ever.
2 As the mountains *are* round about Jerusalem, so
the LORD *is* round about his people from henceforth
even for ever.
3 For the rod of the wicked shall not rest upon the
lot of the righteous; lest the righteous put forth their
hands unto iniquity.
4 Do good, O LORD, unto *those that be* good, and *to*
them that are upright in their hearts.
5 As for such as turn aside unto their crooked ways,
the LORD shall lead them forth with the workers of
iniquity: *but* peace *shall be* upon Israel.

126 *A Song of degrees*

1 When the LORD turned again the captivity of
Zion, we were like them that dream.
2 Then was our mouth filled with laughter, and our
tongue with singing: then said they among the heathen, The LORD hath done great things for them.
3 The LORD hath done great things for us; *whereof*
we are glad.
4 Turn again our captivity, O LORD, as the streams
in the south.
5 They that sow in tears shall reap in joy.
6 He that goeth forth and weepeth, bearing precious seed, shall doubtless come again with rejoicing, bringing his sheaves *with him.*

127 *A Song of degrees for Solomon*

1 Except the LORD build the house, they labour in
vain that build it: except the LORD keep the city, the
watchman waketh *but* in vain.
2 *It is* vain for you to rise up early, to sit up late, to
eat the bread of sorrows: *for* so he giveth his beloved
sleep.

NEW LIVING TRANSLATION

6 Praise the LORD,
who did not let their teeth tear us apart!
7 We escaped like a bird from a hunter's trap.
The trap is broken, and we are free!
8 Our help is from the LORD,
who made heaven and earth.

125 *A song for pilgrims ascending to Jerusalem.*

1 Those who trust in the LORD are as secure
as Mount Zion;
they will not be defeated but will endure
forever.
2 Just as the mountains surround Jerusalem,
so the LORD surrounds his people, both now
and forever.
3 The wicked will not rule the land of the godly,
for then the godly might be tempted to
do wrong.
4 O LORD, do good to those who are good,
whose hearts are in tune with you.
5 But banish those who turn to crooked ways,
O LORD.
Take them away with those who do evil.

May Israel have peace!

126 *A song for pilgrims ascending to Jerusalem.*

1 When the LORD brought back his exiles
to Jerusalem,*
it was like a dream!
2 We were filled with laughter,
and we sang for joy.
And the other nations said,
"What amazing things the LORD has done
for them."
3 Yes, the LORD has done amazing things for us!
What joy!

4 Restore our fortunes, LORD,
as streams renew the desert.
5 Those who plant in tears
will harvest with shouts of joy.
6 They weep as they go to plant their seed,
but they sing as they return with the harvest.

127 *A song for pilgrims ascending to Jerusalem. A psalm of Solomon.*

1 Unless the LORD builds a house,
the work of the builders is wasted.
Unless the LORD protects a city,
guarding it with sentries will do no good.
2 It is useless for you to work so hard
from early morning until late at night,
anxiously working for food to eat;
for God gives rest to his loved ones.

126:1 Hebrew *Zion.*

KING JAMES VERSION

3 Lo, children *are* an heritage of the LORD: *and* the
fruit of the womb *is his* reward.
4 As arrows *are* in the hand of a mighty man; so *are*
children of the youth.
5 Happy *is* the man that hath his quiver full of
them: they shall not be ashamed, but they shall speak
with the enemies in the gate.

128 *A Song of degrees*

1 Blessed *is* every one that feareth the LORD; that
walketh in his ways.
2 For thou shalt eat the labour of thine hands:
happy *shalt* thou *be*, and *it shall be* well with thee.
3 Thy wife *shall be* as a fruitful vine by the sides of
thine house: thy children like olive plants round
about thy table.
4 Behold, that thus shall the man be blessed that
feareth the LORD.
5 The LORD shall bless thee out of Zion: and thou
shalt see the good of Jerusalem all the days of thy life.
6 Yea, thou shalt see thy children's children, *and*
peace upon Israel.

129 *A Song of degrees*

1 Many a time have they afflicted me from my
youth, may Israel now say:
2 Many a time have they afflicted me from my
youth: yet they have not prevailed against me.
3 The plowers plowed upon my back: they made
long their furrows.
4 The LORD *is* righteous: he hath cut asunder the
cords of the wicked.
5 Let them all be confounded and turned back that
hate Zion.
6 Let them be as the grass *upon* the housetops,
which withereth afore it groweth up:
7 Wherewith the mower filleth not his hand; nor
he that bindeth sheaves his bosom.
8 Neither do they which go by say, The blessing of
the LORD *be* upon you: we bless you in the name of
the LORD.

130 *A Song of degrees*

1 Out of the depths have I cried unto thee, O LORD.

NEW LIVING TRANSLATION

3 Children are a gift from the LORD;
they are a reward from him.
4 Children born to a young man
are like arrows in a warrior's hands.
5 How joyful is the man whose quiver is full of them!
He will not be put to shame when he confronts
his accusers at the city gates.

128 *A song for pilgrims ascending to Jerusalem.*

1 How joyful are those who fear the LORD—
all who follow his ways!
2 You will enjoy the fruit of your labor.
How joyful and prosperous you will be!
3 Your wife will be like a fruitful grapevine,
flourishing within your home.
Your children will be like vigorous young
olive trees
as they sit around your table.
4 That is the LORD's blessing
for those who fear him.
5 May the LORD continually bless you from Zion.
May you see Jerusalem prosper as long
as you live.
6 May you live to enjoy your grandchildren.
May Israel have peace!

129 *A song for pilgrims ascending to Jerusalem.*

1 From my earliest youth my enemies have
persecuted me.
Let all Israel repeat this:
2 From my earliest youth my enemies have
persecuted me,
but they have never defeated me.
3 My back is covered with cuts,
as if a farmer had plowed long furrows.
4 But the LORD is good;
he has cut me free from the ropes of
the ungodly.
5 May all who hate Jerusalem*
be turned back in shameful defeat.
6 May they be as useless as grass on a rooftop,
turning yellow when only half grown,
7 ignored by the harvester,
despised by the binder.
8 And may those who pass by
refuse to give them this blessing:
"The LORD bless you;
we bless you in the LORD's name."

130 *A song for pilgrims ascending to Jerusalem.*

1 From the depths of despair, O LORD,
I call for your help.

129:5 Hebrew *Zion.*

KING JAMES VERSION

2 Lord, hear my voice: let thine ears be attentive to the voice of my supplications.

3 If thou, LORD, shouldest mark iniquities, O Lord, who shall stand?

4 But *there is* forgiveness with thee, that thou mayest be feared.

5 I wait for the LORD, my soul doth wait, and in his word do I hope.

6 My soul *waiteth* for the Lord more than they that watch for the morning: *I say, more than* they that watch for the morning.

7 Let Israel hope in the LORD: for with the LORD *there is* mercy, and with him *is* plenteous redemption.

8 And he shall redeem Israel from all his iniquities.

131 *A Song of degrees of David*

1 LORD, my heart is not haughty, nor mine eyes lofty: neither do I exercise myself in great matters, or in things too high for me.

2 Surely I have behaved and quieted myself, as a child that is weaned of his mother: my soul *is* even as a weaned child.

3 Let Israel hope in the LORD from henceforth and for ever.

132 *A Song of degrees*

1 LORD, remember David, *and* all his afflictions:

2 How he sware unto the LORD, *and* vowed unto the mighty *God* of Jacob;

3 Surely I will not come into the tabernacle of my house, nor go up into my bed;

4 I will not give sleep to mine eyes, *or* slumber to mine eyelids,

5 Until I find out a place for the LORD, an habitation for the mighty *God* of Jacob.

6 Lo, we heard of it at Ephratah: we found it in the fields of the wood.

7 We will go into his tabernacles: we will worship at his footstool.

8 Arise, O LORD, into thy rest; thou, and the ark of thy strength.

9 Let thy priests be clothed with righteousness; and let thy saints shout for joy.

10 For thy servant David's sake turn not away the face of thine anointed.

NEW LIVING TRANSLATION

2 Hear my cry, O Lord.
Pay attention to my prayer.

3 LORD, if you kept a record of our sins,
who, O Lord, could ever survive?
4 But you offer forgiveness,
that we might learn to fear you.

5 I am counting on the LORD;
yes, I am counting on him.
I have put my hope in his word.
6 I long for the Lord
more than sentries long for the dawn,
yes, more than sentries long for the dawn.

7 O Israel, hope in the LORD;
for with the LORD there is unfailing love.
His redemption overflows.
8 He himself will redeem Israel
from every kind of sin.

131 *A song for pilgrims ascending to Jerusalem. A psalm of David.*

1 LORD, my heart is not proud;
my eyes are not haughty.
I don't concern myself with matters too great
or too awesome for me to grasp.
2 Instead, I have calmed and quieted myself,
like a weaned child who no longer cries for
its mother's milk.
Yes, like a weaned child is my soul within me.

3 O Israel, put your hope in the LORD—
now and always.

132 *A song for pilgrims ascending to Jerusalem.*

1 LORD, remember David
and all that he suffered.
2 He made a solemn promise to the LORD.
He vowed to the Mighty One of Israel,*
3 "I will not go home;
I will not let myself rest.
4 I will not let my eyes sleep
nor close my eyelids in slumber
5 until I find a place to build a house for the LORD,
a sanctuary for the Mighty One of Israel."

6 We heard that the Ark was in Ephrathah;
then we found it in the distant countryside
of Jaar.
7 Let us go to the sanctuary of the LORD;
let us worship at the footstool of his throne.
8 Arise, O LORD, and enter your resting place,
along with the Ark, the symbol of your power.
9 May your priests be clothed in godliness;
may your loyal servants sing for joy.
10 For the sake of your servant David,
do not reject the king you have anointed.

132:2 Hebrew *of Jacob;* also in 132:5. See note on 44:4.

KING JAMES VERSION

11 The LORD hath sworn *in* truth unto David; he will not turn from it; Of the fruit of thy body will I set upon thy throne.

12 If thy children will keep my covenant and my testimony that I shall teach them, their children shall also sit upon thy throne for evermore.

13 For the LORD hath chosen Zion; he hath desired *it* for his habitation.

14 This *is* my rest for ever: here will I dwell; for I have desired it.

15 I will abundantly bless her provision: I will satisfy her poor with bread.

16 I will also clothe her priests with salvation: and her saints shall shout aloud for joy.

17 There will I make the horn of David to bud: I have ordained a lamp for mine anointed.

18 His enemies will I clothe with shame: but upon himself shall his crown flourish.

133 *A Song of degrees of David*

1 Behold, how good and how pleasant *it is* for brethren to dwell together in unity!

2 *It is* like the precious ointment upon the head, that ran down upon the beard, *even* Aaron's beard: that went down to the skirts of his garments;

3 As the dew of Hermon, *and as the dew* that descended upon the mountains of Zion: for there the LORD commanded the blessing, *even* life for evermore.

134 *A Song of degrees*

1 Behold, bless ye the LORD, all *ye* servants of the LORD, which by night stand in the house of the LORD.

2 Lift up your hands *in* the sanctuary, and bless the LORD.

3 The LORD that made heaven and earth bless thee out of Zion.

135

1 Praise ye the LORD. Praise ye the name of the LORD; praise *him*, O ye servants of the LORD.

2 Ye that stand in the house of the LORD, in the courts of the house of our God,

3 Praise the LORD; for the LORD *is* good: sing praises unto his name; for *it is* pleasant.

4 For the LORD hath chosen Jacob unto himself, *and* Israel for his peculiar treasure.

NEW LIVING TRANSLATION

11 The LORD swore an oath to David
with a promise he will never take back:
"I will place one of your descendants
on your throne.
12 If your descendants obey the terms of
my covenant
and the laws that I teach them,
then your royal line
will continue forever and ever."
13 For the LORD has chosen Jerusalem*;
he has desired it for his home.
14 "This is my resting place forever," he said.
"I will live here, for this is the home I desired.
15 I will bless this city and make it prosperous;
I will satisfy its poor with food.
16 I will clothe its priests with godliness;
its faithful servants will sing for joy.
17 Here I will increase the power of David;
my anointed one will be a light for my people.
18 I will clothe his enemies with shame,
but he will be a glorious king."

133 *A song for pilgrims ascending to Jerusalem. A psalm of David.*

1 How wonderful and pleasant it is
when brothers live together in harmony!
2 For harmony is as precious as the anointing oil
that was poured over Aaron's head,
that ran down his beard
and onto the border of his robe.
3 Harmony is as refreshing as the dew from
Mount Hermon
that falls on the mountains of Zion.
And there the LORD has pronounced his blessing,
even life everlasting.

134 *A song for pilgrims ascending to Jerusalem.*

1 Oh, praise the LORD, all you servants of the LORD,
you who serve at night in the house of the LORD.
2 Lift up holy hands in prayer,
and praise the LORD.

3 May the LORD, who made heaven and earth,
bless you from Jerusalem.*

135

1 Praise the LORD!

Praise the name of the LORD!
Praise him, you who serve the LORD,
2 you who serve in the house of the LORD,
in the courts of the house of our God.
3 Praise the LORD, for the LORD is good;
celebrate his lovely name with music.
4 For the LORD has chosen Jacob for himself,
Israel for his own special treasure.

132:13 Hebrew *Zion*. 134:3 Hebrew *Zion*.

KING JAMES VERSION

5 For I know that the Lord *is* great, and *that* our
LORD *is* above all gods.
6 Whatsoever the LORD pleased, *that* did he in
heaven, and in earth, in the seas, and all deep places.
7 He causeth the vapours to ascend from the ends
of the earth; he maketh lightnings for the rain; he
bringeth the wind out of his treasuries.
8 Who smote the firstborn of Egypt, both of man
and beast.
9 *Who* sent tokens and wonders into the midst
of thee, O Egypt, upon Pharaoh, and upon all his
servants.
10 Who smote great nations, and slew mighty
kings;
11 Sihon king of the Amorites, and Og king of
Bashan, and all the kingdoms of Canaan:
12 And gave their land *for* an heritage, an heritage
unto Israel his people.
13 Thy name, O LORD, *endureth* for ever; *and* thy
memorial, O LORD, throughout all generations.
14 For the LORD will judge his people, and he will
repent himself concerning his servants.
15 The idols of the heathen *are* silver and gold, the
work of men's hands.
16 They have mouths, but they speak not; eyes have
they, but they see not;
17 They have ears, but they hear not; neither is
there *any* breath in their mouths.
18 They that make them are like unto them: *so is*
every one that trusteth in them.
19 Bless the LORD, O house of Israel: bless the LORD,
O house of Aaron:
20 Bless the LORD, O house of Levi: ye that fear the
LORD, bless the LORD.
21 Blessed be the LORD out of Zion, which dwelleth
at Jerusalem. Praise ye the LORD.

136

1 O give thanks unto the LORD; for *he is*
good: for his mercy *endureth* for ever.
2 O give thanks unto the God of gods: for his mercy
endureth for ever.
3 O give thanks to the Lord of lords: for his mercy
endureth for ever.
4 To him who alone doeth great wonders: for his
mercy *endureth* for ever.
5 To him that by wisdom made the heavens: for his
mercy *endureth* for ever.

NEW LIVING TRANSLATION

5 I know the greatness of the LORD—
that our Lord is greater than any other god.
6 The LORD does whatever pleases him
throughout all heaven and earth,
and on the seas and in their depths.
7 He causes the clouds to rise over the whole earth.
He sends the lightning with the rain
and releases the wind from his storehouses.
8 He destroyed the firstborn in each Egyptian home,
both people and animals.
9 He performed miraculous signs and wonders
in Egypt
against Pharaoh and all his people.
10 He struck down great nations
and slaughtered mighty kings—
11 Sihon king of the Amorites,
Og king of Bashan,
and all the kings of Canaan.
12 He gave their land as an inheritance,
a special possession to his people Israel.
13 Your name, O LORD, endures forever;
your fame, O LORD, is known to every
generation.
14 For the LORD will give justice to his people
and have compassion on his servants.
15 The idols of the nations are merely things
of silver and gold,
shaped by human hands.
16 They have mouths but cannot speak,
and eyes but cannot see.
17 They have ears but cannot hear,
and noses but cannot smell.
18 And those who make idols are just like them,
as are all who trust in them.
19 O Israel, praise the LORD!
O priests—descendants of Aaron—praise
the LORD!
20 O Levites, praise the LORD!
All you who fear the LORD, praise the LORD!
21 The LORD be praised from Zion,
for he lives here in Jerusalem.

Praise the LORD!

136

1 Give thanks to the LORD, for he is good!
His faithful love endures forever.
2 Give thanks to the God of gods.
His faithful love endures forever.
3 Give thanks to the Lord of lords.
His faithful love endures forever.
4 Give thanks to him who alone does mighty
miracles.
His faithful love endures forever.
5 Give thanks to him who made the heavens so
skillfully.
His faithful love endures forever.

KING JAMES VERSION

6To him that stretched out the earth above the
waters: for his mercy *endureth* for ever.
7To him that made great lights: for his mercy
endureth for ever:
8The sun to rule by day: for his mercy *endureth*
for ever:
9The moon and stars to rule by night: for his
mercy *endureth* for ever.
10To him that smote Egypt in their firstborn: for
his mercy *endureth* for ever:
11And brought out Israel from among them: for
his mercy *endureth* for ever:
12With a strong hand, and with a stretched out
arm: for his mercy *endureth* for ever.
13To him which divided the Red sea into parts:
for his mercy *endureth* for ever:
14And made Israel to pass through the midst of it:
for his mercy *endureth* for ever:
15But overthrew Pharaoh and his host in the Red
sea: for his mercy *endureth* for ever.
16To him which led his people through the wilderness: for his mercy *endureth* for ever.
17To him which smote great kings: for his mercy
endureth for ever:
18And slew famous kings: for his mercy *endureth*
for ever:
19Sihon king of the Amorites: for his mercy
endureth for ever:
20And Og the king of Bashan: for his mercy
endureth for ever:
21And gave their land for an heritage: for his
mercy *endureth* for ever:
22*Even* an heritage unto Israel his servant: for his
mercy *endureth* for ever.
23Who remembered us in our low estate: for his
mercy *endureth* for ever:
24And hath redeemed us from our enemies: for
his mercy *endureth* for ever.
25Who giveth food to all flesh: for his mercy
endureth for ever.
26O give thanks unto the God of heaven: for his
mercy *endureth* for ever.

137 1By the rivers of Babylon, there we sat
down, yea, we wept, when we remembered Zion.
2We hanged our harps upon the willows in the
midst thereof.

NEW LIVING TRANSLATION

6 Give thanks to him who placed the earth among
the waters.
His faithful love endures forever.
7 Give thanks to him who made the heavenly
lights—
His faithful love endures forever.
8 the sun to rule the day,
His faithful love endures forever.
9 and the moon and stars to rule the night.
His faithful love endures forever.

10 Give thanks to him who killed the firstborn
of Egypt.
His faithful love endures forever.
11 He brought Israel out of Egypt.
His faithful love endures forever.
12 He acted with a strong hand and powerful arm.
His faithful love endures forever.

13 Give thanks to him who parted the Red Sea.*
His faithful love endures forever.
14 He led Israel safely through,
His faithful love endures forever.
15 but he hurled Pharaoh and his army into
the Red Sea.
His faithful love endures forever.

16 Give thanks to him who led his people through
the wilderness.
His faithful love endures forever.

17 Give thanks to him who struck down mighty kings.
His faithful love endures forever.
18 He killed powerful kings—
His faithful love endures forever.
19 Sihon king of the Amorites,
His faithful love endures forever.
20 and Og king of Bashan.
His faithful love endures forever.
21 God gave the land of these kings as an
inheritance—
His faithful love endures forever.
22 a special possession to his servant Israel.
His faithful love endures forever.

23 He remembered us in our weakness.
His faithful love endures forever.
24 He saved us from our enemies.
His faithful love endures forever.
25 He gives food to every living thing.
His faithful love endures forever.
26 Give thanks to the God of heaven.
His faithful love endures forever.

137 1Beside the rivers of Babylon, we sat
and wept
as we thought of Jerusalem.*
2 We put away our harps,
hanging them on the branches of poplar trees.

136:13 Hebrew *sea of reeds;* also in 136:15. **137:1** Hebrew *Zion;* also in 137:3.

KING JAMES VERSION

3 For there they that carried us away captive required of us a song; and they that wasted us *required of us* mirth, *saying,* Sing us *one* of the songs of Zion.

4 How shall we sing the LORD's song in a strange land?

5 If I forget thee, O Jerusalem, let my right hand forget *her cunning.*

6 If I do not remember thee, let my tongue cleave to the roof of my mouth; if I prefer not Jerusalem above my chief joy.

7 Remember, O LORD, the children of Edom in the day of Jerusalem; who said, Rase *it,* rase *it, even* to the foundation thereof.

8 O daughter of Babylon, who art to be destroyed; happy *shall he be,* that rewardeth thee as thou hast served us.

9 Happy *shall he be,* that taketh and dasheth thy little ones against the stones.

138 A Psalm *of David*

1 I will praise thee with my whole heart: before the gods will I sing praise unto thee.

2 I will worship toward thy holy temple, and praise thy name for thy lovingkindness and for thy truth: for thou hast magnified thy word above all thy name.

3 In the day when I cried thou answeredst me, *and* strengthenedst me *with* strength in my soul.

4 All the kings of the earth shall praise thee, O LORD, when they hear the words of thy mouth.

5 Yea, they shall sing in the ways of the LORD: for great *is* the glory of the LORD.

6 Though the LORD *be* high, yet hath he respect unto the lowly: but the proud he knoweth afar off.

7 Though I walk in the midst of trouble, thou wilt revive me: thou shalt stretch forth thine hand against the wrath of mine enemies, and thy right hand shall save me.

8 The LORD will perfect *that which* concerneth me: thy mercy, O LORD, *endureth* for ever: forsake not the works of thine own hands.

139 *To the chief Musician, A Psalm of David*

1 O LORD, thou hast searched me, and known *me.*

2 Thou knowest my downsitting and mine uprising, thou understandest my thought afar off.

NEW LIVING TRANSLATION

3 For our captors demanded a song from us.
Our tormentors insisted on a joyful hymn:
"Sing us one of those songs of Jerusalem!"
4 But how can we sing the songs of the LORD
while in a pagan land?

5 If I forget you, O Jerusalem,
let my right hand forget how to play the harp.
6 May my tongue stick to the roof of my mouth
if I fail to remember you,
if I don't make Jerusalem my greatest joy.

7 O LORD, remember what the Edomites did
on the day the armies of Babylon captured
Jerusalem.
"Destroy it!" they yelled.
"Level it to the ground!"
8 O Babylon, you will be destroyed.
Happy is the one who pays you back
for what you have done to us.
9 Happy is the one who takes your babies
and smashes them against the rocks!

138 *A psalm of David.*

1 I give you thanks, O LORD, with all my heart;
I will sing your praises before the gods.
2 I bow before your holy Temple as I worship.
I praise your name for your unfailing love and
faithfulness;
for your promises are backed
by all the honor of your name.
3 As soon as I pray, you answer me;
you encourage me by giving me strength.

4 Every king in all the earth will thank you, LORD,
for all of them will hear your words.
5 Yes, they will sing about the LORD's ways,
for the glory of the LORD is very great.
6 Though the LORD is great, he cares for
the humble,
but he keeps his distance from the proud.

7 Though I am surrounded by troubles,
you will protect me from the anger
of my enemies.
You reach out your hand,
and the power of your right hand saves me.
8 The LORD will work out his plans for my life—
for your faithful love, O LORD, endures forever.
Don't abandon me, for you made me.

139 *For the choir director: A psalm of David.*

1 O LORD, you have examined my heart
and know everything about me.
2 You know when I sit down or stand up.
You know my thoughts even when I'm
far away.

KING JAMES VERSION

3 Thou compassest my path and my lying down,
and art acquainted *with* all my ways.
4 For *there is* not a word in my tongue, *but*, lo,
O LORD, thou knowest it altogether.
5 Thou hast beset me behind and before, and laid
thine hand upon me.
6 *Such* knowledge *is* too wonderful for me; it is
high, I cannot *attain* unto it.
7 Whither shall I go from thy spirit? or whither
shall I flee from thy presence?
8 If I ascend up into heaven, thou *art* there: if I
make my bed in hell, behold, thou *art there*.
9 *If* I take the wings of the morning, *and* dwell in
the uttermost parts of the sea;
10 Even there shall thy hand lead me, and thy right
hand shall hold me.
11 If I say, Surely the darkness shall cover me; even
the night shall be light about me.
12 Yea, the darkness hideth not from thee; but the
night shineth as the day: the darkness and the light
are both alike *to thee*.
13 For thou hast possessed my reins: thou hast
covered me in my mother's womb.
14 I will praise thee; for I am fearfully *and* wonderfully made: marvellous *are* thy works; and *that* my
soul knoweth right well.
15 My substance was not hid from thee, when I was
made in secret, *and* curiously wrought in the lowest
parts of the earth.
16 Thine eyes did see my substance, yet being
unperfect; and in thy book all *my members* were
written, *which* in continuance were fashioned, when
as yet there was none of them.
17 How precious also are thy thoughts unto me,
O God! how great is the sum of them!
18 *If* I should count them, they are more in number
than the sand: when I awake, I am still with thee.
19 Surely thou wilt slay the wicked, O God: depart
from me therefore, ye bloody men.
20 For they speak against thee wickedly, *and* thine
enemies take *thy name* in vain.
21 Do not I hate them, O LORD, that hate thee? and
am not I grieved with those that rise up against thee?
22 I hate them with perfect hatred: I count them
mine enemies.
23 Search me, O God, and know my heart: try me,
and know my thoughts:
24 And see if *there be any* wicked way in me, and
lead me in the way everlasting.

NEW LIVING TRANSLATION

3 You see me when I travel
and when I rest at home.
You know everything I do.
4 You know what I am going to say
even before I say it, LORD.
5 You go before me and follow me.
You place your hand of blessing on my head.
6 Such knowledge is too wonderful for me,
too great for me to understand!

7 I can never escape from your Spirit!
I can never get away from your presence!
8 If I go up to heaven, you are there;
if I go down to the grave,* you are there.
9 If I ride the wings of the morning,
if I dwell by the farthest oceans,
10 even there your hand will guide me,
and your strength will support me.
11 I could ask the darkness to hide me
and the light around me to become night—
12 but even in darkness I cannot hide from you.
To you the night shines as bright as day.
Darkness and light are the same to you.

13 You made all the delicate, inner parts of my body
and knit me together in my mother's womb.
14 Thank you for making me so wonderfully
complex!
Your workmanship is marvelous—how well
I know it.
15 You watched me as I was being formed in
utter seclusion,
as I was woven together in the dark of
the womb.
16 You saw me before I was born.
Every day of my life was recorded in your book.
Every moment was laid out
before a single day had passed.

17 How precious are your thoughts about me,* O God.
They cannot be numbered!
18 I can't even count them;
they outnumber the grains of sand!
And when I wake up,
you are still with me!

19 O God, if only you would destroy the wicked!
Get out of my life, you murderers!
20 They blaspheme you;
your enemies misuse your name.
21 O LORD, shouldn't I hate those who hate you?
Shouldn't I despise those who oppose you?
22 Yes, I hate them with total hatred,
for your enemies are my enemies.

23 Search me, O God, and know my heart;
test me and know my anxious thoughts.
24 Point out anything in me that offends you,
and lead me along the path of everlasting life.

139:8 Hebrew *to Sheol*. **139:17** Or *How precious to me are your thoughts*.

KING JAMES VERSION

140 *To the chief Musician, A Psalm of David*

1 Deliver me, O LORD, from the evil man: preserve
me from the violent man;
2 Which imagine mischiefs in *their* heart; continually are they gathered together *for* war.
3 They have sharpened their tongues like a serpent; adders' poison *is* under their lips. Selah.
4 Keep me, O LORD, from the hands of the wicked;
preserve me from the violent man; who have purposed to overthrow my goings.
5 The proud have hid a snare for me, and cords;
they have spread a net by the wayside; they have set
gins for me. Selah.
6 I said unto the LORD, Thou *art* my God: hear the
voice of my supplications, O LORD.
7 O GOD the Lord, the strength of my salvation,
thou hast covered my head in the day of battle.
8 Grant not, O LORD, the desires of the wicked: further not his wicked device; *lest* they exalt themselves. Selah.
9 *As for* the head of those that compass me about,
let the mischief of their own lips cover them.
10 Let burning coals fall upon them: let them be
cast into the fire; into deep pits, that they rise not up
again.
11 Let not an evil speaker be established in the
earth: evil shall hunt the violent man to overthrow
him.
12 I know that the LORD will maintain the cause of
the afflicted, *and* the right of the poor.
13 Surely the righteous shall give thanks unto thy
name: the upright shall dwell in thy presence.

141 *A Psalm of David*

1 LORD, I cry unto thee: make haste unto me; give
ear unto my voice, when I cry unto thee.
2 Let my prayer be set forth before thee *as* incense; *and* the lifting up of my hands *as* the evening
sacrifice.
3 Set a watch, O LORD, before my mouth; keep the
door of my lips.
4 Incline not my heart to *any* evil thing, to practise
wicked works with men that work iniquity: and let
me not eat of their dainties.
5 Let the righteous smite me; *it shall be* a kindness:
and let him reprove me; *it shall be* an excellent oil,
which shall not break my head: for yet my prayer also
shall be in their calamities.

NEW LIVING TRANSLATION

140 *For the choir director: A psalm of David.*

1 O LORD, rescue me from evil people.
Protect me from those who are violent,
2 those who plot evil in their hearts
and stir up trouble all day long.
3 Their tongues sting like a snake;
the venom of a viper drips from their lips.
Interlude

4 O LORD, keep me out of the hands of the wicked.
Protect me from those who are violent,
for they are plotting against me.
5 The proud have set a trap to catch me;
they have stretched out a net;
they have placed traps all along the way.
Interlude

6 I said to the LORD, "You are my God!"
Listen, O LORD, to my cries for mercy!
7 O Sovereign LORD, the strong one who rescued me,
you protected me on the day of battle.
8 LORD, do not let evil people have their way.
Do not let their evil schemes succeed,
or they will become proud. *Interlude*

9 Let my enemies be destroyed
by the very evil they have planned for me.
10 Let burning coals fall down on their heads.
Let them be thrown into the fire
or into watery pits from which they can't escape.
11 Don't let liars prosper here in our land.
Cause great disasters to fall on the violent.
12 But I know the LORD will help those they persecute;
he will give justice to the poor.
13 Surely righteous people are praising your name;
the godly will live in your presence.

141 *A psalm of David.*

1 O LORD, I am calling to you. Please hurry!
Listen when I cry to you for help!
2 Accept my prayer as incense offered to you,
and my upraised hands as an evening offering.
3 Take control of what I say, O LORD,
and guard my lips.
4 Don't let me drift toward evil
or take part in acts of wickedness.
Don't let me share in the delicacies
of those who do wrong.

5 Let the godly strike me!
It will be a kindness!
If they correct me, it is soothing medicine.
Don't let me refuse it.

But I pray constantly
against the wicked and their deeds.

6 When their judges are overthrown in stony places, they shall hear my words; for they are sweet.

7 Our bones are scattered at the grave's mouth, as when one cutteth and cleaveth *wood* upon the earth.

8 But mine eyes *are* unto thee, O GOD the Lord: in thee is my trust; leave not my soul destitute.

9 Keep me from the snares *which* they have laid for me, and the gins of the workers of iniquity.

10 Let the wicked fall into their own nets, whilst that I withal escape.

142 *Maschil of David; A Prayer when he was in the cave.*

1 I cried unto the LORD with my voice; with my voice unto the LORD did I make my supplication.

2 I poured out my complaint before him; I shewed before him my trouble.

3 When my spirit was overwhelmed within me, then thou knewest my path. In the way wherein I walked have they privily laid a snare for me.

4 I looked on *my* right hand, and beheld, but *there was* no man that would know me: refuge failed me; no man cared for my soul.

5 I cried unto thee, O LORD: I said, Thou *art* my refuge *and* my portion in the land of the living.

6 Attend unto my cry; for I am brought very low: deliver me from my persecutors; for they are stronger than I.

7 Bring my soul out of prison, that I may praise thy name: the righteous shall compass me about; for thou shalt deal bountifully with me.

143 *A Psalm of David*

1 Hear my prayer, O LORD, give ear to my supplications: in thy faithfulness answer me, *and* in thy righteousness.

2 And enter not into judgment with thy servant: for in thy sight shall no man living be justified.

3 For the enemy hath persecuted my soul; he hath smitten my life down to the ground; he hath made me to dwell in darkness, as those that have been long dead.

4 Therefore is my spirit overwhelmed within me; my heart within me is desolate.

6 When their leaders are thrown down from a cliff,
the wicked will listen to my words and find
them true.
7 Like rocks brought up by a plow,
the bones of the wicked will lie scattered
without burial.*

8 I look to you for help, O Sovereign LORD.
You are my refuge; don't let them kill me.
9 Keep me from the traps they have set for me,
from the snares of those who do wrong.
10 Let the wicked fall into their own nets,
but let me escape.

142 *A psalm* of David, regarding his experience in the cave. A prayer.*

1 I cry out to the LORD;
I plead for the LORD's mercy.
2 I pour out my complaints before him
and tell him all my troubles.
3 When I am overwhelmed,
you alone know the way I should turn.
Wherever I go,
my enemies have set traps for me.
4 I look for someone to come and help me,
but no one gives me a passing thought!
No one will help me;
no one cares a bit what happens to me.
5 Then I pray to you, O LORD.
I say, "You are my place of refuge.
You are all I really want in life.
6 Hear my cry,
for I am very low.
Rescue me from my persecutors,
for they are too strong for me.
7 Bring me out of prison
so I can thank you.
The godly will crowd around me,
for you are good to me."

143 *A psalm of David.*

1 Hear my prayer, O LORD;
listen to my plea!
Answer me because you are faithful
and righteous.
2 Don't put your servant on trial,
for no one is innocent before you.
3 My enemy has chased me.
He has knocked me to the ground
and forces me to live in darkness like
those in the grave.
4 I am losing all hope;
I am paralyzed with fear.

141:7 Hebrew *scattered at the mouth of Sheol.* **142:TITLE** Hebrew *maskil.* This may be a literary or musical term.

KING JAMES VERSION

5 I remember the days of old; I meditate on all thy works; I muse on the work of thy hands.

6 I stretch forth my hands unto thee: my soul *thirsteth* after thee, as a thirsty land. Selah.

7 Hear me speedily, O LORD: my spirit faileth: hide not thy face from me, lest I be like unto them that go down into the pit.

8 Cause me to hear thy lovingkindness in the morning; for in thee do I trust: cause me to know the way wherein I should walk; for I lift up my soul unto thee.

9 Deliver me, O LORD, from mine enemies: I flee unto thee to hide me.

10 Teach me to do thy will; for thou *art* my God: thy spirit *is* good; lead me into the land of uprightness.

11 Quicken me, O LORD, for thy name's sake: for thy righteousness' sake bring my soul out of trouble.

12 And of thy mercy cut off mine enemies, and destroy all them that afflict my soul: for I *am* thy servant.

144 A Psalm *of David*

1 Blessed *be* the LORD my strength, which teacheth my hands to war, *and* my fingers to fight:

2 My goodness, and my fortress; my high tower, and my deliverer; my shield, and *he* in whom I trust; who subdueth my people under me.

3 LORD, what *is* man, that thou takest knowledge of him! *or* the son of man, that thou makest account of him!

4 Man is like to vanity: his days *are* as a shadow that passeth away.

5 Bow thy heavens, O LORD, and come down: touch the mountains, and they shall smoke.

6 Cast forth lightning, and scatter them: shoot out thine arrows, and destroy them.

7 Send thine hand from above; rid me, and deliver me out of great waters, from the hand of strange children;

8 Whose mouth speaketh vanity, and their right hand *is* a right hand of falsehood.

9 I will sing a new song unto thee, O God: upon a psaltery *and* an instrument of ten strings will I sing praises unto thee.

NEW LIVING TRANSLATION

5 I remember the days of old.
I ponder all your great works
and think about what you have done.
6 I lift my hands to you in prayer.
I thirst for you as parched land thirsts for rain.
Interlude

7 Come quickly, LORD, and answer me,
for my depression deepens.
Don't turn away from me,
or I will die.
8 Let me hear of your unfailing love each morning,
for I am trusting you.
Show me where to walk,
for I give myself to you.
9 Rescue me from my enemies, LORD;
I run to you to hide me.
10 Teach me to do your will,
for you are my God.
May your gracious Spirit lead me forward
on a firm footing.
11 For the glory of your name, O LORD,
preserve my life.
Because of your faithfulness, bring me
out of this distress.
12 In your unfailing love, silence all my enemies
and destroy all my foes,
for I am your servant.

144 *A psalm of David.*

1 Praise the LORD, who is my rock.
He trains my hands for war
and gives my fingers skill for battle.
2 He is my loving ally and my fortress,
my tower of safety, my rescuer.
He is my shield, and I take refuge in him.
He makes the nations* submit to me.

3 O LORD, what are human beings that you should
notice them,
mere mortals that you should think about them?
4 For they are like a breath of air;
their days are like a passing shadow.

5 Open the heavens, LORD, and come down.
Touch the mountains so they billow smoke.
6 Hurl your lightning bolts and scatter your
enemies!
Shoot your arrows and confuse them!
7 Reach down from heaven and rescue me;
rescue me from deep waters,
from the power of my enemies.
8 Their mouths are full of lies;
they swear to tell the truth, but they lie instead.

9 I will sing a new song to you, O God!
I will sing your praises with a ten-stringed harp.

144:2 Some manuscripts read *my people*.

KING JAMES VERSION

[10]*It is he* that giveth salvation unto kings: who delivereth David his servant from the hurtful sword.
[11]Rid me, and deliver me from the hand of strange children, whose mouth speaketh vanity, and their right hand *is* a right hand of falsehood:
[12]That our sons *may be* as plants grown up in their youth; *that* our daughters *may be* as corner stones, polished *after* the similitude of a palace:
[13]*That* our garners *may be* full, affording all manner of store: *that* our sheep may bring forth thousands and ten thousands in our streets:
[14]*That* our oxen *may be* strong to labour; *that there be* no breaking in, nor going out; that *there be* no complaining in our streets.
[15]Happy *is that* people, that is in such a case: *yea,* happy *is that* people, whose God *is* the LORD.

145 *David's* Psalm *of praise*

[1]I will extol thee, my God, O king; and I will bless thy name for ever and ever.
[2]Every day will I bless thee; and I will praise thy name for ever and ever.
[3]Great *is* the LORD, and greatly to be praised; and his greatness *is* unsearchable.
[4]One generation shall praise thy works to another, and shall declare thy mighty acts.
[5]I will speak of the glorious honour of thy majesty, and of thy wondrous works.
[6]And *men* shall speak of the might of thy terrible acts: and I will declare thy greatness.
[7]They shall abundantly utter the memory of thy great goodness, and shall sing of thy righteousness.
[8]The LORD *is* gracious, and full of compassion; slow to anger, and of great mercy.
[9]The LORD *is* good to all: and his tender mercies *are* over all his works.
[10]All thy works shall praise thee, O LORD; and thy saints shall bless thee.
[11]They shall speak of the glory of thy kingdom, and talk of thy power;
[12]To make known to the sons of men his mighty acts, and the glorious majesty of his kingdom.

NEW LIVING TRANSLATION

[10] For you grant victory to kings!
You rescued your servant David from the fatal sword.
[11] Save me!
Rescue me from the power of my enemies.
Their mouths are full of lies;
they swear to tell the truth, but they lie instead.

[12] May our sons flourish in their youth
like well-nurtured plants.
May our daughters be like graceful pillars,
carved to beautify a palace.
[13] May our barns be filled
with crops of every kind.
May the flocks in our fields multiply by the thousands,
even tens of thousands,
[14] and may our oxen be loaded down
with produce.
May there be no enemy breaking through our walls,
no going into captivity,
no cries of alarm in our town squares.
[15] Yes, joyful are those who live like this!
Joyful indeed are those whose God is the LORD.

145* *A psalm of praise of David.*

[1] I will exalt you, my God and King,
and praise your name forever and ever.
[2] I will praise you every day;
yes, I will praise you forever.
[3] Great is the LORD! He is most worthy of praise!
No one can measure his greatness.
[4] Let each generation tell its children of your mighty acts;
let them proclaim your power.
[5] I will meditate* on your majestic, glorious splendor
and your wonderful miracles.
[6] Your awe-inspiring deeds will be on every tongue;
I will proclaim your greatness.
[7] Everyone will share the story of your wonderful goodness;
they will sing with joy about your righteousness.
[8] The LORD is merciful and compassionate,
slow to get angry and filled with unfailing love.
[9] The LORD is good to everyone.
He showers compassion on all his creation.
[10] All of your works will thank you, LORD,
and your faithful followers will praise you.
[11] They will speak of the glory of your kingdom;
they will give examples of your power.
[12] They will tell about your mighty deeds
and about the majesty and glory of your reign.

145 This psalm is a Hebrew acrostic poem; each verse (including 13b) begins with a successive letter of the Hebrew alphabet. **145:5** Some manuscripts read *They will speak.*

KING JAMES VERSION

13 Thy kingdom *is* an everlasting kingdom, and thy dominion *endureth* throughout all generations.

14 The LORD upholdeth all that fall, and raiseth up all *those that be* bowed down.

15 The eyes of all wait upon thee; and thou givest them their meat in due season.

16 Thou openest thine hand, and satisfiest the desire of every living thing.

17 The LORD *is* righteous in all his ways, and holy in all his works.

18 The LORD *is* nigh unto all them that call upon him, to all that call upon him in truth.

19 He will fulfil the desire of them that fear him: he also will hear their cry, and will save them.

20 The LORD preserveth all them that love him: but all the wicked will he destroy.

21 My mouth shall speak the praise of the LORD: and let all flesh bless his holy name for ever and ever.

146 1 Praise ye the LORD. Praise the LORD, O my soul.

2 While I live will I praise the LORD: I will sing praises unto my God while I have any being.

3 Put not your trust in princes, *nor* in the son of man, in whom *there is* no help.

4 His breath goeth forth, he returneth to his earth; in that very day his thoughts perish.

5 Happy *is he* that *hath* the God of Jacob for his help, whose hope *is* in the LORD his God:

6 Which made heaven, and earth, the sea, and all that therein *is:* which keepeth truth for ever:

7 Which executeth judgment for the oppressed: which giveth food to the hungry. The LORD looseth the prisoners:

8 The LORD openeth *the eyes of* the blind: the LORD raiseth them that are bowed down: the LORD loveth the righteous:

9 The LORD preserveth the strangers; he relieveth the fatherless and widow: but the way of the wicked he turneth upside down.

10 The LORD shall reign for ever, *even* thy God, O Zion, unto all generations. Praise ye the LORD.

NEW LIVING TRANSLATION

13 For your kingdom is an everlasting kingdom.
You rule throughout all generations.

The LORD always keeps his promises;
he is gracious in all he does.*
14 The LORD helps the fallen
and lifts those bent beneath their loads.
15 The eyes of all look to you in hope;
you give them their food as they need it.
16 When you open your hand,
you satisfy the hunger and thirst of every living thing.
17 The LORD is righteous in everything he does;
he is filled with kindness.
18 The LORD is close to all who call on him,
yes, to all who call on him in truth.
19 He grants the desires of those who fear him;
he hears their cries for help and rescues them.
20 The LORD protects all those who love him,
but he destroys the wicked.

21 I will praise the LORD,
and may everyone on earth bless his holy name forever and ever.

146 1 Praise the LORD!

Let all that I am praise the LORD.
2 I will praise the LORD as long as I live.
I will sing praises to my God with my dying breath.

3 Don't put your confidence in powerful people;
there is no help for you there.
4 When they breathe their last, they return to the earth,
and all their plans die with them.
5 But joyful are those who have the God of Israel* as their helper,
whose hope is in the LORD their God.
6 He made heaven and earth,
the sea, and everything in them.
He keeps every promise forever.
7 He gives justice to the oppressed
and food to the hungry.
The LORD frees the prisoners.
8 The LORD opens the eyes of the blind.
The LORD lifts up those who are weighed down.
The LORD loves the godly.
9 The LORD protects the foreigners among us.
He cares for the orphans and widows,
but he frustrates the plans of the wicked.
10 The LORD will reign forever.
He will be your God, O Jerusalem,* throughout the generations.

Praise the LORD!

145:13 The last two lines of 145:13 are not found in many of the ancient manuscripts. **146:5** Hebrew *of Jacob.* See note on 44:4. **146:10** Hebrew *Zion.*

KING JAMES VERSION

147 1 Praise ye the LORD: for *it is* good to sing
praises unto our God; for *it is* pleasant;
and praise is comely.
2 The LORD doth build up Jerusalem: he gathereth
together the outcasts of Israel.
3 He healeth the broken in heart, and bindeth up
their wounds.
4 He telleth the number of the stars; he calleth
them all by *their* names.
5 Great *is* our LORD, and of great power: his understanding *is* infinite.
6 The LORD lifteth up the meek: he casteth the
wicked down to the ground.
7 Sing unto the LORD with thanksgiving; sing praise
upon the harp unto our God:
8 Who covereth the heaven with clouds, who
prepareth rain for the earth, who maketh grass to
grow upon the mountains.
9 He giveth to the beast his food, *and* to the young
ravens which cry.
10 He delighteth not in the strength of the horse:
he taketh not pleasure in the legs of a man.
11 The LORD taketh pleasure in them that fear him,
in those that hope in his mercy.
12 Praise the LORD, O Jerusalem; praise thy God,
O Zion.
13 For he hath strengthened the bars of thy gates;
he hath blessed thy children within thee.
14 He maketh peace *in* thy borders, *and* filleth thee
with the finest of the wheat.
15 He sendeth forth his commandment *upon*
earth: his word runneth very swiftly.
16 He giveth snow like wool: he scattereth the hoar-
frost like ashes.
17 He casteth forth his ice like morsels: who can
stand before his cold?
18 He sendeth out his word, and melteth them: he
causeth his wind to blow, *and* the waters flow.
19 He sheweth his word unto Jacob, his statutes
and his judgments unto Israel.
20 He hath not dealt so with any nation: and *as for*
his judgments, they have not known them. Praise ye
the LORD.

148 1 Praise ye the LORD. Praise ye the LORD
from the heavens: praise him in the
heights.
2 Praise ye him, all his angels: praise ye him, all
his hosts.
3 Praise ye him, sun and moon: praise him, all ye
stars of light.
4 Praise him, ye heavens of heavens, and ye waters
that *be* above the heavens.

NEW LIVING TRANSLATION

147 1 Praise the LORD!

How good to sing praises to our God!
How delightful and how fitting!
2 The LORD is rebuilding Jerusalem
and bringing the exiles back to Israel.
3 He heals the brokenhearted
and bandages their wounds.
4 He counts the stars
and calls them all by name.
5 How great is our Lord! His power is absolute!
His understanding is beyond comprehension!
6 The LORD supports the humble,
but he brings the wicked down into the dust.

7 Sing out your thanks to the LORD;
sing praises to our God with a harp.
8 He covers the heavens with clouds,
provides rain for the earth,
and makes the grass grow in mountain
pastures.
9 He gives food to the wild animals
and feeds the young ravens when they cry.
10 He takes no pleasure in the strength of a horse
or in human might.
11 No, the LORD's delight is in those who fear him,
those who put their hope in his unfailing love.

12 Glorify the LORD, O Jerusalem!
Praise your God, O Zion!
13 For he has strengthened the bars of your gates
and blessed your children within your walls.
14 He sends peace across your nation
and satisfies your hunger with the finest wheat.
15 He sends his orders to the world—
how swiftly his word flies!
16 He sends the snow like white wool;
he scatters frost upon the ground like ashes.
17 He hurls the hail like stones.*
Who can stand against his freezing cold?
18 Then, at his command, it all melts.
He sends his winds, and the ice thaws.
19 He has revealed his words to Jacob,
his decrees and regulations to Israel.
20 He has not done this for any other nation;
they do not know his regulations.

Praise the LORD!

148 1 Praise the LORD!

Praise the LORD from the heavens!
Praise him from the skies!
2 Praise him, all his angels!
Praise him, all the armies of heaven!
3 Praise him, sun and moon!
Praise him, all you twinkling stars!
4 Praise him, skies above!
Praise him, vapors high above the clouds!

147:17 Hebrew *like bread crumbs.*

KING JAMES VERSION

5 Let them praise the name of the LORD: for he
commanded, and they were created.
6 He hath also stablished them for ever and ever:
he hath made a decree which shall not pass.
7 Praise the LORD from the earth, ye dragons, and
all deeps:
8 Fire, and hail; snow, and vapours; stormy wind
fulfilling his word:
9 Mountains, and all hills; fruitful trees, and all
cedars:
10 Beasts, and all cattle; creeping things, and flying
fowl:
11 Kings of the earth, and all people; princes, and
all judges of the earth:
12 Both young men, and maidens; old men, and
children:
13 Let them praise the name of the LORD: for his
name alone is excellent; his glory *is* above the earth
and heaven.
14 He also exalteth the horn of his people, the
praise of all his saints; *even* of the children of Israel,
a people near unto him. Praise ye the LORD.

149

1 Praise ye the LORD. Sing unto the LORD a
new song, *and* his praise in the congregation of saints.
2 Let Israel rejoice in him that made him: let the
children of Zion be joyful in their King.
3 Let them praise his name in the dance: let them
sing praises unto him with the timbrel and harp.
4 For the LORD taketh pleasure in his people: he will
beautify the meek with salvation.
5 Let the saints be joyful in glory: let them sing
aloud upon their beds.
6 *Let* the high *praises* of God *be* in their mouth, and
a twoedged sword in their hand;
7 To execute vengeance upon the heathen, *and*
punishments upon the people;
8 To bind their kings with chains, and their nobles
with fetters of iron;
9 To execute upon them the judgment written: this
honour have all his saints. Praise ye the LORD.

150

1 Praise ye the LORD. Praise God in his
sanctuary: praise him in the firmament of
his power.
2 Praise him for his mighty acts: praise him according to his excellent greatness.

NEW LIVING TRANSLATION

5 Let every created thing give praise to the LORD,
for he issued his command, and they came
into being.
6 He set them in place forever and ever.
His decree will never be revoked.

7 Praise the LORD from the earth,
you creatures of the ocean depths,
8 fire and hail, snow and clouds,*
wind and weather that obey him,
9 mountains and all hills,
fruit trees and all cedars,
10 wild animals and all livestock,
small scurrying animals and birds,
11 kings of the earth and all people,
rulers and judges of the earth,
12 young men and young women,
old men and children.

13 Let them all praise the name of the LORD.
For his name is very great;
his glory towers over the earth and heaven!
14 He has made his people strong,
honoring his faithful ones—
the people of Israel who are close to him.

Praise the LORD!

149

1 Praise the LORD!

Sing to the LORD a new song.
Sing his praises in the assembly of the faithful.

2 O Israel, rejoice in your Maker.
O people of Jerusalem,* exult in your King.
3 Praise his name with dancing,
accompanied by tambourine and harp.
4 For the LORD delights in his people;
he crowns the humble with victory.
5 Let the faithful rejoice that he honors them.
Let them sing for joy as they lie on their beds.

6 Let the praises of God be in their mouths,
and a sharp sword in their hands—
7 to execute vengeance on the nations
and punishment on the peoples,
8 to bind their kings with shackles
and their leaders with iron chains,
9 to execute the judgment written against them.
This is the glorious privilege of his
faithful ones.

Praise the LORD!

150

1 Praise the LORD!

Praise God in his sanctuary;
praise him in his mighty heaven!
2 Praise him for his mighty works;
praise his unequaled greatness!

148:8 Or *mist*, or *smoke*. **149:2** Hebrew *Zion*.

KING JAMES VERSION

[3]Praise him with the sound of the trumpet: praise
him with the psaltery and harp.
[4]Praise him with the timbrel and dance: praise
him with stringed instruments and organs.
[5]Praise him upon the loud cymbals: praise him
upon the high sounding cymbals.
[6]Let every thing that hath breath praise the LORD.
Praise ye the LORD.

NEW LIVING TRANSLATION

[3] Praise him with a blast of the ram's horn;
praise him with the lyre and harp!
[4] Praise him with the tambourine and dancing;
praise him with strings and flutes!
[5] Praise him with a clash of cymbals;
praise him with loud clanging cymbals.
[6] Let everything that breathes sing praises
to the LORD!

Praise the LORD!

Proverbs

KING JAMES VERSION

1 1 The proverbs of Solomon the son of David, king of Israel;

2 To know wisdom and instruction; to perceive the words of understanding;

3 To receive the instruction of wisdom, justice, and judgment, and equity;

4 To give subtilty to the simple, to the young man knowledge and discretion.

5 A wise *man* will hear, and will increase learning; and a man of understanding shall attain unto wise counsels:

6 To understand a proverb, and the interpretation; the words of the wise, and their dark sayings.

7 The fear of the LORD *is* the beginning of knowledge: *but* fools despise wisdom and instruction.

8 My son, hear the instruction of thy father, and forsake not the law of thy mother:

9 For they *shall be* an ornament of grace unto thy head, and chains about thy neck.

10 My son, if sinners entice thee, consent thou not.

11 If they say, Come with us, let us lay wait for blood, let us lurk privily for the innocent without cause:

12 Let us swallow them up alive as the grave; and whole, as those that go down into the pit:

13 We shall find all precious substance, we shall fill our houses with spoil:

14 Cast in thy lot among us; let us all have one purse:

NEW LIVING TRANSLATION

The Purpose of Proverbs

1 These are the proverbs of Solomon, David's son, king of Israel.

2 Their purpose is to teach people wisdom
and discipline,
to help them understand the insights of
the wise.
3 Their purpose is to teach people to live
disciplined and successful lives,
to help them do what is right, just, and fair.
4 These proverbs will give insight to the simple,
knowledge and discernment to the young.

5 Let the wise listen to these proverbs and become
even wiser.
Let those with understanding receive guidance
6 by exploring the meaning in these proverbs
and parables,
the words of the wise and their riddles.

7 Fear of the LORD is the foundation of
true knowledge,
but fools despise wisdom and discipline.

A Father's Exhortation: Acquire Wisdom

8 My child,* listen when your father corrects you.
Don't neglect your mother's instruction.
9 What you learn from them will crown you
with grace
and be a chain of honor around your neck.

10 My child, if sinners entice you,
turn your back on them!
11 They may say, "Come and join us.
Let's hide and kill someone!
Just for fun, let's ambush the innocent!
12 Let's swallow them alive, like the grave*;
let's swallow them whole, like those who
go down to the pit of death.
13 Think of the great things we'll get!
We'll fill our houses with all the stuff we take.
14 Come, throw in your lot with us;
we'll all share the loot."

1:8 Hebrew *My son;* also in 1:10, 15. **1:12** Hebrew *like Sheol.*

KING JAMES VERSION

15 My son, walk not thou in the way with them; refrain thy foot from their path:
16 For their feet run to evil, and make haste to shed
blood.
17 Surely in vain the net is spread in the sight of any
bird.
18 And they lay wait for their *own* blood; they lurk
privily for their *own* lives.
19 So *are* the ways of every one that is greedy of gain;
which taketh away the life of the owners thereof.

20 Wisdom crieth without; she uttereth her voice
in the streets:
21 She crieth in the chief place of concourse, in the
openings of the gates: in the city she uttereth her
words, *saying,*
22 How long, ye simple ones, will ye love simplicity? and the scorners delight in their scorning, and
fools hate knowledge?
23 Turn you at my reproof: behold, I will pour out
my spirit unto you, I will make known my words
unto you.
24 Because I have called, and ye refused; I have
stretched out my hand, and no man regarded;
25 But ye have set at nought all my counsel, and
would none of my reproof:
26 I also will laugh at your calamity; I will mock
when your fear cometh;
27 When your fear cometh as desolation, and your
destruction cometh as a whirlwind; when distress
and anguish cometh upon you.
28 Then shall they call upon me, but I will not answer; they shall seek me early, but they shall not
find me:
29 For that they hated knowledge, and did not
choose the fear of the LORD:
30 They would none of my counsel: they despised
all my reproof.
31 Therefore shall they eat of the fruit of their own
way, and be filled with their own devices.
32 For the turning away of the simple shall slay
them, and the prosperity of fools shall destroy them.
33 But whoso hearkeneth unto me shall dwell
safely, and shall be quiet from fear of evil.

2 1 My son, if thou wilt receive my words, and hide
my commandments with thee;
2 So that thou incline thine ear unto wisdom, *and*
apply thine heart to understanding;
3 Yea, if thou criest after knowledge, *and* liftest up
thy voice for understanding;
4 If thou seekest her as silver, and searchest for her
as *for* hid treasures;

NEW LIVING TRANSLATION

15 My child, don't go along with them!
Stay far away from their paths.
16 They rush to commit evil deeds.
They hurry to commit murder.
17 If a bird sees a trap being set,
it knows to stay away.
18 But these people set an ambush for themselves;
they are trying to get themselves killed.
19 Such is the fate of all who are greedy for money;
it robs them of life.

Wisdom Shouts in the Streets

20 Wisdom shouts in the streets.
She cries out in the public square.
21 She calls to the crowds along the main street,
to those gathered in front of the city gate:
22 "How long, you simpletons,
will you insist on being simpleminded?
How long will you mockers relish your mocking?
How long will you fools hate knowledge?
23 Come and listen to my counsel.
I'll share my heart with you
and make you wise.
24 "I called you so often, but you wouldn't come.
I reached out to you, but you paid no attention.
25 You ignored my advice
and rejected the correction I offered.
26 So I will laugh when you are in trouble!
I will mock you when disaster overtakes you—
27 when calamity overtakes you like a storm,
when disaster engulfs you like a cyclone,
and anguish and distress overwhelm you.

28 "When they cry for help, I will not answer.
Though they anxiously search for me, they
will not find me.
29 For they hated knowledge
and chose not to fear the LORD.
30 They rejected my advice
and paid no attention when I corrected them.
31 Therefore, they must eat the bitter fruit of living
their own way,
choking on their own schemes.
32 For simpletons turn away from me—to death.
Fools are destroyed by their own complacency.
33 But all who listen to me will live in peace,
untroubled by fear of harm."

The Benefits of Wisdom

2 1 My child,* listen to what I say,
and treasure my commands.
2 Tune your ears to wisdom,
and concentrate on understanding.
3 Cry out for insight,
and ask for understanding.
4 Search for them as you would for silver;
seek them like hidden treasures.

2:1 Hebrew *My son.*

KING JAMES VERSION

5 Then shalt thou understand the fear of the LORD,
and find the knowledge of God.
6 For the LORD giveth wisdom: out of his mouth
cometh knowledge and understanding.
7 He layeth up sound wisdom for the righteous: *he*
is a buckler to them that walk uprightly.
8 He keepeth the paths of judgment, and preserveth the way of his saints.
9 Then shalt thou understand righteousness, and
judgment, and equity; *yea,* every good path.
10 When wisdom entereth into thine heart, and
knowledge is pleasant unto thy soul;
11 Discretion shall preserve thee, understanding
shall keep thee:
12 To deliver thee from the way of the evil *man,*
from the man that speaketh froward things;
13 Who leave the paths of uprightness, to walk in
the ways of darkness;
14 Who rejoice to do evil, *and* delight in the
frowardness of the wicked;
15 Whose ways *are* crooked, and *they* froward in
their paths:
16 To deliver thee from the strange woman, *even*
from the stranger *which* flattereth with her words;
17 Which forsaketh the guide of her youth, and
forgetteth the covenant of her God.
18 For her house inclineth unto death, and her
paths unto the dead.
19 None that go unto her return again, neither take
they hold of the paths of life.
20 That thou mayest walk in the way of good *men,*
and keep the paths of the righteous.
21 For the upright shall dwell in the land, and the
perfect shall remain in it.
22 But the wicked shall be cut off from the earth,
and the transgressors shall be rooted out of it.

3 1 My son, forget not my law; but let thine heart
keep my commandments:
2 For length of days, and long life, and peace, shall
they add to thee.
3 Let not mercy and truth forsake thee: bind them
about thy neck; write them upon the table of thine
heart:
4 So shalt thou find favour and good understanding in the sight of God and man.

NEW LIVING TRANSLATION

5 Then you will understand what it means
to fear the LORD,
and you will gain knowledge of God.
6 For the LORD grants wisdom!
From his mouth come knowledge and
understanding.
7 He grants a treasure of common sense
to the honest.
He is a shield to those who walk with integrity.
8 He guards the paths of the just
and protects those who are faithful to him.

9 Then you will understand what is right,
just, and fair,
and you will find the right way to go.
10 For wisdom will enter your heart,
and knowledge will fill you with joy.
11 Wise choices will watch over you.
Understanding will keep you safe.
12 Wisdom will save you from evil people,
from those whose words are twisted.
13 These men turn from the right way
to walk down dark paths.
14 They take pleasure in doing wrong,
and they enjoy the twisted ways of evil.
15 Their actions are crooked,
and their ways are wrong.

16 Wisdom will save you from the immoral woman,
from the seductive words of the
promiscuous woman.
17 She has abandoned her husband
and ignores the covenant she made before God.
18 Entering her house leads to death;
it is the road to the grave.*
19 The man who visits her is doomed.
He will never reach the paths of life.

20 Follow the steps of good men instead,
and stay on the paths of the righteous.
21 For only the godly will live in the land,
and those with integrity will remain in it.
22 But the wicked will be removed from the land,
and the treacherous will be uprooted.

Trusting in the LORD

3 1 My child,* never forget the things I have
taught you.
Store my commands in your heart.
2 If you do this, you will live many years,
and your life will be satisfying.
3 Never let loyalty and kindness leave you!
Tie them around your neck as a reminder.
Write them deep within your heart.
4 Then you will find favor with both God
and people,
and you will earn a good reputation.

2:18 Hebrew *to the spirits of the dead.* **3:1** Hebrew *My son;* also in 3:11, 21.

KING JAMES VERSION

5 Trust in the LORD with all thine heart; and lean not unto thine own understanding.

6 In all thy ways acknowledge him, and he shall direct thy paths.

7 Be not wise in thine own eyes: fear the LORD, and depart from evil.

8 It shall be health to thy navel, and marrow to thy bones.

9 Honour the LORD with thy substance, and with the firstfruits of all thine increase:

10 So shall thy barns be filled with plenty, and thy presses shall burst out with new wine.

11 My son, despise not the chastening of the LORD; neither be weary of his correction:

12 For whom the LORD loveth he correcteth; even as a father the son *in whom* he delighteth.

13 Happy *is* the man *that* findeth wisdom, and the man *that* getteth understanding.

14 For the merchandise of it *is* better than the merchandise of silver, and the gain thereof than fine gold.

15 She *is* more precious than rubies: and all the things thou canst desire are not to be compared unto her.

16 Length of days *is* in her right hand; *and* in her left hand riches and honour.

17 Her ways *are* ways of pleasantness, and all her paths *are* peace.

18 She *is* a tree of life to them that lay hold upon her: and happy *is every one* that retaineth her.

19 The LORD by wisdom hath founded the earth; by understanding hath he established the heavens.

20 By his knowledge the depths are broken up, and the clouds drop down the dew.

21 My son, let not them depart from thine eyes: keep sound wisdom and discretion:

22 So shall they be life unto thy soul, and grace to thy neck.

23 Then shalt thou walk in thy way safely, and thy foot shall not stumble.

24 When thou liest down, thou shalt not be afraid: yea, thou shalt lie down, and thy sleep shall be sweet.

25 Be not afraid of sudden fear, neither of the desolation of the wicked, when it cometh.

26 For the LORD shall be thy confidence, and shall keep thy foot from being taken.

27 Withhold not good from them to whom it is due, when it is in the power of thine hand to do *it*.

NEW LIVING TRANSLATION

5 Trust in the LORD with all your heart;
do not depend on your own understanding.
6 Seek his will in all you do,
and he will show you which path to take.
7 Don't be impressed with your own wisdom.
Instead, fear the LORD and turn away from evil.
8 Then you will have healing for your body
and strength for your bones.
9 Honor the LORD with your wealth
and with the best part of everything
you produce.
10 Then he will fill your barns with grain,
and your vats will overflow with good wine.
11 My child, don't reject the LORD's discipline,
and don't be upset when he corrects you.
12 For the LORD corrects those he loves,
just as a father corrects a child in whom
he delights.*
13 Joyful is the person who finds wisdom,
the one who gains understanding.
14 For wisdom is more profitable than silver,
and her wages are better than gold.
15 Wisdom is more precious than rubies;
nothing you desire can compare with her.
16 She offers you long life in her right hand,
and riches and honor in her left.
17 She will guide you down delightful paths;
all her ways are satisfying.
18 Wisdom is a tree of life to those who embrace her;
happy are those who hold her tightly.
19 By wisdom the LORD founded the earth;
by understanding he created the heavens.
20 By his knowledge the deep fountains of the earth
burst forth,
and the dew settles beneath the night sky.

21 My child, don't lose sight of common sense
and discernment.
Hang on to them,
22 for they will refresh your soul.
They are like jewels on a necklace.
23 They keep you safe on your way,
and your feet will not stumble.
24 You can go to bed without fear;
you will lie down and sleep soundly.
25 You need not be afraid of sudden disaster
or the destruction that comes upon
the wicked,
26 for the LORD is your security.
He will keep your foot from being caught
in a trap.

27 Do not withhold good from those who deserve it
when it's in your power to help them.

3:12 Greek version reads *And he punishes those he accepts as his children.* Compare Heb 12:6.

KING JAMES VERSION

28 Say not unto thy neighbour, Go, and come again,
and tomorrow I will give; when thou hast it by thee.
29 Devise not evil against thy neighbour, seeing he
dwelleth securely by thee.
30 Strive not with a man without cause, if he have
done thee no harm.
31 Envy thou not the oppressor, and choose none
of his ways.
32 For the froward *is* abomination to the LORD: but
his secret *is* with the righteous.
33 The curse of the LORD *is* in the house of the
wicked: but he blesseth the habitation of the just.
34 Surely he scorneth the scorners: but he giveth
grace unto the lowly.
35 The wise shall inherit glory: but shame shall be
the promotion of fools.

4 1 Hear, ye children, the instruction of a father,
and attend to know understanding.
2 For I give you good doctrine, forsake ye not my
law.
3 For I was my father's son, tender and only *beloved*
in the sight of my mother.
4 He taught me also, and said unto me, Let thine
heart retain my words: keep my commandments,
and live.
5 Get wisdom, get understanding: forget *it* not;
neither decline from the words of my mouth.
6 Forsake her not, and she shall preserve thee: love
her, and she shall keep thee.
7 Wisdom *is* the principal thing; *therefore* get wisdom: and with all thy getting get understanding.
8 Exalt her, and she shall promote thee: she shall
bring thee to honour, when thou dost embrace her.
9 She shall give to thine head an ornament of
grace: a crown of glory shall she deliver to thee.
10 Hear, O my son, and receive my sayings; and the
years of thy life shall be many.
11 I have taught thee in the way of wisdom; I have
led thee in right paths.
12 When thou goest, thy steps shall not be straitened; and when thou runnest, thou shalt not stumble.
13 Take fast hold of instruction; let *her* not go: keep
her; for she *is* thy life.
14 Enter not into the path of the wicked, and go not
in the way of evil *men*.

NEW LIVING TRANSLATION

28 If you can help your neighbor now, don't say,
"Come back tomorrow, and then I'll help you."

29 Don't plot harm against your neighbor,
for those who live nearby trust you.

30 Don't pick a fight without reason,
when no one has done you harm.

31 Don't envy violent people
or copy their ways.

32 Such wicked people are detestable to the LORD,
but he offers his friendship to the godly.

33 The LORD curses the house of the wicked,
but he blesses the home of the upright.

34 The LORD mocks the mockers
but is gracious to the humble.*

35 The wise inherit honor,
but fools are put to shame!

A Father's Wise Advice

4 1 My children,* listen when your father
corrects you.
Pay attention and learn good judgment,
2 for I am giving you good guidance.
Don't turn away from my instructions.
3 For I, too, was once my father's son,
tenderly loved as my mother's only child.

4 My father taught me,
"Take my words to heart.
Follow my commands, and you will live.
5 Get wisdom; develop good judgment.
Don't forget my words or turn away
from them.
6 Don't turn your back on wisdom, for she will
protect you.
Love her, and she will guard you.
7 Getting wisdom is the wisest thing you can do!
And whatever else you do, develop good
judgment.
8 If you prize wisdom, she will make you great.
Embrace her, and she will honor you.
9 She will place a lovely wreath on your head;
she will present you with a beautiful crown."

10 My child,* listen to me and do as I say,
and you will have a long, good life.
11 I will teach you wisdom's ways
and lead you in straight paths.
12 When you walk, you won't be held back;
when you run, you won't stumble.
13 Take hold of my instructions; don't let them go.
Guard them, for they are the key to life.

14 Don't do as the wicked do,
and don't follow the path of evildoers.

3:34 Greek version reads *The LORD opposes the proud / but favors the humble.* Compare Jas 4:6; 1 Pet 5:5. **4:1** Hebrew *My sons.* **4:10** Hebrew *My son;* also in 4:20.

KING JAMES VERSION

15 Avoid it, pass not by it, turn from it, and pass away.

16 For they sleep not, except they have done mischief; and their sleep is taken away, unless they cause *some* to fall.

17 For they eat the bread of wickedness, and drink the wine of violence.

18 But the path of the just *is* as the shining light, that shineth more and more unto the perfect day.

19 The way of the wicked *is* as darkness: they know not at what they stumble.

20 My son, attend to my words; incline thine ear unto my sayings.

21 Let them not depart from thine eyes; keep them in the midst of thine heart.

22 For they *are* life unto those that find them, and health to all their flesh.

23 Keep thy heart with all diligence; for out of it *are* the issues of life.

24 Put away from thee a froward mouth, and perverse lips put far from thee.

25 Let thine eyes look right on, and let thine eyelids look straight before thee.

26 Ponder the path of thy feet, and let all thy ways be established.

27 Turn not to the right hand nor to the left: remove thy foot from evil.

5 1 My son, attend unto my wisdom, *and* bow thine ear to my understanding:

2 That thou mayest regard discretion, and *that* thy lips may keep knowledge.

3 For the lips of a strange woman drop *as* an honeycomb, and her mouth *is* smoother than oil:

4 But her end is bitter as wormwood, sharp as a twoedged sword.

5 Her feet go down to death; her steps take hold on hell.

6 Lest thou shouldest ponder the path of life, her ways are moveable, *that* thou canst not know *them*.

7 Hear me now therefore, O ye children, and depart not from the words of my mouth.

8 Remove thy way far from her, and come not nigh the door of her house:

9 Lest thou give thine honour unto others, and thy years unto the cruel:

NEW LIVING TRANSLATION

15 Don't even think about it; don't go that way.
Turn away and keep moving.
16 For evil people can't sleep until they've done their evil deed for the day.
They can't rest until they've caused someone to stumble.
17 They eat the food of wickedness
and drink the wine of violence!

18 The way of the righteous is like the first gleam of dawn,
which shines ever brighter until the full light of day.
19 But the way of the wicked is like total darkness.
They have no idea what they are stumbling over.

20 My child, pay attention to what I say.
Listen carefully to my words.
21 Don't lose sight of them.
Let them penetrate deep into your heart,
22 for they bring life to those who find them,
and healing to their whole body.

23 Guard your heart above all else,
for it determines the course of your life.

24 Avoid all perverse talk;
stay away from corrupt speech.

25 Look straight ahead,
and fix your eyes on what lies before you.
26 Mark out a straight path for your feet;
stay on the safe path.
27 Don't get sidetracked;
keep your feet from following evil.

Avoid Immoral Women

5 1 My son, pay attention to my wisdom;
listen carefully to my wise counsel.
2 Then you will show discernment,
and your lips will express what you've learned.
3 For the lips of an immoral woman are as sweet as honey,
and her mouth is smoother than oil.
4 But in the end she is as bitter as poison,
as dangerous as a double-edged sword.
5 Her feet go down to death;
her steps lead straight to the grave.*
6 For she cares nothing about the path to life.
She staggers down a crooked trail and doesn't realize it.

7 So now, my sons, listen to me.
Never stray from what I am about to say:
8 Stay away from her!
Don't go near the door of her house!
9 If you do, you will lose your honor
and will lose to merciless people all you have achieved.

5:5 Hebrew *to Sheol*.

KING JAMES VERSION

10 Lest strangers be filled with thy wealth; and thy
labours *be* in the house of a stranger;
11 And thou mourn at the last, when thy flesh and
thy body are consumed,
12 And say, How have I hated instruction, and my
heart despised reproof;
13 And have not obeyed the voice of my teachers,
nor inclined mine ear to them that instructed me!
14 I was almost in all evil in the midst of the congregation and assembly.
15 Drink waters out of thine own cistern, and running waters out of thine own well.
16 Let thy fountains be dispersed abroad, *and*
rivers of waters in the streets.
17 Let them be only thine own, and not strangers'
with thee.
18 Let thy fountain be blessed: and rejoice with the
wife of thy youth.
19 *Let her be as* the loving hind and pleasant roe; let
her breasts satisfy thee at all times; and be thou
ravished always with her love.
20 And why wilt thou, my son, be ravished with
a strange woman, and embrace the bosom of a
stranger?
21 For the ways of man *are* before the eyes of the
LORD, and he pondereth all his goings.
22 His own iniquities shall take the wicked himself,
and he shall be holden with the cords of his sins.
23 He shall die without instruction; and in the
greatness of his folly he shall go astray.

6 1 My son, if thou be surety for thy friend, *if* thou
hast stricken thy hand with a stranger,
2 Thou art snared with the words of thy mouth,
thou art taken with the words of thy mouth.
3 Do this now, my son, and deliver thyself, when
thou art come into the hand of thy friend; go, humble
thyself, and make sure thy friend.
4 Give not sleep to thine eyes, nor slumber to thine
eyelids.
5 Deliver thyself as a roe from the hand *of the*
hunter, and as a bird from the hand of the fowler.
6 Go to the ant, thou sluggard; consider her ways,
and be wise:
7 Which having no guide, overseer, or ruler,
8 Provideth her meat in the summer, *and* gathereth
her food in the harvest.

NEW LIVING TRANSLATION

10 Strangers will consume your wealth,
and someone else will enjoy the fruit of your labor.
11 In the end you will groan in anguish
when disease consumes your body.
12 You will say, "How I hated discipline!
If only I had not ignored all the warnings!
13 Oh, why didn't I listen to my teachers?
Why didn't I pay attention to my instructors?
14 I have come to the brink of utter ruin,
and now I must face public disgrace."

15 Drink water from your own well—
share your love only with your wife.*
16 Why spill the water of your springs in the streets,
having sex with just anyone?*
17 You should reserve it for yourselves.
Never share it with strangers.

18 Let your wife be a fountain of blessing for you.
Rejoice in the wife of your youth.
19 She is a loving deer, a graceful doe.
Let her breasts satisfy you always.
May you always be captivated by her love.
20 Why be captivated, my son, by an immoral woman,
or fondle the breasts of a promiscuous woman?

21 For the LORD sees clearly what a man does,
examining every path he takes.
22 An evil man is held captive by his own sins;
they are ropes that catch and hold him.
23 He will die for lack of self-control;
he will be lost because of his great foolishness.

Lessons for Daily Life

6 1 My child,* if you have put up security for a friend's debt
or agreed to guarantee the debt of a stranger—
2 if you have trapped yourself by your agreement
and are caught by what you said—
3 follow my advice and save yourself,
for you have placed yourself at your friend's mercy.
Now swallow your pride;
go and beg to have your name erased.
4 Don't put it off; do it now!
Don't rest until you do.
5 Save yourself like a gazelle escaping from a hunter,
like a bird fleeing from a net.

6 Take a lesson from the ants, you lazybones.
Learn from their ways and become wise!
7 Though they have no prince
or governor or ruler to make them work,
8 they labor hard all summer,
gathering food for the winter.

5:15 Hebrew *Drink water from your own cistern, / flowing water from your own well.* **5:16** Hebrew *Why spill your springs in the streets, / your streams in the city squares?* **6:1** Hebrew *My son.*

KING JAMES VERSION

9 How long wilt thou sleep, O sluggard? when wilt
thou arise out of thy sleep?
10 *Yet* a little sleep, a little slumber, a little folding of
the hands to sleep:
11 So shall thy poverty come as one that travelleth,
and thy want as an armed man.
12 A naughty person, a wicked man, walketh with a
froward mouth.
13 He winketh with his eyes, he speaketh with his
feet, he teacheth with his fingers;
14 Frowardness *is* in his heart, he deviseth mischief
continually; he soweth discord.
15 Therefore shall his calamity come suddenly;
suddenly shall he be broken without remedy.
16 These six *things* doth the LORD hate: yea, seven
are an abomination unto him:
17 A proud look, a lying tongue, and hands that
shed innocent blood,
18 An heart that deviseth wicked imaginations, feet
that be swift in running to mischief,
19 A false witness *that* speaketh lies, and he that
soweth discord among brethren.
20 My son, keep thy father's commandment, and
forsake not the law of thy mother:
21 Bind them continually upon thine heart, *and* tie
them about thy neck.
22 When thou goest, it shall lead thee; when thou
sleepest, it shall keep thee; and *when* thou awakest,
it shall talk with thee.
23 For the commandment *is* a lamp; and the law *is*
light; and reproofs of instruction *are* the way of life:
24 To keep thee from the evil woman, from the flattery of the tongue of a strange woman.
25 Lust not after her beauty in thine heart; neither
let her take thee with her eyelids.
26 For by means of a whorish woman *a man is*
brought to a piece of bread: and the adulteress will
hunt for the precious life.
27 Can a man take fire in his bosom, and his clothes
not be burned?
28 Can one go upon hot coals, and his feet not be
burned?
29 So he that goeth in to his neighbour's wife; whosoever toucheth her shall not be innocent.
30 *Men* do not despise a thief, if he steal to satisfy
his soul when he is hungry;
31 But *if* he be found, he shall restore sevenfold; he
shall give all the substance of his house.

NEW LIVING TRANSLATION

9 But you, lazybones, how long will you sleep?
When will you wake up?
10 A little extra sleep, a little more slumber,
a little folding of the hands to rest—
11 then poverty will pounce on you like a bandit;
scarcity will attack you like an armed robber.

12 What are worthless and wicked people like?
They are constant liars,
13 signaling their deceit with a wink of the eye,
a nudge of the foot, or the wiggle of fingers.
14 Their perverted hearts plot evil,
and they constantly stir up trouble.
15 But they will be destroyed suddenly,
broken in an instant beyond all hope
of healing.

16 There are six things the LORD hates—
no, seven things he detests:
17 haughty eyes,
a lying tongue,
hands that kill the innocent,
18 a heart that plots evil,
feet that race to do wrong,
19 a false witness who pours out lies,
a person who sows discord in a family.

20 My son, obey your father's commands,
and don't neglect your mother's instruction.
21 Keep their words always in your heart.
Tie them around your neck.
22 When you walk, their counsel will lead you.
When you sleep, they will protect you.
When you wake up, they will advise you.
23 For their command is a lamp
and their instruction a light;
their corrective discipline
is the way to life.
24 It will keep you from the immoral woman,
from the smooth tongue of a promiscuous
woman.
25 Don't lust for her beauty.
Don't let her coy glances seduce you.
26 For a prostitute will bring you to poverty,*
but sleeping with another man's wife will
cost you your life.
27 Can a man scoop a flame into his lap
and not have his clothes catch on fire?
28 Can he walk on hot coals
and not blister his feet?
29 So it is with the man who sleeps with another
man's wife.
He who embraces her will not go unpunished.

30 Excuses might be found for a thief
who steals because he is starving.
31 But if he is caught, he must pay back seven times
what he stole,
even if he has to sell everything in his house.

6:26 Hebrew *to a loaf of bread.*

KING JAMES VERSION

32 *But* whoso committeth adultery with a woman lacketh understanding: he *that* doeth it destroyeth his own soul.

33 A wound and dishonour shall he get; and his reproach shall not be wiped away.

34 For jealousy *is* the rage of a man: therefore he will not spare in the day of vengeance.

35 He will not regard any ransom; neither will he rest content, though thou givest many gifts.

7 1 My son, keep my words, and lay up my commandments with thee.

2 Keep my commandments, and live; and my law as the apple of thine eye.

3 Bind them upon thy fingers, write them upon the table of thine heart.

4 Say unto wisdom, Thou *art* my sister; and call understanding *thy* kinswoman:

5 That they may keep thee from the strange woman, from the stranger *which* flattereth with her words.

6 For at the window of my house I looked through my casement,

7 And beheld among the simple ones, I discerned among the youths, a young man void of understanding,

8 Passing through the street near her corner; and he went the way to her house,

9 In the twilight, in the evening, in the black and dark night:

10 And, behold, there met him a woman *with* the attire of an harlot, and subtil of heart.

11 (She *is* loud and stubborn; her feet abide not in her house:

12 Now *is she* without, now in the streets, and lieth in wait at every corner.)

13 So she caught him, and kissed him, *and* with an impudent face said unto him,

14 *I have* peace offerings with me; this day have I payed my vows.

15 Therefore came I forth to meet thee, diligently to seek thy face, and I have found thee.

16 I have decked my bed with coverings of tapestry, with carved *works,* with fine linen of Egypt.

17 I have perfumed my bed with myrrh, aloes, and cinnamon.

18 Come, let us take our fill of love until the morning: let us solace ourselves with loves.

19 For the goodman *is* not at home, he is gone a long journey:

NEW LIVING TRANSLATION

32 But the man who commits adultery
is an utter fool,
for he destroys himself.
33 He will be wounded and disgraced.
His shame will never be erased.
34 For the woman's jealous husband will be furious,
and he will show no mercy when he takes
revenge.
35 He will accept no compensation,
nor be satisfied with a payoff of any size.

Another Warning about Immoral Women

7 1 Follow my advice, my son;
always treasure my commands.
2 Obey my commands and live!
Guard my instructions as you guard your
own eyes.*
3 Tie them on your fingers as a reminder.
Write them deep within your heart.

4 Love wisdom like a sister;
make insight a beloved member of
your family.
5 Let them protect you from an affair with
an immoral woman,
from listening to the flattery of a
promiscuous woman.

6 While I was at the window of my house,
looking through the curtain,
7 I saw some naive young men,
and one in particular who lacked
common sense.
8 He was crossing the street near the house
of an immoral woman,
strolling down the path by her house.
9 It was at twilight, in the evening,
as deep darkness fell.
10 The woman approached him,
seductively dressed and sly of heart.
11 She was the brash, rebellious type,
never content to stay at home.
12 She is often in the streets and markets,
soliciting at every corner.
13 She threw her arms around him and kissed him,
and with a brazen look she said,
14 "I've just made my peace offerings
and fulfilled my vows.
15 You're the one I was looking for!
I came out to find you, and here you are!
16 My bed is spread with beautiful blankets,
with colored sheets of Egyptian linen.
17 I've perfumed my bed
with myrrh, aloes, and cinnamon.
18 Come, let's drink our fill of love until morning.
Let's enjoy each other's caresses,
19 for my husband is not home.
He's away on a long trip.

7:2 Hebrew *as the pupil of your eye.*

KING JAMES VERSION

20He hath taken a bag of money with him, *and* will come home at the day appointed.

21With her much fair speech she caused him to yield, with the flattering of her lips she forced him.

22He goeth after her straightway, as an ox goeth to the slaughter, or as a fool to the correction of the stocks;

23Till a dart strike through his liver; as a bird hasteth to the snare, and knoweth not that it *is* for his life.

24Hearken unto me now therefore, O ye children, and attend to the words of my mouth.

25Let not thine heart decline to her ways, go not astray in her paths.

26For she hath cast down many wounded: yea, many strong *men* have been slain by her.

27Her house *is* the way to hell, going down to the chambers of death.

8 1Doth not wisdom cry? and understanding put forth her voice?

2She standeth in the top of high places, by the way in the places of the paths.

3She crieth at the gates, at the entry of the city, at the coming in at the doors.

4Unto you, O men, I call; and my voice *is* to the sons of man.

5O ye simple, understand wisdom: and, ye fools, be ye of an understanding heart.

6Hear; for I will speak of excellent things; and the opening of my lips *shall be* right things.

7For my mouth shall speak truth; and wickedness *is* an abomination to my lips.

8All the words of my mouth *are* in righteousness; *there is* nothing froward or perverse in them.

9They *are* all plain to him that understandeth, and right to them that find knowledge.

10Receive my instruction, and not silver; and knowledge rather than choice gold.

11For wisdom *is* better than rubies; and all the things that may be desired are not to be compared to it.

12I wisdom dwell with prudence, and find out knowledge of witty inventions.

13The fear of the LORD *is* to hate evil: pride, and arrogancy, and the evil way, and the froward mouth, do I hate.

14Counsel *is* mine, and sound wisdom: I *am* understanding; I have strength.

15By me kings reign, and princes decree justice.

NEW LIVING TRANSLATION

20 He has taken a wallet full of money with him
and won't return until later this month.*"

21 So she seduced him with her pretty speech
and enticed him with her flattery.
22 He followed her at once,
like an ox going to the slaughter.
He was like a stag caught in a trap,
23 awaiting the arrow that would pierce its heart.
He was like a bird flying into a snare,
little knowing it would cost him his life.

24 So listen to me, my sons,
and pay attention to my words.
25 Don't let your hearts stray away toward her.
Don't wander down her wayward path.
26 For she has been the ruin of many;
many men have been her victims.
27 Her house is the road to the grave.*
Her bedroom is the den of death.

Wisdom Calls for a Hearing

8 1 Listen as Wisdom calls out!
Hear as understanding raises her voice!
2 On the hilltop along the road,
she takes her stand at the crossroads.
3 By the gates at the entrance to the town,
on the road leading in, she cries aloud,
4 "I call to you, to all of you!
I raise my voice to all people.
5 You simple people, use good judgment.
You foolish people, show some understanding.
6 Listen to me! For I have important things
to tell you.
Everything I say is right,
7 for I speak the truth
and detest every kind of deception.
8 My advice is wholesome.
There is nothing devious or crooked in it.
9 My words are plain to anyone with
understanding,
clear to those with knowledge.
10 Choose my instruction rather than silver,
and knowledge rather than pure gold.
11 For wisdom is far more valuable than rubies.
Nothing you desire can compare with it.

12 "I, Wisdom, live together with good judgment.
I know where to discover knowledge and
discernment.
13 All who fear the LORD will hate evil.
Therefore, I hate pride and arrogance,
corruption and perverse speech.
14 Common sense and success belong to me.
Insight and strength are mine.
15 Because of me, kings reign,
and rulers make just decrees.

7:20 Hebrew *until the moon is full.* **7:27** Hebrew *to Sheol.*

KING JAMES VERSION

16 By me princes rule, and nobles, *even* all the
judges of the earth.
17 I love them that love me; and those that seek me
early shall find me.
18 Riches and honour *are* with me; *yea,* durable
riches and righteousness.
19 My fruit *is* better than gold, yea, than fine gold;
and my revenue than choice silver.
20 I lead in the way of righteousness, in the midst of
the paths of judgment:
21 That I may cause those that love me to inherit
substance; and I will fill their treasures.
22 The LORD possessed me in the beginning of his
way, before his works of old.
23 I was set up from everlasting, from the beginning, or ever the earth was.
24 When *there were* no depths, I was brought
forth; when *there were* no fountains abounding
with water.
25 Before the mountains were settled, before the
hills was I brought forth:
26 While as yet he had not made the earth, nor the
fields, nor the highest part of the dust of the world.
27 When he prepared the heavens, I *was* there:
when he set a compass upon the face of the depth:
28 When he established the clouds above: when he
strengthened the fountains of the deep:
29 When he gave to the sea his decree, that the
waters should not pass his commandment: when he
appointed the foundations of the earth:
30 Then I was by him, *as* one brought up *with him:*
and I was daily *his* delight, rejoicing always before
him;
31 Rejoicing in the habitable part of his earth; and
my delights *were* with the sons of men.
32 Now therefore hearken unto me, O ye children:
for blessed *are they that* keep my ways.
33 Hear instruction, and be wise, and refuse it not.
34 Blessed *is* the man that heareth me, watching
daily at my gates, waiting at the posts of my doors.
35 For whoso findeth me findeth life, and shall obtain favour of the LORD.
36 But he that sinneth against me wrongeth his
own soul: all they that hate me love death.

9 1 Wisdom hath builded her house, she hath
hewn out her seven pillars:
2 She hath killed her beasts; she hath mingled her
wine; she hath also furnished her table.
3 She hath sent forth her maidens: she crieth upon
the highest places of the city,

NEW LIVING TRANSLATION

16 Rulers lead with my help,
and nobles make righteous judgments.*
17 "I love all who love me.
Those who search will surely find me.
18 I have riches and honor,
as well as enduring wealth and justice.
19 My gifts are better than gold, even the purest gold,
my wages better than sterling silver!
20 I walk in righteousness,
in paths of justice.
21 Those who love me inherit wealth.
I will fill their treasuries.
22 "The LORD formed me from the beginning,
before he created anything else.
23 I was appointed in ages past,
at the very first, before the earth began.
24 I was born before the oceans were created,
before the springs bubbled forth their waters.
25 Before the mountains were formed,
before the hills, I was born—
26 before he had made the earth and fields
and the first handfuls of soil.
27 I was there when he established the heavens,
when he drew the horizon on the oceans.
28 I was there when he set the clouds above,
when he established springs deep in the earth.
29 I was there when he set the limits of the seas,
so they would not spread beyond their
boundaries.
And when he marked off the earth's foundations,
30 I was the architect at his side.
I was his constant delight,
rejoicing always in his presence.
31 And how happy I was with the world he created;
how I rejoiced with the human family!
32 "And so, my children,* listen to me,
for all who follow my ways are joyful.
33 Listen to my instruction and be wise.
Don't ignore it.
34 Joyful are those who listen to me,
watching for me daily at my gates,
waiting for me outside my home!
35 For whoever finds me finds life
and receives favor from the LORD.
36 But those who miss me injure themselves.
All who hate me love death."

9 1 Wisdom has built her house;
she has carved its seven columns.
2 She has prepared a great banquet,
mixed the wines, and set the table.
3 She has sent her servants to invite everyone
to come.
She calls out from the heights overlooking
the city.

8:16 Some Hebrew manuscripts and Greek version read *and nobles are judges over the earth.* **8:32** Hebrew *my sons.*

KING JAMES VERSION

4 Whoso *is* simple, let him turn in hither: *as for* him
that wanteth understanding, she saith to him,
5 Come, eat of my bread, and drink of the wine
which I have mingled.
6 Forsake the foolish, and live; and go in the way of
understanding.
7 He that reproveth a scorner getteth to himself
shame: and he that rebuketh a wicked *man getteth*
himself a blot.
8 Reprove not a scorner, lest he hate thee: rebuke a
wise man, and he will love thee.
9 Give *instruction* to a wise *man*, and he will be
yet wiser: teach a just *man*, and he will increase in
learning.
10 The fear of the LORD *is* the beginning of wisdom:
and the knowledge of the holy *is* understanding.
11 For by me thy days shall be multiplied, and the
years of thy life shall be increased.
12 If thou be wise, thou shalt be wise for thyself:
but *if* thou scornest, thou alone shalt bear *it*.

13 A foolish woman *is* clamorous: *she is* simple, and
knoweth nothing.
14 For she sitteth at the door of her house, on a seat
in the high places of the city,
15 To call passengers who go right on their ways:
16 Whoso *is* simple, let him turn in hither: and *as*
for him that wanteth understanding, she saith to
him,
17 Stolen waters are sweet, and bread *eaten* in secret is pleasant.
18 But he knoweth not that the dead *are* there; *and*
that her guests *are* in the depths of hell.

10 1 The proverbs of Solomon. A wise son maketh a glad father: but a foolish son *is* the
heaviness of his mother.
2 Treasures of wickedness profit nothing: but righteousness delivereth from death.
3 The LORD will not suffer the soul of the righteous
to famish: but he casteth away the substance of the
wicked.
4 He becometh poor that dealeth *with* a slack
hand: but the hand of the diligent maketh rich.

NEW LIVING TRANSLATION

4 "Come in with me," she urges the simple.
To those who lack good judgment, she says,
5 "Come, eat my food,
and drink the wine I have mixed.
6 Leave your simple ways behind, and begin to live;
learn to use good judgment."
7 Anyone who rebukes a mocker will get an insult
in return.
Anyone who corrects the wicked will get hurt.
8 So don't bother correcting mockers;
they will only hate you.
But correct the wise,
and they will love you.
9 Instruct the wise,
and they will be even wiser.
Teach the righteous,
and they will learn even more.
10 Fear of the LORD is the foundation of wisdom.
Knowledge of the Holy One results in
good judgment.
11 Wisdom will multiply your days
and add years to your life.
12 If you become wise, you will be the one
to benefit.
If you scorn wisdom, you will be the one
to suffer.

Folly Calls for a Hearing

13 The woman named Folly is brash.
She is ignorant and doesn't know it.
14 She sits in her doorway
on the heights overlooking the city.
15 She calls out to men going by
who are minding their own business.
16 "Come in with me," she urges the simple.
To those who lack good judgment, she says,
17 "Stolen water is refreshing;
food eaten in secret tastes the best!"
18 But little do they know that the dead are there.
Her guests are in the depths of the grave.*

The Proverbs of Solomon

10 The proverbs of Solomon:

A wise child* brings joy to a father;
a foolish child brings grief to a mother.

2 Tainted wealth has no lasting value,
but right living can save your life.

3 The LORD will not let the godly go hungry,
but he refuses to satisfy the craving
of the wicked.

4 Lazy people are soon poor;
hard workers get rich.

9:18 Hebrew *in Sheol*. **10:1** Hebrew *son;* also in 10:1b.

KING JAMES VERSION

5 He that gathereth in summer *is* a wise son: *but* he that sleepeth in harvest *is* a son that causeth shame.

6 Blessings *are* upon the head of the just: but violence covereth the mouth of the wicked.

7 The memory of the just *is* blessed: but the name of the wicked shall rot.

8 The wise in heart will receive commandments: but a prating fool shall fall.

9 He that walketh uprightly walketh surely: but he that perverteth his ways shall be known.

10 He that winketh with the eye causeth sorrow: but a prating fool shall fall.

11 The mouth of a righteous *man is* a well of life: but violence covereth the mouth of the wicked.

12 Hatred stirreth up strifes: but love covereth all sins.

13 In the lips of him that hath understanding wisdom is found: but a rod *is* for the back of him that is void of understanding.

14 Wise *men* lay up knowledge: but the mouth of the foolish *is* near destruction.

15 The rich man's wealth *is* his strong city: the destruction of the poor *is* their poverty.

16 The labour of the righteous *tendeth* to life: the fruit of the wicked to sin.

17 He *is in* the way of life that keepeth instruction: but he that refuseth reproof erreth.

18 He that hideth hatred *with* lying lips, and he that uttereth a slander, *is* a fool.

19 In the multitude of words there wanteth not sin: but he that refraineth his lips *is* wise.

20 The tongue of the just *is as* choice silver: the heart of the wicked *is* little worth.

21 The lips of the righteous feed many: but fools die for want of wisdom.

22 The blessing of the LORD, it maketh rich, and he addeth no sorrow with it.

23 *It is* as sport to a fool to do mischief: but a man of understanding hath wisdom.

24 The fear of the wicked, it shall come upon him: but the desire of the righteous shall be granted.

NEW LIVING TRANSLATION

5 A wise youth harvests in the summer,
but one who sleeps during harvest is a disgrace.

6 The godly are showered with blessings;
the words of the wicked conceal violent intentions.

7 We have happy memories of the godly,
but the name of a wicked person rots away.

8 The wise are glad to be instructed,
but babbling fools fall flat on their faces.

9 People with integrity walk safely,
but those who follow crooked paths will slip and fall.

10 People who wink at wrong cause trouble,
but a bold reproof promotes peace.*

11 The words of the godly are a life-giving fountain;
the words of the wicked conceal violent intentions.

12 Hatred stirs up quarrels,
but love makes up for all offenses.

13 Wise words come from the lips of people with understanding,
but those lacking sense will be beaten with a rod.

14 Wise people treasure knowledge,
but the babbling of a fool invites disaster.

15 The wealth of the rich is their fortress;
the poverty of the poor is their destruction.

16 The earnings of the godly enhance their lives,
but evil people squander their money on sin.

17 People who accept discipline are on the pathway to life,
but those who ignore correction will go astray.

18 Hiding hatred makes you a liar;
slandering others makes you a fool.

19 Too much talk leads to sin.
Be sensible and keep your mouth shut.

20 The words of the godly are like sterling silver;
the heart of a fool is worthless.

21 The words of the godly encourage many,
but fools are destroyed by their lack of common sense.

22 The blessing of the LORD makes a person rich,
and he adds no sorrow with it.

23 Doing wrong is fun for a fool,
but living wisely brings pleasure to the sensible.

24 The fears of the wicked will be fulfilled;
the hopes of the godly will be granted.

10:10 As in Greek version; Hebrew reads *but babbling fools fall flat on their faces.*

KING JAMES VERSION

[25]As the whirlwind passeth, so *is* the wicked no
more: but the righteous *is* an everlasting foundation.
[26]As vinegar to the teeth, and as smoke to the eyes,
so *is* the sluggard to them that send him.
[27]The fear of the LORD prolongeth days: but the
years of the wicked shall be shortened.
[28]The hope of the righteous *shall be* gladness: but
the expectation of the wicked shall perish.
[29]The way of the LORD *is* strength to the upright:
but destruction *shall be* to the workers of iniquity.
[30]The righteous shall never be removed: but the
wicked shall not inhabit the earth.
[31]The mouth of the just bringeth forth wisdom:
but the froward tongue shall be cut out.
[32]The lips of the righteous know what is acceptable: but the mouth of the wicked *speaketh*
frowardness.

11 [1]A false balance *is* abomination to the LORD:
but a just weight *is* his delight.
[2]*When* pride cometh, then cometh shame: but
with the lowly *is* wisdom.
[3]The integrity of the upright shall guide them: but
the perverseness of transgressors shall destroy
them.
[4]Riches profit not in the day of wrath: but righteousness delivereth from death.
[5]The righteousness of the perfect shall direct his
way: but the wicked shall fall by his own wickedness.
[6]The righteousness of the upright shall deliver
them: but transgressors shall be taken in *their own*
naughtiness.
[7]When a wicked man dieth, *his* expectation shall
perish: and the hope of unjust *men* perisheth.
[8]The righteous is delivered out of trouble, and the
wicked cometh in his stead.
[9]An hypocrite with *his* mouth destroyeth his
neighbour: but through knowledge shall the just be
delivered.
[10]When it goeth well with the righteous, the city
rejoiceth: and when the wicked perish, *there is*
shouting.
[11]By the blessing of the upright the city is exalted:
but it is overthrown by the mouth of the wicked.
[12]He that is void of wisdom despiseth his neighbour: but a man of understanding holdeth his peace.

NEW LIVING TRANSLATION

[25] When the storms of life come, the wicked are
whirled away,
but the godly have a lasting foundation.

[26] Lazy people irritate their employers,
like vinegar to the teeth or smoke in the eyes.

[27] Fear of the LORD lengthens one's life,
but the years of the wicked are cut short.

[28] The hopes of the godly result in happiness,
but the expectations of the wicked come
to nothing.

[29] The way of the LORD is a stronghold to those
with integrity,
but it destroys the wicked.

[30] The godly will never be disturbed,
but the wicked will be removed from the land.

[31] The mouth of the godly person gives wise advice,
but the tongue that deceives will be cut off.

[32] The lips of the godly speak helpful words,
but the mouth of the wicked speaks
perverse words.

11 [1]The LORD detests the use of
dishonest scales,
but he delights in accurate weights.
[2] Pride leads to disgrace,
but with humility comes wisdom.

[3] Honesty guides good people;
dishonesty destroys treacherous people.

[4] Riches won't help on the day of judgment,
but right living can save you from death.

[5] The godly are directed by honesty;
the wicked fall beneath their load of sin.

[6] The godliness of good people rescues them;
the ambition of treacherous people traps them.

[7] When the wicked die, their hopes die with them,
for they rely on their own feeble strength.

[8] The godly are rescued from trouble,
and it falls on the wicked instead.

[9] With their words, the godless destroy
their friends,
but knowledge will rescue the righteous.

[10] The whole city celebrates when the
godly succeed;
they shout for joy when the wicked die.

[11] Upright citizens are good for a city and make
it prosper,
but the talk of the wicked tears it apart.

[12] It is foolish to belittle one's neighbor;
a sensible person keeps quiet.

KING JAMES VERSION

[13]A talebearer revealeth secrets: but he that is of a
faithful spirit concealeth the matter.
[14]Where no counsel *is,* the people fall: but in the
multitude of counsellors *there is* safety.
[15]He that is surety for a stranger shall smart *for it:*
and he that hateth suretiship is sure.
[16]A gracious woman retaineth honour: and strong
men retain riches.
[17]The merciful man doeth good to his own soul:
but *he that is* cruel troubleth his own flesh.
[18]The wicked worketh a deceitful work: but to him
that soweth righteousness *shall be* a sure reward.
[19]As righteousness *tendeth* to life: so he that
pursueth evil *pursueth it* to his own death.
[20]They that are of a froward heart *are* abomination
to the LORD: but *such as are* upright in *their* way
are his delight.
[21]*Though* hand *join* in hand, the wicked shall not
be unpunished: but the seed of the righteous shall be
delivered.
[22]*As* a jewel of gold in a swine's snout, *so is* a fair
woman which is without discretion.
[23]The desire of the righteous *is* only good: *but* the
expectation of the wicked *is* wrath.
[24]There is that scattereth, and yet increaseth; and
there is that withholdeth more than is meet, but *it*
tendeth to poverty.
[25]The liberal soul shall be made fat: and he that
watereth shall be watered also himself.
[26]He that withholdeth corn, the people shall curse
him: but blessing *shall be* upon the head of him that
selleth *it.*
[27]He that diligently seeketh good procureth favour:
but he that seeketh mischief, it shall come
unto him.
[28]He that trusteth in his riches shall fall: but the
righteous shall flourish as a branch.
[29]He that troubleth his own house shall inherit
the wind: and the fool *shall be* servant to the wise of
heart.
[30]The fruit of the righteous *is* a tree of life; and he
that winneth souls *is* wise.
[31]Behold, the righteous shall be recompensed in
the earth: much more the wicked and the sinner.

12

[1]Whoso loveth instruction loveth knowledge:
but he that hateth reproof *is* brutish.

NEW LIVING TRANSLATION

[13] A gossip goes around telling secrets,
but those who are trustworthy can keep
a confidence.

[14] Without wise leadership, a nation falls;
there is safety in having many advisers.

[15] There's danger in putting up security for
a stranger's debt;
it's safer not to guarantee another
person's debt.

[16] A gracious woman gains respect,
but ruthless men gain only wealth.

[17] Your kindness will reward you,
but your cruelty will destroy you.

[18] Evil people get rich for the moment,
but the reward of the godly will last.

[19] Godly people find life;
evil people find death.

[20] The LORD detests people with crooked hearts,
but he delights in those with integrity.

[21] Evil people will surely be punished,
but the children of the godly will go free.

[22] A beautiful woman who lacks discretion
is like a gold ring in a pig's snout.

[23] The godly can look forward to a reward,
while the wicked can expect only judgment.

[24] Give freely and become more wealthy;
be stingy and lose everything.

[25] The generous will prosper;
those who refresh others will themselves
be refreshed.

[26] People curse those who hoard their grain,
but they bless the one who sells in time of need.

[27] If you search for good, you will find favor;
but if you search for evil, it will find you!

[28] Trust in your money and down you go!
But the godly flourish like leaves in spring.

[29] Those who bring trouble on their families inherit
the wind.
The fool will be a servant to the wise.

[30] The seeds of good deeds become a tree of life;
a wise person wins friends.*

[31] If the righteous are rewarded here on earth,
what will happen to wicked sinners?*

12

[1] To learn, you must love discipline;
it is stupid to hate correction.

11:30 Or *and those who win souls are wise.* 11:31 Greek version reads *If the righteous are barely saved, / what will happen to godless sinners?* Compare 1 Pet 4:18.

KING JAMES VERSION

2 A good *man* obtaineth favour of the LORD: but a
man of wicked devices will he condemn.
3 A man shall not be established by wickedness:
but the root of the righteous shall not be moved.
4 A virtuous woman *is* a crown to her husband: but
she that maketh ashamed *is* as rottenness in his
bones.
5 The thoughts of the righteous *are* right: *but* the
counsels of the wicked *are* deceit.
6 The words of the wicked *are* to lie in wait for
blood: but the mouth of the upright shall deliver
them.
7 The wicked are overthrown, and *are* not: but the
house of the righteous shall stand.
8 A man shall be commended according to his wisdom: but he that is of a perverse heart shall be
despised.
9 *He that is* despised, and hath a servant, *is* better
than he that honoureth himself, and lacketh bread.
10 A righteous *man* regardeth the life of his beast:
but the tender mercies of the wicked *are* cruel.
11 He that tilleth his land shall be satisfied with
bread: but he that followeth vain *persons is* void of
understanding.
12 The wicked desireth the net of evil *men:* but the
root of the righteous yieldeth *fruit.*
13 The wicked is snared by the transgression of *his*
lips: but the just shall come out of trouble.
14 A man shall be satisfied with good by the fruit of
his mouth: and the recompense of a man's hands
shall be rendered unto him.
15 The way of a fool *is* right in his own eyes: but he
that hearkeneth unto counsel *is* wise.
16 A fool's wrath is presently known: but a prudent
man covereth shame.
17 *He that* speaketh truth sheweth forth righteousness: but a false witness deceit.
18 There is that speaketh like the piercings of a
sword: but the tongue of the wise *is* health.
19 The lip of truth shall be established for ever: but
a lying tongue *is* but for a moment.
20 Deceit *is* in the heart of them that imagine evil:
but to the counsellors of peace *is* joy.
21 There shall no evil happen to the just: but the
wicked shall be filled with mischief.
22 Lying lips *are* abomination to the LORD: but they
that deal truly *are* his delight.
23 A prudent man concealeth knowledge: but the
heart of fools proclaimeth foolishness.

NEW LIVING TRANSLATION

2 The LORD approves of those who are good,
but he condemns those who plan wickedness.

3 Wickedness never brings stability,
but the godly have deep roots.

4 A worthy wife is a crown for her husband,
but a disgraceful woman is like cancer
in his bones.

5 The plans of the godly are just;
the advice of the wicked is treacherous.

6 The words of the wicked are like a
murderous ambush,
but the words of the godly save lives.

7 The wicked die and disappear,
but the family of the godly stands firm.

8 A sensible person wins admiration,
but a warped mind is despised.

9 Better to be an ordinary person with a servant
than to be self-important but have no food.

10 The godly care for their animals,
but the wicked are always cruel.

11 A hard worker has plenty of food,
but a person who chases fantasies has no sense.

12 Thieves are jealous of each other's loot,
but the godly are well rooted and bear their
own fruit.

13 The wicked are trapped by their own words,
but the godly escape such trouble.

14 Wise words bring many benefits,
and hard work brings rewards.

15 Fools think their own way is right,
but the wise listen to others.

16 A fool is quick-tempered,
but a wise person stays calm when insulted.

17 An honest witness tells the truth;
a false witness tells lies.

18 Some people make cutting remarks,
but the words of the wise bring healing.

19 Truthful words stand the test of time,
but lies are soon exposed.

20 Deceit fills hearts that are plotting evil;
joy fills hearts that are planning peace!

21 No harm comes to the godly,
but the wicked have their fill of trouble.

22 The LORD detests lying lips,
but he delights in those who tell the truth.

23 The wise don't make a show of their knowledge,
but fools broadcast their foolishness.

KING JAMES VERSION

24 The hand of the diligent shall bear rule: but the slothful shall be under tribute.

25 Heaviness in the heart of man maketh it stoop: but a good word maketh it glad.

26 The righteous *is* more excellent than his neighbour: but the way of the wicked seduceth them.

27 The slothful *man* roasteth not that which he took in hunting: but the substance of a diligent man *is* precious.

28 In the way of righteousness *is* life; and *in* the pathway *thereof there is* no death.

13

1 A wise son *heareth* his father's instruction: but a scorner heareth not rebuke.

2 A man shall eat good by the fruit of *his* mouth: but the soul of the transgressors *shall eat* violence.

3 He that keepeth his mouth keepeth his life: *but* he that openeth wide his lips shall have destruction.

4 The soul of the sluggard desireth, and *hath* nothing: but the soul of the diligent shall be made fat.

5 A righteous *man* hateth lying: but a wicked *man* is loathsome, and cometh to shame.

6 Righteousness keepeth *him that is* upright in the way: but wickedness overthroweth the sinner.

7 There is that maketh himself rich, yet *hath* nothing: *there is* that maketh himself poor, yet *hath* great riches.

8 The ransom of a man's life *are* his riches: but the poor heareth not rebuke.

9 The light of the righteous rejoiceth: but the lamp of the wicked shall be put out.

10 Only by pride cometh contention: but with the well advised *is* wisdom.

11 Wealth *gotten* by vanity shall be diminished: but he that gathereth by labour shall increase.

12 Hope deferred maketh the heart sick: but *when* the desire cometh, *it is* a tree of life.

13 Whoso despiseth the word shall be destroyed: but he that feareth the commandment shall be rewarded.

14 The law of the wise *is* a fountain of life, to depart from the snares of death.

15 Good understanding giveth favour: but the way of transgressors *is* hard.

NEW LIVING TRANSLATION

24 Work hard and become a leader;
be lazy and become a slave.

25 Worry weighs a person down;
an encouraging word cheers a person up.

26 The godly give good advice to their friends;*
the wicked lead them astray.

27 Lazy people don't even cook the game they catch,
but the diligent make use of everything
they find.

28 The way of the godly leads to life;
that path does not lead to death.

13

1 A wise child accepts a parent's discipline;*
a mocker refuses to listen to correction.

2 Wise words will win you a good meal,
but treacherous people have an appetite
for violence.

3 Those who control their tongue will have
a long life;
opening your mouth can ruin everything.

4 Lazy people want much but get little,
but those who work hard will prosper.

5 The godly hate lies;
the wicked cause shame and disgrace.

6 Godliness guards the path of the blameless,
but the evil are misled by sin.

7 Some who are poor pretend to be rich;
others who are rich pretend to be poor.

8 The rich can pay a ransom for their lives,
but the poor won't even get threatened.

9 The life of the godly is full of light and joy,
but the light of the wicked will be snuffed out.

10 Pride leads to conflict;
those who take advice are wise.

11 Wealth from get-rich-quick schemes quickly
disappears;
wealth from hard work grows over time.

12 Hope deferred makes the heart sick,
but a dream fulfilled is a tree of life.

13 People who despise advice are asking for trouble;
those who respect a command will succeed.

14 The instruction of the wise is like a life-giving
fountain;
those who accept it avoid the snares of death.

15 A person with good sense is respected;
a treacherous person is headed for destruction.*

12:26 Or *The godly are cautious in friendship;* or *The godly are freed from evil.* The meaning of the Hebrew is uncertain. **13:1** Hebrew *A wise son accepts his father's discipline.* **13:15** As in Greek version; Hebrew reads *the way of the treacherous is lasting.*

KING JAMES VERSION

16 Every prudent *man* dealeth with knowledge: but a fool layeth open *his* folly.

17 A wicked messenger falleth into mischief: but a faithful ambassador *is* health.

18 Poverty and shame *shall be to* him that refuseth instruction: but he that regardeth reproof shall be honoured.

19 The desire accomplished is sweet to the soul: but *it is* abomination to fools to depart from evil.

20 He that walketh with wise *men* shall be wise: but a companion of fools shall be destroyed.

21 Evil pursueth sinners: but to the righteous good shall be repayed.

22 A good *man* leaveth an inheritance to his children's children: and the wealth of the sinner *is* laid up for the just.

23 Much food *is in* the tillage of the poor: but there is *that is* destroyed for want of judgment.

24 He that spareth his rod hateth his son: but he that loveth him chasteneth him betimes.

25 The righteous eateth to the satisfying of his soul: but the belly of the wicked shall want.

14 1 Every wise woman buildeth her house: but the foolish plucketh it down with her hands.

2 He that walketh in his uprightness feareth the LORD: but *he that is* perverse in his ways despiseth him.

3 In the mouth of the foolish *is* a rod of pride: but the lips of the wise shall preserve them.

4 Where no oxen *are,* the crib *is* clean: but much increase *is* by the strength of the ox.

5 A faithful witness will not lie: but a false witness will utter lies.

6 A scorner seeketh wisdom, and *findeth it* not: but knowledge *is* easy unto him that understandeth.

7 Go from the presence of a foolish man, when thou perceivest not *in him* the lips of knowledge.

8 The wisdom of the prudent *is* to understand his way: but the folly of fools *is* deceit.

9 Fools make a mock at sin: but among the righteous *there is* favour.

NEW LIVING TRANSLATION

16 Wise people think before they act;
fools don't—and even brag about
their foolishness.

17 An unreliable messenger stumbles into trouble,
but a reliable messenger brings healing.

18 If you ignore criticism, you will end in poverty
and disgrace;
if you accept correction, you will be honored.

19 It is pleasant to see dreams come true,
but fools refuse to turn from evil to
attain them.

20 Walk with the wise and become wise;
associate with fools and get in trouble.

21 Trouble chases sinners,
while blessings reward the righteous.

22 Good people leave an inheritance to their
grandchildren,
but the sinner's wealth passes to the godly.

23 A poor person's farm may produce much food,
but injustice sweeps it all away.

24 Those who spare the rod of discipline hate
their children.
Those who love their children care enough
to discipline them.

25 The godly eat to their hearts' content,
but the belly of the wicked goes hungry.

14 1 A wise woman builds her home,
but a foolish woman tears it down
with her own hands.

2 Those who follow the right path fear the LORD;
those who take the wrong path despise him.

3 A fool's proud talk becomes a rod that beats him,
but the words of the wise keep them safe.

4 Without oxen a stable stays clean,
but you need a strong ox for a large harvest.

5 An honest witness does not lie;
a false witness breathes lies.

6 A mocker seeks wisdom and never finds it,
but knowledge comes easily to those
with understanding.

7 Stay away from fools,
for you won't find knowledge on their lips.

8 The prudent understand where they are going,
but fools deceive themselves.

9 Fools make fun of guilt,
but the godly acknowledge it and
seek reconciliation.

KING JAMES VERSION

10 The heart knoweth his own bitterness; and a stranger doth not intermeddle with his joy.

11 The house of the wicked shall be overthrown: but the tabernacle of the upright shall flourish.

12 There is a way which seemeth right unto a man, but the end thereof *are* the ways of death.

13 Even in laughter the heart is sorrowful; and the end of that mirth *is* heaviness.

14 The backslider in heart shall be filled with his own ways: and a good man *shall be satisfied* from himself.

15 The simple believeth every word: but the prudent *man* looketh well to his going.

16 A wise *man* feareth, and departeth from evil: but the fool rageth, and is confident.

17 *He that is* soon angry dealeth foolishly: and a man of wicked devices is hated.

18 The simple inherit folly: but the prudent are crowned with knowledge.

19 The evil bow before the good; and the wicked at the gates of the righteous.

20 The poor is hated even of his own neighbour: but the rich *hath* many friends.

21 He that despiseth his neighbour sinneth: but he that hath mercy on the poor, happy *is* he.

22 Do they not err that devise evil? but mercy and truth *shall be* to them that devise good.

23 In all labour there is profit: but the talk of the lips *tendeth* only to penury.

24 The crown of the wise *is* their riches: *but* the foolishness of fools *is* folly.

25 A true witness delivereth souls: but a deceitful *witness* speaketh lies.

26 In the fear of the LORD *is* strong confidence: and his children shall have a place of refuge.

27 The fear of the LORD *is* a fountain of life, to depart from the snares of death.

28 In the multitude of people *is* the king's honour: but in the want of people *is* the destruction of the prince.

29 *He that is* slow to wrath *is* of great understanding: but *he that is* hasty of spirit exalteth folly.

30 A sound heart *is* the life of the flesh: but envy the rottenness of the bones.

31 He that oppresseth the poor reproacheth his Maker: but he that honoureth him hath mercy on the poor.

NEW LIVING TRANSLATION

10 Each heart knows its own bitterness,
and no one else can fully share its joy.

11 The house of the wicked will be destroyed,
but the tent of the godly will flourish.

12 There is a path before each person that
seems right,
but it ends in death.

13 Laughter can conceal a heavy heart,
but when the laughter ends, the grief remains.

14 Backsliders get what they deserve;
good people receive their reward.

15 Only simpletons believe everything they're told!
The prudent carefully consider their steps.

16 The wise are cautious* and avoid danger;
fools plunge ahead with reckless confidence.

17 Short-tempered people do foolish things,
and schemers are hated.

18 Simpletons are clothed with foolishness,*
but the prudent are crowned with knowledge.

19 Evil people will bow before good people;
the wicked will bow at the gates of the godly.

20 The poor are despised even by their neighbors,
while the rich have many "friends."

21 It is a sin to belittle one's neighbor;
blessed are those who help the poor.

22 If you plan to do evil, you will be lost;
if you plan to do good, you will receive
unfailing love and faithfulness.

23 Work brings profit,
but mere talk leads to poverty!

24 Wealth is a crown for the wise;
the effort of fools yields only foolishness.

25 A truthful witness saves lives,
but a false witness is a traitor.

26 Those who fear the LORD are secure;
he will be a refuge for their children.

27 Fear of the LORD is a life-giving fountain;
it offers escape from the snares of death.

28 A growing population is a king's glory;
a prince without subjects has nothing.

29 People with understanding control their anger;
a hot temper shows great foolishness.

30 A peaceful heart leads to a healthy body;
jealousy is like cancer in the bones.

31 Those who oppress the poor insult their Maker,
but helping the poor honors him.

14:16 Hebrew *The wise fear.* **14:18** Or *inherit foolishness.*

KING JAMES VERSION

32 The wicked is driven away in his wickedness:
but the righteous hath hope in his death.
33 Wisdom resteth in the heart of him that hath
understanding: but *that which is* in the midst of
fools is made known.
34 Righteousness exalteth a nation: but sin *is* a reproach to any people.
35 The king's favour *is* toward a wise servant: but
his wrath is *against* him that causeth shame.

15 1 A soft answer turneth away wrath: but grievous words stir up anger.
2 The tongue of the wise useth knowledge aright:
but the mouth of fools poureth out foolishness.
3 The eyes of the LORD *are* in every place, beholding the evil and the good.
4 A wholesome tongue *is* a tree of life: but perverseness therein *is* a breach in the spirit.
5 A fool despiseth his father's instruction: but he
that regardeth reproof is prudent.
6 In the house of the righteous *is* much treasure:
but in the revenues of the wicked is trouble.
7 The lips of the wise disperse knowledge: but the
heart of the foolish *doeth* not so.
8 The sacrifice of the wicked *is* an abomination to
the LORD: but the prayer of the upright *is* his delight.
9 The way of the wicked *is* an abomination unto
the LORD: but he loveth him that followeth after
righteousness.
10 Correction *is* grievous unto him that forsaketh
the way: *and* he that hateth reproof shall die.
11 Hell and destruction *are* before the LORD: how
much more then the hearts of the children of men?
12 A scorner loveth not one that reproveth him:
neither will he go unto the wise.
13 A merry heart maketh a cheerful countenance:
but by sorrow of the heart the spirit is broken.
14 The heart of him that hath understanding
seeketh knowledge: but the mouth of fools feedeth
on foolishness.
15 All the days of the afflicted *are* evil: but he that is
of a merry heart *hath* a continual feast.
16 Better *is* little with the fear of the LORD than
great treasure and trouble therewith.

NEW LIVING TRANSLATION

32 The wicked are crushed by disaster,
but the godly have a refuge when they die.
33 Wisdom is enshrined in an understanding heart;
wisdom is not* found among fools.
34 Godliness makes a nation great,
but sin is a disgrace to any people.
35 A king rejoices in wise servants
but is angry with those who disgrace him.

15 1 A gentle answer deflects anger,
but harsh words make tempers flare.
2 The tongue of the wise makes knowledge
appealing,
but the mouth of a fool belches out
foolishness.
3 The LORD is watching everywhere,
keeping his eye on both the evil and the good.
4 Gentle words are a tree of life;
a deceitful tongue crushes the spirit.
5 Only a fool despises a parent's* discipline;
whoever learns from correction is wise.
6 There is treasure in the house of the godly,
but the earnings of the wicked bring trouble.
7 The lips of the wise give good advice;
the heart of a fool has none to give.
8 The LORD detests the sacrifice of the wicked,
but he delights in the prayers of the upright.
9 The LORD detests the way of the wicked,
but he loves those who pursue godliness.
10 Whoever abandons the right path will be
severely disciplined;
whoever hates correction will die.
11 Even Death and Destruction* hold no secrets
from the LORD.
How much more does he know the
human heart!
12 Mockers hate to be corrected,
so they stay away from the wise.
13 A glad heart makes a happy face;
a broken heart crushes the spirit.
14 A wise person is hungry for knowledge,
while the fool feeds on trash.
15 For the despondent, every day brings trouble;
for the happy heart, life is a continual feast.
16 Better to have little, with fear for the LORD,
than to have great treasure and inner turmoil.

14:33 As in Greek and Syriac versions; Hebrew lacks *not.* **15:5** Hebrew *father's.* **15:11** Hebrew *Sheol and Abaddon.*

KING JAMES VERSION

17 Better *is* a dinner of herbs where love is, than a stalled ox and hatred therewith.

18 A wrathful man stirreth up strife: but *he that is* slow to anger appeaseth strife.

19 The way of the slothful *man is* as an hedge of thorns: but the way of the righteous *is* made plain.

20 A wise son maketh a glad father: but a foolish man despiseth his mother.

21 Folly *is* joy to *him that is* destitute of wisdom: but a man of understanding walketh uprightly.

22 Without counsel purposes are disappointed: but in the multitude of counsellors they are established.

23 A man hath joy by the answer of his mouth: and a word *spoken* in due season, how good *is it!*

24 The way of life *is* above to the wise, that he may depart from hell beneath.

25 The LORD will destroy the house of the proud: but he will establish the border of the widow.

26 The thoughts of the wicked *are* an abomination to the LORD: but *the words* of the pure *are* pleasant words.

27 He that is greedy of gain troubleth his own house; but he that hateth gifts shall live.

28 The heart of the righteous studieth to answer: but the mouth of the wicked poureth out evil things.

29 The LORD *is* far from the wicked: but he heareth the prayer of the righteous.

30 The light of the eyes rejoiceth the heart: *and* a good report maketh the bones fat.

31 The ear that heareth the reproof of life abideth among the wise.

32 He that refuseth instruction despiseth his own soul: but he that heareth reproof getteth understanding.

33 The fear of the LORD *is* the instruction of wisdom; and before honour *is* humility.

16

1 The preparations of the heart in man, and the answer of the tongue, *is* from the LORD.

2 All the ways of a man *are* clean in his own eyes; but the LORD weigheth the spirits.

3 Commit thy works unto the LORD, and thy thoughts shall be established.

4 The LORD hath made all *things* for himself: yea, even the wicked for the day of evil.

NEW LIVING TRANSLATION

17 A bowl of vegetables with someone you love
is better than steak with someone you hate.

18 A hot-tempered person starts fights;
a cool-tempered person stops them.

19 A lazy person's way is blocked with briers,
but the path of the upright is an open highway.

20 Sensible children bring joy to their father;
foolish children despise their mother.

21 Foolishness brings joy to those with no sense;
a sensible person stays on the right path.

22 Plans go wrong for lack of advice;
many advisers bring success.

23 Everyone enjoys a fitting reply;
it is wonderful to say the right thing
at the right time!

24 The path of life leads upward for the wise;
they leave the grave* behind.

25 The LORD tears down the house of the proud,
but he protects the property of widows.

26 The LORD detests evil plans,
but he delights in pure words.

27 Greed brings grief to the whole family,
but those who hate bribes will live.

28 The heart of the godly thinks carefully before
speaking;
the mouth of the wicked overflows with
evil words.

29 The LORD is far from the wicked,
but he hears the prayers of the righteous.

30 A cheerful look brings joy to the heart;
good news makes for good health.

31 If you listen to constructive criticism,
you will be at home among the wise.

32 If you reject discipline, you only harm yourself;
but if you listen to correction, you grow
in understanding.

33 Fear of the LORD teaches wisdom;
humility precedes honor.

16

1 We can make our own plans,
but the LORD gives the right answer.

2 People may be pure in their own eyes,
but the LORD examines their motives.

3 Commit your actions to the LORD,
and your plans will succeed.

4 The LORD has made everything for his
own purposes,
even the wicked for a day of disaster.

15:24 Hebrew *Sheol*.

KING JAMES VERSION

5 Every one *that is* proud in heart *is* an abomination to the LORD: *though* hand *join* in hand, he shall
not be unpunished.
6 By mercy and truth iniquity is purged: and by the
fear of the LORD *men* depart from evil.
7 When a man's ways please the LORD, he maketh
even his enemies to be at peace with him.
8 Better *is* a little with righteousness than great
revenues without right.
9 A man's heart deviseth his way: but the LORD
directeth his steps.
10 A divine sentence *is* in the lips of the king: his
mouth transgresseth not in judgment.
11 A just weight and balance *are* the LORD's: all the
weights of the bag *are* his work.
12 *It is* an abomination to kings to commit wickedness: for the throne is established by righteousness.
13 Righteous lips *are* the delight of kings; and they
love him that speaketh right.
14 The wrath of a king *is as* messengers of death:
but a wise man will pacify it.
15 In the light of the king's countenance *is* life; and
his favour *is* as a cloud of the latter rain.
16 How much better *is it* to get wisdom than gold!
and to get understanding rather to be chosen than
silver!
17 The highway of the upright *is* to depart from
evil: he that keepeth his way preserveth his soul.
18 Pride *goeth* before destruction, and an haughty
spirit before a fall.
19 Better *it is to be* of an humble spirit with the
lowly, than to divide the spoil with the proud.
20 He that handleth a matter wisely shall find good:
and whoso trusteth in the LORD, happy *is* he.
21 The wise in heart shall be called prudent: and
the sweetness of the lips increaseth learning.
22 Understanding *is* a wellspring of life unto him
that hath it: but the instruction of fools *is* folly.
23 The heart of the wise teacheth his mouth, and
addeth learning to his lips.
24 Pleasant words *are as* an honeycomb, sweet to
the soul, and health to the bones.
25 There is a way that seemeth right unto a man,
but the end thereof *are* the ways of death.
26 He that laboureth laboureth for himself; for his
mouth craveth it of him.

NEW LIVING TRANSLATION

5 The LORD detests the proud;
they will surely be punished.

6 Unfailing love and faithfulness make
atonement for sin.
By fearing the LORD, people avoid evil.

7 When people's lives please the LORD,
even their enemies are at peace with them.

8 Better to have little, with godliness,
than to be rich and dishonest.

9 We can make our plans,
but the LORD determines our steps.

10 The king speaks with divine wisdom;
he must never judge unfairly.

11 The LORD demands accurate scales and balances;
he sets the standards for fairness.

12 A king detests wrongdoing,
for his rule is built on justice.

13 The king is pleased with words from
righteous lips;
he loves those who speak honestly.

14 The anger of the king is a deadly threat;
the wise will try to appease it.

15 When the king smiles, there is life;
his favor refreshes like a spring rain.

16 How much better to get wisdom than gold,
and good judgment than silver!

17 The path of the virtuous leads away from evil;
whoever follows that path is safe.

18 Pride goes before destruction,
and haughtiness before a fall.

19 Better to live humbly with the poor
than to share plunder with the proud.

20 Those who listen to instruction will prosper;
those who trust the LORD will be joyful.

21 The wise are known for their understanding,
and pleasant words are persuasive.

22 Discretion is a life-giving fountain to those
who possess it,
but discipline is wasted on fools.

23 From a wise mind comes wise speech;
the words of the wise are persuasive.

24 Kind words are like honey—
sweet to the soul and healthy for the body.

25 There is a path before each person that
seems right,
but it ends in death.

26 It is good for workers to have an appetite;
an empty stomach drives them on.

KING JAMES VERSION

27 An ungodly man diggeth up evil: and in his lips
there is as a burning fire.
28 A froward man soweth strife: and a whisperer
separateth chief friends.
29 A violent man enticeth his neighbour, and
leadeth him into the way *that is* not good.
30 He shutteth his eyes to devise froward things:
moving his lips he bringeth evil to pass.
31 The hoary head *is* a crown of glory, *if* it be found
in the way of righteousness.
32 *He that is* slow to anger *is* better than the mighty;
and he that ruleth his spirit than he that taketh a city.
33 The lot is cast into the lap; but the whole dispos-
ing thereof *is* of the LORD.

17

1 Better *is* a dry morsel, and quietness therewith, than an house full of sacrifices *with*
strife.
2 A wise servant shall have rule over a son that
causeth shame, and shall have part of the inheritance among the brethren.
3 The fining pot *is* for silver, and the furnace for
gold: but the LORD trieth the hearts.
4 A wicked doer giveth heed to false lips; *and* a liar
giveth ear to a naughty tongue.
5 Whoso mocketh the poor reproacheth his
Maker: *and* he that is glad at calamities shall not be
unpunished.
6 Children's children *are* the crown of old men; and
the glory of children *are* their fathers.
7 Excellent speech becometh not a fool: much less
do lying lips a prince.
8 A gift *is as* a precious stone in the eyes of him that
hath it: whithersoever it turneth, it prospereth.
9 He that covereth a transgression seeketh love; but
he that repeateth a matter separateth *very* friends.
10 A reproof entereth more into a wise man than an
hundred stripes into a fool.
11 An evil *man* seeketh only rebellion: therefore a
cruel messenger shall be sent against him.
12 Let a bear robbed of her whelps meet a man,
rather than a fool in his folly.
13 Whoso rewardeth evil for good, evil shall not
depart from his house.

NEW LIVING TRANSLATION

27 Scoundrels create trouble;
their words are a destructive blaze.

28 A troublemaker plants seeds of strife;
gossip separates the best of friends.

29 Violent people mislead their companions,
leading them down a harmful path.

30 With narrowed eyes, people plot evil;
with a smirk, they plan their mischief.

31 Gray hair is a crown of glory;
it is gained by living a godly life.

32 Better to be patient than powerful;
better to have self-control than to
conquer a city.

33 We may throw the dice,*
but the LORD determines how they fall.

17

1 Better a dry crust eaten in peace
than a house filled with feasting—
and conflict.

2 A wise servant will rule over the master's
disgraceful son
and will share the inheritance of the
master's children.

3 Fire tests the purity of silver and gold,
but the LORD tests the heart.

4 Wrongdoers eagerly listen to gossip;
liars pay close attention to slander.

5 Those who mock the poor insult their Maker;
those who rejoice at the misfortune of others
will be punished.

6 Grandchildren are the crowning glory of
the aged;
parents* are the pride of their children.

7 Eloquent words are not fitting for a fool;
even less are lies fitting for a ruler.

8 A bribe is like a lucky charm;
whoever gives one will prosper!

9 Love prospers when a fault is forgiven,
but dwelling on it separates close friends.

10 A single rebuke does more for a person
of understanding
than a hundred lashes on the back of a fool.

11 Evil people are eager for rebellion,
but they will be severely punished.

12 It is safer to meet a bear robbed of her cubs
than to confront a fool caught in foolishness.

13 If you repay good with evil,
evil will never leave your house.

16:33 Hebrew *We may cast lots.* **17:6** Hebrew *fathers.*

KING JAMES VERSION

14The beginning of strife *is as* when one letteth
out water: therefore leave off contention, before it be
meddled with.
15He that justifieth the wicked, and he that
condemneth the just, even they both *are* abomination to the LORD.
16Wherefore *is there* a price in the hand of a fool
to get wisdom, seeing *he hath* no heart *to it?*
17A friend loveth at all times, and a brother is born
for adversity.
18A man void of understanding striketh hands,
and becometh surety in the presence of his friend.
19He loveth transgression that loveth strife: *and*
he that exalteth his gate seeketh destruction.
20He that hath a froward heart findeth no good:
and he that hath a perverse tongue falleth into
mischief.
21He that begetteth a fool *doeth it* to his sorrow:
and the father of a fool hath no joy.
22A merry heart doeth good *like* a medicine: but a
broken spirit drieth the bones.
23A wicked *man* taketh a gift out of the bosom to
pervert the ways of judgment.
24Wisdom *is* before him that hath understanding;
but the eyes of a fool *are* in the ends of the earth.
25A foolish son *is* a grief to his father, and bitterness to her that bare him.
26Also to punish the just *is* not good, *nor* to strike
princes for equity.
27He that hath knowledge spareth his words: *and*
a man of understanding is of an excellent spirit.
28Even a fool, when he holdeth his peace, is
counted wise: *and* he that shutteth his lips *is esteemed* a man of understanding.

18 1Through desire a man, having separated
himself, seeketh *and* intermeddleth with all
wisdom.
2A fool hath no delight in understanding, but that
his heart may discover itself.
3When the wicked cometh, *then* cometh also contempt, and with ignominy reproach.
4The words of a man's mouth *are as* deep waters,
and the wellspring of wisdom *as* a flowing brook.
5*It is* not good to accept the person of the wicked,
to overthrow the righteous in judgment.

NEW LIVING TRANSLATION

14 Starting a quarrel is like opening a floodgate,
so stop before a dispute breaks out.

15 Acquitting the guilty and condemning
the innocent—
both are detestable to the LORD.

16 It is senseless to pay tuition to educate a fool,
since he has no heart for learning.

17 A friend is always loyal,
and a brother is born to help in time of need.

18 It's poor judgment to guarantee another
person's debt
or put up security for a friend.

19 Anyone who loves to quarrel loves sin;
anyone who trusts in high walls invites disaster.

20 The crooked heart will not prosper;
the lying tongue tumbles into trouble.

21 It is painful to be the parent of a fool;
there is no joy for the father of a rebel.

22 A cheerful heart is good medicine,
but a broken spirit saps a person's strength.

23 The wicked take secret bribes
to pervert the course of justice.

24 Sensible people keep their eyes glued on wisdom,
but a fool's eyes wander to the ends
of the earth.

25 Foolish children* bring grief to their father
and bitterness to the one who gave them birth.

26 It is wrong to punish the godly for being good
or to flog leaders for being honest.

27 A truly wise person uses few words;
a person with understanding is even-tempered.

28 Even fools are thought wise when they
keep silent;
with their mouths shut, they seem intelligent.

18 1 Unfriendly people care only about
themselves;
they lash out at common sense.

2 Fools have no interest in understanding;
they only want to air their own opinions.

3 Doing wrong leads to disgrace,
and scandalous behavior brings contempt.

4 Wise words are like deep waters;
wisdom flows from the wise like
a bubbling brook.

5 It is not right to acquit the guilty
or deny justice to the innocent.

17:25 Hebrew *A foolish son.*

KING JAMES VERSION

6 A fool's lips enter into contention, and his mouth calleth for strokes.

7 A fool's mouth *is* his destruction, and his lips *are* the snare of his soul.

8 The words of a talebearer *are* as wounds, and they go down into the innermost parts of the belly.

9 He also that is slothful in his work is brother to him that is a great waster.

10 The name of the LORD *is* a strong tower: the righteous runneth into it, and is safe.

11 The rich man's wealth *is* his strong city, and as an high wall in his own conceit.

12 Before destruction the heart of man is haughty, and before honour *is* humility.

13 He that answereth a matter before he heareth *it*, it *is* folly and shame unto him.

14 The spirit of a man will sustain his infirmity; but a wounded spirit who can bear?

15 The heart of the prudent getteth knowledge; and the ear of the wise seeketh knowledge.

16 A man's gift maketh room for him, and bringeth him before great men.

17 *He that is* first in his own cause *seemeth* just; but his neighbour cometh and searcheth him.

18 The lot causeth contentions to cease, and parteth between the mighty.

19 A brother offended *is harder to be won* than a strong city: and *their* contentions *are* like the bars of a castle.

20 A man's belly shall be satisfied with the fruit of his mouth; *and* with the increase of his lips shall he be filled.

21 Death and life *are* in the power of the tongue: and they that love it shall eat the fruit thereof.

22 *Whoso* findeth a wife findeth a good *thing*, and obtaineth favour of the LORD.

23 The poor useth intreaties; but the rich answereth roughly.

24 A man *that hath* friends must shew himself friendly: and there is a friend *that* sticketh closer than a brother.

19 1 Better *is* the poor that walketh in his integrity, than *he that is* perverse in his lips, and is a fool.

2 Also, *that* the soul *be* without knowledge, *it is* not good; and he that hasteth with *his* feet sinneth.

NEW LIVING TRANSLATION

6 Fools' words get them into constant quarrels;
they are asking for a beating.

7 The mouths of fools are their ruin;
they trap themselves with their lips.

8 Rumors are dainty morsels
that sink deep into one's heart.

9 A lazy person is as bad as
someone who destroys things.

10 The name of the LORD is a strong fortress;
the godly run to him and are safe.

11 The rich think of their wealth as a strong defense;
they imagine it to be a high wall of safety.

12 Haughtiness goes before destruction;
humility precedes honor.

13 Spouting off before listening to the facts
is both shameful and foolish.

14 The human spirit can endure a sick body,
but who can bear a crushed spirit?

15 Intelligent people are always ready to learn.
Their ears are open for knowledge.

16 Giving a gift can open doors;
it gives access to important people!

17 The first to speak in court sounds right—
until the cross-examination begins.

18 Flipping a coin* can end arguments;
it settles disputes between powerful opponents.

19 An offended friend is harder to win back than a fortified city.
Arguments separate friends like a gate locked with bars.

20 Wise words satisfy like a good meal;
the right words bring satisfaction.

21 The tongue can bring death or life;
those who love to talk will reap the consequences.

22 The man who finds a wife finds a treasure,
and he receives favor from the LORD.

23 The poor plead for mercy;
the rich answer with insults.

24 There are "friends" who destroy each other,
but a real friend sticks closer than a brother.

19 1 Better to be poor and honest
than to be dishonest and a fool.

2 Enthusiasm without knowledge is no good;
haste makes mistakes.

18:18 Hebrew *Casting lots.*

KING JAMES VERSION

3 The foolishness of man perverteth his way: and
his heart fretteth against the LORD.
4 Wealth maketh many friends; but the poor is separated from his neighbour.
5 A false witness shall not be unpunished, and *he*
that speaketh lies shall not escape.
6 Many will intreat the favour of the prince: and
every man *is* a friend to him that giveth gifts.
7 All the brethren of the poor do hate him: how
much more do his friends go far from him? he
pursueth *them with* words, *yet* they *are* wanting *to*
him.
8 He that getteth wisdom loveth his own soul: he
that keepeth understanding shall find good.
9 A false witness shall not be unpunished, and *he*
that speaketh lies shall perish.
10 Delight is not seemly for a fool; much less for a
servant to have rule over princes.
11 The discretion of a man deferreth his anger; and
it is his glory to pass over a transgression.
12 The king's wrath *is* as the roaring of a lion; but
his favour *is* as dew upon the grass.
13 A foolish son *is* the calamity of his father: and
the contentions of a wife *are* a continual dropping.
14 House and riches *are* the inheritance of fathers:
and a prudent wife *is* from the LORD.
15 Slothfulness casteth into a deep sleep; and an
idle soul shall suffer hunger.
16 He that keepeth the commandment keepeth his
own soul; *but* he that despiseth his ways shall die.
17 He that hath pity upon the poor lendeth unto
the LORD; and that which he hath given will he pay
him again.
18 Chasten thy son while there is hope, and let not
thy soul spare for his crying.
19 A man of great wrath shall suffer punishment:
for if thou deliver *him,* yet thou must do it again.
20 Hear counsel, and receive instruction, that thou
mayest be wise in thy latter end.
21 *There are* many devices in a man's heart; nevertheless the counsel of the LORD, that shall stand.

NEW LIVING TRANSLATION

3 People ruin their lives by their own foolishness
and then are angry at the LORD.

4 Wealth makes many "friends";
poverty drives them all away.

5 A false witness will not go unpunished,
nor will a liar escape.

6 Many seek favors from a ruler;
everyone is the friend of a person who
gives gifts!

7 The relatives of the poor despise them;
how much more will their friends avoid them!
Though the poor plead with them,
their friends are gone.

8 To acquire wisdom is to love oneself;
people who cherish understanding
will prosper.

9 A false witness will not go unpunished,
and a liar will be destroyed.

10 It isn't right for a fool to live in luxury
or for a slave to rule over princes!

11 Sensible people control their temper;
they earn respect by overlooking wrongs.

12 The king's anger is like a lion's roar,
but his favor is like dew on the grass.

13 A foolish child* is a calamity to a father;
a quarrelsome wife is as annoying as
constant dripping.

14 Fathers can give their sons an inheritance
of houses and wealth,
but only the LORD can give an
understanding wife.

15 Lazy people sleep soundly,
but idleness leaves them hungry.

16 Keep the commandments and keep your life;
despising them leads to death.

17 If you help the poor, you are lending
to the LORD—
and he will repay you!

18 Discipline your children while there is hope.
Otherwise you will ruin their lives.

19 Hot-tempered people must pay the penalty.
If you rescue them once, you will have
to do it again.

20 Get all the advice and instruction you can,
so you will be wise the rest of your life.

21 You can make many plans,
but the LORD's purpose will prevail.

19:13 Hebrew *son;* also in 19:27.

KING JAMES VERSION

22 The desire of a man *is* his kindness: and a poor
man *is* better than a liar.
23 The fear of the LORD *tendeth* to life: and *he that*
hath it shall abide satisfied; he shall not be visited
with evil.
24 A slothful *man* hideth his hand in *his* bosom,
and will not so much as bring it to his mouth again.
25 Smite a scorner, and the simple will beware: and
reprove one that hath understanding, *and* he will
understand knowledge.
26 He that wasteth *his* father, *and* chaseth away *his*
mother, *is* a son that causeth shame, and bringeth
reproach.
27 Cease, my son, to hear the instruction *that*
causeth to err from the words of knowledge.
28 An ungodly witness scorneth judgment: and the
mouth of the wicked devoureth iniquity.
29 Judgments are prepared for scorners, and
stripes for the back of fools.

20 1 Wine *is* a mocker, strong drink *is* raging:
and whosoever is deceived thereby is not
wise.
2 The fear of a king *is* as the roaring of a lion:
whoso provoketh him to anger sinneth *against* his
own soul.
3 *It is* an honour for a man to cease from strife: but
every fool will be meddling.
4 The sluggard will not plow by reason of the cold;
therefore shall he beg in harvest, and *have* nothing.
5 Counsel in the heart of man *is like* deep water;
but a man of understanding will draw it out.
6 Most men will proclaim every one his own goodness: but a faithful man who can find?
7 The just *man* walketh in his integrity: his children *are* blessed after him.
8 A king that sitteth in the throne of judgment
scattereth away all evil with his eyes.
9 Who can say, I have made my heart clean, I am
pure from my sin?
10 Divers weights, *and* divers measures, both of
them *are* alike abomination to the LORD.
11 Even a child is known by his doings, whether his
work *be* pure, and whether *it be* right.
12 The hearing ear, and the seeing eye, the LORD
hath made even both of them.

NEW LIVING TRANSLATION

22 Loyalty makes a person attractive.
It is better to be poor than dishonest.

23 Fear of the LORD leads to life,
bringing security and protection from harm.

24 Lazy people take food in their hand
but don't even lift it to their mouth.

25 If you punish a mocker, the simpleminded will
learn a lesson;
if you correct the wise, they will be all the wiser.

26 Children who mistreat their father or chase away
their mother
are an embarrassment and a public disgrace.

27 If you stop listening to instruction, my child,
you will turn your back on knowledge.

28 A corrupt witness makes a mockery of justice;
the mouth of the wicked gulps down evil.

29 Punishment is made for mockers,
and the backs of fools are made to be beaten.

20 1 Wine produces mockers; alcohol
leads to brawls.
Those led astray by drink cannot be wise.

2 The king's fury is like a lion's roar;
to rouse his anger is to risk your life.

3 Avoiding a fight is a mark of honor;
only fools insist on quarreling.

4 Those too lazy to plow in the right season
will have no food at the harvest.

5 Though good advice lies deep within the heart,
a person with understanding will draw it out.

6 Many will say they are loyal friends,
but who can find one who is truly reliable?

7 The godly walk with integrity;
blessed are their children who follow them.

8 When a king sits in judgment, he weighs
all the evidence,
distinguishing the bad from the good.

9 Who can say, "I have cleansed my heart;
I am pure and free from sin"?

10 False weights and unequal measures*—
the LORD detests double standards
of every kind.

11 Even children are known by the way they act,
whether their conduct is pure, and
whether it is right.

12 Ears to hear and eyes to see—
both are gifts from the LORD.

20:10 Hebrew *A stone and a stone, an ephah and an ephah.*

KING JAMES VERSION

13 Love not sleep, lest thou come to poverty; open
thine eyes, *and* thou shalt be satisfied with bread.
14 *It is* naught, *it is* naught, saith the buyer: but
when he is gone his way, then he boasteth.
15 There is gold, and a multitude of rubies: but the
lips of knowledge *are* a precious jewel.
16 Take his garment that is surety *for* a stranger:
and take a pledge of him for a strange woman.
17 Bread of deceit *is* sweet to a man; but afterwards
his mouth shall be filled with gravel.
18 *Every* purpose is established by counsel: and
with good advice make war.
19 He that goeth about *as* a talebearer revealeth secrets: therefore meddle not with him that flattereth
with his lips.
20 Whoso curseth his father or his mother, his
lamp shall be put out in obscure darkness.
21 An inheritance *may be* gotten hastily at the beginning; but the end thereof shall not be blessed.
22 Say not thou, I will recompense evil; *but* wait on
the LORD, and he shall save thee.
23 Divers weights *are* an abomination unto the
LORD; and a false balance *is* not good.
24 Man's goings *are* of the LORD; how can a man
then understand his own way?
25 *It is* a snare to the man *who* devoureth *that
which is* holy, and after vows to make inquiry.
26 A wise king scattereth the wicked, and bringeth
the wheel over them.
27 The spirit of man *is* the candle of the LORD,
searching all the inward parts of the belly.
28 Mercy and truth preserve the king: and his
throne is upholden by mercy.
29 The glory of young men *is* their strength: and
the beauty of old men *is* the grey head.
30 The blueness of a wound cleanseth away evil: so
do stripes the inward parts of the belly.

21

1 The king's heart *is* in the hand of the LORD,
as the rivers of water: he turneth it whithersoever he will.
2 Every way of a man *is* right in his own eyes: but
the LORD pondereth the hearts.

NEW LIVING TRANSLATION

13 If you love sleep, you will end in poverty.
Keep your eyes open, and there will be plenty
to eat!

14 The buyer haggles over the price, saying,
"It's worthless,"
then brags about getting a bargain!

15 Wise words are more valuable
than much gold and many rubies.

16 Get security from someone who guarantees
a stranger's debt.
Get a deposit if he does it for foreigners.*

17 Stolen bread tastes sweet,
but it turns to gravel in the mouth.

18 Plans succeed through good counsel;
don't go to war without wise advice.

19 A gossip goes around telling secrets,
so don't hang around with chatterers.

20 If you insult your father or mother,
your light will be snuffed out in total darkness.

21 An inheritance obtained too early in life
is not a blessing in the end.

22 Don't say, "I will get even for this wrong."
Wait for the LORD to handle the matter.

23 The LORD detests double standards;
he is not pleased by dishonest scales.

24 The LORD directs our steps,
so why try to understand everything
along the way?

25 Don't trap yourself by making a rash
promise to God
and only later counting the cost.

26 A wise king scatters the wicked like wheat,
then runs his threshing wheel over them.

27 The LORD's light penetrates the human spirit,*
exposing every hidden motive.

28 Unfailing love and faithfulness protect the king;
his throne is made secure through love.

29 The glory of the young is their strength;
the gray hair of experience is the splendor
of the old.

30 Physical punishment cleanses away evil;*
such discipline purifies the heart.

21

1 The king's heart is like a stream of water
directed by the LORD;
he guides it wherever he pleases.

2 People may be right in their own eyes,
but the LORD examines their heart.

20:16 An alternate reading in the Masoretic Text is *for a promiscuous woman.* **20:27** Or *The human spirit is the LORD's light.* **20:30** The meaning of the Hebrew is uncertain.

KING JAMES VERSION

3 To do justice and judgment *is* more acceptable to
the LORD than sacrifice.
4 An high look, and a proud heart, *and* the plowing
of the wicked, *is* sin.
5 The thoughts of the diligent *tend* only to plenteousness; but of every one *that is* hasty only to want.
6 The getting of treasures by a lying tongue *is* a vanity tossed to and fro of them that seek death.
7 The robbery of the wicked shall destroy them;
because they refuse to do judgment.
8 The way of man *is* froward and strange: but *as for*
the pure, his work *is* right.
9 *It is* better to dwell in a corner of the housetop,
than with a brawling woman in a wide house.
10 The soul of the wicked desireth evil: his neighbour findeth no favour in his eyes.
11 When the scorner is punished, the simple is
made wise: and when the wise is instructed, he
receiveth knowledge.
12 The righteous *man* wisely considereth the
house of the wicked: *but God* overthroweth the
wicked for *their* wickedness.
13 Whoso stoppeth his ears at the cry of the poor,
he also shall cry himself, but shall not be heard.
14 A gift in secret pacifieth anger: and a reward in
the bosom strong wrath.
15 *It is* joy to the just to do judgment: but destruction *shall be* to the workers of iniquity.
16 The man that wandereth out of the way of
understanding shall remain in the congregation of
the dead.
17 He that loveth pleasure *shall be* a poor man: he
that loveth wine and oil shall not be rich.
18 The wicked *shall be* a ransom for the righteous,
and the transgressor for the upright.
19 *It is* better to dwell in the wilderness, than with
a contentious and an angry woman.
20 *There is* treasure to be desired and oil in the
dwelling of the wise; but a foolish man spendeth
it up.
21 He that followeth after righteousness and mercy
findeth life, righteousness, and honour.
22 A wise *man* scaleth the city of the mighty, and
casteth down the strength of the confidence thereof.
23 Whoso keepeth his mouth and his tongue
keepeth his soul from troubles.

NEW LIVING TRANSLATION

3 The LORD is more pleased when we do what
is right and just
than when we offer him sacrifices.

4 Haughty eyes, a proud heart,
and evil actions are all sin.

5 Good planning and hard work lead to prosperity,
but hasty shortcuts lead to poverty.

6 Wealth created by a lying tongue
is a vanishing mist and a deadly trap.*

7 The violence of the wicked sweeps them away,
because they refuse to do what is just.

8 The guilty walk a crooked path;
the innocent travel a straight road.

9 It's better to live alone in the corner of an attic
than with a quarrelsome wife in a lovely home.

10 Evil people desire evil;
their neighbors get no mercy from them.

11 If you punish a mocker, the simpleminded
become wise;
if you instruct the wise, they will be all the wiser.

12 The Righteous One* knows what is going on
in the homes of the wicked;
he will bring disaster on them.

13 Those who shut their ears to the cries of the poor
will be ignored in their own time of need.

14 A secret gift calms anger;
a bribe under the table pacifies fury.

15 Justice is a joy to the godly,
but it terrifies evildoers.

16 The person who strays from common sense
will end up in the company of the dead.

17 Those who love pleasure become poor;
those who love wine and luxury will
never be rich.

18 The wicked are punished in place of the godly,
and traitors in place of the honest.

19 It's better to live alone in the desert
than with a quarrelsome, complaining wife.

20 The wise have wealth and luxury,
but fools spend whatever they get.

21 Whoever pursues righteousness and unfailing love
will find life, righteousness, and honor.

22 The wise conquer the city of the strong
and level the fortress in which they trust.

23 Watch your tongue and keep your mouth shut,
and you will stay out of trouble.

21:6 As in Greek version; Hebrew reads *mist for those who seek death.*
21:12 Or *The righteous man.*

KING JAMES VERSION

24 Proud *and* haughty scorner *is* his name, who dealeth in proud wrath.

25 The desire of the slothful killeth him; for his hands refuse to labour.

26 He coveteth greedily all the day long: but the righteous giveth and spareth not.

27 The sacrifice of the wicked *is* abomination: how much more, *when* he bringeth it with a wicked mind?

28 A false witness shall perish: but the man that heareth speaketh constantly.

29 A wicked man hardeneth his face: but *as for* the upright, he directeth his way.

30 *There is* no wisdom nor understanding nor counsel against the LORD.

31 The horse *is* prepared against the day of battle: but safety *is* of the LORD.

22

1 A *good* name *is* rather to be chosen than great riches, *and* loving favour rather than silver and gold.

2 The rich and poor meet together: the LORD *is* the maker of them all.

3 A prudent *man* foreseeth the evil, and hideth himself: but the simple pass on, and are punished.

4 By humility *and* the fear of the LORD *are* riches, and honour, and life.

5 Thorns *and* snares *are* in the way of the froward: he that doth keep his soul shall be far from them.

6 Train up a child in the way he should go: and when he is old, he will not depart from it.

7 The rich ruleth over the poor, and the borrower *is* servant to the lender.

8 He that soweth iniquity shall reap vanity: and the rod of his anger shall fail.

9 He that hath a bountiful eye shall be blessed; for he giveth of his bread to the poor.

10 Cast out the scorner, and contention shall go out; yea, strife and reproach shall cease.

11 He that loveth pureness of heart, *for* the grace of his lips the king *shall be* his friend.

12 The eyes of the LORD preserve knowledge, and he overthroweth the words of the transgressor.

NEW LIVING TRANSLATION

24 Mockers are proud and haughty;
they act with boundless arrogance.

25 Despite their desires, the lazy will come to ruin,
for their hands refuse to work.

26 Some people are always greedy for more,
but the godly love to give!

27 The sacrifice of an evil person is detestable,
especially when it is offered with wrong motives.

28 A false witness will be cut off,
but a credible witness will be allowed to speak.

29 The wicked bluff their way through,
but the virtuous think before they act.

30 No human wisdom or understanding or plan
can stand against the LORD.

31 The horse is prepared for the day of battle,
but the victory belongs to the LORD.

22

1 Choose a good reputation over great riches;
being held in high esteem is better than silver or gold.

2 The rich and poor have this in common:
The LORD made them both.

3 A prudent person foresees danger and takes precautions.
The simpleton goes blindly on and suffers the consequences.

4 True humility and fear of the LORD
lead to riches, honor, and long life.

5 Corrupt people walk a thorny, treacherous road;
whoever values life will avoid it.

6 Direct your children onto the right path,
and when they are older, they will not leave it.

7 Just as the rich rule the poor,
so the borrower is servant to the lender.

8 Those who plant injustice will harvest disaster,
and their reign of terror will come to an end.*

9 Blessed are those who are generous,
because they feed the poor.

10 Throw out the mocker, and fighting goes, too.
Quarrels and insults will disappear.

11 Whoever loves a pure heart and gracious speech
will have the king as a friend.

12 The LORD preserves those with knowledge,
but he ruins the plans of the treacherous.

22:8 The Greek version includes an additional proverb: *God blesses a man who gives cheerfully, / but his worthless deeds will come to an end.* Compare 2 Cor 9:7.

KING JAMES VERSION

13 The slothful *man* saith, *There is* a lion without, I
shall be slain in the streets.
14 The mouth of strange women *is* a deep pit: he
that is abhorred of the LORD shall fall therein.
15 Foolishness *is* bound in the heart of a child; *but*
the rod of correction shall drive it far from him.
16 He that oppresseth the poor to increase his
riches, and he that giveth to the rich, *shall* surely
come to want.

17 Bow down thine ear, and hear the words of the
wise, and apply thine heart unto my knowledge.
18 For *it is* a pleasant thing if thou keep them
within thee; they shall withal be fitted in thy lips.
19 That thy trust may be in the LORD, I have made
known to thee this day, even to thee.
20 Have not I written to thee excellent things in
counsels and knowledge,
21 That I might make thee know the certainty of
the words of truth; that thou mightest answer the
words of truth to them that send unto thee?
22 Rob not the poor, because he *is* poor: neither
oppress the afflicted in the gate:
23 For the LORD will plead their cause, and spoil the
soul of those that spoiled them.
24 Make no friendship with an angry man; and with
a furious man thou shalt not go:
25 Lest thou learn his ways, and get a snare to thy
soul.
26 Be not thou *one* of them that strike hands, *or* of
them that are sureties for debts.
27 If thou hast nothing to pay, why should he take
away thy bed from under thee?
28 Remove not the ancient landmark, which thy
fathers have set.
29 Seest thou a man diligent in his business? he
shall stand before kings; he shall not stand before
mean *men*.

23 1 When thou sittest to eat with a ruler, consider diligently what *is* before thee:
2 And put a knife to thy throat, if thou *be* a man
given to appetite.
3 Be not desirous of his dainties: for they *are* deceitful meat.
4 Labour not to be rich: cease from thine own
wisdom.

NEW LIVING TRANSLATION

13 The lazy person claims, "There's a lion out there!
If I go outside, I might be killed!"

14 The mouth of an immoral woman is a
dangerous trap;
those who make the LORD angry will fall into it.
15 A youngster's heart is filled with foolishness,
but physical discipline will drive it far away.

16 A person who gets ahead by oppressing the poor
or by showering gifts on the rich will end
in poverty.

Sayings of the Wise
17 Listen to the words of the wise;
apply your heart to my instruction.
18 For it is good to keep these sayings in your heart
and always ready on your lips.
19 I am teaching you today—yes, you—
so you will trust in the LORD.
20 I have written thirty sayings* for you,
filled with advice and knowledge.
21 In this way, you may know the truth
and take an accurate report to those
who sent you.

22 Don't rob the poor just because you can,
or exploit the needy in court.
23 For the LORD is their defender.
He will ruin anyone who ruins them.

24 Don't befriend angry people
or associate with hot-tempered people,
25 or you will learn to be like them
and endanger your soul.

26 Don't agree to guarantee another person's debt
or put up security for someone else.
27 If you can't pay it,
even your bed will be snatched from
under you.

28 Don't cheat your neighbor by moving the
ancient boundary markers
set up by previous generations.

29 Do you see any truly competent workers?
They will serve kings
rather than working for ordinary people.

23 1 While dining with a ruler,
pay attention to what is put before you.
2 If you are a big eater,
put a knife to your throat;
3 don't desire all the delicacies,
for he might be trying to trick you.

4 Don't wear yourself out trying to get rich.
Be wise enough to know when to quit.

22:20 Or *excellent sayings;* the meaning of the Hebrew is uncertain.

KING JAMES VERSION

5 Wilt thou set thine eyes upon that which is not? for *riches* certainly make themselves wings; they fly away as an eagle toward heaven.

6 Eat thou not the bread of *him that hath* an evil eye, neither desire thou his dainty meats:

7 For as he thinketh in his heart, so *is* he: Eat and drink, saith he to thee; but his heart *is* not with thee.

8 The morsel *which* thou hast eaten shalt thou vomit up, and lose thy sweet words.

9 Speak not in the ears of a fool: for he will despise the wisdom of thy words.

10 Remove not the old landmark; and enter not into the fields of the fatherless:

11 For their redeemer *is* mighty; he shall plead their cause with thee.

12 Apply thine heart unto instruction, and thine ears to the words of knowledge.

13 Withhold not correction from the child: for *if* thou beatest him with the rod, he shall not die.

14 Thou shalt beat him with the rod, and shalt deliver his soul from hell.

15 My son, if thine heart be wise, my heart shall rejoice, even mine.

16 Yea, my reins shall rejoice, when thy lips speak right things.

17 Let not thine heart envy sinners: but *be thou* in the fear of the LORD all the day long.

18 For surely there is an end; and thine expectation shall not be cut off.

19 Hear thou, my son, and be wise, and guide thine heart in the way.

20 Be not among winebibbers; among riotous eaters of flesh:

21 For the drunkard and the glutton shall come to poverty: and drowsiness shall clothe *a man* with rags.

22 Hearken unto thy father that begat thee, and despise not thy mother when she is old.

23 Buy the truth, and sell *it* not; *also* wisdom, and instruction, and understanding.

24 The father of the righteous shall greatly rejoice: and he that begetteth a wise *child* shall have joy of him.

25 Thy father and thy mother shall be glad, and she that bare thee shall rejoice.

26 My son, give me thine heart, and let thine eyes observe my ways.

NEW LIVING TRANSLATION

5 In the blink of an eye wealth disappears,
for it will sprout wings
and fly away like an eagle.

6 Don't eat with people who are stingy;
don't desire their delicacies.
7 They are always thinking about how much it costs.*
"Eat and drink," they say, but they don't mean it.
8 You will throw up what little you've eaten,
and your compliments will be wasted.

9 Don't waste your breath on fools,
for they will despise the wisest advice.

10 Don't cheat your neighbor by moving the ancient boundary markers;
don't take the land of defenseless orphans.
11 For their Redeemer* is strong;
he himself will bring their charges against you.

12 Commit yourself to instruction;
listen carefully to words of knowledge.

13 Don't fail to discipline your children.
They won't die if you spank them.
14 Physical discipline
may well save them from death.*

15 My child,* if your heart is wise,
my own heart will rejoice!
16 Everything in me will celebrate
when you speak what is right.

17 Don't envy sinners,
but always continue to fear the LORD.
18 You will be rewarded for this;
your hope will not be disappointed.

19 My child, listen and be wise:
Keep your heart on the right course.
20 Do not carouse with drunkards
or feast with gluttons,
21 for they are on their way to poverty,
and too much sleep clothes them in rags.

22 Listen to your father, who gave you life,
and don't despise your mother when she is old.
23 Get the truth and never sell it;
also get wisdom, discipline, and good judgment.
24 The father of godly children has cause for joy.
What a pleasure to have children who are wise.*
25 So give your father and mother joy!
May she who gave you birth be happy.

26 O my son, give me your heart.
May your eyes take delight in following my ways.

23:7 The meaning of the Hebrew is uncertain. **23:11** Or *redeemer.* **23:14** Hebrew *from Sheol.* **23:15** Hebrew *My son;* also in 23:19. **23:24** Hebrew *to have a wise son.*

KING JAMES VERSION

27 For a whore *is* a deep ditch; and a strange
woman *is* a narrow pit.
28 She also lieth in wait as *for* a prey, and increaseth
the transgressors among men.
29 Who hath woe? who hath sorrow? who hath
contentions? who hath babbling? who hath wounds
without cause? who hath redness of eyes?
30 They that tarry long at the wine; they that go to
seek mixed wine.
31 Look not thou upon the wine when it is red,
when it giveth his colour in the cup, *when* it moveth
itself aright.
32 At the last it biteth like a serpent, and stingeth
like an adder.
33 Thine eyes shall behold strange women, and
thine heart shall utter perverse things.
34 Yea, thou shalt be as he that lieth down in the
midst of the sea, or as he that lieth upon the top of a
mast.
35 They have stricken me, *shalt thou say, and* I was
not sick; they have beaten me, *and* I felt *it* not: when
shall I awake? I will seek it yet again.

24

1 Be not thou envious against evil men, neither desire to be with them.
2 For their heart studieth destruction, and their
lips talk of mischief.
3 Through wisdom is an house builded; and by
understanding it is established:
4 And by knowledge shall the chambers be filled
with all precious and pleasant riches.
5 A wise man *is* strong; yea, a man of knowledge
increaseth strength.
6 For by wise counsel thou shalt make thy war: and
in multitude of counsellors *there is* safety.
7 Wisdom *is* too high for a fool: he openeth not his
mouth in the gate.
8 He that deviseth to do evil shall be called a mischievous person.
9 The thought of foolishness *is* sin: and the scorner
is an abomination to men.
10 *If* thou faint in the day of adversity, thy strength
is small.
11 If thou forbear to deliver *them that are* drawn
unto death, and *those that are* ready to be slain;
12 If thou sayest, Behold, we knew it not; doth not

NEW LIVING TRANSLATION

27 A prostitute is a dangerous trap;
a promiscuous woman is as dangerous
as falling into a narrow well.
28 She hides and waits like a robber,
eager to make more men unfaithful.

29 Who has anguish? Who has sorrow?
Who is always fighting? Who is always
complaining?
Who has unnecessary bruises? Who has
bloodshot eyes?
30 It is the one who spends long hours in the taverns,
trying out new drinks.
31 Don't gaze at the wine, seeing how red it is,
how it sparkles in the cup, how smoothly it
goes down.
32 For in the end it bites like a poisonous snake;
it stings like a viper.
33 You will see hallucinations,
and you will say crazy things.
34 You will stagger like a sailor tossed at sea,
clinging to a swaying mast.
35 And you will say, "They hit me, but I didn't feel it.
I didn't even know it when they beat me up.
When will I wake up
so I can look for another drink?"

24

1 Don't envy evil people
or desire their company.
2 For their hearts plot violence,
and their words always stir up trouble.

3 A house is built by wisdom
and becomes strong through good sense.
4 Through knowledge its rooms are filled
with all sorts of precious riches and valuables.

5 The wise are mightier than the strong,*
and those with knowledge grow stronger
and stronger.
6 So don't go to war without wise guidance;
victory depends on having many advisers.

7 Wisdom is too lofty for fools.
Among leaders at the city gate, they have
nothing to say.

8 A person who plans evil
will get a reputation as a troublemaker.
9 The schemes of a fool are sinful;
everyone detests a mocker.

10 If you fail under pressure,
your strength is too small.

11 Rescue those who are unjustly sentenced to die;
save them as they stagger to their death.
12 Don't excuse yourself by saying, "Look, we
didn't know."
For God understands all hearts, and he sees you.

24:5 As in Greek version; Hebrew reads *A wise man is strength.*

KING JAMES VERSION

he that pondereth the heart consider *it?* and he that
keepeth thy soul, doth *not* he know *it?* and shall *not*
he render to *every* man according to his works?
13My son, eat thou honey, because *it is* good; and
the honeycomb, *which is* sweet to thy taste:
14So *shall* the knowledge of wisdom *be* unto thy
soul: when thou hast found *it,* then there shall be a
reward, and thy expectation shall not be cut off.
15Lay not wait, O wicked *man,* against the dwelling
of the righteous; spoil not his resting place:
16For a just *man* falleth seven times, and riseth up
again: but the wicked shall fall into mischief.
17Rejoice not when thine enemy falleth, and let
not thine heart be glad when he stumbleth:
18Lest the LORD see *it,* and it displease him, and
he turn away his wrath from him.
19Fret not thyself because of evil *men,* neither be
thou envious at the wicked;
20For there shall be no reward to the evil *man;* the
candle of the wicked shall be put out.
21My son, fear thou the LORD and the king: *and*
meddle not with them that are given to change:
22For their calamity shall rise suddenly; and who
knoweth the ruin of them both?

23These *things* also *belong* to the wise. *It is* not
good to have respect of persons in judgment.
24He that saith unto the wicked, Thou *art* righteous; him shall the people curse, nations shall abhor
him:
25But to them that rebuke *him* shall be delight,
and a good blessing shall come upon them.
26*Every man* shall kiss *his* lips that giveth a right
answer.
27Prepare thy work without, and make it fit for thyself in the field; and afterwards build thine house.
28Be not a witness against thy neighbour without
cause; and deceive *not* with thy lips.
29Say not, I will do so to him as he hath done to me:
I will render to the man according to his work.
30I went by the field of the slothful, and by the
vineyard of the man void of understanding;

NEW LIVING TRANSLATION

He who guards your soul knows you knew.
He will repay all people as their
actions deserve.

13 My child,* eat honey, for it is good,
and the honeycomb is sweet to the taste.
14 In the same way, wisdom is sweet to your soul.
If you find it, you will have a bright future,
and your hopes will not be cut short.

15 Don't wait in ambush at the home of the godly,
and don't raid the house where the godly live.
16 The godly may trip seven times, but they will
get up again.
But one disaster is enough to overthrow
the wicked.

17 Don't rejoice when your enemies fall;
don't be happy when they stumble.
18 For the LORD will be displeased with you
and will turn his anger away from them.

19 Don't fret because of evildoers;
don't envy the wicked.
20 For evil people have no future;
the light of the wicked will be snuffed out.

21 My child, fear the LORD and the king.
Don't associate with rebels,
22 for disaster will hit them suddenly.
Who knows what punishment will come
from the LORD and the king?

More Sayings of the Wise

23Here are some further sayings of the wise:

It is wrong to show favoritism when passing
judgment.
24 A judge who says to the wicked, "You are
innocent,"
will be cursed by many people and denounced
by the nations.
25 But it will go well for those who convict
the guilty;
rich blessings will be showered on them.

26 An honest answer
is like a kiss of friendship.

27 Do your planning and prepare your fields
before building your house.

28 Don't testify against your neighbors
without cause;
don't lie about them.
29 And don't say, "Now I can pay them back for
what they've done to me!
I'll get even with them!"

30 I walked by the field of a lazy person,
the vineyard of one with no common sense.

24:13 Hebrew *My son;* also in 24:21.

KING JAMES VERSION

[31]And, lo, it was all grown over with thorns, *and*
nettles had covered the face thereof, and the stone
wall thereof was broken down.
[32]Then I saw, *and* considered *it* well: I looked
upon *it*, *and* received instruction.
[33]*Yet* a little sleep, a little slumber, a little folding of
the hands to sleep:
[34]So shall thy poverty come *as* one that travelleth;
and thy want as an armed man.

25 [1]These *are* also proverbs of Solomon, which
the men of Hezekiah king of Judah copied
out.
[2]*It is* the glory of God to conceal a thing: but the
honour of kings *is* to search out a matter.
[3]The heaven for height, and the earth for depth,
and the heart of kings *is* unsearchable.
[4]Take away the dross from the silver, and there
shall come forth a vessel for the finer.
[5]Take away the wicked *from* before the king, and
his throne shall be established in righteousness.
[6]Put not forth thyself in the presence of the king,
and stand not in the place of great *men*:
[7]For better *it is* that it be said unto thee, Come up
hither; than that thou shouldest be put lower in the
presence of the prince whom thine eyes have seen.
[8]Go not forth hastily to strive, lest *thou know not*
what to do in the end thereof, when thy neighbour
hath put thee to shame.
[9]Debate thy cause with thy neighbour *himself*;
and discover not a secret to another:
[10]Lest he that heareth *it* put thee to shame, and
thine infamy turn not away.
[11]A word fitly spoken *is like* apples of gold in pictures of silver.
[12]*As* an earring of gold, and an ornament of fine
gold, *so is* a wise reprover upon an obedient ear.
[13]As the cold of snow in the time of harvest, *so is* a
faithful messenger to them that send him: for he
refresheth the soul of his masters.
[14]Whoso boasteth himself of a false gift *is like*
clouds and wind without rain.
[15]By long forbearing is a prince persuaded, and a
soft tongue breaketh the bone.
[16]Hast thou found honey? eat so much as is sufficient for thee, lest thou be filled therewith, and
vomit it.

NEW LIVING TRANSLATION

[31] I saw that it was overgrown with nettles.
It was covered with weeds,
and its walls were broken down.
[32] Then, as I looked and thought about it,
I learned this lesson:
[33] A little extra sleep, a little more slumber,
a little folding of the hands to rest—
[34] then poverty will pounce on you like a bandit;
scarcity will attack you like an armed robber.

More Proverbs of Solomon

25 These are more proverbs of Solomon, collected by the advisers of King Hezekiah of Judah.

[2] It is God's privilege to conceal things
and the king's privilege to discover them.

[3] No one can comprehend the height of heaven,
the depth of the earth,
or all that goes on in the king's mind!

[4] Remove the impurities from silver,
and the sterling will be ready for the
silversmith.
[5] Remove the wicked from the king's court,
and his reign will be made secure by justice.

[6] Don't demand an audience with the king
or push for a place among the great.
[7] It's better to wait for an invitation to the
head table
than to be sent away in public disgrace.

Just because you've seen something,
[8] don't be in a hurry to go to court.
For what will you do in the end
if your neighbor deals you a shameful defeat?

[9] When arguing with your neighbor,
don't betray another person's secret.
[10] Others may accuse you of gossip,
and you will never regain your
good reputation.

[11] Timely advice is lovely,
like golden apples in a silver basket.

[12] To one who listens, valid criticism
is like a gold earring or other gold jewelry.

[13] Trustworthy messengers refresh like snow
in summer.
They revive the spirit of their employer.

[14] A person who promises a gift but doesn't give it
is like clouds and wind that bring no rain.

[15] Patience can persuade a prince,
and soft speech can break bones.

[16] Do you like honey?
Don't eat too much, or it will make you sick!

KING JAMES VERSION

17 Withdraw thy foot from thy neighbour's house;
lest he be weary of thee, and *so* hate thee.
18 A man that beareth false witness against his
neighbour *is* a maul, and a sword, and a sharp arrow.
19 Confidence in an unfaithful man in time of
trouble *is like* a broken tooth, and a foot out of joint.
20 *As* he that taketh away a garment in cold weather,
and as vinegar upon nitre, so *is* he that singeth songs
to an heavy heart.
21 If thine enemy be hungry, give him bread to eat;
and if he be thirsty, give him water to drink:
22 For thou shalt heap coals of fire upon his head,
and the LORD shall reward thee.
23 The north wind driveth away rain: so *doth* an
angry countenance a backbiting tongue.
24 *It is* better to dwell in the corner of the housetop,
than with a brawling woman and in a wide house.
25 *As* cold waters to a thirsty soul, so *is* good news
from a far country.
26 A righteous man falling down before the wicked
is as a troubled fountain, and a corrupt spring.
27 *It is* not good to eat much honey: so *for men* to
search their own glory *is not* glory.
28 He that *hath* no rule over his own spirit *is like* a
city *that is* broken down, *and* without walls.

26 1 As snow in summer, and as rain in harvest,
so honour is not seemly for a fool.
2 As the bird by wandering, as the swallow by flying, so the curse causeless shall not come.
3 A whip for the horse, a bridle for the ass, and a
rod for the fool's back.
4 Answer not a fool according to his folly, lest thou
also be like unto him.
5 Answer a fool according to his folly, lest he be
wise in his own conceit.
6 He that sendeth a message by the hand of a fool
cutteth off the feet, *and* drinketh damage.
7 The legs of the lame are not equal: so *is* a parable
in the mouth of fools.

NEW LIVING TRANSLATION

17 Don't visit your neighbors too often,
or you will wear out your welcome.

18 Telling lies about others
is as harmful as hitting them with an ax,
wounding them with a sword,
or shooting them with a sharp arrow.

19 Putting confidence in an unreliable person in times of trouble
is like chewing with a broken tooth or walking on a lame foot.

20 Singing cheerful songs to a person with a heavy heart
is like taking someone's coat in cold weather
or pouring vinegar in a wound.*

21 If your enemies are hungry, give them food to eat.
If they are thirsty, give them water to drink.
22 You will heap burning coals of shame on their heads,
and the LORD will reward you.

23 As surely as a north wind brings rain,
so a gossiping tongue causes anger!

24 It's better to live alone in the corner of an attic
than with a quarrelsome wife in a lovely home.
25 Good news from far away
is like cold water to the thirsty.

26 If the godly give in to the wicked,
it's like polluting a fountain or muddying a spring.

27 It's not good to eat too much honey,
and it's not good to seek honors for yourself.

28 A person without self-control
is like a city with broken-down walls.

26 1 Honor is no more associated with fools
than snow with summer or rain with harvest.

2 Like a fluttering sparrow or a darting swallow,
an undeserved curse will not land on its intended victim.

3 Guide a horse with a whip, a donkey with a bridle,
and a fool with a rod to his back!

4 Don't answer the foolish arguments of fools,
or you will become as foolish as they are.

5 Be sure to answer the foolish arguments of fools,
or they will become wise in their own estimation.

6 Trusting a fool to convey a message
is like cutting off one's feet or drinking poison!

7 A proverb in the mouth of a fool
is as useless as a paralyzed leg.

25:20 As in Greek version; Hebrew reads *pouring vinegar on soda.*

KING JAMES VERSION

8 As he that bindeth a stone in a sling, so *is* he that giveth honour to a fool.

9 *As* a thorn goeth up into the hand of a drunkard, so *is* a parable in the mouth of fools.

10 The great *God* that formed all *things* both rewardeth the fool, and rewardeth transgressors.

11 As a dog returneth to his vomit, *so* a fool returneth to his folly.

12 Seest thou a man wise in his own conceit? *there is* more hope of a fool than of him.

13 The slothful *man* saith, *There is* a lion in the way; a lion *is* in the streets.

14 *As* the door turneth upon his hinges, so *doth* the slothful upon his bed.

15 The slothful hideth his hand in *his* bosom; it grieveth him to bring it again to his mouth.

16 The sluggard *is* wiser in his own conceit than seven men that can render a reason.

17 He that passeth by, *and* meddleth with strife *belonging* not to him, *is like* one that taketh a dog by the ears.

18 As a mad *man* who casteth firebrands, arrows, and death,

19 So *is* the man *that* deceiveth his neighbour, and saith, Am not I in sport?

20 Where no wood is, *there* the fire goeth out: so where *there is* no talebearer, the strife ceaseth.

21 *As* coals *are* to burning coals, and wood to fire; so *is* a contentious man to kindle strife.

22 The words of a talebearer *are* as wounds, and they go down into the innermost parts of the belly.

23 Burning lips and a wicked heart *are like* a potsherd covered with silver dross.

24 He that hateth dissembleth with his lips, and layeth up deceit within him;

25 When he speaketh fair, believe him not: for *there are* seven abominations in his heart.

26 *Whose* hatred is covered by deceit, his wickedness shall be shewed before the *whole* congregation.

27 Whoso diggeth a pit shall fall therein: and he that rolleth a stone, it will return upon him.

28 A lying tongue hateth *those that are* afflicted by it; and a flattering mouth worketh ruin.

NEW LIVING TRANSLATION

8 Honoring a fool
is as foolish as tying a stone to a slingshot.

9 A proverb in the mouth of a fool
is like a thorny branch brandished by a drunk.

10 An employer who hires a fool or a bystander
is like an archer who shoots at random.

11 As a dog returns to its vomit,
so a fool repeats his foolishness.

12 There is more hope for fools
than for people who think they are wise.

13 The lazy person claims, "There's a lion on the road!
Yes, I'm sure there's a lion out there!"

14 As a door swings back and forth on its hinges,
so the lazy person turns over in bed.

15 Lazy people take food in their hand
but don't even lift it to their mouth.

16 Lazy people consider themselves smarter
than seven wise counselors.

17 Interfering in someone else's argument
is as foolish as yanking a dog's ears.

18 Just as damaging
as a madman shooting a deadly weapon
19 is someone who lies to a friend
and then says, "I was only joking."

20 Fire goes out without wood,
and quarrels disappear when gossip stops.

21 A quarrelsome person starts fights
as easily as hot embers light charcoal or fire lights wood.

22 Rumors are dainty morsels
that sink deep into one's heart.

23 Smooth* words may hide a wicked heart,
just as a pretty glaze covers a clay pot.

24 People may cover their hatred with pleasant words,
but they're deceiving you.
25 They pretend to be kind, but don't believe them.
Their hearts are full of many evils.*
26 While their hatred may be concealed by trickery,
their wrongdoing will be exposed in public.

27 If you set a trap for others,
you will get caught in it yourself.
If you roll a boulder down on others,
it will crush you instead.

28 A lying tongue hates its victims,
and flattering words cause ruin.

26:23 As in Greek version; Hebrew reads *Burning.* **26:25** Hebrew *seven evils.*

KING JAMES VERSION

27

1 Boast not thyself of tomorrow; for thou knowest not what a day may bring forth.

2 Let another man praise thee, and not thine own mouth; a stranger, and not thine own lips.

3 A stone *is* heavy, and the sand weighty; but a fool's wrath *is* heavier than them both.

4 Wrath *is* cruel, and anger *is* outrageous; but who *is* able to stand before envy?

5 Open rebuke *is* better than secret love.

6 Faithful *are* the wounds of a friend; but the kisses of an enemy *are* deceitful.

7 The full soul loatheth an honeycomb; but to the hungry soul every bitter thing is sweet.

8 As a bird that wandereth from her nest, so *is* a man that wandereth from his place.

9 Ointment and perfume rejoice the heart: so *doth* the sweetness of a man's friend by hearty counsel.

10 Thine own friend, and thy father's friend, forsake not; neither go into thy brother's house in the day of thy calamity: *for* better *is* a neighbour *that is* near than a brother far off.

11 My son, be wise, and make my heart glad, that I may answer him that reproacheth me.

12 A prudent *man* foreseeth the evil, *and* hideth himself; *but* the simple pass on, *and* are punished.

13 Take his garment that is surety for a stranger, and take a pledge of him for a strange woman.

14 He that blesseth his friend with a loud voice, rising early in the morning, it shall be counted a curse to him.

15 A continual dropping in a very rainy day and a contentious woman are alike.

16 Whosoever hideth her hideth the wind, and the ointment of his right hand, *which* bewrayeth *itself*.

17 Iron sharpeneth iron; so a man sharpeneth the countenance of his friend.

18 Whoso keepeth the fig tree shall eat the fruit thereof: so he that waiteth on his master shall be honoured.

NEW LIVING TRANSLATION

27

1 Don't brag about tomorrow,
since you don't know what
the day will bring.

2 Let someone else praise you, not your own mouth—
a stranger, not your own lips.

3 A stone is heavy and sand is weighty,
but the resentment caused by a fool
is even heavier.

4 Anger is cruel, and wrath is like a flood,
but jealousy is even more dangerous.

5 An open rebuke
is better than hidden love!

6 Wounds from a sincere friend
are better than many kisses from an enemy.

7 A person who is full refuses honey,
but even bitter food tastes sweet to the hungry.

8 A person who strays from home
is like a bird that strays from its nest.

9 The heartfelt counsel of a friend
is as sweet as perfume and incense.

10 Never abandon a friend—
either yours or your father's.
When disaster strikes, you won't have to ask your
brother for assistance.
It's better to go to a neighbor than to a brother
who lives far away.

11 Be wise, my child,* and make my heart glad.
Then I will be able to answer my critics.

12 A prudent person foresees danger and takes
precautions.
The simpleton goes blindly on and suffers
the consequences.

13 Get security from someone who guarantees
a stranger's debt.
Get a deposit if he does it for foreigners.*

14 A loud and cheerful greeting early in the morning
will be taken as a curse!

15 A quarrelsome wife is as annoying
as constant dripping on a rainy day.

16 Stopping her complaints is like trying to stop
the wind
or trying to hold something with greased hands.

17 As iron sharpens iron,
so a friend sharpens a friend.

18 As workers who tend a fig tree are allowed
to eat the fruit,
so workers who protect their employer's
interests will be rewarded.

27:11 Hebrew *my son.* **27:13** As in Greek and Latin versions (see also 20:16); Hebrew reads *for a promiscuous woman.*

19 As in water face *answereth* to face, so the heart of man to man.

20 Hell and destruction are never full; so the eyes of man are never satisfied.

21 *As* the fining pot for silver, and the furnace for gold; so *is* a man to his praise.

22 Though thou shouldest bray a fool in a mortar among wheat with a pestle, *yet* will not his foolishness depart from him.

23 Be thou diligent to know the state of thy flocks, *and* look well to thy herds.

24 For riches *are* not for ever: and doth the crown *endure* to every generation?

25 The hay appeareth, and the tender grass sheweth itself, and herbs of the mountains are gathered.

26 The lambs *are* for thy clothing, and the goats *are* the price of the field.

27 And *thou shalt have* goats' milk enough for thy food, for the food of thy household, and *for* the maintenance for thy maidens.

28

1 The wicked flee when no man pursueth: but the righteous are bold as a lion.

2 For the transgression of a land many *are* the princes thereof: but by a man of understanding *and* knowledge the state *thereof* shall be prolonged.

3 A poor man that oppresseth the poor *is like* a sweeping rain which leaveth no food.

4 They that forsake the law praise the wicked: but such as keep the law contend with them.

5 Evil men understand not judgment: but they that seek the LORD understand all *things*.

6 Better *is* the poor that walketh in his uprightness, than *he that is* perverse *in his* ways, though he *be* rich.

7 Whoso keepeth the law *is* a wise son: but he that is a companion of riotous *men* shameth his father.

8 He that by usury and unjust gain increaseth his substance, he shall gather it for him that will pity the poor.

9 He that turneth away his ear from hearing the law, even his prayer *shall be* abomination.

10 Whoso causeth the righteous to go astray in an evil way, he shall fall himself into his own pit: but the upright shall have good *things* in possession.

19 As a face is reflected in water,
so the heart reflects the real person.

20 Just as Death and Destruction* are never satisfied,
so human desire is never satisfied.

21 Fire tests the purity of silver and gold,
but a person is tested by being praised.*

22 You cannot separate fools from their foolishness,
even though you grind them like grain with
mortar and pestle.

23 Know the state of your flocks,
and put your heart into caring for your herds,
24 for riches don't last forever,
and the crown might not be passed to the
next generation.
25 After the hay is harvested and the new crop
appears
and the mountain grasses are gathered in,
26 your sheep will provide wool for clothing,
and your goats will provide the price of a field.
27 And you will have enough goats' milk for yourself,
your family, and your servant girls.

28

1 The wicked run away when no one
is chasing them,
but the godly are as bold as lions.

2 When there is moral rot within a nation,
its government topples easily.
But wise and knowledgeable leaders
bring stability.

3 A poor person who oppresses the poor
is like a pounding rain that destroys the crops.

4 To reject the law is to praise the wicked;
to obey the law is to fight them.

5 Evil people don't understand justice,
but those who follow the LORD understand
completely.

6 Better to be poor and honest
than to be dishonest and rich.

7 Young people who obey the law are wise;
those with wild friends bring shame
to their parents.*

8 Income from charging high interest rates
will end up in the pocket of someone who is
kind to the poor.

9 God detests the prayers
of a person who ignores the law.

10 Those who lead good people along an evil path
will fall into their own trap,
but the honest will inherit good things.

27:20 Hebrew *Sheol and Abaddon*. **27:21** Or *by flattery*. **28:7** Hebrew *their father*.

KING JAMES VERSION

11 The rich man *is* wise in his own conceit; but the poor that hath understanding searcheth him out.

12 When righteous *men* do rejoice, *there is* great glory: but when the wicked rise, a man is hidden.

13 He that covereth his sins shall not prosper: but whoso confesseth and forsaketh *them* shall have mercy.

14 Happy *is* the man that feareth alway: but he that hardeneth his heart shall fall into mischief.

15 *As* a roaring lion, and a ranging bear; *so is* a wicked ruler over the poor people.

16 The prince that wanteth understanding *is* also a great oppressor: *but* he that hateth covetousness shall prolong *his* days.

17 A man that doeth violence to the blood of *any* person shall flee to the pit; let no man stay him.

18 Whoso walketh uprightly shall be saved: but *he that is* perverse *in his* ways shall fall at once.

19 He that tilleth his land shall have plenty of bread: but he that followeth after vain *persons* shall have poverty enough.

20 A faithful man shall abound with blessings: but he that maketh haste to be rich shall not be innocent.

21 To have respect of persons *is* not good: for for a piece of bread *that* man will transgress.

22 He that hasteth to be rich *hath* an evil eye, and considereth not that poverty shall come upon him.

23 He that rebuketh a man afterwards shall find more favour than he that flattereth with the tongue.

24 Whoso robbeth his father or his mother, and saith, *It is* no transgression; the same *is* the companion of a destroyer.

25 He that is of a proud heart stirreth up strife: but he that putteth his trust in the LORD shall be made fat.

26 He that trusteth in his own heart is a fool: but whoso walketh wisely, he shall be delivered.

27 He that giveth unto the poor shall not lack: but he that hideth his eyes shall have many a curse.

28 When the wicked rise, men hide themselves: but when they perish, the righteous increase.

NEW LIVING TRANSLATION

11 Rich people may think they are wise,
but a poor person with discernment can
see right through them.

12 When the godly succeed, everyone is glad.
When the wicked take charge, people go
into hiding.

13 People who conceal their sins will not prosper,
but if they confess and turn from them, they
will receive mercy.

14 Blessed are those who fear to do wrong,*
but the stubborn are headed for serious trouble.

15 A wicked ruler is as dangerous to the poor
as a roaring lion or an attacking bear.

16 A ruler with no understanding will oppress
his people,
but one who hates corruption will have
a long life.

17 A murderer's tormented conscience will drive
him into the grave.
Don't protect him!

18 The blameless will be rescued from harm,
but the crooked will be suddenly destroyed.

19 A hard worker has plenty of food,
but a person who chases fantasies ends up
in poverty.

20 The trustworthy person will get a rich reward,
but a person who wants quick riches will get
into trouble.

21 Showing partiality is never good,
yet some will do wrong for a mere
piece of bread.

22 Greedy people try to get rich quick
but don't realize they're headed for poverty.

23 In the end, people appreciate honest criticism
far more than flattery.

24 Anyone who steals from his father and mother
and says, "What's wrong with that?"
is no better than a murderer.

25 Greed causes fighting;
trusting the LORD leads to prosperity.

26 Those who trust their own insight are foolish,
but anyone who walks in wisdom is safe.

27 Whoever gives to the poor will lack nothing,
but those who close their eyes to poverty
will be cursed.

28 When the wicked take charge, people
go into hiding.
When the wicked meet disaster,
the godly flourish.

28:14 Or *those who fear the LORD;* Hebrew reads *those who fear.*

KING JAMES VERSION

29 1 He, that being often reproved hardeneth
his neck, shall suddenly be destroyed, and
that without remedy.
2 When the righteous are in authority, the people
rejoice: but when the wicked beareth rule, the people
mourn.
3 Whoso loveth wisdom rejoiceth his father: but
he that keepeth company with harlots spendeth *his*
substance.
4 The king by judgment establisheth the land: but
he that receiveth gifts overthroweth it.
5 A man that flattereth his neighbour spreadeth a
net for his feet.
6 In the transgression of an evil man *there is* a
snare: but the righteous doth sing and rejoice.
7 The righteous considereth the cause of the poor:
but the wicked regardeth not to know *it*.
8 Scornful men bring a city into a snare: but wise
men turn away wrath.
9 *If* a wise man contendeth with a foolish man,
whether he rage or laugh, *there is* no rest.
10 The bloodthirsty hate the upright: but the just
seek his soul.
11 A fool uttereth all his mind: but a wise *man*
keepeth it in till afterwards.
12 If a ruler hearken to lies, all his servants *are*
wicked.
13 The poor and the deceitful man meet together:
the LORD lighteneth both their eyes.
14 The king that faithfully judgeth the poor, his
throne shall be established for ever.
15 The rod and reproof give wisdom: but a child
left *to himself* bringeth his mother to shame.
16 When the wicked are multiplied, transgression
increaseth: but the righteous shall see their fall.
17 Correct thy son, and he shall give thee rest; yea,
he shall give delight unto thy soul.
18 Where *there is* no vision, the people perish: but
he that keepeth the law, happy *is* he.
19 A servant will not be corrected by words: for
though he understand he will not answer.

NEW LIVING TRANSLATION

29 1 Whoever stubbornly refuses to accept
criticism
will suddenly be destroyed beyond recovery.

2 When the godly are in authority, the people
rejoice.
But when the wicked are in power, they groan.

3 The man who loves wisdom brings joy
to his father,
but if he hangs around with prostitutes,
his wealth is wasted.

4 A just king gives stability to his nation,
but one who demands bribes destroys it.

5 To flatter friends
is to lay a trap for their feet.

6 Evil people are trapped by sin,
but the righteous escape, shouting for joy.

7 The godly care about the rights of the poor;
the wicked don't care at all.

8 Mockers can get a whole town agitated,
but the wise will calm anger.

9 If a wise person takes a fool to court,
there will be ranting and ridicule but no
satisfaction.

10 The bloodthirsty hate blameless people,
but the upright seek to help them.*

11 Fools vent their anger,
but the wise quietly hold it back.

12 If a ruler pays attention to liars,
all his advisers will be wicked.

13 The poor and the oppressor have this in common—
the LORD gives sight to the eyes of both.

14 If a king judges the poor fairly,
his throne will last forever.

15 To discipline a child produces wisdom,
but a mother is disgraced by an
undisciplined child.

16 When the wicked are in authority, sin flourishes,
but the godly will live to see their downfall.

17 Discipline your children, and they will give you
peace of mind
and will make your heart glad.

18 When people do not accept divine guidance,
they run wild.
But whoever obeys the law is joyful.

19 Words alone will not discipline a servant;
the words may be understood, but they
are not heeded.

29:10 Or *The bloodthirsty hate blameless people, / and they seek to kill the upright;* Hebrew reads *The bloodthirsty hate blameless people; / as for the upright, they seek their life.*

KING JAMES VERSION

20Seest thou a man *that is* hasty in his words? *there is* more hope of a fool than of him.

21He that delicately bringeth up his servant from a child shall have him become *his* son at the length.

22An angry man stirreth up strife, and a furious man aboundeth in transgression.

23A man's pride shall bring him low: but honour shall uphold the humble in spirit.

24Whoso is partner with a thief hateth his own soul: he heareth cursing, and bewrayeth *it* not.

25The fear of man bringeth a snare: but whoso putteth his trust in the LORD shall be safe.

26Many seek the ruler's favour; but *every* man's judgment *cometh* from the LORD.

27An unjust man *is* an abomination to the just: and *he that is* upright in the way *is* abomination to the wicked.

30 1The words of Agur the son of Jakeh, *even* the prophecy: the man spake unto Ithiel, even unto Ithiel and Ucal,

2Surely I *am* more brutish than *any* man, and have not the understanding of a man.

3I neither learned wisdom, nor have the knowledge of the holy.

4Who hath ascended up into heaven, or descended? who hath gathered the wind in his fists? who hath bound the waters in a garment? who hath established all the ends of the earth? what *is* his name, and what *is* his son's name, if thou canst tell?

5Every word of God *is* pure: he *is* a shield unto them that put their trust in him.

6Add thou not unto his words, lest he reprove thee, and thou be found a liar.

7Two *things* have I required of thee; deny me *them* not before I die:

8Remove far from me vanity and lies: give me neither poverty nor riches; feed me with food convenient for me:

9Lest I be full, and deny *thee,* and say, Who *is* the LORD? or lest I be poor, and steal, and take the name of my God *in vain.*

NEW LIVING TRANSLATION

20 There is more hope for a fool
than for someone who speaks
without thinking.

21 A servant pampered from childhood
will become a rebel.

22 An angry person starts fights;
a hot-tempered person commits all
kinds of sin.

23 Pride ends in humiliation,
while humility brings honor.

24 If you assist a thief, you only hurt yourself.
You are sworn to tell the truth, but you
dare not testify.

25 Fearing people is a dangerous trap,
but trusting the LORD means safety.

26 Many seek the ruler's favor,
but justice comes from the LORD.

27 The righteous despise the unjust;
the wicked despise the godly.

The Sayings of Agur

30 The sayings of Agur son of Jakeh contain this message.*

I am weary, O God;
I am weary and worn out, O God.*

2 I am too stupid to be human,
and I lack common sense.

3 I have not mastered human wisdom,
nor do I know the Holy One.

4 Who but God goes up to heaven and comes
back down?
Who holds the wind in his fists?
Who wraps up the oceans in his cloak?
Who has created the whole wide world?
What is his name—and his son's name?
Tell me if you know!

5 Every word of God proves true.
He is a shield to all who come to him for
protection.

6 Do not add to his words,
or he may rebuke you and expose you as a liar.

7 O God, I beg two favors from you;
let me have them before I die.

8 First, help me never to tell a lie.
Second, give me neither poverty nor riches!
Give me just enough to satisfy my needs.

9 For if I grow rich, I may deny you and say,
"Who is the LORD?"
And if I am too poor, I may steal and thus
insult God's holy name.

30:1a Or *son of Jakeh from Massa;* or *son of Jakeh, an oracle.* **30:1b** The Hebrew can also be translated *The man declares this to Ithiel, / to Ithiel and to Ucal.*

KING JAMES VERSION

10 Accuse not a servant unto his master, lest he curse thee, and thou be found guilty.

11 *There is* a generation *that* curseth their father, and doth not bless their mother.

12 *There is* a generation *that are* pure in their own eyes, and *yet* is not washed from their filthiness.

13 *There is* a generation, O how lofty are their eyes! and their eyelids are lifted up.

14 *There is* a generation, whose teeth *are as* swords, and their jaw teeth *as* knives, to devour the poor from off the earth, and the needy from *among* men.

15 The horseleach hath two daughters, *crying*, Give, give. There are three *things that* are never satisfied, *yea*, four *things* say not, *It is* enough:

16 The grave; and the barren womb; the earth *that* is not filled with water; and the fire *that* saith not, *It is* enough.

17 The eye *that* mocketh at *his* father, and despiseth to obey *his* mother, the ravens of the valley shall pick it out, and the young eagles shall eat it.

18 There be three *things which* are too wonderful for me, yea, four which I know not:

19 The way of an eagle in the air; the way of a serpent upon a rock; the way of a ship in the midst of the sea; and the way of a man with a maid.

20 Such *is* the way of an adulterous woman; she eateth, and wipeth her mouth, and saith, I have done no wickedness.

21 For three *things* the earth is disquieted, and for four *which* it cannot bear:

22 For a servant when he reigneth; and a fool when he is filled with meat;

23 For an odious *woman* when she is married; and an handmaid that is heir to her mistress.

24 There be four *things which are* little upon the earth, but they *are* exceeding wise:

25 The ants *are* a people not strong, yet they prepare their meat in the summer;

26 The conies *are but* a feeble folk, yet make they their houses in the rocks;

27 The locusts have no king, yet go they forth all of them by bands;

28 The spider taketh hold with her hands, and is in kings' palaces.

NEW LIVING TRANSLATION

10 Never slander a worker to the employer,
or the person will curse you, and you
will pay for it.

11 Some people curse their father
and do not thank their mother.
12 They are pure in their own eyes,
but they are filthy and unwashed.
13 They look proudly around,
casting disdainful glances.
14 They have teeth like swords
and fangs like knives.
They devour the poor from the earth
and the needy from among humanity.

15 The leech has two suckers
that cry out, "More, more!"*

There are three things that are never satisfied—
no, four that never say, "Enough!":
16 the grave,*
the barren womb,
the thirsty desert,
the blazing fire.

17 The eye that mocks a father
and despises a mother's instructions
will be plucked out by ravens of the valley
and eaten by vultures.

18 There are three things that amaze me—
no, four things that I don't understand:
19 how an eagle glides through the sky,
how a snake slithers on a rock,
how a ship navigates the ocean,
how a man loves a woman.

20 An adulterous woman consumes a man,
then wipes her mouth and says,
"What's wrong with that?"

21 There are three things that make the
earth tremble—
no, four it cannot endure:
22 a slave who becomes a king,
an overbearing fool who prospers,
23 a bitter woman who finally gets a husband,
a servant girl who supplants her mistress.

24 There are four things on earth that are small
but unusually wise:
25 Ants—they aren't strong,
but they store up food all summer.
26 Hyraxes*—they aren't powerful,
but they make their homes among the rocks.
27 Locusts—they have no king,
but they march in formation.
28 Lizards—they are easy to catch,
but they are found even in kings' palaces.

30:15 Hebrew *two daughters who cry out, "Give, give!"* **30:16** Hebrew *Sheol.* **30:26** Or *Coneys*, or *Rock badgers*.

KING JAMES VERSION

29There be three *things* which go well, yea, four
are comely in going:
30A lion *which is* strongest among beasts, and
turneth not away for any;
31A greyhound; an he goat also; and a king, against
whom *there is* no rising up.
32If thou hast done foolishly in lifting up thyself,
or if thou hast thought evil, *lay* thine hand upon thy
mouth.
33Surely the churning of milk bringeth forth butter, and the wringing of the nose bringeth forth
blood: so the forcing of wrath bringeth forth strife.

31 1The words of king Lemuel, the prophecy
that his mother taught him.
2What, my son? and what, the son of my womb?
and what, the son of my vows?
3Give not thy strength unto women, nor thy ways
to that which destroyeth kings.
4*It is* not for kings, O Lemuel, *it is* not for kings to
drink wine; nor for princes strong drink:
5Lest they drink, and forget the law, and pervert
the judgment of any of the afflicted.
6Give strong drink unto him that is ready to perish, and wine unto those that be of heavy hearts.
7Let him drink, and forget his poverty, and remember his misery no more.
8Open thy mouth for the dumb in the cause of all
such as are appointed to destruction.
9Open thy mouth, judge righteously, and plead the
cause of the poor and needy.

10Who can find a virtuous woman? for her price *is*
far above rubies.
11The heart of her husband doth safely trust in
her, so that he shall have no need of spoil.
12She will do him good and not evil all the days of
her life.
13She seeketh wool, and flax, and worketh willingly with her hands.
14She is like the merchants' ships; she bringeth
her food from afar.
15She riseth also while it is yet night, and giveth
meat to her household, and a portion to her maidens.
16She considereth a field, and buyeth it: with the
fruit of her hands she planteth a vineyard.

NEW LIVING TRANSLATION

29 There are three things that walk with
stately stride—
no, four that strut about:
30 the lion, king of animals, who won't
turn aside for anything,
31 the strutting rooster,
the male goat,
a king as he leads his army.

32 If you have been a fool by being proud
or plotting evil,
cover your mouth in shame.

33 As the beating of cream yields butter
and striking the nose causes bleeding,
so stirring up anger causes quarrels.

The Sayings of King Lemuel

31 The sayings of King Lemuel contain this message,* which his mother taught him.

2 O my son, O son of my womb,
O son of my vows,
3 do not waste your strength on women,
on those who ruin kings.

4 It is not for kings, O Lemuel, to guzzle wine.
Rulers should not crave alcohol.
5 For if they drink, they may forget the law
and not give justice to the oppressed.
6 Alcohol is for the dying,
and wine for those in bitter distress.
7 Let them drink to forget their poverty
and remember their troubles no more.

8 Speak up for those who cannot speak for
themselves;
ensure justice for those being crushed.
9 Yes, speak up for the poor and helpless,
and see that they get justice.

A Wife of Noble Character

10* Who can find a virtuous and capable wife?
She is more precious than rubies.
11 Her husband can trust her,
and she will greatly enrich his life.
12 She brings him good, not harm,
all the days of her life.

13 She finds wool and flax
and busily spins it.
14 She is like a merchant's ship,
bringing her food from afar.
15 She gets up before dawn to prepare breakfast
for her household
and plan the day's work for her servant girls.

16 She goes to inspect a field and buys it;
with her earnings she plants a vineyard.

31:1 Or *of Lemuel, king of Massa;* or *of King Lemuel, an oracle.*
31:10 Verses 10-31 comprise a Hebrew acrostic poem; each verse begins with a successive letter of the Hebrew alphabet.

KING JAMES VERSION

[17]She girdeth her loins with strength, and
strengtheneth her arms.
[18]She perceiveth that her merchandise *is* good:
her candle goeth not out by night.
[19]She layeth her hands to the spindle, and her
hands hold the distaff.
[20]She stretcheth out her hand to the poor; yea, she
reacheth forth her hands to the needy.
[21]She is not afraid of the snow for her household:
for all her household *are* clothed with scarlet.
[22]She maketh herself coverings of tapestry; her
clothing *is* silk and purple.
[23]Her husband is known in the gates, when he
sitteth among the elders of the land.
[24]She maketh fine linen, and selleth *it;* and
delivereth girdles unto the merchant.
[25]Strength and honour *are* her clothing; and she
shall rejoice in time to come.
[26]She openeth her mouth with wisdom; and in her
tongue *is* the law of kindness.
[27]She looketh well to the ways of her household,
and eateth not the bread of idleness.
[28]Her children arise up, and call her blessed; her
husband *also,* and he praiseth her.
[29]Many daughters have done virtuously, but thou
excellest them all.
[30]Favour *is* deceitful, and beauty *is* vain: *but* a
woman *that* feareth the LORD, she shall be praised.
[31]Give her of the fruit of her hands; and let her
own works praise her in the gates.

NEW LIVING TRANSLATION

17 She is energetic and strong,
a hard worker.
18 She makes sure her dealings are profitable;
her lamp burns late into the night.
19 Her hands are busy spinning thread,
her fingers twisting fiber.
20 She extends a helping hand to the poor
and opens her arms to the needy.
21 She has no fear of winter for her household,
for everyone has warm* clothes.
22 She makes her own bedspreads.
She dresses in fine linen and purple gowns.
23 Her husband is well known at the city gates,
where he sits with the other civic leaders.
24 She makes belted linen garments
and sashes to sell to the merchants.
25 She is clothed with strength and dignity,
and she laughs without fear of the future.
26 When she speaks, her words are wise,
and she gives instructions with kindness.
27 She carefully watches everything in her household
and suffers nothing from laziness.
28 Her children stand and bless her.
Her husband praises her:
29 "There are many virtuous and capable women in the world,
but you surpass them all!"
30 Charm is deceptive, and beauty does not last;
but a woman who fears the LORD will be greatly praised.
31 Reward her for all she has done.
Let her deeds publicly declare her praise.

31:21 As in Greek and Latin versions; Hebrew reads *scarlet.*

Ecclesiastes

KING JAMES VERSION

1 1 The words of the Preacher, the son of David, king in Jerusalem.

2 Vanity of vanities, saith the Preacher, vanity of vanities; all *is* vanity.

3 What profit hath a man of all his labour which he taketh under the sun?

4 *One* generation passeth away, and *another* generation cometh: but the earth abideth for ever.

5 The sun also ariseth, and the sun goeth down, and hasteth to his place where he arose.

6 The wind goeth toward the south, and turneth about unto the north; it whirleth about continually, and the wind returneth again according to his circuits.

7 All the rivers run into the sea; yet the sea *is* not full; unto the place from whence the rivers come, thither they return again.

8 All things *are* full of labour; man cannot utter *it:* the eye is not satisfied with seeing, nor the ear filled with hearing.

9 The thing that hath been, it *is that* which shall be; and that which is done *is* that which shall be done: and *there is* no new *thing* under the sun.

10 Is there *any* thing whereof it may be said, See, this *is* new? it hath been already of old time, which was before us.

11 *There is* no remembrance of former *things;* neither shall there be *any* remembrance of *things* that are to come with *those* that shall come after.

12 I the Preacher was king over Israel in Jerusalem.

13 And I gave my heart to seek and search out by wisdom concerning all *things* that are done under heaven: this sore travail hath God given to the sons of man to be exercised therewith.

14 I have seen all the works that are done under the sun; and, behold, all *is* vanity and vexation of spirit.

15 *That which is* crooked cannot be made straight: and that which is wanting cannot be numbered.

16 I communed with mine own heart, saying, Lo, I am come to great estate, and have gotten more wisdom than all *they* that have been before me in Jerusalem: yea, my heart had great experience of wisdom and knowledge.

NEW LIVING TRANSLATION

1 These are the words of the Teacher,* King
David's son, who ruled in Jerusalem.

Everything Is Meaningless

2 "Everything is meaningless," says the Teacher, "completely meaningless!"

3 What do people get for all their hard work under
the sun? 4 Generations come and generations go,
but the earth never changes. 5 The sun rises and the
sun sets, then hurries around to rise again. 6 The
wind blows south, and then turns north. Around and
around it goes, blowing in circles. 7 Rivers run into
the sea, but the sea is never full. Then the water returns again to the rivers and flows out again to the
sea. 8 Everything is wearisome beyond description.
No matter how much we see, we are never satisfied.
No matter how much we hear, we are not content.

9 History merely repeats itself. It has all been done
before. Nothing under the sun is truly new. 10 Sometimes people say, "Here is something new!" But actually it is old; nothing is ever truly new. 11 We don't
remember what happened in the past, and in future
generations, no one will remember what we are
doing now.

The Teacher Speaks: The Futility of Wisdom

12 I, the Teacher, was king of Israel, and I lived in Jerusalem. 13 I devoted myself to search for understanding and to explore by wisdom everything being done
under heaven. I soon discovered that God has dealt
a tragic existence to the human race. 14 I observed
everything going on under the sun, and really, it is all
meaningless—like chasing the wind.

15 What is wrong cannot be made right.
What is missing cannot be recovered.

16 I said to myself, "Look, I am wiser than any of
the kings who ruled in Jerusalem before me. I have
greater wisdom and knowledge than any of them."

1:1 Hebrew *Qoheleth;* this term is rendered "the Teacher" throughout this book.

KING JAMES VERSION

17 And I gave my heart to know wisdom, and to know madness and folly: I perceived that this also is vexation of spirit.

18 For in much wisdom *is* much grief: and he that increaseth knowledge increaseth sorrow.

2 1 I said in mine heart, Go to now, I will prove thee with mirth, therefore enjoy pleasure: and, behold, this also *is* vanity.

2 I said of laughter, *It is* mad: and of mirth, What doeth it?

3 I sought in mine heart to give myself unto wine, yet acquainting mine heart with wisdom; and to lay hold on folly, till I might see what *was* that good for the sons of men, which they should do under the heaven all the days of their life.

4 I made me great works; I builded me houses; I planted me vineyards:

5 I made me gardens and orchards, and I planted trees in them of all *kind of* fruits:

6 I made me pools of water, to water therewith the wood that bringeth forth trees:

7 I got *me* servants and maidens, and had servants born in my house; also I had great possessions of great and small cattle above all that were in Jerusalem before me:

8 I gathered me also silver and gold, and the peculiar treasure of kings and of the provinces: I gat me men singers and women singers, and the delights of the sons of men, *as* musical instruments, and that of all sorts.

9 So I was great, and increased more than all that were before me in Jerusalem: also my wisdom remained with me.

10 And whatsoever mine eyes desired I kept not from them, I withheld not my heart from any joy; for my heart rejoiced in all my labour: and this was my portion of all my labour.

11 Then I looked on all the works that my hands had wrought, and on the labour that I had laboured to do: and, behold, all *was* vanity and vexation of spirit, and *there was* no profit under the sun.

12 And I turned myself to behold wisdom, and madness, and folly: for what *can* the man *do* that cometh after the king? *even* that which hath been already done.

13 Then I saw that wisdom excelleth folly, as far as light excelleth darkness.

14 The wise man's eyes *are* in his head; but the fool walketh in darkness: and I myself perceived also that one event happeneth to them all.

15 Then said I in my heart, As it happeneth to the fool, so it happeneth even to me; and why was I then more wise? Then I said in my heart, that this also *is* vanity.

NEW LIVING TRANSLATION

17 So I set out to learn everything from wisdom to madness and folly. But I learned firsthand that pursuing all this is like chasing the wind.

18 The greater my wisdom, the greater my grief.
To increase knowledge only increases sorrow.

The Futility of Pleasure

2 I said to myself, "Come on, let's try pleasure. Let's look for the 'good things' in life." But I found that this, too, was meaningless. 2 So I said, "Laughter is silly. What good does it do to seek pleasure?" 3 After much thought, I decided to cheer myself with wine. And while still seeking wisdom, I clutched at foolishness. In this way, I tried to experience the only happiness most people find during their brief life in this world.

4 I also tried to find meaning by building huge homes for myself and by planting beautiful vineyards. 5 I made gardens and parks, filling them with all kinds of fruit trees. 6 I built reservoirs to collect the water to irrigate my many flourishing groves. 7 I bought slaves, both men and women, and others were born into my household. I also owned large herds and flocks, more than any of the kings who had lived in Jerusalem before me. 8 I collected great sums of silver and gold, the treasure of many kings and provinces. I hired wonderful singers, both men and women, and had many beautiful concubines. I had everything a man could desire!

9 So I became greater than all who had lived in Jerusalem before me, and my wisdom never failed me. 10 Anything I wanted, I would take. I denied myself no pleasure. I even found great pleasure in hard work, a reward for all my labors. 11 But as I looked at everything I had worked so hard to accomplish, it was all so meaningless—like chasing the wind. There was nothing really worthwhile anywhere.

The Wise and the Foolish

12 So I decided to compare wisdom with foolishness and madness (for who can do this better than I, the king?*). 13 I thought, "Wisdom is better than foolishness, just as light is better than darkness. 14 For the wise can see where they are going, but fools walk in the dark." Yet I saw that the wise and the foolish share the same fate. 15 Both will die. So I said to myself, "Since I will end up the same as the fool, what's the value of all my wisdom? This is all so meaningless!"

2:12 The meaning of the Hebrew is uncertain.

16 For *there is* no remembrance of the wise more than of the fool for ever; seeing that which now *is* in the days to come shall all be forgotten. And how dieth the wise *man?* as the fool.

17 Therefore I hated life; because the work that is wrought under the sun *is* grievous unto me: for all *is* vanity and vexation of spirit.

18 Yea, I hated all my labour which I had taken under the sun: because I should leave it unto the man that shall be after me.

19 And who knoweth whether he shall be a wise *man* or a fool? yet shall he have rule over all my labour wherein I have laboured, and wherein I have shewed myself wise under the sun. This *is* also vanity.

20 Therefore I went about to cause my heart to despair of all the labour which I took under the sun.

21 For there is a man whose labour *is* in wisdom, and in knowledge, and in equity; yet to a man that hath not laboured therein shall he leave it *for* his portion. This also *is* vanity and a great evil.

22 For what hath man of all his labour, and of the vexation of his heart, wherein he hath laboured under the sun?

23 For all his days *are* sorrows, and his travail grief; yea, his heart taketh not rest in the night. This is also vanity.

24 *There is* nothing better for a man, *than* that he should eat and drink, and *that* he should make his soul enjoy good in his labour. This also I saw, that it *was* from the hand of God.

25 For who can eat, or who else can hasten *hereunto,* more than I?

26 For *God* giveth to a man that *is* good in his sight wisdom, and knowledge, and joy: but to the sinner he giveth travail, to gather and to heap up, that he may give to *him that is* good before God. This also *is* vanity and vexation of spirit.

3 1 To every *thing there is* a season, and a time to every purpose under the heaven:

2 A time to be born, and a time to die; a time to plant, and a time to pluck up *that which is* planted;

3 A time to kill, and a time to heal; a time to break down, and a time to build up;

4 A time to weep, and a time to laugh; a time to mourn, and a time to dance;

5 A time to cast away stones, and a time to gather stones together; a time to embrace, and a time to refrain from embracing;

6 A time to get, and a time to lose; a time to keep, and a time to cast away;

7 A time to rend, and a time to sew; a time to keep silence, and a time to speak;

8 A time to love, and a time to hate; a time of war, and a time of peace.

16 For the wise and the foolish both die. The wise will not be remembered any longer than the fool. In the days to come, both will be forgotten.

17 So I came to hate life because everything done here under the sun is so troubling. Everything is meaningless—like chasing the wind.

The Futility of Work

18 I came to hate all my hard work here on earth, for I must leave to others everything I have earned. 19 And who can tell whether my successors will be wise or foolish? Yet they will control everything I have gained by my skill and hard work under the sun. How meaningless! 20 So I gave up in despair, questioning the value of all my hard work in this world.

21 Some people work wisely with knowledge and skill, then must leave the fruit of their efforts to someone who hasn't worked for it. This, too, is meaningless, a great tragedy. 22 So what do people get in this life for all their hard work and anxiety? 23 Their days of labor are filled with pain and grief; even at night their minds cannot rest. It is all meaningless.

24 So I decided there is nothing better than to enjoy food and drink and to find satisfaction in work. Then I realized that these pleasures are from the hand of God. 25 For who can eat or enjoy anything apart from him?* 26 God gives wisdom, knowledge, and joy to those who please him. But if a sinner becomes wealthy, God takes the wealth away and gives it to those who please him. This, too, is meaningless—like chasing the wind.

A Time for Everything

3 1 For everything there is a season,
a time for every activity under heaven.
2 A time to be born and a time to die.
A time to plant and a time to harvest.
3 A time to kill and a time to heal.
A time to tear down and a time to build up.
4 A time to cry and a time to laugh.
A time to grieve and a time to dance.
5 A time to scatter stones and a time to gather stones.
A time to embrace and a time to turn away.
6 A time to search and a time to quit searching.
A time to keep and a time to throw away.
7 A time to tear and a time to mend.
A time to be quiet and a time to speak.
8 A time to love and a time to hate.
A time for war and a time for peace.

2:25 As in Greek and Syriac versions; Hebrew reads *apart from me?*

KING JAMES VERSION

9 What profit hath he that worketh in that wherein
he laboureth?
10 I have seen the travail, which God hath given to
the sons of men to be exercised in it.
11 He hath made every *thing* beautiful in his time:
also he hath set the world in their heart, so that no
man can find out the work that God maketh from the
beginning to the end.
12 I know that *there is* no good in them, but for *a*
man to rejoice, and to do good in his life.
13 And also that every man should eat and drink, and
enjoy the good of all his labour, it *is* the gift of God.
14 I know that, whatsoever God doeth, it shall be
for ever: nothing can be put to it, nor any thing taken
from it: and God doeth *it*, that *men* should fear before him.
15 That which hath been is now; and that which
is to be hath already been; and God requireth that
which is past.
16 And moreover I saw under the sun the place of
judgment, *that* wickedness *was* there; and the place
of righteousness, *that* iniquity *was* there.
17 I said in mine heart, God shall judge the righteous and the wicked: for *there is* a time there for
every purpose and for every work.
18 I said in mine heart concerning the estate of the
sons of men, that God might manifest them, and that
they might see that they themselves are beasts.
19 For that which befalleth the sons of men
befalleth beasts; even one thing befalleth them: as
the one dieth, so dieth the other; yea, they have all
one breath; so that a man hath no preeminence
above a beast: for all *is* vanity.
20 All go unto one place; all are of the dust, and all
turn to dust again.
21 Who knoweth the spirit of man that goeth upward, and the spirit of the beast that goeth downward to the earth?
22 Wherefore I perceive that *there is* nothing
better, than that a man should rejoice in his own
works; for that *is* his portion: for who shall bring him
to see what shall be after him?

4 1 So I returned, and considered all the oppressions that are done under the sun: and behold
the tears of *such as were* oppressed, and they had no
comforter; and on the side of their oppressors *there*
was power; but they had no comforter.
2 Wherefore I praised the dead which are already
dead more than the living which are yet alive.
3 Yea, better *is he* than both they, which hath not
yet been, who hath not seen the evil work that is
done under the sun.
4 Again, I considered all travail, and every right
work, that for this a man is envied of his neighbour.
This *is* also vanity and vexation of spirit.
5 The fool foldeth his hands together, and eateth
his own flesh.

NEW LIVING TRANSLATION

9 What do people really get for all their hard work?
10 I have seen the burden God has placed on us all.
11 Yet God has made everything beautiful for its own
time. He has planted eternity in the human heart, but
even so, people cannot see the whole scope of God's
work from beginning to end. 12 So I concluded there
is nothing better than to be happy and enjoy ourselves as long as we can. 13 And people should eat and
drink and enjoy the fruits of their labor, for these are
gifts from God.
14 And I know that whatever God does is final.
Nothing can be added to it or taken from it. God's
purpose is that people should fear him. 15 What is
happening now has happened before, and what will
happen in the future has happened before, because
God makes the same things happen over and over
again.

The Injustices of Life

16 I also noticed that under the sun there is evil in the
courtroom. Yes, even the courts of law are corrupt!
17 I said to myself, "In due season God will judge
everyone, both good and bad, for all their deeds."
18 I also thought about the human condition—how
God proves to people that they are like animals. 19 For
people and animals share the same fate—both
breathe* and both must die. So people have no real
advantage over the animals. How meaningless!
20 Both go to the same place—they came from dust
and they return to dust. 21 For who can prove that the
human spirit goes up and the spirit of animals goes
down into the earth? 22 So I saw that there is nothing
better for people than to be happy in their work.
That is why we are here! No one will bring us back
from death to enjoy life after we die.

4 Again, I observed all the oppression that takes
place under the sun. I saw the tears of the oppressed, with no one to comfort them. The oppressors have great power, and their victims are helpless.
2 So I concluded that the dead are better off than the
living. 3 But most fortunate of all are those who are
not yet born. For they have not seen all the evil that is
done under the sun.
4 Then I observed that most people are motivated
to success because they envy their neighbors. But
this, too, is meaningless—like chasing the wind.

5 "Fools fold their idle hands,
leading them to ruin."

3:19 Or *both have the same spirit.*

KING JAMES VERSION

6 Better *is* an handful *with* quietness, than both the hands full *with* travail and vexation of spirit.

7 Then I returned, and I saw vanity under the sun.

8 There is one *alone,* and *there is* not a second; yea, he hath neither child nor brother: yet *is there* no end of all his labour; neither is his eye satisfied with riches; neither *saith he,* For whom do I labour, and bereave my soul of good? This *is* also vanity, yea, it *is* a sore travail.

9 Two *are* better than one; because they have a good reward for their labour.

10 For if they fall, the one will lift up his fellow: but woe to him *that is* alone when he falleth; for *he hath* not another to help him up.

11 Again, if two lie together, then they have heat: but how can one be warm *alone?*

12 And if one prevail against him, two shall withstand him; and a threefold cord is not quickly broken.

13 Better *is* a poor and a wise child than an old and foolish king, who will no more be admonished.

14 For out of prison he cometh to reign; whereas also *he that is* born in his kingdom becometh poor.

15 I considered all the living which walk under the sun, with the second child that shall stand up in his stead.

16 *There is* no end of all the people, *even* of all that have been before them: they also that come after shall not rejoice in him. Surely this also *is* vanity and vexation of spirit.

5 1 Keep thy foot when thou goest to the house of God, and be more ready to hear, than to give the sacrifice of fools: for they consider not that they do evil.

2 Be not rash with thy mouth, and let not thine heart be hasty to utter *any* thing before God: for God *is* in heaven, and thou upon earth: therefore let thy words be few.

3 For a dream cometh through the multitude of business; and a fool's voice *is known* by multitude of words.

4 When thou vowest a vow unto God, defer not to pay it; for *he hath* no pleasure in fools: pay that which thou hast vowed.

5 Better *is it* that thou shouldest not vow, than that thou shouldest vow and not pay.

6 Suffer not thy mouth to cause thy flesh to sin; neither say thou before the angel, that it *was* an error: wherefore should God be angry at thy voice, and destroy the work of thine hands?

7 For in the multitude of dreams and many words *there are* also *divers* vanities: but fear thou God.

NEW LIVING TRANSLATION

6 And yet,

"Better to have one handful with quietness
than two handfuls with hard work
and chasing the wind."

The Advantages of Companionship

7 I observed yet another example of something
meaningless under the sun. 8 This is the case of a man
who is all alone, without a child or a brother, yet who
works hard to gain as much wealth as he can. But
then he asks himself, "Who am I working for? Why
am I giving up so much pleasure now?" It is all so
meaningless and depressing.

9 Two people are better off than one, for they can
help each other succeed. 10 If one person falls, the
other can reach out and help. But someone who falls
alone is in real trouble. 11 Likewise, two people lying
close together can keep each other warm. But how
can one be warm alone? 12 A person standing alone
can be attacked and defeated, but two can stand
back-to-back and conquer. Three are even better,
for a triple-braided cord is not easily broken.

The Futility of Political Power

13 It is better to be a poor but wise youth than an old
and foolish king who refuses all advice. 14 Such a
youth could rise from poverty and succeed. He might
even become king, though he has been in prison.
15 But then everyone rushes to the side of yet another
youth* who replaces him. 16 Endless crowds stand
around him,* but then another generation grows
up and rejects him, too. So it is all meaningless—like
chasing the wind.

Approaching God with Care

5 1* As you enter the house of God, keep your ears
open and your mouth shut. It is evil to make
mindless offerings to God. 2* Don't make rash promises, and don't be hasty in bringing matters before
God. After all, God is in heaven, and you are here on
earth. So let your words be few.

3 Too much activity gives you restless dreams; too
many words make you a fool.

4 When you make a promise to God, don't delay in
following through, for God takes no pleasure in fools.
Keep all the promises you make to him. 5 It is better
to say nothing than to make a promise and not keep
it. 6 Don't let your mouth make you sin. And don't defend yourself by telling the Temple messenger that
the promise you made was a mistake. That would
make God angry, and he might wipe out everything
you have achieved.

7 Talk is cheap, like daydreams and other useless
activities. Fear God instead.

4:15 Hebrew *the second youth.* **4:16** Hebrew *There is no end to all the people, to all those who are before them.* **5:1** Verse 5:1 is numbered 4:17 in Hebrew text. **5:2** Verses 5:2-20 are numbered 5:1-19 in Hebrew text.

KING JAMES VERSION

8 If thou seest the oppression of the poor, and violent perverting of judgment and justice in a province, marvel not at the matter: for *he that is* higher than the highest regardeth; and *there be* higher than they.

9 Moreover the profit of the earth is for all: the king *himself* is served by the field.

10 He that loveth silver shall not be satisfied with silver; nor he that loveth abundance with increase: this *is* also vanity.

11 When goods increase, they are increased that eat them: and what good *is there* to the owners thereof, saving the beholding *of them* with their eyes?

12 The sleep of a labouring man *is* sweet, whether he eat little or much: but the abundance of the rich will not suffer him to sleep.

13 There is a sore evil *which* I have seen under the sun, *namely,* riches kept for the owners thereof to their hurt.

14 But those riches perish by evil travail: and he begetteth a son, and *there is* nothing in his hand.

15 As he came forth of his mother's womb, naked shall he return to go as he came, and shall take nothing of his labour, which he may carry away in his hand.

16 And this also *is* a sore evil, *that* in all points as he came, so shall he go: and what profit hath he that hath laboured for the wind?

17 All his days also he eateth in darkness, and *he hath* much sorrow and wrath with his sickness.

18 Behold *that* which I have seen: *it is* good and comely *for one* to eat and to drink, and to enjoy the good of all his labour that he taketh under the sun all the days of his life, which God giveth him: for it *is* his portion.

19 Every man also to whom God hath given riches and wealth, and hath given him power to eat thereof, and to take his portion, and to rejoice in his labour; this *is* the gift of God.

20 For he shall not much remember the days of his life; because God answereth *him* in the joy of his heart.

6 1 There is an evil which I have seen under the sun, and it *is* common among men:

2 A man to whom God hath given riches, wealth, and honour, so that he wanteth nothing for his soul of all that he desireth, yet God giveth him not power to eat thereof, but a stranger eateth it: this *is* vanity, and it *is* an evil disease.

3 If a man beget an hundred *children,* and live many years, so that the days of his years be many, and his soul be not filled with good, and also *that* he have no burial; I say, *that* an untimely birth *is* better than he.

4 For he cometh in with vanity, and departeth in darkness, and his name shall be covered with darkness.

NEW LIVING TRANSLATION

The Futility of Wealth

8 Don't be surprised if you see a poor person being oppressed by the powerful and if justice is being miscarried throughout the land. For every official is under orders from higher up, and matters of justice get lost in red tape and bureaucracy. 9 Even the king milks the land for his own profit!*

10 Those who love money will never have enough. How meaningless to think that wealth brings true happiness! 11 The more you have, the more people come to help you spend it. So what good is wealth—except perhaps to watch it slip through your fingers!

12 People who work hard sleep well, whether they eat little or much. But the rich seldom get a good night's sleep.

13 There is another serious problem I have seen under the sun. Hoarding riches harms the saver. 14 Money is put into risky investments that turn sour, and everything is lost. In the end, there is nothing left to pass on to one's children. 15 We all come to the end of our lives as naked and empty-handed as on the day we were born. We can't take our riches with us.

16 And this, too, is a very serious problem. People leave this world no better off than when they came. All their hard work is for nothing—like working for the wind. 17 Throughout their lives, they live under a cloud—frustrated, discouraged, and angry.

18 Even so, I have noticed one thing, at least, that is good. It is good for people to eat, drink, and enjoy their work under the sun during the short life God has given them, and to accept their lot in life. 19 And it is a good thing to receive wealth from God and the good health to enjoy it. To enjoy your work and accept your lot in life—this is indeed a gift from God. 20 God keeps such people so busy enjoying life that they take no time to brood over the past.

6 There is another serious tragedy I have seen under the sun, and it weighs heavily on humanity. 2 God gives some people great wealth and honor and everything they could ever want, but then he doesn't give them the chance to enjoy these things. They die, and someone else, even a stranger, ends up enjoying their wealth! This is meaningless—a sickening tragedy.

3 A man might have a hundred children and live to be very old. But if he finds no satisfaction in life and doesn't even get a decent burial, it would have been better for him to be born dead. 4 His birth would have been meaningless, and he would have ended in

5:9 The meaning of the Hebrew in verses 8 and 9 is uncertain.

KING JAMES VERSION

5Moreover he hath not seen the sun, nor known
any thing: this hath more rest than the other.
6Yea, though he live a thousand years twice *told,*
yet hath he seen no good: do not all go to one place?
7All the labour of man *is* for his mouth, and yet the
appetite is not filled.
8For what hath the wise more than the fool? what
hath the poor, that knoweth to walk before the
living?
9Better *is* the sight of the eyes than the wandering
of the desire: this *is* also vanity and vexation of spirit.

10That which hath been is named already, and it is
known that it *is* man: neither may he contend with
him that is mightier than he.
11Seeing there be many things that increase vanity,
what *is* man the better?
12For who knoweth what *is* good for man in *this*
life, all the days of his vain life which he spendeth as a
shadow? for who can tell a man what shall be after
him under the sun?

7 1A good name *is* better than precious ointment;
and the day of death than the day of one's birth.
2*It is* better to go to the house of mourning, than to
go to the house of feasting: for that *is* the end of all
men; and the living will lay *it* to his heart.
3Sorrow *is* better than laughter: for by the sadness
of the countenance the heart is made better.
4The heart of the wise *is* in the house of mourning; but the heart of fools *is* in the house of mirth.
5*It is* better to hear the rebuke of the wise, than for
a man to hear the song of fools.
6For as the crackling of thorns under a pot, so *is*
the laughter of the fool: this also *is* vanity.
7Surely oppression maketh a wise man mad; and
a gift destroyeth the heart.
8Better *is* the end of a thing than the beginning
thereof: *and* the patient in spirit *is* better than the
proud in spirit.
9Be not hasty in thy spirit to be angry: for anger
resteth in the bosom of fools.
10Say not thou, What is *the cause* that the former
days were better than these? for thou dost not inquire wisely concerning this.

NEW LIVING TRANSLATION

darkness. He wouldn't even have had a name, 5and
he would never have seen the sun or known of its existence. Yet he would have had more peace than in
growing up to be an unhappy man. 6He might live a
thousand years twice over but still not find contentment. And since he must die like everyone else—
well, what's the use?
7All people spend their lives scratching for food,
but they never seem to have enough. 8So are wise
people really better off than fools? Do poor people
gain anything by being wise and knowing how to act
in front of others?
9Enjoy what you have rather than desiring what
you don't have. Just dreaming about nice things is
meaningless—like chasing the wind.

The Future—Determined and Unknown

10Everything has already been decided. It was known
long ago what each person would be. So there's no
use arguing with God about your destiny.
11The more words you speak, the less they mean.
So what good are they?
12In the few days of our meaningless lives, who
knows how our days can best be spent? Our lives are
like a shadow. Who can tell what will happen on this
earth after we are gone?

Wisdom for Life

7 1A good reputation is more valuable than
costly perfume.
And the day you die is better than the
day you are born.
2 Better to spend your time at funerals than
at parties.
After all, everyone dies—
so the living should take this to heart.
3 Sorrow is better than laughter,
for sadness has a refining influence on us.
4 A wise person thinks a lot about death,
while a fool thinks only about having
a good time.

5 Better to be criticized by a wise person
than to be praised by a fool.
6 A fool's laughter is quickly gone,
like thorns crackling in a fire.
This also is meaningless.
7 Extortion turns wise people into fools,
and bribes corrupt the heart.

8 Finishing is better than starting.
Patience is better than pride.

9 Control your temper,
for anger labels you a fool.

10 Don't long for "the good old days."
This is not wise.

KING JAMES VERSION

11 Wisdom *is* good with an inheritance: and *by it*
there is profit to them that see the sun.
12 For wisdom *is* a defence, *and* money *is* a defence: but the excellency of knowledge *is, that* wisdom giveth life to them that have it.
13 Consider the work of God: for who can make
that straight, which he hath made crooked?
14 In the day of prosperity be joyful, but in the day
of adversity consider: God also hath set the one over
against the other, to the end that man should find
nothing after him.

15 All *things* have I seen in the days of my vanity:
there is a just *man* that perisheth in his righteousness, and there is a wicked *man* that prolongeth *his*
life in his wickedness.
16 Be not righteous over much; neither make thyself over wise: why shouldest thou destroy thyself?
17 Be not over much wicked, neither be thou foolish: why shouldest thou die before thy time?
18 *It is* good that thou shouldest take hold of this;
yea, also from this withdraw not thine hand: for he
that feareth God shall come forth of them all.
19 Wisdom strengtheneth the wise more than ten
mighty *men* which are in the city.
20 For *there is* not a just man upon earth, that doeth
good, and sinneth not.
21 Also take no heed unto all words that are spoken;
lest thou hear thy servant curse thee:
22 For oftentimes also thine own heart knoweth
that thou thyself likewise hast cursed others.
23 All this have I proved by wisdom: I said, I will be
wise; but it *was* far from me.
24 That which is far off, and exceeding deep, who
can find it out?
25 I applied mine heart to know, and to search, and
to seek out wisdom, and the reason *of things*, and to
know the wickedness of folly, even of foolishness
and madness:
26 And I find more bitter than death the woman,
whose heart *is* snares and nets, *and* her hands *as*
bands: whoso pleaseth God shall escape from her;
but the sinner shall be taken by her.
27 Behold, this have I found, saith the preacher,
counting one by one, to find out the account:
28 Which yet my soul seeketh, but I find not: one
man among a thousand have I found; but a woman
among all those have I not found.
29 Lo, this only have I found, that God hath made
man upright; but they have sought out many inventions.

8 1 Who *is* as the wise *man?* and who knoweth the
interpretation of a thing? a man's wisdom

NEW LIVING TRANSLATION

11 Wisdom is even better when you have money.
Both are a benefit as you go through life.
12 Wisdom and money can get you almost anything,
but only wisdom can save your life.

13 Accept the way God does things,
for who can straighten what he has
made crooked?
14 Enjoy prosperity while you can,
but when hard times strike, realize that
both come from God.
Remember that nothing is certain in this life.

The Limits of Human Wisdom

15 I have seen everything in this meaningless life, including the death of good young people and the long
life of wicked people. 16 So don't be too good or too
wise! Why destroy yourself? 17 On the other hand,
don't be too wicked either. Don't be a fool! Why die
before your time? 18 Pay attention to these instructions, for anyone who fears God will avoid both
extremes.*
19 One wise person is stronger than ten leading citizens of a town!
20 Not a single person on earth is always good and
never sins.
21 Don't eavesdrop on others—you may hear your
servant curse you. 22 For you know how often you
yourself have cursed others.
23 I have always tried my best to let wisdom guide
my thoughts and actions. I said to myself, "I am determined to be wise." But it didn't work. 24 Wisdom is
always distant and difficult to find. 25 I searched
everywhere, determined to find wisdom and to understand the reason for things. I was determined to
prove to myself that wickedness is stupid and that
foolishness is madness.
26 I discovered that a seductive woman* is a trap
more bitter than death. Her passion is a snare, and
her soft hands are chains. Those who are pleasing to
God will escape her, but sinners will be caught in her
snare.
27 "This is my conclusion," says the Teacher. "I discovered this after looking at the matter from every
possible angle. 28 Though I have searched repeatedly,
I have not found what I was looking for. Only one out
of a thousand men is virtuous, but not one woman!
29 But I did find this: God created people to be virtuous, but they have each turned to follow their own
downward path."

8 1 How wonderful to be wise,
to analyze and interpret things.

7:18 Or *will follow them both.* **7:26** Hebrew *a woman.*

KING JAMES VERSION

maketh his face to shine, and the boldness of his face shall be changed.

[2]I *counsel thee* to keep the king's commandment, and *that* in regard of the oath of God.

[3]Be not hasty to go out of his sight: stand not in an evil thing; for he doeth whatsoever pleaseth him.

[4]Where the word of a king *is, there is* power: and who may say unto him, What doest thou?

[5]Whoso keepeth the commandment shall feel no evil thing: and a wise man's heart discerneth both time and judgment.

[6]Because to every purpose there is time and judgment, therefore the misery of man *is* great upon him.

[7]For he knoweth not that which shall be: for who can tell him when it shall be?

[8]*There is* no man that hath power over the spirit to retain the spirit; neither *hath he* power in the day of death: and *there is* no discharge in *that* war; neither shall wickedness deliver those that are given to it.

[9]All this have I seen, and applied my heart unto every work that is done under the sun: *there is* a time wherein one man ruleth over another to his own hurt.

[10]And so I saw the wicked buried, who had come and gone from the place of the holy, and they were forgotten in the city where they had so done: this *is* also vanity.

[11]Because sentence against an evil work is not executed speedily, therefore the heart of the sons of men is fully set in them to do evil.

[12]Though a sinner do evil an hundred times, and his *days* be prolonged, yet surely I know that it shall be well with them that fear God, which fear before him:

[13]But it shall not be well with the wicked, neither shall he prolong *his* days, *which are* as a shadow; because he feareth not before God.

[14]There is a vanity which is done upon the earth; that there be just *men,* unto whom it happeneth according to the work of the wicked; again, there be wicked *men,* to whom it happeneth according to the work of the righteous: I said that this also *is* vanity.

[15]Then I commended mirth, because a man hath no better thing under the sun, than to eat, and to drink, and to be merry: for that shall abide with him of his labour the days of his life, which God giveth him under the sun.

[16]When I applied mine heart to know wisdom, and to see the business that is done upon the earth: (for also *there is that* neither day nor night seeth sleep with his eyes:)

[17]Then I beheld all the work of God, that a man cannot find out the work that is done under the sun: because though a man labour to seek *it* out, yet he shall not find *it;* yea farther; though a wise *man* think to know *it,* yet shall he not be able to find *it.*

NEW LIVING TRANSLATION

Wisdom lights up a person's face,
softening its harshness.

Obedience to the King

[2]Obey the king since you vowed to God that you would. [3]Don't try to avoid doing your duty, and don't stand with those who plot evil, for the king can do whatever he wants. [4]His command is backed by great power. No one can resist or question it. [5]Those who obey him will not be punished. Those who are wise will find a time and a way to do what is right, [6]for there is a time and a way for everything, even when a person is in trouble.

[7]Indeed, how can people avoid what they don't know is going to happen? [8]None of us can hold back our spirit from departing. None of us has the power to prevent the day of our death. There is no escaping that obligation, that dark battle. And in the face of death, wickedness will certainly not rescue the wicked.

The Wicked and the Righteous

[9]I have thought deeply about all that goes on here under the sun, where people have the power to hurt each other. [10]I have seen wicked people buried with honor. Yet they were the very ones who frequented the Temple and are now praised* in the same city where they committed their crimes! This, too, is meaningless. [11]When a crime is not punished quickly, people feel it is safe to do wrong. [12]But even though a person sins a hundred times and still lives a long time, I know that those who fear God will be better off. [13]The wicked will not prosper, for they do not fear God. Their days will never grow long like the evening shadows.

[14]And this is not all that is meaningless in our world. In this life, good people are often treated as though they were wicked, and wicked people are often treated as though they were good. This is so meaningless!

[15]So I recommend having fun, because there is nothing better for people in this world than to eat, drink, and enjoy life. That way they will experience some happiness along with all the hard work God gives them under the sun.

[16]In my search for wisdom and in my observation of people's burdens here on earth, I discovered that there is ceaseless activity, day and night. [17]I realized that no one can discover everything God is doing under the sun. Not even the wisest people discover everything, no matter what they claim.

8:10 As in some Hebrew manuscripts and Greek version; many Hebrew manuscripts read *and are forgotten.*

KING JAMES VERSION

9 1 For all this I considered in my heart even to declare all this, that the righteous, and the wise,
and their works, *are* in the hand of God: no man
knoweth either love or hatred *by* all *that is* before
them.
2 All *things come* alike to all: *there is* one event to
the righteous, and to the wicked; to the good and to
the clean, and to the unclean; to him that sacrificeth,
and to him that sacrificeth not: as *is* the good, so *is*
the sinner; *and* he that sweareth, as *he* that feareth
an oath.
3 This *is* an evil among all *things* that are done under the sun, that *there is* one event unto all: yea, also
the heart of the sons of men is full of evil, and madness *is* in their heart while they live, and after that
they go to the dead.
4 For to him that is joined to all the living there is
hope: for a living dog is better than a dead lion.
5 For the living know that they shall die: but the
dead know not any thing, neither have they any more
a reward; for the memory of them is forgotten.
6 Also their love, and their hatred, and their envy, is
now perished; neither have they any more a portion
for ever in any *thing* that is done under the sun.
7 Go thy way, eat thy bread with joy, and drink thy
wine with a merry heart; for God now accepteth thy
works.
8 Let thy garments be always white; and let thy
head lack no ointment.
9 Live joyfully with the wife whom thou lovest all
the days of the life of thy vanity, which he hath given
thee under the sun, all the days of thy vanity: for that
is thy portion in *this* life, and in thy labour which
thou takest under the sun.
10 Whatsoever thy hand findeth to do, do *it* with thy
might; for *there is* no work, nor device, nor knowledge, nor wisdom, in the grave, whither thou goest.
11 I returned, and saw under the sun, that the race
is not to the swift, nor the battle to the strong, neither yet bread to the wise, nor yet riches to men of
understanding, nor yet favour to men of skill; but
time and chance happeneth to them all.
12 For man also knoweth not his time: as the fishes
that are taken in an evil net, and as the birds that are
caught in the snare; so *are* the sons of men snared in
an evil time, when it falleth suddenly upon them.
13 This wisdom have I seen also under the sun, and
it *seemed* great unto me:
14 *There was* a little city, and few men within it; and
there came a great king against it, and besieged it,
and built great bulwarks against it:
15 Now there was found in it a poor wise man, and
he by his wisdom delivered the city; yet no man remembered that same poor man.
16 Then said I, Wisdom *is* better than strength:
nevertheless the poor man's wisdom *is* despised, and
his words are not heard.

NEW LIVING TRANSLATION

Death Comes to All

9 This, too, I carefully explored: Even though the
actions of godly and wise people are in God's
hands, no one knows whether God will show them
favor. 2 The same destiny ultimately awaits everyone,
whether righteous or wicked, good or bad,* ceremonially clean or unclean, religious or irreligious. Good
people receive the same treatment as sinners,
and people who make promises to God are treated
like people who don't.
3 It seems so tragic that everyone under the sun
suffers the same fate. That is why people are not
more careful to be good. Instead, they choose their
own mad course, for they have no hope. There is
nothing ahead but death anyway. 4 There is hope only
for the living. As they say, "It's better to be a live dog
than a dead lion!"
5 The living at least know they will die, but the
dead know nothing. They have no further reward,
nor are they remembered. 6 Whatever they did in
their lifetime—loving, hating, envying—is all long
gone. They no longer play a part in anything here on
earth. 7 So go ahead. Eat your food with joy, and drink
your wine with a happy heart, for God approves of
this! 8 Wear fine clothes, with a splash of cologne!
9 Live happily with the woman you love through all
the meaningless days of life that God has given you
under the sun. The wife God gives you is your reward
for all your earthly toil. 10 Whatever you do, do well.
For when you go to the grave,* there will be no work
or planning or knowledge or wisdom.
11 I have observed something else under the sun.
The fastest runner doesn't always win the race, and
the strongest warrior doesn't always win the battle.
The wise sometimes go hungry, and the skillful are
not necessarily wealthy. And those who are educated
don't always lead successful lives. It is all decided by
chance, by being in the right place at the right time.
12 People can never predict when hard times might
come. Like fish in a net or birds in a trap, people are
caught by sudden tragedy.

Thoughts on Wisdom and Folly

13 Here is another bit of wisdom that has impressed
me as I have watched the way our world works.
14 There was a small town with only a few people, and
a great king came with his army and besieged it. 15 A
poor, wise man knew how to save the town, and so it
was rescued. But afterward no one thought to thank
him. 16 So even though wisdom is better than strength,
those who are wise will be despised if they are poor.
What they say will not be appreciated for long.

9:2 As in Greek and Syriac versions and Latin Vulgate; Hebrew lacks *or bad.*
9:10 Hebrew *to Sheol.*

KING JAMES VERSION

17 The words of wise *men are* heard in quiet more than the cry of him that ruleth among fools.

18 Wisdom *is* better than weapons of war: but one sinner destroyeth much good.

10 1 Dead flies cause the ointment of the apothecary to send forth a stinking savour: *so doth* a little folly him that is in reputation for wisdom *and* honour.

2 A wise man's heart *is* at his right hand; but a fool's heart at his left.

3 Yea also, when he that is a fool walketh by the way, his wisdom faileth *him,* and he saith to every one *that* he *is* a fool.

4 If the spirit of the ruler rise up against thee, leave not thy place; for yielding pacifieth great offences.

5 There is an evil *which* I have seen under the sun, as an error *which* proceedeth from the ruler:

6 Folly is set in great dignity, and the rich sit in low place.

7 I have seen servants upon horses, and princes walking as servants upon the earth.

8 He that diggeth a pit shall fall into it; and whoso breaketh an hedge, a serpent shall bite him.

9 Whoso removeth stones shall be hurt therewith; *and* he that cleaveth wood shall be endangered thereby.

10 If the iron be blunt, and he do not whet the edge, then must he put to more strength: but wisdom *is* profitable to direct.

11 Surely the serpent will bite without enchantment; and a babbler is no better.

12 The words of a wise man's mouth *are* gracious; but the lips of a fool will swallow up himself.

13 The beginning of the words of his mouth *is* foolishness: and the end of his talk *is* mischievous madness.

14 A fool also is full of words: a man cannot tell what shall be; and what shall be after him, who can tell him?

15 The labour of the foolish wearieth every one of them, because he knoweth not how to go to the city.

16 Woe to thee, O land, when thy king *is* a child, and thy princes eat in the morning!

17 Blessed *art* thou, O land, when thy king *is* the son of nobles, and thy princes eat in due season, for strength, and not for drunkenness!

NEW LIVING TRANSLATION

17 Better to hear the quiet words of a wise person
than the shouts of a foolish king.
18 Better to have wisdom than weapons of war,
but one sinner can destroy much that is good.

10 1 As dead flies cause even a bottle of perfume
to stink,
so a little foolishness spoils great wisdom
and honor.

2 A wise person chooses the right road;
a fool takes the wrong one.

3 You can identify fools
just by the way they walk down the street!

4 If your boss is angry at you, don't quit!
A quiet spirit can overcome even great mistakes.

The Ironies of Life

5 There is another evil I have seen under the sun.
Kings and rulers make a grave mistake 6 when they
give great authority to foolish people and low positions to people of proven worth. 7 I have even seen
servants riding horseback like princes—and princes
walking like servants!

8 When you dig a well,
you might fall in.
When you demolish an old wall,
you could be bitten by a snake.
9 When you work in a quarry,
stones might fall and crush you.
When you chop wood,
there is danger with each stroke of your ax.

10 Using a dull ax requires great strength,
so sharpen the blade.
That's the value of wisdom;
it helps you succeed.

11 If a snake bites before you charm it,
what's the use of being a snake charmer?

12 Wise words bring approval,
but fools are destroyed by their own words.

13 Fools base their thoughts on foolish assumptions,
so their conclusions will be wicked madness;
14 they chatter on and on.

No one really knows what is going to happen;
no one can predict the future.

15 Fools are so exhausted by a little work
that they can't even find their way home.

16 What sorrow for the land ruled by a servant,*
the land whose leaders feast in the morning.
17 Happy is the land whose king is a noble leader
and whose leaders feast at the proper time
to gain strength for their work, not to get drunk.

10:16 Or *a child.*

KING JAMES VERSION

18 By much slothfulness the building decayeth;
and through idleness of the hands the house
droppeth through.
19 A feast is made for laughter, and wine maketh
merry: but money answereth all *things*.
20 Curse not the king, no not in thy thought; and
curse not the rich in thy bedchamber: for a bird of
the air shall carry the voice, and that which hath
wings shall tell the matter.

11 1 Cast thy bread upon the waters: for thou shalt
find it after many days.
2 Give a portion to seven, and also to eight; for thou
knowest not what evil shall be upon the earth.
3 If the clouds be full of rain, they empty *them-*
selves upon the earth: and if the tree fall toward the
south, or toward the north, in the place where the
tree falleth, there it shall be.
4 He that observeth the wind shall not sow; and he
that regardeth the clouds shall not reap.
5 As thou knowest not what *is* the way of the spirit,
nor how the bones *do grow* in the womb of her that
is with child: even so thou knowest not the works of
God who maketh all.
6 In the morning sow thy seed, and in the evening
withhold not thine hand: for thou knowest not
whether shall prosper, either this or that, or whether
they both *shall be* alike good.

7 Truly the light *is* sweet, and a pleasant *thing it is*
for the eyes to behold the sun:
8 But if a man live many years, *and* rejoice in them
all; yet let him remember the days of darkness; for
they shall be many. All that cometh *is* vanity.
9 Rejoice, O young man, in thy youth; and let thy
heart cheer thee in the days of thy youth, and walk in
the ways of thine heart, and in the sight of thine eyes:
but know thou, that for all these *things* God will
bring thee into judgment.
10 Therefore remove sorrow from thy heart, and
put away evil from thy flesh: for childhood and youth
are vanity.

12 1 Remember now thy Creator in the days of
thy youth, while the evil days come not, nor
the years draw nigh, when thou shalt say, I have no
pleasure in them;
2 While the sun, or the light, or the moon, or the
stars, be not darkened, nor the clouds return after
the rain:

NEW LIVING TRANSLATION

18 Laziness leads to a sagging roof;
idleness leads to a leaky house.

19 A party gives laughter,
wine gives happiness,
and money gives everything!

20 Never make light of the king, even in
your thoughts.
And don't make fun of the powerful,
even in your own bedroom.
For a little bird might deliver your message
and tell them what you said.

The Uncertainties of Life

11 1 Send your grain across the seas,
and in time, profits will flow back to you.*
2 But divide your investments among
many places,*
for you do not know what risks might lie ahead.

3 When clouds are heavy, the rains come down.
Whether a tree falls north or south, it stays
where it falls.

4 Farmers who wait for perfect weather
never plant.
If they watch every cloud, they never harvest.

5 Just as you cannot understand the path of the
wind or the mystery of a tiny baby growing in its
mother's womb,* so you cannot understand the
activity of God, who does all things.
6 Plant your seed in the morning and keep busy all
afternoon, for you don't know if profit will come
from one activity or another—or maybe both.

Advice for Young and Old

7 Light is sweet; how pleasant to see a new day
dawning.
8 When people live to be very old, let them rejoice
in every day of life. But let them also remember there
will be many dark days. Everything still to come is
meaningless.
9 Young people,* it's wonderful to be young! Enjoy
every minute of it. Do everything you want to do; take
it all in. But remember that you must give an account
to God for everything you do. 10 So refuse to worry,
and keep your body healthy. But remember that
youth, with a whole life before you, is meaningless.

12 Don't let the excitement of youth cause you to
forget your Creator. Honor him in your youth
before you grow old and say, "Life is not pleasant anymore." 2 Remember him before the light of the sun,
moon, and stars is dim to your old eyes, and rain

11:1 Or *Give generously, / for your gifts will return to you later.* Hebrew reads *Throw your bread on the waters, / for after many days you will find it again.* **11:2** Hebrew *among seven or even eight.* **11:5** Some manuscripts read *Just as you cannot understand how breath comes to a tiny baby in its mother's womb.* **11:9** Hebrew *Young man.*

KING JAMES VERSION

3 In the day when the keepers of the house shall tremble, and the strong men shall bow themselves, and the grinders cease because they are few, and those that look out of the windows be darkened,

4 And the doors shall be shut in the streets, when the sound of the grinding is low, and he shall rise up at the voice of the bird, and all the daughters of musick shall be brought low;

5 Also *when* they shall be afraid of *that which is* high, and fears *shall be* in the way, and the almond tree shall flourish, and the grasshopper shall be a burden, and desire shall fail: because man goeth to his long home, and the mourners go about the streets:

6 Or ever the silver cord be loosed, or the golden bowl be broken, or the pitcher be broken at the fountain, or the wheel broken at the cistern.

7 Then shall the dust return to the earth as it was: and the spirit shall return unto God who gave it.

8 Vanity of vanities, saith the preacher; all *is* vanity.

9 And moreover, because the preacher was wise, he still taught the people knowledge; yea, he gave good heed, and sought out, *and* set in order many proverbs.

10 The preacher sought to find out acceptable words: and *that which was* written *was* upright, *even* words of truth.

11 The words of the wise *are* as goads, and as nails fastened *by* the masters of assemblies, *which* are given from one shepherd.

12 And further, by these, my son, be admonished: of making many books *there is* no end; and much study *is* a weariness of the flesh.

13 Let us hear the conclusion of the whole matter: Fear God, and keep his commandments: for this *is* the whole *duty* of man.

14 For God shall bring every work into judgment, with every secret thing, whether *it be* good, or whether *it be* evil.

NEW LIVING TRANSLATION

clouds continually darken your sky. 3 Remember him before your legs—the guards of your house—start to tremble; and before your shoulders—the strong men—stoop. Remember him before your teeth—your few remaining servants—stop grinding; and before your eyes—the women looking through the windows—see dimly.

4 Remember him before the door to life's opportunities is closed and the sound of work fades. Now you rise at the first chirping of the birds, but then all their sounds will grow faint.

5 Remember him before you become fearful of falling and worry about danger in the streets; before your hair turns white like an almond tree in bloom, and you drag along without energy like a dying grasshopper, and the caperberry no longer inspires sexual desire. Remember him before you near the grave, your everlasting home, when the mourners will weep at your funeral.

6 Yes, remember your Creator now while you are young, before the silver cord of life snaps and the golden bowl is broken. Don't wait until the water jar is smashed at the spring and the pulley is broken at the well. 7 For then the dust will return to the earth, and the spirit will return to God who gave it.

Concluding Thoughts about the Teacher

8 "Everything is meaningless," says the Teacher, "completely meaningless."

9 Keep this in mind: The Teacher was considered wise, and he taught the people everything he knew. He listened carefully to many proverbs, studying and classifying them. 10 The Teacher sought to find just the right words to express truths clearly.*

11 The words of the wise are like cattle prods—painful but helpful. Their collected sayings are like a nail-studded stick with which a shepherd* drives the sheep.

12 But, my child,* let me give you some further advice: Be careful, for writing books is endless, and much study wears you out.

13 That's the whole story. Here now is my final conclusion: Fear God and obey his commands, for this is everyone's duty. 14 God will judge us for everything we do, including every secret thing, whether good or bad.

12:10 Or *sought to write what was upright and true.* **12:11** Or *one shepherd.* **12:12** Hebrew *my son.*

Song of Songs

KING JAMES VERSION

1 1 The song of songs, which *is* Solomon's.
2 Let him kiss me with the kisses of his mouth: for thy love *is* better than wine.

3 Because of the savour of thy good ointments thy name *is as* ointment poured forth, therefore do the virgins love thee.

4 Draw me, we will run after thee: the king hath brought me into his chambers: we will be glad and rejoice in thee, we will remember thy love more than wine: the upright love thee.

5 I *am* black, but comely, O ye daughters of Jerusalem, as the tents of Kedar, as the curtains of Solomon.

6 Look not upon me, because I *am* black, because the sun hath looked upon me: my mother's children were angry with me; they made me the keeper of the vineyards; *but* mine own vineyard have I not kept.

7 Tell me, O thou whom my soul loveth, where thou feedest, where thou makest *thy flock* to rest at noon: for why should I be as one that turneth aside by the flocks of thy companions?

8 If thou know not, O thou fairest among women, go thy way forth by the footsteps of the flock, and feed thy kids beside the shepherds' tents.

9 I have compared thee, O my love, to a company of horses in Pharaoh's chariots.

10 Thy cheeks are comely with rows *of jewels,* thy neck with chains *of gold.*

NEW LIVING TRANSLATION

1 This is Solomon's song of songs, more wonderful than any other.

*Young Woman**

2 Kiss me and kiss me again,
for your love is sweeter than wine.
3 How fragrant your cologne;
your name is like its spreading fragrance.
No wonder all the young women love you!
4 Take me with you; come, let's run!
The king has brought me into his bedroom.

Young Women of Jerusalem

How happy we are for you, O king.
We praise your love even more than wine.

Young Woman

How right they are to adore you.
5 I am dark but beautiful,
O women of Jerusalem—
dark as the tents of Kedar,
dark as the curtains of Solomon's tents.
6 Don't stare at me because I am dark—
the sun has darkened my skin.
My brothers were angry with me;
they forced me to care for their vineyards,
so I couldn't care for myself—my own vineyard.
7 Tell me, my love, where are you leading your
flock today?
Where will you rest your sheep at noon?
For why should I wander like a prostitute*
among your friends and their flocks?

Young Man

8 If you don't know, O most beautiful woman,
follow the trail of my flock,
and graze your young goats by the
shepherds' tents.
9 You are as exciting, my darling,
as a mare among Pharaoh's stallions.
10 How lovely are your cheeks;
your earrings set them afire!

1:1 The headings identifying the speakers are not in the original text, though the Hebrew usually gives clues by means of the gender of the person speaking. **1:7** Hebrew *like a veiled woman.*

KING JAMES VERSION

11 We will make thee borders of gold with studs of
silver.
12 While the king *sitteth* at his table, my spikenard
sendeth forth the smell thereof.
13 A bundle of myrrh *is* my wellbeloved unto me;
he shall lie all night betwixt my breasts.
14 My beloved *is* unto me *as* a cluster of camphire
in the vineyards of En-gedi.
15 Behold, thou *art* fair, my love; behold, thou *art*
fair; thou *hast* doves' eyes.
16 Behold, thou *art* fair, my beloved, yea, pleasant:
also our bed *is* green.
17 The beams of our house *are* cedar, *and* our
rafters of fir.

2 1 I *am* the rose of Sharon, *and* the lily of the
valleys.
2 As the lily among thorns, so *is* my love among the
daughters.
3 As the apple tree among the trees of the wood, so
is my beloved among the sons. I sat down under his
shadow with great delight, and his fruit *was* sweet to
my taste.
4 He brought me to the banqueting house, and his
banner over me *was* love.
5 Stay me with flagons, comfort me with apples:
for I *am* sick of love.
6 His left hand *is* under my head, and his right
hand doth embrace me.
7 I charge you, O ye daughters of Jerusalem, by the
roes, and by the hinds of the field, that ye stir not up,
nor awake *my* love, till he please.
8 The voice of my beloved! behold, he cometh leaping upon the mountains, skipping upon the hills.
9 My beloved is like a roe or a young hart: behold,
he standeth behind our wall, he looketh forth at the
windows, shewing himself through the lattice.

NEW LIVING TRANSLATION

How lovely is your neck,
enhanced by a string of jewels.
11 We will make for you earrings of gold
and beads of silver.

Young Woman
12 The king is lying on his couch,
enchanted by the fragrance of my perfume.
13 My lover is like a sachet of myrrh
lying between my breasts.
14 He is like a bouquet of sweet henna blossoms
from the vineyards of En-gedi.

Young Man
15 How beautiful you are, my darling,
how beautiful!
Your eyes are like doves.

Young Woman
16 You are so handsome, my love,
pleasing beyond words!
The soft grass is our bed;
17 fragrant cedar branches are the beams
of our house,
and pleasant smelling firs are the rafters.

Young Woman
2 1 I am the spring crocus blooming
on the Sharon Plain,*
the lily of the valley.

Young Man
2 Like a lily among thistles
is my darling among young women.

Young Woman
3 Like the finest apple tree in the orchard
is my lover among other young men.
I sit in his delightful shade
and taste his delicious fruit.
4 He escorts me to the banquet hall;
it's obvious how much he loves me.
5 Strengthen me with raisin cakes,
refresh me with apples,
for I am weak with love.
6 His left arm is under my head,
and his right arm embraces me.

7 Promise me, O women of Jerusalem,
by the gazelles and wild deer,
not to awaken love until the time is right.*

8 Ah, I hear my lover coming!
He is leaping over the mountains,
bounding over the hills.
9 My lover is like a swift gazelle
or a young stag.
Look, there he is behind the wall,
looking through the window,
peering into the room.

2:1 Traditionally rendered *I am the rose of Sharon.* Sharon Plain is a region in the coastal plain of Palestine. **2:7** Or *not to awaken love until it is ready.*

KING JAMES VERSION

10 My beloved spake, and said unto me, Rise up, my
love, my fair one, and come away.
11 For, lo, the winter is past, the rain is over *and*
gone;
12 The flowers appear on the earth; the time of the
singing *of birds* is come, and the voice of the turtle is
heard in our land;
13 The fig tree putteth forth her green figs, and the
vines *with* the tender grape give a *good* smell. Arise,
my love, my fair one, and come away.
14 O my dove, *that art* in the clefts of the rock, in
the secret *places* of the stairs, let me see thy countenance, let me hear thy voice; for sweet *is* thy voice,
and thy countenance *is* comely.
15 Take us the foxes, the little foxes, that spoil the
vines: for our vines *have* tender grapes.
16 My beloved *is* mine, and I *am* his: he feedeth
among the lilies.
17 Until the day break, and the shadows flee away,
turn, my beloved, and be thou like a roe or a young
hart upon the mountains of Bether.

3 1 By night on my bed I sought him whom my
soul loveth: I sought him, but I found him not.
2 I will rise now, and go about the city in the streets,
and in the broad ways I will seek him whom my soul
loveth: I sought him, but I found him not.
3 The watchmen that go about the city found me:
to whom I said, Saw ye him whom my soul loveth?
4 *It was* but a little that I passed from them, but I
found him whom my soul loveth: I held him, and
would not let him go, until I had brought him into my
mother's house, and into the chamber of her that
conceived me.
5 I charge you, O ye daughters of Jerusalem, by the
roes, and by the hinds of the field, that ye stir not up,
nor awake *my* love, till he please.

NEW LIVING TRANSLATION

10 My lover said to me,
"Rise up, my darling!
Come away with me, my fair one!
11 Look, the winter is past,
and the rains are over and gone.
12 The flowers are springing up,
the season of singing birds* has come,
and the cooing of turtledoves fills the air.
13 The fig trees are forming young fruit,
and the fragrant grapevines are blossoming.
Rise up, my darling!
Come away with me, my fair one!"

Young Man

14 My dove is hiding behind the rocks,
behind an outcrop on the cliff.
Let me see your face;
let me hear your voice.
For your voice is pleasant,
and your face is lovely.

Young Women of Jerusalem

15 Catch all the foxes,
those little foxes,
before they ruin the vineyard of love,
for the grapevines are blossoming!

Young Woman

16 My lover is mine, and I am his.
He browses among the lilies.
17 Before the dawn breezes blow
and the night shadows flee,
return to me, my love, like a gazelle
or a young stag on the rugged mountains.*

Young Woman

3 1 One night as I lay in bed, I yearned
for my lover.
I yearned for him, but he did not come.
2 So I said to myself, "I will get up and roam
the city,
searching in all its streets and squares.
I will search for the one I love."
So I searched everywhere but did not find him.
3 The watchmen stopped me as they made
their rounds,
and I asked, "Have you seen the one I love?"
4 Then scarcely had I left them
when I found my love!
I caught and held him tightly,
then I brought him to my mother's house,
into my mother's bed, where I had
been conceived.

5 Promise me, O women of Jerusalem,
by the gazelles and wild deer,
not to awaken love until the time is right.*

2:12 Or *the season of pruning vines.* **2:17** Or *on the hills of Bether.*
3:5 Or *not to awaken love until it is ready.*

KING JAMES VERSION

6 Who *is* this that cometh out of the wilderness like pillars of smoke, perfumed with myrrh and frankincense, with all powders of the merchant?

7 Behold his bed, which *is* Solomon's; threescore valiant men *are* about it, of the valiant of Israel.

8 They all hold swords, *being* expert in war: every man *hath* his sword upon his thigh because of fear in the night.

9 King Solomon made himself a chariot of the wood of Lebanon.

10 He made the pillars thereof *of* silver, the bottom thereof *of* gold, the covering of it *of* purple, the midst thereof being paved *with* love, for the daughters of Jerusalem.

11 Go forth, O ye daughters of Zion, and behold king Solomon with the crown wherewith his mother crowned him in the day of his espousals, and in the day of the gladness of his heart.

4 1 Behold, thou *art* fair, my love; behold, thou *art* fair; thou *hast* doves' eyes within thy locks: thy hair *is* as a flock of goats, that appear from mount Gilead.

2 Thy teeth *are* like a flock *of sheep that are even* shorn, which came up from the washing; whereof every one bear twins, and none *is* barren among them.

3 Thy lips *are* like a thread of scarlet, and thy speech *is* comely: thy temples *are* like a piece of a pomegranate within thy locks.

4 Thy neck *is* like the tower of David builded for an armoury, whereon there hang a thousand bucklers, all shields of mighty men.

5 Thy two breasts *are* like two young roes that are twins, which feed among the lilies.

6 Until the day break, and the shadows flee away, I will get me to the mountain of myrrh, and to the hill of frankincense.

7 Thou *art* all fair, my love; *there is* no spot in thee.

8 Come with me from Lebanon, *my* spouse, with

NEW LIVING TRANSLATION

Young Women of Jerusalem

6 Who is this sweeping in from the wilderness
like a cloud of smoke?
Who is it, fragrant with myrrh and frankincense
and every kind of spice?
7 Look, it is Solomon's carriage,
surrounded by sixty heroic men,
the best of Israel's soldiers.
8 They are all skilled swordsmen,
experienced warriors.
Each wears a sword on his thigh,
ready to defend the king against an attack
in the night.
9 King Solomon's carriage is built
of wood imported from Lebanon.
10 Its posts are silver,
its canopy gold;
its cushions are purple.
It was decorated with love
by the young women of Jerusalem.

Young Woman

11 Come out to see King Solomon,
young women of Jerusalem.*
He wears the crown his mother gave him
on his wedding day,
his most joyous day.

Young Man

4 1 You are beautiful, my darling,
beautiful beyond words.
Your eyes are like doves
behind your veil.
Your hair falls in waves,
like a flock of goats winding down the
slopes of Gilead.
2 Your teeth are as white as sheep,
recently shorn and freshly washed.
Your smile is flawless,
each tooth matched with its twin.*
3 Your lips are like scarlet ribbon;
your mouth is inviting.
Your cheeks are like rosy pomegranates
behind your veil.
4 Your neck is as beautiful as the tower of David,
jeweled with the shields of a thousand heroes.
5 Your breasts are like two fawns,
twin fawns of a gazelle grazing among the lilies.
6 Before the dawn breezes blow
and the night shadows flee,
I will hurry to the mountain of myrrh
and to the hill of frankincense.
7 You are altogether beautiful, my darling,
beautiful in every way.

8 Come with me from Lebanon, my bride,
come with me from Lebanon.

3:11 Hebrew *of Zion.* **4:2** Hebrew *Not one is missing; each has a twin.*

KING JAMES VERSION

me from Lebanon: look from the top of Amana, from
the top of Shenir and Hermon, from the lions' dens,
from the mountains of the leopards.
9 Thou hast ravished my heart, my sister, *my*
spouse; thou hast ravished my heart with one of
thine eyes, with one chain of thy neck.
10 How fair is thy love, my sister, *my* spouse! how
much better is thy love than wine! and the smell of
thine ointments than all spices!
11 Thy lips, O *my* spouse, drop *as* the honeycomb:
honey and milk *are* under thy tongue; and the smell
of thy garments *is* like the smell of Lebanon.
12 A garden inclosed *is* my sister, *my* spouse; a
spring shut up, a fountain sealed.
13 Thy plants *are* an orchard of pomegranates,
with pleasant fruits; camphire, with spikenard,
14 Spikenard and saffron; calamus and cinnamon,
with all trees of frankincense; myrrh and aloes, with
all the chief spices:
15 A fountain of gardens, a well of living waters,
and streams from Lebanon.
16 Awake, O north wind; and come, thou south;
blow upon my garden, *that* the spices thereof may
flow out. Let my beloved come into his garden, and
eat his pleasant fruits.

5 1 I am come into my garden, my sister, *my*
spouse: I have gathered my myrrh with my
spice; I have eaten my honeycomb with my honey; I
have drunk my wine with my milk: eat, O friends;
drink, yea, drink abundantly, O beloved.
2 I sleep, but my heart waketh: *it is* the voice of my
beloved that knocketh, *saying*, Open to me, my
sister, my love, my dove, my undefiled: for my head
is filled with dew, *and* my locks with the drops of
the night.

NEW LIVING TRANSLATION

Come down* from Mount Amana,
from the peaks of Senir and Hermon,
where the lions have their dens
and leopards live among the hills.
9 You have captured my heart,
my treasure,* my bride.
You hold it hostage with one glance of your eyes,
with a single jewel of your necklace.
10 Your love delights me,
my treasure, my bride.
Your love is better than wine,
your perfume more fragrant than spices.
11 Your lips are as sweet as nectar, my bride.
Honey and milk are under your tongue.
Your clothes are scented
like the cedars of Lebanon.
12 You are my private garden, my treasure,
my bride,
a secluded spring, a hidden fountain.
13 Your thighs shelter a paradise of pomegranates
with rare spices—
henna with nard,
14 nard and saffron,
fragrant calamus and cinnamon,
with all the trees of frankincense, myrrh,
and aloes,
and every other lovely spice.
15 You are a garden fountain,
a well of fresh water
streaming down from Lebanon's mountains.

Young Woman

16 Awake, north wind!
Rise up, south wind!
Blow on my garden
and spread its fragrance all around.
Come into your garden, my love;
taste its finest fruits.

Young Man

5 1 I have entered my garden, my treasure,*
my bride!
I gather myrrh with my spices
and eat honeycomb with my honey.
I drink wine with my milk.

Young Women of Jerusalem

Oh, lover and beloved, eat and drink!
Yes, drink deeply of your love!

Young Woman

2 I slept, but my heart was awake,
when I heard my lover knocking and calling:
"Open to me, my treasure, my darling,
my dove, my perfect one.
My head is drenched with dew,
my hair with the dampness of the night."

4:8 Or *Look down.* **4:9** Hebrew *my sister;* also in 4:10, 12. **5:1** Hebrew *my sister;* also in 5:2.

KING JAMES VERSION

3 I have put off my coat; how shall I put it on? I have
washed my feet; how shall I defile them?
4 My beloved put in his hand by the hole *of the*
door, and my bowels were moved for him.
5 I rose up to open to my beloved; and my hands
dropped *with* myrrh, and my fingers *with* sweet
smelling myrrh, upon the handles of the lock.
6 I opened to my beloved; but my beloved had
withdrawn himself, *and* was gone: my soul failed
when he spake: I sought him, but I could not find
him; I called him, but he gave me no answer.
7 The watchmen that went about the city found
me, they smote me, they wounded me; the keepers of
the walls took away my veil from me.
8 I charge you, O daughters of Jerusalem, if ye find
my beloved, that ye tell him, that I *am* sick of love.
9 What *is* thy beloved more than *another* beloved,
O thou fairest among women? what *is* thy beloved
more than *another* beloved, that thou dost so
charge us?
10 My beloved *is* white and ruddy, the chiefest
among ten thousand.
11 His head *is as* the most fine gold, his locks *are*
bushy, *and* black as a raven.
12 His eyes *are* as *the eyes* of doves by the rivers of
waters, washed with milk, *and* fitly set.
13 His cheeks *are* as a bed of spices, *as* sweet flowers: his lips *like* lilies, dropping sweet smelling
myrrh.
14 His hands *are as* gold rings set with the beryl: his
belly *is as* bright ivory overlaid *with* sapphires.
15 His legs *are as* pillars of marble, set upon sockets
of fine gold: his countenance *is* as Lebanon, excellent as the cedars.
16 His mouth *is* most sweet: yea, he *is* altogether
lovely. This *is* my beloved, and this *is* my friend,
O daughters of Jerusalem.

NEW LIVING TRANSLATION

3 But I responded,
"I have taken off my robe.
Should I get dressed again?
I have washed my feet.
Should I get them soiled?"
4 My lover tried to unlatch the door,
and my heart thrilled within me.
5 I jumped up to open the door for my love,
and my hands dripped with perfume.
My fingers dripped with lovely myrrh
as I pulled back the bolt.
6 I opened to my lover,
but he was gone!
My heart sank.
I searched for him
but could not find him anywhere.
I called to him,
but there was no reply.
7 The night watchmen found me
as they made their rounds.
They beat and bruised me
and stripped off my veil,
those watchmen on the walls.
8 Make this promise, O women of Jerusalem—
If you find my lover,
tell him I am weak with love.

Young Women of Jerusalem

9 Why is your lover better than all others,
O woman of rare beauty?
What makes your lover so special
that we must promise this?

Young Woman

10 My lover is dark and dazzling,
better than ten thousand others!
11 His head is finest gold,
his wavy hair is black as a raven.
12 His eyes sparkle like doves
beside springs of water;
they are set like jewels
washed in milk.
13 His cheeks are like gardens of spices
giving off fragrance.
His lips are like lilies,
perfumed with myrrh.
14 His arms are like rounded bars of gold,
set with beryl.
His body is like bright ivory,
glowing with lapis lazuli.
15 His legs are like marble pillars
set in sockets of finest gold.
His posture is stately,
like the noble cedars of Lebanon.
16 His mouth is sweetness itself;
he is desirable in every way.
Such, O women of Jerusalem,
is my lover, my friend.

O LORD, what a variety of things
you have made!
In wisdom you have made them all.
The earth is full of your creatures.

PSALM 104:24

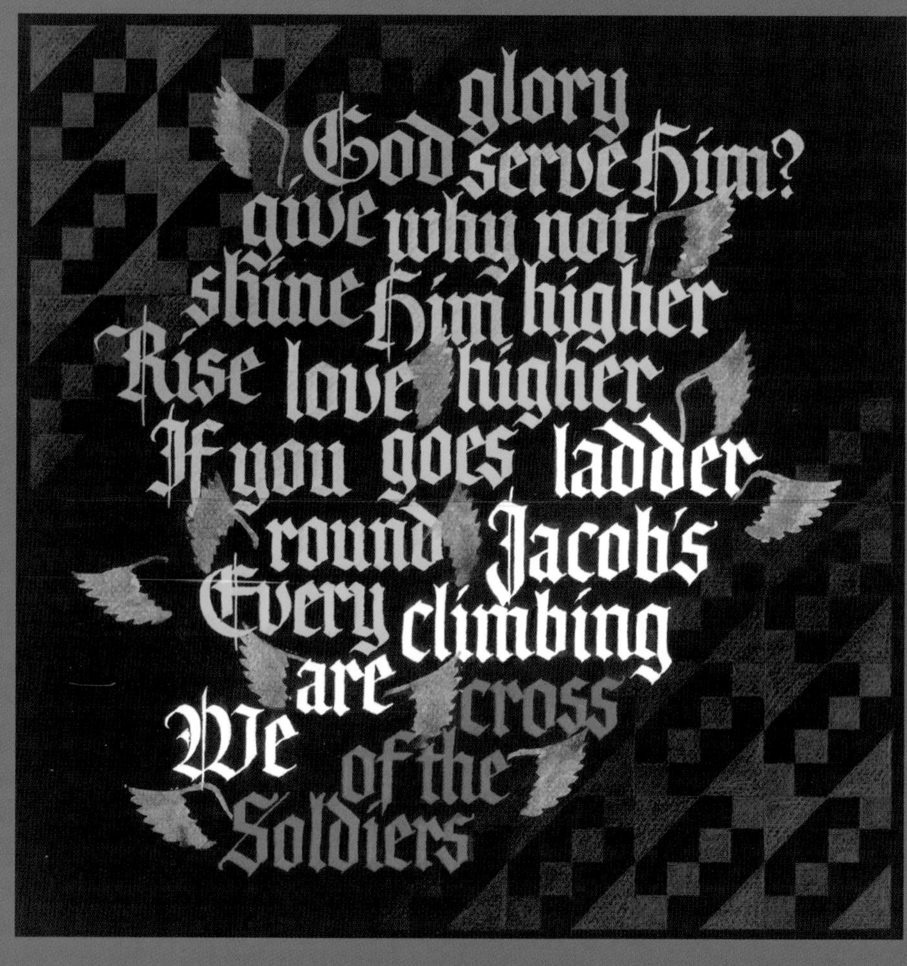

I focus on this one thing:
Forgetting the past and
looking forward to what lies ahead,
I press on to reach the end of the race
and receive the heavenly prize
for which God, through Christ Jesus,
is calling us.

PHILIPPIANS 3:13-14

This is my command—
be strong and courageous!
Do not be afraid or discouraged.
For the LORD your God is with you
wherever you go.

JOSHUA 1:9

He reached down from heaven
and rescued me;
he drew me out of deep waters. . . .
He led me to a place of safety;
he rescued me because
he delights in me.

PSALM 18:16,19

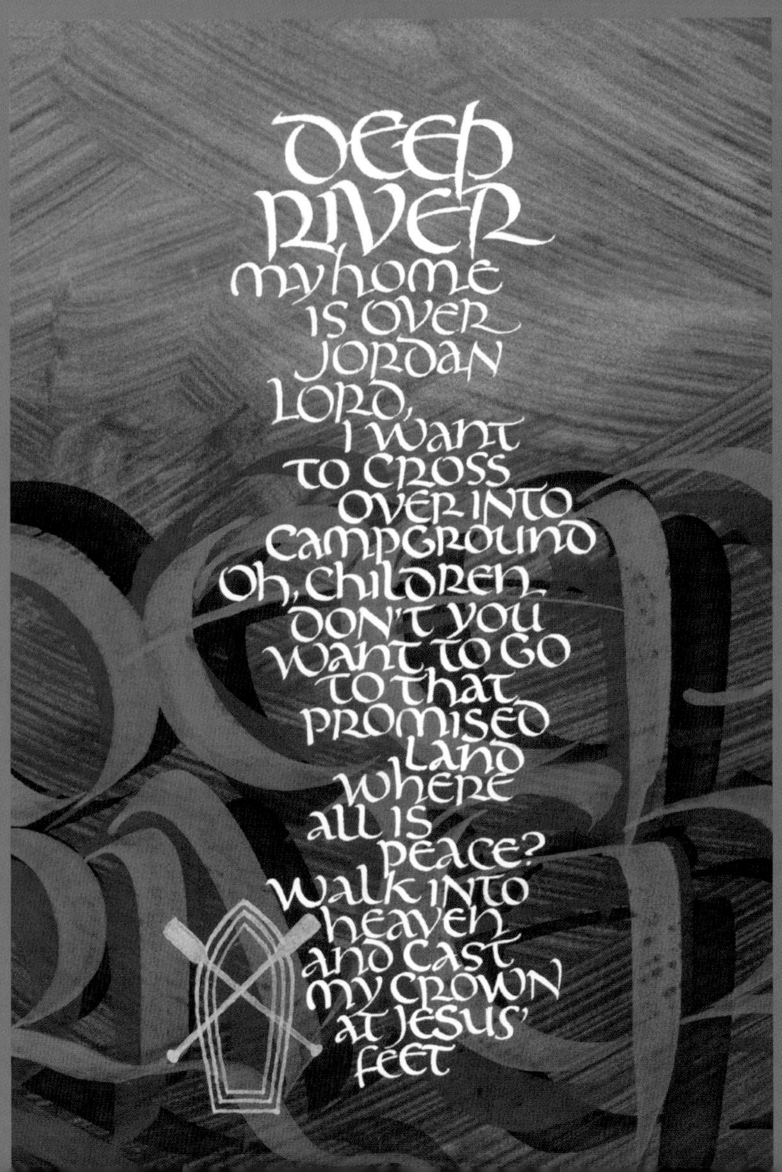
DEEP
RIVER
MY HOME
IS OVER
JORDAN
LORD,
I WANT
TO CROSS
OVER INTO
CAMPGROUND
OH, CHILDREN,
DON'T YOU
WANT TO GO
TO THAT
PROMISED
LAND
WHERE
ALL IS
PEACE?
WALK INTO
HEAVEN
AND CAST
MY CROWN
AT JESUS'
FEET

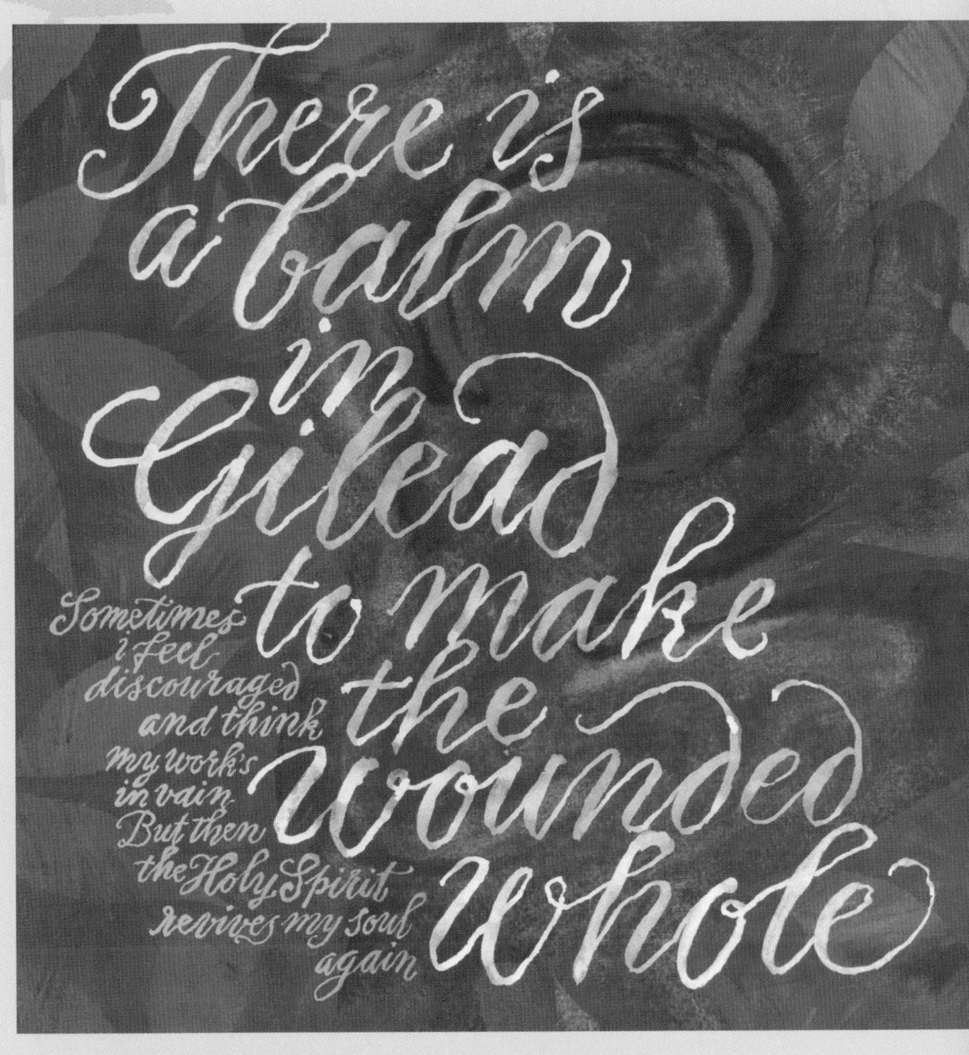

There is a balm in Gilead to make the wounded whole
Sometimes i feel discouraged and think my work's in vain. But then the Holy Spirit revives my soul again

Have compassion on me, LORD,
for I am weak.
Heal me, LORD,
for my bones are in agony. . . .
The LORD has heard my plea;
the LORD will answer my prayer.

PSALM 6:2,9

We never give up.
Though our bodies are dying,
our spirits are being renewed
every day.
So we don't look at the troubles
we can see now;
rather, we fix our gaze
on things that cannot be seen.
For the things we see now
will soon be gone,
but the things we cannot see
will last forever.

2 CORINTHIANS 4:16,18

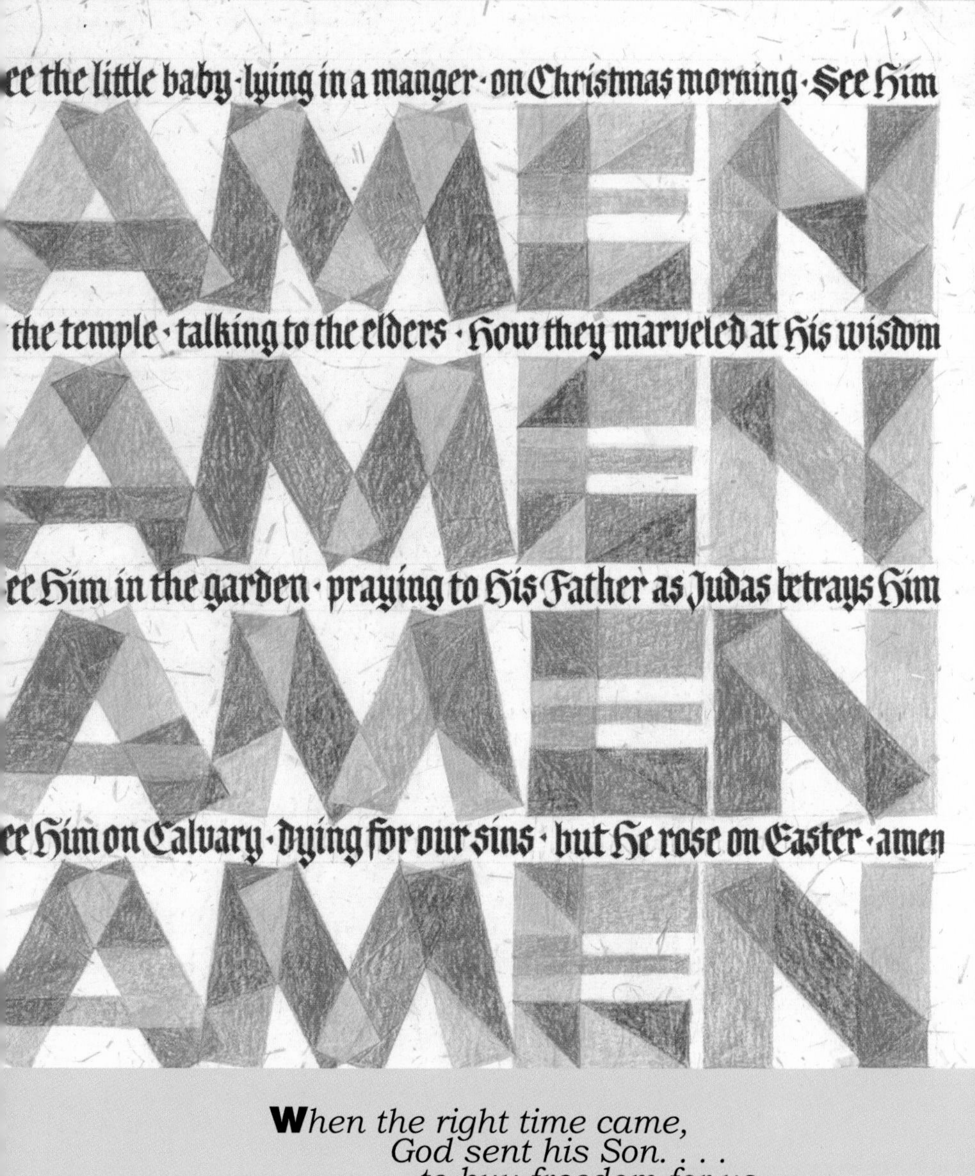

ee the little baby · lying in a manger · on Christmas morning · See Him
AMEN
the temple · talking to the elders · How they marveled at His wisdom
AMEN
ee Him in the garden · praying to His Father as Judas betrays Him
AMEN
ee Him on Calvary · dying for our sins · but He rose on Easter · amen
AMEN

When the right time came,
God sent his Son. . . .
to buy freedom for us. . . .
Now you are no longer a slave
but God's own child.
And . . . God has made
you his heir.

GALATIANS 4:4-5,7

This little light of mine
I'm going to let it shine
down in my heart
all in my house
everywhere I go
Out in the dark
all through the night

You are the light of the world—
like a city on a hilltop
that cannot be hidden.
No one lights a lamp
and then puts it under a basket.
Instead, a lamp is placed on a stand,
where it gives light
to everyone in the house.

MATTHEW 5:14-15

God blesses those
who work for peace,
for they will be called
the children of God.

MATTHEW 5:9

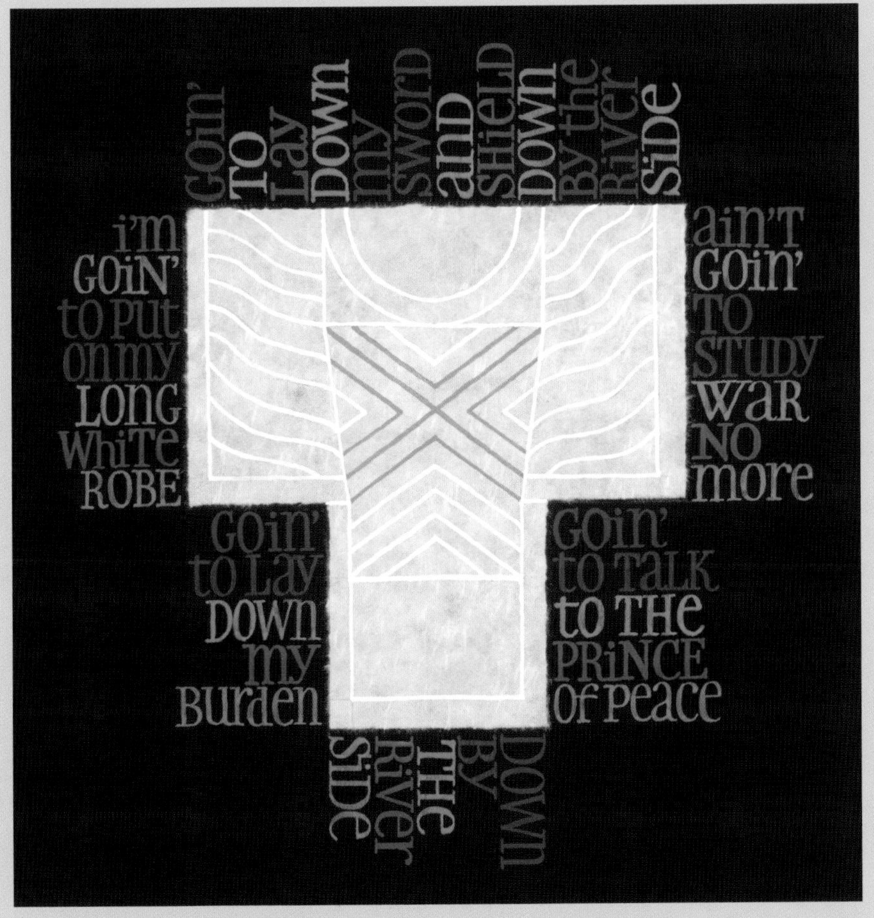

If we confess our sins to him,
he is faithful and just
to forgive us our sins
and to cleanse us
from all wickedness.

1 JOHN 1:9

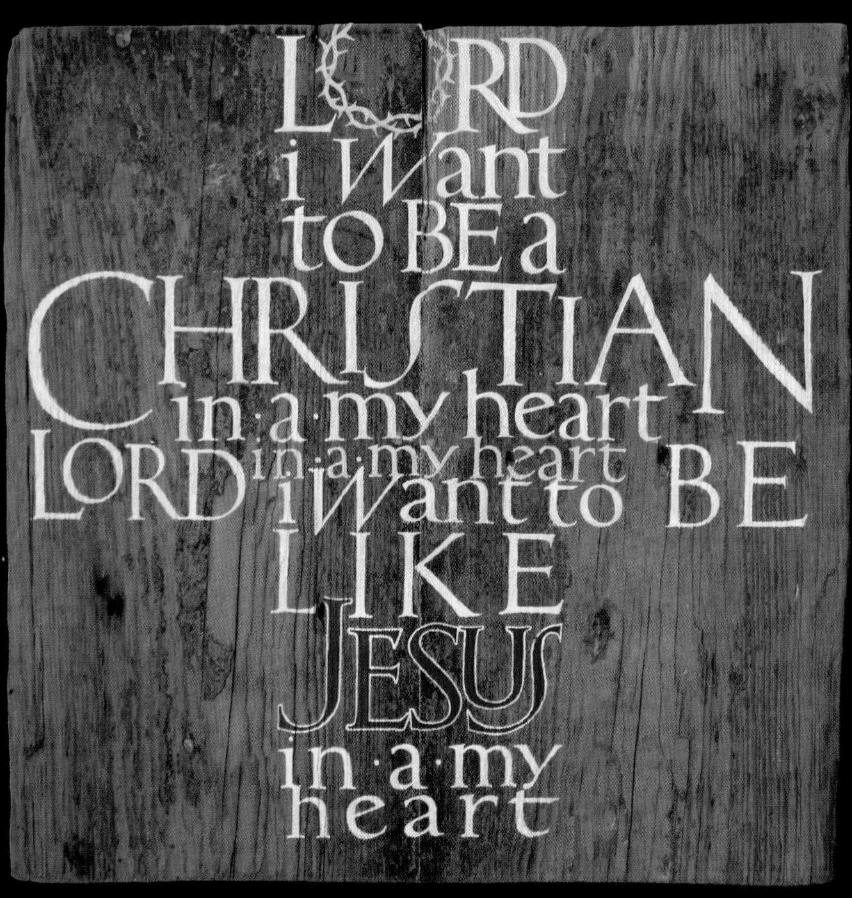

LORD
i Want
to BE a
CHRISTIAN
in a my heart
LORD in a my heart
i Want to BE
LIKE
JESUS
in a my
heart

My old self has been
crucified with Christ.
It is no longer I who live,
but Christ lives in me.
So I live in this earthly body
by trusting in the Son of God,
who loved me and
gave himself for me.

GALATIANS 2:20

I *passed on to you*
what was most important and
what had also been passed on to me.
Christ died for our sins,
just as the Scriptures said.
He was buried,
and he was raised from the dead
on the third day,
just as the Scriptures said.

1 CORINTHIANS 15:3-4

Were you there when they crucified my Lord?
Sometimes it causes me to tremble
tremble
tremble
Were you there when he rose up from the grave
Sometimes I feel like shouting Glory

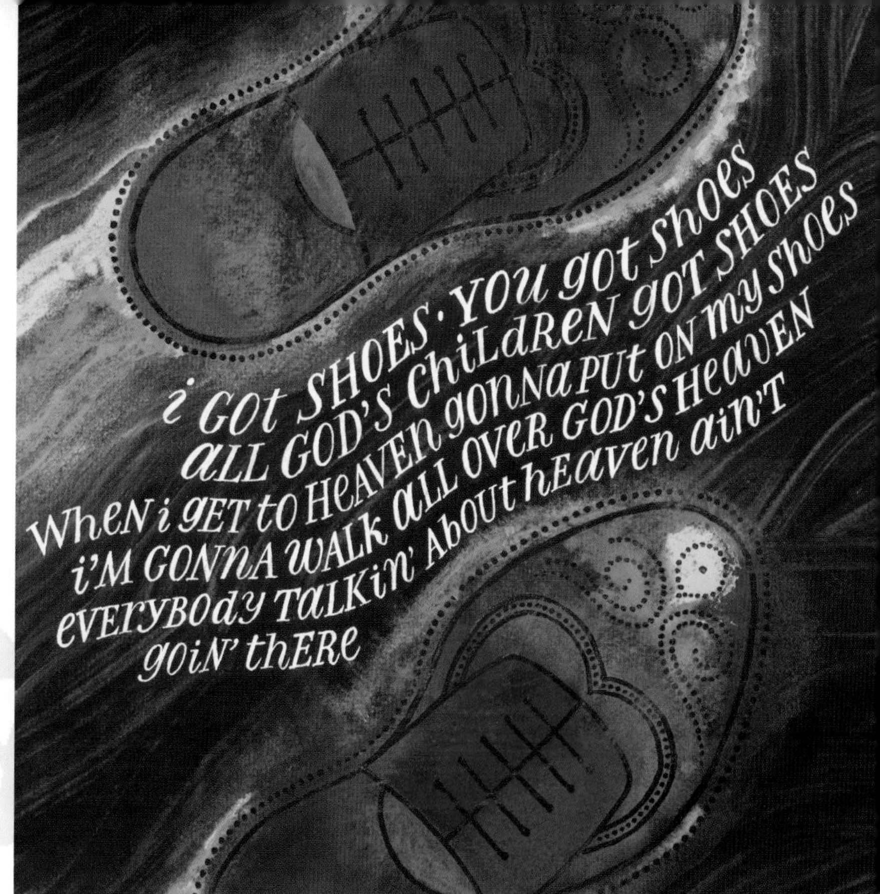

i GOT SHOES · YOU got ShOes
aLL GOD'S ChiLdREN gOT SHOES
WheN i GET to HeAVEN gONNa PUT ON my ShOes
i'M GONNA WALK aLL OVER GOD'S HeaVEN
eVERYBOdY TaLKin' About hEAVEN ain'T
goiN' thERE

N*o eye has seen,*
no ear has heard,
and no mind has imagined
what God has prepared for those
who love him.

1 CORINTHIANS 2:9

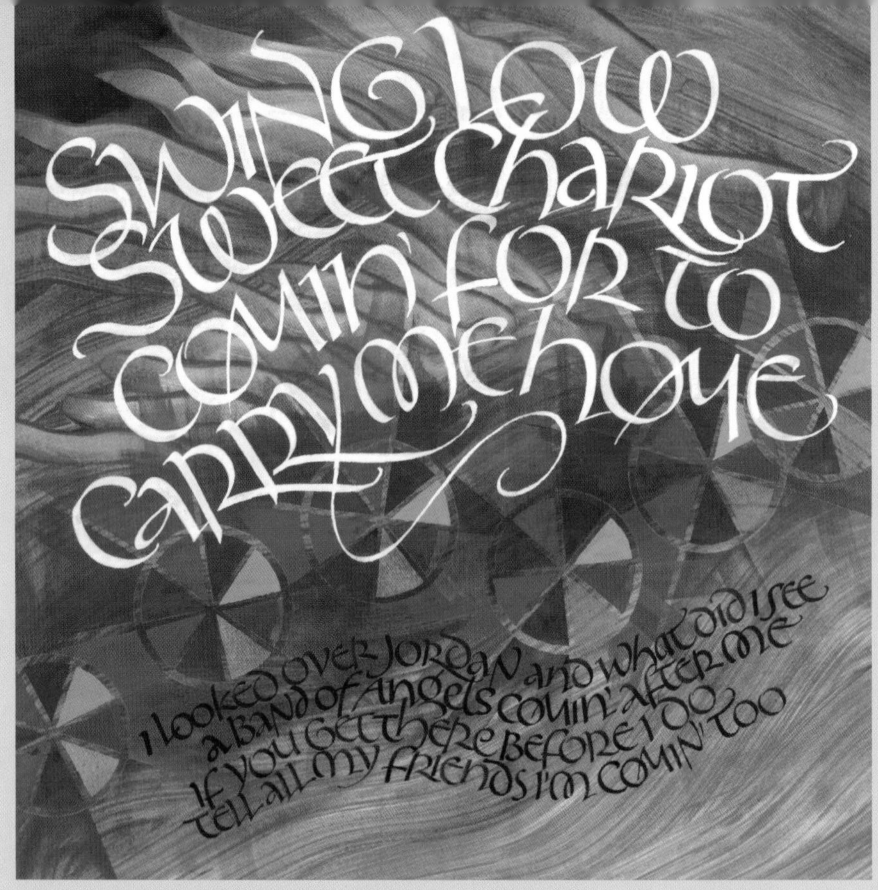

SWING LOW
SWEET CHARIOT
COMIN' FOR TO
CARRY ME HOME
I LOOKED OVER JORDAN AND WHAT DID I SEE
A BAND OF ANGELS COMIN' AFTER ME
IF YOU GET THERE BEFORE I DO
TELL ALL MY FRIENDS I'M COMIN' TOO

As they were walking along
and talking,
suddenly
a chariot of fire appeared,
drawn by horses of fire.
It drove between the two men,
separating them,
and Elijah was carried
by a whirlwind
into heaven.

2 KINGS 2:11

For this world is not
our permanent home;
we are looking forward
to a home yet to come.

HEBREWS 13:14

Lord
I want to be in that number
when the saints
come marchin' in

I saw the dead,
both great and small,
standing before God's throne.
And the books were opened,
including the Book of Life.
And the dead were judged
according to what they had done,
as recorded in the books.

REVELATION 20:12

KING JAMES VERSION

6

[1]Whither is thy beloved gone, O thou fairest
among women? whither is thy beloved turned
aside? that we may seek him with thee.
[2]My beloved is gone down into his garden, to the
beds of spices, to feed in the gardens, and to gather
lilies.
[3]I *am* my beloved's, and my beloved *is* mine: he
feedeth among the lilies.
[4]Thou *art* beautiful, O my love, as Tirzah, comely
as Jerusalem, terrible as *an army* with banners.
[5]Turn away thine eyes from me, for they have overcome me: thy hair *is* as a flock of goats that appear
from Gilead.
[6]Thy teeth *are* as a flock of sheep which go up
from the washing, whereof every one beareth twins,
and *there is* not one barren among them.
[7]As a piece of a pomegranate *are* thy temples
within thy locks.
[8]There are threescore queens, and fourscore concubines, and virgins without number.
[9]My dove, my undefiled is *but* one; she *is* the *only*
one of her mother, she *is* the choice *one* of her that
bare her. The daughters saw her, and blessed her;
yea, the queens and the concubines, and they
praised her.
[10]Who *is* she *that* looketh forth as the morning,
fair as the moon, clear as the sun, *and* terrible as *an
army* with banners?
[11]I went down into the garden of nuts to see the
fruits of the valley, *and* to see whether the vine flourished, *and* the pomegranates budded.
[12]Or ever I was aware, my soul made me *like* the
chariots of Ammi-nadib.

NEW LIVING TRANSLATION

Young Women of Jerusalem

6

[1]Where has your lover gone,
O woman of rare beauty?
Which way did he turn
so we can help you find him?

Young Woman

[2] My lover has gone down to his garden,
to his spice beds,
to browse in the gardens
and gather the lilies.
[3] I am my lover's, and my lover is mine.
He browses among the lilies.

Young Man

[4] You are beautiful, my darling,
like the lovely city of Tirzah.
Yes, as beautiful as Jerusalem,
as majestic as an army with billowing banners.
[5] Turn your eyes away,
for they overpower me.
Your hair falls in waves,
like a flock of goats winding down the
slopes of Gilead.
[6] Your teeth are as white as sheep
that are freshly washed.
Your smile is flawless,
each tooth matched with its twin.*
[7] Your cheeks are like rosy pomegranates
behind your veil.
[8] Even among sixty queens
and eighty concubines
and countless young women,
[9] I would still choose my dove, my perfect one—
the favorite of her mother,
dearly loved by the one who bore her.
The young women see her and praise her;
even queens and royal concubines sing her
praises:
[10] "Who is this, arising like the dawn,
as fair as the moon,
as bright as the sun,
as majestic as an army with billowing
banners?"

Young Woman

[11] I went down to the grove of walnut trees
and out to the valley to see the new
spring growth,
to see whether the grapevines had budded
or the pomegranates were in bloom.
[12] Before I realized it,
my strong desires had taken me to the chariot
of a noble man.*

6:6 Hebrew *Not one is missing; each has a twin.* **6:12** Or *to the royal chariots of my people,* or *to the chariots of Amminadab.* The meaning of the Hebrew is uncertain.

KING JAMES VERSION

13Return, return, O Shulamite; return, return, that
we may look upon thee. What will ye see in the
Shulamite? As it were the company of two armies.

7

1How beautiful are thy feet with shoes,
O prince's daughter! the joints of thy thighs
are like jewels, the work of the hands of a cunning
workman.
2Thy navel *is like* a round goblet, *which* wanteth
not liquor: thy belly *is like* an heap of wheat set about
with lilies.
3Thy two breasts *are* like two young roes *that are*
twins.
4Thy neck *is* as a tower of ivory; thine eyes *like* the
fishpools in Heshbon, by the gate of Bath-rabbim:
thy nose *is* as the tower of Lebanon which looketh toward Damascus.
5Thine head upon thee *is* like Carmel, and the hair
of thine head like purple; the king *is* held in the galleries.
6How fair and how pleasant art thou, O love, for
delights!
7This thy stature is like to a palm tree, and thy
breasts to clusters *of grapes*.
8I said, I will go up to the palm tree, I will take hold
of the boughs thereof: now also thy breasts shall be
as clusters of the vine, and the smell of thy nose like
apples;
9And the roof of thy mouth like the best wine for
my beloved, that goeth *down* sweetly, causing the
lips of those that are asleep to speak.
10I *am* my beloved's, and his desire *is* toward me.
11Come, my beloved, let us go forth into the field;
let us lodge in the villages.
12Let us get up early to the vineyards; let us see if
the vine flourish, *whether* the tender grape appear,
and the pomegranates bud forth: there will I give
thee my loves.
13The mandrakes give a smell, and at our gates *are*
all manner of pleasant *fruits*, new and old, *which* I
have laid up for thee, O my beloved.

NEW LIVING TRANSLATION

Young Women of Jerusalem

13*Return, return to us, O maid of Shulam.
Come back, come back, that we may
see you again.

Young Man

Why do you stare at this young woman
of Shulam,
as she moves so gracefully between
two lines of dancers?*

7

1*How beautiful are your sandaled feet,
O queenly maiden.
Your rounded thighs are like jewels,
the work of a skilled craftsman.
2 Your navel is perfectly formed
like a goblet filled with mixed wine.
Between your thighs lies a mound of wheat
bordered with lilies.
3 Your breasts are like two fawns,
twin fawns of a gazelle.
4 Your neck is as beautiful as an ivory tower.
Your eyes are like the sparkling pools in Heshbon
by the gate of Bath-rabbim.
Your nose is as fine as the tower of Lebanon
overlooking Damascus.
5 Your head is as majestic as Mount Carmel,
and the sheen of your hair radiates royalty.
The king is held captive by its tresses.
6 Oh, how beautiful you are!
How pleasing, my love, how full of delights!
7 You are slender like a palm tree,
and your breasts are like its clusters of fruit.
8 I said, "I will climb the palm tree
and take hold of its fruit."
May your breasts be like grape clusters,
and the fragrance of your breath like apples.
9 May your kisses be as exciting as the best wine,
flowing gently over lips and teeth.*

Young Woman

10 I am my lover's,
and he claims me as his own.
11 Come, my love, let us go out to the fields
and spend the night among the wildflowers.*
12 Let us get up early and go to the vineyards
to see if the grapevines have budded,
if the blossoms have opened,
and if the pomegranates have bloomed.
There I will give you my love.
13 There the mandrakes give off their fragrance,
and the finest fruits are at our door,
new delights as well as old,
which I have saved for you, my lover.

6:13a Verse 6:13 is numbered 7:1 in Hebrew text. **6:13b** Or *as you would at the movements of two armies?* or *as you would at the dance of Mahanaim?* The meaning of the Hebrew is uncertain. **7:1** Verses 7:1-13 are numbered 7:2-14 in Hebrew text. **7:9** As in Greek and Syriac versions and Latin Vulgate; Hebrew reads *over lips of sleepers*. **7:11** Or *in the villages*.

KING JAMES VERSION

8

1 O that thou *wert* as my brother, that sucked
the breasts of my mother! *when* I should find
thee without, I would kiss thee; yea, I should not be
despised.
2 I would lead thee, *and* bring thee into my
mother's house, *who* would instruct me: I would
cause thee to drink of spiced wine of the juice of my
pomegranate.
3 His left hand *should be* under my head, and his
right hand should embrace me.
4 I charge you, O daughters of Jerusalem, that ye
stir not up, nor awake *my* love, until he please.
5 Who *is* this that cometh up from the wilderness,
leaning upon her beloved? I raised thee up under the
apple tree: there thy mother brought thee forth:
there she brought thee forth *that* bare thee.
6 Set me as a seal upon thine heart, as a seal upon
thine arm: for love *is* strong as death; jealousy *is* cruel
as the grave: the coals thereof *are* coals of fire, *which
hath a* most vehement flame.
7 Many waters cannot quench love, neither can the
floods drown it: if *a* man would give all the substance
of his house for love, it would utterly be contemned.
8 We have a little sister, and she hath no breasts:
what shall we do for our sister in the day when she
shall be spoken for?
9 If she *be* a wall, we will build upon her a palace of
silver: and if she *be* a door, we will inclose her with
boards of cedar.
10 I *am* a wall, and my breasts like towers: then was
I in his eyes as one that found favour.
11 Solomon had a vineyard at Baal-hamon; he let
out the vineyard unto keepers; every one for the fruit
thereof was to bring a thousand *pieces* of silver.
12 My vineyard, which *is* mine, *is* before me: thou,

NEW LIVING TRANSLATION

Young Woman

8

1 Oh, I wish you were my brother,
who nursed at my mother's breasts.
Then I could kiss you no matter who
was watching,
and no one would criticize me.
2 I would bring you to my childhood home,
and there you would teach me.*
I would give you spiced wine to drink,
my sweet pomegranate wine.
3 Your left arm would be under my head,
and your right arm would embrace me.

4 Promise me, O women of Jerusalem,
not to awaken love until the time is right.*

Young Women of Jerusalem
5 Who is this sweeping in from the desert,
leaning on her lover?

Young Woman
I aroused you under the apple tree,
where your mother gave you birth,
where in great pain she delivered you.
6 Place me like a seal over your heart,
like a seal on your arm.
For love is as strong as death,
its jealousy* as enduring as the grave.*
Love flashes like fire,
the brightest kind of flame.
7 Many waters cannot quench love,
nor can rivers drown it.
If a man tried to buy love
with all his wealth,
his offer would be utterly scorned.

The Young Woman's Brothers
8 We have a little sister
too young to have breasts.
What will we do for our sister
if someone asks to marry her?
9 If she is a virgin, like a wall,
we will protect her with a silver tower.
But if she is promiscuous, like a swinging door,
we will block her door with a cedar bar.

Young Woman
10 I was a virgin, like a wall;
now my breasts are like towers.
When my lover looks at me,
he is delighted with what he sees.

11 Solomon has a vineyard at Baal-hamon,
which he leases out to tenant farmers.
Each of them pays a thousand pieces of silver*
for harvesting its fruit.
12 But my vineyard is mine to give,
and Solomon need not pay a thousand
pieces of silver.

8:2 Or *there she will teach me;* or *there she bore me.* **8:4** Or *not to awaken love until it is ready.* **8:6a** Or *its passion.* **8:6b** Hebrew *as Sheol.* **8:11** Hebrew *1,000 shekels of silver.*

KING JAMES VERSION

O Solomon, *must have* a thousand, and those that
keep the fruit thereof two hundred.
13 Thou that dwellest in the gardens, the companions hearken to thy voice: cause me to hear *it*.
14 Make haste, my beloved, and be thou like to a roe
or to a young hart upon the mountains of spices.

NEW LIVING TRANSLATION

But I will give two hundred pieces
to those who care for its vines.

Young Man

13 O my darling, lingering in the gardens,
your companions are fortunate to hear
your voice.
Let me hear it, too!

Young Woman

14 Come away, my love! Be like a gazelle
or a young stag on the mountains of spices.

Isaiah

KING JAMES VERSION

1 1 The vision of Isaiah the son of Amoz, which he
saw concerning Judah and Jerusalem in the
days of Uzziah, Jotham, Ahaz, *and* Hezekiah, kings
of Judah.

2 Hear, O heavens, and give ear, O earth: for the
LORD hath spoken, I have nourished and brought up
children, and they have rebelled against me.
3 The ox knoweth his owner, and the ass his master's crib: *but* Israel doth not know, my people doth
not consider.
4 Ah sinful nation, a people laden with iniquity, a
seed of evildoers, children that are corrupters: they
have forsaken the LORD, they have provoked the
Holy One of Israel unto anger, they are gone away
backward.
5 Why should ye be stricken any more? ye will revolt more and more: the whole head is sick, and the
whole heart faint.
6 From the sole of the foot even unto the head
there is no soundness in it; *but* wounds, and bruises,
and putrifying sores: they have not been closed, neither bound up, neither mollified with ointment.
7 Your country *is* desolate, your cities *are* burned
with fire: your land, strangers devour it in your presence, and *it is* desolate, as overthrown by strangers.
8 And the daughter of Zion is left as a cottage in a
vineyard, as a lodge in a garden of cucumbers, as a
besieged city.
9 Except the LORD of hosts had left unto us a very
small remnant, we should have been as Sodom, *and*
we should have been like unto Gomorrah.

NEW LIVING TRANSLATION

1 These are the visions that Isaiah son of Amoz
saw concerning Judah and Jerusalem. He saw
these visions during the years when Uzziah, Jotham,
Ahaz, and Hezekiah were kings of Judah.*

A Message for Rebellious Judah

2 Listen, O heavens! Pay attention, earth!
This is what the LORD says:
"The children I raised and cared for
have rebelled against me.
3 Even an ox knows its owner,
and a donkey recognizes its master's care—
but Israel doesn't know its master.
My people don't recognize my care for them."
4 Oh, what a sinful nation they are—
loaded down with a burden of guilt.
They are evil people,
corrupt children who have rejected the LORD.
They have despised the Holy One of Israel
and turned their backs on him.

5 Why do you continue to invite punishment?
Must you rebel forever?
Your head is injured,
and your heart is sick.
6 You are battered from head to foot—
covered with bruises, welts, and infected
wounds—
without any soothing ointments or bandages.
7 Your country lies in ruins,
and your towns are burned.
Foreigners plunder your fields before your eyes
and destroy everything they see.
8 Beautiful Jerusalem* stands abandoned
like a watchman's shelter in a vineyard,
like a lean-to in a cucumber field after
the harvest,
like a helpless city under siege.
9 If the LORD of Heaven's Armies
had not spared a few of us,*
we would have been wiped out like Sodom,
destroyed like Gomorrah.

1:1 These kings reigned from 792 to 686 B.C. **1:8** Hebrew *The daughter of Zion.* **1:9** Greek version reads *a few of our children.* Compare Rom 9:29.

KING JAMES VERSION

10 Hear the word of the LORD, ye rulers of Sodom; give ear unto the law of our God, ye people of Gomorrah.

11 To what purpose *is* the multitude of your sacrifices unto me? saith the LORD: I am full of the burnt offerings of rams, and the fat of fed beasts; and I delight not in the blood of bullocks, or of lambs, or of he goats.

12 When ye come to appear before me, who hath required this at your hand, to tread my courts?

13 Bring no more vain oblations; incense is an abomination unto me; the new moons and sabbaths, the calling of assemblies, I cannot away with; *it is* iniquity, even the solemn meeting.

14 Your new moons and your appointed feasts my soul hateth: they are a trouble unto me; I am weary to bear *them*.

15 And when ye spread forth your hands, I will hide mine eyes from you: yea, when ye make many prayers, I will not hear: your hands are full of blood.

16 Wash you, make you clean; put away the evil of your doings from before mine eyes; cease to do evil;

17 Learn to do well; seek judgment, relieve the oppressed, judge the fatherless, plead for the widow.

18 Come now, and let us reason together, saith the LORD: though your sins be as scarlet, they shall be as white as snow; though they be red like crimson, they shall be as wool.

19 If ye be willing and obedient, ye shall eat the good of the land:

20 But if ye refuse and rebel, ye shall be devoured with the sword: for the mouth of the LORD hath spoken *it*.

21 How is the faithful city become an harlot! it was full of judgment; righteousness lodged in it; but now murderers.

22 Thy silver is become dross, thy wine mixed with water:

NEW LIVING TRANSLATION

10 Listen to the LORD, you leaders of "Sodom."
Listen to the law of our God, people of "Gomorrah."
11 "What makes you think I want all your sacrifices?"
says the LORD.
"I am sick of your burnt offerings of rams
and the fat of fattened cattle.
I get no pleasure from the blood
of bulls and lambs and goats.
12 When you come to worship me,
who asked you to parade through my courts
with all your ceremony?
13 Stop bringing me your meaningless gifts;
the incense of your offerings disgusts me!
As for your celebrations of the new moon and the Sabbath
and your special days for fasting—
they are all sinful and false.
I want no more of your pious meetings.
14 I hate your new moon celebrations and your annual festivals.
They are a burden to me. I cannot stand them!
15 When you lift up your hands in prayer, I will not look.
Though you offer many prayers, I will not listen,
for your hands are covered with the blood of innocent victims.
16 Wash yourselves and be clean!
Get your sins out of my sight.
Give up your evil ways.
17 Learn to do good.
Seek justice.
Help the oppressed.
Defend the cause of orphans.
Fight for the rights of widows.
18 "Come now, let's settle this,"
says the LORD.
"Though your sins are like scarlet,
I will make them as white as snow.
Though they are red like crimson,
I will make them as white as wool.
19 If you will only obey me,
you will have plenty to eat.
20 But if you turn away and refuse to listen,
you will be devoured by the sword of your enemies.
I, the LORD, have spoken!"

Unfaithful Jerusalem

21 See how Jerusalem, once so faithful,
has become a prostitute.
Once the home of justice and righteousness,
she is now filled with murderers.
22 Once like pure silver,
you have become like worthless slag.
Once so pure,
you are now like watered-down wine.

KING JAMES VERSION

[23]Thy princes *are* rebellious, and companions of
thieves: every one loveth gifts, and followeth after
rewards: they judge not the fatherless, neither doth
the cause of the widow come unto them.
[24]Therefore saith the Lord, the LORD of hosts, the
mighty One of Israel, Ah, I will ease me of mine adversaries, and avenge me of mine enemies:
[25]And I will turn my hand upon thee, and purely
purge away thy dross, and take away all thy tin:
[26]And I will restore thy judges as at the first, and
thy counsellors as at the beginning: afterward thou
shalt be called, The city of righteousness, the faithful
city.
[27]Zion shall be redeemed with judgment, and her
converts with righteousness.
[28]And the destruction of the transgressors and of
the sinners *shall be* together, and they that forsake
the LORD shall be consumed.
[29]For they shall be ashamed of the oaks which ye
have desired, and ye shall be confounded for the gardens that ye have chosen.
[30]For ye shall be as an oak whose leaf fadeth, and
as a garden that hath no water.
[31]And the strong shall be as tow, and the maker of
it as a spark, and they shall both burn together, and
none shall quench *them*.

2 [1]The word that Isaiah the son of Amoz saw concerning Judah and Jerusalem.
[2]And it shall come to pass in the last days, *that* the
mountain of the LORD's house shall be established in
the top of the mountains, and shall be exalted above
the hills; and all nations shall flow unto it.
[3]And many people shall go and say, Come ye, and
let us go up to the mountain of the LORD, to the
house of the God of Jacob; and he will teach us of his
ways, and we will walk in his paths: for out of Zion
shall go forth the law, and the word of the LORD from
Jerusalem.
[4]And he shall judge among the nations, and shall

NEW LIVING TRANSLATION

[23] Your leaders are rebels,
the companions of thieves.
All of them love bribes
and demand payoffs,
but they refuse to defend the cause of orphans
or fight for the rights of widows.
[24] Therefore, the Lord, the LORD of Heaven's Armies,
the Mighty One of Israel, says,
"I will take revenge on my enemies
and pay back my foes!
[25] I will raise my fist against you.
I will melt you down and skim off your slag.
I will remove all your impurities.
[26] Then I will give you good judges again
and wise counselors like you used to have.
Then Jerusalem will again be called the
Home of Justice
and the Faithful City."
[27] Zion will be restored by justice;
those who repent will be revived by
righteousness.
[28] But rebels and sinners will be completely
destroyed,
and those who desert the LORD will
be consumed.
[29] You will be ashamed of your idol worship
in groves of sacred oaks.
You will blush because you worshiped
in gardens dedicated to idols.
[30] You will be like a great tree with withered leaves,
like a garden without water.
[31] The strongest among you will disappear
like straw;
their evil deeds will be the spark that sets
it on fire.
They and their evil works will burn up together,
and no one will be able to put out the fire.

The LORD's Future Reign

2 This is a vision that Isaiah son of Amoz saw
concerning Judah and Jerusalem:
[2] In the last days, the mountain of the LORD's house
will be the highest of all—
the most important place on earth.
It will be raised above the other hills,
and people from all over the world will stream
there to worship.
[3] People from many nations will come and say,
"Come, let us go up to the mountain of the LORD,
to the house of Jacob's God.
There he will teach us his ways,
and we will walk in his paths."
For the LORD's teaching will go out from Zion;
his word will go out from Jerusalem.
[4] The LORD will mediate between nations
and will settle international disputes.

KING JAMES VERSION

rebuke many people: and they shall beat their
swords into plowshares, and their spears into
pruninghooks: nation shall not lift up sword against
nation, neither shall they learn war any more.

5 O house of Jacob, come ye, and let us walk in the
light of the LORD.
6 Therefore thou hast forsaken thy people the
house of Jacob, because they be replenished from
the east, and *are* soothsayers like the Philistines, and
they please themselves in the children of strangers.
7 Their land also is full of silver and gold, neither *is*
there any end of their treasures; their land is also full
of horses, neither *is there any* end of their chariots:
8 Their land also is full of idols; they worship the
work of their own hands, that which their own fingers have made:
9 And the mean man boweth down, and the great
man humbleth himself: therefore forgive them not.
10 Enter into the rock, and hide thee in the dust, for
fear of the LORD, and for the glory of his majesty.
11 The lofty looks of man shall be humbled, and
the haughtiness of men shall be bowed down, and
the LORD alone shall be exalted in that day.
12 For the day of the LORD of hosts *shall be* upon
every *one that is* proud and lofty, and upon every *one*
that is lifted up; and he shall be brought low:
13 And upon all the cedars of Lebanon, *that are*
high and lifted up, and upon all the oaks of Bashan,
14 And upon all the high mountains, and upon all
the hills *that are* lifted up,
15 And upon every high tower, and upon every
fenced wall,
16 And upon all the ships of Tarshish, and upon all
pleasant pictures.
17 And the loftiness of man shall be bowed down,
and the haughtiness of men shall be made low: and
the LORD alone shall be exalted in that day.
18 And the idols he shall utterly abolish.
19 And they shall go into the holes off the rocks,
and into the caves of the earth, for fear of the LORD,
and for the glory of his majesty, when he ariseth to
shake terribly the earth.
20 In that day a man shall cast his idols of silver, and
his idols of gold, which they made *each one* for himself to worship, to the moles and to the bats;

NEW LIVING TRANSLATION

They will hammer their swords into plowshares
and their spears into pruning hooks.
Nation will no longer fight against nation,
nor train for war anymore.

A Warning of Judgment

5 Come, descendants of Jacob,
let us walk in the light of the LORD!
6 For the LORD has rejected his people,
the descendants of Jacob,
because they have filled their land with
practices from the East
and with sorcerers, as the Philistines do.
They have made alliances with pagans.
7 Israel is full of silver and gold;
there is no end to its treasures.
Their land is full of warhorses;
there is no end to its chariots.
8 Their land is full of idols;
the people worship things they have made
with their own hands.
9 So now they will be humbled,
and all will be brought low—
do not forgive them.
10 Crawl into caves in the rocks.
Hide in the dust
from the terror of the LORD
and the glory of his majesty.
11 Human pride will be brought down,
and human arrogance will be humbled.
Only the LORD will be exalted
on that day of judgment.

12 For the LORD of Heaven's Armies
has a day of reckoning.
He will punish the proud and mighty
and bring down everything that is exalted.
13 He will cut down the tall cedars of Lebanon
and all the mighty oaks of Bashan.
14 He will level all the high mountains
and all the lofty hills.
15 He will break down every high tower
and every fortified wall.
16 He will destroy all the great trading ships*
and every magnificent vessel.
17 Human pride will be humbled,
and human arrogance will be brought down.
Only the LORD will be exalted
on that day of judgment.

18 Idols will completely disappear.
19 When the LORD rises to shake the earth,
his enemies will crawl into holes in the ground.
They will hide in caves in the rocks
from the terror of the LORD
and the glory of his majesty.
20 On that day of judgment they will abandon the
gold and silver idols

2:16 Hebrew *every ship of Tarshish.*

KING JAMES VERSION

21 To go into the clefts of the rocks, and into the
tops of the ragged rocks, for fear of the LORD, and for
the glory of his majesty, when he ariseth to shake terribly the earth.
22 Cease ye from man, whose breath *is* in his nostrils: for wherein is he to be accounted of?

3 1 For, behold, the Lord, the LORD of hosts, doth
take away from Jerusalem and from Judah the
stay and the staff, the whole stay of bread, and the
whole stay of water.
2 The mighty man, and the man of war, the judge,
and the prophet, and the prudent, and the ancient,
3 The captain of fifty, and the honourable man,
and the counsellor, and the cunning artificer, and the
eloquent orator.
4 And I will give children *to be* their princes, and
babes shall rule over them.
5 And the people shall be oppressed, every one by
another, and every one by his neighbour: the child
shall behave himself proudly against the ancient,
and the base against the honourable.
6 When a man shall take hold of his brother of the
house of his father, *saying*, Thou hast clothing, be
thou our ruler, and *let* this ruin *be* under thy hand:
7 In that day shall he swear, saying, I will not be an
healer; for in my house *is* neither bread nor clothing:
make me not a ruler of the people.
8 For Jerusalem is ruined, and Judah is fallen: because their tongue and their doings *are* against the
LORD, to provoke the eyes of his glory.
9 The shew of their countenance doth witness
against them; and they declare their sin as Sodom,
they hide *it* not. Woe unto their soul! for they have
rewarded evil unto themselves.
10 Say ye to the righteous, that *it shall be* well *with
him:* for they shall eat the fruit of their doings.
11 Woe unto the wicked! *it shall be* ill *with him:* for
the reward of his hands shall be given him.
12 *As for* my people, children *are* their oppressors,
and women rule over them. O my people, they which

NEW LIVING TRANSLATION

they made for themselves to worship.
They will leave their gods to the rodents and bats,
21 while they crawl away into caverns
and hide among the jagged rocks in the cliffs.
They will try to escape the terror of the LORD
and the glory of his majesty
as he rises to shake the earth.
22 Don't put your trust in mere humans.
They are as frail as breath.
What good are they?

Judgment against Judah

3 1 The Lord, the LORD of Heaven's Armies,
will take away from Jerusalem and Judah
everything they depend on:
every bit of bread
and every drop of water,
2 all their heroes and soldiers,
judges and prophets,
fortune-tellers and elders,
3 army officers and high officials,
advisers, skilled craftsmen, and astrologers.
4 I will make boys their leaders,
and toddlers their rulers.
5 People will oppress each other—
man against man,
neighbor against neighbor.
Young people will insult their elders,
and vulgar people will sneer at the honorable.

6 In those days a man will say to his brother,
"Since you have a coat, you be our leader!
Take charge of this heap of ruins!"
7 But he will reply,
"No! I can't help.
I don't have any extra food or clothes.
Don't put me in charge!"
8 For Jerusalem will stumble,
and Judah will fall,
because they speak out against the LORD and
refuse to obey him.
They provoke him to his face.
9 The very look on their faces gives them away.
They display their sin like the people of Sodom
and don't even try to hide it.
They are doomed!
They have brought destruction upon
themselves.

10 Tell the godly that all will be well for them.
They will enjoy the rich reward they
have earned!
11 But the wicked are doomed,
for they will get exactly what they deserve.
12 Childish leaders oppress my people,
and women rule over them.

KING JAMES VERSION

lead thee cause *thee* to err, and destroy the way of thy paths.

13 The LORD standeth up to plead, and standeth to judge the people.

14 The LORD will enter into judgment with the ancients of his people, and the princes thereof: for ye have eaten up the vineyard; the spoil of the poor *is* in your houses.

15 What mean ye *that* ye beat my people to pieces, and grind the faces of the poor? saith the Lord GOD of hosts.

16 Moreover the LORD saith, Because the daughters of Zion are haughty, and walk with stretched forth necks and wanton eyes, walking and mincing *as* they go, and making a tinkling with their feet:

17 Therefore the Lord will smite with a scab the crown of the head of the daughters of Zion, and the LORD will discover their secret parts.

18 In that day the Lord will take away the bravery of *their* tinkling ornaments *about their feet*, and *their* cauls, and *their* round tires like the moon,

19 The chains, and the bracelets, and the mufflers,

20 The bonnets, and the ornaments of the legs, and the headbands, and the tablets, and the earrings,

21 The rings, and nose jewels,

22 The changeable suits of apparel, and the mantles, and the wimples, and the crisping pins,

23 The glasses, and the fine linen, and the hoods, and the veils.

24 And it shall come to pass, *that* instead of sweet smell there shall be stink; and instead of a girdle a rent; and instead of well set hair baldness; and instead of a stomacher a girding of sackcloth; *and* burning instead of beauty.

25 Thy men shall fall by the sword, and thy mighty in the war.

26 And her gates shall lament and mourn; and she *being* desolate shall sit upon the ground.

4 1 And in that day seven women shall take hold of one man, saying, We will eat our own bread, and wear our own apparel: only let us be called by thy name, to take away our reproach.

2 In that day shall the branch of the LORD be beautiful and glorious, and the fruit of the earth *shall be*

NEW LIVING TRANSLATION

O my people, your leaders mislead you;
they send you down the wrong road.
13 The LORD takes his place in court
and presents his case against his people!
14 The LORD comes forward to pronounce judgment
on the elders and rulers of his people:
"You have ruined Israel, my vineyard.
Your houses are filled with things stolen
from the poor.
15 How dare you crush my people,
grinding the faces of the poor into the dust?"
demands the Lord, the LORD of Heaven's Armies.

A Warning to Jerusalem

16 The LORD says, "Beautiful Zion* is haughty:
craning her elegant neck,
flirting with her eyes,
walking with dainty steps,
tinkling her ankle bracelets.
17 So the Lord will send scabs on her head;
the LORD will make beautiful Zion bald."
18 On that day of judgment
the Lord will strip away everything that
makes her beautiful:
ornaments, headbands, crescent necklaces,
19 earrings, bracelets, and veils;
20 scarves, ankle bracelets, sashes,
perfumes, and charms;
21 rings, jewels,
22 party clothes, gowns, capes, and purses;
23 mirrors, fine linen garments,
head ornaments, and shawls.
24 Instead of smelling of sweet perfume,
she will stink.
She will wear a rope for a sash,
and her elegant hair will fall out.
She will wear rough burlap instead of rich robes.
Shame will replace her beauty.*
25 The men of the city will be killed with the sword,
and her warriors will die in battle.
26 The gates of Zion will weep and mourn.
The city will be like a ravaged woman,
huddled on the ground.

4 In that day so few men will be left that seven women will fight for each man, saying, "Let us all marry you! We will provide our own food and clothing. Only let us take your name so we won't be mocked as old maids."

A Promise of Restoration

2 But in that day, the branch* of the LORD
will be beautiful and glorious;

3:16 Or *The women of Zion* (with corresponding changes to plural forms through verse 24); Hebrew reads *The daughters of Zion;* also in 3:17. **3:24** As in Dead Sea Scrolls; Masoretic Text reads *robes / because instead of beauty.* **4:2** Or *the Branch.*

KING JAMES VERSION

excellent and comely for them that are escaped of
Israel.
3 And it shall come to pass, *that he that is* left in
Zion, and *he that* remaineth in Jerusalem, shall be
called holy, *even* every one that is written among the
living in Jerusalem:
4 When the Lord shall have washed away the filth
of the daughters of Zion, and shall have purged the
blood of Jerusalem from the midst thereof by the
spirit of judgment, and by the spirit of burning.
5 And the LORD will create upon every dwelling
place of mount Zion, and upon her assemblies, a
cloud and smoke by day, and the shining of a flaming
fire by night: for upon all the glory *shall be* a defence.
6 And there shall be a tabernacle for a shadow in
the daytime from the heat, and for a place of refuge,
and for a covert from storm and from rain.

5 1 Now will I sing to my wellbeloved a song of my
beloved touching his vineyard. My wellbeloved
hath a vineyard in a very fruitful hill:
2 And he fenced it, and gathered out the stones
thereof, and planted it with the choicest vine, and
built a tower in the midst of it, and also made a winepress therein: and he looked that it should bring
forth grapes, and it brought forth wild grapes.
3 And now, O inhabitants of Jerusalem, and men of
Judah, judge, I pray you, betwixt me and my vineyard.
4 What could have been done more to my vineyard,
that I have not done in it? wherefore, when I looked
that it should bring forth grapes, brought it forth
wild grapes?
5 And now go to; I will tell you what I will do to my
vineyard: I will take away the hedge thereof, and it
shall be eaten up; *and* break down the wall thereof,
and it shall be trodden down:
6 And I will lay it waste: it shall not be pruned, nor
digged; but there shall come up briers and thorns: I
will also command the clouds that they rain no rain
upon it.
7 For the vineyard of the LORD of hosts *is* the house
of Israel, and the men of Judah his pleasant plant:
and he looked for judgment, but behold oppression;
for righteousness, but behold a cry.

NEW LIVING TRANSLATION

the fruit of the land will be the pride and glory
of all who survive in Israel.
3 All who remain in Zion
will be a holy people—
those who survive the destruction of Jerusalem
and are recorded among the living.
4 The Lord will wash the filth from beautiful Zion*
and cleanse Jerusalem of its bloodstains
with the hot breath of fiery judgment.
5 Then the LORD will provide shade for Mount Zion
and all who assemble there.
He will provide a canopy of cloud during the day
and smoke and flaming fire at night,
covering the glorious land.
6 It will be a shelter from daytime heat
and a hiding place from storms and rain.

A Song about the LORD's Vineyard

5 1 Now I will sing for the one I love
a song about his vineyard:
My beloved had a vineyard
on a rich and fertile hill.
2 He plowed the land, cleared its stones,
and planted it with the best vines.
In the middle he built a watchtower
and carved a winepress in the nearby rocks.
Then he waited for a harvest of sweet grapes,
but the grapes that grew were bitter.

3 Now, you people of Jerusalem and Judah,
you judge between me and my vineyard.
4 What more could I have done for my vineyard
that I have not already done?
When I expected sweet grapes,
why did my vineyard give me bitter grapes?

5 Now let me tell you
what I will do to my vineyard:
I will tear down its hedges
and let it be destroyed.
I will break down its walls
and let the animals trample it.
6 I will make it a wild place
where the vines are not pruned and
the ground is not hoed,
a place overgrown with briers and thorns.
I will command the clouds
to drop no rain on it.

7 The nation of Israel is the vineyard of the LORD
of Heaven's Armies.
The people of Judah are his pleasant garden.
He expected a crop of justice,
but instead he found oppression.
He expected to find righteousness,
but instead he heard cries of violence.

4:4 Or *from the women of Zion;* Hebrew reads *from the daughters of Zion.*

KING JAMES VERSION

8 Woe unto them that join house to house, *that* lay
field to field, till *there be* no place, that they may be
placed alone in the midst of the earth!
9 In mine ears *said* the LORD of hosts, Of a truth
many houses shall be desolate, *even* great and fair,
without inhabitant.
10 Yea, ten acres of vineyard shall yield one bath,
and the seed of an homer shall yield an ephah.
11 Woe unto them that rise up early in the morning, *that* they may follow strong drink; that continue
until night, *till* wine inflame them!
12 And the harp, and the viol, the tabret, and pipe,
and wine, are in their feasts: but they regard not the
work of the LORD, neither consider the operation of
his hands.
13 Therefore my people are gone into captivity, because *they have* no knowledge: and their honourable men *are* famished, and their multitude dried up
with thirst.
14 Therefore hell hath enlarged herself, and
opened her mouth without measure: and their glory,
and their multitude, and their pomp, and he that
rejoiceth, shall descend into it.
15 And the mean man shall be brought down, and
the mighty man shall be humbled, and the eyes of
the lofty shall be humbled:
16 But the LORD of hosts shall be exalted in judgment, and God that is holy shall be sanctified in righteousness.
17 Then shall the lambs feed after their manner,
and the waste places of the fat ones shall strangers
eat.
18 Woe unto them that draw iniquity with cords of
vanity, and sin as it were with a cart rope:
19 That say, Let him make speed, *and* hasten his
work, that we may see *it:* and let the counsel of the
Holy One of Israel draw nigh and come, that we may
know *it!*

NEW LIVING TRANSLATION

Judah's Guilt and Judgment

8 What sorrow for you who buy up house after
house and field after field,
until everyone is evicted and you live alone
in the land.
9 But I have heard the LORD of Heaven's Armies
swear a solemn oath:
"Many houses will stand deserted;
even beautiful mansions will be empty.
10 Ten acres* of vineyard will not produce even
six gallons* of wine.
Ten baskets of seed will yield only one
basket* of grain."

11 What sorrow for those who get up early
in the morning
looking for a drink of alcohol
and spend long evenings drinking wine
to make themselves flaming drunk.
12 They furnish wine and lovely music at their
grand parties—
lyre and harp, tambourine and flute—
but they never think about the LORD
or notice what he is doing.

13 So my people will go into exile far away
because they do not know me.
Those who are great and honored will starve,
and the common people will die of thirst.
14 The grave* is licking its lips in anticipation,
opening its mouth wide.
The great and the lowly
and all the drunken mob will be swallowed up.
15 Humanity will be destroyed, and people
brought down;
even the arrogant will lower their eyes in
humiliation.
16 But the LORD of Heaven's Armies will be exalted
by his justice.
The holiness of God will be displayed by his
righteousness.
17 In that day lambs will find good pastures,
and fattened sheep and young goats* will feed
among the ruins.

18 What sorrow for those who drag their sins
behind them
with ropes made of lies,
who drag wickedness behind them like a cart!
19 They even mock God and say,
"Hurry up and do something!
We want to see what you can do.
Let the Holy One of Israel carry out his plan,
for we want to know what it is."

5:10a Hebrew *A ten yoke,* that is, the area of land plowed by ten teams of oxen in one day. **5:10b** Hebrew *a bath* [21 liters]. **5:10c** Hebrew *A homer* [5 bushels or 182 liters] *of seed will yield only an ephah* [20 quarts or 22 liters]. **5:14** Hebrew *Sheol.* **5:17** As in Greek version; Hebrew reads *and strangers.*

KING JAMES VERSION

20Woe unto them that call evil good, and good evil;
that put darkness for light, and light for darkness;
that put bitter for sweet, and sweet for bitter!
21Woe unto *them that are* wise in their own eyes,
and prudent in their own sight!
22Woe unto *them that are* mighty to drink wine,
and men of strength to mingle strong drink:
23Which justify the wicked for reward, and take
away the righteousness of the righteous from him!
24Therefore as the fire devoureth the stubble,
and the flame consumeth the chaff, *so* their root
shall be as rottenness, and their blossom shall go up
as dust: because they have cast away the law of the
LORD of hosts, and despised the word of the Holy
One of Israel.
25Therefore is the anger of the LORD kindled
against his people, and he hath stretched forth his
hand against them, and hath smitten them: and the
hills did tremble, and their carcases *were* torn in
the midst of the streets. For all this his anger is not
turned away, but his hand *is* stretched out still.
26And he will lift up an ensign to the nations from
far, and will hiss unto them from the end of the earth:
and, behold, they shall come with speed swiftly:
27None shall be weary nor stumble among them;
none shall slumber nor sleep; neither shall the girdle
of their loins be loosed, nor the latchet of their shoes
be broken:
28Whose arrows *are* sharp, and all their bows bent,
their horses' hoofs shall be counted like flint, and
their wheels like a whirlwind.
29Their roaring *shall be* like a lion, they shall roar
like young lions: yea, they shall roar, and lay hold of
the prey, and shall carry *it* away safe, and none shall
deliver *it*.
30And in that day they shall roar against them like
the roaring of the sea: and if *one* look unto the land,
behold darkness *and* sorrow, and the light is darkened in the heavens thereof.

6 1In the year that king Uzziah died I saw also the
Lord sitting upon a throne, high and lifted up,
and his train filled the temple.
2Above it stood the seraphims: each one had six

NEW LIVING TRANSLATION

20 What sorrow for those who say
that evil is good and good is evil,
that dark is light and light is dark,
that bitter is sweet and sweet is bitter.
21 What sorrow for those who are wise in
their own eyes
and think themselves so clever.
22 What sorrow for those who are heroes
at drinking wine
and boast about all the alcohol they can hold.
23 They take bribes to let the wicked go free,
and they punish the innocent.

24 Therefore, just as fire licks up stubble
and dry grass shrivels in the flame,
so their roots will rot
and their flowers wither.
For they have rejected the law of the LORD
of Heaven's Armies;
they have despised the word of the
Holy One of Israel.
25 That is why the LORD's anger burns against
his people,
and why he has raised his fist to crush them.
The mountains tremble,
and the corpses of his people litter the streets
like garbage.
But even then the LORD's anger is not satisfied.
His fist is still poised to strike!
26 He will send a signal to distant nations far away
and whistle to those at the ends of the earth.
They will come racing toward Jerusalem.
27 They will not get tired or stumble.
They will not stop for rest or sleep.
Not a belt will be loose,
not a sandal strap broken.
28 Their arrows will be sharp
and their bows ready for battle.
Sparks will fly from their horses' hooves,
and the wheels of their chariots will spin
like a whirlwind.
29 They will roar like lions,
like the strongest of lions.
Growling, they will pounce on their victims
and carry them off,
and no one will be there to rescue them.
30 They will roar over their victims on that day
of destruction
like the roaring of the sea.
If someone looks across the land,
only darkness and distress will be seen;
even the light will be darkened by clouds.

Isaiah's Cleansing and Call

6 It was in the year King Uzziah died* that I saw
the Lord. He was sitting on a lofty throne, and
the train of his robe filled the Temple. 2Attending

6:1 King Uzziah died in 740 B.C.

KING JAMES VERSION

wings; with twain he covered his face, and with twain
he covered his feet, and with twain he did fly.
3 And one cried unto another, and said, Holy, holy,
holy, *is* the LORD of hosts: the whole earth *is* full of his
glory.
4 And the posts of the door moved at the voice of
him that cried, and the house was filled with smoke.
5 Then said I, Woe *is* me! for I am undone; because
I *am* a man of unclean lips, and I dwell in the midst of
a people of unclean lips: for mine eyes have seen the
King, the LORD of hosts.
6 Then flew one of the seraphims unto me, having
a live coal in his hand, *which* he had taken with the
tongs from off the altar:
7 And he laid *it* upon my mouth, and said, Lo, this
hath touched thy lips; and thine iniquity is taken
away, and thy sin purged.
8 Also I heard the voice of the Lord, saying, Whom
shall I send, and who will go for us? Then said I, Here
am I; send me.
9 And he said, Go, and tell this people, Hear ye indeed, but understand not; and see ye indeed, but
perceive not.
10 Make the heart of this people fat, and make their
ears heavy, and shut their eyes; lest they see with
their eyes, and hear with their ears, and understand
with their heart, and convert, and be healed.
11 Then said I, Lord, how long? And he answered,
Until the cities be wasted without inhabitant, and
the houses without man, and the land be utterly
desolate,
12 And the LORD have removed men far away, and
there be a great forsaking in the midst of the land.
13 But yet in it *shall be* a tenth, and *it* shall return,
and shall be eaten: as a teil tree, and as an oak, whose
substance *is* in them, when they cast *their leaves: so*
the holy seed *shall be* the substance thereof.

7 1 And it came to pass in the days of Ahaz the son
of Jotham, the son of Uzziah, king of Judah, *that*
Rezin the king of Syria, and Pekah the son of Remaliah, king of Israel, went up toward Jerusalem to war
against it, but could not prevail against it.

NEW LIVING TRANSLATION

him were mighty seraphim, each having six wings.
With two wings they covered their faces, with two
they covered their feet, and with two they flew. 3 They
were calling out to each other,

"Holy, holy, holy is the LORD of Heaven's Armies!
The whole earth is filled with his glory!"

4 Their voices shook the Temple to its foundations,
and the entire building was filled with smoke.
5 Then I said, "It's all over! I am doomed, for I am
a sinful man. I have filthy lips, and I live among a
people with filthy lips. Yet I have seen the King, the
LORD of Heaven's Armies."
6 Then one of the seraphim flew to me with a
burning coal he had taken from the altar with a pair
of tongs. 7 He touched my lips with it and said, "See,
this coal has touched your lips. Now your guilt is
removed, and your sins are forgiven."
8 Then I heard the Lord asking, "Whom should
I send as a messenger to this people? Who will go
for us?"
I said, "Here I am. Send me."
9 And he said, "Yes, go, and say to this people,

'Listen carefully, but do not understand.
Watch closely, but learn nothing.'
10 Harden the hearts of these people.
Plug their ears and shut their eyes.
That way, they will not see with their eyes,
nor hear with their ears,
nor understand with their hearts
and turn to me for healing."*

11 Then I said, "Lord, how long will this go on?"
And he replied,

"Until their towns are empty,
their houses are deserted,
and the whole country is a wasteland;
12 until the LORD has sent everyone away,
and the entire land of Israel lies deserted.
13 If even a tenth—a remnant—survive,
it will be invaded again and burned.
But as a terebinth or oak tree leaves a stump
when it is cut down,
so Israel's stump will be a holy seed."

A Message for Ahaz

7 When Ahaz, son of Jotham and grandson of Uzziah, was king of Judah, King Rezin of Syria*
and Pekah son of Remaliah, the king of Israel, set out
to attack Jerusalem. However, they were unable to
carry out their plan.

6:9-10 Greek version reads *And he said, "Go and say to this people, / 'When you hear what I say, you will not understand. / When you see what I do, you will not comprehend.' / For the hearts of these people are hardened, / and their ears cannot hear, and they have closed their eyes— / so their eyes cannot see, / and their ears cannot hear, / and their hearts cannot understand, / and they cannot turn to me and let me heal them."* Compare Matt 13:14-15; Mark 4:12; Luke 8:10; Acts 28:26-27. **7:1** Hebrew *Aram;* also in 7:2, 4, 5, 8.

2 And it was told the house of David, saying, Syria is
confederate with Ephraim. And his heart was moved,
and the heart of his people, as the trees of the wood
are moved with the wind.

3 Then said the LORD unto Isaiah, Go forth now to
meet Ahaz, thou, and Shear-jashub thy son, at the
end of the conduit of the upper pool in the highway
of the fuller's field;

4 And say unto him, Take heed, and be quiet; fear
not, neither be fainthearted for the two tails of these
smoking firebrands, for the fierce anger of Rezin
with Syria, and of the son of Remaliah.

5 Because Syria, Ephraim, and the son of Remaliah,
have taken evil counsel against thee, saying,

6 Let us go up against Judah, and vex it, and let us
make a breach therein for us, and set a king in the
midst of it, *even* the son of Tabeal:

7 Thus saith the Lord GOD, It shall not stand, neither shall it come to pass.

8 For the head of Syria *is* Damascus, and the head
of Damascus *is* Rezin; and within threescore and
five years shall Ephraim be broken, that it be not a
people.

9 And the head of Ephraim *is* Samaria, and the
head of Samaria *is* Remaliah's son. If ye will not believe, surely ye shall not be established.

10 Moreover the LORD spake again unto Ahaz,
saying,

11 Ask thee a sign of the LORD thy God; ask it either
in the depth, or in the height above.

12 But Ahaz said, I will not ask, neither will I tempt
the LORD.

13 And he said, Hear ye now, O house of David; *Is it* a
small thing for you to weary men, but will ye weary
my God also?

14 Therefore the Lord himself shall give you a sign;
Behold, a virgin shall conceive, and bear a son, and
shall call his name Immanuel.

15 Butter and honey shall he eat, that he may know
to refuse the evil, and choose the good.

16 For before the child shall know to refuse the evil,
and choose the good, the land that thou abhorrest
shall be forsaken of both her kings.

17 The LORD shall bring upon thee, and upon thy
people, and upon thy father's house, days that have
not come from the day that Ephraim departed from
Judah; *even* the king of Assyria.

18 And it shall come to pass in that day, *that* the
LORD shall hiss for the fly that *is* in the uttermost part
of the rivers of Egypt, and for the bee that *is* in the
land of Assyria.

2 The news had come to the royal court of Judah:
"Syria is allied with Israel* against us!" So the hearts
of the king and his people trembled with fear, like
trees shaking in a storm.

3 Then the LORD said to Isaiah, "Take your son
Shear-jashub* and go out to meet King Ahaz. You
will find him at the end of the aqueduct that feeds
water into the upper pool, near the road leading to
the field where cloth is washed.* 4 Tell him to stop
worrying. Tell him he doesn't need to fear the fierce
anger of those two burned-out embers, King Rezin
of Syria and Pekah son of Remaliah. 5 Yes, the kings
of Syria and Israel are plotting against him, saying,
6 'We will attack Judah and capture it for ourselves.
Then we will install the son of Tabeel as Judah's king.'
7 But this is what the Sovereign LORD says:

"This invasion will never happen;
it will never take place;
8 for Syria is no stronger than its capital,
Damascus,
and Damascus is no stronger than
its king, Rezin.
As for Israel, within sixty-five years
it will be crushed and completely destroyed.
9 Israel is no stronger than its capital, Samaria,
and Samaria is no stronger than its king, Pekah
son of Remaliah.
Unless your faith is firm,
I cannot make you stand firm."

The Sign of Immanuel

10 Later, the LORD sent this message to King Ahaz:
11 "Ask the LORD your God for a sign of confirmation,
Ahaz. Make it as difficult as you want—as high as
heaven or as deep as the place of the dead.*"

12 But the king refused. "No," he said, "I will not test
the LORD like that."

13 Then Isaiah said, "Listen well, you royal family of
David! Isn't it enough to exhaust human patience?
Must you exhaust the patience of my God as well?
14 All right then, the Lord himself will give you the
sign. Look! The virgin* will conceive a child! She will
give birth to a son and will call him Immanuel (which
means 'God is with us'). 15 By the time this child is old
enough to choose what is right and reject what is
wrong, he will be eating yogurt* and honey. 16 For before the child is that old, the lands of the two kings
you fear so much will both be deserted.

17 "Then the LORD will bring things on you, your
nation, and your family unlike anything since Israel
broke away from Judah. He will bring the king of
Assyria upon you!"

18 In that day the LORD will whistle for the army of
southern Egypt and for the army of Assyria. They will

7:2 Hebrew *Ephraim,* referring to the northern kingdom of Israel; also in 7:5, 8, 9, 17. **7:3a** *Shear-jashub* means "A remnant will return." **7:3b** Or *bleached.* **7:11** Hebrew *as deep as Sheol.* **7:14** Or *young woman.* **7:15** Or *curds;* also in 7:22.

KING JAMES VERSION

19 And they shall come, and shall rest all of them in
the desolate valleys, and in the holes of the rocks,
and upon all thorns, and upon all bushes.
20 In the same day shall the Lord shave with a razor
that is hired, *namely,* by them beyond the river, by
the king of Assyria, the head, and the hair of the feet:
and it shall also consume the beard.
21 And it shall come to pass in that day, *that* a man
shall nourish a young cow, and two sheep;
22 And it shall come to pass, for the abundance of
milk *that* they shall give he shall eat butter: for butter
and honey shall every one eat that is left in the land.
23 And it shall come to pass in that day, *that* every
place shall be, where there were a thousand vines at a
thousand silverlings, it shall *even* be for briers and
thorns.
24 With arrows and with bows shall *men* come
thither; because all the land shall become briers and
thorns.
25 And *on* all hills that shall be digged with the
mattock, there shall not come thither the fear of briers and thorns: but it shall be for the sending forth of
oxen, and for the treading of lesser cattle.

8 1 Moreover the LORD said unto me, Take thee a
great roll, and write in it with a man's pen concerning Maher-shalal-hash-baz.
2 And I took unto me faithful witnesses to record,
Uriah the priest, and Zechariah the son of Jeberechiah.
3 And I went unto the prophetess; and she conceived, and bare a son. Then said the LORD to me, Call
his name Maher-shalal-hash-baz.
4 For before the child shall have knowledge to cry,
My father, and my mother, the riches of Damascus
and the spoil of Samaria shall be taken away before
the king of Assyria.
5 The LORD spake also unto me again, saying,
6 Forasmuch as this people refuseth the waters of
Shiloah that go softly, and rejoice in Rezin and Remaliah's son;
7 Now therefore, behold, the Lord bringeth up
upon them the waters of the river, strong and many,
even the king of Assyria, and all his glory: and he
shall come up over all his channels, and go over all
his banks:
8 And he shall pass through Judah; he shall overflow and go over, he shall reach *even* to the neck; and
the stretching out of his wings shall fill the breadth
of thy land, O Immanuel.
9 Associate yourselves, O ye people, and ye shall be
broken in pieces; and give ear, all ye of far countries:
gird yourselves, and ye shall be broken in pieces; gird
yourselves, and ye shall be broken in pieces.
10 Take counsel together, and it shall come to

NEW LIVING TRANSLATION

swarm around you like flies and bees. 19 They will
come in vast hordes and settle in the fertile areas and
also in the desolate valleys, caves, and thorny places.
20 In that day the Lord will hire a "razor" from beyond
the Euphrates River*—the king of Assyria—and use
it to shave off everything: your land, your crops, and
your people.*
21 In that day a farmer will be fortunate to have a
cow and two sheep or goats left. 22 Nevertheless,
there will be enough milk for everyone because so
few people will be left in the land. They will eat their
fill of yogurt and honey. 23 In that day the lush vineyards, now worth 1,000 pieces of silver,* will become patches of briers and thorns. 24 The entire land
will become a vast expanse of briers and thorns, a
hunting ground overrun by wildlife. 25 No one will go
to the fertile hillsides where the gardens once grew,
for briers and thorns will cover them. Cattle, sheep,
and goats will graze there.

The Coming Assyrian Invasion

8 Then the LORD said to me, "Make a large sign-
board and clearly write this name on it: Maher-
shalal-hash-baz.*" 2 I asked Uriah the priest and
Zechariah son of Jeberekiah, both known as honest
men, to witness my doing this.
3 Then I slept with my wife, and she became pregnant and gave birth to a son. And the LORD said, "Call
him Maher-shalal-hash-baz. 4 For before this child is
old enough to say 'Papa' or 'Mama,' the king of Assyria will carry away both the abundance of Damascus
and the riches of Samaria."
5 Then the LORD spoke to me again and said, 6 "My
care for the people of Judah is like the gently flowing
waters of Shiloah, but they have rejected it. They are
rejoicing over what will happen to* King Rezin and
King Pekah.* 7 Therefore, the Lord will overwhelm
them with a mighty flood from the Euphrates
River*—the king of Assyria and all his glory. This
flood will overflow all its channels 8 and sweep into
Judah until it is chin deep. It will spread its wings,
submerging your land from one end to the other,
O Immanuel.

9 "Huddle together, you nations, and be terrified.
Listen, all you distant lands.
Prepare for battle, but you will be crushed!
Yes, prepare for battle, but you will be crushed!
10 Call your councils of war, but they will be
worthless.

7:20a Hebrew *the river.* **7:20b** Hebrew *shave off the head, the hair of the legs, and the beard.* **7:23** Hebrew *1,000 shekels of silver,* about 25 pounds or 11.4 kilograms in weight. **8:1** *Maher-shalal-hash-baz* means "Swift to plunder and quick to carry away." **8:6a** Or *They are rejoicing because of.* **8:6b** Hebrew *and the son of Remaliah.* **8:7** Hebrew *the river.*

KING JAMES VERSION

nought; speak the word, and it shall not stand: for God *is* with us.

11 For the LORD spake thus to me with a strong hand, and instructed me that I should not walk in the way of this people, saying,

12 Say ye not, A confederacy, to all *them to* whom this people shall say, A confederacy; neither fear ye their fear, nor be afraid.

13 Sanctify the LORD of hosts himself; and *let* him *be* your fear, and *let* him *be* your dread.

14 And he shall be for a sanctuary; but for a stone of stumbling and for a rock of offence to both the houses of Israel, for a gin and for a snare to the inhabitants of Jerusalem.

15 And many among them shall stumble, and fall, and be broken, and be snared, and be taken.

16 Bind up the testimony, seal the law among my disciples.

17 And I will wait upon the LORD, that hideth his face from the house of Jacob, and I will look for him.

18 Behold, I and the children whom the LORD hath given me *are* for signs and for wonders in Israel from the LORD of hosts, which dwelleth in mount Zion.

19 And when they shall say unto you, Seek unto them that have familiar spirits, and unto wizards that peep, and that mutter: should not a people seek unto their God? for the living to the dead?

20 To the law and to the testimony: if they speak not according to this word, *it is* because *there is* no light in them.

21 And they shall pass through it, hardly bestead and hungry: and it shall come to pass, that when they shall be hungry, they shall fret themselves, and curse their king and their God, and look upward.

22 And they shall look unto the earth; and behold trouble and darkness, dimness of anguish; and *they shall be* driven to darkness.

9 1 Nevertheless the dimness *shall* not *be* such as *was* in her vexation, when at the first he lightly afflicted the land of Zebulun and the land of Naphtali, and afterward did more grievously afflict *her by* the way of the sea, beyond Jordan, in Galilee of the nations.

NEW LIVING TRANSLATION

Develop your strategies, but they will
not succeed.
For God is with us!*"

A Call to Trust the LORD

11 The LORD has given me a strong warning not to think like everyone else does. He said,

12 "Don't call everything a conspiracy, like they do,
and don't live in dread of what frightens them.
13 Make the LORD of Heaven's Armies holy in
your life.
He is the one you should fear.
He is the one who should make you tremble.
14 He will keep you safe.
But to Israel and Judah
he will be a stone that makes people stumble,
a rock that makes them fall.
And for the people of Jerusalem
he will be a trap and a snare.
15 Many will stumble and fall,
never to rise again.
They will be snared and captured."

16 Preserve the teaching of God;
entrust his instructions to those who
follow me.
17 I will wait for the LORD,
who has turned away from the descendants
of Jacob.
I will put my hope in him.

18 I and the children the LORD has given me serve as signs and warnings to Israel from the LORD of Heaven's Armies who dwells in his Temple on Mount Zion.

19 Someone may say to you, "Let's ask the mediums and those who consult the spirits of the dead. With their whisperings and mutterings, they will tell us what to do." But shouldn't people ask God for guidance? Should the living seek guidance from the dead?

20 Look to God's instructions and teachings! People who contradict his word are completely in the dark.
21 They will go from one place to another, weary and hungry. And because they are hungry, they will rage and curse their king and their God. They will look up to heaven 22 and down at the earth, but wherever they look, there will be trouble and anguish and dark despair. They will be thrown out into the darkness.

Hope in the Messiah

9 1* Nevertheless, that time of darkness and despair will not go on forever. The land of Zebulun and Naphtali will be humbled, but there will be a time in the future when Galilee of the Gentiles, which lies along the road that runs between the Jordan and the sea, will be filled with glory.

8:10 Hebrew *Immanuel!* **9:1** Verse 9:1 is numbered 8:23 in Hebrew text.

KING JAMES VERSION

2 The people that walked in darkness have seen a great light: they that dwell in the land of the shadow of death, upon them hath the light shined.

3 Thou hast multiplied the nation, *and* not increased the joy: they joy before thee according to the joy in harvest, *and* as *men* rejoice when they divide the spoil.

4 For thou hast broken the yoke of his burden, and the staff of his shoulder, the rod of his oppressor, as in the day of Midian.

5 For every battle of the warrior *is* with confused noise, and garments rolled in blood; but *this* shall be with burning *and* fuel of fire.

6 For unto us a child is born, unto us a son is given: and the government shall be upon his shoulder: and his name shall be called Wonderful, Counsellor, The mighty God, The everlasting Father, The Prince of Peace.

7 Of the increase of *his* government and peace *there shall be* no end, upon the throne of David, and upon his kingdom, to order it, and to establish it with judgment and with justice from henceforth even for ever. The zeal of the LORD of hosts will perform this.

8 The Lord sent a word into Jacob, and it hath lighted upon Israel.

9 And all the people shall know, *even* Ephraim and the inhabitant of Samaria, that say in the pride and stoutness of heart,

10 The bricks are fallen down, but we will build with hewn stones: the sycamores are cut down, but we will change *them into* cedars.

11 Therefore the LORD shall set up the adversaries of Rezin against him, and join his enemies together;

12 The Syrians before, and the Philistines behind; and they shall devour Israel with open mouth. For all this his anger is not turned away, but his hand *is* stretched out still.

NEW LIVING TRANSLATION

2* The people who walk in darkness
will see a great light.
For those who live in a land of deep darkness,*
a light will shine.

3 You will enlarge the nation of Israel,
and its people will rejoice.
They will rejoice before you
as people rejoice at the harvest
and like warriors dividing the plunder.

4 For you will break the yoke of their slavery
and lift the heavy burden from their shoulders.
You will break the oppressor's rod,
just as you did when you destroyed the army
of Midian.

5 The boots of the warrior
and the uniforms bloodstained by war
will all be burned.
They will be fuel for the fire.

6 For a child is born to us,
a son is given to us.
The government will rest on his shoulders.
And he will be called:
Wonderful Counselor,* Mighty God,
Everlasting Father, Prince of Peace.

7 His government and its peace
will never end.
He will rule with fairness and justice from
the throne of his ancestor David
for all eternity.
The passionate commitment of the LORD
of Heaven's Armies
will make this happen!

The LORD's Anger against Israel

8 The Lord has spoken out against Jacob;
his judgment has fallen upon Israel.

9 And the people of Israel* and Samaria,
who spoke with such pride and arrogance,
will soon know it.

10 They said, "We will replace the broken bricks
of our ruins with finished stone,
and replant the felled sycamore-fig trees
with cedars."

11 But the LORD will bring Rezin's enemies
against Israel
and stir up all their foes.

12 The Syrians* from the east and the Philistines
from the west
will bare their fangs and devour Israel.
But even then the LORD's anger will not
be satisfied.
His fist is still poised to strike.

9:2a Verses 9:2-21 are numbered 9:1-20 in Hebrew text. **9:2b** Greek version reads *a land where death casts its shadow.* Compare Matt 4:16. **9:6** Or *Wonderful, Counselor.* **9:9** Hebrew *of Ephraim,* referring to the northern kingdom of Israel. **9:12** Hebrew *Arameans.*

KING JAMES VERSION

13 For the people turneth not unto him that smiteth them, neither do they seek the LORD of hosts.

14 Therefore the LORD will cut off from Israel head and tail, branch and rush, in one day.

15 The ancient and honourable, he *is* the head; and the prophet that teacheth lies, he *is* the tail.

16 For the leaders of this people cause *them* to err; and *they that are* led of them *are* destroyed.

17 Therefore the Lord shall have no joy in their young men, neither shall have mercy on their fatherless and widows: for every one *is* an hypocrite and an evildoer, and every mouth speaketh folly. For all this his anger is not turned away, but his hand *is* stretched out still.

18 For wickedness burneth as the fire: it shall devour the briers and thorns, and shall kindle in the thickets of the forest, and they shall mount up *like* the lifting up of smoke.

19 Through the wrath of the LORD of hosts is the land darkened, and the people shall be as the fuel of the fire: no man shall spare his brother.

20 And he shall snatch on the right hand, and be hungry; and he shall eat on the left hand, and they shall not be satisfied: they shall eat every man the flesh of his own arm:

21 Manasseh, Ephraim; and Ephraim, Manasseh: *and* they together *shall be* against Judah. For all this his anger is not turned away, but his hand *is* stretched out still.

10

1 Woe unto them that decree unrighteous decrees, and that write grievousness *which* they have prescribed;

2 To turn aside the needy from judgment, and to take away the right from the poor of my people, that widows may be their prey, and *that* they may rob the fatherless!

3 And what will ye do in the day of visitation, and in the desolation *which* shall come from far? to whom will ye flee for help? and where will ye leave your glory?

4 Without me they shall bow down under the prisoners, and they shall fall under the slain. For all this

NEW LIVING TRANSLATION

13 For after all this punishment, the people will
still not repent.
They will not seek the LORD of
Heaven's Armies.
14 Therefore, in a single day the LORD will destroy
both the head and the tail,
the noble palm branch and the lowly reed.
15 The leaders of Israel are the head,
and the lying prophets are the tail.
16 For the leaders of the people have misled them.
They have led them down the path
of destruction.
17 That is why the Lord takes no pleasure in the
young men
and shows no mercy even to the widows
and orphans.
For they are all wicked hypocrites,
and they all speak foolishness.
But even then the LORD's anger will not
be satisfied.
His fist is still poised to strike.

18 This wickedness is like a brushfire.
It burns not only briers and thorns
but also sets the forests ablaze.
Its burning sends up clouds of smoke.
19 The land will be blackened
by the fury of the LORD of Heaven's Armies.
The people will be fuel for the fire,
and no one will spare even his own brother.
20 They will attack their neighbor on the right
but will still be hungry.
They will devour their neighbor on the left
but will not be satisfied.
In the end they will even eat their own children.*
21 Manasseh will feed on Ephraim,
Ephraim will feed on Manasseh,
and both will devour Judah.
But even then the LORD's anger will not be
satisfied.
His fist is still poised to strike.

10

1 What sorrow awaits the unjust judges
and those who issue unfair laws.
2 They deprive the poor of justice
and deny the rights of the needy among
my people.
They prey on widows
and take advantage of orphans.
3 What will you do when I punish you,
when I send disaster upon you from
a distant land?
To whom will you turn for help?
Where will your treasures be safe?
4 You will stumble along as prisoners
or lie among the dead.

9:20 Or *eat their own arms.*

KING JAMES VERSION

his anger is not turned away, but his hand *is*
stretched out still.

5O Assyrian, the rod of mine anger, and the staff in
their hand is mine indignation.
6I will send him against an hypocritical nation,
and against the people of my wrath will I give him a
charge, to take the spoil, and to take the prey, and to
tread them down like the mire of the streets.
7Howbeit he meaneth not so, neither doth his
heart think so; but *it is* in his heart to destroy and cut
off nations not a few.
8For he saith, *Are* not my princes altogether kings?
9*Is* not Calno as Carchemish? *is* not Hamath as
Arpad? *is* not Samaria as Damascus?
10As my hand hath found the kingdoms of the
idols, and whose graven images did excel them of
Jerusalem and of Samaria;
11Shall I not, as I have done unto Samaria and her
idols, so do to Jerusalem and her idols?
12Wherefore it shall come to pass, *that* when the
Lord hath performed his whole work upon mount
Zion and on Jerusalem, I will punish the fruit of the
stout heart of the king of Assyria, and the glory of his
high looks.
13For he saith, By the strength of my hand I have
done *it*, and by my wisdom; for I am prudent: and I
have removed the bounds of the people, and have
robbed their treasures, and I have put down the inhabitants like a valiant *man:*
14And my hand hath found as a nest the riches of
the people: and as one gathereth eggs *that are* left,
have I gathered all the earth; and there was none that
moved the wing, or opened the mouth, or peeped.
15Shall the ax boast itself against him that heweth
therewith? *or* shall the saw magnify itself against
him that shaketh it? as if the rod should shake *itself*
against them that lift it up, *or* as if the staff should lift
up *itself, as if it were* no wood.
16Therefore shall the Lord, the Lord of hosts, send
among his fat ones leanness; and under his glory he
shall kindle a burning like the burning of a fire.
17And the light of Israel shall be for a fire, and his
Holy One for a flame: and it shall burn and devour
his thorns and his briers in one day;
18And shall consume the glory of his forest, and of

NEW LIVING TRANSLATION

But even then the LORD's anger will
not be satisfied.
His fist is still poised to strike.

Judgment against Assyria

5 "What sorrow awaits Assyria, the rod of my anger.
I use it as a club to express my anger.
6 I am sending Assyria against a godless nation,
against a people with whom I am angry.
Assyria will plunder them,
trampling them like dirt beneath its feet.
7 But the king of Assyria will not understand that
he is my tool;
his mind does not work that way.
His plan is simply to destroy,
to cut down nation after nation.
8 He will say,
'Each of my princes will soon be a king.
9 We destroyed Calno just as we did Carchemish.
Hamath fell before us as Arpad did.
And we destroyed Samaria just as we
did Damascus.
10 Yes, we have finished off many a kingdom
whose gods were greater than those in
Jerusalem and Samaria.
11 So we will defeat Jerusalem and her gods,
just as we destroyed Samaria with hers.'"

12After the Lord has used the king of Assyria to
accomplish his purposes on Mount Zion and in Jerusalem, he will turn against the king of Assyria and
punish him—for he is proud and arrogant. 13He
boasts,

"By my own powerful arm I have done this.
With my own shrewd wisdom I planned it.
I have broken down the defenses of nations
and carried off their treasures.
I have knocked down their kings like a bull.
14 I have robbed their nests of riches
and gathered up kingdoms as a farmer
gathers eggs.
No one can even flap a wing against me
or utter a peep of protest."
15 But can the ax boast greater power than the
person who uses it?
Is the saw greater than the person who saws?
Can a rod strike unless a hand moves it?
Can a wooden cane walk by itself?
16 Therefore, the Lord, the LORD of Heaven's Armies,
will send a plague among Assyria's proud troops,
and a flaming fire will consume its glory.
17 The LORD, the Light of Israel, will be a fire;
the Holy One will be a flame.
He will devour the thorns and briers with fire,
burning up the enemy in a single night.
18 The LORD will consume Assyria's glory
like a fire consumes a forest in a fruitful land;

KING JAMES VERSION

his fruitful field, both soul and body: and they shall
be as when a standardbearer fainteth.
19 And the rest of the trees of his forest shall be few,
that a child may write them.

20 And it shall come to pass in that day, *that* the
remnant of Israel, and such as are escaped of the
house of Jacob, shall no more again stay upon him
that smote them; but shall stay upon the LORD, the
Holy One of Israel, in truth.
21 The remnant shall return, *even* the remnant of
Jacob, unto the mighty God.
22 For though thy people Israel be as the sand of the
sea, *yet* a remnant of them shall return: the consumption decreed shall overflow with righteousness.
23 For the Lord GOD of hosts shall make a consumption, even determined, in the midst of all the
land.
24 Therefore thus saith the Lord GOD of hosts,
O my people that dwellest in Zion, be not afraid of
the Assyrian: he shall smite thee with a rod, and shall
lift up his staff against thee, after the manner of
Egypt.
25 For yet a very little while, and the indignation
shall cease, and mine anger in their destruction.
26 And the LORD of hosts shall stir up a scourge for
him according to the slaughter of Midian at the rock
of Oreb: and *as* his rod *was* upon the sea, so shall he
lift it up after the manner of Egypt.
27 And it shall come to pass in that day, *that* his
burden shall be taken away from off thy shoulder,
and his yoke from off thy neck, and the yoke shall be
destroyed because of the anointing.
28 He is come to Aiath, he is passed to Migron; at
Michmash he hath laid up his carriages:
29 They are gone over the passage: they have taken
up their lodging at Geba; Ramah is afraid; Gibeah of
Saul is fled.
30 Lift up thy voice, O daughter of Gallim: cause it
to be heard unto Laish, O poor Anathoth.
31 Madmenah is removed; the inhabitants of
Gebim gather themselves to flee.

NEW LIVING TRANSLATION

it will waste away like sick people in a plague.
19 Of all that glorious forest, only a few trees
will survive—
so few that a child could count them!

Hope for the LORD's People

20 In that day the remnant left in Israel,
the survivors in the house of Jacob,
will no longer depend on allies
who seek to destroy them.
But they will faithfully trust the LORD,
the Holy One of Israel.
21 A remnant will return;*
yes, the remnant of Jacob will return
to the Mighty God.
22 But though the people of Israel are as numerous
as the sand of the seashore,
only a remnant of them will return.
The LORD has rightly decided to destroy
his people.
23 Yes, the Lord, the LORD of Heaven's Armies,
has already decided to destroy the
entire land.*

24 So this is what the Lord, the LORD of Heaven's Armies, says: "O my people in Zion, do not be afraid of
the Assyrians when they oppress you with rod and
club as the Egyptians did long ago. 25 In a little while
my anger against you will end, and then my anger
will rise up to destroy them." 26 The LORD of Heaven's
Armies will lash them with his whip, as he did when
Gideon triumphed over the Midianites at the rock of
Oreb, or when the LORD's staff was raised to drown
the Egyptian army in the sea.

27 In that day the LORD will end the bondage
of his people.
He will break the yoke of slavery
and lift it from their shoulders.*
28 Look, the Assyrians are now at Aiath.
They are passing through Migron
and are storing their equipment at Micmash.
29 They are crossing the pass
and are camping at Geba.
Fear strikes the town of Ramah.
All the people of Gibeah, the hometown
of Saul,
are running for their lives.
30 Scream in terror,
you people of Gallim!
Shout out a warning to Laishah.
Oh, poor Anathoth!
31 There go the people of Madmenah, all fleeing.
The citizens of Gebim are trying to hide.

10:21 Hebrew *Shear-jashub;* see 7:3; 8:18. **10:22-23** Greek version reads *only a remnant of them will be saved. / For he will carry out his sentence quickly and with finality and righteousness; / for God will carry out his sentence upon all the world with finality.* Compare Rom 9:27-28. **10:27** As in Greek version; Hebrew reads *The yoke will be broken, / for you have grown so fat.*

KING JAMES VERSION

32 As yet shall he remain at Nob that day: he shall
shake his hand *against* the mount of the daughter of
Zion, the hill of Jerusalem.
33 Behold, the Lord, the LORD of hosts, shall lop the
bough with terror: and the high ones of stature *shall
be* hewn down, and the haughty shall be humbled.
34 And he shall cut down the thickets of the forest
with iron, and Lebanon shall fall by a mighty one.

11 1 And there shall come forth a rod out of the
stem of Jesse, and a Branch shall grow out of
his roots:
2 And the spirit of the LORD shall rest upon him, the
spirit of wisdom and understanding, the spirit of
counsel and might, the spirit of knowledge and of
the fear of the LORD;
3 And shall make him of quick understanding in
the fear of the LORD: and he shall not judge after the
sight of his eyes, neither reprove after the hearing of
his ears:
4 But with righteousness shall he judge the poor,
and reprove with equity for the meek of the earth:
and he shall smite the earth with the rod of his
mouth, and with the breath of his lips shall he slay
the wicked.
5 And righteousness shall be the girdle of his loins,
and faithfulness the girdle of his reins.
6 The wolf also shall dwell with the lamb, and the
leopard shall lie down with the kid; and the calf and
the young lion and the fatling together; and a little
child shall lead them.
7 And the cow and the bear shall feed; their young
ones shall lie down together: and the lion shall eat
straw like the ox.
8 And the sucking child shall play on the hole of
the asp, and the weaned child shall put his hand on
the cockatrice' den.
9 They shall not hurt nor destroy in all my holy
mountain: for the earth shall be full of the knowledge of the LORD, as the waters cover the sea.
10 And in that day there shall be a root of Jesse,
which shall stand for an ensign of the people; to it
shall the Gentiles seek: and his rest shall be glorious.
11 And it shall come to pass in that day, *that* the
Lord shall set his hand again the second time to re-

NEW LIVING TRANSLATION

32 The enemy stops at Nob for the rest of that day.
He shakes his fist at beautiful Mount Zion, the
mountain of Jerusalem.

33 But look! The Lord, the LORD of Heaven's Armies,
will chop down the mighty tree of Assyria
with great power!
He will cut down the proud.
That lofty tree will be brought down.
34 He will cut down the forest trees with an ax.
Lebanon will fall to the Mighty One.*

A Branch from David's Line

11 1 Out of the stump of David's family* will
grow a shoot—
yes, a new Branch bearing fruit from
the old root.
2 And the Spirit of the LORD will rest on him—
the Spirit of wisdom and understanding,
the Spirit of counsel and might,
the Spirit of knowledge and the fear
of the LORD.
3 He will delight in obeying the LORD.
He will not judge by appearance
nor make a decision based on hearsay.
4 He will give justice to the poor
and make fair decisions for the exploited.
The earth will shake at the force of his word,
and one breath from his mouth will destroy
the wicked.
5 He will wear righteousness like a belt
and truth like an undergarment.
6 In that day the wolf and the lamb will live together;
the leopard will lie down with the baby goat.
The calf and the yearling will be safe with the lion,
and a little child will lead them all.
7 The cow will graze near the bear.
The cub and the calf will lie down together.
The lion will eat hay like a cow.
8 The baby will play safely near the hole of a cobra.
Yes, a little child will put its hand in a nest of
deadly snakes without harm.
9 Nothing will hurt or destroy in all my
holy mountain,
for as the waters fill the sea,
so the earth will be filled with people
who know the LORD.

10 In that day the heir to David's throne*
will be a banner of salvation to all the world.
The nations will rally to him,
and the land where he lives will be a
glorious place.*
11 In that day the Lord will reach out his hand
a second time

10:34 Or *with an ax / as even the mighty trees of Lebanon fall.* **11:1** Hebrew *the stump of the line of Jesse.* Jesse was King David's father. **11:10a** Hebrew *the root of Jesse.* **11:10b** Greek version reads *In that day the heir to David's throne* [literally *the root of Jesse*] *will come, / and he will rule over the Gentiles. / They will place their hopes on him.* Compare Rom 15:12.

KING JAMES VERSION

cover the remnant of his people, which shall be left, from Assyria, and from Egypt, and from Pathros, and from Cush, and from Elam, and from Shinar, and from Hamath, and from the islands of the sea.

12 And he shall set up an ensign for the nations, and shall assemble the outcasts of Israel, and gather together the dispersed of Judah from the four corners of the earth.

13 The envy also of Ephraim shall depart, and the adversaries of Judah shall be cut off: Ephraim shall not envy Judah, and Judah shall not vex Ephraim.

14 But they shall fly upon the shoulders of the Philistines toward the west; they shall spoil them of the east together: they shall lay their hand upon Edom and Moab; and the children of Ammon shall obey them.

15 And the LORD shall utterly destroy the tongue of the Egyptian sea; and with his mighty wind shall he shake his hand over the river, and shall smite it in the seven streams, and make *men* go over dryshod.

16 And there shall be an highway for the remnant of his people, which shall be left, from Assyria; like as it was to Israel in the day that he came up out of the land of Egypt.

12 1 And in that day thou shalt say, O LORD, I will praise thee: though thou wast angry with me, thine anger is turned away, and thou comfortedst me.

2 Behold, God *is* my salvation; I will trust, and not be afraid: for the LORD JEHOVAH *is* my strength and *my* song; he also is become my salvation.

3 Therefore with joy shall ye draw water out of the wells of salvation.

4 And in that day shall ye say, Praise the LORD, call upon his name, declare his doings among the people, make mention that his name is exalted.

5 Sing unto the LORD; for he hath done excellent things: this *is* known in all the earth.

6 Cry out and shout, thou inhabitant of Zion: for great *is* the Holy One of Israel in the midst of thee.

NEW LIVING TRANSLATION

to bring back the remnant of his people—
those who remain in Assyria and northern
Egypt;
in southern Egypt, Ethiopia,* and Elam;
in Babylonia,* Hamath, and all the distant
coastlands.
12 He will raise a flag among the nations
and assemble the exiles of Israel.
He will gather the scattered people of Judah
from the ends of the earth.
13 Then at last the jealousy between Israel* and
Judah will end.
They will not be rivals anymore.
14 They will join forces to swoop down on Philistia
to the west.
Together they will attack and plunder the
nations to the east.
They will occupy the lands of Edom and Moab,
and Ammon will obey them.
15 The LORD will make a dry path through
the gulf of the Red Sea.*
He will wave his hand over the
Euphrates River,*
sending a mighty wind to divide it into
seven streams
so it can easily be crossed on foot.
16 He will make a highway for the remnant
of his people,
the remnant coming from Assyria,
just as he did for Israel long ago
when they returned from Egypt.

Songs of Praise for Salvation

12 1 In that day you will sing:
"I will praise you, O LORD!
You were angry with me, but not any more.
Now you comfort me.
2 See, God has come to save me.
I will trust in him and not be afraid.
The LORD GOD is my strength and my song;
he has given me victory."

3 With joy you will drink deeply
from the fountain of salvation!
4 In that wonderful day you will sing:
"Thank the LORD! Praise his name!
Tell the nations what he has done.
Let them know how mighty he is!
5 Sing to the LORD, for he has done
wonderful things.
Make known his praise around the world.
6 Let all the people of Jerusalem* shout his
praise with joy!
For great is the Holy One of Israel who
lives among you."

11:11a Hebrew *in Pathros, Cush.* **11:11b** Hebrew *in Shinar.*
11:13 Hebrew *Ephraim,* referring to the northern kingdom of Israel.
11:15a Hebrew *will destroy the tongue of the sea of Egypt.*
11:15b Hebrew *the river.* **12:6** Hebrew *Zion.*

KING JAMES VERSION

13

1 The burden of Babylon, which Isaiah the son
of Amoz did see.
2 Lift ye up a banner upon the high mountain, exalt
the voice unto them, shake the hand, that they may
go into the gates of the nobles.
3 I have commanded my sanctified ones, I have
also called my mighty ones for mine anger, *even*
them that rejoice in my highness.
4 The noise of a multitude in the mountains, like as
of a great people; a tumultuous noise of the kingdoms of nations gathered together: the LORD of hosts
mustereth the host of the battle.
5 They come from a far country, from the end of
heaven, *even* the LORD, and the weapons of his indignation, to destroy the whole land.
6 Howl ye; for the day of the LORD *is* at hand; it shall
come as a destruction from the Almighty.
7 Therefore shall all hands be faint, and every
man's heart shall melt:
8 And they shall be afraid: pangs and sorrows shall
take hold of them; they shall be in pain as a woman
that travaileth: they shall be amazed one at another;
their faces *shall be as* flames.
9 Behold, the day of the LORD cometh, cruel both
with wrath and fierce anger, to lay the land desolate:
and he shall destroy the sinners thereof out of it.
10 For the stars of heaven and the constellations
thereof shall not give their light: the sun shall be
darkened in his going forth, and the moon shall not
cause her light to shine.
11 And I will punish the world for *their* evil, and the
wicked for their iniquity; and I will cause the
arrogancy of the proud to cease, and will lay low
the haughtiness of the terrible.
12 I will make a man more precious than fine gold;
even a man than the golden wedge of Ophir.
13 Therefore I will shake the heavens, and the earth
shall remove out of her place, in the wrath of the
LORD of hosts, and in the day of his fierce anger.
14 And it shall be as the chased roe, and as a sheep

NEW LIVING TRANSLATION

A Message about Babylon

13

Isaiah son of Amoz received this message concerning the destruction of Babylon:

2 "Raise a signal flag on a bare hilltop.
Call up an army against Babylon.
Wave your hand to encourage them
as they march into the palaces of the high and mighty.
3 I, the LORD, have dedicated these soldiers for this task.
Yes, I have called mighty warriors to express my anger,
and they will rejoice when I am exalted."
4 Hear the noise on the mountains!
Listen, as the vast armies march!
It is the noise and shouting of many nations.
The LORD of Heaven's Armies has called this army together.
5 They come from distant countries,
from beyond the farthest horizons.
They are the LORD's weapons to carry out his anger.
With them he will destroy the whole land.

6 Scream in terror, for the day of the LORD has arrived—
the time for the Almighty to destroy.
7 Every arm is paralyzed with fear.
Every heart melts,
8 and people are terrified.
Pangs of anguish grip them,
like those of a woman in labor.
They look helplessly at one another,
their faces aflame with fear.

9 For see, the day of the LORD is coming—
the terrible day of his fury and fierce anger.
The land will be made desolate,
and all the sinners destroyed with it.
10 The heavens will be black above them;
the stars will give no light.
The sun will be dark when it rises,
and the moon will provide no light.
11 "I, the LORD, will punish the world for its evil
and the wicked for their sin.
I will crush the arrogance of the proud
and humble the pride of the mighty.
12 I will make people scarcer than gold—
more rare than the fine gold of Ophir.
13 For I will shake the heavens.
The earth will move from its place
when the LORD of Heaven's Armies displays his wrath
in the day of his fierce anger."

14 Everyone in Babylon will run about like a hunted gazelle,
like sheep without a shepherd.

KING JAMES VERSION

that no man taketh up: they shall every man turn to
his own people, and flee every one into his own land.
15 Every one that is found shall be thrust through;
and every one that is joined *unto them* shall fall by
the sword.
16 Their children also shall be dashed to pieces before their eyes; their houses shall be spoiled, and
their wives ravished.
17 Behold, I will stir up the Medes against them,
which shall not regard silver; and *as for* gold, they
shall not delight in it.
18 *Their* bows also shall dash the young men to
pieces; and they shall have no pity on the fruit of the
womb; their eye shall not spare children.
19 And Babylon, the glory of kingdoms, the beauty
of the Chaldees' excellency, shall be as when God
overthrew Sodom and Gomorrah.
20 It shall never be inhabited, neither shall it be
dwelt in from generation to generation: neither shall
the Arabian pitch tent there; neither shall the shepherds make their fold there.
21 But wild beasts of the desert shall lie there; and
their houses shall be full of doleful creatures; and
owls shall dwell there, and satyrs shall dance there.
22 And the wild beasts of the islands shall cry in
their desolate houses, and dragons in *their* pleasant
palaces: and her time *is* near to come, and her days
shall not be prolonged.

14 1 For the LORD will have mercy on Jacob, and
will yet choose Israel, and set them in their
own land: and the strangers shall be joined with
them, and they shall cleave to the house of Jacob.
2 And the people shall take them, and bring them
to their place: and the house of Israel shall possess
them in the land of the LORD for servants and handmaids: and they shall take them captives, whose
captives they were; and they shall rule over their
oppressors.
3 And it shall come to pass in the day that the LORD
shall give thee rest from thy sorrow, and from thy
fear, and from the hard bondage wherein thou wast
made to serve,
4 That thou shalt take up this proverb against the
king of Babylon, and say, How hath the oppressor
ceased! the golden city ceased!
5 The LORD hath broken the staff of the wicked,
and the sceptre of the rulers.

NEW LIVING TRANSLATION

They will try to find their own people
and flee to their own land.
15 Anyone who is captured will be cut down—
run through with a sword.
16 Their little children will be dashed to death
before their eyes.
Their homes will be sacked, and their wives
will be raped.
17 "Look, I will stir up the Medes against Babylon.
They cannot be tempted by silver
or bribed with gold.
18 The attacking armies will shoot down the young
men with arrows.
They will have no mercy on helpless babies
and will show no compassion for children."
19 Babylon, the most glorious of kingdoms,
the flower of Chaldean pride,
will be devastated like Sodom and Gomorrah
when God destroyed them.
20 Babylon will never be inhabited again.
It will remain empty for generation
after generation.
Nomads will refuse to camp there,
and shepherds will not bed down their sheep.
21 Desert animals will move into the ruined city,
and the houses will be haunted by
howling creatures.
Owls will live among the ruins,
and wild goats will go there to dance.
22 Hyenas will howl in its fortresses,
and jackals will make dens in its
luxurious palaces.
Babylon's days are numbered;
its time of destruction will soon arrive.

A Taunt for Babylon's King

14 But the LORD will have mercy on the descendants of Jacob. He will choose Israel as his
special people once again. He will bring them back to
settle once again in their own land. And people from
many different nations will come and join them there
and unite with the people of Israel.* 2 The nations of
the world will help the LORD's people to return, and
those who come to live in their land will serve them.
Those who captured Israel will themselves be captured, and Israel will rule over its enemies.
3 In that wonderful day when the LORD gives his people rest from sorrow and fear, from slavery and chains,
4 you will taunt the king of Babylon. You will say,

"The mighty man has been destroyed.
Yes, your insolence* is ended.
5 For the LORD has crushed your wicked power
and broken your evil rule.

14:1 Hebrew *the house of Jacob.* The names "Jacob" and "Israel" are often interchanged throughout the Old Testament, referring sometimes to the individual patriarch and sometimes to the nation. **14:4** As in Dead Sea Scrolls; the meaning of the Masoretic Text is uncertain.

KING JAMES VERSION

6 He who smote the people in wrath with a continual stroke, he that ruled the nations in anger, is persecuted, *and* none hindereth.
7 The whole earth is at rest, *and* is quiet: they break
forth into singing.
8 Yea, the fir trees rejoice at thee, *and* the cedars of
Lebanon, *saying,* Since thou art laid down, no feller
is come up against us.
9 Hell from beneath is moved for thee to meet *thee*
at thy coming: it stirreth up the dead for thee, *even* all
the chief ones of the earth; it hath raised up from
their thrones all the kings of the nations.
10 All they shall speak and say unto thee, Art thou
also become weak as we? art thou become like
unto us?
11 Thy pomp is brought down to the grave, *and* the
noise of thy viols: the worm is spread under thee, and
the worms cover thee.
12 How art thou fallen from heaven, O Lucifer, son
of the morning! *how* art thou cut down to the
ground, which didst weaken the nations!
13 For thou hast said in thine heart, I will ascend
into heaven, I will exalt my throne above the stars of
God: I will sit also upon the mount of the congregation, in the sides of the north:
14 I will ascend above the heights of the clouds; I
will be like the most High.
15 Yet thou shalt be brought down to hell, to the
sides of the pit.
16 They that see thee shall narrowly look upon
thee, *and* consider thee, *saying, Is* this the man that
made the earth to tremble, that did shake kingdoms;
17 *That* made the world as a wilderness, and destroyed the cities thereof; *that* opened not the house
of his prisoners?
18 All the kings of the nations, *even* all of them, lie
in glory, every one in his own house.
19 But thou art cast out of thy grave like an abominable branch, *and as* the raiment of those that are
slain, thrust through with a sword, that go down to
the stones of the pit; as a carcase trodden under feet.
20 Thou shalt not be joined with them in burial,
because thou hast destroyed thy land, *and* slain thy

NEW LIVING TRANSLATION

6 You struck the people with endless blows of rage
and held the nations in your angry grip
with unrelenting tyranny.
7 But finally the earth is at rest and quiet.
Now it can sing again!
8 Even the trees of the forest—
the cypress trees and the cedars of Lebanon—
sing out this joyous song:
'Since you have been cut down,
no one will come now to cut us down!'

9 "In the place of the dead* there is excitement
over your arrival.
The spirits of world leaders and mighty kings
long dead
stand up to see you.
10 With one voice they all cry out,
'Now you are as weak as we are!
11 Your might and power were buried with you.*
The sound of the harp in your palace
has ceased.
Now maggots are your sheet,
and worms your blanket.'
12 "How you are fallen from heaven,
O shining star, son of the morning!
You have been thrown down to the earth,
you who destroyed the nations of the world.
13 For you said to yourself,
'I will ascend to heaven and set my throne
above God's stars.
I will preside on the mountain of the gods
far away in the north.*
14 I will climb to the highest heavens
and be like the Most High.'
15 Instead, you will be brought down to the place
of the dead,
down to its lowest depths.
16 Everyone there will stare at you and ask,
'Can this be the one who shook the earth
and made the kingdoms of the world tremble?
17 Is this the one who destroyed the world
and made it into a wasteland?
Is this the king who demolished the world's
greatest cities
and had no mercy on his prisoners?'

18 "The kings of the nations lie in stately glory,
each in his own tomb,
19 but you will be thrown out of your grave
like a worthless branch.
Like a corpse trampled underfoot,
you will be dumped into a mass grave
with those killed in battle.
You will descend to the pit.
20 You will not be given a proper burial,
for you have destroyed your nation
and slaughtered your people.

14:9 Hebrew *Sheol;* also in 14:15. **14:11** Hebrew *were brought down to Sheol.* **14:13** Or *on the heights of Zaphon.*

KING JAMES VERSION

people: the seed of evildoers shall never be renowned.

21 Prepare slaughter for his children for the iniquity of their fathers; that they do not rise, nor possess the land, nor fill the face of the world with cities.

22 For I will rise up against them, saith the LORD of hosts, and cut off from Babylon the name, and remnant, and son, and nephew, saith the LORD.

23 I will also make it a possession for the bittern, and pools of water: and I will sweep it with the besom of destruction, saith the LORD of hosts.

24 The LORD of hosts hath sworn, saying, Surely as I have thought, so shall it come to pass; and as I have purposed, *so* shall it stand:

25 That I will break the Assyrian in my land, and upon my mountains tread him under foot: then shall his yoke depart from off them, and his burden depart from off their shoulders.

26 This *is* the purpose that is purposed upon the whole earth: and this *is* the hand that is stretched out upon all the nations.

27 For the LORD of hosts hath purposed, and who shall disannul *it?* and his hand *is* stretched out, and who shall turn it back?

28 In the year that king Ahaz died was this burden.

29 Rejoice not thou, whole Palestina, because the rod of him that smote thee is broken: for out of the serpent's root shall come forth a cockatrice, and his fruit *shall be* a fiery flying serpent.

30 And the firstborn of the poor shall feed, and the needy shall lie down in safety: and I will kill thy root with famine, and he shall slay thy remnant.

31 Howl, O gate; cry, O city; thou, whole Palestina, *art* dissolved: for there shall come from the north a smoke, and none *shall be* alone in his appointed times.

32 What shall *one* then answer the messengers of the nation? That the LORD hath founded Zion, and the poor of his people shall trust in it.

NEW LIVING TRANSLATION

The descendants of such an evil person
will never again receive honor.
21 Kill this man's children!
Let them die because of their father's sins!
They must not rise and conquer the earth,
filling the world with their cities."

22 This is what the LORD of Heaven's Armies says:
"I, myself, have risen against Babylon!
I will destroy its children and its children's children,"
says the LORD.
23 "I will make Babylon a desolate place of owls,
filled with swamps and marshes.
I will sweep the land with the broom of destruction.
I, the LORD of Heaven's Armies, have spoken!"

A Message about Assyria

24 The LORD of Heaven's Armies has sworn this oath:

"It will all happen as I have planned.
It will be as I have decided.
25 I will break the Assyrians when they are in Israel;
I will trample them on my mountains.
My people will no longer be their slaves
nor bow down under their heavy loads.
26 I have a plan for the whole earth,
a hand of judgment upon all the nations.
27 The LORD of Heaven's Armies has spoken—
who can change his plans?
When his hand is raised,
who can stop him?"

A Message about Philistia

28 This message came to me the year King Ahaz died:*

29 Do not rejoice, you Philistines,
that the rod that struck you is broken—
that the king who attacked you is dead.
For from that snake a more poisonous snake will be born,
a fiery serpent to destroy you!
30 I will feed the poor in my pasture;
the needy will lie down in peace.
But as for you, I will wipe you out with famine
and destroy the few who remain.
31 Wail at the gates! Weep in the cities!
Melt with fear, you Philistines!
A powerful army comes like smoke from the north.
Each soldier rushes forward eager to fight.

32 What should we tell the Philistine messengers?
Tell them,

"The LORD has built Jerusalem*;
its walls will give refuge to his
oppressed people."

14:28 King Ahaz died in 715 B.C. **14:32** Hebrew *Zion.*

KING JAMES VERSION

15 1 The burden of Moab. Because in the night Ar of Moab is laid waste, *and* brought to silence; because in the night Kir of Moab is laid waste, *and* brought to silence;

2 He is gone up to Bajith, and to Dibon, the high places, to weep: Moab shall howl over Nebo, and over Medeba: on all their heads *shall be* baldness, *and* every beard cut off.

3 In their streets they shall gird themselves with sackcloth: on the tops of their houses, and in their streets, every one shall howl, weeping abundantly.

4 And Heshbon shall cry, and Elealeh: their voice shall be heard *even* unto Jahaz: therefore the armed soldiers of Moab shall cry out; his life shall be grievous unto him.

5 My heart shall cry out for Moab; his fugitives *shall flee* unto Zoar, an heifer of three years old: for by the mounting up of Luhith with weeping shall they go it up; for in the way of Horonaim they shall raise up a cry of destruction.

6 For the waters of Nimrim shall be desolate: for the hay is withered away, the grass faileth, there is no green thing.

7 Therefore the abundance they have gotten, and that which they have laid up, shall they carry away to the brook of the willows.

8 For the cry is gone round about the borders of Moab; the howling thereof unto Eglaim, and the howling thereof unto Beer-elim.

9 For the waters of Dimon shall be full of blood: for I will bring more upon Dimon, lions upon him that escapeth of Moab, and upon the remnant of the land.

16 1 Send ye the lamb to the ruler of the land from Sela to the wilderness, unto the mount of the daughter of Zion.

2 For it shall be, *that,* as a wandering bird cast out of the nest, *so* the daughters of Moab shall be at the fords of Arnon.

3 Take counsel, execute judgment; make thy shadow as the night in the midst of the noonday; hide the outcasts; bewray not him that wandereth.

4 Let mine outcasts dwell with thee, Moab; be thou a covert to them from the face of the spoiler: for the extortioner is at an end, the spoiler ceaseth, the oppressors are consumed out of the land.

NEW LIVING TRANSLATION

A Message about Moab

15 This message came to me concerning Moab:
In one night the town of Ar will be leveled,
and the city of Kir will be destroyed.
2 Your people will go to their temple in Dibon to mourn.
They will go to their sacred shrines to weep.
They will wail for the fate of Nebo and Medeba,
shaving their heads in sorrow and cutting off their beards.
3 They will wear burlap as they wander the streets.
From every home and public square will come the sound of wailing.
4 The people of Heshbon and Elealeh will cry out;
their voices will be heard as far away as Jahaz!
The bravest warriors of Moab will cry out in utter terror.
They will be helpless with fear.

5 My heart weeps for Moab.
Its people flee to Zoar and Eglath-shelishiyah.
Weeping, they climb the road to Luhith.
Their cries of distress can be heard all along the road to Horonaim.
6 Even the waters of Nimrim are dried up!
The grassy banks are scorched.
The tender plants are gone;
nothing green remains.
7 The people grab their possessions
and carry them across the Ravine of Willows.
8 A cry of distress echoes through the land of Moab
from one end to the other—
from Eglaim to Beer-elim.
9 The stream near Dibon* runs red with blood,
but I am still not finished with Dibon!
Lions will hunt down the survivors—
both those who try to escape
and those who remain behind.

16 1 Send lambs from Sela as tribute
to the ruler of the land.
Send them through the desert
to the mountain of beautiful Zion.
2 The women of Moab are left like homeless birds
at the shallow crossings of the Arnon River.
3 "Help us," they cry.
"Defend us against our enemies.
Protect us from their relentless attack.
Do not betray us now that we have escaped.
4 Let our refugees stay among you.
Hide them from our enemies until the terror is past."

When oppression and destruction have ended
and enemy raiders have disappeared,

15:9 As in Dead Sea Scrolls, some Greek manuscripts, and Latin Vulgate; Masoretic Text reads *Dimon;* also in 15:9b.

KING JAMES VERSION

5 And in mercy shall the throne be established:
and he shall sit upon it in truth in the tabernacle of
David, judging, and seeking judgment, and hasting
righteousness.
6 We have heard of the pride of Moab; *he is* very
proud: *even* of his haughtiness, and his pride, and his
wrath: *but* his lies *shall* not *be* so.
7 Therefore shall Moab howl for Moab, every one
shall howl: for the foundations of Kir-hareseth shall
ye mourn; surely *they are* stricken.
8 For the fields of Heshbon languish, *and* the vine
of Sibmah: the lords of the heathen have broken
down the principal plants thereof, they are come
even unto Jazer, they wandered *through* the wilderness: her branches are stretched out, they are gone
over the sea.
9 Therefore I will bewail with the weeping of Jazer
the vine of Sibmah: I will water thee with my tears,
O Heshbon, and Elealeh: for the shouting for thy
summer fruits and for thy harvest is fallen.
10 And gladness is taken away, and joy out of the
plentiful field; and in the vineyards there shall be no
singing, neither shall there be shouting: the treaders
shall tread out no wine in *their* presses; I have made
their vintage shouting to cease.
11 Wherefore my bowels shall sound like an harp
for Moab, and mine inward parts for Kir-haresh.
12 And it shall come to pass, when it is seen that
Moab is weary on the high place, that he shall come
to his sanctuary to pray; but he shall not prevail.
13 This *is* the word that the LORD hath spoken concerning Moab since that time.
14 But now the LORD hath spoken, saying, Within
three years, as the years of an hireling, and the glory of
Moab shall be contemned, with all that great multitude; and the remnant *shall be* very small *and* feeble.

17 1 The burden of Damascus. Behold, Damascus
is taken away from *being* a city, and it shall be
a ruinous heap.
2 The cities of Aroer *are* forsaken: they shall be for
flocks, which shall lie down, and none shall make
them afraid.

NEW LIVING TRANSLATION

5 then God will establish one of David's
descendants as king.
He will rule with mercy and truth.
He will always do what is just
and be eager to do what is right.
6 We have heard about proud Moab—
about its pride and arrogance and rage.
But all that boasting has disappeared.
7 The entire land of Moab weeps.
Yes, everyone in Moab mourns
for the cakes of raisins from Kir-hareseth.
They are all gone now.
8 The farms of Heshbon are abandoned;
the vineyards at Sibmah are deserted.
The rulers of the nations have broken
down Moab—
that beautiful grapevine.
Its tendrils spread north as far as the town of Jazer
and trailed eastward into the wilderness.
Its shoots reached so far west
that they crossed over the Dead Sea.*
9 So now I weep for Jazer and the vineyards
of Sibmah;
my tears will flow for Heshbon and Elealeh.
There are no more shouts of joy
over your summer fruits and harvest.
10 Gone now is the gladness,
gone the joy of harvest.
There will be no singing in the vineyards,
no more happy shouts,
no treading of grapes in the winepresses.
I have ended all their harvest joys.
11 My heart's cry for Moab is like a lament on a harp.
I am filled with anguish for Kir-hareseth.*
12 The people of Moab will worship at their
pagan shrines,
but it will do them no good.
They will cry to the gods in their temples,
but no one will be able to save them.

13 The LORD has already said these things about
Moab in the past. 14 But now the LORD says, "Within
three years, counting each day,* the glory of Moab
will be ended. From its great population, only a few
of its people will be left alive."

A Message about Damascus and Israel

17 This message came to me concerning Damascus:

"Look, the city of Damascus will disappear!
It will become a heap of ruins.
2 The towns of Aroer will be deserted.
Flocks will graze in the streets and lie down
undisturbed,
with no one to chase them away.

16:8 Hebrew *the sea.* **16:11** Hebrew *Kir-heres,* a variant spelling of Kir-hareseth. **16:14** Hebrew *Within three years, as a servant bound by contract would count them.*

KING JAMES VERSION

3 The fortress also shall cease from Ephraim, and the kingdom from Damascus, and the remnant of Syria: they shall be as the glory of the children of Israel, saith the LORD of hosts.

4 And in that day it shall come to pass, *that* the glory of Jacob shall be made thin, and the fatness of his flesh shall wax lean.

5 And it shall be as when the harvestman gathereth the corn, and reapeth the ears with his arm; and it shall be as he that gathereth ears in the valley of Rephaim.

6 Yet gleaning grapes shall be left in it, as the shaking of an olive tree, two *or* three berries in the top of the uppermost bough, four *or* five in the outmost fruitful branches thereof, saith the LORD God of Israel.

7 At that day shall a man look to his Maker, and his eyes shall have respect to the Holy One of Israel.

8 And he shall not look to the altars, the work of his hands, neither shall respect *that* which his fingers have made, either the groves, or the images.

9 In that day shall his strong cities be as a forsaken bough, and an uppermost branch, which they left because of the children of Israel: and there shall be desolation.

10 Because thou hast forgotten the God of thy salvation, and hast not been mindful of the rock of thy strength, therefore shalt thou plant pleasant plants, and shalt set it with strange slips:

11 In the day shalt thou make thy plant to grow, and in the morning shalt thou make thy seed to flourish: *but* the harvest *shall be* a heap in the day of grief and of desperate sorrow.

12 Woe to the multitude of many people, *which* make a noise like the noise of the seas; and to the rushing of nations, *that* make a rushing like the rushing of mighty waters!

13 The nations shall rush like the rushing of many waters: but *God* shall rebuke them, and they shall flee far off, and shall be chased as the chaff of the mountains before the wind, and like a rolling thing before the whirlwind.

14 And behold at eveningtide trouble; *and* before the morning he *is* not. This *is* the portion of them that spoil us, and the lot of them that rob us.

NEW LIVING TRANSLATION

3 The fortified towns of Israel* will also be
destroyed,
and the royal power of Damascus will end.
All that remains of Syria*
will share the fate of Israel's departed glory,"
declares the LORD of Heaven's Armies.

4 "In that day Israel's* glory will grow dim;
its robust body will waste away.
5 The whole land will look like a grainfield
after the harvesters have gathered the grain.
It will be desolate,
like the fields in the valley of Rephaim
after the harvest.
6 Only a few of its people will be left,
like stray olives left on a tree after the harvest.
Only two or three remain in the highest branches,
four or five scattered here and there on
the limbs,"
declares the LORD, the God of Israel.

7 Then at last the people will look to their Creator
and turn their eyes to the Holy One of Israel.
8 They will no longer look to their idols for help
or worship what their own hands have made.
They will never again bow down to their
Asherah poles
or worship at the pagan shrines they have built.
9 Their largest cities will be like a deserted forest,
like the land the Hivites and Amorites
abandoned*
when the Israelites came here so long ago.
It will be utterly desolate.
10 Why? Because you have turned from the God
who can save you.
You have forgotten the Rock who can hide you.
So you may plant the finest grapevines
and import the most expensive seedlings.
11 They may sprout on the day you set them out;
yes, they may blossom on the very morning
you plant them,
but you will never pick any grapes from them.
Your only harvest will be a load of grief and
unrelieved pain.

12 Listen! The armies of many nations
roar like the roaring of the sea.
Hear the thunder of the mighty forces
as they rush forward like thundering waves.
13 But though they thunder like breakers on a beach,
God will silence them, and they will run away.
They will flee like chaff scattered by the wind,
like a tumbleweed whirling before a storm.
14 In the evening Israel waits in terror,
but by dawn its enemies are dead.
This is the just reward of those who plunder us,
a fitting end for those who destroy us.

17:3a Hebrew *of Ephraim,* referring to the northern kingdom of Israel. **17:3b** Hebrew *Aram.* **17:4** Hebrew *Jacob's.* See note on 14:1. **17:9** As in Greek version; Hebrew reads *like places of the wood and the highest bough.*

KING JAMES VERSION

18

1 Woe to the land shadowing with wings, which *is* beyond the rivers of Ethiopia:

2 That sendeth ambassadors by the sea, even in vessels of bulrushes upon the waters, *saying,* Go, ye swift messengers, to a nation scattered and peeled, to a people terrible from their beginning hitherto; a nation meted out and trodden down, whose land the rivers have spoiled!

3 All ye inhabitants of the world, and dwellers on the earth, see ye, when he lifteth up an ensign on the mountains; and when he bloweth a trumpet, hear ye.

4 For so the LORD said unto me, I will take my rest, and I will consider in my dwelling place like a clear heat upon herbs, *and* like a cloud of dew in the heat of harvest.

5 For afore the harvest, when the bud is perfect, and the sour grape is ripening in the flower, he shall both cut off the sprigs with pruning hooks, and take away *and* cut down the branches.

6 They shall be left together unto the fowls of the mountains, and to the beasts of the earth: and the fowls shall summer upon them, and all the beasts of the earth shall winter upon them.

7 In that time shall the present be brought unto the LORD of hosts of a people scattered and peeled, and from a people terrible from their beginning hitherto; a nation meted out and trodden under foot, whose land the rivers have spoiled, to the place of the name of the LORD of hosts, the mount Zion.

19

1 The burden of Egypt. Behold, the LORD rideth upon a swift cloud, and shall come into Egypt: and the idols of Egypt shall be moved at his presence, and the heart of Egypt shall melt in the midst of it.

2 And I will set the Egyptians against the Egyptians: and they shall fight every one against his brother, and every one against his neighbour; city against city, *and* kingdom against kingdom.

3 And the spirit of Egypt shall fail in the midst thereof; and I will destroy the counsel thereof: and

NEW LIVING TRANSLATION

A Message about Ethiopia

18

1 Listen, Ethiopia*—land of fluttering sails*
that lies at the headwaters of the Nile,
2 that sends ambassadors
in swift boats down the river.
Go, swift messengers!
Take a message to a tall, smooth-skinned people,
who are feared far and wide
for their conquests and destruction,
and whose land is divided by rivers.

3 All you people of the world,
everyone who lives on the earth—
when I raise my battle flag on the mountain, look!
When I blow the ram's horn, listen!
4 For the LORD has told me this:
"I will watch quietly from my dwelling place—
as quietly as the heat rises on a summer day,
or as the morning dew forms during
the harvest."
5 Even before you begin your attack,
while your plans are ripening like grapes,
the LORD will cut off your new growth with
pruning shears.
He will snip off and discard your
spreading branches.
6 Your mighty army will be left dead in the fields
for the mountain vultures and wild animals.
The vultures will tear at the corpses all summer.
The wild animals will gnaw at the bones
all winter.

7 At that time the LORD of Heaven's Armies
will receive gifts
from this land divided by rivers,
from this tall, smooth-skinned people,
who are feared far and wide for their
conquests and destruction.
They will bring the gifts to Jerusalem,*
where the LORD of Heaven's Armies dwells.

A Message about Egypt

19

1 This message came to me concerning Egypt:

Look! The LORD is advancing against Egypt,
riding on a swift cloud.
The idols of Egypt tremble.
The hearts of the Egyptians melt with fear.

2 "I will make Egyptian fight against Egyptian—
brother against brother,
neighbor against neighbor,
city against city,
province against province.
3 The Egyptians will lose heart,
and I will confuse their plans.
They will plead with their idols for wisdom

18:1a Hebrew *Cush.* **18:1b** Or *land of many locusts;* Hebrew reads *land of whirring wings.* **18:7** Hebrew *to Mount Zion.*

KING JAMES VERSION

they shall seek to the idols, and to the charmers, and to them that have familiar spirits, and to the wizards.

4 And the Egyptians will I give over into the hand of a cruel lord; and a fierce king shall rule over them, saith the Lord, the LORD of hosts.

5 And the waters shall fail from the sea, and the river shall be wasted and dried up.

6 And they shall turn the rivers far away; *and* the brooks of defence shall be emptied and dried up: the reeds and flags shall wither.

7 The paper reeds by the brooks, by the mouth of the brooks, and every thing sown by the brooks, shall wither, be driven away, and be no *more*.

8 The fishers also shall mourn, and all they that cast angle into the brooks shall lament, and they that spread nets upon the waters shall languish.

9 Moreover they that work in fine flax, and they that weave networks, shall be confounded.

10 And they shall be broken in the purposes thereof, all that make sluices *and* ponds for fish.

11 Surely the princes of Zoan *are* fools, the counsel of the wise counsellors of Pharaoh is become brutish: how say ye unto Pharaoh, I *am* the son of the wise, the son of ancient kings?

12 Where *are* they? where *are* thy wise *men?* and let them tell thee now, and let them know what the LORD of hosts hath purposed upon Egypt.

13 The princes of Zoan are become fools, the princes of Noph are deceived; they have also seduced Egypt, *even they that are* the stay of the tribes thereof.

14 The LORD hath mingled a perverse spirit in the midst thereof: and they have caused Egypt to err in every work thereof, as a drunken *man* staggereth in his vomit.

15 Neither shall there be *any* work for Egypt, which the head or tail, branch or rush, may do.

16 In that day shall Egypt be like unto women: and it shall be afraid and fear because of the shaking of the hand of the LORD of hosts, which he shaketh over it.

17 And the land of Judah shall be a terror unto Egypt, every one that maketh mention thereof shall be afraid in himself, because of the counsel of the LORD of hosts, which he hath determined against it.

18 In that day shall five cities in the land of Egypt speak the language of Canaan, and swear to the LORD of hosts; one shall be called, The city of destruction.

NEW LIVING TRANSLATION

and call on spirits, mediums, and those who
consult the spirits of the dead.
4 I will hand Egypt over
to a hard, cruel master.
A fierce king will rule them,"
says the Lord, the LORD of Heaven's Armies.

5 The waters of the Nile will fail to rise and
flood the fields.
The riverbed will be parched and dry.
6 The canals of the Nile will dry up,
and the streams of Egypt will stink
with rotting reeds and rushes.
7 All the greenery along the riverbank
and all the crops along the river
will dry up and blow away.
8 The fishermen will lament for lack of work.
Those who cast hooks into the Nile will groan,
and those who use nets will lose heart.
9 There will be no flax for the harvesters,
no thread for the weavers.
10 They will be in despair,
and all the workers will be sick at heart.

11 What fools are the officials of Zoan!
Their best counsel to the king of Egypt is
stupid and wrong.
Will they still boast to Pharaoh of their wisdom?
Will they dare brag about all their wise
ancestors?
12 Where are your wise counselors, Pharaoh?
Let them tell you what God plans,
what the LORD of Heaven's Armies is going
to do to Egypt.
13 The officials of Zoan are fools,
and the officials of Memphis* are deluded.
The leaders of the people
have led Egypt astray.
14 The LORD has sent a spirit of foolishness
on them,
so all their suggestions are wrong.
They cause Egypt to stagger
like a drunk in his vomit.
15 There is nothing Egypt can do.
All are helpless—
the head and the tail,
the noble palm branch and the lowly reed.

16 In that day the Egyptians will be as weak as
women. They will cower in fear beneath the upraised
fist of the LORD of Heaven's Armies. 17 Just to speak
the name of Israel will terrorize them, for the LORD
of Heaven's Armies has laid out his plans against
them.

18 In that day five of Egypt's cities will follow the
LORD of Heaven's Armies. They will even begin to
speak Hebrew, the language of Canaan. One of these
cities will be Heliopolis, the City of the Sun.*

19:13 Hebrew *Noph.* **19:18** Or *will be the City of Destruction.*

KING JAMES VERSION

19 In that day shall there be an altar to the LORD in the midst of the land of Egypt, and a pillar at the border thereof to the LORD.

20 And it shall be for a sign and for a witness unto the LORD of hosts in the land of Egypt: for they shall cry unto the LORD because of the oppressors, and he shall send them a saviour, and a great one, and he shall deliver them.

21 And the LORD shall be known to Egypt, and the Egyptians shall know the LORD in that day, and shall do sacrifice and oblation; yea, they shall vow a vow unto the LORD, and perform *it*.

22 And the LORD shall smite Egypt: he shall smite and heal *it*: and they shall return *even* to the LORD, and he shall be intreated of them, and shall heal them.

23 In that day shall there be a highway out of Egypt to Assyria, and the Assyrian shall come into Egypt, and the Egyptian into Assyria, and the Egyptians shall serve with the Assyrians.

24 In that day shall Israel be the third with Egypt and with Assyria, *even* a blessing in the midst of the land:

25 Whom the LORD of hosts shall bless, saying, Blessed *be* Egypt my people, and Assyria the work of my hands, and Israel mine inheritance.

20 1 In the year that Tartan came unto Ashdod (when Sargon the king of Assyria sent him,) and fought against Ashdod, and took it;

2 At the same time spake the LORD by Isaiah the son of Amoz, saying, Go and loose the sackcloth from off thy loins, and put off thy shoe from thy foot. And he did so, walking naked and barefoot.

3 And the LORD said, Like as my servant Isaiah hath walked naked and barefoot three years *for* a sign and wonder upon Egypt and upon Ethiopia;

4 So shall the king of Assyria lead away the Egyptians prisoners, and the Ethiopians captives, young and old, naked and barefoot, even with *their* buttocks uncovered, to the shame of Egypt.

5 And they shall be afraid and ashamed of Ethiopia their expectation, and of Egypt their glory.

6 And the inhabitant of this isle shall say in that day, Behold, such *is* our expectation, whither we flee for help to be delivered from the king of Assyria: and how shall we escape?

21 1 The burden of the desert of the sea. As whirlwinds in the south pass through; *so* it cometh from the desert, from a terrible land.

2 A grievous vision is declared unto me; the treacherous dealer dealeth treacherously, and the spoiler

NEW LIVING TRANSLATION

19 In that day there will be an altar to the LORD in the heart of Egypt, and there will be a monument to the LORD at its border. 20 It will be a sign and a witness that the LORD of Heaven's Armies is worshiped in the land of Egypt. When the people cry to the LORD for help against those who oppress them, he will send them a savior who will rescue them. 21 The LORD will make himself known to the Egyptians. Yes, they will know the LORD and will give their sacrifices and offerings to him. They will make a vow to the LORD and will keep it. 22 The LORD will strike Egypt, and then he will bring healing. For the Egyptians will turn to the LORD, and he will listen to their pleas and heal them.

23 In that day Egypt and Assyria will be connected by a highway. The Egyptians and Assyrians will move freely between their lands, and they will both worship God. 24 And Israel will be their ally. The three will be together, and Israel will be a blessing to them. 25 For the LORD of Heaven's Armies will say, "Blessed be Egypt, my people. Blessed be Assyria, the land I have made. Blessed be Israel, my special possession!"

A Message about Egypt and Ethiopia

20 In the year when King Sargon of Assyria sent his commander in chief to capture the Philistine city of Ashdod,* 2 the LORD told Isaiah son of Amoz, "Take off the burlap you have been wearing, and remove your sandals." Isaiah did as he was told and walked around naked and barefoot.

3 Then the LORD said, "My servant Isaiah has been walking around naked and barefoot for the last three years. This is a sign—a symbol of the terrible troubles I will bring upon Egypt and Ethiopia.* 4 For the king of Assyria will take away the Egyptians and Ethiopians* as prisoners. He will make them walk naked and barefoot, both young and old, their buttocks bared, to the shame of Egypt. 5 Then the Philistines will be thrown into panic, for they counted on the power of Ethiopia and boasted of their allies in Egypt! 6 They will say, 'If this can happen to Egypt, what chance do we have? We were counting on Egypt to protect us from the king of Assyria.'"

A Message about Babylon

21 This message came to me concerning Babylon—the desert by the sea*:

Disaster is roaring down on you from the desert,
  like a whirlwind sweeping in from the Negev.
2 I see a terrifying vision:
  I see the betrayer betraying,
  the destroyer destroying.
Go ahead, you Elamites and Medes,
  attack and lay siege.

20:1 Ashdod was captured by Assyria in 711 B.C. **20:3** Hebrew *Cush;* also in 20:5. **20:4** Hebrew *Cushites.* **21:1** Hebrew *concerning the desert by the sea.*

KING JAMES VERSION

spoileth. Go up, O Elam: besiege, O Media; all the
sighing thereof have I made to cease.
3 Therefore are my loins filled with pain: pangs
have taken hold upon me, as the pangs of a woman
that travaileth: I was bowed down at the hearing *of it;*
I was dismayed at the seeing *of it.*
4 My heart panted, fearfulness affrighted me: the
night of my pleasure hath he turned into fear
unto me.
5 Prepare the table, watch in the watchtower, eat,
drink: arise, ye princes, *and* anoint the shield.
6 For thus hath the Lord said unto me, Go, set a
watchman, let him declare what he seeth.
7 And he saw a chariot *with* a couple of horsemen,
a chariot of asses, *and* a chariot of camels; and he
hearkened diligently with much heed:
8 And he cried, A lion: My lord, I stand continually
upon the watchtower in the daytime, and I am set in
my ward whole nights:
9 And, behold, here cometh a chariot of men, *with*
a couple of horsemen. And he answered and said,
Babylon is fallen, is fallen; and all the graven images
of her gods he hath broken unto the ground.
10 O my threshing, and the corn of my floor: that
which I have heard of the LORD of hosts, the God of
Israel, have I declared unto you.

11 The burden of Dumah. He calleth to me out of
Seir, Watchman, what of the night? Watchman, what
of the night?
12 The watchman said, The morning cometh, and
also the night: if ye will inquire, inquire ye: return,
come.

13 The burden upon Arabia. In the forest in Arabia shall ye lodge, O ye travelling companies of
Dedanim.

NEW LIVING TRANSLATION

I will make an end
to all the groaning Babylon caused.

3 My stomach aches and burns with pain.
Sharp pangs of anguish are upon me,
like those of a woman in labor.
I grow faint when I hear what God is planning;
I am too afraid to look.

4 My mind reels and my heart races.
I longed for evening to come,
but now I am terrified of the dark.

5 Look! They are preparing a great feast.
They are spreading rugs for people to sit on.
Everyone is eating and drinking.
But quick! Grab your shields and prepare
for battle.
You are being attacked!

6 Meanwhile, the Lord said to me,
"Put a watchman on the city wall.
Let him shout out what he sees.

7 He should look for chariots
drawn by pairs of horses,
and for riders on donkeys and camels.
Let the watchman be fully alert."

8 Then the watchman* called out,
"Day after day I have stood on the watchtower,
my lord.
Night after night I have remained at my post.

9 Now at last—look!
Here comes a man in a chariot
with a pair of horses!"
Then the watchman said,
"Babylon is fallen, fallen!
All the idols of Babylon
lie broken on the ground!"

10 O my people, threshed and winnowed,
I have told you everything the LORD of
Heaven's Armies has said,
everything the God of Israel has told me.

A Message about Edom

11 This message came to me concerning Edom*:

Someone from Edom* keeps calling to me,
"Watchman, how much longer until morning?
When will the night be over?"

12 The watchman replies,
"Morning is coming, but night will soon return.
If you wish to ask again, then come back
and ask."

A Message about Arabia

13 This message came to me concerning Arabia:

O caravans from Dedan,
hide in the deserts of Arabia.

21:8 As in Dead Sea Scrolls and Syriac version; Masoretic Text reads *a lion.* **21:11a** Hebrew *Dumah,* which means "silence" or "stillness." It is a wordplay on the word *Edom.* **21:11b** Hebrew *Seir,* another name for Edom.

KING JAMES VERSION

14 The inhabitants of the land of Tema brought water to him that was thirsty, they prevented with their bread him that fled.

15 For they fled from the swords, from the drawn sword, and from the bent bow, and from the grievousness of war.

16 For thus hath the Lord said unto me, Within a year, according to the years of an hireling, and all the glory of Kedar shall fail:

17 And the residue of the number of archers, the mighty men of the children of Kedar, shall be diminished: for the LORD God of Israel hath spoken *it*.

22 1 The burden of the valley of vision. What aileth thee now, that thou art wholly gone up to the housetops?

2 Thou that art full of stirs, a tumultuous city, a joyous city: thy slain *men are* not slain with the sword, nor dead in battle.

3 All thy rulers are fled together, they are bound by the archers: all that are found in thee are bound together, *which* have fled from far.

4 Therefore said I, Look away from me: I will weep bitterly, labour not to comfort me, because of the spoiling of the daughter of my people.

5 For *it is* a day of trouble, and of treading down, and of perplexity by the Lord GOD of hosts in the valley of vision, breaking down the walls, and of crying to the mountains.

6 And Elam bare the quiver with chariots of men *and* horsemen, and Kir uncovered the shield.

7 And it shall come to pass, *that* thy choicest valleys shall be full of chariots, and the horsemen shall set themselves in array at the gate.

8 And he discovered the covering of Judah, and thou didst look in that day to the armour of the house of the forest.

9 Ye have seen also the breaches of the city of David, that they are many: and ye gathered together the waters of the lower pool.

10 And ye have numbered the houses of Jerusalem, and the houses have ye broken down to fortify the wall.

11 Ye made also a ditch between the two walls for the water of the old pool: but ye have not looked unto the maker thereof, neither had respect unto him that fashioned it long ago.

NEW LIVING TRANSLATION

14 O people of Tema,
bring water to these thirsty people,
food to these weary refugees.
15 They have fled from the sword,
from the drawn sword,
from the bent bow
and the terrors of battle.

16 The Lord said to me, "Within a year, counting each day,* all the glory of Kedar will come to an end.
17 Only a few of its courageous archers will survive. I, the LORD, the God of Israel, have spoken!"

A Message about Jerusalem

22 This message came to me concerning Jerusalem—the Valley of Vision*:

What is happening?
Why is everyone running to the rooftops?
2 The whole city is in a terrible uproar.
What do I see in this reveling city?
Bodies are lying everywhere,
killed not in battle but by famine and disease.
3 All your leaders have fled.
They surrendered without resistance.
The people tried to slip away,
but they were captured, too.
4 That's why I said, "Leave me alone to weep;
do not try to comfort me.
Let me cry for my people
as I watch them being destroyed."
5 Oh, what a day of crushing defeat!
What a day of confusion and terror
brought by the Lord, the LORD of
Heaven's Armies,
upon the Valley of Vision!
The walls of Jerusalem have been broken,
and cries of death echo from the mountainsides.
6 Elamites are the archers,
with their chariots and charioteers.
The men of Kir hold up the shields.
7 Chariots fill your beautiful valleys,
and charioteers storm your gates.
8 Judah's defenses have been stripped away.
You run to the armory* for your weapons.
9 You inspect the breaks in the walls of Jerusalem.*
You store up water in the lower pool.
10 You survey the houses and tear some down
for stone to strengthen the walls.
11 Between the city walls, you build a reservoir
for water from the old pool.
But you never ask for help from the One
who did all this.
You never considered the One who planned
this long ago.

21:16 Hebrew *Within a year, as a servant bound by contract would count it.* Some ancient manuscripts read *Within three years,* as in 16:14. **22:1** Hebrew *concerning the Valley of Vision.* **22:8** Hebrew *to the House of the Forest;* see 1 Kgs 7:2-5. **22:9** Hebrew *the city of David.*

KING JAMES VERSION

12 And in that day did the Lord GOD of hosts call to
weeping, and to mourning, and to baldness, and to
girding with sackcloth:

13 And behold joy and gladness, slaying oxen, and
killing sheep, eating flesh, and drinking wine: let us
eat and drink; for tomorrow we shall die.

14 And it was revealed in mine ears by the LORD of
hosts, Surely this iniquity shall not be purged from
you till ye die, saith the Lord GOD of hosts.

15 Thus saith the Lord GOD of hosts, Go, get thee
unto this treasurer, *even* unto Shebna, which *is* over
the house, *and say,*

16 What hast thou here? and whom hast thou here,
that thou hast hewed thee out a sepulchre here, *as* he
that heweth him out a sepulchre on high, *and* that
graveth an habitation for himself in a rock?

17 Behold, the LORD will carry thee away with a
mighty captivity, and will surely cover thee.

18 He will surely violently turn and toss thee *like* a
ball into a large country: there shalt thou die, and
there the chariots of thy glory *shall be* the shame of
thy lord's house.

19 And I will drive thee from thy station, and from
thy state shall he pull thee down.

20 And it shall come to pass in that day, that I will
call my servant Eliakim the son of Hilkiah:

21 And I will clothe him with thy robe, and strength-
en him with thy girdle, and I will commit thy government into his hand: and he shall be a father to the
inhabitants of Jerusalem, and to the house of Judah.

22 And the key of the house of David will I lay upon
his shoulder; so he shall open, and none shall shut;
and he shall shut, and none shall open.

23 And I will fasten him *as* a nail in a sure place; and
he shall be for a glorious throne to his father's house.

24 And they shall hang upon him all the glory of his
father's house, the offspring and the issue, all vessels
of small quantity, from the vessels of cups, even to all
the vessels of flagons.

25 In that day, saith the LORD of hosts, shall the nail
that is fastened in the sure place be removed, and be
cut down, and fall; and the burden that *was* upon it
shall be cut off: for the LORD hath spoken *it*.

NEW LIVING TRANSLATION

12 At that time the Lord, the LORD of
Heaven's Armies,
called you to weep and mourn.
He told you to shave your heads in sorrow
for your sins
and to wear clothes of burlap to show
your remorse.
13 But instead, you dance and play;
you slaughter cattle and kill sheep.
You feast on meat and drink wine.
You say, "Let's feast and drink,
for tomorrow we die!"

14 The LORD of Heaven's Armies has revealed this to
me: "Till the day you die, you will never be forgiven
for this sin." That is the judgment of the Lord, the
LORD of Heaven's Armies.

A Message for Shebna

15 This is what the Lord, the LORD of Heaven's Armies,
said to me: "Confront Shebna, the palace administrator, and give him this message:

16 "Who do you think you are,
and what are you doing here,
building a beautiful tomb for yourself—
a monument high up in the rock?
17 For the LORD is about to hurl you away,
mighty man.
He is going to grab you,
18 crumple you into a ball,
and toss you away into a distant, barren land.
There you will die,
and your glorious chariots will be broken
and useless.
You are a disgrace to your master!

19 "Yes, I will drive you out of office," says the
LORD. "I will pull you down from your high position.
20 And then I will call my servant Eliakim son of Hilkiah to replace you. 21 I will dress him in your royal
robes and will give him your title and your authority.
And he will be a father to the people of Jerusalem
and Judah. 22 I will give him the key to the house of
David—the highest position in the royal court.
When he opens doors, no one will be able to close
them; when he closes doors, no one will be able to
open them. 23 He will bring honor to his family name,
for I will drive him firmly in place like a nail in the
wall. 24 They will give him great responsibility, and
he will bring honor to even the lowliest members of
his family.*"

25 But the LORD of Heaven's Armies also says: "The
time will come when I will pull out the nail that
seemed so firm. It will come out and fall to the
ground. Everything it supports will fall with it. I, the
LORD, have spoken!"

22:24 Hebrew *They will hang on him all the glory of his father's house: its offspring and offshoots, all its lesser vessels, from the bowls to all the jars.*

KING JAMES VERSION

23

1 The burden of Tyre. Howl, ye ships of Tarshish; for it is laid waste, so that there is no house, no entering in: from the land of Chittim it is revealed to them.

2 Be still, ye inhabitants of the isle; thou whom the merchants of Zidon, that pass over the sea, have replenished.

3 And by great waters the seed of Sihor, the harvest of the river, *is* her revenue; and she is a mart of nations.

4 Be thou ashamed, O Zidon: for the sea hath spoken, *even* the strength of the sea, saying, I travail not, nor bring forth children, neither do I nourish up young men, *nor* bring up virgins.

5 As at the report concerning Egypt, *so* shall they be sorely pained at the report of Tyre.

6 Pass ye over to Tarshish; howl, ye inhabitants of the isle.

7 *Is* this your joyous *city*, whose antiquity *is* of ancient days? her own feet shall carry her afar off to sojourn.

8 Who hath taken this counsel against Tyre, the crowning *city*, whose merchants *are* princes, whose traffickers *are* the honourable of the earth?

9 The LORD of hosts hath purposed it, to stain the pride of all glory, *and* to bring into contempt all the honourable of the earth.

10 Pass through thy land as a river, O daughter of Tarshish: *there is* no more strength.

11 He stretched out his hand over the sea, he shook the kingdoms: the LORD hath given a commandment against the merchant *city*, to destroy the strong holds thereof.

12 And he said, Thou shalt no more rejoice, O thou oppressed virgin, daughter of Zidon: arise, pass over to Chittim; there also shalt thou have no rest.

13 Behold the land of the Chaldeans; this people was not, *till* the Assyrian founded it for them that dwell in the wilderness: they set up the towers thereof, they raised up the palaces thereof; *and* he brought it to ruin.

14 Howl, ye ships of Tarshish: for your strength is laid waste.

NEW LIVING TRANSLATION

A Message about Tyre

23

This message came to me concerning Tyre:
Weep, O ships of Tarshish,
for the harbor and houses of Tyre are gone!
The rumors you heard in Cyprus*
are all true.
2 Mourn in silence, you people of the coast
and you merchants of Sidon.
Your traders crossed the sea,
3 sailing over deep waters.
They brought you grain from Egypt*
and harvests from along the Nile.
You were the marketplace of the world.
4 But now you are put to shame, city of Sidon,
for Tyre, the fortress of the sea, says,
"Now I am childless;
I have no sons or daughters."
5 When Egypt hears the news about Tyre,
there will be great sorrow.
6 Send word now to Tarshish!
Wail, you people who live in distant lands!
7 Is this silent ruin all that is left of your once
joyous city?
What a long history was yours!
Think of all the colonists you sent
to distant places.

8 Who has brought this disaster on Tyre,
that great creator of kingdoms?
Her traders were all princes,
her merchants were nobles.
9 The LORD of Heaven's Armies has done it
to destroy your pride
and bring low all earth's nobility.
10 Come, people of Tarshish,
sweep over the land like the flooding Nile,
for Tyre is defenseless.*
11 The LORD held out his hand over the sea
and shook the kingdoms of the earth.
He has spoken out against Phoenicia,*
ordering that her fortresses be destroyed.
12 He says, "Never again will you rejoice,
O daughter of Sidon, for you have been
crushed.
Even if you flee to Cyprus,
you will find no rest."

13 Look at the land of Babylonia*—
the people of that land are gone!
The Assyrians have handed Babylon over
to the wild animals of the desert.
They have built siege ramps against its walls,
torn down its palaces,
and turned it to a heap of rubble.

14 Wail, O ships of Tarshish,
for your harbor is destroyed!

23:1 Hebrew *Kittim;* also in 23:12. **23:3** Hebrew *from Shihor,* a branch of the Nile River. **23:10** The meaning of the Hebrew in this verse is uncertain. **23:11** Hebrew *Canaan.* **23:13** Or *Chaldea.*

KING JAMES VERSION

15 And it shall come to pass in that day, that Tyre shall be forgotten seventy years, according to the days of one king: after the end of seventy years shall Tyre sing as an harlot.

16 Take an harp, go about the city, thou harlot that hast been forgotten; make sweet melody, sing many songs, that thou mayest be remembered.

17 And it shall come to pass after the end of seventy years, that the LORD will visit Tyre, and she shall turn to her hire, and shall commit fornication with all the kingdoms of the world upon the face of the earth.

18 And her merchandise and her hire shall be holiness to the LORD: it shall not be treasured nor laid up; for her merchandise shall be for them that dwell before the LORD, to eat sufficiently, and for durable clothing.

24 1 Behold, the LORD maketh the earth empty, and maketh it waste, and turneth it upside down, and scattereth abroad the inhabitants thereof.

2 And it shall be, as with the people, so with the priest; as with the servant, so with his master; as with the maid, so with her mistress; as with the buyer, so with the seller; as with the lender, so with the borrower; as with the taker of usury, so with the giver of usury to him.

3 The land shall be utterly emptied, and utterly spoiled: for the LORD hath spoken this word.

4 The earth mourneth *and* fadeth away, the world languisheth *and* fadeth away, the haughty people of the earth do languish.

5 The earth also is defiled under the inhabitants thereof; because they have transgressed the laws, changed the ordinance, broken the everlasting covenant.

6 Therefore hath the curse devoured the earth, and they that dwell therein are desolate: therefore the inhabitants of the earth are burned, and few men left.

7 The new wine mourneth, the vine languisheth, all the merryhearted do sigh.

8 The mirth of tabrets ceaseth, the noise of them that rejoice endeth, the joy of the harp ceaseth.

9 They shall not drink wine with a song; strong drink shall be bitter to them that drink it.

10 The city of confusion is broken down: every house is shut up, that no man may come in.

11 *There is* a crying for wine in the streets; all joy is darkened, the mirth of the land is gone.

12 In the city is left desolation, and the gate is smitten with destruction.

NEW LIVING TRANSLATION

15 For seventy years, the length of a king's life, Tyre will be forgotten. But then the city will come back to life as in the song about the prostitute:

16 Take a harp and walk the streets,
you forgotten harlot.
Make sweet melody and sing your songs
so you will be remembered again.

17 Yes, after seventy years the LORD will revive Tyre.
But she will be no different than she was before. She
will again be a prostitute to all kingdoms around the
world. 18 But in the end her profits will be given to the
LORD. Her wealth will not be hoarded but will provide good food and fine clothing for the LORD's
priests.

Destruction of the Earth

24 1 Look! The LORD is about to
destroy the earth
and make it a vast wasteland.
He devastates the surface of the earth
and scatters the people.
2 Priests and laypeople,
servants and masters,
maids and mistresses,
buyers and sellers,
lenders and borrowers,
bankers and debtors—none will be spared.
3 The earth will be completely emptied and looted.
The LORD has spoken!
4 The earth mourns and dries up,
and the crops waste away and wither.
Even the greatest people on earth waste away.
5 The earth suffers for the sins of its people,
for they have twisted God's instructions,
violated his laws,
and broken his everlasting covenant.
6 Therefore, a curse consumes the earth.
Its people must pay the price for their sin.
They are destroyed by fire,
and only a few are left alive.
7 The grapevines waste away,
and there is no new wine.
All the merrymakers sigh and mourn.
8 The cheerful sound of tambourines is stilled;
the happy cries of celebration are heard
no more.
The melodious chords of the harp are silent.
9 Gone are the joys of wine and song;
alcoholic drink turns bitter in the mouth.
10 The city writhes in chaos;
every home is locked to keep out intruders.
11 Mobs gather in the streets, crying out for wine.
Joy has turned to gloom.
Gladness has been banished from the land.
12 The city is left in ruins,
its gates battered down.

KING JAMES VERSION

13 When thus it shall be in the midst of the land
among the people, *there shall be* as the shaking of an
olive tree, *and* as the gleaning grapes when the
vintage is done.
14 They shall lift up their voice, they shall sing for
the majesty of the LORD, they shall cry aloud from the
sea.
15 Wherefore glorify ye the LORD in the fires, *even*
the name of the LORD God of Israel in the isles of
the sea.
16 From the uttermost part of the earth have we
heard songs, *even* glory to the righteous. But I said,
My leanness, my leanness, woe unto me! the treacherous dealers have dealt treacherously; yea, the
treacherous dealers have dealt very treacherously.
17 Fear, and the pit, and the snare, *are* upon thee,
O inhabitant of the earth.
18 And it shall come to pass, *that* he who fleeth
from the noise of the fear shall fall into the pit; and
he that cometh up out of the midst of the pit shall be
taken in the snare: for the windows from on high are
open, and the foundations of the earth do shake.
19 The earth is utterly broken down, the earth is
clean dissolved, the earth is moved exceedingly.
20 The earth shall reel to and fro like a drunkard,
and shall be removed like a cottage; and the transgression thereof shall be heavy upon it; and it shall
fall, and not rise again.
21 And it shall come to pass in that day, *that* the
LORD shall punish the host of the high ones *that are*
on high, and the kings of the earth upon the earth.
22 And they shall be gathered together, *as* prisoners are gathered in the pit, and shall be shut up in the
prison, and after many days shall they be visited.
23 Then the moon shall be confounded, and the
sun ashamed, when the LORD of hosts shall reign in
mount Zion, and in Jerusalem, and before his ancients gloriously.

25 1 O LORD, thou *art* my God; I will exalt thee, I
will praise thy name; for thou hast done
wonderful *things; thy* counsels of old *are* faithfulness *and* truth.
2 For thou hast made of a city an heap; *of* a
defenced city a ruin: a palace of strangers to be no
city; it shall never be built.
3 Therefore shall the strong people glorify thee,
the city of the terrible nations shall fear thee.

NEW LIVING TRANSLATION

13 Throughout the earth the story is the same—
only a remnant is left,
like the stray olives left on the tree
or the few grapes left on the vine after harvest.
14 But all who are left shout and sing for joy.
Those in the west praise the LORD's majesty.
15 In eastern lands, give glory to the LORD.
In the lands beyond the sea, praise the name of
the LORD, the God of Israel.
16 We hear songs of praise from the ends
of the earth,
songs that give glory to the Righteous One!

But my heart is heavy with grief.
Weep for me, for I wither away.
Deceit still prevails,
and treachery is everywhere.
17 Terror and traps and snares will be your lot,
you people of the earth.
18 Those who flee in terror will fall into a trap,
and those who escape the trap will be
caught in a snare.

Destruction falls like rain from the heavens;
the foundations of the earth shake.
19 The earth has broken up.
It has utterly collapsed;
it is violently shaken.
20 The earth staggers like a drunk.
It trembles like a tent in a storm.
It falls and will not rise again,
for the guilt of its rebellion is very heavy.
21 In that day the LORD will punish the gods
in the heavens
and the proud rulers of the nations on earth.
22 They will be rounded up and put in prison.
They will be shut up in prison
and will finally be punished.
23 Then the glory of the moon will wane,
and the brightness of the sun will fade,
for the LORD of Heaven's Armies will rule
on Mount Zion.
He will rule in great glory in Jerusalem,
in the sight of all the leaders of his people.

Praise for Judgment and Salvation

25 1 O LORD, I will honor and praise your name,
for you are my God.
You do such wonderful things!
You planned them long ago,
and now you have accomplished them.
2 You turn mighty cities into heaps of ruins.
Cities with strong walls are turned to rubble.
Beautiful palaces in distant lands disappear
and will never be rebuilt.
3 Therefore, strong nations will declare your glory;
ruthless nations will fear you.

KING JAMES VERSION

4 For thou hast been a strength to the poor, a strength to the needy in his distress, a refuge from the storm, a shadow from the heat, when the blast of the terrible ones *is* as a storm *against* the wall.

5 Thou shalt bring down the noise of strangers, as the heat in a dry place; *even* the heat with the shadow of a cloud: the branch of the terrible ones shall be brought low.

6 And in this mountain shall the LORD of hosts make unto all people a feast of fat things, a feast of wines on the lees, of fat things full of marrow, of wines on the lees well refined.

7 And he will destroy in this mountain the face of the covering cast over all people, and the veil that is spread over all nations.

8 He will swallow up death in victory; and the Lord GOD will wipe away tears from off all faces; and the rebuke of his people shall he take away from off all the earth: for the LORD hath spoken *it*.

9 And it shall be said in that day, Lo, this *is* our God; we have waited for him, and he will save us: this *is* the LORD; we have waited for him, we will be glad and rejoice in his salvation.

10 For in this mountain shall the hand of the LORD rest, and Moab shall be trodden down under him, even as straw is trodden down for the dunghill.

11 And he shall spread forth his hands in the midst of them, as he that swimmeth spreadeth forth *his hands* to swim: and he shall bring down their pride together with the spoils of their hands.

12 And the fortress of the high fort of thy walls shall he bring down, lay low, *and* bring to the ground, *even* to the dust.

26

1 In that day shall this song be sung in the land of Judah; We have a strong city; salvation will *God* appoint *for* walls and bulwarks.

2 Open ye the gates, that the righteous nation which keepeth the truth may enter in.

3 Thou wilt keep *him* in perfect peace, *whose* mind *is* stayed *on thee:* because he trusteth in thee.

4 Trust ye in the LORD for ever: for in the LORD JEHOVAH *is* everlasting strength:

NEW LIVING TRANSLATION

4 But you are a tower of refuge to the poor, O LORD,
a tower of refuge to the needy in distress.
You are a refuge from the storm
and a shelter from the heat.
For the oppressive acts of ruthless people
are like a storm beating against a wall,
5 or like the relentless heat of the desert.
But you silence the roar of foreign nations.
As the shade of a cloud cools relentless heat,
so the boastful songs of ruthless people
are stilled.

6 In Jerusalem,* the LORD of Heaven's Armies
will spread a wonderful feast
for all the people of the world.
It will be a delicious banquet
with clear, well-aged wine and choice meat.
7 There he will remove the cloud of gloom,
the shadow of death that hangs over the earth.
8 He will swallow up death forever!*
The Sovereign LORD will wipe away all tears.
He will remove forever all insults and mockery
against his land and people.
The LORD has spoken!

9 In that day the people will proclaim,
"This is our God!
We trusted in him, and he saved us!
This is the LORD, in whom we trusted.
Let us rejoice in the salvation he brings!"
10 For the LORD's hand of blessing will rest
on Jerusalem.
But Moab will be crushed.
It will be like straw trampled down
and left to rot.
11 God will push down Moab's people
as a swimmer pushes down water
with his hands.
He will end their pride
and all their evil works.
12 The high walls of Moab will be demolished.
They will be brought down to the ground,
down into the dust.

A Song of Praise to the LORD

26

In that day, everyone in the land of Judah will sing this song:

Our city is strong!
We are surrounded by the walls of
God's salvation.
2 Open the gates to all who are righteous;
allow the faithful to enter.
3 You will keep in perfect peace
all who trust in you,
all whose thoughts are fixed on you!
4 Trust in the LORD always,
for the LORD GOD is the eternal Rock.

25:6 Hebrew *On this mountain;* also in 25:10. **25:8** Greek version reads *Death is swallowed up in victory.* Compare 1 Cor 15:54.

KING JAMES VERSION

5 For he bringeth down them that dwell on high; the lofty city, he layeth it low; he layeth it low, *even* to the ground; he bringeth it *even* to the dust.

6 The foot shall tread it down, *even* the feet of the poor, *and* the steps of the needy.

7 The way of the just *is* uprightness: thou, most upright, dost weigh the path of the just.

8 Yea, in the way of thy judgments, O LORD, have we waited for thee; the desire of *our* soul *is* to thy name, and to the remembrance of thee.

9 With my soul have I desired thee in the night; yea, with my spirit within me will I seek thee early: for when thy judgments *are* in the earth, the inhabitants of the world will learn righteousness.

10 Let favour be shewed to the wicked, *yet* will he not learn righteousness: in the land of uprightness will he deal unjustly, and will not behold the majesty of the LORD.

11 LORD, *when* thy hand is lifted up, they will not see: *but* they shall see, and be ashamed for *their* envy at the people; yea, the fire of thine enemies shall devour them.

12 LORD, thou wilt ordain peace for us: for thou also hast wrought all our works in us.

13 O LORD our God, *other* lords beside thee have had dominion over us: *but* by thee only will we make mention of thy name.

14 *They are* dead, they shall not live; *they are* deceased, they shall not rise: therefore hast thou visited and destroyed them, and made all their memory to perish.

15 Thou hast increased the nation, O LORD, thou hast increased the nation: thou art glorified: thou hadst removed *it* far *unto* all the ends of the earth.

16 LORD, in trouble have they visited thee, they poured out a prayer *when* thy chastening *was* upon them.

17 Like as a woman with child, *that* draweth near the time of her delivery, is in pain, *and* crieth out in her pangs; so have we been in thy sight, O LORD.

18 We have been with child, we have been in pain, we have as it were brought forth wind; we have not wrought any deliverance in the earth; neither have the inhabitants of the world fallen.

19 Thy dead *men* shall live, *together with* my dead body shall they arise. Awake and sing, ye that dwell in dust: for thy dew *is as* the dew of herbs, and the earth shall cast out the dead.

NEW LIVING TRANSLATION

5 He humbles the proud
and brings down the arrogant city.
He brings it down to the dust.
6 The poor and oppressed trample it underfoot,
and the needy walk all over it.
7 But for those who are righteous,
the way is not steep and rough.
You are a God who does what is right,
and you smooth out the path ahead of them.
8 LORD, we show our trust in you by obeying
your laws;
our heart's desire is to glorify your name.
9 All night long I search for you;
in the morning I earnestly seek for God.
For only when you come to judge the earth
will people learn what is right.
10 Your kindness to the wicked
does not make them do good.
Although others do right, the wicked
keep doing wrong
and take no notice of the LORD's majesty.
11 O LORD, they pay no attention to your
upraised fist.
Show them your eagerness to defend
your people.
Then they will be ashamed.
Let your fire consume your enemies.

12 LORD, you will grant us peace;
all we have accomplished is really from you.
13 O LORD our God, others have ruled us,
but you alone are the one we worship.
14 Those we served before are dead and gone.
Their departed spirits will never return!
You attacked them and destroyed them,
and they are long forgotten.
15 O LORD, you have made our nation great;
yes, you have made us great.
You have extended our borders,
and we give you the glory!

16 LORD, in distress we searched for you.
We prayed beneath the burden of
your discipline.
17 Just as a pregnant woman
writhes and cries out in pain as she gives birth,
so were we in your presence, LORD.
18 We, too, writhe in agony,
but nothing comes of our suffering.
We have not given salvation to the earth,
nor brought life into the world.
19 But those who die in the LORD will live;
their bodies will rise again!
Those who sleep in the earth
will rise up and sing for joy!
For your life-giving light will fall like dew
on your people in the place of the dead!

KING JAMES VERSION

20Come, my people, enter thou into thy chambers, and shut thy doors about thee: hide thyself as it were for a little moment, until the indignation be overpast.

21For, behold, the LORD cometh out of his place to punish the inhabitants of the earth for their iniquity: the earth also shall disclose her blood, and shall no more cover her slain.

27 1In that day the LORD with his sore and great and strong sword shall punish leviathan the piercing serpent, even leviathan that crooked serpent; and he shall slay the dragon that *is* in the sea.

2In that day sing ye unto her, A vineyard of red wine.

3I the LORD do keep it; I will water it every moment: lest *any* hurt it, I will keep it night and day.

4Fury *is* not in me: who would set the briers *and* thorns against me in battle? I would go through them, I would burn them together.

5Or let him take hold of my strength, *that* he may make peace with me; *and* he shall make peace with me.

6He shall cause them that come of Jacob to take root: Israel shall blossom and bud, and fill the face of the world with fruit.

7Hath he smitten him, as he smote those that smote him? *or* is he slain according to the slaughter of them that are slain by him?

8In measure, when it shooteth forth, thou wilt debate with it: he stayeth his rough wind in the day of the east wind.

9By this therefore shall the iniquity of Jacob be purged; and this *is* all the fruit to take away his sin; when he maketh all the stones of the altar as chalkstones that are beaten in sunder, the groves and images shall not stand up.

10Yet the defenced city *shall be* desolate, *and* the habitation forsaken, and left like a wilderness: there shall the calf feed, and there shall he lie down, and consume the branches thereof.

11When the boughs thereof are withered, they shall be broken off: the women come, *and* set them on fire:

NEW LIVING TRANSLATION

Restoration for Israel

20 Go home, my people,
and lock your doors!
Hide yourselves for a little while
until the LORD's anger has passed.
21 Look! The LORD is coming from heaven
to punish the people of the earth for their sins.
The earth will no longer hide those who have been killed.
They will be brought out for all to see.

27 In that day the LORD will take his terrible, swift sword and punish Leviathan,* the swiftly moving serpent, the coiling, writhing serpent. He will kill the dragon of the sea.

2 "In that day,
sing about the fruitful vineyard.
3 I, the LORD, will watch over it,
watering it carefully.
Day and night I will watch so no one can harm it.
4 My anger will be gone.
If I find briers and thorns growing,
I will attack them;
I will burn them up—
5 unless they turn to me for help.
Let them make peace with me;
yes, let them make peace with me."
6 The time is coming when Jacob's descendants will take root.
Israel will bud and blossom
and fill the whole earth with fruit!
7 Has the LORD struck Israel
as he struck her enemies?
Has he punished her
as he punished them?
8 No, but he exiled Israel to call her to account.
She was exiled from her land
as though blown away in a storm from the east.
9 The LORD did this to purge Israel's* wickedness,
to take away all her sin.
As a result, all the pagan altars will be crushed to dust.
No Asherah pole or pagan shrine will be left standing.
10 The fortified towns will be silent and empty,
the houses abandoned, the streets overgrown with weeds.
Calves will graze there,
chewing on twigs and branches.
11 The people are like the dead branches of a tree,
broken off and used for kindling beneath the cooking pots.
Israel is a foolish and stupid nation,
for its people have turned away from God.

27:1 The identification of Leviathan is disputed, ranging from an earthly creature to a mythical sea monster in ancient literature. **27:9** Hebrew *Jacob's*. See note on 14:1.

for it *is* a people of no understanding: therefore he that made them will not have mercy on them, and he that formed them will shew them no favour.

12 And it shall come to pass in that day, *that* the LORD shall beat off from the channel of the river unto the stream of Egypt, and ye shall be gathered one by one, O ye children of Israel.

13 And it shall come to pass in that day, *that* the great trumpet shall be blown, and they shall come which were ready to perish in the land of Assyria, and the outcasts in the land of Egypt, and shall worship the LORD in the holy mount at Jerusalem.

28 1 Woe to the crown of pride, to the drunkards of Ephraim, whose glorious beauty *is* a fading flower, which *are* on the head of the fat valleys of them that are overcome with wine!

2 Behold, the Lord hath a mighty and strong one, *which* as a tempest of hail *and* a destroying storm, as a flood of mighty waters overflowing, shall cast down to the earth with the hand.

3 The crown of pride, the drunkards of Ephraim, shall be trodden under feet:

4 And the glorious beauty, which *is* on the head of the fat valley, shall be a fading flower, *and* as the hasty fruit before the summer; which *when* he that looketh upon it seeth, while it is yet in his hand he eateth it up.

5 In that day shall the LORD of hosts be for a crown of glory, and for a diadem of beauty, unto the residue of his people,

6 And for a spirit of judgment to him that sitteth in judgment, and for strength to them that turn the battle to the gate.

7 But they also have erred through wine, and through strong drink are out of the way; the priest and the prophet have erred through strong drink, they are swallowed up of wine, they are out of the way through strong drink; they err in vision, they stumble *in* judgment.

8 For all tables are full of vomit *and* filthiness, *so that there is* no place *clean*.

9 Whom shall he teach knowledge? and whom shall he make to understand doctrine? *them that are* weaned from the milk, *and* drawn from the breasts.

10 For precept *must be* upon precept, precept upon

Therefore, the one who made them
will show them no pity or mercy.

12 Yet the time will come when the LORD will
gather them together like handpicked grain. One by
one he will gather them—from the Euphrates River*
in the east to the Brook of Egypt in the west. 13 In that
day the great trumpet will sound. Many who were dying in exile in Assyria and Egypt will return to Jerusalem to worship the LORD on his holy mountain.

A Message about Samaria

28 1 What sorrow awaits the proud city
of Samaria—
the glorious crown of the drunks of Israel.*
It sits at the head of a fertile valley,
but its glorious beauty will fade like a flower.
It is the pride of a people
brought down by wine.
2 For the Lord will send a mighty army against it.
Like a mighty hailstorm and a torrential rain,
they will burst upon it like a surging flood
and smash it to the ground.
3 The proud city of Samaria—
the glorious crown of the drunks of Israel*—
will be trampled beneath its enemies' feet.
4 It sits at the head of a fertile valley,
but its glorious beauty will fade like a flower.
Whoever sees it will snatch it up,
as an early fig is quickly picked and eaten.
5 Then at last the LORD of Heaven's Armies
will himself be Israel's glorious crown.
He will be the pride and joy
of the remnant of his people.
6 He will give a longing for justice
to their judges.
He will give great courage
to their warriors who stand at the gates.
7 Now, however, Israel is led by drunks
who reel with wine and stagger with alcohol.
The priests and prophets stagger with alcohol
and lose themselves in wine.
They reel when they see visions
and stagger as they render decisions.
8 Their tables are covered with vomit;
filth is everywhere.
9 "Who does the LORD think we are?" they ask.
"Why does he speak to us like this?
Are we little children,
just recently weaned?
10 He tells us everything over and over—
one line at a time,
one line at a time,

27:12 Hebrew *the river.* **28:1** Hebrew *What sorrow awaits the crowning glory of the drunks of Ephraim,* referring to Samaria, capital of the northern kingdom of Israel. **28:3** Hebrew *The crowning glory of the drunks of Ephraim;* see note on 28:1.

KING JAMES VERSION

precept; line upon line, line upon line; here a little, *and* there a little:

11For with stammering lips and another tongue will he speak to this people.

12To whom he said, This *is* the rest *wherewith* ye may cause the weary to rest; and this *is* the refreshing: yet they would not hear.

13But the word of the LORD was unto them precept upon precept, precept upon precept; line upon line, line upon line; here a little, *and* there a little; that they might go, and fall backward, and be broken, and snared, and taken.

14Wherefore hear the word of the LORD, ye scornful men, that rule this people which *is* in Jerusalem.

15Because ye have said, We have made a covenant with death, and with hell are we at agreement; when the overflowing scourge shall pass through, it shall not come unto us: for we have made lies our refuge, and under falsehood have we hid ourselves:

16Therefore thus saith the Lord GOD, Behold, I lay in Zion for a foundation a stone, a tried stone, a precious corner *stone,* a sure foundation: he that believeth shall not make haste.

17Judgment also will I lay to the line, and righteousness to the plummet: and the hail shall sweep away the refuge of lies, and the waters shall overflow the hiding place.

18And your covenant with death shall be disannulled, and your agreement with hell shall not stand; when the overflowing scourge shall pass through, then ye shall be trodden down by it.

19From the time that it goeth forth it shall take you: for morning by morning shall it pass over, by day and by night: and it shall be a vexation only *to* understand the report.

20For the bed is shorter than that *a man* can stretch himself *on it:* and the covering narrower than that he can wrap himself *in it.*

21For the LORD shall rise up as *in* mount Perazim, he shall be wroth as *in* the valley of Gibeon, that he

NEW LIVING TRANSLATION

a little here,
and a little there!"

11 So now God will have to speak to his people
through foreign oppressors who speak
a strange language!
12 God has told his people,
"Here is a place of rest;
let the weary rest here.
This is a place of quiet rest."
But they would not listen.
13 So the LORD will spell out his message
for them again,
one line at a time,
one line at a time,
a little here,
and a little there,
so that they will stumble and fall.
They will be injured, trapped, and captured.
14 Therefore, listen to this message from the LORD,
you scoffing rulers in Jerusalem.
15 You boast, "We have struck a bargain to
cheat death
and have made a deal to dodge the grave.*
The coming destruction can never touch us,
for we have built a strong refuge made of lies
and deception."
16 Therefore, this is what the Sovereign LORD says:
"Look! I am placing a foundation stone in
Jerusalem,*
a firm and tested stone.
It is a precious cornerstone that is safe to build on.
Whoever believes need never be shaken.*
17 I will test you with the measuring line of justice
and the plumb line of righteousness.
Since your refuge is made of lies,
a hailstorm will knock it down.
Since it is made of deception,
a flood will sweep it away.
18 I will cancel the bargain you made to cheat death,
and I will overturn your deal to dodge the grave.
When the terrible enemy sweeps through,
you will be trampled into the ground.
19 Again and again that flood will come,
morning after morning,
day and night,
until you are carried away."

This message will bring terror to your people.
20 The bed you have made is too short to lie on.
The blankets are too narrow to cover you.
21 The LORD will come as he did against the
Philistines at Mount Perazim
and against the Amorites at Gibeon.

28:15 Hebrew *Sheol;* also in 28:18. **28:16a** Hebrew *in Zion.*
28:16b Greek version reads *Look! I am placing a stone in the foundation of Jerusalem* [literally *Zion*], */ a precious cornerstone for its foundation, chosen for great honor. / Anyone who trusts in him will never be disgraced.* Compare Rom 9:33; 1 Pet 2:6.

KING JAMES VERSION

may do his work, his strange work; and bring to pass his act, his strange act.

22 Now therefore be ye not mockers, lest your bands be made strong: for I have heard from the Lord God of hosts a consumption, even determined upon the whole earth.

23 Give ye ear, and hear my voice; hearken, and hear my speech.

24 Doth the plowman plow all day to sow? doth he open and break the clods of his ground?

25 When he hath made plain the face thereof, doth he not cast abroad the fitches, and scatter the cummin, and cast in the principal wheat and the appointed barley and the rie in their place?

26 For his God doth instruct him to discretion, *and* doth teach him.

27 For the fitches are not threshed with a threshing instrument, neither is a cart wheel turned about upon the cummin; but the fitches are beaten out with a staff, and the cummin with a rod.

28 Bread *corn* is bruised; because he will not ever be threshing it, nor break *it with* the wheel of his cart, nor bruise it *with* his horsemen.

29 This also cometh forth from the Lord of hosts, *which* is wonderful in counsel, *and* excellent in working.

29 1 Woe to Ariel, to Ariel, the city *where* David dwelt! add ye year to year; let them kill sacrifices.

2 Yet I will distress Ariel, and there shall be heaviness and sorrow: and it shall be unto me as Ariel.

3 And I will camp against thee round about, and will lay siege against thee with a mount, and I will raise forts against thee.

4 And thou shalt be brought down, *and* shalt speak out of the ground, and thy speech shall be low out of the dust, and thy voice shall be, as of one that hath a familiar spirit, out of the ground, and thy speech shall whisper out of the dust.

5 Moreover the multitude of thy strangers shall be like small dust, and the multitude of the terrible ones *shall be* as chaff that passeth away: yea, it shall be at an instant suddenly.

NEW LIVING TRANSLATION

He will come to do a strange thing;
he will come to do an unusual deed:
22 For the Lord, the Lord of Heaven's Armies,
has plainly said that he is determined
to crush the whole land.
So scoff no more,
or your punishment will be even greater.

23 Listen to me;
listen, and pay close attention.
24 Does a farmer always plow and never sow?
Is he forever cultivating the soil and
never planting?
25 Does he not finally plant his seeds—
black cumin, cumin, wheat, barley, and
emmer wheat—
each in its proper way,
and each in its proper place?
26 The farmer knows just what to do,
for God has given him understanding.
27 A heavy sledge is never used to thresh
black cumin;
rather, it is beaten with a light stick.
A threshing wheel is never rolled on cumin;
instead, it is beaten lightly with a flail.
28 Grain for bread is easily crushed,
so he doesn't keep on pounding it.
He threshes it under the wheels of a cart,
but he doesn't pulverize it.
29 The Lord of Heaven's Armies is a wonderful
teacher,
and he gives the farmer great wisdom.

A Message about Jerusalem

29 1 "What sorrow awaits Ariel,* the City
of David.
Year after year you celebrate your feasts.
2 Yet I will bring disaster upon you,
and there will be much weeping and sorrow.
For Jerusalem will become what her name
Ariel means—
an altar covered with blood.
3 I will be your enemy,
surrounding Jerusalem and attacking its walls.
I will build siege towers
and destroy it.
4 Then deep from the earth you will speak;
from low in the dust your words will come.
Your voice will whisper from the ground
like a ghost conjured up from the grave.

5 "But suddenly, your ruthless enemies
will be crushed
like the finest of dust.
Your many attackers will be driven away
like chaff before the wind.
Suddenly, in an instant,

29:1 *Ariel* sounds like a Hebrew term that means "hearth" or "altar."

KING JAMES VERSION

[6]Thou shalt be visited of the LORD of hosts with thunder, and with earthquake, and great noise, with storm and tempest, and the flame of devouring fire.

[7]And the multitude of all the nations that fight against Ariel, even all that fight against her and her munition, and that distress her, shall be as a dream of a night vision.

[8]It shall even be as when an hungry *man* dreameth, and, behold, he eateth; but he awaketh, and his soul is empty: or as when a thirsty man dreameth, and, behold, he drinketh; but he awaketh, and, behold, *he is* faint, and his soul hath appetite: so shall the multitude of all the nations be, that fight against mount Zion.

[9]Stay yourselves, and wonder; cry ye out, and cry: they are drunken, but not with wine; they stagger, but not with strong drink.

[10]For the LORD hath poured out upon you the spirit of deep sleep, and hath closed your eyes: the prophets and your rulers, the seers hath he covered.

[11]And the vision of all is become unto you as the words of a book that is sealed, which *men* deliver to one that is learned, saying, Read this, I pray thee: and he saith, I cannot; for it *is* sealed:

[12]And the book is delivered to him that is not learned, saying, Read this, I pray thee: and he saith, I am not learned.

[13]Wherefore the Lord said, Forasmuch as this people draw near *me* with their mouth, and with their lips do honour me, but have removed their heart far from me, and their fear toward me is taught by the precept of men:

[14]Therefore, behold, I will proceed to do a marvellous work among this people, *even* a marvellous work and a wonder: for the wisdom of their wise *men* shall perish, and the understanding of their prudent *men* shall be hid.

[15]Woe unto them that seek deep to hide their counsel from the LORD, and their works are in the dark, and they say, Who seeth us? and who knoweth us?

[16]Surely your turning of things upside down shall be esteemed as the potter's clay: for shall the work say of him that made it, He made me not? or shall the thing framed say of him that framed it, He had no understanding?

NEW LIVING TRANSLATION

[6] I, the LORD of Heaven's Armies, will act for you
with thunder and earthquake and great noise,
with whirlwind and storm and consuming fire.
[7] All the nations fighting against Jerusalem*
will vanish like a dream!
Those who are attacking her walls
will vanish like a vision in the night.
[8] A hungry person dreams of eating
but wakes up still hungry.
A thirsty person dreams of drinking
but is still faint from thirst when
morning comes.
So it will be with your enemies,
with those who attack Mount Zion."

[9] Are you amazed and incredulous?
Don't you believe it?
Then go ahead and be blind.
You are stupid, but not from wine!
You stagger, but not from liquor!
[10] For the LORD has poured out on you a spirit
of deep sleep.
He has closed the eyes of your prophets
and visionaries.

[11]All the future events in this vision are like a
sealed book to them. When you give it to those who
can read, they will say, "We can't read it because it is
sealed." [12]When you give it to those who cannot
read, they will say, "We don't know how to read."

[13] And so the Lord says,
"These people say they are mine.
They honor me with their lips,
but their hearts are far from me.
And their worship of me
is nothing but man-made rules learned
by rote.*
[14] Because of this, I will once again astound
these hypocrites
with amazing wonders.
The wisdom of the wise will pass away,
and the intelligence of the intelligent
will disappear."
[15] What sorrow awaits those who try to hide
their plans from the LORD,
who do their evil deeds in the dark!
"The LORD can't see us," they say.
"He doesn't know what's going on!"
[16] How foolish can you be?
He is the Potter, and he is certainly greater
than you, the clay!
Should the created thing say of the one
who made it,
"He didn't make me"?
Does a jar ever say,
"The potter who made me is stupid"?

29:7 Hebrew *Ariel*. 29:13 Greek version reads *Their worship is a farce, / for they teach man-made ideas as commands from God*. Compare Mark 7:7.

KING JAMES VERSION

17 *Is* it not yet a very little while, and Lebanon shall be turned into a fruitful field, and the fruitful field shall be esteemed as a forest?

18 And in that day shall the deaf hear the words of the book, and the eyes of the blind shall see out of obscurity, and out of darkness.

19 The meek also shall increase *their* joy in the LORD, and the poor among men shall rejoice in the Holy One of Israel.

20 For the terrible one is brought to nought, and the scorner is consumed, and all that watch for iniquity are cut off:

21 That make a man an offender for a word, and lay a snare for him that reproveth in the gate, and turn aside the just for a thing of nought.

22 Therefore thus saith the LORD, who redeemed Abraham, concerning the house of Jacob, Jacob shall not now be ashamed, neither shall his face now wax pale.

23 But when he seeth his children, the work of mine hands, in the midst of him, they shall sanctify my name, and sanctify the Holy One of Jacob, and shall fear the God of Israel.

24 They also that erred in spirit shall come to understanding, and they that murmured shall learn doctrine.

30 1 Woe to the rebellious children, saith the LORD, that take counsel, but not of me; and that cover with a covering, but not of my spirit, that they may add sin to sin:

2 That walk to go down into Egypt, and have not asked at my mouth; to strengthen themselves in the strength of Pharaoh, and to trust in the shadow of Egypt!

3 Therefore shall the strength of Pharaoh be your shame, and the trust in the shadow of Egypt *your* confusion.

4 For his princes were at Zoan, and his ambassadors came to Hanes.

5 They were all ashamed of a people *that* could not profit them, nor be an help nor profit, but a shame, and also a reproach.

6 The burden of the beasts of the south: into the

NEW LIVING TRANSLATION

17 Soon—and it will not be very long—
the forests of Lebanon will become
a fertile field,
and the fertile field will yield bountiful crops.
18 In that day the deaf will hear words read
from a book,
and the blind will see through the gloom
and darkness.
19 The humble will be filled with fresh joy from
the LORD.
The poor will rejoice in the Holy One of Israel.
20 The scoffer will be gone,
the arrogant will disappear,
and those who plot evil will be killed.
21 Those who convict the innocent
by their false testimony will disappear.
A similar fate awaits those who use trickery to
pervert justice
and who tell lies to destroy the innocent.

22 That is why the LORD, who redeemed Abraham, says to the people of Israel,*

"My people will no longer be ashamed
or turn pale with fear.
23 For when they see their many children
and all the blessings I have given them,
they will recognize the holiness of the
Holy One of Israel.
They will stand in awe of the God of Jacob.
24 Then the wayward will gain understanding,
and complainers will accept instruction.

Judah's Worthless Treaty with Egypt

30 1 "What sorrow awaits my rebellious
children,"
says the LORD.
"You make plans that are contrary to mine.
You make alliances not directed by my Spirit,
thus piling up your sins.
2 For without consulting me,
you have gone down to Egypt for help.
You have put your trust in Pharaoh's protection.
You have tried to hide in his shade.
3 But by trusting Pharaoh, you will be humiliated,
and by depending on him, you will
be disgraced.
4 For though his power extends to Zoan
and his officials have arrived in Hanes,
5 all who trust in him will be ashamed.
He will not help you.
Instead, he will disgrace you."

6 This message came to me concerning the animals in the Negev:

The caravan moves slowly
across the terrible desert to Egypt—
donkeys weighed down with riches

29:22 Hebrew *of Jacob*. See note on 14:1.

KING JAMES VERSION

land of trouble and anguish, from whence *come* the
young and old lion, the viper and fiery flying serpent,
they will carry their riches upon the shoulders of
young asses, and their treasures upon the bunches of
camels, to a people *that* shall not profit *them.*
7 For the Egyptians shall help in vain, and to no
purpose: therefore have I cried concerning this,
Their strength *is* to sit still.

8 Now go, write it before them in a table, and note it
in a book, that it may be for the time to come for ever
and ever:
9 That this *is* a rebellious people, lying children,
children *that* will not hear the law of the LORD:
10 Which say to the seers, See not; and to the
prophets, Prophesy not unto us right things, speak
unto us smooth things, prophesy deceits:
11 Get you out of the way, turn aside out of the path,
cause the Holy One of Israel to cease from before us.
12 Wherefore thus saith the Holy One of Israel, Because ye despise this word, and trust in oppression
and perverseness, and stay thereon:
13 Therefore this iniquity shall be to you as a
breach ready to fall, swelling out in a high wall,
whose breaking cometh suddenly at an instant.
14 And he shall break it as the breaking of the potters' vessel that is broken in pieces; he shall not
spare: so that there shall not be found in the bursting
of it a sherd to take fire from the hearth, or to take
water *withal* out of the pit.
15 For thus saith the Lord GOD, the Holy One of Israel; In returning and rest shall ye be saved; in quietness and in confidence shall be your strength: and ye
would not.
16 But ye said, No; for we will flee upon horses;
therefore shall ye flee: and, We will ride upon the
swift; therefore shall they that pursue you be swift.
17 One thousand *shall flee* at the rebuke of one; at

NEW LIVING TRANSLATION

and camels loaded with treasure—
all to pay for Egypt's protection.
They travel through the wilderness,
a place of lionesses and lions,
a place where vipers and poisonous
snakes live.
All this, and Egypt will give you nothing in return.
7 Egypt's promises are worthless!
Therefore, I call her Rahab—
the Harmless Dragon.*

A Warning for Rebellious Judah

8 Now go and write down these words.
Write them in a book.
They will stand until the end of time
as a witness
9 that these people are stubborn rebels
who refuse to pay attention to the LORD's
instructions.
10 They tell the seers,
"Stop seeing visions!"
They tell the prophets,
"Don't tell us what is right.
Tell us nice things.
Tell us lies.
11 Forget all this gloom.
Get off your narrow path.
Stop telling us about your
'Holy One of Israel.'"

12 This is the reply of the Holy One of Israel:

"Because you despise what I tell you
and trust instead in oppression and lies,
13 calamity will come upon you suddenly—
like a bulging wall that bursts and falls.
In an instant it will collapse
and come crashing down.
14 You will be smashed like a piece of pottery—
shattered so completely that
there won't be a piece big enough
to carry coals from a fireplace
or a little water from the well."
15 This is what the Sovereign LORD,
the Holy One of Israel, says:
"Only in returning to me
and resting in me will you be saved.
In quietness and confidence is your strength.
But you would have none of it.
16 You said, 'No, we will get our help from Egypt.
They will give us swift horses for riding
into battle.'
But the only swiftness you are going to see
is the swiftness of your enemies chasing you!
17 One of them will chase a thousand of you.
Five of them will make all of you flee.

30:7 Hebrew *Rahab who sits still.* Rahab is the name of a mythical sea monster that represents chaos in ancient literature. The name is used here as a poetic name for Egypt.

KING JAMES VERSION

the rebuke of five shall ye flee: till ye be left as a beacon upon the top of a mountain, and as an ensign on an hill.

18 And therefore will the LORD wait, that he may be gracious unto you, and therefore will he be exalted, that he may have mercy upon you: for the LORD *is* a God of judgment: blessed *are* all they that wait for him.

19 For the people shall dwell in Zion at Jerusalem: thou shalt weep no more: he will be very gracious unto thee at the voice of thy cry; when he shall hear it, he will answer thee.

20 And *though* the Lord give you the bread of adversity, and the water of affliction, yet shall not thy teachers be removed into a corner any more, but thine eyes shall see thy teachers:

21 And thine ears shall hear a word behind thee, saying, This *is* the way, walk ye in it, when ye turn to the right hand, and when ye turn to the left.

22 Ye shall defile also the covering of thy graven images of silver, and the ornament of thy molten images of gold: thou shalt cast them away as a menstruous cloth; thou shalt say unto it, Get thee hence.

23 Then shall he give the rain of thy seed, that thou shalt sow the ground withal; and bread of the increase of the earth, and it shall be fat and plenteous: in that day shall thy cattle feed in large pastures.

24 The oxen likewise and the young asses that ear the ground shall eat clean provender, which hath been winnowed with the shovel and with the fan.

25 And there shall be upon every high mountain, and upon every high hill, rivers *and* streams of waters in the day of the great slaughter, when the towers fall.

26 Moreover the light of the moon shall be as the light of the sun, and the light of the sun shall be sevenfold, as the light of seven days, in the day that the LORD bindeth up the breach of his people, and healeth the stroke of their wound.

27 Behold, the name of the LORD cometh from far, burning *with* his anger, and the burden *thereof is* heavy: his lips are full of indignation, and his tongue as a devouring fire:

28 And his breath, as an overflowing stream, shall reach to the midst of the neck, to sift the nations with the sieve of vanity: and *there shall be* a bridle in the jaws of the people, causing *them* to err.

29 Ye shall have a song, as in the night *when* a holy solemnity is kept; and gladness of heart, as when one goeth with a pipe to come into the mountain of the LORD, to the mighty One of Israel.

30 And the LORD shall cause his glorious voice to be heard, and shall shew the lighting down of his arm,

NEW LIVING TRANSLATION

You will be left like a lonely flagpole on a hill
or a tattered banner on a distant
mountaintop."

Blessings for the LORD's People

18 So the LORD must wait for you to come to him
so he can show you his love and compassion.
For the LORD is a faithful God.
Blessed are those who wait for his help.

19 O people of Zion, who live in Jerusalem,
you will weep no more.
He will be gracious if you ask for help.
He will surely respond to the sound
of your cries.

20 Though the Lord gave you adversity for food
and suffering for drink,
he will still be with you to teach you.
You will see your teacher with your own eyes.

21 Your own ears will hear him.
Right behind you a voice will say,
"This is the way you should go,"
whether to the right or to the left.

22 Then you will destroy all your silver idols
and your precious gold images.
You will throw them out like filthy rags,
saying to them, "Good riddance!"

23 Then the LORD will bless you with rain at planting time. There will be wonderful harvests and
plenty of pastureland for your livestock. 24 The oxen
and donkeys that till the ground will eat good grain,
its chaff blown away by the wind. 25 In that day, when
your enemies are slaughtered and the towers fall,
there will be streams of water flowing down every
mountain and hill. 26 The moon will be as bright as
the sun, and the sun will be seven times brighter—
like the light of seven days in one! So it will be when
the LORD begins to heal his people and cure the
wounds he gave them.

27 Look! The LORD is coming from far away,
burning with anger,
surrounded by thick, rising smoke.
His lips are filled with fury;
his words consume like fire.

28 His hot breath pours out like a flood
up to the neck of his enemies.
He will sift out the proud nations for destruction.
He will bridle them and lead them away
to ruin.

29 But the people of God will sing a song of joy,
like the songs at the holy festivals.
You will be filled with joy,
as when a flutist leads a group of pilgrims
to Jerusalem, the mountain of the LORD—
to the Rock of Israel.

30 And the LORD will make his majestic voice heard.
He will display the strength of his mighty arm.

KING JAMES VERSION

with the indignation of *his* anger, and *with* the flame
of a devouring fire, *with* scattering, and tempest, and
hailstones.
31 For through the voice of the LORD shall the Assyrian be beaten down, *which* smote with a rod.
32 And *in* every place where the grounded staff
shall pass, which the LORD shall lay upon him, *it* shall
be with tabrets and harps: and in battles of shaking
will he fight with it.
33 For Tophet *is* ordained of old; yea, for the king it
is prepared; he hath made *it* deep *and* large: the pile
thereof *is* fire and much wood; the breath of the
LORD, like a stream of brimstone, doth kindle it.

31 1 Woe to them that go down to Egypt for help;
and stay on horses, and trust in chariots, because *they are* many; and in horsemen, because they
are very strong; but they look not unto the Holy One
of Israel, neither seek the LORD!
2 Yet he also *is* wise, and will bring evil, and will not
call back his words: but will arise against the house
of the evildoers, and against the help of them that
work iniquity.
3 Now the Egyptians *are* men, and not God; and
their horses flesh, and not spirit. When the LORD
shall stretch out his hand, both he that helpeth shall
fall, and he that is holpen shall fall down, and they all
shall fail together.
4 For thus hath the LORD spoken unto me, Like as
the lion and the young lion roaring on his prey, when
a multitude of shepherds is called forth against him,
he will not be afraid of their voice, nor abase himself
for the noise of them: so shall the LORD of hosts
come down to fight for mount Zion, and for the hill
thereof.
5 As birds flying, so will the LORD of hosts defend
Jerusalem; defending also he will deliver *it; and*
passing over he will preserve it.
6 Turn ye unto *him from* whom the children of Israel have deeply revolted.
7 For in that day every man shall cast away his idols
of silver, and his idols of gold, which your own hands
have made unto you *for* a sin.
8 Then shall the Assyrian fall with the sword, not of
a mighty man; and the sword, not of a mean man,

NEW LIVING TRANSLATION

It will descend with devouring flames,
with cloudbursts, thunderstorms, and huge
hailstones.
31 At the LORD's command, the Assyrians will
be shattered.
He will strike them down with his
royal scepter.
32 And as the LORD strikes them with his rod
of punishment,
his people will celebrate with tambourines
and harps.
Lifting his mighty arm, he will fight
the Assyrians.
33 Topheth—the place of burning—
has long been ready for the Assyrian king;
the pyre is piled high with wood.
The breath of the LORD, like fire from a volcano,
will set it ablaze.

The Futility of Relying on Egypt

31 1 What sorrow awaits those who look to
Egypt for help,
trusting their horses, chariots, and charioteers
and depending on the strength of human armies
instead of looking to the LORD,
the Holy One of Israel.
2 In his wisdom, the LORD will send great disaster;
he will not change his mind.
He will rise against the wicked
and against their helpers.
3 For these Egyptians are mere humans, not God!
Their horses are puny flesh, not mighty spirits!
When the LORD raises his fist against them,
those who help will stumble,
and those being helped will fall.
They will all fall down and die together.

4 But this is what the LORD has told me:

"When a strong young lion
stands growling over a sheep it has killed,
it is not frightened by the shouts and noise
of a whole crowd of shepherds.
In the same way, the LORD of Heaven's Armies
will come down and fight on Mount Zion.
5 The LORD of Heaven's Armies will hover
over Jerusalem
and protect it like a bird protecting its nest.
He will defend and save the city;
he will pass over it and rescue it."

6 Though you are such wicked rebels, my people,
come and return to the LORD. 7 I know the glorious day
will come when each of you will throw away the gold
idols and silver images your sinful hands have made.

8 "The Assyrians will be destroyed,
but not by the swords of men.
The sword of God will strike them,
and they will panic and flee.

KING JAMES VERSION

shall devour him: but he shall flee from the sword,
and his young men shall be discomfited.
9And he shall pass over to his strong hold for fear,
and his princes shall be afraid of the ensign, saith
the LORD, whose fire *is* in Zion, and his furnace in
Jerusalem.

32 1Behold, a king shall reign in righteousness,
and princes shall rule in judgment.
2And a man shall be as an hiding place from the
wind, and a covert from the tempest; as rivers of
water in a dry place, as the shadow of a great rock in a
weary land.
3And the eyes of them that see shall not be dim,
and the ears of them that hear shall hearken.
4The heart also of the rash shall understand
knowledge, and the tongue of the stammerers shall
be ready to speak plainly.
5The vile person shall be no more called liberal,
nor the churl said *to be* bountiful.
6For the vile person will speak villany, and his
heart will work iniquity, to practise hypocrisy, and to
utter error against the LORD, to make empty the soul
of the hungry, and he will cause the drink of the
thirsty to fail.
7The instruments also of the churl *are* evil: he
deviseth wicked devices to destroy the poor with lying words, even when the needy speaketh right.
8But the liberal deviseth liberal things; and by liberal things shall he stand.
9Rise up, ye women that are at ease; hear my voice,
ye careless daughters; give ear unto my speech.
10Many days and years shall ye be troubled, ye
careless women: for the vintage shall fail, the gathering shall not come.
11Tremble, ye women that are at ease; be troubled,
ye careless ones: strip you, and make you bare, and
gird *sackcloth* upon *your* loins.
12They shall lament for the teats, for the pleasant
fields, for the fruitful vine.
13Upon the land of my people shall come up
thorns *and* briers; yea, upon all the houses of joy *in*
the joyous city:
14Because the palaces shall be forsaken; the multitude of the city shall be left; the forts and towers

NEW LIVING TRANSLATION

The strong young Assyrians
will be taken away as captives.
9 Even the strongest will quake with terror,
and princes will flee when they see your
battle flags,"
says the LORD, whose fire burns in Zion,
whose flame blazes from Jerusalem.

Israel's Ultimate Deliverance

32 1 Look, a righteous king is coming!
And honest princes will rule under him.
2 Each one will be like a shelter from the wind
and a refuge from the storm,
like streams of water in the desert
and the shadow of a great rock in
a parched land.
3 Then everyone who has eyes will be able
to see the truth,
and everyone who has ears will be able
to hear it.
4 Even the hotheads will be full of sense
and understanding.
Those who stammer will speak out plainly.
5 In that day ungodly fools will not be heroes.
Scoundrels will not be respected.
6 For fools speak foolishness
and make evil plans.
They practice ungodliness
and spread false teachings about the LORD.
They deprive the hungry of food
and give no water to the thirsty.
7 The smooth tricks of scoundrels are evil.
They plot crooked schemes.
They lie to convict the poor,
even when the cause of the poor is just.
8 But generous people plan to do what is generous,
and they stand firm in their generosity.
9 Listen, you women who lie around in ease.
Listen to me, you who are so smug.
10 In a short time—just a little more than a year—
you careless ones will suddenly begin to care.
For your fruit crops will fail,
and the harvest will never take place.
11 Tremble, you women of ease;
throw off your complacency.
Strip off your pretty clothes,
and put on burlap to show your grief.
12 Beat your breasts in sorrow for your
bountiful farms
and your fruitful grapevines.
13 For your land will be overgrown with
thorns and briers.
Your joyful homes and happy towns
will be gone.
14 The palace and the city will be deserted,
and busy towns will be empty.

KING JAMES VERSION

shall be for dens for ever, a joy of wild asses, a pasture
of flocks;
15 Until the spirit be poured upon us from on high,
and the wilderness be a fruitful field, and the fruitful
field be counted for a forest.
16 Then judgment shall dwell in the wilderness,
and righteousness remain in the fruitful field.
17 And the work of righteousness shall be peace;
and the effect of righteousness quietness and assurance for ever.
18 And my people shall dwell in a peaceable habitation, and in sure dwellings, and in quiet resting
places;
19 When it shall hail, coming down on the forest;
and the city shall be low in a low place.
20 Blessed *are* ye that sow beside all waters, that
send forth *thither* the feet of the ox and the ass.

33 1 Woe to thee that spoilest, and thou *wast*
not spoiled; and dealest treacherously, and
they dealt not treacherously with thee! when thou
shalt cease to spoil, thou shalt be spoiled; *and* when
thou shalt make an end to deal treacherously, they
shall deal treacherously with thee.
2 O LORD, be gracious unto us; we have waited for
thee: be thou their arm every morning, our salvation
also in the time of trouble.
3 At the noise of the tumult the people fled; at the
lifting up of thyself the nations were scattered.
4 And your spoil shall be gathered *like* the gathering of the caterpiller: as the running to and fro of locusts shall he run upon them.
5 The LORD is exalted; for he dwelleth on high: he
hath filled Zion with judgment and righteousness.
6 And wisdom and knowledge shall be the stability
of thy times, *and* strength of salvation: the fear of the
LORD *is* his treasure.
7 Behold, their valiant ones shall cry without: the
ambassadors of peace shall weep bitterly.
8 The highways lie waste, the wayfaring man
ceaseth: he hath broken the covenant, he hath despised the cities, he regardeth no man.

NEW LIVING TRANSLATION

Wild donkeys will frolic and flocks will graze
in the empty forts* and watchtowers
15 until at last the Spirit is poured out
on us from heaven.
Then the wilderness will become a fertile field,
and the fertile field will yield bountiful crops.

16 Justice will rule in the wilderness
and righteousness in the fertile field.
17 And this righteousness will bring peace.
Yes, it will bring quietness and confidence
forever.
18 My people will live in safety, quietly at home.
They will be at rest.
19 Even if the forest should be destroyed
and the city torn down,
20 the LORD will greatly bless his people.
Wherever they plant seed, bountiful crops
will spring up.
Their cattle and donkeys will graze freely.

A Message about Assyria

33 1 What sorrow awaits you Assyrians, who
have destroyed others*
but have never been destroyed yourselves.
You betray others,
but you have never been betrayed.
When you are done destroying,
you will be destroyed.
When you are done betraying,
you will be betrayed.
2 But LORD, be merciful to us,
for we have waited for you.
Be our strong arm each day
and our salvation in times of trouble.
3 The enemy runs at the sound of your voice.
When you stand up, the nations flee!
4 Just as caterpillars and locusts strip the fields
and vines,
so the fallen army of Assyria will be stripped!
5 Though the LORD is very great and lives in heaven,
he will make Jerusalem* his home of justice
and righteousness.
6 In that day he will be your sure foundation,
providing a rich store of salvation, wisdom,
and knowledge.
The fear of the LORD will be your treasure.
7 But now your brave warriors weep in public.
Your ambassadors of peace cry in bitter
disappointment.
8 Your roads are deserted;
no one travels them anymore.
The Assyrians have broken their peace treaty
and care nothing for the promises they made
before witnesses.*

32:14 Hebrew *the Ophel.* **33:1** Hebrew *What sorrow awaits you, O destroyer.* The Hebrew text does not specifically name Assyria as the object of the prophecy in this chapter. **33:5** Hebrew *Zion;* also in 33:14. **33:8** As in Dead Sea Scrolls; Masoretic Text reads *care nothing for the cities.*

KING JAMES VERSION

9 The earth mourneth *and* languisheth: Lebanon is ashamed *and* hewn down: Sharon is like a wilderness; and Bashan and Carmel shake off *their fruits*.

10 Now will I rise, saith the LORD; now will I be exalted; now will I lift up myself.

11 Ye shall conceive chaff, ye shall bring forth stubble: your breath, *as* fire, shall devour you.

12 And the people shall be *as* the burnings of lime: *as* thorns cut up shall they be burned in the fire.

13 Hear, ye *that are* far off, what I have done; and, ye *that are* near, acknowledge my might.

14 The sinners in Zion are afraid; fearfulness hath surprised the hypocrites. Who among us shall dwell with the devouring fire? who among us shall dwell with everlasting burnings?

15 He that walketh righteously, and speaketh uprightly; he that despiseth the gain of oppressions, that shaketh his hands from holding of bribes, that stoppeth his ears from hearing of blood, and shutteth his eyes from seeing evil;

16 He shall dwell on high: his place of defence *shall be* the munitions of rocks: bread shall be given him; his waters *shall be* sure.

17 Thine eyes shall see the king in his beauty: they shall behold the land that is very far off.

18 Thine heart shall meditate terror. Where *is* the scribe? where *is* the receiver? where *is* he that counted the towers?

19 Thou shalt not see a fierce people, a people of a deeper speech than thou canst perceive; of a stammering tongue, *that thou canst* not understand.

20 Look upon Zion, the city of our solemnities: thine eyes shall see Jerusalem a quiet habitation, a tabernacle *that* shall not be taken down; not one of the stakes thereof shall ever be removed, neither shall any of the cords thereof be broken.

21 But there the glorious LORD *will be* unto us a place of broad rivers *and* streams; wherein shall go no galley with oars, neither shall gallant ship pass thereby.

22 For the LORD *is* our judge, the LORD *is* our lawgiver, the LORD *is* our king; he will save us.

23 Thy tacklings are loosed; they could not well strengthen their mast, they could not spread the sail:

NEW LIVING TRANSLATION

They have no respect for anyone.
9 The land of Israel wilts in mourning.
Lebanon withers with shame.
The plain of Sharon is now a wilderness.
Bashan and Carmel have been plundered.

10 But the LORD says: "Now I will stand up.
Now I will show my power and might.
11 You Assyrians produce nothing but dry grass and stubble.
Your own breath will turn to fire and consume you.
12 Your people will be burned up completely,
like thornbushes cut down and tossed in a fire.
13 Listen to what I have done, you nations far away!
And you that are near, acknowledge my might!"
14 The sinners in Jerusalem shake with fear.
Terror seizes the godless.
"Who can live with this devouring fire?" they cry.
"Who can survive this all-consuming fire?"
15 Those who are honest and fair,
who refuse to profit by fraud,
who stay far away from bribes,
who refuse to listen to those who plot murder,
who shut their eyes to all enticement to do wrong—
16 these are the ones who will dwell on high.
The rocks of the mountains will be their fortress.
Food will be supplied to them,
and they will have water in abundance.
17 Your eyes will see the king in all his splendor,
and you will see a land that stretches into the distance.
18 You will think back to this time of terror, asking,
"Where are the Assyrian officers
who counted our towers?
Where are the bookkeepers
who recorded the plunder taken from our fallen city?"
19 You will no longer see these fierce, violent people
with their strange, unknown language.

20 Instead, you will see Zion as a place of holy festivals.
You will see Jerusalem, a city quiet and secure.
It will be like a tent whose ropes are taut
and whose stakes are firmly fixed.
21 The LORD will be our Mighty One.
He will be like a wide river of protection
that no enemy can cross,
that no enemy ship can sail upon.
22 For the LORD is our judge,
our lawgiver, and our king.
He will care for us and save us.
23 The enemies' sails hang loose
on broken masts with useless tackle.

KING JAMES VERSION

then is the prey of a great spoil divided; the lame take the prey.

24 And the inhabitant shall not say, I am sick: the people that dwell therein *shall be* forgiven *their* iniquity.

34

1 Come near, ye nations, to hear; and hearken, ye people: let the earth hear, and all that is therein; the world, and all things that come forth of it.

2 For the indignation of the LORD *is* upon all nations, and *his* fury upon all their armies: he hath utterly destroyed them, he hath delivered them to the slaughter.

3 Their slain also shall be cast out, and their stink shall come up out of their carcases, and the mountains shall be melted with their blood.

4 And all the host of heaven shall be dissolved, and the heavens shall be rolled together as a scroll: and all their host shall fall down, as the leaf falleth off from the vine, and as a falling *fig* from the fig tree.

5 For my sword shall be bathed in heaven: behold, it shall come down upon Idumea, and upon the people of my curse, to judgment.

6 The sword of the LORD is filled with blood, it is made fat with fatness, *and* with the blood of lambs and goats, with the fat of the kidneys of rams: for the LORD hath a sacrifice in Bozrah, and a great slaughter in the land of Idumea.

7 And the unicorns shall come down with them, and the bullocks with the bulls; and their land shall be soaked with blood, and their dust made fat with fatness.

8 For *it is* the day of the LORD's vengeance, *and* the year of recompences for the controversy of Zion.

9 And the streams thereof shall be turned into pitch, and the dust thereof into brimstone, and the land thereof shall become burning pitch.

10 It shall not be quenched night nor day; the smoke thereof shall go up for ever: from generation to generation it shall lie waste; none shall pass through it for ever and ever.

11 But the cormorant and the bittern shall possess it; the owl also and the raven shall dwell in it: and he

NEW LIVING TRANSLATION

Their treasure will be divided by the
people of God.
Even the lame will take their share!
24 The people of Israel will no longer say,
"We are sick and helpless,"
for the LORD will forgive their sins.

A Message for the Nations

34 Come here and listen, O nations
of the earth.
Let the world and everything in it hear
my words.
2 For the LORD is enraged against the nations.
His fury is against all their armies.
He will completely destroy* them,
dooming them to slaughter.
3 Their dead will be left unburied,
and the stench of rotting bodies will
fill the land.
The mountains will flow with their blood.
4 The heavens above will melt away
and disappear like a rolled-up scroll.
The stars will fall from the sky
like withered leaves from a grapevine,
or shriveled figs from a fig tree.
5 And when my sword has finished its work
in the heavens,
it will fall upon Edom,
the nation I have marked for destruction.
6 The sword of the LORD is drenched with blood
and covered with fat—
with the blood of lambs and goats,
with the fat of rams prepared for sacrifice.
Yes, the LORD will offer a sacrifice in the
city of Bozrah.
He will make a mighty slaughter in Edom.
7 Even men as strong as wild oxen will die—
the young men alongside the veterans.
The land will be soaked with blood
and the soil enriched with fat.
8 For it is the day of the LORD's revenge,
the year when Edom will be paid back for
all it did to Israel.*
9 The streams of Edom will be filled with
burning pitch,
and the ground will be covered with fire.
10 This judgment on Edom will never end;
the smoke of its burning will rise forever.
The land will lie deserted from generation
to generation.
No one will live there anymore.
11 It will be haunted by the desert owl and
the screech owl,
the great owl and the raven.*

34:2 The Hebrew term used here refers to the complete consecration of things or people to the LORD, either by destroying them or by giving them as an offering; similarly in 34:5. **34:8** Hebrew *to Zion.* **34:11** The identification of some of these birds is uncertain.

KING JAMES VERSION

shall stretch out upon it the line of confusion, and
the stones of emptiness.
12 They shall call the nobles thereof to the kingdom, but none *shall be* there, and all her princes shall
be nothing.
13 And thorns shall come up in her palaces, nettles
and brambles in the fortresses thereof: and it shall
be an habitation of dragons, *and* a court for owls.
14 The wild beasts of the desert shall also meet
with the wild beasts of the island, and the satyr shall
cry to his fellow; the screech owl also shall rest there,
and find for herself a place of rest.
15 There shall the great owl make her nest, and lay,
and hatch, and gather under her shadow: there shall
the vultures also be gathered, every one with her
mate.
16 Seek ye out of the book of the LORD, and read: no
one of these shall fail, none shall want her mate: for
my mouth it hath commanded, and his spirit it hath
gathered them.
17 And he hath cast the lot for them, and his hand
hath divided it unto them by line: they shall possess
it for ever, from generation to generation shall they
dwell therein.

35 1 The wilderness and the solitary place shall
be glad for them; and the desert shall rejoice,
and blossom as the rose.
2 It shall blossom abundantly, and rejoice even
with joy and singing: the glory of Lebanon shall be
given unto it, the excellency of Carmel and Sharon,
they shall see the glory of the LORD, *and* the excellency of our God.
3 Strengthen ye the weak hands, and confirm the
feeble knees.
4 Say to them *that are* of a fearful heart, Be strong,
fear not: behold, your God will come *with* vengeance, *even* God *with* a recompence; he will come
and save you.
5 Then the eyes of the blind shall be opened, and
the ears of the deaf shall be unstopped.
6 Then shall the lame *man* leap as an hart, and the

NEW LIVING TRANSLATION

For God will measure that land carefully;
he will measure it for chaos and destruction.
12 It will be called the Land of Nothing,
and all its nobles will soon be gone.*
13 Thorns will overrun its palaces;
nettles and thistles will grow in its forts.
The ruins will become a haunt for jackals
and a home for owls.
14 Desert animals will mingle there with hyenas,
their howls filling the night.
Wild goats will bleat at one another among
the ruins,
and night creatures* will come there to rest.
15 There the owl will make her nest and lay
her eggs.
She will hatch her young and cover them
with her wings.
And the buzzards will come,
each one with its mate.

16 Search the book of the LORD,
and see what he will do.
Not one of these birds and animals will be missing,
and none will lack a mate,
for the LORD has promised this.
His Spirit will make it all come true.
17 He has surveyed and divided the land
and deeded it over to those creatures.
They will possess it forever,
from generation to generation.

Hope for Restoration

35 1 Even the wilderness and desert will be
glad in those days.
The wasteland will rejoice and blossom with
spring crocuses.
2 Yes, there will be an abundance of flowers
and singing and joy!
The deserts will become as green as the
mountains of Lebanon,
as lovely as Mount Carmel or the plain
of Sharon.
There the LORD will display his glory,
the splendor of our God.
3 With this news, strengthen those who
have tired hands,
and encourage those who have weak knees.
4 Say to those with fearful hearts,
"Be strong, and do not fear,
for your God is coming to destroy your enemies.
He is coming to save you."
5 And when he comes, he will open the eyes
of the blind
and unplug the ears of the deaf.
6 The lame will leap like a deer,
and those who cannot speak will sing for joy!

34:12 The meaning of the Hebrew is uncertain. 34:14 Hebrew *Lilith*, possibly a reference to a mythical demon of the night.

KING JAMES VERSION

tongue of the dumb sing: for in the wilderness shall
waters break out, and streams in the desert.
7 And the parched ground shall become a pool, and
the thirsty land springs of water: in the habitation of
dragons, where each lay, *shall be* grass with reeds and
rushes.
8 And an highway shall be there, and a way, and it
shall be called The way of holiness; the unclean shall
not pass over it; but it *shall be* for those: the wayfaring men, though fools, shall not err *therein*.
9 No lion shall be there, nor *any* ravenous beast
shall go up thereon, it shall not be found there; but
the redeemed shall walk *there*:
10 And the ransomed of the LORD shall return, and
come to Zion with songs and everlasting joy upon
their heads: they shall obtain joy and gladness, and
sorrow and sighing shall flee away.

36 1 Now it came to pass in the fourteenth year
of king Hezekiah, *that* Sennacherib king of
Assyria came up against all the defenced cities of
Judah, and took them.
2 And the king of Assyria sent Rabshakeh from
Lachish to Jerusalem unto king Hezekiah with a
great army. And he stood by the conduit of the upper
pool in the highway of the fuller's field.
3 Then came forth unto him Eliakim, Hilkiah's son,
which was over the house, and Shebna the scribe,
and Joah, Asaph's son, the recorder.

4 And Rabshakeh said unto them, Say ye now to
Hezekiah, Thus saith the great king, the king of Assyria, What confidence *is* this wherein thou trustest?
5 I say, *sayest thou*, (but *they are but* vain words)
I have counsel and strength for war: now on whom
dost thou trust, that thou rebellest against me?
6 Lo, thou trustest in the staff of this broken reed,
on Egypt; whereon if a man lean, it will go into his
hand, and pierce it: so *is* Pharaoh king of Egypt to all
that trust in him.
7 But if thou say to me, We trust in the LORD our
God: *is it* not he, whose high places and whose altars

NEW LIVING TRANSLATION

Springs will gush forth in the wilderness,
and streams will water the wasteland.
7 The parched ground will become a pool,
and springs of water will satisfy the
thirsty land.
Marsh grass and reeds and rushes will flourish
where desert jackals once lived.
8 And a great road will go through that once
deserted land.
It will be named the Highway of Holiness.
Evil-minded people will never travel on it.
It will be only for those who walk in God's ways;
fools will never walk there.
9 Lions will not lurk along its course,
nor any other ferocious beasts.
There will be no other dangers.
Only the redeemed will walk on it.
10 Those who have been ransomed by the
LORD will return.
They will enter Jerusalem* singing,
crowned with everlasting joy.
Sorrow and mourning will disappear,
and they will be filled with joy and gladness.

Assyria Invades Judah

36 In the fourteenth year of King Hezekiah's
reign,* King Sennacherib of Assyria came to
attack the fortified towns of Judah and conquered
them. 2 Then the king of Assyria sent his chief of
staff* from Lachish with a huge army to confront
King Hezekiah in Jerusalem. The Assyrians took up a
position beside the aqueduct that feeds water into
the upper pool, near the road leading to the field
where cloth is washed.*
3 These are the officials who went out to meet with
them: Eliakim son of Hilkiah, the palace administrator; Shebna the court secretary; and Joah son of
Asaph, the royal historian.

Sennacherib Threatens Jerusalem

4 Then the Assyrian king's chief of staff told them to
give this message to Hezekiah:

"This is what the great king of Assyria says: What
are you trusting in that makes you so confident?
5 Do you think that mere words can substitute for
military skill and strength? Who are you counting
on, that you have rebelled against me? 6 On Egypt?
If you lean on Egypt, it will be like a reed that
splinters beneath your weight and pierces your
hand. Pharaoh, the king of Egypt, is completely
unreliable!
7 "But perhaps you will say to me, 'We are
trusting in the LORD our God!' But isn't he the one
who was insulted by Hezekiah? Didn't Hezekiah
tear down his shrines and altars and make

35:10 Hebrew *Zion*. **36:1** The fourteenth year of Hezekiah's reign was 701 B.C. **36:2a** Or *the rabshakeh;* also in 36:4, 11, 12, 22. **36:2b** Or *bleached.*

KING JAMES VERSION

Hezekiah hath taken away, and said to Judah and to
Jerusalem, Ye shall worship before this altar?
8 Now therefore give pledges, I pray thee, to my
master the king of Assyria, and I will give thee two
thousand horses, if thou be able on thy part to set
riders upon them.
9 How then wilt thou turn away the face of one captain of the least of my master's servants, and put thy
trust on Egypt for chariots and for horsemen?
10 And am I now come up without the LORD against
this land to destroy it? the LORD said unto me, Go up
against this land, and destroy it.
11 Then said Eliakim and Shebna and Joah unto
Rabshakeh, Speak, I pray thee, unto thy servants in
the Syrian language; for we understand *it;* and speak
not to us in the Jews' language, in the ears of the
people that *are* on the wall.
12 But Rabshakeh said, Hath my master sent me to
thy master and to thee to speak these words? *hath he*
not *sent me* to the men that sit upon the wall, that
they may eat their own dung, and drink their own
piss with you?
13 Then Rabshakeh stood, and cried with a loud
voice in the Jews' language, and said, Hear ye the
words of the great king, the king of Assyria.
14 Thus saith the king, Let not Hezekiah deceive
you: for he shall not be able to deliver you.
15 Neither let Hezekiah make you trust in the LORD,
saying, The LORD will surely deliver us: this city shall
not be delivered into the hand of the king of Assyria.
16 Hearken not to Hezekiah: for thus saith the king
of Assyria, Make *an agreement* with me *by* a present,
and come out to me: and eat ye every one of his vine,
and every one of his fig tree, and drink ye every one
the waters of his own cistern;
17 Until I come and take you away to a land like
your own land, a land of corn and wine, a land of
bread and vineyards.
18 *Beware* lest Hezekiah persuade you, saying, The
LORD will deliver us. Hath any of the gods of the nations delivered his land out of the hand of the king of
Assyria?
19 Where *are* the gods of Hamath and Arphad?
where *are* the gods of Sepharvaim? and have they delivered Samaria out of my hand?
20 Who *are they* among all the gods of these lands,
that have delivered their land out of my hand, that
the LORD should deliver Jerusalem out of my hand?
21 But they held their peace, and answered him not
a word: for the king's commandment was, saying,
Answer him not.
22 Then came Eliakim, the son of Hilkiah, that *was*
over the household, and Shebna the scribe, and Joah,
the son of Asaph, the recorder, to Hezekiah with
their clothes rent, and told him the words of
Rabshakeh.

NEW LIVING TRANSLATION

everyone in Judah and Jerusalem worship only
at the altar here in Jerusalem?
8 "I'll tell you what! Strike a bargain with my
master, the king of Assyria. I will give you 2,000
horses if you can find that many men to ride on
them! 9 With your tiny army, how can you think
of challenging even the weakest contingent of
my master's troops, even with the help of Egypt's
chariots and charioteers? 10 What's more, do you
think we have invaded your land without the
LORD's direction? The LORD himself told us,
'Attack this land and destroy it!'"
11 Then Eliakim, Shebna, and Joah said to the Assyrian chief of staff, "Please speak to us in Aramaic,
for we understand it well. Don't speak in Hebrew,*
for the people on the wall will hear."
12 But Sennacherib's chief of staff replied, "Do you
think my master sent this message only to you and
your master? He wants all the people to hear it, for
when we put this city under siege, they will suffer
along with you. They will be so hungry and thirsty
that they will eat their own dung and drink their
own urine."
13 Then the chief of staff stood and shouted in Hebrew to the people on the wall, "Listen to this message from the great king of Assyria! 14 This is what
the king says: Don't let Hezekiah deceive you. He will
never be able to rescue you. 15 Don't let him fool you
into trusting in the LORD by saying, 'The LORD will
surely rescue us. This city will never fall into the
hands of the Assyrian king!'
16 "Don't listen to Hezekiah! These are the terms
the king of Assyria is offering: Make peace with me—
open the gates and come out. Then each of you can
continue eating from your own grapevine and fig
tree and drinking from your own well. 17 Then I will
arrange to take you to another land like this one—a
land of grain and new wine, bread and vineyards.
18 "Don't let Hezekiah mislead you by saying, 'The
LORD will rescue us!' Have the gods of any other nations ever saved their people from the king of Assyria? 19 What happened to the gods of Hamath and
Arpad? And what about the gods of Sepharvaim? Did
any god rescue Samaria from my power? 20 What god
of any nation has ever been able to save its people
from my power? So what makes you think that the
LORD can rescue Jerusalem from me?"
21 But the people were silent and did not utter a
word because Hezekiah had commanded them, "Do
not answer him."
22 Then Eliakim son of Hilkiah, the palace administrator; Shebna the court secretary; and Joah son of
Asaph, the royal historian, went back to Hezekiah.
They tore their clothes in despair, and they went in to
see the king and told him what the Assyrian chief of
staff had said.

36:11 Hebrew *in the dialect of Judah;* also in 36:13.

KING JAMES VERSION

37 1And it came to pass, when king Hezekiah
heard *it,* that he rent his clothes, and covered himself with sackcloth, and went into the house
of the LORD.
2And he sent Eliakim, who *was* over the household, and Shebna the scribe, and the elders of the
priests covered with sackcloth, unto Isaiah the
prophet the son of Amoz.
3And they said unto him, Thus saith Hezekiah,
This day *is* a day of trouble, and of rebuke, and of
blasphemy: for the children are come to the birth,
and *there is* not strength to bring forth.
4It may be the LORD thy God will hear the words of
Rabshakeh, whom the king of Assyria his master
hath sent to reproach the living God, and will reprove
the words which the LORD thy God hath heard:
wherefore lift up *thy* prayer for the remnant that
is left.
5So the servants of king Hezekiah came to Isaiah.
6And Isaiah said unto them, Thus shall ye say unto
your master, Thus saith the LORD, Be not afraid of the
words that thou hast heard, wherewith the servants
of the king of Assyria have blasphemed me.
7Behold, I will send a blast upon him, and he shall
hear a rumour, and return to his own land; and I will
cause him to fall by the sword in his own land.
8So Rabshakeh returned, and found the king of
Assyria warring against Libnah: for he had heard that
he was departed from Lachish.
9And he heard say concerning Tirhakah king of
Ethiopia, He is come forth to make war with thee.
And when he heard *it,* he sent messengers to Hezekiah, saying,
10Thus shall ye speak to Hezekiah king of Judah,
saying, Let not thy God, in whom thou trustest, deceive thee, saying, Jerusalem shall not be given into
the hand of the king of Assyria.
11Behold, thou hast heard what the kings of Assyria have done to all lands by destroying them utterly;
and shalt thou be delivered?
12Have the gods of the nations delivered them
which my fathers have destroyed, *as* Gozan, and Haran, and Rezeph, and the children of Eden which
were in Telassar?
13Where *is* the king of Hamath, and the king of
Arphad, and the king of the city of Sepharvaim,
Hena, and Ivah?
14And Hezekiah received the letter from the hand
of the messengers, and read it: and Hezekiah went
up unto the house of the LORD, and spread it before
the LORD.
15And Hezekiah prayed unto the LORD, saying,
16O LORD of hosts, God of Israel, that dwellest *between* the cherubims, thou *art* the God, *even* thou
alone, of all the kingdoms of the earth: thou hast
made heaven and earth.
17Incline thine ear, O LORD, and hear; open thine

NEW LIVING TRANSLATION

Hezekiah Seeks the LORD's Help

37 When King Hezekiah heard their report, he
tore his clothes and put on burlap and went
into the Temple of the LORD. 2And he sent Eliakim
the palace administrator, Shebna the court secretary,
and the leading priests, all dressed in burlap, to the
prophet Isaiah son of Amoz. 3They told him, "This is
what King Hezekiah says: Today is a day of trouble,
insults, and disgrace. It is like when a child is ready
to be born, but the mother has no strength to deliver
the baby. 4But perhaps the LORD your God has heard
the Assyrian chief of staff,* sent by the king to defy
the living God, and will punish him for his words. Oh,
pray for those of us who are left!"
5After King Hezekiah's officials delivered the
king's message to Isaiah, 6the prophet replied, "Say
to your master, 'This is what the LORD says: Do not be
disturbed by this blasphemous speech against me
from the Assyrian king's messengers. 7Listen! I myself will move against him,* and the king will receive
a message that he is needed at home. So he will return to his land, where I will have him killed with a
sword.'"
8Meanwhile, the Assyrian chief of staff left Jerusalem and went to consult the king of Assyria, who had
left Lachish and was attacking Libnah.
9Soon afterward King Sennacherib received word
that King Tirhakah of Ethiopia* was leading an army
to fight against him. Before leaving to meet the attack, he sent messengers back to Hezekiah in Jerusalem with this message:

10"This message is for King Hezekiah of Judah.
Don't let your God, in whom you trust, deceive
you with promises that Jerusalem will not be
captured by the king of Assyria. 11You know
perfectly well what the kings of Assyria have done
wherever they have gone. They have completely
destroyed everyone who stood in their way! Why
should you be any different? 12Have the gods of
other nations rescued them—such nations as
Gozan, Haran, Rezeph, and the people of Eden
who were in Tel-assar? My predecessors
destroyed them all! 13What happened to the
king of Hamath and the king of Arpad? What
happened to the kings of Sepharvaim, Hena,
and Ivvah?"

14After Hezekiah received the letter from the
messengers and read it, he went up to the LORD's
Temple and spread it out before the LORD. 15And
Hezekiah prayed this prayer before the LORD:
16"O LORD of Heaven's Armies, God of Israel, you are
enthroned between the mighty cherubim! You alone
are God of all the kingdoms of the earth. You alone
created the heavens and the earth. 17Bend down,
O LORD, and listen! Open your eyes, O LORD, and see!

37:4 Or *the rabshakeh;* also in 37:8. 37:7 Hebrew *I will put a spirit in him.* 37:9 Hebrew *of Cush.*

KING JAMES VERSION

eyes, O LORD, and see: and hear all the words of Sennacherib, which hath sent to reproach the living God.
18 Of a truth, LORD, the kings of Assyria have laid
waste all the nations, and their countries,
19 And have cast their gods into the fire: for they
were no gods, but the work of men's hands, wood and
stone: therefore they have destroyed them.
20 Now therefore, O LORD our God, save us from his
hand, that all the kingdoms of the earth may know
that thou *art* the LORD, *even* thou only.

21 Then Isaiah the son of Amoz sent unto Hezekiah, saying, Thus saith the LORD God of Israel,
Whereas thou hast prayed to me against Sennacherib king of Assyria:
22 This *is* the word which the LORD hath spoken
concerning him; The virgin, the daughter of Zion,
hath despised thee, *and* laughed thee to scorn; the
daughter of Jerusalem hath shaken her head at thee.
23 Whom hast thou reproached and blasphemed?
and against whom hast thou exalted *thy* voice, and
lifted up thine eyes on high? *even* against the Holy
One of Israel.
24 By thy servants hast thou reproached the Lord,
and hast said, By the multitude of my chariots am I
come up to the height of the mountains, to the sides
of Lebanon; and I will cut down the tall cedars
thereof, *and* the choice fir trees thereof: and I will
enter into the height of his border, *and* the forest of
his Carmel.
25 I have digged, and drunk water; and with the
sole of my feet have I dried up all the rivers of the besieged places.
26 Hast thou not heard long ago, *how* I have done it;
and of ancient times, that I have formed it? now have
I brought it to pass, that thou shouldest be to lay
waste defenced cities *into* ruinous heaps.
27 Therefore their inhabitants *were* of small power,
they were dismayed and confounded: they were *as*
the grass of the field, and *as* the green herb, *as* the
grass on the housetops, and *as corn* blasted before it
be grown up.
28 But I know thy abode, and thy going out, and thy
coming in, and thy rage against me.

NEW LIVING TRANSLATION

Listen to Sennacherib's words of defiance against
the living God.
18 "It is true, LORD, that the kings of Assyria have destroyed all these nations. 19 And they have thrown the
gods of these nations into the fire and burned them.
But of course the Assyrians could destroy them! They
were not gods at all—only idols of wood and stone
shaped by human hands. 20 Now, O LORD our God, rescue us from his power; then all the kingdoms of the
earth will know that you alone, O LORD, are God.*"

Isaiah Predicts Judah's Deliverance

21 Then Isaiah son of Amoz sent this message to Hezekiah: "This is what the LORD, the God of Israel, says:
Because you prayed about King Sennacherib of Assyria, 22 the LORD has spoken this word against him:

"The virgin daughter of Zion
despises you and laughs at you.
The daughter of Jerusalem
shakes her head in derision as you flee.

23 "Whom have you been defying and ridiculing?
Against whom did you raise your voice?
At whom did you look with such haughty eyes?
It was the Holy One of Israel!
24 By your messengers you have defied the Lord.
You have said, 'With my many chariots
I have conquered the highest mountains—
yes, the remotest peaks of Lebanon.
I have cut down its tallest cedars
and its finest cypress trees.
I have reached its farthest heights
and explored its deepest forests.
25 I have dug wells in many foreign lands*
and refreshed myself with their water.
With the sole of my foot,
I stopped up all the rivers of Egypt!'

26 "But have you not heard?
I decided this long ago.
Long ago I planned it,
and now I am making it happen.
I planned for you to crush fortified cities
into heaps of rubble.
27 That is why their people have so little power
and are so frightened and confused.
They are as weak as grass,
as easily trampled as tender green shoots.
They are like grass sprouting on a housetop,
scorched* before it can grow lush and tall.

28 "But I know you well—
where you stay
and when you come and go.
I know the way you have raged against me.

37:20 As in Dead Sea Scrolls (see also 2 Kgs 19:19); Masoretic Text reads *you alone are the LORD.* **37:25** As in Dead Sea Scrolls (see also 2 Kgs 19:24); Masoretic Text lacks *in many foreign lands.* **37:27** As in Dead Sea Scrolls and some Greek manuscripts (see also 2 Kgs 19:26); most Hebrew manuscripts read *like a terraced field.*

KING JAMES VERSION

29 Because thy rage against me, and thy tumult, is
come up into mine ears, therefore will I put my hook
in thy nose, and my bridle in thy lips, and I will turn
thee back by the way by which thou camest.
30 And this *shall be* a sign unto thee, Ye shall eat
this year such as groweth of itself; and the second
year that which springeth of the same: and in the
third year sow ye, and reap, and plant vineyards, and
eat the fruit thereof.
31 And the remnant that is escaped of the house of
Judah shall again take root downward, and bear fruit
upward:
32 For out of Jerusalem shall go forth a remnant,
and they that escape out of mount Zion: the zeal of
the LORD of hosts shall do this.
33 Therefore thus saith the LORD concerning the
king of Assyria, He shall not come into this city, nor
shoot an arrow there, nor come before it with
shields, nor cast a bank against it.
34 By the way that he came, by the same shall he return, and shall not come into this city, saith the LORD.
35 For I will defend this city to save it for mine own
sake, and for my servant David's sake.
36 Then the angel of the LORD went forth, and
smote in the camp of the Assyrians a hundred and
fourscore and five thousand: and when they arose
early in the morning, behold, they *were* all dead
corpses.
37 So Sennacherib king of Assyria departed, and
went and returned, and dwelt at Nineveh.
38 And it came to pass, as he was worshipping in
the house of Nisroch his god, that Adrammelech
and Sharezer his sons smote him with the sword;
and they escaped into the land of Armenia: and Esarhaddon his son reigned in his stead.

NEW LIVING TRANSLATION

29 And because of your raging against me
and your arrogance, which I have heard
for myself,
I will put my hook in your nose
and my bit in your mouth.
I will make you return
by the same road on which you came."

30 Then Isaiah said to Hezekiah, "Here is the proof
that what I say is true:

"This year you will eat only what grows
up by itself,
and next year you will eat what springs
up from that.
But in the third year you will plant crops and
harvest them;
you will tend vineyards and eat their fruit.
31 And you who are left in Judah,
who have escaped the ravages of the siege,
will put roots down in your own soil
and grow up and flourish.
32 For a remnant of my people will spread
out from Jerusalem,
a group of survivors from Mount Zion.
The passionate commitment of the LORD of
Heaven's Armies
will make this happen!

33 "And this is what the LORD says about the king of
Assyria:

"'His armies will not enter Jerusalem.
They will not even shoot an arrow at it.
They will not march outside its gates with
their shields
nor build banks of earth against its walls.
34 The king will return to his own country
by the same road on which he came.
He will not enter this city,'
says the LORD.
35 'For my own honor and for the sake of
my servant David,
I will defend this city and protect it.'"

36 That night the angel of the LORD went out to the
Assyrian camp and killed 185,000 Assyrian soldiers.
When the surviving Assyrians* woke up the next
morning, they found corpses everywhere. 37 Then
King Sennacherib of Assyria broke camp and returned to his own land. He went home to his capital
of Nineveh and stayed there.
38 One day while he was worshiping in the temple
of his god Nisroch, his sons Adrammelech and Sharezer killed him with their swords. They then escaped to the land of Ararat, and another son,
Esarhaddon, became the next king of Assyria.

37:36 Hebrew *When they.*

KING JAMES VERSION

38 1In those days was Hezekiah sick unto
death. And Isaiah the prophet the son of
Amoz came unto him, and said unto him, Thus saith
the LORD, Set thine house in order: for thou shalt die,
and not live.
2Then Hezekiah turned his face toward the wall,
and prayed unto the LORD,
3And said, Remember now, O LORD, I beseech thee,
how I have walked before thee in truth and with a
perfect heart, and have done *that which is* good in
thy sight. And Hezekiah wept sore.
4Then came the word of the LORD to Isaiah, saying,
5Go, and say to Hezekiah, Thus saith the LORD, the
God of David thy father, I have heard thy prayer, I
have seen thy tears: behold, I will add unto thy days
fifteen years.
6And I will deliver thee and this city out of the
hand of the king of Assyria: and I will defend this
city.
7And this *shall be* a sign unto thee from the LORD,
that the LORD will do this thing that he hath spoken;
8Behold, I will bring again the shadow of the degrees, which is gone down in the sun dial of Ahaz, ten
degrees backward. So the sun returned ten degrees,
by which degrees it was gone down.
9The writing of Hezekiah king of Judah, when he
had been sick, and was recovered of his sickness:
10I said in the cutting off of my days, I shall go to
the gates of the grave: I am deprived of the residue of
my years.
11I said, I shall not see the LORD, *even* the LORD, in
the land of the living: I shall behold man no more
with the inhabitants of the world.
12Mine age is departed, and is removed from me
as a shepherd's tent: I have cut off like a weaver my
life: he will cut me off with pining sickness: from day
even to night wilt thou make an end of me.
13I reckoned till morning, *that,* as a lion, so will he
break all my bones: from day *even* to night wilt thou
make an end of me.
14Like a crane *or* a swallow, so did I chatter: I did
mourn as a dove: mine eyes fail *with looking* upward: O LORD, I am oppressed; undertake for me.
15What shall I say? he hath both spoken unto me,
and himself hath done *it:* I shall go softly all my years
in the bitterness of my soul.
16O Lord, by these *things men* live, and in all these
things is the life of my spirit: so wilt thou recover me,
and make me to live.

NEW LIVING TRANSLATION

Hezekiah's Sickness and Recovery

38 About that time Hezekiah became deathly
ill, and the prophet Isaiah son of Amoz went
to visit him. He gave the king this message: "This is
what the LORD says: 'Set your affairs in order, for you
are going to die. You will not recover from this illness.'"
2When Hezekiah heard this, he turned his face to
the wall and prayed to the LORD, 3"Remember,
O LORD, how I have always been faithful to you and
have served you single-mindedly, always doing what
pleases you." Then he broke down and wept bitterly.
4Then this message came to Isaiah from the LORD:
5"Go back to Hezekiah and tell him, 'This is what the
LORD, the God of your ancestor David, says: I have
heard your prayer and seen your tears. I will add fifteen years to your life, 6and I will rescue you and this
city from the king of Assyria. Yes, I will defend this
city.
7"'And this is the sign from the LORD to prove that
he will do as he promised: 8I will cause the sun's
shadow to move ten steps backward on the sundial*
of Ahaz!'" So the shadow on the sundial moved backward ten steps.

Hezekiah's Poem of Praise

9When King Hezekiah was well again, he wrote this
poem:

10 I said, "In the prime of my life,
must I now enter the place of the dead?*
Am I to be robbed of the rest of my years?"
11 I said, "Never again will I see the LORD GOD
while still in the land of the living.
Never again will I see my friends
or be with those who live in this world.
12 My life has been blown away
like a shepherd's tent in a storm.
It has been cut short,
as when a weaver cuts cloth from a loom.
Suddenly, my life was over.
13 I waited patiently all night,
but I was torn apart as though by lions.
Suddenly, my life was over.
14 Delirious, I chattered like a swallow or a crane,
and then I moaned like a mourning dove.
My eyes grew tired of looking to heaven for help.
I am in trouble, Lord. Help me!"
15 But what could I say?
For he himself sent this sickness.
Now I will walk humbly throughout my years
because of this anguish I have felt.
16 Lord, your discipline is good,
for it leads to life and health.
You restore my health
and allow me to live!

38:8 Hebrew *the steps.* **38:10** Hebrew *enter the gates of Sheol?*

KING JAMES VERSION

17 Behold, for peace I had great bitterness: but
thou hast in love to my soul *delivered it* from the pit
of corruption: for thou hast cast all my sins behind
thy back.
18 For the grave cannot praise thee, death can *not*
celebrate thee: they that go down into the pit cannot
hope for thy truth.
19 The living, the living, he shall praise thee, as I *do*
this day: the father to the children shall make known
thy truth.
20 The LORD *was ready* to save me: therefore we
will sing my songs to the stringed instruments all the
days of our life in the house of the LORD.
21 For Isaiah had said, Let them take a lump of figs,
and lay *it* for a plaster upon the boil, and he shall
recover.
22 Hezekiah also had said, What *is* the sign that I
shall go up to the house of the LORD?

39 1 At that time Merodach-baladan, the son of
Baladan, king of Babylon, sent letters and a
present to Hezekiah: for he had heard that he had
been sick, and was recovered.
2 And Hezekiah was glad of them, and shewed
them the house of his precious things, the silver, and
the gold, and the spices, and the precious ointment,
and all the house of his armour, and all that was
found in his treasures: there was nothing in his
house, nor in all his dominion, that Hezekiah shewed
them not.
3 Then came Isaiah the prophet unto king Hezekiah, and said unto him, What said these men? and
from whence came they unto thee? And Hezekiah
said, They are come from a far country unto me, *even*
from Babylon.
4 Then said he, What have they seen in thine
house? And Hezekiah answered, All that *is* in mine
house have they seen: there is nothing among my
treasures that I have not shewed them.
5 Then said Isaiah to Hezekiah, Hear the word of
the LORD of hosts:
6 Behold, the days come, that all that *is* in thine
house, and *that* which thy fathers have laid up in
store until this day, shall be carried to Babylon: nothing shall be left, saith the LORD.
7 And of thy sons that shall issue from thee, which
thou shalt beget, shall they take away; and they shall
be eunuchs in the palace of the king of Babylon.
8 Then said Hezekiah to Isaiah, Good *is* the word of
the LORD which thou hast spoken. He said moreover,
For there shall be peace and truth in my days.

40 1 Comfort ye, comfort ye my people, saith
your God.

NEW LIVING TRANSLATION

17 Yes, this anguish was good for me,
for you have rescued me from death
and forgiven all my sins.
18 For the dead* cannot praise you;
they cannot raise their voices in praise.
Those who go down to the grave
can no longer hope in your faithfulness.
19 Only the living can praise you as I do today.
Each generation tells of your faithfulness
to the next.
20 Think of it—the LORD is ready to heal me!
I will sing his praises with instruments
every day of my life
in the Temple of the LORD.

21 Isaiah had said to Hezekiah's servants, "Make an
ointment from figs and spread it over the boil, and
Hezekiah will recover."
22 And Hezekiah had asked, "What sign will prove
that I will go to the Temple of the LORD?"

Envoys from Babylon

39 Soon after this, Merodach-baladan son of
Baladan, king of Babylon, sent Hezekiah his
best wishes and a gift. He had heard that Hezekiah
had been very sick and that he had recovered. 2 Hezekiah was delighted with the Babylonian envoys and
showed them everything in his treasure-houses—the
silver, the gold, the spices, and the aromatic oils. He
also took them to see his armory and showed them
everything in his royal treasuries! There was nothing
in his palace or kingdom that Hezekiah did not show
them.
3 Then Isaiah the prophet went to King Hezekiah
and asked him, "What did those men want? Where
were they from?"
Hezekiah replied, "They came from the distant
land of Babylon."
4 "What did they see in your palace?" asked Isaiah.
"They saw everything," Hezekiah replied. "I showed
them everything I own—all my royal treasuries."
5 Then Isaiah said to Hezekiah, "Listen to this message from the LORD of Heaven's Armies: 6 'The time is
coming when everything in your palace—all the treasures stored up by your ancestors until now—will be
carried off to Babylon. Nothing will be left,' says the
LORD. 7 'Some of your very own sons will be taken
away into exile. They will become eunuchs who will
serve in the palace of Babylon's king.'"
8 Then Hezekiah said to Isaiah, "This message you
have given me from the LORD is good." For the king
was thinking, "At least there will be peace and security during my lifetime."

Comfort for God's People

40 1 "Comfort, comfort my people,"
says your God.

38:18 Hebrew *Sheol*.

KING JAMES VERSION

2 Speak ye comfortably to Jerusalem, and cry unto her, that her warfare is accomplished, that her iniquity is pardoned: for she hath received of the LORD's hand double for all her sins.

3 The voice of him that crieth in the wilderness, Prepare ye the way of the LORD, make straight in the desert a highway for our God.

4 Every valley shall be exalted, and every mountain and hill shall be made low: and the crooked shall be made straight, and the rough places plain:

5 And the glory of the LORD shall be revealed, and all flesh shall see *it* together: for the mouth of the LORD hath spoken *it*.

6 The voice said, Cry. And he said, What shall I cry? All flesh *is* grass, and all the goodliness thereof *is* as the flower of the field:

7 The grass withereth, the flower fadeth: because the spirit of the LORD bloweth upon it: surely the people *is* grass.

8 The grass withereth, the flower fadeth: but the word of our God shall stand for ever.

9 O Zion, that bringest good tidings, get thee up into the high mountain; O Jerusalem, that bringest good tidings, lift up thy voice with strength; lift *it* up, be not afraid; say unto the cities of Judah, Behold your God!

10 Behold, the Lord GOD will come with strong *hand,* and his arm shall rule for him: behold, his reward *is* with him, and his work before him.

11 He shall feed his flock like a shepherd: he shall gather the lambs with his arm, and carry *them* in his bosom, *and* shall gently lead those that are with young.

12 Who hath measured the waters in the hollow of his hand, and meted out heaven with the span, and comprehended the dust of the earth in a measure, and weighed the mountains in scales, and the hills in a balance?

NEW LIVING TRANSLATION

2 "Speak tenderly to Jerusalem.
Tell her that her sad days are gone
and her sins are pardoned.
Yes, the LORD has punished her twice over
for all her sins."

3 Listen! It's the voice of someone shouting,
"Clear the way through the wilderness
for the LORD!
Make a straight highway through the wasteland
for our God!
4 Fill in the valleys,
and level the mountains and hills.
Straighten the curves,
and smooth out the rough places.
5 Then the glory of the LORD will be revealed,
and all people will see it together.
The LORD has spoken!"*

6 A voice said, "Shout!"
I asked, "What should I shout?"

"Shout that people are like the grass.
Their beauty fades as quickly
as the flowers in a field.
7 The grass withers and the flowers fade
beneath the breath of the LORD.
And so it is with people.
8 The grass withers and the flowers fade,
but the word of our God stands forever."

9 O Zion, messenger of good news,
shout from the mountaintops!
Shout it louder, O Jerusalem.*
Shout, and do not be afraid.
Tell the towns of Judah,
"Your God is coming!"
10 Yes, the Sovereign LORD is coming in power.
He will rule with a powerful arm.
See, he brings his reward with him as
he comes.
11 He will feed his flock like a shepherd.
He will carry the lambs in his arms,
holding them close to his heart.
He will gently lead the mother sheep
with their young.

The LORD Has No Equal

12 Who else has held the oceans in his hand?
Who has measured off the heavens with
his fingers?
Who else knows the weight of the earth
or has weighed the mountains and hills
on a scale?

40:3-5 Greek version reads *He is a voice shouting in the wilderness, / "Prepare the way for the LORD's coming! / Clear a road for our God! / Fill in the valleys, / and level the mountains and hills. / And then the glory of the LORD will be revealed, / and all people will see the salvation sent from God. / The LORD has spoken!"* Compare Matt 3:3; Mark 1:3; Luke 3:4-6. **40:9** Or *O messenger of good news, shout to Zion from the mountaintops! Shout it louder to Jerusalem.*

KING JAMES VERSION

13 Who hath directed the Spirit of the LORD, or *being* his counsellor hath taught him?

14 With whom took he counsel, and *who* instructed him, and taught him in the path of judgment, and taught him knowledge, and shewed to him the way of understanding?

15 Behold, the nations *are* as a drop of a bucket, and are counted as the small dust of the balance: behold, he taketh up the isles as a very little thing.

16 And Lebanon *is* not sufficient to burn, nor the beasts thereof sufficient for a burnt offering.

17 All nations before him *are* as nothing; and they are counted to him less than nothing, and vanity.

18 To whom then will ye liken God? or what likeness will ye compare unto him?

19 The workman melteth a graven image, and the goldsmith spreadeth it over with gold, and casteth silver chains.

20 He that *is* so impoverished that he hath no oblation chooseth a tree *that* will not rot; he seeketh unto him a cunning workman to prepare a graven image, *that* shall not be moved.

21 Have ye not known? have ye not heard? hath it not been told you from the beginning? have ye not understood from the foundations of the earth?

22 *It is* he that sitteth upon the circle of the earth, and the inhabitants thereof *are* as grasshoppers; that stretcheth out the heavens as a curtain, and spreadeth them out as a tent to dwell in:

23 That bringeth the princes to nothing; he maketh the judges of the earth as vanity.

24 Yea, they shall not be planted; yea, they shall not be sown: yea, their stock shall not take root in the earth: and he shall also blow upon them, and they shall wither, and the whirlwind shall take them away as stubble.

25 To whom then will ye liken me, or shall I be equal? saith the Holy One.

26 Lift up your eyes on high, and behold who hath created these *things,* that bringeth out their host by number: he calleth them all by names by the greatness of his might, for that *he is* strong in power; not one faileth.

NEW LIVING TRANSLATION

13 Who is able to advise the Spirit of the LORD?*
Who knows enough to give him advice or
teach him?
14 Has the LORD ever needed anyone's advice?
Does he need instruction about what is good?
Did someone teach him what is right
or show him the path of justice?

15 No, for all the nations of the world
are but a drop in the bucket.
They are nothing more
than dust on the scales.
He picks up the whole earth
as though it were a grain of sand.
16 All the wood in Lebanon's forests
and all Lebanon's animals would
not be enough
to make a burnt offering worthy of our God.
17 The nations of the world are worth nothing to him.
In his eyes they count for less than nothing—
mere emptiness and froth.

18 To whom can you compare God?
What image can you find to resemble him?
19 Can he be compared to an idol formed in a mold,
overlaid with gold, and decorated with
silver chains?
20 Or if people are too poor for that,
they might at least choose wood that
won't decay
and a skilled craftsman
to carve an image that won't fall down!

21 Haven't you heard? Don't you understand?
Are you deaf to the words of God—
the words he gave before the world began?
Are you so ignorant?
22 God sits above the circle of the earth.
The people below seem like grasshoppers
to him!
He spreads out the heavens like a curtain
and makes his tent from them.
23 He judges the great people of the world
and brings them all to nothing.
24 They hardly get started, barely taking root,
when he blows on them and they wither.
The wind carries them off like chaff.

25 "To whom will you compare me?
Who is my equal?" asks the Holy One.
26 Look up into the heavens.
Who created all the stars?
He brings them out like an army, one after another,
calling each by its name.
Because of his great power and incomparable
strength,
not a single one is missing.

40:13 Greek version reads *Who can know the LORD's thoughts?* Compare Rom 11:34; 1 Cor 2:16.

KING JAMES VERSION

27 Why sayest thou, O Jacob, and speakest, O Israel, My way is hid from the LORD, and my judgment is passed over from my God?

28 Hast thou not known? hast thou not heard, *that* the everlasting God, the LORD, the Creator of the ends of the earth, fainteth not, neither is weary? *there is* no searching of his understanding.

29 He giveth power to the faint; and to *them that have* no might he increaseth strength.

30 Even the youths shall faint and be weary, and the young men shall utterly fall:

31 But they that wait upon the LORD shall renew *their* strength; they shall mount up with wings as eagles; they shall run, and not be weary; *and* they shall walk, and not faint.

41 1 Keep silence before me, O islands; and let the people renew *their* strength: let them come near; then let them speak: let us come near together to judgment.

2 Who raised up the righteous *man* from the east, called him to his foot, gave the nations before him, and made *him* rule over kings? he gave *them* as the dust to his sword, *and* as driven stubble to his bow.

3 He pursued them, *and* passed safely; *even* by the way *that* he had not gone with his feet.

4 Who hath wrought and done *it*, calling the generations from the beginning? I the LORD, the first, and with the last; I *am* he.

5 The isles saw *it*, and feared; the ends of the earth were afraid, drew near, and came.

6 They helped every one his neighbour; and *every one* said to his brother, Be of good courage.

7 So the carpenter encouraged the goldsmith, *and* he that smootheth *with* the hammer him that smote the anvil, saying, It *is* ready for the soldering: and he fastened it with nails, *that* it should not be moved.

8 But thou, Israel, *art* my servant, Jacob whom I have chosen, the seed of Abraham my friend.

NEW LIVING TRANSLATION

27 O Jacob, how can you say the LORD does not
see your troubles?
O Israel, how can you say God ignores
your rights?
28 Have you never heard?
Have you never understood?
The LORD is the everlasting God,
the Creator of all the earth.
He never grows weak or weary.
No one can measure the depths of his
understanding.
29 He gives power to the weak
and strength to the powerless.
30 Even youths will become weak and tired,
and young men will fall in exhaustion.
31 But those who trust in the LORD will find
new strength.
They will soar high on wings like eagles.
They will run and not grow weary.
They will walk and not faint.

God's Help for Israel

41 1 "Listen in silence before me, you lands
beyond the sea.
Bring your strongest arguments.
Come now and speak.
The court is ready for your case.

2 "Who has stirred up this king from the east,
rightly calling him to God's service?
Who gives this man victory over many nations
and permits him to trample their kings
underfoot?
With his sword, he reduces armies to dust.
With his bow, he scatters them like chaff
before the wind.
3 He chases them away and goes on safely,
though he is walking over unfamiliar ground.
4 Who has done such mighty deeds,
summoning each new generation from the
beginning of time?
It is I, the LORD, the First and the Last.
I alone am he."

5 The lands beyond the sea watch in fear.
Remote lands tremble and mobilize for war.
6 The idol makers encourage one another,
saying to each other, "Be strong!"
7 The carver encourages the goldsmith,
and the molder helps at the anvil.
"Good," they say. "It's coming along fine."
Carefully they join the parts together,
then fasten the thing in place so it won't
fall over.

8 "But as for you, Israel my servant,
Jacob my chosen one,
descended from Abraham my friend,

KING JAMES VERSION

9 *Thou* whom I have taken from the ends of the
earth, and called thee from the chief men thereof,
and said unto thee, Thou *art* my servant; I have chosen thee, and not cast thee away.
10 Fear thou not; for I *am* with thee: be not dismayed; for I *am* thy God: I will strengthen thee; yea, I
will help thee; yea, I will uphold thee with the right
hand of my righteousness.
11 Behold, all they that were incensed against thee
shall be ashamed and confounded: they shall be as
nothing; and they that strive with thee shall perish.
12 Thou shalt seek them, and shalt not find them,
even them that contended with thee: they that war
against thee shall be as nothing, and as a thing of
nought.
13 For I the LORD thy God will hold thy right hand,
saying unto thee, Fear not; I will help thee.
14 Fear not, thou worm Jacob, *and* ye men of Israel;
I will help thee, saith the LORD, and thy redeemer, the
Holy One of Israel.
15 Behold, I will make thee a new sharp threshing
instrument having teeth: thou shalt thresh the
mountains, and beat *them* small, and shalt make the
hills as chaff.
16 Thou shalt fan them, and the wind shall carry
them away, and the whirlwind shall scatter them: and
thou shalt rejoice in the LORD, *and* shalt glory in the
Holy One of Israel.
17 *When* the poor and needy seek water, and *there*
is none, *and* their tongue faileth for thirst, I the LORD
will hear them, *I* the God of Israel will not forsake
them.
18 I will open rivers in high places, and fountains in
the midst of the valleys: I will make the wilderness a
pool of water, and the dry land springs of water.
19 I will plant in the wilderness the cedar, the
shittah tree, and the myrtle, and the oil tree; I will set
in the desert the fir tree, *and* the pine, and the box
tree together:
20 That they may see, and know, and consider, and
understand together, that the hand of the LORD hath
done this, and the Holy One of Israel hath created it.
21 Produce your cause, saith the LORD; bring forth
your strong *reasons,* saith the King of Jacob.

NEW LIVING TRANSLATION

9 I have called you back from the ends of the earth,
saying, 'You are my servant.'
For I have chosen you
and will not throw you away.
10 Don't be afraid, for I am with you.
Don't be discouraged, for I am your God.
I will strengthen you and help you.
I will hold you up with my victorious right hand.

11 "See, all your angry enemies lie there,
confused and humiliated.
Anyone who opposes you will die
and come to nothing.
12 You will look in vain
for those who tried to conquer you.
Those who attack you
will come to nothing.
13 For I hold you by your right hand—
I, the LORD your God.
And I say to you,
'Don't be afraid. I am here to help you.
14 Though you are a lowly worm, O Jacob,
don't be afraid, people of Israel, for I will
help you.
I am the LORD, your Redeemer.
I am the Holy One of Israel.'
15 You will be a new threshing instrument
with many sharp teeth.
You will tear your enemies apart,
making chaff of mountains.
16 You will toss them into the air,
and the wind will blow them all away;
a whirlwind will scatter them.
Then you will rejoice in the LORD.
You will glory in the Holy One of Israel.

17 "When the poor and needy search for water
and there is none,
and their tongues are parched from thirst,
then I, the LORD, will answer them.
I, the God of Israel, will never abandon them.
18 I will open up rivers for them on the
high plateaus.
I will give them fountains of water in the valleys.
I will fill the desert with pools of water.
Rivers fed by springs will flow across the
parched ground.
19 I will plant trees in the barren desert—
cedar, acacia, myrtle, olive, cypress, fir, and pine.
20 I am doing this so all who see this miracle
will understand what it means—
that it is the LORD who has done this,
the Holy One of Israel who created it.

21 "Present the case for your idols,"
says the LORD.
"Let them show what they can do,"
says the King of Israel.*

41:21 Hebrew *the King of Jacob.* See note on 14:1.

KING JAMES VERSION

22Let them bring *them* forth, and shew us what
shall happen: let them shew the former things, what
they *be*, that we may consider them, and know the
latter end of them; or declare us things for to come.
23Shew the things that are to come hereafter,
that we may know that ye *are* gods: yea, do good,
or do evil, that we may be dismayed, and behold *it*
together.
24Behold, ye *are* of nothing, and your work of
nought: an abomination *is he that* chooseth you.
25I have raised up *one* from the north, and he shall
come: from the rising of the sun shall he call upon
my name: and he shall come upon princes as *upon*
mortar, and as the potter treadeth clay.
26Who hath declared from the beginning, that we
may know? and beforetime, that we may say, *He is*
righteous? yea, *there is* none that sheweth, yea, *there*
is none that declareth, yea, *there is* none that heareth
your words.
27The first *shall say* to Zion, Behold, behold them:
and I will give to Jerusalem one that bringeth good
tidings.
28For I beheld, and *there was* no man; even among
them, and *there was* no counsellor, that, when I
asked of them, could answer a word.
29Behold, they *are* all vanity; their works *are* nothing: their molten images *are* wind and confusion.

42 1Behold my servant, whom I uphold; mine
elect, *in whom* my soul delighteth; I have
put my spirit upon him: he shall bring forth judgment to the Gentiles.
2He shall not cry, nor lift up, nor cause his voice to
be heard in the street.
3A bruised reed shall he not break, and the smoking flax shall he not quench: he shall bring forth
judgment unto truth.
4He shall not fail nor be discouraged, till he have
set judgment in the earth: and the isles shall wait for
his law.
5Thus saith God the LORD, he that created the
heavens, and stretched them out; he that spread
forth the earth, and that which cometh out of it; he
that giveth breath unto the people upon it, and spirit
to them that walk therein:
6I the LORD have called thee in righteousness, and
will hold thine hand, and will keep thee, and give

NEW LIVING TRANSLATION

22 "Let them try to tell us what happened long ago
so that we may consider the evidence.
Or let them tell us what the future holds,
so we can know what's going to happen.
23 Yes, tell us what will occur in the days ahead.
Then we will know you are gods.
In fact, do anything—good or bad!
Do something that will amaze and frighten us.
24 But no! You are less than nothing and can do
nothing at all.
Those who choose you pollute themselves.

25 "But I have stirred up a leader who will come
from the north.
I have called him by name from the east.
I will give him victory over kings and princes.
He will trample them as a potter treads on clay.
26 "Who told you from the beginning
that this would happen?
Who predicted this,
making you admit that he was right?
No one said a word!
27 I was the first to tell Zion,
'Look! Help is on the way!'*
I will send Jerusalem a messenger with
good news.
28 Not one of your idols told you this.
Not one gave any answer when I asked.
29 See, they are all foolish, worthless things.
All your idols are as empty as the wind.

The LORD's Chosen Servant

42 1 "Look at my servant, whom I strengthen.
He is my chosen one, who pleases me.
I have put my Spirit upon him.
He will bring justice to the nations.
2 He will not shout
or raise his voice in public.
3 He will not crush the weakest reed
or put out a flickering candle.
He will bring justice to all who have
been wronged.
4 He will not falter or lose heart
until justice prevails throughout the earth.
Even distant lands beyond the sea will wait
for his instruction.*"

5 God, the LORD, created the heavens and
stretched them out.
He created the earth and everything in it.
He gives breath to everyone,
life to everyone who walks the earth.
And it is he who says,
6 "I, the LORD, have called you to demonstrate
my righteousness.
I will take you by the hand and guard you,

41:27 Or *'Look! They are coming home.'* **42:4** Greek version reads *And his name will be the hope of all the world.* Compare Matt 12:21.

KING JAMES VERSION

thee for a covenant of the people, for a light of the
Gentiles;
7 To open the blind eyes, to bring out the prisoners
from the prison, *and* them that sit in darkness out of
the prison house.
8 I *am* the LORD: that *is* my name: and my glory will
I not give to another, neither my praise to graven
images.
9 Behold, the former things are come to pass, and
new things do I declare: before they spring forth I tell
you of them.

10 Sing unto the LORD a new song, *and* his praise
from the end of the earth, ye that go down to the sea,
and all that is therein; the isles, and the inhabitants
thereof.
11 Let the wilderness and the cities thereof lift up
their voice, the villages *that* Kedar doth inhabit: let
the inhabitants of the rock sing, let them shout from
the top of the mountains.
12 Let them give glory unto the LORD, and declare
his praise in the islands.
13 The LORD shall go forth as a mighty man, he
shall stir up jealousy like a man of war: he shall cry,
yea, roar; he shall prevail against his enemies.
14 I have long time holden my peace; I have been
still, *and* refrained myself: *now* will I cry like a travailing woman; I will destroy and devour at once.
15 I will make waste mountains and hills, and dry
up all their herbs; and I will make the rivers islands,
and I will dry up the pools.
16 And I will bring the blind by a way *that* they
knew not; I will lead them in paths *that* they have not
known: I will make darkness light before them, and
crooked things straight. These things will I do unto
them, and not forsake them.
17 They shall be turned back, they shall be greatly
ashamed, that trust in graven images, that say to the
molten images, Ye *are* our gods.

18 Hear, ye deaf; and look, ye blind, that ye may see.
19 Who *is* blind, but my servant? or deaf, as my
messenger *that* I sent? who *is* blind as *he that is* perfect, and blind as the LORD's servant?
20 Seeing many things, but thou observest not;
opening the ears, but he heareth not.

NEW LIVING TRANSLATION

and I will give you to my people, Israel,
as a symbol of my covenant with them.
And you will be a light to guide the nations.
7 You will open the eyes of the blind.
You will free the captives from prison,
releasing those who sit in dark dungeons.

8 "I am the LORD; that is my name!
I will not give my glory to anyone else,
nor share my praise with carved idols.
9 Everything I prophesied has come true,
and now I will prophesy again.
I will tell you the future before it happens."

A Song of Praise to the LORD

10 Sing a new song to the LORD!
Sing his praises from the ends of the earth!
Sing, all you who sail the seas,
all you who live in distant coastlands.
11 Join in the chorus, you desert towns;
let the villages of Kedar rejoice!
Let the people of Sela sing for joy;
shout praises from the mountaintops!
12 Let the whole world glorify the LORD;
let it sing his praise.
13 The LORD will march forth like a mighty hero;
he will come out like a warrior, full of fury.
He will shout his battle cry
and crush all his enemies.

14 He will say, "I have long been silent;
yes, I have restrained myself.
But now, like a woman in labor,
I will cry and groan and pant.
15 I will level the mountains and hills
and blight all their greenery.
I will turn the rivers into dry land
and will dry up all the pools.
16 I will lead blind Israel down a new path,
guiding them along an unfamiliar way.
I will brighten the darkness before them
and smooth out the road ahead of them.
Yes, I will indeed do these things;
I will not forsake them.
17 But those who trust in idols,
who say, 'You are our gods,'
will be turned away in shame.

Israel's Failure to Listen and See

18 "Listen, you who are deaf!
Look and see, you blind!
19 Who is as blind as my own people, my servant?
Who is as deaf as my messenger?
Who is as blind as my chosen people,
the servant of the LORD?
20 You see and recognize what is right
but refuse to act on it.
You hear with your ears,
but you don't really listen."

KING JAMES VERSION

21 The LORD is well pleased for his righteousness' sake; he will magnify the law, and make *it* honourable.

22 But this *is* a people robbed and spoiled; *they are* all of them snared in holes, and they are hid in prison houses: they are for a prey, and none delivereth; for a spoil, and none saith, Restore.

23 Who among you will give ear to this? *who* will hearken and hear for the time to come?

24 Who gave Jacob for a spoil, and Israel to the robbers? did not the LORD, he against whom we have sinned? for they would not walk in his ways, neither were they obedient unto his law.

25 Therefore he hath poured upon him the fury of his anger, and the strength of battle: and it hath set him on fire round about, yet he knew not; and it burned him, yet he laid *it* not to heart.

43 1 But now thus saith the LORD that created thee, O Jacob, and he that formed thee, O Israel, Fear not: for I have redeemed thee, I have called *thee* by thy name; thou *art* mine.

2 When thou passest through the waters, I *will be* with thee; and through the rivers, they shall not overflow thee: when thou walkest through the fire, thou shalt not be burned; neither shall the flame kindle upon thee.

3 For I *am* the LORD thy God, the Holy One of Israel, thy Saviour: I gave Egypt *for* thy ransom, Ethiopia and Seba for thee.

4 Since thou wast precious in my sight, thou hast been honourable, and I have loved thee: therefore will I give men for thee, and people for thy life.

5 Fear not: for I *am* with thee: I will bring thy seed from the east, and gather thee from the west;

6 I will say to the north, Give up; and to the south, Keep not back: bring my sons from far, and my daughters from the ends of the earth;

7 *Even* every one that is called by my name: for I have created him for my glory, I have formed him; yea, I have made him.

8 Bring forth the blind people that have eyes, and the deaf that have ears.

9 Let all the nations be gathered together, and let the people be assembled: who among them can

NEW LIVING TRANSLATION

21 Because he is righteous,
the LORD has exalted his glorious law.
22 But his own people have been robbed
and plundered,
enslaved, imprisoned, and trapped.
They are fair game for anyone
and have no one to protect them,
no one to take them back home.

23 Who will hear these lessons from the past
and see the ruin that awaits you in the future?
24 Who allowed Israel to be robbed and hurt?
It was the LORD, against whom we sinned,
for the people would not walk in his path,
nor would they obey his law.
25 Therefore, he poured out his fury on them
and destroyed them in battle.
They were enveloped in flames,
but they still refused to understand.
They were consumed by fire,
but they did not learn their lesson.

The Savior of Israel

43 1 But now, O Jacob, listen to the LORD
who created you.
O Israel, the one who formed you says,
"Do not be afraid, for I have ransomed you.
I have called you by name; you are mine.
2 When you go through deep waters,
I will be with you.
When you go through rivers of difficulty,
you will not drown.
When you walk through the fire of oppression,
you will not be burned up;
the flames will not consume you.
3 For I am the LORD, your God,
the Holy One of Israel, your Savior.
I gave Egypt as a ransom for your freedom;
I gave Ethiopia* and Seba in your place.
4 Others were given in exchange for you.
I traded their lives for yours
because you are precious to me.
You are honored, and I love you.
5 "Do not be afraid, for I am with you.
I will gather you and your children from
east and west.
6 I will say to the north and south,
'Bring my sons and daughters back to Israel
from the distant corners of the earth.
7 Bring all who claim me as their God,
for I have made them for my glory.
It was I who created them.'"

8 Bring out the people who have eyes but are blind,
who have ears but are deaf.
9 Gather the nations together!
Assemble the peoples of the world!

43:3 Hebrew *Cush*.

KING JAMES VERSION

declare this, and shew us former things? let them
bring forth their witnesses, that they may be justified: or let them hear, and say, *It is* truth.
10 Ye *are* my witnesses, saith the LORD, and my servant whom I have chosen: that ye may know and
believe me, and understand that I *am* he: before me
there was no God formed, neither shall there be
after me.
11 I, *even* I, *am* the LORD; and beside me *there is* no
saviour.
12 I have declared, and have saved, and I have
shewed, when *there was* no strange *god* among you:
therefore ye *are* my witnesses, saith the LORD, that I
am God.
13 Yea, before the day *was* I *am* he; and *there is*
none that can deliver out of my hand: I will work, and
who shall let it?

14 Thus saith the LORD, your redeemer, the Holy
One of Israel; For your sake I have sent to Babylon,
and have brought down all their nobles, and the
Chaldeans, whose cry *is* in the ships.
15 I *am* the LORD, your Holy One, the creator of Israel, your King.
16 Thus saith the LORD, which maketh a way in the
sea, and a path in the mighty waters;
17 Which bringeth forth the chariot and horse, the
army and the power; they shall lie down together,
they shall not rise: they are extinct, they are
quenched as tow.
18 Remember ye not the former things, neither
consider the things of old.
19 Behold, I will do a new thing; now it shall spring
forth; shall ye not know it? I will even make a way in
the wilderness, *and* rivers in the desert.
20 The beast of the field shall honour me, the dragons and the owls: because I give waters in the wilderness, *and* rivers in the desert, to give drink to my
people, my chosen.
21 This people have I formed for myself; they shall
shew forth my praise.

NEW LIVING TRANSLATION

Which of their idols has ever foretold such things?
Which can predict what will happen tomorrow?
Where are the witnesses of such predictions?
Who can verify that they spoke the truth?

10 "But you are my witnesses, O Israel!"
says the LORD.
"You are my servant.
You have been chosen to know me, believe in me,
and understand that I alone am God.
There is no other God—
there never has been, and there never will be.
11 I, yes I, am the LORD,
and there is no other Savior.
12 First I predicted your rescue,
then I saved you and proclaimed it
to the world.
No foreign god has ever done this.
You are witnesses that I am the only God,"
says the LORD.
13 "From eternity to eternity I am God.
No one can snatch anyone out of my hand.
No one can undo what I have done."

The LORD's Promise of Victory

14 This is what the LORD says—your Redeemer, the Holy One of Israel:

"For your sakes I will send an army against
Babylon,
forcing the Babylonians* to flee in those
ships they are so proud of.
15 I am the LORD, your Holy One,
Israel's Creator and King.
16 I am the LORD, who opened a way through
the waters,
making a dry path through the sea.
17 I called forth the mighty army of Egypt
with all its chariots and horses.
I drew them beneath the waves, and they
drowned,
their lives snuffed out like a smoldering
candlewick.

18 "But forget all that—
it is nothing compared to what I am going to do.
19 For I am about to do something new.
See, I have already begun! Do you not see it?
I will make a pathway through the wilderness.
I will create rivers in the dry wasteland.
20 The wild animals in the fields will thank me,
the jackals and owls, too,
for giving them water in the desert.
Yes, I will make rivers in the dry wasteland
so my chosen people can be refreshed.
21 I have made Israel for myself,
and they will someday honor me before
the whole world.

43:14 Or *Chaldeans.*

KING JAMES VERSION

[22]But thou hast not called upon me, O Jacob; but thou hast been weary of me, O Israel.
[23]Thou hast not brought me the small cattle of thy burnt offerings; neither hast thou honoured me with thy sacrifices. I have not caused thee to serve with an offering, nor wearied thee with incense.
[24]Thou hast bought me no sweet cane with money, neither hast thou filled me with the fat of thy sacrifices: but thou hast made me to serve with thy sins, thou hast wearied me with thine iniquities.
[25]I, *even* I, *am* he that blotteth out thy transgressions for mine own sake, and will not remember thy sins.
[26]Put me in remembrance: let us plead together: declare thou, that thou mayest be justified.
[27]Thy first father hath sinned, and thy teachers have transgressed against me.
[28]Therefore I have profaned the princes of the sanctuary, and have given Jacob to the curse, and Israel to reproaches.

44 [1]Yet now hear, O Jacob my servant; and Israel, whom I have chosen:
[2]Thus saith the LORD that made thee, and formed thee from the womb, *which* will help thee; Fear not, O Jacob, my servant; and thou, Jesurun, whom I have chosen.
[3]For I will pour water upon him that is thirsty, and floods upon the dry ground: I will pour my spirit upon thy seed, and my blessing upon thine offspring:
[4]And they shall spring up *as* among the grass, as willows by the water courses.
[5]One shall say, I *am* the LORD's; and another shall call *himself* by the name of Jacob; and another shall subscribe *with* his hand unto the LORD, and surname *himself* by the name of Israel.

[6]Thus saith the LORD the King of Israel, and his redeemer the LORD of hosts; I *am* the first, and I *am* the last; and beside me *there is* no God.
[7]And who, as I, shall call, and shall declare it, and set it in order for me, since I appointed the ancient people? and the things that are coming, and shall come, let them shew unto them.

NEW LIVING TRANSLATION

[22] "But, dear family of Jacob, you refuse to ask
for my help.
You have grown tired of me, O Israel!
[23] You have not brought me sheep or goats for
burnt offerings.
You have not honored me with sacrifices,
though I have not burdened and wearied you
with requests for grain offerings and
frankincense.
[24] You have not brought me fragrant calamus
or pleased me with the fat from sacrifices.
Instead, you have burdened me with your sins
and wearied me with your faults.

[25] "I—yes, I alone—will blot out your sins for
my own sake
and will never think of them again.
[26] Let us review the situation together,
and you can present your case to prove
your innocence.
[27] From the very beginning, your first ancestor
sinned against me;
all your leaders broke my laws.
[28] That is why I have disgraced your priests;
I have decreed complete destruction*
for Jacob
and shame for Israel.

44 [1] "But now, listen to me, Jacob my servant,
Israel my chosen one.
[2] The LORD who made you and helps you says:
Do not be afraid, O Jacob, my servant,
O dear Israel,* my chosen one.
[3] For I will pour out water to quench your thirst
and to irrigate your parched fields.
And I will pour out my Spirit on your descendants,
and my blessing on your children.
[4] They will thrive like watered grass,
like willows on a riverbank.
[5] Some will proudly claim, 'I belong to the LORD.'
Others will say, 'I am a descendant of Jacob.'
Some will write the LORD's name on their hands
and will take the name of Israel as their own."

The Foolishness of Idols

[6]This is what the LORD says—Israel's King and Redeemer, the LORD of Heaven's Armies:

"I am the First and the Last;
there is no other God.
[7] Who is like me?
Let him step forward and prove to you
his power.
Let him do as I have done since ancient times
when I established a people and explained
its future.

43:28 The Hebrew term used here refers to the complete consecration of things or people to the LORD, either by destroying them or by giving them as an offering. **44:2** Hebrew *Jeshurun*, a term of endearment for Israel.

KING JAMES VERSION

8 Fear ye not, neither be afraid: have not I told thee from that time, and have declared *it?* ye *are* even my witnesses. Is there a God beside me? yea, *there is* no God; I know not *any*.

9 They that make a graven image *are* all of them vanity; and their delectable things shall not profit; and they *are* their own witnesses; they see not, nor know; that they may be ashamed.

10 Who hath formed a god, or molten a graven image *that* is profitable for nothing?

11 Behold, all his fellows shall be ashamed: and the workmen, they *are* of men: let them all be gathered together, let them stand up; *yet* they shall fear, *and* they shall be ashamed together.

12 The smith with the tongs both worketh in the coals, and fashioneth it with hammers, and worketh it with the strength of his arms: yea, he is hungry, and his strength faileth: he drinketh no water, and is faint.

13 The carpenter stretcheth out *his* rule; he marketh it out with a line; he fitteth it with planes, and he marketh it out with the compass, and maketh it after the figure of a man, according to the beauty of a man; that it may remain in the house.

14 He heweth him down cedars, and taketh the cypress and the oak, which he strengtheneth for himself among the trees of the forest: he planteth an ash, and the rain doth nourish *it*.

15 Then shall it be for a man to burn: for he will take thereof, and warm himself; yea, he kindleth *it,* and baketh bread; yea, he maketh a god, and worshippeth *it;* he maketh it a graven image, and falleth down thereto.

16 He burneth part thereof in the fire; with part thereof he eateth flesh; he roasteth roast, and is satisfied: yea, he warmeth *himself,* and saith, Aha, I am warm, I have seen the fire:

17 And the residue thereof he maketh a god, *even* his graven image: he falleth down unto it, and worshippeth *it,* and prayeth unto it, and saith, Deliver me; for thou *art* my god.

18 They have not known nor understood: for he hath shut their eyes, that they cannot see; *and* their hearts, that they cannot understand.

19 And none considereth in his heart, neither *is there* knowledge nor understanding to say, I have burned part of it in the fire; yea, also I have baked bread upon the coals thereof; I have roasted flesh, and eaten *it:* and shall I make the residue thereof an abomination? shall I fall down to the stock of a tree?

NEW LIVING TRANSLATION

8 Do not tremble; do not be afraid.
Did I not proclaim my purposes for you long ago?
You are my witnesses—is there any other God?
No! There is no other Rock—not one!"

9 How foolish are those who manufacture idols.
These prized objects are really worthless.
The people who worship idols don't know this,
so they are all put to shame.
10 Who but a fool would make his own god—
an idol that cannot help him one bit?
11 All who worship idols will be disgraced
along with all these craftsmen—mere humans—
who claim they can make a god.
They may all stand together,
but they will stand in terror and shame.

12 The blacksmith stands at his forge to make a sharp tool,
pounding and shaping it with all his might.
His work makes him hungry and weak.
It makes him thirsty and faint.
13 Then the wood-carver measures a block of wood
and draws a pattern on it.
He works with chisel and plane
and carves it into a human figure.
He gives it human beauty
and puts it in a little shrine.
14 He cuts down cedars;
he selects the cypress and the oak;
he plants the pine in the forest
to be nourished by the rain.
15 Then he uses part of the wood to make a fire.
With it he warms himself and bakes his bread.
Then—yes, it's true—he takes the rest of it
and makes himself a god to worship!
He makes an idol
and bows down in front of it!
16 He burns part of the tree to roast his meat
and to keep himself warm.
He says, "Ah, that fire feels good."
17 Then he takes what's left
and makes his god: a carved idol!
He falls down in front of it,
worshiping and praying to it.
"Rescue me!" he says.
"You are my god!"

18 Such stupidity and ignorance!
Their eyes are closed, and they cannot see.
Their minds are shut, and they cannot think.
19 The person who made the idol never stops to reflect,
"Why, it's just a block of wood!
I burned half of it for heat
and used it to bake my bread and roast my meat.
How can the rest of it be a god?
Should I bow down to worship a piece of wood?"

KING JAMES VERSION

20He feedeth on ashes: a deceived heart hath turned him aside, that he cannot deliver his soul, nor say, *Is there* not a lie in my right hand?

21Remember these, O Jacob and Israel; for thou *art* my servant: I have formed thee; thou *art* my servant: O Israel, thou shalt not be forgotten of me.

22I have blotted out, as a thick cloud, thy transgressions, and, as a cloud, thy sins: return unto me; for I have redeemed thee.

23Sing, O ye heavens; for the LORD hath done *it:* shout, ye lower parts of the earth: break forth into singing, ye mountains, O forest, and every tree therein: for the LORD hath redeemed Jacob, and glorified himself in Israel.

24Thus saith the LORD, thy redeemer, and he that formed thee from the womb, I *am* the LORD that maketh all *things;* that stretcheth forth the heavens alone; that spreadeth abroad the earth by myself;

25That frustrateth the tokens of the liars, and maketh diviners mad; that turneth wise *men* backward, and maketh their knowledge foolish;

26That confirmeth the word of his servant, and performeth the counsel of his messengers; that saith to Jerusalem, Thou shalt be inhabited; and to the cities of Judah, Ye shall be built, and I will raise up the decayed places thereof:

27That saith to the deep, Be dry, and I will dry up thy rivers:

28That saith of Cyrus, *He is* my shepherd, and shall perform all my pleasure: even saying to Jerusalem, Thou shalt be built; and to the temple, Thy foundation shall be laid.

45 1Thus saith the LORD to his anointed, to Cyrus, whose right hand I have holden, to subdue nations before him; and I will loose the loins of kings, to open before him the two leaved gates; and the gates shall not be shut;

2I will go before thee, and make the crooked

NEW LIVING TRANSLATION

20 The poor, deluded fool feeds on ashes.
He trusts something that can't help him at all.
Yet he cannot bring himself to ask,
"Is this idol that I'm holding in my hand a lie?"

Restoration for Jerusalem

21 "Pay attention, O Jacob,
for you are my servant, O Israel.
I, the LORD, made you,
and I will not forget you.
22 I have swept away your sins like a cloud.
I have scattered your offenses like the
morning mist.
Oh, return to me,
for I have paid the price to set you free."

23 Sing, O heavens, for the LORD has done this
wondrous thing.
Shout for joy, O depths of the earth!
Break into song,
O mountains and forests and every tree!
For the LORD has redeemed Jacob
and is glorified in Israel.

24 This is what the LORD says—
your Redeemer and Creator:
"I am the LORD, who made all things.
I alone stretched out the heavens.
Who was with me
when I made the earth?
25 I expose the false prophets as liars
and make fools of fortune-tellers.
I cause the wise to give bad advice,
thus proving them to be fools.
26 But I carry out the predictions of my prophets!
By them I say to Jerusalem, 'People will live
here again,'
and to the towns of Judah, 'You will be rebuilt;
I will restore all your ruins!'
27 When I speak to the rivers and say, 'Dry up!'
they will be dry.
28 When I say of Cyrus, 'He is my shepherd,'
he will certainly do as I say.
He will command, 'Rebuild Jerusalem';
he will say, 'Restore the Temple.'"

Cyrus, the LORD's Chosen One

45 1 This is what the LORD says to Cyrus,
his anointed one,
whose right hand he will empower.
Before him, mighty kings will be paralyzed
with fear.
Their fortress gates will be opened,
never to shut again.
2 This is what the LORD says:

"I will go before you, Cyrus,
and level the mountains.*

45:2 As in Dead Sea Scrolls and Greek version; Masoretic Text reads *the swellings.*

places straight: I will break in pieces the gates of brass, and cut in sunder the bars of iron:

3 And I will give thee the treasures of darkness, and hidden riches of secret places, that thou mayest know that I, the LORD, which call *thee* by thy name, *am* the God of Israel.

4 For Jacob my servant's sake, and Israel mine elect, I have even called thee by thy name: I have surnamed thee, though thou hast not known me.

5 I *am* the LORD, and *there is* none else, *there is* no God beside me: I girded thee, though thou hast not known me:

6 That they may know from the rising of the sun, and from the west, that *there is* none beside me. I *am* the LORD, and *there is* none else.

7 I form the light, and create darkness: I make peace, and create evil: I the LORD do all these *things*.

8 Drop down, ye heavens, from above, and let the skies pour down righteousness: let the earth open, and let them bring forth salvation, and let righteousness spring up together; I the LORD have created it.

9 Woe unto him that striveth with his Maker! *Let* the potsherd *strive* with the potsherds of the earth. Shall the clay say to him that fashioneth it, What makest thou? or thy work, He hath no hands?

10 Woe unto him that saith unto *his* father, What begettest thou? or to the woman, What hast thou brought forth?

11 Thus saith the LORD, the Holy One of Israel, and his Maker, Ask me of things to come concerning my sons, and concerning the work of my hands command ye me.

12 I have made the earth, and created man upon it: I, *even* my hands, have stretched out the heavens, and all their host have I commanded.

13 I have raised him up in righteousness, and I will direct all his ways: he shall build my city, and he shall

I will smash down gates of bronze
and cut through bars of iron.

3 And I will give you treasures hidden in
the darkness—
secret riches.
I will do this so you may know that I am the LORD,
the God of Israel, the one who calls you by name.

4 "And why have I called you for this work?
Why did I call you by name when you did not
know me?
It is for the sake of Jacob my servant,
Israel my chosen one.

5 I am the LORD;
there is no other God.
I have equipped you for battle,
though you don't even know me,

6 so all the world from east to west
will know there is no other God.
I am the LORD, and there is no other.

7 I create the light and make the darkness.
I send good times and bad times.
I, the LORD, am the one who does
these things.

8 "Open up, O heavens,
and pour out your righteousness.
Let the earth open wide
so salvation and righteousness can
sprout up together.
I, the LORD, created them.

9 "What sorrow awaits those who argue with
their Creator.
Does a clay pot argue with its maker?
Does the clay dispute with the one who
shapes it, saying,
'Stop, you're doing it wrong!'
Does the pot exclaim,
'How clumsy can you be?'

10 How terrible it would be if a newborn baby
said to its father,
'Why was I born?'
or if it said to its mother,
'Why did you make me this way?'"

11 This is what the LORD says—
the Holy One of Israel and your Creator:
"Do you question what I do for my children?
Do you give me orders about the work
of my hands?

12 I am the one who made the earth
and created people to live on it.
With my hands I stretched out the heavens.
All the stars are at my command.

13 I will raise up Cyrus to fulfill my righteous
purpose,
and I will guide his actions.
He will restore my city and free my captive
people—

KING JAMES VERSION

let go my captives, not for price nor reward, saith the LORD of hosts.

14 Thus saith the LORD, The labour of Egypt, and merchandise of Ethiopia and of the Sabeans, men of stature, shall come over unto thee, and they shall be thine: they shall come after thee; in chains they shall come over, and they shall fall down unto thee, they shall make supplication unto thee, *saying,* Surely God *is* in thee; and *there is* none else, *there is* no God.

15 Verily thou *art* a God that hidest thyself, O God of Israel, the Saviour.

16 They shall be ashamed, and also confounded, all of them: they shall go to confusion together *that are* makers of idols.

17 *But* Israel shall be saved in the LORD with an everlasting salvation: ye shall not be ashamed nor confounded world without end.

18 For thus saith the LORD that created the heavens; God himself that formed the earth and made it; he hath established it, he created it not in vain, he formed it to be inhabited: I *am* the LORD; and *there is* none else.

19 I have not spoken in secret, in a dark place of the earth: I said not unto the seed of Jacob, Seek ye me in vain: I the LORD speak righteousness, I declare things that are right.

20 Assemble yourselves and come; draw near together, ye *that are* escaped of the nations: they have no knowledge that set up the wood of their graven image, and pray unto a god *that* cannot save.

21 Tell ye, and bring *them* near; yea, let them take counsel together: who hath declared this from ancient time? *who* hath told it from that time? *have* not I the LORD? and *there is* no God else beside me; a just God and a Saviour; *there is* none beside me.

22 Look unto me, and be ye saved, all the ends of the earth: for I *am* God, and *there is* none else.

23 I have sworn by myself, the word is gone out of

NEW LIVING TRANSLATION

without seeking a reward!
I, the LORD of Heaven's Armies, have spoken!"

Future Conversion of Gentiles

14 This is what the LORD says:

"You will rule the Egyptians,
the Ethiopians,* and the Sabeans.
They will come to you with all their merchandise,
and it will all be yours.
They will follow you as prisoners in chains.
They will fall to their knees in front of you
and say,
'God is with you, and he is the only God.
There is no other.'"
15 Truly, O God of Israel, our Savior,
you work in mysterious ways.
16 All craftsmen who make idols will be humiliated.
They will all be disgraced together.
17 But the LORD will save the people of Israel
with eternal salvation.
Throughout everlasting ages,
they will never again be humiliated
and disgraced.

18 For the LORD is God,
and he created the heavens and earth
and put everything in place.
He made the world to be lived in,
not to be a place of empty chaos.
"I am the LORD," he says,
"and there is no other.
19 I publicly proclaim bold promises.
I do not whisper obscurities in some
dark corner.
I would not have told the people of Israel*
to seek me
if I could not be found.
I, the LORD, speak only what is true
and declare only what is right.
20 "Gather together and come,
you fugitives from surrounding nations.
What fools they are who carry around their
wooden idols
and pray to gods that cannot save!
21 Consult together, argue your case.
Get together and decide what to say.
Who made these things known so long ago?
What idol ever told you they would happen?
Was it not I, the LORD?
For there is no other God but me,
a righteous God and Savior.
There is none but me.
22 Let all the world look to me for salvation!
For I am God; there is no other.
23 I have sworn by my own name;
I have spoken the truth,

45:14 Hebrew *Cushites.* 45:19 Hebrew *of Jacob.* See note on 14:1.

KING JAMES VERSION

my mouth *in* righteousness, and shall not return,
That unto me every knee shall bow, every tongue
shall swear.
24 Surely, shall *one* say, in the LORD have I righteousness and strength: *even* to him shall *men* come;
and all that are incensed against him shall be
ashamed.
25 In the LORD shall all the seed of Israel be justified, and shall glory.

46

1 Bel boweth down, Nebo stoopeth, their
idols were upon the beasts, and upon the
cattle: your carriages *were* heavy loaden; *they are* a
burden to the weary *beast*.
2 They stoop, they bow down together; they could
not deliver the burden, but themselves are gone into
captivity.
3 Hearken unto me, O house of Jacob, and all the
remnant of the house of Israel, which are borne *by*
me from the belly, which are carried from the womb:
4 And *even* to *your* old age I *am* he; and *even* to
hoar hairs will I carry *you:* I have made, and I will
bear; even I will carry, and will deliver *you*.
5 To whom will ye liken me, and make *me* equal,
and compare me, that we may be like?
6 They lavish gold out of the bag, and weigh silver
in the balance, *and* hire a goldsmith; and he maketh
it a god: they fall down, yea, they worship.
7 They bear him upon the shoulder, they carry him,
and set him in his place, and he standeth; from his
place shall he not remove: yea, *one* shall cry unto
him, yet can he not answer, nor save him out of his
trouble.
8 Remember this, and shew yourselves men: bring
it again to mind, O ye transgressors.
9 Remember the former things of old: for I *am*
God, and *there is* none else; *I am* God, and *there is*
none like me,
10 Declaring the end from the beginning, and from
ancient times *the things* that are not *yet* done, saying, My counsel shall stand, and I will do all my pleasure:
11 Calling a ravenous bird from the east, the man
that executeth my counsel from a far country: yea, I
have spoken *it*, I will also bring it to pass; I have purposed *it*, I will also do it.

NEW LIVING TRANSLATION

and I will never go back on my word:
Every knee will bend to me,
and every tongue will confess allegiance to me.*"
24 The people will declare,
"The LORD is the source of all my
righteousness and strength."
And all who were angry with him
will come to him and be ashamed.
25 In the LORD all the generations of Israel
will be justified,
and in him they will boast.

Babylon's False Gods

46

1 Bel and Nebo, the gods of Babylon,
bow as they are lowered to the ground.
They are being hauled away on ox carts.
The poor beasts stagger under the weight.
2 Both the idols and their owners are bowed down.
The gods cannot protect the people,
and the people cannot protect the gods.
They go off into captivity together.
3 "Listen to me, descendants of Jacob,
all you who remain in Israel.
I have cared for you since you were born.
Yes, I carried you before you were born.
4 I will be your God throughout your lifetime—
until your hair is white with age.
I made you, and I will care for you.
I will carry you along and save you.
5 "To whom will you compare me?
Who is my equal?
6 Some people pour out their silver and gold
and hire a craftsman to make a god from it.
Then they bow down and worship it!
7 They carry it around on their shoulders,
and when they set it down, it stays there.
It can't even move!
And when someone prays to it, there is
no answer.
It can't rescue anyone from trouble.

8 "Do not forget this! Keep it in mind!
Remember this, you guilty ones.
9 Remember the things I have done in the past.
For I alone am God!
I am God, and there is none like me.
10 Only I can tell you the future
before it even happens.
Everything I plan will come to pass,
for I do whatever I wish.
11 I will call a swift bird of prey from the east—
a leader from a distant land to come and
do my bidding.
I have said what I would do,
and I will do it.

45:23 Hebrew *will confess;* Greek version reads *will confess and give praise to God*. Compare Rom 14:11.

KING JAMES VERSION

12 Hearken unto me, ye stouthearted, that *are* far from righteousness:

13 I bring near my righteousness: it shall not be far off, and my salvation shall not tarry: and I will place salvation in Zion for Israel my glory.

47 1 Come down, and sit in the dust, O virgin daughter of Babylon, sit on the ground: *there is* no throne, O daughter of the Chaldeans: for thou shalt no more be called tender and delicate.

2 Take the millstones, and grind meal: uncover thy locks, make bare the leg, uncover the thigh, pass over the rivers.

3 Thy nakedness shall be uncovered, yea, thy shame shall be seen: I will take vengeance, and I will not meet *thee as* a man.

4 *As for* our redeemer, the LORD of hosts *is* his name, the Holy One of Israel.

5 Sit thou silent, and get thee into darkness, O daughter of the Chaldeans: for thou shalt no more be called, The lady of kingdoms.

6 I was wroth with my people, I have polluted mine inheritance, and given them into thine hand: thou didst shew them no mercy; upon the ancient hast thou very heavily laid thy yoke.

7 And thou saidst, I shall be a lady for ever: *so* that thou didst not lay these *things* to thy heart, neither didst remember the latter end of it.

8 Therefore hear now this, *thou that art* given to pleasures, that dwellest carelessly, that sayest in thine heart, I *am*, and none else beside me; I shall not sit *as* a widow, neither shall I know the loss of children:

9 But these two *things* shall come to thee in a moment in one day, the loss of children, and widowhood: they shall come upon thee in their perfection for the multitude of thy sorceries, *and* for the great abundance of thine enchantments.

10 For thou hast trusted in thy wickedness: thou hast said, None seeth me. Thy wisdom and thy knowledge, it hath perverted thee; and thou hast said in thine heart, I *am*, and none else beside me.

11 Therefore shall evil come upon thee; thou shalt not know from whence it riseth: and mischief shall fall upon thee; thou shalt not be able to put it off: and desolation shall come upon thee suddenly, *which* thou shalt not know.

NEW LIVING TRANSLATION

12 "Listen to me, you stubborn people
who are so far from doing right.
13 For I am ready to set things right,
not in the distant future, but right now!
I am ready to save Jerusalem*
and show my glory to Israel.

Prediction of Babylon's Fall

47 1 "Come down, virgin daughter of Babylon,
and sit in the dust.
For your days of sitting on a throne have
ended.
O daughter of Babylonia,* never again will you be
the lovely princess, tender and delicate.
2 Take heavy millstones and grind flour.
Remove your veil, and strip off your robe.
Expose yourself to public view.
3 You will be naked and burdened with shame.
I will take vengeance against you without pity."

4 Our Redeemer, whose name is the LORD of
Heaven's Armies,
is the Holy One of Israel.

5 "O beautiful Babylon, sit now in darkness and
silence.
Never again will you be known as the queen
of kingdoms.
6 For I was angry with my chosen people
and punished them by letting them fall into
your hands.
But you, Babylon, showed them no mercy.
You oppressed even the elderly.
7 You said, 'I will reign forever as queen of the world!'
You did not reflect on your actions
or think about their consequences.

8 "Listen to this, you pleasure-loving kingdom,
living at ease and feeling secure.
You say, 'I am the only one, and there is no other.
I will never be a widow or lose my children.'
9 Well, both these things will come upon you
in a moment:
widowhood and the loss of your children.
Yes, these calamities will come upon you,
despite all your witchcraft and magic.

10 "You felt secure in your wickedness.
'No one sees me,' you said.
But your 'wisdom' and 'knowledge' have led
you astray,
and you said, 'I am the only one, and there
is no other.'
11 So disaster will overtake you,
and you won't be able to charm it away.
Calamity will fall upon you,
and you won't be able to buy your way out.
A catastrophe will strike you suddenly,
one for which you are not prepared.

46:13 Hebrew *Zion*. **47:1** Or *Chaldea;* also in 47:5.

KING JAMES VERSION

12 Stand now with thine enchantments, and with the multitude of thy sorceries, wherein thou hast laboured from thy youth; if so be thou shalt be able to profit, if so be thou mayest prevail.

13 Thou art wearied in the multitude of thy counsels. Let now the astrologers, the stargazers, the monthly prognosticators, stand up, and save thee from *these things* that shall come upon thee.

14 Behold, they shall be as stubble; the fire shall burn them; they shall not deliver themselves from the power of the flame: *there shall* not *be* a coal to warm at, *nor* fire to sit before it.

15 Thus shall they be unto thee with whom thou hast laboured, *even* thy merchants, from thy youth: they shall wander every one to his quarter; none shall save thee.

48 1 Hear ye this, O house of Jacob, which are called by the name of Israel, and are come forth out of the waters of Judah, which swear by the name of the LORD, and make mention of the God of Israel, *but* not in truth, nor in righteousness.

2 For they call themselves of the holy city, and stay themselves upon the God of Israel; The LORD of hosts *is* his name.

3 I have declared the former things from the beginning; and they went forth out of my mouth, and I shewed them; I did *them* suddenly, and they came to pass.

4 Because I knew that thou *art* obstinate, and thy neck *is* an iron sinew, and thy brow brass;

5 I have even from the beginning declared *it* to thee; before it came to pass I shewed *it* thee: lest thou shouldest say, Mine idol hath done them, and my graven image, and my molten image, hath commanded them.

6 Thou hast heard, see all this; and will not ye declare *it?* I have shewed thee new things from this time, even hidden things, and thou didst not know them.

7 They are created now, and not from the beginning; even before the day when thou heardest them not; lest thou shouldest say, Behold, I knew them.

8 Yea, thou heardest not; yea, thou knewest not; yea, from that time *that* thine ear was not opened: for I knew that thou wouldest deal very treacherously, and wast called a transgressor from the womb.

9 For my name's sake will I defer mine anger, and for my praise will I refrain for thee, that I cut thee not off.

NEW LIVING TRANSLATION

12 "Now use your magical charms!
Use the spells you have worked at
all these years!
Maybe they will do you some good.
Maybe they can make someone afraid of you.
13 All the advice you receive has made you tired.
Where are all your astrologers,
those stargazers who make predictions
each month?
Let them stand up and save you from what
the future holds.
14 But they are like straw burning in a fire;
they cannot save themselves from the flame.
You will get no help from them at all;
their hearth is no place to sit for warmth.
15 And all your friends,
those with whom you've done business
since childhood,
will go their own ways,
turning a deaf ear to your cries.

God's Stubborn People

48 1 "Listen to me, O family of Jacob,
you who are called by the name
of Israel
and born into the family of Judah.
Listen, you who take oaths in the name of the LORD
and call on the God of Israel.
You don't keep your promises,
2 even though you call yourself the holy city
and talk about depending on the God of Israel,
whose name is the LORD of Heaven's Armies.
3 Long ago I told you what was going to happen.
Then suddenly I took action,
and all my predictions came true.
4 For I know how stubborn and obstinate you are.
Your necks are as unbending as iron.
Your heads are as hard as bronze.
5 That is why I told you what would happen;
I told you beforehand what I was going to do.
Then you could never say, 'My idols did it.
My wooden image and metal god commanded
it to happen!'
6 You have heard my predictions and seen
them fulfilled,
but you refuse to admit it.
Now I will tell you new things,
secrets you have not yet heard.
7 They are brand new, not things from the past.
So you cannot say, 'We knew that all the time!'

8 "Yes, I will tell you of things that are entirely new,
things you never heard of before.
For I know so well what traitors you are.
You have been rebels from birth.
9 Yet for my own sake and for the honor
of my name,
I will hold back my anger and not wipe you out.

KING JAMES VERSION

10Behold, I have refined thee, but not with silver; I have chosen thee in the furnace of affliction.

11For mine own sake, *even* for mine own sake, will I do *it:* for how should *my name* be polluted? and I will not give my glory unto another.

12Hearken unto me, O Jacob and Israel, my called; I *am* he; I *am* the first, I also *am* the last.

13Mine hand also hath laid the foundation of the earth, and my right hand hath spanned the heavens: *when* I call unto them, they stand up together.

14All ye, assemble yourselves, and hear; which among them hath declared these *things?* The LORD hath loved him: he will do his pleasure on Babylon, and his arm *shall be on* the Chaldeans.

15I, *even* I, have spoken; yea, I have called him: I have brought him, and he shall make his way prosperous.

16Come ye near unto me, hear ye this; I have not spoken in secret from the beginning; from the time that it was, there *am* I: and now the Lord GOD, and his Spirit, hath sent me.

17Thus saith the LORD, thy Redeemer, the Holy One of Israel; I *am* the LORD thy God which teacheth thee to profit, which leadeth thee by the way *that* thou shouldest go.

18O that thou hadst hearkened to my commandments! then had thy peace been as a river, and thy righteousness as the waves of the sea:

19Thy seed also had been as the sand, and the offspring of thy bowels like the gravel thereof; his name should not have been cut off nor destroyed from before me.

20Go ye forth of Babylon, flee ye from the Chaldeans, with a voice of singing declare ye, tell this, utter

NEW LIVING TRANSLATION

10 I have refined you, but not as silver is refined.
Rather, I have refined you in the furnace of suffering.
11 I will rescue you for my sake—
yes, for my own sake!
I will not let my reputation be tarnished,
and I will not share my glory with idols!

Freedom from Babylon

12 "Listen to me, O family of Jacob,
Israel my chosen one!
I alone am God,
the First and the Last.
13 It was my hand that laid the foundations of the earth,
my right hand that spread out the heavens above.
When I call out the stars,
they all appear in order."

14 Have any of your idols ever told you this?
Come, all of you, and listen:
The LORD has chosen Cyrus as his ally.
He will use him to put an end to the empire of Babylon
and to destroy the Babylonian* armies.
15 "I have said it: I am calling Cyrus!
I will send him on this errand and will help him succeed.
16 Come closer, and listen to this.
From the beginning I have told you plainly what would happen."

And now the Sovereign LORD and his Spirit
have sent me with this message.
17 This is what the LORD says—
your Redeemer, the Holy One of Israel:
"I am the LORD your God,
who teaches you what is good for you
and leads you along the paths you should follow.
18 Oh, that you had listened to my commands!
Then you would have had peace flowing like a gentle river
and righteousness rolling over you like waves in the sea.
19 Your descendants would have been like the sands along the seashore—
too many to count!
There would have been no need for your destruction,
or for cutting off your family name."
20 Yet even now, be free from your captivity!
Leave Babylon and the Babylonians.*
Sing out this message!
Shout it to the ends of the earth!

48:14 Or *Chaldean.* **48:20a** Or *the Chaldeans.*

KING JAMES VERSION

it *even* to the end of the earth; say ye, The LORD hath
redeemed his servant Jacob.
21 And they thirsted not *when* he led them through
the deserts: he caused the waters to flow out of the
rock for them: he clave the rock also, and the waters
gushed out.
22 *There is* no peace, saith the LORD, unto the
wicked.

49 1 Listen, O isles, unto me; and hearken, ye
people, from far; The LORD hath called me
from the womb; from the bowels of my mother hath
he made mention of my name.
2 And he hath made my mouth like a sharp sword;
in the shadow of his hand hath he hid me, and made
me a polished shaft; in his quiver hath he hid me;
3 And said unto me, Thou *art* my servant, O Israel,
in whom I will be glorified.
4 Then I said, I have laboured in vain, I have spent
my strength for nought, and in vain: *yet* surely my
judgment *is* with the LORD, and my work with my
God.
5 And now, saith the LORD that formed me from the
womb *to be* his servant, to bring Jacob again to him,
Though Israel be not gathered, yet shall I be glorious
in the eyes of the LORD, and my God shall be my
strength.
6 And he said, It is a light thing that thou shouldest
be my servant to raise up the tribes of Jacob, and to
restore the preserved of Israel: I will also give thee for
a light to the Gentiles, that thou mayest be my salvation unto the end of the earth.
7 Thus saith the LORD, the Redeemer of Israel, *and*
his Holy One, to him whom man despiseth, to him
whom the nation abhorreth, to a servant of rulers,
Kings shall see and arise, princes also shall worship,
because of the LORD that is faithful, *and* the Holy
One of Israel, and he shall choose thee.

8 Thus saith the LORD, In an acceptable time have
I heard thee, and in a day of salvation have I helped
thee: and I will preserve thee, and give thee for a

NEW LIVING TRANSLATION

The LORD has redeemed his servants,
the people of Israel.*
21 They were not thirsty
when he led them through the desert.
He divided the rock,
and water gushed out for them to drink.
22 "But there is no peace for the wicked,"
says the LORD.

The LORD's Servant Commissioned

49 1 Listen to me, all you in distant lands!
Pay attention, you who are far away!
The LORD called me before my birth;
from within the womb he called me by name.
2 He made my words of judgment as sharp as
a sword.
He has hidden me in the shadow of his hand.
I am like a sharp arrow in his quiver.
3 He said to me, "You are my servant, Israel,
and you will bring me glory."
4 I replied, "But my work seems so useless!
I have spent my strength for nothing and
to no purpose.
Yet I leave it all in the LORD's hand;
I will trust God for my reward."
5 And now the LORD speaks—
the one who formed me in my mother's womb
to be his servant,
who commissioned me to bring Israel back
to him.
The LORD has honored me,
and my God has given me strength.
6 He says, "You will do more than restore the people
of Israel to me.
I will make you a light to the Gentiles,
and you will bring my salvation to the ends
of the earth."

7 The LORD, the Redeemer
and Holy One of Israel,
says to the one who is despised and rejected
by the nations,
to the one who is the servant of rulers:
"Kings will stand at attention when you pass by.
Princes will also bow low
because of the LORD, the faithful one,
the Holy One of Israel, who has chosen you."

Promises of Israel's Restoration

8 This is what the LORD says:

"At just the right time, I will respond to you.*
On the day of salvation I will help you.
I will protect you and give you to the people
as my covenant with them.

48:20b Hebrew *his servant, Jacob.* See note on 14:1. **49:8** Greek version reads *I heard you.* Compare 2 Cor 6:2.

KING JAMES VERSION

covenant of the people, to establish the earth, to cause to inherit the desolate heritages;

9 That thou mayest say to the prisoners, Go forth; to them that *are* in darkness, Shew yourselves. They shall feed in the ways, and their pastures *shall be* in all high places.

10 They shall not hunger nor thirst; neither shall the heat nor sun smite them: for he that hath mercy on them shall lead them, even by the springs of water shall he guide them.

11 And I will make all my mountains a way, and my highways shall be exalted.

12 Behold, these shall come from far: and, lo, these from the north and from the west; and these from the land of Sinim.

13 Sing, O heavens; and be joyful, O earth; and break forth into singing, O mountains: for the LORD hath comforted his people, and will have mercy upon his afflicted.

14 But Zion said, The LORD hath forsaken me, and my Lord hath forgotten me.

15 Can a woman forget her sucking child, that she should not have compassion on the son of her womb? yea, they may forget, yet will I not forget thee.

16 Behold, I have graven thee upon the palms of *my* hands; thy walls *are* continually before me.

17 Thy children shall make haste; thy destroyers and they that made thee waste shall go forth of thee.

18 Lift up thine eyes round about, and behold: all these gather themselves together, *and* come to thee. *As* I live, saith the LORD, thou shalt surely clothe thee with them all, as with an ornament, and bind them *on thee,* as a bride *doeth.*

19 For thy waste and thy desolate places, and the land of thy destruction, shall even now be too narrow by reason of the inhabitants, and they that swallowed thee up shall be far away.

20 The children which thou shalt have, after thou hast lost the other, shall say again in thine ears, The place *is* too strait for me: give place to me that I may dwell.

21 Then shalt thou say in thine heart, Who hath begotten me these, seeing I have lost my children, and

NEW LIVING TRANSLATION

Through you I will reestablish the land of Israel
and assign it to its own people again.
9 I will say to the prisoners, 'Come out in freedom,'
and to those in darkness, 'Come into the light.'
They will be my sheep, grazing in green pastures
and on hills that were previously bare.
10 They will neither hunger nor thirst.
The searing sun will not reach them anymore.
For the LORD in his mercy will lead them;
he will lead them beside cool waters.
11 And I will make my mountains into level paths
for them.
The highways will be raised above the valleys.
12 See, my people will return from far away,
from lands to the north and west,
and from as far south as Egypt.*"

13 Sing for joy, O heavens!
Rejoice, O earth!
Burst into song, O mountains!
For the LORD has comforted his people
and will have compassion on them in
their suffering.
14 Yet Jerusalem* says, "The LORD has deserted us;
the Lord has forgotten us."

15 "Never! Can a mother forget her nursing child?
Can she feel no love for the child she
has borne?
But even if that were possible,
I would not forget you!
16 See, I have written your name on the palms
of my hands.
Always in my mind is a picture of Jerusalem's
walls in ruins.
17 Soon your descendants will come back,
and all who are trying to destroy you will
go away.
18 Look around you and see,
for all your children will come back to you.
As surely as I live," says the LORD,
"they will be like jewels or bridal ornaments
for you to display.

19 "Even the most desolate parts of your
abandoned land
will soon be crowded with your people.
Your enemies who enslaved you
will be far away.
20 The generations born in exile will return and say,
'We need more room! It's crowded here!'
21 Then you will think to yourself,
'Who has given me all these descendants?
For most of my children were killed,
and the rest were carried away into exile.
I was left here all alone.
Where did all these people come from?

49:12 As in Dead Sea Scrolls, which read *from the region of Aswan,* which is in southern Egypt. Masoretic Text reads *from the region of Sinim.* **49:14** Hebrew *Zion.*

KING JAMES VERSION

am desolate, a captive, and removing to and fro? and who hath brought up these? Behold, I was left alone; these, where *had* they *been?*

22 Thus saith the Lord GOD, Behold, I will lift up mine hand to the Gentiles, and set up my standard to the people: and they shall bring thy sons in *their* arms, and thy daughters shall be carried upon *their* shoulders.

23 And kings shall be thy nursing fathers, and their queens thy nursing mothers: they shall bow down to thee with *their* face toward the earth, and lick up the dust of thy feet; and thou shalt know that I *am* the LORD: for they shall not be ashamed that wait for me.

24 Shall the prey be taken from the mighty, or the lawful captive delivered?

25 But thus saith the LORD, Even the captives of the mighty shall be taken away, and the prey of the terrible shall be delivered: for I will contend with him that contendeth with thee, and I will save thy children.

26 And I will feed them that oppress thee with their own flesh; and they shall be drunken with their own blood, as with sweet wine: and all flesh shall know that I the LORD *am* thy Saviour and thy Redeemer, the mighty One of Jacob.

50 1 Thus saith the LORD, Where *is* the bill of your mother's divorcement, whom I have put away? or which of my creditors *is it* to whom I have sold you? Behold, for your iniquities have ye sold yourselves, and for your transgressions is your mother put away.

2 Wherefore, when I came, *was there* no man? when I called, *was there* none to answer? Is my hand shortened at all, that it cannot redeem? or have I no power to deliver? behold, at my rebuke I dry up the sea, I make the rivers a wilderness: their fish stinketh, because *there is* no water, and dieth for thirst.

3 I clothe the heavens with blackness, and I make sackcloth their covering.

4 The Lord GOD hath given me the tongue of the learned, that I should know how to speak a word in season to *him that is* weary: he wakeneth morning by morning, he wakeneth mine ear to hear as the learned.

NEW LIVING TRANSLATION

Who bore these children?
Who raised them for me?'"

22 This is what the Sovereign LORD says:
"See, I will give a signal to the godless nations.
They will carry your little sons back to you
in their arms;
they will bring your daughters on their
shoulders.
23 Kings and queens will serve you
and care for all your needs.
They will bow to the earth before you
and lick the dust from your feet.
Then you will know that I am the LORD.
Those who trust in me will never be
put to shame."
24 Who can snatch the plunder of war from the
hands of a warrior?
Who can demand that a tyrant* let his
captives go?
25 But the LORD says,
"The captives of warriors will be released,
and the plunder of tyrants will be retrieved.
For I will fight those who fight you,
and I will save your children.
26 I will feed your enemies with their own flesh.
They will be drunk with rivers of their
own blood.
All the world will know that I, the LORD,
am your Savior and your Redeemer,
the Mighty One of Israel.*"

50 This is what the LORD says:
"Was your mother sent away because
I divorced her?
Did I sell you as slaves to my creditors?
No, you were sold because of your sins.
And your mother, too, was taken because
of your sins.
2 Why was no one there when I came?
Why didn't anyone answer when I called?
Is it because I have no power to rescue?
No, that is not the reason!
For I can speak to the sea and make it dry up!
I can turn rivers into deserts covered with
dying fish.
3 I dress the skies in darkness,
covering them with clothes of mourning."

The LORD's Obedient Servant

4 The Sovereign LORD has given me his words
of wisdom,
so that I know how to comfort the weary.
Morning by morning he wakens me
and opens my understanding to his will.

49:24 As in Dead Sea Scrolls, Syriac version, and Latin Vulgate (also see 49:25); Masoretic Text reads *a righteous person.* **49:26** Hebrew *of Jacob.* See note on 14:1.

KING JAMES VERSION

5 The Lord GOD hath opened mine ear, and I was not rebellious, neither turned away back.

6 I gave my back to the smiters, and my cheeks to them that plucked off the hair: I hid not my face from shame and spitting.

7 For the Lord GOD will help me; therefore shall I not be confounded: therefore have I set my face like a flint, and I know that I shall not be ashamed.

8 *He is* near that justifieth me; who will contend with me? let us stand together: who *is* mine adversary? let him come near to me.

9 Behold, the Lord GOD will help me; who *is* he *that* shall condemn me? lo, they all shall wax old as a garment; the moth shall eat them up.

10 Who *is* among you that feareth the LORD, that obeyeth the voice of his servant, that walketh *in* darkness, and hath no light? let him trust in the name of the LORD, and stay upon his God.

11 Behold, all ye that kindle a fire, that compass *yourselves* about with sparks: walk in the light of your fire, and in the sparks *that* ye have kindled. This shall ye have of mine hand; ye shall lie down in sorrow.

51 1 Hearken to me, ye that follow after righteousness, ye that seek the LORD: look unto the rock *whence* ye are hewn, and to the hole of the pit *whence* ye are digged.

2 Look unto Abraham your father, and unto Sarah *that* bare you: for I called him alone, and blessed him, and increased him.

3 For the LORD shall comfort Zion: he will comfort all her waste places; and he will make her wilderness like Eden, and her desert like the garden of the LORD; joy and gladness shall be found therein, thanksgiving, and the voice of melody.

4 Hearken unto me, my people; and give ear unto me, O my nation: for a law shall proceed from me, and I will make my judgment to rest for a light of the people.

NEW LIVING TRANSLATION

5 The Sovereign LORD has spoken to me,
and I have listened.
I have not rebelled or turned away.
6 I offered my back to those who beat me
and my cheeks to those who pulled
out my beard.
I did not hide my face
from mockery and spitting.

7 Because the Sovereign LORD helps me,
I will not be disgraced.
Therefore, I have set my face like a stone,
determined to do his will.
And I know that I will not be put to shame.
8 He who gives me justice is near.
Who will dare to bring charges against
me now?
Where are my accusers?
Let them appear!
9 See, the Sovereign LORD is on my side!
Who will declare me guilty?
All my enemies will be destroyed
like old clothes that have been eaten by moths!

10 Who among you fears the LORD
and obeys his servant?
If you are walking in darkness,
without a ray of light,
trust in the LORD
and rely on your God.
11 But watch out, you who live in your own light
and warm yourselves by your own fires.
This is the reward you will receive from me:
You will soon fall down in great torment.

A Call to Trust the LORD

51 1 "Listen to me, all who hope for
deliverance—
all who seek the LORD!
Consider the rock from which you were cut,
the quarry from which you were mined.
2 Yes, think about Abraham, your ancestor,
and Sarah, who gave birth to your nation.
Abraham was only one man when I called him.
But when I blessed him, he became
a great nation."

3 The LORD will comfort Israel* again
and have pity on her ruins.
Her desert will blossom like Eden,
her barren wilderness like the garden
of the LORD.
Joy and gladness will be found there.
Songs of thanksgiving will fill the air.

4 "Listen to me, my people.
Hear me, Israel,
for my law will be proclaimed,
and my justice will become a light to the nations.

51:3 Hebrew *Zion;* also in 51:16.

5 My righteousness *is* near; my salvation is gone forth, and mine arms shall judge the people; the isles shall wait upon me, and on mine arm shall they trust.

6 Lift up your eyes to the heavens, and look upon the earth beneath: for the heavens shall vanish away like smoke, and the earth shall wax old like a garment, and they that dwell therein shall die in like manner: but my salvation shall be for ever, and my righteousness shall not be abolished.

7 Hearken unto me, ye that know righteousness, the people in whose heart *is* my law; fear ye not the reproach of men, neither be ye afraid of their revilings.

8 For the moth shall eat them up like a garment, and the worm shall eat them like wool: but my righteousness shall be for ever, and my salvation from generation to generation.

9 Awake, awake, put on strength, O arm of the LORD; awake, as in the ancient days, in the generations of old. *Art* thou not it that hath cut Rahab, *and* wounded the dragon?

10 *Art* thou not it which hath dried the sea, the waters of the great deep; that hath made the depths of the sea a way for the ransomed to pass over?

11 Therefore the redeemed of the LORD shall return, and come with singing unto Zion; and everlasting joy *shall be* upon their head: they shall obtain gladness and joy; *and* sorrow and mourning shall flee away.

12 I, *even* I, *am* he that comforteth you: who *art* thou, that thou shouldest be afraid of a man *that* shall die, and of the son of man *which* shall be made *as* grass;

13 And forgettest the LORD thy maker, that hath stretched forth the heavens, and laid the foundations of the earth; and hast feared continually every day because of the fury of the oppressor, as if he were ready to destroy? and where *is* the fury of the oppressor?

14 The captive exile hasteneth that he may be loosed, and that he should not die in the pit, nor that his bread should fail.

5 My mercy and justice are coming soon.
My salvation is on the way.
My strong arm will bring justice to the nations.
All distant lands will look to me
and wait in hope for my powerful arm.
6 Look up to the skies above,
and gaze down on the earth below.
For the skies will disappear like smoke,
and the earth will wear out like a piece
of clothing.
The people of the earth will die like flies,
but my salvation lasts forever.
My righteous rule will never end!

7 "Listen to me, you who know right from wrong,
you who cherish my law in your hearts.
Do not be afraid of people's scorn,
nor fear their insults.
8 For the moth will devour them as it
devours clothing.
The worm will eat at them as it eats wool.
But my righteousness will last forever.
My salvation will continue from generation
to generation."

9 Wake up, wake up, O LORD! Clothe yourself
with strength!
Flex your mighty right arm!
Rouse yourself as in the days of old
when you slew Egypt, the dragon of the Nile.*
10 Are you not the same today,
the one who dried up the sea,
making a path of escape through the depths
so that your people could cross over?
11 Those who have been ransomed by the LORD
will return.
They will enter Jerusalem* singing,
crowned with everlasting joy.
Sorrow and mourning will disappear,
and they will be filled with joy and gladness.

12 "I, yes I, am the one who comforts you.
So why are you afraid of mere humans,
who wither like the grass and disappear?
13 Yet you have forgotten the LORD, your Creator,
the one who stretched out the sky like a canopy
and laid the foundations of the earth.
Will you remain in constant dread of human
oppressors?
Will you continue to fear the anger of
your enemies?
Where is their fury and anger now?
It is gone!
14 Soon all you captives will be released!
Imprisonment, starvation, and death
will not be your fate!

51:9 Hebrew *You slew Rahab; you pierced the dragon*. Rahab is the name of a mythical sea monster that represents chaos in ancient literature. The name is used here as a poetic name for Egypt. **51:11** Hebrew *Zion*.

KING JAMES VERSION

15 But I *am* the LORD thy God, that divided the sea,
whose waves roared: The LORD of hosts *is* his name.
16 And I have put my words in thy mouth, and I
have covered thee in the shadow of mine hand, that I
may plant the heavens, and lay the foundations of the
earth, and say unto Zion, Thou *art* my people.
17 Awake, awake, stand up, O Jerusalem, which hast
drunk at the hand of the LORD the cup of his fury;
thou hast drunken the dregs of the cup of trembling,
and wrung *them* out.
18 *There is* none to guide her among all the sons
whom she hath brought forth; neither *is there any*
that taketh her by the hand of all the sons *that* she
hath brought up.
19 These two *things* are come unto thee; who shall
be sorry for thee? desolation, and destruction, and
the famine, and the sword: by whom shall I comfort
thee?
20 Thy sons have fainted, they lie at the head of all
the streets, as a wild bull in a net: they are full of the
fury of the LORD, the rebuke of thy God.
21 Therefore hear now this, thou afflicted, and
drunken, but not with wine:
22 Thus saith thy Lord the LORD, and thy God *that*
pleadeth the cause of his people, Behold, I have taken
out of thine hand the cup of trembling, *even* the
dregs of the cup of my fury; thou shalt no more drink
it again:
23 But I will put it into the hand of them that afflict
thee; which have said to thy soul, Bow down, that we
may go over: and thou hast laid thy body as the
ground, and as the street, to them that went over.

52 1 Awake, awake; put on thy strength, O Zion;
put on thy beautiful garments, O Jerusalem,
the holy city: for henceforth there shall no more
come into thee the uncircumcised and the unclean.
2 Shake thyself from the dust; arise, *and* sit down,
O Jerusalem: loose thyself from the bands of thy
neck, O captive daughter of Zion.
3 For thus saith the LORD, Ye have sold yourselves
for nought; and ye shall be redeemed without
money.
4 For thus saith the Lord GOD, My people went
down aforetime into Egypt to sojourn there; and the
Assyrian oppressed them without cause.

NEW LIVING TRANSLATION

15 For I am the LORD your God,
who stirs up the sea, causing its waves to roar.
My name is the LORD of Heaven's Armies.
16 And I have put my words in your mouth
and hidden you safely in my hand.
I stretched out* the sky like a canopy
and laid the foundations of the earth.
I am the one who says to Israel,
'You are my people!'"
17 Wake up, wake up, O Jerusalem!
You have drunk the cup of the LORD's fury.
You have drunk the cup of terror,
tipping out its last drops.
18 Not one of your children is left alive
to take your hand and guide you.
19 These two calamities have fallen on you:
desolation and destruction, famine and war.
And who is left to sympathize with you?
Who is left to comfort you?*
20 For your children have fainted and lie
in the streets,
helpless as antelopes caught in a net.
The LORD has poured out his fury;
God has rebuked them.
21 But now listen to this, you afflicted ones
who sit in a drunken stupor,
though not from drinking wine.
22 This is what the Sovereign LORD,
your God and Defender, says:
"See, I have taken the terrible cup from your hands.
You will drink no more of my fury.
23 Instead, I will hand that cup to your tormentors,
those who said, 'We will trample you
into the dust
and walk on your backs.'"

Deliverance for Jerusalem

52 1 Wake up, wake up, O Zion!
Clothe yourself with strength.
Put on your beautiful clothes, O holy city
of Jerusalem,
for unclean and godless people will enter
your gates no longer.
2 Rise from the dust, O Jerusalem.
Sit in a place of honor.
Remove the chains of slavery from your neck,
O captive daughter of Zion.
3 For this is what the LORD says:
"When I sold you into exile,
I received no payment.
Now I can redeem you
without having to pay for you."

4 This is what the Sovereign LORD says: "Long ago
my people chose to live in Egypt. Now they are

51:16 As in Syriac version (see also 51:13); Hebrew reads *planted*.
51:19 As in Dead Sea Scrolls and Greek, Latin, and Syriac versions; Masoretic Text reads *How can I comfort you?*

KING JAMES VERSION

5 Now therefore, what have I here, saith the LORD,
that my people is taken away for nought? they that
rule over them make them to howl, saith the LORD;
and my name continually every day *is* blasphemed.
6 Therefore my people shall know my name: therefore *they shall know* in that day that I *am* he that
doth speak: behold, *it is* I.
7 How beautiful upon the mountains are the feet of
him that bringeth good tidings, that publisheth
peace; that bringeth good tidings of good, that
publisheth salvation; that saith unto Zion, Thy God
reigneth!
8 Thy watchmen shall lift up the voice; with the
voice together shall they sing: for they shall see eye
to eye, when the LORD shall bring again Zion.
9 Break forth into joy, sing together, ye waste places
of Jerusalem: for the LORD hath comforted his
people, he hath redeemed Jerusalem.
10 The LORD hath made bare his holy arm in the
eyes of all the nations; and all the ends of the earth
shall see the salvation of our God.
11 Depart ye, depart ye, go ye out from thence,
touch no unclean *thing;* go ye out of the midst of her;
be ye clean, that bear the vessels of the LORD.
12 For ye shall not go out with haste, nor go by
flight: for the LORD will go before you; and the God of
Israel *will be* your rereward.

13 Behold, my servant shall deal prudently, he shall
be exalted and extolled, and be very high.
14 As many were astonied at thee; his visage was so
marred more than any man, and his form more than
the sons of men:
15 So shall he sprinkle many nations; the kings
shall shut their mouths at him: for *that* which had
not been told them shall they see; and *that* which
they had not heard shall they consider.

53 1 Who hath believed our report? and to
whom is the arm of the LORD revealed?
2 For he shall grow up before him as a tender plant,
and as a root out of a dry ground: he hath no form

NEW LIVING TRANSLATION

oppressed by Assyria. 5 What is this?" asks the LORD.
"Why are my people enslaved again? Those who rule
them shout in exultation. My name is blasphemed all
day long.* 6 But I will reveal my name to my people,
and they will come to know its power. Then at last
they will recognize that I am the one who speaks to
them."

7 How beautiful on the mountains
are the feet of the messenger who
brings good news,
the good news of peace and salvation,
the news that the God of Israel* reigns!
8 The watchmen shout and sing with joy,
for before their very eyes
they see the LORD returning to Jerusalem.*
9 Let the ruins of Jerusalem break into joyful song,
for the LORD has comforted his people.
He has redeemed Jerusalem.
10 The LORD has demonstrated his holy power
before the eyes of all the nations.
All the ends of the earth will see
the victory of our God.

11 Get out! Get out and leave your captivity,
where everything you touch is unclean.
Get out of there and purify yourselves,
you who carry home the sacred objects
of the LORD.
12 You will not leave in a hurry,
running for your lives.
For the LORD will go ahead of you;
yes, the God of Israel will protect you
from behind.

The LORD's Suffering Servant

13 See, my servant will prosper;
he will be highly exalted.
14 But many were amazed when they saw him.*
His face was so disfigured he seemed
hardly human,
and from his appearance, one would scarcely
know he was a man.
15 And he will startle* many nations.
Kings will stand speechless in his presence.
For they will see what they had not been told;
they will understand what they had not
heard about.*

53 1 Who has believed our message?
To whom has the LORD revealed his
powerful arm?
2 My servant grew up in the LORD's presence like
a tender green shoot,
like a root in dry ground.

52:5 Greek version reads *The Gentiles continually blaspheme my name because of you.* Compare Rom 2:24. 52:7 Hebrew *of Zion.* 52:8 Hebrew *to Zion.* 52:14 As in Syriac version; Hebrew reads *you.* 52:15a Or *cleanse.* 52:15b Greek version reads *Those who have never been told about him will see, / and those who have never heard of him will understand.* Compare Rom 15:21.

KING JAMES VERSION

nor comeliness; and when we shall see him, *there is* no beauty that we should desire him.

3 He is despised and rejected of men; a man of sorrows, and acquainted with grief: and we hid as it were *our* faces from him; he was despised, and we esteemed him not.

4 Surely he hath borne our griefs, and carried our sorrows: yet we did esteem him stricken, smitten of God, and afflicted.

5 But he *was* wounded for our transgressions, *he was* bruised for our iniquities: the chastisement of our peace *was* upon him; and with his stripes we are healed.

6 All we like sheep have gone astray; we have turned every one to his own way; and the LORD hath laid on him the iniquity of us all.

7 He was oppressed, and he was afflicted, yet he opened not his mouth: he is brought as a lamb to the slaughter, and as a sheep before her shearers is dumb, so he openeth not his mouth.

8 He was taken from prison and from judgment: and who shall declare his generation? for he was cut off out of the land of the living: for the transgression of my people was he stricken.

9 And he made his grave with the wicked, and with the rich in his death; because he had done no violence, neither *was any* deceit in his mouth.

10 Yet it pleased the LORD to bruise him; he hath put *him* to grief: when thou shalt make his soul an offering for sin, he shall see *his* seed, he shall prolong *his* days, and the pleasure of the LORD shall prosper in his hand.

11 He shall see of the travail of his soul, *and* shall be satisfied: by his knowledge shall my righteous servant justify many; for he shall bear their iniquities.

12 Therefore will I divide him *a portion* with the great, and he shall divide the spoil with the strong; because he hath poured out his soul unto death: and

NEW LIVING TRANSLATION

There was nothing beautiful or majestic about
his appearance,
nothing to attract us to him.
3 He was despised and rejected—
a man of sorrows, acquainted with
deepest grief.
We turned our backs on him and looked
the other way.
He was despised, and we did not care.

4 Yet it was our weaknesses he carried;
it was our sorrows* that weighed him down.
And we thought his troubles were a punishment
from God,
a punishment for his own sins!
5 But he was pierced for our rebellion,
crushed for our sins.
He was beaten so we could be whole.
He was whipped so we could be healed.
6 All of us, like sheep, have strayed away.
We have left God's paths to follow our own.
Yet the LORD laid on him
the sins of us all.
7 He was oppressed and treated harshly,
yet he never said a word.
He was led like a lamb to the slaughter.
And as a sheep is silent before the shearers,
he did not open his mouth.
8 Unjustly condemned,
he was led away.*
No one cared that he died without descendants,
that his life was cut short in midstream.*
But he was struck down
for the rebellion of my people.
9 He had done no wrong
and had never deceived anyone.
But he was buried like a criminal;
he was put in a rich man's grave.

10 But it was the LORD's good plan to crush him
and cause him grief.
Yet when his life is made an offering for sin,
he will have many descendants.
He will enjoy a long life,
and the LORD's good plan will prosper
in his hands.
11 When he sees all that is accomplished
by his anguish,
he will be satisfied.
And because of his experience,
my righteous servant will make it possible
for many to be counted righteous,
for he will bear all their sins.
12 I will give him the honors of a victorious soldier,
because he exposed himself to death.

53:4 Or *Yet it was our sicknesses he carried; / it was our diseases.* **53:8a** Greek version reads *He was humiliated and received no justice.* Compare Acts 8:33. **53:8b** Or *As for his contemporaries, / who cared that his life was cut short in midstream?* Greek version reads *Who can speak of his descendants? / For his life was taken from the earth.* Compare Acts 8:33.

KING JAMES VERSION

he was numbered with the transgressors; and he
bare the sin of many, and made intercession for the
transgressors.

54 1 Sing, O barren, thou *that* didst not bear;
break forth into singing, and cry aloud, thou
that didst not travail with child: for more *are* the children of the desolate than the children of the married
wife, saith the LORD.
2 Enlarge the place of thy tent, and let them stretch
forth the curtains of thine habitations: spare not,
lengthen thy cords, and strengthen thy stakes;
3 For thou shalt break forth on the right hand and
on the left; and thy seed shall inherit the Gentiles,
and make the desolate cities to be inhabited.
4 Fear not; for thou shalt not be ashamed: neither
be thou confounded; for thou shalt not be put to
shame: for thou shalt forget the shame of thy youth,
and shalt not remember the reproach of thy widowhood any more.
5 For thy Maker *is* thine husband; the LORD of hosts
is his name; and thy Redeemer the Holy One of Israel;
The God of the whole earth shall he be called.
6 For the LORD hath called thee as a woman forsaken and grieved in spirit, and a wife of youth, when
thou wast refused, saith thy God.
7 For a small moment have I forsaken thee; but
with great mercies will I gather thee.
8 In a little wrath I hid my face from thee for a moment; but with everlasting kindness will I have mercy
on thee, saith the LORD thy Redeemer.
9 For this *is as* the waters of Noah unto me: for *as* I
have sworn that the waters of Noah should no more
go over the earth; so have I sworn that I would not be
wroth with thee, nor rebuke thee.
10 For the mountains shall depart, and the hills be
removed; but my kindness shall not depart from
thee, neither shall the covenant of my peace be removed, saith the LORD that hath mercy on thee.
11 O thou afflicted, tossed with tempest, *and* not
comforted, behold, I will lay thy stones with fair
colours, and lay thy foundations with sapphires.
12 And I will make thy windows of agates, and thy
gates of carbuncles, and all thy borders of pleasant
stones.

NEW LIVING TRANSLATION

He was counted among the rebels.
He bore the sins of many and interceded
for rebels.

Future Glory for Jerusalem

54 1 "Sing, O childless woman,
you who have never given birth!
Break into loud and joyful song, O Jerusalem,
you who have never been in labor.
For the desolate woman now has more children
than the woman who lives with her husband,"
says the LORD.
2 "Enlarge your house; build an addition.
Spread out your home, and spare no expense!
3 For you will soon be bursting at the seams.
Your descendants will occupy other nations
and resettle the ruined cities.

4 "Fear not; you will no longer live in shame.
Don't be afraid; there is no more disgrace
for you.
You will no longer remember the shame
of your youth
and the sorrows of widowhood.
5 For your Creator will be your husband;
the LORD of Heaven's Armies is his name!
He is your Redeemer, the Holy One of Israel,
the God of all the earth.
6 For the LORD has called you back from
your grief—
as though you were a young wife abandoned
by her husband,"
says your God.
7 "For a brief moment I abandoned you,
but with great compassion I will take you back.
8 In a burst of anger I turned my face away for
a little while.
But with everlasting love I will have
compassion on you,"
says the LORD, your Redeemer.

9 "Just as I swore in the time of Noah
that I would never again let a flood
cover the earth,
so now I swear
that I will never again be angry and punish you.
10 For the mountains may move
and the hills disappear,
but even then my faithful love for you will remain.
My covenant of blessing will never be broken,"
says the LORD, who has mercy on you.

11 "O storm-battered city,
troubled and desolate!
I will rebuild you with precious jewels
and make your foundations from lapis lazuli.
12 I will make your towers of sparkling rubies,
your gates of shining gems,
and your walls of precious stones.

KING JAMES VERSION

13 And all thy children *shall be* taught of the LORD; and great *shall be* the peace of thy children.

14 In righteousness shalt thou be established: thou shalt be far from oppression; for thou shalt not fear: and from terror; for it shall not come near thee.

15 Behold, they shall surely gather together, *but* not by me: whosoever shall gather together against thee shall fall for thy sake.

16 Behold, I have created the smith that bloweth the coals in the fire, and that bringeth forth an instrument for his work; and I have created the waster to destroy.

17 No weapon that is formed against thee shall prosper; and every tongue *that* shall rise against thee in judgment thou shalt condemn. This *is* the heritage of the servants of the LORD, and their righteousness *is* of me, saith the LORD.

55 1 Ho, every one that thirsteth, come ye to the waters, and he that hath no money; come ye, buy, and eat; yea, come, buy wine and milk without money and without price.

2 Wherefore do ye spend money for *that which is* not bread? and your labour for *that which* satisfieth not? hearken diligently unto me, and eat ye *that which is* good, and let your soul delight itself in fatness.

3 Incline your ear, and come unto me: hear, and your soul shall live; and I will make an everlasting covenant with you, *even* the sure mercies of David.

4 Behold, I have given him *for* a witness to the people, a leader and commander to the people.

5 Behold, thou shalt call a nation *that* thou knowest not, and nations *that* knew not thee shall run unto thee because of the LORD thy God, and for the Holy One of Israel; for he hath glorified thee.

6 Seek ye the LORD while he may be found, call ye upon him while he is near:

7 Let the wicked forsake his way, and the unrighteous man his thoughts: and let him return unto the LORD, and he will have mercy upon him; and to our God, for he will abundantly pardon.

NEW LIVING TRANSLATION

13 I will teach all your children,
and they will enjoy great peace.
14 You will be secure under a government
that is just and fair.
Your enemies will stay far away.
You will live in peace,
and terror will not come near.
15 If any nation comes to fight you,
it is not because I sent them.
Whoever attacks you will go down in defeat.

16 "I have created the blacksmith
who fans the coals beneath the forge
and makes the weapons of destruction.
And I have created the armies that destroy.
17 But in that coming day
no weapon turned against you will succeed.
You will silence every voice
raised up to accuse you.
These benefits are enjoyed by the servants
of the LORD;
their vindication will come from me.
I, the LORD, have spoken!

Invitation to the LORD's Salvation

55 1 "Is anyone thirsty?
Come and drink—
even if you have no money!
Come, take your choice of wine or milk—
it's all free!
2 Why spend your money on food that does
not give you strength?
Why pay for food that does you no good?
Listen to me, and you will eat what is good.
You will enjoy the finest food.

3 "Come to me with your ears wide open.
Listen, and you will find life.
I will make an everlasting covenant with you.
I will give you all the unfailing love I
promised to David.
4 See how I used him to display my power
among the peoples.
I made him a leader among the nations.
5 You also will command nations you do not know,
and peoples unknown to you will come
running to obey,
because I, the LORD your God,
the Holy One of Israel, have made
you glorious."

6 Seek the LORD while you can find him.
Call on him now while he is near.
7 Let the wicked change their ways
and banish the very thought of doing wrong.
Let them turn to the LORD that he may have
mercy on them.
Yes, turn to our God, for he will forgive
generously.

KING JAMES VERSION

8 For my thoughts *are* not your thoughts, neither
are your ways my ways, saith the LORD.
9 For *as* the heavens are higher than the earth, so
are my ways higher than your ways, and my thoughts
than your thoughts.
10 For as the rain cometh down, and the snow from
heaven, and returneth not thither, but watereth the
earth, and maketh it bring forth and bud, that it may
give seed to the sower, and bread to the eater:
11 So shall my word be that goeth forth out of my
mouth: it shall not return unto me void, but it shall
accomplish that which I please, and it shall prosper
in the thing whereto I sent it.
12 For ye shall go out with joy, and be led forth with
peace: the mountains and the hills shall break forth
before you into singing, and all the trees of the field
shall clap *their* hands.
13 Instead of the thorn shall come up the fir tree,
and instead of the brier shall come up the myrtle
tree: and it shall be to the LORD for a name, for an
everlasting sign *that* shall not be cut off.

56 1 Thus saith the LORD, Keep ye judgment,
and do justice: for my salvation *is* near to
come, and my righteousness to be revealed.
2 Blessed *is* the man *that* doeth this, and the son of
man *that* layeth hold on it; that keepeth the sabbath
from polluting it, and keepeth his hand from doing
any evil.
3 Neither let the son of the stranger, that hath
joined himself to the LORD, speak, saying, The LORD
hath utterly separated me from his people: neither
let the eunuch say, Behold, I *am* a dry tree.
4 For thus saith the LORD unto the eunuchs that
keep my sabbaths, and choose *the things* that please
me, and take hold of my covenant;
5 Even unto them will I give in mine house and
within my walls a place and a name better than of
sons and of daughters: I will give them an everlasting
name, that shall not be cut off.

NEW LIVING TRANSLATION

8 "My thoughts are nothing like your thoughts,"
says the LORD.
"And my ways are far beyond anything you
could imagine.
9 For just as the heavens are higher than the earth,
so my ways are higher than your ways
and my thoughts higher than your thoughts.

10 "The rain and snow come down from
the heavens
and stay on the ground to water the earth.
They cause the grain to grow,
producing seed for the farmer
and bread for the hungry.
11 It is the same with my word.
I send it out, and it always produces fruit.
It will accomplish all I want it to,
and it will prosper everywhere I send it.
12 You will live in joy and peace.
The mountains and hills will burst into song,
and the trees of the field will clap their hands!
13 Where once there were thorns, cypress trees
will grow.
Where nettles grew, myrtles will sprout up.
These events will bring great honor to the
LORD's name;
they will be an everlasting sign of his power
and love."

Blessings for All Nations

56 This is what the LORD says:
"Be just and fair to all.
Do what is right and good,
for I am coming soon to rescue you
and to display my righteousness among you.
2 Blessed are all those
who are careful to do this.
Blessed are those who honor my Sabbath
days of rest
and keep themselves from doing wrong.
3 "Don't let foreigners who commit themselves
to the LORD say,
'The LORD will never let me be part of
his people.'
And don't let the eunuchs say,
'I'm a dried-up tree with no children
and no future.'
4 For this is what the LORD says:
I will bless those eunuchs
who keep my Sabbath days holy
and who choose to do what pleases me
and commit their lives to me.
5 I will give them—within the walls of my house—
a memorial and a name
far greater than sons and daughters could give.
For the name I give them is an everlasting one.
It will never disappear!

KING JAMES VERSION

6 Also the sons of the stranger, that join themselves
to the LORD, to serve him, and to love the name of the
LORD, to be his servants, every one that keepeth the
sabbath from polluting it, and taketh hold of my
covenant;
7 Even them will I bring to my holy mountain, and
make them joyful in my house of prayer: their burnt
offerings and their sacrifices *shall be* accepted upon
mine altar; for mine house shall be called an house of
prayer for all people.
8 The Lord GOD which gathereth the outcasts of
Israel saith, Yet will I gather *others* to him, beside
those that are gathered unto him.

9 All ye beasts of the field, come to devour, *yea,* all
ye beasts in the forest.
10 His watchmen *are* blind: they are all ignorant,
they *are* all dumb dogs, they cannot bark; sleeping,
lying down, loving to slumber.
11 Yea, *they are* greedy dogs *which* can never have
enough, and they *are* shepherds *that* cannot understand: they all look to their own way, every one for his
gain, from his quarter.
12 Come ye, *say they,* I will fetch wine, and we will
fill ourselves with strong drink; and tomorrow shall
be as this day, *and* much more abundant.

57 1 The righteous perisheth, and no man layeth
it to heart: and merciful men *are* taken away,
none considering that the righteous is taken away
from the evil *to come.*
2 He shall enter into peace: they shall rest in their
beds, *each one* walking *in* his uprightness.

3 But draw near hither, ye sons of the sorceress, the
seed of the adulterer and the whore.
4 Against whom do ye sport yourselves? against
whom make ye a wide mouth, *and* draw out the
tongue? *are* ye not children of transgression, a seed
of falsehood,
5 Enflaming yourselves with idols under every
green tree, slaying the children in the valleys under
the clifts of the rocks?
6 Among the smooth *stones* of the stream *is* thy

NEW LIVING TRANSLATION

6 "I will also bless the foreigners who commit
themselves to the LORD,
who serve him and love his name,
who worship him and do not desecrate the
Sabbath day of rest,
and who hold fast to my covenant.
7 I will bring them to my holy mountain
of Jerusalem
and will fill them with joy in my house
of prayer.
I will accept their burnt offerings and sacrifices,
because my Temple will be called a house of
prayer for all nations.
8 For the Sovereign LORD,
who brings back the outcasts of Israel, says:
I will bring others, too,
besides my people Israel."

Sinful Leaders Condemned

9 Come, wild animals of the field!
Come, wild animals of the forest!
Come and devour my people!
10 For the leaders of my people—
the LORD's watchmen, his shepherds—
are blind and ignorant.
They are like silent watchdogs
that give no warning when danger comes.
They love to lie around, sleeping and dreaming.
11 Like greedy dogs, they are never satisfied.
They are ignorant shepherds,
all following their own path
and intent on personal gain.
12 "Come," they say, "let's get some wine
and have a party.
Let's all get drunk.
Then tomorrow we'll do it again
and have an even bigger party!"

57 1 Good people pass away;
the godly often die before their time.
But no one seems to care or wonder why.
No one seems to understand
that God is protecting them from the
evil to come.
2 For those who follow godly paths
will rest in peace when they die.

Idolatrous Worship Condemned

3 "But you—come here, you witches' children,
you offspring of adulterers and prostitutes!
4 Whom do you mock,
making faces and sticking out your tongues?
You children of sinners and liars!
5 You worship your idols with great passion
beneath the oaks and under every green tree.
You sacrifice your children down in the valleys,
among the jagged rocks in the cliffs.
6 Your gods are the smooth stones in the valleys.

KING JAMES VERSION

portion; they, they *are* thy lot: even to them hast thou
poured a drink offering, thou hast offered a meat
offering. Should I receive comfort in these?
7 Upon a lofty and high mountain hast thou set thy
bed: even thither wentest thou up to offer sacrifice.
8 Behind the doors also and the posts hast thou set
up thy remembrance: for thou hast discovered *thy-*
self to another than me, and art gone up; thou hast
enlarged thy bed, and made thee *a covenant* with
them; thou lovedst their bed where thou sawest *it*.
9 And thou wentest to the king with ointment, and
didst increase thy perfumes, and didst send thy messengers far off, and didst debase *thyself even* unto
hell.
10 Thou art wearied in the greatness of thy way; *yet*
saidst thou not, There is no hope: thou hast found
the life of thine hand; therefore thou wast not
grieved.
11 And of whom hast thou been afraid or feared,
that thou hast lied, and hast not remembered me,
nor laid *it* to thy heart? have not I held my peace even
of old, and thou fearest me not?
12 I will declare thy righteousness, and thy works;
for they shall not profit thee.
13 When thou criest, let thy companies deliver
thee; but the wind shall carry them all away; vanity
shall take *them*: but he that putteth his trust in me
shall possess the land, and shall inherit my holy
mountain;

14 And shall say, Cast ye up, cast ye up, prepare the
way, take up the stumbling block out of the way of my
people.
15 For thus saith the high and lofty One that
inhabiteth eternity, whose name *is* Holy; I dwell in
the high and holy *place*, with him also *that is* of a
contrite and humble spirit, to revive the spirit of the
humble, and to revive the heart of the contrite ones.
16 For I will not contend for ever, neither will I be
always wroth: for the spirit should fail before me, and
the souls *which* I have made.
17 For the iniquity of his covetousness was I wroth,

NEW LIVING TRANSLATION

You worship them with liquid offerings
and grain offerings.
They, not I, are your inheritance.
Do you think all this makes me happy?
7 You have committed adultery on every high
mountain.
There you have worshiped idols
and have been unfaithful to me.
8 You have put pagan symbols
on your doorposts and behind your doors.
You have left me
and climbed into bed with these detestable gods.
You have committed yourselves to them.
You love to look at their naked bodies.
9 You have given olive oil to Molech*
with many gifts of perfume.
You have traveled far,
even into the world of the dead,*
to find new gods to love.
10 You grew weary in your search,
but you never gave up.
Desire gave you renewed strength,
and you did not grow weary.

11 "Are you afraid of these idols?
Do they terrify you?
Is that why you have lied to me
and forgotten me and my words?
Is it because of my long silence
that you no longer fear me?
12 Now I will expose your so-called good deeds.
None of them will help you.
13 Let's see if your idols can save you
when you cry to them for help.
Why, a puff of wind can knock them down!
If you just breathe on them, they fall over!
But whoever trusts in me will inherit the land
and possess my holy mountain."

God Forgives the Repentant

14 God says, "Rebuild the road!
Clear away the rocks and stones
so my people can return from captivity."
15 The high and lofty one who lives in eternity,
the Holy One, says this:
"I live in the high and holy place
with those whose spirits are contrite
and humble.
I restore the crushed spirit of the humble
and revive the courage of those with
repentant hearts.
16 For I will not fight against you forever;
I will not always be angry.
If I were, all people would pass away—
all the souls I have made.
17 I was angry,
so I punished these greedy people.

57:9a Or *to the king*. **57:9b** Hebrew *into Sheol*.

KING JAMES VERSION

and smote him: I hid me, and was wroth, and he went
on frowardly in the way of his heart.
18 I have seen his ways, and will heal him: I will lead
him also, and restore comforts unto him and to his
mourners.
19 I create the fruit of the lips; Peace, peace to *him*
that is far off, and to *him that is* near, saith the LORD;
and I will heal him.
20 But the wicked *are* like the troubled sea, when it
cannot rest, whose waters cast up mire and dirt.
21 *There is* no peace, saith my God, to the wicked.

58 1 Cry aloud, spare not, lift up thy voice like a
trumpet, and shew my people their transgression, and the house of Jacob their sins.
2 Yet they seek me daily, and delight to know my
ways, as a nation that did righteousness, and forsook
not the ordinance of their God: they ask of me the ordinances of justice; they take delight in approaching
to God.
3 Wherefore have we fasted, *say they,* and thou
seest not? *wherefore* have we afflicted our soul, and
thou takest no knowledge? Behold, in the day of your
fast ye find pleasure, and exact all your labours.
4 Behold, ye fast for strife and debate, and to smite
with the fist of wickedness: ye shall not fast as *ye do*
this day, to make your voice to be heard on high.
5 Is it such a fast that I have chosen? a day for a man
to afflict his soul? *is it* to bow down his head as a bul-
rush, and to spread sackcloth and ashes *under him?*
wilt thou call this a fast, and an acceptable day to the
LORD?
6 *Is* not this the fast that I have chosen? to loose the
bands of wickedness, to undo the heavy burdens,
and to let the oppressed go free, and that ye break
every yoke?
7 *Is it* not to deal thy bread to the hungry, and that
thou bring the poor that are cast out to thy house?

NEW LIVING TRANSLATION

I withdrew from them,
but they kept going on their own stubborn way.
18 I have seen what they do,
but I will heal them anyway!
I will lead them.
I will comfort those who mourn,
19 bringing words of praise to their lips.
May they have abundant peace, both near
and far,"
says the LORD, who heals them.
20 "But those who still reject me are like the
restless sea,
which is never still
but continually churns up mud and dirt.
21 There is no peace for the wicked,"
says my God.

True and False Worship

58 1 "Shout with the voice of a trumpet blast.
Shout aloud! Don't be timid.
Tell my people Israel* of their sins!
2 Yet they act so pious!
They come to the Temple every day
and seem delighted to learn all about me.
They act like a righteous nation
that would never abandon the laws of its God.
They ask me to take action on their behalf,
pretending they want to be near me.
3 'We have fasted before you!' they say.
'Why aren't you impressed?
We have been very hard on ourselves,
and you don't even notice it!'

"I will tell you why!" I respond.
"It's because you are fasting to please
yourselves.
Even while you fast,
you keep oppressing your workers.
4 What good is fasting
when you keep on fighting and quarreling?
This kind of fasting
will never get you anywhere with me.
5 You humble yourselves
by going through the motions of penance,
bowing your heads
like reeds bending in the wind.
You dress in burlap
and cover yourselves with ashes.
Is this what you call fasting?
Do you really think this will please the LORD?

6 "No, this is the kind of fasting I want:
Free those who are wrongly imprisoned;
lighten the burden of those who work for you.
Let the oppressed go free,
and remove the chains that bind people.
7 Share your food with the hungry,
and give shelter to the homeless.

58:1 Hebrew *Jacob.* See note on 14:1.

KING JAMES VERSION

when thou seest the naked, that thou cover him; and
that thou hide not thyself from thine own flesh?
8 Then shall thy light break forth as the morning,
and thine health shall spring forth speedily: and thy
righteousness shall go before thee; the glory of the
LORD shall be thy rereward.
9 Then shalt thou call, and the LORD shall answer;
thou shalt cry, and he shall say, Here I *am*. If thou take
away from the midst of thee the yoke, the putting
forth of the finger, and speaking vanity;
10 And *if* thou draw out thy soul to the hungry, and
satisfy the afflicted soul; then shall thy light rise in
obscurity, and thy darkness *be* as the noon day:
11 And the LORD shall guide thee continually, and
satisfy thy soul in drought, and make fat thy bones:
and thou shalt be like a watered garden, and like a
spring of water, whose waters fail not.
12 And *they that shall be* of thee shall build the old
waste places: thou shalt raise up the foundations of
many generations; and thou shalt be called, The re-
pairer of the breach, The restorer of paths to dwell in.
13 If thou turn away thy foot from the sabbath,
from doing thy pleasure on my holy day; and call the
sabbath a delight, the holy of the LORD, honourable;
and shalt honour him, not doing thine own ways, nor
finding thine own pleasure, nor speaking *thine own*
words:
14 Then shalt thou delight thyself in the LORD; and
I will cause thee to ride upon the high places of the
earth, and feed thee with the heritage of Jacob thy
father: for the mouth of the LORD hath spoken *it*.

59 1 Behold, the LORD's hand is not shortened,
that it cannot save; neither his ear heavy, that
it cannot hear:
2 But your iniquities have separated between you
and your God, and your sins have hid *his* face from
you, that he will not hear.
3 For your hands are defiled with blood, and your
fingers with iniquity; your lips have spoken lies, your
tongue hath muttered perverseness.
4 None calleth for justice, nor *any* pleadeth for
truth: they trust in vanity, and speak lies; they conceive mischief, and bring forth iniquity.

NEW LIVING TRANSLATION

Give clothes to those who need them,
and do not hide from relatives who
need your help.
8 "Then your salvation will come like the dawn,
and your wounds will quickly heal.
Your godliness will lead you forward,
and the glory of the LORD will protect you
from behind.
9 Then when you call, the LORD will answer.
'Yes, I am here,' he will quickly reply.

"Remove the heavy yoke of oppression.
Stop pointing your finger and spreading
vicious rumors!
10 Feed the hungry,
and help those in trouble.
Then your light will shine out from the darkness,
and the darkness around you will be as bright
as noon.
11 The LORD will guide you continually,
giving you water when you are dry
and restoring your strength.
You will be like a well-watered garden,
like an ever-flowing spring.
12 Some of you will rebuild the deserted ruins of
your cities.
Then you will be known as a rebuilder of walls
and a restorer of homes.

13 "Keep the Sabbath day holy.
Don't pursue your own interests on that day,
but enjoy the Sabbath
and speak of it with delight as the LORD's
holy day.
Honor the Sabbath in everything you do
on that day,
and don't follow your own desires or talk idly.
14 Then the LORD will be your delight.
I will give you great honor
and satisfy you with the inheritance I promised
to your ancestor Jacob.
I, the LORD, have spoken!"

Warnings against Sin

59 1 Listen! The LORD's arm is not too weak
to save you,
nor is his ear too deaf to hear you call.
2 It's your sins that have cut you off from God.
Because of your sins, he has turned away
and will not listen anymore.
3 Your hands are the hands of murderers,
and your fingers are filthy with sin.
Your lips are full of lies,
and your mouth spews corruption.

4 No one cares about being fair and honest.
The people's lawsuits are based on lies.
They conceive evil deeds
and then give birth to sin.

KING JAMES VERSION

5 They hatch cockatrice' eggs, and weave the spider's web: he that eateth of their eggs dieth, and that
which is crushed breaketh out into a viper.
6 Their webs shall not become garments, neither
shall they cover themselves with their works: their
works *are* works of iniquity, and the act of violence *is*
in their hands.
7 Their feet run to evil, and they make haste to
shed innocent blood: their thoughts *are* thoughts of
iniquity; wasting and destruction *are* in their paths.
8 The way of peace they know not; and *there is* no
judgment in their goings: they have made them
crooked paths: whosoever goeth therein shall not
know peace.
9 Therefore is judgment far from us, neither doth
justice overtake us: we wait for light, but behold obscurity; for brightness, *but* we walk in darkness.
10 We grope for the wall like the blind, and we
grope as if *we had* no eyes: we stumble at noon day as
in the night; *we are* in desolate places as dead *men*.
11 We roar all like bears, and mourn sore like
doves: we look for judgment, but *there is* none; for
salvation, *but* it is far off from us.
12 For our transgressions are multiplied before
thee, and our sins testify against us: for our transgressions *are* with us; and *as for* our iniquities, we
know them;
13 In transgressing and lying against the LORD, and
departing away from our God, speaking oppression
and revolt, conceiving and uttering from the heart
words of falsehood.
14 And judgment is turned away backward, and
justice standeth afar off: for truth is fallen in the
street, and equity cannot enter.
15 Yea, truth faileth; and he *that* departeth from
evil maketh himself a prey: and the LORD saw *it*, and
it displeased him that *there was* no judgment.
16 And he saw that *there was* no man, and wondered that *there was* no intercessor: therefore his
arm brought salvation unto him; and his righteousness, it sustained him.
17 For he put on righteousness as a breastplate, and
an helmet of salvation upon his head; and he put on
the garments of vengeance *for* clothing, and was clad
with zeal as a cloak.

NEW LIVING TRANSLATION

5 They hatch deadly snakes
and weave spiders' webs.
Whoever falls into their webs will die,
and there's danger even in getting near them.
6 Their webs can't be made into clothing,
and nothing they do is productive.
All their activity is filled with sin,
and violence is their trademark.
7 Their feet run to do evil,
and they rush to commit murder.
They think only about sinning.
Misery and destruction always follow them.
8 They don't know where to find peace
or what it means to be just and good.
They have mapped out crooked roads,
and no one who follows them knows
a moment's peace.

9 So there is no justice among us,
and we know nothing about right living.
We look for light but find only darkness.
We look for bright skies but walk in gloom.
10 We grope like the blind along a wall,
feeling our way like people without eyes.
Even at brightest noontime,
we stumble as though it were dark.
Among the living,
we are like the dead.
11 We growl like hungry bears;
we moan like mournful doves.
We look for justice, but it never comes.
We look for rescue, but it is far away from us.
12 For our sins are piled up before God
and testify against us.
Yes, we know what sinners we are.
13 We know we have rebelled and have denied
the LORD.
We have turned our backs on our God.
We know how unfair and oppressive we have been,
carefully planning our deceitful lies.
14 Our courts oppose the righteous,
and justice is nowhere to be found.
Truth stumbles in the streets,
and honesty has been outlawed.
15 Yes, truth is gone,
and anyone who renounces evil is attacked.

The LORD looked and was displeased
to find there was no justice.
16 He was amazed to see that no one intervened
to help the oppressed.
So he himself stepped in to save them with his
strong arm,
and his justice sustained him.
17 He put on righteousness as his body armor
and placed the helmet of salvation on his head.
He clothed himself with a robe of vengeance
and wrapped himself in a cloak of divine
passion.

KING JAMES VERSION

18 According to *their* deeds, accordingly he will repay, fury to his adversaries, recompence to his enemies; to the islands he will repay recompence.

19 So shall they fear the name of the LORD from the west, and his glory from the rising of the sun. When the enemy shall come in like a flood, the Spirit of the LORD shall lift up a standard against him.

20 And the Redeemer shall come to Zion, and unto them that turn from transgression in Jacob, saith the LORD.

21 As for me, this *is* my covenant with them, saith the LORD; My spirit that *is* upon thee, and my words which I have put in thy mouth, shall not depart out of thy mouth, nor out of the mouth of thy seed, nor out of the mouth of thy seed's seed, saith the LORD, from henceforth and for ever.

60 1 Arise, shine; for thy light is come, and the glory of the LORD is risen upon thee.

2 For, behold, the darkness shall cover the earth, and gross darkness the people: but the LORD shall arise upon thee, and his glory shall be seen upon thee.

3 And the Gentiles shall come to thy light, and kings to the brightness of thy rising.

4 Lift up thine eyes round about, and see: all they gather themselves together, they come to thee: thy sons shall come from far, and thy daughters shall be nursed at *thy* side.

5 Then thou shalt see, and flow together, and thine heart shall fear, and be enlarged; because the abundance of the sea shall be converted unto thee, the forces of the Gentiles shall come unto thee.

6 The multitude of camels shall cover thee, the dromedaries of Midian and Ephah; all they from Sheba shall come: they shall bring gold and incense; and they shall shew forth the praises of the LORD.

7 All the flocks of Kedar shall be gathered together unto thee, the rams of Nebaioth shall minister unto thee: they shall come up with acceptance on mine altar, and I will glorify the house of my glory.

8 Who *are* these *that* fly as a cloud, and as the doves to their windows?

9 Surely the isles shall wait for me, and the ships of

NEW LIVING TRANSLATION

18 He will repay his enemies for their evil deeds.
His fury will fall on his foes.
He will pay them back even to the ends
of the earth.
19 In the west, people will respect the name
of the LORD;
in the east, they will glorify him.
For he will come like a raging flood tide
driven by the breath of the LORD.*
20 "The Redeemer will come to Jerusalem
to buy back those in Israel
who have turned from their sins,"*
says the LORD.

21 "And this is my covenant with them," says the LORD. "My Spirit will not leave them, and neither will these words I have given you. They will be on your lips and on the lips of your children and your children's children forever. I, the LORD, have spoken!

Future Glory for Jerusalem

60 1 "Arise, Jerusalem! Let your light shine
for all to see.
For the glory of the LORD rises to shine on you.
2 Darkness as black as night covers all the nations
of the earth,
but the glory of the LORD rises and appears
over you.
3 All nations will come to your light;
mighty kings will come to see your radiance.

4 "Look and see, for everyone is coming home!
Your sons are coming from distant lands;
your little daughters will be carried home.
5 Your eyes will shine,
and your heart will thrill with joy,
for merchants from around the world will
come to you.
They will bring you the wealth of many lands.
6 Vast caravans of camels will converge on you,
the camels of Midian and Ephah.
The people of Sheba will bring gold and
frankincense
and will come worshiping the LORD.
7 The flocks of Kedar will be given to you,
and the rams of Nebaioth will be brought
for my altars.
I will accept their offerings,
and I will make my Temple glorious.

8 "And what do I see flying like clouds to Israel,
like doves to their nests?
9 They are ships from the ends of the earth,
from lands that trust in me,
led by the great ships of Tarshish.

59:19 Or *When the enemy comes like a raging flood tide, / the Spirit of the LORD will drive him back.* 59:20 Hebrew *The Redeemer will come to Zion / to buy back those in Jacob / who have turned from their sins.* Greek version reads *The one who rescues will come on behalf of Zion, / and he will turn Jacob away from ungodliness.* Compare Rom 11:26.

KING JAMES VERSION

Tarshish first, to bring thy sons from far, their silver
and their gold with them, unto the name of the LORD
thy God, and to the Holy One of Israel, because he
hath glorified thee.
10 And the sons of strangers shall build up thy
walls, and their kings shall minister unto thee: for in
my wrath I smote thee, but in my favour have I had
mercy on thee.
11 Therefore thy gates shall be open continually;
they shall not be shut day nor night; that *men* may
bring unto thee the forces of the Gentiles, and *that*
their kings *may be* brought.
12 For the nation and kingdom that will not serve
thee shall perish; yea, *those* nations shall be utterly
wasted.
13 The glory of Lebanon shall come unto thee, the
fir tree, the pine tree, and the box together, to beautify the place of my sanctuary; and I will make the
place of my feet glorious.
14 The sons also of them that afflicted thee shall
come bending unto thee; and all they that despised
thee shall bow themselves down at the soles of thy
feet; and they shall call thee, The city of the LORD, The
Zion of the Holy One of Israel.
15 Whereas thou hast been forsaken and hated, so
that no man went through *thee,* I will make thee an
eternal excellency, a joy of many generations.
16 Thou shalt also suck the milk of the Gentiles,
and shalt suck the breast of kings: and thou shalt
know that I the LORD *am* thy Saviour and thy Redeemer, the mighty One of Jacob.
17 For brass I will bring gold, and for iron I will
bring silver, and for wood brass, and for stones iron: I
will also make thy officers peace, and thine exactors
righteousness.
18 Violence shall no more be heard in thy land,
wasting nor destruction within thy borders; but thou
shalt call thy walls Salvation, and thy gates Praise.
19 The sun shall be no more thy light by day; neither for brightness shall the moon give light unto
thee: but the LORD shall be unto thee an everlasting
light, and thy God thy glory.

NEW LIVING TRANSLATION

They are bringing the people of Israel home
from far away,
carrying their silver and gold.
They will honor the LORD your God,
the Holy One of Israel,
for he has filled you with splendor.

10 "Foreigners will come to rebuild your towns,
and their kings will serve you.
For though I have destroyed you in my anger,
I will now have mercy on you through
my grace.
11 Your gates will stay open day and night
to receive the wealth of many lands.
The kings of the world will be led as captives
in a victory procession.
12 For the nations that refuse to serve you
will be destroyed.

13 "The glory of Lebanon will be yours—
the forests of cypress, fir, and pine—
to beautify my sanctuary.
My Temple will be glorious!
14 The descendants of your tormentors
will come and bow before you.
Those who despised you
will kiss your feet.
They will call you the City of the LORD,
and Zion of the Holy One of Israel.

15 "Though you were once despised and hated,
with no one traveling through you,
I will make you beautiful forever,
a joy to all generations.
16 Powerful kings and mighty nations
will satisfy your every need,
as though you were a child
nursing at the breast of a queen.
You will know at last that I, the LORD,
am your Savior and your Redeemer,
the Mighty One of Israel.*
17 I will exchange your bronze for gold,
your iron for silver,
your wood for bronze,
and your stones for iron.
I will make peace your leader
and righteousness your ruler.
18 Violence will disappear from your land;
the desolation and destruction of war will end.
Salvation will surround you like city walls,
and praise will be on the lips of all who
enter there.

19 "No longer will you need the sun to shine by day,
nor the moon to give its light by night,
for the LORD your God will be your
everlasting light,
and your God will be your glory.

60:16 Hebrew *of Jacob.* See note on 14:1.

KING JAMES VERSION

20 Thy sun shall no more go down; neither shall thy
moon withdraw itself: for the LORD shall be thine
everlasting light, and the days of thy mourning shall
be ended.
21 Thy people also *shall be* all righteous: they shall
inherit the land for ever, the branch of my planting,
the work of my hands, that I may be glorified.
22 A little one shall become a thousand, and a small
one a strong nation: I the LORD will hasten it in his
time.

61 1 The Spirit of the Lord GOD *is* upon me; because the LORD hath anointed me to preach
good tidings unto the meek; he hath sent me to bind
up the brokenhearted, to proclaim liberty to the captives, and the opening of the prison to *them that are*
bound;
2 To proclaim the acceptable year of the LORD, and
the day of vengeance of our God; to comfort all that
mourn;
3 To appoint unto them that mourn in Zion, to give
unto them beauty for ashes, the oil of joy for mourning, the garment of praise for the spirit of heaviness;
that they might be called trees of righteousness, the
planting of the LORD, that he might be glorified.
4 And they shall build the old wastes, they shall
raise up the former desolations, and they shall repair
the waste cities, the desolations of many generations.
5 And strangers shall stand and feed your flocks,
and the sons of the alien *shall be* your plowmen and
your vinedressers.
6 But ye shall be named the Priests of the LORD:
men shall call you the Ministers of our God: ye shall
eat the riches of the Gentiles, and in their glory shall
ye boast yourselves.
7 For your shame *ye shall have* double; and *for*
confusion they shall rejoice in their portion: therefore in their land they shall possess the double: everlasting joy shall be unto them.
8 For I the LORD love judgment, I hate robbery for
burnt offering; and I will direct their work in truth,
and I will make an everlasting covenant with them.

NEW LIVING TRANSLATION

20 Your sun will never set;
your moon will not go down.
For the LORD will be your everlasting light.
Your days of mourning will come to an end.
21 All your people will be righteous.
They will possess their land forever,
for I will plant them there with my own hands
in order to bring myself glory.
22 The smallest family will become
a thousand people,
and the tiniest group will become
a mighty nation.
At the right time, I, the LORD, will make
it happen."

Good News for the Oppressed

61 1 The Spirit of the Sovereign LORD is upon me,
for the LORD has anointed me
to bring good news to the poor.
He has sent me to comfort the brokenhearted
and to proclaim that captives will be released
and prisoners will be freed.*
2 He has sent me to tell those who mourn
that the time of the LORD's favor has come,*
and with it, the day of God's anger against
their enemies.
3 To all who mourn in Israel,*
he will give a crown of beauty for ashes,
a joyous blessing instead of mourning,
festive praise instead of despair.
In their righteousness, they will be like great oaks
that the LORD has planted for his own glory.

4 They will rebuild the ancient ruins,
repairing cities destroyed long ago.
They will revive them,
though they have been deserted for
many generations.
5 Foreigners will be your servants.
They will feed your flocks
and plow your fields
and tend your vineyards.
6 You will be called priests of the LORD,
ministers of our God.
You will feed on the treasures of the nations
and boast in their riches.
7 Instead of shame and dishonor,
you will enjoy a double share of honor.
You will possess a double portion of prosperity
in your land,
and everlasting joy will be yours.

8 "For I, the LORD, love justice.
I hate robbery and wrongdoing.
I will faithfully reward my people for
their suffering
and make an everlasting covenant with them.

61:1 Greek version reads *and the blind will see.* Compare Luke 4:18.
61:2 Or *to proclaim the acceptable year of the LORD.* **61:3** Hebrew *in Zion.*

KING JAMES VERSION

9 And their seed shall be known among the
Gentiles, and their offspring among the people: all
that see them shall acknowledge them, that they *are*
the seed *which* the LORD hath blessed.
10 I will greatly rejoice in the LORD, my soul shall be
joyful in my God; for he hath clothed me with the
garments of salvation, he hath covered me with the
robe of righteousness, as a bridegroom decketh *him-*
self with ornaments, and as a bride adorneth *herself*
with her jewels.
11 For as the earth bringeth forth her bud, and as
the garden causeth the things that are sown in it to
spring forth; so the Lord GOD will cause righteousness and praise to spring forth before all the nations.

62 1 For Zion's sake will I not hold my peace, and
for Jerusalem's sake I will not rest, until the
righteousness thereof go forth as brightness, and the
salvation thereof as a lamp *that* burneth.
2 And the Gentiles shall see thy righteousness, and
all kings thy glory: and thou shalt be called by a new
name, which the mouth of the LORD shall name.
3 Thou shalt also be a crown of glory in the hand of
the LORD, and a royal diadem in the hand of thy God.
4 Thou shalt no more be termed Forsaken; neither
shall thy land any more be termed Desolate: but thou
shalt be called Hephzi-bah, and thy land Beulah: for
the LORD delighteth in thee, and thy land shall be
married.
5 For *as* a young man marrieth a virgin, *so* shall thy
sons marry thee: and *as* the bridegroom rejoiceth
over the bride, *so* shall thy God rejoice over thee.
6 I have set watchmen upon thy walls, O Jerusalem,
which shall never hold their peace day nor night: ye
that make mention of the LORD, keep not silence.
7 And give him no rest, till he establish, and till he
make Jerusalem a praise in the earth.
8 The LORD hath sworn by his right hand, and by

NEW LIVING TRANSLATION

9 Their descendants will be recognized
and honored among the nations.
Everyone will realize that they are a people
the LORD has blessed."
10 I am overwhelmed with joy in the LORD my God!
For he has dressed me with the clothing
of salvation
and draped me in a robe of righteousness.
I am like a bridegroom in his wedding suit
or a bride with her jewels.
11 The Sovereign LORD will show his justice
to the nations of the world.
Everyone will praise him!
His righteousness will be like a garden
in early spring,
with plants springing up everywhere.

Isaiah's Prayer for Jerusalem

62 1 Because I love Zion,
I will not keep still.
Because my heart yearns for Jerusalem,
I cannot remain silent.
I will not stop praying for her
until her righteousness shines like the dawn,
and her salvation blazes like a burning torch.
2 The nations will see your righteousness.
World leaders will be blinded by your glory.
And you will be given a new name
by the LORD's own mouth.
3 The LORD will hold you in his hand for all to see—
a splendid crown in the hand of God.
4 Never again will you be called
"The Forsaken City"*
or "The Desolate Land."*
Your new name will be "The City of
God's Delight"*
and "The Bride of God,"*
for the LORD delights in you
and will claim you as his bride.
5 Your children will commit themselves to you,
O Jerusalem,
just as a young man commits himself
to his bride.
Then God will rejoice over you
as a bridegroom rejoices over his bride.
6 O Jerusalem, I have posted watchmen
on your walls;
they will pray day and night, continually.
Take no rest, all you who pray to the LORD.
7 Give the LORD no rest until he completes his work,
until he makes Jerusalem the pride
of the earth.
8 The LORD has sworn to Jerusalem by his
own strength:

62:4a Hebrew *Azubah,* which means "forsaken." **62:4b** Hebrew *Shemamah,* which means "desolate." **62:4c** Hebrew *Hephzibah,* which means "my delight is in her." **62:4d** Hebrew *Beulah,* which means "married."

KING JAMES VERSION

the arm of his strength, Surely I will no more give thy
corn *to be* meat for thine enemies; and the sons of
the stranger shall not drink thy wine, for the which
thou hast laboured:
9 But they that have gathered it shall eat it and
praise the LORD; and they that have brought it together shall drink it in the courts of my holiness.
10 Go through, go through the gates; prepare ye the
way of the people; cast up, cast up the highway;
gather out the stones; lift up a standard for the
people.
11 Behold, the LORD hath proclaimed unto the end
of the world, Say ye to the daughter of Zion, Behold,
thy salvation cometh; behold, his reward *is* with him,
and his work before him.
12 And they shall call them, The holy people, The
redeemed of the LORD: and thou shalt be called,
Sought out, A city not forsaken.

63 1 Who *is* this that cometh from Edom, with
dyed garments from Bozrah? this *that is*
glorious in his apparel, travelling in the greatness of
his strength? I that speak in righteousness, mighty to
save.
2 Wherefore *art thou* red in thine apparel, and thy
garments like him that treadeth in the winefat?
3 I have trodden the winepress alone; and of the
people *there was* none with me: for I will tread them
in mine anger, and trample them in my fury; and
their blood shall be sprinkled upon my garments,
and I will stain all my raiment.
4 For the day of vengeance *is* in mine heart, and the
year of my redeemed is come.
5 And I looked, and *there was* none to help; and I
wondered that *there was* none to uphold: therefore
mine own arm brought salvation unto me; and my
fury, it upheld me.
6 And I will tread down the people in mine anger,
and make them drunk in my fury, and I will bring
down their strength to the earth.
7 I will mention the lovingkindnesses of the LORD,
and the praises of the LORD, according to all that the
LORD hath bestowed on us, and the great goodness

NEW LIVING TRANSLATION

"I will never again hand you over to
your enemies.
Never again will foreign warriors come
and take away your grain and new wine.
9 You raised the grain, and you will eat it,
praising the LORD.
Within the courtyards of the Temple,
you yourselves will drink the wine you
have pressed."

10 Go out through the gates!
Prepare the highway for my people to return!
Smooth out the road; pull out the boulders;
raise a flag for all the nations to see.
11 The LORD has sent this message to every land:
"Tell the people of Israel,*
'Look, your Savior is coming.
See, he brings his reward with him
as he comes.'"
12 They will be called "The Holy People"
and "The People Redeemed by the LORD."
And Jerusalem will be known as
"The Desirable Place"
and "The City No Longer Forsaken."

Judgment against the LORD's Enemies

63 1 Who is this who comes from Edom,
from the city of Bozrah,
with his clothing stained red?
Who is this in royal robes,
marching in his great strength?

"It is I, the LORD, announcing your salvation!
It is I, the LORD, who has the power to save!"

2 Why are your clothes so red,
as if you have been treading out grapes?
3 "I have been treading the winepress alone;
no one was there to help me.
In my anger I have trampled my enemies
as if they were grapes.
In my fury I have trampled my foes.
Their blood has stained my clothes.
4 For the time has come for me to avenge
my people,
to ransom them from their oppressors.
5 I was amazed to see that no one intervened
to help the oppressed.
So I myself stepped in to save them with
my strong arm,
and my wrath sustained me.
6 I crushed the nations in my anger
and made them stagger and fall to the ground,
spilling their blood upon the earth."

Praise for Deliverance

7 I will tell of the LORD's unfailing love.
I will praise the LORD for all he has done.

62:11 Hebrew *Tell the daughter of Zion.*

toward the house of Israel, which he hath bestowed
on them according to his mercies, and according to
the multitude of his lovingkindnesses.
8 For he said, Surely they *are* my people, children
that will not lie: so he was their Saviour.
9 In all their affliction he was afflicted, and the
angel of his presence saved them: in his love and in
his pity he redeemed them; and he bare them, and
carried them all the days of old.
10 But they rebelled, and vexed his holy Spirit:
therefore he was turned to be their enemy, *and* he
fought against them.
11 Then he remembered the days of old, Moses,
and his people, *saying,* Where *is* he that brought
them up out of the sea with the shepherd of his
flock? where *is* he that put his holy Spirit within him?
12 That led *them* by the right hand of Moses with
his glorious arm, dividing the water before them, to
make himself an everlasting name?
13 That led them through the deep, as an horse in
the wilderness, *that* they should not stumble?
14 As a beast goeth down into the valley, the Spirit
of the LORD caused him to rest: so didst thou lead thy
people, to make thyself a glorious name.

15 Look down from heaven, and behold from the
habitation of thy holiness and of thy glory: where *is*
thy zeal and thy strength, the sounding of thy bowels
and of thy mercies toward me? are they restrained?
16 Doubtless thou *art* our father, though Abraham
be ignorant of us, and Israel acknowledge us not:
thou, O LORD, *art* our father, our redeemer; thy name
is from everlasting.
17 O LORD, why hast thou made us to err from thy
ways, *and* hardened our heart from thy fear? Return
for thy servants' sake, the tribes of thine inheritance.
18 The people of thy holiness have possessed *it* but
a little while: our adversaries have trodden down thy
sanctuary.

I will rejoice in his great goodness to Israel,
which he has granted according to his
mercy and love.
8 He said, "They are my very own people.
Surely they will not betray me again."
And he became their Savior.
9 In all their suffering he also suffered,
and he personally* rescued them.
In his love and mercy he redeemed them.
He lifted them up and carried them
through all the years.
10 But they rebelled against him
and grieved his Holy Spirit.
So he became their enemy
and fought against them.

11 Then they remembered those days of old
when Moses led his people out of Egypt.
They cried out, "Where is the one who brought
Israel through the sea,
with Moses as their shepherd?
Where is the one who sent his Holy Spirit
to be among his people?
12 Where is the one whose power was displayed
when Moses lifted up his hand—
the one who divided the sea before them,
making himself famous forever?
13 Where is the one who led them through the
bottom of the sea?
They were like fine stallions
racing through the desert, never stumbling.
14 As with cattle going down into a peaceful valley,
the Spirit of the LORD gave them rest.
You led your people, LORD,
and gained a magnificent reputation."

Prayer for Mercy and Pardon

15 LORD, look down from heaven;
look from your holy, glorious home,
and see us.
Where is the passion and the might
you used to show on our behalf?
Where are your mercy and compassion now?
16 Surely you are still our Father!
Even if Abraham and Jacob* would disown us,
LORD, you would still be our Father.
You are our Redeemer from ages past.
17 LORD, why have you allowed us to turn from
your path?
Why have you given us stubborn hearts so we
no longer fear you?
Return and help us, for we are your servants,
the tribes that are your special possession.
18 How briefly your holy people possessed your
holy place,
and now our enemies have destroyed it.

63:9 Hebrew *and the angel of his presence.* **63:16** Hebrew *Israel.* See note on 14:1.

KING JAMES VERSION

[19]We are *thine:* thou never barest rule over them;
they were not called by thy name.

64

[1]Oh that thou wouldest rend the heavens,
that thou wouldest come down, that the
mountains might flow down at thy presence.
[2]As *when* the melting fire burneth, the fire
causeth the waters to boil, to make thy name known
to thine adversaries, *that* the nations may tremble at
thy presence!
[3]When thou didst terrible things *which* we
looked not for, thou camest down, the mountains
flowed down at thy presence.
[4]For since the beginning of the world *men* have
not heard, nor perceived by the ear, neither hath the
eye seen, O God, beside thee, *what* he hath prepared
for him that waiteth for him.
[5]Thou meetest him that rejoiceth and worketh
righteousness, *those that* remember thee in thy
ways: behold, thou art wroth; for we have sinned: in
those is continuance, and we shall be saved.
[6]But we are all as an unclean *thing,* and all our
righteousnesses *are* as filthy rags; and we all do fade
as a leaf; and our iniquities, like the wind, have taken
us away.
[7]And *there is* none that calleth upon thy name,
that stirreth up himself to take hold of thee: for thou
hast hid thy face from us, and hast consumed us, because of our iniquities.
[8]But now, O LORD, thou *art* our father; we *are* the
clay, and thou our potter; and we all *are* the work of
thy hand.
[9]Be not wroth very sore, O LORD, neither remember iniquity for ever: behold, see, we beseech thee,
we *are* all thy people.
[10]Thy holy cities are a wilderness, Zion is a wilderness, Jerusalem a desolation.
[11]Our holy and our beautiful house, where our
fathers praised thee, is burned up with fire: and all
our pleasant things are laid waste.
[12]Wilt thou refrain thyself for these *things,*
O LORD? wilt thou hold thy peace, and afflict us very
sore?

NEW LIVING TRANSLATION

[19] Sometimes it seems as though we never
belonged to you,
as though we had never been known
as your people.

64

[1]*Oh, that you would burst from the
heavens and come down!
How the mountains would quake in your
presence!
[2]*As fire causes wood to burn
and water to boil,
your coming would make the nations tremble.
Then your enemies would learn the reason
for your fame!
[3] When you came down long ago,
you did awesome deeds beyond our
highest expectations.
And oh, how the mountains quaked!
[4] For since the world began,
no ear has heard
and no eye has seen a God like you,
who works for those who wait for him!
[5] You welcome those who gladly do good,
who follow godly ways.
But you have been very angry with us,
for we are not godly.
We are constant sinners;
how can people like us be saved?
[6] We are all infected and impure with sin.
When we display our righteous deeds,
they are nothing but filthy rags.
Like autumn leaves, we wither and fall,
and our sins sweep us away like the wind.
[7] Yet no one calls on your name
or pleads with you for mercy.
Therefore, you have turned away from us
and turned us over* to our sins.
[8] And yet, O LORD, you are our Father.
We are the clay, and you are the potter.
We all are formed by your hand.
[9] Don't be so angry with us, LORD.
Please don't remember our sins forever.
Look at us, we pray,
and see that we are all your people.
[10] Your holy cities are destroyed.
Zion is a wilderness;
yes, Jerusalem is a desolate ruin.
[11] The holy and beautiful Temple
where our ancestors praised you
has been burned down,
and all the things of beauty are destroyed.
[12] After all this, LORD, must you still refuse
to help us?
Will you continue to be silent and punish us?

64:1 In the Hebrew text this verse is included in 63:19. **64:2** Verses 64:2-12 are numbered 64:1-11 in Hebrew text. **64:7** As in Greek, Syriac, and Aramaic versions; Hebrew reads *melted us.*

KING JAMES VERSION

65

[1]I am sought of *them that* asked not *for me;*
I am found of *them that* sought me not: I
said, Behold me, behold me, unto a nation *that* was
not called by my name.
[2]I have spread out my hands all the day unto a rebellious people, which walketh in a way *that was* not
good, after their own thoughts;
[3]A people that provoketh me to anger continually
to my face; that sacrificeth in gardens, and burneth
incense upon altars of brick;
[4]Which remain among the graves, and lodge in
the monuments, which eat swine's flesh, and broth
of abominable *things is in* their vessels;
[5]Which say, Stand by thyself, come not near to me;
for I am holier than thou. These *are* a smoke in my
nose, a fire that burneth all the day.
[6]Behold, *it is* written before me: I will not keep silence, but will recompense, even recompense into
their bosom,
[7]Your iniquities, and the iniquities of your fathers
together, saith the LORD, which have burned incense
upon the mountains, and blasphemed me upon the
hills: therefore will I measure their former work into
their bosom.
[8]Thus saith the LORD, As the new wine is found in
the cluster, and *one* saith, Destroy it not; for a blessing *is* in it: so will I do for my servants' sakes, that I
may not destroy them all.
[9]And I will bring forth a seed out of Jacob, and out
of Judah an inheritor of my mountains: and mine
elect shall inherit it, and my servants shall dwell
there.
[10]And Sharon shall be a fold of flocks, and the
valley of Achor a place for the herds to lie down in,
for my people that have sought me.

NEW LIVING TRANSLATION

Judgment and Final Salvation

65

The LORD says,
"I was ready to respond, but no one
asked for help.
I was ready to be found, but no one was
looking for me.
I said, 'Here I am, here I am!'
to a nation that did not call on my name.*
[2] All day long I opened my arms to a
rebellious people.*
But they follow their own evil paths
and their own crooked schemes.
[3] All day long they insult me to my face
by worshiping idols in their sacred gardens.
They burn incense on pagan altars.
[4] At night they go out among the graves,
worshiping the dead.
They eat the flesh of pigs
and make stews with other forbidden foods.
[5] Yet they say to each other,
'Don't come too close or you will defile me!
I am holier than you!'
These people are a stench in my nostrils,
an acrid smell that never goes away.
[6] "Look, my decree is written out* in front of me:
I will not stand silent;
I will repay them in full!
Yes, I will repay them—
[7] both for their own sins
and for those of their ancestors,"
says the LORD.
"For they also burned incense on the mountains
and insulted me on the hills.
I will pay them back in full!
[8] "But I will not destroy them all,"
says the LORD.
"For just as good grapes are found among
a cluster of bad ones
(and someone will say, 'Don't throw them
all away—
some of those grapes are good!'),
so I will not destroy all Israel.
For I still have true servants there.
[9] I will preserve a remnant of the people of Israel*
and of Judah to possess my land.
Those I choose will inherit it,
and my servants will live there.
[10] The plain of Sharon will again be filled
with flocks
for my people who have searched for me,
and the valley of Achor will be a place to
pasture herds.

65:1 Or *to a nation that did not bear my name.* **65:1-2** Greek version reads *I was found by people who were not looking for me. / I showed myself to those who were not asking for me. / All day long I opened my arms to them, / but they were disobedient and rebellious.* Compare Rom 10:20-21.
65:6 Or *their sins are written out;* Hebrew reads *it stands written.*
65:9 Hebrew *remnant of Jacob.* See note on 14:1.

KING JAMES VERSION

11 But ye *are* they that forsake the LORD, that forget my holy mountain, that prepare a table for that troop, and that furnish the drink offering unto that number.

12 Therefore will I number you to the sword, and ye shall all bow down to the slaughter: because when I called, ye did not answer; when I spake, ye did not hear; but did evil before mine eyes, and did choose *that* wherein I delighted not.

13 Therefore thus saith the Lord GOD, Behold, my servants shall eat, but ye shall be hungry: behold, my servants shall drink, but ye shall be thirsty: behold, my servants shall rejoice, but ye shall be ashamed:

14 Behold, my servants shall sing for joy of heart, but ye shall cry for sorrow of heart, and shall howl for vexation of spirit.

15 And ye shall leave your name for a curse unto my chosen: for the Lord GOD shall slay thee, and call his servants by another name:

16 That he who blesseth himself in the earth shall bless himself in the God of truth; and he that sweareth in the earth shall swear by the God of truth; because the former troubles are forgotten, and because they are hid from mine eyes.

17 For, behold, I create new heavens and a new earth: and the former shall not be remembered, nor come into mind.

18 But be ye glad and rejoice for ever *in that* which I create: for, behold, I create Jerusalem a rejoicing, and her people a joy.

19 And I will rejoice in Jerusalem, and joy in my people: and the voice of weeping shall be no more heard in her, nor the voice of crying.

20 There shall be no more thence an infant of days, nor an old man that hath not filled his days: for the child shall die an hundred years old; but the sinner *being* an hundred years old shall be accursed.

21 And they shall build houses, and inhabit *them;* and they shall plant vineyards, and eat the fruit of them.

22 They shall not build, and another inhabit; they shall not plant, and another eat: for as the days of a

NEW LIVING TRANSLATION

11 "But because the rest of you have forsaken
the LORD
and have forgotten his Temple,
and because you have prepared feasts
to honor the god of Fate
and have offered mixed wine to the
god of Destiny,
12 now I will 'destine' you for the sword.
All of you will bow down before the
executioner.
For when I called, you did not answer.
When I spoke, you did not listen.
You deliberately sinned—before my very eyes—
and chose to do what you know I despise."

13 Therefore, this is what the Sovereign LORD says:
"My servants will eat,
but you will starve.
My servants will drink,
but you will be thirsty.
My servants will rejoice,
but you will be sad and ashamed.
14 My servants will sing for joy,
but you will cry in sorrow and despair.
15 Your name will be a curse word among my people,
for the Sovereign LORD will destroy you
and will call his true servants by another name.
16 All who invoke a blessing or take an oath
will do so by the God of truth.
For I will put aside my anger
and forget the evil of earlier days.
17 "Look! I am creating new heavens and
a new earth,
and no one will even think about the
old ones anymore.
18 Be glad; rejoice forever in my creation!
And look! I will create Jerusalem as a place
of happiness.
Her people will be a source of joy.
19 I will rejoice over Jerusalem
and delight in my people.
And the sound of weeping and crying
will be heard in it no more.

20 "No longer will babies die when only
a few days old.
No longer will adults die before they have
lived a full life.
No longer will people be considered old
at one hundred!
Only the cursed will die that young!
21 In those days people will live in the houses
they build
and eat the fruit of their own vineyards.
22 Unlike the past, invaders will not take
their houses
and confiscate their vineyards.
For my people will live as long as trees,

KING JAMES VERSION

tree *are* the days of my people, and mine elect shall
long enjoy the work of their hands.
23 They shall not labour in vain, nor bring forth for
trouble; for they *are* the seed of the blessed of the
LORD, and their offspring with them.
24 And it shall come to pass, that before they call, I
will answer; and while they are yet speaking, I will
hear.
25 The wolf and the lamb shall feed together, and
the lion shall eat straw like the bullock: and dust
shall be the serpent's meat. They shall not hurt nor
destroy in all my holy mountain, saith the LORD.

66 1 Thus saith the LORD, The heaven *is* my
throne, and the earth *is* my footstool: where
is the house that ye build unto me? and where *is* the
place of my rest?
2 For all those *things* hath mine hand made, and all
those *things* have been, saith the LORD: but to this
man will I look, *even* to *him that is* poor and of a contrite spirit, and trembleth at my word.
3 He that killeth an ox *is as if* he slew a man; he that
sacrificeth a lamb, *as if* he cut off a dog's neck; he
that offereth an oblation, *as if he offered* swine's
blood; he that burneth incense, *as if* he blessed an
idol. Yea, they have chosen their own ways, and their
soul delighteth in their abominations.
4 I also will choose their delusions, and will bring
their fears upon them; because when I called, none
did answer; when I spake, they did not hear: but they
did evil before mine eyes, and chose *that* in which I
delighted not.
5 Hear the word of the LORD, ye that tremble at his
word; Your brethren that hated you, that cast you out
for my name's sake, said, Let the LORD be glorified:
but he shall appear to your joy, and they shall be
ashamed.
6 A voice of noise from the city, a voice from the

NEW LIVING TRANSLATION

and my chosen ones will have time to enjoy
their hard-won gains.
23 They will not work in vain,
and their children will not be doomed to
misfortune.
For they are people blessed by the LORD,
and their children, too, will be blessed.
24 I will answer them before they even call to me.
While they are still talking about their needs,
I will go ahead and answer their prayers!
25 The wolf and the lamb will feed together.
The lion will eat hay like a cow.
But the snakes will eat dust.
In those days no one will be hurt or destroyed
on my holy mountain.
I, the LORD, have spoken!"

66 This is what the LORD says:
"Heaven is my throne,
and the earth is my footstool.
Could you build me a temple as good as that?
Could you build me such a resting place?
2 My hands have made both heaven and earth;
they and everything in them are mine.*
I, the LORD, have spoken!
"I will bless those who have humble and
contrite hearts,
who tremble at my word.
3 But those who choose their own ways—
delighting in their detestable sins—
will not have their offerings accepted.
When such people sacrifice a bull,
it is no more acceptable than a human
sacrifice.
When they sacrifice a lamb,
it's as though they had sacrificed a dog!
When they bring an offering of grain,
they might as well offer the blood of a pig.
When they burn frankincense,
it's as if they had blessed an idol.
4 I will send them great trouble—
all the things they feared.
For when I called, they did not answer.
When I spoke, they did not listen.
They deliberately sinned before my very eyes
and chose to do what they know I despise."

5 Hear this message from the LORD,
all you who tremble at his words:
"Your own people hate you
and throw you out for being loyal to my name.
'Let the LORD be honored!' they scoff.
'Be joyful in him!'
But they will be put to shame.
6 What is all the commotion in the city?
What is that terrible noise from the Temple?

66:2 As in Greek, Latin, and Syriac versions; Hebrew reads *these things are.*

KING JAMES VERSION

temple, a voice of the LORD that rendereth recompence to his enemies.
7 Before she travailed, she brought forth; before
her pain came, she was delivered of a man child.
8 Who hath heard such a thing? who hath seen
such things? Shall the earth be made to bring forth
in one day? *or* shall a nation be born at once? for
as soon as Zion travailed, she brought forth her
children.
9 Shall I bring to the birth, and not cause to bring
forth? saith the LORD: shall I cause to bring forth, and
shut *the womb?* saith thy God.
10 Rejoice ye with Jerusalem, and be glad with her,
all ye that love her: rejoice for joy with her, all ye that
mourn for her:
11 That ye may suck, and be satisfied with the
breasts of her consolations; that ye may milk out, and
be delighted with the abundance of her glory.
12 For thus saith the LORD, Behold, I will extend
peace to her like a river, and the glory of the Gentiles
like a flowing stream: then shall ye suck, ye shall be
borne upon *her* sides, and be dandled upon *her*
knees.
13 As one whom his mother comforteth, so will I
comfort you; and ye shall be comforted in Jerusalem.
14 And when ye see *this,* your heart shall rejoice,
and your bones shall flourish like an herb: and the
hand of the LORD shall be known toward his servants,
and *his* indignation toward his enemies.
15 For, behold, the LORD will come with fire, and
with his chariots like a whirlwind, to render his anger with fury, and his rebuke with flames of fire.
16 For by fire and by his sword will the LORD plead
with all flesh: and the slain of the LORD shall be
many.
17 They that sanctify themselves, and purify themselves in the gardens behind one *tree* in the midst,
eating swine's flesh, and the abomination, and the
mouse, shall be consumed together, saith the LORD.
18 For I *know* their works and their thoughts: it
shall come, that I will gather all nations and tongues;
and they shall come, and see my glory.
19 And I will set a sign among them, and I will send
those that escape of them unto the nations, *to* Tarshish, Pul, and Lud, that draw the bow, *to* Tubal, and

NEW LIVING TRANSLATION

It is the voice of the LORD
taking vengeance against his enemies.

7 "Before the birth pains even begin,
Jerusalem gives birth to a son.
8 Who has ever seen anything as strange as this?
Who ever heard of such a thing?
Has a nation ever been born in a single day?
Has a country ever come forth in a mere moment?
But by the time Jerusalem's* birth pains begin,
her children will be born.
9 Would I ever bring this nation to the point of birth
and then not deliver it?" asks the LORD.
"No! I would never keep this nation from being born,"
says your God.

10 "Rejoice with Jerusalem!
Be glad with her, all you who love her
and all you who mourn for her.
11 Drink deeply of her glory
even as an infant drinks at its mother's comforting breasts."

12 This is what the LORD says:
"I will give Jerusalem a river of peace and prosperity.
The wealth of the nations will flow to her.
Her children will be nursed at her breasts,
carried in her arms, and held on her lap.
13 I will comfort you there in Jerusalem
as a mother comforts her child."
14 When you see these things, your heart will rejoice.
You will flourish like the grass!
Everyone will see the LORD's hand of blessing on his servants—
and his anger against his enemies.
15 See, the LORD is coming with fire,
and his swift chariots roar like a whirlwind.
He will bring punishment with the fury of his anger
and the flaming fire of his hot rebuke.
16 The LORD will punish the world by fire
and by his sword.
He will judge the earth,
and many will be killed by him.

17 "Those who 'consecrate' and 'purify' themselves
in a sacred garden with its idol in the center—feasting on pork and rats and other detestable meats—
will come to a terrible end," says the LORD.
18 "I can see what they are doing, and I know what
they are thinking. So I will gather all nations and
peoples together, and they will see my glory. 19 I will
perform a sign among them. And I will send those
who survive to be messengers to the nations—to

66:8 Hebrew *Zion's.*

KING JAMES VERSION

Javan, *to* the isles afar off, that have not heard my
fame, neither have seen my glory; and they shall
declare my glory among the Gentiles.
20 And they shall bring all your brethren *for* an offering unto the LORD out of all nations upon horses,
and in chariots, and in litters, and upon mules, and
upon swift beasts, to my holy mountain Jerusalem,
saith the LORD, as the children of Israel bring an offering in a clean vessel into the house of the LORD.
21 And I will also take of them for priests *and* for
Levites, saith the LORD.
22 For as the new heavens and the new earth, which
I will make, shall remain before me, saith the LORD, so
shall your seed and your name remain.
23 And it shall come to pass, *that* from one new
moon to another, and from one sabbath to another,
shall all flesh come to worship before me, saith the
LORD.
24 And they shall go forth, and look upon the carcases of the men that have transgressed against me:
for their worm shall not die, neither shall their fire
be quenched; and they shall be an abhorring unto
all flesh.

NEW LIVING TRANSLATION

Tarshish, to the Libyans* and Lydians* (who are famous as archers), to Tubal and Greece,* and to all the
lands beyond the sea that have not heard of my fame
or seen my glory. There they will declare my glory to
the nations. 20 They will bring the remnant of your
people back from every nation. They will bring them
to my holy mountain in Jerusalem as an offering to
the LORD. They will ride on horses, in chariots and
wagons, and on mules and camels," says the LORD.
21 "And I will appoint some of them to be my priests
and Levites. I, the LORD, have spoken!

22 "As surely as my new heavens and earth
will remain,
so will you always be my people,
with a name that will never disappear,"
says the LORD.
23 "All humanity will come to worship me
from week to week
and from month to month.
24 And as they go out, they will see
the dead bodies of those who have
rebelled against me.
For the worms that devour them will never die,
and the fire that burns them will never go out.
All who pass by
will view them with utter horror."

66:19a As in some Greek manuscripts, which read *Put* (that is, *Libya*); Hebrew reads *Pul*. **66:19b** Hebrew *Lud*. **66:19c** Hebrew *Javan*.

Jeremiah

KING JAMES VERSION

1 [1]The words of Jeremiah the son of Hilkiah, of the priests that *were* in Anathoth in the land of Benjamin:

[2]To whom the word of the LORD came in the days of Josiah the son of Amon king of Judah, in the thirteenth year of his reign.

[3]It came also in the days of Jehoiakim the son of Josiah king of Judah, unto the end of the eleventh year of Zedekiah the son of Josiah king of Judah, unto the carrying away of Jerusalem captive in the fifth month.

[4]Then the word of the LORD came unto me, saying,

[5]Before I formed thee in the belly I knew thee; and before thou camest forth out of the womb I sanctified thee, *and* I ordained thee a prophet unto the nations.

[6]Then said I, Ah, Lord GOD! behold, I cannot speak: for I *am* a child.

[7]But the LORD said unto me, Say not, I *am* a child: for thou shalt go to all that I shall send thee, and whatsoever I command thee thou shalt speak.

[8]Be not afraid of their faces: for I *am* with thee to deliver thee, saith the LORD.

[9]Then the LORD put forth his hand, and touched my mouth. And the LORD said unto me, Behold, I have put my words in thy mouth.

[10]See, I have this day set thee over the nations and over the kingdoms, to root out, and to pull down, and to destroy, and to throw down, to build, and to plant.

[11]Moreover the word of the LORD came unto me, saying, Jeremiah, what seest thou? And I said, I see a rod of an almond tree.

NEW LIVING TRANSLATION

1 These are the words of Jeremiah son of Hilkiah, one of the priests from the town of Anathoth in the land of Benjamin. [2]The LORD first gave messages to Jeremiah during the thirteenth year of the reign of Josiah son of Amon, king of Judah.* [3]The LORD's messages continued throughout the reign of King Jehoiakim, Josiah's son, until the eleventh year of the reign of King Zedekiah, another of Josiah's sons. In August* of that eleventh year the people of Jerusalem were taken away as captives.

Jeremiah's Call and First Visions

[4]The LORD gave me this message:

[5] "I knew you before I formed you in your
mother's womb.
Before you were born I set you apart
and appointed you as my prophet to
the nations."

[6]"O Sovereign LORD," I said, "I can't speak for you! I'm too young!"

[7]The LORD replied, "Don't say, 'I'm too young,' for you must go wherever I send you and say whatever I tell you. [8]And don't be afraid of the people, for I will be with you and will protect you. I, the LORD, have spoken!" [9]Then the LORD reached out and touched my mouth and said,

"Look, I have put my words in your mouth!
[10] Today I appoint you to stand up
against nations and kingdoms.
Some you must uproot and tear down,
destroy and overthrow.
Others you must build up
and plant."

[11]Then the LORD said to me, "Look, Jeremiah! What do you see?"

And I replied, "I see a branch from an almond tree."

1:2 The thirteenth year of Josiah's reign was 627 B.C. **1:3** Hebrew *In the fifth month,* of the ancient Hebrew lunar calendar. A number of events in Jeremiah can be cross-checked with dates in surviving Babylonian records and related accurately to our modern calendar. The fifth month in the eleventh year of Zedekiah's reign occurred within the months of August and September 586 B.C. Also see 52:12 and the note there.

KING JAMES VERSION

12 Then said the LORD unto me, Thou hast well seen: for I will hasten my word to perform it.

13 And the word of the LORD came unto me the second time, saying, What seest thou? And I said, I see a seething pot; and the face thereof *is* toward the north.

14 Then the LORD said unto me, Out of the north an evil shall break forth upon all the inhabitants of the land.

15 For, lo, I will call all the families of the kingdoms of the north, saith the LORD; and they shall come, and they shall set every one his throne at the entering of the gates of Jerusalem, and against all the walls thereof round about, and against all the cities of Judah.

16 And I will utter my judgments against them touching all their wickedness, who have forsaken me, and have burned incense unto other gods, and worshipped the works of their own hands.

17 Thou therefore gird up thy loins, and arise, and speak unto them all that I command thee: be not dismayed at their faces, lest I confound thee before them.

18 For, behold, I have made thee this day a defenced city, and an iron pillar, and brasen walls against the whole land, against the kings of Judah, against the princes thereof, against the priests thereof, and against the people of the land.

19 And they shall fight against thee; but they shall not prevail against thee; for I *am* with thee, saith the LORD, to deliver thee.

2 1 Moreover the word of the LORD came to me, saying,

2 Go and cry in the ears of Jerusalem, saying, Thus saith the LORD; I remember thee, the kindness of thy youth, the love of thine espousals, when thou wentest after me in the wilderness, in a land *that was* not sown.

3 Israel *was* holiness unto the LORD, *and* the firstfruits of his increase: all that devour him shall offend; evil shall come upon them, saith the LORD.

4 Hear ye the word of the LORD, O house of Jacob, and all the families of the house of Israel:

5 Thus saith the LORD, What iniquity have your

NEW LIVING TRANSLATION

12 And the LORD said, "That's right, and it means that I am watching,* and I will certainly carry out all my plans."

13 Then the LORD spoke to me again and asked, "What do you see now?"

And I replied, "I see a pot of boiling water, spilling from the north."

14 "Yes," the LORD said, "for terror from the north will boil out on the people of this land. 15 Listen! I am calling the armies of the kingdoms of the north to come to Jerusalem. I, the LORD, have spoken!

"They will set their thrones
at the gates of the city.
They will attack its walls
and all the other towns of Judah.
16 I will pronounce judgment
on my people for all their evil—
for deserting me and burning incense
to other gods.
Yes, they worship idols made with
their own hands!

17 "Get up and prepare for action.
Go out and tell them everything I tell
you to say.
Do not be afraid of them,
or I will make you look foolish
in front of them.
18 For see, today I have made you strong
like a fortified city that cannot be captured,
like an iron pillar or a bronze wall.
You will stand against the whole land—
the kings, officials, priests, and people
of Judah.
19 They will fight you, but they will fail.
For I am with you, and I will take care of you.
I, the LORD, have spoken!"

The LORD's Case against His People

2 The LORD gave me another message. He said, 2 "Go and shout this message to Jerusalem. This is what the LORD says:

"I remember how eager you were to please me
as a young bride long ago,
how you loved me and followed me
even through the barren wilderness.
3 In those days Israel was holy to the LORD,
the first of his children.*
All who harmed his people were declared guilty,
and disaster fell on them.
I, the LORD, have spoken!"

4 Listen to the word of the LORD, people of Jacob—all you families of Israel! 5 This is what the LORD says:

"What did your ancestors find wrong with me
that led them to stray so far from me?

1:12 The Hebrew word for "watching" (*shoqed*) sounds like the word for "almond tree" (*shaqed*). **2:3** Hebrew *the firstfruits of his harvest.*

KING JAMES VERSION

fathers found in me, that they are gone far from me,
and have walked after vanity, and are become vain?
6 Neither said they, Where *is* the LORD that brought
us up out of the land of Egypt, that led us through the
wilderness, through a land of deserts and of pits,
through a land of drought, and of the shadow of
death, through a land that no man passed through,
and where no man dwelt?
7 And I brought you into a plentiful country, to eat
the fruit thereof and the goodness thereof; but when
ye entered, ye defiled my land, and made mine heritage an abomination.
8 The priests said not, Where *is* the LORD? and they
that handle the law knew me not: the pastors also
transgressed against me, and the prophets prophesied by Baal, and walked after *things that* do not
profit.
9 Wherefore I will yet plead with you, saith the
LORD, and with your children's children will I plead.
10 For pass over the isles of Chittim, and see; and
send unto Kedar, and consider diligently, and see if
there be such a thing.
11 Hath a nation changed *their* gods, which *are* yet
no gods? but my people have changed their glory for
that which doth not profit.
12 Be astonished, O ye heavens, at this, and be horribly afraid, be ye very desolate, saith the LORD.
13 For my people have committed two evils; they
have forsaken me the fountain of living waters, *and*
hewed them out cisterns, broken cisterns, that can
hold no water.

14 *Is* Israel a servant? *is* he a homeborn *slave?* why
is he spoiled?
15 The young lions roared upon him, *and* yelled,
and they made his land waste: his cities are burned
without inhabitant.
16 Also the children of Noph and Tahapanes have
broken the crown of thy head.
17 Hast thou not procured this unto thyself, in that
thou hast forsaken the LORD thy God, when he led
thee by the way?

NEW LIVING TRANSLATION

They worshiped worthless idols,
only to become worthless themselves.
6 They did not ask, 'Where is the LORD
who brought us safely out of Egypt
and led us through the barren wilderness—
a land of deserts and pits,
a land of drought and death,
where no one lives or even travels?'

7 "And when I brought you into a fruitful land
to enjoy its bounty and goodness,
you defiled my land and
corrupted the possession I had promised you.
8 The priests did not ask,
'Where is the LORD?'
Those who taught my word ignored me,
the rulers turned against me,
and the prophets spoke in the name of Baal,
wasting their time on worthless idols.
9 Therefore, I will bring my case against you,"
says the LORD.
"I will even bring charges against your
children's children
in the years to come.
10 "Go west and look in the land of Cyprus*;
go east and search through the land of Kedar.
Has anyone ever heard of anything
as strange as this?
11 Has any nation ever traded its gods for new ones,
even though they are not gods at all?
Yet my people have exchanged their
glorious God*
for worthless idols!
12 The heavens are shocked at such a thing
and shrink back in horror and dismay,"
says the LORD.
13 "For my people have done two evil things:
They have abandoned me—
the fountain of living water.
And they have dug for themselves
cracked cisterns
that can hold no water at all!

The Results of Israel's Sin

14 "Why has Israel become a slave?
Why has he been carried away as plunder?
15 Strong lions have roared against him,
and the land has been destroyed.
The towns are now in ruins,
and no one lives in them anymore.
16 Egyptians, marching from their cities of
Memphis* and Tahpanhes,
have destroyed Israel's glory and power.
17 And you have brought this upon yourselves
by rebelling against the LORD your God,
even though he was leading you on the way!

2:10 Hebrew *Kittim.* **2:11** Hebrew *their glory.* **2:16** Hebrew *Noph.*

KING JAMES VERSION

18 And now what hast thou to do in the way of
Egypt, to drink the waters of Sihor? or what hast thou
to do in the way of Assyria, to drink the waters of the
river?
19 Thine own wickedness shall correct thee, and
thy backslidings shall reprove thee: know therefore
and see that *it is* an evil *thing* and bitter, that thou
hast forsaken the LORD thy God, and that my fear *is*
not in thee, saith the Lord GOD of hosts.
20 For of old time I have broken thy yoke, *and* burst
thy bands; and thou saidst, I will not transgress;
when upon every high hill and under every green
tree thou wanderest, playing the harlot.
21 Yet I had planted thee a noble vine, wholly a
right seed: how then art thou turned into the degen-
erate plant of a strange vine unto me?
22 For though thou wash thee with nitre, and take
thee much sope, *yet* thine iniquity is marked before
me, saith the Lord GOD.

23 How canst thou say, I am not polluted, I have not
gone after Baalim? see thy way in the valley, know
what thou hast done: *thou art* a swift dromedary
traversing her ways;
24 A wild ass used to the wilderness, *that* snuffeth
up the wind at her pleasure; in her occasion who can
turn her away? all they that seek her will not weary
themselves; in her month they shall find her.
25 Withhold thy foot from being unshod, and thy
throat from thirst: but thou saidst, There is no hope:
no; for I have loved strangers, and after them will I go.
26 As the thief is ashamed when he is found, so is
the house of Israel ashamed; they, their kings, their
princes, and their priests, and their prophets,
27 Saying to a stock, Thou *art* my father; and to a
stone, Thou hast brought me forth: for they have
turned *their* back unto me, and not *their* face: but
in the time of their trouble they will say, Arise, and
save us.

NEW LIVING TRANSLATION

18 "What have you gained by your alliances
with Egypt
and your covenants with Assyria?
What good to you are the streams of the Nile*
or the waters of the Euphrates River?*
19 Your wickedness will bring its own punishment.
Your turning from me will shame you.
You will see what an evil, bitter thing it is
to abandon the LORD your God and not
to fear him.
I, the Lord, the LORD of Heaven's Armies,
have spoken!

20 "Long ago I broke the yoke that oppressed you
and tore away the chains of your slavery,
but still you said,
'I will not serve you.'
On every hill and under every green tree,
you have prostituted yourselves by bowing
down to idols.
21 But I was the one who planted you,
choosing a vine of the purest stock—
the very best.
How did you grow into this corrupt wild vine?
22 No amount of soap or lye can make you clean.
I still see the stain of your guilt.
I, the Sovereign LORD, have spoken!

Israel, an Unfaithful Wife

23 "You say, 'That's not true!
I haven't worshiped the images of Baal!'
But how can you say that?
Go and look in any valley in the land!
Face the awful sins you have done.
You are like a restless female camel
desperately searching for a mate.
24 You are like a wild donkey,
sniffing the wind at mating time.
Who can restrain her lust?
Those who desire her don't need to search,
for she goes running to them!
25 When will you stop running?
When will you stop panting after other gods?
But you say, 'Save your breath.
I'm in love with these foreign gods,
and I can't stop loving them now!'

26 "Israel is like a thief
who feels shame only when he gets caught.
They, their kings, officials, priests, and prophets—
all are alike in this.
27 To an image carved from a piece of wood they say,
'You are my father.'
To an idol chiseled from a block of stone they say,
'You are my mother.'
They turn their backs on me,
but in times of trouble they cry out to me,
'Come and save us!'

2:18a Hebrew *of Shihor*, a branch of the Nile River. **2:18b** Hebrew *the river?*

KING JAMES VERSION

28But where *are* thy gods that thou hast made
thee? let them arise, if they can save thee in the time
of thy trouble: for *according to* the number of thy
cities are thy gods, O Judah.
29Wherefore will ye plead with me? ye all have
transgressed against me, saith the LORD.
30In vain have I smitten your children; they received no correction: your own sword hath devoured
your prophets, like a destroying lion.
31O generation, see ye the word of the LORD. Have I
been a wilderness unto Israel? a land of darkness?
wherefore say my people, We are lords; we will come
no more unto thee?
32Can a maid forget her ornaments, *or* a bride her
attire? yet my people have forgotten me days without
number.
33Why trimmest thou thy way to seek love? therefore hast thou also taught the wicked ones thy ways.
34Also in thy skirts is found the blood of the souls
of the poor innocents: I have not found it by secret
search, but upon all these.
35Yet thou sayest, Because I am innocent, surely
his anger shall turn from me. Behold, I will plead
with thee, because thou sayest, I have not sinned.
36Why gaddest thou about so much to change thy
way? thou also shalt be ashamed of Egypt, as thou
wast ashamed of Assyria.
37Yea, thou shalt go forth from him, and thine
hands upon thine head: for the LORD hath rejected
thy confidences, and thou shalt not prosper in them.

3 1They say, If a man put away his wife, and she go
from him, and become another man's, shall he
return unto her again? shall not that land be greatly
polluted? but thou hast played the harlot with many
lovers; yet return again to me, saith the LORD.
2Lift up thine eyes unto the high places, and see
where thou hast not been lien with. In the ways hast
thou sat for them, as the Arabian in the wilderness;

NEW LIVING TRANSLATION

28 But why not call on these gods you have made?
When trouble comes, let them save you
if they can!
For you have as many gods
as there are towns in Judah.
29 Why do you accuse me of doing wrong?
You are the ones who have rebelled,"
says the LORD.
30 "I have punished your children,
but they did not respond to my discipline.
You yourselves have killed your prophets
as a lion kills its prey.

31 "O my people, listen to the words of the LORD!
Have I been like a desert to Israel?
Have I been to them a land of darkness?
Why then do my people say, 'At last we are
free from God!
We don't need him anymore!'
32 Does a young woman forget her jewelry?
Does a bride hide her wedding dress?
Yet for years on end
my people have forgotten me.

33 "How you plot and scheme to win your lovers.
Even an experienced prostitute could learn
from you!
34 Your clothing is stained with the blood of the
innocent and the poor,
though you didn't catch them breaking into
your houses!
35 And yet you say,
'I have done nothing wrong.
Surely God isn't angry with me!'
But now I will punish you severely
because you claim you have not sinned.
36 First here, then there—
you flit from one ally to another asking for help.
But your new friends in Egypt will let you down,
just as Assyria did before.
37 In despair, you will be led into exile
with your hands on your heads,
for the LORD has rejected the nations you trust.
They will not help you at all.

3 1 "If a man divorces a woman
and she goes and marries someone else,
he will not take her back again,
for that would surely corrupt the land.
But you have prostituted yourself with
many lovers,
so why are you trying to come back to me?"
says the LORD.
2 "Look at the shrines on every hilltop.
Is there any place you have not been defiled
by your adultery with other gods?
You sit like a prostitute beside the road waiting
for a customer.
You sit alone like a nomad in the desert.

KING JAMES VERSION

and thou hast polluted the land with thy whoredoms
and with thy wickedness.
3 Therefore the showers have been withholden,
and there hath been no latter rain; and thou hadst a
whore's forehead, thou refusedst to be ashamed.
4 Wilt thou not from this time cry unto me, My
father, thou *art* the guide of my youth?
5 Will he reserve *his anger* for ever? will he keep *it*
to the end? Behold, thou hast spoken and done evil
things as thou couldest.

6 The LORD said also unto me in the days of Josiah
the king, Hast thou seen *that* which backsliding
Israel hath done? she is gone up upon every high
mountain and under every green tree, and there hath
played the harlot.
7 And I said after she had done all these *things,*
Turn thou unto me. But she returned not. And her
treacherous sister Judah saw *it.*
8 And I saw, when for all the causes whereby backsliding Israel committed adultery I had put her away,
and given her a bill of divorce; yet her treacherous
sister Judah feared not, but went and played the
harlot also.
9 And it came to pass through the lightness of her
whoredom, that she defiled the land, and committed
adultery with stones and with stocks.
10 And yet for all this her treacherous sister Judah
hath not turned unto me with her whole heart, but
feignedly, saith the LORD.
11 And the LORD said unto me, The backsliding
Israel hath justified herself more than treacherous
Judah.
12 Go and proclaim these words toward the north,
and say, Return, thou backsliding Israel, saith the
LORD; *and* I will not cause mine anger to fall upon
you: for I *am* merciful, saith the LORD, *and* I will not
keep *anger* for ever.
13 Only acknowledge thine iniquity, that thou hast
transgressed against the LORD thy God, and hast
scattered thy ways to the strangers under every
green tree, and ye have not obeyed my voice, saith
the LORD.
14 Turn, O backsliding children, saith the LORD; for
I am married unto you: and I will take you one of a
city, and two of a family, and I will bring you to Zion:

NEW LIVING TRANSLATION

You have polluted the land with your prostitution
and your wickedness.
3 That's why even the spring rains have failed.
For you are a brazen prostitute and
completely shameless.
4 Yet you say to me,
'Father, you have been my guide since
my youth.
5 Surely you won't be angry forever!
Surely you can forget about it!'
So you talk,
but you keep on doing all the evil you can."

Judah Follows Israel's Example

6 During the reign of King Josiah, the LORD said to me,
"Have you seen what fickle Israel has done? Like a
wife who commits adultery, Israel has worshiped
other gods on every hill and under every green tree.
7 I thought, 'After she has done all this, she will return
to me.' But she did not return, and her faithless sister
Judah saw this. 8 She saw that I divorced faithless
Israel because of her adultery. But that treacherous
sister Judah had no fear, and now she, too, has left me
and given herself to prostitution. 9 Israel treated it all
so lightly—she thought nothing of committing adultery by worshiping idols made of wood and stone. So
now the land has been polluted. 10 But despite all this,
her faithless sister Judah has never sincerely returned to me. She has only pretended to be sorry. I,
the LORD, have spoken!"

Hope for Wayward Israel

11 Then the LORD said to me, "Even faithless Israel
is less guilty than treacherous Judah! 12 Therefore,
go and give this message to Israel.* This is what the
LORD says:

"O Israel, my faithless people,
come home to me again,
for I am merciful.
I will not be angry with you forever.
13 Only acknowledge your guilt.
Admit that you rebelled against the
LORD your God
and committed adultery against him
by worshiping idols under every green tree.
Confess that you refused to listen to my voice.
I, the LORD, have spoken!

14 "Return home, you wayward children,"
says the LORD,
"for I am your master.
I will bring you back to the land of Israel*—
one from this town and two from
that family—
from wherever you are scattered.

3:12 Hebrew *toward the north.* **3:14** Hebrew *to Zion.*

KING JAMES VERSION

15 And I will give you pastors according to mine heart, which shall feed you with knowledge and understanding.

16 And it shall come to pass, when ye be multiplied and increased in the land, in those days, saith the LORD, they shall say no more, The ark of the covenant of the LORD: neither shall it come to mind: neither shall they remember it; neither shall they visit *it;* neither shall *that* be done any more.

17 At that time they shall call Jerusalem the throne of the LORD; and all the nations shall be gathered unto it, to the name of the LORD, to Jerusalem: neither shall they walk any more after the imagination of their evil heart.

18 In those days the house of Judah shall walk with the house of Israel, and they shall come together out of the land of the north to the land that I have given for an inheritance unto your fathers.

19 But I said, How shall I put thee among the children, and give thee a pleasant land, a goodly heritage of the hosts of nations? and I said, Thou shalt call me, My father; and shalt not turn away from me.

20 Surely *as* a wife treacherously departeth from her husband, so have ye dealt treacherously with me, O house of Israel, saith the LORD.

21 A voice was heard upon the high places, weeping *and* supplications of the children of Israel: for they have perverted their way, *and* they have forgotten the LORD their God.

22 Return, ye backsliding children, *and* I will heal your backslidings. Behold, we come unto thee; for thou *art* the LORD our God.

23 Truly in vain *is salvation hoped for* from the hills, *and from* the multitude of mountains: truly in the LORD our God *is* the salvation of Israel.

24 For shame hath devoured the labour of our fathers from our youth; their flocks and their herds, their sons and their daughters.

25 We lie down in our shame, and our confusion covereth us: for we have sinned against the LORD our God, we and our fathers, from our youth even unto this day, and have not obeyed the voice of the LORD our God.

NEW LIVING TRANSLATION

15 And I will give you shepherds after my own heart,
who will guide you with knowledge and
understanding.

16 "And when your land is once more filled with
people," says the LORD, "you will no longer wish for
'the good old days' when you possessed the Ark of
the LORD's Covenant. You will not miss those days or
even remember them, and there will be no need to
rebuild the Ark. 17 In that day Jerusalem will be
known as 'The Throne of the LORD.' All nations will
come there to honor the LORD. They will no longer
stubbornly follow their own evil desires. 18 In those
days the people of Judah and Israel will return together from exile in the north. They will return to the
land I gave their ancestors as an inheritance forever.

19 "I thought to myself,
'I would love to treat you as my own children!'
I wanted nothing more than to give you this
beautiful land—
the finest possession in the world.
I looked forward to your calling me 'Father,'
and I wanted you never to turn from me.
20 But you have been unfaithful to me, you people
of Israel!
You have been like a faithless wife who leaves
her husband.
I, the LORD, have spoken."

21 Voices are heard high on the windswept
mountains,
the weeping and pleading of Israel's people.
For they have chosen crooked paths
and have forgotten the LORD their God.
22 "My wayward children," says the LORD,
"come back to me, and I will heal your
wayward hearts."

"Yes, we're coming," the people reply,
"for you are the LORD our God.
23 Our worship of idols on the hills
and our religious orgies on the mountains
are a delusion.
Only in the LORD our God
will Israel ever find salvation.
24 From childhood we have watched
as everything our ancestors worked for—
their flocks and herds, their sons
and daughters—
was squandered on a delusion.
25 Let us now lie down in shame
and cover ourselves with dishonor,
for we and our ancestors have sinned
against the LORD our God.
From our childhood to this day
we have never obeyed him."

KING JAMES VERSION

4 [1]If thou wilt return, O Israel, saith the LORD, return unto me: and if thou wilt put away thine abominations out of my sight, then shalt thou not remove.

[2]And thou shalt swear, The LORD liveth, in truth, in judgment, and in righteousness; and the nations shall bless themselves in him, and in him shall they glory.

[3]For thus saith the LORD to the men of Judah and Jerusalem, Break up your fallow ground, and sow not among thorns.

[4]Circumcise yourselves to the LORD, and take away the foreskins of your heart, ye men of Judah and inhabitants of Jerusalem: lest my fury come forth like fire, and burn that none can quench *it*, because of the evil of your doings.

[5]Declare ye in Judah, and publish in Jerusalem; and say, Blow ye the trumpet in the land: cry, gather together, and say, Assemble yourselves, and let us go into the defenced cities.

[6]Set up the standard toward Zion: retire, stay not: for I will bring evil from the north, and a great destruction.

[7]The lion is come up from his thicket, and the destroyer of the Gentiles is on his way; he is gone forth from his place to make thy land desolate; *and* thy cities shall be laid waste, without an inhabitant.

[8]For this gird you with sackcloth, lament and howl: for the fierce anger of the LORD is not turned back from us.

[9]And it shall come to pass at that day, saith the LORD, *that* the heart of the king shall perish, and the heart of the princes; and the priests shall be astonished, and the prophets shall wonder.

[10]Then said I, Ah, Lord GOD! surely thou hast greatly deceived this people and Jerusalem, saying, Ye shall have peace; whereas the sword reacheth unto the soul.

NEW LIVING TRANSLATION

4 [1] "O Israel," says the LORD,
"if you wanted to return to me, you could.
You could throw away your detestable idols
and stray away no more.
[2] Then when you swear by my name, saying,
'As surely as the LORD lives,'
you could do so
with truth, justice, and righteousness.
Then you would be a blessing to the nations
of the world,
and all people would come and praise
my name."

Coming Judgment against Judah

[3]This is what the LORD says to the people of Judah and Jerusalem:

"Plow up the hard ground of your hearts!
Do not waste your good seed among thorns.
[4] O people of Judah and Jerusalem,
surrender your pride and power.
Change your hearts before the LORD,*
or my anger will burn like an
unquenchable fire
because of all your sins.

[5] "Shout to Judah, and broadcast to Jerusalem!
Tell them to sound the alarm throughout
the land:
'Run for your lives!
Flee to the fortified cities!'
[6] Raise a signal flag as a warning for Jerusalem*:
'Flee now! Do not delay!'
For I am bringing terrible destruction upon
you from the north."
[7] A lion stalks from its den,
a destroyer of nations.
It has left its lair and is headed your way.
It's going to devastate your land!
Your towns will lie in ruins,
with no one living in them anymore.
[8] So put on clothes of mourning
and weep with broken hearts,
for the fierce anger of the LORD
is still upon us.

[9] "In that day," says the LORD,
"the king and the officials will tremble in fear.
The priests will be struck with horror,
and the prophets will be appalled."
[10] Then I said, "O Sovereign LORD,
the people have been deceived by what you said,
for you promised peace for Jerusalem.
But the sword is held at their throats!"

4:4 Hebrew *Circumcise yourselves to the LORD, and take away the foreskins of your heart.* **4:6** Hebrew *Zion.*

KING JAMES VERSION

11 At that time shall it be said to this people and to
Jerusalem, A dry wind of the high places in the
wilderness toward the daughter of my people, not to
fan, nor to cleanse,
12 *Even* a full wind from those *places* shall come
unto me: now also will I give sentence against them.
13 Behold, he shall come up as clouds, and his chariots *shall be* as a whirlwind: his horses are swifter
than eagles. Woe unto us! for we are spoiled.
14 O Jerusalem, wash thine heart from wickedness,
that thou mayest be saved. How long shall thy vain
thoughts lodge within thee?
15 For a voice declareth from Dan, and publisheth
affliction from mount Ephraim.
16 Make ye mention to the nations; behold, publish
against Jerusalem, *that* watchers come from a far
country, and give out their voice against the cities
of Judah.
17 As keepers of a field, are they against her round
about; because she hath been rebellious against me,
saith the LORD.
18 Thy way and thy doings have procured these
things unto thee; this *is* thy wickedness, because it is
bitter, because it reacheth unto thine heart.

19 My bowels, my bowels! I am pained at my very
heart; my heart maketh a noise in me; I cannot hold
my peace, because thou hast heard, O my soul, the
sound of the trumpet, the alarm of war.
20 Destruction upon destruction is cried; for the
whole land is spoiled: suddenly are my tents spoiled,
and my curtains in a moment.
21 How long shall I see the standard, *and* hear the
sound of the trumpet?
22 For my people *is* foolish, they have not known
me; they *are* sottish children, and they have none
understanding: they *are* wise to do evil, but to do
good they have no knowledge.

23 I beheld the earth, and, lo, *it was* without form,
and void; and the heavens, and they *had* no light.
24 I beheld the mountains, and, lo, they trembled,
and all the hills moved lightly.
25 I beheld, and, lo, *there was* no man, and all the
birds of the heavens were fled.

NEW LIVING TRANSLATION

11 The time is coming when the LORD will say
to the people of Jerusalem,
"My dear people, a burning wind is blowing
in from the desert,
and it's not a gentle breeze useful for
winnowing grain.
12 It is a roaring blast sent by me!
Now I will pronounce your destruction!"

13 Our enemy rushes down on us like storm clouds!
His chariots are like whirlwinds.
His horses are swifter than eagles.
How terrible it will be, for we are doomed!
14 O Jerusalem, cleanse your heart
that you may be saved.
How long will you harbor
your evil thoughts?
15 Your destruction has been announced
from Dan and the hill country of Ephraim.

16 "Warn the surrounding nations
and announce this to Jerusalem:
The enemy is coming from a distant land,
raising a battle cry against the towns of Judah.
17 They surround Jerusalem like watchmen
around a field,
for my people have rebelled against me,"
says the LORD.
18 "Your own actions have brought this upon you.
This punishment is bitter, piercing you to
the heart!"

Jeremiah Weeps for His People

19 My heart, my heart—I writhe in pain!
My heart pounds within me! I cannot be still.
For I have heard the blast of enemy trumpets
and the roar of their battle cries.
20 Waves of destruction roll over the land,
until it lies in complete desolation.
Suddenly my tents are destroyed;
in a moment my shelters are crushed.
21 How long must I see the battle flags
and hear the trumpets of war?

22 "My people are foolish
and do not know me," says the LORD.
"They are stupid children
who have no understanding.
They are clever enough at doing wrong,
but they have no idea how to do right!"

Jeremiah's Vision of Coming Disaster

23 I looked at the earth, and it was empty
and formless.
I looked at the heavens, and there was no light.
24 I looked at the mountains and hills,
and they trembled and shook.
25 I looked, and all the people were gone.
All the birds of the sky had flown away.

KING JAMES VERSION

[26]I beheld, and, lo, the fruitful place *was* a wilderness, and all the cities thereof were broken down at the presence of the LORD, *and* by his fierce anger.

[27]For thus hath the LORD said, The whole land shall be desolate; yet will I not make a full end.

[28]For this shall the earth mourn, and the heavens above be black: because I have spoken *it*, I have purposed *it*, and will not repent, neither will I turn back from it.

[29]The whole city shall flee for the noise of the horsemen and bowmen; they shall go into thickets, and climb up upon the rocks: every city *shall be* forsaken, and not a man dwell therein.

[30]And *when* thou *art* spoiled, what wilt thou do? Though thou clothest thyself with crimson, though thou deckest thee with ornaments of gold, though thou rentest thy face with painting, in vain shalt thou make thyself fair; *thy* lovers will despise thee, they will seek thy life.

[31]For I have heard a voice as of a woman in travail, *and* the anguish as of her that bringeth forth her first child, the voice of the daughter of Zion, *that* bewaileth herself, *that* spreadeth her hands, *saying*, Woe *is* me now! for my soul is wearied because of murderers.

5 [1]Run ye to and fro through the streets of Jerusalem, and see now, and know, and seek in the broad places thereof, if ye can find a man, if there be *any* that executeth judgment, that seeketh the truth; and I will pardon it.

[2]And though they say, The LORD liveth; surely they swear falsely.

[3]O LORD, *are* not thine eyes upon the truth? thou hast stricken them, but they have not grieved; thou hast consumed them, *but* they have refused to receive correction: they have made their faces harder than a rock; they have refused to return.

[4]Therefore I said, Surely these *are* poor; they are foolish: for they know not the way of the LORD, *nor* the judgment of their God.

NEW LIVING TRANSLATION

26 I looked, and the fertile fields had become
a wilderness.
The towns lay in ruins,
crushed by the LORD's fierce anger.

27 This is what the LORD says:
"The whole land will be ruined,
but I will not destroy it completely.
28 The earth will mourn
and the heavens will be draped in black
because of my decree against my people.
I have made up my mind and will not
change it."
29 At the noise of charioteers and archers,
the people flee in terror.
They hide in the bushes
and run for the mountains.
All the towns have been abandoned—
not a person remains!
30 What are you doing,
you who have been plundered?
Why do you dress up in beautiful clothing
and put on gold jewelry?
Why do you brighten your eyes with mascara?
Your primping will do you no good!
The allies who were your lovers
despise you and seek to kill you.

31 I hear a cry, like that of a woman in labor,
the groans of a woman giving birth to
her first child.
It is beautiful Jerusalem*
gasping for breath and crying out,
"Help! I'm being murdered!"

The Sins of Judah

5 1 "Run up and down every street in
Jerusalem," says the LORD.
"Look high and low; search throughout the city!
If you can find even one just and honest person,
I will not destroy the city.
2 But even when they are under oath,
saying, 'As surely as the LORD lives,'
they are still telling lies!"

3 LORD, you are searching for honesty.
You struck your people,
but they paid no attention.
You crushed them,
but they refused to be corrected.
They are determined, with faces set like stone;
they have refused to repent.

4 Then I said, "But what can we expect from
the poor?
They are ignorant.
They don't know the ways of the LORD.
They don't understand God's laws.

4:31 Hebrew *the daughter of Zion.*

KING JAMES VERSION

5 I will get me unto the great men, and will speak
unto them; for they have known the way of the LORD,
and the judgment of their God: but these have altogether broken the yoke, *and* burst the bonds.
6 Wherefore a lion out of the forest shall slay them,
and a wolf of the evenings shall spoil them, a leopard
shall watch over their cities: every one that goeth
out thence shall be torn in pieces: because their
transgressions are many, *and* their backslidings are
increased.
7 How shall I pardon thee for this? thy children
have forsaken me, and sworn by *them that are* no
gods: when I had fed them to the full, they then
committed adultery, and assembled themselves by
troops in the harlots' houses.
8 They were *as* fed horses in the morning: every
one neighed after his neighbour's wife.
9 Shall I not visit for these *things?* saith the LORD:
and shall not my soul be avenged on such a nation as
this?
10 Go ye up upon her walls, and destroy; but make
not a full end: take away her battlements; for they *are*
not the LORD's.
11 For the house of Israel and the house of Judah
have dealt very treacherously against me, saith the
LORD.
12 They have belied the LORD, and said, *It is* not he;
neither shall evil come upon us; neither shall we see
sword nor famine:
13 And the prophets shall become wind, and the
word *is* not in them: thus shall it be done unto them.
14 Wherefore thus saith the LORD God of hosts,
Because ye speak this word, behold, I will make my
words in thy mouth fire, and this people wood, and it
shall devour them.
15 Lo, I will bring a nation upon you from far,
O house of Israel, saith the LORD: it *is* a mighty nation,
it *is* an ancient nation, a nation whose language thou
knowest not, neither understandest what they say.
16 Their quiver *is* as an open sepulchre, they *are* all
mighty men.
17 And they shall eat up thine harvest, and thy
bread, *which* thy sons and thy daughters should eat:
they shall eat up thy flocks and thine herds: they
shall eat up thy vines and thy fig trees: they shall

NEW LIVING TRANSLATION

5 So I will go and speak to their leaders.
Surely they know the ways of the LORD
and understand God's laws."
But the leaders, too, as one man,
had thrown off God's yoke
and broken his chains.
6 So now a lion from the forest will attack them;
a wolf from the desert will pounce on them.
A leopard will lurk near their towns,
tearing apart any who dare to venture out.
For their rebellion is great,
and their sins are many.

7 "How can I pardon you?
For even your children have turned from me.
They have sworn by gods that are not gods at all!
I fed my people until they were full.
But they thanked me by committing adultery
and lining up at the brothels.
8 They are well-fed, lusty stallions,
each neighing for his neighbor's wife.
9 Should I not punish them for this?" says the LORD.
"Should I not avenge myself against such
a nation?
10 "Go down the rows of the vineyards and destroy
the grapevines,
leaving a scattered few alive.
Strip the branches from the vines,
for these people do not belong to the LORD.
11 The people of Israel and Judah
are full of treachery against me,"
says the LORD.
12 "They have lied about the LORD
and said, 'He won't bother us!
No disasters will come upon us.
There will be no war or famine.
13 God's prophets are all windbags
who don't really speak for him.
Let their predictions of disaster fall
on themselves!'"

14 Therefore, this is what the LORD God of Heaven's
Armies says:

"Because the people are talking like this,
my messages will flame out of your mouth
and burn the people like kindling wood.
15 O Israel, I will bring a distant nation against you,"
says the LORD.
"It is a mighty nation,
an ancient nation,
a people whose language you do not know,
whose speech you cannot understand.
16 Their weapons are deadly;
their warriors are mighty.
17 They will devour the food of your harvest;
they will devour your sons and daughters.
They will devour your flocks and herds;
they will devour your grapes and figs.

KING JAMES VERSION

impoverish thy fenced cities, wherein thou trustedst, with the sword.

18 Nevertheless in those days, saith the LORD, I will not make a full end with you.

19 And it shall come to pass, when ye shall say, Wherefore doeth the LORD our God all these *things* unto us? then shalt thou answer them, Like as ye have forsaken me, and served strange gods in your land, so shall ye serve strangers in a land *that is* not yours.

20 Declare this in the house of Jacob, and publish it in Judah, saying,

21 Hear now this, O foolish people, and without understanding; which have eyes, and see not; which have ears, and hear not:

22 Fear ye not me? saith the LORD: will ye not tremble at my presence, which have placed the sand *for* the bound of the sea by a perpetual decree, that it cannot pass it: and though the waves thereof toss themselves, yet can they not prevail; though they roar, yet can they not pass over it?

23 But this people hath a revolting and a rebellious heart; they are revolted and gone.

24 Neither say they in their heart, Let us now fear the LORD our God, that giveth rain, both the former and the latter, in his season: he reserveth unto us the appointed weeks of the harvest.

25 Your iniquities have turned away these *things*, and your sins have withholden good *things* from you.

26 For among my people are found wicked *men*: they lay wait, as he that setteth snares; they set a trap, they catch men.

27 As a cage is full of birds, so *are* their houses full of deceit: therefore they are become great, and waxen rich.

28 They are waxen fat, they shine: yea, they overpass the deeds of the wicked: they judge not the cause, the cause of the fatherless, yet they prosper; and the right of the needy do they not judge.

29 Shall I not visit for these *things?* saith the LORD: shall not my soul be avenged on such a nation as this?

30 A wonderful and horrible thing is committed in the land;

31 The prophets prophesy falsely, and the priests bear rule by their means; and my people love *to have it* so: and what will ye do in the end thereof?

NEW LIVING TRANSLATION

And they will destroy your fortified towns,
which you think are so safe.

18 "Yet even in those days I will not blot you out completely," says the LORD. 19 "And when your people ask, 'Why did the LORD our God do all this to us?' you must reply, 'You rejected him and gave yourselves to foreign gods in your own land. Now you will serve foreigners in a land that is not your own.'

A Warning for God's People

20 "Make this announcement to Israel,*
and say this to Judah:
21 Listen, you foolish and senseless people,
with eyes that do not see
and ears that do not hear.
22 Have you no respect for me?
Why don't you tremble in my presence?
I, the LORD, define the ocean's sandy shoreline
as an everlasting boundary that the waters
cannot cross.
The waves may toss and roar,
but they can never pass the boundaries I set.
23 But my people have stubborn and rebellious
hearts.
They have turned away and abandoned me.
24 They do not say from the heart,
'Let us live in awe of the LORD our God,
for he gives us rain each spring and fall,
assuring us of a harvest when the time is right.'
25 Your wickedness has deprived you of these
wonderful blessings.
Your sin has robbed you of all these
good things.

26 "Among my people are wicked men
who lie in wait for victims like a hunter
hiding in a blind.
They continually set traps
to catch people.
27 Like a cage filled with birds,
their homes are filled with evil plots.
And now they are great and rich.
28 They are fat and sleek,
and there is no limit to their wicked deeds.
They refuse to provide justice to orphans
and deny the rights of the poor.
29 Should I not punish them for this?" says the LORD.
"Should I not avenge myself against such
a nation?
30 A horrible and shocking thing
has happened in this land—
31 the prophets give false prophecies,
and the priests rule with an iron hand.
Worse yet, my people like it that way!
But what will you do when the end comes?

5:20 Hebrew *to the house of Jacob.* The names "Jacob" and "Israel" are often interchanged throughout the Old Testament, referring sometimes to the individual patriarch and sometimes to the nation.

KING JAMES VERSION

6

1 O ye children of Benjamin, gather yourselves to flee out of the midst of Jerusalem, and blow the trumpet in Tekoa, and set up a sign of fire in Beth-haccerem: for evil appeareth out of the north, and great destruction.

2 I have likened the daughter of Zion to a comely and delicate *woman.*

3 The shepherds with their flocks shall come unto her; they shall pitch *their* tents against her round about; they shall feed every one in his place.

4 Prepare ye war against her; arise, and let us go up at noon. Woe unto us! for the day goeth away, for the shadows of the evening are stretched out.

5 Arise, and let us go by night, and let us destroy her palaces.

6 For thus hath the LORD of hosts said, Hew ye down trees, and cast a mount against Jerusalem: this *is* the city to be visited; she *is* wholly oppression in the midst of her.

7 As a fountain casteth out her waters, so she casteth out her wickedness: violence and spoil is heard in her; before me continually *is* grief and wounds.

8 Be thou instructed, O Jerusalem, lest my soul depart from thee; lest I make thee desolate, a land not inhabited.

9 Thus saith the LORD of hosts, They shall throughly glean the remnant of Israel as a vine: turn back thine hand as a grapegatherer into the baskets.

10 To whom shall I speak, and give warning, that they may hear? behold, their ear *is* uncircumcised, and they cannot hearken: behold, the word of the LORD is unto them a reproach; they have no delight in it.

11 Therefore I am full of the fury of the LORD; I am weary with holding in: I will pour it out upon the children abroad, and upon the assembly of young men together: for even the husband with the wife shall be taken, the aged with *him that is* full of days.

12 And their houses shall be turned unto others,

NEW LIVING TRANSLATION

Jerusalem's Last Warning

6

1 "Run for your lives, you people of Benjamin!
Get out of Jerusalem!
Sound the alarm in Tekoa!
Send up a signal at Beth-hakkerem!
A powerful army is coming from the north,
coming with disaster and destruction.
2 O Jerusalem,* you are my beautiful and
delicate daughter—
but I will destroy you!
3 Enemies will surround you, like shepherds
camped around the city.
Each chooses a place for his troops to devour.
4 They shout, 'Prepare for battle!
Attack at noon!'
'No, it's too late; the day is fading,
and the evening shadows are falling.'
5 'Well then, let's attack at night
and destroy her palaces!'"

6 This is what the LORD of Heaven's Armies says:
"Cut down the trees for battering rams.
Build siege ramps against the walls of Jerusalem.
This is the city to be punished,
for she is wicked through and through.
7 She spouts evil like a fountain.
Her streets echo with the sounds of violence
and destruction.
I always see her sickness and sores.
8 Listen to this warning, Jerusalem,
or I will turn from you in disgust.
Listen, or I will turn you into a heap of ruins,
a land where no one lives."

9 This is what the LORD of Heaven's Armies says:
"Even the few who remain in Israel
will be picked over again,
as when a harvester checks each vine
a second time
to pick the grapes that were missed."

Israel's Constant Rebellion

10 To whom can I give warning?
Who will listen when I speak?
Their ears are closed,
and they cannot hear.
They scorn the word of the LORD.
They don't want to listen at all.
11 So now I am filled with the LORD's fury.
Yes, I am tired of holding it in!

"I will pour out my fury on children playing
in the streets
and on gatherings of young men,
on husbands and wives
and on those who are old and gray.
12 Their homes will be turned over to their enemies,
as will their fields and their wives.

6:2 Hebrew *Daughter of Zion.*

KING JAMES VERSION

with their fields and wives together: for I will stretch out my hand upon the inhabitants of the land, saith the LORD.

13 For from the least of them even unto the greatest of them every one *is* given to covetousness; and from the prophet even unto the priest every one dealeth falsely.

14 They have healed also the hurt *of the daughter* of my people slightly, saying, Peace, peace; when *there is* no peace.

15 Were they ashamed when they had committed abomination? nay, they were not at all ashamed, neither could they blush: therefore they shall fall among them that fall: at the time *that* I visit them they shall be cast down, saith the LORD.

16 Thus saith the LORD, Stand ye in the ways, and see, and ask for the old paths, where *is* the good way, and walk therein, and ye shall find rest for your souls. But they said, We will not walk *therein.*

17 Also I set watchmen over you, *saying,* Hearken to the sound of the trumpet. But they said, We will not hearken.

18 Therefore hear, ye nations, and know, O congregation, what *is* among them.

19 Hear, O earth: behold, I will bring evil upon this people, *even* the fruit of their thoughts, because they have not hearkened unto my words, nor to my law, but rejected it.

20 To what purpose cometh there to me incense from Sheba, and the sweet cane from a far country? your burnt offerings *are* not acceptable, nor your sacrifices sweet unto me.

21 Therefore thus saith the LORD, Behold, I will lay stumblingblocks before this people, and the fathers and the sons together shall fall upon them; the neighbour and his friend shall perish.

22 Thus saith the LORD Behold, a people cometh from the north country, and a great nation shall be raised from the sides of the earth.

23 They shall lay hold on bow and spear; they *are* cruel, and have no mercy; their voice roareth like the sea; and they ride upon horses, set in array as men for war against thee, O daughter of Zion.

NEW LIVING TRANSLATION

For I will raise my powerful fist
against the people of this land,"
says the LORD.

13 "From the least to the greatest,
their lives are ruled by greed.
From prophets to priests,
they are all frauds.
14 They offer superficial treatments
for my people's mortal wound.
They give assurances of peace
when there is no peace.
15 Are they ashamed of their disgusting actions?
Not at all—they don't even know how to blush!
Therefore, they will lie among the slaughtered.
They will be brought down when I punish them,"
says the LORD.

Israel Rejects the LORD's Way

16 This is what the LORD says:
"Stop at the crossroads and look around.
Ask for the old, godly way, and walk in it.
Travel its path, and you will find rest for your souls.
But you reply, 'No, that's not the road we want!'
17 I posted watchmen over you who said,
'Listen for the sound of the alarm.'
But you replied,
'No! We won't pay attention!'

18 "Therefore, listen to this, all you nations.
Take note of my people's situation.
19 Listen, all the earth!
I will bring disaster on my people.
It is the fruit of their own schemes,
because they refuse to listen to me.
They have rejected my word.
20 There's no use offering me sweet frankincense
from Sheba.
Keep your fragrant calamus imported from
distant lands!
I will not accept your burnt offerings.
Your sacrifices have no pleasing aroma for me."

21 Therefore, this is what the LORD says:
"I will put obstacles in my people's path.
Fathers and sons will both fall over them.
Neighbors and friends will die together."

An Invasion from the North

22 This is what the LORD says:
"Look! A great army coming from the north!
A great nation is rising against you from
far-off lands.
23 They are armed with bows and spears.
They are cruel and show no mercy.
They sound like a roaring sea
as they ride forward on horses.
They are coming in battle formation,
planning to destroy you, beautiful Jerusalem.*"

6:23 Hebrew *daughter of Zion.*

KING JAMES VERSION

24 We have heard the fame thereof: our hands wax feeble: anguish hath taken hold of us, *and* pain, as of a woman in travail.

25 Go not forth into the field, nor walk by the way; for the sword of the enemy *and* fear *is* on every side.

26 O daughter of my people, gird *thee* with sackcloth, and wallow thyself in ashes: make thee mourning, *as for* an only son, most bitter lamentation: for the spoiler shall suddenly come upon us.

27 I have set thee *for* a tower *and* a fortress among my people, that thou mayest know and try their way.

28 They *are* all grievous revolters, walking with slanders: *they are* brass and iron; they *are* all corrupters.

29 The bellows are burned, the lead is consumed of the fire; the founder melteth in vain: for the wicked are not plucked away.

30 Reprobate silver shall *men* call them, because the LORD hath rejected them.

7

1 The word that came to Jeremiah from the LORD, saying,

2 Stand in the gate of the LORD's house, and proclaim there this word, and say, Hear the word of the LORD, all *ye of* Judah, that enter in at these gates to worship the LORD.

3 Thus saith the LORD of hosts, the God of Israel, Amend your ways and your doings, and I will cause you to dwell in this place.

4 Trust ye not in lying words, saying, The temple of the LORD, The temple of the LORD, The temple of the LORD, *are* these.

5 For if ye throughly amend your ways and your doings; if ye throughly execute judgment between a man and his neighbour;

6 *If* ye oppress not the stranger, the fatherless, and the widow, and shed not innocent blood in this place, neither walk after other gods to your hurt:

7 Then will I cause you to dwell in this place, in the land that I gave to your fathers, for ever and ever.

8 Behold, ye trust in lying words, that cannot profit.

9 Will ye steal, murder, and commit adultery, and swear falsely, and burn incense unto Baal, and walk after other gods whom ye know not;

10 And come and stand before me in this house, which is called by my name, and say, We are delivered to do all these abominations?

11 Is this house, which is called by my name,

NEW LIVING TRANSLATION

24 We have heard reports about the enemy,
and we wring our hands in fright.
Pangs of anguish have gripped us,
like those of a woman in labor.
25 Don't go out to the fields!
Don't travel on the roads!
The enemy's sword is everywhere
and terrorizes us at every turn!
26 Oh, my people, dress yourselves in burlap
and sit among the ashes.
Mourn and weep bitterly, as for the loss
of an only son.
For suddenly the destroying armies will
be upon you!

27 "Jeremiah, I have made you a tester of metals,*
that you may determine the quality
of my people.
28 They are the worst kind of rebel,
full of slander.
They are as hard as bronze and iron,
and they lead others into corruption.
29 The bellows fiercely fan the flames
to burn out the corruption.
But it does not purify them,
for the wickedness remains.
30 I will label them 'Rejected Silver,'
for I, the LORD, am discarding them."

Jeremiah Speaks at the Temple

7 The LORD gave another message to Jeremiah. He
said, 2 "Go to the entrance of the LORD's Temple,
and give this message to the people: 'O Judah, listen to
this message from the LORD! Listen to it, all of you
who worship here! 3 This is what the LORD of Heaven's
Armies, the God of Israel, says:
"'Even now, if you quit your evil ways, I will let you
stay in your own land. 4 But don't be fooled by those
who promise you safety simply because the LORD's
Temple is here. They chant, "The LORD's Temple is
here! The LORD's Temple is here!" 5 But I will be merciful only if you stop your evil thoughts and deeds
and start treating each other with justice; 6 only if
you stop exploiting foreigners, orphans, and widows;
only if you stop your murdering; and only if you stop
harming yourselves by worshiping idols. 7 Then I will
let you stay in this land that I gave to your ancestors
to keep forever.
8 "'Don't be fooled into thinking that you will
never suffer because the Temple is here. It's a lie!
9 Do you really think you can steal, murder, commit
adultery, lie, and burn incense to Baal and all those
other new gods of yours, 10 and then come here and
stand before me in my Temple and chant, "We are
safe!"—only to go right back to all those evils again?
11 Don't you yourselves admit that this Temple,
which bears my name, has become a den of thieves?

6:27 As in Greek version; Hebrew reads *a tester of my people a fortress.*

KING JAMES VERSION

become a den of robbers in your eyes? Behold, even I have seen *it,* saith the LORD.

12 But go ye now unto my place which *was* in Shiloh, where I set my name at the first, and see what I did to it for the wickedness of my people Israel.

13 And now, because ye have done all these works, saith the LORD, and I spake unto you, rising up early and speaking, but ye heard not; and I called you, but ye answered not;

14 Therefore will I do unto *this* house, which is called by my name, wherein ye trust, and unto the place which I gave to you and to your fathers, as I have done to Shiloh.

15 And I will cast you out of my sight, as I have cast out all your brethren, *even* the whole seed of Ephraim.

16 Therefore pray not thou for this people, neither lift up cry nor prayer for them, neither make intercession to me: for I will not hear thee.

17 Seest thou not what they do in the cities of Judah and in the streets of Jerusalem?

18 The children gather wood, and the fathers kindle the fire, and the women knead *their* dough, to make cakes to the queen of heaven, and to pour out drink offerings unto other gods, that they may provoke me to anger.

19 Do they provoke me to anger? saith the LORD: *do they* not *provoke* themselves to the confusion of their own faces?

20 Therefore thus saith the Lord GOD; Behold, mine anger and my fury shall be poured out upon this place, upon man, and upon beast, and upon the trees of the field, and upon the fruit of the ground; and it shall burn, and shall not be quenched.

21 Thus saith the LORD of hosts, the God of Israel; Put your burnt offerings unto your sacrifices, and eat flesh.

22 For I spake not unto your fathers, nor commanded them in the day that I brought them out of the land of Egypt, concerning burnt offerings or sacrifices:

23 But this thing commanded I them, saying, Obey my voice, and I will be your God, and ye shall be my people: and walk ye in all the ways that I have commanded you, that it may be well unto you.

24 But they hearkened not, nor inclined their ear, but walked in the counsels *and* in the imagination of their evil heart, and went backward, and not forward.

25 Since the day that your fathers came forth out of the land of Egypt unto this day I have even sent unto you all my servants the prophets, daily rising up early and sending *them:*

26 Yet they hearkened not unto me, nor inclined their ear, but hardened their neck: they did worse than their fathers.

27 Therefore thou shalt speak all these words unto them; but they will not hearken to thee: thou shalt also call unto them; but they will not answer thee.

NEW LIVING TRANSLATION

Surely I see all the evil going on there. I, the LORD, have spoken!

12 "Go now to the place at Shiloh where I once put the Tabernacle that bore my name. See what I did there because of all the wickedness of my people, the Israelites. 13 While you were doing these wicked things, says the LORD, I spoke to you about it repeatedly, but you would not listen. I called out to you, but you refused to answer. 14 So just as I destroyed Shiloh, I will now destroy this Temple that bears my name, this Temple that you trust in for help, this place that I gave to you and your ancestors. 15 And I will send you out of my sight into exile, just as I did your relatives, the people of Israel.*'

Judah's Persistent Idolatry

16 "Pray no more for these people, Jeremiah. Do not weep or pray for them, and don't beg me to help them, for I will not listen to you. 17 Don't you see what they are doing throughout the towns of Judah and in the streets of Jerusalem? 18 No wonder I am so angry! Watch how the children gather wood and the fathers build sacrificial fires. See how the women knead dough and make cakes to offer to the Queen of Heaven. And they pour out liquid offerings to their other idol gods! 19 Am I the one they are hurting?" asks the LORD. "Most of all, they hurt themselves, to their own shame."

20 So this is what the Sovereign LORD says: "I will pour out my terrible fury on this place. Its people, animals, trees, and crops will be consumed by the unquenchable fire of my anger."

21 This is what the LORD of Heaven's Armies, the God of Israel, says: "Take your burnt offerings and your other sacrifices and eat them yourselves! 22 When I led your ancestors out of Egypt, it was not burnt offerings and sacrifices I wanted from them. 23 This is what I told them: 'Obey me, and I will be your God, and you will be my people. Do everything as I say, and all will be well!'

24 "But my people would not listen to me. They kept doing whatever they wanted, following the stubborn desires of their evil hearts. They went backward instead of forward. 25 From the day your ancestors left Egypt until now, I have continued to send my servants, the prophets—day in and day out. 26 But my people have not listened to me or even tried to hear. They have been stubborn and sinful—even worse than their ancestors.

27 "Tell them all this, but do not expect them to listen. Shout out your warnings, but do not expect them

7:15 Hebrew *of Ephraim,* referring to the northern kingdom of Israel.

28But thou shalt say unto them, This *is* a nation
that obeyeth not the voice of the LORD their God, nor
receiveth correction: truth is perished, and is cut off
from their mouth.
29Cut off thine hair, *O Jerusalem,* and cast *it* away,
and take up a lamentation on high places; for the
LORD hath rejected and forsaken the generation of
his wrath.

30For the children of Judah have done evil in my
sight, saith the LORD: they have set their abominations in the house which is called by my name, to
pollute it.
31And they have built the high places of Tophet,
which *is* in the valley of the son of Hinnom, to burn
their sons and their daughters in the fire; which I
commanded *them* not, neither came it into my heart.
32Therefore, behold, the days come, saith the
LORD, that it shall no more be called Tophet, nor the
valley of the son of Hinnom, but the valley of slaughter: for they shall bury in Tophet, till there be no
place.
33And the carcases of this people shall be meat for
the fowls of the heaven, and for the beasts of the
earth; and none shall fray *them* away.
34Then will I cause to cease from the cities of
Judah, and from the streets of Jerusalem, the voice
of mirth, and the voice of gladness, the voice of the
bridegroom, and the voice of the bride: for the land
shall be desolate.

8 1At that time, saith the LORD, they shall bring out
the bones of the kings of Judah, and the bones
of his princes, and the bones of the priests, and the
bones of the prophets, and the bones of the inhabitants of Jerusalem, out of their graves:
2And they shall spread them before the sun, and
the moon, and all the host of heaven, whom they
have loved, and whom they have served, and after
whom they have walked, and whom they have
sought, and whom they have worshipped: they shall
not be gathered, nor be buried; they shall be for dung
upon the face of the earth.
3And death shall be chosen rather than life by all
the residue of them that remain of this evil family,
which remain in all the places whither I have driven
them, saith the LORD of hosts.
4Moreover thou shalt say unto them, Thus saith
the LORD; Shall they fall, and not arise? shall he turn
away, and not return?
5Why *then* is this people of Jerusalem slidden

to respond. 28Say to them, 'This is the nation whose
people will not obey the LORD their God and who refuse to be taught. Truth has vanished from among
them; it is no longer heard on their lips. 29Shave your
head in mourning, and weep alone on the mountains. For the LORD has rejected and forsaken this
generation that has provoked his fury.'

The Valley of Slaughter

30"The people of Judah have sinned before my very
eyes," says the LORD. "They have set up their abominable idols right in the Temple that bears my name,
defiling it. 31They have built pagan shrines at
Topheth, the garbage dump in the valley of Ben-
Hinnom, and there they burn their sons and daughters in the fire. I have never commanded such a
horrible deed; it never even crossed my mind to
command such a thing! 32So beware, for the time is
coming," says the LORD, "when that garbage dump
will no longer be called Topheth or the valley of Ben-
Hinnom, but the Valley of Slaughter. They will bury
the bodies in Topheth until there is no more room for
them. 33The bodies of my people will be food for the
vultures and wild animals, and no one will be left to
scare them away. 34I will put an end to the happy
singing and laughter in the streets of Jerusalem. The
joyful voices of bridegrooms and brides will no longer be heard in the towns of Judah. The land will lie
in complete desolation.

8 "In that day," says the LORD, "the enemy will
break open the graves of the kings and officials
of Judah, and the graves of the priests, prophets, and
common people of Jerusalem. 2They will spread out
their bones on the ground before the sun, moon, and
stars—the gods my people have loved, served, and
worshiped. Their bones will not be gathered up
again or buried but will be scattered on the ground
like manure. 3And the people of this evil nation who
survive will wish to die rather than live where I will
send them. I, the LORD of Heaven's Armies, have
spoken!

Deception by False Prophets

4"Jeremiah, say to the people, 'This is what the LORD
says:

"'When people fall down, don't they get
up again?
When they discover they're on the wrong road,
don't they turn back?
5 Then why do these people stay on their
self-destructive path?
Why do the people of Jerusalem refuse
to turn back?

KING JAMES VERSION

back by a perpetual backsliding? they hold fast deceit, they refuse to return.

6 I hearkened and heard, *but* they spake not aright: no man repented him of his wickedness, saying, What have I done? every one turned to his course, as the horse rusheth into the battle.

7 Yea, the stork in the heaven knoweth her appointed times; and the turtle and the crane and the swallow observe the time of their coming; but my people know not the judgment of the LORD.

8 How do ye say, We *are* wise, and the law of the LORD *is* with us? Lo, certainly in vain made he *it;* the pen of the scribes *is* in vain.

9 The wise *men* are ashamed, they are dismayed and taken: lo, they have rejected the word of the LORD; and what wisdom *is* in them?

10 Therefore will I give their wives unto others, *and* their fields to them that shall inherit *them:* for every one from the least even unto the greatest is given to covetousness, from the prophet even unto the priest every one dealeth falsely.

11 For they have healed the hurt of the daughter of my people slightly, saying, Peace, peace; when *there is* no peace.

12 Were they ashamed when they had committed abomination? nay, they were not at all ashamed, neither could they blush: therefore shall they fall among them that fall: in the time of their visitation they shall be cast down, saith the LORD.

13 I will surely consume them, saith the LORD: *there shall be* no grapes on the vine, nor figs on the fig tree, and the leaf shall fade; and *the things that* I have given them shall pass away from them.

14 Why do we sit still? assemble yourselves, and let us enter into the defenced cities, and let us be silent there: for the LORD our God hath put us to silence, and given us water of gall to drink, because we have sinned against the LORD.

15 We looked for peace, but no good *came; and* for a time of health, and behold trouble!

NEW LIVING TRANSLATION

They cling tightly to their lies
and will not turn around.
6 I listen to their conversations
and don't hear a word of truth.
Is anyone sorry for doing wrong?
Does anyone say, "What a terrible thing
I have done"?
No! All are running down the path of sin
as swiftly as a horse galloping into battle!
7 Even the stork that flies across the sky
knows the time of her migration,
as do the turtledove, the swallow, and the crane.*
They all return at the proper time each year.
But not my people!
They do not know the LORD's laws.

8 "'How can you say, "We are wise because
we have the word of the LORD,"
when your teachers have twisted it by
writing lies?
9 These wise teachers will fall
into the trap of their own foolishness,
for they have rejected the word of the LORD.
Are they so wise after all?
10 I will give their wives to others
and their farms to strangers.
From the least to the greatest,
their lives are ruled by greed.
Yes, even my prophets and priests are like that.
They are all frauds.
11 They offer superficial treatments
for my people's mortal wound.
They give assurances of peace
when there is no peace.
12 Are they ashamed of these disgusting actions?
Not at all—they don't even know how to blush!
Therefore, they will lie among the slaughtered.
They will be brought down when I
punish them,
says the LORD.
13 I will surely consume them.
There will be no more harvests of figs
and grapes.
Their fruit trees will all die.
Whatever I gave them will soon be gone.
I, the LORD, have spoken!'

14 "Then the people will say,
'Why should we wait here to die?
Come, let's go to the fortified towns and
die there.
For the LORD our God has decreed our
destruction
and has given us a cup of poison to drink
because we sinned against the LORD.
15 We hoped for peace, but no peace came.
We hoped for a time of healing, but found
only terror.'

8:7 The identification of some of these birds is uncertain.

KING JAMES VERSION

16 The snorting of his horses was heard from Dan:
the whole land trembled at the sound of the neighing of his strong ones; for they are come, and have
devoured the land, and all that is in it; the city, and
those that dwell therein.
17 For, behold, I will send serpents, cockatrices,
among you, which *will* not *be* charmed, and they
shall bite you, saith the LORD.

18 *When* I would comfort myself against sorrow,
my heart *is* faint in me.
19 Behold the voice of the cry of the daughter of
my people because of them that dwell in a far country: *Is* not the LORD in Zion? *is* not her king in her?
Why have they provoked me to anger with their
graven images, *and* with strange vanities?
20 The harvest is past, the summer is ended, and we
are not saved.
21 For the hurt of the daughter of my people am
I hurt; I am black; astonishment hath taken hold
on me.
22 *Is there* no balm in Gilead; *is there* no physician
there? why then is not the health of the daughter of
my people recovered?

9 1 Oh that my head were waters, and mine eyes a
fountain of tears, that I might weep day and
night for the slain of the daughter of my people!
2 Oh that I had in the wilderness a lodging place of
wayfaring men; that I might leave my people, and go
from them! for they *be* all adulterers, an assembly of
treacherous men.

3 And they bend their tongues *like* their bow *for*
lies: but they are not valiant for the truth upon the
earth; for they proceed from evil to evil, and they
know not me, saith the LORD.
4 Take ye heed every one of his neighbour, and
trust ye not in any brother: for every brother will

NEW LIVING TRANSLATION

16 "The snorting of the enemies' warhorses
can be heard
all the way from the land of Dan in the north!
The neighing of their stallions makes the whole
land tremble.
They are coming to devour the land and
everything in it—
cities and people alike.
17 I will send these enemy troops among you
like poisonous snakes you cannot charm.
They will bite you, and you will die.
I, the LORD, have spoken!"

Jeremiah Weeps for Sinful Judah

18 My grief is beyond healing;
my heart is broken.
19 Listen to the weeping of my people;
it can be heard all across the land.
"Has the LORD abandoned Jerusalem?*"
the people ask.
"Is her King no longer there?"
"Oh, why have they provoked my anger with
their carved idols
and their worthless foreign gods?"
says the LORD.
20 "The harvest is finished,
and the summer is gone," the people cry,
"yet we are not saved!"
21 I hurt with the hurt of my people.
I mourn and am overcome with grief.
22 Is there no medicine in Gilead?
Is there no physician there?
Why is there no healing
for the wounds of my people?

9 1* If only my head were a pool of water
and my eyes a fountain of tears,
I would weep day and night
for all my people who have been slaughtered.
2* Oh, that I could go away and forget my people
and live in a travelers' shack in the desert.
For they are all adulterers—
a pack of treacherous liars.

Judgment for Disobedience

3 "My people bend their tongues like bows
to shoot out lies.
They refuse to stand up for the truth.
They only go from bad to worse.
They do not know me,"
says the LORD.

4 "Beware of your neighbor!
Don't even trust your brother!

8:19 Hebrew *Zion?* **9:1** Verse 9:1 is numbered 8:23 in Hebrew text.
9:2 Verses 9:2-26 are numbered 9:1-25 in Hebrew text.

KING JAMES VERSION

utterly supplant, and every neighbour will walk with slanders.

5 And they will deceive every one his neighbour, and will not speak the truth: they have taught their tongue to speak lies, *and* weary themselves to commit iniquity.

6 Thine habitation *is* in the midst of deceit; through deceit they refuse to know me, saith the LORD.

7 Therefore thus saith the LORD of hosts, Behold, I will melt them, and try them; for how shall I do for the daughter of my people?

8 Their tongue *is as* an arrow shot out; it speaketh deceit: *one* speaketh peaceably to his neighbour with his mouth, but in heart he layeth his wait.

9 Shall I not visit them for these *things?* saith the LORD: shall not my soul be avenged on such a nation as this?

10 For the mountains will I take up a weeping and wailing, and for the habitations of the wilderness a lamentation, because they are burned up, so that none can pass through *them;* neither can *men* hear the voice of the cattle; both the fowl of the heavens and the beast are fled; they are gone.

11 And I will make Jerusalem heaps, *and* a den of dragons; and I will make the cities of Judah desolate, without an inhabitant.

12 Who *is* the wise man, that may understand this? and *who is he* to whom the mouth of the LORD hath spoken, that he may declare it, for what the land perisheth *and* is burned up like a wilderness, that none passeth through?

13 And the LORD saith, Because they have forsaken my law which I set before them, and have not obeyed my voice, neither walked therein;

14 But have walked after the imagination of their own heart, and after Baalim, which their fathers taught them:

15 Therefore thus saith the LORD of hosts, the God of Israel; Behold, I will feed them, *even* this people, with wormwood, and give them water of gall to drink.

16 I will scatter them also among the heathen, whom neither they nor their fathers have known: and I will send a sword after them, till I have consumed them.

17 Thus saith the LORD of hosts, Consider ye, and call for the mourning women, that they may come; and send for cunning *women,* that they may come:

18 And let them make haste, and take up a wailing for us, that our eyes may run down with tears, and our eyelids gush out with waters.

NEW LIVING TRANSLATION

For brother takes advantage of brother,
and friend slanders friend.
5 They all fool and defraud each other;
no one tells the truth.
With practiced tongues they tell lies;
they wear themselves out with all their sinning.
6 They pile lie upon lie
and utterly refuse to acknowledge me,"
says the LORD.

7 Therefore, this is what the LORD of Heaven's
Armies says:
"See, I will melt them down in a crucible
and test them like metal.
What else can I do with my people?*
8 For their tongues shoot lies like
poisoned arrows.
They speak friendly words to their neighbors
while scheming in their heart to kill them.
9 Should I not punish them for this?"
says the LORD.
"Should I not avenge myself against
such a nation?"

10 I will weep for the mountains
and wail for the wilderness pastures.
For they are desolate and empty of life;
the lowing of cattle is heard no more;
the birds and wild animals have all fled.

11 "I will make Jerusalem into a heap of ruins,"
says the LORD.
"It will be a place haunted by jackals.
The towns of Judah will be ghost towns,
with no one living in them."

12 Who is wise enough to understand all this? Who
has been instructed by the LORD and can explain it to
others? Why has the land been so ruined that no one
dares to travel through it?
13 The LORD replies, "This has happened because my
people have abandoned my instructions; they have refused to obey what I said. 14 Instead, they have stubbornly followed their own desires and worshiped the
images of Baal, as their ancestors taught them. 15 So
now, this is what the LORD of Heaven's Armies, the God
of Israel, says: Look! I will feed them with bitterness
and give them poison to drink. 16 I will scatter them
around the world, in places they and their ancestors
never heard of, and even there I will chase them with
the sword until I have destroyed them completely."

Weeping in Jerusalem

17 This is what the LORD of Heaven's Armies says:
"Consider all this, and call for the mourners.
Send for the women who mourn at funerals.
18 Quick! Begin your weeping!
Let the tears flow from your eyes.

9:7 Hebrew *with the daughter of my people?* Greek version reads *with the evil daughter of my people?*

KING JAMES VERSION

19 For a voice of wailing is heard out of Zion, How are we spoiled! we are greatly confounded, because we have forsaken the land, because our dwellings have cast *us* out.

20 Yet hear the word of the LORD, O ye women, and let your ear receive the word of his mouth, and teach your daughters wailing, and every one her neighbour lamentation.

21 For death is come up into our windows, *and* is entered into our palaces, to cut off the children from without, *and* the young men from the streets.

22 Speak, Thus saith the LORD, Even the carcases of men shall fall as dung upon the open field, and as the handful after the harvestman, and none shall gather *them*.

23 Thus saith the LORD, Let not the wise *man* glory in his wisdom, neither let the mighty *man* glory in his might, let not the rich *man* glory in his riches:

24 But let him that glorieth glory in this, that he understandeth and knoweth me, that I *am* the LORD which exercise lovingkindness, judgment, and righteousness, in the earth: for in these *things* I delight, saith the LORD.

25 Behold, the days come, saith the LORD, that I will punish all *them which are* circumcised with the uncircumcised;

26 Egypt, and Judah, and Edom, and the children of Ammon, and Moab, and all *that are* in the utmost corners, that dwell in the wilderness: for all *these* nations *are* uncircumcised, and all the house of Israel *are* uncircumcised in the heart.

10 1 Hear ye the word which the LORD speaketh unto you, O house of Israel:

2 Thus saith the LORD, Learn not the way of the heathen, and be not dismayed at the signs of heaven; for the heathen are dismayed at them.

3 For the customs of the people *are* vain: for *one* cutteth a tree out of the forest, the work of the hands of the workman, with the ax.

4 They deck it with silver and with gold; they fasten it with nails and with hammers, that it move not.

NEW LIVING TRANSLATION

19 Hear the people of Jerusalem* crying in despair,
'We are ruined! We are completely humiliated!
We must leave our land,
because our homes have been torn down.'"

20 Listen, you women, to the words of the LORD;
open your ears to what he has to say.
Teach your daughters to wail;
teach one another how to lament.

21 For death has crept in through our windows
and has entered our mansions.
It has killed off the flower of our youth:
Children no longer play in the streets,
and young men no longer gather in
the squares.

22 This is what the LORD says:
"Bodies will be scattered across the fields
like clumps of manure,
like bundles of grain after the harvest.
No one will be left to bury them."

23 This is what the LORD says:
"Don't let the wise boast in their wisdom,
or the powerful boast in their power,
or the rich boast in their riches.

24 But those who wish to boast
should boast in this alone:
that they truly know me and understand
that I am the LORD
who demonstrates unfailing love
and who brings justice and righteousness
to the earth,
and that I delight in these things.
I, the LORD, have spoken!

25 "A time is coming," says the LORD, "when I will
punish all those who are circumcised in body but
not in spirit—26 the Egyptians, Edomites, Ammonites,
Moabites, the people who live in the desert in remote
places,* and yes, even the people of Judah. And like
all these pagan nations, the people of Israel also have
uncircumcised hearts."

Idolatry Brings Destruction

10 Hear the word that the LORD speaks to you, O Israel! 2 This is what the LORD says:

"Do not act like the other nations,
who try to read their future in the stars.
Do not be afraid of their predictions,
even though other nations are terrified by them.

3 Their ways are futile and foolish.
They cut down a tree, and a craftsman carves
an idol.

4 They decorate it with gold and silver
and then fasten it securely with hammer
and nails
so it won't fall over.

9:19 Hebrew *Zion*. **9:26** Or *in the desert and clip the corners of their hair.*

5 They *are* upright as the palm tree, but speak not: they must needs be borne, because they cannot go. Be not afraid of them; for they cannot do evil, neither also *is it* in them to do good.

6 Forasmuch as *there is* none like unto thee, O LORD; thou *art* great, and thy name *is* great in might.

7 Who would not fear thee, O King of nations? for to thee doth it appertain: forasmuch as among all the wise *men* of the nations, and in all their kingdoms, *there is* none like unto thee.

8 But they are altogether brutish and foolish: the stock *is* a doctrine of vanities.

9 Silver spread into plates is brought from Tarshish, and gold from Uphaz, the work of the workman, and of the hands of the founder: blue and purple *is* their clothing: they *are* all the work of cunning *men*.

10 But the LORD *is* the true God, he *is* the living God, and an everlasting king: at his wrath the earth shall tremble, and the nations shall not be able to abide his indignation.

11 Thus shall ye say unto them, The gods that have not made the heavens and the earth, *even* they shall perish from the earth, and from under these heavens.

12 He hath made the earth by his power, he hath established the world by his wisdom, and hath stretched out the heavens by his discretion.

13 When he uttereth his voice, *there is* a multitude of waters in the heavens, and he causeth the vapours to ascend from the ends of the earth; he maketh lightnings with rain, and bringeth forth the wind out of his treasures.

14 Every man is brutish in *his* knowledge: every founder is confounded by the graven image: for his molten image *is* falsehood, and *there is* no breath in them.

15 They *are* vanity, *and* the work of errors: in the time of their visitation they shall perish.

16 The portion of Jacob *is* not like them: for he *is*

5 Their gods are like
helpless scarecrows in a cucumber field!
They cannot speak,
and they need to be carried because they
cannot walk.
Do not be afraid of such gods,
for they can neither harm you nor do you
any good."

6 LORD, there is no one like you!
For you are great, and your name is full
of power.
7 Who would not fear you, O King of nations?
That title belongs to you alone!
Among all the wise people of the earth
and in all the kingdoms of the world,
there is no one like you.
8 People who worship idols are stupid and foolish.
The things they worship are made of wood!
9 They bring beaten sheets of silver from Tarshish
and gold from Uphaz,
and they give these materials to skillful
craftsmen
who make their idols.
Then they dress these gods in royal blue
and purple robes
made by expert tailors.
10 But the LORD is the only true God.
He is the living God and the everlasting King!
The whole earth trembles at his anger.
The nations cannot stand up to his wrath.

11 Say this to those who worship other gods: "Your so-called gods, who did not make the heavens and earth, will vanish from the earth and from under the heavens."*

12 But God made the earth by his power,
and he preserves it by his wisdom.
With his own understanding
he stretched out the heavens.
13 When he speaks in the thunder,
the heavens roar with rain.
He causes the clouds to rise over the earth.
He sends the lightning with the rain
and releases the wind from his storehouses.
14 The whole human race is foolish and has
no knowledge!
The craftsmen are disgraced by the idols
they make,
for their carefully shaped works are a fraud.
These idols have no breath or power.
15 Idols are worthless; they are ridiculous lies!
On the day of reckoning they will all
be destroyed.
16 But the God of Israel* is no idol!
He is the Creator of everything that exists,

10:11 The original text of this verse is in Aramaic. **10:16** Hebrew *the Portion of Jacob*. See note on 5:20.

KING JAMES VERSION

the former of all *things;* and Israel *is* the rod of his
inheritance: The LORD of hosts *is* his name.

17 Gather up thy wares out of the land, O inhabitant of the fortress.
18 For thus saith the LORD, Behold, I will sling out
the inhabitants of the land at this once, and will distress them, that they may find *it so.*
19 Woe is me for my hurt! my wound is grievous:
but I said, Truly this *is* a grief, and I must bear it.
20 My tabernacle is spoiled, and all my cords are
broken: my children are gone forth of me, and they
are not: *there is* none to stretch forth my tent any
more, and to set up my curtains.
21 For the pastors are become brutish, and have not
sought the LORD: therefore they shall not prosper,
and all their flocks shall be scattered.
22 Behold, the noise of the bruit is come, and a
great commotion out of the north country, to make
the cities of Judah desolate, *and* a den of dragons.

23 O LORD, I know that the way of man *is* not in himself: *it is* not in man that walketh to direct his steps.
24 O LORD, correct me, but with judgment; not in
thine anger, lest thou bring me to nothing.
25 Pour out thy fury upon the heathen that know
thee not, and upon the families that call not on thy
name: for they have eaten up Jacob, and devoured
him, and consumed him, and have made his habitation desolate.

11 1 The word that came to Jeremiah from the
LORD, saying,
2 Hear ye the words of this covenant, and speak
unto the men of Judah, and to the inhabitants of
Jerusalem;
3 And say thou unto them, Thus saith the LORD God
of Israel; Cursed *be* the man that obeyeth not the
words of this covenant,
4 Which I commanded your fathers in the day *that*
I brought them forth out of the land of Egypt, from
the iron furnace, saying, Obey my voice, and do them,
according to all which I command you: so shall ye be
my people, and I will be your God:
5 That I may perform the oath which I have sworn

NEW LIVING TRANSLATION

including Israel, his own special possession.
The LORD of Heaven's Armies is his name!

The Coming Destruction

17 Pack your bags and prepare to leave;
the siege is about to begin.
18 For this is what the LORD says:
"Suddenly, I will fling out
all you who live in this land.
I will pour great troubles upon you,
and at last you will feel my anger."

19 My wound is severe,
and my grief is great.
My sickness is incurable,
but I must bear it.
20 My home is gone,
and no one is left to help me rebuild it.
My children have been taken away,
and I will never see them again.
21 The shepherds of my people have lost
their senses.
They no longer seek wisdom from the LORD.
Therefore, they fail completely,
and their flocks are scattered.
22 Listen! Hear the terrifying roar of great armies
as they roll down from the north.
The towns of Judah will be destroyed
and become a haunt for jackals.

Jeremiah's Prayer

23 I know, LORD, that our lives are not our own.
We are not able to plan our own course.
24 So correct me, LORD, but please be gentle.
Do not correct me in anger, for I would die.
25 Pour out your wrath on the nations that refuse
to acknowledge you—
on the peoples that do not call upon
your name.
For they have devoured your people Israel*;
they have devoured and consumed them,
making the land a desolate wilderness.

Judah's Broken Covenant

11 The LORD gave another message to Jeremiah.
He said, 2 "Remind the people of Judah and
Jerusalem about the terms of my covenant with
them. 3 Say to them, 'This is what the LORD, the God of
Israel, says: Cursed is anyone who does not obey the
terms of my covenant! 4 For I said to your ancestors
when I brought them out of the iron-smelting furnace of Egypt, "If you obey me and do whatever I
command you, then you will be my people, and I will
be your God." 5 I said this so I could keep my promise

10:25 Hebrew *devoured Jacob.* See note on 5:20.

unto your fathers, to give them a land flowing with
milk and honey, as *it is* this day. Then answered I, and
said, So be it, O LORD.
6 Then the LORD said unto me, Proclaim all these
words in the cities of Judah, and in the streets of
Jerusalem, saying, Hear ye the words of this covenant, and do them.
7 For I earnestly protested unto your fathers in the
day *that* I brought them up out of the land of Egypt,
even unto this day, rising early and protesting, saying, Obey my voice.
8 Yet they obeyed not, nor inclined their ear, but
walked every one in the imagination of their evil
heart: therefore I will bring upon them all the words
of this covenant, which I commanded *them* to do;
but they did *them* not.
9 And the LORD said unto me, A conspiracy is found
among the men of Judah, and among the inhabitants
of Jerusalem.
10 They are turned back to the iniquities of their
forefathers, which refused to hear my words; and
they went after other gods to serve them: the house
of Israel and the house of Judah have broken my covenant which I made with their fathers.
11 Therefore thus saith the LORD, Behold, I will
bring evil upon them, which they shall not be able to
escape; and though they shall cry unto me, I will not
hearken unto them.
12 Then shall the cities of Judah and inhabitants of
Jerusalem go, and cry unto the gods unto whom they
offer incense: but they shall not save them at all in
the time of their trouble.
13 For *according to* the number of thy cities were
thy gods, O Judah; and *according to* the number of
the streets of Jerusalem have ye set up altars to *that*
shameful thing, *even* altars to burn incense unto
Baal.
14 Therefore pray not thou for this people, neither
lift up a cry or prayer for them: for I will not hear
them in the time that they cry unto me for their
trouble.
15 What hath my beloved to do in mine house, *seeing* she hath wrought lewdness with many, and the
holy flesh is passed from thee? when thou doest evil,
then thou rejoicest.
16 The LORD called thy name, A green olive tree,
fair, *and* of goodly fruit: with the noise of a great tumult he hath kindled fire upon it, and the branches
of it are broken.
17 For the LORD of hosts, that planted thee, hath
pronounced evil against thee, for the evil of the
house of Israel and of the house of Judah, which they
have done against themselves to provoke me to anger in offering incense unto Baal.
18 And the LORD hath given me knowledge *of it*,
and I know *it:* then thou shewedst me their doings.
19 But I *was* like a lamb *or* an ox *that* is brought to
the slaughter; and I knew not that they had devised

to your ancestors to give you a land flowing with milk
and honey—the land you live in today.'"
Then I replied, "Amen, LORD! May it be so."
6 Then the LORD said, "Broadcast this message in
the streets of Jerusalem. Go from town to town
throughout the land and say, 'Remember the ancient
covenant, and do everything it requires. 7 For I solemnly warned your ancestors when I brought them
out of Egypt, "Obey me!" I have repeated this warning
over and over to this day, 8 but your ancestors did not
listen or even pay attention. Instead, they stubbornly
followed their own evil desires. And because they
refused to obey, I brought upon them all the curses
described in this covenant.'"
9 Again the LORD spoke to me and said, "I have discovered a conspiracy against me among the people
of Judah and Jerusalem. 10 They have returned to the
sins of their forefathers. They have refused to listen
to me and are worshiping other gods. Israel and
Judah have both broken the covenant I made with
their ancestors. 11 Therefore, this is what the LORD
says: I am going to bring calamity upon them, and
they will not escape. Though they beg for mercy, I
will not listen to their cries. 12 Then the people of
Judah and Jerusalem will pray to their idols and burn
incense before them. But the idols will not save them
when disaster strikes! 13 Look now, people of Judah;
you have as many gods as you have towns. You have
as many altars of shame—altars for burning incense
to your god Baal—as there are streets in Jerusalem.
14 "Pray no more for these people, Jeremiah. Do not
weep or pray for them, for I will not listen to them
when they cry out to me in distress.

15 "What right do my beloved people have to come
to my Temple,
when they have done so many immoral things?
Can their vows and sacrifices prevent their
destruction?
They actually rejoice in doing evil!
16 I, the LORD, once called them a thriving olive tree,
beautiful to see and full of good fruit.
But now I have sent the fury of their enemies
to burn them with fire,
leaving them charred and broken.

17 "I, the LORD of Heaven's Armies, who planted
this olive tree, have ordered it destroyed. For the people of Israel and Judah have done evil, arousing my
anger by burning incense to Baal."

A Plot against Jeremiah

18 Then the LORD told me about the plots my enemies
were making against me. 19 I was like a lamb being
led to the slaughter. I had no idea that they were
planning to kill me! "Let's destroy this man and all his

KING JAMES VERSION

devices against me, *saying,* Let us destroy the tree
with the fruit thereof, and let us cut him off from the
land of the living, that his name may be no more
remembered.
20 But, O LORD of hosts, that judgest righteously,
that triest the reins and the heart, let me see thy vengeance on them: for unto thee have I revealed my
cause.
21 Therefore thus saith the LORD of the men of Anathoth, that seek thy life, saying, Prophesy not in the
name of the LORD, that thou die not by our hand:
22 Therefore thus saith the LORD of hosts, Behold,
I will punish them: the young men shall die by the
sword; their sons and their daughters shall die by
famine:
23 And there shall be no remnant of them: for I will
bring evil upon the men of Anathoth, *even* the year
of their visitation.

12 1 Righteous *art* thou, O LORD, when I plead
with thee: yet let me talk with thee of *thy* judgments: Wherefore doth the way of the wicked prosper? *wherefore* are all they happy that deal very
treacherously?
2 Thou hast planted them, yea, they have taken
root: they grow, yea, they bring forth fruit: thou *art*
near in their mouth, and far from their reins.
3 But thou, O LORD, knowest me: thou hast seen me,
and tried mine heart toward thee: pull them out like
sheep for the slaughter, and prepare them for the day
of slaughter.
4 How long shall the land mourn, and the herbs of
every field wither, for the wickedness of them that
dwell therein? the beasts are consumed, and the
birds; because they said, He shall not see our last end.

5 If thou hast run with the footmen, and they have
wearied thee, then how canst thou contend with
horses? and *if* in the land of peace, *wherein* thou
trustedst, *they wearied thee,* then how wilt thou do
in the swelling of Jordan?
6 For even thy brethren, and the house of thy father, even they have dealt treacherously with thee;
yea, they have called a multitude after thee: believe
them not, though they speak fair words unto thee.
7 I have forsaken mine house, I have left mine heritage; I have given the dearly beloved of my soul into
the hand of her enemies.

NEW LIVING TRANSLATION

words," they said. "Let's cut him down, so his name
will be forgotten forever."

20 O LORD of Heaven's Armies,
you make righteous judgments,
and you examine the deepest thoughts
and secrets.
Let me see your vengeance against them,
for I have committed my cause to you.

21 This is what the LORD says about the men of Anathoth who wanted me dead. They had said, "We will
kill you if you do not stop prophesying in the LORD's
name." 22 So this is what the LORD of Heaven's Armies
says about them: "I will punish them! Their young
men will die in battle, and their boys and girls will
starve to death. 23 Not one of these plotters from Anathoth will survive, for I will bring disaster upon them
when their time of punishment comes."

Jeremiah Questions the LORD's Justice

12 1 LORD, you always give me justice
when I bring a case before you.
So let me bring you this complaint:
Why are the wicked so prosperous?
Why are evil people so happy?
2 You have planted them,
and they have taken root and prospered.
Your name is on their lips,
but you are far from their hearts.
3 But as for me, LORD, you know my heart.
You see me and test my thoughts.
Drag these people away like sheep to be
butchered!
Set them aside to be slaughtered!
4 How long must this land mourn?
Even the grass in the fields has withered.
The wild animals and birds have disappeared
because of the evil in the land.
For the people have said,
"The LORD doesn't see what's ahead for us!"

The LORD's Reply to Jeremiah

5 "If racing against mere men makes you tired,
how will you race against horses?
If you stumble and fall on open ground,
what will you do in the thickets near
the Jordan?
6 Even your brothers, members of your own family,
have turned against you.
They plot and raise complaints against you.
Do not trust them,
no matter how pleasantly they speak.

7 "I have abandoned my people, my special
possession.
I have surrendered my dearest ones
to their enemies.

KING JAMES VERSION

8 Mine heritage is unto me as a lion in the forest; it crieth out against me: therefore have I hated it.

9 Mine heritage *is* unto me *as* a speckled bird, the birds round about *are* against her; come ye, assemble all the beasts of the field, come to devour.

10 Many pastors have destroyed my vineyard, they have trodden my portion under foot, they have made my pleasant portion a desolate wilderness.

11 They have made it desolate, *and being* desolate it mourneth unto me; the whole land is made desolate, because no man layeth *it* to heart.

12 The spoilers are come upon all high places through the wilderness: for the sword of the LORD shall devour from the *one* end of the land even to the *other* end of the land: no flesh shall have peace.

13 They have sown wheat, but shall reap thorns: they have put themselves to pain, *but* shall not profit: and they shall be ashamed of your revenues because of the fierce anger of the LORD.

NEW LIVING TRANSLATION

8 My chosen people have roared at me like
a lion of the forest,
so I have treated them with contempt.
9 My chosen people act like speckled vultures,*
but they themselves are surrounded
by vultures.
Bring on the wild animals to pick their
corpses clean!

10 "Many rulers have ravaged my vineyard,
trampling down the vines
and turning all its beauty into a barren
wilderness.
11 They have made it an empty wasteland;
I hear its mournful cry.
The whole land is desolate,
and no one even cares.
12 On all the bare hilltops,
destroying armies can be seen.
The sword of the LORD devours people
from one end of the nation to the other.
No one will escape!
13 My people have planted wheat
but are harvesting thorns.
They have worn themselves out,
but it has done them no good.
They will harvest a crop of shame
because of the fierce anger of the LORD."

14 Thus saith the LORD against all mine evil neighbours, that touch the inheritance which I have caused my people Israel to inherit; Behold, I will pluck them out of their land, and pluck out the house of Judah from among them.

15 And it shall come to pass, after that I have plucked them out I will return, and have compassion on them, and will bring them again, every man to his heritage, and every man to his land.

16 And it shall come to pass, if they will diligently learn the ways of my people, to swear by my name, The LORD liveth; as they taught my people to swear by Baal; then shall they be built in the midst of my people.

17 But if they will not obey, I will utterly pluck up and destroy that nation, saith the LORD.

A Message for Israel's Neighbors

14 Now this is what the LORD says: "I will uproot from
their land all the evil nations reaching out for the
possession I gave my people Israel. And I will uproot
Judah from among them. 15 But afterward I will return and have compassion on all of them. I will bring
them home to their own lands again, each nation to
its own possession. 16 And if these nations truly learn
the ways of my people, and if they learn to swear by
my name, saying, 'As surely as the LORD lives' (just as
they taught my people to swear by the name of Baal),
then they will be given a place among my people.
17 But any nation who refuses to obey me will be uprooted and destroyed. I, the LORD, have spoken!"

13 1 Thus saith the LORD unto me, Go and get thee a linen girdle, and put it upon thy loins, and put it not in water.

2 So I got a girdle according to the word of the LORD, and put *it* on my loins.

3 And the word of the LORD came unto me the second time, saying,

4 Take the girdle that thou hast got, which *is* upon thy loins, and arise, go to Euphrates, and hide it there in a hole of the rock.

5 So I went, and hid it by Euphrates, as the LORD commanded me.

Jeremiah's Linen Loincloth

13 This is what the LORD said to me: "Go and buy
a linen loincloth and put it on, but do not wash
it." 2 So I bought the loincloth as the LORD directed
me, and I put it on.
3 Then the LORD gave me another message: 4 "Take
the linen loincloth you are wearing, and go to the Euphrates River.* Hide it there in a hole in the rocks."
5 So I went and hid it by the Euphrates as the LORD
had instructed me.

12:9 Or *speckled hyenas.* **13:4** Hebrew *Perath;* also in 13:5, 6, 7.

KING JAMES VERSION

6And it came to pass after many days, that the
LORD said unto me, Arise, go to Euphrates, and take
the girdle from thence, which I commanded thee to
hide there.
7Then I went to Euphrates, and digged, and took
the girdle from the place where I had hid it: and, behold, the girdle was marred, it was profitable for
nothing.
8Then the word of the LORD came unto me, saying,
9Thus saith the LORD, After this manner will I mar
the pride of Judah, and the great pride of Jerusalem.
10This evil people, which refuse to hear my words,
which walk in the imagination of their heart, and
walk after other gods, to serve them, and to worship
them, shall even be as this girdle, which is good for
nothing.
11For as the girdle cleaveth to the loins of a man, so
have I caused to cleave unto me the whole house of
Israel and the whole house of Judah, saith the LORD;
that they might be unto me for a people, and for a
name, and for a praise, and for a glory: but they would
not hear.
12Therefore thou shalt speak unto them this word;
Thus saith the LORD God of Israel, Every bottle shall
be filled with wine: and they shall say unto thee, Do
we not certainly know that every bottle shall be filled
with wine?
13Then shalt thou say unto them, Thus saith the
LORD, Behold, I will fill all the inhabitants of this land,
even the kings that sit upon David's throne, and the
priests, and the prophets, and all the inhabitants of
Jerusalem, with drunkenness.
14And I will dash them one against another, even
the fathers and the sons together, saith the LORD: I will
not pity, nor spare, nor have mercy, but destroy them.
15Hear ye, and give ear; be not proud: for the LORD
hath spoken.
16Give glory to the LORD your God, before he cause
darkness, and before your feet stumble upon the
dark mountains, and, while ye look for light, he turn
it into the shadow of death, *and* make *it* gross darkness.
17But if ye will not hear it, my soul shall weep in secret places for *your* pride; and mine eye shall weep
sore, and run down with tears, because the LORD's
flock is carried away captive.
18Say unto the king and to the queen, Humble
yourselves, sit down: for your principalities shall
come down, *even* the crown of your glory.
19The cities of the south shall be shut up, and
none shall open *them:* Judah shall be carried away

NEW LIVING TRANSLATION

6A long time afterward the LORD said to me, "Go
back to the Euphrates and get the loincloth I told you
to hide there." 7So I went to the Euphrates and dug it
out of the hole where I had hidden it. But now it was
rotting and falling apart. The loincloth was good for
nothing.
8Then I received this message from the LORD:
9"This is what the LORD says: This shows how I will
rot away the pride of Judah and Jerusalem. 10These
wicked people refuse to listen to me. They stubbornly follow their own desires and worship other
gods. Therefore, they will become like this loincloth—good for nothing! 11As a loincloth clings to a
man's waist, so I created Judah and Israel to cling
to me, says the LORD. They were to be my people,
my pride, my glory—an honor to my name. But they
would not listen to me.
12"So tell them, 'This is what the LORD, the God of
Israel, says: May all your jars be filled with wine.' And
they will reply, 'Of course! Jars are made to be filled
with wine!'
13"Then tell them, 'No, this is what the LORD
means: I will fill everyone in this land with drunkenness—from the king sitting on David's throne to the
priests and the prophets, right down to the common
people of Jerusalem. 14I will smash them against
each other, even parents against children, says the
LORD. I will not let my pity or mercy or compassion
keep me from destroying them.'"

A Warning against Pride

15 Listen and pay attention!
Do not be arrogant, for the LORD has spoken.
16 Give glory to the LORD your God
before it is too late.
Acknowledge him before he brings darkness
upon you,
causing you to stumble and fall on the
darkening mountains.
For then, when you look for light,
you will find only terrible darkness and gloom.
17 And if you still refuse to listen,
I will weep alone because of your pride.
My eyes will overflow with tears,
because the LORD's flock will be led away
into exile.
18 Say to the king and his mother,
"Come down from your thrones
and sit in the dust,
for your glorious crowns
will soon be snatched from your heads."
19 The towns of the Negev will close their gates,
and no one will be able to open them.

KING JAMES VERSION

captive all of it, it shall be wholly carried away
captive.
20 Lift up your eyes, and behold them that come
from the north: where *is* the flock *that* was given
thee, thy beautiful flock?
21 What wilt thou say when he shall punish thee?
for thou hast taught them *to be* captains, *and* as chief
over thee: shall not sorrows take thee, as a woman in
travail?
22 And if thou say in thine heart, Wherefore come
these things upon me? For the greatness of thine iniquity are thy skirts discovered, *and* thy heels made
bare.
23 Can the Ethiopian change his skin, or the leopard his spots? *then* may ye also do good, that are accustomed to do evil.
24 Therefore will I scatter them as the stubble that
passeth away by the wind of the wilderness.
25 This *is* thy lot, the portion of thy measures from
me, saith the LORD; because thou hast forgotten me,
and trusted in falsehood.
26 Therefore will I discover thy skirts upon thy
face, that thy shame may appear.
27 I have seen thine adulteries, and thy neighings,
the lewdness of thy whoredom, *and* thine abominations on the hills in the fields. Woe unto thee, O Jerusalem! wilt thou not be made clean? when *shall it*
once *be?*

14 1 The word of the LORD that came to Jeremiah
concerning the dearth.
2 Judah mourneth, and the gates thereof languish;
they are black unto the ground; and the cry of Jerusalem is gone up.
3 And their nobles have sent their little ones to the
waters: they came to the pits, *and* found no water;
they returned with their vessels empty; they were
ashamed and confounded, and covered their heads.
4 Because the ground is chapt, for there was no rain
in the earth, the plowmen were ashamed, they covered their heads.
5 Yea, the hind also calved in the field, and forsook
it, because there was no grass.

NEW LIVING TRANSLATION

The people of Judah will be taken away as captives.
All will be carried into exile.

20 Open up your eyes and see
the armies marching down from the north!
Where is your flock—
your beautiful flock—
that he gave you to care for?
21 What will you say when the LORD takes the allies
you have cultivated
and appoints them as your rulers?
Pangs of anguish will grip you,
like those of a woman in labor!
22 You may ask yourself,
"Why is all this happening to me?"
It is because of your many sins!
That is why you have been stripped
and raped by invading armies.
23 Can an Ethiopian* change the color of his skin?
Can a leopard take away its spots?
Neither can you start doing good,
for you have always done evil.

24 "I will scatter you like chaff
that is blown away by the desert winds.
25 This is your allotment,
the portion I have assigned to you,"
says the LORD,
"for you have forgotten me,
putting your trust in false gods.
26 I myself will strip you
and expose you to shame.
27 I have seen your adultery and lust,
and your disgusting idol worship out in the
fields and on the hills.
What sorrow awaits you, Jerusalem!
How long before you are pure?"

Judah's Terrible Drought

14 This message came to Jeremiah from the
LORD, explaining why he was holding back the
rain:

2 "Judah wilts;
commerce at the city gates grinds to a halt.
All the people sit on the ground in mourning,
and a great cry rises from Jerusalem.
3 The nobles send servants to get water,
but all the wells are dry.
The servants return with empty pitchers,
confused and desperate,
covering their heads in grief.
4 The ground is parched
and cracked for lack of rain.
The farmers are deeply troubled;
they, too, cover their heads.
5 Even the doe abandons her newborn fawn
because there is no grass in the field.

13:23 Hebrew *a Cushite.*

KING JAMES VERSION

6 And the wild asses did stand in the high places,
they snuffed up the wind like dragons; their eyes did
fail, because *there was* no grass.
7 O LORD, though our iniquities testify against us,
do thou *it* for thy name's sake: for our backslidings
are many; we have sinned against thee.
8 O the hope of Israel, the saviour thereof in time of
trouble, why shouldest thou be as a stranger in the
land, and as a wayfaring man *that* turneth aside to
tarry for a night?
9 Why shouldest thou be as a man astonied, as a
mighty man *that* cannot save? yet thou, O LORD, *art*
in the midst of us, and we are called by thy name;
leave us not.
10 Thus saith the LORD unto this people, Thus have
they loved to wander, they have not refrained their
feet, therefore the LORD doth not accept them; he will
now remember their iniquity, and visit their sins.

11 Then said the LORD unto me, Pray not for this
people for *their* good.
12 When they fast, I will not hear their cry; and
when they offer burnt offering and an oblation, I will
not accept them: but I will consume them by the
sword, and by the famine, and by the pestilence.
13 Then said I, Ah, Lord GOD! behold, the prophets
say unto them, Ye shall not see the sword, neither
shall ye have famine; but I will give you assured peace
in this place.
14 Then the LORD said unto me, The prophets
prophesy lies in my name: I sent them not, neither
have I commanded them, neither spake unto them:
they prophesy unto you a false vision and divination,
and a thing of nought, and the deceit of their heart.
15 Therefore thus saith the LORD concerning the
prophets that prophesy in my name, and I sent them
not, yet they say, Sword and famine shall not be in
this land; By sword and famine shall those prophets
be consumed.
16 And the people to whom they prophesy shall be
cast out in the streets of Jerusalem because of the
famine and the sword; and they shall have none to
bury them, them, their wives, nor their sons, nor
their daughters: for I will pour their wickedness
upon them.
17 Therefore thou shalt say this word unto them;
Let mine eyes run down with tears night and day, and

NEW LIVING TRANSLATION

6 The wild donkeys stand on the bare hills
panting like thirsty jackals.
They strain their eyes looking for grass,
but there is none to be found."

7 The people say, "Our wickedness has caught
up with us, LORD,
but help us for the sake of your own
reputation.
We have turned away from you
and sinned against you again and again.
8 O Hope of Israel, our Savior in times of trouble,
why are you like a stranger to us?
Why are you like a traveler passing through
the land,
stopping only for the night?
9 Are you also confused?
Is our champion helpless to save us?
You are right here among us, LORD.
We are known as your people.
Please don't abandon us now!"

10 So this is what the LORD says to his people:
"You love to wander far from me
and do not restrain yourselves.
Therefore, I will no longer accept you
as my people.
Now I will remember all your wickedness
and will punish you for your sins."

The LORD Forbids Jeremiah to Intercede

11 Then the LORD said to me, "Do not pray for these
people anymore. 12 When they fast, I will pay no attention. When they present their burnt offerings and
grain offerings to me, I will not accept them. Instead, I
will devour them with war, famine, and disease."
13 Then I said, "O Sovereign LORD, their prophets
are telling them, 'All is well—no war or famine will
come. The LORD will surely send you peace.'"
14 Then the LORD said, "These prophets are telling
lies in my name. I did not send them or tell them to
speak. I did not give them any messages. They
prophesy of visions and revelations they have never
seen or heard. They speak foolishness made up in
their own lying hearts. 15 Therefore, this is what the
LORD says: I will punish these lying prophets, for they
have spoken in my name even though I never sent
them. They say that no war or famine will come, but
they themselves will die by war and famine! 16 As
for the people to whom they prophesy—their bodies
will be thrown out into the streets of Jerusalem, victims of famine and war. There will be no one left to
bury them. Husbands, wives, sons, and daughters—
all will be gone. For I will pour out their own wickedness on them. 17 Now, Jeremiah, say this to them:

"Night and day my eyes overflow with tears.
I cannot stop weeping,
for my virgin daughter—my precious people—

KING JAMES VERSION

let them not cease: for the virgin daughter of my people is broken with a great breach, with a very grievous blow.

18If I go forth into the field, then behold the slain with the sword! and if I enter into the city, then behold them that are sick with famine! yea, both the prophet and the priest go about into a land that they know not.

19Hast thou utterly rejected Judah? hath thy soul lothed Zion? why hast thou smitten us, and *there is* no healing for us? we looked for peace, and *there is* no good; and for the time of healing, and behold trouble!

20We acknowledge, O LORD, our wickedness, *and* the iniquity of our fathers: for we have sinned against thee.

21Do not abhor *us*, for thy name's sake, do not disgrace the throne of thy glory: remember, break not thy covenant with us.

22Are there *any* among the vanities of the Gentiles that can cause rain? or can the heavens give showers? *art* not thou he, O LORD our God? therefore we will wait upon thee: for thou hast made all these *things*.

15

1Then said the LORD unto me, Though Moses and Samuel stood before me, *yet* my mind *could* not *be* toward this people: cast *them* out of my sight, and let them go forth.

2And it shall come to pass, if they say unto thee, Whither shall we go forth? then thou shalt tell them, Thus saith the LORD; Such as *are* for death, to death; and such as *are* for the sword, to the sword; and such as *are* for the famine, to the famine; and such as *are* for the captivity, to the captivity.

3And I will appoint over them four kinds, saith the LORD: the sword to slay, and the dogs to tear, and the fowls of the heaven, and the beasts of the earth, to devour and destroy.

4And I will cause them to be removed into all kingdoms of the earth, because of Manasseh the son of Hezekiah king of Judah, for *that* which he did in Jerusalem.

5For who shall have pity upon thee, O Jerusalem? or who shall bemoan thee? or who shall go aside to ask how thou doest?

NEW LIVING TRANSLATION

has been struck down
and lies mortally wounded.
18 If I go out into the fields,
I see the bodies of people slaughtered
by the enemy.
If I walk the city streets,
I see people who have died of starvation.
The prophets and priests continue with their work,
but they don't know what they're doing."

A Prayer for Healing

19 LORD, have you completely rejected Judah?
Do you really hate Jerusalem?*
Why have you wounded us past all hope
of healing?
We hoped for peace, but no peace came.
We hoped for a time of healing, but found
only terror.
20 LORD, we confess our wickedness
and that of our ancestors, too.
We all have sinned against you.
21 For the sake of your reputation, LORD, do not
abandon us.
Do not disgrace your own glorious throne.
Please remember us,
and do not break your covenant with us.

22 Can any of the worthless foreign gods send
us rain?
Does it fall from the sky by itself?
No, you are the one, O LORD our God!
Only you can do such things.
So we will wait for you to help us.

Judah's Inevitable Doom

15 Then the LORD said to me, "Even if Moses and
Samuel stood before me pleading for these
people, I wouldn't help them. Away with them! Get
them out of my sight! 2And if they say to you, 'But
where can we go?' tell them, 'This is what the LORD
says:

"'Those who are destined for death, to death;
those who are destined for war, to war;
those who are destined for famine, to famine;
those who are destined for captivity,
to captivity.'

3"I will send four kinds of destroyers against
them," says the LORD. "I will send the sword to kill,
the dogs to drag away, the vultures to devour, and the
wild animals to finish up what is left. 4Because of the
wicked things Manasseh son of Hezekiah, king of
Judah, did in Jerusalem, I will make my people an
object of horror to all the kingdoms of the earth.

5 "Who will feel sorry for you, Jerusalem?
Who will weep for you?
Who will even bother to ask how you are?

14:19 Hebrew *Zion?*

KING JAMES VERSION

6 Thou hast forsaken me, saith the LORD, thou art gone backward: therefore will I stretch out my hand against thee, and destroy thee; I am weary with repenting.

7 And I will fan them with a fan in the gates of the land; I will bereave *them* of children, I will destroy my people, *since* they return not from their ways.

8 Their widows are increased to me above the sand of the seas: I have brought upon them against the mother of the young men a spoiler at noonday: I have caused *him* to fall upon it suddenly, and terrors upon the city.

9 She that hath borne seven languisheth: she hath given up the ghost; her sun is gone down while *it was* yet day: she hath been ashamed and confounded: and the residue of them will I deliver to the sword before their enemies, saith the LORD.

10 Woe is me, my mother, that thou hast borne me a man of strife and a man of contention to the whole earth! I have neither lent on usury, nor men have lent to me on usury; *yet* every one of them doth curse me.

11 The LORD said, Verily it shall be well with thy remnant; verily I will cause the enemy to entreat thee *well* in the time of evil and in the time of affliction.

12 Shall iron break the northern iron and the steel?

13 Thy substance and thy treasures will I give to the spoil without price, and *that* for all thy sins, even in all thy borders.

14 And I will make *thee* to pass with thine enemies into a land *which* thou knowest not: for a fire is kindled in mine anger, *which* shall burn upon you.

15 O LORD, thou knowest: remember me, and visit me, and revenge me of my persecutors; take me not away in thy longsuffering: know that for thy sake I have suffered rebuke.

NEW LIVING TRANSLATION

6 You have abandoned me
and turned your back on me,"
says the LORD.
"Therefore, I will raise my fist to destroy you.
I am tired of always giving you another chance.
7 I will winnow you like grain at the gates of your cities
and take away the children you hold dear.
I will destroy my own people,
because they refuse to change their evil ways.
8 There will be more widows
than the grains of sand on the seashore.
At noontime I will bring a destroyer
against the mothers of young men.
I will cause anguish and terror
to come upon them suddenly.
9 The mother of seven grows faint and gasps for breath;
her sun has gone down while it is still day.
She sits childless now,
disgraced and humiliated.
And I will hand over those who are left
to be killed by the enemy.
I, the LORD, have spoken!"

Jeremiah's Complaint

10 Then I said,

"What sorrow is mine, my mother.
Oh, that I had died at birth!
I am hated everywhere I go.
I am neither a lender who threatens to foreclose
nor a borrower who refuses to pay—
yet they all curse me."

11 The LORD replied,

"I will take care of you, Jeremiah.
Your enemies will ask you to plead on their behalf
in times of trouble and distress.
12 Can a man break a bar of iron from the north,
or a bar of bronze?
13 At no cost to them,
I will hand over your wealth and treasures
as plunder to your enemies,
for sin runs rampant in your land.
14 I will tell your enemies to take you
as captives to a foreign land.
For my anger blazes like a fire
that will burn forever.*"

15 Then I said,

"LORD, you know what's happening to me.
Please step in and help me. Punish my persecutors!
Please give me time; don't let me die young.
It's for your sake that I am suffering.

15:14 As in some Hebrew manuscripts (see also 17:4); most Hebrew manuscripts read *will burn against you.*

KING JAMES VERSION

16 Thy words were found, and I did eat them; and thy word was unto me the joy and rejoicing of mine heart: for I am called by thy name, O LORD God of hosts.

17 I sat not in the assembly of the mockers, nor rejoiced; I sat alone because of thy hand: for thou hast filled me with indignation.

18 Why is my pain perpetual, and my wound incurable, *which* refuseth to be healed? wilt thou be altogether unto me as a liar, *and as* waters *that* fail?

19 Therefore thus saith the LORD, If thou return, then will I bring thee again, *and* thou shalt stand before me: and if thou take forth the precious from the vile, thou shalt be as my mouth: let them return unto thee; but return not thou unto them.

20 And I will make thee unto this people a fenced brasen wall: and they shall fight against thee, but they shall not prevail against thee: for I *am* with thee to save thee and to deliver thee, saith the LORD.

21 And I will deliver thee out of the hand of the wicked, and I will redeem thee out of the hand of the terrible.

16 1 The word of the LORD came also unto me, saying,

2 Thou shalt not take thee a wife, neither shalt thou have sons or daughters in this place.

3 For thus saith the LORD concerning the sons and concerning the daughters that are born in this place, and concerning their mothers that bare them, and concerning their fathers that begat them in this land;

4 They shall die of grievous deaths; they shall not be lamented; neither shall they be buried; *but* they shall be as dung upon the face of the earth: and they shall be consumed by the sword, and by famine; and their carcases shall be meat for the fowls of heaven, and for the beasts of the earth.

5 For thus saith the LORD, Enter not into the house of mourning, neither go to lament nor bemoan them: for I have taken away my peace from this people, saith the LORD, *even* lovingkindness and mercies.

6 Both the great and the small shall die in this land: they shall not be buried, neither shall *men* lament for them, nor cut themselves, nor make themselves bald for them:

7 Neither shall *men* tear *themselves* for them in mourning, to comfort them for the dead; neither shall *men* give them the cup of consolation to drink for their father or for their mother.

NEW LIVING TRANSLATION

16 When I discovered your words, I devoured them.
They are my joy and my heart's delight,
for I bear your name,
O LORD God of Heaven's Armies.
17 I never joined the people in their merry feasts.
I sat alone because your hand was on me.
I was filled with indignation at their sins.
18 Why then does my suffering continue?
Why is my wound so incurable?
Your help seems as uncertain as a seasonal brook,
like a spring that has gone dry."

19 This is how the LORD responds:

"If you return to me, I will restore you
so you can continue to serve me.
If you speak good words rather than
worthless ones,
you will be my spokesman.
You must influence them;
do not let them influence you!
20 They will fight against you like an attacking army,
but I will make you as secure as a fortified
wall of bronze.
They will not conquer you,
for I am with you to protect and rescue you.
I, the LORD, have spoken!
21 Yes, I will certainly keep you safe from these
wicked men.
I will rescue you from their cruel hands."

Jeremiah Forbidden to Marry

16 The LORD gave me another message. He said,
2 "Do not get married or have children in this
place. 3 For this is what the LORD says about the children born here in this city and about their mothers
and fathers: 4 They will die from terrible diseases. No
one will mourn for them or bury them, and they will
lie scattered on the ground like manure. They will die
from war and famine, and their bodies will be food for
the vultures and wild animals."

Judah's Coming Punishment

5 This is what the LORD says: "Do not go to funerals to
mourn and show sympathy for these people, for I
have removed my protection and peace from them. I
have taken away my unfailing love and my mercy.
6 Both the great and the lowly will die in this land. No
one will bury them or mourn for them. Their friends
will not cut themselves in sorrow or shave their
heads in sadness. 7 No one will offer a meal to comfort those who mourn for the dead—not even at the
death of a mother or father. No one will send a cup of
wine to console them.

KING JAMES VERSION

8 Thou shalt not also go into the house of feasting,
to sit with them to eat and to drink.

9 For thus saith the LORD of hosts, the God of Israel;
Behold, I will cause to cease out of this place in your
eyes, and in your days, the voice of mirth, and the
voice of gladness, the voice of the bridegroom, and
the voice of the bride.

10 And it shall come to pass, when thou shalt shew
this people all these words, and they shall say unto
thee, Wherefore hath the LORD pronounced all this
great evil against us? or what *is* our iniquity? or what
is our sin that we have committed against the LORD
our God?

11 Then shalt thou say unto them, Because your
fathers have forsaken me, saith the LORD, and have
walked after other gods, and have served them, and
have worshipped them, and have forsaken me, and
have not kept my law;

12 And ye have done worse than your fathers; for,
behold, ye walk every one after the imagination of
his evil heart, that they may not hearken unto me:

13 Therefore will I cast you out of this land into a
land that ye know not, *neither* ye nor your fathers;
and there shall ye serve other gods day and night;
where I will not shew you favour.

14 Therefore, behold, the days come, saith the
LORD, that it shall no more be said, The LORD liveth,
that brought up the children of Israel out of the land
of Egypt;

15 But, The LORD liveth, that brought up the children of Israel from the land of the north, and from all
the lands whither he had driven them: and I will
bring them again into their land that I gave unto
their fathers.

16 Behold, I will send for many fishers, saith the
LORD, and they shall fish them; and after will I send
for many hunters, and they shall hunt them from
every mountain, and from every hill, and out of the
holes of the rocks.

17 For mine eyes *are* upon all their ways: they are
not hid from my face, neither is their iniquity hid
from mine eyes.

18 And first I will recompense their iniquity and
their sin double; because they have defiled my land,
they have filled mine inheritance with the carcases
of their detestable and abominable things.

19 O LORD, my strength, and my fortress, and my
refuge in the day of affliction, the Gentiles shall
come unto thee from the ends of the earth, and shall
say, Surely our fathers have inherited lies, vanity, and
things wherein *there is* no profit.

20 Shall a man make gods unto himself, and they
are no gods?

21 Therefore, behold, I will this once cause them to

NEW LIVING TRANSLATION

8 "And do not go to their feasts and parties. Do not
eat and drink with them at all. 9 For this is what the
LORD of Heaven's Armies, the God of Israel, says: In
your own lifetime, before your very eyes, I will put an
end to the happy singing and laughter in this land.
The joyful voices of bridegrooms and brides will no
longer be heard.

10 "When you tell the people all these things, they
will ask, 'Why has the LORD decreed such terrible
things against us? What have we done to deserve
such treatment? What is our sin against the LORD
our God?'

11 "Then you will give them the LORD's reply: 'It is
because your ancestors were unfaithful to me. They
worshiped other gods and served them. They abandoned me and did not obey my word. 12 And you are
even worse than your ancestors! You stubbornly follow your own evil desires and refuse to listen to me.
13 So I will throw you out of this land and send you
into a foreign land where you and your ancestors
have never been. There you can worship idols day
and night—and I will grant you no favors!'

Hope despite the Disaster

14 "But the time is coming," says the LORD, "when
people who are taking an oath will no longer say, 'As
surely as the LORD lives, who rescued the people of
Israel from the land of Egypt.' 15 Instead, they will say,
'As surely as the LORD lives, who brought the people
of Israel back to their own land from the land of the
north and from all the countries to which he had exiled them.' For I will bring them back to this land that
I gave their ancestors.

16 "But now I am sending for many fishermen who
will catch them," says the LORD. "I am sending for
hunters who will hunt them down in the mountains,
hills, and caves. 17 I am watching them closely, and I
see every sin. They cannot hope to hide from me.
18 I will double their punishment for all their sins, because they have defiled my land with lifeless images
of their detestable gods and have filled my territory
with their evil deeds."

Jeremiah's Prayer of Confidence

19 LORD, you are my strength and fortress,
my refuge in the day of trouble!
Nations from around the world
will come to you and say,
"Our ancestors left us a foolish heritage,
for they worshiped worthless idols.
20 Can people make their own gods?
These are not real gods at all!"

21 The LORD says,
"Now I will show them my power;
now I will show them my might.

KING JAMES VERSION

know, I will cause them to know mine hand and my
might; and they shall know that my name *is* The LORD.

17 1 The sin of Judah *is* written with a pen of iron,
and with the point of a diamond: *it is* graven
upon the table of their heart, and upon the horns of
your altars;
2 Whilst their children remember their altars and
their groves by the green trees upon the high hills.
3 O my mountain in the field, I will give thy substance *and* all thy treasures to the spoil, *and* thy high
places for sin, throughout all thy borders.
4 And thou, even thyself, shalt discontinue from
thine heritage that I gave thee; and I will cause thee
to serve thine enemies in the land which thou
knowest not: for ye have kindled a fire in mine anger,
which shall burn for ever.

5 Thus saith the LORD; Cursed *be* the man that
trusteth in man, and maketh flesh his arm, and
whose heart departeth from the LORD.
6 For he shall be like the heath in the desert, and
shall not see when good cometh; but shall inhabit
the parched places in the wilderness, *in* a salt land
and not inhabited.
7 Blessed *is* the man that trusteth in the LORD, and
whose hope the LORD is.
8 For he shall be as a tree planted by the waters, and
that spreadeth out her roots by the river, and shall
not see when heat cometh, but her leaf shall be
green; and shall not be careful in the year of drought,
neither shall cease from yielding fruit.
9 The heart *is* deceitful above all *things*, and desperately wicked: who can know it?
10 I the LORD search the heart, *I* try the reins, even
to give every man according to his ways, *and* according to the fruit of his doings.

11 *As* the partridge sitteth *on eggs*, and hatcheth
them not; *so* he that getteth riches, and not by right,

NEW LIVING TRANSLATION

At last they will know and understand
that I am the LORD.

Judah's Sin and Punishment

17 1 "The sin of Judah
is inscribed with an iron chisel—
engraved with a diamond point on their
stony hearts
and on the corners of their altars.
2 Even their children go to worship
at their pagan altars and Asherah poles,
beneath every green tree
and on every high hill.
3 So I will hand over my holy mountain—
along with all your wealth and treasures
and your pagan shrines—
as plunder to your enemies,
for sin runs rampant in your land.
4 The wonderful possession I have reserved for you
will slip from your hands.
I will tell your enemies to take you
as captives to a foreign land.
For my anger blazes like a fire
that will burn forever."

Wisdom from the LORD

5 This is what the LORD says:
"Cursed are those who put their trust
in mere humans,
who rely on human strength
and turn their hearts away from the LORD.
6 They are like stunted shrubs in the desert,
with no hope for the future.
They will live in the barren wilderness,
in an uninhabited salty land.
7 "But blessed are those who trust in the LORD
and have made the LORD their hope
and confidence.
8 They are like trees planted along a riverbank,
with roots that reach deep into the water.
Such trees are not bothered by the heat
or worried by long months of drought.
Their leaves stay green,
and they never stop producing fruit.
9 "The human heart is the most deceitful
of all things,
and desperately wicked.
Who really knows how bad it is?
10 But I, the LORD, search all hearts
and examine secret motives.
I give all people their due rewards,
according to what their actions deserve."

Jeremiah's Trust in the LORD

11 Like a partridge that hatches eggs she
has not laid,

shall leave them in the midst of his days, and at his end shall be a fool.

12 A glorious high throne from the beginning *is* the place of our sanctuary.

13 O LORD, the hope of Israel, all that forsake thee shall be ashamed, *and* they that depart from me shall be written in the earth, because they have forsaken the LORD, the fountain of living waters.

14 Heal me, O LORD, and I shall be healed; save me, and I shall be saved: for thou *art* my praise.

15 Behold, they say unto me, Where *is* the word of the LORD? let it come now.

16 As for me, I have not hastened from *being* a pastor to follow thee: neither have I desired the woeful day; thou knowest: that which came out of my lips was *right* before thee.

17 Be not a terror unto me: thou *art* my hope in the day of evil.

18 Let them be confounded that persecute me, but let not me be confounded: let them be dismayed, but let not me be dismayed: bring upon them the day of evil, and destroy them with double destruction.

19 Thus said the LORD unto me; Go and stand in the gate of the children of the people, whereby the kings of Judah come in, and by the which they go out, and in all the gates of Jerusalem;

20 And say unto them, Hear ye the word of the LORD, ye kings of Judah, and all Judah, and all the inhabitants of Jerusalem, that enter in by these gates:

21 Thus saith the LORD; Take heed to yourselves, and bear no burden on the sabbath day, nor bring *it* in by the gates of Jerusalem;

22 Neither carry forth a burden out of your houses on the sabbath day, neither do ye any work, but hallow ye the sabbath day, as I commanded your fathers.

23 But they obeyed not, neither inclined their ear, but made their neck stiff, that they might not hear, nor receive instruction.

24 And it shall come to pass, if ye diligently hearken unto me, saith the LORD, to bring in no burden through the gates of this city on the sabbath day, but hallow the sabbath day, to do no work therein;

25 Then shall there enter into the gates of this city kings and princes sitting upon the throne of David, riding in chariots and on horses, they, and their princes, the men of Judah, and the inhabitants of Jerusalem: and this city shall remain for ever.

so are those who get their wealth by
unjust means.
At midlife they will lose their riches;
in the end, they will become poor old fools.
12 But we worship at your throne—
eternal, high, and glorious!
13 O LORD, the hope of Israel,
all who turn away from you will be disgraced.
They will be buried in the dust of the earth,
for they have abandoned the LORD, the
fountain of living water.
14 O LORD, if you heal me, I will be truly healed;
if you save me, I will be truly saved.
My praises are for you alone!
15 People scoff at me and say,
"What is this 'message from the LORD'
you talk about?
Why don't your predictions come true?"

16 LORD, I have not abandoned my job
as a shepherd for your people.
I have not urged you to send disaster.
You have heard everything I've said.
17 LORD, don't terrorize me!
You alone are my hope in the day of disaster.
18 Bring shame and dismay on all who
persecute me,
but don't let me experience shame
and dismay.
Bring a day of terror on them.
Yes, bring double destruction upon them!

Observing the Sabbath

19 This is what the LORD said to me: "Go and stand in
the gates of Jerusalem, first in the gate where the
king goes in and out, and then in each of the other
gates. 20 Say to all the people, 'Listen to this message
from the LORD, you kings of Judah and all you people
of Judah and everyone living in Jerusalem. 21 This is
what the LORD says: Listen to my warning! Stop carrying on your trade at Jerusalem's gates on the Sabbath
day. 22 Do not do your work on the Sabbath, but make
it a holy day. I gave this command to your ancestors,
23 but they did not listen or obey. They stubbornly refused to pay attention or accept my discipline.

24 "'But if you obey me, says the LORD, and do not
carry on your trade at the gates or work on the Sabbath day, and if you keep it holy, 25 then kings and
their officials will go in and out of these gates forever.
There will always be a descendant of David sitting on
the throne here in Jerusalem. Kings and their officials
will always ride in and out among the people of Judah
in chariots and on horses, and this city will remain

KING JAMES VERSION

26 And they shall come from the cities of Judah, and from the places about Jerusalem, and from the land of Benjamin, and from the plain, and from the mountains, and from the south, bringing burnt offerings, and sacrifices, and meat offerings, and incense, and bringing sacrifices of praise, unto the house of the LORD.

27 But if ye will not hearken unto me to hallow the sabbath day, and not to bear a burden, even entering in at the gates of Jerusalem on the sabbath day; then will I kindle a fire in the gates thereof, and it shall devour the palaces of Jerusalem, and it shall not be quenched.

18 1 The word which came to Jeremiah from the LORD, saying,

2 Arise, and go down to the potter's house, and there I will cause thee to hear my words.

3 Then I went down to the potter's house, and, behold, he wrought a work on the wheels.

4 And the vessel that he made of clay was marred in the hand of the potter: so he made it again another vessel, as seemed good to the potter to make *it*.

5 Then the word of the LORD came to me, saying,

6 O house of Israel, cannot I do with you as this potter? saith the LORD. Behold, as the clay *is* in the potter's hand, so *are* ye in mine hand, O house of Israel.

7 *At what* instant I shall speak concerning a nation, and concerning a kingdom, to pluck up, and to pull down, and to destroy *it;*

8 If that nation, against whom I have pronounced, turn from their evil, I will repent of the evil that I thought to do unto them.

9 And *at what* instant I shall speak concerning a nation, and concerning a kingdom, to build and to plant *it;*

10 If it do evil in my sight, that it obey not my voice, then I will repent of the good, wherewith I said I would benefit them.

11 Now therefore go to, speak to the men of Judah, and to the inhabitants of Jerusalem, saying, Thus saith the LORD; Behold, I frame evil against you, and devise a device against you: return ye now every one from his evil way, and make your ways and your doings good.

12 And they said, There is no hope: but we will walk after our own devices, and we will every one do the imagination of his evil heart.

13 Therefore thus saith the LORD; Ask ye now among the heathen, who hath heard such things: the virgin of Israel hath done a very horrible thing.

14 Will *a man* leave the snow of Lebanon *which cometh* from the rock of the field? *or* shall the cold flowing waters that come from another place be forsaken?

15 Because my people hath forgotten me, they have burned incense to vanity, and they have caused them to stumble in their ways *from* the ancient paths, to walk in paths, *in* a way not cast up;

NEW LIVING TRANSLATION

forever. 26 And from all around Jerusalem, from the towns of Judah and Benjamin, from the western foothills* and the hill country and the Negev, the people will come with their burnt offerings and sacrifices. They will bring their grain offerings, frankincense, and thanksgiving offerings to the LORD's Temple.

27 "'But if you do not listen to me and refuse to keep the Sabbath holy, and if on the Sabbath day you bring loads of merchandise through the gates of Jerusalem just as on other days, then I will set fire to these gates. The fire will spread to the palaces, and no one will be able to put out the roaring flames.'"

The Potter and the Clay

18 The LORD gave another message to Jeremiah. He said, 2 "Go down to the potter's shop, and I will speak to you there." 3 So I did as he told me and found the potter working at his wheel. 4 But the jar he was making did not turn out as he had hoped, so he crushed it into a lump of clay again and started over.

5 Then the LORD gave me this message: 6 "O Israel, can I not do to you as this potter has done to his clay? As the clay is in the potter's hand, so are you in my hand. 7 If I announce that a certain nation or kingdom is to be uprooted, torn down, and destroyed, 8 but then that nation renounces its evil ways, I will not destroy it as I had planned. 9 And if I announce that I will plant and build up a certain nation or kingdom, 10 but then that nation turns to evil and refuses to obey me, I will not bless it as I said I would.

11 "Therefore, Jeremiah, go and warn all Judah and Jerusalem. Say to them, 'This is what the LORD says: I am planning disaster for you instead of good. So turn from your evil ways, each of you, and do what is right.'"

12 But the people replied, "Don't waste your breath. We will continue to live as we want to, stubbornly following our own evil desires."

13 So this is what the LORD says:

"Has anyone ever heard of such a thing,
even among the pagan nations?
My virgin daughter Israel
has done something terrible!
14 Does the snow ever disappear from the
mountaintops of Lebanon?
Do the cold streams flowing from those distant
mountains ever run dry?
15 But my people are not so reliable, for they have
deserted me;
they burn incense to worthless idols.
They have stumbled off the ancient highways
and walk in muddy paths.

17:26 Hebrew *the Shephelah.*

KING JAMES VERSION

16 To make their land desolate, *and* a perpetual hissing; every one that passeth thereby shall be astonished, and wag his head.

17 I will scatter them as with an east wind before the enemy; I will shew them the back, and not the face, in the day of their calamity.

18 Then said they, Come, and let us devise devices against Jeremiah; for the law shall not perish from the priest, nor counsel from the wise, nor the word from the prophet. Come, and let us smite him with the tongue, and let us not give heed to any of his words.

19 Give heed to me, O LORD, and hearken to the voice of them that contend with me.

20 Shall evil be recompensed for good? for they have digged a pit for my soul. Remember that I stood before thee to speak good for them, *and* to turn away thy wrath from them.

21 Therefore deliver up their children to the famine, and pour out their *blood* by the force of the sword; and let their wives be bereaved of their children, and *be* widows; and let their men be put to death; *let* their young men *be* slain by the sword in battle.

22 Let a cry be heard from their houses, when thou shalt bring a troop suddenly upon them: for they have digged a pit to take me, and hid snares for my feet.

23 Yet, LORD, thou knowest all their counsel against me to slay *me*: forgive not their iniquity, neither blot out their sin from thy sight, but let them be overthrown before thee; deal *thus* with them in the time of thine anger.

19 1 Thus saith the LORD, Go and get a potter's earthen bottle, and *take* of the ancients of the people, and of the ancients of the priests;

2 And go forth unto the valley of the son of Hinnom, which *is* by the entry of the east gate, and proclaim there the words that I shall tell thee,

3 And say, Hear ye the word of the LORD, O kings of Judah, and inhabitants of Jerusalem; Thus saith the LORD of hosts, the God of Israel; Behold, I will bring evil upon this place, the which whosoever heareth, his ears shall tingle.

4 Because they have forsaken me, and have estranged this place, and have burned incense in it unto other gods, whom neither they nor their fathers have known, nor the kings of Judah, and have filled this place with the blood of innocents;

5 They have built also the high places of Baal, to burn their sons with fire *for* burnt offerings unto Baal, which I commanded not, nor spake *it*, neither came *it* into my mind:

NEW LIVING TRANSLATION

16 Therefore, their land will become desolate,
a monument to their stupidity.
All who pass by will be astonished
and will shake their heads in amazement.
17 I will scatter my people before their enemies
as the east wind scatters dust.
And in all their trouble I will turn my back on them
and refuse to notice their distress."

A Plot against Jeremiah

18 Then the people said, "Come on, let's plot a way to stop Jeremiah. We have plenty of priests and wise men and prophets. We don't need him to teach the word and give us advice and prophecies. Let's spread rumors about him and ignore what he says."

19 LORD, hear me and help me!
Listen to what my enemies are saying.
20 Should they repay evil for good?
They have dug a pit to kill me,
though I pleaded for them
and tried to protect them from your anger.
21 So let their children starve!
Let them die by the sword!
Let their wives become childless widows.
Let their old men die in a plague,
and let their young men be killed in battle!
22 Let screaming be heard from their homes
as warriors come suddenly upon them.
For they have dug a pit for me
and have hidden traps along my path.
23 LORD, you know all about their murderous plots
against me.
Don't forgive their crimes and blot out their sins.
Let them die before you.
Deal with them in your anger.

Jeremiah's Shattered Jar

19 This is what the LORD said to me: "Go and buy
a clay jar. Then ask some of the leaders of the
people and of the priests to follow you. 2 Go out
through the Gate of Broken Pots to the garbage
dump in the valley of Ben-Hinnom, and give them
this message. 3 Say to them, 'Listen to this message
from the LORD, you kings of Judah and citizens of Jerusalem! This is what the LORD of Heaven's Armies,
the God of Israel, says: I will bring a terrible disaster
on this place, and the ears of those who hear about it
will ring!
4 " 'For Israel has forsaken me and turned this
valley into a place of wickedness. The people burn
incense to foreign gods—idols never before acknowledged by this generation, by their ancestors,
or by the kings of Judah. And they have filled this
place with the blood of innocent children. 5 They
have built pagan shrines to Baal, and there they burn
their sons as sacrifices to Baal. I have never commanded such a horrible deed; it never even crossed

KING JAMES VERSION

6 Therefore, behold, the days come, saith the LORD, that this place shall no more be called Tophet, nor The valley of the son of Hinnom, but The valley of slaughter.

7 And I will make void the counsel of Judah and Jerusalem in this place; and I will cause them to fall by the sword before their enemies, and by the hands of them that seek their lives: and their carcases will I give to be meat for the fowls of the heaven, and for the beasts of the earth.

8 And I will make this city desolate, and an hissing; every one that passeth thereby shall be astonished and hiss because of all the plagues thereof.

9 And I will cause them to eat the flesh of their sons and the flesh of their daughters, and they shall eat every one the flesh of his friend in the siege and straitness, wherewith their enemies, and they that seek their lives, shall straiten them.

10 Then shalt thou break the bottle in the sight of the men that go with thee.

11 And shalt say unto them, Thus saith the LORD of hosts; Even so will I break this people and this city, as *one* breaketh a potter's vessel, that cannot be made whole again: and they shall bury *them* in Tophet, till *there be* no place to bury.

12 Thus will I do unto this place, saith the LORD, and to the inhabitants thereof, and *even* make this city as Tophet:

13 And the houses of Jerusalem, and the houses of the kings of Judah, shall be defiled as the place of Tophet, because of all the houses upon whose roofs they have burned incense unto all the host of heaven, and have poured out drink offerings unto other gods.

14 Then came Jeremiah from Tophet, whither the LORD had sent him to prophesy; and he stood in the court of the LORD's house; and said to all the people,

15 Thus saith the LORD of hosts, the God of Israel; Behold, I will bring upon this city and upon all her towns all the evil that I have pronounced against it, because they have hardened their necks, that they might not hear my words.

20 1 Now Pashur the son of Immer the priest, who *was* also chief governor in the house of the LORD, heard that Jeremiah prophesied these things.

2 Then Pashur smote Jeremiah the prophet, and put him in the stocks that *were* in the high gate of Benjamin, which *was* by the house of the LORD.

3 And it came to pass on the morrow, that Pashur brought forth Jeremiah out of the stocks. Then said Jeremiah unto him, The LORD hath not called thy name Pashur, but Magor-missabib.

4 For thus saith the LORD, Behold, I will make thee a terror to thyself, and to all thy friends: and they shall fall by the sword of their enemies, and thine eyes shall behold *it:* and I will give all Judah into the hand of the king of Babylon, and he shall carry them captive into Babylon, and shall slay them with the sword.

NEW LIVING TRANSLATION

my mind to command such a thing! 6 So beware, for the time is coming, says the LORD, when this garbage dump will no longer be called Topheth or the valley of Ben-Hinnom, but the Valley of Slaughter.

7 "'For I will upset the careful plans of Judah and Jerusalem. I will allow the people to be slaughtered by invading armies, and I will leave their dead bodies as food for the vultures and wild animals. 8 I will reduce Jerusalem to ruins, making it a monument to their stupidity. All who pass by will be astonished and will gasp at the destruction they see there. 9 I will see to it that your enemies lay siege to the city until all the food is gone. Then those trapped inside will eat their own sons and daughters and friends. They will be driven to utter despair.'

10 "As these men watch you, Jeremiah, smash the jar you brought. 11 Then say to them, 'This is what the LORD of Heaven's Armies says: As this jar lies shattered, so I will shatter the people of Judah and Jerusalem beyond all hope of repair. They will bury the bodies here in Topheth, the garbage dump, until there is no more room for them. 12 This is what I will do to this place and its people, says the LORD. I will cause this city to become defiled like Topheth. 13 Yes, all the houses in Jerusalem, including the palace of Judah's kings, will become like Topheth—all the houses where you burned incense on the rooftops to your star gods, and where liquid offerings were poured out to your idols.'"

14 Then Jeremiah returned from Topheth, the garbage dump where he had delivered this message, and he stopped in front of the Temple of the LORD. He said to the people there, 15 "This is what the LORD of Heaven's Armies, the God of Israel, says: 'I will bring disaster upon this city and its surrounding towns as I promised, because you have stubbornly refused to listen to me.'"

Jeremiah and Pashhur

20 Now Pashhur son of Immer, the priest in charge of the Temple of the LORD, heard what Jeremiah was prophesying. 2 So he arrested Jeremiah the prophet and had him whipped and put in stocks at the Benjamin Gate of the LORD's Temple.

3 The next day, when Pashhur finally released him, Jeremiah said, "Pashhur, the LORD has changed your name. From now on you are to be called 'The Man Who Lives in Terror.'* 4 For this is what the LORD says: 'I will send terror upon you and all your friends, and you will watch as they are slaughtered by the swords of the enemy. I will hand the people of Judah over to the king of Babylon. He will take them captive to Babylon or run them through with the sword.

20:3 Hebrew *Magor-missabib,* which means "surrounded by terror"; also in 20:10.

KING JAMES VERSION

5 Moreover I will deliver all the strength of this city,
and all the labours thereof, and all the precious things
thereof, and all the treasures of the kings of Judah will
I give into the hand of their enemies, which shall spoil
them, and take them, and carry them to Babylon.
6 And thou, Pashur, and all that dwell in thine
house shall go into captivity: and thou shalt come to
Babylon, and there thou shalt die, and shalt be buried
there, thou, and all thy friends, to whom thou hast
prophesied lies.
7 O LORD, thou hast deceived me, and I was deceived: thou art stronger than I, and hast prevailed: I
am in derision daily, every one mocketh me.
8 For since I spake, I cried out, I cried violence and
spoil; because the word of the LORD was made a reproach unto me, and a derision, daily.
9 Then I said, I will not make mention of him, nor
speak any more in his name. But *his word* was in
mine heart as a burning fire shut up in my bones, and
I was weary with forbearing, and I could not *stay*.
10 For I heard the defaming of many, fear on every
side. Report, *say they*, and we will report it. All
my familiars watched for my halting, *saying*, Peradventure he will be enticed, and we shall prevail
against him, and we shall take our revenge on him.
11 But the LORD *is* with me as a mighty terrible one:
therefore my persecutors shall stumble, and they
shall not prevail: they shall be greatly ashamed; for
they shall not prosper: *their* everlasting confusion
shall never be forgotten.
12 But, O LORD of hosts, that triest the righteous,
and seest the reins and the heart, let me see thy vengeance on them: for unto thee have I opened my
cause.
13 Sing unto the LORD, praise ye the LORD: for he
hath delivered the soul of the poor from the hand of
evildoers.
14 Cursed *be* the day wherein I was born: let not the
day wherein my mother bare me be blessed.
15 Cursed *be* the man who brought tidings to my
father, saying, A man child is born unto thee; making
him very glad.
16 And let that man be as the cities which the LORD
overthrew, and repented not: and let him hear the cry
in the morning, and the shouting at noontide;
17 Because he slew me not from the womb; or that

NEW LIVING TRANSLATION

5 And I will let your enemies plunder Jerusalem. All
the famed treasures of the city—the precious jewels
and gold and silver of your kings—will be carried off
to Babylon. 6 As for you, Pashhur, you and all your
household will go as captives to Babylon. There you
will die and be buried, you and all your friends to
whom you prophesied that everything would be all
right.'"

Jeremiah's Complaint

7 O LORD, you misled me,
and I allowed myself to be misled.
You are stronger than I am,
and you overpowered me.
Now I am mocked every day;
everyone laughs at me.
8 When I speak, the words burst out.
"Violence and destruction!" I shout.
So these messages from the LORD
have made me a household joke.
9 But if I say I'll never mention the LORD
or speak in his name,
his word burns in my heart like a fire.
It's like a fire in my bones!
I am worn out trying to hold it in!
I can't do it!
10 I have heard the many rumors about me.
They call me "The Man Who Lives in Terror."
They threaten, "If you say anything, we will
report it."
Even my old friends are watching me,
waiting for a fatal slip.
"He will trap himself," they say,
"and then we will get our revenge on him."

11 But the LORD stands beside me like a great warrior.
Before him my persecutors will stumble.
They cannot defeat me.
They will fail and be thoroughly humiliated.
Their dishonor will never be forgotten.
12 O LORD of Heaven's Armies,
you test those who are righteous,
and you examine the deepest thoughts
and secrets.
Let me see your vengeance against them,
for I have committed my cause to you.
13 Sing to the LORD!
Praise the LORD!
For though I was poor and needy,
he rescued me from my oppressors.
14 Yet I curse the day I was born!
May no one celebrate the day of my birth.
15 I curse the messenger who told my father,
"Good news—you have a son!"
16 Let him be destroyed like the cities of old
that the LORD overthrew without mercy.
Terrify him all day long with battle shouts,
17 because he did not kill me at birth.

my mother might have been my grave, and her womb *to be* always great *with me.*

18 Wherefore came I forth out of the womb to see labour and sorrow, that my days should be consumed with shame?

21

1 The word which came unto Jeremiah from the LORD, when king Zedekiah sent unto him Pashur the son of Melchiah, and Zephaniah the son of Maaseiah the priest, saying,

2 Inquire, I pray thee, of the LORD for us; for Nebuchadrezzar king of Babylon maketh war against us; if so be that the LORD will deal with us according to all his wondrous works, that he may go up from us.

3 Then said Jeremiah unto them, Thus shall ye say to Zedekiah:

4 Thus saith the LORD God of Israel; Behold, I will turn back the weapons of war that *are* in your hands, wherewith ye fight against the king of Babylon, and *against* the Chaldeans, which besiege you without the walls, and I will assemble them into the midst of this city.

5 And I myself will fight against you with an outstretched hand and with a strong arm, even in anger, and in fury, and in great wrath.

6 And I will smite the inhabitants of this city, both man and beast: they shall die of a great pestilence.

7 And afterward, saith the LORD, I will deliver Zedekiah king of Judah, and his servants, and the people, and such as are left in this city from the pestilence, from the sword, and from the famine, into the hand of Nebuchadrezzar king of Babylon, and into the hand of their enemies, and into the hand of those that seek their life: and he shall smite them with the edge of the sword; he shall not spare them, neither have pity, nor have mercy.

8 And unto this people thou shalt say, Thus saith the LORD; Behold, I set before you the way of life, and the way of death.

9 He that abideth in this city shall die by the sword, and by the famine, and by the pestilence: but he that goeth out, and falleth to the Chaldeans that besiege you, he shall live, and his life shall be unto him for a prey.

10 For I have set my face against this city for evil, and not for good, saith the LORD: it shall be given into the hand of the king of Babylon, and he shall burn it with fire.

11 And touching the house of the king of Judah, *say,* Hear ye the word of the LORD;

12 O house of David, thus saith the LORD; Execute judgment in the morning, and deliver *him that is*

Oh, that I had died in my mother's womb,
  that her body had been my grave!
18 Why was I ever born?
  My entire life has been filled
  with trouble, sorrow, and shame.

No Deliverance from Babylon

21

The LORD spoke through Jeremiah when King Zedekiah sent Pashhur son of Malkijah and Zephaniah son of Maaseiah, the priest, to speak with him. They begged Jeremiah, 2 "Please speak to the LORD for us and ask him to help us. King Nebuchadnezzar* of Babylon is attacking Judah. Perhaps the LORD will be gracious and do a mighty miracle as he has done in the past. Perhaps he will force Nebuchadnezzar to withdraw his armies."

3 Jeremiah replied, "Go back to King Zedekiah and tell him, 4 'This is what the LORD, the God of Israel, says: I will make your weapons useless against the king of Babylon and the Babylonians* who are outside your walls attacking you. In fact, I will bring your enemies right into the heart of this city. 5 I myself will fight against you with a strong hand and a powerful arm, for I am very angry. You have made me furious! 6 I will send a terrible plague upon this city, and both people and animals will die. 7 And after all that, says the LORD, I will hand over King Zedekiah, his staff, and everyone else in the city who survives the disease, war, and famine. I will hand them over to King Nebuchadnezzar of Babylon and to their other enemies. He will slaughter them and show them no mercy, pity, or compassion.'

8 "Tell all the people, 'This is what the LORD says: Take your choice of life or death! 9 Everyone who stays in Jerusalem will die from war, famine, or disease, but those who go out and surrender to the Babylonians will live. Their reward will be life! 10 For I have decided to bring disaster and not good upon this city, says the LORD. It will be handed over to the king of Babylon, and he will reduce it to ashes.'

Judgment on Judah's Kings

11 "Say to the royal family of Judah, 'Listen to this message from the LORD! 12 This is what the LORD says to the dynasty of David:

"'Give justice each morning to the people
  you judge!
Help those who have been robbed;
  rescue them from their oppressors.

21:2 Hebrew *Nebuchadrezzar,* a variant spelling of Nebuchadnezzar; also in 21:7. **21:4** Or *Chaldeans;* also in 21:9.

KING JAMES VERSION

spoiled out of the hand of the oppressor, lest my fury go out like fire, and burn that none can quench *it*, because of the evil of your doings.

13 Behold, I *am* against thee, O inhabitant of the valley, *and* rock of the plain, saith the LORD; which say, Who shall come down against us? or who shall enter into our habitations?

14 But I will punish you according to the fruit of your doings, saith the LORD: and I will kindle a fire in the forest thereof, and it shall devour all things round about it.

22

1 Thus saith the LORD; Go down to the house of the king of Judah, and speak there this word,

2 And say, Hear the word of the LORD, O king of Judah, that sittest upon the throne of David, thou, and thy servants, and thy people that enter in by these gates:

3 Thus saith the LORD; Execute ye judgment and righteousness, and deliver the spoiled out of the hand of the oppressor: and do no wrong, do no violence to the stranger, the fatherless, nor the widow, neither shed innocent blood in this place.

4 For if ye do this thing indeed, then shall there enter in by the gates of this house kings sitting upon the throne of David, riding in chariots and on horses, he, and his servants, and his people.

5 But if ye will not hear these words, I swear by myself, saith the LORD, that this house shall become a desolation.

6 For thus saith the LORD unto the king's house of Judah; Thou *art* Gilead unto me, *and* the head of Lebanon: *yet* surely I will make thee a wilderness, *and* cities *which* are not inhabited.

7 And I will prepare destroyers against thee, every one with his weapons: and they shall cut down thy choice cedars, and cast *them* into the fire.

8 And many nations shall pass by this city, and they shall say every man to his neighbour, Wherefore hath the LORD done thus unto this great city?

9 Then they shall answer, Because they have forsaken the covenant of the LORD their God, and worshipped other gods, and served them.

10 Weep ye not for the dead, neither bemoan him: *but* weep sore for him that goeth away: for he shall return no more, nor see his native country.

NEW LIVING TRANSLATION

Otherwise, my anger will burn like an
unquenchable fire
because of all your sins.
13 I will personally fight against the people
in Jerusalem,
that mighty fortress—
the people who boast, "No one can touch us here.
No one can break in here."
14 And I myself will punish you for your sinfulness,
says the LORD.
I will light a fire in your forests
that will burn up everything around you.'"

A Message for Judah's Kings

22

This is what the LORD said to me: "Go over and speak directly to the king of Judah. Say to him, 2 'Listen to this message from the LORD, you king of Judah, sitting on David's throne. Let your attendants and your people listen, too. 3 This is what the LORD says: Be fair-minded and just. Do what is right! Help those who have been robbed; rescue them from their oppressors. Quit your evil deeds! Do not mistreat foreigners, orphans, and widows. Stop murdering the innocent! 4 If you obey me, there will always be a descendant of David sitting on the throne here in Jerusalem. The king will ride through the palace gates in chariots and on horses, with his parade of attendants and subjects. 5 But if you refuse to pay attention to this warning, I swear by my own name, says the LORD, that this palace will become a pile of rubble.'"

A Message about the Palace

6 Now this is what the LORD says concerning Judah's royal palace:

"I love you as much as fruitful Gilead
and the green forests of Lebanon.
But I will turn you into a desert,
with no one living within your walls.
7 I will call for wreckers,
who will bring out their tools to
dismantle you.
They will tear out all your fine cedar beams
and throw them on the fire.

8 "People from many nations will pass by the ruins of this city and say to one another, 'Why did the LORD destroy such a great city?' 9 And the answer will be, 'Because they violated their covenant with the LORD their God by worshiping other gods.'"

A Message about Jehoahaz

10 Do not weep for the dead king or mourn his loss.
Instead, weep for the captive king being
led away!
For he will never return to see his native
land again.

KING JAMES VERSION

11For thus saith the LORD touching Shallum the son of Josiah king of Judah, which reigned instead of Josiah his father, which went forth out of this place; He shall not return thither any more:

12But he shall die in the place whither they have led him captive, and shall see this land no more.

13Woe unto him that buildeth his house by unrighteousness, and his chambers by wrong; *that* useth his neighbour's service without wages, and giveth him not for his work;

14That saith, I will build me a wide house and large chambers, and cutteth him out windows; and *it is* cieled with cedar, and painted with vermilion.

15Shalt thou reign, because thou closest *thyself* in cedar? did not thy father eat and drink, and do judgment and justice, *and* then *it was* well with him?

16He judged the cause of the poor and needy; then *it was* well *with him: was* not this to know me? saith the LORD.

17But thine eyes and thine heart *are* not but for thy covetousness, and for to shed innocent blood, and for oppression, and for violence, to do *it*.

18Therefore thus saith the LORD concerning Jehoiakim the son of Josiah king of Judah; They shall not lament for him, *saying,* Ah my brother! or, Ah sister! they shall not lament for him, *saying,* Ah lord! or, Ah his glory!

19He shall be buried with the burial of an ass, drawn and cast forth beyond the gates of Jerusalem.

20Go up to Lebanon, and cry; and lift up thy voice in Bashan, and cry from the passages: for all thy lovers are destroyed.

21I spake unto thee in thy prosperity; *but* thou saidst, I will not hear. This *hath been* thy manner from thy youth, that thou obeyedst not my voice.

22The wind shall eat up all thy pastors, and thy lovers shall go into captivity: surely then shalt thou be ashamed and confounded for all thy wickedness.

NEW LIVING TRANSLATION

11For this is what the LORD says about Jehoahaz,*
who succeeded his father, King Josiah, and was taken
away as a captive: "He will never return. 12He will
die in a distant land and will never again see his own
country."

A Message about Jehoiakim

13 And the LORD says, "What sorrow awaits
Jehoiakim,*
who builds his palace with forced labor.*
He builds injustice into its walls,
for he makes his neighbors work for nothing.
He does not pay them for their labor.
14 He says, 'I will build a magnificent palace
with huge rooms and many windows.
I will panel it throughout with fragrant cedar
and paint it a lovely red.'
15 But a beautiful cedar palace does not make
a great king!
Your father, Josiah, also had plenty to eat
and drink.
But he was just and right in all his dealings.
That is why God blessed him.
16 He gave justice and help to the poor and needy,
and everything went well for him.
Isn't that what it means to know me?"
says the LORD.
17 "But you! You have eyes only for greed
and dishonesty!
You murder the innocent,
oppress the poor, and reign ruthlessly."

18Therefore, this is what the LORD says about Jehoiakim, son of King Josiah:

"The people will not mourn for him, crying
to one another,
'Alas, my brother! Alas, my sister!'
His subjects will not mourn for him, crying,
'Alas, our master is dead! Alas, his splendor
is gone!'
19 He will be buried like a dead donkey—
dragged out of Jerusalem and dumped
outside the gates!
20 Weep for your allies in Lebanon.
Shout for them in Bashan.
Search for them in the regions east of the river.*
See, they are all destroyed.
Not one is left to help you.
21 I warned you when you were prosperous,
but you replied, 'Don't bother me.'
You have been that way since childhood—
you simply will not obey me!
22 And now the wind will blow away your allies.
All your friends will be taken away as captives.
Surely then you will see your wickedness
and be ashamed.

22:11 Hebrew *Shallum,* another name for Jehoahaz. **22:13a** The brother and successor of the exiled Jehoahaz. See 22:18. **22:13b** Hebrew *by unrighteousness.* **22:20** Or *in Abarim.*

KING JAMES VERSION

23 O inhabitant of Lebanon, that makest thy nest in
the cedars, how gracious shalt thou be when pangs
come upon thee, the pain as of a woman in travail!

24 *As* I live, saith the LORD, though Coniah the son
of Jehoiakim king of Judah were the signet upon my
right hand, yet would I pluck thee thence;
25 And I will give thee into the hand of them that
seek thy life, and into the hand *of them* whose face
thou fearest, even into the hand of Nebuchadrezzar
king of Babylon, and into the hand of the Chaldeans.
26 And I will cast thee out, and thy mother that bare
thee, into another country, where ye were not born;
and there shall ye die.
27 But to the land whereunto they desire to return,
thither shall they not return.
28 *Is* this man Coniah a despised broken idol? *is he*
a vessel wherein *is* no pleasure? wherefore are they
cast out, he and his seed, and are cast into a land
which they know not?
29 O earth, earth, earth, hear the word of the LORD.
30 Thus saith the LORD, Write ye this man childless,
a man *that* shall not prosper in his days: for no man
of his seed shall prosper, sitting upon the throne of
David, and ruling any more in Judah.

23 1 Woe be unto the pastors that destroy and
scatter the sheep of my pasture! saith the
LORD.
2 Therefore thus saith the LORD God of Israel
against the pastors that feed my people; Ye have scattered my flock, and driven them away, and have not
visited them: behold, I will visit upon you the evil of
your doings, saith the LORD.
3 And I will gather the remnant of my flock out of
all countries whither I have driven them, and will
bring them again to their folds; and they shall be
fruitful and increase.
4 And I will set up shepherds over them which shall
feed them: and they shall fear no more, nor be dismayed, neither shall they be lacking, saith the LORD.
5 Behold, the days come, saith the LORD, that I will
raise unto David a righteous Branch, and a King shall

NEW LIVING TRANSLATION

23 It may be nice to live in a beautiful palace
paneled with wood from the cedars
of Lebanon,
but soon you will groan with pangs of anguish—
anguish like that of a woman in labor.

A Message for Jehoiachin

24 "As surely as I live," says the LORD, "I will abandon
you, Jehoiachin* son of Jehoiakim, king of Judah.
Even if you were the signet ring on my right hand,
I would pull you off. 25 I will hand you over to those
who seek to kill you, those you so desperately fear—
to King Nebuchadnezzar* of Babylon and the mighty
Babylonian* army. 26 I will expel you and your mother
from this land, and you will die in a foreign country,
not in your native land. 27 You will never again return
to the land you yearn for.

28 "Why is this man Jehoiachin like a discarded,
broken jar?
Why are he and his children to be exiled
to a foreign land?
29 O earth, earth, earth!
Listen to this message from the LORD!
30 This is what the LORD says:
'Let the record show that this man Jehoiachin
was childless.
He is a failure,
for none of his children will succeed him
on the throne of David
to rule over Judah.'

The Righteous Descendant

23 "What sorrow awaits the leaders of my people—the shepherds of my sheep—for they
have destroyed and scattered the very ones they were
expected to care for," says the LORD.
2 Therefore, this is what the LORD, the God of Israel,
says to these shepherds: "Instead of caring for my
flock and leading them to safety, you have deserted
them and driven them to destruction. Now I will
pour out judgment on you for the evil you have done
to them. 3 But I will gather together the remnant of
my flock from the countries where I have driven
them. I will bring them back to their own sheepfold,
and they will be fruitful and increase in number.
4 Then I will appoint responsible shepherds who will
care for them, and they will never be afraid again.
Not a single one will be lost or missing. I, the LORD,
have spoken!

5 "For the time is coming,"
says the LORD,
"when I will raise up a righteous descendant*
from King David's line.
He will be a King who rules with wisdom.

22:24 Hebrew *Coniah,* a variant spelling of Jehoiachin; also 22:28.
22:25a Hebrew *Nebuchadrezzar,* a variant spelling of Nebuchadnezzar.
22:25b Or *Chaldean.* **23:5** Hebrew *a righteous branch.*

KING JAMES VERSION

reign and prosper, and shall execute judgment and justice in the earth.

6 In his days Judah shall be saved, and Israel shall dwell safely: and this *is* his name whereby he shall be called, THE LORD OUR RIGHTEOUSNESS.

7 Therefore, behold, the days come, saith the LORD, that they shall no more say, The LORD liveth, which brought up the children of Israel out of the land of Egypt;

8 But, The LORD liveth, which brought up and which led the seed of the house of Israel out of the north country, and from all countries whither I had driven them; and they shall dwell in their own land.

9 Mine heart within me is broken because of the prophets; all my bones shake; I am like a drunken man, and like a man whom wine hath overcome, because of the LORD, and because of the words of his holiness.

10 For the land is full of adulterers; for because of swearing the land mourneth; the pleasant places of the wilderness are dried up, and their course is evil, and their force *is* not right.

11 For both prophet and priest are profane; yea, in my house have I found their wickedness, saith the LORD.

12 Wherefore their way shall be unto them as slippery *ways* in the darkness: they shall be driven on, and fall therein: for I will bring evil upon them, *even* the year of their visitation, saith the LORD.

13 And I have seen folly in the prophets of Samaria; they prophesied in Baal, and caused my people Israel to err.

14 I have seen also in the prophets of Jerusalem an horrible thing: they commit adultery, and walk in lies: they strengthen also the hands of evildoers, that none doth return from his wickedness: they are all of them unto me as Sodom, and the inhabitants thereof as Gomorrah.

15 Therefore thus saith the LORD of hosts concerning the prophets; Behold, I will feed them with

NEW LIVING TRANSLATION

He will do what is just and right
throughout the land.
6 And this will be his name:
'The LORD Is Our Righteousness.'*
In that day Judah will be saved,
and Israel will live in safety.

7 "In that day," says the LORD, "when people are
taking an oath, they will no longer say, 'As surely as
the LORD lives, who rescued the people of Israel from
the land of Egypt.' 8 Instead, they will say, 'As surely
as the LORD lives, who brought the people of Israel
back to their own land from the land of the north and
from all the countries to which he had exiled them.'
Then they will live in their own land."

Judgment on False Prophets

9 My heart is broken because of the false prophets,
and my bones tremble.
I stagger like a drunkard,
like someone overcome by wine,
because of the holy words
the LORD has spoken against them.
10 For the land is full of adultery,
and it lies under a curse.
The land itself is in mourning—
its wilderness pastures are dried up.
For they all do evil
and abuse what power they have.

11 "Even the priests and prophets
are ungodly, wicked men.
I have seen their despicable acts
right here in my own Temple,"
says the LORD.
12 "Therefore, the paths they take
will become slippery.
They will be chased through the dark,
and there they will fall.
For I will bring disaster upon them
at the time fixed for their punishment.
I, the LORD, have spoken!

13 "I saw that the prophets of Samaria were
terribly evil,
for they prophesied in the name of Baal
and led my people of Israel into sin.
14 But now I see that the prophets of Jerusalem
are even worse!
They commit adultery and love dishonesty.
They encourage those who are doing evil
so that no one turns away from their sins.
These prophets are as wicked
as the people of Sodom and Gomorrah
once were."

15 Therefore, this is what the LORD of Heaven's Armies says concerning the prophets:

23:6 Hebrew *Yahweh Tsidqenu.*

KING JAMES VERSION

wormwood, and make them drink the water of gall:
for from the prophets of Jerusalem is profaneness
gone forth into all the land.

16 Thus saith the LORD of hosts, Hearken not unto
the words of the prophets that prophesy unto you:
they make you vain: they speak a vision of their own
heart, *and* not out of the mouth of the LORD.

17 They say still unto them that despise me, The
LORD hath said, Ye shall have peace; and they say
unto every one that walketh after the imagination of
his own heart, No evil shall come upon you.

18 For who hath stood in the counsel of the LORD,
and hath perceived and heard his word? who hath
marked his word, and heard *it?*

19 Behold, a whirlwind of the LORD is gone forth in
fury, even a grievous whirlwind: it shall fall grievously upon the head of the wicked.

20 The anger of the LORD shall not return, until
he have executed, and till he have performed the
thoughts of his heart: in the latter days ye shall consider it perfectly.

21 I have not sent these prophets, yet they ran: I
have not spoken to them, yet they prophesied.

22 But if they had stood in my counsel, and had
caused my people to hear my words, then they
should have turned them from their evil way, and
from the evil of their doings.

23 *Am* I a God at hand, saith the LORD, and not a God
afar off?

24 Can any hide himself in secret places that I shall
not see him? saith the LORD. Do not I fill heaven and
earth? saith the LORD.

25 I have heard what the prophets said, that prophesy lies in my name, saying, I have dreamed, I have
dreamed.

26 How long shall *this* be in the heart of the prophets that prophesy lies? yea, *they are* prophets of the
deceit of their own heart;

27 Which think to cause my people to forget my
name by their dreams which they tell every man to
his neighbour, as their fathers have forgotten my
name for Baal.

28 The prophet that hath a dream, let him tell a
dream; and he that hath my word, let him speak my
word faithfully. What *is* the chaff to the wheat? saith
the LORD.

NEW LIVING TRANSLATION

"I will feed them with bitterness
and give them poison to drink.
For it is because of Jerusalem's prophets
that wickedness has filled this land."

16 This is what the LORD of Heaven's Armies says to
his people:

"Do not listen to these prophets when they
prophesy to you,
filling you with futile hopes.
They are making up everything they say.
They do not speak for the LORD!
17 They keep saying to those who despise my word,
'Don't worry! The LORD says you will
have peace!'
And to those who stubbornly follow their
own desires,
they say, 'No harm will come your way!'
18 "Have any of these prophets been in the
LORD's presence
to hear what he is really saying?
Has even one of them cared enough to listen?
19 Look! The LORD's anger bursts out like a storm,
a whirlwind that swirls down on the heads of
the wicked.
20 The anger of the LORD will not diminish
until it has finished all he has planned.
In the days to come
you will understand all this very clearly.
21 "I have not sent these prophets,
yet they run around claiming to speak for me.
I have given them no message,
yet they go on prophesying.
22 If they had stood before me and listened to me,
they would have spoken my words,
and they would have turned my people
from their evil ways and deeds.
23 Am I a God who is only close at hand?"
says the LORD.
"No, I am far away at the same time.
24 Can anyone hide from me in a secret place?
Am I not everywhere in all the heavens
and earth?"
says the LORD.

25 "I have heard these prophets say, 'Listen to the
dream I had from God last night.' And then they proceed to tell lies in my name.
26 How long will this go
on? If they are prophets, they are prophets of deceit,
inventing everything they say.
27 By telling these false
dreams, they are trying to get my people to forget me,
just as their ancestors did by worshiping the idols
of Baal.

28 "Let these false prophets tell their dreams,
but let my true messengers faithfully proclaim
my every word.
There is a difference between straw and grain!

KING JAMES VERSION

29 *Is* not my word like as a fire? saith the LORD; and
like a hammer *that* breaketh the rock in pieces?

30 Therefore, behold, I *am* against the prophets,
saith the LORD, that steal my words every one from
his neighbour.

31 Behold, I *am* against the prophets, saith the
LORD, that use their tongues, and say, He saith.

32 Behold, I *am* against them that prophesy false
dreams, saith the LORD, and do tell them, and cause
my people to err by their lies, and by their lightness;
yet I sent them not, nor commanded them: therefore
they shall not profit this people at all, saith the LORD.

33 And when this people, or the prophet, or a priest,
shall ask thee, saying, What *is* the burden of the
LORD? thou shalt then say unto them, What burden?
I will even forsake you, saith the LORD.

34 And *as for* the prophet, and the priest, and the
people, that shall say, The burden of the LORD, I will
even punish that man and his house.

35 Thus shall ye say every one to his neighbour, and
every one to his brother, What hath the LORD answered? and, What hath the LORD spoken?

36 And the burden of the LORD shall ye mention no
more: for every man's word shall be his burden; for
ye have perverted the words of the living God, of the
LORD of hosts our God.

37 Thus shalt thou say to the prophet, What hath
the LORD answered thee? and, What hath the LORD
spoken?

38 But since ye say, The burden of the LORD; therefore thus saith the LORD; Because ye say this word,
The burden of the LORD, and I have sent unto you,
saying, Ye shall not say, The burden of the LORD;

39 Therefore, behold, I, even I, will utterly forget
you, and I will forsake you, and the city that I gave you
and your fathers, *and cast you* out of my presence:

40 And I will bring an everlasting reproach upon
you, and a perpetual shame, which shall not be forgotten.

24 1 The LORD shewed me, and, behold, two baskets of figs *were* set before the temple of the
LORD, after that Nebuchadrezzar king of Babylon had
carried away captive Jeconiah the son of Jehoiakim
king of Judah, and the princes of Judah, with the carpenters and smiths, from Jerusalem, and had brought
them to Babylon.

2 One basket *had* very good figs, *even* like the figs
that are first ripe: and the other basket *had* very
naughty figs, which could not be eaten, they were
so bad.

3 Then said the LORD unto me, What seest thou, Jeremiah? And I said, Figs; the good figs, very good; and
the evil, very evil, that cannot be eaten, they are so evil.

NEW LIVING TRANSLATION

29 Does not my word burn like fire?"
says the LORD.
"Is it not like a mighty hammer
that smashes a rock to pieces?

30 "Therefore," says the LORD, "I am against these
prophets who steal messages from each other and
claim they are from me.
31 I am against these smooth-tongued prophets who say, 'This prophecy is from
the LORD!'
32 I am against these false prophets. Their
imaginary dreams are flagrant lies that lead my
people into sin. I did not send or appoint them, and
they have no message at all for my people. I, the LORD,
have spoken!

False Prophecies and False Prophets

33 "Suppose one of the people or one of the prophets
or priests asks you, 'What prophecy has the LORD
burdened you with now?' You must reply, 'You are the
burden!* The LORD says he will abandon you!'

34 "If any prophet, priest, or anyone else says, 'I
have a prophecy from the LORD,' I will punish that
person along with his entire family.
35 You should
keep asking each other, 'What is the LORD's answer?'
or 'What is the LORD saying?'
36 But stop using this
phrase, 'prophecy from the LORD.' For people are using it to give authority to their own ideas, turning upside down the words of our God, the living God, the
LORD of Heaven's Armies.

37 "This is what you should say to the prophets:
'What is the LORD's answer?' or 'What is the LORD
saying?'
38 But suppose they respond, 'This is a
prophecy from the LORD!' Then you should say, 'This
is what the LORD says: Because you have used this
phrase, "prophecy from the LORD," even though I
warned you not to use it,
39 I will forget you completely.* I will expel you from my presence, along
with this city that I gave to you and your ancestors.
40 And I will make you an object of ridicule, and your
name will be infamous throughout the ages.'"

Good and Bad Figs

24 After King Nebuchadnezzar* of Babylon exiled Jehoiachin* son of Jehoiakim, king of
Judah, to Babylon along with the officials of Judah
and all the craftsmen and artisans, the LORD gave me
this vision. I saw two baskets of figs placed in front of
the LORD's Temple in Jerusalem.
2 One basket was
filled with fresh, ripe figs, while the other was filled
with bad figs that were too rotten to eat.

3 Then the LORD said to me, "What do you see,
Jeremiah?"

I replied, "Figs, some very good and some very bad,
too rotten to eat."

23:33 As in Greek version and Latin Vulgate; Hebrew reads *What burden?*
23:39 Some Hebrew manuscripts and Greek version read *I will surely lift you up.*
24:1a Hebrew *Nebuchadrezzar,* a variant spelling of Nebuchadnezzar.
24:1b Hebrew *Jeconiah,* a variant spelling of Jehoiachin.

KING JAMES VERSION

4 Again the word of the LORD came unto me, saying,

5 Thus saith the LORD, the God of Israel; Like these good figs, so will I acknowledge them that are carried away captive of Judah, whom I have sent out of this place into the land of the Chaldeans for *their* good.

6 For I will set mine eyes upon them for good, and I will bring them again to this land: and I will build them, and not pull *them* down; and I will plant them, and not pluck *them* up.

7 And I will give them an heart to know me, that I *am* the LORD: and they shall be my people, and I will be their God: for they shall return unto me with their whole heart.

8 And as the evil figs, which cannot be eaten, they are so evil; surely thus saith the LORD, So will I give Zedekiah the king of Judah, and his princes, and the residue of Jerusalem, that remain in this land, and them that dwell in the land of Egypt:

9 And I will deliver them to be removed into all the kingdoms of the earth for *their* hurt, *to be* a reproach and a proverb, a taunt and a curse, in all places whither I shall drive them.

10 And I will send the sword, the famine, and the pestilence, among them, till they be consumed from off the land that I gave unto them and to their fathers.

25 1 The word that came to Jeremiah concerning all the people of Judah in the fourth year of Jehoiakim the son of Josiah king of Judah, that *was* the first year of Nebuchadrezzar king of Babylon;

2 The which Jeremiah the prophet spake unto all the people of Judah, and to all the inhabitants of Jerusalem, saying,

3 From the thirteenth year of Josiah the son of Amon king of Judah, even unto this day, that *is* the three and twentieth year, the word of the LORD hath come unto me, and I have spoken unto you, rising early and speaking; but ye have not hearkened.

4 And the LORD hath sent unto you all his servants the prophets, rising early and sending *them;* but ye have not hearkened, nor inclined your ear to hear.

5 They said, Turn ye again now every one from his evil way, and from the evil of your doings, and dwell in the land that the LORD hath given unto you and to your fathers for ever and ever:

6 And go not after other gods to serve them, and to worship them, and provoke me not to anger with the works of your hands; and I will do you no hurt.

7 Yet ye have not hearkened unto me, saith the LORD; that ye might provoke me to anger with the works of your hands to your own hurt.

8 Therefore thus saith the LORD of hosts; Because ye have not heard my words,

9 Behold, I will send and take all the families of the north, saith the LORD, and Nebuchadrezzar the king

NEW LIVING TRANSLATION

4 Then the LORD gave me this message: 5 "This is
what the LORD, the God of Israel, says: The good figs
represent the exiles I sent from Judah to the land of
the Babylonians.* 6 I will watch over and care for
them, and I will bring them back here again. I will
build them up and not tear them down. I will plant
them and not uproot them. 7 I will give them hearts
that recognize me as the LORD. They will be my
people, and I will be their God, for they will return to
me wholeheartedly.

8 "But the bad figs," the LORD said, "represent King
Zedekiah of Judah, his officials, all the people left in
Jerusalem, and those who live in Egypt. I will treat
them like bad figs, too rotten to eat. 9 I will make
them an object of horror and a symbol of evil to
every nation on earth. They will be disgraced and
mocked, taunted and cursed, wherever I scatter
them. 10 And I will send war, famine, and disease until
they have vanished from the land of Israel, which I
gave to them and their ancestors."

Seventy Years of Captivity

25 This message for all the people of Judah
came to Jeremiah from the LORD during the
fourth year of Jehoiakim's reign over Judah.* This was
the year when King Nebuchadnezzar* of Babylon began his reign.

2 Jeremiah the prophet said to all the people in
Judah and Jerusalem, 3 "For the past twenty-three
years—from the thirteenth year of the reign of Josiah
son of Amon,* king of Judah, until now—the LORD
has been giving me his messages. I have faithfully
passed them on to you, but you have not listened.

4 "Again and again the LORD has sent you his servants, the prophets, but you have not listened or even
paid attention. 5 Each time the message was this:
'Turn from the evil road you are traveling and from
the evil things you are doing. Only then will I let you
live in this land that the LORD gave to you and your
ancestors forever. 6 Do not provoke my anger by worshiping idols you made with your own hands. Then I
will not harm you.'

7 "But you would not listen to me," says the LORD.
"You made me furious by worshiping idols you made
with your own hands, bringing on yourselves all the
disasters you now suffer. 8 And now the LORD of
Heaven's Armies says: Because you have not listened
to me, 9 I will gather together all the armies of the
north under King Nebuchadnezzar of Babylon,

24:5 Or *Chaldeans.* **25:1a** The fourth year of Jehoiakim's reign and the accession year of Nebuchadnezzar's reign was 605 B.C. **25:1b** Hebrew *Nebuchadrezzar,* a variant spelling of Nebuchadnezzar; also in 25:9. **25:3** The thirteenth year of Josiah's reign was 627 B.C.

KING JAMES VERSION

of Babylon, my servant, and will bring them against this land, and against the inhabitants thereof, and against all these nations round about, and will utterly destroy them, and make them an astonishment, and an hissing, and perpetual desolations.

10 Moreover I will take from them the voice of mirth, and the voice of gladness, the voice of the bridegroom, and the voice of the bride, the sound of the millstones, and the light of the candle.

11 And this whole land shall be a desolation, *and* an astonishment; and these nations shall serve the king of Babylon seventy years.

12 And it shall come to pass, when seventy years are accomplished, *that* I will punish the king of Babylon, and that nation, saith the LORD, for their iniquity, and the land of the Chaldeans, and will make it perpetual desolations.

13 And I will bring upon that land all my words which I have pronounced against it, *even* all that is written in this book, which Jeremiah hath prophesied against all the nations.

14 For many nations and great kings shall serve themselves of them also: and I will recompense them according to their deeds, and according to the works of their own hands.

15 For thus saith the LORD God of Israel unto me; Take the wine cup of this fury at my hand, and cause all the nations, to whom I send thee, to drink it.

16 And they shall drink, and be moved, and be mad, because of the sword that I will send among them.

17 Then took I the cup at the LORD's hand, and made all the nations to drink, unto whom the LORD had sent me:

18 *To wit,* Jerusalem, and the cities of Judah, and the kings thereof, and the princes thereof, to make them a desolation, an astonishment, an hissing, and a curse; as *it is* this day;

19 Pharaoh king of Egypt, and his servants, and his princes, and all his people;

20 And all the mingled people, and all the kings of the land of Uz, and all the kings of the land of the Philistines, and Ashkelon, and Azzah, and Ekron, and the remnant of Ashdod,

21 Edom, and Moab, and the children of Ammon,

22 And all the kings of Tyrus, and all the kings of Zidon, and the kings of the isles which *are* beyond the sea,

23 Dedan, and Tema, and Buz, and all *that are* in the utmost corners,

24 And all the kings of Arabia, and all the kings of the mingled people that dwell in the desert,

25 And all the kings of Zimri, and all the kings of Elam, and all the kings of the Medes,

26 And all the kings of the north, far and near, one with another, and all the kingdoms of the world, which *are* upon the face of the earth: and the king of Sheshach shall drink after them.

27 Therefore thou shalt say unto them, Thus saith

NEW LIVING TRANSLATION

whom I have appointed as my deputy. I will bring them all against this land and its people and against the surrounding nations. I will completely destroy* you and make you an object of horror and contempt and a ruin forever. 10 I will take away your happy singing and laughter. The joyful voices of bridegrooms and brides will no longer be heard. Your millstones will fall silent, and the lights in your homes will go out. 11 This entire land will become a desolate wasteland. Israel and her neighboring lands will serve the king of Babylon for seventy years.

12 "Then, after the seventy years of captivity are over, I will punish the king of Babylon and his people for their sins," says the LORD. "I will make the country of the Babylonians* a wasteland forever. 13 I will bring upon them all the terrors I have promised in this book—all the penalties announced by Jeremiah against the nations. 14 Many nations and great kings will enslave the Babylonians, just as they enslaved my people. I will punish them in proportion to the suffering they cause my people."

The Cup of the LORD's Anger

15 This is what the LORD, the God of Israel, said to me: "Take from my hand this cup filled to the brim with my anger, and make all the nations to whom I send you drink from it. 16 When they drink from it, they will stagger, crazed by the warfare I will send against them."

17 So I took the cup of anger from the LORD and made all the nations drink from it—every nation to which the LORD sent me. 18 I went to Jerusalem and the other towns of Judah, and their kings and officials drank from the cup. From that day until this, they have been a desolate ruin, an object of horror, contempt, and cursing. 19 I gave the cup to Pharaoh, king of Egypt, his attendants, his officials, and all his people, 20 along with all the foreigners living in that land. I also gave it to all the kings of the land of Uz and the kings of the Philistine cities of Ashkelon, Gaza, Ekron, and what remains of Ashdod. 21 Then I gave the cup to the nations of Edom, Moab, and Ammon, 22 and the kings of Tyre and Sidon, and the kings of the regions across the sea. 23 I gave it to Dedan, Tema, and Buz, and to the people who live in distant places.* 24 I gave it to the kings of Arabia, the kings of the nomadic tribes of the desert, 25 and to the kings of Zimri, Elam, and Media. 26 And I gave it to the kings of the northern countries, far and near, one after the other—all the kingdoms of the world. And finally, the king of Babylon* himself drank from the cup of the LORD's anger.

27 Then the LORD said to me, "Now tell them, 'This

25:9 The Hebrew term used here refers to the complete consecration of things or people to the LORD, either by destroying them or by giving them as an offering. 25:12 Or *Chaldeans.* 25:23 Or *who clip the corners of their hair.* 25:26 Hebrew *of Sheshach,* a code name for Babylon.

KING JAMES VERSION

the LORD of hosts, the God of Israel; Drink ye, and be
drunken, and spue, and fall, and rise no more, because of the sword which I will send among you.
28 And it shall be, if they refuse to take the cup at
thine hand to drink, then shalt thou say unto them,
Thus saith the LORD of hosts; Ye shall certainly drink.
29 For, lo, I begin to bring evil on the city which
is called by my name, and should ye be utterly
unpunished? Ye shall not be unpunished: for I will
call for a sword upon all the inhabitants of the earth,
saith the LORD of hosts.
30 Therefore prophesy thou against them all these
words, and say unto them, The LORD shall roar from
on high, and utter his voice from his holy habitation;
he shall mightily roar upon his habitation; he shall
give a shout, as they that tread *the grapes,* against all
the inhabitants of the earth.
31 A noise shall come *even* to the ends of the earth;
for the LORD hath a controversy with the nations, he
will plead with all flesh; he will give them *that are*
wicked to the sword, saith the LORD.
32 Thus saith the LORD of hosts, Behold, evil shall
go forth from nation to nation, and a great whirlwind
shall be raised up from the coasts of the earth.
33 And the slain of the LORD shall be at that day
from *one* end of the earth even unto the *other* end of
the earth: they shall not be lamented, neither gathered, nor buried; they shall be dung upon the ground.
34 Howl, ye shepherds, and cry; and wallow yourselves *in the ashes,* ye principal of the flock: for the
days of your slaughter and of your dispersions are
accomplished; and ye shall fall like a pleasant vessel.
35 And the shepherds shall have no way to flee, nor
the principal of the flock to escape.
36 A voice of the cry of the shepherds, and an howling of the principal of the flock, *shall be heard:* for
the LORD hath spoiled their pasture.
37 And the peaceable habitations are cut down because of the fierce anger of the LORD.
38 He hath forsaken his covert, as the lion: for their
land is desolate because of the fierceness of the oppressor, and because of his fierce anger.

26 1 In the beginning of the reign of Jehoiakim
the son of Josiah king of Judah came this
word from the LORD, saying,
2 Thus saith the LORD; Stand in the court of the

NEW LIVING TRANSLATION

is what the LORD of Heaven's Armies, the God of Israel, says: Drink from this cup of my anger. Get drunk
and vomit; fall to rise no more, for I am sending terrible wars against you.' 28 And if they refuse to accept
the cup, tell them, 'The LORD of Heaven's Armies
says: You have no choice but to drink from it. 29 I have
begun to punish Jerusalem, the city that bears my
name. Now should I let you go unpunished? No, you
will not escape disaster. I will call for war against all
the nations of the earth. I, the LORD of Heaven's Armies, have spoken!'

30 "Now prophesy all these things, and say to them,

"'The LORD will roar against his own land
from his holy dwelling in heaven.
He will shout like those who tread grapes;
he will shout against everyone on earth.
31 His cry of judgment will reach the ends
of the earth,
for the LORD will bring his case against
all the nations.
He will judge all the people of the earth,
slaughtering the wicked with the sword.
I, the LORD, have spoken!'"

32 This is what the LORD of Heaven's Armies says:
"Look! Disaster will fall upon nation
after nation!
A great whirlwind of fury is rising
from the most distant corners of the earth!"

33 In that day those the LORD has slaughtered will
fill the earth from one end to the other. No one will
mourn for them or gather up their bodies to bury
them. They will be scattered on the ground like
manure.

34 Weep and moan, you evil shepherds!
Roll in the dust, you leaders of the flock!
The time of your slaughter has arrived;
you will fall and shatter like a fragile vase.
35 You will find no place to hide;
there will be no way to escape.
36 Listen to the frantic cries of the shepherds.
The leaders of the flock are wailing in despair,
for the LORD is ruining their pastures.
37 Peaceful meadows will be turned into
a wasteland
by the LORD's fierce anger.
38 He has left his den like a strong lion
seeking its prey,
and their land will be made desolate
by the sword of the enemy
and the LORD's fierce anger.

Jeremiah's Escape from Death

26 This message came to Jeremiah from the
LORD early in the reign of Jehoiakim son of
Josiah,* king of Judah. 2 "This is what the LORD says:

26:1 The first year of Jehoiakim's reign was 608 B.C.

KING JAMES VERSION

LORD's house, and speak unto all the cities of Judah,
which come to worship in the LORD's house, all the
words that I command thee to speak unto them;
diminish not a word:
3If so be they will hearken, and turn every man
from his evil way, that I may repent me of the evil,
which I purpose to do unto them because of the evil
of their doings.
4And thou shalt say unto them, Thus saith the
LORD; If ye will not hearken to me, to walk in my law,
which I have set before you,
5To hearken to the words of my servants the
prophets, whom I sent unto you, both rising up early,
and sending *them*, but ye have not hearkened;
6Then will I make this house like Shiloh, and will
make this city a curse to all the nations of the earth.
7So the priests and the prophets and all the people
heard Jeremiah speaking these words in the house of
the LORD.
8Now it came to pass, when Jeremiah had made an
end of speaking all that the LORD had commanded
him to speak unto all the people, that the priests and
the prophets and all the people took him, saying,
Thou shalt surely die.
9Why hast thou prophesied in the name of the
LORD, saying, This house shall be like Shiloh, and this
city shall be desolate without an inhabitant? And all
the people were gathered against Jeremiah in the
house of the LORD.
10When the princes of Judah heard these things,
then they came up from the king's house unto the
house of the LORD, and sat down in the entry of the
new gate of the LORD's *house*.
11Then spake the priests and the prophets unto
the princes and to all the people, saying, This man *is*
worthy to die; for he hath prophesied against this
city, as ye have heard with your ears.
12Then spake Jeremiah unto all the princes and to
all the people, saying, The LORD sent me to prophesy
against this house and against this city all the words
that ye have heard.
13Therefore now amend your ways and your doings, and obey the voice of the LORD your God; and
the LORD will repent him of the evil that he hath pronounced against you.
14As for me, behold, I *am* in your hand: do with me
as seemeth good and meet unto you.
15But know ye for certain, that if ye put me to
death, ye shall surely bring innocent blood upon
yourselves, and upon this city, and upon the inhabitants thereof: for of a truth the LORD hath sent me
unto you to speak all these words in your ears.
16Then said the princes and all the people unto
the priests and to the prophets; This man *is* not worthy to die: for he hath spoken to us in the name of the
LORD our God.
17Then rose up certain of the elders of the land,
and spake to all the assembly of the people, saying,

NEW LIVING TRANSLATION

Stand in the courtyard in front of the Temple of the
LORD, and make an announcement to the people who
have come there to worship from all over Judah. Give
them my entire message; include every word. 3Per-
haps they will listen and turn from their evil ways.
Then I will change my mind about the disaster I am
ready to pour out on them because of their sins.
4"Say to them, 'This is what the LORD says: If you
will not listen to me and obey my word I have given
you, 5and if you will not listen to my servants, the
prophets—for I sent them again and again to warn
you, but you would not listen to them—6then I will
destroy this Temple as I destroyed Shiloh, the place
where the Tabernacle was located. And I will make
Jerusalem an object of cursing in every nation on
earth.'"
7The priests, the prophets, and all the people listened to Jeremiah as he spoke in front of the LORD's
Temple. 8But when Jeremiah had finished his message, saying everything the LORD had told him to
say, the priests and prophets and all the people at
the Temple mobbed him. "Kill him!" they shouted.
9"What right do you have to prophesy in the LORD's
name that this Temple will be destroyed like Shiloh?
What do you mean, saying that Jerusalem will be destroyed and left with no inhabitants?" And all the
people threatened him as he stood in front of the
Temple.
10When the officials of Judah heard what was
happening, they rushed over from the palace and sat
down at the New Gate of the Temple to hold court.
11The priests and prophets presented their accusations to the officials and the people. "This man
should die!" they said. "You have heard with your
own ears what a traitor he is, for he has prophesied
against this city."
12Then Jeremiah spoke to the officials and the
people in his own defense. "The LORD sent me to
prophesy against this Temple and this city," he said.
"The LORD gave me every word that I have spoken.
13But if you stop your sinning and begin to obey the
LORD your God, he will change his mind about this
disaster that he has announced against you. 14As for
me, I am in your hands—do with me as you think
best. 15But if you kill me, rest assured that you will be
killing an innocent man! The responsibility for such
a deed will lie on you, on this city, and on every person living in it. For it is absolutely true that the LORD
sent me to speak every word you have heard."
16Then the officials and the people said to the
priests and prophets, "This man does not deserve
the death sentence, for he has spoken to us in the
name of the LORD our God."
17Then some of the wise old men stood and spoke

KING JAMES VERSION

18 Micah the Morasthite prophesied in the days of
Hezekiah king of Judah, and spake to all the people
of Judah, saying, Thus saith the LORD of hosts; Zion
shall be plowed *like* a field, and Jerusalem shall become heaps, and the mountain of the house as the
high places of a forest.
19 Did Hezekiah king of Judah and all Judah put
him at all to death? did he not fear the LORD, and besought the LORD, and the LORD repented him of the
evil which he had pronounced against them? Thus
might we procure great evil against our souls.
20 And there was also a man that prophesied in the
name of the LORD, Urijah the son of Shemaiah of
Kirjath-jearim, who prophesied against this city
and against this land according to all the words of
Jeremiah:
21 And when Jehoiakim the king, with all his
mighty men, and all the princes, heard his words, the
king sought to put him to death: but when Urijah
heard it, he was afraid, and fled, and went into Egypt;
22 And Jehoiakim the king sent men into Egypt,
namely, Elnathan the son of Achbor, and *certain*
men with him into Egypt.
23 And they fetched forth Urijah out of Egypt, and
brought him unto Jehoiakim the king; who slew him
with the sword, and cast his dead body into the
graves of the common people.
24 Nevertheless the hand of Ahikam the son of
Shaphan was with Jeremiah, that they should not
give him into the hand of the people to put him to
death.

27

1 In the beginning of the reign of Jehoiakim
the son of Josiah king of Judah came this
word unto Jeremiah from the LORD, saying,
2 Thus saith the LORD to me; Make thee bonds and
yokes, and put them upon thy neck,
3 And send them to the king of Edom, and to the
king of Moab, and to the king of the Ammonites, and
to the king of Tyrus, and to the king of Zidon, by the
hand of the messengers which come to Jerusalem
unto Zedekiah king of Judah;
4 And command them to say unto their masters,
Thus saith the LORD of hosts, the God of Israel; Thus
shall ye say unto your masters;
5 I have made the earth, the man and the beast that
are upon the ground, by my great power and by my
outstretched arm, and have given it unto whom it
seemed meet unto me.
6 And now have I given all these lands into the
hand of Nebuchadnezzar the king of Babylon, my
servant; and the beasts of the field have I given him
also to serve him.
7 And all nations shall serve him, and his son, and
his son's son, until the very time of his land come:
and then many nations and great kings shall serve
themselves of him.

NEW LIVING TRANSLATION

to all the people assembled there. 18 They said, "Remember when Micah of Moresheth prophesied
during the reign of King Hezekiah of Judah. He told
the people of Judah,

> 'This is what the LORD of Heaven's Armies says:
> Mount Zion will be plowed like an open field;
> Jerusalem will be reduced to ruins!
> A thicket will grow on the heights
> where the Temple now stands.'*

19 But did King Hezekiah and the people kill him for
saying this? No, they turned from their sins and worshiped the LORD. They begged him for mercy. Then
the LORD changed his mind about the terrible disaster he had pronounced against them. So we are about
to do ourselves great harm."
20 At this time Uriah son of Shemaiah from Kiriath-jearim was also prophesying for the LORD. And he
predicted the same terrible disaster against the city
and nation as Jeremiah did. 21 When King Jehoiakim
and the army officers and officials heard what he was
saying, the king sent someone to kill him. But Uriah
heard about the plan and escaped in fear to Egypt.
22 Then King Jehoiakim sent Elnathan son of Acbor to
Egypt along with several other men to capture Uriah.
23 They took him prisoner and brought him back to
King Jehoiakim. The king then killed Uriah with a
sword and had him buried in an unmarked grave.
24 Nevertheless, Ahikam son of Shaphan stood up
for Jeremiah and persuaded the court not to turn
him over to the mob to be killed.

Jeremiah Wears an Ox Yoke

27

This message came to Jeremiah from the
LORD early in the reign of Zedekiah* son of
Josiah, king of Judah.
2 This is what the LORD said to me: "Make a yoke,
and fasten it on your neck with leather straps.
3 Then send messages to the kings of Edom, Moab,
Ammon, Tyre, and Sidon through their ambassadors
who have come to see King Zedekiah in Jerusalem.
4 Give them this message for their masters: 'This is
what the LORD of Heaven's Armies, the God of Israel,
says: 5 With my great strength and powerful arm I
made the earth and all its people and every animal.
I can give these things of mine to anyone I choose.
6 Now I will give your countries to King Nebuchadnezzar of Babylon, who is my servant. I have put
everything, even the wild animals, under his control.
7 All the nations will serve him, his son, and his grandson until his time is up. Then many nations and great

26:18 Mic 3:12. **27:1** As in some Hebrew manuscripts and Syriac version (see also 27:3, 12); most Hebrew manuscripts read *Jehoiakim*.

KING JAMES VERSION

8 And it shall come to pass, *that* the nation and kingdom which will not serve the same Nebuchadnezzar the king of Babylon, and that will not put their neck under the yoke of the king of Babylon, that nation will I punish, saith the LORD, with the sword, and with the famine, and with the pestilence, until I have consumed them by his hand.

9 Therefore hearken not ye to your prophets, nor to your diviners, nor to your dreamers, nor to your enchanters, nor to your sorcerers, which speak unto you, saying, Ye shall not serve the king of Babylon:

10 For they prophesy a lie unto you, to remove you far from your land; and that I should drive you out, and ye should perish.

11 But the nations that bring their neck under the yoke of the king of Babylon, and serve him, those will I let remain still in their own land, saith the LORD; and they shall till it, and dwell therein.

12 I spake also to Zedekiah king of Judah according to all these words, saying, Bring your necks under the yoke of the king of Babylon, and serve him and his people, and live.

13 Why will ye die, thou and thy people, by the sword, by the famine, and by the pestilence, as the LORD hath spoken against the nation that will not serve the king of Babylon?

14 Therefore hearken not unto the words of the prophets that speak unto you, saying, Ye shall not serve the king of Babylon: for they prophesy a lie unto you.

15 For I have not sent them, saith the LORD, yet they prophesy a lie in my name; that I might drive you out, and that ye might perish, ye, and the prophets that prophesy unto you.

16 Also I spake to the priests and to all this people, saying, Thus saith the LORD; Hearken not to the words of your prophets that prophesy unto you, saying, Behold, the vessels of the LORD's house shall now shortly be brought again from Babylon: for they prophesy a lie unto you.

17 Hearken not unto them; serve the king of Babylon, and live: wherefore should this city be laid waste?

18 But if they *be* prophets, and if the word of the LORD be with them, let them now make intercession to the LORD of hosts, that the vessels which are left in the house of the LORD, and *in* the house of the king of Judah, and at Jerusalem, go not to Babylon.

19 For thus saith the LORD of hosts concerning the pillars, and concerning the sea, and concerning the bases, and concerning the residue of the vessels that remain in this city,

20 Which Nebuchadnezzar king of Babylon took not, when he carried away captive Jeconiah the son of Jehoiakim king of Judah from Jerusalem to Babylon, and all the nobles of Judah and Jerusalem;

21 Yea, thus saith the LORD of hosts, the God of Israel, concerning the vessels that remain *in* the house of

NEW LIVING TRANSLATION

kings will conquer and rule over Babylon. 8 So you must submit to Babylon's king and serve him; put your neck under Babylon's yoke! I will punish any nation that refuses to be his slave, says the LORD. I will send war, famine, and disease upon that nation until Babylon has conquered it.

9 "'Do not listen to your false prophets, fortune-tellers, interpreters of dreams, mediums, and sorcerers who say, "The king of Babylon will not conquer you." 10 They are all liars, and their lies will lead to your being driven out of your land. I will drive you out and send you far away to die. 11 But the people of any nation that submits to the king of Babylon will be allowed to stay in their own country to farm the land as usual. I, the LORD, have spoken!'"

12 Then I repeated this same message to King Zedekiah of Judah. "If you want to live, submit to the yoke of the king of Babylon and his people. 13 Why do you insist on dying—you and your people? Why should you choose war, famine, and disease, which the LORD will bring against every nation that refuses to submit to Babylon's king? 14 Do not listen to the false prophets who keep telling you, 'The king of Babylon will not conquer you.' They are liars. 15 This is what the LORD says: 'I have not sent these prophets! They are telling you lies in my name, so I will drive you from this land. You will all die—you and all these prophets, too.'"

16 Then I spoke to the priests and the people and said, "This is what the LORD says: 'Do not listen to your prophets who claim that soon the gold articles taken from my Temple will be returned from Babylon. It is all a lie! 17 Do not listen to them. Surrender to the king of Babylon, and you will live. Why should this whole city be destroyed? 18 If they really are prophets and speak the LORD's messages, let them pray to the LORD of Heaven's Armies. Let them pray that the articles remaining in the LORD's Temple and in the king's palace and in the palaces of Jerusalem will not be carried away to Babylon!'

19 "For the LORD of Heaven's Armies has spoken about the pillars in front of the Temple, the great bronze basin called the Sea, the water carts, and all the other ceremonial articles. 20 King Nebuchadnezzar of Babylon left them here when he exiled Jehoiachin* son of Jehoiakim, king of Judah, to Babylon, along with all the other nobles of Judah and Jerusalem. 21 Yes, this is what the LORD of Heaven's Armies,

27:20 Hebrew *Jeconiah*, a variant spelling of Jehoiachin.

KING JAMES VERSION

the LORD, and *in* the house of the king of Judah and
of Jerusalem;
22They shall be carried to Babylon, and there shall
they be until the day that I visit them, saith the LORD;
then will I bring them up, and restore them to this
place.

28 1And it came to pass the same year, in the
beginning of the reign of Zedekiah king of
Judah, in the fourth year, *and* in the fifth month, *that*
Hananiah the son of Azur the prophet, which *was* of
Gibeon, spake unto me in the house of the LORD, in
the presence of the priests and of all the people,
saying,
2Thus speaketh the LORD of hosts, the God of Israel, saying, I have broken the yoke of the king of
Babylon.
3Within two full years will I bring again into this
place all the vessels of the LORD's house, that Nebuchadnezzar king of Babylon took away from this
place, and carried them to Babylon:
4And I will bring again to this place Jeconiah the
son of Jehoiakim king of Judah, with all the captives
of Judah, that went into Babylon, saith the LORD: for I
will break the yoke of the king of Babylon.
5Then the prophet Jeremiah said unto the
prophet Hananiah in the presence of the priests, and
in the presence of all the people that stood in the
house of the LORD,
6Even the prophet Jeremiah said, Amen: the LORD
do so: the LORD perform thy words which thou hast
prophesied, to bring again the vessels of the LORD's
house, and all that is carried away captive, from Babylon into this place.
7Nevertheless hear thou now this word that I
speak in thine ears, and in the ears of all the people;
8The prophets that have been before me and before thee of old prophesied both against many countries, and against great kingdoms, of war, and of evil,
and of pestilence.
9The prophet which prophesieth of peace, when
the word of the prophet shall come to pass, *then*
shall the prophet be known, that the LORD hath truly
sent him.
10Then Hananiah the prophet took the yoke from
off the prophet Jeremiah's neck, and brake it.
11And Hananiah spake in the presence of all the
people, saying, Thus saith the LORD; Even so will I
break the yoke of Nebuchadnezzar king of Babylon
from the neck of all nations within the space of two
full years. And the prophet Jeremiah went his way.
12Then the word of the LORD came unto Jeremiah
the prophet, after that Hananiah the prophet had
broken the yoke from off the neck of the prophet Jeremiah, saying,
13Go and tell Hananiah, saying, Thus saith the
LORD; Thou hast broken the yokes of wood; but thou
shalt make for them yokes of iron.

NEW LIVING TRANSLATION

the God of Israel, says about the precious things still
in the Temple and in the palace of Judah's king:
22'They will all be carried away to Babylon and will
stay there until I send for them,' says the LORD. 'Then
I will bring them back to Jerusalem again.'"

Jeremiah Condemns Hananiah

28 One day in late summer* of that same
year—the fourth year of the reign of Zedekiah, king of Judah—Hananiah son of Azzur, a
prophet from Gibeon, addressed me publicly in the
Temple while all the priests and people listened. He
said, 2"This is what the LORD of Heaven's Armies, the
God of Israel, says: 'I will remove the yoke of the king
of Babylon from your necks. 3Within two years I will
bring back all the Temple treasures that King Nebuchadnezzar carried off to Babylon. 4And I will bring
back Jehoiachin* son of Jehoiakim, king of Judah,
and all the other captives that were taken to Babylon.
I will surely break the yoke that the king of Babylon
has put on your necks. I, the LORD, have spoken!'"
5Jeremiah responded to Hananiah as they stood in
front of all the priests and people at the Temple. 6He
said, "Amen! May your prophecies come true! I hope
the LORD does everything you say. I hope he does
bring back from Babylon the treasures of this Temple
and all the captives. 7But listen now to the solemn
words I speak to you in the presence of all these people. 8The ancient prophets who preceded you and
me spoke against many nations, always warning of
war, disaster, and disease. 9So a prophet who predicts
peace must show he is right. Only when his predictions come true can we know that he is really from
the LORD."
10Then Hananiah the prophet took the yoke off
Jeremiah's neck and broke it in pieces. 11And Hananiah said again to the crowd that had gathered, "This
is what the LORD says: 'Just as this yoke has been broken, within two years I will break the yoke of oppression from all the nations now subject to King
Nebuchadnezzar of Babylon.'" With that, Jeremiah
left the Temple area.
12Soon after this confrontation with Hananiah,
the LORD gave this message to Jeremiah: 13"Go and
tell Hananiah, 'This is what the LORD says: You have
broken a wooden yoke, but you have replaced it with

28:1 Hebrew *In the fifth month,* of the ancient Hebrew lunar calendar. The fifth month in the fourth year of Zedekiah's reign occurred within the months of August and September 593 B.C. Also see note on 1:3.
28:4 Hebrew *Jeconiah,* a variant spelling of Jehoiachin.

KING JAMES VERSION

14 For thus saith the LORD of hosts, the God of Israel; I have put a yoke of iron upon the neck of all these nations, that they may serve Nebuchadnezzar king of Babylon; and they shall serve him: and I have given him the beasts of the field also.

15 Then said the prophet Jeremiah unto Hananiah the prophet, Hear now, Hananiah; The LORD hath not sent thee; but thou makest this people to trust in a lie.

16 Therefore thus saith the LORD; Behold, I will cast thee from off the face of the earth: this year thou shalt die, because thou hast taught rebellion against the LORD.

17 So Hananiah the prophet died the same year in the seventh month.

29 1 Now these *are* the words of the letter that Jeremiah the prophet sent from Jerusalem unto the residue of the elders which were carried away captives, and to the priests, and to the prophets, and to all the people whom Nebuchadnezzar had carried away captive from Jerusalem to Babylon;

2 (After that Jeconiah the king, and the queen, and the eunuchs, the princes of Judah and Jerusalem, and the carpenters, and the smiths, were departed from Jerusalem;)

3 By the hand of Elasah the son of Shaphan, and Gemariah the son of Hilkiah, (whom Zedekiah king of Judah sent unto Babylon to Nebuchadnezzar king of Babylon) saying,

4 Thus saith the LORD of hosts, the God of Israel, unto all that are carried away captives, whom I have caused to be carried away from Jerusalem unto Babylon;

5 Build ye houses, and dwell *in them;* and plant gardens, and eat the fruit of them;

6 Take ye wives, and beget sons and daughters; and take wives for your sons, and give your daughters to husbands, that they may bear sons and daughters; that ye may be increased there, and not diminished.

7 And seek the peace of the city whither I have caused you to be carried away captives, and pray unto the LORD for it: for in the peace thereof shall ye have peace.

8 For thus saith the LORD of hosts, the God of Israel; Let not your prophets and your diviners, that *be* in the midst of you, deceive you, neither hearken to your dreams which ye cause to be dreamed.

9 For they prophesy falsely unto you in my name: I have not sent them, saith the LORD.

10 For thus saith the LORD, That after seventy years be accomplished at Babylon I will visit you, and perform my good word toward you, in causing you to return to this place.

11 For I know the thoughts that I think toward you, saith the LORD, thoughts of peace, and not of evil, to give you an expected end.

12 Then shall ye call upon me, and ye shall go and pray unto me, and I will hearken unto you.

NEW LIVING TRANSLATION

a yoke of iron. 14 The LORD of Heaven's Armies, the God of Israel, says: I have put a yoke of iron on the necks of all these nations, forcing them into slavery under King Nebuchadnezzar of Babylon. I have put everything, even the wild animals, under his control.'"

15 Then Jeremiah the prophet said to Hananiah, "Listen, Hananiah! The LORD has not sent you, but the people believe your lies. 16 Therefore, this is what the LORD says: 'You must die. Your life will end this very year because you have rebelled against the LORD.'"

17 Two months later* the prophet Hananiah died.

A Letter to the Exiles

29 Jeremiah wrote a letter from Jerusalem to the elders, priests, prophets, and all the people who had been exiled to Babylon by King Nebuchadnezzar. 2 This was after King Jehoiachin,* the queen mother, the court officials, the other officials of Judah, and all the craftsmen and artisans had been deported from Jerusalem. 3 He sent the letter with Elasah son of Shaphan and Gemariah son of Hilkiah when they went to Babylon as King Zedekiah's ambassadors to Nebuchadnezzar. This is what Jeremiah's letter said:

4 This is what the LORD of Heaven's Armies, the
God of Israel, says to all the captives he has exiled
to Babylon from Jerusalem: 5 "Build homes, and
plan to stay. Plant gardens, and eat the food they
produce. 6 Marry and have children. Then find
spouses for them so that you may have many
grandchildren. Multiply! Do not dwindle away!
7 And work for the peace and prosperity of the city
where I sent you into exile. Pray to the LORD for it,
for its welfare will determine your welfare."

8 This is what the LORD of Heaven's Armies, the
God of Israel, says: "Do not let your prophets and
fortune-tellers who are with you in the land of
Babylon trick you. Do not listen to their dreams,
9 because they are telling you lies in my name.
I have not sent them," says the LORD.

10 This is what the LORD says: "You will be in
Babylon for seventy years. But then I will come
and do for you all the good things I have
promised, and I will bring you home again.
11 For I know the plans I have for you," says the
LORD. "They are plans for good and not for
disaster, to give you a future and a hope. 12 In

28:17 Hebrew *In the seventh month of that same year.* See 28:1 and the note there. **29:2** Hebrew *Jeconiah,* a variant spelling of Jehoiachin.

KING JAMES VERSION

13 And ye shall seek me, and find *me,* when ye shall search for me with all your heart.

14 And I will be found of you, saith the LORD: and I will turn away your captivity, and I will gather you from all the nations, and from all the places whither I have driven you, saith the LORD; and I will bring you again into the place whence I caused you to be carried away captive.

15 Because ye have said, The LORD hath raised us up prophets in Babylon;

16 *Know* that thus saith the LORD of the king that sitteth upon the throne of David, and of all the people that dwelleth in this city, *and* of your brethren that are not gone forth with you into captivity;

17 Thus saith the LORD of hosts; Behold, I will send upon them the sword, the famine, and the pestilence, and will make them like vile figs, that cannot be eaten, they are so evil.

18 And I will persecute them with the sword, with the famine, and with the pestilence, and will deliver them to be removed to all the kingdoms of the earth, to be a curse, and an astonishment, and an hissing, and a reproach, among all the nations whither I have driven them:

19 Because they have not hearkened to my words, saith the LORD, which I sent unto them by my servants the prophets, rising up early and sending *them;* but ye would not hear, saith the LORD.

20 Hear ye therefore the word of the LORD, all ye of the captivity, whom I have sent from Jerusalem to Babylon:

21 Thus saith the LORD of hosts, the God of Israel, of Ahab the son of Kolaiah, and of Zedekiah the son of Maaseiah, which prophesy a lie unto you in my name; Behold, I will deliver them into the hand of Nebuchadrezzar king of Babylon; and he shall slay them before your eyes;

22 And of them shall be taken up a curse by all the captivity of Judah which *are* in Babylon, saying, The LORD make thee like Zedekiah and like Ahab, whom the king of Babylon roasted in the fire;

23 Because they have committed villany in Israel, and have committed adultery with their neighbours' wives, and have spoken lying words in my name, which I have not commanded them; even I know, and *am* a witness, saith the LORD.

24 *Thus* shalt thou also speak to Shemaiah the Nehelamite, saying,

25 Thus speaketh the LORD of hosts, the God of Israel, saying, Because thou hast sent letters in thy name unto all the people that *are* at Jerusalem, and to Zephaniah the son of Maaseiah the priest, and to all the priests, saying,

26 The LORD hath made thee priest in the stead of Jehoiada the priest, that ye should be officers in the house of the LORD, for every man *that is* mad, and maketh himself a prophet, that thou shouldest put him in prison, and in the stocks.

NEW LIVING TRANSLATION

those days when you pray, I will listen. 13 If you look for me wholeheartedly, you will find me. 14 I will be found by you," says the LORD. "I will end your captivity and restore your fortunes. I will gather you out of the nations where I sent you and will bring you home again to your own land."

15 You claim that the LORD has raised up prophets for you in Babylon. 16 But this is what the LORD says about the king who sits on David's throne and all those still living here in Jerusalem—your relatives who were not exiled to Babylon. 17 This is what the LORD of Heaven's Armies says: "I will send war, famine, and disease upon them and make them like bad figs, too rotten to eat. 18 Yes, I will pursue them with war, famine, and disease, and I will scatter them around the world. In every nation where I send them, I will make them an object of damnation, horror, contempt, and mockery. 19 For they refuse to listen to me, though I have spoken to them repeatedly through the prophets I sent. And you who are in exile have not listened either," says the LORD.

20 Therefore, listen to this message from the LORD, all you captives there in Babylon. 21 This is what the LORD of Heaven's Armies, the God of Israel, says about your prophets—Ahab son of Kolaiah and Zedekiah son of Maaseiah—who are telling you lies in my name: "I will turn them over to Nebuchadnezzar* for execution before your eyes. 22 Their terrible fate will become proverbial, so that the Judean exiles will curse someone by saying, 'May the LORD make you like Zedekiah and Ahab, whom the king of Babylon burned alive!' 23 For these men have done terrible things among my people. They have committed adultery with their neighbors' wives and have lied in my name, saying things I did not command. I am a witness to this. I, the LORD, have spoken."

A Message for Shemaiah

24 The LORD sent this message to Shemaiah the Nehelamite in Babylon: 25 "This is what the LORD of Heaven's Armies, the God of Israel, says: You wrote a letter on your own authority to Zephaniah son of Maaseiah, the priest, and you sent copies to the other priests and people in Jerusalem. You wrote to Zephaniah,

26 "The LORD has appointed you to replace Jehoiada as the priest in charge of the house of the LORD. You are responsible to put into stocks and neck irons any crazy man who claims to be a

29:21 Hebrew *Nebuchadrezzar,* a variant spelling of Nebuchadnezzar.

KING JAMES VERSION

27 Now therefore why hast thou not reproved Jeremiah of Anathoth, which maketh himself a prophet
to you?
28 For therefore he sent unto us *in* Babylon, saying,
This *captivity is* long: build ye houses, and dwell *in*
them; and plant gardens, and eat the fruit of them.
29 And Zephaniah the priest read this letter in the
ears of Jeremiah the prophet.
30 Then came the word of the LORD unto Jeremiah,
saying,
31 Send to all them of the captivity, saying, Thus
saith the LORD concerning Shemaiah the Nehelamite; Because that Shemaiah hath prophesied unto
you, and I sent him not, and he caused you to trust in
a lie:
32 Therefore thus saith the LORD; Behold, I will
punish Shemaiah the Nehelamite, and his seed: he
shall not have a man to dwell among this people; neither shall he behold the good that I will do for my
people, saith the LORD; because he hath taught rebellion against the LORD.

30 1 The word that came to Jeremiah from the
LORD, saying,
2 Thus speaketh the LORD God of Israel, saying,
Write thee all the words that I have spoken unto thee
in a book.
3 For, lo, the days come, saith the LORD, that I will
bring again the captivity of my people Israel and
Judah, saith the LORD: and I will cause them to return
to the land that I gave to their fathers, and they shall
possess it.
4 And these *are* the words that the LORD spake concerning Israel and concerning Judah.
5 For thus saith the LORD; We have heard a voice of
trembling, of fear, and not of peace.
6 Ask ye now, and see whether a man doth travail
with child? wherefore do I see every man with his
hands on his loins, as a woman in travail, and all faces
are turned into paleness?
7 Alas! for that day *is* great, so that none *is* like it: it
is even the time of Jacob's trouble; but he shall be
saved out of it.
8 For it shall come to pass in that day, saith the
LORD of hosts, *that* I will break his yoke from off thy
neck, and will burst thy bonds, and strangers shall no
more serve themselves of him:
9 But they shall serve the LORD their God, and
David their king, whom I will raise up unto them.
10 Therefore fear thou not, O my servant Jacob,
saith the LORD; neither be dismayed, O Israel: for, lo, I

NEW LIVING TRANSLATION

prophet. 27 So why have you done nothing to stop
Jeremiah from Anathoth, who pretends to be a
prophet among you? 28 Jeremiah sent a letter here
to Babylon, predicting that our captivity will be a
long one. He said, 'Build homes, and plan to stay.
Plant gardens, and eat the food they produce.'"

29 But when Zephaniah the priest received Shemaiah's letter, he took it to Jeremiah and read it to him.
30 Then the LORD gave this message to Jeremiah:
31 "Send an open letter to all the exiles in Babylon.
Tell them, 'This is what the LORD says concerning
Shemaiah the Nehelamite: Since he has prophesied
to you when I did not send him and has tricked you
into believing his lies, 32 I will punish him and his
family. None of his descendants will see the good
things I will do for my people, for he has incited you
to rebel against me. I, the LORD, have spoken!'"

Promises of Deliverance

30 The LORD gave another message to Jeremiah. He said, 2 "This is what the LORD, the God
of Israel, says: Write down for the record everything I
have said to you, Jeremiah. 3 For the time is coming
when I will restore the fortunes of my people of Israel
and Judah. I will bring them home to this land that I
gave to their ancestors, and they will possess it again.
I, the LORD, have spoken!"
4 This is the message the LORD gave concerning
Israel and Judah. 5 This is what the LORD says:

"I hear cries of fear;
there is terror and no peace.
6 Now let me ask you a question:
Do men give birth to babies?
Then why do they stand there, ashen-faced,
hands pressed against their sides
like a woman in labor?
7 In all history there has never been such
a time of terror.
It will be a time of trouble for my people Israel.*
Yet in the end they will be saved!
8 For in that day,"
says the LORD of Heaven's Armies,
"I will break the yoke from their necks
and snap their chains.
Foreigners will no longer be their masters.
9 For my people will serve the LORD their God
and their king descended from David—
the king I will raise up for them.

10 "So do not be afraid, Jacob, my servant;
do not be dismayed, Israel,"
says the LORD.
"For I will bring you home again from distant lands,
and your children will return from their exile.

30:7 Hebrew *Jacob;* also in 30:10b, 18. See note on 5:20.

KING JAMES VERSION

will save thee from afar, and thy seed from the land of their captivity; and Jacob shall return, and shall be in rest, and be quiet, and none shall make *him* afraid.

11 For I *am* with thee, saith the LORD, to save thee: though I make a full end of all nations whither I have scattered thee, yet will I not make a full end of thee: but I will correct thee in measure, and will not leave thee altogether unpunished.

12 For thus saith the LORD, Thy bruise *is* incurable, *and* thy wound *is* grievous.

13 *There is* none to plead thy cause, that thou mayest be bound up: thou hast no healing medicines.

14 All thy lovers have forgotten thee; they seek thee not; for I have wounded thee with the wound of an enemy, with the chastisement of a cruel one, for the multitude of thine iniquity; *because* thy sins were increased.

15 Why criest thou for thine affliction? thy sorrow *is* incurable for the multitude of thine iniquity: *because* thy sins were increased, I have done these things unto thee.

16 Therefore all they that devour thee shall be devoured; and all thine adversaries, every one of them, shall go into captivity; and they that spoil thee shall be a spoil, and all that prey upon thee will I give for a prey.

17 For I will restore health unto thee, and I will heal thee of thy wounds, saith the LORD; because they called thee an Outcast, *saying,* This *is* Zion, whom no man seeketh after.

18 Thus saith the LORD; Behold, I will bring again the captivity of Jacob's tents, and have mercy on his dwellingplaces; and the city shall be builded upon her own heap, and the palace shall remain after the manner thereof.

19 And out of them shall proceed thanksgiving and the voice of them that make merry: and I will multiply them, and they shall not be few; I will also glorify them, and they shall not be small.

20 Their children also shall be as aforetime, and their congregation shall be established before me, and I will punish all that oppress them.

21 And their nobles shall be of themselves, and their governor shall proceed from the midst of them; and I will cause him to draw near, and he shall approach unto me: for who *is* this that engaged his heart to approach unto me? saith the LORD.

22 And ye shall be my people, and I will be your God.

23 Behold, the whirlwind of the LORD goeth forth with fury, a continuing whirlwind: it shall fall with pain upon the head of the wicked.

NEW LIVING TRANSLATION

Israel will return to a life of peace and quiet,
and no one will terrorize them.
11 For I am with you and will save you,"
says the LORD.
"I will completely destroy the nations where
I have scattered you,
but I will not completely destroy you.
I will discipline you, but with justice;
I cannot let you go unpunished."

12 This is what the LORD says:
"Your injury is incurable—
a terrible wound.
13 There is no one to help you
or to bind up your injury.
No medicine can heal you.
14 All your lovers—your allies—have left you
and do not care about you anymore.
I have wounded you cruelly,
as though I were your enemy.
For your sins are many,
and your guilt is great.
15 Why do you protest your punishment—
this wound that has no cure?
I have had to punish you
because your sins are many
and your guilt is great.

16 "But all who devour you will be devoured,
and all your enemies will be sent into exile.
All who plunder you will be plundered,
and all who attack you will be attacked.
17 I will give you back your health
and heal your wounds," says the LORD.
"For you are called an outcast—
'Jerusalem* for whom no one cares.'"

18 This is what the LORD says:
"When I bring Israel home again from captivity
and restore their fortunes,
Jerusalem will be rebuilt on its ruins,
and the palace reconstructed as before.
19 There will be joy and songs of thanksgiving,
and I will multiply my people, not
diminish them;
I will honor them, not despise them.
20 Their children will prosper as they did long ago.
I will establish them as a nation before me,
and I will punish anyone who hurts them.
21 They will have their own ruler again,
and he will come from their own people.
I will invite him to approach me," says the LORD,
"for who would dare to come unless invited?
22 You will be my people,
and I will be your God."

23 Look! The LORD's anger bursts out like a storm,
a driving wind that swirls down on the heads
of the wicked.

30:17 Hebrew *Zion.*

KING JAMES VERSION

24 The fierce anger of the LORD shall not return, until he have done *it,* and until he have performed the intents of his heart: in the latter days ye shall consider it.

31 1 At the same time, saith the LORD, will I be the God of all the families of Israel, and they shall be my people.

2 Thus saith the LORD, The people *which were* left of the sword found grace in the wilderness; *even* Israel, when I went to cause him to rest.

3 The LORD hath appeared of old unto me, *saying,* Yea, I have loved thee with an everlasting love: therefore with lovingkindness have I drawn thee.

4 Again I will build thee, and thou shalt be built, O virgin of Israel: thou shalt again be adorned with thy tabrets, and shalt go forth in the dances of them that make merry.

5 Thou shalt yet plant vines upon the mountains of Samaria: the planters shall plant, and shall eat *them* as common things.

6 For there shall be a day, *that* the watchmen upon the mount Ephraim shall cry, Arise ye, and let us go up to Zion unto the LORD our God.

7 For thus saith the LORD; Sing with gladness for Jacob, and shout among the chief of the nations: publish ye, praise ye, and say, O LORD, save thy people, the remnant of Israel.

8 Behold, I will bring them from the north country, and gather them from the coasts of the earth, *and* with them the blind and the lame, the woman with child and her that travaileth with child together: a great company shall return thither.

9 They shall come with weeping, and with supplications will I lead them: I will cause them to walk by the rivers of waters in a straight way, wherein they shall not stumble: for I am a father to Israel, and Ephraim *is* my firstborn.

10 Hear the word of the LORD, O ye nations, and declare *it* in the isles afar off, and say, He that scattered Israel will gather him, and keep him, as a shepherd *doth* his flock.

11 For the LORD hath redeemed Jacob, and ransomed him from the hand of *him that was* stronger than he.

12 Therefore they shall come and sing in the height

NEW LIVING TRANSLATION

24 The fierce anger of the LORD will not diminish
until it has finished all he has planned.
In the days to come
you will understand all this.

Hope for Restoration

31 "In that day," says the LORD, "I will be the God of all the families of Israel, and they will be my people. 2 This is what the LORD says:

"Those who survive the coming destruction
will find blessings even in the barren land,
for I will give rest to the people of Israel."

3 Long ago the LORD said to Israel:
"I have loved you, my people, with an
everlasting love.
With unfailing love I have drawn you to myself.
4 I will rebuild you, my virgin Israel.
You will again be happy
and dance merrily with your tambourines.
5 Again you will plant your vineyards on the
mountains of Samaria
and eat from your own gardens there.
6 The day will come when watchmen will shout
from the hill country of Ephraim,
'Come, let us go up to Jerusalem*
to worship the LORD our God.'"
7 Now this is what the LORD says:
"Sing with joy for Israel.*
Shout for the greatest of nations!
Shout out with praise and joy:
'Save your people, O LORD,
the remnant of Israel!'
8 For I will bring them from the north
and from the distant corners of the earth.
I will not forget the blind and lame,
the expectant mothers and women in labor.
A great company will return!
9 Tears of joy will stream down their faces,
and I will lead them home with great care.
They will walk beside quiet streams
and on smooth paths where they will
not stumble.
For I am Israel's father,
and Ephraim is my oldest child.

10 "Listen to this message from the LORD,
you nations of the world;
proclaim it in distant coastlands:
The LORD, who scattered his people,
will gather them and watch over them
as a shepherd does his flock.
11 For the LORD has redeemed Israel
from those too strong for them.
12 They will come home and sing songs of joy
on the heights of Jerusalem.

31:6 Hebrew *Zion;* also in 31:12. **31:7** Hebrew *Jacob;* also in 31:11. See note on 5:20.

KING JAMES VERSION

of Zion, and shall flow together to the goodness of
the LORD, for wheat, and for wine, and for oil, and for
the young of the flock and of the herd: and their soul
shall be as a watered garden; and they shall not sorrow any more at all.
13 Then shall the virgin rejoice in the dance, both
young men and old together: for I will turn their
mourning into joy, and will comfort them, and make
them rejoice from their sorrow.
14 And I will satiate the soul of the priests with
fatness, and my people shall be satisfied with my
goodness, saith the LORD.

15 Thus saith the LORD; A voice was heard in Ramah, lamentation, *and* bitter weeping; Rahel weeping for her children refused to be comforted for her
children, because they *were* not.
16 Thus saith the LORD; Refrain thy voice from
weeping, and thine eyes from tears: for thy work
shall be rewarded, saith the LORD; and they shall
come again from the land of the enemy.
17 And there is hope in thine end, saith the LORD,
that thy children shall come again to their own
border.
18 I have surely heard Ephraim bemoaning himself
thus; Thou hast chastised me, and I was chastised, as
a bullock unaccustomed *to the yoke:* turn thou me,
and I shall be turned; for thou *art* the LORD my God.
19 Surely after that I was turned, I repented; and
after that I was instructed, I smote upon *my* thigh: I
was ashamed, yea, even confounded, because I did
bear the reproach of my youth.
20 *Is* Ephraim my dear son? *is he* a pleasant child?
for since I spake against him, I do earnestly remember him still: therefore my bowels are troubled for
him; I will surely have mercy upon him, saith the
LORD.
21 Set thee up waymarks, make thee high heaps: set
thine heart toward the highway, *even* the way *which*
thou wentest: turn again, O virgin of Israel, turn again
to these thy cities.

NEW LIVING TRANSLATION

They will be radiant because of the
LORD's good gifts—
the abundant crops of grain, new wine,
and olive oil,
and the healthy flocks and herds.
Their life will be like a watered garden,
and all their sorrows will be gone.
13 The young women will dance for joy,
and the men—old and young—will join
in the celebration.
I will turn their mourning into joy.
I will comfort them and exchange their
sorrow for rejoicing.
14 The priests will enjoy abundance,
and my people will feast on my good gifts.
I, the LORD, have spoken!"

Rachel's Sadness Turns to Joy

15 This is what the LORD says:

"A cry is heard in Ramah—
deep anguish and bitter weeping.
Rachel weeps for her children,
refusing to be comforted—
for her children are gone."

16 But now this is what the LORD says:
"Do not weep any longer,
for I will reward you," says the LORD.
"Your children will come back to you
from the distant land of the enemy.
17 There is hope for your future," says the LORD.
"Your children will come again to their
own land.
18 I have heard Israel* saying,
'You disciplined me severely,
like a calf that needs training for the yoke.
Turn me again to you and restore me,
for you alone are the LORD my God.
19 I turned away from God,
but then I was sorry.
I kicked myself for my stupidity!
I was thoroughly ashamed of all I did
in my younger days.'
20 "Is not Israel still my son,
my darling child?" says the LORD.
"I often have to punish him,
but I still love him.
That's why I long for him
and surely will have mercy on him.
21 Set up road signs;
put up guideposts.
Mark well the path
by which you came.
Come back again, my virgin Israel;
return to your towns here.

31:18 Hebrew *Ephraim,* referring to the northern kingdom of Israel; also in 31:20.

KING JAMES VERSION

22How long wilt thou go about, O thou backsliding
daughter? for the LORD hath created a new thing in
the earth, A woman shall compass a man.
23 Thus saith the LORD of hosts, the God of Israel;
As yet they shall use this speech in the land of Judah
and in the cities thereof, when I shall bring again
their captivity; The LORD bless thee, O habitation of
justice, *and* mountain of holiness.
24And there shall dwell in Judah itself, and in all
the cities thereof together, husbandmen, and they
that go forth with flocks.
25For I have satiated the weary soul, and I have
replenished every sorrowful soul.
26Upon this I awaked, and beheld; and my sleep
was sweet unto me.
27Behold, the days come, saith the LORD, that I will
sow the house of Israel and the house of Judah with
the seed of man, and with the seed of beast.
28And it shall come to pass, *that* like as I have
watched over them, to pluck up, and to break down,
and to throw down, and to destroy, and to afflict; so
will I watch over them, to build, and to plant, saith
the LORD.
29In those days they shall say no more, The fathers
have eaten a sour grape, and the children's teeth are
set on edge.
30But every one shall die for his own iniquity:
every man that eateth the sour grape, his teeth shall
be set on edge.
31Behold, the days come, saith the LORD, that I will
make a new covenant with the house of Israel, and
with the house of Judah:
32Not according to the covenant that I made with
their fathers in the day *that* I took them by the hand
to bring them out of the land of Egypt; which my covenant they brake, although I was an husband unto
them, saith the LORD:
33But this *shall be* the covenant that I will make
with the house of Israel; After those days, saith the
LORD, I will put my law in their inward parts, and
write it in their hearts; and will be their God, and
they shall be my people.
34And they shall teach no more every man his
neighbour, and every man his brother, saying, Know
the LORD: for they shall all know me, from the least of
them unto the greatest of them, saith the LORD: for I
will forgive their iniquity, and I will remember their
sin no more.
35Thus saith the LORD, which giveth the sun for a
light by day, *and* the ordinances of the moon and of
the stars for a light by night, which divideth the sea
when the waves thereof roar; The LORD of hosts *is*
his name:
36If those ordinances depart from before me, saith
the LORD, *then* the seed of Israel also shall cease from
being a nation before me for ever.

NEW LIVING TRANSLATION

22 How long will you wander,
my wayward daughter?
For the LORD will cause something
new to happen—
Israel will embrace her God.*"

23This is what the LORD of Heaven's Armies, the
God of Israel, says: "When I bring them back from
captivity, the people of Judah and its towns will again
say, 'The LORD bless you, O righteous home, O holy
mountain!' 24Townspeople and farmers and shepherds alike will live together in peace and happiness.
25For I have given rest to the weary and joy to the
sorrowing."
26At this, I woke up and looked around. My sleep
had been very sweet.
27"The day is coming," says the LORD, "when I will
greatly increase the human population and the number of animals here in Israel and Judah. 28In the past
I deliberately uprooted and tore down this nation. I
overthrew it, destroyed it, and brought disaster upon
it. But in the future I will just as deliberately plant it
and build it up. I, the LORD, have spoken!
29"The people will no longer quote this proverb:

'The parents have eaten sour grapes,
but their children's mouths pucker
at the taste.'

30All people will die for their own sins—those who
eat the sour grapes will be the ones whose mouths
will pucker.
31"The day is coming," says the LORD, "when I will
make a new covenant with the people of Israel and
Judah. 32This covenant will not be like the one I
made with their ancestors when I took them by the
hand and brought them out of the land of Egypt.
They broke that covenant, though I loved them as a
husband loves his wife," says the LORD.
33"But this is the new covenant I will make with
the people of Israel on that day," says the LORD. "I will
put my instructions deep within them, and I will
write them on their hearts. I will be their God, and
they will be my people. 34And they will not need to
teach their neighbors, nor will they need to teach
their relatives, saying, 'You should know the LORD.'
For everyone, from the least to the greatest, will
know me already," says the LORD. "And I will forgive
their wickedness, and I will never again remember
their sins."

35 It is the LORD who provides the sun
to light the day
and the moon and stars to light the night,
and who stirs the sea into roaring waves.
His name is the LORD of Heaven's Armies,
and this is what he says:
36 "I am as likely to reject my people Israel
as I am to abolish the laws of nature!"

31:22 Hebrew *a woman will surround a man.*

KING JAMES VERSION

37 Thus saith the LORD; If heaven above can be measured, and the foundations of the earth searched out
beneath, I will also cast off all the seed of Israel for all
that they have done, saith the LORD.
38 Behold, the days come, saith the LORD, that the
city shall be built to the LORD from the tower of
Hananeel unto the gate of the corner.
39 And the measuring line shall yet go forth over
against it upon the hill Gareb, and shall compass
about to Goath.
40 And the whole valley of the dead bodies, and of
the ashes, and all the fields unto the brook of Kidron,
unto the corner of the horse gate toward the east,
shall be holy unto the LORD; it shall not be plucked
up, nor thrown down any more for ever.

32 1 The word that came to Jeremiah from the
LORD in the tenth year of Zedekiah king of
Judah, which *was* the eighteenth year of Nebuchadrezzar.
2 For then the king of Babylon's army besieged
Jerusalem: and Jeremiah the prophet was shut up in
the court of the prison, which *was* in the king of
Judah's house.
3 For Zedekiah king of Judah had shut him up, saying, Wherefore dost thou prophesy, and say, Thus
saith the LORD, Behold, I will give this city into the
hand of the king of Babylon, and he shall take it;
4 And Zedekiah king of Judah shall not escape out
of the hand of the Chaldeans, but shall surely be
delivered into the hand of the king of Babylon, and
shall speak with him mouth to mouth, and his eyes
shall behold his eyes;
5 And he shall lead Zedekiah to Babylon, and there
shall he be until I visit him, saith the LORD: though ye
fight with the Chaldeans, ye shall not prosper.
6 And Jeremiah said, The word of the LORD came
unto me, saying,
7 Behold, Hanameel the son of Shallum thine
uncle shall come unto thee, saying, Buy thee my field
that *is* in Anathoth: for the right of redemption *is*
thine to buy *it*.
8 So Hanameel mine uncle's son came to me in
the court of the prison according to the word of the
LORD, and said unto me, Buy my field, I pray thee, that
is in Anathoth, which *is* in the country of Benjamin:
for the right of inheritance *is* thine, and the redemption *is* thine; buy *it* for thyself. Then I knew that this
was the word of the LORD.
9 And I bought the field of Hanameel my uncle's
son, that *was* in Anathoth, and weighed him the
money, *even* seventeen shekels of silver.
10 And I subscribed the evidence, and sealed *it*,
and took witnesses, and weighed *him* the money in
the balances.

NEW LIVING TRANSLATION

37 This is what the LORD says:
"Just as the heavens cannot bes measured
and the foundations of the earth cannot
be explored,
so I will not consider casting them away
for the evil they have done.
I, the LORD, have spoken!

38 "The day is coming," says the LORD, "when all
Jerusalem will be rebuilt for me, from the Tower of
Hananel to the Corner Gate. 39 A measuring line will
be stretched out over the hill of Gareb and across to
Goah. 40 And the entire area—including the graveyard
and ash dump in the valley, and all the fields out to
the Kidron Valley on the east as far as the Horse
Gate—will be holy to the LORD. The city will never
again be captured or destroyed."

Jeremiah's Land Purchase

32 The following message came to Jeremiah
from the LORD in the tenth year of the reign
of Zedekiah,* king of Judah. This was also the eighteenth year of the reign of King Nebuchadnezzar.*
2 Jerusalem was then under siege from the Babylonian army, and Jeremiah was imprisoned in the
courtyard of the guard in the royal palace. 3 King
Zedekiah had put him there, asking why he kept giving this prophecy: "This is what the LORD says: 'I am
about to hand this city over to the king of Babylon,
and he will take it. 4 King Zedekiah will be captured
by the Babylonians* and taken to meet the king of
Babylon face to face. 5 He will take Zedekiah to Babylon, and I will deal with him there,' says the LORD. 'If
you fight against the Babylonians, you will never
succeed.'"
6 At that time the LORD sent me a message. He said,
7 "Your cousin Hanamel son of Shallum will come
and say to you, 'Buy my field at Anathoth. By law you
have the right to buy it before it is offered to anyone
else.'"
8 Then, just as the LORD had said he would, my
cousin Hanamel came and visited me in the prison.
He said, "Please buy my field at Anathoth in the land
of Benjamin. By law you have the right to buy it before it is offered to anyone else, so buy it for yourself." Then I knew that the message I had heard was
from the LORD.
9 So I bought the field at Anathoth, paying Hanamel seventeen pieces* of silver for it. 10 I signed and
sealed the deed of purchase before witnesses,

32:1a The tenth year of Zedekiah's reign and the eighteenth year of Nebuchadnezzar's reign was 587 B.C. **32:1b** Hebrew *Nebuchadrezzar,* a variant spelling of Nebuchadnezzar; also in 32:28. **32:4** Or *Chaldeans;* also in 32:5, 24, 25, 28, 29, 43. **32:9** Hebrew *17 shekels,* about 7 ounces or 194 grams in weight.

KING JAMES VERSION

11So I took the evidence of the purchase, *both* that which was sealed *according* to the law and custom, and that which was open:

12And I gave the evidence of the purchase unto Baruch the son of Neriah, the son of Maaseiah, in the sight of Hanameel mine uncle's *son*, and in the presence of the witnesses that subscribed the book of the purchase, before all the Jews that sat in the court of the prison.

13And I charged Baruch before them, saying,

14Thus saith the LORD of hosts, the God of Israel; Take these evidences, this evidence of the purchase, both which is sealed, and this evidence which is open; and put them in an earthen vessel, that they may continue many days.

15For thus saith the LORD of hosts, the God of Israel; Houses and fields and vineyards shall be possessed again in this land.

16Now when I had delivered the evidence of the purchase unto Baruch the son of Neriah, I prayed unto the LORD, saying,

17Ah Lord GOD! behold, thou hast made the heaven and the earth by thy great power and stretched out arm, *and* there is nothing too hard for thee:

18Thou shewest lovingkindness unto thousands, and recompensest the iniquity of the fathers into the bosom of their children after them: the Great, the Mighty God, the LORD of hosts, *is* his name,

19Great in counsel, and mighty in work: for thine eyes *are* open upon all the ways of the sons of men: to give every one according to his ways, and according to the fruit of his doings:

20Which hast set signs and wonders in the land of Egypt, *even* unto this day, and in Israel, and among *other* men; and hast made thee a name, as at this day;

21And hast brought forth thy people Israel out of the land of Egypt with signs, and with wonders, and with a strong hand, and with a stretched out arm, and with great terror;

22And hast given them this land, which thou didst swear to their fathers to give them, a land flowing with milk and honey;

23And they came in, and possessed it; but they obeyed not thy voice, neither walked in thy law; they have done nothing of all that thou commandedst them to do: therefore thou hast caused all this evil to come upon them:

24Behold the mounts, they are come unto the city to take it; and the city is given into the hand of the Chaldeans, that fight against it, because of the sword, and of the famine, and of the pestilence: and what thou hast spoken is come to pass; and, behold, thou seest *it*.

25And thou hast said unto me, O Lord GOD, Buy thee the field for money, and take witnesses; for the city is given into the hand of the Chaldeans.

NEW LIVING TRANSLATION

weighed out the silver, and paid him. 11Then I took
the sealed deed and an unsealed copy of the deed,
which contained the terms and conditions of the
purchase, 12and I handed them to Baruch son of Neriah and grandson of Mahseiah. I did all this in the
presence of my cousin Hanamel, the witnesses who
had signed the deed, and all the men of Judah who
were there in the courtyard of the guardhouse.
13Then I said to Baruch as they all listened, 14"This
is what the LORD of Heaven's Armies, the God of Israel, says: 'Take both this sealed deed and the unsealed
copy, and put them into a pottery jar to preserve
them for a long time.' 15For this is what the LORD of
Heaven's Armies, the God of Israel, says: 'Someday
people will again own property here in this land and
will buy and sell houses and vineyards and fields.'"

Jeremiah's Prayer

16Then after I had given the papers to Baruch, I
prayed to the LORD:

17"O Sovereign LORD! You made the heavens and
earth by your strong hand and powerful arm.
Nothing is too hard for you! 18You show unfailing
love to thousands, but you also bring the
consequences of one generation's sin upon the
next. You are the great and powerful God, the
LORD of Heaven's Armies. 19You have all wisdom
and do great and mighty miracles. You see the
conduct of all people, and you give them what
they deserve. 20You performed miraculous signs
and wonders in the land of Egypt—things still
remembered to this day! And you have continued
to do great miracles in Israel and all around the
world. You have made your name famous to
this day.

21"You brought Israel out of Egypt with mighty
signs and wonders, with a strong hand and
powerful arm, and with overwhelming terror.
22You gave the people of Israel this land that you
had promised their ancestors long before—a land
flowing with milk and honey. 23Our ancestors
came and conquered it and lived in it, but they
refused to obey you or follow your word. They
have not done anything you commanded. That
is why you have sent this terrible disaster upon
them.

24"See how the siege ramps have been built
against the city walls! Through war, famine,
and disease, the city will be handed over to the
Babylonians, who will conquer it. Everything has
happened just as you said. 25And yet, O Sovereign
LORD, you have told me to buy the field—paying
good money for it before these witnesses—even
though the city will soon be handed over to the
Babylonians."

KING JAMES VERSION

26 Then came the word of the LORD unto Jeremiah, saying,

27 Behold, I *am* the LORD, the God of all flesh: is there any thing too hard for me?

28 Therefore thus saith the LORD; Behold, I will give this city into the hand of the Chaldeans, and into the hand of Nebuchadrezzar king of Babylon, and he shall take it:

29 And the Chaldeans, that fight against this city, shall come and set fire on this city, and burn it with the houses, upon whose roofs they have offered incense unto Baal, and poured out drink offerings unto other gods, to provoke me to anger.

30 For the children of Israel and the children of Judah have only done evil before me from their youth: for the children of Israel have only provoked me to anger with the work of their hands, saith the LORD.

31 For this city hath been to me *as* a provocation of mine anger and of my fury from the day that they built it even unto this day; that I should remove it from before my face,

32 Because of all the evil of the children of Israel and of the children of Judah, which they have done to provoke me to anger, they, their kings, their princes, their priests, and their prophets, and the men of Judah, and the inhabitants of Jerusalem.

33 And they have turned unto me the back, and not the face: though I taught them, rising up early and teaching *them*, yet they have not hearkened to receive instruction.

34 But they set their abominations in the house, which is called by my name, to defile it.

35 And they built the high places of Baal, which *are* in the valley of the son of Hinnom, to cause their sons and their daughters to pass through *the fire* unto Molech; which I commanded them not, neither came it into my mind, that they should do this abomination, to cause Judah to sin.

36 And now therefore thus saith the LORD, the God of Israel, concerning this city, whereof ye say, It shall be delivered into the hand of the king of Babylon by the sword, and by the famine, and by the pestilence;

37 Behold, I will gather them out of all countries, whither I have driven them in mine anger, and in my fury, and in great wrath; and I will bring them again unto this place, and I will cause them to dwell safely:

38 And they shall be my people, and I will be their God:

39 And I will give them one heart, and one way, that they may fear me for ever, for the good of them, and of their children after them:

40 And I will make an everlasting covenant with them, that I will not turn away from them, to do them good; but I will put my fear in their hearts, that they shall not depart from me.

41 Yea, I will rejoice over them to do them good,

NEW LIVING TRANSLATION

A Prediction of Jerusalem's Fall

26 Then this message came to Jeremiah from the
LORD: 27 "I am the LORD, the God of all the peoples of
the world. Is anything too hard for me? 28 Therefore,
this is what the LORD says: I will hand this city over to
the Babylonians and to Nebuchadnezzar, king of
Babylon, and he will capture it. 29 The Babylonians
outside the walls will come in and set fire to the city.
They will burn down all these houses where the people provoked my anger by burning incense to Baal on
the rooftops and by pouring out liquid offerings to
other gods. 30 Israel and Judah have done nothing but
wrong since their earliest days. They have infuriated
me with all their evil deeds," says the LORD. 31 "From
the time this city was built until now, it has done
nothing but anger me, so I am determined to get
rid of it.

32 "The sins of Israel and Judah—the sins of the
people of Jerusalem, the kings, the officials, the
priests, and the prophets—have stirred up my anger.
33 My people have turned their backs on me and have
refused to return. Even though I diligently taught
them, they would not receive instruction or obey.
34 They have set up their abominable idols right in
my own Temple, defiling it. 35 They have built pagan
shrines to Baal in the valley of Ben-Hinnom, and
there they sacrifice their sons and daughters to
Molech. I have never commanded such a horrible
deed; it never even crossed my mind to command
such a thing. What an incredible evil, causing Judah
to sin so greatly!

A Promise of Restoration

36 "Now I want to say something more about this city.
You have been saying, 'It will fall to the king of Babylon through war, famine, and disease.' But this is
what the LORD, the God of Israel, says: 37 I will certainly bring my people back again from all the countries where I will scatter them in my fury. I will bring
them back to this very city and let them live in peace
and safety. 38 They will be my people, and I will be
their God. 39 And I will give them one heart and one
purpose: to worship me forever, for their own good
and for the good of all their descendants. 40 And I will
make an everlasting covenant with them: I will never
stop doing good for them. I will put a desire in their
hearts to worship me, and they will never leave me.
41 I will find joy doing good for them and will faithfully and wholeheartedly replant them in this land.

42 "This is what the LORD says: Just as I have
brought all these calamities on them, so I will do all
the good I have promised them. 43 Fields will again be

and I will plant them in this land assuredly with my whole heart and with my whole soul.

42For thus saith the LORD; Like as I have brought all this great evil upon this people, so will I bring upon them all the good that I have promised them.

43And fields shall be bought in this land, whereof ye say, *It is* desolate without man or beast; it is given into the hand of the Chaldeans.

44Men shall buy fields for money, and subscribe evidences, and seal *them,* and take witnesses in the land of Benjamin, and in the places about Jerusalem, and in the cities of Judah, and in the cities of the mountains, and in the cities of the valley, and in the cities of the south: for I will cause their captivity to return, saith the LORD.

33 1Moreover the word of the LORD came unto Jeremiah the second time, while he was yet shut up in the court of the prison, saying,

2Thus saith the LORD the maker thereof, the LORD that formed it, to establish it; the LORD *is* his name;

3Call unto me, and I will answer thee, and shew thee great and mighty things, which thou knowest not.

4For thus saith the LORD, the God of Israel, concerning the houses of this city, and concerning the houses of the kings of Judah, which are thrown down by the mounts, and by the sword;

5They come to fight with the Chaldeans, but *it is* to fill them with the dead bodies of men, whom I have slain in mine anger and in my fury, and for all whose wickedness I have hid my face from this city.

6Behold, I will bring it health and cure, and I will cure them, and will reveal unto them the abundance of peace and truth.

7And I will cause the captivity of Judah and the captivity of Israel to return, and will build them, as at the first.

8And I will cleanse them from all their iniquity, whereby they have sinned against me; and I will pardon all their iniquities, whereby they have sinned, and whereby they have transgressed against me.

9And it shall be to me a name of joy, a praise and an honour before all the nations of the earth, which shall hear all the good that I do unto them: and they shall fear and tremble for all the goodness and for all the prosperity that I procure unto it.

10Thus saith the LORD; Again there shall be heard in this place, which ye say *shall be* desolate without man and without beast, *even* in the cities of Judah, and in the streets of Jerusalem, that are desolate, without man, and without inhabitant, and without beast,

11The voice of joy, and the voice of gladness, the voice of the bridegroom, and the voice of the bride, the voice of them that shall say, Praise the LORD of hosts: for the LORD *is* good; for his mercy *endureth* for ever: *and* of them that shall bring the sacrifice of praise into

bought and sold in this land about which you now say, 'It has been ravaged by the Babylonians, a desolate land where people and animals have all disappeared.' 44Yes, fields will once again be bought and sold—deeds signed and sealed and witnessed—in the land of Benjamin and here in Jerusalem, in the towns of Judah and in the hill country, in the foothills of Judah* and in the Negev, too. For someday I will restore prosperity to them. I, the LORD, have spoken!"

Promises of Peace and Prosperity

33 While Jeremiah was still confined in the courtyard of the guard, the LORD gave him this second message: 2"This is what the LORD says—the LORD who made the earth, who formed and established it, whose name is the LORD: 3Ask me and I will tell you remarkable secrets you do not know about things to come. 4For this is what the LORD, the God of Israel, says: You have torn down the houses of this city and even the king's palace to get materials to strengthen the walls against the siege ramps and swords of the enemy. 5You expect to fight the Babylonians,* but the men of this city are already as good as dead, for I have determined to destroy them in my terrible anger. I have abandoned them because of all their wickedness.

6"Nevertheless, the time will come when I will heal Jerusalem's wounds and give it prosperity and true peace. 7I will restore the fortunes of Judah and Israel and rebuild their towns. 8I will cleanse them of their sins against me and forgive all their sins of rebellion. 9Then this city will bring me joy, glory, and honor before all the nations of the earth! The people of the world will see all the good I do for my people, and they will tremble with awe at the peace and prosperity I provide for them.

10"This is what the LORD says: You have said, 'This is a desolate land where people and animals have all disappeared.' Yet in the empty streets of Jerusalem and Judah's other towns, there will be heard once more 11the sounds of joy and laughter. The joyful voices of bridegrooms and brides will be heard again, along with the joyous songs of people bringing thanksgiving offerings to the LORD. They will sing,

'Give thanks to the LORD of Heaven's Armies,
for the LORD is good.
His faithful love endures forever!'

32:44 Hebrew *the Shephelah.* **33:5** Or *Chaldeans.*

KING JAMES VERSION

the house of the LORD. For I will cause to return the
captivity of the land, as at the first, saith the LORD.
12 Thus saith the LORD of hosts; Again in this place,
which is desolate without man and without beast,
and in all the cities thereof, shall be an habitation of
shepherds causing *their* flocks to lie down.
13 In the cities of the mountains, in the cities of the
vale, and in the cities of the south, and in the land of
Benjamin, and in the places about Jerusalem, and in
the cities of Judah, shall the flocks pass again under
the hands of him that telleth *them,* saith the LORD.
14 Behold, the days come, saith the LORD, that I will
perform that good thing which I have promised unto
the house of Israel and to the house of Judah.
15 In those days, and at that time, will I cause the
Branch of righteousness to grow up unto David; and he
shall execute judgment and righteousness in the land.
16 In those days shall Judah be saved, and Jerusalem shall dwell safely: and this *is the name* wherewith she shall be called, The LORD our righteousness.
17 For thus saith the LORD; David shall never want a
man to sit upon the throne of the house of Israel;
18 Neither shall the priests the Levites want a man
before me to offer burnt offerings, and to kindle
meat offerings, and to do sacrifice continually.
19 And the word of the LORD came unto Jeremiah,
saying,
20 Thus saith the LORD; If ye can break my covenant
of the day, and my covenant of the night, and that
there should not be day and night in their season;
21 *Then* may also my covenant be broken with
David my servant, that he should not have a son to
reign upon his throne; and with the Levites the
priests, my ministers.
22 As the host of heaven cannot be numbered, neither the sand of the sea measured: so will I multiply
the seed of David my servant, and the Levites that
minister unto me.
23 Moreover the word of the LORD came to Jeremiah, saying,
24 Considerest thou not what this people have
spoken, saying, The two families which the LORD
hath chosen, he hath even cast them off? thus they
have despised my people, that they should be no
more a nation before them.
25 Thus saith the LORD; If my covenant *be* not with
day and night, *and if* I have not appointed the ordinances of heaven and earth;
26 Then will I cast away the seed of Jacob, and
David my servant, *so* that I will not take *any* of his
seed *to be* rulers over the seed of Abraham, Isaac, and
Jacob: for I will cause their captivity to return, and
have mercy on them.

34 1 The word which came unto Jeremiah from
the LORD, when Nebuchadnezzar king of
Babylon, and all his army, and all the kingdoms of the

NEW LIVING TRANSLATION

For I will restore the prosperity of this land to what it
was in the past, says the LORD.
12 "This is what the LORD of Heaven's Armies says:
This land—though it is now desolate and has no
people and animals—will once more have pastures
where shepherds can lead their flocks. 13 Once again
shepherds will count their flocks in the towns of the
hill country, the foothills of Judah,* the Negev, the
land of Benjamin, the vicinity of Jerusalem, and all
the towns of Judah. I, the LORD, have spoken!
14 "The day will come, says the LORD, when I will do
for Israel and Judah all the good things I have promised them.

15 "In those days and at that time
I will raise up a righteous descendant*
from King David's line.
He will do what is just and right
throughout the land.
16 In that day Judah will be saved,
and Jerusalem will live in safety.
And this will be its name:
'The LORD Is Our Righteousness.'*

17 For this is what the LORD says: David will have a
descendant sitting on the throne of Israel forever.
18 And there will always be Levitical priests to offer
burnt offerings and grain offerings and sacrifices
to me."
19 Then this message came to Jeremiah from the
LORD: 20 "This is what the LORD says: If you can break
my covenant with the day and the night so that one
does not follow the other, 21 only then will my covenant with my servant David be broken. Only then
will he no longer have a descendant to reign on his
throne. The same is true for my covenant with the
Levitical priests who minister before me. 22 And as
the stars of the sky cannot be counted and the sand
on the seashore cannot be measured, so I will multiply the descendants of my servant David and the
Levites who minister before me."
23 The LORD gave another message to Jeremiah. He
said, 24 "Have you noticed what people are saying?—
'The LORD chose Judah and Israel and then abandoned them!' They are sneering and saying that Israel
is not worthy to be counted as a nation. 25 But this is
what the LORD says: I would no more reject my people
than I would change my laws that govern night and
day, earth and sky. 26 I will never abandon the descendants of Jacob or David, my servant, or change the
plan that David's descendants will rule the descendants of Abraham, Isaac, and Jacob. Instead, I will restore them to their land and have mercy on them."

A Warning for Zedekiah

34 King Nebuchadnezzar of Babylon came
with all the armies from the kingdoms he

33:13 Hebrew *the Shephelah.* 33:15 Hebrew *a righteous branch.*
33:16 Hebrew *Yahweh Tsidqenu.*

KING JAMES VERSION

earth of his dominion, and all the people, fought
against Jerusalem, and against all the cities thereof,
saying,
2 Thus saith the LORD, the God of Israel; Go and
speak to Zedekiah king of Judah, and tell him, Thus
saith the LORD; Behold, I will give this city into the
hand of the king of Babylon, and he shall burn it
with fire:
3 And thou shalt not escape out of his hand, but
shalt surely be taken, and delivered into his hand;
and thine eyes shall behold the eyes of the king of
Babylon, and he shall speak with thee mouth to
mouth, and thou shalt go to Babylon.
4 Yet hear the word of the LORD, O Zedekiah king of
Judah; Thus saith the LORD of thee, Thou shalt not
die by the sword:
5 *But* thou shalt die in peace: and with the burnings of thy fathers, the former kings which were before thee, so shall they burn *odours* for thee; and they
will lament thee, *saying,* Ah lord! for I have pronounced the word, saith the LORD.
6 Then Jeremiah the prophet spake all these words
unto Zedekiah king of Judah in Jerusalem,
7 When the king of Babylon's army fought against
Jerusalem, and against all the cities of Judah that
were left, against Lachish, and against Azekah: for
these defenced cities remained of the cities of
Judah.
8 *This is* the word that came unto Jeremiah from
the LORD, after that the king Zedekiah had made a
covenant with all the people which *were* at Jerusalem, to proclaim liberty unto them;
9 That every man should let his manservant, and
every man his maidservant, *being* an Hebrew or an
Hebrewess, go free; that none should serve himself
of them, *to wit,* of a Jew his brother.
10 Now when all the princes, and all the people,
which had entered into the covenant, heard that
every one should let his manservant, and every one
his maidservant, go free, that none should serve
themselves of them any more, then they obeyed, and
let *them* go.
11 But afterward they turned, and caused the servants and the handmaids, whom they had let go free,
to return, and brought them into subjection for servants and for handmaids.
12 Therefore the word of the LORD came to Jeremiah from the LORD, saying,
13 Thus saith the LORD, the God of Israel; I made a
covenant with your fathers in the day that I brought
them forth out of the land of Egypt, out of the house
of bondmen, saying,
14 At the end of seven years let ye go every man his
brother an Hebrew, which hath been sold unto thee;
and when he hath served thee six years, thou shalt let
him go free from thee: but your fathers hearkened
not unto me, neither inclined their ear.
15 And ye were now turned, and had done right in

NEW LIVING TRANSLATION

ruled, and he fought against Jerusalem and the towns
of Judah. At that time this message came to Jeremiah
from the LORD: 2 "Go to King Zedekiah of Judah, and
tell him, 'This is what the LORD, the God of Israel, says:
I am about to hand this city over to the king of Babylon, and he will burn it down. 3 You will not escape
his grasp but will be captured and taken to meet the
king of Babylon face to face. Then you will be exiled
to Babylon.
4 "'But listen to this promise from the LORD, O Zedekiah, king of Judah. This is what the LORD says:
You will not be killed in war 5 but will die peacefully.
People will burn incense in your memory, just as they
did for your ancestors, the kings who preceded you.
They will mourn for you, crying, "Alas, our master is
dead!" This I have decreed, says the LORD.'"
6 So Jeremiah the prophet delivered the message
to King Zedekiah of Judah. 7 At this time the Babylonian army was besieging Jerusalem, Lachish, and
Azekah—the only fortified cities of Judah not yet
captured.

Freedom for Hebrew Slaves

8 This message came to Jeremiah from the LORD after
King Zedekiah made a covenant with the people,
proclaiming freedom for the slaves. 9 He had ordered
all the people to free their Hebrew slaves—both
men and women. No one was to keep a fellow Judean
in bondage. 10 The officials and all the people had
obeyed the king's command, 11 but later they
changed their minds. They took back the men and
women they had freed, forcing them to be slaves
again.
12 So the LORD gave them this message through
Jeremiah: 13 "This is what the LORD, the God of Israel,
says: I made a covenant with your ancestors long ago
when I rescued them from their slavery in Egypt. 14 I
told them that every Hebrew slave must be freed after serving six years. But your ancestors paid no attention to me. 15 Recently you repented and did what

KING JAMES VERSION

my sight, in proclaiming liberty every man to his neighbour; and ye had made a covenant before me in the house which is called by my name:

16 But ye turned and polluted my name, and caused every man his servant, and every man his handmaid, whom he had set at liberty at their pleasure, to return, and brought them into subjection, to be unto you for servants and for handmaids.

17 Therefore thus saith the LORD; Ye have not hearkened unto me, in proclaiming liberty, every one to his brother, and every man to his neighbour: behold, I proclaim a liberty for you, saith the LORD, to the sword, to the pestilence, and to the famine; and I will make you to be removed into all the kingdoms of the earth.

18 And I will give the men that have transgressed my covenant, which have not performed the words of the covenant which they had made before me, when they cut the calf in twain, and passed between the parts thereof.

19 The princes of Judah, and the princes of Jerusalem, the eunuchs, and the priests, and all the people of the land, which passed between the parts of the calf;

20 I will even give them into the hand of their enemies, and into the hand of them that seek their life: and their dead bodies shall be for meat unto the fowls of the heaven, and to the beasts of the earth.

21 And Zedekiah king of Judah and his princes will I give into the hand of their enemies, and into the hand of them that seek their life, and into the hand of the king of Babylon's army, which are gone up from you.

22 Behold, I will command, saith the LORD, and cause them to return to this city; and they shall fight against it, and take it, and burn it with fire: and I will make the cities of Judah a desolation without an inhabitant.

35 1 The word which came unto Jeremiah from the LORD in the days of Jehoiakim the son of Josiah king of Judah, saying,

2 Go unto the house of the Rechabites, and speak unto them, and bring them into the house of the LORD, into one of the chambers, and give them wine to drink.

3 Then I took Jaazaniah the son of Jeremiah, the son of Habaziniah, and his brethren, and all his sons, and the whole house of the Rechabites;

4 And I brought them into the house of the LORD, into the chamber of the sons of Hanan, the son of Igdaliah, a man of God, which *was* by the chamber of the princes, which *was* above the chamber of Maaseiah the son of Shallum, the keeper of the door:

5 And I set before the sons of the house of the Rechabites pots full of wine, and cups, and I said unto them, Drink ye wine.

6 But they said, We will drink no wine: for Jonadab the son of Rechab our father commanded us, saying,

NEW LIVING TRANSLATION

was right, following my command. You freed your slaves and made a solemn covenant with me in the Temple that bears my name. 16 But now you have shrugged off your oath and defiled my name by taking back the men and women you had freed, forcing them to be slaves once again.

17 "Therefore, this is what the LORD says: Since you have not obeyed me by setting your countrymen free, I will set you free to be destroyed by war, disease, and famine. You will be an object of horror to all the nations of the earth. 18 Because you have broken the terms of our covenant, I will cut you apart just as you cut apart the calf when you walked between its halves to solemnize your vows. 19 Yes, I will cut you apart, whether you are officials of Judah or Jerusalem, court officials, priests, or common people—for you have broken your oath. 20 I will give you to your enemies, and they will kill you. Your bodies will be food for the vultures and wild animals.

21 "I will hand over King Zedekiah of Judah and his officials to the army of the king of Babylon. And although Babylon's king has left Jerusalem for a while, 22 I will call the Babylonian armies back again. They will fight against this city and will capture it and burn it down. I will see to it that all the towns of Judah are destroyed, with no one living there."

The Faithful Recabites

35 This is the message the LORD gave Jeremiah when Jehoiakim son of Josiah was king of Judah: 2 "Go to the settlement where the families of the Recabites live, and invite them to the LORD's Temple. Take them into one of the inner rooms, and offer them some wine."

3 So I went to see Jaazaniah son of Jeremiah and grandson of Habazziniah and all his brothers and sons—representing all the Recabite families. 4 I took them to the Temple, and we went into the room assigned to the sons of Hanan son of Igdaliah, a man of God. This room was located next to the one used by the Temple officials, directly above the room of Maaseiah son of Shallum, the Temple gatekeeper.

5 I set cups and jugs of wine before them and invited them to have a drink, 6 but they refused. "No," they said, "we don't drink wine, because our ancestor Jehonadab* son of Recab gave us this command:

35:6 Hebrew *Jonadab*, a variant spelling of Jehonadab; also in 35:10, 14, 16, 18, 19. See 2 Kgs 10:15.

Ye shall drink no wine, *neither ye*, nor your sons for ever:

7Neither shall ye build house, nor sow seed, nor plant vineyard, nor have *any:* but all your days ye shall dwell in tents; that ye may live many days in the land where ye *be* strangers.

8Thus have we obeyed the voice of Jonadab the son of Rechab our father in all that he hath charged us, to drink no wine all our days, we, our wives, our sons, nor our daughters;

9Nor to build houses for us to dwell in: neither have we vineyard, nor field, nor seed:

10But we have dwelt in tents, and have obeyed, and done according to all that Jonadab our father commanded us.

11But it came to pass, when Nebuchadrezzar king of Babylon came up into the land, that we said, Come, and let us go to Jerusalem for fear of the army of the Chaldeans, and for fear of the army of the Syrians: so we dwell at Jerusalem.

12Then came the word of the LORD unto Jeremiah, saying,

13Thus saith the LORD of hosts, the God of Israel; Go and tell the men of Judah and the inhabitants of Jerusalem, Will ye not receive instruction to hearken to my words? saith the LORD.

14The words of Jonadab the son of Rechab, that he commanded his sons not to drink wine, are performed; for unto this day they drink none, but obey their father's commandment: notwithstanding I have spoken unto you, rising early and speaking; but ye hearkened not unto me.

15I have sent also unto you all my servants the prophets, rising up early and sending *them,* saying, Return ye now every man from his evil way, and amend your doings, and go not after other gods to serve them, and ye shall dwell in the land which I have given to you and to your fathers: but ye have not inclined your ear, nor hearkened unto me.

16Because the sons of Jonadab the son of Rechab have performed the commandment of their father, which he commanded them; but this people hath not hearkened unto me:

17Therefore thus saith the LORD God of hosts, the God of Israel; Behold, I will bring upon Judah and upon all the inhabitants of Jerusalem all the evil that I have pronounced against them: because I have spoken unto them, but they have not heard; and I have called unto them, but they have not answered.

18And Jeremiah said unto the house of the Rechabites, Thus saith the LORD of hosts, the God of Israel; Because ye have obeyed the commandment of Jonadab your father, and kept all his precepts, and done according unto all that he hath commanded you:

19Therefore thus saith the LORD of hosts, the God of Israel; Jonadab the son of Rechab shall not want a man to stand before me for ever.

'You and your descendants must never drink wine. 7And do not build houses or plant crops or vineyards, but always live in tents. If you follow these commands, you will live long, good lives in the land.' 8So we have obeyed him in all these things. We have never had a drink of wine to this day, nor have our wives, our sons, or our daughters. 9We haven't built houses or owned vineyards or farms or planted crops. 10We have lived in tents and have fully obeyed all the commands of Jehonadab, our ancestor. 11But when King Nebuchadnezzar* of Babylon attacked this country, we were afraid of the Babylonian and Syrian* armies. So we decided to move to Jerusalem. That is why we are here."

12Then the LORD gave this message to Jeremiah: 13"This is what the LORD of Heaven's Armies, the God of Israel, says: Go and say to the people in Judah and Jerusalem, 'Come and learn a lesson about how to obey me. 14The Recabites do not drink wine to this day because their ancestor Jehonadab told them not to. But I have spoken to you again and again, and you refuse to obey me. 15Time after time I sent you prophets, who told you, "Turn from your wicked ways, and start doing things right. Stop worshiping other gods so that you might live in peace here in the land I have given to you and your ancestors." But you would not listen to me or obey me. 16The descendants of Jehonadab son of Recab have obeyed their ancestor completely, but you have refused to listen to me.'

17"Therefore, this is what the LORD God of Heaven's Armies, the God of Israel, says: 'Because you refuse to listen or answer when I call, I will send upon Judah and Jerusalem all the disasters I have threatened.'"

18Then Jeremiah turned to the Recabites and said, "This is what the LORD of Heaven's Armies, the God of Israel, says: 'You have obeyed your ancestor Jehonadab in every respect, following all his instructions.' 19Therefore, this is what the LORD of Heaven's Armies, the God of Israel, says: 'Jehonadab son of Recab will always have descendants who serve me.'"

35:11a Hebrew *Nebuchadrezzar*, a variant spelling of Nebuchadnezzar.
35:11b Or *Chaldean and Aramean*.

KING JAMES VERSION

36 1 And it came to pass in the fourth year of Jehoiakim the son of Josiah king of Judah, *that* this word came unto Jeremiah from the LORD, saying,

2 Take thee a roll of a book, and write therein all the words that I have spoken unto thee against Israel, and against Judah, and against all the nations, from the day I spake unto thee, from the days of Josiah, even unto this day.

3 It may be that the house of Judah will hear all the evil which I purpose to do unto them; that they may return every man from his evil way; that I may forgive their iniquity and their sin.

4 Then Jeremiah called Baruch the son of Neriah: and Baruch wrote from the mouth of Jeremiah all the words of the LORD, which he had spoken unto him, upon a roll of a book.

5 And Jeremiah commanded Baruch, saying, I *am* shut up; I cannot go into the house of the LORD:

6 Therefore go thou, and read in the roll, which thou hast written from my mouth, the words of the LORD in the ears of the people in the LORD's house upon the fasting day: and also thou shalt read them in the ears of all Judah that come out of their cities.

7 It may be they will present their supplication before the LORD, and will return every one from his evil way: for great *is* the anger and the fury that the LORD hath pronounced against this people.

8 And Baruch the son of Neriah did according to all that Jeremiah the prophet commanded him, reading in the book the words of the LORD in the LORD's house.

9 And it came to pass in the fifth year of Jehoiakim the son of Josiah king of Judah, in the ninth month, *that* they proclaimed a fast before the LORD to all the people in Jerusalem, and to all the people that came from the cities of Judah unto Jerusalem.

10 Then read Baruch in the book the words of Jeremiah in the house of the LORD, in the chamber of Gemariah the son of Shaphan the scribe, in the higher court, at the entry of the new gate of the LORD's house, in the ears of all the people.

11 When Michaiah the son of Gemariah, the son of Shaphan, had heard out of the book all the words of the LORD,

12 Then he went down into the king's house, into the scribe's chamber: and, lo, all the princes sat there, *even* Elishama the scribe, and Delaiah the son of Shemaiah, and Elnathan the son of Achbor, and Gemariah the son of Shaphan, and Zedekiah the son of Hananiah, and all the princes.

13 Then Michaiah declared unto them all the words that he had heard, when Baruch read the book in the ears of the people.

14 Therefore all the princes sent Jehudi the son of Nethaniah, the son of Shelemiah, the son of Cushi, unto Baruch, saying, Take in thine hand the roll

NEW LIVING TRANSLATION

Baruch Reads the LORD's Messages

36 During the fourth year that Jehoiakim son of Josiah was king in Judah,* the LORD gave this message to Jeremiah: 2 "Get a scroll, and write down all my messages against Israel, Judah, and the other nations. Begin with the first message back in the days of Josiah, and write down every message, right up to the present time. 3 Perhaps the people of Judah will repent when they hear again all the terrible things I have planned for them. Then I will be able to forgive their sins and wrongdoings."

4 So Jeremiah sent for Baruch son of Neriah, and as Jeremiah dictated all the prophecies that the LORD had given him, Baruch wrote them on a scroll. 5 Then Jeremiah said to Baruch, "I am a prisoner here and unable to go to the Temple. 6 So you go to the Temple on the next day of fasting, and read the messages from the LORD that I have had you write on this scroll. Read them so the people who are there from all over Judah will hear them. 7 Perhaps even yet they will turn from their evil ways and ask the LORD's forgiveness before it is too late. For the LORD has threatened them with his terrible anger."

8 Baruch did as Jeremiah told him and read these messages from the LORD to the people at the Temple. 9 He did this on a day of sacred fasting held in late autumn,* during the fifth year of the reign of Jehoiakim son of Josiah. People from all over Judah had come to Jerusalem to attend the services at the Temple on that day. 10 Baruch read Jeremiah's words on the scroll to all the people. He stood in front of the Temple room of Gemariah, son of Shaphan the secretary. This room was just off the upper courtyard of the Temple, near the New Gate entrance.

11 When Micaiah son of Gemariah and grandson of Shaphan heard the messages from the LORD, 12 he went down to the secretary's room in the palace where the administrative officials were meeting. Elishama the secretary was there, along with Delaiah son of Shemaiah, Elnathan son of Acbor, Gemariah son of Shaphan, Zedekiah son of Hananiah, and all the other officials. 13 When Micaiah told them about the messages Baruch was reading to the people, 14 the officials sent Jehudi son of Nethaniah, grandson of Shelemiah and great-grandson of Cushi, to

36:1 The fourth year of Jehoiakim's reign was 605 B.C. **36:9** Hebrew *in the ninth month,* of the ancient Hebrew lunar calendar (also in 36:22). The ninth month in the fifth year of Jehoiakim's reign occurred within the months of November and December 604 B.C. Also see note on 1:3.

KING JAMES VERSION

wherein thou hast read in the ears of the people, and
come. So Baruch the son of Neriah took the roll in
his hand, and came unto them.
15 And they said unto him, Sit down now, and read
it in our ears. So Baruch read *it* in their ears.
16 Now it came to pass, when they had heard all the
words, they were afraid both one and other, and said
unto Baruch, We will surely tell the king of all these
words.
17 And they asked Baruch, saying, Tell us now, How
didst thou write all these words at his mouth?
18 Then Baruch answered them, He pronounced all
these words unto me with his mouth, and I wrote
them with ink in the book.
19 Then said the princes unto Baruch, Go, hide
thee, thou and Jeremiah; and let no man know where
ye be.
20 And they went in to the king into the court, but
they laid up the roll in the chamber of Elishama the
scribe, and told all the words in the ears of the king.
21 So the king sent Jehudi to fetch the roll: and he
took it out of Elishama the scribe's chamber. And Jehudi read it in the ears of the king, and in the ears of
all the princes which stood beside the king.
22 Now the king sat in the winterhouse in the ninth
month: and *there was a fire* on the hearth burning
before him.
23 And it came to pass, *that* when Jehudi had read
three or four leaves, he cut it with the penknife, and
cast *it* into the fire that *was* on the hearth, until all the
roll was consumed in the fire that *was* on the hearth.
24 Yet they were not afraid, nor rent their garments,
neither the king, nor any of his servants that heard
all these words.
25 Nevertheless Elnathan and Delaiah and Gemariah had made intercession to the king that he would
not burn the roll: but he would not hear them.
26 But the king commanded Jerahmeel the son of
Hammelech, and Seraiah the son of Azriel, and Shelemiah the son of Abdeel, to take Baruch the scribe
and Jeremiah the prophet: but the LORD hid them.
27 Then the word of the LORD came to Jeremiah, after that the king had burned the roll, and the words
which Baruch wrote at the mouth of Jeremiah, saying,
28 Take thee again another roll, and write in it all
the former words that were in the first roll, which
Jehoiakim the king of Judah hath burned.
29 And thou shalt say to Jehoiakim king of Judah,
Thus saith the LORD; Thou hast burned this roll, saying, Why hast thou written therein, saying, The king
of Babylon shall certainly come and destroy this land,
and shall cause to cease from thence man and beast?
30 Therefore thus saith the LORD of Jehoiakim king
of Judah; He shall have none to sit upon the throne of
David: and his dead body shall be cast out in the day
to the heat, and in the night to the frost.
31 And I will punish him and his seed and his servants for their iniquity; and I will bring upon them,

NEW LIVING TRANSLATION

ask Baruch to come and read the messages to them,
too. So Baruch took the scroll and went to them.
15 "Sit down and read the scroll to us," the officials
said, and Baruch did as they requested.
16 When they heard all the messages, they looked
at one another in alarm. "We must tell the king what
we have heard," they said to Baruch. 17 "But first, tell
us how you got these messages. Did they come directly from Jeremiah?"
18 So Baruch explained, "Jeremiah dictated them,
and I wrote them down in ink, word for word, on this
scroll."
19 "You and Jeremiah should both hide," the officials told Baruch. "Don't tell anyone where you are!"
20 Then the officials left the scroll for safekeeping in
the room of Elishama the secretary and went to tell
the king what had happened.

King Jehoiakim Burns the Scroll

21 The king sent Jehudi to get the scroll. Jehudi
brought it from Elishama's room and read it to the
king as all his officials stood by. 22 It was late autumn,
and the king was in a winterized part of the palace,
sitting in front of a fire to keep warm. 23 Each time
Jehudi finished reading three or four columns, the
king took a knife and cut off that section of the scroll.
He then threw it into the fire, section by section, until
the whole scroll was burned up. 24 Neither the king
nor his attendants showed any signs of fear or repentance at what they heard. 25 Even when Elnathan,
Delaiah, and Gemariah begged the king not to burn
the scroll, he wouldn't listen.
26 Then the king commanded his son Jerahmeel,
Seraiah son of Azriel, and Shelemiah son of Abdeel
to arrest Baruch and Jeremiah. But the LORD had
hidden them.

Jeremiah Rewrites the Scroll

27 After the king had burned the scroll on which Baruch had written Jeremiah's words, the LORD gave
Jeremiah another message. He said, 28 "Get another
scroll, and write everything again just as you did on
the scroll King Jehoiakim burned. 29 Then say to the
king, 'This is what the LORD says: You burned the
scroll because it said the king of Babylon would destroy this land and empty it of people and animals.
30 Now this is what the LORD says about King Jehoiakim of Judah: He will have no heirs to sit on the
throne of David. His dead body will be thrown out to
lie unburied—exposed to the heat of the day and the
frost of the night. 31 I will punish him and his family
and his attendants for their sins. I will pour out on

KING JAMES VERSION

and upon the inhabitants of Jerusalem, and upon the
men of Judah, all the evil that I have pronounced
against them; but they hearkened not.
32 Then took Jeremiah another roll, and gave it to
Baruch the scribe, the son of Neriah; who wrote
therein from the mouth of Jeremiah all the words of
the book which Jehoiakim king of Judah had burned
in the fire: and there were added besides unto them
many like words.

37 1 And king Zedekiah the son of Josiah reigned
instead of Coniah the son of Jehoiakim,
whom Nebuchadrezzar king of Babylon made king in
the land of Judah.
2 But neither he, nor his servants, nor the people of
the land, did hearken unto the words of the LORD,
which he spake by the prophet Jeremiah.
3 And Zedekiah the king sent Jehucal the son of
Shelemiah and Zephaniah the son of Maaseiah the
priest to the prophet Jeremiah, saying, Pray now unto
the LORD our God for us.
4 Now Jeremiah came in and went out among the
people: for they had not put him into prison.
5 Then Pharaoh's army was come forth out of
Egypt: and when the Chaldeans that besieged Jerusalem
heard tidings of them, they departed from
Jerusalem.
6 Then came the word of the LORD unto the
prophet Jeremiah, saying,
7 Thus saith the LORD, the God of Israel; Thus shall
ye say to the king of Judah, that sent you unto me to
inquire of me; Behold, Pharaoh's army, which is
come forth to help you, shall return to Egypt into
their own land.
8 And the Chaldeans shall come again, and fight
against this city, and take it, and burn it with fire.
9 Thus saith the LORD; Deceive not yourselves, saying,
The Chaldeans shall surely depart from us: for
they shall not depart.
10 For though ye had smitten the whole army of the
Chaldeans that fight against you, and there remained
but wounded men among them, *yet* should they rise
up every man in his tent, and burn this city with fire.
11 And it came to pass, that when the army of the
Chaldeans was broken up from Jerusalem for fear of
Pharaoh's army,
12 Then Jeremiah went forth out of Jerusalem to go
into the land of Benjamin, to separate himself thence
in the midst of the people.
13 And when he was in the gate of Benjamin, a captain
of the ward *was* there, whose name *was* Irijah,
the son of Shelemiah, the son of Hananiah; and he
took Jeremiah the prophet, saying, Thou fallest away
to the Chaldeans.
14 Then said Jeremiah, *It is* false; I fall not away to
the Chaldeans. But he hearkened not to him: so Irijah
took Jeremiah, and brought him to the princes.

NEW LIVING TRANSLATION

them and on all the people of Jerusalem and Judah all
the disasters I promised, for they would not listen to
my warnings.'"
32 So Jeremiah took another scroll and dictated
again to his secretary, Baruch. He wrote everything
that had been on the scroll King Jehoiakim had
burned in the fire. Only this time he added much
more!

Zedekiah Calls for Jeremiah

37 Zedekiah son of Josiah succeeded Jehoiachin*
son of Jehoiakim as the king of Judah.
He was appointed by King Nebuchadnezzar* of Babylon.
2 But neither King Zedekiah nor his attendants
nor the people who were left in the land listened to
what the LORD said through Jeremiah.
3 Nevertheless, King Zedekiah sent Jehucal son of
Shelemiah, and Zephaniah the priest, son of Maaseiah,
to ask Jeremiah, "Please pray to the LORD our God
for us." 4 Jeremiah had not yet been imprisoned, so
he could come and go among the people as he
pleased.
5 At this time the army of Pharaoh Hophra* of
Egypt appeared at the southern border of Judah.
When the Babylonian* army heard about it, they
withdrew from their siege of Jerusalem.
6 Then the LORD gave this message to Jeremiah:
7 "This is what the LORD, the God of Israel, says: The
king of Judah sent you to ask me what is going to
happen. Tell him, 'Pharaoh's army is about to return
to Egypt, though he came here to help you. 8 Then the
Babylonians* will come back and capture this city
and burn it to the ground.'
9 "This is what the LORD says: Do not fool yourselves
into thinking that the Babylonians are gone
for good. They aren't! 10 Even if you were to destroy
the entire Babylonian army, leaving only a handful of
wounded survivors, they would still stagger from
their tents and burn this city to the ground!"

Jeremiah Is Imprisoned

11 When the Babylonian army left Jerusalem because
of Pharaoh's approaching army, 12 Jeremiah started to
leave the city on his way to the territory of Benjamin,
to claim his share of the property among his relatives
there.* 13 But as he was walking through the Benjamin
Gate, a sentry arrested him and said, "You are defecting
to the Babylonians!" The sentry making the arrest
was Irijah son of Shelemiah, grandson of Hananiah.
14 "That's not true!" Jeremiah protested. "I had no
intention of doing any such thing." But Irijah
wouldn't listen, and he took Jeremiah before the

37:1a Hebrew *Coniah*, a variant spelling of Jehoiachin. **37:1b** Hebrew *Nebuchadrezzar*, a variant spelling of Nebuchadnezzar. **37:5a** Hebrew *army of Pharaoh;* see 44:30. **37:5b** Or *Chaldean;* also in 37:10, 11. **37:8** Or *Chaldeans;* also in 37:9, 13. **37:12** Hebrew *to separate from there in the midst of the people.*

KING JAMES VERSION

15 Wherefore the princes were wroth with Jeremiah, and smote him, and put him in prison in the
house of Jonathan the scribe: for they had made that
the prison.
16 When Jeremiah was entered into the dungeon,
and into the cabins, and Jeremiah had remained
there many days;
17 Then Zedekiah the king sent, and took him out:
and the king asked him secretly in his house, and
said, Is there *any* word from the LORD? And Jeremiah
said, There is: for, said he, thou shalt be delivered into
the hand of the king of Babylon.
18 Moreover Jeremiah said unto king Zedekiah,
What have I offended against thee, or against thy servants, or against this people, that ye have put me in
prison?
19 Where *are* now your prophets which prophesied unto you, saying, The king of Babylon shall not
come against you, nor against this land?
20 Therefore hear now, I pray thee, O my lord the
king: let my supplication, I pray thee, be accepted before thee; that thou cause me not to return to the
house of Jonathan the scribe, lest I die there.
21 Then Zedekiah the king commanded that they
should commit Jeremiah into the court of the prison,
and that they should give him daily a piece of bread
out of the bakers' street, until all the bread in the city
were spent. Thus Jeremiah remained in the court of
the prison.

38 1 Then Shephatiah the son of Mattan, and
Gedaliah the son of Pashur, and Jucal the
son of Shelemiah, and Pashur the son of Malchiah,
heard the words that Jeremiah had spoken unto all
the people, saying,
2 Thus saith the LORD, He that remaineth in this city
shall die by the sword, by the famine, and by the pestilence: but he that goeth forth to the Chaldeans shall
live; for he shall have his life for a prey, and shall live.
3 Thus saith the LORD, This city shall surely be
given into the hand of the king of Babylon's army,
which shall take it.
4 Therefore the princes said unto the king, We beseech thee, let this man be put to death: for thus he
weakeneth the hands of the men of war that remain
in this city, and the hands of all the people, in speaking such words unto them: for this man seeketh not
the welfare of this people, but the hurt.
5 Then Zedekiah the king said, Behold, he *is* in
your hand: for the king *is* not *he that* can do *any*
thing against you.
6 Then took they Jeremiah, and cast him into the
dungeon of Malchiah the son of Hammelech, that
was in the court of the prison: and they let down Jeremiah with cords. And in the dungeon *there was* no
water, but mire: so Jeremiah sunk in the mire.
7 Now when Ebed-melech the Ethiopian, one of
the eunuchs which was in the king's house, heard

NEW LIVING TRANSLATION

officials. 15 They were furious with Jeremiah and had
him flogged and imprisoned in the house of Jonathan
the secretary. Jonathan's house had been converted
into a prison. 16 Jeremiah was put into a dungeon cell,
where he remained for many days.
17 Later King Zedekiah secretly requested that
Jeremiah come to the palace, where the king asked
him, "Do you have any messages from the LORD?"
"Yes, I do!" said Jeremiah. "You will be defeated by
the king of Babylon."
18 Then Jeremiah asked the king, "What crime
have I committed? What have I done against you,
your attendants, or the people that I should be imprisoned like this? 19 Where are your prophets now
who told you the king of Babylon would not attack
you or this land? 20 Listen, my lord the king, I beg you.
Don't send me back to the dungeon in the house of
Jonathan the secretary, for I will die there."
21 So King Zedekiah commanded that Jeremiah
not be returned to the dungeon. Instead, he was imprisoned in the courtyard of the guard in the royal
palace. The king also commanded that Jeremiah be
given a loaf of fresh bread every day as long as there
was any left in the city. So Jeremiah was put in the
palace prison.

Jeremiah in a Cistern

38 Now Shephatiah son of Mattan, Gedaliah
son of Pashhur, Jehucal* son of Shelemiah,
and Pashhur son of Malkijah heard what Jeremiah
had been telling the people. He had been saying,
2 "This is what the LORD says: 'Everyone who stays in
Jerusalem will die from war, famine, or disease, but
those who surrender to the Babylonians* will live.
Their reward will be life. They will live!' 3 The LORD
also says: 'The city of Jerusalem will certainly be
handed over to the army of the king of Babylon, who
will capture it.'"
4 So these officials went to the king and said, "Sir,
this man must die! That kind of talk will undermine
the morale of the few fighting men we have left, as
well as that of all the people. This man is a traitor!"
5 King Zedekiah agreed. "All right," he said. "Do as
you like. I can't stop you."
6 So the officials took Jeremiah from his cell and
lowered him by ropes into an empty cistern in the
prison yard. It belonged to Malkijah, a member of
the royal family. There was no water in the cistern,
but there was a thick layer of mud at the bottom, and
Jeremiah sank down into it.
7 But Ebed-melech the Ethiopian,* an important
court official, heard that Jeremiah was in the cistern.

38:1 Hebrew *Jucal,* a variant spelling of Jehucal; see 37:3. **38:2** Or *Chaldeans;* also in 38:18, 19, 23. **38:7** Hebrew *the Cushite.*

that they had put Jeremiah in the dungeon; the king then sitting in the gate of Benjamin;

8 Ebed-melech went forth out of the king's house, and spake to the king, saying,

9 My lord the king, these men have done evil in all that they have done to Jeremiah the prophet, whom they have cast into the dungeon; and he is like to die for hunger in the place where he is: for *there is* no more bread in the city.

10 Then the king commanded Ebed-melech the Ethiopian, saying, Take from hence thirty men with thee, and take up Jeremiah the prophet out of the dungeon, before he die.

11 So Ebed-melech took the men with him, and went into the house of the king under the treasury, and took thence old cast clouts and old rotten rags, and let them down by cords into the dungeon to Jeremiah.

12 And Ebed-melech the Ethiopian said unto Jeremiah, Put now *these* old cast clouts and rotten rags under thine armholes under the cords. And Jeremiah did so.

13 So they drew up Jeremiah with cords, and took him up out of the dungeon: and Jeremiah remained in the court of the prison.

14 Then Zedekiah the king sent, and took Jeremiah the prophet unto him into the third entry that *is* in the house of the LORD: and the king said unto Jeremiah, I will ask thee a thing; hide nothing from me.

15 Then Jeremiah said unto Zedekiah, If I declare *it* unto thee, wilt thou not surely put me to death? and if I give thee counsel, wilt thou not hearken unto me?

16 So Zedekiah the king sware secretly unto Jeremiah, saying, *As* the LORD liveth, that made us this soul, I will not put thee to death, neither will I give thee into the hand of these men that seek thy life.

17 Then said Jeremiah unto Zedekiah, Thus saith the LORD, the God of hosts, the God of Israel; If thou wilt assuredly go forth unto the king of Babylon's princes, then thy soul shall live, and this city shall not be burned with fire; and thou shalt live, and thine house:

18 But if thou wilt not go forth to the king of Babylon's princes, then shall this city be given into the hand of the Chaldeans, and they shall burn it with fire, and thou shalt not escape out of their hand.

19 And Zedekiah the king said unto Jeremiah, I am afraid of the Jews that are fallen to the Chaldeans, lest they deliver me into their hand, and they mock me.

20 But Jeremiah said, They shall not deliver *thee*. Obey, I beseech thee, the voice of the LORD, which I speak unto thee: so it shall be well unto thee, and thy soul shall live.

21 But if thou refuse to go forth, this *is* the word that the LORD hath shewed me:

22 And, behold, all the women that are left in the king of Judah's house *shall be* brought forth to the king of Babylon's princes, and those *women* shall say, Thy friends have set thee on, and have prevailed against thee: thy feet are sunk in the mire, *and* they are turned away back.

At that time the king was holding court at the Benjamin Gate, 8 so Ebed-melech rushed from the palace
to speak with him. 9 "My lord the king," he said,
"these men have done a very evil thing in putting
Jeremiah the prophet into the cistern. He will soon
die of hunger, for almost all the bread in the city is
gone."

10 So the king told Ebed-melech, "Take thirty of my
men with you, and pull Jeremiah out of the cistern
before he dies."

11 So Ebed-melech took the men with him and
went to a room in the palace beneath the treasury,
where he found some old rags and discarded clothing. He carried these to the cistern and lowered
them to Jeremiah on a rope. 12 Ebed-melech called
down to Jeremiah, "Put these rags under your arm-
pits to protect you from the ropes." Then when Jeremiah was ready, 13 they pulled him out. So Jeremiah
was returned to the courtyard of the guard—the palace prison—where he remained.

Zedekiah Questions Jeremiah

14 One day King Zedekiah sent for Jeremiah and had
him brought to the third entrance of the LORD's
Temple. "I want to ask you something," the king said.
"And don't try to hide the truth."

15 Jeremiah said, "If I tell you the truth, you will kill
me. And if I give you advice, you won't listen to me
anyway."

16 So King Zedekiah secretly promised him, "As
surely as the LORD our Creator lives, I will not kill you
or hand you over to the men who want you dead."

17 Then Jeremiah said to Zedekiah, "This is what
the LORD God of Heaven's Armies, the God of Israel,
says: 'If you surrender to the Babylonian officers, you
and your family will live, and the city will not be
burned down. 18 But if you refuse to surrender, you
will not escape! This city will be handed over to the
Babylonians, and they will burn it to the ground.'"

19 "But I am afraid to surrender," the king said, "for
the Babylonians may hand me over to the Judeans
who have defected to them. And who knows what
they will do to me!"

20 Jeremiah replied, "You won't be handed over to
them if you choose to obey the LORD. Your life will be
spared, and all will go well for you. 21 But if you refuse
to surrender, this is what the LORD has revealed to
me: 22 All the women left in your palace will be
brought out and given to the officers of the Babylonian army. Then the women will taunt you, saying,

'What fine friends you have!
They have betrayed and misled you.
When your feet sank in the mud,
they left you to your fate!'

KING JAMES VERSION

23 So they shall bring out all thy wives and thy children to the Chaldeans: and thou shalt not escape out
of their hand, but shalt be taken by the hand of the
king of Babylon: and thou shalt cause this city to be
burned with fire.
24 Then said Zedekiah unto Jeremiah, Let no man
know of these words, and thou shalt not die.
25 But if the princes hear that I have talked with
thee, and they come unto thee, and say unto thee,
Declare unto us now what thou hast said unto the
king, hide it not from us, and we will not put thee to
death; also what the king said unto thee:
26 Then thou shalt say unto them, I presented my
supplication before the king, that he would not
cause me to return to Jonathan's house, to die there.
27 Then came all the princes unto Jeremiah, and
asked him: and he told them according to all these
words that the king had commanded. So they left off
speaking with him; for the matter was not perceived.
28 So Jeremiah abode in the court of the prison
until the day that Jerusalem was taken: and he was
there when Jerusalem was taken.

39 1 In the ninth year of Zedekiah king of Judah, in the tenth month, came Nebuchadrezzar king of Babylon and all his army against
Jerusalem, and they besieged it.
2 *And* in the eleventh year of Zedekiah, in the
fourth month, the ninth *day* of the month, the city
was broken up.
3 And all the princes of the king of Babylon came
in, and sat in the middle gate, *even* Nergal-sharezer,
Samgar-nebo, Sarsechim, Rab-saris, Nergal-sharezer,
Rab-mag, with all the residue of the princes of the
king of Babylon.
4 And it came to pass, *that* when Zedekiah the king
of Judah saw them, and all the men of war, then they
fled, and went forth out of the city by night, by the
way of the king's garden, by the gate betwixt the two
walls: and he went out the way of the plain.
5 But the Chaldeans' army pursued after them, and
overtook Zedekiah in the plains of Jericho: and when
they had taken him, they brought him up to Nebuchadnezzar king of Babylon to Riblah in the land of
Hamath, where he gave judgment upon him.
6 Then the king of Babylon slew the sons of Zedekiah in Riblah before his eyes: also the king of Babylon slew all the nobles of Judah.
7 Moreover he put out Zedekiah's eyes, and bound
him with chains, to carry him to Babylon.
8 And the Chaldeans burned the king's house, and
the houses of the people, with fire, and brake down
the walls of Jerusalem.
9 Then Nebuzar-adan the captain of the guard carried away captive into Babylon the remnant of the
people that remained in the city, and those that fell
away, that fell to him, with the rest of the people that
remained.

NEW LIVING TRANSLATION

23 All your wives and children will be led out to the
Babylonians, and you will not escape. You will be
seized by the king of Babylon, and this city will be
burned down."
24 Then Zedekiah said to Jeremiah, "Don't tell anyone you told me this, or you will die! 25 My officials
may hear that I spoke to you, and they may say, 'Tell
us what you and the king were talking about. If you
don't tell us, we will kill you.' 26 If this happens, just
tell them you begged me not to send you back to
Jonathan's dungeon, for fear you would die there."
27 Sure enough, it wasn't long before the king's officials came to Jeremiah and asked him why the king
had called for him. But Jeremiah followed the king's
instructions, and they left without finding out the
truth. No one had overheard the conversation between Jeremiah and the king. 28 And Jeremiah remained a prisoner in the courtyard of the guard until
the day Jerusalem was captured.

The Fall of Jerusalem

39 In January* of the ninth year of King Zedekiah's reign, King Nebuchadnezzar* came
with his army to besiege Jerusalem. 2 Two and a half
years later, on July 18* in the eleventh year of Zedekiah's reign, the Babylonians broke through the wall,
and the city fell. 3 All the officers of the Babylonian
army came in and sat in triumph at the Middle Gate:
Nergal-sharezer of Samgar, and Nebo-sarsekim,* a
chief officer, and Nergal-sharezer, the king's adviser,
and all the other officers.
4 When King Zedekiah and all the soldiers saw that
the Babylonians had broken into the city, they fled.
They waited for nightfall and then slipped through
the gate between the two walls behind the king's garden and headed toward the Jordan Valley.*
5 But the Babylonian* troops chased the king and
caught him on the plains of Jericho. They took him
to King Nebuchadnezzar of Babylon, who was at Riblah in the land of Hamath. There the king of Babylon
pronounced judgment upon Zedekiah. 6 He made
Zedekiah watch as they slaughtered his sons and all
the nobles of Judah. 7 Then they gouged out Zedekiah's eyes, bound him in bronze chains, and led him
away to Babylon.
8 Meanwhile, the Babylonians burned Jerusalem,
including the palace, and tore down the walls of the
city. 9 Then Nebuzaradan, the captain of the guard,
sent to Babylon the rest of the people who remained
in the city as well as those who had defected to him.

39:1a Hebrew *in the tenth month,* of the ancient Hebrew lunar calendar. A number of events in Jeremiah can be cross-checked with dates in surviving Babylonian records and related accurately to our modern calendar. This event occurred on January 15, 588 B.C.; see 52:4a and the note there. **39:1b** Hebrew *Nebuchadrezzar,* a variant spelling of Nebuchadnezzar; also in 39:11. **39:2** Hebrew *On the ninth day of the fourth month.* This day was July 18, 586 B.C.; also see note on 39:1a. **39:3** Or *Nergal-sharezer, Samgar-nebo, Sarsekim.* **39:4** Hebrew *the Arabah.* **39:5** Or *Chaldean;* similarly in 39:8.

KING JAMES VERSION

10 But Nebuzar-adan the captain of the guard left of the poor of the people, which had nothing, in the land of Judah, and gave them vineyards and fields at the same time.

11 Now Nebuchadrezzar king of Babylon gave charge concerning Jeremiah to Nebuzar-adan the captain of the guard, saying,

12 Take him, and look well to him, and do him no harm; but do unto him even as he shall say unto thee.

13 So Nebuzar-adan the captain of the guard sent, and Nebushasban, Rab-saris, and Nergal-sharezer, Rab-mag, and all the king of Babylon's princes;

14 Even they sent, and took Jeremiah out of the court of the prison, and committed him unto Gedaliah the son of Ahikam the son of Shaphan, that he should carry him home: so he dwelt among the people.

15 Now the word of the LORD came unto Jeremiah, while he was shut up in the court of the prison, saying,

16 Go and speak to Ebed-melech the Ethiopian, saying, Thus saith the LORD of hosts, the God of Isral; Behold, I will bring my words upon this city for evil, and not for good; and they shall be *accomplished* in that day before thee.

17 But I will deliver thee in that day, saith the LORD: and thou shalt not be given into the hand of the men of whom thou *art* afraid.

18 For I will surely deliver thee, and thou shalt not fall by the sword, but thy life shall be for a prey unto thee: because thou hast put thy trust in me, saith the LORD.

40 1 The word that came to Jeremiah from the LORD, after that Nebuzar-adan the captain of the guard had let him go from Ramah, when he had taken him being bound in chains among all that were carried away captive of Jerusalem and Judah, which were carried away captive unto Babylon.

2 And the captain of the guard took Jeremiah, and said unto him, The LORD thy God hath pronounced this evil upon this place.

3 Now the LORD hath brought *it*, and done according as he hath said: because ye have sinned against the LORD, and have not obeyed his voice, therefore this thing is come upon you.

4 And now, behold, I loose thee this day from the chains which *were* upon thine hand. If it seem good unto thee to come with me into Babylon, come; and I will look well unto thee: but if it seem ill unto thee to come with me into Babylon, forbear: behold, all the land *is* before thee: whither it seemeth good and convenient for thee to go, thither go.

5 Now while he was not yet gone back, *he said,* Go back also to Gedaliah the son of Ahikam the son of Shaphan, whom the king of Babylon hath made governor over the cities of Judah, and dwell with him among the people: or go wheresoever it seemeth

NEW LIVING TRANSLATION

10 But Nebuzaradan left a few of the poorest people in Judah, and he assigned them vineyards and fields to care for.

Jeremiah Remains in Judah

11 King Nebuchadnezzar had told Nebuzaradan, the captain of the guard, to find Jeremiah. 12 "See that he isn't hurt," he said. "Look after him well, and give him anything he wants." 13 So Nebuzaradan, the captain of the guard; Nebushazban, a chief officer; Nergal-sharezer, the king's adviser; and the other officers of Babylon's king 14 sent messengers to bring Jeremiah out of the prison. They put him under the care of Gedaliah son of Ahikam and grandson of Shaphan, who took him back to his home. So Jeremiah stayed in Judah among his own people.

15 The LORD had given the following message to Jeremiah while he was still in prison: 16 "Say to Ebed-melech the Ethiopian,* 'This is what the LORD of Heaven's Armies, the God of Israel, says: I will do to this city everything I have threatened. I will send disaster, not prosperity. You will see its destruction, 17 but I will rescue you from those you fear so much. 18 Because you trusted me, I will give you your life as a reward. I will rescue you and keep you safe. I, the LORD, have spoken!'"

40 The LORD gave a message to Jeremiah after Nebuzaradan, the captain of the guard, had released him at Ramah. He had found Jeremiah bound in chains among all the other captives of Jerusalem and Judah who were being sent to exile in Babylon.

2 The captain of the guard called for Jeremiah and said, "The LORD your God has brought this disaster on this land, 3 just as he said he would. For these people have sinned against the LORD and disobeyed him. That is why it happened. 4 But I am going to take off your chains and let you go. If you want to come with me to Babylon, you are welcome. I will see that you are well cared for. But if you don't want to come, you may stay here. The whole land is before you—go wherever you like. 5 If you decide to stay, then return to Gedaliah son of Ahikam and grandson of Shaphan. He has been appointed governor of Judah by the king of Babylon. Stay there with the people he rules. But it's up to you; go wherever you like."

39:16 Hebrew *the Cushite.*

KING JAMES VERSION

convenient unto thee to go. So the captain of the
guard gave him victuals and a reward, and let him go.
6 Then went Jeremiah unto Gedaliah the son of
Ahikam to Mizpah; and dwelt with him among the
people that were left in the land.

7 Now when all the captains of the forces which
were in the fields, *even* they and their men, heard
that the king of Babylon had made Gedaliah the son
of Ahikam governor in the land, and had committed
unto him men, and women, and children, and of the
poor of the land, of them that were not carried away
captive to Babylon;
8 Then they came to Gedaliah to Mizpah, even
Ishmael the son of Nethaniah, and Johanan and
Jonathan the sons of Kareah, and Seraiah the son of
Tanhumeth, and the sons of Ephai the Netophathite,
and Jezaniah the son of a Maachathite, they and
their men.
9 And Gedaliah the son of Ahikam the son of
Shaphan sware unto them and to their men, saying,
Fear not to serve the Chaldeans: dwell in the land,
and serve the king of Babylon, and it shall be well
with you.
10 As for me, behold, I will dwell at Mizpah, to serve
the Chaldeans, which will come unto us: but ye,
gather ye wine, and summer fruits, and oil, and put
them in your vessels, and dwell in your cities that ye
have taken.
11 Likewise when all the Jews that *were* in Moab,
and among the Ammonites, and in Edom, and that
were in all the countries, heard that the king of Babylon had left a remnant of Judah, and that he had set
over them Gedaliah the son of Ahikam the son of
Shaphan;
12 Even all the Jews returned out of all places
whither they were driven, and came to the land of
Judah, to Gedaliah, unto Mizpah, and gathered wine
and summer fruits very much.
13 Moreover Johanan the son of Kareah, and all the
captains of the forces that *were* in the fields, came to
Gedaliah to Mizpah,
14 And said unto him, Dost thou certainly know
that Baalis the king of the Ammonites hath sent Ishmael the son of Nethaniah to slay thee? But Gedaliah
the son of Ahikam believed them not.
15 Then Johanan the son of Kareah spake to Gedaliah in Mizpah secretly, saying, Let me go, I pray thee,
and I will slay Ishmael the son of Nethaniah, and no
man shall know *it:* wherefore should he slay thee,
that all the Jews which are gathered unto thee should
be scattered, and the remnant in Judah perish?
16 But Gedaliah the son of Ahikam said unto Johanan the son of Kareah, Thou shalt not do this thing:
for thou speakest falsely of Ishmael.

NEW LIVING TRANSLATION

Then Nebuzaradan, the captain of the guard, gave
Jeremiah some food and money and let him go. 6 So
Jeremiah returned to Gedaliah son of Ahikam at
Mizpah, and he lived in Judah with the few who were
still left in the land.

Gedaliah Governs in Judah

7 The leaders of the Judean guerrilla bands in the
countryside heard that the king of Babylon had appointed Gedaliah son of Ahikam as governor over
the poor people who were left behind in Judah—the
men, women, and children who hadn't been exiled to
Babylon. 8 So they went to see Gedaliah at Mizpah.
These included: Ishmael son of Nethaniah, Johanan
and Jonathan sons of Kareah, Seraiah son of Tanhumeth, the sons of Ephai the Netophathite, Jezaniah
son of the Maacathite, and all their men.
9 Gedaliah vowed to them that the Babylonians*
meant them no harm. "Don't be afraid to serve them.
Live in the land and serve the king of Babylon, and
all will go well for you," he promised. 10 "As for me, I
will stay at Mizpah to represent you before the Babylonians who come to meet with us. Settle in the
towns you have taken, and live off the land. Harvest
the grapes and summer fruits and olives, and store
them away."
11 When the Judeans in Moab, Ammon, Edom, and
the other nearby countries heard that the king of
Babylon had left a few people in Judah and that Gedaliah was the governor, 12 they began to return to
Judah from the places to which they had fled. They
stopped at Mizpah to meet with Gedaliah and then
went into the Judean countryside to gather a great
harvest of grapes and other crops.

A Plot against Gedaliah

13 Soon after this, Johanan son of Kareah and the
other guerrilla leaders came to Gedaliah at Mizpah.
14 They said to him, "Did you know that Baalis, king of
Ammon, has sent Ishmael son of Nethaniah to assassinate you?" But Gedaliah refused to believe them.
15 Later Johanan had a private conference with
Gedaliah and volunteered to kill Ishmael secretly.
"Why should we let him come and murder you?"
Johanan asked. "What will happen then to the Judeans who have returned? Why should the few of us
who are still left be scattered and lost?"
16 But Gedaliah said to Johanan, "I forbid you to do
any such thing, for you are lying about Ishmael."

40:9 Or *Chaldeans;* also in 40:10.

KING JAMES VERSION

41 1Now it came to pass in the seventh month,
that Ishmael the son of Nethaniah the son of
Elishama, of the seed royal, and the princes of the
king, even ten men with him, came unto Gedaliah the
son of Ahikam to Mizpah; and there they did eat
bread together in Mizpah.
2Then arose Ishmael the son of Nethaniah, and
the ten men that were with him, and smote Gedaliah
the son of Ahikam the son of Shaphan with the
sword, and slew him, whom the king of Babylon had
made governor over the land.
3Ishmael also slew all the Jews that were with him,
even with Gedaliah, at Mizpah, and the Chaldeans
that were found there, *and* the men of war.
4And it came to pass the second day after he had
slain Gedaliah, and no man knew *it*,
5That there came certain from Shechem, from
Shiloh, and from Samaria, *even* fourscore men, having their beards shaven, and their clothes rent, and
having cut themselves, with offerings and incense in
their hand, to bring *them* to the house of the LORD.
6And Ishmael the son of Nethaniah went forth
from Mizpah to meet them, weeping all along as he
went: and it came to pass, as he met them, he said
unto them, Come to Gedaliah the son of Ahikam.
7And it was *so*, when they came into the midst of
the city, that Ishmael the son of Nethaniah slew
them, *and cast them* into the midst of the pit, he, and
the men that *were* with him.
8But ten men were found among them that said
unto Ishmael, Slay us not: for we have treasures in
the field, of wheat, and of barley, and of oil, and of
honey. So he forbare, and slew them not among their
brethren.
9Now the pit wherein Ishmael had cast all the
dead bodies of the men, whom he had slain because
of Gedaliah, *was* it which Asa the king had made for
fear of Baasha king of Israel: *and* Ishmael the son of
Nethaniah filled it with *them that were* slain.
10Then Ishmael carried away captive all the residue
of the people that *were* in Mizpah, *even* the king's
daughters, and all the people that remained in
Mizpah, whom Nebuzar-adan the captain of the
guard had committed to Gedaliah the son of Ahikam:
and Ishmael the son of Nethaniah carried them away
captive, and departed to go over to the Ammonites.
11But when Johanan the son of Kareah, and all
the captains of the forces that *were* with him, heard
of all the evil that Ishmael the son of Nethaniah
had done,
12Then they took all the men, and went to fight
with Ishmael the son of Nethaniah, and found him
by the great waters that *are* in Gibeon.
13Now it came to pass, *that* when all the people
which *were* with Ishmael saw Johanan the son of
Kareah, and all the captains of the forces that *were*
with him, then they were glad.

NEW LIVING TRANSLATION

The Murder of Gedaliah

41 But in midautumn,* Ishmael son of Nethaniah and grandson of Elishama, who was a
member of the royal family and had been one of the
king's high officials, went to Mizpah with ten men to
meet Gedaliah. While they were eating together,
2Ishmael and his ten men suddenly jumped up, drew
their swords, and killed Gedaliah, whom the king of
Babylon had appointed governor. 3Ishmael also killed
all the Judeans and the Babylonian* soldiers who
were with Gedaliah at Mizpah.
4The next day, before anyone had heard about
Gedaliah's murder, 5eighty men arrived from Shechem, Shiloh, and Samaria to worship at the Temple
of the LORD. They had shaved off their beards, torn
their clothes, and cut themselves, and had brought
along grain offerings and frankincense. 6Ishmael
left Mizpah to meet them, weeping as he went.
When he reached them, he said, "Oh, come and see
what has happened to Gedaliah!"
7But as soon as they were all inside the town, Ishmael and his men killed all but ten of them and
threw their bodies into a cistern. 8The other ten had
talked Ishmael into letting them go by promising to
bring him their stores of wheat, barley, olive oil, and
honey that they had hidden away. 9The cistern
where Ishmael dumped the bodies of the men he
murdered was the large one dug by King Asa when
he fortified Mizpah to protect himself against King
Baasha of Israel. Ishmael son of Nethaniah filled it
with corpses.
10Then Ishmael made captives of the king's
daughters and the other people who had been left
under Gedaliah's care in Mizpah by Nebuzaradan,
the captain of the guard. Taking them with him, he
started back toward the land of Ammon.
11But when Johanan son of Kareah and the other
guerrilla leaders heard about Ishmael's crimes,
12they took all their men and set out to stop him.
They caught up with him at the large pool near Gibeon. 13The people Ishmael had captured shouted for
joy when they saw Johanan and the other guerrilla

41:1 Hebrew *in the seventh month,* of the ancient Hebrew lunar calendar. This month occurred within the months of October and November 586 B.C; also see note on 39:1a. 41:3 Or *Chaldean.*

KING JAMES VERSION

14So all the people that Ishmael had carried away captive from Mizpah cast about and returned, and went unto Johanan the son of Kareah.

15But Ishmael the son of Nethaniah escaped from Johanan with eight men, and went to the Ammonites.

16Then took Johanan the son of Kareah, and all the captains of the forces that *were* with him, all the remnant of the people whom he had recovered from Ishmael the son of Nethaniah, from Mizpah, after *that* he had slain Gedaliah the son of Ahikam, *even* mighty men of war, and the women, and the children, and the eunuchs, whom he had brought again from Gibeon:

17And they departed, and dwelt in the habitation of Chimham, which is by Bethlehem, to go to enter into Egypt,

18Because of the Chaldeans: for they were afraid of them, because Ishmael the son of Nethaniah had slain Gedaliah the son of Ahikam, whom the king of Babylon made governor in the land.

42 1Then all the captains of the forces, and Johanan the son of Kareah, and Jezaniah the son of Hoshaiah, and all the people from the least even unto the greatest, came near,

2And said unto Jeremiah the prophet, Let, we beseech thee, our supplication be accepted before thee, and pray for us unto the LORD thy God, *even* for all this remnant; (for we are left *but* a few of many, as thine eyes do behold us:)

3That the LORD thy God may shew us the way wherein we may walk, and the thing that we may do.

4Then Jeremiah the prophet said unto them, I have heard *you;* behold, I will pray unto the LORD your God according to your words; and it shall come to pass, *that* whatsoever thing the LORD shall answer you, I will declare *it* unto you; I will keep nothing back from you.

5Then they said to Jeremiah, The LORD be a true and faithful witness between us, if we do not even according to all things for the which the LORD thy God shall send thee to us.

6Whether *it be* good, or whether *it be* evil, we will obey the voice of the LORD our God, to whom we send thee; that it may be well with us, when we obey the voice of the LORD our God.

7And it came to pass after ten days, that the word of the LORD came unto Jeremiah.

8Then called he Johanan the son of Kareah, and all the captains of the forces which *were* with him, and all the people from the least even to the greatest,

9And said unto them, Thus saith the LORD, the God of Israel, unto whom ye sent me to present your supplication before him;

10If ye will still abide in this land, then will I build you, and not pull *you* down, and I will plant you, and not pluck *you* up: for I repent me of the evil that I have done unto you.

NEW LIVING TRANSLATION

leaders. 14And all the captives from Mizpah escaped
and began to help Johanan. 15Meanwhile, Ishmael
and eight of his men escaped from Johanan into the
land of Ammon.
16Then Johanan son of Kareah and the other guerrilla leaders took all the people they had rescued in
Gibeon—the soldiers, women, children, and court
officials* whom Ishmael had captured after he
killed Gedaliah. 17They took them all to the village of
Geruth-kimham near Bethlehem, where they prepared to leave for Egypt. 18They were afraid of what
the Babylonians* would do when they heard that
Ishmael had killed Gedaliah, the governor appointed by the Babylonian king.

Warning to Stay in Judah

42 Then all the guerrilla leaders, including
Johanan son of Kareah and Jezaniah* son of
Hoshaiah, and all the people, from the least to the
greatest, approached 2Jeremiah the prophet. They
said, "Please pray to the LORD your God for us. As you
can see, we are only a tiny remnant compared to what
we were before. 3Pray that the LORD your God will
show us what to do and where to go."
4"All right," Jeremiah replied. "I will pray to the
LORD your God, as you have asked, and I will tell you
everything he says. I will hide nothing from you."
5Then they said to Jeremiah, "May the LORD your
God be a faithful witness against us if we refuse to
obey whatever he tells us to do! 6Whether we like it
or not, we will obey the LORD our God to whom we
are sending you with our plea. For if we obey him,
everything will turn out well for us."
7Ten days later the LORD gave his reply to Jeremiah. 8So he called for Johanan son of Kareah and the
other guerrilla leaders, and for all the people, from
the least to the greatest. 9He said to them, "You sent
me to the LORD, the God of Israel, with your request,
and this is his reply: 10'Stay here in this land. If you
do, I will build you up and not tear you down; I will
plant you and not uproot you. For I am sorry about
all the punishment I have had to bring upon you.

41:16 Or *eunuchs.* **41:18** Or *Chaldeans.* **42:1** Greek version reads *Azariah;* compare 43:2.

KING JAMES VERSION

11 Be not afraid of the king of Babylon, of whom ye are afraid; be not afraid of him, saith the LORD: for I *am* with you to save you, and to deliver you from his hand.

12 And I will shew mercies unto you, that he may have mercy upon you, and cause you to return to your own land.

13 But if ye say, We will not dwell in this land, neither obey the voice of the LORD your God,

14 Saying, No; but we will go into the land of Egypt, where we shall see no war, nor hear the sound of the trumpet, nor have hunger of bread; and there will we dwell:

15 And now therefore hear the word of the LORD, ye remnant of Judah; Thus saith the LORD of hosts, the God of Israel; If ye wholly set your faces to enter into Egypt, and go to sojourn there;

16 Then it shall come to pass, *that* the sword, which ye feared, shall overtake you there in the land of Egypt, and the famine, whereof ye were afraid, shall follow close after you there in Egypt; and there ye shall die.

17 So shall it be with all the men that set their faces to go into Egypt to sojourn there; they shall die by the sword, by the famine, and by the pestilence: and none of them shall remain or escape from the evil that I will bring upon them.

18 For thus saith the LORD of hosts, the God of Israel; As mine anger and my fury hath been poured forth upon the inhabitants of Jerusalem; so shall my fury be poured forth upon you, when ye shall enter into Egypt: and ye shall be an execration, and an astonishment, and a curse, and a reproach; and ye shall see this place no more.

19 The LORD hath said concerning you, O ye remnant of Judah; Go ye not into Egypt: know certainly that I have admonished you this day.

20 For ye dissembled in your hearts, when ye sent me unto the LORD your God, saying, Pray for us unto the LORD our God; and according unto all that the LORD our God shall say, so declare unto us, and we will do *it*.

21 And *now* I have this day declared *it* to you; but ye have not obeyed the voice of the LORD your God, nor any *thing* for the which he hath sent me unto you.

22 Now therefore know certainly that ye shall die by the sword, by the famine, and by the pestilence, in the place whither ye desire to go *and* to sojourn.

43 1 And it came to pass, *that* when Jeremiah had made an end of speaking unto all the people all the words of the LORD their God, for which the LORD their God had sent him to them, *even* all these words,

2 Then spake Azariah the son of Hoshaiah, and Johanan the son of Kareah, and all the proud men, saying unto Jeremiah, Thou speakest falsely: the LORD our God hath not sent thee to say, Go not into Egypt to sojourn there:

NEW LIVING TRANSLATION

11 Do not fear the king of Babylon anymore,' says the LORD. 'For I am with you and will save you and rescue you from his power. 12 I will be merciful to you by making him kind, so he will let you stay here in your land.'

13 "But if you refuse to obey the LORD your God, and if you say, 'We will not stay here; 14 instead, we will go to Egypt where we will be free from war, the call to arms, and hunger,' 15 then hear the LORD's message to the remnant of Judah. This is what the LORD of Heaven's Armies, the God of Israel, says: 'If you are determined to go to Egypt and live there, 16 the very war and famine you fear will catch up to you, and you will die there. 17 That is the fate awaiting every one of you who insists on going to live in Egypt. Yes, you will die from war, famine, and disease. None of you will escape the disaster I will bring upon you there.'

18 "This is what the LORD of Heaven's Armies, the God of Israel, says: 'Just as my anger and fury have been poured out on the people of Jerusalem, so they will be poured out on you when you enter Egypt. You will be an object of damnation, horror, cursing, and mockery. And you will never see your homeland again.'

19 "Listen, you remnant of Judah. The LORD has told you: 'Do not go to Egypt!' Don't forget this warning I have given you today. 20 For you were not being honest when you sent me to pray to the LORD your God for you. You said, 'Just tell us what the LORD our God says, and we will do it!' 21 And today I have told you exactly what he said, but you will not obey the LORD your God any better now than you have in the past. 22 So you can be sure that you will die from war, famine, and disease in Egypt, where you insist on going."

Jeremiah Taken to Egypt

43 When Jeremiah had finished giving this message from the LORD their God to all the people, 2 Azariah son of Hoshaiah and Johanan son of Kareah and all the other proud men said to Jeremiah, "You lie! The LORD our God hasn't forbidden us to go

KING JAMES VERSION

3But Baruch the son of Neriah setteth thee on against us, for to deliver us into the hand of the Chaldeans, that they might put us to death, and carry us away captives into Babylon.

4So Johanan the son of Kareah, and all the captains of the forces, and all the people, obeyed not the voice of the LORD, to dwell in the land of Judah.

5But Johanan the son of Kareah, and all the captains of the forces, took all the remnant of Judah, that were returned from all nations, whither they had been driven, to dwell in the land of Judah;

6*Even* men, and women, and children, and the king's daughters, and every person that Nebuzaradan the captain of the guard had left with Gedaliah the son of Ahikam the son of Shaphan, and Jeremiah the prophet, and Baruch the son of Neriah.

7So they came into the land of Egypt: for they obeyed not the voice of the LORD: thus came they *even* to Tahpanhes.

8Then came the word of the LORD unto Jeremiah in Tahpanhes, saying,

9Take great stones in thine hand, and hide them in the clay in the brickkiln, which *is* at the entry of Pharaoh's house in Tahpanhes, in the sight of the men of Judah;

10And say unto them, Thus saith the LORD of hosts, the God of Israel; Behold, I will send and take Nebuchadrezzar the king of Babylon, my servant, and will set his throne upon these stones that I have hid; and he shall spread his royal pavilion over them.

11And when he cometh, he shall smite the land of Egypt, *and deliver* such *as are* for death to death; and such *as are* for captivity to captivity; and such *as are* for the sword to the sword.

12And I will kindle a fire in the houses of the gods of Egypt; and he shall burn them, and carry them away captives: and he shall array himself with the land of Egypt, as a shepherd putteth on his garment; and he shall go forth from thence in peace.

13He shall break also the images of Beth-shemesh, that *is* in the land of Egypt; and the houses of the gods of the Egyptians shall he burn with fire.

44 1The word that came to Jeremiah concerning all the Jews which dwell in the land of Egypt, which dwell at Migdol, and at Tahpanhes, and at Noph, and in the country of Pathros, saying,

2Thus saith the LORD of hosts, the God of Israel; Ye have seen all the evil that I have brought upon Jerusalem, and upon all the cities of Judah; and, behold, this day they *are* a desolation, and no man dwelleth therein,

3Because of their wickedness which they have committed to provoke me to anger, in that they went to burn incense, *and* to serve other gods, whom they knew not, *neither* they, ye, nor your fathers.

4Howbeit I sent unto you all my servants the

NEW LIVING TRANSLATION

to Egypt! 3Baruch son of Neriah has convinced you to say this, because he wants us to stay here and be killed by the Babylonians* or be carried off into exile."

4So Johanan and the other guerrilla leaders and all the people refused to obey the LORD's command to stay in Judah. 5Johanan and the other leaders took with them all the people who had returned from the nearby countries to which they had fled. 6In the crowd were men, women, and children, the king's daughters, and all those whom Nebuzaradan, the captain of the guard, had left with Gedaliah. The prophet Jeremiah and Baruch were also included. 7The people refused to obey the voice of the LORD and went to Egypt, going as far as the city of Tahpanhes.

8Then at Tahpanhes, the LORD gave another message to Jeremiah. He said, 9"While the people of Judah are watching, take some large rocks and bury them under the pavement stones at the entrance of Pharaoh's palace here in Tahpanhes. 10Then say to the people of Judah, 'This is what the LORD of Heaven's Armies, the God of Israel, says: I will certainly bring my servant Nebuchadnezzar,* king of Babylon, here to Egypt. I will set his throne over these stones that I have hidden. He will spread his royal canopy over them. 11And when he comes, he will destroy the land of Egypt. He will bring death to those destined for death, captivity to those destined for captivity, and war to those destined for war. 12He will set fire to the temples of Egypt's gods; he will burn the temples and carry the idols away as plunder. He will pick clean the land of Egypt as a shepherd picks fleas from his cloak. And he himself will leave unharmed. 13He will break down the sacred pillars standing in the temple of the sun* in Egypt, and he will burn down the temples of Egypt's gods.'"

Judgment for Idolatry

44 This is the message Jeremiah received concerning the Judeans living in northern Egypt in the cities of Migdol, Tahpanhes, and Memphis,* and in southern Egypt* as well: 2"This is what the LORD of Heaven's Armies, the God of Israel, says: You saw the calamity I brought on Jerusalem and all the towns of Judah. They now lie deserted and in ruins. 3They provoked my anger with all their wickedness. They burned incense and worshiped other gods—gods that neither they nor you nor any of your ancestors had ever even known.

4"Again and again I sent my servants, the prophets,

43:3 Or *Chaldeans.* **43:10** Hebrew *Nebuchadrezzar,* a variant spelling of Nebuchadnezzar. **43:13** Or *in Heliopolis.* **44:1a** Hebrew *Noph.* **44:1b** Hebrew *in Pathros.*

prophets, rising early and sending *them*, saying, Oh, do not this abominable thing that I hate.

5 But they hearkened not, nor inclined their ear to turn from their wickedness, to burn no incense unto other gods.

6 Wherefore my fury and mine anger was poured forth, and was kindled in the cities of Judah and in the streets of Jerusalem; and they are wasted *and* desolate, as at this day.

7 Therefore now thus saith the LORD, the God of hosts, the God of Israel; Wherefore commit ye *this* great evil against your souls, to cut off from you man and woman, child and suckling, out of Judah, to leave you none to remain;

8 In that ye provoke me unto wrath with the works of your hands, burning incense unto other gods in the land of Egypt, whither ye be gone to dwell, that ye might cut yourselves off, and that ye might be a curse and a reproach among all the nations of the earth?

9 Have ye forgotten the wickedness of your fathers, and the wickedness of the kings of Judah, and the wickedness of their wives, and your own wickedness, and the wickedness of your wives, which they have committed in the land of Judah, and in the streets of Jerusalem?

10 They are not humbled *even* unto this day, neither have they feared, nor walked in my law, nor in my statutes, that I set before you and before your fathers.

11 Therefore thus saith the LORD of hosts, the God of Israel; Behold, I will set my face against you for evil, and to cut off all Judah.

12 And I will take the remnant of Judah, that have set their faces to go into the land of Egypt to sojourn there, and they shall all be consumed, *and* fall in the land of Egypt; they shall *even* be consumed by the sword *and* by the famine: they shall die, from the least even unto the greatest, by the sword and by the famine: and they shall be an execration, *and* an astonishment, and a curse, and a reproach.

13 For I will punish them that dwell in the land of Egypt, as I have punished Jerusalem, by the sword, by the famine, and by the pestilence:

14 So that none of the remnant of Judah, which are gone into the land of Egypt to sojourn there, shall escape or remain, that they should return into the land of Judah, to the which they have a desire to return to dwell there: for none shall return but such as shall escape.

15 Then all the men which knew that their wives had burned incense unto other gods, and all the women that stood by, a great multitude, even all the people that dwelt in the land of Egypt, in Pathros, answered Jeremiah, saying,

16 *As for* the word that thou hast spoken unto us in the name of the LORD, we will not hearken unto thee.

17 But we will certainly do whatsoever thing goeth forth out of our own mouth, to burn incense unto the

to plead with them, 'Don't do these horrible things that I hate so much.' 5 But my people would not listen or turn back from their wicked ways. They kept on burning incense to these gods. 6 And so my fury boiled over and fell like fire on the towns of Judah and into the streets of Jerusalem, and they are still a desolate ruin today.

7 "And now the LORD God of Heaven's Armies, the God of Israel, asks you: Why are you destroying yourselves? For not one of you will survive—not a man, woman, or child among you who has come here from Judah, not even the babies in your arms. 8 Why provoke my anger by burning incense to the idols you have made here in Egypt? You will only destroy yourselves and make yourselves an object of cursing and mockery for all the nations of the earth. 9 Have you forgotten the sins of your ancestors, the sins of the kings and queens of Judah, and the sins you and your wives committed in Judah and Jerusalem? 10 To this very hour you have shown no remorse or reverence. No one has chosen to follow my word and the decrees I gave to you and your ancestors before you.

11 "Therefore, this is what the LORD of Heaven's Armies, the God of Israel, says: I am determined to destroy every one of you! 12 I will take this remnant of Judah—those who were determined to come here and live in Egypt—and I will consume them. They will fall here in Egypt, killed by war and famine. All will die, from the least to the greatest. They will be an object of damnation, horror, cursing, and mockery. 13 I will punish them in Egypt just as I punished them in Jerusalem, by war, famine, and disease. 14 Of that remnant who fled to Egypt, hoping someday to return to Judah, there will be no survivors. Even though they long to return home, only a handful will do so."

15 Then all the women present and all the men who knew that their wives had burned incense to idols—a great crowd of all the Judeans living in northern Egypt and southern Egypt*—answered Jeremiah, 16 "We will not listen to your messages from the LORD! 17 We will do whatever we want. We will burn incense and pour out liquid offerings to the Queen

44:15 Hebrew *in Egypt, in Pathros.*

KING JAMES VERSION

queen of heaven, and to pour out drink offerings
unto her, as we have done, we, and our fathers, our
kings, and our princes, in the cities of Judah, and in
the streets of Jerusalem: for *then* had we plenty of
victuals, and were well, and saw no evil.
18But since we left off to burn incense to the
queen of heaven, and to pour out drink offerings
unto her, we have wanted all *things*, and have been
consumed by the sword and by the famine.
19And when we burned incense to the queen of
heaven, and poured out drink offerings unto her, did
we make her cakes to worship her, and pour out
drink offerings unto her, without our men?
20Then Jeremiah said unto all the people, to the
men, and to the women, and to all the people which
had given him *that* answer, saying,
21The incense that ye burned in the cities of Judah,
and in the streets of Jerusalem, ye, and your fathers,
your kings, and your princes, and the people of the
land, did not the LORD remember them, and came it
not into his mind?
22So that the LORD could no longer bear, because
of the evil of your doings, *and* because of the abominations which ye have committed; therefore is your
land a desolation, and an astonishment, and a curse,
without an inhabitant, as at this day.
23Because ye have burned incense, and because ye
have sinned against the LORD, and have not obeyed
the voice of the LORD, nor walked in his law, nor in his
statutes, nor in his testimonies; therefore this evil is
happened unto you, as at this day.
24Moreover Jeremiah said unto all the people, and
to all the women, Hear the word of the LORD, all
Judah that *are* in the land of Egypt:
25Thus saith the LORD of hosts, the God of Israel,
saying; Ye and your wives have both spoken with
your mouths, and fulfilled with your hand, saying,
We will surely perform our vows that we have vowed,
to burn incense to the queen of heaven, and to pour
out drink offerings unto her: ye will surely accomplish your vows, and surely perform your vows.
26Therefore hear ye the word of the LORD, all Judah that dwell in the land of Egypt; Behold, I have
sworn by my great name, saith the LORD, that my
name shall no more be named in the mouth of any
man of Judah in all the land of Egypt, saying, The
Lord GOD liveth.
27Behold, I will watch over them for evil, and not
for good: and all the men of Judah that *are* in the land
of Egypt shall be consumed by the sword and by the
famine, until there be an end of them.
28Yet a small number that escape the sword shall
return out of the land of Egypt into the land of Judah,
and all the remnant of Judah, that are gone into the
land of Egypt to sojourn there, shall know whose
words shall stand, mine, or theirs.
29And this *shall be* a sign unto you, saith the LORD,

NEW LIVING TRANSLATION

of Heaven just as much as we like—just as we, and
our ancestors, and our kings and officials have always done in the towns of Judah and in the streets
of Jerusalem. For in those days we had plenty to eat,
and we were well off and had no troubles! 18But ever
since we quit burning incense to the Queen of
Heaven and stopped worshiping her with liquid offerings, we have been in great trouble and have been
dying from war and famine."
19"Besides," the women added, "do you suppose
that we were burning incense and pouring out liquid
offerings to the Queen of Heaven, and making cakes
marked with her image, without our husbands
knowing it and helping us? Of course not!"
20Then Jeremiah said to all of them, men and
women alike, who had given him that answer, 21"Do
you think the LORD did not know that you and your
ancestors, your kings and officials, and all the people
were burning incense to idols in the towns of Judah
and in the streets of Jerusalem? 22It was because the
LORD could no longer bear all the disgusting things
you were doing that he made your land an object of
cursing—a desolate ruin without inhabitants—as it
is today. 23All these terrible things happened to you
because you have burned incense to idols and
sinned against the LORD. You have refused to obey
him and have not followed his instructions, his decrees, and his laws."
24Then Jeremiah said to them all, including the
women, "Listen to this message from the LORD, all
you citizens of Judah who live in Egypt. 25This is
what the LORD of Heaven's Armies, the God of Israel,
says: 'You and your wives have said, "We will keep
our promises to burn incense and pour out liquid offerings to the Queen of Heaven," and you have
proved by your actions that you meant it. So go
ahead and carry out your promises and vows to her!'
26"But listen to this message from the LORD, all you
Judeans now living in Egypt: 'I have sworn by my
great name,' says the LORD, 'that my name will no longer be spoken by any of the Judeans in the land of
Egypt. None of you may invoke my name or use this
oath: "As surely as the Sovereign LORD lives." 27For I
will watch over you to bring you disaster and not
good. Everyone from Judah who is now living in
Egypt will suffer war and famine until all of you are
dead. 28Only a small number will escape death and
return to Judah from Egypt. Then all those who came
to Egypt will find out whose words are true—mine
or theirs!
29"'And this is the proof I give you,' says the LORD,

KING JAMES VERSION

that I will punish you in this place, that ye may know
that my words shall surely stand against you for evil:
30 Thus saith the LORD; Behold, I will give Pharaoh-
hophra king of Egypt into the hand of his enemies,
and into the hand of them that seek his life; as I gave
Zedekiah king of Judah into the hand of Nebuchadrezzar king of Babylon, his enemy, and that sought
his life.

45 1 The word that Jeremiah the prophet spake
unto Baruch the son of Neriah, when he had
written these words in a book at the mouth of Jeremiah, in the fourth year of Jehoiakim the son of Josiah
king of Judah, saying,
2 Thus saith the LORD, the God of Israel, unto thee,
O Baruch;
3 Thou didst say, Woe is me now! for the LORD hath
added grief to my sorrow; I fainted in my sighing,
and I find no rest.
4 Thus shalt thou say unto him, The LORD saith
thus; Behold, *that* which I have built will I break
down, and that which I have planted I will pluck up,
even this whole land.
5 And seekest thou great things for thyself? seek
them not: for, behold, I will bring evil upon all flesh,
saith the LORD: but thy life will I give unto thee for a
prey in all places whither thou goest.

46 1 The word of the LORD which came to Jeremiah the prophet against the Gentiles;

2 Against Egypt, against the army of Pharaoh-
necho king of Egypt, which was by the river Euphrates in Carchemish, which Nebuchadrezzar king of
Babylon smote in the fourth year of Jehoiakim the
son of Josiah king of Judah.
3 Order ye the buckler and shield, and draw near
to battle.
4 Harness the horses; and get up, ye horsemen, and
stand forth with *your* helmets; furbish the spears,
and put on the brigandines.
5 Wherefore have I seen them dismayed *and*
turned away back? and their mighty ones are beaten
down, and are fled apace, and look not back: *for* fear
was round about, saith the LORD.

NEW LIVING TRANSLATION

'that all I have threatened will happen to you and that
I will punish you here.' 30 This is what the LORD says: 'I
will turn Pharaoh Hophra, king of Egypt, over to his
enemies who want to kill him, just as I turned King
Zedekiah of Judah over to King Nebuchadnezzar* of
Babylon.'"

A Message for Baruch

45 The prophet Jeremiah gave a message to
Baruch son of Neriah in the fourth year of
the reign of Jehoiakim son of Josiah,* after Baruch
had written down everything Jeremiah had dictated
to him. He said, 2 "This is what the LORD, the God of
Israel, says to you, Baruch: 3 You have said, 'I am overwhelmed with trouble! Haven't I had enough pain already? And now the LORD has added more! I am worn
out from sighing and can find no rest.'
4 "Baruch, this is what the LORD says: 'I will destroy
this nation that I built. I will uproot what I planted.
5 Are you seeking great things for yourself? Don't do
it! I will bring great disaster upon all these people;
but I will give you your life as a reward wherever you
go. I, the LORD, have spoken!'"

Messages for the Nations

46 The following messages were given to Jeremiah the prophet from the LORD concerning foreign nations.

Messages about Egypt

2 This message concerning Egypt was given in the
fourth year of the reign of Jehoiakim son of Josiah,
the king of Judah, on the occasion of the battle of
Carchemish* when Pharaoh Neco, king of Egypt, and
his army were defeated beside the Euphrates River
by King Nebuchadnezzar* of Babylon.

3 "Prepare your shields,
 and advance into battle!
4 Harness the horses,
 and mount the stallions.
Take your positions.
 Put on your helmets.
Sharpen your spears,
 and prepare your armor.
5 But what do I see?
 The Egyptian army flees in terror.
The bravest of its fighting men run
 without a backward glance.
They are terrorized at every turn,"
 says the LORD.

44:30 Hebrew *Nebuchadrezzar,* a variant spelling of Nebuchadnezzar.
45:1 The fourth year of Jehoiakim's reign was 605 B.C. **46:2a** This event occurred in 605 B.C., during the fourth year of Jehoiakim's reign (according to the calendar system in which the new year begins in the spring).
46:2b Hebrew *Nebuchadrezzar,* a variant spelling of Nebuchadnezzar; also in 46:13, 26.

KING JAMES VERSION

6Let not the swift flee away, nor the mighty man
escape; they shall stumble, and fall toward the north
by the river Euphrates.
7Who *is* this *that* cometh up as a flood, whose
waters are moved as the rivers?
8Egypt riseth up like a flood, and *his* waters are
moved like the rivers; and he saith, I will go up, *and*
will cover the earth; I will destroy the city and the
inhabitants thereof.
9Come up, ye horses; and rage, ye chariots; and let
the mighty men come forth; the Ethiopians and the
Libyans, that handle the shield; and the Lydians, that
handle *and* bend the bow.
10For this *is* the day of the Lord GOD of hosts, a day
of vengeance, that he may avenge him of his adversaries: and the sword shall devour, and it shall be satiate and made drunk with their blood: for the Lord
GOD of hosts hath a sacrifice in the north country by
the river Euphrates.
11Go up into Gilead, and take balm, O virgin, the
daughter of Egypt: in vain shalt thou use many medicines; *for* thou shalt not be cured.
12The nations have heard of thy shame, and thy
cry hath filled the land: for the mighty man hath
stumbled against the mighty, *and* they are fallen
both together.
13The word that the LORD spake to Jeremiah the
prophet, how Nebuchadrezzar king of Babylon
should come *and* smite the land of Egypt.
14Declare ye in Egypt, and publish in Migdol, and
publish in Noph and in Tahpanhes: say ye, Stand fast,
and prepare thee; for the sword shall devour round
about thee.
15Why are thy valiant *men* swept away? they stood
not, because the LORD did drive them.
16He made many to fall, yea, one fell upon another:
and they said, Arise, and let us go again to our own
people, and to the land of our nativity, from the oppressing sword.
17They did cry there, Pharaoh king of Egypt *is but* a
noise; he hath passed the time appointed.
18*As* I live, saith the King, whose name *is* the LORD

NEW LIVING TRANSLATION

6 "The swiftest runners cannot flee;
the mightiest warriors cannot escape.
By the Euphrates River to the north,
they stumble and fall.

7 "Who is this, rising like the Nile at floodtime,
overflowing all the land?
8 It is the Egyptian army,
overflowing all the land,
boasting that it will cover the earth like a flood,
destroying cities and their people.
9 Charge, you horses and chariots;
attack, you mighty warriors of Egypt!
Come, all you allies from Ethiopia, Libya,
and Lydia*
who are skilled with the shield and bow!
10 For this is the day of the Lord, the LORD of
Heaven's Armies,
a day of vengeance on his enemies.
The sword will devour until it is satisfied,
yes, until it is drunk with your blood!
The Lord, the LORD of Heaven's Armies,
will receive a sacrifice today
in the north country beside the
Euphrates River.

11 "Go up to Gilead to get medicine,
O virgin daughter of Egypt!
But your many treatments
will bring you no healing.
12 The nations have heard of your shame.
The earth is filled with your cries of despair.
Your mightiest warriors will run into each other
and fall down together."

13Then the LORD gave the prophet Jeremiah this message about King Nebuchadnezzar's plans to attack Egypt.

14 "Shout it out in Egypt!
Publish it in the cities of Migdol, Memphis,*
and Tahpanhes!
Mobilize for battle,
for the sword will devour everyone
around you.
15 Why have your warriors fallen?
They cannot stand, for the LORD has knocked
them down.
16 They stumble and fall over each other
and say among themselves,
'Come, let's go back to our people,
to the land of our birth.
Let's get away from the sword of the enemy!'
17 There they will say,
'Pharaoh, the king of Egypt, is a loudmouth
who missed his opportunity!'

18 "As surely as I live," says the King,
whose name is the LORD of Heaven's Armies,

46:9 Hebrew *from Cush, Put, and Lud.* **46:14** Hebrew *Noph;* also in 46:19.

KING JAMES VERSION

of hosts, Surely as Tabor *is* among the mountains,
and as Carmel by the sea, *so* shall he come.
19 O thou daughter dwelling in Egypt, furnish thyself to go into captivity: for Noph shall be waste and
desolate without an inhabitant.
20 Egypt *is like* a very fair heifer, *but* destruction
cometh; it cometh out of the north.
21 Also her hired men *are* in the midst of her like
fatted bullocks; for they also are turned back, *and* are
fled away together: they did not stand, because the
day of their calamity was come upon them, *and* the
time of their visitation.
22 The voice thereof shall go like a serpent; for they
shall march with an army, and come against her with
axes, as hewers of wood.
23 They shall cut down her forest, saith the LORD,
though it cannot be searched; because they are more
than the grasshoppers, and *are* innumerable.
24 The daughter of Egypt shall be confounded; she
shall be delivered into the hand of the people of the
north.
25 The LORD of hosts, the God of Israel, saith; Behold, I will punish the multitude of No, and Pharaoh,
and Egypt, with their gods, and their kings; even
Pharaoh, and *all* them that trust in him:
26 And I will deliver them into the hand of those
that seek their lives, and into the hand of Nebuchadrezzar king of Babylon, and into the hand of his servants: and afterward it shall be inhabited, as in the
days of old, saith the LORD.
27 But fear not thou, O my servant Jacob, and be not
dismayed, O Israel: for, behold, I will save thee from
afar off, and thy seed from the land of their captivity;
and Jacob shall return, and be in rest and at ease, and
none shall make *him* afraid.
28 Fear thou not, O Jacob my servant, saith the
LORD: for I *am* with thee; for I will make a full end of
all the nations whither I have driven thee: but I will
not make a full end of thee, but correct thee in measure; yet will I not leave thee wholly unpunished.

47 1 The word of the LORD that came to Jeremiah the prophet against the Philistines,
before that Pharaoh smote Gaza.
2 Thus saith the LORD; Behold, waters rise up out of
the north, and shall be an overflowing flood, and
shall overflow the land, and all that is therein; the

NEW LIVING TRANSLATION

"one is coming against Egypt
who is as tall as Mount Tabor,
or as Mount Carmel by the sea!
19 Pack up! Get ready to leave for exile,
you citizens of Egypt!
The city of Memphis will be destroyed,
without a single inhabitant.
20 Egypt is as sleek as a beautiful young cow,
but a horsefly from the north is on its way!
21 Egypt's mercenaries have become like
fattened calves.
They, too, will turn and run,
for it is a day of great disaster for Egypt,
a time of great punishment.
22 Egypt flees, silent as a serpent gliding away.
The invading army marches in;
they come against her with axes like
woodsmen.
23 They will cut down her people like trees,"
says the LORD,
"for they are more numerous than locusts.
24 Egypt will be humiliated;
she will be handed over to people from
the north."

25 The LORD of Heaven's Armies, the God of Israel,
says: "I will punish Amon, the god of Thebes,* and all
the other gods of Egypt. I will punish its rulers and
Pharaoh, too, and all who trust in him. 26 I will hand
them over to those who want them killed—to King
Nebuchadnezzar of Babylon and his army. But afterward the land will recover from the ravages of war. I,
the LORD, have spoken!

27 "But do not be afraid, Jacob, my servant;
do not be dismayed, Israel.
For I will bring you home again from distant lands,
and your children will return from their exile.
Israel* will return to a life of peace and quiet,
and no one will terrorize them.
28 Do not be afraid, Jacob, my servant,
for I am with you," says the LORD.
"I will completely destroy the nations to
which I have exiled you,
but I will not completely destroy you.
I will discipline you, but with justice;
I cannot let you go unpunished."

A Message about Philistia

47 This is the LORD's message to the prophet
Jeremiah concerning the Philistines of Gaza,
before it was captured by the Egyptian army. 2 This is
what the LORD says:

"A flood is coming from the north
to overflow the land.
It will destroy the land and everything in it—
cities and people alike.

46:25 Hebrew *of No.* **46:27** Hebrew *Jacob.* See note on 5:20.

city, and them that dwell therein: then the men shall
cry, and all the inhabitants of the land shall howl.
3 At the noise of the stamping of the hoofs of his
strong *horses*, at the rushing of his chariots, *and at*
the rumbling of his wheels, the fathers shall not look
back to *their* children for feebleness of hands;
4 Because of the day that cometh to spoil all the Philistines, *and* to cut off from Tyrus and Zidon every
helper that remaineth: for the LORD will spoil the Philistines, the remnant of the country of Caphtor.
5 Baldness is come upon Gaza; Ashkelon is cut off
with the remnant of their valley: how long wilt thou
cut thyself?
6 O thou sword of the LORD, how long *will it be* ere
thou be quiet? put up thyself into thy scabbard, rest,
and be still.
7 How can it be quiet, seeing the LORD hath given it
a charge against Ashkelon, and against the sea shore?
there hath he appointed it.

48 1 Against Moab thus saith the LORD of hosts,
the God of Israel; Woe unto Nebo! for it is
spoiled: Kiriathaim is confounded *and* taken: Misgab
is confounded and dismayed.
2 *There shall be* no more praise of Moab: in Heshbon they have devised evil against it; come, and let us
cut it off from *being* a nation. Also thou shalt be cut
down, O Madmen; the sword shall pursue thee.
3 A voice of crying *shall be* from Horonaim, spoiling and great destruction.
4 Moab is destroyed; her little ones have caused a
cry to be heard.
5 For in the going up of Luhith continual weeping
shall go up; for in the going down of Horonaim the
enemies have heard a cry of destruction.

People will scream in terror,
and everyone in the land will wail.
3 Hear the clatter of stallions' hooves
and the rumble of wheels as the
chariots rush by.
Terrified fathers run madly,
without a backward glance at their
helpless children.
4 "The time has come for the Philistines
to be destroyed,
along with their allies from Tyre and Sidon.
Yes, the LORD is destroying the remnant of
the Philistines,
those colonists from the island of Crete.*
5 Gaza will be humiliated, its head shaved bald;
Ashkelon will lie silent.
You remnant from the Mediterranean coast,*
how long will you lament and mourn?
6 "Now, O sword of the LORD,
when will you be at rest again?
Go back into your sheath;
rest and be still.
7 "But how can it be still
when the LORD has sent it on a mission?
For the city of Ashkelon
and the people living along the sea
must be destroyed."

A Message about Moab

48 This message was given concerning Moab.
This is what the LORD of Heaven's Armies,
the God of Israel, says:

"What sorrow awaits the city of Nebo;
it will soon lie in ruins.
The city of Kiriathaim will be humiliated
and captured;
the fortress will be humiliated and
broken down.
2 No one will ever brag about Moab again,
for in Heshbon there is a plot to destroy her.
'Come,' they say, 'we will cut her off from
being a nation.'
The town of Madmen,* too, will be silenced;
the sword will follow you there.
3 Listen to the cries from Horonaim,
cries of devastation and great destruction.
4 All Moab is destroyed.
Her little ones will cry out.*
5 Her refugees weep bitterly,
climbing the slope to Luhith.
They cry out in terror,
descending the slope to Horonaim.

47:4 Hebrew *from Caphtor.* **47:5** Hebrew *the plain.* **48:2** *Madmen* sounds like the Hebrew word for "silence"; it should not be confused with the English word *madmen.* **48:4** Greek version reads *Her cries are heard as far away as Zoar.*

KING JAMES VERSION

6 Flee, save your lives, and be like the heath in the wilderness.

7 For because thou hast trusted in thy works and in thy treasures, thou shalt also be taken: and Chemosh shall go forth into captivity *with* his priests and his princes together.

8 And the spoiler shall come upon every city, and no city shall escape: the valley also shall perish, and the plain shall be destroyed, as the LORD hath spoken.

9 Give wings unto Moab, that it may flee and get away: for the cities thereof shall be desolate, without any to dwell therein.

10 Cursed *be* he that doeth the work of the LORD deceitfully, and cursed *be* he that keepeth back his sword from blood.

11 Moab hath been at ease from his youth, and he hath settled on his lees, and hath not been emptied from vessel to vessel, neither hath he gone into captivity: therefore his taste remained in him, and his scent is not changed.

12 Therefore, behold, the days come, saith the LORD, that I will send unto him wanderers, that shall cause him to wander, and shall empty his vessels, and break their bottles.

13 And Moab shall be ashamed of Chemosh, as the house of Israel was ashamed of Bethel their confidence.

14 How say ye, We *are* mighty and strong men for the war?

15 Moab is spoiled, and gone up *out of* her cities, and his chosen young men are gone down to the slaughter, saith the King, whose name *is* the LORD of hosts.

16 The calamity of Moab *is* near to come, and his affliction hasteth fast.

17 All ye that are about him, bemoan him; and all ye that know his name, say, How is the strong staff broken, *and* the beautiful rod!

18 Thou daughter that dost inhabit Dibon, come down from *thy* glory, and sit in thirst; for the spoiler of Moab shall come upon thee, *and* he shall destroy thy strong holds.

19 O inhabitant of Aroer, stand by the way, and

NEW LIVING TRANSLATION

6 Flee for your lives!
Hide* in the wilderness!
7 Because you have trusted in your wealth and skill,
you will be taken captive.
Your god Chemosh, with his priests and officials,
will be hauled off to distant lands!
8 "All the towns will be destroyed,
and no one will escape—
either on the plateaus or in the valleys,
for the LORD has spoken.
9 Oh, that Moab had wings
so she could fly away,*
for her towns will be left empty,
with no one living in them.
10 Cursed are those who refuse to do the LORD's work,
who hold back their swords from
shedding blood!
11 "From his earliest history, Moab has lived
in peace,
never going into exile.
He is like wine that has been allowed to settle.
He has not been poured from flask to flask,
and he is now fragrant and smooth.
12 But the time is coming soon," says the LORD,
"when I will send men to pour him
from his jar.
They will pour him out,
then shatter the jar!
13 At last Moab will be ashamed of his
idol Chemosh,
as the people of Israel were ashamed
of their gold calf at Bethel.*
14 "You used to boast, 'We are heroes,
mighty men of war.'
15 But now Moab and his towns will be destroyed.
His most promising youth are doomed
to slaughter,"
says the King, whose name is the LORD
of Heaven's Armies.
16 "Destruction is coming fast for Moab;
calamity threatens ominously.
17 You friends of Moab,
weep for him and cry!
See how the strong scepter is broken,
how the beautiful staff is shattered!

18 "Come down from your glory
and sit in the dust, you people of Dibon,
for those who destroy Moab will shatter
Dibon, too.
They will tear down all your towers.
19 You people of Aroer,
stand beside the road and watch.

48:6 Or *Hide like a wild donkey;* or *Hide like a juniper shrub;* or *Be like* [the town of] *Aroer.* The meaning of the Hebrew is uncertain. **48:9** Or *Put salt on Moab, / for she will be laid waste.* **48:13** Hebrew *ashamed when they trusted in Bethel.*

espy; ask him that fleeth, and her that escapeth, *and*
say, What is done?
20 Moab is confounded; for it is broken down: howl
and cry; tell ye it in Arnon, that Moab is spoiled,
21 And judgment is come upon the plain country;
upon Holon, and upon Jahazah, and upon Mephaath,
22 And upon Dibon, and upon Nebo, and upon
Beth-diblathaim,
23 And upon Kiriathaim, and upon Beth-gamul,
and upon Beth-meon,
24 And upon Kerioth, and upon Bozrah, and upon
all the cities of the land of Moab, far or near.
25 The horn of Moab is cut off, and his arm is
broken, saith the LORD.
26 Make ye him drunken: for he magnified *himself*
against the LORD: Moab also shall wallow in his
vomit, and he also shall be in derision.
27 For was not Israel a derision unto thee? was he
found among thieves? for since thou spakest of him,
thou skippedst for joy.
28 O ye that dwell in Moab, leave the cities, and
dwell in the rock, and be like the dove *that* maketh
her nest in the sides of the hole's mouth.
29 We have heard the pride of Moab, (he is exceeding proud) his loftiness, and his arrogancy, and his
pride, and the haughtiness of his heart.
30 I know his wrath, saith the LORD; but *it shall* not
be so; his lies shall not so effect *it*.
31 Therefore will I howl for Moab, and I will cry out
for all Moab; *mine heart* shall mourn for the men of
Kir-heres.
32 O vine of Sibmah, I will weep for thee with the
weeping of Jazer: thy plants are gone over the sea,
they reach *even* to the sea of Jazer: the spoiler is
fallen upon thy summer fruits and upon thy vintage.
33 And joy and gladness is taken from the plentiful
field, and from the land of Moab; and I have caused
wine to fail from the winepresses: none shall tread
with shouting; *their* shouting *shall be* no shouting.
34 From the cry of Heshbon *even* unto Elealeh, *and*
even unto Jahaz, have they uttered their voice, from

Shout to those who flee from Moab,
'What has happened there?'
20 "And the reply comes back,
'Moab lies in ruins, disgraced;
weep and wail!
Tell it by the banks of the Arnon River:
Moab has been destroyed!'
21 Judgment has been poured out on the towns
of the plateau—
on Holon and Jahaz* and Mephaath,
22 on Dibon and Nebo and Beth-diblathaim,
23 on Kiriathaim and Beth-gamul and Beth-meon,
24 on Kerioth and Bozrah—
all the towns of Moab, far and near.
25 "The strength of Moab has ended.
His arm has been broken," says the LORD.
26 "Let him stagger and fall like a drunkard,
for he has rebelled against the LORD.
Moab will wallow in his own vomit,
ridiculed by all.
27 Did you not ridicule the people of Israel?
Were they caught in the company of thieves
that you should despise them as you do?
28 "You people of Moab,
flee from your towns and live in the caves.
Hide like doves that nest
in the clefts of the rocks.
29 We have all heard of the pride of Moab,
for his pride is very great.
We know of his lofty pride,
his arrogance, and his haughty heart.
30 I know about his insolence,"
says the LORD,
"but his boasts are empty—
as empty as his deeds.
31 So now I wail for Moab;
yes, I will mourn for Moab.
My heart is broken for the men
of Kir-hareseth.*
32 "You people of Sibmah, rich in vineyards,
I will weep for you even more than
I did for Jazer.
Your spreading vines once reached as far
as the Dead Sea,*
but the destroyer has stripped you bare!
He has harvested your grapes and
summer fruits.
33 Joy and gladness are gone from fruitful Moab.
The presses yield no wine.
No one treads the grapes with shouts of joy.
There is shouting, yes, but not of joy.

34 "Instead, their awful cries of terror can be heard
from Heshbon clear across to Elealeh and Jahaz; from

48:21 Hebrew *Jahzah*, a variant spelling of Jahaz. **48:31** Hebrew *Kir-heres*, a variant spelling of Kir-hareseth; also in 48:36. **48:32** Hebrew *the sea of Jazer.*

KING JAMES VERSION

Zoar *even* unto Horonaim, *as* an heifer of three years
old: for the waters also of Nimrim shall be desolate.
35 Moreover I will cause to cease in Moab, saith the
LORD, him that offereth in the high places, and him
that burneth incense to his gods.
36 Therefore mine heart shall sound for Moab like
pipes, and mine heart shall sound like pipes for the
men of Kir-heres: because the riches *that* he hath
gotten are perished.
37 For every head *shall be* bald, and every beard
clipped: upon all the hands *shall be* cuttings, and
upon the loins sackcloth.
38 *There shall be* lamentation generally upon all the
housetops of Moab, and in the streets thereof: for I
have broken Moab like a vessel wherein *is* no pleasure, saith the LORD.
39 They shall howl, *saying,* How is it broken down!
how hath Moab turned the back with shame! so shall
Moab be a derision and a dismaying to all them
about him.
40 For thus saith the LORD; Behold, he shall fly as an
eagle, and shall spread his wings over Moab.
41 Kerioth is taken, and the strong holds are surprised, and the mighty men's hearts in Moab at that
day shall be as the heart of a woman in her pangs.
42 And Moab shall be destroyed from *being* a
people, because he hath magnified *himself* against
the LORD.
43 Fear, and the pit, and the snare, *shall be* upon
thee, O inhabitant of Moab, saith the LORD.
44 He that fleeth from the fear shall fall into the pit;
and he that getteth up out of the pit shall be taken in
the snare: for I will bring upon it, *even* upon Moab,
the year of their visitation, saith the LORD.
45 They that fled stood under the shadow of Heshbon because of the force: but a fire shall come forth
out of Heshbon, and a flame from the midst of Sihon,
and shall devour the corner of Moab, and the crown
of the head of the tumultuous ones.
46 Woe be unto thee, O Moab! the people of
Chemosh perisheth: for thy sons are taken captives,
and thy daughters captives.
47 Yet will I bring again the captivity of Moab in the
latter days, saith the LORD. Thus far *is* the judgment
of Moab.

49

1 Concerning the Ammonites, thus saith the
LORD; Hath Israel no sons? hath he no heir?
why *then* doth their king inherit Gad, and his people
dwell in his cities?

NEW LIVING TRANSLATION

Zoar all the way to Horonaim and Eglath-shelishiyah.
Even the waters of Nimrim are dried up now.
35 "I will put an end to Moab," says the LORD, "for the
people offer sacrifices at the pagan shrines and burn
incense to their false gods. 36 My heart moans like a
flute for Moab and Kir-hareseth, for all their wealth has
disappeared. 37 The people shave their heads and
beards in mourning. They slash their hands and put on
clothes made of burlap. 38 There is crying and sorrow in
every Moabite home and on every street. For I have
smashed Moab like an old, unwanted jar. 39 How it is
shattered! Hear the wailing! See the shame of Moab! It
has become an object of ridicule, an example of ruin to
all its neighbors."
40 This is what the LORD says:

"Look! The enemy swoops down like an eagle,
spreading his wings over Moab.
41 Its cities will fall,
and its strongholds will be seized.
Even the mightiest warriors will be in anguish
like a woman in labor.
42 Moab will no longer be a nation,
for it has boasted against the LORD.
43 "Terror and traps and snares will be your lot,
O Moab," says the LORD.
44 "Those who flee in terror will fall into a trap,
and those who escape the trap will step
into a snare.
I will see to it that you do not get away,
for the time of your judgment has come,"
says the LORD.
45 "The people flee as far as Heshbon
but are unable to go on.
For a fire comes from Heshbon,
King Sihon's ancient home,
to devour the entire land
with all its rebellious people.

46 "O Moab, they weep for you!
The people of the god Chemosh are destroyed!
Your sons and your daughters
have been taken away as captives.
47 But I will restore the fortunes of Moab
in days to come.
I, the LORD, have spoken!"

This is the end of Jeremiah's prophecy concerning
Moab.

A Message about Ammon

49

This message was given concerning the
Ammonites. This is what the LORD says:

"Are there no descendants of Israel
to inherit the land of Gad?
Why are you, who worship Molech,*
living in its towns?

49:1 Hebrew *Malcam,* a variant spelling of Molech; also in 49:3.

2 Therefore, behold, the days come, saith the LORD, that I will cause an alarm of war to be heard in Rabbah of the Ammonites; and it shall be a desolate heap, and her daughters shall be burned with fire: then shall Israel be heir unto them that were his heirs, saith the LORD.

3 Howl, O Heshbon, for Ai is spoiled: cry, ye daughters of Rabbah, gird you with sackcloth; lament, and run to and fro by the hedges; for their king shall go into captivity, *and* his priests and his princes together.

4 Wherefore gloriest thou in the valleys, thy flowing valley, O backsliding daughter? that trusted in her treasures, *saying,* Who shall come unto me?

5 Behold, I will bring a fear upon thee, saith the Lord GOD of hosts, from all those that be about thee; and ye shall be driven out every man right forth; and none shall gather up him that wandereth.

6 And afterward I will bring again the captivity of the children of Ammon, saith the LORD.

7 Concerning Edom, thus saith the LORD of hosts; *Is* wisdom no more in Teman? is counsel perished from the prudent? is their wisdom vanished?

8 Flee ye, turn back, dwell deep, O inhabitants of Dedan; for I will bring the calamity of Esau upon him, the time *that* I will visit him.

9 If grapegatherers come to thee, would they not leave *some* gleaning grapes? if thieves by night, they will destroy till they have enough.

10 But I have made Esau bare, I have uncovered his secret places, and he shall not be able to hide himself: his seed is spoiled, and his brethren, and his neighbours, and he *is* not.

11 Leave thy fatherless children, I will preserve *them* alive; and let thy widows trust in me.

12 For thus saith the LORD; Behold, they whose judgment *was* not to drink of the cup have assuredly drunken; and *art* thou he *that* shall altogether go unpunished? thou shalt not go unpunished, but thou shalt surely drink *of it.*

13 For I have sworn by myself, saith the LORD, that Bozrah shall become a desolation, a reproach, a

2 In the days to come," says the LORD,
"I will sound the battle cry against your
city of Rabbah.
It will become a desolate heap of ruins,
and the neighboring towns will be burned.
Then Israel will take back the land
you took from her," says the LORD.

3 "Cry out, O Heshbon,
for the town of Ai is destroyed.
Weep, O people of Rabbah!
Put on your clothes of mourning.
Weep and wail, hiding in the hedges,
for your god Molech, with his priests
and officials,
will be hauled off to distant lands.
4 You are proud of your fertile valleys,
but they will soon be ruined.
You trusted in your wealth,
you rebellious daughter,
and thought no one could ever harm you.
5 But look! I will bring terror upon you,"
says the Lord, the LORD of Heaven's Armies.
"Your neighbors will chase you from your land,
and no one will help your exiles as they flee.
6 But I will restore the fortunes of the Ammonites
in days to come.
I, the LORD, have spoken."

Messages about Edom

7 This message was given concerning Edom. This is what the LORD of Heaven's Armies says:

"Is there no wisdom in Teman?
Is no one left to give wise counsel?
8 Turn and flee!
Hide in deep caves, you people of Dedan!
For when I bring disaster on Edom,*
I will punish you, too!
9 Those who harvest grapes
always leave a few for the poor.
If thieves came at night,
they would not take everything.
10 But I will strip bare the land of Edom,
and there will be no place left to hide.
Its children, its brothers, and its neighbors
will all be destroyed,
and Edom itself will be no more.
11 But I will protect the orphans who remain
among you.
Your widows, too, can depend on me for help."

12 And this is what the LORD says: "If the innocent
must suffer, how much more must you! You will not
go unpunished! You must drink this cup of judgment! 13 For I have sworn by my own name," says the
LORD, "that Bozrah will become an object of horror

49:8 Hebrew *Esau;* also in 49:10.

KING JAMES VERSION

waste, and a curse; and all the cities thereof shall be
perpetual wastes.
14I have heard a rumour from the LORD, and an
ambassador is sent unto the heathen, *saying*, Gather
ye together, and come against her, and rise up to the
battle.
15For, lo, I will make thee small among the heathen, *and* despised among men.
16Thy terribleness hath deceived thee, *and* the
pride of thine heart, O thou that dwellest in the clefts
of the rock, that holdest the height of the hill: though
thou shouldest make thy nest as high as the eagle, I
will bring thee down from thence, saith the LORD.
17Also Edom shall be a desolation: every one that
goeth by it shall be astonished, and shall hiss at all
the plagues thereof.
18As in the overthrow of Sodom and Gomorrah
and the neighbour *cities* thereof, saith the LORD, no
man shall abide there, neither shall a son of man
dwell in it.
19Behold, he shall come up like a lion from the
swelling of Jordan against the habitation of the
strong: but I will suddenly make him run away from
her: and who *is* a chosen *man, that* I may appoint
over her? for who *is* like me? and who will appoint
me the time? and who *is* that shepherd that will
stand before me?
20Therefore hear the counsel of the LORD, that he
hath taken against Edom; and his purposes, that he
hath purposed against the inhabitants of Teman:
Surely the least of the flock shall draw them out:
surely he shall make their habitations desolate with
them.
21The earth is moved at the noise of their fall, at
the cry the noise thereof was heard in the Red sea.
22Behold, he shall come up and fly as the eagle,
and spread his wings over Bozrah: and at that day
shall the heart of the mighty men of Edom be as the
heart of a woman in her pangs.

23Concerning Damascus. Hamath is confounded,
and Arpad: for they have heard evil tidings: they are

NEW LIVING TRANSLATION

and a heap of ruins; it will be mocked and cursed. All its towns and villages will be desolate forever."

14 I have heard a message from the LORD
that an ambassador was sent to the nations to say,
"Form a coalition against Edom,
and prepare for battle!"
15 The LORD says to Edom,
"I will cut you down to size among the nations.
You will be despised by all.
16 You have been deceived
by the fear you inspire in others
and by your own pride.
You live in a rock fortress
and control the mountain heights.
But even if you make your nest among the peaks with the eagles,
I will bring you crashing down,"
says the LORD.

17 "Edom will be an object of horror.
All who pass by will be appalled
and will gasp at the destruction they see there.
18 It will be like the destruction of Sodom and Gomorrah
and their neighboring towns," says the LORD.
"No one will live there;
no one will inhabit it.
19 I will come like a lion from the thickets of the Jordan,
leaping on the sheep in the pasture.
I will chase Edom from its land,
and I will appoint the leader of my choice.
For who is like me, and who can challenge me?
What ruler can oppose my will?"
20 Listen to the LORD's plans against Edom
and the people of Teman.
Even the little children will be dragged off like sheep,
and their homes will be destroyed.
21 The earth will shake with the noise of Edom's fall,
and its cry of despair will be heard all the way to the Red Sea.*
22 Look! The enemy swoops down like an eagle,
spreading his wings over Bozrah.
Even the mightiest warriors will be in anguish
like a woman in labor.

A Message about Damascus

23 This message was given concerning Damascus. This is what the LORD says:

"The towns of Hamath and Arpad are struck with fear,
for they have heard the news of their destruction.

49:21 Hebrew *sea of reeds.*

fainthearted; *there is* sorrow on the sea; it cannot be quiet.

24 Damascus is waxed feeble, *and* turneth herself to flee, and fear hath seized on *her:* anguish and sorrows have taken her, as a woman in travail.

25 How is the city of praise not left, the city of my joy!

26 Therefore her young men shall fall in her streets, and all the men of war shall be cut off in that day, saith the LORD of hosts.

27 And I will kindle a fire in the wall of Damascus, and it shall consume the palaces of Ben-hadad.

28 Concerning Kedar, and concerning the kingdoms of Hazor, which Nebuchadrezzar king of Babylon shall smite, thus saith the LORD; Arise ye, go up to Kedar, and spoil the men of the east.

29 Their tents and their flocks shall they take away: they shall take to themselves their curtains, and all their vessels, and their camels; and they shall cry unto them, Fear *is* on every side.

30 Flee, get you far off, dwell deep, O ye inhabitants of Hazor, saith the LORD; for Nebuchadrezzar king of Babylon hath taken counsel against you, and hath conceived a purpose against you.

31 Arise, get you up unto the wealthy nation, that dwelleth without care, saith the LORD, which have neither gates nor bars, *which* dwell alone.

32 And their camels shall be a booty, and the multitude of their cattle a spoil: and I will scatter into all winds them *that are* in the utmost corners; and I will bring their calamity from all sides thereof, saith the LORD.

33 And Hazor shall be a dwelling for dragons, *and* a desolation for ever: there shall no man abide there, nor *any* son of man dwell in it.

34 The word of the LORD that came to Jeremiah the prophet against Elam in the beginning of the reign of Zedekiah king of Judah, saying,

35 Thus saith the LORD of hosts; Behold, I will break the bow of Elam, the chief of their might.

36 And upon Elam will I bring the four winds from

Their hearts are troubled
like a wild sea in a raging storm.
24 Damascus has become feeble,
and all her people turn to flee.
Fear, anguish, and pain have gripped her
as they grip a woman in labor.
25 That famous city, a city of joy,
will be forsaken!
26 Her young men will fall in the streets and die.
Her soldiers will all be killed,"
says the LORD of Heaven's Armies.
27 "And I will set fire to the walls of Damascus
that will burn up the palaces of Ben-hadad."

A Message about Kedar and Hazor

28 This message was given concerning Kedar and the kingdoms of Hazor, which were attacked by King Nebuchadnezzar* of Babylon. This is what the LORD says:

"Advance against Kedar!
Destroy the warriors from the East!
29 Their flocks and tents will be captured,
and their household goods and camels
will be taken away.
Everywhere shouts of panic will be heard:
'We are terrorized at every turn!'
30 Run for your lives," says the LORD.
"Hide yourselves in deep caves, you people
of Hazor,
for King Nebuchadnezzar of Babylon has
plotted against you
and is preparing to destroy you.

31 "Go up and attack that complacent nation,"
says the LORD.
"Its people live alone in the desert
without walls or gates.
32 Their camels and other livestock will all be yours.
I will scatter to the winds these people
who live in remote places.*
I will bring calamity upon them
from every direction," says the LORD.
33 "Hazor will be inhabited by jackals,
and it will be desolate forever.
No one will live there;
no one will inhabit it."

A Message about Elam

34 This message concerning Elam came to the prophet Jeremiah from the LORD at the beginning of the reign of King Zedekiah of Judah. 35 This is what the LORD of Heaven's Armies says:

"I will destroy the archers of Elam—
the best of their forces.
36 I will bring enemies from all directions,

49:28 Hebrew *Nebuchadrezzar,* a variant spelling of Nebuchadnezzar; also in 49:30. **49:32** Or *who clip the corners of their hair.*

KING JAMES VERSION

the four quarters of heaven, and will scatter them
toward all those winds; and there shall be no nation
whither the outcasts of Elam shall not come.
37 For I will cause Elam to be dismayed before their
enemies, and before them that seek their life: and I
will bring evil upon them, *even* my fierce anger, saith
the LORD; and I will send the sword after them, till I
have consumed them:
38 And I will set my throne in Elam, and will destroy
from thence the king and the princes, saith the LORD.
39 But it shall come to pass in the latter days, *that* I
will bring again the captivity of Elam, saith the LORD.

50 1 The word that the LORD spake against Babylon *and* against the land of the Chaldeans
by Jeremiah the prophet.
2 Declare ye among the nations, and publish, and
set up a standard; publish, *and* conceal not: say, Babylon is taken, Bel is confounded, Merodach is broken
in pieces; her idols are confounded, her images are
broken in pieces.
3 For out of the north there cometh up a nation
against her, which shall make her land desolate, and
none shall dwell therein: they shall remove, they
shall depart, both man and beast.

4 In those days, and in that time, saith the LORD, the
children of Israel shall come, they and the children
of Judah together, going and weeping: they shall go,
and seek the LORD their God.
5 They shall ask the way to Zion with their faces
thitherward, *saying*, Come, and let us join ourselves
to the LORD in a perpetual covenant *that* shall not be
forgotten.
6 My people hath been lost sheep: their shepherds
have caused them to go astray, they have turned
them away *on* the mountains: they have gone from
mountain to hill, they have forgotten their resting-
place.
7 All that found them have devoured them: and
their adversaries said, We offend not, because they

NEW LIVING TRANSLATION

and I will scatter the people of Elam
to the four winds.
They will be exiled to countries around
the world.
37 I myself will go with Elam's enemies to shatter it.
In my fierce anger, I will bring great disaster
upon the people of Elam," says the LORD.
"Their enemies will chase them with the sword
until I have destroyed them completely.
38 I will set my throne in Elam," says the LORD,
"and I will destroy its king and officials.
39 But I will restore the fortunes of Elam
in days to come.
I, the LORD, have spoken!"

A Message about Babylon

50 The LORD gave Jeremiah the prophet this
message concerning Babylon and the land
of the Babylonians.* 2 This is what the LORD says:

"Tell the whole world,
and keep nothing back.
Raise a signal flag
to tell everyone that Babylon will fall!
Her images and idols* will be shattered.
Her gods Bel and Marduk will be
utterly disgraced.
3 For a nation will attack her from the north
and bring such destruction that no one
will live there again.
Everything will be gone;
both people and animals will flee.

Hope for Israel and Judah

4 "In those coming days,"
says the LORD,
"the people of Israel will return home
together with the people of Judah.
They will come weeping
and seeking the LORD their God.
5 They will ask the way to Jerusalem*
and will start back home again.
They will bind themselves to the LORD
with an eternal covenant that will never
be forgotten.

6 "My people have been lost sheep.
Their shepherds have led them astray
and turned them loose in the mountains.
They have lost their way
and can't remember how to get back
to the sheepfold.
7 All who found them devoured them.
Their enemies said,
'We did nothing wrong in attacking them,
for they sinned against the LORD,

50:1 Or *Chaldeans;* also in 50:8, 25, 35, 45. **50:2** The Hebrew term (literally *round things*) probably alludes to dung. **50:5** Hebrew *Zion;* also in 50:28.

KING JAMES VERSION

have sinned against the LORD, the habitation of justice, even the LORD, the hope of their fathers.
8Remove out of the midst of Babylon, and go forth
out of the land of the Chaldeans, and be as the he
goats before the flocks.
9For, lo, I will raise and cause to come up against
Babylon an assembly of great nations from the north
country: and they shall set themselves in array
against her; from thence she shall be taken: their arrows *shall be* as of a mighty expert man; none shall
return in vain.
10And Chaldea shall be a spoil: all that spoil her
shall be satisfied, saith the LORD.

11Because ye were glad, because ye rejoiced, O ye
destroyers of mine heritage, because ye are grown fat
as the heifer at grass, and bellow as bulls;
12Your mother shall be sore confounded; she that
bare you shall be ashamed: behold, the hindermost
of the nations *shall be* a wilderness, a dry land, and
a desert.
13Because of the wrath of the LORD it shall not be
inhabited, but it shall be wholly desolate: every one
that goeth by Babylon shall be astonished, and hiss at
all her plagues.
14Put yourselves in array against Babylon round
about: all ye that bend the bow, shoot at her, spare no
arrows: for she hath sinned against the LORD.
15Shout against her round about: she hath given
her hand: her foundations are fallen, her walls are
thrown down: for it *is* the vengeance of the LORD:
take vengeance upon her; as she hath done, do unto
her.
16Cut off the sower from Babylon, and him that
handleth the sickle in the time of harvest: for fear of
the oppressing sword they shall turn every one to his
people, and they shall flee every one to his own land.

17Israel *is* a scattered sheep; the lions have driven
him away: first the king of Assyria hath devoured
him; and last this Nebuchadrezzar king of Babylon
hath broken his bones.
18Therefore thus saith the LORD of hosts, the God

NEW LIVING TRANSLATION

their true place of rest,
and the hope of their ancestors.'

8 "But now, flee from Babylon!
Leave the land of the Babylonians.
Like male goats at the head of the flock,
lead my people home again.
9 For I am raising up an army
of great nations from the north.
They will join forces to attack Babylon,
and she will be captured.
The enemies' arrows will go straight to the mark;
they will not miss!
10 Babylonia* will be looted
until the attackers are glutted with loot.
I, the LORD, have spoken!

Babylon's Sure Fall

11 "You rejoice and are glad,
you who plundered my chosen people.
You frisk about like a calf in a meadow
and neigh like a stallion.
12 But your homeland* will be overwhelmed
with shame and disgrace.
You will become the least of nations—
a wilderness, a dry and desolate land.
13 Because of the LORD's anger,
Babylon will become a deserted wasteland.
All who pass by will be horrified
and will gasp at the destruction they see there.

14 "Yes, prepare to attack Babylon,
all you surrounding nations.
Let your archers shoot at her; spare no arrows.
For she has sinned against the LORD.
15 Shout war cries against her from every side.
Look! She surrenders!
Her walls have fallen.
It is the LORD's vengeance,
so take vengeance on her.
Do to her as she has done to others!
16 Take from Babylon all those who plant crops;
send all the harvesters away.
Because of the sword of the enemy,
everyone will run away and rush back
to their own lands.

Hope for God's People

17 "The Israelites are like sheep
that have been scattered by lions.
First the king of Assyria ate them up.
Then King Nebuchadnezzar* of Babylon
cracked their bones."
18 Therefore, this is what the LORD of
Heaven's Armies,
the God of Israel, says:

50:10 Or *Chaldea.* **50:12** Hebrew *your mother.* **50:17** Hebrew *Nebuchadrezzar*, a variant spelling of Nebuchadnezzar.

KING JAMES VERSION

of Israel; Behold, I will punish the king of Babylon
and his land, as I have punished the king of Assyria.
19 And I will bring Israel again to his habitation,
and he shall feed on Carmel and Bashan, and his soul
shall be satisfied upon mount Ephraim and Gilead.
20 In those days, and in that time, saith the LORD,
the iniquity of Israel shall be sought for, and *there*
shall be none; and the sins of Judah, and they shall
not be found: for I will pardon them whom I reserve.

21 Go up against the land of Merathaim, *even*
against it, and against the inhabitants of Pekod:
waste and utterly destroy after them, saith the LORD,
and do according to all that I have commanded thee.
22 A sound of battle *is* in the land, and of great
destruction.
23 How is the hammer of the whole earth cut asunder and broken! how is Babylon become a desolation
among the nations!
24 I have laid a snare for thee, and thou art also
taken, O Babylon, and thou wast not aware: thou art
found, and also caught, because thou hast striven
against the LORD.
25 The LORD hath opened his armoury, and hath
brought forth the weapons of his indignation: for
this *is* the work of the Lord GOD of hosts in the land
of the Chaldeans.
26 Come against her from the utmost border, open
her storehouses: cast her up as heaps, and destroy
her utterly: let nothing of her be left.
27 Slay all her bullocks; let them go down to the
slaughter: woe unto them! for their day is come, the
time of their visitation.
28 The voice of them that flee and escape out of the
land of Babylon, to declare in Zion the vengeance of
the LORD our God, the vengeance of his temple.
29 Call together the archers against Babylon: all ye
that bend the bow, camp against it round about; let
none thereof escape: recompense her according to
her work; according to all that she hath done, do
unto her: for she hath been proud against the LORD,
against the Holy One of Israel.
30 Therefore shall her young men fall in the streets,
and all her men of war shall be cut off in that day,
saith the LORD.
31 Behold, I *am* against thee, *O thou* most proud,
saith the Lord GOD of hosts: for thy day is come, the
time *that* I will visit thee.

NEW LIVING TRANSLATION

"Now I will punish the king of Babylon and
his land,
just as I punished the king of Assyria.
19 And I will bring Israel home again to its own land,
to feed in the fields of Carmel and Bashan,
and to be satisfied once more
in the hill country of Ephraim and Gilead.
20 In those days," says the LORD,
"no sin will be found in Israel or in Judah,
for I will forgive the remnant I preserve.

The LORD's Judgment on Babylon

21 "Go up, my warriors, against the land of Merathaim
and against the people of Pekod.
Pursue, kill, and completely destroy* them,
as I have commanded you," says the LORD.
22 "Let the battle cry be heard in the land,
a shout of great destruction.
23 Babylon, the mightiest hammer in all the earth,
lies broken and shattered.
Babylon is desolate among the nations!
24 Listen, Babylon, for I have set a trap for you.
You are caught, for you have fought against
the LORD.
25 The LORD has opened his armory
and brought out weapons to vent his fury.
The terror that falls upon the Babylonians
will be the work of the Sovereign LORD of
Heaven's Armies.
26 Yes, come against her from distant lands.
Break open her granaries.
Crush her walls and houses into heaps of rubble.
Destroy her completely, and leave nothing!
27 Destroy even her young bulls—
it will be terrible for them, too!
Slaughter them all!
For Babylon's day of reckoning has come.
28 Listen to the people who have escaped
from Babylon,
as they tell in Jerusalem
how the LORD our God has taken vengeance
against those who destroyed his Temple.

29 "Send out a call for archers to come to Babylon.
Surround the city so none can escape.
Do to her as she has done to others,
for she has defied the LORD, the Holy One
of Israel.
30 Her young men will fall in the streets and die.
Her soldiers will all be killed,"
says the LORD.

31 "See, I am your enemy, you arrogant people,"
says the Lord, the LORD of Heaven's Armies.
"Your day of reckoning has arrived—
the day when I will punish you.

50:21 The Hebrew term used here refers to the complete consecration of things or people to the LORD, either by destroying them or by giving them as an offering.

KING JAMES VERSION

32And the most proud shall stumble and fall, and
none shall raise him up: and I will kindle a fire in his
cities, and it shall devour all round about him.
33Thus saith the LORD of hosts; The children of
Israel and the children of Judah *were* oppressed
together: and all that took them captives held them
fast; they refused to let them go.
34Their Redeemer *is* strong; the LORD of hosts *is*
his name: he shall throughly plead their cause, that
he may give rest to the land, and disquiet the inhabitants of Babylon.
35A sword *is* upon the Chaldeans, saith the LORD,
and upon the inhabitants of Babylon, and upon her
princes, and upon her wise *men.*
36A sword *is* upon the liars; and they shall dote: a
sword *is* upon her mighty men; and they shall be
dismayed.
37A sword *is* upon their horses, and upon their
chariots, and upon all the mingled people that *are* in
the midst of her; and they shall become as women: a
sword *is* upon her treasures; and they shall be
robbed.
38A drought *is* upon her waters; and they shall be
dried up: for it *is* the land of graven images, and they
are mad upon *their* idols.
39Therefore the wild beasts of the desert with the
wild beasts of the islands shall dwell *there,* and the
owls shall dwell therein: and it shall be no more inhabited for ever; neither shall it be dwelt in from
generation to generation.
40As God overthrew Sodom and Gomorrah and
the neighbour *cities* thereof, saith the LORD; *so* shall
no man abide there, neither shall any son of man
dwell therein.
41Behold, a people shall come from the north, and
a great nation, and many kings shall be raised up
from the coasts of the earth.
42They shall hold the bow and the lance: they *are*
cruel, and will not shew mercy: their voice shall roar
like the sea, and they shall ride upon horses, *every
one* put in array, like a man to the battle, against thee,
O daughter of Babylon.

NEW LIVING TRANSLATION

32 O land of arrogance, you will stumble and fall,
and no one will raise you up.
For I will light a fire in the cities of Babylon
that will burn up everything around them."

33 This is what the LORD of Heaven's Armies says:
"The people of Israel and Judah have
been wronged.
Their captors hold them and refuse
to let them go.
34 But the one who redeems them is strong.
His name is the LORD of Heaven's Armies.
He will defend them
and give them rest again in Israel.
But for the people of Babylon
there will be no rest!

35 "The sword of destruction will strike
the Babylonians,"
says the LORD.
"It will strike the people of Babylon—
her officials and wise men, too.
36 The sword will strike her wise counselors,
and they will become fools.
The sword will strike her mightiest warriors,
and panic will seize them.
37 The sword will strike her horses and chariots
and her allies from other lands,
and they will all become like women.
The sword will strike her treasures,
and they all will be plundered.
38 The sword will even strike her water supply,
causing it to dry up.
And why? Because the whole land is filled
with idols,
and the people are madly in love with them.

39 "Soon Babylon will be inhabited by desert
animals and hyenas.
It will be a home for owls.
Never again will people live there;
it will lie desolate forever.
40 I will destroy it as I* destroyed Sodom
and Gomorrah
and their neighboring towns," says the LORD.
"No one will live there;
no one will inhabit it.

41 "Look! A great army is coming from the north.
A great nation and many kings
are rising against you from far-off lands.
42 They are armed with bows and spears.
They are cruel and show no mercy.
As they ride forward on horses,
they sound like a roaring sea.
They are coming in battle formation,
planning to destroy you, Babylon.

50:40 Hebrew *as God.*

KING JAMES VERSION

43 The king of Babylon hath heard the report of
them, and his hands waxed feeble: anguish took hold
of him, *and* pangs as of a woman in travail.
44 Behold, he shall come up like a lion from the
swelling of Jordan unto the habitation of the strong:
but I will make them suddenly run away from her: and
who *is* a chosen *man, that* I may appoint over her? for
who *is* like me? and who will appoint me the time?
and who *is* that shepherd that will stand before me?
45 Therefore hear ye the counsel of the LORD, that
he hath taken against Babylon; and his purposes, that
he hath purposed against the land of the Chaldeans:
Surely the least of the flock shall draw them out:
surely he shall make *their* habitation desolate with
them.
46 At the noise of the taking of Babylon the earth is
moved, and the cry is heard among the nations.

51 1 Thus saith the LORD; Behold, I will raise up
against Babylon, and against them that dwell
in the midst of them that rise up against me, a destroying wind;
2 And will send unto Babylon fanners, that shall
fan her, and shall empty her land: for in the day of
trouble they shall be against her round about.
3 Against *him that* bendeth let the archer bend his
bow, and against *him that* lifteth himself up in his
brigandine: and spare ye not her young men; destroy
ye utterly all her host.
4 Thus the slain shall fall in the land of the Chaldeans, and *they that are* thrust through in her streets.
5 For Israel *hath* not *been* forsaken, nor Judah of
his God, of the LORD of hosts; though their land was
filled with sin against the Holy One of Israel.
6 Flee out of the midst of Babylon, and deliver
every man his soul: be not cut off in her iniquity; for
this *is* the time of the LORD's vengeance; he will render unto her a recompence.
7 Babylon *hath been* a golden cup in the LORD's
hand, that made all the earth drunken: the nations
have drunken of her wine; therefore the nations are
mad.
8 Babylon is suddenly fallen and destroyed: howl
for her; take balm for her pain, if so be she may be
healed.

NEW LIVING TRANSLATION

43 The king of Babylon has heard reports
about the enemy,
and he is weak with fright.
Pangs of anguish have gripped him,
like those of a woman in labor.

44 "I will come like a lion from the thickets
of the Jordan,
leaping on the sheep in the pasture.
I will chase Babylon from its land,
and I will appoint the leader of my choice.
For who is like me, and who can challenge me?
What ruler can oppose my will?"
45 Listen to the LORD's plans against Babylon
and the land of the Babylonians.
Even the little children will be dragged off
like sheep,
and their homes will be destroyed.
46 The earth will shake with the shout, "Babylon
has been taken!"
and its cry of despair will be heard around
the world.

51 1 This is what the LORD says:
"I will stir up a destroyer against Babylon
and the people of Babylonia.*
2 Foreigners will come and winnow her,
blowing her away as chaff.
They will come from every side
to rise against her in her day of trouble.
3 Don't let the archers put on their armor
or draw their bows.
Don't spare even her best soldiers!
Let her army be completely destroyed.*
4 They will fall dead in the land of the
Babylonians,*
slashed to death in her streets.
5 For the LORD of Heaven's Armies
has not abandoned Israel and Judah.
He is still their God,
even though their land was filled with sin
against the Holy One of Israel."

6 Flee from Babylon! Save yourselves!
Don't get trapped in her punishment!
It is the LORD's time for vengeance;
he will repay her in full.
7 Babylon has been a gold cup in the LORD's hands,
a cup that made the whole earth drunk.
The nations drank Babylon's wine,
and it drove them all mad.
8 But suddenly Babylon, too, has fallen.
Weep for her.
Give her medicine.
Perhaps she can yet be healed.

51:1 Hebrew *of Leb-kamai,* a code name for Babylonia. **51:3** The Hebrew term used here refers to the complete consecration of things or people to the LORD, either by destroying them or by giving them as an offering. **51:4** Or *Chaldeans;* also in 51:54.

KING JAMES VERSION

9 We would have healed Babylon, but she is not healed: forsake her, and let us go every one into his own country: for her judgment reacheth unto heaven, and is lifted up *even* to the skies.

10 The LORD hath brought forth our righteousness: come, and let us declare in Zion the work of the LORD our God.

11 Make bright the arrows; gather the shields: the LORD hath raised up the spirit of the kings of the Medes: for his device *is* against Babylon, to destroy it; because it *is* the vengeance of the LORD, the vengeance of his temple.

12 Set up the standard upon the walls of Babylon, make the watch strong, set up the watchmen, prepare the ambushes: for the LORD hath both devised and done that which he spake against the inhabitants of Babylon.

13 O thou that dwellest upon many waters, abundant in treasures, thine end is come, *and* the measure of thy covetousness.

14 The LORD of hosts hath sworn by himself, *saying,* Surely I will fill thee with men, as with caterpillers; and they shall lift up a shout against thee.

15 He hath made the earth by his power, he hath established the world by his wisdom, and hath stretched out the heaven by his understanding.

16 When he uttereth *his* voice, *there is* a multitude of waters in the heavens; and he causeth the vapours to ascend from the ends of the earth: he maketh lightnings with rain, and bringeth forth the wind out of his treasures.

17 Every man is brutish by *his* knowledge; every founder is confounded by the graven image: for his molten image *is* falsehood, and *there is* no breath in them.

18 They *are* vanity, the work of errors: in the time of their visitation they shall perish.

19 The portion of Jacob *is* not like them; for he *is* the former of all things: and *Israel is* the rod of his inheritance: the LORD of hosts *is* his name.

NEW LIVING TRANSLATION

9 We would have helped her if we could,
but nothing can save her now.
Let her go; abandon her.
Return now to your own land.
For her punishment reaches to the heavens;
it is so great it cannot be measured.
10 The LORD has vindicated us.
Come, let us announce in Jerusalem*
everything the LORD our God has done.

11 Sharpen the arrows!
Lift up the shields!*
For the LORD has inspired the kings of the Medes
to march against Babylon and destroy her.
This is his vengeance against those
who desecrated his Temple.
12 Raise the battle flag against Babylon!
Reinforce the guard and station
the watchmen.
Prepare an ambush,
for the LORD will fulfill all his plans
against Babylon.
13 You are a city by a great river,
a great center of commerce,
but your end has come.
The thread of your life is cut.
14 The LORD of Heaven's Armies has taken this vow
and has sworn to it by his own name:
"Your cities will be filled with enemies,
like fields swarming with locusts,
and they will shout in triumph over you."

A Hymn of Praise to the LORD

15 The LORD made the earth by his power,
and he preserves it by his wisdom.
With his own understanding
he stretched out the heavens.
16 When he speaks in the thunder,
the heavens are filled with water.
He causes the clouds to rise over the earth.
He sends the lightning with the rain
and releases the wind from his storehouses.

17 The whole human race is foolish and has
no knowledge!
The craftsmen are disgraced by the idols
they make,
for their carefully shaped works are a fraud.
These idols have no breath or power.
18 Idols are worthless; they are ridiculous lies!
On the day of reckoning they will all
be destroyed.
19 But the God of Israel* is no idol!
He is the Creator of everything that exists,
including his people, his own special possession.
The LORD of Heaven's Armies is his name!

51:10 Hebrew *Zion;* also in 51:24. **51:11** Greek version reads *Fill up the quivers.* **51:19** Hebrew *the Portion of Jacob.* See note on 5:20.

KING JAMES VERSION

20 Thou *art* my battle ax *and* weapons of war: for
with thee will I break in pieces the nations, and with
thee will I destroy kingdoms;
21 And with thee will I break in pieces the horse
and his rider; and with thee will I break in pieces the
chariot and his rider;
22 With thee also will I break in pieces man and
woman; and with thee will I break in pieces old and
young; and with thee will I break in pieces the young
man and the maid;
23 I will also break in pieces with thee the shepherd
and his flock; and with thee will I break in pieces the
husbandman and his yoke of oxen; and with thee will
I break in pieces captains and rulers.
24 And I will render unto Babylon and to all the inhabitants of Chaldea all their evil that they have done
in Zion in your sight, saith the LORD.
25 Behold, I *am* against thee, O destroying mountain, saith the LORD, which destroyest all the earth:
and I will stretch out mine hand upon thee, and roll
thee down from the rocks, and will make thee a
burnt mountain.
26 And they shall not take of thee a stone for a corner, nor a stone for foundations; but thou shalt be
desolate for ever, saith the LORD.
27 Set ye up a standard in the land, blow the trumpet among the nations, prepare the nations against
her, call together against her the kingdoms of Ararat,
Minni, and Ashchenaz; appoint a captain against
her; cause the horses to come up as the rough caterpillers.
28 Prepare against her the nations with the kings of
the Medes, the captains thereof, and all the rulers
thereof, and all the land of his dominion.
29 And the land shall tremble and sorrow: for every
purpose of the LORD shall be performed against Babylon, to make the land of Babylon a desolation without an inhabitant.
30 The mighty men of Babylon have forborn to
fight, they have remained in *their* holds: their might
hath failed; they became as women: they have
burned her dwellingplaces; her bars are broken.
31 One post shall run to meet another, and one
messenger to meet another, to shew the king of Babylon that his city is taken at *one* end,

NEW LIVING TRANSLATION

Babylon's Great Punishment

20 "You* are my battle-ax and sword,"
says the LORD.
"With you I will shatter nations
and destroy many kingdoms.
21 With you I will shatter armies—
destroying the horse and rider,
the chariot and charioteer.
22 With you I will shatter men and women,
old people and children,
young men and maidens.
23 With you I will shatter shepherds and flocks,
farmers and oxen,
captains and officers.

24 "I will repay Babylon
and the people of Babylonia*
for all the wrong they have done
to my people in Jerusalem," says the LORD.
25 "Look, O mighty mountain, destroyer of the earth!
I am your enemy," says the LORD.
"I will raise my fist against you,
to knock you down from the heights.
When I am finished,
you will be nothing but a heap of burnt rubble.
26 You will be desolate forever.
Even your stones will never again be used
for building.
You will be completely wiped out,"
says the LORD.

27 Raise a signal flag to the nations.
Sound the battle cry!
Mobilize them all against Babylon.
Prepare them to fight against her!
Bring out the armies of Ararat, Minni, and
Ashkenaz.
Appoint a commander,
and bring a multitude of horses like
swarming locusts!
28 Bring against her the armies of the nations—
led by the kings of the Medes
and all their captains and officers.
29 The earth trembles and writhes in pain,
for everything the LORD has planned against
Babylon stands unchanged.
Babylon will be left desolate without a single
inhabitant.
30 Her mightiest warriors no longer fight.
They stay in their barracks, their courage gone.
They have become like women.
The invaders have burned the houses
and broken down the city gates.
31 The news is passed from one runner to the next
as the messengers hurry to tell the king
that his city has been captured.

51:20 Possibly Cyrus, whom God used to conquer Babylon. Compare Isa 44:28; 45:1. **51:24** Or *Chaldea;* also in 51:35.

KING JAMES VERSION

32 And that the passages are stopped, and the reeds they have burned with fire, and the men of war are affrighted.

33 For thus saith the LORD of hosts, the God of Israel; The daughter of Babylon *is* like a threshingfloor, *it is* time to thresh her: yet a little while, and the time of her harvest shall come.

34 Nebuchadrezzar the king of Babylon hath devoured me, he hath crushed me, he hath made me an empty vessel, he hath swallowed me up like a dragon, he hath filled his belly with my delicates, he hath cast me out.

35 The violence done to me and to my flesh *be* upon Babylon, shall the inhabitant of Zion say; and my blood upon the inhabitants of Chaldea, shall Jerusalem say.

36 Therefore thus saith the LORD; Behold, I will plead thy cause, and take vengeance for thee; and I will dry up her sea, and make her springs dry.

37 And Babylon shall become heaps, a dwellingplace for dragons, and astonishment, and an hissing, without an inhabitant.

38 They shall roar together like lions: they shall yell as lions' whelps.

39 In their heat I will make their feasts, and I will make them drunken, that they may rejoice, and sleep a perpetual sleep, and not wake, saith the LORD.

40 I will bring them down like lambs to the slaughter, like rams with he goats.

41 How is Sheshach taken! and how is the praise of the whole earth surprised! how is Babylon become an astonishment among the nations!

42 The sea is come up upon Babylon: she is covered with the multitude of the waves thereof.

43 Her cities are a desolation, a dry land, and a wilderness, a land wherein no man dwelleth, neither doth *any* son of man pass thereby.

44 And I will punish Bel in Babylon, and I will bring forth out of his mouth that which he hath swallowed up: and the nations shall not flow together any more unto him: yea, the wall of Babylon shall fall.

NEW LIVING TRANSLATION

32 All the escape routes are blocked.
The marshes have been set aflame,
and the army is in a panic.

33 This is what the LORD of Heaven's Armies,
the God of Israel, says:
"Babylon is like wheat on a threshing floor,
about to be trampled.
In just a little while
her harvest will begin."

34 "King Nebuchadnezzar* of Babylon has
eaten and crushed us
and drained us of strength.
He has swallowed us like a great monster
and filled his belly with our riches.
He has thrown us out of our own country.
35 Make Babylon suffer as she made us suffer,"
say the people of Zion.
"Make the people of Babylonia pay for spilling
our blood,"
says Jerusalem.

The LORD's Vengeance on Babylon

36 This is what the LORD says to Jerusalem:

"I will be your lawyer to plead your case,
and I will avenge you.
I will dry up her river,
as well as her springs,
37 and Babylon will become a heap of ruins,
haunted by jackals.
She will be an object of horror and contempt,
a place where no one lives.
38 Her people will roar together like strong lions.
They will growl like lion cubs.
39 And while they lie inflamed with all their wine,
I will prepare a different kind of feast for them.
I will make them drink until they fall asleep,
and they will never wake up again,"
says the LORD.
40 "I will bring them down
like lambs to the slaughter,
like rams and goats to be sacrificed.

41 "How Babylon* is fallen—
great Babylon, praised throughout the earth!
Now she has become an object of horror
among the nations.
42 The sea has risen over Babylon;
she is covered by its crashing waves.
43 Her cities now lie in ruins;
she is a dry wasteland
where no one lives or even passes by.
44 And I will punish Bel, the god of Babylon,
and make him vomit up all he has eaten.
The nations will no longer come and worship him.
The wall of Babylon has fallen!

51:34 Hebrew *Nebuchadrezzar*, a variant spelling of Nebuchadnezzar.
51:41 Hebrew *Sheshach*, a code name for Babylon.

KING JAMES VERSION

45 My people, go ye out of the midst of her, and deliver ye every man his soul from the fierce anger of the LORD.

46 And lest your heart faint, and ye fear for the rumour that shall be heard in the land; a rumour shall both come *one* year, and after that in *another* year *shall come* a rumour, and violence in the land, ruler against ruler.

47 Therefore, behold, the days come, that I will do judgment upon the graven images of Babylon: and her whole land shall be confounded, and all her slain shall fall in the midst of her.

48 Then the heaven and the earth, and all that *is* therein, shall sing for Babylon: for the spoilers shall come unto her from the north, saith the LORD.

49 As Babylon *hath caused* the slain of Israel to fall, so at Babylon shall fall the slain of all the earth.

50 Ye that have escaped the sword, go away, stand not still: remember the LORD afar off, and let Jerusalem come into your mind.

51 We are confounded, because we have heard reproach: shame hath covered our faces: for strangers are come into the sanctuaries of the LORD's house.

52 Wherefore, behold, the days come, saith the LORD, that I will do judgment upon her graven images: and through all her land the wounded shall groan.

53 Though Babylon should mount up to heaven, and though she should fortify the height of her strength, *yet* from me shall spoilers come unto her, saith the LORD.

54 A sound of a cry *cometh* from Babylon, and great destruction from the land of the Chaldeans:

55 Because the LORD hath spoiled Babylon, and destroyed out of her the great voice; when her waves do roar like great waters, a noise of their voice is uttered:

56 Because the spoiler is come upon her, *even* upon Babylon, and her mighty men are taken, every one of their bows is broken: for the LORD God of recompences shall surely requite.

57 And I will make drunk her princes, and her wise *men,* her captains, and her rulers, and her mighty men: and they shall sleep a perpetual sleep, and not

NEW LIVING TRANSLATION

A Message for the Exiles

45 "Come out, my people, flee from Babylon.
Save yourselves! Run from the LORD's
fierce anger.
46 But do not panic; don't be afraid
when you hear the first rumor of
approaching forces.
For rumors will keep coming year by year.
Violence will erupt in the land
as the leaders fight against each other.
47 For the time is surely coming
when I will punish this great city and all
her idols.
Her whole land will be disgraced,
and her dead will lie in the streets.
48 Then the heavens and earth will rejoice,
for out of the north will come
destroying armies
against Babylon," says the LORD.
49 "Just as Babylon killed the people of Israel
and others throughout the world,
so must her people be killed.
50 Get out, all you who have escaped the sword!
Do not stand and watch—flee while you can!
Remember the LORD, though you are in
a far-off land,
and think about your home in Jerusalem."
51 "We are ashamed," the people say.
"We are insulted and disgraced
because the LORD's Temple
has been defiled by foreigners."
52 "Yes," says the LORD, "but the time is coming
when I will destroy Babylon's idols.
The groans of her wounded people
will be heard throughout the land.
53 Though Babylon reaches as high as the heavens
and makes her fortifications incredibly strong,
I will still send enemies to plunder her.
I, the LORD, have spoken!

Babylon's Complete Destruction

54 "Listen! Hear the cry of Babylon,
the sound of great destruction from the land
of the Babylonians.
55 For the LORD is destroying Babylon.
He will silence her loud voice.
Waves of enemies pound against her;
the noise of battle rings through the city.
56 Destroying armies come against Babylon.
Her mighty men are captured,
and their weapons break in their hands.
For the LORD is a God who gives just punishment;
he always repays in full.
57 I will make her officials and wise men drunk,
along with her captains, officers, and warriors.
They will fall asleep
and never wake up again!"

KING JAMES VERSION

wake, saith the King, whose name *is* the LORD of hosts.

58 Thus saith the LORD of hosts; The broad walls of Babylon shall be utterly broken, and her high gates shall be burned with fire; and the people shall labour in vain, and the folk in the fire, and they shall be weary.

59 The word which Jeremiah the prophet commanded Seraiah the son of Neriah, the son of Maaseiah, when he went with Zedekiah the king of Judah into Babylon in the fourth year of his reign. And *this* Seraiah *was* a quiet prince.

60 So Jeremiah wrote in a book all the evil that should come upon Babylon, *even* all these words that are written against Babylon.

61 And Jeremiah said to Seraiah, When thou comest to Babylon, and shalt see, and shalt read all these words;

62 Then shalt thou say, O LORD, thou hast spoken against this place, to cut it off, that none shall remain in it, neither man nor beast, but that it shall be desolate for ever.

63 And it shall be, when thou hast made an end of reading this book, *that* thou shalt bind a stone to it, and cast it into the midst of Euphrates:

64 And thou shalt say, Thus shall Babylon sink, and shall not rise from the evil that I will bring upon her: and they shall be weary. Thus far *are* the words of Jeremiah.

52 1 Zedekiah *was* one and twenty years old when he began to reign, and he reigned eleven years in Jerusalem. And his mother's name *was* Hamutal the daughter of Jeremiah of Libnah.

2 And he did *that which was* evil in the eyes of the LORD, according to all that Jehoiakim had done.

3 For through the anger of the LORD it came to pass in Jerusalem and Judah, till he had cast them out from his presence, that Zedekiah rebelled against the king of Babylon.

4 And it came to pass in the ninth year of his reign, in the tenth month, in the tenth *day* of the month, *that* Nebuchadrezzar king of Babylon came, he and all his army, against Jerusalem, and pitched against it, and built forts against it round about.

5 So the city was besieged unto the eleventh year of king Zedekiah.

6 And in the fourth month, in the ninth *day* of the

NEW LIVING TRANSLATION

says the King, whose name is
the LORD of Heaven's Armies.

58 This is what the LORD of Heaven's Armies says:
"The thick walls of Babylon will be leveled
to the ground,
and her massive gates will be burned.
The builders from many lands have
worked in vain,
for their work will be destroyed by fire!"

Jeremiah's Message Sent to Babylon

59 The prophet Jeremiah gave this message to Seraiah son of Neriah and grandson of Mahseiah, a staff officer, when Seraiah went to Babylon with King Zedekiah of Judah. This was during the fourth year of Zedekiah's reign.* 60 Jeremiah had recorded on a scroll all the terrible disasters that would soon come upon Babylon—all the words written here. 61 He said to Seraiah, "When you get to Babylon, read aloud everything on this scroll. 62 Then say, 'LORD, you have said that you will destroy Babylon so that neither people nor animals will remain here. She will lie empty and abandoned forever.' 63 When you have finished reading the scroll, tie it to a stone and throw it into the Euphrates River. 64 Then say, 'In this same way Babylon and her people will sink, never again to rise, because of the disasters I will bring upon her.'"

This is the end of Jeremiah's messages.

The Fall of Jerusalem

52 Zedekiah was twenty-one years old when he became king, and he reigned in Jerusalem eleven years. His mother was Hamutal, the daughter of Jeremiah from Libnah. 2 But Zedekiah did what was evil in the LORD's sight, just as Jehoiakim had done. 3 These things happened because of the LORD's anger against the people of Jerusalem and Judah, until he finally banished them from his presence and sent them into exile.

Zedekiah rebelled against the king of Babylon. 4 So on January 15,* during the ninth year of Zedekiah's reign, King Nebuchadnezzar* of Babylon led his entire army against Jerusalem. They surrounded the city and built siege ramps against its walls. 5 Jerusalem was kept under siege until the eleventh year of King Zedekiah's reign.

6 By July 18 in the eleventh year of Zedekiah's reign,* the famine in the city had become very

51:59 The fourth year of Zedekiah's reign was 593 B.C. **52:4a** Hebrew *on the tenth day of the tenth month,* of the ancient Hebrew lunar calendar. A number of events in Jeremiah can be cross-checked with dates in surviving Babylonian records and related accurately to our modern calendar. This day was January 15, 588 B.C. **52:4b** Hebrew *Nebuchadrezzar,* a variant spelling of Nebuchadnezzar; also in 52:12, 28, 29, 30. **52:6** Hebrew *By the ninth day of the fourth month* [in the eleventh year of Zedekiah's reign]. This day was July 18, 586 B.C.; also see note on 52:4a.

KING JAMES VERSION

month, the famine was sore in the city, so that there was no bread for the people of the land.

7 Then the city was broken up, and all the men of war fled, and went forth out of the city by night by the way of the gate between the two walls, which *was* by the king's garden; (now the Chaldeans *were* by the city round about:) and they went by the way of the plain.

8 But the army of the Chaldeans pursued after the king, and overtook Zedekiah in the plains of Jericho; and all his army was scattered from him.

9 Then they took the king, and carried him up unto the king of Babylon to Riblah in the land of Hamath; where he gave judgment upon him.

10 And the king of Babylon slew the sons of Zedekiah before his eyes: he slew also all the princes of Judah in Riblah.

11 Then he put out the eyes of Zedekiah; and the king of Babylon bound him in chains, and carried him to Babylon, and put him in prison till the day of his death.

12 Now in the fifth month, in the tenth *day* of the month, which *was* the nineteenth year of Nebuchadrezzar king of Babylon, came Nebuzar-adan, captain of the guard, *which* served the king of Babylon, into Jerusalem,

13 And burned the house of the LORD, and the king's house; and all the houses of Jerusalem, and all the houses of the great *men,* burned he with fire:

14 And all the army of the Chaldeans, that *were* with the captain of the guard, brake down all the walls of Jerusalem round about.

15 Then Nebuzar-adan the captain of the guard carried away captive *certain* of the poor of the people, and the residue of the people that remained in the city, and those that fell away, that fell to the king of Babylon, and the rest of the multitude.

16 But Nebuzar-adan the captain of the guard left *certain* of the poor of the land for vinedressers and for husbandmen.

17 Also the pillars of brass that *were* in the house of the LORD, and the bases, and the brasen sea that *was* in the house of the LORD, the Chaldeans brake, and carried all the brass of them to Babylon.

18 The caldrons also, and the shovels, and the snuffers, and the bowls, and the spoons, and all the vessels of brass wherewith they ministered, took they away.

19 And the basins, and the firepans, and the bowls, and the caldrons, and the candlesticks, and the spoons, and the cups; *that* which *was* of gold *in* gold, and *that* which *was* of silver *in* silver, took the captain of the guard away.

20 The two pillars, one sea, and twelve brasen bulls that *were* under the bases, which king Solomon had made in the house of the LORD: the brass of all these vessels was without weight.

21 And *concerning* the pillars, the height of one

NEW LIVING TRANSLATION

severe, and the last of the food was entirely gone.
7 Then a section of the city wall was broken down,
and all the soldiers fled. Since the city was surrounded by the Babylonians,* they waited for nightfall. Then they slipped through the gate between the
two walls behind the king's garden and headed toward the Jordan Valley.*

8 But the Babylonian troops chased King Zedekiah
and caught him on the plains of Jericho, for his men
had all deserted him and scattered. 9 They took him
to the king of Babylon at Riblah in the land of
Hamath. There the king of Babylon pronounced
judgment upon Zedekiah. 10 He made Zedekiah
watch as they slaughtered his sons and all the other
officials of Judah. 11 Then they gouged out Zedekiah's eyes, bound him in bronze chains, and led him
away to Babylon. Zedekiah remained there in prison
until the day of his death.

The Temple Destroyed

12 On August 17 of that year,* which was the nineteenth year of King Nebuchadnezzar's reign, Nebuzaradan, the captain of the guard and an official of
the Babylonian king, arrived in Jerusalem. 13 He
burned down the Temple of the LORD, the royal palace, and all the houses of Jerusalem. He destroyed all
the important buildings* in the city. 14 Then he supervised the entire Babylonian* army as they tore
down the walls of Jerusalem on every side. 15 Nebuzaradan, the captain of the guard, then took as exiles
some of the poorest of the people, the rest of the people who remained in the city, the defectors who had
declared their allegiance to the king of Babylon, and
the rest of the craftsmen. 16 But Nebuzaradan allowed some of the poorest people to stay behind in
Judah to care for the vineyards and fields.

17 The Babylonians broke up the bronze pillars in
front of the LORD's Temple, the bronze water carts,
and the great bronze basin called the Sea, and they
carried all the bronze away to Babylon. 18 They also
took all the ash buckets, shovels, lamp snuffers, basins, dishes, and all the other bronze articles used for
making sacrifices at the Temple. 19 Nebuzaradan, the
captain of the guard, also took the small bowls, incense burners, basins, pots, lampstands, dishes,
bowls used for liquid offerings, and all the other articles made of pure gold or silver.

20 The weight of the bronze from the two pillars,
the Sea with the twelve bronze oxen beneath it, and
the water carts was too great to be measured. These
things had been made for the LORD's Temple in
the days of King Solomon. 21 Each of the pillars was

52:7a Or *the Chaldeans;* similarly in 52:8, 17. **52:7b** Hebrew *the Arabah.* **52:12** Hebrew *On the tenth day of the fifth month,* of the ancient Hebrew lunar calendar. This day was August 17, 586 B.C.; also see note on 52:4a. **52:13** Or *destroyed the houses of all the important people.* **52:14** Or *Chaldean.*

KING JAMES VERSION

pillar *was* eighteen cubits; and a fillet of twelve cubits did compass it; and the thickness thereof *was* four fingers: *it was* hollow.

22 And a chapiter of brass *was* upon it; and the height of one chapiter *was* five cubits, with network and pomegranates upon the chapiters round about, all *of* brass. The second pillar also and the pomegranates *were* like unto these.

23 And there were ninety and six pomegranates on a side; *and* all the pomegranates upon the network *were* an hundred round about.

24 And the captain of the guard took Seraiah the chief priest, and Zephaniah the second priest, and the three keepers of the door:

25 He took also out of the city an eunuch, which had the charge of the men of war; and seven men of them that were near the king's person, which were found in the city; and the principal scribe of the host, who mustered the people of the land; and threescore men of the people of the land, that were found in the midst of the city.

26 So Nebuzar-adan the captain of the guard took them, and brought them to the king of Babylon to Riblah.

27 And the king of Babylon smote them, and put them to death in Riblah in the land of Hamath. Thus Judah was carried away captive out of his own land.

28 This *is* the people whom Nebuchadrezzar carried away captive: in the seventh year three thousand Jews and three and twenty:

29 In the eighteenth year of Nebuchadrezzar he carried away captive from Jerusalem eight hundred thirty and two persons:

30 In the three and twentieth year of Nebuchadrezzar Nebuzar-adan the captain of the guard carried away captive of the Jews seven hundred forty and five persons: all the persons *were* four thousand and six hundred.

31 And it came to pass in the seven and thirtieth year of the captivity of Jehoiachin king of Judah, in the twelfth month, in the five and twentieth *day* of the month, *that* Evil-merodach king of Babylon in the *first* year of his reign lifted up the head of Jehoiachin king of Judah, and brought him forth out of prison,

32 And spake kindly unto him, and set his throne above the throne of the kings that *were* with him in Babylon,

33 And changed his prison garments: and he did continually eat bread before him all the days of his life.

34 And *for* his diet, there was a continual diet given him of the king of Babylon, every day a portion until the day of his death, all the days of his life.

NEW LIVING TRANSLATION

27 feet tall and 18 feet in circumference.* They were
hollow, with walls 3 inches thick.* 22 The bronze capital on top of each pillar was 7½ feet* high and was
decorated with a network of bronze pomegranates all
the way around. 23 There were 96 pomegranates on
the sides, and a total of 100 on the network around
the top.

24 Nebuzaradan, the captain of the guard, took
with him as prisoners Seraiah the high priest, Zephaniah the priest of the second rank, and the three
chief gatekeepers. 25 And from among the people
still hiding in the city, he took an officer who had
been in charge of the Judean army; seven of the
king's personal advisers; the army commander's
chief secretary, who was in charge of recruitment;
and sixty other citizens. 26 Nebuzaradan, the captain
of the guard, took them all to the king of Babylon at
Riblah. 27 And there at Riblah, in the land of Hamath,
the king of Babylon had them all put to death. So the
people of Judah were sent into exile from their land.

28 The number of captives taken to Babylon in the
seventh year of Nebuchadnezzar's reign* was 3,023.
29 Then in Nebuchadnezzar's eighteenth year* he
took 832 more. 30 In Nebuchadnezzar's twenty-third
year* he sent Nebuzaradan, the captain of the guard,
who took 745 more—a total of 4,600 captives in all.

Hope for Israel's Royal Line

31 In the thirty-seventh year of the exile of King Jehoiachin of Judah, Evil-merodach ascended to the Babylonian throne. He was kind to* Jehoiachin and
released him from prison on March 31 of that year.*
32 He spoke kindly to Jehoiachin and gave him a
higher place than all the other exiled kings in Babylon. 33 He supplied Jehoiachin with new clothes to
replace his prison garb and allowed him to dine in
the king's presence for the rest of his life. 34 So the
Babylonian king gave him a regular food allowance
as long as he lived. This continued until the day of his
death.

52:21a Hebrew *18 cubits* [8.1 meters] *tall and 12 cubits* [5.4 meters] *in circumference.* **52:21b** Hebrew *4 fingers thick* [8 centimeters]. **52:22** Hebrew *5 cubits* [2.3 meters]. **52:28** This exile in the seventh year of Nebuchadnezzar's reign occurred in 597 B.C. **52:29** This exile in the eighteenth year of Nebuchadnezzar's reign occurred in 586 B.C. **52:30** This exile in the twenty-third year of Nebuchadnezzar's reign occurred in 581 B.C. **52:31a** Hebrew *He raised the head of.* **52:31b** Hebrew *on the twenty-fifth day of the twelfth month,* of the ancient Hebrew lunar calendar. This day was March 31, 561 B.C.; also see note on 52:4a.

Lamentations

KING JAMES VERSION

1 1How doth the city sit solitary, *that was* full of people! *how* is she become as a widow! she *that was* great among the nations, *and* princess among the provinces, *how* is she become tributary!

2She weepeth sore in the night, and her tears *are* on her cheeks: among all her lovers she hath none to comfort *her:* all her friends have dealt treacherously with her, they are become her enemies.

3Judah is gone into captivity because of affliction, and because of great servitude: she dwelleth among the heathen, she findeth no rest: all her persecutors overtook her between the straits.

4The ways of Zion do mourn, because none come to the solemn feasts: all her gates are desolate: her priests sigh, her virgins are afflicted, and she *is* in bitterness.

5Her adversaries are the chief, her enemies prosper; for the LORD hath afflicted her for the multitude of her transgressions: her children are gone into captivity before the enemy.

6And from the daughter of Zion all her beauty is departed: her princes are become like harts *that* find no pasture, and they are gone without strength before the pursuer.

NEW LIVING TRANSLATION

Sorrow in Jerusalem

1* 1Jerusalem, once so full of people,
is now deserted.
She who was once great among the nations
now sits alone like a widow.
Once the queen of all the earth,
she is now a slave.

2 She sobs through the night;
tears stream down her cheeks.
Among all her lovers,
there is no one left to comfort her.
All her friends have betrayed her
and become her enemies.

3 Judah has been led away into captivity,
oppressed with cruel slavery.
She lives among foreign nations
and has no place of rest.
Her enemies have chased her down,
and she has nowhere to turn.

4 The roads to Jerusalem* are in mourning,
for crowds no longer come to celebrate
the festivals.
The city gates are silent,
her priests groan,
her young women are crying—
how bitter is her fate!

5 Her oppressors have become her masters,
and her enemies prosper,
for the LORD has punished Jerusalem
for her many sins.
Her children have been captured
and taken away to distant lands.

6 All the majesty of beautiful Jerusalem*
has been stripped away.
Her princes are like starving deer
searching for pasture.
They are too weak to run
from the pursuing enemy.

1 Each of the first four chapters of this book is an acrostic, laid out in the order of the Hebrew alphabet. The first word of each verse begins with a successive Hebrew letter. Chapters 1, 2, and 4 have one verse for each of the 22 Hebrew letters. Chapter 3 contains 22 stanzas of three verses each. Though chapter 5 has 22 verses, it is not an acrostic. **1:4** Hebrew *Zion;* also in 1:17. **1:6** Hebrew *of the daughter of Zion.*

KING JAMES VERSION

7 Jerusalem remembered in the days of her affliction and of her miseries all her pleasant things that she had in the days of old, when her people fell into the hand of the enemy, and none did help her: the adversaries saw her, *and* did mock at her sabbaths.

8 Jerusalem hath grievously sinned; therefore she is removed: all that honoured her despise her, because they have seen her nakedness: yea, she sigheth, and turneth backward.

9 Her filthiness *is* in her skirts; she remembereth not her last end; therefore she came down wonderfully: she had no comforter. O LORD, behold my affliction: for the enemy hath magnified *himself.*

10 The adversary hath spread out his hand upon all her pleasant things: for she hath seen *that* the heathen entered into her sanctuary, whom thou didst command *that* they should not enter into thy congregation.

11 All her people sigh, they seek bread; they have given their pleasant things for meat to relieve the soul: see, O LORD, and consider; for I am become vile.

12 *Is it* nothing to you, all ye that pass by? behold, and see if there be any sorrow like unto my sorrow, which is done unto me, wherewith the LORD hath afflicted *me* in the day of his fierce anger.

13 From above hath he sent fire into my bones, and it prevaileth against them: he hath spread a net for my feet, he hath turned me back: he hath made me desolate *and* faint all the day.

14 The yoke of my transgressions is bound by his hand: they are wreathed, *and* come up upon my neck: he hath made my strength to fall, the Lord hath delivered me into *their* hands, *from whom* I am not able to rise up.

15 The Lord hath trodden under foot all my mighty *men* in the midst of me: he hath called an assembly against me to crush my young men: the Lord hath trodden the virgin, the daughter of Judah, *as* in a winepress.

NEW LIVING TRANSLATION

7 In the midst of her sadness and wandering,
Jerusalem remembers her ancient splendor.
But now she has fallen to her enemy,
and there is no one to help her.
Her enemy struck her down
and laughed as she fell.

8 Jerusalem has sinned greatly,
so she has been tossed away like a filthy rag.
All who once honored her now despise her,
for they have seen her stripped naked
and humiliated.
All she can do is groan
and hide her face.

9 She defiled herself with immorality
and gave no thought to her future.
Now she lies in the gutter
with no one to lift her out.
"LORD, see my misery," she cries.
"The enemy has triumphed."

10 The enemy has plundered her completely,
taking every precious thing she owns.
She has seen foreigners violate her
sacred Temple,
the place the LORD had forbidden
them to enter.

11 Her people groan as they search for bread.
They have sold their treasures for food
to stay alive.
"O LORD, look," she mourns,
"and see how I am despised.

12 "Does it mean nothing to you, all you who pass by?
Look around and see if there is any suffering
like mine,
which the LORD brought on me
when he erupted in fierce anger.

13 "He has sent fire from heaven that burns
in my bones.
He has placed a trap in my path and
turned me back.
He has left me devastated,
racked with sickness all day long.

14 "He wove my sins into ropes
to hitch me to a yoke of captivity.
The Lord sapped my strength and turned me over
to my enemies;
I am helpless in their hands.

15 "The Lord has treated my mighty men
with contempt.
At his command a great army has come
to crush my young warriors.
The Lord has trampled his beloved city*
like grapes are trampled in a winepress.

1:15 Hebrew *the virgin daughter of Judah.*

KING JAMES VERSION

16 For these *things* I weep; mine eye, mine eye runneth down with water, because the comforter that should relieve my soul is far from me: my children are desolate, because the enemy prevailed.

17 Zion spreadeth forth her hands, *and there is* none to comfort her: the LORD hath commanded concerning Jacob, *that* his adversaries *should be* round about him: Jerusalem is as a menstruous woman among them.

18 The LORD is righteous; for I have rebelled against his commandment: hear, I pray you, all people, and behold my sorrow: my virgins and my young men are gone into captivity.

19 I called for my lovers, *but* they deceived me: my priests and mine elders gave up the ghost in the city, while they sought their meat to relieve their souls.

20 Behold, O LORD; for I *am* in distress: my bowels are troubled; mine heart is turned within me; for I have grievously rebelled: abroad the sword bereaveth, at home *there is* as death.

21 They have heard that I sigh: *there is* none to comfort me: all mine enemies have heard of my trouble; they are glad that thou hast done *it:* thou wilt bring the day *that* thou hast called, and they shall be like unto me.

22 Let all their wickedness come before thee; and do unto them, as thou hast done unto me for all my transgressions: for my sighs *are* many, and my heart *is* faint.

2 1 How hath the Lord covered the daughter of Zion with a cloud in his anger, *and* cast down from heaven unto the earth the beauty of Israel, and remembered not his footstool in the day of his anger!

NEW LIVING TRANSLATION

16 "For all these things I weep;
tears flow down my cheeks.
No one is here to comfort me;
any who might encourage me are far away.
My children have no future,
for the enemy has conquered us."

17 Jerusalem reaches out for help,
but no one comforts her.
Regarding his people Israel,*
the LORD has said,
"Let their neighbors be their enemies!
Let them be thrown away like a filthy rag!"

18 "The LORD is right," Jerusalem says,
"for I rebelled against him.
Listen, people everywhere;
look upon my anguish and despair,
for my sons and daughters
have been taken captive to distant lands.

19 "I begged my allies for help,
but they betrayed me.
My priests and leaders
starved to death in the city,
even as they searched for food
to save their lives.

20 "LORD, see my anguish!
My heart is broken
and my soul despairs,
for I have rebelled against you.
In the streets the sword kills,
and at home there is only death.

21 "Others heard my groans,
but no one turned to comfort me.
When my enemies heard about my troubles,
they were happy to see what you had done.
Oh, bring the day you promised,
when they will suffer as I have suffered.

22 "Look at all their evil deeds, LORD.
Punish them,
as you have punished me
for all my sins.
My groans are many,
and I am sick at heart."

God's Anger at Sin

2 1 The Lord in his anger
has cast a dark shadow over
beautiful Jerusalem.*
The fairest of Israel's cities lies in the dust,
thrown down from the heights of heaven.
In his day of great anger,
the Lord has shown no mercy even
to his Temple.*

1:17 Hebrew *Jacob.* The names "Jacob" and "Israel" are often interchanged throughout the Old Testament, referring sometimes to the individual patriarch and sometimes to the nation. **2:1a** Hebrew *the daughter of Zion;* also in 2:8, 10, 18. **2:1b** Hebrew *his footstool.*

KING JAMES VERSION

2 The Lord hath swallowed up all the habitations
of Jacob, and hath not pitied: he hath thrown down in
his wrath the strong holds of the daughter of Judah;
he hath brought *them* down to the ground: he hath
polluted the kingdom and the princes thereof.
3 He hath cut off in *his* fierce anger all the horn of
Israel: he hath drawn back his right hand from before the enemy, and he burned against Jacob like a
flaming fire, *which* devoureth round about.
4 He hath bent his bow like an enemy: he stood
with his right hand as an adversary, and slew all *that*
were pleasant to the eye in the tabernacle of the
daughter of Zion: he poured out his fury like fire.
5 The Lord was as an enemy: he hath swallowed up
Israel, he hath swallowed up all her palaces: he hath
destroyed his strong holds, and hath increased in the
daughter of Judah mourning and lamentation.
6 And he hath violently taken away his tabernacle,
as *if it were of* a garden: he hath destroyed his places
of the assembly: the LORD hath caused the solemn
feasts and sabbaths to be forgotten in Zion, and hath
despised in the indignation of his anger the king and
the priest.
7 The Lord hath cast off his altar, he hath abhorred
his sanctuary, he hath given up into the hand of the
enemy the walls of her palaces; they have made a
noise in the house of the LORD, as in the day of a solemn feast.
8 The LORD hath purposed to destroy the wall of
the daughter of Zion: he hath stretched out a line, he
hath not withdrawn his hand from destroying: therefore he made the rampart and the wall to lament;
they languished together.
9 Her gates are sunk into the ground; he hath destroyed and broken her bars: her king and her
princes *are* among the Gentiles: the law *is* no *more;*
her prophets also find no vision from the LORD.
10 The elders of the daughter of Zion sit upon the
ground, *and* keep silence: they have cast up dust

NEW LIVING TRANSLATION

2 Without mercy the Lord has destroyed
every home in Israel.*
In his anger he has broken down
the fortress walls of beautiful Jerusalem.*
He has brought them to the ground,
dishonoring the kingdom and its rulers.

3 All the strength of Israel
vanishes beneath his fierce anger.
The Lord has withdrawn his protection
as the enemy attacks.
He consumes the whole land of Israel
like a raging fire.

4 He bends his bow against his people,
as though he were their enemy.
His strength is used against them
to kill their finest youth.
His fury is poured out like fire
on beautiful Jerusalem.*

5 Yes, the Lord has vanquished Israel
like an enemy.
He has destroyed her palaces
and demolished her fortresses.
He has brought unending sorrow and tears
upon beautiful Jerusalem.

6 He has broken down his Temple
as though it were merely a garden shelter.
The LORD has blotted out all memory
of the holy festivals and Sabbath days.
Kings and priests fall together
before his fierce anger.

7 The Lord has rejected his own altar;
he despises his own sanctuary.
He has given Jerusalem's palaces
to her enemies.
They shout in the LORD's Temple
as though it were a day of celebration.

8 The LORD was determined
to destroy the walls of beautiful Jerusalem.
He made careful plans for their destruction,
then did what he had planned.
Therefore, the ramparts and walls
have fallen down before him.

9 Jerusalem's gates have sunk into the ground.
He has smashed their locks and bars.
Her kings and princes have been exiled
to distant lands;
her law has ceased to exist.
Her prophets receive
no more visions from the LORD.

10 The leaders of beautiful Jerusalem
sit on the ground in silence.

2:2a Hebrew *Jacob;* also in 2:3b. See note on 1:17. **2:2b** Hebrew *the daughter of Judah;* also in 2:5. **2:4** Hebrew *on the tent of the daughter of Zion.*

KING JAMES VERSION

upon their heads; they have girded themselves with
sackcloth: the virgins of Jerusalem hang down their
heads to the ground.
11 Mine eyes do fail with tears, my bowels are
troubled, my liver is poured upon the earth, for the
destruction of the daughter of my people; because
the children and the sucklings swoon in the streets
of the city.
12 They say to their mothers, Where *is* corn and
wine? when they swooned as the wounded in the
streets of the city, when their soul was poured out
into their mothers' bosom.
13 What thing shall I take to witness for thee? what
thing shall I liken to thee, O daughter of Jerusalem?
what shall I equal to thee, that I may comfort thee,
O virgin daughter of Zion? for thy breach *is* great like
the sea: who can heal thee?
14 Thy prophets have seen vain and foolish things
for thee: and they have not discovered thine iniquity,
to turn away thy captivity; but have seen for thee
false burdens and causes of banishment.
15 All that pass by clap *their* hands at thee; they hiss
and wag their head at the daughter of Jerusalem,
saying, Is this the city that *men* call The perfection of
beauty, The joy of the whole earth?
16 All thine enemies have opened their mouth
against thee: they hiss and gnash the teeth: they say,
We have swallowed *her* up: certainly this *is* the day
that we looked for; we have found, we have seen *it*.
17 The LORD hath done *that* which he had devised;
he hath fulfilled his word that he had commanded in
the days of old: he hath thrown down, and hath not
pitied: and he hath caused *thine* enemy to rejoice
over thee, he hath set up the horn of thine adversaries.
18 Their heart cried unto the Lord, O wall of the
daughter of Zion, let tears run down like a river day
and night: give thyself no rest; let not the apple of
thine eye cease.

NEW LIVING TRANSLATION

They are clothed in burlap
and throw dust on their heads.
The young women of Jerusalem
hang their heads in shame.

11 I have cried until the tears no longer come;
my heart is broken.
My spirit is poured out in agony
as I see the desperate plight of my people.
Little children and tiny babies
are fainting and dying in the streets.

12 They cry out to their mothers,
"We need food and drink!"
Their lives ebb away in the streets
like the life of a warrior wounded in battle.
They gasp for life
as they collapse in their mothers' arms.

13 What can I say about you?
Who has ever seen such sorrow?
O daughter of Jerusalem,
to what can I compare your anguish?
O virgin daughter of Zion,
how can I comfort you?
For your wound is as deep as the sea.
Who can heal you?

14 Your prophets have said
so many foolish things, false to the core.
They did not save you from exile
by pointing out your sins.
Instead, they painted false pictures,
filling you with false hope.

15 All who pass by jeer at you.
They scoff and insult beautiful Jerusalem,*
saying,
"Is this the city called 'Most Beautiful in
All the World'
and 'Joy of All the Earth'?"

16 All your enemies mock you.
They scoff and snarl and say,
"We have destroyed her at last!
We have long waited for this day,
and it is finally here!"

17 But it is the LORD who did just as he planned.
He has fulfilled the promises of disaster
he made long ago.
He has destroyed Jerusalem without mercy.
He has caused her enemies to gloat over her
and has given them power over her.

18 Cry aloud* before the Lord,
O walls of beautiful Jerusalem!
Let your tears flow like a river
day and night.
Give yourselves no rest;
give your eyes no relief.

2:15 Hebrew *the daughter of Jerusalem.* **2:18** Hebrew *Their heart cried.*

KING JAMES VERSION

19 Arise, cry out in the night: in the beginning of the watches pour out thine heart like water before the face of the Lord: lift up thy hands toward him for the life of thy young children, that faint for hunger in the top of every street.

20 Behold, O LORD, and consider to whom thou hast done this. Shall the women eat their fruit, *and* children of a span long? shall the priest and the prophet be slain in the sanctuary of the Lord?

21 The young and the old lie on the ground in the streets: my virgins and my young men are fallen by the sword; thou hast slain *them* in the day of thine anger; thou hast killed, *and* not pitied.

22 Thou hast called as in a solemn day my terrors round about, so that in the day of the LORD's anger none escaped nor remained: those that I have swaddled and brought up hath mine enemy consumed.

3 1 I *am* the man *that* hath seen affliction by the rod of his wrath.

2 He hath led me, and brought *me into* darkness, but not *into* light.

3 Surely against me is he turned; he turneth his hand *against me* all the day.

4 My flesh and my skin hath he made old: he hath broken my bones.

5 He hath builded against me, and compassed *me* with gall and travail.

6 He hath set me in dark places, as *they that be* dead of old.

7 He hath hedged me about, that I cannot get out: he hath made my chain heavy.

8 Also when I cry and shout, he shutteth out my prayer.

9 He hath inclosed my ways with hewn stone, he hath made my paths crooked.

10 He *was* unto me *as* a bear lying in wait, *and as* a lion in secret places.

11 He hath turned aside my ways, and pulled me in pieces: he hath made me desolate.

12 He hath bent his bow, and set me as a mark for the arrow.

13 He hath caused the arrows of his quiver to enter into my reins.

NEW LIVING TRANSLATION

19 Rise during the night and cry out.
Pour out your hearts like water to the Lord.
Lift up your hands to him in prayer,
pleading for your children,
for in every street
they are faint with hunger.

20 "O LORD, think about this!
Should you treat your own people this way?
Should mothers eat their own children,
those they once bounced on their knees?
Should priests and prophets be killed
within the Lord's Temple?

21 "See them lying in the streets—
young and old,
boys and girls,
killed by the swords of the enemy.
You have killed them in your anger,
slaughtering them without mercy.

22 "You have invited terrors from all around,
as though you were calling them to
a day of feasting.
In the day of the LORD's anger,
no one has escaped or survived.
The enemy has killed all the children
whom I carried and raised."

Hope in the LORD's Faithfulness

3 1 I am the one who has seen the afflictions
that come from the rod of the LORD's anger.
2 He has led me into darkness,
shutting out all light.
3 He has turned his hand against me
again and again, all day long.
4 He has made my skin and flesh grow old.
He has broken my bones.
5 He has besieged and surrounded me
with anguish and distress.
6 He has buried me in a dark place,
like those long dead.

7 He has walled me in, and I cannot escape.
He has bound me in heavy chains.
8 And though I cry and shout,
he has shut out my prayers.
9 He has blocked my way with a high stone wall;
he has made my road crooked.

10 He has hidden like a bear or a lion,
waiting to attack me.
11 He has dragged me off the path and torn
me in pieces,
leaving me helpless and devastated.
12 He has drawn his bow
and made me the target for his arrows.

13 He shot his arrows
deep into my heart.

KING JAMES VERSION

14 I was a derision to all my people; *and* their song
all the day.
15 He hath filled me with bitterness, he hath made
me drunken with wormwood.
16 He hath also broken my teeth with gravel stones,
he hath covered me with ashes.
17 And thou hast removed my soul far off from
peace: I forgat prosperity.
18 And I said, My strength and my hope is perished
from the LORD:
19 Remembering mine affliction and my misery,
the wormwood and the gall.
20 My soul hath *them* still in remembrance, and is
humbled in me.
21 This I recall to my mind, therefore have I hope.
22 *It is of* the LORD's mercies that we are not consumed, because his compassions fail not.
23 *They are* new every morning: great *is* thy faithfulness.
24 The LORD *is* my portion, saith my soul; therefore
will I hope in him.
25 The LORD *is* good unto them that wait for him, to
the soul *that* seeketh him.
26 *It is* good that *a man* should both hope and
quietly wait for the salvation of the LORD.
27 *It is* good for a man that he bear the yoke in his
youth.
28 He sitteth alone and keepeth silence, because he
hath borne *it* upon him.
29 He putteth his mouth in the dust; if so be there
may be hope.
30 He giveth *his* cheek to him that smiteth him: he
is filled full with reproach.
31 For the Lord will not cast off for ever:
32 But though he cause grief, yet will he have compassion according to the multitude of his mercies.
33 For he doth not afflict willingly nor grieve the
children of men.
34 To crush under his feet all the prisoners of the
earth,
35 To turn aside the right of a man before the face
of the most High,
36 To subvert a man in his cause, the Lord approv-
eth not.
37 Who *is* he *that* saith, and it cometh to pass,
when the Lord commandeth *it* not?

NEW LIVING TRANSLATION

14 My own people laugh at me.
All day long they sing their mocking songs.
15 He has filled me with bitterness
and given me a bitter cup of sorrow to drink.

16 He has made me chew on gravel.
He has rolled me in the dust.
17 Peace has been stripped away,
and I have forgotten what prosperity is.
18 I cry out, "My splendor is gone!
Everything I had hoped for from the
LORD is lost!"
19 The thought of my suffering and homelessness
is bitter beyond words.*
20 I will never forget this awful time,
as I grieve over my loss.
21 Yet I still dare to hope
when I remember this:

22 The faithful love of the LORD never ends!*
His mercies never cease.
23 Great is his faithfulness;
his mercies begin afresh each morning.
24 I say to myself, "The LORD is my inheritance;
therefore, I will hope in him!"

25 The LORD is good to those who depend on him,
to those who search for him.
26 So it is good to wait quietly
for salvation from the LORD.
27 And it is good for people to submit at an early age
to the yoke of his discipline:
28 Let them sit alone in silence
beneath the LORD's demands.
29 Let them lie face down in the dust,
for there may be hope at last.
30 Let them turn the other cheek to those
who strike them
and accept the insults of their enemies.
31 For no one is abandoned
by the Lord forever.
32 Though he brings grief, he also shows
compassion
because of the greatness of his unfailing love.
33 For he does not enjoy hurting people
or causing them sorrow.

34 If people crush underfoot
all the prisoners of the land,
35 if they deprive others of their rights
in defiance of the Most High,
36 if they twist justice in the courts—
doesn't the Lord see all these things?

37 Who can command things to happen
without the Lord's permission?

3:19 Or *is wormwood and gall.* **3:22** As in Syriac version; Hebrew reads *of the LORD keeps us from destruction.*

KING JAMES VERSION

38 Out of the mouth of the most High proceedeth
not evil and good?
39 Wherefore doth a living man complain, a man
for the punishment of his sins?
40 Let us search and try our ways, and turn again to
the LORD.
41 Let us lift up our heart with *our* hands unto God
in the heavens.
42 We have transgressed and have rebelled: thou
hast not pardoned.
43 Thou hast covered with anger, and persecuted
us: thou hast slain, thou hast not pitied.
44 Thou hast covered thyself with a cloud, that *our*
prayer should not pass through.
45 Thou hast made us *as* the offscouring and refuse in the midst of the people.
46 All our enemies have opened their mouths
against us.
47 Fear and a snare is come upon us, desolation
and destruction.
48 Mine eye runneth down with rivers of water for
the destruction of the daughter of my people.
49 Mine eye trickleth down, and ceaseth not, without any intermission,
50 Till the LORD look down, and behold from
heaven.
51 Mine eye affecteth mine heart because of all the
daughters of my city.
52 Mine enemies chased me sore, like a bird, without cause.
53 They have cut off my life in the dungeon, and
cast a stone upon me.
54 Waters flowed over mine head; *then* I said, I am
cut off.
55 I called upon thy name, O LORD, out of the low
dungeon.
56 Thou hast heard my voice: hide not thine ear at
my breathing, at my cry.
57 Thou drewest near in the day *that* I called upon
thee: thou saidst, Fear not.
58 O Lord, thou hast pleaded the causes of my soul;
thou hast redeemed my life.
59 O LORD, thou hast seen my wrong: judge thou
my cause.
60 Thou hast seen all their vengeance *and* all their
imaginations against me.
61 Thou hast heard their reproach, O LORD, *and* all
their imaginations against me;
62 The lips of those that rose up against me, and
their device against me all the day.

NEW LIVING TRANSLATION

38 Does not the Most High
send both calamity and good?
39 Then why should we, mere humans, complain
when we are punished for our sins?

40 Instead, let us test and examine our ways.
Let us turn back to the LORD.
41 Let us lift our hearts and hands
to God in heaven and say,
42 "We have sinned and rebelled,
and you have not forgiven us.

43 "You have engulfed us with your anger,
chased us down,
and slaughtered us without mercy.
44 You have hidden yourself in a cloud
so our prayers cannot reach you.
45 You have discarded us as refuse and garbage
among the nations.
46 "All our enemies
have spoken out against us.
47 We are filled with fear,
for we are trapped, devastated, and ruined."
48 Tears stream from my eyes
because of the destruction of my people!
49 My tears flow endlessly;
they will not stop
50 until the LORD looks down
from heaven and sees.
51 My heart is breaking
over the fate of all the women of Jerusalem.
52 My enemies, whom I have never harmed,
hunted me down like a bird.
53 They threw me into a pit
and dropped stones on me.
54 The water rose over my head,
and I cried out, "This is the end!"
55 But I called on your name, LORD,
from deep within the pit.
56 You heard me when I cried, "Listen to my
pleading!
Hear my cry for help!"
57 Yes, you came when I called;
you told me, "Do not fear."

58 Lord, you are my lawyer! Plead my case!
For you have redeemed my life.
59 You have seen the wrong they have done
to me, LORD.
Be my judge, and prove me right.
60 You have seen the vengeful plots
my enemies have laid against me.

61 LORD, you have heard the vile names they call me.
You know all about the plans they have made.
62 My enemies whisper and mutter
as they plot against me all day long.

KING JAMES VERSION

[63]Behold their sitting down, and their rising up; I *am* their musick.

[64]Render unto them a recompence, O LORD, according to the work of their hands.

[65]Give them sorrow of heart, thy curse unto them.

[66]Persecute and destroy them in anger from under the heavens of the LORD.

4 [1]How is the gold become dim! *how* is the most fine gold changed! the stones of the sanctuary are poured out in the top of every street.

[2]The precious sons of Zion, comparable to fine gold, how are they esteemed as earthen pitchers, the work of the hands of the potter!

[3]Even the sea monsters draw out the breast, they give suck to their young ones: the daughter of my people *is become* cruel, like the ostriches in the wilderness.

[4]The tongue of the sucking child cleaveth to the roof of his mouth for thirst: the young children ask bread, *and* no man breaketh *it* unto them.

[5]They that did feed delicately are desolate in the streets: they that were brought up in scarlet embrace dunghills.

[6]For the punishment of the iniquity of the daughter of my people is greater than the punishment of the sin of Sodom, that was overthrown as in a moment, and no hands stayed on her.

[7]Her Nazarites were purer than snow, they were whiter than milk, they were more ruddy in body than rubies, their polishing *was* of sapphire:

[8]Their visage is blacker than a coal; they are not known in the streets: their skin cleaveth to their bones; it is withered, it is become like a stick.

[9]*They that be* slain with the sword are better than *they that be* slain with hunger: for these pine away, stricken through for *want of* the fruits of the field.

[10]The hands of the pitiful women have sodden their own children: they were their meat in the destruction of the daughter of my people.

NEW LIVING TRANSLATION

63 Look at them! Whether they sit or stand,
I am the object of their mocking songs.
64 Pay them back, LORD,
for all the evil they have done.
65 Give them hard and stubborn hearts,
and then let your curse fall on them!
66 Chase them down in your anger,
destroying them beneath the LORD's heavens.

God's Anger Satisfied

4 [1]How the gold has lost its luster!
Even the finest gold has become dull.
The sacred gemstones
lie scattered in the streets!

2 See how the precious children of Jerusalem,*
worth their weight in fine gold,
are now treated like pots of clay
made by a common potter.

3 Even the jackals feed their young,
but not my people Israel.
They ignore their children's cries,
like ostriches in the desert.

4 The parched tongues of their little ones
stick to the roofs of their mouths in thirst.
The children cry for bread,
but no one has any to give them.

5 The people who once ate the richest foods
now beg in the streets for anything
they can get.
Those who once wore the finest clothes
now search the garbage dumps for food.

6 The guilt* of my people
is greater than that of Sodom,
where utter disaster struck in a moment
and no hand offered help.

7 Our princes once glowed with health—
brighter than snow, whiter than milk.
Their faces were as ruddy as rubies,
their appearance like fine jewels.*

8 But now their faces are blacker than soot.
No one recognizes them in the streets.
Their skin sticks to their bones;
it is as dry and hard as wood.

9 Those killed by the sword are better off
than those who die of hunger.
Starving, they waste away
for lack of food from the fields.

10 Tenderhearted women
have cooked their own children.
They have eaten them
to survive the siege.

4:2 Hebrew *precious sons of Zion.* **4:6** Or *punishment.* **4:7** Hebrew *like lapis lazuli.*

KING JAMES VERSION

[11]The LORD hath accomplished his fury; he hath poured out his fierce anger, and hath kindled a fire in Zion, and it hath devoured the foundations thereof.
[12]The kings of the earth, and all the inhabitants of the world, would not have believed that the adversary and the enemy should have entered into the gates of Jerusalem.
[13]For the sins of her prophets, *and* the iniquities of her priests, that have shed the blood of the just in the midst of her,
[14]They have wandered *as* blind *men* in the streets, they have polluted themselves with blood, so that men could not touch their garments.
[15]They cried unto them, Depart ye; *it is* unclean; depart, depart, touch not: when they fled away and wandered, they said among the heathen, They shall no more sojourn *there*.
[16]The anger of the LORD hath divided them; he will no more regard them: they respected not the persons of the priests, they favoured not the elders.
[17]As for us, our eyes as yet failed for our vain help: in our watching we have watched for a nation *that* could not save *us*.
[18]They hunt our steps, that we cannot go in our streets: our end is near, our days are fulfilled; for our end is come.
[19]Our persecutors are swifter than the eagles of the heaven: they pursued us upon the mountains, they laid wait for us in the wilderness.
[20]The breath of our nostrils, the anointed of the LORD, was taken in their pits, of whom we said, Under his shadow we shall live among the heathen.
[21]Rejoice and be glad, O daughter of Edom, that dwellest in the land of Uz; the cup also shall pass through unto thee: thou shalt be drunken, and shalt make thyself naked.
[22]The punishment of thine iniquity is accomplished, O daughter of Zion; he will no more carry

NEW LIVING TRANSLATION

11 But now the anger of the LORD is satisfied.
His fierce anger has been poured out.
He started a fire in Jerusalem*
that burned the city to its foundations.

12 Not a king in all the earth—
no one in all the world—
would have believed that an enemy
could march through the gates of Jerusalem.

13 Yet it happened because of the sins of
her prophets
and the sins of her priests,
who defiled the city
by shedding innocent blood.

14 They wandered blindly
through the streets,
so defiled by blood
that no one dared touch them.

15 "Get away!" the people shouted at them.
"You're defiled! Don't touch us!"
So they fled to distant lands
and wandered among foreign nations,
but none would let them stay.

16 The LORD himself has scattered them,
and he no longer helps them.
People show no respect for the priests
and no longer honor the leaders.

17 We looked in vain for our allies
to come and save us,
but we were looking to nations
that could not help us.

18 We couldn't go into the streets
without danger to our lives.
Our end was near; our days were numbered.
We were doomed!

19 Our enemies were swifter than eagles in flight.
If we fled to the mountains, they found us.
If we hid in the wilderness,
they were waiting for us there.

20 Our king—the LORD's anointed, the very life
of our nation—
was caught in their snares.
We had thought that his shadow
would protect us against any nation on earth!

21 Are you rejoicing in the land of Uz,
O people of Edom?
But you, too, must drink from the cup of the
LORD's anger.
You, too, will be stripped naked in your
drunkenness.

22 O beautiful Jerusalem,* your punishment
will end;

4:11 Hebrew *in Zion.* **4:22** Hebrew *O daughter of Zion.*

KING JAMES VERSION

thee away into captivity: he will visit thine iniquity, O daughter of Edom; he will discover thy sins.

5

1 Remember, O LORD, what is come upon us: consider, and behold our reproach.

2 Our inheritance is turned to strangers, our houses to aliens.

3 We are orphans and fatherless, our mothers *are* as widows.

4 We have drunken our water for money; our wood is sold unto us.

5 Our necks *are* under persecution: we labour, *and* have no rest.

6 We have given the hand *to* the Egyptians, *and to* the Assyrians, to be satisfied with bread.

7 Our fathers have sinned, *and are* not; and we have borne their iniquities.

8 Servants have ruled over us: *there is* none that doth deliver *us* out of their hand.

9 We gat our bread with *the peril of* our lives because of the sword of the wilderness.

10 Our skin was black like an oven because of the terrible famine.

11 They ravished the women in Zion, *and* the maids in the cities of Judah.

12 Princes are hanged up by their hand: the faces of elders were not honoured.

13 They took the young men to grind, and the children fell under the wood.

14 The elders have ceased from the gate, the young men from their musick.

15 The joy of our heart is ceased; our dance is turned into mourning.

16 The crown is fallen *from* our head: woe unto us, that we have sinned!

17 For this our heart is faint; for these *things* our eyes are dim.

18 Because of the mountain of Zion, which is desolate, the foxes walk upon it.

19 Thou, O LORD, remainest for ever; thy throne from generation to generation.

20 Wherefore dost thou forget us for ever, *and* forsake us so long time?

21 Turn thou us unto thee, O LORD, and we shall be turned; renew our days as of old.

22 But thou hast utterly rejected us; thou art very wrath against us.

NEW LIVING TRANSLATION

you will soon return from exile.
But Edom, your punishment is just beginning;
soon your many sins will be exposed.

Prayer for Restoration

5

1 O LORD, remember what has happened to us.
See how we have been disgraced!
2 Our inheritance has been turned over to strangers,
our homes to foreigners.
3 We are orphaned and fatherless.
Our mothers are widowed.
4 We have to pay for water to drink,
and even firewood is expensive.
5 Those who pursue us are at our heels;
we are exhausted but are given no rest.
6 We submitted to Egypt and Assyria
to get enough food to survive.
7 Our ancestors sinned, but they have died—
and we are suffering the punishment they deserved!
8 Slaves have now become our masters;
there is no one left to rescue us.
9 We hunt for food at the risk of our lives,
for violence rules the countryside.
10 The famine has blackened our skin
as though baked in an oven.
11 Our enemies rape the women in Jerusalem*
and the young girls in all the towns of Judah.
12 Our princes are being hanged by their thumbs,
and our elders are treated with contempt.
13 Young men are led away to work at millstones,
and boys stagger under heavy loads of wood.
14 The elders no longer sit in the city gates;
the young men no longer dance and sing.
15 Joy has left our hearts;
our dancing has turned to mourning.
16 The garlands have* fallen from our heads.
Weep for us because we have sinned.
17 Our hearts are sick and weary,
and our eyes grow dim with tears.
18 For Jerusalem* is empty and desolate,
a place haunted by jackals.

19 But LORD, you remain the same forever!
Your throne continues from generation to generation.
20 Why do you continue to forget us?
Why have you abandoned us for so long?
21 Restore us, O LORD, and bring us back to you again!
Give us back the joys we once had!
22 Or have you utterly rejected us?
Are you angry with us still?

5:11 Hebrew *in Zion.* **5:16** Or *The crown has.* **5:18** Hebrew *Mount Zion.*

Ezekiel

KING JAMES VERSION

1 1 Now it came to pass in the thirtieth year, in the fourth *month,* in the fifth *day* of the month, as I *was* among the captives by the river of Chebar, *that* the heavens were opened, and I saw visions of God.

2 In the fifth *day* of the month, which *was* the fifth year of king Jehoiachin's captivity,

3 The word of the LORD came expressly unto Ezekiel the priest, the son of Buzi, in the land of the Chaldeans by the river Chebar; and the hand of the LORD was there upon him.

4 And I looked, and, behold, a whirlwind came out of the north, a great cloud, and a fire infolding itself, and a brightness *was* about it, and out of the midst thereof as the colour of amber, out of the midst of the fire.

5 Also out of the midst thereof *came* the likeness of four living creatures. And this *was* their appearance; they had the likeness of a man.

6 And every one had four faces, and every one had four wings.

7 And their feet *were* straight feet; and the sole of their feet *was* like the sole of a calf's foot: and they sparkled like the colour of burnished brass.

8 And *they had* the hands of a man under their wings on their four sides; and they four had their faces and their wings.

9 Their wings *were* joined one to another; they turned not when they went; they went every one straight forward.

10 As for the likeness of their faces, they four had the face of a man, and the face of a lion, on the right side: and they four had the face of an ox on the left side; they four also had the face of an eagle.

11 Thus *were* their faces: and their wings *were* stretched upward; two *wings* of every one *were* joined one to another, and two covered their bodies.

12 And they went every one straight forward: whither the spirit was to go, they went; *and* they turned not when they went.

13 As for the likeness of the living creatures, their appearance *was* like burning coals of fire, *and* like the appearance of lamps: it went up and down among the living creatures; and the fire was bright, and out of the fire went forth lightning.

NEW LIVING TRANSLATION

A Vision of Living Beings

1 On July 31* of my thirtieth year,* while I was with the Judean exiles beside the Kebar River in Babylon, the heavens were opened and I saw visions of God. 2 This happened during the fifth year of King Jehoiachin's captivity. 3 (The LORD gave this message to Ezekiel son of Buzi, a priest, beside the Kebar River in the land of the Babylonians,* and he felt the hand of the LORD take hold of him.)

4 As I looked, I saw a great storm coming from the north, driving before it a huge cloud that flashed with lightning and shone with brilliant light. There was fire inside the cloud, and in the middle of the fire glowed something like gleaming amber.* 5 From the center of the cloud came four living beings that looked human, 6 except that each had four faces and four wings. 7 Their legs were straight, and their feet had hooves like those of a calf and shone like burnished bronze. 8 Under each of their four wings I could see human hands. So each of the four beings had four faces and four wings. 9 The wings of each living being touched the wings of the beings beside it. Each one moved straight forward in any direction without turning around.

10 Each had a human face in the front, the face of a lion on the right side, the face of an ox on the left side, and the face of an eagle at the back. 11 Each had two pairs of outstretched wings—one pair stretched out to touch the wings of the living beings on either side of it, and the other pair covered its body. 12 They went in whatever direction the spirit chose, and they moved straight forward in any direction without turning around.

13 The living beings looked like bright coals of fire or brilliant torches, and lightning seemed to flash

1:1a Hebrew *On the fifth day of the fourth month,* of the ancient Hebrew lunar calendar. A number of dates in Ezekiel can be cross-checked with dates in surviving Babylonian records and related accurately to our modern calendar. This event occurred on July 31, 593 B.C. **1:1b** Or *in the thirtieth year.* **1:3** Or *Chaldeans.* **1:4** Or *like burnished metal;* also in 1:27.

KING JAMES VERSION

14 And the living creatures ran and returned as the
appearance of a flash of lightning.
15 Now as I beheld the living creatures, behold one
wheel upon the earth by the living creatures, with his
four faces.
16 The appearance of the wheels and their work
was like unto the colour of a beryl: and they four had
one likeness: and their appearance and their work
was as it were a wheel in the middle of a wheel.
17 When they went, they went upon their four
sides: *and* they turned not when they went.
18 As for their rings, they were so high that they
were dreadful; and their rings *were* full of eyes round
about them four.
19 And when the living creatures went, the wheels
went by them: and when the living creatures were
lifted up from the earth, the wheels were lifted up.
20 Whithersoever the spirit was to go, they went,
thither *was their* spirit to go; and the wheels were
lifted up over against them: for the spirit of the living
creature *was* in the wheels.
21 When those went, *these* went; and when those
stood, *these* stood; and when those were lifted up
from the earth, the wheels were lifted up over
against them: for the spirit of the living creature *was*
in the wheels.
22 And the likeness of the firmament upon the
heads of the living creature *was* as the colour of the
terrible crystal, stretched forth over their heads
above.
23 And under the firmament *were* their wings
straight, the one toward the other: every one had two,
which covered on this side, and every one had two,
which covered on that side, their bodies.
24 And when they went, I heard the noise of their
wings, like the noise of great waters, as the voice of
the Almighty, the voice of speech, as the noise of an
host: when they stood, they let down their wings.
25 And there was a voice from the firmament that
was over their heads, when they stood, *and* had let
down their wings.
26 And above the firmament that *was* over their
heads *was* the likeness of a throne, as the appearance of a sapphire stone: and upon the likeness of
the throne *was* the likeness as the appearance of a
man above upon it.
27 And I saw as the colour of amber, as the appearance of fire round about within it, from the appearance of his loins even upward, and from the
appearance of his loins even downward, I saw as it
were the appearance of fire, and it had brightness
round about.
28 As the appearance of the bow that is in the cloud
in the day of rain, so *was* the appearance of the
brightness round about. This *was* the appearance of
the likeness of the glory of the LORD. And when I saw
it, I fell upon my face, and I heard a voice of one that
spake.

NEW LIVING TRANSLATION

back and forth among them. 14 And the living beings
darted to and fro like flashes of lightning.
15 As I looked at these beings, I saw four wheels
touching the ground beside them, one wheel belonging to each. 16 The wheels sparkled as if made of
beryl. All four wheels looked alike and were made
the same; each wheel had a second wheel turning
crosswise within it. 17 The beings could move in any
of the four directions they faced, without turning as
they moved. 18 The rims of the four wheels were tall
and frightening, and they were covered with eyes all
around.
19 When the living beings moved, the wheels
moved with them. When they flew upward, the
wheels went up, too. 20 The spirit of the living beings
was in the wheels. So wherever the spirit went, the
wheels and the living beings also went. 21 When the
beings moved, the wheels moved. When the beings
stopped, the wheels stopped. When the beings flew
upward, the wheels rose up, for the spirit of the living
beings was in the wheels.
22 Spread out above them was a surface like the sky,
glittering like crystal. 23 Beneath this surface the
wings of each living being stretched out to touch the
others' wings, and each had two wings covering its
body. 24 As they flew, their wings sounded to me like
waves crashing against the shore or like the voice of
the Almighty* or like the shouting of a mighty army.
When they stopped, they let down their wings. 25 As
they stood with wings lowered, a voice spoke from
beyond the crystal surface above them.
26 Above this surface was something that looked
like a throne made of blue lapis lazuli. And on this
throne high above was a figure whose appearance
resembled a man. 27 From what appeared to be his
waist up, he looked like gleaming amber, flickering
like a fire. And from his waist down, he looked like a
burning flame, shining with splendor. 28 All around
him was a glowing halo, like a rainbow shining in the
clouds on a rainy day. This is what the glory of the
LORD looked like to me. When I saw it, I fell face
down on the ground, and I heard someone's voice
speaking to me.

1:24 Hebrew *Shaddai*.

KING JAMES VERSION

2 1And he said unto me, Son of man, stand upon
thy feet, and I will speak unto thee.
2And the spirit entered into me when he spake
unto me, and set me upon my feet, that I heard him
that spake unto me.
3And he said unto me, Son of man, I send thee to
the children of Israel, to a rebellious nation that hath
rebelled against me: they and their fathers have
transgressed against me, *even* unto this very day.
4For *they are* impudent children and stiffhearted.
I do send thee unto them; and thou shalt say unto
them, Thus saith the Lord GOD.
5And they, whether they will hear, or whether they
will forbear, (for they *are* a rebellious house,) yet shall
know that there hath been a prophet among them.
6And thou, son of man, be not afraid of them,
neither be afraid of their words, though briers and
thorns *be* with thee, and thou dost dwell among scorpions: be not afraid of their words, nor be dismayed
at their looks, though they *be* a rebellious house.
7And thou shalt speak my words unto them,
whether they will hear, or whether they will forbear:
for they *are* most rebellious.
8But thou, son of man, hear what I say unto thee;
Be not thou rebellious like that rebellious house:
open thy mouth, and eat that I give thee.
9And when I looked, behold, an hand *was* sent
unto me; and, lo, a roll of a book *was* therein;
10And he spread it before me; and it *was* written
within and without: and *there was* written therein
lamentations, and mourning, and woe.

3 1Moreover he said unto me, Son of man, eat
that thou findest; eat this roll, and go speak
unto the house of Israel.
2So I opened my mouth, and he caused me to eat
that roll.
3And he said unto me, Son of man, cause thy belly
to eat, and fill thy bowels with this roll that I give
thee. Then did I eat *it;* and it was in my mouth as
honey for sweetness.
4And he said unto me, Son of man, go, get thee
unto the house of Israel, and speak with my words
unto them.
5For thou *art* not sent to a people of a strange
speech and of an hard language, *but* to the house
of Israel;
6Not to many people of a strange speech and of an
hard language, whose words thou canst not understand. Surely, had I sent thee to them, they would
have hearkened unto thee.
7But the house of Israel will not hearken unto
thee; for they will not hearken unto me: for all the
house of Israel *are* impudent and hardhearted.
8Behold, I have made thy face strong against their
faces, and thy forehead strong against their foreheads.

NEW LIVING TRANSLATION

Ezekiel's Call and Commission

2 "Stand up, son of man," said the voice. "I want
to speak with you." 2The Spirit came into me as
he spoke, and he set me on my feet. I listened carefully to his words. 3"Son of man," he said, "I am sending you to the nation of Israel, a rebellious nation
that has rebelled against me. They and their ancestors have been rebelling against me to this very day.
4They are a stubborn and hard-hearted people. But I
am sending you to say to them, 'This is what the Sovereign LORD says!' 5And whether they listen or refuse
to listen—for remember, they are rebels—at least
they will know they have had a prophet among them.
6"Son of man, do not fear them or their words.
Don't be afraid even though their threats surround
you like nettles and briers and stinging scorpions. Do
not be dismayed by their dark scowls, even though
they are rebels. 7You must give them my messages
whether they listen or not. But they won't listen, for
they are completely rebellious! 8Son of man, listen to
what I say to you. Do not join them in their rebellion.
Open your mouth, and eat what I give you."
9Then I looked and saw a hand reaching out to me.
It held a scroll, 10which he unrolled. And I saw that
both sides were covered with funeral songs, words of
sorrow, and pronouncements of doom.

3 The voice said to me, "Son of man, eat what I am
giving you—eat this scroll! Then go and give its
message to the people of Israel." 2So I opened my
mouth, and he fed me the scroll. 3"Fill your stomach
with this," he said. And when I ate it, it tasted as
sweet as honey in my mouth.
4Then he said, "Son of man, go to the people of Israel and give them my messages. 5I am not sending
you to a foreign people whose language you cannot
understand. 6No, I am not sending you to people with
strange and difficult speech. If I did, they would listen! 7But the people of Israel won't listen to you any
more than they listen to me! For the whole lot of them
are hard-hearted and stubborn. 8But look, I have
made you as obstinate and hard-hearted as they are.

KING JAMES VERSION

[9]As an adamant harder than flint have I made thy forehead: fear them not, neither be dismayed at their looks, though they *be* a rebellious house.

[10]Moreover he said unto me, Son of man, all my words that I shall speak unto thee receive in thine heart, and hear with thine ears.

[11]And go, get thee to them of the captivity, unto the children of thy people, and speak unto them, and tell them, Thus saith the Lord GOD; whether they will hear, or whether they will forbear.

[12]Then the spirit took me up, and I heard behind me a voice of a great rushing, *saying,* Blessed *be* the glory of the LORD from his place.

[13]*I heard* also the noise of the wings of the living creatures that touched one another, and the noise of the wheels over against them, and a noise of a great rushing.

[14]So the spirit lifted me up, and took me away, and I went in bitterness, in the heat of my spirit; but the hand of the LORD was strong upon me.

[15]Then I came to them of the captivity at Tel-abib, that dwelt by the river of Chebar, and I sat where they sat, and remained there astonished among them seven days.

[16]And it came to pass at the end of seven days, that the word of the LORD came unto me, saying,

[17]Son of man, I have made thee a watchman unto the house of Israel: therefore hear the word at my mouth, and give them warning from me.

[18]When I say unto the wicked, Thou shalt surely die; and thou givest him not warning, nor speakest to warn the wicked from his wicked way, to save his life; the same wicked *man* shall die in his iniquity; but his blood will I require at thine hand.

[19]Yet if thou warn the wicked, and he turn not from his wickedness, nor from his wicked way, he shall die in his iniquity; but thou hast delivered thy soul.

[20]Again, When a righteous *man* doth turn from his righteousness, and commit iniquity, and I lay a stumblingblock before him, he shall die: because thou hast not given him warning, he shall die in his sin, and his righteousness which he hath done shall not be remembered; but his blood will I require at thine hand.

[21]Nevertheless if thou warn the righteous *man,* that the righteous sin not, and he doth not sin, he shall surely live, because he is warned; also thou hast delivered thy soul.

[22]And the hand of the LORD was there upon me; and he said unto me, Arise, go forth into the plain, and I will there talk with thee.

[23]Then I arose, and went forth into the plain: and, behold, the glory of the LORD stood there, as the glory which I saw by the river of Chebar: and I fell on my face.

[24]Then the spirit entered into me, and set me upon my feet, and spake with me, and said unto me, Go, shut thyself within thine house.

NEW LIVING TRANSLATION

[9]I have made your forehead as hard as the hardest rock! So don't be afraid of them or fear their angry looks, even though they are rebels."

[10]Then he added, "Son of man, let all my words sink deep into your own heart first. Listen to them carefully for yourself. [11]Then go to your people in exile and say to them, 'This is what the Sovereign LORD says!' Do this whether they listen to you or not."

[12]Then the Spirit lifted me up, and I heard a loud rumbling sound behind me. (May the glory of the LORD be praised in his place!)* [13]It was the sound of the wings of the living beings as they brushed against each other and the rumbling of their wheels beneath them.

[14]The Spirit lifted me up and took me away. I went in bitterness and turmoil, but the LORD's hold on me was strong. [15]Then I came to the colony of Judean exiles in Tel-abib, beside the Kebar River. I was overwhelmed and sat among them for seven days.

A Watchman for Israel

[16]After seven days the LORD gave me a message. He said, [17]"Son of man, I have appointed you as a watchman for Israel. Whenever you receive a message from me, warn people immediately. [18]If I warn the wicked, saying, 'You are under the penalty of death,' but you fail to deliver the warning, they will die in their sins. And I will hold you responsible for their deaths. [19]If you warn them and they refuse to repent and keep on sinning, they will die in their sins. But you will have saved yourself because you obeyed me.

[20]"If righteous people turn away from their righteous behavior and ignore the obstacles I put in their way, they will die. And if you do not warn them, they will die in their sins. None of their righteous acts will be remembered, and I will hold you responsible for their deaths. [21]But if you warn righteous people not to sin and they listen to you and do not sin, they will live, and you will have saved yourself, too."

[22]Then the LORD took hold of me and said, "Get up and go out into the valley, and I will speak to you there." [23]So I got up and went, and there I saw the glory of the LORD, just as I had seen in my first vision by the Kebar River. And I fell face down on the ground.

[24]Then the Spirit came into me and set me on my feet. He spoke to me and said, "Go to your house and

3:12 A possible reading for this verse is *Then the Spirit lifted me up, and as the glory of the LORD rose from its place, I heard a loud rumbling sound behind me.*

KING JAMES VERSION

25 But thou, O son of man, behold, they shall put bands upon thee, and shall bind thee with them, and thou shalt not go out among them:

26 And I will make thy tongue cleave to the roof of thy mouth, that thou shalt be dumb, and shalt not be to them a reprover: for they *are* a rebellious house.

27 But when I speak with thee, I will open thy mouth, and thou shalt say unto them, Thus saith the Lord GOD; He that heareth, let him hear; and he that forbeareth, let him forbear: for they *are* a rebellious house.

4 1 Thou also, son of man, take thee a tile, and lay it before thee, and pourtray upon it the city, *even* Jerusalem:

2 And lay siege against it, and build a fort against it, and cast a mount against it; set the camp also against it, and set *battering* rams against it round about.

3 Moreover take thou unto thee an iron pan, and set it *for* a wall of iron between thee and the city: and set thy face against it, and it shall be besieged, and thou shalt lay siege against it. This *shall be* a sign to the house of Israel.

4 Lie thou also upon thy left side, and lay the iniquity of the house of Israel upon it: *according* to the number of the days that thou shalt lie upon it thou shalt bear their iniquity.

5 For I have laid upon thee the years of their iniquity, according to the number of the days, three hundred and ninety days: so shalt thou bear the iniquity of the house of Israel.

6 And when thou hast accomplished them, lie again on thy right side, and thou shalt bear the iniquity of the house of Judah forty days: I have appointed thee each day for a year.

7 Therefore thou shalt set thy face toward the siege of Jerusalem, and thine arm *shall be* uncovered, and thou shalt prophesy against it.

8 And, behold, I will lay bands upon thee, and thou shalt not turn thee from one side to another, till thou hast ended the days of thy siege.

9 Take thou also unto thee wheat, and barley, and beans, and lentiles, and millet, and fitches, and put them in one vessel, and make thee bread thereof, *according* to the number of the days that thou shalt lie upon thy side, three hundred and ninety days shalt thou eat thereof.

10 And thy meat which thou shalt eat *shall be* by weight, twenty shekels a day: from time to time shalt thou eat it.

11 Thou shalt drink also water by measure, the sixth part of an hin: from time to time shalt thou drink.

12 And thou shalt eat it *as* barley cakes, and thou shalt bake it with dung that cometh out of man, in their sight.

13 And the LORD said, Even thus shall the children of Israel eat their defiled bread among the Gentiles, whither I will drive them.

NEW LIVING TRANSLATION

shut yourself in. 25 There, son of man, you will be tied with ropes so you cannot go out among the people. 26 And I will make your tongue stick to the roof of your mouth so that you will be speechless and unable to rebuke them, for they are rebels. 27 But when I give you a message, I will loosen your tongue and let you speak. Then you will say to them, 'This is what the Sovereign LORD says!' Those who choose to listen will listen, but those who refuse will refuse, for they are rebels.

A Sign of the Coming Siege

4 "And now, son of man, take a large clay brick and set it down in front of you. Then draw a map of the city of Jerusalem on it. 2 Show the city under siege. Build a wall around it so no one can escape. Set up the enemy camp, and surround the city with siege ramps and battering rams. 3 Then take an iron griddle and place it between you and the city. Turn toward the city and demonstrate how harsh the siege will be against Jerusalem. This will be a warning to the people of Israel.

4 "Now lie on your left side and place the sins of Israel on yourself. You are to bear their sins for the number of days you lie there on your side. 5 I am requiring you to bear Israel's sins for 390 days—one day for each year of their sin. 6 After that, turn over and lie on your right side for 40 days—one day for each year of Judah's sin.

7 "Meanwhile, keep staring at the siege of Jerusalem. Lie there with your arm bared and prophesy her destruction. 8 I will tie you up with ropes so you won't be able to turn from side to side until the days of your siege have been completed.

9 "Now go and get some wheat, barley, beans, lentils, millet, and emmer wheat, and mix them together in a storage jar. Use them to make bread for yourself during the 390 days you will be lying on your side. 10 Ration this out to yourself, eight ounces* of food for each day, and eat it at set times. 11 Then measure out a jar* of water for each day, and drink it at set times. 12 Prepare and eat this food as you would barley cakes. While all the people are watching, bake it over a fire using dried human dung as fuel and then eat the bread." 13 Then the LORD said, "This is how Israel will eat defiled bread in the Gentile lands to which I will banish them!"

4:10 Hebrew *20 shekels* [228 grams]. **4:11** Hebrew ⅙ *of a hin* [about 1 pint or 0.6 liters].

KING JAMES VERSION

14 Then said I, Ah Lord GOD! behold, my soul hath
not been polluted: for from my youth up even till
now have I not eaten of that which dieth of itself,
or is torn in pieces; neither came there abominable
flesh into my mouth.
15 Then he said unto me, Lo, I have given thee cow's
dung for man's dung, and thou shalt prepare thy
bread therewith.
16 Moreover he said unto me, Son of man, behold,
I will break the staff of bread in Jerusalem: and they
shall eat bread by weight, and with care; and they
shall drink water by measure, and with astonishment:
17 That they may want bread and water, and be
astonied one with another, and consume away for
their iniquity.

5 1 And thou, son of man, take thee a sharp knife,
take thee a barber's razor, and cause *it* to pass
upon thine head and upon thy beard: then take thee
balances to weigh, and divide the *hair.*
2 Thou shalt burn with fire a third part in the midst
of the city, when the days of the siege are fulfilled:
and thou shalt take a third part, *and* smite about it
with a knife: and a third part thou shalt scatter in the
wind; and I will draw out a sword after them.
3 Thou shalt also take thereof a few in number, and
bind them in thy skirts.
4 Then take of them again, and cast them into
the midst of the fire, and burn them in the fire; *for*
thereof shall a fire come forth into all the house of
Israel.
5 Thus saith the Lord GOD; This *is* Jerusalem: I have
set it in the midst of the nations and countries *that*
are round about her.
6 And she hath changed my judgments into wickedness more than the nations, and my statutes more
than the countries that *are* round about her: for they
have refused my judgments and my statutes, they
have not walked in them.
7 Therefore thus saith the Lord GOD; Because ye
multiplied more than the nations that *are* round
about you, *and* have not walked in my statutes, neither have kept my judgments, neither have done according to the judgments of the nations that *are*
round about you;
8 Therefore thus saith the Lord GOD; Behold, I, even
I, *am* against thee, and will execute judgments in the
midst of thee in the sight of the nations.
9 And I will do in thee that which I have not done,
and whereunto I will not do any more the like, because of all thine abominations.
10 Therefore the fathers shall eat the sons in the
midst of thee, and the sons shall eat their fathers;
and I will execute judgments in thee, and the whole
remnant of thee will I scatter into all the winds.
11 Wherefore, *as* I live, saith the Lord GOD; Surely,
because thou hast defiled my sanctuary with all thy

NEW LIVING TRANSLATION

14 Then I said, "O Sovereign LORD, must I be defiled
by using human dung? For I have never been defiled
before. From the time I was a child until now I have
never eaten any animal that died of sickness or was
killed by other animals. I have never eaten any meat
forbidden by the law."
15 "All right," the LORD said. "You may bake your
bread with cow dung instead of human dung."
16 Then he told me, "Son of man, I will make food very
scarce in Jerusalem. It will be weighed out with great
care and eaten fearfully. The water will be rationed
out drop by drop, and the people will drink it with
dismay. 17 Lacking food and water, people will look at
one another in terror, and they will waste away under
their punishment.

A Sign of the Coming Judgment

5 "Son of man, take a sharp sword and use it as a
razor to shave your head and beard. Use a scale
to weigh the hair into three equal parts. 2 Place a
third of it at the center of your map of Jerusalem. After acting out the siege, burn it there. Scatter another
third across your map and chop it with a sword. Scatter the last third to the wind, for I will scatter my people with the sword. 3 Keep just a bit of the hair and tie
it up in your robe. 4 Then take some of these hairs out
and throw them into the fire, burning them up. A fire
will then spread from this remnant and destroy all of
Israel.
5 "This is what the Sovereign LORD says: This is
an illustration of what will happen to Jerusalem. I
placed her at the center of the nations, 6 but she has
rebelled against my regulations and decrees and has
been even more wicked than the surrounding nations. She has refused to obey the regulations and
decrees I gave her to follow.
7 "Therefore, this is what the Sovereign LORD says:
You people have behaved worse than your neighbors
and have refused to obey my decrees and regulations. You have not even lived up to the standards
of the nations around you. 8 Therefore, I myself, the
Sovereign LORD, am now your enemy. I will punish
you publicly while all the nations watch. 9 Because of
your detestable idols, I will punish you like I have
never punished anyone before or ever will again.
10 Parents will eat their own children, and children
will eat their parents. I will punish you and scatter to
the winds the few who survive.
11 "As surely as I live, says the Sovereign LORD, I will
cut you off completely. I will show you no pity at all

KING JAMES VERSION

detestable things, and with all thine abominations,
therefore will I also diminish *thee;* neither shall
mine eye spare, neither will I have any pity.
12A third part of thee shall die with the pestilence,
and with famine shall they be consumed in the midst
of thee: and a third part shall fall by the sword round
about thee; and I will scatter a third part into all the
winds, and I will draw out a sword after them.
13Thus shall mine anger be accomplished, and I
will cause my fury to rest upon them, and I will be
comforted: and they shall know that I the LORD have
spoken *it* in my zeal, when I have accomplished my
fury in them.
14Moreover I will make thee waste, and a reproach
among the nations that *are* round about thee, in the
sight of all that pass by.
15So it shall be a reproach and a taunt, an instruction and an astonishment unto the nations that *are*
round about thee, when I shall execute judgments in
thee in anger and in fury and in furious rebukes. I
the LORD have spoken *it.*
16When I shall send upon them the evil arrows
of famine, which shall be for *their* destruction, *and*
which I will send to destroy you: and I will increase
the famine upon you, and will break your staff of
bread:
17So will I send upon you famine and evil beasts,
and they shall bereave thee; and pestilence and
blood shall pass through thee; and I will bring the
sword upon thee. I the LORD have spoken *it.*

6 1And the word of the LORD came unto me,
saying,
2Son of man, set thy face toward the mountains of
Israel, and prophesy against them,
3And say, Ye mountains of Israel, hear the word of
the Lord GOD; Thus saith the Lord GOD to the mountains, and to the hills, to the rivers, and to the valleys;
Behold, I, *even* I, will bring a sword upon you, and
I will destroy your high places.
4And your altars shall be desolate, and your images shall be broken: and I will cast down your slain
men before your idols.
5And I will lay the dead carcases of the children of
Israel before their idols; and I will scatter your bones
round about your altars.
6In all your dwellingplaces the cities shall be laid
waste, and the high places shall be desolate; that
your altars may be laid waste and made desolate, and
your idols may be broken and cease, and your images
may be cut down, and your works may be abolished.
7And the slain shall fall in the midst of you, and ye
shall know that I *am* the LORD.
8Yet will I leave a remnant, that ye may have *some*
that shall escape the sword among the nations, when
ye shall be scattered through the countries.
9And they that escape of you shall remember me
among the nations whither they shall be carried

NEW LIVING TRANSLATION

because you have defiled my Temple with your vile
images and detestable sins. 12A third of your people
will die in the city from disease and famine. A third
of them will be slaughtered by the enemy outside the
city walls. And I will scatter a third to the winds, chasing them with my sword. 13Then at last my anger will
be spent, and I will be satisfied. And when my fury
against them has subsided, all Israel will know that I,
the LORD, have spoken to them in my jealous anger.
14"So I will turn you into a ruin, a mockery in the
eyes of the surrounding nations and to all who pass
by. 15You will become an object of mockery and
taunting and horror. You will be a warning to all the
nations around you. They will see what happens
when the LORD punishes a nation in anger and rebukes it, says the LORD.
16"I will shower you with the deadly arrows of
famine to destroy you. The famine will become more
and more severe until every crumb of food is gone.
17And along with the famine, wild animals will attack
you and rob you of your children. Disease and war
will stalk your land, and I will bring the sword of the
enemy against you. I, the LORD, have spoken!"

Judgment against Israel's Mountains

6 Again a message came to me from the LORD:
2"Son of man, turn and face the mountains of
Israel and prophesy against them. 3Proclaim this
message from the Sovereign LORD against the mountains of Israel. This is what the Sovereign LORD says
to the mountains and hills and to the ravines and valleys: I am about to bring war upon you, and I will
smash your pagan shrines. 4All your altars will be
demolished, and your places of worship will be destroyed. I will kill your people in front of your idols.*
5I will lay your corpses in front of your idols and scatter your bones around your altars. 6Wherever you
live there will be desolation, and I will destroy your
pagan shrines. Your altars will be demolished, your
idols will be smashed, your places of worship will
be torn down, and all the religious objects you have
made will be destroyed. 7The place will be littered
with corpses, and you will know that I alone am the
LORD.
8"But I will let a few of my people escape destruction, and they will be scattered among the nations
of the world. 9Then when they are exiled among the

6:4 The Hebrew term (literally *round things*) probably alludes to dung; also in 6:5, 6, 9, 13.

KING JAMES VERSION

captives, because I am broken with their whorish
heart, which hath departed from me, and with their
eyes, which go a whoring after their idols: and they
shall lothe themselves for the evils which they have
committed in all their abominations.
10And they shall know that I *am* the LORD, *and that*
I have not said in vain that I would do this evil unto
them.
11Thus saith the Lord GOD; Smite with thine
hand, and stamp with thy foot, and say, Alas for all
the evil abominations of the house of Israel! for they
shall fall by the sword, by the famine, and by the
pestilence.
12He that is far off shall die of the pestilence; and
he that is near shall fall by the sword; and he that
remaineth and is besieged shall die by the famine:
thus will I accomplish my fury upon them.
13Then shall ye know that I *am* the LORD, when
their slain *men* shall be among their idols round
about their altars, upon every high hill, in all the tops
of the mountains, and under every green tree, and
under every thick oak, the place where they did offer
sweet savour to all their idols.
14So will I stretch out my hand upon them, and
make the land desolate, yea, more desolate than the
wilderness toward Diblath, in all their habitations:
and they shall know that I *am* the LORD.

7 1Moreover the word of the LORD came unto me,
saying,
2Also, thou son of man, thus saith the Lord GOD
unto the land of Israel; An end, the end is come upon
the four corners of the land.
3Now *is* the end *come* upon thee, and I will send
mine anger upon thee, and will judge thee according
to thy ways, and will recompense upon thee all thine
abominations.
4And mine eye shall not spare thee, neither will I
have pity: but I will recompense thy ways upon thee,
and thine abominations shall be in the midst of thee:
and ye shall know that I *am* the LORD.
5Thus saith the Lord GOD; An evil, an only evil,
behold, is come.
6An end is come, the end is come: it watcheth for
thee; behold, it is come.
7The morning is come unto thee, O thou that
dwellest in the land: the time is come, the day of
trouble *is* near, and not the sounding again of the
mountains.
8Now will I shortly pour out my fury upon thee,
and accomplish mine anger upon thee: and I will

NEW LIVING TRANSLATION

nations, they will remember me. They will recognize
how hurt I am by their unfaithful hearts and lustful
eyes that long for their idols. Then at last they will
hate themselves for all their detestable sins. 10They
will know that I alone am the LORD and that I was
serious when I said I would bring this calamity on
them.
11"This is what the Sovereign LORD says: Clap your
hands in horror, and stamp your feet. Cry out because of all the detestable sins the people of Israel
have committed. Now they are going to die from war
and famine and disease. 12Disease will strike down
those who are far away in exile. War will destroy
those who are nearby. And anyone who survives will
be killed by famine. So at last I will spend my fury on
them. 13They will know that I am the LORD when
their dead lie scattered among their idols and altars
on every hill and mountain and under every green
tree and every great shade tree—the places where
they offered sacrifices to their idols. 14I will crush
them and make their cities desolate from the wilderness in the south to Riblah* in the north. Then they
will know that I am the LORD."

The Coming of the End

7 Then this message came to me from the LORD:
2"Son of man, this is what the Sovereign LORD
says to Israel:

"The end is here!
Wherever you look—
east, west, north, or south—
your land is finished.
3 No hope remains,
for I will unleash my anger against you.
I will call you to account
for all your detestable sins.
4 I will turn my eyes away and show no pity.
I will repay you for all your detestable sins.
Then you will know that I am the LORD.

5 "This is what the Sovereign LORD says:
Disaster after disaster
is coming your way!
6 The end has come.
It has finally arrived.
Your final doom is waiting!
7 O people of Israel, the day of your destruction
is dawning.
The time has come; the day of trouble is near.
Shouts of anguish will be heard on the mountains,
not shouts of joy.
8 Soon I will pour out my fury on you
and unleash my anger against you.

6:14 As in some Hebrew manuscripts; most Hebrew manuscripts read *Diblah*.

KING JAMES VERSION

judge thee according to thy ways, and will recompense thee for all thine abominations.
9And mine eye shall not spare, neither will I have
pity: I will recompense thee according to thy ways
and thine abominations *that* are in the midst of thee;
and ye shall know that I *am* the LORD that smiteth.
10Behold the day, behold, it is come: the morning
is gone forth; the rod hath blossomed, pride hath
budded.
11Violence is risen up into a rod of wickedness:
none of them *shall remain,* nor of their multitude,
nor of any of theirs: neither *shall there be* wailing
for them.
12The time is come, the day draweth near: let not
the buyer rejoice, nor the seller mourn: for wrath
is upon all the multitude thereof.
13For the seller shall not return to that which is
sold, although they were yet alive: for the vision *is*
touching the whole multitude thereof, *which* shall
not return; neither shall any strengthen himself in
the iniquity of his life.

14They have blown the trumpet, even to make all
ready; but none goeth to the battle: for my wrath *is*
upon all the multitude thereof.
15The sword *is* without, and the pestilence and the
famine within: he that *is* in the field shall die with the
sword; and he that *is* in the city, famine and pestilence shall devour him.
16But they that escape of them shall escape, and
shall be on the mountains like doves of the valleys, all
of them mourning, every one for his iniquity.
17All hands shall be feeble, and all knees shall be
weak *as* water.
18They shall also gird *themselves* with sackcloth,
and horror shall cover them; and shame *shall be*
upon all faces, and baldness upon all their heads.
19They shall cast their silver in the streets, and
their gold shall be removed: their silver and their
gold shall not be able to deliver them in the day of
the wrath of the LORD: they shall not satisfy their
souls, neither fill their bowels: because it is the
stumblingblock of their iniquity.
20As for the beauty of his ornament, he set it in
majesty: but they made the images of their abominations *and* of their detestable things therein: therefore have I set it far from them.

NEW LIVING TRANSLATION

I will call you to account
for all your detestable sins.
9 I will turn my eyes away and show no pity.
I will repay you for all your detestable sins.
Then you will know that it is I, the LORD,
who is striking the blow.

10 "The day of judgment is here;
your destruction awaits!
The people's wickedness and pride
have blossomed to full flower.
11 Their violence has grown into a rod
that will beat them for their wickedness.
None of these proud and wicked people
will survive.
All their wealth and prestige will be swept away.
12 Yes, the time has come;
the day is here!
Buyers should not rejoice over bargains,
nor sellers grieve over losses,
for all of them will fall
under my terrible anger.
13 Even if the merchants survive,
they will never return to their business.
For what God has said applies to everyone—
it will not be changed!
Not one person whose life is twisted by sin
will ever recover.

The Desolation of Israel

14 "The trumpet calls Israel's army to mobilize,
but no one listens,
for my fury is against them all.
15 There is war outside the city
and disease and famine within.
Those outside the city walls
will be killed by enemy swords.
Those inside the city
will die of famine and disease.
16 The survivors who escape to the mountains
will moan like doves, weeping for their sins.
17 Their hands will hang limp,
their knees will be weak as water.
18 They will dress themselves in burlap;
horror and shame will cover them.
They will shave their heads
in sorrow and remorse.

19 "They will throw their money in the streets,
tossing it out like worthless trash.
Their silver and gold won't save them
on that day of the LORD's anger.
It will neither satisfy nor feed them,
for their greed can only trip them up.
20 They were proud of their beautiful jewelry
and used it to make detestable idols and
vile images.
Therefore, I will make all their wealth
disgusting to them.

KING JAMES VERSION

21 And I will give it into the hands of the strangers
for a prey, and to the wicked of the earth for a spoil;
and they shall pollute it.
22 My face will I turn also from them, and they shall
pollute my secret *place:* for the robbers shall enter
into it, and defile it.
23 Make a chain: for the land is full of bloody
crimes, and the city is full of violence.
24 Wherefore I will bring the worst of the heathen,
and they shall possess their houses: I will also make
the pomp of the strong to cease; and their holy
places shall be defiled.
25 Destruction cometh; and they shall seek peace,
and *there shall be* none.
26 Mischief shall come upon mischief, and rumour
shall be upon rumour; then shall they seek a vision of
the prophet; but the law shall perish from the priest,
and counsel from the ancients.
27 The king shall mourn, and the prince shall be
clothed with desolation, and the hands of the people
of the land shall be troubled: I will do unto them
after their way, and according to their deserts will I
judge them; and they shall know that I *am* the LORD.

8 1 And it came to pass in the sixth year, in the
sixth *month,* in the fifth *day* of the month, *as* I
sat in mine house, and the elders of Judah sat before
me, that the hand of the Lord GOD fell there upon me.
2 Then I beheld, and lo a likeness as the appearance
of fire: from the appearance of his loins even downward, fire; and from his loins even upward, as the appearance of brightness, as the colour of amber.
3 And he put forth the form of an hand, and took me
by a lock of mine head; and the spirit lifted me up between the earth and the heaven, and brought me in the
visions of God to Jerusalem, to the door of the inner
gate that looketh toward the north; where *was* the seat
of the image of jealousy, which provoketh to jealousy.
4 And, behold, the glory of the God of Israel *was*
there, according to the vision that I saw in the plain.
5 Then said he unto me, Son of man, lift up thine
eyes now the way toward the north. So I lifted up
mine eyes the way toward the north, and behold
northward at the gate of the altar this image of jealousy in the entry.
6 He said furthermore unto me, Son of man, seest
thou what they do? *even* the great abominations that
the house of Israel committeth here, that I should go

NEW LIVING TRANSLATION

21 I will give it as plunder to foreigners,
to the most wicked of nations,
and they will defile it.
22 I will turn my eyes from them
as these robbers invade and defile
my treasured land.
23 "Prepare chains for my people,
for the land is bloodied by terrible crimes.
Jerusalem is filled with violence.
24 I will bring the most ruthless of nations
to occupy their homes.
I will break down their proud fortresses
and defile their sanctuaries.
25 Terror and trembling will overcome my people.
They will look for peace but not find it.
26 Calamity will follow calamity;
rumor will follow rumor.
They will look in vain
for a vision from the prophets.
They will receive no teaching from the priests
and no counsel from the leaders.
27 The king and the prince will stand helpless,
weeping in despair,
and the people's hands
will tremble with fear.
I will bring on them
the evil they have done to others,
and they will receive the punishment
they so richly deserve.
Then they will know that I am the LORD."

Idolatry in the Temple

8 Then on September 17,* during the sixth year
of King Jehoiachin's captivity, while the leaders
of Judah were in my home, the Sovereign LORD took
hold of me. 2 I saw a figure that appeared to be a man.
From what appeared to be his waist down, he looked
like a burning flame. From the waist up he looked
like gleaming amber.* 3 He reached out what seemed
to be a hand and took me by the hair. Then the Spirit
lifted me up into the sky and transported me to Jerusalem in a vision from God. I was taken to the north
gate of the inner courtyard of the Temple, where
there is a large idol that has made the LORD very jealous. 4 Suddenly, the glory of the God of Israel was
there, just as I had seen it before in the valley.
5 Then the LORD said to me, "Son of man, look toward the north." So I looked, and there to the north,
beside the entrance to the gate near the altar, stood
the idol that had made the LORD so jealous.
6 "Son of man," he said, "do you see what they are
doing? Do you see the detestable sins the people of

8:1 Hebrew *on the fifth day of the sixth month,* of the ancient Hebrew lunar calendar. This event occurred on September 17, 592 B.C.; also see note on 1:1. **8:2** Or *like burnished metal.*

KING JAMES VERSION

far off from my sanctuary? but turn thee yet again,
and thou shalt see greater abominations.
7 And he brought me to the door of the court; and
when I looked, behold a hole in the wall.
8 Then said he unto me, Son of man, dig now in the
wall: and when I had digged in the wall, behold a door.
9 And he said unto me, Go in, and behold the
wicked abominations that they do here.
10 So I went in and saw; and behold every form of
creeping things, and abominable beasts, and all the
idols of the house of Israel, pourtrayed upon the wall
round about.
11 And there stood before them seventy men of the
ancients of the house of Israel, and in the midst of
them stood Jaazaniah the son of Shaphan, with every
man his censer in his hand; and a thick cloud of incense went up.
12 Then said he unto me, Son of man, hast thou
seen what the ancients of the house of Israel do in
the dark, every man in the chambers of his imagery?
for they say, The LORD seeth us not; the LORD hath
forsaken the earth.
13 He said also unto me, Turn thee yet again, *and*
thou shalt see greater abominations that they do.
14 Then he brought me to the door of the gate of
the LORD's house which *was* toward the north; and,
behold, there sat women weeping for Tammuz.
15 Then said he unto me, Hast thou seen *this,* O son
of man? turn thee yet again, *and* thou shalt see
greater abominations than these.
16 And he brought me into the inner court of the
LORD's house, and, behold, at the door of the temple
of the LORD, between the porch and the altar, *were*
about five and twenty men, with their backs toward
the temple of the LORD, and their faces toward the
east; and they worshipped the sun toward the east.
17 Then he said unto me, Hast thou seen *this,* O son
of man? Is it a light thing to the house of Judah that
they commit the abominations which they commit
here? for they have filled the land with violence,
and have returned to provoke me to anger: and, lo,
they put the branch to their nose.
18 Therefore will I also deal in fury: mine eye shall
not spare, neither will I have pity: and though they cry
in mine ears with a loud voice, *yet* will I not hear them.

9
1 He cried also in mine ears with a loud voice,
saying, Cause them that have charge over the
city to draw near, even every man *with* his destroying
weapon in his hand.
2 And, behold, six men came from the way of the
higher gate, which lieth toward the north, and every
man a slaughter weapon in his hand; and one man
among them *was* clothed with linen, with a writer's
inkhorn by his side: and they went in, and stood
beside the brasen altar.
3 And the glory of the God of Israel was gone up
from the cherub, whereupon he was, to the threshold

NEW LIVING TRANSLATION

Israel are committing to drive me from my Temple?
But come, and you will see even more detestable
sins than these!" 7 Then he brought me to the door
of the Temple courtyard, where I could see a hole in
the wall. 8 He said to me, "Now, son of man, dig into
the wall." So I dug into the wall and found a hidden
doorway.
9 "Go in," he said, "and see the wicked and detestable sins they are committing in there!" 10 So I went
in and saw the walls engraved with all kinds of crawling animals and detestable creatures. I also saw the
various idols* worshiped by the people of Israel.
11 Seventy leaders of Israel were standing there with
Jaazaniah son of Shaphan in the center. Each of
them held an incense burner, from which a cloud of
incense rose above their heads.
12 Then the LORD said to me, "Son of man, have you
seen what the leaders of Israel are doing with their
idols in dark rooms? They are saying, 'The LORD
doesn't see us; he has deserted our land!'" 13 Then the
LORD added, "Come, and I will show you even more
detestable sins than these!"
14 He brought me to the north gate of the LORD's
Temple, and some women were sitting there, weeping for the god Tammuz. 15 "Have you seen this?" he
asked. "But I will show you even more detestable sins
than these!"
16 Then he brought me into the inner courtyard of
the LORD's Temple. At the entrance to the sanctuary,
between the entry room and the bronze altar, there
were about twenty-five men with their backs to the
sanctuary of the LORD. They were facing east, bowing
low to the ground, worshiping the sun!
17 "Have you seen this, son of man?" he asked. "Is it
nothing to the people of Judah that they commit
these detestable sins, leading the whole nation into
violence, thumbing their noses at me, and provoking
my anger? 18 Therefore, I will respond in fury. I will
neither pity nor spare them. And though they cry for
mercy, I will not listen."

The Slaughter of Idolaters

9
Then the LORD thundered, "Bring on the men
appointed to punish the city! Tell them to bring
their weapons with them!" 2 Six men soon appeared
from the upper gate that faces north, each carrying a
deadly weapon in his hand. With them was a man
dressed in linen, who carried a writer's case at his
side. They all went into the Temple courtyard and
stood beside the bronze altar.
3 Then the glory of the God of Israel rose up from
between the cherubim, where it had rested, and

8:10 The Hebrew term (literally *round things*) probably alludes to dung.

KING JAMES VERSION

of the house. And he called to the man clothed with linen, which *had* the writer's inkhorn by his side;

4 And the LORD said unto him, Go through the midst of the city, through the midst of Jerusalem, and set a mark upon the foreheads of the men that sigh and that cry for all the abominations that be done in the midst thereof.

5 And to the others he said in mine hearing, Go ye after him through the city, and smite: let not your eye spare, neither have ye pity:

6 Slay utterly old *and* young, both maids, and little children, and women: but come not near any man upon whom *is* the mark; and begin at my sanctuary. Then they began at the ancient men which *were* before the house.

7 And he said unto them, Defile the house, and fill the courts with the slain: go ye forth. And they went forth, and slew in the city.

8 And it came to pass, while they were slaying them, and I was left, that I fell upon my face, and cried, and said, Ah Lord GOD! wilt thou destroy all the residue of Israel in thy pouring out of thy fury upon Jerusalem?

9 Then said he unto me, The iniquity of the house of Israel and Judah *is* exceeding great, and the land is full of blood, and the city full of perverseness: for they say, The LORD hath forsaken the earth, and the LORD seeth not.

10 And as for me also, mine eye shall not spare, neither will I have pity, *but* I will recompense their way upon their head.

11 And, behold, the man clothed with linen, which *had* the inkhorn by his side, reported the matter, saying, I have done as thou hast commanded me.

10 1 Then I looked, and, behold, in the firmament that was above the head of the cherubims there appeared over them as it were a sapphire stone, as the appearance of the likeness of a throne.

2 And he spake unto the man clothed with linen, and said, Go in between the wheels, *even* under the cherub, and fill thine hand with coals of fire from between the cherubims, and scatter *them* over the city. And he went in in my sight.

3 Now the cherubims stood on the right side of the house, when the man went in; and the cloud filled the inner court.

4 Then the glory of the LORD went up from the cherub, *and stood* over the threshold of the house; and the house was filled with the cloud, and the court was full of the brightness of the LORD's glory.

5 And the sound of the cherubims' wings was heard *even* to the outer court, as the voice of the Almighty God when he speaketh.

6 And it came to pass, *that* when he had commanded the man clothed with linen, saying, Take fire from between the wheels, from between the cherubims; then he went in, and stood beside the wheels.

NEW LIVING TRANSLATION

moved to the entrance of the Temple. And the LORD called to the man dressed in linen who was carrying the writer's case. 4 He said to him, "Walk through the streets of Jerusalem and put a mark on the foreheads of all who weep and sigh because of the detestable sins being committed in their city."

5 Then I heard the LORD say to the other men, "Follow him through the city and kill everyone whose forehead is not marked. Show no mercy; have no pity! 6 Kill them all—old and young, girls and women and little children. But do not touch anyone with the mark. Begin right here at the Temple." So they began by killing the seventy leaders.

7 "Defile the Temple!" the LORD commanded. "Fill its courtyards with corpses. Go!" So they went and began killing throughout the city.

8 While they were out killing, I was all alone. I fell face down on the ground and cried out, "O Sovereign LORD! Will your fury against Jerusalem wipe out everyone left in Israel?"

9 Then he said to me, "The sins of the people of Israel and Judah are very, very great. The entire land is full of murder; the city is filled with injustice. They are saying, 'The LORD doesn't see it! The LORD has abandoned the land!' 10 So I will not spare them or have any pity on them. I will fully repay them for all they have done."

11 Then the man in linen clothing, who carried the writer's case, reported back and said, "I have done as you commanded."

The LORD's Glory Leaves the Temple

10 In my vision I saw what appeared to be a throne of blue lapis lazuli above the crystal surface over the heads of the cherubim. 2 Then the LORD spoke to the man in linen clothing and said, "Go between the whirling wheels beneath the cherubim, and take a handful of burning coals and scatter them over the city." He did this as I watched.

3 The cherubim were standing at the south end of the Temple when the man went in, and the cloud of glory filled the inner courtyard. 4 Then the glory of the LORD rose up from above the cherubim and went over to the door of the Temple. The Temple was filled with this cloud of glory, and the courtyard glowed brightly with the glory of the LORD. 5 The moving wings of the cherubim sounded like the voice of God Almighty* and could be heard even in the outer courtyard.

6 The LORD said to the man in linen clothing, "Go between the cherubim and take some burning coals from between the wheels." So the man went in and

10:5 Hebrew *El-Shaddai.*

KING JAMES VERSION

7And *one* cherub stretched forth his hand from between the cherubims unto the fire that *was* between the cherubims, and took *thereof,* and put *it* into the hands of *him that was* clothed with linen: who took *it,* and went out.

8And there appeared in the cherubims the form of a man's hand under their wings.

9And when I looked, behold the four wheels by the cherubims, one wheel by one cherub, and another wheel by another cherub: and the appearance of the wheels *was* as the colour of a beryl stone.

10And *as for* their appearances, they four had one likeness, as if a wheel had been in the midst of a wheel.

11When they went, they went upon their four sides; they turned not as they went, but to the place whither the head looked they followed it; they turned not as they went.

12And their whole body, and their backs, and their hands, and their wings, and the wheels, *were* full of eyes round about, *even* the wheels that they four had.

13As for the wheels, it was cried unto them in my hearing, O wheel.

14And every one had four faces: the first face *was* the face of a cherub, and the second face *was* the face of a man, and the third the face of a lion, and the fourth the face of an eagle.

15And the cherubims were lifted up. This *is* the living creature that I saw by the river of Chebar.

16And when the cherubims went, the wheels went by them: and when the cherubims lifted up their wings to mount up from the earth, the same wheels also turned not from beside them.

17When they stood, *these* stood; and when they were lifted up, *these* lifted up themselves *also:* for the spirit of the living creature *was* in them.

18Then the glory of the LORD departed from off the threshold of the house, and stood over the cherubims.

19And the cherubims lifted up their wings, and mounted up from the earth in my sight: when they went out, the wheels also *were* beside them, and *every one* stood at the door of the east gate of the LORD'S house; and the glory of the God of Israel *was* over them above.

20This *is* the living creature that I saw under the God of Israel by the river of Chebar; and I knew that they *were* the cherubims.

21Every one had four faces apiece, and every one four wings; and the likeness of the hands of a man *was* under their wings.

22And the likeness of their faces *was* the same faces which I saw by the river of Chebar, their appearances and themselves: they went every one straight forward.

NEW LIVING TRANSLATION

stood beside one of the wheels. 7Then one of the cherubim reached out his hand and took some live coals from the fire burning among them. He put the coals into the hands of the man in linen clothing, and the man took them and went out. 8(All the cherubim had what looked like human hands under their wings.)

9I looked, and each of the four cherubim had a wheel beside him, and the wheels sparkled like beryl. 10All four wheels looked alike and were made the same; each wheel had a second wheel turning crosswise within it. 11The cherubim could move in any of the four directions they faced, without turning as they moved. They went straight in the direction they faced, never turning aside. 12Both the cherubim and the wheels were covered with eyes. The cherubim had eyes all over their bodies, including their hands, their backs, and their wings. 13I heard someone refer to the wheels as "the whirling wheels." 14Each of the four cherubim had four faces: the first was the face of an ox,* the second was a human face, the third was the face of a lion, and the fourth was the face of an eagle.

15Then the cherubim rose upward. These were the same living beings I had seen beside the Kebar River. 16When the cherubim moved, the wheels moved with them. When they lifted their wings to fly, the wheels stayed beside them. 17When the cherubim stopped, the wheels stopped. When they flew upward, the wheels rose up, for the spirit of the living beings was in the wheels.

18Then the glory of the LORD moved out from the door of the Temple and hovered above the cherubim. 19And as I watched, the cherubim flew with their wheels to the east gate of the LORD'S Temple. And the glory of the God of Israel hovered above them.

20These were the same living beings I had seen beneath the God of Israel when I was by the Kebar River. I knew they were cherubim, 21for each had four faces and four wings and what looked like human hands under their wings. 22And their faces were just like the faces of the beings I had seen at the Kebar, and they traveled straight ahead, just as the others had.

10:14 Hebrew *the face of a cherub;* compare 1:10.

KING JAMES VERSION

11

1 Moreover the spirit lifted me up, and brought me unto the east gate of the LORD's house, which looketh eastward: and behold at the door of the gate five and twenty men; among whom I saw Jaazaniah the son of Azur, and Pelatiah the son of Benaiah, princes of the people.

2 Then said he unto me, Son of man, these *are* the men that devise mischief, and give wicked counsel in this city:

3 Which say, *It is* not near; let us build houses: this *city is* the caldron, and we *be* the flesh.

4 Therefore prophesy against them, prophesy, O son of man.

5 And the Spirit of the LORD fell upon me, and said unto me, Speak; Thus saith the LORD; Thus have ye said, O house of Israel: for I know the things that come into your mind, *every one of* them.

6 Ye have multiplied your slain in this city, and ye have filled the streets thereof with the slain.

7 Therefore thus saith the Lord GOD; Your slain whom ye have laid in the midst of it, they *are* the flesh, and this *city is* the caldron: but I will bring you forth out of the midst of it.

8 Ye have feared the sword; and I will bring a sword upon you, saith the Lord GOD.

9 And I will bring you out of the midst thereof, and deliver you into the hands of strangers, and will execute judgments among you.

10 Ye shall fall by the sword; I will judge you in the border of Israel; and ye shall know that I *am* the LORD.

11 This *city* shall not be your caldron, neither shall ye be the flesh in the midst thereof; *but* I will judge you in the border of Israel:

12 And ye shall know that I *am* the LORD: for ye have not walked in my statutes, neither executed my judgments, but have done after the manners of the heathen that *are* round about you.

13 And it came to pass, when I prophesied, that Pelatiah the son of Benaiah died. Then fell I down upon my face, and cried with a loud voice, and said, Ah Lord GOD! wilt thou make a full end of the remnant of Israel?

14 Again the word of the LORD came unto me, saying,

15 Son of man, thy brethren, *even* thy brethren, the men of thy kindred, and all the house of Israel wholly, *are* they unto whom the inhabitants of Jerusalem have said, Get you far from the LORD: unto us is this land given in possession.

16 Therefore say, Thus saith the Lord GOD; Although I have cast them far off among the heathen, and although I have scattered them among the countries, yet will I be to them as a little sanctuary in the countries where they shall come.

17 Therefore say, Thus saith the Lord GOD; I will even gather you from the people, and assemble you out of the countries where ye have been scattered, and I will give you the land of Israel.

NEW LIVING TRANSLATION

Judgment on Israel's Leaders

11

Then the Spirit lifted me and brought me to the east gateway of the LORD's Temple, where I saw twenty-five prominent men of the city. Among them were Jaazaniah son of Azzur and Pelatiah son of Benaiah, who were leaders among the people.

2 The Spirit said to me, "Son of man, these are the men who are planning evil and giving wicked counsel in this city. 3 They say to the people, 'Is it not a good time to build houses? This city is like an iron pot. We are safe inside it like meat in a pot.*' 4 Therefore, son of man, prophesy against them loudly and clearly."

5 Then the Spirit of the LORD came upon me, and he told me to say, "This is what the LORD says to the people of Israel: I know what you are saying, for I know every thought that comes into your minds. 6 You have murdered many in this city and filled its streets with the dead.

7 "Therefore, this is what the Sovereign LORD says: This city is an iron pot all right, but the pieces of meat are the victims of your injustice. As for you, I will soon drag you from this pot. 8 I will bring on you the sword of war you so greatly fear, says the Sovereign LORD. 9 I will drive you out of Jerusalem and hand you over to foreigners, who will carry out my judgments against you. 10 You will be slaughtered all the way to the borders of Israel. I will execute judgment on you, and you will know that I am the LORD. 11 No, this city will not be an iron pot for you, and you will not be like meat safe inside it. I will judge you even to the borders of Israel, 12 and you will know that I am the LORD. For you have refused to obey my decrees and regulations; instead, you have copied the standards of the nations around you."

13 While I was still prophesying, Pelatiah son of Benaiah suddenly died. Then I fell face down on the ground and cried out, "O Sovereign LORD, are you going to kill everyone in Israel?"

Hope for Exiled Israel

14 Then this message came to me from the LORD: 15 "Son of man, the people still left in Jerusalem are talking about you and your relatives and all the people of Israel who are in exile. They are saying, 'Those people are far away from the LORD, so now he has given their land to us!'

16 "Therefore, tell the exiles, 'This is what the Sovereign LORD says: Although I have scattered you in the countries of the world, I will be a sanctuary to you during your time in exile. 17 I, the Sovereign LORD, will gather you back from the nations where you have been scattered, and I will give you the land of Israel once again.'

11:3 Hebrew *This city is the pot, and we are the meat.*

KING JAMES VERSION

18 And they shall come thither, and they shall take
away all the detestable things thereof and all the
abominations thereof from thence.
19 And I will give them one heart, and I will put a
new spirit within you; and I will take the stony heart
out of their flesh, and will give them an heart of flesh:
20 That they may walk in my statutes, and keep
mine ordinances, and do them: and they shall be my
people, and I will be their God.
21 But *as for them* whose heart walketh after the
heart of their detestable things and their abominations, I will recompense their way upon their own
heads, saith the Lord GOD.
22 Then did the cherubims lift up their wings, and
the wheels beside them; and the glory of the God of
Israel *was* over them above.
23 And the glory of the LORD went up from the
midst of the city, and stood upon the mountain
which *is* on the east side of the city.
24 Afterwards the spirit took me up, and brought
me in a vision by the Spirit of God into Chaldea, to
them of the captivity. So the vision that I had seen
went up from me.
25 Then I spake unto them of the captivity all the
things that the LORD had shewed me.

12 1 The word of the LORD also came unto me,
saying,
2 Son of man, thou dwellest in the midst of a rebellious house, which have eyes to see, and see not; they
have ears to hear, and hear not: for they *are* a rebellious house.
3 Therefore, thou son of man, prepare thee stuff
for removing, and remove by day in their sight; and
thou shalt remove from thy place to another place in
their sight: it may be they will consider, though they
be a rebellious house.
4 Then shalt thou bring forth thy stuff by day in
their sight, as stuff for removing: and thou shalt go
forth at even in their sight, as they that go forth into
captivity.
5 Dig thou through the wall in their sight, and carry
out thereby.
6 In their sight shalt thou bear *it* upon *thy* shoulders, *and* carry *it* forth in the twilight: thou shalt
cover thy face, that thou see not the ground: for I
have set thee *for* a sign unto the house of Israel.
7 And I did so as I was commanded: I brought forth
my stuff by day, as stuff for captivity, and in the even I
digged through the wall with mine hand; I brought *it*
forth in the twilight, *and* I bare *it* upon *my* shoulder
in their sight.
8 And in the morning came the word of the LORD
unto me, saying,
9 Son of man, hath not the house of Israel, the rebellious house, said unto thee, What doest thou?
10 Say thou unto them, Thus saith the Lord GOD;

NEW LIVING TRANSLATION

18 "When the people return to their homeland,
they will remove every trace of their vile images and
detestable idols. 19 And I will give them singleness
of heart and put a new spirit within them. I will take
away their stony, stubborn heart and give them a
tender, responsive heart,* 20 so they will obey my
decrees and regulations. Then they will truly be my
people, and I will be their God. 21 But as for those who
long for vile images and detestable idols, I will repay
them fully for their sins. I, the Sovereign LORD, have
spoken!"

The LORD's Glory Leaves Jerusalem

22 Then the cherubim lifted their wings and rose into
the air with their wheels beside them, and the glory
of the God of Israel hovered above them. 23 Then the
glory of the LORD went up from the city and stopped
above the mountain to the east.
24 Afterward the Spirit of God carried me back
again to Babylonia,* to the people in exile there. And
so ended the vision of my visit to Jerusalem. 25 And I
told the exiles everything the LORD had shown me.

Signs of the Coming Exile

12 Again a message came to me from the LORD:
2 "Son of man, you live among rebels who
have eyes but refuse to see. They have ears but refuse
to hear. For they are a rebellious people.
3 "So now, son of man, pretend you are being sent
into exile. Pack the few items an exile could carry,
and leave your home to go somewhere else. Do this
right in front of the people so they can see you. For
perhaps they will pay attention to this, even though
they are such rebels. 4 Bring your baggage outside
during the day so they can watch you. Then in the
evening, as they are watching, leave your house as
captives do when they begin a long march to distant
lands. 5 Dig a hole through the wall while they are
watching and go out through it. 6 As they watch, lift
your pack to your shoulders and walk away into the
night. Cover your face so you cannot see the land you
are leaving. For I have made you a sign for the people
of Israel."
7 So I did as I was told. In broad daylight I brought
my pack outside, filled with the things I might carry
into exile. Then in the evening while the people
looked on, I dug through the wall with my hands and
went out into the night with my pack on my shoulder.
8 The next morning this message came to me from
the LORD: 9 "Son of man, these rebels, the people of
Israel, have asked you what all this means. 10 Say to
them, 'This is what the Sovereign LORD says: These

11:19 Hebrew *a heart of flesh.* **11:24** Or *Chaldea.*

KING JAMES VERSION

This burden *concerneth* the prince in Jerusalem, and
all the house of Israel that *are* among them.
11 Say, I *am* your sign: like as I have done, so shall it
be done unto them: they shall remove *and* go into
captivity.
12 And the prince that *is* among them shall bear
upon *his* shoulder in the twilight, and shall go forth:
they shall dig through the wall to carry out thereby:
he shall cover his face, that he see not the ground
with *his* eyes.
13 My net also will I spread upon him, and he shall
be taken in my snare: and I will bring him to Babylon
to the land of the Chaldeans; yet shall he not see it,
though he shall die there.
14 And I will scatter toward every wind all that *are*
about him to help him, and all his bands; and I will
draw out the sword after them.
15 And they shall know that I *am* the LORD, when I
shall scatter them among the nations, and disperse
them in the countries.
16 But I will leave a few men of them from the
sword, from the famine, and from the pestilence;
that they may declare all their abominations among
the heathen whither they come; and they shall know
that I *am* the LORD.
17 Moreover the word of the LORD came to me,
saying,
18 Son of man, eat thy bread with quaking, and
drink thy water with trembling and with carefulness;
19 And say unto the people of the land, Thus saith
the Lord GOD of the inhabitants of Jerusalem, *and* of
the land of Israel; They shall eat their bread with
carefulness, and drink their water with astonishment, that her land may be desolate from all that is
therein, because of the violence of all them that
dwell therein.
20 And the cities that are inhabited shall be laid
waste, and the land shall be desolate; and ye shall
know that I *am* the LORD.
21 And the word of the LORD came unto me, saying,
22 Son of man, what *is* that proverb *that* ye have in
the land of Israel, saying, The days are prolonged,
and every vision faileth?
23 Tell them therefore, Thus saith the Lord GOD;
I will make this proverb to cease, and they shall no
more use it as a proverb in Israel; but say unto them,
The days are at hand, and the effect of every vision.
24 For there shall be no more any vain vision nor
flattering divination within the house of Israel.
25 For I *am* the LORD: I will speak, and the word that
I shall speak shall come to pass; it shall be no more
prolonged: for in your days, O rebellious house, will
I say the word, and will perform it, saith the Lord GOD.
26 Again the word of the LORD came to me, saying,
27 Son of man, behold, *they of* the house of Israel
say, The vision that he seeth *is* for many days *to come*,
and he prophesieth of the times *that are* far off.
28 Therefore say unto them, Thus saith the Lord

NEW LIVING TRANSLATION

actions contain a message for King Zedekiah in Jerusalem* and for all the people of Israel.' 11 Explain that
your actions are a sign to show what will soon happen to them, for they will be driven into exile as
captives.
12 "Even Zedekiah will leave Jerusalem at night
through a hole in the wall, taking only what he can
carry with him. He will cover his face, and his eyes
will not see the land he is leaving. 13 Then I will throw
my net over him and capture him in my snare. I will
bring him to Babylon, the land of the Babylonians,*
though he will never see it, and he will die there. 14 I
will scatter his servants and warriors to the four
winds and send the sword after them. 15 And when I
scatter them among the nations, they will know that
I am the LORD. 16 But I will spare a few of them from
death by war, famine, or disease, so they can confess
all their detestable sins to their captors. Then they
will know that I am the LORD."
17 Then this message came to me from the LORD:
18 "Son of man, tremble as you eat your food. Shake
with fear as you drink your water. 19 Tell the people,
'This is what the Sovereign LORD says concerning
those living in Israel and Jerusalem: They will eat
their food with trembling and sip their water in despair, for their land will be stripped bare because of
their violence. 20 The cities will be destroyed and the
farmland made desolate. Then you will know that I
am the LORD.'"

A New Proverb for Israel

21 Again a message came to me from the LORD: 22 "Son
of man, you've heard that proverb they quote in Israel: 'Time passes, and prophecies come to nothing.'
23 Tell the people, 'This is what the Sovereign LORD
says: I will put an end to this proverb, and you will
soon stop quoting it.' Now give them this new proverb to replace the old one: 'The time has come for
every prophecy to be fulfilled!'
24 "There will be no more false visions and flattering
predictions in Israel. 25 For I am the LORD! If I say it, it
will happen. There will be no more delays, you rebels
of Israel. I will fulfill my threat of destruction in your
own lifetime. I, the Sovereign LORD, have spoken!"
26 Then this message came to me from the LORD:
27 "Son of man, the people of Israel are saying, 'He's
talking about the distant future. His visions won't
come true for a long, long time.' 28 Therefore, tell

12:10 Hebrew *the prince in Jerusalem;* similarly in 12:12. **12:13** Or *Chaldeans.*

KING JAMES VERSION

GOD; There shall none of my words be prolonged any
more, but the word which I have spoken shall be
done, saith the Lord GOD.

13 1 And the word of the LORD came unto me,
saying,
2 Son of man, prophesy against the prophets of
Israel that prophesy, and say thou unto them that
prophesy out of their own hearts, Hear ye the word
of the LORD;
3 Thus saith the Lord GOD; Woe unto the foolish
prophets, that follow their own spirit, and have seen
nothing!
4 O Israel, thy prophets are like the foxes in the
deserts.
5 Ye have not gone up into the gaps, neither made
up the hedge for the house of Israel to stand in the
battle in the day of the LORD.
6 They have seen vanity and lying divination, saying, The LORD saith: and the LORD hath not sent
them: and they have made *others* to hope that they
would confirm the word.
7 Have ye not seen a vain vision, and have ye not
spoken a lying divination, whereas ye say, The LORD
saith *it;* albeit I have not spoken?
8 Therefore thus saith the Lord GOD; Because ye
have spoken vanity, and seen lies, therefore, behold,
I *am* against you, saith the Lord GOD.
9 And mine hand shall be upon the prophets that
see vanity, and that divine lies: they shall not be in the
assembly of my people, neither shall they be written
in the writing of the house of Israel, neither shall
they enter into the land of Israel; and ye shall know
that I *am* the Lord GOD.
10 Because, even because they have seduced my
people, saying, Peace; and *there was* no peace; and
one built up a wall, and, lo, others daubed it with
untempered *mortar:*
11 Say unto them which daub *it* with untempered
mortar, that it shall fall: there shall be an overflowing shower; and ye, O great hailstones, shall fall;
and a stormy wind shall rend *it.*
12 Lo, when the wall is fallen, shall it not be said
unto you, Where *is* the daubing wherewith ye have
daubed *it?*
13 Therefore thus saith the Lord GOD; I will even
rend *it* with a stormy wind in my fury; and there shall
be an overflowing shower in mine anger, and great
hailstones in *my* fury to consume *it.*
14 So will I break down the wall that ye have
daubed with untempered *mortar,* and bring it down
to the ground, so that the foundation thereof shall be
discovered, and it shall fall, and ye shall be consumed in the midst thereof: and ye shall know that I
am the LORD.
15 Thus will I accomplish my wrath upon the wall,
and upon them that have daubed it with untempered

NEW LIVING TRANSLATION

them, 'This is what the Sovereign LORD says: No more
delay! I will now do everything I have threatened. I,
the Sovereign LORD, have spoken!'"

Judgment against False Prophets

13 Then this message came to me from the
LORD: 2 "Son of man, prophesy against the
false prophets of Israel who are inventing their own
prophecies. Say to them, 'Listen to the word of the
LORD. 3 This is what the Sovereign LORD says: What
sorrow awaits the false prophets who are following
their own imaginations and have seen nothing at all!'
4 "O people of Israel, these prophets of yours are
like jackals digging in the ruins. 5 They have done
nothing to repair the breaks in the walls around the
nation. They have not helped it to stand firm in battle on the day of the LORD. 6 Instead, they have told
lies and made false predictions. They say, 'This message is from the LORD,' even though the LORD never
sent them. And yet they expect him to fulfill their
prophecies! 7 Can your visions be anything but false
if you claim, 'This message is from the LORD,' when I
have not even spoken to you?
8 "Therefore, this is what the Sovereign LORD says:
Because what you say is false and your visions are a
lie, I will stand against you, says the Sovereign LORD.
9 I will raise my fist against all the prophets who see
false visions and make lying predictions, and they
will be banished from the community of Israel. I will
blot their names from Israel's record books, and they
will never again set foot in their own land. Then you
will know that I am the Sovereign LORD.
10 "This will happen because these evil prophets
deceive my people by saying, 'All is peaceful' when
there is no peace at all! It's as if the people have built
a flimsy wall, and these prophets are trying to reinforce it by covering it with whitewash! 11 Tell these
whitewashers that their wall will soon fall down. A
heavy rainstorm will undermine it; great hailstones
and mighty winds will knock it down. 12 And when
the wall falls, the people will cry out, 'What happened to your whitewash?'
13 "Therefore, this is what the Sovereign LORD says:
I will sweep away your whitewashed wall with a
storm of indignation, with a great flood of anger, and
with hailstones of fury. 14 I will break down your wall
right to its foundation, and when it falls, it will crush
you. Then you will know that I am the LORD. 15 At last
my anger against the wall and those who covered

mortar, and will say unto you, The wall *is* no *more,* neither they that daubed it;

16*To wit,* the prophets of Israel which prophesy concerning Jerusalem, and which see visions of peace for her, and *there is* no peace, saith the Lord GOD.

17Likewise, thou son of man, set thy face against the daughters of thy people, which prophesy out of their own heart; and prophesy thou against them,

18And say, Thus saith the Lord GOD; Woe to the *women* that sew pillows to all armholes, and make kerchiefs upon the head of every stature to hunt souls! Will ye hunt the souls of my people, and will ye save the souls alive *that come* unto you?

19And will ye pollute me among my people for handfuls of barley and for pieces of bread, to slay the souls that should not die, and to save the souls alive that should not live, by your lying to my people that hear *your* lies?

20Wherefore thus saith the Lord GOD; Behold, I *am* against your pillows, wherewith ye there hunt the souls to make *them* fly, and I will tear them from your arms, and will let the souls go, *even* the souls that ye hunt to make *them* fly.

21Your kerchiefs also will I tear, and deliver my people out of your hand, and they shall be no more in your hand to be hunted; and ye shall know that I *am* the LORD.

22Because with lies ye have made the heart of the righteous sad, whom I have not made sad; and strengthened the hands of the wicked, that he should not return from his wicked way, by promising him life:

23Therefore ye shall see no more vanity, nor divine divinations: for I will deliver my people out of your hand: and ye shall know that I *am* the LORD.

14 1Then came certain of the elders of Israel unto me, and sat before me.

2And the word of the LORD came unto me, saying,

3Son of man, these men have set up their idols in their heart, and put the stumblingblock of their iniquity before their face: should I be inquired of at all by them?

4Therefore speak unto them, and say unto them, Thus saith the Lord GOD; Every man of the house of Israel that setteth up his idols in his heart, and putteth the stumblingblock of his iniquity before his face, and cometh to the prophet; I the LORD will answer him that cometh according to the multitude of his idols;

5That I may take the house of Israel in their own heart, because they are all estranged from me through their idols.

6Therefore say unto the house of Israel, Thus saith the Lord GOD; Repent, and turn *yourselves* from your idols; and turn away your faces from all your abominations.

it with whitewash will be satisfied. Then I will say to you: 'The wall and those who whitewashed it are both gone. 16They were lying prophets who claimed peace would come to Jerusalem when there was no peace. I, the Sovereign LORD, have spoken!'

Judgment against False Women Prophets

17"Now, son of man, speak out against the women who prophesy from their own imaginations. 18This is what the Sovereign LORD says: What sorrow awaits you women who are ensnaring the souls of my people, young and old alike. You tie magic charms on their wrists and furnish them with magic veils. Do you think you can trap others without bringing destruction on yourselves? 19You bring shame on me among my people for a few handfuls of barley or a piece of bread. By lying to my people who love to listen to lies, you kill those who should not die, and you promise life to those who should not live.

20"This is what the Sovereign LORD says: I am against all your magic charms, which you use to ensnare my people like birds. I will tear them from your arms, setting my people free like birds set free from a cage. 21I will tear off the magic veils and save my people from your grasp. They will no longer be your victims. Then you will know that I am the LORD. 22You have discouraged the righteous with your lies, but I didn't want them to be sad. And you have encouraged the wicked by promising them life, even though they continue in their sins. 23Because of all this, you will no longer talk of seeing visions that you never saw, nor will you make predictions. For I will rescue my people from your grasp. Then you will know that I am the LORD."

The Idolatry of Israel's Leaders

14 Then some of the leaders of Israel visited me, and while they were sitting with me, 2this message came to me from the LORD: 3"Son of man, these leaders have set up idols* in their hearts. They have embraced things that will make them fall into sin. Why should I listen to their requests? 4Tell them, 'This is what the Sovereign LORD says: The people of Israel have set up idols in their hearts and fallen into sin, and then they go to a prophet asking for a message. So I, the LORD, will give them the kind of answer their great idolatry deserves. 5I will do this to capture the minds and hearts of all my people who have turned from me to worship their detestable idols.'

6"Therefore, tell the people of Israel, 'This is what the Sovereign LORD says: Repent and turn away from

14:3 The Hebrew term (literally *round things*) probably alludes to dung; also in 14:4, 5, 6, 7.

KING JAMES VERSION

7 For every one of the house of Israel, or of the stranger that sojourneth in Israel, which separateth himself from me, and setteth up his idols in his heart, and putteth the stumblingblock of his iniquity before his face, and cometh to a prophet to inquire of him concerning me; I the LORD will answer him by myself:

8 And I will set my face against that man, and will make him a sign and a proverb, and I will cut him off from the midst of my people; and ye shall know that I *am* the LORD.

9 And if the prophet be deceived when he hath spoken a thing, I the LORD have deceived that prophet, and I will stretch out my hand upon him, and will destroy him from the midst of my people Israel.

10 And they shall bear the punishment of their iniquity: the punishment of the prophet shall be even as the punishment of him that seeketh *unto him;*

11 That the house of Israel may go no more astray from me, neither be polluted any more with all their transgressions; but that they may be my people, and I may be their God, saith the Lord GOD.

12 The word of the LORD came again to me, saying,

13 Son of man, when the land sinneth against me by trespassing grievously, then will I stretch out mine hand upon it, and will break the staff of the bread thereof, and will send famine upon it, and will cut off man and beast from it:

14 Though these three men, Noah, Daniel, and Job, were in it, they should deliver *but* their own souls by their righteousness, saith the Lord GOD.

15 If I cause noisome beasts to pass through the land, and they spoil it, so that it be desolate, that no man may pass through because of the beasts:

16 *Though* these three men *were* in it, *as* I live, saith the Lord GOD, they shall deliver neither sons nor daughters; they only shall be delivered, but the land shall be desolate.

17 Or *if* I bring a sword upon that land, and say, Sword, go through the land; so that I cut off man and beast from it:

18 Though these three men *were* in it, *as* I live, saith the Lord GOD, they shall deliver neither sons nor daughters, but they only shall be delivered themselves.

19 Or *if* I send a pestilence into that land, and pour out my fury upon it in blood, to cut off from it man and beast:

20 Though Noah, Daniel, and Job, *were* in it, *as* I live, saith the Lord GOD, they shall deliver neither son nor daughter; they shall *but* deliver their own souls by their righteousness.

21 For thus saith the Lord GOD; How much more when I send my four sore judgments upon Jerusalem, the sword, and the famine, and the noisome beast, and the pestilence, to cut off from it man and beast?

22 Yet, behold, therein shall be left a remnant that shall be brought forth, *both* sons and daughters:

NEW LIVING TRANSLATION

your idols, and stop all your detestable sins. 7 I, the
LORD, will answer all those, both Israelites and foreigners, who reject me and set up idols in their
hearts and so fall into sin, and who then come to a
prophet asking for my advice. 8 I will turn against
such people and make a terrible example of them,
eliminating them from among my people. Then you
will know that I am the LORD.

9 "'And if a prophet is deceived into giving a message, it is because I, the LORD, have deceived that
prophet. I will lift my fist against such prophets and
cut them off from the community of Israel. 10 False
prophets and those who seek their guidance will all
be punished for their sins. 11 In this way, the people of
Israel will learn not to stray from me, polluting themselves with sin. They will be my people, and I will be
their God. I, the Sovereign LORD, have spoken!'"

The Certainty of the LORD's Judgment

12 Then this message came to me from the LORD:
13 "Son of man, suppose the people of a country were
to sin against me, and I lifted my fist to crush them,
cutting off their food supply and sending a famine
to destroy both people and animals. 14 Even if Noah,
Daniel, and Job were there, their righteousness
would save no one but themselves, says the Sovereign LORD.

15 "Or suppose I were to send wild animals to invade the country, kill the people, and make the land
too desolate and dangerous to pass through. 16 As
surely as I live, says the Sovereign LORD, even if those
three men were there, they wouldn't be able to save
their own sons or daughters. They alone would be
saved, but the land would be made desolate.

17 "Or suppose I were to bring war against the land,
and I sent enemy armies to destroy both people and
animals. 18 As surely as I live, says the Sovereign LORD,
even if those three men were there, they wouldn't be
able to save their own sons or daughters. They alone
would be saved.

19 "Or suppose I were to pour out my fury by sending an epidemic into the land, and the disease killed
people and animals alike. 20 As surely as I live, says
the Sovereign LORD, even if Noah, Daniel, and Job
were there, they wouldn't be able to save their own
sons or daughters. They alone would be saved by
their righteousness.

21 "Now this is what the Sovereign LORD says:
How terrible it will be when all four of these dreadful
punishments fall upon Jerusalem—war, famine, wild
animals, and disease—destroying all her people and
animals. 22 Yet there will be survivors, and they will

KING JAMES VERSION

behold, they shall come forth unto you, and ye shall
see their way and their doings: and ye shall be comforted concerning the evil that I have brought upon
Jerusalem, *even* concerning all that I have brought
upon it.
23And they shall comfort you, when ye see their
ways and their doings: and ye shall know that I have
not done without cause all that I have done in it, saith
the Lord GOD.

15 1And the word of the LORD came unto me,
saying,
2Son of man, What is the vine tree more than any
tree, *or than* a branch which is among the trees of the
forest?
3Shall wood be taken thereof to do any work? or
will *men* take a pin of it to hang any vessel thereon?
4Behold, it is cast into the fire for fuel; the fire
devoureth both the ends of it, and the midst of it is
burned. Is it meet for *any* work?
5Behold, when it was whole, it was meet for no
work: how much less shall it be meet yet for *any* work,
when the fire hath devoured it, and it is burned?
6Therefore thus saith the Lord GOD; As the vine
tree among the trees of the forest, which I have given
to the fire for fuel, so will I give the inhabitants of
Jerusalem.
7And I will set my face against them; they shall
go out from *one* fire, and *another* fire shall devour
them; and ye shall know that I *am* the LORD, when I
set my face against them.
8And I will make the land desolate, because they
have committed a trespass, saith the Lord GOD.

16 1Again the word of the LORD came unto me,
saying,
2Son of man, cause Jerusalem to know her abominations,
3And say, Thus saith the Lord GOD unto Jerusalem;
Thy birth and thy nativity *is* of the land of Canaan;
thy father *was* an Amorite, and thy mother an Hittite.
4And *as for* thy nativity, in the day thou wast born
thy navel was not cut, neither wast thou washed in
water to supple *thee;* thou wast not salted at all, nor
swaddled at all.
5None eye pitied thee, to do any of these unto thee,
to have compassion upon thee; but thou wast cast
out in the open field, to the lothing of thy person, in
the day that thou wast born.
6And when I passed by thee, and saw thee polluted
in thine own blood, I said unto thee *when thou wast*
in thy blood, Live; yea, I said unto thee *when thou
wast* in thy blood, Live.
7I have caused thee to multiply as the bud of the
field, and thou hast increased and waxen great, and
thou art come to excellent ornaments: *thy* breasts
are fashioned, and thine hair is grown, whereas thou
wast naked and bare.

NEW LIVING TRANSLATION

come here to join you as exiles in Babylon. You will
see with your own eyes how wicked they are, and
then you will feel better about what I have done to
Jerusalem. 23When you meet them and see their behavior, you will understand that these things are not
being done to Israel without cause. I, the Sovereign
LORD, have spoken!"

Jerusalem—a Useless Vine

15 Then this message came to me from the
LORD: 2"Son of man, how does a grapevine
compare to a tree? Is a vine's wood as useful as the
wood of a tree? 3Can its wood be used for making
things, like pegs to hang up pots and pans? 4No, it can
only be used for fuel, and even as fuel, it burns too
quickly. 5Vines are useless both before and after being put into the fire!
6"And this is what the Sovereign LORD says: The
people of Jerusalem are like grapevines growing
among the trees of the forest. Since they are useless, I
have thrown them on the fire to be burned. 7And I
will see to it that if they escape from one fire, they
will fall into another. When I turn against them,
you will know that I am the LORD. 8And I will make
the land desolate because my people have been unfaithful to me. I, the Sovereign LORD, have spoken!"

Jerusalem—an Unfaithful Wife

16 Then another message came to me from the
LORD: 2"Son of man, confront Jerusalem with
her detestable sins. 3Give her this message from the
Sovereign LORD: You are nothing but a Canaanite!
Your father was an Amorite and your mother a Hittite. 4On the day you were born, no one cared about
you. Your umbilical cord was not cut, and you were
never washed, rubbed with salt, and wrapped in
cloth. 5No one had the slightest interest in you; no
one pitied you or cared for you. On the day you were
born, you were unwanted, dumped in a field and left
to die.
6"But I came by and saw you there, helplessly kicking about in your own blood. As you lay there, I said,
'Live!' 7And I helped you to thrive like a plant in the
field. You grew up and became a beautiful jewel.
Your breasts became full, and your body hair grew,

8 Now when I passed by thee, and looked upon thee, behold, thy time *was* the time of love; and I spread my skirt over thee, and covered thy nakedness: yea, I sware unto thee, and entered into a covenant with thee, saith the Lord GOD, and thou becamest mine.

9 Then washed I thee with water; yea, I throughly washed away thy blood from thee, and I anointed thee with oil.

10 I clothed thee also with broidered work, and shod thee with badgers' skin, and I girded thee about with fine linen, and I covered thee with silk.

11 I decked thee also with ornaments, and I put bracelets upon thy hands, and a chain on thy neck.

12 And I put a jewel on thy forehead, and earrings in thine ears, and a beautiful crown upon thine head.

13 Thus wast thou decked with gold and silver; and thy raiment *was of* fine linen, and silk, and broidered work; thou didst eat fine flour, and honey, and oil: and thou wast exceeding beautiful, and thou didst prosper into a kingdom.

14 And thy renown went forth among the heathen for thy beauty: for it *was* perfect through my comeliness, which I had put upon thee, saith the Lord GOD.

15 But thou didst trust in thine own beauty, and playedst the harlot because of thy renown, and pouredst out thy fornications on every one that passed by; his it was.

16 And of thy garments thou didst take, and deckedst thy high places with divers colours, and playedst the harlot thereupon: *the like things* shall not come, neither shall it be *so.*

17 Thou hast also taken thy fair jewels of my gold and of my silver, which I had given thee, and madest to thyself images of men, and didst commit whoredom with them,

18 And tookest thy broidered garments, and coveredst them: and thou hast set mine oil and mine incense before them.

19 My meat also which I gave thee, fine flour, and oil, and honey, *wherewith* I fed thee, thou hast even set it before them for a sweet savour: and *thus* it was, saith the Lord GOD.

20 Moreover thou hast taken thy sons and thy daughters, whom thou hast borne unto me, and these hast thou sacrificed unto them to be devoured. *Is this* of thy whoredoms a small matter,

21 That thou hast slain my children, and delivered them to cause them to pass through *the fire* for them?

22 And in all thine abominations and thy whoredoms thou hast not remembered the days of thy youth, when thou wast naked and bare, *and* wast polluted in thy blood.

23 And it came to pass after all thy wickedness, (woe, woe unto thee! saith the Lord GOD;)

24 *That* thou hast also built unto thee an eminent place, and hast made thee an high place in every street.

but you were still naked. 8 And when I passed by again, I saw that you were old enough for love. So I wrapped my cloak around you to cover your nakedness and declared my marriage vows. I made a covenant with you, says the Sovereign LORD, and you became mine.

9 "Then I bathed you and washed off your blood, and I rubbed fragrant oils into your skin. 10 I gave you expensive clothing of fine linen and silk, beautifully embroidered, and sandals made of fine goatskin leather. 11 I gave you lovely jewelry, bracelets, beautiful necklaces, 12 a ring for your nose, earrings for your ears, and a lovely crown for your head. 13 And so you were adorned with gold and silver. Your clothes were made of fine linen and were beautifully embroidered. You ate the finest foods—choice flour, honey, and olive oil—and became more beautiful than ever. You looked like a queen, and so you were! 14 Your fame soon spread throughout the world because of your beauty. I dressed you in my splendor and perfected your beauty, says the Sovereign LORD.

15 "But you thought your fame and beauty were your own. So you gave yourself as a prostitute to every man who came along. Your beauty was theirs for the asking. 16 You used the lovely things I gave you to make shrines for idols, where you played the prostitute. Unbelievable! How could such a thing ever happen? 17 You took the very jewels and gold and silver ornaments I had given you and made statues of men and worshiped them. This is adultery against me! 18 You used the beautifully embroidered clothes I gave you to dress your idols. Then you used my special oil and my incense to worship them. 19 Imagine it! You set before them as a sacrifice the choice flour, olive oil, and honey I had given you, says the Sovereign LORD.

20 "Then you took your sons and daughters—the children you had borne to me—and sacrificed them to your gods. Was your prostitution not enough? 21 Must you also slaughter my children by sacrificing them to idols? 22 In all your years of adultery and detestable sin, you have not once remembered the days long ago when you lay naked in a field, kicking about in your own blood.

23 "What sorrow awaits you, says the Sovereign LORD. In addition to all your other wickedness, 24 you built a pagan shrine and put altars to idols in every

KING JAMES VERSION

[25]Thou hast built thy high place at every head of the way, and hast made thy beauty to be abhorred, and hast opened thy feet to every one that passed by, and multiplied thy whoredoms.

[26]Thou hast also committed fornication with the Egyptians thy neighbours, great of flesh; and hast increased thy whoredoms, to provoke me to anger.

[27]Behold, therefore I have stretched out my hand over thee, and have diminished thine ordinary *food,* and delivered thee unto the will of them that hate thee, the daughters of the Philistines, which are ashamed of thy lewd way.

[28]Thou hast played the whore also with the Assyrians, because thou wast unsatiable; yea, thou hast played the harlot with them, and yet couldest not be satisfied.

[29]Thou hast moreover multiplied thy fornication in the land of Canaan unto Chaldea; and yet thou wast not satisfied herewith.

[30]How weak is thine heart, saith the Lord GOD, seeing thou doest all these *things,* the work of an imperious whorish woman;

[31]In that thou buildest thine eminent place in the head of every way, and makest thine high place in every street; and hast not been as an harlot, in that thou scornest hire;

[32]*But as* a wife that committeth adultery, *which* taketh strangers instead of her husband!

[33]They give gifts to all whores: but thou givest thy gifts to all thy lovers, and hirest them, that they may come unto thee on every side for thy whoredom.

[34]And the contrary is in thee from *other* women in thy whoredoms, whereas none followeth thee to commit whoredoms: and in that thou givest a reward, and no reward is given unto thee, therefore thou art contrary.

[35]Wherefore, O harlot, hear the word of the LORD:

[36]Thus saith the Lord GOD; Because thy filthiness was poured out, and thy nakedness discovered through thy whoredoms with thy lovers, and with all the idols of thy abominations, and by the blood of thy children, which thou didst give unto them;

[37]Behold, therefore I will gather all thy lovers, with whom thou hast taken pleasure, and all *them* that thou hast loved, with all *them* that thou hast hated; I will even gather them round about against thee, and will discover thy nakedness unto them, that they may see all thy nakedness.

[38]And I will judge thee, as women that break wedlock and shed blood are judged; and I will give thee blood in fury and jealousy.

[39]And I will also give thee into their hand, and they shall throw down thine eminent place, and shall break down thy high places: they shall strip thee also of thy clothes, and shall take thy fair jewels, and leave thee naked and bare.

[40]They shall also bring up a company against thee,

NEW LIVING TRANSLATION

town square. [25]On every street corner you defiled
your beauty, offering your body to every passerby in
an endless stream of prostitution. [26]Then you added
lustful Egypt to your lovers, provoking my anger with
your increasing promiscuity. [27]That is why I struck
you with my fist and reduced your boundaries. I
handed you over to your enemies, the Philistines,
and even they were shocked by your lewd conduct.
[28]You have prostituted yourself with the Assyrians,
too. It seems you can never find enough new lovers!
And after your prostitution there, you still were not
satisfied. [29]You added to your lovers by embracing
Babylonia,* the land of merchants, but you still
weren't satisfied.

[30]"What a sick heart you have, says the Sovereign
LORD, to do such things as these, acting like a shameless prostitute. [31]You build your pagan shrines on
every street corner and your altars to idols in every
square. In fact, you have been worse than a prostitute, so eager for sin that you have not even demanded payment. [32]Yes, you are an adulterous wife
who takes in strangers instead of her own husband.
[33]Prostitutes charge for their services—but not you!
You give gifts to your lovers, bribing them to come
and have sex with you. [34]So you are the opposite of
other prostitutes. You pay your lovers instead of
their paying you!

Judgment on Jerusalem's Prostitution

[35]"Therefore, you prostitute, listen to this message
from the LORD! [36]This is what the Sovereign LORD
says: Because you have poured out your lust and exposed yourself in prostitution to all your lovers, and
because you have worshiped detestable idols,* and
because you have slaughtered your children as sacrifices to your gods, [37]this is what I am going to do. I
will gather together all your allies—the lovers with
whom you have sinned, both those you loved and
those you hated—and I will strip you naked in front
of them so they can stare at you. [38]I will punish you
for your murder and adultery. I will cover you with
blood in my jealous fury. [39]Then I will give you to
these many nations who are your lovers, and they
will destroy you. They will knock down your pagan
shrines and the altars to your idols. They will strip
you and take your beautiful jewels, leaving you stark
naked. [40]They will band together in a mob to stone

16:29 Or *Chaldea.* **16:36** The Hebrew term (literally *round things*) probably alludes to dung.

KING JAMES VERSION

and they shall stone thee with stones, and thrust thee
through with their swords.
41 And they shall burn thine houses with fire, and
execute judgments upon thee in the sight of many
women: and I will cause thee to cease from playing
the harlot, and thou also shalt give no hire any more.
42 So will I make my fury toward thee to rest, and
my jealousy shall depart from thee, and I will be
quiet, and will be no more angry.
43 Because thou hast not remembered the days of
thy youth, but hast fretted me in all these *things;* behold, therefore I also will recompense thy way upon
thine head, saith the Lord GOD: and thou shalt not
commit this lewdness above all thine abominations.
44 Behold, every one that useth proverbs shall use
this proverb against thee, saying, As *is* the mother, *so*
is her daughter.
45 Thou *art* thy mother's daughter, that lotheth her
husband and her children; and thou *art* the sister of
thy sisters, which lothed their husbands and their
children: your mother *was* an Hittite, and your father
an Amorite.

46 And thine elder sister *is* Samaria, she and her
daughters that dwell at thy left hand: and thy younger sister, that dwelleth at thy right hand, *is* Sodom
and her daughters.

47 Yet hast thou not walked after their ways, nor
done after their abominations: but, as *if that were* a
very little *thing,* thou wast corrupted more than they
in all thy ways.
48 *As* I live, saith the Lord GOD, Sodom thy sister
hath not done, she nor her daughters, as thou hast
done, thou and thy daughters.
49 Behold, this was the iniquity of thy sister Sodom, pride, fulness of bread, and abundance of idleness was in her and in her daughters, neither did she
strengthen the hand of the poor and needy.
50 And they were haughty, and committed abomination before me: therefore I took them away as I saw
good.
51 Neither hath Samaria committed half of thy
sins; but thou hast multiplied thine abominations
more than they, and hast justified thy sisters in all
thine abominations which thou hast done.
52 Thou also, which hast judged thy sisters, bear
thine own shame for thy sins that thou hast committed more abominable than they: they are more righteous than thou: yea, be thou confounded also, and
bear thy shame, in that thou hast justified thy sisters.
53 When I shall bring again their captivity, the captivity of Sodom and her daughters, and the captivity
of Samaria and her daughters, then *will I bring again*
the captivity of thy captives in the midst of them:
54 That thou mayest bear thine own shame, and
mayest be confounded in all that thou hast done, in
that thou art a comfort unto them.
55 When thy sisters, Sodom and her daughters, shall
return to their former estate, and Samaria and her

NEW LIVING TRANSLATION

you and cut you up with swords. 41 They will burn
your homes and punish you in front of many women.
I will stop your prostitution and end your payments
to your many lovers.
42 "Then at last my fury against you will be spent,
and my jealous anger will subside. I will be calm and
will not be angry with you anymore. 43 But first, because you have not remembered your youth but have
angered me by doing all these evil things, I will fully
repay you for all of your sins, says the Sovereign
LORD. For you have added lewd acts to all your detestable sins. 44 Everyone who makes up proverbs
will say of you, 'Like mother, like daughter.' 45 For
your mother loathed her husband and her children,
and so do you. And you are exactly like your sisters,
for they despised their husbands and their children.
Truly your mother was a Hittite and your father an
Amorite.
46 "Your older sister was Samaria, who lived with
her daughters in the north. Your younger sister was
Sodom, who lived with her daughters in the south.
47 But you have not merely sinned as they did. You
quickly surpassed them in corruption. 48 As surely as
I live, says the Sovereign LORD, Sodom and her
daughters were never as wicked as you and your
daughters. 49 Sodom's sins were pride, gluttony, and
laziness, while the poor and needy suffered outside
her door. 50 She was proud and committed detestable
sins, so I wiped her out, as you have seen.*
51 "Even Samaria did not commit half your sins.
You have done far more detestable things than your
sisters ever did. They seem righteous compared to
you. 52 Shame on you! Your sins are so terrible that
you make your sisters seem righteous, even virtuous.
53 "But someday I will restore the fortunes of Sodom and Samaria, and I will restore you, too. 54 Then
you will be truly ashamed of everything you have
done, for your sins make them feel good in comparison. 55 Yes, your sisters, Sodom and Samaria, and all

16:50 As in a few Hebrew manuscripts and Greek version; Masoretic Text reads *as I have seen.*

KING JAMES VERSION

daughters shall return to their former estate, then thou and thy daughters shall return to your former estate.

56 For thy sister Sodom was not mentioned by thy mouth in the day of thy pride,

57 Before thy wickedness was discovered, as at the time of *thy* reproach of the daughters of Syria, and all *that are* round about her, the daughters of the Philistines, which despise thee round about.

58 Thou hast borne thy lewdness and thine abominations, saith the LORD.

59 For thus saith the Lord GOD; I will even deal with thee as thou hast done, which hast despised the oath in breaking the covenant.

60 Nevertheless I will remember my covenant with thee in the days of thy youth, and I will establish unto thee an everlasting covenant.

61 Then thou shalt remember thy ways, and be ashamed, when thou shalt receive thy sisters, thine elder and thy younger: and I will give them unto thee for daughters, but not by thy covenant.

62 And I will establish my covenant with thee; and thou shalt know that I *am* the LORD:

63 That thou mayest remember, and be confounded, and never open thy mouth any more because of thy shame, when I am pacified toward thee for all that thou hast done, saith the Lord GOD.

17 1 And the word of the LORD came unto me, saying,

2 Son of man, put forth a riddle, and speak a parable unto the house of Israel;

3 And say, Thus saith the Lord GOD; A great eagle with great wings, longwinged, full of feathers, which had divers colours, came unto Lebanon, and took the highest branch of the cedar:

4 He cropped off the top of his young twigs, and carried it into a land of traffick; he set it in a city of merchants.

5 He took also of the seed of the land, and planted it in a fruitful field; he placed *it* by great waters, *and* set it *as* a willow tree.

6 And it grew, and became a spreading vine of low stature, whose branches turned toward him, and the roots thereof were under him: so it became a vine, and brought forth branches, and shot forth sprigs.

7 There was also another great eagle with great wings and many feathers: and, behold, this vine did bend her roots toward him, and shot forth her branches toward him, that he might water it by the furrows of her plantation.

8 It was planted in a good soil by great waters, that it might bring forth branches, and that it might bear fruit, that it might be a goodly vine.

NEW LIVING TRANSLATION

their people will be restored, and at that time you also will be restored. 56 In your proud days you held Sodom in contempt. 57 But now your greater wickedness has been exposed to all the world, and you are the one who is scorned—by Edom* and all her neighbors and by Philistia. 58 This is your punishment for all your lewdness and detestable sins, says the LORD.

59 "Now this is what the Sovereign LORD says: I will give you what you deserve, for you have taken your solemn vows lightly by breaking your covenant. 60 Yet I will remember the covenant I made with you when you were young, and I will establish an everlasting covenant with you. 61 Then you will remember with shame all the evil you have done. I will make your sisters, Samaria and Sodom, to be your daughters, even though they are not part of our covenant. 62 And I will reaffirm my covenant with you, and you will know that I am the LORD. 63 You will remember your sins and cover your mouth in silent shame when I forgive you of all that you have done. I, the Sovereign LORD, have spoken!"

A Story of Two Eagles

17 Then this message came to me from the LORD: 2 "Son of man, give this riddle, and tell this story to the people of Israel. 3 Give them this message from the Sovereign LORD:

"A great eagle with broad wings and long feathers,
covered with many-colored plumage,
came to Lebanon.
He seized the top of a cedar tree
4 and plucked off its highest branch.
He carried it away to a city filled with merchants.
He planted it in a city of traders.
5 He also took a seedling from the land
and planted it in fertile soil.
He placed it beside a broad river,
where it could grow like a willow tree.
6 It took root there and
grew into a low, spreading vine.
Its branches turned up toward the eagle,
and its roots grew down into the ground.
It produced strong branches
and put out shoots.
7 But then another great eagle came
with broad wings and full plumage.
So the vine now sent its roots and branches
toward him for water,
8 even though it was already planted in good soil
and had plenty of water
so it could grow into a splendid vine
and produce rich leaves and luscious fruit.

16:57 As in many Hebrew manuscripts and Syriac version; Masoretic Text reads *Aram.*

KING JAMES VERSION

9 Say thou, Thus saith the Lord GOD; Shall it prosper? shall he not pull up the roots thereof, and cut off the fruit thereof, that it wither? it shall wither in all the leaves of her spring, even without great power or many people to pluck it up by the roots thereof.

10 Yea, behold, *being* planted, shall it prosper? shall it not utterly wither, when the east wind toucheth it? it shall wither in the furrows where it grew.

11 Moreover the word of the LORD came unto me, saying,

12 Say now to the rebellious house, Know ye not what these *things mean?* tell *them,* Behold, the king of Babylon is come to Jerusalem, and hath taken the king thereof, and the princes thereof, and led them with him to Babylon;

13 And hath taken of the king's seed, and made a covenant with him, and hath taken an oath of him: he hath also taken the mighty of the land:

14 That the kingdom might be base, that it might not lift itself up, *but* that by keeping of his covenant it might stand.

15 But he rebelled against him in sending his ambassadors into Egypt, that they might give him horses and much people. Shall he prosper? shall he escape that doeth such *things?* or shall he break the covenant, and be delivered?

16 *As* I live, saith the Lord GOD, surely in the place *where* the king *dwelleth* that made him king, whose oath he despised, and whose covenant he brake, *even* with him in the midst of Babylon he shall die.

17 Neither shall Pharaoh with *his* mighty army and great company make for him in the war, by casting up mounts, and building forts, to cut off many persons:

18 Seeing he despised the oath by breaking the covenant, when, lo, he had given his hand, and hath done all these *things,* he shall not escape.

19 Therefore thus saith the Lord GOD; *As* I live, surely mine oath that he hath despised, and my covenant that he hath broken, even it will I recompense upon his own head.

20 And I will spread my net upon him, and he shall be taken in my snare, and I will bring him to Babylon, and will plead with him there for his trespass that he hath trespassed against me.

21 And all his fugitives with all his bands shall fall by the sword, and they that remain shall be scattered toward all winds: and ye shall know that I the LORD have spoken *it.*

22 Thus saith the Lord GOD; I will also take of the highest branch of the high cedar, and will set *it;* I will crop off from the top of his young twigs a tender one,

NEW LIVING TRANSLATION

9 "So now the Sovereign LORD asks:
Will this vine grow and prosper?
No! I will pull it up, roots and all!
I will cut off its fruit
and let its leaves wither and die.
I will pull it up easily
without a strong arm or a large army.
10 But when the vine is transplanted,
will it thrive?
No, it will wither away
when the east wind blows against it.
It will die in the same good soil
where it had grown so well."

The Riddle Explained

11 Then this message came to me from the LORD: 12 "Say to these rebels of Israel: Don't you understand the meaning of this riddle of the eagles? The king of Babylon came to Jerusalem, took away her king and princes, and brought them to Babylon. 13 He made a treaty with a member of the royal family and forced him to take an oath of loyalty. He also exiled Israel's most influential leaders, 14 so Israel would not become strong again and revolt. Only by keeping her treaty with Babylon could Israel survive.

15 "Nevertheless, this man of Israel's royal family rebelled against Babylon, sending ambassadors to Egypt to request a great army and many horses. Can Israel break her sworn treaties like that and get away with it? 16 No! For as surely as I live, says the Sovereign LORD, the king of Israel will die in Babylon, the land of the king who put him in power and whose treaty he disregarded and broke. 17 Pharaoh and all his mighty army will fail to help Israel when the king of Babylon lays siege to Jerusalem again and destroys many lives. 18 For the king of Israel disregarded his treaty and broke it after swearing to obey; therefore, he will not escape.

19 "So this is what the Sovereign LORD says: As surely as I live, I will punish him for breaking my covenant and disregarding the solemn oath he made in my name. 20 I will throw my net over him and capture him in my snare. I will bring him to Babylon and put him on trial for this treason against me. 21 And all his best warriors* will be killed in battle, and those who survive will be scattered to the four winds. Then you will know that I, the LORD, have spoken.

22 "This is what the Sovereign LORD says: I will take

17:21 Or *his fleeing warriors.* The meaning of the Hebrew is uncertain.

KING JAMES VERSION

and will plant *it* upon an high mountain and eminent:

23In the mountain of the height of Israel will I plant it: and it shall bring forth boughs, and bear fruit, and be a goodly cedar: and under it shall dwell all fowl of every wing; in the shadow of the branches thereof shall they dwell.

24And all the trees of the field shall know that I the LORD have brought down the high tree, have exalted the low tree, have dried up the green tree, and have made the dry tree to flourish: I the LORD have spoken and have done *it*.

18 1The word of the LORD came unto me again, saying,

2What mean ye, that ye use this proverb concerning the land of Israel, saying, The fathers have eaten sour grapes, and the children's teeth are set on edge?

3*As* I live, saith the Lord GOD, ye shall not have *occasion* any more to use this proverb in Israel.

4Behold, all souls are mine; as the soul of the father, so also the soul of the son is mine: the soul that sinneth, it shall die.

5But if a man be just, and do that which is lawful and right,

6*And* hath not eaten upon the mountains, neither hath lifted up his eyes to the idols of the house of Israel, neither hath defiled his neighbour's wife, neither hath come near to a menstruous woman,

7And hath not oppressed any, *but* hath restored to the debtor his pledge, hath spoiled none by violence, hath given his bread to the hungry, and hath covered the naked with a garment;

8He *that* hath not given forth upon usury, neither hath taken any increase, *that* hath withdrawn his hand from iniquity, hath executed true judgment between man and man,

9Hath walked in my statutes, and hath kept my judgments, to deal truly; he *is* just, he shall surely live, saith the Lord GOD.

10If he beget a son *that is* a robber, a shedder of blood, and *that* doeth the like to *any* one of these *things*,

11And that doeth not any of those *duties*, but even hath eaten upon the mountains, and defiled his neighbour's wife,

12Hath oppressed the poor and needy, hath spoiled by violence, hath not restored the pledge, and hath lifted up his eyes to the idols, hath committed abomination,

13Hath given forth upon usury, and hath taken increase: shall he then live? he shall not live: he hath done all these abominations; he shall surely die; his blood shall be upon him.

14Now, lo, *if* he beget a son, that seeth all his father's sins which he hath done, and considereth, and doeth not such like,

15*That* hath not eaten upon the mountains, neither

NEW LIVING TRANSLATION

a branch from the top of a tall cedar, and I will plant it
on the top of Israel's highest mountain. 23It will become a majestic cedar, sending forth its branches
and producing seed. Birds of every sort will nest in it,
finding shelter in the shade of its branches. 24And all
the trees will know that it is I, the LORD, who cuts the
tall tree down and makes the short tree grow tall. It is
I who makes the green tree wither and gives the dead
tree new life. I, the LORD, have spoken, and I will do
what I said!"

The Justice of a Righteous God

18 Then another message came to me from the
LORD: 2"Why do you quote this proverb concerning the land of Israel: 'The parents have eaten
sour grapes, but their children's mouths pucker at
the taste'? 3As surely as I live, says the Sovereign
LORD, you will not quote this proverb anymore in Israel. 4For all people are mine to judge—both parents
and children alike. And this is my rule: The person
who sins is the one who will die.

5"Suppose a certain man is righteous and does
what is just and right. 6He does not feast in the
mountains before Israel's idols* or worship them.
He does not commit adultery or have intercourse
with a woman during her menstrual period. 7He is
a merciful creditor, not keeping the items given as
security by poor debtors. He does not rob the poor
but instead gives food to the hungry and provides
clothes for the needy. 8He grants loans without interest, stays away from injustice, is honest and fair when
judging others, 9and faithfully obeys my decrees and
regulations. Anyone who does these things is just
and will surely live, says the Sovereign LORD.

10"But suppose that man has a son who grows up
to be a robber or murderer and refuses to do what is
right. 11And that son does all the evil things his father would never do—he worships idols on the
mountains, commits adultery, 12oppresses the poor
and helpless, steals from debtors by refusing to let
them redeem their security, worships idols, commits
detestable sins, 13and lends money at excessive interest. Should such a sinful person live? No! He must
die and must take full blame.

14"But suppose that sinful son, in turn, has a son
who sees his father's wickedness and decides against
that kind of life. 15This son refuses to worship idols

18:6 The Hebrew term (literally *round things*) probably alludes to dung; also in 18:12, 15.

hath lifted up his eyes to the idols of the house of Israel, hath not defiled his neighbour's wife,

16 Neither hath oppressed any, hath not withholden the pledge, neither hath spoiled by violence, *but* hath given his bread to the hungry, and hath covered the naked with a garment,

17 *That* hath taken off his hand from the poor, *that* hath not received usury nor increase, hath executed my judgments, hath walked in my statutes; he shall not die for the iniquity of his father, he shall surely live.

18 *As for* his father, because he cruelly oppressed, spoiled his brother by violence, and did *that* which *is* not good among his people, lo, even he shall die in his iniquity.

19 Yet say ye, Why? doth not the son bear the iniquity of the father? When the son hath done that which is lawful and right, *and* hath kept all my statutes, and hath done them, he shall surely live.

20 The soul that sinneth, it shall die. The son shall not bear the iniquity of the father, neither shall the father bear the iniquity of the son: the righteousness of the righteous shall be upon him, and the wickedness of the wicked shall be upon him.

21 But if the wicked will turn from all his sins that he hath committed, and keep all my statutes, and do that which is lawful and right, he shall surely live, he shall not die.

22 All his transgressions that he hath committed, they shall not be mentioned unto him: in his righteousness that he hath done he shall live.

23 Have I any pleasure at all that the wicked should die? saith the Lord GOD: *and* not that he should return from his ways, and live?

24 But when the righteous turneth away from his righteousness, and committeth iniquity, *and* doeth according to all the abominations that the wicked *man* doeth, shall he live? All his righteousness that he hath done shall not be mentioned: in his trespass that he hath trespassed, and in his sin that he hath sinned, in them shall he die.

25 Yet ye say, The way of the LORD is not equal. Hear now, O house of Israel; Is not my way equal? are not your ways unequal?

26 When a righteous *man* turneth away from his righteousness, and committeth iniquity, and dieth in them; for his iniquity that he hath done shall he die.

27 Again, when the wicked *man* turneth away from his wickedness that he hath committed, and doeth that which is lawful and right, he shall save his soul alive.

28 Because he considereth, and turneth away from all his transgressions that he hath committed, he shall surely live, he shall not die.

29 Yet saith the house of Israel, The way of the LORD is not equal. O house of Israel, are not my ways equal? are not your ways unequal?

30 Therefore I will judge you, O house of Israel,

on the mountains and does not commit adultery.
16 He does not exploit the poor, but instead is fair to
debtors and does not rob them. He gives food to the
hungry and provides clothes for the needy. 17 He
helps the poor,* does not lend money at interest, and
obeys all my regulations and decrees. Such a person
will not die because of his father's sins; he will surely
live. 18 But the father will die for his many sins—for
being cruel, robbing people, and doing what was
clearly wrong among his people.

19 "'What?' you ask. 'Doesn't the child pay for the
parent's sins?' No! For if the child does what is just
and right and keeps my decrees, that child will surely
live. 20 The person who sins is the one who will die.
The child will not be punished for the parent's sins,
and the parent will not be punished for the child's
sins. Righteous people will be rewarded for their
own righteous behavior, and wicked people will be
punished for their own wickedness. 21 But if wicked
people turn away from all their sins and begin to
obey my decrees and do what is just and right, they
will surely live and not die. 22 All their past sins will be
forgotten, and they will live because of the righteous
things they have done.

23 "Do you think that I like to see wicked people
die? says the Sovereign LORD. Of course not! I want
them to turn from their wicked ways and live.
24 However, if righteous people turn from their righteous behavior and start doing sinful things and act
like other sinners, should they be allowed to live?
No, of course not! All their righteous acts will be forgotten, and they will die for their sins.

25 "Yet you say, 'The Lord isn't doing what's right!'
Listen to me, O people of Israel. Am I the one not
doing what's right, or is it you? 26 When righteous
people turn from their righteous behavior and start
doing sinful things, they will die for it. Yes, they will
die because of their sinful deeds. 27 And if wicked
people turn from their wickedness, obey the law, and
do what is just and right, they will save their lives.
28 They will live because they thought it over and decided to turn from their sins. Such people will not
die. 29 And yet the people of Israel keep saying, 'The
Lord isn't doing what's right!' O people of Israel, it is
you who are not doing what's right, not I.

30 "Therefore, I will judge each of you, O people of

18:17 Greek version reads *He refuses to do evil.*

KING JAMES VERSION

every one according to his ways, saith the Lord GOD.
Repent, and turn *yourselves* from all your transgressions; so iniquity shall not be your ruin.
31 Cast away from you all your transgressions,
whereby ye have transgressed; and make you a new
heart and a new spirit: for why will ye die, O house of
Israel?
32 For I have no pleasure in the death of him that
dieth, saith the Lord GOD: wherefore turn *yourselves*,
and live ye.

19 1 Moreover take thou up a lamentation for the
princes of Israel,
2 And say, What *is* thy mother? A lioness: she lay
down among lions, she nourished her whelps among
young lions.
3 And she brought up one of her whelps: it became
a young lion, and it learned to catch the prey; it devoured men.
4 The nations also heard of him; he was taken in
their pit, and they brought him with chains unto the
land of Egypt.
5 Now when she saw that she had waited, *and* her
hope was lost, then she took another of her whelps,
and made him a young lion.
6 And he went up and down among the lions, he
became a young lion, and learned to catch the prey,
and devoured men.
7 And he knew their desolate palaces, and he laid
waste their cities; and the land was desolate, and the
fulness thereof, by the noise of his roaring.
8 Then the nations set against him on every side
from the provinces, and spread their net over him:
he was taken in their pit.
9 And they put him in ward in chains, and brought
him to the king of Babylon: they brought him into
holds, that his voice should no more be heard upon
the mountains of Israel.
10 Thy mother *is* like a vine in thy blood, planted
by the waters: she was fruitful and full of branches
by reason of many waters.
11 And she had strong rods for the sceptres of
them that bare rule, and her stature was exalted

NEW LIVING TRANSLATION

Israel, according to your actions, says the Sovereign
LORD. Repent, and turn from your sins. Don't let
them destroy you! 31 Put all your rebellion behind
you, and find yourselves a new heart and a new spirit.
For why should you die, O people of Israel? 32 I don't
want you to die, says the Sovereign LORD. Turn back
and live!

A Funeral Song for Israel's Kings

19 "Sing this funeral song for the princes of Israel:
2 "What is your mother?
A lioness among lions!
She lay down among the young lions
and reared her cubs.
3 She raised one of her cubs
to become a strong young lion.
He learned to hunt and devour prey,
and he became a man-eater.
4 Then the nations heard about him,
and he was trapped in their pit.
They led him away with hooks
to the land of Egypt.

5 "When the lioness saw
that her hopes for him were gone,
she took another of her cubs
and taught him to be a strong young lion.
6 He prowled among the other lions
and stood out among them in his strength.
He learned to hunt and devour prey,
and he, too, became a man-eater.
7 He demolished fortresses*
and destroyed their towns and cities.
Their farms were desolated,
and their crops were destroyed.
The land and its people trembled in fear
when they heard him roar.
8 Then the armies of the nations attacked him,
surrounding him from every direction.
They threw a net over him
and captured him in their pit.
9 With hooks, they dragged him into a cage
and brought him before the king of Babylon.
They held him in captivity,
so his voice could never again be heard
on the mountains of Israel.

10 "Your mother was like a vine
planted by the water's edge.
It had lush, green foliage
because of the abundant water.
11 Its branches became strong—
strong enough to be a ruler's scepter.
It grew very tall,
towering above all others.

19:7 As in Greek version; Hebrew reads *He knew widows*.

KING JAMES VERSION

among the thick branches, and she appeared in her
height with the multitude of her branches.
12But she was plucked up in fury, she was cast
down to the ground, and the east wind dried up her
fruit: her strong rods were broken and withered;
the fire consumed them.
13And now she *is* planted in the wilderness, in a
dry and thirsty ground.
14And fire is gone out of a rod of her branches,
which hath devoured her fruit, so that she hath no
strong rod *to be* a sceptre to rule. This *is* a lamentation, and shall be for a lamentation.

20 1And it came to pass in the seventh year,
in the fifth *month*, the tenth *day* of the
month, *that* certain of the elders of Israel came to
inquire of the LORD, and sat before me.
2Then came the word of the LORD unto me, saying,
3Son of man, speak unto the elders of Israel, and
say unto them, Thus saith the Lord GOD; Are ye come
to inquire of me? *As* I live, saith the Lord GOD, I will
not be inquired of by you.
4Wilt thou judge them, son of man, wilt thou judge
them? cause them to know the abominations of their
fathers:
5And say unto them, Thus saith the Lord GOD; In the
day when I chose Israel, and lifted up mine hand unto
the seed of the house of Jacob, and made myself
known unto them in the land of Egypt, when I lifted up
mine hand unto them, saying, I *am* the LORD your God;
6In the day *that* I lifted up mine hand unto them,
to bring them forth of the land of Egypt into a land
that I had espied for them, flowing with milk and
honey, which *is* the glory of all lands:
7Then said I unto them, Cast ye away every man the
abominations of his eyes, and defile not yourselves
with the idols of Egypt: I *am* the LORD your God.
8But they rebelled against me, and would not hearken unto me: they did not every man cast away the
abominations of their eyes, neither did they forsake
the idols of Egypt: then I said, I will pour out my fury
upon them, to accomplish my anger against them in
the midst of the land of Egypt.
9But I wrought for my name's sake, that it should
not be polluted before the heathen, among whom
they *were*, in whose sight I made myself known unto
them, in bringing them forth out of the land of
Egypt.
10Wherefore I caused them to go forth out of the
land of Egypt, and brought them into the wilderness.
11And I gave them my statutes, and shewed them
my judgments, which *if* a man do, he shall even live
in them.

NEW LIVING TRANSLATION

It stood out because of its height
and its many lush branches.
12 But the vine was uprooted in fury
and thrown down to the ground.
The desert wind dried up its fruit
and tore off its strong branches,
so that it withered
and was destroyed by fire.
13 Now the vine is transplanted to the wilderness,
where the ground is hard and dry.
14 A fire has burst out from its branches
and devoured its fruit.
Its remaining limbs are not
strong enough to be a ruler's scepter.
"This is a funeral song, and it will be used in a funeral."

The Rebellion of Israel

20 On August 14,* during the seventh year of
King Jehoiachin's captivity, some of the
leaders of Israel came to request a message from the
LORD. They sat down in front of me to wait for his reply. 2Then this message came to me from the LORD:
3"Son of man, tell the leaders of Israel, 'This is what
the Sovereign LORD says: How dare you come to ask
me for a message? As surely as I live, says the Sovereign LORD, I will tell you nothing!'
4"Son of man, bring charges against them and
condemn them. Make them realize how detestable
the sins of their ancestors really were. 5Give them
this message from the Sovereign LORD: When I
chose Israel—when I revealed myself to the descendants of Jacob in Egypt—I took a solemn oath that I,
the LORD, would be their God. 6I took a solemn oath
that day that I would bring them out of Egypt to a
land I had discovered and explored for them—a good
land, a land flowing with milk and honey, the best of
all lands anywhere. 7Then I said to them, 'Each of
you, get rid of the vile images you are so obsessed
with. Do not defile yourselves with the idols* of
Egypt, for I am the LORD your God.'
8"But they rebelled against me and would not listen. They did not get rid of the vile images they were
obsessed with, or forsake the idols of Egypt. Then I
threatened to pour out my fury on them to satisfy my
anger while they were still in Egypt. 9But I didn't do it,
for I acted to protect the honor of my name. I would
not allow shame to be brought on my name among
the surrounding nations who saw me reveal myself by
bringing the Israelites out of Egypt. 10So I brought
them out of Egypt and led them into the wilderness.
11There I gave them my decrees and regulations so

20:1 Hebrew *In the fifth month, on the tenth day,* of the ancient Hebrew lunar calendar. This day was August 14, 591 B.C.; also see note on 1:1. **20:7** The Hebrew term (literally *round things*) probably alludes to dung; also in 20:8, 16, 18, 24, 31, 39.

KING JAMES VERSION

12Moreover also I gave them my sabbaths, to be a sign between me and them, that they might know that I *am* the Lord that sanctify them.

13But the house of Israel rebelled against me in the wilderness: they walked not in my statutes, and they despised my judgments, which *if* a man do, he shall even live in them; and my sabbaths they greatly polluted: then I said, I would pour out my fury upon them in the wilderness, to consume them.

14But I wrought for my name's sake, that it should not be polluted before the heathen, in whose sight I brought them out.

15Yet also I lifted up my hand unto them in the wilderness, that I would not bring them into the land which I had given *them,* flowing with milk and honey, which *is* the glory of all lands;

16Because they despised my judgments, and walked not in my statutes, but polluted my sabbaths: for their heart went after their idols.

17Nevertheless mine eye spared them from destroying them, neither did I make an end of them in the wilderness.

18But I said unto their children in the wilderness, Walk ye not in the statutes of your fathers, neither observe their judgments, nor defile yourselves with their idols:

19I *am* the Lord your God; walk in my statutes, and keep my judgments, and do them;

20And hallow my sabbaths; and they shall be a sign between me and you, that ye may know that I *am* the Lord your God.

21Notwithstanding the children rebelled against me: they walked not in my statutes, neither kept my judgments to do them, which *if* a man do, he shall even live in them; they polluted my sabbaths: then I said, I would pour out my fury upon them, to accomplish my anger against them in the wilderness.

22Nevertheless I withdrew mine hand, and wrought for my name's sake, that it should not be polluted in the sight of the heathen, in whose sight I brought them forth.

23I lifted up mine hand unto them also in the wilderness, that I would scatter them among the heathen, and disperse them through the countries;

24Because they had not executed my judgments, but had despised my statutes, and had polluted my sabbaths, and their eyes were after their fathers' idols.

25Wherefore I gave them also statutes *that were* not good, and judgments whereby they should not live;

26And I polluted them in their own gifts, in that they caused to pass through *the fire* all that openeth the womb, that I might make them desolate, to the end that they might know that I *am* the Lord.

27Therefore, son of man, speak unto the house of Israel, and say unto them, Thus saith the Lord God; Yet in this your fathers have blasphemed me, in that they have committed a trespass against me.

NEW LIVING TRANSLATION

they could find life by keeping them. 12And I gave them my Sabbath days of rest as a sign between them and me. It was to remind them that I am the Lord, who had set them apart to be holy.

13"But the people of Israel rebelled against me, and they refused to obey my decrees there in the wilderness. They wouldn't obey my regulations even though obedience would have given them life. They also violated my Sabbath days. So I threatened to pour out my fury on them, and I made plans to utterly consume them in the wilderness. 14But again I held back in order to protect the honor of my name before the nations who had seen my power in bringing Israel out of Egypt. 15But I took a solemn oath against them in the wilderness. I swore I would not bring them into the land I had given them, a land flowing with milk and honey, the most beautiful place on earth. 16For they had rejected my regulations, refused to follow my decrees, and violated my Sabbath days. Their hearts were given to their idols. 17Nevertheless, I took pity on them and held back from destroying them in the wilderness.

18"Then I warned their children not to follow in their parents' footsteps, defiling themselves with their idols. 19'I am the Lord your God,' I told them. 'Follow my decrees, pay attention to my regulations, 20and keep my Sabbath days holy, for they are a sign to remind you that I am the Lord your God.'

21"But their children, too, rebelled against me. They refused to keep my decrees and follow my regulations, even though obedience would have given them life. And they also violated my Sabbath days. So again I threatened to pour out my fury on them in the wilderness. 22Nevertheless, I withdrew my judgment against them to protect the honor of my name before the nations that had seen my power in bringing them out of Egypt. 23But I took a solemn oath against them in the wilderness. I swore I would scatter them among all the nations 24because they did not obey my regulations. They scorned my decrees by violating my Sabbath days and longing for the idols of their ancestors. 25I gave them over to worthless decrees and regulations that would not lead to life. 26I let them pollute themselves* with the very gifts I had given them, and I allowed them to give their firstborn children as offerings to their gods—so I might devastate them and remind them that I alone am the Lord.

Judgment and Restoration

27"Therefore, son of man, give the people of Israel this message from the Sovereign Lord: Your ancestors

20:25-26 Or *I gave them worthless decrees and regulations. . . . I polluted them.*

28*For* when I had brought them into the land, *for* the which I lifted up mine hand to give it to them, then they saw every high hill, and all the thick trees, and they offered there their sacrifices, and there they presented the provocation of their offering: there also they made their sweet savour, and poured out there their drink offerings.

29Then I said unto them, What *is* the high place whereunto ye go? And the name thereof is called Bamah unto this day.

30Wherefore say unto the house of Israel, Thus saith the Lord GOD; Are ye polluted after the manner of your fathers? and commit ye whoredom after their abominations?

31For when ye offer your gifts, when ye make your sons to pass through the fire, ye pollute yourselves with all your idols, even unto this day: and shall I be inquired of by you, O house of Israel? *As* I live, saith the Lord GOD, I will not be inquired of by you.

32And that which cometh into your mind shall not be at all, that ye say, We will be as the heathen, as the families of the countries, to serve wood and stone.

33*As* I live, saith the Lord GOD, surely with a mighty hand, and with a stretched out arm, and with fury poured out, will I rule over you:

34And I will bring you out from the people, and will gather you out of the countries wherein ye are scattered, with a mighty hand, and with a stretched out arm, and with fury poured out.

35And I will bring you into the wilderness of the people, and there will I plead with you face to face.

36Like as I pleaded with your fathers in the wilderness of the land of Egypt, so will I plead with you, saith the Lord GOD.

37And I will cause you to pass under the rod, and I will bring you into the bond of the covenant:

38And I will purge out from among you the rebels, and them that transgress against me: I will bring them forth out of the country where they sojourn, and they shall not enter into the land of Israel: and ye shall know that I *am* the LORD.

39As for you, O house of Israel, thus saith the Lord GOD; Go ye, serve ye every one his idols, and hereafter *also,* if ye will not hearken unto me: but pollute ye my holy name no more with your gifts, and with your idols.

40For in mine holy mountain, in the mountain of the height of Israel, saith the Lord GOD, there shall all the house of Israel, all of them in the land, serve me: there will I accept them, and there will I require your offerings, and the firstfruits of your oblations, with all your holy things.

41I will accept you with your sweet savour, when I bring you out from the people, and gather you out of the countries wherein ye have been scattered; and I will be sanctified in you before the heathen.

42And ye shall know that I *am* the LORD, when I shall bring you into the land of Israel, into the

continued to blaspheme and betray me, 28for when I
brought them into the land I had promised them, they
offered sacrifices on every high hill and under every
green tree they saw! They roused my fury as they offered up sacrifices to their gods. They brought their
perfumes and incense and poured out their liquid
offerings to them. 29I said to them, 'What is this high
place where you are going?' (This kind of pagan shrine
has been called Bamah—'high place'—ever since.)
30"Therefore, give the people of Israel this message from the Sovereign LORD: Do you plan to pollute
yourselves just as your ancestors did? Do you intend
to keep prostituting yourselves by worshiping vile
images? 31For when you offer gifts to them and give
your little children to be burned as sacrifices,* you
continue to pollute yourselves with idols to this day.
Should I allow you to ask for a message from me,
O people of Israel? As surely as I live, says the Sovereign LORD, I will tell you nothing.
32"You say, 'We want to be like the nations all
around us, who serve idols of wood and stone.' But
what you have in mind will never happen. 33As surely
as I live, says the Sovereign LORD, I will rule over you
with an iron fist in great anger and with awesome
power. 34And in anger I will reach out with my strong
hand and powerful arm, and I will bring you back*
from the lands where you are scattered. 35I will bring
you into the wilderness of the nations, and there I
will judge you face to face. 36I will judge you there
just as I did your ancestors in the wilderness after
bringing them out of Egypt, says the Sovereign LORD.
37I will examine you carefully and hold you to the
terms of the covenant. 38I will purge you of all those
who rebel and revolt against me. I will bring them
out of the countries where they are in exile, but they
will never enter the land of Israel. Then you will
know that I am the LORD.
39"As for you, O people of Israel, this is what the
Sovereign LORD says: Go right ahead and worship
your idols, but sooner or later you will obey me and
will stop bringing shame on my holy name by worshiping idols. 40For on my holy mountain, the great
mountain of Israel, says the Sovereign LORD, the
people of Israel will someday worship me, and I will
accept them. There I will require that you bring me
all your offerings and choice gifts and sacrifices.
41When I bring you home from exile, you will be like
a pleasing sacrifice to me. And I will display my holiness through you as all the nations watch. 42Then

20:31 Or *and make your little children pass through the fire.* **20:34** Greek version reads *I will welcome you.* Compare 2 Cor 6:17.

KING JAMES VERSION

country *for* the which I lifted up mine hand to give it to your fathers.

43 And there shall ye remember your ways, and all your doings, wherein ye have been defiled; and ye shall lothe yourselves in your own sight for all your evils that ye have committed.

44 And ye shall know that I *am* the LORD, when I have wrought with you for my name's sake, not according to your wicked ways, nor according to your corrupt doings, O ye house of Israel, saith the Lord GOD.

45 Moreover the word of the LORD came unto me, saying,

46 Son of man, set thy face toward the south, and drop *thy word* toward the south, and prophesy against the forest of the south field;

47 And say to the forest of the south, Hear the word of the LORD; Thus saith the Lord GOD; Behold, I will kindle a fire in thee, and it shall devour every green tree in thee, and every dry tree: the flaming flame shall not be quenched, and all faces from the south to the north shall be burned therein.

48 And all flesh shall see that I the LORD have kindled it: it shall not be quenched.

49 Then said I, Ah Lord GOD! they say of me, Doth he not speak parables?

21 1 And the word of the LORD came unto me, saying,

2 Son of man, set thy face toward Jerusalem, and drop *thy word* toward the holy places, and prophesy against the land of Israel,

3 And say to the land of Israel, Thus saith the LORD; Behold, I *am* against thee, and will draw forth my sword out of his sheath, and will cut off from thee the righteous and the wicked.

4 Seeing then that I will cut off from thee the righteous and the wicked, therefore shall my sword go forth out of his sheath against all flesh from the south to the north:

5 That all flesh may know that I the LORD have drawn forth my sword out of his sheath: it shall not return any more.

6 Sigh therefore, thou son of man, with the breaking of *thy* loins; and with bitterness sigh before their eyes.

7 And it shall be, when they say unto thee, Wherefore sighest thou? that thou shalt answer, For the tidings; because it cometh: and every heart shall melt, and all hands shall be feeble, and every spirit shall faint, and all knees shall be weak *as* water: behold, it cometh, and shall be brought to pass, saith the Lord GOD.

8 Again the word of the LORD came unto me, saying,

9 Son of man, prophesy, and say, Thus saith the LORD; Say, A sword, a sword is sharpened, and also furbished:

NEW LIVING TRANSLATION

when I have brought you home to the land I promised with a solemn oath to give to your ancestors, you will know that I am the LORD. 43 You will look back on all the ways you defiled yourselves and will hate yourselves because of the evil you have done. 44 You will know that I am the LORD, O people of Israel, when I have honored my name by treating you mercifully in spite of your wickedness. I, the Sovereign LORD, have spoken!"

Judgment against the Negev

45* Then this message came to me from the LORD: 46 "Son of man, turn and face the south* and speak out against it; prophesy against the brushlands of the Negev. 47 Tell the southern wilderness, 'This is what the Sovereign LORD says: Hear the word of the LORD! I will set you on fire, and every tree, both green and dry, will be burned. The terrible flames will not be quenched and will scorch everything from south to north. 48 And everyone in the world will see that I, the LORD, have set this fire. It will not be put out.'"

49 Then I said, "O Sovereign LORD, they are saying of me, 'He only talks in riddles!'"

The LORD's Sword of Judgment

21 1* Then this message came to me from the LORD: 2 "Son of man, turn and face Jerusalem and prophesy against Israel and her sanctuaries. 3 Tell her, 'This is what the LORD says: I am your enemy, O Israel, and I am about to unsheath my sword to destroy your people—the righteous and the wicked alike. 4 Yes, I will cut off both the righteous and the wicked! I will draw my sword against everyone in the land from south to north. 5 Everyone in the world will know that I am the LORD. My sword is in my hand, and it will not return to its sheath until its work is finished.'

6 "Son of man, groan before the people! Groan before them with bitter anguish and a broken heart. 7 When they ask why you are groaning, tell them, 'I groan because of the terrifying news I have heard. When it comes true, the boldest heart will melt with fear; all strength will disappear. Every spirit will faint; strong knees will become as weak as water. And the Sovereign LORD says: It is coming! It's on its way!'"

8 Then the LORD said to me, 9 "Son of man, give the people this message from the Lord:

"A sword, a sword
is being sharpened and polished.

20:45 Verses 20:45-49 are numbered 21:1-5 in Hebrew text. **20:46** Hebrew *toward Teman.* **21:1** Verses 21:1-32 are numbered 21:6-37 in Hebrew text.

KING JAMES VERSION

[10]It is sharpened to make a sore slaughter; it is
furbished that it may glitter: should we then make
mirth? it contemneth the rod of my son, *as* every tree.
[11]And he hath given it to be furbished, that it may
be handled: this sword is sharpened, and it is furbished, to give it into the hand of the slayer.
[12]Cry and howl, son of man: for it shall be upon my
people, it *shall be* upon all the princes of Israel: terrors by reason of the sword shall be upon my people:
smite therefore upon *thy* thigh.
[13]Because *it is* a trial, and what if *the sword*
contemn even the rod? it shall be no *more,* saith the
Lord GOD.
[14]Thou therefore, son of man, prophesy, and smite
thine hands together, and let the sword be doubled
the third time, the sword of the slain: it *is* the sword of
the great *men that are* slain, which entereth into their
privy chambers.
[15]I have set the point of the sword against all their
gates, that *their* heart may faint, and *their* ruins be
multiplied: ah! *it is* made bright, *it is* wrapped up for
the slaughter.
[16]Go thee one way or other, *either* on the right
hand, *or* on the left, whithersoever thy face *is* set.
[17]I will also smite mine hands together, and I will
cause my fury to rest: I the LORD have said *it.*

[18]The word of the LORD came unto me again,
saying,
[19]Also, thou son of man, appoint thee two ways,
that the sword of the king of Babylon may come:
both twain shall come forth out of one land: and
choose thou a place, choose *it* at the head of the way
to the city.
[20]Appoint a way, that the sword may come to
Rabbath of the Ammonites, and to Judah in Jerusalem the defenced.
[21]For the king of Babylon stood at the parting of
the way, at the head of the two ways, to use divination: he made *his* arrows bright, he consulted with
images, he looked in the liver.
[22]At his right hand was the divination for Jerusalem, to appoint captains, to open the mouth in
the slaughter, to lift up the voice with shouting, to
appoint *battering* rams against the gates, to cast a
mount, *and* to build a fort.
[23]And it shall be unto them as a false divination
in their sight, to them that have sworn oaths: but he

NEW LIVING TRANSLATION

[10] It is sharpened for terrible slaughter
and polished to flash like lightning!
Now will you laugh?
Those far stronger than you have fallen
beneath its power!*
[11] Yes, the sword is now being sharpened
and polished;
it is being prepared for the executioner.

[12] "Son of man, cry out and wail;
pound your thighs in anguish,
for that sword will slaughter my people and
their leaders—
everyone will die!
[13] It will put them all to the test.
What chance do they have?*
says the Sovereign LORD.

[14] "Son of man, prophesy to them
and clap your hands.
Then take the sword and brandish it twice,
even three times,
to symbolize the great massacre,
the great massacre facing them on every side.
[15] Let their hearts melt with terror,
for the sword glitters at every gate.
It flashes like lightning
and is polished for slaughter!
[16] O sword, slash to the right,
then slash to the left,
wherever you will,
wherever you want.
[17] I, too, will clap my hands,
and I will satisfy my fury.
I, the LORD, have spoken!"

Omens for Babylon's King

[18]Then this message came to me from the LORD:
[19]"Son of man, make a map and trace two routes on it
for the sword of Babylon's king to follow. Put a signpost on the road that comes out of Babylon where
the road forks into two—[20]one road going to Ammon
and its capital, Rabbah, and the other to Judah and
fortified Jerusalem. [21]The king of Babylon now
stands at the fork, uncertain whether to attack Jerusalem or Rabbah. He calls his magicians to look for
omens. They cast lots by shaking arrows from the
quiver. They inspect the livers of animal sacrifices.
[22]The omen in his right hand says, 'Jerusalem!' With
battering rams his soldiers will go against the gates,
shouting for the kill. They will put up siege towers
and build ramps against the walls. [23]The people
of Jerusalem will think it is a false omen, because of
their treaty with the Babylonians. But the king of

21:10 The meaning of the Hebrew is uncertain. **21:13** The meaning of the Hebrew is uncertain.

KING JAMES VERSION

will call to remembrance the iniquity, that they may
be taken.
24 Therefore thus saith the Lord GOD; Because ye
have made your iniquity to be remembered, in that
your transgressions are discovered, so that in all your
doings your sins do appear; because, *I say,* that ye are
come to remembrance, ye shall be taken with the
hand.
25 And thou, profane wicked prince of Israel,
whose day is come, when iniquity *shall have* an end,
26 Thus saith the Lord GOD; Remove the diadem,
and take off the crown: this *shall* not *be* the same:
exalt *him that is* low, and abase *him that is* high.
27 I will overturn, overturn, overturn, it: and it shall
be no *more,* until he come whose right it is; and I will
give it *him.*

28 And thou, son of man, prophesy and say, Thus
saith the Lord GOD concerning the Ammonites, and
concerning their reproach; even say thou, The sword,
the sword *is* drawn: for the slaughter *it is* furbished,
to consume because of the glittering:
29 Whiles they see vanity unto thee, whiles they
divine a lie unto thee, to bring thee upon the necks
of *them that are* slain, of the wicked, whose day is
come, when their iniquity *shall have* an end.
30 Shall I cause *it* to return into his sheath? I will
judge thee in the place where thou wast created, in
the land of thy nativity.
31 And I will pour out mine indignation upon thee,
I will blow against thee in the fire of my wrath, and
deliver thee into the hand of brutish men, *and* skilful
to destroy.
32 Thou shalt be for fuel to the fire; thy blood shall
be in the midst of the land; thou shalt be no *more*
remembered: for I the LORD have spoken *it.*

22 1 Moreover the word of the LORD came unto
me, saying,
2 Now, thou son of man, wilt thou judge, wilt thou
judge the bloody city? yea, thou shalt shew her all her
abominations.
3 Then say thou, Thus saith the Lord GOD, The city
sheddeth blood in the midst of it, that her time may
come, and maketh idols against herself to defile
herself.

NEW LIVING TRANSLATION

Babylon will remind the people of their rebellion.
Then he will attack and capture them.
24 "Therefore, this is what the Sovereign LORD says:
Again and again you remind me of your sin and your
guilt. You don't even try to hide it! In everything you
do, your sins are obvious for all to see. So now the
time of your punishment has come!
25 "O you corrupt and wicked prince of Israel, your
final day of reckoning is here! 26 This is what the Sovereign LORD says:

"Take off your jeweled crown,
for the old order changes.
Now the lowly will be exalted,
and the mighty will be brought down.
27 Destruction! Destruction!
I will surely destroy the kingdom.
And it will not be restored until the one appears
who has the right to judge it.
Then I will hand it over to him.

A Message for the Ammonites

28 "And now, son of man, prophesy concerning the
Ammonites and their mockery. Give them this message from the Sovereign LORD:

"A sword, a sword
is drawn for your slaughter.
It is polished to destroy,
flashing like lightning!
29 Your prophets have given false visions,
and your fortune-tellers have told lies.
The sword will fall on the necks of the wicked
for whom the day of final reckoning has come.

30 "Now return the sword to its sheath,
for in your own country,
the land of your birth,
I will pass judgment upon you.
31 I will pour out my fury on you
and blow on you with the fire of my anger.
I will hand you over to cruel men
who are skilled in destruction.
32 You will be fuel for the fire,
and your blood will be spilled in your own land.
You will be utterly wiped out,
your memory lost to history,
for I, the LORD, have spoken!"

The Sins of Jerusalem

22 Now this message came to me from the
LORD: 2 "Son of man, are you ready to judge
Jerusalem? Are you ready to judge this city of murderers? Publicly denounce her detestable sins, 3 and give
her this message from the Sovereign LORD: O city of
murderers, doomed and damned—city of idols,* filthy

22:3 The Hebrew term (literally *round things*) probably alludes to dung; also in 22:4.

KING JAMES VERSION

4 Thou art become guilty in thy blood that thou
hast shed; and hast defiled thyself in thine idols
which thou hast made; and thou hast caused thy days
to draw near, and art come *even* unto thy years:
therefore have I made thee a reproach unto the
heathen, and a mocking to all countries.
5 *Those that be* near, and *those that be* far from thee,
shall mock thee, *which art* infamous *and* much vexed.
6 Behold, the princes of Israel, every one were in
thee to their power to shed blood.
7 In thee have they set light by father and mother:
in the midst of thee have they dealt by oppression
with the stranger: in thee have they vexed the fatherless and the widow.
8 Thou hast despised mine holy things, and hast
profaned my sabbaths.
9 In thee are men that carry tales to shed blood:
and in thee they eat upon the mountains: in the
midst of thee they commit lewdness.
10 In thee have they discovered their fathers'
nakedness: in thee have they humbled her that was
set apart for pollution.
11 And one hath committed abomination with his
neighbour's wife; and another hath lewdly defiled
his daughter in law; and another in thee hath
humbled his sister, his father's daughter.
12 In thee have they taken gifts to shed blood; thou
hast taken usury and increase, and thou hast greedily
gained of thy neighbours by extortion, and hast forgotten me, saith the Lord GOD.
13 Behold, therefore I have smitten mine hand at
thy dishonest gain which thou hast made, and at thy
blood which hath been in the midst of thee.
14 Can thine heart endure, or can thine hands be
strong, in the days that I shall deal with thee? I the
LORD have spoken *it,* and will do *it.*
15 And I will scatter thee among the heathen, and
disperse thee in the countries, and will consume thy
filthiness out of thee.
16 And thou shalt take thine inheritance in thyself
in the sight of the heathen, and thou shalt know that
I *am* the LORD.
17 And the word of the LORD came unto me, saying,
18 Son of man, the house of Israel is to me become
dross: all they *are* brass, and tin, and iron, and lead, in
the midst of the furnace; they are *even* the dross of
silver.
19 Therefore thus saith the Lord GOD; Because ye
are all become dross, behold, therefore I will gather
you into the midst of Jerusalem.
20 *As* they gather silver, and brass, and iron, and
lead, and tin, into the midst of the furnace, to blow
the fire upon it, to melt *it;* so will I gather *you* in mine
anger and in my fury, and I will leave *you there,* and
melt you.
21 Yea, I will gather you, and blow upon you in the
fire of my wrath, and ye shall be melted in the midst
thereof.

NEW LIVING TRANSLATION

and foul—4 you are guilty because of the blood you
have shed. You are defiled because of the idols
you have made. Your day of destruction has come!
You have reached the end of your years. I will make you
an object of mockery throughout the world. 5 O infamous city, filled with confusion, you will be mocked
by people far and near.
6 "Every leader in Israel who lives within your walls
is bent on murder. 7 Fathers and mothers are treated
with contempt. Foreigners are forced to pay for protection. Orphans and widows are wronged and oppressed among you. 8 You despise my holy things and
violate my Sabbath days of rest. 9 People accuse others falsely and send them to their death. You are
filled with idol worshipers and people who do obscene things. 10 Men sleep with their fathers' wives
and have intercourse with women who are menstru-
ating. 11 Within your walls live men who commit
adultery with their neighbors' wives, who defile their
daughters-in-law, or who rape their own sisters.
12 There are hired murderers, loan racketeers, and
extortioners everywhere. They never even think of
me and my commands, says the Sovereign LORD.
13 "But now I clap my hands in indignation over
your dishonest gain and bloodshed. 14 How strong
and courageous will you be in my day of reckoning?
I, the LORD, have spoken, and I will do what I said. 15 I
will scatter you among the nations and purge you
of your wickedness. 16 And when I have been dishonored among the nations because of you,* you will
know that I am the LORD."

The LORD's Refining Furnace

17 Then this message came to me from the LORD:
18 "Son of man, the people of Israel are the worthless
slag that remains after silver is smelted. They are the
dross that is left over—a useless mixture of copper,
tin, iron, and lead. 19 So tell them, 'This is what the
Sovereign LORD says: Because you are all worthless
slag, I will bring you to my crucible in Jerusalem.
20 Just as copper, iron, lead, and tin are melted down
in a furnace, I will melt you down in the heat of my
fury. 21 I will gather you together and blow the fire of

22:16 Or *when you have been dishonored among the nations.*

KING JAMES VERSION

22As silver is melted in the midst of the furnace,
so shall ye be melted in the midst thereof; and ye
shall know that I the LORD have poured out my fury
upon you.

23And the word of the LORD came unto me, saying,
24Son of man, say unto her, Thou *art* the land
that is not cleansed, nor rained upon in the day of
indignation.

25*There is* a conspiracy of her prophets in the
midst thereof, like a roaring lion ravening the prey;
they have devoured souls; they have taken the treasure and precious things; they have made her many
widows in the midst thereof.

26Her priests have violated my law, and have profaned mine holy things: they have put no difference
between the holy and profane, neither have they
shewed *difference* between the unclean and the
clean, and have hid their eyes from my sabbaths, and
I am profaned among them.

27Her princes in the midst thereof *are* like wolves
ravening the prey, to shed blood, *and* to destroy
souls, to get dishonest gain.

28And her prophets have daubed them with untempered *mortar*, seeing vanity, and divining lies
unto them, saying, Thus saith the Lord GOD, when
the LORD hath not spoken.

29The people of the land have used oppression,
and exercised robbery, and have vexed the poor and
needy: yea, they have oppressed the stranger wrongfully.

30And I sought for a man among them, that should
make up the hedge, and stand in the gap before me
for the land, that I should not destroy it: but I found
none.

31Therefore have I poured out mine indignation
upon them; I have consumed them with the fire of
my wrath: their own way have I recompensed upon
their heads, saith the Lord GOD.

23 1The word of the LORD came again unto me,
saying,
2Son of man, there were two women, the daughters of one mother:
3And they committed whoredoms in Egypt; they
committed whoredoms in their youth: there were
their breasts pressed, and there they bruised the
teats of their virginity.
4And the names of them *were* Aholah the elder,
and Aholibah her sister: and they were mine, and
they bare sons and daughters. Thus *were* their
names; Samaria *is* Aholah, and Jerusalem Aholibah.
5And Aholah played the harlot when she was
mine; and she doted on her lovers, on the Assyrians
her neighbours,
6*Which were* clothed with blue, captains and
rulers, all of them desirable young men, horsemen
riding upon horses.

NEW LIVING TRANSLATION

my anger upon you, 22and you will melt like silver in
fierce heat. Then you will know that I, the LORD, have
poured out my fury on you.'"

The Sins of Israel's Leaders

23Again a message came to me from the LORD: 24"Son
of man, give the people of Israel this message: In the
day of my indignation, you will be like a polluted
land, a land without rain. 25Your princes* plot con-
spiracies just as lions stalk their prey. They devour
innocent people, seizing treasures and extorting
wealth. They make many widows in the land. 26Your
priests have violated my instructions and defiled my
holy things. They make no distinction between what
is holy and what is not. And they do not teach my
people the difference between what is ceremonially
clean and unclean. They disregard my Sabbath days
so that I am dishonored among them. 27Your leaders
are like wolves who tear apart their victims. They
actually destroy people's lives for money! 28And your
prophets cover up for them by announcing false
visions and making lying predictions. They say, 'My
message is from the Sovereign LORD,' when the LORD
hasn't spoken a single word to them. 29Even common people oppress the poor, rob the needy, and
deprive foreigners of justice.

30"I looked for someone who might rebuild the
wall of righteousness that guards the land. I searched
for someone to stand in the gap in the wall so I
wouldn't have to destroy the land, but I found no one.
31So now I will pour out my fury on them, consuming
them with the fire of my anger. I will heap on their
heads the full penalty for all their sins. I, the Sovereign LORD, have spoken!"

The Adultery of Two Sisters

23 This message came to me from the LORD:
2"Son of man, once there were two sisters
who were daughters of the same mother. 3They became prostitutes in Egypt. Even as young girls, they
allowed men to fondle their breasts. 4The older girl
was named Oholah, and her sister was Oholibah. I
married them, and they bore me sons and daughters.
I am speaking of Samaria and Jerusalem, for Oholah
is Samaria and Oholibah is Jerusalem.

5"Then Oholah lusted after other lovers instead of
me, and she gave her love to the Assyrian officers.
6They were all attractive young men, captains and
commanders dressed in handsome blue, charioteers

22:25 As in Greek version; Hebrew reads *prophets*.

KING JAMES VERSION

7 Thus she committed her whoredoms with them, with all them *that were* the chosen men of Assyria, and with all on whom she doted: with all their idols she defiled herself.

8 Neither left she her whoredoms *brought* from Egypt: for in her youth they lay with her, and they bruised the breasts of her virginity, and poured their whoredom upon her.

9 Wherefore I have delivered her into the hand of her lovers, into the hand of the Assyrians, upon whom she doted.

10 These discovered her nakedness: they took her sons and her daughters, and slew her with the sword: and she became famous among women; for they had executed judgment upon her.

11 And when her sister Aholibah saw *this,* she was more corrupt in her inordinate love than she, and in her whoredoms more than her sister in *her* whoredoms.

12 She doted upon the Assyrians *her* neighbours, captains and rulers clothed most gorgeously, horsemen riding upon horses, all of them desirable young men.

13 Then I saw that she was defiled, *that* they *took* both one way,

14 And *that* she increased her whoredoms: for when she saw men pourtrayed upon the wall, the images of the Chaldeans pourtrayed with vermilion,

15 Girded with girdles upon their loins, exceeding in dyed attire upon their heads, all of them princes to look to, after the manner of the Babylonians of Chaldea, the land of their nativity:

16 And as soon as she saw them with her eyes, she doted upon them, and sent messengers unto them into Chaldea.

17 And the Babylonians came to her into the bed of love, and they defiled her with their whoredom, and she was polluted with them, and her mind was alienated from them.

18 So she discovered her whoredoms, and discovered her nakedness: then my mind was alienated from her, like as my mind was alienated from her sister.

19 Yet she multiplied her whoredoms, in calling to remembrance the days of her youth, wherein she had played the harlot in the land of Egypt.

20 For she doted upon their paramours, whose flesh *is as* the flesh of asses, and whose issue *is like* the issue of horses.

21 Thus thou calledst to remembrance the lewdness of thy youth, in bruising thy teats by the Egyptians for the paps of thy youth.

22 Therefore, O Aholibah, thus saith the Lord GOD; Behold, I will raise up thy lovers against thee, from whom thy mind is alienated, and I will bring them against thee on every side;

23 The Babylonians, and all the Chaldeans, Pekod, and Shoa, and Koa, *and* all the Assyrians with them:

NEW LIVING TRANSLATION

driving their horses. 7 And so she prostituted herself
with the most desirable men of Assyria, worshiping
their idols* and defiling herself. 8 For when she left
Egypt, she did not leave her spirit of prostitution behind. She was still as lewd as in her youth, when the
Egyptians slept with her, fondled her breasts, and
used her as a prostitute.
9 "And so I handed her over to her Assyrian lovers,
whom she desired so much. 10 They stripped her,
took away her children as their slaves, and then
killed her. After she received her punishment, her
reputation was known to every woman in the land.
11 "Yet even though Oholibah saw what had happened to Oholah, her sister, she followed right in her
footsteps. And she was even more depraved, abandoning herself to her lust and prostitution. 12 She
fawned over all the Assyrian officers—those captains and commanders in handsome uniforms, those
charioteers driving their horses—all of them attractive young men. 13 I saw the way she was going, defiling herself just like her older sister.
14 "Then she carried her prostitution even further.
She fell in love with pictures that were painted on a
wall—pictures of Babylonian* military officers, out-
fitted in striking red uniforms. 15 Handsome belts
encircled their waists, and flowing turbans crowned
their heads. They were dressed like chariot officers
from the land of Babylonia.* 16 When she saw these
paintings, she longed to give herself to them, so she
sent messengers to Babylonia to invite them to come
to her. 17 So they came and committed adultery with
her, defiling her in the bed of love. After being defiled, however, she rejected them in disgust.
18 "In the same way, I became disgusted with Oholibah and rejected her, just as I had rejected her sister,
because she flaunted herself before them and gave
herself to satisfy their lusts. 19 Yet she turned to even
greater prostitution, remembering her youth when
she was a prostitute in Egypt. 20 She lusted after lovers with genitals as large as a donkey's and emissions
like those of a horse. 21 And so, Oholibah, you relived
your former days as a young girl in Egypt, when you
first allowed your breasts to be fondled.

The LORD's Judgment of Oholibah

22 "Therefore, Oholibah, this is what the Sovereign
LORD says: I will send your lovers against you from
every direction—those very nations from which you
turned away in disgust. 23 For the Babylonians will

23:7 The Hebrew term (literally *round things*) probably alludes to dung; also in 23:30, 37, 39, 49. **23:14** Or *Chaldean.* **23:15** Or *Chaldea;* also in 23:16.

KING JAMES VERSION

all of them desirable young men, captains and rulers, great lords and renowned, all of them riding upon horses.

24 And they shall come against thee with chariots, wagons, and wheels, and with an assembly of people, *which* shall set against thee buckler and shield and helmet round about: and I will set judgment before them, and they shall judge thee according to their judgments.

25 And I will set my jealousy against thee, and they shall deal furiously with thee: they shall take away thy nose and thine ears; and thy remnant shall fall by the sword: they shall take thy sons and thy daughters; and thy residue shall be devoured by the fire.

26 They shall also strip thee out of thy clothes, and take away thy fair jewels.

27 Thus will I make thy lewdness to cease from thee, and thy whoredom *brought* from the land of Egypt: so that thou shalt not lift up thine eyes unto them, nor remember Egypt any more.

28 For thus saith the Lord GOD; Behold, I will deliver thee into the hand *of them* whom thou hatest, into the hand *of them* from whom thy mind is alienated:

29 And they shall deal with thee hatefully, and shall take away all thy labour, and shall leave thee naked and bare: and the nakedness of thy whoredoms shall be discovered, both thy lewdness and thy whoredoms.

30 I will do these *things* unto thee, because thou hast gone a whoring after the heathen, *and* because thou art polluted with their idols.

31 Thou hast walked in the way of thy sister; therefore will I give her cup into thine hand.

32 Thus saith the Lord GOD; Thou shalt drink of thy sister's cup deep and large: thou shalt be laughed to scorn and had in derision; it containeth much.

33 Thou shalt be filled with drunkenness and sorrow, with the cup of astonishment and desolation, with the cup of thy sister Samaria.

34 Thou shalt even drink it and suck *it* out, and thou shalt break the sherds thereof, and pluck off thine own breasts: for I have spoken *it,* saith the Lord GOD.

35 Therefore thus saith the Lord GOD; Because thou hast forgotten me, and cast me behind thy back, therefore bear thou also thy lewdness and thy whoredoms.

36 The LORD said moreover unto me; Son of man, wilt thou judge Aholah and Aholibah? yea, declare unto them their abominations;

37 That they have committed adultery, and blood *is* in their hands, and with their idols have they committed adultery, and have also caused their sons,

NEW LIVING TRANSLATION

come with all the Chaldeans from Pekod and Shoa
and Koa. And all the Assyrians will come with them—
handsome young captains, commanders, chariot
officers, and other high-ranking officers, all riding
their horses. 24 They will all come against you from
the north* with chariots, wagons, and a great army
prepared for attack. They will take up positions
on every side, surrounding you with men armed
with shields and helmets. And I will hand you over to
them for punishment so they can do with you as they
please. 25 I will turn my jealous anger against you, and
they will deal harshly with you. They will cut off your
nose and ears, and any survivors will then be slaughtered by the sword. Your children will be taken away
as captives, and everything that is left will be burned.
26 They will strip you of your beautiful clothes and
jewels. 27 In this way, I will put a stop to the lewdness
and prostitution you brought from Egypt. You will
never again cast longing eyes on those things or
fondly remember your time in Egypt.

28 "For this is what the Sovereign LORD says: I will
surely hand you over to your enemies, to those you
loathe, those you rejected. 29 They will treat you with
hatred and rob you of all you own, leaving you stark
naked. The shame of your prostitution will be exposed to all the world. 30 You brought all this on yourself by prostituting yourself to other nations, defiling
yourself with all their idols. 31 Because you have followed in your sister's footsteps, I will force you to
drink the same cup of terror she drank.

32 "Yes, this is what the Sovereign LORD says:

"You will drink from your sister's cup of terror,
a cup that is large and deep.
It is filled to the brim
with scorn and derision.
33 Drunkenness and anguish will fill you,
for your cup is filled to the brim with distress
and desolation,
the same cup your sister Samaria drank.
34 You will drain that cup of terror
to the very bottom.
Then you will smash it to pieces
and beat your breast in anguish.
I, the Sovereign LORD, have spoken!

35 "And because you have forgotten me and turned
your back on me, this is what the Sovereign LORD
says: You must bear the consequences of all your
lewdness and prostitution."

The LORD's Judgment on Both Sisters

36 The LORD said to me, "Son of man, you must accuse
Oholah and Oholibah of all their detestable sins.
37 They have committed both adultery and murder—

23:24 As in Greek version; the meaning of the Hebrew is uncertain.

whom they bare unto me, to pass for them through
the fire, to devour *them.*
38 Moreover this they have done unto me: they
have defiled my sanctuary in the same day, and have
profaned my sabbaths.
39 For when they had slain their children to their
idols, then they came the same day into my sanctuary
to profane it; and, lo, thus have they done in the midst
of mine house.
40 And furthermore, that ye have sent for men to
come from far, unto whom a messenger *was* sent;
and, lo, they came: for whom thou didst wash thyself, paintedst thy eyes, and deckedst thyself with
ornaments,
41 And satest upon a stately bed, and a table prepared before it, whereupon thou hast set mine incense and mine oil.
42 And a voice of a multitude being at ease *was*
with her: and with the men of the common sort *were*
brought Sabeans from the wilderness, which put
bracelets upon their hands, and beautiful crowns
upon their heads.
43 Then said I unto *her that was* old in adulteries,
Will they now commit whoredoms with her, and she
with them?
44 Yet they went in unto her, as they go in unto a
woman that playeth the harlot: so went they in unto
Aholah and unto Aholibah, the lewd women.
45 And the righteous men, they shall judge them
after the manner of adulteresses, and after the manner of women that shed blood; because they *are*
adulteresses, and blood *is* in their hands.
46 For thus saith the Lord GOD; I will bring up a
company upon them, and will give them to be removed and spoiled.
47 And the company shall stone them with stones,
and dispatch them with their swords; they shall slay
their sons and their daughters, and burn up their
houses with fire.
48 Thus will I cause lewdness to cease out of the
land, that all women may be taught not to do after
your lewdness.
49 And they shall recompense your lewdness upon
you, and ye shall bear the sins of your idols: and ye
shall know that I *am* the Lord GOD.

24 1 Again in the ninth year, in the tenth month,
in the tenth *day* of the month, the word of
the LORD came unto me, saying,
2 Son of man, write thee the name of the day, *even*
of this same day: the king of Babylon set himself
against Jerusalem this same day.
3 And utter a parable unto the rebellious house,
and say unto them, Thus saith the Lord GOD; Set on a
pot, set *it* on, and also pour water into it:

adultery by worshiping idols and murder by burning
as sacrifices the children they bore to me. 38 Furthermore, they have defiled my Temple and violated my
Sabbath day! 39 On the very day that they sacrificed
their children to their idols, they boldly came into
my Temple to worship! They came in and defiled
my house.
40 "You sisters sent messengers to distant lands to
get men. Then when they arrived, you bathed yourselves, painted your eyelids, and put on your finest
jewels for them. 41 You sat with them on a beautifully
embroidered couch and put my incense and my special oil on a table that was spread before you. 42 From
your room came the sound of many men carousing.
They were lustful men and drunkards* from the
wilderness, who put bracelets on your wrists and
beautiful crowns on your heads. 43 Then I said, 'If
they really want to have sex with old worn-out prostitutes like these, let them!' 44 And that is what they did.
They had sex with Oholah and Oholibah, these
shameless prostitutes. 45 But righteous people will
judge these sister cities for what they really are—
adulterers and murderers.
46 "Now this is what the Sovereign LORD says: Bring
an army against them and hand them over to be terrorized and plundered. 47 For their enemies will
stone them and kill them with swords. They will
butcher their sons and daughters and burn their
homes. 48 In this way, I will put an end to lewdness
and idolatry in the land, and my judgment will be a
warning to others not to follow their wicked example. 49 You will be fully repaid for all your prostitution—your worship of idols. Yes, you will suffer the
full penalty. Then you will know that I am the Sovereign LORD."

The Sign of the Cooking Pot

24 On January 15,* during the ninth year of
King Jehoiachin's captivity, this message
came to me from the LORD: 2 "Son of man, write down
today's date, because on this very day the king of
Babylon is beginning his attack against Jerusalem.
3 Then give these rebels an illustration with this
message from the Sovereign LORD:

"Put a pot on the fire,
and pour in some water.

23:42 Or *Sabeans.* **24:1** Hebrew *On the tenth day of the tenth month,* of the ancient Hebrew lunar calendar. This event occurred on January 15, 588 B.C.; also see note on 1:1.

KING JAMES VERSION

4 Gather the pieces thereof into it, *even* every good
piece, the thigh, and the shoulder; fill *it* with the
choice bones.
5 Take the choice of the flock, and burn also the
bones under it, *and* make it boil well, and let them
seethe the bones of it therein.
6 Wherefore thus saith the Lord GOD; Woe to the
bloody city, to the pot whose scum *is* therein, and
whose scum is not gone out of it! bring it out piece by
piece; let no lot fall upon it.
7 For her blood is in the midst of her; she set it
upon the top of a rock; she poured it not upon the
ground, to cover it with dust;
8 That it might cause fury to come up to take vengeance; I have set her blood upon the top of a rock,
that it should not be covered.
9 Therefore thus saith the Lord GOD; Woe to the
bloody city! I will even make the pile for fire great.
10 Heap on wood, kindle the fire, consume the
flesh, and spice it well, and let the bones be burned.
11 Then set it empty upon the coals thereof, that
the brass of it may be hot, and may burn, and *that* the
filthiness of it may be molten in it, *that* the scum of it
may be consumed.
12 She hath wearied *herself* with lies, and her great
scum went not forth out of her: her scum *shall be* in
the fire.
13 In thy filthiness *is* lewdness: because I have
purged thee, and thou wast not purged, thou shalt
not be purged from thy filthiness any more, till I have
caused my fury to rest upon thee.
14 I the LORD have spoken *it*: it shall come to pass,
and I will do *it*; I will not go back, neither will I spare,
neither will I repent; according to thy ways, and according to thy doings, shall they judge thee, saith the
Lord GOD.

15 Also the word of the LORD came unto me, saying,
16 Son of man, behold, I take away from thee the
desire of thine eyes with a stroke: yet neither shalt
thou mourn nor weep, neither shall thy tears run
down.
17 Forbear to cry, make no mourning for the dead,
bind the tire of thine head upon thee, and put on thy

NEW LIVING TRANSLATION

4 Fill it with choice pieces of meat—
the rump and the shoulder
and all the most tender cuts.
5 Use only the best sheep from the flock,
and heap fuel on the fire beneath the pot.
Bring the pot to a boil,
and cook the bones along with the meat.
6 "Now this is what the Sovereign LORD says:
What sorrow awaits Jerusalem,
the city of murderers!
She is a cooking pot
whose corruption can't be cleaned out.
Take the meat out in random order,
for no piece is better than another.
7 For the blood of her murders
is splashed on the rocks.
It isn't even spilled on the ground,
where the dust could cover it!
8 So I will splash her blood on a rock
for all to see,
an expression of my anger
and vengeance against her.
9 "This is what the Sovereign LORD says:
What sorrow awaits Jerusalem,
the city of murderers!
I myself will pile up the fuel beneath her.
10 Yes, heap on the wood!
Let the fire roar to make the pot boil.
Cook the meat with many spices,
and afterward burn the bones.
11 Now set the empty pot on the coals.
Heat it red hot!
Burn away the filth and corruption.
12 But it's hopeless;
the corruption can't be cleaned out.
So throw it into the fire.
13 Your impurity is your lewdness
and the corruption of your idolatry.
I tried to cleanse you,
but you refused.
So now you will remain in your filth
until my fury against you has been satisfied.

14 "I, the LORD, have spoken! The time has come,
and I won't hold back. I will not change my mind, and
I will have no pity on you. You will be judged on the
basis of all your wicked actions, says the Sovereign
LORD."

The Death of Ezekiel's Wife

15 Then this message came to me from the LORD:
16 "Son of man, with one blow I will take away your
dearest treasure. Yet you must not show any sorrow
at her death. Do not weep; let there be no tears.
17 Groan silently, but let there be no wailing at her
grave. Do not uncover your head or take off your sandals. Do not perform the usual rituals of mourning

KING JAMES VERSION

shoes upon thy feet, and cover not *thy* lips, and eat
not the bread of men.

18So I spake unto the people in the morning: and
at even my wife died; and I did in the morning as I
was commanded.

19And the people said unto me, Wilt thou not tell
us what these *things are* to us, that thou doest *so*?

20Then I answered them, The word of the LORD
came unto me, saying,

21Speak unto the house of Israel, Thus saith the
Lord GOD; Behold, I will profane my sanctuary, the
excellency of your strength, the desire of your eyes,
and that which your soul pitieth; and your sons and
your daughters whom ye have left shall fall by the
sword.

22And ye shall do as I have done: ye shall not cover
your lips, nor eat the bread of men.

23And your tires *shall be* upon your heads, and
your shoes upon your feet: ye shall not mourn nor
weep; but ye shall pine away for your iniquities, and
mourn one toward another.

24Thus Ezekiel is unto you a sign: according to all
that he hath done shall ye do: and when this cometh,
ye shall know that I *am* the Lord GOD.

25Also, thou son of man, *shall it* not *be* in the day
when I take from them their strength, the joy of their
glory, the desire of their eyes, and that whereupon
they set their minds, their sons and their daughters,

26*That* he that escapeth in that day shall come
unto thee, to cause *thee* to hear *it* with *thine* ears?

27In that day shall thy mouth be opened to him
which is escaped, and thou shalt speak, and be no
more dumb: and thou shalt be a sign unto them; and
they shall know that I *am* the LORD.

25 1The word of the LORD came again unto me,
saying,

2Son of man, set thy face against the Ammonites,
and prophesy against them;

3And say unto the Ammonites, Hear the word of
the Lord GOD; Thus saith the Lord GOD; Because thou
saidst, Aha, against my sanctuary, when it was profaned; and against the land of Israel, when it was desolate; and against the house of Judah, when they
went into captivity;

4Behold, therefore I will deliver thee to the men of
the east for a possession, and they shall set their palaces in thee, and make their dwellings in thee: they
shall eat thy fruit, and they shall drink thy milk.

5And I will make Rabbah a stable for camels, and
the Ammonites a couchingplace for flocks: and ye
shall know that I *am* the LORD.

6For thus saith the Lord GOD; Because thou hast
clapped *thine* hands, and stamped with the feet, and
rejoiced in heart with all thy despite against the land
of Israel;

7Behold, therefore I will stretch out mine hand
upon thee, and will deliver thee for a spoil to the

NEW LIVING TRANSLATION

or accept any food brought to you by consoling
friends."

18So I proclaimed this to the people the next
morning, and in the evening my wife died. The next
morning I did everything I had been told to do.
19Then the people asked, "What does all this mean?
What are you trying to tell us?"

20So I said to them, "A message came to me from
the LORD, 21and I was told to give this message to the
people of Israel. This is what the Sovereign LORD
says: I will defile my Temple, the source of your security and pride, the place your heart delights in. Your
sons and daughters whom you left behind in Judea
will be slaughtered by the sword. 22Then you will do
as Ezekiel has done. You will not mourn in public or
console yourselves by eating the food brought by
friends. 23Your heads will remain covered, and your
sandals will not be taken off. You will not mourn or
weep, but you will waste away because of your sins.
You will mourn privately for all the evil you have
done. 24Ezekiel is an example for you; you will do just
as he has done. And when that time comes, you will
know that I am the Sovereign LORD."

25Then the LORD said to me, "Son of man, on the
day I take away their stronghold—their joy and glory,
their heart's desire, their dearest treasure—I will also
take away their sons and daughters. 26And on that
day a survivor from Jerusalem will come to you in
Babylon and tell you what has happened. 27And
when he arrives, your voice will suddenly return so
you can talk to him, and you will be a symbol for
these people. Then they will know that I am the
LORD."

A Message for Ammon

25 Then this message came to me from the
LORD: 2"Son of man, turn and face the land
of Ammon and prophesy against its people. 3Give the
Ammonites this message from the Sovereign LORD:
Hear the word of the Sovereign LORD! Because you
cheered when my Temple was defiled, mocked Israel
in her desolation, and laughed at Judah as she went
away into exile, 4I will allow nomads from the eastern
deserts to overrun your country. They will set up
their camps among you and pitch their tents on your
land. They will harvest all your fruit and drink the
milk from your livestock. 5And I will turn the city of
Rabbah into a pasture for camels, and all the land of
the Ammonites into a resting place for sheep and
goats. Then you will know that I am the LORD.

6"This is what the Sovereign LORD says: Because
you clapped and danced and cheered with glee at the
destruction of my people, 7I will raise my fist of judgment against you. I will give you as plunder to many
nations. I will cut you off from being a nation and

KING JAMES VERSION

heathen; and I will cut thee off from the people, and I will cause thee to perish out of the countries: I will destroy thee; and thou shalt know that I *am* the LORD.

8 Thus saith the Lord GOD; Because that Moab and Seir do say, Behold, the house of Judah *is* like unto all the heathen;

9 Therefore, behold, I will open the side of Moab from the cities, from his cities *which are* on his frontiers, the glory of the country, Beth-jeshimoth, Baal-meon, and Kiriathaim,

10 Unto the men of the east with the Ammonites, and will give them in possession, that the Ammonites may not be remembered among the nations.

11 And I will execute judgments upon Moab; and they shall know that I *am* the LORD.

12 Thus saith the Lord GOD; Because that Edom hath dealt against the house of Judah by taking vengeance, and hath greatly offended, and revenged himself upon them;

13 Therefore thus saith the Lord GOD; I will also stretch out mine hand upon Edom, and will cut off man and beast from it; and I will make it desolate from Teman; and they of Dedan shall fall by the sword.

14 And I will lay my vengeance upon Edom by the hand of my people Israel: and they shall do in Edom according to mine anger and according to my fury; and they shall know my vengeance, saith the Lord GOD.

15 Thus saith the Lord GOD; Because the Philistines have dealt by revenge, and have taken vengeance with a despiteful heart, to destroy *it* for the old hatred;

16 Therefore thus saith the Lord GOD; Behold, I will stretch out mine hand upon the Philistines, and I will cut off the Cherethims, and destroy the remnant of the sea coast.

17 And I will execute great vengeance upon them with furious rebukes; and they shall know that I *am* the LORD, when I shall lay my vengeance upon them.

26 1 And it came to pass in the eleventh year, in the first *day* of the month, *that* the word of the LORD came unto me, saying,

2 Son of man, because that Tyrus hath said against Jerusalem, Aha, she is broken *that was* the gates of the people: she is turned unto me: I shall be replenished, *now* she is laid waste:

3 Therefore thus saith the Lord GOD; Behold, I *am* against thee, O Tyrus, and will cause many nations to come up against thee, as the sea causeth his waves to come up.

4 And they shall destroy the walls of Tyrus, and break down her towers: I will also scrape her dust from her, and make her like the top of a rock.

5 It shall be *a place for* the spreading of nets in the

NEW LIVING TRANSLATION

destroy you completely. Then you will know that I am the LORD.

A Message for Moab

8 "This is what the Sovereign LORD says: Because the people of Moab have said that Judah is just like all the other nations, 9 I will open up their eastern flank and wipe out their glorious frontier towns—Beth-jeshimoth, Baal-meon, and Kiriathaim. 10 And I will hand Moab over to nomads from the eastern deserts, just as I handed over Ammon. Yes, the Ammonites will no longer be counted among the nations. 11 In the same way, I will bring my judgment down on the Moabites. Then they will know that I am the LORD.

A Message for Edom

12 "This is what the Sovereign LORD says: The people of Edom have sinned greatly by avenging themselves against the people of Judah. 13 Therefore, says the Sovereign LORD, I will raise my fist of judgment against Edom. I will wipe out its people and animals with the sword. I will make a wasteland of everything from Teman to Dedan. 14 I will accomplish this by the hand of my people of Israel. They will carry out my vengeance with anger, and Edom will know that this vengeance is from me. I, the Sovereign LORD, have spoken!

A Message for Philistia

15 "This is what the Sovereign LORD says: The people of Philistia have acted against Judah out of bitter revenge and long-standing contempt. 16 Therefore, this is what the Sovereign LORD says: I will raise my fist of judgment against the land of the Philistines. I will wipe out the Kerethites and utterly destroy the people who live by the sea. 17 I will execute terrible vengeance against them to punish them for what they have done. And when I have inflicted my revenge, they will know that I am the LORD."

A Message for Tyre

26 On February 3, during the twelfth year of King Jehoiachin's captivity,* this message came to me from the LORD: 2 "Son of man, Tyre has rejoiced over the fall of Jerusalem, saying, 'Ha! She who was the gateway to the rich trade routes to the east has been broken, and I am the heir! Because she has been made desolate, I will become wealthy!'

3 "Therefore, this is what the Sovereign LORD says: I am your enemy, O Tyre, and I will bring many nations against you, like the waves of the sea crashing against your shoreline. 4 They will destroy the walls of Tyre and tear down its towers. I will scrape away its soil and make it a bare rock! 5 It will be just a rock

26:1 Hebrew *In the eleventh year, on the first day of the month,* of the ancient Hebrew lunar calendar year. Since an element is missing in the date formula here, scholars have reconstructed this probable reading: *In the eleventh [month of the twelfth] year, on the first day of the month.* This reading would put this message on February 3, 585 B.C.; also see note on 1:1.

KING JAMES VERSION

midst of the sea: for I have spoken *it,* saith the Lord
GOD: and it shall become a spoil to the nations.
6And her daughters which *are* in the field shall be
slain by the sword; and they shall know that I *am* the
LORD.
7For thus saith the Lord GOD; Behold, I will bring
upon Tyrus Nebuchadrezzar king of Babylon, a king
of kings, from the north, with horses, and with chariots, and with horsemen, and companies, and much
people.
8He shall slay with the sword thy daughters in the
field: and he shall make a fort against thee, and cast a
mount against thee, and lift up the buckler against
thee.
9And he shall set engines of war against thy walls,
and with his axes he shall break down thy towers.
10By reason of the abundance of his horses their
dust shall cover thee: thy walls shall shake at the
noise of the horsemen, and of the wheels, and of the
chariots, when he shall enter into thy gates, as men
enter into a city wherein is made a breach.
11With the hoofs of his horses shall he tread down
all thy streets: he shall slay thy people by the sword,
and thy strong garrisons shall go down to the
ground.
12And they shall make a spoil of thy riches, and
make a prey of thy merchandise: and they shall break
down thy walls, and destroy thy pleasant houses: and
they shall lay thy stones and thy timber and thy dust
in the midst of the water.
13And I will cause the noise of thy songs to cease;
and the sound of thy harps shall be no more heard.
14And I will make thee like the top of a rock: thou
shalt be *a place* to spread nets upon; thou shalt be
built no more: for I the LORD have spoken *it,* saith the
Lord GOD.
15Thus saith the Lord GOD to Tyrus; Shall not
the isles shake at the sound of thy fall, when the
wounded cry, when the slaughter is made in the
midst of thee?
16Then all the princes of the sea shall come down
from their thrones, and lay away their robes, and put
off their broidered garments: they shall clothe themselves with trembling; they shall sit upon the ground,
and shall tremble at *every* moment, and be astonished at thee.
17And they shall take up a lamentation for thee,
and say to thee, How art thou destroyed, *that wast* inhabited of seafaring men, the renowned city, which
wast strong in the sea, she and her inhabitants,
which cause their terror *to be* on all that haunt it!
18Now shall the isles tremble in the day of thy fall;
yea, the isles that *are* in the sea shall be troubled at
thy departure.
19For thus saith the Lord GOD; When I shall make
thee a desolate city, like the cities that are not inhabited; when I shall bring up the deep upon thee, and
great waters shall cover thee;

NEW LIVING TRANSLATION

in the sea, a place for fishermen to spread their nets,
for I have spoken, says the Sovereign LORD. Tyre will
become the prey of many nations, 6and its mainland
villages will be destroyed by the sword. Then they
will know that I am the LORD.
7"This is what the Sovereign LORD says: From
the north I will bring King Nebuchadnezzar* of Babylon against Tyre. He is king of kings and brings his
horses, chariots, charioteers, and great army. 8First
he will destroy your mainland villages. Then he will
attack you by building a siege wall, constructing a
ramp, and raising a roof of shields against you. 9He
will pound your walls with battering rams and demolish your towers with sledgehammers. 10The
hooves of his horses will choke the city with dust,
and the noise of the charioteers and chariot wheels
will shake your walls as they storm through your
broken gates. 11His horsemen will trample through
every street in the city. They will butcher your
people, and your strong pillars will topple.
12"They will plunder all your riches and merchandise and break down your walls. They will destroy
your lovely homes and dump your stones and timbers and even your dust into the sea. 13I will stop the
music of your songs. No more will the sound of harps
be heard among your people. 14I will make your island a bare rock, a place for fishermen to spread
their nets. You will never be rebuilt, for I, the LORD,
have spoken. Yes, the Sovereign LORD has spoken!

The Effect of Tyre's Destruction

15"This is what the Sovereign LORD says to Tyre: The
whole coastline will tremble at the sound of your fall,
as the screams of the wounded echo in the continuing slaughter. 16All the seaport rulers will step down
from their thrones and take off their royal robes and
beautiful clothing. They will sit on the ground trembling with horror at your destruction. 17Then they
will wail for you, singing this funeral song:

"O famous island city,
  once ruler of the sea,
  how you have been destroyed!
Your people, with their naval power,
  once spread fear around the world.
18 Now the coastlands tremble at your fall.
  The islands are dismayed as you disappear.

19"This is what the Sovereign LORD says: I will
make Tyre an uninhabited ruin, like many others. I
will bury you beneath the terrible waves of enemy

26:7 Hebrew *Nebuchadrezzar,* a variant spelling of Nebuchadnezzar.

KING JAMES VERSION

20 When I shall bring thee down with them that
descend into the pit, with the people of old time, and
shall set thee in the low parts of the earth, in places
desolate of old, with them that go down to the pit,
that thou be not inhabited; and I shall set glory in the
land of the living;
21 I will make thee a terror, and thou *shalt be* no
more: though thou be sought for, yet shalt thou never
be found again, saith the Lord God.

27 1 The word of the Lord came again unto me,
saying,
2 Now, thou son of man, take up a lamentation for
Tyrus;
3 And say unto Tyrus, O thou that art situate at the
entry of the sea, *which art* a merchant of the people
for many isles, Thus saith the Lord God; O Tyrus,
thou hast said, I *am* of perfect beauty.
4 Thy borders *are* in the midst of the seas, thy
builders have perfected thy beauty.
5 They have made all thy *ship* boards of fir trees of
Senir: they have taken cedars from Lebanon to make
masts for thee.
6 *Of* the oaks of Bashan have they made thine oars;
the company of the Ashurites have made thy
benches *of* ivory, *brought* out of the isles of Chittim.
7 Fine linen with broidered work from Egypt was
that which thou spreadest forth to be thy sail; blue
and purple from the isles of Elishah was that which
covered thee.
8 The inhabitants of Zidon and Arvad were thy
mariners: thy wise *men,* O Tyrus, *that* were in thee,
were thy pilots.
9 The ancients of Gebal and the wise *men* thereof
were in thee thy calkers: all the ships of the sea with
their mariners were in thee to occupy thy merchandise.
10 They of Persia and of Lud and of Phut were in
thine army, thy men of war: they hanged the shield
and helmet in thee; they set forth thy comeliness.
11 The men of Arvad with thine army *were* upon
thy walls round about, and the Gammadims were in
thy towers: they hanged their shields upon thy walls
round about; they have made thy beauty perfect.
12 Tarshish *was* thy merchant by reason of the
multitude of all *kind of* riches; with silver, iron, tin,
and lead, they traded in thy fairs.
13 Javan, Tubal, and Meshech, they *were* thy merchants: they traded the persons of men and vessels
of brass in thy market.
14 They of the house of Togarmah traded in thy
fairs with horses and horsemen and mules.
15 The men of Dedan *were* thy merchants; many
isles *were* the merchandise of thine hand: they
brought thee *for* a present horns of ivory and ebony.

NEW LIVING TRANSLATION

attack. Great seas will swallow you. 20 I will send you
to the pit to join those who descended there long
ago. Your city will lie in ruins, buried beneath the
earth, like those in the pit who have entered the
world of the dead. You will have no place of respect
here in the land of the living. 21 I will bring you to a
terrible end, and you will exist no more. You will be
looked for, but you will never again be found. I, the
Sovereign Lord, have spoken!"

The End of Tyre's Glory

27 Then this message came to me from the
Lord: 2 "Son of man, sing a funeral song
for Tyre, 3 that mighty gateway to the sea, the trading
center of the world. Give Tyre this message from the
Sovereign Lord:

"You boasted, O Tyre,
'My beauty is perfect!'
4 You extended your boundaries into the sea.
Your builders made your beauty perfect.
5 You were like a great ship
built of the finest cypress from Senir.*
They took a cedar from Lebanon
to make a mast for you.
6 They carved your oars
from the oaks of Bashan.
Your deck of pine from the coasts of Cyprus*
was inlaid with ivory.
7 Your sails were made of Egypt's finest linen,
and they flew as a banner above you.
You stood beneath blue and purple awnings
made bright with dyes from the coasts
of Elishah.
8 Your oarsmen came from Sidon and Arvad;
your helmsmen were skilled men from
Tyre itself.
9 Wise old craftsmen from Gebal did the caulking.
Ships from every land came with goods to
barter for your trade.

10 "Men from distant Persia, Lydia, and Libya*
served in your great army. They hung their shields and
helmets on your walls, giving you great honor. 11 Men
from Arvad and Helech stood on your walls. Your
towers were manned by men from Gammad. Their
shields hung on your walls, completing your beauty.
12 "Tarshish sent merchants to buy your wares in
exchange for silver, iron, tin, and lead. 13 Merchants
from Greece,* Tubal, and Meshech brought slaves
and articles of bronze to trade with you.
14 "From Beth-togarmah came riding horses, chariot horses, and mules, all in exchange for your goods.
15 Merchants came to you from Dedan.* Numerous
coastlands were your captive markets; they brought
payment in ivory tusks and ebony wood.

27:5 Or *Hermon.* **27:6** Hebrew *Kittim.* **27:10** Hebrew *Paras, Lud, and Put.* **27:13** Hebrew *Javan.* **27:15** Greek version reads *Rhodes.*

16 Syria *was* thy merchant by reason of the multitude of the wares of thy making: they occupied in thy
fairs with emeralds, purple, and broidered work, and
fine linen, and coral, and agate.

17 Judah, and the land of Israel, they *were* thy merchants: they traded in thy market wheat of Minnith,
and Pannag, and honey, and oil, and balm.

18 Damascus *was* thy merchant in the multitude
of the wares of thy making, for the multitude of all
riches; in the wine of Helbon, and white wool.

19 Dan also and Javan going to and fro occupied
in thy fairs: bright iron, cassia, and calamus, were in
thy market.

20 Dedan *was* thy merchant in precious clothes for
chariots.

21 Arabia, and all the princes of Kedar, they occupied with thee in lambs, and rams, and goats: in these
were they thy merchants.

22 The merchants of Sheba and Raamah, they *were*
thy merchants: they occupied in thy fairs with chief
of all spices, and with all precious stones, and gold.

23 Haran, and Canneh, and Eden, the merchants of
Sheba, Asshur, *and* Chilmad, *were* thy merchants.

24 These *were* thy merchants in all sorts *of things*,
in blue clothes, and broidered work, and in chests of
rich apparel, bound with cords, and made of cedar,
among thy merchandise.

25 The ships of Tarshish did sing of thee in thy
market: and thou wast replenished, and made very
glorious in the midst of the seas.

26 Thy rowers have brought thee into great waters:
the east wind hath broken thee in the midst of the
seas.

27 Thy riches, and thy fairs, thy merchandise, thy
mariners, and thy pilots, thy calkers, and the occupi-
ers of thy merchandise, and all thy men of war, that
are in thee, and in all thy company which *is* in the
midst of thee, shall fall into the midst of the seas in
the day of thy ruin.

28 The suburbs shall shake at the sound of the cry
of thy pilots.

29 And all that handle the oar, the mariners, *and* all
the pilots of the sea, shall come down from their
ships, they shall stand upon the land;

30 And shall cause their voice to be heard against
thee, and shall cry bitterly, and shall cast up dust
upon their heads, they shall wallow themselves in
the ashes:

31 And they shall make themselves utterly bald for
thee, and gird them with sackcloth, and they shall
weep for thee with bitterness of heart *and* bitter
wailing.

32 And in their wailing they shall take up a lamentation for thee, and lament over thee, *saying*, What
city is like Tyrus, like the destroyed in the midst of
the sea?

16 "Syria* sent merchants to buy your rich variety
of goods. They traded turquoise, purple dyes, embroidery, fine linen, and jewelry of coral and rubies.
17 Judah and Israel traded for your wares, offering
wheat from Minnith, figs,* honey, olive oil, and balm.

18 "Damascus sent merchants to buy your rich variety of goods, bringing wine from Helbon and white
wool from Zahar. 19 Greeks from Uzal* came to trade
for your merchandise. Wrought iron, cassia, and fragrant calamus were bartered for your wares.

20 "Dedan sent merchants to trade their expensive
saddle blankets with you. 21 The Arabians and the
princes of Kedar sent merchants to trade lambs and
rams and male goats in exchange for your goods.
22 The merchants of Sheba and Raamah came with
all kinds of spices, jewels, and gold in exchange for
your wares.

23 "Haran, Canneh, Eden, Sheba, Asshur, and Kil-
mad came with their merchandise, too. 24 They
brought choice fabrics to trade—blue cloth, embroidery, and multicolored carpets rolled up and bound
with cords. 25 The ships of Tarshish were your ocean
caravans. Your island warehouse was filled to the
brim!

The Destruction of Tyre

26 "But look! Your oarsmen
have taken you into stormy seas!
A mighty eastern gale
has wrecked you in the heart of the sea!
27 Everything is lost—
your riches and wares,
your sailors and pilots,
your ship builders, merchants, and warriors.
On the day of your ruin,
everyone on board sinks into the depths
of the sea.
28 Your cities by the sea tremble
as your pilots cry out in terror.
29 All the oarsmen abandon their ships;
the sailors and pilots on shore come to stand
on the beach.
30 They cry aloud over you
and weep bitterly.
They throw dust on their heads
and roll in ashes.
31 They shave their heads in grief for you
and dress themselves in burlap.
They weep for you with bitter anguish
and deep mourning.
32 As they wail and mourn over you,
they sing this sad funeral song:

27:16 Hebrew *Aram;* some manuscripts read *Edom.* **27:17** The meaning of the Hebrew is uncertain. **27:19** Hebrew *Vedan and Javan from Uzal.* The meaning of the Hebrew is uncertain.

KING JAMES VERSION

33 When thy wares went forth out of the seas, thou filledst many people; thou didst enrich the kings of the earth with the multitude of thy riches and of thy merchandise.

34 In the time *when* thou shalt be broken by the seas in the depths of the waters thy merchandise and all thy company in the midst of thee shall fall.

35 All the inhabitants of the isles shall be astonished at thee, and their kings shall be sore afraid, they shall be troubled in *their* countenance.

36 The merchants among the people shall hiss at thee; thou shalt be a terror, and never *shalt be* any more.

28 1 The word of the LORD came again unto me, saying,

2 Son of man, say unto the prince of Tyrus, Thus saith the Lord GOD; Because thine heart *is* lifted up, and thou hast said, I *am* a God, I sit *in* the seat of God, in the midst of the seas; yet thou *art* a man, and not God, though thou set thine heart as the heart of God:

3 Behold, thou *art* wiser than Daniel; there is no secret that they can hide from thee:

4 With thy wisdom and with thine understanding thou hast gotten thee riches, and hast gotten gold and silver into thy treasures:

5 By thy great wisdom *and* by thy traffick hast thou increased thy riches, and thine heart is lifted up because of thy riches:

6 Therefore thus saith the Lord GOD; Because thou hast set thine heart as the heart of God;

7 Behold, therefore I will bring strangers upon thee, the terrible of the nations: and they shall draw their swords against the beauty of thy wisdom, and they shall defile thy brightness.

8 They shall bring thee down to the pit, and thou shalt die the deaths of *them that are* slain in the midst of the seas.

9 Wilt thou yet say before him that slayeth thee, I *am* God? but thou *shalt be* a man, and no God, in the hand of him that slayeth thee.

10 Thou shalt die the deaths of the uncircumcised by the hand of strangers: for I have spoken *it,* saith the Lord GOD.

11 Moreover the word of the LORD came unto me, saying,

12 Son of man, take up a lamentation upon the king of Tyrus, and say unto him, Thus saith the Lord GOD;

NEW LIVING TRANSLATION

'Was there ever such a city as Tyre,
now silent at the bottom of the sea?
33 The merchandise you traded
satisfied the desires of many nations.
Kings at the ends of the earth
were enriched by your trade.
34 Now you are a wrecked ship,
broken at the bottom of the sea.
All your merchandise and crew
have gone down with you.
35 All who live along the coastlands
are appalled at your terrible fate.
Their kings are filled with horror
and look on with twisted faces.
36 The merchants among the nations
shake their heads at the sight of you,*
for you have come to a horrible end
and will exist no more.'"

A Message for Tyre's King

28 Then this message came to me from the
LORD: 2 "Son of man, give the prince of Tyre
this message from the Sovereign LORD:

"In your great pride you claim, 'I am a god!
I sit on a divine throne in the heart of the sea.'
But you are only a man and not a god,
though you boast that you are a god.
3 You regard yourself as wiser than Daniel
and think no secret is hidden from you.
4 With your wisdom and understanding you have
amassed great wealth—
gold and silver for your treasuries.
5 Yes, your wisdom has made you very rich,
and your riches have made you very proud.
6 "Therefore, this is what the Sovereign LORD says:
Because you think you are as wise as a god,
7 I will now bring against you a foreign army,
the terror of the nations.
They will draw their swords against your
marvelous wisdom
and defile your splendor!
8 They will bring you down to the pit,
and you will die in the heart of the sea,
pierced with many wounds.
9 Will you then boast, 'I am a god!'
to those who kill you?
To them you will be no god
but merely a man!
10 You will die like an outcast*
at the hands of foreigners.
I, the Sovereign LORD, have spoken!"

11 Then this further message came to me from
the LORD: 12 "Son of man, sing this funeral song for
the king of Tyre. Give him this message from the
Sovereign LORD:

27:36 Hebrew *hiss at you.* **28:10** Hebrew *will die the death of the uncircumcised.*

KING JAMES VERSION

Thou sealest up the sum, full of wisdom, and perfect in beauty.

13 Thou hast been in Eden the garden of God; every precious stone *was* thy covering, the sardius, topaz, and the diamond, the beryl, the onyx, and the jasper, the sapphire, the emerald, and the carbuncle, and gold: the workmanship of thy tabrets and of thy pipes was prepared in thee in the day that thou wast created.

14 Thou *art* the anointed cherub that covereth; and I have set thee *so:* thou wast upon the holy mountain of God; thou hast walked up and down in the midst of the stones of fire.

15 Thou *wast* perfect in thy ways from the day that thou wast created, till iniquity was found in thee.

16 By the multitude of thy merchandise they have filled the midst of thee with violence, and thou hast sinned: therefore I will cast thee as profane out of the mountain of God: and I will destroy thee, O covering cherub, from the midst of the stones of fire.

17 Thine heart was lifted up because of thy beauty, thou hast corrupted thy wisdom by reason of thy brightness: I will cast thee to the ground, I will lay thee before kings, that they may behold thee.

18 Thou hast defiled thy sanctuaries by the multitude of thine iniquities, by the iniquity of thy traffick; therefore will I bring forth a fire from the midst of thee, it shall devour thee, and I will bring thee to ashes upon the earth in the sight of all them that behold thee.

19 All they that know thee among the people shall be astonished at thee: thou shalt be a terror, and never *shalt* thou *be* any more.

20 Again the word of the LORD came unto me, saying,

21 Son of man, set thy face against Zidon, and prophesy against it,

22 And say, Thus saith the Lord GOD; Behold, I *am* against thee, O Zidon; and I will be glorified in the midst of thee: and they shall know that I *am* the LORD, when I shall have executed judgments in her, and shall be sanctified in her.

23 For I will send into her pestilence, and blood into

NEW LIVING TRANSLATION

"You were the model of perfection,
full of wisdom and exquisite in beauty.
13 You were in Eden,
the garden of God.
Your clothing was adorned with every
precious stone*—
red carnelian, pale-green peridot, white
moonstone,
blue-green beryl, onyx, green jasper,
blue lapis lazuli, turquoise, and emerald—
all beautifully crafted for you
and set in the finest gold.
They were given to you
on the day you were created.
14 I ordained and anointed you
as the mighty angelic guardian.*
You had access to the holy mountain of God
and walked among the stones of fire.

15 "You were blameless in all you did
from the day you were created
until the day evil was found in you.
16 Your rich commerce led you to violence,
and you sinned.
So I banished you in disgrace
from the mountain of God.
I expelled you, O mighty guardian,
from your place among the stones of fire.
17 Your heart was filled with pride
because of all your beauty.
Your wisdom was corrupted
by your love of splendor.
So I threw you to the ground
and exposed you to the curious gaze of kings.
18 You defiled your sanctuaries
with your many sins and your dishonest trade.
So I brought fire out from within you,
and it consumed you.
I reduced you to ashes on the ground
in the sight of all who were watching.
19 All who knew you are appalled at your fate.
You have come to a terrible end,
and you will exist no more."

A Message for Sidon

20 Then another message came to me from the LORD:
21 "Son of man, turn and face the city of Sidon and
prophesy against it. 22 Give the people of Sidon this
message from the Sovereign LORD:

"I am your enemy, O Sidon,
and I will reveal my glory by what I do to you.
When I bring judgment against you
and reveal my holiness among you,
everyone watching will know
that I am the LORD.
23 I will send a plague against you,

28:13 The identification of some of these gemstones is uncertain.
28:14 Hebrew *guardian cherub;* similarly in 28:16.

KING JAMES VERSION

her streets; and the wounded shall be judged in the midst of her by the sword upon her on every side; and they shall know that I *am* the LORD.

24 And there shall be no more a pricking brier unto the house of Israel, nor *any* grieving thorn of all *that are* round about them, that despised them; and they shall know that I *am* the Lord GOD.

25 Thus saith the Lord GOD; When I shall have gathered the house of Israel from the people among whom they are scattered, and shall be sanctified in them in the sight of the heathen, then shall they dwell in their land that I have given to my servant Jacob.

26 And they shall dwell safely therein, and shall build houses, and plant vineyards; yea, they shall dwell with confidence, when I have executed judgments upon all those that despise them round about them; and they shall know that I *am* the LORD their God.

29 1 In the tenth year, in the tenth *month*, in the twelfth *day* of the month, the word of the LORD came unto me, saying,

2 Son of man, set thy face against Pharaoh king of Egypt, and prophesy against him, and against all Egypt:

3 Speak, and say, Thus saith the Lord GOD; Behold, I *am* against thee, Pharaoh king of Egypt, the great dragon that lieth in the midst of his rivers, which hath said, My river *is* mine own, and I have made *it* for myself.

4 But I will put hooks in thy jaws, and I will cause the fish of thy rivers to stick unto thy scales, and I will bring thee up out of the midst of thy rivers, and all the fish of thy rivers shall stick unto thy scales.

5 And I will leave thee *thrown* into the wilderness, thee and all the fish of thy rivers: thou shalt fall upon the open fields; thou shalt not be brought together, nor gathered: I have given thee for meat to the beasts of the field and to the fowls of the heaven.

6 And all the inhabitants of Egypt shall know that I *am* the LORD, because they have been a staff of reed to the house of Israel.

7 When they took hold of thee by thy hand, thou didst break, and rend all their shoulder: and when they leaned upon thee, thou brakest, and madest all their loins to be at a stand.

8 Therefore thus saith the Lord GOD; Behold, I will bring a sword upon thee, and cut off man and beast out of thee.

9 And the land of Egypt shall be desolate and waste; and they shall know that I *am* the LORD: because he hath said, The river *is* mine, and I have made *it*.

NEW LIVING TRANSLATION

and blood will be spilled in your streets.
The attack will come from every direction,
and your people will lie slaughtered within
your walls.
Then everyone will know
that I am the LORD.
24 No longer will Israel's scornful neighbors
prick and tear at her like briers and thorns.
For then they will know
that I am the Sovereign LORD.

Restoration for Israel

25 "This is what the Sovereign LORD says: The people of Israel will again live in their own land, the land I gave my servant Jacob. For I will gather them from the distant lands where I have scattered them. I will reveal to the nations of the world my holiness among my people. 26 They will live safely in Israel and build homes and plant vineyards. And when I punish the neighboring nations that treated them with contempt, they will know that I am the LORD their God."

A Message for Egypt

29 On January 7,* during the tenth year of King Jehoiachin's captivity, this message came to me from the LORD: 2 "Son of man, turn and face Egypt and prophesy against Pharaoh the king and all the people of Egypt. 3 Give them this message from the Sovereign LORD:

"I am your enemy, O Pharaoh, king of Egypt—
you great monster, lurking in the streams
of the Nile.
For you have said, 'The Nile River is mine;
I made it for myself.'
4 I will put hooks in your jaws
and drag you out on the land
with fish sticking to your scales.
5 I will leave you and all your fish
stranded in the wilderness to die.
You will lie unburied on the open ground,
for I have given you as food to the
wild animals and birds.
6 All the people of Egypt will know that I am the
LORD,
for to Israel you were just a staff made of reeds.
7 When Israel leaned on you,
you splintered and broke
and stabbed her in the armpit.
When she put her weight on you, you gave way,
and her back was thrown out of joint.

8 "Therefore, this is what the Sovereign LORD says: I will bring an army against you, O Egypt, and destroy both people and animals. 9 The land of Egypt will become a desolate wasteland, and the Egyptians will know that I am the LORD.

29:1 Hebrew *On the twelfth day of the tenth month,* of the ancient Hebrew lunar calendar. This event occurred on January 7, 587 B.C.; also see note on 1:1.

KING JAMES VERSION

10Behold, therefore I *am* against thee, and against
thy rivers, and I will make the land of Egypt utterly
waste *and* desolate, from the tower of Syene even
unto the border of Ethiopia.
11No foot of man shall pass through it, nor foot of
beast shall pass through it, neither shall it be inhabited forty years.
12And I will make the land of Egypt desolate in the
midst of the countries *that are* desolate, and her
cities among the cities *that are* laid waste shall be
desolate forty years: and I will scatter the Egyptians
among the nations, and will disperse them through
the countries.
13Yet thus saith the Lord GOD; At the end of forty
years will I gather the Egyptians from the people
whither they were scattered:
14And I will bring again the captivity of Egypt, and
will cause them to return *into* the land of Pathros,
into the land of their habitation; and they shall be
there a base kingdom.
15It shall be the basest of the kingdoms; neither
shall it exalt itself any more above the nations: for I
will diminish them, that they shall no more rule over
the nations.
16And it shall be no more the confidence of the
house of Israel, which bringeth *their* iniquity to remembrance, when they shall look after them: but
they shall know that I *am* the Lord GOD.
17And it came to pass in the seven and twentieth
year, in the first *month,* in the first *day* of the month,
the word of the LORD came unto me, saying,
18Son of man, Nebuchadrezzar king of Babylon
caused his army to serve a great service against
Tyrus: every head *was* made bald, and every shoulder
was peeled: yet had he no wages, nor his army, for
Tyrus, for the service that he had served against it:
19Therefore thus saith the Lord GOD; Behold, I will
give the land of Egypt unto Nebuchadrezzar king of
Babylon; and he shall take her multitude, and take
her spoil, and take her prey; and it shall be the wages
for his army.
20I have given him the land of Egypt *for* his labour
wherewith he served against it, because they
wrought for me, saith the Lord GOD.
21In that day will I cause the horn of the house of
Israel to bud forth, and I will give thee the opening of
the mouth in the midst of them; and they shall know
that I *am* the LORD.

30 1The word of the LORD came again unto me,
saying,
2Son of man, prophesy and say, Thus saith the
Lord GOD; Howl ye, Woe worth the day!

NEW LIVING TRANSLATION

"Because you said, 'The Nile River is mine; I made
it,' 10I am now the enemy of both you and your river. I
will make the land of Egypt a totally desolate wasteland, from Migdol to Aswan, as far south as the border of Ethiopia.* 11For forty years not a soul will pass
that way, neither people nor animals. It will be completely uninhabited. 12I will make Egypt desolate,
and it will be surrounded by other desolate nations.
Its cities will be empty and desolate for forty years,
surrounded by other ruined cities. I will scatter the
Egyptians to distant lands.
13"But this is what the Sovereign LORD also says: At
the end of the forty years I will bring the Egyptians
home again from the nations to which they have
been scattered. 14I will restore the prosperity of
Egypt and bring its people back to the land of Pathros in southern Egypt from which they came. But
Egypt will remain an unimportant, minor kingdom.
15It will be the lowliest of all the nations, never again
great enough to rise above its neighbors.
16"Then Israel will no longer be tempted to trust
in Egypt for help. Egypt's shattered condition will
remind Israel of how sinful she was to trust Egypt in
earlier days. Then Israel will know that I am the
Sovereign LORD."

Nebuchadnezzar to Conquer Egypt

17On April 26, the first day of the new year,* during
the twenty-seventh year of King Jehoiachin's captivity, this message came to me from the LORD: 18"Son
of man, the army of King Nebuchadnezzar* of Babylon fought so hard against Tyre that the warriors'
heads were rubbed bare and their shoulders were
raw and blistered. Yet Nebuchadnezzar and his army
won no plunder to compensate them for all their
work. 19Therefore, this is what the Sovereign LORD
says: I will give the land of Egypt to Nebuchadnezzar,
king of Babylon. He will carry off its wealth, plunder-
ing everything it has so he can pay his army. 20Yes, I
have given him the land of Egypt as a reward for his
work, says the Sovereign LORD, because he was working for me when he destroyed Tyre.
21"And the day will come when I will cause the ancient glory of Israel to revive,* and then, Ezekiel, your
words will be respected. Then they will know that I
am the LORD."

A Sad Day for Egypt

30 This is another message that came to me
from the LORD: 2"Son of man, prophesy and
give this message from the Sovereign LORD:

"Weep and wail
for that day,

29:10 Hebrew *from Migdol to Syene as far as the border of Cush.*
29:17 Hebrew *On the first day of the first month,* of the ancient Hebrew lunar calendar. This event occurred on April 26, 571 B.C.; also see note on 1:1.
29:18 Hebrew *Nebuchadrezzar,* a variant spelling of Nebuchadnezzar; also in 29:19. **29:21** Hebrew *I will cause a horn to sprout for the house of Israel.*

KING JAMES VERSION

3 For the day *is* near, even the day of the LORD *is* near, a cloudy day; it shall be the time of the heathen.

4 And the sword shall come upon Egypt, and great pain shall be in Ethiopia, when the slain shall fall in Egypt, and they shall take away her multitude, and her foundations shall be broken down.

5 Ethiopia, and Libya, and Lydia, and all the mingled people, and Chub, and the men of the land that is in league, shall fall with them by the sword.

6 Thus saith the LORD; They also that uphold Egypt shall fall; and the pride of her power shall come down: from the tower of Syene shall they fall in it by the sword, saith the Lord GOD.

7 And they shall be desolate in the midst of the countries *that are* desolate, and her cities shall be in the midst of the cities *that are* wasted.

8 And they shall know that I *am* the LORD, when I have set a fire in Egypt, and *when* all her helpers shall be destroyed.

9 In that day shall messengers go forth from me in ships to make the careless Ethiopians afraid, and great pain shall come upon them, as in the day of Egypt: for, lo, it cometh.

10 Thus saith the Lord GOD; I will also make the multitude of Egypt to cease by the hand of Nebuchadrezzar king of Babylon.

11 He and his people with him, the terrible of the nations, shall be brought to destroy the land: and they shall draw their swords against Egypt, and fill the land with the slain.

12 And I will make the rivers dry, and sell the land into the hand of the wicked: and I will make the land waste, and all that is therein, by the hand of strangers: I the LORD have spoken *it*.

13 Thus saith the Lord GOD; I will also destroy the idols, and I will cause *their* images to cease out of Noph; and there shall be no more a prince of the land of Egypt: and I will put a fear in the land of Egypt.

NEW LIVING TRANSLATION

3 for the terrible day is almost here—
the day of the LORD!
It is a day of clouds and gloom,
a day of despair for the nations.
4 A sword will come against Egypt,
and those who are slaughtered will
cover the ground.
Its wealth will be carried away
and its foundations destroyed.
The land of Ethiopia* will be ravished.
5 Ethiopia, Libya, Lydia, all Arabia,*
and all their other allies
will be destroyed in that war.

6 "For this is what the LORD says:
All of Egypt's allies will fall,
and the pride of her power will end.
From Migdol to Aswan*
they will be slaughtered by the sword,
says the Sovereign LORD.
7 Egypt will be desolate,
surrounded by desolate nations,
and its cities will be in ruins,
surrounded by other ruined cities.
8 And the people of Egypt will know that
I am the LORD
when I have set Egypt on fire
and destroyed all their allies.
9 At that time I will send swift messengers
in ships
to terrify the complacent Ethiopians.
Great panic will come upon them
on that day of Egypt's certain destruction.
Watch for it!
It is sure to come!
10 "For this is what the Sovereign LORD says:
By the power of King Nebuchadnezzar*
of Babylon,
I will destroy the hordes of Egypt.
11 He and his armies—the most ruthless of all—
will be sent to demolish the land.
They will make war against Egypt
until slaughtered Egyptians cover the ground.
12 I will dry up the Nile River
and sell the land to wicked men.
I will destroy the land of Egypt and
everything in it
by the hands of foreigners.
I, the LORD, have spoken!

13 "This is what the Sovereign LORD says:
I will smash the idols* of Egypt
and the images at Memphis.*
There will be no rulers left in Egypt;
terror will sweep the land.

30:4 Hebrew *Cush;* similarly in 30:9. **30:5** Hebrew *Cush, Put, Lud, all Arabia, Cub. Cub* is otherwise unknown and may be another spelling for *Lub* (Libya). **30:6** Hebrew *to Syene.* **30:10** Hebrew *Nebuchadrezzar*, a variant spelling of Nebuchadnezzar. **30:13a** The Hebrew term (literally *round things*) probably alludes to dung. **30:13b** Hebrew *Noph;* also in 30:16.

KING JAMES VERSION

14 And I will make Pathros desolate, and will set fire in Zoan, and will execute judgments in No.

15 And I will pour my fury upon Sin, the strength of Egypt; and I will cut off the multitude of No.

16 And I will set fire in Egypt: Sin shall have great pain, and No shall be rent asunder, and Noph *shall have* distresses daily.

17 The young men of Aven and of Pi-beseth shall fall by the sword: and these *cities* shall go into captivity.

18 At Tehaphnehes also the day shall be darkened, when I shall break there the yokes of Egypt: and the pomp of her strength shall cease in her: as for her, a cloud shall cover her, and her daughters shall go into captivity.

19 Thus will I execute judgments in Egypt: and they shall know that I *am* the LORD.

20 And it came to pass in the eleventh year, in the first *month,* in the seventh *day* of the month, *that* the word of the LORD came unto me, saying,

21 Son of man, I have broken the arm of Pharaoh king of Egypt; and, lo, it shall not be bound up to be healed, to put a roller to bind it, to make it strong to hold the sword.

22 Therefore thus saith the Lord GOD; Behold, I *am* against Pharaoh king of Egypt, and will break his arms, the strong, and that which was broken; and I will cause the sword to fall out of his hand.

23 And I will scatter the Egyptians among the nations, and will disperse them through the countries.

24 And I will strengthen the arms of the king of Babylon, and put my sword in his hand: but I will break Pharaoh's arms, and he shall groan before him with the groanings of a deadly wounded *man.*

25 But I will strengthen the arms of the king of Babylon, and the arms of Pharaoh shall fall down; and they shall know that I *am* the LORD, when I shall put my sword into the hand of the king of Babylon, and he shall stretch it out upon the land of Egypt.

26 And I will scatter the Egyptians among the nations, and disperse them among the countries; and they shall know that I *am* the LORD.

31 1 And it came to pass in the eleventh year, in the third *month,* in the first *day* of the month, *that* the word of the LORD came unto me, saying,

2 Son of man, speak unto Pharaoh king of Egypt,

NEW LIVING TRANSLATION

14 I will destroy southern Egypt,*
set fire to Zoan,
and bring judgment against Thebes.*
15 I will pour out my fury on Pelusium,*
the strongest fortress of Egypt,
and I will stamp out
the hordes of Thebes.
16 Yes, I will set fire to all Egypt!
Pelusium will be racked with pain;
Thebes will be torn apart;
Memphis will live in constant terror.
17 The young men of Heliopolis and Bubastis*
will die in battle,
and the women* will be taken away as slaves.
18 When I come to break the proud strength
of Egypt,
it will be a dark day for Tahpanhes, too.
A dark cloud will cover Tahpanhes,
and its daughters will be led away as captives.
19 And so I will greatly punish Egypt,
and they will know that I am the LORD."

The Broken Arms of Pharaoh

20 On April 29,* during the eleventh year of King
Jehoiachin's captivity, this message came to me from
the LORD: 21 "Son of man, I have broken the arm of
Pharaoh, the king of Egypt. His arm has not been put
in a cast so that it may heal. Neither has it been
bound up with a splint to make it strong enough to
hold a sword. 22 Therefore, this is what the Sovereign
LORD says: I am the enemy of Pharaoh, the king of
Egypt! I will break both of his arms—the good arm
along with the broken one—and I will make his
sword clatter to the ground. 23 I will scatter the Egyptians to many lands throughout the world. 24 I will
strengthen the arms of Babylon's king and put my
sword in his hand. But I will break the arms of Pharaoh, king of Egypt, and he will lie there mortally
wounded, groaning in pain. 25 I will strengthen the
arms of the king of Babylon, while the arms of Pharaoh fall useless to his sides. And when I put my
sword in the hand of Babylon's king and he brings it
against the land of Egypt, Egypt will know that I am
the LORD. 26 I will scatter the Egyptians among the nations, dispersing them throughout the earth. Then
they will know that I am the LORD."

Egypt Compared to Fallen Assyria

31 On June 21,* during the eleventh year of
King Jehoiachin's captivity, this message
came to me from the LORD: 2 "Son of man, give this
message to Pharaoh, king of Egypt, and all his hordes:

30:14a Hebrew *Pathros.* **30:14b** Hebrew *No;* also in 30:15, 16. **30:15** Hebrew *Sin;* also in 30:16. **30:17a** Hebrew *of Awen and Pi-beseth.* **30:17b** Or *and her cities.* **30:20** Hebrew *On the seventh day of the first month,* of the ancient Hebrew lunar calendar. This event occurred on April 29, 587 B.C.; also see note on 1:1. **31:1** Hebrew *On the first day of the third month,* of the ancient Hebrew lunar calendar. This event occurred on June 21, 587 B.C.; also see note on 1:1.

KING JAMES VERSION

and to his multitude; Whom art thou like in thy greatness?

3 Behold, the Assyrian *was* a cedar in Lebanon with fair branches, and with a shadowing shroud, and of an high stature; and his top was among the thick boughs.

4 The waters made him great, the deep set him up on high with her rivers running round about his plants, and sent out her little rivers unto all the trees of the field.

5 Therefore his height was exalted above all the trees of the field, and his boughs were multiplied, and his branches became long because of the multitude of waters, when he shot forth.

6 All the fowls of heaven made their nests in his boughs, and under his branches did all the beasts of the field bring forth their young, and under his shadow dwelt all great nations.

7 Thus was he fair in his greatness, in the length of his branches: for his root was by great waters.

8 The cedars in the garden of God could not hide him: the fir trees were not like his boughs, and the chestnut trees were not like his branches; nor any tree in the garden of God was like unto him in his beauty.

9 I have made him fair by the multitude of his branches: so that all the trees of Eden, that *were* in the garden of God, envied him.

10 Therefore thus saith the Lord God; Because thou hast lifted up thyself in height, and he hath shot up his top among the thick boughs, and his heart is lifted up in his height;

11 I have therefore delivered him into the hand of the mighty one of the heathen; he shall surely deal with him: I have driven him out for his wickedness.

12 And strangers, the terrible of the nations, have cut him off, and have left him: upon the mountains and in all the valleys his branches are fallen, and his boughs are broken by all the rivers of the land; and all the people of the earth are gone down from his shadow, and have left him.

13 Upon his ruin shall all the fowls of the heaven remain, and all the beasts of the field shall be upon his branches:

14 To the end that none of all the trees by the waters exalt themselves for their height, neither shoot up their top among the thick boughs, neither their trees stand up in their height, all that drink water: for they are all delivered unto death, to the nether parts of the earth, in the midst of the children of men, with them that go down to the pit.

15 Thus saith the Lord God; In the day when he went down to the grave I caused a mourning: I covered the deep for him, and I restrained the floods thereof, and the great waters were stayed: and I

NEW LIVING TRANSLATION

"To whom would you compare your greatness?
3 You are like mighty Assyria,
which was once like a cedar of Lebanon,
with beautiful branches that cast deep forest shade
and with its top high among the clouds.
4 Deep springs watered it
and helped it to grow tall and luxuriant.
The water flowed around it like a river,
streaming to all the trees nearby.
5 This great tree towered high,
higher than all the other trees around it.
It prospered and grew long thick branches
because of all the water at its roots.
6 The birds nested in its branches,
and in its shade all the wild animals gave birth.
All the great nations of the world
lived in its shadow.
7 It was strong and beautiful,
with wide-spreading branches,
for its roots went deep
into abundant water.
8 No other cedar in the garden of God
could rival it.
No cypress had branches to equal it;
no plane tree had boughs to compare.
No tree in the garden of God
came close to it in beauty.
9 Because I made this tree so beautiful,
and gave it such magnificent foliage,
it was the envy of all the other trees of Eden,
the garden of God.

10 "Therefore, this is what the Sovereign Lord says:
Because Egypt* became proud and arrogant, and because it set itself so high above the others, with its
top reaching to the clouds, 11 I will hand it over to a
mighty nation that will destroy it as its wickedness
deserves. I have already discarded it. 12 A foreign
army—the terror of the nations—has cut it down and
left it fallen on the ground. Its branches are scattered
across the mountains and valleys and ravines of the
land. All those who lived in its shadow have gone
away and left it lying there.

13 "The birds roost on its fallen trunk,
and the wild animals lie among its branches.
14 Let the tree of no other nation
proudly exult in its own prosperity,
though it be higher than the clouds
and it be watered from the depths.
For all are doomed to die,
to go down to the depths of the earth.
They will land in the pit
along with everyone else on earth.

15 "This is what the Sovereign Lord says: When
Assyria went down to the grave,* I made the deep
springs mourn. I stopped its rivers and dried up its

31:10 Hebrew *you.* **31:15** Hebrew *to Sheol;* also in 31:16, 17.

KING JAMES VERSION

caused Lebanon to mourn for him, and all the trees
of the field fainted for him.
16 I made the nations to shake at the sound of his
fall, when I cast him down to hell with them that
descend into the pit: and all the trees of Eden, the
choice and best of Lebanon, all that drink water, shall
be comforted in the nether parts of the earth.
17 They also went down into hell with him unto
them that be slain with the sword; and *they that*
were his arm, *that* dwelt under his shadow in the
midst of the heathen.
18 To whom art thou thus like in glory and in
greatness among the trees of Eden? yet shalt thou
be brought down with the trees of Eden unto the
nether parts of the earth: thou shalt lie in the midst
of the uncircumcised with *them that be* slain by the
sword. This *is* Pharaoh and all his multitude, saith
the Lord GOD.

32 1 And it came to pass in the twelfth year,
in the twelfth month, in the first *day* of the
month, *that* the word of the LORD came unto me,
saying,
2 Son of man, take up a lamentation for Pharaoh
king of Egypt, and say unto him, Thou art like a young
lion of the nations, and thou *art* as a whale in the
seas: and thou camest forth with thy rivers, and
troubledst the waters with thy feet, and fouledst
their rivers.
3 Thus saith the Lord GOD; I will therefore spread
out my net over thee with a company of many
people; and they shall bring thee up in my net.
4 Then will I leave thee upon the land, I will cast
thee forth upon the open field, and will cause all the
fowls of the heaven to remain upon thee, and I will
fill the beasts of the whole earth with thee.
5 And I will lay thy flesh upon the mountains, and
fill the valleys with thy height.
6 I will also water with thy blood the land wherein
thou swimmest, *even* to the mountains; and the
rivers shall be full of thee.
7 And when I shall put thee out, I will cover the
heaven, and make the stars thereof dark; I will cover
the sun with a cloud, and the moon shall not give her
light.
8 All the bright lights of heaven will I make dark
over thee, and set darkness upon thy land, saith the
Lord GOD.
9 I will also vex the hearts of many people, when I
shall bring thy destruction among the nations, into
the countries which thou hast not known.
10 Yea, I will make many people amazed at thee,
and their kings shall be horribly afraid for thee,
when I shall brandish my sword before them; and
they shall tremble at *every* moment, every man for
his own life, in the day of thy fall.

NEW LIVING TRANSLATION

abundant water. I clothed Lebanon in black and
caused the trees of the field to wilt. 16 I made the nations shake with fear at the sound of its fall, for I sent
it down to the grave with all the others who descend
to the pit. And all the other proud trees of Eden, the
most beautiful and the best of Lebanon, the ones
whose roots went deep into the water, took comfort
to find it there with them in the depths of the earth.
17 Its allies, too, were all destroyed and had passed
away. They had gone down to the grave—all those
nations that had lived in its shade.
18 "O Egypt, to which of the trees of Eden will you
compare your strength and glory? You, too, will be
brought down to the depths with all these other nations. You will lie there among the outcasts* who
have died by the sword. This will be the fate of Pharaoh and all his hordes. I, the Sovereign LORD, have
spoken!"

A Warning for Pharaoh

32 On March 3,* during the twelfth year of
King Jehoiachin's captivity, this message
came to me from the LORD: 2 "Son of man, mourn for
Pharaoh, king of Egypt, and give him this message:

"You think of yourself as a strong young lion
among the nations,
but you are really just a sea monster,
heaving around in your own rivers,
stirring up mud with your feet.
3 Therefore, this is what the Sovereign LORD says:
I will send many people
to catch you in my net
and haul you out of the water.
4 I will leave you stranded on the land to die.
All the birds of the heavens will land on you,
and the wild animals of the whole earth
will gorge themselves on you.
5 I will scatter your flesh on the hills
and fill the valleys with your bones.
6 I will drench the earth with your gushing blood
all the way to the mountains,
filling the ravines to the brim.
7 When I blot you out,
I will veil the heavens and darken the stars.
I will cover the sun with a cloud,
and the moon will not give you its light.
8 I will darken the bright stars overhead
and cover your land in darkness.
I, the Sovereign LORD, have spoken!

9 "I will disturb many hearts when I bring news of
your downfall to distant nations you have never seen.
10 Yes, I will shock many lands, and their kings will
be terrified at your fate. They will shudder in fear for
their lives as I brandish my sword before them on the

31:18 Hebrew *among the uncircumcised.* **32:1** Hebrew *On the first day of the twelfth month,* of the ancient Hebrew lunar calendar. This event occurred on March 3, 585 B.C.; also see note on 1:1.

KING JAMES VERSION

11 For thus saith the Lord GOD; The sword of the king of Babylon shall come upon thee.

12 By the swords of the mighty will I cause thy multitude to fall, the terrible of the nations, all of them: and they shall spoil the pomp of Egypt, and all the multitude thereof shall be destroyed.

13 I will destroy also all the beasts thereof from beside the great waters; neither shall the foot of man trouble them any more, nor the hoofs of beasts trouble them.

14 Then will I make their waters deep, and cause their rivers to run like oil, saith the Lord GOD.

15 When I shall make the land of Egypt desolate, and the country shall be destitute of that whereof it was full, when I shall smite all them that dwell therein, then shall they know that I *am* the LORD.

16 This *is* the lamentation wherewith they shall lament her: the daughters of the nations shall lament her: they shall lament for her, *even* for Egypt, and for all her multitude, saith the Lord GOD.

17 It came to pass also in the twelfth year, in the fifteenth *day* of the month, *that* the word of the LORD came unto me, saying,

18 Son of man, wail for the multitude of Egypt, and cast them down, *even* her, and the daughters of the famous nations, unto the nether parts of the earth, with them that go down into the pit.

19 Whom dost thou pass in beauty? go down, and be thou laid with the uncircumcised.

20 They shall fall in the midst of *them that are* slain by the sword: she is delivered to the sword: draw her and all her multitudes.

21 The strong among the mighty shall speak to him out of the midst of hell with them that help him: they are gone down, they lie uncircumcised, slain by the sword.

22 Asshur *is* there and all her company: his graves *are* about him: all of them slain, fallen by the sword:

23 Whose graves are set in the sides of the pit, and her company is round about her grave: all of them slain, fallen by the sword, which caused terror in the land of the living.

NEW LIVING TRANSLATION

day of your fall. 11 For this is what the Sovereign LORD says:

"The sword of the king of Babylon
will come against you.
12 I will destroy your hordes with the swords
of mighty warriors—
the terror of the nations.
They will shatter the pride of Egypt,
and all its hordes will be destroyed.
13 I will destroy all your flocks and herds
that graze beside the streams.
Never again will people or animals
muddy those waters with their feet.
14 Then I will let the waters of Egypt become
calm again,
and they will flow as smoothly as olive oil,
says the Sovereign LORD.
15 And when I destroy Egypt
and strip you of everything you own
and strike down all your people,
then you will know that I am the LORD.
16 Yes, this is the funeral song
they will sing for Egypt.
Let all the nations mourn.
Let them mourn for Egypt and its hordes.
I, the Sovereign LORD, have spoken!"

Egypt Falls into the Pit

17 On March 17,* during the twelfth year, another message came to me from the LORD: 18 "Son of man, weep for the hordes of Egypt and for the other mighty nations.* For I will send them down to the world below in company with those who descend to the pit. 19 Say to them,

'O Egypt, are you lovelier than the other nations?
No! So go down to the pit and lie there among
the outcasts.*'

20 The Egyptians will fall with the many who have died by the sword, for the sword is drawn against them. Egypt and its hordes will be dragged away to their judgment. 21 Down in the grave* mighty leaders will mockingly welcome Egypt and its allies, saying, 'They have come down; they lie among the outcasts, hordes slaughtered by the sword.'

22 "Assyria lies there surrounded by the graves of its army, those who were slaughtered by the sword. 23 Their graves are in the depths of the pit, and they are surrounded by their allies. They struck terror in the hearts of people everywhere, but now they have been slaughtered by the sword.

32:17 Hebrew *On the fifteenth day of the month,* presumably in the twelfth month of the ancient Hebrew lunar calendar (see 32:1). This would put this message at the end of King Jehoiachin's twelfth year of captivity, on March 17, 585 B.C.; also see note on 1:1. Greek version reads *On the fifteenth day of the first month,* which would put this message on April 27, 586 B.C., at the beginning of Jehoiachin's twelfth year. **32:18** The meaning of the Hebrew is uncertain. **32:19** Hebrew *the uncircumcised;* also in 32:21, 24, 25, 26, 28, 29, 30, 32. **32:21** Hebrew *in Sheol.*

KING JAMES VERSION

24 There *is* Elam and all her multitude round about her grave, all of them slain, fallen by the sword, which are gone down uncircumcised into the nether parts of the earth, which caused their terror in the land of the living; yet have they borne their shame with them that go down to the pit.

25 They have set her a bed in the midst of the slain with all her multitude: her graves *are* round about him: all of them uncircumcised, slain by the sword: though their terror was caused in the land of the living, yet have they borne their shame with them that go down to the pit: he is put in the midst of *them that be* slain.

26 There *is* Meshech, Tubal, and all her multitude: her graves *are* round about him: all of them uncircumcised, slain by the sword, though they caused their terror in the land of the living.

27 And they shall not lie with the mighty *that are* fallen of the uncircumcised, which are gone down to hell with their weapons of war: and they have laid their swords under their heads, but their iniquities shall be upon their bones, though *they were* the terror of the mighty in the land of the living.

28 Yea, thou shalt be broken in the midst of the uncircumcised, and shalt lie with *them that are* slain with the sword.

29 There *is* Edom, her kings, and all her princes, which with their might are laid by *them that were* slain by the sword: they shall lie with the uncircumcised, and with them that go down to the pit.

30 There *be* the princes of the north, all of them, and all the Zidonians, which are gone down with the slain; with their terror they are ashamed of their might; and they lie uncircumcised with *them that be* slain by the sword, and bear their shame with them that go down to the pit.

31 Pharaoh shall see them, and shall be comforted over all his multitude, *even* Pharaoh and all his army slain by the sword, saith the Lord GOD.

32 For I have caused my terror in the land of the living: and he shall be laid in the midst of the uncircumcised with *them that are* slain with the sword, *even* Pharaoh and all his multitude, saith the Lord GOD.

33 1 Again the word of the LORD came unto me, saying,

2 Son of man, speak to the children of thy people, and say unto them, When I bring the sword upon a land, if the people of the land take a man of their coasts, and set him for their watchman:

3 If when he seeth the sword come upon the land, he blow the trumpet, and warn the people;

4 Then whosoever heareth the sound of the trumpet, and taketh not warning; if the sword come, and take him away, his blood shall be upon his own head.

5 He heard the sound of the trumpet, and took not warning; his blood shall be upon him. But he that taketh warning shall deliver his soul.

NEW LIVING TRANSLATION

24 "Elam lies there surrounded by the graves of all
its hordes, those who were slaughtered by the sword.
They struck terror in the hearts of people everywhere, but now they have descended as outcasts to
the world below. Now they lie in the pit and share the
shame of those who have gone before them. 25 They
have a resting place among the slaughtered, surrounded by the graves of all their hordes. Yes, they
terrorized the nations while they lived, but now they
lie in shame with others in the pit, all of them outcasts, slaughtered by the sword.

26 "Meshech and Tubal are there, surrounded by
the graves of all their hordes. They once struck terror
in the hearts of people everywhere. But now they
are outcasts, all slaughtered by the sword. 27 They are
not buried in honor like their fallen heroes, who
went down to the grave* with their weapons—their
shields covering their bodies* and their swords beneath their heads. Their guilt rests upon them because they brought terror to everyone while they
were still alive.

28 "You too, Egypt, will lie crushed and broken
among the outcasts, all slaughtered by the sword.

29 "Edom is there with its kings and princes. Mighty
as they were, they also lie among those slaughtered
by the sword, with the outcasts who have gone down
to the pit.

30 "All the princes of the north and the Sidonians
are there with others who have died. Once a terror,
they have been put to shame. They lie there as outcasts with others who were slaughtered by the
sword. They share the shame of all who have descended to the pit.

31 "When Pharaoh and his entire army arrive, he
will take comfort that he is not alone in having his
hordes killed, says the Sovereign LORD. 32 Although
I have caused his terror to fall upon all the living,
Pharaoh and his hordes will lie there among the
outcasts who were slaughtered by the sword. I, the
Sovereign LORD, have spoken!"

Ezekiel as Israel's Watchman

33 Once again a message came to me from the
LORD: 2 "Son of man, give your people this
message: 'When I bring an army against a country,
the people of that land choose one of their own to be
a watchman. 3 When the watchman sees the enemy
coming, he sounds the alarm to warn the people.
4 Then if those who hear the alarm refuse to take action, it is their own fault if they die. 5 They heard the
alarm but ignored it, so the responsibility is theirs. If
they had listened to the warning, they could have

32:27a Hebrew *to Sheol.* **32:27b** The meaning of the Hebrew is uncertain.

KING JAMES VERSION

6But if the watchman see the sword come, and
blow not the trumpet, and the people be not warned;
if the sword come, and take *any* person from among
them, he is taken away in his iniquity; but his blood
will I require at the watchman's hand.
7So thou, O son of man, I have set thee a watchman
unto the house of Israel; therefore thou shalt hear
the word at my mouth, and warn them from me.
8When I say unto the wicked, O wicked *man*, thou
shalt surely die; if thou dost not speak to warn the
wicked from his way, that wicked *man* shall die in his
iniquity; but his blood will I require at thine hand.
9Nevertheless, if thou warn the wicked of his way
to turn from it; if he do not turn from his way, he shall
die in his iniquity; but thou hast delivered thy soul.
10Therefore, O thou son of man, speak unto the
house of Israel; Thus ye speak, saying, If our transgressions and our sins *be* upon us, and we pine away
in them, how should we then live?
11Say unto them, *As* I live, saith the Lord GOD, I
have no pleasure in the death of the wicked; but that
the wicked turn from his way and live: turn ye, turn
ye from your evil ways; for why will ye die, O house of
Israel?
12Therefore, thou son of man, say unto the children
of thy people, The righteousness of the righteous shall
not deliver him in the day of his transgression: as for
the wickedness of the wicked, he shall not fall thereby
in the day that he turneth from his wickedness; neither shall the righteous be able to live for his *righteousness* in the day that he sinneth.
13When I shall say to the righteous, *that* he shall
surely live; if he trust to his own righteousness, and
commit iniquity, all his righteousnesses shall not be
remembered; but for his iniquity that he hath committed, he shall die for it.
14Again, when I say unto the wicked, Thou shalt
surely die; if he turn from his sin, and do that which
is lawful and right;
15*If* the wicked restore the pledge, give again that
he had robbed, walk in the statutes of life, without
committing iniquity; he shall surely live, he shall
not die.
16None of his sins that he hath committed shall
be mentioned unto him: he hath done that which is
lawful and right; he shall surely live.
17Yet the children of thy people say, The way of the
Lord is not equal: but as for them, their way is not
equal.
18When the righteous turneth from his righteousness, and committeth iniquity, he shall even die
thereby.
19But if the wicked turn from his wickedness,
and do that which is lawful and right, he shall live
thereby.
20Yet ye say, The way of the LORD is not equal. O ye
house of Israel, I will judge you every one after his
ways.

NEW LIVING TRANSLATION

saved their lives. 6But if the watchman sees the enemy coming and doesn't sound the alarm to warn the
people, he is responsible for their captivity. They will
die in their sins, but I will hold the watchman responsible for their deaths.'
7"Now, son of man, I am making you a watchman
for the people of Israel. Therefore, listen to what I say
and warn them for me. 8If I announce that some
wicked people are sure to die and you fail to tell them
to change their ways, then they will die in their sins,
and I will hold you responsible for their deaths. 9But if
you warn them to repent and they don't repent, they
will die in their sins, but you will have saved yourself.

The Watchman's Message

10"Son of man, give the people of Israel this message:
You are saying, 'Our sins are heavy upon us; we are
wasting away! How can we survive?' 11As surely as I
live, says the Sovereign LORD, I take no pleasure in the
death of wicked people. I only want them to turn
from their wicked ways so they can live. Turn! Turn
from your wickedness, O people of Israel! Why
should you die?
12"Son of man, give your people this message: The
righteous behavior of righteous people will not save
them if they turn to sin, nor will the wicked behavior
of wicked people destroy them if they repent and
turn from their sins. 13When I tell righteous people
that they will live, but then they sin, expecting their
past righteousness to save them, then none of their
righteous acts will be remembered. I will destroy
them for their sins. 14And suppose I tell some wicked
people that they will surely die, but then they turn
from their sins and do what is just and right. 15For instance, they might give back a debtor's security, return what they have stolen, and obey my life-giving
laws, no longer doing what is evil. If they do this, then
they will surely live and not die. 16None of their past
sins will be brought up again, for they have done
what is just and right, and they will surely live.
17"Your people are saying, 'The Lord isn't doing
what's right,' but it is they who are not doing what's
right. 18For again I say, when righteous people turn
away from their righteous behavior and turn to evil,
they will die. 19But if wicked people turn from their
wickedness and do what is just and right, they will
live. 20O people of Israel, you are saying, 'The Lord
isn't doing what's right.' But I judge each of you according to your deeds."

KING JAMES VERSION

21 And it came to pass in the twelfth year of our captivity, in the tenth *month,* in the fifth *day* of the month, *that* one that had escaped out of Jerusalem came unto me, saying, The city is smitten.

22 Now the hand of the LORD was upon me in the evening, afore he that was escaped came; and had opened my mouth, until he came to me in the morning; and my mouth was opened, and I was no more dumb.

23 Then the word of the LORD came unto me, saying,

24 Son of man, they that inhabit those wastes of the land of Israel speak, saying, Abraham was one, and he inherited the land: but we *are* many; the land is given us for inheritance.

25 Wherefore say unto them, Thus saith the Lord GOD; Ye eat with the blood, and lift up your eyes toward your idols, and shed blood: and shall ye possess the land?

26 Ye stand upon your sword, ye work abomination, and ye defile every one his neighbour's wife: and shall ye possess the land?

27 Say thou thus unto them, Thus saith the Lord GOD; *As* I live, surely they that *are* in the wastes shall fall by the sword, and him that *is* in the open field will I give to the beasts to be devoured, and they that *be* in the forts and in the caves shall die of the pestilence.

28 For I will lay the land most desolate, and the pomp of her strength shall cease; and the mountains of Israel shall be desolate, that none shall pass through.

29 Then shall they know that I *am* the LORD, when I have laid the land most desolate because of all their abominations which they have committed.

30 Also, thou son of man, the children of thy people still are talking against thee by the walls and in the doors of the houses, and speak one to another, every one to his brother, saying, Come, I pray you, and hear what is the word that cometh forth from the LORD.

31 And they come unto thee as the people cometh, and they sit before thee *as* my people, and they hear thy words, but they will not do them: for with their mouth they shew much love, *but* their heart goeth after their covetousness.

32 And, lo, thou *art* unto them as a very lovely song of one that hath a pleasant voice, and can play well on an instrument: for they hear thy words, but they do them not.

33 And when this cometh to pass, (lo, it will come,) then shall they know that a prophet hath been among them.

34 1 And the word of the LORD came unto me, saying,

2 Son of man, prophesy against the shepherds of Israel, prophesy, and say unto them, Thus saith the

NEW LIVING TRANSLATION

Explanation of Jerusalem's Fall

21 On January 8,* during the twelfth year of our captivity, a survivor from Jerusalem came to me and said, "The city has fallen!" 22 The previous evening the LORD had taken hold of me and given me back my voice. So I was able to speak when this man arrived the next morning.

23 Then this message came to me from the LORD: 24 "Son of man, the scattered remnants of Judah living among the ruined cities keep saying, 'Abraham was only one man, yet he gained possession of the entire land. We are many; surely the land has been given to us as a possession.' 25 So tell these people, 'This is what the Sovereign LORD says: You eat meat with blood in it, you worship idols,* and you murder the innocent. Do you really think the land should be yours? 26 Murderers! Idolaters! Adulterers! Should the land belong to you?'

27 "Say to them, 'This is what the Sovereign LORD says: As surely as I live, those living in the ruins will die by the sword. And I will send wild animals to eat those living in the open fields. Those hiding in the forts and caves will die of disease. 28 I will completely destroy the land and demolish her pride. Her arrogant power will come to an end. The mountains of Israel will be so desolate that no one will even travel through them. 29 When I have completely destroyed the land because of their detestable sins, then they will know that I am the LORD.'

30 "Son of man, your people talk about you in their houses and whisper about you at the doors. They say to each other, 'Come on, let's go hear the prophet tell us what the LORD is saying!' 31 So my people come pretending to be sincere and sit before you. They listen to your words, but they have no intention of doing what you say. Their mouths are full of lustful words, and their hearts seek only after money. 32 You are very entertaining to them, like someone who sings love songs with a beautiful voice or plays fine music on an instrument. They hear what you say, but they don't act on it! 33 But when all these terrible things happen to them—as they certainly will—then they will know a prophet has been among them."

The Shepherds of Israel

34 Then this message came to me from the LORD: 2 "Son of man, prophesy against the

33:21 Hebrew *On the fifth day of the tenth month,* of the ancient Hebrew lunar calendar. This event occurred on January 8, 585 B.C.; also see note on 1:1. **33:25** The Hebrew term (literally *round things*) probably alludes to dung.

KING JAMES VERSION

Lord GOD unto the shepherds; Woe *be* to the shepherds of Israel that do feed themselves! should not
the shepherds feed the flocks?
3 Ye eat the fat, and ye clothe you with the wool, ye
kill them that are fed: *but* ye feed not the flock.
4 The diseased have ye not strengthened, neither
have ye healed that which was sick, neither have ye
bound up *that which was* broken, neither have ye
brought again that which was driven away, neither
have ye sought that which was lost; but with force
and with cruelty have ye ruled them.
5 And they were scattered, because *there is* no
shepherd: and they became meat to all the beasts of
the field, when they were scattered.
6 My sheep wandered through all the mountains,
and upon every high hill: yea, my flock was scattered
upon all the face of the earth, and none did search or
seek *after them.*
7 Therefore, ye shepherds, hear the word of the
LORD;
8 *As* I live, saith the Lord GOD, surely because my
flock became a prey, and my flock became meat to
every beast of the field, because *there was* no shepherd, neither did my shepherds search for my flock,
but the shepherds fed themselves, and fed not my
flock;
9 Therefore, O ye shepherds, hear the word of
theLORD;
10 Thus saith the Lord GOD; Behold, I *am* against
the shepherds; and I will require my flock at their
hand, and cause them to cease from feeding the
flock; neither shall the shepherds feed themselves
any more; for I will deliver my flock from their
mouth, that they may not be meat for them.
11 For thus saith the Lord GOD; Behold, I, *even* I, will
both search my sheep, and seek them out.
12 As a shepherd seeketh out his flock in the day
that he is among his sheep *that are* scattered; so will
I seek out my sheep, and will deliver them out of all
places where they have been scattered in the cloudy
and dark day.
13 And I will bring them out from the people, and
gather them from the countries, and will bring them
to their own land, and feed them upon the mountains of Israel by the rivers, and in all the inhabited
places of the country.
14 I will feed them in a good pasture, and upon the
high mountains of Israel shall their fold be: there
shall they lie in a good fold, and *in* a fat pasture shall
they feed upon the mountains of Israel.
15 I will feed my flock, and I will cause them to lie
down, saith the Lord GOD.
16 I will seek that which was lost, and bring again
that which was driven away, and will bind up *that
which was* broken, and will strengthen that which
was sick: but I will destroy the fat and the strong; I
will feed them with judgment.
17 And *as for* you, O my flock, thus saith the Lord

NEW LIVING TRANSLATION

shepherds, the leaders of Israel. Give them this message from the Sovereign LORD: What sorrow awaits
you shepherds who feed yourselves instead of your
flocks. Shouldn't shepherds feed their sheep? 3 You
drink the milk, wear the wool, and butcher the best
animals, but you let your flocks starve. 4 You have not
taken care of the weak. You have not tended the sick
or bound up the injured. You have not gone looking
for those who have wandered away and are lost. Instead, you have ruled them with harshness and cruelty. 5 So my sheep have been scattered without a
shepherd, and they are easy prey for any wild animal.
6 They have wandered through all the mountains and
all the hills, across the face of the earth, yet no one
has gone to search for them.
7 "Therefore, you shepherds, hear the word of the
LORD: 8 As surely as I live, says the Sovereign LORD,
you abandoned my flock and left them to be attacked by every wild animal. And though you were
my shepherds, you didn't search for my sheep when
they were lost. You took care of yourselves and left
the sheep to starve. 9 Therefore, you shepherds, hear
the word of the LORD. 10 This is what the Sovereign
LORD says: I now consider these shepherds my enemies, and I will hold them responsible for what has
happened to my flock. I will take away their right to
feed the flock, and I will stop them from feeding
themselves. I will rescue my flock from their
mouths; the sheep will no longer be their prey.

The Good Shepherd

11 "For this is what the Sovereign LORD says: I myself
will search and find my sheep. 12 I will be like a shepherd looking for his scattered flock. I will find my
sheep and rescue them from all the places where
they were scattered on that dark and cloudy day. 13 I
will bring them back home to their own land of Israel from among the peoples and nations. I will feed
them on the mountains of Israel and by the rivers
and in all the places where people live. 14 Yes, I will
give them good pastureland on the high hills of Israel. There they will lie down in pleasant places and
feed in the lush pastures of the hills. 15 I myself will
tend my sheep and give them a place to lie down in
peace, says the Sovereign LORD. 16 I will search for my
lost ones who strayed away, and I will bring them
safely home again. I will bandage the injured and
strengthen the weak. But I will destroy those who are
fat and powerful. I will feed them, yes—feed them
justice!
17 "And as for you, my flock, this is what the Sovereign LORD says to his people: I will judge between one

KING JAMES VERSION

GOD; Behold, I judge between cattle and cattle, between the rams and the he goats.
18 *Seemeth it* a small thing unto you to have eaten
up the good pasture, but ye must tread down with
your feet the residue of your pastures? and to have
drunk of the deep waters, but ye must foul the residue with your feet?
19 And *as for* my flock, they eat that which ye have
trodden with your feet; and they drink that which ye
have fouled with your feet.
20 Therefore thus saith the Lord GOD unto them;
Behold, I, *even* I, will judge between the fat cattle and
between the lean cattle.
21 Because ye have thrust with side and with shoulder, and pushed all the diseased with your horns, till
ye have scattered them abroad;
22 Therefore will I save my flock, and they shall no
more be a prey; and I will judge between cattle and
cattle.
23 And I will set up one shepherd over them, and he
shall feed them, *even* my servant David; he shall feed
them, and he shall be their shepherd.
24 And I the LORD will be their God, and my servant
David a prince among them; I the LORD have spoken *it*.
25 And I will make with them a covenant of peace,
and will cause the evil beasts to cease out of the land:
and they shall dwell safely in the wilderness, and
sleep in the woods.
26 And I will make them and the places round about
my hill a blessing; and I will cause the shower to come
down in his season; there shall be showers of blessing.
27 And the tree of the field shall yield her fruit, and
the earth shall yield her increase, and they shall be
safe in their land, and shall know that I *am* the LORD,
when I have broken the bands of their yoke, and delivered them out of the hand of those that served
themselves of them.
28 And they shall no more be a prey to the heathen,
neither shall the beast of the land devour them; but
they shall dwell safely, and none shall make *them*
afraid.
29 And I will raise up for them a plant of renown, and
they shall be no more consumed with hunger in the
land, neither bear the shame of the heathen any more.
30 Thus shall they know that I the LORD their God
am with them, and *that* they, *even* the house of Israel, *are* my people, saith the Lord GOD.
31 And ye my flock, the flock of my pasture, *are*
men, *and* I *am* your God, saith the Lord GOD.

35 1 Moreover the word of the LORD came unto
me, saying,
2 Son of man, set thy face against mount Seir, and
prophesy against it,
3 And say unto it, Thus saith the Lord GOD; Behold,
O mount Seir, I *am* against thee, and I will stretch out
mine hand against thee, and I will make thee most
desolate.

NEW LIVING TRANSLATION

animal of the flock and another, separating the sheep
from the goats. 18 Isn't it enough for you to keep the
best of the pastures for yourselves? Must you also
trample down the rest? Isn't it enough for you to
drink clear water for yourselves? Must you also
muddy the rest with your feet? 19 Why must my flock
eat what you have trampled down and drink water
you have fouled?
20 "Therefore, this is what the Sovereign LORD says:
I will surely judge between the fat sheep and the
scrawny sheep. 21 For you fat sheep pushed and
butted and crowded my sick and hungry flock until
you scattered them to distant lands. 22 So I will rescue
my flock, and they will no longer be abused. I will
judge between one animal of the flock and another.
23 And I will set over them one shepherd, my servant
David. He will feed them and be a shepherd to them.
24 And I, the LORD, will be their God, and my servant
David will be a prince among my people. I, the LORD,
have spoken!

The LORD's Covenant of Peace

25 "I will make a covenant of peace with my people
and drive away the dangerous animals from the land.
Then they will be able to camp safely in the wildest
places and sleep in the woods without fear. 26 I will
bless my people and their homes around my holy
hill. And in the proper season I will send the showers
they need. There will be showers of blessing. 27 The
orchards and fields of my people will yield bumper
crops, and everyone will live in safety. When I have
broken their chains of slavery and rescued them
from those who enslaved them, then they will know
that I am the LORD. 28 They will no longer be prey for
other nations, and wild animals will no longer devour them. They will live in safety, and no one will
frighten them.
29 "And I will make their land famous for its crops,
so my people will never again suffer from famines or
the insults of foreign nations. 30 In this way, they will
know that I, the LORD their God, am with them. And
they will know that they, the people of Israel, are my
people, says the Sovereign LORD. 31 You are my flock,
the sheep of my pasture. You are my people, and I am
your God. I, the Sovereign LORD, have spoken!"

A Message for Edom

35 Again a message came to me from the LORD:
2 "Son of man, turn and face Mount Seir, and
prophesy against its people. 3 Give them this message
from the Sovereign LORD:

"I am your enemy, O Mount Seir,
and I will raise my fist against you
to destroy you completely.

KING JAMES VERSION

4 I will lay thy cities waste, and thou shalt be desolate, and thou shalt know that I *am* the LORD.

5 Because thou hast had a perpetual hatred, and hast shed *the blood of* the children of Israel by the force of the sword in the time of their calamity, in the time *that their* iniquity *had* an end:

6 Therefore, *as* I live, saith the Lord GOD, I will prepare thee unto blood, and blood shall pursue thee: sith thou hast not hated blood, even blood shall pursue thee.

7 Thus will I make mount Seir most desolate, and cut off from it him that passeth out and him that returneth.

8 And I will fill his mountains with his slain *men:* in thy hills, and in thy valleys, and in all thy rivers, shall they fall that are slain with the sword.

9 I will make thee perpetual desolations, and thy cities shall not return: and ye shall know that I *am* the LORD.

10 Because thou hast said, These two nations and these two countries shall be mine, and we will possess it; whereas the LORD was there:

11 Therefore, *as* I live, saith the Lord GOD, I will even do according to thine anger, and according to thine envy which thou hast used out of thy hatred against them; and I will make myself known among them, when I have judged thee.

12 And thou shalt know that I *am* the LORD, *and that* I have heard all thy blasphemies which thou hast spoken against the mountains of Israel, saying, They are laid desolate, they are given us to consume.

13 Thus with your mouth ye have boasted against me, and have multiplied your words against me: I have heard *them.*

14 Thus saith the Lord GOD; When the whole earth rejoiceth, I will make thee desolate.

15 As thou didst rejoice at the inheritance of the house of Israel, because it was desolate, so will I do unto thee: thou shalt be desolate, O mount Seir, and all Idumea, *even* all of it: and they shall know that I *am* the LORD.

36 1 Also, thou son of man, prophesy unto the mountains of Israel, and say, Ye mountains of Israel, hear the word of the LORD:

2 Thus saith the Lord GOD; Because the enemy hath said against you, Aha, even the ancient high places are ours in possession:

3 Therefore prophesy and say, Thus saith the Lord GOD; Because they have made *you* desolate, and swallowed you up on every side, that ye might be a possession unto the residue of the heathen, and ye are taken up in the lips of talkers, and *are* an infamy of the people:

4 Therefore, ye mountains of Israel, hear the word of the Lord GOD; Thus saith the Lord GOD to the mountains, and to the hills, to the rivers, and to the valleys, to the desolate wastes, and to the cities that

NEW LIVING TRANSLATION

4 I will demolish your cities
and make you desolate.
Then you will know that I am the LORD.

5 "Your eternal hatred for the people of Israel led
you to butcher them when they were helpless, when I
had already punished them for all their sins. 6 As
surely as I live, says the Sovereign LORD, since you
show no distaste for blood, I will give you a blood-
bath of your own. Your turn has come! 7 I will make
Mount Seir utterly desolate, killing off all who try to
escape and any who return. 8 I will fill your mountains with the dead. Your hills, your valleys, and your
ravines will be filled with people slaughtered by the
sword. 9 I will make you desolate forever. Your cities
will never be rebuilt. Then you will know that I am
the LORD.

10 "For you said, 'The lands of Israel and Judah will
be ours. We will take possession of them. What do
we care that the LORD is there!' 11 Therefore, as surely
as I live, says the Sovereign LORD, I will pay back your
angry deeds with my own. I will punish you for all
your acts of anger, envy, and hatred. And I will make
myself known to Israel* by what I do to you. 12 Then
you will know that I, the LORD, have heard every con-
temptuous word you spoke against the mountains of
Israel. For you said, 'They are desolate; they have
been given to us as food to eat!' 13 In saying that, you
boasted proudly against me, and I have heard it all!

14 "This is what the Sovereign LORD says: The
whole world will rejoice when I make you desolate.
15 You rejoiced at the desolation of Israel's territory.
Now I will rejoice at yours! You will be wiped out, you
people of Mount Seir and all who live in Edom! Then
you will know that I am the LORD.

Restoration for Israel

36 "Son of man, prophesy to Israel's mountains. Give them this message: O mountains
of Israel, hear the word of the LORD! 2 This is what the
Sovereign LORD says: Your enemies have taunted
you, saying, 'Aha! Now the ancient heights belong to
us!' 3 Therefore, son of man, give the mountains of Israel this message from the Sovereign LORD: Your enemies have attacked you from all directions, making
you the property of many nations and the object of
much mocking and slander. 4 Therefore, O mountains of Israel, hear the word of the Sovereign LORD.
He speaks to the hills and mountains, ravines and

35:11 Hebrew *to them;* Greek version reads *to you.*

KING JAMES VERSION

are forsaken, which became a prey and derision to
the residue of the heathen that *are* round about;
[5]Therefore thus saith the Lord GOD; Surely in the
fire of my jealousy have I spoken against the residue
of the heathen, and against all Idumea, which have
appointed my land into their possession with the joy
of all *their* heart, with despiteful minds, to cast it out
for a prey.
[6]Prophesy therefore concerning the land of Israel,
and say unto the mountains, and to the hills, to the
rivers, and to the valleys, Thus saith the Lord GOD;
Behold, I have spoken in my jealousy and in my fury,
because ye have borne the shame of the heathen:
[7]Therefore thus saith the Lord GOD; I have lifted
up mine hand, Surely the heathen that *are* about you,
they shall bear their shame.
[8]But ye, O mountains of Israel, ye shall shoot forth
your branches, and yield your fruit to my people of
Israel; for they are at hand to come.
[9]For, behold, I *am* for you, and I will turn unto you,
and ye shall be tilled and sown:
[10]And I will multiply men upon you, all the house
of Israel, *even* all of it: and the cities shall be inhabited, and the wastes shall be builded:
[11]And I will multiply upon you man and beast; and
they shall increase and bring fruit: and I will settle
you after your old estates, and will do better *unto*
you than at your beginnings: and ye shall know that I
am the LORD.
[12]Yea, I will cause men to walk upon you, *even* my
people Israel; and they shall possess thee, and thou
shalt be their inheritance, and thou shalt no more
henceforth bereave them *of men*.
[13]Thus saith the Lord GOD; Because they say unto
you, Thou *land* devourest up men, and hast bereaved
thy nations;
[14]Therefore thou shalt devour men no more,
neither bereave thy nations any more, saith the
Lord GOD.
[15]Neither will I cause *men* to hear in thee the
shame of the heathen any more, neither shalt thou
bear the reproach of the people any more, neither
shalt thou cause thy nations to fall any more, saith
the Lord GOD.
[16]Moreover the word of the LORD came unto me,
saying,
[17]Son of man, when the house of Israel dwelt in
their own land, they defiled it by their own way and
by their doings: their way was before me as the uncleanness of a removed woman.
[18]Wherefore I poured my fury upon them for the
blood that they had shed upon the land, and for their
idols *wherewith* they had polluted it:
[19]And I scattered them among the heathen, and
they were dispersed through the countries: according to their way and according to their doings I
judged them.
[20]And when they entered unto the heathen,

NEW LIVING TRANSLATION

valleys, and to ruined wastes and long-deserted cities that have been destroyed and mocked by the surrounding nations. [5]This is what the Sovereign LORD
says: My jealous anger burns against these nations,
especially Edom, because they have shown utter
contempt for me by gleefully taking my land for
themselves as plunder.
[6]"Therefore, prophesy to the hills and mountains,
the ravines and valleys of Israel. This is what the Sovereign LORD says: I am furious that you have suffered
shame before the surrounding nations. [7]Therefore,
this is what the Sovereign LORD says: I have taken a
solemn oath that those nations will soon have their
own shame to endure.
[8]"But the mountains of Israel will produce heavy
crops of fruit for my people—for they will be coming
home again soon! [9]See, I care about you, and I will
pay attention to you. Your ground will be plowed and
your crops planted. [10]I will greatly increase the population of Israel, and the ruined cities will be rebuilt
and filled with people. [11]I will increase not only the
people, but also your animals. O mountains of Israel,
I will bring people to live on you once again. I will
make you even more prosperous than you were before. Then you will know that I am the LORD. [12]I will
cause my people to walk on you once again, and you
will be their territory. You will never again rob them
of their children.
[13]"This is what the Sovereign LORD says: The other
nations taunt you, saying, 'Israel is a land that devours its own people and robs them of their children!' [14]But you will never again devour your people
or rob them of their children, says the Sovereign
LORD. [15]I will not let you hear those other nations
insult you, and you will no longer be mocked by
them. You will not be a land that causes its nation to
fall, says the Sovereign LORD."
[16]Then this further message came to me from the
LORD: [17]"Son of man, when the people of Israel were
living in their own land, they defiled it by the evil way
they lived. To me their conduct was as unclean as a
woman's menstrual cloth. [18]They polluted the land
with murder and the worship of idols,* so I poured
out my fury on them. [19]I scattered them to many
lands to punish them for the evil way they had lived.
[20]But when they were scattered among the nations,

36:18 The Hebrew term (literally *round things*) probably alludes to dung; also in 36:25.

whither they went, they profaned my holy name, when they said to them, These *are* the people of the LORD, and are gone forth out of his land.

21 But I had pity for mine holy name, which the house of Israel had profaned among the heathen, whither they went.

22 Therefore say unto the house of Israel, Thus saith the Lord GOD; I do not *this* for your sakes, O house of Israel, but for mine holy name's sake, which ye have profaned among the heathen, whither ye went.

23 And I will sanctify my great name, which was profaned among the heathen, which ye have profaned in the midst of them; and the heathen shall know that I *am* the LORD, saith the Lord GOD, when I shall be sanctified in you before their eyes.

24 For I will take you from among the heathen, and gather you out of all countries, and will bring you into your own land.

25 Then will I sprinkle clean water upon you, and ye shall be clean: from all your filthiness, and from all your idols, will I cleanse you.

26 A new heart also will I give you, and a new spirit will I put within you: and I will take away the stony heart out of your flesh, and I will give you an heart of flesh.

27 And I will put my spirit within you, and cause you to walk in my statutes, and ye shall keep my judgments, and do *them*.

28 And ye shall dwell in the land that I gave to your fathers; and ye shall be my people, and I will be your God.

29 I will also save you from all your uncleannesses: and I will call for the corn, and will increase it, and lay no famine upon you.

30 And I will multiply the fruit of the tree, and the increase of the field, that ye shall receive no more reproach of famine among the heathen.

31 Then shall ye remember your own evil ways, and your doings that *were* not good, and shall lothe yourselves in your own sight for your iniquities and for your abominations.

32 Not for your sakes do I *this*, saith the Lord GOD, be it known unto you: be ashamed and confounded for your own ways, O house of Israel.

33 Thus saith the Lord GOD; In the day that I shall have cleansed you from all your iniquities I will also cause *you* to dwell in the cities, and the wastes shall be builded.

34 And the desolate land shall be tilled, whereas it lay desolate in the sight of all that passed by.

35 And they shall say, This land that was desolate is become like the garden of Eden; and the waste and desolate and ruined cities *are become* fenced, *and* are inhabited.

36 Then the heathen that are left round about you shall know that I the LORD build the ruined *places*,

they brought shame on my holy name. For the nations said, 'These are the people of the LORD, but he
couldn't keep them safe in his own land!' 21 Then I
was concerned for my holy name, on which my
people brought shame among the nations.

22 "Therefore, give the people of Israel this message from the Sovereign LORD: I am bringing you
back, but not because you deserve it. I am doing it to
protect my holy name, on which you brought shame
while you were scattered among the nations. 23 I will
show how holy my great name is—the name on
which you brought shame among the nations. And
when I reveal my holiness through you before their
very eyes, says the Sovereign LORD, then the nations
will know that I am the LORD. 24 For I will gather you
up from all the nations and bring you home again to
your land.

25 "Then I will sprinkle clean water on you, and
you will be clean. Your filth will be washed away, and
you will no longer worship idols. 26 And I will give you
a new heart, and I will put a new spirit in you. I will
take out your stony, stubborn heart and give you a
tender, responsive heart.* 27 And I will put my Spirit
in you so that you will follow my decrees and be careful to obey my regulations.

28 "And you will live in Israel, the land I gave your
ancestors long ago. You will be my people, and I will
be your God. 29 I will cleanse you of your filthy behavior. I will give you good crops of grain, and I will send
no more famines on the land. 30 I will give you great
harvests from your fruit trees and fields, and never
again will the surrounding nations be able to scoff at
your land for its famines. 31 Then you will remember
your past sins and despise yourselves for all the detestable things you did. 32 But remember, says the
Sovereign LORD, I am not doing this because you deserve it. O my people of Israel, you should be utterly
ashamed of all you have done!

33 "This is what the Sovereign LORD says: When I
cleanse you from your sins, I will repopulate your cities, and the ruins will be rebuilt. 34 The fields that
used to lie empty and desolate in plain view of everyone will again be farmed. 35 And when I bring you
back, people will say, 'This former wasteland is now
like the Garden of Eden! The abandoned and ruined
cities now have strong walls and are filled with
people!' 36 Then the surrounding nations that survive
will know that I, the LORD, have rebuilt the ruins and

36:26 Hebrew *a heart of flesh.*

KING JAMES VERSION

and plant that that was desolate: I the LORD have
spoken *it*, and I will do *it*.
37 Thus saith the Lord GOD; I will yet *for* this be
inquired of by the house of Israel, to do *it* for them; I
will increase them with men like a flock.
38 As the holy flock, as the flock of Jerusalem in
her solemn feasts; so shall the waste cities be filled
with flocks of men: and they shall know that I *am*
the LORD.

37 1 The hand of the LORD was upon me, and
carried me out in the spirit of the LORD, and
set me down in the midst of the valley which *was* full
of bones,
2 And caused me to pass by them round about: and,
behold, *there were* very many in the open valley; and,
lo, *they were* very dry.
3 And he said unto me, Son of man, can these bones
live? And I answered, O Lord GOD, thou knowest.
4 Again he said unto me, Prophesy upon these
bones, and say unto them, O ye dry bones, hear the
word of the LORD.
5 Thus saith the Lord GOD unto these bones; Behold, I will cause breath to enter into you, and ye
shall live:
6 And I will lay sinews upon you, and will bring up
flesh upon you, and cover you with skin, and put
breath in you, and ye shall live; and ye shall know that
I *am* the LORD.
7 So I prophesied as I was commanded: and as I
prophesied, there was a noise, and behold a shaking,
and the bones came together, bone to his bone.
8 And when I beheld, lo, the sinews and the flesh
came up upon them, and the skin covered them
above: but *there was* no breath in them.
9 Then said he unto me, Prophesy unto the wind,
prophesy, son of man, and say to the wind, Thus saith
the Lord GOD; Come from the four winds, O breath,
and breathe upon these slain, that they may live.
10 So I prophesied as he commanded me, and the
breath came into them, and they lived, and stood up
upon their feet, an exceeding great army.
11 Then he said unto me, Son of man, these bones
are the whole house of Israel: behold, they say, Our
bones are dried, and our hope is lost: we are cut off
for our parts.
12 Therefore prophesy and say unto them, Thus
saith the Lord GOD; Behold, O my people, I will open
your graves, and cause you to come up out of your
graves, and bring you into the land of Israel.
13 And ye shall know that I *am* the LORD, when I
have opened your graves, O my people, and brought
you up out of your graves,
14 And shall put my spirit in you, and ye shall live,
and I shall place you in your own land: then shall ye
know that I the LORD have spoken *it*, and performed
it, saith the LORD.

NEW LIVING TRANSLATION

replanted the wasteland. For I, the LORD, have spoken, and I will do what I say.
37 "This is what the Sovereign LORD says: I am
ready to hear Israel's prayers and to increase their
numbers like a flock. 38 They will be as numerous as
the sacred flocks that fill Jerusalem's streets at the
time of her festivals. The ruined cities will be
crowded with people once more, and everyone will
know that I am the LORD."

A Valley of Dry Bones

37 The LORD took hold of me, and I was carried
away by the Spirit of the LORD to a valley
filled with bones. 2 He led me all around among the
bones that covered the valley floor. They were scattered everywhere across the ground and were completely dried out. 3 Then he asked me, "Son of man,
can these bones become living people again?"
"O Sovereign LORD," I replied, "you alone know the
answer to that."
4 Then he said to me, "Speak a prophetic message
to these bones and say, 'Dry bones, listen to the word
of the LORD! 5 This is what the Sovereign LORD says:
Look! I am going to put breath into you and make you
live again! 6 I will put flesh and muscles on you and
cover you with skin. I will put breath into you, and
you will come to life. Then you will know that I am
the LORD.'"
7 So I spoke this message, just as he told me. Suddenly as I spoke, there was a rattling noise all across
the valley. The bones of each body came together
and attached themselves as complete skeletons.
8 Then as I watched, muscles and flesh formed over
the bones. Then skin formed to cover their bodies,
but they still had no breath in them.
9 Then he said to me, "Speak a prophetic message
to the winds, son of man. Speak a prophetic message
and say, 'This is what the Sovereign LORD says: Come,
O breath, from the four winds! Breathe into these
dead bodies so they may live again.'"
10 So I spoke the message as he commanded me,
and breath came into their bodies. They all came to
life and stood up on their feet—a great army.
11 Then he said to me, "Son of man, these bones
represent the people of Israel. They are saying, 'We
have become old, dry bones—all hope is gone. Our
nation is finished.' 12 Therefore, prophesy to them
and say, 'This is what the Sovereign LORD says: O my
people, I will open your graves of exile and cause you
to rise again. Then I will bring you back to the land of
Israel. 13 When this happens, O my people, you will
know that I am the LORD. 14 I will put my Spirit in you,
and you will live again and return home to your own
land. Then you will know that I, the LORD, have spoken, and I have done what I said. Yes, the LORD has
spoken!'"

KING JAMES VERSION

15 The word of the LORD came again unto me, saying,

16 Moreover, thou son of man, take thee one stick, and write upon it, For Judah, and for the children of Israel his companions: then take another stick, and write upon it, For Joseph, the stick of Ephraim, and *for* all the house of Israel his companions:

17 And join them one to another into one stick; and they shall become one in thine hand.

18 And when the children of thy people shall speak unto thee, saying, Wilt thou not shew us what thou *meanest* by these?

19 Say unto them, Thus saith the Lord GOD; Behold, I will take the stick of Joseph, which *is* in the hand of Ephraim, and the tribes of Israel his fellows, and will put them with him, *even* with the stick of Judah, and make them one stick, and they shall be one in mine hand.

20 And the sticks whereon thou writest shall be in thine hand before their eyes.

21 And say unto them, Thus saith the Lord GOD; Behold, I will take the children of Israel from among the heathen, whither they be gone, and will gather them on every side, and bring them into their own land:

22 And I will make them one nation in the land upon the mountains of Israel; and one king shall be king to them all: and they shall be no more two nations, neither shall they be divided into two kingdoms any more at all:

23 Neither shall they defile themselves any more with their idols, nor with their detestable things, nor with any of their transgressions: but I will save them out of all their dwellingplaces, wherein they have sinned, and will cleanse them: so shall they be my people, and I will be their God.

24 And David my servant *shall be* king over them; and they all shall have one shepherd: they shall also walk in my judgments, and observe my statutes, and do them.

25 And they shall dwell in the land that I have given unto Jacob my servant, wherein your fathers have dwelt; and they shall dwell therein, *even* they, and their children, and their children's children for ever: and my servant David *shall be* their prince for ever.

26 Moreover I will make a covenant of peace with them; it shall be an everlasting covenant with them: and I will place them, and multiply them, and will set my sanctuary in the midst of them for evermore.

27 My tabernacle also shall be with them: yea, I will be their God, and they shall be my people.

28 And the heathen shall know that I the LORD do sanctify Israel, when my sanctuary shall be in the midst of them for evermore.

NEW LIVING TRANSLATION

Reunion of Israel and Judah

15 Again a message came to me from the LORD: 16 "Son
of man, take a piece of wood and carve on it these
words: 'This represents Judah and its allied tribes.'
Then take another piece and carve these words on it:
'This represents Ephraim and the northern tribes of
Israel.'* 17 Now hold them together in your hand as if
they were one piece of wood. 18 When your people
ask you what your actions mean, 19 say to them, 'This
is what the Sovereign LORD says: I will take Ephraim
and the northern tribes and join them to Judah. I will
make them one piece of wood in my hand.'

20 "Then hold out the pieces of wood you have inscribed, so the people can see them. 21 And give them
this message from the Sovereign LORD: I will gather
the people of Israel from among the nations. I will
bring them home to their own land from the places
where they have been scattered. 22 I will unify them
into one nation on the mountains of Israel. One king
will rule them all; no longer will they be divided into
two nations or into two kingdoms. 23 They will never
again pollute themselves with their idols* and vile
images and rebellion, for I will save them from their
sinful backsliding. I will cleanse them. Then they
will truly be my people, and I will be their God.

24 "My servant David will be their king, and they
will have only one shepherd. They will obey my regulations and be careful to keep my decrees. 25 They
will live in the land I gave my servant Jacob, the land
where their ancestors lived. They and their children
and their grandchildren after them will live there
forever, generation after generation. And my servant
David will be their prince forever. 26 And I will make
a covenant of peace with them, an everlasting covenant. I will give them their land and increase their
numbers,* and I will put my Temple among them
forever. 27 I will make my home among them. I will be
their God, and they will be my people. 28 And when
my Temple is among them forever, the nations will
know that I am the LORD, who makes Israel holy."

37:16 Hebrew *This is Ephraim's wood, representing Joseph and all the house of Israel.* **37:23** The Hebrew term (literally *round things*) probably alludes to dung. **37:26** Hebrew reads *I will give them and increase their numbers;* Greek version lacks the entire phrase.

KING JAMES VERSION

38 1 And the word of the LORD came unto me, saying,

2 Son of man, set thy face against Gog, the land of Magog, the chief prince of Meshech and Tubal, and prophesy against him,

3 And say, Thus saith the Lord GOD; Behold, I *am* against thee, O Gog, the chief prince of Meshech and Tubal:

4 And I will turn thee back, and put hooks into thy jaws, and I will bring thee forth, and all thine army, horses and horsemen, all of them clothed with all sorts *of armour, even* a great company *with* bucklers and shields, all of them handling swords:

5 Persia, Ethiopia, and Libya with them; all of them with shield and helmet:

6 Gomer, and all his bands; the house of Togarmah of the north quarters, and all his bands: *and* many people with thee.

7 Be thou prepared, and prepare for thyself, thou, and all thy company that are assembled unto thee, and be thou a guard unto them.

8 After many days thou shalt be visited: in the latter years thou shalt come into the land *that is* brought back from the sword, *and is* gathered out of many people, against the mountains of Israel, which have been always waste: but it is brought forth out of the nations, and they shall dwell safely all of them.

9 Thou shalt ascend and come like a storm, thou shalt be like a cloud to cover the land, thou, and all thy bands, and many people with thee.

10 Thus saith the Lord GOD; It shall also come to pass, *that* at the same time shall things come into thy mind, and thou shalt think an evil thought:

11 And thou shalt say, I will go up to the land of unwalled villages; I will go to them that are at rest, that dwell safely, all of them dwelling without walls, and having neither bars nor gates,

12 To take a spoil, and to take a prey; to turn thine hand upon the desolate places *that are now* inhabited, and upon the people *that are* gathered out of the nations, which have gotten cattle and goods, that dwell in the midst of the land.

13 Sheba, and Dedan, and the merchants of Tarshish, with all the young lions thereof, shall say unto thee, Art thou come to take a spoil? hast thou gathered thy company to take a prey? to carry away silver and gold, to take away cattle and goods, to take a great spoil?

14 Therefore, son of man, prophesy and say unto Gog, Thus saith the Lord GOD; In that day when my people of Israel dwelleth safely, shalt thou not know *it?*

15 And thou shalt come from thy place out of the north parts, thou, and many people with thee, all of them riding upon horses, a great company, and a mighty army:

16 And thou shalt come up against my people of

NEW LIVING TRANSLATION

A Message for Gog

38 This is another message that came to me
from the LORD: 2 "Son of man, turn and face
Gog of the land of Magog, the prince who rules over
the nations of Meshech and Tubal, and prophesy
against him. 3 Give him this message from the Sovereign LORD: Gog, I am your enemy! 4 I will turn you
around and put hooks in your jaws to lead you out
with your whole army—your horses and charioteers
in full armor and a great horde armed with shields
and swords. 5 Persia, Ethiopia, and Libya* will join
you, too, with all their weapons. 6 Gomer and all its armies will also join you, along with the armies of Bethtogarmah from the distant north, and many others.

7 "Get ready; be prepared! Keep all the armies
around you mobilized, and take command of them.
8 A long time from now you will be called into action.
In the distant future you will swoop down on the
land of Israel, which will be enjoying peace after
recovering from war and after its people have returned from many lands to the mountains of Israel.
9 You and all your allies—a vast and awesome army—
will roll down on them like a storm and cover the
land like a cloud.

10 "This is what the Sovereign LORD says: At that
time evil thoughts will come to your mind, and you
will devise a wicked scheme. 11 You will say, 'Israel is
an unprotected land filled with unwalled villages! I
will march against her and destroy these people who
live in such confidence! 12 I will go to those formerly
desolate cities that are now filled with people who
have returned from exile in many nations. I will capture vast amounts of plunder, for the people are rich
with livestock and other possessions now. They
think the whole world revolves around them!' 13 But
Sheba and Dedan and the merchants of Tarshish will
ask, 'Do you really think the armies you have gathered can rob them of silver and gold? Do you think
you can drive away their livestock and seize their
goods and carry off plunder?'

14 "Therefore, son of man, prophesy against Gog.
Give him this message from the Sovereign LORD:
When my people are living in peace in their land,
then you will rouse yourself.* 15 You will come from
your homeland in the distant north with your vast
cavalry and your mighty army, 16 and you will attack
my people Israel, covering their land like a cloud. At

38:5 Hebrew *Paras, Cush, and Put.* **38:14** As in Greek version; Hebrew reads *then you will know.*

KING JAMES VERSION

Israel, as a cloud to cover the land; it shall be in the
latter days, and I will bring thee against my land, that
the heathen may know me, when I shall be sanctified
in thee, O Gog, before their eyes.
17Thus saith the Lord God; *Art* thou he of whom I
have spoken in old time by my servants the prophets
of Israel, which prophesied in those days *many* years
that I would bring thee against them?
18And it shall come to pass at the same time when
Gog shall come against the land of Israel, saith the
Lord God, *that* my fury shall come up in my face.
19For in my jealousy *and* in the fire of my wrath
have I spoken, Surely in that day there shall be a great
shaking in the land of Israel;
20So that the fishes of the sea, and the fowls of the
heaven, and the beasts of the field, and all creeping
things that creep upon the earth, and all the men that
are upon the face of the earth, shall shake at my presence, and the mountains shall be thrown down, and
the steep places shall fall, and every wall shall fall to
the ground.
21And I will call for a sword against him throughout all my mountains, saith the Lord God: every
man's sword shall be against his brother.
22And I will plead against him with pestilence and
with blood; and I will rain upon him, and upon his
bands, and upon the many people that *are* with him,
an overflowing rain, and great hailstones, fire, and
brimstone.
23Thus will I magnify myself, and sanctify myself;
and I will be known in the eyes of many nations, and
they shall know that I *am* the Lord.

39 1Therefore, thou son of man, prophesy
against Gog, and say, Thus saith the Lord
God; Behold, I *am* against thee, O Gog, the chief
prince of Meshech and Tubal:
2And I will turn thee back, and leave but the sixth
part of thee, and will cause thee to come up from the
north parts, and will bring thee upon the mountains
of Israel:
3And I will smite thy bow out of thy left hand, and
will cause thine arrows to fall out of thy right hand.
4Thou shalt fall upon the mountains of Israel,
thou, and all thy bands, and the people that *is* with
thee: I will give thee unto the ravenous birds of every
sort, and *to* the beasts of the field to be devoured.
5Thou shalt fall upon the open field: for I have
spoken *it*, saith the Lord God.
6And I will send a fire on Magog, and among them
that dwell carelessly in the isles: and they shall know
that I *am* the Lord.
7So will I make my holy name known in the midst
of my people Israel; and I will not *let them* pollute my
holy name any more: and the heathen shall know
that I *am* the Lord, the Holy One in Israel.
8Behold, it is come, and it is done, saith the Lord
God; this *is* the day whereof I have spoken.

NEW LIVING TRANSLATION

that time in the distant future, I will bring you against
my land as everyone watches, and my holiness will
be displayed by what happens to you, Gog. Then all
the nations will know that I am the Lord.
17"This is what the Sovereign Lord asks: Are you
the one I was talking about long ago, when I announced through Israel's prophets that in the future
I would bring you against my people? 18But this is
what the Sovereign Lord says: When Gog invades
the land of Israel, my fury will boil over! 19In my jealousy and blazing anger, I promise a mighty shaking
in the land of Israel on that day. 20All living things—
the fish in the sea, the birds of the sky, the animals of
the field, the small animals that scurry along the
ground, and all the people on earth—will quake in
terror at my presence. Mountains will be thrown
down; cliffs will crumble; walls will fall to the earth.
21I will summon the sword against you on all the hills
of Israel, says the Sovereign Lord. Your men will turn
their swords against each other. 22I will punish you
and your armies with disease and bloodshed; I will
send torrential rain, hailstones, fire, and burning sulfur! 23In this way, I will show my greatness and holiness, and I will make myself known to all the nations
of the world. Then they will know that I am the Lord.

The Slaughter of Gog's Hordes

39 "Son of man, prophesy against Gog. Give
him this message from the Sovereign Lord:
I am your enemy, O Gog, ruler of the nations of Meshech and Tubal. 2I will turn you around and drive
you toward the mountains of Israel, bringing you
from the distant north. 3I will knock the bow from
your left hand and the arrows from your right hand,
and I will leave you helpless. 4You and your army and
your allies will all die on the mountains. I will feed
you to the vultures and wild animals. 5You will fall in
the open fields, for I have spoken, says the Sovereign
Lord. 6And I will rain down fire on Magog and on all
your allies who live safely on the coasts. Then they
will know that I am the Lord.
7"In this way, I will make known my holy name
among my people of Israel. I will not let anyone bring
shame on it. And the nations, too, will know that I am
the Lord, the Holy One of Israel. 8That day of judgment will come, says the Sovereign Lord. Everything
will happen just as I have declared it.

KING JAMES VERSION

9And they that dwell in the cities of Israel shall go
forth, and shall set on fire and burn the weapons,
both the shields and the bucklers, the bows and the
arrows, and the handstaves, and the spears, and they
shall burn them with fire seven years:
10So that they shall take no wood out of the field,
neither cut down *any* out of the forests; for they shall
burn the weapons with fire: and they shall spoil
those that spoiled them, and rob those that robbed
them, saith the Lord GOD.
11And it shall come to pass in that day, *that* I will
give unto Gog a place there of graves in Israel, the
valley of the passengers on the east of the sea: and it
shall stop the *noses* of the passengers: and there shall
they bury Gog and all his multitude: and they shall
call *it* The valley of Hamon-gog.
12And seven months shall the house of Israel be
burying of them, that they may cleanse the land.
13Yea, all the people of the land shall bury *them;*
and it shall be to them a renown the day that I shall
be glorified, saith the Lord GOD.
14And they shall sever out men of continual em-
ployment, passing through the land to bury with the
passengers those that remain upon the face of the
earth, to cleanse it: after the end of seven months
shall they search.
15And the passengers *that* pass through the land,
when *any* seeth a man's bone, then shall he set up a
sign by it, till the buriers have buried it in the valley
of Hamon-gog.
16And also the name of the city *shall be* Hamonah.
Thus shall they cleanse the land.
17And, thou son of man, thus saith the Lord GOD;
Speak unto every feathered fowl, and to every beast
of the field, Assemble yourselves, and come; gather
yourselves on every side to my sacrifice that I do sacrifice for you, *even* a great sacrifice upon the mountains of Israel, that ye may eat flesh, and drink blood.
18Ye shall eat the flesh of the mighty, and drink the
blood of the princes of the earth, of rams, of lambs,
and of goats, of bullocks, all of them fatlings of
Bashan.
19And ye shall eat fat till ye be full, and drink blood
till ye be drunken, of my sacrifice which I have sacrificed for you.
20Thus ye shall be filled at my table with horses
and chariots, with mighty men, and with all men of
war, saith the Lord GOD.
21And I will set my glory among the heathen, and
all the heathen shall see my judgment that I have executed, and my hand that I have laid upon them.
22So the house of Israel shall know that I *am* the
LORD their God from that day and forward.
23And the heathen shall know that the house of
Israel went into captivity for their iniquity: because
they trespassed against me, therefore hid I my face
from them, and gave them into the hand of their enemies: so fell they all by the sword.

NEW LIVING TRANSLATION

9"Then the people in the towns of Israel will go
out and pick up your small and large shields, bows
and arrows, javelins and spears, and they will use
them for fuel. There will be enough to last them
seven years! 10They won't need to cut wood from the
fields or forests, for these weapons will give them all
the fuel they need. They will plunder those who
planned to plunder them, and they will rob those
who planned to rob them, says the Sovereign LORD.
11"And I will make a vast graveyard for Gog and his
hordes in the Valley of the Travelers, east of the Dead
Sea.* It will block the way of those who travel there,
and they will change the name of the place to the Valley of Gog's Hordes. 12It will take seven months for
the people of Israel to bury the bodies and cleanse
the land. 13Everyone in Israel will help, for it will be
a glorious victory for Israel when I demonstrate my
glory on that day, says the Sovereign LORD.
14"After seven months, teams of men will be appointed to search the land for skeletons to bury,
so the land will be made clean again. 15Whenever
bones are found, a marker will be set up so the burial
crews will take them to be buried in the Valley of
Gog's Hordes. 16(There will be a town there named
Hamonah, which means 'horde.') And so the land
will finally be cleansed.
17"And now, son of man, this is what the Sovereign
LORD says: Call all the birds and wild animals. Say to
them: Gather together for my great sacrificial feast.
Come from far and near to the mountains of Israel,
and there eat flesh and drink blood! 18Eat the flesh of
mighty men and drink the blood of princes as
though they were rams, lambs, goats, and bulls—all
fattened animals from Bashan! 19Gorge yourselves
with flesh until you are glutted; drink blood until you
are drunk. This is the sacrificial feast I have prepared
for you. 20Feast at my banquet table—feast on horses
and charioteers, on mighty men and all kinds of valiant warriors, says the Sovereign LORD.
21"In this way, I will demonstrate my glory to the
nations. Everyone will see the punishment I have inflicted on them and the power of my fist when I
strike. 22And from that time on the people of Israel
will know that I am the LORD their God. 23The nations
will then know why Israel was sent away to exile—it
was punishment for sin, for they were unfaithful to
their God. Therefore, I turned away from them and

39:11 Hebrew *the sea.*

KING JAMES VERSION

[24]According to their uncleanness and according to their transgressions have I done unto them, and hid my face from them.

[25]Therefore thus saith the Lord GOD; Now will I bring again the captivity of Jacob, and have mercy upon the whole house of Israel, and will be jealous for my holy name;

[26]After that they have borne their shame, and all their trespasses whereby they have trespassed against me, when they dwelt safely in their land, and none made *them* afraid.

[27]When I have brought them again from the people, and gathered them out of their enemies' lands, and am sanctified in them in the sight of many nations;

[28]Then shall they know that I *am* the LORD their God, which caused them to be led into captivity among the heathen: but I have gathered them unto their own land, and have left none of them any more there.

[29]Neither will I hide my face any more from them: for I have poured out my spirit upon the house of Israel, saith the Lord GOD.

40 [1]In the five and twentieth year of our captivity, in the beginning of the year, in the tenth *day* of the month, in the fourteenth year after that the city was smitten, in the selfsame day the hand of the LORD was upon me, and brought me thither.

[2]In the visions of God brought he me into the land of Israel, and set me upon a very high mountain, by which *was* as the frame of a city on the south.

[3]And he brought me thither, and, behold, *there was* a man, whose appearance *was* like the appearance of brass, with a line of flax in his hand, and a measuring reed; and he stood in the gate.

[4]And the man said unto me, Son of man, behold with thine eyes, and hear with thine ears, and set thine heart upon all that I shall shew thee; for to the intent that I might shew *them* unto thee *art* thou brought hither: declare all that thou seest to the house of Israel.

[5]And behold a wall on the outside of the house round about, and in the man's hand a measuring reed of six cubits *long* by the cubit and an hand breadth: so he measured the breadth of the building, one reed; and the height, one reed.

[6]Then came he unto the gate which looketh toward the east, and went up the stairs thereof, and measured the threshold of the gate, *which was* one reed broad; and the other threshold *of the gate, which was* one reed broad.

[7]And *every* little chamber *was* one reed long, and one reed broad; and between the little chambers

NEW LIVING TRANSLATION

let their enemies destroy them. [24]I turned my face away and punished them because of their defilement and their sins.

Restoration for God's People

[25]"So now, this is what the Sovereign LORD says: I will end the captivity of my people*; I will have mercy on all Israel, for I jealously guard my holy reputation! [26]They will accept responsibility for* their past shame and unfaithfulness after they come home to live in peace in their own land, with no one to bother them. [27]When I bring them home from the lands of their enemies, I will display my holiness among them for all the nations to see. [28]Then my people will know that I am the LORD their God, because I sent them away to exile and brought them home again. I will leave none of my people behind. [29]And I will never again turn my face from them, for I will pour out my Spirit upon the people of Israel. I, the Sovereign LORD, have spoken!"

The New Temple Area

40 On April 28,* during the twenty-fifth year of our captivity—fourteen years after the fall of Jerusalem—the LORD took hold of me. [2]In a vision from God he took me to the land of Israel and set me down on a very high mountain. From there I could see toward the south what appeared to be a city. [3]As he brought me nearer, I saw a man whose face shone like bronze standing beside a gateway entrance. He was holding in his hand a linen measuring cord and a measuring rod.

[4]He said to me, "Son of man, watch and listen. Pay close attention to everything I show you. You have been brought here so I can show you many things. Then you will return to the people of Israel and tell them everything you have seen."

The East Gateway

[5]I could see a wall completely surrounding the Temple area. The man took a measuring rod that was 10½ feet* long and measured the wall, and the wall was 10½ feet* thick and 10½ feet high.

[6]Then he went over to the eastern gateway. He climbed the steps and measured the threshold of the gateway; it was 10½ feet front to back.* [7]There were guard alcoves on each side built into the gateway

39:25 Hebrew *of Jacob.* **39:26** A few Hebrew manuscripts read *They will forget.* **40:1** Hebrew *At the beginning of the year, on the tenth day of the month,* of the ancient Hebrew lunar calendar. This event occurred on April 28, 573 B.C.; also see note on 1:1. **40:5a** Hebrew *6 long cubits* [3.2 meters], *each being a cubit* [18 inches or 45 centimeters] *and a handbreadth* [3 inches or 8 centimeters] *in length.* **40:5b** Hebrew *1 rod* [3.2 meters]; also in 40:5c, 7. **40:6** As in Greek version, which reads *1 rod* [3.2 meters] *deep;* Hebrew reads *1 rod deep, and 1 threshold, 1 rod deep.*

KING JAMES VERSION

were five cubits; and the threshold of the gate by the porch of the gate within *was* one reed.

8He measured also the porch of the gate within, one reed.

9Then measured he the porch of the gate, eight cubits; and the posts thereof, two cubits; and the porch of the gate *was* inward.

10And the little chambers of the gate eastward *were* three on this side, and three on that side; they three *were* of one measure: and the posts had one measure on this side and on that side.

11And he measured the breadth of the entry of the gate, ten cubits; *and* the length of the gate, thirteen cubits.

12The space also before the little chambers *was* one cubit *on this side,* and the space *was* one cubit on that side: and the little chambers *were* six cubits on this side, and six cubits on that side.

13He measured then the gate from the roof of *one* little chamber to the roof of another: the breadth *was* five and twenty cubits, door against door.

14He made also posts of threescore cubits, even unto the post of the court round about the gate.

15And from the face of the gate of the entrance unto the face of the porch of the inner gate *were* fifty cubits.

16And *there were* narrow windows to the little chambers, and to their posts within the gate round about, and likewise to the arches: and windows *were* round about inward: and upon *each* post *were* palm trees.

17Then brought he me into the outward court, and, lo, *there were* chambers, and a pavement made for the court round about: thirty chambers *were* upon the pavement.

18And the pavement by the side of the gates over against the length of the gates *was* the lower pavement.

19Then he measured the breadth from the forefront of the lower gate unto the forefront of the inner court without, an hundred cubits eastward and northward.

20And the gate of the outward court that looked toward the north, he measured the length thereof, and the breadth thereof.

21And the little chambers thereof *were* three on this side and three on that side; and the posts thereof and the arches thereof were after the measure of the first gate: the length thereof *was* fifty cubits, and the breadth five and twenty cubits.

22And their windows, and their arches, and their

NEW LIVING TRANSLATION

passage. Each of these alcoves was 10½ feet square,
with a distance between them of 8¾ feet* along the
passage wall. The gateway's inner threshold, which
led to the entry room at the inner end of the gateway
passage, was 10½ feet front to back. 8He also measured the entry room of the gateway.* 9It was
14 feet* across, with supporting columns 3½ feet*
thick. This entry room was at the inner end of the
gateway structure, facing toward the Temple.

10There were three guard alcoves on each side of
the gateway passage. Each had the same measurements, and the dividing walls separating them were
also identical. 11The man measured the gateway entrance, which was 17½ feet* wide at the opening and
22¾ feet* wide in the gateway passage. 12In front of
each of the guard alcoves was a 21-inch* curb. The
alcoves themselves were 10½ feet* on each side.

13Then he measured the entire width of the gateway, measuring the distance between the back walls
of facing guard alcoves; this distance was 43¾ feet.*
14He measured the dividing walls all along the inside
of the gateway up to the entry room of the gateway;
this distance was 105 feet.* 15The full length of the
gateway passage was 87½ feet* from one end to the
other. 16There were recessed windows that narrowed inward through the walls of the guard alcoves
and their dividing walls. There were also windows in
the entry room. The surfaces of the dividing walls
were decorated with carved palm trees.

The Outer Courtyard

17Then the man brought me through the gateway
into the outer courtyard of the Temple. A stone pavement ran along the walls of the courtyard, and thirty
rooms were built against the walls, opening onto the
pavement. 18This pavement flanked the gates and
extended out from the walls into the courtyard the
same distance as the gateway entrance. This was the
lower pavement. 19Then the man measured across
the Temple's outer courtyard between the outer and
inner gateways; the distance was 175 feet.*

The North Gateway

20The man measured the gateway on the north just
like the one on the east. 21Here, too, there were three
guard alcoves on each side, with dividing walls and
an entry room. All the measurements matched those
of the east gateway. The gateway passage was 87½
feet long and 43¾ feet wide between the back walls
of facing guard alcoves. 22The windows, the entry

40:7 Hebrew *5 cubits* [2.7 meters]; also in 40:48. **40:8** Many Hebrew manuscripts add *which faced inward toward the Temple; it was 1 rod* [10.5 feet or 3.2 meters] *deep.* [9]*Then he measured the entry room of the gateway.* **40:9a** Hebrew *8 cubits* [4.2 meters]. **40:9b** Hebrew *2 cubits* [1.1 meters]. **40:11a** Hebrew *10 cubits* [5.3 meters]. **40:11b** Hebrew *13 cubits* [6.9 meters]. **40:12a** Hebrew *1 cubit* [53 centimeters]. **40:12b** Hebrew *6 cubits* [3.2 meters]. **40:13** Hebrew *25 cubits* [13.3meters]; also in 40:21, 25, 29, 30, 33, 36. **40:14** Hebrew *60 cubits* [31.8 meters]. Greek version reads *20 cubits* [35 feet or 10.6 meters]. The meaning of the Hebrew in this verse is uncertain. **40:15** Hebrew *50 cubits* [26.5 meters]; also in 40:21, 25, 29, 33, 36. **40:19** Hebrew *100 cubits* [53 meters]; also in 40:23, 27, 47.

KING JAMES VERSION

palm trees, *were* after the measure of the gate that looketh toward the east; and they went up unto it by seven steps; and the arches thereof *were* before them.

23 And the gate of the inner court *was* over against the gate toward the north, and toward the east; and he measured from gate to gate an hundred cubits.

24 After that he brought me toward the south, and behold a gate toward the south: and he measured the posts thereof and the arches thereof according to these measures.

25 And *there were* windows in it and in the arches thereof round about, like those windows: the length *was* fifty cubits, and the breadth five and twenty cubits.

26 And *there were* seven steps to go up to it, and the arches thereof *were* before them: and it had palm trees, one on this side, and another on that side, upon the posts thereof.

27 And *there was* a gate in the inner court toward the south: and he measured from gate to gate toward the south an hundred cubits.

28 And he brought me to the inner court by the south gate: and he measured the south gate according to these measures;

29 And the little chambers thereof, and the posts thereof, and the arches thereof, according to these measures: and *there were* windows in it and in the arches thereof round about: *it was* fifty cubits long, and five and twenty cubits broad.

30 And the arches round about *were* five and twenty cubits long, and five cubits broad.

31 And the arches thereof *were* toward the utter court; and palm trees *were* upon the posts thereof: and the going up to it *had* eight steps.

32 And he brought me into the inner court toward the east: and he measured the gate according to these measures.

33 And the little chambers thereof, and the posts thereof, and the arches thereof, *were* according to these measures: and *there were* windows therein and in the arches thereof round about: *it was* fifty cubits long, and five and twenty cubits broad.

34 And the arches thereof *were* toward the outward court; and palm trees *were* upon the posts thereof, on this side, and on that side: and the going up to it *had* eight steps.

35 And he brought me to the north gate, and measured *it* according to these measures;

36 The little chambers thereof, the posts thereof, and the arches thereof, and the windows to it round

NEW LIVING TRANSLATION

room, and the palm tree decorations were identical
to those in the east gateway. There were seven steps
leading up to the gateway entrance, and the entry
room was at the inner end of the gateway passage.
23 Here on the north side, just as on the east, there was
another gateway leading to the Temple's inner courtyard directly opposite this outer gateway. The distance between the two gateways was 175 feet.

The South Gateway

24 Then the man took me around to the south gateway and measured its various parts, and they were
exactly the same as in the others. 25 It had windows
along the walls as the others did, and there was an
entry room where the gateway passage opened into
the outer courtyard. And like the others, the gateway
passage was 87½ feet long and 43¾ feet wide between the back walls of facing guard alcoves. 26 This
gateway also had a stairway of seven steps leading up
to it, and an entry room at the inner end, and palm
tree decorations along the dividing walls. 27 And here
again, directly opposite the outer gateway, was another gateway that led into the inner courtyard. The
distance between the two gateways was 175 feet.

Gateways to the Inner Courtyard

28 Then the man took me to the south gateway leading into the inner courtyard. He measured it, and it
had the same measurements as the other gateways.
29 Its guard alcoves, dividing walls, and entry room
were the same size as those in the others. It also had
windows along its walls and in the entry room. And
like the others, the gateway passage was 87½ feet
long and 43¾ feet wide. 30 (The entry rooms of the
gateways leading into the inner courtyard were
14 feet* across and 43¾ feet wide.) 31 The entry
room to the south gateway faced into the outer
courtyard. It had palm tree decorations on its columns, and there were eight steps leading to its
entrance.

32 Then he took me to the east gateway leading
to the inner courtyard. He measured it, and it had
the same measurements as the other gateways. 33 Its
guard alcoves, dividing walls, and entry room were
the same size as those of the others, and there were
windows along the walls and in the entry room. The
gateway passage measured 87½ feet long and 43¾
feet wide. 34 Its entry room faced into the outer courtyard. It had palm tree decorations on its columns, and
there were eight steps leading to its entrance.

35 Then he took me around to the north gateway
leading to the inner courtyard. He measured it, and it
had the same measurements as the other gateways.
36 The guard alcoves, dividing walls, and entry room
of this gateway had the same measurements as in the

40:30 As in 40:9, which reads *8 cubits* [14 feet or 4.2 meters]; here the Hebrew reads *5 cubits* [8¾ feet or 2.7 meters]. Some Hebrew manuscripts and the Greek version lack this entire verse.

KING JAMES VERSION

about: the length *was* fifty cubits, and the breadth five and twenty cubits.

37 And the posts thereof *were* toward the utter court; and palm trees *were* upon the posts thereof, on this side, and on that side: and the going up to it *had* eight steps.

38 And the chambers and the entries thereof *were* by the posts of the gates, where they washed the burnt offering.

39 And in the porch of the gate *were* two tables on this side, and two tables on that side, to slay thereon the burnt offering and the sin offering and the trespass offering.

40 And at the side without, as one goeth up to the entry of the north gate, *were* two tables; and on the other side, which *was* at the porch of the gate, *were* two tables.

41 Four tables *were* on this side, and four tables on that side, by the side of the gate; eight tables, whereupon they slew *their sacrifices*.

42 And the four tables *were* of hewn stone for the burnt offering, of a cubit and an half long, and a cubit and an half broad, and one cubit high: whereupon also they laid the instruments wherewith they slew the burnt offering and the sacrifice.

43 And within *were* hooks, an hand broad, fastened round about: and upon the tables *was* the flesh of the offering.

44 And without the inner gate *were* the chambers of the singers in the inner court, which *was* at the side of the north gate; and their prospect *was* toward the south: one at the side of the east gate *having* the prospect toward the north.

45 And he said unto me, This chamber, whose prospect *is* toward the south, *is* for the priests, the keepers of the charge of the house.

46 And the chamber whose prospect *is* toward the north *is* for the priests, the keepers of the charge of the altar: these *are* the sons of Zadok among the sons of Levi, which come near to the LORD to minister unto him.

47 So he measured the court, an hundred cubits long, and an hundred cubits broad, foursquare; and the altar *that was* before the house.

48 And he brought me to the porch of the house, and measured *each* post of the porch, five cubits on this side, and five cubits on that side: and the breadth of the gate *was* three cubits on this side, and three cubits on that side.

49 The length of the porch *was* twenty cubits, and the breadth eleven cubits; and *he brought me* by the steps whereby they went up to it: and *there were*

NEW LIVING TRANSLATION

others and the same window arrangements. The
gateway passage measured 87½ feet long and 43¾
feet wide.
37 Its entry room faced into the outer
courtyard, and it had palm tree decorations on the
columns. There were eight steps leading to its
entrance.

Rooms for Preparing Sacrifices

38 A door led from the entry room of one of the inner
gateways into a side room, where the meat for sacrifices was washed.
39 On each side of this entry room
were two tables, where the sacrificial animals were
slaughtered for the burnt offerings, sin offerings,
and guilt offerings.
40 Outside the entry room, on
each side of the stairs going up to the north entrance,
were two more tables.
41 So there were eight tables
in all—four inside and four outside—where the sacrifices were cut up and prepared.
42 There were
also four tables of finished stone for preparation
of the burnt offerings, each 31½ inches square and
21 inches high.* On these tables were placed the
butchering knives and other implements for slaughtering the sacrificial animals.
43 There were hooks,
each 3 inches* long, fastened to the foyer walls. The
sacrificial meat was laid on the tables.

Rooms for the Priests

44 Inside the inner courtyard were two rooms,* one
beside the north gateway, facing south, and the other
beside the south* gateway, facing north.
45 And the
man said to me, "The room beside the north inner
gate is for the priests who supervise the Temple
maintenance.
46 The room beside the south inner
gate is for the priests in charge of the altar—the descendants of Zadok—for they alone of all the Levites
may approach the LORD to minister to him."

The Inner Courtyard and Temple

47 Then the man measured the inner courtyard, and
it was a square, 175 feet wide and 175 feet across.
The altar stood in the courtyard in front of the
Temple.
48 Then he brought me to the entry room of
the Temple. He measured the walls on either side of
the opening to the entry room, and they were 8¾ feet
thick. The entrance itself was 24½ feet wide, and
the walls on each side of the entrance were an additional 5¼ feet long.*
49 The entry room was 35 feet*

40:42 Hebrew *1½ cubits* [80 centimeters] *long and 1½ cubits wide and 1 cubit* [53 centimeters] *high.* **40:43** Hebrew *a handbreadth* [8 centimeters]. **40:44a** As in Greek version; Hebrew reads *rooms for singers.* **40:44b** As in Greek version; Hebrew reads *east.* **40:48** As in Greek version, which reads *The entrance was 14 cubits* [7.4 meters] *wide, and the walls of the entrance were 3 cubits* [1.6 meters] *on each side;* Hebrew lacks *14 cubits wide, and the walls of the entrance were.* **40:49a** Hebrew *20 cubits* [10.6 meters].

KING JAMES VERSION

pillars by the posts, one on this side, and another on that side.

41

1 Afterward he brought me to the temple, and measured the posts, six cubits broad on the one side, and six cubits broad on the other side, *which was* the breadth of the tabernacle.

2 And the breadth of the door *was* ten cubits: and the sides of the door *were* five cubits on the one side, and five cubits on the other side: and he measured the length thereof, forty cubits: and the breadth, twenty cubits.

3 Then went he inward, and measured the post of the door, two cubits; and the door, six cubits; and the breadth of the door, seven cubits.

4 So he measured the length thereof, twenty cubits; and the breadth, twenty cubits, before the temple: and he said unto me, This *is* the most holy *place*.

5 After he measured the wall of the house, six cubits; and the breadth of *every* side chamber, four cubits, round about the house on every side.

6 And the side chambers *were* three, one over another, and thirty in order; and they entered into the wall which *was* of the house for the side chambers round about, that they might have hold, but they had not hold in the wall of the house.

7 And *there was* an enlarging, and a winding about still upward to the side chambers: for the winding about of the house went still upward round about the house: therefore the breadth of the house *was still* upward, and so increased *from* the lowest *chamber* to the highest by the midst.

8 I saw also the height of the house round about: the foundations of the side chambers *were* a full reed of six great cubits.

9 The thickness of the wall, which *was* for the side chamber without, *was* five cubits: and *that* which *was* left *was* the place of the side chambers that *were* within.

10 And between the chambers *was* the wideness of twenty cubits round about the house on every side.

11 And the doors of the side chambers *were* toward *the place that was* left, one door toward the north, and another door toward the south: and the breadth of the place that was left *was* five cubits round about.

12 Now the building that *was* before the separate place at the end toward the west *was* seventy cubits broad; and the wall of the building *was* five cubits thick round about, and the length thereof ninety cubits.

13 So he measured the house, an hundred cubits long; and the separate place, and the building, with the walls thereof, an hundred cubits long;

14 Also the breadth of the face of the house, and of the separate place toward the east, an hundred cubits.

15 And he measured the length of the building over against the separate place which *was* behind it, and the galleries thereof on the one side and on the other

NEW LIVING TRANSLATION

wide and 21 feet* deep. There were ten steps leading up to it, with a column on each side.

41

After that, the man brought me into the sanctuary of the Temple. He measured the walls on either side of its doorway, and they were 10½ feet* thick. 2 The doorway was 17½ feet* wide, and the walls on each side of it were 8¾ feet* long. The sanctuary itself was 70 feet long and 35 feet wide.*

3 Then he went beyond the sanctuary into the inner room. He measured the walls on either side of its entrance, and they were 3½ feet* thick. The entrance was 10½ feet wide, and the walls on each side of the entrance were 12¼ feet* long. 4 The inner room of the sanctuary was 35 feet* long and 35 feet wide. "This," he told me, "is the Most Holy Place."

5 Then he measured the wall of the Temple, and it was 10½ feet thick. There was a row of rooms along the outside wall; each room was 7 feet* wide. 6 These side rooms were built in three levels, one above the other, with thirty rooms on each level. The supports for these side rooms rested on exterior ledges on the Temple wall; they did not extend into the wall. 7 Each level was wider than the one below it, corresponding to the narrowing of the Temple wall as it rose higher. A stairway led up from the bottom level through the middle level to the top level.

8 I saw that the Temple was built on a terrace, which provided a foundation for the side rooms. This terrace was 10½ feet* high. 9 The outer wall of the Temple's side rooms was 8¾ feet thick. This left an open area between these side rooms 10 and the row of rooms along the outer wall of the inner courtyard. This open area was 35 feet wide, and it went all the way around the Temple. 11 Two doors opened from the side rooms into the terrace yard, which was 8¾ feet wide. One door faced north and the other south.

12 A large building stood on the west, facing the Temple courtyard. It was 122½ feet wide and 157½ feet long, and its walls were 8¾ feet* thick. 13 Then the man measured the Temple, and it was 175 feet* long. The courtyard around the building, including its walls, was an additional 175 feet in length. 14 The inner courtyard to the east of the Temple was also 175 feet wide. 15 The building to the west, including its two walls, was also 175 feet wide.

The sanctuary, the inner room, and the entry room

40:49b As in Greek version, which reads *12 cubits* [21 feet or 6.4 meters]; Hebrew reads *11 cubits* [19¼ feet or 5.8 meters]. **41:1** Hebrew *6 cubits* [3.2 meters]; also in 41:3, 5. **41:2a** Hebrew *10 cubits* [5.3 meters]. **41:2b** Hebrew *5 cubits* [2.7 meters]; also in 41:9, 11. **41:2c** Hebrew *40 cubits* [21.2 meters] *long and 20 cubits* [10.6 meters] *wide*. **41:3a** Hebrew *2 cubits* [1.1 meters]. **41:3b** Hebrew *7 cubits* [3.7 meters]. **41:4** Hebrew *20 cubits* [10.6 meters]; also in 41:4b, 10. **41:5** Hebrew *4 cubits* [2.1 meters]. **41:8** Hebrew *1 rod, 6 cubits* [3.2 meters]. **41:12** Hebrew *70 cubits* [37.1 meters] *wide and 90 cubits* [47.7 meters] *long, and its walls were 5 cubits* [2.7 meters] *thick*. **41:13** Hebrew *100 cubits* [53 meters]; also in 41:13b, 14, 15.

KING JAMES VERSION

side, an hundred cubits, with the inner temple, and
the porches of the court;
16The door posts, and the narrow windows, and
the galleries round about on their three stories, over
against the door, cieled with wood round about,
and from the ground up to the windows, and the
windows *were* covered;
17To that above the door, even unto the inner
house, and without, and by all the wall round about
within and without, by measure.
18And *it was* made with cherubims and palm
trees, so that a palm tree *was* between a cherub and
a cherub; and *every* cherub had two faces;
19So that the face of a man *was* toward the palm
tree on the one side, and the face of a young lion toward the palm tree on the other side: *it was* made
through all the house round about.
20From the ground unto above the door *were*
cherubims and palm trees made, and *on* the wall of
the temple.
21The posts of the temple *were* squared, *and* the
face of the sanctuary; the appearance *of the one* as
the appearance *of the other.*
22The altar of wood *was* three cubits high, and the
length thereof two cubits; and the corners thereof,
and the length thereof, and the walls thereof, *were*
of wood: and he said unto me, This *is* the table that *is*
before the LORD.
23And the temple and the sanctuary had two doors.
24And the doors had two leaves *apiece,* two turning leaves; two *leaves* for the one door, and two leaves
for the other *door.*
25And *there were* made on them, on the doors of
the temple, cherubims and palm trees, like as *were*
made upon the walls; and *there were* thick planks
upon the face of the porch without.
26And *there were* narrow windows and palm trees
on the one side and on the other side, on the sides of
the porch, and *upon* the side chambers of the house,
and thick planks.

42 1Then he brought me forth into the utter
court, the way toward the north: and he
brought me into the chamber that *was* over against
the separate place, and which *was* before the building toward the north.
2Before the length of an hundred cubits *was* the
north door, and the breadth *was* fifty cubits.
3Over against the twenty *cubits* which *were* for the
inner court, and over against the pavement which
was for the utter court, *was* gallery against gallery in
three *stories.*
4And before the chambers *was* a walk of ten cubits breadth inward, a way of one cubit; and their
doors toward the north.

NEW LIVING TRANSLATION

of the Temple 16were all paneled with wood, as were
the frames of the recessed windows. The inner walls
of the Temple were paneled with wood above and
below the windows. 17The space above the door
leading into the inner room, and its walls inside and
out, were also paneled. 18All the walls were decorated with carvings of cherubim, each with two
faces, and there was a carving of a palm tree between
each of the cherubim. 19One face—that of a man—
looked toward the palm tree on one side. The other
face—that of a young lion—looked toward the palm
tree on the other side. The figures were carved all
along the inside of the Temple, 20from the floor to
the top of the walls, including the outer wall of the
sanctuary.
21There were square columns at the entrance to
the sanctuary, and the ones at the entrance of the
Most Holy Place were similar. 22There was an altar
made of wood, 5¼ feet high and 3½ feet across.* Its
corners, base, and sides were all made of wood.
"This," the man told me, "is the table that stands in
the LORD's presence."
23Both the sanctuary and the Most Holy Place had
double doorways, 24each with two swinging doors.
25The doors leading into the sanctuary were decorated with carved cherubim and palm trees, just as
on the walls. And there was a wooden roof at the
front of the entry room to the Temple. 26On both
sides of the entry room were recessed windows decorated with carved palm trees. The side rooms along
the outside wall also had roofs.

Rooms for the Priests

42 Then the man led me out of the Temple
courtyard by way of the north gateway. We
entered the outer courtyard and came to a group of
rooms against the north wall of the inner courtyard.
2This structure, whose entrance opened toward the
north, was 175 feet* long and 87½ feet* wide. 3One
block of rooms overlooked the 35-foot* width of the
inner courtyard. Another block of rooms looked out
onto the pavement of the outer courtyard. The two
blocks were built three levels high and stood across
from each other. 4Between the two blocks of rooms
ran a walkway 17½ feet* wide. It extended the entire
175 feet of the complex,* and all the doors faced

41:22 Hebrew *3 cubits* [1.6 meters] *high and 2 cubits* [1.1 meters] *across.*
42:2a Hebrew *100 cubits* [53 meters]; also in 42:8. **42:2b** Hebrew *50 cubits* [26.5 meters]; also in 42:7, 8. **42:3** Hebrew *20-cubit* [10.6-meter]. **42:4a** Hebrew *10 cubits* [5.3 meters]. **42:4b** As in Greek and Syriac versions, which read *Its length was 100 cubits* [53 meters]; Hebrew reads *and a passage 1 cubit* [18 inches or 53 centimeters] *wide.*

KING JAMES VERSION

5 Now the upper chambers *were* shorter: for the
galleries were higher than these, than the lower, and
than the middlemost of the building.
6 For they *were* in three *stories,* but had not pillars
as the pillars of the courts: therefore *the building*
was straitened more than the lowest and the
middlemost from the ground.
7 And the wall that *was* without over against the
chambers, toward the utter court on the forepart of
the chambers, the length thereof *was* fifty cubits.
8 For the length of the chambers that *were* in the
utter court *was* fifty cubits: and, lo, before the temple
were an hundred cubits.
9 And from under these chambers *was* the entry
on the east side, as one goeth into them from the
utter court.
10 The chambers *were* in the thickness of the wall
of the court toward the east, over against the separate place, and over against the building.
11 And the way before them *was* like the appearance of the chambers which *were* toward the north,
as long as they, *and* as broad as they: and all their
goings out *were* both according to their fashions,
and according to their doors.
12 And according to the doors of the chambers that
were toward the south *was* a door in the head of the
way, *even* the way directly before the wall toward the
east, as one entereth into them.
13 Then said he unto me, The north chambers *and*
the south chambers, which *are* before the separate
place, they *be* holy chambers, where the priests that
approach unto the LORD shall eat the most holy
things: there shall they lay the most holy things, and
the meat offering, and the sin offering, and the trespass offering; for the place *is* holy.
14 When the priests enter therein, then shall they
not go out of the holy *place* into the utter court, but
there they shall lay their garments wherein they minister; for they *are* holy; and shall put on other garments, and shall approach to *those things* which *are*
for the people.
15 Now when he had made an end of measuring
the inner house, he brought me forth toward the gate
whose prospect *is* toward the east, and measured it
round about.
16 He measured the east side with the measuring
reed, five hundred reeds, with the measuring reed
round about.
17 He measured the north side, five hundred reeds,
with the measuring reed round about.
18 He measured the south side, five hundred reeds,
with the measuring reed.
19 He turned about to the west side, *and* measured
five hundred reeds with the measuring reed.
20 He measured it by the four sides: it had a wall
round about, five hundred *reeds* long, and five hundred broad, to make a separation between the sanctuary and the profane place.

NEW LIVING TRANSLATION

north. 5 Each of the two upper levels of rooms was
narrower than the one beneath it because the upper
levels had to allow space for walkways in front of
them. 6 Since there were three levels and they did not
have supporting columns as in the courtyards, each
of the upper levels was set back from the level beneath it. 7 There was an outer wall that separated the
rooms from the outer courtyard; it was 87½ feet
long. 8 This wall added length to the outer block of
rooms, which extended for only 87½ feet, while the
inner block—the rooms toward the Temple—extended for 175 feet. 9 There was an eastern entrance
from the outer courtyard to these rooms.
10 On the south* side of the Temple there were two
blocks of rooms just south of the inner courtyard
between the Temple and the outer courtyard. These
rooms were arranged just like the rooms on the
north. 11 There was a walkway between the two
blocks of rooms just like the complex on the north
side of the Temple. This complex of rooms was the
same length and width as the other one, and it had
the same entrances and doors. The dimensions of
each were identical. 12 So there was an entrance in
the wall facing the doors of the inner block of rooms,
and another on the east at the end of the interior
walkway.
13 Then the man told me, "These rooms that overlook the Temple from the north and south are holy.
Here the priests who offer sacrifices to the LORD will
eat the most holy offerings. And because these
rooms are holy, they will be used to store the sacred
offerings—the grain offerings, sin offerings, and
guilt offerings. 14 When the priests leave the sanctuary, they must not go directly to the outer courtyard.
They must first take off the clothes they wore while
ministering, because these clothes are holy. They
must put on other clothes before entering the parts
of the building complex open to the public."
15 When the man had finished measuring the inside of the Temple area, he led me out through the
east gateway to measure the entire perimeter. 16 He
measured the east side with his measuring rod, and
it was 875 feet long.* 17 Then he measured the north
side, and it was also 875 feet. 18 The south side was
also 875 feet, 19 and the west side was also 875 feet.
20 So the area was 875 feet on each side with a wall all
around it to separate what was holy from what was
common.

42:10 As in Greek version; Hebrew reads *east.* **42:16** As in 45:2 and in Greek version at 42:17, which reads *500 cubits* [265 meters]; Hebrew reads *500 rods* [5,250 feet or 1,590 meters]; similarly in 42:17, 18, 19, 20.

KING JAMES VERSION

43

1Afterward he brought me to the gate, *even* the gate that looketh toward the east:

2And, behold, the glory of the God of Israel came from the way of the east: and his voice *was* like a noise of many waters: and the earth shined with his glory.

3And *it was* according to the appearance of the vision which I saw, *even* according to the vision that I saw when I came to destroy the city: and the visions *were* like the vision that I saw by the river Chebar; and I fell upon my face.

4And the glory of the LORD came into the house by the way of the gate whose prospect *is* toward the east.

5So the spirit took me up, and brought me into the inner court; and, behold, the glory of the LORD filled the house.

6And I heard *him* speaking unto me out of the house; and the man stood by me.

7And he said unto me, Son of man, the place of my throne, and the place of the soles of my feet, where I will dwell in the midst of the children of Israel for ever, and my holy name, shall the house of Israel no more defile, *neither* they, nor their kings, by their whoredom, nor by the carcases of their kings in their high places.

8In their setting of their threshold by my thresholds, and their post by my posts, and the wall between me and them, they have even defiled my holy name by their abominations that they have committed: wherefore I have consumed them in mine anger.

9Now let them put away their whoredom, and the carcases of their kings, far from me, and I will dwell in the midst of them for ever.

10Thou son of man, shew the house to the house of Israel, that they may be ashamed of their iniquities: and let them measure the pattern.

11And if they be ashamed of all that they have done, shew them the form of the house, and the fashion thereof, and the goings out thereof, and the comings in thereof, and all the forms thereof, and all the ordinances thereof, and all the forms thereof, and all the laws thereof: and write *it* in their sight, that they may keep the whole form thereof, and all the ordinances thereof, and do them.

12This *is* the law of the house; Upon the top of the mountain the whole limit thereof round about *shall be* most holy. Behold, this *is* the law of the house.

13And these *are* the measures of the altar after the cubits: The cubit *is* a cubit and an hand breadth; even the bottom *shall be* a cubit, and the breadth a cubit, and the border thereof by the edge thereof round about *shall be* a span: and this *shall be* the higher place of the altar.

14And from the bottom *upon* the ground *even* to the lower settle *shall be* two cubits, and the breadth one cubit; and from the lesser settle *even* to the

NEW LIVING TRANSLATION

The LORD's Glory Returns

43

After this, the man brought me back around to the east gateway. 2Suddenly, the glory of the God of Israel appeared from the east. The sound of his coming was like the roar of rushing waters, and the whole landscape shone with his glory. 3This vision was just like the others I had seen, first by the Kebar River and then when he came to destroy Jerusalem. I fell face down on the ground. 4And the glory of the LORD came into the Temple through the east gateway.

5Then the Spirit took me up and brought me into the inner courtyard, and the glory of the LORD filled the Temple. 6And I heard someone speaking to me from within the Temple, while the man who had been measuring stood beside me. 7The LORD said to me, "Son of man, this is the place of my throne and the place where I will rest my feet. I will live here forever among the people of Israel. They and their kings will not defile my holy name any longer by their adulterous worship of other gods or by honoring the relics of their kings who have died. 8They put their idol altars right next to mine with only a wall between them and me. They defiled my holy name by such detestable sin, so I consumed them in my anger. 9Now let them stop worshiping other gods and honoring the relics of their kings, and I will live among them forever.

10"Son of man, describe to the people of Israel the Temple I have shown you, so they will be ashamed of all their sins. Let them study its plan, 11and they will be ashamed* of what they have done. Describe to them all the specifications of the Temple—including its entrances and exits—and everything else about it. Tell them about its decrees and laws. Write down all these specifications and decrees as they watch so they will be sure to remember and follow them. 12And this is the basic law of the Temple: absolute holiness! The entire top of the mountain where the Temple is built is holy. Yes, this is the basic law of the Temple.

The Altar

13"These are the measurements of the altar*: There is a gutter all around the altar 21 inches deep and 21 inches wide,* with a curb 9 inches* wide around its edge. And this is the height* of the altar: 14From the gutter the altar rises 3½ feet* to a lower ledge that

43:11 As in Greek version; Hebrew reads *if they are ashamed.*
43:13a Hebrew *measurements of the altar in long cubits, each being a cubit* [18 inches or 45 centimeters] *and a handbreadth* [3 inches or 8 centimeters] *in length.* **43:13b** Hebrew *a cubit* [53 centimeters] *deep and a cubit wide.* **43:13c** Hebrew *1 span* [23 centimeters]. **43:13d** As in Greek version; Hebrew reads *base.* **43:14a** Hebrew *2 cubits* [1.1 meters].

KING JAMES VERSION

greater settle *shall be* four cubits, and the breadth *one* cubit.

15 So the altar *shall be* four cubits; and from the altar and upward *shall be* four horns.

16 And the altar *shall be* twelve *cubits* long, twelve broad, square in the four squares thereof.

17 And the settle *shall be* fourteen *cubits* long and fourteen broad in the four squares thereof; and the border about it *shall be* half a cubit; and the bottom thereof *shall be* a cubit about; and his stairs shall look toward the east.

18 And he said unto me, Son of man, thus saith the Lord GOD; These *are* the ordinances of the altar in the day when they shall make it, to offer burnt offerings thereon, and to sprinkle blood thereon.

19 And thou shalt give to the priests the Levites that be of the seed of Zadok, which approach unto me, to minister unto me, saith the Lord GOD, a young bullock for a sin offering.

20 And thou shalt take of the blood thereof, and put *it* on the four horns of it, and on the four corners of the settle, and upon the border round about: thus shalt thou cleanse and purge it.

21 Thou shalt take the bullock also of the sin offering, and he shall burn it in the appointed place of the house, without the sanctuary.

22 And on the second day thou shalt offer a kid of the goats without blemish for a sin offering; and they shall cleanse the altar, as they did cleanse *it* with the bullock.

23 When thou hast made an end of cleansing *it*, thou shalt offer a young bullock without blemish, and a ram out of the flock without blemish.

24 And thou shalt offer them before the LORD, and the priests shall cast salt upon them, and they shall offer them up *for* a burnt offering unto the LORD.

25 Seven days shalt thou prepare every day a goat *for* a sin offering: they shall also prepare a young bullock, and a ram out of the flock, without blemish.

26 Seven days shall they purge the altar and purify it; and they shall consecrate themselves.

27 And when these days are expired, it shall be, *that* upon the eighth day, and *so* forward, the priests shall make your burnt offerings upon the altar, and your peace offerings; and I will accept you, saith the Lord GOD.

44 1 Then he brought me back the way of the gate of the outward sanctuary which looketh toward the east; and it *was* shut.

2 Then said the LORD unto me; This gate shall be shut, it shall not be opened, and no man shall enter in by it; because the LORD, the God of Israel, hath entered in by it, therefore it shall be shut.

3 *It is* for the prince; the prince, he shall sit in it to

NEW LIVING TRANSLATION

surrounds the altar and is 21 inches* wide. From the lower ledge the altar rises 7 feet* to the upper ledge that is also 21 inches wide. 15 The top of the altar, the hearth, rises another 7 feet higher, with a horn rising up from each of the four corners. 16 The top of the altar is square, measuring 21 feet by 21 feet.* 17 The upper ledge also forms a square, measuring 24½ feet by 24½ feet,* with a 21-inch gutter and a 10½-inch curb* all around the edge. There are steps going up the east side of the altar."

18 Then he said to me, "Son of man, this is what the Sovereign LORD says: These will be the regulations for the burning of offerings and the sprinkling of blood when the altar is built. 19 At that time, the Levitical priests of the family of Zadok, who minister before me, are to be given a young bull for a sin offering, says the Sovereign LORD. 20 You will take some of its blood and smear it on the four horns of the altar, the four corners of the upper ledge, and the curb that runs around that ledge. This will cleanse and make atonement for the altar. 21 Then take the young bull for the sin offering and burn it at the appointed place outside the Temple area.

22 "On the second day, sacrifice as a sin offering a young male goat that has no physical defects. Then cleanse and make atonement for the altar again, just as you did with the young bull. 23 When you have finished the cleansing ceremony, offer another young bull that has no defects and a perfect ram from the flock. 24 You are to present them to the LORD, and the priests are to sprinkle salt on them and offer them as a burnt offering to the LORD.

25 "Every day for seven days a male goat, a young bull, and a ram from the flock will be sacrificed as a sin offering. None of these animals may have physical defects of any kind. 26 Do this each day for seven days to cleanse and make atonement for the altar, thus setting it apart for holy use. 27 On the eighth day, and on each day afterward, the priests will sacrifice on the altar the burnt offerings and peace offerings of the people. Then I will accept you. I, the Sovereign LORD, have spoken!"

The Prince, Levites, and Priests

44 Then the man brought me back to the east gateway in the outer wall of the Temple area, but it was closed. 2 And the LORD said to me, "This gate must remain closed; it will never again be opened. No one will ever open it and pass through, for the LORD, the God of Israel, has entered here. Therefore, it must always remain shut. 3 Only the

43:14b Hebrew *1 cubit* [53 centimeters]; also in 43:14d. **43:14c** Hebrew *4 cubits* [2.1 meters]; also in 43:15. **43:16** Hebrew *12 cubits* [6.4 meters] *long and 12 cubits wide.* **43:17a** Hebrew *14 cubits* [7.4 meters] *long and 14 cubits wide.* **43:17b** Hebrew *a gutter of 1 cubit* [53 centimeters] *and a curb of ½ a cubit* [27 centimeters].

KING JAMES VERSION

eat bread before the LORD; he shall enter by the way of the porch of *that* gate, and shall go out by the way of the same.

4 Then brought he me the way of the north gate before the house: and I looked, and, behold, the glory of the LORD filled the house of the LORD: and I fell upon my face.

5 And the LORD said unto me, Son of man, mark well, and behold with thine eyes, and hear with thine ears all that I say unto thee concerning all the ordinances of the house of the LORD, and all the laws thereof; and mark well the entering in of the house, with every going forth of the sanctuary.

6 And thou shalt say to the rebellious, *even* to the house of Israel, Thus saith the Lord GOD; O ye house of Israel, let it suffice you of all your abominations,

7 In that ye have brought *into my sanctuary* strangers, uncircumcised in heart, and uncircumcised in flesh, to be in my sanctuary, to pollute it, *even* my house, when ye offer my bread, the fat and the blood, and they have broken my covenant because of all your abominations.

8 And ye have not kept the charge of mine holy things: but ye have set keepers of my charge in my sanctuary for yourselves.

9 Thus saith the Lord GOD; No stranger, uncircumcised in heart, nor uncircumcised in flesh, shall enter into my sanctuary, of any stranger that *is* among the children of Israel.

10 And the Levites that are gone away far from me, when Israel went astray, which went astray away from me after their idols; they shall even bear their iniquity.

11 Yet they shall be ministers in my sanctuary, *having* charge at the gates of the house, and ministering to the house: they shall slay the burnt offering and the sacrifice for the people, and they shall stand before them to minister unto them.

12 Because they ministered unto them before their idols, and caused the house of Israel to fall into iniquity; therefore have I lifted up mine hand against them, saith the Lord GOD, and they shall bear their iniquity.

13 And they shall not come near unto me, to do the office of a priest unto me, nor to come near to any of my holy things, in the most holy *place:* but they shall bear their shame, and their abominations which they have committed.

14 But I will make them keepers of the charge of the house, for all the service thereof, and for all that shall be done therein.

15 But the priests the Levites, the sons of Zadok, that kept the charge of my sanctuary when the children of Israel went astray from me, they shall come near to me to minister unto me, and they shall stand before me to offer unto me the fat and the blood, saith the Lord GOD:

16 They shall enter into my sanctuary, and they

NEW LIVING TRANSLATION

prince himself may sit inside this gateway to feast in the LORD's presence. But he may come and go only through the entry room of the gateway."

4 Then the man brought me through the north gateway to the front of the Temple. I looked and saw that the glory of the LORD filled the Temple of the LORD, and I fell face down on the ground.

5 And the LORD said to me, "Son of man, take careful notice. Use your eyes and ears, and listen to everything I tell you about the regulations concerning the LORD's Temple. Take careful note of the procedures for using the Temple's entrances and exits. 6 And give these rebels, the people of Israel, this message from the Sovereign LORD: O people of Israel, enough of your detestable sins! 7 You have brought uncircumcised foreigners into my sanctuary—people who have no heart for God. In this way, you defiled my Temple even as you offered me my food, the fat and blood of sacrifices. In addition to all your other detestable sins, you have broken my covenant. 8 Instead of safeguarding my sacred rituals, you have hired foreigners to take charge of my sanctuary.

9 "So this is what the Sovereign LORD says: No foreigners, including those who live among the people of Israel, will enter my sanctuary if they have not been circumcised and have not surrendered themselves to the LORD. 10 And the men of the tribe of Levi who abandoned me when Israel strayed away from me to worship idols* must bear the consequences of their unfaithfulness. 11 They may still be Temple guards and gatekeepers, and they may slaughter the animals brought for burnt offerings and be present to help the people. 12 But they encouraged my people to worship idols, causing Israel to fall into deep sin. So I have taken a solemn oath that they must bear the consequences for their sins, says the Sovereign LORD. 13 They may not approach me to minister as priests. They may not touch any of my holy things or the holy offerings, for they must bear the shame of all the detestable sins they have committed. 14 They are to serve as the Temple caretakers, taking charge of the maintenance work and performing general duties.

15 "However, the Levitical priests of the family of Zadok continued to minister faithfully in the Temple when Israel abandoned me for idols. These men will serve as my ministers. They will stand in my presence and offer the fat and blood of the sacrifices, says the Sovereign LORD. 16 They alone will enter my

44:10 The Hebrew term (literally *round things*) probably alludes to dung; also in 44:12.

KING JAMES VERSION

shall come near to my table, to minister unto me, and
they shall keep my charge.
17 And it shall come to pass, *that* when they enter
in at the gates of the inner court, they shall be
clothed with linen garments; and no wool shall come
upon them, whiles they minister in the gates of the
inner court, and within.
18 They shall have linen bonnets upon their heads,
and shall have linen breeches upon their loins; they
shall not gird *themselves* with any thing that causeth
sweat.
19 And when they go forth into the utter court,
even into the utter court to the people, they shall put
off their garments wherein they ministered, and lay
them in the holy chambers, and they shall put on
other garments; and they shall not sanctify the people with their garments.
20 Neither shall they shave their heads, nor suffer
their locks to grow long; they shall only poll their
heads.
21 Neither shall any priest drink wine, when they
enter into the inner court.
22 Neither shall they take for their wives a widow,
nor her that is put away: but they shall take maidens
of the seed of the house of Israel, or a widow that had
a priest before.
23 And they shall teach my people *the difference*
between the holy and profane, and cause them to
discern between the unclean and the clean.
24 And in controversy they shall stand in judgment;
and they shall judge it according to my judgments:
and they shall keep my laws and my statutes in all
mine assemblies; and they shall hallow my sabbaths.
25 And they shall come at no dead person to defile
themselves: but for father, or for mother, or for son,
or for daughter, for brother, or for sister that hath
had no husband, they may defile themselves.
26 And after he is cleansed, they shall reckon unto
him seven days.
27 And in the day that he goeth into the sanctuary,
unto the inner court, to minister in the sanctuary, he
shall offer his sin offering, saith the Lord GOD.
28 And it shall be unto them for an inheritance: I
am their inheritance: and ye shall give them no possession in Israel: I *am* their possession.
29 They shall eat the meat offering, and the sin
offering, and the trespass offering: and every dedicated thing in Israel shall be theirs.
30 And the first of all the firstfruits of all *things*,
and every oblation of all, of every *sort* of your oblations, shall be the priest's: ye shall also give unto the
priest the first of your dough, that he may cause the
blessing to rest in thine house.
31 The priests shall not eat of any thing that is dead
of itself, or torn, whether it be fowl or beast.

NEW LIVING TRANSLATION

sanctuary and approach my table to serve me. They
will fulfill all my requirements.
17 "When they enter the gateway to the inner
courtyard, they must wear only linen clothing. They
must wear no wool while on duty in the inner courtyard or in the Temple itself. 18 They must wear linen
turbans and linen undergarments. They must not
wear anything that would cause them to perspire.
19 When they return to the outer courtyard where
the people are, they must take off the clothes they
wear while ministering to me. They must leave them
in the sacred rooms and put on other clothes so they
do not endanger anyone by transmitting holiness to
them through this clothing.
20 "They must neither shave their heads nor let
their hair grow too long. Instead, they must trim it
regularly. 21 The priests must not drink wine before
entering the inner courtyard. 22 They may choose
their wives only from among the virgins of Israel or
the widows of the priests. They may not marry other
widows or divorced women. 23 They will teach my
people the difference between what is holy and
what is common, what is ceremonially clean and
unclean.
24 "They will serve as judges to resolve any dis-
agreements among my people. Their decisions must
be based on my regulations. And the priests themselves must obey my instructions and decrees at all
the sacred festivals, and see to it that the Sabbaths
are set apart as holy days.
25 "A priest must not defile himself by being in the
presence of a dead person unless it is his father,
mother, child, brother, or unmarried sister. In such
cases it is permitted. 26 Even then, he can return to
his Temple duties only after being ceremonially
cleansed and then waiting for seven days. 27 The first
day he returns to work and enters the inner courtyard and the sanctuary, he must offer a sin offering
for himself, says the Sovereign LORD.
28 "The priests will not have any property or possession of land, for I alone am their special possession. 29 Their food will come from the gifts and
sacrifices brought to the Temple by the people—the
grain offerings, the sin offerings, and the guilt offerings. Whatever anyone sets apart* for the LORD will
belong to the priests. 30 The first of the ripe fruits
and all the gifts brought to the LORD will go to the
priests. The first samples of each grain harvest and
the first of your flour must also be given to the
priests so the LORD will bless your homes. 31 The
priests may not eat meat from any bird or animal
that dies a natural death or that dies after being
attacked by another animal.

44:29 The Hebrew term used here refers to the complete consecration of things or people to the LORD, either by destroying them or by giving them as an offering.

KING JAMES VERSION

45 [1]Moreover, when ye shall divide by lot the
land for inheritance, ye shall offer an oblation unto the LORD, an holy portion of the land: the
length *shall be* the length of five and twenty thousand *reeds,* and the breadth *shall be* ten thousand.
This *shall be* holy in all the borders thereof round
about.
[2]Of this there shall be for the sanctuary five hundred *in length,* with five hundred *in breadth,* square
round about; and fifty cubits round about for the
suburbs thereof.
[3]And of this measure shalt thou measure the
length of five and twenty thousand, and the breadth
of ten thousand: and in it shall be the sanctuary *and*
the most holy *place.*
[4]The holy *portion* of the land shall be for the priests
the ministers of the sanctuary, which shall come near
to minister unto the LORD: and it shall be a place for
their houses, and an holy place for the sanctuary.
[5]And the five and twenty thousand of length, and
the ten thousand of breadth, shall also the Levites,
the ministers of the house, have for themselves, for
a possession for twenty chambers.
[6]And ye shall appoint the possession of the city
five thousand broad, and five and twenty thousand
long, over against the oblation of the holy *portion:*
it shall be for the whole house of Israel.
[7]And a *portion shall be* for the prince on the one
side and on the other side of the oblation of the holy
portion, and of the possession of the city, before the
oblation of the holy *portion,* and before the possession of the city, from the west side westward, and
from the east side eastward: and the length *shall be*
over against one of the portions, from the west border unto the east border.
[8]In the land shall be his possession in Israel: and
my princes shall no more oppress my people; and *the*
rest of the land shall they give to the house of Israel
according to their tribes.
[9]Thus saith the Lord GOD; Let it suffice you,
O princes of Israel: remove violence and spoil, and
execute judgment and justice, take away your exac-
tions from my people, saith the Lord GOD.
[10]Ye shall have just balances, and a just ephah, and
a just bath.
[11]The ephah and the bath shall be of one measure,
that the bath may contain the tenth part of an homer,
and the ephah the tenth part of an homer: the measure thereof shall be after the homer.
[12]And the shekel *shall be* twenty gerahs: twenty

NEW LIVING TRANSLATION

Division of the Land

45 "When you divide the land among the
tribes of Israel, you must set aside a section
for the LORD as his holy portion. This piece of land
will be 8⅓ miles long and 6⅔ miles wide.* The entire area will be holy. [2]A section of this land, measuring 875 feet by 875 feet,* will be set aside for the
Temple. An additional strip of land 87½ feet* wide
is to be left empty all around it. [3]Within the larger
sacred area, measure out a portion of land 8⅓ miles
long and 3⅓ miles wide.* Within it the sanctuary of
the Most Holy Place will be located. [4]This area will
be holy, set aside for the priests who minister to the
LORD in the sanctuary. They will use it for their
homes, and my Temple will be located within it.
[5]The strip of sacred land next to it, also 8⅓ miles
long and 3⅓ miles wide, will be a living area for the
Levites who work at the Temple. It will be their possession and a place for their towns.*
[6]"Adjacent to the larger sacred area will be a section of land 8⅓ miles long and 1⅔ miles wide.* This
will be set aside for a city where anyone in Israel
can live.
[7]"Two special sections of land will be set apart for
the prince. One section will share a border with the
east side of the sacred lands and city, and the second
section will share a border on the west side. Then the
far eastern and western borders of the prince's lands
will line up with the eastern and western boundaries
of the tribal areas. [8]These sections of land will be the
prince's allotment. Then my princes will no longer
oppress and rob my people; they will assign the rest
of the land to the people, giving an allotment to each
tribe.

Rules for the Princes

[9]"For this is what the Sovereign LORD says: Enough,
you princes of Israel! Stop your violence and oppression and do what is just and right. Quit robbing and
cheating my people out of their land. Stop expelling
them from their homes, says the Sovereign LORD.
[10]Use only honest weights and scales and honest
measures, both dry and liquid.* [11]The homer* will
be your standard unit for measuring volume. The
ephah and the bath* will each measure one-tenth of
a homer. [12]The standard unit for weight will be the

45:1 As in Greek version, which reads *25,000 cubits* [13.3 kilometers] *long and 20,000 cubits* [10.6 kilometers] *wide;* Hebrew reads *25,000 cubits long and 10,000 cubits* [3⅓ miles or 5.3 kilometers] *wide.* Compare 45:3, 5; 48:9. **45:2a** Hebrew *500 cubits* [265 meters] *by 500 cubits, a square.* **45:2b** Hebrew *50 cubits* [26.5 meters]. **45:3** Hebrew *25,000 cubits* [13.3 kilometers] *long and 10,000 cubits* [5.3 kilometers] *wide;* also in 45:5. **45:5** As in Greek version; Hebrew reads *They will have as their possession 20 rooms.* **45:6** Hebrew *25,000 cubits* [13.3 kilometers] *long and 5,000 cubits* [2.65 kilometers] *wide.* **45:10** Hebrew *use honest scales, an honest ephah, and an honest bath.* **45:11a** The *homer* measures about 40 gallons or 182 liters. **45:11b** The *ephah* is a dry measure; the *bath* is a liquid measure.

KING JAMES VERSION

shekels, five and twenty shekels, fifteen shekels, shall be your maneh.

13 This *is* the oblation that ye shall offer; the sixth part of an ephah of an homer of wheat, and ye shall give the sixth part of an ephah of an homer of barley:

14 Concerning the ordinance of oil, the bath of oil, *ye shall offer* the tenth part of a bath out of the cor, *which is* an homer of ten baths; for ten baths *are* an homer:

15 And one lamb out of the flock, out of two hundred, out of the fat pastures of Israel; for a meat offering, and for a burnt offering, and for peace offerings, to make reconciliation for them, saith the Lord GOD.

16 All the people of the land shall give this oblation for the prince in Israel.

17 And it shall be the prince's part *to give* burnt offerings, and meat offerings, and drink offerings, in the feasts, and in the new moons, and in the sabbaths, in all solemnities of the house of Israel: he shall prepare the sin offering, and the meat offering, and the burnt offering, and the peace offerings, to make reconciliation for the house of Israel.

18 Thus saith the Lord GOD; In the first *month,* in the first *day* of the month, thou shalt take a young bullock without blemish, and cleanse the sanctuary:

19 And the priest shall take of the blood of the sin offering, and put *it* upon the posts of the house, and upon the four corners of the settle of the altar, and upon the posts of the gate of the inner court.

20 And so thou shalt do the seventh *day* of the month for every one that erreth, and for *him that is* simple: so shall ye reconcile the house.

21 In the first *month,* in the fourteenth day of the month, ye shall have the passover, a feast of seven days; unleavened bread shall be eaten.

22 And upon that day shall the prince prepare for himself and for all the people of the land a bullock *for* a sin offering.

23 And seven days of the feast he shall prepare a burnt offering to the LORD, seven bullocks and seven rams without blemish daily the seven days; and a kid of the goats daily *for* a sin offering.

24 And he shall prepare a meat offering of an ephah for a bullock, and an ephah for a ram, and an hin of oil for an ephah.

25 In the seventh *month,* in the fifteenth day of the month, shall he do the like in the feast of the seven days, according to the sin offering, according to the burnt offering, and according to the meat offering, and according to the oil.

NEW LIVING TRANSLATION

silver shekel.* One shekel will consist of twenty gerahs, and sixty shekels will be equal to one mina.*

Special Offerings and Celebrations

13 "You must give this tax to the prince: one bushel of
wheat or barley for every 60* you harvest, 14 one percent of your olive oil,* 15 and one sheep or goat for
every 200 in your flocks in Israel. These will be the
grain offerings, burnt offerings, and peace offerings
that will make atonement for the people who bring
them, says the Sovereign LORD. 16 All the people of Israel must join in bringing these offerings to the
prince. 17 The prince will be required to provide offerings that are given at the religious festivals, the
new moon celebrations, the Sabbath days, and all
other similar occasions. He will provide the sin offerings, burnt offerings, grain offerings, liquid offerings, and peace offerings to purify the people of Israel, making them right with the LORD.*

18 "This is what the Sovereign LORD says: In early
spring, on the first day of each new year,* sacrifice a
young bull with no defects to purify the Temple.
19 The priest will take blood from this sin offering
and put it on the doorposts of the Temple, the four
corners of the upper ledge of the altar, and the gate-
posts at the entrance to the inner courtyard. 20 Do
this also on the seventh day of the new year for anyone who has sinned through error or ignorance. In this way, you will purify* the Temple.

21 "On the fourteenth day of the first month,* you
must celebrate the Passover. This festival will last for
seven days. The bread you eat during that time must
be made without yeast. 22 On the day of Passover the
prince will provide a young bull as a sin offering for
himself and the people of Israel. 23 On each of the
seven days of the feast he will prepare a burnt offering to the LORD, consisting of seven young bulls and
seven rams without defects. A male goat will also be
given each day for a sin offering. 24 The prince will
provide a basket of flour as a grain offering and a gallon of olive oil* with each young bull and ram.

25 "During the seven days of the Festival of Shelters, which occurs every year in early autumn,* the prince will provide these same sacrifices for the sin offering, the burnt offering, and the grain offering, along with the required olive oil.

45:12a The *shekel* weighs about 0.4 ounces or 11 grams. **45:12b** Elsewhere the *mina* is equated to 50 shekels. **45:13** Hebrew *1/6 of an ephah from each homer of wheat and 1/6 of an ephah from each homer of barley.* **45:14** Hebrew *the portion of oil, measured by the bath, is 1/10 of a bath from each cor, which consists of 10 baths or 1 homer, for 10 baths are equivalent to a homer.* **45:17** Or *to make atonement for the people of Israel.* **45:18** Hebrew *On the first day of the first month,* of the Hebrew calendar. This day in the ancient Hebrew lunar calendar occurred in March or April. **45:20** Or *will make atonement for.* **45:21** This day in the ancient Hebrew lunar calendar occurred in late March, April, or early May. **45:24** Hebrew *an ephah* [20 quarts or 22 liters] *of flour . . . and a hin* [3.8 liters] *of olive oil.* **45:25** Hebrew *the festival which begins on the fifteenth day of the seventh month* (see Lev 23:34). This day in the ancient Hebrew lunar calendar occurred in late September, October, or early November.

KING JAMES VERSION

46 1 Thus saith the Lord GOD; The gate of the
inner court that looketh toward the east
shall be shut the six working days; but on the sabbath it shall be opened, and in the day of the new
moon it shall be opened.
2 And the prince shall enter by the way of the porch
of *that* gate without, and shall stand by the post of
the gate, and the priests shall prepare his burnt offering and his peace offerings, and he shall worship
at the threshold of the gate: then he shall go forth;
but the gate shall not be shut until the evening.
3 Likewise the people of the land shall worship at
the door of this gate before the LORD in the sabbaths
and in the new moons.
4 And the burnt offering that the prince shall offer
unto the LORD in the sabbath day *shall be* six lambs
without blemish, and a ram without blemish.
5 And the meat offering *shall be* an ephah for a
ram, and the meat offering for the lambs as he shall
be able to give, and an hin of oil to an ephah.
6 And in the day of the new moon *it shall be* a
young bullock without blemish, and six lambs, and
a ram: they shall be without blemish.
7 And he shall prepare a meat offering, an ephah
for a bullock, and an ephah for a ram, and for the
lambs according as his hand shall attain unto, and an
hin of oil to an ephah.
8 And when the prince shall enter, he shall go in by
the way of the porch of *that* gate, and he shall go
forth by the way thereof.
9 But when the people of the land shall come before
the LORD in the solemn feasts, he that entereth in by
the way of the north gate to worship shall go out by the
way of the south gate; and he that entereth by the way
of the south gate shall go forth by the way of the north
gate: he shall not return by the way of the gate
whereby he came in, but shall go forth over against it.
10 And the prince in the midst of them, when they go
in, shall go in; and when they go forth, shall go forth.
11 And in the feasts and in the solemnities the meat
offering shall be an ephah to a bullock, and an ephah
to a ram, and to the lambs as he is able to give, and an
hin of oil to an ephah.
12 Now when the prince shall prepare a voluntary
burnt offering or peace offerings voluntarily unto
the LORD, *one* shall then open him the gate that
looketh toward the east, and he shall prepare his
burnt offering and his peace offerings, as he did on
the sabbath day: then he shall go forth; and after his
going forth *one* shall shut the gate.
13 Thou shalt daily prepare a burnt offering unto
the LORD *of* a lamb of the first year without blemish:
thou shalt prepare it every morning.
14 And thou shalt prepare a meat offering for it
every morning, the sixth part of an ephah, and the
third part of an hin of oil, to temper with the fine
flour; a meat offering continually by a perpetual ordinance unto the LORD.

NEW LIVING TRANSLATION

46 "This is what the Sovereign LORD says: The
east gateway of the inner courtyard will be
closed during the six workdays each week, but it will
be open on Sabbath days and the days of new moon
celebrations. 2 The prince will enter the entry room of
the gateway from the outside. Then he will stand by
the gatepost while the priest offers his burnt offering
and peace offering. He will bow down in worship inside the gateway passage and then go back out the
way he came. The gateway will not be closed until
evening. 3 The common people will bow down and
worship the LORD in front of this gateway on Sabbath
days and the days of new moon celebrations.
4 "Each Sabbath day the prince will present to the
LORD a burnt offering of six lambs and one ram, all
with no defects. 5 He will present a grain offering of a
basket of choice flour to go with the ram and whatever amount of flour he chooses to go with each
lamb, and he is to offer one gallon of olive oil* for
each basket of flour. 6 At the new moon celebrations,
he will bring one young bull, six lambs, and one ram,
all with no defects. 7 With the young bull he must
bring a basket of choice flour for a grain offering.
With the ram he must bring another basket of flour.
And with each lamb he is to bring whatever amount
of flour he chooses to give. With each basket of flour
he must offer one gallon of olive oil.
8 "The prince must enter the gateway through the
entry room, and he must leave the same way. 9 But
when the people come in through the north gateway
to worship the LORD during the religious festivals,
they must leave by the south gateway. And those who
entered through the south gateway must leave by the
north gateway. They must never leave by the same
gateway they came in, but must always use the opposite gateway. 10 The prince will enter and leave with
the people on these occasions.
11 "So at the special feasts and sacred festivals, the
grain offering will be a basket of choice flour with
each young bull, another basket of flour with each
ram, and as much flour as the prince chooses to give
with each lamb. Give one gallon of olive oil with each
basket of flour. 12 When the prince offers a voluntary
burnt offering or peace offering to the LORD, the east
gateway to the inner courtyard will be opened for
him, and he will offer his sacrifices as he does on
Sabbath days. Then he will leave, and the gateway
will be shut behind him.
13 "Each morning you must sacrifice a one-year-
old lamb with no defects as a burnt offering to the
LORD. 14 With the lamb, a grain offering must also be
given to the LORD—about three quarts of flour with a
third of a gallon of olive oil* to moisten the choice

46:5 Hebrew *an ephah* [20 quarts or 22 liters] *of choice flour . . . a hin* [3.8 liters] *of olive oil;* similarly in 46:7, 11. **46:14** Hebrew ⅙ *of an ephah* [3.7 liters] *of flour with* ⅓ *of a hin* [1.3 liters] *of olive oil.*

KING JAMES VERSION

15Thus shall they prepare the lamb, and the meat
offering, and the oil, every morning *for* a continual
burnt offering.
16Thus saith the Lord GOD; If the prince give a gift
unto any of his sons, the inheritance thereof shall be
his sons'; it *shall be* their possession by inheritance.
17But if he give a gift of his inheritance to one of
his servants, then it shall be his to the year of liberty;
after it shall return to the prince: but his inheritance
shall be his sons' for them.
18Moreover the prince shall not take of the people's
inheritance by oppression, to thrust them out of their
possession; *but* he shall give his sons inheritance out
of his own possession: that my people be not scattered every man from his possession.

19After he brought me through the entry, which
was at the side of the gate, into the holy chambers
of the priests, which looked toward the north: and,
behold, there *was* a place on the two sides westward.
20Then said he unto me, This *is* the place where
the priests shall boil the trespass offering and the sin
offering, where they shall bake the meat offering;
that they bear *them* not out into the utter court, to
sanctify the people.
21Then he brought me forth into the utter court,
and caused me to pass by the four corners of the
court; and, behold, in every corner of the court *there
was* a court.
22In the four corners of the court *there were*
courts joined of forty *cubits* long and thirty broad:
these four corners *were* of one measure.
23And *there was* a row *of building* round about in
them, round about them four, and *it was* made with
boiling places under the rows round about.
24Then said he unto me, These *are* the places of
them that boil, where the ministers of the house
shall boil the sacrifice of the people.

47 1Afterward he brought me again unto the
door of the house; and, behold, waters issued out from under the threshold of the house eastward: for the forefront of the house *stood toward* the
east, and the waters came down from under from the
right side of the house, at the south *side* of the altar.
2Then brought he me out of the way of the gate
northward, and led me about the way without unto
the utter gate by the way that looketh eastward; and,
behold, there ran out waters on the right side.
3And when the man that had the line in his hand
went forth eastward, he measured a thousand cubits,
and he brought me through the waters; the waters
were to the ancles.
4Again he measured a thousand, and brought me
through the waters; the waters *were* to the knees.

NEW LIVING TRANSLATION

flour. This will be a permanent law for you. 15The
lamb, the grain offering, and the olive oil must be
given as a daily sacrifice every morning without fail.
16"This is what the Sovereign LORD says: If the
prince gives a gift of land to one of his sons as his inheritance, it will belong to him and his descendants
forever. 17But if the prince gives a gift of land from
his inheritance to one of his servants, the servant
may keep it only until the Year of Jubilee, which
comes every fiftieth year.* At that time the land will
return to the prince. But when the prince gives gifts
to his sons, those gifts will be permanent. 18And the
prince may never take anyone's property by force. If
he gives property to his sons, it must be from his own
land, for I do not want any of my people unjustly
evicted from their property."

The Temple Kitchens

19In my vision, the man brought me through the entrance beside the gateway and led me to the sacred
rooms assigned to the priests, which faced toward
the north. He showed me a place at the extreme west
end of these rooms. 20He explained, "This is where
the priests will cook the meat from the guilt offerings and sin offerings and bake the flour from the
grain offerings into bread. They will do it here to
avoid carrying the sacrifices through the outer
courtyard and endangering the people by transmitting holiness to them."
21Then he brought me back to the outer courtyard
and led me to each of its four corners. In each corner
I saw an enclosure. 22Each of these enclosures was
70 feet long and 52½ feet wide,* surrounded by
walls. 23Along the inside of these walls was a ledge of
stone with fireplaces under the ledge all the way
around. 24The man said to me, "These are the kitchens to be used by the Temple assistants to boil the
sacrifices offered by the people."

The River of Healing

47 In my vision, the man brought me back to
the entrance of the Temple. There I saw a
stream flowing east from beneath the door of the
Temple and passing to the right of the altar on its
south side. 2The man brought me outside the wall
through the north gateway and led me around to the
eastern entrance. There I could see the water flowing out through the south side of the east gateway.
3Measuring as he went, he took me along the
stream for 1,750 feet* and then led me across. The
water was up to my ankles. 4He measured off another 1,750 feet and led me across again. This time

46:17 Hebrew *until the Year of Release;* see Lev 25:8-17. **46:22** Hebrew *40 cubits* [21.2 meters] *long and 30 cubits* [15.9 meters] *wide.*
47:3 Hebrew *1,000 cubits* [530 meters]; also in 47:4, 5.

KING JAMES VERSION

Again he measured a thousand, and brought me through; the waters *were* to the loins.

5Afterward he measured a thousand; *and it was* a river that I could not pass over: for the waters were risen, waters to swim in, a river that could not be passed over.

6And he said unto me, Son of man, hast thou seen *this?* Then he brought me, and caused me to return to the brink of the river.

7Now when I had returned, behold, at the bank of the river *were* very many trees on the one side and on the other.

8Then said he unto me, These waters issue out toward the east country, and go down into the desert, and go into the sea: *which being* brought forth into the sea, the waters shall be healed.

9And it shall come to pass, *that* every thing that liveth, which moveth, whithersoever the rivers shall come, shall live: and there shall be a very great multitude of fish, because these waters shall come thither: for they shall be healed; and every thing shall live whither the river cometh.

10And it shall come to pass, *that* the fishers shall stand upon it from En-gedi even unto En-eglaim; they shall be a *place* to spread forth nets; their fish shall be according to their kinds, as the fish of the great sea, exceeding many.

11But the miry places thereof and the marishes thereof shall not be healed; they shall be given to salt.

12And by the river upon the bank thereof, on this side and on that side, shall grow all trees for meat, whose leaf shall not fade, neither shall the fruit thereof be consumed: it shall bring forth new fruit according to his months, because their waters they issued out of the sanctuary: and the fruit thereof shall be for meat, and the leaf thereof for medicine.

13Thus saith the Lord GOD; This *shall be* the border, whereby ye shall inherit the land according to the twelve tribes of Israel: Joseph *shall have two* portions.

14And ye shall inherit it, one as well as another: *concerning* the which I lifted up mine hand to give it unto your fathers: and this land shall fall unto you for inheritance.

15And this *shall be* the border of the land toward the north side, from the great sea, the way of Hethlon, as men go to Zedad;

16Hamath, Berothah, Sibraim, which *is* between the border of Damascus and the border of Hamath; Hazar-hatticon, which *is* by the coast of Hauran.

17And the border from the sea shall be Hazar-enan, the border of Damascus, and the north northward, and the border of Hamath. And *this is* the north side.

18And the east side ye shall measure from Hauran,

NEW LIVING TRANSLATION

the water was up to my knees. After another 1,750 feet, it was up to my waist. 5Then he measured another 1,750 feet, and the river was too deep to walk across. It was deep enough to swim in, but too deep to walk through.

6He asked me, "Have you been watching, son of man?" Then he led me back along the riverbank. 7When I returned, I was surprised by the sight of many trees growing on both sides of the river. 8Then he said to me, "This river flows east through the desert into the valley of the Dead Sea.* The waters of this stream will make the salty waters of the Dead Sea fresh and pure. 9There will be swarms of living things wherever the water of this river flows. Fish will abound in the Dead Sea, for its waters will become fresh. Life will flourish wherever this water flows. 10Fishermen will stand along the shores of the Dead Sea. All the way from En-gedi to En-eglaim, the shores will be covered with nets drying in the sun. Fish of every kind will fill the Dead Sea, just as they fill the Mediterranean.* 11But the marshes and swamps will not be purified; they will still be salty. 12Fruit trees of all kinds will grow along both sides of the river. The leaves of these trees will never turn brown and fall, and there will always be fruit on their branches. There will be a new crop every month, for they are watered by the river flowing from the Temple. The fruit will be for food and the leaves for healing."

Boundaries for the Land

13This is what the Sovereign LORD says: "Divide the land in this way for the twelve tribes of Israel: The descendants of Joseph will be given two shares of land.* 14Otherwise each tribe will receive an equal share. I took a solemn oath and swore that I would give this land to your ancestors, and it will now come to you as your possession.

15"These are the boundaries of the land: The northern border will run from the Mediterranean toward Hethlon, then on through Lebo-hamath to Zedad; 16then it will run to Berothah and Sibraim, which are on the border between Damascus and Hamath, and finally to Hazer-hatticon, on the border of Hauran. 17So the northern border will run from the Mediterranean to Hazar-enan, on the border between Hamath to the north and Damascus to the south.

18"The eastern border starts at a point

47:8 Hebrew *the sea.* **47:10** Hebrew *the great sea;* also in 47:15, 17, 19, 20. **47:13** It was important to retain twelve portions of land. Since Levi had no portion, the descendants of Joseph's sons, Ephraim and Manasseh, received land as two tribes.

KING JAMES VERSION

and from Damascus, and from Gilead, and from the land of Israel *by* Jordan, from the border unto the east sea. And *this is* the east side.

19 And the south side southward, from Tamar *even* to the waters of strife *in* Kadesh, the river to the great sea. And *this is* the south side southward.

20 The west side also *shall be* the great sea from the border, till a man come over against Hamath. This *is* the west side.

21 So shall ye divide this land unto you according to the tribes of Israel.

22 And it shall come to pass, *that* ye shall divide it by lot for an inheritance unto you, and to the strangers that sojourn among you, which shall beget children among you: and they shall be unto you as born in the country among the children of Israel; they shall have inheritance with you among the tribes of Israel.

23 And it shall come to pass, *that* in what tribe the stranger sojourneth, there shall ye give *him* his inheritance, saith the Lord GOD.

48 1 Now these *are* the names of the tribes. From the north end to the coast of the way of Hethlon, as one goeth to Hamath, Hazar-enan, the border of Damascus northward, to the coast of Hamath; for these are his sides east *and* west; a *portion for* Dan.

2 And by the border of Dan, from the east side unto the west side, a *portion for* Asher.

3 And by the border of Asher, from the east side even unto the west side, a *portion for* Naphtali.

4 And by the border of Naphtali, from the east side unto the west side, a *portion for* Manasseh.

5 And by the border of Manasseh, from the east side unto the west side, a *portion for* Ephraim.

6 And by the border of Ephraim, from the east side even unto the west side, a *portion for* Reuben.

7 And by the border of Reuben, from the east side unto the west side, a *portion for* Judah.

8 And by the border of Judah, from the east side unto the west side, shall be the offering which ye shall offer of five and twenty thousand *reeds in* breadth, and *in* length as one of the *other* parts, from the east side unto the west side: and the sanctuary shall be in the midst of it.

9 The oblation that ye shall offer unto the LORD *shall be* of five and twenty thousand in length, and of ten thousand in breadth.

10 And for them, *even* for the priests, shall be *this* holy oblation; toward the north five and twenty thousand *in length,* and toward the west ten thousand in breadth, and toward the east ten thousand in breadth, and toward the south five and twenty

NEW LIVING TRANSLATION

between Hauran and Damascus and runs south along the Jordan River between Israel and Gilead, past the Dead Sea* and as far south as Tamar.* This will be the eastern border.

19 "The southern border will go west from Tamar to the waters of Meribah at Kadesh* and then follow the course of the Brook of Egypt to the Mediterranean. This will be the southern border.

20 "On the west side, the Mediterranean itself will be your border from the southern border to the point where the northern border begins, opposite Lebo-hamath.

21 "Divide the land within these boundaries among
the tribes of Israel. 22 Distribute the land as an allotment for yourselves and for the foreigners who have
joined you and are raising their families among you.
They will be like native-born Israelites to you and will
receive an allotment among the tribes. 23 These foreigners are to be given land within the territory of
the tribe with whom they now live. I, the Sovereign
LORD, have spoken!

Division of the Land

48 "Here is the list of the tribes of Israel and the territory each is to receive. The territory of Dan is in the extreme north. Its boundary line follows the Hethlon road to Lebo-hamath and then runs on to Hazar-enan on the border of Damascus, with Hamath to the north. Dan's territory extends all the way across the land of Israel from east to west.

2 "Asher's territory lies south of Dan's and also extends from east to west. 3 Naphtali's land lies south of
Asher's, also extending from east to west. 4 Then
comes Manasseh south of Naphtali, and its territory
also extends from east to west. 5 South of Manasseh
is Ephraim, 6 and then Reuben, 7 and then Judah, all of
whose boundaries extend from east to west.

8 "South of Judah is the land set aside for a special purpose. It will be 8⅓ miles* wide and will extend as far east and west as the tribal territories, with the Temple at the center.

9 "The area set aside for the LORD's Temple will be
8⅓ miles long and 6⅔ miles wide.* 10 For the priests
there will be a strip of land measuring 8⅓ miles long
by 3⅓ miles wide,* with the LORD's Temple at the

47:18a Hebrew *the eastern sea.* **47:18b** As in Greek version; Hebrew reads *you will measure.* **47:19** Hebrew *waters of Meribath-kadesh.* **48:8** Hebrew *25,000 cubits* [13.3 kilometers]. **48:9** As in one Greek manuscript and the Greek reading in 45:1: *25,000 cubits* [13.3 kilometers] *long and 20,000 cubits* [10.6 kilometers] *wide;* Hebrew reads *25,000 cubits long and 10,000 cubits* [3⅓ miles or 5.3 kilometers] *wide.* Similarly in 48:13b. Compare 45:1-5; 48:10-13. **48:10** Hebrew *25,000 cubits* [13.3 kilometers] *long by 10,000 cubits* [5.3 kilometers] *wide;* also in 48:13a.

KING JAMES VERSION

thousand in length: and the sanctuary of the LORD shall be in the midst thereof.

11*It shall be* for the priests that are sanctified of the sons of Zadok; which have kept my charge, which went not astray when the children of Israel went astray, as the Levites went astray.

12And *this* oblation of the land that is offered shall be unto them a thing most holy by the border of the Levites.

13And over against the border of the priests the Levites *shall have* five and twenty thousand in length, and ten thousand in breadth: all the length *shall be* five and twenty thousand, and the breadth ten thousand.

14And they shall not sell of it, neither exchange, nor alienate the firstfruits of the land: for *it is* holy unto the LORD.

15And the five thousand, that are left in the breadth over against the five and twenty thousand, shall be a profane *place* for the city, for dwelling, and for suburbs: and the city shall be in the midst thereof.

16And these *shall be* the measures thereof; the north side four thousand and five hundred, and the south side four thousand and five hundred, and on the east side four thousand and five hundred, and the west side four thousand and five hundred.

17And the suburbs of the city shall be toward the north two hundred and fifty, and toward the south two hundred and fifty, and toward the east two hundred and fifty, and toward the west two hundred and fifty.

18And the residue in length over against the oblation of the holy *portion shall be* ten thousand eastward, and ten thousand westward: and it shall be over against the oblation of the holy *portion;* and the increase thereof shall be for food unto them that serve the city.

19And they that serve the city shall serve it out of all the tribes of Israel.

20All the oblation *shall be* five and twenty thousand by five and twenty thousand: ye shall offer the holy oblation foursquare, with the possession of the city.

21And the residue *shall be* for the prince, on the one side and on the other of the holy oblation, and of the possession of the city, over against the five and twenty thousand of the oblation toward the east border, and westward over against the five and twenty thousand toward the west border, over against the portions for the prince: and it shall be the holy oblation; and the sanctuary of the house *shall be* in the midst thereof.

22Moreover from the possession of the Levites, and from the possession of the city, *being* in the midst *of that* which is the prince's, between the border of Judah and the border of Benjamin, shall be for the prince.

NEW LIVING TRANSLATION

center. 11This area is set aside for the ordained priests, the descendants of Zadok who served me faithfully and did not go astray with the people of Israel and the rest of the Levites. 12It will be their special portion when the land is distributed, the most sacred land of all. Next to the priests' territory will lie the land where the other Levites will live.

13"The land allotted to the Levites will be the same size and shape as that belonging to the priests—8⅓ miles long and 3⅓ miles wide. Together these portions of land will measure 8⅓ miles long by 6⅔ miles wide.* 14None of this special land may ever be sold or traded or used by others, for it belongs to the LORD; it is set apart as holy.

15"An additional strip of land 8⅓ miles long by 1⅔ miles wide,* south of the sacred Temple area, will be allotted for public use—homes, pasturelands, and common lands, with a city at the center. 16The city will measure 1½ miles* on each side—north, south, east, and west. 17Open lands will surround the city for 150 yards* in every direction. 18Outside the city there will be a farming area that stretches 3⅓ miles to the east and 3⅓ miles to the west* along the border of the sacred area. This farmland will produce food for the people working in the city. 19Those who come from the various tribes to work in the city may farm it. 20This entire area—including the sacred lands and the city—is a square that measures 8⅓ miles* on each side.

21"The areas that remain, to the east and to the west of the sacred lands and the city, will belong to the prince. Each of these areas will be 8⅓ miles wide, extending in opposite directions to the eastern and western borders of Israel, with the sacred lands and the sanctuary of the Temple in the center. 22So the prince's land will include everything between the territories allotted to Judah and Benjamin, except for the areas set aside for the sacred lands and the city.

48:13 See note on 48:9. **48:15** Hebrew *25,000 cubits* [13.3 kilometers] *long by 5,000 cubits* [2.65 kilometers] *wide.* **48:16** Hebrew *4,500 cubits* [2.4 kilometers]; also in 48:30, 32, 33, 34. **48:17** Hebrew *250 cubits* [133 meters]. **48:18** Hebrew *10,000 cubits* [5.3 kilometers] *to the east and 10,000 cubits to the west.* **48:20** Hebrew *25,000 cubits* [13.3 kilometers]; also in 48:21.

KING JAMES VERSION

23 As for the rest of the tribes, from the east side unto the west side, Benjamin *shall have* a *portion.*

24 And by the border of Benjamin, from the east side unto the west side, Simeon *shall have* a *portion.*

25 And by the border of Simeon, from the east side unto the west side, Issachar a *portion.*

26 And by the border of Issachar, from the east side unto the west side, Zebulun a *portion.*

27 And by the border of Zebulun, from the east side unto the west side, Gad a *portion.*

28 And by the border of Gad, at the south side southward, the border shall be even from Tamar *unto* the waters of strife *in* Kadesh, *and* to the river toward the great sea.

29 This *is* the land which ye shall divide by lot unto the tribes of Israel for inheritance, and these *are* their portions, saith the Lord GOD.

30 And these *are* the goings out of the city on the north side, four thousand and five hundred measures.

31 And the gates of the city *shall be* after the names of the tribes of Israel: three gates northward; one gate of Reuben, one gate of Judah, one gate of Levi.

32 And at the east side four thousand and five hundred: and three gates; and one gate of Joseph, one gate of Benjamin, one gate of Dan.

33 And at the south side four thousand and five hundred measures: and three gates; one gate of Simeon, one gate of Issachar, one gate of Zebulun.

34 At the west side four thousand and five hundred, *with* their three gates; one gate of Gad, one gate of Asher, one gate of Naphtali.

35 *It was* round about eighteen thousand *measures:* and the name of the city from *that* day *shall be,* The LORD *is* there.

NEW LIVING TRANSLATION

23 "These are the territories allotted to the rest of
the tribes. Benjamin's territory lies just south of the
prince's lands, and it extends across the entire land
of Israel from east to west. 24 South of Benjamin's territory lies that of Simeon, also extending across the
land from east to west. 25 Next is the territory of Issachar with the same eastern and western boundaries.

26 "Then comes the territory of Zebulun, which
also extends across the land from east to west. 27 The
territory of Gad is just south of Zebulun with the
same borders to the east and west. 28 The southern
border of Gad runs from Tamar to the waters of Meribah at Kadesh* and then follows the Brook of Egypt
to the Mediterranean.*

29 "These are the allotments that will be set aside
for each tribe's exclusive possession. I, the Sovereign
LORD, have spoken!

The Gates of the City

30 "These will be the exits to the city: On the north
wall, which is 1½ miles long, 31 there will be three
gates, each one named after a tribe of Israel. The first
will be named for Reuben, the second for Judah, and
the third for Levi. 32 On the east wall, also 1½ miles
long, the gates will be named for Joseph, Benjamin,
and Dan. 33 The south wall, also 1½ miles long, will
have gates named for Simeon, Issachar, and Zebulun.
34 And on the west wall, also 1½ miles long, the gates
will be named for Gad, Asher, and Naphtali.

35 "The distance around the entire city will be
6 miles.* And from that day the name of the city will
be 'The LORD Is There.'*"

48:28a Hebrew *waters of Meribath-kadesh.* **48:28b** Hebrew *the great sea.* **48:35a** Hebrew *18,000 cubits* [9.6 kilometers]. **48:35b** Hebrew *Yahweh Shammah.*

Daniel

KING JAMES VERSION

1 [1]In the third year of the reign of Jehoiakim king of Judah came Nebuchadnezzar king of Babylon unto Jerusalem, and besieged it.

[2]And the Lord gave Jehoiakim king of Judah into his hand, with part of the vessels of the house of God: which he carried into the land of Shinar to the house of his god; and he brought the vessels into the treasure house of his god.

[3]And the king spake unto Ashpenaz the master of his eunuchs, that he should bring *certain* of the children of Israel, and of the king's seed, and of the princes;

[4]Children in whom *was* no blemish, but well favoured, and skilful in all wisdom, and cunning in knowledge, and understanding science, and such as *had* ability in them to stand in the king's palace, and whom they might teach the learning and the tongue of the Chaldeans.

[5]And the king appointed them a daily provision of the king's meat, and of the wine which he drank: so nourishing them three years, that at the end thereof they might stand before the king.

[6]Now among these were of the children of Judah, Daniel, Hananiah, Mishael, and Azariah:

[7]Unto whom the prince of the eunuchs gave names: for he gave unto Daniel *the name* of Belteshazzar; and to Hananiah, of Shadrach; and to Mishael, of Meshach; and to Azariah, of Abed-nego.

[8]But Daniel purposed in his heart that he would not defile himself with the portion of the king's meat, nor with the wine which he drank: therefore he requested of the prince of the eunuchs that he might not defile himself.

[9]Now God had brought Daniel into favour and tender love with the prince of the eunuchs.

[10]And the prince of the eunuchs said unto Daniel, I fear my lord the king, who hath appointed your meat and your drink: for why should he see your faces worse liking than the children which *are* of your sort? then shall ye make *me* endanger my head to the king.

[11]Then said Daniel to Melzar, whom the prince of

NEW LIVING TRANSLATION

Daniel in Nebuchadnezzar's Court

1 During the third year of King Jehoiakim's reign in Judah,* King Nebuchadnezzar of Babylon came to Jerusalem and besieged it. [2]The Lord gave him victory over King Jehoiakim of Judah and permitted him to take some of the sacred objects from the Temple of God. So Nebuchadnezzar took them back to the land of Babylonia* and placed them in the treasure-house of his god.

[3]Then the king ordered Ashpenaz, his chief of staff, to bring to the palace some of the young men of Judah's royal family and other noble families, who had been brought to Babylon as captives. [4]"Select only strong, healthy, and good-looking young men," he said. "Make sure they are well versed in every branch of learning, are gifted with knowledge and good judgment, and are suited to serve in the royal palace. Train these young men in the language and literature of Babylon.*" [5]The king assigned them a daily ration of food and wine from his own kitchens. They were to be trained for three years, and then they would enter the royal service.

[6]Daniel, Hananiah, Mishael, and Azariah were four of the young men chosen, all from the tribe of Judah. [7]The chief of staff renamed them with these Babylonian names:

Daniel was called Belteshazzar.
Hananiah was called Shadrach.
Mishael was called Meshach.
Azariah was called Abednego.

[8]But Daniel was determined not to defile himself by eating the food and wine given to them by the king. He asked the chief of staff for permission not to eat these unacceptable foods. [9]Now God had given the chief of staff both respect and affection for Daniel. [10]But he responded, "I am afraid of my lord the king, who has ordered that you eat this food and wine. If you become pale and thin compared to the other youths your age, I am afraid the king will have me beheaded."

[11]Daniel spoke with the attendant who had been

1:1 This event occurred in 605 B.C., during the third year of Jehoiakim's reign (according to the calendar system in which the new year begins in the spring). **1:2** Hebrew *the land of Shinar.* **1:4** Or *of the Chaldeans.*

KING JAMES VERSION

the eunuchs had set over Daniel, Hananiah, Mishael, and Azariah,

12 Prove thy servants, I beseech thee, ten days; and let them give us pulse to eat, and water to drink.

13 Then let our countenances be looked upon before thee, and the countenance of the children that eat of the portion of the king's meat: and as thou seest, deal with thy servants.

14 So he consented to them in this matter, and proved them ten days.

15 And at the end of ten days their countenances appeared fairer and fatter in flesh than all the children which did eat the portion of the king's meat.

16 Thus Melzar took away the portion of their meat, and the wine that they should drink; and gave them pulse.

17 As for these four children, God gave them knowledge and skill in all learning and wisdom: and Daniel had understanding in all visions and dreams.

18 Now at the end of the days that the king had said he should bring them in, then the prince of the eunuchs brought them in before Nebuchadnezzar.

19 And the king communed with them; and among them all was found none like Daniel, Hananiah, Mishael, and Azariah: therefore stood they before the king.

20 And in all matters of wisdom *and* understanding, that the king inquired of them, he found them ten times better than all the magicians *and* astrologers that *were* in all his realm.

21 And Daniel continued *even* unto the first year of king Cyrus.

2 1 And in the second year of the reign of Nebuchadnezzar, Nebuchadnezzar dreamed dreams, wherewith his spirit was troubled, and his sleep brake from him.

2 Then the king commanded to call the magicians, and the astrologers, and the sorcerers, and the Chaldeans, for to shew the king his dreams. So they came and stood before the king.

3 And the king said unto them, I have dreamed a dream, and my spirit was troubled to know the dream.

4 Then spake the Chaldeans to the king in Syriack, O king, live for ever: tell thy servants the dream, and we will shew the interpretation.

5 The king answered and said to the Chaldeans, The thing is gone from me: if ye will not make known unto me the dream, with the interpretation thereof, ye shall be cut in pieces, and your houses shall be made a dunghill.

6 But if ye shew the dream, and the interpretation thereof, ye shall receive of me gifts and rewards and great honour: therefore shew me the dream, and the interpretation thereof.

7 They answered again and said, Let the king tell his servants the dream, and we will shew the interpretation of it.

NEW LIVING TRANSLATION

appointed by the chief of staff to look after Daniel, Hananiah, Mishael, and Azariah. 12 "Please test us for ten days on a diet of vegetables and water," Daniel said. 13 "At the end of the ten days, see how we look compared to the other young men who are eating the king's food. Then make your decision in light of what you see." 14 The attendant agreed to Daniel's suggestion and tested them for ten days.

15 At the end of the ten days, Daniel and his three friends looked healthier and better nourished than the young men who had been eating the food assigned by the king. 16 So after that, the attendant fed them only vegetables instead of the food and wine provided for the others.

17 God gave these four young men an unusual aptitude for understanding every aspect of literature and wisdom. And God gave Daniel the special ability to interpret the meanings of visions and dreams.

18 When the training period ordered by the king was completed, the chief of staff brought all the young men to King Nebuchadnezzar. 19 The king talked with them, and no one impressed him as much as Daniel, Hananiah, Mishael, and Azariah. So they entered the royal service. 20 Whenever the king consulted them in any matter requiring wisdom and balanced judgment, he found them ten times more capable than any of the magicians and enchanters in his entire kingdom.

21 Daniel remained in the royal service until the first year of the reign of King Cyrus.*

Nebuchadnezzar's Dream

2 One night during the second year of his reign,* Nebuchadnezzar had such disturbing dreams that he couldn't sleep. 2 He called in his magicians, enchanters, sorcerers, and astrologers,* and he demanded that they tell him what he had dreamed. As they stood before the king, 3 he said, "I have had a dream that deeply troubles me, and I must know what it means."

4 Then the astrologers answered the king in Aramaic,* "Long live the king! Tell us the dream, and we will tell you what it means."

5 But the king said to the astrologers, "I am serious about this. If you don't tell me what my dream was and what it means, you will be torn limb from limb, and your houses will be turned into heaps of rubble! 6 But if you tell me what I dreamed and what the dream means, I will give you many wonderful gifts and honors. Just tell me the dream and what it means!"

7 They said again, "Please, Your Majesty. Tell us the dream, and we will tell you what it means."

1:21 Cyrus began his reign (over Babylon) in 539 B.C. **2:1** The second year of Nebuchadnezzar's reign was 603 B.C. **2:2** Or *Chaldeans;* also in 2:4, 5, 10. **2:4** The original text from this point through chapter 7 is in Aramaic.

KING JAMES VERSION

8The king answered and said, I know of certainty that ye would gain the time, because ye see the thing is gone from me.

9But if ye will not make known unto me the dream, *there is but* one decree for you: for ye have prepared lying and corrupt words to speak before me, till the time be changed: therefore tell me the dream, and I shall know that ye can shew me the interpretation thereof.

10The Chaldeans answered before the king, and said, There is not a man upon the earth that can shew the king's matter: therefore *there is* no king, lord, nor ruler, *that* asked such things at any magician, or astrologer, or Chaldean.

11And *it is* a rare thing that the king requireth, and there is none other that can shew it before the king, except the gods, whose dwelling is not with flesh.

12For this cause the king was angry and very furious, and commanded to destroy all the wise *men* of Babylon.

13And the decree went forth that the wise *men* should be slain; and they sought Daniel and his fellows to be slain.

14Then Daniel answered with counsel and wisdom to Arioch the captain of the king's guard, which was gone forth to slay the wise *men* of Babylon:

15He answered and said to Arioch the king's captain, Why *is* the decree *so* hasty from the king? Then Arioch made the thing known to Daniel.

16Then Daniel went in, and desired of the king that he would give him time, and that he would shew the king the interpretation.

17Then Daniel went to his house, and made the thing known to Hananiah, Mishael, and Azariah, his companions:

18That they would desire mercies of the God of heaven concerning this secret; that Daniel and his fellows should not perish with the rest of the wise *men* of Babylon.

19Then was the secret revealed unto Daniel in a night vision. Then Daniel blessed the God of heaven.

20Daniel answered and said, Blessed be the name of God for ever and ever: for wisdom and might are his:

21And he changeth the times and the seasons: he removeth kings, and setteth up kings: he giveth wisdom unto the wise, and knowledge to them that know understanding:

22He revealeth the deep and secret things: he knoweth what *is* in the darkness, and the light dwelleth with him.

23I thank thee, and praise thee, O thou God of my fathers, who hast given me wisdom and might, and hast made known unto me now what we desired of thee: for thou hast *now* made known unto us the king's matter.

24Therefore Daniel went in unto Arioch, whom the king had ordained to destroy the wise *men* of

NEW LIVING TRANSLATION

8The king replied, "I know what you are doing! You're stalling for time because you know I am serious when I say, 9'If you don't tell me the dream, you are doomed.' So you have conspired to tell me lies, hoping I will change my mind. But tell me the dream, and then I'll know that you can tell me what it means."

10The astrologers replied to the king, "No one on earth can tell the king his dream! And no king, however great and powerful, has ever asked such a thing of any magician, enchanter, or astrologer! 11The king's demand is impossible. No one except the gods can tell you your dream, and they do not live here among people."

12The king was furious when he heard this, and he ordered that all the wise men of Babylon be executed. 13And because of the king's decree, men were sent to find and kill Daniel and his friends.

14When Arioch, the commander of the king's guard, came to kill them, Daniel handled the situation with wisdom and discretion. 15He asked Arioch, "Why has the king issued such a harsh decree?" So Arioch told him all that had happened. 16Daniel went at once to see the king and requested more time to tell the king what the dream meant.

17Then Daniel went home and told his friends Hananiah, Mishael, and Azariah what had happened. 18He urged them to ask the God of heaven to show them his mercy by telling them the secret, so they would not be executed along with the other wise men of Babylon. 19That night the secret was revealed to Daniel in a vision. Then Daniel praised the God of heaven. 20He said,

"Praise the name of God forever and ever,
  for he has all wisdom and power.
21 He controls the course of world events;
  he removes kings and sets up other kings.
He gives wisdom to the wise
  and knowledge to the scholars.
22 He reveals deep and mysterious things
  and knows what lies hidden in darkness,
  though he is surrounded by light.
23 I thank and praise you, God of my ancestors,
  for you have given me wisdom and strength.
You have told me what we asked of you
  and revealed to us what the king demanded."

Daniel Interprets the Dream

24Then Daniel went in to see Arioch, whom the king had ordered to execute the wise men of Babylon.

KING JAMES VERSION

Babylon: he went and said thus unto him; Destroy not
the wise *men* of Babylon: bring me in before the king,
and I will shew unto the king the interpretation.
25 Then Arioch brought in Daniel before the king
in haste, and said thus unto him, I have found a man
of the captives of Judah, that will make known unto
the king the interpretation.
26 The king answered and said to Daniel, whose
name *was* Belteshazzar, Art thou able to make known
unto me the dream which I have seen, and the interpretation thereof?
27 Daniel answered in the presence of the king, and
said, The secret which the king hath demanded cannot the wise *men,* the astrologers, the magicians, the
soothsayers, shew unto the king;
28 But there is a God in heaven that revealeth
secrets, and maketh known to the king Nebuchadnezzar what shall be in the latter days. Thy dream,
and the visions of thy head upon thy bed, are these;
29 As for thee, O king, thy thoughts came *into thy*
mind upon thy bed, what should come to pass hereafter: and he that revealeth secrets maketh known to
thee what shall come to pass.
30 But as for me, this secret is not revealed to me for
any wisdom that I have more than any living, but for
their sakes that shall make known the interpretation
to the king, and that thou mightest know the
thoughts of thy heart.
31 Thou, O king, sawest, and behold a great image.
This great image, whose brightness *was* excellent,
stood before thee; and the form thereof *was* terrible.
32 This image's head *was* of fine gold, his breast
and his arms of silver, his belly and his thighs of
brass,
33 His legs of iron, his feet part of iron and part
of clay.
34 Thou sawest till that a stone was cut out without
hands, which smote the image upon his feet *that*
were of iron and clay, and brake them to pieces.
35 Then was the iron, the clay, the brass, the silver,
and the gold, broken to pieces together, and became
like the chaff of the summer threshingfloors; and
the wind carried them away, that no place was found
for them: and the stone that smote the image became a great mountain, and filled the whole earth.
36 This *is* the dream; and we will tell the interpretation thereof before the king.
37 Thou, O king, *art* a king of kings: for the God of
heaven hath given thee a kingdom, power, and
strength, and glory.
38 And wheresoever the children of men dwell, the
beasts of the field and the fowls of the heaven hath
he given into thine hand, and hath made thee ruler
over them all. Thou *art* this head of gold.
39 And after thee shall arise another kingdom inferior to thee, and another third kingdom of brass,
which shall bear rule over all the earth.
40 And the fourth kingdom shall be strong as iron:

NEW LIVING TRANSLATION

Daniel said to him, "Don't kill the wise men. Take me
to the king, and I will tell him the meaning of his
dream."
25 Arioch quickly took Daniel to the king and said,
"I have found one of the captives from Judah who
will tell the king the meaning of his dream!"
26 The king said to Daniel (also known as Belteshazzar), "Is this true? Can you tell me what my
dream was and what it means?"
27 Daniel replied, "There are no wise men, enchanters, magicians, or fortune-tellers who can reveal the king's secret. 28 But there is a God in heaven
who reveals secrets, and he has shown King Nebuchadnezzar what will happen in the future. Now I
will tell you your dream and the visions you saw as
you lay on your bed.
29 "While Your Majesty was sleeping, you dreamed
about coming events. He who reveals secrets has
shown you what is going to happen. 30 And it is not
because I am wiser than anyone else that I know the
secret of your dream, but because God wants you to
understand what was in your heart.
31 "In your vision, Your Majesty, you saw standing
before you a huge, shining statue of a man. It was a
frightening sight. 32 The head of the statue was made
of fine gold. Its chest and arms were silver, its belly
and thighs were bronze, 33 its legs were iron, and its
feet were a combination of iron and baked clay. 34 As
you watched, a rock was cut from a mountain, but
not by human hands. It struck the feet of iron and
clay, smashing them to bits. 35 The whole statue was
crushed into small pieces of iron, clay, bronze, silver,
and gold. Then the wind blew them away without a
trace, like chaff on a threshing floor. But the rock that
knocked the statue down became a great mountain
that covered the whole earth.
36 "That was the dream. Now we will tell the king
what it means. 37 Your Majesty, you are the greatest of
kings. The God of heaven has given you sovereignty,
power, strength, and honor. 38 He has made you the
ruler over all the inhabited world and has put even
the wild animals and birds under your control. You
are the head of gold.
39 "But after your kingdom comes to an end, another kingdom, inferior to yours, will rise to take
your place. After that kingdom has fallen, yet a third
kingdom, represented by bronze, will rise to rule the
world. 40 Following that kingdom, there will be a

KING JAMES VERSION

forasmuch as iron breaketh in pieces and subdueth all *things:* and as iron that breaketh all these, shall it break in pieces and bruise.

41 And whereas thou sawest the feet and toes, part of potter's clay, and part of iron, the kingdom shall be divided; but there shall be in it of the strength of the iron, forasmuch as thou sawest the iron mixed with miry clay.

42 And *as* the toes of the feet *were* part of iron, and part of clay, *so* the kingdom shall be partly strong, and partly broken.

43 And whereas thou sawest iron mixed with miry clay, they shall mingle themselves with the seed of men: but they shall not cleave one to another, even as iron is not mixed with clay.

44 And in the days of these kings shall the God of heaven set up a kingdom, which shall never be destroyed: and the kingdom shall not be left to other people, *but* it shall break in pieces and consume all these kingdoms, and it shall stand for ever.

45 Forasmuch as thou sawest that the stone was cut out of the mountain without hands, and that it brake in pieces the iron, the brass, the clay, the silver, and the gold; the great God hath made known to the king what shall come to pass hereafter: and the dream *is* certain, and the interpretation thereof sure.

46 Then the king Nebuchadnezzar fell upon his face, and worshipped Daniel, and commanded that they should offer an oblation and sweet odours unto him.

47 The king answered unto Daniel, and said, Of a truth *it is,* that your God *is* a God of gods, and a Lord of kings, and a revealer of secrets, seeing thou couldest reveal this secret.

48 Then the king made Daniel a great man, and gave him many great gifts, and made him ruler over the whole province of Babylon, and chief of the governors over all the wise *men* of Babylon.

49 Then Daniel requested of the king, and he set Shadrach, Meshach, and Abed-nego, over the affairs of the province of Babylon: but Daniel *sat* in the gate of the king.

3

1 Nebuchadnezzar the king made an image of gold, whose height *was* threescore cubits, *and* the breadth thereof six cubits: he set it up in the plain of Dura, in the province of Babylon.

2 Then Nebuchadnezzar the king sent to gather together the princes, the governors, and the captains, the judges, the treasurers, the counsellors, the sheriffs, and all the rulers of the provinces, to come to the dedication of the image which Nebuchadnezzar the king had set up.

3 Then the princes, the governors, and captains, the judges, the treasurers, the counsellors, the sheriffs, and all the rulers of the provinces, were gathered together unto the dedication of the image that

NEW LIVING TRANSLATION

fourth one, as strong as iron. That kingdom will smash and crush all previous empires, just as iron smashes and crushes everything it strikes. 41 The feet and toes you saw were a combination of iron and baked clay, showing that this kingdom will be divided. Like iron mixed with clay, it will have some of the strength of iron. 42 But while some parts of it will be as strong as iron, other parts will be as weak as clay. 43 This mixture of iron and clay also shows that these kingdoms will try to strengthen themselves by forming alliances with each other through intermarriage. But they will not hold together, just as iron and clay do not mix.

44 "During the reigns of those kings, the God of heaven will set up a kingdom that will never be destroyed or conquered. It will crush all these kingdoms into nothingness, and it will stand forever. 45 That is the meaning of the rock cut from the mountain, though not by human hands, that crushed to pieces the statue of iron, bronze, clay, silver, and gold. The great God was showing the king what will happen in the future. The dream is true, and its meaning is certain."

Nebuchadnezzar Rewards Daniel

46 Then King Nebuchadnezzar threw himself down before Daniel and worshiped him, and he commanded his people to offer sacrifices and burn sweet incense before him. 47 The king said to Daniel, "Truly, your God is the greatest of gods, the Lord over kings, a revealer of mysteries, for you have been able to reveal this secret."

48 Then the king appointed Daniel to a high position and gave him many valuable gifts. He made Daniel ruler over the whole province of Babylon, as well as chief over all his wise men. 49 At Daniel's request, the king appointed Shadrach, Meshach, and Abednego to be in charge of all the affairs of the province of Babylon, while Daniel remained in the king's court.

Nebuchadnezzar's Gold Statue

3

King Nebuchadnezzar made a gold statue ninety feet tall and nine feet wide* and set it up on the plain of Dura in the province of Babylon. 2 Then he sent messages to the high officers, officials, governors, advisers, treasurers, judges, magistrates, and all the provincial officials to come to the dedication of the statue he had set up. 3 So all these

3:1 Aramaic *60 cubits* [27 meters] *tall and 6 cubits* [2.7 meters] *wide.*

KING JAMES VERSION

Nebuchadnezzar the king had set up; and they stood
before the image that Nebuchadnezzar had set up.
4Then an herald cried aloud, To you it is commanded, O people, nations, and languages,
5*That* at what time ye hear the sound of the cornet,
flute, harp, sackbut, psaltery, dulcimer, and all kinds
of musick, ye fall down and worship the golden image that Nebuchadnezzar the king hath set up:
6And whoso falleth not down and worshippeth
shall the same hour be cast into the midst of a burning fiery furnace.
7Therefore at that time, when all the people heard
the sound of the cornet, flute, harp, sackbut, psaltery, and all kinds of musick, all the people, the nations, and the languages, fell down *and* worshipped
the golden image that Nebuchadnezzar the king had
set up.
8Wherefore at that time certain Chaldeans came
near, and accused the Jews.
9They spake and said to the king Nebuchadnezzar, O king, live for ever.
10Thou, O king, hast made a decree, that every
man that shall hear the sound of the cornet, flute,
harp, sackbut, psaltery, and dulcimer, and all kinds of
musick, shall fall down and worship the golden
image:
11And whoso falleth not down and worshippeth,
that he should be cast into the midst of a burning
fiery furnace.
12There are certain Jews whom thou hast set over
the affairs of the province of Babylon, Shadrach,
Meshach, and Abed-nego; these men, O king, have
not regarded thee: they serve not thy gods, nor worship the golden image which thou hast set up.
13Then Nebuchadnezzar in *his* rage and fury
commanded to bring Shadrach, Meshach, and Abed-
nego. Then they brought these men before the king.
14Nebuchadnezzar spake and said unto them, *Is it*
true, O Shadrach, Meshach, and Abed-nego, do not ye
serve my gods, nor worship the golden image which I
have set up?
15Now if ye be ready that at what time ye hear the
sound of the cornet, flute, harp, sackbut, psaltery,
and dulcimer, and all kinds of musick, ye fall down
and worship the image which I have made; *well:* but
if ye worship not, ye shall be cast the same hour into
the midst of a burning fiery furnace; and who *is* that
God that shall deliver you out of my hands?
16Shadrach, Meshach, and Abed-nego, answered
and said to the king, O Nebuchadnezzar, we *are* not
careful to answer thee in this matter.
17If it be *so,* our God whom we serve is able to deliver us from the burning fiery furnace, and he will
deliver *us* out of thine hand, O king.
18But if not, be it known unto thee, O king, that we
will not serve thy gods, nor worship the golden image which thou hast set up.

NEW LIVING TRANSLATION

officials* came and stood before the statue King
Nebuchadnezzar had set up.
4Then a herald shouted out, "People of all races
and nations and languages, listen to the king's command! 5When you hear the sound of the horn, flute,
zither, lyre, harp, pipes, and other musical instruments,* bow to the ground to worship King Nebuchadnezzar's gold statue. 6Anyone who refuses to
obey will immediately be thrown into a blazing
furnace."
7So at the sound of the musical instruments,* all
the people, whatever their race or nation or language, bowed to the ground and worshiped the gold
statue that King Nebuchadnezzar had set up.
8But some of the astrologers* went to the king and
informed on the Jews. 9They said to King Nebuchadnezzar, "Long live the king! 10You issued a decree requiring all the people to bow down and worship the
gold statue when they hear the sound of the horn,
flute, zither, lyre, harp, pipes, and other musical instruments. 11That decree also states that those who
refuse to obey must be thrown into a blazing furnace. 12But there are some Jews—Shadrach, Meshach, and Abednego—whom you have put in charge
of the province of Babylon. They pay no attention to
you, Your Majesty. They refuse to serve your gods and
do not worship the gold statue you have set up."
13Then Nebuchadnezzar flew into a rage and ordered that Shadrach, Meshach, and Abednego be
brought before him. When they were brought in,
14Nebuchadnezzar said to them, "Is it true, Shadrach, Meshach, and Abednego, that you refuse to
serve my gods or to worship the gold statue I have set
up? 15I will give you one more chance to bow down
and worship the statue I have made when you hear
the sound of the musical instruments.* But if you refuse, you will be thrown immediately into the blazing furnace. And then what god will be able to rescue
you from my power?"
16Shadrach, Meshach, and Abednego replied,
"O Nebuchadnezzar, we do not need to defend ourselves before you. 17If we are thrown into the blazing
furnace, the God whom we serve is able to save us.
He will rescue us from your power, Your Majesty.
18But even if he doesn't, we want to make it clear to
you, Your Majesty, that we will never serve your gods
or worship the gold statue you have set up."

3:3 Aramaic *the high officers, officials, governors, advisers, treasurers, judges, magistrates, and all the provincial officials.* **3:5** The identification of some of these musical instruments is uncertain. **3:7** Aramaic *the horn, flute, zither, lyre, harp, and other musical instruments.* **3:8** Aramaic *Chaldeans.* **3:15** Aramaic *the horn, flute, zither, lyre, harp, pipes, and other musical instruments.*

KING JAMES VERSION

19 Then was Nebuchadnezzar full of fury, and the
form of his visage was changed against Shadrach,
Meshach, and Abed-nego: *therefore* he spake, and
commanded that they should heat the furnace one
seven times more than it was wont to be heated.

20 And he commanded the most mighty men that
were in his army to bind Shadrach, Meshach, and
Abed-nego, *and* to cast *them* into the burning fiery
furnace.

21 Then these men were bound in their coats, their
hosen, and their hats, and their *other* garments, and
were cast into the midst of the burning fiery furnace.

22 Therefore because the king's commandment
was urgent, and the furnace exceeding hot, the flame
of the fire slew those men that took up Shadrach,
Meshach, and Abed-nego.

23 And these three men, Shadrach, Meshach, and
Abed-nego, fell down bound into the midst of the
burning fiery furnace.

24 Then Nebuchadnezzar the king was astonied,
and rose up in haste, *and* spake, and said unto his
counsellors, Did not we cast three men bound into
the midst of the fire? They answered and said unto
the king, True, O king.

25 He answered and said, Lo, I see four men loose,
walking in the midst of the fire, and they have no hurt;
and the form of the fourth is like the Son of God.

26 Then Nebuchadnezzar came near to the mouth
of the burning fiery furnace, *and* spake, and said,
Shadrach, Meshach, and Abed-nego, ye servants of
the most high God, come forth, and come *hither*.
Then Shadrach, Meshach, and Abed-nego, came
forth of the midst of the fire.

27 And the princes, governors, and captains, and
the king's counsellors, being gathered together, saw
these men, upon whose bodies the fire had no power,
nor was an hair of their head singed, neither were
their coats changed, nor the smell of fire had passed
on them.

28 *Then* Nebuchadnezzar spake, and said, Blessed
be the God of Shadrach, Meshach, and Abed-nego,
who hath sent his angel, and delivered his servants
that trusted in him, and have changed the king's
word, and yielded their bodies, that they might not
serve nor worship any god, except their own God.

29 Therefore I make a decree, That every people,
nation, and language, which speak any thing amiss
against the God of Shadrach, Meshach, and Abed-
nego, shall be cut in pieces, and their houses shall be
made a dunghill: because there is no other God that
can deliver after this sort.

30 Then the king promoted Shadrach, Meshach,
and Abed-nego, in the province of Babylon.

NEW LIVING TRANSLATION

The Blazing Furnace

19 Nebuchadnezzar was so furious with Shadrach,
Meshach, and Abednego that his face became dis-
torted with rage. He commanded that the furnace be
heated seven times hotter than usual. 20 Then he ordered some of the strongest men of his army to bind
Shadrach, Meshach, and Abednego and throw them
into the blazing furnace. 21 So they tied them up and
threw them into the furnace, fully dressed in their
pants, turbans, robes, and other garments. 22 And because the king, in his anger, had demanded such a
hot fire in the furnace, the flames killed the soldiers
as they threw the three men in. 23 So Shadrach,
Meshach, and Abednego, securely tied, fell into the
roaring flames.

24 But suddenly, Nebuchadnezzar jumped up in
amazement and exclaimed to his advisers, "Didn't
we tie up three men and throw them into the
furnace?"

"Yes, Your Majesty, we certainly did," they replied.

25 "Look!" Nebuchadnezzar shouted. "I see four
men, unbound, walking around in the fire unharmed! And the fourth looks like a god*!"

26 Then Nebuchadnezzar came as close as he could
to the door of the flaming furnace and shouted:
"Shadrach, Meshach, and Abednego, servants of the
Most High God, come out! Come here!"

So Shadrach, Meshach, and Abednego stepped
out of the fire. 27 Then the high officers, officials,
governors, and advisers crowded around them and
saw that the fire had not touched them. Not a hair on
their heads was singed, and their clothing was not
scorched. They didn't even smell of smoke!

28 Then Nebuchadnezzar said, "Praise to the God
of Shadrach, Meshach, and Abednego! He sent his
angel to rescue his servants who trusted in him. They
defied the king's command and were willing to die
rather than serve or worship any god except their
own God. 29 Therefore, I make this decree: If any
people, whatever their race or nation or language,
speak a word against the God of Shadrach, Meshach,
and Abednego, they will be torn limb from limb, and
their houses will be turned into heaps of rubble.
There is no other god who can rescue like this!"

30 Then the king promoted Shadrach, Meshach,
and Abednego to even higher positions in the province of Babylon.

3:25 Aramaic *like a son of the gods.*

KING JAMES VERSION

4

1Nebuchadnezzar the king, unto all people, nations, and languages, that dwell in all the earth; Peace be multiplied unto you.

2I thought it good to shew the signs and wonders that the high God hath wrought toward me.

3How great *are* his signs! and how mighty *are* his wonders! his kingdom *is* an everlasting kingdom, and his dominion *is* from generation to generation.

4I Nebuchadnezzar was at rest in mine house, and flourishing in my palace:

5I saw a dream which made me afraid, and the thoughts upon my bed and the visions of my head troubled me.

6Therefore made I a decree to bring in all the wise *men* of Babylon before me, that they might make known unto me the interpretation of the dream.

7Then came in the magicians, the astrologers, the Chaldeans, and the soothsayers: and I told the dream before them; but they did not make known unto me the interpretation thereof.

8But at the last Daniel came in before me, whose name *was* Belteshazzar, according to the name of my god, and in whom *is* the spirit of the holy gods: and before him I told the dream, *saying*,

9O Belteshazzar, master of the magicians, because I know that the spirit of the holy gods *is* in thee, and no secret troubleth thee, tell me the visions of my dream that I have seen, and the interpretation thereof.

10Thus *were* the visions of mine head in my bed; I saw, and behold, a tree in the midst of the earth, and the height thereof *was* great.

11The tree grew, and was strong, and the height thereof reached unto heaven, and the sight thereof to the end of all the earth:

12The leaves thereof *were* fair, and the fruit thereof much, and in it *was* meat for all: the beasts of the field had shadow under it, and the fowls of the heaven dwelt in the boughs thereof, and all flesh was fed of it.

13I saw in the visions of my head upon my bed, and, behold, a watcher and an holy one came down from heaven;

14He cried aloud, and said thus, Hew down the tree, and cut off his branches, shake off his leaves, and scatter his fruit: let the beasts get away from under it, and the fowls from his branches:

15Nevertheless leave the stump of his roots in the earth, even with a band of iron and brass, in the tender grass of the field; and let it be wet with the dew of heaven, and *let* his portion *be* with the beasts in the grass of the earth:

16Let his heart be changed from man's, and let a

NEW LIVING TRANSLATION

Nebuchadnezzar's Dream about a Tree

4

1*King Nebuchadnezzar sent this message to the people of every race and nation and language throughout the world:

"Peace and prosperity to you!

2"I want you all to know about the miraculous signs and wonders the Most High God has performed for me.

3 How great are his signs,
how powerful his wonders!
His kingdom will last forever,
his rule through all generations.

4*"I, Nebuchadnezzar, was living in my palace in comfort and prosperity. 5But one night I had a dream that frightened me; I saw visions that terrified me as I lay in my bed. 6So I issued an order calling in all the wise men of Babylon, so they could tell me what my dream meant. 7When all the magicians, enchanters, astrologers,* and fortune-tellers came in, I told them the dream, but they could not tell me what it meant. 8At last Daniel came in before me, and I told him the dream. (He was named Belteshazzar after my god, and the spirit of the holy gods is in him.)

9"I said to him, 'Belteshazzar, chief of the magicians, I know that the spirit of the holy gods is in you and that no mystery is too great for you to solve. Now tell me what my dream means.

10"'While I was lying in my bed, this is what I dreamed. I saw a large tree in the middle of the earth. 11The tree grew very tall and strong, reaching high into the heavens for all the world to see. 12It had fresh green leaves, and it was loaded with fruit for all to eat. Wild animals lived in its shade, and birds nested in its branches. All the world was fed from this tree.

13"'Then as I lay there dreaming, I saw a messenger,* a holy one, coming down from heaven. 14The messenger shouted,

"Cut down the tree and lop off its branches!
Shake off its leaves and scatter its fruit!
Chase the wild animals from its shade
and the birds from its branches.
15 But leave the stump and the roots in the ground,
bound with a band of iron and bronze
and surrounded by tender grass.
Now let him be drenched with the dew
of heaven,
and let him live with the wild animals
among the plants of the field.
16 For seven periods of time,
let him have the mind of a wild animal

4:1 Verses 4:1-3 are numbered 3:31-33 in Aramaic text. **4:4** Verses 4:4-37 are numbered 4:1-34 in Aramaic text. **4:7** Or *Chaldeans.* **4:13** Aramaic *a watcher;* also in 4:23.

KING JAMES VERSION

beast's heart be given unto him: and let seven times pass over him.

17 This matter *is* by the decree of the watchers, and the demand by the word of the holy ones: to the intent that the living may know that the most High ruleth in the kingdom of men, and giveth it to whomsoever he will, and setteth up over it the basest of men.

18 This dream I king Nebuchadnezzar have seen. Now thou, O Belteshazzar, declare the interpretation thereof, forasmuch as all the wise *men* of my kingdom are not able to make known unto me the interpretation: but thou *art* able; for the spirit of the holy gods *is* in thee.

19 Then Daniel, whose name *was* Belteshazzar, was astonied for one hour, and his thoughts troubled him. The king spake, and said, Belteshazzar, let not the dream, or the interpretation thereof, trouble thee. Belteshazzar answered and said, My lord, the dream *be* to them that hate thee, and the interpretation thereof to thine enemies.

20 The tree that thou sawest, which grew, and was strong, whose height reached unto the heaven, and the sight thereof to all the earth;

21 Whose leaves *were* fair, and the fruit thereof much, and in it *was* meat for all; under which the beasts of the field dwelt, and upon whose branches the fowls of the heaven had their habitation:

22 It *is* thou, O king, that art grown and become strong: for thy greatness is grown, and reacheth unto heaven, and thy dominion to the end of the earth.

23 And whereas the king saw a watcher and an holy one coming down from heaven, and saying, Hew the tree down, and destroy it; yet leave the stump of the roots thereof in the earth, even with a band of iron and brass, in the tender grass of the field; and let it be wet with the dew of heaven, and *let* his portion *be* with the beasts of the field, till seven times pass over him;

24 This *is* the interpretation, O king, and this *is* the decree of the most High, which is come upon my lord the king:

25 That they shall drive thee from men, and thy dwelling shall be with the beasts of the field, and they shall make thee to eat grass as oxen, and they shall wet thee with the dew of heaven, and seven times shall pass over thee, till thou know that the most High ruleth in the kingdom of men, and giveth it to whomsoever he will.

26 And whereas they commanded to leave the stump of the tree roots; thy kingdom shall be sure unto thee, after that thou shalt have known that the heavens do rule.

27 Wherefore, O king, let my counsel be acceptable unto thee, and break off thy sins by righteousness, and thine iniquities by shewing mercy to the poor; if it may be a lengthening of thy tranquillity.

NEW LIVING TRANSLATION

instead of the mind of a human.
17 For this has been decreed by the messengers*;
it is commanded by the holy ones,
so that everyone may know
that the Most High rules over the kingdoms
of the world.
He gives them to anyone he chooses—
even to the lowliest of people."

18 "'Belteshazzar, that was the dream that I, King Nebuchadnezzar, had. Now tell me what it means, for none of the wise men of my kingdom can do so. But you can tell me because the spirit of the holy gods is in you.'

Daniel Explains the Dream

19 "Upon hearing this, Daniel (also known as Belteshazzar) was overcome for a time, frightened by the meaning of the dream. Then the king said to him, 'Belteshazzar, don't be alarmed by the dream and what it means.'

"Belteshazzar replied, 'I wish the events foreshadowed in this dream would happen to your enemies, my lord, and not to you! 20 The tree you saw was growing very tall and strong, reaching high into the heavens for all the world to see. 21 It had fresh green leaves and was loaded with fruit for all to eat. Wild animals lived in its shade, and birds nested in its branches. 22 That tree, Your Majesty, is you. For you have grown strong and great; your greatness reaches up to heaven, and your rule to the ends of the earth.

23 "'Then you saw a messenger, a holy one, coming down from heaven and saying, "Cut down the tree and destroy it. But leave the stump and the roots in the ground, bound with a band of iron and bronze and surrounded by tender grass. Let him be drenched with the dew of heaven. Let him live with the animals of the field for seven periods of time."

24 "'This is what the dream means, Your Majesty, and what the Most High has declared will happen to my lord the king. 25 You will be driven from human society, and you will live in the fields with the wild animals. You will eat grass like a cow, and you will be drenched with the dew of heaven. Seven periods of time will pass while you live this way, until you learn that the Most High rules over the kingdoms of the world and gives them to anyone he chooses. 26 But the stump and roots of the tree were left in the ground. This means that you will receive your kingdom back again when you have learned that heaven rules.

27 "'King Nebuchadnezzar, please accept my advice. Stop sinning and do what is right. Break from your wicked past and be merciful to the poor. Perhaps then you will continue to prosper.'

4:17 Aramaic *the watchers*.

KING JAMES VERSION

28 All this came upon the king Nebuchadnezzar.
29 At the end of twelve months he walked in the
palace of the kingdom of Babylon.
30 The king spake, and said, Is not this great Babylon, that I have built for the house of the kingdom
by the might of my power, and for the honour of my
majesty?
31 While the word *was* in the king's mouth, there
fell a voice from heaven, *saying*, O king Nebuchadnezzar, to thee it is spoken; The kingdom is departed
from thee.
32 And they shall drive thee from men, and thy
dwelling *shall be* with the beasts of the field: they
shall make thee to eat grass as oxen, and seven times
shall pass over thee, until thou know that the most
High ruleth in the kingdom of men, and giveth it to
whomsoever he will.
33 The same hour was the thing fulfilled upon
Nebuchadnezzar: and he was driven from men, and
did eat grass as oxen, and his body was wet with the
dew of heaven, till his hairs were grown like eagles'
feathers, and his nails like birds' *claws*.

34 And at the end of the days I Nebuchadnezzar
lifted up mine eyes unto heaven, and mine understanding returned unto me, and I blessed the most
High, and I praised and honoured him that liveth for
ever, whose dominion *is* an everlasting dominion,
and his kingdom *is* from generation to generation:
35 And all the inhabitants of the earth *are* reputed
as nothing: and he doeth according to his will in the
army of heaven, and *among* the inhabitants of the
earth: and none can stay his hand, or say unto him,
What doest thou?
36 At the same time my reason returned unto me;
and for the glory of my kingdom, mine honour and
brightness returned unto me; and my counsellors
and my lords sought unto me; and I was established
in my kingdom, and excellent majesty was added
unto me.
37 Now I Nebuchadnezzar praise and extol and
honour the King of heaven, all whose works *are*
truth, and his ways judgment: and those that walk in
pride he is able to abase.

5 1 Belshazzar the king made a great feast to a
thousand of his lords, and drank wine before
the thousand.
2 Belshazzar, whiles he tasted the wine, commanded to bring the golden and silver vessels which
his father Nebuchadnezzar had taken out of the
temple which *was* in Jerusalem; that the king, and his

NEW LIVING TRANSLATION

The Dream's Fulfillment

28 "But all these things did happen to King
Nebuchadnezzar. 29 Twelve months later he was
taking a walk on the flat roof of the royal palace
in Babylon. 30 As he looked out across the city, he
said, 'Look at this great city of Babylon! By my
own mighty power, I have built this beautiful
city as my royal residence to display my majestic
splendor.'
31 "While these words were still in his mouth,
a voice called down from heaven, 'O King
Nebuchadnezzar, this message is for you! You are
no longer ruler of this kingdom. 32 You will be
driven from human society. You will live in the
fields with the wild animals, and you will eat
grass like a cow. Seven periods of time will pass
while you live this way, until you learn that the
Most High rules over the kingdoms of the world
and gives them to anyone he chooses.'
33 "That same hour the judgment was fulfilled,
and Nebuchadnezzar was driven from human
society. He ate grass like a cow, and he was
drenched with the dew of heaven. He lived this
way until his hair was as long as eagles' feathers
and his nails were like birds' claws.

Nebuchadnezzar Praises God

34 "After this time had passed, I, Nebuchadnezzar,
looked up to heaven. My sanity returned, and
I praised and worshiped the Most High and
honored the one who lives forever.

His rule is everlasting,
and his kingdom is eternal.
35 All the people of the earth
are nothing compared to him.
He does as he pleases
among the angels of heaven
and among the people of the earth.
No one can stop him or say to him,
'What do you mean by doing these things?'

36 "When my sanity returned to me, so did my
honor and glory and kingdom. My advisers and
nobles sought me out, and I was restored as head
of my kingdom, with even greater honor than
before.
37 "Now I, Nebuchadnezzar, praise and glorify
and honor the King of heaven. All his acts are just
and true, and he is able to humble the proud."

The Writing on the Wall

5 Many years later King Belshazzar gave a great
feast for 1,000 of his nobles, and he drank
wine with them. 2 While Belshazzar was drinking the
wine, he gave orders to bring in the gold and silver
cups that his predecessor,* Nebuchadnezzar, had
taken from the Temple in Jerusalem. He wanted to

5:2 Aramaic *father;* also in 5:11, 13, 18.

KING JAMES VERSION

princes, his wives, and his concubines, might drink
therein.
3 Then they brought the golden vessels that were
taken out of the temple of the house of God which
was at Jerusalem; and the king, and his princes, his
wives, and his concubines, drank in them.
4 They drank wine, and praised the gods of gold,
and of silver, of brass, of iron, of wood, and of stone.
5 In the same hour came forth fingers of a man's
hand, and wrote over against the candlestick upon
the plaster of the wall of the king's palace: and the
king saw the part of the hand that wrote.
6 Then the king's countenance was changed, and his
thoughts troubled him, so that the joints of his loins
were loosed, and his knees smote one against another.
7 The king cried aloud to bring in the astrologers,
the Chaldeans, and the soothsayers. *And* the king
spake, and said to the wise *men* of Babylon, Whosoever shall read this writing, and shew me the interpretation thereof, shall be clothed with scarlet, and
have a chain of gold about his neck, and shall be the
third ruler in the kingdom.
8 Then came in all the king's wise *men:* but they
could not read the writing, nor make known to the
king the interpretation thereof.
9 Then was king Belshazzar greatly troubled, and
his countenance was changed in him, and his lords
were astonied.
10 *Now* the queen by reason of the words of the
king and his lords came into the banquet house: *and*
the queen spake and said, O king, live for ever: let not
thy thoughts trouble thee, nor let thy countenance
be changed:
11 There is a man in thy kingdom, in whom *is* the
spirit of the holy gods; and in the days of thy father
light and understanding and wisdom, like the wisdom of the gods, was found in him; whom the king
Nebuchadnezzar thy father, the king, *I say,* thy father, made master of the magicians, astrologers,
Chaldeans, *and* soothsayers;
12 Forasmuch as an excellent spirit, and knowledge, and understanding, interpreting of dreams,
and shewing of hard sentences, and dissolving of
doubts, were found in the same Daniel, whom the
king named Belteshazzar: now let Daniel be called,
and he will shew the interpretation.
13 Then was Daniel brought in before the king. *And*
the king spake and said unto Daniel, *Art* thou that
Daniel, which *art* of the children of the captivity of
Judah, whom the king my father brought out of Jewry?
14 I have even heard of thee, that the spirit of the
gods *is* in thee, and *that* light and understanding and
excellent wisdom is found in thee.
15 And now the wise *men,* the astrologers, have
been brought in before me, that they should read
this writing, and make known unto me the interpretation thereof: but they could not shew the interpretation of the thing:

NEW LIVING TRANSLATION

drink from them with his nobles, his wives, and his
concubines. 3 So they brought these gold cups taken
from the Temple, the house of God in Jerusalem,
and the king and his nobles, his wives, and his concubines drank from them. 4 While they drank from
them they praised their idols made of gold, silver,
bronze, iron, wood, and stone.
5 Suddenly, they saw the fingers of a human hand
writing on the plaster wall of the king's palace, near
the lampstand. The king himself saw the hand as it
wrote, 6 and his face turned pale with fright. His
knees knocked together in fear and his legs gave way
beneath him.
7 The king shouted for the enchanters, astrologers,* and fortune-tellers to be brought before him.
He said to these wise men of Babylon, "Whoever can
read this writing and tell me what it means will be
dressed in purple robes of royal honor and will have
a gold chain placed around his neck. He will become
the third highest ruler in the kingdom!"
8 But when all the king's wise men had come in,
none of them could read the writing or tell him what
it meant. 9 So the king grew even more alarmed, and
his face turned pale. His nobles, too, were shaken.
10 But when the queen mother heard what was
happening, she hurried to the banquet hall. She said
to Belshazzar, "Long live the king! Don't be so pale
and frightened. 11 There is a man in your kingdom
who has within him the spirit of the holy gods. During Nebuchadnezzar's reign, this man was found to
have insight, understanding, and wisdom like that of
the gods. Your predecessor, the king—your predecessor King Nebuchadnezzar—made him chief over
all the magicians, enchanters, astrologers, and fortune-tellers of Babylon. 12 This man Daniel, whom
the king named Belteshazzar, has exceptional ability
and is filled with divine knowledge and understanding. He can interpret dreams, explain riddles, and
solve difficult problems. Call for Daniel, and he will
tell you what the writing means."

Daniel Explains the Writing

13 So Daniel was brought in before the king. The king
asked him, "Are you Daniel, one of the exiles brought
from Judah by my predecessor, King Nebuchadnezzar? 14 I have heard that you have the spirit of the
gods within you and that you are filled with insight,
understanding, and wisdom. 15 My wise men and enchanters have tried to read the words on the wall and

5:7 Or *Chaldeans;* also in 5:11.

KING JAMES VERSION

16 And I have heard of thee, that thou canst make interpretations, and dissolve doubts: now if thou canst read the writing, and make known to me the interpretation thereof, thou shalt be clothed with scarlet, and *have* a chain of gold about thy neck, and shalt be the third ruler in the kingdom.

17 Then Daniel answered and said before the king, Let thy gifts be to thyself, and give thy rewards to another; yet I will read the writing unto the king, and make known to him the interpretation.

18 O thou king, the most high God gave Nebuchadnezzar thy father a kingdom, and majesty, and glory, and honour:

19 And for the majesty that he gave him, all people, nations, and languages, trembled and feared before him: whom he would he slew; and whom he would he kept alive; and whom he would he set up; and whom he would he put down.

20 But when his heart was lifted up, and his mind hardened in pride, he was deposed from his kingly throne, and they took his glory from him:

21 And he was driven from the sons of men; and his heart was made like the beasts, and his dwelling *was* with the wild asses: they fed him with grass like oxen, and his body was wet with the dew of heaven; till he knew that the most high God ruled in the kingdom of men, and *that* he appointeth over it whomsoever he will.

22 And thou his son, O Belshazzar, hast not humbled thine heart, though thou knewest all this;

23 But hast lifted up thyself against the Lord of heaven; and they have brought the vessels of his house before thee, and thou, and thy lords, thy wives, and thy concubines, have drunk wine in them; and thou hast praised the gods of silver, and gold, of brass, iron, wood, and stone, which see not, nor hear, nor know: and the God in whose hand thy breath *is,* and whose *are* all thy ways, hast thou not glorified:

24 Then was the part of the hand sent from him; and this writing was written.

25 And this *is* the writing that was written, MENE, MENE, TEKEL, UPHARSIN.

26 This *is* the interpretation of the thing: MENE; God hath numbered thy kingdom, and finished it.

27 TEKEL; Thou art weighed in the balances, and art found wanting.

28 PERES; Thy kingdom is divided, and given to the Medes and Persians.

29 Then commanded Belshazzar, and they clothed Daniel with scarlet, and *put* a chain of gold about his neck, and made a proclamation concerning him, that he should be the third ruler in the kingdom.

30 In that night was Belshazzar the king of the Chaldeans slain.

31 And Darius the Median took the kingdom, *being* about threescore and two years old.

NEW LIVING TRANSLATION

tell me their meaning, but they cannot do it. 16 I am told that you can give interpretations and solve difficult problems. If you can read these words and tell me their meaning, you will be clothed in purple robes of royal honor, and you will have a gold chain placed around your neck. You will become the third highest ruler in the kingdom."

17 Daniel answered the king, "Keep your gifts or give them to someone else, but I will tell you what the writing means. 18 Your Majesty, the Most High God gave sovereignty, majesty, glory, and honor to your predecessor, Nebuchadnezzar. 19 He made him so great that people of all races and nations and languages trembled before him in fear. He killed those he wanted to kill and spared those he wanted to spare. He honored those he wanted to honor and disgraced those he wanted to disgrace. 20 But when his heart and mind were puffed up with arrogance, he was brought down from his royal throne and stripped of his glory. 21 He was driven from human society. He was given the mind of a wild animal, and he lived among the wild donkeys. He ate grass like a cow, and he was drenched with the dew of heaven, until he learned that the Most High God rules over the kingdoms of the world and appoints anyone he desires to rule over them.

22 "You are his successor,* O Belshazzar, and you knew all this, yet you have not humbled yourself. 23 For you have proudly defied the Lord of heaven and have had these cups from his Temple brought before you. You and your nobles and your wives and concubines have been drinking wine from them while praising gods of silver, gold, bronze, iron, wood, and stone—gods that neither see nor hear nor know anything at all. But you have not honored the God who gives you the breath of life and controls your destiny! 24 So God has sent this hand to write this message.

25 "This is the message that was written: MENE, MENE, TEKEL, and PARSIN. 26 This is what these words mean:

Mene means 'numbered'—God has numbered the days of your reign and has brought it to an end.

27 *Tekel* means 'weighed'—you have been weighed on the balances and have not measured up.

28 *Parsin** means 'divided'—your kingdom has been divided and given to the Medes and Persians."

29 Then at Belshazzar's command, Daniel was dressed in purple robes, a gold chain was hung around his neck, and he was proclaimed the third highest ruler in the kingdom.

30 That very night Belshazzar, the Babylonian* king, was killed.*

31 *And Darius the Mede took over the kingdom at the age of sixty-two.

5:22 Aramaic *son.* **5:28** Aramaic *Peres,* the singular of *Parsin.* **5:30a** Or *Chaldean.* **5:30b** The Persians and Medes conquered Babylon in October 539 B.C. **5:31** Verse 5:31 is numbered 6:1 in Aramaic text.

KING JAMES VERSION

6 1It pleased Darius to set over the kingdom an hundred and twenty princes, which should be over the whole kingdom;

2And over these three presidents; of whom Daniel *was* first: that the princes might give accounts unto them, and the king should have no damage.

3Then this Daniel was preferred above the presidents and princes, because an excellent spirit *was* in him; and the king thought to set him over the whole realm.

4Then the presidents and princes sought to find occasion against Daniel concerning the kingdom; but they could find none occasion nor fault; forasmuch as he *was* faithful, neither was there any error or fault found in him.

5Then said these men, We shall not find any occasion against this Daniel, except we find *it* against him concerning the law of his God.

6Then these presidents and princes assembled together to the king, and said thus unto him, King Darius, live for ever.

7All the presidents of the kingdom, the governors, and the princes, the counsellors, and the captains, have consulted together to establish a royal statute, and to make a firm decree, that whosoever shall ask a petition of any God or man for thirty days, save of thee, O king, he shall be cast into the den of lions.

8Now, O king, establish the decree, and sign the writing, that it be not changed, according to the law of the Medes and Persians, which altereth not.

9Wherefore king Darius signed the writing and the decree.

10Now when Daniel knew that the writing was signed, he went into his house; and his windows being open in his chamber toward Jerusalem, he kneeled upon his knees three times a day, and prayed, and gave thanks before his God, as he did aforetime.

11Then these men assembled, and found Daniel praying and making supplication before his God.

12Then they came near, and spake before the king concerning the king's decree; Hast thou not signed a decree, that every man that shall ask *a petition* of any God or man within thirty days, save of thee, O king, shall be cast into the den of lions? The king answered and said, The thing *is* true, according to the law of the Medes and Persians, which altereth not.

13Then answered they and said before the king, That Daniel, which *is* of the children of the captivity of Judah, regardeth not thee, O king, nor the decree that thou hast signed, but maketh his petition three times a day.

14Then the king, when he heard *these* words, was sore displeased with himself, and set *his* heart on Daniel to deliver him: and he laboured till the going down of the sun to deliver him.

15Then these men assembled unto the king, and

NEW LIVING TRANSLATION

Daniel in the Lions' Den

6 1*Darius the Mede decided to divide the kingdom into 120 provinces, and he appointed a
high officer to rule over each province. 2The king
also chose Daniel and two others as administrators
to supervise the high officers and protect the king's
interests. 3Daniel soon proved himself more capable
than all the other administrators and high officers.
Because of Daniel's great ability, the king made plans
to place him over the entire empire.

4Then the other administrators and high officers
began searching for some fault in the way Daniel was
handling government affairs, but they couldn't find
anything to criticize or condemn. He was faithful,
always responsible, and completely trustworthy.
5So they concluded, "Our only chance of finding
grounds for accusing Daniel will be in connection
with the rules of his religion."

6So the administrators and high officers went to
the king and said, "Long live King Darius! 7We are all
in agreement—we administrators, officials, high officers, advisers, and governors—that the king should
make a law that will be strictly enforced. Give orders
that for the next thirty days any person who prays to
anyone, divine or human—except to you, Your Majesty—will be thrown into the den of lions. 8And now,
Your Majesty, issue and sign this law so it cannot be
changed, an official law of the Medes and Persians
that cannot be revoked." 9So King Darius signed
the law.

10But when Daniel learned that the law had been
signed, he went home and knelt down as usual in his
upstairs room, with its windows open toward Jerusalem. He prayed three times a day, just as he had
always done, giving thanks to his God. 11Then the
officials went together to Daniel's house and found
him praying and asking for God's help. 12So they
went straight to the king and reminded him about
his law. "Did you not sign a law that for the next
thirty days any person who prays to anyone, divine
or human—except to you, Your Majesty—will be
thrown into the den of lions?"

"Yes," the king replied, "that decision stands; it is
an official law of the Medes and Persians that cannot
be revoked."

13Then they told the king, "That man Daniel, one
of the captives from Judah, is ignoring you and your
law. He still prays to his God three times a day."

14Hearing this, the king was deeply troubled, and
he tried to think of a way to save Daniel. He spent the
rest of the day looking for a way to get Daniel out of
this predicament.

15In the evening the men went together to the king

6:1 Verses 6:1-28 are numbered 6:2-29 in Aramaic text.

KING JAMES VERSION

said unto the king, Know, O king, that the law of the
Medes and Persians *is,* That no decree nor statute
which the king establisheth may be changed.
16 Then the king commanded, and they brought
Daniel, and cast *him* into the den of lions. *Now* the
king spake and said unto Daniel, Thy God whom
thou servest continually, he will deliver thee.
17 And a stone was brought, and laid upon the
mouth of the den; and the king sealed it with his own
signet, and with the signet of his lords; that the purpose might not be changed concerning Daniel.
18 Then the king went to his palace, and passed the
night fasting: neither were instruments of musick
brought before him: and his sleep went from him.
19 Then the king arose very early in the morning,
and went in haste unto the den of lions.
20 And when he came to the den, he cried with a la-
mentable voice unto Daniel: *and* the king spake and
said to Daniel, O Daniel, servant of the living God, is
thy God, whom thou servest continually, able to deliver thee from the lions?
21 Then said Daniel unto the king, O king, live for
ever.
22 My God hath sent his angel, and hath shut the
lions' mouths, that they have not hurt me: forasmuch
as before him innocency was found in me; and also
before thee, O king, have I done no hurt.
23 Then was the king exceeding glad for him, and
commanded that they should take Daniel up out of
the den. So Daniel was taken up out of the den, and
no manner of hurt was found upon him, because he
believed in his God.
24 And the king commanded, and they brought
those men which had accused Daniel, and they cast
them into the den of lions, them, their children, and
their wives; and the lions had the mastery of them,
and brake all their bones in pieces or ever they came
at the bottom of the den.
25 Then king Darius wrote unto all people, nations,
and languages, that dwell in all the earth; Peace be
multiplied unto you.
26 I make a decree, That in every dominion of my
kingdom men tremble and fear before the God of
Daniel: for he *is* the living God, and stedfast for ever,
and his kingdom *that* which shall not be destroyed,
and his dominion *shall be even* unto the end.
27 He delivereth and rescueth, and he worketh
signs and wonders in heaven and in earth, who hath
delivered Daniel from the power of the lions.
28 So this Daniel prospered in the reign of Darius,
and in the reign of Cyrus the Persian.

7 1 In the first year of Belshazzar king of Babylon
Daniel had a dream and visions of his head

NEW LIVING TRANSLATION

and said, "Your Majesty, you know that according to
the law of the Medes and the Persians, no law that the
king signs can be changed."
16 So at last the king gave orders for Daniel to be arrested and thrown into the den of lions. The king
said to him, "May your God, whom you serve so faithfully, rescue you."
17 A stone was brought and placed over the mouth
of the den. The king sealed the stone with his own
royal seal and the seals of his nobles, so that no one
could rescue Daniel. 18 Then the king returned to his
palace and spent the night fasting. He refused his
usual entertainment and couldn't sleep at all that
night.
19 Very early the next morning, the king got up and
hurried out to the lions' den. 20 When he got there, he
called out in anguish, "Daniel, servant of the living
God! Was your God, whom you serve so faithfully,
able to rescue you from the lions?"
21 Daniel answered, "Long live the king! 22 My God
sent his angel to shut the lions' mouths so that they
would not hurt me, for I have been found innocent in
his sight. And I have not wronged you, Your Majesty."
23 The king was overjoyed and ordered that Daniel
be lifted from the den. Not a scratch was found on
him, for he had trusted in his God.
24 Then the king gave orders to arrest the men who
had maliciously accused Daniel. He had them
thrown into the lions' den, along with their wives and
children. The lions leaped on them and tore them
apart before they even hit the floor of the den.
25 Then King Darius sent this message to the people
of every race and nation and language throughout
the world:

"Peace and prosperity to you!
26 "I decree that everyone throughout my
kingdom should tremble with fear before the
God of Daniel.

For he is the living God,
and he will endure forever.
His kingdom will never be destroyed,
and his rule will never end.
27 He rescues and saves his people;
he performs miraculous signs and wonders
in the heavens and on earth.
He has rescued Daniel
from the power of the lions."

28 So Daniel prospered during the reign of Darius
and the reign of Cyrus the Persian.*

Daniel's Vision of Four Beasts

7 Earlier, during the first year of King Belshazzar's reign in Babylon,* Daniel had a dream and

6:28 Or *of Darius, that is, the reign of Cyrus the Persian.* 7:1 The first year of Belshazzar's reign (who was co-regent with his father, Nabonidus) was 556 B.C. (or perhaps as late as 553 B.C.).

KING JAMES VERSION

upon his bed: then he wrote the dream, *and* told the
sum of the matters.
2 Daniel spake and said, I saw in my vision by night,
and, behold, the four winds of the heaven strove
upon the great sea.
3 And four great beasts came up from the sea, diverse one from another.
4 The first *was* like a lion, and had eagle's wings: I
beheld till the wings thereof were plucked, and it was
lifted up from the earth, and made stand upon the
feet as a man, and a man's heart was given to it.
5 And behold another beast, a second, like to a
bear, and it raised up itself on one side, and *it had*
three ribs in the mouth of it between the teeth of it:
and they said thus unto it, Arise, devour much flesh.
6 After this I beheld, and lo another, like a leopard,
which had upon the back of it four wings of a fowl;
the beast had also four heads; and dominion was
given to it.
7 After this I saw in the night visions, and behold a
fourth beast, dreadful and terrible, and strong exceedingly; and it had great iron teeth: it devoured
and brake in pieces, and stamped the residue with
the feet of it: and it *was* diverse from all the beasts
that *were* before it; and it had ten horns.
8 I considered the horns, and, behold, there came
up among them another little horn, before whom
there were three of the first horns plucked up by the
roots: and, behold, in this horn *were* eyes like the
eyes of man, and a mouth speaking great things.
9 I beheld till the thrones were cast down, and the
Ancient of days did sit, whose garment *was* white as
snow, and the hair of his head like the pure wool: his
throne *was like* the fiery flame, *and* his wheels *as*
burning fire.
10 A fiery stream issued and came forth from before him: thousand thousands ministered unto him,
and ten thousand times ten thousand stood before
him: the judgment was set, and the books were
opened.
11 I beheld then because of the voice of the great
words which the horn spake: I beheld *even* till the
beast was slain, and his body destroyed, and given to
the burning flame.
12 As concerning the rest of the beasts, they had
their dominion taken away: yet their lives were prolonged for a season and time.
13 I saw in the night visions, and, behold, *one* like
the Son of man came with the clouds of heaven, and
came to the Ancient of days, and they brought him
near before him.
14 And there was given him dominion, and glory,
and a kingdom, that all people, nations, and languages, should serve him: his dominion *is* an everlasting dominion, which shall not pass away, and his
kingdom *that* which shall not be destroyed.

NEW LIVING TRANSLATION

saw visions as he lay in his bed. He wrote down the
dream, and this is what he saw.
2 In my vision that night, I, Daniel, saw a great
storm churning the surface of a great sea, with
strong winds blowing from every direction. 3 Then
four huge beasts came up out of the water, each different from the others.
4 The first beast was like a lion with eagles' wings.
As I watched, its wings were pulled off, and it was left
standing with its two hind feet on the ground, like a
human being. And it was given a human mind.
5 Then I saw a second beast, and it looked like a
bear. It was rearing up on one side, and it had three
ribs in its mouth between its teeth. And I heard a voice
saying to it, "Get up! Devour the flesh of many people!"
6 Then the third of these strange beasts appeared,
and it looked like a leopard. It had four bird's wings
on its back, and it had four heads. Great authority
was given to this beast.
7 Then in my vision that night, I saw a fourth beast—
terrifying, dreadful, and very strong. It devoured and
crushed its victims with huge iron teeth and trampled
their remains beneath its feet. It was different from
any of the other beasts, and it had ten horns.
8 As I was looking at the horns, suddenly another
small horn appeared among them. Three of the first
horns were torn out by the roots to make room for
it. This little horn had eyes like human eyes and a
mouth that was boasting arrogantly.

9 I watched as thrones were put in place
   and the Ancient One* sat down to judge.
His clothing was as white as snow,
   his hair like purest wool.
He sat on a fiery throne
   with wheels of blazing fire,
10 and a river of fire was pouring out,
   flowing from his presence.
Millions of angels ministered to him;
   many millions stood to attend him.
Then the court began its session,
   and the books were opened.

11 I continued to watch because I could hear the
little horn's boastful speech. I kept watching until the
fourth beast was killed and its body was destroyed
by fire. 12 The other three beasts had their authority
taken from them, but they were allowed to live a
while longer.*
13 As my vision continued that night, I saw someone like a son of man* coming with the clouds of
heaven. He approached the Ancient One and was led
into his presence. 14 He was given authority, honor,
and sovereignty over all the nations of the world, so
that people of every race and nation and language
would obey him. His rule is eternal—it will never
end. His kingdom will never be destroyed.

7:9 Aramaic *an Ancient of Days;* also in 7:13, 22. **7:12** Aramaic *for a season and a time.* **7:13** Or *like a Son of Man.*

KING JAMES VERSION

15 I Daniel was grieved in my spirit in the midst of *my* body, and the visions of my head troubled me.

16 I came near unto one of them that stood by, and asked him the truth of all this. So he told me, and made me know the interpretation of the things.

17 These great beasts, which are four, *are* four kings, *which* shall arise out of the earth.

18 But the saints of the most High shall take the kingdom, and possess the kingdom for ever, even for ever and ever.

19 Then I would know the truth of the fourth beast, which was diverse from all the others, exceeding dreadful, whose teeth *were of* iron, and his nails *of* brass; *which* devoured, brake in pieces, and stamped the residue with his feet;

20 And of the ten horns that *were* in his head, and *of* the other which came up, and before whom three fell; even *of* that horn that had eyes, and a mouth that spake very great things, whose look *was* more stout than his fellows.

21 I beheld, and the same horn made war with the saints, and prevailed against them;

22 Until the Ancient of days came, and judgment was given to the saints of the most High; and the time came that the saints possessed the kingdom.

23 Thus he said, The fourth beast shall be the fourth kingdom upon earth, which shall be diverse from all kingdoms, and shall devour the whole earth, and shall tread it down, and break it in pieces.

24 And the ten horns out of this kingdom *are* ten kings *that* shall arise: and another shall rise after them; and he shall be diverse from the first, and he shall subdue three kings.

25 And he shall speak *great* words against the most High, and shall wear out the saints of the most High, and think to change times and laws: and they shall be given into his hand until a time and times and the dividing of time.

26 But the judgment shall sit, and they shall take away his dominion, to consume and to destroy *it* unto the end.

27 And the kingdom and dominion, and the greatness of the kingdom under the whole heaven, shall be given to the people of the saints of the most High, whose kingdom *is* an everlasting kingdom, and all dominions shall serve and obey him.

28 Hitherto *is* the end of the matter. As for me Daniel, my cogitations much troubled me, and my countenance changed in me: but I kept the matter in my heart.

8 1 In the third year of the reign of king Belshazzar a vision appeared unto me, *even unto* me Daniel, after that which appeared unto me at the first.

2 And I saw in a vision; and it came to pass, when I saw, that I *was* at Shushan *in* the palace, which *is* in

NEW LIVING TRANSLATION

The Vision Is Explained

15 I, Daniel, was troubled by all I had seen, and my visions terrified me. 16 So I approached one of those standing beside the throne and asked him what it all meant. He explained it to me like this: 17 "These four huge beasts represent four kingdoms that will arise from the earth. 18 But in the end, the holy people of the Most High will be given the kingdom, and they will rule forever and ever."

19 Then I wanted to know the true meaning of the fourth beast, the one so different from the others and so terrifying. It had devoured and crushed its victims with iron teeth and bronze claws, trampling their remains beneath its feet. 20 I also asked about the ten horns on the fourth beast's head and the little horn that came up afterward and destroyed three of the other horns. This horn had seemed greater than the others, and it had human eyes and a mouth that was boasting arrogantly. 21 As I watched, this horn was waging war against God's holy people and was defeating them, 22 until the Ancient One—the Most High—came and judged in favor of his holy people. Then the time arrived for the holy people to take over the kingdom.

23 Then he said to me, "This fourth beast is the fourth world power that will rule the earth. It will be different from all the others. It will devour the whole world, trampling and crushing everything in its path. 24 Its ten horns are ten kings who will rule that empire. Then another king will arise, different from the other ten, who will subdue three of them. 25 He will defy the Most High and oppress the holy people of the Most High. He will try to change their sacred festivals and laws, and they will be placed under his control for a time, times, and half a time.

26 "But then the court will pass judgment, and all his power will be taken away and completely destroyed. 27 Then the sovereignty, power, and greatness of all the kingdoms under heaven will be given to the holy people of the Most High. His kingdom will last forever, and all rulers will serve and obey him."

28 That was the end of the vision. I, Daniel, was terrified by my thoughts and my face was pale with fear, but I kept these things to myself.

Daniel's Vision of a Ram and Goat

8 1 *During the third year of King Belshazzar's reign, I, Daniel, saw another vision, following the one that had already appeared to me. 2 In this

8:1 The original text from this point through chapter 12 is in Hebrew. See note at 2:4.

KING JAMES VERSION

the province of Elam; and I saw in a vision, and I was
by the river of Ulai.

3 Then I lifted up mine eyes, and saw, and, behold,
there stood before the river a ram which had *two*
horns: and the *two* horns *were* high; but one *was*
higher than the other, and the higher came up last.

4 I saw the ram pushing westward, and northward,
and southward; so that no beasts might stand before
him, neither *was there any* that could deliver out of
his hand; but he did according to his will, and became great.

5 And as I was considering, behold, an he goat
came from the west on the face of the whole earth,
and touched not the ground: and the goat *had* a
notable horn between his eyes.

6 And he came to the ram that had *two* horns,
which I had seen standing before the river, and ran
unto him in the fury of his power.

7 And I saw him come close unto the ram, and he
was moved with choler against him, and smote the
ram, and brake his two horns: and there was no
power in the ram to stand before him, but he cast
him down to the ground, and stamped upon him:
and there was none that could deliver the ram out of
his hand.

8 Therefore the he goat waxed very great: and when
he was strong, the great horn was broken; and for it
came up four notable ones toward the four winds of
heaven.

9 And out of one of them came forth a little horn,
which waxed exceeding great, toward the south, and
toward the east, and toward the pleasant *land*.

10 And it waxed great, *even* to the host of heaven;
and it cast down *some* of the host and of the stars to
the ground, and stamped upon them.

11 Yea, he magnified *himself* even to the prince of
the host, and by him the daily *sacrifice* was taken
away, and the place of his sanctuary was cast down.

12 And an host was given *him* against the daily *sacrifice* by reason of transgression, and it cast down the
truth to the ground; and it practised, and prospered.

13 Then I heard one saint speaking, and another
saint said unto that certain *saint* which spake, How
long *shall be* the vision *concerning* the daily *sacrifice*, and the transgression of desolation, to give both
the sanctuary and the host to be trodden under foot?

14 And he said unto me, Unto two thousand and
three hundred days; then shall the sanctuary be
cleansed.

15 And it came to pass, when I, *even* I Daniel, had
seen the vision, and sought for the meaning, then,
behold, there stood before me as the appearance of a
man.

16 And I heard a man's voice between *the banks of*
Ulai, which called, and said, Gabriel, make this *man*
to understand the vision.

17 So he came near where I stood: and when he
came, I was afraid, and fell upon my face: but he said

NEW LIVING TRANSLATION

vision I was at the fortress of Susa, in the province of
Elam, standing beside the Ulai River.*

3 As I looked up, I saw a ram with two long horns
standing beside the river.* One of the horns was longer than the other, even though it had grown later
than the other one. 4 The ram butted everything out
of his way to the west, to the north, and to the south,
and no one could stand against him or help his victims. He did as he pleased and became very great.

5 While I was watching, suddenly a male goat appeared from the west, crossing the land so swiftly
that he didn't even touch the ground. This goat,
which had one very large horn between its eyes,
6 headed toward the two-horned ram that I had seen
standing beside the river, rushing at him in a rage.
7 The goat charged furiously at the ram and struck
him, breaking off both his horns. Now the ram was
helpless, and the goat knocked him down and
trampled him. No one could rescue the ram from the
goat's power.

8 The goat became very powerful. But at the height
of his power, his large horn was broken off. In the
large horn's place grew four prominent horns pointing in the four directions of the earth. 9 Then from
one of the prominent horns came a small horn
whose power grew very great. It extended toward the
south and the east and toward the glorious land of
Israel. 10 Its power reached to the heavens, where it
attacked the heavenly army, throwing some of the
heavenly beings and some of the stars to the ground
and trampling them. 11 It even challenged the Commander of heaven's army by canceling the daily sacrifices offered to him and by destroying his Temple.
12 The army of heaven was restrained from responding to this rebellion. So the daily sacrifice was halted,
and truth was overthrown. The horn succeeded in
everything it did.*

13 Then I heard two holy ones talking to each other.
One of them asked, "How long will the events of this
vision last? How long will the rebellion that causes
desecration stop the daily sacrifices? How long will
the Temple and heaven's army be trampled on?"

14 The other replied, "It will take 2,300 evenings
and mornings; then the Temple will be made right
again."

Gabriel Explains the Vision

15 As I, Daniel, was trying to understand the meaning
of this vision, someone who looked like a man stood
in front of me. 16 And I heard a human voice calling
out from the Ulai River, "Gabriel, tell this man the
meaning of his vision."

17 As Gabriel approached the place where I was
standing, I became so terrified that I fell with my

8:2 Or *the Ulai Gate;* also in 8:16. **8:3** Or *the gate;* also in 8:6.
8:11-12 The meaning of the Hebrew for these verses is uncertain.

KING JAMES VERSION

unto me, Understand, O son of man: for at the time of
the end *shall be* the vision.
18 Now as he was speaking with me, I was in a deep
sleep on my face toward the ground: but he touched
me, and set me upright.
19 And he said, Behold, I will make thee know what
shall be in the last end of the indignation: for at the
time appointed the end *shall be*.
20 The ram which thou sawest having *two* horns
are the kings of Media and Persia.
21 And the rough goat *is* the king of Grecia: and the
great horn that *is* between his eyes *is* the first king.
22 Now that being broken, whereas four stood up
for it, four kingdoms shall stand up out of the nation,
but not in his power.
23 And in the latter time of their kingdom, when
the transgressors are come to the full, a king of fierce
countenance, and understanding dark sentences,
shall stand up.
24 And his power shall be mighty, but not by his
own power: and he shall destroy wonderfully, and
shall prosper, and practise, and shall destroy the
mighty and the holy people.
25 And through his policy also he shall cause craft
to prosper in his hand; and he shall magnify *himself*
in his heart, and by peace shall destroy many: he
shall also stand up against the Prince of princes; but
he shall be broken without hand.
26 And the vision of the evening and the morning
which was told *is* true: wherefore shut thou up the
vision; for it *shall be* for many days.
27 And I Daniel fainted, and was sick *certain* days;
afterward I rose up, and did the king's business; and I
was astonished at the vision, but none understood *it*.

9 1 In the first year of Darius the son of Ahasuerus, of the seed of the Medes, which was made
king over the realm of the Chaldeans;
2 In the first year of his reign I Daniel understood
by books the number of the years, whereof the word
of the LORD came to Jeremiah the prophet, that he
would accomplish seventy years in the desolations
of Jerusalem.
3 And I set my face unto the Lord God, to seek by
prayer and supplications, with fasting, and sackcloth, and ashes:
4 And I prayed unto the LORD my God, and made
my confession, and said, O Lord, the great and dreadful God, keeping the covenant and mercy to them
that love him, and to them that keep his commandments;
5 We have sinned, and have committed iniquity,
and have done wickedly, and have rebelled, even by
departing from thy precepts and from thy judgments:
6 Neither have we hearkened unto thy servants the
prophets, which spake in thy name to our kings,
our princes, and our fathers, and to all the people of
the land.

NEW LIVING TRANSLATION

face to the ground. "Son of man," he said, "you must
understand that the events you have seen in your
vision relate to the time of the end."
18 While he was speaking, I fainted and lay there
with my face to the ground. But Gabriel roused me
with a touch and helped me to my feet.
19 Then he said, "I am here to tell you what will
happen later in the time of wrath. What you have
seen pertains to the very end of time. 20 The two-
horned ram represents the kings of Media and Persia. 21 The shaggy male goat represents the king of
Greece,* and the large horn between his eyes represents the first king of the Greek Empire. 22 The four
prominent horns that replaced the one large horn
show that the Greek Empire will break into four
kingdoms, but none as great as the first.
23 "At the end of their rule, when their sin is at its
height, a fierce king, a master of intrigue, will rise to
power. 24 He will become very strong, but not by his
own power. He will cause a shocking amount of destruction and succeed in everything he does. He will
destroy powerful leaders and devastate the holy
people. 25 He will be a master of deception and will become arrogant; he will destroy many without warning.
He will even take on the Prince of princes in battle, but
he will be broken, though not by human power.
26 "This vision about the 2,300 evenings and
mornings* is true. But none of these things will happen for a long time, so keep this vision a secret."
27 Then I, Daniel, was overcome and lay sick for
several days. Afterward I got up and performed my
duties for the king, but I was greatly troubled by the
vision and could not understand it.

Daniel's Prayer for His People

9 It was the first year of the reign of Darius the
Mede, the son of Ahasuerus, who became king
of the Babylonians.* 2 During the first year of his
reign, I, Daniel, learned from reading the word of the
LORD, as revealed to Jeremiah the prophet, that
Jerusalem must lie desolate for seventy years.* 3 So
I turned to the Lord God and pleaded with him in
prayer and fasting. I also wore rough burlap and
sprinkled myself with ashes.
4 I prayed to the LORD my God and confessed:

"O Lord, you are a great and awesome God!
You always fulfill your covenant and keep your
promises of unfailing love to those who love
you and obey your commands. 5 But we have
sinned and done wrong. We have rebelled
against you and scorned your commands and
regulations. 6 We have refused to listen to your
servants the prophets, who spoke on your
authority to our kings and princes and ancestors
and to all the people of the land.
7 "Lord, you are in the right; but as you see,

8:21 Hebrew *of Javan.* **8:26** Hebrew *about the evenings and mornings;* compare 8:14. **9:1** Or *the Chaldeans.* **9:2** See Jer 25:11-12; 29:10.

KING JAMES VERSION

7 O Lord, righteousness *belongeth* unto thee, but
unto us confusion of faces, as at this day; to the men
of Judah, and to the inhabitants of Jerusalem, and
unto all Israel, *that are* near, and *that are* far off,
through all the countries whither thou hast driven
them, because of their trespass that they have trespassed against thee.
8 O Lord, to us *belongeth* confusion of face, to our
kings, to our princes, and to our fathers, because we
have sinned against thee.
9 To the Lord our God *belong* mercies and forgive-
nesses, though we have rebelled against him;
10 Neither have we obeyed the voice of the LORD
our God, to walk in his laws, which he set before us by
his servants the prophets.
11 Yea, all Israel have transgressed thy law, even by
departing, that they might not obey thy voice; therefore the curse is poured upon us, and the oath that *is*
written in the law of Moses the servant of God, because we have sinned against him.
12 And he hath confirmed his words, which he
spake against us, and against our judges that judged
us, by bringing upon us a great evil: for under the
whole heaven hath not been done as hath been done
upon Jerusalem.
13 As *it is* written in the law of Moses, all this evil is
come upon us: yet made we not our prayer before the
LORD our God, that we might turn from our iniquities, and understand thy truth.
14 Therefore hath the LORD watched upon the evil,
and brought it upon us: for the LORD our God *is* righteous in all his works which he doeth: for we obeyed
not his voice.
15 And now, O Lord our God, that hast brought thy
people forth out of the land of Egypt with a mighty
hand, and hast gotten thee renown, as at this day;
we have sinned, we have done wickedly.
16 O Lord, according to all thy righteousness, I
beseech thee, let thine anger and thy fury be turned
away from thy city Jerusalem, thy holy mountain:
because for our sins, and for the iniquities of our
fathers, Jerusalem and thy people *are become* a
reproach to all *that are* about us.
17 Now therefore, O our God, hear the prayer of thy
servant, and his supplications, and cause thy face to
shine upon thy sanctuary that is desolate, for the
Lord's sake.
18 O my God, incline thine ear, and hear; open thine
eyes, and behold our desolations, and the city which
is called by thy name: for we do not present our supplications before thee for our righteousnesses, but
for thy great mercies.
19 O Lord, hear; O Lord, forgive; O Lord, hearken
and do; defer not, for thine own sake, O my God: for
thy city and thy people are called by thy name.
20 And whiles I *was* speaking, and praying, and
confessing my sin and the sin of my people Israel,

NEW LIVING TRANSLATION

our faces are covered with shame. This is true
of all of us, including the people of Judah and
Jerusalem and all Israel, scattered near and far,
wherever you have driven us because of our
disloyalty to you. 8 O LORD, we and our kings,
princes, and ancestors are covered with shame
because we have sinned against you. 9 But the
Lord our God is merciful and forgiving, even
though we have rebelled against him. 10 We have
not obeyed the LORD our God, for we have not
followed the instructions he gave us through his
servants the prophets. 11 All Israel has disobeyed
your instruction and turned away, refusing to
listen to your voice.
"So now the solemn curses and judgments
written in the Law of Moses, the servant of God,
have been poured down on us because of our
sin. 12 You have kept your word and done to us
and our rulers exactly as you warned. Never
has there been such a disaster as happened in
Jerusalem. 13 Every curse written against us in
the Law of Moses has come true. Yet we have
refused to seek mercy from the LORD our God by
turning from our sins and recognizing his truth.
14 Therefore, the LORD has brought upon us the
disaster he prepared. The LORD our God was
right to do all of these things, for we did not
obey him.
15 "O Lord our God, you brought lasting honor
to your name by rescuing your people from Egypt
in a great display of power. But we have sinned
and are full of wickedness. 16 In view of all your
faithful mercies, Lord, please turn your furious
anger away from your city Jerusalem, your holy
mountain. All the neighboring nations mock
Jerusalem and your people because of our sins
and the sins of our ancestors.
17 "O our God, hear your servant's prayer! Listen
as I plead. For your own sake, Lord, smile again on
your desolate sanctuary.
18 "O my God, lean down and listen to me.
Open your eyes and see our despair. See how
your city—the city that bears your name—lies in
ruins. We make this plea, not because we deserve
help, but because of your mercy.
19 "O Lord, hear. O Lord, forgive. O Lord, listen
and act! For your own sake, do not delay, O my
God, for your people and your city bear your
name."

Gabriel's Message about the Anointed One

20 I went on praying and confessing my sin and the
sin of my people, pleading with the LORD my God for

KING JAMES VERSION

and presenting my supplication before the LORD my God for the holy mountain of my God;

21 Yea, whiles I *was* speaking in prayer, even the man Gabriel, whom I had seen in the vision at the beginning, being caused to fly swiftly, touched me about the time of the evening oblation.

22 And he informed *me,* and talked with me, and said, O Daniel, I am now come forth to give thee skill and understanding.

23 At the beginning of thy supplications the commandment came forth, and I am come to shew *thee;* for thou *art* greatly beloved: therefore understand the matter, and consider the vision.

24 Seventy weeks are determined upon thy people and upon thy holy city, to finish the transgression, and to make an end of sins, and to make reconciliation for iniquity, and to bring in everlasting righteousness, and to seal up the vision and prophecy, and to anoint the most Holy.

25 Know therefore and understand, *that* from the going forth of the commandment to restore and to build Jerusalem unto the Messiah the Prince *shall be* seven weeks, and threescore and two weeks: the street shall be built again, and the wall, even in troublous times.

26 And after threescore and two weeks shall Messiah be cut off, but not for himself: and the people of the prince that shall come shall destroy the city and the sanctuary; and the end thereof *shall be* with a flood, and unto the end of the war desolations are determined.

27 And he shall confirm the covenant with many for one week: and in the midst of the week he shall cause the sacrifice and the oblation to cease, and for the overspreading of abominations he shall make *it* desolate, even until the consummation, and that determined shall be poured upon the desolate.

10 1 In the third year of Cyrus king of Persia a thing was revealed unto Daniel, whose name was called Belteshazzar; and the thing *was* true, but the time appointed *was* long: and he understood the thing, and had understanding of the vision.

2 In those days I Daniel was mourning three full weeks.

3 I ate no pleasant bread, neither came flesh nor wine in my mouth, neither did I anoint myself at all, till three whole weeks were fulfilled.

4 And in the four and twentieth day of the first month, as I was by the side of the great river, which *is* Hiddekel;

5 Then I lifted up mine eyes, and looked, and behold a certain man clothed in linen, whose loins *were* girded with fine gold of Uphaz:

NEW LIVING TRANSLATION

Jerusalem, his holy mountain. 21 As I was praying, Gabriel, whom I had seen in the earlier vision, came
swiftly to me at the time of the evening sacrifice.
22 He explained to me, "Daniel, I have come here to
give you insight and understanding. 23 The moment
you began praying, a command was given. And now I
am here to tell you what it was, for you are very precious to God. Listen carefully so that you can understand the meaning of your vision.

24 "A period of seventy sets of seven* has been decreed for your people and your holy city to finish
their rebellion, to put an end to their sin, to atone for
their guilt, to bring in everlasting righteousness, to
confirm the prophetic vision, and to anoint the Most
Holy Place.* 25 Now listen and understand! Seven
sets of seven plus sixty-two sets of seven* will pass
from the time the command is given to rebuild Jerusalem until a ruler—the Anointed One*—comes.
Jerusalem will be rebuilt with streets and strong
defenses,* despite the perilous times.

26 "After this period of sixty-two sets of seven,* the
Anointed One will be killed, appearing to have accomplished nothing, and a ruler will arise whose armies will destroy the city and the Temple. The end
will come with a flood, and war and its miseries are
decreed from that time to the very end. 27 The ruler
will make a treaty with the people for a period of one
set of seven,* but after half this time, he will put an
end to the sacrifices and offerings. And as a climax
to all his terrible deeds,* he will set up a sacrilegious
object that causes desecration,* until the fate decreed for this defiler is finally poured out on him."

Daniel's Vision of a Messenger

10 In the third year of the reign of King Cyrus of Persia,* Daniel (also known as Belteshazzar) had another vision. He understood that the vision concerned events certain to happen in the future—times of war and great hardship.

2 When this vision came to me, I, Daniel, had been
in mourning for three whole weeks. 3 All that time I
had eaten no rich food. No meat or wine crossed my
lips, and I used no fragrant lotions until those three
weeks had passed.

4 On April 23,* as I was standing on the bank of
the great Tigris River, 5 I looked up and saw a man
dressed in linen clothing, with a belt of pure gold

9:24a Hebrew *seventy sevens.* **9:24b** Or *the Most Holy One.* **9:25a** Hebrew *Seven sevens plus sixty-two sevens.* **9:25b** Or *an anointed one;* similarly in 9:26. Hebrew reads *a messiah.* **9:25c** Or *and a moat,* or *and trenches.* **9:26** Hebrew *After sixty-two sevens.* **9:27a** Hebrew *for one seven.* **9:27b** Hebrew *And on the wing of abominations;* the meaning of the Hebrew is uncertain. **9:27c** Hebrew *an abomination of desolation.* **10:1** The third year of Cyrus's reign was 536 B.C. **10:4** Hebrew *On the twenty-fourth day of the first month,* of the ancient Hebrew lunar calendar. This date in the book of Daniel can be cross-checked with dates in surviving Persian records and can be related accurately to our modern calendar. This event occurred on April 23, 536 B.C.

KING JAMES VERSION

6 His body also *was* like the beryl, and his face as the appearance of lightning, and his eyes as lamps of fire, and his arms and his feet like in colour to polished brass, and the voice of his words like the voice of a multitude.

7 And I Daniel alone saw the vision: for the men that were with me saw not the vision; but a great quaking fell upon them, so that they fled to hide themselves.

8 Therefore I was left alone, and saw this great vision, and there remained no strength in me: for my comeliness was turned in me into corruption, and I retained no strength.

9 Yet heard I the voice of his words: and when I heard the voice of his words, then was I in a deep sleep on my face, and my face toward the ground.

10 And, behold, an hand touched me, which set me upon my knees and *upon* the palms of my hands.

11 And he said unto me, O Daniel, a man greatly beloved, understand the words that I speak unto thee, and stand upright: for unto thee am I now sent. And when he had spoken this word unto me, I stood trembling.

12 Then said he unto me, Fear not, Daniel: for from the first day that thou didst set thine heart to understand, and to chasten thyself before thy God, thy words were heard, and I am come for thy words.

13 But the prince of the kingdom of Persia withstood me one and twenty days: but, lo, Michael, one of the chief princes, came to help me; and I remained there with the kings of Persia.

14 Now I am come to make thee understand what shall befall thy people in the latter days: for yet the vision *is* for *many* days.

15 And when he had spoken such words unto me, I set my face toward the ground, and I became dumb.

16 And, behold, *one* like the similitude of the sons of men touched my lips: then I opened my mouth, and spake, and said unto him that stood before me, O my lord, by the vision my sorrows are turned upon me, and I have retained no strength.

17 For how can the servant of this my lord talk with this my lord? for as for me, straightway there remained no strength in me, neither is there breath left in me.

18 Then there came again and touched me *one* like the appearance of a man, and he strengthened me,

19 And said, O man greatly beloved, fear not: peace *be* unto thee, be strong, yea, be strong. And when he had spoken unto me, I was strengthened, and said, Let my lord speak; for thou hast strengthened me.

20 Then said he, Knowest thou wherefore I come unto thee? and now will I return to fight with the prince of Persia: and when I am gone forth, lo, the prince of Grecia shall come.

21 But I will shew thee that which is noted in the

NEW LIVING TRANSLATION

around his waist. 6 His body looked like a precious gem. His face flashed like lightning, and his eyes flamed like torches. His arms and feet shone like polished bronze, and his voice roared like a vast multitude of people.

7 Only I, Daniel, saw this vision. The men with me saw nothing, but they were suddenly terrified and ran away to hide. 8 So I was left there all alone to see this amazing vision. My strength left me, my face grew deathly pale, and I felt very weak. 9 Then I heard the man speak, and when I heard the sound of his voice, I fainted and lay there with my face to the ground.

10 Just then a hand touched me and lifted me, still trembling, to my hands and knees. 11 And the man said to me, "Daniel, you are very precious to God, so listen carefully to what I have to say to you. Stand up, for I have been sent to you." When he said this to me, I stood up, still trembling.

12 Then he said, "Don't be afraid, Daniel. Since the first day you began to pray for understanding and to humble yourself before your God, your request has been heard in heaven. I have come in answer to your prayer. 13 But for twenty-one days the spirit prince* of the kingdom of Persia blocked my way. Then Michael, one of the archangels,* came to help me, and I left him there with the spirit prince of the kingdom of Persia.* 14 Now I am here to explain what will happen to your people in the future, for this vision concerns a time yet to come."

15 While he was speaking to me, I looked down at the ground, unable to say a word. 16 Then the one who looked like a man* touched my lips, and I opened my mouth and began to speak. I said to the one standing in front of me, "I am filled with anguish because of the vision I have seen, my lord, and I am very weak. 17 How can someone like me, your servant, talk to you, my lord? My strength is gone, and I can hardly breathe."

18 Then the one who looked like a man touched me again, and I felt my strength returning. 19 "Don't be afraid," he said, "for you are very precious to God. Peace! Be encouraged! Be strong!"

As he spoke these words to me, I suddenly felt stronger and said to him, "Please speak to me, my lord, for you have strengthened me."

20 He replied, "Do you know why I have come? Soon I must return to fight against the spirit prince of the kingdom of Persia, and after that the spirit prince of the kingdom of Greece* will come. 21 Meanwhile, I will tell you what is written in the Book of Truth. (No one helps me against these spirit princes except Michael, your spirit prince.* 11:1 I have been standing beside Michael* to support and

10:13a Hebrew *the prince;* also in 10:13c, 20. **10:13b** Hebrew *the chief princes.* **10:13c** As in one Greek version; Hebrew reads *and I was left there with the kings of Persia.* The meaning of the Hebrew is uncertain. **10:16** As in most manuscripts of the Masoretic Text; one manuscript of the Masoretic Text and one Greek version read *Then something that looked like a human hand.* **10:20** Hebrew *of Javan.* **10:21** Hebrew *against these except Michael, your prince.* **11:1** Hebrew *him.*

KING JAMES VERSION

scripture of truth: and *there is* none that holdeth with me in these things, but Michael your prince.

11 1Also I in the first year of Darius the Mede, *even* I, stood to confirm and to strengthen him.

2And now will I shew thee the truth. Behold, there shall stand up yet three kings in Persia; and the fourth shall be far richer than *they* all: and by his strength through his riches he shall stir up all against the realm of Grecia.

3And a mighty king shall stand up, that shall rule with great dominion, and do according to his will.

4And when he shall stand up, his kingdom shall be broken, and shall be divided toward the four winds of heaven; and not to his posterity, nor according to his dominion which he ruled: for his kingdom shall be plucked up, even for others beside those.

5And the king of the south shall be strong, and *one* of his princes; and he shall be strong above him, and have dominion; his dominion *shall be* a great dominion.

6And in the end of years they shall join themselves together; for the king's daughter of the south shall come to the king of the north to make an agreement: but she shall not retain the power of the arm; neither shall he stand, nor his arm: but she shall be given up, and they that brought her, and he that begat her, and he that strengthened her in *these* times.

7But out of a branch of her roots shall *one* stand up in his estate, which shall come with an army, and shall enter into the fortress of the king of the north, and shall deal against them, and shall prevail:

8And shall also carry captives into Egypt their gods, with their princes, *and* with their precious vessels of silver and of gold; and he shall continue *more* years than the king of the north.

9So the king of the south shall come into *his* kingdom, and shall return into his own land.

10But his sons shall be stirred up, and shall assemble a multitude of great forces: and *one* shall certainly come, and overflow, and pass through: then shall he return, and be stirred up, *even* to his fortress.

11And the king of the south shall be moved with choler, and shall come forth and fight with him, *even* with the king of the north: and he shall set forth a great multitude; but the multitude shall be given into his hand.

12*And* when he hath taken away the multitude, his heart shall be lifted up; and he shall cast down *many* ten thousands: but he shall not be strengthened *by it*.

13For the king of the north shall return, and shall set forth a multitude greater than the former, and shall certainly come after certain years with a great army and with much riches.

14And in those times there shall many stand up against the king of the south: also the robbers of thy

NEW LIVING TRANSLATION

strengthen him since the first year of the reign of Darius the Mede.)

Kings of the South and North

11 2"Now then, I will reveal the truth to you. Three more Persian kings will reign, to be succeeded by a fourth, far richer than the others. He will use his wealth to stir up everyone to fight against the kingdom of Greece.*

3"Then a mighty king will rise to power who will rule with great authority and accomplish everything he sets out to do. 4But at the height of his power, his kingdom will be broken apart and divided into four parts. It will not be ruled by the king's descendants, nor will the kingdom hold the authority it once had. For his empire will be uprooted and given to others.

5"The king of the south will increase in power, but one of his own officials will become more powerful than he and will rule his kingdom with great strength.

6"Some years later an alliance will be formed between the king of the north and the king of the south. The daughter of the king of the south will be given in marriage to the king of the north to secure the alliance, but she will lose her influence over him, and so will her father. She will be abandoned along with her supporters. 7But when one of her relatives* becomes king of the south, he will raise an army and enter the fortress of the king of the north and defeat him. 8When he returns to Egypt, he will carry back their idols with him, along with priceless articles of gold and silver. For some years afterward he will leave the king of the north alone.

9"Later the king of the north will invade the realm of the king of the south but will soon return to his own land. 10However, the sons of the king of the north will assemble a mighty army that will advance like a flood and carry the battle as far as the enemy's fortress.

11"Then, in a rage, the king of the south will rally against the vast forces assembled by the king of the north and will defeat them. 12After the enemy army is swept away, the king of the south will be filled with pride and will execute many thousands of his enemies. But his success will be short lived.

13"A few years later the king of the north will return with a fully equipped army far greater than before. 14At that time there will be a general uprising

11:2 Hebrew *of Javan.* 11:7 Hebrew *a branch from her roots.*

KING JAMES VERSION

people shall exalt themselves to establish the vision;
but they shall fall.
15 So the king of the north shall come, and cast up
a mount, and take the most fenced cities: and the
arms of the south shall not withstand, neither his
chosen people, neither *shall there be any* strength to
withstand.
16 But he that cometh against him shall do according to his own will, and none shall stand before him:
and he shall stand in the glorious land, which by his
hand shall be consumed.
17 He shall also set his face to enter with the
strength of his whole kingdom, and upright ones
with him; thus shall he do: and he shall give him the
daughter of women, corrupting her: but she shall not
stand *on his side*, neither be for him.
18 After this shall he turn his face unto the isles,
and shall take many: but a prince for his own behalf
shall cause the reproach offered by him to cease;
without his own reproach he shall cause *it* to turn
upon him.
19 Then he shall turn his face toward the fort of his
own land: but he shall stumble and fall, and not be
found.
20 Then shall stand up in his estate a raiser of taxes
in the glory of the kingdom: but within few days he
shall be destroyed, neither in anger, nor in battle.
21 And in his estate shall stand up a vile person, to
whom they shall not give the honour of the kingdom:
but he shall come in peaceably, and obtain the kingdom by flatteries.
22 And with the arms of a flood shall they be overflown from before him, and shall be broken; yea, also
the prince of the covenant.
23 And after the league *made* with him he shall
work deceitfully: for he shall come up, and shall become strong with a small people.
24 He shall enter peaceably even upon the fattest
places of the province; and he shall do *that* which
his fathers have not done, nor his fathers' fathers;
he shall scatter among them the prey, and spoil, and
riches: *yea*, and he shall forecast his devices against
the strong holds, even for a time.
25 And he shall stir up his power and his courage
against the king of the south with a great army; and
the king of the south shall be stirred up to battle with
a very great and mighty army; but he shall not stand:
for they shall forecast devices against him.
26 Yea, they that feed of the portion of his meat
shall destroy him, and his army shall overflow: and
many shall fall down slain.
27 And both these kings' hearts *shall be* to do mischief, and they shall speak lies at one table; but it
shall not prosper: for yet the end *shall be* at the time
appointed.
28 Then shall he return into his land with great
riches; and his heart *shall be* against the holy

NEW LIVING TRANSLATION

against the king of the south. Violent men among
your own people will join them in fulfillment of this
vision, but they will not succeed. 15 Then the king of
the north will come and lay siege to a fortified city
and capture it. The best troops of the south will not
be able to stand in the face of the onslaught.
16 "The king of the north will march onward un-
opposed; none will be able to stop him. He will pause
in the glorious land of Israel,* intent on destroying it.
17 He will make plans to come with the might of his
entire kingdom and will form an alliance with the
king of the south. He will give him a daughter in
marriage in order to overthrow the kingdom from
within, but his plan will fail.
18 "After this, he will turn his attention to the
coastland and conquer many cities. But a commander from another land will put an end to his insolence and cause him to retreat in shame. 19 He will
take refuge in his own fortresses but will stumble
and fall and be seen no more.
20 "His successor will send out a tax collector to
maintain the royal splendor. But after a very brief
reign, he will die, though not from anger or in battle.
21 "The next to come to power will be a despicable
man who is not in line for royal succession. He will
slip in when least expected and take over the kingdom by flattery and intrigue. 22 Before him great
armies will be swept away, including a covenant
prince. 23 With deceitful promises, he will make various alliances. He will become strong despite having
only a handful of followers. 24 Without warning he
will enter the richest areas of the land. Then he will
distribute among his followers the plunder and
wealth of the rich—something his predecessors had
never done. He will plot the overthrow of strongholds, but this will last for only a short while.
25 "Then he will stir up his courage and raise a
great army against the king of the south. The king of
the south will go to battle with a mighty army, but to
no avail, for there will be plots against him. 26 His own
household will cause his downfall. His army will be
swept away, and many will be killed. 27 Seeking nothing but each other's harm, these kings will plot
against each other at the conference table, attempt-
ing to deceive each other. But it will make no difference, for the end will come at the appointed time.
28 "The king of the north will then return home
with great riches. On the way he will set himself

11:16 Hebrew *the glorious land*.

KING JAMES VERSION

covenant; and he shall do *exploits,* and return to his own land.

29At the time appointed he shall return, and come toward the south; but it shall not be as the former, or as the latter.

30For the ships of Chittim shall come against him: therefore he shall be grieved, and return, and have indignation against the holy covenant: so shall he do; he shall even return, and have intelligence with them that forsake the holy covenant.

31And arms shall stand on his part, and they shall pollute the sanctuary of strength, and shall take away the daily *sacrifice*, and they shall place the abomination that maketh desolate.

32And such as do wickedly against the covenant shall he corrupt by flatteries: but the people that do know their God shall be strong, and do *exploits*.

33And they that understand among the people shall instruct many: yet they shall fall by the sword, and by flame, by captivity, and by spoil, *many* days.

34Now when they shall fall, they shall be holpen with a little help: but many shall cleave to them with flatteries.

35And *some* of them of understanding shall fall, to try them, and to purge, and to make *them* white, *even* to the time of the end: because *it is* yet for a time appointed.

36And the king shall do according to his will; and he shall exalt himself, and magnify himself above every god, and shall speak marvellous things against the God of gods, and shall prosper till the indignation be accomplished: for that that is determined shall be done.

37Neither shall he regard the God of his fathers, nor the desire of women, nor regard any god: for he shall magnify himself above all.

38But in his estate shall he honour the God of forces: and a god whom his fathers knew not shall he honour with gold, and silver, and with precious stones, and pleasant things.

39Thus shall he do in the most strong holds with a strange god, whom he shall acknowledge *and* increase with glory: and he shall cause them to rule over many, and shall divide the land for gain.

40And at the time of the end shall the king of the south push at him: and the king of the north shall come against him like a whirlwind, with chariots, and with horsemen, and with many ships; and he shall enter into the countries, and shall overflow and pass over.

41He shall enter also into the glorious land, and many *countries* shall be overthrown: but these shall escape out of his hand, *even* Edom, and Moab, and the chief of the children of Ammon.

42He shall stretch forth his hand also upon the countries: and the land of Egypt shall not escape.

43But he shall have power over the treasures of gold and of silver, and over all the precious things of

NEW LIVING TRANSLATION

against the people of the holy covenant, doing much
damage before continuing his journey.
29"Then at the appointed time he will once again
invade the south, but this time the result will be
different. 30For warships from western coastlands*
will scare him off, and he will withdraw and return
home. But he will vent his anger against the people
of the holy covenant and reward those who forsake
the covenant.
31"His army will take over the Temple fortress, pollute the sanctuary, put a stop to the daily sacrifices,
and set up the sacrilegious object that causes desecration.* 32He will flatter and win over those who
have violated the covenant. But the people who know
their God will be strong and will resist him.
33"Wise leaders will give instruction to many, but
these teachers will die by fire and sword, or they will
be jailed and robbed. 34During these persecutions,
little help will arrive, and many who join them will
not be sincere. 35And some of the wise will fall victim
to persecution. In this way, they will be refined and
cleansed and made pure until the time of the end, for
the appointed time is still to come.
36"The king will do as he pleases, exalting himself
and claiming to be greater than every god, even blaspheming the God of gods. He will succeed, but only
until the time of wrath is completed. For what has
been determined will surely take place. 37He will
have no respect for the gods of his ancestors, or for
the god loved by women, or for any other god, for he
will boast that he is greater than them all. 38Instead
of these, he will worship the god of fortresses—a god
his ancestors never knew—and lavish on him gold,
silver, precious stones, and expensive gifts. 39Claiming this foreign god's help, he will attack the strongest fortresses. He will honor those who submit to
him, appointing them to positions of authority and
dividing the land among them as their reward.*
40"Then at the time of the end, the king of the
south will attack the king of the north. The king of
the north will storm out with chariots, charioteers,
and a vast navy. He will invade various lands and
sweep through them like a flood. 41He will enter the
glorious land of Israel,* and many nations will fall,
but Moab, Edom, and the best part of Ammon will escape. 42He will conquer many countries, and even
Egypt will not escape. 43He will gain control over the

11:30 Hebrew *from Kittim.* **11:31** Hebrew *the abomination of desolation.* **11:39** Or *at a price.* **11:41** Hebrew *the glorious land.*

KING JAMES VERSION

Egypt: and the Libyans and the Ethiopians *shall be* at his steps.

44But tidings out of the east and out of the north shall trouble him: therefore he shall go forth with great fury to destroy, and utterly to make away many.

45And he shall plant the tabernacles of his palace between the seas in the glorious holy mountain; yet he shall come to his end, and none shall help him.

12

1And at that time shall Michael stand up, the great prince which standeth for the children of thy people: and there shall be a time of trouble, such as never was since there was a nation *even* to that same time: and at that time thy people shall be delivered, every one that shall be found written in the book.

2And many of them that sleep in the dust of the earth shall awake, some to everlasting life, and some to shame *and* everlasting contempt.

3And they that be wise shall shine as the brightness of the firmament; and they that turn many to righteousness as the stars for ever and ever.

4But thou, O Daniel, shut up the words, and seal the book, *even* to the time of the end: many shall run to and fro, and knowledge shall be increased.

5Then I Daniel looked, and, behold, there stood other two, the one on this side of the bank of the river, and the other on that side of the bank of the river.

6And *one* said to the man clothed in linen, which *was* upon the waters of the river, How long *shall it be to* the end of these wonders?

7And I heard the man clothed in linen, which *was* upon the waters of the river, when he held up his right hand and his left hand unto heaven, and sware by him that liveth for ever that *it shall be* for a time, times, and an half; and when he shall have accomplished to scatter the power of the holy people, all these *things* shall be finished.

8And I heard, but I understood not: then said I, O my Lord, what *shall be* the end of these *things?*

9And he said, Go thy way, Daniel: for the words *are* closed up and sealed till the time of the end.

10Many shall be purified, and made white, and tried; but the wicked shall do wickedly: and none of the wicked shall understand; but the wise shall understand.

11And from the time *that* the daily *sacrifice* shall be taken away, and the abomination that maketh desolate set up, *there shall be* a thousand two hundred and ninety days.

12Blessed *is* he that waiteth, and cometh to the thousand three hundred and five and thirty days.

13But go thou thy way till the end *be:* for thou shalt rest, and stand in thy lot at the end of the days.

NEW LIVING TRANSLATION

gold, silver, and treasures of Egypt, and the Libyans and Ethiopians* will be his servants.

44"But then news from the east and the north will alarm him, and he will set out in great anger to destroy and obliterate many. 45He will stop between the glorious holy mountain and the sea and will pitch his royal tents. But while he is there, his time will suddenly run out, and no one will help him.

The Time of the End

12

"At that time Michael, the archangel* who stands guard over your nation, will arise. Then there will be a time of anguish greater than any since nations first came into existence. But at that time every one of your people whose name is written in the book will be rescued. 2Many of those whose bodies lie dead and buried will rise up, some to everlasting life and some to shame and everlasting disgrace. 3Those who are wise will shine as bright as the sky, and those who lead many to righteousness will shine like the stars forever. 4But you, Daniel, keep this prophecy a secret; seal up the book until the time of the end, when many will rush here and there, and knowledge will increase."

5Then I, Daniel, looked and saw two others standing on opposite banks of the river. 6One of them asked the man dressed in linen, who was now standing above the river, "How long will it be until these shocking events are over?"

7The man dressed in linen, who was standing above the river, raised both his hands toward heaven and took a solemn oath by the One who lives forever, saying, "It will go on for a time, times, and half a time. When the shattering of the holy people has finally come to an end, all these things will have happened."

8I heard what he said, but I did not understand what he meant. So I asked, "How will all this finally end, my lord?"

9But he said, "Go now, Daniel, for what I have said is kept secret and sealed until the time of the end. 10Many will be purified, cleansed, and refined by these trials. But the wicked will continue in their wickedness, and none of them will understand. Only those who are wise will know what it means.

11"From the time the daily sacrifice is stopped and the sacrilegious object that causes desecration* is set up to be worshiped, there will be 1,290 days. 12And blessed are those who wait and remain until the end of the 1,335 days!

13"As for you, go your way until the end. You will rest, and then at the end of the days, you will rise again to receive the inheritance set aside for you."

11:43 Hebrew *Cushites.* **12:1** Hebrew *the great prince.* **12:11** Hebrew *the abomination of desolation.*

Hosea

KING JAMES VERSION

1 1 The word of the LORD that came unto Hosea,
the son of Beeri, in the days of Uzziah, Jotham,
Ahaz, *and* Hezekiah, kings of Judah, and in the days
of Jeroboam the son of Joash, king of Israel.

2 The beginning of the word of the LORD by Hosea.
And the LORD said to Hosea, Go, take unto thee a wife
of whoredoms and children of whoredoms: for the
land hath committed great whoredom, *departing*
from the LORD.
3 So he went and took Gomer the daughter of
Diblaim; which conceived, and bare him a son.
4 And the LORD said unto him, Call his name Jezreel; for yet a little *while,* and I will avenge the blood
of Jezreel upon the house of Jehu, and will cause to
cease the kingdom of the house of Israel.
5 And it shall come to pass at that day, that I will
break the bow of Israel in the valley of Jezreel.
6 And she conceived again, and bare a daughter.
And *God* said unto him, Call her name Lo-ruhamah:
for I will no more have mercy upon the house of Israel; but I will utterly take them away.
7 But I will have mercy upon the house of Judah,
and will save them by the LORD their God, and will
not save them by bow, nor by sword, nor by battle, by
horses, nor by horsemen.
8 Now when she had weaned Lo-ruhamah, she
conceived, and bare a son.
9 Then said *God,* Call his name Lo-ammi: for ye *are*
not my people, and I will not be your *God.*
10 Yet the number of the children of Israel shall be
as the sand of the sea, which cannot be measured nor
numbered; and it shall come to pass, *that* in the
place where it was said unto them, Ye *are* not my
people, *there* it shall be said unto them, *Ye are* the
sons of the living God.
11 Then shall the children of Judah and the children of Israel be gathered together, and appoint

NEW LIVING TRANSLATION

1 The LORD gave this message to Hosea son of
Beeri during the years when Uzziah, Jotham,
Ahaz, and Hezekiah were kings of Judah, and Jero-
boam son of Jehoash* was king of Israel.

Hosea's Wife and Children

2 When the LORD first began speaking to Israel
through Hosea, he said to him, "Go and marry a prostitute,* so that some of her children will be conceived in prostitution. This will illustrate how Israel
has acted like a prostitute by turning against the
LORD and worshiping other gods."
3 So Hosea married Gomer, the daughter of Diblaim, and she became pregnant and gave Hosea a son.
4 And the LORD said, "Name the child Jezreel, for I am
about to punish King Jehu's dynasty to avenge the
murders he committed at Jezreel. In fact, I will bring
an end to Israel's independence. 5 I will break its
military power in the Jezreel Valley."
6 Soon Gomer became pregnant again and gave
birth to a daughter. And the LORD said to Hosea,
"Name your daughter Lo-ruhamah—'Not loved'—for
I will no longer show love to the people of Israel or
forgive them. 7 But I will show love to the people of
Judah. I will free them from their enemies—not with
weapons and armies or horses and charioteers, but
by my power as the LORD their God."
8 After Gomer had weaned Lo-ruhamah, she again
became pregnant and gave birth to a second son.
9 And the LORD said, "Name him Lo-ammi—'Not my
people'—for Israel is not my people, and I am not
their God.
10* "Yet the time will come when Israel's people
will be like the sands of the seashore—too many to
count! Then, at the place where they were told, 'You
are not my people,' it will be said, 'You are children of
the living God.' 11 Then the people of Judah and Israel
will unite together. They will choose one leader for
themselves, and they will return from exile together.
What a day that will be—the day of Jezreel*—when
God will again plant his people in his land.

1:1 Hebrew *Joash,* a variant spelling of Jehoash. 1:2 Or *a promiscuous woman.* 1:10 Verses 1:10-11 are numbered 2:1-2 in Hebrew text.
1:11 *Jezreel* means "God plants."

KING JAMES VERSION

themselves one head, and they shall come up out of
the land: for great *shall be* the day of Jezreel.

2

1 Say ye unto your brethren, Ammi; and to your
sisters, Ruhamah.
2 Plead with your mother, plead: for she *is* not my
wife, neither *am* I her husband: let her therefore put
away her whoredoms out of her sight, and her adulteries from between her breasts;
3 Lest I strip her naked, and set her as in the day
that she was born, and make her as a wilderness, and
set her like a dry land, and slay her with thirst.
4 And I will not have mercy upon her children; for
they *be* the children of whoredoms.
5 For their mother hath played the harlot: she that
conceived them hath done shamefully: for she said, I
will go after my lovers, that give *me* my bread and my
water, my wool and my flax, mine oil and my drink.
6 Therefore, behold, I will hedge up thy way with
thorns, and make a wall, that she shall not find her
paths.
7 And she shall follow after her lovers, but she shall
not overtake them; and she shall seek them, but shall
not find *them:* then shall she say, I will go and return
to my first husband; for then *was it* better with me
than now.
8 For she did not know that I gave her corn, and
wine, and oil, and multiplied her silver and gold,
which they prepared for Baal.
9 Therefore will I return, and take away my corn in
the time thereof, and my wine in the season thereof,
and will recover my wool and my flax *given* to cover
her nakedness.
10 And now will I discover her lewdness in the
sight of her lovers, and none shall deliver her out of
mine hand.
11 I will also cause all her mirth to cease, her feast
days, her new moons, and her sabbaths, and all her
solemn feasts.
12 And I will destroy her vines and her fig trees,
whereof she hath said, These *are* my rewards that my

NEW LIVING TRANSLATION

2:1 *"In that day you will call your brothers Ammi—
'My people.' And you will call your sisters Ruhamah—'The ones I love.'

Charges against an Unfaithful Wife

2

2 "But now bring charges against Israel—your
mother—
for she is no longer my wife,
and I am no longer her husband.
Tell her to remove the prostitute's makeup
from her face
and the clothing that exposes her breasts.
3 Otherwise, I will strip her as naked
as she was on the day she was born.
I will leave her to die of thirst,
as in a dry and barren wilderness.
4 And I will not love her children,
for they were conceived in prostitution.
5 Their mother is a shameless prostitute
and became pregnant in a shameful way.
She said, 'I'll run after other lovers
and sell myself to them for food and water,
for clothing of wool and linen,
and for olive oil and drinks.'

6 "For this reason I will fence her in with
thornbushes.
I will block her path with a wall
to make her lose her way.
7 When she runs after her lovers,
she won't be able to catch them.
She will search for them
but not find them.
Then she will think,
'I might as well return to my husband,
for I was better off with him than I am now.'
8 She doesn't realize it was I who gave her
everything she has—
the grain, the new wine, the olive oil;
I even gave her silver and gold.
But she gave all my gifts to Baal.

9 "But now I will take back the ripened grain
and new wine
I generously provided each harvest season.
I will take away the wool and linen clothing
I gave her to cover her nakedness.
10 I will strip her naked in public,
while all her lovers look on.
No one will be able
to rescue her from my hands.
11 I will put an end to her annual festivals,
her new moon celebrations, and her
Sabbath days—
all her appointed festivals.
12 I will destroy her grapevines and fig trees,
things she claims her lovers gave her.

2:1 Verses 2:1-23 are numbered 2:3-25 in Hebrew text.

KING JAMES VERSION

lovers have given me: and I will make them a forest,
and the beasts of the field shall eat them.
13And I will visit upon her the days of Baalim,
wherein she burned incense to them, and she decked
herself with her earrings and her jewels, and she went
after her lovers, and forgat me, saith the LORD.

14Therefore, behold, I will allure her, and bring her
into the wilderness, and speak comfortably unto her.
15And I will give her her vineyards from thence,
and the valley of Achor for a door of hope: and she
shall sing there, as in the days of her youth, and as in
the day when she came up out of the land of Egypt.
16And it shall be at that day, saith the LORD, *that*
thou shalt call me Ishi; and shalt call me no more
Baali.
17For I will take away the names of Baalim out of
her mouth, and they shall no more be remembered
by their name.
18And in that day will I make a covenant for them
with the beasts of the field, and with the fowls of
heaven, and *with* the creeping things of the ground:
and I will break the bow and the sword and the battle
out of the earth, and will make them to lie down
safely.
19And I will betroth thee unto me for ever; yea, I
will betroth thee unto me in righteousness, and in
judgment, and in lovingkindness, and in mercies.
20I will even betroth thee unto me in faithfulness:
and thou shalt know the LORD.
21And it shall come to pass in that day, I will hear,
saith the LORD, I will hear the heavens, and they shall
hear the earth;
22And the earth shall hear the corn, and the wine,
and the oil; and they shall hear Jezreel.
23And I will sow her unto me in the earth; and I will
have mercy upon her that had not obtained mercy;
and I will say to *them which were* not my people,
Thou *art* my people; and they shall say, *Thou art*
my God.

NEW LIVING TRANSLATION

I will let them grow into tangled thickets,
where only wild animals will eat the fruit.
13 I will punish her for all those times
when she burned incense to her images
of Baal,
when she put on her earrings and jewels
and went out to look for her lovers
but forgot all about me,"
says the LORD.

The LORD's Love for Unfaithful Israel

14 "But then I will win her back once again.
I will lead her into the desert
and speak tenderly to her there.
15 I will return her vineyards to her
and transform the Valley of Trouble* into
a gateway of hope.
She will give herself to me there,
as she did long ago when she was young,
when I freed her from her captivity in Egypt.
16 When that day comes," says the LORD,
"you will call me 'my husband'
instead of 'my master.'*
17 O Israel, I will wipe the many names of Baal
from your lips,
and you will never mention them again.
18 On that day I will make a covenant
with all the wild animals and the birds
of the sky
and the animals that scurry along the ground
so they will not harm you.
I will remove all weapons of war from the land,
all swords and bows,
so you can live unafraid
in peace and safety.
19 I will make you my wife forever,
showing you righteousness and justice,
unfailing love and compassion.
20 I will be faithful to you and make you mine,
and you will finally know me as the LORD.

21 "In that day, I will answer,"
says the LORD.
"I will answer the sky as it pleads for clouds.
And the sky will answer the earth with rain.
22 Then the earth will answer the thirsty cries
of the grain, the grapevines, and the olive trees.
And they in turn will answer,
'Jezreel'—'God plants!'
23 At that time I will plant a crop of Israelites
and raise them for myself.
I will show love
to those I called 'Not loved.'*
And to those I called 'Not my people,'*
I will say, 'Now you are my people.'
And they will reply, 'You are our God!'"

2:15 Hebrew *valley of Achor.* **2:16** Hebrew *'my baal.'* **2:23a** Hebrew *Lo-ruhamah;* see 1:6. **2:23b** Hebrew *Lo-ammi;* see 1:9.

KING JAMES VERSION

3 1Then said the LORD unto me, Go yet, love a woman beloved of *her* friend, yet an adulteress, according to the love of the LORD toward the children of Israel, who look to other gods, and love flagons of wine.

2So I bought her to me for fifteen *pieces* of silver, and *for* an homer of barley, and an half homer of barley:

3And I said unto her, Thou shalt abide for me many days; thou shalt not play the harlot, and thou shalt not be for *another* man: so *will* I also *be* for thee.

4For the children of Israel shall abide many days without a king, and without a prince, and without a sacrifice, and without an image, and without an ephod, and *without* teraphim:

5Afterward shall the children of Israel return, and seek the LORD their God, and David their king; and shall fear the LORD and his goodness in the latter days.

4 1Hear the word of the LORD, ye children of Israel: for the LORD hath a controversy with the inhabitants of the land, because *there is* no truth, nor mercy, nor knowledge of God in the land.

2By swearing, and lying, and killing, and stealing, and committing adultery, they break out, and blood toucheth blood.

3Therefore shall the land mourn, and every one that dwelleth therein shall languish, with the beasts of the field, and with the fowls of heaven; yea, the fishes of the sea also shall be taken away.

4Yet let no man strive, nor reprove another: for thy people *are* as they that strive with the priest.

5Therefore shalt thou fall in the day, and the prophet also shall fall with thee in the night, and I will destroy thy mother.

6My people are destroyed for lack of knowledge: because thou hast rejected knowledge, I will also reject thee, that thou shalt be no priest to me: seeing thou hast forgotten the law of thy God, I will also forget thy children.

7As they were increased, so they sinned against me: *therefore* will I change their glory into shame.

NEW LIVING TRANSLATION

Hosea's Wife Is Redeemed

3 Then the LORD said to me, "Go and love your wife again, even though she* commits adultery with another lover. This will illustrate that the LORD still loves Israel, even though the people have turned to other gods and love to worship them.*"

2So I bought her back for fifteen pieces of silver* and five bushels of barley and a measure of wine.* 3Then I said to her, "You must live in my house for many days and stop your prostitution. During this time, you will not have sexual relations with anyone, not even with me.*"

4This shows that Israel will go a long time without
a king or prince, and without sacrifices, sacred pillars, priests,* or even idols!
5But afterward the
people will return and devote themselves to the LORD their God and to David's descendant, their king.* In the last days, they will tremble in awe of the LORD and of his goodness.

The LORD's Case against Israel

4 1Hear the word of the LORD, O people of Israel!
The LORD has brought charges against you, saying:
"There is no faithfulness, no kindness,
no knowledge of God in your land.
2 You make vows and break them;
you kill and steal and commit adultery.
There is violence everywhere—
one murder after another.
3 That is why your land is in mourning,
and everyone is wasting away.
Even the wild animals, the birds of the sky,
and the fish of the sea are disappearing.

4 "Don't point your finger at someone else
and try to pass the blame!
My complaint, you priests,
is with you.*
5 So you will stumble in broad daylight,
and your false prophets will fall with you in the night.
And I will destroy Israel, your mother.
6 My people are being destroyed
because they don't know me.
Since you priests refuse to know me,
I refuse to recognize you as my priests.
Since you have forgotten the laws of your God,
I will forget to bless your children.
7 The more priests there are,
the more they sin against me.
They have exchanged the glory of God
for the shame of idols.*

3:1a Or *Go and love a woman who.* **3:1b** Hebrew *love their raisin cakes.* **3:2a** Hebrew *15 shekels of silver,* about 6 ounces or 171 grams in weight. **3:2b** As in Greek version, which reads *a homer of barley and a wineskin full of wine;* Hebrew reads *a homer* [5 bushels or 182 liters] *of barley and a lethech* [2.5 bushels or 91 liters] *of barley.* **3:3** Or *and I will live with you.* **3:4** Hebrew *ephod,* the vest worn by the priest. **3:5** Hebrew *to David their king.* **4:4** Hebrew *Your people are like those with a complaint against the priests.* **4:7** As in Syriac version and an ancient Hebrew tradition; Masoretic Text reads *I will turn their glory into shame.*

KING JAMES VERSION

8 They eat up the sin of my people, and they set
their heart on their iniquity.
9 And there shall be, like people, like priest: and I
will punish them for their ways, and reward them
their doings.
10 For they shall eat, and not have enough: they
shall commit whoredom, and shall not increase: because they have left off to take heed to the LORD.
11 Whoredom and wine and new wine take away
the heart.
12 My people ask counsel at their stocks, and their
staff declareth unto them: for the spirit of whoredoms hath caused *them* to err, and they have gone a
whoring from under their God.
13 They sacrifice upon the tops of the mountains,
and burn incense upon the hills, under oaks and
poplars and elms, because the shadow thereof *is*
good: therefore your daughters shall commit whoredom, and your spouses shall commit adultery.
14 I will not punish your daughters when they
commit whoredom, nor your spouses when they
commit adultery: for themselves are separated with
whores, and they sacrifice with harlots: therefore the
people *that* doth not understand shall fall.
15 Though thou, Israel, play the harlot, *yet* let not
Judah offend; and come not ye unto Gilgal, neither
go ye up to Beth-aven, nor swear, The LORD liveth.
16 For Israel slideth back as a backsliding heifer:
now the LORD will feed them as a lamb in a large
place.
17 Ephraim *is* joined to idols: let him alone.
18 Their drink is sour: they have committed whoredom continually: her rulers *with* shame do love,
Give ye.
19 The wind hath bound her up in her wings, and
they shall be ashamed because of their sacrifices.

5 1 Hear ye this, O priests; and hearken, ye house
of Israel; and give ye ear, O house of the king;

NEW LIVING TRANSLATION

8 "When the people bring their sin offerings,
the priests get fed.
So the priests are glad when the people sin!
9 'And what the priests do, the people also do.'
So now I will punish both priests and people
for their wicked deeds.
10 They will eat and still be hungry.
They will play the prostitute and gain
nothing from it,
for they have deserted the LORD
11 to worship other gods.

"Wine has robbed my people
of their understanding.
12 They ask a piece of wood for advice!
They think a stick can tell them the future!
Longing after idols
has made them foolish.
They have played the prostitute,
serving other gods and deserting their God.
13 They offer sacrifices to idols on the mountaintops.
They go up into the hills to burn incense
in the pleasant shade of oaks, poplars, and
terebinth trees.

"That is why your daughters turn to prostitution,
and your daughters-in-law commit adultery.
14 But why should I punish them
for their prostitution and adultery?
For your men are doing the same thing,
sinning with whores and shrine prostitutes.
O foolish people! You refuse to understand,
so you will be destroyed.

15 "Though you, Israel, are a prostitute,
may Judah avoid such guilt.
Do not join the false worship at Gilgal
or Beth-aven,*
even though they take oaths there in the
LORD's name.
16 Israel is stubborn,
like a stubborn heifer.
So should the LORD feed her
like a lamb in a lush pasture?
17 Leave Israel* alone,
because she is married to idolatry.
18 When the rulers of Israel finish their drinking,
off they go to find some prostitutes.
They love shame more than honor.*
19 So a mighty wind will sweep them away.
Their sacrifices to idols will bring them shame.

The Failure of Israel's Leaders

5 1 "Hear this, you priests.
Pay attention, you leaders of Israel.
Listen, you members of the royal family.
Judgment has been handed down against you.

4:15 *Beth-aven* means "house of wickedness"; it is being used as another name for Bethel, which means "house of God." **4:17** Hebrew *Ephraim*, referring to the northern kingdom of Israel. **4:18** As in Greek version; the meaning of the Hebrew is uncertain.

KING JAMES VERSION

for judgment *is* toward you, because ye have been a
snare on Mizpah, and a net spread upon Tabor.
2 And the revolters are profound to make slaughter, though I *have been* a rebuker of them all.
3 I know Ephraim, and Israel is not hid from me: for
now, O Ephraim, thou committest whoredom, *and*
Israel is defiled.
4 They will not frame their doings to turn unto
their God: for the spirit of whoredoms *is* in the midst
of them, and they have not known the LORD.
5 And the pride of Israel doth testify to his face:
therefore shall Israel and Ephraim fall in their iniquity; Judah also shall fall with them.
6 They shall go with their flocks and with their
herds to seek the LORD; but they shall not find *him;*
he hath withdrawn himself from them.
7 They have dealt treacherously against the LORD:
for they have begotten strange children: now shall a
month devour them with their portions.
8 Blow ye the cornet in Gibeah, *and* the trumpet
in Ramah: cry aloud *at* Beth-aven, after thee, O Benjamin.
9 Ephraim shall be desolate in the day of rebuke:
among the tribes of Israel have I made known that
which shall surely be.
10 The princes of Judah were like them that remove
the bound: *therefore* I will pour out my wrath upon
them like water.
11 Ephraim *is* oppressed *and* broken in judgment,
because he willingly walked after the commandment.
12 Therefore *will* I *be* unto Ephraim as a moth, and
to the house of Judah as rottenness.
13 When Ephraim saw his sickness, and Judah *saw*
his wound, then went Ephraim to the Assyrian, and
sent to king Jareb: yet could he not heal you, nor cure
you of your wound.
14 For I *will be* unto Ephraim as a lion, and as a
young lion to the house of Judah: I, *even* I, will tear
and go away; I will take away, and none shall rescue
him.

NEW LIVING TRANSLATION

For you have led the people into a snare
by worshiping the idols at Mizpah and Tabor.
2 You have dug a deep pit to trap them at
Acacia Grove.*
But I will settle with you for what you
have done.
3 I know what you are like, O Ephraim.
You cannot hide yourself from me, O Israel.
You have left me as a prostitute leaves
her husband;
you are utterly defiled.
4 Your deeds won't let you return to your God.
You are a prostitute through and through,
and you do not know the LORD.

5 "The arrogance of Israel testifies against her;
Israel and Ephraim will stumble under their
load of guilt.
Judah, too, will fall with them.
6 When they come with their flocks and herds
to offer sacrifices to the LORD,
they will not find him,
because he has withdrawn from them.
7 They have betrayed the honor of the LORD,
bearing children that are not his.
Now their false religion will devour them
along with their wealth.*

8 "Sound the alarm in Gibeah!
Blow the trumpet in Ramah!
Raise the battle cry in Beth-aven*!
Lead on into battle, O warriors of Benjamin!
9 One thing is certain, Israel*:
On your day of punishment,
you will become a heap of rubble.

10 "The leaders of Judah have become like thieves.*
So I will pour my anger on them like
a waterfall.
11 The people of Israel will be crushed and broken
by my judgment
because they are determined to worship
idols.*
12 I will destroy Israel as a moth consumes wool.
I will make Judah as weak as rotten wood.

13 "When Israel and Judah saw how sick they were,
Israel turned to Assyria—
to the great king there—
but he could neither help nor cure them.
14 I will be like a lion to Israel,
like a strong young lion to Judah.
I will tear them to pieces!
I will carry them off,
and no one will be left to rescue them.

5:2 Hebrew *at Shittim.* The meaning of the Hebrew for this sentence is uncertain. **5:7** The meaning of the Hebrew is uncertain. **5:8** *Beth-aven* means "house of wickedness"; it is being used as another name for Bethel, which means "house of God." **5:9** Hebrew *Ephraim,* referring to the northern kingdom of Israel; also in 5:11, 12, 13, 14. **5:10** Hebrew *like those who move a boundary marker.* **5:11** Or *determined to follow human commands.* The meaning of the Hebrew is uncertain.

KING JAMES VERSION

15 I will go *and* return to my place, till they acknowledge their offence, and seek my face: in their
affliction they will seek me early.

6 1 Come, and let us return unto the LORD: for he
hath torn, and he will heal us; he hath smitten,
and he will bind us up.
2 After two days will he revive us: in the third day
he will raise us up, and we shall live in his sight.
3 Then shall we know, *if* we follow on to know the
LORD: his going forth is prepared as the morning; and
he shall come unto us as the rain, as the latter *and*
former rain unto the earth.
4 O Ephraim, what shall I do unto thee? O Judah,
what shall I do unto thee? for your goodness *is* as a
morning cloud, and as the early dew it goeth away.
5 Therefore have I hewed *them* by the prophets; I
have slain them by the words of my mouth: and thy
judgments *are as* the light *that* goeth forth.
6 For I desired mercy, and not sacrifice; and the
knowledge of God more than burnt offerings.
7 But they like men have transgressed the covenant:
there have they dealt treacherously against me.
8 Gilead *is* a city of them that work iniquity, *and is*
polluted with blood.
9 And as troops of robbers wait for a man, *so* the
company of priests murder in the way by consent:
for they commit lewdness.
10 I have seen an horrible thing in the house of
Israel: there *is* the whoredom of Ephraim, Israel is
defiled.
11 Also, O Judah, he hath set an harvest for thee,
when I returned the captivity of my people.

7 1 When I would have healed Israel, then the
iniquity of Ephraim was discovered, and the
wickedness of Samaria: for they commit falsehood;
and the thief cometh in, *and* the troop of robbers
spoileth without.
2 And they consider not in their hearts *that* I

NEW LIVING TRANSLATION

15 Then I will return to my place
until they admit their guilt and turn to me.
For as soon as trouble comes,
they will earnestly search for me."

A Call to Repentance

6 1 "Come, let us return to the LORD.
He has torn us to pieces;
now he will heal us.
He has injured us;
now he will bandage our wounds.
2 In just a short time he will restore us,
so that we may live in his presence.
3 Oh, that we might know the LORD!
Let us press on to know him.
He will respond to us as surely as the arrival
of dawn
or the coming of rains in early spring."

4 "O Israel* and Judah,
what should I do with you?" asks the LORD.
"For your love vanishes like the morning mist
and disappears like dew in the sunlight.
5 I sent my prophets to cut you to pieces—
to slaughter you with my words,
with judgments as inescapable as light.
6 I want you to show love,*
not offer sacrifices.
I want you to know me*
more than I want burnt offerings.
7 But like Adam,* you broke my covenant
and betrayed my trust.
8 "Gilead is a city of sinners,
tracked with footprints of blood.
9 Priests form bands of robbers,
waiting in ambush for their victims.
They murder travelers along the road to Shechem
and practice every kind of sin.
10 Yes, I have seen something horrible in Ephraim
and Israel:
My people are defiled by prostituting
themselves with other gods!

11 "O Judah, a harvest of punishment is also
waiting for you,
though I wanted to restore the fortunes
of my people.

Israel's Love for Wickedness

7 1 "I want to heal Israel,* but its sins are too great.
Samaria is filled with liars.
Thieves are on the inside
and bandits on the outside!
2 Its people don't realize
that I am watching them.

6:4 Hebrew *Ephraim,* referring to the northern kingdom of Israel.
6:6a Greek version translates this Hebrew term as *to show mercy.* Compare Matt 9:13; 12:7. **6:6b** Hebrew *to know God.* **6:7** Or *But at Adam.*
7:1 Hebrew *Ephraim,* referring to the northern kingdom of Israel; also in 7:8, 11.

KING JAMES VERSION

remember all their wickedness: now their own doings have beset them about; they are before my face.
3 They make the king glad with their wickedness,
and the princes with their lies.
4 They *are* all adulterers, as an oven heated by the
baker, *who* ceaseth from raising after he hath
kneaded the dough, until it be leavened.
5 In the day of our king the princes have made *him*
sick with bottles of wine; he stretched out his hand
with scorners.
6 For they have made ready their heart like an oven,
whiles they lie in wait: their baker sleepeth all the
night; in the morning it burneth as a flaming fire.
7 They are all hot as an oven, and have devoured
their judges; all their kings are fallen: *there is* none
among them that calleth unto me.
8 Ephraim, he hath mixed himself among the
people; Ephraim is a cake not turned.
9 Strangers have devoured his strength, and he
knoweth *it* not: yea, gray hairs are here and there
upon him, yet he knoweth not.
10 And the pride of Israel testifieth to his face: and
they do not return to the LORD their God, nor seek
him for all this.
11 Ephraim also is like a silly dove without heart:
they call to Egypt, they go to Assyria.
12 When they shall go, I will spread my net upon
them; I will bring them down as the fowls of the
heaven; I will chastise them, as their congregation
hath heard.
13 Woe unto them! for they have fled from me: destruction unto them! because they have transgressed
against me: though I have redeemed them, yet they
have spoken lies against me.
14 And they have not cried unto me with their
heart, when they howled upon their beds: they assemble themselves for corn and wine, *and* they rebel
against me.
15 Though I have bound *and* strengthened their
arms, yet do they imagine mischief against me.
16 They return, *but* not to the most High: they are

NEW LIVING TRANSLATION

Their sinful deeds are all around them,
and I see them all.

3 "The people entertain the king with their
wickedness,
and the princes laugh at their lies.
4 They are all adulterers,
always aflame with lust.
They are like an oven that is kept hot
while the baker is kneading the dough.
5 On royal holidays, the princes get drunk
with wine,
carousing with those who mock them.
6 Their hearts are like an oven
blazing with intrigue.
Their plot smolders* through the night,
and in the morning it breaks out like
a raging fire.
7 Burning like an oven,
they consume their leaders.
They kill their kings one after another,
and no one cries to me for help.
8 "The people of Israel mingle with godless
foreigners,
making themselves as worthless as
a half-baked cake!
9 Worshiping foreign gods has sapped
their strength,
but they don't even know it.
Their hair is gray,
but they don't realize they're old and weak.
10 Their arrogance testifies against them,
yet they don't return to the LORD their God
or even try to find him.

11 "The people of Israel have become like silly,
witless doves,
first calling to Egypt, then flying to Assyria
for help.
12 But as they fly about,
I will throw my net over them
and bring them down like a bird from the sky.
I will punish them for all the evil they do.*

13 "What sorrow awaits those who have deserted me!
Let them die, for they have rebelled against me.
I wanted to redeem them,
but they have told lies about me.
14 They do not cry out to me with sincere hearts.
Instead, they sit on their couches and wail.
They cut themselves,* begging foreign gods for
grain and new wine,
and they turn away from me.
15 I trained them and made them strong,
yet now they plot evil against me.
16 They look everywhere except to the Most High.
They are as useless as a crooked bow.

7:6 Hebrew *Their baker sleeps.* **7:12** Hebrew *I will punish them because of what was reported against them in the assembly.* **7:14** As in Greek version; Hebrew reads *They gather together.*

KING JAMES VERSION

like a deceitful bow: their princes shall fall by the
sword for the rage of their tongue: this *shall be* their
derision in the land of Egypt.

8 1 *Set* the trumpet to thy mouth. *He shall come* as
an eagle against the house of the LORD, because
they have transgressed my covenant, and trespassed
against my law.
2 Israel shall cry unto me, My God, we know thee.
3 Israel hath cast off *the thing that is* good: the enemy shall pursue him.
4 They have set up kings, but not by me: they have
made princes, and I knew *it* not: of their silver and
their gold have they made them idols, that they may
be cut off.
5 Thy calf, O Samaria, hath cast *thee* off; mine anger is kindled against them: how long *will it be* ere
they attain to innocency?
6 For from Israel *was* it also: the workman made it;
therefore it *is* not God: but the calf of Samaria shall
be broken in pieces.
7 For they have sown the wind, and they shall reap
the whirlwind: it hath no stalk: the bud shall yield
no meal: if so be it yield, the strangers shall swallow
it up.
8 Israel is swallowed up: now shall they be among
the Gentiles as a vessel wherein *is* no pleasure.
9 For they are gone up to Assyria, a wild ass alone
by himself: Ephraim hath hired lovers.
10 Yea, though they have hired among the nations,
now will I gather them, and they shall sorrow a little
for the burden of the king of princes.
11 Because Ephraim hath made many altars to sin,
altars shall be unto him to sin.
12 I have written to him the great things of my law,
but they were counted as a strange thing.
13 They sacrifice flesh *for* the sacrifices of mine
offerings, and eat *it; but* the LORD accepteth them

NEW LIVING TRANSLATION

Their leaders will be killed by their enemies
because of their insolence toward me.
Then the people of Egypt
will laugh at them.

Israel Harvests the Whirlwind

8 1 "Sound the alarm!
The enemy descends like an eagle
on the people of the LORD,
for they have broken my covenant
and revolted against my law.
2 Now Israel pleads with me,
'Help us, for you are our God!'
3 But it is too late.
The people of Israel have rejected what is good,
and now their enemies will chase after them.
4 The people have appointed kings without
my consent,
and princes without my knowledge.
By making idols for themselves from their
silver and gold,
they have brought about their own destruction.

5 "O Samaria, I reject this calf—
this idol you have made.
My fury burns against you.
How long will you be incapable of innocence?
6 This calf you worship, O Israel,
was crafted by your own hands!
It is not God!
Therefore, it must be smashed to bits.

7 "They have planted the wind
and will harvest the whirlwind.
The stalks of grain wither
and produce nothing to eat.
And even if there is any grain,
foreigners will eat it.
8 The people of Israel have been swallowed up;
they lie among the nations like an old
discarded pot.
9 Like a wild donkey looking for a mate,
they have gone up to Assyria.
The people of Israel* have sold themselves—
sold themselves to many lovers.
10 But though they have sold themselves to
many allies,
I will now gather them together for judgment.
Then they will writhe
under the burden of the great king.

11 "Israel has built many altars to take away sin,
but these very altars became places for
sinning!
12 Even though I gave them all my laws,
they act as if those laws don't apply to them.
13 The people of Israel love their rituals of sacrifice,
but to me their sacrifices are all meaningless.

8:9 Hebrew *Ephraim*, referring to the northern kingdom of Israel;
also in 8:11.

KING JAMES VERSION

not; now will he remember their iniquity, and visit
their sins: they shall return to Egypt.
14 For Israel hath forgotten his Maker, and buildeth
temples; and Judah hath multiplied fenced cities:
but I will send a fire upon his cities, and it shall devour the palaces thereof.

9 1 Rejoice not, O Israel, for joy, as *other* people:
for thou hast gone a whoring from thy God,
thou hast loved a reward upon every cornfloor.
2 The floor and the winepress shall not feed them,
and the new wine shall fail in her.
3 They shall not dwell in the LORD's land; but
Ephraim shall return to Egypt, and they shall eat unclean *things* in Assyria.
4 They shall not offer wine *offerings* to the LORD,
neither shall they be pleasing unto him: their sacrifices *shall be* unto them as the bread of mourners; all
that eat thereof shall be polluted: for their bread for
their soul shall not come into the house of the LORD.
5 What will ye do in the solemn day, and in the day
of the feast of the LORD?
6 For, lo, they are gone because of destruction:
Egypt shall gather them up, Memphis shall bury
them: the pleasant *places* for their silver, nettles shall
possess them: thorns *shall be* in their tabernacles.
7 The days of visitation are come, the days of
recompence are come; Israel shall know *it:* the
prophet *is* a fool, the spiritual man *is* mad, for the
multitude of thine iniquity, and the great hatred.
8 The watchman of Ephraim *was* with my God: *but*
the prophet *is* a snare of a fowler in all his ways, *and*
hatred in the house of his God.
9 They have deeply corrupted *themselves,* as in the
days of Gibeah: *therefore* he will remember their
iniquity, he will visit their sins.
10 I found Israel like grapes in the wilderness; I saw
your fathers as the firstripe in the fig tree at her first

NEW LIVING TRANSLATION

I will hold my people accountable for their sins,
and I will punish them.
They will return to Egypt.
14 Israel has forgotten its Maker and built
great palaces,
and Judah has fortified its cities.
Therefore, I will send down fire on their cities
and will burn up their fortresses."

Hosea Announces Israel's Punishment

9 1 O people of Israel,
do not rejoice as other nations do.
For you have been unfaithful to your God,
hiring yourselves out like prostitutes,
worshiping other gods on every threshing floor.
2 So now your harvests will be too small to feed you.
There will be no grapes for making new wine.
3 You may no longer stay here in the LORD's land.
Instead, you will return to Egypt,
and in Assyria you will eat food
that is ceremonially unclean.
4 There you will make no offerings of wine
to the LORD.
None of your sacrifices there will please him.
They will be unclean, like food touched by a
person in mourning.
All who present such sacrifices will be defiled.
They may eat this food themselves,
but they may not offer it to the LORD.
5 What then will you do on festival days?
How will you observe the LORD's festivals?
6 Even if you escape destruction from Assyria,
Egypt will conquer you, and Memphis* will
bury you.
Nettles will take over your treasures of silver;
thistles will invade your ruined homes.

7 The time of Israel's punishment has come;
the day of payment is here.
Soon Israel will know this all too well.
Because of your great sin and hostility,
you say, "The prophets are crazy
and the inspired men are fools!"
8 The prophet is a watchman over Israel*
for my God,
yet traps are laid for him wherever he goes.
He faces hostility even in the house of God.
9 The things my people do are as depraved
as what they did in Gibeah long ago.
God will not forget.
He will surely punish them for their sins.

10 The LORD says, "O Israel, when I first found you,
it was like finding fresh grapes in the desert.
When I saw your ancestors,
it was like seeing the first ripe figs
of the season.

9:6 Memphis was the capital of northern Egypt. **9:8** Hebrew *Ephraim,* referring to the northern kingdom of Israel; also in 9:11, 13, 16.

KING JAMES VERSION

time: *but* they went to Baal-peor, and separated themselves unto *that* shame; and *their* abominations were according as they loved.

11 *As for* Ephraim, their glory shall fly away like a bird, from the birth, and from the womb, and from the conception.

12 Though they bring up their children, yet will I bereave them, *that there shall* not *be* a man *left:* yea, woe also to them when I depart from them!

13 Ephraim, as I saw Tyrus, *is* planted in a pleasant place: but Ephraim shall bring forth his children to the murderer.

14 Give them, O LORD: what wilt thou give? give them a miscarrying womb and dry breasts.

15 All their wickedness *is* in Gilgal: for there I hated them: for the wickedness of their doings I will drive them out of mine house, I will love them no more: all their princes *are* revolters.

16 Ephraim is smitten, their root is dried up, they shall bear no fruit: yea, though they bring forth, yet will I slay *even* the beloved *fruit* of their womb.

17 My God will cast them away, because they did not hearken unto him: and they shall be wanderers among the nations.

10 1 Israel *is* an empty vine, he bringeth forth fruit unto himself: according to the multitude of his fruit he hath increased the altars; according to the goodness of his land they have made goodly images.

2 Their heart is divided; now shall they be found faulty: he shall break down their altars, he shall spoil their images.

3 For now they shall say, We have no king, because we feared not the LORD; what then should a king do to us?

4 They have spoken words, swearing falsely in making a covenant: thus judgment springeth up as hemlock in the furrows of the field.

NEW LIVING TRANSLATION

But then they deserted me for Baal-peor,
giving themselves to that shameful idol.
Soon they became vile,
as vile as the god they worshiped.
11 The glory of Israel will fly away like a bird,
for your children will not be born
or grow in the womb
or even be conceived.
12 Even if you do have children who grow up,
I will take them from you.
It will be a terrible day when I turn away
and leave you alone.
13 I have watched Israel become as beautiful as Tyre.
But now Israel will bring out her children
for slaughter."

14 O LORD, what should I request for your people?
I will ask for wombs that don't give birth
and breasts that give no milk.
15 The LORD says, "All their wickedness began
at Gilgal;
there I began to hate them.
I will drive them from my land
because of their evil actions.
I will love them no more
because all their leaders are rebels.
16 The people of Israel are struck down.
Their roots are dried up,
and they will bear no more fruit.
And if they give birth,
I will slaughter their beloved children."
17 My God will reject the people of Israel
because they will not listen or obey.
They will be wanderers,
homeless among the nations.

The LORD's Judgment against Israel

10 1 How prosperous Israel is—
a luxuriant vine loaded with fruit.
But the richer the people get,
the more pagan altars they build.
The more bountiful their harvests,
the more beautiful their sacred pillars.
2 The hearts of the people are fickle;
they are guilty and must be punished.
The LORD will break down their altars
and smash their sacred pillars.
3 Then they will say, "We have no king
because we didn't fear the LORD.
But even if we had a king,
what could he do for us anyway?"
4 They spout empty words
and make covenants they don't intend
to keep.
So injustice springs up among them
like poisonous weeds in a farmer's field.

KING JAMES VERSION

[5]The inhabitants of Samaria shall fear because of
the calves of Beth-aven: for the people thereof shall
mourn over it, and the priests thereof *that* rejoiced
on it, for the glory thereof, because it is departed
from it.
[6]It shall be also carried unto Assyria *for* a present
to king Jareb: Ephraim shall receive shame, and Israel shall be ashamed of his own counsel.
[7]*As for* Samaria, her king is cut off as the foam
upon the water.
[8]The high places also of Aven, the sin of Israel,
shall be destroyed: the thorn and the thistle shall
come up on their altars; and they shall say to the
mountains, Cover us; and to the hills, Fall on us.
[9]O Israel, thou hast sinned from the days of Gibeah: there they stood: the battle in Gibeah against the
children of iniquity did not overtake them.
[10]*It is* in my desire that I should chastise them; and
the people shall be gathered against them, when they
shall bind themselves in their two furrows.
[11]And Ephraim *is as* an heifer *that is* taught, *and*
loveth to tread out *the corn;* but I passed over upon
her fair neck: I will make Ephraim to ride; Judah shall
plow, *and* Jacob shall break his clods.
[12]Sow to yourselves in righteousness, reap in
mercy; break up your fallow ground: for *it is* time to
seek the LORD, till he come and rain righteousness
upon you.
[13]Ye have plowed wickedness, ye have reaped iniquity; ye have eaten the fruit of lies: because thou
didst trust in thy way, in the multitude of thy mighty
men.
[14]Therefore shall a tumult arise among thy people,
and all thy fortresses shall be spoiled, as Shalman
spoiled Beth-arbel in the day of battle: the mother
was dashed in pieces upon *her* children.

NEW LIVING TRANSLATION

[5] The people of Samaria tremble in fear
for what might happen to their calf idol
at Beth-aven.*
The people mourn and the priests wail,
because its glory will be stripped away.*
[6] This idol will be carted away to Assyria,
a gift to the great king there.
Ephraim will be ridiculed and Israel will
be shamed,
because its people have trusted in this idol.
[7] Samaria and its king will be cut off;
they will float away like driftwood on an
ocean wave.
[8] And the pagan shrines of Aven,* the place
of Israel's sin, will crumble.
Thorns and thistles will grow up around
their altars.
They will beg the mountains, "Bury us!"
and plead with the hills, "Fall on us!"

[9] The LORD says, "O Israel, ever since Gibeah,
there has been only sin and more sin!
You have made no progress whatsoever.
Was it not right that the wicked men of Gibeah
were attacked?
[10] Now whenever it fits my plan,
I will attack you, too.
I will call out the armies of the nations
to punish you for your multiplied sins.

[11] "Israel* is like a trained heifer treading out
the grain—
an easy job she loves.
But I will put a heavy yoke on her tender neck.
I will force Judah to pull the plow
and Israel* to break up the hard ground.
[12] I said, 'Plant the good seeds of righteousness,
and you will harvest a crop of love.
Plow up the hard ground of your hearts,
for now is the time to seek the LORD,
that he may come
and shower righteousness upon you.'

[13] "But you have cultivated wickedness
and harvested a thriving crop of sins.
You have eaten the fruit of lies—
trusting in your military might,
believing that great armies
could make your nation safe.
[14] Now the terrors of war
will rise among your people.
All your fortifications will fall,
just as when Shalman destroyed Beth-arbel.
Even mothers and children
were dashed to death there.

10:5a *Beth-aven* means "house of wickedness"; it is being used as another name for Bethel, which means "house of God." **10:5b** Or *will be taken away into exile.* **10:8** *Aven* is a reference to Beth-aven; see 10:5a and the note there. **10:11a** Hebrew *Ephraim,* referring to the northern kingdom of Israel. **10:11b** Hebrew *Jacob.* The names "Jacob" and "Israel" are often interchanged throughout the Old Testament, referring sometimes to the individual patriarch and sometimes to the nation.

KING JAMES VERSION

15 So shall Bethel do unto you because of your
great wickedness: in a morning shall the king of Israel utterly be cut off.

11

1 When Israel *was* a child, then I loved him,
and called my son out of Egypt.
2 *As* they called them, so they went from them: they
sacrificed unto Baalim, and burned incense to
graven images.
3 I taught Ephraim also to go, taking them by their
arms; but they knew not that I healed them.
4 I drew them with cords of a man, with bands of
love: and I was to them as they that take off the yoke
on their jaws, and I laid meat unto them.
5 He shall not return into the land of Egypt, but the
Assyrian shall be his king, because they refused to
return.
6 And the sword shall abide on his cities, and shall
consume his branches, and devour *them*, because of
their own counsels.
7 And my people are bent to backsliding from me:
though they called them to the most High, none at all
would exalt *him*.
8 How shall I give thee up, Ephraim? *how* shall I
deliver thee, Israel? how shall I make thee as Admah?
how shall I set thee as Zeboim? mine heart is turned
within me, my repentings are kindled together.
9 I will not execute the fierceness of mine anger, I
will not return to destroy Ephraim: for I *am* God, and
not man; the Holy One in the midst of thee: and I will
not enter into the city.
10 They shall walk after the LORD: he shall roar like
a lion: when he shall roar, then the children shall
tremble from the west.
11 They shall tremble as a bird out of Egypt, and as
a dove out of the land of Assyria: and I will place
them in their houses, saith the LORD.

NEW LIVING TRANSLATION

15 You will share that fate, Bethel,
because of your great wickedness.
When the day of judgment dawns,
the king of Israel will be completely
destroyed.

The LORD's Love for Israel

11

1 "When Israel was a child, I loved him,
and I called my son out of Egypt.
2 But the more I* called to him,
the farther he moved from me,
offering sacrifices to the images of Baal
and burning incense to idols.
3 I myself taught Israel* how to walk,
leading him along by the hand.
But he doesn't know or even care
that it was I who took care of him.
4 I led Israel along
with my ropes of kindness and love.
I lifted the yoke from his neck,
and I myself stooped to feed him.

5 "But since my people refuse to return to me,
they will return to Egypt
and will be forced to serve Assyria.
6 War will swirl through their cities;
their enemies will crash through their gates.
They will destroy them,
trapping them in their own evil plans.
7 For my people are determined to desert me.
They call me the Most High,
but they don't truly honor me.

8 "Oh, how can I give you up, Israel?
How can I let you go?
How can I destroy you like Admah
or demolish you like Zeboiim?
My heart is torn within me,
and my compassion overflows.
9 No, I will not unleash my fierce anger.
I will not completely destroy Israel,
for I am God and not a mere mortal.
I am the Holy One living among you,
and I will not come to destroy.
10 For someday the people will follow me.
I, the LORD, will roar like a lion.
And when I roar,
my people will return trembling from
the west.
11 Like a flock of birds, they will come
from Egypt.
Trembling like doves, they will return
from Assyria.
And I will bring them home again,"
says the LORD.

11:2 As in Greek version; Hebrew reads *they*. **11:3** Hebrew *Ephraim*, referring to the northern kingdom of Israel; also in 11:8, 9, 12.

KING JAMES VERSION

12 Ephraim compasseth me about with lies, and
the house of Israel with deceit: but Judah yet ruleth
with God, and is faithful with the saints.

12

1 Ephraim feedeth on wind, and followeth
after the east wind: he daily increaseth lies
and desolation; and they do make a covenant with
the Assyrians, and oil is carried into Egypt.
2 The LORD hath also a controversy with Judah, and
will punish Jacob according to his ways; according to
his doings will he recompense him.
3 He took his brother by the heel in the womb, and
by his strength he had power with God:
4 Yea, he had power over the angel, and prevailed:
he wept, and made supplication unto him: he found
him *in* Bethel, and there he spake with us;
5 Even the LORD God of hosts; the LORD *is* his
memorial.
6 Therefore turn thou to thy God: keep mercy and
judgment, and wait on thy God continually.
7 *He is* a merchant, the balances of deceit *are* in his
hand: he loveth to oppress.
8 And Ephraim said, Yet I am become rich, I have
found me out substance: *in* all my labours they shall
find none iniquity in me that *were* sin.
9 And I *that am* the LORD thy God from the land of
Egypt will yet make thee to dwell in tabernacles, as
in the days of the solemn feast.
10 I have also spoken by the prophets, and I have
multiplied visions, and used similitudes, by the ministry of the prophets.
11 *Is there* iniquity *in* Gilead? surely they are vanity:
they sacrifice bullocks in Gilgal; yea, their altars *are*
as heaps in the furrows of the fields.

NEW LIVING TRANSLATION

Charges against Israel and Judah

12* Israel surrounds me with lies and deceit,
but Judah still obeys God
and is faithful to the Holy One.*

12

1* The people of Israel* feed on the wind;
they chase after the east wind all
day long.
They pile up lies and violence;
they are making an alliance with Assyria
while sending olive oil to buy support
from Egypt.

2 Now the LORD is bringing charges against Judah.
He is about to punish Jacob* for all his
deceitful ways,
and pay him back for all he has done.
3 Even in the womb,
Jacob struggled with his brother;
when he became a man,
he even fought with God.
4 Yes, he wrestled with the angel and won.
He wept and pleaded for a blessing
from him.
There at Bethel he met God face to face,
and God spoke to him*—
5 the LORD God of Heaven's Armies,
the LORD is his name!
6 So now, come back to your God.
Act with love and justice,
and always depend on him.

7 But no, the people are like crafty merchants
selling from dishonest scales—
they love to cheat.
8 Israel boasts, "I am rich!
I've made a fortune all by myself!
No one has caught me cheating!
My record is spotless!"
9 "But I am the LORD your God,
who rescued you from slavery in Egypt.
And I will make you live in tents again,
as you do each year at the Festival
of Shelters.*
10 I sent my prophets to warn you
with many visions and parables."
11 But the people of Gilead are worthless
because of their idol worship.
And in Gilgal, too, they sacrifice bulls;
their altars are lined up like the
heaps of stone
along the edges of a plowed field.

11:12a Verse 11:12 is numbered 12:1 in Hebrew text. **11:12b** Or *and Judah is unruly against God, the faithful Holy One.* The meaning of the Hebrew is uncertain. **12:1a** Verses 12:1-14 are numbered 12:2-15 in Hebrew text. **12:1b** Hebrew *Ephraim,* referring to the northern kingdom of Israel; also in 12:8, 14. **12:2** *Jacob* sounds like the Hebrew word for "deceiver." **12:4** As in Greek and Syriac versions; Hebrew reads *to us.* **12:9** Hebrew *as in the days of your appointed feast.*

KING JAMES VERSION

[12]And Jacob fled into the country of Syria, and Israel served for a wife, and for a wife he kept *sheep.*
[13]And by a prophet the LORD brought Israel out of Egypt, and by a prophet was he preserved.
[14]Ephraim provoked *him* to anger most bitterly: therefore shall he leave his blood upon him, and his reproach shall his Lord return unto him.

13 [1]When Ephraim spake trembling, he exalted himself in Israel; but when he offended in Baal, he died.
[2]And now they sin more and more, and have made them molten images of their silver, *and* idols according to their own understanding, all of it the work of the craftsmen: they say of them, Let the men that sacrifice kiss the calves.
[3]Therefore they shall be as the morning cloud, and as the early dew that passeth away, as the chaff *that* is driven with the whirlwind out of the floor, and as the smoke out of the chimney.
[4]Yet I *am* the LORD thy God from the land of Egypt, and thou shalt know no god but me: for *there is* no saviour beside me.
[5]I did know thee in the wilderness, in the land of great drought.
[6]According to their pasture, so were they filled; they were filled, and their heart was exalted; therefore have they forgotten me.
[7]Therefore I will be unto them as a lion: as a leopard by the way will I observe *them:*
[8]I will meet them as a bear *that is* bereaved *of her whelps,* and will rend the caul of their heart, and there will I devour them like a lion: the wild beast shall tear them.
[9]O Israel, thou hast destroyed thyself; but in me *is* thine help.
[10]I will be thy king: where *is any other* that may save thee in all thy cities? and thy judges of whom thou saidst, Give me a king and princes?
[11]I gave thee a king in mine anger, and took *him* away in my wrath.
[12]The iniquity of Ephraim *is* bound up; his sin *is* hid.

NEW LIVING TRANSLATION

[12] Jacob fled to the land of Aram,
and there he* earned a wife by tending sheep.
[13] Then by a prophet
the LORD brought Jacob's descendants*
out of Egypt;
and by that prophet
they were protected.
[14] But the people of Israel
have bitterly provoked the LORD,
so their Lord will now sentence them to death
in payment for their sins.

The LORD's Anger against Israel

13 [1]When the tribe of Ephraim spoke,
the people shook with fear,
for that tribe was important in Israel.
But the people of Ephraim sinned by
worshiping Baal
and thus sealed their destruction.
[2] Now they continue to sin by making silver idols,
images shaped skillfully with human hands.
"Sacrifice to these," they cry,
"and kiss the calf idols!"
[3] Therefore, they will disappear like the
morning mist,
like dew in the morning sun,
like chaff blown by the wind,
like smoke from a chimney.

[4] "I have been the LORD your God
ever since I brought you out of Egypt.
You must acknowledge no God but me,
for there is no other savior.
[5] I took care of you in the wilderness,
in that dry and thirsty land.
[6] But when you had eaten and were satisfied,
you became proud and forgot me.
[7] So now I will attack you like a lion,
like a leopard that lurks along the road.
[8] Like a bear whose cubs have been taken away,
I will tear out your heart.
I will devour you like a hungry lioness
and mangle you like a wild animal.

[9] "You are about to be destroyed, O Israel—
yes, by me, your only helper.
[10] Now where is* your king?
Let him save you!
Where are all the leaders of the land,
the king and the officials you demanded
of me?
[11] In my anger I gave you kings,
and in my fury I took them away.

[12] "Ephraim's guilt has been collected,
and his sin has been stored up for punishment.

12:12 Hebrew *Israel.* See note on 10:11b. **12:13** Hebrew *brought Israel.* See note on 10:11b. **13:10** As in Greek and Syriac versions and Latin Vulgate; Hebrew reads *I will be.*

KING JAMES VERSION

[13]The sorrows of a travailing woman shall come
upon him: he *is* an unwise son; for he should not stay
long in *the place of* the breaking forth of children.
[14]I will ransom them from the power of the grave;
I will redeem them from death: O death, I will be thy
plagues; O grave, I will be thy destruction: repentance shall be hid from mine eyes.
[15]Though he be fruitful among *his* brethren, an
east wind shall come, the wind of the LORD shall
come up from the wilderness, and his spring shall
become dry, and his fountain shall be dried up: he
shall spoil the treasure of all pleasant vessels.
[16]Samaria shall become desolate; for she hath rebelled against her God: they shall fall by the sword:
their infants shall be dashed in pieces, and their
women with child shall be ripped up.

NEW LIVING TRANSLATION

13 Pain has come to the people
like the pain of childbirth,
but they are like a child
who resists being born.
The moment of birth has arrived,
but they stay in the womb!
14 "Should I ransom them from the grave*?
Should I redeem them from death?
O death, bring on your terrors!
O grave, bring on your plagues!*
For I will not take pity on them.
15 Ephraim was the most fruitful of all his brothers,
but the east wind—a blast from the LORD—
will arise in the desert.
All their flowing springs will run dry,
and all their wells will disappear.
Every precious thing they own
will be plundered and carried away.
16 *The people of Samaria
must bear the consequences of their guilt
because they rebelled against their God.
They will be killed by an invading army,
their little ones dashed to death against
the ground,
their pregnant women ripped open
by swords."

14 [1]O Israel, return unto the LORD thy God; for
thou hast fallen by thine iniquity.
[2]Take with you words, and turn to the LORD: say
unto him, Take away all iniquity, and receive *us* graciously: so will we render the calves of our lips.
[3]Asshur shall not save us; we will not ride upon
horses: neither will we say any more to the work of
our hands, *Ye are* our gods: for in thee the fatherless
findeth mercy.
[4]I will heal their backsliding, I will love them
freely: for mine anger is turned away from him.
[5]I will be as the dew unto Israel: he shall grow as
the lily, and cast forth his roots as Lebanon.
[6]His branches shall spread, and his beauty shall be
as the olive tree, and his smell as Lebanon.

Healing for the Repentant

14 1 *Return, O Israel, to the LORD your God,
for your sins have brought you down.
2 Bring your confessions, and return to the LORD.
Say to him,
"Forgive all our sins and graciously receive us,
so that we may offer you our praises.*
3 Assyria cannot save us,
nor can our warhorses.
Never again will we say to the idols we
have made,
'You are our gods.'
No, in you alone
do the orphans find mercy."

4 The LORD says,
"Then I will heal you of your faithlessness;
my love will know no bounds,
for my anger will be gone forever.
5 I will be to Israel
like a refreshing dew from heaven.
Israel will blossom like the lily;
it will send roots deep into the soil
like the cedars in Lebanon.
6 Its branches will spread out like beautiful
olive trees,
as fragrant as the cedars of Lebanon.

13:14a Hebrew *Sheol;* also in 13:14b. **13:14b** Greek version reads *O death, where is your punishment? / O grave* [Hades], *where is your sting?* Compare 1 Cor 15:55. **13:16** Verse 16 is numbered 14:1 in Hebrew text. **14:1** Verses 14:1-9 are numbered 14:2-10 in Hebrew text. **14:2** As in Greek and Syriac versions, which read *may repay the fruit of our lips;* Hebrew reads *may repay the bulls of our lips.*

KING JAMES VERSION

[7]They that dwell under his shadow shall return; they shall revive *as* the corn, and grow as the vine: the scent thereof *shall be* as the wine of Lebanon.

[8]Ephraim *shall say,* What have I to do any more with idols? I have heard *him,* and observed him: I *am* like a green fir tree. From me is thy fruit found.

[9]Who *is* wise, and he shall understand these *things?* prudent, and he shall know them? for the ways of the LORD *are* right, and the just shall walk in them: but the transgressors shall fall therein.

NEW LIVING TRANSLATION

[7] My people will again live under my shade.
They will flourish like grain and blossom like grapevines.
They will be as fragrant as the wines of Lebanon.

[8] "O Israel,* stay away from idols!
I am the one who answers your prayers and cares for you.
I am like a tree that is always green;
all your fruit comes from me."

[9] Let those who are wise understand these things.
Let those with discernment listen carefully.
The paths of the LORD are true and right,
and righteous people live by walking in them.
But in those paths sinners stumble and fall.

14:8 Hebrew *Ephraim,* referring to the northern kingdom of Israel.

Joel

KING JAMES VERSION

1 1The word of the LORD that came to Joel the son of Pethuel.

2Hear this, ye old men, and give ear, all ye inhabitants of the land. Hath this been in your days, or even in the days of your fathers?

3Tell ye your children of it, and *let* your children *tell* their children, and their children another generation.

4That which the palmerworm hath left hath the locust eaten; and that which the locust hath left hath the cankerworm eaten; and that which the cankerworm hath left hath the caterpiller eaten.

5Awake, ye drunkards, and weep; and howl, all ye drinkers of wine, because of the new wine; for it is cut off from your mouth.

6For a nation is come up upon my land, strong, and without number, whose teeth *are* the teeth of a lion, and he hath the cheek teeth of a great lion.

7He hath laid my vine waste, and barked my fig tree: he hath made it clean bare, and cast *it* away; the branches thereof are made white.

8Lament like a virgin girded with sackcloth for the husband of her youth.

9The meat offering and the drink offering is cut off from the house of the LORD; the priests, the LORD's ministers, mourn.

10The field is wasted, the land mourneth; for the corn is wasted: the new wine is dried up, the oil languisheth.

11Be ye ashamed, O ye husbandmen; howl, O ye

NEW LIVING TRANSLATION

1 The LORD gave this message to Joel son of Pethuel.

Mourning over the Locust Plague

2 Hear this, you leaders of the people.
Listen, all who live in the land.
In all your history,
has anything like this happened before?
3 Tell your children about it in the years to come,
and let your children tell their children.
Pass the story down from generation to generation.
4 After the cutting locusts finished eating the crops,
the swarming locusts took what was left!
After them came the hopping locusts,
and then the stripping locusts,* too!

5 Wake up, you drunkards, and weep!
Wail, all you wine-drinkers!
All the grapes are ruined,
and all your sweet wine is gone.
6 A vast army of locusts* has invaded my land,
a terrible army too numerous to count.
Its teeth are like lions' teeth,
its fangs like those of a lioness.
7 It has destroyed my grapevines
and ruined my fig trees,
stripping their bark and destroying it,
leaving the branches white and bare.

8 Weep like a bride dressed in black,
mourning the death of her husband.
9 For there is no grain or wine
to offer at the Temple of the LORD.
So the priests are in mourning.
The ministers of the LORD are weeping.
10 The fields are ruined,
the land is stripped bare.
The grain is destroyed,
the grapes have shriveled,
and the olive oil is gone.
11 Despair, all you farmers!
Wail, all you vine growers!

1:4 The precise identification of the four kinds of locusts mentioned here is uncertain. **1:6** Hebrew *A nation.*

KING JAMES VERSION

vinedressers, for the wheat and for the barley; because the harvest of the field is perished.

12 The vine is dried up, and the fig tree languisheth; the pomegranate tree, the palm tree also, and the apple tree, *even* all the trees of the field, are withered: because joy is withered away from the sons of men.

13 Gird yourselves, and lament, ye priests: howl, ye ministers of the altar: come, lie all night in sackcloth, ye ministers of my God: for the meat offering and the drink offering is withholden from the house of your God.

14 Sanctify ye a fast, call a solemn assembly, gather the elders *and* all the inhabitants of the land *into* the house of the LORD your God, and cry unto the LORD.

15 Alas for the day! for the day of the LORD *is* at hand, and as a destruction from the Almighty shall it come.

16 Is not the meat cut off before our eyes, *yea,* joy and gladness from the house of our God?

17 The seed is rotten under their clods, the garners are laid desolate, the barns are broken down; for the corn is withered.

18 How do the beasts groan! the herds of cattle are perplexed, because they have no pasture; yea, the flocks of sheep are made desolate.

19 O LORD, to thee will I cry: for the fire hath devoured the pastures of the wilderness, and the flame hath burned all the trees of the field.

20 The beasts of the field cry also unto thee: for the rivers of waters are dried up, and the fire hath devoured the pastures of the wilderness.

2 1 Blow ye the trumpet in Zion, and sound an alarm in my holy mountain: let all the inhabitants of the land tremble: for the day of the LORD cometh, for *it is* nigh at hand;

2 A day of darkness and of gloominess, a day of clouds and of thick darkness, as the morning spread upon the mountains: a great people and a strong; there hath not been ever the like, neither shall be any more after it, *even* to the years of many generations.

NEW LIVING TRANSLATION

Weep, because the wheat and barley—
all the crops of the field—are ruined.
12 The grapevines have dried up,
and the fig trees have withered.
The pomegranate trees, palm trees, and
apple trees—
all the fruit trees—have dried up.
And the people's joy has dried up with them.

13 Dress yourselves in burlap and weep, you priests!
Wail, you who serve before the altar!
Come, spend the night in burlap,
you ministers of my God.
For there is no grain or wine
to offer at the Temple of your God.
14 Announce a time of fasting;
call the people together for a solemn meeting.
Bring the leaders
and all the people of the land
into the Temple of the LORD your God,
and cry out to him there.
15 The day of the LORD is near,
the day when destruction comes from
the Almighty.
How terrible that day will be!
16 Our food disappears before our very eyes.
No joyful celebrations are held in the house
of our God.
17 The seeds die in the parched ground,
and the grain crops fail.
The barns stand empty,
and granaries are abandoned.
18 How the animals moan with hunger!
The herds of cattle wander about confused,
because they have no pasture.
The flocks of sheep and goats bleat in misery.

19 LORD, help us!
The fire has consumed the wilderness pastures,
and flames have burned up all the trees.
20 Even the wild animals cry out to you
because the streams have dried up,
and fire has consumed the wilderness
pastures.

Locusts Invade like an Army

2 1 Sound the alarm in Jerusalem*!
Raise the battle cry on my holy mountain!
Let everyone tremble in fear
because the day of the LORD is upon us.
2 It is a day of darkness and gloom,
a day of thick clouds and deep blackness.
Suddenly, like dawn spreading across
the mountains,
a great and mighty army appears.
Nothing like it has been seen before
or will ever be seen again.

2:1 Hebrew *Zion;* also in 2:15, 23.

KING JAMES VERSION

3 A fire devoureth before them; and behind them a flame burneth: the land *is* as the garden of Eden before them, and behind them a desolate wilderness; yea, and nothing shall escape them.

4 The appearance of them *is* as the appearance of horses; and as horsemen, so shall they run.

5 Like the noise of chariots on the tops of mountains shall they leap, like the noise of a flame of fire that devoureth the stubble, as a strong people set in battle array.

6 Before their face the people shall be much pained: all faces shall gather blackness.

7 They shall run like mighty men; they shall climb the wall like men of war; and they shall march every one on his ways, and they shall not break their ranks:

8 Neither shall one thrust another; they shall walk every one in his path: and *when* they fall upon the sword, they shall not be wounded.

9 They shall run to and fro in the city; they shall run upon the wall, they shall climb up upon the houses; they shall enter in at the windows like a thief.

10 The earth shall quake before them; the heavens shall tremble: the sun and the moon shall be dark, and the stars shall withdraw their shining:

11 And the LORD shall utter his voice before his army: for his camp *is* very great: for *he is* strong that executeth his word: for the day of the LORD *is* great and very terrible; and who can abide it?

12 Therefore also now, saith the LORD, turn ye *even* to me with all your heart, and with fasting, and with weeping, and with mourning:

13 And rend your heart, and not your garments, and turn unto the LORD your God: for he *is* gracious and merciful, slow to anger, and of great kindness, and repenteth him of the evil.

14 Who knoweth *if* he will return and repent, and leave a blessing behind him; *even* a meat offering and a drink offering unto the LORD your God?

NEW LIVING TRANSLATION

3 Fire burns in front of them,
and flames follow after them.
Ahead of them the land lies
as beautiful as the Garden of Eden.
Behind them is nothing but desolation;
not one thing escapes.
4 They look like horses;
they charge forward like warhorses.*
5 Look at them as they leap along the
mountaintops.
Listen to the noise they make—like the
rumbling of chariots,
like the roar of fire sweeping across a field
of stubble,
or like a mighty army moving into battle.

6 Fear grips all the people;
every face grows pale with terror.
7 The attackers march like warriors
and scale city walls like soldiers.
Straight forward they march,
never breaking rank.
8 They never jostle each other;
each moves in exactly the right position.
They break through defenses
without missing a step.
9 They swarm over the city
and run along its walls.
They enter all the houses,
climbing like thieves through the windows.
10 The earth quakes as they advance,
and the heavens tremble.
The sun and moon grow dark,
and the stars no longer shine.

11 The LORD is at the head of the column.
He leads them with a shout.
This is his mighty army,
and they follow his orders.
The day of the LORD is an awesome,
terrible thing.
Who can possibly survive?

A Call to Repentance

12 That is why the LORD says,
"Turn to me now, while there is time.
Give me your hearts.
Come with fasting, weeping, and mourning.
13 Don't tear your clothing in your grief,
but tear your hearts instead."
Return to the LORD your God,
for he is merciful and compassionate,
slow to get angry and filled with unfailing love.
He is eager to relent and not punish.
14 Who knows? Perhaps he will give you a reprieve,
sending you a blessing instead of this curse.
Perhaps you will be able to offer grain and wine
to the LORD your God as before.

2:4 Or *like charioteers.*

KING JAMES VERSION

15 Blow the trumpet in Zion, sanctify a fast, call a solemn assembly:

16 Gather the people, sanctify the congregation, assemble the elders, gather the children, and those that suck the breasts: let the bridegroom go forth of his chamber, and the bride out of her closet.

17 Let the priests, the ministers of the LORD, weep between the porch and the altar, and let them say, Spare thy people, O LORD, and give not thine heritage to reproach, that the heathen should rule over them: wherefore should they say among the people, Where *is* their God?

18 Then will the LORD be jealous for his land, and pity his people.

19 Yea, the LORD will answer and say unto his people, Behold, I will send you corn, and wine, and oil, and ye shall be satisfied therewith: and I will no more make you a reproach among the heathen:

20 But I will remove far off from you the northern *army*, and will drive him into a land barren and desolate, with his face toward the east sea, and his hinder part toward the utmost sea, and his stink shall come up, and his ill savour shall come up, because he hath done great things.

21 Fear not, O land; be glad and rejoice: for the LORD will do great things.

22 Be not afraid, ye beasts of the field: for the pastures of the wilderness do spring, for the tree beareth her fruit, the fig tree and the vine do yield their strength.

23 Be glad then, ye children of Zion, and rejoice in the LORD your God: for he hath given you the former rain moderately, and he will cause to come down for you the rain, the former rain, and the latter rain in the first *month*.

24 And the floors shall be full of wheat, and the fats shall overflow with wine and oil.

25 And I will restore to you the years that the locust

NEW LIVING TRANSLATION

15 Blow the ram's horn in Jerusalem!
Announce a time of fasting;
call the people together
for a solemn meeting.
16 Gather all the people—
the elders, the children, and even the babies.
Call the bridegroom from his quarters
and the bride from her private room.
17 Let the priests, who minister in the LORD's presence,
stand and weep between the entry room
to the Temple and the altar.
Let them pray, "Spare your people, LORD!
Don't let your special possession become
an object of mockery.
Don't let them become a joke for unbelieving
foreigners who say,
'Has the God of Israel left them?'"

The LORD's Promise of Restoration

18 Then the LORD will pity his people
and jealously guard the honor of his land.
19 The LORD will reply,
"Look! I am sending you grain and new wine
and olive oil,
enough to satisfy your needs.
You will no longer be an object of mockery
among the surrounding nations.
20 I will drive away these armies from the north.
I will send them into the parched wastelands.
Those in the front will be driven into the
Dead Sea,
and those at the rear into the Mediterranean.*
The stench of their rotting bodies will rise over
the land."

Surely the LORD has done great things!
21 Don't be afraid, my people.
Be glad now and rejoice,
for the LORD has done great things.
22 Don't be afraid, you animals of the field,
for the wilderness pastures will soon be green.
The trees will again be filled with fruit;
fig trees and grapevines will be loaded down
once more.
23 Rejoice, you people of Jerusalem!
Rejoice in the LORD your God!
For the rain he sends demonstrates his
faithfulness.
Once more the autumn rains will come,
as well as the rains of spring.
24 The threshing floors will again be piled high
with grain,
and the presses will overflow with new wine
and olive oil.

25 The LORD says, "I will give you back what you lost
to the swarming locusts, the hopping locusts,

2:20 Hebrew *into the eastern sea, . . . into the western sea.*

KING JAMES VERSION

hath eaten, the cankerworm, and the caterpiller, and
the palmerworm, my great army which I sent among
you.
26 And ye shall eat in plenty, and be satisfied, and
praise the name of the LORD your God, that hath
dealt wondrously with you: and my people shall
never be ashamed.
27 And ye shall know that I *am* in the midst of Israel, and *that* I *am* the LORD your God, and none else:
and my people shall never be ashamed.

28 And it shall come to pass afterward, *that* I will
pour out my spirit upon all flesh; and your sons and
your daughters shall prophesy, your old men shall
dream dreams, your young men shall see visions:
29 And also upon the servants and upon the handmaids in those days will I pour out my spirit.
30 And I will shew wonders in the heavens and in
the earth, blood, and fire, and pillars of smoke.
31 The sun shall be turned into darkness, and the
moon into blood, before the great and the terrible
day of the LORD come.
32 And it shall come to pass, *that* whosoever shall
call on the name of the LORD shall be delivered: for in
mount Zion and in Jerusalem shall be deliverance,
as the LORD hath said, and in the remnant whom the
LORD shall call.

3 1 For, behold, in those days, and in that time,
when I shall bring again the captivity of Judah
and Jerusalem,
2 I will also gather all nations, and will bring them
down into the valley of Jehoshaphat, and will plead
with them there for my people and *for* my heritage
Israel, whom they have scattered among the nations,
and parted my land.
3 And they have cast lots for my people; and have
given a boy for an harlot, and sold a girl for wine, that
they might drink.
4 Yea, and what have ye to do with me, O Tyre, and
Zidon, and all the coasts of Palestine? will ye render
me a recompence? and if ye recompense me, swiftly
and speedily will I return your recompence upon
your own head;
5 Because ye have taken my silver and my gold, and

NEW LIVING TRANSLATION

the stripping locusts, and the cutting locusts.*
It was I who sent this great destroying army
against you.
26 Once again you will have all the food you want,
and you will praise the LORD your God,
who does these miracles for you.
Never again will my people be disgraced.
27 Then you will know that I am among my
people Israel,
that I am the LORD your God, and there
is no other.
Never again will my people be disgraced.

The LORD's Promise of His Spirit

28* "Then, after doing all those things,
I will pour out my Spirit upon all people.
Your sons and daughters will prophesy.
Your old men will dream dreams,
and your young men will see visions.
29 In those days I will pour out my Spirit
even on servants—men and women alike.
30 And I will cause wonders in the heavens and
on the earth—
blood and fire and columns of smoke.
31 The sun will become dark,
and the moon will turn blood red
before that great and terrible* day of the
LORD arrives.
32 But everyone who calls on the name of the LORD
will be saved,
for some on Mount Zion in Jerusalem will escape,
just as the LORD has said.
These will be among the survivors
whom the LORD has called.

Judgment against Enemy Nations

3 1* "At the time of those events," says the LORD,
"when I restore the prosperity of Judah
and Jerusalem,
2 I will gather the armies of the world
into the valley of Jehoshaphat.*
There I will judge them
for harming my people, my special possession,
for scattering my people among the nations,
and for dividing up my land.
3 They threw dice* to decide which of my people
would be their slaves.
They traded boys to obtain prostitutes
and sold girls for enough wine to get drunk.

4 "What do you have against me, Tyre and Sidon
and you cities of Philistia? Are you trying to take revenge on me? If you are, then watch out! I will strike
swiftly and pay you back for everything you have
done. 5 You have taken my silver and gold and all my

2:25 The precise identification of the four kinds of locusts mentioned here is uncertain. **2:28** Verses 2:28-32 are numbered 3:1-5 in Hebrew text. **2:31** Greek version reads *glorious.* **3:1** Verses 3:1-21 are numbered 4:1-21 in Hebrew text. **3:2** *Jehoshaphat* means "the LORD judges." **3:3** Hebrew *They cast lots.*

KING JAMES VERSION

have carried into your temples my goodly pleasant
things:
6 The children also of Judah and the children of Jerusalem have ye sold unto the Grecians, that ye might
remove them far from their border.
7 Behold, I will raise them out of the place whither
ye have sold them, and will return your recompense
upon your own head:
8 And I will sell your sons and your daughters into
the hand of the children of Judah, and they shall sell
them to the Sabeans, to a people far off: for the LORD
hath spoken *it*.
9 Proclaim ye this among the Gentiles; Prepare war,
wake up the mighty men, let all the men of war draw
near; let them come up:
10 Beat your plowshares into swords, and your
pruninghooks into spears: let the weak say, I *am*
strong.
11 Assemble yourselves, and come, all ye heathen,
and gather yourselves together round about: thither
cause thy mighty ones to come down, O LORD.
12 Let the heathen be wakened, and come up to the
valley of Jehoshaphat: for there will I sit to judge all
the heathen round about.
13 Put ye in the sickle, for the harvest is ripe: come,
get you down; for the press is full, the fats overflow;
for their wickedness *is* great.
14 Multitudes, multitudes in the valley of decision:
for the day of the LORD *is* near in the valley of decision.
15 The sun and the moon shall be darkened, and
the stars shall withdraw their shining.
16 The LORD also shall roar out of Zion, and utter
his voice from Jerusalem; and the heavens and the
earth shall shake: but the LORD *will be* the hope of his
people, and the strength of the children of Israel.

17 So shall ye know that I *am* the LORD your God
dwelling in Zion, my holy mountain: then shall Jerusalem be holy, and there shall no strangers pass
through her any more.
18 And it shall come to pass in that day, *that* the
mountains shall drop down new wine, and the hills
shall flow with milk, and all the rivers of Judah shall
flow with waters, and a fountain shall come forth of
the house of the LORD, and shall water the valley of
Shittim.

NEW LIVING TRANSLATION

precious treasures, and have carried them off to your
pagan temples. 6 You have sold the people of Judah
and Jerusalem to the Greeks,* so they could take
them far from their homeland.
7 "But I will bring them back from all the places to
which you sold them, and I will pay you back for
everything you have done. 8 I will sell your sons and
daughters to the people of Judah, and they will sell
them to the people of Arabia,* a nation far away. I,
the LORD, have spoken!"

9 Say to the nations far and wide:
"Get ready for war!
Call out your best warriors.
Let all your fighting men advance for the attack.
10 Hammer your plowshares into swords
and your pruning hooks into spears.
Train even your weaklings to be warriors.
11 Come quickly, all you nations everywhere.
Gather together in the valley."

And now, O LORD, call out your warriors!

12 "Let the nations be called to arms.
Let them march to the valley of Jehoshaphat.
There I, the LORD, will sit
to pronounce judgment on them all.
13 Swing the sickle,
for the harvest is ripe.*
Come, tread the grapes,
for the winepress is full.
The storage vats are overflowing
with the wickedness of these people."

14 Thousands upon thousands are waiting in the
valley of decision.
There the day of the LORD will soon arrive.
15 The sun and moon will grow dark,
and the stars will no longer shine.
16 The LORD's voice will roar from Zion
and thunder from Jerusalem,
and the heavens and the earth will shake.
But the LORD will be a refuge for his people,
a strong fortress for the people of Israel.

Blessings for God's People
17 "Then you will know that I, the LORD your God,
live in Zion, my holy mountain.
Jerusalem will be holy forever,
and foreign armies will never conquer her again.
18 In that day the mountains will drip with sweet
wine,
and the hills will flow with milk.
Water will fill the streambeds of Judah,
and a fountain will burst forth from the
LORD's Temple,
watering the arid valley of acacias.*

3:6 Hebrew *to the peoples of Javan.* **3:8** Hebrew *to the Sabeans.*
3:13 Greek version reads *for the harvest time has come.* Compare Mark 4:29.
3:18 Hebrew *valley of Shittim.*

KING JAMES VERSION

[19]Egypt shall be a desolation, and Edom shall be a
desolate wilderness, for the violence *against* the
children of Judah, because they have shed innocent
blood in their land.
[20]But Judah shall dwell for ever, and Jerusalem
from generation to generation.
[21]For I will cleanse their blood *that* I have not
cleansed: for the LORD dwelleth in Zion.

NEW LIVING TRANSLATION

[19] But Egypt will become a wasteland
and Edom will become a wilderness,
because they attacked the people of Judah
and killed innocent people in their land.

[20] "But Judah will be filled with people forever,
and Jerusalem will endure through all
generations.
[21] I will pardon my people's crimes,
which I have not yet pardoned;
and I, the LORD, will make my home
in Jerusalem* with my people."

3:21 Hebrew *Zion.*

Amos

KING JAMES VERSION

1 [1]The words of Amos, who was among the
herdmen of Tekoa, which he saw concerning
Israel in the days of Uzziah king of Judah, and in the
days of Jeroboam the son of Joash king of Israel, two
years before the earthquake.
2And he said, The LORD will roar from Zion, and
utter his voice from Jerusalem; and the habitations
of the shepherds shall mourn, and the top of Carmel
shall wither.

3Thus saith the LORD; For three transgressions of
Damascus, and for four, I will not turn away *the punishment* thereof; because they have threshed Gilead
with threshing instruments of iron:
4But I will send a fire into the house of Hazael,
which shall devour the palaces of Ben-hadad.
5I will break also the bar of Damascus, and cut off
the inhabitant from the plain of Aven, and him that
holdeth the sceptre from the house of Eden: and the
people of Syria shall go into captivity unto Kir, saith
the LORD.
6Thus saith the LORD; For three transgressions of
Gaza, and for four, I will not turn away *the punishment* thereof; because they carried away captive the
whole captivity, to deliver *them* up to Edom:
7But I will send a fire on the wall of Gaza, which
shall devour the palaces thereof:
8And I will cut off the inhabitant from Ashdod,
and him that holdeth the sceptre from Ashkelon,

NEW LIVING TRANSLATION

1 This message was given to Amos, a shepherd
from the town of Tekoa in Judah. He received
this message in visions two years before the earthquake, when Uzziah was king of Judah and Jeroboam II, the son of Jehoash,* was king of Israel.
2This is what he saw and heard:

"The LORD's voice will roar from Zion
and thunder from Jerusalem!
The lush pastures of the shepherds will
dry up;
the grass on Mount Carmel will wither
and die."

God's Judgment on Israel's Neighbors

3This is what the LORD says:

"The people of Damascus have sinned again
and again,*
and I will not let them go unpunished!
They beat down my people in Gilead
as grain is threshed with iron sledges.
4 So I will send down fire on King Hazael's palace,
and the fortresses of King Ben-hadad will be
destroyed.
5 I will break down the gates of Damascus
and slaughter the people in the valley of Aven.
I will destroy the ruler in Beth-eden,
and the people of Aram will go as captives
to Kir,"
says the LORD.

6This is what the LORD says:

"The people of Gaza have sinned again and again,
and I will not let them go unpunished!
They sent whole villages into exile,
selling them as slaves to Edom.
7 So I will send down fire on the walls of Gaza,
and all its fortresses will be destroyed.
8 I will slaughter the people of Ashdod
and destroy the king of Ashkelon.
Then I will turn to attack Ekron,

1:1 Hebrew *Joash*, a variant spelling of Jehoash. **1:3** Hebrew *have committed three sins, even four;* also in 1:6, 9, 11, 13.

KING JAMES VERSION

and I will turn mine hand against Ekron: and the remnant of the Philistines shall perish, saith the Lord GOD.

9 Thus saith the LORD; For three transgressions of Tyrus, and for four, I will not turn away *the punishment* thereof; because they delivered up the whole captivity to Edom, and remembered not the brotherly covenant:

10 But I will send a fire on the wall of Tyrus, which shall devour the palaces thereof.

11 Thus saith the LORD; For three transgressions of Edom, and for four, I will not turn away *the punishment* thereof; because he did pursue his brother with the sword, and did cast off all pity, and his anger did tear perpetually, and he kept his wrath for ever:

12 But I will send a fire upon Teman, which shall devour the palaces of Bozrah.

13 Thus saith the LORD; For three transgressions of the children of Ammon, and for four, I will not turn away *the punishment* thereof; because they have ripped up the women with child of Gilead, that they might enlarge their border:

14 But I will kindle a fire in the wall of Rabbah, and it shall devour the palaces thereof, with shouting in the day of battle, with a tempest in the day of the whirlwind:

15 And their king shall go into captivity, he and his princes together, saith the LORD.

2

1 Thus saith the LORD; For three transgressions of Moab, and for four, I will not turn away *the punishment* thereof; because he burned the bones of the king of Edom into lime:

2 But I will send a fire upon Moab, and it shall devour the palaces of Kirioth: and Moab shall die with tumult, with shouting, *and* with the sound of the trumpet:

3 And I will cut off the judge from the midst thereof, and will slay all the princes thereof with him, saith the LORD.

NEW LIVING TRANSLATION

and the few Philistines still left will be killed,"
says the Sovereign LORD.

9 This is what the LORD says:

"The people of Tyre have sinned again and again,
and I will not let them go unpunished!
They broke their treaty of brotherhood
with Israel,
selling whole villages as slaves to Edom.
10 So I will send down fire on the walls of Tyre,
and all its fortresses will be destroyed."

11 This is what the LORD says:

"The people of Edom have sinned again
and again,
and I will not let them go unpunished!
They chased down their relatives, the Israelites,
with swords,
showing them no mercy.
In their rage, they slashed them continually
and were unrelenting in their anger.
12 So I will send down fire on Teman,
and the fortresses of Bozrah will be
destroyed."

13 This is what the LORD says:

"The people of Ammon have sinned again
and again,
and I will not let them go unpunished!
When they attacked Gilead to extend their
borders,
they ripped open pregnant women with
their swords.
14 So I will send down fire on the walls of Rabbah,
and all its fortresses will be destroyed.
The battle will come upon them with shouts,
like a whirlwind in a mighty storm.
15 And their king* and his princes will go into
exile together,"
says the LORD.

2

This is what the LORD says:

"The people of Moab have sinned again
and again,*
and I will not let them go unpunished!
They desecrated the bones of Edom's king,
burning them to ashes.
2 So I will send down fire on the land of Moab,
and all the fortresses in Kerioth will be
destroyed.
The people will fall in the noise of battle,
as the warriors shout and the ram's horn sounds.
3 And I will destroy their king
and slaughter all their princes,"
says the LORD.

1:15 Hebrew *malcam,* possibly referring to their god Molech. **2:1** Hebrew *have committed three sins, even four;* also in 2:4, 6.

KING JAMES VERSION

4Thus saith the LORD; For three transgressions of
Judah, and for four, I will not turn away *the punishment* thereof; because they have despised the law of
the LORD, and have not kept his commandments, and
their lies caused them to err, after the which their
fathers have walked:
5But I will send a fire upon Judah, and it shall devour the palaces of Jerusalem.
6Thus saith the LORD; For three transgressions of
Israel, and for four, I will not turn away *the punishment* thereof; because they sold the righteous for
silver, and the poor for a pair of shoes;
7That pant after the dust of the earth on the head
of the poor, and turn aside the way of the meek: and a
man and his father will go in unto the *same* maid, to
profane my holy name:
8And they lay *themselves* down upon clothes laid
to pledge by every altar, and they drink the wine of
the condemned *in* the house of their god.
9Yet destroyed I the Amorite before them, whose
height *was* like the height of the cedars, and he *was*
strong as the oaks; yet I destroyed his fruit from
above, and his roots from beneath.
10Also I brought you up from the land of Egypt,
and led you forty years through the wilderness, to
possess the land of the Amorite.
11And I raised up of your sons for prophets, and of
your young men for Nazarites. *Is it* not even thus,
O ye children of Israel? saith the LORD.
12But ye gave the Nazarites wine to drink; and
commanded the prophets, saying, Prophesy not.
13Behold, I am pressed under you, as a cart is
pressed *that is* full of sheaves.
14Therefore the flight shall perish from the swift,
and the strong shall not strengthen his force, neither
shall the mighty deliver himself:
15Neither shall he stand that handleth the bow;
and *he that is* swift of foot shall not deliver *himself:*
neither shall he that rideth the horse deliver himself.

NEW LIVING TRANSLATION

God's Judgment on Judah and Israel

4This is what the LORD says:

"The people of Judah have sinned again and again,
and I will not let them go unpunished!
They have rejected the instruction of the LORD,
refusing to obey his decrees.
They have been led astray by the same lies
that deceived their ancestors.
5 So I will send down fire on Judah,
and all the fortresses of Jerusalem will
be destroyed."

6This is what the LORD says:

"The people of Israel have sinned again
and again,
and I will not let them go unpunished!
They sell honorable people for silver
and poor people for a pair of sandals.
7 They trample helpless people in the dust
and shove the oppressed out of the way.
Both father and son sleep with the same woman,
corrupting my holy name.
8 At their religious festivals,
they lounge in clothing their debtors put
up as security.
In the house of their gods,
they drink wine bought with unjust fines.

9 "But as my people watched,
I destroyed the Amorites,
though they were as tall as cedars
and as strong as oaks.
I destroyed the fruit on their branches
and dug out their roots.
10 It was I who rescued you from Egypt
and led you through the desert for forty years,
so you could possess the land of the Amorites.
11 I chose some of your sons to be prophets
and others to be Nazirites.
Can you deny this, my people of Israel?"
asks the LORD.
12 "But you caused the Nazirites to sin by making
them drink wine,
and you commanded the prophets, 'Shut up!'

13 "So I will make you groan
like a wagon loaded down with sheaves
of grain.
14 Your fastest runners will not get away.
The strongest among you will become weak.
Even mighty warriors will be unable to save
themselves.
15 The archers will not stand their ground.
The swiftest runners won't be fast enough
to escape.
Even those riding horses won't be able
to save themselves.

2:8 Or *their God.*

KING JAMES VERSION

16 And *he that is* courageous among the mighty
shall flee away naked in that day, saith the LORD.

3

1 Hear this word that the LORD hath spoken
against you, O children of Israel, against the
whole family which I brought up from the land of
Egypt, saying,
2 You only have I known of all the families of the
earth: therefore I will punish you for all your iniquities.

3 Can two walk together, except they be agreed?
4 Will a lion roar in the forest, when he hath no
prey? will a young lion cry out of his den, if he have
taken nothing?
5 Can a bird fall in a snare upon the earth, where no
gin *is* for him? shall *one* take up a snare from the
earth, and have taken nothing at all?
6 Shall a trumpet be blown in the city, and the
people not be afraid? shall there be evil in a city, and
the LORD hath not done *it*?
7 Surely the Lord GOD will do nothing, but he
revealeth his secret unto his servants the prophets.
8 The lion hath roared, who will not fear? the Lord
GOD hath spoken, who can but prophesy?
9 Publish in the palaces at Ashdod, and in the palaces in the land of Egypt, and say, Assemble yourselves upon the mountains of Samaria, and behold
the great tumults in the midst thereof, and the oppressed in the midst thereof.
10 For they know not to do right, saith the LORD,
who store up violence and robbery in their palaces.
11 Therefore thus saith the Lord GOD; An adversary
there shall be even round about the land; and he shall
bring down thy strength from thee, and thy palaces
shall be spoiled.
12 Thus saith the LORD; As the shepherd taketh out
of the mouth of the lion two legs, or a piece of an ear;
so shall the children of Israel be taken out that dwell

NEW LIVING TRANSLATION

16 On that day the most courageous of your
fighting men
will drop their weapons and run for their lives,"
says the LORD.

3

Listen to this message that the LORD has spoken
against you, O people of Israel and Judah—
against the entire family I rescued from Egypt:

2 "From among all the families on the earth,
I have been intimate with you alone.
That is why I must punish you
for all your sins."

Witnesses against Guilty Israel

3 Can two people walk together
without agreeing on the direction?
4 Does a lion ever roar in a thicket
without first finding a victim?
Does a young lion growl in its den
without first catching its prey?
5 Does a bird ever get caught in a trap
that has no bait?
Does a trap spring shut
when there's nothing to catch?
6 When the ram's horn blows a warning,
shouldn't the people be alarmed?
Does disaster come to a city
unless the LORD has planned it?
7 Indeed, the Sovereign LORD never does anything
until he reveals his plans to his servants
the prophets.

8 The lion has roared—
so who isn't frightened?
The Sovereign LORD has spoken—
so who can refuse to proclaim his message?
9 Announce this to the leaders of Philistia*
and to the great ones of Egypt:
"Take your seats now on the hills around Samaria,
and witness the chaos and oppression in Israel."

10 "My people have forgotten how to do right,"
says the LORD.
"Their fortresses are filled with wealth
taken by theft and violence.
11 Therefore," says the Sovereign LORD,
"an enemy is coming!
He will surround them and shatter their defenses.
Then he will plunder all their fortresses."

12 This is what the LORD says:

"A shepherd who tries to rescue a sheep from
a lion's mouth
will recover only two legs or a piece of an ear.
So it will be for the Israelites in Samaria lying
on luxurious beds,

3:9 Hebrew *Ashdod*.

KING JAMES VERSION

in Samaria in the corner of a bed, and in Damascus *in*
a couch.
13Hear ye, and testify in the house of Jacob, saith
the Lord GOD, the God of hosts,
14That in the day that I shall visit the transgressions of Israel upon him I will also visit the altars of
Bethel: and the horns of the altar shall be cut off, and
fall to the ground.
15And I will smite the winter house with the summer house; and the houses of ivory shall perish, and
the great houses shall have an end, saith the LORD.

4 1Hear this word, ye kine of Bashan, that *are* in
the mountain of Samaria, which oppress the
poor, which crush the needy, which say to their masters, Bring, and let us drink.
2The Lord GOD hath sworn by his holiness, that, lo,
the days shall come upon you, that he will take you
away with hooks, and your posterity with fishhooks.
3And ye shall go out at the breaches, every *cow at*
that which is before her; and ye shall cast *them* into
the palace, saith the LORD.
4Come to Bethel, and transgress; at Gilgal multiply
transgression; and bring your sacrifices every morning, *and* your tithes after three years:
5And offer a sacrifice of thanksgiving with leaven,
and proclaim *and* publish the free offerings: for this
liketh you, O ye children of Israel, saith the Lord GOD.
6And I also have given you cleanness of teeth in all
your cities, and want of bread in all your places: yet
have ye not returned unto me, saith the LORD.
7And also I have withholden the rain from you,
when *there were* yet three months to the harvest: and
I caused it to rain upon one city, and caused it not to
rain upon another city: one piece was rained upon,
and the piece whereupon it rained not withered.

NEW LIVING TRANSLATION

and for the people of Damascus reclining
on couches.*

13"Now listen to this, and announce it throughout all Israel,*" says the Lord, the LORD God of Heaven's Armies.

14 "On the very day I punish Israel for its sins,
I will destroy the pagan altars at Bethel.
The horns of the altar will be cut off
and fall to the ground.
15 And I will destroy the beautiful homes of
the wealthy—
their winter mansions and their summer
houses, too—
all their palaces filled with ivory,"
says the LORD.

Israel's Failure to Learn

4 1Listen to me, you fat cows*
living in Samaria,
you women who oppress the poor
and crush the needy,
and who are always calling to your husbands,
"Bring us another drink!"
2 The Sovereign LORD has sworn this by his holiness:
"The time will come when you will be led away
with hooks in your noses.
Every last one of you will be dragged away
like a fish on a hook!
3 You will be led out through the ruins of the wall;
you will be thrown from your fortresses,*"
says the LORD.
4 "Go ahead and offer sacrifices to the idols
at Bethel.
Keep on disobeying at Gilgal.
Offer sacrifices each morning,
and bring your tithes every three days.
5 Present your bread made with yeast
as an offering of thanksgiving.
Then give your extra voluntary offerings
so you can brag about it everywhere!
This is the kind of thing you Israelites love to do,"
says the Sovereign LORD.

6 "I brought hunger to every city
and famine to every town.
But still you would not return to me,"
says the LORD.

7 "I kept the rain from falling
when your crops needed it the most.
I sent rain on one town
but withheld it from another.
Rain fell on one field,
while another field withered away.

3:12 The meaning of the Hebrew in this sentence is uncertain. **3:13** Hebrew *the house of Jacob.* The names "Jacob" and "Israel" are often interchanged throughout the Old Testament, referring sometimes to the individual patriarch and sometimes to the nation. **4:1** Hebrew *you cows of Bashan.* **4:3** Or *thrown out toward Harmon,* possibly a reference to Mount Hermon.

KING JAMES VERSION

8So two *or* three cities wandered unto one city, to
drink water; but they were not satisfied: yet have ye
not returned unto me, saith the LORD.
9I have smitten you with blasting and mildew:
when your gardens and your vineyards and your fig
trees and your olive trees increased, the palmerworm
devoured *them:* yet have ye not returned unto me,
saith the LORD.
10I have sent among you the pestilence after the
manner of Egypt: your young men have I slain with
the sword, and have taken away your horses; and I
have made the stink of your camps to come up unto
your nostrils: yet have ye not returned unto me, saith
the LORD.
11I have overthrown *some* of you, as God overthrew Sodom and Gomorrah, and ye were as a firebrand plucked out of the burning: yet have ye not
returned unto me, saith the LORD.
12Therefore thus will I do unto thee, O Israel: *and*
because I will do this unto thee, prepare to meet thy
God, O Israel.
13For, lo, he that formeth the mountains, and
createth the wind, and declareth unto man what *is*
his thought, that maketh the morning darkness, and
treadeth upon the high places of the earth, The LORD,
The God of hosts, *is* his name.

5 1Hear ye this word which I take up against you,
even a lamentation, O house of Israel.
2The virgin of Israel is fallen; she shall no more
rise: she is forsaken upon her land; *there is* none to
raise her up.
3For thus saith the Lord GOD; The city that went
out *by* a thousand shall leave an hundred, and that
which went forth *by* an hundred shall leave ten, to
the house of Israel.
4For thus saith the LORD unto the house of Israel,
Seek ye me, and ye shall live:
5But seek not Bethel, nor enter into Gilgal, and

NEW LIVING TRANSLATION

8 People staggered from town to town
looking for water,
but there was never enough.
But still you would not return to me,"
says the LORD.

9 "I struck your farms and vineyards with blight
and mildew.
Locusts devoured all your fig and olive trees.
But still you would not return to me,"
says the LORD.

10 "I sent plagues on you
like the plagues I sent on Egypt long ago.
I killed your young men in war
and led all your horses away.*
The stench of death filled the air!
But still you would not return to me,"
says the LORD.

11 "I destroyed some of your cities,
as I destroyed* Sodom and Gomorrah.
Those of you who survived
were like charred sticks pulled from a fire.
But still you would not return to me,"
says the LORD.

12 "Therefore, I will bring upon you all the disasters
I have announced.
Prepare to meet your God in judgment, you
people of Israel!"

13 For the LORD is the one who shaped the mountains,
stirs up the winds, and reveals his thoughts
to mankind.
He turns the light of dawn into darkness
and treads on the heights of the earth.
The LORD God of Heaven's Armies is his name!

A Call to Repentance

5 Listen, you people of Israel! Listen to this funeral song I am singing:

2 "The virgin Israel has fallen,
never to rise again!
She lies abandoned on the ground,
with no one to help her up."

3 The Sovereign LORD says:

"When a city sends a thousand men to battle,
only a hundred will return.
When a town sends a hundred,
only ten will come back alive."

4 Now this is what the LORD says to the family of Israel:

"Come back to me and live!
5 Don't worship at the pagan altars at Bethel;
don't go to the shrines at Gilgal or Beersheba.
For the people of Gilgal will be dragged off
into exile,

4:10 Or *and slaughtered your captured horses.* **4:11** Hebrew *as when God destroyed.*

KING JAMES VERSION

pass not to Beer-sheba: for Gilgal shall surely go into
captivity, and Bethel shall come to nought.
6 Seek the LORD, and ye shall live; lest he break out
like fire in the house of Joseph, and devour *it*, and
there be none to quench *it* in Bethel.
7 Ye who turn judgment to wormwood, and leave
off righteousness in the earth,
8 *Seek him* that maketh the seven stars and Orion,
and turneth the shadow of death into the morning,
and maketh the day dark with night: that calleth for
the waters of the sea, and poureth them out upon the
face of the earth: The LORD *is* his name:
9 That strengtheneth the spoiled against the strong,
so that the spoiled shall come against the fortress.
10 They hate him that rebuketh in the gate, and
they abhor him that speaketh uprightly.
11 Forasmuch therefore as your treading *is* upon
the poor, and ye take from him burdens of wheat:
ye have built houses of hewn stone, but ye shall not
dwell in them; ye have planted pleasant vineyards,
but ye shall not drink wine of them.
12 For I know your manifold transgressions and
your mighty sins: they afflict the just, they take a
bribe, and they turn aside the poor in the gate *from
their right*.
13 Therefore the prudent shall keep silence in that
time; for it *is* an evil time.
14 Seek good, and not evil, that ye may live: and so
the LORD, the God of hosts, shall be with you, as ye
have spoken.
15 Hate the evil, and love the good, and establish
judgment in the gate: it may be that the LORD God of
hosts will be gracious unto the remnant of Joseph.
16 Therefore the LORD, the God of hosts, the Lord,
saith thus; Wailing *shall be* in all streets; and they
shall say in all the highways, Alas! alas! and they shall
call the husbandman to mourning, and such as are
skilful of lamentation to wailing.
17 And in all vineyards *shall be* wailing: for I will
pass through thee, saith the LORD.

NEW LIVING TRANSLATION

and the people of Bethel will be reduced
to nothing."
6 Come back to the LORD and live!
Otherwise, he will roar through Israel* like a fire,
devouring you completely.
Your gods in Bethel
won't be able to quench the flames.
7 You twist justice, making it a bitter pill for
the oppressed.
You treat the righteous like dirt.

8 It is the LORD who created the stars,
the Pleiades and Orion.
He turns darkness into morning
and day into night.
He draws up water from the oceans
and pours it down as rain on the land.
The LORD is his name!
9 With blinding speed and power he destroys
the strong,
crushing all their defenses.

10 How you hate honest judges!
How you despise people who tell the truth!
11 You trample the poor,
stealing their grain through taxes and unfair
rent.
Therefore, though you build beautiful stone
houses,
you will never live in them.
Though you plant lush vineyards,
you will never drink wine from them.
12 For I know the vast number of your sins
and the depth of your rebellions.
You oppress good people by taking bribes
and deprive the poor of justice in the courts.
13 So those who are smart keep their mouths shut,
for it is an evil time.

14 Do what is good and run from evil
so that you may live!
Then the LORD God of Heaven's Armies will be
your helper,
just as you have claimed.
15 Hate evil and love what is good;
turn your courts into true halls of justice.
Perhaps even yet the LORD God of Heaven's Armies
will have mercy on the remnant of his people.*

16 Therefore, this is what the Lord, the LORD God of
Heaven's Armies, says:

"There will be crying in all the public squares
and mourning in every street.
Call for the farmers to weep with you,
and summon professional mourners to wail.
17 There will be wailing in every vineyard,
for I will destroy them all,"
says the LORD.

5:6 Hebrew *the house of Joseph*. 5:15 Hebrew *the remnant of Joseph*.

KING JAMES VERSION

18Woe unto you that desire the day of the LORD! to what end *is* it for you? the day of the LORD *is* darkness, and not light.

19As if a man did flee from a lion, and a bear met him; or went into the house, and leaned his hand on the wall, and a serpent bit him.

20*Shall* not the day of the LORD *be* darkness, and not light? even very dark, and no brightness in it?

21I hate, I despise your feast days, and I will not smell in your solemn assemblies.

22Though ye offer me burnt offerings and your meat offerings, I will not accept *them:* neither will I regard the peace offerings of your fat beasts.

23Take thou away from me the noise of thy songs; for I will not hear the melody of thy viols.

24But let judgment run down as waters, and righteousness as a mighty stream.

25Have ye offered unto me sacrifices and offerings in the wilderness forty years, O house of Israel?

26But ye have borne the tabernacle of your Moloch and Chiun your images, the star of your god, which ye made to yourselves.

27Therefore will I cause you to go into captivity beyond Damascus, saith the LORD, whose name *is* The God of hosts.

6 1Woe to them *that are* at ease in Zion, and trust in the mountain of Samaria, *which are* named chief of the nations, to whom the house of Israel came!

2Pass ye unto Calneh, and see; and from thence go ye to Hamath the great: then go down to Gath of the Philistines: *be they* better than these kingdoms? or their border greater than your border?

3Ye that put far away the evil day, and cause the seat of violence to come near;

4That lie upon beds of ivory, and stretch themselves upon their couches, and eat the lambs out of the flock, and the calves out of the midst of the stall;

5That chant to the sound of the viol, *and* invent to themselves instruments of musick, like David;

NEW LIVING TRANSLATION

Warning of Coming Judgment

18 What sorrow awaits you who say,
"If only the day of the LORD were here!"
You have no idea what you are wishing for.
That day will bring darkness, not light.
19 In that day you will be like a man who runs
from a lion—
only to meet a bear.
Escaping from the bear, he leans his hand against
a wall in his house—
and he's bitten by a snake.
20 Yes, the day of the LORD will be dark and
hopeless,
without a ray of joy or hope.

21 "I hate all your show and pretense—
the hypocrisy of your religious festivals and
solemn assemblies.
22 I will not accept your burnt offerings and grain
offerings.
I won't even notice all your choice peace
offerings.
23 Away with your noisy hymns of praise!
I will not listen to the music of your harps.
24 Instead, I want to see a mighty flood of justice,
an endless river of righteous living.

25"Was it to me you were bringing sacrifices and
offerings during the forty years in the wilderness,
Israel? 26No, you served your pagan gods—Sakkuth
your king god and Kaiwan your star god—the images
you made for yourselves. 27So I will send you into
exile, to a land east of Damascus,*" says the LORD,
whose name is the God of Heaven's Armies.

6 1What sorrow awaits you who lounge in
luxury in Jerusalem,*
and you who feel secure in Samaria!
You are famous and popular in Israel,
and people go to you for help.
2 But go over to Calneh
and see what happened there.
Then go to the great city of Hamath
and down to the Philistine city of Gath.
You are no better than they were,
and look at how they were destroyed.
3 You push away every thought of coming disaster,
but your actions only bring the day of
judgment closer.
4 How terrible for you who sprawl on ivory beds
and lounge on your couches,
eating the meat of tender lambs from the flock
and of choice calves fattened in the stall.
5 You sing trivial songs to the sound of the harp
and fancy yourselves to be great musicians
like David.

5:26-27 Greek version reads *No, you carried your pagan gods—the shrine of Molech, the star of your god Rephan, and the images you made for yourselves. So I will send you into exile, to a land east of Damascus.* Compare Acts 7:43. **6:1** Hebrew *in Zion.*

KING JAMES VERSION

6 That drink wine in bowls, and anoint themselves with the chief ointments: but they are not grieved for the affliction of Joseph.

7 Therefore now shall they go captive with the first that go captive, and the banquet of them that stretched themselves shall be removed.

8 The Lord God hath sworn by himself, saith the Lord the God of hosts, I abhor the excellency of Jacob, and hate his palaces: therefore will I deliver up the city with all that is therein.

9 And it shall come to pass, if there remain ten men in one house, that they shall die.

10 And a man's uncle shall take him up, and he that burneth him, to bring out the bones out of the house, and shall say unto him that *is* by the sides of the house, *Is there* yet *any* with thee? and he shall say, No. Then shall he say, Hold thy tongue: for we may not make mention of the name of the Lord.

11 For, behold, the Lord commandeth, and he will smite the great house with breaches, and the little house with clefts.

12 Shall horses run upon the rock? will *one* plow *there* with oxen? for ye have turned judgment into gall, and the fruit of righteousness into hemlock:

13 Ye which rejoice in a thing of nought, which say, Have we not taken to us horns by our own strength?

14 But, behold, I will raise up against you a nation, O house of Israel, saith the Lord the God of hosts; and they shall afflict you from the entering in of Hemath unto the river of the wilderness.

7 1 Thus hath the Lord God shewed unto me; and, behold, he formed grasshoppers in the beginning of the shooting up of the latter growth; and, lo, *it was* the latter growth after the king's mowings.

2 And it came to pass, *that* when they had made an end of eating the grass of the land, then I said, O Lord God, forgive, I beseech thee: by whom shall Jacob arise? for he *is* small.

3 The Lord repented for this: It shall not be, saith the Lord.

NEW LIVING TRANSLATION

6 You drink wine by the bowlful
and perfume yourselves with fragrant lotions.
You care nothing about the ruin of your
nation.*
7 Therefore, you will be the first to be led away
as captives.
Suddenly, all your parties will end.

8 The Sovereign Lord has sworn by his own name,
and this is what he, the Lord God of Heaven's Armies,
says:

"I despise the arrogance of Israel,*
and I hate their fortresses.
I will give this city
and everything in it to their enemies."

9 (If there are ten men left in one house, they will all
die. 10 And when a relative who is responsible to dis-
pose of the dead* goes into the house to carry out the
bodies, he will ask the last survivor, "Is anyone else
with you?" When the person begins to swear, "No,
by . . . ," he will interrupt and say, "Stop! Don't even
mention the name of the Lord.")

11 When the Lord gives the command,
homes both great and small will be smashed
to pieces.

12 Can horses gallop over boulders?
Can oxen be used to plow them?
But that's how foolish you are when you turn
justice into poison
and the sweet fruit of righteousness into
bitterness.
13 And you brag about your conquest of Lo-debar.*
You boast, "Didn't we take Karnaim* by our
own strength?"
14 "O people of Israel, I am about to bring an enemy
nation against you,"
says the Lord God of Heaven's Armies.
"They will oppress you throughout your land—
from Lebo-hamath in the north
to the Arabah Valley in the south."

A Vision of Locusts

7 The Sovereign Lord showed me a vision. I saw
him preparing to send a vast swarm of locusts
over the land. This was after the king's share had
been harvested from the fields and as the main crop
was coming up. 2 In my vision the locusts ate every
green plant in sight. Then I said, "O Sovereign Lord,
please forgive us or we will not survive, for Israel* is
so small."

3 So the Lord relented from this plan. "I will not do
it," he said.

6:6 Hebrew *of Joseph.* **6:8** Hebrew *Jacob.* See note on 3:13. **6:10** Or *to burn the dead.* The meaning of the Hebrew is uncertain. **6:13a** *Lo-debar* means "nothing." **6:13b** *Karnaim* means "horns," a term that symbolizes strength. **7:2** Hebrew *Jacob;* also in 7:5. See note on 3:13.

KING JAMES VERSION

4 Thus hath the Lord GOD shewed unto me: and,
behold, the Lord GOD called to contend by fire, and
it devoured the great deep, and did eat up a part.
5 Then said I, O Lord GOD, cease, I beseech thee: by
whom shall Jacob arise? for he *is* small.
6 The LORD repented for this: This also shall not be,
saith the Lord GOD.

7 Thus he shewed me: and, behold, the Lord stood
upon a wall *made* by a plumbline, with a plumbline
in his hand.
8 And the LORD said unto me, Amos, what seest
thou? And I said, A plumbline. Then said the Lord,
Behold, I will set a plumbline in the midst of my
people Israel: I will not again pass by them any more:
9 And the high places of Isaac shall be desolate, and
the sanctuaries of Israel shall be laid waste; and I will
rise against the house of Jeroboam with the sword.

10 Then Amaziah the priest of Bethel sent to Jeroboam king of Israel, saying, Amos hath conspired
against thee in the midst of the house of Israel: the
land is not able to bear all his words.
11 For thus Amos saith, Jeroboam shall die by the
sword, and Israel shall surely be led away captive out
of their own land.
12 Also Amaziah said unto Amos, O thou seer, go,
flee thee away into the land of Judah, and there eat
bread, and prophesy there:
13 But prophesy not again any more at Bethel: for it
is the king's chapel, and it *is* the king's court.
14 Then answered Amos, and said to Amaziah, I
was no prophet, neither *was* I a prophet's son; but
I *was* an herdman, and a gatherer of sycamore fruit:
15 And the LORD took me as I followed the flock,
and the LORD said unto me, Go, prophesy unto my
people Israel.
16 Now therefore hear thou the word of the LORD:
Thou sayest, Prophesy not against Israel, and drop
not *thy word* against the house of Isaac.
17 Therefore thus saith the LORD; Thy wife shall be
an harlot in the city, and thy sons and thy daughters
shall fall by the sword, and thy land shall be divided
by line; and thou shalt die in a polluted land: and
Israel shall surely go into captivity forth of his land.

NEW LIVING TRANSLATION

A Vision of Fire

4 Then the Sovereign LORD showed me another vision. I saw him preparing to punish his people with a
great fire. The fire had burned up the depths of the
sea and was devouring the entire land. 5 Then I said,
"O Sovereign LORD, please stop or we will not survive,
for Israel is so small."
6 Then the LORD relented from this plan, too. "I will
not do that either," said the Sovereign LORD.

A Vision of a Plumb Line

7 Then he showed me another vision. I saw the Lord
standing beside a wall that had been built using a
plumb line. He was using a plumb line to see if it was
still straight. 8 And the LORD said to me, "Amos, what
do you see?"
I answered, "A plumb line."
And the Lord replied, "I will test my people with
this plumb line. I will no longer ignore all their sins.
9 The pagan shrines of your ancestors* will be
ruined, and the temples of Israel will be destroyed;
I will bring the dynasty of King Jeroboam to a sudden end."

Amos and Amaziah

10 Then Amaziah, the priest of Bethel, sent a message
to Jeroboam, king of Israel: "Amos is hatching a plot
against you right here on your very doorstep! What
he is saying is intolerable. 11 He is saying, 'Jeroboam
will soon be killed, and the people of Israel will be
sent away into exile.'"
12 Then Amaziah sent orders to Amos: "Get out of
here, you prophet! Go on back to the land of Judah,
and earn your living by prophesying there! 13 Don't
bother us with your prophecies here in Bethel. This
is the king's sanctuary and the national place of
worship!"
14 But Amos replied, "I'm not a professional
prophet, and I was never trained to be one.* I'm just
a shepherd, and I take care of sycamore-fig trees.
15 But the LORD called me away from my flock and
told me, 'Go and prophesy to my people in Israel.'
16 Now then, listen to this message from the LORD:

"You say,
'Don't prophesy against Israel.
Stop preaching against my people.*'
17 But this is what the LORD says:
'Your wife will become a prostitute in this city,
and your sons and daughters will be killed.
Your land will be divided up,
and you yourself will die in a foreign land.
And the people of Israel will certainly become
captives in exile,
far from their homeland.'"

7:9 Hebrew *of Isaac.* **7:14** Or *I'm not a prophet nor the son of a prophet.*
7:16 Hebrew *against the house of Isaac.*

KING JAMES VERSION

8 1 Thus hath the Lord GOD shewed unto me: and
behold a basket of summer fruit.
2 And he said, Amos, what seest thou? And I said, A
basket of summer fruit. Then said the LORD unto me,
The end is come upon my people of Israel; I will not
again pass by them any more.
3 And the songs of the temple shall be howlings in
that day, saith the Lord GOD: *there shall be* many dead
bodies in every place; they shall cast *them* forth with
silence.
4 Hear this, O ye that swallow up the needy, even to
make the poor of the land to fail,
5 Saying, When will the new moon be gone, that
we may sell corn? and the sabbath, that we may set
forth wheat, making the ephah small, and the shekel
great, and falsifying the balances by deceit?
6 That we may buy the poor for silver, and the
needy for a pair of shoes; *yea,* and sell the refuse of
the wheat?
7 The LORD hath sworn by the excellency of Jacob,
Surely I will never forget any of their works.
8 Shall not the land tremble for this, and every
one mourn that dwelleth therein? and it shall rise
up wholly as a flood; and it shall be cast out and
drowned, as *by* the flood of Egypt.
9 And it shall come to pass in that day, saith the
Lord GOD, that I will cause the sun to go down at
noon, and I will darken the earth in the clear day:
10 And I will turn your feasts into mourning, and all
your songs into lamentation; and I will bring up sackcloth upon all loins, and baldness upon every head;
and I will make it as the mourning of an only *son,* and
the end thereof as a bitter day.
11 Behold, the days come, saith the Lord GOD, that I
will send a famine in the land, not a famine of bread,
nor a thirst for water, but of hearing the words of the
LORD:
12 And they shall wander from sea to sea, and from
the north even to the east, they shall run to and fro to
seek the word of the LORD, and shall not find *it.*
13 In that day shall the fair virgins and young men
faint for thirst.

NEW LIVING TRANSLATION

A Vision of Ripe Fruit

8 Then the Sovereign LORD showed me another
vision. In it I saw a basket filled with ripe fruit.
2 "What do you see, Amos?" he asked.
I replied, "A basket full of ripe fruit."
Then the LORD said, "Like this fruit, Israel is ripe
for punishment! I will not delay their punishment
again. 3 In that day the singing in the Temple will turn
to wailing. Dead bodies will be scattered everywhere.
They will be carried out of the city in silence. I, the
Sovereign LORD, have spoken!"

4 Listen to this, you who rob the poor
and trample down the needy!
5 You can't wait for the Sabbath day to be over
and the religious festivals to end
so you can get back to cheating the helpless.
You measure out grain with dishonest measures
and cheat the buyer with dishonest scales.*
6 And you mix the grain you sell
with chaff swept from the floor.
Then you enslave poor people
for one piece of silver or a pair of sandals.

7 Now the LORD has sworn this oath
by his own name, the Pride of Israel*:
"I will never forget
the wicked things you have done!
8 The earth will tremble for your deeds,
and everyone will mourn.
The ground will rise like the Nile River
at floodtime;
it will heave up, then sink again.

9 "In that day," says the Sovereign LORD,
"I will make the sun go down at noon
and darken the earth while it is still day.
10 I will turn your celebrations into times of
mourning
and your singing into weeping.
You will wear funeral clothes
and shave your heads to show your sorrow—
as if your only son had died.
How very bitter that day will be!

11 "The time is surely coming," says the
Sovereign LORD,
"when I will send a famine on the land—
not a famine of bread or water
but of hearing the words of the LORD.
12 People will stagger from sea to sea
and wander from border to border*
searching for the word of the LORD,
but they will not find it.
13 Beautiful girls and strong young men
will grow faint in that day,
thirsting for the LORD's word.

8:5 Hebrew *You make the ephah* [a unit for measuring grain] *small and the shekel* [a unit of weight] *great, and you deal falsely by using deceitful balances.* **8:7** Hebrew *the pride of Jacob.* See note on 3:13. **8:12** Hebrew *from north to east.*

KING JAMES VERSION

14 They that swear by the sin of Samaria, and say, Thy god, O Dan, liveth; and, The manner of Beer-sheba liveth; even they shall fall, and never rise up again.

9 1 I saw the Lord standing upon the altar: and he said, Smite the lintel of the door, that the posts may shake: and cut them in the head, all of them; and I will slay the last of them with the sword: he that fleeth of them shall not flee away, and he that escapeth of them shall not be delivered.

2 Though they dig into hell, thence shall mine hand take them; though they climb up to heaven, thence will I bring them down:

3 And though they hide themselves in the top of Carmel, I will search and take them out thence; and though they be hid from my sight in the bottom of the sea, thence will I command the serpent, and he shall bite them:

4 And though they go into captivity before their enemies, thence will I command the sword, and it shall slay them: and I will set mine eyes upon them for evil, and not for good.

5 And the Lord GOD of hosts *is* he that toucheth the land, and it shall melt, and all that dwell therein shall mourn: and it shall rise up wholly like a flood; and shall be drowned, as *by* the flood of Egypt.

6 *It is* he that buildeth his stories in the heaven, and hath founded his troop in the earth; he that calleth for the waters of the sea, and poureth them out upon the face of the earth: The LORD *is* his name.

7 *Are* ye not as children of the Ethiopians unto me, O children of Israel? saith the LORD. Have not I brought up Israel out of the land of Egypt? and the Philistines from Caphtor, and the Syrians from Kir?

8 Behold, the eyes of the Lord GOD *are* upon the sinful kingdom, and I will destroy it from off the face of the earth; saving that I will not utterly destroy the house of Jacob, saith the LORD.

NEW LIVING TRANSLATION

14 And those who swear by the shameful idols
of Samaria—
who take oaths in the name of the god of Dan
and make vows in the name of the god of
Beersheba*—
they will all fall down,
never to rise again."

A Vision of God at the Altar

9 Then I saw a vision of the Lord standing beside the altar. He said,

"Strike the tops of the Temple columns,
so that the foundation will shake.
Bring down the roof
on the heads of the people below.
I will kill with the sword those who survive.
No one will escape!
2 "Even if they dig down to the place of the dead,*
I will reach down and pull them up.
Even if they climb up into the heavens,
I will bring them down.
3 Even if they hide at the very top of Mount Carmel,
I will search them out and capture them.
Even if they hide at the bottom of the ocean,
I will send the sea serpent after them to
bite them.
4 Even if their enemies drive them into exile,
I will command the sword to kill them there.
I am determined to bring disaster upon them
and not to help them."

5 The Lord, the LORD of Heaven's Armies,
touches the land and it melts,
and all its people mourn.
The ground rises like the Nile River at floodtime,
and then it sinks again.
6 The LORD's home reaches up to the heavens,
while its foundation is on the earth.
He draws up water from the oceans
and pours it down as rain on the land.
The LORD is his name!

7 "Are you Israelites more important to me
than the Ethiopians?*" asks the LORD.
"I brought Israel out of Egypt,
but I also brought the Philistines from Crete*
and led the Arameans out of Kir.

8 "I, the Sovereign LORD,
am watching this sinful nation of Israel.
I will destroy it
from the face of the earth.
But I will never completely destroy the family
of Israel,*"
says the LORD.

8:14 Hebrew *the way of Beersheba.* **9:2** Hebrew *to Sheol.* **9:7a** Hebrew *the Cushites?* **9:7b** Hebrew *Caphtor.* **9:8** Hebrew *the house of Jacob.* See note on 3:13.

KING JAMES VERSION

9For, lo, I will command, and I will sift the house of
Israel among all nations, like as *corn* is sifted in a
sieve, yet shall not the least grain fall upon the earth.
10All the sinners of my people shall die by the
sword, which say, The evil shall not overtake nor prevent us.

11In that day will I raise up the tabernacle of David
that is fallen, and close up the breaches thereof; and I
will raise up his ruins, and I will build it as in the days
of old:
12That they may possess the remnant of Edom,
and of all the heathen, which are called by my name,
saith the LORD that doeth this.
13Behold, the days come, saith the LORD, that the
plowman shall overtake the reaper, and the treader
of grapes him that soweth seed; and the mountains
shall drop sweet wine, and all the hills shall melt.
14And I will bring again the captivity of my people
of Israel, and they shall build the waste cities, and inhabit *them;* and they shall plant vineyards, and drink
the wine thereof; they shall also make gardens, and
eat the fruit of them.
15And I will plant them upon their land, and they
shall no more be pulled up out of their land which I
have given them, saith the LORD thy God.

NEW LIVING TRANSLATION

9 "For I will give the command
and will shake Israel along with the
other nations
as grain is shaken in a sieve,
yet not one true kernel will be lost.
10 But all the sinners will die by the sword—
all those who say, 'Nothing bad will
happen to us.'

A Promise of Restoration

11 "In that day I will restore the fallen house*
of David.
I will repair its damaged walls.
From the ruins I will rebuild it
and restore its former glory.
12 And Israel will possess what is left of Edom
and all the nations I have called to be mine.*"
The LORD has spoken,
and he will do these things.

13 "The time will come," says the LORD,
"when the grain and grapes will grow faster
than they can be harvested.
Then the terraced vineyards on the hills
of Israel
will drip with sweet wine!
14 I will bring my exiled people of Israel
back from distant lands,
and they will rebuild their ruined cities
and live in them again.
They will plant vineyards and gardens;
they will eat their crops and drink their wine.
15 I will firmly plant them there
in their own land.
They will never again be uprooted
from the land I have given them,"
says the LORD your God.

9:11a Or *kingdom;* Hebrew reads *tent.* **9:11b-12** Greek version reads *and restore its former glory, / so that the rest of humanity, including the Gentiles— / all those I have called to be mine—might seek me.* Compare Acts 15:16-17.

Obadiah

KING JAMES VERSION

1 The vision of Obadiah. Thus saith the Lord GOD concerning Edom; We have heard a rumour from the
LORD, and an ambassador is sent among the heathen,
Arise ye, and let us rise up against her in battle.
2 Behold, I have made thee small among the heathen: thou art greatly despised.
3 The pride of thine heart hath deceived thee, thou
that dwellest in the clefts of the rock, whose habitation *is* high; that saith in his heart, Who shall bring
me down to the ground?
4 Though thou exalt *thyself* as the eagle, and
though thou set thy nest among the stars, thence will
I bring thee down, saith the LORD.
5 If thieves came to thee, if robbers by night, (how
art thou cut off!) would they not have stolen till they
had enough? if the grapegatherers came to thee,
would they not leave *some* grapes?
6 How are *the things* of Esau searched out! *how* are
his hidden things sought up!
7 All the men of thy confederacy have brought thee
even to the border: the men that were at peace with
thee have deceived thee, *and* prevailed against thee;
they that eat thy bread have laid a wound under
thee: *there is* none understanding in him.
8 Shall I not in that day, saith the LORD, even destroy the wise *men* out of Edom, and understanding
out of the mount of Esau?

NEW LIVING TRANSLATION

This is the vision that the Sovereign LORD revealed to Obadiah concerning the land of Edom.

Edom's Judgment Announced

We have heard a message from the LORD
that an ambassador was sent to the nations
to say,
"Get ready, everyone!
Let's assemble our armies and attack Edom!"

2 The LORD says to Edom,
"I will cut you down to size among the nations;
you will be greatly despised.
3 You have been deceived by your own pride
because you live in a rock fortress
and make your home high in the mountains.
'Who can ever reach us way up here?'
you ask boastfully.
4 But even if you soar as high as eagles
and build your nest among the stars,
I will bring you crashing down,"
says the LORD.

5 "If thieves came at night and robbed you
(what a disaster awaits you!),
they would not take everything.
Those who harvest grapes
always leave a few for the poor.
But your enemies will wipe you out completely!
6 Every nook and cranny of Edom*
will be searched and looted.
Every treasure will be found and taken.

7 "All your allies will turn against you.
They will help to chase you from your land.
They will promise you peace
while plotting to deceive and destroy you.
Your trusted friends will set traps for you,
and you won't even know about it.
8 At that time not a single wise person
will be left in the whole land of Edom,"
says the LORD.
"For on the mountains of Edom
I will destroy everyone who has understanding.

6 Hebrew *Esau;* also in 8b, 9, 18, 19, 21.

KING JAMES VERSION

9 And thy mighty *men*, O Teman, shall be dismayed, to the end that every one of the mount of Esau may be cut off by slaughter.

10 For *thy* violence against thy brother Jacob shame shall cover thee, and thou shalt be cut off for ever.

11 In the day that thou stoodest on the other side, in the day that the strangers carried away captive his forces, and foreigners entered into his gates, and cast lots upon Jerusalem, even thou *wast* as one of them.

12 But thou shouldest not have looked on the day of thy brother in the day that he became a stranger; neither shouldest thou have rejoiced over the children of Judah in the day of their destruction; neither shouldest thou have spoken proudly in the day of distress.

13 Thou shouldest not have entered into the gate of my people in the day of their calamity; yea, thou shouldest not have looked on their affliction in the day of their calamity, nor have laid *hands* on their substance in the day of their calamity;

14 Neither shouldest thou have stood in the crossway, to cut off those of his that did escape; neither shouldest thou have delivered up those of his that did remain in the day of distress.

15 For the day of the LORD *is* near upon all the heathen: as thou hast done, it shall be done unto thee: thy reward shall return upon thine own head.

16 For as ye have drunk upon my holy mountain, *so* shall all the heathen drink continually, yea, they shall drink, and they shall swallow down, and they shall be as though they had not been.

17 But upon mount Zion shall be deliverance, and there shall be holiness; and the house of Jacob shall possess their possessions.

NEW LIVING TRANSLATION

9 The mightiest warriors of Teman
will be terrified,
and everyone on the mountains of Edom
will be cut down in the slaughter.

Reasons for Edom's Punishment

10 "Because of the violence you did
to your close relatives in Israel,*
you will be filled with shame
and destroyed forever.
11 When they were invaded,
you stood aloof, refusing to help them.
Foreign invaders carried off their wealth
and cast lots to divide up Jerusalem,
but you acted like one of Israel's enemies.

12 "You should not have gloated
when they exiled your relatives
to distant lands.
You should not have rejoiced
when the people of Judah suffered such
misfortune.
You should not have spoken arrogantly
in that terrible time of trouble.
13 You should not have plundered the land of Israel
when they were suffering such calamity.
You should not have gloated over their
destruction
when they were suffering such calamity.
You should not have seized their wealth
when they were suffering such calamity.
14 You should not have stood at the crossroads,
killing those who tried to escape.
You should not have captured the survivors
and handed them over in their terrible time
of trouble.

Edom Destroyed, Israel Restored

15 "The day is near when I, the LORD,
will judge all godless nations!
As you have done to Israel,
so it will be done to you.
All your evil deeds
will fall back on your own heads.
16 Just as you swallowed up my people
on my holy mountain,
so you and the surrounding nations
will swallow the punishment I pour out on you.
Yes, all you nations will drink and stagger
and disappear from history.

17 "But Jerusalem* will become a refuge for those
who escape;
it will be a holy place.
And the people of Israel* will come back
to reclaim their inheritance.

10 Hebrew *your brother Jacob.* The names "Jacob" and "Israel" are often interchanged throughout the Old Testament, referring sometimes to the individual patriarch and sometimes to the nation. **17a** Hebrew *Mount Zion.* **17b** Hebrew *house of Jacob;* also in 18. See note on 10.

KING JAMES VERSION

18 And the house of Jacob shall be a fire, and the
house of Joseph a flame, and the house of Esau for
stubble, and they shall kindle in them, and devour
them; and there shall not be *any* remaining of the
house of Esau; for the LORD hath spoken *it*.
19 And *they of* the south shall possess the mount of
Esau; and *they of* the plain the Philistines: and they
shall possess the fields of Ephraim, and the fields of
Samaria: and Benjamin *shall possess* Gilead.
20 And the captivity of this host of the children of
Israel *shall possess* that of the Canaanites, *even* unto
Zarephath; and the captivity of Jerusalem, which *is* in
Sepharad, shall possess the cities of the south.
21 And saviours shall come up on mount Zion to
judge the mount of Esau; and the kingdom shall be
the LORD'S.

NEW LIVING TRANSLATION

18 The people of Israel will be a raging fire,
and Edom a field of dry stubble.
The descendants of Joseph will be a flame
roaring across the field, devouring everything.
There will be no survivors in Edom.
I, the LORD, have spoken!

19 "Then my people living in the Negev
will occupy the mountains of Edom.
Those living in the foothills of Judah*
will possess the Philistine plains
and take over the fields of Ephraim
and Samaria.
And the people of Benjamin
will occupy the land of Gilead.
20 The exiles of Israel will return to their land
and occupy the Phoenician coast as far north
as Zarephath.
The captives from Jerusalem exiled in the north*
will return home and resettle the towns
of the Negev.
21 Those who have been rescued* will go up to*
Mount Zion in Jerusalem
to rule over the mountains of Edom.
And the LORD himself will be king!"

19 Hebrew *the Shephelah.* **20** Hebrew *in Sepharad.* **21a** As in Greek and Syriac versions; Hebrew reads *Rescuers.* **21b** Or *from.*

Jonah

KING JAMES VERSION

1 [1]Now the word of the LORD came unto Jonah the
son of Amittai, saying,
[2]Arise, go to Nineveh, that great city, and cry against
it; for their wickedness is come up before me.
[3]But Jonah rose up to flee unto Tarshish from the
presence of the LORD, and went down to Joppa; and
he found a ship going to Tarshish: so he paid the fare
thereof, and went down into it, to go with them unto
Tarshish from the presence of the LORD.
[4]But the LORD sent out a great wind into the sea,
and there was a mighty tempest in the sea, so that the
ship was like to be broken.
[5]Then the mariners were afraid, and cried every
man unto his god, and cast forth the wares that *were*
in the ship into the sea, to lighten *it* of them. But Jonah was gone down into the sides of the ship; and he
lay, and was fast asleep.
[6]So the shipmaster came to him, and said unto
him, What meanest thou, O sleeper? arise, call upon
thy God, if so be that God will think upon us, that we
perish not.
[7]And they said every one to his fellow, Come, and
let us cast lots, that we may know for whose cause
this evil *is* upon us. So they cast lots, and the lot fell
upon Jonah.
[8]Then said they unto him, Tell us, we pray thee, for
whose cause this evil *is* upon us; What *is* thine occupation? and whence comest thou? what *is* thy country? and of what people *art* thou?
[9]And he said unto them, I *am* an Hebrew; and I fear
the LORD, the God of heaven, which hath made the
sea and the dry *land*.
[10]Then were the men exceedingly afraid, and said
unto him, Why hast thou done this? For the men
knew that he fled from the presence of the LORD, because he had told them.
[11]Then said they unto him, What shall we do unto
thee, that the sea may be calm unto us? for the sea
wrought, and was tempestuous.
[12]And he said unto them, Take me up, and cast me
forth into the sea; so shall the sea be calm unto you:
for I know that for my sake this great tempest *is*
upon you.

NEW LIVING TRANSLATION

Jonah Runs from the LORD

1 The LORD gave this message to Jonah son of
Amittai: [2]"Get up and go to the great city of Nineveh. Announce my judgment against it because I
have seen how wicked its people are."
[3]But Jonah got up and went in the opposite direction to get away from the LORD. He went down to the
port of Joppa, where he found a ship leaving for Tarshish. He bought a ticket and went on board, hoping
to escape from the LORD by sailing to Tarshish.
[4]But the LORD hurled a powerful wind over the sea,
causing a violent storm that threatened to break the
ship apart. [5]Fearing for their lives, the desperate sailors shouted to their gods for help and threw the
cargo overboard to lighten the ship.
But all this time Jonah was sound asleep down in
the hold. [6]So the captain went down after him. "How
can you sleep at a time like this?" he shouted. "Get up
and pray to your god! Maybe he will pay attention to
us and spare our lives."
[7]Then the crew cast lots to see which of them had
offended the gods and caused the terrible storm.
When they did this, the lots identified Jonah as the
culprit. [8]"Why has this awful storm come down on
us?" they demanded. "Who are you? What is your
line of work? What country are you from? What is
your nationality?"
[9]Jonah answered, "I am a Hebrew, and I worship
the LORD, the God of heaven, who made the sea and
the land."
[10]The sailors were terrified when they heard this,
for he had already told them he was running away
from the LORD. "Oh, why did you do it?" they
groaned. [11]And since the storm was getting worse all
the time, they asked him, "What should we do to you
to stop this storm?"
[12]"Throw me into the sea," Jonah said, "and it will
become calm again. I know that this terrible storm is
all my fault."

KING JAMES VERSION

13 Nevertheless the men rowed hard to bring *it* to
the land; but they could not: for the sea wrought, and
was tempestuous against them.
14 Wherefore they cried unto the LORD, and said,
We beseech thee, O LORD, we beseech thee, let us not
perish for this man's life, and lay not upon us innocent blood: for thou, O LORD, hast done as it pleased
thee.
15 So they took up Jonah, and cast him forth into
the sea: and the sea ceased from her raging.
16 Then the men feared the LORD exceedingly, and
offered a sacrifice unto the LORD, and made vows.
17 Now the LORD had prepared a great fish to swallow up Jonah. And Jonah was in the belly of the fish
three days and three nights.

2 1 Then Jonah prayed unto the LORD his God out
of the fish's belly,
2 And said, I cried by reason of mine affliction unto
the LORD, and he heard me; out of the belly of hell
cried I, *and* thou heardest my voice.
3 For thou hadst cast me into the deep, in the midst
of the seas; and the floods compassed me about: all
thy billows and thy waves passed over me.
4 Then I said, I am cast out of thy sight; yet I will
look again toward thy holy temple.
5 The waters compassed me about, *even* to the
soul: the depth closed me round about, the weeds
were wrapped about my head.
6 I went down to the bottoms of the mountains; the
earth with her bars *was* about me for ever: yet hast
thou brought up my life from corruption, O LORD
my God.
7 When my soul fainted within me I remembered
the LORD: and my prayer came in unto thee, into
thine holy temple.
8 They that observe lying vanities forsake their own
mercy.
9 But I will sacrifice unto thee with the voice of
thanksgiving; I will pay *that* that I have vowed. Salvation *is* of the LORD.
10 And the LORD spake unto the fish, and it vomited
out Jonah upon the dry *land*.

NEW LIVING TRANSLATION

13 Instead, the sailors rowed even harder to get the
ship to the land. But the stormy sea was too violent
for them, and they couldn't make it.
14 Then they
cried out to the LORD, Jonah's God. "O LORD," they
pleaded, "don't make us die for this man's sin. And
don't hold us responsible for his death. O LORD, you
have sent this storm upon him for your own good
reasons."
15 Then the sailors picked Jonah up and threw him
into the raging sea, and the storm stopped at once!
16 The sailors were awestruck by the LORD's great
power, and they offered him a sacrifice and vowed
to serve him.
17 *Now the LORD had arranged for a great fish to
swallow Jonah. And Jonah was inside the fish for
three days and three nights.

Jonah's Prayer

2 1 *Then Jonah prayed to the LORD his God from
inside the fish.
2 He said,

"I cried out to the LORD in my great trouble,
and he answered me.
I called to you from the land of the dead,*
and LORD, you heard me!
3 You threw me into the ocean depths,
and I sank down to the heart of the sea.
The mighty waters engulfed me;
I was buried beneath your wild and
stormy waves.
4 Then I said, 'O LORD, you have driven me
from your presence.
Yet I will look once more toward your
holy Temple.'
5 "I sank beneath the waves,
and the waters closed over me.
Seaweed wrapped itself around my head.
6 I sank down to the very roots of the mountains.
I was imprisoned in the earth,
whose gates lock shut forever.
But you, O LORD my God,
snatched me from the jaws of death!
7 As my life was slipping away,
I remembered the LORD.
And my earnest prayer went out to you
in your holy Temple.
8 Those who worship false gods
turn their backs on all God's mercies.
9 But I will offer sacrifices to you with songs
of praise,
and I will fulfill all my vows.
For my salvation comes from the LORD alone."

10 Then the LORD ordered the fish to spit Jonah out
onto the beach.

1:17 Verse 1:17 is numbered 2:1 in Hebrew text. **2:1** Verses 2:1-10 are numbered 2:2-11 in Hebrew text. **2:2** Hebrew *from Sheol.*

KING JAMES VERSION

3 1 And the word of the LORD came unto Jonah the second time, saying,

2 Arise, go unto Nineveh, that great city, and preach unto it the preaching that I bid thee.

3 So Jonah arose, and went unto Nineveh, according to the word of the LORD. Now Nineveh was an exceeding great city of three days' journey.

4 And Jonah began to enter into the city a day's journey, and he cried, and said, Yet forty days, and Nineveh shall be overthrown.

5 So the people of Nineveh believed God, and proclaimed a fast, and put on sackcloth, from the greatest of them even to the least of them.

6 For word came unto the king of Nineveh, and he arose from his throne, and he laid his robe from him, and covered *him* with sackcloth, and sat in ashes.

7 And he caused *it* to be proclaimed and published through Nineveh by the decree of the king and his nobles, saying, Let neither man nor beast, herd nor flock, taste any thing: let them not feed, nor drink water:

8 But let man and beast be covered with sackcloth, and cry mightily unto God: yea, let them turn every one from his evil way, and from the violence that *is* in their hands.

9 Who can tell *if* God will turn and repent, and turn away from his fierce anger, that we perish not?

10 And God saw their works, that they turned from their evil way; and God repented of the evil, that he had said that he would do unto them; and he did *it* not.

4 1 But it displeased Jonah exceedingly, and he was very angry.

2 And he prayed unto the LORD, and said, I pray thee, O LORD, *was* not this my saying, when I was yet in my country? Therefore I fled before unto Tarshish: for I knew that thou *art* a gracious God, and merciful, slow to anger, and of great kindness, and repentest thee of the evil.

3 Therefore now, O LORD, take, I beseech thee, my life from me; for *it is* better for me to die than to live.

4 Then said the LORD, Doest thou well to be angry?

5 So Jonah went out of the city, and sat on the east side of the city, and there made him a booth, and sat under it in the shadow, till he might see what would become of the city.

6 And the LORD God prepared a gourd, and made *it* to come up over Jonah, that it might be a shadow over his head, to deliver him from his grief. So Jonah was exceeding glad of the gourd.

7 But God prepared a worm when the morning rose the next day, and it smote the gourd that it withered.

8 And it came to pass, when the sun did arise, that God prepared a vehement east wind; and the sun beat upon the head of Jonah, that he fainted, and

NEW LIVING TRANSLATION

Jonah Goes to Nineveh

3 Then the LORD spoke to Jonah a second time:
2 "Get up and go to the great city of Nineveh,
and deliver the message I have given you."
3 This time Jonah obeyed the LORD's command and
went to Nineveh, a city so large that it took three days
to see it all.* 4 On the day Jonah entered the city, he
shouted to the crowds: "Forty days from now Nineveh will be destroyed!" 5 The people of Nineveh believed God's message, and from the greatest to the
least, they declared a fast and put on burlap to show
their sorrow.
6 When the king of Nineveh heard what Jonah was
saying, he stepped down from his throne and took
off his royal robes. He dressed himself in burlap and
sat on a heap of ashes. 7 Then the king and his nobles
sent this decree throughout the city:

"No one, not even the animals from your herds
and flocks, may eat or drink anything at all.
8 People and animals alike must wear garments
of mourning, and everyone must pray earnestly
to God. They must turn from their evil ways and
stop all their violence. 9 Who can tell? Perhaps
even yet God will change his mind and hold back
his fierce anger from destroying us."

10 When God saw what they had done and how
they had put a stop to their evil ways, he changed his
mind and did not carry out the destruction he had
threatened.

Jonah's Anger at the LORD's Mercy

4 This change of plans greatly upset Jonah, and
he became very angry. 2 So he complained to
the LORD about it: "Didn't I say before I left home that
you would do this, LORD? That is why I ran away to
Tarshish! I knew that you are a merciful and compassionate God, slow to get angry and filled with unfailing love. You are eager to turn back from destroying
people. 3 Just kill me now, LORD! I'd rather be dead
than alive if what I predicted will not happen."
4 The LORD replied, "Is it right for you to be angry
about this?"
5 Then Jonah went out to the east side of the city
and made a shelter to sit under as he waited to see
what would happen to the city. 6 And the LORD God
arranged for a leafy plant to grow there, and soon it
spread its broad leaves over Jonah's head, shading
him from the sun. This eased his discomfort, and
Jonah was very grateful for the plant.
7 But God also arranged for a worm! The next
morning at dawn the worm ate through the stem of
the plant so that it withered away. 8 And as the sun
grew hot, God arranged for a scorching east wind to
blow on Jonah. The sun beat down on his head until

3:3 Hebrew *a great city to God, of three days' journey.*

KING JAMES VERSION

wished in himself to die, and said, *It is* better for me
to die than to live.
9And God said to Jonah, Doest thou well to be angry for the gourd? And he said, I do well to be angry,
even unto death.
10Then said the LORD, Thou hast had pity on the
gourd, for the which thou hast not laboured, neither
madest it grow; which came up in a night, and perished in a night:
11And should not I spare Nineveh, that great city,
wherein are more than sixscore thousand persons
that cannot discern between their right hand and
their left hand; and *also* much cattle?

NEW LIVING TRANSLATION

he grew faint and wished to die. "Death is certainly
better than living like this!" he exclaimed.
9Then God said to Jonah, "Is it right for you to be
angry because the plant died?"
"Yes," Jonah retorted, "even angry enough to die!"
10Then the LORD said, "You feel sorry about the
plant, though you did nothing to put it there. It came
quickly and died quickly. 11But Nineveh has more
than 120,000 people living in spiritual darkness,*
not to mention all the animals. Shouldn't I feel sorry
for such a great city?"

4:11 Hebrew *people who don't know their right hand from their left.*

Micah

KING JAMES VERSION

1 [1]The word of the LORD that came to Micah the Morasthite in the days of Jotham, Ahaz, *and* Hezekiah, kings of Judah, which he saw concerning Samaria and Jerusalem.

[2]Hear, all ye people; hearken, O earth, and all that therein is: and let the Lord GOD be witness against you, the LORD from his holy temple.

[3]For, behold, the LORD cometh forth out of his place, and will come down, and tread upon the high places of the earth.

[4]And the mountains shall be molten under him, and the valleys shall be cleft, as wax before the fire, *and* as the waters *that are* poured down a steep place.

[5]For the transgression of Jacob *is* all this, and for the sins of the house of Israel. What *is* the transgression of Jacob? *is it* not Samaria? and what *are* the high places of Judah? *are they* not Jerusalem?

[6]Therefore I will make Samaria as an heap of the field, *and* as plantings of a vineyard: and I will pour down the stones thereof into the valley, and I will discover the foundations thereof.

[7]And all the graven images thereof shall be beaten to pieces, and all the hires thereof shall be burned with the fire, and all the idols thereof will I lay desolate: for she gathered *it* of the hire of an harlot, and they shall return to the hire of an harlot.

[8]Therefore I will wail and howl, I will go stripped

NEW LIVING TRANSLATION

1 The LORD gave this message to Micah of Moresheth during the years when Jotham, Ahaz, and Hezekiah were kings of Judah. The visions he saw concerned both Samaria and Jerusalem.

Grief over Samaria and Jerusalem

2 Attention! Let all the people of the world listen!
  Let the earth and everything in it hear.
The Sovereign LORD is making accusations
    against you;
  the Lord speaks from his holy Temple.
3 Look! The LORD is coming!
  He leaves his throne in heaven
  and tramples the heights of the earth.
4 The mountains melt beneath his feet
  and flow into the valleys
like wax in a fire,
  like water pouring down a hill.
5 And why is this happening?
  Because of the rebellion of Israel*—
  yes, the sins of the whole nation.
Who is to blame for Israel's rebellion?
  Samaria, its capital city!
Where is the center of idolatry in Judah?
  In Jerusalem, its capital!

6 "So I, the LORD, will make the city of Samaria
  a heap of ruins.
Her streets will be plowed up
  for planting vineyards.
I will roll the stones of her walls into the
    valley below,
  exposing her foundations.
7 All her carved images will be smashed.
  All her sacred treasures will be burned.
These things were bought with the money
  earned by her prostitution,
and they will now be carried away
  to pay prostitutes elsewhere."

8 Therefore, I will mourn and lament.
  I will walk around barefoot and naked.

1:5 Hebrew *Jacob;* also in 1:5b. The names "Jacob" and "Israel" are often interchanged throughout the Old Testament, referring sometimes to the individual patriarch and sometimes to the nation.

KING JAMES VERSION

and naked: I will make a wailing like the dragons, and mourning as the owls.

9 For her wound *is* incurable; for it is come unto Judah; he is come unto the gate of my people, *even* to Jerusalem.

10 Declare ye *it* not at Gath, weep ye not at all: in the house of Aphrah roll thyself in the dust.

11 Pass ye away, thou inhabitant of Saphir, having thy shame naked: the inhabitant of Zaanan came not forth in the mourning of Beth-ezel; he shall receive of you his standing.

12 For the inhabitant of Maroth waited carefully for good: but evil came down from the LORD unto the gate of Jerusalem.

13 O thou inhabitant of Lachish, bind the chariot to the swift beast: she *is* the beginning of the sin to the daughter of Zion: for the transgressions of Israel were found in thee.

14 Therefore shalt thou give presents to Moresheth-gath: the houses of Achzib *shall be* a lie to the kings of Israel.

15 Yet will I bring an heir unto thee, O inhabitant of Mareshah: he shall come unto Adullam the glory of Israel.

16 Make thee bald, and poll thee for thy delicate children; enlarge thy baldness as the eagle; for they are gone into captivity from thee.

2 1 Woe to them that devise iniquity, and work evil upon their beds! when the morning is light, they practise it, because it is in the power of their hand.

2 And they covet fields, and take *them* by violence; and houses, and take *them* away: so they oppress a man and his house, even a man and his heritage.

NEW LIVING TRANSLATION

I will howl like a jackal
and moan like an owl.
9 For my people's wound
is too deep to heal.
It has reached into Judah,
even to the gates of Jerusalem.
10 Don't tell our enemies in Gath*;
don't weep at all.
You people in Beth-leaphrah,*
roll in the dust to show your despair.
11 You people in Shaphir,*
go as captives into exile—naked and ashamed.
The people of Zaanan*
dare not come outside their walls.
The people of Beth-ezel* mourn,
for their house has no support.
12 The people of Maroth* anxiously wait for relief,
but only bitterness awaits them
as the LORD's judgment reaches
even to the gates of Jerusalem.
13 Harness your chariot horses and flee,
you people of Lachish.*
You were the first city in Judah
to follow Israel in her rebellion,
and you led Jerusalem* into sin.
14 Send farewell gifts to Moresheth-gath*;
there is no hope of saving it.
The town of Aczib*
has deceived the kings of Israel.
15 O people of Mareshah,*
I will bring a conqueror to capture your town.
And the leaders* of Israel
will go to Adullam.
16 Oh, people of Judah, shave your heads in sorrow,
for the children you love will be snatched away.
Make yourselves as bald as a vulture,
for your little ones will be exiled to
distant lands.

Judgment against Wealthy Oppressors

2 1 What sorrow awaits you who lie awake
at night,
thinking up evil plans.
You rise at dawn and hurry to carry them out,
simply because you have the power to do so.
2 When you want a piece of land,
you find a way to seize it.
When you want someone's house,
you take it by fraud and violence.
You cheat a man of his property,
stealing his family's inheritance.

1:10a *Gath* sounds like the Hebrew term for "tell." **1:10b** *Beth-leaphrah* means "house of dust." **1:11a** *Shaphir* means "pleasant." **1:11b** *Zaanan* sounds like the Hebrew term for "come out." **1:11c** *Beth-ezel* means "adjoining house." **1:12** *Maroth* sounds like the Hebrew term for "bitter." **1:13a** *Lachish* sounds like the Hebrew term for "team of horses." **1:13b** Hebrew *the daughter of Zion.* **1:14a** *Moresheth* sounds like the Hebrew term for "gift" or "dowry." **1:14b** *Aczib* means "deception." **1:15a** *Mareshah* sounds like the Hebrew term for "conqueror." **1:15b** Hebrew *the glory.*

KING JAMES VERSION

3 Therefore thus saith the LORD; Behold, against this family do I devise an evil, from which ye shall not remove your necks; neither shall ye go haughtily: for this time *is* evil.

4 In that day shall *one* take up a parable against you, and lament with a doleful lamentation, *and* say, We be utterly spoiled: he hath changed the portion of my people: how hath he removed *it* from me! turning away he hath divided our fields.

5 Therefore thou shalt have none that shall cast a cord by lot in the congregation of the LORD.

6 Prophesy ye not, *say they to them that* prophesy: they shall not prophesy to them, *that* they shall not take shame.

7 O *thou that art* named the house of Jacob, is the spirit of the LORD straitened? *are* these his doings? do not my words do good to him that walketh uprightly?

8 Even of late my people is risen up as an enemy: ye pull off the robe with the garment from them that pass by securely as men averse from war.

9 The women of my people have ye cast out from their pleasant houses; from their children have ye taken away my glory for ever.

10 Arise ye, and depart; for this *is* not *your* rest: because it is polluted, it shall destroy *you,* even with a sore destruction.

11 If a man walking in the spirit and falsehood do lie, *saying,* I will prophesy unto thee of wine and of strong drink; he shall even be the prophet of this people.

12 I will surely assemble, O Jacob, all of thee; I will surely gather the remnant of Israel; I will put them together as the sheep of Bozrah, as the flock in the midst of their fold: they shall make great noise by reason of *the multitude of* men.

NEW LIVING TRANSLATION

3 But this is what the LORD says:
"I will reward your evil with evil;
you won't be able to pull your neck out
of the noose.
You will no longer walk around proudly,
for it will be a terrible time."

4 In that day your enemies will make fun of you
by singing this song of despair about you:
"We are finished,
completely ruined!
God has confiscated our land,
taking it from us.
He has given our fields
to those who betrayed us.*"
5 Others will set your boundaries then,
and the LORD's people will have no say
in how the land is divided.

True and False Prophets

6 "Don't say such things,"
the people respond.*
"Don't prophesy like that.
Such disasters will never come our way!"

7 Should you talk that way, O family of Israel?*
Will the LORD's Spirit have patience with
such behavior?
If you would do what is right,
you would find my words comforting.
8 Yet to this very hour
my people rise against me like an enemy!
You steal the shirts right off the backs
of those who trusted you,
making them as ragged as men
returning from battle.
9 You have evicted women from their
pleasant homes
and forever stripped their children of all
that God would give them.
10 Up! Begone!
This is no longer your land and home,
for you have filled it with sin
and ruined it completely.
11 Suppose a prophet full of lies would say to you,
"I'll preach to you the joys of wine and
alcohol!"
That's just the kind of prophet you would like!

Hope for Restoration

12 "Someday, O Israel, I will gather you;
I will gather the remnant who are left.
I will bring you together again like sheep in a pen,
like a flock in its pasture.
Yes, your land will again
be filled with noisy crowds!

2:4 Or *to those who took us captive.* **2:6** Or *the prophets respond;* Hebrew reads *they prophesy.* **2:7** Hebrew *O house of Jacob?* See note on 1:5a.

KING JAMES VERSION

13 The breaker is come up before them: they have
broken up, and have passed through the gate, and are
gone out by it: and their king shall pass before them,
and the LORD on the head of them.

3 1 And I said, Hear, I pray you, O heads of Jacob,
and ye princes of the house of Israel; *Is it* not
for you to know judgment?
2 Who hate the good, and love the evil; who pluck
off their skin from off them, and their flesh from off
their bones;
3 Who also eat the flesh of my people, and flay
their skin from off them; and they break their bones,
and chop them in pieces, as for the pot, and as flesh
within the caldron.
4 Then shall they cry unto the LORD, but he will not
hear them: he will even hide his face from them at
that time, as they have behaved themselves ill in their
doings.
5 Thus saith the LORD concerning the prophets
that make my people err, that bite with their teeth,
and cry, Peace; and he that putteth not into their
mouths, they even prepare war against him.
6 Therefore night *shall be* unto you, that ye shall not
have a vision; and it shall be dark unto you, that ye
shall not divine; and the sun shall go down over the
prophets, and the day shall be dark over them.
7 Then shall the seers be ashamed, and the diviners
confounded: yea, they shall all cover their lips; for
there is no answer of God.
8 But truly I am full of power by the spirit of the
LORD, and of judgment, and of might, to declare unto
Jacob his transgression, and to Israel his sin.
9 Hear this, I pray you, ye heads of the house of Jacob, and princes of the house of Israel, that abhor
judgment, and pervert all equity.
10 They build up Zion with blood, and Jerusalem
with iniquity.
11 The heads thereof judge for reward, and the
priests thereof teach for hire, and the prophets
thereof divine for money: yet will they lean upon the
LORD, and say, *Is* not the LORD among us? none evil
can come upon us.

NEW LIVING TRANSLATION

13 Your leader will break out
and lead you out of exile,
out through the gates of the enemy cities,
back to your own land.
Your king will lead you;
the LORD himself will guide you."

Judgment against Israel's Leaders

3 1 I said, "Listen, you leaders of Israel!
You are supposed to know right
from wrong,
2 but you are the very ones
who hate good and love evil.
You skin my people alive
and tear the flesh from their bones.
3 Yes, you eat my people's flesh,
strip off their skin,
and break their bones.
You chop them up
like meat for the cooking pot.
4 Then you beg the LORD for help in times
of trouble!
Do you really expect him to answer?
After all the evil you have done,
he won't even look at you!"

5 This is what the LORD says:
"You false prophets are leading my
people astray!
You promise peace for those who give you food,
but you declare war on those who refuse to
feed you.
6 Now the night will close around you,
cutting off all your visions.
Darkness will cover you,
putting an end to your predictions.
The sun will set for you prophets,
and your day will come to an end.
7 Then you seers will be put to shame,
and you fortune-tellers will be disgraced.
And you will cover your faces
because there is no answer from God."
8 But as for me, I am filled with power—
with the Spirit of the LORD.
I am filled with justice and strength
to boldly declare Israel's sin and rebellion.
9 Listen to me, you leaders of Israel!
You hate justice and twist all that is right.
10 You are building Jerusalem
on a foundation of murder and corruption.
11 You rulers make decisions based on bribes;
you priests teach God's laws only for a price;
you prophets won't prophesy unless you
are paid.
Yet all of you claim to depend on the LORD.
"No harm can come to us," you say,
"for the LORD is here among us."

KING JAMES VERSION

12 Therefore shall Zion for your sake be plowed
as a field, and Jerusalem shall become heaps, and
the mountain of the house as the high places of the
forest.

4 1 But in the last days it shall come to pass, *that*
the mountain of the house of the LORD shall be
established in the top of the mountains, and it shall
be exalted above the hills; and people shall flow
unto it.
2 And many nations shall come, and say, Come, and
let us go up to the mountain of the LORD, and to the
house of the God of Jacob; and he will teach us of his
ways, and we will walk in his paths: for the law shall
go forth of Zion, and the word of the LORD from
Jerusalem.
3 And he shall judge among many people, and rebuke strong nations afar off; and they shall beat their
swords into plowshares, and their spears into
pruninghooks: nation shall not lift up a sword
against nation, neither shall they learn war any more.
4 But they shall sit every man under his vine and
under his fig tree; and none shall make *them* afraid:
for the mouth of the LORD of hosts hath spoken *it*.
5 For all people will walk every one in the name of
his god, and we will walk in the name of the LORD our
God for ever and ever.

6 In that day, saith the LORD, will I assemble her that
halteth, and I will gather her that is driven out, and
her that I have afflicted;
7 And I will make her that halted a remnant, and
her that was cast far off a strong nation: and the LORD
shall reign over them in mount Zion from henceforth, even for ever.
8 And thou, O tower of the flock, the strong hold of
the daughter of Zion, unto thee shall it come, even
the first dominion; the kingdom shall come to the
daughter of Jerusalem.
9 Now why dost thou cry out aloud? *is there* no king

NEW LIVING TRANSLATION

12 Because of you, Mount Zion will be plowed like
an open field;
Jerusalem will be reduced to ruins!
A thicket will grow on the heights
where the Temple now stands.

The LORD's Future Reign

4 1 In the last days, the mountain of the
LORD's house
will be the highest of all—
the most important place on earth.
It will be raised above the other hills,
and people from all over the world will stream
there to worship.
2 People from many nations will come and say,
"Come, let us go up to the mountain of the LORD,
to the house of Jacob's God.
There he will teach us his ways,
and we will walk in his paths."
For the LORD's teaching will go out from Zion;
his word will go out from Jerusalem.
3 The LORD will mediate between peoples
and will settle disputes between strong nations
far away.
They will hammer their swords into plowshares
and their spears into pruning hooks.
Nation will no longer fight against nation,
nor train for war anymore.
4 Everyone will live in peace and prosperity,
enjoying their own grapevines and fig trees,
for there will be nothing to fear.
The LORD of Heaven's Armies
has made this promise!
5 Though the nations around us follow their idols,
we will follow the LORD our God forever and
ever.

Israel's Return from Exile

6 "In that coming day," says the LORD,
"I will gather together those who are lame,
those who have been exiles,
and those whom I have filled with grief.
7 Those who are weak will survive as a remnant;
those who were exiles will become a
strong nation.
Then I, the LORD, will rule from Jerusalem*
as their king forever."
8 As for you, Jerusalem,
the citadel of God's people,*
your royal might and power
will come back to you again.
The kingship will be restored
to my precious Jerusalem.

9 But why are you now screaming in terror?
Have you no king to lead you?

4:7 Hebrew *Mount Zion.* **4:8** Hebrew *As for you, Migdal-eder, / the Ophel of the daughter of Zion.*

KING JAMES VERSION

in thee? is thy counsellor perished? for pangs have taken thee as a woman in travail.

10 Be in pain, and labour to bring forth, O daughter of Zion, like a woman in travail: for now shalt thou go forth out of the city, and thou shalt dwell in the field, and thou shalt go *even* to Babylon; there shalt thou be delivered; there the LORD shall redeem thee from the hand of thine enemies.

11 Now also many nations are gathered against thee, that say, Let her be defiled, and let our eye look upon Zion.

12 But they know not the thoughts of the LORD, neither understand they his counsel: for he shall gather them as the sheaves into the floor.

13 Arise and thresh, O daughter of Zion: for I will make thine horn iron, and I will make thy hoofs brass: and thou shalt beat in pieces many people: and I will consecrate their gain unto the LORD, and their substance unto the Lord of the whole earth.

5

1 Now gather thyself in troops, O daughter of troops: he hath laid siege against us: they shall smite the judge of Israel with a rod upon the cheek.

2 But thou, Bethlehem Ephratah, *though* thou be little among the thousands of Judah, *yet* out of thee shall he come forth unto me *that is* to be ruler in Israel; whose goings forth *have been* from of old, from everlasting.

3 Therefore will he give them up, until the time *that* she which travaileth hath brought forth: then the remnant of his brethren shall return unto the children of Israel.

4 And he shall stand and feed in the strength of the LORD, in the majesty of the name of the LORD his God; and they shall abide: for now shall he be great unto the ends of the earth.

5 And this *man* shall be the peace, when the Assyrian shall come into our land: and when he shall tread

NEW LIVING TRANSLATION

Have your wise people all died?
Pain has gripped you like a woman
in childbirth.
10 Writhe and groan like a woman in labor,
you people of Jerusalem,*
for now you must leave this city
to live in the open country.
You will soon be sent in exile
to distant Babylon.
But the LORD will rescue you there;
he will redeem you from the grip
of your enemies.

11 Now many nations have gathered against you.
"Let her be desecrated," they say.
"Let us see the destruction of Jerusalem.*"
12 But they do not know the LORD's thoughts
or understand his plan.
These nations don't know
that he is gathering them together
to be beaten and trampled
like sheaves of grain on a threshing floor.
13 "Rise up and crush the nations, O Jerusalem!"*
says the LORD.
"For I will give you iron horns and bronze hooves,
so you can trample many nations to pieces.
You will present their stolen riches to the LORD,
their wealth to the LORD of all the earth."

5

1* Mobilize! Marshal your troops!
The enemy is laying siege to Jerusalem.
They will strike Israel's leader
in the face with a rod.

A Ruler from Bethlehem

2* But you, O Bethlehem Ephrathah,
are only a small village among all the people
of Judah.
Yet a ruler of Israel will come from you,
one whose origins are from the distant past.
3 The people of Israel will be abandoned to
their enemies
until the woman in labor gives birth.
Then at last his fellow countrymen
will return from exile to their own land.
4 And he will stand to lead his flock with the
LORD's strength,
in the majesty of the name of the LORD
his God.
Then his people will live there undisturbed,
for he will be highly honored around
the world.
5 And he will be the source of peace.

When the Assyrians invade our land
and break through our defenses,

4:10 Hebrew *O daughter of Zion.* **4:11** Hebrew *of Zion.* **4:13** Hebrew *"Rise up and thresh, O daughter of Zion."* **5:1** Verse 5:1 is numbered 4:14 in Hebrew text. **5:2** Verses 5:2-15 are numbered 5:1-14 in Hebrew text.

KING JAMES VERSION

in our palaces, then shall we raise against him seven
shepherds, and eight principal men.
6 And they shall waste the land of Assyria with the
sword, and the land of Nimrod in the entrances
thereof: thus shall he deliver *us* from the Assyrian,
when he cometh into our land, and when he treadeth
within our borders.

7 And the remnant of Jacob shall be in the midst of
many people as a dew from the LORD, as the showers
upon the grass, that tarrieth not for man, nor waiteth
for the sons of men.
8 And the remnant of Jacob shall be among the
Gentiles in the midst of many people as a lion among
the beasts of the forest, as a young lion among the
flocks of sheep: who, if he go through, both treadeth
down, and teareth in pieces, and none can deliver.
9 Thine hand shall be lifted up upon thine adversaries, and all thine enemies shall be cut off.
10 And it shall come to pass in that day, saith the
LORD, that I will cut off thy horses out of the midst of
thee, and I will destroy thy chariots:
11 And I will cut off the cities of thy land, and throw
down all thy strong holds:
12 And I will cut off witchcrafts out of thine hand;
and thou shalt have no *more* soothsayers:
13 Thy graven images also will I cut off, and thy
standing images out of the midst of thee; and thou
shalt no more worship the work of thine hands.
14 And I will pluck up thy groves out of the midst of
thee: so will I destroy thy cities.
15 And I will execute vengeance in anger and fury
upon the heathen, such as they have not heard.

6 1 Hear ye now what the LORD saith; Arise, contend thou before the mountains, and let the
hills hear thy voice.
2 Hear ye, O mountains, the LORD's controversy,
and ye strong foundations of the earth: for the LORD
hath a controversy with his people, and he will plead
with Israel.
3 O my people, what have I done unto thee? and
wherein have I wearied thee? testify against me.
4 For I brought thee up out of the land of Egypt, and

NEW LIVING TRANSLATION

we will appoint seven rulers to watch over us,
eight princes to lead us.
6 They will rule Assyria with drawn swords
and enter the gates of the land of Nimrod.
He will rescue us from the Assyrians
when they pour over the borders to invade
our land.

The Remnant Purified

7 Then the remnant left in Israel*
will take their place among the nations.
They will be like dew sent by the LORD
or like rain falling on the grass,
which no one can hold back
and no one can restrain.
8 The remnant left in Israel
will take their place among the nations.
They will be like a lion among the animals
of the forest,
like a strong young lion among flocks
of sheep and goats,
pouncing and tearing as they go
with no rescuer in sight.
9 The people of Israel will stand up to their foes,
and all their enemies will be wiped out.

10 "In that day," says the LORD,
"I will slaughter your horses
and destroy your chariots.
11 I will tear down your walls
and demolish your defenses.
12 I will put an end to all witchcraft,
and there will be no more fortune-tellers.
13 I will destroy all your idols and sacred pillars,
so you will never again worship the work of
your own hands.
14 I will abolish your idol shrines with their
Asherah poles
and destroy your pagan cities.
15 I will pour out my vengeance
on all the nations that refuse to obey me."

The LORD's Case against Israel

6 Listen to what the LORD is saying:
"Stand up and state your case against me.
Let the mountains and hills be called to
witness your complaints.
2 And now, O mountains,
listen to the LORD's complaint!
He has a case against his people.
He will bring charges against Israel.

3 "O my people, what have I done to you?
What have I done to make you tired of me?
Answer me!
4 For I brought you out of Egypt
and redeemed you from slavery.

5:7 Hebrew *in Jacob;* also in 5:8. See note on 1:5a.

KING JAMES VERSION

redeemed thee out of the house of servants; and I sent before thee Moses, Aaron, and Miriam.

5 O my people, remember now what Balak king of Moab consulted, and what Balaam the son of Beor answered him from Shittim unto Gilgal; that ye may know the righteousness of the LORD.

6 Wherewith shall I come before the LORD, *and* bow myself before the high God? shall I come before him with burnt offerings, with calves of a year old?

7 Will the LORD be pleased with thousands of rams, *or* with ten thousands of rivers of oil? shall I give my firstborn *for* my transgression, the fruit of my body *for* the sin of my soul?

8 He hath shewed thee, O man, what *is* good; and what doth the LORD require of thee, but to do justly, and to love mercy, and to walk humbly with thy God?

9 The LORD's voice crieth unto the city, and *the man of* wisdom shall see thy name: hear ye the rod, and who hath appointed it.

10 Are there yet the treasures of wickedness in the house of the wicked, and the scant measure *that is* abominable?

11 Shall I count *them* pure with the wicked balances, and with the bag of deceitful weights?

12 For the rich men thereof are full of violence, and the inhabitants thereof have spoken lies, and their tongue *is* deceitful in their mouth.

13 Therefore also will I make *thee* sick in smiting thee, in making *thee* desolate because of thy sins.

14 Thou shalt eat, but not be satisfied; and thy casting down *shall be* in the midst of thee; and thou shalt take hold, but shalt not deliver; and *that* which thou deliverest will I give up to the sword.

15 Thou shalt sow, but thou shalt not reap; thou shalt tread the olives, but thou shalt not anoint thee with oil; and sweet wine, but shalt not drink wine.

NEW LIVING TRANSLATION

I sent Moses, Aaron, and Miriam to help you.
5 Don't you remember, my people,
how King Balak of Moab tried to have
you cursed
and how Balaam son of Beor blessed
you instead?
And remember your journey from Acacia Grove*
to Gilgal,
when I, the LORD, did everything I could
to teach you about my faithfulness."

6 What can we bring to the LORD?
What kind of offerings should we give him?
Should we bow before God
with offerings of yearling calves?
7 Should we offer him thousands of rams
and ten thousand rivers of olive oil?
Should we sacrifice our firstborn children
to pay for our sins?
8 No, O people, the LORD has told you what is good,
and this is what he requires of you:
to do what is right, to love mercy,
and to walk humbly with your God.

Israel's Guilt and Punishment

9 Fear the LORD if you are wise!
His voice calls to everyone in Jerusalem:
"The armies of destruction are coming;
the LORD is sending them.*
10 What shall I say about the homes of the wicked
filled with treasures gained by cheating?
What about the disgusting practice
of measuring out grain with dishonest
measures?*
11 How can I tolerate your merchants
who use dishonest scales and weights?
12 The rich among you have become wealthy
through extortion and violence.
Your citizens are so used to lying
that their tongues can no longer tell the truth.

13 "Therefore, I will wound you!
I will bring you to ruin for all your sins.
14 You will eat but never have enough.
Your hunger pangs and emptiness will remain.
And though you try to save your money,
it will come to nothing in the end.
You will save a little,
but I will give it to those who conquer you.
15 You will plant crops
but not harvest them.
You will press your olives
but not get enough oil to anoint yourselves.
You will trample the grapes
but get no juice to make your wine.

6:5 Hebrew *Shittim.* **6:9** Hebrew *"Listen to the rod. / Who appointed it?"*
6:10 Hebrew *of using the short ephah?* The ephah was a unit for measuring grain.

KING JAMES VERSION

16 For the statutes of Omri are kept, and all the
works of the house of Ahab, and ye walk in their
counsels; that I should make thee a desolation, and
the inhabitants thereof an hissing: therefore ye shall
bear the reproach of my people.

7 1 Woe is me! for I am as when they have gathered the summer fruits, as the grapegleanings
of the vintage: *there is* no cluster to eat: my soul desired the firstripe fruit.
2 The good *man* is perished out of the earth: and
there is none upright among men: they all lie in wait
for blood; they hunt every man his brother with a net.
3 That they may do evil with both hands earnestly,
the prince asketh, and the judge *asketh* for a reward;
and the great *man*, he uttereth his mischievous desire: so they wrap it up.
4 The best of them *is* as a brier: the most upright *is*
sharper than a thorn hedge: the day of thy watchmen *and* thy visitation cometh; now shall be their
perplexity.
5 Trust ye not in a friend, put ye not confidence in a
guide: keep the doors of thy mouth from her that
lieth in thy bosom.
6 For the son dishonoureth the father, the daughter
riseth up against her mother, the daughter in law
against her mother in law; a man's enemies *are* the
men of his own house.
7 Therefore I will look unto the LORD; I will wait for
the God of my salvation: my God will hear me.
8 Rejoice not against me, O mine enemy: when I
fall, I shall arise; when I sit in darkness, the LORD *shall*
be a light unto me.
9 I will bear the indignation of the LORD, because I
have sinned against him, until he plead my cause, and
execute judgment for me: he will bring me forth to
the light, *and* I shall behold his righteousness.
10 Then *she that is* mine enemy shall see *it*, and
shame shall cover her which said unto me, Where is
the LORD thy God? mine eyes shall behold her: now
shall she be trodden down as the mire of the streets.

NEW LIVING TRANSLATION

16 You keep only the laws of evil King Omri;
you follow only the example of wicked
King Ahab!
Therefore, I will make an example of you,
bringing you to complete ruin.
You will be treated with contempt,
mocked by all who see you."

Misery Turned to Hope

7 1 How miserable I am!
I feel like the fruit picker after the harvest
who can find nothing to eat.
Not a cluster of grapes or a single early fig
can be found to satisfy my hunger.
2 The godly people have all disappeared;
not one honest person is left on the earth.
They are all murderers,
setting traps even for their own brothers.
3 Both their hands are equally skilled at doing evil!
Officials and judges alike demand bribes.
The people with influence get what they want,
and together they scheme to twist justice.
4 Even the best of them is like a brier;
the most honest is as dangerous as a hedge
of thorns.
But your judgment day is coming swiftly now.
Your time of punishment is here, a time
of confusion.
5 Don't trust anyone—
not your best friend or even your wife!
6 For the son despises his father.
The daughter defies her mother.
The daughter-in-law defies her mother-in-law.
Your enemies are right in your own household!
7 As for me, I look to the LORD for help.
I wait confidently for God to save me,
and my God will certainly hear me.
8 Do not gloat over me, my enemies!
For though I fall, I will rise again.
Though I sit in darkness,
the LORD will be my light.
9 I will be patient as the LORD punishes me,
for I have sinned against him.
But after that, he will take up my case
and give me justice for all I have suffered
from my enemies.
The LORD will bring me into the light,
and I will see his righteousness.
10 Then my enemies will see that the LORD
is on my side.
They will be ashamed that they taunted me,
saying,
"So where is the LORD—
that God of yours?"
With my own eyes I will see their downfall;
they will be trampled like mud in the streets.

KING JAMES VERSION

[11]*In* the day that thy walls are to be built, *in* that
day shall the decree be far removed.
[12]*In* that day *also* he shall come even to thee from
Assyria, and *from* the fortified cities, and from the
fortress even to the river, and from sea to sea, and
from mountain to mountain.
[13]Notwithstanding the land shall be desolate because of them that dwell therein, for the fruit of their
doings.

[14]Feed thy people with thy rod, the flock of thine
heritage, which dwell solitarily *in* the wood, in the
midst of Carmel: let them feed *in* Bashan and Gilead,
as in the days of old.
[15]According to the days of thy coming out of the
land of Egypt will I shew unto him marvellous *things*.
[16]The nations shall see and be confounded at all
their might: they shall lay *their* hand upon *their*
mouth, their ears shall be deaf.
[17]They shall lick the dust like a serpent, they shall
move out of their holes like worms of the earth: they
shall be afraid of the LORD our God, and shall fear because of thee.
[18]Who *is* a God like unto thee, that pardoneth iniquity, and passeth by the transgression of the remnant
of his heritage? he retaineth not his anger for ever,
because he delighteth *in* mercy.
[19]He will turn again, he will have compassion upon
us; he will subdue our iniquities; and thou wilt cast
all their sins into the depths of the sea.
[20]Thou wilt perform the truth to Jacob, *and* the
mercy to Abraham, which thou hast sworn unto our
fathers from the days of old.

NEW LIVING TRANSLATION

[11] In that day, Israel, your cities will be rebuilt,
and your borders will be extended.
[12] People from many lands will come and
honor you—
from Assyria all the way to the towns of Egypt,
from Egypt all the way to the Euphrates River,*
and from distant seas and mountains.
[13] But the land* will become empty and desolate
because of the wickedness of those who
live there.

The LORD's Compassion on Israel

[14] O LORD, protect your people with your
shepherd's staff;
lead your flock, your special possession.
Though they live alone in a thicket
on the heights of Mount Carmel,*
let them graze in the fertile pastures of Bashan
and Gilead
as they did long ago.
[15] "Yes," says the LORD,
"I will do mighty miracles for you,
like those I did when I rescued you
from slavery in Egypt."
[16] All the nations of the world will stand amazed
at what the LORD will do for you.
They will be embarrassed
at their feeble power.
They will cover their mouths in silent awe,
deaf to everything around them.
[17] Like snakes crawling from their holes,
they will come out to meet the LORD our God.
They will fear him greatly,
trembling in terror at his presence.
[18] Where is another God like you,
who pardons the guilt of the remnant,
overlooking the sins of his special people?
You will not stay angry with your people forever,
because you delight in showing unfailing love.
[19] Once again you will have compassion on us.
You will trample our sins under your feet
and throw them into the depths of the ocean!
[20] You will show us your faithfulness and
unfailing love
as you promised to our ancestors Abraham
and Jacob long ago.

7:12 Hebrew *the river.* **7:13** Or *earth.* **7:14** Or *surrounded by a fruitful land.*

Nahum

KING JAMES VERSION

1 1 The burden of Nineveh. The book of the vision
of Nahum the Elkoshite.

2 God *is* jealous, and the LORD revengeth; the LORD
revengeth, and *is* furious; the LORD will take vengeance on his adversaries, and he reserveth *wrath*
for his enemies.
3 The LORD *is* slow to anger, and great in power, and
will not at all acquit *the wicked:* the LORD *hath* his
way in the whirlwind and in the storm, and the
clouds *are* the dust of his feet.
4 He rebuketh the sea, and maketh it dry, and drieth
up all the rivers: Bashan languisheth, and Carmel,
and the flower of Lebanon languisheth.
5 The mountains quake at him, and the hills melt,
and the earth is burned at his presence, yea, the
world, and all that dwell therein.
6 Who can stand before his indignation? and who
can abide in the fierceness of his anger? his fury is
poured out like fire, and the rocks are thrown down
by him.
7 The LORD *is* good, a strong hold in the day of trouble; and he knoweth them that trust in him.
8 But with an overrunning flood he will make an utter end of the place thereof, and darkness shall pursue his enemies.
9 What do ye imagine against the LORD? he will
make an utter end: affliction shall not rise up the
second time.
10 For while *they be* folden together *as* thorns, and
while they are drunken *as* drunkards, they shall be
devoured as stubble fully dry.
11 There is *one* come out of thee, that imagineth
evil against the LORD, a wicked counsellor.

NEW LIVING TRANSLATION

1 This message concerning Nineveh came as a vision to Nahum, who lived in Elkosh.

The LORD's Anger against Nineveh

2 The LORD is a jealous God,
filled with vengeance and rage.
He takes revenge on all who oppose him
and continues to rage against his enemies!
3 The LORD is slow to get angry, but his power
is great,
and he never lets the guilty go unpunished.
He displays his power in the whirlwind and
the storm.
The billowing clouds are the dust beneath
his feet.
4 At his command the oceans dry up,
and the rivers disappear.
The lush pastures of Bashan and Carmel fade,
and the green forests of Lebanon wither.
5 In his presence the mountains quake,
and the hills melt away;
the earth trembles,
and its people are destroyed.
6 Who can stand before his fierce anger?
Who can survive his burning fury?
His rage blazes forth like fire,
and the mountains crumble to dust
in his presence.

7 The LORD is good,
a strong refuge when trouble comes.
He is close to those who trust in him.
8 But he will sweep away his enemies
in an overwhelming flood.
He will pursue his foes
into the darkness of night.

9 Why are you scheming against the LORD?
He will destroy you with one blow;
he won't need to strike twice!
10 His enemies, tangled like thornbushes
and staggering like drunks,
will be burned up like dry stubble in a field.
11 Who is this wicked counselor of yours
who plots evil against the LORD?

KING JAMES VERSION

12 Thus saith the LORD; Though *they be* quiet, and
likewise many, yet thus shall they be cut down, when
he shall pass through. Though I have afflicted thee,
I will afflict thee no more.
13 For now will I break his yoke from off thee, and
will burst thy bonds in sunder.
14 And the LORD hath given a commandment concerning thee, *that* no more of thy name be sown: out
of the house of thy gods will I cut off the graven image and the molten image: I will make thy grave; for
thou art vile.
15 Behold upon the mountains the feet of him that
bringeth good tidings, that publisheth peace! O Judah, keep thy solemn feasts, perform thy vows: for
the wicked shall no more pass through thee; he is
utterly cut off.

2 1 He that dasheth in pieces is come up before
thy face: keep the munition, watch the way,
make *thy* loins strong, fortify *thy* power mightily.
2 For the LORD hath turned away the excellency of
Jacob, as the excellency of Israel: for the emptiers
have emptied them out, and marred their vine
branches.
3 The shield of his mighty men is made red, the
valiant men *are* in scarlet: the chariots *shall be* with
flaming torches in the day of his preparation, and the
fir trees shall be terribly shaken.
4 The chariots shall rage in the streets, they shall
justle one against another in the broad ways: they
shall seem like torches, they shall run like the
lightnings.
5 He shall recount his worthies: they shall stumble
in their walk; they shall make haste to the wall
thereof, and the defence shall be prepared.
6 The gates of the rivers shall be opened, and the
palace shall be dissolved.
7 And Huzzab shall be led away captive, she shall
be brought up, and her maids shall lead *her* as with
the voice of doves, tabering upon their breasts.

NEW LIVING TRANSLATION

12 This is what the LORD says:
"Though the Assyrians have many allies,
they will be destroyed and disappear.
O my people, I have punished you before,
but I will not punish you again.
13 Now I will break the yoke of bondage from
your neck
and tear off the chains of Assyrian
oppression."

14 And this is what the LORD says concerning the
Assyrians in Nineveh:
"You will have no more children to carry on your
name.
I will destroy all the idols in the temples
of your gods.
I am preparing a grave for you
because you are despicable!"

15 *Look! A messenger is coming over the
mountains with good news!
He is bringing a message of peace.
Celebrate your festivals, O people of Judah,
and fulfill all your vows,
for your wicked enemies will never invade your
land again.
They will be completely destroyed!

The Fall of Nineveh

2 1 *Your enemy is coming to crush you,
Nineveh.
Man the ramparts! Watch the roads!
Prepare your defenses! Call out your forces!

2 Even though the destroyer has destroyed Judah,
the LORD will restore its honor.
Israel's vine has been stripped of branches,
but he will restore its splendor.

3 Shields flash red in the sunlight!
See the scarlet uniforms of the
valiant troops!
Watch as their glittering chariots move into
position,
with a forest of spears waving above them.*
4 The chariots race recklessly along the streets
and rush wildly through the squares.
They flash like firelight
and move as swiftly as lightning.
5 The king shouts to his officers;
they stumble in their haste,
rushing to the walls to set up their defenses.
6 The river gates have been torn open!
The palace is about to collapse!
7 Nineveh's exile has been decreed,
and all the servant girls mourn its capture.
They moan like doves
and beat their breasts in sorrow.

1:15 Verse 1:15 is numbered 2:1 in Hebrew text. **2:1** Verses 2:1-13 are numbered 2:2-14 in Hebrew text. **2:3** Greek and Syriac versions read *into position, / the horses whipped into a frenzy.*

KING JAMES VERSION

8 But Nineveh *is* of old like a pool of water: yet they
shall flee away. Stand, stand, *shall they cry;* but none
shall look back.
9 Take ye the spoil of silver, take the spoil of gold:
for *there is* none end of the store *and* glory out of all
the pleasant furniture.
10 She is empty, and void, and waste: and the heart
melteth, and the knees smite together, and much
pain *is* in all loins, and the faces of them all gather
blackness.
11 Where *is* the dwelling of the lions, and the
feedingplace of the young lions, where the lion, *even*
the old lion, walked, *and* the lion's whelp, and none
made *them* afraid?
12 The lion did tear in pieces enough for his
whelps, and strangled for his lionesses, and filled his
holes with prey, and his dens with ravin.
13 Behold, I *am* against thee, saith the LORD of
hosts, and I will burn her chariots in the smoke, and
the sword shall devour thy young lions: and I will cut
off thy prey from the earth, and the voice of thy
messengers shall no more be heard.

3 1 Woe to the bloody city! it *is* all full of lies *and*
robbery; the prey departeth not;
2 The noise of a whip, and the noise of the rattling
of the wheels, and of the pransing horses, and of the
jumping chariots.
3 The horseman lifteth up both the bright sword
and the glittering spear: and *there is* a multitude of
slain, and a great number of carcases; and *there is*
none end of *their* corpses; they stumble upon their
corpses:
4 Because of the multitude of the whoredoms of
the wellfavoured harlot, the mistress of witchcrafts,
that selleth nations through her whoredoms, and
families through her witchcrafts.
5 Behold, I *am* against thee, saith the LORD of hosts;
and I will discover thy skirts upon thy face, and I will
shew the nations thy nakedness, and the kingdoms
thy shame.

NEW LIVING TRANSLATION

8 Nineveh is like a leaking water reservoir!
The people are slipping away.
"Stop, stop!" someone shouts,
but no one even looks back.
9 Loot the silver!
Plunder the gold!
There's no end to Nineveh's treasures—
its vast, uncounted wealth.
10 Soon the city is plundered, empty, and ruined.
Hearts melt and knees shake.
The people stand aghast,
their faces pale and trembling.
11 Where now is that great Nineveh,
that den filled with young lions?
It was a place where people—like lions and
their cubs—
walked freely and without fear.
12 The lion tore up meat for his cubs
and strangled prey for his mate.
He filled his den with prey,
his caverns with his plunder.

13 "I am your enemy!"
says the LORD of Heaven's Armies.
"Your chariots will soon go up in smoke.
Your young men* will be killed in battle.
Never again will you plunder conquered
nations.
The voices of your proud messengers will
be heard no more."

The LORD's Judgment against Nineveh

3 1 What sorrow awaits Nineveh,
the city of murder and lies!
She is crammed with wealth
and is never without victims.
2 Hear the crack of whips,
the rumble of wheels!
Horses' hooves pound,
and chariots clatter wildly.
3 See the flashing swords and glittering spears
as the charioteers charge past!
There are countless casualties,
heaps of bodies—
so many bodies that
people stumble over them.
4 All this because Nineveh,
the beautiful and faithless city,
mistress of deadly charms,
enticed the nations with her beauty.
She taught them all her magic,
enchanting people everywhere.

5 "I am your enemy!"
says the LORD of Heaven's Armies.
"And now I will lift your skirts
and show all the earth your nakedness
and shame.

2:13 Hebrew *young lions.*

KING JAMES VERSION

6 And I will cast abominable filth upon thee, and
make thee vile, and will set thee as a gazingstock.
7 And it shall come to pass, *that* all they that look
upon thee shall flee from thee, and say, Nineveh is
laid waste: who will bemoan her? whence shall I seek
comforters for thee?
8 Art thou better than populous No, that was situate among the rivers, *that had* the waters round
about it, whose rampart *was* the sea, *and* her wall
was from the sea?
9 Ethiopia and Egypt *were* her strength, and *it was*
infinite; Put and Lubim were thy helpers.
10 Yet *was* she carried away, she went into captivity: her young children also were dashed in pieces at
the top of all the streets: and they cast lots for her
honourable men, and all her great men were bound
in chains.
11 Thou also shalt be drunken: thou shalt be hid,
thou also shalt seek strength because of the enemy.
12 All thy strong holds *shall be like* fig trees with
the firstripe figs: if they be shaken, they shall even
fall into the mouth of the eater.
13 Behold, thy people in the midst of thee *are*
women: the gates of thy land shall be set wide open
unto thine enemies: the fire shall devour thy bars.
14 Draw thee waters for the siege, fortify thy strong
holds: go into clay, and tread the mortar, make strong
the brickkiln.
15 There shall the fire devour thee; the sword shall
cut thee off, it shall eat thee up like the cankerworm:
make thyself many as the cankerworm, make thyself
many as the locusts.
16 Thou hast multiplied thy merchants above the
stars of heaven: the cankerworm spoileth, and fleeth
away.
17 Thy crowned *are* as the locusts, and thy captains
as the great grasshoppers, which camp in the hedges
in the cold day, *but* when the sun ariseth they flee
away, and their place is not known where they *are*.

NEW LIVING TRANSLATION

6 I will cover you with filth
and show the world how vile you really are.
7 All who see you will shrink back and say,
'Nineveh lies in ruins.
Where are the mourners?'
Does anyone regret your destruction?"

8 Are you any better than the city of Thebes,*
situated on the Nile River, surrounded by water?
She was protected by the river on all sides,
walled in by water.
9 Ethiopia* and the land of Egypt
gave unlimited assistance.
The nations of Put and Libya
were among her allies.
10 Yet Thebes fell,
and her people were led away as captives.
Her babies were dashed to death
against the stones of the streets.
Soldiers threw dice* to get Egyptian officers
as servants.
All their leaders were bound in chains.

11 And you, Nineveh, will also stagger like
a drunkard.
You will hide for fear of the attacking enemy.
12 All your fortresses will fall.
They will be devoured like the ripe figs
that fall into the mouths
of those who shake the trees.
13 Your troops will be as weak
and helpless as women.
The gates of your land will be opened wide
to the enemy
and set on fire and burned.
14 Get ready for the siege!
Store up water!
Strengthen the defenses!
Go into the pits to trample clay,
and pack it into molds,
making bricks to repair the walls.

15 But the fire will devour you;
the sword will cut you down.
The enemy will consume you like locusts,
devouring everything they see.
There will be no escape,
even if you multiply like swarming locusts.
16 Your merchants have multiplied
until they outnumber the stars.
But like a swarm of locusts,
they strip the land and fly away.
17 Your guards* and officials are also like
swarming locusts
that crowd together in the hedges on a cold day.
But like locusts that fly away when the sun
comes up,
all of them will fly away and disappear.

3:8 Hebrew *No-amon;* also in 3:10. **3:9** Hebrew *Cush.* **3:10** Hebrew *They cast lots.* **3:17** Or *princes.*

KING JAMES VERSION

18Thy shepherds slumber, O king of Assyria: thy
nobles shall dwell *in the dust:* thy people is scattered
upon the mountains, and no man gathereth *them.*
19*There is* no healing of thy bruise; thy wound
is grievous: all that hear the bruit of thee shall clap
the hands over thee: for upon whom hath not thy
wickedness passed continually?

NEW LIVING TRANSLATION

18 Your shepherds are asleep, O Assyrian king;
your princes lie dead in the dust.
Your people are scattered across the mountains
with no one to gather them together.
19 There is no healing for your wound;
your injury is fatal.
All who hear of your destruction
will clap their hands for joy.
Where can anyone be found
who has not suffered from your
continual cruelty?

Habakkuk

KING JAMES VERSION

1 1 The burden which Habakkuk the prophet
did see.

2 O LORD, how long shall I cry, and thou wilt not
hear! *even* cry out unto thee *of* violence, and thou wilt
not save!
3 Why dost thou shew me iniquity, and cause *me* to
behold grievance? for spoiling and violence *are*
before me: and there are *that* raise up strife and
contention.
4 Therefore the law is slacked, and judgment
doth never go forth: for the wicked doth compass
about the righteous; therefore wrong judgment
proceedeth.

5 Behold ye among the heathen, and regard, and
wonder marvellously: for *I* will work a work in your
days, *which* ye will not believe, though it be told *you*.
6 For, lo, I raise up the Chaldeans, *that* bitter and
hasty nation, which shall march through the breadth
of the land, to possess the dwellingplaces *that are*
not theirs.
7 They *are* terrible and dreadful: their judgment
and their dignity shall proceed of themselves.
8 Their horses also are swifter than the leopards,
and are more fierce than the evening wolves: and
their horsemen shall spread themselves, and their
horsemen shall come from far; they shall fly as the
eagle *that* hasteth to eat.
9 They shall come all for violence: their faces shall
sup up *as* the east wind, and they shall gather the
captivity as the sand.
10 And they shall scoff at the kings, and the princes

NEW LIVING TRANSLATION

1 This is the message that the prophet Habakkuk
received in a vision.

Habakkuk's Complaint

2 How long, O LORD, must I call for help?
But you do not listen!
"Violence is everywhere!" I cry,
but you do not come to save.
3 Must I forever see these evil deeds?
Why must I watch all this misery?
Wherever I look,
I see destruction and violence.
I am surrounded by people
who love to argue and fight.
4 The law has become paralyzed,
and there is no justice in the courts.
The wicked far outnumber the righteous,
so that justice has become perverted.

The LORD's Reply

5 The LORD replied,

"Look around at the nations;
look and be amazed!*
For I am doing something in your own day,
something you wouldn't believe
even if someone told you about it.
6 I am raising up the Babylonians,*
a cruel and violent people.
They will march across the world
and conquer other lands.
7 They are notorious for their cruelty
and do whatever they like.
8 Their horses are swifter than cheetahs*
and fiercer than wolves at dusk.
Their charioteers charge from far away.
Like eagles, they swoop down to devour
their prey.

9 "On they come, all bent on violence.
Their hordes advance like a desert wind,
sweeping captives ahead of them like sand.
10 They scoff at kings and princes
and scorn all their fortresses.

1:5 Greek version reads *Look, you mockers; / look and be amazed and die.* Compare Acts 13:41. **1:6** Or *Chaldeans.* **1:8** Or *leopards.*

KING JAMES VERSION

shall be a scorn unto them: they shall deride every
strong hold; for they shall heap dust, and take it.
11 Then shall *his* mind change, and he shall pass
over, and offend, *imputing* this his power unto
his god.

12 *Art* thou not from everlasting, O LORD my God,
mine Holy One? we shall not die. O LORD, thou hast
ordained them for judgment; and, O mighty God,
thou hast established them for correction.
13 *Thou art* of purer eyes than to behold evil, and
canst not look on iniquity: wherefore lookest thou
upon them that deal treacherously, *and* holdest thy
tongue when the wicked devoureth *the man that is*
more righteous than he?
14 And makest men as the fishes of the sea, as the
creeping things, *that have* no ruler over them?
15 They take up all of them with the angle, they
catch them in their net, and gather them in their
drag: therefore they rejoice and are glad.
16 Therefore they sacrifice unto their net, and burn
incense unto their drag; because by them their portion *is* fat, and their meat plenteous.
17 Shall they therefore empty their net, and not
spare continually to slay the nations?

2 1 I will stand upon my watch, and set me upon
the tower, and will watch to see what he will
say unto me, and what I shall answer when I am
reproved.

2 And the LORD answered me, and said, Write the
vision, and make *it* plain upon tables, that he may
run that readeth it.
3 For the vision *is* yet for an appointed time, but at
the end it shall speak, and not lie: though it tarry, wait
for it; because it will surely come, it will not tarry.
4 Behold, his soul *which* is lifted up is not upright
in him: but the just shall live by his faith.

NEW LIVING TRANSLATION

They simply pile ramps of earth
against their walls and capture them!
11 They sweep past like the wind
and are gone.
But they are deeply guilty,
for their own strength is their god."

Habakkuk's Second Complaint

12 O LORD my God, my Holy One, you who
are eternal—
surely you do not plan to wipe us out?
O LORD, our Rock, you have sent these
Babylonians to correct us,
to punish us for our many sins.
13 But you are pure and cannot stand the
sight of evil.
Will you wink at their treachery?
Should you be silent while the wicked
swallow up people more righteous than they?
14 Are we only fish to be caught and killed?
Are we only sea creatures that have no leader?
15 Must we be strung up on their hooks
and caught in their nets while they rejoice
and celebrate?
16 Then they will worship their nets
and burn incense in front of them.
"These nets are the gods who have made
us rich!"
they will claim.
17 Will you let them get away with this forever?
Will they succeed forever in their heartless
conquests?

2 1 I will climb up to my watchtower
and stand at my guardpost.
There I will wait to see what the LORD says
and how he* will answer my complaint.

The LORD's Second Reply

2 Then the LORD said to me,
"Write my answer plainly on tablets,
so that a runner can carry the correct message
to others.
3 This vision is for a future time.
It describes the end, and it will be fulfilled.
If it seems slow in coming, wait patiently,
for it will surely take place.
It will not be delayed.
4 "Look at the proud!
They trust in themselves, and their lives
are crooked.
But the righteous will live by their faithfulness
to God.*

2:1 As in Syriac version; Hebrew reads *I.* **2:3b-4** Greek version reads *If the vision is delayed, wait patiently, / for it will surely come and not delay. / [4] I will take no pleasure in anyone who turns away. / But the righteous person will live by my faith.* Compare Rom 1:17; Gal 3:11; Heb 10:37-38.

KING JAMES VERSION

[5] Yea also, because he transgresseth by wine, *he is* a
proud man, neither keepeth at home, who enlargeth
his desire as hell, and *is* as death, and cannot be satisfied, but gathereth unto him all nations, and heapeth
unto him all people:
[6] Shall not all these take up a parable against him,
and a taunting proverb against him, and say, Woe to
him that increaseth *that which is* not his! how long?
and to him that ladeth himself with thick clay!
[7] Shall they not rise up suddenly that shall bite
thee, and awake that shall vex thee, and thou shalt be
for booties unto them?
[8] Because thou hast spoiled many nations, all the
remnant of the people shall spoil thee; because of
men's blood, and *for* the violence of the land, of the
city, and of all that dwell therein.
[9] Woe to him that coveteth an evil covetousness to
his house, that he may set his nest on high, that he
may be delivered from the power of evil!
[10] Thou hast consulted shame to thy house by
cutting off many people, and hast sinned *against*
thy soul.
[11] For the stone shall cry out of the wall, and the
beam out of the timber shall answer it.
[12] Woe to him that buildeth a town with blood, and
stablisheth a city by iniquity!
[13] Behold, *is it* not of the LORD of hosts that the people shall labour in the very fire, and the people shall
weary themselves for very vanity?
[14] For the earth shall be filled with the knowledge
of the glory of the LORD, as the waters cover the sea.
[15] Woe unto him that giveth his neighbour drink,
that puttest thy bottle to *him*, and makest *him*
drunken also, that thou mayest look on their nakedness!
[16] Thou art filled with shame for glory: drink thou
also, and let thy foreskin be uncovered: the cup of the
LORD's right hand shall be turned unto thee, and
shameful spewing *shall be* on thy glory.
[17] For the violence of Lebanon shall cover thee, and

NEW LIVING TRANSLATION

[5] Wealth* is treacherous,
and the arrogant are never at rest.
They open their mouths as wide as the grave,*
and like death, they are never satisfied.
In their greed they have gathered up
many nations
and swallowed many peoples.

[6] "But soon their captives will taunt them.
They will mock them, saying,
'What sorrow awaits you thieves!
Now you will get what you deserve!
You've become rich by extortion,
but how much longer can this go on?'
[7] Suddenly, your debtors will take action.
They will turn on you and take all you have,
while you stand trembling and helpless.
[8] Because you have plundered many nations,
now all the survivors will plunder you.
You committed murder throughout
the countryside
and filled the towns with violence.

[9] "What sorrow awaits you who build big houses
with money gained dishonestly!
You believe your wealth will buy security,
putting your family's nest beyond the reach
of danger.
[10] But by the murders you committed,
you have shamed your name and forfeited
your lives.
[11] The very stones in the walls cry out against you,
and the beams in the ceilings echo the
complaint.

[12] "What sorrow awaits you who build cities
with money gained through murder and
corruption!
[13] Has not the LORD of Heaven's Armies promised
that the wealth of nations will turn to ashes?
They work so hard,
but all in vain!
[14] For as the waters fill the sea,
the earth will be filled with an awareness
of the glory of the LORD.

[15] "What sorrow awaits you who make your
neighbors drunk!
You force your cup on them
so you can gloat over their shameful nakedness.
[16] But soon it will be your turn to be disgraced.
Come, drink and be exposed!*
Drink from the cup of the LORD's judgment,
and all your glory will be turned to shame.
[17] You cut down the forests of Lebanon.
Now you will be cut down.
You destroyed the wild animals,
so now their terror will be yours.

2:5a As in Dead Sea Scroll 1QpHab; other Hebrew manuscripts read *Wine*. **2:5b** Hebrew *as Sheol*. **2:16** Dead Sea Scrolls and Greek and Syriac versions read *and stagger!*

KING JAMES VERSION

the spoil of beasts, *which* made them afraid, because
of men's blood, and for the violence of the land, of
the city, and of all that dwell therein.
18What profiteth the graven image that the maker
thereof hath graven it; the molten image, and a
teacher of lies, that the maker of his work trusteth
therein, to make dumb idols?
19Woe unto him that saith to the wood, Awake; to
the dumb stone, Arise, it shall teach! Behold, it *is* laid
over with gold and silver, and *there is* no breath at all
in the midst of it.
20But the LORD *is* in his holy temple: let all the
earth keep silence before him.

3 1A prayer of Habakkuk the prophet upon Shigionoth.
2O LORD, I have heard thy speech, *and* was afraid:
O LORD, revive thy work in the midst of the years, in
the midst of the years make known; in wrath remember mercy.
3God came from Teman, and the Holy One from
mount Paran. Selah. His glory covered the heavens,
and the earth was full of his praise.
4And *his* brightness was as the light; he had horns
coming out of his hand: and there *was* the hiding of
his power.
5Before him went the pestilence, and burning
coals went forth at his feet.
6He stood, and measured the earth: he beheld, and
drove asunder the nations; and the everlasting
mountains were scattered, the perpetual hills did
bow: his ways *are* everlasting.
7I saw the tents of Cushan in affliction: *and* the
curtains of the land of Midian did tremble.
8Was the LORD displeased against the rivers? *was*
thine anger against the rivers? *was* thy wrath against
the sea, that thou didst ride upon thine horses *and*
thy chariots of salvation?
9Thy bow was made quite naked, *according* to the
oaths of the tribes, *even thy* word. Selah. Thou didst
cleave the earth with rivers.
10The mountains saw thee, *and* they trembled: the

NEW LIVING TRANSLATION

You committed murder throughout
the countryside
and filled the towns with violence.
18 "What good is an idol carved by man,
or a cast image that deceives you?
How foolish to trust in your own creation—
a god that can't even talk!
19 What sorrow awaits you who say to wooden idols,
'Wake up and save us!'
To speechless stone images you say,
'Rise up and teach us!'
Can an idol tell you what to do?
They may be overlaid with gold and silver,
but they are lifeless inside.
20 But the LORD is in his holy Temple.
Let all the earth be silent before him."

Habakkuk's Prayer

3 This prayer was sung by the prophet Habakkuk*:
2 I have heard all about you, LORD.
I am filled with awe by your amazing works.
In this time of our deep need,
help us again as you did in years gone by.
And in your anger,
remember your mercy.

3 I see God moving across the deserts from Edom,*
the Holy One coming from Mount Paran.*
His brilliant splendor fills the heavens,
and the earth is filled with his praise.
4 His coming is as brilliant as the sunrise.
Rays of light flash from his hands,
where his awesome power is hidden.
5 Pestilence marches before him;
plague follows close behind.
6 When he stops, the earth shakes.
When he looks, the nations tremble.
He shatters the everlasting mountains
and levels the eternal hills.
He is the Eternal One!
7 I see the people of Cushan in distress,
and the nation of Midian trembling in terror.

8 Was it in anger, LORD, that you struck the rivers
and parted the sea?
Were you displeased with them?
No, you were sending your chariots
of salvation!
9 You brandished your bow
and your quiver of arrows.
You split open the earth with flowing rivers.
10 The mountains watched and trembled.
Onward swept the raging waters.

3:1 Hebrew adds *according to shigionoth,* probably indicating the musical setting for the prayer. **3:3a** Hebrew *Teman.* **3:3b** Hebrew adds *selah;* also in 3:9, 13. The meaning of this Hebrew term is uncertain; it is probably a musical or literary term.

KING JAMES VERSION

overflowing of the water passed by: the deep uttered his voice, *and* lifted up his hands on high.

11 The sun *and* moon stood still in their habitation: at the light of thine arrows they went, *and* at the shining of thy glittering spear.

12 Thou didst march through the land in indignation, thou didst thresh the heathen in anger.

13 Thou wentest forth for the salvation of thy people, *even* for salvation with thine anointed; thou woundedst the head out of the house of the wicked, by discovering the foundation unto the neck. Selah.

14 Thou didst strike through with his staves the head of his villages: they came out as a whirlwind to scatter me: their rejoicing *was* as to devour the poor secretly.

15 Thou didst walk through the sea with thine horses, *through* the heap of great waters.

16 When I heard, my belly trembled; my lips quivered at the voice: rottenness entered into my bones, and I trembled in myself, that I might rest in the day of trouble: when he cometh up unto the people, he will invade them with his troops.

17 Although the fig tree shall not blossom, neither *shall* fruit *be* in the vines; the labour of the olive shall fail, and the fields shall yield no meat; the flock shall be cut off from the fold, and *there shall be* no herd in the stalls:

18 Yet I will rejoice in the LORD, I will joy in the God of my salvation.

19 The LORD God *is* my strength, and he will make my feet like hinds' *feet*, and he will make me to walk upon mine high places. To the chief singer on my stringed instruments.

NEW LIVING TRANSLATION

The mighty deep cried out,
lifting its hands to the LORD.
11 The sun and moon stood still in the sky
as your brilliant arrows flew
and your glittering spear flashed.

12 You marched across the land in anger
and trampled the nations in your fury.
13 You went out to rescue your chosen people,
to save your anointed ones.
You crushed the heads of the wicked
and stripped their bones from head to toe.
14 With his own weapons,
you destroyed the chief of those
who rushed out like a whirlwind,
thinking Israel would be easy prey.
15 You trampled the sea with your horses,
and the mighty waters piled high.

16 I trembled inside when I heard this;
my lips quivered with fear.
My legs gave way beneath me,*
and I shook in terror.
I will wait quietly for the coming day
when disaster will strike the people who invade us.
17 Even though the fig trees have no blossoms,
and there are no grapes on the vines;
even though the olive crop fails,
and the fields lie empty and barren;
even though the flocks die in the fields,
and the cattle barns are empty,
18 yet I will rejoice in the LORD!
I will be joyful in the God of my salvation!
19 The Sovereign LORD is my strength!
He makes me as surefooted as a deer,*
able to tread upon the heights.
(For the choir director: This prayer is to be accompanied by stringed instruments.)

3:16 Hebrew *Decay entered my bones.* 3:19 Or *He gives me the speed of a deer.*

Zephaniah

KING JAMES VERSION

1 1 The word of the LORD which came unto Zephaniah the son of Cushi, the son of Gedaliah, the
son of Amariah, the son of Hizkiah, in the days of
Josiah the son of Amon, king of Judah.

2 I will utterly consume all *things* from off the land,
saith the LORD.
3 I will consume man and beast; I will consume the
fowls of the heaven, and the fishes of the sea, and the
stumblingblocks with the wicked; and I will cut off
man from off the land, saith the LORD.
4 I will also stretch out mine hand upon Judah, and
upon all the inhabitants of Jerusalem; and I will cut
off the remnant of Baal from this place, *and* the
name of the Chemarims with the priests;
5 And them that worship the host of heaven upon
the housetops; and them that worship *and* that
swear by the LORD, and that swear by Malcham;
6 And them that are turned back from the LORD;
and *those* that have not sought the LORD, nor inquired for him.
7 Hold thy peace at the presence of the Lord GOD:
for the day of the LORD *is* at hand: for the LORD hath
prepared a sacrifice, he hath bid his guests.
8 And it shall come to pass in the day of the LORD's
sacrifice, that I will punish the princes, and the king's
children, and all such as are clothed with strange
apparel.
9 In the same day also will I punish all those that

NEW LIVING TRANSLATION

1 The LORD gave this message to Zephaniah when Josiah son of Amon was king of Judah. Zephaniah was the son of Cushi, son of Gedaliah, son of Amariah, son of Hezekiah.

Coming Judgment against Judah

2 "I will sweep away everything
from the face of the earth," says the LORD.
3 "I will sweep away people and animals alike.
I will sweep away the birds of the sky and
the fish in the sea.
I will reduce the wicked to heaps of rubble,*
and I will wipe humanity from the face of
the earth," says the LORD.
4 "I will crush Judah and Jerusalem with my fist
and destroy every last trace of their Baal
worship.
I will put an end to all the idolatrous priests,
so that even the memory of them will
disappear.
5 For they go up to their roofs
and bow down to the sun, moon, and stars.
They claim to follow the LORD,
but then they worship Molech,* too.
6 And I will destroy those who used to worship me
but now no longer do.
They no longer ask for the LORD's guidance
or seek my blessings."

7 Stand in silence in the presence of the
Sovereign LORD,
for the awesome day of the LORD's judgment
is near.
The LORD has prepared his people for a
great slaughter
and has chosen their executioners.*
8 "On that day of judgment,"
says the LORD,
"I will punish the leaders and princes of Judah
and all those following pagan customs.
9 Yes, I will punish those who participate in pagan
worship ceremonies,

1:3 The meaning of the Hebrew is uncertain. **1:5** Hebrew *Malcam,* a variant spelling of Molech; or it could possibly mean *their king.* **1:7** Hebrew *has prepared a sacrifice and sanctified his guests.*

leap on the threshold, which fill their masters'
houses with violence and deceit.
10 And it shall come to pass in that day, saith the
LORD, *that there shall be* the noise of a cry from the
fish gate, and an howling from the second, and a
great crashing from the hills.
11 Howl, ye inhabitants of Maktesh, for all the merchant people are cut down; all they that bear silver
are cut off.
12 And it shall come to pass at that time, *that* I will
search Jerusalem with candles, and punish the men
that are settled on their lees: that say in their heart,
The LORD will not do good, neither will he do evil.
13 Therefore their goods shall become a booty, and
their houses a desolation: they shall also build
houses, but not inhabit *them;* and they shall plant
vineyards, but not drink the wine thereof.
14 The great day of the LORD *is* near, *it is* near, and
hasteth greatly, *even* the voice of the day of the LORD:
the mighty man shall cry there bitterly.
15 That day *is* a day of wrath, a day of trouble and
distress, a day of wasteness and desolation, a day of
darkness and gloominess, a day of clouds and thick
darkness,
16 A day of the trumpet and alarm against the
fenced cities, and against the high towers.
17 And I will bring distress upon men, that they
shall walk like blind men, because they have sinned
against the LORD: and their blood shall be poured out
as dust, and their flesh as the dung.
18 Neither their silver nor their gold shall be able to
deliver them in the day of the LORD's wrath; but the
whole land shall be devoured by the fire of his jealousy: for he shall make even a speedy riddance of all
them that dwell in the land.

2 1 Gather yourselves together, yea, gather together, O nation not desired;
2 Before the decree bring forth, *before* the day pass
as the chaff, before the fierce anger of the LORD

and those who fill their masters' houses
with violence and deceit.

10 "On that day," says the LORD,
"a cry of alarm will come from the Fish Gate
and echo throughout the New Quarter of
the city.*
And a great crash will sound from the hills.
11 Wail in sorrow, all you who live in the
market area,
for all the merchants and traders will
be destroyed.
12 "I will search with lanterns in Jerusalem's
darkest corners
to punish those who sit complacent in
their sins.
They think the LORD will do nothing to them,
either good or bad.
13 So their property will be plundered,
their homes will be ransacked.
They will build new homes
but never live in them.
They will plant vineyards
but never drink wine from them.

14 "That terrible day of the LORD is near.
Swiftly it comes—
a day of bitter tears,
a day when even strong men will cry out.
15 It will be a day when the LORD's anger is
poured out—
a day of terrible distress and anguish,
a day of ruin and desolation,
a day of darkness and gloom,
a day of clouds and blackness,
16 a day of trumpet calls and battle cries.
Down go the walled cities
and the strongest battlements!
17 "Because you have sinned against the LORD,
I will make you grope around like the blind.
Your blood will be poured into the dust,
and your bodies will lie rotting on the ground."

18 Your silver and gold will not save you
on that day of the LORD's anger.
For the whole land will be devoured
by the fire of his jealousy.
He will make a terrifying end
of all the people on earth.*

A Call to Repentance

2 1 Gather together—yes, gather together,
you shameless nation.
2 Gather before judgment begins,
before your time to repent is blown away
like chaff.

1:10 Or *the Second Quarter,* a newer section of Jerusalem. Hebrew reads *the Mishneh.* **1:18** Or *the people living in the land.*

KING JAMES VERSION

come upon you, before the day of the LORD's anger
come upon you.
3 Seek ye the LORD, all ye meek of the earth, which
have wrought his judgment; seek righteousness,
seek meekness: it may be ye shall be hid in the day of
the LORD's anger.

4 For Gaza shall be forsaken, and Ashkelon a desolation: they shall drive out Ashdod at the noon day,
and Ekron shall be rooted up.
5 Woe unto the inhabitants of the sea coast, the
nation of the Cherethites! the word of the LORD *is*
against you; O Canaan, the land of the Philistines,
I will even destroy thee, that there shall be no inhabitant.
6 And the sea coast shall be dwellings *and* cottages
for shepherds, and folds for flocks.
7 And the coast shall be for the remnant of the
house of Judah; they shall feed thereupon: in the
houses of Ashkelon shall they lie down in the evening: for the LORD their God shall visit them, and
turn away their captivity.

8 I have heard the reproach of Moab, and the
revilings of the children of Ammon, whereby they
have reproached my people, and magnified *themselves* against their border.
9 Therefore *as* I live, saith the LORD of hosts, the
God of Israel, Surely Moab shall be as Sodom, and the
children of Ammon as Gomorrah, *even* the breeding
of nettles, and saltpits, and a perpetual desolation:
the residue of my people shall spoil them, and the
remnant of my people shall possess them.
10 This shall they have for their pride, because they
have reproached and magnified *themselves* against
the people of the LORD of hosts.
11 The LORD *will be* terrible unto them: for he will
famish all the gods of the earth; and *men* shall
worship him, every one from his place, *even* all the
isles of the heathen.

NEW LIVING TRANSLATION

Act now, before the fierce fury of the LORD falls
and the terrible day of the LORD's anger begins.
3 Seek the LORD, all who are humble,
and follow his commands.
Seek to do what is right
and to live humbly.
Perhaps even yet the LORD will protect you—
protect you from his anger on that day
of destruction.

Judgment against Philistia

4 Gaza and Ashkelon will be abandoned,
Ashdod and Ekron torn down.
5 And what sorrow awaits you Philistines*
who live along the coast and in the land
of Canaan,
for this judgment is against you, too!
The LORD will destroy you
until not one of you is left.
6 The Philistine coast will become
a wilderness pasture,
a place of shepherd camps
and enclosures for sheep and goats.
7 The remnant of the tribe of Judah will
pasture there.
They will rest at night in the abandoned
houses in Ashkelon.
For the LORD their God will visit his people
in kindness
and restore their prosperity again.

Judgment against Moab and Ammon

8 "I have heard the taunts of the Moabites
and the insults of the Ammonites,
mocking my people
and invading their borders.
9 Now, as surely as I live,"
says the LORD of Heaven's Armies, the God
of Israel,
"Moab and Ammon will be destroyed—
destroyed as completely as Sodom and
Gomorrah.
Their land will become a place of stinging nettles,
salt pits, and eternal desolation.
The remnant of my people will plunder them
and take their land."

10 They will receive the wages of their pride,
for they have scoffed at the people of the
LORD of Heaven's Armies.
11 The LORD will terrify them
as he destroys all the gods in the land.
Then nations around the world will worship
the LORD,
each in their own land.

2:5 Hebrew *Kerethites*.

KING JAMES VERSION

[12]Ye Ethiopians also, ye *shall be* slain by my sword.
[13]And he will stretch out his hand against the
north, and destroy Assyria; and will make Nineveh a
desolation, *and* dry like a wilderness.
[14]And flocks shall lie down in the midst of her,
all the beasts of the nations: both the cormorant and
the bittern shall lodge in the upper lintels of it; *their*
voice shall sing in the windows; desolation *shall be* in
the thresholds: for he shall uncover the cedar work.
[15]This *is* the rejoicing city that dwelt carelessly,
that said in her heart, I *am*, and *there is* none beside
me: how is she become a desolation, a place for
beasts to lie down in! every one that passeth by her
shall hiss, *and* wag his hand.

3 [1]Woe to her that is filthy and polluted, to the
oppressing city!
[2]She obeyed not the voice; she received not correction; she trusted not in the LORD; she drew not
near to her God.
[3]Her princes within her *are* roaring lions; her
judges *are* evening wolves; they gnaw not the bones
till the morrow.
[4]Her prophets *are* light *and* treacherous persons:
her priests have polluted the sanctuary, they have
done violence to the law.
[5]The just LORD *is* in the midst thereof; he will not
do iniquity: every morning doth he bring his judgment to light, he faileth not; but the unjust knoweth
no shame.
[6]I have cut off the nations: their towers are desolate; I made their streets waste, that none passeth by:
their cities are destroyed, so that there is no man,
that there is none inhabitant.

NEW LIVING TRANSLATION

Judgment against Ethiopia and Assyria

[12] "You Ethiopians* will also be slaughtered
by my sword," says the LORD.

[13] And the LORD will strike the lands of the north
with his fist,
destroying the land of Assyria.
He will make its great capital, Nineveh, a desolate
wasteland,
parched like a desert.
[14] The proud city will become a pasture for flocks
and herds,
and all sorts of wild animals will settle there.
The desert owl and screech owl will roost on its
ruined columns,
their calls echoing through the gaping windows.
Rubble will block all the doorways,
and the cedar paneling will be exposed
to the weather.
[15] This is the boisterous city,
once so secure.
"I am the greatest!" it boasted.
"No other city can compare with me!"
But now, look how it has become an utter ruin,
a haven for wild animals.
Everyone passing by will laugh in derision
and shake a defiant fist.

Jerusalem's Rebellion and Redemption

3 [1]What sorrow awaits rebellious, polluted
Jerusalem,
the city of violence and crime!
[2] No one can tell it anything;
it refuses all correction.
It does not trust in the LORD
or draw near to its God.
[3] Its leaders are like roaring lions
hunting for their victims.
Its judges are like ravenous wolves
at evening time,
who by dawn have left no trace of their prey.
[4] Its prophets are arrogant liars seeking their
own gain.
Its priests defile the Temple by disobeying
God's instructions.
[5] But the LORD is still there in the city,
and he does no wrong.
Day by day he hands down justice,
and he does not fail.
But the wicked know no shame.

[6] "I have wiped out many nations,
devastating their fortress walls and towers.
Their streets are now deserted;
their cities lie in silent ruin.
There are no survivors—
none at all.

2:12 Hebrew *Cushites.*

KING JAMES VERSION

7 I said, Surely thou wilt fear me, thou wilt receive
instruction; so their dwelling should not be cut off,
howsoever I punished them: but they rose early, *and*
corrupted all their doings.
8 Therefore wait ye upon me, saith the LORD, until
the day that I rise up to the prey: for my determination *is* to gather the nations, that I may assemble the
kingdoms, to pour upon them mine indignation,
even all my fierce anger: for all the earth shall be devoured with the fire of my jealousy.
9 For then will I turn to the people a pure language,
that they may all call upon the name of the LORD, to
serve him with one consent.
10 From beyond the rivers of Ethiopia my suppli-
ants, *even* the daughter of my dispersed, shall bring
mine offering.
11 In that day shalt thou not be ashamed for all thy
doings, wherein thou hast transgressed against me:
for then I will take away out of the midst of thee them
that rejoice in thy pride, and thou shalt no more be
haughty because of my holy mountain.
12 I will also leave in the midst of thee an afflicted
and poor people, and they shall trust in the name of
the LORD.
13 The remnant of Israel shall not do iniquity, nor
speak lies; neither shall a deceitful tongue be found
in their mouth: for they shall feed and lie down, and
none shall make *them* afraid.
14 Sing, O daughter of Zion; shout, O Israel; be
glad and rejoice with all the heart, O daughter of
Jerusalem.
15 The LORD hath taken away thy judgments, he
hath cast out thine enemy: the king of Israel, *even*
the LORD, *is* in the midst of thee: thou shalt not see
evil any more.
16 In that day it shall be said to Jerusalem, Fear thou
not: *and to* Zion, Let not thine hands be slack.
17 The LORD thy God in the midst of thee *is* mighty;
he will save, he will rejoice over thee with joy; he will
rest in his love, he will joy over thee with singing.

NEW LIVING TRANSLATION

7 I thought, 'Surely they will have reverence
for me now!
Surely they will listen to my warnings.
Then I won't need to strike again,
destroying their homes.'
But no, they get up early
to continue their evil deeds.
8 Therefore, be patient," says the LORD.
"Soon I will stand and accuse these evil
nations.
For I have decided to gather the kingdoms
of the earth
and pour out my fiercest anger and fury
on them.
All the earth will be devoured
by the fire of my jealousy.

9 "Then I will purify the speech of all people,
so that everyone can worship the LORD
together.
10 My scattered people who live beyond the rivers of
Ethiopia*
will come to present their offerings.
11 On that day you will no longer need to be
ashamed,
for you will no longer be rebels against me.
I will remove all proud and arrogant people
from among you.
There will be no more haughtiness on my
holy mountain.
12 Those who are left will be the lowly and humble,
for it is they who trust in the name of
the LORD.
13 The remnant of Israel will do no wrong;
they will never tell lies or deceive one another.
They will eat and sleep in safety,
and no one will make them afraid."
14 Sing, O daughter of Zion;
shout aloud, O Israel!
Be glad and rejoice with all your heart,
O daughter of Jerusalem!
15 For the LORD will remove his hand of judgment
and will disperse the armies of your enemy.
And the LORD himself, the King of Israel,
will live among you!
At last your troubles will be over,
and you will never again fear disaster.
16 On that day the announcement to Jerusalem
will be,
"Cheer up, Zion! Don't be afraid!
17 For the LORD your God is living among you.
He is a mighty savior.
He will take delight in you with gladness.
With his love, he will calm all your fears.*
He will rejoice over you with joyful songs."

3:10 Hebrew *Cush.* **3:17** Or *He will be silent in his love.* Greek and Syriac versions read *He will renew you with his love.*

KING JAMES VERSION

18I will gather *them that are* sorrowful for the
solemn assembly, *who* are of thee, *to whom* the reproach of it *was* a burden.
19Behold, at that time I will undo all that afflict
thee: and I will save her that halteth, and gather her
that was driven out; and I will get them praise and
fame in every land where they have been put to
shame.
20At that time will I bring you *again*, even in the
time that I gather you: for I will make you a name and
a praise among all people of the earth, when I turn
back your captivity before your eyes, saith the LORD.

NEW LIVING TRANSLATION

18 "I will gather you who mourn for the appointed
festivals;
you will be disgraced no more.*
19 And I will deal severely with all who have
oppressed you.
I will save the weak and helpless ones;
I will bring together
those who were chased away.
I will give glory and fame to my former exiles,
wherever they have been mocked and shamed.
20 On that day I will gather you together
and bring you home again.
I will give you a good name, a name of distinction,
among all the nations of the earth,
as I restore your fortunes before their very eyes.
I, the LORD, have spoken!"

3:18 The meaning of the Hebrew for this verse is uncertain.

Haggai

KING JAMES VERSION

1 1 In the second year of Darius the king, in the
sixth month, in the first day of the month, came
the word of the LORD by Haggai the prophet unto Zerubbabel the son of Shealtiel, governor of Judah, and
to Joshua the son of Josedech, the high priest, saying,
2 Thus speaketh the LORD of hosts, saying, This
people say, The time is not come, the time that the
LORD's house should be built.
3 Then came the word of the LORD by Haggai the
prophet, saying,
4 *Is it* time for you, O ye, to dwell in your cieled
houses, and this house *lie* waste?
5 Now therefore thus saith the LORD of hosts; Consider your ways.
6 Ye have sown much, and bring in little; ye eat, but
ye have not enough; ye drink, but ye are not filled
with drink; ye clothe you, but there is none warm;
and he that earneth wages earneth wages *to put it*
into a bag with holes.
7 Thus saith the LORD of hosts; Consider your ways.
8 Go up to the mountain, and bring wood, and
build the house; and I will take pleasure in it, and I
will be glorified, saith the LORD.
9 Ye looked for much, and, lo, *it came* to little; and
when ye brought *it* home, I did blow upon it. Why?
saith the LORD of hosts. Because of mine house that
is waste, and ye run every man unto his own house.
10 Therefore the heaven over you is stayed from
dew, and the earth is stayed *from* her fruit.
11 And I called for a drought upon the land, and
upon the mountains, and upon the corn, and upon
the new wine, and upon the oil, and upon *that* which
the ground bringeth forth, and upon men, and upon
cattle, and upon all the labour of the hands.
12 Then Zerubbabel the son of Shealtiel, and Joshua the son of Josedech, the high priest, with all the
remnant of the people, obeyed the voice of the LORD
their God, and the words of Haggai the prophet, as
the LORD their God had sent him, and the people did
fear before the LORD.
13 Then spake Haggai the LORD's messenger in the

NEW LIVING TRANSLATION

A Call to Rebuild the Temple

1 On August 29* of the second year of King Darius's reign, the LORD gave a message through the
prophet Haggai to Zerubbabel son of Shealtiel,
governor of Judah, and to Jeshua* son of Jehozadak,
the high priest.
2 "This is what the LORD of Heaven's Armies says:
The people are saying, 'The time has not yet come to
rebuild the house of the LORD.'"
3 Then the LORD sent this message through the
prophet Haggai: 4 "Why are you living in luxurious
houses while my house lies in ruins? 5 This is what
the LORD of Heaven's Armies says: Look at what's
happening to you! 6 You have planted much but harvest little. You eat but are not satisfied. You drink but
are still thirsty. You put on clothes but cannot keep
warm. Your wages disappear as though you were
putting them in pockets filled with holes!
7 "This is what the LORD of Heaven's Armies says:
Look at what's happening to you! 8 Now go up into the
hills, bring down timber, and rebuild my house. Then
I will take pleasure in it and be honored, says the
LORD. 9 You hoped for rich harvests, but they were
poor. And when you brought your harvest home, I
blew it away. Why? Because my house lies in ruins,
says the LORD of Heaven's Armies, while all of you are
busy building your own fine houses. 10 It's because of
you that the heavens withhold the dew and the earth
produces no crops. 11 I have called for a drought on
your fields and hills—a drought to wither the grain
and grapes and olive trees and all your other crops, a
drought to starve you and your livestock and to ruin
everything you have worked so hard to get."

Obedience to God's Call

12 Then Zerubbabel son of Shealtiel, and Jeshua son
of Jehozadak, the high priest, and the whole remnant
of God's people began to obey the message from the
LORD their God. When they heard the words of the
prophet Haggai, whom the LORD their God had sent,
the people feared the LORD. 13 Then Haggai, the

1:1a Hebrew *On the first day of the sixth month,* of the ancient Hebrew lunar calendar. A number of dates in Haggai can be cross-checked with dates in surviving Persian records and related accurately to our modern calendar. This event occurred on August 29, 520 B.C. **1:1b** Hebrew *Joshua,* a variant spelling of Jeshua; also in 1:12, 14.

KING JAMES VERSION

LORD's message unto the people, saying, I *am* with you, saith the LORD.

14 And the LORD stirred up the spirit of Zerubbabel the son of Shealtiel, governor of Judah, and the spirit of Joshua the son of Josedech, the high priest, and the spirit of all the remnant of the people; and they came and did work in the house of the LORD of hosts, their God,

15 In the four and twentieth day of the sixth month, in the second year of Darius the king.

2 1 In the seventh *month,* in the one and twentieth *day* of the month, came the word of the LORD by the prophet Haggai, saying,

2 Speak now to Zerubbabel the son of Shealtiel, governor of Judah, and to Joshua the son of Josedech, the high priest, and to the residue of the people, saying,

3 Who *is* left among you that saw this house in her first glory? and how do ye see it now? *is it* not in your eyes in comparison of it as nothing?

4 Yet now be strong, O Zerubbabel, saith the LORD; and be strong, O Joshua, son of Josedech, the high priest; and be strong, all ye people of the land, saith the LORD, and work: for I *am* with you, saith the LORD of hosts:

5 *According to* the word that I covenanted with you when ye came out of Egypt, so my spirit remaineth among you: fear ye not.

6 For thus saith the LORD of hosts; Yet once, it *is* a little while, and I will shake the heavens, and the earth, and the sea, and the dry *land;*

7 And I will shake all nations, and the desire of all nations shall come: and I will fill this house with glory, saith the LORD of hosts.

8 The silver *is* mine, and the gold *is* mine, saith the LORD of hosts.

9 The glory of this latter house shall be greater than of the former, saith the LORD of hosts: and in this place will I give peace, saith the LORD of hosts.

10 In the four and twentieth *day* of the ninth *month,* in the second year of Darius, came the word of the LORD by Haggai the prophet, saying,

11 Thus saith the LORD of hosts; Ask now the priests *concerning* the law, saying,

12 If one bear holy flesh in the skirt of his garment, and with his skirt do touch bread, or pottage, or wine, or oil, or any meat, shall it be holy? And the priests answered and said, No.

13 Then said Haggai, If *one that is* unclean by a dead body touch any of these, shall it be unclean? And the priests answered and said, It shall be unclean.

NEW LIVING TRANSLATION

LORD's messenger, gave the people this message from the LORD: "I am with you, says the LORD!"

14 So the LORD sparked the enthusiasm of Zerubbabel son of Shealtiel, governor of Judah, and the enthusiasm of Jeshua son of Jehozadak, the high priest, and the enthusiasm of the whole remnant of God's people. They began to work on the house of their God, the LORD of Heaven's Armies, 15 on September 21* of the second year of King Darius's reign.

The New Temple's Diminished Splendor

2 Then on October 17 of that same year,* the LORD sent another message through the prophet Haggai. 2 "Say this to Zerubbabel son of Shealtiel, governor of Judah, and to Jeshua* son of Jehozadak, the high priest, and to the remnant of God's people there in the land: 3 'Does anyone remember this house—this Temple—in its former splendor? How, in comparison, does it look to you now? It must seem like nothing at all! 4 But now the LORD says: Be strong, Zerubbabel. Be strong, Jeshua son of Jehozadak, the high priest. Be strong, all you people still left in the land. And now get to work, for I am with you, says the LORD of Heaven's Armies. 5 My Spirit remains among you, just as I promised when you came out of Egypt. So do not be afraid.'

6 "For this is what the LORD of Heaven's Armies says: In just a little while I will again shake the heavens and the earth, the oceans and the dry land. 7 I will shake all the nations, and the treasures of all the nations will be brought to this Temple. I will fill this place with glory, says the LORD of Heaven's Armies. 8 The silver is mine, and the gold is mine, says the LORD of Heaven's Armies. 9 The future glory of this Temple will be greater than its past glory, says the LORD of Heaven's Armies. And in this place I will bring peace. I, the LORD of Heaven's Armies, have spoken!"

Blessings Promised for Obedience

10 On December 18* of the second year of King Darius's reign, the LORD sent this message to the prophet Haggai: 11 "This is what the LORD of Heaven's Armies says. Ask the priests this question about the law: 12 'If one of you is carrying some meat from a holy sacrifice in his robes and his robe happens to brush against some bread or stew, wine or olive oil, or any other kind of food, will it also become holy?'"

The priests replied, "No."

13 Then Haggai asked, "If someone becomes ceremonially unclean by touching a dead person and then touches any of these foods, will the food be defiled?"

And the priests answered, "Yes."

1:15 Hebrew *on the twenty-fourth day of the sixth month,* of the ancient Hebrew lunar calendar. This event occurred on September 21, 520 B.C.; also see note on 1:1a. **2:1** Hebrew *on the twenty-first day of the seventh month,* of the ancient Hebrew lunar calendar. This event (in the second year of Darius's reign) occurred on October 17, 520 B.C.; also see note on 1:1a. **2:2** Hebrew *Joshua,* a variant spelling of Jeshua; also in 2:4. **2:10** Hebrew *On the twenty-fourth day of the ninth month,* of the ancient Hebrew lunar calendar (similarly in 2:18). This event occurred on December 18, 520 B.C.; also see note on 1:1a.

KING JAMES VERSION

14Then answered Haggai, and said, So *is* this people, and so *is* this nation before me, saith the LORD; and so *is* every work of their hands; and that which they offer there *is* unclean.

15And now, I pray you, consider from this day and upward, from before a stone was laid upon a stone in the temple of the LORD:

16Since those *days* were, when *one* came to an heap of twenty *measures*, there were *but* ten: when *one* came to the pressfat for to draw out fifty *vessels* out of the press, there were *but* twenty.

17I smote you with blasting and with mildew and with hail in all the labours of your hands; yet ye *turned* not to me, saith the LORD.

18Consider now from this day and upward, from the four and twentieth day of the ninth *month, even* from the day that the foundation of the LORD's temple was laid, consider *it*.

19Is the seed yet in the barn? yea, as yet the vine, and the fig tree, and the pomegranate, and the olive tree, hath not brought forth: from this day will I bless *you*.

20And again the word of the LORD came unto Haggai in the four and twentieth *day* of the month, saying,

21Speak to Zerubbabel, governor of Judah, saying, I will shake the heavens and the earth;

22And I will overthrow the throne of kingdoms, and I will destroy the strength of the kingdoms of the heathen; and I will overthrow the chariots, and those that ride in them; and the horses and their riders shall come down, every one by the sword of his brother.

23In that day, saith the LORD of hosts, will I take thee, O Zerubbabel, my servant, the son of Shealtiel, saith the LORD, and will make thee as a signet: for I have chosen thee, saith the LORD of hosts.

NEW LIVING TRANSLATION

14Then Haggai responded, "That is how it is with
this people and this nation, says the LORD. Everything they do and everything they offer is defiled by
their sin. 15Look at what was happening to you before you began to lay the foundation of the LORD's
Temple. 16When you hoped for a twenty-bushel
crop, you harvested only ten. When you expected to
draw fifty gallons from the winepress, you found
only twenty. 17I sent blight and mildew and hail to
destroy everything you worked so hard to produce.
Even so, you refused to return to me, says the LORD.

18"Think about this eighteenth day of December,
the day* when the foundation of the LORD's Temple
was laid. Think carefully. 19I am giving you a promise
now while the seed is still in the barn.* You have not
yet harvested your grain, and your grapevines, fig
trees, pomegranates, and olive trees have not yet produced their crops. But from this day onward I will
bless you."

Promises for Zerubbabel

20On that same day, December 18,* the LORD sent
this second message to Haggai: 21"Tell Zerubbabel,
the governor of Judah, that I am about to shake the
heavens and the earth. 22I will overthrow royal
thrones and destroy the power of foreign kingdoms.
I will overturn their chariots and riders. The horses
will fall, and their riders will kill each other.

23"But when this happens, says the LORD of
Heaven's Armies, I will honor you, Zerubbabel son of
Shealtiel, my servant. I will make you like a signet
ring on my finger, says the LORD, for I have chosen
you. I, the LORD of Heaven's Armies, have spoken!"

2:18 Or *On this eighteenth day of December, think about the day.* **2:19** Hebrew *Is the seed yet in the barn?* **2:20** Hebrew *On the twenty-fourth day of the [ninth] month;* see note on 2:10.

Zechariah

KING JAMES VERSION

1 1 In the eighth month, in the second year of Darius, came the word of the LORD unto Zechariah, the son of Berechiah, the son of Iddo the prophet, saying,

2 The LORD hath been sore displeased with your fathers.

3 Therefore say thou unto them, Thus saith the LORD of hosts; Turn ye unto me, saith the LORD of hosts, and I will turn unto you, saith the LORD of hosts.

4 Be ye not as your fathers, unto whom the former prophets have cried, saying, Thus saith the LORD of hosts; Turn ye now from your evil ways, and *from* your evil doings: but they did not hear, nor hearken unto me, saith the LORD.

5 Your fathers, where *are* they? and the prophets, do they live for ever?

6 But my words and my statutes, which I commanded my servants the prophets, did they not take hold of your fathers? and they returned and said, Like as the LORD of hosts thought to do unto us, according to our ways, and according to our doings, so hath he dealt with us.

7 Upon the four and twentieth day of the eleventh month, which *is* the month Sebat, in the second year of Darius, came the word of the LORD unto Zechariah, the son of Berechiah, the son of Iddo the prophet, saying,

8 I saw by night, and behold a man riding upon a red horse, and he stood among the myrtle trees that *were* in the bottom; and behind him *were there* red horses, speckled, and white.

9 Then said I, O my lord, what *are* these? And the angel that talked with me said unto me, I will shew thee what these *be*.

10 And the man that stood among the myrtle trees answered and said, These *are they* whom the LORD hath sent to walk to and fro through the earth.

11 And they answered the angel of the LORD that stood among the myrtle trees, and said, We have

NEW LIVING TRANSLATION

A Call to Return to the LORD

1 In November* of the second year of King Darius's reign, the LORD gave this message to the prophet Zechariah son of Berekiah and grandson of Iddo:

2 "I, the LORD, was very angry with your ancestors. 3 Therefore, say to the people, 'This is what the LORD of Heaven's Armies says: Return to me, and I will return to you, says the LORD of Heaven's Armies.' 4 Don't be like your ancestors who would not listen or pay attention when the earlier prophets said to them, 'This is what the LORD of Heaven's Armies says: Turn from your evil ways, and stop all your evil practices.'

5 "Where are your ancestors now? They and the prophets are long dead. 6 But everything I said through my servants the prophets happened to your ancestors, just as I said. As a result, they repented and said, 'We have received what we deserved from the LORD of Heaven's Armies. He has done what he said he would do.'"

A Man among the Myrtle Trees

7 Three months later, on February 15,* the LORD sent another message to the prophet Zechariah son of Berekiah and grandson of Iddo.

8 In a vision during the night, I saw a man sitting on a red horse that was standing among some myrtle trees in a small valley. Behind him were riders on red, brown, and white horses. 9 I asked the angel who was talking with me, "My lord, what do these horses mean?"

"I will show you," the angel replied.

10 The rider standing among the myrtle trees then explained, "They are the ones the LORD has sent out to patrol the earth."

11 Then the other riders reported to the angel of the LORD, who was standing among the myrtle trees,

1:1 Hebrew *In the eighth month.* A number of dates in Zechariah can be cross-checked with dates in surviving Persian records and related accurately to our modern calendar. This month of the ancient Hebrew lunar calendar occurred within the months of October and November 520 B.C. **1:7** Hebrew *On the twenty-fourth day of the eleventh month, the month of Shebat, in the second year of Darius.* This event occurred on February 15, 519 B.C.; also see note on 1:1.

KING JAMES VERSION

walked to and fro through the earth, and, behold,
all the earth sitteth still, and is at rest.
12 Then the angel of the LORD answered and said,
O LORD of hosts, how long wilt thou not have mercy
on Jerusalem and on the cities of Judah, against
which thou hast had indignation these threescore
and ten years?
13 And the LORD answered the angel that talked
with me *with* good words *and* comfortable words.
14 So the angel that communed with me said unto
me, Cry thou, saying, Thus saith the LORD of hosts; I
am jealous for Jerusalem and for Zion with a great
jealousy.
15 And I am very sore displeased with the heathen
that are at ease: for I was but a little displeased, and
they helped forward the affliction.
16 Therefore thus saith the LORD; I am returned to
Jerusalem with mercies: my house shall be built in it,
saith the LORD of hosts, and a line shall be stretched
forth upon Jerusalem.
17 Cry yet, saying, Thus saith the LORD of hosts; My
cities through prosperity shall yet be spread abroad;
and the LORD shall yet comfort Zion, and shall yet
choose Jerusalem.

18 Then lifted I up mine eyes, and saw, and behold
four horns.
19 And I said unto the angel that talked with me,
What *be* these? And he answered me, These *are*
the horns which have scattered Judah, Israel, and
Jerusalem.
20 And the LORD shewed me four carpenters.
21 Then said I, What come these to do? And he
spake, saying, These *are* the horns which have scattered Judah, so that no man did lift up his head: but
these are come to fray them, to cast out the horns of
the Gentiles, which lifted up *their* horn over the land
of Judah to scatter it.

2 1 I lifted up mine eyes again, and looked, and behold a man with a measuring line in his hand.
2 Then said I, Whither goest thou? And he said
unto me, To measure Jerusalem, to see what *is* the
breadth thereof, and what *is* the length thereof.
3 And, behold, the angel that talked with me went
forth, and another angel went out to meet him,
4 And said unto him, Run, speak to this young man,
saying, Jerusalem shall be inhabited *as* towns without walls for the multitude of men and cattle therein:
5 For I, saith the LORD, will be unto her a wall of fire
round about, and will be the glory in the midst of her.

NEW LIVING TRANSLATION

"We have been patrolling the earth, and the whole
earth is at peace."
12 Upon hearing this, the angel of the LORD prayed
this prayer: "O LORD of Heaven's Armies, for seventy
years now you have been angry with Jerusalem and
the towns of Judah. How long until you again show
mercy to them?" 13 And the LORD spoke kind and
comforting words to the angel who talked with me.
14 Then the angel said to me, "Shout this message
for all to hear: 'This is what the LORD of Heaven's
Armies says: My love for Jerusalem and Mount Zion
is passionate and strong. 15 But I am very angry with
the other nations that are now enjoying peace and
security. I was only a little angry with my people, but
the nations inflicted harm on them far beyond my
intentions.
16 "'Therefore, this is what the LORD says: I have returned to show mercy to Jerusalem. My Temple will
be rebuilt, says the LORD of Heaven's Armies, and
measurements will be taken for the reconstruction
of Jerusalem.*'
17 "Say this also: 'This is what the LORD of Heaven's
Armies says: The towns of Israel will again overflow
with prosperity, and the LORD will again comfort
Zion and choose Jerusalem as his own.'"

Four Horns and Four Blacksmiths

18 *Then I looked up and saw four animal horns.
19 "What are these?" I asked the angel who was talking with me.
He replied, "These horns represent the nations
that scattered Judah, Israel, and Jerusalem."
20 Then the LORD showed me four blacksmiths.
21 "What are these men coming to do?" I asked.
The angel replied, "These four horns—these nations—scattered and humbled Judah. Now these
blacksmiths have come to terrify those nations and
throw them down and destroy them."

Future Prosperity of Jerusalem

2 1 *When I looked again, I saw a man with a
measuring line in his hand. 2 "Where are you
going?" I asked.
He replied, "I am going to measure Jerusalem, to
see how wide and how long it is."
3 Then the angel who was with me went to meet a
second angel who was coming toward him. 4 The
other angel said, "Hurry, and say to that young man,
'Jerusalem will someday be so full of people and livestock that there won't be room enough for everyone!
Many will live outside the city walls. 5 Then I, myself,
will be a protective wall of fire around Jerusalem,
says the LORD. And I will be the glory inside the city!'"

1:16 Hebrew *and the measuring line will be stretched out over Jerusalem.*
1:18 Verses 1:18-21 are numbered 2:1-4 in Hebrew text. **2:1** Verses
2:1-13 are numbered 2:5-17 in Hebrew text.

KING JAMES VERSION

[6]Ho, ho, *come forth,* and flee from the land of the north, saith the LORD: for I have spread you abroad as the four winds of the heaven, saith the LORD.

[7]Deliver thyself, O Zion, that dwellest *with* the daughter of Babylon.

[8]For thus saith the LORD of hosts; After the glory hath he sent me unto the nations which spoiled you: for he that toucheth you toucheth the apple of his eye.

[9]For, behold, I will shake mine hand upon them, and they shall be a spoil to their servants: and ye shall know that the LORD of hosts hath sent me.

[10]Sing and rejoice, O daughter of Zion: for, lo, I come, and I will dwell in the midst of thee, saith the LORD.

[11]And many nations shall be joined to the LORD in that day, and shall be my people: and I will dwell in the midst of thee, and thou shalt know that the LORD of hosts hath sent me unto thee.

[12]And the LORD shall inherit Judah his portion in the holy land, and shall choose Jerusalem again.

[13]Be silent, O all flesh, before the LORD: for he is raised up out of his holy habitation.

3 [1]And he shewed me Joshua the high priest standing before the angel of the LORD, and Satan standing at his right hand to resist him.

[2]And the LORD said unto Satan, The LORD rebuke thee, O Satan; even the LORD that hath chosen Jerusalem rebuke thee: *is* not this a brand plucked out of the fire?

[3]Now Joshua was clothed with filthy garments, and stood before the angel.

[4]And he answered and spake unto those that stood before him, saying, Take away the filthy garments from him. And unto him he said, Behold, I have caused thine iniquity to pass from thee, and I will clothe thee with change of raiment.

[5]And I said, Let them set a fair mitre upon his head. So they set a fair mitre upon his head, and clothed him with garments. And the angel of the LORD stood by.

[6]And the angel of the LORD protested unto Joshua, saying,

[7]Thus saith the LORD of hosts; If thou wilt walk in my ways, and if thou wilt keep my charge, then thou shalt also judge my house, and shalt also keep my courts, and I will give thee places to walk among these that stand by.

[8]Hear now, O Joshua the high priest, thou, and thy fellows that sit before thee: for they *are* men wondered at: for, behold, I will bring forth my servant the BRANCH.

[9]For behold the stone that I have laid before Joshua; upon one stone *shall be* seven eyes: behold, I will engrave the graving thereof, saith the LORD of hosts, and I will remove the iniquity of that land in one day.

NEW LIVING TRANSLATION

The Exiles Are Called Home

[6]The LORD says, "Come away! Flee from Babylon in the land of the north, for I have scattered you to the four winds. [7]Come away, people of Zion, you who are exiled in Babylon!"

[8]After a period of glory, the LORD of Heaven's Armies sent me* against the nations who plundered you. For he said, "Anyone who harms you harms my most precious possession.* [9]I will raise my fist to crush them, and their own slaves will plunder them." Then you will know that the LORD of Heaven's Armies has sent me.

[10]The LORD says, "Shout and rejoice, O beautiful Jerusalem,* for I am coming to live among you. [11]Many nations will join themselves to the LORD on that day, and they, too, will be my people. I will live among you, and you will know that the LORD of Heaven's Armies sent me to you. [12]The land of Judah will be the LORD's special possession in the holy land, and he will once again choose Jerusalem to be his own city. [13]Be silent before the LORD, all humanity, for he is springing into action from his holy dwelling."

Cleansing for the High Priest

3 Then the angel showed me Jeshua* the high priest standing before the angel of the LORD. The Accuser, Satan,* was there at the angel's right hand, making accusations against Jeshua. [2]And the LORD said to Satan, "I, the LORD, reject your accusations, Satan. Yes, the LORD, who has chosen Jerusalem, rebukes you. This man is like a burning stick that has been snatched from the fire."

[3]Jeshua's clothing was filthy as he stood there before the angel. [4]So the angel said to the others standing there, "Take off his filthy clothes." And turning to Jeshua he said, "See, I have taken away your sins, and now I am giving you these fine new clothes."

[5]Then I said, "They should also place a clean turban on his head." So they put a clean priestly turban on his head and dressed him in new clothes while the angel of the LORD stood by.

[6]Then the angel of the LORD spoke very solemnly to Jeshua and said, [7]"This is what the LORD of Heaven's Armies says: If you follow my ways and carefully serve me, then you will be given authority over my Temple and its courtyards. I will let you walk among these others standing here.

[8]"Listen to me, O Jeshua the high priest, and all you other priests. You are symbols of things to come. Soon I am going to bring my servant, the Branch. [9]Now look at the jewel I have set before Jeshua, a single stone with seven facets.* I will engrave an inscription on it, says the LORD of Heaven's Armies, and I will remove the sins of this land in a single day.

2:8a The meaning of the Hebrew is uncertain. **2:8b** Hebrew *Anyone who touches you touches the pupil of his eye.* **2:10** Hebrew *O daughter of Zion.* **3:1a** Hebrew *Joshua,* a variant spelling of Jeshua; also in 3:3, 4, 6, 8, 9. **3:1b** Hebrew *The satan;* similarly in 3:2. **3:9** Hebrew *seven eyes.*

KING JAMES VERSION

10In that day, saith the LORD of hosts, shall ye call every man his neighbour under the vine and under the fig tree.

4

1And the angel that talked with me came again, and waked me, as a man that is wakened out of his sleep,

2And said unto me, What seest thou? And I said, I have looked, and behold a candlestick all *of* gold, with a bowl upon the top of it, and his seven lamps thereon, and seven pipes to the seven lamps, which *are* upon the top thereof:

3And two olive trees by it, one upon the right *side* of the bowl, and the other upon the left *side* thereof.

4So I answered and spake to the angel that talked with me, saying, What *are* these, my lord?

5Then the angel that talked with me answered and said unto me, Knowest thou not what these be? And I said, No, my lord.

6Then he answered and spake unto me, saying, This *is* the word of the LORD unto Zerubbabel, saying, Not by might, nor by power, but by my spirit, saith the LORD of hosts.

7Who *art* thou, O great mountain? before Zerubbabel *thou shalt become* a plain: and he shall bring forth the headstone *thereof with* shoutings, *crying,* Grace, grace unto it.

8Moreover the word of the LORD came unto me, saying,

9The hands of Zerubbabel have laid the foundation of this house; his hands shall also finish it; and thou shalt know that the LORD of hosts hath sent me unto you.

10For who hath despised the day of small things? for they shall rejoice, and shall see the plummet in the hand of Zerubbabel *with* those seven; they *are* the eyes of the LORD, which run to and fro through the whole earth.

11Then answered I, and said unto him, What *are* these two olive trees upon the right *side* of the candlestick and upon the left *side* thereof?

12And I answered again, and said unto him, What *be these* two olive branches which through the two golden pipes empty the golden *oil* out of themselves?

13And he answered me and said, Knowest thou not what these *be?* And I said, No, my lord.

14Then said he, These *are* the two anointed ones, that stand by the Lord of the whole earth.

5

1Then I turned, and lifted up mine eyes, and looked, and behold a flying roll.

2And he said unto me, What seest thou? And I answered, I see a flying roll; the length thereof *is* twenty cubits, and the breadth thereof ten cubits.

NEW LIVING TRANSLATION

10"And on that day, says the LORD of Heaven's Armies, each of you will invite your neighbor to sit with you peacefully under your own grapevine and fig tree."

A Lampstand and Two Olive Trees

4

Then the angel who had been talking with me returned and woke me, as though I had been asleep. 2"What do you see now?" he asked.

I answered, "I see a solid gold lampstand with a bowl of oil on top of it. Around the bowl are seven lamps, each having seven spouts with wicks. 3And I see two olive trees, one on each side of the bowl." 4Then I asked the angel, "What are these, my lord? What do they mean?"

5"Don't you know?" the angel asked.

"No, my lord," I replied.

6Then he said to me, "This is what the LORD says to Zerubbabel: It is not by force nor by strength, but by my Spirit, says the LORD of Heaven's Armies. 7Nothing, not even a mighty mountain, will stand in Zerubbabel's way; it will become a level plain before him! And when Zerubbabel sets the final stone of the Temple in place, the people will shout: 'May God bless it! May God bless it!'*"

8Then another message came to me from the LORD: 9"Zerubbabel is the one who laid the foundation of this Temple, and he will complete it. Then you will know that the LORD of Heaven's Armies has sent me. 10Do not despise these small beginnings, for the LORD rejoices to see the work begin, to see the plumb line in Zerubbabel's hand."

(The seven lamps* represent the eyes of the LORD that search all around the world.)

11Then I asked the angel, "What are these two olive trees on each side of the lampstand, 12and what are the two olive branches that pour out golden oil through two gold tubes?"

13"Don't you know?" he asked.

"No, my lord," I replied.

14Then he said to me, "They represent the two heavenly beings who stand in the court of the Lord of all the earth."

A Flying Scroll

5

I looked up again and saw a scroll flying through the air.

2"What do you see?" the angel asked.

"I see a flying scroll," I replied. "It appears to be about 30 feet long and 15 feet wide.*"

4:7 Hebrew *'Grace, grace to it.'* 4:10 Or *The seven facets* (see 3:9); Hebrew reads *These seven.* 5:2 Hebrew *20 cubits* [9 meters] *long and 10 cubits* [4.5 meters] *wide.*

KING JAMES VERSION

3 Then said he unto me, This *is* the curse that goeth forth over the face of the whole earth: for every one that stealeth shall be cut off *as* on this side according to it; and every one that sweareth shall be cut off *as* on that side according to it.

4 I will bring it forth, saith the LORD of hosts, and it shall enter into the house of the thief, and into the house of him that sweareth falsely by my name: and it shall remain in the midst of his house, and shall consume it with the timber thereof and the stones thereof.

5 Then the angel that talked with me went forth, and said unto me, Lift up now thine eyes, and see what *is* this that goeth forth.

6 And I said, What *is* it? And he said, This *is* an ephah that goeth forth. He said moreover, This *is* their resemblance through all the earth.

7 And, behold, there was lifted up a talent of lead: and this *is* a woman that sitteth in the midst of the ephah.

8 And he said, This *is* wickedness. And he cast it into the midst of the ephah; and he cast the weight of lead upon the mouth thereof.

9 Then lifted I up mine eyes, and looked, and, behold, there came out two women, and the wind *was* in their wings; for they had wings like the wings of a stork: and they lifted up the ephah between the earth and the heaven.

10 Then said I to the angel that talked with me, Whither do these bear the ephah?

11 And he said unto me, To build it an house in the land of Shinar: and it shall be established, and set there upon her own base.

6 1 And I turned, and lifted up mine eyes, and looked, and, behold, there came four chariots out from between two mountains; and the mountains *were* mountains of brass.

2 In the first chariot *were* red horses; and in the second chariot black horses;

3 And in the third chariot white horses; and in the fourth chariot grisled and bay horses.

4 Then I answered and said unto the angel that talked with me, What *are* these, my lord?

5 And the angel answered and said unto me, These *are* the four spirits of the heavens, which go forth from standing before the Lord of all the earth.

6 The black horses which *are* therein go forth into the north country; and the white go forth after them; and the grisled go forth toward the south country.

7 And the bay went forth, and sought to go that they might walk to and fro through the earth: and he said, Get you hence, walk to and fro through the earth. So they walked to and fro through the earth.

8 Then cried he upon me, and spake unto me,

NEW LIVING TRANSLATION

3 Then he said to me, "This scroll contains the
curse that is going out over the entire land. One side
of the scroll says that those who steal will be banished from the land; the other side says that those
who swear falsely will be banished from the land.
4 And this is what the LORD of Heaven's Armies says:
I am sending this curse into the house of every thief
and into the house of everyone who swears falsely
using my name. And my curse will remain in that
house and completely destroy it—even its timbers
and stones."

A Woman in a Basket

5 Then the angel who was talking with me came forward and said, "Look up and see what's coming."
6 "What is it?" I asked.
He replied, "It is a basket for measuring grain,*
and it's filled with the sins* of everyone throughout
the land."
7 Then the heavy lead cover was lifted off the basket, and there was a woman sitting inside it. 8 The
angel said, "The woman's name is Wickedness," and
he pushed her back into the basket and closed the
heavy lid again.
9 Then I looked up and saw two women flying toward us, gliding on the wind. They had wings like a
stork, and they picked up the basket and flew into
the sky.
10 "Where are they taking the basket?" I asked the
angel.
11 He replied, "To the land of Babylonia,* where
they will build a temple for the basket. And when the
temple is ready, they will set the basket there on its
pedestal."

Four Chariots

6 Then I looked up again and saw four chariots
coming from between two bronze mountains.
2 The first chariot was pulled by red horses, the second by black horses, 3 the third by white horses, and
the fourth by powerful dappled-gray horses. 4 "And
what are these, my lord?" I asked the angel who was
talking with me.
5 The angel replied, "These are the four spirits* of
heaven who stand before the Lord of all the earth.
They are going out to do his work. 6 The chariot with
black horses is going north, the chariot with white
horses is going west,* and the chariot with dappled-
gray horses is going south."
7 The powerful horses were eager to set out to patrol the earth. And the LORD said, "Go and patrol the
earth!" So they left at once on their patrol.
8 Then the LORD summoned me and said, "Look,

5:6a Hebrew *an ephah* [20 quarts or 22 liters]; also in 5:7, 8, 9, 10, 11. **5:6b** As in Greek version; Hebrew reads *the appearance.* **5:11** Hebrew *the land of Shinar.* **6:5** Or *the four winds.* **6:6** Hebrew *is going after them.*

KING JAMES VERSION

saying, Behold, these that go toward the north country have quieted my spirit in the north country.

9 And the word of the LORD came unto me, saying,
10 Take of *them of* the captivity, *even* of Heldai, of
Tobijah, and of Jedaiah, which are come from Babylon, and come thou the same day, and go into the
house of Josiah the son of Zephaniah;
11 Then take silver and gold, and make crowns, and
set *them* upon the head of Joshua the son of
Josedech, the high priest;
12 And speak unto him, saying, Thus speaketh the
LORD of hosts, saying, Behold the man whose name *is*
The BRANCH; and he shall grow up out of his place,
and he shall build the temple of the LORD:
13 Even he shall build the temple of the LORD; and
he shall bear the glory, and shall sit and rule upon his
throne; and he shall be a priest upon his throne: and
the counsel of peace shall be between them both.
14 And the crowns shall be to Helem, and to Tobijah, and to Jedaiah, and to Hen the son of Zephaniah,
for a memorial in the temple of the LORD.
15 And they *that are* far off shall come and build in
the temple of the LORD, and ye shall know that the
LORD of hosts hath sent me unto you. And *this* shall
come to pass, if ye will diligently obey the voice of
the LORD your God.

7 1 And it came to pass in the fourth year of king
Darius, *that* the word of the LORD came unto
Zechariah in the fourth *day* of the ninth month, *even*
in Chisleu;
2 When they had sent unto the house of God
Sherezer and Regem-melech, and their men, to pray
before the LORD,
3 *And* to speak unto the priests which *were* in the
house of the LORD of hosts, and to the prophets, saying, Should I weep in the fifth month, separating
myself, as I have done these so many years?
4 Then came the word of the LORD of hosts unto
me, saying,
5 Speak unto all the people of the land, and to the
priests, saying, When ye fasted and mourned in the
fifth and seventh *month*, even those seventy years,
did ye at all fast unto me, *even* to me?
6 And when ye did eat, and when ye did drink, did
not ye eat *for yourselves*, and drink *for yourselves?*
7 *Should ye* not *hear* the words which the LORD
hath cried by the former prophets, when Jerusalem
was inhabited and in prosperity, and the cities

NEW LIVING TRANSLATION

those who went north have vented the anger of my
Spirit* there in the land of the north."

The Crowning of Jeshua

9 Then I received another message from the LORD:
10 "Heldai, Tobijah, and Jedaiah will bring gifts of silver and gold from the Jews exiled in Babylon. As soon
as they arrive, meet them at the home of Josiah son of
Zephaniah. 11 Accept their gifts, and make a crown*
from the silver and gold. Then put the crown on the
head of Jeshua* son of Jehozadak, the high priest.
12 Tell him, 'This is what the LORD of Heaven's Armies
says: Here is the man called the Branch. He will
branch out from where he is and build the Temple of
the LORD. 13 Yes, he will build the Temple of the LORD.
Then he will receive royal honor and will rule as king
from his throne. He will also serve as priest from his
throne,* and there will be perfect harmony between
his two roles.'
14 "The crown will be a memorial in the Temple of
the LORD to honor those who gave it—Heldai,* Tobijah, Jedaiah, and Josiah* son of Zephaniah."
15 People will come from distant lands to rebuild
the Temple of the LORD. And when this happens, you
will know that my messages have been from the
LORD of Heaven's Armies. All this will happen if you
carefully obey what the LORD your God says.

A Call to Justice and Mercy

7 On December 7* of the fourth year of King
Darius's reign, another message came to Zechariah from the LORD. 2 The people of Bethel had sent
Sharezer and Regemmelech,* along with their attendants, to seek the LORD's favor. 3 They were to ask
this question of the prophets and the priests at the
Temple of the LORD of Heaven's Armies: "Should we
continue to mourn and fast each summer on the
anniversary of the Temple's destruction,* as we have
done for so many years?"
4 The LORD of Heaven's Armies sent me this message in reply: 5 "Say to all your people and your
priests, 'During these seventy years of exile, when
you fasted and mourned in the summer and in early
autumn,* was it really for me that you were fasting?
6 And even now in your holy festivals, aren't you eating and drinking just to please yourselves? 7 Isn't this
the same message the LORD proclaimed through the
prophets in years past when Jerusalem and the towns

6:8 Hebrew *have given my Spirit rest.* **6:11a** As in Greek and Syriac versions; Hebrew reads *crowns.* **6:11b** Hebrew *Joshua,* a variant spelling of Jeshua. **6:13** Or *There will be a priest by his throne.* **6:14a** As in Syriac version (compare 6:10); Hebrew reads *Helem.* **6:14b** As in Syriac version (compare 6:10); Hebrew reads *Hen.* **7:1** Hebrew *On the fourth day of the ninth month, the month of Kislev,* of the ancient Hebrew lunar calendar. This event occurred on December 7, 518 B.C.; also see note on 1:1. **7:2** Or *Bethel-sharezer had sent Regemmelech.* **7:3** Hebrew *mourn and fast in the fifth month.* The Temple had been destroyed in the fifth month of the ancient Hebrew lunar calendar (August 586 B.C.); see 2 Kgs 25:8. **7:5** Hebrew *fasted and mourned in the fifth and seventh months.* The fifth month of the ancient Hebrew lunar calendar usually occurs within the months of July and August. The seventh month usually occurs within the months of September and October; both the Day of Atonement and the Festival of Shelters were celebrated in the seventh month.

KING JAMES VERSION

thereof round about her, when *men* inhabited the south and the plain?

8 And the word of the LORD came unto Zechariah, saying,

9 Thus speaketh the LORD of hosts, saying, Execute true judgment, and shew mercy and compassions every man to his brother:

10 And oppress not the widow, nor the fatherless, the stranger, nor the poor; and let none of you imagine evil against his brother in your heart.

11 But they refused to hearken, and pulled away the shoulder, and stopped their ears, that they should not hear.

12 Yea, they made their hearts *as* an adamant stone, lest they should hear the law, and the words which the LORD of hosts hath sent in his spirit by the former prophets: therefore came a great wrath from the LORD of hosts.

13 Therefore it is come to pass, *that* as he cried, and they would not hear; so they cried, and I would not hear, saith the LORD of hosts:

14 But I scattered them with a whirlwind among all the nations whom they knew not. Thus the land was desolate after them, that no man passed through nor returned: for they laid the pleasant land desolate.

8 1 Again the word of the LORD of hosts came *to me,* saying,

2 Thus saith the LORD of hosts; I was jealous for Zion with great jealousy, and I was jealous for her with great fury.

3 Thus saith the LORD; I am returned unto Zion, and will dwell in the midst of Jerusalem: and Jerusalem shall be called a city of truth; and the mountain of the LORD of hosts the holy mountain.

4 Thus saith the LORD of hosts; There shall yet old men and old women dwell in the streets of Jerusalem, and every man with his staff in his hand for very age.

5 And the streets of the city shall be full of boys and girls playing in the streets thereof.

6 Thus saith the LORD of hosts; If it be marvellous in the eyes of the remnant of this people in these days, should it also be marvellous in mine eyes? saith the LORD of hosts.

7 Thus saith the LORD of hosts; Behold, I will save my people from the east country, and from the west country;

8 And I will bring them, and they shall dwell in the midst of Jerusalem: and they shall be my people, and I will be their God, in truth and in righteousness.

9 Thus saith the LORD of hosts; Let your hands be strong, ye that hear in these days these words by the mouth of the prophets, which *were* in the day *that* the foundation of the house of the LORD of hosts was laid, that the temple might be built.

10 For before these days there was no hire for man, nor any hire for beast; neither *was there any* peace

NEW LIVING TRANSLATION

of Judah were bustling with people, and the Negev and the foothills of Judah* were well populated?'"

8 Then this message came to Zechariah from the LORD: 9 "This is what the LORD of Heaven's Armies says: Judge fairly, and show mercy and kindness to one another. 10 Do not oppress widows, orphans, foreigners, and the poor. And do not scheme against each other.

11 "Your ancestors refused to listen to this message. They stubbornly turned away and put their fingers in their ears to keep from hearing. 12 They made their hearts as hard as stone, so they could not hear the instructions or the messages that the LORD of Heaven's Armies had sent them by his Spirit through the earlier prophets. That is why the LORD of Heaven's Armies was so angry with them.

13 "Since they refused to listen when I called to them, I would not listen when they called to me, says the LORD of Heaven's Armies. 14 As with a whirlwind, I scattered them among the distant nations, where they lived as strangers. Their land became so desolate that no one even traveled through it. They turned their pleasant land into a desert."

Promised Blessings for Jerusalem

8 Then another message came to me from the LORD of Heaven's Armies: 2 "This is what the LORD of Heaven's Armies says: My love for Mount Zion is passionate and strong; I am consumed with passion for Jerusalem!

3 "And now the LORD says: I am returning to Mount Zion, and I will live in Jerusalem. Then Jerusalem will be called the Faithful City; the mountain of the LORD of Heaven's Armies will be called the Holy Mountain.

4 "This is what the LORD of Heaven's Armies says: Once again old men and women will walk Jerusalem's streets with their canes and will sit together in the city squares. 5 And the streets of the city will be filled with boys and girls at play.

6 "This is what the LORD of Heaven's Armies says: All this may seem impossible to you now, a small remnant of God's people. But is it impossible for me? says the LORD of Heaven's Armies.

7 "This is what the LORD of Heaven's Armies says: You can be sure that I will rescue my people from the east and from the west. 8 I will bring them home again to live safely in Jerusalem. They will be my people, and I will be faithful and just toward them as their God.

9 "This is what the LORD of Heaven's Armies says: Be strong and finish the task! Ever since the laying of the foundation of the Temple of the LORD of Heaven's Armies, you have heard what the prophets have been saying about completing the building. 10 Before the work on the Temple began, there were no jobs and no money to hire people or animals. No

7:7 Hebrew *the Shephelah.*

KING JAMES VERSION

to him that went out or came in because of the affliction: for I set all men every one against his neighbour.
11But now I *will* not *be* unto the residue of this
people as in the former days, saith the LORD of hosts.
12For the seed *shall be* prosperous; the vine shall
give her fruit, and the ground shall give her increase,
and the heavens shall give their dew; and I will cause
the remnant of this people to possess all these
things.
13And it shall come to pass, *that* as ye were a curse
among the heathen, O house of Judah, and house of
Israel; so will I save you, and ye shall be a blessing:
fear not, *but* let your hands be strong.
14For thus saith the LORD of hosts; As I thought to
punish you, when your fathers provoked me to
wrath, saith the LORD of hosts, and I repented not:
15So again have I thought in these days to do well
unto Jerusalem and to the house of Judah: fear ye
not.
16These *are* the things that ye shall do; Speak ye
every man the truth to his neighbour; execute the
judgment of truth and peace in your gates:
17And let none of you imagine evil in your hearts
against his neighbour; and love no false oath: for all
these *are things* that I hate, saith the LORD.
18And the word of the LORD of hosts came unto
me, saying,
19Thus saith the LORD of hosts; The fast of the
fourth *month,* and the fast of the fifth, and the fast of
the seventh, and the fast of the tenth, shall be to the
house of Judah joy and gladness, and cheerful feasts;
therefore love the truth and peace.
20Thus saith the LORD of hosts; *It shall* yet *come to*
pass, that there shall come people, and the inhabitants of many cities:
21And the inhabitants of one *city* shall go to another, saying, Let us go speedily to pray before the
LORD, and to seek the LORD of hosts: I will go also.
22Yea, many people and strong nations shall come
to seek the LORD of hosts in Jerusalem, and to pray
before the LORD.
23Thus saith the LORD of hosts; In those days *it*
shall come to pass, that ten men shall take hold out of
all languages of the nations, even shall take hold of
the skirt of him that is a Jew, saying, We will go with
you: for we have heard *that* God *is* with you.

9 1The burden of the word of the LORD in the
land of Hadrach, and Damascus *shall be* the

NEW LIVING TRANSLATION

traveler was safe from the enemy, for there were enemies on all sides. I had turned everyone against each
other.
11"But now I will not treat the remnant of my people as I treated them before, says the LORD of
Heaven's Armies. 12For I am planting seeds of peace
and prosperity among you. The grapevines will be
heavy with fruit. The earth will produce its crops, and
the heavens will release the dew. Once more I will
cause the remnant in Judah and Israel to inherit
these blessings. 13Among the other nations, Judah
and Israel became symbols of a cursed nation. But no
longer! Now I will rescue you and make you both a
symbol and a source of blessing. So don't be afraid.
Be strong, and get on with rebuilding the Temple!
14"For this is what the LORD of Heaven's Armies
says: I was determined to punish you when your ancestors angered me, and I did not change my mind,
says the LORD of Heaven's Armies. 15But now I am determined to bless Jerusalem and the people of Judah.
So don't be afraid. 16But this is what you must do: Tell
the truth to each other. Render verdicts in your
courts that are just and that lead to peace. 17Don't
scheme against each other. Stop your love of telling
lies that you swear are the truth. I hate all these
things, says the LORD."
18Here is another message that came to me from
the LORD of Heaven's Armies. 19"This is what the
LORD of Heaven's Armies says: The traditional fasts
and times of mourning you have kept in early
summer, midsummer, autumn, and winter* are now
ended. They will become festivals of joy and celebration for the people of Judah. So love truth and peace.
20"This is what the LORD of Heaven's Armies says:
People from nations and cities around the world will
travel to Jerusalem. 21The people of one city will say
to the people of another, 'Come with us to Jerusalem
to ask the LORD to bless us. Let's worship the LORD
of Heaven's Armies. I'm determined to go.' 22Many
peoples and powerful nations will come to Jerusalem
to seek the LORD of Heaven's Armies and to ask for
his blessing.
23"This is what the LORD of Heaven's Armies says:
In those days ten men from different nations and
languages of the world will clutch at the sleeve of one
Jew. And they will say, 'Please let us walk with you, for
we have heard that God is with you.'"

Judgment against Israel's Enemies

9 This is the message* from the LORD against the
land of Aram* and the city of Damascus, for the

8:19 Hebrew *in the fourth, fifth, seventh, and tenth months.* The fourth month of the ancient Hebrew lunar calendar usually occurs within the months of June and July. The fifth month usually occurs within the months of July and August. The seventh month usually occurs within the months of September and October. The tenth month usually occurs within the months of December and January. **9:1a** Hebrew *An Oracle: The message.* **9:1b** Hebrew *land of Hadrach.*

KING JAMES VERSION

rest thereof: when the eyes of man, as of all the tribes
of Israel, *shall be* toward the LORD.
2 And Hamath also shall border thereby; Tyrus, and
Zidon, though it be very wise.
3 And Tyrus did build herself a strong hold, and
heaped up silver as the dust, and fine gold as the
mire of the streets.
4 Behold, the Lord will cast her out, and he will
smite her power in the sea; and she shall be devoured
with fire.
5 Ashkelon shall see *it,* and fear; Gaza also *shall see*
it, and be very sorrowful, and Ekron; for her expectation shall be ashamed; and the king shall perish from
Gaza, and Ashkelon shall not be inhabited.
6 And a bastard shall dwell in Ashdod, and I will cut
off the pride of the Philistines.
7 And I will take away his blood out of his mouth,
and his abominations from between his teeth: but
he that remaineth, even he, *shall be* for our God, and
he shall be as a governor in Judah, and Ekron as a
Jebusite.
8 And I will encamp about mine house because of
the army, because of him that passeth by, and because of him that returneth: and no oppressor shall
pass through them any more: for now have I seen
with mine eyes.

9 Rejoice greatly, O daughter of Zion; shout,
O daughter of Jerusalem: behold, thy King cometh
unto thee: he *is* just, and having salvation; lowly, and
riding upon an ass, and upon a colt the foal of an ass.
10 And I will cut off the chariot from Ephraim, and
the horse from Jerusalem, and the battle bow shall
be cut off: and he shall speak peace unto the heathen: and his dominion *shall be* from sea *even* to sea,
and from the river *even* to the ends of the earth.
11 As for thee also, by the blood of thy covenant I
have sent forth thy prisoners out of the pit wherein *is*
no water.

NEW LIVING TRANSLATION

eyes of humanity, including all the tribes of Israel,
are on the LORD.

2 Doom is certain for Hamath,
near Damascus,
and for the cities of Tyre and Sidon,
though they are so clever.
3 Tyre has built a strong fortress
and has made silver and gold
as plentiful as dust in the streets!
4 But now the Lord will strip away Tyre's
possessions
and hurl its fortifications into the sea,
and it will be burned to the ground.
5 The city of Ashkelon will see Tyre fall
and will be filled with fear.
Gaza will shake with terror,
as will Ekron, for their hopes will be dashed.
Gaza's king will be killed,
and Ashkelon will be deserted.
6 Foreigners will occupy the city of Ashdod.
I will destroy the pride of the Philistines.
7 I will grab the bloody meat from their mouths
and snatch the detestable sacrifices from
their teeth.
Then the surviving Philistines will worship
our God
and become like a clan in Judah.*
The Philistines of Ekron will join my people,
as the ancient Jebusites once did.
8 I will guard my Temple
and protect it from invading armies.
I am watching closely to ensure
that no more foreign oppressors overrun
my people's land.

Zion's Coming King

9 Rejoice, O people of Zion!*
Shout in triumph, O people of Jerusalem!
Look, your king is coming to you.
He is righteous and victorious,*
yet he is humble, riding on a donkey—
riding on a donkey's colt.
10 I will remove the battle chariots from Israel*
and the warhorses from Jerusalem.
I will destroy all the weapons used in battle,
and your king will bring peace to the
nations.
His realm will stretch from sea to sea
and from the Euphrates River* to the ends
of the earth.*
11 Because of the covenant I made with you,
sealed with blood,
I will free your prisoners
from death in a waterless dungeon.

9:7 Hebrew *and will become a leader in Judah.* **9:9a** Hebrew *O daughter of Zion!* **9:9b** Hebrew *and is being vindicated.* **9:10a** Hebrew *Ephraim,* referring to the northern kingdom of Israel; also in 9:13. **9:10b** Hebrew *the river.* **9:10c** Or *the end of the land.*

KING JAMES VERSION

[12]Turn you to the strong hold, ye prisoners of
hope: even today do I declare *that* I will render double unto thee;
[13]When I have bent Judah for me, filled the bow
with Ephraim, and raised up thy sons, O Zion, against
thy sons, O Greece, and made thee as the sword of a
mighty man.
[14]And the LORD shall be seen over them, and his
arrow shall go forth as the lightning: and the Lord
GOD shall blow the trumpet, and shall go with whirlwinds of the south.
[15]The LORD of hosts shall defend them; and they
shall devour, and subdue with sling stones; and they
shall drink, *and* make a noise as through wine; and
they shall be filled like bowls, *and* as the corners of
the altar.
[16]And the LORD their God shall save them in that
day as the flock of his people: for they *shall be as*
the stones of a crown, lifted up as an ensign upon his
land.
[17]For how great *is* his goodness, and how great *is*
his beauty! corn shall make the young men cheerful,
and new wine the maids.

10 [1]Ask ye of the LORD rain in the time of the
latter rain; *so* the LORD shall make bright
clouds, and give them showers of rain, to every one
grass in the field.
[2]For the idols have spoken vanity, and the diviners
have seen a lie, and have told false dreams; they comfort in vain: therefore they went their way as a flock,
they were troubled, because *there was* no shepherd.
[3]Mine anger was kindled against the shepherds,
and I punished the goats: for the LORD of hosts hath
visited his flock the house of Judah, and hath made
them as his goodly horse in the battle.
[4]Out of him came forth the corner, out of him the
nail, out of him the battle bow, out of him every oppressor together.

NEW LIVING TRANSLATION

[12] Come back to the place of safety,
all you prisoners who still have hope!
I promise this very day
that I will repay two blessings for each
of your troubles.
[13] Judah is my bow,
and Israel is my arrow.
Jerusalem* is my sword,
and like a warrior, I will brandish it against
the Greeks.*
[14] The LORD will appear above his people;
his arrows will fly like lightning!
The Sovereign LORD will sound the ram's horn
and attack like a whirlwind from the
southern desert.
[15] The LORD of Heaven's Armies will protect
his people,
and they will defeat their enemies by hurling
great stones.
They will shout in battle as though drunk
with wine.
They will be filled with blood like a bowl,
drenched with blood like the corners of
the altar.
[16] On that day the LORD their God will rescue
his people,
just as a shepherd rescues his sheep.
They will sparkle in his land
like jewels in a crown.
[17] How wonderful and beautiful they will be!
The young men will thrive on abundant grain,
and the young women will flourish on new wine.

The LORD Will Restore His People

10 [1] Ask the LORD for rain in the spring,
for he makes the storm clouds.
And he will send showers of rain
so every field becomes a lush pasture.
[2] Household gods give worthless advice,
fortune-tellers predict only lies,
and interpreters of dreams pronounce
falsehoods that give no comfort.
So my people are wandering like lost sheep;
they are attacked because they have
no shepherd.

[3] "My anger burns against your shepherds,
and I will punish these leaders.*
For the LORD of Heaven's Armies has arrived
to look after Judah, his flock.
He will make them strong and glorious,
like a proud warhorse in battle.
[4] From Judah will come the cornerstone,
the tent peg,
the bow for battle,
and all the rulers.

9:13a Hebrew *Zion.* **9:13b** Hebrew *the sons of Javan.* **10:3** Or *these male goats.*

KING JAMES VERSION

5And they shall be as mighty *men,* which tread
down *their enemies* in the mire of the streets in the
battle: and they shall fight, because the LORD *is* with
them, and the riders on horses shall be confounded.
6And I will strengthen the house of Judah, and I
will save the house of Joseph, and I will bring them
again to place them; for I have mercy upon them: and
they shall be as though I had not cast them off: for I
am the LORD their God, and will hear them.
7And *they of* Ephraim shall be like a mighty *man,*
and their heart shall rejoice as through wine: yea,
their children shall see *it,* and be glad; their heart
shall rejoice in the LORD.
8I will hiss for them, and gather them; for I have redeemed them: and they shall increase as they have
increased.
9And I will sow them among the people: and they
shall remember me in far countries; and they shall
live with their children, and turn again.
10I will bring them again also out of the land of
Egypt, and gather them out of Assyria; and I will
bring them into the land of Gilead and Lebanon; and
place shall not be found for them.
11And he shall pass through the sea with affliction,
and shall smite the waves in the sea, and all the deeps
of the river shall dry up: and the pride of Assyria shall
be brought down, and the sceptre of Egypt shall depart away.
12And I will strengthen them in the LORD; and they
shall walk up and down in his name, saith the LORD.

11 1Open thy doors, O Lebanon, that the fire may
devour thy cedars.
2Howl, fir tree; for the cedar is fallen; because the
mighty are spoiled: howl, O ye oaks of Bashan; for the
forest of the vintage is come down.
3*There is* a voice of the howling of the shepherds;
for their glory is spoiled: a voice of the roaring of
young lions; for the pride of Jordan is spoiled.
4Thus saith the LORD my God; Feed the flock of
the slaughter;
5Whose possessors slay them, and hold themselves

NEW LIVING TRANSLATION

5 They will be like mighty warriors in battle,
trampling their enemies in the mud under
their feet.
Since the LORD is with them as they fight,
they will overthrow even the enemy's horsemen.
6 "I will strengthen Judah and save Israel*;
I will restore them because of my compassion.
It will be as though I had never rejected them,
for I am the LORD their God, who will hear
their cries.
7 The people of Israel* will become like mighty
warriors,
and their hearts will be made happy as
if by wine.
Their children, too, will see it and be glad;
their hearts will rejoice in the LORD.
8 When I whistle to them, they will come running,
for I have redeemed them.
From the few who are left,
they will grow as numerous as they were before.
9 Though I have scattered them like seeds among
the nations,
they will still remember me in distant lands.
They and their children will survive
and return again to Israel.
10 I will bring them back from Egypt
and gather them from Assyria.
I will resettle them in Gilead and Lebanon
until there is no more room for them all.
11 They will pass safely through the sea of distress,*
for the waves of the sea will be held back,
and the waters of the Nile will dry up.
The pride of Assyria will be crushed,
and the rule of Egypt will end.
12 By my power* I will make my people strong,
and by my authority they will go wherever
they wish.
I, the LORD, have spoken!"

11 1Open your doors, Lebanon,
so that fire may devour your cedar
forests.
2 Weep, you cypress trees, for all the ruined cedars;
the most majestic ones have fallen.
Weep, you oaks of Bashan,
for the thick forests have been cut down.
3 Listen to the wailing of the shepherds,
for their rich pastures are destroyed.
Hear the young lions roaring,
for their thickets in the Jordan Valley
are ruined.

The Good and Evil Shepherds

4This is what the LORD my God says: "Go and care for
the flock that is intended for slaughter. 5The buyers

10:6 Hebrew *save the house of Joseph.* **10:7** Hebrew *of Ephraim.*
10:11 Or *the sea of Egypt,* referring to the Red Sea. **10:12** Hebrew
In the LORD.

KING JAMES VERSION

not guilty: and they that sell them say, Blessed *be* the LORD; for I am rich: and their own shepherds pity them not.

6 For I will no more pity the inhabitants of the land, saith the LORD: but, lo, I will deliver the men every one into his neighbour's hand, and into the hand of his king: and they shall smite the land, and out of their hand I will not deliver *them*.

7 And I will feed the flock of slaughter, *even* you, O poor of the flock. And I took unto me two staves; the one I called Beauty, and the other I called Bands; and I fed the flock.

8 Three shepherds also I cut off in one month; and my soul lothed them, and their soul also abhorred me.

9 Then said I, I will not feed you: that that dieth, let it die; and that that is to be cut off, let it be cut off; and let the rest eat every one the flesh of another.

10 And I took my staff, *even* Beauty, and cut it asunder, that I might break my covenant which I had made with all the people.

11 And it was broken in that day: and so the poor of the flock that waited upon me knew that it *was* the word of the LORD.

12 And I said unto them, If ye think good, give *me* my price; and if not, forbear. So they weighed for my price thirty *pieces* of silver.

13 And the LORD said unto me, Cast it unto the potter: a goodly price that I was prised at of them. And I took the thirty *pieces* of silver, and cast them to the potter in the house of the LORD.

14 Then I cut asunder mine other staff, *even* Bands, that I might break the brotherhood between Judah and Israel.

15 And the LORD said unto me, Take unto thee yet the instruments of a foolish shepherd.

16 For, lo, I will raise up a shepherd in the land, *which* shall not visit those that be cut off, neither shall seek the young one, nor heal that that is broken, nor feed that that standeth still: but he shall eat the flesh of the fat, and tear their claws in pieces.

17 Woe to the idol shepherd that leaveth the flock! the sword *shall be* upon his arm, and upon his right eye: his arm shall be clean dried up, and his right eye shall be utterly darkened.

12 1 The burden of the word of the LORD for Israel, saith the LORD, which stretcheth forth the heavens, and layeth the foundation of the earth, and formeth the spirit of man within him.

2 Behold, I will make Jerusalem a cup of trembling unto all the people round about, when they shall be in the siege both against Judah *and* against Jerusalem.

NEW LIVING TRANSLATION

slaughter their sheep without remorse. The sellers say, 'Praise the LORD! Now I'm rich!' Even the shepherds have no compassion for them. 6 Likewise, I will no longer have pity on the people of the land," says the LORD. "I will let them fall into each other's hands and into the hands of their king. They will turn the land into a wilderness, and I will not rescue them."

7 So I cared for the flock intended for slaughter—the flock that was oppressed. Then I took two shepherd's staffs and named one Favor and the other Union. 8 I got rid of their three evil shepherds in a single month.

But I became impatient with these sheep, and they hated me, too. 9 So I told them, "I won't be your shepherd any longer. If you die, you die. If you are killed, you are killed. And let those who remain devour each other!"

10 Then I took my staff called Favor and cut it in two, showing that I had revoked the covenant I had made with all the nations. 11 That was the end of my covenant with them. The suffering flock was watching me, and they knew that the LORD was speaking through my actions.

12 And I said to them, "If you like, give me my wages, whatever I am worth; but only if you want to." So they counted out for my wages thirty pieces of silver.

13 And the LORD said to me, "Throw it to the potter*"—this magnificent sum at which they valued me! So I took the thirty coins and threw them to the potter in the Temple of the LORD.

14 Then I took my other staff, Union, and cut it in two, showing that the bond of unity between Judah and Israel was broken.

15 Then the LORD said to me, "Go again and play the part of a worthless shepherd. 16 This illustrates how I will give this nation a shepherd who will not care for those who are dying, nor look after the young,* nor heal the injured, nor feed the healthy. Instead, this shepherd will eat the meat of the fattest sheep and tear off their hooves.

17 "What sorrow awaits this worthless shepherd
who abandons the flock!
The sword will cut his arm
and pierce his right eye.
His arm will become useless,
and his right eye completely blind."

Future Deliverance for Jerusalem

12 This* message concerning the fate of Israel came from the LORD: "This message is from the LORD, who stretched out the heavens, laid the foundations of the earth, and formed the human spirit. 2 I will make Jerusalem like an intoxicating drink that makes the nearby nations stagger when they send their armies to besiege Jerusalem and

11:13 Syriac version reads *into the treasury;* also in 11:13b. Compare Matt 27:6-10. 11:16 Or *the scattered.* 12:1 Hebrew *An Oracle: This.*

KING JAMES VERSION

3And in that day will I make Jerusalem a burdensome stone for all people: all that burden themselves
with it shall be cut in pieces, though all the people of
the earth be gathered together against it.
4In that day, saith the LORD, I will smite every
horse with astonishment, and his rider with madness: and I will open mine eyes upon the house of
Judah, and will smite every horse of the people with
blindness.
5And the governors of Judah shall say in their
heart, The inhabitants of Jerusalem *shall be* my
strength in the LORD of hosts their God.
6In that day will I make the governors of Judah like
an hearth of fire among the wood, and like a torch of
fire in a sheaf; and they shall devour all the people
round about, on the right hand and on the left: and
Jerusalem shall be inhabited again in her own place,
even in Jerusalem.
7The LORD also shall save the tents of Judah first,
that the glory of the house of David and the glory of
the inhabitants of Jerusalem do not magnify *them-*
selves against Judah.
8In that day shall the LORD defend the inhabitants
of Jerusalem; and he that is feeble among them at
that day shall be as David; and the house of David
shall be as God, as the angel of the LORD before them.
9And it shall come to pass in that day, *that* I will
seek to destroy all the nations that come against
Jerusalem.
10And I will pour upon the house of David, and
upon the inhabitants of Jerusalem, the spirit of grace
and of supplications: and they shall look upon me
whom they have pierced, and they shall mourn for
him, as one mourneth for *his* only *son,* and shall be in
bitterness for him, as one that is in bitterness for *his*
firstborn.
11In that day shall there be a great mourning in
Jerusalem, as the mourning of Hadadrimmon in the
valley of Megiddon.
12And the land shall mourn, every family apart; the
family of the house of David apart, and their wives
apart; the family of the house of Nathan apart, and
their wives apart;
13The family of the house of Levi apart, and their
wives apart; the family of Shimei apart, and their
wives apart;
14All the families that remain, every family apart,
and their wives apart.

13 1In that day there shall be a fountain opened
to the house of David and to the inhabitants
of Jerusalem for sin and for uncleanness.
2And it shall come to pass in that day, saith the
LORD of hosts, *that* I will cut off the names of the
idols out of the land, and they shall no more be remembered: and also I will cause the prophets and
the unclean spirit to pass out of the land.

NEW LIVING TRANSLATION

Judah. 3On that day I will make Jerusalem an immovable rock. All the nations will gather against it to try
to move it, but they will only hurt themselves.
4"On that day," says the LORD, "I will cause every
horse to panic and every rider to lose his nerve. I will
watch over the people of Judah, but I will blind all
the horses of their enemies. 5And the clans of Judah
will say to themselves, 'The people of Jerusalem have
found strength in the LORD of Heaven's Armies,
their God.'
6"On that day I will make the clans of Judah like a
flame that sets a woodpile ablaze or like a burning
torch among sheaves of grain. They will burn up all
the neighboring nations right and left, while the
people living in Jerusalem remain secure.
7"The LORD will give victory to the rest of Judah
first, before Jerusalem, so that the people of Jerusalem and the royal line of David will not have greater
honor than the rest of Judah. 8On that day the LORD
will defend the people of Jerusalem; the weakest
among them will be as mighty as King David! And the
royal descendants will be like God, like the angel of
the LORD who goes before them! 9For on that day I
will begin to destroy all the nations that come
against Jerusalem.
10"Then I will pour out a spirit* of grace and
prayer on the family of David and on the people of Jerusalem. They will look on me whom they have
pierced and mourn for him as for an only son. They
will grieve bitterly for him as for a firstborn son who
has died. 11The sorrow and mourning in Jerusalem
on that day will be like the great mourning for Hadadrimmon in the valley of Megiddo.
12"All Israel will mourn, each clan by itself, and
with the husbands separate from their wives. The
clan of David will mourn alone, as will the clan of Nathan, 13the clan of Levi, and the clan of Shimei.
14Each of the surviving clans from Judah will mourn
separately, and with the husbands separate from
their wives.

A Fountain of Cleansing

13 "On that day a fountain will be opened for the
dynasty of David and for the people of Jerusalem, a fountain to cleanse them from all their sins
and impurity.
2"And on that day," says the LORD of Heaven's Armies, "I will erase idol worship throughout the land,
so that even the names of the idols will be forgotten.
I will remove from the land both the false prophets

12:10 Or *the Spirit*.

KING JAMES VERSION

3 And it shall come to pass, *that* when any shall yet
prophesy, then his father and his mother that begat
him shall say unto him, Thou shalt not live; for thou
speakest lies in the name of the LORD: and his father
and his mother that begat him shall thrust him
through when he prophesieth.

4 And it shall come to pass in that day, *that* the
prophets shall be ashamed every one of his vision,
when he hath prophesied; neither shall they wear a
rough garment to deceive:

5 But he shall say, I *am* no prophet, I *am* an husbandman; for man taught me to keep cattle from my
youth.

6 And *one* shall say unto him, What *are* these
wounds in thine hands? Then he shall answer, *Those*
with which I was wounded *in* the house of my
friends.

7 Awake, O sword, against my shepherd, and
against the man *that is* my fellow, saith the LORD of
hosts: smite the shepherd, and the sheep shall be
scattered: and I will turn mine hand upon the little
ones.

8 And it shall come to pass, *that* in all the land,
saith the LORD, two parts therein shall be cut off *and*
die; but the third shall be left therein.

9 And I will bring the third part through the fire,
and will refine them as silver is refined, and will try
them as gold is tried: they shall call on my name, and
I will hear them: I will say, It *is* my people: and they
shall say, The LORD *is* my God.

14 1 Behold, the day of the LORD cometh, and thy
spoil shall be divided in the midst of thee.

2 For I will gather all nations against Jerusalem to
battle; and the city shall be taken, and the houses ri-
fled, and the women ravished; and half of the city
shall go forth into captivity, and the residue of the
people shall not be cut off from the city.

3 Then shall the LORD go forth, and fight against
those nations, as when he fought in the day of battle.

4 And his feet shall stand in that day upon the
mount of Olives, which *is* before Jerusalem on the
east, and the mount of Olives shall cleave in the midst
thereof toward the east and toward the west, *and
there shall be* a very great valley; and half of the mountain shall remove toward the north, and half of it toward the south.

5 And ye shall flee *to* the valley of the mountains;
for the valley of the mountains shall reach unto Azal:
yea, ye shall flee, like as ye fled from before the
earthquake in the days of Uzziah king of Judah: and
the LORD my God shall come, *and* all the saints
with thee.

NEW LIVING TRANSLATION

and the spirit of impurity that came with them. 3 If
anyone continues to prophesy, his own father and
mother will tell him, 'You must die, for you have
prophesied lies in the name of the LORD.' And as
he prophesies, his own father and mother will
stab him.

4 "On that day people will be ashamed to claim
the prophetic gift. No one will pretend to be a
prophet by wearing prophet's clothes. 5 He will say,
'I'm no prophet; I'm a farmer. I began working for a
farmer as a boy.' 6 And if someone asks, 'Then what
about those wounds on your chest?*' he will say, 'I
was wounded at my friends' house!'

The Scattering of the Sheep

7 "Awake, O sword, against my shepherd,
the man who is my partner,"
says the LORD of Heaven's Armies.
"Strike down the shepherd,
and the sheep will be scattered,
and I will turn against the lambs.
8 Two-thirds of the people in the land
will be cut off and die," says the LORD.
"But one-third will be left in the land.
9 I will bring that group through the fire
and make them pure.
I will refine them like silver
and purify them like gold.
They will call on my name,
and I will answer them.
I will say, 'These are my people,'
and they will say, 'The LORD is our God.'"

The LORD Will Rule the Earth

14 Watch, for the day of the LORD is coming
when your possessions will be plundered
right in front of you! 2 I will gather all the nations to
fight against Jerusalem. The city will be taken, the
houses looted, and the women raped. Half the population will be taken into captivity, and the rest will
be left among the ruins of the city.

3 Then the LORD will go out to fight against those
nations, as he has fought in times past. 4 On that day
his feet will stand on the Mount of Olives, east of
Jerusalem. And the Mount of Olives will split apart,
making a wide valley running from east to west.
Half the mountain will move toward the north and
half toward the south. 5 You will flee through this
valley, for it will reach across to Azal.* Yes, you will
flee as you did from the earthquake in the days of
King Uzziah of Judah. Then the LORD my God will
come, and all his holy ones with him.*

13:6 Hebrew *wounds between your hands?* 14:5a The meaning of the Hebrew is uncertain. 14:5b As in Greek version; Hebrew reads *with you.*

KING JAMES VERSION

6 And it shall come to pass in that day, *that* the light
shall not be clear, *nor* dark:
7 But it shall be one day which shall be known to
the LORD, not day, nor night: but it shall come to pass,
that at evening time it shall be light.
8 And it shall be in that day, *that* living waters shall
go out from Jerusalem; half of them toward the former sea, and half of them toward the hinder sea: in
summer and in winter shall it be.
9 And the LORD shall be king over all the earth: in
that day shall there be one LORD, and his name one.
10 All the land shall be turned as a plain from Geba
to Rimmon south of Jerusalem: and it shall be lifted
up, and inhabited in her place, from Benjamin's gate
unto the place of the first gate, unto the corner gate,
and *from* the tower of Hananeel unto the king's
winepresses.
11 And *men* shall dwell in it, and there shall be no
more utter destruction; but Jerusalem shall be safely
inhabited.
12 And this shall be the plague wherewith the LORD
will smite all the people that have fought against
Jerusalem; Their flesh shall consume away while
they stand upon their feet, and their eyes shall consume away in their holes, and their tongue shall consume away in their mouth.
13 And it shall come to pass in that day, *that* a great
tumult from the LORD shall be among them; and they
shall lay hold every one on the hand of his neighbour,
and his hand shall rise up against the hand of his
neighbour.
14 And Judah also shall fight at Jerusalem; and the
wealth of all the heathen round about shall be gathered together, gold, and silver, and apparel, in great
abundance.
15 And so shall be the plague of the horse, of the
mule, of the camel, and of the ass, and of all the
beasts that shall be in these tents, as this plague.
16 And it shall come to pass, *that* every one that is
left of all the nations which came against Jerusalem
shall even go up from year to year to worship the
King, the LORD of hosts, and to keep the feast of
tabernacles.
17 And it shall be, *that* whoso will not come up of
all the families of the earth unto Jerusalem to worship the King, the LORD of hosts, even upon them
shall be no rain.
18 And if the family of Egypt go not up, and come
not, that *have* no *rain;* there shall be the plague,
wherewith the LORD will smite the heathen that
come not up to keep the feast of tabernacles.
19 This shall be the punishment of Egypt, and the
punishment of all nations that come not up to keep
the feast of tabernacles.
20 In that day shall there be upon the bells of the
horses, HOLINESS UNTO THE LORD; and the pots
in the LORD's house shall be like the bowls before the
altar.

NEW LIVING TRANSLATION

6 On that day the sources of light will no longer
shine,* 7 yet there will be continuous day! Only the
LORD knows how this could happen. There will be no
normal day and night, for at evening time it will still
be light.
8 On that day life-giving waters will flow out from
Jerusalem, half toward the Dead Sea and half toward
the Mediterranean,* flowing continuously in both
summer and winter.
9 And the LORD will be king over all the earth. On
that day there will be one LORD—his name alone will
be worshiped.
10 All the land from Geba, north of Judah, to Rimmon, south of Jerusalem, will become one vast plain.
But Jerusalem will be raised up in its original place
and will be inhabited all the way from the Benjamin
Gate over to the site of the old gate, then to the
Corner Gate, and from the Tower of Hananel to the
king's winepresses. 11 And Jerusalem will be filled,
safe at last, never again to be cursed and destroyed.
12 And the LORD will send a plague on all the nations that fought against Jerusalem. Their people
will become like walking corpses, their flesh rotting
away. Their eyes will rot in their sockets, and their
tongues will rot in their mouths. 13 On that day they
will be terrified, stricken by the LORD with great
panic. They will fight their neighbors hand to hand.
14 Judah, too, will be fighting at Jerusalem. The
wealth of all the neighboring nations will be captured—great quantities of gold and silver and fine
clothing. 15 This same plague will strike the horses,
mules, camels, donkeys, and all the other animals in
the enemy camps.
16 In the end, the enemies of Jerusalem who survive the plague will go up to Jerusalem each year to
worship the King, the LORD of Heaven's Armies, and
to celebrate the Festival of Shelters. 17 Any nation in
the world that refuses to come to Jerusalem to worship the King, the LORD of Heaven's Armies, will have
no rain. 18 If the people of Egypt refuse to attend the
festival, the LORD will punish them with the same
plague that he sends on the other nations who refuse to go. 19 Egypt and the other nations will all be
punished if they don't go to celebrate the Festival of
Shelters.
20 On that day even the harness bells of the horses
will be inscribed with these words: HOLY TO THE
LORD. And the cooking pots in the Temple of the
LORD will be as sacred as the basins used beside the

14:6 Hebrew *there will be no light, no cold or frost.* The meaning of the Hebrew is uncertain. **14:8** Hebrew *half toward the eastern sea and half toward the western sea.*

KING JAMES VERSION

[21]Yea, every pot in Jerusalem and in Judah shall be holiness unto the LORD of hosts: and all they that sacrifice shall come and take of them, and seethe therein: and in that day there shall be no more the Canaanite in the house of the LORD of hosts.

NEW LIVING TRANSLATION

altar. [21]In fact, every cooking pot in Jerusalem and Judah will be holy to the LORD of Heaven's Armies. All who come to worship will be free to use any of these pots to boil their sacrifices. And on that day there will no longer be traders* in the Temple of the LORD of Heaven's Armies.

14:21 Hebrew *Canaanites.*

Malachi

KING JAMES VERSION

1 1The burden of the word of the LORD to Israel
by Malachi.

2I have loved you, saith the LORD. Yet ye say,
Wherein hast thou loved us? *Was* not Esau Jacob's
brother? saith the LORD: yet I loved Jacob,
3And I hated Esau, and laid his mountains and his
heritage waste for the dragons of the wilderness.
4Whereas Edom saith, We are impoverished, but
we will return and build the desolate places. Thus
saith the Lord of hosts, They shall build, but I will
throw down; and they shall call them, The border of
wickedness, and, The people against whom the LORD
hath indignation for ever.
5And your eyes shall see, and ye shall say, The LORD
will be magnified from the border of Israel.

6A son honoureth *his* father, and a servant his
master: if then I *be* a father, where *is* mine honour?
and if I *be* a master, where *is* my fear? saith the LORD
of hosts unto you, O priests, that despise my name.
And ye say, Wherein have we despised thy name?
7Ye offer polluted bread upon mine altar. And ye
say, Wherein have we polluted thee? In that ye say,
The table of the LORD *is* contemptible.
8And if ye offer the blind for sacrifice, *is it* not evil?
and if ye offer the lame and sick, *is it* not evil? offer it
now unto thy governor; will he be pleased with thee,
or accept thy person? saith the LORD of hosts.
9And now, I pray you, beseech God that he will be

NEW LIVING TRANSLATION

1 This is the message* that the LORD gave to Israel
through the prophet Malachi.*

The LORD's Love for Israel

2"I have always loved you," says the LORD.
But you retort, "Really? How have you loved us?"
And the LORD replies, "This is how I showed my
love for you: I loved your ancestor Jacob, 3but I rejected his brother, Esau, and devastated his hill
country. I turned Esau's inheritance into a desert for
jackals."
4Esau's descendants in Edom may say, "We have
been shattered, but we will rebuild the ruins."
But the LORD of Heaven's Armies replies, "They
may try to rebuild, but I will demolish them again.
Their country will be known as 'The Land of Wickedness,' and their people will be called 'The People with
Whom the LORD Is Forever Angry.' 5When you see
the destruction for yourselves, you will say, 'Truly,
the LORD's greatness reaches far beyond Israel's
borders!'"

Unworthy Sacrifices

6The LORD of Heaven's Armies says to the priests:
"A son honors his father, and a servant respects his
master. If I am your father and master, where are the
honor and respect I deserve? You have shown contempt for my name!
"But you ask, 'How have we ever shown contempt
for your name?'
7"You have shown contempt by offering defiled
sacrifices on my altar.
"Then you ask, 'How have we defiled the sacrifices?*'
"You defile them by saying the altar of the LORD
deserves no respect. 8When you give blind animals
as sacrifices, isn't that wrong? And isn't it wrong to
offer animals that are crippled and diseased? Try
giving gifts like that to your governor, and see how
pleased he is!" says the LORD of Heaven's Armies.
9"Go ahead, beg God to be merciful to you! But
when you bring that kind of offering, why should he

1:1a Hebrew *An Oracle: The message.* **1:1b** *Malachi* means "my messenger." **1:7** As in Greek version; Hebrew reads *defiled you?*

KING JAMES VERSION

gracious unto us: this hath been by your means: will
he regard your persons? saith the LORD of hosts.
10 Who *is there* even among you that would shut
the doors *for nought?* neither do ye kindle *fire* on
mine altar for nought. I have no pleasure in you, saith
the LORD of hosts, neither will I accept an offering at
your hand.
11 For from the rising of the sun even unto the going down of the same my name *shall be* great among
the Gentiles; and in every place incense *shall be*
offered unto my name, and a pure offering: for my
name *shall be* great among the heathen, saith the
LORD of hosts.
12 But ye have profaned it, in that ye say, The table
of the LORD *is* polluted; and the fruit thereof, *even* his
meat, *is* contemptible.
13 Ye said also, Behold, what a weariness *is it!* and
ye have snuffed at it, saith the LORD of hosts; and ye
brought *that which was* torn, and the lame, and the
sick; thus ye brought an offering: should I accept this
of your hand? saith the LORD.
14 But cursed *be* the deceiver, which hath in his
flock a male, and voweth, and sacrificeth unto the
LORD a corrupt thing: for I *am* a great King, saith the
LORD of hosts, and my name *is* dreadful among
the heathen.

2 1 And now, O ye priests, this commandment *is*
for you.
2 If ye will not hear, and if ye will not lay *it* to heart,
to give glory unto my name, saith the LORD of hosts, I
will even send a curse upon you, and I will curse your
blessings: yea, I have cursed them already, because ye
do not lay *it* to heart.
3 Behold, I will corrupt your seed, and spread dung
upon your faces, *even* the dung of your solemn
feasts; and *one* shall take you away with it.
4 And ye shall know that I have sent this commandment unto you, that my covenant might be with Levi,
saith the LORD of hosts.
5 My covenant was with him of life and peace; and I
gave them to him *for* the fear wherewith he feared
me, and was afraid before my name.
6 The law of truth was in his mouth, and iniquity
was not found in his lips: he walked with me in peace
and equity, and did turn many away from iniquity.
7 For the priest's lips should keep knowledge, and
they should seek the law at his mouth: for he *is* the
messenger of the LORD of hosts.
8 But ye are departed out of the way; ye have caused
many to stumble at the law; ye have corrupted the
covenant of Levi, saith the LORD of hosts.
9 Therefore have I also made you contemptible

NEW LIVING TRANSLATION

show you any favor at all?" asks the LORD of Heaven's
Armies.
10 "How I wish one of you would shut the Temple
doors so that these worthless sacrifices could not be
offered! I am not pleased with you," says the LORD of
Heaven's Armies, "and I will not accept your offerings. 11 But my name is honored* by people of other
nations from morning till night. All around the world
they offer* sweet incense and pure offerings in
honor of my name. For my name is great among the
nations," says the LORD of Heaven's Armies.
12 "But you dishonor my name with your actions.
By bringing contemptible food, you are saying it's all
right to defile the Lord's table. 13 You say, 'It's too
hard to serve the LORD,' and you turn up your noses at
my commands," says the LORD of Heaven's Armies.
"Think of it! Animals that are stolen and crippled
and sick are being presented as offerings! Should I
accept from you such offerings as these?" asks the
LORD.
14 "Cursed is the cheat who promises to give a fine
ram from his flock but then sacrifices a defective
one to the Lord. For I am a great king," says the LORD
of Heaven's Armies, "and my name is feared among
the nations!

A Warning to the Priests

2 "Listen, you priests—this command is for you!
2 Listen to me and make up your minds to honor
my name," says the LORD of Heaven's Armies, "or I
will bring a terrible curse against you. I will curse
even the blessings you receive. Indeed, I have already
cursed them, because you have not taken my warning to heart. 3 I will punish your descendants and
splatter your faces with the manure from your festival sacrifices, and I will throw you on the manure
pile. 4 Then at last you will know it was I who sent you
this warning so that my covenant with the Levites
can continue," says the LORD of Heaven's Armies.
5 "The purpose of my covenant with the Levites
was to bring life and peace, and that is what I gave
them. This required reverence from them, and they
greatly revered me and stood in awe of my name.
6 They passed on to the people the truth of the instructions they received from me. They did not lie or
cheat; they walked with me, living good and righteous lives, and they turned many from lives of sin.
7 "The words of a priest's lips should preserve
knowledge of God, and people should go to him for
instruction, for the priest is the messenger of the
LORD of Heaven's Armies. 8 But you priests have left
God's paths. Your instructions have caused many to
stumble into sin. You have corrupted the covenant I
made with the Levites," says the LORD of Heaven's Armies. 9 "So I have made you despised and humiliated
in the eyes of all the people. For you have not obeyed

1:11a Or *will be honored.* **1:11b** Or *will offer.*

KING JAMES VERSION

and base before all the people, according as ye have not kept my ways, but have been partial in the law.

10 Have we not all one father? hath not one God created us? why do we deal treacherously every man against his brother, by profaning the covenant of our fathers?

11 Judah hath dealt treacherously, and an abomination is committed in Israel and in Jerusalem; for Judah hath profaned the holiness of the LORD which he loved, and hath married the daughter of a strange god.

12 The LORD will cut off the man that doeth this, the master and the scholar, out of the tabernacles of Jacob, and him that offereth an offering unto the LORD of hosts.

13 And this have ye done again, covering the altar of the LORD with tears, with weeping, and with crying out, insomuch that he regardeth not the offering any more, or receiveth *it* with good will at your hand.

14 Yet ye say, Wherefore? Because the LORD hath been witness between thee and the wife of thy youth, against whom thou hast dealt treacherously: yet *is* she thy companion, and the wife of thy covenant.

15 And did not he make one? Yet had he the residue of the spirit. And wherefore one? That he might seek a godly seed. Therefore take heed to your spirit, and let none deal treacherously against the wife of his youth.

16 For the LORD, the God of Israel, saith that he hateth putting away: for *one* covereth violence with his garment, saith the LORD of hosts: therefore take heed to your spirit, that ye deal not treacherously.

17 Ye have wearied the LORD with your words. Yet ye say, Wherein have we wearied *him?* When ye say, Every one that doeth evil *is* good in the sight of the LORD, and he delighteth in them; or, Where *is* the God of judgment?

3 1 Behold, I will send my messenger, and he shall prepare the way before me: and the Lord, whom ye seek, shall suddenly come to his temple, even the messenger of the covenant, whom ye delight in: behold, he shall come, saith the LORD of hosts.

2 But who may abide the day of his coming? and who shall stand when he appeareth? for he *is* like a refiner's fire, and like fullers' sope:

3 And he shall sit *as* a refiner and purifier of silver: and he shall purify the sons of Levi, and purge them as gold and silver, that they may offer unto the LORD an offering in righteousness.

NEW LIVING TRANSLATION

me but have shown favoritism in the way you carry
out my instructions."

A Call to Faithfulness

10 Are we not all children of the same Father? Are we
not all created by the same God? Then why do we
betray each other, violating the covenant of our ancestors?

11 Judah has been unfaithful, and a detestable
thing has been done in Israel and in Jerusalem. The
men of Judah have defiled the LORD's beloved sanctuary by marrying women who worship idols. 12 May
the LORD cut off from the nation of Israel* every last
man who has done this and yet brings an offering to
the LORD of Heaven's Armies.

13 Here is another thing you do. You cover the
LORD's altar with tears, weeping and groaning because he pays no attention to your offerings and
doesn't accept them with pleasure. 14 You cry out,
"Why doesn't the LORD accept my worship?" I'll tell
you why! Because the LORD witnessed the vows you
and your wife made when you were young. But you
have been unfaithful to her, though she remained
your faithful partner, the wife of your marriage
vows.

15 Didn't the LORD make you one with your wife? In
body and spirit you are his.* And what does he want?
Godly children from your union. So guard your
heart; remain loyal to the wife of your youth. 16 "For I
hate divorce!" says the LORD, the God of Israel. "To divorce your wife is to overwhelm her with cruelty,*"
says the LORD of Heaven's Armies. "So guard your
heart; do not be unfaithful to your wife."

17 You have wearied the LORD with your words.

"How have we wearied him?" you ask.

You have wearied him by saying that all who do
evil are good in the LORD's sight, and he is pleased
with them. You have wearied him by asking, "Where
is the God of justice?"

The Coming Day of Judgment

3 "Look! I am sending my messenger, and he will
prepare the way before me. Then the Lord you
are seeking will suddenly come to his Temple. The
messenger of the covenant, whom you look for so
eagerly, is surely coming," says the LORD of Heaven's
Armies.

2 "But who will be able to endure it when he
comes? Who will be able to stand and face him when
he appears? For he will be like a blazing fire that refines metal, or like a strong soap that bleaches
clothes. 3 He will sit like a refiner of silver, burning
away the dross. He will purify the Levites, refining
them like gold and silver, so that they may once again

2:12 Hebrew *from the tents of Jacob.* The names "Jacob" and "Israel" are often interchanged throughout the Old Testament, referring sometimes to the individual patriarch and sometimes to the nation. **2:15** Or *Didn't the one LORD make us and preserve our life and breath?* or *Didn't the one LORD make her, both flesh and spirit?* The meaning of the Hebrew is uncertain. **2:16** Hebrew *to cover one's garment with violence.*

KING JAMES VERSION

4Then shall the offering of Judah and Jerusalem
be pleasant unto the LORD, as in the days of old, and
as in former years.
5And I will come near to you to judgment; and I
will be a swift witness against the sorcerers, and
against the adulterers, and against false swearers,
and against those that oppress the hireling in *his*
wages, the widow, and the fatherless, and that turn
aside the stranger *from his right,* and fear not me,
saith the LORD of hosts.

6For I *am* the LORD, I change not; therefore ye sons
of Jacob are not consumed.
7Even from the days of your fathers ye are gone
away from mine ordinances, and have not kept *them.*
Return unto me, and I will return unto you, saith the
LORD of hosts. But ye said, Wherein shall we return?
8Will a man rob God? Yet ye have robbed me. But
ye say, Wherein have we robbed thee? In tithes and
offerings.
9Ye *are* cursed with a curse: for ye have robbed
me, *even* this whole nation.
10Bring ye all the tithes into the storehouse, that
there may be meat in mine house, and prove me now
herewith, saith the LORD of hosts, if I will not open
you the windows of heaven, and pour you out a blessing, that *there shall* not *be room* enough *to receive it.*
11And I will rebuke the devourer for your sakes,
and he shall not destroy the fruits of your ground;
neither shall your vine cast her fruit before the time
in the field, saith the LORD of hosts.
12And all nations shall call you blessed: for ye shall
be a delightsome land, saith the LORD of hosts.
13Your words have been stout against me, saith
the LORD. Yet ye say, What have we spoken *so much*
against thee?
14Ye have said, It *is* vain to serve God: and what
profit *is it* that we have kept his ordinance, and that
we have walked mournfully before the LORD of
hosts?
15And now we call the proud happy; yea, they that
work wickedness are set up; yea, *they that* tempt God
are even delivered.

16Then they that feared the LORD spake often one
to another: and the LORD hearkened, and heard *it,*
and a book of remembrance was written before him
for them that feared the LORD, and that thought upon
his name.

NEW LIVING TRANSLATION

offer acceptable sacrifices to the LORD. 4Then once
more the LORD will accept the offerings brought to
him by the people of Judah and Jerusalem, as he did
in the past.
5"At that time I will put you on trial. I am eager to
witness against all sorcerers and adulterers and liars.
I will speak against those who cheat employees of
their wages, who oppress widows and orphans, or
who deprive the foreigners living among you of justice, for these people do not fear me," says the LORD
of Heaven's Armies.

A Call to Repentance

6"I am the LORD, and I do not change. That is why you
descendants of Jacob are not already destroyed.
7Ever since the days of your ancestors, you have
scorned my decrees and failed to obey them. Now
return to me, and I will return to you," says the LORD
of Heaven's Armies.
"But you ask, 'How can we return when we have
never gone away?'
8"Should people cheat God? Yet you have cheated
me!
"But you ask, 'What do you mean? When did we
ever cheat you?'
"You have cheated me of the tithes and offerings
due to me. 9You are under a curse, for your whole nation has been cheating me. 10Bring all the tithes into
the storehouse so there will be enough food in my
Temple. If you do," says the LORD of Heaven's Armies,
"I will open the windows of heaven for you. I will
pour out a blessing so great you won't have enough
room to take it in! Try it! Put me to the test! 11Your
crops will be abundant, for I will guard them from
insects and disease.* Your grapes will not fall from
the vine before they are ripe," says the LORD of
Heaven's Armies. 12"Then all nations will call you
blessed, for your land will be such a delight," says the
LORD of Heaven's Armies.
13"You have said terrible things about me," says
the LORD.
"But you say, 'What do you mean? What have we
said against you?'
14"You have said, 'What's the use of serving God?
What have we gained by obeying his commands or
by trying to show the LORD of Heaven's Armies that
we are sorry for our sins? 15From now on we will call
the arrogant blessed. For those who do evil get rich,
and those who dare God to punish them suffer no
harm.'"

The LORD's Promise of Mercy

16Then those who feared the LORD spoke with each
other, and the LORD listened to what they said. In his
presence, a scroll of remembrance was written to record the names of those who feared him and always
thought about the honor of his name.

3:11 Hebrew *from the devourer.*

KING JAMES VERSION

17 And they shall be mine, saith the LORD of hosts, in that day when I make up my jewels; and I will spare them, as a man spareth his own son that serveth him.

18 Then shall ye return, and discern between the righteous and the wicked, between him that serveth God and him that serveth him not.

4 1 For, behold, the day cometh, that shall burn as an oven; and all the proud, yea, and all that do wickedly, shall be stubble: and the day that cometh shall burn them up, saith the LORD of hosts, that it shall leave them neither root nor branch.

2 But unto you that fear my name shall the Sun of righteousness arise with healing in his wings; and ye shall go forth, and grow up as calves of the stall.

3 And ye shall tread down the wicked; for they shall be ashes under the soles of your feet in the day that I shall do *this,* saith the LORD of hosts.

4 Remember ye the law of Moses my servant, which I commanded unto him in Horeb for all Israel, *with* the statutes and judgments.

5 Behold, I will send you Elijah the prophet before the coming of the great and dreadful day of the LORD:

6 And he shall turn the heart of the fathers to the children, and the heart of the children to their fathers, lest I come and smite the earth with a curse.

NEW LIVING TRANSLATION

17 "They will be my people," says the LORD of Heaven's Armies. "On the day when I act in judgment, they will be my own special treasure. I will spare them as a father spares an obedient child. 18 Then you will again see the difference between the righteous and the wicked, between those who serve God and those who do not."

The Coming Day of Judgment

4 1 *The LORD of Heaven's Armies says, "The day of judgment is coming, burning like a furnace. On that day the arrogant and the wicked will be burned up like straw. They will be consumed—roots, branches, and all.

2 "But for you who fear my name, the Sun of Righteousness will rise with healing in his wings.* And you will go free, leaping with joy like calves let out to pasture. 3 On the day when I act, you will tread upon the wicked as if they were dust under your feet," says the LORD of Heaven's Armies.

4 "Remember to obey the Law of Moses, my servant—all the decrees and regulations that I gave him on Mount Sinai* for all Israel.

5 "Look, I am sending you the prophet Elijah before the great and dreadful day of the LORD arrives. 6 His preaching will turn the hearts of fathers to their children, and the hearts of children to their fathers. Otherwise I will come and strike the land with a curse."

4:1 Verses 4:1-6 are numbered 3:19-24 in Hebrew text. **4:2** Or *the sun of righteousness will rise with healing in its wings.* **4:4** Hebrew *Horeb,* another name for Sinai.

NEW TESTAMENT

Matthew

KING JAMES VERSION

1 1 The book of the generation of Jesus Christ, the
son of David, the son of Abraham.
2 Abraham begat Isaac; and Isaac begat Jacob; and
Jacob begat Judas and his brethren;
3 And Judas begat Phares and Zara of Thamar; and
Phares begat Esrom; and Esrom begat Aram;
4 And Aram begat Aminadab; and Aminadab begat
Naasson; and Naasson begat Salmon;
5 And Salmon begat Booz of Rachab; and Booz
begat Obed of Ruth; and Obed begat Jesse;
6 And Jesse begat David the king; and David the
king begat Solomon of her *that had been the wife*
of Urias;
7 And Solomon begat Roboam; and Roboam begat
Abia; and Abia begat Asa;
8 And Asa begat Josaphat; and Josaphat begat Joram; and Joram begat Ozias;
9 And Ozias begat Joatham; and Joatham begat
Achaz; and Achaz begat Ezekias;
10 And Ezekias begat Manasses; and Manasses
begat Amon; and Amon begat Josias;
11 And Josias begat Jechonias and his brethren,
about the time they were carried away to Babylon:
12 And after they were brought to Babylon, Jechonias begat Salathiel; and Salathiel begat Zorobabel;

NEW LIVING TRANSLATION

The Ancestors of Jesus the Messiah

1 This is a record of the ancestors of Jesus the Messiah, a descendant of David* and of Abraham:

2 Abraham was the father of Isaac.
Isaac was the father of Jacob.
Jacob was the father of Judah and his brothers.
3 Judah was the father of Perez and Zerah (whose mother was Tamar).
Perez was the father of Hezron.
Hezron was the father of Ram.*
4 Ram was the father of Amminadab.
Amminadab was the father of Nahshon.
Nahshon was the father of Salmon.
5 Salmon was the father of Boaz (whose mother was Rahab).
Boaz was the father of Obed (whose mother was Ruth).
Obed was the father of Jesse.
6 Jesse was the father of King David.
David was the father of Solomon (whose mother was Bathsheba, the widow of Uriah).
7 Solomon was the father of Rehoboam.
Rehoboam was the father of Abijah.
Abijah was the father of Asa.*
8 Asa was the father of Jehoshaphat.
Jehoshaphat was the father of Jehoram.*
Jehoram was the father* of Uzziah.
9 Uzziah was the father of Jotham.
Jotham was the father of Ahaz.
Ahaz was the father of Hezekiah.
10 Hezekiah was the father of Manasseh.
Manasseh was the father of Amon.*
Amon was the father of Josiah.
11 Josiah was the father of Jehoiachin* and his brothers (born at the time of the exile to Babylon).
12 After the Babylonian exile:
Jehoiachin was the father of Shealtiel.
Shealtiel was the father of Zerubbabel.

1:1 Greek *Jesus the Messiah, son of David.* **1:3** Greek *Aram,* a variant spelling of Ram; also in 1:4. See 1 Chr 2:9-10. **1:7** Greek *Asaph,* a variant spelling of Asa; also in 1:8. See 1 Chr 3:10. **1:8a** Greek *Joram,* a variant spelling of Jehoram; also in 1:8b. See 1 Kgs 22:50 and note at 1 Chr 3:11. **1:8b** Or *ancestor;* also in 1:11. **1:10** Greek *Amos,* a variant spelling of Amon; also in 1:10b. See 1 Chr 3:14. **1:11** Greek *Jeconiah,* a variant spelling of Jehoiachin; also in 1:12. See 2 Kgs 24:6 and note at 1 Chr 3:16.

KING JAMES VERSION

13 And Zorobabel begat Abiud; and Abiud begat
Eliakim; and Eliakim begat Azor;
14 And Azor begat Sadoc; and Sadoc begat Achim;
and Achim begat Eliud;
15 And Eliud begat Eleazar; and Eleazar begat Matthan; and Matthan begat Jacob;
16 And Jacob begat Joseph the husband of Mary,
of whom was born Jesus, who is called Christ.
17 So all the generations from Abraham to David
are fourteen generations; and from David until the
carrying away into Babylon *are* fourteen generations; and from the carrying away into Babylon unto
Christ *are* fourteen generations.

18 Now the birth of Jesus Christ was on this wise:
When as his mother Mary was espoused to Joseph,
before they came together, she was found with child
of the Holy Ghost.
19 Then Joseph her husband, being a just *man*, and
not willing to make her a publick example, was
minded to put her away privily.
20 But while he thought on these things, behold,
the angel of the Lord appeared unto him in a dream,
saying, Joseph, thou son of David, fear not to take
unto thee Mary thy wife: for that which is conceived
in her is of the Holy Ghost.
21 And she shall bring forth a son, and thou shalt
call his name JESUS: for he shall save his people from
their sins.
22 Now all this was done, that it might be fulfilled
which was spoken of the Lord by the prophet, saying,
23 Behold, a virgin shall be with child, and shall
bring forth a son, and they shall call his name Em-
manuel, which being interpreted is, God with us.
24 Then Joseph being raised from sleep did as the
angel of the Lord had bidden him, and took unto him
his wife:
25 And knew her not till she had brought forth her
firstborn son: and he called his name JESUS.

2 1 Now when Jesus was born in Bethlehem of
Judaea in the days of Herod the king, behold,
there came wise men from the east to Jerusalem,
2 Saying, Where is he that is born King of the Jews?
for we have seen his star in the east, and are come to
worship him.
3 When Herod the king had heard *these things*, he
was troubled, and all Jerusalem with him.
4 And when he had gathered all the chief priests
and scribes of the people together, he demanded of
them where Christ should be born.

NEW LIVING TRANSLATION

13 Zerubbabel was the father of Abiud.
Abiud was the father of Eliakim.
Eliakim was the father of Azor.
14 Azor was the father of Zadok.
Zadok was the father of Akim.
Akim was the father of Eliud.
15 Eliud was the father of Eleazar.
Eleazar was the father of Matthan.
Matthan was the father of Jacob.
16 Jacob was the father of Joseph, the husband
of Mary.
Mary gave birth to Jesus, who is called the Messiah.

17 All those listed above include fourteen generations
from Abraham to David, fourteen from David to the
Babylonian exile, and fourteen from the Babylonian
exile to the Messiah.

The Birth of Jesus the Messiah

18 This is how Jesus the Messiah was born. His
mother, Mary, was engaged to be married to Joseph.
But before the marriage took place, while she was
still a virgin, she became pregnant through the
power of the Holy Spirit. 19 Joseph, her fiancé, was a
good man and did not want to disgrace her publicly,
so he decided to break the engagement* quietly.
20 As he considered this, an angel of the Lord appeared to him in a dream. "Joseph, son of David," the
angel said, "do not be afraid to take Mary as your wife.
For the child within her was conceived by the Holy
Spirit. 21 And she will have a son, and you are to name
him Jesus,* for he will save his people from their sins."
22 All of this occurred to fulfill the Lord's message
through his prophet:

23 "Look! The virgin will conceive a child!
She will give birth to a son,
and they will call him Immanuel,*
which means 'God is with us.'"

24 When Joseph woke up, he did as the angel of the
Lord commanded and took Mary as his wife. 25 But he
did not have sexual relations with her until her son
was born. And Joseph named him Jesus.

Visitors from the East

2 Jesus was born in Bethlehem in Judea, during
the reign of King Herod. About that time some
wise men* from eastern lands arrived in Jerusalem,
asking, 2 "Where is the newborn king of the Jews?
We saw his star as it rose,* and we have come to worship him."
3 King Herod was deeply disturbed when he heard
this, as was everyone in Jerusalem. 4 He called a meeting of the leading priests and teachers of religious
law and asked, "Where is the Messiah supposed to
be born?"

1:19 Greek *to divorce her.* **1:21** *Jesus* means "The LORD saves." **1:23** Isa 7:14; 8:8, 10 (Greek version). **2:1** Or *royal astrologers;* Greek reads *magi;* also in 2:7, 16. **2:2** Or *star in the east.*

KING JAMES VERSION

5And they said unto him, In Bethlehem of Judaea:
for thus it is written by the prophet,
6And thou Bethlehem, *in* the land of Judah, art not
the least among the princes of Judah: for out of thee
shall come a Governor, that shall rule my people
Israel.
7Then Herod, when he had privily called the wise
men, inquired of them diligently what time the star
appeared.
8And he sent them to Bethlehem, and said, Go and
search diligently for the young child; and when ye
have found *him,* bring me word again, that I may
come and worship him also.
9When they had heard the king, they departed;
and, lo, the star, which they saw in the east, went before them, till it came and stood over where the
young child was.
10When they saw the star, they rejoiced with exceeding great joy.
11And when they were come into the house, they
saw the young child with Mary his mother, and fell
down, and worshipped him: and when they had
opened their treasures, they presented unto him
gifts; gold, and frankincense, and myrrh.
12And being warned of God in a dream that they
should not return to Herod, they departed into their
own country another way.
13And when they were departed, behold, the angel
of the Lord appeareth to Joseph in a dream, saying,
Arise, and take the young child and his mother,
and flee into Egypt, and be thou there until I bring
thee word: for Herod will seek the young child to destroy him.
14When he arose, he took the young child and his
mother by night, and departed into Egypt:
15And was there until the death of Herod: that it
might be fulfilled which was spoken of the Lord by
the prophet, saying, Out of Egypt have I called my son.
16Then Herod, when he saw that he was mocked of
the wise men, was exceeding wroth, and sent forth,
and slew all the children that were in Bethlehem, and
in all the coasts thereof, from two years old and under, according to the time which he had diligently
inquired of the wise men.
17Then was fulfilled that which was spoken by
Jeremy the prophet, saying,
18In Rama was there a voice heard, lamentation,
and weeping, and great mourning, Rachel weeping
for her children, and would not be comforted, because they are not.

19But when Herod was dead, behold, an angel of
the Lord appeareth in a dream to Joseph in Egypt,
20Saying, Arise, and take the young child and his
mother, and go into the land of Israel: for they are
dead which sought the young child's life.

NEW LIVING TRANSLATION

5"In Bethlehem in Judea," they said, "for this is
what the prophet wrote:

6 'And you, O Bethlehem in the land of Judah,
are not least among the ruling cities* of Judah,
for a ruler will come from you
who will be the shepherd for my people Israel.'*"

7Then Herod called for a private meeting with the
wise men, and he learned from them the time when
the star first appeared. 8Then he told them, "Go to
Bethlehem and search carefully for the child. And
when you find him, come back and tell me so that
I can go and worship him, too!"
9After this interview the wise men went their way.
And the star they had seen in the east guided them to
Bethlehem. It went ahead of them and stopped over
the place where the child was. 10When they saw the
star, they were filled with joy! 11They entered the
house and saw the child with his mother, Mary, and
they bowed down and worshiped him. Then they
opened their treasure chests and gave him gifts of
gold, frankincense, and myrrh.
12When it was time to leave, they returned to their
own country by another route, for God had warned
them in a dream not to return to Herod.

The Escape to Egypt

13After the wise men were gone, an angel of the Lord
appeared to Joseph in a dream. "Get up! Flee to Egypt
with the child and his mother," the angel said. "Stay
there until I tell you to return, because Herod is going to search for the child to kill him."
14That night Joseph left for Egypt with the child
and Mary, his mother, 15and they stayed there until
Herod's death. This fulfilled what the Lord had spoken through the prophet: "I called my Son out of
Egypt."*
16Herod was furious when he realized that the
wise men had outwitted him. He sent soldiers to kill
all the boys in and around Bethlehem who were two
years old and under, based on the wise men's report
of the star's first appearance. 17Herod's brutal action
fulfilled what God had spoken through the prophet
Jeremiah:

18 "A cry was heard in Ramah—
weeping and great mourning.
Rachel weeps for her children,
refusing to be comforted,
for they are dead."*

The Return to Nazareth

19When Herod died, an angel of the Lord appeared
in a dream to Joseph in Egypt. 20"Get up!" the angel
said. "Take the child and his mother back to the land
of Israel, because those who were trying to kill the
child are dead."

2:6a Greek *the rulers.* **2:6b** Mic 5:2; 2 Sam 5:2. **2:15** Hos 11:1.
2:18 Jer 31:15.

KING JAMES VERSION

21And he arose, and took the young child and his mother, and came into the land of Israel.

22But when he heard that Archelaus did reign in Judaea in the room of his father Herod, he was afraid to go thither: notwithstanding, being warned of God in a dream, he turned aside into the parts of Galilee:

23And he came and dwelt in a city called Nazareth: that it might be fulfilled which was spoken by the prophets, He shall be called a Nazarene.

3 1In those days came John the Baptist, preaching in the wilderness of Judaea,

2And saying, Repent ye: for the kingdom of heaven is at hand.

3For this is he that was spoken of by the prophet Esaias, saying, The voice of one crying in the wilderness, Prepare ye the way of the Lord, make his paths straight.

4And the same John had his raiment of camel's hair, and a leathern girdle about his loins; and his meat was locusts and wild honey.

5Then went out to him Jerusalem, and all Judaea, and all the region round about Jordan,

6And were baptized of him in Jordan, confessing their sins.

7But when he saw many of the Pharisees and Sadducees come to his baptism, he said unto them, O generation of vipers, who hath warned you to flee from the wrath to come?

8Bring forth therefore fruits meet for repentance:

9And think not to say within yourselves, We have Abraham to *our* father: for I say unto you, that God is able of these stones to raise up children unto Abraham.

10And now also the ax is laid unto the root of the trees: therefore every tree which bringeth not forth good fruit is hewn down, and cast into the fire.

11I indeed baptize you with water unto repentance: but he that cometh after me is mightier than I, whose shoes I am not worthy to bear: he shall baptize you with the Holy Ghost, and *with* fire:

12Whose fan *is* in his hand, and he will throughly purge his floor, and gather his wheat into the garner; but he will burn up the chaff with unquenchable fire.

13Then cometh Jesus from Galilee to Jordan unto John, to be baptized of him.

14But John forbad him, saying, I have need to be baptized of thee, and comest thou to me?

15And Jesus answering said unto him, Suffer *it to be so* now: for thus it becometh us to fulfil all righteousness. Then he suffered him.

NEW LIVING TRANSLATION

21So Joseph got up and returned to the land of Israel with Jesus and his mother. 22But when he learned that the new ruler of Judea was Herod's son Archelaus, he was afraid to go there. Then, after being warned in a dream, he left for the region of Galilee. 23So the family went and lived in a town called Nazareth. This fulfilled what the prophets had said: "He will be called a Nazarene."

John the Baptist Prepares the Way

3 In those days John the Baptist came to the Judean wilderness and began preaching. His message was, 2"Repent of your sins and turn to God, for the Kingdom of Heaven is near.*" 3The prophet Isaiah was speaking about John when he said,

"He is a voice shouting in the wilderness,
'Prepare the way for the LORD's coming!
Clear the road for him!'"*

4John's clothes were woven from coarse camel hair, and he wore a leather belt around his waist. For food he ate locusts and wild honey. 5People from Jerusalem and from all of Judea and all over the Jordan Valley went out to see and hear John. 6And when they confessed their sins, he baptized them in the Jordan River.

7But when he saw many Pharisees and Sadducees coming to watch him baptize,* he denounced them. "You brood of snakes!" he exclaimed. "Who warned you to flee God's coming wrath? 8Prove by the way you live that you have repented of your sins and turned to God. 9Don't just say to each other, 'We're safe, for we are descendants of Abraham.' That means nothing, for I tell you, God can create children of Abraham from these very stones. 10Even now the ax of God's judgment is poised, ready to sever the roots of the trees. Yes, every tree that does not produce good fruit will be chopped down and thrown into the fire.

11"I baptize with* water those who repent of their sins and turn to God. But someone is coming soon who is greater than I am—so much greater that I'm not worthy even to be his slave and carry his sandals. He will baptize you with the Holy Spirit and with fire.* 12He is ready to separate the chaff from the wheat with his winnowing fork. Then he will clean up the threshing area, gathering the wheat into his barn but burning the chaff with never-ending fire."

The Baptism of Jesus

13Then Jesus went from Galilee to the Jordan River to be baptized by John. 14But John tried to talk him out of it. "I am the one who needs to be baptized by you," he said, "so why are you coming to me?"

15But Jesus said, "It should be done, for we must carry out all that God requires.*" So John agreed to baptize him.

3:2 Or *has come*, or *is coming soon*. **3:3** Isa 40:3 (Greek version). **3:7** Or *coming to be baptized*. **3:11a** Or *in*. **3:11b** Or *in the Holy Spirit and in fire*. **3:15** Or *for we must fulfill all righteousness*.

KING JAMES VERSION

[16]And Jesus, when he was baptized, went up straightway out of the water: and, lo, the heavens were opened unto him, and he saw the Spirit of God descending like a dove, and lighting upon him:

[17]And lo a voice from heaven, saying, This is my beloved Son, in whom I am well pleased.

4 [1]Then was Jesus led up of the Spirit into the wilderness to be tempted of the devil.

[2]And when he had fasted forty days and forty nights, he was afterward an hungred.

[3]And when the tempter came to him, he said, If thou be the Son of God, command that these stones be made bread.

[4]But he answered and said, It is written, Man shall not live by bread alone, but by every word that proceedeth out of the mouth of God.

[5]Then the devil taketh him up into the holy city, and setteth him on a pinnacle of the temple,

[6]And saith unto him, If thou be the Son of God, cast thyself down: for it is written, He shall give his angels charge concerning thee: and in *their* hands they shall bear thee up, lest at any time thou dash thy foot against a stone.

[7]Jesus said unto him, It is written again, Thou shalt not tempt the Lord thy God.

[8]Again, the devil taketh him up into an exceeding high mountain, and sheweth him all the kingdoms of the world, and the glory of them;

[9]And saith unto him, All these things will I give thee, if thou wilt fall down and worship me.

[10]Then saith Jesus unto him, Get thee hence, Satan: for it is written, Thou shalt worship the Lord thy God, and him only shalt thou serve.

[11]Then the devil leaveth him, and, behold, angels came and ministered unto him.

[12]Now when Jesus had heard that John was cast into prison, he departed into Galilee;

[13]And leaving Nazareth, he came and dwelt in Capernaum, which is upon the sea coast, in the borders of Zabulon and Nephthalim:

[14]That it might be fulfilled which was spoken by Esaias the prophet, saying,

[15]The land of Zabulon, and the land of Nephthalim, *by* the way of the sea, beyond Jordan, Galilee of the Gentiles;

[16]The people which sat in darkness saw great light; and to them which sat in the region and shadow of death light is sprung up.

NEW LIVING TRANSLATION

[16]After his baptism, as Jesus came up out of the water, the heavens were opened* and he saw the Spirit of God descending like a dove and settling on him. [17]And a voice from heaven said, "This is my dearly loved Son, who brings me great joy."

The Temptation of Jesus

4 Then Jesus was led by the Spirit into the wilderness to be tempted there by the devil. [2]For forty days and forty nights he fasted and became very hungry.

[3]During that time the devil* came and said to him, "If you are the Son of God, tell these stones to become loaves of bread."

[4]But Jesus told him, "No! The Scriptures say,

'People do not live by bread alone,
but by every word that comes from the mouth of God.'*"

[5]Then the devil took him to the holy city, Jerusalem, to the highest point of the Temple, [6]and said, "If you are the Son of God, jump off! For the Scriptures say,

'He will order his angels to protect you.
And they will hold you up with their hands
so you won't even hurt your foot on a stone.'*"

[7]Jesus responded, "The Scriptures also say, 'You must not test the LORD your God.'*"

[8]Next the devil took him to the peak of a very high mountain and showed him all the kingdoms of the world and their glory. [9]"I will give it all to you," he said, "if you will kneel down and worship me."

[10]"Get out of here, Satan," Jesus told him. "For the Scriptures say,

'You must worship the LORD your God
and serve only him.'*"

[11]Then the devil went away, and angels came and took care of Jesus.

The Ministry of Jesus Begins

[12]When Jesus heard that John had been arrested, he left Judea and returned to Galilee. [13]He went first to Nazareth, then left there and moved to Capernaum, beside the Sea of Galilee, in the region of Zebulun and Naphtali. [14]This fulfilled what God said through the prophet Isaiah:

[15] "In the land of Zebulun and of Naphtali,
beside the sea, beyond the Jordan River,
in Galilee where so many Gentiles live,
[16] the people who sat in darkness
have seen a great light.
And for those who lived in the land where
death casts its shadow,
a light has shined."*

3:16 Some manuscripts read *opened to him.* **4:3** Greek *the tempter.* **4:4** Deut 8:3. **4:6** Ps 91:11-12. **4:7** Deut 6:16. **4:10** Deut 6:13. **4:15-16** Isa 9:1-2 (Greek version).

KING JAMES VERSION

17From that time Jesus began to preach, and to say,
Repent: for the kingdom of heaven is at hand.

18And Jesus, walking by the sea of Galilee, saw
two brethren, Simon called Peter, and Andrew his
brother, casting a net into the sea: for they were
fishers.
19And he saith unto them, Follow me, and I will
make you fishers of men.
20And they straightway left *their* nets, and followed him.
21And going on from thence, he saw other two
brethren, James *the son* of Zebedee, and John his
brother, in a ship with Zebedee their father, mending
their nets; and he called them.
22And they immediately left the ship and their
father, and followed him.
23And Jesus went about all Galilee, teaching in
their synagogues, and preaching the gospel of the
kingdom, and healing all manner of sickness and all
manner of disease among the people.
24And his fame went throughout all Syria: and
they brought unto him all sick people that were
taken with divers diseases and torments, and those
which were possessed with devils, and those which
were lunatick, and those that had the palsy; and he
healed them.
25And there followed him great multitudes of
people from Galilee, and *from* Decapolis, and *from*
Jerusalem, and *from* Judaea, and *from* beyond Jordan.

5 1And seeing the multitudes, he went up into a
mountain: and when he was set, his disciples
came unto him:
2And he opened his mouth, and taught them,
saying,

3Blessed *are* the poor in spirit: for theirs is the
kingdom of heaven.
4Blessed *are* they that mourn: for they shall be
comforted.
5Blessed *are* the meek: for they shall inherit the
earth.
6Blessed *are* they which do hunger and thirst after
righteousness: for they shall be filled.
7Blessed *are* the merciful: for they shall obtain
mercy.
8Blessed *are* the pure in heart: for they shall see
God.
9Blessed *are* the peacemakers: for they shall be
called the children of God.

NEW LIVING TRANSLATION

17From then on Jesus began to preach, "Repent
of your sins and turn to God, for the Kingdom of
Heaven is near.*"

The First Disciples

18One day as Jesus was walking along the shore of the
Sea of Galilee, he saw two brothers—Simon, also
called Peter, and Andrew—throwing a net into the
water, for they fished for a living. 19Jesus called out
to them, "Come, follow me, and I will show you how
to fish for people!" 20And they left their nets at once
and followed him.
21A little farther up the shore he saw two other
brothers, James and John, sitting in a boat with their
father, Zebedee, repairing their nets. And he called
them to come, too. 22They immediately followed
him, leaving the boat and their father behind.

Crowds Follow Jesus

23Jesus traveled throughout the region of Galilee,
teaching in the synagogues and announcing the
Good News about the Kingdom. And he healed every
kind of disease and illness. 24News about him spread
as far as Syria, and people soon began bringing to
him all who were sick. And whatever their sickness
or disease, or if they were demon possessed or epi-
leptic or paralyzed—he healed them all. 25Large
crowds followed him wherever he went—people
from Galilee, the Ten Towns,* Jerusalem, from all
over Judea, and from east of the Jordan River.

The Sermon on the Mount

5 One day as he saw the crowds gathering, Jesus
went up on the mountainside and sat down.
His disciples gathered around him, 2and he began
to teach them.

The Beatitudes

3 "God blesses those who are poor and realize their
need for him,*
for the Kingdom of Heaven is theirs.
4 God blesses those who mourn,
for they will be comforted.
5 God blesses those who are humble,
for they will inherit the whole earth.
6 God blesses those who hunger and thirst
for justice,*
for they will be satisfied.
7 God blesses those who are merciful,
for they will be shown mercy.
8 God blesses those whose hearts are pure,
for they will see God.
9 God blesses those who work for peace,
for they will be called the children of God.

4:17 Or *has come,* or *is coming soon.* **4:25** Greek *Decapolis.* **5:3** Greek *poor in spirit.* **5:6** Or *for righteousness.*

KING JAMES VERSION

10 Blessed *are* they which are persecuted for righteousness' sake: for theirs is the kingdom of heaven.

11 Blessed are ye, when *men* shall revile you, and persecute *you,* and shall say all manner of evil against you falsely, for my sake.

12 Rejoice, and be exceeding glad: for great *is* your reward in heaven: for so persecuted they the prophets which were before you.

13 Ye are the salt of the earth: but if the salt have lost his savour, wherewith shall it be salted? it is thenceforth good for nothing, but to be cast out, and to be trodden under foot of men.

14 Ye are the light of the world. A city that is set on an hill cannot be hid.

15 Neither do men light a candle, and put it under a bushel, but on a candlestick; and it giveth light unto all that are in the house.

16 Let your light so shine before men, that they may see your good works, and glorify your Father which is in heaven.

17 Think not that I am come to destroy the law, or the prophets: I am not come to destroy, but to fulfil.

18 For verily I say unto you, Till heaven and earth pass, one jot or one tittle shall in no wise pass from the law, till all be fulfilled.

19 Whosoever therefore shall break one of these least commandments, and shall teach men so, he shall be called the least in the kingdom of heaven: but whosoever shall do and teach *them,* the same shall be called great in the kingdom of heaven.

20 For I say unto you, That except your righteousness shall exceed *the righteousness* of the scribes and Pharisees, ye shall in no case enter into the kingdom of heaven.

21 Ye have heard that it was said by them of old time, Thou shalt not kill; and whosoever shall kill shall be in danger of the judgment:

22 But I say unto you, That whosoever is angry with his brother without a cause shall be in danger of the judgment: and whosoever shall say to his brother, Raca, shall be in danger of the council: but whosoever shall say, Thou fool, shall be in danger of hell fire.

23 Therefore if thou bring thy gift to the altar, and there rememberest that thy brother hath aught against thee;

24 Leave there thy gift before the altar, and go thy way; first be reconciled to thy brother, and then come and offer thy gift.

NEW LIVING TRANSLATION

10 God blesses those who are persecuted
for doing right,
for the Kingdom of Heaven is theirs.

11 "God blesses you when people mock you and persecute you and lie about you* and say all sorts of evil things against you because you are my followers. 12 Be happy about it! Be very glad! For a great reward awaits you in heaven. And remember, the ancient prophets were persecuted in the same way.

Teaching about Salt and Light

13 "You are the salt of the earth. But what good is salt if it has lost its flavor? Can you make it salty again? It will be thrown out and trampled underfoot as worthless.

14 "You are the light of the world—like a city on a hilltop that cannot be hidden. 15 No one lights a lamp and then puts it under a basket. Instead, a lamp is placed on a stand, where it gives light to everyone in the house. 16 In the same way, let your good deeds shine out for all to see, so that everyone will praise your heavenly Father.

Teaching about the Law

17 "Don't misunderstand why I have come. I did not come to abolish the law of Moses or the writings of the prophets. No, I came to accomplish their purpose. 18 I tell you the truth, until heaven and earth disappear, not even the smallest detail of God's law will disappear until its purpose is achieved. 19 So if you ignore the least commandment and teach others to do the same, you will be called the least in the Kingdom of Heaven. But anyone who obeys God's laws and teaches them will be called great in the Kingdom of Heaven.

20 "But I warn you—unless your righteousness is better than the righteousness of the teachers of religious law and the Pharisees, you will never enter the Kingdom of Heaven!

Teaching about Anger

21 "You have heard that our ancestors were told, 'You must not murder. If you commit murder, you are subject to judgment.'* 22 But I say, if you are even angry with someone,* you are subject to judgment! If you call someone an idiot,* you are in danger of being brought before the court. And if you curse someone,* you are in danger of the fires of hell.*

23 "So if you are presenting a sacrifice* at the altar in the Temple and you suddenly remember that someone has something against you, 24 leave your sacrifice there at the altar. Go and be reconciled to that person. Then come and offer your sacrifice to God.

5:11 Some manuscripts do not include *and lie about you.* **5:21** Exod 20:13; Deut 5:17. **5:22a** Some manuscripts add *without cause.* **5:22b** Greek uses an Aramaic term of contempt: *If you say to your brother, 'Raca.'* **5:22c** Greek *if you say, 'You fool.'* **5:22d** Greek *Gehenna;* also in 5:29, 30. **5:23** Greek *gift;* also in 5:24.

KING JAMES VERSION

25 Agree with thine adversary quickly, whiles thou
art in the way with him; lest at any time the adversary
deliver thee to the judge, and the judge deliver thee
to the officer, and thou be cast into prison.
26 Verily I say unto thee, Thou shalt by no means
come out thence, till thou hast paid the uttermost
farthing.

27 Ye have heard that it was said by them of old
time, Thou shalt not commit adultery:
28 But I say unto you, That whosoever looketh on a
woman to lust after her hath committed adultery
with her already in his heart.
29 And if thy right eye offend thee, pluck it out, and
cast *it* from thee: for it is profitable for thee that one
of thy members should perish, and not *that* thy
whole body should be cast into hell.
30 And if thy right hand offend thee, cut it off, and
cast *it* from thee: for it is profitable for thee that one
of thy members should perish, and not *that* thy
whole body should be cast into hell.

31 It hath been said, Whosoever shall put away his
wife, let him give her a writing of divorcement:
32 But I say unto you, That whosoever shall put
away his wife, saving for the cause of fornication,
causeth her to commit adultery: and whosoever shall
marry her that is divorced committeth adultery.

33 Again, ye have heard that it hath been said by
them of old time, Thou shalt not forswear thyself,
but shalt perform unto the Lord thine oaths:
34 But I say unto you, Swear not at all; neither by
heaven; for it is God's throne:
35 Nor by the earth; for it is his footstool: neither by
Jerusalem; for it is the city of the great King.
36 Neither shalt thou swear by thy head, because
thou canst not make one hair white or black.
37 But let your communication be, Yea, yea; Nay,
nay: for whatsoever is more than these cometh of
evil.

38 Ye have heard that it hath been said, An eye for
an eye, and a tooth for a tooth:
39 But I say unto you, That ye resist not evil: but
whosoever shall smite thee on thy right cheek, turn
to him the other also.
40 And if any man will sue thee at the law, and take
away thy coat, let him have *thy* cloak also.
41 And whosoever shall compel thee to go a mile,
go with him twain.
42 Give to him that asketh thee, and from him that
would borrow of thee turn not thou away.

NEW LIVING TRANSLATION

25 "When you are on the way to court with your adversary, settle your differences quickly. Otherwise,
your accuser may hand you over to the judge, who
will hand you over to an officer, and you will be
thrown into prison. 26 And if that happens, you surely
won't be free again until you have paid the last
penny.*

Teaching about Adultery

27 "You have heard the commandment that says,
'You must not commit adultery.'* 28 But I say, anyone
who even looks at a woman with lust has already
committed adultery with her in his heart. 29 So if
your eye—even your good eye*—causes you to lust,
gouge it out and throw it away. It is better for you to
lose one part of your body than for your whole body
to be thrown into hell. 30 And if your hand—even
your stronger hand*—causes you to sin, cut it off
and throw it away. It is better for you to lose one part
of your body than for your whole body to be thrown
into hell.

Teaching about Divorce

31 "You have heard the law that says, 'A man can divorce his wife by merely giving her a written notice
of divorce.'* 32 But I say that a man who divorces his
wife, unless she has been unfaithful, causes her to
commit adultery. And anyone who marries a divorced woman also commits adultery.

Teaching about Vows

33 "You have also heard that our ancestors were told,
'You must not break your vows; you must carry out
the vows you make to the LORD.'* 34 But I say, do not
make any vows! Do not say, 'By heaven!' because
heaven is God's throne. 35 And do not say, 'By the
earth!' because the earth is his footstool. And do not
say, 'By Jerusalem!' for Jerusalem is the city of the
great King. 36 Do not even say, 'By my head!' for you
can't turn one hair white or black. 37 Just say a simple,
'Yes, I will,' or 'No, I won't.' Anything beyond this is
from the evil one.

Teaching about Revenge

38 "You have heard the law that says the punishment
must match the injury: 'An eye for an eye, and a tooth
for a tooth.'* 39 But I say, do not resist an evil person!
If someone slaps you on the right cheek, offer the
other cheek also. 40 If you are sued in court and your
shirt is taken from you, give your coat, too. 41 If a soldier demands that you carry his gear for a mile,*
carry it two miles. 42 Give to those who ask, and don't
turn away from those who want to borrow.

5:26 Greek *the last kodrantes* [i.e., quadrans]. **5:27** Exod 20:14; Deut 5:18. **5:29** Greek *your right eye*. **5:30** Greek *your right hand*. **5:31** Deut 24:1. **5:33** Num 30:2. **5:38** Greek *the law that says: 'An eye for an eye and a tooth for a tooth.'* Exod 21:24; Lev 24:20; Deut 19:21. **5:41** Greek *milion* [4,854 feet or 1,478 meters].

KING JAMES VERSION

43 Ye have heard that it hath been said, Thou shalt love thy neighbour, and hate thine enemy.

44 But I say unto you, Love your enemies, bless them that curse you, do good to them that hate you, and pray for them which despitefully use you, and persecute you;

45 That ye may be the children of your Father which is in heaven: for he maketh his sun to rise on the evil and on the good, and sendeth rain on the just and on the unjust.

46 For if ye love them which love you, what reward have ye? do not even the publicans the same?

47 And if ye salute your brethren only, what do ye more *than others?* do not even the publicans so?

48 Be ye therefore perfect, even as your Father which is in heaven is perfect.

6 1 Take heed that ye do not your alms before men, to be seen of them: otherwise ye have no reward of your Father which is in heaven.

2 Therefore when thou doest *thine* alms, do not sound a trumpet before thee, as the hypocrites do in the synagogues and in the streets, that they may have glory of men. Verily I say unto you, They have their reward.

3 But when thou doest alms, let not thy left hand know what thy right hand doeth:

4 That thine alms may be in secret: and thy Father which seeth in secret himself shall reward thee openly.

5 And when thou prayest, thou shalt not be as the hypocrites *are:* for they love to pray standing in the synagogues and in the corners of the streets, that they may be seen of men. Verily I say unto you, They have their reward.

6 But thou, when thou prayest, enter into thy closet, and when thou hast shut thy door, pray to thy Father which is in secret; and thy Father which seeth in secret shall reward thee openly.

7 But when ye pray, use not vain repetitions, as the heathen *do:* for they think that they shall be heard for their much speaking.

8 Be not ye therefore like unto them: for your Father knoweth what things ye have need of, before ye ask him.

9 After this manner therefore pray ye: Our Father which art in heaven, Hallowed be thy name.

10 Thy kingdom come. Thy will be done in earth, as *it is* in heaven.

11 Give us this day our daily bread.

12 And forgive us our debts, as we forgive our debtors.

NEW LIVING TRANSLATION

Teaching about Love for Enemies

43 "You have heard the law that says, 'Love your
neighbor'* and hate your enemy. 44 But I say, love
your enemies!* Pray for those who persecute you!
45 In that way, you will be acting as true children of
your Father in heaven. For he gives his sunlight to
both the evil and the good, and he sends rain on the
just and the unjust alike. 46 If you love only those who
love you, what reward is there for that? Even corrupt
tax collectors do that much. 47 If you are kind only to
your friends,* how are you different from anyone
else? Even pagans do that. 48 But you are to be perfect,
even as your Father in heaven is perfect.

Teaching about Giving to the Needy

6 "Watch out! Don't do your good deeds publicly,
to be admired by others, for you will lose the reward from your Father in heaven. 2 When you give to
someone in need, don't do as the hypocrites do—
blowing trumpets in the synagogues and streets to
call attention to their acts of charity! I tell you the
truth, they have received all the reward they will ever
get. 3 But when you give to someone in need, don't let
your left hand know what your right hand is doing.
4 Give your gifts in private, and your Father, who sees
everything, will reward you.

Teaching about Prayer and Fasting

5 "When you pray, don't be like the hypocrites who
love to pray publicly on street corners and in the
synagogues where everyone can see them. I tell you
the truth, that is all the reward they will ever get.
6 But when you pray, go away by yourself, shut the
door behind you, and pray to your Father in private.
Then your Father, who sees everything, will reward
you.

7 "When you pray, don't babble on and on as
people of other religions do. They think their prayers
are answered merely by repeating their words again
and again. 8 Don't be like them, for your Father knows
exactly what you need even before you ask him! 9 Pray
like this:

Our Father in heaven,
may your name be kept holy.
10 May your Kingdom come soon.
May your will be done on earth,
as it is in heaven.
11 Give us today the food we need,*
12 and forgive us our sins,
as we have forgiven those who sin
against us.

5:43 Lev 19:18. **5:44** Some manuscripts add *Bless those who curse you. Do good to those who hate you.* Compare Luke 6:27-28. **5:47** Greek *your brothers.* **6:11** Or *Give us today our food for the day;* or *Give us today our food for tomorrow.*

KING JAMES VERSION

13 And lead us not into temptation, but deliver us from evil: For thine is the kingdom, and the power, and the glory, for ever. Amen.

14 For if ye forgive men their trespasses, your heavenly Father will also forgive you:

15 But if ye forgive not men their trespasses, neither will your Father forgive your trespasses.

16 Moreover when ye fast, be not, as the hypocrites, of a sad countenance: for they disfigure their faces, that they may appear unto men to fast. Verily I say unto you, They have their reward.

17 But thou, when thou fastest, anoint thine head, and wash thy face;

18 That thou appear not unto men to fast, but unto thy Father which is in secret: and thy Father, which seeth in secret, shall reward thee openly.

19 Lay not up for yourselves treasures upon earth, where moth and rust doth corrupt, and where thieves break through and steal:

20 But lay up for yourselves treasures in heaven, where neither moth nor rust doth corrupt, and where thieves do not break through nor steal:

21 For where your treasure is, there will your heart be also.

22 The light of the body is the eye: if therefore thine eye be single, thy whole body shall be full of light.

23 But if thine eye be evil, thy whole body shall be full of darkness. If therefore the light that is in thee be darkness, how great *is* that darkness!

24 No man can serve two masters: for either he will hate the one, and love the other; or else he will hold to the one, and despise the other. Ye cannot serve God and mammon.

25 Therefore I say unto you, Take no thought for your life, what ye shall eat, or what ye shall drink; nor yet for your body, what ye shall put on. Is not the life more than meat, and the body than raiment?

26 Behold the fowls of the air: for they sow not, neither do they reap, nor gather into barns; yet your heavenly Father feedeth them. Are ye not much better than they?

27 Which of you by taking thought can add one cubit unto his stature?

28 And why take ye thought for raiment? Consider the lilies of the field, how they grow; they toil not, neither do they spin:

29 And yet I say unto you, That even Solomon in all his glory was not arrayed like one of these.

30 Wherefore, if God so clothe the grass of the field, which today is, and tomorrow is cast into the oven, *shall he* not much more *clothe* you, O ye of little faith?

31 Therefore take no thought, saying, What shall we eat? or, What shall we drink? or, Wherewithal shall we be clothed?

32 (For after all these things do the Gentiles seek:)

NEW LIVING TRANSLATION

13 And don't let us yield to temptation,*
but rescue us from the evil one.*

14 "If you forgive those who sin against you, your heavenly Father will forgive you. 15 But if you refuse to forgive others, your Father will not forgive your sins.

16 "And when you fast, don't make it obvious, as the hypocrites do, for they try to look miserable and disheveled so people will admire them for their fasting. I tell you the truth, that is the only reward they will ever get. 17 But when you fast, comb your hair and wash your face. 18 Then no one will notice that you are fasting, except your Father, who knows what you do in private. And your Father, who sees everything, will reward you.

Teaching about Money and Possessions

19 "Don't store up treasures here on earth, where moths eat them and rust destroys them, and where thieves break in and steal. 20 Store your treasures in heaven, where moths and rust cannot destroy, and thieves do not break in and steal. 21 Wherever your treasure is, there the desires of your heart will also be.

22 "Your eye is a lamp that provides light for your body. When your eye is good, your whole body is filled with light. 23 But when your eye is bad, your whole body is filled with darkness. And if the light you think you have is actually darkness, how deep that darkness is!

24 "No one can serve two masters. For you will hate one and love the other; you will be devoted to one and despise the other. You cannot serve both God and money.

25 "That is why I tell you not to worry about everyday life—whether you have enough food and drink, or enough clothes to wear. Isn't life more than food, and your body more than clothing? 26 Look at the birds. They don't plant or harvest or store food in barns, for your heavenly Father feeds them. And aren't you far more valuable to him than they are? 27 Can all your worries add a single moment to your life?

28 "And why worry about your clothing? Look at the lilies of the field and how they grow. They don't work or make their clothing, 29 yet Solomon in all his glory was not dressed as beautifully as they are. 30 And if God cares so wonderfully for wildflowers that are here today and thrown into the fire tomorrow, he will certainly care for you. Why do you have so little faith?

31 "So don't worry about these things, saying, 'What will we eat? What will we drink? What will we wear?' 32 These things dominate the thoughts

6:13a Or *And keep us from being tested.* **6:13b** Or *from evil.* Some manuscripts add *For yours is the kingdom and the power and the glory forever. Amen.*

KING JAMES VERSION

for your heavenly Father knoweth that ye have need
of all these things.
33 But seek ye first the kingdom of God, and his
righteousness; and all these things shall be added
unto you.
34 Take therefore no thought for the morrow: for
the morrow shall take thought for the things of itself.
Sufficient unto the day *is* the evil thereof.

7 1 Judge not, that ye be not judged.
2 For with what judgment ye judge, ye shall be
judged: and with what measure ye mete, it shall be
measured to you again.
3 And why beholdest thou the mote that is in thy
brother's eye, but considerest not the beam that is in
thine own eye?
4 Or how wilt thou say to thy brother, Let me pull
out the mote out of thine eye; and, behold, a beam *is*
in thine own eye?
5 Thou hypocrite, first cast out the beam out of
thine own eye; and then shalt thou see clearly to cast
out the mote out of thy brother's eye.
6 Give not that which is holy unto the dogs, neither
cast ye your pearls before swine, lest they trample
them under their feet, and turn again and rend you.
7 Ask, and it shall be given you; seek, and ye shall
find; knock, and it shall be opened unto you:
8 For every one that asketh receiveth; and he that
seeketh findeth; and to him that knocketh it shall be
opened.
9 Or what man is there of you, whom if his son ask
bread, will he give him a stone?
10 Or if he ask a fish, will he give him a serpent?
11 If ye then, being evil, know how to give good
gifts unto your children, how much more shall your
Father which is in heaven give good things to them
that ask him?

12 Therefore all things whatsoever ye would that
men should do to you, do ye even so to them: for this
is the law and the prophets.

13 Enter ye in at the strait gate: for wide *is* the gate,
and broad *is* the way, that leadeth to destruction, and
many there be which go in thereat:
14 Because strait *is* the gate, and narrow *is* the way,
which leadeth unto life, and few there be that find it.

15 Beware of false prophets, which come to you in
sheep's clothing, but inwardly they are ravening
wolves.
16 Ye shall know them by their fruits. Do men
gather grapes of thorns, or figs of thistles?

NEW LIVING TRANSLATION

of unbelievers, but your heavenly Father already
knows all your needs. 33 Seek the Kingdom of God*
above all else, and live righteously, and he will give
you everything you need.
34 "So don't worry about tomorrow, for tomorrow
will bring its own worries. Today's trouble is enough
for today.

Do Not Judge Others

7 "Do not judge others, and you will not be
judged. 2 For you will be treated as you treat
others.* The standard you use in judging is the standard by which you will be judged.*
3 "And why worry about a speck in your friend's
eye* when you have a log in your own? 4 How can you
think of saying to your friend,* 'Let me help you get
rid of that speck in your eye,' when you can't see past
the log in your own eye? 5 Hypocrite! First get rid of
the log in your own eye; then you will see well
enough to deal with the speck in your friend's eye.
6 "Don't waste what is holy on people who are
unholy.* Don't throw your pearls to pigs! They will
trample the pearls, then turn and attack you.

Effective Prayer

7 "Keep on asking, and you will receive what you ask
for. Keep on seeking, and you will find. Keep on
knocking, and the door will be opened to you. 8 For
everyone who asks, receives. Everyone who seeks,
finds. And to everyone who knocks, the door will
be opened.
9 "You parents—if your children ask for a loaf of
bread, do you give them a stone instead? 10 Or if they
ask for a fish, do you give them a snake? Of course
not! 11 So if you sinful people know how to give good
gifts to your children, how much more will your
heavenly Father give good gifts to those who ask him.

The Golden Rule

12 "Do to others whatever you would like them to do
to you. This is the essence of all that is taught in the
law and the prophets.

The Narrow Gate

13 "You can enter God's Kingdom only through the
narrow gate. The highway to hell* is broad, and its
gate is wide for the many who choose that way. 14 But
the gateway to life is very narrow and the road is
difficult, and only a few ever find it.

The Tree and Its Fruit

15 "Beware of false prophets who come disguised as
harmless sheep but are really vicious wolves. 16 You
can identify them by their fruit, that is, by the way

6:33 Some manuscripts do not include *of God.* **7:2a** Or *For God will judge you as you judge others.* **7:2b** Or *The measure you give will be the measure you get back.* **7:3** Greek *your brother's eye;* also in 7:5. **7:4** Greek *your brother.* **7:6** Greek *Don't give the sacred to dogs.* **7:13** Greek *The road that leads to destruction.*

KING JAMES VERSION

17 Even so every good tree bringeth forth good fruit; but a corrupt tree bringeth forth evil fruit.

18 A good tree cannot bring forth evil fruit, neither *can* a corrupt tree bring forth good fruit.

19 Every tree that bringeth not forth good fruit is hewn down, and cast into the fire.

20 Wherefore by their fruits ye shall know them.

21 Not every one that saith unto me, Lord, Lord, shall enter into the kingdom of heaven; but he that doeth the will of my Father which is in heaven.

22 Many will say to me in that day, Lord, Lord, have we not prophesied in thy name? and in thy name have cast out devils? and in thy name done many wonderful works?

23 And then will I profess unto them, I never knew you: depart from me, ye that work iniquity.

24 Therefore whosoever heareth these sayings of mine, and doeth them, I will liken him unto a wise man, which built his house upon a rock:

25 And the rain descended, and the floods came, and the winds blew, and beat upon that house; and it fell not: for it was founded upon a rock.

26 And every one that heareth these sayings of mine, and doeth them not, shall be likened unto a foolish man, which built his house upon the sand:

27 And the rain descended, and the floods came, and the winds blew, and beat upon that house; and it fell: and great was the fall of it.

28 And it came to pass, when Jesus had ended these sayings, the people were astonished at his doctrine:

29 For he taught them as *one* having authority, and not as the scribes.

8 1 When he was come down from the mountain, great multitudes followed him.

2 And, behold, there came a leper and worshipped him, saying, Lord, if thou wilt, thou canst make me clean.

3 And Jesus put forth *his* hand, and touched him, saying, I will; be thou clean. And immediately his leprosy was cleansed.

4 And Jesus saith unto him, See thou tell no man; but go thy way, shew thyself to the priest, and offer the gift that Moses commanded, for a testimony unto them.

5 And when Jesus was entered into Capernaum, there came unto him a centurion, beseeching him,

6 And saying, Lord, my servant lieth at home sick of the palsy, grievously tormented.

7 And Jesus saith unto him, I will come and heal him.

NEW LIVING TRANSLATION

they act. Can you pick grapes from thornbushes, or figs from thistles? 17 A good tree produces good fruit, and a bad tree produces bad fruit. 18 A good tree can't produce bad fruit, and a bad tree can't produce good fruit. 19 So every tree that does not produce good fruit is chopped down and thrown into the fire. 20 Yes, just as you can identify a tree by its fruit, so you can identify people by their actions.

True Disciples

21 "Not everyone who calls out to me, 'Lord! Lord!' will enter the Kingdom of Heaven. Only those who actually do the will of my Father in heaven will enter. 22 On judgment day many will say to me, 'Lord! Lord! We prophesied in your name and cast out demons in your name and performed many miracles in your name.' 23 But I will reply, 'I never knew you. Get away from me, you who break God's laws.'

Building on a Solid Foundation

24 "Anyone who listens to my teaching and follows it is wise, like a person who builds a house on solid rock. 25 Though the rain comes in torrents and the floodwaters rise and the winds beat against that house, it won't collapse because it is built on bedrock. 26 But anyone who hears my teaching and doesn't obey it is foolish, like a person who builds a house on sand. 27 When the rains and floods come and the winds beat against that house, it will collapse with a mighty crash."

28 When Jesus had finished saying these things, the crowds were amazed at his teaching, 29 for he taught with real authority—quite unlike their teachers of religious law.

Jesus Heals a Man with Leprosy

8 Large crowds followed Jesus as he came down the mountainside. 2 Suddenly, a man with leprosy approached him and knelt before him. "Lord," the man said, "if you are willing, you can heal me and make me clean."

3 Jesus reached out and touched him. "I am willing," he said. "Be healed!" And instantly the leprosy disappeared. 4 Then Jesus said to him, "Don't tell anyone about this. Instead, go to the priest and let him examine you. Take along the offering required in the law of Moses for those who have been healed of leprosy.* This will be a public testimony that you have been cleansed."

The Faith of a Roman Officer

5 When Jesus returned to Capernaum, a Roman officer* came and pleaded with him, 6 "Lord, my young servant* lies in bed, paralyzed and in terrible pain."

7 Jesus said, "I will come and heal him."

8:4 See Lev 14:2-32. **8:5** Greek *a centurion;* similarly in 8:8, 13. **8:6** Or *child;* also in 8:13.

KING JAMES VERSION

8The centurion answered and said, Lord, I am not
worthy that thou shouldest come under my roof: but
speak the word only, and my servant shall be healed.
9For I am a man under authority, having soldiers
under me: and I say to this *man,* Go, and he goeth;
and to another, Come, and he cometh; and to my servant, Do this, and he doeth *it.*
10When Jesus heard *it,* he marvelled, and said to
them that followed, Verily I say unto you, I have not
found so great faith, no, not in Israel.
11And I say unto you, That many shall come from
the east and west, and shall sit down with Abraham,
and Isaac, and Jacob, in the kingdom of heaven.
12But the children of the kingdom shall be cast out
into outer darkness: there shall be weeping and
gnashing of teeth.
13And Jesus said unto the centurion, Go thy way;
and as thou hast believed, *so* be it done unto thee.
And his servant was healed in the selfsame hour.

14And when Jesus was come into Peter's house, he
saw his wife's mother laid, and sick of a fever.
15And he touched her hand, and the fever left her:
and she arose, and ministered unto them.
16When the even was come, they brought unto
him many that were possessed with devils: and he
cast out the spirits with *his* word, and healed all that
were sick:
17That it might be fulfilled which was spoken by
Esaias the prophet, saying, Himself took our infirmities, and bare *our* sicknesses.

18Now when Jesus saw great multitudes about
him, he gave commandment to depart unto the other
side.
19And a certain scribe came, and said unto him,
Master, I will follow thee whithersoever thou goest.
20And Jesus saith unto him, The foxes have holes,
and the birds of the air *have* nests; but the Son of
man hath not where to lay *his* head.
21And another of his disciples said unto him, Lord,
suffer me first to go and bury my father.
22But Jesus said unto him, Follow me; and let the
dead bury their dead.

23And when he was entered into a ship, his disciples followed him.
24And, behold, there arose a great tempest in the
sea, insomuch that the ship was covered with the
waves: but he was asleep.
25And his disciples came to *him,* and awoke him,
saying, Lord, save us: we perish.

NEW LIVING TRANSLATION

8But the officer said, "Lord, I am not worthy to have
you come into my home. Just say the word from
where you are, and my servant will be healed. 9I know
this because I am under the authority of my superior
officers, and I have authority over my soldiers. I only
need to say, 'Go,' and they go, or 'Come,' and they
come. And if I say to my slaves, 'Do this,' they do it."
10When Jesus heard this, he was amazed. Turning
to those who were following him, he said, "I tell you
the truth, I haven't seen faith like this in all Israel!
11And I tell you this, that many Gentiles will come
from all over the world—from east and west—and sit
down with Abraham, Isaac, and Jacob at the feast in
the Kingdom of Heaven. 12But many Israelites—
those for whom the Kingdom was prepared—will be
thrown into outer darkness, where there will be
weeping and gnashing of teeth."
13Then Jesus said to the Roman officer, "Go back
home. Because you believed, it has happened." And
the young servant was healed that same hour.

Jesus Heals Many People

14When Jesus arrived at Peter's house, Peter's
mother-in-law was sick in bed with a high fever.
15But when Jesus touched her hand, the fever left
her. Then she got up and prepared a meal for him.
16That evening many demon-possessed people
were brought to Jesus. He cast out the evil spirits
with a simple command, and he healed all the sick.
17This fulfilled the word of the Lord through the
prophet Isaiah, who said,

"He took our sicknesses
and removed our diseases."*

The Cost of Following Jesus

18When Jesus saw the crowd around him, he instructed his disciples to cross to the other side of
the lake.
19Then one of the teachers of religious law said to
him, "Teacher, I will follow you wherever you go."
20But Jesus replied, "Foxes have dens to live in, and
birds have nests, but the Son of Man* has no place
even to lay his head."
21Another of his disciples said, "Lord, first let me
return home and bury my father."
22But Jesus told him, "Follow me now. Let the spiritually dead bury their own dead.*"

Jesus Calms the Storm

23Then Jesus got into the boat and started across the
lake with his disciples. 24Suddenly, a fierce storm
struck the lake, with waves breaking into the boat.
But Jesus was sleeping. 25The disciples went and
woke him up, shouting, "Lord, save us! We're going
to drown!"

8:17 Isa 53:4. **8:20** "Son of Man" is a title Jesus used for himself.
8:22 Greek *Let the dead bury their own dead.*

KING JAMES VERSION

26 And he saith unto them, Why are ye fearful, O ye
of little faith? Then he arose, and rebuked the winds
and the sea; and there was a great calm.
27 But the men marvelled, saying, What manner of
man is this, that even the winds and the sea obey him!

28 And when he was come to the other side into the
country of the Gergesenes, there met him two possessed with devils, coming out of the tombs, exceeding fierce, so that no man might pass by that way.
29 And, behold, they cried out, saying, What have
we to do with thee, Jesus, thou Son of God? art thou
come hither to torment us before the time?
30 And there was a good way off from them an herd
of many swine feeding.
31 So the devils besought him, saying, If thou cast
us out, suffer us to go away into the herd of swine.
32 And he said unto them, Go. And when they were
come out, they went into the herd of swine: and, behold, the whole herd of swine ran violently down a
steep place into the sea, and perished in the waters.
33 And they that kept them fled, and went their
ways into the city, and told every thing, and what was
befallen to the possessed of the devils.
34 And, behold, the whole city came out to meet
Jesus: and when they saw him, they besought *him*
that he would depart out of their coasts.

9 1 And he entered into a ship, and passed over,
and came into his own city.
2 And, behold, they brought to him a man sick of
the palsy, lying on a bed: and Jesus seeing their faith
said unto the sick of the palsy; Son, be of good cheer;
thy sins be forgiven thee.
3 And, behold, certain of the scribes said within
themselves, This *man* blasphemeth.
4 And Jesus knowing their thoughts said, Wherefore think ye evil in your hearts?
5 For whether is easier, to say, *Thy* sins be forgiven
thee; or to say, Arise, and walk?
6 But that ye may know that the Son of man hath
power on earth to forgive sins, (then saith he to the
sick of the palsy,) Arise, take up thy bed, and go unto
thine house.
7 And he arose, and departed to his house.
8 But when the multitude saw *it,* they marvelled,
and glorified God, which had given such power unto
men.

9 And as Jesus passed forth from thence, he saw a
man, named Matthew, sitting at the receipt of custom: and he saith unto him, Follow me. And he arose,
and followed him.

NEW LIVING TRANSLATION

26 Jesus responded, "Why are you afraid? You have
so little faith!" Then he got up and rebuked the wind
and waves, and suddenly there was a great calm.
27 The disciples were amazed. "Who is this man?"
they asked. "Even the winds and waves obey him!"

Jesus Heals Two Demon-Possessed Men

28 When Jesus arrived on the other side of the lake, in
the region of the Gadarenes,* two men who were
possessed by demons met him. They lived in a cemetery and were so violent that no one could go
through that area.
29 They began screaming at him, "Why are you
interfering with us, Son of God? Have you come here
to torture us before God's appointed time?"
30 There happened to be a large herd of pigs feeding in the distance. 31 So the demons begged, "If you
cast us out, send us into that herd of pigs."
32 "All right, go!" Jesus commanded them. So the
demons came out of the men and entered the pigs,
and the whole herd plunged down the steep hillside
into the lake and drowned in the water.
33 The herdsmen fled to the nearby town, telling
everyone what happened to the demon-possessed
men. 34 Then the entire town came out to meet Jesus,
but they begged him to go away and leave them
alone.

Jesus Heals a Paralyzed Man

9 Jesus climbed into a boat and went back across
the lake to his own town. 2 Some people
brought to him a paralyzed man on a mat. Seeing
their faith, Jesus said to the paralyzed man, "Be encouraged, my child! Your sins are forgiven."
3 But some of the teachers of religious law said to
themselves, "That's blasphemy! Does he think he's
God?"
4 Jesus knew* what they were thinking, so he
asked them, "Why do you have such evil thoughts in
your hearts? 5 Is it easier to say 'Your sins are forgiven,' or 'Stand up and walk'? 6 So I will prove to you
that the Son of Man* has the authority on earth to
forgive sins." Then Jesus turned to the paralyzed
man and said, "Stand up, pick up your mat, and go
home!"
7 And the man jumped up and went home! 8 Fear
swept through the crowd as they saw this happen.
And they praised God for sending a man with such
great authority.*

Jesus Calls Matthew

9 As Jesus was walking along, he saw a man named
Matthew sitting at his tax collector's booth. "Follow
me and be my disciple," Jesus said to him. So Matthew got up and followed him.

8:28 Other manuscripts read *Gerasenes;* still others read *Gergesenes.* Compare Mark 5:1; Luke 8:26. **9:4** Some manuscripts read *saw.* **9:6** "Son of Man" is a title Jesus used for himself. **9:8** Greek *for giving such authority to human beings.*

KING JAMES VERSION

10And it came to pass, as Jesus sat at meat in the
house, behold, many publicans and sinners came
and sat down with him and his disciples.
11And when the Pharisees saw *it,* they said unto
his disciples, Why eateth your Master with publicans
and sinners?
12But when Jesus heard *that,* he said unto them,
They that be whole need not a physician, but they
that are sick.
13But go ye and learn what *that* meaneth, I will
have mercy, and not sacrifice: for I am not come to
call the righteous, but sinners to repentance.

14Then came to him the disciples of John, saying,
Why do we and the Pharisees fast oft, but thy disciples fast not?
15And Jesus said unto them, Can the children of
the bridechamber mourn, as long as the bridegroom
is with them? but the days will come, when the bridegroom shall be taken from them, and then shall
they fast.
16No man putteth a piece of new cloth unto an old
garment, for that which is put in to fill it up taketh
from the garment, and the rent is made worse.
17Neither do men put new wine into old bottles:
else the bottles break, and the wine runneth out, and
the bottles perish: but they put new wine into new
bottles, and both are preserved.

18While he spake these things unto them, behold,
there came a certain ruler, and worshipped him, saying, My daughter is even now dead: but come and lay
thy hand upon her, and she shall live.
19And Jesus arose, and followed him, and *so did* his
disciples.
20And, behold, a woman, which was diseased with
an issue of blood twelve years, came behind *him,* and
touched the hem of his garment:
21For she said within herself, If I may but touch his
garment, I shall be whole.
22But Jesus turned him about, and when he saw
her, he said, Daughter, be of good comfort; thy faith
hath made thee whole. And the woman was made
whole from that hour.
23And when Jesus came into the ruler's house, and
saw the minstrels and the people making a noise,
24He said unto them, Give place: for the maid is not
dead, but sleepeth. And they laughed him to scorn.
25But when the people were put forth, he went in,
and took her by the hand, and the maid arose.
26And the fame hereof went abroad into all that
land.
27And when Jesus departed thence, two blind men
followed him, crying, and saying, *Thou* son of David,
have mercy on us.

NEW LIVING TRANSLATION

10Later, Matthew invited Jesus and his disciples to
his home as dinner guests, along with many tax collectors and other disreputable sinners. 11But when
the Pharisees saw this, they asked his disciples,
"Why does your teacher eat with such scum?*"
12When Jesus heard this, he said, "Healthy people
don't need a doctor—sick people do." 13Then he
added, "Now go and learn the meaning of this Scripture: 'I want you to show mercy, not offer sacrifices.'*
For I have come to call not those who think they are
righteous, but those who know they are sinners."

A Discussion about Fasting

14One day the disciples of John the Baptist came to
Jesus and asked him, "Why don't your disciples fast*
like we do and the Pharisees do?"
15Jesus replied, "Do wedding guests mourn while
celebrating with the groom? Of course not. But
someday the groom will be taken away from them,
and then they will fast.
16"Besides, who would patch old clothing with
new cloth? For the new patch would shrink and rip
away from the old cloth, leaving an even bigger tear
than before.
17"And no one puts new wine into old wineskins.
For the old skins would burst from the pressure,
spilling the wine and ruining the skins. New wine is
stored in new wineskins so that both are preserved."

Jesus Heals in Response to Faith

18As Jesus was saying this, the leader of a synagogue
came and knelt before him. "My daughter has just
died," he said, "but you can bring her back to life
again if you just come and lay your hand on her."
19So Jesus and his disciples got up and went with
him. 20Just then a woman who had suffered for
twelve years with constant bleeding came up behind
him. She touched the fringe of his robe, 21for she
thought, "If I can just touch his robe, I will be healed."
22Jesus turned around, and when he saw her he
said, "Daughter, be encouraged! Your faith has made
you well." And the woman was healed at that moment.
23When Jesus arrived at the official's home, he
saw the noisy crowd and heard the funeral music.
24"Get out!" he told them. "The girl isn't dead; she's
only asleep." But the crowd laughed at him. 25After
the crowd was put outside, however, Jesus went in
and took the girl by the hand, and she stood up!
26The report of this miracle swept through the entire
countryside.

Jesus Heals the Blind

27After Jesus left the girl's home, two blind men followed along behind him, shouting, "Son of David,
have mercy on us!"

9:11 Greek *with tax collectors and sinners?* **9:13** Hos 6:6 (Greek version).
9:14 Some manuscripts read *fast often.*

KING JAMES VERSION

28 And when he was come into the house, the blind
men came to him: and Jesus saith unto them, Believe
ye that I am able to do this? They said unto him, Yea,
Lord.
29 Then touched he their eyes, saying, According
to your faith be it unto you.
30 And their eyes were opened; and Jesus straitly
charged them, saying, See *that* no man know *it*.
31 But they, when they were departed, spread
abroad his fame in all that country.
32 As they went out, behold, they brought to him a
dumb man possessed with a devil.
33 And when the devil was cast out, the dumb
spake: and the multitudes marvelled, saying, It was
never so seen in Israel.
34 But the Pharisees said, He casteth out devils
through the prince of the devils.

35 And Jesus went about all the cities and villages,
teaching in their synagogues, and preaching the gospel of the kingdom, and healing every sickness and
every disease among the people.
36 But when he saw the multitudes, he was moved
with compassion on them, because they fainted, and
were scattered abroad, as sheep having no shepherd.
37 Then saith he unto his disciples, The harvest
truly *is* plenteous, but the labourers *are* few;
38 Pray ye therefore the Lord of the harvest, that he
will send forth labourers into his harvest.

10 1 And when he had called unto *him* his twelve
disciples, he gave them power *against* unclean spirits, to cast them out, and to heal all manner
of sickness and all manner of disease.
2 Now the names of the twelve apostles are these;
The first, Simon, who is called Peter, and Andrew his
brother; James *the son* of Zebedee, and John his
brother;
3 Philip, and Bartholomew; Thomas, and Matthew
the publican; James *the son* of Alphaeus, and
Lebbaeus, whose surname was Thaddaeus;
4 Simon the Canaanite, and Judas Iscariot, who also
betrayed him.
5 These twelve Jesus sent forth, and commanded
them, saying, Go not into the way of the Gentiles, and
into *any* city of the Samaritans enter ye not:
6 But go rather to the lost sheep of the house of
Israel.
7 And as ye go, preach, saying, The kingdom of
heaven is at hand.
8 Heal the sick, cleanse the lepers, raise the dead,
cast out devils: freely ye have received, freely give.

NEW LIVING TRANSLATION

28 They went right into the house where he was
staying, and Jesus asked them, "Do you believe I can
make you see?"
"Yes, Lord," they told him, "we do."
29 Then he touched their eyes and said, "Because
of your faith, it will happen." 30 Then their eyes were
opened, and they could see! Jesus sternly warned
them, "Don't tell anyone about this." 31 But instead,
they went out and spread his fame all over the region.
32 When they left, a demon-possessed man who
couldn't speak was brought to Jesus. 33 So Jesus cast
out the demon, and then the man began to speak.
The crowds were amazed. "Nothing like this has ever
happened in Israel!" they exclaimed.
34 But the Pharisees said, "He can cast out demons
because he is empowered by the prince of demons."

The Need for Workers

35 Jesus traveled through all the towns and villages of
that area, teaching in the synagogues and announcing the Good News about the Kingdom. And he
healed every kind of disease and illness. 36 When he
saw the crowds, he had compassion on them because they were confused and helpless, like sheep
without a shepherd. 37 He said to his disciples, "The
harvest is great, but the workers are few. 38 So pray to
the Lord who is in charge of the harvest; ask him to
send more workers into his fields."

Jesus Sends Out the Twelve Apostles

10 Jesus called his twelve disciples together
and gave them authority to cast out evil*
spirits and to heal every kind of disease and illness.
2 Here are the names of the twelve apostles:

first, Simon (also called Peter),
then Andrew (Peter's brother),
James (son of Zebedee),
John (James's brother),
3 Philip,
Bartholomew,
Thomas,
Matthew (the tax collector),
James (son of Alphaeus),
Thaddaeus,*
4 Simon (the zealot*),
Judas Iscariot (who later betrayed him).

5 Jesus sent out the twelve apostles with these instructions: "Don't go to the Gentiles or the Samaritans, 6 but only to the people of Israel—God's lost
sheep. 7 Go and announce to them that the Kingdom
of Heaven is near.* 8 Heal the sick, raise the dead,
cure those with leprosy, and cast out demons. Give
as freely as you have received!

10:1 Greek *unclean*. **10:3** Other manuscripts read *Lebbaeus;* still others read *Lebbaeus who is called Thaddaeus*. **10:4** Greek *the Cananean*, an Aramaic term for Jewish nationalists. **10:7** Or *has come*, or *is coming soon*.

KING JAMES VERSION

9 Provide neither gold, nor silver, nor brass in your purses,

10 Nor scrip for *your* journey, neither two coats, neither shoes, nor yet staves: for the workman is worthy of his meat.

11 And into whatsoever city or town ye shall enter, inquire who in it is worthy; and there abide till ye go thence.

12 And when ye come into an house, salute it.

13 And if the house be worthy, let your peace come upon it: but if it be not worthy, let your peace return to you.

14 And whosoever shall not receive you, nor hear your words, when ye depart out of that house or city, shake off the dust of your feet.

15 Verily I say unto you, It shall be more tolerable for the land of Sodom and Gomorrha in the day of judgment, than for that city.

16 Behold, I send you forth as sheep in the midst of wolves: be ye therefore wise as serpents, and harmless as doves.

17 But beware of men: for they will deliver you up to the councils, and they will scourge you in their synagogues;

18 And ye shall be brought before governors and kings for my sake, for a testimony against them and the Gentiles.

19 But when they deliver you up, take no thought how or what ye shall speak: for it shall be given you in that same hour what ye shall speak.

20 For it is not ye that speak, but the Spirit of your Father which speaketh in you.

21 And the brother shall deliver up the brother to death, and the father the child: and the children shall rise up against *their* parents, and cause them to be put to death.

22 And ye shall be hated of all *men* for my name's sake: but he that endureth to the end shall be saved.

23 But when they persecute you in this city, flee ye into another: for verily I say unto you, Ye shall not have gone over the cities of Israel, till the Son of man be come.

24 The disciple is not above *his* master, nor the servant above his lord.

25 It is enough for the disciple that he be as his master, and the servant as his lord. If they have called the master of the house Beelzebub, how much more *shall they call* them of his household?

26 Fear them not therefore: for there is nothing covered, that shall not be revealed; and hid, that shall not be known.

27 What I tell you in darkness, *that* speak ye in light: and what ye hear in the ear, *that* preach ye upon the housetops.

28 And fear not them which kill the body, but are not able to kill the soul: but rather fear him which is able to destroy both soul and body in hell.

29 Are not two sparrows sold for a farthing? and

NEW LIVING TRANSLATION

9 "Don't take any money in your money belts—no
gold, silver, or even copper coins. 10 Don't carry a traveler's bag with a change of clothes and sandals or
even a walking stick. Don't hesitate to accept hospitality, because those who work deserve to be fed.

11 "Whenever you enter a city or village, search for
a worthy person and stay in his home until you leave
town. 12 When you enter the home, give it your blessing. 13 If it turns out to be a worthy home, let your
blessing stand; if it is not, take back the blessing. 14 If
any household or town refuses to welcome you or
listen to your message, shake its dust from your feet
as you leave. 15 I tell you the truth, the wicked cities of
Sodom and Gomorrah will be better off than such a
town on the judgment day.

16 "Look, I am sending you out as sheep among
wolves. So be as shrewd as snakes and harmless as
doves. 17 But beware! For you will be handed over to
the courts and will be flogged with whips in the synagogues. 18 You will stand trial before governors and
kings because you are my followers. But this will
be your opportunity to tell the rulers and other unbelievers about me.* 19 When you are arrested, don't
worry about how to respond or what to say. God will
give you the right words at the right time. 20 For it is
not you who will be speaking—it will be the Spirit of
your Father speaking through you.

21 "A brother will betray his brother to death, a father will betray his own child, and children will rebel
against their parents and cause them to be killed.
22 And all nations will hate you because you are my
followers.* But everyone who endures to the end will
be saved. 23 When you are persecuted in one town,
flee to the next. I tell you the truth, the Son of Man*
will return before you have reached all the towns
of Israel.

24 "Students* are not greater than their teacher,
and slaves are not greater than their master. 25 Students are to be like their teacher, and slaves are to be
like their master. And since I, the master of the
household, have been called the prince of demons,*
the members of my household will be called by even
worse names!

26 "But don't be afraid of those who threaten you.
For the time is coming when everything that is covered will be revealed, and all that is secret will be
made known to all. 27 What I tell you now in the darkness, shout abroad when daybreak comes. What I
whisper in your ear, shout from the housetops for all
to hear!

28 "Don't be afraid of those who want to kill your
body; they cannot touch your soul. Fear only God,
who can destroy both soul and body in hell.* 29 What
is the price of two sparrows—one copper coin*? But

10:18 Or *But this will be your testimony against the rulers and other unbelievers.* **10:22** Greek *on account of my name.* **10:23** "Son of Man" is a title Jesus used for himself. **10:24** Or *Disciples.* **10:25** Greek *Beelzeboul;* other manuscripts read *Beezeboul;* Latin version reads *Beelzebub.* **10:28** Greek *Gehenna.* **10:29** Greek *one assarion* [i.e., one "as," a Roman coin equal to 1/16 of a denarius].

KING JAMES VERSION

one of them shall not fall on the ground without your
Father.
30 But the very hairs of your head are all numbered.
31 Fear ye not therefore, ye are of more value than
many sparrows.
32 Whosoever therefore shall confess me before
men, him will I confess also before my Father which
is in heaven.
33 But whosoever shall deny me before men, him
will I also deny before my Father which is in heaven.
34 Think not that I am come to send peace on
earth: I came not to send peace, but a sword.
35 For I am come to set a man at variance against
his father, and the daughter against her mother, and
the daughter in law against her mother in law.
36 And a man's foes *shall be* they of his own household.
37 He that loveth father or mother more than me is
not worthy of me: and he that loveth son or daughter
more than me is not worthy of me.
38 And he that taketh not his cross, and followeth
after me, is not worthy of me.
39 He that findeth his life shall lose it: and he that
loseth his life for my sake shall find it.
40 He that receiveth you receiveth me, and he that
receiveth me receiveth him that sent me.
41 He that receiveth a prophet in the name of a
prophet shall receive a prophet's reward; and he that
receiveth a righteous man in the name of a righteous
man shall receive a righteous man's reward.
42 And whosoever shall give to drink unto one of
these little ones a cup of cold *water* only in the name
of a disciple, verily I say unto you, he shall in no wise
lose his reward.

11 1 And it came to pass, when Jesus had made an
end of commanding his twelve disciples, he
departed thence to teach and to preach in their
cities.
2 Now when John had heard in the prison the
works of Christ, he sent two of his disciples,
3 And said unto him, Art thou he that should come,
or do we look for another?
4 Jesus answered and said unto them, Go and shew
John again those things which ye do hear and see:
5 The blind receive their sight, and the lame walk,
the lepers are cleansed, and the deaf hear, the dead
are raised up, and the poor have the gospel preached
to them.
6 And blessed is *he,* whosoever shall not be offended in me.
7 And as they departed, Jesus began to say unto the
multitudes concerning John, What went ye out into
the wilderness to see? A reed shaken with the wind?
8 But what went ye out for to see? A man clothed in
soft raiment? behold, they that wear soft *clothing* are
in kings' houses.

NEW LIVING TRANSLATION

not a single sparrow can fall to the ground without
your Father knowing it. 30 And the very hairs on your
head are all numbered. 31 So don't be afraid; you are
more valuable to God than a whole flock of sparrows.
32 "Everyone who acknowledges me publicly here
on earth, I will also acknowledge before my Father in
heaven. 33 But everyone who denies me here on earth,
I will also deny before my Father in heaven.
34 "Don't imagine that I came to bring peace to the
earth! I came not to bring peace, but a sword.

35 'I have come to set a man against his father,
a daughter against her mother,
and a daughter-in-law against her mother-in-law.
36 Your enemies will be right in your own
household!'*

37 "If you love your father or mother more than you
love me, you are not worthy of being mine; or if you
love your son or daughter more than me, you are not
worthy of being mine. 38 If you refuse to take up your
cross and follow me, you are not worthy of being
mine. 39 If you cling to your life, you will lose it; but if
you give up your life for me, you will find it.
40 "Anyone who receives you receives me, and anyone who receives me receives the Father who sent
me. 41 If you receive a prophet as one who speaks for
God,* you will be given the same reward as a
prophet. And if you receive righteous people because of their righteousness, you will be given a reward like theirs. 42 And if you give even a cup of cold
water to one of the least of my followers, you will
surely be rewarded."

Jesus and John the Baptist

11 When Jesus had finished giving these instructions to his twelve disciples, he went out
to teach and preach in towns throughout the region.
2 John the Baptist, who was in prison, heard about
all the things the Messiah was doing. So he sent his
disciples to ask Jesus, 3 "Are you the Messiah we've
been expecting,* or should we keep looking for
someone else?"
4 Jesus told them, "Go back to John and tell him
what you have heard and seen—5 the blind see, the
lame walk, the lepers are cured, the deaf hear, the
dead are raised to life, and the Good News is being
preached to the poor. 6 And tell him, 'God blesses
those who do not turn away because of me.*'"
7 As John's disciples were leaving, Jesus began talking about him to the crowds. "What kind of man did
you go into the wilderness to see? Was he a weak
reed, swayed by every breath of wind? 8 Or were you
expecting to see a man dressed in expensive clothes?
No, people with expensive clothes live in palaces.

10:35-36 Mic 7:6. **10:41** Greek *receive a prophet in the name of a prophet.*
11:3 Greek *Are you the one who is coming?* **11:6** Or *who are not offended by me.*

KING JAMES VERSION

9 But what went ye out for to see? A prophet? yea, I say unto you, and more than a prophet.
10 For this is *he,* of whom it is written, Behold, I send my messenger before thy face, which shall prepare thy way before thee.
11 Verily I say unto you, Among them that are born of women there hath not risen a greater than John the Baptist: notwithstanding he that is least in the kingdom of heaven is greater than he.
12 And from the days of John the Baptist until now the kingdom of heaven suffereth violence, and the violent take it by force.
13 For all the prophets and the law prophesied until John.
14 And if ye will receive *it,* this is Elias, which was for to come.
15 He that hath ears to hear, let him hear.
16 But whereunto shall I liken this generation? It is like unto children sitting in the markets, and calling unto their fellows,
17 And saying, We have piped unto you, and ye have not danced; we have mourned unto you, and ye have not lamented.
18 For John came neither eating nor drinking, and they say, He hath a devil.
19 The Son of man came eating and drinking, and they say, Behold a man gluttonous, and a winebibber, a friend of publicans and sinners. But wisdom is justified of her children.

20 Then began he to upbraid the cities wherein most of his mighty works were done, because they repented not:
21 Woe unto thee, Chorazin! woe unto thee, Bethsaida! for if the mighty works, which were done in you, had been done in Tyre and Sidon, they would have repented long ago in sackcloth and ashes.
22 But I say unto you, It shall be more tolerable for Tyre and Sidon at the day of judgment, than for you.
23 And thou, Capernaum, which art exalted unto heaven, shalt be brought down to hell: for if the mighty works, which have been done in thee, had been done in Sodom, it would have remained until this day.
24 But I say unto you, That it shall be more tolerable for the land of Sodom in the day of judgment, than for thee.

25 At that time Jesus answered and said, I thank thee, O Father, Lord of heaven and earth, because thou hast hid these things from the wise and prudent, and hast revealed them unto babes.

NEW LIVING TRANSLATION

9 Were you looking for a prophet? Yes, and he is more
than a prophet. 10 John is the man to whom the Scriptures refer when they say,

'Look, I am sending my messenger ahead of you,
and he will prepare your way before you.'*

11 "I tell you the truth, of all who have ever lived, none is greater than John the Baptist. Yet even the least person in the Kingdom of Heaven is greater
than he is! 12 And from the time John the Baptist began preaching until now, the Kingdom of Heaven has been forcefully advancing,* and violent people
are attacking it. 13 For before John came, all the prophets and the law of Moses looked forward to this
present time. 14 And if you are willing to accept what I say, he is Elijah, the one the prophets said would
come.* 15 Anyone with ears to hear should listen and understand!

16 "To what can I compare this generation? It is like children playing a game in the public square. They complain to their friends,

17 'We played wedding songs,
and you didn't dance,
so we played funeral songs,
and you didn't mourn.'

18 For John didn't spend his time eating and drinking,
and you say, 'He's possessed by a demon.' 19 The Son
of Man,* on the other hand, feasts and drinks, and you say, 'He's a glutton and a drunkard, and a friend of tax collectors and other sinners!' But wisdom is shown to be right by its results."

Judgment for the Unbelievers

20 Then Jesus began to denounce the towns where he had done so many of his miracles, because they hadn't repented of their sins and turned to God.
21 "What sorrow awaits you, Korazin and Bethsaida! For if the miracles I did in you had been done in wicked Tyre and Sidon, their people would have repented of their sins long ago, clothing themselves in burlap and throwing ashes on their heads to show
their remorse. 22 I tell you, Tyre and Sidon will be better off on judgment day than you.

23 "And you people of Capernaum, will you be honored in heaven? No, you will go down to the place of the dead.* For if the miracles I did for you had been done in wicked Sodom, it would still be here today.
24 I tell you, even Sodom will be better off on judgment day than you."

Jesus' Prayer of Thanksgiving

25 At that time Jesus prayed this prayer: "O Father, Lord of heaven and earth, thank you for hiding these things from those who think themselves wise and

11:10 Mal 3:1. **11:12** Or *the Kingdom of Heaven has suffered from violence.* **11:14** See Mal 4:5. **11:19** "Son of Man" is a title Jesus used for himself. **11:23** Greek *to Hades.*

KING JAMES VERSION

26 Even so, Father: for so it seemed good in thy
sight.
27 All things are delivered unto me of my Father:
and no man knoweth the Son, but the Father; neither
knoweth any man the Father, save the Son, and *he*
to whomsoever the Son will reveal *him*.
28 Come unto me, all *ye* that labour and are heavy
laden, and I will give you rest.
29 Take my yoke upon you, and learn of me; for I am
meek and lowly in heart: and ye shall find rest unto
your souls.
30 For my yoke *is* easy, and my burden is light.

12 1 At that time Jesus went on the sabbath day
through the corn; and his disciples were an
hungred, and began to pluck the ears of corn, and
to eat.
2 But when the Pharisees saw *it*, they said unto
him, Behold, thy disciples do that which is not lawful
to do upon the sabbath day.
3 But he said unto them, Have ye not read what
David did, when he was an hungred, and they that
were with him;
4 How he entered into the house of God, and did
eat the shewbread, which was not lawful for him to
eat, neither for them which were with him, but only
for the priests?
5 Or have ye not read in the law, how that on the
sabbath days the priests in the temple profane the
sabbath, and are blameless?
6 But I say unto you, That in this place is *one*
greater than the temple.
7 But if ye had known what *this* meaneth, I will
have mercy, and not sacrifice, ye would not have condemned the guiltless.
8 For the Son of man is Lord even of the sabbath day.
9 And when he was departed thence, he went into
their synagogue:
10 And, behold, there was a man which had *his*
hand withered. And they asked him, saying, Is it lawful to heal on the sabbath days? that they might
accuse him.
11 And he said unto them, What man shall there be
among you, that shall have one sheep, and if it fall
into a pit on the sabbath day, will he not lay hold on
it, and lift *it* out?
12 How much then is a man better than a sheep?
Wherefore it is lawful to do well on the sabbath days.
13 Then saith he to the man, Stretch forth thine
hand. And he stretched *it* forth; and it was restored
whole, like as the other.
14 Then the Pharisees went out, and held a council
against him, how they might destroy him.
15 But when Jesus knew *it*, he withdrew himself
from thence: and great multitudes followed him, and
he healed them all;

NEW LIVING TRANSLATION

clever, and for revealing them to the childlike. 26 Yes,
Father, it pleased you to do it this way!
27 "My Father has entrusted everything to me. No
one truly knows the Son except the Father, and no
one truly knows the Father except the Son and those
to whom the Son chooses to reveal him."
28 Then Jesus said, "Come to me, all of you who are
weary and carry heavy burdens, and I will give you
rest. 29 Take my yoke upon you. Let me teach you, because I am humble and gentle at heart, and you will
find rest for your souls. 30 For my yoke is easy to bear,
and the burden I give you is light."

A Discussion about the Sabbath

12 At about that time Jesus was walking through
some grainfields on the Sabbath. His disciples were hungry, so they began breaking off some
heads of grain and eating them. 2 But some Pharisees
saw them do it and protested, "Look, your disciples
are breaking the law by harvesting grain on the
Sabbath."
3 Jesus said to them, "Haven't you read in the Scriptures what David did when he and his companions
were hungry? 4 He went into the house of God, and he
and his companions broke the law by eating the sacred loaves of bread that only the priests are allowed
to eat. 5 And haven't you read in the law of Moses that
the priests on duty in the Temple may work on the
Sabbath? 6 I tell you, there is one here who is even
greater than the Temple! 7 But you would not have
condemned my innocent disciples if you knew the
meaning of this Scripture: 'I want you to show mercy,
not offer sacrifices.'* 8 For the Son of Man* is Lord,
even over the Sabbath!"

Jesus Heals on the Sabbath

9 Then Jesus went over to their synagogue, 10 where he
noticed a man with a deformed hand. The Pharisees
asked Jesus, "Does the law permit a person to work by
healing on the Sabbath?" (They were hoping he would
say yes, so they could bring charges against him.)
11 And he answered, "If you had a sheep that fell
into a well on the Sabbath, wouldn't you work to pull
it out? Of course you would. 12 And how much more
valuable is a person than a sheep! Yes, the law permits a person to do good on the Sabbath."
13 Then he said to the man, "Hold out your hand."
So the man held out his hand, and it was restored, just
like the other one! 14 Then the Pharisees called a
meeting to plot how to kill Jesus.

Jesus, God's Chosen Servant

15 But Jesus knew what they were planning. So he left
that area, and many people followed him. He healed

12:7 Hos 6:6 (Greek version). **12:8** "Son of Man" is a title Jesus used for himself.

KING JAMES VERSION

16And charged them that they should not make
him known:
17That it might be fulfilled which was spoken by
Esaias the prophet, saying,
18Behold my servant, whom I have chosen; my
beloved, in whom my soul is well pleased: I will put
my spirit upon him, and he shall shew judgment to
the Gentiles.
19He shall not strive, nor cry; neither shall any man
hear his voice in the streets.
20A bruised reed shall he not break, and smoking
flax shall he not quench, till he send forth judgment
unto victory.
21And in his name shall the Gentiles trust.

22Then was brought unto him one possessed with
a devil, blind, and dumb: and he healed him, insomuch that the blind and dumb both spake and saw.
23And all the people were amazed, and said, Is not
this the son of David?
24But when the Pharisees heard *it,* they said, This
fellow doth not cast out devils, but by Beelzebub the
prince of the devils.
25And Jesus knew their thoughts, and said unto
them, Every kingdom divided against itself is brought
to desolation; and every city or house divided against
itself shall not stand:
26And if Satan cast out Satan, he is divided against
himself; how shall then his kingdom stand?
27And if I by Beelzebub cast out devils, by whom
do your children cast *them* out? therefore they shall
be your judges.
28But if I cast out devils by the Spirit of God, then
the kingdom of God is come unto you.
29Or else how can one enter into a strong man's
house, and spoil his goods, except he first bind the
strong man? and then he will spoil his house.
30He that is not with me is against me; and he that
gathereth not with me scattereth abroad.
31Wherefore I say unto you, All manner of sin and
blasphemy shall be forgiven unto men: but the blasphemy *against* the *Holy* Ghost shall not be forgiven
unto men.
32And whosoever speaketh a word against the Son
of man, it shall be forgiven him: but whosoever speaketh against the Holy Ghost, it shall not be forgiven him,
neither in this world, neither in the *world* to come.
33Either make the tree good, and his fruit good; or
else make the tree corrupt, and his fruit corrupt: for
the tree is known by *his* fruit.
34O generation of vipers, how can ye, being evil,
speak good things? for out of the abundance of the
heart the mouth speaketh.
35A good man out of the good treasure of the heart
bringeth forth good things: and an evil man out of
the evil treasure bringeth forth evil things.

NEW LIVING TRANSLATION

all the sick among them, 16but he warned them not
to reveal who he was. 17This fulfilled the prophecy
of Isaiah concerning him:

18 "Look at my Servant, whom I have chosen.
He is my Beloved, who pleases me.
I will put my Spirit upon him,
and he will proclaim justice to the nations.
19 He will not fight or shout
or raise his voice in public.
20 He will not crush the weakest reed
or put out a flickering candle.
Finally he will cause justice to be victorious.
21 And his name will be the hope
of all the world."*

Jesus and the Prince of Demons

22Then a demon-possessed man, who was blind and
couldn't speak, was brought to Jesus. He healed the
man so that he could both speak and see. 23The
crowd was amazed and asked, "Could it be that Jesus
is the Son of David, the Messiah?"
24But when the Pharisees heard about the miracle,
they said, "No wonder he can cast out demons. He
gets his power from Satan,* the prince of demons."
25Jesus knew their thoughts and replied, "Any
kingdom divided by civil war is doomed. A town or
family splintered by feuding will fall apart. 26And if
Satan is casting out Satan, he is divided and fighting
against himself. His own kingdom will not survive.
27And if I am empowered by Satan, what about your
own exorcists? They cast out demons, too, so they
will condemn you for what you have said. 28But if I
am casting out demons by the Spirit of God, then the
Kingdom of God has arrived among you. 29For who is
powerful enough to enter the house of a strong man
like Satan and plunder his goods? Only someone
even stronger—someone who could tie him up and
then plunder his house.
30"Anyone who isn't with me opposes me, and anyone who isn't working with me is actually working
against me.
31"So I tell you, every sin and blasphemy can be
forgiven—except blasphemy against the Holy Spirit,
which will never be forgiven. 32Anyone who speaks
against the Son of Man can be forgiven, but anyone
who speaks against the Holy Spirit will never be forgiven, either in this world or in the world to come.
33"A tree is identified by its fruit. If a tree is good,
its fruit will be good. If a tree is bad, its fruit will be
bad. 34You brood of snakes! How could evil men like
you speak what is good and right? For whatever is in
your heart determines what you say. 35A good person
produces good things from the treasury of a good
heart, and an evil person produces evil things from

12:18-21 Isa 42:1-4 (Greek version for 42:4). **12:24** Greek *Beelzeboul;* also in 12:27. Other manuscripts read *Beezeboul;* Latin version reads *Beelzebub.*

KING JAMES VERSION

36But I say unto you, That every idle word that men
shall speak, they shall give account thereof in the day
of judgment.
37For by thy words thou shalt be justified, and by
thy words thou shalt be condemned.

38Then certain of the scribes and of the Pharisees
answered, saying, Master, we would see a sign from
thee.
39But he answered and said unto them, An evil and
adulterous generation seeketh after a sign; and there
shall no sign be given to it, but the sign of the
prophet Jonas:
40For as Jonas was three days and three nights in
the whale's belly; so shall the Son of man be three
days and three nights in the heart of the earth.
41The men of Nineveh shall rise in judgment with
this generation, and shall condemn it: because they
repented at the preaching of Jonas; and, behold, a
greater than Jonas *is* here.
42The queen of the south shall rise up in the judgment with this generation, and shall condemn it: for
she came from the uttermost parts of the earth to
hear the wisdom of Solomon; and, behold, a greater
than Solomon *is* here.
43When the unclean spirit is gone out of a man, he
walketh through dry places, seeking rest, and findeth
none.
44Then he saith, I will return into my house from
whence I came out; and when he is come, he findeth
it empty, swept, and garnished.
45Then goeth he, and taketh with himself seven
other spirits more wicked than himself, and they enter in and dwell there: and the last *state* of that man
is worse than the first. Even so shall it be also unto
this wicked generation.
46While he yet talked to the people, behold, *his*
mother and his brethren stood without, desiring to
speak with him.
47Then one said unto him, Behold, thy mother
and thy brethren stand without, desiring to speak
with thee.
48But he answered and said unto him that told
him, Who is my mother? and who are my brethren?
49And he stretched forth his hand toward his disciples, and said, Behold my mother and my brethren!
50For whosoever shall do the will of my Father
which is in heaven, the same is my brother, and sister,
and mother.

13 1The same day went Jesus out of the house,
and sat by the sea side.
2And great multitudes were gathered together
unto him, so that he went into a ship, and sat; and the
whole multitude stood on the shore.
3And he spake many things unto them in parables,
saying, Behold, a sower went forth to sow;

NEW LIVING TRANSLATION

the treasury of an evil heart. 36And I tell you this, you
must give an account on judgment day for every idle
word you speak. 37The words you say will either acquit you or condemn you."

The Sign of Jonah

38One day some teachers of religious law and Pharisees came to Jesus and said, "Teacher, we want you to
show us a miraculous sign to prove your authority."
39But Jesus replied, "Only an evil, adulterous generation would demand a miraculous sign; but the
only sign I will give them is the sign of the prophet
Jonah. 40For as Jonah was in the belly of the great fish
for three days and three nights, so will the Son of
Man be in the heart of the earth for three days and
three nights.
41"The people of Nineveh will stand up against
this generation on judgment day and condemn it, for
they repented of their sins at the preaching of Jonah.
Now someone greater than Jonah is here—but you
refuse to repent. 42The queen of Sheba* will also
stand up against this generation on judgment day
and condemn it, for she came from a distant land to
hear the wisdom of Solomon. Now someone greater
than Solomon is here—but you refuse to listen.
43"When an evil* spirit leaves a person, it goes
into the desert, seeking rest but finding none.
44Then it says, 'I will return to the person I came
from.' So it returns and finds its former home empty,
swept, and in order. 45Then the spirit finds seven
other spirits more evil than itself, and they all enter
the person and live there. And so that person is
worse off than before. That will be the experience of
this evil generation."

The True Family of Jesus

46As Jesus was speaking to the crowd, his mother and
brothers stood outside, asking to speak to him.
47Someone told Jesus, "Your mother and your brothers are outside, and they want to speak to you."*
48Jesus asked, "Who is my mother? Who are my
brothers?" 49Then he pointed to his disciples and
said, "Look, these are my mother and brothers.
50Anyone who does the will of my Father in heaven is
my brother and sister and mother!"

Parable of the Farmer Scattering Seed

13 Later that same day Jesus left the house and
sat beside the lake. 2A large crowd soon gathered around him, so he got into a boat. Then he sat
there and taught as the people stood on the shore.
3He told many stories in the form of parables, such
as this one:

12:42 Greek *The queen of the south.* **12:43** Greek *unclean.* **12:47** Some manuscripts do not include verse 47. Compare Mark 3:32 and Luke 8:20.

KING JAMES VERSION

4And when he sowed, some *seeds* fell by the way side, and the fowls came and devoured them up:
5Some fell upon stony places, where they had not much earth: and forthwith they sprung up, because they had no deepness of earth:
6And when the sun was up, they were scorched; and because they had no root, they withered away.

7And some fell among thorns; and the thorns sprung up, and choked them:
8But other fell into good ground, and brought forth fruit, some an hundredfold, some sixtyfold, some thirtyfold.
9Who hath ears to hear, let him hear.
10And the disciples came, and said unto him, Why speakest thou unto them in parables?
11He answered and said unto them, Because it is given unto you to know the mysteries of the kingdom of heaven, but to them it is not given.
12For whosoever hath, to him shall be given, and he shall have more abundance: but whosoever hath not, from him shall be taken away even that he hath.
13Therefore speak I to them in parables: because they seeing see not; and hearing they hear not, neither do they understand.
14And in them is fulfilled the prophecy of Esaias, which saith, By hearing ye shall hear, and shall not understand; and seeing ye shall see, and shall not perceive:
15For this people's heart is waxed gross, and *their* ears are dull of hearing, and their eyes they have closed; lest at any time they should see with *their* eyes and hear with *their* ears, and should understand with *their* heart, and should be converted, and I should heal them.

16But blessed *are* your eyes, for they see: and your ears, for they hear.
17For verily I say unto you, That many prophets and righteous *men* have desired to see *those things* which ye see, and have not seen *them;* and to hear *those things* which ye hear, and have not heard *them.*
18Hear ye therefore the parable of the sower.
19When any one heareth the word of the kingdom, and understandeth *it* not, then cometh the wicked *one,* and catcheth away that which was sown in his heart. This is he which received seed by the way side.
20But he that received the seed into stony places, the same is he that heareth the word, and anon with joy receiveth it;
21Yet hath he not root in himself, but dureth for a while: for when tribulation or persecution ariseth because of the word, by and by he is offended.
22He also that received seed among the thorns is

NEW LIVING TRANSLATION

"Listen! A farmer went out to plant some seeds. 4As he scattered them across his field, some seeds fell on a footpath, and the birds came and ate them. 5Other seeds fell on shallow soil with underlying rock. The seeds sprouted quickly because the soil was shallow. 6But the plants soon wilted under the hot sun, and since they didn't have deep roots, they died. 7Other seeds fell among thorns that grew up and choked out the tender plants. 8Still other seeds fell on fertile soil, and they produced a crop that was thirty, sixty, and even a hundred times as much as had been planted! 9Anyone with ears to hear should listen and understand."

10His disciples came and asked him, "Why do you use parables when you talk to the people?"

11He replied, "You are permitted to understand the secrets* of the Kingdom of Heaven, but others are not. 12To those who listen to my teaching, more understanding will be given, and they will have an abundance of knowledge. But for those who are not listening, even what little understanding they have will be taken away from them. 13That is why I use these parables,

For they look, but they don't really see.
They hear, but they don't really listen
or understand.

14This fulfills the prophecy of Isaiah that says,

'When you hear what I say,
you will not understand.
When you see what I do,
you will not comprehend.
15 For the hearts of these people are hardened,
and their ears cannot hear,
and they have closed their eyes—
so their eyes cannot see,
and their ears cannot hear,
and their hearts cannot understand,
and they cannot turn to me
and let me heal them.'*

16"But blessed are your eyes, because they see; and your ears, because they hear. 17I tell you the truth, many prophets and righteous people longed to see what you see, but they didn't see it. And they longed to hear what you hear, but they didn't hear it.

18"Now listen to the explanation of the parable about the farmer planting seeds: 19The seed that fell on the footpath represents those who hear the message about the Kingdom and don't understand it. Then the evil one comes and snatches away the seed that was planted in their hearts. 20The seed on the rocky soil represents those who hear the message and immediately receive it with joy. 21But since they don't have deep roots, they don't last long. They fall away as soon as they have problems or are persecuted for believing God's word. 22The seed that fell

13:11 Greek *the mysteries.* **13:14-15** Isa 6:9-10 (Greek version).

he that heareth the word; and the care of this world, and the deceitfulness of riches, choke the word, and he becometh unfruitful.

23 But he that received seed into the good ground is he that heareth the word, and understandeth *it;* which also beareth fruit, and bringeth forth, some an hundredfold, some sixty, some thirty.

24 Another parable put he forth unto them, saying, The kingdom of heaven is likened unto a man which sowed good seed in his field:

25 But while men slept, his enemy came and sowed tares among the wheat, and went his way.

26 But when the blade was sprung up, and brought forth fruit, then appeared the tares also.

27 So the servants of the householder came and said unto him, Sir, didst not thou sow good seed in thy field? from whence then hath it tares?

28 He said unto them, An enemy hath done this. The servants said unto him, Wilt thou then that we go and gather them up?

29 But he said, Nay; lest while ye gather up the tares, ye root up also the wheat with them.

30 Let both grow together until the harvest: and in the time of harvest I will say to the reapers, Gather ye together first the tares, and bind them in bundles to burn them: but gather the wheat into my barn.

31 Another parable put he forth unto them, saying, The kingdom of heaven is like to a grain of mustard seed, which a man took, and sowed in his field:

32 Which indeed is the least of all seeds: but when it is grown, it is the greatest among herbs, and becometh a tree, so that the birds of the air come and lodge in the branches thereof.

33 Another parable spake he unto them; The kingdom of heaven is like unto leaven, which a woman took, and hid in three measures of meal, till the whole was leavened.

34 All these things spake Jesus unto the multitude in parables; and without a parable spake he not unto them:

35 That it might be fulfilled which was spoken by the prophet, saying, I will open my mouth in parables; I will utter things which have been kept secret from the foundation of the world.

36 Then Jesus sent the multitude away, and went into the house: and his disciples came unto him, saying, Declare unto us the parable of the tares of the field.

37 He answered and said unto them, He that soweth the good seed is the Son of man;

38 The field is the world; the good seed are the children of the kingdom; but the tares are the children of the wicked *one;*

among the thorns represents those who hear God's word, but all too quickly the message is crowded out by the worries of this life and the lure of wealth, so no fruit is produced. 23 The seed that fell on good soil represents those who truly hear and understand God's word and produce a harvest of thirty, sixty, or even a hundred times as much as had been planted!"

Parable of the Wheat and Weeds

24 Here is another story Jesus told: "The Kingdom of Heaven is like a farmer who planted good seed in his field. 25 But that night as the workers slept, his enemy came and planted weeds among the wheat, then slipped away. 26 When the crop began to grow and produce grain, the weeds also grew.

27 "The farmer's workers went to him and said, 'Sir, the field where you planted that good seed is full of weeds! Where did they come from?'

28 "'An enemy has done this!' the farmer exclaimed.

"'Should we pull out the weeds?' they asked.

29 "'No,' he replied, 'you'll uproot the wheat if you do. 30 Let both grow together until the harvest. Then I will tell the harvesters to sort out the weeds, tie them into bundles, and burn them, and to put the wheat in the barn.'"

Parable of the Mustard Seed

31 Here is another illustration Jesus used: "The Kingdom of Heaven is like a mustard seed planted in a field. 32 It is the smallest of all seeds, but it becomes the largest of garden plants; it grows into a tree, and birds come and make nests in its branches."

Parable of the Yeast

33 Jesus also used this illustration: "The Kingdom of Heaven is like the yeast a woman used in making bread. Even though she put only a little yeast in three measures of flour, it permeated every part of the dough."

34 Jesus always used stories and illustrations like these when speaking to the crowds. In fact, he never spoke to them without using such parables. 35 This fulfilled what God had spoken through the prophet:

"I will speak to you in parables.
I will explain things hidden since the creation of the world.*"

Parable of the Wheat and Weeds Explained

36 Then, leaving the crowds outside, Jesus went into the house. His disciples said, "Please explain to us the story of the weeds in the field."

37 Jesus replied, "The Son of Man* is the farmer who plants the good seed. 38 The field is the world, and the good seed represents the people of the Kingdom. The weeds are the people who belong to the

13:35 Some manuscripts do not include *of the world.* Ps 78:2. **13:37** "Son of Man" is a title Jesus used for himself.

KING JAMES VERSION

39 The enemy that sowed them is the devil; the harvest is the end of the world; and the reapers are the angels.

40 As therefore the tares are gathered and burned in the fire; so shall it be in the end of this world.

41 The Son of man shall send forth his angels, and they shall gather out of his kingdom all things that offend, and them which do iniquity;

42 And shall cast them into a furnace of fire: there shall be wailing and gnashing of teeth.

43 Then shall the righteous shine forth as the sun in the kingdom of their Father. Who hath ears to hear, let him hear.

44 Again, the kingdom of heaven is like unto treasure hid in a field; the which when a man hath found, he hideth, and for joy thereof goeth and selleth all that he hath, and buyeth that field.

45 Again, the kingdom of heaven is like unto a merchant man, seeking goodly pearls:

46 Who, when he had found one pearl of great price, went and sold all that he had, and bought it.

47 Again, the kingdom of heaven is like unto a net, that was cast into the sea, and gathered of every kind:

48 Which, when it was full, they drew to shore, and sat down, and gathered the good into vessels, but cast the bad away.

49 So shall it be at the end of the world: the angels shall come forth, and sever the wicked from among the just,

50 And shall cast them into the furnace of fire: there shall be wailing and gnashing of teeth.

51 Jesus saith unto them, Have ye understood all these things? They say unto him, Yea, Lord.

52 Then said he unto them, Therefore every scribe *which is* instructed unto the kingdom of heaven is like unto a man *that is* an householder, which bringeth forth out of his treasure *things* new and old.

53 And it came to pass, *that* when Jesus had finished these parables, he departed thence.

54 And when he was come into his own country, he taught them in their synagogue, insomuch that they were astonished, and said, Whence hath this *man* this wisdom, and *these* mighty works?

55 Is not this the carpenter's son? is not his mother called Mary? and his brethren, James, and Joses, and Simon, and Judas?

56 And his sisters, are they not all with us? Whence then hath this *man* all these things?

57 And they were offended in him. But Jesus said unto them, A prophet is not without honour, save in his own country, and in his own house.

58 And he did not many mighty works there because of their unbelief.

NEW LIVING TRANSLATION

evil one. 39 The enemy who planted the weeds among the wheat is the devil. The harvest is the end of the world,* and the harvesters are the angels.

40 "Just as the weeds are sorted out and burned in the fire, so it will be at the end of the world. 41 The Son of Man will send his angels, and they will remove from his Kingdom everything that causes sin and all who do evil. 42 And the angels will throw them into the fiery furnace, where there will be weeping and gnashing of teeth. 43 Then the righteous will shine like the sun in their Father's Kingdom. Anyone with ears to hear should listen and understand!

Parables of the Hidden Treasure and the Pearl

44 "The Kingdom of Heaven is like a treasure that a man discovered hidden in a field. In his excitement, he hid it again and sold everything he owned to get enough money to buy the field.

45 "Again, the Kingdom of Heaven is like a merchant on the lookout for choice pearls. 46 When he discovered a pearl of great value, he sold everything he owned and bought it!

Parable of the Fishing Net

47 "Again, the Kingdom of Heaven is like a fishing net that was thrown into the water and caught fish of every kind. 48 When the net was full, they dragged it up onto the shore, sat down, and sorted the good fish into crates, but threw the bad ones away. 49 That is the way it will be at the end of the world. The angels will come and separate the wicked people from the righteous, 50 throwing the wicked into the fiery furnace, where there will be weeping and gnashing of teeth. 51 Do you understand all these things?"

"Yes," they said, "we do."

52 Then he added, "Every teacher of religious law who becomes a disciple in the Kingdom of Heaven is like a homeowner who brings from his storeroom new gems of truth as well as old."

Jesus Rejected at Nazareth

53 When Jesus had finished telling these stories and illustrations, he left that part of the country. 54 He returned to Nazareth, his hometown. When he taught there in the synagogue, everyone was amazed and said, "Where does he get this wisdom and the power to do miracles?" 55 Then they scoffed, "He's just the carpenter's son, and we know Mary, his mother, and his brothers—James, Joseph,* Simon, and Judas. 56 All his sisters live right here among us. Where did he learn all these things?" 57 And they were deeply offended and refused to believe in him.

Then Jesus told them, "A prophet is honored everywhere except in his own hometown and among his own family." 58 And so he did only a few miracles there because of their unbelief.

13:39 Or *the age;* also in 13:40, 49. **13:55** Other manuscripts read *Joses;* still others read *John.*

KING JAMES VERSION

14 1 At that time Herod the tetrarch heard of the fame of Jesus,

2 And said unto his servants, This is John the Baptist; he is risen from the dead; and therefore mighty works do shew forth themselves in him.

3 For Herod had laid hold on John, and bound him, and put *him* in prison for Herodias' sake, his brother Philip's wife.

4 For John said unto him, It is not lawful for thee to have her.

5 And when he would have put him to death, he feared the multitude, because they counted him as a prophet.

6 But when Herod's birthday was kept, the daughter of Herodias danced before them, and pleased Herod.

7 Whereupon he promised with an oath to give her whatsoever she would ask.

8 And she, being before instructed of her mother, said, Give me here John Baptist's head in a charger.

9 And the king was sorry: nevertheless for the oath's sake, and them which sat with him at meat, he commanded *it* to be given *her.*

10 And he sent, and beheaded John in the prison.

11 And his head was brought in a charger, and given to the damsel: and she brought *it* to her mother.

12 And his disciples came, and took up the body, and buried it, and went and told Jesus.

13 When Jesus heard *of it,* he departed thence by ship into a desert place apart: and when the people had heard *thereof,* they followed him on foot out of the cities.

14 And Jesus went forth, and saw a great multitude, and was moved with compassion toward them, and he healed their sick.

15 And when it was evening, his disciples came to him, saying, This is a desert place, and the time is now past; send the multitude away, that they may go into the villages, and buy themselves victuals.

16 But Jesus said unto them, They need not depart; give ye them to eat.

17 And they say unto him, We have here but five loaves, and two fishes.

18 He said, Bring them hither to me.

19 And he commanded the multitude to sit down on the grass, and took the five loaves, and the two fishes, and looking up to heaven, he blessed, and brake, and gave the loaves to *his* disciples, and the disciples to the multitude.

20 And they did all eat, and were filled: and they took up of the fragments that remained twelve baskets full.

21 And they that had eaten were about five thousand men, beside women and children.

22 And straightway Jesus constrained his disciples to get into a ship, and to go before him unto the other side, while he sent the multitudes away.

NEW LIVING TRANSLATION

The Death of John the Baptist

14 When Herod Antipas, the ruler of Galilee,*
heard about Jesus, 2 he said to his advisers,
"This must be John the Baptist raised from the dead!
That is why he can do such miracles."

3 For Herod had arrested and imprisoned John as a
favor to his wife Herodias (the former wife of Herod's
brother Philip). 4 John had been telling Herod, "It is
against God's law for you to marry her." 5 Herod
wanted to kill John, but he was afraid of a riot, because all the people believed John was a prophet.

6 But at a birthday party for Herod, Herodias's
daughter performed a dance that greatly pleased him,
7 so he promised with a vow to give her anything she
wanted. 8 At her mother's urging, the girl said, "I want
the head of John the Baptist on a tray!" 9 Then the king
regretted what he had said; but because of the vow he
had made in front of his guests, he issued the necessary orders. 10 So John was beheaded in the prison,
11 and his head was brought on a tray and given to the
girl, who took it to her mother. 12 Later, John's disciples came for his body and buried it. Then they went
and told Jesus what had happened.

Jesus Feeds Five Thousand

13 As soon as Jesus heard the news, he left in a boat
to a remote area to be alone. But the crowds heard
where he was headed and followed on foot from
many towns. 14 Jesus saw the huge crowd as he
stepped from the boat, and he had compassion on
them and healed their sick.

15 That evening the disciples came to him and said,
"This is a remote place, and it's already getting late.
Send the crowds away so they can go to the villages
and buy food for themselves."

16 But Jesus said, "That isn't necessary—you feed
them."

17 "But we have only five loaves of bread and two
fish!" they answered.

18 "Bring them here," he said. 19 Then he told the
people to sit down on the grass. Jesus took the five
loaves and two fish, looked up toward heaven, and
blessed them. Then, breaking the loaves into pieces,
he gave the bread to the disciples, who distributed it
to the people. 20 They all ate as much as they wanted,
and afterward, the disciples picked up twelve baskets of leftovers. 21 About 5,000 men were fed that
day, in addition to all the women and children!

Jesus Walks on Water

22 Immediately after this, Jesus insisted that his disciples get back into the boat and cross to the other

14:1 Greek *Herod the tetrarch.* Herod Antipas was a son of King Herod and was ruler over Galilee.

KING JAMES VERSION

23 And when he had sent the multitudes away, he went up into a mountain apart to pray: and when the evening was come, he was there alone.

24 But the ship was now in the midst of the sea, tossed with waves: for the wind was contrary.

25 And in the fourth watch of the night Jesus went unto them, walking on the sea.

26 And when the disciples saw him walking on the sea, they were troubled, saying, It is a spirit; and they cried out for fear.

27 But straightway Jesus spake unto them, saying, Be of good cheer; it is I; be not afraid.

28 And Peter answered him and said, Lord, if it be thou, bid me come unto thee on the water.

29 And he said, Come. And when Peter was come down out of the ship, he walked on the water, to go to Jesus.

30 But when he saw the wind boisterous, he was afraid; and beginning to sink, he cried, saying, Lord, save me.

31 And immediately Jesus stretched forth *his* hand, and caught him, and said unto him, O thou of little faith, wherefore didst thou doubt?

32 And when they were come into the ship, the wind ceased.

33 Then they that were in the ship came and worshipped him, saying, Of a truth thou art the Son of God.

34 And when they were gone over, they came into the land of Gennesaret.

35 And when the men of that place had knowledge of him, they sent out into all that country round about, and brought unto him all that were diseased;

36 And besought him that they might only touch the hem of his garment: and as many as touched were made perfectly whole.

15 1 Then came to Jesus scribes and Pharisees, which were of Jerusalem, saying,

2 Why do thy disciples transgress the tradition of the elders? for they wash not their hands when they eat bread.

3 But he answered and said unto them, Why do ye also transgress the commandment of God by your tradition?

4 For God commanded, saying, Honour thy father and mother: and, He that curseth father or mother, let him die the death.

5 But ye say, Whosoever shall say to *his* father or *his* mother, *It is* a gift, by whatsoever thou mightest be profited by me;

6 And honour not his father or his mother, *he shall be free*. Thus have ye made the commandment of God of none effect by your tradition.

7 *Ye* hypocrites, well did Esaias prophesy of you, saying,

NEW LIVING TRANSLATION

side of the lake, while he sent the people home. 23 After sending them home, he went up into the hills by himself to pray. Night fell while he was there alone.

24 Meanwhile, the disciples were in trouble far away from land, for a strong wind had risen, and they were fighting heavy waves. 25 About three o'clock in the morning* Jesus came toward them, walking on the water. 26 When the disciples saw him walking on the water, they were terrified. In their fear, they cried out, "It's a ghost!"

27 But Jesus spoke to them at once. "Don't be afraid," he said. "Take courage. I am here!*"

28 Then Peter called to him, "Lord, if it's really you, tell me to come to you, walking on the water."

29 "Yes, come," Jesus said.

So Peter went over the side of the boat and walked on the water toward Jesus. 30 But when he saw the strong* wind and the waves, he was terrified and began to sink. "Save me, Lord!" he shouted.

31 Jesus immediately reached out and grabbed him. "You have so little faith," Jesus said. "Why did you doubt me?"

32 When they climbed back into the boat, the wind stopped. 33 Then the disciples worshiped him. "You really are the Son of God!" they exclaimed.

34 After they had crossed the lake, they landed at Gennesaret. 35 When the people recognized Jesus, the news of his arrival spread quickly throughout the whole area, and soon people were bringing all their sick to be healed. 36 They begged him to let the sick touch at least the fringe of his robe, and all who touched him were healed.

Jesus Teaches about Inner Purity

15 1 Some Pharisees and teachers of religious law now arrived from Jerusalem to see Jesus. They asked him, 2 "Why do your disciples disobey our age-old tradition? For they ignore our tradition of ceremonial hand washing before they eat."

3 Jesus replied, "And why do you, by your traditions, violate the direct commandments of God? 4 For instance, God says, 'Honor your father and mother,'* and 'Anyone who speaks disrespectfully of father or mother must be put to death.'* 5 But you say it is all right for people to say to their parents, 'Sorry, I can't help you. For I have vowed to give to God what I would have given to you.' 6 In this way, you say they don't need to honor their parents.* And so you cancel the word of God for the sake of your own tradition. 7 You hypocrites! Isaiah was right when he prophesied about you, for he wrote,

14:25 Greek *In the fourth watch of the night.* **14:27** Or *The 'I AM' is here;* Greek reads *I am.* See Exod 3:14. **14:30** Some manuscripts do not include *strong.* **15:4a** Exod 20:12; Deut 5:16. **15:4b** Exod 21:17 (Greek version); Lev 20:9 (Greek version). **15:6** Greek *their father;* other manuscripts read *their father or their mother.*

KING JAMES VERSION

8 This people draweth nigh unto me with their mouth, and honoureth me with *their* lips; but their heart is far from me.

9 But in vain they do worship me, teaching *for* doctrines the commandments of men.

10 And he called the multitude, and said unto them, Hear, and understand:

11 Not that which goeth into the mouth defileth a man; but that which cometh out of the mouth, this defileth a man.

12 Then came his disciples, and said unto him, Knowest thou that the Pharisees were offended, after they heard this saying?

13 But he answered and said, Every plant, which my heavenly Father hath not planted, shall be rooted up.

14 Let them alone: they be blind leaders of the blind. And if the blind lead the blind, both shall fall into the ditch.

15 Then answered Peter and said unto him, Declare unto us this parable.

16 And Jesus said, Are ye also yet without understanding?

17 Do not ye yet understand, that whatsoever entereth in at the mouth goeth into the belly, and is cast out into the draught?

18 But those things which proceed out of the mouth come forth from the heart; and they defile the man.

19 For out of the heart proceed evil thoughts, murders, adulteries, fornications, thefts, false witness, blasphemies:

20 These are *the things* which defile a man: but to eat with unwashen hands defileth not a man.

21 Then Jesus went thence, and departed into the coasts of Tyre and Sidon.

22 And, behold, a woman of Canaan came out of the same coasts, and cried unto him, saying, Have mercy on me, O Lord, *thou* son of David; my daughter is grievously vexed with a devil.

23 But he answered her not a word. And his disciples came and besought him, saying, Send her away; for she crieth after us.

24 But he answered and said, I am not sent but unto the lost sheep of the house of Israel.

25 Then came she and worshipped him, saying, Lord, help me.

26 But he answered and said, It is not meet to take the children's bread, and cast *it* to dogs.

27 And she said, Truth, Lord: yet the dogs eat of the crumbs which fall from their masters' table.

28 Then Jesus answered and said unto her, O woman, great *is* thy faith: be it unto thee even as thou wilt. And her daughter was made whole from that very hour.

NEW LIVING TRANSLATION

8 'These people honor me with their lips,
but their hearts are far from me.
9 Their worship is a farce,
for they teach man-made ideas as commands
from God.'*"

10 Then Jesus called to the crowd to come and
hear. "Listen," he said, "and try to understand. 11 It's
not what goes into your mouth that defiles you; you
are defiled by the words that come out of your
mouth."

12 Then the disciples came to him and asked, "Do
you realize you offended the Pharisees by what you
just said?"

13 Jesus replied, "Every plant not planted by my
heavenly Father will be uprooted, 14 so ignore them.
They are blind guides leading the blind, and if one
blind person guides another, they will both fall into
a ditch."

15 Then Peter said to Jesus, "Explain to us the parable that says people aren't defiled by what they eat."

16 "Don't you understand yet?" Jesus asked. 17 "Anything you eat passes through the stomach and then
goes into the sewer. 18 But the words you speak come
from the heart—that's what defiles you. 19 For from
the heart come evil thoughts, murder, adultery, all
sexual immorality, theft, lying, and slander. 20 These
are what defile you. Eating with unwashed hands will
never defile you."

The Faith of a Gentile Woman

21 Then Jesus left Galilee and went north to the region of Tyre and Sidon. 22 A Gentile* woman who
lived there came to him, pleading, "Have mercy on
me, O Lord, Son of David! For my daughter is possessed by a demon that torments her severely."

23 But Jesus gave her no reply, not even a word.
Then his disciples urged him to send her away. "Tell
her to go away," they said. "She is bothering us with
all her begging."

24 Then Jesus said to the woman, "I was sent only
to help God's lost sheep—the people of Israel."

25 But she came and worshiped him, pleading
again, "Lord, help me!"

26 Jesus responded, "It isn't right to take food from
the children and throw it to the dogs."

27 She replied, "That's true, Lord, but even dogs are
allowed to eat the scraps that fall beneath their
masters' table."

28 "Dear woman," Jesus said to her, "your faith
is great. Your request is granted." And her daughter
was instantly healed.

15:8-9 Isa 29:13 (Greek version). **15:22** Greek *Canaanite*.

KING JAMES VERSION

29 And Jesus departed from thence, and came nigh unto the sea of Galilee; and went up into a mountain, and sat down there.

30 And great multitudes came unto him, having with them *those that were* lame, blind, dumb, maimed, and many others, and cast them down at Jesus' feet; and he healed them:

31 Insomuch that the multitude wondered, when they saw the dumb to speak, the maimed to be whole, the lame to walk, and the blind to see: and they glorified the God of Israel.

32 Then Jesus called his disciples *unto him,* and said, I have compassion on the multitude, because they continue with me now three days, and have nothing to eat: and I will not send them away fasting, lest they faint in the way.

33 And his disciples say unto him, Whence should we have so much bread in the wilderness, as to fill so great a multitude?

34 And Jesus saith unto them, How many loaves have ye? And they said, Seven, and a few little fishes.

35 And he commanded the multitude to sit down on the ground.

36 And he took the seven loaves and the fishes, and gave thanks, and brake *them,* and gave to his disciples, and the disciples to the multitude.

37 And they did all eat, and were filled: and they took up of the broken *meat* that was left seven baskets full.

38 And they that did eat were four thousand men, beside women and children.

39 And he sent away the multitude, and took ship, and came into the coasts of Magdala.

16 1 The Pharisees also with the Sadducees came, and tempting desired him that he would shew them a sign from heaven.

2 He answered and said unto them, When it is evening, ye say, *It will be* fair weather: for the sky is red.

3 And in the morning, *It will be* foul weather today: for the sky is red and lowring. O *ye* hypocrites, ye can discern the face of the sky; but can ye not *discern* the signs of the times?

4 A wicked and adulterous generation seeketh after a sign; and there shall no sign be given unto it, but the sign of the prophet Jonas. And he left them, and departed.

5 And when his disciples were come to the other side, they had forgotten to take bread.

6 Then Jesus said unto them, Take heed and beware of the leaven of the Pharisees and of the Sadducees.

7 And they reasoned among themselves, saying, *It is* because we have taken no bread.

8 *Which* when Jesus perceived, he said unto them, O ye of little faith, why reason ye among yourselves, because ye have brought no bread?

NEW LIVING TRANSLATION

Jesus Heals Many People

29 Jesus returned to the Sea of Galilee and climbed a
hill and sat down. 30 A vast crowd brought to him
people who were lame, blind, crippled, those who
couldn't speak, and many others. They laid them before Jesus, and he healed them all. 31 The crowd was
amazed! Those who hadn't been able to speak were
talking, the crippled were made well, the lame were
walking, and the blind could see again! And they
praised the God of Israel.

Jesus Feeds Four Thousand

32 Then Jesus called his disciples and told them, "I
feel sorry for these people. They have been here with
me for three days, and they have nothing left to eat. I
don't want to send them away hungry, or they will
faint along the way."

33 The disciples replied, "Where would we get
enough food here in the wilderness for such a huge
crowd?"

34 Jesus asked, "How much bread do you have?"

They replied, "Seven loaves, and a few small fish."

35 So Jesus told all the people to sit down on the
ground. 36 Then he took the seven loaves and the
fish, thanked God for them, and broke them into
pieces. He gave them to the disciples, who distributed the food to the crowd.

37 They all ate as much as they wanted. Afterward,
the disciples picked up seven large baskets of leftover food. 38 There were 4,000 men who were fed
that day, in addition to all the women and children.
39 Then Jesus sent the people home, and he got into
a boat and crossed over to the region of Magadan.

Leaders Demand a Miraculous Sign

16 One day the Pharisees and Sadducees came
to test Jesus, demanding that he show them a
miraculous sign from heaven to prove his authority.

2 He replied, "You know the saying, 'Red sky at night
means fair weather tomorrow; 3 red sky in the morning
means foul weather all day.' You know how to interpret
the weather signs in the sky, but you don't know how to
interpret the signs of the times!* 4 Only an evil, adulterous generation would demand a miraculous sign, but
the only sign I will give them is the sign of the prophet
Jonah.*" Then Jesus left them and went away.

Yeast of the Pharisees and Sadducees

5 Later, after they crossed to the other side of the lake,
the disciples discovered they had forgotten to bring
any bread. 6 "Watch out!" Jesus warned them. "Beware of the yeast of the Pharisees and Sadducees."

7 At this they began to argue with each other because they hadn't brought any bread. 8 Jesus knew
what they were saying, so he said, "You have so little
faith! Why are you arguing with each other about

16:2-3 Several manuscripts do not include any of the words in 16:2-3 after *He replied.* **16:4** Greek *the sign of Jonah.*

KING JAMES VERSION

9 Do ye not yet understand, neither remember the
five loaves of the five thousand, and how many
baskets ye took up?
10 Neither the seven loaves of the four thousand,
and how many baskets ye took up?
11 How is it that ye do not understand that I spake
it not to you concerning bread, that ye should beware
of the leaven of the Pharisees and of the Sadducees?
12 Then understood they how that he bade *them*
not beware of the leaven of bread, but of the doctrine
of the Pharisees and of the Sadducees.

13 When Jesus came into the coasts of Caesarea
Philippi, he asked his disciples, saying, Whom do
men say that I the Son of man am?
14 And they said, Some *say that thou art* John the
Baptist: some, Elias; and others, Jeremias, or one of
the prophets.
15 He saith unto them, But whom say ye that I am?
16 And Simon Peter answered and said, Thou art
the Christ, the Son of the living God.
17 And Jesus answered and said unto him, Blessed
art thou, Simon Bar-jona: for flesh and blood hath
not revealed *it* unto thee, but my Father which is in
heaven.
18 And I say also unto thee, That thou art Peter, and
upon this rock I will build my church; and the gates
of hell shall not prevail against it.
19 And I will give unto thee the keys of the kingdom
of heaven: and whatsoever thou shalt bind on earth
shall be bound in heaven: and whatsoever thou shalt
loose on earth shall be loosed in heaven.
20 Then charged he his disciples that they should
tell no man that he was Jesus the Christ.

21 From that time forth began Jesus to shew unto
his disciples, how that he must go unto Jerusalem,
and suffer many things of the elders and chief
priests and scribes, and be killed, and be raised again
the third day.
22 Then Peter took him, and began to rebuke him,
saying, Be it far from thee, Lord: this shall not be
unto thee.
23 But he turned, and said unto Peter, Get thee behind me, Satan: thou art an offence unto me: for thou
savourest not the things that be of God, but those
that be of men.
24 Then said Jesus unto his disciples, If any *man*
will come after me, let him deny himself, and take up
his cross, and follow me.
25 For whosoever will save his life shall lose it: and
whosoever will lose his life for my sake shall find it.

NEW LIVING TRANSLATION

having no bread? 9 Don't you understand even yet?
Don't you remember the 5,000 I fed with five loaves,
and the baskets of leftovers you picked up? 10 Or
the 4,000 I fed with seven loaves, and the large baskets of leftovers you picked up? 11 Why can't you
understand that I'm not talking about bread? So
again I say, 'Beware of the yeast of the Pharisees and
Sadducees.'"
12 Then at last they understood that he wasn't
speaking about the yeast in bread, but about the
deceptive teaching of the Pharisees and Sadducees.

Peter's Declaration about Jesus

13 When Jesus came to the region of Caesarea Philippi, he asked his disciples, "Who do people say that
the Son of Man is?"*
14 "Well," they replied, "some say John the Baptist,
some say Elijah, and others say Jeremiah or one of
the other prophets."
15 Then he asked them, "But who do you say I am?"
16 Simon Peter answered, "You are the Messiah,*
the Son of the living God."
17 Jesus replied, "You are blessed, Simon son of
John,* because my Father in heaven has revealed this
to you. You did not learn this from any human being.
18 Now I say to you that you are Peter (which means
'rock'),* and upon this rock I will build my church,
and all the powers of hell* will not conquer it. 19 And
I will give you the keys of the Kingdom of Heaven.
Whatever you forbid* on earth will be forbidden in
heaven, and whatever you permit* on earth will be
permitted in heaven."
20 Then he sternly warned the disciples not to tell
anyone that he was the Messiah.

Jesus Predicts His Death

21 From then on Jesus* began to tell his disciples
plainly that it was necessary for him to go to Jerusalem, and that he would suffer many terrible things at
the hands of the elders, the leading priests, and the
teachers of religious law. He would be killed, but on
the third day he would be raised from the dead.
22 But Peter took him aside and began to reprimand him* for saying such things. "Heaven forbid,
Lord," he said. "This will never happen to you!"
23 Jesus turned to Peter and said, "Get away from
me, Satan! You are a dangerous trap to me. You are
seeing things merely from a human point of view, not
from God's."
24 Then Jesus said to his disciples, "If any of you
wants to be my follower, you must turn from your
selfish ways, take up your cross, and follow me. 25 If
you try to hang on to your life, you will lose it. But if
you give up your life for my sake, you will save it.

16:13 "Son of Man" is a title Jesus used for himself. **16:16** Or *the Christ.* *Messiah* (a Hebrew term) and *Christ* (a Greek term) both mean "the anointed one." **16:17** Greek *Simon bar-Jonah;* see John 1:42; 21:15-17. **16:18a** Greek *that you are Peter.* **16:18b** Greek *and the gates of Hades.* **16:19a** Or *bind,* or *lock.* **16:19b** Or *loose,* or *open.* **16:21** Some manuscripts read *Jesus the Messiah.* **16:22** Or *began to correct him.*

KING JAMES VERSION

26For what is a man profited, if he shall gain the
whole world, and lose his own soul? or what shall a
man give in exchange for his soul?
27For the Son of man shall come in the glory of his
Father with his angels; and then he shall reward
every man according to his works.
28Verily I say unto you, There be some standing
here, which shall not taste of death, till they see the
Son of man coming in his kingdom.

17 1And after six days Jesus taketh Peter, James,
and John his brother, and bringeth them up
into an high mountain apart,
2And was transfigured before them: and his face
did shine as the sun, and his raiment was white as the
light.
3And, behold, there appeared unto them Moses
and Elias talking with him.
4Then answered Peter, and said unto Jesus, Lord, it
is good for us to be here: if thou wilt, let us make here
three tabernacles; one for thee, and one for Moses,
and one for Elias.
5While he yet spake, behold, a bright cloud overshadowed them: and behold a voice out of the cloud,
which said, This is my beloved Son, in whom I am
well pleased; hear ye him.
6And when the disciples heard *it,* they fell on their
face, and were sore afraid.
7And Jesus came and touched them, and said,
Arise, and be not afraid.
8And when they had lifted up their eyes, they saw
no man, save Jesus only.
9And as they came down from the mountain, Jesus
charged them, saying, Tell the vision to no man, until
the Son of man be risen again from the dead.
10And his disciples asked him, saying, Why then
say the scribes that Elias must first come?
11And Jesus answered and said unto them, Elias
truly shall first come, and restore all things.
12But I say unto you, That Elias is come already,
and they knew him not, but have done unto him
whatsoever they listed. Likewise shall also the Son
of man suffer of them.
13Then the disciples understood that he spake
unto them of John the Baptist.
14And when they were come to the multitude,
there came to him a *certain* man, kneeling down to
him, and saying,
15Lord, have mercy on my son: for he is a lunatick,
and sore vexed: for ofttimes he falleth into the fire,
and oft into the water.
16And I brought him to thy disciples, and they
could not cure him.
17Then Jesus answered and said, O faithless and
perverse generation, how long shall I be with you?
how long shall I suffer you? bring him hither to me.
18And Jesus rebuked the devil; and he departed

NEW LIVING TRANSLATION

26And what do you benefit if you gain the whole
world but lose your own soul?* Is anything worth
more than your soul? 27For the Son of Man will come
with his angels in the glory of his Father and will
judge all people according to their deeds. 28And I tell
you the truth, some standing here right now will not
die before they see the Son of Man coming in his
Kingdom."

The Transfiguration

17 Six days later Jesus took Peter and the two
brothers, James and John, and led them up a
high mountain to be alone. 2As the men watched,
Jesus' appearance was transformed so that his face
shone like the sun, and his clothes became as white
as light. 3Suddenly, Moses and Elijah appeared and
began talking with Jesus.
4Peter exclaimed, "Lord, it's wonderful for us to be
here! If you want, I'll make three shelters as
memorials*—one for you, one for Moses, and one
for Elijah."
5But even as he spoke, a bright cloud overshadowed them, and a voice from the cloud said,
"This is my dearly loved Son, who brings me great
joy. Listen to him." 6The disciples were terrified and
fell face down on the ground.
7Then Jesus came over and touched them. "Get
up," he said. "Don't be afraid." 8And when they
looked up, Moses and Elijah were gone, and they
saw only Jesus.
9As they went back down the mountain, Jesus
commanded them, "Don't tell anyone what you have
seen until the Son of Man* has been raised from the
dead."
10Then his disciples asked him, "Why do the
teachers of religious law insist that Elijah must return before the Messiah comes?*"
11Jesus replied, "Elijah is indeed coming first to
get everything ready. 12But I tell you, Elijah has already come, but he wasn't recognized, and they
chose to abuse him. And in the same way they will
also make the Son of Man suffer." 13Then the disciples realized he was talking about John the Baptist.

Jesus Heals a Demon-Possessed Boy

14At the foot of the mountain, a large crowd was waiting for them. A man came and knelt before Jesus and
said, 15"Lord, have mercy on my son. He has seizures
and suffers terribly. He often falls into the fire or into
the water. 16So I brought him to your disciples, but
they couldn't heal him."
17Jesus said, "You faithless and corrupt people!
How long must I be with you? How long must I put
up with you? Bring the boy here to me." 18Then Jesus

16:26 Or *your self?* also in 16:26b. **17:4** Greek *three tabernacles.*
17:9 "Son of Man" is a title Jesus used for himself. **17:10** Greek *that Elijah must come first?*

out of him: and the child was cured from that very
hour.
19Then came the disciples to Jesus apart, and said,
Why could not we cast him out?
20And Jesus said unto them, Because of your unbelief: for verily I say unto you, If ye have faith as a
grain of mustard seed, ye shall say unto this mountain, Remove hence to yonder place; and it shall remove; and nothing shall be impossible unto you.
21Howbeit this kind goeth not out but by prayer
and fasting.
22And while they abode in Galilee, Jesus said unto
them, The Son of man shall be betrayed into the
hands of men:
23And they shall kill him, and the third day he shall
be raised again. And they were exceeding sorry.

24And when they were come to Capernaum, they
that received tribute *money* came to Peter, and said,
Doth not your master pay tribute?
25He saith, Yes. And when he was come into the
house, Jesus prevented him, saying, What thinkest
thou, Simon? of whom do the kings of the earth take
custom or tribute? of their own children, or of
strangers?
26Peter saith unto him, Of strangers. Jesus saith
unto him, Then are the children free.
27Notwithstanding, lest we should offend them,
go thou to the sea, and cast an hook, and take up the
fish that first cometh up; and when thou hast
opened his mouth, thou shalt find a piece of money:
that take, and give unto them for me and thee.

18 1At the same time came the disciples unto
Jesus, saying, Who is the greatest in the kingdom of heaven?
2And Jesus called a little child unto him, and set
him in the midst of them,
3And said, Verily I say unto you, Except ye be converted, and become as little children, ye shall not enter into the kingdom of heaven.
4Whosoever therefore shall humble himself as
this little child, the same is greatest in the kingdom
of heaven.
5And whoso shall receive one such little child in
my name receiveth me.
6But whoso shall offend one of these little ones
which believe in me, it were better for him that a
millstone were hanged about his neck, and *that* he
were drowned in the depth of the sea.
7Woe unto the world because of offences! for it
must needs be that offences come; but woe to that
man by whom the offence cometh!
8Wherefore if thy hand or thy foot offend thee, cut
them off, and cast *them* from thee: it is better for

rebuked the demon in the boy, and it left him. From
that moment the boy was well.
19Afterward the disciples asked Jesus privately,
"Why couldn't we cast out that demon?"
20"You don't have enough faith," Jesus told them.
"I tell you the truth, if you had faith even as small as a
mustard seed, you could say to this mountain, 'Move
from here to there,' and it would move. Nothing
would be impossible.*"

Jesus Again Predicts His Death

22After they gathered again in Galilee, Jesus told
them, "The Son of Man is going to be betrayed into
the hands of his enemies. 23He will be killed, but
on the third day he will be raised from the dead."
And the disciples were filled with grief.

Payment of the Temple Tax

24On their arrival in Capernaum, the collectors of the
Temple tax* came to Peter and asked him, "Doesn't
your teacher pay the Temple tax?"
25"Yes, he does," Peter replied. Then he went into
the house.
But before he had a chance to speak, Jesus asked
him, "What do you think, Peter?* Do kings tax their
own people or the people they have conquered?*"
26"They tax the people they have conquered,"
Peter replied.
"Well, then," Jesus said, "the citizens are free!
27However, we don't want to offend them, so go down
to the lake and throw in a line. Open the mouth of
the first fish you catch, and you will find a large silver
coin.* Take it and pay the tax for both of us."

The Greatest in the Kingdom

18 About that time the disciples came to Jesus
and asked, "Who is greatest in the Kingdom
of Heaven?"
2Jesus called a little child to him and put the child
among them. 3Then he said, "I tell you the truth, unless you turn from your sins and become like little
children, you will never get into the Kingdom of
Heaven. 4So anyone who becomes as humble as this
little child is the greatest in the Kingdom of Heaven.
5"And anyone who welcomes a little child like this
on my behalf* is welcoming me. 6But if you cause
one of these little ones who trusts in me to fall into
sin, it would be better for you to have a large millstone tied around your neck and be drowned in the
depths of the sea.
7"What sorrow awaits the world, because it
tempts people to sin. Temptations are inevitable, but
what sorrow awaits the person who does the tempting. 8So if your hand or foot causes you to sin, cut it

17:20 Some manuscripts add verse 21, *But this kind of demon won't leave except by prayer and fasting.* Compare Mark 9:29. **17:24** Greek *the two-drachma [tax];* also in 17:24b. See Exod 30:13-16; Neh 10:32-33. **17:25a** Greek *Simon?* **17:25b** Greek *their sons or others?* **17:27** Greek *a stater* [a Greek coin equivalent to four drachmas]. **18:5** Greek *in my name.*

KING JAMES VERSION

thee to enter into life halt or maimed, rather than having two hands or two feet to be cast into everlasting fire.

9And if thine eye offend thee, pluck it out, and cast *it* from thee: it is better for thee to enter into life with one eye, rather than having two eyes to be cast into hell fire.

10Take heed that ye despise not one of these little ones; for I say unto you, That in heaven their angels do always behold the face of my Father which is in heaven.

11For the Son of man is come to save that which was lost.

12How think ye? if a man have an hundred sheep, and one of them be gone astray, doth he not leave the ninety and nine, and goeth into the mountains, and seeketh that which is gone astray?

13And if so be that he find it, verily I say unto you, he rejoiceth more of that *sheep*, than of the ninety and nine which went not astray.

14Even so it is not the will of your Father which is in heaven, that one of these little ones should perish.

15Moreover if thy brother shall trespass against thee, go and tell him his fault between thee and him alone: if he shall hear thee, thou hast gained thy brother.

16But if he will not hear *thee, then* take with thee one or two more, that in the mouth of two or three witnesses every word may be established.

17And if he shall neglect to hear them, tell *it* unto the church: but if he neglect to hear the church, let him be unto thee as a heathen man and a publican.

18Verily I say unto you, Whatsoever ye shall bind on earth shall be bound in heaven: and whatsoever ye shall loose on earth shall be loosed in heaven.

19Again I say unto you, That if two of you shall agree on earth as touching any thing that they shall ask, it shall be done for them of my Father which is in heaven.

20For where two or three are gathered together in my name, there am I in the midst of them.

21Then came Peter to him, and said, Lord, how oft shall my brother sin against me, and I forgive him? till seven times?

22Jesus saith unto him, I say not unto thee, Until seven times: but, Until seventy times seven.

23Therefore is the kingdom of heaven likened unto a certain king, which would take account of his servants.

24And when he had begun to reckon, one was brought unto him, which owed him ten thousand talents.

NEW LIVING TRANSLATION

off and throw it away. It's better to enter eternal life
with only one hand or one foot than to be thrown
into eternal fire with both of your hands and feet.
9And if your eye causes you to sin, gouge it out and
throw it away. It's better to enter eternal life with only
one eye than to have two eyes and be thrown into the
fire of hell.*

10"Beware that you don't look down on any of
these little ones. For I tell you that in heaven their
angels are always in the presence of my heavenly
Father.*

Parable of the Lost Sheep

12"If a man has a hundred sheep and one of them
wanders away, what will he do? Won't he leave the
ninety-nine others on the hills and go out to search
for the one that is lost? 13And if he finds it, I tell you
the truth, he will rejoice over it more than over the
ninety-nine that didn't wander away! 14In the same
way, it is not my heavenly Father's will that even one
of these little ones should perish.

Correcting Another Believer

15"If another believer* sins against you,* go privately
and point out the offense. If the other person listens
and confesses it, you have won that person back.
16But if you are unsuccessful, take one or two others
with you and go back again, so that everything you
say may be confirmed by two or three witnesses. 17If
the person still refuses to listen, take your case to the
church. Then if he or she won't accept the church's
decision, treat that person as a pagan or a corrupt tax
collector.

18"I tell you the truth, whatever you forbid* on
earth will be forbidden in heaven, and whatever you
permit* on earth will be permitted in heaven.

19"I also tell you this: If two of you agree here on
earth concerning anything you ask, my Father in
heaven will do it for you. 20For where two or three
gather together as my followers,* I am there among
them."

Parable of the Unforgiving Debtor

21Then Peter came to him and asked, "Lord, how
often should I forgive someone* who sins against
me? Seven times?"

22"No, not seven times," Jesus replied, "but seventy
times seven!*

23"Therefore, the Kingdom of Heaven can be
compared to a king who decided to bring his accounts up to date with servants who had borrowed
money from him. 24In the process, one of his debtors
was brought in who owed him millions of dollars.*

18:9 Greek *the Gehenna of fire.* **18:10** Some manuscripts add verse 11, *And the Son of Man came to save those who are lost.* Compare Luke 19:10. **18:15a** Greek *If your brother.* **18:15b** Some manuscripts do not include *against you.* **18:18a** Or *bind,* or *lock.* **18:18b** Or *loose,* or *open.* **18:20** Greek *gather together in my name.* **18:21** Greek *my brother.* **18:22** Or *seventy-seven times.* **18:24** Greek *10,000 talents* [375 tons or 340 metric tons of silver].

KING JAMES VERSION

25 But forasmuch as he had not to pay, his lord commanded him to be sold, and his wife, and children, and all that he had, and payment to be made.

26 The servant therefore fell down, and worshipped him, saying, Lord, have patience with me, and I will pay thee all.

27 Then the lord of that servant was moved with compassion, and loosed him, and forgave him the debt.

28 But the same servant went out, and found one of his fellowservants, which owed him an hundred pence: and he laid hands on him, and took *him* by the throat, saying, Pay me that thou owest.

29 And his fellowservant fell down at his feet, and besought him, saying, Have patience with me, and I will pay thee all.

30 And he would not: but went and cast him into prison, till he should pay the debt.

31 So when his fellowservants saw what was done, they were very sorry, and came and told unto their lord all that was done.

32 Then his lord, after that he had called him, said unto him, O thou wicked servant, I forgave thee all that debt, because thou desiredst me:

33 Shouldest not thou also have had compassion on thy fellowservant, even as I had pity on thee?

34 And his lord was wroth, and delivered him to the tormentors, till he should pay all that was due unto him.

35 So likewise shall my heavenly Father do also unto you, if ye from your hearts forgive not every one his brother their trespasses.

19 1 And it came to pass, *that* when Jesus had finished these sayings, he departed from Galilee, and came into the coasts of Judaea beyond Jordan;

2 And great multitudes followed him; and he healed them there.

3 The Pharisees also came unto him, tempting him, and saying unto him, Is it lawful for a man to put away his wife for every cause?

4 And he answered and said unto them, Have ye not read, that he which made *them* at the beginning made them male and female,

5 And said, For this cause shall a man leave father and mother, and shall cleave to his wife: and they twain shall be one flesh?

6 Wherefore they are no more twain, but one flesh. What therefore God hath joined together, let not man put asunder.

7 They say unto him, Why did Moses then command to give a writing of divorcement, and to put her away?

8 He saith unto them, Moses because of the hardness of your hearts suffered you to put away your wives: but from the beginning it was not so.

9 And I say unto you, Whosoever shall put away his wife, except *it be* for fornication, and shall marry

NEW LIVING TRANSLATION

25 He couldn't pay, so his master ordered that he be sold—along with his wife, his children, and everything he owned—to pay the debt.

26 "But the man fell down before his master and begged him, 'Please, be patient with me, and I will pay it all.' 27 Then his master was filled with pity for him, and he released him and forgave his debt.

28 "But when the man left the king, he went to a fellow servant who owed him a few thousand dollars.* He grabbed him by the throat and demanded instant payment.

29 "His fellow servant fell down before him and begged for a little more time. 'Be patient with me, and I will pay it,' he pleaded. 30 But his creditor wouldn't wait. He had the man arrested and put in prison until the debt could be paid in full.

31 "When some of the other servants saw this, they were very upset. They went to the king and told him everything that had happened. 32 Then the king called in the man he had forgiven and said, 'You evil servant! I forgave you that tremendous debt because you pleaded with me. 33 Shouldn't you have mercy on your fellow servant, just as I had mercy on you?' 34 Then the angry king sent the man to prison to be tortured until he had paid his entire debt.

35 "That's what my heavenly Father will do to you if you refuse to forgive your brothers and sisters* from your heart."

Discussion about Divorce and Marriage

19 When Jesus had finished saying these things, he left Galilee and went down to the region of Judea east of the Jordan River. 2 Large crowds followed him there, and he healed their sick.

3 Some Pharisees came and tried to trap him with this question: "Should a man be allowed to divorce his wife for just any reason?"

4 "Haven't you read the Scriptures?" Jesus replied. "They record that from the beginning 'God made them male and female.'* 5 And he said, 'This explains why a man leaves his father and mother and is joined to his wife, and the two are united into one.'* 6 Since they are no longer two but one, let no one split apart what God has joined together."

7 "Then why did Moses say in the law that a man could give his wife a written notice of divorce and send her away?"* they asked.

8 Jesus replied, "Moses permitted divorce only as a concession to your hard hearts, but it was not what God had originally intended. 9 And I tell you this, whoever divorces his wife and marries someone

18:28 Greek *100 denarii.* A denarius was equivalent to a laborer's full day's wage. **18:35** Greek *your brother.* **19:4** Gen 1:27; 5:2. **19:5** Gen 2:24. **19:7** See Deut 24:1.

KING JAMES VERSION

another, committeth adultery: and whoso marrieth her which is put away doth commit adultery.

10His disciples say unto him, If the case of the man be so with *his* wife, it is not good to marry.

11But he said unto them, All *men* cannot receive this saying, save *they* to whom it is given.

12For there are some eunuchs, which were so born from *their* mother's womb: and there are some eunuchs, which were made eunuchs of men: and there be eunuchs, which have made themselves eunuchs for the kingdom of heaven's sake. He that is able to receive *it*, let him receive *it*.

13Then were there brought unto him little children, that he should put *his* hands on them, and pray: and the disciples rebuked them.

14But Jesus said, Suffer little children, and forbid them not, to come unto me: for of such is the kingdom of heaven.

15And he laid *his* hands on them, and departed thence.

16And, behold, one came and said unto him, Good Master, what good thing shall I do, that I may have eternal life?

17And he said unto him, Why callest thou me good? *there is* none good but one, *that is*, God: but if thou wilt enter into life, keep the commandments.

18He saith unto him, Which? Jesus said, Thou shalt do no murder, Thou shalt not commit adultery, Thou shalt not steal, Thou shalt not bear false witness,

19Honour thy father and *thy* mother: and, Thou shalt love thy neighbour as thyself.

20The young man saith unto him, All these things have I kept from my youth up: what lack I yet?

21Jesus said unto him, If thou wilt be perfect, go *and* sell that thou hast, and give to the poor, and thou shalt have treasure in heaven: and come *and* follow me.

22But when the young man heard that saying, he went away sorrowful: for he had great possessions.

23Then said Jesus unto his disciples, Verily I say unto you, That a rich man shall hardly enter into the kingdom of heaven.

24And again I say unto you, It is easier for a camel to go through the eye of a needle, than for a rich man to enter into the kingdom of God.

25When his disciples heard *it*, they were exceedingly amazed, saying, Who then can be saved?

26But Jesus beheld *them*, and said unto them, With men this is impossible; but with God all things are possible.

NEW LIVING TRANSLATION

else commits adultery—unless his wife has been unfaithful.*"

10Jesus' disciples then said to him, "If this is the case, it is better not to marry!"

11"Not everyone can accept this statement," Jesus said. "Only those whom God helps. 12Some are born as eunuchs, some have been made eunuchs by others, and some choose not to marry* for the sake of the Kingdom of Heaven. Let anyone accept this who can."

Jesus Blesses the Children

13One day some parents brought their children to Jesus so he could lay his hands on them and pray for them. But the disciples scolded the parents for bothering him.

14But Jesus said, "Let the children come to me. Don't stop them! For the Kingdom of Heaven belongs to those who are like these children." 15And he placed his hands on their heads and blessed them before he left.

The Rich Man

16Someone came to Jesus with this question: "Teacher,* what good deed must I do to have eternal life?"

17"Why ask me about what is good?" Jesus replied. "There is only One who is good. But to answer your question—if you want to receive eternal life, keep* the commandments."

18"Which ones?" the man asked.

And Jesus replied: "'You must not murder. You must not commit adultery. You must not steal. You must not testify falsely. 19Honor your father and mother. Love your neighbor as yourself.'*"

20"I've obeyed all these commandments," the young man replied. "What else must I do?"

21Jesus told him, "If you want to be perfect, go and sell all your possessions and give the money to the poor, and you will have treasure in heaven. Then come, follow me."

22But when the young man heard this, he went away sad, for he had many possessions.

23Then Jesus said to his disciples, "I tell you the truth, it is very hard for a rich person to enter the Kingdom of Heaven. 24I'll say it again—it is easier for a camel to go through the eye of a needle than for a rich person to enter the Kingdom of God!"

25The disciples were astounded. "Then who in the world can be saved?" they asked.

26Jesus looked at them intently and said, "Humanly speaking, it is impossible. But with God everything is possible."

19:9 Some manuscripts add *And anyone who marries a divorced woman commits adultery.* Compare Matt 5:32. **19:12** Greek *and some make themselves eunuchs.* **19:16** Some manuscripts read *Good Teacher.* **19:17** Some manuscripts read *continue to keep.* **19:18-19** Exod 20:12-16; Deut 5:16-20; Lev 19:18.

KING JAMES VERSION

27 Then answered Peter and said unto him, Behold,
we have forsaken all, and followed thee; what shall
we have therefore?
28 And Jesus said unto them, Verily I say unto you,
That ye which have followed me, in the regeneration
when the Son of man shall sit in the throne of his
glory, ye also shall sit upon twelve thrones, judging
the twelve tribes of Israel.
29 And every one that hath forsaken houses, or
brethren, or sisters, or father, or mother, or wife, or
children, or lands, for my name's sake, shall receive
an hundredfold, and shall inherit everlasting life.
30 But many *that are* first shall be last; and the last
shall be first.

20 1 For the kingdom of heaven is like unto
a man *that is* an householder, which went
out early in the morning to hire labourers into his
vineyard.
2 And when he had agreed with the labourers for
a penny a day, he sent them into his vineyard.
3 And he went out about the third hour, and saw
others standing idle in the marketplace,
4 And said unto them; Go ye also into the vineyard,
and whatsoever is right I will give you. And they went
their way.
5 Again he went out about the sixth and ninth hour,
and did likewise.
6 And about the eleventh hour he went out, and
found others standing idle, and saith unto them,
Why stand ye here all the day idle?
7 They say unto him, Because no man hath hired
us. He saith unto them, Go ye also into the vineyard;
and whatsoever is right, *that* shall ye receive.
8 So when even was come, the lord of the vineyard
saith unto his steward, Call the labourers, and give
them *their* hire, beginning from the last unto the
first.
9 And when they came that *were hired* about the
eleventh hour, they received every man a penny.
10 But when the first came, they supposed that they
should have received more; and they likewise received every man a penny.
11 And when they had received *it*, they murmured
against the goodman of the house,
12 Saying, These last have wrought *but* one hour,
and thou hast made them equal unto us, which have
borne the burden and heat of the day.
13 But he answered one of them, and said, Friend, I
do thee no wrong: didst not thou agree with me for
a penny?
14 Take *that* thine *is*, and go thy way: I will give
unto this last, even as unto thee.
15 Is it not lawful for me to do what I will with mine
own? Is thine eye evil, because I am good?
16 So the last shall be first, and the first last: for
many be called, but few chosen.

NEW LIVING TRANSLATION

27 Then Peter said to him, "We've given up everything to follow you. What will we get?"
28 Jesus replied, "I assure you that when the world
is made new* and the Son of Man* sits upon his glorious throne, you who have been my followers will
also sit on twelve thrones, judging the twelve tribes
of Israel. 29 And everyone who has given up houses or
brothers or sisters or father or mother or children or
property, for my sake, will receive a hundred times as
much in return and will inherit eternal life. 30 But
many who are the greatest now will be least important then, and those who seem least important now
will be the greatest then.*

Parable of the Vineyard Workers

20 "For the Kingdom of Heaven is like the
landowner who went out early one morn-
ing to hire workers for his vineyard. 2 He agreed to
pay the normal daily wage* and sent them out to
work.
3 "At nine o'clock in the morning he was passing
through the marketplace and saw some people
standing around doing nothing. 4 So he hired them,
telling them he would pay them whatever was right
at the end of the day. 5 So they went to work in the
vineyard. At noon and again at three o'clock he did
the same thing.
6 "At five o'clock that afternoon he was in town
again and saw some more people standing around.
He asked them, 'Why haven't you been working
today?'
7 "They replied, 'Because no one hired us.'
"The landowner told them, 'Then go out and join
the others in my vineyard.'
8 "That evening he told the foreman to call the
workers in and pay them, beginning with the last
workers first. 9 When those hired at five o'clock were
paid, each received a full day's wage. 10 When those
hired first came to get their pay, they assumed they
would receive more. But they, too, were paid a day's
wage. 11 When they received their pay, they protested
to the owner, 12 'Those people worked only one hour,
and yet you've paid them just as much as you paid us
who worked all day in the scorching heat.'
13 "He answered one of them, 'Friend, I haven't
been unfair! Didn't you agree to work all day for the
usual wage? 14 Take your money and go. I wanted to
pay this last worker the same as you. 15 Is it against
the law for me to do what I want with my money?
Should you be jealous because I am kind to others?'
16 "So those who are last now will be first then, and
those who are first will be last."

19:28a Or *in the regeneration.* **19:28b** "Son of Man" is a title Jesus used for himself. **19:30** Greek *But many who are first will be last; and the last, first.* **20:2** Greek *a denarius,* the payment for a full day's labor; similarly in 20:9, 10, 13.

KING JAMES VERSION

17 And Jesus going up to Jerusalem took the twelve disciples apart in the way, and said unto them,

18 Behold, we go up to Jerusalem; and the Son of man shall be betrayed unto the chief priests and unto the scribes, and they shall condemn him to death,

19 And shall deliver him to the Gentiles to mock, and to scourge, and to crucify *him:* and the third day he shall rise again.

20 Then came to him the mother of Zebedee's children with her sons, worshipping *him,* and desiring a certain thing of him.

21 And he said unto her, What wilt thou? She saith unto him, Grant that these my two sons may sit, the one on thy right hand, and the other on the left, in thy kingdom.

22 But Jesus answered and said, Ye know not what ye ask. Are ye able to drink of the cup that I shall drink of, and to be baptized with the baptism that I am baptized with? They say unto him, We are able.

23 And he saith unto them, Ye shall drink indeed of my cup, and be baptized with the baptism that I am baptized with: but to sit on my right hand, and on my left, is not mine to give, but *it shall be given to them* for whom it is prepared of my Father.

24 And when the ten heard *it,* they were moved with indignation against the two brethren.

25 But Jesus called them *unto him,* and said, Ye know that the princes of the Gentiles exercise dominion over them, and they that are great exercise authority upon them.

26 But it shall not be so among you: but whosoever will be great among you, let him be your minister;

27 And whosoever will be chief among you, let him be your servant:

28 Even as the Son of man came not to be ministered unto, but to minister, and to give his life a ransom for many.

29 And as they departed from Jericho, a great multitude followed him.

30 And, behold, two blind men sitting by the way side, when they heard that Jesus passed by, cried out, saying, Have mercy on us, O Lord, *thou* son of David.

31 And the multitude rebuked them, because they should hold their peace: but they cried the more, saying, Have mercy on us, O Lord, *thou* son of David.

32 And Jesus stood still, and called them, and said, What will ye that I shall do unto you?

33 They say unto him, Lord, that our eyes may be opened.

34 So Jesus had compassion *on them,* and touched their eyes: and immediately their eyes received sight, and they followed him.

NEW LIVING TRANSLATION

Jesus Again Predicts His Death

17 As Jesus was going up to Jerusalem, he took the twelve disciples aside privately and told them what was going to happen to him. 18 "Listen," he said, "we're going up to Jerusalem, where the Son of Man* will be betrayed to the leading priests and the teachers of religious law. They will sentence him to die. 19 Then they will hand him over to the Romans* to be mocked, flogged with a whip, and crucified. But on the third day he will be raised from the dead."

Jesus Teaches about Serving Others

20 Then the mother of James and John, the sons of Zebedee, came to Jesus with her sons. She knelt respectfully to ask a favor. 21 "What is your request?" he asked.

She replied, "In your Kingdom, please let my two sons sit in places of honor next to you, one on your right and the other on your left."

22 But Jesus answered by saying to them, "You don't know what you are asking! Are you able to drink from the bitter cup of suffering I am about to drink?"

"Oh yes," they replied, "we are able!"

23 Jesus told them, "You will indeed drink from my bitter cup. But I have no right to say who will sit on my right or my left. My Father has prepared those places for the ones he has chosen."

24 When the ten other disciples heard what James and John had asked, they were indignant. 25 But Jesus called them together and said, "You know that the rulers in this world lord it over their people, and officials flaunt their authority over those under them. 26 But among you it will be different. Whoever wants to be a leader among you must be your servant, 27 and whoever wants to be first among you must become your slave. 28 For even the Son of Man came not to be served but to serve others and to give his life as a ransom for many."

Jesus Heals Two Blind Men

29 As Jesus and the disciples left the town of Jericho, a large crowd followed behind. 30 Two blind men were sitting beside the road. When they heard that Jesus was coming that way, they began shouting, "Lord, Son of David, have mercy on us!"

31 "Be quiet!" the crowd yelled at them.

But they only shouted louder, "Lord, Son of David, have mercy on us!"

32 When Jesus heard them, he stopped and called, "What do you want me to do for you?"

33 "Lord," they said, "we want to see!" 34 Jesus felt sorry for them and touched their eyes. Instantly they could see! Then they followed him.

20:18 "Son of Man" is a title Jesus used for himself. **20:19** Greek *the Gentiles.*

KING JAMES VERSION

21 1 And when they drew nigh unto Jerusalem, and were come to Bethphage, unto the mount of Olives, then sent Jesus two disciples,

2 Saying unto them, Go into the village over against you, and straightway ye shall find an ass tied, and a colt with her: loose *them,* and bring *them* unto me.

3 And if any *man* say aught unto you, ye shall say, The Lord hath need of them; and straightway he will send them.

4 All this was done, that it might be fulfilled which was spoken by the prophet, saying,

5 Tell ye the daughter of Sion, Behold, thy King cometh unto thee, meek, and sitting upon an ass, and a colt the foal of an ass.

6 And the disciples went, and did as Jesus commanded them,

7 And brought the ass, and the colt, and put on them their clothes, and they set *him* thereon.

8 And a very great multitude spread their garments in the way; others cut down branches from the trees, and strawed *them* in the way.

9 And the multitudes that went before, and that followed, cried, saying, Hosanna to the son of David: Blessed *is* he that cometh in the name of the Lord; Hosanna in the highest.

10 And when he was come into Jerusalem, all the city was moved, saying, Who is this?

11 And the multitude said, This is Jesus the prophet of Nazareth of Galilee.

12 And Jesus went into the temple of God, and cast out all them that sold and bought in the temple, and overthrew the tables of the moneychangers, and the seats of them that sold doves,

13 And said unto them, It is written, My house shall be called the house of prayer; but ye have made it a den of thieves.

14 And the blind and the lame came to him in the temple; and he healed them.

15 And when the chief priests and scribes saw the wonderful things that he did, and the children crying in the temple, and saying, Hosanna to the son of David; they were sore displeased,

16 And said unto him, Hearest thou what these say? And Jesus saith unto them, Yea; have ye never read, Out of the mouth of babes and sucklings thou hast perfected praise?

17 And he left them, and went out of the city into Bethany; and he lodged there.

NEW LIVING TRANSLATION

Jesus' Triumphant Entry

21 As Jesus and the disciples approached Jerusalem, they came to the town of Bethphage
on the Mount of Olives. Jesus sent two of them on
ahead. 2 "Go into the village over there," he said. "As
soon as you enter it, you will see a donkey tied there,
with its colt beside it. Untie them and bring them to
me. 3 If anyone asks what you are doing, just say, 'The
Lord needs them,' and he will immediately let you
take them."

4 This took place to fulfill the prophecy that said,

5 "Tell the people of Jerusalem,*
'Look, your King is coming to you.
He is humble, riding on a donkey—
riding on a donkey's colt.'"*

6 The two disciples did as Jesus commanded.
7 They brought the donkey and the colt to him and
threw their garments over the colt, and he sat on it.*
8 Most of the crowd spread their garments on the
road ahead of him, and others cut branches from the
trees and spread them on the road. 9 Jesus was in
the center of the procession, and the people all
around him were shouting,

"Praise God* for the Son of David!
Blessings on the one who comes in the
name of the LORD!
Praise God in highest heaven!"*

10 The entire city of Jerusalem was in an uproar as
he entered. "Who is this?" they asked.

11 And the crowds replied, "It's Jesus, the prophet
from Nazareth in Galilee."

Jesus Clears the Temple

12 Jesus entered the Temple and began to drive out all
the people buying and selling animals for sacrifice.
He knocked over the tables of the money changers
and the chairs of those selling doves. 13 He said to
them, "The Scriptures declare, 'My Temple will be
called a house of prayer,' but you have turned it into
a den of thieves!"*

14 The blind and the lame came to him in the
Temple, and he healed them. 15 The leading priests
and the teachers of religious law saw these wonder-
ful miracles and heard even the children in the
Temple shouting, "Praise God for the Son of David."
But the leaders were indignant. 16 They asked
Jesus, "Do you hear what these children are saying?"
"Yes," Jesus replied. "Haven't you ever read the
Scriptures? For they say, 'You have taught children
and infants to give you praise.'*" 17 Then he returned
to Bethany, where he stayed overnight.

21:5a Greek *Tell the daughter of Zion.* Isa 62:11. **21:5b** Zech 9:9. **21:7** Greek *over them, and he sat on them.* **21:9a** Greek *Hosanna,* an exclamation of praise that literally means "save now"; also in 21:9b, 15. **21:9b** Pss 118:25-26; 148:1. **21:13** Isa 56:7; Jer 7:11. **21:16** Ps 8:2.

KING JAMES VERSION

18Now in the morning as he returned into the city,
he hungered.
19And when he saw a fig tree in the way, he came to
it, and found nothing thereon, but leaves only, and
said unto it, Let no fruit grow on thee henceforward
for ever. And presently the fig tree withered away.
20And when the disciples saw *it,* they marvelled,
saying, How soon is the fig tree withered away!
21Jesus answered and said unto them, Verily I say
unto you, If ye have faith, and doubt not, ye shall not
only do this *which is done* to the fig tree, but also if ye
shall say unto this mountain, Be thou removed, and
be thou cast into the sea; it shall be done.
22And all things, whatsoever ye shall ask in prayer,
believing, ye shall receive.

23And when he was come into the temple, the
chief priests and the elders of the people came unto
him as he was teaching, and said, By what authority
doest thou these things? and who gave thee this
authority?
24And Jesus answered and said unto them, I also
will ask you one thing, which if ye tell me, I in like
wise will tell you by what authority I do these things.
25The baptism of John, whence was it? from
heaven, or of men? And they reasoned with themselves, saying, If we shall say, From heaven; he will say
unto us, Why did ye not then believe him?
26But if we shall say, Of men; we fear the people;
for all hold John as a prophet.
27And they answered Jesus, and said, We cannot
tell. And he said unto them, Neither tell I you by what
authority I do these things.
28But what think ye? A *certain* man had two sons;
and he came to the first, and said, Son, go work today
in my vineyard.
29He answered and said, I will not: but afterward
he repented, and went.
30And he came to the second, and said likewise.
And he answered and said, I *go,* sir: and went not.
31Whether of them twain did the will of *his* father? They say unto him, The first. Jesus saith unto
them, Verily I say unto you, That the publicans and
the harlots go into the kingdom of God before you.
32For John came unto you in the way of righteousness, and ye believed him not: but the publicans and
the harlots believed him: and ye, when ye had seen *it,*
repented not afterward, that ye might believe him.

33Hear another parable: There was a certain
householder, which planted a vineyard, and hedged
it round about, and digged a winepress in it, and built
a tower, and let it out to husbandmen, and went into
a far country:

NEW LIVING TRANSLATION

Jesus Curses the Fig Tree

18In the morning, as Jesus was returning to Jerusalem, he was hungry, 19and he noticed a fig tree beside
the road. He went over to see if there were any figs,
but there were only leaves. Then he said to it, "May
you never bear fruit again!" And immediately the fig
tree withered up.
20The disciples were amazed when they saw this
and asked, "How did the fig tree wither so quickly?"
21Then Jesus told them, "I tell you the truth, if you
have faith and don't doubt, you can do things like
this and much more. You can even say to this mountain, 'May you be lifted up and thrown into the sea,'
and it will happen. 22You can pray for anything, and
if you have faith, you will receive it."

The Authority of Jesus Challenged

23When Jesus returned to the Temple and began
teaching, the leading priests and elders came up to
him. They demanded, "By what authority are you
doing all these things? Who gave you the right?"
24"I'll tell you by what authority I do these things
if you answer one question," Jesus replied. 25"Did
John's authority to baptize come from heaven, or
was it merely human?"
They talked it over among themselves. "If we say it
was from heaven, he will ask us why we didn't believe
John. 26But if we say it was merely human, we'll be
mobbed because the people believe John was a
prophet." 27So they finally replied, "We don't know."
And Jesus responded, "Then I won't tell you by
what authority I do these things.

Parable of the Two Sons

28"But what do you think about this? A man with two
sons told the older boy, 'Son, go out and work in the
vineyard today.' 29The son answered, 'No, I won't go,'
but later he changed his mind and went anyway.
30Then the father told the other son, 'You go,' and he
said, 'Yes, sir, I will.' But he didn't go.
31"Which of the two obeyed his father?"
They replied, "The first."*
Then Jesus explained his meaning: "I tell you the
truth, corrupt tax collectors and prostitutes will get
into the Kingdom of God before you do. 32For John the
Baptist came and showed you the right way to live, but
you didn't believe him, while tax collectors and prostitutes did. And even when you saw this happening, you
refused to believe him and repent of your sins.

Parable of the Evil Farmers

33"Now listen to another story. A certain landowner
planted a vineyard, built a wall around it, dug a pit
for pressing out the grape juice, and built a lookout
tower. Then he leased the vineyard to tenant farmers

21:29-31 Other manuscripts read *"The second."* In still other manuscripts the first son says "Yes" but does nothing, the second son says "No" but then repents and goes, and the answer to Jesus' question is that the second son obeyed his father.

KING JAMES VERSION

34 And when the time of the fruit drew near, he sent his servants to the husbandmen, that they might receive the fruits of it.

35 And the husbandmen took his servants, and beat one, and killed another, and stoned another.

36 Again, he sent other servants more than the first: and they did unto them likewise.

37 But last of all he sent unto them his son, saying, They will reverence my son.

38 But when the husbandmen saw the son, they said among themselves, This is the heir; come, let us kill him, and let us seize on his inheritance.

39 And they caught him, and cast *him* out of the vineyard, and slew *him*.

40 When the lord therefore of the vineyard cometh, what will he do unto those husbandmen?

41 They say unto him, He will miserably destroy those wicked men, and will let out *his* vineyard unto other husbandmen, which shall render him the fruits in their seasons.

42 Jesus saith unto them, Did ye never read in the scriptures, The stone which the builders rejected, the same is become the head of the corner: this is the Lord's doing, and it is marvellous in our eyes?

43 Therefore say I unto you, The kingdom of God shall be taken from you, and given to a nation bringing forth the fruits thereof.

44 And whosoever shall fall on this stone shall be broken: but on whomsoever it shall fall, it will grind him to powder.

45 And when the chief priests and Pharisees had heard his parables, they perceived that he spake of them.

46 But when they sought to lay hands on him, they feared the multitude, because they took him for a prophet.

22 1 And Jesus answered and spake unto them again by parables, and said,

2 The kingdom of heaven is like unto a certain king, which made a marriage for his son,

3 And sent forth his servants to call them that were bidden to the wedding: and they would not come.

4 Again, he sent forth other servants, saying, Tell them which are bidden, Behold, I have prepared my dinner: my oxen and *my* fatlings *are* killed, and all things *are* ready: come unto the marriage.

5 But they made light of *it*, and went their ways, one to his farm, another to his merchandise:

6 And the remnant took his servants, and entreated *them* spitefully, and slew *them*.

7 But when the king heard *thereof*, he was wroth: and he sent forth his armies, and destroyed those murderers, and burned up their city.

8 Then saith he to his servants, The wedding is ready, but they which were bidden were not worthy.

NEW LIVING TRANSLATION

and moved to another country. 34 At the time of the
grape harvest, he sent his servants to collect his
share of the crop. 35 But the farmers grabbed his servants, beat one, killed one, and stoned another. 36 So
the landowner sent a larger group of his servants to
collect for him, but the results were the same.

37 "Finally, the owner sent his son, thinking, 'Surely
they will respect my son.'

38 "But when the tenant farmers saw his son coming, they said to one another, 'Here comes the heir to
this estate. Come on, let's kill him and get the estate
for ourselves!' 39 So they grabbed him, dragged him
out of the vineyard, and murdered him.

40 "When the owner of the vineyard returns,"
Jesus asked, "what do you think he will do to those
farmers?"

41 The religious leaders replied, "He will put the
wicked men to a horrible death and lease the vineyard to others who will give him his share of the crop
after each harvest."

42 Then Jesus asked them, "Didn't you ever read
this in the Scriptures?

'The stone that the builders rejected
has now become the cornerstone.
This is the LORD's doing,
and it is wonderful to see.'*

43 I tell you, the Kingdom of God will be taken away
from you and given to a nation that will produce the
proper fruit. 44 Anyone who stumbles over that stone
will be broken to pieces, and it will crush anyone it
falls on.*"

45 When the leading priests and Pharisees heard
this parable, they realized he was telling the story
against them—they were the wicked farmers. 46 They
wanted to arrest him, but they were afraid of the
crowds, who considered Jesus to be a prophet.

Parable of the Great Feast

22 Jesus also told them other parables. He
said, 2 "The Kingdom of Heaven can be illustrated by the story of a king who prepared a great
wedding feast for his son. 3 When the banquet was
ready, he sent his servants to notify those who were
invited. But they all refused to come!

4 "So he sent other servants to tell them, 'The feast
has been prepared. The bulls and fattened cattle
have been killed, and everything is ready. Come to
the banquet!' 5 But the guests he had invited ignored
them and went their own way, one to his farm, another to his business. 6 Others seized his messengers
and insulted them and killed them.

7 "The king was furious, and he sent out his army
to destroy the murderers and burn their town. 8 And
he said to his servants, 'The wedding feast is ready,
and the guests I invited aren't worthy of the honor.

21:42 Ps 118:22-23. **21:44** This verse is not included in some early manuscripts. Compare Luke 20:18.

KING JAMES VERSION

9 Go ye therefore into the highways, and as many as ye shall find, bid to the marriage.

10 So those servants went out into the highways, and gathered together all as many as they found, both bad and good: and the wedding was furnished with guests.

11 And when the king came in to see the guests, he saw there a man which had not on a wedding garment:

12 And he saith unto him, Friend, how camest thou in hither not having a wedding garment? And he was speechless.

13 Then said the king to the servants, Bind him hand and foot, and take him away, and cast *him* into outer darkness; there shall be weeping and gnashing of teeth.

14 For many are called, but few *are* chosen.

15 Then went the Pharisees, and took counsel how they might entangle him in *his* talk.

16 And they sent out unto him their disciples with the Herodians, saying, Master, we know that thou art true, and teachest the way of God in truth, neither carest thou for any *man:* for thou regardest not the person of men.

17 Tell us therefore, What thinkest thou? Is it lawful to give tribute unto Caesar, or not?

18 But Jesus perceived their wickedness, and said, Why tempt ye me, *ye* hypocrites?

19 Shew me the tribute money. And they brought unto him a penny.

20 And he saith unto them, Whose *is* this image and superscription?

21 They say unto him, Caesar's. Then saith he unto them, Render therefore unto Caesar the things which are Caesar's; and unto God the things that are God's.

22 When they had heard *these words,* they marvelled, and left him, and went their way.

23 The same day came to him the Sadducees, which say that there is no resurrection, and asked him,

24 Saying, Master, Moses said, If a man die, having no children, his brother shall marry his wife, and raise up seed unto his brother.

25 Now there were with us seven brethren: and the first, when he had married a wife, deceased, and, having no issue, left his wife unto his brother:

26 Likewise the second also, and the third, unto the seventh.

27 And last of all the woman died also.

28 Therefore in the resurrection whose wife shall she be of the seven? for they all had her.

29 Jesus answered and said unto them, Ye do err, not knowing the scriptures, nor the power of God.

30 For in the resurrection they neither marry, nor are given in marriage, but are as the angels of God in heaven.

NEW LIVING TRANSLATION

9 Now go out to the street corners and invite everyone
you see.' 10 So the servants brought in everyone they
could find, good and bad alike, and the banquet hall
was filled with guests.

11 "But when the king came in to meet the guests,
he noticed a man who wasn't wearing the proper
clothes for a wedding. 12 'Friend,' he asked, 'how is it
that you are here without wedding clothes?' But the
man had no reply. 13 Then the king said to his aides,
'Bind his hands and feet and throw him into the
outer darkness, where there will be weeping and
gnashing of teeth.'

14 "For many are called, but few are chosen."

Taxes for Caesar

15 Then the Pharisees met together to plot how to
trap Jesus into saying something for which he could
be arrested. 16 They sent some of their disciples,
along with the supporters of Herod, to meet with
him. "Teacher," they said, "we know how honest you
are. You teach the way of God truthfully. You are impartial
and don't play favorites. 17 Now tell us what
you think about this: Is it right to pay taxes to Caesar
or not?"

18 But Jesus knew their evil motives. "You hypocrites!"
he said. "Why are you trying to trap me?
19 Here, show me the coin used for the tax." When
they handed him a Roman coin,* 20 he asked,
"Whose picture and title are stamped on it?"

21 "Caesar's," they replied.

"Well, then," he said, "give to Caesar what belongs
to Caesar, and give to God what belongs to God."

22 His reply amazed them, and they went away.

Discussion about Resurrection

23 That same day Jesus was approached by some Sadducees—religious
leaders who say there is no resurrection
from the dead. They posed this question:
24 "Teacher, Moses said, 'If a man dies without children,
his brother should marry the widow and have a
child who will carry on the brother's name.'* 25 Well,
suppose there were seven brothers. The oldest one
married and then died without children, so his
brother married the widow. 26 But the second
brother also died, and the third brother married her.
This continued with all seven of them. 27 Last of all,
the woman also died. 28 So tell us, whose wife will she
be in the resurrection? For all seven were married
to her."

29 Jesus replied, "Your mistake is that you don't
know the Scriptures, and you don't know the power
of God. 30 For when the dead rise, they will neither
marry nor be given in marriage. In this respect they
will be like the angels in heaven.

22:19 Greek *a denarius.* **22:24** Deut 25:5-6.

KING JAMES VERSION

31 But as touching the resurrection of the dead, have ye not read that which was spoken unto you by God, saying,

32 I am the God of Abraham, and the God of Isaac, and the God of Jacob? God is not the God of the dead, but of the living.

33 And when the multitude heard *this,* they were astonished at his doctrine.

34 But when the Pharisees had heard that he had put the Sadducees to silence, they were gathered together.

35 Then one of them, *which was* a lawyer, asked *him a question,* tempting him, and saying,

36 Master, which *is* the great commandment in the law?

37 Jesus said unto him, Thou shalt love the Lord thy God with all thy heart, and with all thy soul, and with all thy mind.

38 This is the first and great commandment.

39 And the second *is* like unto it, Thou shalt love thy neighbour as thyself.

40 On these two commandments hang all the law and the prophets.

41 While the Pharisees were gathered together, Jesus asked them,

42 Saying, What think ye of Christ? whose son is he? They say unto him, *The son* of David.

43 He saith unto them, How then doth David in spirit call him Lord, saying,

44 The LORD said unto my Lord, Sit thou on my right hand, till I make thine enemies thy footstool?

45 If David then call him Lord, how is he his son?

46 And no man was able to answer him a word, neither durst any *man* from that day forth ask him any more *questions.*

23 1 Then spake Jesus to the multitude, and to his disciples,

2 Saying, The scribes and the Pharisees sit in Moses' seat:

3 All therefore whatsoever they bid you observe, *that* observe and do; but do not ye after their works: for they say, and do not.

4 For they bind heavy burdens and grievous to be borne, and lay *them* on men's shoulders; but they *themselves* will not move them with one of their fingers.

5 But all their works they do for to be seen of men: they make broad their phylacteries, and enlarge the borders of their garments,

NEW LIVING TRANSLATION

31 "But now, as to whether there will be a resurrection of the dead—haven't you ever read about this in
the Scriptures? Long after Abraham, Isaac, and Jacob
had died, God said,* 32 'I am the God of Abraham,
the God of Isaac, and the God of Jacob.'* So he is the
God of the living, not the dead."
33 When the crowds heard him, they were astounded at his teaching.

The Most Important Commandment

34 But when the Pharisees heard that he had silenced
the Sadducees with his reply, they met together to
question him again. 35 One of them, an expert in religious law, tried to trap him with this question:
36 "Teacher, which is the most important commandment in the law of Moses?"
37 Jesus replied, "'You must love the LORD your
God with all your heart, all your soul, and all your
mind.'* 38 This is the first and greatest commandment. 39 A second is equally important: 'Love your
neighbor as yourself.'* 40 The entire law and all the
demands of the prophets are based on these two
commandments."

Whose Son Is the Messiah?

41 Then, surrounded by the Pharisees, Jesus asked
them a question: 42 "What do you think about the
Messiah? Whose son is he?"
They replied, "He is the son of David."
43 Jesus responded, "Then why does David, speaking under the inspiration of the Spirit, call the
Messiah 'my Lord'? For David said,

44 'The LORD said to my Lord,
Sit in the place of honor at my right hand
until I humble your enemies beneath
your feet.'*

45 Since David called the Messiah 'my Lord,' how can
the Messiah be his son?"
46 No one could answer him. And after that, no one
dared to ask him any more questions.

Jesus Criticizes the Religious Leaders

23 Then Jesus said to the crowds and to his
disciples, 2 "The teachers of religious law
and the Pharisees are the official interpreters of the
law of Moses.* 3 So practice and obey whatever they
tell you, but don't follow their example. For they
don't practice what they teach. 4 They crush people
with unbearable religious demands and never lift a
finger to ease the burden.
5 "Everything they do is for show. On their arms
they wear extra wide prayer boxes with Scripture
verses inside, and they wear robes with extra long

22:31 Greek *read about this? God said.* 22:32 Exod 3:6. 22:37 Deut 6:5. 22:39 Lev 19:18. 22:44 Ps 110:1. 23:2 Greek *and the Pharisees sit in the seat of Moses.*

KING JAMES VERSION

6 And love the uppermost rooms at feasts, and the chief seats in the synagogues,

7 And greetings in the markets, and to be called of men, Rabbi, Rabbi.

8 But be not ye called Rabbi: for one is your Master, *even* Christ; and all ye are brethren.

9 And call no *man* your father upon the earth: for one is your Father, which is in heaven.

10 Neither be ye called masters: for one is your Master, *even* Christ.

11 But he that is greatest among you shall be your servant.

12 And whosoever shall exalt himself shall be abased; and he that shall humble himself shall be exalted.

13 But woe unto you, scribes and Pharisees, hypocrites! for ye shut up the kingdom of heaven against men: for ye neither go in *yourselves,* neither suffer ye them that are entering to go in.

14 Woe unto you, scribes and Pharisees, hypocrites! for ye devour widows' houses, and for a pretence make long prayer: therefore ye shall receive the greater damnation.

15 Woe unto you, scribes and Pharisees, hypocrites! for ye compass sea and land to make one proselyte, and when he is made, ye make him twofold more the child of hell than yourselves.

16 Woe unto you, *ye* blind guides, which say, Whosoever shall swear by the temple, it is nothing; but whosoever shall swear by the gold of the temple, he is a debtor!

17 *Ye* fools and blind: for whether is greater, the gold, or the temple that sanctifieth the gold?

18 And, Whosoever shall swear by the altar, it is nothing; but whosoever sweareth by the gift that is upon it, he is guilty.

19 *Ye* fools and blind: for whether *is* greater, the gift, or the altar that sanctifieth the gift?

20 Whoso therefore shall swear by the altar, sweareth by it, and by all things thereon.

21 And whoso shall swear by the temple, sweareth by it, and by him that dwelleth therein.

22 And he that shall swear by heaven, sweareth by the throne of God, and by him that sitteth thereon.

23 Woe unto you, scribes and Pharisees, hypocrites! for ye pay tithe of mint and anise and cummin, and have omitted the weightier *matters* of the law, judgment, mercy, and faith: these ought ye to have done, and not to leave the other undone.

24 *Ye* blind guides, which strain at a gnat, and swallow a camel.

25 Woe unto you, scribes and Pharisees, hypocrites! for ye make clean the outside of the cup and of the platter, but within they are full of extortion and excess.

NEW LIVING TRANSLATION

tassels.* 6 And they love to sit at the head table at banquets and in the seats of honor in the synagogues. 7 They love to receive respectful greetings as they walk in the marketplaces, and to be called 'Rabbi.'*

8 "Don't let anyone call you 'Rabbi,' for you have only one teacher, and all of you are equal as brothers and sisters.* 9 And don't address anyone here on earth as 'Father,' for only God in heaven is your spiritual Father. 10 And don't let anyone call you 'Teacher,' for you have only one teacher, the Messiah. 11 The greatest among you must be a servant. 12 But those who exalt themselves will be humbled, and those who humble themselves will be exalted.

13 "What sorrow awaits you teachers of religious law and you Pharisees. Hypocrites! For you shut the door of the Kingdom of Heaven in people's faces. You won't go in yourselves, and you don't let others enter either.*

15 "What sorrow awaits you teachers of religious law and you Pharisees. Hypocrites! For you cross land and sea to make one convert, and then you turn that person into twice the child of hell* you yourselves are!

16 "Blind guides! What sorrow awaits you! For you say that it means nothing to swear 'by God's Temple,' but that it is binding to swear 'by the gold in the Temple.' 17 Blind fools! Which is more important—the gold or the Temple that makes the gold sacred? 18 And you say that to swear 'by the altar' is not binding, but to swear 'by the gifts on the altar' is binding. 19 How blind! For which is more important—the gift on the altar or the altar that makes the gift sacred? 20 When you swear 'by the altar,' you are swearing by it and by everything on it. 21 And when you swear 'by the Temple,' you are swearing by it and by God, who lives in it. 22 And when you swear 'by heaven,' you are swearing by the throne of God and by God, who sits on the throne.

23 "What sorrow awaits you teachers of religious law and you Pharisees. Hypocrites! For you are careful to tithe even the tiniest income from your herb gardens,* but you ignore the more important aspects of the law—justice, mercy, and faith. You should tithe, yes, but do not neglect the more important things. 24 Blind guides! You strain your water so you won't accidentally swallow a gnat, but you swallow a camel!*

25 "What sorrow awaits you teachers of religious law and you Pharisees. Hypocrites! For you are so careful to clean the outside of the cup and the dish, but inside you are filthy—full of greed and

23:5 Greek *They enlarge their phylacteries and lengthen their tassels.* **23:7** *Rabbi,* from Aramaic, means "master" or "teacher." **23:8** Greek *brothers.* **23:13** Some manuscripts add verse 14, *What sorrow awaits you teachers of religious law and you Pharisees. Hypocrites! You shamelessly cheat widows out of their property and then pretend to be pious by making long prayers in public. Because of this, you will be severely punished.* Compare Mark 12:40 and Luke 20:47. **23:15** Greek *of Gehenna;* also in 23:33. **23:23** Greek *tithe the mint, the dill, and the cumin.* **23:24** See Lev 11:4, 23, where gnats and camels are both forbidden as food.

KING JAMES VERSION

26 *Thou* blind Pharisee, cleanse first that *which is* within the cup and platter, that the outside of them may be clean also.

27 Woe unto you, scribes and Pharisees, hypocrites! for ye are like unto whited sepulchres, which indeed appear beautiful outward, but are within full of dead *men's* bones, and of all uncleanness.

28 Even so ye also outwardly appear righteous unto men, but within ye are full of hypocrisy and iniquity.

29 Woe unto you, scribes and Pharisees, hypocrites! because ye build the tombs of the prophets, and garnish the sepulchres of the righteous,

30 And say, If we had been in the days of our fathers, we would not have been partakers with them in the blood of the prophets.

31 Wherefore ye be witnesses unto yourselves, that ye are the children of them which killed the prophets.

32 Fill ye up then the measure of your fathers.

33 *Ye* serpents, *ye* generation of vipers, how can ye escape the damnation of hell?

34 Wherefore, behold, I send unto you prophets, and wise men, and scribes: and *some* of them ye shall kill and crucify; and *some* of them shall ye scourge in your synagogues, and persecute *them* from city to city:

35 That upon you may come all the righteous blood shed upon the earth, from the blood of righteous Abel unto the blood of Zacharias son of Barachias, whom ye slew between the temple and the altar.

36 Verily I say unto you, All these things shall come upon this generation.

37 O Jerusalem, Jerusalem, *thou* that killest the prophets, and stonest them which are sent unto thee, how often would I have gathered thy children together, even as a hen gathereth her chickens under *her* wings, and ye would not!

38 Behold, your house is left unto you desolate.

39 For I say unto you, Ye shall not see me henceforth, till ye shall say, Blessed *is* he that cometh in the name of the Lord.

24 1 And Jesus went out, and departed from the temple: and his disciples came to *him* for to shew him the buildings of the temple.

2 And Jesus said unto them, See ye not all these things? verily I say unto you, There shall not be left here one stone upon another, that shall not be thrown down.

3 And as he sat upon the mount of Olives, the disciples came unto him privately, saying, Tell us, when shall these things be? and what *shall be* the sign of thy coming, and of the end of the world?

4 And Jesus answered and said unto them, Take heed that no man deceive you.

NEW LIVING TRANSLATION

self-indulgence! 26 You blind Pharisee! First wash the inside of the cup and the dish,* and then the outside will become clean, too.

27 "What sorrow awaits you teachers of religious law and you Pharisees. Hypocrites! For you are like whitewashed tombs—beautiful on the outside but filled on the inside with dead people's bones and all sorts of impurity. 28 Outwardly you look like righteous people, but inwardly your hearts are filled with hypocrisy and lawlessness.

29 "What sorrow awaits you teachers of religious law and you Pharisees. Hypocrites! For you build tombs for the prophets your ancestors killed, and you decorate the monuments of the godly people your ancestors destroyed. 30 Then you say, 'If we had lived in the days of our ancestors, we would never have joined them in killing the prophets.'

31 "But in saying that, you testify against yourselves that you are indeed the descendants of those who murdered the prophets. 32 Go ahead and finish what your ancestors started. 33 Snakes! Sons of vipers! How will you escape the judgment of hell?

34 "Therefore, I am sending you prophets and wise men and teachers of religious law. But you will kill some by crucifixion, and you will flog others with whips in your synagogues, chasing them from city to city. 35 As a result, you will be held responsible for the murder of all godly people of all time—from the murder of righteous Abel to the murder of Zechariah son of Barachiah, whom you killed in the Temple between the sanctuary and the altar. 36 I tell you the truth, this judgment will fall on this very generation.

Jesus Grieves over Jerusalem

37 "O Jerusalem, Jerusalem, the city that kills the prophets and stones God's messengers! How often I have wanted to gather your children together as a hen protects her chicks beneath her wings, but you wouldn't let me. 38 And now, look, your house is abandoned and desolate.* 39 For I tell you this, you will never see me again until you say, 'Blessings on the one who comes in the name of the LORD!'*"

Jesus Foretells the Future

24 As Jesus was leaving the Temple grounds, his disciples pointed out to him the various Temple buildings. 2 But he responded, "Do you see all these buildings? I tell you the truth, they will be completely demolished. Not one stone will be left on top of another!"

3 Later, Jesus sat on the Mount of Olives. His disciples came to him privately and said, "Tell us, when will all this happen? What sign will signal your return and the end of the world?*"

4 Jesus told them, "Don't let anyone mislead you,

23:26 Some manuscripts do not include *and the dish*. 23:38 Some manuscripts do not include *and desolate*. 23:39 Ps 118:26. 24:3 Or *the age?*

KING JAMES VERSION

5 For many shall come in my name, saying, I am Christ; and shall deceive many.

6 And ye shall hear of wars and rumours of wars: see that ye be not troubled: for all *these things* must come to pass, but the end is not yet.

7 For nation shall rise against nation, and kingdom against kingdom: and there shall be famines, and pestilences, and earthquakes, in divers places.

8 All these *are* the beginning of sorrows.

9 Then shall they deliver you up to be afflicted, and shall kill you: and ye shall be hated of all nations for my name's sake.

10 And then shall many be offended, and shall betray one another, and shall hate one another.

11 And many false prophets shall rise, and shall deceive many.

12 And because iniquity shall abound, the love of many shall wax cold.

13 But he that shall endure unto the end, the same shall be saved.

14 And this gospel of the kingdom shall be preached in all the world for a witness unto all nations; and then shall the end come.

15 When ye therefore shall see the abomination of desolation, spoken of by Daniel the prophet, stand in the holy place, (whoso readeth, let him understand:)

16 Then let them which be in Judaea flee into the mountains:

17 Let him which is on the housetop not come down to take any thing out of his house:

18 Neither let him which is in the field return back to take his clothes.

19 And woe unto them that are with child, and to them that give suck in those days!

20 But pray ye that your flight be not in the winter, neither on the sabbath day:

21 For then shall be great tribulation, such as was not since the beginning of the world to this time, no, nor ever shall be.

22 And except those days should be shortened, there should no flesh be saved: but for the elect's sake those days shall be shortened.

23 Then if any man shall say unto you, Lo, here *is* Christ, or there; believe *it* not.

24 For there shall arise false Christs, and false prophets, and shall shew great signs and wonders; insomuch that, if *it were* possible, they shall deceive the very elect.

25 Behold, I have told you before.

26 Wherefore if they shall say unto you, Behold, he is in the desert; go not forth: behold, *he is* in the secret chambers; believe *it* not.

27 For as the lightning cometh out of the east, and shineth even unto the west; so shall also the coming of the Son of man be.

28 For wheresoever the carcase is, there will the eagles be gathered together.

29 Immediately after the tribulation of those days

NEW LIVING TRANSLATION

5 for many will come in my name, claiming, 'I am the
Messiah.' They will deceive many. 6 And you will hear
of wars and threats of wars, but don't panic. Yes,
these things must take place, but the end won't follow immediately. 7 Nation will go to war against nation, and kingdom against kingdom. There will be
famines and earthquakes in many parts of the world.
8 But all this is only the first of the birth pains, with
more to come.

9 "Then you will be arrested, persecuted, and
killed. You will be hated all over the world because
you are my followers.* 10 And many will turn away
from me and betray and hate each other. 11 And many
false prophets will appear and will deceive many
people. 12 Sin will be rampant everywhere, and the
love of many will grow cold. 13 But the one who endures to the end will be saved. 14 And the Good News
about the Kingdom will be preached throughout the
whole world, so that all nations* will hear it; and then
the end will come.

15 "The day is coming when you will see what Daniel the prophet spoke about—the sacrilegious object
that causes desecration* standing in the Holy Place."
(Reader, pay attention!) 16 "Then those in Judea must
flee to the hills. 17 A person out on the deck of a roof
must not go down into the house to pack. 18 A person
out in the field must not return even to get a coat.
19 How terrible it will be for pregnant women and for
nursing mothers in those days. 20 And pray that your
flight will not be in winter or on the Sabbath. 21 For
there will be greater anguish than at any time since
the world began. And it will never be so great again.
22 In fact, unless that time of calamity is shortened,
not a single person will survive. But it will be shortened for the sake of God's chosen ones.

23 "Then if anyone tells you, 'Look, here is the Messiah,' or 'There he is,' don't believe it. 24 For false messiahs and false prophets will rise up and perform
great signs and wonders so as to deceive, if possible,
even God's chosen ones. 25 See, I have warned you
about this ahead of time.

26 "So if someone tells you, 'Look, the Messiah is
out in the desert,' don't bother to go and look. Or,
'Look, he is hiding here,' don't believe it! 27 For as the
lightning flashes in the east and shines to the west,
so it will be when the Son of Man* comes. 28 Just as
the gathering of vultures shows there is a carcass
nearby, so these signs indicate that the end is near.*

29 "Immediately after the anguish of those days,

the sun will be darkened,
 the moon will give no light,

24:9 Greek *on account of my name.* **24:14** Or *all peoples.* **24:15** Greek *the abomination of desolation.* See Dan 9:27; 11:31; 12:11. **24:27** "Son of Man" is a title Jesus used for himself. **24:28** Greek *Wherever the carcass is, the vultures gather.*

KING JAMES VERSION

shall the sun be darkened, and the moon shall not give her light, and the stars shall fall from heaven, and the powers of the heavens shall be shaken:

30 And then shall appear the sign of the Son of man in heaven: and then shall all the tribes of the earth mourn, and they shall see the Son of man coming in the clouds of heaven with power and great glory.

31 And he shall send his angels with a great sound of a trumpet, and they shall gather together his elect from the four winds, from one end of heaven to the other.

32 Now learn a parable of the fig tree; When his branch is yet tender, and putteth forth leaves, ye know that summer *is* nigh:

33 So likewise ye, when ye shall see all these things, know that it is near, *even* at the doors.

34 Verily I say unto you, This generation shall not pass, till all these things be fulfilled.

35 Heaven and earth shall pass away, but my words shall not pass away.

36 But of that day and hour knoweth no *man*, no, not the angels of heaven, but my Father only.

37 But as the days of Noe *were*, so shall also the coming of the Son of man be.

38 For as in the days that were before the flood they were eating and drinking, marrying and giving in marriage, until the day that Noe entered into the ark,

39 And knew not until the flood came, and took them all away; so shall also the coming of the Son of man be.

40 Then shall two be in the field; the one shall be taken, and the other left.

41 Two *women shall be* grinding at the mill; the one shall be taken, and the other left.

42 Watch therefore: for ye know not what hour your Lord doth come.

43 But know this, that if the goodman of the house had known in what watch the thief would come, he would have watched, and would not have suffered his house to be broken up.

44 Therefore be ye also ready: for in such an hour as ye think not the Son of man cometh.

45 Who then is a faithful and wise servant, whom his lord hath made ruler over his household, to give them meat in due season?

46 Blessed *is* that servant, whom his lord when he cometh shall find so doing.

47 Verily I say unto you, That he shall make him ruler over all his goods.

48 But and if that evil servant shall say in his heart, My lord delayeth his coming;

49 And shall begin to smite *his* fellowservants, and to eat and drink with the drunken;

50 The lord of that servant shall come in a day when he looketh not for *him*, and in an hour that he is not aware of,

51 And shall cut him asunder, and appoint *him* his portion with the hypocrites: there shall be weeping and gnashing of teeth.

NEW LIVING TRANSLATION

the stars will fall from the sky,
and the powers in the heavens will be shaken.*

30 And then at last, the sign that the Son of Man is
coming will appear in the heavens, and there will be
deep mourning among all the peoples of the earth.
And they will see the Son of Man coming on the
clouds of heaven with power and great glory.* 31 And
he will send out his angels with the mighty blast of a
trumpet, and they will gather his chosen ones from
all over the world*—from the farthest ends of the
earth and heaven.

32 "Now learn a lesson from the fig tree. When its
branches bud and its leaves begin to sprout, you
know that summer is near. 33 In the same way, when
you see all these things, you can know his return is
very near, right at the door. 34 I tell you the truth, this
generation* will not pass from the scene until all
these things take place. 35 Heaven and earth will disappear, but my words will never disappear.

36 "However, no one knows the day or hour when
these things will happen, not even the angels in
heaven or the Son himself.* Only the Father knows.

37 "When the Son of Man returns, it will be like it
was in Noah's day. 38 In those days before the flood,
the people were enjoying banquets and parties and
weddings right up to the time Noah entered his boat.
39 People didn't realize what was going to happen until the flood came and swept them all away. That is
the way it will be when the Son of Man comes.

40 "Two men will be working together in the field;
one will be taken, the other left. 41 Two women will
be grinding flour at the mill; one will be taken, the
other left.

42 "So you, too, must keep watch! For you don't
know what day your Lord is coming. 43 Understand
this: If a homeowner knew exactly when a burglar
was coming, he would keep watch and not permit his
house to be broken into. 44 You also must be ready all
the time, for the Son of Man will come when least
expected.

45 "A faithful, sensible servant is one to whom the
master can give the responsibility of managing his
other household servants and feeding them. 46 If the
master returns and finds that the servant has done a
good job, there will be a reward. 47 I tell you the truth,
the master will put that servant in charge of all he
owns. 48 But what if the servant is evil and thinks, 'My
master won't be back for a while,' 49 and he begins
beating the other servants, partying, and getting
drunk? 50 The master will return unannounced and
unexpected, 51 and he will cut the servant to pieces
and assign him a place with the hypocrites. In that
place there will be weeping and gnashing of teeth.

24:29 See Isa 13:10; 34:4; Joel 2:10. **24:30** See Dan 7:13. **24:31** Greek *from the four winds.* **24:34** Or *this age,* or *this nation.* **24:36** Some manuscripts do not include *or the Son himself.*

KING JAMES VERSION

25

1Then shall the kingdom of heaven be likened unto ten virgins, which took their lamps, and went forth to meet the bridegroom.

2And five of them were wise, and five *were* foolish.

3They that *were* foolish took their lamps, and took no oil with them:

4But the wise took oil in their vessels with their lamps.

5While the bridegroom tarried, they all slumbered and slept.

6And at midnight there was a cry made, Behold, the bridegroom cometh; go ye out to meet him.

7Then all those virgins arose, and trimmed their lamps.

8And the foolish said unto the wise, Give us of your oil; for our lamps are gone out.

9But the wise answered, saying, *Not so;* lest there be not enough for us and you: but go ye rather to them that sell, and buy for yourselves.

10And while they went to buy, the bridegroom came; and they that were ready went in with him to the marriage: and the door was shut.

11Afterward came also the other virgins, saying, Lord, Lord, open to us.

12But he answered and said, Verily I say unto you, I know you not.

13Watch therefore, for ye know neither the day nor the hour wherein the Son of man cometh.

14For *the kingdom of heaven is* as a man travelling into a far country, *who* called his own servants, and delivered unto them his goods.

15And unto one he gave five talents, to another two, and to another one; to every man according to his several ability; and straightway took his journey.

16Then he that had received the five talents went and traded with the same, and made *them* other five talents.

17And likewise he that *had received* two, he also gained other two.

18But he that had received one went and digged in the earth, and hid his lord's money.

19After a long time the lord of those servants cometh, and reckoneth with them.

20And so he that had received five talents came and brought other five talents, saying, Lord, thou deliveredst unto me five talents: behold, I have gained beside them five talents more.

21His lord said unto him, Well done, *thou* good and faithful servant: thou hast been faithful over a few things, I will make thee ruler over many things: enter thou into the joy of thy lord.

NEW LIVING TRANSLATION

Parable of the Ten Bridesmaids

25

"Then the Kingdom of Heaven will be like
ten bridesmaids* who took their lamps and
went to meet the bridegroom. 2Five of them were
foolish, and five were wise. 3The five who were foolish didn't take enough olive oil for their lamps, 4but
the other five were wise enough to take along extra
oil. 5When the bridegroom was delayed, they all became drowsy and fell asleep.

6"At midnight they were roused by the shout,
'Look, the bridegroom is coming! Come out and
meet him!'

7"All the bridesmaids got up and prepared their
lamps. 8Then the five foolish ones asked the others,
'Please give us some of your oil because our lamps
are going out.'

9"But the others replied, 'We don't have enough
for all of us. Go to a shop and buy some for yourselves.'

10"But while they were gone to buy oil, the bridegroom came. Then those who were ready went in
with him to the marriage feast, and the door was
locked. 11Later, when the other five bridesmaids returned, they stood outside, calling, 'Lord! Lord! Open
the door for us!'

12"But he called back, 'Believe me, I don't know
you!'

13"So you, too, must keep watch! For you do not
know the day or hour of my return.

Parable of the Three Servants

14"Again, the Kingdom of Heaven can be illustrated
by the story of a man going on a long trip. He called
together his servants and entrusted his money to
them while he was gone. 15He gave five bags of silver* to one, two bags of silver to another, and one bag
of silver to the last—dividing it in proportion to their
abilities. He then left on his trip.

16"The servant who received the five bags of silver
began to invest the money and earned five more.
17The servant with two bags of silver also went to
work and earned two more. 18But the servant who received the one bag of silver dug a hole in the ground
and hid the master's money.

19"After a long time their master returned from his
trip and called them to give an account of how they
had used his money. 20The servant to whom he had
entrusted the five bags of silver came forward with
five more and said, 'Master, you gave me five bags of
silver to invest, and I have earned five more.'

21"The master was full of praise. 'Well done, my
good and faithful servant. You have been faithful
in handling this small amount, so now I will give
you many more responsibilities. Let's celebrate
together!*'

25:1 Or *virgins;* also in 25:7, 11. **25:15** Greek *talents;* also throughout the story. A talent is equal to 75 pounds or 34 kilograms. **25:21** Greek *Enter into the joy of your master* [or *your Lord*]; also in 25:23.

KING JAMES VERSION

22He also that had received two talents came and
said, Lord, thou deliveredst unto me two talents: behold, I have gained two other talents beside them.
23His lord said unto him, Well done, good and
faithful servant; thou hast been faithful over a few
things, I will make thee ruler over many things: enter
thou into the joy of thy lord.
24Then he which had received the one talent came
and said, Lord, I knew thee that thou art an hard man,
reaping where thou hast not sown, and gathering
where thou hast not strawed:
25And I was afraid, and went and hid thy talent in
the earth: lo, *there* thou hast *that is* thine.
26His lord answered and said unto him, *Thou*
wicked and slothful servant, thou knewest that I reap
where I sowed not, and gather where I have not
strawed:
27Thou oughtest therefore to have put my money
to the exchangers, and *then* at my coming I should
have received mine own with usury.
28Take therefore the talent from him, and give *it*
unto him which hath ten talents.
29For unto every one that hath shall be given, and
he shall have abundance: but from him that hath not
shall be taken away even that which he hath.
30And cast ye the unprofitable servant into outer
darkness: there shall be weeping and gnashing of
teeth.

31When the Son of man shall come in his glory,
and all the holy angels with him, then shall he sit
upon the throne of his glory:
32And before him shall be gathered all nations:
and he shall separate them one from another, as a
shepherd divideth *his* sheep from the goats:
33And he shall set the sheep on his right hand, but
the goats on the left.
34Then shall the King say unto them on his right
hand, Come, ye blessed of my Father, inherit the
kingdom prepared for you from the foundation of
the world:
35For I was an hungred, and ye gave me meat: I was
thirsty, and ye gave me drink: I was a stranger, and ye
took me in:
36Naked, and ye clothed me: I was sick, and ye
visited me: I was in prison, and ye came unto me.
37Then shall the righteous answer him, saying,
Lord, when saw we thee an hungred, and fed *thee?* or
thirsty, and gave *thee* drink?
38When saw we thee a stranger, and took *thee* in?
or naked, and clothed *thee?*
39Or when saw we thee sick, or in prison, and
came unto thee?
40And the King shall answer and say unto them,
Verily I say unto you, Inasmuch as ye have done *it*
unto one of the least of these my brethren, ye have
done *it* unto me.
41Then shall he say also unto them on the left

NEW LIVING TRANSLATION

22"The servant who had received the two bags of
silver came forward and said, 'Master, you gave me
two bags of silver to invest, and I have earned two
more.'
23"The master said, 'Well done, my good and
faithful servant. You have been faithful in handling
this small amount, so now I will give you many more
responsibilities. Let's celebrate together!'
24"Then the servant with the one bag of silver
came and said, 'Master, I knew you were a harsh man,
harvesting crops you didn't plant and gathering
crops you didn't cultivate. 25I was afraid I would lose
your money, so I hid it in the earth. Look, here is your
money back.'
26"But the master replied, 'You wicked and lazy
servant! If you knew I harvested crops I didn't plant
and gathered crops I didn't cultivate, 27why didn't
you deposit my money in the bank? At least I could
have gotten some interest on it.'
28"Then he ordered, 'Take the money from this
servant, and give it to the one with the ten bags of silver. 29To those who use well what they are given,
even more will be given, and they will have an abundance. But from those who do nothing, even what
little they have will be taken away. 30Now throw this
useless servant into outer darkness, where there will
be weeping and gnashing of teeth.'

The Final Judgment

31"But when the Son of Man* comes in his glory, and
all the angels with him, then he will sit upon his glorious throne. 32All the nations* will be gathered in
his presence, and he will separate the people as a
shepherd separates the sheep from the goats. 33He
will place the sheep at his right hand and the goats at
his left.
34"Then the King will say to those on his right,
'Come, you who are blessed by my Father, inherit the
Kingdom prepared for you from the creation of the
world. 35For I was hungry, and you fed me. I was
thirsty, and you gave me a drink. I was a stranger, and
you invited me into your home. 36I was naked, and
you gave me clothing. I was sick, and you cared for
me. I was in prison, and you visited me.'
37"Then these righteous ones will reply, 'Lord,
when did we ever see you hungry and feed you?
Or thirsty and give you something to drink? 38Or a
stranger and show you hospitality? Or naked and
give you clothing? 39When did we ever see you sick
or in prison and visit you?'
40"And the King will say, 'I tell you the truth, when
you did it to one of the least of these my brothers and
sisters,* you were doing it to me!'
41"Then the King will turn to those on the left and

25:31 "Son of Man" is a title Jesus used for himself. **25:32** Or *peoples.*
25:40 Greek *my brothers.*

KING JAMES VERSION

hand, Depart from me, ye cursed, into everlasting
fire, prepared for the devil and his angels:
42 For I was an hungred, and ye gave me no meat:
I was thirsty, and ye gave me no drink:
43 I was a stranger, and ye took me not in: naked,
and ye clothed me not: sick, and in prison, and ye
visited me not.
44 Then shall they also answer him, saying, Lord,
when saw we thee an hungred, or athirst, or a
stranger, or naked, or sick, or in prison, and did not
minister unto thee?
45 Then shall he answer them, saying, Verily I say
unto you, Inasmuch as ye did *it* not to one of the least
of these, ye did *it* not to me.
46 And these shall go away into everlasting punishment: but the righteous into life eternal.

26 1 And it came to pass, when Jesus had finished all these sayings, he said unto his
disciples,
2 Ye know that after two days is *the feast of* the
passover, and the Son of man is betrayed to be
crucified.
3 Then assembled together the chief priests, and
the scribes, and the elders of the people, unto the
palace of the high priest, who was called Caiaphas,
4 And consulted that they might take Jesus by
subtilty, and kill *him.*
5 But they said, Not on the feast *day,* lest there be
an uproar among the people.
6 Now when Jesus was in Bethany, in the house of
Simon the leper,
7 There came unto him a woman having an alabaster box of very precious ointment, and poured it on
his head, as he sat *at meat.*
8 But when his disciples saw *it,* they had indignation, saying, To what purpose *is* this waste?
9 For this ointment might have been sold for much,
and given to the poor.
10 When Jesus understood *it,* he said unto them,
Why trouble ye the woman? for she hath wrought a
good work upon me.
11 For ye have the poor always with you; but me ye
have not always.
12 For in that she hath poured this ointment on my
body, she did *it* for my burial.
13 Verily I say unto you, Wheresoever this gospel
shall be preached in the whole world, *there* shall also
this, that this woman hath done, be told for a memorial of her.
14 Then one of the twelve, called Judas Iscariot,
went unto the chief priests,
15 And said *unto them,* What will ye give me, and I
will deliver him unto you? And they covenanted with
him for thirty pieces of silver.
16 And from that time he sought opportunity to
betray him.

NEW LIVING TRANSLATION

say, 'Away with you, you cursed ones, into the eternal
fire prepared for the devil and his demons.* 42 For I
was hungry, and you didn't feed me. I was thirsty, and
you didn't give me a drink. 43 I was a stranger, and you
didn't invite me into your home. I was naked, and you
didn't give me clothing. I was sick and in prison, and
you didn't visit me.'
44 "Then they will reply, 'Lord, when did we ever
see you hungry or thirsty or a stranger or naked or
sick or in prison, and not help you?'
45 "And he will answer, 'I tell you the truth, when
you refused to help the least of these my brothers
and sisters, you were refusing to help me.'
46 "And they will go away into eternal punishment,
but the righteous will go into eternal life."

The Plot to Kill Jesus

26 When Jesus had finished saying all these
things, he said to his disciples, 2 "As you
know, Passover begins in two days, and the Son of
Man* will be handed over to be crucified."
3 At that same time the leading priests and elders
were meeting at the residence of Caiaphas, the high
priest, 4 plotting how to capture Jesus secretly and
kill him. 5 "But not during the Passover celebration,"
they agreed, "or the people may riot."

Jesus Anointed at Bethany

6 Meanwhile, Jesus was in Bethany at the home of
Simon, a man who had previously had leprosy.
7 While he was eating,* a woman came in with a
beautiful alabaster jar of expensive perfume and
poured it over his head.
8 The disciples were indignant when they saw this.
"What a waste!" they said. 9 "It could have been sold
for a high price and the money given to the poor."
10 But Jesus, aware of this, replied, "Why criticize
this woman for doing such a good thing to me? 11 You
will always have the poor among you, but you will not
always have me. 12 She has poured this perfume on
me to prepare my body for burial. 13 I tell you the
truth, wherever the Good News is preached throughout the world, this woman's deed will be remembered and discussed."

Judas Agrees to Betray Jesus

14 Then Judas Iscariot, one of the twelve disciples,
went to the leading priests 15 and asked, "How much
will you pay me to betray Jesus to you?" And they
gave him thirty pieces of silver. 16 From that time on,
Judas began looking for an opportunity to betray
Jesus.

25:41 Greek *his angels.* **26:2** "Son of Man" is a title Jesus used for himself.
26:7 Or *reclining.*

KING JAMES VERSION

17 Now the first *day* of the *feast of* unleavened bread the disciples came to Jesus, saying unto him, Where wilt thou that we prepare for thee to eat the passover?

18 And he said, Go into the city to such a man, and say unto him, The Master saith, My time is at hand; I will keep the passover at thy house with my disciples.

19 And the disciples did as Jesus had appointed them; and they made ready the passover.

20 Now when the even was come, he sat down with the twelve.

21 And as they did eat, he said, Verily I say unto you, that one of you shall betray me.

22 And they were exceeding sorrowful, and began every one of them to say unto him, Lord, is it I?

23 And he answered and said, He that dippeth *his* hand with me in the dish, the same shall betray me.

24 The Son of man goeth as it is written of him: but woe unto that man by whom the Son of man is betrayed! it had been good for that man if he had not been born.

25 Then Judas, which betrayed him, answered and said, Master, is it I? He said unto him, Thou hast said.

26 And as they were eating, Jesus took bread, and blessed *it,* and brake *it,* and gave *it* to the disciples, and said, Take, eat; this is my body.

27 And he took the cup, and gave thanks, and gave *it* to them, saying, Drink ye all of it;

28 For this is my blood of the new testament, which is shed for many for the remission of sins.

29 But I say unto you, I will not drink henceforth of this fruit of the vine, until that day when I drink it new with you in my Father's kingdom.

30 And when they had sung an hymn, they went out into the mount of Olives.

31 Then saith Jesus unto them, All ye shall be offended because of me this night: for it is written, I will smite the shepherd, and the sheep of the flock shall be scattered abroad.

32 But after I am risen again, I will go before you into Galilee.

33 Peter answered and said unto him, Though all *men* shall be offended because of thee, *yet* will I never be offended.

34 Jesus said unto him, Verily I say unto thee, That this night, before the cock crow, thou shalt deny me thrice.

35 Peter said unto him, Though I should die with thee, yet will I not deny thee. Likewise also said all the disciples.

NEW LIVING TRANSLATION

The Last Supper

17 On the first day of the Festival of Unleavened Bread, the disciples came to Jesus and asked, "Where do you want us to prepare the Passover meal for you?"

18 "As you go into the city," he told them, "you will see a certain man. Tell him, 'The Teacher says: My time has come, and I will eat the Passover meal with my disciples at your house.'" 19 So the disciples did as Jesus told them and prepared the Passover meal there.

20 When it was evening, Jesus sat down at the table* with the twelve disciples.* 21 While they were eating, he said, "I tell you the truth, one of you will betray me."

22 Greatly distressed, each one asked in turn, "Am I the one, Lord?"

23 He replied, "One of you who has just eaten from this bowl with me will betray me. 24 For the Son of Man must die, as the Scriptures declared long ago. But how terrible it will be for the one who betrays him. It would be far better for that man if he had never been born!"

25 Judas, the one who would betray him, also asked, "Rabbi, am I the one?"

And Jesus told him, "You have said it."

26 As they were eating, Jesus took some bread and blessed it. Then he broke it in pieces and gave it to the disciples, saying, "Take this and eat it, for this is my body."

27 And he took a cup of wine and gave thanks to God for it. He gave it to them and said, "Each of you drink from it, 28 for this is my blood, which confirms the covenant* between God and his people. It is poured out as a sacrifice to forgive the sins of many. 29 Mark my words—I will not drink wine again until the day I drink it new with you in my Father's Kingdom."

30 Then they sang a hymn and went out to the Mount of Olives.

Jesus Predicts Peter's Denial

31 On the way, Jesus told them, "Tonight all of you will desert me. For the Scriptures say,

'God will strike* the Shepherd,
and the sheep of the flock will be scattered.'

32 But after I have been raised from the dead, I will go ahead of you to Galilee and meet you there."

33 Peter declared, "Even if everyone else deserts you, I will never desert you."

34 Jesus replied, "I tell you the truth, Peter—this very night, before the rooster crows, you will deny three times that you even know me."

35 "No!" Peter insisted. "Even if I have to die with you, I will never deny you!" And all the other disciples vowed the same.

26:20a Or *Jesus reclined.* **26:20b** Some manuscripts read *the Twelve.* **26:28** Some manuscripts read *the new covenant.* **26:31** Greek *I will strike.* Zech 13:7.

KING JAMES VERSION

36 Then cometh Jesus with them unto a place
called Gethsemane, and saith unto the disciples, Sit
ye here, while I go and pray yonder.
37 And he took with him Peter and the two sons of
Zebedee, and began to be sorrowful and very heavy.
38 Then saith he unto them, My soul is exceeding
sorrowful, even unto death: tarry ye here, and watch
with me.
39 And he went a little farther, and fell on his face,
and prayed, saying, O my Father, if it be possible, let
this cup pass from me: nevertheless not as I will, but
as thou *wilt*.
40 And he cometh unto the disciples, and findeth
them asleep, and saith unto Peter, What, could ye not
watch with me one hour?
41 Watch and pray, that ye enter not into temptation: the spirit indeed *is* willing, but the flesh *is* weak.
42 He went away again the second time, and prayed,
saying, O my Father, if this cup may not pass away
from me, except I drink it, thy will be done.
43 And he came and found them asleep again: for
their eyes were heavy.
44 And he left them, and went away again, and
prayed the third time, saying the same words.
45 Then cometh he to his disciples, and saith unto
them, Sleep on now, and take *your* rest: behold, the
hour is at hand, and the Son of man is betrayed into
the hands of sinners.
46 Rise, let us be going: behold, he is at hand that
doth betray me.
47 And while he yet spake, lo, Judas, one of the
twelve, came, and with him a great multitude with
swords and staves, from the chief priests and elders
of the people.
48 Now he that betrayed him gave them a sign, saying, Whomsoever I shall kiss, that same is he: hold
him fast.
49 And forthwith he came to Jesus, and said, Hail,
master; and kissed him.
50 And Jesus said unto him, Friend, wherefore art
thou come? Then came they, and laid hands on Jesus,
and took him.
51 And, behold, one of them which were with Jesus
stretched out *his* hand, and drew his sword, and
struck a servant of the high priest's, and smote off
his ear.
52 Then said Jesus unto him, Put up again thy
sword into his place: for all they that take the sword
shall perish with the sword.
53 Thinkest thou that I cannot now pray to my
Father, and he shall presently give me more than
twelve legions of angels?
54 But how then shall the scriptures be fulfilled,
that thus it must be?
55 In that same hour said Jesus to the multitudes,
Are ye come out as against a thief with swords and

NEW LIVING TRANSLATION

Jesus Prays in Gethsemane

36 Then Jesus went with them to the olive grove
called Gethsemane, and he said, "Sit here while I go
over there to pray." 37 He took Peter and Zebedee's
two sons, James and John, and he became anguished
and distressed. 38 He told them, "My soul is crushed
with grief to the point of death. Stay here and keep
watch with me."
39 He went on a little farther and bowed with his
face to the ground, praying, "My Father! If it is
possible, let this cup of suffering be taken away from
me. Yet I want your will to be done, not mine."
40 Then he returned to the disciples and found
them asleep. He said to Peter, "Couldn't you watch
with me even one hour? 41 Keep watch and pray, so
that you will not give in to temptation. For the spirit
is willing, but the body is weak!"
42 Then Jesus left them a second time and prayed,
"My Father! If this cup cannot be taken away* unless
I drink it, your will be done." 43 When he returned
to them again, he found them sleeping, for they
couldn't keep their eyes open.
44 So he went to pray a third time, saying the same
things again. 45 Then he came to the disciples and
said, "Go ahead and sleep. Have your rest. But look—
the time has come. The Son of Man is betrayed into
the hands of sinners. 46 Up, let's be going. Look,
my betrayer is here!"

Jesus Is Betrayed and Arrested

47 And even as Jesus said this, Judas, one of the twelve
disciples, arrived with a crowd of men armed with
swords and clubs. They had been sent by the leading
priests and elders of the people. 48 The traitor, Judas,
had given them a prearranged signal: "You will know
which one to arrest when I greet him with a kiss."
49 So Judas came straight to Jesus. "Greetings, Rabbi!"
he exclaimed and gave him the kiss.
50 Jesus said, "My friend, go ahead and do what you
have come for."
Then the others grabbed Jesus and arrested him.
51 But one of the men with Jesus pulled out his sword
and struck the high priest's slave, slashing off his ear.
52 "Put away your sword," Jesus told him. "Those
who use the sword will die by the sword. 53 Don't you
realize that I could ask my Father for thousands* of
angels to protect us, and he would send them instantly? 54 But if I did, how would the Scriptures be
fulfilled that describe what must happen now?"
55 Then Jesus said to the crowd, "Am I some dangerous revolutionary, that you come with swords and

26:42 Greek *If this cannot pass.* **26:53** Greek *twelve legions.*

KING JAMES VERSION

staves for to take me? I sat daily with you teaching in
the temple, and ye laid no hold on me.
56But all this was done, that the scriptures of the
prophets might be fulfilled. Then all the disciples
forsook him, and fled.

57And they that had laid hold on Jesus led *him*
away to Caiaphas the high priest, where the scribes
and the elders were assembled.
58But Peter followed him afar off unto the high
priest's palace, and went in, and sat with the servants,
to see the end.
59Now the chief priests, and elders, and all the
council, sought false witness against Jesus, to put
him to death;
60But found none: yea, though many false witnesses came, *yet* found they none. At the last came
two false witnesses,
61And said, This *fellow* said, I am able to destroy
the temple of God, and to build it in three days.
62And the high priest arose, and said unto him,
Answerest thou nothing? what *is it which* these
witness against thee?
63But Jesus held his peace. And the high priest
answered and said unto him, I adjure thee by the living God, that thou tell us whether thou be the Christ,
the Son of God.
64Jesus saith unto him, Thou hast said: nevertheless I say unto you, Hereafter shall ye see the Son of
man sitting on the right hand of power, and coming
in the clouds of heaven.
65Then the high priest rent his clothes, saying, He
hath spoken blasphemy; what further need have
we of witnesses? behold, now ye have heard his
blasphemy.
66What think ye? They answered and said, He is
guilty of death.
67Then did they spit in his face, and buffeted him;
and others smote *him* with the palms of their hands,
68Saying, Prophesy unto us, thou Christ, Who is he
that smote thee?
69Now Peter sat without in the palace: and a damsel came unto him, saying, Thou also wast with Jesus
of Galilee.
70But he denied before *them* all, saying, I know not
what thou sayest.
71And when he was gone out into the porch, another *maid* saw him, and said unto them that were
there, This *fellow* was also with Jesus of Nazareth.
72And again he denied with an oath, I do not know
the man.
73And after a while came unto *him* they that stood
by, and said to Peter, Surely thou also art *one* of them;
for thy speech bewrayeth thee.

NEW LIVING TRANSLATION

clubs to arrest me? Why didn't you arrest me in the
Temple? I was there teaching every day. 56But this is
all happening to fulfill the words of the prophets as
recorded in the Scriptures." At that point, all the disciples deserted him and fled.

Jesus before the Council

57Then the people who had arrested Jesus led him to
the home of Caiaphas, the high priest, where the
teachers of religious law and the elders had gathered.
58Meanwhile, Peter followed him at a distance and
came to the high priest's courtyard. He went in and sat
with the guards and waited to see how it would all end.
59Inside, the leading priests and the entire high
council* were trying to find witnesses who would lie
about Jesus, so they could put him to death. 60But
even though they found many who agreed to give
false witness, they could not use anyone's testimony.
Finally, two men came forward 61who declared,
"This man said, 'I am able to destroy the Temple of
God and rebuild it in three days.'"
62Then the high priest stood up and said to Jesus,
"Well, aren't you going to answer these charges?
What do you have to say for yourself?" 63But Jesus remained silent. Then the high priest said to him, "I
demand in the name of the living God—tell us if you
are the Messiah, the Son of God."
64Jesus replied, "You have said it. And in the future
you will see the Son of Man seated in the place of
power at God's right hand* and coming on the
clouds of heaven."*
65Then the high priest tore his clothing to show
his horror and said, "Blasphemy! Why do we need
other witnesses? You have all heard his blasphemy.
66What is your verdict?"
"Guilty!" they shouted. "He deserves to die!"
67Then they began to spit in Jesus' face and beat
him with their fists. And some slapped him, 68jeer-
ing, "Prophesy to us, you Messiah! Who hit you that
time?"

Peter Denies Jesus

69Meanwhile, Peter was sitting outside in the courtyard. A servant girl came over and said to him, "You
were one of those with Jesus the Galilean."
70But Peter denied it in front of everyone. "I don't
know what you're talking about," he said.
71Later, out by the gate, another servant girl noticed him and said to those standing around, "This
man was with Jesus of Nazareth.*"
72Again Peter denied it, this time with an oath.
"I don't even know the man," he said.
73A little later some of the other bystanders came
over to Peter and said, "You must be one of them;
we can tell by your Galilean accent."

26:59 Greek *the Sanhedrin.* **26:64a** Greek *seated at the right hand of the power.* See Ps 110:1. **26:64b** See Dan 7:13. **26:71** Or *Jesus the Nazarene.*

KING JAMES VERSION

74 Then began he to curse and to swear, *saying,* I
know not the man. And immediately the cock crew.
75 And Peter remembered the word of Jesus, which
said unto him, Before the cock crow, thou shalt deny
me thrice. And he went out, and wept bitterly.

27 1 When the morning was come, all the chief
priests and elders of the people took counsel against Jesus to put him to death:
2 And when they had bound him, they led *him* away,
and delivered him to Pontius Pilate the governor.
3 Then Judas, which had betrayed him, when he
saw that he was condemned, repented himself, and
brought again the thirty pieces of silver to the chief
priests and elders,
4 Saying, I have sinned in that I have betrayed the
innocent blood. And they said, What *is that* to us?
see thou *to that.*
5 And he cast down the pieces of silver in the
temple, and departed, and went and hanged himself.
6 And the chief priests took the silver pieces, and
said, It is not lawful for to put them into the treasury,
because it is the price of blood.
7 And they took counsel, and bought with them the
potter's field, to bury strangers in.
8 Wherefore that field was called, The field of
blood, unto this day.
9 Then was fulfilled that which was spoken by
Jeremy the prophet, saying, And they took the thirty
pieces of silver, the price of him that was valued,
whom they of the children of Israel did value;
10 And gave them for the potter's field, as the Lord
appointed me.

11 And Jesus stood before the governor: and the
governor asked him, saying, Art thou the King of the
Jews? And Jesus said unto him, Thou sayest.
12 And when he was accused of the chief priests
and elders, he answered nothing.
13 Then said Pilate unto him, Hearest thou not how
many things they witness against thee?
14 And he answered him to never a word; insomuch that the governor marvelled greatly.
15 Now at *that* feast the governor was wont to release unto the people a prisoner, whom they would.
16 And they had then a notable prisoner, called
Barabbas.
17 Therefore when they were gathered together,
Pilate said unto them, Whom will ye that I release
unto you? Barabbas, or Jesus which is called Christ?

NEW LIVING TRANSLATION

74 Peter swore, "A curse on me if I'm lying—I don't
know the man!" And immediately the rooster
crowed.
75 Suddenly, Jesus' words flashed through Peter's
mind: "Before the rooster crows, you will deny three
times that you even know me." And he went away,
weeping bitterly.

Judas Hangs Himself

27 Very early in the morning the leading
priests and the elders of the people met
again to lay plans for putting Jesus to death. 2 Then
they bound him, led him away, and took him to Pilate,
the Roman governor.
3 When Judas, who had betrayed him, realized that
Jesus had been condemned to die, he was filled with
remorse. So he took the thirty pieces of silver back to
the leading priests and the elders. 4 "I have sinned,"
he declared, "for I have betrayed an innocent man."
"What do we care?" they retorted. "That's your
problem."
5 Then Judas threw the silver coins down in the
Temple and went out and hanged himself.
6 The leading priests picked up the coins. "It
wouldn't be right to put this money in the Temple
treasury," they said, "since it was payment for murder."* 7 After some discussion they finally decided to
buy the potter's field, and they made it into a cemetery for foreigners. 8 That is why the field is still
called the Field of Blood. 9 This fulfilled the prophecy of Jeremiah that says,

"They took* the thirty pieces of silver—
the price at which he was valued by the people
of Israel,
10 and purchased the potter's field,
as the LORD directed.*"

Jesus' Trial before Pilate

11 Now Jesus was standing before Pilate, the Roman
governor. "Are you the king of the Jews?" the governor asked him.
Jesus replied, "You have said it."
12 But when the leading priests and the elders
made their accusations against him, Jesus remained
silent. 13 "Don't you hear all these charges they are
bringing against you?" Pilate demanded. 14 But Jesus
made no response to any of the charges, much to the
governor's surprise.
15 Now it was the governor's custom each year during the Passover celebration to release one prisoner
to the crowd—anyone they wanted. 16 This year there
was a notorious prisoner, a man named Barabbas.*
17 As the crowds gathered before Pilate's house that
morning, he asked them, "Which one do you want
me to release to you—Barabbas, or Jesus who is

27:6 Greek *since it is the price for blood.* **27:9** Or *I took.* **27:9-10** Greek *as the LORD directed me.* Zech 11:12-13; Jer 32:6-9. **27:16** Some manuscripts read *Jesus Barabbas;* also in 27:17.

KING JAMES VERSION

18 For he knew that for envy they had delivered him.

19 When he was set down on the judgment seat, his wife sent unto him, saying, Have thou nothing to do with that just man: for I have suffered many things this day in a dream because of him.

20 But the chief priests and elders persuaded the multitude that they should ask Barabbas, and destroy Jesus.

21 The governor answered and said unto them, Whether of the twain will ye that I release unto you? They said, Barabbas.

22 Pilate saith unto them, What shall I do then with Jesus which is called Christ? *They* all say unto him, Let him be crucified.

23 And the governor said, Why, what evil hath he done? But they cried out the more, saying, Let him be crucified.

24 When Pilate saw that he could prevail nothing, but *that* rather a tumult was made, he took water, and washed *his* hands before the multitude, saying, I am innocent of the blood of this just person: see ye *to it.*

25 Then answered all the people, and said, His blood *be* on us, and on our children.

26 Then released he Barabbas unto them: and when he had scourged Jesus, he delivered *him* to be crucified.

27 Then the soldiers of the governor took Jesus into the common hall, and gathered unto him the whole band *of soldiers.*

28 And they stripped him, and put on him a scarlet robe.

29 And when they had platted a crown of thorns, they put *it* upon his head, and a reed in his right hand: and they bowed the knee before him, and mocked him, saying, Hail, King of the Jews!

30 And they spit upon him, and took the reed, and smote him on the head.

31 And after that they had mocked him, they took the robe off from him, and put his own raiment on him, and led him away to crucify *him.*

32 And as they came out, they found a man of Cyrene, Simon by name: him they compelled to bear his cross.

33 And when they were come unto a place called Golgotha, that is to say, a place of a skull,

34 They gave him vinegar to drink mingled with gall: and when he had tasted *thereof,* he would not drink.

35 And they crucified him, and parted his garments, casting lots: that it might be fulfilled which was spoken by the prophet, They parted my garments among them, and upon my vesture did they cast lots.

36 And sitting down they watched him there;

NEW LIVING TRANSLATION

called the Messiah?" 18 (He knew very well that the religious leaders had arrested Jesus out of envy.)

19 Just then, as Pilate was sitting on the judgment seat, his wife sent him this message: "Leave that innocent man alone. I suffered through a terrible nightmare about him last night."

20 Meanwhile, the leading priests and the elders persuaded the crowd to ask for Barabbas to be released and for Jesus to be put to death. 21 So the governor asked again, "Which of these two do you want me to release to you?"

The crowd shouted back, "Barabbas!"

22 Pilate responded, "Then what should I do with Jesus who is called the Messiah?"

They shouted back, "Crucify him!"

23 "Why?" Pilate demanded. "What crime has he committed?"

But the mob roared even louder, "Crucify him!"

24 Pilate saw that he wasn't getting anywhere and that a riot was developing. So he sent for a bowl of water and washed his hands before the crowd, saying, "I am innocent of this man's blood. The responsibility is yours!"

25 And all the people yelled back, "We will take responsibility for his death—we and our children!"*

26 So Pilate released Barabbas to them. He ordered Jesus flogged with a lead-tipped whip, then turned him over to the Roman soldiers to be crucified.

The Soldiers Mock Jesus

27 Some of the governor's soldiers took Jesus into their headquarters* and called out the entire regiment. 28 They stripped him and put a scarlet robe on him. 29 They wove thorn branches into a crown and put it on his head, and they placed a reed stick in his right hand as a scepter. Then they knelt before him in mockery and taunted, "Hail! King of the Jews!" 30 And they spit on him and grabbed the stick and struck him on the head with it. 31 When they were finally tired of mocking him, they took off the robe and put his own clothes on him again. Then they led him away to be crucified.

The Crucifixion

32 Along the way, they came across a man named Simon, who was from Cyrene,* and the soldiers forced him to carry Jesus' cross. 33 And they went out to a place called Golgotha (which means "Place of the Skull"). 34 The soldiers gave him wine mixed with bitter gall, but when he had tasted it, he refused to drink it.

35 After they had nailed him to the cross, the soldiers gambled for his clothes by throwing dice.* 36 Then they sat around and kept guard as he hung

27:25 Greek *"His blood be on us and on our children."* **27:27** Or *into the Praetorium.* **27:32** *Cyrene* was a city in northern Africa. **27:35** Greek *by casting lots.* A few late manuscripts add *This fulfilled the word of the prophet: "They divided my garments among themselves and cast lots for my robe."* See Ps 22:18.

KING JAMES VERSION

37 And set up over his head his accusation written, THIS IS JESUS THE KING OF THE JEWS.

38 Then were there two thieves crucified with him, one on the right hand, and another on the left.

39 And they that passed by reviled him, wagging their heads,

40 And saying, Thou that destroyest the temple, and buildest *it* in three days, save thyself. If thou be the Son of God, come down from the cross.

41 Likewise also the chief priests mocking *him,* with the scribes and elders, said,

42 He saved others; himself he cannot save. If he be the King of Israel, let him now come down from the cross, and we will believe him.

43 He trusted in God; let him deliver him now, if he will have him: for he said, I am the Son of God.

44 The thieves also, which were crucified with him, cast the same in his teeth.

45 Now from the sixth hour there was darkness over all the land unto the ninth hour.

46 And about the ninth hour Jesus cried with a loud voice, saying, Eli, Eli, lama sabachthani? that is to say, My God, my God, why hast thou forsaken me?

47 Some of them that stood there, when they heard *that,* said, This *man* calleth for Elias.

48 And straightway one of them ran, and took a spunge, and filled *it* with vinegar, and put *it* on a reed, and gave him to drink.

49 The rest said, Let be, let us see whether Elias will come to save him.

50 Jesus, when he had cried again with a loud voice, yielded up the ghost.

51 And, behold, the veil of the temple was rent in twain from the top to the bottom; and the earth did quake, and the rocks rent;

52 And the graves were opened; and many bodies of the saints which slept arose,

53 And came out of the graves after his resurrection, and went into the holy city, and appeared unto many.

54 Now when the centurion, and they that were with him, watching Jesus, saw the earthquake, and those things that were done, they feared greatly, saying, Truly this was the Son of God.

55 And many women were there beholding afar off, which followed Jesus from Galilee, ministering unto him:

56 Among which was Mary Magdalene, and Mary the mother of James and Joses, and the mother of Zebedee's children.

57 When the even was come, there came a rich man of Arimathaea, named Joseph, who also himself was Jesus' disciple:

NEW LIVING TRANSLATION

there. 37 A sign was fastened above Jesus' head, announcing the charge against him. It read: "This is
Jesus, the King of the Jews." 38 Two revolutionaries*
were crucified with him, one on his right and one on
his left.

39 The people passing by shouted abuse, shaking
their heads in mockery. 40 "Look at you now!" they
yelled at him. "You said you were going to destroy
the Temple and rebuild it in three days. Well then,
if you are the Son of God, save yourself and come
down from the cross!"

41 The leading priests, the teachers of religious law,
and the elders also mocked Jesus. 42 "He saved others," they scoffed, "but he can't save himself! So he is
the King of Israel, is he? Let him come down from
the cross right now, and we will believe in him! 43 He
trusted God, so let God rescue him now if he wants
him! For he said, 'I am the Son of God.'" 44 Even the
revolutionaries who were crucified with him ridiculed him in the same way.

The Death of Jesus

45 At noon, darkness fell across the whole land until
three o'clock. 46 At about three o'clock, Jesus called
out with a loud voice, *"Eli, Eli,* lema sabachthani?"*
which means "My God, my God, why have you abandoned me?"*

47 Some of the bystanders misunderstood and
thought he was calling for the prophet Elijah. 48 One
of them ran and filled a sponge with sour wine, holding it up to him on a reed stick so he could drink.
49 But the rest said, "Wait! Let's see whether Elijah
comes to save him."*

50 Then Jesus shouted out again, and he released
his spirit. 51 At that moment the curtain in the sanctuary of the Temple was torn in two, from top to bottom. The earth shook, rocks split apart, 52 and tombs
opened. The bodies of many godly men and women
who had died were raised from the dead. 53 They left
the cemetery after Jesus' resurrection, went into the
holy city of Jerusalem, and appeared to many people.

54 The Roman officer* and the other soldiers at
the crucifixion were terrified by the earthquake and
all that had happened. They said, "This man truly
was the Son of God!"

55 And many women who had come from Galilee
with Jesus to care for him were watching from a distance. 56 Among them were Mary Magdalene, Mary
(the mother of James and Joseph), and the mother of
James and John, the sons of Zebedee.

The Burial of Jesus

57 As evening approached, Joseph, a rich man from
Arimathea who had become a follower of Jesus,

27:38 Or *criminals;* also in 27:44. **27:46a** Some manuscripts read *Eloi, Eloi.* **27:46b** Ps 22:1. **27:49** Some manuscripts add *And another took a spear and pierced his side, and out flowed water and blood.* Compare John 19:34. **27:54** Greek *The centurion.*

KING JAMES VERSION

58 He went to Pilate, and begged the body of Jesus. Then Pilate commanded the body to be delivered.

59 And when Joseph had taken the body, he wrapped it in a clean linen cloth,

60 And laid it in his own new tomb, which he had hewn out in the rock: and he rolled a great stone to the door of the sepulchre, and departed.

61 And there was Mary Magdalene, and the other Mary, sitting over against the sepulchre.

62 Now the next day, that followed the day of the preparation, the chief priests and Pharisees came together unto Pilate,

63 Saying, Sir, we remember that that deceiver said, while he was yet alive, After three days I will rise again.

64 Command therefore that the sepulchre be made sure until the third day, lest his disciples come by night, and steal him away, and say unto the people, He is risen from the dead: so the last error shall be worse than the first.

65 Pilate said unto them, Ye have a watch: go your way, make *it* as sure as ye can.

66 So they went, and made the sepulchre sure, sealing the stone, and setting a watch.

28 1 In the end of the sabbath, as it began to dawn toward the first *day* of the week, came Mary Magdalene and the other Mary to see the sepulchre.

2 And, behold, there was a great earthquake: for the angel of the Lord descended from heaven, and came and rolled back the stone from the door, and sat upon it.

3 His countenance was like lightning, and his raiment white as snow:

4 And for fear of him the keepers did shake, and became as dead *men*.

5 And the angel answered and said unto the women, Fear not ye: for I know that ye seek Jesus, which was crucified.

6 He is not here: for he is risen, as he said. Come, see the place where the Lord lay.

7 And go quickly, and tell his disciples that he is risen from the dead; and, behold, he goeth before you into Galilee; there shall ye see him: lo, I have told you.

8 And they departed quickly from the sepulchre with fear and great joy; and did run to bring his disciples word.

9 And as they went to tell his disciples, behold, Jesus met them, saying, All hail. And they came and held him by the feet, and worshipped him.

10 Then said Jesus unto them, Be not afraid: go tell my brethren that they go into Galilee, and there shall they see me.

11 Now when they were going, behold, some of the watch came into the city, and shewed unto the chief priests all the things that were done.

NEW LIVING TRANSLATION

58 went to Pilate and asked for Jesus' body. And Pilate issued an order to release it to him. 59 Joseph took the body and wrapped it in a long sheet of clean linen cloth. 60 He placed it in his own new tomb, which had been carved out of the rock. Then he rolled a great stone across the entrance and left. 61 Both Mary Magdalene and the other Mary were sitting across from the tomb and watching.

The Guard at the Tomb

62 The next day, on the Sabbath,* the leading priests and Pharisees went to see Pilate. 63 They told him, "Sir, we remember what that deceiver once said while he was still alive: 'After three days I will rise from the dead.' 64 So we request that you seal the tomb until the third day. This will prevent his disciples from coming and stealing his body and then telling everyone he was raised from the dead! If that happens, we'll be worse off than we were at first."

65 Pilate replied, "Take guards and secure it the best you can." 66 So they sealed the tomb and posted guards to protect it.

The Resurrection

28 Early on Sunday morning,* as the new day was dawning, Mary Magdalene and the other Mary went out to visit the tomb.

2 Suddenly there was a great earthquake! For an angel of the Lord came down from heaven, rolled aside the stone, and sat on it. 3 His face shone like lightning, and his clothing was as white as snow. 4 The guards shook with fear when they saw him, and they fell into a dead faint.

5 Then the angel spoke to the women. "Don't be afraid!" he said. "I know you are looking for Jesus, who was crucified. 6 He isn't here! He is risen from the dead, just as he said would happen. Come, see where his body was lying. 7 And now, go quickly and tell his disciples that he has risen from the dead, and he is going ahead of you to Galilee. You will see him there. Remember what I have told you."

8 The women ran quickly from the tomb. They were very frightened but also filled with great joy, and they rushed to give the disciples the angel's message. 9 And as they went, Jesus met them and greeted them. And they ran to him, grasped his feet, and worshiped him. 10 Then Jesus said to them, "Don't be afraid! Go tell my brothers to leave for Galilee, and they will see me there."

The Report of the Guard

11 As the women were on their way, some of the guards went into the city and told the leading priests

27:62 Or *On the next day, which is after the Preparation.* **28:1** Greek *After the Sabbath, on the first day of the week.*

KING JAMES VERSION

12 And when they were assembled with the elders, and had taken counsel, they gave large money unto the soldiers,

13 Saying, Say ye, His disciples came by night, and stole him *away* while we slept.

14 And if this come to the governor's ears, we will persuade him, and secure you.

15 So they took the money, and did as they were taught: and this saying is commonly reported among the Jews until this day.

16 Then the eleven disciples went away into Galilee, into a mountain where Jesus had appointed them.

17 And when they saw him, they worshipped him: but some doubted.

18 And Jesus came and spake unto them, saying, All power is given unto me in heaven and in earth.

19 Go ye therefore, and teach all nations, baptizing them in the name of the Father, and of the Son, and of the Holy Ghost:

20 Teaching them to observe all things whatsoever I have commanded you: and, lo, I am with you alway, *even* unto the end of the world. Amen.

NEW LIVING TRANSLATION

what had happened. 12 A meeting with the elders was
called, and they decided to give the soldiers a large
bribe. 13 They told the soldiers, "You must say, 'Jesus'
disciples came during the night while we were sleeping, and they stole his body.' 14 If the governor hears
about it, we'll stand up for you so you won't get in
trouble." 15 So the guards accepted the bribe and
said what they were told to say. Their story spread
widely among the Jews, and they still tell it today.

The Great Commission

16 Then the eleven disciples left for Galilee, going to
the mountain where Jesus had told them to go.
17 When they saw him, they worshiped him—but
some of them doubted!

18 Jesus came and told his disciples, "I have been
given all authority in heaven and on earth. 19 Therefore, go and make disciples of all the nations,* baptizing them in the name of the Father and the Son
and the Holy Spirit. 20 Teach these new disciples to
obey all the commands I have given you. And be sure
of this: I am with you always, even to the end of
the age."

28:19 Or *all peoples.*

Mark

KING JAMES VERSION

1 1 The beginning of the gospel of Jesus Christ, the Son of God;

2 As it is written in the prophets, Behold, I send my messenger before thy face, which shall prepare thy way before thee.

3 The voice of one crying in the wilderness, Prepare ye the way of the Lord, make his paths straight.

4 John did baptize in the wilderness, and preach the baptism of repentance for the remission of sins.

5 And there went out unto him all the land of Judaea, and they of Jerusalem, and were all baptized of him in the river of Jordan, confessing their sins.

6 And John was clothed with camel's hair, and with a girdle of a skin about his loins; and he did eat locusts and wild honey;

7 And preached, saying, There cometh one mightier than I after me, the latchet of whose shoes I am not worthy to stoop down and unloose.

8 I indeed have baptized you with water: but he shall baptize you with the Holy Ghost.

9 And it came to pass in those days, that Jesus came from Nazareth of Galilee, and was baptized of John in Jordan.

10 And straightway coming up out of the water, he saw the heavens opened, and the Spirit like a dove descending upon him:

11 And there came a voice from heaven, *saying,* Thou art my beloved Son, in whom I am well pleased.

12 And immediately the Spirit driveth him into the wilderness.

13 And he was there in the wilderness forty days, tempted of Satan; and was with the wild beasts; and the angels ministered unto him.

14 Now after that John was put in prison, Jesus came into Galilee, preaching the gospel of the kingdom of God,

15 And saying, The time is fulfilled, and the kingdom of God is at hand: repent ye, and believe the gospel.

NEW LIVING TRANSLATION

John the Baptist Prepares the Way

1 This is the Good News about Jesus the Messiah, the Son of God.* It began 2 just as the prophet Isaiah had written:

"Look, I am sending my messenger ahead of you,
and he will prepare your way.*
3 He is a voice shouting in the wilderness,
'Prepare the way for the LORD's coming!
Clear the road for him!'*"

4 This messenger was John the Baptist. He was in the wilderness and preached that people should be baptized to show that they had repented of their sins and turned to God to be forgiven. 5 All of Judea, including all the people of Jerusalem, went out to see and hear John. And when they confessed their sins, he baptized them in the Jordan River. 6 His clothes were woven from coarse camel hair, and he wore a leather belt around his waist. For food he ate locusts and wild honey.

7 John announced: "Someone is coming soon who is greater than I am—so much greater that I'm not even worthy to stoop down like a slave and untie the straps of his sandals. 8 I baptize you with* water, but he will baptize you with the Holy Spirit!"

The Baptism and Temptation of Jesus

9 One day Jesus came from Nazareth in Galilee, and John baptized him in the Jordan River. 10 As Jesus came up out of the water, he saw the heavens splitting apart and the Holy Spirit descending on him* like a dove. 11 And a voice from heaven said, "You are my dearly loved Son, and you bring me great joy."

12 The Spirit then compelled Jesus to go into the wilderness, 13 where he was tempted by Satan for forty days. He was out among the wild animals, and angels took care of him.

14 Later on, after John was arrested, Jesus went into Galilee, where he preached God's Good News.* 15 "The time promised by God has come at last!" he announced. "The Kingdom of God is near! Repent of your sins and believe the Good News!"

1:1 Some manuscripts do not include *the Son of God.* **1:2** Mal 3:1. **1:3** Isa 40:3 (Greek version). **1:8** Or *in;* also in 1:8b. **1:10** Or *toward him,* or *into him.* **1:14** Some manuscripts read *the Good News of the Kingdom of God.*

KING JAMES VERSION

[16]Now as he walked by the sea of Galilee, he saw Simon and Andrew his brother casting a net into the sea: for they were fishers.

[17]And Jesus said unto them, Come ye after me, and I will make you to become fishers of men.

[18]And straightway they forsook their nets, and followed him.

[19]And when he had gone a little farther thence, he saw James the *son* of Zebedee, and John his brother, who also were in the ship mending their nets.

[20]And straightway he called them: and they left their father Zebedee in the ship with the hired servants, and went after him.

[21]And they went into Capernaum; and straightway on the sabbath day he entered into the synagogue, and taught.

[22]And they were astonished at his doctrine: for he taught them as one that had authority, and not as the scribes.

[23]And there was in their synagogue a man with an unclean spirit; and he cried out,

[24]Saying, Let *us* alone; what have we to do with thee, thou Jesus of Nazareth? art thou come to destroy us? I know thee who thou art, the Holy One of God.

[25]And Jesus rebuked him, saying, Hold thy peace, and come out of him.

[26]And when the unclean spirit had torn him, and cried with a loud voice, he came out of him.

[27]And they were all amazed, insomuch that they questioned among themselves, saying, What thing is this? what new doctrine *is* this? for with authority commandeth he even the unclean spirits, and they do obey him.

[28]And immediately his fame spread abroad throughout all the region round about Galilee.

[29]And forthwith, when they were come out of the synagogue, they entered into the house of Simon and Andrew, with James and John.

[30]But Simon's wife's mother lay sick of a fever, and anon they tell him of her.

[31]And he came and took her by the hand, and lifted her up; and immediately the fever left her, and she ministered unto them.

[32]And at even, when the sun did set, they brought unto him all that were diseased, and them that were possessed with devils.

[33]And all the city was gathered together at the door.

[34]And he healed many that were sick of divers diseases, and cast out many devils; and suffered not the devils to speak, because they knew him.

[35]And in the morning, rising up a great while before day, he went out, and departed into a solitary place, and there prayed.

[36]And Simon and they that were with him followed after him.

NEW LIVING TRANSLATION

The First Disciples

[16]One day as Jesus was walking along the shore of the
Sea of Galilee, he saw Simon* and his brother
Andrew throwing a net into the water, for they fished
for a living. [17]Jesus called out to them, "Come, follow
me, and I will show you how to fish for people!"
[18]And they left their nets at once and followed him.
[19]A little farther up the shore Jesus saw Zebedee's
sons, James and John, in a boat repairing their nets.
[20]He called them at once, and they also followed him,
leaving their father, Zebedee, in the boat with the
hired men.

Jesus Casts Out an Evil Spirit

[21]Jesus and his companions went to the town of
Capernaum. When the Sabbath day came, he went
into the synagogue and began to teach. [22]The people
were amazed at his teaching, for he taught with real
authority—quite unlike the teachers of religious law.
[23]Suddenly, a man in the synagogue who was possessed by an evil* spirit began shouting, [24]"Why are
you interfering with us, Jesus of Nazareth? Have you
come to destroy us? I know who you are—the Holy
One of God!"
[25]Jesus cut him short. "Be quiet! Come out of the
man," he ordered. [26]At that, the evil spirit screamed,
threw the man into a convulsion, and then came out
of him.
[27]Amazement gripped the audience, and they
began to discuss what had happened. "What sort of
new teaching is this?" they asked excitedly. "It has
such authority! Even evil spirits obey his orders!"
[28]The news about Jesus spread quickly throughout
the entire region of Galilee.

Jesus Heals Many People

[29]After Jesus left the synagogue with James and John,
they went to Simon and Andrew's home. [30]Now
Simon's mother-in-law was sick in bed with a high
fever. They told Jesus about her right away. [31]So
he went to her bedside, took her by the hand, and
helped her sit up. Then the fever left her, and she
prepared a meal for them.
[32]That evening after sunset, many sick and demon-
possessed people were brought to Jesus. [33]The whole
town gathered at the door to watch. [34]So Jesus healed
many people who were sick with various diseases, and
he cast out many demons. But because the demons
knew who he was, he did not allow them to speak.

Jesus Preaches in Galilee

[35]Before daybreak the next morning, Jesus got up and
went out to an isolated place to pray. [36]Later Simon

1:16 *Simon* is called "Peter" in 3:16 and thereafter. **1:23** Greek *unclean;* also in 1:26, 27.

KING JAMES VERSION

37 And when they had found him, they said unto him, All *men* seek for thee.

38 And he said unto them, Let us go into the next towns, that I may preach there also: for therefore came I forth.

39 And he preached in their synagogues throughout all Galilee, and cast out devils.

40 And there came a leper to him, beseeching him, and kneeling down to him, and saying unto him, If thou wilt, thou canst make me clean.

41 And Jesus, moved with compassion, put forth *his* hand, and touched him, and saith unto him, I will; be thou clean.

42 And as soon as he had spoken, immediately the leprosy departed from him, and he was cleansed.

43 And he straitly charged him, and forthwith sent him away;

44 And saith unto him, See thou say nothing to any man: but go thy way, shew thyself to the priest, and offer for thy cleansing those things which Moses commanded, for a testimony unto them.

45 But he went out, and began to publish *it* much, and to blaze abroad the matter, insomuch that Jesus could no more openly enter into the city, but was without in desert places: and they came to him from every quarter.

2 1 And again he entered into Capernaum after *some* days; and it was noised that he was in the house.

2 And straightway many were gathered together, insomuch that there was no room to receive *them,* no, not so much as about the door: and he preached the word unto them.

3 And they come unto him, bringing one sick of the palsy, which was borne of four.

4 And when they could not come nigh unto him for the press, they uncovered the roof where he was: and when they had broken *it* up, they let down the bed wherein the sick of the palsy lay.

5 When Jesus saw their faith, he said unto the sick of the palsy, Son, thy sins be forgiven thee.

6 But there were certain of the scribes sitting there, and reasoning in their hearts,

7 Why doth this *man* thus speak blasphemies? who can forgive sins but God only?

8 And immediately when Jesus perceived in his spirit that they so reasoned within themselves, he said unto them, Why reason ye these things in your hearts?

9 Whether is it easier to say to the sick of the palsy, *Thy* sins be forgiven thee; or to say, Arise, and take up thy bed, and walk?

10 But that ye may know that the Son of man hath power on earth to forgive sins, (he saith to the sick of the palsy,)

NEW LIVING TRANSLATION

and the others went out to find him. 37 When they found him, they said, "Everyone is looking for you."

38 But Jesus replied, "We must go on to other towns as well, and I will preach to them, too. That is why I came." 39 So he traveled throughout the region of Galilee, preaching in the synagogues and casting out demons.

Jesus Heals a Man with Leprosy

40 A man with leprosy came and knelt in front of Jesus, begging to be healed. "If you are willing, you can heal me and make me clean," he said.

41 Moved with compassion,* Jesus reached out and touched him. "I am willing," he said. "Be healed!" 42 Instantly the leprosy disappeared, and the man was healed. 43 Then Jesus sent him on his way with a stern warning: 44 "Don't tell anyone about this. Instead, go to the priest and let him examine you. Take along the offering required in the law of Moses for those who have been healed of leprosy.* This will be a public testimony that you have been cleansed."

45 But the man went and spread the word, proclaiming to everyone what had happened. As a result, large crowds soon surrounded Jesus, and he couldn't publicly enter a town anywhere. He had to stay out in the secluded places, but people from everywhere kept coming to him.

Jesus Heals a Paralyzed Man

2 When Jesus returned to Capernaum several days later, the news spread quickly that he was back home. 2 Soon the house where he was staying was so packed with visitors that there was no more room, even outside the door. While he was preaching God's word to them, 3 four men arrived carrying a paralyzed man on a mat. 4 They couldn't bring him to Jesus because of the crowd, so they dug a hole through the roof above his head. Then they lowered the man on his mat, right down in front of Jesus. 5 Seeing their faith, Jesus said to the paralyzed man, "My child, your sins are forgiven."

6 But some of the teachers of religious law who were sitting there thought to themselves, 7 "What is he saying? This is blasphemy! Only God can forgive sins!"

8 Jesus knew immediately what they were thinking, so he asked them, "Why do you question this in your hearts? 9 Is it easier to say to the paralyzed man 'Your sins are forgiven,' or 'Stand up, pick up your mat, and walk'? 10 So I will prove to you that the Son of Man* has the authority on earth to forgive sins." Then Jesus

1:41 Some manuscripts read *Moved with anger.* **1:44** See Lev 14:2-32.
2:10 "Son of Man" is a title Jesus used for himself.

KING JAMES VERSION

11 I say unto thee, Arise, and take up thy bed, and go thy way into thine house.

12 And immediately he arose, took up the bed, and went forth before them all; insomuch that they were all amazed, and glorified God, saying, We never saw it on this fashion.

13 And he went forth again by the sea side; and all the multitude resorted unto him, and he taught them.

14 And as he passed by, he saw Levi the *son* of Alphaeus sitting at the receipt of custom, and said unto him, Follow me. And he arose and followed him.

15 And it came to pass, that, as Jesus sat at meat in his house, many publicans and sinners sat also together with Jesus and his disciples: for there were many, and they followed him.

16 And when the scribes and Pharisees saw him eat with publicans and sinners, they said unto his disciples, How is it that he eateth and drinketh with publicans and sinners?

17 When Jesus heard *it,* he saith unto them, They that are whole have no need of the physician, but they that are sick: I came not to call the righteous, but sinners to repentance.

18 And the disciples of John and of the Pharisees used to fast: and they come and say unto him, Why do the disciples of John and of the Pharisees fast, but thy disciples fast not?

19 And Jesus said unto them, Can the children of the bridechamber fast, while the bridegroom is with them? as long as they have the bridegroom with them, they cannot fast.

20 But the days will come, when the bridegroom shall be taken away from them, and then shall they fast in those days.

21 No man also seweth a piece of new cloth on an old garment: else the new piece that filled it up taketh away from the old, and the rent is made worse.

22 And no man putteth new wine into old bottles: else the new wine doth burst the bottles, and the wine is spilled, and the bottles will be marred: but new wine must be put into new bottles.

23 And it came to pass, that he went through the corn fields on the sabbath day; and his disciples began, as they went, to pluck the ears of corn.

24 And the Pharisees said unto him, Behold, why do they on the sabbath day that which is not lawful?

25 And he said unto them, Have ye never read what David did, when he had need, and was an hungred, he, and they that were with him?

26 How he went into the house of God in the days of Abiathar the high priest, and did eat the shewbread,

NEW LIVING TRANSLATION

turned to the paralyzed man and said, 11 "Stand up,
pick up your mat, and go home!"

12 And the man jumped up, grabbed his mat, and walked out through the stunned onlookers. They were all amazed and praised God, exclaiming, "We've never seen anything like this before!"

Jesus Calls Levi (Matthew)

13 Then Jesus went out to the lakeshore again and
taught the crowds that were coming to him. 14 As he
walked along, he saw Levi son of Alphaeus sitting
at his tax collector's booth. "Follow me and be my
disciple," Jesus said to him. So Levi got up and followed him.

15 Later, Levi invited Jesus and his disciples to his home as dinner guests, along with many tax collectors and other disreputable sinners. (There were many people of this kind among Jesus' followers.)

16 But when the teachers of religious law who were Pharisees* saw him eating with tax collectors and other sinners, they asked his disciples, "Why does he eat with such scum?*"

17 When Jesus heard this, he told them, "Healthy people don't need a doctor—sick people do. I have come to call not those who think they are righteous, but those who know they are sinners."

A Discussion about Fasting

18 Once when John's disciples and the Pharisees were fasting, some people came to Jesus and asked, "Why don't your disciples fast like John's disciples and the Pharisees do?"

19 Jesus replied, "Do wedding guests fast while celebrating with the groom? Of course not. They can't
fast while the groom is with them. 20 But someday the
groom will be taken away from them, and then they
will fast.

21 "Besides, who would patch old clothing with new cloth? For the new patch would shrink and rip away from the old cloth, leaving an even bigger tear than before.

22 "And no one puts new wine into old wineskins. For the wine would burst the wineskins, and the wine and the skins would both be lost. New wine calls for new wineskins."

A Discussion about the Sabbath

23 One Sabbath day as Jesus was walking through
some grainfields, his disciples began breaking off
heads of grain to eat. 24 But the Pharisees said to
Jesus, "Look, why are they breaking the law by harvesting grain on the Sabbath?"

25 Jesus said to them, "Haven't you ever read in the
Scriptures what David did when he and his companions were hungry? 26 He went into the house of God
(during the days when Abiathar was high priest) and

2:16a Greek *the scribes of the Pharisees.* **2:16b** Greek *with tax collectors and sinners?*

KING JAMES VERSION

which is not lawful to eat but for the priests, and gave also to them which were with him?

27 And he said unto them, The sabbath was made for man, and not man for the sabbath:

28 Therefore the Son of man is Lord also of the sabbath.

3 1 And he entered again into the synagogue; and there was a man there which had a withered hand.

2 And they watched him, whether he would heal him on the sabbath day; that they might accuse him.

3 And he saith unto the man which had the withered hand, Stand forth.

4 And he saith unto them, Is it lawful to do good on the sabbath days, or to do evil? to save life, or to kill? But they held their peace.

5 And when he had looked round about on them with anger, being grieved for the hardness of their hearts, he saith unto the man, Stretch forth thine hand. And he stretched *it* out: and his hand was restored whole as the other.

6 And the Pharisees went forth, and straightway took counsel with the Herodians against him, how they might destroy him.

7 But Jesus withdrew himself with his disciples to the sea: and a great multitude from Galilee followed him, and from Judaea,

8 And from Jerusalem, and from Idumaea, and *from* beyond Jordan; and they about Tyre and Sidon, a great multitude, when they had heard what great things he did, came unto him.

9 And he spake to his disciples, that a small ship should wait on him because of the multitude, lest they should throng him.

10 For he had healed many; insomuch that they pressed upon him for to touch him, as many as had plagues.

11 And unclean spirits, when they saw him, fell down before him, and cried, saying, Thou art the Son of God.

12 And he straitly charged them that they should not make him known.

13 And he goeth up into a mountain, and calleth *unto him* whom he would: and they came unto him.

14 And he ordained twelve, that they should be with him, and that he might send them forth to preach,

15 And to have power to heal sicknesses, and to cast out devils:

16 And Simon he surnamed Peter;

17 And James the *son* of Zebedee, and John the brother of James; and he surnamed them Boanerges, which is, The sons of thunder:

NEW LIVING TRANSLATION

broke the law by eating the sacred loaves of bread that only the priests are allowed to eat. He also gave some to his companions."

27 Then Jesus said to them, "The Sabbath was made to meet the needs of people, and not people to meet the requirements of the Sabbath. 28 So the Son of Man is Lord, even over the Sabbath!"

Jesus Heals on the Sabbath

3 Jesus went into the synagogue again and noticed a man with a deformed hand. 2 Since it was the Sabbath, Jesus' enemies watched him closely. If he healed the man's hand, they planned to accuse him of working on the Sabbath.

3 Jesus said to the man with the deformed hand, "Come and stand in front of everyone." 4 Then he turned to his critics and asked, "Does the law permit good deeds on the Sabbath, or is it a day for doing evil? Is this a day to save life or to destroy it?" But they wouldn't answer him.

5 He looked around at them angrily and was deeply saddened by their hard hearts. Then he said to the man, "Hold out your hand." So the man held out his hand, and it was restored! 6 At once the Pharisees went away and met with the supporters of Herod to plot how to kill Jesus.

Crowds Follow Jesus

7 Jesus went out to the lake with his disciples, and a large crowd followed him. They came from all over Galilee, Judea, 8 Jerusalem, Idumea, from east of the Jordan River, and even from as far north as Tyre and Sidon. The news about his miracles had spread far and wide, and vast numbers of people came to see him.

9 Jesus instructed his disciples to have a boat ready so the crowd would not crush him. 10 He had healed many people that day, so all the sick people eagerly pushed forward to touch him. 11 And whenever those possessed by evil* spirits caught sight of him, the spirits would throw them to the ground in front of him shrieking, "You are the Son of God!" 12 But Jesus sternly commanded the spirits not to reveal who he was.

Jesus Chooses the Twelve Apostles

13 Afterward Jesus went up on a mountain and called out the ones he wanted to go with him. And they came to him. 14 Then he appointed twelve of them and called them his apostles.* They were to accompany him, and he would send them out to preach, 15 giving them authority to cast out demons. 16 These are the twelve he chose:

Simon (whom he named Peter),

17 James and John (the sons of Zebedee, but Jesus nicknamed them "Sons of Thunder"*),

3:11 Greek *unclean;* also in 3:30. **3:14** Some manuscripts do not include *and called them his apostles.* **3:17** Greek *whom he named Boanerges, which means Sons of Thunder.*

KING JAMES VERSION

18And Andrew, and Philip, and Bartholomew, and Matthew, and Thomas, and James the *son* of Alphaeus, and Thaddaeus, and Simon the Canaanite,

19And Judas Iscariot, which also betrayed him: and they went into an house.

20And the multitude cometh together again, so that they could not so much as eat bread.

21And when his friends heard *of it,* they went out to lay hold on him: for they said, He is beside himself.

22And the scribes which came down from Jerusalem said, He hath Beelzebub, and by the prince of the devils casteth he out devils.

23And he called them *unto him,* and said unto them in parables, How can Satan cast out Satan?

24And if a kingdom be divided against itself, that kingdom cannot stand.

25And if a house be divided against itself, that house cannot stand.

26And if Satan rise up against himself, and be divided, he cannot stand, but hath an end.

27No man can enter into a strong man's house, and spoil his goods, except he will first bind the strong man; and then he will spoil his house.

28Verily I say unto you, All sins shall be forgiven unto the sons of men, and blasphemies wherewith soever they shall blaspheme:

29But he that shall blaspheme against the Holy Ghost hath never forgiveness, but is in danger of eternal damnation:

30Because they said, He hath an unclean spirit.

31There came then his brethren and his mother, and, standing without, sent unto him, calling him.

32And the multitude sat about him, and they said unto him, Behold, thy mother and thy brethren without seek for thee.

33And he answered them, saying, Who is my mother, or my brethren?

34And he looked round about on them which sat about him, and said, Behold my mother and my brethren!

35For whosoever shall do the will of God, the same is my brother, and my sister, and mother.

4 1And he began again to teach by the sea side: and there was gathered unto him a great multitude, so that he entered into a ship, and sat in the sea; and the whole multitude was by the sea on the land.

2And he taught them many things by parables, and said unto them in his doctrine,

NEW LIVING TRANSLATION

18 Andrew,
Philip,
Bartholomew,
Matthew,
Thomas,
James (son of Alphaeus),
Thaddaeus,
Simon (the zealot*),
19 Judas Iscariot (who later betrayed him).

Jesus and the Prince of Demons

20One time Jesus entered a house, and the crowds
began to gather again. Soon he and his disciples
couldn't even find time to eat. 21When his family
heard what was happening, they tried to take him
away. "He's out of his mind," they said.

22But the teachers of religious law who had arrived from Jerusalem said, "He's possessed by Satan,* the prince of demons. That's where he gets the power to cast out demons."

23Jesus called them over and responded with an illustration. "How can Satan cast out Satan?" he asked.
24"A kingdom divided by civil war will collapse. 25Sim-
ilarly, a family splintered by feuding will fall apart.
26And if Satan is divided and fights against himself,
how can he stand? He would never survive. 27Let me
illustrate this further. Who is powerful enough to enter the house of a strong man like Satan and plunder his goods? Only someone even stronger—someone who could tie him up and then plunder his house.

28"I tell you the truth, all sin and blasphemy can be
forgiven, 29but anyone who blasphemes the Holy
Spirit will never be forgiven. This is a sin with eternal
consequences." 30He told them this because they
were saying, "He's possessed by an evil spirit."

The True Family of Jesus

31Then Jesus' mother and brothers came to see him.
They stood outside and sent word for him to come
out and talk with them. 32There was a crowd sitting
around Jesus, and someone said, "Your mother and
your brothers* are outside asking for you."

33Jesus replied, "Who is my mother? Who are my
brothers?" 34Then he looked at those around him
and said, "Look, these are my mother and brothers.
35Anyone who does God's will is my brother and
sister and mother."

Parable of the Farmer Scattering Seed

4 Once again Jesus began teaching by the lakeshore. A very large crowd soon gathered around him, so he got into a boat. Then he sat in the boat while all the people remained on the shore. 2He
taught them by telling many stories in the form of
parables, such as this one:

3:18 Greek *the Cananean,* an Aramaic term for Jewish nationalists.
3:22 Greek *Beelzeboul;* other manuscripts read *Beezeboul;* Latin version reads *Beelzebub.* **3:32** Some manuscripts add *and sisters.*

KING JAMES VERSION

3 Hearken; Behold, there went out a sower to sow:

4 And it came to pass, as he sowed, some fell by the way side, and the fowls of the air came and devoured it up.

5 And some fell on stony ground, where it had not much earth; and immediately it sprang up, because it had no depth of earth:

6 But when the sun was up, it was scorched; and because it had no root, it withered away.

7 And some fell among thorns, and the thorns grew up, and choked it, and it yielded no fruit.

8 And other fell on good ground, and did yield fruit that sprang up and increased; and brought forth, some thirty, and some sixty, and some an hundred.

9 And he said unto them, He that hath ears to hear, let him hear.

10 And when he was alone, they that were about him with the twelve asked of him the parable.

11 And he said unto them, Unto you it is given to know the mystery of the kingdom of God: but unto them that are without, all *these* things are done in parables:

12 That seeing they may see, and not perceive; and hearing they may hear, and not understand; lest at any time they should be converted, and *their* sins should be forgiven them.

13 And he said unto them, Know ye not this parable? and how then will ye know all parables?

14 The sower soweth the word.

15 And these are they by the way side, where the word is sown; but when they have heard, Satan cometh immediately, and taketh away the word that was sown in their hearts.

16 And these are they likewise which are sown on stony ground; who, when they have heard the word, immediately receive it with gladness;

17 And have no root in themselves, and so endure but for a time: afterward, when affliction or persecution ariseth for the word's sake, immediately they are offended.

18 And these are they which are sown among thorns; such as hear the word,

19 And the cares of this world, and the deceitfulness of riches, and the lusts of other things entering in, choke the word, and it becometh unfruitful.

20 And these are they which are sown on good ground; such as hear the word, and receive *it*, and bring forth fruit, some thirtyfold, some sixty, and some an hundred.

21 And he said unto them, Is a candle brought to be put under a bushel, or under a bed? and not to be set on a candlestick?

22 For there is nothing hid, which shall not be manifested; neither was any thing kept secret, but that it should come abroad.

23 If any man have ears to hear, let him hear.

NEW LIVING TRANSLATION

3 "Listen! A farmer went out to plant some seed. 4 As he scattered it across his field, some of the seed fell on a footpath, and the birds came and ate it. 5 Other seed fell on shallow soil with underlying rock. The seed sprouted quickly because the soil was shallow. 6 But the plant soon wilted under the hot sun, and since it didn't have deep roots, it died. 7 Other seed fell among thorns that grew up and choked out the tender plants so they produced no grain. 8 Still other seeds fell on fertile soil, and they sprouted, grew, and produced a crop that was thirty, sixty, and even a hundred times as much as had been planted!" 9 Then he said, "Anyone with ears to hear should listen and understand."

10 Later, when Jesus was alone with the twelve disciples and with the others who were gathered around, they asked him what the parables meant.

11 He replied, "You are permitted to understand the secret* of the Kingdom of God. But I use parables for everything I say to outsiders, 12 so that the Scriptures might be fulfilled:

'When they see what I do,
they will learn nothing.
When they hear what I say,
they will not understand.
Otherwise, they will turn to me
and be forgiven.'*"

13 Then Jesus said to them, "If you can't understand the meaning of this parable, how will you understand all the other parables? 14 The farmer plants seed by taking God's word to others. 15 The seed that fell on the footpath represents those who hear the message, only to have Satan come at once and take it away. 16 The seed on the rocky soil represents those who hear the message and immediately receive it with joy. 17 But since they don't have deep roots, they don't last long. They fall away as soon as they have problems or are persecuted for believing God's word. 18 The seed that fell among the thorns represents others who hear God's word, 19 but all too quickly the message is crowded out by the worries of this life, the lure of wealth, and the desire for other things, so no fruit is produced. 20 And the seed that fell on good soil represents those who hear and accept God's word and produce a harvest of thirty, sixty, or even a hundred times as much as had been planted!"

Parable of the Lamp

21 Then Jesus asked them, "Would anyone light a lamp and then put it under a basket or under a bed? Of course not! A lamp is placed on a stand, where its light will shine. 22 For everything that is hidden will eventually be brought into the open, and every secret will be brought to light. 23 Anyone with ears to hear should listen and understand."

4:11 Greek *mystery*. **4:12** Isa 6:9-10 (Greek version).

KING JAMES VERSION

24And he said unto them, Take heed what ye hear: with what measure ye mete, it shall be measured to you: and unto you that hear shall more be given.

25For he that hath, to him shall be given: and he that hath not, from him shall be taken even that which he hath.

26And he said, So is the kingdom of God, as if a man should cast seed into the ground;

27And should sleep, and rise night and day, and the seed should spring and grow up, he knoweth not how.

28For the earth bringeth forth fruit of herself; first the blade, then the ear, after that the full corn in the ear.

29But when the fruit is brought forth, immediately he putteth in the sickle, because the harvest is come.

30And he said, Whereunto shall we liken the kingdom of God? or with what comparison shall we compare it?

31*It is* like a grain of mustard seed, which, when it is sown in the earth, is less than all the seeds that be in the earth:

32But when it is sown, it groweth up, and becometh greater than all herbs, and shooteth out great branches; so that the fowls of the air may lodge under the shadow of it.

33And with many such parables spake he the word unto them, as they were able to hear *it*.

34But without a parable spake he not unto them: and when they were alone, he expounded all things to his disciples.

35And the same day, when the even was come, he saith unto them, Let us pass over unto the other side.

36And when they had sent away the multitude, they took him even as he was in the ship. And there were also with him other little ships.

37And there arose a great storm of wind, and the waves beat into the ship, so that it was now full.

38And he was in the hinder part of the ship, asleep on a pillow: and they awake him, and say unto him, Master, carest thou not that we perish?

39And he arose, and rebuked the wind, and said unto the sea, Peace, be still. And the wind ceased, and there was a great calm.

40And he said unto them, Why are ye so fearful? how is it that ye have no faith?

41And they feared exceedingly, and said one to another, What manner of man is this, that even the wind and the sea obey him?

NEW LIVING TRANSLATION

24Then he added, "Pay close attention to what you hear. The closer you listen, the more understanding you will be given*—and you will receive even more.
25To those who listen to my teaching, more understanding will be given. But for those who are not listening, even what little understanding they have will be taken away from them."

Parable of the Growing Seed

26Jesus also said, "The Kingdom of God is like a farmer who scatters seed on the ground. 27Night and day, while he's asleep or awake, the seed sprouts and grows, but he does not understand how it happens. 28The earth produces the crops on its own. First a leaf blade pushes through, then the heads of wheat are formed, and finally the grain ripens.
29And as soon as the grain is ready, the farmer comes and harvests it with a sickle, for the harvest time has come."

Parable of the Mustard Seed

30Jesus said, "How can I describe the Kingdom of God? What story should I use to illustrate it? 31It is like a mustard seed planted in the ground. It is the smallest of all seeds, 32but it becomes the largest of all garden plants; it grows long branches, and birds can make nests in its shade."

33Jesus used many similar stories and illustrations to teach the people as much as they could understand. 34In fact, in his public ministry he never taught without using parables; but afterward, when he was alone with his disciples, he explained everything to them.

Jesus Calms the Storm

35As evening came, Jesus said to his disciples, "Let's cross to the other side of the lake." 36So they took Jesus in the boat and started out, leaving the crowds behind (although other boats followed). 37But soon a fierce storm came up. High waves were breaking into the boat, and it began to fill with water.

38Jesus was sleeping at the back of the boat with his head on a cushion. The disciples woke him up, shouting, "Teacher, don't you care that we're going to drown?"

39When Jesus woke up, he rebuked the wind and said to the waves, "Silence! Be still!" Suddenly the wind stopped, and there was a great calm. 40Then he asked them, "Why are you afraid? Do you still have no faith?"

41The disciples were absolutely terrified. "Who is this man?" they asked each other. "Even the wind and waves obey him!"

4:24 Or *The measure you give will be the measure you get back.*

KING JAMES VERSION

5

1 And they came over unto the other side of the sea, into the country of the Gadarenes.

2 And when he was come out of the ship, immediately there met him out of the tombs a man with an unclean spirit,

3 Who had *his* dwelling among the tombs; and no man could bind him, no, not with chains:

4 Because that he had been often bound with fetters and chains, and the chains had been plucked asunder by him, and the fetters broken in pieces: neither could any *man* tame him.

5 And always, night and day, he was in the mountains, and in the tombs, crying, and cutting himself with stones.

6 But when he saw Jesus afar off, he ran and worshipped him,

7 And cried with a loud voice, and said, What have I to do with thee, Jesus, *thou* Son of the most high God? I adjure thee by God, that thou torment me not.

8 For he said unto him, Come out of the man, *thou* unclean spirit.

9 And he asked him, What *is* thy name? And he answered, saying, My name *is* Legion: for we are many.

10 And he besought him much that he would not send them away out of the country.

11 Now there was there nigh unto the mountains a great herd of swine feeding.

12 And all the devils besought him, saying, Send us into the swine, that we may enter into them.

13 And forthwith Jesus gave them leave. And the unclean spirits went out, and entered into the swine: and the herd ran violently down a steep place into the sea, (they were about two thousand;) and were choked in the sea.

14 And they that fed the swine fled, and told *it* in the city, and in the country. And they went out to see what it was that was done.

15 And they come to Jesus, and see him that was possessed with the devil, and had the legion, sitting, and clothed, and in his right mind: and they were afraid.

16 And they that saw *it* told them how it befell to him that was possessed with the devil, and *also* concerning the swine.

17 And they began to pray him to depart out of their coasts.

18 And when he was come into the ship, he that had been possessed with the devil prayed him that he might be with him.

19 Howbeit Jesus suffered him not, but saith unto him, Go home to thy friends, and tell them how great things the Lord hath done for thee, and hath had compassion on thee.

20 And he departed, and began to publish in Decapolis how great things Jesus had done for him: and all *men* did marvel.

NEW LIVING TRANSLATION

Jesus Heals a Demon-Possessed Man

5

So they arrived at the other side of the lake,
in the region of the Gerasenes.* 2 When Jesus
climbed out of the boat, a man possessed by an evil*
spirit came out from a cemetery to meet him. 3 This
man lived among the burial caves and could no longer be restrained, even with a chain. 4 Whenever he
was put into chains and shackles—as he often was—
he snapped the chains from his wrists and smashed
the shackles. No one was strong enough to subdue
him. 5 Day and night he wandered among the burial
caves and in the hills, howling and cutting himself
with sharp stones.

6 When Jesus was still some distance away, the
man saw him, ran to meet him, and bowed low before
him. 7 With a shriek, he screamed, "Why are you interfering with me, Jesus, Son of the Most High God?
In the name of God, I beg you, don't torture me!" 8 For
Jesus had already said to the spirit, "Come out of the
man, you evil spirit."

9 Then Jesus demanded, "What is your name?"

And he replied, "My name is Legion, because there
are many of us inside this man." 10 Then the evil spirits begged him again and again not to send them to
some distant place.

11 There happened to be a large herd of pigs feeding on the hillside nearby. 12 "Send us into those
pigs," the spirits begged. "Let us enter them."

13 So Jesus gave them permission. The evil spirits
came out of the man and entered the pigs, and the
entire herd of about 2,000 pigs plunged down the
steep hillside into the lake and drowned in the water.

14 The herdsmen fled to the nearby town and the
surrounding countryside, spreading the news as they
ran. People rushed out to see what had happened.
15 A crowd soon gathered around Jesus, and they saw
the man who had been possessed by the legion of
demons. He was sitting there fully clothed and perfectly sane, and they were all afraid. 16 Then those
who had seen what happened told the others about
the demon-possessed man and the pigs. 17 And the
crowd began pleading with Jesus to go away and
leave them alone.

18 As Jesus was getting into the boat, the man who
had been demon possessed begged to go with him.
19 But Jesus said, "No, go home to your family, and tell
them everything the Lord has done for you and how
merciful he has been." 20 So the man started off to
visit the Ten Towns* of that region and began to proclaim the great things Jesus had done for him; and
everyone was amazed at what he told them.

5:1 Other manuscripts read *Gadarenes;* still others read *Gergesenes.* See Matt 8:28; Luke 8:26. **5:2** Greek *unclean;* also in 5:8, 13.
5:20 Greek *Decapolis.*

21 And when Jesus was passed over again by ship unto the other side, much people gathered unto him: and he was nigh unto the sea.

22 And, behold, there cometh one of the rulers of the synagogue, Jairus by name; and when he saw him, he fell at his feet,

23 And besought him greatly, saying, My little daughter lieth at the point of death: *I pray thee*, come and lay thy hands on her, that she may be healed; and she shall live.

24 And *Jesus* went with him; and much people followed him, and thronged him.

25 And a certain woman, which had an issue of blood twelve years,

26 And had suffered many things of many physicians, and had spent all that she had, and was nothing bettered, but rather grew worse,

27 When she had heard of Jesus, came in the press behind, and touched his garment.

28 For she said, If I may touch but his clothes, I shall be whole.

29 And straightway the fountain of her blood was dried up; and she felt in *her* body that she was healed of that plague.

30 And Jesus, immediately knowing in himself that virtue had gone out of him, turned him about in the press, and said, Who touched my clothes?

31 And his disciples said unto him, Thou seest the multitude thronging thee, and sayest thou, Who touched me?

32 And he looked round about to see her that had done this thing.

33 But the woman fearing and trembling, knowing what was done in her, came and fell down before him, and told him all the truth.

34 And he said unto her, Daughter, thy faith hath made thee whole; go in peace, and be whole of thy plague.

35 While he yet spake, there came from the ruler of the synagogue's *house certain* which said, Thy daughter is dead: why troublest thou the Master any further?

36 As soon as Jesus heard the word that was spoken, he saith unto the ruler of the synagogue, Be not afraid, only believe.

37 And he suffered no man to follow him, save Peter, and James, and John the brother of James.

38 And he cometh to the house of the ruler of the synagogue, and seeth the tumult, and them that wept and wailed greatly.

39 And when he was come in, he saith unto them, Why make ye this ado, and weep? the damsel is not dead, but sleepeth.

40 And they laughed him to scorn. But when he had put them all out, he taketh the father and the mother of the damsel, and them that were with him, and entereth in where the damsel was lying.

Jesus Heals in Response to Faith

21 Jesus got into the boat again and went back to the other side of the lake, where a large crowd gathered around him on the shore. 22 Then a leader of the local synagogue, whose name was Jairus, arrived. When he saw Jesus, he fell at his feet, 23 pleading fervently with him. "My little daughter is dying," he said. "Please come and lay your hands on her; heal her so she can live."

24 Jesus went with him, and all the people followed, crowding around him. 25 A woman in the crowd had suffered for twelve years with constant bleeding. 26 She had suffered a great deal from many doctors, and over the years she had spent everything she had to pay them, but she had gotten no better. In fact, she had gotten worse. 27 She had heard about Jesus, so she came up behind him through the crowd and touched his robe. 28 For she thought to herself, "If I can just touch his robe, I will be healed." 29 Immediately the bleeding stopped, and she could feel in her body that she had been healed of her terrible condition.

30 Jesus realized at once that healing power had gone out from him, so he turned around in the crowd and asked, "Who touched my robe?"

31 His disciples said to him, "Look at this crowd pressing around you. How can you ask, 'Who touched me?'"

32 But he kept on looking around to see who had done it. 33 Then the frightened woman, trembling at the realization of what had happened to her, came and fell to her knees in front of him and told him what she had done. 34 And he said to her, "Daughter, your faith has made you well. Go in peace. Your suffering is over."

35 While he was still speaking to her, messengers arrived from the home of Jairus, the leader of the synagogue. They told him, "Your daughter is dead. There's no use troubling the Teacher now."

36 But Jesus overheard* them and said to Jairus, "Don't be afraid. Just have faith."

37 Then Jesus stopped the crowd and wouldn't let anyone go with him except Peter, James, and John (the brother of James). 38 When they came to the home of the synagogue leader, Jesus saw much commotion and weeping and wailing. 39 He went inside and asked, "Why all this commotion and weeping? The child isn't dead; she's only asleep."

40 The crowd laughed at him. But he made them all leave, and he took the girl's father and mother and his three disciples into the room where the girl was

5:36 Or *ignored.*

KING JAMES VERSION

41And he took the damsel by the hand, and said unto her, Talitha cumi; which is, being interpreted, Damsel, I say unto thee, arise.

42And straightway the damsel arose, and walked; for she was *of the age* of twelve years. And they were astonished with a great astonishment.

43And he charged them straitly that no man should know it; and commanded that something should be given her to eat.

6 1And he went out from thence, and came into his own country; and his disciples follow him.

2And when the sabbath day was come, he began to teach in the synagogue: and many hearing *him* were astonished, saying, From whence hath this *man* these things? and what wisdom *is* this which is given unto him, that even such mighty works are wrought by his hands?

3Is not this the carpenter, the son of Mary, the brother of James, and Joses, and of Judah, and Simon? and are not his sisters here with us? And they were offended at him.

4But Jesus said unto them, A prophet is not without honour, but in his own country, and among his own kin, and in his own house.

5And he could there do no mighty work, save that he laid his hands upon a few sick folk, and healed *them.*

6And he marvelled because of their unbelief. And he went round about the villages, teaching.

7And he called *unto him* the twelve, and began to send them forth by two and two; and gave them power over unclean spirits;

8And commanded them that they should take nothing for *their* journey, save a staff only; no scrip, no bread, no money in *their* purse:

9But *be* shod with sandals; and not put on two coats.

10And he said unto them, In what place soever ye enter into an house, there abide till ye depart from that place.

11And whosoever shall not receive you, nor hear you, when ye depart thence, shake off the dust under your feet for a testimony against them. Verily I say unto you, It shall be more tolerable for Sodom and Gomorrha in the day of judgment, than for that city.

12And they went out, and preached that men should repent.

13And they cast out many devils, and anointed with oil many that were sick, and healed *them.*

14And king Herod heard *of him;* (for his name was spread abroad:) and he said, That John the Baptist was risen from the dead, and therefore mighty works do shew forth themselves in him.

NEW LIVING TRANSLATION

lying. 41Holding her hand, he said to her, "Talitha koum," which means "Little girl, get up!" 42And the girl, who was twelve years old, immediately stood up and walked around! They were overwhelmed and totally amazed. 43Jesus gave them strict orders not to tell anyone what had happened, and then he told them to give her something to eat.

Jesus Rejected at Nazareth

6 Jesus left that part of the country and returned with his disciples to Nazareth, his hometown. 2The next Sabbath he began teaching in the synagogue, and many who heard him were amazed. They asked, "Where did he get all this wisdom and the power to perform such miracles?" 3Then they scoffed, "He's just a carpenter, the son of Mary* and the brother of James, Joseph,* Judas, and Simon. And his sisters live right here among us." They were deeply offended and refused to believe in him.

4Then Jesus told them, "A prophet is honored everywhere except in his own hometown and among his relatives and his own family." 5And because of their unbelief, he couldn't do any miracles among them except to place his hands on a few sick people and heal them. 6And he was amazed at their unbelief.

Jesus Sends Out the Twelve Disciples

Then Jesus went from village to village, teaching the people. 7And he called his twelve disciples together and began sending them out two by two, giving them authority to cast out evil* spirits. 8He told them to take nothing for their journey except a walking stick—no food, no traveler's bag, no money.* 9He allowed them to wear sandals but not to take a change of clothes.

10"Wherever you go," he said, "stay in the same house until you leave town. 11But if any place refuses to welcome you or listen to you, shake its dust from your feet as you leave to show that you have abandoned those people to their fate."

12So the disciples went out, telling everyone they met to repent of their sins and turn to God. 13And they cast out many demons and healed many sick people, anointing them with olive oil.

The Death of John the Baptist

14Herod Antipas, the king, soon heard about Jesus, because everyone was talking about him. Some were saying,* "This must be John the Baptist raised from the dead. That is why he can do such miracles."

6:3a Some manuscripts read *He's just the son of the carpenter and of Mary.* **6:3b** Most manuscripts read *Joses;* see Matt 13:55. **6:7** Greek *unclean.* **6:8** Greek *no copper coins in their money belts.* **6:14** Some manuscripts read *He was saying.*

KING JAMES VERSION

15Others said, That it is Elias. And others said, That
it is a prophet, or as one of the prophets.

16But when Herod heard *thereof,* he said, It is
John, whom I beheaded: he is risen from the dead.

17For Herod himself had sent forth and laid hold
upon John, and bound him in prison for Herodias'
sake, his brother Philip's wife: for he had married her.

18For John had said unto Herod, It is not lawful for
thee to have thy brother's wife.

19Therefore Herodias had a quarrel against him,
and would have killed him; but she could not:

20For Herod feared John, knowing that he was a
just man and an holy, and observed him; and when
he heard him, he did many things, and heard him
gladly.

21And when a convenient day was come, that Herod on his birthday made a supper to his lords, high
captains, and chief *estates* of Galilee;

22And when the daughter of the said Herodias
came in, and danced, and pleased Herod and them
that sat with him, the king said unto the damsel, Ask
of me whatsoever thou wilt, and I will give *it* thee.

23And he sware unto her, Whatsoever thou shalt
ask of me, I will give *it* thee, unto the half of my
kingdom.

24And she went forth, and said unto her mother,
What shall I ask? And she said, The head of John the
Baptist.

25And she came in straightway with haste unto
the king, and asked, saying, I will that thou give me
by and by in a charger the head of John the Baptist.

26And the king was exceeding sorry; *yet* for his
oath's sake, and for their sakes which sat with him, he
would not reject her.

27And immediately the king sent an executioner,
and commanded his head to be brought: and he
went and beheaded him in the prison,

28And brought his head in a charger, and gave it to
the damsel: and the damsel gave it to her mother.

29And when his disciples heard *of it,* they came
and took up his corpse, and laid it in a tomb.

30And the apostles gathered themselves together
unto Jesus, and told him all things, both what they
had done, and what they had taught.

31And he said unto them, Come ye yourselves
apart into a desert place, and rest a while: for there
were many coming and going, and they had no lei-
sure so much as to eat.

32And they departed into a desert place by ship
privately.

33And the people saw them departing, and many
knew him, and ran afoot thither out of all cities, and
outwent them, and came together unto him.

34And Jesus, when he came out, saw much people,
and was moved with compassion toward them,

NEW LIVING TRANSLATION

15Others said, "He's the prophet Elijah." Still others
said, "He's a prophet like the other great prophets of
the past."

16When Herod heard about Jesus, he said, "John,
the man I beheaded, has come back from the dead."

17For Herod had sent soldiers to arrest and imprison John as a favor to Herodias. She had been his
brother Philip's wife, but Herod had married her.
18John had been telling Herod, "It is against God's
law for you to marry your brother's wife." 19So Herodias bore a grudge against John and wanted to kill
him. But without Herod's approval she was powerless, 20for Herod respected John; and knowing that
he was a good and holy man, he protected him. Herod was greatly disturbed whenever he talked with
John, but even so, he liked to listen to him.

21Herodias's chance finally came on Herod's
birthday. He gave a party for his high government
officials, army officers, and the leading citizens of
Galilee. 22Then his daughter, also named Herodias,*
came in and performed a dance that greatly pleased
Herod and his guests. "Ask me for anything you like,"
the king said to the girl, "and I will give it to you."
23He even vowed, "I will give you whatever you ask,
up to half my kingdom!"

24She went out and asked her mother, "What
should I ask for?"

Her mother told her, "Ask for the head of John the
Baptist!"

25So the girl hurried back to the king and told him,
"I want the head of John the Baptist, right now, on a
tray!"

26Then the king deeply regretted what he had
said; but because of the vows he had made in front of
his guests, he couldn't refuse her. 27So he immediately sent an executioner to the prison to cut off
John's head and bring it to him. The soldier beheaded John in the prison, 28brought his head on a
tray, and gave it to the girl, who took it to her mother.
29When John's disciples heard what had happened,
they came to get his body and buried it in a tomb.

Jesus Feeds Five Thousand

30The apostles returned to Jesus from their ministry
tour and told him all they had done and taught.
31Then Jesus said, "Let's go off by ourselves to a quiet
place and rest awhile." He said this because there
were so many people coming and going that Jesus
and his apostles didn't even have time to eat.

32So they left by boat for a quiet place, where they
could be alone. 33But many people recognized them
and saw them leaving, and people from many towns
ran ahead along the shore and got there ahead of
them. 34Jesus saw the huge crowd as he stepped
from the boat, and he had compassion on them

6:22 Some manuscripts read *the daughter of Herodias herself.*

KING JAMES VERSION

because they were as sheep not having a shepherd:
and he began to teach them many things.
35And when the day was now far spent, his disciples came unto him, and said, This is a desert place,
and now the time *is* far passed:
36Send them away, that they may go into the country round about, and into the villages, and buy themselves bread: for they have nothing to eat.
37He answered and said unto them, Give ye them
to eat. And they say unto him, Shall we go and buy
two hundred pennyworth of bread, and give them
to eat?
38He saith unto them, How many loaves have ye?
go and see. And when they knew, they say, Five, and
two fishes.
39And he commanded them to make all sit down
by companies upon the green grass.
40And they sat down in ranks, by hundreds, and
by fifties.
41And when he had taken the five loaves and the
two fishes, he looked up to heaven, and blessed, and
brake the loaves, and gave *them* to his disciples to set
before them; and the two fishes divided he among
them all.
42And they did all eat, and were filled.
43And they took up twelve baskets full of the fragments, and of the fishes.
44And they that did eat of the loaves were about
five thousand men.
45And straightway he constrained his disciples to
get into the ship, and to go to the other side before
unto Bethsaida, while he sent away the people.
46And when he had sent them away, he departed
into a mountain to pray.
47And when even was come, the ship was in the
midst of the sea, and he alone on the land.
48And he saw them toiling in rowing; for the wind
was contrary unto them: and about the fourth watch
of the night he cometh unto them, walking upon the
sea, and would have passed by them.
49But when they saw him walking upon the sea,
they supposed it had been a spirit, and cried out:
50For they all saw him, and were troubled. And immediately he talked with them, and saith unto them,
Be of good cheer: it is I; be not afraid.
51And he went up unto them into the ship; and the
wind ceased: and they were sore amazed in themselves beyond measure, and wondered.
52For they considered not *the miracle* of the
loaves: for their heart was hardened.
53And when they had passed over, they came into
the land of Gennesaret, and drew to the shore.
54And when they were come out of the ship,
straightway they knew him,
55And ran through that whole region round about,
and began to carry about in beds those that were
sick, where they heard he was.
56And whithersoever he entered, into villages, or

NEW LIVING TRANSLATION

because they were like sheep without a shepherd. So
he began teaching them many things.
35Late in the afternoon his disciples came to him
and said, "This is a remote place, and it's already getting late. 36Send the crowds away so they can go to
the nearby farms and villages and buy something
to eat."
37But Jesus said, "You feed them."
"With what?" they asked. "We'd have to work for
months to earn enough money* to buy food for all
these people!"
38"How much bread do you have?" he asked. "Go
and find out."
They came back and reported, "We have five
loaves of bread and two fish."
39Then Jesus told the disciples to have the people
sit down in groups on the green grass. 40So they sat
down in groups of fifty or a hundred.
41Jesus took the five loaves and two fish, looked
up toward heaven, and blessed them. Then, breaking
the loaves into pieces, he kept giving the bread to the
disciples so they could distribute it to the people. He
also divided the fish for everyone to share. 42They all
ate as much as they wanted, 43and afterward, the disciples picked up twelve baskets of leftover bread and
fish. 44A total of 5,000 men and their families were
fed from those loaves!

Jesus Walks on Water

45Immediately after this, Jesus insisted that his disciples get back into the boat and head across the lake
to Bethsaida, while he sent the people home. 46After
telling everyone good-bye, he went up into the hills
by himself to pray.
47Late that night, the disciples were in their boat
in the middle of the lake, and Jesus was alone on
land. 48He saw that they were in serious trouble, rowing hard and struggling against the wind and waves.
About three o'clock in the morning* Jesus came toward them, walking on the water. He intended to
go past them, 49but when they saw him walking on
the water, they cried out in terror, thinking he was a
ghost. 50They were all terrified when they saw him.
But Jesus spoke to them at once. "Don't be afraid,"
he said. "Take courage! I am here!*" 51Then he
climbed into the boat, and the wind stopped. They
were totally amazed, 52for they still didn't understand the significance of the miracle of the loaves.
Their hearts were too hard to take it in.
53After they had crossed the lake, they landed
at Gennesaret. They brought the boat to shore
54and climbed out. The people recognized Jesus
at once, 55and they ran throughout the whole area,
carrying sick people on mats to wherever they
heard he was. 56Wherever he went—in villages,

6:37 Greek *It would take 200 denarii.* A denarius was equivalent to a laborer's full day's wage. **6:48** Greek *About the fourth watch of the night.* **6:50** Or *The 'I AM' is here;* Greek reads *I am.* See Exod 3:14.

KING JAMES VERSION

cities, or country, they laid the sick in the streets, and
besought him that they might touch if it were but the
border of his garment: and as many as touched him
were made whole.

7 1Then came together unto him the Pharisees,
and certain of the scribes, which came from
Jerusalem.
2And when they saw some of his disciples eat
bread with defiled, that is to say, with unwashen,
hands, they found fault.
3For the Pharisees, and all the Jews, except they
wash *their* hands oft, eat not, holding the tradition
of the elders.
4And *when they come* from the market, except
they wash, they eat not. And many other things there
be, which they have received to hold, *as* the washing
of cups, and pots, brasen vessels, and of tables.
5Then the Pharisees and scribes asked him, Why
walk not thy disciples according to the tradition of
the elders, but eat bread with unwashen hands?
6He answered and said unto them, Well hath
Esaias prophesied of you hypocrites, as it is written,
This people honoureth me with *their* lips, but their
heart is far from me.
7Howbeit in vain do they worship me, teaching
for doctrines the commandments of men.
8For laying aside the commandment of God, ye
hold the tradition of men, *as* the washing of pots
and cups: and many other such like things ye do.
9And he said unto them, Full well ye reject the
commandment of God, that ye may keep your own
tradition.
10For Moses said, Honour thy father and thy
mother; and, Whoso curseth father or mother, let
him die the death:
11But ye say, If a man shall say to his father or
mother, *It is* Corban, that is to say, a gift, by whatsoever thou mightest be profited by me; *he shall
be free*.
12And ye suffer him no more to do aught for his father or his mother;
13Making the word of God of none effect through
your tradition, which ye have delivered: and many
such like things do ye.
14And when he had called all the people *unto him,*
he said unto them, Hearken unto me every one *of
you,* and understand:
15There is nothing from without a man, that entering into him can defile him: but the things which
come out of him, those are they that defile the man.
16If any man have ears to hear, let him hear.
17And when he was entered into the house from
the people, his disciples asked him concerning the
parable.
18And he saith unto them, Are ye so without understanding also? Do ye not perceive, that whatsoever

NEW LIVING TRANSLATION

cities, or the countryside—they brought the sick out
to the marketplaces. They begged him to let the sick
touch at least the fringe of his robe, and all who
touched him were healed.

Jesus Teaches about Inner Purity

7 One day some Pharisees and teachers of religious law arrived from Jerusalem to see Jesus.
2They noticed that some of his disciples failed to follow the Jewish ritual of hand washing before eating.
3(The Jews, especially the Pharisees, do not eat until
they have poured water over their cupped hands,* as
required by their ancient traditions. 4Similarly, they
don't eat anything from the market until they im-
merse their hands* in water. This is but one of many
traditions they have clung to—such as their ceremonial washing of cups, pitchers, and kettles.*)
5So the Pharisees and teachers of religious law
asked him, "Why don't your disciples follow our age-
old tradition? They eat without first performing the
hand-washing ceremony."
6Jesus replied, "You hypocrites! Isaiah was right
when he prophesied about you, for he wrote,

'These people honor me with their lips,
but their hearts are far from me.
7 Their worship is a farce,
for they teach man-made ideas as
commands from God.'*

8For you ignore God's law and substitute your own
tradition."
9Then he said, "You skillfully sidestep God's law
in order to hold on to your own tradition. 10For instance, Moses gave you this law from God: 'Honor
your father and mother,'* and 'Anyone who speaks
disrespectfully of father or mother must be put to
death.'* 11But you say it is all right for people to say
to their parents, 'Sorry, I can't help you. For I have
vowed to give to God what I would have given to
you.'* 12In this way, you let them disregard their
needy parents. 13And so you cancel the word of God
in order to hand down your own tradition. And this
is only one example among many others."
14Then Jesus called to the crowd to come and
hear. "All of you listen," he said, "and try to understand. 15It's not what goes into your body that defiles
you; you are defiled by what comes from your
heart.*"
17Then Jesus went into a house to get away from
the crowd, and his disciples asked him what he
meant by the parable he had just used. 18"Don't you

7:3 Greek *have washed with the fist.* **7:4a** Some manuscripts read *sprinkle themselves.* **7:4b** Some manuscripts add *and dining couches.* **7:7** Isa 29:13 (Greek version). **7:10a** Exod 20:12; Deut 5:16. **7:10b** Exod 21:17 (Greek version); Lev 20:9 (Greek version). **7:11** Greek *'What I would have given to you is Corban' (that is, a gift).* **7:15** Some manuscripts add verse 16, *Anyone with ears to hear should listen and understand.* Compare 4:9, 23.

KING JAMES VERSION

thing from without entereth into the man, *it* cannot defile him;

19 Because it entereth not into his heart, but into the belly, and goeth out into the draught, purging all meats?

20 And he said, That which cometh out of the man, that defileth the man.

21 For from within, out of the heart of men, proceed evil thoughts, adulteries, fornications, murders,

22 Thefts, covetousness, wickedness, deceit, lasciviousness, an evil eye, blasphemy, pride, foolishness:

23 All these evil things come from within, and defile the man.

24 And from thence he arose, and went into the borders of Tyre and Sidon, and entered into an house, and would have no man know *it:* but he could not be hid.

25 For a *certain* woman, whose young daughter had an unclean spirit, heard of him, and came and fell at his feet:

26 The woman was a Greek, a Syrophenician by nation; and she besought him that he would cast forth the devil out of her daughter.

27 But Jesus said unto her, Let the children first be filled: for it is not meet to take the children's bread, and to cast *it* unto the dogs.

28 And she answered and said unto him, Yes, Lord: yet the dogs under the table eat of the children's crumbs.

29 And he said unto her, For this saying go thy way; the devil is gone out of thy daughter.

30 And when she was come to her house, she found the devil gone out, and her daughter laid upon the bed.

31 And again, departing from the coasts of Tyre and Sidon, he came unto the sea of Galilee, through the midst of the coasts of Decapolis.

32 And they bring unto him one that was deaf, and had an impediment in his speech; and they beseech him to put his hand upon him.

33 And he took him aside from the multitude, and put his fingers into his ears, and he spit, and touched his tongue;

34 And looking up to heaven, he sighed, and saith unto him, Ephphatha, that is, Be opened.

35 And straightway his ears were opened, and the string of his tongue was loosed, and he spake plain.

36 And he charged them that they should tell no man: but the more he charged them, so much the more a great deal they published *it;*

37 And were beyond measure astonished, saying, He hath done all things well: he maketh both the deaf to hear, and the dumb to speak.

NEW LIVING TRANSLATION

understand either?" he asked. "Can't you see that the food you put into your body cannot defile you? 19 Food doesn't go into your heart, but only passes through the stomach and then goes into the sewer." (By saying this, he declared that every kind of food is acceptable in God's eyes.)

20 And then he added, "It is what comes from inside that defiles you. 21 For from within, out of a person's heart, come evil thoughts, sexual immorality, theft, murder, 22 adultery, greed, wickedness, deceit, lustful desires, envy, slander, pride, and foolishness. 23 All these vile things come from within; they are what defile you."

The Faith of a Gentile Woman

24 Then Jesus left Galilee and went north to the region of Tyre.* He didn't want anyone to know which house he was staying in, but he couldn't keep it a secret. 25 Right away a woman who had heard about him came and fell at his feet. Her little girl was possessed by an evil* spirit, 26 and she begged him to cast out the demon from her daughter.

Since she was a Gentile, born in Syrian Phoenicia, 27 Jesus told her, "First I should feed the children—my own family, the Jews.* It isn't right to take food from the children and throw it to the dogs."

28 She replied, "That's true, Lord, but even the dogs under the table are allowed to eat the scraps from the children's plates."

29 "Good answer!" he said. "Now go home, for the demon has left your daughter." 30 And when she arrived home, she found her little girl lying quietly in bed, and the demon was gone.

Jesus Heals a Deaf Man

31 Jesus left Tyre and went up to Sidon before going back to the Sea of Galilee and the region of the Ten Towns.* 32 A deaf man with a speech impediment was brought to him, and the people begged Jesus to lay his hands on the man to heal him.

33 Jesus led him away from the crowd so they could be alone. He put his fingers into the man's ears. Then, spitting on his own fingers, he touched the man's tongue. 34 Looking up to heaven, he sighed and said, *"Ephphatha,"* which means, "Be opened!" 35 Instantly the man could hear perfectly, and his tongue was freed so he could speak plainly!

36 Jesus told the crowd not to tell anyone, but the more he told them not to, the more they spread the news. 37 They were completely amazed and said again and again, "Everything he does is wonderful. He even makes the deaf to hear and gives speech to those who cannot speak."

7:24 Some manuscripts add *and Sidon.* **7:25** Greek *unclean.* **7:27** Greek *Let the children eat first.* **7:31** Greek *Decapolis.*

KING JAMES VERSION

8 1In those days the multitude being very great, and having nothing to eat, Jesus called his disciples *unto him,* and saith unto them,

2I have compassion on the multitude, because they have now been with me three days, and have nothing to eat:

3And if I send them away fasting to their own houses, they will faint by the way: for divers of them came from far.

4And his disciples answered him, From whence can a man satisfy these *men* with bread here in the wilderness?

5And he asked them, How many loaves have ye? And they said, Seven.

6And he commanded the people to sit down on the ground: and he took the seven loaves, and gave thanks, and brake, and gave to his disciples to set before *them;* and they did set *them* before the people.

7And they had a few small fishes: and he blessed, and commanded to set them also before *them.*

8So they did eat, and were filled: and they took up of the broken *meat* that was left seven baskets.

9And they that had eaten were about four thousand: and he sent them away.

10And straightway he entered into a ship with his disciples, and came into the parts of Dalmanutha.

11And the Pharisees came forth, and began to question with him, seeking of him a sign from heaven, tempting him.

12And he sighed deeply in his spirit, and saith, Why doth this generation seek after a sign? verily I say unto you, There shall no sign be given unto this generation.

13And he left them, and entering into the ship again departed to the other side.

14Now *the disciples* had forgotten to take bread, neither had they in the ship with them more than one loaf.

15And he charged them, saying, Take heed, beware of the leaven of the Pharisees, and *of* the leaven of Herod.

16And they reasoned among themselves, saying, *It is* because we have no bread.

17And when Jesus knew *it,* he saith unto them, Why reason ye, because ye have no bread? perceive ye not yet, neither understand? have ye your heart yet hardened?

18Having eyes, see ye not? and having ears, hear ye not? and do ye not remember?

19When I brake the five loaves among five thousand, how many baskets full of fragments took ye up? They say unto him, Twelve.

NEW LIVING TRANSLATION

Jesus Feeds Four Thousand

8 About this time another large crowd had gathered, and the people ran out of food again. Jesus called his disciples and told them, 2"I feel sorry for these people. They have been here with me for three days, and they have nothing left to eat. 3If I send them home hungry, they will faint along the way. For some of them have come a long distance."

4His disciples replied, "How are we supposed to find enough food to feed them out here in the wilderness?"

5Jesus asked, "How much bread do you have?"

"Seven loaves," they replied.

6So Jesus told all the people to sit down on the ground. Then he took the seven loaves, thanked God for them, and broke them into pieces. He gave them to his disciples, who distributed the bread to the crowd. 7A few small fish were found, too, so Jesus also blessed these and told the disciples to distribute them.

8They ate as much as they wanted. Afterward, the disciples picked up seven large baskets of leftover food. 9There were about 4,000 people in the crowd that day, and Jesus sent them home after they had eaten. 10Immediately after this, he got into a boat with his disciples and crossed over to the region of Dalmanutha.

Pharisees Demand a Miraculous Sign

11When the Pharisees heard that Jesus had arrived, they came and started to argue with him. Testing him, they demanded that he show them a miraculous sign from heaven to prove his authority.

12When he heard this, he sighed deeply in his spirit and said, "Why do these people keep demanding a miraculous sign? I tell you the truth, I will not give this generation any such sign." 13So he got back into the boat and left them, and he crossed to the other side of the lake.

Yeast of the Pharisees and Herod

14But the disciples had forgotten to bring any food. They had only one loaf of bread with them in the boat. 15As they were crossing the lake, Jesus warned them, "Watch out! Beware of the yeast of the Pharisees and of Herod."

16At this they began to argue with each other because they hadn't brought any bread. 17Jesus knew what they were saying, so he said, "Why are you arguing about having no bread? Don't you know or understand even yet? Are your hearts too hard to take it in? 18'You have eyes—can't you see? You have ears—can't you hear?'* Don't you remember anything at all? 19When I fed the 5,000 with five loaves of bread, how many baskets of leftovers did you pick up afterward?"

"Twelve," they said.

8:18 Jer 5:21.

KING JAMES VERSION

20 And when the seven among four thousand, how many baskets full of fragments took ye up? And they said, Seven.

21 And he said unto them, How is it that ye do not understand?

22 And he cometh to Bethsaida; and they bring a blind man unto him, and besought him to touch him.

23 And he took the blind man by the hand, and led him out of the town; and when he had spit on his eyes, and put his hands upon him, he asked him if he saw aught.

24 And he looked up, and said, I see men as trees, walking.

25 After that he put *his* hands again upon his eyes, and made him look up: and he was restored, and saw every man clearly.

26 And he sent him away to his house, saying, Neither go into the town, nor tell *it* to any in the town.

27 And Jesus went out, and his disciples, into the towns of Caesarea Philippi: and by the way he asked his disciples, saying unto them, Whom do men say that I am?

28 And they answered, John the Baptist: but some *say,* Elias; and others, One of the prophets.

29 And he saith unto them, But whom say ye that I am? And Peter answereth and saith unto him, Thou art the Christ.

30 And he charged them that they should tell no man of him.

31 And he began to teach them, that the Son of man must suffer many things, and be rejected of the elders, and *of* the chief priests, and scribes, and be killed, and after three days rise again.

32 And he spake that saying openly. And Peter took him, and began to rebuke him.

33 But when he had turned about and looked on his disciples, he rebuked Peter, saying, Get thee behind me, Satan: for thou savourest not the things that be of God, but the things that be of men.

34 And when he had called the people *unto him* with his disciples also, he said unto them, Whosoever will come after me, let him deny himself, and take up his cross, and follow me.

35 For whosoever will save his life shall lose it; but whosoever shall lose his life for my sake and the gospel's, the same shall save it.

36 For what shall it profit a man, if he shall gain the whole world, and lose his own soul?

37 Or what shall a man give in exchange for his soul?

38 Whosoever therefore shall be ashamed of me and of my words in this adulterous and sinful generation;

NEW LIVING TRANSLATION

20 "And when I fed the 4,000 with seven loaves, how many large baskets of leftovers did you pick up?"

"Seven," they said.

21 "Don't you understand yet?" he asked them.

Jesus Heals a Blind Man

22 When they arrived at Bethsaida, some people brought a blind man to Jesus, and they begged him to touch the man and heal him. 23 Jesus took the blind man by the hand and led him out of the village. Then, spitting on the man's eyes, he laid his hands on him and asked, "Can you see anything now?"

24 The man looked around. "Yes," he said, "I see people, but I can't see them very clearly. They look like trees walking around."

25 Then Jesus placed his hands on the man's eyes again, and his eyes were opened. His sight was completely restored, and he could see everything clearly. 26 Jesus sent him away, saying, "Don't go back into the village on your way home."

Peter's Declaration about Jesus

27 Jesus and his disciples left Galilee and went up to the villages near Caesarea Philippi. As they were walking along, he asked them, "Who do people say I am?"

28 "Well," they replied, "some say John the Baptist, some say Elijah, and others say you are one of the other prophets."

29 Then he asked them, "But who do you say I am?"

Peter replied, "You are the Messiah.*"

30 But Jesus warned them not to tell anyone about him.

Jesus Predicts His Death

31 Then Jesus began to tell them that the Son of Man* must suffer many terrible things and be rejected by the elders, the leading priests, and the teachers of religious law. He would be killed, but three days later he would rise from the dead. 32 As he talked about this openly with his disciples, Peter took him aside and began to reprimand him for saying such things.*

33 Jesus turned around and looked at his disciples, then reprimanded Peter. "Get away from me, Satan!" he said. "You are seeing things merely from a human point of view, not from God's."

34 Then, calling the crowd to join his disciples, he said, "If any of you wants to be my follower, you must turn from your selfish ways, take up your cross, and follow me. 35 If you try to hang on to your life, you will lose it. But if you give up your life for my sake and for the sake of the Good News, you will save it. 36 And what do you benefit if you gain the whole world but lose your own soul?* 37 Is anything worth more than your soul? 38 If anyone is ashamed of me and my message in these adulterous and sinful days, the Son

8:29 Or *the Christ. Messiah* (a Hebrew term) and *Christ* (a Greek term) both mean "the anointed one." **8:31** "Son of Man" is a title Jesus used for himself. **8:32** Or *began to correct him.* **8:36** Or *your self?* also in 8:37.

KING JAMES VERSION

of him also shall the Son of man be ashamed, when he
cometh in the glory of his Father with the holy angels.

9 1And he said unto them, Verily I say unto you,
That there be some of them that stand here,
which shall not taste of death, till they have seen the
kingdom of God come with power.

2And after six days Jesus taketh *with him* Peter,
and James, and John, and leadeth them up into an
high mountain apart by themselves: and he was
transfigured before them.

3And his raiment became shining, exceeding
white as snow; so as no fuller on earth can white
them.

4And there appeared unto them Elias with Moses:
and they were talking with Jesus.

5And Peter answered and said to Jesus, Master, it is
good for us to be here: and let us make three tabernacles; one for thee, and one for Moses, and one for
Elias.

6For he wist not what to say; for they were sore
afraid.

7And there was a cloud that overshadowed them:
and a voice came out of the cloud, saying, This is my
beloved Son: hear him.

8And suddenly, when they had looked round
about, they saw no man any more, save Jesus only
with themselves.

9And as they came down from the mountain, he
charged them that they should tell no man what
things they had seen, till the Son of man were risen
from the dead.

10And they kept that saying with themselves, questioning one with another what the rising from the
dead should mean.

11And they asked him, saying, Why say the scribes
that Elias must first come?

12And he answered and told them, Elias verily
cometh first, and restoreth all things; and how it is
written of the Son of man, that he must suffer many
things, and be set at nought.

13But I say unto you, That Elias is indeed come, and
they have done unto him whatsoever they listed, as
it is written of him.

14And when he came to *his* disciples, he saw a
great multitude about them, and the scribes questioning with them.

15And straightway all the people, when they beheld him, were greatly amazed, and running to *him*
saluted him.

16And he asked the scribes, What question ye with
them?

17And one of the multitude answered and said,
Master, I have brought unto thee my son, which hath
a dumb spirit;

18And wheresoever he taketh him, he teareth him:
and he foameth, and gnasheth with his teeth, and

NEW LIVING TRANSLATION

of Man will be ashamed of that person when he returns in the glory of his Father with the holy angels."

9 Jesus went on to say, "I tell you the truth, some
standing here right now will not die before they
see the Kingdom of God arrive in great power!"

The Transfiguration

2Six days later Jesus took Peter, James, and John, and
led them up a high mountain to be alone. As the men
watched, Jesus' appearance was transformed, 3and
his clothes became dazzling white, far whiter than
any earthly bleach could ever make them. 4Then Elijah and Moses appeared and began talking with
Jesus.

5Peter exclaimed, "Rabbi, it's wonderful for us to
be here! Let's make three shelters as memorials*—
one for you, one for Moses, and one for Elijah." 6He
said this because he didn't really know what else to
say, for they were all terrified.

7Then a cloud overshadowed them, and a voice
from the cloud said, "This is my dearly loved Son.
Listen to him." 8Suddenly, when they looked around,
Moses and Elijah were gone, and they saw only Jesus
with them.

9As they went back down the mountain, he told
them not to tell anyone what they had seen until the
Son of Man* had risen from the dead. 10So they kept
it to themselves, but they often asked each other
what he meant by "rising from the dead."

11Then they asked him, "Why do the teachers of
religious law insist that Elijah must return before the
Messiah comes?*"

12Jesus responded, "Elijah is indeed coming first
to get everything ready. Yet why do the Scriptures say
that the Son of Man must suffer greatly and be
treated with utter contempt? 13But I tell you, Elijah
has already come, and they chose to abuse him, just
as the Scriptures predicted."

Jesus Heals a Demon-Possessed Boy

14When they returned to the other disciples, they
saw a large crowd surrounding them, and some
teachers of religious law were arguing with them.
15When the crowd saw Jesus, they were overwhelmed with awe, and they ran to greet him.

16"What is all this arguing about?" Jesus asked.

17One of the men in the crowd spoke up and said,
"Teacher, I brought my son so you could heal him.
He is possessed by an evil spirit that won't let him
talk. 18And whenever this spirit seizes him, it throws
him violently to the ground. Then he foams at the

9:5 Greek *three tabernacles.* **9:9** "Son of Man" is a title Jesus used for himself. **9:11** Greek *that Elijah must come first?*

KING JAMES VERSION

pineth away: and I spake to thy disciples that they
should cast him out; and they could not.
19He answereth him, and saith, O faithless generation, how long shall I be with you? how long shall I
suffer you? bring him unto me.
20And they brought him unto him: and when he
saw him, straightway the spirit tare him; and he fell
on the ground, and wallowed foaming.
21And he asked his father, How long is it ago since
this came unto him? And he said, Of a child.
22And ofttimes it hath cast him into the fire, and
into the waters, to destroy him: but if thou canst
do any thing, have compassion on us, and help us.
23Jesus said unto him, If thou canst believe, all
things *are* possible to him that believeth.
24And straightway the father of the child cried out,
and said with tears, Lord, I believe; help thou mine
unbelief.
25When Jesus saw that the people came running
together, he rebuked the foul spirit, saying unto him,
Thou dumb and deaf spirit, I charge thee, come out
of him, and enter no more into him.
26And *the spirit* cried, and rent him sore, and came
out of him: and he was as one dead; insomuch that
many said, He is dead.
27But Jesus took him by the hand, and lifted him
up; and he arose.
28And when he was come into the house, his disciples asked him privately, Why could not we cast
him out?
29And he said unto them, This kind can come
forth by nothing, but by prayer and fasting.

30And they departed thence, and passed through
Galilee; and he would not that any man should
know *it*.
31For he taught his disciples, and said unto them,
The Son of man is delivered into the hands of men,
and they shall kill him; and after that he is killed, he
shall rise the third day.
32But they understood not that saying, and were
afraid to ask him.

33And he came to Capernaum: and being in the
house he asked them, What was it that ye disputed
among yourselves by the way?
34But they held their peace: for by the way they
had disputed among themselves, who *should be* the
greatest.
35And he sat down, and called the twelve, and saith
unto them, If any man desire to be first, *the same*
shall be last of all, and servant of all.

NEW LIVING TRANSLATION

mouth and grinds his teeth and becomes rigid.* So I
asked your disciples to cast out the evil spirit, but
they couldn't do it."
19Jesus said to them,* "You faithless people! How
long must I be with you? How long must I put up with
you? Bring the boy to me."
20So they brought the boy. But when the evil spirit
saw Jesus, it threw the child into a violent convulsion,
and he fell to the ground, writhing and foaming at
the mouth.
21"How long has this been happening?" Jesus
asked the boy's father.
He replied, "Since he was a little boy. 22The spirit
often throws him into the fire or into water, trying to
kill him. Have mercy on us and help us, if you can."
23"What do you mean, 'If I can'?" Jesus asked.
"Anything is possible if a person believes."
24The father instantly cried out, "I do believe, but
help me overcome my unbelief!"
25When Jesus saw that the crowd of onlookers
was growing, he rebuked the evil* spirit. "Listen, you
spirit that makes this boy unable to hear and speak,"
he said. "I command you to come out of this child
and never enter him again!"
26Then the spirit screamed and threw the boy
into another violent convulsion and left him. The
boy appeared to be dead. A murmur ran through
the crowd as people said, "He's dead." 27But Jesus
took him by the hand and helped him to his feet,
and he stood up.
28Afterward, when Jesus was alone in the house
with his disciples, they asked him, "Why couldn't we
cast out that evil spirit?"
29Jesus replied, "This kind can be cast out only by
prayer.*"

Jesus Again Predicts His Death

30Leaving that region, they traveled through Galilee.
Jesus didn't want anyone to know he was there, 31for
he wanted to spend more time with his disciples and
teach them. He said to them, "The Son of Man is going to be betrayed into the hands of his enemies. He
will be killed, but three days later he will rise from
the dead." 32They didn't understand what he was
saying, however, and they were afraid to ask him
what he meant.

The Greatest in the Kingdom

33After they arrived at Capernaum and settled in a
house, Jesus asked his disciples, "What were you discussing out on the road?" 34But they didn't answer,
because they had been arguing about which of them
was the greatest. 35He sat down, called the twelve disciples over to him, and said, "Whoever wants to be
first must take last place and be the servant of everyone else."

9:18 Or *becomes weak.* **9:19** Or *said to his disciples.* **9:25** Greek *unclean.*
9:29 Some manuscripts read *by prayer and fasting.*

KING JAMES VERSION

36 And he took a child, and set him in the midst of them: and when he had taken him in his arms, he said unto them,

37 Whosoever shall receive one of such children in my name, receiveth me: and whosoever shall receive me, receiveth not me, but him that sent me.

38 And John answered him, saying, Master, we saw one casting out devils in thy name, and he followeth not us: and we forbad him, because he followeth not us.

39 But Jesus said, Forbid him not: for there is no man which shall do a miracle in my name, that can lightly speak evil of me.

40 For he that is not against us is on our part.

41 For whosoever shall give you a cup of water to drink in my name, because ye belong to Christ, verily I say unto you, he shall not lose his reward.

42 And whosoever shall offend one of *these* little ones that believe in me, it is better for him that a millstone were hanged about his neck, and he were cast into the sea.

43 And if thy hand offend thee, cut it off: it is better for thee to enter into life maimed, than having two hands to go into hell, into the fire that never shall be quenched:

44 Where their worm dieth not, and the fire is not quenched.

45 And if thy foot offend thee, cut it off: it is better for thee to enter halt into life, than having two feet to be cast into hell, into the fire that never shall be quenched:

46 Where their worm dieth not, and the fire is not quenched.

47 And if thine eye offend thee, pluck it out: it is better for thee to enter into the kingdom of God with one eye, than having two eyes to be cast into hell fire:

48 Where their worm dieth not, and the fire is not quenched.

49 For every one shall be salted with fire, and every sacrifice shall be salted with salt.

50 Salt *is* good: but if the salt have lost his saltness, wherewith will ye season it? Have salt in yourselves, and have peace one with another.

10 1 And he arose from thence, and cometh into the coasts of Judaea by the farther side of Jordan: and the people resort unto him again; and, as he was wont, he taught them again.

2 And the Pharisees came to him, and asked him, Is it lawful for a man to put away *his* wife? tempting him.

3 And he answered and said unto them, What did Moses command you?

NEW LIVING TRANSLATION

36 Then he put a little child among them. Taking
the child in his arms, he said to them, 37 "Anyone who
welcomes a little child like this on my behalf* welcomes me, and anyone who welcomes me welcomes
not only me but also my Father who sent me."

Using the Name of Jesus

38 John said to Jesus, "Teacher, we saw someone using
your name to cast out demons, but we told him to
stop because he wasn't in our group."
39 "Don't stop him!" Jesus said. "No one who performs a miracle in my name will soon be able to
speak evil of me. 40 Anyone who is not against us is
for us. 41 If anyone gives you even a cup of water because you belong to the Messiah, I tell you the truth,
that person will surely be rewarded.
42 "But if you cause one of these little ones who
trusts in me to fall into sin, it would be better for you
to be thrown into the sea with a large millstone hung
around your neck. 43 If your hand causes you to sin,
cut it off. It's better to enter eternal life with only one
hand than to go into the unquenchable fires of hell*
with two hands.* 45 If your foot causes you to sin, cut
it off. It's better to enter eternal life with only one
foot than to be thrown into hell with two feet.* 47 And
if your eye causes you to sin, gouge it out. It's better
to enter the Kingdom of God with only one eye than
to have two eyes and be thrown into hell, 48 'where
the maggots never die and the fire never goes out.'*
49 "For everyone will be tested with fire.* 50 Salt is
good for seasoning. But if it loses its flavor, how do
you make it salty again? You must have the qualities
of salt among yourselves and live in peace with each
other."

Discussion about Divorce and Marriage

10 Then Jesus left Capernaum and went down
to the region of Judea and into the area east
of the Jordan River. Once again crowds gathered
around him, and as usual he was teaching them.
2 Some Pharisees came and tried to trap him with
this question: "Should a man be allowed to divorce
his wife?"
3 Jesus answered them with a question: "What did
Moses say in the law about divorce?"

9:37 Greek *in my name.* **9:43a** Greek *Gehenna;* also in 9:45, 47. **9:43b** Some manuscripts add verse 44, *'where the maggots never die and the fire never goes out.'* See 9:48. **9:45** Some manuscripts add verse 46, *'where the maggots never die and the fire never goes out.'* See 9:48. **9:48** Isa 66:24. **9:49** Greek *salted with fire;* other manuscripts add *and every sacrifice will be salted with salt.*

KING JAMES VERSION

4 And they said, Moses suffered to write a bill of divorcement, and to put *her* away.

5 And Jesus answered and said unto them, For the hardness of your heart he wrote you this precept.

6 But from the beginning of the creation God made them male and female.

7 For this cause shall a man leave his father and mother, and cleave to his wife;

8 And they twain shall be one flesh: so then they are no more twain, but one flesh.

9 What therefore God hath joined together, let not man put asunder.

10 And in the house his disciples asked him again of the same *matter.*

11 And he saith unto them, Whosoever shall put away his wife, and marry another, committeth adultery against her.

12 And if a woman shall put away her husband, and be married to another, she committeth adultery.

13 And they brought young children to him, that he should touch them: and *his* disciples rebuked those that brought *them.*

14 But when Jesus saw *it,* he was much displeased, and said unto them, Suffer the little children to come unto me, and forbid them not: for of such is the kingdom of God.

15 Verily I say unto you, Whosoever shall not receive the kingdom of God as a little child, he shall not enter therein.

16 And he took them up in his arms, put *his* hands upon them, and blessed them.

17 And when he was gone forth into the way, there came one running, and kneeled to him, and asked him, Good Master, what shall I do that I may inherit eternal life?

18 And Jesus said unto him, Why callest thou me good? *there is* none good but one, *that is,* God.

19 Thou knowest the commandments, Do not commit adultery, Do not kill, Do not steal, Do not bear false witness, Defraud not, Honour thy father and mother.

20 And he answered and said unto him, Master, all these have I observed from my youth.

21 Then Jesus beholding him loved him, and said unto him, One thing thou lackest: go thy way, sell whatsoever thou hast, and give to the poor, and thou shalt have treasure in heaven: and come, take up the cross, and follow me.

22 And he was sad at that saying, and went away grieved: for he had great possessions.

23 And Jesus looked round about, and saith unto his disciples, How hardly shall they that have riches enter into the kingdom of God!

24 And the disciples were astonished at his words. But Jesus answereth again, and saith unto them, Children, how hard is it for them that trust in riches to enter into the kingdom of God!

NEW LIVING TRANSLATION

4 "Well, he permitted it," they replied. "He said a
man can give his wife a written notice of divorce and
send her away."*

5 But Jesus responded, "He wrote this commandment only as a concession to your hard hearts. 6 But
'God made them male and female'* from the beginning of creation. 7 "This explains why a man leaves
his father and mother and is joined to his wife,* 8 and
the two are united into one.'* Since they are no longer two but one, 9 let no one split apart what God has
joined together."

10 Later, when he was alone with his disciples in
the house, they brought up the subject again. 11 He
told them, "Whoever divorces his wife and marries
someone else commits adultery against her. 12 And if
a woman divorces her husband and marries someone else, she commits adultery."

Jesus Blesses the Children

13 One day some parents brought their children to
Jesus so he could touch and bless them. But the disciples scolded the parents for bothering him.

14 When Jesus saw what was happening, he was
angry with his disciples. He said to them, "Let the
children come to me. Don't stop them! For the Kingdom of God belongs to those who are like these children. 15 I tell you the truth, anyone who doesn't
receive the Kingdom of God like a child will never
enter it." 16 Then he took the children in his arms and
placed his hands on their heads and blessed them.

The Rich Man

17 As Jesus was starting out on his way to Jerusalem, a
man came running up to him, knelt down, and asked,
"Good Teacher, what must I do to inherit eternal
life?"

18 "Why do you call me good?" Jesus asked. "Only
God is truly good. 19 But to answer your question, you
know the commandments: 'You must not murder.
You must not commit adultery. You must not steal.
You must not testify falsely. You must not cheat any-
one. Honor your father and mother.'*"

20 "Teacher," the man replied, "I've obeyed all
these commandments since I was young."

21 Looking at the man, Jesus felt genuine love for
him. "There is still one thing you haven't done," he
told him. "Go and sell all your possessions and give
the money to the poor, and you will have treasure in
heaven. Then come, follow me."

22 At this the man's face fell, and he went away sad,
for he had many possessions.

23 Jesus looked around and said to his disciples,
"How hard it is for the rich to enter the Kingdom of
God!" 24 This amazed them. But Jesus said again,
"Dear children, it is very hard* to enter the Kingdom

10:4 See Deut 24:1. **10:6** Gen 1:27; 5:2. **10:7** Some manuscripts do not include *and is joined to his wife.* **10:7-8** Gen 2:24. **10:19** Exod 20:12-16; Deut 5:16-20. **10:24** Some manuscripts read *very hard for those who trust in riches.*

KING JAMES VERSION

25 It is easier for a camel to go through the eye of a needle, than for a rich man to enter into the kingdom of God.

26 And they were astonished out of measure, saying among themselves, Who then can be saved?

27 And Jesus looking upon them saith, With men *it is* impossible, but not with God: for with God all things are possible.

28 Then Peter began to say unto him, Lo, we have left all, and have followed thee.

29 And Jesus answered and said, Verily I say unto you, There is no man that hath left house, or brethren, or sisters, or father, or mother, or wife, or children, or lands, for my sake, and the gospel's,

30 But he shall receive an hundredfold now in this time, houses, and brethren, and sisters, and mothers, and children, and lands, with persecutions; and in the world to come eternal life.

31 But many *that are* first shall be last; and the last first.

32 And they were in the way going up to Jerusalem; and Jesus went before them: and they were amazed; and as they followed, they were afraid. And he took again the twelve, and began to tell them what things should happen unto him,

33 *Saying,* Behold, we go up to Jerusalem; and the Son of man shall be delivered unto the chief priests, and unto the scribes; and they shall condemn him to death, and shall deliver him to the Gentiles:

34 And they shall mock him, and shall scourge him, and shall spit upon him, and shall kill him: and the third day he shall rise again.

35 And James and John, the sons of Zebedee, come unto him, saying, Master, we would that thou shouldest do for us whatsoever we shall desire.

36 And he said unto them, What would ye that I should do for you?

37 They said unto him, Grant unto us that we may sit, one on thy right hand, and the other on thy left hand, in thy glory.

38 But Jesus said unto them, Ye know not what ye ask: can ye drink of the cup that I drink of? and be baptized with the baptism that I am baptized with?

39 And they said unto him, We can. And Jesus said unto them, Ye shall indeed drink of the cup that I drink of; and with the baptism that I am baptized withal shall ye be baptized:

40 But to sit on my right hand and on my left hand is not mine to give; but *it shall be given to them* for whom it is prepared.

NEW LIVING TRANSLATION

of God. 25 In fact, it is easier for a camel to go through
the eye of a needle than for a rich person to enter the
Kingdom of God!"

26 The disciples were astounded. "Then who in
the world can be saved?" they asked.

27 Jesus looked at them intently and said, "Humanly speaking, it is impossible. But not with God.
Everything is possible with God."

28 Then Peter began to speak up. "We've given up
everything to follow you," he said.

29 "Yes," Jesus replied, "and I assure you that everyone who has given up house or brothers or sisters or
mother or father or children or property, for my sake
and for the Good News, 30 will receive now in return
a hundred times as many houses, brothers, sisters,
mothers, children, and property—along with persecution. And in the world to come that person will
have eternal life. 31 But many who are the greatest
now will be least important then, and those who
seem least important now will be the greatest then.*"

Jesus Again Predicts His Death

32 They were now on the way up to Jerusalem, and
Jesus was walking ahead of them. The disciples were
filled with awe, and the people following behind
were overwhelmed with fear. Taking the twelve disciples aside, Jesus once more began to describe
everything that was about to happen to him. 33 "Listen," he said, "we're going up to Jerusalem, where the
Son of Man* will be betrayed to the leading priests
and the teachers of religious law. They will sentence
him to die and hand him over to the Romans.*
34 They will mock him, spit on him, flog him with a
whip, and kill him, but after three days he will rise
again."

Jesus Teaches about Serving Others

35 Then James and John, the sons of Zebedee, came
over and spoke to him. "Teacher," they said, "we want
you to do us a favor."

36 "What is your request?" he asked.

37 They replied, "When you sit on your glorious
throne, we want to sit in places of honor next to you,
one on your right and the other on your left."

38 But Jesus said to them, "You don't know what
you are asking! Are you able to drink from the bitter
cup of suffering I am about to drink? Are you able
to be baptized with the baptism of suffering I must
be baptized with?"

39 "Oh yes," they replied, "we are able!"

Then Jesus told them, "You will indeed drink from
my bitter cup and be baptized with my baptism of
suffering. 40 But I have no right to say who will sit on
my right or my left. God has prepared those places
for the ones he has chosen."

10:31 Greek *But many who are first will be last; and the last, first.*
10:33a "Son of Man" is a title Jesus used for himself. **10:33b** Greek *the Gentiles.*

KING JAMES VERSION

41 And when the ten heard *it,* they began to be
much displeased with James and John.
42 But Jesus called them *to him,* and saith unto
them, Ye know that they which are accounted to rule
over the Gentiles exercise lordship over them; and
their great ones exercise authority upon them.
43 But so shall it not be among you: but whosoever
will be great among you, shall be your minister:
44 And whosoever of you will be the chiefest, shall
be servant of all.
45 For even the Son of man came not to be ministered unto, but to minister, and to give his life a ransom for many.
46 And they came to Jericho: and as he went out of
Jericho with his disciples and a great number of
people, blind Bartimaeus, the son of Timaeus, sat by
the highway side begging.
47 And when he heard that it was Jesus of Nazareth,
he began to cry out, and say, Jesus, *thou* son of David,
have mercy on me.
48 And many charged him that he should hold his
peace: but he cried the more a great deal, *Thou* son of
David, have mercy on me.
49 And Jesus stood still, and commanded him to be
called. And they call the blind man, saying unto him,
Be of good comfort, rise; he calleth thee.
50 And he, casting away his garment, rose, and
came to Jesus.
51 And Jesus answered and said unto him, What
wilt thou that I should do unto thee? The blind man
said unto him, Lord, that I might receive my sight.
52 And Jesus said unto him, Go thy way; thy faith
hath made thee whole. And immediately he received
his sight, and followed Jesus in the way.

11 1 And when they came nigh to Jerusalem,
unto Bethphage and Bethany, at the mount of
Olives, he sendeth forth two of his disciples,
2 And saith unto them, Go your way into the village
over against you: and as soon as ye be entered into it,
ye shall find a colt tied, whereon never man sat; loose
him, and bring *him.*
3 And if any man say unto you, Why do ye this? say
ye that the Lord hath need of him; and straightway
he will send him hither.
4 And they went their way, and found the colt tied
by the door without in a place where two ways met;
and they loose him.
5 And certain of them that stood there said unto
them, What do ye, loosing the colt?
6 And they said unto them even as Jesus had commanded: and they let them go.
7 And they brought the colt to Jesus, and cast their
garments on him; and he sat upon him.
8 And many spread their garments in the way: and
others cut down branches off the trees, and strawed
them in the way.
9 And they that went before, and they that followed,

NEW LIVING TRANSLATION

41 When the ten other disciples heard what James
and John had asked, they were indignant. 42 So Jesus
called them together and said, "You know that the
rulers in this world lord it over their people, and officials flaunt their authority over those under them.
43 But among you it will be different. Whoever wants
to be a leader among you must be your servant, 44 and
whoever wants to be first among you must be the
slave of everyone else. 45 For even the Son of Man
came not to be served but to serve others and to give
his life as a ransom for many."

Jesus Heals Blind Bartimaeus

46 Then they reached Jericho, and as Jesus and his disciples left town, a large crowd followed him. A blind
beggar named Bartimaeus (son of Timaeus) was sitting beside the road. 47 When Bartimaeus heard that
Jesus of Nazareth was nearby, he began to shout,
"Jesus, Son of David, have mercy on me!"
48 "Be quiet!" many of the people yelled at him.
But he only shouted louder, "Son of David, have
mercy on me!"
49 When Jesus heard him, he stopped and said,
"Tell him to come here."
So they called the blind man. "Cheer up," they
said. "Come on, he's calling you!" 50 Bartimaeus threw
aside his coat, jumped up, and came to Jesus.
51 "What do you want me to do for you?" Jesus
asked.
"My rabbi,*" the blind man said, "I want to see!"
52 And Jesus said to him, "Go, for your faith has
healed you." Instantly the man could see, and he
followed Jesus down the road.*

Jesus' Triumphant Entry

11 As Jesus and his disciples approached Jerusalem, they came to the towns of Bethphage and
Bethany on the Mount of Olives. Jesus sent two of
them on ahead. 2 "Go into that village over there," he
told them. "As soon as you enter it, you will see a
young donkey tied there that no one has ever ridden.
Untie it and bring it here. 3 If anyone asks, 'What are
you doing?' just say, 'The Lord needs it and will return it soon.'"
4 The two disciples left and found the colt standing in the street, tied outside the front door. 5 As they
were untying it, some bystanders demanded, "What
are you doing, untying that colt?" 6 They said what
Jesus had told them to say, and they were permitted
to take it. 7 Then they brought the colt to Jesus and
threw their garments over it, and he sat on it.
8 Many in the crowd spread their garments on the
road ahead of him, and others spread leafy branches
they had cut in the fields. 9 Jesus was in the center of
the procession, and the people all around him were
shouting,

10:51 Greek uses the Hebrew term *Rabboni.* **10:52** Or *on the way.*

KING JAMES VERSION

cried, saying, Hosanna; Blessed *is* he that cometh in
the name of the Lord:
10Blessed *be* the kingdom of our father David,
that cometh in the name of the Lord: Hosanna in
the highest.
11And Jesus entered into Jerusalem, and into the
temple: and when he had looked round about upon
all things, and now the eventide was come, he went
out unto Bethany with the twelve.

12And on the morrow, when they were come from
Bethany, he was hungry:
13And seeing a fig tree afar off having leaves, he
came, if haply he might find any thing thereon: and
when he came to it, he found nothing but leaves; for
the time of figs was not *yet*.
14And Jesus answered and said unto it, No man eat
fruit of thee hereafter for ever. And his disciples
heard *it*.
15And they come to Jerusalem: and Jesus went into
the temple, and began to cast out them that sold and
bought in the temple, and overthrew the tables of the
moneychangers, and the seats of them that sold
doves;
16And would not suffer that any man should carry
any vessel through the temple.
17And he taught, saying unto them, Is it not written, My house shall be called of all nations the house
of prayer? but ye have made it a den of thieves.
18And the scribes and chief priests heard *it*, and
sought how they might destroy him: for they feared
him, because all the people was astonished at his
doctrine.
19And when even was come, he went out of the city.
20And in the morning, as they passed by, they saw
the fig tree dried up from the roots.
21And Peter calling to remembrance saith unto
him, Master, behold, the fig tree which thou cursedst
is withered away.
22And Jesus answering saith unto them, Have faith
in God.
23For verily I say unto you, That whosoever shall say
unto this mountain, Be thou removed, and be thou
cast into the sea; and shall not doubt in his heart, but
shall believe that those things which he saith shall
come to pass; he shall have whatsoever he saith.
24Therefore I say unto you, What things soever ye
desire, when ye pray, believe that ye receive *them*,
and ye shall have *them*.
25And when ye stand praying, forgive, if ye have
aught against any: that your Father also which is in
heaven may forgive you your trespasses.
26But if ye do not forgive, neither will your Father
which is in heaven forgive your trespasses.

NEW LIVING TRANSLATION

"Praise God!*
Blessings on the one who comes in the
name of the LORD!
10 Blessings on the coming Kingdom of our
ancestor David!
Praise God in highest heaven!"*

11So Jesus came to Jerusalem and went into the
Temple. After looking around carefully at everything, he left because it was late in the afternoon.
Then he returned to Bethany with the twelve
disciples.

Jesus Curses the Fig Tree

12The next morning as they were leaving Bethany,
Jesus was hungry. 13He noticed a fig tree in full leaf a
little way off, so he went over to see if he could find
any figs. But there were only leaves because it was too
early in the season for fruit. 14Then Jesus said to the
tree, "May no one ever eat your fruit again!" And the
disciples heard him say it.

Jesus Clears the Temple

15When they arrived back in Jerusalem, Jesus
entered the Temple and began to drive out the
people buying and selling animals for sacrifices. He
knocked over the tables of the money changers and
the chairs of those selling doves, 16and he stopped
everyone from using the Temple as a marketplace.*
17He said to them, "The Scriptures declare, 'My
Temple will be called a house of prayer for all nations,' but you have turned it into a den of thieves."*
18When the leading priests and teachers of religious law heard what Jesus had done, they began
planning how to kill him. But they were afraid of him
because the people were so amazed at his teaching.
19That evening Jesus and the disciples left* the
city.
20The next morning as they passed by the fig tree
he had cursed, the disciples noticed it had withered
from the roots up. 21Peter remembered what Jesus
had said to the tree on the previous day and exclaimed, "Look, Rabbi! The fig tree you cursed has
withered and died!"
22Then Jesus said to the disciples, "Have faith in
God. 23I tell you the truth, you can say to this mountain, 'May you be lifted up and thrown into the sea,'
and it will happen. But you must really believe it will
happen and have no doubt in your heart. 24I tell you,
you can pray for anything, and if you believe that
you've received it, it will be yours. 25But when you are
praying, first forgive anyone you are holding a
grudge against, so that your Father in heaven will
forgive your sins, too.*"

11:9 Greek *Hosanna*, an exclamation of praise that literally means "save now"; also in 11:10. **11:9-10** Pss 118:25-26; 148:1. **11:16** Or *from carrying merchandise through the Temple.* **11:17** Isa 56:7; Jer 7:11. **11:19** Greek *they left;* other manuscripts read *he left.* **11:25** Some manuscripts add verse 26, *But if you refuse to forgive, your Father in heaven will not forgive your sins.* Compare Matt 6:15.

KING JAMES VERSION

27 And they come again to Jerusalem: and as he was walking in the temple, there come to him the chief priests, and the scribes, and the elders,

28 And say unto him, By what authority doest thou these things? and who gave thee this authority to do these things?

29 And Jesus answered and said unto them, I will also ask of you one question, and answer me, and I will tell you by what authority I do these things.

30 The baptism of John, was *it* from heaven, or of men? answer me.

31 And they reasoned with themselves, saying, If we shall say, From heaven; he will say, Why then did ye not believe him?

32 But if we shall say, Of men; they feared the people: for all *men* counted John, that he was a prophet indeed.

33 And they answered and said unto Jesus, We cannot tell. And Jesus answering saith unto them, Neither do I tell you by what authority I do these things.

12 1 And he began to speak unto them by parables. A *certain* man planted a vineyard, and set an hedge about *it,* and digged *a place for* the winefat, and built a tower, and let it out to husbandmen, and went into a far country.

2 And at the season he sent to the husbandmen a servant, that he might receive from the husbandmen of the fruit of the vineyard.

3 And they caught *him,* and beat him, and sent *him* away empty.

4 And again he sent unto them another servant; and at him they cast stones, and wounded *him* in the head, and sent *him* away shamefully handled.

5 And again he sent another; and him they killed, and many others; beating some, and killing some.

6 Having yet therefore one son, his wellbeloved, he sent him also last unto them, saying, They will reverence my son.

7 But those husbandmen said among themselves, This is the heir; come, let us kill him, and the inheritance shall be ours.

8 And they took him, and killed *him,* and cast *him* out of the vineyard.

9 What shall therefore the lord of the vineyard do? he will come and destroy the husbandmen, and will give the vineyard unto others.

10 And have ye not read this scripture; The stone which the builders rejected is become the head of the corner:

11 This was the Lord's doing, and it is marvellous in our eyes?

12 And they sought to lay hold on him, but feared the people: for they knew that he had spoken the parable against them: and they left him, and went their way.

NEW LIVING TRANSLATION

The Authority of Jesus Challenged

27 Again they entered Jerusalem. As Jesus was walking through the Temple area, the leading priests, the teachers of religious law, and the elders came up to him. 28 They demanded, "By what authority are you doing all these things? Who gave you the right to do them?"

29 "I'll tell you by what authority I do these things if you answer one question," Jesus replied. 30 "Did John's authority to baptize come from heaven, or was it merely human? Answer me!"

31 They talked it over among themselves. "If we say it was from heaven, he will ask why we didn't believe John. 32 But do we dare say it was merely human?" For they were afraid of what the people would do, because everyone believed that John was a prophet. 33 So they finally replied, "We don't know."

And Jesus responded, "Then I won't tell you by what authority I do these things."

Parable of the Evil Farmers

12 Then Jesus began teaching them with stories: "A man planted a vineyard. He built a wall around it, dug a pit for pressing out the grape juice, and built a lookout tower. Then he leased the vineyard to tenant farmers and moved to another country. 2 At the time of the grape harvest, he sent one of his servants to collect his share of the crop. 3 But the farmers grabbed the servant, beat him up, and sent him back empty-handed. 4 The owner then sent another servant, but they insulted him and beat him over the head. 5 The next servant he sent was killed. Others he sent were either beaten or killed, 6 until there was only one left—his son whom he loved dearly. The owner finally sent him, thinking, 'Surely they will respect my son.'

7 "But the tenant farmers said to one another, 'Here comes the heir to this estate. Let's kill him and get the estate for ourselves!' 8 So they grabbed him and murdered him and threw his body out of the vineyard.

9 "What do you suppose the owner of the vineyard will do?" Jesus asked. "I'll tell you—he will come and kill those farmers and lease the vineyard to others. 10 Didn't you ever read this in the Scriptures?

'The stone that the builders rejected
has now become the cornerstone.
11 This is the LORD's doing,
and it is wonderful to see.'*"

12 The religious leaders* wanted to arrest Jesus because they realized he was telling the story against them—they were the wicked farmers. But they were afraid of the crowd, so they left him and went away.

12:10-11 Ps 118:22-23. **12:12** Greek *They.*

KING JAMES VERSION

13And they send unto him certain of the Pharisees and of the Herodians, to catch him in *his* words.

14And when they were come, they say unto him, Master, we know that thou art true, and carest for no man: for thou regardest not the person of men, but teachest the way of God in truth: Is it lawful to give tribute to Caesar, or not?

15Shall we give, or shall we not give? But he, knowing their hypocrisy, said unto them, Why tempt ye me? bring me a penny, that I may see *it*.

16And they brought *it*. And he saith unto them, Whose *is* this image and superscription? And they said unto him, Caesar's.

17And Jesus answering said unto them, Render to Caesar the things that are Caesar's, and to God the things that are God's. And they marvelled at him.

18Then come unto him the Sadducees, which say there is no resurrection; and they asked him, saying,

19Master, Moses wrote unto us, If a man's brother die, and leave *his* wife *behind him,* and leave no children, that his brother should take his wife, and raise up seed unto his brother.

20Now there were seven brethren: and the first took a wife, and dying left no seed.

21And the second took her, and died, neither left he any seed: and the third likewise.

22And the seven had her, and left no seed: last of all the woman died also.

23In the resurrection therefore, when they shall rise, whose wife shall she be of them? for the seven had her to wife.

24And Jesus answering said unto them, Do ye not therefore err, because ye know not the scriptures, neither the power of God?

25For when they shall rise from the dead, they neither marry, nor are given in marriage; but are as the angels which are in heaven.

26And as touching the dead, that they rise: have ye not read in the book of Moses, how in the bush God spake unto him, saying, I *am* the God of Abraham, and the God of Isaac, and the God of Jacob?

27He is not the God of the dead, but the God of the living: ye therefore do greatly err.

28And one of the scribes came, and having heard them reasoning together, and perceiving that he had answered them well, asked him, Which is the first commandment of all?

29And Jesus answered him, The first of all the commandments *is,* Hear, O Israel; The Lord our God is one Lord:

30And thou shalt love the Lord thy God with all thy heart, and with all thy soul, and with all thy mind, and with all thy strength: this *is* the first commandment.

31And the second *is* like, *namely* this, Thou shalt

NEW LIVING TRANSLATION

Taxes for Caesar

13Later the leaders sent some Pharisees and supporters of Herod to trap Jesus into saying something for
which he could be arrested. 14"Teacher," they said,
"we know how honest you are. You are impartial and don't play favorites. You teach the way of God truthfully. Now tell us—is it right to pay taxes to Caesar or
not? 15Should we pay them, or shouldn't we?"

Jesus saw through their hypocrisy and said, "Why are you trying to trap me? Show me a Roman coin,*
and I'll tell you." 16When they handed it to him, he
asked, "Whose picture and title are stamped on it?"

"Caesar's," they replied.

17"Well, then," Jesus said, "give to Caesar what belongs to Caesar, and give to God what belongs to God."

His reply completely amazed them.

Discussion about Resurrection

18Then Jesus was approached by some Sadducees—religious leaders who say there is no resurrection
from the dead. They posed this question: 19"Teacher,
Moses gave us a law that if a man dies, leaving a wife without children, his brother should marry the widow and have a child who will carry on the
brother's name.* 20Well, suppose there were seven
brothers. The oldest one married and then died
without children. 21So the second brother married
the widow, but he also died without children. Then
the third brother married her. 22This continued with
all seven of them, and still there were no children.
Last of all, the woman also died. 23So tell us, whose
wife will she be in the resurrection? For all seven were married to her."

24Jesus replied, "Your mistake is that you don't know the Scriptures, and you don't know the power
of God. 25For when the dead rise, they will neither marry nor be given in marriage. In this respect they will be like the angels in heaven.

26"But now, as to whether the dead will be raised—haven't you ever read about this in the writings of Moses, in the story of the burning bush? Long after Abraham, Isaac, and Jacob had died, God said to Moses,* 'I am the God of Abraham, the God of Isaac,
and the God of Jacob.'* 27So he is the God of the living, not the dead. You have made a serious error."

The Most Important Commandment

28One of the teachers of religious law was standing there listening to the debate. He realized that Jesus had answered well, so he asked, "Of all the commandments, which is the most important?"

29Jesus replied, "The most important commandment is this: 'Listen, O Israel! The LORD our God is the
one and only LORD. 30And you must love the LORD
your God with all your heart, all your soul, all your mind, and all your strength.'* 31The second is equally

12:15 Greek *a denarius.* **12:19** See Deut 25:5-6. **12:26a** Greek *in the story of the bush? God said to him.* **12:26b** Exod 3:6. **12:29-30** Deut 6:4-5.

KING JAMES VERSION

love thy neighbour as thyself. There is none other
commandment greater than these.
32 And the scribe said unto him, Well, Master, thou
hast said the truth: for there is one God; and there is
none other but he:
33 And to love him with all the heart, and with all
the understanding, and with all the soul, and with all
the strength, and to love *his* neighbour as himself, is
more than all whole burnt offerings and sacrifices.
34 And when Jesus saw that he answered discreetly,
he said unto him, Thou art not far from the kingdom
of God. And no man after that durst ask him *any
question.*

35 And Jesus answered and said, while he taught in
the temple, How say the scribes that Christ is the son
of David?
36 For David himself said by the Holy Ghost, The
LORD said to my Lord, Sit thou on my right hand, till
I make thine enemies thy footstool.
37 David therefore himself calleth him Lord; and
whence is he *then* his son? And the common people
heard him gladly.
38 And he said unto them in his doctrine, Beware
of the scribes, which love to go in long clothing, and
love salutations in the marketplaces,
39 And the chief seats in the synagogues, and the
uppermost rooms at feasts:
40 Which devour widows' houses, and for a pretence make long prayers: these shall receive greater
damnation.

41 And Jesus sat over against the treasury, and beheld how the people cast money into the treasury:
and many that were rich cast in much.
42 And there came a certain poor widow, and she
threw in two mites, which make a farthing.
43 And he called *unto him* his disciples, and saith
unto them, Verily I say unto you, That this poor
widow hath cast more in, than all they which have
cast into the treasury:
44 For all *they* did cast in of their abundance; but
she of her want did cast in all that she had, *even* all
her living.

13 1 And as he went out of the temple, one of his
disciples saith unto him, Master, see what
manner of stones and what buildings *are here!*

NEW LIVING TRANSLATION

important: 'Love your neighbor as yourself.'* No
other commandment is greater than these."
32 The teacher of religious law replied, "Well said,
Teacher. You have spoken the truth by saying that
there is only one God and no other.
33 And I know it
is important to love him with all my heart and all
my understanding and all my strength, and to love
my neighbor as myself. This is more important than
to offer all of the burnt offerings and sacrifices required in the law."
34 Realizing how much the man understood, Jesus
said to him, "You are not far from the Kingdom of
God." And after that, no one dared to ask him any
more questions.

Whose Son Is the Messiah?

35 Later, as Jesus was teaching the people in the
Temple, he asked, "Why do the teachers of religious
law claim that the Messiah is the son of David?
36 For
David himself, speaking under the inspiration of the
Holy Spirit, said,

'The LORD said to my Lord,
Sit in the place of honor at my right hand
until I humble your enemies beneath your feet.'*

37 Since David himself called the Messiah 'my Lord,'
how can the Messiah be his son?" The large crowd
listened to him with great delight.
38 Jesus also taught: "Beware of these teachers of
religious law! For they like to parade around in flowing robes and receive respectful greetings as they
walk in the marketplaces.
39 And how they love the
seats of honor in the synagogues and the head table
at banquets.
40 Yet they shamelessly cheat widows
out of their property and then pretend to be pious by
making long prayers in public. Because of this, they
will be more severely punished."

The Widow's Offering

41 Jesus sat down near the collection box in the
Temple and watched as the crowds dropped in their
money. Many rich people put in large amounts.
42 Then a poor widow came and dropped in two
small coins.*
43 Jesus called his disciples to him and said, "I tell
you the truth, this poor widow has given more than
all the others who are making contributions.
44 For
they gave a tiny part of their surplus, but she, poor as
she is, has given everything she had to live on."

Jesus Foretells the Future

13 As Jesus was leaving the Temple that day, one
of his disciples said, "Teacher, look at these
magnificent buildings! Look at the impressive stones
in the walls."

12:31 Lev 19:18. **12:36** Ps 110:1. **12:42** Greek *two lepta, which is a kodrantes* [i.e., a quadrans].

KING JAMES VERSION

2 And Jesus answering said unto him, Seest thou these great buildings? there shall not be left one stone upon another, that shall not be thrown down.

3 And as he sat upon the mount of Olives over against the temple, Peter and James and John and Andrew asked him privately,

4 Tell us, when shall these things be? and what *shall be* the sign when all these things shall be fulfilled?

5 And Jesus answering them began to say, Take heed lest any *man* deceive you:

6 For many shall come in my name, saying, I am *Christ;* and shall deceive many.

7 And when ye shall hear of wars and rumours of wars, be ye not troubled: for *such things* must needs be; but the end *shall* not *be* yet.

8 For nation shall rise against nation, and kingdom against kingdom: and there shall be earthquakes in divers places, and there shall be famines and troubles: these *are* the beginnings of sorrows.

9 But take heed to yourselves: for they shall deliver you up to councils; and in the synagogues ye shall be beaten: and ye shall be brought before rulers and kings for my sake, for a testimony against them.

10 And the gospel must first be published among all nations.

11 But when they shall lead *you,* and deliver you up, take no thought beforehand what ye shall speak, neither do ye premeditate: but whatsoever shall be given you in that hour, that speak ye: for it is not ye that speak, but the Holy Ghost.

12 Now the brother shall betray the brother to death, and the father the son; and children shall rise up against *their* parents, and shall cause them to be put to death.

13 And ye shall be hated of all *men* for my name's sake: but he that shall endure unto the end, the same shall be saved.

14 But when ye shall see the abomination of desolation, spoken of by Daniel the prophet, standing where it ought not, (let him that readeth understand,) then let them that be in Judaea flee to the mountains:

15 And let him that is on the housetop not go down into the house, neither enter *therein,* to take any thing out of his house:

16 And let him that is in the field not turn back again for to take up his garment.

17 But woe to them that are with child, and to them that give suck in those days!

18 And pray ye that your flight be not in the winter.

19 For *in* those days shall be affliction, such as was not from the beginning of the creation which God created unto this time, neither shall be.

20 And except that the Lord had shortened those days, no flesh should be saved: but for the elect's sake, whom he hath chosen, he hath shortened the days.

21 And then if any man shall say to you, Lo, here *is* Christ; or, lo, *he is* there; believe *him* not:

NEW LIVING TRANSLATION

2 Jesus replied, "Yes, look at these great buildings. But they will be completely demolished. Not one stone will be left on top of another!"

3 Later, Jesus sat on the Mount of Olives across the valley from the Temple. Peter, James, John, and Andrew came to him privately and asked him, 4 "Tell us, when will all this happen? What sign will show us that these things are about to be fulfilled?"

5 Jesus replied, "Don't let anyone mislead you, 6 for many will come in my name, claiming, 'I am the Messiah.'* They will deceive many. 7 And you will hear of wars and threats of wars, but don't panic. Yes, these things must take place, but the end won't follow immediately. 8 Nation will go to war against nation, and kingdom against kingdom. There will be earthquakes in many parts of the world, as well as famines. But this is only the first of the birth pains, with more to come.

9 "When these things begin to happen, watch out! You will be handed over to the local councils and beaten in the synagogues. You will stand trial before governors and kings because you are my followers. But this will be your opportunity to tell them about me.* 10 For the Good News must first be preached to all nations.* 11 But when you are arrested and stand trial, don't worry in advance about what to say. Just say what God tells you at that time, for it is not you who will be speaking, but the Holy Spirit.

12 "A brother will betray his brother to death, a father will betray his own child, and children will rebel against their parents and cause them to be killed. 13 And everyone will hate you because you are my followers.* But the one who endures to the end will be saved.

14 "The day is coming when you will see the sacrilegious object that causes desecration* standing where he* should not be." (Reader, pay attention!) "Then those in Judea must flee to the hills. 15 A person out on the deck of a roof must not go down into the house to pack. 16 A person out in the field must not return even to get a coat. 17 How terrible it will be for pregnant women and for nursing mothers in those days. 18 And pray that your flight will not be in winter. 19 For there will be greater anguish in those days than at any time since God created the world. And it will never be so great again. 20 In fact, unless the Lord shortens that time of calamity, not a single person will survive. But for the sake of his chosen ones he has shortened those days.

21 "Then if anyone tells you, 'Look, here is the

13:6 Greek *claiming, 'I am.'* **13:9** Or *But this will be your testimony against them.* **13:10** Or *all peoples.* **13:13** Greek *on account of my name.* **13:14a** Greek *the abomination of desolation.* See Dan 9:27; 11:31; 12:11. **13:14b** Or *it.*

KING JAMES VERSION

22For false Christs and false prophets shall rise,
and shall shew signs and wonders, to seduce, if *it*
were possible, even the elect.
23But take ye heed: behold, I have foretold you
all things.
24But in those days, after that tribulation, the sun
shall be darkened, and the moon shall not give her
light,
25And the stars of heaven shall fall, and the powers
that are in heaven shall be shaken.
26And then shall they see the Son of man coming
in the clouds with great power and glory.
27And then shall he send his angels, and shall
gather together his elect from the four winds, from
the uttermost part of the earth to the uttermost part
of heaven.
28Now learn a parable of the fig tree; When her
branch is yet tender, and putteth forth leaves, ye
know that summer is near:
29So ye in like manner, when ye shall see these
things come to pass, know that it is nigh, *even* at
the doors.
30Verily I say unto you, that this generation shall
not pass, till all these things be done.
31Heaven and earth shall pass away: but my words
shall not pass away.
32But of that day and *that* hour knoweth no man,
no, not the angels which are in heaven, neither the
Son, but the Father.
33Take ye heed, watch and pray: for ye know not
when the time is.
34*For the Son of man is* as a man taking a far journey, who left his house, and gave authority to his servants, and to every man his work, and commanded
the porter to watch.
35Watch ye therefore: for ye know not when the
master of the house cometh, at even, or at midnight,
or at the cockcrowing, or in the morning:
36Lest coming suddenly he find you sleeping.
37And what I say unto you I say unto all, Watch.

14 1After two days was *the feast of* the passover,
and of unleavened bread: and the chief
priests and the scribes sought how they might take
him by craft, and put *him* to death.
2But they said, Not on the feast *day,* lest there be
an uproar of the people.
3And being in Bethany in the house of Simon the
leper, as he sat at meat, there came a woman having
an alabaster box of ointment of spikenard very precious; and she brake the box, and poured *it* on his
head.

NEW LIVING TRANSLATION

Messiah,' or 'There he is,' don't believe it. 22For false
messiahs and false prophets will rise up and perform signs and wonders so as to deceive, if possible,
even God's chosen ones. 23Watch out! I have warned
you about this ahead of time!
24"At that time, after the anguish of those days,

the sun will be darkened,
the moon will give no light,
25 the stars will fall from the sky,
and the powers in the heavens will be shaken.*

26Then everyone will see the Son of Man* coming on
the clouds with great power and glory.* 27And he will
send out his angels to gather his chosen ones from all
over the world*—from the farthest ends of the earth
and heaven.
28"Now learn a lesson from the fig tree. When its
branches bud and its leaves begin to sprout, you
know that summer is near. 29In the same way, when
you see all these things taking place, you can know
that his return is very near, right at the door. 30I tell
you the truth, this generation* will not pass from the
scene before all these things take place. 31Heaven
and earth will disappear, but my words will never
disappear.
32"However, no one knows the day or hour when
these things will happen, not even the angels in
heaven or the Son himself. Only the Father knows.
33And since you don't know when that time will
come, be on guard! Stay alert*!
34"The coming of the Son of Man can be illustrated by the story of a man going on a long trip.
When he left home, he gave each of his slaves instructions about the work they were to do, and he
told the gatekeeper to watch for his return. 35You,
too, must keep watch! For you don't know when
the master of the household will return—in the evening, at midnight, before dawn, or at daybreak.
36Don't let him find you sleeping when he arrives
without warning. 37I say to you what I say to everyone: Watch for him!"

Jesus Anointed at Bethany

14 It was now two days before Passover and
the Festival of Unleavened Bread. The leading priests and the teachers of religious law were still
looking for an opportunity to capture Jesus secretly
and kill him. 2"But not during the Passover celebration," they agreed, "or the people may riot."
3Meanwhile, Jesus was in Bethany at the home of
Simon, a man who had previously had leprosy. While
he was eating,* a woman came in with a beautiful alabaster jar of expensive perfume made from essence
of nard. She broke open the jar and poured the perfume over his head.

13:24-25 See Isa 13:10; 34:4; Joel 2:10. **13:26a** "Son of Man" is a title Jesus used for himself. **13:26b** See Dan 7:13. **13:27** Greek *from the four winds.* **13:30** Or *this age,* or *this nation.* **13:33** Some manuscripts add *and pray.* **14:3** Or *reclining.*

KING JAMES VERSION

4 And there were some that had indignation within themselves, and said, Why was this waste of the ointment made?

5 For it might have been sold for more than three hundred pence, and have been given to the poor. And they murmured against her.

6 And Jesus said, Let her alone; why trouble ye her? she hath wrought a good work on me.

7 For ye have the poor with you always, and whensoever ye will ye may do them good: but me ye have not always.

8 She hath done what she could: she is come aforehand to anoint my body to the burying.

9 Verily I say unto you, Wheresoever this gospel shall be preached throughout the whole world, *this* also that she hath done shall be spoken of for a memorial of her.

10 And Judas Iscariot, one of the twelve, went unto the chief priests, to betray him unto them.

11 And when they heard *it,* they were glad, and promised to give him money. And he sought how he might conveniently betray him.

12 And the first day of unleavened bread, when they killed the passover, his disciples said unto him, Where wilt thou that we go and prepare that thou mayest eat the passover?

13 And he sendeth forth two of his disciples, and saith unto them, Go ye into the city, and there shall meet you a man bearing a pitcher of water: follow him.

14 And wheresoever he shall go in, say ye to the goodman of the house, The Master saith, Where is the guestchamber, where I shall eat the passover with my disciples?

15 And he will shew you a large upper room furnished *and* prepared: there make ready for us.

16 And his disciples went forth, and came into the city, and found as he had said unto them: and they made ready the passover.

17 And in the evening he cometh with the twelve.

18 And as they sat and did eat, Jesus said, Verily I say unto you, One of you which eateth with me shall betray me.

19 And they began to be sorrowful, and to say unto him one by one, *Is* it I? and another *said, Is* it I?

20 And he answered and said unto them, *It is* one of the twelve, that dippeth with me in the dish.

21 The Son of man indeed goeth, as it is written of him: but woe to that man by whom the Son of man is betrayed! good were it for that man if he had never been born.

22 And as they did eat, Jesus took bread, and blessed, and brake *it,* and gave to them, and said, Take, eat: this is my body.

23 And he took the cup, and when he had given thanks, he gave *it* to them: and they all drank of it.

NEW LIVING TRANSLATION

4 Some of those at the table were indignant. "Why waste such expensive perfume?" they asked.
5 "It could have been sold for a year's wages* and the money given to the poor!" So they scolded her harshly.

6 But Jesus replied, "Leave her alone. Why criticize her for doing such a good thing to me?
7 You will always have the poor among you, and you can help them whenever you want to. But you will not always have me.
8 She has done what she could and has anointed my body for burial ahead of time.
9 I tell you the truth, wherever the Good News is preached throughout the world, this woman's deed will be remembered and discussed."

Judas Agrees to Betray Jesus

10 Then Judas Iscariot, one of the twelve disciples, went to the leading priests to arrange to betray Jesus to them.
11 They were delighted when they heard why he had come, and they promised to give him money. So he began looking for an opportunity to betray Jesus.

The Last Supper

12 On the first day of the Festival of Unleavened Bread, when the Passover lamb is sacrificed, Jesus' disciples asked him, "Where do you want us to go to prepare the Passover meal for you?"

13 So Jesus sent two of them into Jerusalem with these instructions: "As you go into the city, a man carrying a pitcher of water will meet you. Follow him.
14 At the house he enters, say to the owner, 'The Teacher asks: Where is the guest room where I can eat the Passover meal with my disciples?'
15 He will take you upstairs to a large room that is already set up. That is where you should prepare our meal."
16 So the two disciples went into the city and found everything just as Jesus had said, and they prepared the Passover meal there.

17 In the evening Jesus arrived with the twelve disciples.*
18 As they were at the table* eating, Jesus said, "I tell you the truth, one of you eating with me here will betray me."

19 Greatly distressed, each one asked in turn, "Am I the one?"

20 He replied, "It is one of you twelve who is eating from this bowl with me.
21 For the Son of Man* must die, as the Scriptures declared long ago. But how terrible it will be for the one who betrays him. It would be far better for that man if he had never been born!"

22 As they were eating, Jesus took some bread and blessed it. Then he broke it in pieces and gave it to the disciples, saying, "Take it, for this is my body."

23 And he took a cup of wine and gave thanks to

14:5 Greek *for 300 denarii.* A denarius was equivalent to a laborer's full day's wage. **14:17** Greek *the Twelve.* **14:18** Or *As they reclined.* **14:21** "Son of Man" is a title Jesus used for himself.

KING JAMES VERSION

24 And he said unto them, This is my blood of the new testament, which is shed for many.

25 Verily I say unto you, I will drink no more of the fruit of the vine, until that day that I drink it new in the kingdom of God.

26 And when they had sung an hymn, they went out into the mount of Olives.

27 And Jesus saith unto them, All ye shall be offended because of me this night: for it is written, I will smite the shepherd, and the sheep shall be scattered.

28 But after that I am risen, I will go before you into Galilee.

29 But Peter said unto him, Although all shall be offended, yet *will* not I.

30 And Jesus saith unto him, Verily I say unto thee, That this day, *even* in this night, before the cock crow twice, thou shalt deny me thrice.

31 But he spake the more vehemently, If I should die with thee, I will not deny thee in any wise. Likewise also said they all.

32 And they came to a place which was named Gethsemane: and he saith to his disciples, Sit ye here, while I shall pray.

33 And he taketh with him Peter and James and John, and began to be sore amazed, and to be very heavy;

34 And saith unto them, My soul is exceeding sorrowful unto death: tarry ye here, and watch.

35 And he went forward a little, and fell on the ground, and prayed that, if it were possible, the hour might pass from him.

36 And he said, Abba, Father, all things *are* possible unto thee; take away this cup from me: nevertheless not what I will, but what thou wilt.

37 And he cometh, and findeth them sleeping, and saith unto Peter, Simon, sleepest thou? couldest not thou watch one hour?

38 Watch ye and pray, lest ye enter into temptation. The spirit truly *is* ready, but the flesh *is* weak.

39 And again he went away, and prayed, and spake the same words.

40 And when he returned, he found them asleep again, (for their eyes were heavy,) neither wist they what to answer him.

41 And he cometh the third time, and saith unto them, Sleep on now, and take *your* rest: it is enough, the hour is come; behold, the Son of man is betrayed into the hands of sinners.

42 Rise up, let us go; lo, he that betrayeth me is at hand.

NEW LIVING TRANSLATION

God for it. He gave it to them, and they all drank from it. 24 And he said to them, "This is my blood, which confirms the covenant* between God and his people. It is poured out as a sacrifice for many. 25 I tell you the truth, I will not drink wine again until the day I drink it new in the Kingdom of God."

26 Then they sang a hymn and went out to the Mount of Olives.

Jesus Predicts Peter's Denial

27 On the way, Jesus told them, "All of you will desert me. For the Scriptures say,

'God will strike* the Shepherd,
and the sheep will be scattered.'

28 But after I am raised from the dead, I will go ahead of you to Galilee and meet you there."

29 Peter said to him, "Even if everyone else deserts you, I never will."

30 Jesus replied, "I tell you the truth, Peter—this very night, before the rooster crows twice, you will deny three times that you even know me."

31 "No!" Peter declared emphatically. "Even if I have to die with you, I will never deny you!" And all the others vowed the same.

Jesus Prays in Gethsemane

32 They went to the olive grove called Gethsemane, and Jesus said, "Sit here while I go and pray." 33 He took Peter, James, and John with him, and he became deeply troubled and distressed. 34 He told them, "My soul is crushed with grief to the point of death. Stay here and keep watch with me."

35 He went on a little farther and fell to the ground. He prayed that, if it were possible, the awful hour awaiting him might pass him by. 36 "Abba, Father,"* he cried out, "everything is possible for you. Please take this cup of suffering away from me. Yet I want your will to be done, not mine."

37 Then he returned and found the disciples asleep. He said to Peter, "Simon, are you asleep? Couldn't you watch with me even one hour? 38 Keep watch and pray, so that you will not give in to temptation. For the spirit is willing, but the body is weak."

39 Then Jesus left them again and prayed the same prayer as before. 40 When he returned to them again, he found them sleeping, for they couldn't keep their eyes open. And they didn't know what to say.

41 When he returned to them the third time, he said, "Go ahead and sleep. Have your rest. But no—the time has come. The Son of Man is betrayed into the hands of sinners. 42 Up, let's be going. Look, my betrayer is here!"

14:24 Some manuscripts read *the new covenant*. **14:27** Greek *I will strike*. Zech 13:7. **14:36** *Abba* is an Aramaic term for "father."

KING JAMES VERSION

43 And immediately, while he yet spake, cometh Judas, one of the twelve, and with him a great multitude with swords and staves, from the chief priests and the scribes and the elders.

44 And he that betrayed him had given them a token, saying, Whomsoever I shall kiss, that same is he; take him, and lead *him* away safely.

45 And as soon as he was come, he goeth straightway to him, and saith, Master, master; and kissed him.

46 And they laid their hands on him, and took him.

47 And one of them that stood by drew a sword, and smote a servant of the high priest, and cut off his ear.

48 And Jesus answered and said unto them, Are ye come out, as against a thief, with swords and *with* staves to take me?

49 I was daily with you in the temple teaching, and ye took me not: but the scriptures must be fulfilled.

50 And they all forsook him, and fled.

51 And there followed him a certain young man, having a linen cloth cast about *his* naked *body;* and the young men laid hold on him:

52 And he left the linen cloth, and fled from them naked.

53 And they led Jesus away to the high priest: and with him were assembled all the chief priests and the elders and the scribes.

54 And Peter followed him afar off, even into the palace of the high priest: and he sat with the servants, and warmed himself at the fire.

55 And the chief priests and all the council sought for witness against Jesus to put him to death; and found none.

56 For many bare false witness against him, but their witness agreed not together.

57 And there arose certain, and bare false witness against him, saying,

58 We heard him say, I will destroy this temple that is made with hands, and within three days I will build another made without hands.

59 But neither so did their witness agree together.

60 And the high priest stood up in the midst, and asked Jesus, saying, Answerest thou nothing? what *is it which* these witness against thee?

61 But he held his peace, and answered nothing. Again the high priest asked him, and said unto him, Art thou the Christ, the Son of the Blessed?

62 And Jesus said, I am: and ye shall see the Son of man sitting on the right hand of power, and coming in the clouds of heaven.

63 Then the high priest rent his clothes, and saith, What need we any further witnesses?

NEW LIVING TRANSLATION

Jesus Is Betrayed and Arrested

43 And immediately, even as Jesus said this, Judas, one
of the twelve disciples, arrived with a crowd of men
armed with swords and clubs. They had been sent by
the leading priests, the teachers of religious law, and
the elders. 44 The traitor, Judas, had given them a prearranged signal: "You will know which one to arrest
when I greet him with a kiss. Then you can take him
away under guard." 45 As soon as they arrived, Judas
walked up to Jesus. "Rabbi!" he exclaimed, and gave
him the kiss.

46 Then the others grabbed Jesus and arrested
him. 47 But one of the men with Jesus pulled out his
sword and struck the high priest's slave, slashing off
his ear.

48 Jesus asked them, "Am I some dangerous revolutionary, that you come with swords and clubs to arrest me? 49 Why didn't you arrest me in the Temple? I
was there among you teaching every day. But these
things are happening to fulfill what the Scriptures
say about me."

50 Then all his disciples deserted him and ran
away. 51 One young man following behind was
clothed only in a long linen shirt. When the mob
tried to grab him, 52 he slipped out of his shirt and
ran away naked.

Jesus before the Council

53 They took Jesus to the high priest's home where
the leading priests, the elders, and the teachers of
religious law had gathered. 54 Meanwhile, Peter followed him at a distance and went right into the high
priest's courtyard. There he sat with the guards,
warming himself by the fire.

55 Inside, the leading priests and the entire high
council* were trying to find evidence against Jesus,
so they could put him to death. But they couldn't
find any. 56 Many false witnesses spoke against him,
but they contradicted each other. 57 Finally, some
men stood up and gave this false testimony: 58 "We
heard him say, 'I will destroy this Temple made with
human hands, and in three days I will build another,
made without human hands.'" 59 But even then they
didn't get their stories straight!

60 Then the high priest stood up before the others
and asked Jesus, "Well, aren't you going to answer
these charges? What do you have to say for yourself?" 61 But Jesus was silent and made no reply. Then
the high priest asked him, "Are you the Messiah, the
Son of the Blessed One?"

62 Jesus said, "I AM.* And you will see the Son of
Man seated in the place of power at God's right
hand* and coming on the clouds of heaven.*"

63 Then the high priest tore his clothing to show his
horror and said, "Why do we need other witnesses?

14:55 Greek *the Sanhedrin.* **14:62a** Or *The 'I AM' is here;* or *I am the LORD.* See Exod 3:14. **14:62b** Greek *at the right hand of the power.* See Ps 110:1. **14:62c** See Dan 7:13.

KING JAMES VERSION

64Ye have heard the blasphemy: what think ye? And they all condemned him to be guilty of death.

65And some began to spit on him, and to cover his face, and to buffet him, and to say unto him, Prophesy: and the servants did strike him with the palms of their hands.

66And as Peter was beneath in the palace, there cometh one of the maids of the high priest:

67And when she saw Peter warming himself, she looked upon him, and said, And thou also wast with Jesus of Nazareth.

68But he denied, saying, I know not, neither understand I what thou sayest. And he went out into the porch; and the cock crew.

69And a maid saw him again, and began to say to them that stood by, This is *one* of them.

70And he denied it again. And a little after, they that stood by said again to Peter, Surely thou art *one* of them: for thou art a Galilaean, and thy speech agreeth *thereto*.

71But he began to curse and to swear, *saying*, I know not this man of whom ye speak.

72And the second time the cock crew. And Peter called to mind the word that Jesus said unto him, Before the cock crow twice, thou shalt deny me thrice. And when he thought thereon, he wept.

15 1And straightway in the morning the chief priests held a consultation with the elders and scribes and the whole council, and bound Jesus, and carried *him* away, and delivered *him* to Pilate.

2And Pilate asked him, Art thou the King of the Jews? And he answering said unto him, Thou sayest *it*.

3And the chief priests accused him of many things: but he answered nothing.

4And Pilate asked him again, saying, Answerest thou nothing? behold how many things they witness against thee.

5But Jesus yet answered nothing; so that Pilate marvelled.

6Now at *that* feast he released unto them one prisoner, whomsoever they desired.

7And there was *one* named Barabbas, *which lay* bound with them that had made insurrection with him, who had committed murder in the insurrection.

8And the multitude crying aloud began to desire *him to do* as he had ever done unto them.

9But Pilate answered them, saying, Will ye that I release unto you the King of the Jews?

10For he knew that the chief priests had delivered him for envy.

11But the chief priests moved the people, that he should rather release Barabbas unto them.

NEW LIVING TRANSLATION

64You have all heard his blasphemy. What is your verdict?"

"Guilty!" they all cried. "He deserves to die!"

65Then some of them began to spit at him, and they blindfolded him and beat him with their fists. "Prophesy to us," they jeered. And the guards slapped him as they took him away.

Peter Denies Jesus

66Meanwhile, Peter was in the courtyard below. One of the servant girls who worked for the high priest came by 67and noticed Peter warming himself at the fire. She looked at him closely and said, "You were one of those with Jesus of Nazareth.*"

68But Peter denied it. "I don't know what you're talking about," he said, and he went out into the entryway. Just then, a rooster crowed.*

69When the servant girl saw him standing there, she began telling the others, "This man is definitely one of them!" 70But Peter denied it again.

A little later some of the other bystanders confronted Peter and said, "You must be one of them, because you are a Galilean."

71Peter swore, "A curse on me if I'm lying—I don't know this man you're talking about!" 72And immediately the rooster crowed the second time.

Suddenly, Jesus' words flashed through Peter's mind: "Before the rooster crows twice, you will deny three times that you even know me." And he broke down and wept.

Jesus' Trial before Pilate

15 Very early in the morning the leading priests, the elders, and the teachers of religious law—the entire high council*—met to discuss their next step. They bound Jesus, led him away, and took him to Pilate, the Roman governor.

2Pilate asked Jesus, "Are you the king of the Jews?"

Jesus replied, "You have said it."

3Then the leading priests kept accusing him of many crimes, 4and Pilate asked him, "Aren't you going to answer them? What about all these charges they are bringing against you?" 5But Jesus said nothing, much to Pilate's surprise.

6Now it was the governor's custom each year during the Passover celebration to release one prisoner—anyone the people requested. 7One of the prisoners at that time was Barabbas, a revolutionary who had committed murder in an uprising. 8The crowd went to Pilate and asked him to release a prisoner as usual.

9"Would you like me to release to you this 'King of the Jews'?" Pilate asked. 10(For he realized by now that the leading priests had arrested Jesus out of envy.) 11But at this point the leading priests stirred up the crowd to demand the release of Barabbas instead

14:67 Or *Jesus the Nazarene.* **14:68** Some manuscripts do not include *Just then, a rooster crowed.* **15:1** Greek *the Sanhedrin;* also in 15:43.

KING JAMES VERSION

12 And Pilate answered and said again unto them,
What will ye then that I shall do *unto him* whom ye
call the King of the Jews?
13 And they cried out again, Crucify him.
14 Then Pilate said unto them, Why, what evil hath
he done? And they cried out the more exceedingly,
Crucify him.
15 And *so* Pilate, willing to content the people, released Barabbas unto them, and delivered Jesus,
when he had scourged *him,* to be crucified.

16 And the soldiers led him away into the hall,
called Praetorium; and they call together the whole
band.
17 And they clothed him with purple, and platted a
crown of thorns, and put it about his *head,*
18 And began to salute him, Hail, King of the Jews!
19 And they smote him on the head with a reed, and
did spit upon him, and bowing *their* knees worshipped him.
20 And when they had mocked him, they took off
the purple from him, and put his own clothes on
him, and led him out to crucify him.

21 And they compel one Simon a Cyrenian, who
passed by, coming out of the country, the father of
Alexander and Rufus, to bear his cross.
22 And they bring him unto the place Golgotha,
which is, being interpreted, The place of a skull.
23 And they gave him to drink wine mingled with
myrrh: but he received *it* not.
24 And when they had crucified him, they parted
his garments, casting lots upon them, what every
man should take.
25 And it was the third hour, and they crucified him.
26 And the superscription of his accusation was
written over, THE KING OF THE JEWS.
27 And with him they crucify two thieves; the one
on his right hand, and the other on his left.
28 And the scripture was fulfilled, which saith, And
he was numbered with the transgressors.
29 And they that passed by railed on him, wagging
their heads, and saying, Ah, thou that destroyest
the temple, and buildest *it* in three days,
30 Save thyself, and come down from the cross.
31 Likewise also the chief priests mocking said
among themselves with the scribes, He saved others;
himself he cannot save.
32 Let Christ the King of Israel descend now from
the cross, that we may see and believe. And they that
were crucified with him reviled him.
33 And when the sixth hour was come, there was
darkness over the whole land until the ninth hour.
34 And at the ninth hour Jesus cried with a loud

NEW LIVING TRANSLATION

of Jesus. 12 Pilate asked them, "Then what should I do
with this man you call the king of the Jews?"
13 They shouted back, "Crucify him!"
14 "Why?" Pilate demanded. "What crime has he
committed?"
But the mob roared even louder, "Crucify him!"
15 So to pacify the crowd, Pilate released Barabbas
to them. He ordered Jesus flogged with a lead-tipped
whip, then turned him over to the Roman soldiers to
be crucified.

The Soldiers Mock Jesus

16 The soldiers took Jesus into the courtyard of the
governor's headquarters (called the Praetorium) and
called out the entire regiment. 17 They dressed him in
a purple robe, and they wove thorn branches into a
crown and put it on his head. 18 Then they saluted
him and taunted, "Hail! King of the Jews!" 19 And they
struck him on the head with a reed stick, spit on him,
and dropped to their knees in mock worship.
20 When they were finally tired of mocking him, they
took off the purple robe and put his own clothes on
him again. Then they led him away to be crucified.

The Crucifixion

21 A passerby named Simon, who was from Cyrene,*
was coming in from the countryside just then, and
the soldiers forced him to carry Jesus' cross. (Simon
was the father of Alexander and Rufus.) 22 And they
brought Jesus to a place called Golgotha (which
means "Place of the Skull"). 23 They offered him wine
drugged with myrrh, but he refused it.
24 Then the soldiers nailed him to the cross. They
divided his clothes and threw dice* to decide who
would get each piece. 25 It was nine o'clock in the
morning when they crucified him. 26 A sign announced the charge against him. It read, "The King
of the Jews." 27 Two revolutionaries* were crucified
with him, one on his right and one on his left.*
29 The people passing by shouted abuse, shaking
their heads in mockery. "Ha! Look at you now!" they
yelled at him. "You said you were going to destroy
the Temple and rebuild it in three days. 30 Well then,
save yourself and come down from the cross!"
31 The leading priests and teachers of religious law
also mocked Jesus. "He saved others," they scoffed,
"but he can't save himself! 32 Let this Messiah, this
King of Israel, come down from the cross so we can
see it and believe him!" Even the men who were crucified with Jesus ridiculed him.

The Death of Jesus

33 At noon, darkness fell across the whole land until
three o'clock. 34 Then at three o'clock Jesus called out

15:21 *Cyrene* was a city in northern Africa. **15:24** Greek *cast lots.* See Ps 22:18. **15:27a** Or *Two criminals.* **15:27b** Some manuscripts add verse 28, *And the Scripture was fulfilled that said, "He was counted among those who were rebels."* See Isa 53:12; also compare Luke 22:37.

KING JAMES VERSION

voice, saying, Eloi, Eloi, lama sabachthani? which is, being interpreted, My God, my God, why hast thou forsaken me?

35 And some of them that stood by, when they heard *it,* said, Behold, he calleth Elias.

36 And one ran and filled a spunge full of vinegar, and put *it* on a reed, and gave him to drink, saying, Let alone; let us see whether Elias will come to take him down.

37 And Jesus cried with a loud voice, and gave up the ghost.

38 And the veil of the temple was rent in twain from the top to the bottom.

39 And when the centurion, which stood over against him, saw that he so cried out, and gave up the ghost, he said, Truly this man was the Son of God.

40 There were also women looking on afar off: among whom was Mary Magdalene, and Mary the mother of James the less and of Joses, and Salome;

41 (Who also, when he was in Galilee, followed him, and ministered unto him;) and many other women which came up with him unto Jerusalem.

42 And now when the even was come, because it was the preparation, that is, the day before the sabbath,

43 Joseph of Arimathaea, an honourable counsellor, which also waited for the kingdom of God, came, and went in boldly unto Pilate, and craved the body of Jesus.

44 And Pilate marvelled if he were already dead: and calling *unto him* the centurion, he asked him whether he had been any while dead.

45 And when he knew *it* of the centurion, he gave the body to Joseph.

46 And he bought fine linen, and took him down, and wrapped him in the linen, and laid him in a sepulchre which was hewn out of a rock, and rolled a stone unto the door of the sepulchre.

47 And Mary Magdalene and Mary *the mother* of Joses beheld where he was laid.

16 1 And when the sabbath was past, Mary Magdalene, and Mary the *mother* of James, and Salome, had bought sweet spices, that they might come and anoint him.

2 And very early in the morning the first *day* of the week, they came unto the sepulchre at the rising of the sun.

3 And they said among themselves, Who shall roll us away the stone from the door of the sepulchre?

4 And when they looked, they saw that the stone was rolled away: for it was very great.

5 And entering into the sepulchre, they saw a young man sitting on the right side, clothed in a long white garment; and they were affrighted.

6 And he saith unto them, Be not affrighted: Ye seek Jesus of Nazareth, which was crucified: he is

NEW LIVING TRANSLATION

with a loud voice, *"Eloi, Eloi, lema sabachthani?"* which means "My God, my God, why have you abandoned me?"*

35 Some of the bystanders misunderstood and thought he was calling for the prophet Elijah. 36 One of them ran and filled a sponge with sour wine, holding it up to him on a reed stick so he could drink. "Wait!" he said. "Let's see whether Elijah comes to take him down!"

37 Then Jesus uttered another loud cry and breathed his last. 38 And the curtain in the sanctuary of the Temple was torn in two, from top to bottom.

39 When the Roman officer* who stood facing him* saw how he had died, he exclaimed, "This man truly was the Son of God!"

40 Some women were there, watching from a distance, including Mary Magdalene, Mary (the mother of James the younger and of Joseph*), and Salome. 41 They had been followers of Jesus and had cared for him while he was in Galilee. Many other women who had come with him to Jerusalem were also there.

The Burial of Jesus

42 This all happened on Friday, the day of preparation,* the day before the Sabbath. As evening approached, 43 Joseph of Arimathea took a risk and went to Pilate and asked for Jesus' body. (Joseph was an honored member of the high council, and he was waiting for the Kingdom of God to come.) 44 Pilate couldn't believe that Jesus was already dead, so he called for the Roman officer and asked if he had died yet. 45 The officer confirmed that Jesus was dead, so Pilate told Joseph he could have the body. 46 Joseph bought a long sheet of linen cloth. Then he took Jesus' body down from the cross, wrapped it in the cloth, and laid it in a tomb that had been carved out of the rock. Then he rolled a stone in front of the entrance. 47 Mary Magdalene and Mary the mother of Joseph saw where Jesus' body was laid.

The Resurrection

16 Saturday evening, when the Sabbath ended, Mary Magdalene, Mary the mother of James, and Salome went out and purchased burial spices so they could anoint Jesus' body. 2 Very early on Sunday morning,* just at sunrise, they went to the tomb. 3 On the way they were asking each other, "Who will roll away the stone for us from the entrance to the tomb?" 4 But as they arrived, they looked up and saw that the stone, which was very large, had already been rolled aside.

5 When they entered the tomb, they saw a young man clothed in a white robe sitting on the right side. The women were shocked, 6 but the angel said, "Don't

15:34 Ps 22:1. **15:39a** Greek *the centurion;* similarly in 15:44, 45. **15:39b** Some manuscripts add *heard his cry and.* **15:40** Greek *Joses;* also in 15:47. See Matt 27:56. **15:42** Greek *It was the day of preparation.* **16:2** Greek *on the first day of the week;* also in 16:9.

KING JAMES VERSION

risen; he is not here: behold the place where they laid
him.
7But go your way, tell his disciples and Peter that
he goeth before you into Galilee: there shall ye see
him, as he said unto you.
8And they went out quickly, and fled from the sepulchre; for they trembled and were amazed: neither
said they any thing to any *man;* for they were afraid.
9Now when *Jesus* was risen early the first *day* of
the week, he appeared first to Mary Magdalene, out
of whom he had cast seven devils.
10*And* she went and told them that had been with
him, as they mourned and wept.
11And they, when they had heard that he was alive,
and had been seen of her, believed not.
12After that he appeared in another form unto two
of them, as they walked, and went into the country.
13And they went and told *it* unto the residue: neither believed they them.
14Afterward he appeared unto the eleven as they
sat at meat, and upbraided them with their unbelief
and hardness of heart, because they believed not
them which had seen him after he was risen.
15And he said unto them, Go ye into all the world,
and preach the gospel to every creature.
16He that believeth and is baptized shall be saved;
but he that believeth not shall be damned.
17And these signs shall follow them that believe;
In my name shall they cast out devils; they shall
speak with new tongues;
18They shall take up serpents; and if they drink
any deadly thing, it shall not hurt them; they shall lay
hands on the sick, and they shall recover.
19So then after the Lord had spoken unto them, he
was received up into heaven, and sat on the right
hand of God.
20And they went forth, and preached every where,
the Lord working with *them,* and confirming the
word with signs following. Amen.

NEW LIVING TRANSLATION

be alarmed. You are looking for Jesus of Nazareth,*
who was crucified. He isn't here! He is risen from the
dead! Look, this is where they laid his body. 7Now go
and tell his disciples, including Peter, that Jesus is
going ahead of you to Galilee. You will see him there,
just as he told you before he died."
8The women fled from the tomb, trembling and
bewildered, and they said nothing to anyone because
they were too frightened.*

[*Shorter Ending of Mark*]

Then they briefly reported all this to Peter and his
companions. Afterward Jesus himself sent them out
from east to west with the sacred and unfailing message of salvation that gives eternal life. Amen.

[*Longer Ending of Mark*]

9After Jesus rose from the dead early on Sunday
morning, the first person who saw him was Mary
Magdalene, the woman from whom he had cast out
seven demons. 10She went to the disciples, who were
grieving and weeping, and told them what had happened. 11But when she told them that Jesus was alive
and she had seen him, they didn't believe her.
12Afterward he appeared in a different form to
two of his followers who were walking from Jerusalem into the country. 13They rushed back to tell the
others, but no one believed them.
14Still later he appeared to the eleven disciples as
they were eating together. He rebuked them for their
stubborn unbelief because they refused to believe
those who had seen him after he had been raised
from the dead.*
15And then he told them, "Go into all the world and
preach the Good News to everyone. 16Anyone who believes and is baptized will be saved. But anyone who
refuses to believe will be condemned. 17These miraculous signs will accompany those who believe: They
will cast out demons in my name, and they will speak
in new languages.* 18They will be able to handle
snakes with safety, and if they drink anything poisonous, it won't hurt them. They will be able to place their
hands on the sick, and they will be healed."
19When the Lord Jesus had finished talking with
them, he was taken up into heaven and sat down in
the place of honor at God's right hand. 20And the disciples went everywhere and preached, and the Lord
worked through them, confirming what they said by
many miraculous signs.

16:6 Or *Jesus the Nazarene.* **16:8** The most reliable early manuscripts of the Gospel of Mark end at verse 8. Other manuscripts include various endings to the Gospel. A few include both the "shorter ending" and the "longer ending." The majority of manuscripts include the "longer ending" immediately after verse 8. **16:14** Some early manuscripts add: *And they excused themselves, saying, "This age of lawlessness and unbelief is under Satan, who does not permit God's truth and power to conquer the evil [unclean] spirits. Therefore, reveal your justice now." This is what they said to Christ. And Christ replied to them, "The period of years of Satan's power has been fulfilled, but other dreadful things will happen soon. And I was handed over to death for those who have sinned, so that they may return to the truth and sin no more, and so they may inherit the spiritual, incorruptible, and righteous glory in heaven."* **16:17** Or *new tongues;* some manuscripts do not include *new.*

Luke

KING JAMES VERSION

1 1Forasmuch as many have taken in hand to set forth in order a declaration of those things which are most surely believed among us,

2Even as they delivered them unto us, which from the beginning were eyewitnesses, and ministers of the word;

3It seemed good to me also, having had perfect understanding of all things from the very first, to write unto thee in order, most excellent Theophilus,

4That thou mightest know the certainty of those things, wherein thou hast been instructed.

5There was in the days of Herod, the king of Judaea, a certain priest named Zacharias, of the course of Abia: and his wife *was* of the daughters of Aaron, and her name *was* Elisabeth.

6And they were both righteous before God, walking in all the commandments and ordinances of the Lord blameless.

7And they had no child, because that Elisabeth was barren, and they both were *now* well stricken in years.

8And it came to pass, that while he executed the priest's office before God in the order of his course,

9According to the custom of the priest's office, his lot was to burn incense when he went into the temple of the Lord.

10And the whole multitude of the people were praying without at the time of incense.

11And there appeared unto him an angel of the Lord standing on the right side of the altar of incense.

12And when Zacharias saw *him,* he was troubled, and fear fell upon him.

13But the angel said unto him, Fear not, Zacharias: for thy prayer is heard; and thy wife Elisabeth shall bear thee a son, and thou shalt call his name John.

14And thou shalt have joy and gladness; and many shall rejoice at his birth.

15For he shall be great in the sight of the Lord, and shall drink neither wine nor strong drink; and he shall be filled with the Holy Ghost, even from his mother's womb.

16And many of the children of Israel shall he turn to the Lord their God.

NEW LIVING TRANSLATION

Introduction

1 Many people have set out to write accounts about the events that have been fulfilled among us. 2They used the eyewitness reports circulating among us from the early disciples.* 3Having carefully investigated everything from the beginning, I also have decided to write a careful account for you, most honorable Theophilus, 4so you can be certain of the truth of everything you were taught.

The Birth of John the Baptist Foretold

5When Herod was king of Judea, there was a Jewish priest named Zechariah. He was a member of the priestly order of Abijah, and his wife, Elizabeth, was also from the priestly line of Aaron. 6Zechariah and Elizabeth were righteous in God's eyes, careful to obey all of the Lord's commandments and regulations. 7They had no children because Elizabeth was unable to conceive, and they were both very old.

8One day Zechariah was serving God in the Temple, for his order was on duty that week. 9As was the custom of the priests, he was chosen by lot to enter the sanctuary of the Lord and burn incense. 10While the incense was being burned, a great crowd stood outside, praying.

11While Zechariah was in the sanctuary, an angel of the Lord appeared to him, standing to the right of the incense altar. 12Zechariah was shaken and overwhelmed with fear when he saw him. 13But the angel said, "Don't be afraid, Zechariah! God has heard your prayer. Your wife, Elizabeth, will give you a son, and you are to name him John. 14You will have great joy and gladness, and many will rejoice at his birth, 15for he will be great in the eyes of the Lord. He must never touch wine or other alcoholic drinks. He will be filled with the Holy Spirit, even before his birth.* 16And he will turn many Israelites to the Lord their

1:2 Greek *from those who from the beginning were servants of the word.*
1:15 Or *even from birth.*

KING JAMES VERSION

17And he shall go before him in the spirit and power of Elias, to turn the hearts of the fathers to the children, and the disobedient to the wisdom of the just; to make ready a people prepared for the Lord.

18And Zacharias said unto the angel, Whereby shall I know this? for I am an old man, and my wife well stricken in years.

19And the angel answering said unto him, I am Gabriel, that stand in the presence of God; and am sent to speak unto thee, and to shew thee these glad tidings.

20And, behold, thou shalt be dumb, and not able to speak, until the day that these things shall be performed, because thou believest not my words, which shall be fulfilled in their season.

21And the people waited for Zacharias, and marvelled that he tarried so long in the temple.

22And when he came out, he could not speak unto them: and they perceived that he had seen a vision in the temple: for he beckoned unto them, and remained speechless.

23And it came to pass, that, as soon as the days of his ministration were accomplished, he departed to his own house.

24And after those days his wife Elisabeth conceived, and hid herself five months, saying,

25Thus hath the Lord dealt with me in the days wherein he looked on *me,* to take away my reproach among men.

26And in the sixth month the angel Gabriel was sent from God unto a city of Galilee, named Nazareth,

27To a virgin espoused to a man whose name was Joseph, of the house of David; and the virgin's name *was* Mary.

28And the angel came in unto her, and said, Hail, *thou that art* highly favoured, the Lord *is* with thee: blessed *art* thou among women.

29And when she saw *him,* she was troubled at his saying, and cast in her mind what manner of salutation this should be.

30And the angel said unto her, Fear not, Mary: for thou hast found favour with God.

31And, behold, thou shalt conceive in thy womb, and bring forth a son, and shalt call his name JESUS.

32He shall be great, and shall be called the Son of the Highest: and the Lord God shall give unto him the throne of his father David:

33And he shall reign over the house of Jacob for ever; and of his kingdom there shall be no end.

34Then said Mary unto the angel, How shall this be, seeing I know not a man?

35And the angel answered and said unto her, The Holy Ghost shall come upon thee, and the power of the Highest shall overshadow thee: therefore also that holy thing which shall be born of thee shall be called the Son of God.

36And, behold, thy cousin Elisabeth, she hath also conceived a son in her old age: and this is the sixth month with her, who was called barren.

NEW LIVING TRANSLATION

God. 17He will be a man with the spirit and power of Elijah. He will prepare the people for the coming of the Lord. He will turn the hearts of the fathers to their children,* and he will cause those who are rebellious to accept the wisdom of the godly."

18Zechariah said to the angel, "How can I be sure this will happen? I'm an old man now, and my wife is also well along in years."

19Then the angel said, "I am Gabriel! I stand in the very presence of God. It was he who sent me to bring you this good news! 20But now, since you didn't believe what I said, you will be silent and unable to speak until the child is born. For my words will certainly be fulfilled at the proper time."

21Meanwhile, the people were waiting for Zechariah to come out of the sanctuary, wondering why he was taking so long. 22When he finally did come out, he couldn't speak to them. Then they realized from his gestures and his silence that he must have seen a vision in the sanctuary.

23When Zechariah's week of service in the Temple was over, he returned home. 24Soon afterward his wife, Elizabeth, became pregnant and went into seclusion for five months. 25"How kind the Lord is!" she exclaimed. "He has taken away my disgrace of having no children."

The Birth of Jesus Foretold

26In the sixth month of Elizabeth's pregnancy, God sent the angel Gabriel to Nazareth, a village in Galilee, 27to a virgin named Mary. She was engaged to be married to a man named Joseph, a descendant of King David. 28Gabriel appeared to her and said, "Greetings, favored woman! The Lord is with you!*"

29Confused and disturbed, Mary tried to think what the angel could mean. 30"Don't be afraid, Mary," the angel told her, "for you have found favor with God! 31You will conceive and give birth to a son, and you will name him Jesus. 32He will be very great and will be called the Son of the Most High. The Lord God will give him the throne of his ancestor David. 33And he will reign over Israel* forever; his Kingdom will never end!"

34Mary asked the angel, "But how can this happen? I am a virgin."

35The angel replied, "The Holy Spirit will come upon you, and the power of the Most High will overshadow you. So the baby to be born will be holy, and he will be called the Son of God. 36What's more, your relative Elizabeth has become pregnant in her old age! People used to say she was barren, but she has

1:17 See Mal 4:5-6. **1:28** Some manuscripts add *Blessed are you among women.* **1:33** Greek *over the house of Jacob.*

KING JAMES VERSION

37 For with God nothing shall be impossible.

38 And Mary said, Behold the handmaid of the Lord; be it unto me according to thy word. And the angel departed from her.

39 And Mary arose in those days, and went into the hill country with haste, into a city of Judah;

40 And entered into the house of Zacharias, and saluted Elisabeth.

41 And it came to pass, that, when Elisabeth heard the salutation of Mary, the babe leaped in her womb; and Elisabeth was filled with the Holy Ghost:

42 And she spake out with a loud voice, and said, Blessed *art* thou among women, and blessed *is* the fruit of thy womb.

43 And whence *is* this to me, that the mother of my Lord should come to me?

44 For, lo, as soon as the voice of thy salutation sounded in mine ears, the babe leaped in my womb for joy.

45 And blessed *is* she that believed: for there shall be a performance of those things which were told her from the Lord.

46 And Mary said, My soul doth magnify the Lord,

47 And my spirit hath rejoiced in God my Saviour.

48 For he hath regarded the low estate of his handmaiden: for, behold, from henceforth all generations shall call me blessed.

49 For he that is mighty hath done to me great things; and holy *is* his name.

50 And his mercy *is* on them that fear him from generation to generation.

51 He hath shewed strength with his arm; he hath scattered the proud in the imagination of their hearts.

52 He hath put down the mighty from *their* seats, and exalted them of low degree.

53 He hath filled the hungry with good things; and the rich he hath sent empty away.

54 He hath holpen his servant Israel, in remembrance of *his* mercy;

55 As he spake to our fathers, to Abraham, and to his seed for ever.

56 And Mary abode with her about three months, and returned to her own house.

57 Now Elisabeth's full time came that she should be delivered; and she brought forth a son.

58 And her neighbours and her cousins heard how the Lord had shewed great mercy upon her; and they rejoiced with her.

59 And it came to pass, that on the eighth day they came to circumcise the child; and they called him Zacharias, after the name of his father.

NEW LIVING TRANSLATION

conceived a son and is now in her sixth month. 37 For nothing is impossible with God.*"

38 Mary responded, "I am the Lord's servant. May everything you have said about me come true." And then the angel left her.

Mary Visits Elizabeth

39 A few days later Mary hurried to the hill country of Judea, to the town 40 where Zechariah lived. She entered the house and greeted Elizabeth. 41 At the sound of Mary's greeting, Elizabeth's child leaped within her, and Elizabeth was filled with the Holy Spirit.

42 Elizabeth gave a glad cry and exclaimed to Mary, "God has blessed you above all women, and your child is blessed. 43 Why am I so honored, that the mother of my Lord should visit me? 44 When I heard your greeting, the baby in my womb jumped for joy. 45 You are blessed because you believed that the Lord would do what he said."

The Magnificat: Mary's Song of Praise

46 Mary responded,

"Oh, how my soul praises the Lord.
47 How my spirit rejoices in God my Savior!
48 For he took notice of his lowly servant girl,
and from now on all generations will call
me blessed.
49 For the Mighty One is holy,
and he has done great things for me.
50 He shows mercy from generation to generation
to all who fear him.
51 His mighty arm has done tremendous things!
He has scattered the proud and haughty ones.
52 He has brought down princes from their thrones
and exalted the humble.
53 He has filled the hungry with good things
and sent the rich away with empty hands.
54 He has helped his servant Israel
and remembered to be merciful.
55 For he made this promise to our ancestors,
to Abraham and his children forever."

56 Mary stayed with Elizabeth about three months and then went back to her own home.

The Birth of John the Baptist

57 When it was time for Elizabeth's baby to be born, she gave birth to a son. 58 And when her neighbors and relatives heard that the Lord had been very merciful to her, everyone rejoiced with her.

59 When the baby was eight days old, they all came for the circumcision ceremony. They wanted to

1:37 Some manuscripts read *For the word of God will never fail.*

KING JAMES VERSION

60 And his mother answered and said, Not *so;* but
he shall be called John.
61 And they said unto her, There is none of thy
kindred that is called by this name.
62 And they made signs to his father, how he would
have him called.
63 And he asked for a writing table, and wrote,
saying, His name is John. And they marvelled all.
64 And his mouth was opened immediately, and
his tongue *loosed,* and he spake, and praised God.
65 And fear came on all that dwelt round about
them: and all these sayings were noised abroad
throughout all the hill country of Judaea.
66 And all they that heard *them* laid *them* up in
their hearts, saying, What manner of child shall this
be! And the hand of the Lord was with him.
67 And his father Zacharias was filled with the Holy
Ghost, and prophesied, saying,
68 Blessed *be* the Lord God of Israel; for he hath visited and redeemed his people,
69 And hath raised up an horn of salvation for us
in the house of his servant David;
70 As he spake by the mouth of his holy prophets,
which have been since the world began:
71 That we should be saved from our enemies, and
from the hand of all that hate us;
72 To perform the mercy *promised* to our fathers,
and to remember his holy covenant;
73 The oath which he sware to our father Abraham,
74 That he would grant unto us, that we being delivered out of the hand of our enemies might serve
him without fear,
75 In holiness and righteousness before him, all
the days of our life.
76 And thou, child, shalt be called the prophet of
the Highest: for thou shalt go before the face of the
Lord to prepare his ways;
77 To give knowledge of salvation unto his people
by the remission of their sins,
78 Through the tender mercy of our God; whereby
the dayspring from on high hath visited us,
79 To give light to them that sit in darkness and *in*
the shadow of death, to guide our feet into the way of
peace.
80 And the child grew, and waxed strong in spirit,
and was in the deserts till the day of his shewing unto
Israel.

2 1 And it came to pass in those days, that there
went out a decree from Caesar Augustus, that
all the world should be taxed.
2 (*And* this taxing was first made when Cyrenius
was governor of Syria.)

NEW LIVING TRANSLATION

name him Zechariah, after his father. 60 But Elizabeth
said, "No! His name is John!"
61 "What?" they exclaimed. "There is no one in all
your family by that name." 62 So they used gestures to
ask the baby's father what he wanted to name him.
63 He motioned for a writing tablet, and to everyone's
surprise he wrote, "His name is John." 64 Instantly Zechariah could speak again, and he began praising God.
65 Awe fell upon the whole neighborhood, and the
news of what had happened spread throughout the
Judean hills. 66 Everyone who heard about it reflected on these events and asked, "What will this
child turn out to be?" For the hand of the Lord was
surely upon him in a special way.

Zechariah's Prophecy

67 Then his father, Zechariah, was filled with the Holy
Spirit and gave this prophecy:

68 "Praise the Lord, the God of Israel,
because he has visited and redeemed
his people.
69 He has sent us a mighty Savior*
from the royal line of his servant David,
70 just as he promised
through his holy prophets long ago.
71 Now we will be saved from our enemies
and from all who hate us.
72 He has been merciful to our ancestors
by remembering his sacred covenant—
73 the covenant he swore with an oath
to our ancestor Abraham.
74 We have been rescued from our enemies
so we can serve God without fear,
75 in holiness and righteousness
for as long as we live.
76 "And you, my little son,
will be called the prophet of the Most High,
because you will prepare the way for the Lord.
77 You will tell his people how to find salvation
through forgiveness of their sins.
78 Because of God's tender mercy,
the morning light from heaven is about
to break upon us,*
79 to give light to those who sit in darkness and
in the shadow of death,
and to guide us to the path of peace."

80 John grew up and became strong in spirit. And
he lived in the wilderness until he began his public
ministry to Israel.

The Birth of Jesus

2 At that time the Roman emperor, Augustus, decreed that a census should be taken throughout the Roman Empire. 2 (This was the first census

1:69 Greek *has raised up a horn of salvation for us.* **1:78** Or *the Morning Light from Heaven is about to visit us.*

KING JAMES VERSION

3And all went to be taxed, every one into his own
city.
4And Joseph also went up from Galilee, out of the
city of Nazareth, into Judaea, unto the city of David,
which is called Bethlehem; (because he was of the
house and lineage of David:)
5To be taxed with Mary his espoused wife, being
great with child.
6And so it was, that, while they were there, the days
were accomplished that she should be delivered.
7And she brought forth her firstborn son, and
wrapped him in swaddling clothes, and laid him in
a manger; because there was no room for them in
the inn.
8And there were in the same country shepherds
abiding in the field, keeping watch over their flock
by night.
9And, lo, the angel of the Lord came upon them,
and the glory of the Lord shone round about them:
and they were sore afraid.
10And the angel said unto them, Fear not: for, behold, I bring you good tidings of great joy, which shall
be to all people.
11For unto you is born this day in the city of David
a Saviour, which is Christ the Lord.
12And this *shall be* a sign unto you; Ye shall find
the babe wrapped in swaddling clothes, lying in a
manger.
13And suddenly there was with the angel a multitude of the heavenly host praising God, and saying,
14Glory to God in the highest, and on earth peace,
good will toward men.
15And it came to pass, as the angels were gone
away from them into heaven, the shepherds said one
to another, Let us now go even unto Bethlehem, and
see this thing which is come to pass, which the Lord
hath made known unto us.
16And they came with haste, and found Mary, and
Joseph, and the babe lying in a manger.
17And when they had seen *it*, they made known
abroad the saying which was told them concerning
this child.
18And all they that heard *it* wondered at those
things which were told them by the shepherds.
19But Mary kept all these things, and pondered
them in her heart.
20And the shepherds returned, glorifying and
praising God for all the things that they had heard
and seen, as it was told unto them.
21And when eight days were accomplished for the
circumcising of the child, his name was called JESUS,
which was so named of the angel before he was conceived in the womb.
22And when the days of her purification according
to the law of Moses were accomplished, they brought
him to Jerusalem, to present *him* to the Lord;
23(As it is written in the law of the Lord, Every male

NEW LIVING TRANSLATION

taken when Quirinius was governor of Syria.) 3All returned to their own ancestral towns to register for
this census. 4And because Joseph was a descendant
of King David, he had to go to Bethlehem in Judea,
David's ancient home. He traveled there from the village of Nazareth in Galilee. 5He took with him Mary,
his fiancée, who was now obviously pregnant.
6And while they were there, the time came for her
baby to be born. 7She gave birth to her first child, a
son. She wrapped him snugly in strips of cloth and
laid him in a manger, because there was no lodging
available for them.

The Shepherds and Angels

8That night there were shepherds staying in the
fields nearby, guarding their flocks of sheep. 9Sud-
denly, an angel of the Lord appeared among them,
and the radiance of the Lord's glory surrounded
them. They were terrified, 10but the angel reassured
them. "Don't be afraid!" he said. "I bring you good
news that will bring great joy to all people. 11The Savior—yes, the Messiah, the Lord—has been born today
in Bethlehem, the city of David! 12And you will recognize him by this sign: You will find a baby wrapped
snugly in strips of cloth, lying in a manger."
13Suddenly, the angel was joined by a vast host of
others—the armies of heaven—praising God and
saying,
14 "Glory to God in highest heaven,
and peace on earth to those with whom
God is pleased."
15When the angels had returned to heaven, the
shepherds said to each other, "Let's go to Bethlehem!
Let's see this thing that has happened, which the
Lord has told us about."
16They hurried to the village and found Mary and
Joseph. And there was the baby, lying in the manger.
17After seeing him, the shepherds told everyone
what had happened and what the angel had said to
them about this child. 18All who heard the shepherds' story were astonished, 19but Mary kept all
these things in her heart and thought about them
often. 20The shepherds went back to their flocks,
glorifying and praising God for all they had heard
and seen. It was just as the angel had told them.

Jesus Is Presented in the Temple

21Eight days later, when the baby was circumcised, he
was named Jesus, the name given him by the angel
even before he was conceived.
22Then it was time for their purification offering,
as required by the law of Moses after the birth of a
child; so his parents took him to Jerusalem to present him to the Lord. 23The law of the Lord says, "If a

that openeth the womb shall be called holy to the Lord;)

24And to offer a sacrifice according to that which is said in the law of the Lord, A pair of turtledoves, or two young pigeons.

25And, behold, there was a man in Jerusalem, whose name *was* Simeon; and the same man *was* just and devout, waiting for the consolation of Israel: and the Holy Ghost was upon him.

26And it was revealed unto him by the Holy Ghost, that he should not see death, before he had seen the Lord's Christ.

27And he came by the Spirit into the temple: and when the parents brought in the child Jesus, to do for him after the custom of the law,

28Then took he him up in his arms, and blessed God, and said,

29Lord, now lettest thou thy servant depart in peace, according to thy word:

30For mine eyes have seen thy salvation,

31Which thou hast prepared before the face of all people;

32A light to lighten the Gentiles, and the glory of thy people Israel.

33And Joseph and his mother marvelled at those things which were spoken of him.

34And Simeon blessed them, and said unto Mary his mother, Behold, this *child* is set for the fall and rising again of many in Israel; and for a sign which shall be spoken against;

35(Yea, a sword shall pierce through thy own soul also,) that the thoughts of many hearts may be revealed.

36And there was one Anna, a prophetess, the daughter of Phanuel, of the tribe of Aser: she was of a great age, and had lived with an husband seven years from her virginity;

37And she *was* a widow of about fourscore and four years, which departed not from the temple, but served *God* with fastings and prayers night and day.

38And she coming in that instant gave thanks likewise unto the Lord, and spake of him to all them that looked for redemption in Jerusalem.

39And when they had performed all things according to the law of the Lord, they returned into Galilee, to their own city Nazareth.

40And the child grew, and waxed strong in spirit, filled with wisdom: and the grace of God was upon him.

41Now his parents went to Jerusalem every year at the feast of the passover.

42And when he was twelve years old, they went up to Jerusalem after the custom of the feast.

43And when they had fulfilled the days, as they

woman's first child is a boy, he must be dedicated to the LORD."* 24So they offered the sacrifice required in the law of the Lord—"either a pair of turtledoves or two young pigeons."*

The Prophecy of Simeon

25At that time there was a man in Jerusalem named Simeon. He was righteous and devout and was eagerly waiting for the Messiah to come and rescue Israel. The Holy Spirit was upon him 26and had revealed to him that he would not die until he had seen the Lord's Messiah. 27That day the Spirit led him to the Temple. So when Mary and Joseph came to present the baby Jesus to the Lord as the law required, 28Simeon was there. He took the child in his arms and praised God, saying,

29 "Sovereign Lord, now let your servant die
in peace,
as you have promised.
30 I have seen your salvation,
31 which you have prepared for all people.
32 He is a light to reveal God to the nations,
and he is the glory of your people Israel!"

33Jesus' parents were amazed at what was being said about him. 34Then Simeon blessed them, and he said to Mary, the baby's mother, "This child is destined to cause many in Israel to fall, but he will be a joy to many others. He has been sent as a sign from God, but many will oppose him. 35As a result, the deepest thoughts of many hearts will be revealed. And a sword will pierce your very soul."

The Prophecy of Anna

36Anna, a prophet, was also there in the Temple. She was the daughter of Phanuel from the tribe of Asher, and she was very old. Her husband died when they had been married only seven years. 37Then she lived as a widow to the age of eighty-four.* She never left the Temple but stayed there day and night, worshiping God with fasting and prayer. 38She came along just as Simeon was talking with Mary and Joseph, and she began praising God. She talked about the child to everyone who had been waiting expectantly for God to rescue Jerusalem.

39When Jesus' parents had fulfilled all the requirements of the law of the Lord, they returned home to Nazareth in Galilee. 40There the child grew up healthy and strong. He was filled with wisdom, and God's favor was on him.

Jesus Speaks with the Teachers

41Every year Jesus' parents went to Jerusalem for the Passover festival. 42When Jesus was twelve years old, they attended the festival as usual. 43After the

2:23 Exod 13:2. **2:24** Lev 12:8. **2:37** Or *She had been a widow for eighty-four years.*

KING JAMES VERSION

returned, the child Jesus tarried behind in Jerusalem; and Joseph and his mother knew not *of it*.

44But they, supposing him to have been in the company, went a day's journey; and they sought him among *their* kinsfolk and acquaintance.

45And when they found him not, they turned back again to Jerusalem, seeking him.

46And it came to pass, that after three days they found him in the temple, sitting in the midst of the doctors, both hearing them, and asking them questions.

47And all that heard him were astonished at his understanding and answers.

48And when they saw him, they were amazed: and his mother said unto him, Son, why hast thou thus dealt with us? behold, thy father and I have sought thee sorrowing.

49And he said unto them, How is it that ye sought me? wist ye not that I must be about my Father's business?

50And they understood not the saying which he spake unto them.

51And he went down with them, and came to Nazareth, and was subject unto them: but his mother kept all these sayings in her heart.

52And Jesus increased in wisdom and stature, and in favour with God and man.

3 1Now in the fifteenth year of the reign of Tiberius Caesar, Pontius Pilate being governor of Judaea, and Herod being tetrarch of Galilee, and his brother Philip tetrarch of Ituraea and of the region of Trachonitis, and Lysanias the tetrarch of Abilene,

2Annas and Caiaphas being the high priests, the word of God came unto John the son of Zacharias in the wilderness.

3And he came into all the country about Jordan, preaching the baptism of repentance for the remission of sins;

4As it is written in the book of the words of Esaias the prophet, saying, The voice of one crying in the wilderness, Prepare ye the way of the Lord, make his paths straight.

5Every valley shall be filled, and every mountain and hill shall be brought low; and the crooked shall be made straight, and the rough ways *shall be* made smooth;

6And all flesh shall see the salvation of God.

7Then said he to the multitude that came forth to be baptized of him, O generation of vipers, who hath warned you to flee from the wrath to come?

8Bring forth therefore fruits worthy of repentance, and begin not to say within yourselves, We have Abraham to *our* father: for I say unto you, That

NEW LIVING TRANSLATION

celebration was over, they started home to Nazareth, but Jesus stayed behind in Jerusalem. His parents didn't miss him at first, 44because they assumed he was among the other travelers. But when he didn't show up that evening, they started looking for him among their relatives and friends.

45When they couldn't find him, they went back to Jerusalem to search for him there. 46Three days later they finally discovered him in the Temple, sitting among the religious teachers, listening to them and asking questions. 47All who heard him were amazed at his understanding and his answers.

48His parents didn't know what to think. "Son," his mother said to him, "why have you done this to us? Your father and I have been frantic, searching for you everywhere."

49"But why did you need to search?" he asked. "Didn't you know that I must be in my Father's house?"* 50But they didn't understand what he meant.

51Then he returned to Nazareth with them and was obedient to them. And his mother stored all these things in her heart.

52Jesus grew in wisdom and in stature and in favor with God and all the people.

John the Baptist Prepares the Way

3 It was now the fifteenth year of the reign of Tiberius, the Roman emperor. Pontius Pilate was governor over Judea; Herod Antipas was ruler* over Galilee; his brother Philip was ruler* over Iturea and Traconitis; Lysanias was ruler over Abilene. 2Annas and Caiaphas were the high priests. At this time a message from God came to John son of Zechariah, who was living in the wilderness. 3Then John went from place to place on both sides of the Jordan River, preaching that people should be baptized to show that they had repented of their sins and turned to God to be forgiven. 4Isaiah had spoken of John when he said,

"He is a voice shouting in the wilderness,
'Prepare the way for the LORD's coming!
Clear the road for him!
5 The valleys will be filled,
and the mountains and hills made level.
The curves will be straightened,
and the rough places made smooth.
6 And then all people will see
the salvation sent from God.'"*

7When the crowds came to John for baptism, he said, "You brood of snakes! Who warned you to flee God's coming wrath? 8Prove by the way you live that you have repented of your sins and turned to God. Don't just say to each other, 'We're safe, for we are

2:49 Or *"Didn't you realize that I should be involved with my Father's affairs?"* **3:1a** Greek *Herod was tetrarch.* Herod Antipas was a son of King Herod. **3:1b** Greek *tetrarch;* also in 3:1c. **3:4-6** Isa 40:3-5 (Greek version).

KING JAMES VERSION

God is able of these stones to raise up children unto
Abraham.
9And now also the ax is laid unto the root of the
trees: every tree therefore which bringeth not forth
good fruit is hewn down, and cast into the fire.
10And the people asked him, saying, What shall we
do then?
11He answereth and saith unto them, He that hath
two coats, let him impart to him that hath none; and
he that hath meat, let him do likewise.
12Then came also publicans to be baptized, and
said unto him, Master, what shall we do?
13And he said unto them, Exact no more than that
which is appointed you.
14And the soldiers likewise demanded of him, saying, And what shall we do? And he said unto them,
Do violence to no man, neither accuse *any* falsely;
and be content with your wages.
15And as the people were in expectation, and all
men mused in their hearts of John, whether he were
the Christ, or not;
16John answered, saying unto *them* all, I indeed
baptize you with water; but one mightier than I cometh, the latchet of whose shoes I am not worthy to
unloose: he shall baptize you with the Holy Ghost
and with fire:
17Whose fan *is* in his hand, and he will throughly
purge his floor, and will gather the wheat into
his garner; but the chaff he will burn with fire
unquenchable.
18And many other things in his exhortation
preached he unto the people.
19But Herod the tetrarch, being reproved by him
for Herodias his brother Philip's wife, and for all the
evils which Herod had done,
20Added yet this above all, that he shut up John
in prison.

21Now when all the people were baptized, it came
to pass, that Jesus also being baptized, and praying,
the heaven was opened,
22And the Holy Ghost descended in a bodily shape
like a dove upon him, and a voice came from heaven,
which said, Thou art my beloved Son; in thee I am
well pleased.

23And Jesus himself began to be about thirty years
of age, being (as was supposed) the son of Joseph,
which was *the son* of Heli,
24Which was *the son* of Matthat, which was *the
son* of Levi, which was *the son* of Melchi, which was
the son of Janna, which was *the son* of Joseph,

NEW LIVING TRANSLATION

descendants of Abraham.' That means nothing, for I
tell you, God can create children of Abraham from
these very stones. 9Even now the ax of God's judgment is poised, ready to sever the roots of the trees.
Yes, every tree that does not produce good fruit will
be chopped down and thrown into the fire."
10The crowds asked, "What should we do?"
11John replied, "If you have two shirts, give one to
the poor. If you have food, share it with those who
are hungry."
12Even corrupt tax collectors came to be baptized
and asked, "Teacher, what should we do?"
13He replied, "Collect no more taxes than the
government requires."
14"What should we do?" asked some soldiers.
John replied, "Don't extort money or make false
accusations. And be content with your pay."
15Everyone was expecting the Messiah to come
soon, and they were eager to know whether John
might be the Messiah. 16John answered their questions by saying, "I baptize you with* water; but someone is coming soon who is greater than I am—so
much greater that I'm not even worthy to be his slave
and untie the straps of his sandals. He will baptize
you with the Holy Spirit and with fire.* 17He is ready
to separate the chaff from the wheat with his winnowing fork. Then he will clean up the threshing
area, gathering the wheat into his barn but burning
the chaff with never-ending fire." 18John used many
such warnings as he announced the Good News to
the people.
19John also publicly criticized Herod Antipas,
the ruler of Galilee,* for marrying Herodias, his
brother's wife, and for many other wrongs he had
done. 20So Herod put John in prison, adding this sin
to his many others.

The Baptism of Jesus

21One day when the crowds were being baptized,
Jesus himself was baptized. As he was praying, the
heavens opened, 22and the Holy Spirit, in bodily
form, descended on him like a dove. And a voice
from heaven said, "You are my dearly loved Son,
and you bring me great joy.*"

The Ancestors of Jesus

23Jesus was about thirty years old when he began his
public ministry.

Jesus was known as the son of Joseph.
Joseph was the son of Heli.
24 Heli was the son of Matthat.
Matthat was the son of Levi.
Levi was the son of Melki.
Melki was the son of Jannai.
Jannai was the son of Joseph.

3:16a Or *in.* **3:16b** Or *in the Holy Spirit and in fire.* **3:19** Greek *Herod the tetrarch.* **3:22** Some manuscripts read *my Son, and today I have become your Father.*

KING JAMES VERSION

25 Which was *the son* of Mattathias, which was *the*
son of Amos, which was *the son* of Naum, which was
the son of Esli, which was *the son* of Nagge,
26 Which was *the son* of Maath, which was *the son*
of Mattathias, which was *the son* of Semei, which
was *the son* of Joseph, which was *the son* of Judah,
27 Which was *the son* of Joanna, which was *the son*
of Rhesa, which was *the son* of Zorobabel, which was
the son of Salathiel, which was *the son* of Neri,
28 Which was *the son* of Melchi, which was *the son*
of Addi, which was *the son* of Cosam, which was *the*
son of Elmodam, which was *the son* of Er,
29 Which was *the son* of Jose, which was *the son* of
Eliezer, which was *the son* of Jorim, which was *the*
son of Matthat, which was *the son* of Levi,
30 Which was *the son* of Simeon, which was *the son*
of Judah, which was *the son* of Joseph, which was *the*
son of Jonan, which was *the son* of Eliakim,
31 Which was *the son* of Melea, which was *the son*
of Menan, which was *the son* of Mattatha, which was
the son of Nathan, which was *the son* of David,
32 Which was *the son* of Jesse, which was *the son* of
Obed, which was *the son* of Booz, which was *the son*
of Salmon, which was *the son* of Naasson,
33 Which was *the son* of Aminadab, which was *the*
son of Aram, which was *the son* of Esrom, which was
the son of Phares, which was *the son* of Judah,
34 Which was *the son* of Jacob, which was *the son*
of Isaac, which was *the son* of Abraham, which was
the son of Thara, which was *the son* of Nachor,
35 Which was *the son* of Saruch, which was *the son*
of Ragau, which was *the son* of Phalec, which was *the*
son of Heber, which was *the son* of Sala,

NEW LIVING TRANSLATION

25 Joseph was the son of Mattathias.
Mattathias was the son of Amos.
Amos was the son of Nahum.
Nahum was the son of Esli.
Esli was the son of Naggai.
26 Naggai was the son of Maath.
Maath was the son of Mattathias.
Mattathias was the son of Semein.
Semein was the son of Josech.
Josech was the son of Joda.
27 Joda was the son of Joanan.
Joanan was the son of Rhesa.
Rhesa was the son of Zerubbabel.
Zerubbabel was the son of Shealtiel.
Shealtiel was the son of Neri.
28 Neri was the son of Melki.
Melki was the son of Addi.
Addi was the son of Cosam.
Cosam was the son of Elmadam.
Elmadam was the son of Er.
29 Er was the son of Joshua.
Joshua was the son of Eliezer.
Eliezer was the son of Jorim.
Jorim was the son of Matthat.
Matthat was the son of Levi.
30 Levi was the son of Simeon.
Simeon was the son of Judah.
Judah was the son of Joseph.
Joseph was the son of Jonam.
Jonam was the son of Eliakim.
31 Eliakim was the son of Melea.
Melea was the son of Menna.
Menna was the son of Mattatha.
Mattatha was the son of Nathan.
Nathan was the son of David.
32 David was the son of Jesse.
Jesse was the son of Obed.
Obed was the son of Boaz.
Boaz was the son of Salmon.*
Salmon was the son of Nahshon.
33 Nahshon was the son of Amminadab.
Amminadab was the son of Admin.
Admin was the son of Arni.*
Arni was the son of Hezron.
Hezron was the son of Perez.
Perez was the son of Judah.
34 Judah was the son of Jacob.
Jacob was the son of Isaac.
Isaac was the son of Abraham.
Abraham was the son of Terah.
Terah was the son of Nahor.
35 Nahor was the son of Serug.
Serug was the son of Reu.
Reu was the son of Peleg.
Peleg was the son of Eber.
Eber was the son of Shelah.

3:32 Greek *Sala*, a variant spelling of Salmon; also in 3:32b. See Ruth 4:22.
3:33 Some manuscripts read *Amminadab was the son of Aram*. *Arni* and *Aram* are alternate spellings of Ram. See 1 Chr 2:9-10.

KING JAMES VERSION

36 Which was *the son* of Cainan, which was *the son* of Arphaxad, which was *the son* of Sem, which was *the son* of Noe, which was *the son* of Lamech,

37 Which was *the son* of Mathusala, which was *the son* of Enoch, which was *the son* of Jared, which was *the son* of Maleleel, which was *the son* of Cainan,

38 Which was *the son* of Enos, which was *the son* of Seth, which was *the son* of Adam, which was *the son* of God.

4 1 And Jesus being full of the Holy Ghost returned from Jordan, and was led by the Spirit into the wilderness,

2 Being forty days tempted of the devil. And in those days he did eat nothing: and when they were ended, he afterward hungered.

3 And the devil said unto him, If thou be the Son of God, command this stone that it be made bread.

4 And Jesus answered him, saying, It is written, That man shall not live by bread alone, but by every word of God.

5 And the devil, taking him up into an high mountain, shewed unto him all the kingdoms of the world in a moment of time.

6 And the devil said unto him, All this power will I give thee, and the glory of them: for that is delivered unto me; and to whomsoever I will I give it.

7 If thou therefore wilt worship me, all shall be thine.

8 And Jesus answered and said unto him, Get thee behind me, Satan: for it is written, Thou shalt worship the Lord thy God, and him only shalt thou serve.

9 And he brought him to Jerusalem, and set him on a pinnacle of the temple, and said unto him, If thou be the Son of God, cast thyself down from hence:

10 For it is written, He shall give his angels charge over thee, to keep thee:

11 And in *their* hands they shall bear thee up, lest at any time thou dash thy foot against a stone.

12 And Jesus answering said unto him, It is said, Thou shalt not tempt the Lord thy God.

13 And when the devil had ended all the temptation, he departed from him for a season.

14 And Jesus returned in the power of the Spirit into Galilee: and there went out a fame of him through all the region round about.

15 And he taught in their synagogues, being glorified of all.

16 And he came to Nazareth, where he had been brought up: and, as his custom was, he went into the synagogue on the sabbath day, and stood up for to read.

NEW LIVING TRANSLATION

36 Shelah was the son of Cainan.
Cainan was the son of Arphaxad.
Arphaxad was the son of Shem.
Shem was the son of Noah.
Noah was the son of Lamech.
37 Lamech was the son of Methuselah.
Methuselah was the son of Enoch.
Enoch was the son of Jared.
Jared was the son of Mahalalel.
Mahalalel was the son of Kenan.
38 Kenan was the son of Enosh.*
Enosh was the son of Seth.
Seth was the son of Adam.
Adam was the son of God.

The Temptation of Jesus

4 Then Jesus, full of the Holy Spirit, returned from the Jordan River. He was led by the Spirit in the wilderness,* 2 where he was tempted by the devil for forty days. Jesus ate nothing all that time and became very hungry.

3 Then the devil said to him, "If you are the Son of God, tell this stone to become a loaf of bread."

4 But Jesus told him, "No! The Scriptures say, 'People do not live by bread alone.'*"

5 Then the devil took him up and revealed to him all the kingdoms of the world in a moment of time. 6 "I will give you the glory of these kingdoms and authority over them," the devil said, "because they are mine to give to anyone I please. 7 I will give it all to you if you will worship me."

8 Jesus replied, "The Scriptures say,

'You must worship the LORD your God
and serve only him.'*"

9 Then the devil took him to Jerusalem, to the highest point of the Temple, and said, "If you are the Son of God, jump off! 10 For the Scriptures say,

'He will order his angels to protect and guard you.
11 And they will hold you up with their hands
so you won't even hurt your foot on a stone.'*"

12 Jesus responded, "The Scriptures also say, 'You must not test the LORD your God.'*"

13 When the devil had finished tempting Jesus, he left him until the next opportunity came.

Jesus Rejected at Nazareth

14 Then Jesus returned to Galilee, filled with the Holy Spirit's power. Reports about him spread quickly through the whole region. 15 He taught regularly in their synagogues and was praised by everyone.

16 When he came to the village of Nazareth, his boyhood home, he went as usual to the synagogue on the Sabbath and stood up to read the Scriptures.

3:38 Greek *Enos*, a variant spelling of Enosh; also in 3:38b. See Gen 5:6. **4:1** Some manuscripts read *into the wilderness*. **4:4** Deut 8:3. **4:8** Deut 6:13. **4:10-11** Ps 91:11-12. **4:12** Deut 6:16.

KING JAMES VERSION

17And there was delivered unto him the book of the prophet Esaias. And when he had opened the book, he found the place where it was written,

18The Spirit of the Lord *is* upon me, because he hath anointed me to preach the gospel to the poor; he hath sent me to heal the brokenhearted, to preach deliverance to the captives, and recovering of sight to the blind, to set at liberty them that are bruised,

19To preach the acceptable year of the Lord.

20And he closed the book, and he gave *it* again to the minister, and sat down. And the eyes of all them that were in the synagogue were fastened on him.

21And he began to say unto them, This day is this scripture fulfilled in your ears.

22And all bare him witness, and wondered at the gracious words which proceeded out of his mouth. And they said, Is not this Joseph's son?

23And he said unto them, Ye will surely say unto me this proverb, Physician, heal thyself: whatsoever we have heard done in Capernaum, do also here in thy country.

24And he said, Verily, I say unto you, No prophet is accepted in his own country.

25But I tell you of a truth, many widows were in Israel in the days of Elias, when the heaven was shut up three years and six months, when great famine was throughout all the land;

26But unto none of them was Elias sent, save unto Sarepta, *a city* of Sidon, unto a woman *that was* a widow.

27And many lepers were in Israel in the time of Eliseus the prophet; and none of them was cleansed, saving Naaman the Syrian.

28And all they in the synagogue, when they heard these things, were filled with wrath,

29And rose up, and thrust him out of the city, and led him unto the brow of the hill whereon their city was built, that they might cast him down headlong.

30But he passing through the midst of them went his way,

31And came down to Capernaum, a city of Galilee, and taught them on the sabbath days.

32And they were astonished at his doctrine: for his word was with power.

33And in the synagogue there was a man, which had a spirit of an unclean devil, and cried out with a loud voice,

34Saying, Let *us* alone; what have we to do with thee, *thou* Jesus of Nazareth? art thou come to destroy us? I know thee who thou art; the Holy One of God.

35And Jesus rebuked him, saying, Hold thy peace, and come out of him. And when the devil had thrown him in the midst, he came out of him, and hurt him not.

36And they were all amazed, and spake among themselves, saying, What a word *is* this! for with

NEW LIVING TRANSLATION

17The scroll of Isaiah the prophet was handed to
him. He unrolled the scroll and found the place
where this was written:

18 "The Spirit of the LORD is upon me,
for he has anointed me to bring Good News
to the poor.
He has sent me to proclaim that captives will
be released,
that the blind will see,
that the oppressed will be set free,
19 and that the time of the LORD's favor
has come.*"

20He rolled up the scroll, handed it back to the attendant, and sat down. All eyes in the synagogue
looked at him intently. 21Then he began to speak to
them. "The Scripture you've just heard has been fulfilled this very day!"

22Everyone spoke well of him and was amazed by
the gracious words that came from his lips. "How
can this be?" they asked. "Isn't this Joseph's son?"

23Then he said, "You will undoubtedly quote me
this proverb: 'Physician, heal yourself'—meaning,
'Do miracles here in your hometown like those you
did in Capernaum.' 24But I tell you the truth, no
prophet is accepted in his own hometown.

25"Certainly there were many needy widows in
Israel in Elijah's time, when the heavens were closed
for three and a half years, and a severe famine devastated the land. 26Yet Elijah was not sent to any of
them. He was sent instead to a foreigner—a widow of
Zarephath in the land of Sidon. 27And there were
many lepers in Israel in the time of the prophet Elisha, but the only one healed was Naaman, a Syrian."

28When they heard this, the people in the synagogue were furious. 29Jumping up, they mobbed him
and forced him to the edge of the hill on which the
town was built. They intended to push him over the
cliff, 30but he passed right through the crowd and
went on his way.

Jesus Casts Out a Demon

31Then Jesus went to Capernaum, a town in Galilee,
and taught there in the synagogue every Sabbath day.
32There, too, the people were amazed at his teaching,
for he spoke with authority.

33Once when he was in the synagogue, a man possessed by a demon—an evil* spirit—began shouting
at Jesus, 34"Go away! Why are you interfering with us,
Jesus of Nazareth? Have you come to destroy us? I
know who you are—the Holy One of God!"

35Jesus cut him short. "Be quiet! Come out of the
man," he ordered. At that, the demon threw the man
to the floor as the crowd watched; then it came out of
him without hurting him further.

36Amazed, the people exclaimed, "What authority

4:18-19 Or *and to proclaim the acceptable year of the LORD.* Isa 61:1-2 (Greek version); 58:6. **4:33** Greek *unclean;* also in 4:36.

KING JAMES VERSION

authority and power he commandeth the unclean spirits, and they come out.

37 And the fame of him went out into every place of the country round about.

38 And he arose out of the synagogue, and entered into Simon's house. And Simon's wife's mother was taken with a great fever; and they besought him for her.

39 And he stood over her, and rebuked the fever; and it left her: and immediately she arose and ministered unto them.

40 Now when the sun was setting, all they that had any sick with divers diseases brought them unto him; and he laid his hands on every one of them, and healed them.

41 And devils also came out of many, crying out, and saying, Thou art Christ the Son of God. And he rebuking *them* suffered them not to speak: for they knew that he was Christ.

42 And when it was day, he departed and went into a desert place: and the people sought him, and came unto him, and stayed him, that he should not depart from them.

43 And he said unto them, I must preach the kingdom of God to other cities also: for therefore am I sent.

44 And he preached in the synagogues of Galilee.

5 1 And it came to pass, that, as the people pressed upon him to hear the word of God, he stood by the lake of Gennesaret,

2 And saw two ships standing by the lake: but the fishermen were gone out of them, and were washing *their* nets.

3 And he entered into one of the ships, which was Simon's, and prayed him that he would thrust out a little from the land. And he sat down, and taught the people out of the ship.

4 Now when he had left speaking, he said unto Simon, Launch out into the deep, and let down your nets for a draught.

5 And Simon answering said unto him, Master, we have toiled all the night, and have taken nothing: nevertheless at thy word I will let down the net.

6 And when they had this done, they inclosed a great multitude of fishes: and their net brake.

7 And they beckoned unto *their* partners, which were in the other ship, that they should come and help them. And they came, and filled both the ships, so that they began to sink.

8 When Simon Peter saw *it,* he fell down at Jesus' knees, saying, Depart from me; for I am a sinful man, O Lord.

NEW LIVING TRANSLATION

and power this man's words possess! Even evil spirits obey him, and they flee at his command!" 37 The news about Jesus spread through every village in the entire region.

Jesus Heals Many People

38 After leaving the synagogue that day, Jesus went to Simon's home, where he found Simon's mother-in-law very sick with a high fever. "Please heal her," everyone begged. 39 Standing at her bedside, he rebuked the fever, and it left her. And she got up at once and prepared a meal for them.

40 As the sun went down that evening, people throughout the village brought sick family members to Jesus. No matter what their diseases were, the touch of his hand healed every one. 41 Many were possessed by demons; and the demons came out at his command, shouting, "You are the Son of God!" But because they knew he was the Messiah, he rebuked them and refused to let them speak.

Jesus Continues to Preach

42 Early the next morning Jesus went out to an isolated place. The crowds searched everywhere for him, and when they finally found him, they begged him not to leave them. 43 But he replied, "I must preach the Good News of the Kingdom of God in other towns, too, because that is why I was sent." 44 So he continued to travel around, preaching in synagogues throughout Judea.*

The First Disciples

5 One day as Jesus was preaching on the shore of the Sea of Galilee,* great crowds pressed in on him to listen to the word of God. 2 He noticed two empty boats at the water's edge, for the fishermen had left them and were washing their nets. 3 Stepping into one of the boats, Jesus asked Simon,* its owner, to push it out into the water. So he sat in the boat and taught the crowds from there.

4 When he had finished speaking, he said to Simon, "Now go out where it is deeper, and let down your nets to catch some fish."

5 "Master," Simon replied, "we worked hard all last night and didn't catch a thing. But if you say so, I'll let the nets down again." 6 And this time their nets were so full of fish they began to tear! 7 A shout for help brought their partners in the other boat, and soon both boats were filled with fish and on the verge of sinking.

8 When Simon Peter realized what had happened, he fell to his knees before Jesus and said, "Oh, Lord, please leave me—I'm too much of a sinner to be

4:44 Some manuscripts read *Galilee.* **5:1** Greek *Lake Gennesaret,* another name for the Sea of Galilee. **5:3** *Simon* is called "Peter" in 6:14 and thereafter.

KING JAMES VERSION

9 For he was astonished, and all that were with him, at the draught of the fishes which they had taken:

10 And so *was* also James, and John, the sons of Zebedee, which were partners with Simon. And Jesus said unto Simon, Fear not; from henceforth thou shalt catch men.

11 And when they had brought their ships to land, they forsook all, and followed him.

12 And it came to pass, when he was in a certain city, behold a man full of leprosy: who seeing Jesus fell on *his* face, and besought him, saying, Lord, if thou wilt, thou canst make me clean.

13 And he put forth *his* hand, and touched him, saying, I will: be thou clean. And immediately the leprosy departed from him.

14 And he charged him to tell no man: but go, and shew thyself to the priest, and offer for thy cleansing, according as Moses commanded, for a testimony unto them.

15 But so much the more went there a fame abroad of him: and great multitudes came together to hear, and to be healed by him of their infirmities.

16 And he withdrew himself into the wilderness, and prayed.

17 And it came to pass on a certain day, as he was teaching, that there were Pharisees and doctors of the law sitting by, which were come out of every town of Galilee, and Judaea, and Jerusalem: and the power of the Lord was *present* to heal them.

18 And, behold, men brought in a bed a man which was taken with a palsy: and they sought *means* to bring him in, and to lay *him* before him.

19 And when they could not find by what *way* they might bring him in because of the multitude, they went upon the housetop, and let him down through the tiling with *his* couch into the midst before Jesus.

20 And when he saw their faith, he said unto him, Man, thy sins are forgiven thee.

21 And the scribes and the Pharisees began to reason, saying, Who is this which speaketh blasphemies? Who can forgive sins, but God alone?

22 But when Jesus perceived their thoughts, he answering said unto them, What reason ye in your hearts?

23 Whether is easier, to say, Thy sins be forgiven thee; or to say, Rise up and walk?

24 But that ye may know that the Son of man hath power upon earth to forgive sins, (he said unto the sick of the palsy,) I say unto thee, Arise, and take up thy couch, and go into thine house.

25 And immediately he rose up before them, and took up that whereon he lay, and departed to his own house, glorifying God.

NEW LIVING TRANSLATION

around you." 9 For he was awestruck by the number of fish they had caught, as were the others with him. 10 His partners, James and John, the sons of Zebedee, were also amazed.

Jesus replied to Simon, "Don't be afraid! From now on you'll be fishing for people!" 11 And as soon as they landed, they left everything and followed Jesus.

Jesus Heals a Man with Leprosy

12 In one of the villages, Jesus met a man with an advanced case of leprosy. When the man saw Jesus, he bowed with his face to the ground, begging to be healed. "Lord," he said, "if you are willing, you can heal me and make me clean."

13 Jesus reached out and touched him. "I am willing," he said. "Be healed!" And instantly the leprosy disappeared. 14 Then Jesus instructed him not to tell anyone what had happened. He said, "Go to the priest and let him examine you. Take along the offering required in the law of Moses for those who have been healed of leprosy.* This will be a public testimony that you have been cleansed."

15 But despite Jesus' instructions, the report of his power spread even faster, and vast crowds came to hear him preach and to be healed of their diseases. 16 But Jesus often withdrew to the wilderness for prayer.

Jesus Heals a Paralyzed Man

17 One day while Jesus was teaching, some Pharisees and teachers of religious law were sitting nearby. (It seemed that these men showed up from every village in all Galilee and Judea, as well as from Jerusalem.) And the Lord's healing power was strongly with Jesus.

18 Some men came carrying a paralyzed man on a sleeping mat. They tried to take him inside to Jesus, 19 but they couldn't reach him because of the crowd. So they went up to the roof and took off some tiles. Then they lowered the sick man on his mat down into the crowd, right in front of Jesus. 20 Seeing their faith, Jesus said to the man, "Young man, your sins are forgiven."

21 But the Pharisees and teachers of religious law said to themselves, "Who does he think he is? That's blasphemy! Only God can forgive sins!"

22 Jesus knew what they were thinking, so he asked them, "Why do you question this in your hearts? 23 Is it easier to say 'Your sins are forgiven,' or 'Stand up and walk'? 24 So I will prove to you that the Son of Man* has the authority on earth to forgive sins." Then Jesus turned to the paralyzed man and said, "Stand up, pick up your mat, and go home!"

25 And immediately, as everyone watched, the man jumped up, picked up his mat, and went home

5:14 See Lev 14:2-32. **5:24** "Son of Man" is a title Jesus used for himself.

KING JAMES VERSION

26 And they were all amazed, and they glorified God, and were filled with fear, saying, We have seen strange things today.

27 And after these things he went forth, and saw a publican, named Levi, sitting at the receipt of custom: and he said unto him, Follow me.

28 And he left all, rose up, and followed him.

29 And Levi made him a great feast in his own house: and there was a great company of publicans and of others that sat down with them.

30 But their scribes and Pharisees murmured against his disciples, saying, Why do ye eat and drink with publicans and sinners?

31 And Jesus answering said unto them, They that are whole need not a physician; but they that are sick.

32 I came not to call the righteous, but sinners to repentance.

33 And they said unto him, Why do the disciples of John fast often, and make prayers, and likewise *the disciples* of the Pharisees; but thine eat and drink?

34 And he said unto them, Can ye make the children of the bridechamber fast, while the bridegroom is with them?

35 But the days will come, when the bridegroom shall be taken away from them, and then shall they fast in those days.

36 And he spake also a parable unto them; No man putteth a piece of a new garment upon an old; if otherwise, then both the new maketh a rent, and the piece that was *taken* out of the new agreeth not with the old.

37 And no man putteth new wine into old bottles; else the new wine will burst the bottles, and be spilled, and the bottles shall perish.

38 But new wine must be put into new bottles; and both are preserved.

39 No man also having drunk old *wine* straightway desireth new: for he saith, The old is better.

6 1 And it came to pass on the second sabbath after the first, that he went through the corn fields; and his disciples plucked the ears of corn, and did eat, rubbing *them* in *their* hands.

2 And certain of the Pharisees said unto them, Why do ye that which is not lawful to do on the sabbath days?

3 And Jesus answering them said, Have ye not read so much as this, what David did, when himself was an hungred, and they which were with him;

4 How he went into the house of God, and did take and eat the shewbread, and gave also to them that were with him; which it is not lawful to eat but for the priests alone?

5 And he said unto them, That the Son of man is Lord also of the sabbath.

NEW LIVING TRANSLATION

praising God. 26 Everyone was gripped with great wonder and awe, and they praised God, exclaiming, "We have seen amazing things today!"

Jesus Calls Levi (Matthew)

27 Later, as Jesus left the town, he saw a tax collector named Levi sitting at his tax collector's booth. "Follow me and be my disciple," Jesus said to him. 28 So Levi got up, left everything, and followed him.

29 Later, Levi held a banquet in his home with Jesus as the guest of honor. Many of Levi's fellow tax collectors and other guests also ate with them. 30 But the Pharisees and their teachers of religious law complained bitterly to Jesus' disciples, "Why do you eat and drink with such scum?*"

31 Jesus answered them, "Healthy people don't need a doctor—sick people do. 32 I have come to call not those who think they are righteous, but those who know they are sinners and need to repent."

A Discussion about Fasting

33 One day some people said to Jesus, "John the Baptist's disciples fast and pray regularly, and so do the disciples of the Pharisees. Why are your disciples always eating and drinking?"

34 Jesus responded, "Do wedding guests fast while celebrating with the groom? Of course not. 35 But someday the groom will be taken away from them, and then they will fast."

36 Then Jesus gave them this illustration: "No one tears a piece of cloth from a new garment and uses it to patch an old garment. For then the new garment would be ruined, and the new patch wouldn't even match the old garment.

37 "And no one puts new wine into old wineskins. For the new wine would burst the wineskins, spilling the wine and ruining the skins. 38 New wine must be stored in new wineskins. 39 But no one who drinks the old wine seems to want the new wine. 'The old is just fine,' they say."

A Discussion about the Sabbath

6 One Sabbath day as Jesus was walking through some grainfields, his disciples broke off heads of grain, rubbed off the husks in their hands, and ate the grain. 2 But some Pharisees said, "Why are you breaking the law by harvesting grain on the Sabbath?"

3 Jesus replied, "Haven't you read in the Scriptures what David did when he and his companions were hungry? 4 He went into the house of God and broke the law by eating the sacred loaves of bread that only the priests can eat. He also gave some to his companions." 5 And Jesus added, "The Son of Man* is Lord, even over the Sabbath."

5:30 Greek *with tax collectors and sinners?* **6:5** "Son of Man" is a title Jesus used for himself.

KING JAMES VERSION

6And it came to pass also on another sabbath, that
he entered into the synagogue and taught: and there
was a man whose right hand was withered.
7And the scribes and Pharisees watched him,
whether he would heal on the sabbath day; that they
might find an accusation against him.
8But he knew their thoughts, and said to the man
which had the withered hand, Rise up, and stand
forth in the midst. And he arose and stood forth.
9Then said Jesus unto them, I will ask you one
thing; Is it lawful on the sabbath days to do good, or
to do evil? to save life, or to destroy *it?*
10And looking round about upon them all, he said
unto the man, Stretch forth thy hand. And he did so:
and his hand was restored whole as the other.
11And they were filled with madness; and communed one with another what they might do to
Jesus.

12And it came to pass in those days, that he went
out into a mountain to pray, and continued all night
in prayer to God.
13And when it was day, he called *unto him* his
disciples: and of them he chose twelve, whom also
he named apostles;
14Simon, (whom he also named Peter,) and Andrew
his brother, James and John, Philip and Bartholomew,
15Matthew and Thomas, James the *son* of Alphaeus, and Simon called Zelotes,
16And Judas *the brother* of James, and Judas Iscariot, which also was the traitor.

17And he came down with them, and stood in the
plain, and the company of his disciples, and a great
multitude of people out of all Judaea and Jerusalem,
and from the sea coast of Tyre and Sidon, which
came to hear him, and to be healed of their diseases;
18And they that were vexed with unclean spirits:
and they were healed.
19And the whole multitude sought to touch him:
for there went virtue out of him, and healed *them* all.

20And he lifted up his eyes on his disciples, and
said, Blessed *be ye* poor: for yours is the kingdom
of God.
21Blessed *are ye* that hunger now: for ye shall be

NEW LIVING TRANSLATION

Jesus Heals on the Sabbath

6On another Sabbath day, a man with a deformed
right hand was in the synagogue while Jesus was
teaching. 7The teachers of religious law and the
Pharisees watched Jesus closely. If he healed the
man's hand, they planned to accuse him of working
on the Sabbath.
8But Jesus knew their thoughts. He said to the
man with the deformed hand, "Come and stand in
front of everyone." So the man came forward. 9Then
Jesus said to his critics, "I have a question for you.
Does the law permit good deeds on the Sabbath, or
is it a day for doing evil? Is this a day to save life or to
destroy it?"
10He looked around at them one by one and then
said to the man, "Hold out your hand." So the man
held out his hand, and it was restored! 11At this, the
enemies of Jesus were wild with rage and began to
discuss what to do with him.

Jesus Chooses the Twelve Apostles

12One day soon afterward Jesus went up on a moun-
tain to pray, and he prayed to God all night. 13At day-
break he called together all of his disciples and chose
twelve of them to be apostles. Here are their names:
14 Simon (whom he named Peter),
Andrew (Peter's brother),
James,
John,
Philip,
Bartholomew,
15 Matthew,
Thomas,
James (son of Alphaeus),
Simon (who was called the zealot),
16 Judas (son of James),
Judas Iscariot (who later betrayed him).

Crowds Follow Jesus

17When they came down from the mountain, the disciples stood with Jesus on a large, level area, surrounded by many of his followers and by the crowds.
There were people from all over Judea and from Jerusalem and from as far north as the seacoasts of Tyre
and Sidon. 18They had come to hear him and to be
healed of their diseases; and those troubled by evil*
spirits were healed. 19Everyone tried to touch him,
because healing power went out from him, and he
healed everyone.

The Beatitudes

20Then Jesus turned to his disciples and said,
"God blesses you who are poor,
for the Kingdom of God is yours.
21 God blesses you who are hungry now,
for you will be satisfied.

6:18 Greek *unclean.*

KING JAMES VERSION

filled. Blessed *are ye* that weep now: for ye shall
laugh.
22Blessed are ye, when men shall hate you, and
when they shall separate you *from their company,*
and shall reproach *you,* and cast out your name as
evil, for the Son of man's sake.
23Rejoice ye in that day, and leap for joy: for, behold, your reward *is* great in heaven: for in the like
manner did their fathers unto the prophets.

24But woe unto you that are rich! for ye have received your consolation.
25Woe unto you that are full! for ye shall hunger.
Woe unto you that laugh now! for ye shall mourn
and weep.
26Woe unto you, when all men shall speak well of
you! for so did their fathers to the false prophets.

27But I say unto you which hear, Love your enemies, do good to them which hate you,
28Bless them that curse you, and pray for them
which despitefully use you.
29And unto him that smiteth thee on the *one*
cheek offer also the other; and him that taketh away
thy cloak forbid not *to take thy* coat also.
30Give to every man that asketh of thee; and of him
that taketh away thy goods ask *them* not again.
31And as ye would that men should do to you, do ye
also to them likewise.
32For if ye love them which love you, what thank
have ye? for sinners also love those that love them.
33And if ye do good to them which do good to you,
what thank have ye? for sinners also do even the
same.
34And if ye lend *to them* of whom ye hope to receive, what thank have ye? for sinners also lend to
sinners, to receive as much again.
35But love ye your enemies, and do good, and lend,
hoping for nothing again; and your reward shall be
great, and ye shall be the children of the Highest: for
he is kind unto the unthankful and *to* the evil.
36Be ye therefore merciful, as your Father also is
merciful.
37Judge not, and ye shall not be judged: condemn
not, and ye shall not be condemned: forgive, and ye
shall be forgiven:
38Give, and it shall be given unto you; good measure, pressed down, and shaken together, and running over, shall men give into your bosom. For with
the same measure that ye mete withal it shall be
measured to you again.

NEW LIVING TRANSLATION

God blesses you who weep now,
for in due time you will laugh.
22What blessings await you when people hate you
and exclude you and mock you and curse you as evil
because you follow the Son of Man. 23When that
happens, be happy! Yes, leap for joy! For a great reward awaits you in heaven. And remember, their ancestors treated the ancient prophets that same way.

Sorrows Foretold

24 "What sorrow awaits you who are rich,
for you have your only happiness now.
25 What sorrow awaits you who are fat and
prosperous now,
for a time of awful hunger awaits you.
What sorrow awaits you who laugh now,
for your laughing will turn to mourning
and sorrow.
26 What sorrow awaits you who are praised by
the crowds,
for their ancestors also praised false prophets.

Love for Enemies

27"But to you who are willing to listen, I say, love your
enemies! Do good to those who hate you. 28Bless
those who curse you. Pray for those who hurt you.
29If someone slaps you on one cheek, offer the other
cheek also. If someone demands your coat, offer
your shirt also. 30Give to anyone who asks; and when
things are taken away from you, don't try to get them
back. 31Do to others as you would like them to do
to you.
32"If you love only those who love you, why should
you get credit for that? Even sinners love those who
love them! 33And if you do good only to those who do
good to you, why should you get credit? Even sinners
do that much! 34And if you lend money only to those
who can repay you, why should you get credit? Even
sinners will lend to other sinners for a full return.
35"Love your enemies! Do good to them. Lend to
them without expecting to be repaid. Then your reward from heaven will be very great, and you will
truly be acting as children of the Most High, for he
is kind to those who are unthankful and wicked.
36You must be compassionate, just as your Father is
compassionate.

Do Not Judge Others

37"Do not judge others, and you will not be judged.
Do not condemn others, or it will all come back
against you. Forgive others, and you will be forgiven.
38Give, and you will receive. Your gift will return to
you in full—pressed down, shaken together to make
room for more, running over, and poured into your
lap. The amount you give will determine the amount
you get back.*"

6:38 Or *The measure you give will be the measure you get back.*

KING JAMES VERSION

39 And he spake a parable unto them, Can the blind lead the blind? shall they not both fall into the ditch?

40 The disciple is not above his master: but every one that is perfect shall be as his master.

41 And why beholdest thou the mote that is in thy brother's eye, but perceivest not the beam that is in thine own eye?

42 Either how canst thou say to thy brother, Brother, let me pull out the mote that is in thine eye, when thou thyself beholdest not the beam that is in thine own eye? Thou hypocrite, cast out first the beam out of thine own eye, and then shalt thou see clearly to pull out the mote that is in thy brother's eye.

43 For a good tree bringeth not forth corrupt fruit; neither doth a corrupt tree bring forth good fruit.

44 For every tree is known by his own fruit. For of thorns men do not gather figs, nor of a bramble bush gather they grapes.

45 A good man out of the good treasure of his heart bringeth forth that which is good; and an evil man out of the evil treasure of his heart bringeth forth that which is evil: for of the abundance of the heart his mouth speaketh.

46 And why call ye me, Lord, Lord, and do not the things which I say?

47 Whosoever cometh to me, and heareth my sayings, and doeth them, I will shew you to whom he is like:

48 He is like a man which built an house, and digged deep, and laid the foundation on a rock: and when the flood arose, the stream beat vehemently upon that house, and could not shake it: for it was founded upon a rock.

49 But he that heareth, and doeth not, is like a man that without a foundation built an house upon the earth; against which the stream did beat vehemently, and immediately it fell; and the ruin of that house was great.

7 1 Now when he had ended all his sayings in the audience of the people, he entered into Capernaum.

2 And a certain centurion's servant, who was dear unto him, was sick, and ready to die.

3 And when he heard of Jesus, he sent unto him the elders of the Jews, beseeching him that he would come and heal his servant.

4 And when they came to Jesus, they besought him instantly, saying, That he was worthy for whom he should do this:

5 For he loveth our nation, and he hath built us a synagogue.

6 Then Jesus went with them. And when he was now not far from the house, the centurion sent friends to him, saying unto him, Lord, trouble not thyself: for I am not worthy that thou shouldest enter under my roof:

NEW LIVING TRANSLATION

39 Then Jesus gave the following illustration: "Can one blind person lead another? Won't they both fall into a ditch? 40 Students* are not greater than their teacher. But the student who is fully trained will become like the teacher.

41 "And why worry about a speck in your friend's eye* when you have a log in your own? 42 How can you think of saying, 'Friend,* let me help you get rid of that speck in your eye,' when you can't see past the log in your own eye? Hypocrite! First get rid of the log in your own eye; then you will see well enough to deal with the speck in your friend's eye.

The Tree and Its Fruit

43 "A good tree can't produce bad fruit, and a bad tree can't produce good fruit. 44 A tree is identified by its fruit. Figs are never gathered from thornbushes, and grapes are not picked from bramble bushes. 45 A good person produces good things from the treasury of a good heart, and an evil person produces evil things from the treasury of an evil heart. What you say flows from what is in your heart.

Building on a Solid Foundation

46 "So why do you keep calling me 'Lord, Lord!' when you don't do what I say? 47 I will show you what it's like when someone comes to me, listens to my teaching, and then follows it. 48 It is like a person building a house who digs deep and lays the foundation on solid rock. When the floodwaters rise and break against that house, it stands firm because it is well built. 49 But anyone who hears and doesn't obey is like a person who builds a house without a foundation. When the floods sweep down against that house, it will collapse into a heap of ruins."

The Faith of a Roman Officer

7 When Jesus had finished saying all this to the people, he returned to Capernaum. 2 At that time the highly valued slave of a Roman officer* was sick and near death. 3 When the officer heard about Jesus, he sent some respected Jewish elders to ask him to come and heal his slave. 4 So they earnestly begged Jesus to help the man. "If anyone deserves your help, he does," they said, 5 "for he loves the Jewish people and even built a synagogue for us."

6 So Jesus went with them. But just before they arrived at the house, the officer sent some friends to say, "Lord, don't trouble yourself by coming to my

6:40 Or *Disciples.* **6:41** Greek *your brother's eye;* also in 6:42.
6:42 Greek *Brother.* **7:2** Greek *a centurion;* similarly in 7:6.

KING JAMES VERSION

7 Wherefore neither thought I myself worthy to
come unto thee: but say in a word, and my servant
shall be healed.

8 For I also am a man set under authority, having
under me soldiers, and I say unto one, Go, and he
goeth; and to another, Come, and he cometh; and to
my servant, Do this, and he doeth *it*.

9 When Jesus heard these things, he marvelled at
him, and turned him about, and said unto the people
that followed him, I say unto you, I have not found so
great faith, no, not in Israel.

10 And they that were sent, returning to the house,
found the servant whole that had been sick.

11 And it came to pass the day after, that he went
into a city called Nain; and many of his disciples
went with him, and much people.

12 Now when he came nigh to the gate of the city,
behold, there was a dead man carried out, the only
son of his mother, and she was a widow: and much
people of the city was with her.

13 And when the Lord saw her, he had compassion
on her, and said unto her, Weep not.

14 And he came and touched the bier: and they that
bare *him* stood still. And he said, Young man, I say
unto thee, Arise.

15 And he that was dead sat up, and began to speak.
And he delivered him to his mother.

16 And there came a fear on all: and they glorified
God, saying, That a great prophet is risen up among
us; and, That God hath visited his people.

17 And this rumour of him went forth throughout
all Judaea, and throughout all the region round
about.

18 And the disciples of John shewed him of all
these things.

19 And John calling *unto him* two of his disciples
sent *them* to Jesus, saying, Art thou he that should
come? or look we for another?

20 When the men were come unto him, they said,
John Baptist hath sent us unto thee, saying, Art thou
he that should come? or look we for another?

21 And in that same hour he cured many of *their*
infirmities and plagues, and of evil spirits; and unto
many *that were* blind he gave sight.

22 Then Jesus answering said unto them, Go your
way, and tell John what things ye have seen and
heard; how that the blind see, the lame walk, the lepers are cleansed, the deaf hear, the dead are raised,
to the poor the gospel is preached.

23 And blessed is *he*, whosoever shall not be offended in me.

24 And when the messengers of John were departed, he began to speak unto the people concerning John, What went ye out into the wilderness for to
see? A reed shaken with the wind?

NEW LIVING TRANSLATION

home, for I am not worthy of such an honor. 7 I am
not even worthy to come and meet you. Just say the
word from where you are, and my servant will be
healed. 8 I know this because I am under the authority of my superior officers, and I have authority over
my soldiers. I only need to say, 'Go,' and they go, or
'Come,' and they come. And if I say to my slaves, 'Do
this,' they do it."

9 When Jesus heard this, he was amazed. Turning
to the crowd that was following him, he said, "I tell
you, I haven't seen faith like this in all Israel!" 10 And
when the officer's friends returned to his house, they
found the slave completely healed.

Jesus Raises a Widow's Son

11 Soon afterward Jesus went with his disciples to
the village of Nain, and a large crowd followed him.
12 A funeral procession was coming out as he approached the village gate. The young man who had
died was a widow's only son, and a large crowd from
the village was with her. 13 When the Lord saw her,
his heart overflowed with compassion. "Don't cry!"
he said. 14 Then he walked over to the coffin and
touched it, and the bearers stopped. "Young man,"
he said, "I tell you, get up." 15 Then the dead boy
sat up and began to talk! And Jesus gave him back to
his mother.

16 Great fear swept the crowd, and they praised
God, saying, "A mighty prophet has risen among us,"
and "God has visited his people today." 17 And the
news about Jesus spread throughout Judea and the
surrounding countryside.

Jesus and John the Baptist

18 The disciples of John the Baptist told John about
everything Jesus was doing. So John called for two of
his disciples, 19 and he sent them to the Lord to ask
him, "Are you the Messiah we've been expecting,* or
should we keep looking for someone else?"

20 John's two disciples found Jesus and said to him,
"John the Baptist sent us to ask, 'Are you the Messiah
we've been expecting, or should we keep looking for
someone else?'"

21 At that very time, Jesus cured many people of
their diseases, illnesses, and evil spirits, and he restored sight to many who were blind. 22 Then he told
John's disciples, "Go back to John and tell him what
you have seen and heard—the blind see, the lame
walk, the lepers are cured, the deaf hear, the dead
are raised to life, and the Good News is being
preached to the poor. 23 And tell him, 'God blesses
those who do not turn away because of me.*'"

24 After John's disciples left, Jesus began talking
about him to the crowds. "What kind of man did you
go into the wilderness to see? Was he a weak reed,

7:19 Greek *Are you the one who is coming?* Also in 7:20. **7:23** Or *who are not offended by me.*

KING JAMES VERSION

25 But what went ye out for to see? A man clothed in soft raiment? Behold, they which are gorgeously apparelled, and live delicately, are in kings' courts.

26 But what went ye out for to see? A prophet? Yea, I say unto you, and much more than a prophet.

27 This is *he,* of whom it is written, Behold, I send my messenger before thy face, which shall prepare thy way before thee.

28 For I say unto you, Among those that are born of women there is not a greater prophet than John the Baptist: but he that is least in the kingdom of God is greater than he.

29 And all the people that heard *him,* and the publicans, justified God, being baptized with the baptism of John.

30 But the Pharisees and lawyers rejected the counsel of God against themselves, being not baptized of him.

31 And the Lord said, Whereunto then shall I liken the men of this generation? and to what are they like?

32 They are like unto children sitting in the marketplace, and calling one to another, and saying, We have piped unto you, and ye have not danced; we have mourned to you, and ye have not wept.

33 For John the Baptist came neither eating bread nor drinking wine; and ye say, He hath a devil.

34 The Son of man is come eating and drinking; and ye say, Behold a gluttonous man, and a winebibber, a friend of publicans and sinners!

35 But wisdom is justified of all her children.

36 And one of the Pharisees desired him that he would eat with him. And he went into the Pharisee's house, and sat down to meat.

37 And, behold, a woman in the city, which was a sinner, when she knew that *Jesus* sat at meat in the Pharisee's house, brought an alabaster box of ointment,

38 And stood at his feet behind *him* weeping, and began to wash his feet with tears, and did wipe *them* with the hairs of her head, and kissed his feet, and anointed *them* with the ointment.

39 Now when the Pharisee which had bidden him saw *it,* he spake within himself, saying, This man, if he were a prophet, would have known who and what manner of woman *this is* that toucheth him: for she is a sinner.

40 And Jesus answering said unto him, Simon, I have somewhat to say unto thee. And he saith, Master, say on.

41 There was a certain creditor which had two debtors: the one owed five hundred pence, and the other fifty.

NEW LIVING TRANSLATION

swayed by every breath of wind? 25 Or were you expecting to see a man dressed in expensive clothes? No, people who wear beautiful clothes and live in luxury are found in palaces. 26 Were you looking for a prophet? Yes, and he is more than a prophet. 27 John is the man to whom the Scriptures refer when they say,

'Look, I am sending my messenger ahead of you,
and he will prepare your way before you.'*

28 I tell you, of all who have ever lived, none is greater than John. Yet even the least person in the Kingdom of God is greater than he is!"

29 When they heard this, all the people—even the tax collectors—agreed that God's way was right,* for they had been baptized by John. 30 But the Pharisees and experts in religious law rejected God's plan for them, for they had refused John's baptism.

31 "To what can I compare the people of this generation?" Jesus asked. "How can I describe them? 32 They are like children playing a game in the public square. They complain to their friends,

'We played wedding songs,
and you didn't dance,
so we played funeral songs,
and you didn't weep.'

33 For John the Baptist didn't spend his time eating bread or drinking wine, and you say, 'He's possessed by a demon.' 34 The Son of Man,* on the other hand, feasts and drinks, and you say, 'He's a glutton and a drunkard, and a friend of tax collectors and other sinners!' 35 But wisdom is shown to be right by the lives of those who follow it.*"

Jesus Anointed by a Sinful Woman

36 One of the Pharisees asked Jesus to have dinner with him, so Jesus went to his home and sat down to eat.* 37 When a certain immoral woman from that city heard he was eating there, she brought a beautiful alabaster jar filled with expensive perfume. 38 Then she knelt behind him at his feet, weeping. Her tears fell on his feet, and she wiped them off with her hair. Then she kept kissing his feet and putting perfume on them.

39 When the Pharisee who had invited him saw this, he said to himself, "If this man were a prophet, he would know what kind of woman is touching him. She's a sinner!"

40 Then Jesus answered his thoughts. "Simon," he said to the Pharisee, "I have something to say to you."

"Go ahead, Teacher," Simon replied.

41 Then Jesus told him this story: "A man loaned money to two people—500 pieces of silver* to one

7:27 Mal 3:1. **7:29** Or *praised God for his justice.* **7:34** "Son of Man" is a title Jesus used for himself. **7:35** Or *But wisdom is justified by all her children.* **7:36** Or *and reclined.* **7:41** Greek *500 denarii.* A denarius was equivalent to a laborer's full day's wage.

KING JAMES VERSION

42 And when they had nothing to pay, he frankly forgave them both. Tell me therefore, which of them will love him most?

43 Simon answered and said, I suppose that *he*, to whom he forgave most. And he said unto him, Thou hast rightly judged.

44 And he turned to the woman, and said unto Simon, Seest thou this woman? I entered into thine house, thou gavest me no water for my feet: but she hath washed my feet with tears, and wiped *them* with the hairs of her head.

45 Thou gavest me no kiss: but this woman since the time I came in hath not ceased to kiss my feet.

46 My head with oil thou didst not anoint: but this woman hath anointed my feet with ointment.

47 Wherefore I say unto thee, Her sins, which are many, are forgiven; for she loved much: but to whom little is forgiven, *the same* loveth little.

48 And he said unto her, Thy sins are forgiven.

49 And they that sat at meat with him began to say within themselves, Who is this that forgiveth sins also?

50 And he said to the woman, Thy faith hath saved thee; go in peace.

8 1 And it came to pass afterward, that he went throughout every city and village, preaching and shewing the glad tidings of the kingdom of God: and the twelve *were* with him,

2 And certain women, which had been healed of evil spirits and infirmities, Mary called Magdalene, out of whom went seven devils,

3 And Joanna the wife of Chuza Herod's steward, and Susanna, and many others, which ministered unto him of their substance.

4 And when much people were gathered together, and were come to him out of every city, he spake by a parable:

5 A sower went out to sow his seed: and as he sowed, some fell by the way side; and it was trodden down, and the fowls of the air devoured it.

6 And some fell upon a rock; and as soon as it was sprung up, it withered away, because it lacked moisture.

7 And some fell among thorns; and the thorns sprang up with it, and choked it.

8 And other fell on good ground, and sprang up, and bare fruit an hundredfold. And when he had said these things, he cried, He that hath ears to hear, let him hear.

9 And his disciples asked him, saying, What might this parable be?

10 And he said, Unto you it is given to know the

NEW LIVING TRANSLATION

and 50 pieces to the other. 42 But neither of them
could repay him, so he kindly forgave them both,
canceling their debts. Who do you suppose loved
him more after that?"

43 Simon answered, "I suppose the one for whom
he canceled the larger debt."

"That's right," Jesus said. 44 Then he turned to the
woman and said to Simon, "Look at this woman
kneeling here. When I entered your home, you didn't
offer me water to wash the dust from my feet, but
she has washed them with her tears and wiped them
with her hair. 45 You didn't greet me with a kiss, but
from the time I first came in, she has not stopped
kissing my feet. 46 You neglected the courtesy of olive
oil to anoint my head, but she has anointed my feet
with rare perfume.

47 "I tell you, her sins—and they are many—have
been forgiven, so she has shown me much love. But
a person who is forgiven little shows only little
love." 48 Then Jesus said to the woman, "Your sins are
forgiven."

49 The men at the table said among themselves,
"Who is this man, that he goes around forgiving
sins?"

50 And Jesus said to the woman, "Your faith has
saved you; go in peace."

Women Who Followed Jesus

8 Soon afterward Jesus began a tour of the
nearby towns and villages, preaching and announcing the Good News about the Kingdom of God.
He took his twelve disciples with him, 2 along with
some women who had been cured of evil spirits and
diseases. Among them were Mary Magdalene, from
whom he had cast out seven demons; 3 Joanna, the
wife of Chuza, Herod's business manager; Susanna;
and many others who were contributing from their
own resources to support Jesus and his disciples.

Parable of the Farmer Scattering Seed

4 One day Jesus told a story in the form of a parable
to a large crowd that had gathered from many towns
to hear him: 5 "A farmer went out to plant his seed.
As he scattered it across his field, some seed fell on a
footpath, where it was stepped on, and the birds ate
it. 6 Other seed fell among rocks. It began to grow,
but the plant soon wilted and died for lack of moisture. 7 Other seed fell among thorns that grew up
with it and choked out the tender plants. 8 Still other
seed fell on fertile soil. This seed grew and produced a crop that was a hundred times as much as
had been planted!" When he had said this, he called
out, "Anyone with ears to hear should listen and
understand."

9 His disciples asked him what this parable meant.
10 He replied, "You are permitted to understand the

KING JAMES VERSION

mysteries of the kingdom of God: but to others in
parables; that seeing they might not see, and hearing
they might not understand.
11Now the parable is this: The seed is the word
of God.
12Those by the way side are they that hear; then
cometh the devil, and taketh away the word out of
their hearts, lest they should believe and be saved.
13They on the rock *are they,* which, when they
hear, receive the word with joy; and these have no
root, which for a while believe, and in time of temptation fall away.
14And that which fell among thorns are they,
which, when they have heard, go forth, and are
choked with cares and riches and pleasures of *this*
life, and bring no fruit to perfection.
15But that on the good ground are they, which in
an honest and good heart, having heard the word,
keep *it,* and bring forth fruit with patience.

16No man, when he hath lighted a candle, covereth
it with a vessel, or putteth *it* under a bed; but setteth
it on a candlestick, that they which enter in may see
the light.
17For nothing is secret, that shall not be made
manifest; neither *any thing* hid, that shall not be
known and come abroad.
18Take heed therefore how ye hear: for whosoever
hath, to him shall be given; and whosoever hath not,
from him shall be taken even that which he seemeth
to have.

19Then came to him *his* mother and his brethren,
and could not come at him for the press.
20And it was told him *by certain* which said, Thy
mother and thy brethren stand without, desiring to
see thee.
21And he answered and said unto them, My
mother and my brethren are these which hear the
word of God, and do it.
22Now it came to pass on a certain day, that he
went into a ship with his disciples: and he said unto
them, Let us go over unto the other side of the lake.
And they launched forth.
23But as they sailed he fell asleep: and there came
down a storm of wind on the lake; and they were
filled *with water,* and were in jeopardy.
24And they came to him, and awoke him, saying,
Master, master, we perish. Then he arose, and rebuked the wind and the raging of the water: and they
ceased, and there was a calm.
25And he said unto them, Where is your faith? And

NEW LIVING TRANSLATION

secrets* of the Kingdom of God. But I use parables
to teach the others so that the Scriptures might be
fulfilled:

'When they look, they won't really see.
When they hear, they won't understand.'*

11"This is the meaning of the parable: The seed is
God's word. 12The seeds that fell on the footpath represent those who hear the message, only to have the
devil come and take it away from their hearts and
prevent them from believing and being saved. 13The
seeds on the rocky soil represent those who hear the
message and receive it with joy. But since they don't
have deep roots, they believe for a while, then they
fall away when they face temptation. 14The seeds
that fell among the thorns represent those who hear
the message, but all too quickly the message is
crowded out by the cares and riches and pleasures of
this life. And so they never grow into maturity. 15And
the seeds that fell on the good soil represent honest,
good-hearted people who hear God's word, cling to
it, and patiently produce a huge harvest.

Parable of the Lamp

16"No one lights a lamp and then covers it with a bowl
or hides it under a bed. A lamp is placed on a stand,
where its light can be seen by all who enter the house.
17For all that is secret will eventually be brought into
the open, and everything that is concealed will be
brought to light and made known to all.
18"So pay attention to how you hear. To those who
listen to my teaching, more understanding will be
given. But for those who are not listening, even what
they think they understand will be taken away from
them."

The True Family of Jesus

19Then Jesus' mother and brothers came to see him,
but they couldn't get to him because of the crowd.
20Someone told Jesus, "Your mother and your brothers are outside, and they want to see you."
21Jesus replied, "My mother and my brothers are
all those who hear God's word and obey it."

Jesus Calms the Storm

22One day Jesus said to his disciples, "Let's cross to
the other side of the lake." So they got into a boat
and started out. 23As they sailed across, Jesus settled
down for a nap. But soon a fierce storm came down
on the lake. The boat was filling with water, and they
were in real danger.
24The disciples went and woke him up, shouting,
"Master, Master, we're going to drown!"
When Jesus woke up, he rebuked the wind and the
raging waves. Suddenly the storm stopped and all was
calm. 25Then he asked them, "Where is your faith?"

8:10a Greek *mysteries.* **8:10b** Isa 6:9 (Greek version).

KING JAMES VERSION

they being afraid wondered, saying one to another, What manner of man is this! for he commandeth even the winds and water, and they obey him.

26And they arrived at the country of the Gadarenes, which is over against Galilee.

27And when he went forth to land, there met him out of the city a certain man, which had devils long time, and ware no clothes, neither abode in *any* house, but in the tombs.

28When he saw Jesus, he cried out, and fell down before him, and with a loud voice said, What have I to do with thee, Jesus, *thou* Son of God most high? I beseech thee, torment me not.

29(For he had commanded the unclean spirit to come out of the man. For oftentimes it had caught him: and he was kept bound with chains and in fetters; and he brake the bands, and was driven of the devil into the wilderness.)

30And Jesus asked him, saying, What is thy name? And he said, Legion: because many devils were entered into him.

31And they besought him that he would not command them to go out into the deep.

32And there was there an herd of many swine feeding on the mountain: and they besought him that he would suffer them to enter into them. And he suffered them.

33Then went the devils out of the man, and entered into the swine: and the herd ran violently down a steep place into the lake, and were choked.

34When they that fed *them* saw what was done, they fled, and went and told *it* in the city and in the country.

35Then they went out to see what was done; and came to Jesus, and found the man, out of whom the devils were departed, sitting at the feet of Jesus, clothed, and in his right mind: and they were afraid.

36They also which saw *it* told them by what means he that was possessed of the devils was healed.

37Then the whole multitude of the country of the Gadarenes round about besought him to depart from them; for they were taken with great fear: and he went up into the ship, and returned back again.

38Now the man out of whom the devils were departed besought him that he might be with him: but Jesus sent him away, saying,

39Return to thine own house, and shew how great things God hath done unto thee. And he went his way, and published throughout the whole city how great things Jesus had done unto him.

40And it came to pass, that, when Jesus was returned, the people *gladly* received him: for they were all waiting for him.

41And, behold, there came a man named Jairus, and he was a ruler of the synagogue: and he fell down

NEW LIVING TRANSLATION

The disciples were terrified and amazed. "Who is this man?" they asked each other. "When he gives a command, even the wind and waves obey him!"

Jesus Heals a Demon-Possessed Man

26So they arrived in the region of the Gerasenes,* across the lake from Galilee. 27As Jesus was climbing out of the boat, a man who was possessed by demons came out to meet him. For a long time he had been homeless and naked, living in a cemetery outside the town.

28As soon as he saw Jesus, he shrieked and fell down in front of him. Then he screamed, "Why are you interfering with me, Jesus, Son of the Most High God? Please, I beg you, don't torture me!" 29For Jesus had already commanded the evil* spirit to come out of him. This spirit had often taken control of the man. Even when he was placed under guard and put in chains and shackles, he simply broke them and rushed out into the wilderness, completely under the demon's power.

30Jesus demanded, "What is your name?"

"Legion," he replied, for he was filled with many demons. 31The demons kept begging Jesus not to send them into the bottomless pit.*

32There happened to be a large herd of pigs feeding on the hillside nearby, and the demons begged him to let them enter into the pigs.

So Jesus gave them permission. 33Then the demons came out of the man and entered the pigs, and the entire herd plunged down the steep hillside into the lake and drowned.

34When the herdsmen saw it, they fled to the nearby town and the surrounding countryside, spreading the news as they ran. 35People rushed out to see what had happened. A crowd soon gathered around Jesus, and they saw the man who had been freed from the demons. He was sitting at Jesus' feet, fully clothed and perfectly sane, and they were all afraid. 36Then those who had seen what happened told the others how the demon-possessed man had been healed. 37And all the people in the region of the Gerasenes begged Jesus to go away and leave them alone, for a great wave of fear swept over them.

So Jesus returned to the boat and left, crossing back to the other side of the lake. 38The man who had been freed from the demons begged to go with him. But Jesus sent him home, saying, 39"No, go back to your family, and tell them everything God has done for you." So he went all through the town proclaiming the great things Jesus had done for him.

Jesus Heals in Response to Faith

40On the other side of the lake the crowds welcomed Jesus, because they had been waiting for him. 41Then

8:26 Other manuscripts read *Gadarenes;* still others read *Gergesenes;* also in 8:37. See Matt 8:28; Mark 5:1. **8:29** Greek *unclean.* **8:31** Or *the abyss,* or *the underworld.*

KING JAMES VERSION

at Jesus' feet, and besought him that he would come into his house:

42For he had one only daughter, about twelve years of age, and she lay a dying. But as he went the people thronged him.

43And a woman having an issue of blood twelve years, which had spent all her living upon physicians, neither could be healed of any,

44Came behind *him,* and touched the border of his garment: and immediately her issue of blood stanched.

45And Jesus said, Who touched me? When all denied, Peter and they that were with him said, Master, the multitude throng thee and press *thee,* and sayest thou, Who touched me?

46And Jesus said, Somebody hath touched me: for I perceive that virtue is gone out of me.

47And when the woman saw that she was not hid, she came trembling, and falling down before him, she declared unto him before all the people for what cause she had touched him, and how she was healed immediately.

48And he said unto her, Daughter, be of good comfort: thy faith hath made thee whole; go in peace.

49While he yet spake, there cometh one from the ruler of the synagogue's *house,* saying to him, Thy daughter is dead; trouble not the Master.

50But when Jesus heard *it,* he answered him, saying, Fear not: believe only, and she shall be made whole.

51And when he came into the house, he suffered no man to go in, save Peter, and James, and John, and the father and the mother of the maiden.

52And all wept, and bewailed her: but he said, Weep not; she is not dead, but sleepeth.

53And they laughed him to scorn, knowing that she was dead.

54And he put them all out, and took her by the hand, and called, saying, Maid, arise.

55And her spirit came again, and she arose straightway: and he commanded to give her meat.

56And her parents were astonished: but he charged them that they should tell no man what was done.

9 1Then he called his twelve disciples together, and gave them power and authority over all devils, and to cure diseases.

2And he sent them to preach the kingdom of God, and to heal the sick.

3And he said unto them, Take nothing for *your* journey, neither staves, nor scrip, neither bread, neither money; neither have two coats apiece.

4And whatsoever house ye enter into, there abide, and thence depart.

5And whosoever will not receive you, when ye go out of that city, shake off the very dust from your feet for a testimony against them.

NEW LIVING TRANSLATION

a man named Jairus, a leader of the local synagogue, came and fell at Jesus' feet, pleading with him to come home with him. 42His only daughter,* who was about twelve years old, was dying.

As Jesus went with him, he was surrounded by the crowds. 43A woman in the crowd had suffered for twelve years with constant bleeding,* and she could find no cure. 44Coming up behind Jesus, she touched the fringe of his robe. Immediately, the bleeding stopped.

45"Who touched me?" Jesus asked.

Everyone denied it, and Peter said, "Master, this whole crowd is pressing up against you."

46But Jesus said, "Someone deliberately touched me, for I felt healing power go out from me." 47When the woman realized that she could not stay hidden, she began to tremble and fell to her knees in front of him. The whole crowd heard her explain why she had touched him and that she had been immediately healed. 48"Daughter," he said to her, "your faith has made you well. Go in peace."

49While he was still speaking to her, a messenger arrived from the home of Jairus, the leader of the synagogue. He told him, "Your daughter is dead. There's no use troubling the Teacher now."

50But when Jesus heard what had happened, he said to Jairus, "Don't be afraid. Just have faith, and she will be healed."

51When they arrived at the house, Jesus wouldn't let anyone go in with him except Peter, John, James, and the little girl's father and mother. 52The house was filled with people weeping and wailing, but he said, "Stop the weeping! She isn't dead; she's only asleep."

53But the crowd laughed at him because they all knew she had died. 54Then Jesus took her by the hand and said in a loud voice, "My child, get up!" 55And at that moment her life* returned, and she immediately stood up! Then Jesus told them to give her something to eat. 56Her parents were overwhelmed, but Jesus insisted that they not tell anyone what had happened.

Jesus Sends Out the Twelve Disciples

9 One day Jesus called together his twelve disciples* and gave them power and authority to cast out all demons and to heal all diseases. 2Then he sent them out to tell everyone about the Kingdom of God and to heal the sick. 3"Take nothing for your journey," he instructed them. "Don't take a walking stick, a traveler's bag, food, money,* or even a change of clothes. 4Wherever you go, stay in the same house until you leave town. 5And if a town refuses to welcome you, shake its dust from your feet as you leave to show that you have abandoned those people to their fate."

8:42 Or *His only child, a daughter.* **8:43** Some manuscripts add *having spent everything she had on doctors.* **8:55** Or *her spirit.* **9:1** Greek *the Twelve;* other manuscripts read *the twelve apostles.* **9:3** Or *silver coins.*

KING JAMES VERSION

6 And they departed, and went through the towns,
preaching the gospel, and healing every where.

7 Now Herod the tetrarch heard of all that was
done by him: and he was perplexed, because that it
was said of some, that John was risen from the dead;
8 And of some, that Elias had appeared; and of others, that one of the old prophets was risen again.
9 And Herod said, John have I beheaded: but who is
this, of whom I hear such things? And he desired to
see him.

10 And the apostles, when they were returned, told
him all that they had done. And he took them, and
went aside privately into a desert place belonging to
the city called Bethsaida.
11 And the people, when they knew *it*, followed
him: and he received them, and spake unto them of
the kingdom of God, and healed them that had need
of healing.
12 And when the day began to wear away, then
came the twelve, and said unto him, Send the multitude away, that they may go into the towns and country round about, and lodge, and get victuals: for we
are here in a desert place.
13 But he said unto them, Give ye them to eat. And
they said, We have no more but five loaves and two
fishes; except we should go and buy meat for all this
people.
14 For they were about five thousand men. And he
said to his disciples, Make them sit down by fifties in
a company.
15 And they did so, and made them all sit down.
16 Then he took the five loaves and the two fishes,
and looking up to heaven, he blessed them, and
brake, and gave to the disciples to set before the
multitude.
17 And they did eat, and were all filled: and there
was taken up of fragments that remained to them
twelve baskets.
18 And it came to pass, as he was alone praying, his
disciples were with him: and he asked them, saying,
Whom say the people that I am?
19 They answering said, John the Baptist; but some
say, Elias; and others *say*, that one of the old prophets is risen again.
20 He said unto them, But whom say ye that I am?
Peter answering said, The Christ of God.

21 And he straitly charged them, and commanded
them to tell no man that thing;
22 Saying, The Son of man must suffer many things,

NEW LIVING TRANSLATION

6 So they began their circuit of the villages, preaching the Good News and healing the sick.

Herod's Confusion

7 When Herod Antipas, the ruler of Galilee,* heard
about everything Jesus was doing, he was puzzled.
Some were saying that John the Baptist had been
raised from the dead. 8 Others thought Jesus was Elijah or one of the other prophets risen from the dead.
9 "I beheaded John," Herod said, "so who is this
man about whom I hear such stories?" And he kept
trying to see him.

Jesus Feeds Five Thousand

10 When the apostles returned, they told Jesus everything they had done. Then he slipped quietly away
with them toward the town of Bethsaida. 11 But the
crowds found out where he was going, and they
followed him. He welcomed them and taught them
about the Kingdom of God, and he healed those who
were sick.
12 Late in the afternoon the twelve disciples came
to him and said, "Send the crowds away to the nearby
villages and farms, so they can find food and lodging
for the night. There is nothing to eat here in this
remote place."
13 But Jesus said, "You feed them."
"But we have only five loaves of bread and two
fish," they answered. "Or are you expecting us to go
and buy enough food for this whole crowd?" 14 For
there were about 5,000 men there.
Jesus replied, "Tell them to sit down in groups
of about fifty each." 15 So the people all sat down.
16 Jesus took the five loaves and two fish, looked up
toward heaven, and blessed them. Then, breaking
the loaves into pieces, he kept giving the bread and
fish to the disciples so they could distribute it to the
people. 17 They all ate as much as they wanted, and
afterward, the disciples picked up twelve baskets of
leftovers!

Peter's Declaration about Jesus

18 One day Jesus left the crowds to pray alone. Only
his disciples were with him, and he asked them,
"Who do people say I am?"
19 "Well," they replied, "some say John the Baptist,
some say Elijah, and others say you are one of the
other ancient prophets risen from the dead."
20 Then he asked them, "But who do you say I am?"
Peter replied, "You are the Messiah* sent from God!"

Jesus Predicts His Death

21 Jesus warned his disciples not to tell anyone
who he was. 22 "The Son of Man* must suffer many
terrible things," he said. "He will be rejected by the

9:7 Greek *Herod the tetrarch.* Herod Antipas was a son of King Herod and was ruler over Galilee. **9:20** Or *the Christ. Messiah* (a Hebrew term) and *Christ* (a Greek term) both mean "the anointed one." **9:22** "Son of Man" is a title Jesus used for himself.

KING JAMES VERSION

and be rejected of the elders and chief priests and scribes, and be slain, and be raised the third day.

23 And he said to *them* all, If any *man* will come after me, let him deny himself, and take up his cross daily, and follow me.

24 For whosoever will save his life shall lose it: but whosoever will lose his life for my sake, the same shall save it.

25 For what is a man advantaged, if he gain the whole world, and lose himself, or be cast away?

26 For whosoever shall be ashamed of me and of my words, of him shall the Son of man be ashamed, when he shall come in his own glory, and *in his* Father's, and of the holy angels.

27 But I tell you of a truth, there be some standing here, which shall not taste of death, till they see the kingdom of God.

28 And it came to pass about an eight days after these sayings, he took Peter and John and James, and went up into a mountain to pray.

29 And as he prayed, the fashion of his countenance was altered, and his raiment *was* white *and* glistering.

30 And, behold, there talked with him two men, which were Moses and Elias:

31 Who appeared in glory, and spake of his decease which he should accomplish at Jerusalem.

32 But Peter and they that were with him were heavy with sleep: and when they were awake, they saw his glory, and the two men that stood with him.

33 And it came to pass, as they departed from him, Peter said unto Jesus, Master, it is good for us to be here: and let us make three tabernacles; one for thee, and one for Moses, and one for Elias: not knowing what he said.

34 While he thus spake, there came a cloud, and overshadowed them: and they feared as they entered into the cloud.

35 And there came a voice out of the cloud, saying, This is my beloved Son: hear him.

36 And when the voice was past, Jesus was found alone. And they kept *it* close, and told no man in those days any of those things which they had seen.

37 And it came to pass, that on the next day, when they were come down from the hill, much people met him.

38 And, behold, a man of the company cried out, saying, Master, I beseech thee, look upon my son: for he is mine only child.

39 And, lo, a spirit taketh him, and he suddenly crieth out; and it teareth him that he foameth again, and bruising him hardly departeth from him.

40 And I besought thy disciples to cast him out; and they could not.

41 And Jesus answering said, O faithless and perverse generation, how long shall I be with you, and suffer you? Bring thy son hither.

NEW LIVING TRANSLATION

elders, the leading priests, and the teachers of religious law. He will be killed, but on the third day he will be raised from the dead."

23 Then he said to the crowd, "If any of you wants
to be my follower, you must turn from your selfish
ways, take up your cross daily, and follow me. 24 If you
try to hang on to your life, you will lose it. But if you
give up your life for my sake, you will save it. 25 And
what do you benefit if you gain the whole world
but are yourself lost or destroyed? 26 If anyone is
ashamed of me and my message, the Son of Man will
be ashamed of that person when he returns in his
glory and in the glory of the Father and the holy
angels. 27 I tell you the truth, some standing here
right now will not die before they see the Kingdom
of God."

The Transfiguration

28 About eight days later Jesus took Peter, John, and
James up on a mountain to pray. 29 And as he was
praying, the appearance of his face was transformed,
and his clothes became dazzling white. 30 Suddenly,
two men, Moses and Elijah, appeared and began talking with Jesus. 31 They were glorious to see. And they
were speaking about his exodus from this world,
which was about to be fulfilled in Jerusalem.

32 Peter and the others had fallen asleep. When
they woke up, they saw Jesus' glory and the two men
standing with him. 33 As Moses and Elijah were starting to leave, Peter, not even knowing what he was
saying, blurted out, "Master, it's wonderful for us to
be here! Let's make three shelters as memorials*—
one for you, one for Moses, and one for Elijah." 34 But
even as he was saying this, a cloud overshadowed
them, and terror gripped them as the cloud covered
them.

35 Then a voice from the cloud said, "This is my
Son, my Chosen One.* Listen to him." 36 When the
voice finished, Jesus was there alone. They didn't tell
anyone at that time what they had seen.

Jesus Heals a Demon-Possessed Boy

37 The next day, after they had come down the mountain, a large crowd met Jesus. 38 A man in the crowd
called out to him, "Teacher, I beg you to look at my
son, my only child. 39 An evil spirit keeps seizing him,
making him scream. It throws him into convulsions
so that he foams at the mouth. It batters him and
hardly ever leaves him alone. 40 I begged your disciples to cast out the spirit, but they couldn't do it."

41 Jesus said, "You faithless and corrupt people!
How long must I be with you and put up with you?"
Then he said to the man, "Bring your son here."

9:33 Greek *three tabernacles.* 9:35 Some manuscripts read *This is my dearly loved Son.*

KING JAMES VERSION

42 And as he was yet a coming, the devil threw him down, and tare *him.* And Jesus rebuked the unclean spirit, and healed the child, and delivered him again to his father.

43 And they were all amazed at the mighty power of God. But while they wondered every one at all things which Jesus did, he said unto his disciples,

44 Let these sayings sink down into your ears: for the Son of man shall be delivered into the hands of men.

45 But they understood not this saying, and it was hid from them, that they perceived it not: and they feared to ask him of that saying.

46 Then there arose a reasoning among them, which of them should be greatest.

47 And Jesus, perceiving the thought of their heart, took a child, and set him by him,

48 And said unto them, Whosoever shall receive this child in my name receiveth me: and whosoever shall receive me receiveth him that sent me: for he that is least among you all, the same shall be great.

49 And John answered and said, Master, we saw one casting out devils in thy name; and we forbad him, because he followeth not with us.

50 And Jesus said unto him, Forbid *him* not: for he that is not against us is for us.

51 And it came to pass, when the time was come that he should be received up, he stedfastly set his face to go to Jerusalem,

52 And sent messengers before his face: and they went, and entered into a village of the Samaritans, to make ready for him.

53 And they did not receive him, because his face was as though he would go to Jerusalem.

54 And when his disciples James and John saw *this,* they said, Lord, wilt thou that we command fire to come down from heaven, and consume them, even as Elias did?

55 But he turned, and rebuked them, and said, Ye know not what manner of spirit ye are of.

56 For the Son of man is not come to destroy men's lives, but to save *them.* And they went to another village.

57 And it came to pass, that, as they went in the way, a certain *man* said unto him, Lord, I will follow thee whithersoever thou goest.

58 And Jesus said unto him, Foxes have holes, and

NEW LIVING TRANSLATION

42 As the boy came forward, the demon knocked him to the ground and threw him into a violent convulsion. But Jesus rebuked the evil* spirit and healed the boy. Then he gave him back to his father. 43 Awe gripped the people as they saw this majestic display of God's power.

Jesus Again Predicts His Death

While everyone was marveling at everything he was doing, Jesus said to his disciples, 44 "Listen to me and remember what I say. The Son of Man is going to be betrayed into the hands of his enemies." 45 But they didn't know what he meant. Its significance was hidden from them, so they couldn't understand it, and they were afraid to ask him about it.

The Greatest in the Kingdom

46 Then his disciples began arguing about which of them was the greatest. 47 But Jesus knew their thoughts, so he brought a little child to his side. 48 Then he said to them, "Anyone who welcomes a little child like this on my behalf* welcomes me, and anyone who welcomes me also welcomes my Father who sent me. Whoever is the least among you is the greatest."

Using the Name of Jesus

49 John said to Jesus, "Master, we saw someone using your name to cast out demons, but we told him to stop because he isn't in our group."

50 But Jesus said, "Don't stop him! Anyone who is not against you is for you."

Opposition from Samaritans

51 As the time drew near for him to ascend to heaven, Jesus resolutely set out for Jerusalem. 52 He sent messengers ahead to a Samaritan village to prepare for his arrival. 53 But the people of the village did not welcome Jesus because he was on his way to Jerusalem. 54 When James and John saw this, they said to Jesus, "Lord, should we call down fire from heaven to burn them up*?" 55 But Jesus turned and rebuked them.* 56 So they went on to another village.

The Cost of Following Jesus

57 As they were walking along, someone said to Jesus, "I will follow you wherever you go."

58 But Jesus replied, "Foxes have dens to live in, and

9:42 Greek *unclean.* **9:48** Greek *in my name.* **9:54** Some manuscripts add *as Elijah did.* **9:55** Some manuscripts add an expanded conclusion to verse 55 and an additional sentence in verse 56: *And he said, "You don't realize what your hearts are like. [56] For the Son of Man has not come to destroy people's lives, but to save them."*

KING JAMES VERSION

birds of the air *have* nests; but the Son of man hath
not where to lay *his* head.
59And he said unto another, Follow me. But he
said, Lord, suffer me first to go and bury my father.
60Jesus said unto him, Let the dead bury their
dead: but go thou and preach the kingdom of God.
61And another also said, Lord, I will follow thee;
but let me first go bid them farewell, which are at
home at my house.
62And Jesus said unto him, No man, having put his
hand to the plough, and looking back, is fit for the
kingdom of God.

10 1After these things the Lord appointed other
seventy also, and sent them two and two before his face into every city and place, whither he
himself would come.
2Therefore said he unto them, The harvest truly *is*
great, but the labourers *are* few: pray ye therefore the
Lord of the harvest, that he would send forth
labourers into his harvest.
3Go your ways: behold, I send you forth as lambs
among wolves.
4Carry neither purse, nor scrip, nor shoes: and salute no man by the way.
5And into whatsoever house ye enter, first say,
Peace *be* to this house.
6And if the son of peace be there, your peace shall
rest upon it: if not, it shall turn to you again.
7And in the same house remain, eating and drinking such things as they give: for the labourer is worthy of his hire. Go not from house to house.
8And into whatsoever city ye enter, and they receive you, eat such things as are set before you:
9And heal the sick that are therein, and say unto
them, The kingdom of God is come nigh unto you.
10But into whatsoever city ye enter, and they receive you not, go your ways out into the streets of the
same, and say,
11Even the very dust of your city, which cleaveth
on us, we do wipe off against you: notwithstanding
be ye sure of this, that the kingdom of God is come
nigh unto you.
12But I say unto you, that it shall be more tolerable
in that day for Sodom, than for that city.
13Woe unto thee, Chorazin! woe unto thee, Bethsaida! for if the mighty works had been done in Tyre and
Sidon, which have been done in you, they had a great
while ago repented, sitting in sackcloth and ashes.
14But it shall be more tolerable for Tyre and Sidon
at the judgment, than for you.
15And thou, Capernaum, which art exalted to
heaven, shalt be thrust down to hell.
16He that heareth you heareth me; and he that
despiseth you despiseth me; and he that despiseth
me despiseth him that sent me.

NEW LIVING TRANSLATION

birds have nests, but the Son of Man has no place
even to lay his head."
59He said to another person, "Come, follow me."
The man agreed, but he said, "Lord, first let me
return home and bury my father."
60But Jesus told him, "Let the spiritually dead bury
their own dead!* Your duty is to go and preach about
the Kingdom of God."
61Another said, "Yes, Lord, I will follow you, but
first let me say good-bye to my family."
62But Jesus told him, "Anyone who puts a hand to
the plow and then looks back is not fit for the Kingdom of God."

Jesus Sends Out His Disciples

10 The Lord now chose seventy-two* other disciples and sent them ahead in pairs to all the
towns and places he planned to visit. 2These were his
instructions to them: "The harvest is great, but the
workers are few. So pray to the Lord who is in charge
of the harvest; ask him to send more workers into his
fields. 3Now go, and remember that I am sending you
out as lambs among wolves. 4Don't take any money
with you, nor a traveler's bag, nor an extra pair of sandals. And don't stop to greet anyone on the road.
5"Whenever you enter someone's home, first say,
'May God's peace be on this house.' 6If those who live
there are peaceful, the blessing will stand; if they are
not, the blessing will return to you. 7Don't move
around from home to home. Stay in one place, eating
and drinking what they provide. Don't hesitate to
accept hospitality, because those who work deserve
their pay.
8"If you enter a town and it welcomes you, eat
whatever is set before you. 9Heal the sick, and tell
them, 'The Kingdom of God is near you now.' 10But if
a town refuses to welcome you, go out into its streets
and say, 11'We wipe even the dust of your town from
our feet to show that we have abandoned you to your
fate. And know this—the Kingdom of God is near!'
12I assure you, even wicked Sodom will be better off
than such a town on judgment day.
13"What sorrow awaits you, Korazin and Bethsaida! For if the miracles I did in you had been done
in wicked Tyre and Sidon, their people would have
repented of their sins long ago, clothing themselves
in burlap and throwing ashes on their heads to show
their remorse. 14Yes, Tyre and Sidon will be better off
on judgment day than you. 15And you people of
Capernaum, will you be honored in heaven? No, you
will go down to the place of the dead.*"
16Then he said to the disciples, "Anyone who accepts your message is also accepting me. And anyone who rejects you is rejecting me. And anyone who
rejects me is rejecting God, who sent me."

9:60 Greek *Let the dead bury their own dead.* **10:1** Some manuscripts read *seventy;* also in 10:17. **10:15** Greek *to Hades.*

KING JAMES VERSION

17 And the seventy returned again with joy, saying,
Lord, even the devils are subject unto us through thy
name.
18 And he said unto them, I beheld Satan as lightning fall from heaven.
19 Behold, I give unto you power to tread on serpents and scorpions, and over all the power of the
enemy: and nothing shall by any means hurt you.
20 Notwithstanding in this rejoice not, that the
spirits are subject unto you; but rather rejoice, because your names are written in heaven.

21 In that hour Jesus rejoiced in spirit, and said, I
thank thee, O Father, Lord of heaven and earth, that
thou hast hid these things from the wise and prudent, and hast revealed them unto babes: even so,
Father; for so it seemed good in thy sight.
22 All things are delivered to me of my Father: and
no man knoweth who the Son is, but the Father; and
who the Father is, but the Son, and *he* to whom the
Son will reveal *him.*
23 And he turned him unto *his* disciples, and said
privately, Blessed *are* the eyes which see the things
that ye see:
24 For I tell you, that many prophets and kings have
desired to see those things which ye see, and have
not seen *them;* and to hear those things which ye
hear, and have not heard *them.*

25 And, behold, a certain lawyer stood up, and
tempted him, saying, Master, what shall I do to inherit eternal life?
26 He said unto him, What is written in the law?
how readest thou?
27 And he answering said, Thou shalt love the Lord
thy God with all thy heart, and with all thy soul, and
with all thy strength, and with all thy mind; and thy
neighbour as thyself.
28 And he said unto him, Thou hast answered right:
this do, and thou shalt live.
29 But he, willing to justify himself, said unto Jesus,
And who is my neighbour?

30 And Jesus answering said, A certain *man* went
down from Jerusalem to Jericho, and fell among
thieves, which stripped him of his raiment, and
wounded *him,* and departed, leaving *him* half dead.
31 And by chance there came down a certain priest
that way: and when he saw him, he passed by on the
other side.
32 And likewise a Levite, when he was at the place,
came and looked *on him,* and passed by on the other
side.
33 But a certain Samaritan, as he journeyed, came
where he was: and when he saw him, he had compassion *on him,*

NEW LIVING TRANSLATION

17 When the seventy-two disciples returned, they
joyfully reported to him, "Lord, even the demons
obey us when we use your name!"
18 "Yes," he told them, "I saw Satan fall from
heaven like lightning! 19 Look, I have given you authority over all the power of the enemy, and you can
walk among snakes and scorpions and crush them.
Nothing will injure you. 20 But don't rejoice because
evil spirits obey you; rejoice because your names are
registered in heaven."

Jesus' Prayer of Thanksgiving

21 At that same time Jesus was filled with the joy of
the Holy Spirit, and he said, "O Father, Lord of heaven
and earth, thank you for hiding these things from
those who think themselves wise and clever, and for
revealing them to the childlike. Yes, Father, it pleased
you to do it this way.
22 "My Father has entrusted everything to me. No
one truly knows the Son except the Father, and no
one truly knows the Father except the Son and those
to whom the Son chooses to reveal him."
23 Then when they were alone, he turned to the
disciples and said, "Blessed are the eyes that see what
you have seen. 24 I tell you, many prophets and kings
longed to see what you see, but they didn't see it. And
they longed to hear what you hear, but they didn't
hear it."

The Most Important Commandment

25 One day an expert in religious law stood up to test
Jesus by asking him this question: "Teacher, what
should I do to inherit eternal life?"
26 Jesus replied, "What does the law of Moses say?
How do you read it?"
27 The man answered, " 'You must love the LORD
your God with all your heart, all your soul, all your
strength, and all your mind.' And, 'Love your neighbor as yourself.' "*
28 "Right!" Jesus told him. "Do this and you will live!"
29 The man wanted to justify his actions, so he
asked Jesus, "And who is my neighbor?"

Parable of the Good Samaritan

30 Jesus replied with a story: "A Jewish man was traveling from Jerusalem down to Jericho, and he was
attacked by bandits. They stripped him of his
clothes, beat him up, and left him half dead beside
the road.
31 "By chance a priest came along. But when he saw
the man lying there, he crossed to the other side of
the road and passed him by. 32 A Temple assistant*
walked over and looked at him lying there, but he
also passed by on the other side.
33 "Then a despised Samaritan came along, and
when he saw the man, he felt compassion for him.

10:27 Deut 6:5; Lev 19:18. **10:32** Greek *A Levite.*

KING JAMES VERSION

34 And went to *him*, and bound up his wounds, pouring in oil and wine, and set him on his own beast, and brought him to an inn, and took care of him.

35 And on the morrow when he departed, he took out two pence, and gave *them* to the host, and said unto him, Take care of him; and whatsoever thou spendest more, when I come again, I will repay thee.

36 Which now of these three, thinkest thou, was neighbour unto him that fell among the thieves?

37 And he said, He that shewed mercy on him. Then said Jesus unto him, Go, and do thou likewise.

38 Now it came to pass, as they went, that he entered into a certain village: and a certain woman named Martha received him into her house.

39 And she had a sister called Mary, which also sat at Jesus' feet, and heard his word.

40 But Martha was cumbered about much serving, and came to him, and said, Lord, dost thou not care that my sister hath left me to serve alone? bid her therefore that she help me.

41 And Jesus answered and said unto her, Martha, Martha, thou art careful and troubled about many things:

42 But one thing is needful: and Mary hath chosen that good part, which shall not be taken away from her.

11 1 And it came to pass, that, as he was praying in a certain place, when he ceased, one of his disciples said unto him, Lord, teach us to pray, as John also taught his disciples.

2 And he said unto them, When ye pray, say, Our Father which art in heaven, Hallowed be thy name. Thy kingdom come. Thy will be done, as in heaven, so in earth.

3 Give us day by day our daily bread.

4 And forgive us our sins; for we also forgive every one that is indebted to us. And lead us not into temptation; but deliver us from evil.

5 And he said unto them, Which of you shall have a friend, and shall go unto him at midnight, and say unto him, Friend, lend me three loaves;

6 For a friend of mine in his journey is come to me, and I have nothing to set before him?

7 And he from within shall answer and say, Trouble me not: the door is now shut, and my children are with me in bed; I cannot rise and give thee.

8 I say unto you, Though he will not rise and give him, because he is his friend, yet because of his importunity he will rise and give him as many as he needeth.

NEW LIVING TRANSLATION

34 Going over to him, the Samaritan soothed his wounds with olive oil and wine and bandaged them. Then he put the man on his own donkey and took him to an inn, where he took care of him. 35 The next day he handed the innkeeper two silver coins,* telling him, 'Take care of this man. If his bill runs higher than this, I'll pay you the next time I'm here.'

36 "Now which of these three would you say was a neighbor to the man who was attacked by bandits?" Jesus asked.

37 The man replied, "The one who showed him mercy."

Then Jesus said, "Yes, now go and do the same."

Jesus Visits Martha and Mary

38 As Jesus and the disciples continued on their way to Jerusalem, they came to a certain village where a woman named Martha welcomed him into her home. 39 Her sister, Mary, sat at the Lord's feet, listening to what he taught. 40 But Martha was distracted by the big dinner she was preparing. She came to Jesus and said, "Lord, doesn't it seem unfair to you that my sister just sits here while I do all the work? Tell her to come and help me."

41 But the Lord said to her, "My dear Martha, you are worried and upset over all these details! 42 There is only one thing worth being concerned about. Mary has discovered it, and it will not be taken away from her."

Teaching about Prayer

11 Once Jesus was in a certain place praying. As he finished, one of his disciples came to him and said, "Lord, teach us to pray, just as John taught his disciples."

2 Jesus said, "This is how you should pray:*

"Father, may your name be kept holy.
May your Kingdom come soon.
3 Give us each day the food we need,*
4 and forgive us our sins,
as we forgive those who sin against us.
And don't let us yield to temptation.*"

5 Then, teaching them more about prayer, he used this story: "Suppose you went to a friend's house at midnight, wanting to borrow three loaves of bread. You say to him, 6 'A friend of mine has just arrived for a visit, and I have nothing for him to eat.' 7 And suppose he calls out from his bedroom, 'Don't bother me. The door is locked for the night, and my family and I are all in bed. I can't help you.' 8 But I tell you this—though he won't do it for friendship's sake, if you keep knocking long enough, he will get up and give you whatever you need because of your shameless persistence.*

10:35 Greek *two denarii.* A denarius was equivalent to a laborer's full day's wage. **11:2** Some manuscripts add additional phrases from the Lord's Prayer as it reads in Matt 6:9-13. **11:3** Or *Give us each day our food for the day;* or *Give us each day our food for tomorrow.* **11:4** Or *And keep us from being tested.* **11:8** Or *in order to avoid shame, or so his reputation won't be damaged.*

KING JAMES VERSION

9 And I say unto you, Ask, and it shall be given you;
seek, and ye shall find; knock, and it shall be opened
unto you.
10 For every one that asketh receiveth; and he that
seeketh findeth; and to him that knocketh it shall be
opened.
11 If a son shall ask bread of any of you that is a
father, will he give him a stone? or if *he ask* a fish, will
he for a fish give him a serpent?
12 Or if he shall ask an egg, will he offer him a
scorpion?
13 If ye then, being evil, know how to give good gifts
unto your children: how much more shall *your* heavenly Father give the Holy Spirit to them that ask him?
14 And he was casting out a devil, and it was dumb.
And it came to pass, when the devil was gone out, the
dumb spake; and the people wondered.
15 But some of them said, He casteth out devils
through Beelzebub the chief of the devils.
16 And others, tempting *him,* sought of him a sign
from heaven.
17 But he, knowing their thoughts, said unto them,
Every kingdom divided against itself is brought to
desolation; and a house *divided* against a house
falleth.
18 If Satan also be divided against himself, how
shall his kingdom stand? because ye say that I cast
out devils through Beelzebub.
19 And if I by Beelzebub cast out devils, by whom
do your sons cast *them* out? therefore shall they be
your judges.
20 But if I with the finger of God cast out devils, no
doubt the kingdom of God is come upon you.
21 When a strong man armed keepeth his palace,
his goods are in peace:
22 But when a stronger than he shall come upon
him, and overcome him, he taketh from him all his
armour wherein he trusted, and divideth his spoils.
23 He that is not with me is against me: and he that
gathereth not with me scattereth.
24 When the unclean spirit is gone out of a man, he
walketh through dry places, seeking rest; and finding
none, he saith, I will return unto my house whence I
came out.
25 And when he cometh, he findeth *it* swept and
garnished.
26 Then goeth he, and taketh *to him* seven other
spirits more wicked than himself; and they enter in,
and dwell there: and the last *state* of that man is
worse than the first.
27 And it came to pass, as he spake these things, a
certain woman of the company lifted up her voice,
and said unto him, Blessed *is* the womb that bare
thee, and the paps which thou hast sucked.
28 But he said, Yea rather, blessed *are* they that hear
the word of God, and keep it.

NEW LIVING TRANSLATION

9 "And so I tell you, keep on asking, and you will receive what you ask for. Keep on seeking, and you will
find. Keep on knocking, and the door will be opened
to you. 10 For everyone who asks, receives. Everyone
who seeks, finds. And to everyone who knocks, the
door will be opened.
11 "You fathers—if your children ask* for a fish, do
you give them a snake instead? 12 Or if they ask for an
egg, do you give them a scorpion? Of course not!
13 So if you sinful people know how to give good gifts
to your children, how much more will your heavenly
Father give the Holy Spirit to those who ask him."

Jesus and the Prince of Demons

14 One day Jesus cast out a demon from a man who
couldn't speak, and when the demon was gone, the
man began to speak. The crowds were amazed, 15 but
some of them said, "No wonder he can cast out demons. He gets his power from Satan,* the prince of
demons." 16 Others, trying to test Jesus, demanded
that he show them a miraculous sign from heaven
to prove his authority.
17 He knew their thoughts, so he said, "Any kingdom divided by civil war is doomed. A family splintered by feuding will fall apart. 18 You say I am
empowered by Satan. But if Satan is divided and
fighting against himself, how can his kingdom survive? 19 And if I am empowered by Satan, what about
your own exorcists? They cast out demons, too, so
they will condemn you for what you have said. 20 But
if I am casting out demons by the power of God,*
then the Kingdom of God has arrived among you.
21 For when a strong man like Satan is fully armed
and guards his palace, his possessions are safe—
22 until someone even stronger attacks and over-
powers him, strips him of his weapons, and carries
off his belongings.
23 "Anyone who isn't with me opposes me, and anyone who isn't working with me is actually working
against me.
24 "When an evil* spirit leaves a person, it goes
into the desert, searching for rest. But when it finds
none, it says, 'I will return to the person I came from.'
25 So it returns and finds that its former home is all
swept and in order. 26 Then the spirit finds seven
other spirits more evil than itself, and they all enter
the person and live there. And so that person is
worse off than before."
27 As he was speaking, a woman in the crowd
called out, "God bless your mother—the womb from
which you came, and the breasts that nursed you!"
28 Jesus replied, "But even more blessed are all who
hear the word of God and put it into practice."

11:11 Some manuscripts add *for bread, do you give them a stone? Or [if they ask].* **11:15** Greek *Beelzeboul;* also in 11:18, 19. Other manuscripts read *Beezeboul;* Latin version reads *Beelzebub.* **11:20** Greek *by the finger of God.* **11:24** Greek *unclean.*

KING JAMES VERSION

29 And when the people were gathered thick together, he began to say, This is an evil generation: they seek a sign; and there shall no sign be given it, but the sign of Jonas the prophet.

30 For as Jonas was a sign unto the Ninevites, so shall also the Son of man be to this generation.

31 The queen of the south shall rise up in the judgment with the men of this generation, and condemn them: for she came from the utmost parts of the earth to hear the wisdom of Solomon; and, behold, a greater than Solomon *is* here.

32 The men of Nineve shall rise up in the judgment with this generation, and shall condemn it: for they repented at the preaching of Jonas; and, behold, a greater than Jonas *is* here.

33 No man, when he hath lighted a candle, putteth *it* in a secret place, neither under a bushel, but on a candlestick, that they which come in may see the light.

34 The light of the body is the eye: therefore when thine eye is single, thy whole body also is full of light; but when *thine eye* is evil, thy body also *is* full of darkness.

35 Take heed therefore that the light which is in thee be not darkness.

36 If thy whole body therefore *be* full of light, having no part dark, the whole shall be full of light, as when the bright shining of a candle doth give thee light.

37 And as he spake, a certain Pharisee besought him to dine with him: and he went in, and sat down to meat.

38 And when the Pharisee saw *it,* he marvelled that he had not first washed before dinner.

39 And the Lord said unto him, Now do ye Pharisees make clean the outside of the cup and the platter; but your inward part is full of ravening and wickedness.

40 *Ye* fools, did not he that made that which is without make that which is within also?

41 But rather give alms of such things as ye have; and, behold, all things are clean unto you.

42 But woe unto you, Pharisees! for ye tithe mint and rue and all manner of herbs, and pass over judgment and the love of God: these ought ye to have done, and not to leave the other undone.

43 Woe unto you, Pharisees! for ye love the uppermost seats in the synagogues, and greetings in the markets.

44 Woe unto you, scribes and Pharisees, hypocrites! for ye are as graves which appear not, and the men that walk over *them* are not aware *of them.*

NEW LIVING TRANSLATION

The Sign of Jonah

29 As the crowd pressed in on Jesus, he said, "This evil
generation keeps asking me to show them a miraculous sign. But the only sign I will give them is the sign
of Jonah.
30 What happened to him was a sign to the
people of Nineveh that God had sent him. What happens to the Son of Man* will be a sign to these people
that he was sent by God.

31 "The queen of Sheba* will stand up against this
generation on judgment day and condemn it, for she
came from a distant land to hear the wisdom of Solomon. Now someone greater than Solomon is here—
but you refuse to listen.
32 The people of Nineveh will
also stand up against this generation on judgment
day and condemn it, for they repented of their sins at
the preaching of Jonah. Now someone greater than
Jonah is here—but you refuse to repent.

Receiving the Light

33 "No one lights a lamp and then hides it or puts it
under a basket.* Instead, a lamp is placed on a stand,
where its light can be seen by all who enter the
house.

34 "Your eye is a lamp that provides light for your
body. When your eye is good, your whole body is
filled with light. But when it is bad, your body is filled
with darkness.
35 Make sure that the light you think
you have is not actually darkness.
36 If you are filled
with light, with no dark corners, then your whole life
will be radiant, as though a floodlight were filling
you with light."

Jesus Criticizes the Religious Leaders

37 As Jesus was speaking, one of the Pharisees invited
him home for a meal. So he went in and took his
place at the table.*
38 His host was amazed to see that
he sat down to eat without first performing the
hand-washing ceremony required by Jewish custom.
39 Then the Lord said to him, "You Pharisees are so
careful to clean the outside of the cup and the dish,
but inside you are filthy—full of greed and wickedness!
40 Fools! Didn't God make the inside as well as
the outside?
41 So clean the inside by giving gifts to
the poor, and you will be clean all over.

42 "What sorrow awaits you Pharisees! For you are
careful to tithe even the tiniest income from your
herb gardens,* but you ignore justice and the love of
God. You should tithe, yes, but do not neglect the
more important things.

43 "What sorrow awaits you Pharisees! For you love
to sit in the seats of honor in the synagogues and receive respectful greetings as you walk in the marketplaces.
44 Yes, what sorrow awaits you! For you are like
hidden graves in a field. People walk over them without knowing the corruption they are stepping on."

11:30 "Son of Man" is a title Jesus used for himself. **11:31** Greek *The queen of the south.* **11:33** Some manuscripts do not include *or puts it under a basket.* **11:37** Or *and reclined.* **11:42** Greek *tithe the mint, the rue, and every herb.*

KING JAMES VERSION

45 Then answered one of the lawyers, and said unto him, Master, thus saying thou reproachest us also.

46 And he said, Woe unto you also, *ye* lawyers! for ye lade men with burdens grievous to be borne, and ye yourselves touch not the burdens with one of your fingers.

47 Woe unto you! for ye build the sepulchres of the prophets, and your fathers killed them.

48 Truly ye bear witness that ye allow the deeds of your fathers: for they indeed killed them, and ye build their sepulchres.

49 Therefore also said the wisdom of God, I will send them prophets and apostles, and *some* of them they shall slay and persecute:

50 That the blood of all the prophets, which was shed from the foundation of the world, may be required of this generation;

51 From the blood of Abel unto the blood of Zacharias, which perished between the altar and the temple: verily I say unto you, It shall be required of this generation.

52 Woe unto you, lawyers! for ye have taken away the key of knowledge: ye entered not in yourselves, and them that were entering in ye hindered.

53 And as he said these things unto them, the scribes and the Pharisees began to urge *him* vehemently, and to provoke him to speak of many things:

54 Laying wait for him, and seeking to catch something out of his mouth, that they might accuse him.

12 1 In the mean time, when there were gathered together an innumerable multitude of people, insomuch that they trode one upon another, he began to say unto his disciples first of all, Beware ye of the leaven of the Pharisees, which is hypocrisy.

2 For there is nothing covered, that shall not be revealed; neither hid, that shall not be known.

3 Therefore whatsoever ye have spoken in darkness shall be heard in the light; and that which ye have spoken in the ear in closets shall be proclaimed upon the housetops.

4 And I say unto you my friends, Be not afraid of them that kill the body, and after that have no more that they can do.

5 But I will forewarn you whom ye shall fear: Fear him, which after he hath killed hath power to cast into hell; yea, I say unto you, Fear him.

6 Are not five sparrows sold for two farthings, and not one of them is forgotten before God?

7 But even the very hairs of your head are all numbered. Fear not therefore: ye are of more value than many sparrows.

8 Also I say unto you, Whosoever shall confess me before men, him shall the Son of man also confess before the angels of God:

9 But he that denieth me before men shall be denied before the angels of God.

NEW LIVING TRANSLATION

45 "Teacher," said an expert in religious law, "you have insulted us, too, in what you just said."

46 "Yes," said Jesus, "what sorrow also awaits you experts in religious law! For you crush people with unbearable religious demands, and you never lift a finger to ease the burden. 47 What sorrow awaits you! For you build monuments for the prophets your own ancestors killed long ago. 48 But in fact, you stand as witnesses who agree with what your ancestors did. They killed the prophets, and you join in their crime by building the monuments! 49 This is what God in his wisdom said about you:* 'I will send prophets and apostles to them, but they will kill some and persecute the others.'

50 "As a result, this generation will be held responsible for the murder of all God's prophets from the creation of the world—51 from the murder of Abel to the murder of Zechariah, who was killed between the altar and the sanctuary. Yes, it will certainly be charged against this generation.

52 "What sorrow awaits you experts in religious law! For you remove the key to knowledge from the people. You don't enter the Kingdom yourselves, and you prevent others from entering."

53 As Jesus was leaving, the teachers of religious law and the Pharisees became hostile and tried to provoke him with many questions. 54 They wanted to trap him into saying something they could use against him.

A Warning against Hypocrisy

12 Meanwhile, the crowds grew until thousands were milling about and stepping on each other. Jesus turned first to his disciples and warned them, "Beware of the yeast of the Pharisees—their hypocrisy. 2 The time is coming when everything that is covered up will be revealed, and all that is secret will be made known to all. 3 Whatever you have said in the dark will be heard in the light, and what you have whispered behind closed doors will be shouted from the housetops for all to hear!

4 "Dear friends, don't be afraid of those who want to kill your body; they cannot do any more to you after that. 5 But I'll tell you whom to fear. Fear God, who has the power to kill you and then throw you into hell.* Yes, he's the one to fear.

6 "What is the price of five sparrows—two copper coins*? Yet God does not forget a single one of them. 7 And the very hairs on your head are all numbered. So don't be afraid; you are more valuable to God than a whole flock of sparrows.

8 "I tell you the truth, everyone who acknowledges me publicly here on earth, the Son of Man* will also acknowledge in the presence of God's angels. 9 But anyone who denies me here on earth will be denied

11:49 Greek *Therefore, the wisdom of God said.* **12:5** Greek *Gehenna.* **12:6** Greek *two assaria* [Roman coins equal to 1/16 of a denarius]. **12:8** "Son of Man" is a title Jesus used for himself.

KING JAMES VERSION

10 And whosoever shall speak a word against the
Son of man, it shall be forgiven him: but unto him
that blasphemeth against the Holy Ghost it shall not
be forgiven.
11 And when they bring you unto the synagogues,
and *unto* magistrates, and powers, take ye no thought
how or what thing ye shall answer, or what ye shall
say:
12 For the Holy Ghost shall teach you in the same
hour what ye ought to say.
13 And one of the company said unto him, Master,
speak to my brother, that he divide the inheritance
with me.
14 And he said unto him, Man, who made me a
judge or a divider over you?
15 And he said unto them, Take heed, and beware
of covetousness: for a man's life consisteth not in the
abundance of the things which he possesseth.
16 And he spake a parable unto them, saying, The
ground of a certain rich man brought forth plentifully:
17 And he thought within himself, saying, What
shall I do, because I have no room where to bestow
my fruits?
18 And he said, This will I do: I will pull down my
barns, and build greater; and there will I bestow all
my fruits and my goods.
19 And I will say to my soul, Soul, thou hast much
goods laid up for many years; take thine ease, eat,
drink, *and* be merry.
20 But God said unto him, *Thou* fool, this night thy
soul shall be required of thee: then whose shall those
things be, which thou hast provided?
21 So *is* he that layeth up treasure for himself, and is
not rich toward God.
22 And he said unto his disciples, Therefore I say
unto you, Take no thought for your life, what ye shall
eat; neither for the body, what ye shall put on.
23 The life is more than meat, and the body *is more*
than raiment.
24 Consider the ravens: for they neither sow nor
reap; which neither have storehouse nor barn; and
God feedeth them: how much more are ye better
than the fowls?
25 And which of you with taking thought can add
to his stature one cubit?
26 If ye then be not able to do that thing which is
least, why take ye thought for the rest?
27 Consider the lilies how they grow: they toil not,
they spin not; and yet I say unto you, that Solomon in
all his glory was not arrayed like one of these.
28 If then God so clothe the grass, which is today in
the field, and tomorrow is cast into the oven; how
much more *will he clothe* you, O ye of little faith?
29 And seek not ye what ye shall eat, or what ye
shall drink, neither be ye of doubtful mind.
30 For all these things do the nations of the world

NEW LIVING TRANSLATION

before God's angels. 10 Anyone who speaks against
the Son of Man can be forgiven, but anyone who
blasphemes the Holy Spirit will not be forgiven.
11 "And when you are brought to trial in the synagogues and before rulers and authorities, don't
worry about how to defend yourself or what to say,
12 for the Holy Spirit will teach you at that time what
needs to be said."

Parable of the Rich Fool

13 Then someone called from the crowd, "Teacher,
please tell my brother to divide our father's estate
with me."
14 Jesus replied, "Friend, who made me a judge
over you to decide such things as that?" 15 Then he
said, "Beware! Guard against every kind of greed. Life
is not measured by how much you own."
16 Then he told them a story: "A rich man had a fertile farm that produced fine crops. 17 He said to himself, 'What should I do? I don't have room for all my
crops.' 18 Then he said, 'I know! I'll tear down my
barns and build bigger ones. Then I'll have room
enough to store all my wheat and other goods. 19 And
I'll sit back and say to myself, "My friend, you have
enough stored away for years to come. Now take it
easy! Eat, drink, and be merry!"'
20 "But God said to him, 'You fool! You will die this
very night. Then who will get everything you worked
for?'
21 "Yes, a person is a fool to store up earthly wealth
but not have a rich relationship with God."

Teaching about Money and Possessions

22 Then, turning to his disciples, Jesus said, "That is
why I tell you not to worry about everyday life—
whether you have enough food to eat or enough
clothes to wear. 23 For life is more than food, and your
body more than clothing. 24 Look at the ravens. They
don't plant or harvest or store food in barns, for God
feeds them. And you are far more valuable to him
than any birds! 25 Can all your worries add a single
moment to your life? 26 And if worry can't accomplish
a little thing like that, what's the use of worrying over
bigger things?
27 "Look at the lilies and how they grow. They don't
work or make their clothing, yet Solomon in all his
glory was not dressed as beautifully as they are.
28 And if God cares so wonderfully for flowers that
are here today and thrown into the fire tomorrow, he
will certainly care for you. Why do you have so little
faith?
29 "And don't be concerned about what to eat and
what to drink. Don't worry about such things.
30 These things dominate the thoughts of unbelievers

KING JAMES VERSION

seek after: and your Father knoweth that ye have need of these things.

31 But rather seek ye the kingdom of God; and all these things shall be added unto you.

32 Fear not, little flock; for it is your Father's good pleasure to give you the kingdom.

33 Sell that ye have, and give alms; provide yourselves bags which wax not old, a treasure in the heavens that faileth not, where no thief approacheth, neither moth corrupteth.

34 For where your treasure is, there will your heart be also.

35 Let your loins be girded about, and *your* lights burning;

36 And ye yourselves like unto men that wait for their lord, when he will return from the wedding; that when he cometh and knocketh, they may open unto him immediately.

37 Blessed *are* those servants, whom the lord when he cometh shall find watching: verily I say unto you, that he shall gird himself, and make them to sit down to meat, and will come forth and serve them.

38 And if he shall come in the second watch, or come in the third watch, and find *them* so, blessed are those servants.

39 And this know, that if the goodman of the house had known what hour the thief would come, he would have watched, and not have suffered his house to be broken through.

40 Be ye therefore ready also: for the Son of man cometh at an hour when ye think not.

41 Then Peter said unto him, Lord, speakest thou this parable unto us, or even to all?

42 And the Lord said, Who then is that faithful and wise steward, whom *his* lord shall make ruler over his household, to give *them their* portion of meat in due season?

43 Blessed *is* that servant, whom his lord when he cometh shall find so doing.

44 Of a truth I say unto you, that he will make him ruler over all that he hath.

45 But and if that servant say in his heart, My lord delayeth his coming; and shall begin to beat the menservants and maidens, and to eat and drink, and to be drunken;

46 The lord of that servant will come in a day when he looketh not for *him,* and at an hour when he is not aware, and will cut him in sunder, and will appoint him his portion with the unbelievers.

47 And that servant, which knew his lord's will, and prepared not *himself,* neither did according to his will, shall be beaten with many *stripes.*

48 But he that knew not, and did commit things worthy of stripes, shall be beaten with few *stripes.* For unto whomsoever much is given, of him shall be much required: and to whom men have committed much, of him they will ask the more.

NEW LIVING TRANSLATION

all over the world, but your Father already knows
your needs. 31 Seek the Kingdom of God above all
else, and he will give you everything you need.

32 "So don't be afraid, little flock. For it gives your
Father great happiness to give you the Kingdom.

33 "Sell your possessions and give to those in need.
This will store up treasure for you in heaven! And the
purses of heaven never get old or develop holes. Your
treasure will be safe; no thief can steal it and no moth
can destroy it. 34 Wherever your treasure is, there the
desires of your heart will also be.

Be Ready for the Lord's Coming

35 "Be dressed for service and keep your lamps burning, 36 as though you were waiting for your master to
return from the wedding feast. Then you will be
ready to open the door and let him in the moment he
arrives and knocks. 37 The servants who are ready
and waiting for his return will be rewarded. I tell you
the truth, he himself will seat them, put on an apron,
and serve them as they sit and eat! 38 He may come in
the middle of the night or just before dawn.* But
whenever he comes, he will reward the servants who
are ready.

39 "Understand this: If a homeowner knew exactly
when a burglar was coming, he would not permit his
house to be broken into. 40 You also must be ready all
the time, for the Son of Man will come when least
expected."

41 Peter asked, "Lord, is that illustration just for us
or for everyone?"

42 And the Lord replied, "A faithful, sensible servant is one to whom the master can give the responsibility of managing his other household servants
and feeding them. 43 If the master returns and finds
that the servant has done a good job, there will be a
reward. 44 I tell you the truth, the master will put that
servant in charge of all he owns. 45 But what if the
servant thinks, 'My master won't be back for a while,'
and he begins beating the other servants, partying,
and getting drunk? 46 The master will return unannounced and unexpected, and he will cut the servant in pieces and banish him with the unfaithful.

47 "And a servant who knows what the master
wants, but isn't prepared and doesn't carry out those
instructions, will be severely punished. 48 But someone who does not know, and then does something
wrong, will be punished only lightly. When someone
has been given much, much will be required in return; and when someone has been entrusted with
much, even more will be required.

12:38 Greek *in the second or third watch.*

KING JAMES VERSION

49 I am come to send fire on the earth; and what will I, if it be already kindled?

50 But I have a baptism to be baptized with; and how am I straitened till it be accomplished!

51 Suppose ye that I am come to give peace on earth? I tell you, Nay; but rather division:

52 For from henceforth there shall be five in one house divided, three against two, and two against three.

53 The father shall be divided against the son, and the son against the father; the mother against the daughter, and the daughter against the mother; the mother in law against her daughter in law, and the daughter in law against her mother in law.

54 And he said also to the people, When ye see a cloud rise out of the west, straightway ye say, There cometh a shower; and so it is.

55 And when *ye see* the south wind blow, ye say, There will be heat; and it cometh to pass.

56 *Ye* hypocrites, ye can discern the face of the sky and of the earth; but how is it that ye do not discern this time?

57 Yea, and why even of yourselves judge ye not what is right?

58 When thou goest with thine adversary to the magistrate, *as thou art* in the way, give diligence that thou mayest be delivered from him; lest he hale thee to the judge, and the judge deliver thee to the officer, and the officer cast thee into prison.

59 I tell thee, thou shalt not depart thence, till thou hast paid the very last mite.

13 1 There were present at that season some that told him of the Galilaeans, whose blood Pilate had mingled with their sacrifices.

2 And Jesus answering said unto them, Suppose ye that these Galilaeans were sinners above all the Galilaeans, because they suffered such things?

3 I tell you, Nay: but, except ye repent, ye shall all likewise perish.

4 Or those eighteen, upon whom the tower in Siloam fell, and slew them, think ye that they were sinners above all men that dwelt in Jerusalem?

5 I tell you, Nay: but, except ye repent, ye shall all likewise perish.

6 He spake also this parable; A certain *man* had a fig tree planted in his vineyard; and he came and sought fruit thereon, and found none.

7 Then said he unto the dresser of his vineyard, Behold, these three years I come seeking fruit on this fig tree, and find none: cut it down; why cumbereth it the ground?

8 And he answering said unto him, Lord, let it alone this year also, till I shall dig about it, and dung *it:*

9 And if it bear fruit, *well:* and if not, *then* after that thou shalt cut it down.

NEW LIVING TRANSLATION

Jesus Causes Division

49 "I have come to set the world on fire, and I wish it were already burning! 50 I have a terrible baptism of suffering ahead of me, and I am under a heavy burden until it is accomplished. 51 Do you think I have come to bring peace to the earth? No, I have come to divide people against each other! 52 From now on families will be split apart, three in favor of me, and two against—or two in favor and three against.

53 'Father will be divided against son
and son against father;
mother against daughter
and daughter against mother;
and mother-in-law against daughter-in-law
and daughter-in-law against mother-in-law.'*"

54 Then Jesus turned to the crowd and said, "When you see clouds beginning to form in the west, you say, 'Here comes a shower.' And you are right. 55 When the south wind blows, you say, 'Today will be a scorcher.' And it is. 56 You fools! You know how to interpret the weather signs of the earth and sky, but you don't know how to interpret the present times.

57 "Why can't you decide for yourselves what is right? 58 When you are on the way to court with your accuser, try to settle the matter before you get there. Otherwise, your accuser may drag you before the judge, who will hand you over to an officer, who will throw you into prison. 59 And if that happens, you won't be free again until you have paid the very last penny.*"

A Call to Repentance

13 About this time Jesus was informed that Pilate had murdered some people from Galilee as they were offering sacrifices at the Temple. 2 "Do you think those Galileans were worse sinners than all the other people from Galilee?" Jesus asked. "Is that why they suffered? 3 Not at all! And you will perish, too, unless you repent of your sins and turn to God. 4 And what about the eighteen people who died when the tower in Siloam fell on them? Were they the worst sinners in Jerusalem? 5 No, and I tell you again that unless you repent, you will perish, too."

Parable of the Barren Fig Tree

6 Then Jesus told this story: "A man planted a fig tree in his garden and came again and again to see if there was any fruit on it, but he was always disappointed. 7 Finally, he said to his gardener, 'I've waited three years, and there hasn't been a single fig! Cut it down. It's just taking up space in the garden.'

8 "The gardener answered, 'Sir, give it one more chance. Leave it another year, and I'll give it special attention and plenty of fertilizer. 9 If we get figs next year, fine. If not, then you can cut it down.'"

12:53 Mic 7:6. **12:59** Greek *last lepton* [the smallest Jewish coin].

10And he was teaching in one of the synagogues
on the sabbath.
11And, behold, there was a woman which had a
spirit of infirmity eighteen years, and was bowed
together, and could in no wise lift up *herself*.
12And when Jesus saw her, he called *her to him*,
and said unto her, Woman, thou art loosed from
thine infirmity.
13And he laid *his* hands on her: and immediately
she was made straight, and glorified God.
14And the ruler of the synagogue answered with
indignation, because that Jesus had healed on the
sabbath day, and said unto the people, There are six
days in which men ought to work: in them therefore
come and be healed, and not on the sabbath day.
15The Lord then answered him, and said, *Thou*
hypocrite, doth not each one of you on the sabbath
loose his ox or *his* ass from the stall, and lead *him*
away to watering?
16And ought not this woman, being a daughter of
Abraham, whom Satan hath bound, lo, these eighteen years, be loosed from this bond on the sabbath
day?
17And when he had said these things, all his adversaries were ashamed: and all the people rejoiced for
all the glorious things that were done by him.
18Then said he, Unto what is the kingdom of God
like? and whereunto shall I resemble it?
19It is like a grain of mustard seed, which a man
took, and cast into his garden; and it grew, and waxed
a great tree; and the fowls of the air lodged in the
branches of it.
20And again he said, Whereunto shall I liken the
kingdom of God?
21It is like leaven, which a woman took and hid in
three measures of meal, till the whole was leavened.

22And he went through the cities and villages,
teaching, and journeying toward Jerusalem.
23Then said one unto him, Lord, are there few that
be saved? And he said unto them,
24Strive to enter in at the strait gate: for many, I say
unto you, will seek to enter in, and shall not be able.
25When once the master of the house is risen up,
and hath shut to the door, and ye begin to stand without, and to knock at the door, saying, Lord, Lord,
open unto us; and he shall answer and say unto you, I
know you not whence ye are:
26Then shall ye begin to say, We have eaten and
drunk in thy presence, and thou hast taught in our
streets.
27But he shall say, I tell you, I know you not whence
ye are; depart from me, all ye workers of iniquity.
28There shall be weeping and gnashing of teeth,
when ye shall see Abraham, and Isaac, and Jacob, and

Jesus Heals on the Sabbath

10One Sabbath day as Jesus was teaching in a synagogue, 11he saw a woman who had been crippled by
an evil spirit. She had been bent double for eighteen
years and was unable to stand up straight. 12When
Jesus saw her, he called her over and said, "Dear
woman, you are healed of your sickness!" 13Then he
touched her, and instantly she could stand straight.
How she praised God!
14But the leader in charge of the synagogue was
indignant that Jesus had healed her on the Sabbath
day. "There are six days of the week for working," he
said to the crowd. "Come on those days to be healed,
not on the Sabbath."
15But the Lord replied, "You hypocrites! Each of
you works on the Sabbath day! Don't you untie your
ox or your donkey from its stall on the Sabbath and
lead it out for water? 16This dear woman, a daughter
of Abraham, has been held in bondage by Satan for
eighteen years. Isn't it right that she be released,
even on the Sabbath?"
17This shamed his enemies, but all the people
rejoiced at the wonderful things he did.

Parable of the Mustard Seed

18Then Jesus said, "What is the Kingdom of God like?
How can I illustrate it? 19It is like a tiny mustard seed
that a man planted in a garden; it grows and becomes
a tree, and the birds make nests in its branches."

Parable of the Yeast

20He also asked, "What else is the Kingdom of God
like? 21It is like the yeast a woman used in making
bread. Even though she put only a little yeast in three
measures of flour, it permeated every part of the
dough."

The Narrow Door

22Jesus went through the towns and villages, teaching as he went, always pressing on toward Jerusalem.
23Someone asked him, "Lord, will only a few be
saved?"
He replied, 24"Work hard to enter the narrow door
to God's Kingdom, for many will try to enter but will
fail. 25When the master of the house has locked the
door, it will be too late. You will stand outside knocking and pleading, 'Lord, open the door for us!' But he
will reply, 'I don't know you or where you come from.'
26Then you will say, 'But we ate and drank with you,
and you taught in our streets.' 27And he will reply, 'I
tell you, I don't know you or where you come from.
Get away from me, all you who do evil.'
28"There will be weeping and gnashing of teeth,
for you will see Abraham, Isaac, Jacob, and all the

KING JAMES VERSION

all the prophets, in the kingdom of God, and you *yourselves* thrust out.

29 And they shall come from the east, and *from* the west, and from the north, and *from* the south, and shall sit down in the kingdom of God.

30 And, behold, there are last which shall be first, and there are first which shall be last.

31 The same day there came certain of the Pharisees, saying unto him, Get thee out, and depart hence: for Herod will kill thee.

32 And he said unto them, Go ye, and tell that fox, Behold, I cast out devils, and I do cures today and tomorrow, and the third *day* I shall be perfected.

33 Nevertheless I must walk today, and tomorrow, and the *day* following: for it cannot be that a prophet perish out of Jerusalem.

34 O Jerusalem, Jerusalem, which killest the prophets, and stonest them that are sent unto thee; how often would I have gathered thy children together, as a hen *doth gather* her brood under *her* wings, and ye would not!

35 Behold, your house is left unto you desolate: and verily I say unto you, Ye shall not see me, until *the time* come when ye shall say, Blessed *is* he that cometh in the name of the Lord.

14 1 And it came to pass, as he went into the house of one of the chief Pharisees to eat bread on the sabbath day, that they watched him.

2 And, behold, there was a certain man before him which had the dropsy.

3 And Jesus answering spake unto the lawyers and Pharisees, saying, Is it lawful to heal on the sabbath day?

4 And they held their peace. And he took *him,* and healed him, and let him go;

5 And answered them, saying, Which of you shall have an ass or an ox fallen into a pit, and will not straightway pull him out on the sabbath day?

6 And they could not answer him again to these things.

7 And he put forth a parable to those which were bidden, when he marked how they chose out the chief rooms; saying unto them,

8 When thou art bidden of any *man* to a wedding, sit not down in the highest room; lest a more honourable man than thou be bidden of him;

9 And he that bade thee and him come and say to thee, Give this man place; and thou begin with shame to take the lowest room.

10 But when thou art bidden, go and sit down in the lowest room; that when he that bade thee cometh, he may say unto thee, Friend, go up higher: then shalt thou have worship in the presence of them that sit at meat with thee.

NEW LIVING TRANSLATION

prophets in the Kingdom of God, but you will be thrown out. 29 And people will come from all over the world—from east and west, north and south—to take their places in the Kingdom of God. 30 And note this: Some who seem least important now will be the greatest then, and some who are the greatest now will be least important then.*"

Jesus Grieves over Jerusalem

31 At that time some Pharisees said to him, "Get away from here if you want to live! Herod Antipas wants to kill you!"

32 Jesus replied, "Go tell that fox that I will keep on casting out demons and healing people today and tomorrow; and the third day I will accomplish my purpose. 33 Yes, today, tomorrow, and the next day I must proceed on my way. For it wouldn't do for a prophet of God to be killed except in Jerusalem!

34 "O Jerusalem, Jerusalem, the city that kills the prophets and stones God's messengers! How often I have wanted to gather your children together as a hen protects her chicks beneath her wings, but you wouldn't let me. 35 And now, look, your house is abandoned. And you will never see me again until you say, 'Blessings on the one who comes in the name of the LORD!'*"

Jesus Heals on the Sabbath

14 One Sabbath day Jesus went to eat dinner in the home of a leader of the Pharisees, and the people were watching him closely. 2 There was a man there whose arms and legs were swollen.* 3 Jesus asked the Pharisees and experts in religious law, "Is it permitted in the law to heal people on the Sabbath day, or not?" 4 When they refused to answer, Jesus touched the sick man and healed him and sent him away. 5 Then he turned to them and said, "Which of you doesn't work on the Sabbath? If your son* or your cow falls into a pit, don't you rush to get him out?" 6 Again they could not answer.

Jesus Teaches about Humility

7 When Jesus noticed that all who had come to the dinner were trying to sit in the seats of honor near the head of the table, he gave them this advice: 8 "When you are invited to a wedding feast, don't sit in the seat of honor. What if someone who is more distinguished than you has also been invited? 9 The host will come and say, 'Give this person your seat.' Then you will be embarrassed, and you will have to take whatever seat is left at the foot of the table!

10 "Instead, take the lowest place at the foot of the table. Then when your host sees you, he will come and say, 'Friend, we have a better place for you!' Then you will be honored in front of all the other guests.

13:30 Greek *Some are last who will be first, and some are first who will be last.* **13:35** Ps 118:26. **14:2** Or *who had dropsy.* **14:5** Some manuscripts read *donkey.*

KING JAMES VERSION

11 For whosoever exalteth himself shall be abased; and he that humbleth himself shall be exalted.

12 Then said he also to him that bade him, When thou makest a dinner or a supper, call not thy friends, nor thy brethren, neither thy kinsmen, nor *thy* rich neighbours; lest they also bid thee again, and a recompense be made thee.

13 But when thou makest a feast, call the poor, the maimed, the lame, the blind:

14 And thou shalt be blessed; for they cannot recompence thee: for thou shalt be recompensed at the resurrection of the just.

15 And when one of them that sat at meat with him heard these things, he said unto him, Blessed *is* he that shall eat bread in the kingdom of God.

16 Then said he unto him, A certain man made a great supper, and bade many:

17 And sent his servant at supper time to say to them that were bidden, Come; for all things are now ready.

18 And they all with one *consent* began to make excuse. The first said unto him, I have bought a piece of ground, and I must needs go and see it: I pray thee have me excused.

19 And another said, I have bought five yoke of oxen, and I go to prove them: I pray thee have me excused.

20 And another said, I have married a wife, and therefore I cannot come.

21 So that servant came, and shewed his lord these things. Then the master of the house being angry said to his servant, Go out quickly into the streets and lanes of the city, and bring in hither the poor, and the maimed, and the halt, and the blind.

22 And the servant said, Lord, it is done as thou hast commanded, and yet there is room.

23 And the lord said unto the servant, Go out into the highways and hedges, and compel *them* to come in, that my house may be filled.

24 For I say unto you, That none of those men which were bidden shall taste of my supper.

25 And there went great multitudes with him: and he turned, and said unto them,

26 If any *man* come to me, and hate not his father, and mother, and wife, and children, and brethren, and sisters, yea, and his own life also, he cannot be my disciple.

27 And whosoever doth not bear his cross, and come after me, cannot be my disciple.

28 For which of you, intending to build a tower, sitteth not down first, and counteth the cost, whether he have *sufficient* to finish *it?*

29 Lest haply, after he hath laid the foundation, and is not able to finish *it,* all that behold *it* begin to mock him,

30 Saying, This man began to build, and was not able to finish.

31 Or what king, going to make war against another king, sitteth not down first, and consulteth whether

NEW LIVING TRANSLATION

11 For those who exalt themselves will be humbled,
and those who humble themselves will be exalted."

12 Then he turned to his host. "When you put on a
luncheon or a banquet," he said, "don't invite your
friends, brothers, relatives, and rich neighbors. For
they will invite you back, and that will be your only
reward. 13 Instead, invite the poor, the crippled, the
lame, and the blind. 14 Then at the resurrection of the
righteous, God will reward you for inviting those
who could not repay you."

Parable of the Great Feast

15 Hearing this, a man sitting at the table with Jesus
exclaimed, "What a blessing it will be to attend a
banquet* in the Kingdom of God!"

16 Jesus replied with this story: "A man prepared a
great feast and sent out many invitations. 17 When
the banquet was ready, he sent his servant to tell the
guests, 'Come, the banquet is ready.' 18 But they all
began making excuses. One said, 'I have just bought
a field and must inspect it. Please excuse me.' 19 Another said, 'I have just bought five pairs of oxen, and I
want to try them out. Please excuse me.' 20 Another
said, 'I now have a wife, so I can't come.'

21 "The servant returned and told his master what
they had said. His master was furious and said, 'Go
quickly into the streets and alleys of the town and invite the poor, the crippled, the blind, and the lame.'
22 After the servant had done this, he reported, 'There
is still room for more.' 23 So his master said, 'Go out
into the country lanes and behind the hedges and
urge anyone you find to come, so that the house will
be full. 24 For none of those I first invited will get even
the smallest taste of my banquet.'"

The Cost of Being a Disciple

25 A large crowd was following Jesus. He turned
around and said to them, 26 "If you want to be my disciple, you must hate everyone else by comparison—
your father and mother, wife and children, brothers
and sisters—yes, even your own life. Otherwise, you
cannot be my disciple. 27 And if you do not carry your
own cross and follow me, you cannot be my disciple.

28 "But don't begin until you count the cost. For
who would begin construction of a building without
first calculating the cost to see if there is enough
money to finish it? 29 Otherwise, you might complete
only the foundation before running out of money,
and then everyone would laugh at you. 30 They would
say, 'There's the person who started that building
and couldn't afford to finish it!'

31 "Or what king would go to war against another
king without first sitting down with his counselors to

14:15 Greek *to eat bread.*

KING JAMES VERSION

he be able with ten thousand to meet him that cometh against him with twenty thousand?
32 Or else, while the other is yet a great way off, he
sendeth an ambassage, and desireth conditions of
peace.
33 So likewise, whosoever he be of you that
forsaketh not all that he hath, he cannot be my
disciple.
34 Salt *is* good: but if the salt have lost his savour,
wherewith shall it be seasoned?
35 It is neither fit for the land, nor yet for the dunghill; *but* men cast it out. He that hath ears to hear, let
him hear.

15 1 Then drew near unto him all the publicans
and sinners for to hear him.
2 And the Pharisees and scribes murmured, saying,
This man receiveth sinners, and eateth with them.
3 And he spake this parable unto them, saying,
4 What man of you, having an hundred sheep, if he
lose one of them, doth not leave the ninety and nine
in the wilderness, and go after that which is lost, until he find it?
5 And when he hath found *it*, he layeth *it* on his
shoulders, rejoicing.
6 And when he cometh home, he calleth together
his friends and neighbours, saying unto them,
Rejoice with me; for I have found my sheep which
was lost.
7 I say unto you, that likewise joy shall be in heaven
over one sinner that repenteth, more than over ninety
and nine just persons, which need no repentance.

8 Either what woman having ten pieces of silver, if
she lose one piece, doth not light a candle, and sweep
the house, and seek diligently till she find *it?*
9 And when she hath found *it*, she calleth *her*
friends and *her* neighbours together, saying, Rejoice
with me; for I have found the piece which I had lost.
10 Likewise, I say unto you, there is joy in the presence of the angels of God over one sinner that
repenteth.

11 And he said, A certain man had two sons:
12 And the younger of them said to *his* father,
Father, give me the portion of goods that falleth *to*
me. And he divided unto them *his* living.
13 And not many days after the younger son gathered all together, and took his journey into a far country, and there wasted his substance with riotous living.
14 And when he had spent all, there arose a mighty
famine in that land; and he began to be in want.
15 And he went and joined himself to a citizen of
that country; and he sent him into his fields to feed
swine.
16 And he would fain have filled his belly with the
husks that the swine did eat: and no man gave unto
him.

NEW LIVING TRANSLATION

discuss whether his army of 10,000 could defeat the
20,000 soldiers marching against him? 32 And if he
can't, he will send a delegation to discuss terms of
peace while the enemy is still far away. 33 So you cannot become my disciple without giving up everything you own.
34 "Salt is good for seasoning. But if it loses its flavor, how do you make it salty again? 35 Flavorless salt
is good neither for the soil nor for the manure pile.
It is thrown away. Anyone with ears to hear should
listen and understand!"

Parable of the Lost Sheep

15 Tax collectors and other notorious sinners
often came to listen to Jesus teach. 2 This
made the Pharisees and teachers of religious law
complain that he was associating with such sinful
people—even eating with them!
3 So Jesus told them this story: 4 "If a man has a
hundred sheep and one of them gets lost, what will
he do? Won't he leave the ninety-nine others in the
wilderness and go to search for the one that is lost
until he finds it? 5 And when he has found it, he will
joyfully carry it home on his shoulders. 6 When he arrives, he will call together his friends and neighbors,
saying, 'Rejoice with me because I have found my
lost sheep.' 7 In the same way, there is more joy in
heaven over one lost sinner who repents and returns
to God than over ninety-nine others who are righteous and haven't strayed away!

Parable of the Lost Coin

8 "Or suppose a woman has ten silver coins* and
loses one. Won't she light a lamp and sweep the
entire house and search carefully until she finds it?
9 And when she finds it, she will call in her friends
and neighbors and say, 'Rejoice with me because I
have found my lost coin.' 10 In the same way, there is
joy in the presence of God's angels when even one
sinner repents."

Parable of the Lost Son

11 To illustrate the point further, Jesus told them this
story: "A man had two sons. 12 The younger son told
his father, 'I want my share of your estate now before
you die.' So his father agreed to divide his wealth
between his sons.
13 "A few days later this younger son packed all his
belongings and moved to a distant land, and there he
wasted all his money in wild living. 14 About the time
his money ran out, a great famine swept over the
land, and he began to starve. 15 He persuaded a local
farmer to hire him, and the man sent him into his
fields to feed the pigs. 16 The young man became so
hungry that even the pods he was feeding the pigs
looked good to him. But no one gave him anything.

15:8 Greek *ten drachmas*. A drachma was the equivalent of a full day's wage.

KING JAMES VERSION

17And when he came to himself, he said, How many hired servants of my father's have bread enough and to spare, and I perish with hunger!

18I will arise and go to my father, and will say unto him, Father, I have sinned against heaven, and before thee,

19And am no more worthy to be called thy son: make me as one of thy hired servants.

20And he arose, and came to his father. But when he was yet a great way off, his father saw him, and had compassion, and ran, and fell on his neck, and kissed him.

21And the son said unto him, Father, I have sinned against heaven, and in thy sight, and am no more worthy to be called thy son.

22But the father said to his servants, Bring forth the best robe, and put *it* on him; and put a ring on his hand, and shoes on *his* feet:

23And bring hither the fatted calf, and kill *it;* and let us eat, and be merry:

24For this my son was dead, and is alive again; he was lost, and is found. And they began to be merry.

25Now his elder son was in the field: and as he came and drew nigh to the house, he heard musick and dancing.

26And he called one of the servants, and asked what these things meant.

27And he said unto him, Thy brother is come; and thy father hath killed the fatted calf, because he hath received him safe and sound.

28And he was angry, and would not go in: therefore came his father out, and intreated him.

29And he answering said to *his* father, Lo, these many years do I serve thee, neither transgressed I at any time thy commandment: and yet thou never gavest me a kid, that I might make merry with my friends:

30But as soon as this thy son was come, which hath devoured thy living with harlots, thou hast killed for him the fatted calf.

31And he said unto him, Son, thou art ever with me, and all that I have is thine.

32It was meet that we should make merry, and be glad: for this thy brother was dead, and is alive again; and was lost, and is found.

16 1And he said also unto his disciples, There was a certain rich man, which had a steward; and the same was accused unto him that he had wasted his goods.

2And he called him, and said unto him, How is it that I hear this of thee? give an account of thy stewardship; for thou mayest be no longer steward.

3Then the steward said within himself, What shall I do? for my lord taketh away from me the stewardship: I cannot dig; to beg I am ashamed.

4I am resolved what to do, that, when I am put out

NEW LIVING TRANSLATION

17"When he finally came to his senses, he said to
himself, 'At home even the hired servants have food
enough to spare, and here I am dying of hunger! 18I
will go home to my father and say, "Father, I have
sinned against both heaven and you, 19and I am no
longer worthy of being called your son. Please take
me on as a hired servant."'

20"So he returned home to his father. And while
he was still a long way off, his father saw him coming. Filled with love and compassion, he ran to his
son, embraced him, and kissed him. 21His son said
to him, 'Father, I have sinned against both heaven
and you, and I am no longer worthy of being called
your son.*'

22"But his father said to the servants, 'Quick! Bring
the finest robe in the house and put it on him. Get a
ring for his finger and sandals for his feet. 23And kill
the calf we have been fattening. We must celebrate
with a feast, 24for this son of mine was dead and
has now returned to life. He was lost, but now he is
found.' So the party began.

25"Meanwhile, the older son was in the fields
working. When he returned home, he heard music
and dancing in the house, 26and he asked one of the
servants what was going on. 27'Your brother is back,'
he was told, 'and your father has killed the fattened
calf. We are celebrating because of his safe return.'

28"The older brother was angry and wouldn't go
in. His father came out and begged him, 29but he replied, 'All these years I've slaved for you and never
once refused to do a single thing you told me to. And
in all that time you never gave me even one young
goat for a feast with my friends. 30Yet when this son
of yours comes back after squandering your money
on prostitutes, you celebrate by killing the fattened
calf!'

31"His father said to him, 'Look, dear son, you have
always stayed by me, and everything I have is yours.
32We had to celebrate this happy day. For your
brother was dead and has come back to life! He was
lost, but now he is found!'"

Parable of the Shrewd Manager

16 Jesus told this story to his disciples: "There
was a certain rich man who had a manager
handling his affairs. One day a report came that the
manager was wasting his employer's money. 2So the
employer called him in and said, 'What's this I hear
about you? Get your report in order, because you are
going to be fired.'

3"The manager thought to himself, 'Now what?
My boss has fired me. I don't have the strength to dig
ditches, and I'm too proud to beg. 4Ah, I know how to

15:21 Some manuscripts add *Please take me on as a hired servant.*

KING JAMES VERSION

of the stewardship, they may receive me into their houses.

5 So he called every one of his lord's debtors *unto him,* and said unto the first, How much owest thou unto my lord?

6 And he said, An hundred measures of oil. And he said unto him, Take thy bill, and sit down quickly, and write fifty.

7 Then said he to another, And how much owest thou? And he said, An hundred measures of wheat. And he said unto him, Take thy bill, and write fourscore.

8 And the lord commended the unjust steward, because he had done wisely: for the children of this world are in their generation wiser than the children of light.

9 And I say unto you, Make to yourselves friends of the mammon of unrighteousness; that, when ye fail, they may receive you into everlasting habitations.

10 He that is faithful in that which is least is faithful also in much: and he that is unjust in the least is unjust also in much.

11 If therefore ye have not been faithful in the unrighteous mammon, who will commit to your trust the true *riches?*

12 And if ye have not been faithful in that which is another man's, who shall give you that which is your own?

13 No servant can serve two masters: for either he will hate the one, and love the other; or else he will hold to the one, and despise the other. Ye cannot serve God and mammon.

14 And the Pharisees also, who were covetous, heard all these things: and they derided him.

15 And he said unto them, Ye are they which justify yourselves before men; but God knoweth your hearts: for that which is highly esteemed among men is abomination in the sight of God.

16 The law and the prophets *were* until John: since that time the kingdom of God is preached, and every man presseth into it.

17 And it is easier for heaven and earth to pass, than one tittle of the law to fail.

18 Whosoever putteth away his wife, and marrieth another, committeth adultery: and whosoever marrieth her that is put away from *her* husband committeth adultery.

19 There was a certain rich man, which was clothed in purple and fine linen, and fared sumptuously every day:

20 And there was a certain beggar named Lazarus, which was laid at his gate, full of sores,

21 And desiring to be fed with the crumbs which fell from the rich man's table: moreover the dogs came and licked his sores.

NEW LIVING TRANSLATION

ensure that I'll have plenty of friends who will give me a home when I am fired.'

5 "So he invited each person who owed money to his employer to come and discuss the situation. He asked the first one, 'How much do you owe him?' 6 The man replied, 'I owe him 800 gallons of olive oil.' So the manager told him, 'Take the bill and quickly change it to 400 gallons.*'

7 " 'And how much do you owe my employer?' he asked the next man. 'I owe him 1,000 bushels of wheat,' was the reply. 'Here,' the manager said, 'take the bill and change it to 800 bushels.*'

8 "The rich man had to admire the dishonest rascal for being so shrewd. And it is true that the children of this world are more shrewd in dealing with the world around them than are the children of the light. 9 Here's the lesson: Use your worldly resources to benefit others and make friends. Then, when your earthly possessions are gone, they will welcome you to an eternal home.*

10 "If you are faithful in little things, you will be faithful in large ones. But if you are dishonest in little things, you won't be honest with greater responsibilities. 11 And if you are untrustworthy about worldly wealth, who will trust you with the true riches of heaven? 12 And if you are not faithful with other people's things, why should you be trusted with things of your own?

13 "No one can serve two masters. For you will hate one and love the other; you will be devoted to one and despise the other. You cannot serve both God and money."

14 The Pharisees, who dearly loved their money, heard all this and scoffed at him. 15 Then he said to them, "You like to appear righteous in public, but God knows your hearts. What this world honors is detestable in the sight of God.

16 "Until John the Baptist, the law of Moses and the messages of the prophets were your guides. But now the Good News of the Kingdom of God is preached, and everyone is eager to get in.* 17 But that doesn't mean that the law has lost its force. It is easier for heaven and earth to disappear than for the smallest point of God's law to be overturned.

18 "For example, a man who divorces his wife and marries someone else commits adultery. And anyone who marries a woman divorced from her husband commits adultery."

Parable of the Rich Man and Lazarus

19 Jesus said, "There was a certain rich man who was splendidly clothed in purple and fine linen and who lived each day in luxury. 20 At his gate lay a poor man named Lazarus who was covered with sores. 21 As Lazarus lay there longing for scraps from the rich man's table, the dogs would come and lick his open sores.

16:6 Greek *100 baths . . . 50 [baths].* **16:7** Greek *100 korous . . . 80 [korous].* **16:9** Or *you will be welcomed into eternal homes.* **16:16** Or *everyone is urged to enter in.*

KING JAMES VERSION

22And it came to pass, that the beggar died, and
was carried by the angels into Abraham's bosom: the
rich man also died, and was buried;
23And in hell he lift up his eyes, being in torments,
and seeth Abraham afar off, and Lazarus in his
bosom.
24And he cried and said, Father Abraham, have
mercy on me, and send Lazarus, that he may dip the
tip of his finger in water, and cool my tongue; for I
am tormented in this flame.
25But Abraham said, Son, remember that thou in
thy lifetime receivedst thy good things, and likewise
Lazarus evil things: but now he is comforted, and
thou art tormented.
26And beside all this, between us and you there is a
great gulf fixed: so that they which would pass from
hence to you cannot; neither can they pass to us, that
would come from thence.
27Then he said, I pray thee therefore, father, that
thou wouldest send him to my father's house:
28For I have five brethren; that he may testify unto
them, lest they also come into this place of torment.
29Abraham saith unto him, They have Moses and
the prophets; let them hear them.
30And he said, Nay, father Abraham: but if one
went unto them from the dead, they will repent.
31And he said unto him, If they hear not Moses
and the prophets, neither will they be persuaded,
though one rose from the dead.

17 1Then said he unto the disciples, It is impossible but that offences will come: but woe
unto him, through whom they come!
2It were better for him that a millstone were
hanged about his neck, and he cast into the sea, than
that he should offend one of these little ones.
3Take heed to yourselves: If thy brother trespass
against thee, rebuke him; and if he repent, forgive
him.
4And if he trespass against thee seven times in a
day, and seven times in a day turn again to thee, saying, I repent; thou shalt forgive him.
5And the apostles said unto the Lord, Increase our
faith.
6And the Lord said, If ye had faith as a grain of
mustard seed, ye might say unto this sycamine tree,
Be thou plucked up by the root, and be thou planted
in the sea; and it should obey you.
7But which of you, having a servant ploughing or
feeding cattle, will say unto him by and by, when he is
come from the field, Go and sit down to meat?
8And will not rather say unto him, Make ready
wherewith I may sup, and gird thyself, and serve me,
till I have eaten and drunken; and afterward thou
shalt eat and drink?
9Doth he thank that servant because he did the
things that were commanded him? I trow not.

NEW LIVING TRANSLATION

22"Finally, the poor man died and was carried by
the angels to be with Abraham.* The rich man also
died and was buried, 23and his soul went to the place
of the dead.* There, in torment, he saw Abraham in
the far distance with Lazarus at his side.
24"The rich man shouted, 'Father Abraham, have
some pity! Send Lazarus over here to dip the tip of
his finger in water and cool my tongue. I am in anguish in these flames.'
25"But Abraham said to him, 'Son, remember that
during your lifetime you had everything you wanted,
and Lazarus had nothing. So now he is here being
comforted, and you are in anguish. 26And besides,
there is a great chasm separating us. No one can
cross over to you from here, and no one can cross
over to us from there.'
27"Then the rich man said, 'Please, Father Abraham, at least send him to my father's home. 28For I
have five brothers, and I want him to warn them so
they don't end up in this place of torment.'
29"But Abraham said, 'Moses and the prophets
have warned them. Your brothers can read what they
wrote.'
30"The rich man replied, 'No, Father Abraham! But
if someone is sent to them from the dead, then they
will repent of their sins and turn to God.'
31"But Abraham said, 'If they won't listen to Moses
and the prophets, they won't listen even if someone
rises from the dead.'"

Teachings about Forgiveness and Faith

17 One day Jesus said to his disciples, "There
will always be temptations to sin, but what
sorrow awaits the person who does the tempting! 2It
would be better to be thrown into the sea with a millstone hung around your neck than to cause one of
these little ones to fall into sin. 3So watch yourselves!
"If another believer* sins, rebuke that person;
then if there is repentance, forgive. 4Even if that person wrongs you seven times a day and each time
turns again and asks forgiveness, you must forgive."
5The apostles said to the Lord, "Show us how to increase our faith."
6The Lord answered, "If you had faith even as
small as a mustard seed, you could say to this mulberry tree, 'May you be uprooted and thrown into the
sea,' and it would obey you!
7"When a servant comes in from plowing or taking care of sheep, does his master say, 'Come in and
eat with me'? 8No, he says, 'Prepare my meal, put on
your apron, and serve me while I eat. Then you can
eat later.' 9And does the master thank the servant for

16:22 Greek *into Abraham's bosom.* **16:23** Greek *to Hades.* **17:3** Greek *If your brother.*

KING JAMES VERSION

10So likewise ye, when ye shall have done all those things which are commanded you, say, We are unprofitable servants: we have done that which was our duty to do.

11And it came to pass, as he went to Jerusalem, that he passed through the midst of Samaria and Galilee.

12And as he entered into a certain village, there met him ten men that were lepers, which stood afar off:

13And they lifted up *their* voices, and said, Jesus, Master, have mercy on us.

14And when he saw *them,* he said unto them, Go shew yourselves unto the priests. And it came to pass, that, as they went, they were cleansed.

15And one of them, when he saw that he was healed, turned back, and with a loud voice glorified God,

16And fell down on *his* face at his feet, giving him thanks: and he was a Samaritan.

17And Jesus answering said, Were there not ten cleansed? but where *are* the nine?

18There are not found that returned to give glory to God, save this stranger.

19And he said unto him, Arise, go thy way: thy faith hath made thee whole.

20And when he was demanded of the Pharisees, when the kingdom of God should come, he answered them and said, The kingdom of God cometh not with observation:

21Neither shall they say, Lo here! or, lo there! for, behold, the kingdom of God is within you.

22And he said unto the disciples, The days will come, when ye shall desire to see one of the days of the Son of man, and ye shall not see *it.*

23And they shall say to you, See here; or, see there: go not after *them,* nor follow *them.*

24For as the lightning, that lighteneth out of the one *part* under heaven, shineth unto the other *part* under heaven; so shall also the Son of man be in his day.

25But first must he suffer many things, and be rejected of this generation.

26And as it was in the days of Noe, so shall it be also in the days of the Son of man.

27They did eat, they drank, they married wives, they were given in marriage, until the day that Noe entered into the ark, and the flood came, and destroyed them all.

28Likewise also as it was in the days of Lot; they did eat, they drank, they bought, they sold, they planted, they builded;

29But the same day that Lot went out of Sodom it rained fire and brimstone from heaven, and destroyed *them* all.

30Even thus shall it be in the day when the Son of man is revealed.

31In that day, he which shall be upon the housetop, and his stuff in the house, let him not come down to

NEW LIVING TRANSLATION

doing what he was told to do? Of course not. 10In the same way, when you obey me you should say, 'We are unworthy servants who have simply done our duty.'"

Ten Healed of Leprosy

11As Jesus continued on toward Jerusalem, he reached the border between Galilee and Samaria. 12As he entered a village there, ten lepers stood at a distance, 13crying out, "Jesus, Master, have mercy on us!"

14He looked at them and said, "Go show yourselves to the priests."* And as they went, they were cleansed of their leprosy.

15One of them, when he saw that he was healed, came back to Jesus, shouting, "Praise God!" 16He fell to the ground at Jesus' feet, thanking him for what he had done. This man was a Samaritan.

17Jesus asked, "Didn't I heal ten men? Where are the other nine? 18Has no one returned to give glory to God except this foreigner?" 19And Jesus said to the man, "Stand up and go. Your faith has healed you.*"

The Coming of the Kingdom

20One day the Pharisees asked Jesus, "When will the Kingdom of God come?"

Jesus replied, "The Kingdom of God can't be detected by visible signs.* 21You won't be able to say, 'Here it is!' or 'It's over there!' For the Kingdom of God is already among you.*"

22Then he said to his disciples, "The time is coming when you will long to see the day when the Son of Man returns,* but you won't see it. 23People will tell you, 'Look, there is the Son of Man,' or 'Here he is,' but don't go out and follow them. 24For as the lightning flashes and lights up the sky from one end to the other, so it will be on the day when the Son of Man comes. 25But first the Son of Man must suffer terribly* and be rejected by this generation.

26"When the Son of Man returns, it will be like it was in Noah's day. 27In those days, the people enjoyed banquets and parties and weddings right up to the time Noah entered his boat and the flood came and destroyed them all.

28"And the world will be as it was in the days of Lot. People went about their daily business—eating and drinking, buying and selling, farming and building—29until the morning Lot left Sodom. Then fire and burning sulfur rained down from heaven and destroyed them all. 30Yes, it will be 'business as usual' right up to the day when the Son of Man is revealed. 31On that day a person out on the deck of a roof must

17:14 See Lev 14:2-32. **17:19** Or *Your faith has saved you.* **17:20** Or *by your speculations.* **17:21** Or *is within you,* or *is in your grasp.* **17:22** Or *long for even one day with the Son of Man.* "Son of Man" is a title Jesus used for himself. **17:25** Or *suffer many things.*

KING JAMES VERSION

take it away: and he that is in the field, let him likewise not return back.

32 Remember Lot's wife.

33 Whosoever shall seek to save his life shall lose it; and whosoever shall lose his life shall preserve it.

34 I tell you, in that night there shall be two *men* in one bed; the one shall be taken, and the other shall be left.

35 Two *women* shall be grinding together; the one shall be taken, and the other left.

36 Two *men* shall be in the field; the one shall be taken, and the other left.

37 And they answered and said unto him, Where, Lord? And he said unto them, Wheresoever the body *is,* thither will the eagles be gathered together.

18 1 And he spake a parable unto them *to this end,* that men ought always to pray, and not to faint;

2 Saying, There was in a city a judge, which feared not God, neither regarded man:

3 And there was a widow in that city; and she came unto him, saying, Avenge me of mine adversary.

4 And he would not for a while: but afterward he said within himself, Though I fear not God, nor regard man;

5 Yet because this widow troubleth me, I will avenge her, lest by her continual coming she weary me.

6 And the Lord said, Hear what the unjust judge saith.

7 And shall not God avenge his own elect, which cry day and night unto him, though he bear long with them?

8 I tell you that he will avenge them speedily. Nevertheless when the Son of man cometh, shall he find faith on the earth?

9 And he spake this parable unto certain which trusted in themselves that they were righteous, and despised others:

10 Two men went up into the temple to pray; the one a Pharisee, and the other a publican.

11 The Pharisee stood and prayed thus with himself, God, I thank thee, that I am not as other men *are,* extortioners, unjust, adulterers, or even as this publican.

12 I fast twice in the week, I give tithes of all that I possess.

13 And the publican, standing afar off, would not lift up so much as *his* eyes unto heaven, but smote upon his breast, saying, God be merciful to me a sinner.

14 I tell you, this man went down to his house justified *rather* than the other: for every one that exalteth himself shall be abased; and he that humbleth himself shall be exalted.

NEW LIVING TRANSLATION

not go down into the house to pack. A person out in
the field must not return home. 32 Remember what
happened to Lot's wife! 33 If you cling to your life, you
will lose it, and if you let your life go, you will save it.
34 That night two people will be asleep in one bed;
one will be taken, the other left. 35 Two women will
be grinding flour together at the mill; one will be
taken, the other left.*

37 "Where will this happen, Lord?"* the disciples asked.

Jesus replied, "Just as the gathering of vultures shows there is a carcass nearby, so these signs indicate that the end is near."*

Parable of the Persistent Widow

18 One day Jesus told his disciples a story to
show that they should always pray and never
give up. 2 "There was a judge in a certain city," he said,
"who neither feared God nor cared about people. 3 A
widow of that city came to him repeatedly, saying,
'Give me justice in this dispute with my enemy.' 4 The
judge ignored her for a while, but finally he said to
himself, 'I don't fear God or care about people, 5 but
this woman is driving me crazy. I'm going to see that
she gets justice, because she is wearing me out with
her constant requests!'"

6 Then the Lord said, "Learn a lesson from this unjust judge. 7 Even he rendered a just decision in the
end. So don't you think God will surely give justice to
his chosen people who cry out to him day and night?
Will he keep putting them off? 8 I tell you, he will
grant justice to them quickly! But when the Son of
Man* returns, how many will he find on the earth
who have faith?"

Parable of the Pharisee and Tax Collector

9 Then Jesus told this story to some who had great
confidence in their own righteousness and scorned
everyone else: 10 "Two men went to the Temple to
pray. One was a Pharisee, and the other was a despised tax collector. 11 The Pharisee stood by himself
and prayed this prayer*: 'I thank you, God, that I am
not a sinner like everyone else. For I don't cheat, I
don't sin, and I don't commit adultery. I'm certainly
not like that tax collector! 12 I fast twice a week, and
I give you a tenth of my income.'

13 "But the tax collector stood at a distance and
dared not even lift his eyes to heaven as he prayed. Instead, he beat his chest in sorrow, saying, 'O God, be
merciful to me, for I am a sinner.' 14 I tell you, this sinner, not the Pharisee, returned home justified before
God. For those who exalt themselves will be humbled,
and those who humble themselves will be exalted."

17:35 Some manuscripts add verse 36, *Two men will be working in the field; one will be taken, the other left.* Compare Matt 24:40. **17:37a** Greek *"Where, Lord?"* **17:37b** Greek *"Wherever the carcass is, the vultures gather."* **18:8** "Son of Man" is a title Jesus used for himself. **18:11** Some manuscripts read *stood and prayed this prayer to himself.*

15 And they brought unto him also infants, that he
would touch them: but when *his* disciples saw *it*,
they rebuked them.
16 But Jesus called them *unto him*, and said, Suffer
little children to come unto me, and forbid them not:
for of such is the kingdom of God.
17 Verily I say unto you, Whosoever shall not receive the kingdom of God as a little child shall in no
wise enter therein.

18 And a certain ruler asked him, saying, Good
Master, what shall I do to inherit eternal life?
19 And Jesus said unto him, Why callest thou me
good? none *is* good, save one, *that is*, God.
20 Thou knowest the commandments, Do not commit adultery, Do not kill, Do not steal, Do not bear
false witness, Honour thy father and thy mother.
21 And he said, All these have I kept from my
youth up.
22 Now when Jesus heard these things, he said unto
him, Yet lackest thou one thing: sell all that thou hast,
and distribute unto the poor, and thou shalt have
treasure in heaven: and come, follow me.
23 And when he heard this, he was very sorrowful:
for he was very rich.
24 And when Jesus saw that he was very sorrowful,
he said, How hardly shall they that have riches enter
into the kingdom of God!
25 For it is easier for a camel to go through a
needle's eye, than for a rich man to enter into the
kingdom of God.
26 And they that heard *it* said, Who then can be
saved?
27 And he said, The things which are impossible
with men are possible with God.
28 Then Peter said, Lo, we have left all, and followed
thee.
29 And he said unto them, Verily I say unto you,
There is no man that hath left house, or parents, or
brethren, or wife, or children, for the kingdom of
God's sake,
30 Who shall not receive manifold more in this present time, and in the world to come life everlasting.
31 Then he took *unto him* the twelve, and said unto
them, Behold, we go up to Jerusalem, and all things
that are written by the prophets concerning the Son
of man shall be accomplished.
32 For he shall be delivered unto the Gentiles, and
shall be mocked, and spitefully entreated, and spit-
ted on:
33 And they shall scourge *him*, and put him to
death: and the third day he shall rise again.
34 And they understood none of these things: and
this saying was hid from them, neither knew they the
things which were spoken.

Jesus Blesses the Children

15 One day some parents brought their little children
to Jesus so he could touch and bless them. But when
the disciples saw this, they scolded the parents for
bothering him.
16 Then Jesus called for the children and said to
the disciples, "Let the children come to me. Don't
stop them! For the Kingdom of God belongs to those
who are like these children. 17 I tell you the truth,
anyone who doesn't receive the Kingdom of God like
a child will never enter it."

The Rich Man

18 Once a religious leader asked Jesus this question:
"Good Teacher, what should I do to inherit eternal
life?"
19 "Why do you call me good?" Jesus asked him.
"Only God is truly good. 20 But to answer your question, you know the commandments: 'You must not
commit adultery. You must not murder. You must
not steal. You must not testify falsely. Honor your
father and mother.'*"
21 The man replied, "I've obeyed all these commandments since I was young."
22 When Jesus heard his answer, he said, "There is
still one thing you haven't done. Sell all your possessions and give the money to the poor, and you will
have treasure in heaven. Then come, follow me."
23 But when the man heard this he became very
sad, for he was very rich.
24 When Jesus saw this,* he said, "How hard it is
for the rich to enter the Kingdom of God! 25 In fact, it
is easier for a camel to go through the eye of a needle
than for a rich person to enter the Kingdom of God!"
26 Those who heard this said, "Then who in the
world can be saved?"
27 He replied, "What is impossible for people is
possible with God."
28 Peter said, "We've left our homes to follow you."
29 "Yes," Jesus replied, "and I assure you that everyone who has given up house or wife or brothers or
parents or children, for the sake of the Kingdom of
God, 30 will be repaid many times over in this life, and
will have eternal life in the world to come."

Jesus Again Predicts His Death

31 Taking the twelve disciples aside, Jesus said, "Listen, we're going up to Jerusalem, where all the predictions of the prophets concerning the Son of Man
will come true. 32 He will be handed over to the Romans,* and he will be mocked, treated shamefully,
and spit upon. 33 They will flog him with a whip and
kill him, but on the third day he will rise again."
34 But they didn't understand any of this. The significance of his words was hidden from them, and
they failed to grasp what he was talking about.

18:20 Exod 20:12-16; Deut 5:16-20. **18:24** Some manuscripts read *When Jesus saw how sad the man was.* **18:32** Greek *the Gentiles.*

KING JAMES VERSION

35 And it came to pass, that as he was come nigh unto Jericho, a certain blind man sat by the way side begging:

36 And hearing the multitude pass by, he asked what it meant.

37 And they told him, that Jesus of Nazareth passeth by.

38 And he cried, saying, Jesus, *thou* son of David, have mercy on me.

39 And they which went before rebuked him, that he should hold his peace: but he cried so much the more, *Thou* son of David, have mercy on me.

40 And Jesus stood, and commanded him to be brought unto him: and when he was come near, he asked him,

41 Saying, What wilt thou that I shall do unto thee? And he said, Lord, that I may receive my sight.

42 And Jesus said unto him, Receive thy sight: thy faith hath saved thee.

43 And immediately he received his sight, and followed him, glorifying God: and all the people, when they saw *it*, gave praise unto God.

19 1 And *Jesus* entered and passed through Jericho.

2 And, behold, *there was* a man named Zacchaeus, which was the chief among the publicans, and he was rich.

3 And he sought to see Jesus who he was; and could not for the press, because he was little of stature.

4 And he ran before, and climbed up into a sycamore tree to see him: for he was to pass that *way*.

5 And when Jesus came to the place, he looked up, and saw him, and said unto him, Zacchaeus, make haste, and come down; for today I must abide at thy house.

6 And he made haste, and came down, and received him joyfully.

7 And when they saw *it*, they all murmured, saying, That he was gone to be guest with a man that is a sinner.

8 And Zacchaeus stood, and said unto the Lord; Behold, Lord, the half of my goods I give to the poor; and if I have taken any thing from any man by false accusation, I restore *him* fourfold.

9 And Jesus said unto him, This day is salvation come to this house, forsomuch as he also is a son of Abraham.

10 For the Son of man is come to seek and to save that which was lost.

11 And as they heard these things, he added and spake a parable, because he was nigh to Jerusalem, and because they thought that the kingdom of God should immediately appear.

12 He said therefore, A certain nobleman went into a far country to receive for himself a kingdom, and to return.

NEW LIVING TRANSLATION

Jesus Heals a Blind Beggar

35 As Jesus approached Jericho, a blind beggar was sitting beside the road.
36 When he heard the noise of a
crowd going past, he asked what was happening.
37 They told him that Jesus the Nazarene* was going
by.
38 So he began shouting, "Jesus, Son of David, have
mercy on me!"
39 "Be quiet!" the people in front yelled at him.
But he only shouted louder, "Son of David, have
mercy on me!"
40 When Jesus heard him, he stopped and ordered
that the man be brought to him. As the man came
near, Jesus asked him,
41 "What do you want me to do
for you?"
"Lord," he said, "I want to see!"
42 And Jesus said, "All right, receive your sight! Your
faith has healed you."
43 Instantly the man could see,
and he followed Jesus, praising God. And all who saw
it praised God, too.

Jesus and Zacchaeus

19 Jesus entered Jericho and made his way
through the town.
2 There was a man there
named Zacchaeus. He was the chief tax collector in
the region, and he had become very rich.
3 He tried to
get a look at Jesus, but he was too short to see over the
crowd.
4 So he ran ahead and climbed a sycamore-
fig tree beside the road, for Jesus was going to pass
that way.
5 When Jesus came by, he looked up at Zacchaeus
and called him by name. "Zacchaeus!" he said.
"Quick, come down! I must be a guest in your home
today."
6 Zacchaeus quickly climbed down and took Jesus
to his house in great excitement and joy.
7 But the
people were displeased. "He has gone to be the guest
of a notorious sinner," they grumbled.
8 Meanwhile, Zacchaeus stood before the Lord and
said, "I will give half my wealth to the poor, Lord, and
if I have cheated people on their taxes, I will give
them back four times as much!"
9 Jesus responded, "Salvation has come to this
home today, for this man has shown himself to be a
true son of Abraham.
10 For the Son of Man* came to
seek and save those who are lost."

Parable of the Ten Servants

11 The crowd was listening to everything Jesus said.
And because he was nearing Jerusalem, he told them
a story to correct the impression that the Kingdom
of God would begin right away.
12 He said, "A noble-
man was called away to a distant empire to be

18:37 Or *Jesus of Nazareth.* **19:10** "Son of Man" is a title Jesus used for himself.

KING JAMES VERSION

13 And he called his ten servants, and delivered them ten pounds, and said unto them, Occupy till I come.

14 But his citizens hated him, and sent a message after him, saying, We will not have this *man* to reign over us.

15 And it came to pass, that when he was returned, having received the kingdom, then he commanded these servants to be called unto him, to whom he had given the money, that he might know how much every man had gained by trading.

16 Then came the first, saying, Lord, thy pound hath gained ten pounds.

17 And he said unto him, Well, thou good servant: because thou hast been faithful in a very little, have thou authority over ten cities.

18 And the second came, saying, Lord, thy pound hath gained five pounds.

19 And he said likewise to him, Be thou also over five cities.

20 And another came, saying, Lord, behold, *here is* thy pound, which I have kept laid up in a napkin:

21 For I feared thee, because thou art an austere man: thou takest up that thou layedst not down, and reapest that thou didst not sow.

22 And he saith unto him, Out of thine own mouth will I judge thee, *thou* wicked servant. Thou knewest that I was an austere man, taking up that I laid not down, and reaping that I did not sow:

23 Wherefore then gavest not thou my money into the bank, that at my coming I might have required mine own with usury?

24 And he said unto them that stood by, Take from him the pound, and give *it* to him that hath ten pounds.

25 (And they said unto him, Lord, he hath ten pounds.)

26 For I say unto you, That unto every one which hath shall be given; and from him that hath not, even that he hath shall be taken away from him.

27 But those mine enemies, which would not that I should reign over them, bring hither, and slay *them* before me.

28 And when he had thus spoken, he went before, ascending up to Jerusalem.

29 And it came to pass, when he was come nigh to Bethphage and Bethany, at the mount called *the mount* of Olives, he sent two of his disciples,

30 Saying, Go ye into the village over against *you;* in the which at your entering ye shall find a colt tied, whereon yet never man sat: loose him, and bring *him hither.*

31 And if any man ask you, Why do ye loose *him?* thus shall ye say unto him, Because the Lord hath need of him.

NEW LIVING TRANSLATION

crowned king and then return. 13 Before he left, he called together ten of his servants and divided among them ten pounds of silver,* saying, 'Invest this for me while I am gone.' 14 But his people hated him and sent a delegation after him to say, 'We do not want him to be our king.'

15 "After he was crowned king, he returned and called in the servants to whom he had given the money. He wanted to find out what their profits were. 16 The first servant reported, 'Master, I invested your money and made ten times the original amount!'

17 " 'Well done!' the king exclaimed. 'You are a good servant. You have been faithful with the little I entrusted to you, so you will be governor of ten cities as your reward.'

18 "The next servant reported, 'Master, I invested your money and made five times the original amount.'

19 " 'Well done!' the king said. 'You will be governor over five cities.'

20 "But the third servant brought back only the original amount of money and said, 'Master, I hid your money and kept it safe. 21 I was afraid because you are a hard man to deal with, taking what isn't yours and harvesting crops you didn't plant.'

22 " 'You wicked servant!' the king roared. 'Your own words condemn you. If you knew that I'm a hard man who takes what isn't mine and harvests crops I didn't plant, 23 why didn't you deposit my money in the bank? At least I could have gotten some interest on it.'

24 "Then, turning to the others standing nearby, the king ordered, 'Take the money from this servant, and give it to the one who has ten pounds.'

25 " 'But, master,' they said, 'he already has ten pounds!'

26 " 'Yes,' the king replied, 'and to those who use well what they are given, even more will be given. But from those who do nothing, even what little they have will be taken away. 27 And as for these enemies of mine who didn't want me to be their king—bring them in and execute them right here in front of me.' "

Jesus' Triumphant Entry

28 After telling this story, Jesus went on toward Jerusalem, walking ahead of his disciples. 29 As he came to the towns of Bethphage and Bethany on the Mount of Olives, he sent two disciples ahead. 30 "Go into that village over there," he told them. "As you enter it, you will see a young donkey tied there that no one has ever ridden. Untie it and bring it here. 31 If anyone asks, 'Why are you untying that colt?' just say, 'The Lord needs it.' "

19:13 Greek *ten minas;* one mina was worth about three months' wages.

KING JAMES VERSION

32 And they that were sent went their way, and found even as he had said unto them.

33 And as they were loosing the colt, the owners thereof said unto them, Why loose ye the colt?

34 And they said, The Lord hath need of him.

35 And they brought him to Jesus: and they cast their garments upon the colt, and they set Jesus thereon.

36 And as he went, they spread their clothes in the way.

37 And when he was come nigh, even now at the descent of the mount of Olives, the whole multitude of the disciples began to rejoice and praise God with a loud voice for all the mighty works that they had seen;

38 Saying, Blessed *be* the King that cometh in the name of the Lord: peace in heaven, and glory in the highest.

39 And some of the Pharisees from among the multitude said unto him, Master, rebuke thy disciples.

40 And he answered and said unto them, I tell you that, if these should hold their peace, the stones would immediately cry out.

41 And when he was come near, he beheld the city, and wept over it,

42 Saying, If thou hadst known, even thou, at least in this thy day, the things *which belong* unto thy peace! but now they are hid from thine eyes.

43 For the days shall come upon thee, that thine enemies shall cast a trench about thee, and compass thee round, and keep thee in on every side,

44 And shall lay thee even with the ground, and thy children within thee; and they shall not leave in thee one stone upon another; because thou knewest not the time of thy visitation.

45 And he went into the temple, and began to cast out them that sold therein, and them that bought;

46 Saying unto them, It is written, My house is the house of prayer: but ye have made it a den of thieves.

47 And he taught daily in the temple. But the chief priests and the scribes and the chief of the people sought to destroy him,

48 And could not find what they might do: for all the people were very attentive to hear him.

20 1 And it came to pass, *that* on one of those days, as he taught the people in the temple, and preached the gospel, the chief priests and the scribes came upon *him* with the elders,

2 And spake unto him, saying, Tell us, by what authority doest thou these things? or who is he that gave thee this authority?

3 And he answered and said unto them, I will also ask you one thing; and answer me:

NEW LIVING TRANSLATION

32 So they went and found the colt, just as Jesus had
said. 33 And sure enough, as they were untying it, the
owners asked them, "Why are you untying that colt?"
34 And the disciples simply replied, "The Lord
needs it." 35 So they brought the colt to Jesus and
threw their garments over it for him to ride on.

36 As he rode along, the crowds spread out their
garments on the road ahead of him. 37 When he
reached the place where the road started down the
Mount of Olives, all of his followers began to shout
and sing as they walked along, praising God for all
the wonderful miracles they had seen.

38 "Blessings on the King who comes in the name
of the LORD!
Peace in heaven, and glory in highest heaven!"*

39 But some of the Pharisees among the crowd
said, "Teacher, rebuke your followers for saying
things like that!"

40 He replied, "If they kept quiet, the stones along
the road would burst into cheers!"

Jesus Weeps over Jerusalem

41 But as he came closer to Jerusalem and saw the
city ahead, he began to weep. 42 "How I wish today
that you of all people would understand the way to
peace. But now it is too late, and peace is hidden
from your eyes. 43 Before long your enemies will
build ramparts against your walls and encircle you
and close in on you from every side. 44 They will
crush you into the ground, and your children with
you. Your enemies will not leave a single stone in
place, because you did not accept your opportunity
for salvation."

Jesus Clears the Temple

45 Then Jesus entered the Temple and began to drive
out the people selling animals for sacrifices. 46 He
said to them, "The Scriptures declare, 'My Temple
will be a house of prayer,' but you have turned it into a
den of thieves."*

47 After that, he taught daily in the Temple, but the
leading priests, the teachers of religious law, and the
other leaders of the people began planning how to
kill him. 48 But they could think of nothing, because
all the people hung on every word he said.

The Authority of Jesus Challenged

20 One day as Jesus was teaching the people
and preaching the Good News in the
Temple, the leading priests, the teachers of religious
law, and the elders came up to him. 2 They demanded, "By what authority are you doing all these
things? Who gave you the right?"

3 "Let me ask you a question first," he replied.

19:38 Pss 118:26; 148:1. **19:46** Isa 56:7; Jer 7:11.

KING JAMES VERSION

4 The baptism of John, was it from heaven, or of men?

5 And they reasoned with themselves, saying, If we shall say, From heaven; he will say, Why then believed ye him not?

6 But and if we say, Of men; all the people will stone us: for they be persuaded that John was a prophet.

7 And they answered, that they could not tell whence *it was*.

8 And Jesus said unto them, Neither tell I you by what authority I do these things.

9 Then began he to speak to the people this parable; A certain man planted a vineyard, and let it forth to husbandmen, and went into a far country for a long time.

10 And at the season he sent a servant to the husbandmen, that they should give him of the fruit of the vineyard: but the husbandmen beat him, and sent *him* away empty.

11 And again he sent another servant: and they beat him also, and entreated *him* shamefully, and sent *him* away empty.

12 And again he sent a third: and they wounded him also, and cast *him* out.

13 Then said the lord of the vineyard, What shall I do? I will send my beloved son: it may be they will reverence *him* when they see him.

14 But when the husbandmen saw him, they reasoned among themselves, saying, This is the heir: come, let us kill him, that the inheritance may be ours.

15 So they cast him out of the vineyard, and killed *him*. What therefore shall the lord of the vineyard do unto them?

16 He shall come and destroy these husbandmen, and shall give the vineyard to others. And when they heard *it*, they said, God forbid.

17 And he beheld them, and said, What is this then that is written, The stone which the builders rejected, the same is become the head of the corner?

18 Whosoever shall fall upon that stone shall be broken; but on whomsoever it shall fall, it will grind him to powder.

19 And the chief priests and the scribes the same hour sought to lay hands on him; and they feared the people: for they perceived that he had spoken this parable against them.

20 And they watched *him*, and sent forth spies, which should feign themselves just men, that they might take hold of his words, that so they might deliver him unto the power and authority of the governor.

21 And they asked him, saying, Master, we know

NEW LIVING TRANSLATION

4 "Did John's authority to baptize come from heaven, or was it merely human?"

5 They talked it over among themselves. "If we say it was from heaven, he will ask why we didn't believe John. 6 But if we say it was merely human, the people will stone us because they are convinced John was a prophet." 7 So they finally replied that they didn't know.

8 And Jesus responded, "Then I won't tell you by what authority I do these things."

Parable of the Evil Farmers

9 Now Jesus turned to the people again and told them this story: "A man planted a vineyard, leased it to tenant farmers, and moved to another country to live for several years. 10 At the time of the grape harvest, he sent one of his servants to collect his share of the crop. But the farmers attacked the servant, beat him up, and sent him back empty-handed. 11 So the owner sent another servant, but they also insulted him, beat him up, and sent him away empty-handed. 12 A third man was sent, and they wounded him and chased him away.

13 "'What will I do?' the owner asked himself. 'I know! I'll send my cherished son. Surely they will respect him.'

14 "But when the tenant farmers saw his son, they said to each other, 'Here comes the heir to this estate. Let's kill him and get the estate for ourselves!' 15 So they dragged him out of the vineyard and murdered him.

"What do you suppose the owner of the vineyard will do to them?" Jesus asked. 16 "I'll tell you—he will come and kill those farmers and lease the vineyard to others."

"How terrible that such a thing should ever happen," his listeners protested.

17 Jesus looked at them and said, "Then what does this Scripture mean?

'The stone that the builders rejected
has now become the cornerstone.'*

18 Everyone who stumbles over that stone will be broken to pieces, and it will crush anyone it falls on."

19 The teachers of religious law and the leading priests wanted to arrest Jesus immediately because they realized he was telling the story against them—they were the wicked farmers. But they were afraid of the people's reaction.

Taxes for Caesar

20 Watching for their opportunity, the leaders sent spies pretending to be honest men. They tried to get Jesus to say something that could be reported to the Roman governor so he would arrest Jesus. 21 "Teacher," they said, "we know that you speak and

20:17 Ps 118:22.

that thou sayest and teachest rightly, neither ac-
ceptest thou the person *of any*, but teachest the way
of God truly:

22 Is it lawful for us to give tribute unto Caesar,
or no?

23 But he perceived their craftiness, and said unto
them, Why tempt ye me?

24 Shew me a penny. Whose image and superscription hath it? They answered and said, Caesar's.

25 And he said unto them, Render therefore unto
Caesar the things which be Caesar's, and unto God
the things which be God's.

26 And they could not take hold of his words before
the people: and they marvelled at his answer, and
held their peace.

27 Then came to *him* certain of the Sadducees,
which deny that there is any resurrection; and they
asked him,

28 Saying, Master, Moses wrote unto us, If any
man's brother die, having a wife, and he die without
children, that his brother should take his wife, and
raise up seed unto his brother.

29 There were therefore seven brethren: and the
first took a wife, and died without children.

30 And the second took her to wife, and he died
childless.

31 And the third took her; and in like manner the
seven also: and they left no children, and died.

32 Last of all the woman died also.

33 Therefore in the resurrection whose wife of
them is she? for seven had her to wife.

34 And Jesus answering said unto them, The children of this world marry, and are given in marriage:

35 But they which shall be accounted worthy to
obtain that world, and the resurrection from the
dead, neither marry, nor are given in marriage:

36 Neither can they die any more: for they are equal
unto the angels; and are the children of God, being
the children of the resurrection.

37 Now that the dead are raised, even Moses
shewed at the bush, when he calleth the Lord the
God of Abraham, and the God of Isaac, and the God
of Jacob.

38 For he is not a God of the dead, but of the living:
for all live unto him.

39 Then certain of the scribes answering said,
Master, thou hast well said.

40 And after that they durst not ask him any *question at all*.

41 And he said unto them, How say they that Christ
is David's son?

42 And David himself saith in the book of Psalms,
The LORD said unto my Lord, Sit thou on my right
hand,

teach what is right and are not influenced by what
others think. You teach the way of God truthfully.
22 Now tell us—is it right for us to pay taxes to Caesar
or not?"

23 He saw through their trickery and said, 24 "Show
me a Roman coin.* Whose picture and title are
stamped on it?"

"Caesar's," they replied.

25 "Well then," he said, "give to Caesar what belongs to Caesar, and give to God what belongs to
God."

26 So they failed to trap him by what he said in
front of the people. Instead, they were amazed by his
answer, and they became silent.

Discussion about Resurrection

27 Then Jesus was approached by some Sadducees—
religious leaders who say there is no resurrection
from the dead. 28 They posed this question: "Teacher,
Moses gave us a law that if a man dies, leaving a wife
but no children, his brother should marry the widow
and have a child who will carry on the brother's
name.* 29 Well, suppose there were seven brothers.
The oldest one married and then died without children. 30 So the second brother married the widow,
but he also died. 31 Then the third brother married
her. This continued with all seven of them, who died
without children. 32 Finally, the woman also died.
33 So tell us, whose wife will she be in the resurrection? For all seven were married to her!"

34 Jesus replied, "Marriage is for people here on
earth. 35 But in the age to come, those worthy of being raised from the dead will neither marry nor be
given in marriage. 36 And they will never die again. In
this respect they will be like angels. They are children of God and children of the resurrection.

37 "But now, as to whether the dead will be raised—
even Moses proved this when he wrote about the
burning bush. Long after Abraham, Isaac, and Jacob
had died, he referred to the Lord* as 'the God of
Abraham, the God of Isaac, and the God of Jacob.'*
38 So he is the God of the living, not the dead, for they
are all alive to him."

39 "Well said, Teacher!" remarked some of the
teachers of religious law who were standing there.
40 And then no one dared to ask him any more
questions.

Whose Son Is the Messiah?

41 Then Jesus presented them with a question. "Why
is it," he asked, "that the Messiah is said to be the son
of David? 42 For David himself wrote in the book of
Psalms:

'The LORD said to my Lord,
Sit in the place of honor at my right hand

20:24 Greek *a denarius*. **20:28** See Deut 25:5-6. **20:37a** Greek *when he wrote about the bush. He referred to the Lord*. **20:37b** Exod 3:6.

43 Till I make thine enemies thy footstool.
44 David therefore calleth him Lord, how is he then
his son?
45 Then in the audience of all the people he said
unto his disciples,
46 Beware of the scribes, which desire to walk in
long robes, and love greetings in the markets, and the
highest seats in the synagogues, and the chief rooms
at feasts;
47 Which devour widows' houses, and for a shew
make long prayers: the same shall receive greater
damnation.

21 1 And he looked up, and saw the rich men
casting their gifts into the treasury.
2 And he saw also a certain poor widow casting in
thither two mites.
3 And he said, Of a truth I say unto you, that this
poor widow hath cast in more than they all:
4 For all these have of their abundance cast in unto
the offerings of God: but she of her penury hath cast
in all the living that she had.

5 And as some spake of the temple, how it was
adorned with goodly stones and gifts, he said,
6 *As for* these things which ye behold, the days will
come, in the which there shall not be left one stone
upon another, that shall not be thrown down.
7 And they asked him, saying, Master, but when
shall these things be? and what sign *will there be*
when these things shall come to pass?
8 And he said, Take heed that ye be not deceived:
for many shall come in my name, saying, I am *Christ;*
and the time draweth near: go ye not therefore after
them.
9 But when ye shall hear of wars and commotions,
be not terrified: for these things must first come to
pass; but the end *is* not by and by.
10 Then said he unto them, Nation shall rise
against nation, and kingdom against kingdom:
11 And great earthquakes shall be in divers places,
and famines, and pestilences; and fearful sights and
great signs shall there be from heaven.
12 But before all these, they shall lay their hands on
you, and persecute *you,* delivering *you* up to the synagogues, and into prisons, being brought before
kings and rulers for my name's sake.
13 And it shall turn to you for a testimony.
14 Settle *it* therefore in your hearts, not to meditate
before what ye shall answer:
15 For I will give you a mouth and wisdom, which
all your adversaries shall not be able to gainsay nor
resist.
16 And ye shall be betrayed both by parents, and

43 until I humble your enemies,
making them a footstool under your feet.'*

44 Since David called the Messiah 'Lord,' how can the
Messiah be his son?"
45 Then, with the crowds listening, he turned to his
disciples and said, 46 "Beware of these teachers of religious law! For they like to parade around in flowing
robes and love to receive respectful greetings as they
walk in the marketplaces. And how they love the
seats of honor in the synagogues and the head table
at banquets. 47 Yet they shamelessly cheat widows
out of their property and then pretend to be pious by
making long prayers in public. Because of this, they
will be severely punished."

The Widow's Offering

21 While Jesus was in the Temple, he watched
the rich people dropping their gifts in the
collection box. 2 Then a poor widow came by and
dropped in two small coins.*
3 "I tell you the truth," Jesus said, "this poor widow
has given more than all the rest of them. 4 For they
have given a tiny part of their surplus, but she, poor
as she is, has given everything she has."

Jesus Foretells the Future

5 Some of his disciples began talking about the majestic stonework of the Temple and the memorial
decorations on the walls. But Jesus said, 6 "The time
is coming when all these things will be completely
demolished. Not one stone will be left on top of
another!"
7 "Teacher," they asked, "when will all this happen?
What sign will show us that these things are about to
take place?"
8 He replied, "Don't let anyone mislead you, for
many will come in my name, claiming, 'I am the Messiah,'* and saying, 'The time has come!' But don't believe them. 9 And when you hear of wars and
insurrections, don't panic. Yes, these things must take
place first, but the end won't follow immediately."
10 Then he added, "Nation will go to war against nation, and kingdom against kingdom. 11 There will be
great earthquakes, and there will be famines and
plagues in many lands, and there will be terrifying
things and great miraculous signs from heaven.
12 "But before all this occurs, there will be a time of
great persecution. You will be dragged into synagogues and prisons, and you will stand trial before
kings and governors because you are my followers.
13 But this will be your opportunity to tell them about
me.* 14 So don't worry in advance about how to answer the charges against you, 15 for I will give you the
right words and such wisdom that none of your opponents will be able to reply or refute you! 16 Even

20:42-43 Ps 110:1. **21:2** Greek *two lepta* [the smallest of Jewish coins]. **21:8** Greek *claiming, 'I am.'* **21:13** Or *This will be your testimony against them.*

brethren, and kinsfolks, and friends; and *some* of you
shall they cause to be put to death.
17 And ye shall be hated of all *men* for my name's
sake.
18 But there shall not an hair of your head perish.
19 In your patience possess ye your souls.
20 And when ye shall see Jerusalem compassed with
armies, then know that the desolation thereof is nigh.
21 Then let them which are in Judaea flee to the
mountains; and let them which are in the midst of it
depart out; and let not them that are in the countries
enter thereinto.
22 For these be the days of vengeance, that all
things which are written may be fulfilled.
23 But woe unto them that are with child, and to
them that give suck, in those days! for there shall be
great distress in the land, and wrath upon this people.
24 And they shall fall by the edge of the sword, and
shall be led away captive into all nations: and Jerusalem shall be trodden down of the Gentiles, until the
times of the Gentiles be fulfilled.
25 And there shall be signs in the sun, and in the
moon, and in the stars; and upon the earth distress
of nations, with perplexity; the sea and the waves
roaring;
26 Men's hearts failing them for fear, and for looking after those things which are coming on the earth:
for the powers of heaven shall be shaken.
27 And then shall they see the Son of man coming
in a cloud with power and great glory.
28 And when these things begin to come to pass,
then look up, and lift up your heads; for your redemption draweth nigh.
29 And he spake to them a parable; Behold the fig
tree, and all the trees;
30 When they now shoot forth, ye see and know of
your own selves that summer is now nigh at hand.
31 So likewise ye, when ye see these things come to
pass, know ye that the kingdom of God is nigh at hand.
32 Verily I say unto you, This generation shall not
pass away, till all be fulfilled.
33 Heaven and earth shall pass away: but my words
shall not pass away.
34 And take heed to yourselves, lest at any time
your hearts be overcharged with surfeiting, and
drunkenness, and cares of this life, and *so* that day
come upon you unawares.
35 For as a snare shall it come on all them that dwell
on the face of the whole earth.
36 Watch ye therefore, and pray always, that ye
may be accounted worthy to escape all these things
that shall come to pass, and to stand before the Son
of man.
37 And in the day time he was teaching in the temple; and at night he went out, and abode in the mount
that is called *the mount* of Olives.
38 And all the people came early in the morning to
him in the temple, for to hear him.

those closest to you—your parents, brothers, relatives, and friends—will betray you. They will even kill
some of you.
17 And everyone will hate you because
you are my followers.*
18 But not a hair of your head
will perish!
19 By standing firm, you will win your
souls.
20 "And when you see Jerusalem surrounded by armies, then you will know that the time of its destruction has arrived.
21 Then those in Judea must flee to
the hills. Those in Jerusalem must get out, and those
out in the country should not return to the city.
22 For
those will be days of God's vengeance, and the prophetic words of the Scriptures will be fulfilled.
23 How terrible it will be for pregnant women and for
nursing mothers in those days. For there will be disaster in the land and great anger against this people.
24 They will be killed by the sword or sent away as
captives to all the nations of the world. And Jerusalem will be trampled down by the Gentiles until the
period of the Gentiles comes to an end.
25 "And there will be strange signs in the sun,
moon, and stars. And here on earth the nations will
be in turmoil, perplexed by the roaring seas and
strange tides.
26 People will be terrified at what they
see coming upon the earth, for the powers in the
heavens will be shaken.
27 Then everyone will see the
Son of Man* coming on a cloud with power and
great glory.*
28 So when all these things begin to happen, stand and look up, for your salvation is near!"
29 Then he gave them this illustration: "Notice the
fig tree, or any other tree.
30 When the leaves come
out, you know without being told that summer is
near.
31 In the same way, when you see all these things
taking place, you can know that the Kingdom of God
is near.
32 I tell you the truth, this generation will not
pass from the scene until all these things have taken
place.
33 Heaven and earth will disappear, but my
words will never disappear.
34 "Watch out! Don't let your hearts be dulled by
carousing and drunkenness, and by the worries of
this life. Don't let that day catch you unaware,
35 like a
trap. For that day will come upon everyone living on
the earth.
36 Keep alert at all times. And pray that you
might be strong enough to escape these coming horrors and stand before the Son of Man."
37 Every day Jesus went to the Temple to teach, and
each evening he returned to spend the night on the
Mount of Olives.
38 The crowds gathered at the
Temple early each morning to hear him.

21:17 Greek *on account of my name.* **21:27a** "Son of Man" is a title Jesus used for himself. **21:27b** See Dan 7:13.

KING JAMES VERSION

22

1 Now the feast of unleavened bread drew nigh, which is called the Passover.

2 And the chief priests and scribes sought how they might kill him; for they feared the people.

3 Then entered Satan into Judas surnamed Iscariot, being of the number of the twelve.

4 And he went his way, and communed with the chief priests and captains, how he might betray him unto them.

5 And they were glad, and covenanted to give him money.

6 And he promised, and sought opportunity to betray him unto them in the absence of the multitude.

7 Then came the day of unleavened bread, when the passover must be killed.

8 And he sent Peter and John, saying, Go and prepare us the passover, that we may eat.

9 And they said unto him, Where wilt thou that we prepare?

10 And he said unto them, Behold, when ye are entered into the city, there shall a man meet you, bearing a pitcher of water; follow him into the house where he entereth in.

11 And ye shall say unto the goodman of the house, The Master saith unto thee, Where is the guestchamber, where I shall eat the passover with my disciples?

12 And he shall shew you a large upper room furnished: there make ready.

13 And they went, and found as he had said unto them: and they made ready the passover.

14 And when the hour was come, he sat down, and the twelve apostles with him.

15 And he said unto them, With desire I have desired to eat this passover with you before I suffer:

16 For I say unto you, I will not any more eat thereof, until it be fulfilled in the kingdom of God.

17 And he took the cup, and gave thanks, and said, Take this, and divide *it* among yourselves:

18 For I say unto you, I will not drink of the fruit of the vine, until the kingdom of God shall come.

19 And he took bread, and gave thanks, and brake *it*, and gave unto them, saying, This is my body which is given for you: this do in remembrance of me.

20 Likewise also the cup after supper, saying, This cup *is* the new testament in my blood, which is shed for you.

21 But, behold, the hand of him that betrayeth me *is* with me on the table.

22 And truly the Son of man goeth, as it was determined: but woe unto that man by whom he is betrayed!

23 And they began to inquire among themselves, which of them it was that should do this thing.

NEW LIVING TRANSLATION

Judas Agrees to Betray Jesus

22

The Festival of Unleavened Bread, which is also called Passover, was approaching. 2 The leading priests and teachers of religious law were plotting how to kill Jesus, but they were afraid of the people's reaction.

3 Then Satan entered into Judas Iscariot, who was one of the twelve disciples, 4 and he went to the leading priests and captains of the Temple guard to discuss the best way to betray Jesus to them. 5 They were delighted, and they promised to give him money. 6 So he agreed and began looking for an opportunity to betray Jesus so they could arrest him when the crowds weren't around.

The Last Supper

7 Now the Festival of Unleavened Bread arrived, when the Passover lamb is sacrificed. 8 Jesus sent Peter and John ahead and said, "Go and prepare the Passover meal, so we can eat it together."

9 "Where do you want us to prepare it?" they asked him.

10 He replied, "As soon as you enter Jerusalem, a man carrying a pitcher of water will meet you. Follow him. At the house he enters, 11 say to the owner, 'The Teacher asks: Where is the guest room where I can eat the Passover meal with my disciples?' 12 He will take you upstairs to a large room that is already set up. That is where you should prepare our meal." 13 They went off to the city and found everything just as Jesus had said, and they prepared the Passover meal there.

14 When the time came, Jesus and the apostles sat down together at the table.* 15 Jesus said, "I have been very eager to eat this Passover meal with you before my suffering begins. 16 For I tell you now that I won't eat this meal again until its meaning is fulfilled in the Kingdom of God."

17 Then he took a cup of wine and gave thanks to God for it. Then he said, "Take this and share it among yourselves. 18 For I will not drink wine again until the Kingdom of God has come."

19 He took some bread and gave thanks to God for it. Then he broke it in pieces and gave it to the disciples, saying, "This is my body, which is given for you. Do this to remember me."

20 After supper he took another cup of wine and said, "This cup is the new covenant between God and his people—an agreement confirmed with my blood, which is poured out as a sacrifice for you.*

21 "But here at this table, sitting among us as a friend, is the man who will betray me. 22 For it has been determined that the Son of Man* must die. But what sorrow awaits the one who betrays him." 23 The disciples began to ask each other which of them would ever do such a thing.

22:14 Or *reclined together.* **22:19-20** Some manuscripts do not include 22:19b-20, *which is given for you . . . which is poured out as a sacrifice for you.* **22:22** "Son of Man" is a title Jesus used for himself.

KING JAMES VERSION

24 And there was also a strife among them, which of them should be accounted the greatest.

25 And he said unto them, The kings of the Gentiles exercise lordship over them; and they that exercise authority upon them are called benefactors.

26 But ye *shall* not *be* so: but he that is greatest among you, let him be as the younger; and he that is chief, as he that doth serve.

27 For whether *is* greater, he that sitteth at meat, or he that serveth? *is* not he that sitteth at meat? but I am among you as he that serveth.

28 Ye are they which have continued with me in my temptations.

29 And I appoint unto you a kingdom, as my Father hath appointed unto me;

30 That ye may eat and drink at my table in my kingdom, and sit on thrones judging the twelve tribes of Israel.

31 And the Lord said, Simon, Simon, behold, Satan hath desired *to have* you, that he may sift *you* as wheat:

32 But I have prayed for thee, that thy faith fail not: and when thou art converted, strengthen thy brethren.

33 And he said unto him, Lord, I am ready to go with thee, both into prison, and to death.

34 And he said, I tell thee, Peter, the cock shall not crow this day, before that thou shalt thrice deny that thou knowest me.

35 And he said unto them, When I sent you without purse, and scrip, and shoes, lacked ye any thing? And they said, Nothing.

36 Then said he unto them, But now, he that hath a purse, let him take *it,* and likewise *his* scrip: and he that hath no sword, let him sell his garment, and buy one.

37 For I say unto you, that this that is written must yet be accomplished in me, And he was reckoned among the transgressors: for the things concerning me have an end.

38 And they said, Lord, behold, here *are* two swords. And he said unto them, It is enough.

39 And he came out, and went, as he was wont, to the mount of Olives; and his disciples also followed him.

40 And when he was at the place, he said unto them, Pray that ye enter not into temptation.

41 And he was withdrawn from them about a stone's cast, and kneeled down, and prayed,

42 Saying, Father, if thou be willing, remove this cup from me: nevertheless not my will, but thine, be done.

43 And there appeared an angel unto him from heaven, strengthening him.

44 And being in an agony he prayed more earnestly: and his sweat was as it were great drops of blood falling down to the ground.

NEW LIVING TRANSLATION

24 Then they began to argue among themselves about who would be the greatest among them. 25 Jesus told them, "In this world the kings and great men lord it over their people, yet they are called 'friends of the people.' 26 But among you it will be different. Those who are the greatest among you should take the lowest rank, and the leader should be like a servant. 27 Who is more important, the one who sits at the table or the one who serves? The one who sits at the table, of course. But not here! For I am among you as one who serves.

28 "You have stayed with me in my time of trial. 29 And just as my Father has granted me a Kingdom, I now grant you the right 30 to eat and drink at my table in my Kingdom. And you will sit on thrones, judging the twelve tribes of Israel.

Jesus Predicts Peter's Denial

31 "Simon, Simon, Satan has asked to sift each of you like wheat. 32 But I have pleaded in prayer for you, Simon, that your faith should not fail. So when you have repented and turned to me again, strengthen your brothers."

33 Peter said, "Lord, I am ready to go to prison with you, and even to die with you."

34 But Jesus said, "Peter, let me tell you something. Before the rooster crows tomorrow morning, you will deny three times that you even know me."

35 Then Jesus asked them, "When I sent you out to preach the Good News and you did not have money, a traveler's bag, or an extra pair of sandals, did you need anything?"

"No," they replied.

36 "But now," he said, "take your money and a traveler's bag. And if you don't have a sword, sell your cloak and buy one! 37 For the time has come for this prophecy about me to be fulfilled: 'He was counted among the rebels.'* Yes, everything written about me by the prophets will come true."

38 "Look, Lord," they replied, "we have two swords among us."

"That's enough," he said.

Jesus Prays on the Mount of Olives

39 Then, accompanied by the disciples, Jesus left the upstairs room and went as usual to the Mount of Olives. 40 There he told them, "Pray that you will not give in to temptation."

41 He walked away, about a stone's throw, and knelt down and prayed, 42 "Father, if you are willing, please take this cup of suffering away from me. Yet I want your will to be done, not mine." 43 Then an angel from heaven appeared and strengthened him. 44 He prayed more fervently, and he was in such agony of spirit that his sweat fell to the ground like great drops of blood.*

22:37 Isa 53:12. **22:43-44** Verses 43 and 44 are not included in many ancient manuscripts.

KING JAMES VERSION

45 And when he rose up from prayer, and was come to his disciples, he found them sleeping for sorrow,

46 And said unto them, Why sleep ye? rise and pray, lest ye enter into temptation.

47 And while he yet spake, behold a multitude, and he that was called Judas, one of the twelve, went before them, and drew near unto Jesus to kiss him.

48 But Jesus said unto him, Judas, betrayest thou the Son of man with a kiss?

49 When they which were about him saw what would follow, they said unto him, Lord, shall we smite with the sword?

50 And one of them smote the servant of the high priest, and cut off his right ear.

51 And Jesus answered and said, Suffer ye thus far. And he touched his ear, and healed him.

52 Then Jesus said unto the chief priests, and captains of the temple, and the elders, which were come to him, Be ye come out, as against a thief, with swords and staves?

53 When I was daily with you in the temple, ye stretched forth no hands against me: but this is your hour, and the power of darkness.

54 Then took they him, and led *him,* and brought him into the high priest's house. And Peter followed afar off.

55 And when they had kindled a fire in the midst of the hall, and were set down together, Peter sat down among them.

56 But a certain maid beheld him as he sat by the fire, and earnestly looked upon him, and said, This man was also with him.

57 And he denied him, saying, Woman, I know him not.

58 And after a little while another saw him, and said, Thou art also of them. And Peter said, Man, I am not.

59 And about the space of one hour after another confidently affirmed, saying, Of a truth this *fellow* also was with him: for he is a Galilaean.

60 And Peter said, Man, I know not what thou sayest. And immediately, while he yet spake, the cock crew.

61 And the Lord turned, and looked upon Peter. And Peter remembered the word of the Lord, how he had said unto him, Before the cock crow, thou shalt deny me thrice.

62 And Peter went out, and wept bitterly.

63 And the men that held Jesus mocked him, and smote *him.*

64 And when they had blindfolded him, they struck him on the face, and asked him, saying, Prophesy, who is it that smote thee?

65 And many other things blasphemously spake they against him.

66 And as soon as it was day, the elders of the people and the chief priests and the scribes came together, and led him into their council, saying,

NEW LIVING TRANSLATION

45 At last he stood up again and returned to the disciples, only to find them asleep, exhausted from grief.
46 "Why are you sleeping?" he asked them. "Get up and
pray, so that you will not give in to temptation."

Jesus Is Betrayed and Arrested

47 But even as Jesus said this, a crowd approached, led
by Judas, one of the twelve disciples. Judas walked
over to Jesus to greet him with a kiss. 48 But Jesus said,
"Judas, would you betray the Son of Man with a kiss?"
49 When the other disciples saw what was about to
happen, they exclaimed, "Lord, should we fight? We
brought the swords!" 50 And one of them struck at the
high priest's slave, slashing off his right ear.
51 But Jesus said, "No more of this." And he
touched the man's ear and healed him.
52 Then Jesus spoke to the leading priests, the captains of the Temple guard, and the elders who had
come for him. "Am I some dangerous revolutionary,"
he asked, "that you come with swords and clubs
to arrest me? 53 Why didn't you arrest me in the
Temple? I was there every day. But this is your moment, the time when the power of darkness reigns."

Peter Denies Jesus

54 So they arrested him and led him to the high
priest's home. And Peter followed at a distance.
55 The guards lit a fire in the middle of the courtyard
and sat around it, and Peter joined them there. 56 A
servant girl noticed him in the firelight and began
staring at him. Finally she said, "This man was one of
Jesus' followers!"
57 But Peter denied it. "Woman," he said, "I don't
even know him!"
58 After a while someone else looked at him and
said, "You must be one of them!"
"No, man, I'm not!" Peter retorted.
59 About an hour later someone else insisted, "This
must be one of them, because he is a Galilean, too."
60 But Peter said, "Man, I don't know what you are
talking about." And immediately, while he was still
speaking, the rooster crowed.
61 At that moment the Lord turned and looked at
Peter. Suddenly, the Lord's words flashed through
Peter's mind: "Before the rooster crows tomorrow
morning, you will deny three times that you even know
me." 62 And Peter left the courtyard, weeping bitterly.
63 The guards in charge of Jesus began mocking
and beating him. 64 They blindfolded him and said,
"Prophesy to us! Who hit you that time?" 65 And they
hurled all sorts of terrible insults at him.

Jesus before the Council

66 At daybreak all the elders of the people assembled,
including the leading priests and the teachers of religious law. Jesus was led before this high council,*

22:66 Greek *before their Sanhedrin.*

KING JAMES VERSION

67 Art thou the Christ? tell us. And he said unto them, If I tell you, ye will not believe:

68 And if I also ask *you*, ye will not answer me, nor let *me* go.

69 Hereafter shall the Son of man sit on the right hand of the power of God.

70 Then said they all, Art thou then the Son of God? And he said unto them, Ye say that I am.

71 And they said, What need we any further witness? for we ourselves have heard of his own mouth.

23 1 And the whole multitude of them arose, and led him unto Pilate.

2 And they began to accuse him, saying, We found this *fellow* perverting the nation, and forbidding to give tribute to Caesar, saying that he himself is Christ a King.

3 And Pilate asked him, saying, Art thou the King of the Jews? And he answered him and said, Thou sayest *it*.

4 Then said Pilate to the chief priests and *to* the people, I find no fault in this man.

5 And they were the more fierce, saying, He stirreth up the people, teaching throughout all Jewry, beginning from Galilee to this place.

6 When Pilate heard of Galilee, he asked whether the man were a Galilaean.

7 And as soon as he knew that he belonged unto Herod's jurisdiction, he sent him to Herod, who himself also was at Jerusalem at that time.

8 And when Herod saw Jesus, he was exceeding glad: for he was desirous to see him of a long *season*, because he had heard many things of him; and he hoped to have seen some miracle done by him.

9 Then he questioned with him in many words; but he answered him nothing.

10 And the chief priests and scribes stood and vehemently accused him.

11 And Herod with his men of war set him at nought, and mocked *him*, and arrayed him in a gorgeous robe, and sent him again to Pilate.

12 And the same day Pilate and Herod were made friends together: for before they were at enmity between themselves.

13 And Pilate, when he had called together the chief priests and the rulers and the people,

14 Said unto them, Ye have brought this man unto me, as one that perverteth the people: and, behold, I, having examined *him* before you, have found no fault in this man touching those things whereof ye accuse him:

15 No, nor yet Herod: for I sent you to him; and, lo, nothing worthy of death is done unto him.

16 I will therefore chastise him, and release *him*.

17 (For of necessity he must release one unto them at the feast.)

NEW LIVING TRANSLATION

67 and they said, "Tell us, are you the Messiah?"

But he replied, "If I tell you, you won't believe me. 68 And if I ask you a question, you won't answer. 69 But from now on the Son of Man will be seated in the place of power at God's right hand.*"

70 They all shouted, "So, are you claiming to be the Son of God?"

And he replied, "You say that I am."

71 "Why do we need other witnesses?" they said. "We ourselves heard him say it."

Jesus' Trial before Pilate

23 Then the entire council took Jesus to Pilate, the Roman governor. 2 They began to state their case: "This man has been leading our people astray by telling them not to pay their taxes to the Roman government and by claiming he is the Messiah, a king."

3 So Pilate asked him, "Are you the king of the Jews?"

Jesus replied, "You have said it."

4 Pilate turned to the leading priests and to the crowd and said, "I find nothing wrong with this man!"

5 Then they became insistent. "But he is causing riots by his teaching wherever he goes—all over Judea, from Galilee to Jerusalem!"

6 "Oh, is he a Galilean?" Pilate asked. 7 When they said that he was, Pilate sent him to Herod Antipas, because Galilee was under Herod's jurisdiction, and Herod happened to be in Jerusalem at the time.

8 Herod was delighted at the opportunity to see Jesus, because he had heard about him and had been hoping for a long time to see him perform a miracle. 9 He asked Jesus question after question, but Jesus refused to answer. 10 Meanwhile, the leading priests and the teachers of religious law stood there shouting their accusations. 11 Then Herod and his soldiers began mocking and ridiculing Jesus. Finally, they put a royal robe on him and sent him back to Pilate. 12 (Herod and Pilate, who had been enemies before, became friends that day.)

13 Then Pilate called together the leading priests and other religious leaders, along with the people, 14 and he announced his verdict. "You brought this man to me, accusing him of leading a revolt. I have examined him thoroughly on this point in your presence and find him innocent. 15 Herod came to the same conclusion and sent him back to us. Nothing this man has done calls for the death penalty. 16 So I will have him flogged, and then I will release him."*

22:69 See Ps 110:1. **23:16** Some manuscripts add verse 17, *Now it was necessary for him to release one prisoner to them during the Passover celebration.* Compare Matt 27:15; Mark 15:6; John 18:39.

KING JAMES VERSION

18 And they cried out all at once, saying, Away with
this *man,* and release unto us Barabbas:
19 (Who for a certain sedition made in the city, and
for murder, was cast into prison.)
20 Pilate therefore, willing to release Jesus, spake
again to them.
21 But they cried, saying, Crucify *him,* crucify him.
22 And he said unto them the third time, Why, what
evil hath he done? I have found no cause of death in
him: I will therefore chastise him, and let *him* go.
23 And they were instant with loud voices, requiring that he might be crucified. And the voices of
them and of the chief priests prevailed.
24 And Pilate gave sentence that it should be as
they required.
25 And he released unto them him that for sedition
and murder was cast into prison, whom they had
desired; but he delivered Jesus to their will.

26 And as they led him away, they laid hold upon
one Simon, a Cyrenian, coming out of the country,
and on him they laid the cross, that he might bear *it*
after Jesus.
27 And there followed him a great company of
people, and of women, which also bewailed and
lamented him.
28 But Jesus turning unto them said, Daughters of
Jerusalem, weep not for me, but weep for yourselves,
and for your children.
29 For, behold, the days are coming, in the which
they shall say, Blessed *are* the barren, and the wombs
that never bare, and the paps which never gave suck.
30 Then shall they begin to say to the mountains,
Fall on us; and to the hills, Cover us.
31 For if they do these things in a green tree, what
shall be done in the dry?
32 And there were also two other, malefactors, led
with him to be put to death.
33 And when they were come to the place, which is
called Calvary, there they crucified him, and the malefactors, one on the right hand, and the other on the left.
34 Then said Jesus, Father, forgive them; for they
know not what they do. And they parted his raiment,
and cast lots.
35 And the people stood beholding. And the rulers
also with them derided *him,* saying, He saved others; let
him save himself, if he be Christ, the chosen of God.
36 And the soldiers also mocked him, coming to
him, and offering him vinegar,
37 And saying, If thou be the king of the Jews, save
thyself.
38 And a superscription also was written over him
in letters of Greek, and Latin, and Hebrew, THIS IS
THE KING OF THE JEWS.
39 And one of the malefactors which were hanged
railed on him, saying, If thou be Christ, save thyself
and us.

NEW LIVING TRANSLATION

18 Then a mighty roar rose from the crowd, and
with one voice they shouted, "Kill him, and release
Barabbas to us!" 19 (Barabbas was in prison for taking
part in an insurrection in Jerusalem against the
government, and for murder.) 20 Pilate argued with
them, because he wanted to release Jesus. 21 But they
kept shouting, "Crucify him! Crucify him!"
22 For the third time he demanded, "Why? What
crime has he committed? I have found no reason to
sentence him to death. So I will have him flogged,
and then I will release him."
23 But the mob shouted louder and louder, demanding that Jesus be crucified, and their voices
prevailed. 24 So Pilate sentenced Jesus to die as they
demanded. 25 As they had requested, he released
Barabbas, the man in prison for insurrection and
murder. But he turned Jesus over to them to do as
they wished.

The Crucifixion

26 As they led Jesus away, a man named Simon, who
was from Cyrene,* happened to be coming in from
the countryside. The soldiers seized him and put the
cross on him and made him carry it behind Jesus. 27 A
large crowd trailed behind, including many grief-
stricken women. 28 But Jesus turned and said to
them, "Daughters of Jerusalem, don't weep for me,
but weep for yourselves and for your children. 29 For
the days are coming when they will say, 'Fortunate indeed are the women who are childless, the wombs
that have not borne a child and the breasts that have
never nursed.' 30 People will beg the mountains, 'Fall
on us,' and plead with the hills, 'Bury us.'* 31 For if
these things are done when the tree is green, what
will happen when it is dry?*"
32 Two others, both criminals, were led out to be
executed with him. 33 When they came to a place
called The Skull,* they nailed him to the cross. And
the criminals were also crucified—one on his right
and one on his left.
34 Jesus said, "Father, forgive them, for they don't
know what they are doing."* And the soldiers
gambled for his clothes by throwing dice.*
35 The crowd watched and the leaders scoffed. "He
saved others," they said, "let him save himself if he is
really God's Messiah, the Chosen One." 36 The soldiers mocked him, too, by offering him a drink of
sour wine. 37 They called out to him, "If you are the
King of the Jews, save yourself!" 38 A sign was fastened above him with these words: "This is the King
of the Jews."
39 One of the criminals hanging beside him
scoffed, "So you're the Messiah, are you? Prove it by
saving yourself—and us, too, while you're at it!"

23:26 *Cyrene* was a city in northern Africa. **23:30** Hos 10:8. **23:31** Or *If these things are done to me, the living tree, what will happen to you, the dry tree?* **23:33** Sometimes rendered *Calvary,* which comes from the Latin word for "skull." **23:34a** This sentence is not included in many ancient manuscripts. **23:34b** Greek *by casting lots.* See Ps 22:18.

KING JAMES VERSION

40 But the other answering rebuked him, saying, Dost not thou fear God, seeing thou art in the same condemnation?

41 And we indeed justly; for we receive the due reward of our deeds: but this man hath done nothing amiss.

42 And he said unto Jesus, Lord, remember me when thou comest into thy kingdom.

43 And Jesus said unto him, Verily I say unto thee, Today shalt thou be with me in paradise.

44 And it was about the sixth hour, and there was a darkness over all the earth until the ninth hour.

45 And the sun was darkened, and the veil of the temple was rent in the midst.

46 And when Jesus had cried with a loud voice, he said, Father, into thy hands I commend my spirit: and having said thus, he gave up the ghost.

47 Now when the centurion saw what was done, he glorified God, saying, Certainly this was a righteous man.

48 And all the people that came together to that sight, beholding the things which were done, smote their breasts, and returned.

49 And all his acquaintance, and the women that followed him from Galilee, stood afar off, beholding these things.

50 And, behold, *there was* a man named Joseph, a counsellor; *and he was* a good man, and a just:

51 (The same had not consented to the counsel and deed of them;) *he was* of Arimathaea, a city of the Jews: who also himself waited for the kingdom of God.

52 This *man* went unto Pilate, and begged the body of Jesus.

53 And he took it down, and wrapped it in linen, and laid it in a sepulchre that was hewn in stone, wherein never man before was laid.

54 And that day was the preparation, and the sabbath drew on.

55 And the women also, which came with him from Galilee, followed after, and beheld the sepulchre, and how his body was laid.

56 And they returned, and prepared spices and ointments; and rested the sabbath day according to the commandment.

24 1 Now upon the first *day* of the week, very early in the morning, they came unto the sepulchre, bringing the spices which they had prepared, and certain *others* with them.

2 And they found the stone rolled away from the sepulchre.

3 And they entered in, and found not the body of the Lord Jesus.

4 And it came to pass, as they were much perplexed thereabout, behold, two men stood by them in shining garments:

NEW LIVING TRANSLATION

40 But the other criminal protested, "Don't you fear
God even when you have been sentenced to die?
41 We deserve to die for our crimes, but this man
hasn't done anything wrong." 42 Then he said, "Jesus,
remember me when you come into your Kingdom."

43 And Jesus replied, "I assure you, today you will be
with me in paradise."

The Death of Jesus

44 By this time it was about noon, and darkness fell
across the whole land until three o'clock. 45 The light
from the sun was gone. And suddenly, the curtain in
the sanctuary of the Temple was torn down the middle. 46 Then Jesus shouted, "Father, I entrust my spirit
into your hands!"* And with those words he breathed
his last.

47 When the Roman officer* overseeing the execution saw what had happened, he worshiped God
and said, "Surely this man was innocent.*" 48 And
when all the crowd that came to see the crucifixion
saw what had happened, they went home in deep
sorrow.* 49 But Jesus' friends, including the women
who had followed him from Galilee, stood at a distance watching.

The Burial of Jesus

50 Now there was a good and righteous man named
Joseph. He was a member of the Jewish high council,
51 but he had not agreed with the decision and actions of the other religious leaders. He was from the
town of Arimathea in Judea, and he was waiting for
the Kingdom of God to come. 52 He went to Pilate and
asked for Jesus' body. 53 Then he took the body down
from the cross and wrapped it in a long sheet of linen
cloth and laid it in a new tomb that had been carved
out of rock. 54 This was done late on Friday afternoon, the day of preparation,* as the Sabbath was
about to begin.

55 As his body was taken away, the women from
Galilee followed and saw the tomb where his body
was placed. 56 Then they went home and prepared
spices and ointments to anoint his body. But by the
time they were finished the Sabbath had begun, so
they rested as required by the law.

The Resurrection

24 But very early on Sunday morning* the
women went to the tomb, taking the spices
they had prepared. 2 They found that the stone had
been rolled away from the entrance. 3 So they went in,
but they didn't find the body of the Lord Jesus. 4 As
they stood there puzzled, two men suddenly appeared to them, clothed in dazzling robes.

23:46 Ps 31:5. **23:47a** Greek *the centurion.* **23:47b** Or *righteous.* **23:48** Greek *went home beating their breasts.* **23:54** Greek *It was the day of preparation.* **24:1** Greek *But on the first day of the week, very early in the morning.*

KING JAMES VERSION

5 And as they were afraid, and bowed down *their* faces to the earth, they said unto them, Why seek ye the living among the dead?

6 He is not here, but is risen: remember how he spake unto you when he was yet in Galilee,

7 Saying, The Son of man must be delivered into the hands of sinful men, and be crucified, and the third day rise again.

8 And they remembered his words,

9 And returned from the sepulchre, and told all these things unto the eleven, and to all the rest.

10 It was Mary Magdalene, and Joanna, and Mary *the mother* of James, and other *women that were* with them, which told these things unto the apostles.

11 And their words seemed to them as idle tales, and they believed them not.

12 Then arose Peter, and ran unto the sepulchre; and stooping down, he beheld the linen clothes laid by themselves, and departed, wondering in himself at that which was come to pass.

13 And, behold, two of them went that same day to a village called Emmaus, which was from Jerusalem *about* threescore furlongs.

14 And they talked together of all these things which had happened.

15 And it came to pass, that, while they communed *together* and reasoned, Jesus himself drew near, and went with them.

16 But their eyes were holden that they should not know him.

17 And he said unto them, What manner of communications *are* these that ye have one to another, as ye walk, and are sad?

18 And the one of them, whose name was Cleopas, answering said unto him, Art thou only a stranger in Jerusalem, and hast not known the things which are come to pass there in these days?

19 And he said unto them, What things? And they said unto him, Concerning Jesus of Nazareth, which was a prophet mighty in deed and word before God and all the people:

20 And how the chief priests and our rulers delivered him to be condemned to death, and have crucified him.

21 But we trusted that it had been he which should have redeemed Israel: and beside all this, today is the third day since these things were done.

22 Yea, and certain women also of our company made us astonished, which were early at the sepulchre;

23 And when they found not his body, they came, saying, that they had also seen a vision of angels, which said that he was alive.

24 And certain of them which were with us went to the sepulchre, and found *it* even so as the women had said: but him they saw not.

NEW LIVING TRANSLATION

5 The women were terrified and bowed with their
faces to the ground. Then the men asked, "Why are
you looking among the dead for someone who is
alive? 6 He isn't here! He is risen from the dead! Remember what he told you back in Galilee, 7 that the
Son of Man* must be betrayed into the hands of sinful men and be crucified, and that he would rise
again on the third day."

8 Then they remembered that he had said this. 9 So
they rushed back from the tomb to tell his eleven
disciples—and everyone else—what had happened.
10 It was Mary Magdalene, Joanna, Mary the mother
of James, and several other women who told the
apostles what had happened. 11 But the story
sounded like nonsense to the men, so they didn't believe it. 12 However, Peter jumped up and ran to the
tomb to look. Stooping, he peered in and saw the
empty linen wrappings; then he went home again,
wondering what had happened.

The Walk to Emmaus

13 That same day two of Jesus' followers were walking
to the village of Emmaus, seven miles* from Jerusalem. 14 As they walked along they were talking about
everything that had happened. 15 As they talked and
discussed these things, Jesus himself suddenly came
and began walking with them. 16 But God kept them
from recognizing him.

17 He asked them, "What are you discussing so
intently as you walk along?"

They stopped short, sadness written across their
faces. 18 Then one of them, Cleopas, replied, "You
must be the only person in Jerusalem who hasn't
heard about all the things that have happened there
the last few days."

19 "What things?" Jesus asked.

"The things that happened to Jesus, the man from
Nazareth," they said. "He was a prophet who did
powerful miracles, and he was a mighty teacher in
the eyes of God and all the people. 20 But our leading
priests and other religious leaders handed him over
to be condemned to death, and they crucified him.
21 We had hoped he was the Messiah who had come
to rescue Israel. This all happened three days ago.

22 "Then some women from our group of his followers were at his tomb early this morning, and they
came back with an amazing report. 23 They said his
body was missing, and they had seen angels who told
them Jesus is alive! 24 Some of our men ran out to see,
and sure enough, his body was gone, just as the
women had said."

24:7 "Son of Man" is a title Jesus used for himself. **24:13** Greek *60 stadia* [11.1 kilometers].

KING JAMES VERSION

25 Then he said unto them, O fools, and slow of
heart to believe all that the prophets have spoken:
26 Ought not Christ to have suffered these things,
and to enter into his glory?
27 And beginning at Moses and all the prophets, he
expounded unto them in all the scriptures the things
concerning himself.
28 And they drew nigh unto the village, whither
they went: and he made as though he would have
gone further.
29 But they constrained him, saying, Abide with us:
for it is toward evening, and the day is far spent. And
he went in to tarry with them.
30 And it came to pass, as he sat at meat with them, he
took bread, and blessed *it,* and brake, and gave to them.
31 And their eyes were opened, and they knew him;
and he vanished out of their sight.
32 And they said one to another, Did not our heart
burn within us, while he talked with us by the way,
and while he opened to us the scriptures?
33 And they rose up the same hour, and returned to
Jerusalem, and found the eleven gathered together,
and them that were with them,
34 Saying, The Lord is risen indeed, and hath appeared to Simon.
35 And they told what things *were done* in the way,
and how he was known of them in breaking of bread.
36 And as they thus spake, Jesus himself stood in
the midst of them, and saith unto them, Peace *be*
unto you.
37 But they were terrified and affrighted, and
supposed that they had seen a spirit.
38 And he said unto them, Why are ye troubled?
and why do thoughts arise in your hearts?
39 Behold my hands and my feet, that it is I myself:
handle me, and see; for a spirit hath not flesh and
bones, as ye see me have.
40 And when he had thus spoken, he shewed them
his hands and *his* feet.
41 And while they yet believed not for joy, and wondered, he said unto them, Have ye here any meat?
42 And they gave him a piece of a broiled fish, and
of an honeycomb.
43 And he took *it,* and did eat before them.
44 And he said unto them, These *are* the words
which I spake unto you, while I was yet with you, that
all things must be fulfilled, which were written in the
law of Moses, and *in* the prophets, and *in* the psalms,
concerning me.
45 Then opened he their understanding, that they
might understand the scriptures,
46 And said unto them, Thus it is written, and thus
it behoved Christ to suffer, and to rise from the dead
the third day:
47 And that repentance and remission of sins
should be preached in his name among all nations,
beginning at Jerusalem.
48 And ye are witnesses of these things.

NEW LIVING TRANSLATION

25 Then Jesus said to them, "You foolish people!
You find it so hard to believe all that the prophets
wrote in the Scriptures. 26 Wasn't it clearly predicted
that the Messiah would have to suffer all these things
before entering his glory?" 27 Then Jesus took them
through the writings of Moses and all the prophets,
explaining from all the Scriptures the things concerning himself.
28 By this time they were nearing Emmaus and the
end of their journey. Jesus acted as if he were going
on, 29 but they begged him, "Stay the night with us,
since it is getting late." So he went home with them.
30 As they sat down to eat,* he took the bread and
blessed it. Then he broke it and gave it to them.
31 Suddenly, their eyes were opened, and they recognized him. And at that moment he disappeared!
32 They said to each other, "Didn't our hearts burn
within us as he talked with us on the road and explained the Scriptures to us?" 33 And within the hour
they were on their way back to Jerusalem. There they
found the eleven disciples and the others who had
gathered with them, 34 who said, "The Lord has really
risen! He appeared to Peter.*"

Jesus Appears to the Disciples

35 Then the two from Emmaus told their story of how
Jesus had appeared to them as they were walking
along the road, and how they had recognized him as
he was breaking the bread. 36 And just as they were
telling about it, Jesus himself was suddenly standing
there among them. "Peace be with you," he said.
37 But the whole group was startled and frightened,
thinking they were seeing a ghost!
38 "Why are you frightened?" he asked. "Why are
your hearts filled with doubt? 39 Look at my hands.
Look at my feet. You can see that it's really me. Touch
me and make sure that I am not a ghost, because
ghosts don't have bodies, as you see that I do." 40 As
he spoke, he showed them his hands and his feet.
41 Still they stood there in disbelief, filled with joy
and wonder. Then he asked them, "Do you have anything here to eat?" 42 They gave him a piece of broiled
fish, 43 and he ate it as they watched.
44 Then he said, "When I was with you before, I
told you that everything written about me in the law
of Moses and the prophets and in the Psalms must be
fulfilled." 45 Then he opened their minds to understand the Scriptures. 46 And he said, "Yes, it was written long ago that the Messiah would suffer and die
and rise from the dead on the third day. 47 It was also
written that this message would be proclaimed in the
authority of his name to all the nations,* beginning
in Jerusalem: 'There is forgiveness of sins for all who
repent.' 48 You are witnesses of all these things.

24:30 Or *As they reclined.* **24:34** Greek *Simon.* **24:47** Or *all peoples.*

KING JAMES VERSION

49And, behold, I send the promise of my Father upon you: but tarry ye in the city of Jerusalem, until ye be endued with power from on high.

50And he led them out as far as to Bethany, and he lifted up his hands, and blessed them.

51And it came to pass, while he blessed them, he was parted from them, and carried up into heaven.

52And they worshipped him, and returned to Jerusalem with great joy:

53And were continually in the temple, praising and blessing God. Amen.

NEW LIVING TRANSLATION

49"And now I will send the Holy Spirit, just as my Father promised. But stay here in the city until the Holy Spirit comes and fills you with power from heaven."

The Ascension

50Then Jesus led them to Bethany, and lifting his
hands to heaven, he blessed them. 51While he was
blessing them, he left them and was taken up to
heaven. 52So they worshiped him and then returned
to Jerusalem filled with great joy. 53And they spent all
of their time in the Temple, praising God.

John

KING JAMES VERSION

1 1 In the beginning was the Word, and the Word
was with God, and the Word was God.
2 The same was in the beginning with God.
3 All things were made by him; and without him
was not any thing made that was made.
4 In him was life; and the life was the light of men.
5 And the light shineth in darkness; and the darkness comprehended it not.
6 There was a man sent from God, whose name *was*
John.
7 The same came for a witness, to bear witness of
the Light, that all *men* through him might believe.
8 He was not that Light, but *was sent* to bear witness of that Light.
9 *That* was the true Light, which lighteth every man
that cometh into the world.
10 He was in the world, and the world was made
by him, and the world knew him not.
11 He came unto his own, and his own received
him not.
12 But as many as received him, to them gave he
power to become the sons of God, *even* to them that
believe on his name:
13 Which were born, not of blood, nor of the will of
the flesh, nor of the will of man, but of God.
14 And the Word was made flesh, and dwelt among
us, (and we beheld his glory, the glory as of the only
begotten of the Father,) full of grace and truth.
15 John bare witness of him, and cried, saying, This
was he of whom I spake, He that cometh after me is
preferred before me: for he was before me.
16 And of his fulness have all we received, and
grace for grace.
17 For the law was given by Moses, *but* grace and
truth came by Jesus Christ.
18 No man hath seen God at any time; the only
begotten Son, which is in the bosom of the Father,
he hath declared *him*.

NEW LIVING TRANSLATION

Prologue: Christ, the Eternal Word

1 1 In the beginning the Word already existed.
The Word was with God,
and the Word was God.
2 He existed in the beginning with God.
3 God created everything through him,
and nothing was created except through him.
4 The Word gave life to everything that was created,*
and his life brought light to everyone.
5 The light shines in the darkness,
and the darkness can never extinguish it.*

6 God sent a man, John the Baptist,* 7 to tell about
the light so that everyone might believe because of
his testimony. 8 John himself was not the light; he
was simply a witness to tell about the light. 9 The one
who is the true light, who gives light to everyone,
was coming into the world.
10 He came into the very world he created, but the
world didn't recognize him. 11 He came to his own
people, and even they rejected him. 12 But to all who
believed him and accepted him, he gave the right to
become children of God. 13 They are reborn—not
with a physical birth resulting from human passion
or plan, but a birth that comes from God.
14 So the Word became human* and made his
home among us. He was full of unfailing love and
faithfulness.* And we have seen his glory, the glory
of the Father's one and only Son.
15 John testified about him when he shouted to the
crowds, "This is the one I was talking about when I
said, 'Someone is coming after me who is far greater
than I am, for he existed long before me.'"
16 From his abundance we have all received one
gracious blessing after another.* 17 For the law was
given through Moses, but God's unfailing love and
faithfulness came through Jesus Christ. 18 No one has
ever seen God. But the unique One, who is himself
God,* is near to the Father's heart. He has revealed
God to us.

1:3-4 Or *and nothing that was created was created except through him. The Word gave life to everything.* **1:5** Or *and the darkness has not understood it.* **1:6** Greek *a man named John.* **1:14a** Greek *became flesh.* **1:14b** Or *grace and truth;* also in 1:17. **1:16** Or *received the grace of Christ rather than the grace of the law;* Greek reads *received grace upon grace.* **1:18** Some manuscripts read *But the one and only Son.*

KING JAMES VERSION

19And this is the record of John, when the Jews sent priests and Levites from Jerusalem to ask him, Who art thou?

20And he confessed, and denied not; but confessed, I am not the Christ.

21And they asked him, What then? Art thou Elias? And he saith, I am not. Art thou that prophet? And he answered, No.

22Then said they unto him, Who art thou? that we may give an answer to them that sent us. What sayest thou of thyself?

23He said, I *am* the voice of one crying in the wilderness, Make straight the way of the Lord, as said the prophet Esaias.

24And they which were sent were of the Pharisees.

25And they asked him, and said unto him, Why baptizest thou then, if thou be not that Christ, nor Elias, neither that prophet?

26John answered them, saying, I baptize with water: but there standeth one among you, whom ye know not;

27He it is, who coming after me is preferred before me, whose shoe's latchet I am not worthy to unloose.

28These things were done in Bethabara beyond Jordan, where John was baptizing.

29The next day John seeth Jesus coming unto him, and saith, Behold the Lamb of God, which taketh away the sin of the world.

30This is he of whom I said, After me cometh a man which is preferred before me: for he was before me.

31And I knew him not: but that he should be made manifest to Israel, therefore am I come baptizing with water.

32And John bare record, saying, I saw the Spirit descending from heaven like a dove, and it abode upon him.

33And I knew him not: but he that sent me to baptize with water, the same said unto me, Upon whom thou shalt see the Spirit descending, and remaining on him, the same is he which baptizeth with the Holy Ghost.

34And I saw, and bare record that this is the Son of God.

35Again the next day after John stood, and two of his disciples;

36And looking upon Jesus as he walked, he saith, Behold the Lamb of God!

37And the two disciples heard him speak, and they followed Jesus.

38Then Jesus turned, and saw them following, and saith unto them, What seek ye? They said unto him, Rabbi, (which is to say, being interpreted, Master,) where dwellest thou?

NEW LIVING TRANSLATION

The Testimony of John the Baptist

19This was John's testimony when the Jewish leaders
sent priests and Temple assistants* from Jerusalem
to ask John, "Who are you?" 20He came right out and
said, "I am not the Messiah."

21"Well then, who are you?" they asked. "Are you
Elijah?"

"No," he replied.

"Are you the Prophet we are expecting?"*

"No."

22"Then who are you? We need an answer for
those who sent us. What do you have to say about
yourself?"

23John replied in the words of the prophet Isaiah:

"I am a voice shouting in the wilderness,
'Clear the way for the LORD's coming!'"*

24Then the Pharisees who had been sent 25asked
him, "If you aren't the Messiah or Elijah or the
Prophet, what right do you have to baptize?"

26John told them, "I baptize with* water, but right
here in the crowd is someone you do not recognize.
27Though his ministry follows mine, I'm not even
worthy to be his slave and untie the straps of his
sandal."

28This encounter took place in Bethany, an area
east of the Jordan River, where John was baptizing.

Jesus, the Lamb of God

29The next day John saw Jesus coming toward him
and said, "Look! The Lamb of God who takes away the
sin of the world! 30He is the one I was talking about
when I said, 'A man is coming after me who is far
greater than I am, for he existed long before me.' 31I
did not recognize him as the Messiah, but I have
been baptizing with water so that he might be revealed to Israel."

32Then John testified, "I saw the Holy Spirit descending like a dove from heaven and resting upon
him. 33I didn't know he was the one, but when God
sent me to baptize with water, he told me, 'The one
on whom you see the Spirit descend and rest is the
one who will baptize with the Holy Spirit.' 34I saw
this happen to Jesus, so I testify that he is the Chosen
One of God.*"

The First Disciples

35The following day John was again standing with
two of his disciples. 36As Jesus walked by, John
looked at him and declared, "Look! There is the Lamb
of God!" 37When John's two disciples heard this, they
followed Jesus.

38Jesus looked around and saw them following.
"What do you want?" he asked them.

They replied, "Rabbi" (which means "Teacher"),
"where are you staying?"

1:19 Greek *and Levites.* **1:21** Greek *Are you the Prophet?* See Deut 18:15, 18; Mal 4:5-6. **1:23** Isa 40:3. **1:26** Or *in;* also in 1:31, 33. **1:34** Some manuscripts read *the Son of God.*

KING JAMES VERSION

39 He saith unto them, Come and see. They came
and saw where he dwelt, and abode with him that
day: for it was about the tenth hour.
40 One of the two which heard John *speak*, and
followed him, was Andrew, Simon Peter's brother.
41 He first findeth his own brother Simon, and
saith unto him, We have found the Messias, which is,
being interpreted, the Christ.
42 And he brought him to Jesus. And when Jesus
beheld him, he said, Thou art Simon the son of Jona:
thou shalt be called Cephas, which is by interpretation, A stone.
43 The day following Jesus would go forth into
Galilee, and findeth Philip, and saith unto him,
Follow me.
44 Now Philip was of Bethsaida, the city of Andrew
and Peter.
45 Philip findeth Nathanael, and saith unto him,
We have found him, of whom Moses in the law, and
the prophets, did write, Jesus of Nazareth, the son
of Joseph.
46 And Nathanael said unto him, Can there any
good thing come out of Nazareth? Philip saith unto
him, Come and see.
47 Jesus saw Nathanael coming to him, and saith of
him, Behold an Israelite indeed, in whom is no guile!
48 Nathanael saith unto him, Whence knowest
thou me? Jesus answered and said unto him, Before
that Philip called thee, when thou wast under the fig
tree, I saw thee.
49 Nathanael answered and saith unto him, Rabbi,
thou art the Son of God; thou art the King of Israel.
50 Jesus answered and said unto him, Because I
said unto thee, I saw thee under the fig tree, believest
thou? thou shalt see greater things than these.
51 And he saith unto him, Verily, verily, I say unto
you, Hereafter ye shall see heaven open, and the
angels of God ascending and descending upon the
Son of man.

2 1 And the third day there was a marriage in
Cana of Galilee; and the mother of Jesus was
there:
2 And both Jesus was called, and his disciples, to
the marriage.
3 And when they wanted wine, the mother of Jesus
saith unto him, They have no wine.
4 Jesus saith unto her, Woman, what have I to do
with thee? mine hour is not yet come.
5 His mother saith unto the servants, Whatsoever
he saith unto you, do *it*.
6 And there were set there six waterpots of stone,
after the manner of the purifying of the Jews, containing two or three firkins apiece.
7 Jesus saith unto them, Fill the waterpots with
water. And they filled them up to the brim.

NEW LIVING TRANSLATION

39 "Come and see," he said. It was about four
o'clock in the afternoon when they went with him to
the place where he was staying, and they remained
with him the rest of the day.
40 Andrew, Simon Peter's brother, was one of these
men who heard what John said and then followed
Jesus. 41 Andrew went to find his brother, Simon, and
told him, "We have found the Messiah" (which
means "Christ"*).
42 Then Andrew brought Simon to meet Jesus.
Looking intently at Simon, Jesus said, "Your name is
Simon, son of John—but you will be called Cephas"
(which means "Peter"*).
43 The next day Jesus decided to go to Galilee. He
found Philip and said to him, "Come, follow me."
44 Philip was from Bethsaida, Andrew and Peter's
hometown.
45 Philip went to look for Nathanael and told him,
"We have found the very person Moses* and the
prophets wrote about! His name is Jesus, the son of
Joseph from Nazareth."
46 "Nazareth!" exclaimed Nathanael. "Can anything good come from Nazareth?"
"Come and see for yourself," Philip replied.
47 As they approached, Jesus said, "Now here is a
genuine son of Israel—a man of complete integrity."
48 "How do you know about me?" Nathanael asked.
Jesus replied, "I could see you under the fig tree
before Philip found you."
49 Then Nathanael exclaimed, "Rabbi, you are the
Son of God—the King of Israel!"
50 Jesus asked him, "Do you believe this just because I told you I had seen you under the fig tree?
You will see greater things than this." 51 Then he said,
"I tell you the truth, you will all see heaven open and
the angels of God going up and down on the Son of
Man, the one who is the stairway between heaven
and earth.*"

The Wedding at Cana

2 The next day* there was a wedding celebration
in the village of Cana in Galilee. Jesus' mother
was there, 2 and Jesus and his disciples were also invited to the celebration. 3 The wine supply ran out
during the festivities, so Jesus' mother told him,
"They have no more wine."
4 "Dear woman, that's not our problem," Jesus replied. "My time has not yet come."
5 But his mother told the servants, "Do whatever
he tells you."
6 Standing nearby were six stone water jars, used
for Jewish ceremonial washing. Each could hold
twenty to thirty gallons.* 7 Jesus told the servants,
"Fill the jars with water." When the jars had been

1:41 *Messiah* (a Hebrew term) and *Christ* (a Greek term) both mean "the anointed one." **1:42** The names *Cephas* (from Aramaic) and *Peter* (from Greek) both mean "rock." **1:45** Greek *Moses in the law.* **1:51** Greek *going up and down on the Son of Man;* see Gen 28:10-17. "Son of Man" is a title Jesus used for himself. **2:1** Greek *On the third day;* see 1:35, 43. **2:6** Greek *2 or 3 measures* [75 to 113 liters].

KING JAMES VERSION

8 And he saith unto them, Draw out now, and bear unto the governor of the feast. And they bare *it*.

9 When the ruler of the feast had tasted the water that was made wine, and knew not whence it was: (but the servants which drew the water knew;) the governor of the feast called the bridegroom,

10 And saith unto him, Every man at the beginning doth set forth good wine; and when men have well drunk, then that which is worse: *but* thou hast kept the good wine until now.

11 This beginning of miracles did Jesus in Cana of Galilee, and manifested forth his glory; and his disciples believed on him.

12 After this he went down to Capernaum, he, and his mother, and his brethren, and his disciples: and they continued there not many days.

13 And the Jews' passover was at hand, and Jesus went up to Jerusalem,

14 And found in the temple those that sold oxen and sheep and doves, and the changers of money sitting:

15 And when he had made a scourge of small cords, he drove them all out of the temple, and the sheep, and the oxen; and poured out the changers' money, and overthrew the tables;

16 And said unto them that sold doves, Take these things hence; make not my Father's house an house of merchandise.

17 And his disciples remembered that it was written, The zeal of thine house hath eaten me up.

18 Then answered the Jews and said unto him, What sign shewest thou unto us, seeing that thou doest these things?

19 Jesus answered and said unto them, Destroy this temple, and in three days I will raise it up.

20 Then said the Jews, Forty and six years was this temple in building, and wilt thou rear it up in three days?

21 But he spake of the temple of his body.

22 When therefore he was risen from the dead, his disciples remembered that he had said this unto them; and they believed the scripture, and the word which Jesus had said.

23 Now when he was in Jerusalem at the passover, in the feast *day*, many believed in his name, when they saw the miracles which he did.

24 But Jesus did not commit himself unto them, because he knew all *men*,

25 And needed not that any should testify of man: for he knew what was in man.

3 1 There was a man of the Pharisees, named Nicodemus, a ruler of the Jews:

2 The same came to Jesus by night, and said unto

NEW LIVING TRANSLATION

filled, 8 he said, "Now dip some out, and take it to the master of ceremonies." So the servants followed his instructions.

9 When the master of ceremonies tasted the water that was now wine, not knowing where it had come from (though, of course, the servants knew), he called the bridegroom over. 10 "A host always serves the best wine first," he said. "Then, when everyone has had a lot to drink, he brings out the less expensive wine. But you have kept the best until now!"

11 This miraculous sign at Cana in Galilee was the first time Jesus revealed his glory. And his disciples believed in him.

12 After the wedding he went to Capernaum for a few days with his mother, his brothers, and his disciples.

Jesus Clears the Temple

13 It was nearly time for the Jewish Passover celebration, so Jesus went to Jerusalem. 14 In the Temple area he saw merchants selling cattle, sheep, and doves for sacrifices; he also saw dealers at tables exchanging foreign money. 15 Jesus made a whip from some ropes and chased them all out of the Temple. He drove out the sheep and cattle, scattered the money changers' coins over the floor, and turned over their tables. 16 Then, going over to the people who sold doves, he told them, "Get these things out of here. Stop turning my Father's house into a marketplace!"

17 Then his disciples remembered this prophecy from the Scriptures: "Passion for God's house will consume me."*

18 But the Jewish leaders demanded, "What are you doing? If God gave you authority to do this, show us a miraculous sign to prove it."

19 "All right," Jesus replied. "Destroy this temple, and in three days I will raise it up."

20 "What!" they exclaimed. "It has taken forty-six years to build this Temple, and you can rebuild it in three days?" 21 But when Jesus said "this temple," he meant his own body. 22 After he was raised from the dead, his disciples remembered he had said this, and they believed both the Scriptures and what Jesus had said.

Jesus and Nicodemus

23 Because of the miraculous signs Jesus did in Jerusalem at the Passover celebration, many began to trust in him. 24 But Jesus didn't trust them, because he knew human nature. 25 No one needed to tell him what mankind is really like.

3 There was a man named Nicodemus, a Jewish religious leader who was a Pharisee. 2 After dark one evening, he came to speak with Jesus. "Rabbi," he

2:17 Or *"Concern for God's house will be my undoing."* Ps 69:9.

him, Rabbi, we know that thou art a teacher come from God: for no man can do these miracles that thou doest, except God be with him.

3 Jesus answered and said unto him, Verily, verily, I say unto thee, Except a man be born again, he cannot see the kingdom of God.

4 Nicodemus saith unto him, How can a man be born when he is old? can he enter the second time into his mother's womb, and be born?

5 Jesus answered, Verily, verily, I say unto thee, Except a man be born of water and *of* the Spirit, he cannot enter into the kingdom of God.

6 That which is born of the flesh is flesh; and that which is born of the Spirit is spirit.

7 Marvel not that I said unto thee, Ye must be born again.

8 The wind bloweth where it listeth, and thou hearest the sound thereof, but canst not tell whence it cometh, and whither it goeth: so is every one that is born of the Spirit.

9 Nicodemus answered and said unto him, How can these things be?

10 Jesus answered and said unto him, Art thou a master of Israel, and knowest not these things?

11 Verily, verily, I say unto thee, We speak that we do know, and testify that we have seen; and ye receive not our witness.

12 If I have told you earthly things, and ye believe not, how shall ye believe, if I tell you *of* heavenly things?

13 And no man hath ascended up to heaven, but he that came down from heaven, *even* the Son of man which is in heaven.

14 And as Moses lifted up the serpent in the wilderness, even so must the Son of man be lifted up:

15 That whosoever believeth in him should not perish, but have eternal life.

16 For God so loved the world, that he gave his only begotten Son, that whosoever believeth in him should not perish, but have everlasting life.

17 For God sent not his Son into the world to condemn the world; but that the world through him might be saved.

18 He that believeth on him is not condemned: but he that believeth not is condemned already, because he hath not believed in the name of the only begotten Son of God.

19 And this is the condemnation, that light is come into the world, and men loved darkness rather than light, because their deeds were evil.

20 For every one that doeth evil hateth the light, neither cometh to the light, lest his deeds should be reproved.

21 But he that doeth truth cometh to the light, that his deeds may be made manifest, that they are wrought in God.

said, "we all know that God has sent you to teach us. Your miraculous signs are evidence that God is with you."

3 Jesus replied, "I tell you the truth, unless you are born again,* you cannot see the Kingdom of God."

4 "What do you mean?" exclaimed Nicodemus. "How can an old man go back into his mother's womb and be born again?"

5 Jesus replied, "I assure you, no one can enter the Kingdom of God without being born of water and the Spirit.* 6 Humans can reproduce only human life, but the Holy Spirit gives birth to spiritual life.* 7 So don't be surprised when I say, 'You* must be born again.' 8 The wind blows wherever it wants. Just as you can hear the wind but can't tell where it comes from or where it is going, so you can't explain how people are born of the Spirit."

9 "How are these things possible?" Nicodemus asked.

10 Jesus replied, "You are a respected Jewish teacher, and yet you don't understand these things? 11 I assure you, we tell you what we know and have seen, and yet you won't believe our testimony. 12 But if you don't believe me when I tell you about earthly things, how can you possibly believe if I tell you about heavenly things? 13 No one has ever gone to heaven and returned. But the Son of Man* has come down from heaven. 14 And as Moses lifted up the bronze snake on a pole in the wilderness, so the Son of Man must be lifted up, 15 so that everyone who believes in him will have eternal life.*

16 "For God loved the world so much that he gave his one and only Son, so that everyone who believes in him will not perish but have eternal life. 17 God sent his Son into the world not to judge the world, but to save the world through him.

18 "There is no judgment against anyone who believes in him. But anyone who does not believe in him has already been judged for not believing in God's one and only Son. 19 And the judgment is based on this fact: God's light came into the world, but people loved the darkness more than the light, for their actions were evil. 20 All who do evil hate the light and refuse to go near it for fear their sins will be exposed. 21 But those who do what is right come to the light so others can see that they are doing what God wants.*"

3:3 Or *born from above;* also in 3:7. **3:5** Or *and spirit.* The Greek word for *Spirit* can also be translated *wind;* see 3:8. **3:6** Greek *what is born of the Spirit is spirit.* **3:7** The Greek word for *you* is plural; also in 3:12. **3:13** Some manuscripts add *who lives in heaven.* "Son of Man" is a title Jesus used for himself. **3:15** Or *everyone who believes will have eternal life in him.* **3:21** Or *can see God at work in what he is doing.*

KING JAMES VERSION

22 After these things came Jesus and his disciples into the land of Judaea; and there he tarried with them, and baptized.

23 And John also was baptizing in Aenon near to Salim, because there was much water there: and they came, and were baptized.

24 For John was not yet cast into prison.

25 Then there arose a question between *some* of John's disciples and the Jews about purifying.

26 And they came unto John, and said unto him, Rabbi, he that was with thee beyond Jordan, to whom thou barest witness, behold, the same baptizeth, and all *men* come to him.

27 John answered and said, A man can receive nothing, except it be given him from heaven.

28 Ye yourselves bear me witness, that I said, I am not the Christ, but that I am sent before him.

29 He that hath the bride is the bridegroom: but the friend of the bridegroom, which standeth and heareth him, rejoiceth greatly because of the bridegroom's voice: this my joy therefore is fulfilled.

30 He must increase, but I *must* decrease.

31 He that cometh from above is above all: he that is of the earth is earthly, and speaketh of the earth: he that cometh from heaven is above all.

32 And what he hath seen and heard, that he testifieth; and no man receiveth his testimony.

33 He that hath received his testimony hath set to his seal that God is true.

34 For he whom God hath sent speaketh the words of God: for God giveth not the Spirit by measure *unto him.*

35 The Father loveth the Son, and hath given all things into his hand.

36 He that believeth on the Son hath everlasting life: and he that believeth not the Son shall not see life; but the wrath of God abideth on him.

4 1 When therefore the Lord knew how the Pharisees had heard that Jesus made and baptized more disciples than John,

2 (Though Jesus himself baptized not, but his disciples,)

3 He left Judaea, and departed again into Galilee.

4 And he must needs go through Samaria.

5 Then cometh he to a city of Samaria, which is called Sychar, near to the parcel of ground that Jacob gave to his son Joseph.

6 Now Jacob's well was there. Jesus therefore, being wearied with *his* journey, sat thus on the well: *and* it was about the sixth hour.

7 There cometh a woman of Samaria to draw water: Jesus saith unto her, Give me to drink.

8 (For his disciples were gone away unto the city to buy meat.)

9 Then saith the woman of Samaria unto him, How is it that thou, being a Jew, askest drink of me, which

NEW LIVING TRANSLATION

John the Baptist Exalts Jesus

22 Then Jesus and his disciples left Jerusalem and went into the Judean countryside. Jesus spent some time with them there, baptizing people.

23 At this time John the Baptist was baptizing at Aenon, near Salim, because there was plenty of water there; and people kept coming to him for baptism. 24 (This was before John was thrown into prison.) 25 A debate broke out between John's disciples and a certain Jew* over ceremonial cleansing. 26 So John's disciples came to him and said, "Rabbi, the man you met on the other side of the Jordan River, the one you identified as the Messiah, is also baptizing people. And everybody is going to him instead of coming to us."

27 John replied, "No one can receive anything unless God gives it from heaven. 28 You yourselves know how plainly I told you, 'I am not the Messiah. I am only here to prepare the way for him.' 29 It is the bridegroom who marries the bride, and the best man is simply glad to stand with him and hear his vows. Therefore, I am filled with joy at his success. 30 He must become greater and greater, and I must become less and less.

31 "He has come from above and is greater than anyone else. We are of the earth, and we speak of earthly things, but he has come from heaven and is greater than anyone else.* 32 He testifies about what he has seen and heard, but how few believe what he tells them! 33 Anyone who accepts his testimony can affirm that God is true. 34 For he is sent by God. He speaks God's words, for God gives him the Spirit without limit. 35 The Father loves his Son and has put everything into his hands. 36 And anyone who believes in God's Son has eternal life. Anyone who doesn't obey the Son will never experience eternal life but remains under God's angry judgment."

Jesus and the Samaritan Woman

4 Jesus* knew the Pharisees had heard that he was baptizing and making more disciples than John 2 (though Jesus himself didn't baptize them—his disciples did). 3 So he left Judea and returned to Galilee.

4 He had to go through Samaria on the way. 5 Eventually he came to the Samaritan village of Sychar, near the field that Jacob gave to his son Joseph. 6 Jacob's well was there; and Jesus, tired from the long walk, sat wearily beside the well about noontime. 7 Soon a Samaritan woman came to draw water, and Jesus said to her, "Please give me a drink." 8 He was alone at the time because his disciples had gone into the village to buy some food.

9 The woman was surprised, for Jews refuse to have anything to do with Samaritans.* She said to

3:25 Some manuscripts read *some Jews.* **3:31** Some manuscripts do not include *and is greater than anyone else.* **4:1** Some manuscripts read *The Lord.* **4:9** Some manuscripts do not include this sentence.

KING JAMES VERSION

am a woman of Samaria? for the Jews have no dealings with the Samaritans.

10 Jesus answered and said unto her, If thou knewest the gift of God, and who it is that saith to thee, Give me to drink; thou wouldest have asked of him, and he would have given thee living water.

11 The woman saith unto him, Sir, thou hast nothing to draw with, and the well is deep: from whence then hast thou that living water?

12 Art thou greater than our father Jacob, which gave us the well, and drank thereof himself, and his children, and his cattle?

13 Jesus answered and said unto her, Whosoever drinketh of this water shall thirst again:

14 But whosoever drinketh of the water that I shall give him shall never thirst; but the water that I shall give him shall be in him a well of water springing up into everlasting life.

15 The woman saith unto him, Sir, give me this water, that I thirst not, neither come hither to draw.

16 Jesus saith unto her, Go, call thy husband, and come hither.

17 The woman answered and said, I have no husband. Jesus said unto her, Thou hast well said, I have no husband:

18 For thou hast had five husbands; and he whom thou now hast is not thy husband: in that saidst thou truly.

19 The woman saith unto him, Sir, I perceive that thou art a prophet.

20 Our fathers worshipped in this mountain; and ye say, that in Jerusalem is the place where men ought to worship.

21 Jesus saith unto her, Woman, believe me, the hour cometh, when ye shall neither in this mountain, nor yet at Jerusalem, worship the Father.

22 Ye worship ye know not what: we know what we worship: for salvation is of the Jews.

23 But the hour cometh, and now is, when the true worshippers shall worship the Father in spirit and in truth: for the Father seeketh such to worship him.

24 God *is* a Spirit: and they that worship him must worship *him* in spirit and in truth.

25 The woman saith unto him, I know that Messias cometh, which is called Christ: when he is come, he will tell us all things.

26 Jesus saith unto her, I that speak unto thee am *he*.

27 And upon this came his disciples, and marvelled that he talked with the woman: yet no man said, What seekest thou? or, Why talkest thou with her?

28 The woman then left her waterpot, and went her way into the city, and saith to the men,

29 Come, see a man, which told me all things that ever I did: is not this the Christ?

30 Then they went out of the city, and came unto him.

31 In the mean while his disciples prayed him, saying, Master, eat.

NEW LIVING TRANSLATION

Jesus, "You are a Jew, and I am a Samaritan woman. Why are you asking me for a drink?"

10 Jesus replied, "If you only knew the gift God has for you and who you are speaking to, you would ask me, and I would give you living water."

11 "But sir, you don't have a rope or a bucket," she said, "and this well is very deep. Where would you get this living water? 12 And besides, do you think you're greater than our ancestor Jacob, who gave us this well? How can you offer better water than he and his sons and his animals enjoyed?"

13 Jesus replied, "Anyone who drinks this water will soon become thirsty again. 14 But those who drink the water I give will never be thirsty again. It becomes a fresh, bubbling spring within them, giving them eternal life."

15 "Please, sir," the woman said, "give me this water! Then I'll never be thirsty again, and I won't have to come here to get water."

16 "Go and get your husband," Jesus told her.

17 "I don't have a husband," the woman replied.

Jesus said, "You're right! You don't have a husband— 18 for you have had five husbands, and you aren't even married to the man you're living with now. You certainly spoke the truth!"

19 "Sir," the woman said, "you must be a prophet. 20 So tell me, why is it that you Jews insist that Jerusalem is the only place of worship, while we Samaritans claim it is here at Mount Gerizim,* where our ancestors worshiped?"

21 Jesus replied, "Believe me, dear woman, the time is coming when it will no longer matter whether you worship the Father on this mountain or in Jerusalem. 22 You Samaritans know very little about the one you worship, while we Jews know all about him, for salvation comes through the Jews. 23 But the time is coming—indeed it's here now—when true worshipers will worship the Father in spirit and in truth. The Father is looking for those who will worship him that way. 24 For God is Spirit, so those who worship him must worship in spirit and in truth."

25 The woman said, "I know the Messiah is coming—the one who is called Christ. When he comes, he will explain everything to us."

26 Then Jesus told her, "I AM the Messiah!"*

27 Just then his disciples came back. They were shocked to find him talking to a woman, but none of them had the nerve to ask, "What do you want with her?" or "Why are you talking to her?" 28 The woman left her water jar beside the well and ran back to the village, telling everyone, 29 "Come and see a man who told me everything I ever did! Could he possibly be the Messiah?" 30 So the people came streaming from the village to see him.

31 Meanwhile, the disciples were urging Jesus, "Rabbi, eat something."

4:20 Greek *on this mountain.* **4:26** Or *"The 'I AM' is here"*; or *"I am the LORD"*; Greek reads *"I am, the one speaking to you."* See Exod 3:14.

KING JAMES VERSION

32But he said unto them, I have meat to eat that ye know not of.

33Therefore said the disciples one to another, Hath any man brought him *aught* to eat?

34Jesus saith unto them, My meat is to do the will of him that sent me, and to finish his work.

35Say not ye, There are yet four months, and *then* cometh harvest? behold, I say unto you, Lift up your eyes, and look on the fields; for they are white already to harvest.

36And he that reapeth receiveth wages, and gathereth fruit unto life eternal: that both he that soweth and he that reapeth may rejoice together.

37And herein is that saying true, One soweth, and another reapeth.

38I sent you to reap that whereon ye bestowed no labour: other men laboured, and ye are entered into their labours.

39And many of the Samaritans of that city believed on him for the saying of the woman, which testified, He told me all that ever I did.

40So when the Samaritans were come unto him, they besought him that he would tarry with them: and he abode there two days.

41And many more believed because of his own word;

42And said unto the woman, Now we believe, not because of thy saying: for we have heard *him* ourselves, and know that this is indeed the Christ, the Saviour of the world.

43Now after two days he departed thence, and went into Galilee.

44For Jesus himself testified, that a prophet hath no honour in his own country.

45Then when he was come into Galilee, the Galilaeans received him, having seen all the things that he did at Jerusalem at the feast: for they also went unto the feast.

46So Jesus came again into Cana of Galilee, where he made the water wine. And there was a certain nobleman, whose son was sick at Capernaum.

47When he heard that Jesus was come out of Judaea into Galilee, he went unto him, and besought him that he would come down, and heal his son: for he was at the point of death.

48Then said Jesus unto him, Except ye see signs and wonders, ye will not believe.

49The nobleman saith unto him, Sir, come down ere my child die.

50Jesus saith unto him, Go thy way; thy son liveth. And the man believed the word that Jesus had spoken unto him, and he went his way.

51And as he was now going down, his servants met him, and told *him,* saying, Thy son liveth.

52Then inquired he of them the hour when he began to amend. And they said unto him, Yesterday at the seventh hour the fever left him.

NEW LIVING TRANSLATION

32But Jesus replied, "I have a kind of food you know nothing about."

33"Did someone bring him food while we were gone?" the disciples asked each other.

34Then Jesus explained: "My nourishment comes from doing the will of God, who sent me, and from finishing his work. 35You know the saying, 'Four months between planting and harvest.' But I say, wake up and look around. The fields are already ripe* for harvest. 36The harvesters are paid good wages, and the fruit they harvest is people brought to eternal life. What joy awaits both the planter and the harvester alike! 37You know the saying, 'One plants and another harvests.' And it's true. 38I sent you to harvest where you didn't plant; others had already done the work, and now you will get to gather the harvest."

Many Samaritans Believe

39Many Samaritans from the village believed in Jesus because the woman had said, "He told me everything I ever did!" 40When they came out to see him, they begged him to stay in their village. So he stayed for two days, 41long enough for many more to hear his message and believe. 42Then they said to the woman, "Now we believe, not just because of what you told us, but because we have heard him ourselves. Now we know that he is indeed the Savior of the world."

Jesus Heals an Official's Son

43At the end of the two days, Jesus went on to Galilee. 44He himself had said that a prophet is not honored in his own hometown. 45Yet the Galileans welcomed him, for they had been in Jerusalem at the Passover celebration and had seen everything he did there.

46As he traveled through Galilee, he came to Cana, where he had turned the water into wine. There was a government official in nearby Capernaum whose son was very sick. 47When he heard that Jesus had come from Judea to Galilee, he went and begged Jesus to come to Capernaum to heal his son, who was about to die.

48Jesus asked, "Will you never believe in me unless you see miraculous signs and wonders?"

49The official pleaded, "Lord, please come now before my little boy dies."

50Then Jesus told him, "Go back home. Your son will live!" And the man believed what Jesus said and started home.

51While the man was on his way, some of his servants met him with the news that his son was alive and well. 52He asked them when the boy had begun to get better, and they replied, "Yesterday afternoon at one o'clock his fever suddenly disappeared!"

4:35 Greek *white.*

KING JAMES VERSION

53 So the father knew that *it was* at the same hour, in the which Jesus said unto him, Thy son liveth: and himself believed, and his whole house.

54 This *is* again the second miracle *that* Jesus did, when he was come out of Judaea into Galilee.

5

1 After this there was a feast of the Jews; and Jesus went up to Jerusalem.

2 Now there is at Jerusalem by the sheep *market* a pool, which is called in the Hebrew tongue Bethesda, having five porches.

3 In these lay a great multitude of impotent folk, of blind, halt, withered, waiting for the moving of the water.

4 For an angel went down at a certain season into the pool, and troubled the water: whosoever then first after the troubling of the water stepped in was made whole of whatsoever disease he had.

5 And a certain man was there, which had an infirmity thirty and eight years.

6 When Jesus saw him lie, and knew that he had been now a long time *in that case*, he saith unto him, Wilt thou be made whole?

7 The impotent man answered him, Sir, I have no man, when the water is troubled, to put me into the pool: but while I am coming, another steppeth down before me.

8 Jesus saith unto him, Rise, take up thy bed, and walk.

9 And immediately the man was made whole, and took up his bed, and walked: and on the same day was the sabbath.

10 The Jews therefore said unto him that was cured, It is the sabbath day: it is not lawful for thee to carry *thy* bed.

11 He answered them, He that made me whole, the same said unto me, Take up thy bed, and walk.

12 Then asked they him, What man is that which said unto thee, Take up thy bed, and walk?

13 And he that was healed wist not who it was: for Jesus had conveyed himself away, a multitude being in *that* place.

14 Afterward Jesus findeth him in the temple, and said unto him, Behold, thou art made whole: sin no more, lest a worse thing come unto thee.

15 The man departed, and told the Jews that it was Jesus, which had made him whole.

16 And therefore did the Jews persecute Jesus, and sought to slay him, because he had done these things on the sabbath day.

17 But Jesus answered them, My Father worketh hitherto, and I work.

18 Therefore the Jews sought the more to kill him, because he not only had broken the sabbath, but said also that God was his Father, making himself equal with God.

NEW LIVING TRANSLATION

53 Then the father realized that that was the very time
Jesus had told him, "Your son will live." And he and
his entire household believed in Jesus. 54 This was
the second miraculous sign Jesus did in Galilee after
coming from Judea.

Jesus Heals a Lame Man

5 Afterward Jesus returned to Jerusalem for one
of the Jewish holy days. 2 Inside the city, near
the Sheep Gate, was the pool of Bethesda,* with five
covered porches. 3 Crowds of sick people—blind,
lame, or paralyzed—lay on the porches.* 5 One of the
men lying there had been sick for thirty-eight years.
6 When Jesus saw him and knew he had been ill for
a long time, he asked him, "Would you like to get
well?"

7 "I can't, sir," the sick man said, "for I have no one
to put me into the pool when the water bubbles up.
Someone else always gets there ahead of me."

8 Jesus told him, "Stand up, pick up your mat, and
walk!"

9 Instantly, the man was healed! He rolled up his
sleeping mat and began walking! But this miracle
happened on the Sabbath, 10 so the Jewish leaders
objected. They said to the man who was cured, "You
can't work on the Sabbath! The law doesn't allow you
to carry that sleeping mat!"

11 But he replied, "The man who healed me told
me, 'Pick up your mat and walk.'"

12 "Who said such a thing as that?" they demanded.

13 The man didn't know, for Jesus had disappeared
into the crowd. 14 But afterward Jesus found him in
the Temple and told him, "Now you are well; so stop
sinning, or something even worse may happen to
you." 15 Then the man went and told the Jewish leaders that it was Jesus who had healed him.

Jesus Claims to Be the Son of God

16 So the Jewish leaders began harassing* Jesus for
breaking the Sabbath rules. 17 But Jesus replied, "My
Father is always working, and so am I." 18 So the Jewish
leaders tried all the harder to find a way to kill him.
For he not only broke the Sabbath, he called God his
Father, thereby making himself equal with God.

5:2 Other manuscripts read *Beth-zatha;* still others read *Bethsaida*.
5:3 Some manuscripts add an expanded conclusion to verse 3 and all of verse 4: *waiting for a certain movement of the water, [4] for an angel of the Lord came from time to time and stirred up the water. And the first person to step in after the water was stirred was healed of whatever disease he had.*
5:16 Or *persecuting*.

KING JAMES VERSION

19 Then answered Jesus and said unto them, Verily, verily, I say unto you, The Son can do nothing of himself, but what he seeth the Father do: for what things soever he doeth, these also doeth the Son likewise.

20 For the Father loveth the Son, and sheweth him all things that himself doeth: and he will shew him greater works than these, that ye may marvel.

21 For as the Father raiseth up the dead, and quickeneth *them;* even so the Son quickeneth whom he will.

22 For the Father judgeth no man, but hath committed all judgment unto the Son:

23 That all *men* should honour the Son, even as they honour the Father. He that honoureth not the Son honoureth not the Father which hath sent him.

24 Verily, verily, I say unto you, He that heareth my word, and believeth on him that sent me, hath everlasting life, and shall not come into condemnation; but is passed from death unto life.

25 Verily, verily, I say unto you, The hour is coming, and now is, when the dead shall hear the voice of the Son of God: and they that hear shall live.

26 For as the Father hath life in himself; so hath he given to the Son to have life in himself;

27 And hath given him authority to execute judgment also, because he is the Son of man.

28 Marvel not at this: for the hour is coming, in the which all that are in the graves shall hear his voice,

29 And shall come forth; they that have done good, unto the resurrection of life; and they that have done evil, unto the resurrection of damnation.

30 I can of mine own self do nothing: as I hear, I judge: and my judgment is just; because I seek not mine own will, but the will of the Father which hath sent me.

31 If I bear witness of myself, my witness is not true.

32 There is another that beareth witness of me; and I know that the witness which he witnesseth of me is true.

33 Ye sent unto John, and he bare witness unto the truth.

34 But I receive not testimony from man: but these things I say, that ye might be saved.

35 He was a burning and a shining light: and ye were willing for a season to rejoice in his light.

36 But I have greater witness than *that* of John: for the works which the Father hath given me to finish, the same works that I do, bear witness of me, that the Father hath sent me.

37 And the Father himself, which hath sent me, hath borne witness of me. Ye have neither heard his voice at any time, nor seen his shape.

38 And ye have not his word abiding in you: for whom he hath sent, him ye believe not.

39 Search the scriptures; for in them ye think ye have eternal life: and they are they which testify of me.

NEW LIVING TRANSLATION

19 So Jesus explained, "I tell you the truth, the Son can do nothing by himself. He does only what he sees the Father doing. Whatever the Father does, the Son also does. 20 For the Father loves the Son and shows him everything he is doing. In fact, the Father will show him how to do even greater works than healing this man. Then you will truly be astonished. 21 For just as the Father gives life to those he raises from the dead, so the Son gives life to anyone he wants. 22 In addition, the Father judges no one. Instead, he has given the Son absolute authority to judge, 23 so that everyone will honor the Son, just as they honor the Father. Anyone who does not honor the Son is certainly not honoring the Father who sent him.

24 "I tell you the truth, those who listen to my message and believe in God who sent me have eternal life. They will never be condemned for their sins, but they have already passed from death into life.

25 "And I assure you that the time is coming, indeed it's here now, when the dead will hear my voice—the voice of the Son of God. And those who listen will live. 26 The Father has life in himself, and he has granted that same life-giving power to his Son. 27 And he has given him authority to judge everyone because he is the Son of Man.* 28 Don't be so surprised! Indeed, the time is coming when all the dead in their graves will hear the voice of God's Son, 29 and they will rise again. Those who have done good will rise to experience eternal life, and those who have continued in evil will rise to experience judgment. 30 I can do nothing on my own. I judge as God tells me. Therefore, my judgment is just, because I carry out the will of the one who sent me, not my own will.

Witnesses to Jesus

31 "If I were to testify on my own behalf, my testimony would not be valid. 32 But someone else is also testifying about me, and I assure you that everything he says about me is true. 33 In fact, you sent investigators to listen to John the Baptist, and his testimony about me was true. 34 Of course, I have no need of human witnesses, but I say these things so you might be saved. 35 John was like a burning and shining lamp, and you were excited for a while about his message. 36 But I have a greater witness than John—my teachings and my miracles. The Father gave me these works to accomplish, and they prove that he sent me. 37 And the Father who sent me has testified about me himself. You have never heard his voice or seen him face to face, 38 and you do not have his message in your hearts, because you do not believe me—the one he sent to you.

39 "You search the Scriptures because you think they give you eternal life. But the Scriptures point to

5:27 "Son of Man" is a title Jesus used for himself.

KING JAMES VERSION

40 And ye will not come to me, that ye might have life.

41 I receive not honour from men.

42 But I know you, that ye have not the love of God in you.

43 I am come in my Father's name, and ye receive me not: if another shall come in his own name, him ye will receive.

44 How can ye believe, which receive honour one of another, and seek not the honour that *cometh* from God only?

45 Do not think that I will accuse you to the Father: there is *one* that accuseth you, *even* Moses, in whom ye trust.

46 For had ye believed Moses, ye would have believed me: for he wrote of me.

47 But if ye believe not his writings, how shall ye believe my words?

6 1 After these things Jesus went over the sea of Galilee, which is *the sea* of Tiberias.

2 And a great multitude followed him, because they saw his miracles which he did on them that were diseased.

3 And Jesus went up into a mountain, and there he sat with his disciples.

4 And the passover, a feast of the Jews, was nigh.

5 When Jesus then lifted up *his* eyes, and saw a great company come unto him, he saith unto Philip, Whence shall we buy bread, that these may eat?

6 And this he said to prove him: for he himself knew what he would do.

7 Philip answered him, Two hundred pennyworth of bread is not sufficient for them, that every one of them may take a little.

8 One of his disciples, Andrew, Simon Peter's brother, saith unto him,

9 There is a lad here, which hath five barley loaves, and two small fishes: but what are they among so many?

10 And Jesus said, Make the men sit down. Now there was much grass in the place. So the men sat down, in number about five thousand.

11 And Jesus took the loaves; and when he had given thanks, he distributed to the disciples, and the disciples to them that were set down; and likewise of the fishes as much as they would.

12 When they were filled, he said unto his disciples, Gather up the fragments that remain, that nothing be lost.

13 Therefore they gathered *them* together, and filled twelve baskets with the fragments of the five barley loaves, which remained over and above unto them that had eaten.

14 Then those men, when they had seen the miracle that Jesus did, said, This is of a truth that prophet that should come into the world.

15 When Jesus therefore perceived that they would

NEW LIVING TRANSLATION

me! 40 Yet you refuse to come to me to receive this
life.

41 "Your approval means nothing to me, 42 because
I know you don't have God's love within you. 43 For I
have come to you in my Father's name, and you have
rejected me. Yet if others come in their own name,
you gladly welcome them. 44 No wonder you can't believe! For you gladly honor each other, but you don't
care about the honor that comes from the one who
alone is God.*

45 "Yet it isn't I who will accuse you before the Father. Moses will accuse you! Yes, Moses, in whom you
put your hopes. 46 If you really believed Moses, you
would believe me, because he wrote about me. 47 But
since you don't believe what he wrote, how will you
believe what I say?"

Jesus Feeds Five Thousand

6 After this, Jesus crossed over to the far side of
the Sea of Galilee, also known as the Sea of Tiberias. 2 A huge crowd kept following him wherever
he went, because they saw his miraculous signs as
he healed the sick. 3 Then Jesus climbed a hill and sat
down with his disciples around him. 4 (It was nearly
time for the Jewish Passover celebration.) 5 Jesus
soon saw a huge crowd of people coming to look for
him. Turning to Philip, he asked, "Where can we
buy bread to feed all these people?" 6 He was testing
Philip, for he already knew what he was going to do.

7 Philip replied, "Even if we worked for months, we
wouldn't have enough money* to feed them!"

8 Then Andrew, Simon Peter's brother, spoke up.
9 "There's a young boy here with five barley loaves
and two fish. But what good is that with this huge
crowd?"

10 "Tell everyone to sit down," Jesus said. So they
all sat down on the grassy slopes. (The men alone
numbered about 5,000.) 11 Then Jesus took the
loaves, gave thanks to God, and distributed them to
the people. Afterward he did the same with the fish.
And they all ate as much as they wanted. 12 After
everyone was full, Jesus told his disciples, "Now
gather the leftovers, so that nothing is wasted." 13 So
they picked up the pieces and filled twelve baskets
with scraps left by the people who had eaten from
the five barley loaves.

14 When the people saw him* do this miraculous
sign, they exclaimed, "Surely, he is the Prophet we
have been expecting!"* 15 When Jesus saw that they

5:44 Some manuscripts read *from the only One*. **6:7** Greek *Two hundred denarii would not be enough*. A denarius was equivalent to a laborer's full day's wage. **6:14a** Some manuscripts read *Jesus*. **6:14b** See Deut 18:15, 18; Mal 4:5-6.

KING JAMES VERSION

come and take him by force, to make him a king,
he departed again into a mountain himself alone.

16And when even was *now* come, his disciples
went down unto the sea,
17And entered into a ship, and went over the
sea toward Capernaum. And it was now dark, and
Jesus was not come to them.
18And the sea arose by reason of a great wind that
blew.
19So when they had rowed about five and twenty
or thirty furlongs, they see Jesus walking on the sea,
and drawing nigh unto the ship: and they were
afraid.
20But he saith unto them, It is I; be not afraid.
21Then they willingly received him into the ship:
and immediately the ship was at the land whither
they went.
22The day following, when the people which
stood on the other side of the sea saw that there was
none other boat there, save that one whereinto his
disciples were entered, and that Jesus went not with
his disciples into the boat, but *that* his disciples were
gone away alone;
23(Howbeit there came other boats from Tiberias
nigh unto the place where they did eat bread, after
that the Lord had given thanks:)
24When the people therefore saw that Jesus was
not there, neither his disciples, they also took ship-
ping, and came to Capernaum, seeking for Jesus.
25And when they had found him on the other side
of the sea, they said unto him, Rabbi, when camest
thou hither?
26Jesus answered them and said, Verily, verily, I say
unto you, Ye seek me, not because ye saw the miracles, but because ye did eat of the loaves, and were
filled.
27Labour not for the meat which perisheth, but for
that meat which endureth unto everlasting life,
which the Son of man shall give unto you: for him
hath God the Father sealed.
28Then said they unto him, What shall we do, that
we might work the works of God?
29Jesus answered and said unto them, This is the
work of God, that ye believe on him whom he hath
sent.
30They said therefore unto him, What sign
shewest thou then, that we may see, and believe
thee? what dost thou work?
31Our fathers did eat manna in the desert; as it is
written, He gave them bread from heaven to eat.
32Then Jesus said unto them, Verily, verily, I say
unto you, Moses gave you not that bread from
heaven; but my Father giveth you the true bread from
heaven.
33For the bread of God is he which cometh down
from heaven, and giveth life unto the world.

NEW LIVING TRANSLATION

were ready to force him to be their king, he slipped
away into the hills by himself.

Jesus Walks on Water

16That evening Jesus' disciples went down to the
shore to wait for him. 17But as darkness fell and Jesus
still hadn't come back, they got into the boat and
headed across the lake toward Capernaum. 18Soon a
gale swept down upon them, and the sea grew very
rough. 19They had rowed three or four miles* when
suddenly they saw Jesus walking on the water toward
the boat. They were terrified, 20but he called out to
them, "Don't be afraid. I am here!*" 21Then they were
eager to let him in the boat, and immediately they
arrived at their destination!

Jesus, the Bread of Life

22The next day the crowd that had stayed on the far
shore saw that the disciples had taken the only boat,
and they realized Jesus had not gone with them.
23Several boats from Tiberias landed near the place
where the Lord had blessed the bread and the people
had eaten. 24So when the crowd saw that neither
Jesus nor his disciples were there, they got into the
boats and went across to Capernaum to look for him.
25They found him on the other side of the lake and
asked, "Rabbi, when did you get here?"
26Jesus replied, "I tell you the truth, you want to be
with me because I fed you, not because you understood the miraculous signs. 27But don't be so concerned about perishable things like food. Spend
your energy seeking the eternal life that the Son of
Man* can give you. For God the Father has given me
the seal of his approval."
28They replied, "We want to perform God's works,
too. What should we do?"
29Jesus told them, "This is the only work God
wants from you: Believe in the one he has sent."
30They answered, "Show us a miraculous sign if
you want us to believe in you. What can you do?
31After all, our ancestors ate manna while they journeyed through the wilderness! The Scriptures say,
'Moses gave them bread from heaven to eat.'*"
32Jesus said, "I tell you the truth, Moses didn't give
you bread from heaven. My Father did. And now he
offers you the true bread from heaven. 33The true
bread of God is the one who comes down from
heaven and gives life to the world."

6:19 Greek *25 or 30 stadia* [4.6 or 5.5 kilometers]. **6:20** Or *The 'I AM' is here;* Greek reads *I am.* See Exod 3:14. **6:27** "Son of Man" is a title Jesus used for himself. **6:31** Exod 16:4; Ps 78:24.

KING JAMES VERSION

34 Then said they unto him, Lord, evermore give us
this bread.
35 And Jesus said unto them, I am the bread of life:
he that cometh to me shall never hunger; and he that
believeth on me shall never thirst.
36 But I said unto you, That ye also have seen me,
and believe not.
37 All that the Father giveth me shall come to me;
and him that cometh to me I will in no wise cast out.
38 For I came down from heaven, not to do mine
own will, but the will of him that sent me.
39 And this is the Father's will which hath sent me,
that of all which he hath given me I should lose nothing, but should raise it up again at the last day.
40 And this is the will of him that sent me, that
every one which seeth the Son, and believeth on him,
may have everlasting life: and I will raise him up at
the last day.
41 The Jews then murmured at him, because he
said, I am the bread which came down from heaven.
42 And they said, Is not this Jesus, the son of Joseph,
whose father and mother we know? how is it then
that he saith, I came down from heaven?
43 Jesus therefore answered and said unto them,
Murmur not among yourselves.
44 No man can come to me, except the Father
which hath sent me draw him: and I will raise him up
at the last day.
45 It is written in the prophets, And they shall be all
taught of God. Every man therefore that hath heard,
and hath learned of the Father, cometh unto me.
46 Not that any man hath seen the Father, save he
which is of God, he hath seen the Father.
47 Verily, verily, I say unto you, He that believeth on
me hath everlasting life.
48 I am that bread of life.
49 Your fathers did eat manna in the wilderness,
and are dead.
50 This is the bread which cometh down from
heaven, that a man may eat thereof, and not die.
51 I am the living bread which came down from
heaven: if any man eat of this bread, he shall live for
ever: and the bread that I will give is my flesh, which
I will give for the life of the world.
52 The Jews therefore strove among themselves,
saying, How can this man give us *his* flesh to eat?
53 Then Jesus said unto them, Verily, verily, I say
unto you, Except ye eat the flesh of the Son of man,
and drink his blood, ye have no life in you.
54 Whoso eateth my flesh, and drinketh my blood,
hath eternal life; and I will raise him up at the last day.
55 For my flesh is meat indeed, and my blood is
drink indeed.
56 He that eateth my flesh, and drinketh my blood,
dwelleth in me, and I in him.
57 As the living Father hath sent me, and I live by
the Father: so he that eateth me, even he shall live
by me.

NEW LIVING TRANSLATION

34 "Sir," they said, "give us that bread every day."
35 Jesus replied, "I am the bread of life. Whoever
comes to me will never be hungry again. Whoever
believes in me will never be thirsty.
36 But you haven't
believed in me even though you have seen me.
37 However, those the Father has given me will come
to me, and I will never reject them.
38 For I have come
down from heaven to do the will of God who sent me,
not to do my own will.
39 And this is the will of God,
that I should not lose even one of all those he has
given me, but that I should raise them up at the last
day.
40 For it is my Father's will that all who see his Son
and believe in him should have eternal life. I will
raise them up at the last day."
41 Then the people* began to murmur in disagreement because he had said, "I am the bread that came
down from heaven."
42 They said, "Isn't this Jesus, the
son of Joseph? We know his father and mother. How
can he say, 'I came down from heaven'?"
43 But Jesus replied, "Stop complaining about what
I said.
44 For no one can come to me unless the Father
who sent me draws them to me, and at the last day
I will raise them up.
45 As it is written in the Scrip-
tures,* 'They will all be taught by God.' Everyone who
listens to the Father and learns from him comes to
me.
46 (Not that anyone has ever seen the Father; only
I, who was sent from God, have seen him.)
47 "I tell you the truth, anyone who believes has
eternal life.
48 Yes, I am the bread of life!
49 Your an-
cestors ate manna in the wilderness, but they all
died.
50 Anyone who eats the bread from heaven,
however, will never die.
51 I am the living bread that
came down from heaven. Anyone who eats this
bread will live forever; and this bread, which I will
offer so the world may live, is my flesh."
52 Then the people began arguing with each other
about what he meant. "How can this man give us his
flesh to eat?" they asked.
53 So Jesus said again, "I tell you the truth, unless
you eat the flesh of the Son of Man and drink his
blood, you cannot have eternal life within you.
54 But
anyone who eats my flesh and drinks my blood has
eternal life, and I will raise that person at the last day.
55 For my flesh is true food, and my blood is true
drink.
56 Anyone who eats my flesh and drinks my
blood remains in me, and I in him.
57 I live because
of the living Father who sent me; in the same way,

6:41 Greek *Jewish people;* also in 6:52. **6:45** Greek *in the prophets.* Isa 54:13.

KING JAMES VERSION

58This is that bread which came down from heaven: not as your fathers did eat manna, and are dead: he that eateth of this bread shall live for ever.

59These things said he in the synagogue, as he taught in Capernaum.

60Many therefore of his disciples, when they had heard *this*, said, This is an hard saying; who can hear it?

61When Jesus knew in himself that his disciples murmured at it, he said unto them, Doth this offend you?

62*What* and if ye shall see the Son of man ascend up where he was before?

63It is the spirit that quickeneth; the flesh profiteth nothing: the words that I speak unto you, *they* are spirit, and *they* are life.

64But there are some of you that believe not. For Jesus knew from the beginning who they were that believed not, and who should betray him.

65And he said, Therefore said I unto you, that no man can come unto me, except it were given unto him of my Father.

66From that *time* many of his disciples went back, and walked no more with him.

67Then said Jesus unto the twelve, Will ye also go away?

68Then Simon Peter answered him, Lord, to whom shall we go? thou hast the words of eternal life.

69And we believe and are sure that thou art that Christ, the Son of the living God.

70Jesus answered them, Have not I chosen you twelve, and one of you is a devil?

71He spake of Judas Iscariot *the son* of Simon: for he it was that should betray him, being one of the twelve.

7 1After these things Jesus walked in Galilee: for he would not walk in Jewry, because the Jews sought to kill him.

2Now the Jews' feast of tabernacles was at hand.

3His brethren therefore said unto him, Depart hence, and go into Judaea, that thy disciples also may see the works that thou doest.

4For *there is* no man *that* doeth any thing in secret, and he himself seeketh to be known openly. If thou do these things, shew thyself to the world.

5For neither did his brethren believe in him.

6Then Jesus said unto them, My time is not yet come: but your time is alway ready.

7The world cannot hate you; but me it hateth, because I testify of it, that the works thereof are evil.

8Go ye up unto this feast: I go not up yet unto this feast: for my time is not yet full come.

9When he had said these words unto them, he abode *still* in Galilee.

NEW LIVING TRANSLATION

anyone who feeds on me will live because of me. 58I
am the true bread that came down from heaven.
Anyone who eats this bread will not die as your ancestors did (even though they ate the manna) but
will live forever."

59He said these things while he was teaching in
the synagogue in Capernaum.

Many Disciples Desert Jesus

60Many of his disciples said, "This is very hard to
understand. How can anyone accept it?"

61Jesus was aware that his disciples were complaining, so he said to them, "Does this offend you?
62Then what will you think if you see the Son of Man
ascend to heaven again? 63The Spirit alone gives
eternal life. Human effort accomplishes nothing.
And the very words I have spoken to you are spirit
and life. 64But some of you do not believe me." (For
Jesus knew from the beginning which ones didn't
believe, and he knew who would betray him.) 65Then
he said, "That is why I said that people can't come to
me unless the Father gives them to me."

66At this point many of his disciples turned away
and deserted him. 67Then Jesus turned to the Twelve
and asked, "Are you also going to leave?"

68Simon Peter replied, "Lord, to whom would we
go? You have the words that give eternal life. 69We
believe, and we know you are the Holy One of God.*"

70Then Jesus said, "I chose the twelve of you, but
one is a devil." 71He was speaking of Judas, son of
Simon Iscariot, one of the Twelve, who would later
betray him.

Jesus and His Brothers

7 After this, Jesus traveled around Galilee. He
wanted to stay out of Judea, where the Jewish
leaders were plotting his death. 2But soon it was time
for the Jewish Festival of Shelters, 3and Jesus' brothers said to him, "Leave here and go to Judea, where
your followers can see your miracles! 4You can't become famous if you hide like this! If you can do such
wonderful things, show yourself to the world!" 5For
even his brothers didn't believe in him.

6Jesus replied, "Now is not the right time for me to
go, but you can go anytime. 7The world can't hate
you, but it does hate me because I accuse it of doing
evil. 8You go on. I'm not going* to this festival, because my time has not yet come." 9After saying these
things, Jesus remained in Galilee.

6:69 Other manuscripts read *you are the Christ, the Holy One of God;* still others read *you are the Christ, the Son of God;* and still others read *you are the Christ, the Son of the living God.* **7:8** Some manuscripts read *not yet going.*

KING JAMES VERSION

10But when his brethren were gone up, then went
he also up unto the feast, not openly, but as it were in
secret.
11Then the Jews sought him at the feast, and said,
Where is he?
12And there was much murmuring among the
people concerning him: for some said, He is a good
man: others said, Nay; but he deceiveth the people.
13Howbeit no man spake openly of him for fear of
the Jews.
14Now about the midst of the feast Jesus went up
into the temple, and taught.
15And the Jews marvelled, saying, How knoweth
this man letters, having never learned?
16Jesus answered them, and said, My doctrine is
not mine, but his that sent me.
17If any man will do his will, he shall know of the
doctrine, whether it be of God, or *whether* I speak of
myself.
18He that speaketh of himself seeketh his own
glory: but he that seeketh his glory that sent him, the
same is true, and no unrighteousness is in him.
19Did not Moses give you the law, and *yet* none of
you keepeth the law? Why go ye about to kill me?
20The people answered and said, Thou hast a
devil: who goeth about to kill thee?
21Jesus answered and said unto them, I have done
one work, and ye all marvel.
22Moses therefore gave unto you circumcision;
(not because it is of Moses, but of the fathers;) and ye
on the sabbath day circumcise a man.
23If a man on the sabbath day receive circumcision, that the law of Moses should not be broken; are
ye angry at me, because I have made a man every
whit whole on the sabbath day?
24Judge not according to the appearance, but
judge righteous judgment.

25Then said some of them of Jerusalem, Is not this
he, whom they seek to kill?
26But, lo, he speaketh boldly, and they say nothing
unto him. Do the rulers know indeed that this is the
very Christ?
27Howbeit we know this man whence he is: but
when Christ cometh, no man knoweth whence he is.
28Then cried Jesus in the temple as he taught, saying, Ye both know me, and ye know whence I am: and
I am not come of myself, but he that sent me is true,
whom ye know not.
29But I know him: for I am from him, and he hath
sent me.
30Then they sought to take him: but no man laid
hands on him, because his hour was not yet come.
31And many of the people believed on him, and

NEW LIVING TRANSLATION

Jesus Teaches Openly at the Temple

10But after his brothers left for the festival, Jesus also
went, though secretly, staying out of public view.
11The Jewish leaders tried to find him at the festival
and kept asking if anyone had seen him. 12There was
a lot of grumbling about him among the crowds.
Some argued, "He's a good man," but others said,
"He's nothing but a fraud who deceives the people."
13But no one had the courage to speak favorably
about him in public, for they were afraid of getting
in trouble with the Jewish leaders.
14Then, midway through the festival, Jesus went
up to the Temple and began to teach. 15The people*
were surprised when they heard him. "How does he
know so much when he hasn't been trained?" they
asked.
16So Jesus told them, "My message is not my own;
it comes from God who sent me. 17Anyone who
wants to do the will of God will know whether my
teaching is from God or is merely my own. 18Those
who speak for themselves want glory only for themselves, but a person who seeks to honor the one who
sent him speaks truth, not lies. 19Moses gave you the
law, but none of you obeys it! In fact, you are trying
to kill me."
20The crowd replied, "You're demon possessed!
Who's trying to kill you?"
21Jesus replied, "I did one miracle on the Sabbath,
and you were amazed. 22But you work on the Sabbath, too, when you obey Moses' law of circumcision.
(Actually, this tradition of circumcision began with
the patriarchs, long before the law of Moses.) 23For
if the correct time for circumcising your son falls on
the Sabbath, you go ahead and do it so as not to break
the law of Moses. So why should you be angry with
me for healing a man on the Sabbath? 24Look beneath the surface so you can judge correctly."

Is Jesus the Messiah?

25Some of the people who lived in Jerusalem started
to ask each other, "Isn't this the man they are trying
to kill? 26But here he is, speaking in public, and they
say nothing to him. Could our leaders possibly believe that he is the Messiah? 27But how could he be?
For we know where this man comes from. When the
Messiah comes, he will simply appear; no one will
know where he comes from."
28While Jesus was teaching in the Temple, he called
out, "Yes, you know me, and you know where I come
from. But I'm not here on my own. The one who sent
me is true, and you don't know him. 29But I know him
because I come from him, and he sent me to you."
30Then the leaders tried to arrest him; but no one laid
a hand on him, because his time* had not yet come.
31Many among the crowds at the Temple believed
in him. "After all," they said, "would you expect the

7:15 Greek *Jewish people.* **7:30** Greek *his hour.*

KING JAMES VERSION

said, When Christ cometh, will he do more miracles than these which this *man* hath done?

32 The Pharisees heard that the people murmured such things concerning him; and the Pharisees and the chief priests sent officers to take him.

33 Then said Jesus unto them, Yet a little while am I with you, and *then* I go unto him that sent me.

34 Ye shall seek me, and shall not find *me:* and where I am, *thither* ye cannot come.

35 Then said the Jews among themselves, Whither will he go, that we shall not find him? will he go unto the dispersed among the Gentiles, and teach the Gentiles?

36 What *manner of* saying is this that he said, Ye shall seek me, and shall not find *me:* and where I am, *thither* ye cannot come?

37 In the last day, that great *day* of the feast, Jesus stood and cried, saying, If any man thirst, let him come unto me, and drink.

38 He that believeth on me, as the scripture hath said, out of his belly shall flow rivers of living water.

39 (But this spake he of the Spirit, which they that believe on him should receive: for the Holy Ghost was not yet *given;* because that Jesus was not yet glorified.)

40 Many of the people therefore, when they heard this saying, said, Of a truth this is the Prophet.

41 Others said, This is the Christ. But some said, Shall Christ come out of Galilee?

42 Hath not the scripture said, That Christ cometh of the seed of David, and out of the town of Bethlehem, where David was?

43 So there was a division among the people because of him.

44 And some of them would have taken him; but no man laid hands on him.

45 Then came the officers to the chief priests and Pharisees; and they said unto them, Why have ye not brought him?

46 The officers answered, Never man spake like this man.

47 Then answered them the Pharisees, Are ye also deceived?

48 Have any of the rulers or of the Pharisees believed on him?

49 But this people who knoweth not the law are cursed.

50 Nicodemus saith unto them, (he that came to Jesus by night, being one of them,)

51 Doth our law judge *any* man, before it hear him, and know what he doeth?

52 They answered and said unto him, Art thou also

NEW LIVING TRANSLATION

Messiah to do more miraculous signs than this man
has done?"
32 When the Pharisees heard that the crowds were
whispering such things, they and the leading priests
sent Temple guards to arrest Jesus. 33 But Jesus told
them, "I will be with you only a little longer. Then I
will return to the one who sent me. 34 You will search
for me but not find me. And you cannot go where
I am going."
35 The Jewish leaders were puzzled by this statement.
"Where is he planning to go?" they asked. "Is
he thinking of leaving the country and going to the
Jews in other lands?* Maybe he will even teach the
Greeks! 36 What does he mean when he says, 'You will
search for me but not find me,' and 'You cannot
go where I am going'?"

Jesus Promises Living Water

37 On the last day, the climax of the festival, Jesus
stood and shouted to the crowds, "Anyone who is
thirsty may come to me! 38 Anyone who believes in
me may come and drink! For the Scriptures declare,
'Rivers of living water will flow from his heart.' "*
39 (When he said "living water," he was speaking of
the Spirit, who would be given to everyone believing
in him. But the Spirit had not yet been given,* because
Jesus had not yet entered into his glory.)

Division and Unbelief

40 When the crowds heard him say this, some of them
declared, "Surely this man is the Prophet we've been
expecting."* 41 Others said, "He is the Messiah." Still
others said, "But he can't be! Will the Messiah come
from Galilee? 42 For the Scriptures clearly state that
the Messiah will be born of the royal line of David, in
Bethlehem, the village where King David was born."*
43 So the crowd was divided about him. 44 Some even
wanted him arrested, but no one laid a hand on him.
45 When the Temple guards returned without having
arrested Jesus, the leading priests and Pharisees
demanded, "Why didn't you bring him in?"
46 "We have never heard anyone speak like this!"
the guards responded.
47 "Have you been led astray, too?" the Pharisees
mocked. 48 "Is there a single one of us rulers or Pharisees
who believes in him? 49 This foolish crowd follows
him, but they are ignorant of the law. God's
curse is on them!"
50 Then Nicodemus, the leader who had met with
Jesus earlier, spoke up. 51 "Is it legal to convict a man
before he is given a hearing?" he asked.
52 They replied, "Are you from Galilee, too? Search
the Scriptures and see for yourself—no prophet ever
comes* from Galilee!"

7:35 Or *the Jews who live among the Greeks?* **7:37-38** Or *"Let anyone who is thirsty come to me and drink. [38] For the Scriptures declare, 'Rivers of living water will flow from the heart of anyone who believes in me.'"* **7:39** Some manuscripts read *But as yet there was no Spirit.* Still others read *But as yet there was no Holy Spirit.* **7:40** See Deut 18:15, 18; Mal 4:5-6. **7:42** See Mic 5:2. **7:52** Some manuscripts read *the prophet does not come.*

KING JAMES VERSION

of Galilee? Search, and look: for out of Galilee ariseth
no prophet.
[53]And every man went unto his own house.

8 [1]Jesus went unto the mount of Olives.
[2]And early in the morning he came again into
the temple, and all the people came unto him; and he
sat down, and taught them.
[3]And the scribes and Pharisees brought unto him
a woman taken in adultery; and when they had set
her in the midst,
[4]They say unto him, Master, this woman was taken
in adultery, in the very act.
[5]Now Moses in the law commanded us, that such
should be stoned: but what sayest thou?
[6]This they said, tempting him, that they might
have to accuse him. But Jesus stooped down, and
with *his* finger wrote on the ground, *as though he
heard them not*.
[7]So when they continued asking him, he lifted up
himself, and said unto them, He that is without sin
among you, let him first cast a stone at her.
[8]And again he stooped down, and wrote on the
ground.
[9]And they which heard *it*, being convicted by *their
own* conscience, went out one by one, beginning at
the eldest, *even* unto the last: and Jesus was left
alone, and the woman standing in the midst.
[10]When Jesus had lifted up himself, and saw none
but the woman, he said unto her, Woman, where are
those thine accusers? hath no man condemned
thee?
[11]She said, No man, Lord. And Jesus said unto her,
Neither do I condemn thee: go, and sin no more.
[12]Then spake Jesus again unto them, saying, I am
the light of the world: he that followeth me shall not
walk in darkness, but shall have the light of life.
[13]The Pharisees therefore said unto him, Thou
bearest record of thyself; thy record is not true.
[14]Jesus answered and said unto them, Though
I bear record of myself, *yet* my record is true: for I
know whence I came, and whither I go; but ye cannot
tell whence I come, and whither I go.
[15]Ye judge after the flesh; I judge no man.
[16]And yet if I judge, my judgment is true: for I am
not alone, but I and the Father that sent me.
[17]It is also written in your law, that the testimony
of two men is true.
[18]I am one that bear witness of myself, and the
Father that sent me beareth witness of me.
[19]Then said they unto him, Where is thy Father?
Jesus answered, Ye neither know me, nor my Father:
if ye had known me, ye should have known my
Father also.

NEW LIVING TRANSLATION

[*The most ancient Greek manuscripts do not include John 7:53–8:11.*]

[53]Then the meeting broke up, and everybody went
home.

A Woman Caught in Adultery

8 Jesus returned to the Mount of Olives, [2]but
early the next morning he was back again at the
Temple. A crowd soon gathered, and he sat down and
taught them. [3]As he was speaking, the teachers of religious law and the Pharisees brought a woman who
had been caught in the act of adultery. They put her
in front of the crowd.
[4]"Teacher," they said to Jesus, "this woman was
caught in the act of adultery. [5]The law of Moses says
to stone her. What do you say?"
[6]They were trying to trap him into saying something they could use against him, but Jesus stooped
down and wrote in the dust with his finger. [7]They
kept demanding an answer, so he stood up again and
said, "All right, but let the one who has never sinned
throw the first stone!" [8]Then he stooped down again
and wrote in the dust.
[9]When the accusers heard this, they slipped away
one by one, beginning with the oldest, until only
Jesus was left in the middle of the crowd with the
woman. [10]Then Jesus stood up again and said to the
woman, "Where are your accusers? Didn't even one
of them condemn you?"
[11]"No, Lord," she said.
And Jesus said, "Neither do I. Go and sin no more."

Jesus, the Light of the World

[12]Jesus spoke to the people once more and said, "I
am the light of the world. If you follow me, you won't
have to walk in darkness, because you will have the
light that leads to life."
[13]The Pharisees replied, "You are making those
claims about yourself! Such testimony is not valid."
[14]Jesus told them, "These claims are valid even
though I make them about myself. For I know where I
came from and where I am going, but you don't know
this about me. [15]You judge me by human standards,
but I do not judge anyone. [16]And if I did, my judgment
would be correct in every respect because I am not
alone. The Father* who sent me is with me. [17]Your
own law says that if two people agree about something, their witness is accepted as fact.* [18]I am one
witness, and my Father who sent me is the other."
[19]"Where is your father?" they asked.
Jesus answered, "Since you don't know who I am,
you don't know who my Father is. If you knew me,

8:16 Some manuscripts read *The One*. **8:17** See Deut 19:15.

20 These words spake Jesus in the treasury, as he taught in the temple: and no man laid hands on him; for his hour was not yet come.

21 Then said Jesus again unto them, I go my way, and ye shall seek me, and shall die in your sins: whither I go, ye cannot come.

22 Then said the Jews, Will he kill himself? because he saith, Whither I go, ye cannot come.

23 And he said unto them, Ye are from beneath; I am from above: ye are of this world; I am not of this world.

24 I said therefore unto you, that ye shall die in your sins: for if ye believe not that I am *he*, ye shall die in your sins.

25 Then said they unto him, Who art thou? And Jesus saith unto them, Even *the same* that I said unto you from the beginning.

26 I have many things to say and to judge of you: but he that sent me is true; and I speak to the world those things which I have heard of him.

27 They understood not that he spake to them of the Father.

28 Then said Jesus unto them, When ye have lifted up the Son of man, then shall ye know that I am *he*, and *that* I do nothing of myself; but as my Father hath taught me, I speak these things.

29 And he that sent me is with me: the Father hath not left me alone; for I do always those things that please him.

30 As he spake these words, many believed on him.

31 Then said Jesus to those Jews which believed on him, If ye continue in my word, *then* are ye my disciples indeed;

32 And ye shall know the truth, and the truth shall make you free.

33 They answered him, We be Abraham's seed, and were never in bondage to any man: how sayest thou, Ye shall be made free?

34 Jesus answered them, Verily, verily, I say unto you, Whosoever committeth sin is the servant of sin.

35 And the servant abideth not in the house for ever: *but* the Son abideth ever.

36 If the Son therefore shall make you free, ye shall be free indeed.

37 I know that ye are Abraham's seed; but ye seek to kill me, because my word hath no place in you.

38 I speak that which I have seen with my Father: and ye do that which ye have seen with your father.

39 They answered and said unto him, Abraham is our father. Jesus saith unto them, If ye were Abraham's children, ye would do the works of Abraham.

40 But now ye seek to kill me, a man that hath told you the truth, which I have heard of God: this did not Abraham.

you would also know my Father." 20 Jesus made these statements while he was teaching in the section of the Temple known as the Treasury. But he was not arrested, because his time* had not yet come.

The Unbelieving People Warned

21 Later Jesus said to them again, "I am going away. You will search for me but will die in your sin. You cannot come where I am going."

22 The people* asked, "Is he planning to commit suicide? What does he mean, 'You cannot come where I am going'?"

23 Jesus continued, "You are from below; I am from above. You belong to this world; I do not. 24 That is why I said that you will die in your sins; for unless you believe that I AM who I claim to be,* you will die in your sins."

25 "Who are you?" they demanded.

Jesus replied, "The one I have always claimed to be.* 26 I have much to say about you and much to condemn, but I won't. For I say only what I have heard from the one who sent me, and he is completely truthful." 27 But they still didn't understand that he was talking about his Father.

28 So Jesus said, "When you have lifted up the Son of Man on the cross, then you will understand that I AM he.* I do nothing on my own but say only what the Father taught me. 29 And the one who sent me is with me—he has not deserted me. For I always do what pleases him." 30 Then many who heard him say these things believed in him.

Jesus and Abraham

31 Jesus said to the people who believed in him, "You are truly my disciples if you remain faithful to my teachings. 32 And you will know the truth, and the truth will set you free."

33 "But we are descendants of Abraham," they said. "We have never been slaves to anyone. What do you mean, 'You will be set free'?"

34 Jesus replied, "I tell you the truth, everyone who sins is a slave of sin. 35 A slave is not a permanent member of the family, but a son is part of the family forever. 36 So if the Son sets you free, you are truly free. 37 Yes, I realize that you are descendants of Abraham. And yet some of you are trying to kill me because there's no room in your hearts for my message. 38 I am telling you what I saw when I was with my Father. But you are following the advice of your father."

39 "Our father is Abraham!" they declared.

"No," Jesus replied, "for if you were really the children of Abraham, you would follow his example.* 40 Instead, you are trying to kill me because I told you the truth, which I heard from God. Abraham never

8:20 Greek *his hour.* **8:22** Greek *Jewish people;* also in 8:31, 48, 52, 57. **8:24** Greek *unless you believe that I am.* See Exod 3:14. **8:25** Or *Why do I speak to you at all?* **8:28** Greek *When you have lifted up the Son of Man, then you will know that I am.* "Son of Man" is a title Jesus used for himself. **8:39** Some manuscripts read *if you are really the children of Abraham, follow his example.*

KING JAMES VERSION

41 Ye do the deeds of your father. Then said they to him, We be not born of fornication; we have one Father, *even* God.

42 Jesus said unto them, If God were your Father, ye would love me: for I proceeded forth and came from God; neither came I of myself, but he sent me.

43 Why do ye not understand my speech? *even* because ye cannot hear my word.

44 Ye are of *your* father the devil, and the lusts of your father ye will do. He was a murderer from the beginning, and abode not in the truth, because there is no truth in him. When he speaketh a lie, he speaketh of his own: for he is a liar, and the father of it.

45 And because I tell *you* the truth, ye believe me not.

46 Which of you convinceth me of sin? And if I say the truth, why do ye not believe me?

47 He that is of God heareth God's words: ye therefore hear *them* not, because ye are not of God.

48 Then answered the Jews, and said unto him, Say we not well that thou art a Samaritan, and hast a devil?

49 Jesus answered, I have not a devil; but I honour my Father, and ye do dishonour me.

50 And I seek not mine own glory: there is one that seeketh and judgeth.

51 Verily, verily, I say unto you, If a man keep my saying, he shall never see death.

52 Then said the Jews unto him, Now we know that thou hast a devil. Abraham is dead, and the prophets; and thou sayest, If a man keep my saying, he shall never taste of death.

53 Art thou greater than our father Abraham, which is dead? and the prophets are dead: whom makest thou thyself?

54 Jesus answered, If I honour myself, my honour is nothing: it is my Father that honoureth me; of whom ye say, that he is your God:

55 Yet ye have not known him; but I know him: and if I should say, I know him not, I shall be a liar like unto you: but I know him, and keep his saying.

56 Your father Abraham rejoiced to see my day: and he saw *it*, and was glad.

57 Then said the Jews unto him, Thou art not yet fifty years old, and hast thou seen Abraham?

58 Jesus said unto them, Verily, verily, I say unto you, Before Abraham was, I am.

59 Then took they up stones to cast at him: but Jesus hid himself, and went out of the temple, going through the midst of them, and so passed by.

9 1 And as *Jesus* passed by, he saw a man which was blind from *his* birth.

2 And his disciples asked him, saying, Master, who did sin, this man, or his parents, that he was born blind?

NEW LIVING TRANSLATION

did such a thing. 41 No, you are imitating your real father."

They replied, "We aren't illegitimate children! God himself is our true Father."

42 Jesus told them, "If God were your Father, you would love me, because I have come to you from God. I am not here on my own, but he sent me. 43 Why can't you understand what I am saying? It's because you can't even hear me! 44 For you are the children of your father the devil, and you love to do the evil things he does. He was a murderer from the beginning. He has always hated the truth, because there is no truth in him. When he lies, it is consistent with his character; for he is a liar and the father of lies. 45 So when I tell the truth, you just naturally don't believe me! 46 Which of you can truthfully accuse me of sin? And since I am telling you the truth, why don't you believe me? 47 Anyone who belongs to God listens gladly to the words of God. But you don't listen because you don't belong to God."

48 The people retorted, "You Samaritan devil! Didn't we say all along that you were possessed by a demon?"

49 "No," Jesus said, "I have no demon in me. For I honor my Father—and you dishonor me. 50 And though I have no wish to glorify myself, God is going to glorify me. He is the true judge. 51 I tell you the truth, anyone who obeys my teaching will never die!"

52 The people said, "Now we know you are possessed by a demon. Even Abraham and the prophets died, but you say, 'Anyone who obeys my teaching will never die!' 53 Are you greater than our father Abraham? He died, and so did the prophets. Who do you think you are?"

54 Jesus answered, "If I want glory for myself, it doesn't count. But it is my Father who will glorify me. You say, 'He is our God,*' 55 but you don't even know him. I know him. If I said otherwise, I would be as great a liar as you! But I do know him and obey him. 56 Your father Abraham rejoiced as he looked forward to my coming. He saw it and was glad."

57 The people said, "You aren't even fifty years old. How can you say you have seen Abraham?*"

58 Jesus answered, "I tell you the truth, before Abraham was even born, I AM!*" 59 At that point they picked up stones to throw at him. But Jesus was hidden from them and left the Temple.

Jesus Heals a Man Born Blind

9 As Jesus was walking along, he saw a man who had been blind from birth. 2 "Rabbi," his disciples asked him, "why was this man born blind? Was it because of his own sins or his parents' sins?"

8:54 Some manuscripts read *your God.* **8:57** Some manuscripts read *How can you say Abraham has seen you?* **8:58** Or *before Abraham was even born, I have always been alive;* Greek reads *before Abraham was, I am.* See Exod 3:14.

KING JAMES VERSION

3 Jesus answered, Neither hath this man sinned, nor his parents: but that the works of God should be made manifest in him.

4 I must work the works of him that sent me, while it is day: the night cometh, when no man can work.

5 As long as I am in the world, I am the light of the world.

6 When he had thus spoken, he spat on the ground, and made clay of the spittle, and he anointed the eyes of the blind man with the clay,

7 And said unto him, Go, wash in the pool of Siloam, (which is by interpretation, Sent.) He went his way therefore, and washed, and came seeing.

8 The neighbours therefore, and they which before had seen him that he was blind, said, Is not this he that sat and begged?

9 Some said, This is he: others *said,* He is like him: *but* he said, I am *he.*

10 Therefore said they unto him, How were thine eyes opened?

11 He answered and said, A man that is called Jesus made clay, and anointed mine eyes, and said unto me, Go to the pool of Siloam, and wash: and I went and washed, and I received sight.

12 Then said they unto him, Where is he? He said, I know not.

13 They brought to the Pharisees him that aforetime was blind.

14 And it was the sabbath day when Jesus made the clay, and opened his eyes.

15 Then again the Pharisees also asked him how he had received his sight. He said unto them, He put clay upon mine eyes, and I washed, and do see.

16 Therefore said some of the Pharisees, This man is not of God, because he keepeth not the sabbath day. Others said, How can a man that is a sinner do such miracles? And there was a division among them.

17 They say unto the blind man again, What sayest thou of him, that he hath opened thine eyes? He said, He is a prophet.

18 But the Jews did not believe concerning him, that he had been blind, and received his sight, until they called the parents of him that had received his sight.

19 And they asked them, saying, Is this your son, who ye say was born blind? how then doth he now see?

20 His parents answered them and said, We know that this is our son, and that he was born blind:

21 But by what means he now seeth, we know not; or who hath opened his eyes, we know not: he is of age; ask him: he shall speak for himself.

22 These *words* spake his parents, because they feared the Jews: for the Jews had agreed already, that if any man did confess that he was Christ, he should be put out of the synagogue.

23 Therefore said his parents, He is of age; ask him.

24 Then again called they the man that was blind, and said unto him, Give God the praise: we know that this man is a sinner.

NEW LIVING TRANSLATION

3 "It was not because of his sins or his parents' sins," Jesus answered. "This happened so the power of God could be seen in him. 4 We must quickly carry out the tasks assigned us by the one who sent us.* The night is coming, and then no one can work. 5 But while I am here in the world, I am the light of the world."

6 Then he spit on the ground, made mud with the saliva, and spread the mud over the blind man's eyes. 7 He told him, "Go wash yourself in the pool of Siloam" (Siloam means "sent"). So the man went and washed and came back seeing!

8 His neighbors and others who knew him as a blind beggar asked each other, "Isn't this the man who used to sit and beg?" 9 Some said he was, and others said, "No, he just looks like him!"

But the beggar kept saying, "Yes, I am the same one!"

10 They asked, "Who healed you? What happened?"

11 He told them, "The man they call Jesus made mud and spread it over my eyes and told me, 'Go to the pool of Siloam and wash yourself.' So I went and washed, and now I can see!"

12 "Where is he now?" they asked.

"I don't know," he replied.

13 Then they took the man who had been blind to the Pharisees, 14 because it was on the Sabbath that Jesus had made the mud and healed him. 15 The Pharisees asked the man all about it. So he told them, "He put the mud over my eyes, and when I washed it away, I could see!"

16 Some of the Pharisees said, "This man Jesus is not from God, for he is working on the Sabbath." Others said, "But how could an ordinary sinner do such miraculous signs?" So there was a deep division of opinion among them.

17 Then the Pharisees again questioned the man who had been blind and demanded, "What's your opinion about this man who healed you?"

The man replied, "I think he must be a prophet."

18 The Jewish leaders still refused to believe the man had been blind and could now see, so they called in his parents. 19 They asked them, "Is this your son? Was he born blind? If so, how can he now see?"

20 His parents replied, "We know this is our son and that he was born blind, 21 but we don't know how he can see or who healed him. Ask him. He is old enough to speak for himself." 22 His parents said this because they were afraid of the Jewish leaders, who had announced that anyone saying Jesus was the Messiah would be expelled from the synagogue. 23 That's why they said, "He is old enough. Ask him."

24 So for the second time they called in the man who had been blind and told him, "God should get the glory for this,* because we know this man Jesus is a sinner."

9:4 Other manuscripts read *I must quickly carry out the tasks assigned me by the one who sent me;* still others read *We must quickly carry out the tasks assigned us by the one who sent me.* **9:24** Or *Give glory to God, not to Jesus;* Greek reads *Give glory to God.*

KING JAMES VERSION

25 He answered and said, Whether he be a sinner *or no,* I know not: one thing I know, that, whereas I was blind, now I see.

26 Then said they to him again, What did he to thee? how opened he thine eyes?

27 He answered them, I have told you already, and ye did not hear: wherefore would ye hear *it* again? will ye also be his disciples?

28 Then they reviled him, and said, Thou art his disciple; but we are Moses' disciples.

29 We know that God spake unto Moses: *as for* this *fellow,* we know not from whence he is.

30 The man answered and said unto them, Why herein is a marvellous thing, that ye know not from whence he is, and *yet* he hath opened mine eyes.

31 Now we know that God heareth not sinners: but if any man be a worshipper of God, and doeth his will, him he heareth.

32 Since the world began was it not heard that any man opened the eyes of one that was born blind.

33 If this man were not of God, he could do nothing.

34 They answered and said unto him, Thou wast altogether born in sins, and dost thou teach us? And they cast him out.

35 Jesus heard that they had cast him out; and when he had found him, he said unto him, Dost thou believe on the Son of God?

36 He answered and said, Who is he, Lord, that I might believe on him?

37 And Jesus said unto him, Thou hast both seen him, and it is he that talketh with thee.

38 And he said, Lord, I believe. And he worshipped him.

39 And Jesus said, For judgment I am come into this world, that they which see not might see; and that they which see might be made blind.

40 And *some* of the Pharisees which were with him heard these words, and said unto him, Are we blind also?

41 Jesus said unto them, If ye were blind, ye should have no sin: but now ye say, We see; therefore your sin remaineth.

10 1 Verily, verily, I say unto you, He that entereth not by the door into the sheepfold, but climbeth up some other way, the same is a thief and a robber.

2 But he that entereth in by the door is the shepherd of the sheep.

3 To him the porter openeth; and the sheep hear his voice: and he calleth his own sheep by name, and leadeth them out.

4 And when he putteth forth his own sheep, he goeth before them, and the sheep follow him: for they know his voice.

5 And a stranger will they not follow, but will flee from him: for they know not the voice of strangers.

NEW LIVING TRANSLATION

25 "I don't know whether he is a sinner," the man replied. "But I know this: I was blind, and now I can see!"

26 "But what did he do?" they asked. "How did he heal you?"

27 "Look!" the man exclaimed. "I told you once. Didn't you listen? Why do you want to hear it again? Do you want to become his disciples, too?"

28 Then they cursed him and said, "You are his disciple, but we are disciples of Moses!
29 We know God spoke to Moses, but we don't even know where this man comes from."

30 "Why, that's very strange!" the man replied. "He healed my eyes, and yet you don't know where he
comes from? 31 We know that God doesn't listen to sinners, but he is ready to hear those who worship
him and do his will. 32 Ever since the world began, no one has been able to open the eyes of someone born
blind. 33 If this man were not from God, he couldn't have done it."

34 "You were born a total sinner!" they answered. "Are you trying to teach us?" And they threw him out of the synagogue.

Spiritual Blindness

35 When Jesus heard what had happened, he found the man and asked, "Do you believe in the Son of Man?*"

36 The man answered, "Who is he, sir? I want to believe in him."

37 "You have seen him," Jesus said, "and he is speaking to you!"

38 "Yes, Lord, I believe!" the man said. And he worshiped Jesus.

39 Then Jesus told him,* "I entered this world to render judgment—to give sight to the blind and to show those who think they see* that they are blind."

40 Some Pharisees who were standing nearby heard him and asked, "Are you saying we're blind?"

41 "If you were blind, you wouldn't be guilty," Jesus replied. "But you remain guilty because you claim you can see.

The Good Shepherd and His Sheep

10 "I tell you the truth, anyone who sneaks over the wall of a sheepfold, rather than going through the gate, must surely be a thief and a robber!
2 But the one who enters through the gate is the shepherd of the sheep. 3 The gatekeeper opens the gate for
him, and the sheep recognize his voice and come to him. He calls his own sheep by name and leads them
out. 4 After he has gathered his own flock, he walks ahead of them, and they follow him because they
know his voice. 5 They won't follow a stranger; they will run from him because they don't know his voice."

9:35 Some manuscripts read *the Son of God?* "Son of Man" is a title Jesus used for himself. **9:38-39a** Some manuscripts do not include *"Yes, Lord, I believe!" the man said. And he worshiped Jesus. Then Jesus told him.* **9:39b** Greek *those who see.*

KING JAMES VERSION

6 This parable spake Jesus unto them: but they understood not what things they were which he spake unto them.

7 Then said Jesus unto them again, Verily, verily, I say unto you, I am the door of the sheep.

8 All that ever came before me are thieves and robbers: but the sheep did not hear them.

9 I am the door: by me if any man enter in, he shall be saved, and shall go in and out, and find pasture.

10 The thief cometh not, but for to steal, and to kill, and to destroy: I am come that they might have life, and that they might have *it* more abundantly.

11 I am the good shepherd: the good shepherd giveth his life for the sheep.

12 But he that is an hireling, and not the shepherd, whose own the sheep are not, seeth the wolf coming, and leaveth the sheep, and fleeth: and the wolf catcheth them, and scattereth the sheep.

13 The hireling fleeth, because he is an hireling, and careth not for the sheep.

14 I am the good shepherd, and know my *sheep*, and am known of mine.

15 As the Father knoweth me, even so know I the Father: and I lay down my life for the sheep.

16 And other sheep I have, which are not of this fold: them also I must bring, and they shall hear my voice; and there shall be one fold, *and* one shepherd.

17 Therefore doth my Father love me, because I lay down my life, that I might take it again.

18 No man taketh it from me, but I lay it down of myself. I have power to lay it down, and I have power to take it again. This commandment have I received of my Father.

19 There was a division therefore again among the Jews for these sayings.

20 And many of them said, He hath a devil, and is mad; why hear ye him?

21 Others said, These are not the words of him that hath a devil. Can a devil open the eyes of the blind?

22 And it was at Jerusalem the feast of the dedication, and it was winter.

23 And Jesus walked in the temple in Solomon's porch.

24 Then came the Jews round about him, and said unto him, How long dost thou make us to doubt? If thou be the Christ, tell us plainly.

25 Jesus answered them, I told you, and ye believed not: the works that I do in my Father's name, they bear witness of me.

26 But ye believe not, because ye are not of my sheep, as I said unto you.

27 My sheep hear my voice, and I know them, and they follow me:

28 And I give unto them eternal life; and they shall never perish, neither shall any *man* pluck them out of my hand.

29 My Father, which gave *them* me, is greater than

NEW LIVING TRANSLATION

6 Those who heard Jesus use this illustration didn't
understand what he meant, 7 so he explained it to
them: "I tell you the truth, I am the gate for the sheep.
8 All who came before me* were thieves and robbers.
But the true sheep did not listen to them. 9 Yes, I
am the gate. Those who come in through me will be
saved.* They will come and go freely and will find
good pastures. 10 The thief's purpose is to steal and
kill and destroy. My purpose is to give them a rich
and satisfying life.

11 "I am the good shepherd. The good shepherd
sacrifices his life for the sheep. 12 A hired hand will
run when he sees a wolf coming. He will abandon the
sheep because they don't belong to him and he isn't
their shepherd. And so the wolf attacks them and
scatters the flock. 13 The hired hand runs away because he's working only for the money and doesn't
really care about the sheep.

14 "I am the good shepherd; I know my own sheep,
and they know me, 15 just as my Father knows me and
I know the Father. So I sacrifice my life for the sheep.
16 I have other sheep, too, that are not in this
sheepfold. I must bring them also. They will listen
to my voice, and there will be one flock with one
shepherd.

17 "The Father loves me because I sacrifice my life
so I may take it back again. 18 No one can take my life
from me. I sacrifice it voluntarily. For I have the
authority to lay it down when I want to and also to
take it up again. For this is what my Father has commanded."

19 When he said these things, the people* were
again divided in their opinions about him. 20 Some
said, "He's demon possessed and out of his mind.
Why listen to a man like that?" 21 Others said, "This
doesn't sound like a man possessed by a demon!
Can a demon open the eyes of the blind?"

Jesus Claims to Be the Son of God

22 It was now winter, and Jesus was in Jerusalem at the
time of Hanukkah, the Festival of Dedication. 23 He
was in the Temple, walking through the section
known as Solomon's Colonnade. 24 The people surrounded him and asked, "How long are you going to
keep us in suspense? If you are the Messiah, tell us
plainly."

25 Jesus replied, "I have already told you, and you
don't believe me. The proof is the work I do in my
Father's name. 26 But you don't believe me because
you are not my sheep. 27 My sheep listen to my voice;
I know them, and they follow me. 28 I give them eternal life, and they will never perish. No one can snatch
them away from me, 29 for my Father has given them
to me, and he is more powerful than anyone else.*

10:8 Some manuscripts do not include *before me.* **10:9** Or *will find safety.* **10:19** Greek *Jewish people;* also in 10:24, 31. **10:29** Other manuscripts read *for what my Father has given me is more powerful than anything;* still others read *for regarding that which my Father has given me, he is greater than all.*

KING JAMES VERSION

all; and no *man* is able to pluck *them* out of my Father's hand.

30 I and *my* Father are one.

31 Then the Jews took up stones again to stone him.

32 Jesus answered them, Many good works have I shewed you from my Father; for which of those works do ye stone me?

33 The Jews answered him, saying, For a good work we stone thee not; but for blasphemy; and because that thou, being a man, makest thyself God.

34 Jesus answered them, Is it not written in your law, I said, Ye are gods?

35 If he called them gods, unto whom the word of God came, and the scripture cannot be broken;

36 Say ye of him, whom the Father hath sanctified, and sent into the world, Thou blasphemest; because I said, I am the Son of God?

37 If I do not the works of my Father, believe me not.

38 But if I do, though ye believe not me, believe the works: that ye may know, and believe, that the Father *is* in me, and I in him.

39 Therefore they sought again to take him: but he escaped out of their hand,

40 And went away again beyond Jordan into the place where John at first baptized; and there he abode.

41 And many resorted unto him, and said, John did no miracle: but all things that John spake of this man were true.

42 And many believed on him there.

11 1 Now a certain *man* was sick, *named* Lazarus, of Bethany, the town of Mary and her sister Martha.

2 (It was *that* Mary which anointed the Lord with ointment, and wiped his feet with her hair, whose brother Lazarus was sick.)

3 Therefore his sisters sent unto him, saying, Lord, behold, he whom thou lovest is sick.

4 When Jesus heard *that,* he said, This sickness is not unto death, but for the glory of God, that the Son of God might be glorified thereby.

5 Now Jesus loved Martha, and her sister, and Lazarus.

6 When he had heard therefore that he was sick, he abode two days still in the same place where he was.

7 Then after that saith he to *his* disciples, Let us go into Judaea again.

8 *His* disciples say unto him, Master, the Jews of late sought to stone thee; and goest thou thither again?

9 Jesus answered, Are there not twelve hours in the day? If any man walk in the day, he stumbleth not, because he seeth the light of this world.

10 But if a man walk in the night, he stumbleth, because there is no light in him.

NEW LIVING TRANSLATION

No one can snatch them from the Father's hand. 30 The Father and I are one."

31 Once again the people picked up stones to kill him. 32 Jesus said, "At my Father's direction I have done many good works. For which one are you going to stone me?"

33 They replied, "We're stoning you not for any good work, but for blasphemy! You, a mere man, claim to be God."

34 Jesus replied, "It is written in your own Scriptures* that God said to certain leaders of the people, 'I say, you are gods!'* 35 And you know that the Scriptures cannot be altered. So if those people who received God's message were called 'gods,' 36 why do you call it blasphemy when I say, 'I am the Son of God'? After all, the Father set me apart and sent me into the world. 37 Don't believe me unless I carry out my Father's work. 38 But if I do his work, believe in the evidence of the miraculous works I have done, even if you don't believe me. Then you will know and understand that the Father is in me, and I am in the Father."

39 Once again they tried to arrest him, but he got away and left them. 40 He went beyond the Jordan River near the place where John was first baptizing and stayed there awhile. 41 And many followed him. "John didn't perform miraculous signs," they remarked to one another, "but everything he said about this man has come true." 42 And many who were there believed in Jesus.

The Raising of Lazarus

11 A man named Lazarus was sick. He lived in Bethany with his sisters, Mary and Martha. 2 This is the Mary who later poured the expensive perfume on the Lord's feet and wiped them with her hair.* Her brother, Lazarus, was sick. 3 So the two sisters sent a message to Jesus telling him, "Lord, your dear friend is very sick."

4 But when Jesus heard about it he said, "Lazarus's sickness will not end in death. No, it happened for the glory of God so that the Son of God will receive glory from this." 5 So although Jesus loved Martha, Mary, and Lazarus, 6 he stayed where he was for the next two days. 7 Finally, he said to his disciples, "Let's go back to Judea."

8 But his disciples objected. "Rabbi," they said, "only a few days ago the people* in Judea were trying to stone you. Are you going there again?"

9 Jesus replied, "There are twelve hours of daylight every day. During the day people can walk safely. They can see because they have the light of this world. 10 But at night there is danger of stumbling

10:34a Greek *your own law.* **10:34b** Ps 82:6. **11:2** This incident is recorded in chapter 12. **11:8** Greek *Jewish people;* also in 11:19, 31, 33, 36, 45, 54.

KING JAMES VERSION

11 These things said he: and after that he saith unto them, Our friend Lazarus sleepeth; but I go, that I may awake him out of sleep.

12 Then said his disciples, Lord, if he sleep, he shall do well.

13 Howbeit Jesus spake of his death: but they thought that he had spoken of taking of rest in sleep.

14 Then said Jesus unto them plainly, Lazarus is dead.

15 And I am glad for your sakes that I was not there, to the intent ye may believe; nevertheless let us go unto him.

16 Then said Thomas, which is called Didymus, unto his fellowdisciples, Let us also go, that we may die with him.

17 Then when Jesus came, he found that he had *lain* in the grave four days already.

18 Now Bethany was nigh unto Jerusalem, about fifteen furlongs off:

19 And many of the Jews came to Martha and Mary, to comfort them concerning their brother.

20 Then Martha, as soon as she heard that Jesus was coming, went and met him: but Mary sat *still* in the house.

21 Then said Martha unto Jesus, Lord, if thou hadst been here, my brother had not died.

22 But I know, that even now, whatsoever thou wilt ask of God, God will give *it* thee.

23 Jesus saith unto her, Thy brother shall rise again.

24 Martha saith unto him, I know that he shall rise again in the resurrection at the last day.

25 Jesus said unto her, I am the resurrection, and the life: he that believeth in me, though he were dead, yet shall he live:

26 And whosoever liveth and believeth in me shall never die. Believest thou this?

27 She saith unto him, Yea, Lord: I believe that thou art the Christ, the Son of God, which should come into the world.

28 And when she had so said, she went her way, and called Mary her sister secretly, saying, The Master is come, and calleth for thee.

29 As soon as she heard *that,* she arose quickly, and came unto him.

30 Now Jesus was not yet come into the town, but was in that place where Martha met him.

31 The Jews then which were with her in the house, and comforted her, when they saw Mary, that she rose up hastily and went out, followed her, saying, She goeth unto the grave to weep there.

32 Then when Mary was come where Jesus was, and saw him, she fell down at his feet, saying unto him, Lord, if thou hadst been here, my brother had not died.

33 When Jesus therefore saw her weeping, and the Jews also weeping which came with her, he groaned in the spirit, and was troubled,

NEW LIVING TRANSLATION

because they have no light." 11 Then he said, "Our
friend Lazarus has fallen asleep, but now I will go
and wake him up."

12 The disciples said, "Lord, if he is sleeping, he
will soon get better!" 13 They thought Jesus meant
Lazarus was simply sleeping, but Jesus meant Lazarus had died.

14 So he told them plainly, "Lazarus is dead. 15 And
for your sakes, I'm glad I wasn't there, for now you
will really believe. Come, let's go see him."

16 Thomas, nicknamed the Twin,* said to his fellow disciples, "Let's go, too—and die with Jesus."

17 When Jesus arrived at Bethany, he was told that
Lazarus had already been in his grave for four days.
18 Bethany was only a few miles* down the road from
Jerusalem, 19 and many of the people had come
to console Martha and Mary in their loss. 20 When
Martha got word that Jesus was coming, she went to
meet him. But Mary stayed in the house. 21 Martha
said to Jesus, "Lord, if only you had been here, my
brother would not have died. 22 But even now I know
that God will give you whatever you ask."

23 Jesus told her, "Your brother will rise again."

24 "Yes," Martha said, "he will rise when everyone
else rises, at the last day."

25 Jesus told her, "I am the resurrection and the
life.* Anyone who believes in me will live, even after
dying. 26 Everyone who lives in me and believes in me
will never ever die. Do you believe this, Martha?"

27 "Yes, Lord," she told him. "I have always believed
you are the Messiah, the Son of God, the one who has
come into the world from God." 28 Then she returned
to Mary. She called Mary aside from the mourners
and told her, "The Teacher is here and wants to see
you." 29 So Mary immediately went to him.

30 Jesus had stayed outside the village, at the place
where Martha met him. 31 When the people who
were at the house consoling Mary saw her leave so
hastily, they assumed she was going to Lazarus's
grave to weep. So they followed her there. 32 When
Mary arrived and saw Jesus, she fell at his feet and
said, "Lord, if only you had been here, my brother
would not have died."

33 When Jesus saw her weeping and saw the other
people wailing with her, a deep anger welled up

11:16 Greek *Thomas, who was called Didymus.* **11:18** Greek *was about 15 stadia* [about 2.8 kilometers]. **11:25** Some manuscripts do not include *and the life.*

KING JAMES VERSION

34 And said, Where have ye laid him? They said unto him, Lord, come and see.

35 Jesus wept.

36 Then said the Jews, Behold how he loved him!

37 And some of them said, Could not this man, which opened the eyes of the blind, have caused that even this man should not have died?

38 Jesus therefore again groaning in himself cometh to the grave. It was a cave, and a stone lay upon it.

39 Jesus said, Take ye away the stone. Martha, the sister of him that was dead, saith unto him, Lord, by this time he stinketh: for he hath been *dead* four days.

40 Jesus saith unto her, Said I not unto thee, that, if thou wouldest believe, thou shouldest see the glory of God?

41 Then they took away the stone *from the place* where the dead was laid. And Jesus lifted up *his* eyes, and said, Father, I thank thee that thou hast heard me.

42 And I knew that thou hearest me always: but because of the people which stand by I said *it*, that they may believe that thou hast sent me.

43 And when he thus had spoken, he cried with a loud voice, Lazarus, come forth.

44 And he that was dead came forth, bound hand and foot with graveclothes: and his face was bound about with a napkin. Jesus saith unto them, Loose him, and let him go.

45 Then many of the Jews which came to Mary, and had seen the things which Jesus did, believed on him.

46 But some of them went their ways to the Pharisees, and told them what things Jesus had done.

47 Then gathered the chief priests and the Pharisees a council, and said, What do we? for this man doeth many miracles.

48 If we let him thus alone, all *men* will believe on him: and the Romans shall come and take away both our place and nation.

49 And one of them, *named* Caiaphas, being the high priest that same year, said unto them, Ye know nothing at all,

50 Nor consider that it is expedient for us, that one man should die for the people, and that the whole nation perish not.

51 And this spake he not of himself: but being high priest that year, he prophesied that Jesus should die for that nation;

52 And not for that nation only, but that also he should gather together in one the children of God that were scattered abroad.

53 Then from that day forth they took counsel together for to put him to death.

54 Jesus therefore walked no more openly among the Jews; but went thence unto a country near to the wilderness, into a city called Ephraim, and there continued with his disciples.

55 And the Jews' passover was nigh at hand: and

NEW LIVING TRANSLATION

within him,* and he was deeply troubled. 34 "Where have you put him?" he asked them.

They told him, "Lord, come and see." 35 Then Jesus wept. 36 The people who were standing nearby said, "See how much he loved him!" 37 But some said, "This man healed a blind man. Couldn't he have kept Lazarus from dying?"

38 Jesus was still angry as he arrived at the tomb, a cave with a stone rolled across its entrance. 39 "Roll the stone aside," Jesus told them.

But Martha, the dead man's sister, protested, "Lord, he has been dead for four days. The smell will be terrible."

40 Jesus responded, "Didn't I tell you that you would see God's glory if you believe?" 41 So they rolled the stone aside. Then Jesus looked up to heaven and said, "Father, thank you for hearing me. 42 You always hear me, but I said it out loud for the sake of all these people standing here, so that they will believe you sent me." 43 Then Jesus shouted, "Lazarus, come out!" 44 And the dead man came out, his hands and feet bound in graveclothes, his face wrapped in a headcloth. Jesus told them, "Unwrap him and let him go!"

The Plot to Kill Jesus

45 Many of the people who were with Mary believed in Jesus when they saw this happen. 46 But some went to the Pharisees and told them what Jesus had done. 47 Then the leading priests and Pharisees called the high council* together. "What are we going to do?" they asked each other. "This man certainly performs many miraculous signs. 48 If we allow him to go on like this, soon everyone will believe in him. Then the Roman army will come and destroy both our Temple* and our nation."

49 Caiaphas, who was high priest at that time,* said, "You don't know what you're talking about! 50 You don't realize that it's better for you that one man should die for the people than for the whole nation to be destroyed."

51 He did not say this on his own; as high priest at that time he was led to prophesy that Jesus would die for the entire nation. 52 And not only for that nation, but to bring together and unite all the children of God scattered around the world.

53 So from that time on, the Jewish leaders began to plot Jesus' death. 54 As a result, Jesus stopped his public ministry among the people and left Jerusalem. He went to a place near the wilderness, to the village of Ephraim, and stayed there with his disciples.

55 It was now almost time for the Jewish Passover celebration, and many people from all over the country arrived in Jerusalem several days early so

11:33 Or *he was angry in his spirit.* **11:47** Greek *the Sanhedrin.* **11:48** Or *our position;* Greek reads *our place.* **11:49** Greek *that year;* also in 11:51.

many went out of the country up to Jerusalem before
the passover, to purify themselves.

56 Then sought they for Jesus, and spake among
themselves, as they stood in the temple, What think
ye, that he will not come to the feast?

57 Now both the chief priests and the Pharisees
had given a commandment, that, if any man knew
where he were, he should shew *it,* that they might
take him.

12 1 Then Jesus six days before the passover came
to Bethany, where Lazarus was which had
been dead, whom he raised from the dead.

2 There they made him a supper; and Martha
served: but Lazarus was one of them that sat at the
table with him.

3 Then took Mary a pound of ointment of spikenard, very costly, and anointed the feet of Jesus, and
wiped his feet with her hair: and the house was filled
with the odour of the ointment.

4 Then saith one of his disciples, Judas Iscariot,
Simon's *son,* which should betray him,

5 Why was not this ointment sold for three hundred pence, and given to the poor?

6 This he said, not that he cared for the poor; but
because he was a thief, and had the bag, and bare
what was put therein.

7 Then said Jesus, Let her alone: against the day of
my burying hath she kept this.

8 For the poor always ye have with you; but me ye
have not always.

9 Much people of the Jews therefore knew that he
was there: and they came not for Jesus' sake only, but
that they might see Lazarus also, whom he had raised
from the dead.

10 But the chief priests consulted that they might
put Lazarus also to death;

11 Because that by reason of him many of the Jews
went away, and believed on Jesus.

12 On the next day much people that were come
to the feast, when they heard that Jesus was coming
to Jerusalem,

13 Took branches of palm trees, and went forth to
meet him, and cried, Hosanna: Blessed *is* the King of
Israel that cometh in the name of the Lord.

14 And Jesus, when he had found a young ass, sat
thereon; as it is written,

15 Fear not, daughter of Sion: behold, thy King
cometh, sitting on an ass's colt.

they could go through the purification ceremony
before Passover began. 56 They kept looking for
Jesus, but as they stood around in the Temple, they
said to each other, "What do you think? He won't
come for Passover, will he?" 57 Meanwhile, the leading priests and Pharisees had publicly ordered that
anyone seeing Jesus must report it immediately so
they could arrest him.

Jesus Anointed at Bethany

12 Six days before the Passover celebration began, Jesus arrived in Bethany, the home of
Lazarus—the man he had raised from the dead. 2 A
dinner was prepared in Jesus' honor. Martha served,
and Lazarus was among those who ate* with him.
3 Then Mary took a twelve-ounce jar* of expensive
perfume made from essence of nard, and she
anointed Jesus' feet with it, wiping his feet with her
hair. The house was filled with the fragrance.

4 But Judas Iscariot, the disciple who would soon
betray him, said, 5 "That perfume was worth a year's
wages.* It should have been sold and the money
given to the poor." 6 Not that he cared for the poor—
he was a thief, and since he was in charge of the disciples' money, he often stole some for himself.

7 Jesus replied, "Leave her alone. She did this in
preparation for my burial. 8 You will always have the
poor among you, but you will not always have me."

9 When all the people* heard of Jesus' arrival, they
flocked to see him and also to see Lazarus, the man
Jesus had raised from the dead. 10 Then the leading
priests decided to kill Lazarus, too, 11 for it was because of him that many of the people had deserted
them* and believed in Jesus.

Jesus' Triumphant Entry

12 The next day, the news that Jesus was on the way
to Jerusalem swept through the city. A large crowd
of Passover visitors 13 took palm branches and went
down the road to meet him. They shouted,

"Praise God!*
Blessings on the one who comes in the name
of the LORD!
Hail to the King of Israel!"*

14 Jesus found a young donkey and rode on it, fulfilling the prophecy that said:

15 "Don't be afraid, people of Jerusalem.*
Look, your King is coming,
riding on a donkey's colt."*

12:2 Or *who reclined.* **12:3** Greek *took 1 litra* [327 grams]. **12:5** Greek *worth 300 denarii.* A denarius was equivalent to a laborer's full day's wage. **12:9** Greek *Jewish people;* also in 12:11. **12:11** Or *had deserted their traditions;* Greek reads *had deserted.* **12:13a** Greek *Hosanna,* an exclamation of praise adapted from a Hebrew expression that means "save now." **12:13b** Ps 118:25-26; Zeph 3:15. **12:15a** Greek *daughter of Zion.* **12:15b** Zech 9:9.

KING JAMES VERSION

16 These things understood not his disciples at the first: but when Jesus was glorified, then remembered they that these things were written of him, and *that* they had done these things unto him.

17 The people therefore that was with him when he called Lazarus out of his grave, and raised him from the dead, bare record.

18 For this cause the people also met him, for that they heard that he had done this miracle.

19 The Pharisees therefore said among themselves, Perceive ye how ye prevail nothing? behold, the world is gone after him.

20 And there were certain Greeks among them that came up to worship at the feast:

21 The same came therefore to Philip, which was of Bethsaida of Galilee, and desired him, saying, Sir, we would see Jesus.

22 Philip cometh and telleth Andrew: and again Andrew and Philip tell Jesus.

23 And Jesus answered them, saying, The hour is come, that the Son of man should be glorified.

24 Verily, verily, I say unto you, Except a corn of wheat fall into the ground and die, it abideth alone: but if it die, it bringeth forth much fruit.

25 He that loveth his life shall lose it; and he that hateth his life in this world shall keep it unto life eternal.

26 If any man serve me, let him follow me; and where I am, there shall also my servant be: if any man serve me, him will *my* Father honour.

27 Now is my soul troubled; and what shall I say? Father, save me from this hour: but for this cause came I unto this hour.

28 Father, glorify thy name. Then came there a voice from heaven, *saying*, I have both glorified *it*, and will glorify *it* again.

29 The people therefore, that stood by, and heard *it*, said that it thundered: others said, An angel spake to him.

30 Jesus answered and said, This voice came not because of me, but for your sakes.

31 Now is the judgment of this world: now shall the prince of this world be cast out.

32 And I, if I be lifted up from the earth, will draw all *men* unto me.

33 This he said, signifying what death he should die.

34 The people answered him, We have heard out of the law that Christ abideth for ever: and how sayest thou, The Son of man must be lifted up? who is this Son of man?

35 Then Jesus said unto them, Yet a little while is the light with you. Walk while ye have the light, lest darkness come upon you: for he that walketh in darkness knoweth not whither he goeth.

36 While ye have light, believe in the light, that ye

NEW LIVING TRANSLATION

16 His disciples didn't understand at the time that this was a fulfillment of prophecy. But after Jesus entered into his glory, they remembered what had happened and realized that these things had been written about him.

17 Many in the crowd had seen Jesus call Lazarus from the tomb, raising him from the dead, and they were telling others* about it. 18 That was the reason so many went out to meet him—because they had heard about this miraculous sign. 19 Then the Pharisees said to each other, "There's nothing we can do. Look, everyone* has gone after him!"

Jesus Predicts His Death

20 Some Greeks who had come to Jerusalem for the Passover celebration 21 paid a visit to Philip, who was from Bethsaida in Galilee. They said, "Sir, we want to meet Jesus." 22 Philip told Andrew about it, and they went together to ask Jesus.

23 Jesus replied, "Now the time has come for the Son of Man* to enter into his glory. 24 I tell you the truth, unless a kernel of wheat is planted in the soil and dies, it remains alone. But its death will produce many new kernels—a plentiful harvest of new lives. 25 Those who love their life in this world will lose it. Those who care nothing for their life in this world will keep it for eternity. 26 Anyone who wants to be my disciple must follow me, because my servants must be where I am. And the Father will honor anyone who serves me.

27 "Now my soul is deeply troubled. Should I pray, 'Father, save me from this hour'? But this is the very reason I came! 28 Father, bring glory to your name."

Then a voice spoke from heaven, saying, "I have already brought glory to my name, and I will do so again." 29 When the crowd heard the voice, some thought it was thunder, while others declared an angel had spoken to him.

30 Then Jesus told them, "The voice was for your benefit, not mine. 31 The time for judging this world has come, when Satan, the ruler of this world, will be cast out. 32 And when I am lifted up from the earth, I will draw everyone to myself." 33 He said this to indicate how he was going to die.

34 The crowd responded, "We understood from Scripture* that the Messiah would live forever. How can you say the Son of Man will die? Just who is this Son of Man, anyway?"

35 Jesus replied, "My light will shine for you just a little longer. Walk in the light while you can, so the darkness will not overtake you. Those who walk in the darkness cannot see where they are going. 36 Put your trust in the light while there is still time; then you will become children of the light."

12:17 Greek *were testifying.* **12:19** Greek *the world.* **12:23** "Son of Man" is a title Jesus used for himself. **12:34** Greek *from the law.*

KING JAMES VERSION

may be the children of light. These things spake Jesus,
and departed, and did hide himself from them.

37But though he had done so many miracles before them, yet they believed not on him:
38That the saying of Esaias the prophet might be
fulfilled, which he spake, Lord, who hath believed
our report? and to whom hath the arm of the Lord
been revealed?
39Therefore they could not believe, because that
Esaias said again,
40He hath blinded their eyes, and hardened their
heart; that they should not see with *their* eyes, nor
understand with *their* heart, and be converted, and
I should heal them.
41These things said Esaias, when he saw his glory,
and spake of him.
42Nevertheless among the chief rulers also many
believed on him; but because of the Pharisees they
did not confess *him*, lest they should be put out of
the synagogue:
43For they loved the praise of men more than the
praise of God.
44Jesus cried and said, He that believeth on me,
believeth not on me, but on him that sent me.
45And he that seeth me seeth him that sent me.
46I am come a light into the world, that whosoever
believeth on me should not abide in darkness.
47And if any man hear my words, and believe not, I
judge him not: for I came not to judge the world, but
to save the world.
48He that rejecteth me, and receiveth not my
words, hath one that judgeth him: the word that I
have spoken, the same shall judge him in the last day.
49For I have not spoken of myself; but the Father
which sent me, he gave me a commandment, what I
should say, and what I should speak.
50And I know that his commandment is life everlasting: whatsoever I speak therefore, even as the
Father said unto me, so I speak.

13 1Now before the feast of the passover, when
Jesus knew that his hour was come that he
should depart out of this world unto the Father, having
loved his own which were in the world, he loved them
unto the end.
2And supper being ended, the devil having now
put into the heart of Judas Iscariot, Simon's *son*, to
betray him;
3Jesus knowing that the Father had given all
things into his hands, and that he was come from
God, and went to God;
4He riseth from supper, and laid aside his garments; and took a towel, and girded himself.
5After that he poureth water into a basin, and

NEW LIVING TRANSLATION

After saying these things, Jesus went away and was
hidden from them.

The Unbelief of the People

37But despite all the miraculous signs Jesus had done,
most of the people still did not believe in him. 38This
is exactly what Isaiah the prophet had predicted:

"LORD, who has believed our message?
To whom has the LORD revealed his
powerful arm?"*

39But the people couldn't believe, for as Isaiah also
said,

40 "The Lord has blinded their eyes
and hardened their hearts—
so that their eyes cannot see,
and their hearts cannot understand,
and they cannot turn to me
and have me heal them."*

41Isaiah was referring to Jesus when he said this, because he saw the future and spoke of the Messiah's
glory. 42Many people did believe in him, however,
including some of the Jewish leaders. But they
wouldn't admit it for fear that the Pharisees would
expel them from the synagogue. 43For they loved
human praise more than the praise of God.
44Jesus shouted to the crowds, "If you trust me,
you are trusting not only me, but also God who sent
me. 45For when you see me, you are seeing the one
who sent me. 46I have come as a light to shine in this
dark world, so that all who put their trust in me will
no longer remain in the dark. 47I will not judge those
who hear me but don't obey me, for I have come to
save the world and not to judge it. 48But all who reject
me and my message will be judged on the day of
judgment by the truth I have spoken. 49I don't speak
on my own authority. The Father who sent me has
commanded me what to say and how to say it. 50And
I know his commands lead to eternal life; so I say
whatever the Father tells me to say."

Jesus Washes His Disciples' Feet

13 Before the Passover celebration, Jesus knew
that his hour had come to leave this world and
return to his Father. He had loved his disciples during
his ministry on earth, and now he loved them to the
very end.* 2It was time for supper, and the devil had
already prompted Judas,* son of Simon Iscariot, to betray Jesus. 3Jesus knew that the Father had given him
authority over everything and that he had come from
God and would return to God. 4So he got up from the
table, took off his robe, wrapped a towel around his
waist, 5and poured water into a basin. Then he began

12:38 Isa 53:1. **12:40** Isa 6:10. **13:1** Or *he showed them the full extent of his love.* **13:2** Or *the devil had already intended for Judas.*

KING JAMES VERSION

began to wash the disciples' feet, and to wipe *them* with the towel wherewith he was girded.

6 Then cometh he to Simon Peter: and Peter saith unto him, Lord, dost thou wash my feet?

7 Jesus answered and said unto him, What I do thou knowest not now; but thou shalt know hereafter.

8 Peter saith unto him, Thou shalt never wash my feet. Jesus answered him, If I wash thee not, thou hast no part with me.

9 Simon Peter saith unto him, Lord, not my feet only, but also *my* hands and *my* head.

10 Jesus saith to him, He that is washed needeth not save to wash *his* feet, but is clean every whit: and ye are clean, but not all.

11 For he knew who should betray him; therefore said he, Ye are not all clean.

12 So after he had washed their feet, and had taken his garments, and was set down again, he said unto them, Know ye what I have done to you?

13 Ye call me Master and Lord: and ye say well; for *so* I am.

14 If I then, *your* Lord and Master, have washed your feet; ye also ought to wash one another's feet.

15 For I have given you an example, that ye should do as I have done to you.

16 Verily, verily, I say unto you, The servant is not greater than his lord; neither he that is sent greater than he that sent him.

17 If ye know these things, happy are ye if ye do them.

18 I speak not of you all: I know whom I have chosen: but that the scripture may be fulfilled, He that eateth bread with me hath lifted up his heel against me.

19 Now I tell you before it come, that, when it is come to pass, ye may believe that I am *he*.

20 Verily, verily, I say unto you, He that receiveth whomsoever I send receiveth me; and he that receiveth me receiveth him that sent me.

21 When Jesus had thus said, he was troubled in spirit, and testified, and said, Verily, verily, I say unto you, that one of you shall betray me.

22 Then the disciples looked one on another, doubting of whom he spake.

23 Now there was leaning on Jesus' bosom one of his disciples, whom Jesus loved.

24 Simon Peter therefore beckoned to him, that he should ask who it should be of whom he spake.

25 He then lying on Jesus' breast saith unto him, Lord, who is it?

26 Jesus answered, He it is, to whom I shall give a sop, when I have dipped *it*. And when he had dipped the sop, he gave *it* to Judas Iscariot, *the son* of Simon.

27 And after the sop Satan entered into him. Then said Jesus unto him, That thou doest, do quickly.

28 Now no man at the table knew for what intent he spake this unto him.

NEW LIVING TRANSLATION

to wash the disciples' feet, drying them with the towel
he had around him.
6 When Jesus came to Simon Peter, Peter said to
him, "Lord, are you going to wash my feet?"
7 Jesus replied, "You don't understand now what I
am doing, but someday you will."
8 "No," Peter protested, "you will never ever wash
my feet!"
Jesus replied, "Unless I wash you, you won't belong
to me."
9 Simon Peter exclaimed, "Then wash my hands
and head as well, Lord, not just my feet!"
10 Jesus replied, "A person who has bathed all over
does not need to wash, except for the feet,* to be entirely clean. And you disciples are clean, but not all
of you." 11 For Jesus knew who would betray him.
That is what he meant when he said, "Not all of you
are clean."
12 After washing their feet, he put on his robe again
and sat down and asked, "Do you understand what I
was doing? 13 You call me 'Teacher' and 'Lord,' and
you are right, because that's what I am. 14 And since I,
your Lord and Teacher, have washed your feet, you
ought to wash each other's feet. 15 I have given you an
example to follow. Do as I have done to you. 16 I tell
you the truth, slaves are not greater than their master. Nor is the messenger more important than the
one who sends the message. 17 Now that you know
these things, God will bless you for doing them.

Jesus Predicts His Betrayal

18 "I am not saying these things to all of you; I know
the ones I have chosen. But this fulfills the Scripture
that says, 'The one who eats my food has turned
against me.'* 19 I tell you this beforehand, so that
when it happens you will believe that I AM the Messiah.* 20 I tell you the truth, anyone who welcomes
my messenger is welcoming me, and anyone who
welcomes me is welcoming the Father who sent me."
21 Now Jesus was deeply troubled,* and he exclaimed, "I tell you the truth, one of you will betray me!"
22 The disciples looked at each other, wondering
whom he could mean. 23 The disciple Jesus loved was
sitting next to Jesus at the table.* 24 Simon Peter motioned to him to ask, "Who's he talking about?" 25 So
that disciple leaned over to Jesus and asked, "Lord,
who is it?"
26 Jesus responded, "It is the one to whom I give the
bread I dip in the bowl." And when he had dipped it,
he gave it to Judas, son of Simon Iscariot. 27 When
Judas had eaten the bread, Satan entered into him.
Then Jesus told him, "Hurry and do what you're going to do." 28 None of the others at the table knew

13:10 Some manuscripts do not include *except for the feet.* **13:18** Ps 41:9. **13:19** Or *that the 'I AM' has come;* or *that I am the LORD;* Greek reads *that I am.* See Exod 3:14. **13:21** Greek *was troubled in his spirit.* **13:23** Greek *was reclining on Jesus' bosom.* The "disciple Jesus loved" was probably John.

KING JAMES VERSION

29For some *of them* thought, because Judas had the bag, that Jesus had said unto him, Buy *those things* that we have need of against the feast; or, that he should give something to the poor.

30He then having received the sop went immediately out: and it was night.

31Therefore, when he was gone out, Jesus said, Now is the Son of man glorified, and God is glorified in him.

32If God be glorified in him, God shall also glorify him in himself, and shall straightway glorify him.

33Little children, yet a little while I am with you. Ye shall seek me: and as I said unto the Jews, Whither I go, ye cannot come; so now I say to you.

34A new commandment I give unto you, That ye love one another; as I have loved you, that ye also love one another.

35By this shall all *men* know that ye are my disciples, if ye have love one to another.

36Simon Peter said unto him, Lord, whither goest thou? Jesus answered him, Whither I go, thou canst not follow me now; but thou shalt follow me afterwards.

37Peter said unto him, Lord, why cannot I follow thee now? I will lay down my life for thy sake.

38Jesus answered him, Wilt thou lay down thy life for my sake? Verily, verily, I say unto thee, The cock shall not crow, till thou hast denied me thrice.

14 1Let not your heart be troubled: ye believe in God, believe also in me.

2In my Father's house are many mansions: if *it were* not *so,* I would have told you. I go to prepare a place for you.

3And if I go and prepare a place for you, I will come again, and receive you unto myself; that where I am, *there* ye may be also.

4And whither I go ye know, and the way ye know.

5Thomas saith unto him, Lord, we know not whither thou goest; and how can we know the way?

6Jesus saith unto him, I am the way, the truth, and the life: no man cometh unto the Father, but by me.

7If ye had known me, ye should have known my Father also: and from henceforth ye know him, and have seen him.

8Philip saith unto him, Lord, shew us the Father, and it sufficeth us.

9Jesus saith unto him, Have I been so long time with you, and yet hast thou not known me, Philip? he that hath seen me hath seen the Father; and how sayest thou *then,* Shew us the Father?

10Believest thou not that I am in the Father, and the Father in me? the words that I speak unto you I speak not of myself: but the Father that dwelleth in me, he doeth the works.

11Believe me that I *am* in the Father, and the

NEW LIVING TRANSLATION

what Jesus meant. 29Since Judas was their treasurer, some thought Jesus was telling him to go and pay for the food or to give some money to the poor. 30So Judas left at once, going out into the night.

Jesus Predicts Peter's Denial

31As soon as Judas left the room, Jesus said, "The time has come for the Son of Man* to enter into his glory, and God will be glorified because of him. 32And since God receives glory because of the Son,* he will soon give glory to the Son. 33Dear children, I will be with you only a little longer. And as I told the Jewish leaders, you will search for me, but you can't come where I am going. 34So now I am giving you a new commandment: Love each other. Just as I have loved you, you should love each other. 35Your love for one another will prove to the world that you are my disciples."

36Simon Peter asked, "Lord, where are you going?"

And Jesus replied, "You can't go with me now, but you will follow me later."

37"But why can't I come now, Lord?" he asked. "I'm ready to die for you."

38Jesus answered, "Die for me? I tell you the truth, Peter—before the rooster crows tomorrow morning, you will deny three times that you even know me.

Jesus, the Way to the Father

14 "Don't let your hearts be troubled. Trust in God, and trust also in me. 2There is more than enough room in my Father's home.* If this were not so, would I have told you that I am going to prepare a place for you?* 3When everything is ready, I will come and get you, so that you will always be with me where I am. 4And you know the way to where I am going."

5"No, we don't know, Lord," Thomas said. "We have no idea where you are going, so how can we know the way?"

6Jesus told him, "I am the way, the truth, and the life. No one can come to the Father except through me. 7If you had really known me, you would know who my Father is.* From now on, you do know him and have seen him!"

8Philip said, "Lord, show us the Father, and we will be satisfied."

9Jesus replied, "Have I been with you all this time, Philip, and yet you still don't know who I am? Anyone who has seen me has seen the Father! So why are you asking me to show him to you? 10Don't you believe that I am in the Father and the Father is in me? The words I speak are not my own, but my Father who lives in me does his work through me. 11Just believe that I

13:31 "Son of Man" is a title Jesus used for himself. **13:32** Some manuscripts do not include *And since God receives glory because of the Son.* **14:2a** Or *There are many rooms in my Father's house.* **14:2b** Or *If this were not so, I would have told you that I am going to prepare a place for you.* Some manuscripts read *If this were not so, I would have told you. I am going to prepare a place for you.* **14:7** Some manuscripts read *If you have really known me, you will know who my Father is.*

KING JAMES VERSION

Father in me: or else believe me for the very works'
sake.

12 Verily, verily, I say unto you, He that believeth on
me, the works that I do shall he do also; and greater
works than these shall he do; because I go unto my
Father.

13 And whatsoever ye shall ask in my name, that
will I do, that the Father may be glorified in the Son.

14 If ye shall ask any thing in my name, I will do *it*.

15 If ye love me, keep my commandments.

16 And I will pray the Father, and he shall give
you another Comforter, that he may abide with you
for ever;

17 *Even* the Spirit of truth; whom the world cannot
receive, because it seeth him not, neither knoweth
him: but ye know him; for he dwelleth with you, and
shall be in you.

18 I will not leave you comfortless: I will come
to you.

19 Yet a little while, and the world seeth me no
more; but ye see me: because I live, ye shall live also.

20 At that day ye shall know that I *am* in my Father,
and ye in me, and I in you.

21 He that hath my commandments, and keepeth
them, he it is that loveth me: and he that loveth me
shall be loved of my Father, and I will love him, and
will manifest myself to him.

22 Judas saith unto him, not Iscariot, Lord, how is it
that thou wilt manifest thyself unto us, and not unto
the world?

23 Jesus answered and said unto him, If a man love
me, he will keep my words: and my Father will love
him, and we will come unto him, and make our
abode with him.

24 He that loveth me not keepeth not my sayings:
and the word which ye hear is not mine, but the
Father's which sent me.

25 These things have I spoken unto you, being *yet*
present with you.

26 But the Comforter, *which is* the Holy Ghost,
whom the Father will send in my name, he shall
teach you all things, and bring all things to your remembrance, whatsoever I have said unto you.

27 Peace I leave with you, my peace I give unto you:
not as the world giveth, give I unto you. Let not your
heart be troubled, neither let it be afraid.

28 Ye have heard how I said unto you, I go away,
and come *again* unto you. If ye loved me, ye would
rejoice, because I said, I go unto the Father: for my
Father is greater than I.

29 And now I have told you before it come to pass,
that, when it is come to pass, ye might believe.

30 Hereafter I will not talk much with you: for the
prince of this world cometh, and hath nothing in me.

31 But that the world may know that I love the Father; and as the Father gave me commandment, even
so I do. Arise, let us go hence.

NEW LIVING TRANSLATION

am in the Father and the Father is in me. Or at least believe because of the work you have seen me do.

12 "I tell you the truth, anyone who believes in me
will do the same works I have done, and even greater
works, because I am going to be with the Father.
13 You can ask for anything in my name, and I will do
it, so that the Son can bring glory to the Father. 14 Yes,
ask me for anything in my name, and I will do it!

Jesus Promises the Holy Spirit

15 "If you love me, obey* my commandments. 16 And I
will ask the Father, and he will give you another Advocate,* who will never leave you. 17 He is the Holy
Spirit, who leads into all truth. The world cannot
receive him, because it isn't looking for him and
doesn't recognize him. But you know him, because
he lives with you now and later will be in you.* 18 No, I
will not abandon you as orphans—I will come to you.
19 Soon the world will no longer see me, but you will
see me. Since I live, you also will live. 20 When I am
raised to life again, you will know that I am in my
Father, and you are in me, and I am in you. 21 Those
who accept my commandments and obey them are
the ones who love me. And because they love me, my
Father will love them. And I will love them and reveal
myself to each of them."

22 Judas (not Judas Iscariot, but the other disciple
with that name) said to him, "Lord, why are you going
to reveal yourself only to us and not to the world at
large?"

23 Jesus replied, "All who love me will do what I say.
My Father will love them, and we will come and make
our home with each of them. 24 Anyone who doesn't
love me will not obey me. And remember, my words
are not my own. What I am telling you is from the
Father who sent me. 25 I am telling you these things
now while I am still with you. 26 But when the Father
sends the Advocate as my representative—that is, the
Holy Spirit—he will teach you everything and will remind you of everything I have told you.

27 "I am leaving you with a gift—peace of mind
and heart. And the peace I give is a gift the world
cannot give. So don't be troubled or afraid. 28 Remember what I told you: I am going away, but I will
come back to you again. If you really loved me, you
would be happy that I am going to the Father, who is
greater than I am. 29 I have told you these things before they happen so that when they do happen, you
will believe.

30 "I don't have much more time to talk to you, because the ruler of this world approaches. He has no
power over me, 31 but I will do what the Father requires of me, so that the world will know that I love
the Father. Come, let's be going.

14:15 Other manuscripts read *you will obey;* still others read *you should obey.* **14:16** Or *Comforter,* or *Encourager,* or *Counselor.* Greek reads *Paraclete;* also in 14:26. **14:17** Some manuscripts read *and is in you.*

KING JAMES VERSION

15 1I am the true vine, and my Father is the husbandman.

2Every branch in me that beareth not fruit he taketh away: and every *branch* that beareth fruit, he purgeth it, that it may bring forth more fruit.

3Now ye are clean through the word which I have spoken unto you.

4Abide in me, and I in you. As the branch cannot bear fruit of itself, except it abide in the vine; no more can ye, except ye abide in me.

5I am the vine, ye *are* the branches: He that abideth in me, and I in him, the same bringeth forth much fruit: for without me ye can do nothing.

6If a man abide not in me, he is cast forth as a branch, and is withered; and men gather them, and cast *them* into the fire, and they are burned.

7If ye abide in me, and my words abide in you, ye shall ask what ye will, and it shall be done unto you.

8Herein is my Father glorified, that ye bear much fruit; so shall ye be my disciples.

9As the Father hath loved me, so have I loved you: continue ye in my love.

10If ye keep my commandments, ye shall abide in my love; even as I have kept my Father's commandments, and abide in his love.

11These things have I spoken unto you, that my joy might remain in you, and *that* your joy might be full.

12This is my commandment, That ye love one another, as I have loved you.

13Greater love hath no man than this, that a man lay down his life for his friends.

14Ye are my friends, if ye do whatsoever I command you.

15Henceforth I call you not servants; for the servant knoweth not what his lord doeth: but I have called you friends; for all things that I have heard of my Father I have made known unto you.

16Ye have not chosen me, but I have chosen you, and ordained you, that ye should go and bring forth fruit, and *that* your fruit should remain: that whatsoever ye shall ask of the Father in my name, he may give it you.

17These things I command you, that ye love one another.

18If the world hate you, ye know that it hated me before *it hated* you.

19If ye were of the world, the world would love his own: but because ye are not of the world, but I have chosen you out of the world, therefore the world hateth you.

20Remember the word that I said unto you, The servant is not greater than his lord. If they have persecuted me, they will also persecute you; if they have kept my saying, they will keep yours also.

21But all these things will they do unto you for my name's sake, because they know not him that sent me.

22If I had not come and spoken unto them, they

NEW LIVING TRANSLATION

Jesus, the True Vine

15 "I am the true grapevine, and my Father is the
gardener. 2He cuts off every branch of mine
that doesn't produce fruit, and he prunes the
branches that do bear fruit so they will produce even
more. 3You have already been pruned and purified by
the message I have given you. 4Remain in me, and I
will remain in you. For a branch cannot produce fruit
if it is severed from the vine, and you cannot be fruitful unless you remain in me.

5"Yes, I am the vine; you are the branches. Those
who remain in me, and I in them, will produce much
fruit. For apart from me you can do nothing. 6Anyone who does not remain in me is thrown away like
a useless branch and withers. Such branches are
gathered into a pile to be burned. 7But if you remain
in me and my words remain in you, you may ask for
anything you want, and it will be granted! 8When you
produce much fruit, you are my true disciples. This
brings great glory to my Father.

9"I have loved you even as the Father has loved me.
Remain in my love. 10When you obey my commandments, you remain in my love, just as I obey my Father's commandments and remain in his love. 11I
have told you these things so that you will be filled
with my joy. Yes, your joy will overflow! 12This is my
commandment: Love each other in the same way I
have loved you. 13There is no greater love than to lay
down one's life for one's friends. 14You are my
friends if you do what I command. 15I no longer call
you slaves, because a master doesn't confide in his
slaves. Now you are my friends, since I have told you
everything the Father told me. 16You didn't choose
me. I chose you. I appointed you to go and produce
lasting fruit, so that the Father will give you whatever
you ask for, using my name. 17This is my command:
Love each other.

The World's Hatred

18"If the world hates you, remember that it hated me
first. 19The world would love you as one of its own if
you belonged to it, but you are no longer part of the
world. I chose you to come out of the world, so it
hates you. 20Do you remember what I told you? 'A
slave is not greater than the master.' Since they persecuted me, naturally they will persecute you. And if
they had listened to me, they would listen to you.
21They will do all this to you because of me, for they
have rejected the one who sent me. 22They would

KING JAMES VERSION

had not had sin: but now they have no cloak for their sin.

23 He that hateth me hateth my Father also.

24 If I had not done among them the works which none other man did, they had not had sin: but now have they both seen and hated both me and my Father.

25 But *this cometh to pass,* that the word might be fulfilled that is written in their law, They hated me without a cause.

26 But when the Comforter is come, whom I will send unto you from the Father, *even* the Spirit of truth, which proceedeth from the Father, he shall testify of me:

27 And ye also shall bear witness, because ye have been with me from the beginning.

16

1 These things have I spoken unto you, that ye should not be offended.

2 They shall put you out of the synagogues: yea, the time cometh, that whosoever killeth you will think that he doeth God service.

3 And these things will they do unto you, because they have not known the Father, nor me.

4 But these things have I told you, that when the time shall come, ye may remember that I told you of them. And these things I said not unto you at the beginning, because I was with you.

5 But now I go my way to him that sent me; and none of you asketh me, Whither goest thou?

6 But because I have said these things unto you, sorrow hath filled your heart.

7 Nevertheless I tell you the truth; It is expedient for you that I go away: for if I go not away, the Comforter will not come unto you; but if I depart, I will send him unto you.

8 And when he is come, he will reprove the world of sin, and of righteousness, and of judgment:

9 Of sin, because they believe not on me;

10 Of righteousness, because I go to my Father, and ye see me no more;

11 Of judgment, because the prince of this world is judged.

12 I have yet many things to say unto you, but ye cannot bear them now.

13 Howbeit when he, the Spirit of truth, is come, he will guide you into all truth: for he shall not speak of himself; but whatsoever he shall hear, *that* shall he speak: and he will shew you things to come.

14 He shall glorify me: for he shall receive of mine, and shall shew *it* unto you.

15 All things that the Father hath are mine: therefore said I, that he shall take of mine, and shall shew *it* unto you.

16 A little while, and ye shall not see me: and again, a little while, and ye shall see me, because I go to the Father.

NEW LIVING TRANSLATION

not be guilty if I had not come and spoken to them. But now they have no excuse for their sin. 23 Anyone who hates me also hates my Father. 24 If I hadn't done such miraculous signs among them that no one else could do, they would not be guilty. But as it is, they have seen everything I did, yet they still hate me and my Father. 25 This fulfills what is written in their Scriptures*: 'They hated me without cause.'

26 "But I will send you the Advocate*—the Spirit of truth. He will come to you from the Father and will testify all about me. 27 And you must also testify about me because you have been with me from the beginning of my ministry.

16

"I have told you these things so that you won't abandon your faith. 2 For you will be expelled from the synagogues, and the time is coming when those who kill you will think they are doing a holy service for God. 3 This is because they have never known the Father or me. 4 Yes, I'm telling you these things now, so that when they happen, you will remember my warning. I didn't tell you earlier because I was going to be with you for a while longer.

The Work of the Holy Spirit

5 "But now I am going away to the one who sent me, and not one of you is asking where I am going. 6 Instead, you grieve because of what I've told you. 7 But in fact, it is best for you that I go away, because if I don't, the Advocate* won't come. If I do go away, then I will send him to you. 8 And when he comes, he will convict the world of its sin, and of God's righteousness, and of the coming judgment. 9 The world's sin is that it refuses to believe in me. 10 Righteousness is available because I go to the Father, and you will see me no more. 11 Judgment will come because the ruler of this world has already been judged.

12 "There is so much more I want to tell you, but you can't bear it now. 13 When the Spirit of truth comes, he will guide you into all truth. He will not speak on his own but will tell you what he has heard. He will tell you about the future. 14 He will bring me glory by telling you whatever he receives from me. 15 All that belongs to the Father is mine; this is why I said, 'The Spirit will tell you whatever he receives from me.'

Sadness Will Be Turned to Joy

16 "In a little while you won't see me anymore. But a little while after that, you will see me again."

15:25 Greek *in their law.* Pss 35:19; 69:4. **15:26** Or *Comforter,* or *Encourager,* or *Counselor.* Greek reads *Paraclete.* **16:7** Or *Comforter,* or *Encourager,* or *Counselor.* Greek reads *Paraclete.*

KING JAMES VERSION

17 Then said *some* of his disciples among themselves, What is this that he saith unto us, A little while, and ye shall not see me: and again, a little while, and ye shall see me: and, Because I go to the Father?

18 They said therefore, What is this that he saith, A little while? we cannot tell what he saith.

19 Now Jesus knew that they were desirous to ask him, and said unto them, Do ye inquire among yourselves of that I said, A little while, and ye shall not see me: and again, a little while, and ye shall see me?

20 Verily, verily, I say unto you, That ye shall weep and lament, but the world shall rejoice: and ye shall be sorrowful, but your sorrow shall be turned into joy.

21 A woman when she is in travail hath sorrow, because her hour is come: but as soon as she is delivered of the child, she remembereth no more the anguish, for joy that a man is born into the world.

22 And ye now therefore have sorrow: but I will see you again, and your heart shall rejoice, and your joy no man taketh from you.

23 And in that day ye shall ask me nothing. Verily, verily, I say unto you, Whatsoever ye shall ask the Father in my name, he will give *it* you.

24 Hitherto have ye asked nothing in my name: ask, and ye shall receive, that your joy may be full.

25 These things have I spoken unto you in proverbs: but the time cometh, when I shall no more speak unto you in proverbs, but I shall shew you plainly of the Father.

26 At that day ye shall ask in my name: and I say not unto you, that I will pray the Father for you:

27 For the Father himself loveth you, because ye have loved me, and have believed that I came out from God.

28 I came forth from the Father, and am come into the world: again, I leave the world, and go to the Father.

29 His disciples said unto him, Lo, now speakest thou plainly, and speakest no proverb.

30 Now are we sure that thou knowest all things, and needest not that any man should ask thee: by this we believe that thou camest forth from God.

31 Jesus answered them, Do ye now believe?

32 Behold, the hour cometh, yea, is now come, that ye shall be scattered, every man to his own, and shall leave me alone: and yet I am not alone, because the Father is with me.

33 These things I have spoken unto you, that in me ye might have peace. In the world ye shall have tribulation: but be of good cheer; I have overcome the world.

17 1 These words spake Jesus, and lifted up his eyes to heaven, and said, Father, the hour is come; glorify thy Son, that thy Son also may glorify thee:

NEW LIVING TRANSLATION

17 Some of the disciples asked each other, "What does he mean when he says, 'In a little while you won't see me, but then you will see me,' and 'I am going to the Father'? 18 And what does he mean by 'a little while'? We don't understand."

19 Jesus realized they wanted to ask him about it, so he said, "Are you asking yourselves what I meant? I said in a little while you won't see me, but a little while after that you will see me again. 20 I tell you the truth, you will weep and mourn over what is going to happen to me, but the world will rejoice. You will grieve, but your grief will suddenly turn to wonderful joy. 21 It will be like a woman suffering the pains of labor. When her child is born, her anguish gives way to joy because she has brought a new baby into the world. 22 So you have sorrow now, but I will see you again; then you will rejoice, and no one can rob you of that joy. 23 At that time you won't need to ask me for anything. I tell you the truth, you will ask the Father directly, and he will grant your request because you use my name. 24 You haven't done this before. Ask, using my name, and you will receive, and you will have abundant joy.

25 "I have spoken of these matters in figures of speech, but soon I will stop speaking figuratively and will tell you plainly all about the Father. 26 Then you will ask in my name. I'm not saying I will ask the Father on your behalf, 27 for the Father himself loves you dearly because you love me and believe that I came from God.* 28 Yes, I came from the Father into the world, and now I will leave the world and return to the Father."

29 Then his disciples said, "At last you are speaking plainly and not figuratively. 30 Now we understand that you know everything, and there's no need to question you. From this we believe that you came from God."

31 Jesus asked, "Do you finally believe? 32 But the time is coming—indeed it's here now—when you will be scattered, each one going his own way, leaving me alone. Yet I am not alone because the Father is with me. 33 I have told you all this so that you may have peace in me. Here on earth you will have many trials and sorrows. But take heart, because I have overcome the world."

The Prayer of Jesus

17 After saying all these things, Jesus looked up to heaven and said, "Father, the hour has come. Glorify your Son so he can give glory back to

16:27 Some manuscripts read *from the Father.*

KING JAMES VERSION

2As thou hast given him power over all flesh, that he should give eternal life to as many as thou hast given him.

3And this is life eternal, that they might know thee the only true God, and Jesus Christ, whom thou hast sent.

4I have glorified thee on the earth: I have finished the work which thou gavest me to do.

5And now, O Father, glorify thou me with thine own self with the glory which I had with thee before the world was.

6I have manifested thy name unto the men which thou gavest me out of the world: thine they were, and thou gavest them me; and they have kept thy word.

7Now they have known that all things whatsoever thou hast given me are of thee.

8For I have given unto them the words which thou gavest me; and they have received *them,* and have known surely that I came out from thee, and they have believed that thou didst send me.

9I pray for them: I pray not for the world, but for them which thou hast given me; for they are thine.

10And all mine are thine, and thine are mine; and I am glorified in them.

11And now I am no more in the world, but these are in the world, and I come to thee. Holy Father, keep through thine own name those whom thou hast given me, that they may be one, as we *are.*

12While I was with them in the world, I kept them in thy name: those that thou gavest me I have kept, and none of them is lost, but the son of perdition; that the scripture might be fulfilled.

13And now come I to thee; and these things I speak in the world, that they might have my joy fulfilled in themselves.

14I have given them thy word; and the world hath hated them, because they are not of the world, even as I am not of the world.

15I pray not that thou shouldest take them out of the world, but that thou shouldest keep them from the evil.

16They are not of the world, even as I am not of the world.

17Sanctify them through thy truth: thy word is truth.

18As thou hast sent me into the world, even so have I also sent them into the world.

19And for their sakes I sanctify myself, that they also might be sanctified through the truth.

20Neither pray I for these alone, but for them also which shall believe on me through their word;

21That they all may be one; as thou, Father, *art* in me, and I in thee, that they also may be one in us: that the world may believe that thou hast sent me.

22And the glory which thou gavest me I have given them; that they may be one, even as we are one:

23I in them, and thou in me, that they may be made perfect in one; and that the world may know that

NEW LIVING TRANSLATION

you. 2For you have given him authority over everyone.
He gives eternal life to each one you have given him.
3And this is the way to have eternal life—to know you,
the only true God, and Jesus Christ, the one you sent
to earth. 4I brought glory to you here on earth by completing the work you gave me to do. 5Now, Father,
bring me into the glory we shared before the world
began.

6"I have revealed you* to the ones you gave me
from this world. They were always yours. You gave
them to me, and they have kept your word. 7Now
they know that everything I have is a gift from you,
8for I have passed on to them the message you gave
me. They accepted it and know that I came from you,
and they believe you sent me.

9"My prayer is not for the world, but for those you
have given me, because they belong to you. 10All who
are mine belong to you, and you have given them to
me, so they bring me glory. 11Now I am departing
from the world; they are staying in this world, but
I am coming to you. Holy Father, you have given me
your name;* now protect them by the power of your
name so that they will be united just as we are.
12During my time here, I protected them by the
power of the name you gave me.* I guarded them so
that not one was lost, except the one headed for
destruction, as the Scriptures foretold.

13"Now I am coming to you. I told them many
things while I was with them in this world so they
would be filled with my joy. 14I have given them your
word. And the world hates them because they do not
belong to the world, just as I do not belong to the
world. 15I'm not asking you to take them out of the
world, but to keep them safe from the evil one.
16They do not belong to this world any more than I
do. 17Make them holy by your truth; teach them your
word, which is truth. 18Just as you sent me into the
world, I am sending them into the world. 19And I give
myself as a holy sacrifice for them so they can be
made holy by your truth.

20"I am praying not only for these disciples but
also for all who will ever believe in me through their
message. 21I pray that they will all be one, just as you
and I are one—as you are in me, Father, and I am in
you. And may they be in us so that the world will believe you sent me.

22"I have given them the glory you gave me, so they
may be one as we are one. 23I am in them and you are

17:6 Greek *have revealed your name;* also in 17:26. **17:11** Some manuscripts read *you have given me these [disciples].* **17:12** Some manuscripts read *I protected those you gave me, by the power of your name.*

KING JAMES VERSION

thou hast sent me, and hast loved them, as thou hast
loved me.
24 Father, I will that they also, whom thou hast
given me, be with me where I am; that they may behold my glory, which thou hast given me: for thou
lovedst me before the foundation of the world.
25 O righteous Father, the world hath not known
thee: but I have known thee, and these have known
that thou hast sent me.
26 And I have declared unto them thy name, and
will declare *it:* that the love wherewith thou hast
loved me may be in them, and I in them.

18 1 When Jesus had spoken these words, he
went forth with his disciples over the brook
Cedron, where was a garden, into the which he entered, and his disciples.
2 And Judas also, which betrayed him, knew the
place: for Jesus ofttimes resorted thither with his
disciples.
3 Judas then, having received a band *of men* and
officers from the chief priests and Pharisees, cometh thither with lanterns and torches and weapons.
4 Jesus therefore, knowing all things that should
come upon him, went forth, and said unto them,
Whom seek ye?
5 They answered him, Jesus of Nazareth. Jesus
saith unto them, I am *he.* And Judas also, which betrayed him, stood with them.
6 As soon then as he had said unto them, I am *he,*
they went backward, and fell to the ground.
7 Then asked he them again, Whom seek ye? And
they said, Jesus of Nazareth.
8 Jesus answered, I have told you that I am *he:* if
therefore ye seek me, let these go their way:
9 That the saying might be fulfilled, which he spake,
Of them which thou gavest me have I lost none.
10 Then Simon Peter having a sword drew it, and
smote the high priest's servant, and cut off his right
ear. The servant's name was Malchus.
11 Then said Jesus unto Peter, Put up thy sword into
the sheath: the cup which my Father hath given me,
shall I not drink it?
12 Then the band and the captain and officers of
the Jews took Jesus, and bound him,
13 And led him away to Annas first; for he was father in law to Caiaphas, which was the high priest
that same year.
14 Now Caiaphas was he, which gave counsel to the
Jews, that it was expedient that one man should die
for the people.
15 And Simon Peter followed Jesus, and *so did* another disciple: that disciple was known unto the
high priest, and went in with Jesus into the palace of
the high priest.
16 But Peter stood at the door without. Then went
out that other disciple, which was known unto the

NEW LIVING TRANSLATION

in me. May they experience such perfect unity that
the world will know that you sent me and that you
love them as much as you love me. 24 Father, I want
these whom you have given me to be with me where I
am. Then they can see all the glory you gave me because you loved me even before the world began!
25 "O righteous Father, the world doesn't know you,
but I do; and these disciples know you sent me. 26 I
have revealed you to them, and I will continue to do
so. Then your love for me will be in them, and I will
be in them."

Jesus Is Betrayed and Arrested

18 After saying these things, Jesus crossed the
Kidron Valley with his disciples and entered a
grove of olive trees. 2 Judas, the betrayer, knew this
place, because Jesus had often gone there with his disciples. 3 The leading priests and Pharisees had given
Judas a contingent of Roman soldiers and Temple
guards to accompany him. Now with blazing torches,
lanterns, and weapons, they arrived at the olive grove.
4 Jesus fully realized all that was going to happen
to him, so he stepped forward to meet them. "Who
are you looking for?" he asked.
5 "Jesus the Nazarene,"* they replied.
"I AM he,"* Jesus said. (Judas, who betrayed him,
was standing with them.) 6 As Jesus said "I AM he,"
they all drew back and fell to the ground! 7 Once more
he asked them, "Who are you looking for?"
And again they replied, "Jesus the Nazarene."
8 "I told you that I AM he," Jesus said. "And since I
am the one you want, let these others go." 9 He did
this to fulfill his own statement: "I did not lose a
single one of those you have given me."*
10 Then Simon Peter drew a sword and slashed off
the right ear of Malchus, the high priest's slave. 11 But
Jesus said to Peter, "Put your sword back into its
sheath. Shall I not drink from the cup of suffering
the Father has given me?"

Jesus at the High Priest's House

12 So the soldiers, their commanding officer, and the
Temple guards arrested Jesus and tied him up. 13 First
they took him to Annas, the father-in-law of Caiaphas, the high priest at that time.* 14 Caiaphas was
the one who had told the other Jewish leaders, "It's
better that one man should die for the people."

Peter's First Denial

15 Simon Peter followed Jesus, as did another of the
disciples. That other disciple was acquainted with
the high priest, so he was allowed to enter the high
priest's courtyard with Jesus. 16 Peter had to stay

18:5a Or *Jesus of Nazareth;* also in 18:7. **18:5b** Or *"The 'I AM' is here";* or *"I am the LORD";* Greek reads *I am;* also in 18:6, 8. See Exod 3:14. **18:9** See John 6:39 and 17:12. **18:13** Greek *that year.*

KING JAMES VERSION

high priest, and spake unto her that kept the door,
and brought in Peter.
17 Then saith the damsel that kept the door unto
Peter, Art not thou also *one* of this man's disciples?
He saith, I am not.
18 And the servants and officers stood there, who
had made a fire of coals; for it was cold: and they
warmed themselves: and Peter stood with them, and
warmed himself.

19 The high priest then asked Jesus of his disciples,
and of his doctrine.
20 Jesus answered him, I spake openly to the world;
I ever taught in the synagogue, and in the temple,
whither the Jews always resort; and in secret have I
said nothing.
21 Why askest thou me? ask them which heard me,
what I have said unto them: behold, they know what
I said.
22 And when he had thus spoken, one of the officers which stood by struck Jesus with the palm of his
hand, saying, Answerest thou the high priest so?
23 Jesus answered him, If I have spoken evil, bear
witness of the evil: but if well, why smitest thou me?
24 Now Annas had sent him bound unto Caiaphas
the high priest.

25 And Simon Peter stood and warmed himself.
They said therefore unto him, Art not thou also *one*
of his disciples? He denied *it,* and said, I am not.
26 One of the servants of the high priest, being *his*
kinsman whose ear Peter cut off, saith, Did not I see
thee in the garden with him?
27 Peter then denied again: and immediately the
cock crew.

28 Then led they Jesus from Caiaphas unto the hall
of judgment: and it was early; and they themselves
went not into the judgment hall, lest they should be
defiled; but that they might eat the passover.
29 Pilate then went out unto them, and said, What
accusation bring ye against this man?
30 They answered and said unto him, If he were not
a malefactor, we would not have delivered him up
unto thee.
31 Then said Pilate unto them, Take ye him, and
judge him according to your law. The Jews therefore
said unto him, It is not lawful for us to put any man to
death:
32 That the saying of Jesus might be fulfilled,
which he spake, signifying what death he should die.
33 Then Pilate entered into the judgment hall
again, and called Jesus, and said unto him, Art thou
the King of the Jews?

NEW LIVING TRANSLATION

outside the gate. Then the disciple who knew the
high priest spoke to the woman watching at the gate,
and she let Peter in. 17 The woman asked Peter,
"You're not one of that man's disciples, are you?"
"No," he said, "I am not."
18 Because it was cold, the household servants and
the guards had made a charcoal fire. They stood
around it, warming themselves, and Peter stood with
them, warming himself.

The High Priest Questions Jesus

19 Inside, the high priest began asking Jesus about
his followers and what he had been teaching them.
20 Jesus replied, "Everyone knows what I teach. I have
preached regularly in the synagogues and the
Temple, where the people* gather. I have not spoken
in secret. 21 Why are you asking me this question?
Ask those who heard me. They know what I said."
22 Then one of the Temple guards standing nearby
slapped Jesus across the face. "Is that the way to answer the high priest?" he demanded.
23 Jesus replied, "If I said anything wrong, you
must prove it. But if I'm speaking the truth, why are
you beating me?"
24 Then Annas bound Jesus and sent him to Caiaphas, the high priest.

Peter's Second and Third Denials

25 Meanwhile, as Simon Peter was standing by the
fire warming himself, they asked him again, "You're
not one of his disciples, are you?"
He denied it, saying, "No, I am not."
26 But one of the household slaves of the high
priest, a relative of the man whose ear Peter had cut
off, asked, "Didn't I see you out there in the olive
grove with Jesus?" 27 Again Peter denied it. And immediately a rooster crowed.

Jesus' Trial before Pilate

28 Jesus' trial before Caiaphas ended in the early
hours of the morning. Then he was taken to the
headquarters of the Roman governor.* His accusers
didn't go inside because it would defile them, and
they wouldn't be allowed to celebrate the Passover.
29 So Pilate, the governor, went out to them and
asked, "What is your charge against this man?"
30 "We wouldn't have handed him over to you if he
weren't a criminal!" they retorted.
31 "Then take him away and judge him by your own
law," Pilate told them.
"Only the Romans are permitted to execute someone," the Jewish leaders replied. 32 (This fulfilled
Jesus' prediction about the way he would die.*)
33 Then Pilate went back into his headquarters and
called for Jesus to be brought to him. "Are you the
king of the Jews?" he asked him.

18:20 Greek *Jewish people;* also in 18:38. **18:28** Greek *to the Praetorium;* also in 18:33. **18:32** See John 12:32-33.

KING JAMES VERSION

34 Jesus answered him, Sayest thou this thing of thyself, or did others tell it thee of me?

35 Pilate answered, Am I a Jew? Thine own nation and the chief priests have delivered thee unto me: what hast thou done?

36 Jesus answered, My kingdom is not of this world: if my kingdom were of this world, then would my servants fight, that I should not be delivered to the Jews: but now is my kingdom not from hence.

37 Pilate therefore said unto him, Art thou a king then? Jesus answered, Thou sayest that I am a king. To this end was I born, and for this cause came I into the world, that I should bear witness unto the truth. Every one that is of the truth heareth my voice.

38 Pilate saith unto him, What is truth? And when he had said this, he went out again unto the Jews, and saith unto them, I find in him no fault *at all.*

39 But ye have a custom, that I should release unto you one at the passover: will ye therefore that I release unto you the King of the Jews?

40 Then cried they all again, saying, Not this man, but Barabbas. Now Barabbas was a robber.

19 1 Then Pilate therefore took Jesus, and scourged *him.*

2 And the soldiers platted a crown of thorns, and put *it* on his head, and they put on him a purple robe,

3 And said, Hail, King of the Jews! and they smote him with their hands.

4 Pilate therefore went forth again, and saith unto them, Behold, I bring him forth to you, that ye may know that I find no fault in him.

5 Then came Jesus forth, wearing the crown of thorns, and the purple robe. And *Pilate* saith unto them, Behold the man!

6 When the chief priests therefore and officers saw him, they cried out, saying, Crucify *him,* crucify *him.* Pilate saith unto them, Take ye him, and crucify *him:* for I find no fault in him.

7 The Jews answered him, We have a law, and by our law he ought to die, because he made himself the Son of God.

8 When Pilate therefore heard that saying, he was the more afraid;

9 And went again into the judgment hall, and saith unto Jesus, Whence art thou? But Jesus gave him no answer.

10 Then saith Pilate unto him, Speakest thou not unto me? knowest thou not that I have power to crucify thee, and have power to release thee?

11 Jesus answered, Thou couldest have no power *at all* against me, except it were given thee from above: therefore he that delivered me unto thee hath the greater sin.

12 And from thenceforth Pilate sought to release him: but the Jews cried out, saying, If thou let this man go, thou art not Caesar's friend: whosoever maketh himself a king speaketh against Caesar.

NEW LIVING TRANSLATION

34 Jesus replied, "Is this your own question, or did
others tell you about me?"
35 "Am I a Jew?" Pilate retorted. "Your own people
and their leading priests brought you to me for trial.
Why? What have you done?"
36 Jesus answered, "My Kingdom is not an earthly
kingdom. If it were, my followers would fight to keep
me from being handed over to the Jewish leaders.
But my Kingdom is not of this world."
37 Pilate said, "So you are a king?"
Jesus responded, "You say I am a king. Actually, I
was born and came into the world to testify to the
truth. All who love the truth recognize that what I say
is true."
38 "What is truth?" Pilate asked. Then he went out
again to the people and told them, "He is not guilty of
any crime. 39 But you have a custom of asking me
to release one prisoner each year at Passover. Would
you like me to release this 'King of the Jews'?"
40 But they shouted back, "No! Not this man. We
want Barabbas!" (Barabbas was a revolutionary.)

Jesus Sentenced to Death

19 Then Pilate had Jesus flogged with a lead-
tipped whip. 2 The soldiers wove a crown of
thorns and put it on his head, and they put a purple
robe on him. 3 "Hail! King of the Jews!" they mocked,
as they slapped him across the face.
4 Pilate went outside again and said to the people,
"I am going to bring him out to you now, but understand clearly that I find him not guilty." 5 Then Jesus
came out wearing the crown of thorns and the purple robe. And Pilate said, "Look, here is the man!"
6 When they saw him, the leading priests and
Temple guards began shouting, "Crucify him! Crucify him!"
"Take him yourselves and crucify him," Pilate
said. "I find him not guilty."
7 The Jewish leaders replied, "By our law he ought
to die because he called himself the Son of God."
8 When Pilate heard this, he was more frightened
than ever. 9 He took Jesus back into the headquarters* again and asked him, "Where are you
from?" But Jesus gave no answer. 10 "Why don't you
talk to me?" Pilate demanded. "Don't you realize that
I have the power to release you or crucify you?"
11 Then Jesus said, "You would have no power over
me at all unless it were given to you from above. So
the one who handed me over to you has the greater
sin."
12 Then Pilate tried to release him, but the Jewish
leaders shouted, "If you release this man, you are no
'friend of Caesar.'* Anyone who declares himself a
king is a rebel against Caesar."

19:9 Greek *the Praetorium.* **19:12** "Friend of Caesar" is a technical term that refers to an ally of the emperor.

KING JAMES VERSION

13 When Pilate therefore heard that saying, he brought Jesus forth, and sat down in the judgment seat in a place that is called the Pavement, but in the Hebrew, Gabbatha.

14 And it was the preparation of the passover, and about the sixth hour: and he saith unto the Jews, Behold your King!

15 But they cried out, Away with *him,* away with *him,* crucify him. Pilate saith unto them, Shall I crucify your King? The chief priests answered, We have no king but Caesar.

16 Then delivered he him therefore unto them to be crucified. And they took Jesus, and led *him* away.

17 And he bearing his cross went forth into a place called *the place* of a skull, which is called in the Hebrew Golgotha:

18 Where they crucified him, and two others with him, on either side one, and Jesus in the midst.

19 And Pilate wrote a title, and put *it* on the cross. And the writing was, JESUS OF NAZARETH THE KING OF THE JEWS.

20 This title then read many of the Jews: for the place where Jesus was crucified was nigh to the city: and it was written in Hebrew, *and* Greek, *and* Latin.

21 Then said the chief priests of the Jews to Pilate, Write not, The King of the Jews; but that he said, I am King of the Jews.

22 Pilate answered, What I have written I have written.

23 Then the soldiers, when they had crucified Jesus, took his garments, and made four parts, to every soldier a part; and also *his* coat: now the coat was without seam, woven from the top throughout.

24 They said therefore among themselves, Let us not rend it, but cast lots for it, whose it shall be: that the scripture might be fulfilled, which saith, They parted my raiment among them, and for my vesture they did cast lots. These things therefore the soldiers did.

25 Now there stood by the cross of Jesus his mother, and his mother's sister, Mary the *wife* of Cleophas, and Mary Magdalene.

26 When Jesus therefore saw his mother, and the disciple standing by, whom he loved, he saith unto his mother, Woman, behold thy son!

27 Then saith he to the disciple, Behold thy mother! And from that hour that disciple took her unto his own *home.*

28 After this, Jesus knowing that all things were now accomplished, that the scripture might be fulfilled, saith, I thirst.

29 Now there was set a vessel full of vinegar: and they filled a spunge with vinegar, and put *it* upon hyssop, and put *it* to his mouth.

30 When Jesus therefore had received the vinegar, he said, It is finished: and he bowed his head, and gave up the ghost.

NEW LIVING TRANSLATION

13 When they said this, Pilate brought Jesus out to them again. Then Pilate sat down on the judgment seat on the platform that is called the Stone Pavement (in Hebrew, *Gabbatha*). 14 It was now about noon on the day of preparation for the Passover. And Pilate said to the people,* "Look, here is your king!"

15 "Away with him," they yelled. "Away with him! Crucify him!"

"What? Crucify your king?" Pilate asked.

"We have no king but Caesar," the leading priests shouted back.

16 Then Pilate turned Jesus over to them to be crucified.

The Crucifixion

So they took Jesus away. 17 Carrying the cross by himself, he went to the place called Place of the Skull (in Hebrew, *Golgotha*). 18 There they nailed him to the cross. Two others were crucified with him, one on either side, with Jesus between them. 19 And Pilate posted a sign on the cross that read, "Jesus of Nazareth,* the King of the Jews." 20 The place where Jesus was crucified was near the city, and the sign was written in Hebrew, Latin, and Greek, so that many people could read it.

21 Then the leading priests objected and said to Pilate, "Change it from 'The King of the Jews' to 'He said, I am King of the Jews.'"

22 Pilate replied, "No, what I have written, I have written."

23 When the soldiers had crucified Jesus, they divided his clothes among the four of them. They also took his robe, but it was seamless, woven in one piece from top to bottom. 24 So they said, "Rather than tearing it apart, let's throw dice* for it." This fulfilled the Scripture that says, "They divided my garments among themselves and threw dice for my clothing."* So that is what they did.

25 Standing near the cross were Jesus' mother, and his mother's sister, Mary (the wife of Clopas), and Mary Magdalene. 26 When Jesus saw his mother standing there beside the disciple he loved, he said to her, "Dear woman, here is your son." 27 And he said to this disciple, "Here is your mother." And from then on this disciple took her into his home.

The Death of Jesus

28 Jesus knew that his mission was now finished, and to fulfill Scripture he said, "I am thirsty."* 29 A jar of sour wine was sitting there, so they soaked a sponge in it, put it on a hyssop branch, and held it up to his lips. 30 When Jesus had tasted it, he said, "It is finished!" Then he bowed his head and released his spirit.

19:14 Greek *Jewish people;* also in 19:20. **19:19** Or *Jesus the Nazarene.* **19:24a** Greek *cast lots.* **19:24b** Ps 22:18. **19:28** See Pss 22:15; 69:21.

KING JAMES VERSION

31The Jews therefore, because it was the preparation, that the bodies should not remain upon the cross on the sabbath day, (for that sabbath day was an high day,) besought Pilate that their legs might be broken, and *that* they might be taken away.

32Then came the soldiers, and brake the legs of the first, and of the other which was crucified with him.

33But when they came to Jesus, and saw that he was dead already, they brake not his legs:

34But one of the soldiers with a spear pierced his side, and forthwith came there out blood and water.

35And he that saw *it* bare record, and his record is true: and he knoweth that he saith true, that ye might believe.

36For these things were done, that the scripture should be fulfilled, A bone of him shall not be broken.

37And again another scripture saith, They shall look on him whom they pierced.

38And after this Joseph of Arimathaea, being a disciple of Jesus, but secretly for fear of the Jews, besought Pilate that he might take away the body of Jesus: and Pilate gave *him* leave. He came therefore, and took the body of Jesus.

39And there came also Nicodemus, which at the first came to Jesus by night, and brought a mixture of myrrh and aloes, about an hundred pound *weight*.

40Then took they the body of Jesus, and wound it in linen clothes with the spices, as the manner of the Jews is to bury.

41Now in the place where he was crucified there was a garden; and in the garden a new sepulchre, wherein was never man yet laid.

42There laid they Jesus therefore because of the Jews' preparation *day;* for the sepulchre was nigh at hand.

20 1The first *day* of the week cometh Mary Magdalene early, when it was yet dark, unto the sepulchre, and seeth the stone taken away from the sepulchre.

2Then she runneth, and cometh to Simon Peter, and to the other disciple, whom Jesus loved, and saith unto them, They have taken away the Lord out of the sepulchre, and we know not where they have laid him.

3Peter therefore went forth, and that other disciple, and came to the sepulchre.

4So they ran both together: and the other disciple did outrun Peter, and came first to the sepulchre.

5And he stooping down, *and looking in,* saw the linen clothes lying; yet went he not in.

6Then cometh Simon Peter following him, and went into the sepulchre, and seeth the linen clothes lie,

7And the napkin, that was about his head, not lying with the linen clothes, but wrapped together in a place by itself.

NEW LIVING TRANSLATION

31It was the day of preparation, and the Jewish
leaders didn't want the bodies hanging there the
next day, which was the Sabbath (and a very special
Sabbath, because it was the Passover). So they asked
Pilate to hasten their deaths by ordering that their
legs be broken. Then their bodies could be taken
down. 32So the soldiers came and broke the legs of
the two men crucified with Jesus. 33But when they
came to Jesus, they saw that he was already dead, so
they didn't break his legs. 34One of the soldiers, however, pierced his side with a spear, and immediately
blood and water flowed out. 35(This report is from an
eyewitness giving an accurate account. He speaks
the truth so that you also can believe.*) 36These
things happened in fulfillment of the Scriptures that
say, "Not one of his bones will be broken,"* 37and
"They will look on the one they pierced."*

The Burial of Jesus

38Afterward Joseph of Arimathea, who had been a
secret disciple of Jesus (because he feared the Jewish
leaders), asked Pilate for permission to take down
Jesus' body. When Pilate gave permission, Joseph
came and took the body away. 39With him came
Nicodemus, the man who had come to Jesus at night.
He brought about seventy-five pounds* of perfumed
ointment made from myrrh and aloes. 40Following
Jewish burial custom, they wrapped Jesus' body
with the spices in long sheets of linen cloth. 41The
place of crucifixion was near a garden, where there
was a new tomb, never used before. 42And so, because it was the day of preparation for the Jewish
Passover* and since the tomb was close at hand,
they laid Jesus there.

The Resurrection

20 Early on Sunday morning,* while it was
still dark, Mary Magdalene came to the
tomb and found that the stone had been rolled away
from the entrance. 2She ran and found Simon Peter
and the other disciple, the one whom Jesus loved.
She said, "They have taken the Lord's body out of the
tomb, and we don't know where they have put him!"
3Peter and the other disciple started out for the
tomb. 4They were both running, but the other disciple outran Peter and reached the tomb first. 5He
stooped and looked in and saw the linen wrappings
lying there, but he didn't go in. 6Then Simon Peter
arrived and went inside. He also noticed the linen
wrappings lying there, 7while the cloth that had covered Jesus' head was folded up and lying apart from

19:35 Some manuscripts read *can continue to believe.* **19:36** Exod 12:46; Num 9:12; Ps 34:20. **19:37** Zech 12:10. **19:39** Greek *100 litras* [32.7 kilograms]. **19:42** Greek *because of the Jewish day of preparation.* **20:1** Greek *On the first day of the week.*

KING JAMES VERSION

8 Then went in also that other disciple, which came
first to the sepulchre, and he saw, and believed.
9 For as yet they knew not the scripture, that he
must rise again from the dead.
10 Then the disciples went away again unto their
own home.

11 But Mary stood without at the sepulchre weeping: and as she wept, she stooped down, *and looked*
into the sepulchre,
12 And seeth two angels in white sitting, the one at
the head, and the other at the feet, where the body of
Jesus had lain.
13 And they say unto her, Woman, why weepest
thou? She saith unto them, Because they have taken
away my Lord, and I know not where they have laid
him.
14 And when she had thus said, she turned herself
back, and saw Jesus standing, and knew not that it
was Jesus.
15 Jesus saith unto her, Woman, why weepest thou?
whom seekest thou? She, supposing him to be the
gardener, saith unto him, Sir, if thou have borne him
hence, tell me where thou hast laid him, and I will
take him away.
16 Jesus saith unto her, Mary. She turned herself,
and saith unto him, Rabboni; which is to say, Master.
17 Jesus saith unto her, Touch me not; for I am not
yet ascended to my Father: but go to my brethren,
and say unto them, I ascend unto my Father, and your
Father; and *to* my God, and your God.
18 Mary Magdalene came and told the disciples
that she had seen the Lord, and *that* he had spoken
these things unto her.
19 Then the same day at evening, being the first
day of the week, when the doors were shut where the
disciples were assembled for fear of the Jews, came
Jesus and stood in the midst, and saith unto them,
Peace *be* unto you.
20 And when he had so said, he shewed unto them
his hands and his side. Then were the disciples glad,
when they saw the Lord.
21 Then said Jesus to them again, Peace *be* unto
you: as *my* Father hath sent me, even so send I you.
22 And when he had said this, he breathed on *them*,
and saith unto them, Receive ye the Holy Ghost:
23 Whose soever sins ye remit, they are remitted
unto them; *and* whose soever *sins* ye retain, they are
retained.
24 But Thomas, one of the twelve, called Didymus,
was not with them when Jesus came.
25 The other disciples therefore said unto him, We
have seen the Lord. But he said unto them, Except I
shall see in his hands the print of the nails, and put
my finger into the print of the nails, and thrust my
hand into his side, I will not believe.
26 And after eight days again his disciples were

NEW LIVING TRANSLATION

the other wrappings. 8 Then the disciple who had
reached the tomb first also went in, and he saw and
believed—9 for until then they still hadn't understood the Scriptures that said Jesus must rise from
the dead. 10 Then they went home.

Jesus Appears to Mary Magdalene

11 Mary was standing outside the tomb crying, and as
she wept, she stooped and looked in. 12 She saw two
white-robed angels, one sitting at the head and the
other at the foot of the place where the body of Jesus
had been lying. 13 "Dear woman, why are you crying?"
the angels asked her.

"Because they have taken away my Lord," she replied, "and I don't know where they have put him."
14 She turned to leave and saw someone standing
there. It was Jesus, but she didn't recognize him.
15 "Dear woman, why are you crying?" Jesus asked
her. "Who are you looking for?"

She thought he was the gardener. "Sir," she said, "if you have taken him away, tell me where you have put him, and I will go and get him."

16 "Mary!" Jesus said.

She turned to him and cried out, "Rabboni!" (which is Hebrew for "Teacher").

17 "Don't cling to me," Jesus said, "for I haven't yet
ascended to the Father. But go find my brothers and
tell them, 'I am ascending to my Father and your
Father, to my God and your God.'"
18 Mary Magdalene found the disciples and told
them, "I have seen the Lord!" Then she gave them his
message.

Jesus Appears to His Disciples

19 That Sunday evening* the disciples were meeting
behind locked doors because they were afraid of the
Jewish leaders. Suddenly, Jesus was standing there
among them! "Peace be with you," he said. 20 As he
spoke, he showed them the wounds in his hands and
his side. They were filled with joy when they saw the
Lord! 21 Again he said, "Peace be with you. As the
Father has sent me, so I am sending you." 22 Then he
breathed on them and said, "Receive the Holy Spirit.
23 If you forgive anyone's sins, they are forgiven. If you
do not forgive them, they are not forgiven."

Jesus Appears to Thomas

24 One of the twelve disciples, Thomas (nicknamed
the Twin),* was not with the others when Jesus came.
25 They told him, "We have seen the Lord!"

But he replied, "I won't believe it unless I see the nail wounds in his hands, put my fingers into them, and place my hand into the wound in his side."

26 Eight days later the disciples were together

20:19 Greek *In the evening of that day, the first day of the week.*
20:24 Greek *Thomas, who was called Didymus.*

KING JAMES VERSION

within, and Thomas with them: *then* came Jesus, the
doors being shut, and stood in the midst, and said,
Peace *be* unto you.
27 Then saith he to Thomas, Reach hither thy finger, and behold my hands; and reach hither thy hand,
and thrust *it* into my side: and be not faithless, but
believing.
28 And Thomas answered and said unto him, My
Lord and my God.
29 Jesus saith unto him, Thomas, because thou hast
seen me, thou hast believed: blessed *are* they that
have not seen, and *yet* have believed.
30 And many other signs truly did Jesus in the presence of his disciples, which are not written in this
book:
31 But these are written, that ye might believe that
Jesus is the Christ, the Son of God; and that believing
ye might have life through his name.

21 1 After these things Jesus shewed himself
again to the disciples at the sea of Tiberias;
and on this wise shewed he *himself.*
2 There were together Simon Peter, and Thomas
called Didymus, and Nathanael of Cana in Galilee, and
the *sons* of Zebedee, and two other of his disciples.
3 Simon Peter saith unto them, I go a fishing. They
say unto him, We also go with thee. They went forth,
and entered into a ship immediately; and that night
they caught nothing.
4 But when the morning was now come, Jesus
stood on the shore: but the disciples knew not that it
was Jesus.
5 Then Jesus saith unto them, Children, have ye any
meat? They answered him, No.
6 And he said unto them, Cast the net on the right
side of the ship, and ye shall find. They cast therefore, and now they were not able to draw it for the
multitude of fishes.
7 Therefore that disciple whom Jesus loved saith
unto Peter, It is the Lord. Now when Simon Peter
heard that it was the Lord, he girt *his* fisher's coat
unto him, (for he was naked,) and did cast himself
into the sea.
8 And the other disciples came in a little ship;
(for they were not far from land, but as it were two
hundred cubits,) dragging the net with fishes.
9 As soon then as they were come to land, they saw
a fire of coals there, and fish laid thereon, and bread.
10 Jesus saith unto them, Bring of the fish which
ye have now caught.
11 Simon Peter went up, and drew the net to land
full of great fishes, an hundred and fifty and three:
and for all there were so many, yet was not the net
broken.
12 Jesus saith unto them, Come *and* dine. And
none of the disciples durst ask him, Who art thou?
knowing that it was the Lord.

NEW LIVING TRANSLATION

again, and this time Thomas was with them. The
doors were locked; but suddenly, as before, Jesus was
standing among them. "Peace be with you," he said.
27 Then he said to Thomas, "Put your finger here, and
look at my hands. Put your hand into the wound in
my side. Don't be faithless any longer. Believe!"
28 "My Lord and my God!" Thomas exclaimed.
29 Then Jesus told him, "You believe because you
have seen me. Blessed are those who believe without
seeing me."

Purpose of the Book

30 The disciples saw Jesus do many other miraculous
signs in addition to the ones recorded in this book.
31 But these are written so that you may continue to
believe* that Jesus is the Messiah, the Son of God,
and that by believing in him you will have life by the
power of his name.

Epilogue: Jesus Appears to Seven Disciples

21 Later, Jesus appeared again to the disciples
beside the Sea of Galilee.* This is how it
happened. 2 Several of the disciples were there—
Simon Peter, Thomas (nicknamed the Twin),* Nathanael from Cana in Galilee, the sons of Zebedee,
and two other disciples.
3 Simon Peter said, "I'm going fishing."
"We'll come, too," they all said. So they went out in
the boat, but they caught nothing all night.
4 At dawn Jesus was standing on the beach, but the
disciples couldn't see who he was. 5 He called out,
"Fellows,* have you caught any fish?"
"No," they replied.
6 Then he said, "Throw out your net on the right-
hand side of the boat, and you'll get some!" So they
did, and they couldn't haul in the net because there
were so many fish in it.
7 Then the disciple Jesus loved said to Peter, "It's
the Lord!" When Simon Peter heard that it was the
Lord, he put on his tunic (for he had stripped for
work), jumped into the water, and headed to shore.
8 The others stayed with the boat and pulled the
loaded net to the shore, for they were only about a
hundred yards* from shore. 9 When they got there,
they found breakfast waiting for them—fish cooking
over a charcoal fire, and some bread.
10 "Bring some of the fish you've just caught," Jesus
said. 11 So Simon Peter went aboard and dragged the
net to the shore. There were 153 large fish, and yet
the net hadn't torn.
12 "Now come and have some breakfast!" Jesus
said. None of the disciples dared to ask him, "Who

20:31 Some manuscripts read *that you may believe.* **21:1** Greek *Sea of Tiberias,* another name for the Sea of Galilee. **21:2** Greek *Thomas, who was called Didymus.* **21:5** Greek *Children.* **21:8** Greek *200 cubits* [90 meters].

KING JAMES VERSION

13 Jesus then cometh, and taketh bread, and giveth them, and fish likewise.

14 This is now the third time that Jesus shewed himself to his disciples, after that he was risen from the dead.

15 So when they had dined, Jesus saith to Simon Peter, Simon, *son* of Jonas, lovest thou me more than these? He saith unto him, Yea, Lord; thou knowest that I love thee. He saith unto him, Feed my lambs.

16 He saith to him again the second time, Simon, *son* of Jonas, lovest thou me? He saith unto him, Yea, Lord; thou knowest that I love thee. He saith unto him, Feed my sheep.

17 He saith unto him the third time, Simon, *son* of Jonas, lovest thou me? Peter was grieved because he said unto him the third time, Lovest thou me? And he said unto him, Lord, thou knowest all things; thou knowest that I love thee. Jesus saith unto him, Feed my sheep.

18 Verily, verily, I say unto thee, When thou wast young, thou girdedst thyself, and walkedst whither thou wouldest: but when thou shalt be old, thou shalt stretch forth thy hands, and another shall gird thee, and carry *thee* whither thou wouldest not.

19 This spake he, signifying by what death he should glorify God. And when he had spoken this, he saith unto him, Follow me.

20 Then Peter, turning about, seeth the disciple whom Jesus loved following; which also leaned on his breast at supper, and said, Lord, which is he that betrayeth thee?

21 Peter seeing him saith to Jesus, Lord, and what *shall* this man *do?*

22 Jesus saith unto him, If I will that he tarry till I come, what *is that* to thee? follow thou me.

23 Then went this saying abroad among the brethren, that that disciple should not die: yet Jesus said not unto him, He shall not die; but, If I will that he tarry till I come, what *is that* to thee?

24 This is the disciple which testifieth of these things, and wrote these things: and we know that his testimony is true.

25 And there are also many other things which Jesus did, the which, if they should be written every one, I suppose that even the world itself could not contain the books that should be written. Amen.

NEW LIVING TRANSLATION

are you?" They knew it was the Lord.
13 Then Jesus served them the bread and the fish.
14 This was the third time Jesus had appeared to his disciples since he had been raised from the dead.

15 After breakfast Jesus asked Simon Peter, "Simon son of John, do you love me more than these?*"

"Yes, Lord," Peter replied, "you know I love you."

"Then feed my lambs," Jesus told him.

16 Jesus repeated the question: "Simon son of John, do you love me?"

"Yes, Lord," Peter said, "you know I love you."

"Then take care of my sheep," Jesus said.

17 A third time he asked him, "Simon son of John, do you love me?"

Peter was hurt that Jesus asked the question a third time. He said, "Lord, you know everything. You know that I love you."

Jesus said, "Then feed my sheep.

18 "I tell you the truth, when you were young, you were able to do as you liked; you dressed yourself and went wherever you wanted to go. But when you are old, you will stretch out your hands, and others* will dress you and take you where you don't want to go."
19 Jesus said this to let him know by what kind of death he would glorify God. Then Jesus told him, "Follow me."

20 Peter turned around and saw behind them the disciple Jesus loved—the one who had leaned over to Jesus during supper and asked, "Lord, who will betray you?"
21 Peter asked Jesus, "What about him, Lord?"

22 Jesus replied, "If I want him to remain alive until I return, what is that to you? As for you, follow me."
23 So the rumor spread among the community of believers* that this disciple wouldn't die. But that isn't what Jesus said at all. He only said, "If I want him to remain alive until I return, what is that to you?"

24 This disciple is the one who testifies to these events and has recorded them here. And we know that his account of these things is accurate.

25 Jesus also did many other things. If they were all written down, I suppose the whole world could not contain the books that would be written.

21:15 Or *more than these others do?* **21:18** Some manuscripts read *and another one.* **21:23** Greek *the brothers.*

Acts

KING JAMES VERSION

1 1The former treatise have I made, O Theophilus, of all that Jesus began both to do and teach,

2Until the day in which he was taken up, after that he through the Holy Ghost had given commandments unto the apostles whom he had chosen:

3To whom also he shewed himself alive after his passion by many infallible proofs, being seen of them forty days, and speaking of the things pertaining to the kingdom of God:

4And, being assembled together with *them,* commanded them that they should not depart from Jerusalem, but wait for the promise of the Father, which, *saith he,* ye have heard of me.

5For John truly baptized with water; but ye shall be baptized with the Holy Ghost not many days hence.

6When they therefore were come together, they asked of him, saying, Lord, wilt thou at this time restore again the kingdom to Israel?

7And he said unto them, It is not for you to know the times or the seasons, which the Father hath put in his own power.

8But ye shall receive power, after that the Holy Ghost is come upon you: and ye shall be witnesses unto me both in Jerusalem, and in all Judaea, and in Samaria, and unto the uttermost part of the earth.

9And when he had spoken these things, while they beheld, he was taken up; and a cloud received him out of their sight.

10And while they looked stedfastly toward heaven as he went up, behold, two men stood by them in white apparel;

11Which also said, Ye men of Galilee, why stand ye gazing up into heaven? this same Jesus, which is taken up from you into heaven, shall so come in like manner as ye have seen him go into heaven.

12Then returned they unto Jerusalem from the mount called Olivet, which is from Jerusalem a sabbath day's journey.

13And when they were come in, they went up into an upper room, where abode both Peter, and James, and John, and Andrew, Philip, and Thomas, Bartholomew,

NEW LIVING TRANSLATION

The Promise of the Holy Spirit

1 In my first book* I told you, Theophilus, about everything Jesus began to do and teach 2until the day he was taken up to heaven after giving his chosen apostles further instructions through the Holy Spirit. 3During the forty days after his crucifixion, he appeared to the apostles from time to time, and he proved to them in many ways that he was actually alive. And he talked to them about the Kingdom of God.

4Once when he was eating with them, he commanded them, "Do not leave Jerusalem until the Father sends you the gift he promised, as I told you before. 5John baptized with* water, but in just a few days you will be baptized with the Holy Spirit."

The Ascension of Jesus

6So when the apostles were with Jesus, they kept asking him, "Lord, has the time come for you to free Israel and restore our kingdom?"

7He replied, "The Father alone has the authority to set those dates and times, and they are not for you to know. 8But you will receive power when the Holy Spirit comes upon you. And you will be my witnesses, telling people about me everywhere—in Jerusalem, throughout Judea, in Samaria, and to the ends of the earth."

9After saying this, he was taken up into a cloud while they were watching, and they could no longer see him. 10As they strained to see him rising into heaven, two white-robed men suddenly stood among them. 11"Men of Galilee," they said, "why are you standing here staring into heaven? Jesus has been taken from you into heaven, but someday he will return from heaven in the same way you saw him go!"

Matthias Replaces Judas

12Then the apostles returned to Jerusalem from the Mount of Olives, a distance of half a mile.* 13When they arrived, they went to the upstairs room of the house where they were staying.

Here are the names of those who were present:

1:1 The reference is to the Gospel of Luke. **1:5** Or *in;* also in 1:5b.
1:12 Greek *a Sabbath day's journey.*

and Matthew, James *the son* of Alphaeus, and Simon Zelotes, and Judas *the brother* of James.

14 These all continued with one accord in prayer and supplication, with the women, and Mary the mother of Jesus, and with his brethren.

15 And in those days Peter stood up in the midst of the disciples, and said, (the number of names together were about an hundred and twenty,)

16 Men *and* brethren, this scripture must needs have been fulfilled, which the Holy Ghost by the mouth of David spake before concerning Judas, which was guide to them that took Jesus.

17 For he was numbered with us, and had obtained part of this ministry.

18 Now this man purchased a field with the reward of iniquity; and falling headlong, he burst asunder in the midst, and all his bowels gushed out.

19 And it was known unto all the dwellers at Jerusalem; insomuch as that field is called in their proper tongue, Aceldama, that is to say, The field of blood.

20 For it is written in the book of Psalms, Let his habitation be desolate, and let no man dwell therein: and his bishoprick let another take.

21 Wherefore of these men which have companied with us all the time that the Lord Jesus went in and out among us,

22 Beginning from the baptism of John, unto that same day that he was taken up from us, must one be ordained to be a witness with us of his resurrection.

23 And they appointed two, Joseph called Barsabas, who was surnamed Justus, and Matthias.

24 And they prayed, and said, Thou, Lord, which knowest the hearts of all *men,* shew whether of these two thou hast chosen,

25 That he may take part of this ministry and apostleship, from which Judas by transgression fell, that he might go to his own place.

26 And they gave forth their lots; and the lot fell upon Matthias; and he was numbered with the eleven apostles.

2 1 And when the day of Pentecost was fully come, they were all with one accord in one place.

2 And suddenly there came a sound from heaven as of a rushing mighty wind, and it filled all the house where they were sitting.

3 And there appeared unto them cloven tongues like as of fire, and it sat upon each of them.

4 And they were all filled with the Holy Ghost, and began to speak with other tongues, as the Spirit gave them utterance.

5 And there were dwelling at Jerusalem Jews, devout men, out of every nation under heaven.

6 Now when this was noised abroad, the multitude came together, and were confounded, because that every man heard them speak in his own language.

7 And they were all amazed and marvelled, saying

Peter, John, James, Andrew, Philip, Thomas, Bartholomew, Matthew, James (son of Alphaeus), Simon (the
Zealot), and Judas (son of James). 14 They all met together and were constantly united in prayer, along
with Mary the mother of Jesus, several other women,
and the brothers of Jesus.

15 During this time, when about 120 believers*
were together in one place, Peter stood up and addressed them. 16 "Brothers," he said, "the Scriptures
had to be fulfilled concerning Judas, who guided
those who arrested Jesus. This was predicted long
ago by the Holy Spirit, speaking through King David.
17 Judas was one of us and shared in the ministry
with us."

18 (Judas had bought a field with the money he received for his treachery. Falling headfirst there, his
body split open, spilling out all his intestines. 19 The
news of his death spread to all the people of Jerusalem, and they gave the place the Aramaic name *Akel-
dama,* which means "Field of Blood.")

20 Peter continued, "This was written in the book
of Psalms, where it says, 'Let his home become desolate, with no one living in it.' It also says, 'Let someone
else take his position.'*

21 "So now we must choose a replacement for Judas
from among the men who were with us the entire
time we were traveling with the Lord Jesus— 22 from
the time he was baptized by John until the day he was
taken from us. Whoever is chosen will join us as a
witness of Jesus' resurrection."

23 So they nominated two men: Joseph called Barsabbas (also known as Justus) and Matthias. 24 Then
they all prayed, "O Lord, you know every heart. Show
us which of these men you have chosen 25 as an apostle to replace Judas in this ministry, for he has deserted us and gone where he belongs." 26 Then they
cast lots, and Matthias was selected to become an
apostle with the other eleven.

The Holy Spirit Comes

2 On the day of Pentecost* all the believers were
meeting together in one place. 2 Suddenly, there
was a sound from heaven like the roaring of a mighty
windstorm, and it filled the house where they were
sitting. 3 Then, what looked like flames or tongues of
fire appeared and settled on each of them. 4 And
everyone present was filled with the Holy Spirit and
began speaking in other languages,* as the Holy
Spirit gave them this ability.

5 At that time there were devout Jews from every
nation living in Jerusalem. 6 When they heard the
loud noise, everyone came running, and they were
bewildered to hear their own languages being spoken by the believers.

7 They were completely amazed. "How can this

1:15 Greek *brothers.* **1:20** Pss 69:25; 109:8. **2:1** The Festival of Pentecost came 50 days after Passover (when Jesus was crucified). **2:4** Or *in other tongues.*

KING JAMES VERSION

one to another, Behold, are not all these which speak Galilaeans?

8 And how hear we every man in our own tongue, wherein we were born?

9 Parthians, and Medes, and Elamites, and the dwellers in Mesopotamia, and in Judaea, and Cappadocia, in Pontus, and Asia,

10 Phrygia, and Pamphylia, in Egypt, and in the parts of Libya about Cyrene, and strangers of Rome, Jews and proselytes,

11 Cretes and Arabians, we do hear them speak in our tongues the wonderful works of God.

12 And they were all amazed, and were in doubt, saying one to another, What meaneth this?

13 Others mocking said, These men are full of new wine.

14 But Peter, standing up with the eleven, lifted up his voice, and said unto them, Ye men of Judaea, and all *ye* that dwell at Jerusalem, be this known unto you, and hearken to my words:

15 For these are not drunken, as ye suppose, seeing it is *but* the third hour of the day.

16 But this is that which was spoken by the prophet Joel;

17 And it shall come to pass in the last days, saith God, I will pour out of my Spirit upon all flesh: and your sons and your daughters shall prophesy, and your young men shall see visions, and your old men shall dream dreams:

18 And on my servants and on my handmaidens I will pour out in those days of my Spirit; and they shall prophesy:

19 And I will shew wonders in heaven above, and signs in the earth beneath; blood, and fire, and vapour of smoke:

20 The sun shall be turned into darkness, and the moon into blood, before that great and notable day of the Lord come:

21 And it shall come to pass, *that* whosoever shall call on the name of the Lord shall be saved.

22 Ye men of Israel, hear these words; Jesus of Nazareth, a man approved of God among you by miracles and wonders and signs, which God did by him in the midst of you, as ye yourselves also know:

23 Him, being delivered by the determinate counsel and foreknowledge of God, ye have taken, and by wicked hands have crucified and slain:

24 Whom God hath raised up, having loosed the pains of death: because it was not possible that he should be holden of it.

25 For David speaketh concerning him, I foresaw the Lord always before my face, for he is on my right hand, that I should not be moved:

26 Therefore did my heart rejoice, and my tongue was glad; moreover also my flesh shall rest in hope:

NEW LIVING TRANSLATION

be?" they exclaimed. "These people are all from Galilee,
8 and yet we hear them speaking in our own
native languages!
9 Here we are—Parthians, Medes,
Elamites, people from Mesopotamia, Judea, Cappadocia, Pontus, the province of Asia,
10 Phrygia, Pamphylia, Egypt, and the areas of Libya around Cyrene,
visitors from Rome
11 (both Jews and converts to
Judaism), Cretans, and Arabs. And we all hear these
people speaking in our own languages about the
wonderful things God has done!"
12 They stood there
amazed and perplexed. "What can this mean?" they
asked each other.

13 But others in the crowd ridiculed them, saying,
"They're just drunk, that's all!"

Peter Preaches to the Crowd

14 Then Peter stepped forward with the eleven other
apostles and shouted to the crowd, "Listen carefully,
all of you, fellow Jews and residents of Jerusalem!
Make no mistake about this.
15 These people are not
drunk, as some of you are assuming. Nine o'clock in
the morning is much too early for that.
16 No, what
you see was predicted long ago by the prophet Joel:

17 'In the last days,' God says,
'I will pour out my Spirit upon all people.
Your sons and daughters will prophesy.
Your young men will see visions,
and your old men will dream dreams.
18 In those days I will pour out my Spirit
even on my servants—men and women alike—
and they will prophesy.
19 And I will cause wonders in the heavens above
and signs on the earth below—
blood and fire and clouds of smoke.
20 The sun will become dark,
and the moon will turn blood red
before that great and glorious day of the
LORD arrives.
21 But everyone who calls on the name of the
LORD will be saved.'*

22 "People of Israel, listen! God publicly endorsed
Jesus the Nazarene* by doing powerful miracles,
wonders, and signs through him, as you well know.
23 But God knew what would happen, and his prearranged plan was carried out when Jesus was betrayed. With the help of lawless Gentiles, you nailed
him to a cross and killed him.
24 But God released him
from the horrors of death and raised him back to life,
for death could not keep him in its grip.
25 King David
said this about him:

'I see that the LORD is always with me.
I will not be shaken, for he is right beside me.
26 No wonder my heart is glad,
and my tongue shouts his praises!
My body rests in hope.

2:17-21 Joel 2:28-32. **2:22** Or *Jesus of Nazareth.*

KING JAMES VERSION

27 Because thou wilt not leave my soul in hell, neither wilt thou suffer thine Holy One to see corruption.

28 Thou hast made known to me the ways of life; thou shalt make me full of joy with thy countenance.

29 Men *and* brethren, let me freely speak unto you of the patriarch David, that he is both dead and buried, and his sepulchre is with us unto this day.

30 Therefore being a prophet, and knowing that God had sworn with an oath to him, that of the fruit of his loins, according to the flesh, he would raise up Christ to sit on his throne;

31 He seeing this before spake of the resurrection of Christ, that his soul was not left in hell, neither his flesh did see corruption.

32 This Jesus hath God raised up, whereof we all are witnesses.

33 Therefore being by the right hand of God exalted, and having received of the Father the promise of the Holy Ghost, he hath shed forth this, which ye now see and hear.

34 For David is not ascended into the heavens: but he saith himself, The Lord said unto my Lord, Sit thou on my right hand,

35 Until I make thy foes thy footstool.

36 Therefore let all the house of Israel know assuredly, that God hath made that same Jesus, whom ye have crucified, both Lord and Christ.

37 Now when they heard *this,* they were pricked in their heart, and said unto Peter and to the rest of the apostles, Men *and* brethren, what shall we do?

38 Then Peter said unto them, Repent, and be baptized every one of you in the name of Jesus Christ for the remission of sins, and ye shall receive the gift of the Holy Ghost.

39 For the promise is unto you, and to your children, and to all that are afar off, *even* as many as the Lord our God shall call.

40 And with many other words did he testify and exhort, saying, Save yourselves from this untoward generation.

41 Then they that gladly received his word were baptized: and the same day there were added *unto them* about three thousand souls.

42 And they continued stedfastly in the apostles' doctrine and fellowship, and in breaking of bread, and in prayers.

43 And fear came upon every soul: and many wonders and signs were done by the apostles.

44 And all that believed were together, and had all things common;

45 And sold their possessions and goods, and parted them to all *men,* as every man had need.

NEW LIVING TRANSLATION

27 For you will not leave my soul among the dead*
or allow your Holy One to rot in the grave.
28 You have shown me the way of life,
and you will fill me with the joy of your
presence.'*

29 "Dear brothers, think about this! You can be sure
that the patriarch David wasn't referring to himself,
for he died and was buried, and his tomb is still here
among us. 30 But he was a prophet, and he knew God
had promised with an oath that one of David's own
descendants would sit on his throne. 31 David was
looking into the future and speaking of the Messiah's
resurrection. He was saying that God would not leave
him among the dead or allow his body to rot in the
grave.
32 "God raised Jesus from the dead, and we are all
witnesses of this. 33 Now he is exalted to the place of
highest honor in heaven, at God's right hand. And the
Father, as he had promised, gave him the Holy Spirit
to pour out upon us, just as you see and hear today.
34 For David himself never ascended into heaven, yet
he said,

'The LORD said to my Lord,
"Sit in the place of honor at my right hand
35 until I humble your enemies,
making them a footstool under your feet."'*

36 "So let everyone in Israel know for certain that
God has made this Jesus, whom you crucified, to be
both Lord and Messiah!"
37 Peter's words pierced their hearts, and they said
to him and to the other apostles, "Brothers, what
should we do?"
38 Peter replied, "Each of you must repent of your
sins and turn to God, and be baptized in the name of
Jesus Christ for the forgiveness of your sins. Then
you will receive the gift of the Holy Spirit. 39 This
promise is to you, and to your children, and even to
the Gentiles*—all who have been called by the Lord
our God." 40 Then Peter continued preaching for a
long time, strongly urging all his listeners, "Save
yourselves from this crooked generation!"
41 Those who believed what Peter said were baptized and added to the church that day—about 3,000
in all.

The Believers Form a Community

42 All the believers devoted themselves to the apostles' teaching, and to fellowship, and to sharing in
meals (including the Lord's Supper*), and to prayer.
43 A deep sense of awe came over them all, and the
apostles performed many miraculous signs and
wonders. 44 And all the believers met together in one
place and shared everything they had. 45 They sold
their property and possessions and shared the

2:27 Greek *in Hades;* also in 2:31. **2:25-28** Ps 16:8-11 (Greek version). **2:34-35** Ps 110:1. **2:39** Or *and to people far in the future;* Greek reads *and to those far away.* **2:42** Greek *the breaking of bread;* also in 2:46.

KING JAMES VERSION

46And they, continuing daily with one accord in the temple, and breaking bread from house to house, did eat their meat with gladness and singleness of heart,

47Praising God, and having favour with all the people. And the Lord added to the church daily such as should be saved.

3 1Now Peter and John went up together into the temple at the hour of prayer, *being* the ninth *hour.*

2And a certain man lame from his mother's womb was carried, whom they laid daily at the gate of the temple which is called Beautiful, to ask alms of them that entered into the temple;

3Who seeing Peter and John about to go into the temple asked an alms.

4And Peter, fastening his eyes upon him with John, said, Look on us.

5And he gave heed unto them, expecting to receive something of them.

6Then Peter said, Silver and gold have I none; but such as I have give I thee: In the name of Jesus Christ of Nazareth rise up and walk.

7And he took him by the right hand, and lifted *him* up: and immediately his feet and ancle bones received strength.

8And he leaping up stood, and walked, and entered with them into the temple, walking, and leaping, and praising God.

9And all the people saw him walking and praising God:

10And they knew that it was he which sat for alms at the Beautiful gate of the temple: and they were filled with wonder and amazement at that which had happened unto him.

11And as the lame man which was healed held Peter and John, all the people ran together unto them in the porch that is called Solomon's, greatly wondering.

12And when Peter saw *it,* he answered unto the people, Ye men of Israel, why marvel ye at this? or why look ye so earnestly on us, as though by our own power or holiness we had made this man to walk?

13The God of Abraham, and of Isaac, and of Jacob, the God of our fathers, hath glorified his Son Jesus; whom ye delivered up, and denied him in the presence of Pilate, when he was determined to let *him* go.

14But ye denied the Holy One and the Just, and desired a murderer to be granted unto you;

15And killed the Prince of life, whom God hath raised from the dead; whereof we are witnesses.

16And his name through faith in his name hath made this man strong, whom ye see and know: yea, the faith which is by him hath given him this perfect soundness in the presence of you all.

NEW LIVING TRANSLATION

money with those in need. 46They worshiped together at the Temple each day, met in homes for the Lord's Supper, and shared their meals with great joy and generosity*—47all the while praising God and enjoying the goodwill of all the people. And each day the Lord added to their fellowship those who were being saved.

Peter Heals a Crippled Beggar

3 Peter and John went to the Temple one afternoon to take part in the three o'clock prayer service. 2As they approached the Temple, a man lame from birth was being carried in. Each day he was put beside the Temple gate, the one called the Beautiful Gate, so he could beg from the people going into the Temple. 3When he saw Peter and John about to enter, he asked them for some money.

4Peter and John looked at him intently, and Peter said, "Look at us!" 5The lame man looked at them eagerly, expecting some money. 6But Peter said, "I don't have any silver or gold for you. But I'll give you what I have. In the name of Jesus Christ the Nazarene,* get up and* walk!"

7Then Peter took the lame man by the right hand and helped him up. And as he did, the man's feet and ankles were instantly healed and strengthened. 8He jumped up, stood on his feet, and began to walk! Then, walking, leaping, and praising God, he went into the Temple with them.

9All the people saw him walking and heard him praising God. 10When they realized he was the lame beggar they had seen so often at the Beautiful Gate, they were absolutely astounded! 11They all rushed out in amazement to Solomon's Colonnade, where the man was holding tightly to Peter and John.

Peter Preaches in the Temple

12Peter saw his opportunity and addressed the crowd. "People of Israel," he said, "what is so surprising about this? And why stare at us as though we had made this man walk by our own power or godliness? 13For it is the God of Abraham, Isaac, and Jacob—the God of all our ancestors—who has brought glory to his servant Jesus by doing this. This is the same Jesus whom you handed over and rejected before Pilate, despite Pilate's decision to release him. 14You rejected this holy, righteous one and instead demanded the release of a murderer. 15You killed the author of life, but God raised him from the dead. And we are witnesses of this fact!

16"Through faith in the name of Jesus, this man was healed—and you know how crippled he was before. Faith in Jesus' name has healed him before your very eyes.

2:46 Or *and sincere hearts.* **3:6a** Or *Jesus Christ of Nazareth.* **3:6b** Some manuscripts do not include *get up and.*

KING JAMES VERSION

17 And now, brethren, I wot that through ignorance ye did *it*, as *did* also your rulers.

18 But those things, which God before had shewed by the mouth of all his prophets, that Christ should suffer, he hath so fulfilled.

19 Repent ye therefore, and be converted, that your sins may be blotted out, when the times of refreshing shall come from the presence of the Lord;

20 And he shall send Jesus Christ, which before was preached unto you:

21 Whom the heaven must receive until the times of restitution of all things, which God hath spoken by the mouth of all his holy prophets since the world began.

22 For Moses truly said unto the fathers, A prophet shall the Lord your God raise up unto you of your brethren, like unto me; him shall ye hear in all things whatsoever he shall say unto you.

23 And it shall come to pass, *that* every soul, which will not hear that prophet, shall be destroyed from among the people.

24 Yea, and all the prophets from Samuel and those that follow after, as many as have spoken, have likewise foretold of these days.

25 Ye are the children of the prophets, and of the covenant which God made with our fathers, saying unto Abraham, And in thy seed shall all the kindreds of the earth be blessed.

26 Unto you first God, having raised up his Son Jesus, sent him to bless you, in turning away every one of you from his iniquities.

4 1 And as they spake unto the people, the priests, and the captain of the temple, and the Sadducees, came upon them,

2 Being grieved that they taught the people, and preached through Jesus the resurrection from the dead.

3 And they laid hands on them, and put *them* in hold unto the next day: for it was now eventide.

4 Howbeit many of them which heard the word believed; and the number of the men was about five thousand.

5 And it came to pass on the morrow, that their rulers, and elders, and scribes,

6 And Annas the high priest, and Caiaphas, and John, and Alexander, and as many as were of the kindred of the high priest, were gathered together at Jerusalem.

7 And when they had set them in the midst, they asked, By what power, or by what name, have ye done this?

8 Then Peter, filled with the Holy Ghost, said unto them, Ye rulers of the people, and elders of Israel,

9 If we this day be examined of the good deed done to the impotent man, by what means he is made whole;

10 Be it known unto you all, and to all the people of Israel, that by the name of Jesus Christ of Nazareth,

NEW LIVING TRANSLATION

17 "Friends,* I realize that what you and your leaders did to Jesus was done in ignorance. 18 But God was fulfilling what all the prophets had foretold about the Messiah—that he must suffer these things. 19 Now repent of your sins and turn to God, so that your sins may be wiped away. 20 Then times of refreshment will come from the presence of the Lord, and he will again send you Jesus, your appointed Messiah. 21 For he must remain in heaven until the time for the final restoration of all things, as God promised long ago through his holy prophets. 22 Moses said, 'The LORD your God will raise up for you a Prophet like me from among your own people. Listen carefully to everything he tells you.'* 23 Then Moses said, 'Anyone who will not listen to that Prophet will be completely cut off from God's people.'*

24 "Starting with Samuel, every prophet spoke about what is happening today. 25 You are the children of those prophets, and you are included in the covenant God promised to your ancestors. For God said to Abraham, 'Through your descendants* all the families on earth will be blessed.' 26 When God raised up his servant, Jesus, he sent him first to you people of Israel, to bless you by turning each of you back from your sinful ways."

Peter and John before the Council

4 While Peter and John were speaking to the people, they were confronted by the priests, the captain of the Temple guard, and some of the Sadducees. 2 These leaders were very disturbed that Peter and John were teaching the people that through Jesus there is a resurrection of the dead. 3 They arrested them and, since it was already evening, put them in jail until morning. 4 But many of the people who heard their message believed it, so the number of believers now totaled about 5,000 men, not counting women and children.*

5 The next day the council of all the rulers and elders and teachers of religious law met in Jerusalem. 6 Annas the high priest was there, along with Caiaphas, John, Alexander, and other relatives of the high priest. 7 They brought in the two disciples and demanded, "By what power, or in whose name, have you done this?"

8 Then Peter, filled with the Holy Spirit, said to them, "Rulers and elders of our people, 9 are we being questioned today because we've done a good deed for a crippled man? Do you want to know how he was healed? 10 Let me clearly state to all of you and to all

3:17 Greek *Brothers.* **3:22** Deut 18:15. **3:23** Deut 18:19; Lev 23:29. **3:25** Greek *your seed;* see Gen 12:3; 22:18. **4:4** Greek *5,000 adult males.*

KING JAMES VERSION

whom ye crucified, whom God raised from the dead, *even* by him doth this man stand here before you whole.

11This is the stone which was set at nought of you builders, which is become the head of the corner.

12Neither is there salvation in any other: for there is none other name under heaven given among men, whereby we must be saved.

13Now when they saw the boldness of Peter and John, and perceived that they were unlearned and ignorant men, they marvelled; and they took knowledge of them, that they had been with Jesus.

14And beholding the man which was healed standing with them, they could say nothing against it.

15But when they had commanded them to go aside out of the council, they conferred among themselves,

16Saying, What shall we do to these men? for that indeed a notable miracle hath been done by them *is* manifest to all them that dwell in Jerusalem; and we cannot deny *it*.

17But that it spread no further among the people, let us straitly threaten them, that they speak henceforth to no man in this name.

18And they called them, and commanded them not to speak at all nor teach in the name of Jesus.

19But Peter and John answered and said unto them, Whether it be right in the sight of God to hearken unto you more than unto God, judge ye.

20For we cannot but speak the things which we have seen and heard.

21So when they had further threatened them, they let them go, finding nothing how they might punish them, because of the people: for all *men* glorified God for that which was done.

22For the man was above forty years old, on whom this miracle of healing was shewed.

23And being let go, they went to their own company, and reported all that the chief priests and elders had said unto them.

24And when they heard that, they lifted up their voice to God with one accord, and said, Lord, thou *art* God, which hast made heaven, and earth, and the sea, and all that in them is:

25Who by the mouth of thy servant David hast said, Why did the heathen rage, and the people imagine vain things?

26The kings of the earth stood up, and the rulers were gathered together against the Lord, and against his Christ.

NEW LIVING TRANSLATION

the people of Israel that he was healed by the powerful name of Jesus Christ the Nazarene,* the man you crucified but whom God raised from the dead. 11For Jesus is the one referred to in the Scriptures, where it says,

'The stone that you builders rejected
has now become the cornerstone.'*

12There is salvation in no one else! God has given no other name under heaven by which we must be saved."

13The members of the council were amazed when they saw the boldness of Peter and John, for they could see that they were ordinary men with no special training in the Scriptures. They also recognized them as men who had been with Jesus. 14But since they could see the man who had been healed standing right there among them, there was nothing the council could say. 15So they ordered Peter and John out of the council chamber* and conferred among themselves.

16"What should we do with these men?" they asked each other. "We can't deny that they have performed a miraculous sign, and everybody in Jerusalem knows about it. 17But to keep them from spreading their propaganda any further, we must warn them not to speak to anyone in Jesus' name again." 18So they called the apostles back in and commanded them never again to speak or teach in the name of Jesus.

19But Peter and John replied, "Do you think God wants us to obey you rather than him? 20We cannot stop telling about everything we have seen and heard."

21The council then threatened them further, but they finally let them go because they didn't know how to punish them without starting a riot. For everyone was praising God 22for this miraculous sign—the healing of a man who had been lame for more than forty years.

The Believers Pray for Courage

23As soon as they were freed, Peter and John returned to the other believers and told them what the leading priests and elders had said. 24When they heard the report, all the believers lifted their voices together in prayer to God: "O Sovereign Lord, Creator of heaven and earth, the sea, and everything in them—25you spoke long ago by the Holy Spirit through our ancestor David, your servant, saying,

'Why were the nations so angry?
Why did they waste their time with futile plans?
26 The kings of the earth prepared for battle;
the rulers gathered together
against the LORD
and against his Messiah.'*

4:10 Or *Jesus Christ of Nazareth.* **4:11** Ps 118:22. **4:15** Greek *the Sanhedrin.* **4:25-26** Or *his anointed one;* or *his Christ.* Ps 2:1-2.

KING JAMES VERSION

27 For of a truth against thy holy child Jesus, whom
thou hast anointed, both Herod, and Pontius Pilate,
with the Gentiles, and the people of Israel, were gathered together,
28 For to do whatsoever thy hand and thy counsel
determined before to be done.
29 And now, Lord, behold their threatenings: and
grant unto thy servants, that with all boldness they
may speak thy word,
30 By stretching forth thine hand to heal; and that
signs and wonders may be done by the name of thy
holy child Jesus.
31 And when they had prayed, the place was shaken
where they were assembled together; and they were
all filled with the Holy Ghost, and they spake the
word of God with boldness.
32 And the multitude of them that believed were of
one heart and of one soul: neither said any *of them*
that aught of the things which he possessed was his
own; but they had all things common.
33 And with great power gave the apostles witness
of the resurrection of the Lord Jesus: and great grace
was upon them all.
34 Neither was there any among them that lacked:
for as many as were possessors of lands or houses
sold them, and brought the prices of the things that
were sold,
35 And laid *them* down at the apostles' feet: and
distribution was made unto every man according
as he had need.
36 And Joses, who by the apostles was surnamed
Barnabas, (which is, being interpreted, The son of
consolation,) a Levite, *and* of the country of Cyprus,
37 Having land, sold *it*, and brought the money, and
laid *it* at the apostles' feet.

5 1 But a certain man named Ananias, with Sapphira his wife, sold a possession,
2 And kept back *part* of the price, his wife also being privy *to it*, and brought a certain part, and laid
it at the apostles' feet.
3 But Peter said, Ananias, why hath Satan filled
thine heart to lie to the Holy Ghost, and to keep back
part of the price of the land?
4 Whiles it remained, was it not thine own? and after it was sold, was it not in thine own power? why
hast thou conceived this thing in thine heart? thou
hast not lied unto men, but unto God.
5 And Ananias hearing these words fell down, and
gave up the ghost: and great fear came on all them
that heard these things.
6 And the young men arose, wound him up, and
carried *him* out, and buried *him*.
7 And it was about the space of three hours after,
when his wife, not knowing what was done, came in.
8 And Peter answered unto her, Tell me whether ye
sold the land for so much? And she said, Yea, for so
much.

NEW LIVING TRANSLATION

27 "In fact, this has happened here in this very
city! For Herod Antipas, Pontius Pilate the governor,
the Gentiles, and the people of Israel were all united
against Jesus, your holy servant, whom you anointed.
28 But everything they did was determined beforehand according to your will. 29 And now, O Lord, hear
their threats, and give us, your servants, great boldness in preaching your word. 30 Stretch out your hand
with healing power; may miraculous signs and wonders be done through the name of your holy servant
Jesus."
31 After this prayer, the meeting place shook, and
they were all filled with the Holy Spirit. Then they
preached the word of God with boldness.

The Believers Share Their Possessions

32 All the believers were united in heart and mind.
And they felt that what they owned was not their
own, so they shared everything they had. 33 The apostles testified powerfully to the resurrection of the
Lord Jesus, and God's great blessing was upon them
all. 34 There were no needy people among them, because those who owned land or houses would sell
them 35 and bring the money to the apostles to give to
those in need.
36 For instance, there was Joseph, the one the apostles nicknamed Barnabas (which means "Son of Encouragement"). He was from the tribe of Levi and
came from the island of Cyprus. 37 He sold a field he
owned and brought the money to the apostles.

Ananias and Sapphira

5 But there was a certain man named Ananias
who, with his wife, Sapphira, sold some property. 2 He brought part of the money to the apostles,
claiming it was the full amount. With his wife's consent, he kept the rest.
3 Then Peter said, "Ananias, why have you let Satan
fill your heart? You lied to the Holy Spirit, and you
kept some of the money for yourself. 4 The property
was yours to sell or not sell, as you wished. And after
selling it, the money was also yours to give away. How
could you do a thing like this? You weren't lying to us
but to God!"
5 As soon as Ananias heard these words, he fell to
the floor and died. Everyone who heard about it was
terrified. 6 Then some young men got up, wrapped
him in a sheet, and took him out and buried him.
7 About three hours later his wife came in, not
knowing what had happened. 8 Peter asked her, "Was
this the price you and your husband received for
your land?"
"Yes," she replied, "that was the price."

KING JAMES VERSION

[9]Then Peter said unto her, How is it that ye have agreed together to tempt the Spirit of the Lord? behold, the feet of them which have buried thy husband *are* at the door, and shall carry thee out.

[10]Then fell she down straightway at his feet, and yielded up the ghost: and the young men came in, and found her dead, and, carrying *her* forth, buried *her* by her husband.

[11]And great fear came upon all the church, and upon as many as heard these things.

[12]And by the hands of the apostles were many signs and wonders wrought among the people; (and they were all with one accord in Solomon's porch.

[13]And of the rest durst no man join himself to them: but the people magnified them.

[14]And believers were the more added to the Lord, multitudes both of men and women.)

[15]Insomuch that they brought forth the sick into the streets, and laid *them* on beds and couches, that at the least the shadow of Peter passing by might overshadow some of them.

[16]There came also a multitude *out* of the cities round about unto Jerusalem, bringing sick folks, and them which were vexed with unclean spirits: and they were healed every one.

[17]Then the high priest rose up, and all they that were with him, (which is the sect of the Sadducees,) and were filled with indignation,

[18]And laid their hands on the apostles, and put them in the common prison.

[19]But the angel of the Lord by night opened the prison doors, and brought them forth, and said,

[20]Go, stand and speak in the temple to the people all the words of this life.

[21]And when they heard *that,* they entered into the temple early in the morning, and taught. But the high priest came, and they that were with him, and called the council together, and all the senate of the children of Israel, and sent to the prison to have them brought.

[22]But when the officers came, and found them not in the prison, they returned, and told,

[23]Saying, The prison truly found we shut with all safety, and the keepers standing without before the doors: but when we had opened, we found no man within.

[24]Now when the high priest and the captain of the temple and the chief priests heard these things, they doubted of them whereunto this would grow.

[25]Then came one and told them, saying, Behold, the men whom ye put in prison are standing in the temple, and teaching the people.

[26]Then went the captain with the officers, and brought them without violence: for they feared the people, lest they should have been stoned.

[27]And when they had brought them, they set *them* before the council: and the high priest asked them,

NEW LIVING TRANSLATION

[9]And Peter said, "How could the two of you even think of conspiring to test the Spirit of the Lord like this? The young men who buried your husband are just outside the door, and they will carry you out, too."

[10]Instantly, she fell to the floor and died. When the young men came in and saw that she was dead, they carried her out and buried her beside her husband. [11]Great fear gripped the entire church and everyone else who heard what had happened.

The Apostles Heal Many

[12]The apostles were performing many miraculous signs and wonders among the people. And all the believers were meeting regularly at the Temple in the area known as Solomon's Colonnade. [13]But no one else dared to join them, even though all the people had high regard for them. [14]Yet more and more people believed and were brought to the Lord—crowds of both men and women. [15]As a result of the apostles' work, sick people were brought out into the streets on beds and mats so that Peter's shadow might fall across some of them as he went by. [16]Crowds came from the villages around Jerusalem, bringing their sick and those possessed by evil* spirits, and they were all healed.

The Apostles Meet Opposition

[17]The high priest and his officials, who were Sadducees, were filled with jealousy. [18]They arrested the apostles and put them in the public jail. [19]But an angel of the Lord came at night, opened the gates of the jail, and brought them out. Then he told them, [20]"Go to the Temple and give the people this message of life!"

[21]So at daybreak the apostles entered the Temple, as they were told, and immediately began teaching.

When the high priest and his officials arrived, they convened the high council*—the full assembly of the elders of Israel. Then they sent for the apostles to be brought from the jail for trial. [22]But when the Temple guards went to the jail, the men were gone. So they returned to the council and reported, [23]"The jail was securely locked, with the guards standing outside, but when we opened the gates, no one was there!"

[24]When the captain of the Temple guard and the leading priests heard this, they were perplexed, wondering where it would all end. [25]Then someone arrived with startling news: "The men you put in jail are standing in the Temple, teaching the people!"

[26]The captain went with his Temple guards and arrested the apostles, but without violence, for they were afraid the people would stone them. [27]Then they brought the apostles before the high council,

5:16 Greek *unclean.* **5:21** Greek *Sanhedrin;* also in 5:27, 41.

KING JAMES VERSION

28 Saying, Did not we straitly command you that ye should not teach in this name? and, behold, ye have filled Jerusalem with your doctrine, and intend to bring this man's blood upon us.

29 Then Peter and the *other* apostles answered and said, We ought to obey God rather than men.

30 The God of our fathers raised up Jesus, whom ye slew and hanged on a tree.

31 Him hath God exalted with his right hand *to be* a Prince and a Saviour, for to give repentance to Israel, and forgiveness of sins.

32 And we are his witnesses of these things; and *so is* also the Holy Ghost, whom God hath given to them that obey him.

33 When they heard *that,* they were cut *to the heart,* and took counsel to slay them.

34 Then stood there up one in the council, a Pharisee, named Gamaliel, a doctor of the law, had in reputation among all the people, and commanded to put the apostles forth a little space;

35 And said unto them, Ye men of Israel, take heed to yourselves what ye intend to do as touching these men.

36 For before these days rose up Theudas, boasting himself to be somebody; to whom a number of men, about four hundred, joined themselves: who was slain; and all, as many as obeyed him, were scattered, and brought to nought.

37 After this man rose up Judas of Galilee in the days of the taxing, and drew away much people after him: he also perished; and all, *even* as many as obeyed him, were dispersed.

38 And now I say unto you, Refrain from these men, and let them alone: for if this counsel or this work be of men, it will come to nought:

39 But if it be of God, ye cannot overthrow it; lest haply ye be found even to fight against God.

40 And to him they agreed: and when they had called the apostles, and beaten *them,* they commanded that they should not speak in the name of Jesus, and let them go.

41 And they departed from the presence of the council, rejoicing that they were counted worthy to suffer shame for his name.

42 And daily in the temple, and in every house, they ceased not to teach and preach Jesus Christ.

6 1 And in those days, when the number of the disciples was multiplied, there arose a murmuring of the Grecians against the Hebrews, because their widows were neglected in the daily ministration.

2 Then the twelve called the multitude of the disciples *unto them,* and said, It is not reason that we should leave the word of God, and serve tables.

3 Wherefore, brethren, look ye out among you seven men of honest report, full of the Holy Ghost

NEW LIVING TRANSLATION

where the high priest confronted them. 28 "Didn't we tell you never again to teach in this man's name?" he demanded. "Instead, you have filled all Jerusalem with your teaching about him, and you want to make us responsible for his death!"

29 But Peter and the apostles replied, "We must obey God rather than any human authority. 30 The God of our ancestors raised Jesus from the dead after you killed him by hanging him on a cross.* 31 Then God put him in the place of honor at his right hand as Prince and Savior. He did this so the people of Israel would repent of their sins and be forgiven. 32 We are witnesses of these things and so is the Holy Spirit, who is given by God to those who obey him."

33 When they heard this, the high council was furious and decided to kill them. 34 But one member, a Pharisee named Gamaliel, who was an expert in religious law and respected by all the people, stood up and ordered that the men be sent outside the council chamber for a while. 35 Then he said to his colleagues, "Men of Israel, take care what you are planning to do to these men! 36 Some time ago there was that fellow Theudas, who pretended to be someone great. About 400 others joined him, but he was killed, and all his followers went their various ways. The whole movement came to nothing. 37 After him, at the time of the census, there was Judas of Galilee. He got people to follow him, but he was killed, too, and all his followers were scattered.

38 "So my advice is, leave these men alone. Let them go. If they are planning and doing these things merely on their own, it will soon be overthrown. 39 But if it is from God, you will not be able to overthrow them. You may even find yourselves fighting against God!"

40 The others accepted his advice. They called in the apostles and had them flogged. Then they ordered them never again to speak in the name of Jesus, and they let them go.

41 The apostles left the high council rejoicing that God had counted them worthy to suffer disgrace for the name of Jesus.* 42 And every day, in the Temple and from house to house, they continued to teach and preach this message: "Jesus is the Messiah."

Seven Men Chosen to Serve

6 But as the believers* rapidly multiplied, there were rumblings of discontent. The Greek-speaking believers complained about the Hebrew-speaking believers, saying that their widows were being discriminated against in the daily distribution of food.

2 So the Twelve called a meeting of all the believers. They said, "We apostles should spend our time teaching the word of God, not running a food program. 3 And so, brothers, select seven men who are

5:30 Greek *on a tree.* **5:41** Greek *for the name.* **6:1** Greek *disciples;* also in 6:2, 7.

KING JAMES VERSION

and wisdom, whom we may appoint over this business.

4 But we will give ourselves continually to prayer, and to the ministry of the word.

5 And the saying pleased the whole multitude: and they chose Stephen, a man full of faith and of the Holy Ghost, and Philip, and Prochorus, and Nicanor, and Timon, and Parmenas, and Nicolas a proselyte of Antioch:

6 Whom they set before the apostles: and when they had prayed, they laid *their* hands on them.

7 And the word of God increased; and the number of the disciples multiplied in Jerusalem greatly; and a great company of the priests were obedient to the faith.

8 And Stephen, full of faith and power, did great wonders and miracles among the people.

9 Then there arose certain of the synagogue, which is called *the synagogue* of the Libertines, and Cyrenians, and Alexandrians, and of them of Cilicia and of Asia, disputing with Stephen.

10 And they were not able to resist the wisdom and the spirit by which he spake.

11 Then they suborned men, which said, We have heard him speak blasphemous words against Moses, and *against* God.

12 And they stirred up the people, and the elders, and the scribes, and came upon *him,* and caught him, and brought *him* to the council,

13 And set up false witnesses, which said, This man ceaseth not to speak blasphemous words against this holy place, and the law:

14 For we have heard him say, that this Jesus of Nazareth shall destroy this place, and shall change the customs which Moses delivered us.

15 And all that sat in the council, looking stedfastly on him, saw his face as it had been the face of an angel.

7 1 Then said the high priest, Are these things so?

2 And he said, Men, brethren, and fathers, hearken; The God of glory appeared unto our father Abraham, when he was in Mesopotamia, before he dwelt in Charran,

3 And said unto him, Get thee out of thy country, and from thy kindred, and come into the land which I shall shew thee.

4 Then came he out of the land of the Chaldaeans, and dwelt in Charran: and from thence, when his father was dead, he removed him into this land, wherein ye now dwell.

5 And he gave him none inheritance in it, no, not *so much as* to set his foot on: yet he promised that he would give it to him for a possession, and to his seed after him, when *as yet* he had no child.

6 And God spake on this wise, That his seed should sojourn in a strange land; and that they should bring

NEW LIVING TRANSLATION

well respected and are full of the Spirit and wisdom.
We will give them this responsibility. 4 Then we
apostles can spend our time in prayer and teaching
the word."

5 Everyone liked this idea, and they chose the following: Stephen (a man full of faith and the Holy
Spirit), Philip, Procorus, Nicanor, Timon, Parmenas,
and Nicolas of Antioch (an earlier convert to the
Jewish faith). 6 These seven were presented to the
apostles, who prayed for them as they laid their
hands on them.

7 So God's message continued to spread. The number of believers greatly increased in Jerusalem, and
many of the Jewish priests were converted, too.

Stephen Is Arrested

8 Stephen, a man full of God's grace and power, performed amazing miracles and signs among the
people. 9 But one day some men from the Synagogue
of Freed Slaves, as it was called, started to debate
with him. They were Jews from Cyrene, Alexandria,
Cilicia, and the province of Asia. 10 None of them
could stand against the wisdom and the Spirit with
which Stephen spoke.

11 So they persuaded some men to lie about Stephen, saying, "We heard him blaspheme Moses, and
even God." 12 This roused the people, the elders, and
the teachers of religious law. So they arrested Stephen and brought him before the high council.*

13 The lying witnesses said, "This man is always
speaking against the holy Temple and against the law
of Moses. 14 We have heard him say that this Jesus of
Nazareth* will destroy the Temple and change the
customs Moses handed down to us."

15 At this point everyone in the high council stared
at Stephen, because his face became as bright as an
angel's.

Stephen Addresses the Council

7 Then the high priest asked Stephen, "Are these accusations true?"

2 This was Stephen's reply: "Brothers and fathers,
listen to me. Our glorious God appeared to our ancestor Abraham in Mesopotamia before he settled in
Haran.* 3 God told him, 'Leave your native land and
your relatives, and come into the land that I will show
you.'* 4 So Abraham left the land of the Chaldeans
and lived in Haran until his father died. Then God
brought him here to the land where you now live.

5 "But God gave him no inheritance here, not even
one square foot of land. God did promise, however,
that eventually the whole land would belong to Abraham and his descendants—even though he had no
children yet. 6 God also told him that his descendants

6:12 Greek *Sanhedrin;* also in 6:15. **6:14** Or *Jesus the Nazarene.* **7:2** *Mesopotamia* was the region now called Iraq. *Haran* was a city in what is now called Syria. **7:3** Gen 12:1.

KING JAMES VERSION

them into bondage, and entreat *them* evil four hundred years.

7And the nation to whom they shall be in bondage will I judge, said God: and after that shall they come forth, and serve me in this place.

8And he gave him the covenant of circumcision: and so *Abraham* begat Isaac, and circumcised him the eighth day; and Isaac *begat* Jacob; and Jacob *begat* the twelve patriarchs.

9And the patriarchs, moved with envy, sold Joseph into Egypt: but God was with him,

10And delivered him out of all his afflictions, and gave him favour and wisdom in the sight of Pharaoh king of Egypt; and he made him governor over Egypt and all his house.

11Now there came a dearth over all the land of Egypt and Chanaan, and great affliction: and our fathers found no sustenance.

12But when Jacob heard that there was corn in Egypt, he sent out our fathers first.

13And at the second *time* Joseph was made known to his brethren; and Joseph's kindred was made known unto Pharaoh.

14Then sent Joseph, and called his father Jacob to *him,* and all his kindred, threescore and fifteen souls.

15So Jacob went down into Egypt, and died, he, and our fathers,

16And were carried over into Sychem, and laid in the sepulchre that Abraham bought for a sum of money of the sons of Emmor *the father* of Sychem.

17But when the time of the promise drew nigh, which God had sworn to Abraham, the people grew and multiplied in Egypt,

18Till another king arose, which knew not Joseph.

19The same dealt subtilly with our kindred, and evil entreated our fathers, so that they cast out their young children, to the end they might not live.

20In which time Moses was born, and was exceeding fair, and nourished up in his father's house three months:

21And when he was cast out, Pharaoh's daughter took him up, and nourished him for her own son.

22And Moses was learned in all the wisdom of the Egyptians, and was mighty in words and in deeds.

23And when he was full forty years old, it came into his heart to visit his brethren the children of Israel.

24And seeing one *of them* suffer wrong, he defended *him,* and avenged him that was oppressed, and smote the Egyptian:

25For he supposed his brethren would have understood how that God by his hand would deliver them: but they understood not.

26And the next day he shewed himself unto them as they strove, and would have set them at one again, saying, Sirs, ye are brethren; why do ye wrong one to another?

NEW LIVING TRANSLATION

would live in a foreign land, where they would be
oppressed as slaves for 400 years. 7'But I will punish
the nation that enslaves them,' God said, 'and in the
end they will come out and worship me here in this
place.'*

8"God also gave Abraham the covenant of circumcision at that time. So when Abraham became the father of Isaac, he circumcised him on the eighth day.
And the practice was continued when Isaac became
the father of Jacob, and when Jacob became the father of the twelve patriarchs of the Israelite nation.

9"These patriarchs were jealous of their brother
Joseph, and they sold him to be a slave in Egypt. But
God was with him 10and rescued him from all his
troubles. And God gave him favor before Pharaoh,
king of Egypt. God also gave Joseph unusual wisdom,
so that Pharaoh appointed him governor over all of
Egypt and put him in charge of the palace.

11"But a famine came upon Egypt and Canaan.
There was great misery, and our ancestors ran out
of food. 12Jacob heard that there was still grain in
Egypt, so he sent his sons—our ancestors—to buy
some. 13The second time they went, Joseph revealed
his identity to his brothers,* and they were introduced to Pharaoh. 14Then Joseph sent for his father,
Jacob, and all his relatives to come to Egypt, seventy-
five persons in all. 15So Jacob went to Egypt. He died
there, as did our ancestors. 16Their bodies were
taken to Shechem and buried in the tomb Abraham
had bought for a certain price from Hamor's sons
in Shechem.

17"As the time drew near when God would fulfill
his promise to Abraham, the number of our people
in Egypt greatly increased. 18But then a new king
came to the throne of Egypt who knew nothing
about Joseph. 19This king exploited our people and
oppressed them, forcing parents to abandon their
newborn babies so they would die.

20"At that time Moses was born—a beautiful child
in God's eyes. His parents cared for him at home for
three months. 21When they had to abandon him,
Pharaoh's daughter adopted him and raised him as
her own son. 22Moses was taught all the wisdom of
the Egyptians, and he was powerful in both speech
and action.

23"One day when Moses was forty years old, he decided to visit his relatives, the people of Israel. 24He
saw an Egyptian mistreating an Israelite. So Moses
came to the man's defense and avenged him, killing
the Egyptian. 25Moses assumed his fellow Israelites
would realize that God had sent him to rescue them,
but they didn't.

26"The next day he visited them again and saw two
men of Israel fighting. He tried to be a peacemaker.
'Men,' he said, 'you are brothers. Why are you fighting each other?'

7:5-7 Gen 12:7; 15:13-14; Exod 3:12. **7:13** Other manuscripts read *Joseph was recognized by his brothers.*

KING JAMES VERSION

27 But he that did his neighbour wrong thrust him
away, saying, Who made thee a ruler and a judge
over us?
28 Wilt thou kill me, as thou diddest the Egyptian
yesterday?
29 Then fled Moses at this saying, and was a
stranger in the land of Madian, where he begat two
sons.
30 And when forty years were expired, there appeared to him in the wilderness of mount Sina an
angel of the Lord in a flame of fire in a bush.
31 When Moses saw *it,* he wondered at the sight:
and as he drew near to behold *it,* the voice of the
Lord came unto him,
32 *Saying,* I *am* the God of thy fathers, the God of
Abraham, and the God of Isaac, and the God of Jacob.
Then Moses trembled, and durst not behold.
33 Then said the Lord to him, Put off thy shoes
from thy feet: for the place where thou standest is
holy ground.
34 I have seen, I have seen the affliction of my
people which is in Egypt, and I have heard their
groaning, and am come down to deliver them. And
now come, I will send thee into Egypt.
35 This Moses whom they refused, saying, Who
made thee a ruler and a judge? the same did God
send *to be* a ruler and a deliverer by the hand of the
angel which appeared to him in the bush.
36 He brought them out, after that he had shewed
wonders and signs in the land of Egypt, and in the
Red sea, and in the wilderness forty years.
37 This is that Moses, which said unto the children
of Israel, A prophet shall the Lord your God raise up
unto you of your brethren, like unto me; him shall
ye hear.
38 This is he, that was in the church in the wilderness with the angel which spake to him in the mount
Sina, and *with* our fathers: who received the lively
oracles to give unto us:
39 To whom our fathers would not obey, but thrust
him from them, and in their hearts turned back
again into Egypt,
40 Saying unto Aaron, Make us gods to go before us:
for *as for* this Moses, which brought us out of the
land of Egypt, we wot not what is become of him.
41 And they made a calf in those days, and offered
sacrifice unto the idol, and rejoiced in the works of
their own hands.
42 Then God turned, and gave them up to worship
the host of heaven; as it is written in the book of the
prophets, O ye house of Israel, have ye offered to me
slain beasts and sacrifices *by the space of* forty years
in the wilderness?
43 Yea, ye took up the tabernacle of Moloch, and
the star of your god Remphan, figures which ye
made to worship them: and I will carry you away
beyond Babylon.

NEW LIVING TRANSLATION

27 "But the man in the wrong pushed Moses aside.
'Who made you a ruler and judge over us?' he asked.
28 'Are you going to kill me as you killed that Egyptian
yesterday?' 29 When Moses heard that, he fled the
country and lived as a foreigner in the land of Midian. There his two sons were born.
30 "Forty years later, in the desert near Mount Sinai,
an angel appeared to Moses in the flame of a burning
bush. 31 When Moses saw it, he was amazed at the
sight. As he went to take a closer look, the voice of
the LORD called out to him, 32 'I am the God of your
ancestors—the God of Abraham, Isaac, and Jacob.'
Moses shook with terror and did not dare to look.
33 "Then the LORD said to him, 'Take off your sandals, for you are standing on holy ground. 34 I have
certainly seen the oppression of my people in Egypt.
I have heard their groans and have come down to
rescue them. Now go, for I am sending you back to
Egypt.'*
35 "So God sent back the same man his people had
previously rejected when they demanded, 'Who
made you a ruler and judge over us?' Through the
angel who appeared to him in the burning bush,
God sent Moses to be their ruler and savior. 36 And
by means of many wonders and miraculous signs,
he led them out of Egypt, through the Red Sea, and
through the wilderness for forty years.
37 "Moses himself told the people of Israel, 'God
will raise up for you a Prophet like me from among
your own people.'* 38 Moses was with our ancestors,
the assembly of God's people in the wilderness,
when the angel spoke to him at Mount Sinai. And
there Moses received life-giving words to pass on
to us.*
39 "But our ancestors refused to listen to Moses.
They rejected him and wanted to return to Egypt.
40 They told Aaron, 'Make us some gods who can lead
us, for we don't know what has become of this
Moses, who brought us out of Egypt.' 41 So they made
an idol shaped like a calf, and they sacrificed to it and
celebrated over this thing they had made. 42 Then
God turned away from them and abandoned them
to serve the stars of heaven as their gods! In the book
of the prophets it is written,

'Was it to me you were bringing sacrifices
and offerings
during those forty years in the wilderness,
Israel?
43 No, you carried your pagan gods—
the shrine of Molech,
the star of your god Rephan,
and the images you made to worship them.
So I will send you into exile
as far away as Babylon.'*

7:31-34 Exod 3:5-10. **7:37** Deut 18:15. **7:38** Some manuscripts read *to you.* **7:42-43** Amos 5:25-27 (Greek version).

KING JAMES VERSION

44Our fathers had the tabernacle of witness in the wilderness, as he had appointed, speaking unto Moses, that he should make it according to the fashion that he had seen.

45Which also our fathers that came after brought in with Jesus into the possession of the Gentiles, whom God drave out before the face of our fathers, unto the days of David;

46Who found favour before God, and desired to find a tabernacle for the God of Jacob.

47But Solomon built him an house.

48Howbeit the most High dwelleth not in temples made with hands; as saith the prophet,

49Heaven *is* my throne, and earth *is* my footstool: what house will ye build me? saith the Lord: or what *is* the place of my rest?

50Hath not my hand made all these things?

51Ye stiffnecked and uncircumcised in heart and ears, ye do always resist the Holy Ghost: as your fathers *did*, so *do* ye.

52Which of the prophets have not your fathers persecuted? and they have slain them which shewed before of the coming of the Just One; of whom ye have been now the betrayers and murderers:

53Who have received the law by the disposition of angels, and have not kept *it*.

54When they heard these things, they were cut to the heart, and they gnashed on him with *their* teeth.

55But he, being full of the Holy Ghost, looked up stedfastly into heaven, and saw the glory of God, and Jesus standing on the right hand of God,

56And said, Behold, I see the heavens opened, and the Son of man standing on the right hand of God.

57Then they cried out with a loud voice, and stopped their ears, and ran upon him with one accord,

58And cast *him* out of the city, and stoned *him*: and the witnesses laid down their clothes at a young man's feet, whose name was Saul.

59And they stoned Stephen, calling upon *God*, and saying, Lord Jesus, receive my spirit.

60And he kneeled down, and cried with a loud voice, Lord, lay not this sin to their charge. And when he had said this, he fell asleep.

8 1And Saul was consenting unto his death. And at that time there was a great persecution against the church which was at Jerusalem; and they were all scattered abroad throughout the regions of Judaea and Samaria, except the apostles.

2And devout men carried Stephen *to his burial*, and made great lamentation over him.

NEW LIVING TRANSLATION

44"Our ancestors carried the Tabernacle* with them through the wilderness. It was constructed according to the plan God had shown to Moses. 45Years later, when Joshua led our ancestors in battle against the nations that God drove out of this land, the Tabernacle was taken with them into their new territory. And it stayed there until the time of King David.

46"David found favor with God and asked for the privilege of building a permanent Temple for the God of Jacob.* 47But it was Solomon who actually built it. 48However, the Most High doesn't live in temples made by human hands. As the prophet says,

49 'Heaven is my throne,
and the earth is my footstool.
Could you build me a temple as good as that?'
asks the LORD.
'Could you build me such a resting place?
50 Didn't my hands make both heaven
and earth?'*

51"You stubborn people! You are heathen* at heart and deaf to the truth. Must you forever resist the Holy Spirit? That's what your ancestors did, and so do you! 52Name one prophet your ancestors didn't persecute! They even killed the ones who predicted the coming of the Righteous One—the Messiah whom you betrayed and murdered. 53You deliberately disobeyed God's law, even though you received it from the hands of angels."

54The Jewish leaders were infuriated by Stephen's accusation, and they shook their fists at him in rage.* 55But Stephen, full of the Holy Spirit, gazed steadily into heaven and saw the glory of God, and he saw Jesus standing in the place of honor at God's right hand. 56And he told them, "Look, I see the heavens opened and the Son of Man standing in the place of honor at God's right hand!"

57Then they put their hands over their ears and began shouting. They rushed at him 58and dragged him out of the city and began to stone him. His accusers took off their coats and laid them at the feet of a young man named Saul.*

59As they stoned him, Stephen prayed, "Lord Jesus, receive my spirit." 60He fell to his knees, shouting, "Lord, don't charge them with this sin!" And with that, he died.

8 Saul was one of the witnesses, and he agreed completely with the killing of Stephen.

Persecution Scatters the Believers

A great wave of persecution began that day, sweeping over the church in Jerusalem; and all the believers except the apostles were scattered through the regions of Judea and Samaria. 2(Some devout men came and buried Stephen with great mourning.)

7:44 Greek *the tent of witness.* **7:46** Some manuscripts read *the house of Jacob.* **7:49-50** Isa 66:1-2. **7:51** Greek *uncircumcised.* **7:54** Greek *they were grinding their teeth against him.* **7:58** *Saul* is later called Paul; see 13:9.

KING JAMES VERSION

3 As for Saul, he made havock of the church, entering into every house, and haling men and women committed *them* to prison.

4 Therefore they that were scattered abroad went every where preaching the word.

5 Then Philip went down to the city of Samaria, and preached Christ unto them.

6 And the people with one accord gave heed unto those things which Philip spake, hearing and seeing the miracles which he did.

7 For unclean spirits, crying with loud voice, came out of many that were possessed *with them:* and many taken with palsies, and that were lame, were healed.

8 And there was great joy in that city.

9 But there was a certain man, called Simon, which beforetime in the same city used sorcery, and bewitched the people of Samaria, giving out that himself was some great one:

10 To whom they all gave heed, from the least to the greatest, saying, This man is the great power of God.

11 And to him they had regard, because that of long time he had bewitched them with sorceries.

12 But when they believed Philip preaching the things concerning the kingdom of God, and the name of Jesus Christ, they were baptized, both men and women.

13 Then Simon himself believed also: and when he was baptized, he continued with Philip, and wondered, beholding the miracles and signs which were done.

14 Now when the apostles which were at Jerusalem heard that Samaria had received the word of God, they sent unto them Peter and John:

15 Who, when they were come down, prayed for them, that they might receive the Holy Ghost:

16 (For as yet he was fallen upon none of them: only they were baptized in the name of the Lord Jesus.)

17 Then laid they *their* hands on them, and they received the Holy Ghost.

18 And when Simon saw that through laying on of the apostles' hands the Holy Ghost was given, he offered them money,

19 Saying, Give me also this power, that on whomsoever I lay hands, he may receive the Holy Ghost.

20 But Peter said unto him, Thy money perish with thee, because thou hast thought that the gift of God may be purchased with money.

21 Thou hast neither part nor lot in this matter: for thy heart is not right in the sight of God.

22 Repent therefore of this thy wickedness, and pray God, if perhaps the thought of thine heart may be forgiven thee.

23 For I perceive that thou art in the gall of bitterness, and *in* the bond of iniquity.

24 Then answered Simon, and said, Pray ye to the

NEW LIVING TRANSLATION

3 But Saul was going everywhere to destroy the
church. He went from house to house, dragging out
both men and women to throw them into prison.

Philip Preaches in Samaria

4 But the believers who were scattered preached the
Good News about Jesus wherever they went. 5 Philip,
for example, went to the city of Samaria and told the
people there about the Messiah. 6 Crowds listened intently to Philip because they were eager to hear his
message and see the miraculous signs he did. 7 Many
evil* spirits were cast out, screaming as they left their
victims. And many who had been paralyzed or lame
were healed. 8 So there was great joy in that city.

9 A man named Simon had been a sorcerer there
for many years, amazing the people of Samaria and
claiming to be someone great. 10 Everyone, from the
least to the greatest, often spoke of him as "the Great
One—the Power of God." 11 They listened closely to
him because for a long time he had astounded them
with his magic.

12 But now the people believed Philip's message
of Good News concerning the Kingdom of God and
the name of Jesus Christ. As a result, many men
and women were baptized. 13 Then Simon himself
believed and was baptized. He began following Philip wherever he went, and he was amazed by the
signs and great miracles Philip performed.

14 When the apostles in Jerusalem heard that the
people of Samaria had accepted God's message, they
sent Peter and John there. 15 As soon as they arrived,
they prayed for these new believers to receive the
Holy Spirit. 16 The Holy Spirit had not yet come upon
any of them, for they had only been baptized in the
name of the Lord Jesus. 17 Then Peter and John laid
their hands upon these believers, and they received
the Holy Spirit.

18 When Simon saw that the Spirit was given when
the apostles laid their hands on people, he offered
them money to buy this power. 19 "Let me have this
power, too," he exclaimed, "so that when I lay my
hands on people, they will receive the Holy Spirit!"

20 But Peter replied, "May your money be destroyed
with you for thinking God's gift can be bought! 21 You
can have no part in this, for your heart is not right
with God. 22 Repent of your wickedness and pray to
the Lord. Perhaps he will forgive your evil thoughts,
23 for I can see that you are full of bitter jealousy and
are held captive by sin."

24 "Pray to the Lord for me," Simon exclaimed,

8:7 Greek *unclean.*

KING JAMES VERSION

Lord for me, that none of these things which ye have
spoken come upon me.
25 And they, when they had testified and preached
the word of the Lord, returned to Jerusalem, and
preached the gospel in many villages of the Samaritans.

26 And the angel of the Lord spake unto Philip, saying, Arise, and go toward the south unto the way that
goeth down from Jerusalem unto Gaza, which is
desert.
27 And he arose and went: and, behold, a man of
Ethiopia, an eunuch of great authority under Can-
dace queen of the Ethiopians, who had the charge
of all her treasure, and had come to Jerusalem for to
worship,
28 Was returning, and sitting in his chariot read
Esaias the prophet.
29 Then the Spirit said unto Philip, Go near, and
join thyself to this chariot.
30 And Philip ran thither to *him,* and heard him
read the prophet Esaias, and said, Understandest
thou what thou readest?
31 And he said, How can I, except some man should
guide me? And he desired Philip that he would come
up and sit with him.
32 The place of the scripture which he read was
this, He was led as a sheep to the slaughter; and like
a lamb dumb before his shearer, so opened he not his
mouth:
33 In his humiliation his judgment was taken away:
and who shall declare his generation? for his life is
taken from the earth.
34 And the eunuch answered Philip, and said, I pray
thee, of whom speaketh the prophet this? of himself,
or of some other man?
35 Then Philip opened his mouth, and began at the
same scripture, and preached unto him Jesus.
36 And as they went on *their* way, they came unto a
certain water: and the eunuch said, See, *here is* water;
what doth hinder me to be baptized?
37 And Philip said, If thou believest with all thine
heart, thou mayest. And he answered and said, I believe that Jesus Christ is the Son of God.
38 And he commanded the chariot to stand still:
and they went down both into the water, both Philip
and the eunuch; and he baptized him.
39 And when they were come up out of the water,
the Spirit of the Lord caught away Philip, that the
eunuch saw him no more: and he went on his way
rejoicing.
40 But Philip was found at Azotus: and passing
through he preached in all the cities, till he came to
Caesarea.

NEW LIVING TRANSLATION

"that these terrible things you've said won't happen
to me!"
25 After testifying and preaching the word of the
Lord in Samaria, Peter and John returned to Jerusalem. And they stopped in many Samaritan villages
along the way to preach the Good News.

Philip and the Ethiopian Eunuch

26 As for Philip, an angel of the Lord said to him, "Go
south* down the desert road that runs from Jerusalem to Gaza." 27 So he started out, and he met the treasurer of Ethiopia, a eunuch of great authority under
the Kandake, the queen of Ethiopia. The eunuch had
gone to Jerusalem to worship, 28 and he was now returning. Seated in his carriage, he was reading aloud
from the book of the prophet Isaiah.
29 The Holy Spirit said to Philip, "Go over and walk
along beside the carriage."
30 Philip ran over and heard the man reading from
the prophet Isaiah. Philip asked, "Do you understand
what you are reading?"
31 The man replied, "How can I, unless someone
instructs me?" And he urged Philip to come up into
the carriage and sit with him.
32 The passage of Scripture he had been reading
was this:

"He was led like a sheep to the slaughter.
  And as a lamb is silent before the shearers,
  he did not open his mouth.
33 He was humiliated and received no justice.
  Who can speak of his descendants?
  For his life was taken from the earth."*

34 The eunuch asked Philip, "Tell me, was the
prophet talking about himself or someone else?"
35 So beginning with this same Scripture, Philip told
him the Good News about Jesus.
36 As they rode along, they came to some water,
and the eunuch said, "Look! There's some water!
Why can't I be baptized?"* 38 He ordered the carriage to stop, and they went down into the water, and
Philip baptized him.
39 When they came up out of the water, the Spirit
of the Lord snatched Philip away. The eunuch never
saw him again but went on his way rejoicing.
40 Meanwhile, Philip found himself farther north at
the town of Azotus. He preached the Good News
there and in every town along the way until he came
to Caesarea.

8:26 Or *Go at noon.* **8:32-33** Isa 53:7-8 (Greek version). **8:36** Some manuscripts add verse 37, *"You can," Philip answered, "if you believe with all your heart." And the eunuch replied, "I believe that Jesus Christ is the Son of God."*

KING JAMES VERSION

9 [1]And Saul, yet breathing out threatenings and slaughter against the disciples of the Lord, went unto the high priest,

[2]And desired of him letters to Damascus to the synagogues, that if he found any of this way, whether they were men or women, he might bring them bound unto Jerusalem.

[3]And as he journeyed, he came near Damascus: and suddenly there shined round about him a light from heaven:

[4]And he fell to the earth, and heard a voice saying unto him, Saul, Saul, why persecutest thou me?

[5]And he said, Who art thou, Lord? And the Lord said, I am Jesus whom thou persecutest: *it is* hard for thee to kick against the pricks.

[6]And he trembling and astonished said, Lord, what wilt thou have me to do? And the Lord *said* unto him, Arise, and go into the city, and it shall be told thee what thou must do.

[7]And the men which journeyed with him stood speechless, hearing a voice, but seeing no man.

[8]And Saul arose from the earth; and when his eyes were opened, he saw no man: but they led him by the hand, and brought *him* into Damascus.

[9]And he was three days without sight, and neither did eat nor drink.

[10]And there was a certain disciple at Damascus, named Ananias; and to him said the Lord in a vision, Ananias. And he said, Behold, I *am here,* Lord.

[11]And the Lord *said* unto him, Arise, and go into the street which is called Straight, and inquire in the house of Judas for *one* called Saul, of Tarsus: for, behold, he prayeth,

[12]And hath seen in a vision a man named Ananias coming in, and putting *his* hand on him, that he might receive his sight.

[13]Then Ananias answered, Lord, I have heard by many of this man, how much evil he hath done to thy saints at Jerusalem:

[14]And here he hath authority from the chief priests to bind all that call on thy name.

[15]But the Lord said unto him, Go thy way: for he is a chosen vessel unto me, to bear my name before the Gentiles, and kings, and the children of Israel:

[16]For I will shew him how great things he must suffer for my name's sake.

[17]And Ananias went his way, and entered into the house; and putting his hands on him said, Brother Saul, the Lord, *even* Jesus, that appeared unto thee in the way as thou camest, hath sent me, that thou mightest receive thy sight, and be filled with the Holy Ghost.

[18]And immediately there fell from his eyes as it had been scales: and he received sight forthwith, and arose, and was baptized.

[19]And when he had received meat, he was strengthened. Then was Saul certain days with the disciples which were at Damascus.

NEW LIVING TRANSLATION

Saul's Conversion

9 Meanwhile, Saul was uttering threats with every breath and was eager to kill the Lord's followers.* So he went to the high priest. [2]He requested letters addressed to the synagogues in Damascus, asking for their cooperation in the arrest of any followers of the Way he found there. He wanted to bring them—both men and women—back to Jerusalem in chains.

[3]As he was approaching Damascus on this mission, a light from heaven suddenly shone down around him. [4]He fell to the ground and heard a voice saying to him, "Saul! Saul! Why are you persecuting me?"

[5]"Who are you, lord?" Saul asked.

And the voice replied, "I am Jesus, the one you are persecuting! [6]Now get up and go into the city, and you will be told what you must do."

[7]The men with Saul stood speechless, for they heard the sound of someone's voice but saw no one! [8]Saul picked himself up off the ground, but when he opened his eyes he was blind. So his companions led him by the hand to Damascus. [9]He remained there blind for three days and did not eat or drink.

[10]Now there was a believer* in Damascus named Ananias. The Lord spoke to him in a vision, calling, "Ananias!"

"Yes, Lord!" he replied.

[11]The Lord said, "Go over to Straight Street, to the house of Judas. When you get there, ask for a man from Tarsus named Saul. He is praying to me right now. [12]I have shown him a vision of a man named Ananias coming in and laying hands on him so he can see again."

[13]"But Lord," exclaimed Ananias, "I've heard many people talk about the terrible things this man has done to the believers* in Jerusalem! [14]And he is authorized by the leading priests to arrest everyone who calls upon your name."

[15]But the Lord said, "Go, for Saul is my chosen instrument to take my message to the Gentiles and to kings, as well as to the people of Israel. [16]And I will show him how much he must suffer for my name's sake."

[17]So Ananias went and found Saul. He laid his hands on him and said, "Brother Saul, the Lord Jesus, who appeared to you on the road, has sent me so that you might regain your sight and be filled with the Holy Spirit." [18]Instantly something like scales fell from Saul's eyes, and he regained his sight. Then he got up and was baptized. [19]Afterward he ate some food and regained his strength.

9:1 Greek *disciples.* 9:10 Greek *disciple;* also in 9:26, 36. 9:13 Greek *God's holy people;* also in 9:32, 41.

KING JAMES VERSION

20 And straightway he preached Christ in the synagogues, that he is the Son of God.
21 But all that heard *him* were amazed, and said; Is
not this he that destroyed them which called on this
name in Jerusalem, and came hither for that intent,
that he might bring them bound unto the chief
priests?
22 But Saul increased the more in strength, and
confounded the Jews which dwelt at Damascus,
proving that this is very Christ.
23 And after that many days were fulfilled, the Jews
took counsel to kill him:
24 But their laying await was known of Saul. And
they watched the gates day and night to kill him.
25 Then the disciples took him by night, and let
him down by the wall in a basket.
26 And when Saul was come to Jerusalem, he assayed to join himself to the disciples: but they were
all afraid of him, and believed not that he was a
disciple.
27 But Barnabas took him, and brought *him* to the
apostles, and declared unto them how he had seen
the Lord in the way, and that he had spoken to him,
and how he had preached boldly at Damascus in the
name of Jesus.
28 And he was with them coming in and going out
at Jerusalem.
29 And he spake boldly in the name of the Lord
Jesus, and disputed against the Grecians: but they
went about to slay him.
30 *Which* when the brethren knew, they brought
him down to Caesarea, and sent him forth to Tarsus.
31 Then had the churches rest throughout all Judaea and Galilee and Samaria, and were edified; and
walking in the fear of the Lord, and in the comfort of
the Holy Ghost, were multiplied.

32 And it came to pass, as Peter passed throughout
all *quarters,* he came down also to the saints which
dwelt at Lydda.
33 And there he found a certain man named Aeneas, which had kept his bed eight years, and was sick
of the palsy.
34 And Peter said unto him, Aeneas, Jesus Christ
maketh thee whole: arise, and make thy bed. And he
arose immediately.
35 And all that dwelt at Lydda and Saron saw him,
and turned to the Lord.
36 Now there was at Joppa a certain disciple named
Tabitha, which by interpretation is called Dorcas:
this woman was full of good works and almsdeeds
which she did.
37 And it came to pass in those days, that she was

NEW LIVING TRANSLATION

Saul in Damascus and Jerusalem

Saul stayed with the believers* in Damascus for a few
days. 20 And immediately he began preaching about
Jesus in the synagogues, saying, "He is indeed the Son
of God!"
21 All who heard him were amazed. "Isn't this the
same man who caused such devastation among
Jesus' followers in Jerusalem?" they asked. "And
didn't he come here to arrest them and take them in
chains to the leading priests?"
22 Saul's preaching became more and more powerful, and the Jews in Damascus couldn't refute his
proofs that Jesus was indeed the Messiah. 23 After a
while some of the Jews plotted together to kill him.
24 They were watching for him day and night at the
city gate so they could murder him, but Saul was told
about their plot. 25 So during the night, some of the
other believers* lowered him in a large basket
through an opening in the city wall.
26 When Saul arrived in Jerusalem, he tried to meet
with the believers, but they were all afraid of him.
They did not believe he had truly become a believer!
27 Then Barnabas brought him to the apostles and
told them how Saul had seen the Lord on the way to
Damascus and how the Lord had spoken to Saul. He
also told them that Saul had preached boldly in the
name of Jesus in Damascus.
28 So Saul stayed with the apostles and went all
around Jerusalem with them, preaching boldly in
the name of the Lord. 29 He debated with some
Greek-speaking Jews, but they tried to murder him.
30 When the believers* heard about this, they took
him down to Caesarea and sent him away to Tarsus,
his hometown.
31 The church then had peace throughout Judea,
Galilee, and Samaria, and it became stronger as the
believers lived in the fear of the Lord. And with the
encouragement of the Holy Spirit, it also grew in
numbers.

Peter Heals Aeneas and Raises Dorcas

32 Meanwhile, Peter traveled from place to place, and
he came down to visit the believers in the town of
Lydda. 33 There he met a man named Aeneas, who
had been paralyzed and bedridden for eight years.
34 Peter said to him, "Aeneas, Jesus Christ heals you!
Get up, and roll up your sleeping mat!" And he was
healed instantly. 35 Then the whole population of
Lydda and Sharon saw Aeneas walking around, and
they turned to the Lord.
36 There was a believer in Joppa named Tabitha
(which in Greek is Dorcas*). She was always doing
kind things for others and helping the poor. 37 About

9:19 Greek *disciples;* also in 9:26, 38. **9:25** Greek *his disciples.* **9:30** Greek *brothers.* **9:36** The names *Tabitha* in Aramaic and *Dorcas* in Greek both mean "gazelle."

KING JAMES VERSION

sick, and died: whom when they had washed, they
laid *her* in an upper chamber.
38 And forasmuch as Lydda was nigh to Joppa, and
the disciples had heard that Peter was there, they
sent unto him two men, desiring *him* that he would
not delay to come to them.
39 Then Peter arose and went with them. When he
was come, they brought him into the upper chamber: and all the widows stood by him weeping, and
shewing the coats and garments which Dorcas
made, while she was with them.
40 But Peter put them all forth, and kneeled down,
and prayed; and turning *him* to the body said, Tabitha, arise. And she opened her eyes: and when she
saw Peter, she sat up.
41 And he gave her *his* hand, and lifted her up, and
when he had called the saints and widows, presented
her alive.
42 And it was known throughout all Joppa; and
many believed in the Lord.
43 And it came to pass, that he tarried many days
in Joppa with one Simon a tanner.

10 1 There was a certain man in Caesarea called
Cornelius, a centurion of the band called the
Italian *band,*
2 *A* devout *man,* and one that feared God with all
his house, which gave much alms to the people, and
prayed to God alway.
3 He saw in a vision evidently about the ninth hour
of the day an angel of God coming in to him, and saying unto him, Cornelius.
4 And when he looked on him, he was afraid, and
said, What is it, Lord? And he said unto him, Thy
prayers and thine alms are come up for a memorial
before God.
5 And now send men to Joppa, and call for *one*
Simon, whose surname is Peter:
6 He lodgeth with one Simon a tanner, whose
house is by the sea side: he shall tell thee what thou
oughtest to do.
7 And when the angel which spake unto Cornelius
was departed, he called two of his household servants, and a devout soldier of them that waited on
him continually;
8 And when he had declared all *these* things unto
them, he sent them to Joppa.
9 On the morrow, as they went on their journey,
and drew nigh unto the city, Peter went up upon the
housetop to pray about the sixth hour:
10 And he became very hungry, and would have
eaten: but while they made ready, he fell into a trance,
11 And saw heaven opened, and a certain vessel descending unto him, as it had been a great sheet knit
at the four corners, and let down to the earth:
12 Wherein were all manner of fourfooted beasts
of the earth, and wild beasts, and creeping things,
and fowls of the air.

NEW LIVING TRANSLATION

this time she became ill and died. Her body was
washed for burial and laid in an upstairs room. 38 But
the believers had heard that Peter was nearby at
Lydda, so they sent two men to beg him, "Please
come as soon as possible!"
39 So Peter returned with them; and as soon as he
arrived, they took him to the upstairs room. The
room was filled with widows who were weeping and
showing him the coats and other clothes Dorcas had
made for them. 40 But Peter asked them all to leave the
room; then he knelt and prayed. Turning to the body
he said, "Get up, Tabitha." And she opened her eyes!
When she saw Peter, she sat up! 41 He gave her his
hand and helped her up. Then he called in the widows and all the believers, and he presented her
to them alive.
42 The news spread through the whole town, and
many believed in the Lord. 43 And Peter stayed a long
time in Joppa, living with Simon, a tanner of hides.

Cornelius Calls for Peter

10 In Caesarea there lived a Roman army officer* named Cornelius, who was a captain of
the Italian Regiment. 2 He was a devout, God-fearing
man, as was everyone in his household. He gave
generously to the poor and prayed regularly to God.
3 One afternoon about three o'clock, he had a vision
in which he saw an angel of God coming toward him.
"Cornelius!" the angel said.
4 Cornelius stared at him in terror. "What is it, sir?"
he asked the angel.
And the angel replied, "Your prayers and gifts to
the poor have been received by God as an offering!
5 Now send some men to Joppa, and summon a man
named Simon Peter. 6 He is staying with Simon, a tanner who lives near the seashore."
7 As soon as the angel was gone, Cornelius called
two of his household servants and a devout soldier,
one of his personal attendants. 8 He told them what
had happened and sent them off to Joppa.

Peter Visits Cornelius

9 The next day as Cornelius's messengers were nearing the town, Peter went up on the flat roof to pray. It
was about noon, 10 and he was hungry. But while a
meal was being prepared, he fell into a trance. 11 He
saw the sky open, and something like a large sheet
was let down by its four corners. 12 In the sheet were

10:1 Greek *a centurion;* similarly in 10:22.

KING JAMES VERSION

13 And there came a voice to him, Rise, Peter; kill, and eat.

14 But Peter said, Not so, Lord; for I have never eaten any thing that is common or unclean.

15 And the voice *spake* unto him again the second time, What God hath cleansed, *that* call not thou common.

16 This was done thrice: and the vessel was received up again into heaven.

17 Now while Peter doubted in himself what this vision which he had seen should mean, behold, the men which were sent from Cornelius had made inquiry for Simon's house, and stood before the gate,

18 And called, and asked whether Simon, which was surnamed Peter, were lodged there.

19 While Peter thought on the vision, the Spirit said unto him, Behold, three men seek thee.

20 Arise therefore, and get thee down, and go with them, doubting nothing: for I have sent them.

21 Then Peter went down to the men which were sent unto him from Cornelius; and said, Behold, I am he whom ye seek: what *is* the cause wherefore ye are come?

22 And they said, Cornelius the centurion, a just man, and one that feareth God, and of good report among all the nation of the Jews, was warned from God by an holy angel to send for thee into his house, and to hear words of thee.

23 Then called he them in, and lodged *them.* And on the morrow Peter went away with them, and certain brethren from Joppa accompanied him.

24 And the morrow after they entered into Caesarea. And Cornelius waited for them, and had called together his kinsmen and near friends.

25 And as Peter was coming in, Cornelius met him, and fell down at his feet, and worshipped *him.*

26 But Peter took him up, saying, Stand up; I myself also am a man.

27 And as he talked with him, he went in, and found many that were come together.

28 And he said unto them, Ye know how that it is an unlawful thing for a man that is a Jew to keep company, or come unto one of another nation; but God hath shewed me that I should not call any man common or unclean.

29 Therefore came I *unto you* without gainsaying, as soon as I was sent for: I ask therefore for what intent ye have sent for me?

30 And Cornelius said, Four days ago I was fasting until this hour; and at the ninth hour I prayed in my house, and, behold, a man stood before me in bright clothing,

31 And said, Cornelius, thy prayer is heard, and thine alms are had in remembrance in the sight of God.

32 Send therefore to Joppa, and call hither Simon, whose surname is Peter; he is lodged in the house of *one* Simon a tanner by the sea side: who, when he cometh, shall speak unto thee.

NEW LIVING TRANSLATION

all sorts of animals, reptiles, and birds. 13 Then a voice
said to him, "Get up, Peter; kill and eat them."
14 "No, Lord," Peter declared. "I have never eaten
anything that our Jewish laws have declared impure
and unclean.*"
15 But the voice spoke again: "Do not call something unclean if God has made it clean." 16 The same
vision was repeated three times. Then the sheet was
suddenly pulled up to heaven.
17 Peter was very perplexed. What could the vision
mean? Just then the men sent by Cornelius found Simon's house. Standing outside the gate, 18 they asked
if a man named Simon Peter was staying there.
19 Meanwhile, as Peter was puzzling over the vision, the Holy Spirit said to him, "Three men have
come looking for you. 20 Get up, go downstairs, and
go with them without hesitation. Don't worry, for I
have sent them."
21 So Peter went down and said, "I'm the man you
are looking for. Why have you come?"
22 They said, "We were sent by Cornelius, a Roman
officer. He is a devout and God-fearing man, well respected by all the Jews. A holy angel instructed him
to summon you to his house so that he can hear your
message." 23 So Peter invited the men to stay for the
night. The next day he went with them, accompanied
by some of the brothers from Joppa.
24 They arrived in Caesarea the following day. Cornelius was waiting for them and had called together
his relatives and close friends. 25 As Peter entered his
home, Cornelius fell at his feet and worshiped him.
26 But Peter pulled him up and said, "Stand up! I'm a
human being just like you!" 27 So they talked together
and went inside, where many others were assembled.
28 Peter told them, "You know it is against our laws
for a Jewish man to enter a Gentile home like this or
to associate with you. But God has shown me that
I should no longer think of anyone as impure or unclean. 29 So I came without objection as soon as I was
sent for. Now tell me why you sent for me."
30 Cornelius replied, "Four days ago I was praying
in my house about this same time, three o'clock in
the afternoon. Suddenly, a man in dazzling clothes
was standing in front of me. 31 He told me, 'Cornelius,
your prayer has been heard, and your gifts to the
poor have been noticed by God! 32 Now send messengers to Joppa, and summon a man named Simon
Peter. He is staying in the home of Simon, a tanner

10:14 Greek *anything common and unclean.*

KING JAMES VERSION

33 Immediately therefore I sent to thee; and thou
hast well done that thou art come. Now therefore are
we all here present before God, to hear all things that
are commanded thee of God.

34 Then Peter opened *his* mouth, and said, Of a
truth I perceive that God is no respecter of persons:
35 But in every nation he that feareth him, and
worketh righteousness, is accepted with him.
36 The word which *God* sent unto the children of Israel, preaching peace by Jesus Christ: (he is Lord of all:)
37 That word, *I say,* ye know, which was published
throughout all Judaea, and began from Galilee, after
the baptism which John preached;
38 How God anointed Jesus of Nazareth with the
Holy Ghost and with power: who went about doing
good, and healing all that were oppressed of the
devil; for God was with him.
39 And we are witnesses of all things which he did
both in the land of the Jews, and in Jerusalem; whom
they slew and hanged on a tree:
40 Him God raised up the third day, and shewed
him openly;
41 Not to all the people, but unto witnesses chosen
before of God, *even* to us, who did eat and drink with
him after he rose from the dead.
42 And he commanded us to preach unto the
people, and to testify that it is he which was ordained
of God *to be* the Judge of quick and dead.
43 To him give all the prophets witness, that
through his name whosoever believeth in him shall
receive remission of sins.
44 While Peter yet spake these words, the Holy
Ghost fell on all them which heard the word.
45 And they of the circumcision which believed
were astonished, as many as came with Peter, because that on the Gentiles also was poured out the
gift of the Holy Ghost.
46 For they heard them speak with tongues, and
magnify God. Then answered Peter,
47 Can any man forbid water, that these should not
be baptized, which have received the Holy Ghost as
well as we?
48 And he commanded them to be baptized in the
name of the Lord. Then prayed they him to tarry
certain days.

11 1 And the apostles and brethren that were in
Judaea heard that the Gentiles had also received the word of God.
2 And when Peter was come up to Jerusalem, they
that were of the circumcision contended with him,
3 Saying, Thou wentest in to men uncircumcised,
and didst eat with them.
4 But Peter rehearsed *the matter* from the beginning, and expounded *it* by order unto them, saying,

NEW LIVING TRANSLATION

who lives near the seashore.' 33 So I sent for you at
once, and it was good of you to come. Now we are
all here, waiting before God to hear the message the
Lord has given you."

The Gentiles Hear the Good News

34 Then Peter replied, "I see very clearly that God
shows no favoritism. 35 In every nation he accepts
those who fear him and do what is right. 36 This is the
message of Good News for the people of Israel—that
there is peace with God through Jesus Christ, who is
Lord of all. 37 You know what happened throughout
Judea, beginning in Galilee, after John began preaching his message of baptism. 38 And you know that
God anointed Jesus of Nazareth with the Holy Spirit
and with power. Then Jesus went around doing good
and healing all who were oppressed by the devil, for
God was with him.
39 "And we apostles are witnesses of all he did
throughout Judea and in Jerusalem. They put him to
death by hanging him on a cross,* 40 but God raised
him to life on the third day. Then God allowed him to
appear, 41 not to the general public,* but to us whom
God had chosen in advance to be his witnesses. We
were those who ate and drank with him after he rose
from the dead. 42 And he ordered us to preach everywhere and to testify that Jesus is the one appointed
by God to be the judge of all—the living and the dead.
43 He is the one all the prophets testified about, saying that everyone who believes in him will have their
sins forgiven through his name."

The Gentiles Receive the Holy Spirit

44 Even as Peter was saying these things, the Holy
Spirit fell upon all who were listening to the message.
45 The Jewish believers* who came with Peter were
amazed that the gift of the Holy Spirit had been
poured out on the Gentiles, too. 46 For they heard
them speaking in other tongues* and praising God.
Then Peter asked, 47 "Can anyone object to their
being baptized, now that they have received the Holy
Spirit just as we did?" 48 So he gave orders for them to
be baptized in the name of Jesus Christ. Afterward
Cornelius asked him to stay with them for several
days.

Peter Explains His Actions

11 Soon the news reached the apostles and other
believers* in Judea that the Gentiles had received the word of God. 2 But when Peter arrived back
in Jerusalem, the Jewish believers* criticized him.
3 "You entered the home of Gentiles* and even ate
with them!" they said.
4 Then Peter told them exactly what had happened.

10:39 Greek *on a tree.* **10:41** Greek *the people.* **10:45** Greek *The faithful ones of the circumcision.* **10:46** Or *in other languages.* **11:1** Greek *brothers.* **11:2** Greek *those of the circumcision.* **11:3** Greek *of uncircumcised men.*

KING JAMES VERSION

5 I was in the city of Joppa praying: and in a trance I saw a vision, A certain vessel descend, as it had been a great sheet, let down from heaven by four corners; and it came even to me:

6 Upon the which when I had fastened mine eyes, I considered, and saw fourfooted beasts of the earth, and wild beasts, and creeping things, and fowls of the air.

7 And I heard a voice saying unto me, Arise, Peter; slay and eat.

8 But I said, Not so, Lord: for nothing common or unclean hath at any time entered into my mouth.

9 But the voice answered me again from heaven, What God hath cleansed, *that* call not thou common.

10 And this was done three times: and all were drawn up again into heaven.

11 And, behold, immediately there were three men already come unto the house where I was, sent from Caesarea unto me.

12 And the Spirit bade me go with them, nothing doubting. Moreover these six brethren accompanied me, and we entered into the man's house:

13 And he shewed us how he had seen an angel in his house, which stood and said unto him, Send men to Joppa, and call for Simon, whose surname is Peter;

14 Who shall tell thee words, whereby thou and all thy house shall be saved.

15 And as I began to speak, the Holy Ghost fell on them, as on us at the beginning.

16 Then remembered I the word of the Lord, how that he said, John indeed baptized with water; but ye shall be baptized with the Holy Ghost.

17 Forasmuch then as God gave them the like gift as *he did* unto us, who believed on the Lord Jesus Christ; what was I, that I could withstand God?

18 When they heard these things, they held their peace, and glorified God, saying, Then hath God also to the Gentiles granted repentance unto life.

19 Now they which were scattered abroad upon the persecution that arose about Stephen travelled as far as Phenice, and Cyprus, and Antioch, preaching the word to none but unto the Jews only.

20 And some of them were men of Cyprus and Cyrene, which, when they were come to Antioch, spake unto the Grecians, preaching the Lord Jesus.

21 And the hand of the Lord was with them: and a great number believed, and turned unto the Lord.

22 Then tidings of these things came unto the ears of the church which was in Jerusalem: and they sent forth Barnabas, that he should go as far as Antioch.

23 Who, when he came, and had seen the grace of God, was glad, and exhorted them all, that with purpose of heart they would cleave unto the Lord.

24 For he was a good man, and full of the Holy Ghost and of faith: and much people was added unto the Lord.

NEW LIVING TRANSLATION

5 "I was in the town of Joppa," he said, "and while I was praying, I went into a trance and saw a vision. Something like a large sheet was let down by its four corners from the sky. And it came right down to me. 6 When I looked inside the sheet, I saw all sorts of tame and wild animals, reptiles, and birds. 7 And I heard a voice say, 'Get up, Peter; kill and eat them.'

8 "'No, Lord,' I replied. 'I have never eaten anything that our Jewish laws have declared impure or unclean.*'

9 "But the voice from heaven spoke again: 'Do not call something unclean if God has made it clean.' 10 This happened three times before the sheet and all it contained was pulled back up to heaven.

11 "Just then three men who had been sent from Caesarea arrived at the house where we were staying. 12 The Holy Spirit told me to go with them and not to worry that they were Gentiles. These six brothers here accompanied me, and we soon entered the home of the man who had sent for us. 13 He told us how an angel had appeared to him in his home and had told him, 'Send messengers to Joppa, and summon a man named Simon Peter. 14 He will tell you how you and everyone in your household can be saved!'

15 "As I began to speak," Peter continued, "the Holy Spirit fell on them, just as he fell on us at the beginning. 16 Then I thought of the Lord's words when he said, 'John baptized with* water, but you will be baptized with the Holy Spirit.' 17 And since God gave these Gentiles the same gift he gave us when we believed in the Lord Jesus Christ, who was I to stand in God's way?"

18 When the others heard this, they stopped objecting and began praising God. They said, "We can see that God has also given the Gentiles the privilege of repenting of their sins and receiving eternal life."

The Church in Antioch of Syria

19 Meanwhile, the believers who had been scattered during the persecution after Stephen's death traveled as far as Phoenicia, Cyprus, and Antioch of Syria. They preached the word of God, but only to Jews. 20 However, some of the believers who went to Antioch from Cyprus and Cyrene began preaching to the Gentiles* about the Lord Jesus. 21 The power of the Lord was with them, and a large number of these Gentiles believed and turned to the Lord.

22 When the church at Jerusalem heard what had happened, they sent Barnabas to Antioch. 23 When he arrived and saw this evidence of God's blessing, he was filled with joy, and he encouraged the believers to stay true to the Lord. 24 Barnabas was a good man, full of the Holy Spirit and strong in faith. And many people were brought to the Lord.

11:8 Greek *anything common or unclean.* **11:16** Or *in;* also in 11:16b. **11:20** Greek *the Hellenists* (i.e., those who speak Greek); other manuscripts read *the Greeks.*

KING JAMES VERSION

25 Then departed Barnabas to Tarsus, for to seek Saul:

26 And when he had found him, he brought him unto Antioch. And it came to pass, that a whole year they assembled themselves with the church, and taught much people. And the disciples were called Christians first in Antioch.

27 And in these days came prophets from Jerusalem unto Antioch.

28 And there stood up one of them named Agabus, and signified by the Spirit that there should be great dearth throughout all the world: which came to pass in the days of Claudius Caesar.

29 Then the disciples, every man according to his ability, determined to send relief unto the brethren which dwelt in Judaea:

30 Which also they did, and sent it to the elders by the hands of Barnabas and Saul.

12 1 Now about that time Herod the king stretched forth *his* hands to vex certain of the church.

2 And he killed James the brother of John with the sword.

3 And because he saw it pleased the Jews, he proceeded further to take Peter also. (Then were the days of unleavened bread.)

4 And when he had apprehended him, he put *him* in prison, and delivered *him* to four quaternions of soldiers to keep him; intending after Easter to bring him forth to the people.

5 Peter therefore was kept in prison: but prayer was made without ceasing of the church unto God for him.

6 And when Herod would have brought him forth, the same night Peter was sleeping between two soldiers, bound with two chains: and the keepers before the door kept the prison.

7 And, behold, the angel of the Lord came upon *him,* and a light shined in the prison: and he smote Peter on the side, and raised him up, saying, Arise up quickly. And his chains fell off from *his* hands.

8 And the angel said unto him, Gird thyself, and bind on thy sandals. And so he did. And he saith unto him, Cast thy garment about thee, and follow me.

9 And he went out, and followed him; and wist not that it was true which was done by the angel; but thought he saw a vision.

10 When they were past the first and the second ward, they came unto the iron gate that leadeth unto the city; which opened to them of his own accord: and they went out, and passed on through one street; and forthwith the angel departed from him.

11 And when Peter was come to himself, he said, Now I know of a surety, that the Lord hath sent his angel, and hath delivered me out of the hand of Herod, and *from* all the expectation of the people of the Jews.

NEW LIVING TRANSLATION

25 Then Barnabas went on to Tarsus to look for Saul. 26 When he found him, he brought him back to Antioch. Both of them stayed there with the church for a full year, teaching large crowds of people. (It was at Antioch that the believers* were first called Christians.)

27 During this time some prophets traveled from Jerusalem to Antioch. 28 One of them named Agabus stood up in one of the meetings and predicted by the Spirit that a great famine was coming upon the entire Roman world. (This was fulfilled during the reign of Claudius.) 29 So the believers in Antioch decided to send relief to the brothers and sisters* in Judea, everyone giving as much as they could. 30 This they did, entrusting their gifts to Barnabas and Saul to take to the elders of the church in Jerusalem.

James Is Killed and Peter Is Imprisoned

12 About that time King Herod Agrippa* began to persecute some believers in the church. 2 He had the apostle James (John's brother) killed with a sword. 3 When Herod saw how much this pleased the Jewish people, he also arrested Peter. (This took place during the Passover celebration.*) 4 Then he imprisoned him, placing him under the guard of four squads of four soldiers each. Herod intended to bring Peter out for public trial after the Passover. 5 But while Peter was in prison, the church prayed very earnestly for him.

Peter's Miraculous Escape from Prison

6 The night before Peter was to be placed on trial, he was asleep, fastened with two chains between two soldiers. Others stood guard at the prison gate. 7 Suddenly, there was a bright light in the cell, and an angel of the Lord stood before Peter. The angel struck him on the side to awaken him and said, "Quick! Get up!" And the chains fell off his wrists. 8 Then the angel told him, "Get dressed and put on your sandals." And he did. "Now put on your coat and follow me," the angel ordered.

9 So Peter left the cell, following the angel. But all the time he thought it was a vision. He didn't realize it was actually happening. 10 They passed the first and second guard posts and came to the iron gate leading to the city, and this opened for them all by itself. So they passed through and started walking down the street, and then the angel suddenly left him.

11 Peter finally came to his senses. "It's really true!" he said. "The Lord has sent his angel and saved me from Herod and from what the Jewish leaders* had planned to do to me!"

11:26 Greek *disciples;* also in 11:29. **11:29** Greek *the brothers.* **12:1** Greek *Herod the king.* He was the nephew of Herod Antipas and a grandson of Herod the Great. **12:3** Greek *the days of unleavened bread.* **12:11** Or *the Jewish people.*

KING JAMES VERSION

12And when he had considered *the thing,* he came to the house of Mary the mother of John, whose surname was Mark; where many were gathered together praying.

13And as Peter knocked at the door of the gate, a damsel came to hearken, named Rhoda.

14And when she knew Peter's voice, she opened not the gate for gladness, but ran in, and told how Peter stood before the gate.

15And they said unto her, Thou art mad. But she constantly affirmed that it was even so. Then said they, It is his angel.

16But Peter continued knocking: and when they had opened *the door,* and saw him, they were astonished.

17But he, beckoning unto them with the hand to hold their peace, declared unto them how the Lord had brought him out of the prison. And he said, Go shew these things unto James, and to the brethren. And he departed, and went into another place.

18Now as soon as it was day, there was no small stir among the soldiers, what was become of Peter.

19And when Herod had sought for him, and found him not, he examined the keepers, and commanded that *they* should be put to death. And he went down from Judaea to Caesarea, and *there* abode.

20And Herod was highly displeased with them of Tyre and Sidon: but they came with one accord to him, and, having made Blastus the king's chamberlain their friend, desired peace; because their country was nourished by the king's *country.*

21And upon a set day Herod, arrayed in royal apparel, sat upon his throne, and made an oration unto them.

22And the people gave a shout, *saying, It is* the voice of a god, and not of a man.

23And immediately the angel of the Lord smote him, because he gave not God the glory: and he was eaten of worms, and gave up the ghost.

24But the word of God grew and multiplied.

25And Barnabas and Saul returned from Jerusalem, when they had fulfilled *their* ministry, and took with them John, whose surname was Mark.

13 1Now there were in the church that was at Antioch certain prophets and teachers; as Barnabas, and Simeon that was called Niger, and Lucius of Cyrene, and Manaen, which had been brought up with Herod the tetrarch, and Saul.

2As they ministered to the Lord, and fasted, the Holy Ghost said, Separate me Barnabas and Saul for the work whereunto I have called them.

NEW LIVING TRANSLATION

12When he realized this, he went to the home of Mary, the mother of John Mark, where many were gathered for prayer. 13He knocked at the door in the gate, and a servant girl named Rhoda came to open it. 14When she recognized Peter's voice, she was so overjoyed that, instead of opening the door, she ran back inside and told everyone, "Peter is standing at the door!"

15"You're out of your mind!" they said. When she insisted, they decided, "It must be his angel."

16Meanwhile, Peter continued knocking. When they finally opened the door and saw him, they were amazed. 17He motioned for them to quiet down and told them how the Lord had led him out of prison. "Tell James and the other brothers what happened," he said. And then he went to another place.

18At dawn there was a great commotion among the soldiers about what had happened to Peter. 19Herod Agrippa ordered a thorough search for him. When he couldn't be found, Herod interrogated the guards and sentenced them to death. Afterward Herod left Judea to stay in Caesarea for a while.

The Death of Herod Agrippa

20Now Herod was very angry with the people of Tyre and Sidon. So they sent a delegation to make peace with him because their cities were dependent upon Herod's country for food. The delegates won the support of Blastus, Herod's personal assistant, 21and an appointment with Herod was granted. When the day arrived, Herod put on his royal robes, sat on his throne, and made a speech to them. 22The people gave him a great ovation, shouting, "It's the voice of a god, not of a man!"

23Instantly, an angel of the Lord struck Herod with a sickness, because he accepted the people's worship instead of giving the glory to God. So he was consumed with worms and died.

24Meanwhile, the word of God continued to spread, and there were many new believers.

25When Barnabas and Saul had finished their mission to Jerusalem, they returned,* taking John Mark with them.

Barnabas and Saul Are Commissioned

13 Among the prophets and teachers of the church at Antioch of Syria were Barnabas, Simeon (called "the black man"*), Lucius (from Cyrene), Manaen (the childhood companion of King Herod Antipas*), and Saul. 2One day as these men were worshiping the Lord and fasting, the Holy Spirit said, "Dedicate Barnabas and Saul for the special

12:25 Or *mission, they returned to Jerusalem.* Other manuscripts read *mission, they returned from Jerusalem;* still others read *mission, they returned from Jerusalem to Antioch.* **13:1a** Greek *who was called Niger.* **13:1b** Greek *Herod the tetrarch.*

KING JAMES VERSION

3 And when they had fasted and prayed, and laid *their* hands on them, they sent *them* away.

4 So they, being sent forth by the Holy Ghost, departed unto Seleucia; and from thence they sailed to Cyprus.

5 And when they were at Salamis, they preached the word of God in the synagogues of the Jews: and they had also John to *their* minister.

6 And when they had gone through the isle unto Paphos, they found a certain sorcerer, a false prophet, a Jew, whose name *was* Bar-jesus:

7 Which was with the deputy of the country, Sergius Paulus, a prudent man; who called for Barnabas and Saul, and desired to hear the word of God.

8 But Elymas the sorcerer (for so is his name by interpretation) withstood them, seeking to turn away the deputy from the faith.

9 Then Saul, (who also *is called* Paul,) filled with the Holy Ghost, set his eyes on him,

10 And said, O full of all subtilty and all mischief, *thou* child of the devil, *thou* enemy of all righteousness, wilt thou not cease to pervert the right ways of the Lord?

11 And now, behold, the hand of the Lord *is* upon thee, and thou shalt be blind, not seeing the sun for a season. And immediately there fell on him a mist and a darkness; and he went about seeking some to lead him by the hand.

12 Then the deputy, when he saw what was done, believed, being astonished at the doctrine of the Lord.

13 Now when Paul and his company loosed from Paphos, they came to Perga in Pamphylia: and John departing from them returned to Jerusalem.

14 But when they departed from Perga, they came to Antioch in Pisidia, and went into the synagogue on the sabbath day, and sat down.

15 And after the reading of the law and the prophets the rulers of the synagogue sent unto them, saying, *Ye* men *and* brethren, if ye have any word of exhortation for the people, say on.

16 Then Paul stood up, and beckoning with *his* hand said, Men of Israel, and ye that fear God, give audience.

17 The God of this people of Israel chose our fathers, and exalted the people when they dwelt as strangers in the land of Egypt, and with an high arm brought he them out of it.

18 And about the time of forty years suffered he their manners in the wilderness.

NEW LIVING TRANSLATION

work to which I have called them." 3 So after more fasting and prayer, the men laid their hands on them and sent them on their way.

Paul's First Missionary Journey

4 So Barnabas and Saul were sent out by the Holy Spirit. They went down to the seaport of Seleucia and then sailed for the island of Cyprus. 5 There, in the town of Salamis, they went to the Jewish synagogues and preached the word of God. John Mark went with them as their assistant.

6 Afterward they traveled from town to town across the entire island until finally they reached Paphos, where they met a Jewish sorcerer, a false prophet named Bar-Jesus. 7 He had attached himself to the governor, Sergius Paulus, who was an intelligent man. The governor invited Barnabas and Saul to visit him, for he wanted to hear the word of God. 8 But Elymas, the sorcerer (as his name means in Greek), interfered and urged the governor to pay no attention to what Barnabas and Saul said. He was trying to keep the governor from believing.

9 Saul, also known as Paul, was filled with the Holy Spirit, and he looked the sorcerer in the eye. 10 Then he said, "You son of the devil, full of every sort of deceit and fraud, and enemy of all that is good! Will you never stop perverting the true ways of the Lord? 11 Watch now, for the Lord has laid his hand of punishment upon you, and you will be struck blind. You will not see the sunlight for some time." Instantly mist and darkness came over the man's eyes, and he began groping around begging for someone to take his hand and lead him.

12 When the governor saw what had happened, he became a believer, for he was astonished at the teaching about the Lord.

Paul Preaches in Antioch of Pisidia

13 Paul and his companions then left Paphos by ship for Pamphylia, landing at the port town of Perga. There John Mark left them and returned to Jerusalem. 14 But Paul and Barnabas traveled inland to Antioch of Pisidia.*

On the Sabbath they went to the synagogue for the services. 15 After the usual readings from the books of Moses* and the prophets, those in charge of the service sent them this message: "Brothers, if you have any word of encouragement for the people, come and give it."

16 So Paul stood, lifted his hand to quiet them, and started speaking. "Men of Israel," he said, "and you God-fearing Gentiles, listen to me.

17 "The God of this nation of Israel chose our ancestors and made them multiply and grow strong during their stay in Egypt. Then with a powerful arm he led them out of their slavery. 18 He put up with them*

13:13-14 *Pamphylia* and *Pisidia* were districts in what is now Turkey. **13:15** Greek *from the law.* **13:18** Some manuscripts read *He cared for them;* compare Deut 1:31.

KING JAMES VERSION

19 And when he had destroyed seven nations in the land of Chanaan, he divided their land to them by lot.

20 And after that he gave *unto them* judges about the space of four hundred and fifty years, until Samuel the prophet.

21 And afterward they desired a king: and God gave unto them Saul the son of Cis, a man of the tribe of Benjamin, by the space of forty years.

22 And when he had removed him, he raised up unto them David to be their king; to whom also he gave testimony, and said, I have found David the *son* of Jesse, a man after mine own heart, which shall fulfil all my will.

23 Of this man's seed hath God according to *his* promise raised unto Israel a Saviour, Jesus:

24 When John had first preached before his coming the baptism of repentance to all the people of Israel.

25 And as John fulfilled his course, he said, Whom think ye that I am? I am not *he*. But, behold, there cometh one after me, whose shoes of *his* feet I am not worthy to loose.

26 Men *and* brethren, children of the stock of Abraham, and whosoever among you feareth God, to you is the word of this salvation sent.

27 For they that dwell at Jerusalem, and their rulers, because they knew him not, nor yet the voices of the prophets which are read every sabbath day, they have fulfilled *them* in condemning *him*.

28 And though they found no cause of death *in him*, yet desired they Pilate that he should be slain.

29 And when they had fulfilled all that was written of him, they took *him* down from the tree, and laid *him* in a sepulchre.

30 But God raised him from the dead:

31 And he was seen many days of them which came up with him from Galilee to Jerusalem, who are his witnesses unto the people.

32 And we declare unto you glad tidings, how that the promise which was made unto the fathers,

33 God hath fulfilled the same unto us their children, in that he hath raised up Jesus again; as it is also written in the second psalm, Thou art my Son, this day have I begotten thee.

34 And as concerning that he raised him up from the dead, *now* no more to return to corruption, he said on this wise, I will give you the sure mercies of David.

35 Wherefore he saith also in another *psalm*, Thou shalt not suffer thine Holy One to see corruption.

36 For David, after he had served his own generation by the will of God, fell on sleep, and was laid unto his fathers, and saw corruption:

37 But he, whom God raised again, saw no corruption.

NEW LIVING TRANSLATION

through forty years of wandering in the wilderness. 19 Then he destroyed seven nations in Canaan and gave their land to Israel as an inheritance. 20 All this took about 450 years.

"After that, God gave them judges to rule until the time of Samuel the prophet. 21 Then the people begged for a king, and God gave them Saul son of Kish, a man of the tribe of Benjamin, who reigned for forty years. 22 But God removed Saul and replaced him with David, a man about whom God said, 'I have found David son of Jesse, a man after my own heart. He will do everything I want him to do.'*

23 "And it is one of King David's descendants, Jesus, who is God's promised Savior of Israel! 24 Before he came, John the Baptist preached that all the people of Israel needed to repent of their sins and turn to God and be baptized. 25 As John was finishing his ministry he asked, 'Do you think I am the Messiah? No, I am not! But he is coming soon—and I'm not even worthy to be his slave and untie the sandals on his feet.'

26 "Brothers—you sons of Abraham, and also you God-fearing Gentiles—this message of salvation has been sent to us! 27 The people in Jerusalem and their leaders did not recognize Jesus as the one the prophets had spoken about. Instead, they condemned him, and in doing this they fulfilled the prophets' words that are read every Sabbath. 28 They found no legal reason to execute him, but they asked Pilate to have him killed anyway.

29 "When they had done all that the prophecies said about him, they took him down from the cross* and placed him in a tomb. 30 But God raised him from the dead! 31 And over a period of many days he appeared to those who had gone with him from Galilee to Jerusalem. They are now his witnesses to the people of Israel.

32 "And now we are here to bring you this Good News. The promise was made to our ancestors, 33 and God has now fulfilled it for us, their descendants, by raising Jesus. This is what the second psalm says about Jesus:

'You are my Son.
Today I have become your Father.'*

34 For God had promised to raise him from the dead, not leaving him to rot in the grave. He said, 'I will give you the sacred blessings I promised to David.'* 35 Another psalm explains it more fully: 'You will not allow your Holy One to rot in the grave.'* 36 This is not a reference to David, for after David had done the will of God in his own generation, he died and was buried with his ancestors, and his body decayed. 37 No, it was a reference to someone else—someone whom God raised and whose body did not decay.

13:22 1 Sam 13:14. **13:29** Greek *from the tree.* **13:33** Or *Today I reveal you as my Son.* Ps 2:7. **13:34** Isa 55:3. **13:35** Ps 16:10.

KING JAMES VERSION

38 Be it known unto you therefore, men *and* brethren, that through this man is preached unto you the
forgiveness of sins:

39 And by him all that believe are justified from all
things, from which ye could not be justified by the
law of Moses.

40 Beware therefore, lest that come upon you,
which is spoken of in the prophets;

41 Behold, ye despisers, and wonder, and perish: for
I work a work in your days, a work which ye shall in
no wise believe, though a man declare it unto you.

42 And when the Jews were gone out of the synagogue, the Gentiles besought that these words might
be preached to them the next sabbath.

43 Now when the congregation was broken up,
many of the Jews and religious proselytes followed
Paul and Barnabas: who, speaking to them, persuaded them to continue in the grace of God.

44 And the next sabbath day came almost the
whole city together to hear the word of God.

45 But when the Jews saw the multitudes, they were
filled with envy, and spake against those things
which were spoken by Paul, contradicting and blaspheming.

46 Then Paul and Barnabas waxed bold, and said, It
was necessary that the word of God should first have
been spoken to you: but seeing ye put it from you,
and judge yourselves unworthy of everlasting life, lo,
we turn to the Gentiles.

47 For so hath the Lord commanded us, *saying*, I
have set thee to be a light of the Gentiles, that thou
shouldest be for salvation unto the ends of the earth.

48 And when the Gentiles heard this, they were
glad, and glorified the word of the Lord: and as many
as were ordained to eternal life believed.

49 And the word of the Lord was published throughout all the region.

50 But the Jews stirred up the devout and honourable women, and the chief men of the city, and raised
persecution against Paul and Barnabas, and expelled
them out of their coasts.

51 But they shook off the dust of their feet against
them, and came unto Iconium.

52 And the disciples were filled with joy, and with
the Holy Ghost.

14 1 And it came to pass in Iconium, that they
went both together into the synagogue of the
Jews, and so spake, that a great multitude both of the
Jews and also of the Greeks believed.

2 But the unbelieving Jews stirred up the Gentiles,
and made their minds evil affected against the
brethren.

NEW LIVING TRANSLATION

38 *"Brothers, listen! We are here to proclaim that
through this man Jesus there is forgiveness for your
sins. 39 Everyone who believes in him is declared
right with God—something the law of Moses could
never do. 40 Be careful! Don't let the prophets' words
apply to you. For they said,

41 'Look, you mockers,
be amazed and die!
For I am doing something in your own day,
something you wouldn't believe
even if someone told you about it.'*"

42 As Paul and Barnabas left the synagogue that day,
the people begged them to speak about these things
again the next week. 43 Many Jews and devout converts to Judaism followed Paul and Barnabas, and the
two men urged them to continue to rely on the grace
of God.

Paul Turns to the Gentiles

44 The following week almost the entire city turned
out to hear them preach the word of the Lord. 45 But
when some of the Jews saw the crowds, they were
jealous; so they slandered Paul and argued against
whatever he said.

46 Then Paul and Barnabas spoke out boldly and
declared, "It was necessary that we first preach the
word of God to you Jews. But since you have rejected
it and judged yourselves unworthy of eternal life,
we will offer it to the Gentiles. 47 For the Lord gave us
this command when he said,

'I have made you a light to the Gentiles,
to bring salvation to the farthest corners
of the earth.'*"

48 When the Gentiles heard this, they were very
glad and thanked the Lord for his message; and all
who were chosen for eternal life became believers.
49 So the Lord's message spread throughout that
region.

50 Then the Jews stirred up the influential religious
women and the leaders of the city, and they incited a
mob against Paul and Barnabas and ran them out of
town. 51 So they shook the dust from their feet as a
sign of rejection and went to the town of Iconium.
52 And the believers* were filled with joy and with the
Holy Spirit.

Paul and Barnabas in Iconium

14 The same thing happened in Iconium.* Paul
and Barnabas went to the Jewish synagogue
and preached with such power that a great number
of both Jews and Greeks became believers. 2 Some
of the Jews, however, spurned God's message and
poisoned the minds of the Gentiles against Paul and

13:38 English translations divide verses 38 and 39 in various ways.
13:41 Hab 1:5 (Greek version). **13:47** Isa 49:6. **13:52** Greek *the disciples.* **14:1** *Iconium,* as well as *Lystra* and *Derbe* (14:6), were towns in what is now Turkey.

3 Long time therefore abode they speaking boldly
in the Lord, which gave testimony unto the word of
his grace, and granted signs and wonders to be done
by their hands.
4 But the multitude of the city was divided: and
part held with the Jews, and part with the apostles.
5 And when there was an assault made both of the
Gentiles, and also of the Jews with their rulers, to use
them despitefully, and to stone them,
6 They were ware of *it,* and fled unto Lystra and
Derbe, cities of Lycaonia, and unto the region that
lieth round about:
7 And there they preached the gospel.

8 And there sat a certain man at Lystra, impotent in
his feet, being a cripple from his mother's womb,
who never had walked:
9 The same heard Paul speak: who stedfastly beholding him, and perceiving that he had faith to be
healed,
10 Said with a loud voice, Stand upright on thy feet.
And he leaped and walked.
11 And when the people saw what Paul had done,
they lifted up their voices, saying in the speech of
Lycaonia, The gods are come down to us in the likeness of men.
12 And they called Barnabas, Jupiter; and Paul,
Mercurius, because he was the chief speaker.
13 Then the priest of Jupiter, which was before
their city, brought oxen and garlands unto the gates,
and would have done sacrifice with the people.
14 *Which* when the apostles, Barnabas and Paul,
heard *of,* they rent their clothes, and ran in among
the people, crying out,
15 And saying, Sirs, why do ye these things? We also
are men of like passions with you, and preach unto
you that ye should turn from these vanities unto the
living God, which made heaven, and earth, and the
sea, and all things that are therein:
16 Who in times past suffered all nations to walk
in their own ways.
17 Nevertheless he left not himself without witness, in that he did good, and gave us rain from
heaven, and fruitful seasons, filling our hearts with
food and gladness.
18 And with these sayings scarce restrained they the
people, that they had not done sacrifice unto them.
19 And there came thither *certain* Jews from Antioch and Iconium, who persuaded the people, and,
having stoned Paul, drew *him* out of the city, supposing he had been dead.
20 Howbeit, as the disciples stood round about
him, he rose up, and came into the city: and the next
day he departed with Barnabas to Derbe.
21 And when they had preached the gospel to that
city, and had taught many, they returned again to
Lystra, and *to* Iconium, and Antioch,

Barnabas. 3 But the apostles stayed there a long time,
preaching boldly about the grace of the Lord. And
the Lord proved their message was true by giving
them power to do miraculous signs and wonders.
4 But the people of the town were divided in their
opinion about them. Some sided with the Jews, and
some with the apostles.
5 Then a mob of Gentiles and Jews, along with their
leaders, decided to attack and stone them. 6 When
the apostles learned of it, they fled to the region of
Lycaonia—to the towns of Lystra and Derbe and the
surrounding area. 7 And there they preached the
Good News.

Paul and Barnabas in Lystra and Derbe

8 While they were at Lystra, Paul and Barnabas came
upon a man with crippled feet. He had been that way
from birth, so he had never walked. He was sitting
9 and listening as Paul preached. Looking straight at
him, Paul realized he had faith to be healed. 10 So Paul
called to him in a loud voice, "Stand up!" And the man
jumped to his feet and started walking.
11 When the crowd saw what Paul had done, they
shouted in their local dialect, "These men are gods in
human form!" 12 They decided that Barnabas was the
Greek god Zeus and that Paul was Hermes, since he
was the chief speaker. 13 Now the temple of Zeus was
located just outside the town. So the priest of the
temple and the crowd brought bulls and wreaths of
flowers to the town gates, and they prepared to offer
sacrifices to the apostles.
14 But when the apostles Barnabas and Paul heard
what was happening, they tore their clothing in dismay and ran out among the people, shouting,
15 "Friends,* why are you doing this? We are merely
human beings—just like you! We have come to bring
you the Good News that you should turn from these
worthless things and turn to the living God, who
made heaven and earth, the sea, and everything in
them. 16 In the past he permitted all the nations to go
their own ways, 17 but he never left them without evidence of himself and his goodness. For instance, he
sends you rain and good crops and gives you food
and joyful hearts." 18 But even with these words, Paul
and Barnabas could scarcely restrain the people
from sacrificing to them.
19 Then some Jews arrived from Antioch and Iconium and won the crowds to their side. They stoned
Paul and dragged him out of town, thinking he was
dead. 20 But as the believers* gathered around him,
he got up and went back into the town. The next day
he left with Barnabas for Derbe.

Paul and Barnabas Return to Antioch of Syria

21 After preaching the Good News in Derbe and making many disciples, Paul and Barnabas returned to

14:15 Greek *Men.* **14:20** Greek *disciples;* also in 14:22, 28.

KING JAMES VERSION

22Confirming the souls of the disciples, *and* exhorting them to continue in the faith, and that we must through much tribulation enter into the kingdom of God.

23And when they had ordained them elders in every church, and had prayed with fasting, they commended them to the Lord, on whom they believed.

24And after they had passed throughout Pisidia, they came to Pamphylia.

25And when they had preached the word in Perga, they went down into Attalia:

26And thence sailed to Antioch, from whence they had been recommended to the grace of God for the work which they fulfilled.

27And when they were come, and had gathered the church together, they rehearsed all that God had done with them, and how he had opened the door of faith unto the Gentiles.

28And there they abode long time with the disciples.

15 1And certain men which came down from Judaea taught the brethren, *and said,* Except ye be circumcised after the manner of Moses, ye cannot be saved.

2When therefore Paul and Barnabas had no small dissension and disputation with them, they determined that Paul and Barnabas, and certain other of them, should go up to Jerusalem unto the apostles and elders about this question.

3And being brought on their way by the church, they passed through Phenice and Samaria, declaring the conversion of the Gentiles: and they caused great joy unto all the brethren.

4And when they were come to Jerusalem, they were received of the church, and *of* the apostles and elders, and they declared all things that God had done with them.

5But there rose up certain of the sect of the Pharisees which believed, saying, That it was needful to circumcise them, and to command *them* to keep the law of Moses.

6And the apostles and elders came together for to consider of this matter.

7And when there had been much disputing, Peter rose up, and said unto them, Men *and* brethren, ye know how that a good while ago God made choice among us, that the Gentiles by my mouth should hear the word of the gospel, and believe.

8And God, which knoweth the hearts, bare them witness, giving them the Holy Ghost, even as *he did* unto us;

9And put no difference between us and them, purifying their hearts by faith.

10Now therefore why tempt ye God, to put a yoke upon the neck of the disciples, which neither our fathers nor we were able to bear?

NEW LIVING TRANSLATION

Lystra, Iconium, and Antioch of Pisidia, 22where they strengthened the believers. They encouraged them to continue in the faith, reminding them that we must suffer many hardships to enter the Kingdom of God. 23Paul and Barnabas also appointed elders in every church. With prayer and fasting, they turned the elders over to the care of the Lord, in whom they had put their trust. 24Then they traveled back through Pisidia to Pamphylia. 25They preached the word in Perga, then went down to Attalia.

26Finally, they returned by ship to Antioch of Syria, where their journey had begun. The believers there had entrusted them to the grace of God to do the work they had now completed. 27Upon arriving in Antioch, they called the church together and reported everything God had done through them and how he had opened the door of faith to the Gentiles, too. 28And they stayed there with the believers for a long time.

The Council at Jerusalem

15 While Paul and Barnabas were at Antioch of Syria, some men from Judea arrived and began to teach the believers*: "Unless you are circumcised as required by the law of Moses, you cannot be saved." 2Paul and Barnabas disagreed with them, arguing vehemently. Finally, the church decided to send Paul and Barnabas to Jerusalem, accompanied by some local believers, to talk to the apostles and elders about this question. 3The church sent the delegates to Jerusalem, and they stopped along the way in Phoenicia and Samaria to visit the believers. They told them—much to everyone's joy—that the Gentiles, too, were being converted.

4When they arrived in Jerusalem, Barnabas and Paul were welcomed by the whole church, including the apostles and elders. They reported everything God had done through them. 5But then some of the believers who belonged to the sect of the Pharisees stood up and insisted, "The Gentile converts must be circumcised and required to follow the law of Moses."

6So the apostles and elders met together to resolve this issue. 7At the meeting, after a long discussion, Peter stood and addressed them as follows: "Brothers, you all know that God chose me from among you some time ago to preach to the Gentiles so that they could hear the Good News and believe. 8God knows people's hearts, and he confirmed that he accepts Gentiles by giving them the Holy Spirit, just as he did to us. 9He made no distinction between us and them, for he cleansed their hearts through faith. 10So why are you now challenging God by burdening the Gentile believers* with a yoke that neither we nor our ancestors were able to bear?

15:1 Greek *brothers;* also in 15:3, 23, 32, 33, 36, 40. **15:10** Greek *disciples.*

KING JAMES VERSION

11But we believe that through the grace of the Lord
Jesus Christ we shall be saved, even as they.
12Then all the multitude kept silence, and gave
audience to Barnabas and Paul, declaring what
miracles and wonders God had wrought among the
Gentiles by them.
13And after they had held their peace, James answered, saying, Men *and* brethren, hearken unto me:
14Simeon hath declared how God at the first did
visit the Gentiles, to take out of them a people for his
name.
15And to this agree the words of the prophets; as it
is written,
16After this I will return, and will build again the
tabernacle of David, which is fallen down; and I will
build again the ruins thereof, and I will set it up:
17That the residue of men might seek after the
Lord, and all the Gentiles, upon whom my name is
called, saith the Lord, who doeth all these things.
18Known unto God are all his works from the beginning of the world.
19Wherefore my sentence is, that we trouble not
them, which from among the Gentiles are turned to
God:
20But that we write unto them, that they abstain
from pollutions of idols, and *from* fornication, and
from things strangled, and *from* blood.
21For Moses of old time hath in every city them
that preach him, being read in the synagogues every
sabbath day.
22Then pleased it the apostles and elders, with the
whole church, to send chosen men of their own company to Antioch with Paul and Barnabas; *namely*, Judas surnamed Barsabas, and Silas, chief men among
the brethren:
23And they wrote *letters* by them after this manner; The apostles and elders and brethren *send*
greeting unto the brethren which are of the Gentiles
in Antioch and Syria and Cilicia:
24Forasmuch as we have heard, that certain which
went out from us have troubled you with words, subverting your souls, saying, *Ye must* be circumcised,
and keep the law: to whom we gave no *such* commandment:
25It seemed good unto us, being assembled with
one accord, to send chosen men unto you with our
beloved Barnabas and Paul,
26Men that have hazarded their lives for the name
of our Lord Jesus Christ.
27We have sent therefore Judas and Silas, who
shall also tell *you* the same things by mouth.
28For it seemed good to the Holy Ghost, and to us,
to lay upon you no greater burden than these necessary things;
29That ye abstain from meats offered to idols,
and from blood, and from things strangled, and from
fornication: from which if ye keep yourselves, ye
shall do well. Fare ye well.

NEW LIVING TRANSLATION

11We believe that we are all saved the same way, by
the undeserved grace of the Lord Jesus."
12Everyone listened quietly as Barnabas and Paul
told about the miraculous signs and wonders God
had done through them among the Gentiles.
13When they had finished, James stood and said,
"Brothers, listen to me. 14Peter* has told you about the
time God first visited the Gentiles to take from them a
people for himself. 15And this conversion of Gentiles
is exactly what the prophets predicted. As it is written:

16 'Afterward I will return
and restore the fallen house* of David.
I will rebuild its ruins
and restore it,
17 so that the rest of humanity might seek the LORD,
including the Gentiles—
all those I have called to be mine.
The LORD has spoken—
18 he who made these things known so long ago.'*

19"And so my judgment is that we should not make
it difficult for the Gentiles who are turning to God.
20Instead, we should write and tell them to abstain
from eating food offered to idols, from sexual immorality, from eating the meat of strangled animals, and
from consuming blood. 21For these laws of Moses
have been preached in Jewish synagogues in every
city on every Sabbath for many generations."

The Letter for Gentile Believers

22Then the apostles and elders together with the
whole church in Jerusalem chose delegates, and they
sent them to Antioch of Syria with Paul and Barnabas
to report on this decision. The men chosen were two
of the church leaders*—Judas (also called Barsabbas)
and Silas. 23This is the letter they took with them:

"This letter is from the apostles and elders, your
brothers in Jerusalem. It is written to the Gentile
believers in Antioch, Syria, and Cilicia. Greetings!
24"We understand that some men from here
have troubled you and upset you with their
teaching, but we did not send them! 25So we
decided, having come to complete agreement, to
send you official representatives, along with our
beloved Barnabas and Paul, 26who have risked
their lives for the name of our Lord Jesus Christ.
27We are sending Judas and Silas to confirm what
we have decided concerning your question.
28"For it seemed good to the Holy Spirit and to
us to lay no greater burden on you than these few
requirements: 29You must abstain from eating
food offered to idols, from consuming blood or
the meat of strangled animals, and from sexual
immorality. If you do this, you will do well.
Farewell."

15:14 Greek *Symeon.* **15:16** Or *kingdom;* Greek reads *tent.*
15:16-18 Amos 9:11-12 (Greek version); Isa 45:21. **15:22** Greek *were leaders among the brothers.*

KING JAMES VERSION

30 So when they were dismissed, they came to Antioch: and when they had gathered the multitude together, they delivered the epistle:

31 *Which* when they had read, they rejoiced for the consolation.

32 And Judas and Silas, being prophets also themselves, exhorted the brethren with many words, and confirmed *them*.

33 And after they had tarried *there* a space, they were let go in peace from the brethren unto the apostles.

34 Notwithstanding it pleased Silas to abide there still.

35 Paul also and Barnabas continued in Antioch, teaching and preaching the word of the Lord, with many others also.

36 And some days after Paul said unto Barnabas, Let us go again and visit our brethren in every city where we have preached the word of the Lord, *and see* how they do.

37 And Barnabas determined to take with them John, whose surname was Mark.

38 But Paul thought not good to take him with them, who departed from them from Pamphylia, and went not with them to the work.

39 And the contention was so sharp between them, that they departed asunder one from the other: and so Barnabas took Mark, and sailed unto Cyprus;

40 And Paul chose Silas, and departed, being recommended by the brethren unto the grace of God.

41 And he went through Syria and Cilicia, confirming the churches.

16 1 Then came he to Derbe and Lystra: and, behold, a certain disciple was there, named Timotheus, the son of a certain woman, which was a Jewess, and believed; but his father *was* a Greek:

2 Which was well reported of by the brethren that were at Lystra and Iconium.

3 Him would Paul have to go forth with him; and took and circumcised him because of the Jews which were in those quarters: for they knew all that his father was a Greek.

4 And as they went through the cities, they delivered them the decrees for to keep, that were ordained of the apostles and elders which were at Jerusalem.

5 And so were the churches established in the faith, and increased in number daily.

6 Now when they had gone throughout Phrygia and the region of Galatia, and were forbidden of the Holy Ghost to preach the word in Asia,

7 After they were come to Mysia, they assayed to go into Bithynia: but the Spirit suffered them not.

NEW LIVING TRANSLATION

30 The messengers went at once to Antioch, where
they called a general meeting of the believers and delivered the letter. 31 And there was great joy throughout the church that day as they read this encouraging
message.
32 Then Judas and Silas, both being prophets,
spoke at length to the believers, encouraging and
strengthening their faith. 33 They stayed for a while,
and then the believers sent them back to the church
in Jerusalem with a blessing of peace.* 35 Paul and
Barnabas stayed in Antioch. They and many others
taught and preached the word of the Lord there.

Paul and Barnabas Separate

36 After some time Paul said to Barnabas, "Let's go
back and visit each city where we previously
preached the word of the Lord, to see how the new
believers are doing." 37 Barnabas agreed and wanted
to take along John Mark. 38 But Paul disagreed
strongly, since John Mark had deserted them in Pamphylia and had not continued with them in their
work. 39 Their disagreement was so sharp that they
separated. Barnabas took John Mark with him and
sailed for Cyprus. 40 Paul chose Silas, and as he left,
the believers entrusted him to the Lord's gracious
care. 41 Then he traveled throughout Syria and Cilicia,
strengthening the churches there.

Paul's Second Missionary Journey

16 Paul went first to Derbe and then to Lystra,
where there was a young disciple named
Timothy. His mother was a Jewish believer, but his
father was a Greek. 2 Timothy was well thought of by
the believers* in Lystra and Iconium, 3 so Paul
wanted him to join them on their journey. In deference to the Jews of the area, he arranged for Timothy
to be circumcised before they left, for everyone
knew that his father was a Greek. 4 Then they went
from town to town, instructing the believers to follow the decisions made by the apostles and elders
in Jerusalem. 5 So the churches were strengthened
in their faith and grew larger every day.

A Call from Macedonia

6 Next Paul and Silas traveled through the area of
Phrygia and Galatia, because the Holy Spirit had prevented them from preaching the word in the province of Asia at that time. 7 Then coming to the
borders of Mysia, they headed north for the province
of Bithynia,* but again the Spirit of Jesus did not

15:33 Some manuscripts add verse 34, *But Silas decided to stay there.*
16:2 Greek *brothers;* also in 16:40. **16:6-7** *Phrygia, Galatia, Asia, Mysia,* and *Bithynia* were all districts in what is now Turkey.

KING JAMES VERSION

8And they passing by Mysia came down to Troas.

9And a vision appeared to Paul in the night; There stood a man of Macedonia, and prayed him, saying, Come over into Macedonia, and help us.

10And after he had seen the vision, immediately we endeavoured to go into Macedonia, assuredly gathering that the Lord had called us for to preach the gospel unto them.

11Therefore loosing from Troas, we came with a straight course to Samothracia, and the next *day* to Neapolis;

12And from thence to Philippi, which is the chief city of that part of Macedonia, *and* a colony: and we were in that city abiding certain days.

13And on the sabbath we went out of the city by a river side, where prayer was wont to be made; and we sat down, and spake unto the women which resorted *thither.*

14And a certain woman named Lydia, a seller of purple, of the city of Thyatira, which worshipped God, heard *us:* whose heart the Lord opened, that she attended unto the things which were spoken of Paul.

15And when she was baptized, and her household, she besought *us,* saying, If ye have judged me to be faithful to the Lord, come into my house, and abide *there*. And she constrained us.

16And it came to pass, as we went to prayer, a certain damsel possessed with a spirit of divination met us, which brought her masters much gain by soothsaying:

17The same followed Paul and us, and cried, saying, These men are the servants of the most high God, which shew unto us the way of salvation.

18And this did she many days. But Paul, being grieved, turned and said to the spirit, I command thee in the name of Jesus Christ to come out of her. And he came out the same hour.

19And when her masters saw that the hope of their gains was gone, they caught Paul and Silas, and drew *them* into the marketplace unto the rulers,

20And brought them to the magistrates, saying, These men, being Jews, do exceedingly trouble our city,

21And teach customs, which are not lawful for us to receive, neither to observe, being Romans.

22And the multitude rose up together against them: and the magistrates rent off their clothes, and commanded to beat *them.*

23And when they had laid many stripes upon them, they cast *them* into prison, charging the jailor to keep them safely:

24Who, having received such a charge, thrust them into the inner prison, and made their feet fast in the stocks.

25And at midnight Paul and Silas prayed, and sang praises unto God: and the prisoners heard them.

NEW LIVING TRANSLATION

allow them to go there. 8So instead, they went on
through Mysia to the seaport of Troas.

9That night Paul had a vision: A man from Macedonia in northern Greece was standing there, pleading with him, "Come over to Macedonia and help us!"
10So we* decided to leave for Macedonia at once,
having concluded that God was calling us to preach
the Good News there.

Lydia of Philippi Believes in Jesus

11We boarded a boat at Troas and sailed straight
across to the island of Samothrace, and the next day
we landed at Neapolis. 12From there we reached Philippi, a major city of that district of Macedonia and a
Roman colony. And we stayed there several days.

13On the Sabbath we went a little way outside the
city to a riverbank, where we thought people would
be meeting for prayer, and we sat down to speak with
some women who had gathered there. 14One of them
was Lydia from Thyatira, a merchant of expensive
purple cloth, who worshiped God. As she listened to
us, the Lord opened her heart, and she accepted
what Paul was saying. 15She was baptized along with
other members of her household, and she asked us
to be her guests. "If you agree that I am a true believer in the Lord," she said, "come and stay at my
home." And she urged us until we agreed.

Paul and Silas in Prison

16One day as we were going down to the place of
prayer, we met a demon-possessed slave girl. She was
a fortune-teller who earned a lot of money for her
masters. 17She followed Paul and the rest of us,
shouting, "These men are servants of the Most High
God, and they have come to tell you how to be saved."

18This went on day after day until Paul got so exas-
perated that he turned and said to the demon within
her, "I command you in the name of Jesus Christ to
come out of her." And instantly it left her.

19Her masters' hopes of wealth were now shattered, so they grabbed Paul and Silas and dragged
them before the authorities at the marketplace.
20"The whole city is in an uproar because of these
Jews!" they shouted to the city officials. 21"They are
teaching customs that are illegal for us Romans to
practice."

22A mob quickly formed against Paul and Silas,
and the city officials ordered them stripped and
beaten with wooden rods. 23They were severely
beaten, and then they were thrown into prison. The
jailer was ordered to make sure they didn't escape.
24So the jailer put them into the inner dungeon and
clamped their feet in the stocks.

25Around midnight Paul and Silas were praying
and singing hymns to God, and the other prisoners

16:10 Luke, the writer of this book, here joined Paul and accompanied him on his journey.

KING JAMES VERSION

26And suddenly there was a great earthquake, so that the foundations of the prison were shaken: and immediately all the doors were opened, and every one's bands were loosed.

27And the keeper of the prison awaking out of his sleep, and seeing the prison doors open, he drew out his sword, and would have killed himself, supposing that the prisoners had been fled.

28But Paul cried with a loud voice, saying, Do thyself no harm: for we are all here.

29Then he called for a light, and sprang in, and came trembling, and fell down before Paul and Silas,

30And brought them out, and said, Sirs, what must I do to be saved?

31And they said, Believe on the Lord Jesus Christ, and thou shalt be saved, and thy house.

32And they spake unto him the word of the Lord, and to all that were in his house.

33And he took them the same hour of the night, and washed *their* stripes; and was baptized, he and all his, straightway.

34And when he had brought them into his house, he set meat before them, and rejoiced, believing in God with all his house.

35And when it was day, the magistrates sent the serjeants, saying, Let those men go.

36And the keeper of the prison told this saying to Paul, The magistrates have sent to let you go: now therefore depart, and go in peace.

37But Paul said unto them, They have beaten us openly uncondemned, being Romans, and have cast *us* into prison; and now do they thrust us out privily? nay verily; but let them come themselves and fetch us out.

38And the serjeants told these words unto the magistrates: and they feared, when they heard that they were Romans.

39And they came and besought them, and brought *them* out, and desired *them* to depart out of the city.

40And they went out of the prison, and entered into *the house of* Lydia: and when they had seen the brethren, they comforted them, and departed.

17 1Now when they had passed through Amphipolis and Apollonia, they came to Thessalonica, where was a synagogue of the Jews:

2And Paul, as his manner was, went in unto them, and three sabbath days reasoned with them out of the scriptures,

3Opening and alleging, that Christ must needs have suffered, and risen again from the dead; and that this Jesus, whom I preach unto you, is Christ.

4And some of them believed, and consorted with Paul and Silas; and of the devout Greeks a great multitude, and of the chief women not a few.

5But the Jews which believed not, moved with envy, took unto them certain lewd fellows of the baser sort, and gathered a company, and set all the

NEW LIVING TRANSLATION

were listening. 26Suddenly, there was a massive
earthquake, and the prison was shaken to its foundations. All the doors immediately flew open, and the
chains of every prisoner fell off! 27The jailer woke up
to see the prison doors wide open. He assumed the prisoners had escaped, so he drew his sword to kill
himself. 28But Paul shouted to him, "Stop! Don't kill yourself! We are all here!"

29The jailer called for lights and ran to the dungeon and fell down trembling before Paul and Silas.
30Then he brought them out and asked, "Sirs, what must I do to be saved?"

31They replied, "Believe in the Lord Jesus and you will be saved, along with everyone in your household." 32And they shared the word of the Lord with
him and with all who lived in his household. 33Even
at that hour of the night, the jailer cared for them and washed their wounds. Then he and everyone in his household were immediately baptized. 34He
brought them into his house and set a meal before them, and he and his entire household rejoiced because they all believed in God.

35The next morning the city officials sent the police to tell the jailer, "Let those men go!" 36So the
jailer told Paul, "The city officials have said you and Silas are free to leave. Go in peace."

37But Paul replied, "They have publicly beaten us without a trial and put us in prison—and we are Roman citizens. So now they want us to leave secretly? Certainly not! Let them come themselves to release us!"

38When the police reported this, the city officials were alarmed to learn that Paul and Silas were Roman citizens. 39So they came to the jail and apologized to them. Then they brought them out and
begged them to leave the city. 40When Paul and Silas
left the prison, they returned to the home of Lydia. There they met with the believers and encouraged them once more. Then they left town.

Paul Preaches in Thessalonica

17 Paul and Silas then traveled through the towns of Amphipolis and Apollonia and came to Thessalonica, where there was a Jewish synagogue. 2As was Paul's custom, he went to the synagogue service, and for three Sabbaths in a row he
used the Scriptures to reason with the people. 3He
explained the prophecies and proved that the Messiah must suffer and rise from the dead. He said, "This Jesus I'm telling you about is the Messiah."
4Some of the Jews who listened were persuaded and joined Paul and Silas, along with many God-fearing Greek men and quite a few prominent women.*

5But some of the Jews were jealous, so they gathered some troublemakers from the marketplace to form a

17:4 Some manuscripts read *quite a few of the wives of the leading men.*

city on an uproar, and assaulted the house of Jason, and sought to bring them out to the people.

6And when they found them not, they drew Jason and certain brethren unto the rulers of the city, crying, These that have turned the world upside down are come hither also;

7Whom Jason hath received: and these all do contrary to the decrees of Caesar, saying that there is another king, *one* Jesus.

8And they troubled the people and the rulers of the city, when they heard these things.

9And when they had taken security of Jason, and of the other, they let them go.

10And the brethren immediately sent away Paul and Silas by night unto Berea: who coming *thither* went into the synagogue of the Jews.

11These were more noble than those in Thessalonica, in that they received the word with all readiness of mind, and searched the scriptures daily, whether those things were so.

12Therefore many of them believed; also of honourable women which were Greeks, and of men, not a few.

13But when the Jews of Thessalonica had knowledge that the word of God was preached of Paul at Berea, they came thither also, and stirred up the people.

14And then immediately the brethren sent away Paul to go as it were to the sea: but Silas and Timotheus abode there still.

15And they that conducted Paul brought him unto Athens: and receiving a commandment unto Silas and Timotheus for to come to him with all speed, they departed.

16Now while Paul waited for them at Athens, his spirit was stirred in him, when he saw the city wholly given to idolatry.

17Therefore disputed he in the synagogue with the Jews, and with the devout persons, and in the market daily with them that met with him.

18Then certain philosophers of the Epicureans, and of the Stoicks, encountered him. And some said, What will this babbler say? other some, He seemeth to be a setter forth of strange gods: because he preached unto them Jesus, and the resurrection.

19And they took him, and brought him unto Areopagus, saying, May we know what this new doctrine, whereof thou speakest, *is?*

20For thou bringest certain strange things to our ears: we would know therefore what these things mean.

21(For all the Athenians and strangers which were there spent their time in nothing else, but either to tell, or to hear some new thing.)

mob and start a riot. They attacked the home of Jason,
searching for Paul and Silas so they could drag them
out to the crowd.* 6Not finding them there, they
dragged out Jason and some of the other believers* instead and took them before the city council. "Paul and
Silas have caused trouble all over the world," they
shouted, "and now they are here disturbing our city,
too. 7And Jason has welcomed them into his home.
They are all guilty of treason against Caesar, for they
profess allegiance to another king, named Jesus."
8The people of the city, as well as the city council,
were thrown into turmoil by these reports. 9So the
officials forced Jason and the other believers to post
bond, and then they released them.

Paul and Silas in Berea

10That very night the believers sent Paul and Silas to
Berea. When they arrived there, they went to the Jewish synagogue. 11And the people of Berea were more
open-minded than those in Thessalonica, and they
listened eagerly to Paul's message. They searched the
Scriptures day after day to see if Paul and Silas were
teaching the truth. 12As a result, many Jews believed,
as did many of the prominent Greek women and
men.
13But when some Jews in Thessalonica learned
that Paul was preaching the word of God in Berea,
they went there and stirred up trouble. 14The believers acted at once, sending Paul on to the coast, while
Silas and Timothy remained behind. 15Those escort-
ing Paul went with him all the way to Athens; then
they returned to Berea with instructions for Silas and
Timothy to hurry and join him.

Paul Preaches in Athens

16While Paul was waiting for them in Athens, he was
deeply troubled by all the idols he saw everywhere in
the city. 17He went to the synagogue to reason with the
Jews and the God-fearing Gentiles, and he spoke daily
in the public square to all who happened to be there.
18He also had a debate with some of the Epicurean
and Stoic philosophers. When he told them about
Jesus and his resurrection, they said, "What's this
babbler trying to say with these strange ideas he's
picked up?" Others said, "He seems to be preaching
about some foreign gods."
19Then they took him to the high council of the
city.* "Come and tell us about this new teaching,"
they said. 20"You are saying some rather strange
things, and we want to know what it's all about." 21(It
should be explained that all the Athenians as well as
the foreigners in Athens seemed to spend all their
time discussing the latest ideas.)

17:5 Or *the city council.* **17:6** Greek *brothers;* also in 17:10, 14.
17:19 Or *the most learned society of philosophers in the city.* Greek reads *the Areopagus.*

KING JAMES VERSION

22Then Paul stood in the midst of Mars' hill, and
said, *Ye* men of Athens, I perceive that in all things ye
are too superstitious.

23For as I passed by, and beheld your devotions, I
found an altar with this inscription, TO THE
UNKNOWN GOD. Whom therefore ye ignorantly
worship, him declare I unto you.

24God that made the world and all things therein,
seeing that he is Lord of heaven and earth, dwelleth
not in temples made with hands;

25Neither is worshipped with men's hands, as
though he needed any thing, seeing he giveth to all
life, and breath, and all things;

26And hath made of one blood all nations of men
for to dwell on all the face of the earth, and hath
determined the times before appointed, and the
bounds of their habitation;

27That they should seek the Lord, if haply they
might feel after him, and find him, though he be not
far from every one of us:

28For in him we live, and move, and have our being;
as certain also of your own poets have said, For we
are also his offspring.

29Forasmuch then as we are the offspring of God,
we ought not to think that the Godhead is like unto
gold, or silver, or stone, graven by art and man's
device.

30And the times of this ignorance God winked at;
but now commandeth all men every where to repent:

31Because he hath appointed a day, in the which
he will judge the world in righteousness by *that* man
whom he hath ordained; *whereof* he hath given
assurance unto all *men*, in that he hath raised him
from the dead.

32And when they heard of the resurrection of the
dead, some mocked: and others said, We will hear
thee again of this *matter*.

33So Paul departed from among them.

34Howbeit certain men clave unto him, and believed: among the which *was* Dionysius the Areopagite, and a woman named Damaris, and others with
them.

18 1After these things Paul departed from Athens, and came to Corinth;

2And found a certain Jew named Aquila, born in
Pontus, lately come from Italy, with his wife Priscilla;
(because that Claudius had commanded all Jews to
depart from Rome:) and came unto them.

3And because he was of the same craft, he abode
with them, and wrought: for by their occupation they
were tentmakers.

4And he reasoned in the synagogue every sabbath,
and persuaded the Jews and the Greeks.

5And when Silas and Timotheus were come from
Macedonia, Paul was pressed in the spirit, and testified to the Jews *that* Jesus *was* Christ.

NEW LIVING TRANSLATION

22So Paul, standing before the council,* addressed
them as follows: "Men of Athens, I notice that you are
very religious in every way, 23for as I was walking
along I saw your many shrines. And one of your altars had this inscription on it: 'To an Unknown God.'
This God, whom you worship without knowing, is
the one I'm telling you about.

24"He is the God who made the world and everything in it. Since he is Lord of heaven and earth, he
doesn't live in man-made temples, 25and human
hands can't serve his needs—for he has no needs. He
himself gives life and breath to everything, and he
satisfies every need. 26From one man* he created all
the nations throughout the whole earth. He decided
beforehand when they should rise and fall, and he
determined their boundaries.

27"His purpose was for the nations to seek after
God and perhaps feel their way toward him and find
him—though he is not far from any one of us. 28For
in him we live and move and exist. As some of your*
own poets have said, 'We are his offspring.' 29And
since this is true, we shouldn't think of God as an idol
designed by craftsmen from gold or silver or stone.

30"God overlooked people's ignorance about
these things in earlier times, but now he commands
everyone everywhere to repent of their sins and turn
to him. 31For he has set a day for judging the world
with justice by the man he has appointed, and he
proved to everyone who this is by raising him from
the dead."

32When they heard Paul speak about the resurrection of the dead, some laughed in contempt, but
others said, "We want to hear more about this later."
33That ended Paul's discussion with them, 34but
some joined him and became believers. Among
them were Dionysius, a member of the council,* a
woman named Damaris, and others with them.

Paul Meets Priscilla and Aquila in Corinth

18 Then Paul left Athens and went to Corinth.*
2There he became acquainted with a Jew
named Aquila, born in Pontus, who had recently arrived from Italy with his wife, Priscilla. They had left
Italy when Claudius Caesar deported all Jews from
Rome. 3Paul lived and worked with them, for they
were tentmakers* just as he was.

4Each Sabbath found Paul at the synagogue, trying
to convince the Jews and Greeks alike. 5And after
Silas and Timothy came down from Macedonia, Paul
spent all his time preaching the word. He testified to

17:22 Traditionally rendered *standing in the middle of Mars Hill;* Greek reads *standing in the middle of the Areopagus.* **17:26** Greek *From one;* other manuscripts read *From one blood.* **17:28** Some manuscripts read *our.* **17:34** Greek *an Areopagite.* **18:1** *Athens* and *Corinth* were major cities in Achaia, the region in the southern portion of the Greek peninsula. **18:3** Or *leatherworkers.*

KING JAMES VERSION

6 And when they opposed themselves, and blasphemed, he shook *his* raiment, and said unto them, Your blood *be* upon your own heads; I *am* clean: from henceforth I will go unto the Gentiles.

7 And he departed thence, and entered into a certain *man's* house, named Justus, *one* that worshipped God, whose house joined hard to the synagogue.

8 And Crispus, the chief ruler of the synagogue, believed on the Lord with all his house; and many of the Corinthians hearing believed, and were baptized.

9 Then spake the Lord to Paul in the night by a vision, Be not afraid, but speak, and hold not thy peace:

10 For I am with thee, and no man shall set on thee to hurt thee: for I have much people in this city.

11 And he continued *there* a year and six months, teaching the word of God among them.

12 And when Gallio was the deputy of Achaia, the Jews made insurrection with one accord against Paul, and brought him to the judgment seat,

13 Saying, This *fellow* persuadeth men to worship God contrary to the law.

14 And when Paul was now about to open *his* mouth, Gallio said unto the Jews, If it were a matter of wrong or wicked lewdness, O *ye* Jews, reason would that I should bear with you:

15 But if it be a question of words and names, and *of* your law, look ye *to it;* for I will be no judge of such *matters.*

16 And he drave them from the judgment seat.

17 Then all the Greeks took Sosthenes, the chief ruler of the synagogue, and beat *him* before the judgment seat. And Gallio cared for none of those things.

18 And Paul *after this* tarried *there* yet a good while, and then took his leave of the brethren, and sailed thence into Syria, and with him Priscilla and Aquila; having shorn *his* head in Cenchrea: for he had a vow.

19 And he came to Ephesus, and left them there: but he himself entered into the synagogue, and reasoned with the Jews.

20 When they desired *him* to tarry longer time with them, he consented not;

21 But bade them farewell, saying, I must by all means keep this feast that cometh in Jerusalem: but I will return again unto you, if God will. And he sailed from Ephesus.

22 And when he had landed at Caesarea, and gone up, and saluted the church, he went down to Antioch.

23 And after he had spent some time *there,* he departed, and went over *all* the country of Galatia and Phrygia in order, strengthening all the disciples.

NEW LIVING TRANSLATION

the Jews that Jesus was the Messiah. 6 But when they
opposed and insulted him, Paul shook the dust from
his clothes and said, "Your blood is upon your own
heads—I am innocent. From now on I will go preach
to the Gentiles."

7 Then he left and went to the home of Titius
Justus, a Gentile who worshiped God and lived next
door to the synagogue. 8 Crispus, the leader of the
synagogue, and everyone in his household believed
in the Lord. Many others in Corinth also heard Paul,
became believers, and were baptized.

9 One night the Lord spoke to Paul in a vision and
told him, "Don't be afraid! Speak out! Don't be silent!
10 For I am with you, and no one will attack and harm
you, for many people in this city belong to me." 11 So
Paul stayed there for the next year and a half, teaching the word of God.

12 But when Gallio became governor of Achaia,
some Jews rose up together against Paul and brought
him before the governor for judgment. 13 They accused Paul of "persuading people to worship God in
ways that are contrary to our law."
14 But just as Paul started to make his defense,
Gallio turned to Paul's accusers and said, "Listen, you
Jews, if this were a case involving some wrongdoing
or a serious crime, I would have a reason to accept
your case. 15 But since it is merely a question of
words and names and your Jewish law, take care of it
yourselves. I refuse to judge such matters." 16 And he
threw them out of the courtroom.

17 The crowd* then grabbed Sosthenes, the leader
of the synagogue, and beat him right there in the
courtroom. But Gallio paid no attention.

Paul Returns to Antioch of Syria

18 Paul stayed in Corinth for some time after that,
then said good-bye to the brothers and sisters* and
went to nearby Cenchrea. There he shaved his head
according to Jewish custom, marking the end of a
vow. Then he set sail for Syria, taking Priscilla and
Aquila with him.
19 They stopped first at the port of Ephesus, where
Paul left the others behind. While he was there, he
went to the synagogue to reason with the Jews.
20 They asked him to stay longer, but he declined.
21 As he left, however, he said, "I will come back later,*
God willing." Then he set sail from Ephesus. 22 The
next stop was at the port of Caesarea. From there he
went up and visited the church at Jerusalem* and
then went back to Antioch.

23 After spending some time in Antioch, Paul went
back through Galatia and Phrygia, visiting and
strengthening all the believers.*

18:17 Greek *Everyone;* other manuscripts read *All the Greeks.* **18:18** Greek *brothers;* also in 18:27. **18:21** Some manuscripts read *"I must by all means be at Jerusalem for the upcoming festival, but I will come back later."* **18:22** Greek *the church.* **18:23** Greek *disciples;* also in 18:27.

KING JAMES VERSION

24 And a certain Jew named Apollos, born at Alexandria, an eloquent man, *and* mighty in the scriptures, came to Ephesus.

25 This man was instructed in the way of the Lord; and being fervent in the spirit, he spake and taught diligently the things of the Lord, knowing only the baptism of John.

26 And he began to speak boldly in the synagogue: whom when Aquila and Priscilla had heard, they took him unto *them,* and expounded unto him the way of God more perfectly.

27 And when he was disposed to pass into Achaia, the brethren wrote, exhorting the disciples to receive him: who, when he was come, helped them much which had believed through grace:

28 For he mightily convinced the Jews, *and that* publickly, shewing by the scriptures that Jesus was Christ.

19

1 And it came to pass, that, while Apollos was at Corinth, Paul having passed through the upper coasts came to Ephesus: and finding certain disciples,

2 He said unto them, Have ye received the Holy Ghost since ye believed? And they said unto him, We have not so much as heard whether there be any Holy Ghost.

3 And he said unto them, Unto what then were ye baptized? And they said, Unto John's baptism.

4 Then said Paul, John verily baptized with the baptism of repentance, saying unto the people, that they should believe on him which should come after him, that is, on Christ Jesus.

5 When they heard *this,* they were baptized in the name of the Lord Jesus.

6 And when Paul had laid *his* hands upon them, the Holy Ghost came on them; and they spake with tongues, and prophesied.

7 And all the men were about twelve.

8 And he went into the synagogue, and spake boldly for the space of three months, disputing and persuading the things concerning the kingdom of God.

9 But when divers were hardened, and believed not, but spake evil of that way before the multitude, he departed from them, and separated the disciples, disputing daily in the school of one Tyrannus.

10 And this continued by the space of two years; so that all they which dwelt in Asia heard the word of the Lord Jesus, both Jews and Greeks.

11 And God wrought special miracles by the hands of Paul:

12 So that from his body were brought unto the sick handkerchiefs or aprons, and the diseases departed from them, and the evil spirits went out of them.

NEW LIVING TRANSLATION

Apollos Instructed at Ephesus

24 Meanwhile, a Jew named Apollos, an eloquent speaker who knew the Scriptures well, had arrived in Ephesus from Alexandria in Egypt. 25 He had been taught the way of the Lord, and he taught others about Jesus with an enthusiastic spirit* and with accuracy. However, he knew only about John's baptism. 26 When Priscilla and Aquila heard him preaching boldly in the synagogue, they took him aside and explained the way of God even more accurately.

27 Apollos had been thinking about going to Achaia, and the brothers and sisters in Ephesus encouraged him to go. They wrote to the believers in Achaia, asking them to welcome him. When he arrived there, he proved to be of great benefit to those who, by God's grace, had believed. 28 He refuted the Jews with powerful arguments in public debate. Using the Scriptures, he explained to them that Jesus was the Messiah.

Paul's Third Missionary Journey

19

While Apollos was in Corinth, Paul traveled through the interior regions until he reached Ephesus, on the coast, where he found several believers.* 2 "Did you receive the Holy Spirit when you believed?" he asked them.

"No," they replied, "we haven't even heard that there is a Holy Spirit."

3 "Then what baptism did you experience?" he asked.

And they replied, "The baptism of John."

4 Paul said, "John's baptism called for repentance from sin. But John himself told the people to believe in the one who would come later, meaning Jesus."

5 As soon as they heard this, they were baptized in the name of the Lord Jesus. 6 Then when Paul laid his hands on them, the Holy Spirit came on them, and they spoke in other tongues* and prophesied. 7 There were about twelve men in all.

Paul Ministers in Ephesus

8 Then Paul went to the synagogue and preached boldly for the next three months, arguing persuasively about the Kingdom of God. 9 But some became stubborn, rejecting his message and publicly speaking against the Way. So Paul left the synagogue and took the believers with him. Then he held daily discussions at the lecture hall of Tyrannus. 10 This went on for the next two years, so that people throughout the province of Asia—both Jews and Greeks—heard the word of the Lord.

11 God gave Paul the power to perform unusual miracles. 12 When handkerchiefs or aprons that had merely touched his skin were placed on sick people, they were healed of their diseases, and evil spirits were expelled.

18:25 Or *with enthusiasm in the Spirit.* **19:1** Greek *disciples;* also in 19:9, 30. **19:6** Or *in other languages.*

KING JAMES VERSION

13 Then certain of the vagabond Jews, exorcists,
took upon them to call over them which had evil
spirits the name of the Lord Jesus, saying, We adjure
you by Jesus whom Paul preacheth.
14 And there were seven sons of *one* Sceva, a Jew,
and chief of the priests, which did so.
15 And the evil spirit answered and said, Jesus I
know, and Paul I know; but who are ye?
16 And the man in whom the evil spirit was leaped
on them, and overcame them, and prevailed against
them, so that they fled out of that house naked and
wounded.
17 And this was known to all the Jews and Greeks
also dwelling at Ephesus; and fear fell on them all,
and the name of the Lord Jesus was magnified.
18 And many that believed came, and confessed,
and shewed their deeds.
19 Many of them also which used curious arts
brought their books together, and burned them before all *men:* and they counted the price of them, and
found *it* fifty thousand *pieces* of silver.
20 So mightily grew the word of God and prevailed.
21 After these things were ended, Paul purposed in
the spirit, when he had passed through Macedonia
and Achaia, to go to Jerusalem, saying, After I have
been there, I must also see Rome.
22 So he sent into Macedonia two of them that
ministered unto him, Timotheus and Erastus; but he
himself stayed in Asia for a season.
23 And the same time there arose no small stir
about that way.
24 For a certain *man* named Demetrius, a silversmith, which made silver shrines for Diana, brought
no small gain unto the craftsmen;
25 Whom he called together with the workmen of
like occupation, and said, Sirs, ye know that by this
craft we have our wealth.
26 Moreover ye see and hear, that not alone at Ephesus, but almost throughout all Asia, this Paul hath
persuaded and turned away much people, saying
that they be no gods, which are made with hands:
27 So that not only this our craft is in danger to be
set at nought; but also that the temple of the great
goddess Diana should be despised, and her magnifi-
cence should be destroyed, whom all Asia and the
world worshippeth.
28 And when they heard *these sayings,* they were
full of wrath, and cried out, saying, Great *is* Diana of
the Ephesians.
29 And the whole city was filled with confusion:
and having caught Gaius and Aristarchus, men of
Macedonia, Paul's companions in travel, they rushed
with one accord into the theatre.
30 And when Paul would have entered in unto the
people, the disciples suffered him not.
31 And certain of the chief of Asia, which were his

NEW LIVING TRANSLATION

13 A group of Jews was traveling from town to town
casting out evil spirits. They tried to use the name of
the Lord Jesus in their incantation, saying, "I command you in the name of Jesus, whom Paul preaches,
to come out!" 14 Seven sons of Sceva, a leading priest,
were doing this. 15 But one time when they tried it,
the evil spirit replied, "I know Jesus, and I know Paul,
but who are you?" 16 Then the man with the evil spirit
leaped on them, overpowered them, and attacked
them with such violence that they fled from the
house, naked and battered.
17 The story of what happened spread quickly all
through Ephesus, to Jews and Greeks alike. A solemn
fear descended on the city, and the name of the Lord
Jesus was greatly honored. 18 Many who became believers confessed their sinful practices. 19 A number
of them who had been practicing sorcery brought
their incantation books and burned them at a public
bonfire. The value of the books was several million
dollars.* 20 So the message about the Lord spread
widely and had a powerful effect.
21 Afterward Paul felt compelled by the Spirit* to
go over to Macedonia and Achaia before going to
Jerusalem. "And after that," he said, "I must go on
to Rome!" 22 He sent his two assistants, Timothy and
Erastus, ahead to Macedonia while he stayed awhile
longer in the province of Asia.

The Riot in Ephesus

23 About that time, serious trouble developed in Ephesus concerning the Way. 24 It began with Demetrius,
a silversmith who had a large business manufactur-
ing silver shrines of the Greek goddess Artemis.*
He kept many craftsmen busy. 25 He called them together, along with others employed in similar trades,
and addressed them as follows:
"Gentlemen, you know that our wealth comes
from this business. 26 But as you have seen and heard,
this man Paul has persuaded many people that hand-
made gods aren't really gods at all. And he's done this
not only here in Ephesus but throughout the entire
province! 27 Of course, I'm not just talking about the
loss of public respect for our business. I'm also concerned that the temple of the great goddess Artemis
will lose its influence and that Artemis—this magnificent goddess worshiped throughout the province of
Asia and all around the world—will be robbed of her
great prestige!"
28 At this their anger boiled, and they began shouting, "Great is Artemis of the Ephesians!" 29 Soon the
whole city was filled with confusion. Everyone
rushed to the amphitheater, dragging along Gaius
and Aristarchus, who were Paul's traveling companions from Macedonia. 30 Paul wanted to go in, too,
but the believers wouldn't let him. 31 Some of the
officials of the province, friends of Paul, also sent a

19:19 Greek *50,000 pieces of silver,* each of which was the equivalent of a day's wage. **19:21** Or *decided in his spirit.* **19:24** *Artemis* is otherwise known as Diana.

KING JAMES VERSION

friends, sent unto him, desiring *him* that he would not adventure himself into the theatre.

[32]Some therefore cried one thing, and some another: for the assembly was confused; and the more part knew not wherefore they were come together.

[33]And they drew Alexander out of the multitude, the Jews putting him forward. And Alexander beckoned with the hand, and would have made his defence unto the people.

[34]But when they knew that he was a Jew, all with one voice about the space of two hours cried out, Great *is* Diana of the Ephesians.

[35]And when the townclerk had appeased the people, he said, *Ye* men of Ephesus, what man is there that knoweth not how that the city of the Ephesians is a worshipper of the great goddess Diana, and of the *image* which fell down from Jupiter?

[36]Seeing then that these things cannot be spoken against, ye ought to be quiet, and to do nothing rashly.

[37]For ye have brought hither these men, which are neither robbers of churches, nor yet blasphemers of your goddess.

[38]Wherefore if Demetrius, and the craftsmen which are with him, have a matter against any man, the law is open, and there are deputies: let them implead one another.

[39]But if ye inquire any thing concerning other matters, it shall be determined in a lawful assembly.

[40]For we are in danger to be called in question for this day's uproar, there being no cause whereby we may give an account of this concourse.

[41]And when he had thus spoken, he dismissed the assembly.

20 [1]And after the uproar was ceased, Paul called unto *him* the disciples, and embraced *them*, and departed for to go into Macedonia.

[2]And when he had gone over those parts, and had given them much exhortation, he came into Greece,

[3]And *there* abode three months. And when the Jews laid wait for him, as he was about to sail into Syria, he purposed to return through Macedonia.

[4]And there accompanied him into Asia Sopater of Berea; and of the Thessalonians, Aristarchus and Secundus; and Gaius of Derbe, and Timotheus; and of Asia, Tychicus and Trophimus.

[5]These going before tarried for us at Troas.

[6]And we sailed away from Philippi after the days of unleavened bread, and came unto them to Troas in five days; where we abode seven days.

[7]And upon the first *day* of the week, when the disciples came together to break bread, Paul preached

NEW LIVING TRANSLATION

message to him, begging him not to risk his life by entering the amphitheater.

[32]Inside, the people were all shouting, some one thing and some another. Everything was in confusion. In fact, most of them didn't even know why they were there. [33]The Jews in the crowd pushed Alexander forward and told him to explain the situation. He motioned for silence and tried to speak. [34]But when the crowd realized he was a Jew, they started shouting again and kept it up for about two hours: "Great is Artemis of the Ephesians! Great is Artemis of the Ephesians!"

[35]At last the mayor was able to quiet them down enough to speak. "Citizens of Ephesus," he said. "Everyone knows that Ephesus is the official guardian of the temple of the great Artemis, whose image fell down to us from heaven. [36]Since this is an undeniable fact, you should stay calm and not do anything rash. [37]You have brought these men here, but they have stolen nothing from the temple and have not spoken against our goddess.

[38]"If Demetrius and the craftsmen have a case against them, the courts are in session and the officials can hear the case at once. Let them make formal charges. [39]And if there are complaints about other matters, they can be settled in a legal assembly. [40]I am afraid we are in danger of being charged with rioting by the Roman government, since there is no cause for all this commotion. And if Rome demands an explanation, we won't know what to say." [41]*Then he dismissed them, and they dispersed.

Paul Goes to Macedonia and Greece

20 When the uproar was over, Paul sent for the believers* and encouraged them. Then he said good-bye and left for Macedonia. [2]While there, he encouraged the believers in all the towns he passed through. Then he traveled down to Greece, [3]where he stayed for three months. He was preparing to sail back to Syria when he discovered a plot by some Jews against his life, so he decided to return through Macedonia.

[4]Several men were traveling with him. They were Sopater son of Pyrrhus from Berea; Aristarchus and Secundus from Thessalonica; Gaius from Derbe; Timothy; and Tychicus and Trophimus from the province of Asia. [5]They went on ahead and waited for us at Troas. [6]After the Passover* ended, we boarded a ship at Philippi in Macedonia and five days later joined them in Troas, where we stayed a week.

Paul's Final Visit to Troas

[7]On the first day of the week, we gathered with the local believers to share in the Lord's Supper.* Paul

19:41 Some translations include verse 41 as part of verse 40. **20:1** Greek *disciples.* **20:6** Greek *the days of unleavened bread.* **20:7** Greek *to break bread.*

KING JAMES VERSION

unto them, ready to depart on the morrow; and continued his speech until midnight.

8And there were many lights in the upper chamber, where they were gathered together.

9And there sat in a window a certain young man named Eutychus, being fallen into a deep sleep: and as Paul was long preaching, he sunk down with sleep, and fell down from the third loft, and was taken up dead.

10And Paul went down, and fell on him, and embracing *him* said, Trouble not yourselves; for his life is in him.

11When he therefore was come up again, and had broken bread, and eaten, and talked a long while, even till break of day, so he departed.

12And they brought the young man alive, and were not a little comforted.

13And we went before to ship, and sailed unto Assos, there intending to take in Paul: for so had he appointed, minding himself to go afoot.

14And when he met with us at Assos, we took him in, and came to Mitylene.

15And we sailed thence, and came the next *day* over against Chios; and the next *day* we arrived at Samos, and tarried at Trogyllium; and the next *day* we came to Miletus.

16For Paul had determined to sail by Ephesus, because he would not spend the time in Asia: for he hasted, if it were possible for him, to be at Jerusalem the day of Pentecost.

17And from Miletus he sent to Ephesus, and called the elders of the church.

18And when they were come to him, he said unto them, Ye know, from the first day that I came into Asia, after what manner I have been with you at all seasons,

19Serving the Lord with all humility of mind, and with many tears, and temptations, which befell me by the lying in wait of the Jews:

20*And* how I kept back nothing that was profitable *unto you,* but have shewed you, and have taught you publickly, and from house to house,

21Testifying both to the Jews, and also to the Greeks, repentance toward God, and faith toward our Lord Jesus Christ.

22And now, behold, I go bound in the spirit unto Jerusalem, not knowing the things that shall befall me there:

23Save that the Holy Ghost witnesseth in every city, saying that bonds and afflictions abide me.

24But none of these things move me, neither count I my life dear unto myself, so that I might finish my course with joy, and the ministry, which I have received of the Lord Jesus, to testify the gospel of the grace of God.

25And now, behold, I know that ye all, among whom I have gone preaching the kingdom of God, shall see my face no more.

NEW LIVING TRANSLATION

was preaching to them, and since he was leaving the
next day, he kept talking until midnight. 8The upstairs room where we met was lighted with many
flickering lamps. 9As Paul spoke on and on, a young
man named Eutychus, sitting on the windowsill, became very drowsy. Finally, he fell sound asleep and
dropped three stories to his death below. 10Paul went
down, bent over him, and took him into his arms.
"Don't worry," he said, "he's alive!" 11Then they all
went back upstairs, shared in the Lord's Supper,* and
ate together. Paul continued talking to them until
dawn, and then he left. 12Meanwhile, the young
man was taken home unhurt, and everyone was
greatly relieved.

Paul Meets the Ephesian Elders

13Paul went by land to Assos, where he had arranged
for us to join him, while we traveled by ship. 14He
joined us there, and we sailed together to Mitylene.
15The next day we sailed past the island of Kios. The
following day we crossed to the island of Samos,
and* a day later we arrived at Miletus.

16Paul had decided to sail on past Ephesus, for he
didn't want to spend any more time in the province
of Asia. He was hurrying to get to Jerusalem, if possible, in time for the Festival of Pentecost. 17But when
we landed at Miletus, he sent a message to the elders
of the church at Ephesus, asking them to come and
meet him.

18When they arrived he declared, "You know that
from the day I set foot in the province of Asia until
now 19I have done the Lord's work humbly and with
many tears. I have endured the trials that came to
me from the plots of the Jews. 20I never shrank back
from telling you what you needed to hear, either
publicly or in your homes. 21I have had one message
for Jews and Greeks alike—the necessity of repenting
from sin and turning to God, and of having faith in
our Lord Jesus.

22"And now I am bound by the Spirit* to go to Jerusalem. I don't know what awaits me, 23except that
the Holy Spirit tells me in city after city that jail and
suffering lie ahead. 24But my life is worth nothing to
me unless I use it for finishing the work assigned me
by the Lord Jesus—the work of telling others the
Good News about the wonderful grace of God.

25"And now I know that none of you to whom I
have preached the Kingdom will ever see me again.

20:11 Greek *broke the bread.* **20:15** Some manuscripts read *and having stayed at Trogyllium.* **20:22** Or *by my spirit,* or *by an inner compulsion;* Greek reads *by the spirit.*

KING JAMES VERSION

26 Wherefore I take you to record this day, that I
am pure from the blood of all *men*.
27 For I have not shunned to declare unto you all
the counsel of God.
28 Take heed therefore unto yourselves, and to all
the flock, over the which the Holy Ghost hath made
you overseers, to feed the church of God, which he
hath purchased with his own blood.
29 For I know this, that after my departing shall
grievous wolves enter in among you, not sparing the
flock.
30 Also of your own selves shall men arise, speaking
perverse things, to draw away disciples after them.
31 Therefore watch, and remember, that by the
space of three years I ceased not to warn every one
night and day with tears.
32 And now, brethren, I commend you to God, and
to the word of his grace, which is able to build you up,
and to give you an inheritance among all them which
are sanctified.
33 I have coveted no man's silver, or gold, or apparel.
34 Yea, ye yourselves know, that these hands have
ministered unto my necessities, and to them that
were with me.
35 I have shewed you all things, how that so labouring ye ought to support the weak, and to remember
the words of the Lord Jesus, how he said, It is more
blessed to give than to receive.
36 And when he had thus spoken, he kneeled down,
and prayed with them all.
37 And they all wept sore, and fell on Paul's neck,
and kissed him,
38 Sorrowing most of all for the words which he
spake, that they should see his face no more. And
they accompanied him unto the ship.

21 1 And it came to pass, that after we were gotten from them, and had launched, we came
with a straight course unto Coos, and the *day* following unto Rhodes, and from thence unto Patara:
2 And finding a ship sailing over unto Phenicia, we
went aboard, and set forth.
3 Now when we had discovered Cyprus, we left it
on the left hand, and sailed into Syria, and landed at
Tyre: for there the ship was to unlade her burden.
4 And finding disciples, we tarried there seven
days: who said to Paul through the Spirit, that he
should not go up to Jerusalem.
5 And when we had accomplished those days, we
departed and went our way; and they all brought us
on our way, with wives and children, till *we were* out
of the city: and we kneeled down on the shore, and
prayed.
6 And when we had taken our leave one of another,
we took ship; and they returned home again.
7 And when we had finished *our* course from Tyre,
we came to Ptolemais, and saluted the brethren, and
abode with them one day.

NEW LIVING TRANSLATION

26 I declare today that I have been faithful. If anyone
suffers eternal death, it's not my fault,* 27 for I didn't
shrink from declaring all that God wants you to
know.
28 "So guard yourselves and God's people. Feed
and shepherd God's flock—his church, purchased
with his own blood*—over which the Holy Spirit has
appointed you as elders.* 29 I know that false teachers, like vicious wolves, will come in among you after
I leave, not sparing the flock. 30 Even some men from
your own group will rise up and distort the truth in
order to draw a following. 31 Watch out! Remember
the three years I was with you—my constant watch
and care over you night and day, and my many tears
for you.
32 "And now I entrust you to God and the message
of his grace that is able to build you up and give
you an inheritance with all those he has set apart for
himself.
33 "I have never coveted anyone's silver or gold or
fine clothes. 34 You know that these hands of mine
have worked to supply my own needs and even the
needs of those who were with me. 35 And I have been
a constant example of how you can help those in
need by working hard. You should remember the
words of the Lord Jesus: 'It is more blessed to give
than to receive.'"
36 When he had finished speaking, he knelt and
prayed with them. 37 They all cried as they embraced
and kissed him good-bye. 38 They were sad most of
all because he had said that they would never see
him again. Then they escorted him down to the ship.

Paul's Journey to Jerusalem

21 After saying farewell to the Ephesian elders,
we sailed straight to the island of Cos. The
next day we reached Rhodes and then went to Patara.
2 There we boarded a ship sailing for Phoenicia. 3 We
sighted the island of Cyprus, passed it on our left, and
landed at the harbor of Tyre, in Syria, where the ship
was to unload its cargo.
4 We went ashore, found the local believers,* and
stayed with them a week. These believers prophesied through the Holy Spirit that Paul should not go
on to Jerusalem. 5 When we returned to the ship at
the end of the week, the entire congregation, including women* and children, left the city and came
down to the shore with us. There we knelt, prayed,
6 and said our farewells. Then we went aboard, and
they returned home.
7 The next stop after leaving Tyre was Ptolemais,
where we greeted the brothers and sisters* and

20:26 Greek *I am innocent of the blood of all.* **20:28a** Or *with the blood of his own [Son].* **20:28b** Greek *overseers.* **21:4** Greek *disciples;* also in 21:16. **21:5** Or *wives.* **21:7** Greek *brothers;* also in 21:17.

KING JAMES VERSION

8 And the next *day* we that were of Paul's company
departed, and came unto Caesarea: and we entered
into the house of Philip the evangelist, which was
one of the seven; and abode with him.
9 And the same man had four daughters, virgins,
which did prophesy.
10 And as we tarried *there* many days, there came
down from Judaea a certain prophet, named Agabus.
11 And when he was come unto us, he took Paul's
girdle, and bound his own hands and feet, and said,
Thus saith the Holy Ghost, So shall the Jews at Jerusalem bind the man that owneth this girdle, and shall
deliver *him* into the hands of the Gentiles.
12 And when we heard these things, both we, and
they of that place, besought him not to go up to
Jerusalem.
13 Then Paul answered, What mean ye to weep and
to break mine heart? for I am ready not to be bound
only, but also to die at Jerusalem for the name of the
Lord Jesus.
14 And when he would not be persuaded, we
ceased, saying, The will of the Lord be done.
15 And after those days we took up our carriages,
and went up to Jerusalem.
16 There went with us also *certain* of the disciples
of Caesarea, and brought with them one Mnason of
Cyprus, an old disciple, with whom we should lodge.
17 And when we were come to Jerusalem, the
brethren received us gladly.
18 And the *day* following Paul went in with us unto
James; and all the elders were present.
19 And when he had saluted them, he declared particularly what things God had wrought among the
Gentiles by his ministry.
20 And when they heard *it,* they glorified the Lord,
and said unto him, Thou seest, brother, how many
thousands of Jews there are which believe; and they
are all zealous of the law:
21 And they are informed of thee, that thou
teachest all the Jews which are among the Gentiles to
forsake Moses, saying that they ought not to circumcise *their* children, neither to walk after the customs.
22 What is it therefore? the multitude must needs
come together: for they will hear that thou art come.
23 Do therefore this that we say to thee: We have
four men which have a vow on them;
24 Them take, and purify thyself with them, and be
at charges with them, that they may shave *their*
heads: and all may know that those things, whereof
they were informed concerning thee, are nothing;
but *that* thou thyself also walkest orderly, and
keepest the law.
25 As touching the Gentiles which believe, we have
written *and* concluded that they observe no such
thing, save only that they keep themselves from
things offered to idols, and from blood, and from
strangled, and from fornication.

NEW LIVING TRANSLATION

stayed for one day. 8 The next day we went on to
Caesarea and stayed at the home of Philip the Evangelist, one of the seven men who had been chosen to
distribute food. 9 He had four unmarried daughters
who had the gift of prophecy.
10 Several days later a man named Agabus, who
also had the gift of prophecy, arrived from Judea.
11 He came over, took Paul's belt, and bound his
own feet and hands with it. Then he said, "The Holy
Spirit declares, 'So shall the owner of this belt be
bound by the Jewish leaders in Jerusalem and
turned over to the Gentiles.'" 12 When we heard this,
we and the local believers all begged Paul not to go
on to Jerusalem.
13 But he said, "Why all this weeping? You are
breaking my heart! I am ready not only to be jailed at
Jerusalem but even to die for the sake of the Lord
Jesus." 14 When it was clear that we couldn't persuade
him, we gave up and said, "The Lord's will be done."

Paul Arrives at Jerusalem

15 After this we packed our things and left for Jerusalem. 16 Some believers from Caesarea accompanied
us, and they took us to the home of Mnason, a man
originally from Cyprus and one of the early believers.
17 When we arrived, the brothers and sisters in Jerusalem welcomed us warmly.
18 The next day Paul went with us to meet with
James, and all the elders of the Jerusalem church
were present. 19 After greeting them, Paul gave a de-
tailed account of the things God had accomplished
among the Gentiles through his ministry.
20 After hearing this, they praised God. And then
they said, "You know, dear brother, how many thousands of Jews have also believed, and they all follow
the law of Moses very seriously. 21 But the Jewish believers here in Jerusalem have been told that you are
teaching all the Jews who live among the Gentiles to
turn their backs on the laws of Moses. They've heard
that you teach them not to circumcise their children
or follow other Jewish customs. 22 What should we
do? They will certainly hear that you have come.
23 "Here's what we want you to do. We have four
men here who have completed their vow. 24 Go with
them to the Temple and join them in the purification
ceremony, paying for them to have their heads ritu-
ally shaved. Then everyone will know that the rumors are all false and that you yourself observe the
Jewish laws.
25 "As for the Gentile believers, they should do
what we already told them in a letter: They should
abstain from eating food offered to idols, from consuming blood or the meat of strangled animals, and
from sexual immorality."

KING JAMES VERSION

26 Then Paul took the men, and the next day purifying himself with them entered into the temple, to signify the accomplishment of the days of purification, until that an offering should be offered for every one of them.

27 And when the seven days were almost ended, the Jews which were of Asia, when they saw him in the temple, stirred up all the people, and laid hands on him,

28 Crying out, Men of Israel, help: This is the man, that teacheth all *men* every where against the people, and the law, and this place: and further brought Greeks also into the temple, and hath polluted this holy place.

29 (For they had seen before with him in the city Trophimus an Ephesian, whom they supposed that Paul had brought into the temple.)

30 And all the city was moved, and the people ran together: and they took Paul, and drew him out of the temple: and forthwith the doors were shut.

31 And as they went about to kill him, tidings came unto the chief captain of the band, that all Jerusalem was in an uproar.

32 Who immediately took soldiers and centurions, and ran down unto them: and when they saw the chief captain and the soldiers, they left beating of Paul.

33 Then the chief captain came near, and took him, and commanded *him* to be bound with two chains; and demanded who he was, and what he had done.

34 And some cried one thing, some another, among the multitude: and when he could not know the certainty for the tumult, he commanded him to be carried into the castle.

35 And when he came upon the stairs, so it was, that he was borne of the soldiers for the violence of the people.

36 For the multitude of the people followed after, crying, Away with him.

37 And as Paul was to be led into the castle, he said unto the chief captain, May I speak unto thee? Who said, Canst thou speak Greek?

38 Art not thou that Egyptian, which before these days madest an uproar, and leddest out into the wilderness four thousand men that were murderers?

39 But Paul said, I am a man *which am* a Jew of Tarsus, *a city* in Cilicia, a citizen of no mean city: and, I beseech thee, suffer me to speak unto the people.

40 And when he had given him licence, Paul stood on the stairs, and beckoned with the hand unto the people. And when there was made a great silence, he spake unto *them* in the Hebrew tongue, saying,

22 1 Men, brethren, and fathers, hear ye my defence *which I make* now unto you.

2 (And when they heard that he spake in the Hebrew

NEW LIVING TRANSLATION

Paul Is Arrested

26 So Paul went to the Temple the next day with the other men. They had already started the purification ritual, so he publicly announced the date when their vows would end and sacrifices would be offered for each of them.

27 The seven days were almost ended when some Jews from the province of Asia saw Paul in the Temple and roused a mob against him. They grabbed him, 28 yelling, "Men of Israel, help us! This is the man who preaches against our people everywhere and tells everybody to disobey the Jewish laws. He speaks against the Temple—and even defiles this holy place by bringing in Gentiles.*" 29 (For earlier that day they had seen him in the city with Trophimus, a Gentile from Ephesus,* and they assumed Paul had taken him into the Temple.)

30 The whole city was rocked by these accusations, and a great riot followed. Paul was grabbed and dragged out of the Temple, and immediately the gates were closed behind him. 31 As they were trying to kill him, word reached the commander of the Roman regiment that all Jerusalem was in an uproar. 32 He immediately called out his soldiers and officers* and ran down among the crowd. When the mob saw the commander and the troops coming, they stopped beating Paul.

33 Then the commander arrested him and ordered him bound with two chains. He asked the crowd who he was and what he had done. 34 Some shouted one thing and some another. Since he couldn't find out the truth in all the uproar and confusion, he ordered that Paul be taken to the fortress. 35 As Paul reached the stairs, the mob grew so violent the soldiers had to lift him to their shoulders to protect him. 36 And the crowd followed behind, shouting, "Kill him, kill him!"

Paul Speaks to the Crowd

37 As Paul was about to be taken inside, he said to the commander, "May I have a word with you?"

"Do you know Greek?" the commander asked, surprised. 38 "Aren't you the Egyptian who led a rebellion some time ago and took 4,000 members of the Assassins out into the desert?"

39 "No," Paul replied, "I am a Jew and a citizen of Tarsus in Cilicia, which is an important city. Please, let me talk to these people." 40 The commander agreed, so Paul stood on the stairs and motioned to the people to be quiet. Soon a deep silence enveloped the crowd, and he addressed them in their own language, Aramaic.*

22 "Brothers and esteemed fathers," Paul said, "listen to me as I offer my defense." 2 When

21:28 Greek *Greeks.* 21:29 Greek *Trophimus, the Ephesian.* 21:32 Greek *centurions.* 21:40 Or *Hebrew.*

KING JAMES VERSION

tongue to them, they kept the more silence: and he saith,)

3 I am verily a man *which am* a Jew, born in Tarsus, *a city* in Cilicia, yet brought up in this city at the feet of Gamaliel, *and* taught according to the perfect manner of the law of the fathers, and was zealous toward God, as ye all are this day.

4 And I persecuted this way unto the death, binding and delivering into prisons both men and women.

5 As also the high priest doth bear me witness, and all the estate of the elders: from whom also I received letters unto the brethren, and went to Damascus, to bring them which were there bound unto Jerusalem, for to be punished.

6 And it came to pass, that, as I made my journey, and was come nigh unto Damascus about noon, suddenly there shone from heaven a great light round about me.

7 And I fell unto the ground, and heard a voice saying unto me, Saul, Saul, why persecutest thou me?

8 And I answered, Who art thou, Lord? And he said unto me, I am Jesus of Nazareth, whom thou persecutest.

9 And they that were with me saw indeed the light, and were afraid; but they heard not the voice of him that spake to me.

10 And I said, What shall I do, Lord? And the Lord said unto me, Arise, and go into Damascus; and there it shall be told thee of all things which are appointed for thee to do.

11 And when I could not see for the glory of that light, being led by the hand of them that were with me, I came into Damascus.

12 And one Ananias, a devout man according to the law, having a good report of all the Jews which dwelt *there,*

13 Came unto me, and stood, and said unto me, Brother Saul, receive thy sight. And the same hour I looked up upon him.

14 And he said, The God of our fathers hath chosen thee, that thou shouldest know his will, and see that Just One, and shouldest hear the voice of his mouth.

15 For thou shalt be his witness unto all men of what thou hast seen and heard.

16 And now why tarriest thou? arise, and be baptized, and wash away thy sins, calling on the name of the Lord.

17 And it came to pass, that, when I was come again to Jerusalem, even while I prayed in the temple, I was in a trance;

18 And saw him saying unto me, Make haste, and get thee quickly out of Jerusalem: for they will not receive thy testimony concerning me.

19 And I said, Lord, they know that I imprisoned and beat in every synagogue them that believed on thee:

20 And when the blood of thy martyr Stephen was

NEW LIVING TRANSLATION

they heard him speaking in their own language,* the silence was even greater.

3 Then Paul said, "I am a Jew, born in Tarsus, a city
in Cilicia, and I was brought up and educated here in
Jerusalem under Gamaliel. As his student, I was carefully trained in our Jewish laws and customs. I became very zealous to honor God in everything I did,
just like all of you today.
4 And I persecuted the fol-
lowers of the Way, hounding some to death, arresting
both men and women and throwing them in prison.
5 The high priest and the whole council of elders can
testify that this is so. For I received letters from them
to our Jewish brothers in Damascus, authorizing me
to bring the Christians from there to Jerusalem, in
chains, to be punished.

6 "As I was on the road, approaching Damascus
about noon, a very bright light from heaven suddenly
shone down around me.
7 I fell to the ground and
heard a voice saying to me, 'Saul, Saul, why are you
persecuting me?'

8 "'Who are you, lord?' I asked.

"And the voice replied, 'I am Jesus the Nazarene,*
the one you are persecuting.'
9 The people with me
saw the light but didn't understand the voice speaking to me.

10 "I asked, 'What should I do, Lord?'

"And the Lord told me, 'Get up and go into Damascus, and there you will be told everything you are to do.'

11 "I was blinded by the intense light and had to be
led by the hand to Damascus by my companions.
12 A
man named Ananias lived there. He was a godly man,
deeply devoted to the law, and well regarded by all
the Jews of Damascus.
13 He came and stood beside
me and said, 'Brother Saul, regain your sight.' And
that very moment I could see him!

14 "Then he told me, 'The God of our ancestors has
chosen you to know his will and to see the Righteous
One and hear him speak.
15 For you are to be his wit-
ness, telling everyone what you have seen and heard.
16 What are you waiting for? Get up and be baptized.
Have your sins washed away by calling on the name
of the Lord.'

17 "After I returned to Jerusalem, I was praying in
the Temple and fell into a trance.
18 I saw a vision of
Jesus* saying to me, 'Hurry! Leave Jerusalem, for the
people here won't accept your testimony about me.'

19 "'But Lord,' I argued, 'they certainly know that in
every synagogue I imprisoned and beat those who
believed in you.
20 And I was in complete agreement

22:2 Greek *in Aramaic,* or *in Hebrew.* 22:8 Or *Jesus of Nazareth.*
22:18 Greek *him.*

KING JAMES VERSION

shed, I also was standing by, and consenting unto his death, and kept the raiment of them that slew him.

21 And he said unto me, Depart: for I will send thee far hence unto the Gentiles.

22 And they gave him audience unto this word, and *then* lifted up their voices, and said, Away with such a *fellow* from the earth: for it is not fit that he should live.

23 And as they cried out, and cast off *their* clothes, and threw dust into the air,

24 The chief captain commanded him to be brought into the castle, and bade that he should be examined by scourging; that he might know wherefore they cried so against him.

25 And as they bound him with thongs, Paul said unto the centurion that stood by, Is it lawful for you to scourge a man that is a Roman, and uncondemned?

26 When the centurion heard *that,* he went and told the chief captain, saying, Take heed what thou doest: for this man is a Roman.

27 Then the chief captain came, and said unto him, Tell me, art thou a Roman? He said, Yea.

28 And the chief captain answered, With a great sum obtained I this freedom. And Paul said, But I was *free* born.

29 Then straightway they departed from him which should have examined him: and the chief captain also was afraid, after he knew that he was a Roman, and because he had bound him.

30 On the morrow, because he would have known the certainty wherefore he was accused of the Jews, he loosed him from *his* bands, and commanded the chief priests and all their council to appear, and brought Paul down, and set him before them.

23

1 And Paul, earnestly beholding the council, said, Men *and* brethren, I have lived in all good conscience before God until this day.

2 And the high priest Ananias commanded them that stood by him to smite him on the mouth.

3 Then said Paul unto him, God shall smite thee, *thou* whited wall: for sittest thou to judge me after the law, and commandest me to be smitten contrary to the law?

4 And they that stood by said, Revilest thou God's high priest?

5 Then said Paul, I wist not, brethren, that he was the high priest: for it is written, Thou shalt not speak evil of the ruler of thy people.

6 But when Paul perceived that the one part were Sadducees, and the other Pharisees, he cried out in the council, Men *and* brethren, I am a Pharisee, the son of a Pharisee: of the hope and resurrection of the dead I am called in question.

NEW LIVING TRANSLATION

when your witness Stephen was killed. I stood by and kept the coats they took off when they stoned him.'

21 "But the Lord said to me, 'Go, for I will send you far away to the Gentiles!'"

22 The crowd listened until Paul said that word. Then they all began to shout, "Away with such a fellow! He isn't fit to live!" 23 They yelled, threw off their coats, and tossed handfuls of dust into the air.

Paul Reveals His Roman Citizenship

24 The commander brought Paul inside and ordered him lashed with whips to make him confess his crime. He wanted to find out why the crowd had become so furious. 25 When they tied Paul down to lash him, Paul said to the officer* standing there, "Is it legal for you to whip a Roman citizen who hasn't even been tried?"

26 When the officer heard this, he went to the commander and asked, "What are you doing? This man is a Roman citizen!"

27 So the commander went over and asked Paul, "Tell me, are you a Roman citizen?"

"Yes, I certainly am," Paul replied.

28 "I am, too," the commander muttered, "and it cost me plenty!"

Paul answered, "But I am a citizen by birth!"

29 The soldiers who were about to interrogate Paul quickly withdrew when they heard he was a Roman citizen, and the commander was frightened because he had ordered him bound and whipped.

Paul before the High Council

30 The next day the commander ordered the leading priests into session with the Jewish high council.* He wanted to find out what the trouble was all about, so he released Paul to have him stand before them.

23

Gazing intently at the high council,* Paul began: "Brothers, I have always lived before God with a clear conscience!"

2 Instantly Ananias the high priest commanded those close to Paul to slap him on the mouth. 3 But Paul said to him, "God will slap you, you corrupt hypocrite!* What kind of judge are you to break the law yourself by ordering me struck like that?"

4 Those standing near Paul said to him, "Do you dare to insult God's high priest?"

5 "I'm sorry, brothers. I didn't realize he was the high priest," Paul replied, "for the Scriptures say, 'You must not speak evil of any of your rulers.'*"

6 Paul realized that some members of the high council were Sadducees and some were Pharisees, so he shouted, "Brothers, I am a Pharisee, as were my ancestors! And I am on trial because my hope is in the resurrection of the dead!"

22:25 Greek *the centurion;* also in 22:26. **22:30** Greek *Sanhedrin.* **23:1** Greek *Sanhedrin;* also in 23:6, 15, 20, 28. **23:3** Greek *you whitewashed wall.* **23:5** Exod 22:28.

KING JAMES VERSION

7And when he had so said, there arose a dissension between the Pharisees and the Sadducees: and
the multitude was divided.
8For the Sadducees say that there is no resurrection, neither angel, nor spirit: but the Pharisees confess both.
9And there arose a great cry: and the scribes *that*
were of the Pharisees' part arose, and strove, saying,
We find no evil in this man: but if a spirit or an angel
hath spoken to him, let us not fight against God.
10And when there arose a great dissension, the
chief captain, fearing lest Paul should have been
pulled in pieces of them, commanded the soldiers to
go down, and to take him by force from among them,
and to bring *him* into the castle.
11And the night following the Lord stood by him,
and said, Be of good cheer, Paul: for as thou hast testified of me in Jerusalem, so must thou bear witness
also at Rome.
12And when it was day, certain of the Jews banded
together, and bound themselves under a curse, saying that they would neither eat nor drink till they had
killed Paul.
13And they were more than forty which had made
this conspiracy.
14And they came to the chief priests and elders, and
said, We have bound ourselves under a great curse,
that we will eat nothing until we have slain Paul.
15Now therefore ye with the council signify to
the chief captain that he bring him down unto you
tomorrow, as though ye would inquire something
more perfectly concerning him: and we, or ever he
come near, are ready to kill him.
16And when Paul's sister's son heard of their lying
in wait, he went and entered into the castle, and told
Paul.
17Then Paul called one of the centurions unto
him, and said, Bring this young man unto the chief
captain: for he hath a certain thing to tell him.
18So he took him, and brought *him* to the chief
captain, and said, Paul the prisoner called me unto
him, and prayed me to bring this young man unto
thee, who hath something to say unto thee.
19Then the chief captain took him by the hand,
and went *with him* aside privately, and asked *him,*
What is that thou hast to tell me?
20And he said, The Jews have agreed to desire thee
that thou wouldest bring down Paul tomorrow into
the council, as though they would inquire somewhat
of him more perfectly.
21But do not thou yield unto them: for there lie in
wait for him of them more than forty men, which
have bound themselves with an oath, that they will
neither eat nor drink till they have killed him: and
now are they ready, looking for a promise from thee.
22So the chief captain *then* let the young man depart, and charged *him, See thou* tell no man that thou
hast shewed these things to me.

NEW LIVING TRANSLATION

7This divided the council—the Pharisees against
the Sadducees—8for the Sadducees say there is no
resurrection or angels or spirits, but the Pharisees
believe in all of these. 9So there was a great uproar.
Some of the teachers of religious law who were
Pharisees jumped up and began to argue forcefully.
"We see nothing wrong with him," they shouted.
"Perhaps a spirit or an angel spoke to him." 10As the
conflict grew more violent, the commander was
afraid they would tear Paul apart. So he ordered his
soldiers to go and rescue him by force and take him
back to the fortress.
11That night the Lord appeared to Paul and said,
"Be encouraged, Paul. Just as you have been a witness
to me here in Jerusalem, you must preach the Good
News in Rome as well."

The Plan to Kill Paul

12The next morning a group of Jews* got together
and bound themselves with an oath not to eat or
drink until they had killed Paul. 13There were more
than forty of them in the conspiracy. 14They went to
the leading priests and elders and told them, "We
have bound ourselves with an oath to eat nothing until we have killed Paul. 15So you and the high council
should ask the commander to bring Paul back to the
council again. Pretend you want to examine his case
more fully. We will kill him on the way."
16But Paul's nephew—his sister's son—heard of
their plan and went to the fortress and told Paul.
17Paul called for one of the Roman officers* and said,
"Take this young man to the commander. He has
something important to tell him."
18So the officer did, explaining, "Paul, the prisoner, called me over and asked me to bring this
young man to you because he has something to tell
you."
19The commander took his hand, led him aside,
and asked, "What is it you want to tell me?"
20Paul's nephew told him, "Some Jews are going to
ask you to bring Paul before the high council tomorrow, pretending they want to get some more information. 21But don't do it! There are more than forty
men hiding along the way ready to ambush him.
They have vowed not to eat or drink anything until
they have killed him. They are ready now, just waiting
for your consent."
22"Don't let anyone know you told me this," the
commander warned the young man.

23:12 Greek *the Jews.* 23:17 Greek *centurions;* also in 23:23.

KING JAMES VERSION

23And he called unto *him* two centurions, saying, Make ready two hundred soldiers to go to Caesarea, and horsemen threescore and ten, and spearmen two hundred, at the third hour of the night;

24And provide *them* beasts, that they may set Paul on, and bring *him* safe unto Felix the governor.

25And he wrote a letter after this manner:

26Claudius Lysias unto the most excellent governor Felix *sendeth* greeting.

27This man was taken of the Jews, and should have been killed of them: then came I with an army, and rescued him, having understood that he was a Roman.

28And when I would have known the cause wherefore they accused him, I brought him forth into their council:

29Whom I perceived to be accused of questions of their law, but to have nothing laid to his charge worthy of death or of bonds.

30And when it was told me how that the Jews laid wait for the man, I sent straightway to thee, and gave commandment to his accusers also to say before thee what *they had* against him. Farewell.

31Then the soldiers, as it was commanded them, took Paul, and brought *him* by night to Antipatris.

32On the morrow they left the horsemen to go with him, and returned to the castle:

33Who, when they came to Caesarea, and delivered the epistle to the governor, presented Paul also before him.

34And when the governor had read *the letter*, he asked of what province he was. And when he understood that *he was* of Cilicia;

35I will hear thee, said he, when thine accusers are also come. And he commanded him to be kept in Herod's judgment hall.

24 1And after five days Ananias the high priest descended with the elders, and *with* a certain orator *named* Tertullus, who informed the governor against Paul.

2And when he was called forth, Tertullus began to accuse *him*, saying, Seeing that by thee we enjoy great quietness, and that very worthy deeds are done unto this nation by thy providence,

3We accept *it* always, and in all places, most noble Felix, with all thankfulness.

4Notwithstanding, that I be not further tedious unto thee, I pray thee that thou wouldest hear us of thy clemency a few words.

5For we have found this man *a* pestilent *fellow*, and a mover of sedition among all the Jews throughout the world, and a ringleader of the sect of the Nazarenes:

6Who also hath gone about to profane the temple: whom we took, and would have judged according to our law.

NEW LIVING TRANSLATION

Paul Is Sent to Caesarea

23Then the commander called two of his officers and
ordered, "Get 200 soldiers ready to leave for Caesarea at nine o'clock tonight. Also take 200 spearmen
and 70 mounted troops. 24Provide horses for Paul to
ride, and get him safely to Governor Felix." 25Then he
wrote this letter to the governor:

26"From Claudius Lysias, to his Excellency,
Governor Felix: Greetings!

27"This man was seized by some Jews, and they
were about to kill him when I arrived with the
troops. When I learned that he was a Roman
citizen, I removed him to safety. 28Then I took
him to their high council to try to learn the
basis of the accusations against him. 29I soon
discovered the charge was something regarding
their religious law—certainly nothing worthy
of imprisonment or death. 30But when I was
informed of a plot to kill him, I immediately sent
him on to you. I have told his accusers to bring
their charges before you."

31So that night, as ordered, the soldiers took Paul
as far as Antipatris. 32They returned to the fortress
the next morning, while the mounted troops took
him on to Caesarea. 33When they arrived in Caesarea, they presented Paul and the letter to Governor
Felix. 34He read it and then asked Paul what province
he was from. "Cilicia," Paul answered.

35"I will hear your case myself when your accusers
arrive," the governor told him. Then the governor
ordered him kept in the prison at Herod's headquarters.*

Paul Appears before Felix

24 Five days later Ananias, the high priest, arrived with some of the Jewish elders and the
lawyer* Tertullus, to present their case against Paul
to the governor. 2When Paul was called in, Tertullus
presented the charges against Paul in the following
address to the governor:

"You have provided a long period of peace for us
Jews and with foresight have enacted reforms for us.
3For all of this, Your Excellency, we are very grateful
to you. 4But I don't want to bore you, so please give
me your attention for only a moment. 5We have
found this man to be a troublemaker who is constantly stirring up riots among the Jews all over the
world. He is a ringleader of the cult known as the
Nazarenes. 6Furthermore, he was trying to desecrate

23:35 Greek *Herod's Praetorium.* **24:1** Greek *some elders and an orator.*

KING JAMES VERSION

7 But the chief captain Lysias came *upon us,* and with great violence took *him* away out of our hands,

8 Commanding his accusers to come unto thee: by examining of whom thyself mayest take knowledge of all these things, whereof we accuse him.

9 And the Jews also assented, saying that these things were so.

10 Then Paul, after that the governor had beckoned unto him to speak, answered, Forasmuch as I know that thou hast been of many years a judge unto this nation, I do the more cheerfully answer for myself:

11 Because that thou mayest understand, that there are yet but twelve days since I went up to Jerusalem for to worship.

12 And they neither found me in the temple disputing with any man, neither raising up the people, neither in the synagogues, nor in the city:

13 Neither can they prove the things whereof they now accuse me.

14 But this I confess unto thee, that after the way which they call heresy, so worship I the God of my fathers, believing all things which are written in the law and in the prophets:

15 And have hope toward God, which they themselves also allow, that there shall be a resurrection of the dead, both of the just and unjust.

16 And herein do I exercise myself, to have always a conscience void of offence toward God, and *toward* men.

17 Now after many years I came to bring alms to my nation, and offerings.

18 Whereupon certain Jews from Asia found me purified in the temple, neither with multitude, nor with tumult.

19 Who ought to have been here before thee, and object, if they had aught against me.

20 Or else let these same *here* say, if they have found any evil doing in me, while I stood before the council,

21 Except it be for this one voice, that I cried standing among them, Touching the resurrection of the dead I am called in question by you this day.

22 And when Felix heard these things, having more perfect knowledge of *that* way, he deferred them, and said, When Lysias the chief captain shall come down, I will know the uttermost of your matter.

23 And he commanded a centurion to keep Paul, and to let *him* have liberty, and that he should forbid none of his acquaintance to minister or come unto him.

24 And after certain days, when Felix came with his wife Drusilla, which was a Jewess, he sent for Paul, and heard him concerning the faith in Christ.

25 And as he reasoned of righteousness, temperance, and judgment to come, Felix trembled, and answered, Go thy way for this time; when I have a convenient season, I will call for thee.

NEW LIVING TRANSLATION

the Temple when we arrested him.* 8 You can find
out the truth of our accusations by examining him
yourself." 9 Then the other Jews chimed in, declaring
that everything Tertullus said was true.

10 The governor then motioned for Paul to speak.
Paul said, "I know, sir, that you have been a judge of
Jewish affairs for many years, so I gladly present my
defense before you. 11 You can quickly discover that I
arrived in Jerusalem no more than twelve days ago to
worship at the Temple. 12 My accusers never found
me arguing with anyone in the Temple, nor stirring
up a riot in any synagogue or on the streets of the
city. 13 These men cannot prove the things they accuse me of doing.

14 "But I admit that I follow the Way, which they
call a cult. I worship the God of our ancestors, and I
firmly believe the Jewish law and everything written
in the prophets. 15 I have the same hope in God that
these men have, that he will raise both the righteous
and the unrighteous. 16 Because of this, I always try
to maintain a clear conscience before God and all
people.

17 "After several years away, I returned to Jerusalem with money to aid my people and to offer sacrifices to God. 18 My accusers saw me in the Temple as
I was completing a purification ceremony. There
was no crowd around me and no rioting. 19 But some
Jews from the province of Asia were there—and they
ought to be here to bring charges if they have anything against me! 20 Ask these men here what crime
the Jewish high council* found me guilty of, 21 except for the one time I shouted out, 'I am on trial before you today because I believe in the resurrection
of the dead!'"

22 At that point Felix, who was quite familiar with
the Way, adjourned the hearing and said, "Wait until
Lysias, the garrison commander, arrives. Then I will
decide the case." 23 He ordered an officer* to keep
Paul in custody but to give him some freedom and
allow his friends to visit him and take care of his
needs.

24 A few days later Felix came back with his wife,
Drusilla, who was Jewish. Sending for Paul, they listened as he told them about faith in Christ Jesus.
25 As he reasoned with them about righteousness and
self-control and the coming day of judgment, Felix
became frightened. "Go away for now," he replied.
"When it is more convenient, I'll call for you again."

24:6 Some manuscripts add an expanded conclusion to verse 6, all of verse 7, and an additional phrase in verse 8: *We would have judged him by our law, [7]but Lysias, the commander of the garrison, came and violently took him away from us, [8]commanding his accusers to come before you.* **24:20** Greek *Sanhedrin.* **24:23** Greek *a centurion.*

KING JAMES VERSION

26He hoped also that money should have been
given him of Paul, that he might loose him: wherefore he sent for him the oftener, and communed
with him.
27But after two years Porcius Festus came into
Felix' room: and Felix, willing to shew the Jews a
pleasure, left Paul bound.

25 1Now when Festus was come into the province, after three days he ascended from
Caesarea to Jerusalem.
2Then the high priest and the chief of the Jews
informed him against Paul, and besought him,
3And desired favour against him, that he would
send for him to Jerusalem, laying wait in the way to
kill him.
4But Festus answered, that Paul should be kept at
Caesarea, and that he himself would depart shortly
thither.
5Let them therefore, said he, which among you are
able, go down with *me,* and accuse this man, if there
be any wickedness in him.
6And when he had tarried among them more than
ten days, he went down unto Caesarea; and the next
day sitting on the judgment seat commanded Paul
to be brought.
7And when he was come, the Jews which came
down from Jerusalem stood round about, and laid
many and grievous complaints against Paul, which
they could not prove.
8While he answered for himself, Neither against
the law of the Jews, neither against the temple, nor
yet against Caesar, have I offended any thing at all.
9But Festus, willing to do the Jews a pleasure, answered Paul, and said, Wilt thou go up to Jerusalem,
and there be judged of these things before me?
10Then said Paul, I stand at Caesar's judgment seat,
where I ought to be judged: to the Jews have I done
no wrong, as thou very well knowest.
11For if I be an offender, or have committed any
thing worthy of death, I refuse not to die: but if there
be none of these things whereof these accuse me, no
man may deliver me unto them. I appeal unto Caesar.
12Then Festus, when he had conferred with the
council, answered, Hast thou appealed unto Caesar?
unto Caesar shalt thou go.
13And after certain days king Agrippa and Bernice
came unto Caesarea to salute Festus.
14And when they had been there many days, Festus declared Paul's cause unto the king, saying, There
is a certain man left in bonds by Felix:
15About whom, when I was at Jerusalem, the chief
priests and the elders of the Jews informed *me,* desiring *to have* judgment against him.
16To whom I answered, It is not the manner of the
Romans to deliver any man to die, before that he
which is accused have the accusers face to face, and

NEW LIVING TRANSLATION

26He also hoped that Paul would bribe him, so he
sent for him quite often and talked with him.
27After two years went by in this way, Felix was
succeeded by Porcius Festus. And because Felix
wanted to gain favor with the Jewish people, he left
Paul in prison.

Paul Appears before Festus

25 Three days after Festus arrived in Caesarea
to take over his new responsibilities, he left
for Jerusalem, 2where the leading priests and other
Jewish leaders met with him and made their accusations against Paul. 3They asked Festus as a favor to
transfer Paul to Jerusalem (planning to ambush and
kill him on the way). 4But Festus replied that Paul was
at Caesarea and he himself would be returning there
soon. 5So he said, "Those of you in authority can return with me. If Paul has done anything wrong, you
can make your accusations."
6About eight or ten days later Festus returned to
Caesarea, and on the following day he took his seat in
court and ordered that Paul be brought in. 7When
Paul arrived, the Jewish leaders from Jerusalem gathered around and made many serious accusations
they couldn't prove.
8Paul denied the charges. "I am not guilty of any
crime against the Jewish laws or the Temple or the
Roman government," he said.
9Then Festus, wanting to please the Jews, asked
him, "Are you willing to go to Jerusalem and stand
trial before me there?"
10But Paul replied, "No! This is the official Roman
court, so I ought to be tried right here. You know very
well I am not guilty of harming the Jews. 11If I have
done something worthy of death, I don't refuse to
die. But if I am innocent, no one has a right to turn
me over to these men to kill me. I appeal to Caesar!"
12Festus conferred with his advisers and then replied, "Very well! You have appealed to Caesar, and to
Caesar you will go!"
13A few days later King Agrippa arrived with his
sister, Bernice,* to pay their respects to Festus.
14During their stay of several days, Festus discussed
Paul's case with the king. "There is a prisoner here,"
he told him, "whose case was left for me by Felix.
15When I was in Jerusalem, the leading priests and
Jewish elders pressed charges against him and asked
me to condemn him. 16I pointed out to them that
Roman law does not convict people without a trial.

25:13 Greek *Agrippa the king and Bernice arrived.*

have licence to answer for himself concerning the
crime laid against him.
17 Therefore, when they were come hither, without
any delay on the morrow I sat on the judgment seat,
and commanded the man to be brought forth.
18 Against whom when the accusers stood up, they
brought none accusation of such things as I supposed:
19 But had certain questions against him of their
own superstition, and of one Jesus, which was dead,
whom Paul affirmed to be alive.
20 And because I doubted of such manner of questions, I asked *him* whether he would go to Jerusalem,
and there be judged of these matters.
21 But when Paul had appealed to be reserved unto
the hearing of Augustus, I commanded him to be
kept till I might send him to Caesar.
22 Then Agrippa said unto Festus, I would also hear
the man myself. Tomorrow, said he, thou shalt hear
him.
23 And on the morrow, when Agrippa was come,
and Bernice, with great pomp, and was entered into
the place of hearing, with the chief captains, and
principal men of the city, at Festus' commandment
Paul was brought forth.
24 And Festus said, King Agrippa, and all men
which are here present with us, ye see this man,
about whom all the multitude of the Jews have dealt
with me, both at Jerusalem, and *also* here, crying that
he ought not to live any longer.
25 But when I found that he had committed nothing worthy of death, and that he himself hath appealed to Augustus, I have determined to send him.
26 Of whom I have no certain thing to write unto my
lord. Wherefore I have brought him forth before you,
and specially before thee, O king Agrippa, that, after
examination had, I might have somewhat to write.
27 For it seemeth to me unreasonable to send a
prisoner, and not withal to signify the crimes *laid*
against him.

26 1 Then Agrippa said unto Paul, Thou art permitted to speak for thyself. Then Paul
stretched forth the hand, and answered for himself:
2 I think myself happy, king Agrippa, because I
shall answer for myself this day before thee touching
all the things whereof I am accused of the Jews:
3 Especially *because I know* thee to be expert in all
customs and questions which are among the Jews:
wherefore I beseech thee to hear me patiently.
4 My manner of life from my youth, which was at
the first among mine own nation at Jerusalem, know
all the Jews;
5 Which knew me from the beginning, if they
would testify, that after the most straitest sect of our
religion I lived a Pharisee.
6 And now I stand and am judged for the hope of
the promise made of God unto our fathers:

They must be given an opportunity to confront their
accusers and defend themselves.
17 "When his accusers came here for the trial, I
didn't delay. I called the case the very next day and
ordered Paul brought in. 18 But the accusations made
against him weren't any of the crimes I expected.
19 Instead, it was something about their religion and
a dead man named Jesus, who Paul insists is alive. 20 I
was at a loss to know how to investigate these things,
so I asked him whether he would be willing to stand
trial on these charges in Jerusalem. 21 But Paul appealed to have his case decided by the emperor. So
I ordered that he be held in custody until I could
arrange to send him to Caesar."
22 "I'd like to hear the man myself," Agrippa said.
And Festus replied, "You will—tomorrow!"

Paul Speaks to Agrippa

23 So the next day Agrippa and Bernice arrived at the
auditorium with great pomp, accompanied by military officers and prominent men of the city. Festus
ordered that Paul be brought in. 24 Then Festus said,
"King Agrippa and all who are here, this is the man
whose death is demanded by all the Jews, both here
and in Jerusalem. 25 But in my opinion he has done
nothing deserving death. However, since he appealed his case to the emperor, I have decided to
send him to Rome.
26 "But what shall I write the emperor? For there is
no clear charge against him. So I have brought him
before all of you, and especially you, King Agrippa, so
that after we examine him, I might have something
to write. 27 For it makes no sense to send a prisoner to
the emperor without specifying the charges against
him!"

26 Then Agrippa said to Paul, "You may speak
in your defense."
So Paul, gesturing with his hand, started his defense: 2 "I am fortunate, King Agrippa, that you are
the one hearing my defense today against all these
accusations made by the Jewish leaders, 3 for I know
you are an expert on all Jewish customs and controversies. Now please listen to me patiently!
4 "As the Jewish leaders are well aware, I was given
a thorough Jewish training from my earliest childhood among my own people and in Jerusalem. 5 If
they would admit it, they know that I have been a
member of the Pharisees, the strictest sect of our religion. 6 Now I am on trial because of my hope in the
fulfillment of God's promise made to our ancestors.

KING JAMES VERSION

7 Unto which *promise* our twelve tribes, instantly serving *God* day and night, hope to come. For which hope's sake, king Agrippa, I am accused of the Jews.

8 Why should it be thought a thing incredible with you, that God should raise the dead?

9 I verily thought with myself, that I ought to do many things contrary to the name of Jesus of Nazareth.

10 Which thing I also did in Jerusalem: and many of the saints did I shut up in prison, having received authority from the chief priests; and when they were put to death, I gave my voice against *them*.

11 And I punished them oft in every synagogue, and compelled *them* to blaspheme; and being exceedingly mad against them, I persecuted *them* even unto strange cities.

12 Whereupon as I went to Damascus with authority and commission from the chief priests,

13 At midday, O king, I saw in the way a light from heaven, above the brightness of the sun, shining round about me and them which journeyed with me.

14 And when we were all fallen to the earth, I heard a voice speaking unto me, and saying in the Hebrew tongue, Saul, Saul, why persecutest thou me? *it is* hard for thee to kick against the pricks.

15 And I said, Who art thou, Lord? And he said, I am Jesus whom thou persecutest.

16 But rise, and stand upon thy feet: for I have appeared unto thee for this purpose, to make thee a minister and a witness both of these things which thou hast seen, and of those things in the which I will appear unto thee;

17 Delivering thee from the people, and *from* the Gentiles, unto whom now I send thee,

18 To open their eyes, *and* to turn *them* from darkness to light, and *from* the power of Satan unto God, that they may receive forgiveness of sins, and inheritance among them which are sanctified by faith that is in me.

19 Whereupon, O king Agrippa, I was not disobedient unto the heavenly vision:

20 But shewed first unto them of Damascus, and at Jerusalem, and throughout all the coasts of Judaea, and *then* to the Gentiles, that they should repent and turn to God, and do works meet for repentance.

21 For these causes the Jews caught me in the temple, and went about to kill *me*.

22 Having therefore obtained help of God, I continue unto this day, witnessing both to small and great, saying none other things than those which the prophets and Moses did say should come:

23 That Christ should suffer, *and* that he should be the first that should rise from the dead, and should shew light unto the people, and to the Gentiles.

24 And as he thus spake for himself, Festus said with a loud voice, Paul, thou art beside thyself; much learning doth make thee mad.

NEW LIVING TRANSLATION

7 In fact, that is why the twelve tribes of Israel zealously worship God night and day, and they share the
same hope I have. Yet, Your Majesty, they accuse me
for having this hope! 8 Why does it seem incredible
to any of you that God can raise the dead?
9 "I used to believe that I ought to do everything
I could to oppose the very name of Jesus the Nazarene.* 10 Indeed, I did just that in Jerusalem. Authorized by the leading priests, I caused many
believers* there to be sent to prison. And I cast my
vote against them when they were condemned to
death. 11 Many times I had them punished in the synagogues to get them to curse Jesus.* I was so violently opposed to them that I even chased them
down in foreign cities.
12 "One day I was on such a mission to Damascus,
armed with the authority and commission of the
leading priests. 13 About noon, Your Majesty, as I was
on the road, a light from heaven brighter than the
sun shone down on me and my companions. 14 We all
fell down, and I heard a voice saying to me in Aramaic,* 'Saul, Saul, why are you persecuting me? It is useless for you to fight against my will.*'
15 "'Who are you, lord?' I asked.
"And the Lord replied, 'I am Jesus, the one you are
persecuting. 16 Now get to your feet! For I have appeared to you to appoint you as my servant and witness. You are to tell the world what you have seen
and what I will show you in the future. 17 And I will
rescue you from both your own people and the Gentiles. Yes, I am sending you to the Gentiles 18 to open
their eyes, so they may turn from darkness to light
and from the power of Satan to God. Then they will
receive forgiveness for their sins and be given a
place among God's people, who are set apart by faith
in me.'
19 "And so, King Agrippa, I obeyed that vision from
heaven. 20 I preached first to those in Damascus, then
in Jerusalem and throughout all Judea, and also to
the Gentiles, that all must repent of their sins and
turn to God—and prove they have changed by the
good things they do. 21 Some Jews arrested me in the
Temple for preaching this, and they tried to kill me.
22 But God has protected me right up to this present
time so I can testify to everyone, from the least to the
greatest. I teach nothing except what the prophets
and Moses said would happen—23 that the Messiah
would suffer and be the first to rise from the dead,
and in this way announce God's light to Jews and
Gentiles alike."
24 Suddenly, Festus shouted, "Paul, you are insane.
Too much study has made you crazy!"

26:9 Or *Jesus of Nazareth.* **26:10** Greek *many of God's holy people.* **26:11** Greek *to blaspheme.* **26:14a** Or *Hebrew.* **26:14b** Greek *It is hard for you to kick against the oxgoads.*

KING JAMES VERSION

25 But he said, I am not mad, most noble Festus; but speak forth the words of truth and soberness.

26 For the king knoweth of these things, before whom also I speak freely: for I am persuaded that none of these things are hidden from him; for this thing was not done in a corner.

27 King Agrippa, believest thou the prophets? I know that thou believest.

28 Then Agrippa said unto Paul, Almost thou persuadest me to be a Christian.

29 And Paul said, I would to God, that not only thou, but also all that hear me this day, were both almost, and altogether such as I am, except these bonds.

30 And when he had thus spoken, the king rose up, and the governor, and Bernice, and they that sat with them:

31 And when they were gone aside, they talked between themselves, saying, This man doeth nothing worthy of death or of bonds.

32 Then said Agrippa unto Festus, This man might have been set at liberty, if he had not appealed unto Caesar.

27 1 And when it was determined that we should sail into Italy, they delivered Paul and certain other prisoners unto *one* named Julius, a centurion of Augustus' band.

2 And entering into a ship of Adramyttium, we launched, meaning to sail by the coasts of Asia; *one* Aristarchus, a Macedonian of Thessalonica, being with us.

3 And the next *day* we touched at Sidon. And Julius courteously entreated Paul, and gave *him* liberty to go unto his friends to refresh himself.

4 And when we had launched from thence, we sailed under Cyprus, because the winds were contrary.

5 And when we had sailed over the sea of Cilicia and Pamphylia, we came to Myra, *a city* of Lycia.

6 And there the centurion found a ship of Alexandria sailing into Italy; and he put us therein.

7 And when we had sailed slowly many days, and scarce were come over against Cnidus, the wind not suffering us, we sailed under Crete, over against Salmone;

8 And, hardly passing it, came unto a place which is called The Fair Havens; nigh whereunto was the city *of* Lasea.

9 Now when much time was spent, and when sailing was now dangerous, because the fast was now already past, Paul admonished *them*,

NEW LIVING TRANSLATION

25 But Paul replied, "I am not insane, Most Excellent Festus. What I am saying is the sober truth.
26 And King Agrippa knows about these things. I
speak boldly, for I am sure these events are all familiar to him, for they were not done in a corner! 27 King
Agrippa, do you believe the prophets? I know you do—"

28 Agrippa interrupted him. "Do you think you can persuade me to become a Christian so quickly?"*

29 Paul replied, "Whether quickly or not, I pray to God that both you and everyone here in this audience might become the same as I am, except for these chains."

30 Then the king, the governor, Bernice, and all the
others stood and left. 31 As they went out, they talked
it over and agreed, "This man hasn't done anything to deserve death or imprisonment."

32 And Agrippa said to Festus, "He could have been set free if he hadn't appealed to Caesar."

Paul Sails for Rome

27 When the time came, we set sail for Italy. Paul and several other prisoners were placed in the custody of a Roman officer* named
Julius, a captain of the Imperial Regiment. 2 Aristar-
chus, a Macedonian from Thessalonica, was also with us. We left on a ship whose home port was Adramyttium on the northwest coast of the province of Asia;* it was scheduled to make several stops at ports along the coast of the province.

3 The next day when we docked at Sidon, Julius was very kind to Paul and let him go ashore to visit with friends so they could provide for his needs.
4 Putting out to sea from there, we encountered strong headwinds that made it difficult to keep the ship on course, so we sailed north of Cyprus between
the island and the mainland. 5 Keeping to the open
sea, we passed along the coast of Cilicia and Pamphylia, landing at Myra, in the province of Lycia.
6 There the commanding officer found an Egyptian ship from Alexandria that was bound for Italy, and he put us on board.

7 We had several days of slow sailing, and after great difficulty we finally neared Cnidus. But the wind was against us, so we sailed across to Crete and along the sheltered coast of the island, past the cape
of Salmone. 8 We struggled along the coast with great difficulty and finally arrived at Fair Havens, near
the town of Lasea. 9 We had lost a lot of time. The
weather was becoming dangerous for sea travel because it was so late in the fall,* and Paul spoke to the ship's officers about it.

26:28 Or *"A little more, and your arguments would make me a Christian."* **27:1** Greek *centurion;* similarly in 27:6, 11, 31, 43. **27:2** *Asia* was a Roman province in what is now western Turkey. **27:9** Greek *because the fast was now already gone by.* This fast was associated with the Day of Atonement (*Yom Kippur*), which occurred in late September or early October.

KING JAMES VERSION

10 And said unto them, Sirs, I perceive that this voyage will be with hurt and much damage, not only of the lading and ship, but also of our lives.

11 Nevertheless the centurion believed the master and the owner of the ship, more than those things which were spoken by Paul.

12 And because the haven was not commodious to winter in, the more part advised to depart thence also, if by any means they might attain to Phenice, *and there* to winter; *which is* an haven of Crete, and lieth toward the south west and north west.

13 And when the south wind blew softly, supposing that they had obtained *their* purpose, loosing *thence*, they sailed close by Crete.

14 But not long after there arose against it a tempestuous wind, called Euroclydon.

15 And when the ship was caught, and could not bear up into the wind, we let *her* drive.

16 And running under a certain island which is called Clauda, we had much work to come by the boat:

17 Which when they had taken up, they used helps, undergirding the ship; and, fearing lest they should fall into the quicksands, strake sail, and so were driven.

18 And we being exceedingly tossed with a tempest, the next *day* they lightened the ship;

19 And the third *day* we cast out with our own hands the tackling of the ship.

20 And when neither sun nor stars in many days appeared, and no small tempest lay on *us*, all hope that we should be saved was then taken away.

21 But after long abstinence Paul stood forth in the midst of them, and said, Sirs, ye should have hearkened unto me, and not have loosed from Crete, and to have gained this harm and loss.

22 And now I exhort you to be of good cheer: for there shall be no loss of *any man's* life among you, but of the ship.

23 For there stood by me this night the angel of God, whose I am, and whom I serve,

24 Saying, Fear not, Paul; thou must be brought before Caesar: and, lo, God hath given thee all them that sail with thee.

25 Wherefore, sirs, be of good cheer: for I believe God, that it shall be even as it was told me.

26 Howbeit we must be cast upon a certain island.

27 But when the fourteenth night was come, as we were driven up and down in Adria, about midnight the shipmen deemed that they drew near to some country;

28 And sounded, and found *it* twenty fathoms: and when they had gone a little further, they sounded again, and found *it* fifteen fathoms.

29 Then fearing lest we should have fallen upon

NEW LIVING TRANSLATION

10 "Men," he said, "I believe there is trouble ahead if we go on—shipwreck, loss of cargo, and danger to our lives as well." 11 But the officer in charge of the prisoners listened more to the ship's captain and the owner than to Paul. 12 And since Fair Havens was an exposed harbor—a poor place to spend the winter—most of the crew wanted to go on to Phoenix, farther up the coast of Crete, and spend the winter there. Phoenix was a good harbor with only a southwest and northwest exposure.

The Storm at Sea

13 When a light wind began blowing from the south, the sailors thought they could make it. So they pulled up anchor and sailed close to the shore of Crete. 14 But the weather changed abruptly, and a wind of typhoon strength (called a "northeaster") burst across the island and blew us out to sea. 15 The sailors couldn't turn the ship into the wind, so they gave up and let it run before the gale.

16 We sailed along the sheltered side of a small island named Cauda,* where with great difficulty we hoisted aboard the lifeboat being towed behind us. 17 Then the sailors bound ropes around the hull of the ship to strengthen it. They were afraid of being driven across to the sandbars of Syrtis off the African coast, so they lowered the sea anchor to slow the ship and were driven before the wind.

18 The next day, as gale-force winds continued to batter the ship, the crew began throwing the cargo overboard. 19 The following day they even took some of the ship's gear and threw it overboard. 20 The terrible storm raged for many days, blotting out the sun and the stars, until at last all hope was gone.

21 No one had eaten for a long time. Finally, Paul called the crew together and said, "Men, you should have listened to me in the first place and not left Crete. You would have avoided all this damage and loss. 22 But take courage! None of you will lose your lives, even though the ship will go down. 23 For last night an angel of the God to whom I belong and whom I serve stood beside me, 24 and he said, 'Don't be afraid, Paul, for you will surely stand trial before Caesar! What's more, God in his goodness has granted safety to everyone sailing with you.' 25 So take courage! For I believe God. It will be just as he said. 26 But we will be shipwrecked on an island."

The Shipwreck

27 About midnight on the fourteenth night of the storm, as we were being driven across the Sea of Adria,* the sailors sensed land was near. 28 They dropped a weighted line and found that the water was 120 feet deep. But a little later they measured again and found it was only 90 feet deep.* 29 At this rate they were afraid we would soon be driven

27:16 Some manuscripts read *Clauda*. **27:27** The *Sea of Adria* includes the central portion of the Mediterranean. **27:28** Greek *20 fathoms . . . 15 fathoms* [37 meters . . . 27 meters].

KING JAMES VERSION

rocks, they cast four anchors out of the stern, and wished for the day.

30And as the shipmen were about to flee out of the ship, when they had let down the boat into the sea, under colour as though they would have cast anchors out of the foreship,

31Paul said to the centurion and to the soldiers, Except these abide in the ship, ye cannot be saved.

32Then the soldiers cut off the ropes of the boat, and let her fall off.

33And while the day was coming on, Paul besought *them* all to take meat, saying, This day is the fourteenth day that ye have tarried and continued fasting, having taken nothing.

34Wherefore I pray you to take *some* meat: for this is for your health: for there shall not an hair fall from the head of any of you.

35And when he had thus spoken, he took bread, and gave thanks to God in presence of them all: and when he had broken *it,* he began to eat.

36Then were they all of good cheer, and they also took *some* meat.

37And we were in all in the ship two hundred threescore and sixteen souls.

38And when they had eaten enough, they lightened the ship, and cast out the wheat into the sea.

39And when it was day, they knew not the land: but they discovered a certain creek with a shore, into the which they were minded, if it were possible, to thrust in the ship.

40And when they had taken up the anchors, they committed *themselves* unto the sea, and loosed the rudder bands, and hoisted up the mainsail to the wind, and made toward shore.

41And falling into a place where two seas met, they ran the ship aground; and the forepart stuck fast, and remained unmoveable, but the hinder part was broken with the violence of the waves.

42And the soldiers' counsel was to kill the prisoners, lest any of them should swim out, and escape.

43But the centurion, willing to save Paul, kept them from *their* purpose; and commanded that they which could swim should cast *themselves* first *into the sea,* and get to land:

44And the rest, some on boards, and some on *broken pieces* of the ship. And so it came to pass, that they escaped all safe to land.

28 1And when they were escaped, then they knew that the island was called Melita.

2And the barbarous people shewed us no little kindness: for they kindled a fire, and received us every one, because of the present rain, and because of the cold.

3And when Paul had gathered a bundle of sticks, and laid *them* on the fire, there came a viper out of the heat, and fastened on his hand.

4And when the barbarians saw the *venomous* beast

NEW LIVING TRANSLATION

against the rocks along the shore, so they threw out
four anchors from the back of the ship and prayed
for daylight.
30Then the sailors tried to abandon the ship; they
lowered the lifeboat as though they were going to put
out anchors from the front of the ship. 31But Paul
said to the commanding officer and the soldiers,
"You will all die unless the sailors stay aboard." 32So
the soldiers cut the ropes to the lifeboat and let it
drift away.
33Just as day was dawning, Paul urged everyone to
eat. "You have been so worried that you haven't
touched food for two weeks," he said. 34"Please eat
something now for your own good. For not a hair of
your heads will perish." 35Then he took some bread,
gave thanks to God before them all, and broke off a
piece and ate it. 36Then everyone was encouraged
and began to eat—37all 276 of us who were on board.
38After eating, the crew lightened the ship further by
throwing the cargo of wheat overboard.
39When morning dawned, they didn't recognize
the coastline, but they saw a bay with a beach and
wondered if they could get to shore by running the
ship aground. 40So they cut off the anchors and left
them in the sea. Then they lowered the rudders,
raised the foresail, and headed toward shore. 41But
they hit a shoal and ran the ship aground too soon.
The bow of the ship stuck fast, while the stern was
repeatedly smashed by the force of the waves and
began to break apart.
42The soldiers wanted to kill the prisoners to
make sure they didn't swim ashore and escape. 43But
the commanding officer wanted to spare Paul, so he
didn't let them carry out their plan. Then he ordered
all who could swim to jump overboard first and
make for land. 44The others held on to planks or
debris from the broken ship.* So everyone escaped
safely to shore.

Paul on the Island of Malta

28 Once we were safe on shore, we learned
that we were on the island of Malta. 2The
people of the island were very kind to us. It was cold
and rainy, so they built a fire on the shore to welcome us.
3As Paul gathered an armful of sticks and was laying them on the fire, a poisonous snake, driven out
by the heat, bit him on the hand. 4The people of the

27:44 Or *or were helped by members of the ship's crew.*

KING JAMES VERSION

hang on his hand, they said among themselves, No
doubt this man is a murderer, whom, though he hath
escaped the sea, yet vengeance suffereth not to live.
5 And he shook off the beast into the fire, and felt
no harm.
6 Howbeit they looked when he should have swollen, or fallen down dead suddenly: but after they had
looked a great while, and saw no harm come to him,
they changed their minds, and said that he was a god.
7 In the same quarters were possessions of the chief
man of the island, whose name was Publius; who received us, and lodged us three days courteously.
8 And it came to pass, that the father of Publius lay
sick of a fever and of a bloody flux: to whom Paul entered in, and prayed, and laid his hands on him, and
healed him.
9 So when this was done, others also, which had
diseases in the island, came, and were healed:
10 Who also honoured us with many honours; and
when we departed, they laded *us* with such things as
were necessary.
11 And after three months we departed in a ship of
Alexandria, which had wintered in the isle, whose
sign was Castor and Pollux.
12 And landing at Syracuse, we tarried *there* three
days.
13 And from thence we fetched a compass, and
came to Rhegium: and after one day the south wind
blew, and we came the next day to Puteoli:
14 Where we found brethren, and were desired to
tarry with them seven days: and so we went toward
Rome.
15 And from thence, when the brethren heard of us,
they came to meet us as far as Appii forum, and The
Three Taverns: whom when Paul saw, he thanked
God, and took courage.
16 And when we came to Rome, the centurion delivered the prisoners to the captain of the guard: but
Paul was suffered to dwell by himself with a soldier
that kept him.
17 And it came to pass, that after three days Paul
called the chief of the Jews together: and when they
were come together, he said unto them, Men *and*
brethren, though I have committed nothing against
the people, or customs of our fathers, yet was I delivered prisoner from Jerusalem into the hands of the
Romans.
18 Who, when they had examined me, would have
let *me* go, because there was no cause of death in me.
19 But when the Jews spake against *it,* I was constrained to appeal unto Caesar; not that I had aught
to accuse my nation of.
20 For this cause therefore have I called for you, to
see *you,* and to speak with *you:* because that for the
hope of Israel I am bound with this chain.

NEW LIVING TRANSLATION

island saw it hanging from his hand and said to each
other, "A murderer, no doubt! Though he escaped the
sea, justice will not permit him to live." 5 But Paul
shook off the snake into the fire and was unharmed.
6 The people waited for him to swell up or suddenly
drop dead. But when they had waited a long time and
saw that he wasn't harmed, they changed their
minds and decided he was a god.
7 Near the shore where we landed was an estate belonging to Publius, the chief official of the island. He
welcomed us and treated us kindly for three days.
8 As it happened, Publius's father was ill with fever
and dysentery. Paul went in and prayed for him, and
laying his hands on him, he healed him. 9 Then all
the other sick people on the island came and were
healed. 10 As a result we were showered with honors,
and when the time came to sail, people supplied us
with everything we would need for the trip.

Paul Arrives at Rome

11 It was three months after the shipwreck that we set
sail on another ship that had wintered at the island—
an Alexandrian ship with the twin gods* as its figure-
head. 12 Our first stop was Syracuse,* where we
stayed three days. 13 From there we sailed across to
Rhegium.* A day later a south wind began blowing,
so the following day we sailed up the coast to Puteoli.
14 There we found some believers,* who invited us to
spend a week with them. And so we came to Rome.
15 The brothers and sisters* in Rome had heard
we were coming, and they came to meet us at the
Forum* on the Appian Way. Others joined us at
The Three Taverns.* When Paul saw them, he was
encouraged and thanked God.
16 When we arrived in Rome, Paul was permitted
to have his own private lodging, though he was
guarded by a soldier.

Paul Preaches at Rome under Guard

17 Three days after Paul's arrival, he called together
the local Jewish leaders. He said to them, "Brothers, I
was arrested in Jerusalem and handed over to the Roman government, even though I had done nothing
against our people or the customs of our ancestors.
18 The Romans tried me and wanted to release me,
because they found no cause for the death sentence.
19 But when the Jewish leaders protested the decision,
I felt it necessary to appeal to Caesar, even though I
had no desire to press charges against my own people.
20 I asked you to come here today so we could get acquainted and so I could explain to you that I am bound
with this chain because I believe that the hope of Israel—the Messiah—has already come."

28:11 The *twin gods* were the Roman gods Castor and Pollux.
28:12 *Syracuse* was on the island of Sicily. **28:13** *Rhegium* was on the southern tip of Italy. **28:14** Greek *brothers.* **28:15a** Greek *brothers.*
28:15b *The Forum* was about 43 miles (70 kilometers) from Rome.
28:15c *The Three Taverns* was about 35 miles (57 kilometers) from Rome.

KING JAMES VERSION

[21]And they said unto him, We neither received letters out of Judaea concerning thee, neither any of the brethren that came shewed or spake any harm of thee.

[22]But we desire to hear of thee what thou thinkest: for as concerning this sect, we know that every where it is spoken against.

[23]And when they had appointed him a day, there came many to him into *his* lodging; to whom he expounded and testified the kingdom of God, persuading them concerning Jesus, both out of the law of Moses, and *out of* the prophets, from morning till evening.

[24]And some believed the things which were spoken, and some believed not.

[25]And when they agreed not among themselves, they departed, after that Paul had spoken one word, Well spake the Holy Ghost by Esaias the prophet unto our fathers,

[26]Saying, Go unto this people, and say, Hearing ye shall hear, and shall not understand; and seeing ye shall see, and not perceive:

[27]For the heart of this people is waxed gross, and their ears are dull of hearing, and their eyes have they closed; lest they should see with *their* eyes, and hear with *their* ears, and understand with *their* heart, and should be converted, and I should heal them.

[28]Be it known therefore unto you, that the salvation of God is sent unto the Gentiles, and *that* they will hear it.

[29]And when he had said these words, the Jews departed, and had great reasoning among themselves.

[30]And Paul dwelt two whole years in his own hired house, and received all that came in unto him,

[31]Preaching the kingdom of God, and teaching those things which concern the Lord Jesus Christ, with all confidence, no man forbidding him.

NEW LIVING TRANSLATION

[21]They replied, "We have had no letters from Judea or reports against you from anyone who has
come here. [22]But we want to hear what you believe,
for the only thing we know about this movement is
that it is denounced everywhere."

[23]So a time was set, and on that day a large number
of people came to Paul's lodging. He explained and
testified about the Kingdom of God and tried to persuade them about Jesus from the Scriptures. Using
the law of Moses and the books of the prophets, he
spoke to them from morning until evening. [24]Some
were persuaded by the things he said, but others did
not believe. [25]And after they had argued back and
forth among themselves, they left with this final
word from Paul: "The Holy Spirit was right when he
said to your ancestors through Isaiah the prophet,

[26] 'Go and say to this people:
When you hear what I say,
you will not understand.
When you see what I do,
you will not comprehend.
[27] For the hearts of these people are hardened,
and their ears cannot hear,
and they have closed their eyes—
so their eyes cannot see,
and their ears cannot hear,
and their hearts cannot understand,
and they cannot turn to me
and let me heal them.'*

[28]So I want you to know that this salvation from God
has also been offered to the Gentiles, and they will
accept it."*

[30]For the next two years, Paul lived in Rome at his
own expense.* He welcomed all who visited him,
[31]boldly proclaiming the Kingdom of God and
teaching about the Lord Jesus Christ. And no one
tried to stop him.

28:26-27 Isa 6:9-10 (Greek version). **28:28** Some manuscripts add verse 29, *And when he had said these words, the Jews departed, greatly disagreeing with each other.* **28:30** Or *in his own rented quarters.*

Romans

KING JAMES VERSION

1 1Paul, a servant of Jesus Christ, called *to be* an apostle, separated unto the gospel of God,

2(Which he had promised afore by his prophets in the holy scriptures,)

3Concerning his Son Jesus Christ our Lord, which was made of the seed of David according to the flesh;

4And declared *to be* the Son of God with power, according to the spirit of holiness, by the resurrection from the dead:

5By whom we have received grace and apostleship, for obedience to the faith among all nations, for his name:

6Among whom are ye also the called of Jesus Christ:

7To all that be in Rome, beloved of God, called *to be* saints: Grace to you and peace from God our Father, and the Lord Jesus Christ.

8First, I thank my God through Jesus Christ for you all, that your faith is spoken of throughout the whole world.

9For God is my witness, whom I serve with my spirit in the gospel of his Son, that without ceasing I make mention of you always in my prayers;

10Making request, if by any means now at length I might have a prosperous journey by the will of God to come unto you.

11For I long to see you, that I may impart unto you some spiritual gift, to the end ye may be established;

12That is, that I may be comforted together with you by the mutual faith both of you and me.

13Now I would not have you ignorant, brethren, that oftentimes I purposed to come unto you, (but was let hitherto,) that I might have some fruit among you also, even as among other Gentiles.

14I am debtor both to the Greeks, and to the Barbarians; both to the wise, and to the unwise.

15So, as much as in me is, I am ready to preach the gospel to you that are at Rome also.

NEW LIVING TRANSLATION

Greetings from Paul

1 This letter is from Paul, a slave of Christ Jesus, chosen by God to be an apostle and sent out to preach his Good News. 2God promised this Good News long ago through his prophets in the holy Scriptures. 3The Good News is about his Son. In his earthly life he was born into King David's family line, 4and he was shown to be* the Son of God when he was raised from the dead by the power of the Holy Spirit.* He is Jesus Christ our Lord. 5Through Christ, God has given us the privilege* and authority as apostles to tell Gentiles everywhere what God has done for them, so that they will believe and obey him, bringing glory to his name.

6And you are included among those Gentiles who have been called to belong to Jesus Christ. 7I am writing to all of you in Rome who are loved by God and are called to be his own holy people.

May God our Father and the Lord Jesus Christ give you grace and peace.

God's Good News

8Let me say first that I thank my God through Jesus Christ for all of you, because your faith in him is being talked about all over the world. 9God knows how often I pray for you. Day and night I bring you and your needs in prayer to God, whom I serve with all my heart* by spreading the Good News about his Son.

10One of the things I always pray for is the opportunity, God willing, to come at last to see you. 11For I long to visit you so I can bring you some spiritual gift that will help you grow strong in the Lord. 12When we get together, I want to encourage you in your faith, but I also want to be encouraged by yours.

13I want you to know, dear brothers and sisters,* that I planned many times to visit you, but I was prevented until now. I want to work among you and see spiritual fruit, just as I have seen among other Gentiles. 14For I have a great sense of obligation to people in both the civilized world and the rest of the world,* to the educated and uneducated alike. 15So I am eager to come to you in Rome, too, to preach the Good News.

1:4a Or *and was designated.* **1:4b** Or *by the Spirit of holiness;* or *in the new realm of the Spirit.* **1:5** Or *the grace.* **1:9** Or *in my spirit.* **1:13** Greek *brothers.* **1:14** Greek *to Greeks and barbarians.*

KING JAMES VERSION

16 For I am not ashamed of the gospel of Christ: for it is the power of God unto salvation to every one that believeth; to the Jew first, and also to the Greek.

17 For therein is the righteousness of God revealed from faith to faith: as it is written, The just shall live by faith.

18 For the wrath of God is revealed from heaven against all ungodliness and unrighteousness of men, who hold the truth in unrighteousness;

19 Because that which may be known of God is manifest in them; for God hath shewed *it* unto them.

20 For the invisible things of him from the creation of the world are clearly seen, being understood by the things that are made, *even* his eternal power and Godhead; so that they are without excuse:

21 Because that, when they knew God, they glorified *him* not as God, neither were thankful; but became vain in their imaginations, and their foolish heart was darkened.

22 Professing themselves to be wise, they became fools,

23 And changed the glory of the uncorruptible God into an image made like to corruptible man, and to birds, and fourfooted beasts, and creeping things.

24 Wherefore God also gave them up to uncleanness through the lusts of their own hearts, to dishonour their own bodies between themselves:

25 Who changed the truth of God into a lie, and worshipped and served the creature more than the Creator, who is blessed for ever. Amen.

26 For this cause God gave them up unto vile affections: for even their women did change the natural use into that which is against nature:

27 And likewise also the men, leaving the natural use of the woman, burned in their lust one toward another; men with men working that which is unseemly, and receiving in themselves that recompence of their error which was meet.

28 And even as they did not like to retain God in *their* knowledge, God gave them over to a reprobate mind, to do those things which are not convenient;

29 Being filled with all unrighteousness, fornication, wickedness, covetousness, maliciousness; full of envy, murder, debate, deceit, malignity; whisperers,

30 Backbiters, haters of God, despiteful, proud, boasters, inventors of evil things, disobedient to parents,

31 Without understanding, covenantbreakers, without natural affection, implacable, unmerciful:

32 Who knowing the judgment of God, that they which commit such things are worthy of death, not only do the same, but have pleasure in them that do them.

NEW LIVING TRANSLATION

16 For I am not ashamed of this Good News about
Christ. It is the power of God at work, saving everyone who believes—the Jew first and also the Gentile.* 17 This Good News tells us how God makes us
right in his sight. This is accomplished from start to
finish by faith. As the Scriptures say, "It is through
faith that a righteous person has life."*

God's Anger at Sin

18 But God shows his anger from heaven against all
sinful, wicked people who suppress the truth by
their wickedness.* 19 They know the truth about God
because he has made it obvious to them. 20 For ever
since the world was created, people have seen the
earth and sky. Through everything God made, they
can clearly see his invisible qualities—his eternal
power and divine nature. So they have no excuse for
not knowing God.

21 Yes, they knew God, but they wouldn't worship
him as God or even give him thanks. And they began
to think up foolish ideas of what God was like. As
a result, their minds became dark and confused.
22 Claiming to be wise, they instead became utter
fools. 23 And instead of worshiping the glorious, ever-
living God, they worshiped idols made to look like
mere people and birds and animals and reptiles.

24 So God abandoned them to do whatever shameful things their hearts desired. As a result, they did
vile and degrading things with each other's bodies.
25 They traded the truth about God for a lie. So they
worshiped and served the things God created instead of the Creator himself, who is worthy of eternal praise! Amen. 26 That is why God abandoned
them to their shameful desires. Even the women
turned against the natural way to have sex and instead indulged in sex with each other. 27 And the
men, instead of having normal sexual relations with
women, burned with lust for each other. Men did
shameful things with other men, and as a result of
this sin, they suffered within themselves the penalty
they deserved.

28 Since they thought it foolish to acknowledge
God, he abandoned them to their foolish thinking
and let them do things that should never be done.
29 Their lives became full of every kind of wickedness, sin, greed, hate, envy, murder, quarreling, deception, malicious behavior, and gossip. 30 They are
backstabbers, haters of God, insolent, proud, and
boastful. They invent new ways of sinning, and they
disobey their parents. 31 They refuse to understand,
break their promises, are heartless, and have no
mercy. 32 They know God's justice requires that those
who do these things deserve to die, yet they do them
anyway. Worse yet, they encourage others to do
them, too.

1:16 Greek *also the Greek.* **1:17** Or *"The righteous will live by faith."* Hab 2:4. **1:18** Or *who, by their wickedness, prevent the truth from being known.*

KING JAMES VERSION

2 1 Therefore thou art inexcusable, O man, whosoever thou art that judgest: for wherein thou judgest another, thou condemnest thyself; for thou that judgest doest the same things.

2 But we are sure that the judgment of God is according to truth against them which commit such things.

3 And thinkest thou this, O man, that judgest them which do such things, and doest the same, that thou shalt escape the judgment of God?

4 Or despisest thou the riches of his goodness and forbearance and longsuffering; not knowing that the goodness of God leadeth thee to repentance?

5 But after thy hardness and impenitent heart treasurest up unto thyself wrath against the day of wrath and revelation of the righteous judgment of God;

6 Who will render to every man according to his deeds:

7 To them who by patient continuance in well doing seek for glory and honour and immortality, eternal life:

8 But unto them that are contentious, and do not obey the truth, but obey unrighteousness, indignation and wrath,

9 Tribulation and anguish, upon every soul of man that doeth evil, of the Jew first, and also of the Gentile;

10 But glory, honour, and peace, to every man that worketh good, to the Jew first, and also to the Gentile:

11 For there is no respect of persons with God.

12 For as many as have sinned without law shall also perish without law: and as many as have sinned in the law shall be judged by the law;

13 (For not the hearers of the law *are* just before God, but the doers of the law shall be justified.

14 For when the Gentiles, which have not the law, do by nature the things contained in the law, these, having not the law, are a law unto themselves:

15 Which shew the work of the law written in their hearts, their conscience also bearing witness, and *their* thoughts the mean while accusing or else excusing one another;)

16 In the day when God shall judge the secrets of men by Jesus Christ according to my gospel.

17 Behold, thou art called a Jew, and restest in the law, and makest thy boast of God,

18 And knowest *his* will, and approvest the things that are more excellent, being instructed out of the law;

19 And art confident that thou thyself art a guide of the blind, a light of them which are in darkness,

20 An instructor of the foolish, a teacher of babes, which hast the form of knowledge and of the truth in the law.

21 Thou therefore which teachest another, teachest

NEW LIVING TRANSLATION

God's Judgment of Sin

2 You may think you can condemn such people,
but you are just as bad, and you have no excuse!
When you say they are wicked and should be punished, you are condemning yourself, for you who
judge others do these very same things. 2 And we
know that God, in his justice, will punish anyone who
does such things. 3 Since you judge others for doing
these things, why do you think you can avoid God's
judgment when you do the same things? 4 Don't you
see how wonderfully kind, tolerant, and patient God
is with you? Does this mean nothing to you? Can't
you see that his kindness is intended to turn you
from your sin?

5 But because you are stubborn and refuse to turn
from your sin, you are storing up terrible punishment for yourself. For a day of anger is coming, when
God's righteous judgment will be revealed. 6 He will
judge everyone according to what they have done.
7 He will give eternal life to those who keep on doing
good, seeking after the glory and honor and immortality that God offers. 8 But he will pour out his anger
and wrath on those who live for themselves, who
refuse to obey the truth and instead live lives of
wickedness. 9 There will be trouble and calamity for
everyone who keeps on doing what is evil—for the
Jew first and also for the Gentile.* 10 But there will be
glory and honor and peace from God for all who do
good—for the Jew first and also for the Gentile. 11 For
God does not show favoritism.

12 When the Gentiles sin, they will be destroyed,
even though they never had God's written law. And
the Jews, who do have God's law, will be judged by
that law when they fail to obey it. 13 For merely listening to the law doesn't make us right with God. It is
obeying the law that makes us right in his sight.
14 Even Gentiles, who do not have God's written law,
show that they know his law when they instinctively
obey it, even without having heard it. 15 They demonstrate that God's law is written in their hearts, for
their own conscience and thoughts either accuse
them or tell them they are doing right. 16 And this
is the message I proclaim—that the day is coming
when God, through Christ Jesus, will judge everyone's secret life.

The Jews and the Law

17 You who call yourselves Jews are relying on God's
law, and you boast about your special relationship
with him. 18 You know what he wants; you know what
is right because you have been taught his law. 19 You
are convinced that you are a guide for the blind and a
light for people who are lost in darkness. 20 You think
you can instruct the ignorant and teach children the
ways of God. For you are certain that God's law gives
you complete knowledge and truth.

21 Well then, if you teach others, why don't you

2:9 Greek *also for the Greek;* also in 2:10.

KING JAMES VERSION

thou not thyself? thou that preachest a man should not steal, dost thou steal?

22 Thou that sayest a man should not commit adultery, dost thou commit adultery? thou that abhorrest idols, dost thou commit sacrilege?

23 Thou that makest thy boast of the law, through breaking the law dishonourest thou God?

24 For the name of God is blasphemed among the Gentiles through you, as it is written.

25 For circumcision verily profiteth, if thou keep the law: but if thou be a breaker of the law, thy circumcision is made uncircumcision.

26 Therefore if the uncircumcision keep the righteousness of the law, shall not his uncircumcision be counted for circumcision?

27 And shall not uncircumcision which is by nature, if it fulfil the law, judge thee, who by the letter and circumcision dost transgress the law?

28 For he is not a Jew, which is one outwardly; neither *is that* circumcision, which is outward in the flesh:

29 But he *is* a Jew, which is one inwardly; and circumcision *is that* of the heart, in the spirit, *and* not in the letter; whose praise *is* not of men, but of God.

3 1 What advantage then hath the Jew? or what profit *is there* of circumcision?

2 Much every way: chiefly, because that unto them were committed the oracles of God.

3 For what if some did not believe? shall their unbelief make the faith of God without effect?

4 God forbid: yea, let God be true, but every man a liar; as it is written, That thou mightest be justified in thy sayings, and mightest overcome when thou art judged.

5 But if our unrighteousness commend the righteousness of God, what shall we say? *Is* God unrighteous who taketh vengeance? (I speak as a man)

6 God forbid: for then how shall God judge the world?

7 For if the truth of God hath more abounded through my lie unto his glory; why yet am I also judged as a sinner?

8 And not *rather*, (as we be slanderously reported, and as some affirm that we say,) Let us do evil, that good may come? whose damnation is just.

9 What then? are we better *than they*? No, in no wise: for we have before proved both Jews and Gentiles, that they are all under sin;

10 As it is written, There is none righteous, no, not one:

NEW LIVING TRANSLATION

teach yourself? You tell others not to steal, but do
you steal? 22 You say it is wrong to commit adultery,
but do you commit adultery? You condemn idolatry,
but do you use items stolen from pagan temples?*
23 You are so proud of knowing the law, but you dishonor God by breaking it. 24 No wonder the Scriptures say, "The Gentiles blaspheme the name of God
because of you."*

25 The Jewish ceremony of circumcision has value
only if you obey God's law. But if you don't obey God's
law, you are no better off than an uncircumcised
Gentile. 26 And if the Gentiles obey God's law, won't
God declare them to be his own people? 27 In fact,
uncircumcised Gentiles who keep God's law will
condemn you Jews who are circumcised and possess
God's law but don't obey it.

28 For you are not a true Jew just because you were
born of Jewish parents or because you have gone
through the ceremony of circumcision. 29 No, a true
Jew is one whose heart is right with God. And true
circumcision is not merely obeying the letter of the
law; rather, it is a change of heart produced by God's
Spirit. And a person with a changed heart seeks
praise* from God, not from people.

God Remains Faithful

3 Then what's the advantage of being a Jew?
Is there any value in the ceremony of circumcision? 2 Yes, there are great benefits! First of all,
the Jews were entrusted with the whole revelation
of God.*

3 True, some of them were unfaithful; but just because they were unfaithful, does that mean God will
be unfaithful? 4 Of course not! Even if everyone else
is a liar, God is true. As the Scriptures say about him,

"You will be proved right in what you say,
and you will win your case in court."*

5 "But," some might say, "our sinfulness serves a
good purpose, for it helps people see how righteous
God is. Isn't it unfair, then, for him to punish us?"
(This is merely a human point of view.) 6 Of course
not! If God were not entirely fair, how would he
be qualified to judge the world? 7 "But," someone
might still argue, "how can God condemn me as a
sinner if my dishonesty highlights his truthfulness
and brings him more glory?" 8 And some people even
slander us by claiming that we say, "The more we sin,
the better it is!" Those who say such things deserve to
be condemned.

All People Are Sinners

9 Well then, should we conclude that we Jews are
better than others? No, not at all, for we have already
shown that all people, whether Jews or Gentiles,* are
under the power of sin. 10 As the Scriptures say,

2:22 Greek *do you steal from temples?* **2:24** Isa 52:5 (Greek version). **2:29** Or *receives praise.* **3:2** Greek *the oracles of God.* **3:4** Ps 51:4 (Greek version). **3:9** Greek *or Greeks.*

KING JAMES VERSION

11 There is none that understandeth, there is none
that seeketh after God.
12 They are all gone out of the way, they are together become unprofitable; there is none that
doeth good, no, not one.
13 Their throat *is* an open sepulchre; with their
tongues they have used deceit; the poison of asps *is*
under their lips:
14 Whose mouth *is* full of cursing and bitterness:
15 Their feet *are* swift to shed blood:
16 Destruction and misery *are* in their ways:
17 And the way of peace have they not known:
18 There is no fear of God before their eyes.
19 Now we know that what things soever the law
saith, it saith to them who are under the law: that
every mouth may be stopped, and all the world may
become guilty before God.
20 Therefore by the deeds of the law there shall no
flesh be justified in his sight: for by the law *is* the
knowledge of sin.

21 But now the righteousness of God without the
law is manifested, being witnessed by the law and the
prophets;
22 Even the righteousness of God *which is* by faith
of Jesus Christ unto all and upon all them that believe: for there is no difference:
23 For all have sinned, and come short of the glory
of God;
24 Being justified freely by his grace through the
redemption that is in Christ Jesus:
25 Whom God hath set forth *to be* a propitiation
through faith in his blood, to declare his righteousness for the remission of sins that are past, through
the forbearance of God;
26 To declare, *I say,* at this time his righteousness:
that he might be just, and the justifier of him which
believeth in Jesus.
27 Where *is* boasting then? It is excluded. By what
law? of works? Nay: but by the law of faith.
28 Therefore we conclude that a man is justified by
faith without the deeds of the law.
29 *Is he* the God of the Jews only? *is he* not also of
the Gentiles? Yes, of the Gentiles also:
30 Seeing *it is* one God, which shall justify the circumcision by faith, and uncircumcision through
faith.

NEW LIVING TRANSLATION

"No one is righteous—
not even one.
11 No one is truly wise;
no one is seeking God.
12 All have turned away;
all have become useless.
No one does good,
not a single one."*
13 "Their talk is foul, like the stench from
an open grave.
Their tongues are filled with lies."
"Snake venom drips from their lips."*
14 "Their mouths are full of cursing and
bitterness."*
15 "They rush to commit murder.
16 Destruction and misery always follow them.
17 They don't know where to find peace."*
18 "They have no fear of God at all."*

19 Obviously, the law applies to those to whom it
was given, for its purpose is to keep people from having excuses, and to show that the entire world is
guilty before God. 20 For no one can ever be made
right with God by doing what the law commands.
The law simply shows us how sinful we are.

Christ Took Our Punishment

21 But now God has shown us a way to be made right
with him without keeping the requirements of the
law, as was promised in the writings of Moses* and
the prophets long ago. 22 We are made right with God
by placing our faith in Jesus Christ. And this is true
for everyone who believes, no matter who we are.
23 For everyone has sinned; we all fall short of God's
glorious standard. 24 Yet God, with undeserved kindness, declares that we are righteous. He did this
through Christ Jesus when he freed us from the penalty for our sins. 25 For God presented Jesus as the sacrifice for sin. People are made right with God when
they believe that Jesus sacrificed his life, shedding his
blood. This sacrifice shows that God was being fair
when he held back and did not punish those who
sinned in times past, 26 for he was looking ahead and
including them in what he would do in this present
time. God did this to demonstrate his righteousness,
for he himself is fair and just, and he declares sinners
to be right in his sight when they believe in Jesus.
27 Can we boast, then, that we have done anything
to be accepted by God? No, because our acquittal is
not based on obeying the law. It is based on faith.
28 So we are made right with God through faith and
not by obeying the law.
29 After all, is God the God of the Jews only? Isn't he
also the God of the Gentiles? Of course he is. 30 There
is only one God, and he makes people right with himself only by faith, whether they are Jews or Gentiles.*

3:10-12 Pss 14:1-3; 53:1-3 (Greek version). **3:13** Pss 5:9 (Greek version); 140:3. **3:14** Ps 10:7 (Greek version). **3:15-17** Isa 59:7-8. **3:18** Ps 36:1. **3:21** Greek *in the law.* **3:30** Greek *whether they are circumcised or uncircumcised.*

KING JAMES VERSION

31 Do we then make void the law through faith? God forbid: yea, we establish the law.

4

1 What shall we say then that Abraham our father, as pertaining to the flesh, hath found?

2 For if Abraham were justified by works, he hath *whereof* to glory; but not before God.

3 For what saith the scripture? Abraham believed God, and it was counted unto him for righteousness.

4 Now to him that worketh is the reward not reckoned of grace, but of debt.

5 But to him that worketh not, but believeth on him that justifieth the ungodly, his faith is counted for righteousness.

6 Even as David also describeth the blessedness of the man, unto whom God imputeth righteousness without works,

7 *Saying,* Blessed *are* they whose iniquities are forgiven, and whose sins are covered.

8 Blessed *is* the man to whom the Lord will not impute sin.

9 *Cometh* this blessedness then upon the circumcision *only,* or upon the uncircumcision also? for we say that faith was reckoned to Abraham for righteousness.

10 How was it then reckoned? when he was in circumcision, or in uncircumcision? Not in circumcision, but in uncircumcision.

11 And he received the sign of circumcision, a seal of the righteousness of the faith which *he had yet* being uncircumcised: that he might be the father of all them that believe, though they be not circumcised; that righteousness might be imputed unto them also:

12 And the father of circumcision to them who are not of the circumcision only, but who also walk in the steps of that faith of our father Abraham, which *he had* being *yet* uncircumcised.

13 For the promise, that he should be the heir of the world, *was* not to Abraham, or to his seed, through the law, but through the righteousness of faith.

14 For if they which are of the law *be* heirs, faith is made void, and the promise made of none effect:

15 Because the law worketh wrath: for where no law is, *there is* no transgression.

16 Therefore *it is* of faith, that *it might be* by grace; to the end the promise might be sure to all the seed; not to that only which is of the law, but to that also

NEW LIVING TRANSLATION

31 Well then, if we emphasize faith, does this mean that we can forget about the law? Of course not! In fact, only when we have faith do we truly fulfill the law.

The Faith of Abraham

4 Abraham was, humanly speaking, the founder of our Jewish nation. What did he discover
about being made right with God?
2 If his good deeds
had made him acceptable to God, he would have had
something to boast about. But that was not God's
way.
3 For the Scriptures tell us, "Abraham believed
God, and God counted him as righteous because of
his faith."*
4 When people work, their wages are not a gift, but
something they have earned.
5 But people are
counted as righteous, not because of their work, but
because of their faith in God who forgives sinners.
6 David also spoke of this when he described the happiness of those who are declared righteous without
working for it:

7 "Oh, what joy for those
whose disobedience is forgiven,
whose sins are put out of sight.
8 Yes, what joy for those
whose record the LORD has cleared of sin."*

9 Now, is this blessing only for the Jews, or is it also
for uncircumcised Gentiles?* Well, we have been
saying that Abraham was counted as righteous by
God because of his faith.
10 But how did this happen?
Was he counted as righteous only after he was
circumcised, or was it before he was circumcised?
Clearly, God accepted Abraham before he was
circumcised!
11 Circumcision was a sign that Abraham already
had faith and that God had already accepted him and
declared him to be righteous—even before he was
circumcised. So Abraham is the spiritual father of
those who have faith but have not been circumcised.
They are counted as righteous because of their faith.
12 And Abraham is also the spiritual father of those
who have been circumcised, but only if they have
the same kind of faith Abraham had before he was
circumcised.
13 Clearly, God's promise to give the whole earth to
Abraham and his descendants was based not on his
obedience to God's law, but on a right relationship
with God that comes by faith.
14 If God's promise is
only for those who obey the law, then faith is not necessary and the promise is pointless.
15 For the law always brings punishment on those who try to obey it.
(The only way to avoid breaking the law is to have no
law to break!)
16 So the promise is received by faith. It is given
as a free gift. And we are all certain to receive it,

4:3 Gen 15:6. **4:7-8** Ps 32:1-2 (Greek version). **4:9** Greek *is this blessing only for the circumcised, or is it also for the uncircumcised?*

KING JAMES VERSION

which is of the faith of Abraham; who is the father of us all,

17(As it is written, I have made thee a father of many nations,) before him whom he believed, *even* God, who quickeneth the dead, and calleth those things which be not as though they were.

18Who against hope believed in hope, that he might become the father of many nations, according to that which was spoken, So shall thy seed be.

19And being not weak in faith, he considered not his own body now dead, when he was about an hundred years old, neither yet the deadness of Sarah's womb:

20He staggered not at the promise of God through unbelief; but was strong in faith, giving glory to God;

21And being fully persuaded that, what he had promised, he was able also to perform.

22And therefore it was imputed to him for righteousness.

23Now it was not written for his sake alone, that it was imputed to him;

24But for us also, to whom it shall be imputed, if we believe on him that raised up Jesus our Lord from the dead;

25Who was delivered for our offences, and was raised again for our justification.

5 1Therefore being justified by faith, we have peace with God through our Lord Jesus Christ:

2By whom also we have access by faith into this grace wherein we stand, and rejoice in hope of the glory of God.

3And not only *so,* but we glory in tribulations also: knowing that tribulation worketh patience;

4And patience, experience; and experience, hope:

5And hope maketh not ashamed; because the love of God is shed abroad in our hearts by the Holy Ghost which is given unto us.

6For when we were yet without strength, in due time Christ died for the ungodly.

7For scarcely for a righteous man will one die: yet peradventure for a good man some would even dare to die.

8But God commendeth his love toward us, in that, while we were yet sinners, Christ died for us.

9Much more then, being now justified by his blood, we shall be saved from wrath through him.

10For if, when we were enemies, we were reconciled to God by the death of his Son, much more, being reconciled, we shall be saved by his life.

11And not only *so,* but we also joy in God through

NEW LIVING TRANSLATION

whether or not we live according to the law of Moses, if we have faith like Abraham's. For Abraham is the father of all who believe. 17That is what the Scriptures mean when God told him, "I have made you the father of many nations."* This happened because Abraham believed in the God who brings the dead back to life and who creates new things out of nothing.

18Even when there was no reason for hope, Abraham kept hoping—believing that he would become the father of many nations. For God had said to him, "That's how many descendants you will have!"* 19And Abraham's faith did not weaken, even though, at about 100 years of age, he figured his body was as good as dead—and so was Sarah's womb.

20Abraham never wavered in believing God's promise. In fact, his faith grew stronger, and in this he brought glory to God. 21He was fully convinced that God is able to do whatever he promises. 22And because of Abraham's faith, God counted him as righteous. 23And when God counted him as righteous, it wasn't just for Abraham's benefit. It was recorded 24for our benefit, too, assuring us that God will also count us as righteous if we believe in him, the one who raised Jesus our Lord from the dead. 25He was handed over to die because of our sins, and he was raised to life to make us right with God.

Faith Brings Joy

5 Therefore, since we have been made right in God's sight by faith, we have peace with God because of what Jesus Christ our Lord has done for us. 2Because of our faith, Christ has brought us into this place of undeserved privilege where we now stand, and we confidently and joyfully look forward to sharing God's glory.

3We can rejoice, too, when we run into problems and trials, for we know that they help us develop endurance. 4And endurance develops strength of character, and character strengthens our confident hope of salvation. 5And this hope will not lead to disappointment. For we know how dearly God loves us, because he has given us the Holy Spirit to fill our hearts with his love.

6When we were utterly helpless, Christ came at just the right time and died for us sinners. 7Now, most people would not be willing to die for an upright person, though someone might perhaps be willing to die for a person who is especially good. 8But God showed his great love for us by sending Christ to die for us while we were still sinners. 9And since we have been made right in God's sight by the blood of Christ, he will certainly save us from God's condemnation. 10For since our friendship with God was restored by the death of his Son while we were still his enemies, we will certainly be saved through the life of his Son. 11So now we can rejoice in our

4:17 Gen 17:5. **4:18** Gen 15:5.

KING JAMES VERSION

our Lord Jesus Christ, by whom we have now received the atonement.

12 Wherefore, as by one man sin entered into the world, and death by sin; and so death passed upon all men, for that all have sinned:

13 (For until the law sin was in the world: but sin is not imputed when there is no law.

14 Nevertheless death reigned from Adam to Moses, even over them that had not sinned after the similitude of Adam's transgression, who is the figure of him that was to come.

15 But not as the offence, so also *is* the free gift. For if through the offence of one many be dead, much more the grace of God, and the gift by grace, *which is* by one man, Jesus Christ, hath abounded unto many.

16 And not as *it was* by one that sinned, *so is* the gift: for the judgment *was* by one to condemnation, but the free gift *is* of many offences unto justification.

17 For if by one man's offence death reigned by one; much more they which receive abundance of grace and of the gift of righteousness shall reign in life by one, Jesus Christ.)

18 Therefore as by the offence of one *judgment came* upon all men to condemnation; even so by the righteousness of one *the free gift came* upon all men unto justification of life.

19 For as by one man's disobedience many were made sinners, so by the obedience of one shall many be made righteous.

20 Moreover the law entered, that the offence might abound. But where sin abounded, grace did much more abound:

21 That as sin hath reigned unto death, even so might grace reign through righteousness unto eternal life by Jesus Christ our Lord.

6 1 What shall we say then? Shall we continue in sin, that grace may abound?

2 God forbid. How shall we, that are dead to sin, live any longer therein?

3 Know ye not, that so many of us as were baptized into Jesus Christ were baptized into his death?

4 Therefore we are buried with him by baptism into death: that like as Christ was raised up from the dead by the glory of the Father, even so we also should walk in newness of life.

5 For if we have been planted together in the likeness of his death, we shall be also *in the likeness* of *his* resurrection:

6 Knowing this, that our old man is crucified with

NEW LIVING TRANSLATION

wonderful new relationship with God because our Lord Jesus Christ has made us friends of God.

Adam and Christ Contrasted

12 When Adam sinned, sin entered the world. Adam's
sin brought death, so death spread to everyone, for
everyone sinned. 13 Yes, people sinned even before
the law was given. But it was not counted as sin because there was not yet any law to break. 14 Still,
everyone died—from the time of Adam to the time of
Moses—even those who did not disobey an explicit
commandment of God, as Adam did. Now Adam is
a symbol, a representation of Christ, who was yet to
come. 15 But there is a great difference between
Adam's sin and God's gracious gift. For the sin of this
one man, Adam, brought death to many. But even
greater is God's wonderful grace and his gift of forgiveness to many through this other man, Jesus
Christ. 16 And the result of God's gracious gift is very
different from the result of that one man's sin. For
Adam's sin led to condemnation, but God's free gift
leads to our being made right with God, even though
we are guilty of many sins. 17 For the sin of this one
man, Adam, caused death to rule over many. But even
greater is God's wonderful grace and his gift of righteousness, for all who receive it will live in triumph
over sin and death through this one man, Jesus
Christ.

18 Yes, Adam's one sin brings condemnation for
everyone, but Christ's one act of righteousness
brings a right relationship with God and new life for
everyone. 19 Because one person disobeyed God,
many became sinners. But because one other person
obeyed God, many will be made righteous.

20 God's law was given so that all people could see
how sinful they were. But as people sinned more and
more, God's wonderful grace became more abundant. 21 So just as sin ruled over all people and
brought them to death, now God's wonderful grace
rules instead, giving us right standing with God and
resulting in eternal life through Jesus Christ our
Lord.

Sin's Power Is Broken

6 Well then, should we keep on sinning so that
God can show us more and more of his wonderful grace? 2 Of course not! Since we have died to
sin, how can we continue to live in it? 3 Or have you
forgotten that when we were joined with Christ Jesus
in baptism, we joined him in his death? 4 For we died
and were buried with Christ by baptism. And just as
Christ was raised from the dead by the glorious
power of the Father, now we also may live new lives.

5 Since we have been united with him in his death,
we will also be raised to life as he was. 6 We know that

KING JAMES VERSION

him, that the body of sin might be destroyed, that henceforth we should not serve sin.

7For he that is dead is freed from sin.

8Now if we be dead with Christ, we believe that we shall also live with him:

9Knowing that Christ being raised from the dead dieth no more; death hath no more dominion over him.

10For in that he died, he died unto sin once: but in that he liveth, he liveth unto God.

11Likewise reckon ye also yourselves to be dead indeed unto sin, but alive unto God through Jesus Christ our Lord.

12Let not sin therefore reign in your mortal body, that ye should obey it in the lusts thereof.

13Neither yield ye your members *as* instruments of unrighteousness unto sin: but yield yourselves unto God, as those that are alive from the dead, and your members *as* instruments of righteousness unto God.

14For sin shall not have dominion over you: for ye are not under the law, but under grace.

15What then? shall we sin, because we are not under the law, but under grace? God forbid.

16Know ye not, that to whom ye yield yourselves servants to obey, his servants ye are to whom ye obey; whether of sin unto death, or of obedience unto righteousness?

17But God be thanked, that ye were the servants of sin, but ye have obeyed from the heart that form of doctrine which was delivered you.

18Being then made free from sin, ye became the servants of righteousness.

19I speak after the manner of men because of the infirmity of your flesh: for as ye have yielded your members servants to uncleanness and to iniquity unto iniquity; even so now yield your members servants to righteousness unto holiness.

20For when ye were the servants of sin, ye were free from righteousness.

21What fruit had ye then in those things whereof ye are now ashamed? for the end of those things *is* death.

22But now being made free from sin, and become servants to God, ye have your fruit unto holiness, and the end everlasting life.

23For the wages of sin *is* death; but the gift of God *is* eternal life through Jesus Christ our Lord.

7 1Know ye not, brethren, (for I speak to them that know the law,) how that the law hath dominion over a man as long as he liveth?

2For the woman which hath an husband is bound by the law to *her* husband so long as he liveth; but if the husband be dead, she is loosed from the law of *her* husband.

3So then if, while *her* husband liveth, she be married to another man, she shall be called an adulteress:

NEW LIVING TRANSLATION

our old sinful selves were crucified with Christ so that sin might lose its power in our lives. We are no longer slaves to sin. 7For when we died with Christ we were set free from the power of sin. 8And since we died with Christ, we know we will also live with him. 9We are sure of this because Christ was raised from the dead, and he will never die again. Death no longer has any power over him. 10When he died, he died once to break the power of sin. But now that he lives, he lives for the glory of God. 11So you also should consider yourselves to be dead to the power of sin and alive to God through Christ Jesus.

12Do not let sin control the way you live;* do not give in to sinful desires. 13Do not let any part of your body become an instrument of evil to serve sin. Instead, give yourselves completely to God, for you were dead, but now you have new life. So use your whole body as an instrument to do what is right for the glory of God. 14Sin is no longer your master, for you no longer live under the requirements of the law. Instead, you live under the freedom of God's grace.

15Well then, since God's grace has set us free from the law, does that mean we can go on sinning? Of course not! 16Don't you realize that you become the slave of whatever you choose to obey? You can be a slave to sin, which leads to death, or you can choose to obey God, which leads to righteous living. 17Thank God! Once you were slaves of sin, but now you wholeheartedly obey this teaching we have given you. 18Now you are free from your slavery to sin, and you have become slaves to righteous living.

19Because of the weakness of your human nature, I am using the illustration of slavery to help you understand all this. Previously, you let yourselves be slaves to impurity and lawlessness, which led ever deeper into sin. Now you must give yourselves to be slaves to righteous living so that you will become holy.

20When you were slaves to sin, you were free from the obligation to do right. 21And what was the result? You are now ashamed of the things you used to do, things that end in eternal doom. 22But now you are free from the power of sin and have become slaves of God. Now you do those things that lead to holiness and result in eternal life. 23For the wages of sin is death, but the free gift of God is eternal life through Christ Jesus our Lord.

No Longer Bound to the Law

7 Now, dear brothers and sisters*—you who are familiar with the law—don't you know that the law applies only while a person is living? 2For example, when a woman marries, the law binds her to her husband as long as he is alive. But if he dies, the laws of marriage no longer apply to her. 3So while her husband is alive, she would be committing adultery

6:12 Or *Do not let sin reign in your body, which is subject to death.*
7:1 Greek *brothers;* also in 7:4.

KING JAMES VERSION

but if her husband be dead, she is free from that law;
so that she is no adulteress, though she be married
to another man.
4 Wherefore, my brethren, ye also are become
dead to the law by the body of Christ; that ye should
be married to another, *even* to him who is raised
from the dead, that we should bring forth fruit unto
God.
5 For when we were in the flesh, the motions of
sins, which were by the law, did work in our members to bring forth fruit unto death.
6 But now we are delivered from the law, that being
dead wherein we were held; that we should serve in
newness of spirit, and not *in* the oldness of the letter.

7 What shall we say then? *Is* the law sin? God forbid. Nay, I had not known sin, but by the law: for I had
not known lust, except the law had said, Thou shalt
not covet.
8 But sin, taking occasion by the commandment,
wrought in me all manner of concupiscence. For
without the law sin *was* dead.
9 For I was alive without the law once: but when the
commandment came, sin revived, and I died.
10 And the commandment, which *was ordained*
to life, I found *to be* unto death.
11 For sin, taking occasion by the commandment,
deceived me, and by it slew *me*.
12 Wherefore the law *is* holy, and the commandment holy, and just, and good.
13 Was then that which is good made death unto
me? God forbid. But sin, that it might appear sin,
working death in me by that which is good; that sin
by the commandment might become exceeding
sinful.

14 For we know that the law is spiritual: but I am
carnal, sold under sin.
15 For that which I do I allow not: for what I would,
that do I not; but what I hate, that do I.
16 If then I do that which I would not, I consent
unto the law that *it is* good.
17 Now then it is no more I that do it, but sin that
dwelleth in me.
18 For I know that in me (that is, in my flesh,)
dwelleth no good thing: for to will is present with
me; but *how* to perform that which is good I find not.
19 For the good that I would I do not: but the evil
which I would not, that I do.
20 Now if I do that I would not, it is no more I that
do it, but sin that dwelleth in me.
21 I find then a law, that, when I would do good, evil
is present with me.

NEW LIVING TRANSLATION

if she married another man. But if her husband dies,
she is free from that law and does not commit adultery when she remarries.
4 So, my dear brothers and sisters, this is the point:
You died to the power of the law when you died with
Christ. And now you are united with the one who was
raised from the dead. As a result, we can produce
a harvest of good deeds for God. 5 When we were
controlled by our old nature,* sinful desires were at
work within us, and the law aroused these evil desires that produced a harvest of sinful deeds, resulting in death. 6 But now we have been released from
the law, for we died to it and are no longer captive to
its power. Now we can serve God, not in the old way
of obeying the letter of the law, but in the new way of
living in the Spirit.

God's Law Reveals Our Sin

7 Well then, am I suggesting that the law of God is sinful? Of course not! In fact, it was the law that showed
me my sin. I would never have known that coveting is
wrong if the law had not said, "You must not covet."*
8 But sin used this command to arouse all kinds of
covetous desires within me! If there were no law, sin
would not have that power. 9 At one time I lived without understanding the law. But when I learned the
command not to covet, for instance, the power of sin
came to life, 10 and I died. So I discovered that the
law's commands, which were supposed to bring life,
brought spiritual death instead. 11 Sin took advantage of those commands and deceived me; it used
the commands to kill me. 12 But still, the law itself is
holy, and its commands are holy and right and good.
13 But how can that be? Did the law, which is good,
cause my death? Of course not! Sin used what was
good to bring about my condemnation to death. So
we can see how terrible sin really is. It uses God's
good commands for its own evil purposes.

Struggling with Sin

14 So the trouble is not with the law, for it is spiritual
and good. The trouble is with me, for I am all too
human, a slave to sin. 15 I don't really understand myself, for I want to do what is right, but I don't do it. Instead, I do what I hate. 16 But if I know that what I am
doing is wrong, this shows that I agree that the law is
good. 17 So I am not the one doing wrong; it is sin
living in me that does it.
18 And I know that nothing good lives in me, that is,
in my sinful nature.* I want to do what is right, but I
can't. 19 I want to do what is good, but I don't. I don't
want to do what is wrong, but I do it anyway. 20 But if
I do what I don't want to do, I am not really the one
doing wrong; it is sin living in me that does it.
21 I have discovered this principle of life—that
when I want to do what is right, I inevitably do what is

7:5 Greek *When we were in the flesh.* 7:7 Exod 20:17; Deut 5:21.
7:18 Greek *my flesh;* also in 7:25.

KING JAMES VERSION

22For I delight in the law of God after the inward man:

23But I see another law in my members, warring against the law of my mind, and bringing me into captivity to the law of sin which is in my members.

24O wretched man that I am! who shall deliver me from the body of this death?

25I thank God through Jesus Christ our Lord. So then with the mind I myself serve the law of God; but with the flesh the law of sin.

8 1*There is* therefore now no condemnation to them which are in Christ Jesus, who walk not after the flesh, but after the Spirit.

2For the law of the Spirit of life in Christ Jesus hath made me free from the law of sin and death.

3For what the law could not do, in that it was weak through the flesh, God sending his own Son in the likeness of sinful flesh, and for sin, condemned sin in the flesh:

4That the righteousness of the law might be fulfilled in us, who walk not after the flesh, but after the Spirit.

5For they that are after the flesh do mind the things of the flesh; but they that are after the Spirit the things of the Spirit.

6For to be carnally minded *is* death; but to be spiritually minded *is* life and peace.

7Because the carnal mind *is* enmity against God: for it is not subject to the law of God, neither indeed can be.

8So then they that are in the flesh cannot please God.

9But ye are not in the flesh, but in the Spirit, if so be that the Spirit of God dwell in you. Now if any man have not the Spirit of Christ, he is none of his.

10And if Christ *be* in you, the body *is* dead because of sin; but the Spirit *is* life because of righteousness.

11But if the Spirit of him that raised up Jesus from the dead dwell in you, he that raised up Christ from the dead shall also quicken your mortal bodies by his Spirit that dwelleth in you.

12Therefore, brethren, we are debtors, not to the flesh, to live after the flesh.

13For if ye live after the flesh, ye shall die: but if ye through the Spirit do mortify the deeds of the body, ye shall live.

14For as many as are led by the Spirit of God, they are the sons of God.

15For ye have not received the spirit of bondage again to fear; but ye have received the Spirit of adoption, whereby we cry, Abba, Father.

16The Spirit itself beareth witness with our spirit, that we are the children of God:

NEW LIVING TRANSLATION

wrong. 22I love God's law with all my heart. 23But there is another power* within me that is at war with my mind. This power makes me a slave to the sin that is still within me. 24Oh, what a miserable person I am! Who will free me from this life that is dominated by sin and death? 25Thank God! The answer is in Jesus Christ our Lord. So you see how it is: In my mind I really want to obey God's law, but because of my sinful nature I am a slave to sin.

Life in the Spirit

8 So now there is no condemnation for those who belong to Christ Jesus. 2And because you belong to him, the power* of the life-giving Spirit has freed you* from the power of sin that leads to death. 3The law of Moses was unable to save us because of the weakness of our sinful nature.* So God did what the law could not do. He sent his own Son in a body like the bodies we sinners have. And in that body God declared an end to sin's control over us by giving his Son as a sacrifice for our sins. 4He did this so that the just requirement of the law would be fully satisfied for us, who no longer follow our sinful nature but instead follow the Spirit.

5Those who are dominated by the sinful nature think about sinful things, but those who are controlled by the Holy Spirit think about things that please the Spirit. 6So letting your sinful nature control your mind leads to death. But letting the Spirit control your mind leads to life and peace. 7For the sinful nature is always hostile to God. It never did obey God's laws, and it never will. 8That's why those who are still under the control of their sinful nature can never please God.

9But you are not controlled by your sinful nature. You are controlled by the Spirit if you have the Spirit of God living in you. (And remember that those who do not have the Spirit of Christ living in them do not belong to him at all.) 10And Christ lives within you, so even though your body will die because of sin, the Spirit gives you life* because you have been made right with God. 11The Spirit of God, who raised Jesus from the dead, lives in you. And just as God raised Christ Jesus from the dead, he will give life to your mortal bodies by this same Spirit living within you.

12Therefore, dear brothers and sisters,* you have no obligation to do what your sinful nature urges you to do. 13For if you live by its dictates, you will die. But if through the power of the Spirit you put to death the deeds of your sinful nature,* you will live. 14For all who are led by the Spirit of God are children* of God.

15So you have not received a spirit that makes you fearful slaves. Instead, you received God's Spirit when he adopted you as his own children.* Now we call him, "Abba, Father."* 16For his Spirit joins with

7:23 Greek *law;* also in 7:23b. **8:2a** Greek *the law;* also in 8:2b. **8:2b** Some manuscripts read *me.* **8:3** Greek *our flesh;* similarly in 8:4, 5, 6, 7, 8, 9, 12. **8:10** Or *your spirit is alive.* **8:12** Greek *brothers;* also in 8:29. **8:13** Greek *deeds of the body.* **8:14** Greek *sons;* also in 8:19. **8:15a** Greek *you received a spirit of sonship.* **8:15b** *Abba* is an Aramaic term for "father."

KING JAMES VERSION

17And if children, then heirs; heirs of God, and joint-heirs with Christ; if so be that we suffer with *him,* that we may be also glorified together.

18For I reckon that the sufferings of this present time *are* not worthy *to be compared* with the glory which shall be revealed in us.

19For the earnest expectation of the creature waiteth for the manifestation of the sons of God.

20For the creature was made subject to vanity, not willingly, but by reason of him who hath subjected *the same* in hope,

21Because the creature itself also shall be delivered from the bondage of corruption into the glorious liberty of the children of God.

22For we know that the whole creation groaneth and travaileth in pain together until now.

23And not only *they,* but ourselves also, which have the firstfruits of the Spirit, even we ourselves groan within ourselves, waiting for the adoption, *to wit,* the redemption of our body.

24For we are saved by hope: but hope that is seen is not hope: for what a man seeth, why doth he yet hope for?

25But if we hope for that we see not, *then* do we with patience wait for *it.*

26Likewise the Spirit also helpeth our infirmities: for we know not what we should pray for as we ought: but the Spirit itself maketh intercession for us with groanings which cannot be uttered.

27And he that searcheth the hearts knoweth what *is* the mind of the Spirit, because he maketh intercession for the saints according to *the will of* God.

28And we know that all things work together for good to them that love God, to them who are the called according to *his* purpose.

29For whom he did foreknow, he also did predestinate *to be* conformed to the image of his Son, that he might be the firstborn among many brethren.

30Moreover whom he did predestinate, them he also called: and whom he called, them he also justified: and whom he justified, them he also glorified.

31What shall we then say to these things? If God *be* for us, who *can be* against us?

32He that spared not his own Son, but delivered him up for us all, how shall he not with him also freely give us all things?

33Who shall lay any thing to the charge of God's elect? *It is* God that justifieth.

34Who *is* he that condemneth? *It is* Christ that died, yea rather, that is risen again, who is even at the right hand of God, who also maketh intercession for us.

NEW LIVING TRANSLATION

our spirit to affirm that we are God's children. 17And since we are his children, we are his heirs. In fact, together with Christ we are heirs of God's glory. But if we are to share his glory, we must also share his suffering.

The Future Glory

18Yet what we suffer now is nothing compared to the glory he will reveal to us later. 19For all creation is waiting eagerly for that future day when God will reveal who his children really are. 20Against its will, all creation was subjected to God's curse. But with eager hope, 21the creation looks forward to the day when it will join God's children in glorious freedom from death and decay. 22For we know that all creation has been groaning as in the pains of childbirth right up to the present time. 23And we believers also groan, even though we have the Holy Spirit within us as a foretaste of future glory, for we long for our bodies to be released from sin and suffering. We, too, wait with eager hope for the day when God will give us our full rights as his adopted children,* including the new bodies he has promised us. 24We were given this hope when we were saved. (If we already have something, we don't need to hope* for it. 25But if we look forward to something we don't yet have, we must wait patiently and confidently.)

26And the Holy Spirit helps us in our weakness. For example, we don't know what God wants us to pray for. But the Holy Spirit prays for us with groanings that cannot be expressed in words. 27And the Father who knows all hearts knows what the Spirit is saying, for the Spirit pleads for us believers* in harmony with God's own will. 28And we know that God causes everything to work together* for the good of those who love God and are called according to his purpose for them. 29For God knew his people in advance, and he chose them to become like his Son, so that his Son would be the firstborn* among many brothers and sisters. 30And having chosen them, he called them to come to him. And having called them, he gave them right standing with himself. And having given them right standing, he gave them his glory.

Nothing Can Separate Us from God's Love

31What shall we say about such wonderful things as these? If God is for us, who can ever be against us? 32Since he did not spare even his own Son but gave him up for us all, won't he also give us everything else? 33Who dares accuse us whom God has chosen for his own? No one—for God himself has given us right standing with himself. 34Who then will condemn us? No one—for Christ Jesus died for us and was raised to life for us, and he is sitting in the place of honor at God's right hand, pleading for us.

8:23 Greek *wait anxiously for sonship.* **8:24** Some manuscripts read *wait.* **8:27** Greek *for God's holy people.* **8:28** Some manuscripts read *And we know that everything works together.* **8:29** Or *would be supreme.*

KING JAMES VERSION

35 Who shall separate us from the love of Christ? *shall* tribulation, or distress, or persecution, or famine, or nakedness, or peril, or sword?

36 As it is written, For thy sake we are killed all the day long; we are accounted as sheep for the slaughter.

37 Nay, in all these things we are more than conquerors through him that loved us.

38 For I am persuaded, that neither death, nor life, nor angels, nor principalities, nor powers, nor things present, nor things to come,

39 Nor height, nor depth, nor any other creature, shall be able to separate us from the love of God, which is in Christ Jesus our Lord.

9 1 I say the truth in Christ, I lie not, my conscience also bearing me witness in the Holy Ghost,

2 That I have great heaviness and continual sorrow in my heart.

3 For I could wish that myself were accursed from Christ for my brethren, my kinsmen according to the flesh:

4 Who are Israelites; to whom *pertaineth* the adoption, and the glory, and the covenants, and the giving of the law, and the service *of God,* and the promises;

5 Whose *are* the fathers, and of whom as concerning the flesh Christ *came,* who is over all, God blessed for ever. Amen.

6 Not as though the word of God hath taken none effect. For they *are* not all Israel, which are of Israel:

7 Neither, because they are the seed of Abraham, *are they* all children: but, In Isaac shall thy seed be called.

8 That is, They which are the children of the flesh, these *are* not the children of God: but the children of the promise are counted for the seed.

9 For this *is* the word of promise, At this time will I come, and Sarah shall have a son.

10 And not only *this;* but when Rebecca also had conceived by one, *even* by our father Isaac;

11 (For *the children* being not yet born, neither having done any good or evil, that the purpose of God according to election might stand, not of works, but of him that calleth;)

12 It was said unto her, The elder shall serve the younger.

13 As it is written, Jacob have I loved, but Esau have I hated.

NEW LIVING TRANSLATION

35 Can anything ever separate us from Christ's love? Does it mean he no longer loves us if we have trouble or calamity, or are persecuted, or hungry, or destitute, or in danger, or threatened with death? 36 (As the Scriptures say, "For your sake we are killed every day; we are being slaughtered like sheep."*) 37 No, despite all these things, overwhelming victory is ours through Christ, who loved us.

38 And I am convinced that nothing can ever separate us from God's love. Neither death nor life, neither angels nor demons,* neither our fears for today nor our worries about tomorrow—not even the powers of hell can separate us from God's love. 39 No power in the sky above or in the earth below—indeed, nothing in all creation will ever be able to separate us from the love of God that is revealed in Christ Jesus our Lord.

God's Selection of Israel

9 With Christ as my witness, I speak with utter truthfulness. My conscience and the Holy Spirit confirm it. 2 My heart is filled with bitter sorrow and unending grief 3 for my people, my Jewish brothers and sisters.* I would be willing to be forever cursed—cut off from Christ!—if that would save them. 4 They are the people of Israel, chosen to be God's adopted children.* God revealed his glory to them. He made covenants with them and gave them his law. He gave them the privilege of worshiping him and receiving his wonderful promises. 5 Abraham, Isaac, and Jacob are their ancestors, and Christ himself was an Israelite as far as his human nature is concerned. And he is God, the one who rules over everything and is worthy of eternal praise! Amen.*

6 Well then, has God failed to fulfill his promise to Israel? No, for not all who are born into the nation of Israel are truly members of God's people! 7 Being descendants of Abraham doesn't make them truly Abraham's children. For the Scriptures say, "Isaac is the son through whom your descendants will be counted,"* though Abraham had other children, too. 8 This means that Abraham's physical descendants are not necessarily children of God. Only the children of the promise are considered to be Abraham's children. 9 For God had promised, "I will return about this time next year, and Sarah will have a son."*

10 This son was our ancestor Isaac. When he married Rebekah, she gave birth to twins.* 11 But before they were born, before they had done anything good or bad, she received a message from God. (This message shows that God chooses people according to his own purposes; 12 he calls people, but not according to their good or bad works.) She was told, "Your older son will serve your younger son."* 13 In the words of the Scriptures, "I loved Jacob, but I rejected Esau."*

8:36 Ps 44:22. **8:38** Greek *nor rulers.* **9:3** Greek *my brothers.* **9:4** Greek *chosen for sonship.* **9:5** Or *May God, the one who rules over everything, be praised forever. Amen.* **9:7** Gen 21:12. **9:9** Gen 18:10, 14. **9:10** Greek *she conceived children through this one man.* **9:12** Gen 25:23. **9:13** Mal 1:2-3.

KING JAMES VERSION

14 What shall we say then? *Is there* unrighteousness with God? God forbid.
15 For he saith to Moses, I will have mercy on whom
I will have mercy, and I will have compassion on
whom I will have compassion.
16 So then *it is* not of him that willeth, nor of him
that runneth, but of God that sheweth mercy.
17 For the scripture saith unto Pharaoh, Even for
this same purpose have I raised thee up, that I might
shew my power in thee, and that my name might be
declared throughout all the earth.
18 Therefore hath he mercy on whom he will *have*
mercy, and whom he will he hardeneth.
19 Thou wilt say then unto me, Why doth he yet
find fault? For who hath resisted his will?
20 Nay but, O man, who art thou that repliest
against God? Shall the thing formed say to him that
formed *it,* Why hast thou made me thus?
21 Hath not the potter power over the clay, of the
same lump to make one vessel unto honour, and
another unto dishonour?
22 *What* if God, willing to shew *his* wrath, and to
make his power known, endured with much longsuffering the vessels of wrath fitted to destruction:
23 And that he might make known the riches of his
glory on the vessels of mercy, which he had afore prepared unto glory,
24 Even us, whom he hath called, not of the Jews
only, but also of the Gentiles?
25 As he saith also in Osee, I will call them my
people, which were not my people; and her beloved,
which was not beloved.
26 And it shall come to pass, *that* in the place where
it was said unto them, Ye *are* not my people; there
shall they be called the children of the living God.
27 Esaias also crieth concerning Israel, Though the
number of the children of Israel be as the sand of the
sea, a remnant shall be saved:
28 For he will finish the work, and cut *it* short in
righteousness: because a short work will the Lord
make upon the earth.
29 And as Esaias said before, Except the Lord of
Sabaoth had left us a seed, we had been as Sodoma,
and been made like unto Gomorrha.

NEW LIVING TRANSLATION

14 Are we saying, then, that God was unfair? Of
course not! 15 For God said to Moses,

"I will show mercy to anyone I choose,
and I will show compassion to anyone I choose."*

16 So it is God who decides to show mercy. We can
neither choose it nor work for it.
17 For the Scriptures say that God told Pharaoh, "I
have appointed you for the very purpose of display-
ing my power in you and to spread my fame throughout the earth."* 18 So you see, God chooses to show
mercy to some, and he chooses to harden the hearts
of others so they refuse to listen.
19 Well then, you might say, "Why does God blame
people for not responding? Haven't they simply done
what he makes them do?"
20 No, don't say that. Who are you, a mere human
being, to argue with God? Should the thing that was
created say to the one who created it, "Why have you
made me like this?" 21 When a potter makes jars out of
clay, doesn't he have a right to use the same lump
of clay to make one jar for decoration and another
to throw garbage into? 22 In the same way, even though
God has the right to show his anger and his power,
he is very patient with those on whom his anger falls,
who are destined for destruction. 23 He does this to
make the riches of his glory shine even brighter on
those to whom he shows mercy, who were prepared in
advance for glory. 24 And we are among those whom he
selected, both from the Jews and from the Gentiles.
25 Concerning the Gentiles, God says in the prophecy of Hosea,

"Those who were not my people,
I will now call my people.
And I will love those
whom I did not love before."*

26 And,

"Then, at the place where they were told,
'You are not my people,'
there they will be called
'children of the living God.'"*

27 And concerning Israel, Isaiah the prophet cried out,

"Though the people of Israel are as numerous
as the sand of the seashore,
only a remnant will be saved.
28 For the LORD will carry out his sentence
upon the earth
quickly and with finality."*

29 And Isaiah said the same thing in another place:

"If the LORD of Heaven's Armies
had not spared a few of our children,
we would have been wiped out like Sodom,
destroyed like Gomorrah."*

9:15 Exod 33:19. **9:17** Exod 9:16 (Greek version). **9:25** Hos 2:23. **9:26** Greek *sons of the living God.* Hos 1:10. **9:27-28** Isa 10:22-23 (Greek version). **9:29** Isa 1:9.

KING JAMES VERSION

30 What shall we say then? That the Gentiles, which followed not after righteousness, have attained to righteousness, even the righteousness which is of faith.

31 But Israel, which followed after the law of righteousness, hath not attained to the law of righteousness.

32 Wherefore? Because *they sought it* not by faith, but as it were by the works of the law. For they stumbled at that stumblingstone;

33 As it is written, Behold, I lay in Sion a stumblingstone and rock of offence: and whosoever believeth on him shall not be ashamed.

10 1 Brethren, my heart's desire and prayer to God for Israel is, that they might be saved.

2 For I bear them record that they have a zeal of God, but not according to knowledge.

3 For they being ignorant of God's righteousness, and going about to establish their own righteousness, have not submitted themselves unto the righteousness of God.

4 For Christ *is* the end of the law for righteousness to every one that believeth.

5 For Moses describeth the righteousness which is of the law, That the man which doeth those things shall live by them.

6 But the righteousness which is of faith speaketh on this wise, Say not in thine heart, Who shall ascend into heaven? (that is, to bring Christ down *from above:*)

7 Or, Who shall descend into the deep? (that is, to bring up Christ again from the dead.)

8 But what saith it? The word is nigh thee, *even* in thy mouth, and in thy heart: that is, the word of faith, which we preach;

9 That if thou shalt confess with thy mouth the Lord Jesus, and shalt believe in thine heart that God hath raised him from the dead, thou shalt be saved.

10 For with the heart man believeth unto righteousness; and with the mouth confession is made unto salvation.

11 For the scripture saith, Whosoever believeth on him shall not be ashamed.

12 For there is no difference between the Jew and the Greek: for the same Lord over all is rich unto all that call upon him.

13 For whosoever shall call upon the name of the Lord shall be saved.

14 How then shall they call on him in whom they have not believed? and how shall they believe in him

NEW LIVING TRANSLATION

Israel's Unbelief

30 What does all this mean? Even though the Gentiles
were not trying to follow God's standards, they were
made right with God. And it was by faith that this
took place. 31 But the people of Israel, who tried so
hard to get right with God by keeping the law, never
succeeded. 32 Why not? Because they were trying to
get right with God by keeping the law* instead of by
trusting in him. They stumbled over the great rock in
their path. 33 God warned them of this in the Scriptures when he said,

"I am placing a stone in Jerusalem* that makes
people stumble,
a rock that makes them fall.
But anyone who trusts in him
will never be disgraced."*

10 Dear brothers and sisters,* the longing of my
heart and my prayer to God is for the people
of Israel to be saved. 2 I know what enthusiasm they
have for God, but it is misdirected zeal. 3 For they
don't understand God's way of making people right
with himself. Refusing to accept God's way, they
cling to their own way of getting right with God by
trying to keep the law. 4 For Christ has already accomplished the purpose for which the law was given.*
As a result, all who believe in him are made right
with God.

Salvation Is for Everyone

5 For Moses writes that the law's way of making a person right with God requires obedience to all of its
commands.* 6 But faith's way of getting right with
God says, "Don't say in your heart, 'Who will go up to
heaven?' (to bring Christ down to earth). 7 And don't
say, 'Who will go down to the place of the dead?' (to
bring Christ back to life again)." 8 In fact, it says,

"The message is very close at hand;
it is on your lips and in your heart."*

And that message is the very message about faith
that we preach: 9 If you confess with your mouth that
Jesus is Lord and believe in your heart that God
raised him from the dead, you will be saved. 10 For it is
by believing in your heart that you are made right
with God, and it is by confessing with your mouth
that you are saved. 11 As the Scriptures tell us, "Anyone
who trusts in him will never be disgraced."* 12 Jew
and Gentile* are the same in this respect. They have
the same Lord, who gives generously to all who call
on him. 13 For "Everyone who calls on the name of the
LORD will be saved."*

14 But how can they call on him to save them unless
they believe in him? And how can they believe in him

9:32 Greek *by works.* **9:33a** Greek *in Zion.* **9:33b** Isa 8:14; 28:16 (Greek version). **10:1** Greek *Brothers.* **10:4** Or *For Christ is the end of the law.* **10:5** See Lev 18:5. **10:6-8** Deut 30:12-14. **10:11** Isa 28:16 (Greek version). **10:12** Greek *and Greek.* **10:13** Joel 2:32.

KING JAMES VERSION

of whom they have not heard? and how shall they hear without a preacher?

15 And how shall they preach, except they be sent? as it is written, How beautiful are the feet of them that preach the gospel of peace, and bring glad tidings of good things!

16 But they have not all obeyed the gospel. For Esaias saith, Lord, who hath believed our report?

17 So then faith *cometh* by hearing, and hearing by the word of God.

18 But I say, Have they not heard? Yes verily, their sound went into all the earth, and their words unto the ends of the world.

19 But I say, Did not Israel know? First Moses saith, I will provoke you to jealousy by *them that are* no people, *and* by a foolish nation I will anger you.

20 But Esaias is very bold, and saith, I was found of them that sought me not; I was made manifest unto them that asked not after me.

21 But to Israel he saith, All day long I have stretched forth my hands unto a disobedient and gainsaying people.

11 1 I say then, Hath God cast away his people? God forbid. For I also am an Israelite, of the seed of Abraham, *of* the tribe of Benjamin.

2 God hath not cast away his people which he foreknew. Wot ye not what the scripture saith of Elias? how he maketh intercession to God against Israel, saying,

3 Lord, they have killed thy prophets, and digged down thine altars; and I am left alone, and they seek my life.

4 But what saith the answer of God unto him? I have reserved to myself seven thousand men, who have not bowed the knee to *the image of* Baal.

5 Even so then at this present time also there is a remnant according to the election of grace.

6 And if by grace, then *is it* no more of works: otherwise grace is no more grace. But if *it be* of works, then is it no more grace: otherwise work is no more work.

7 What then? Israel hath not obtained that which

NEW LIVING TRANSLATION

if they have never heard about him? And how can they hear about him unless someone tells them? 15 And how will anyone go and tell them without being sent? That is why the Scriptures say, "How beautiful are the feet of messengers who bring good news!"*

16 But not everyone welcomes the Good News, for Isaiah the prophet said, "LORD, who has believed our message?"* 17 So faith comes from hearing, that is, hearing the Good News about Christ. 18 But I ask, have the people of Israel actually heard the message? Yes, they have:

"The message has gone throughout the earth,
and the words to all the world."*

19 But I ask, did the people of Israel really understand? Yes, they did, for even in the time of Moses, God said,

"I will rouse your jealousy through people who
are not even a nation.
I will provoke your anger through the foolish
Gentiles."*

20 And later Isaiah spoke boldly for God, saying,

"I was found by people who were not looking
for me.
I showed myself to those who were not
asking for me."*

21 But regarding Israel, God said,

"All day long I opened my arms to them,
but they were disobedient and rebellious."*

God's Mercy on Israel

11 I ask, then, has God rejected his own people, the nation of Israel? Of course not! I myself am an Israelite, a descendant of Abraham and a member of the tribe of Benjamin.

2 No, God has not rejected his own people, whom he chose from the very beginning. Do you realize what the Scriptures say about this? Elijah the prophet complained to God about the people of Israel and said, 3 "LORD, they have killed your prophets and torn down your altars. I am the only one left, and now they are trying to kill me, too."*

4 And do you remember God's reply? He said, "No, I have 7,000 others who have never bowed down to Baal!"*

5 It is the same today, for a few of the people of Israel* have remained faithful because of God's grace—his undeserved kindness in choosing them. 6 And since it is through God's kindness, then it is not by their good works. For in that case, God's grace would not be what it really is—free and undeserved.

7 So this is the situation: Most of the people of Israel have not found the favor of God they are looking

10:15 Isa 52:7. **10:16** Isa 53:1. **10:18** Ps 19:4. **10:19** Deut 32:21. **10:20** Isa 65:1 (Greek version). **10:21** Isa 65:2 (Greek version). **11:3** 1 Kgs 19:10, 14. **11:4** 1 Kgs 19:18. **11:5** Greek *for a remnant.*

KING JAMES VERSION

he seeketh for; but the election hath obtained it, and the rest were blinded

8 (According as it is written, God hath given them the spirit of slumber, eyes that they should not see, and ears that they should not hear;) unto this day.

9 And David saith, Let their table be made a snare, and a trap, and a stumblingblock, and a recompence unto them:

10 Let their eyes be darkened that they may not see, and bow down their back alway.

11 I say then, Have they stumbled that they should fall? God forbid: but *rather* through their fall salvation *is come* unto the Gentiles, for to provoke them to jealousy.

12 Now if the fall of them *be* the riches of the world, and the diminishing of them the riches of the Gentiles; how much more their fulness?

13 For I speak to you Gentiles, inasmuch as I am the apostle of the Gentiles, I magnify mine office:

14 If by any means I may provoke to emulation *them which are* my flesh, and might save some of them.

15 For if the casting away of them *be* the reconciling of the world, what *shall* the receiving *of them be*, but life from the dead?

16 For if the firstfruit *be* holy, the lump *is* also *holy:* and if the root *be* holy, so *are* the branches.

17 And if some of the branches be broken off, and thou, being a wild olive tree, wert graffed in among them, and with them partakest of the root and fatness of the olive tree;

18 Boast not against the branches. But if thou boast, thou bearest not the root, but the root thee.

19 Thou wilt say then, The branches were broken off, that I might be graffed in.

20 Well; because of unbelief they were broken off, and thou standest by faith. Be not highminded, but fear:

21 For if God spared not the natural branches, *take heed* lest he also spare not thee.

NEW LIVING TRANSLATION

for so earnestly. A few have—the ones God has chosen—but the hearts of the rest were hardened.
8 As the Scriptures say,

"God has put them into a deep sleep.
To this day he has shut their eyes so they
do not see,
and closed their ears so they do not hear."*

9 Likewise, David said,

"Let their bountiful table become a snare,
a trap that makes them think all is well.
Let their blessings cause them to stumble,
and let them get what they deserve.
10 Let their eyes go blind so they cannot see,
and let their backs be bent forever."*

11 Did God's people stumble and fall beyond recovery? Of course not! They were disobedient, so God
made salvation available to the Gentiles. But he
wanted his own people to become jealous and claim
it for themselves. 12 Now if the Gentiles were enriched because the people of Israel turned down
God's offer of salvation, think how much greater a
blessing the world will share when they finally accept it.
13 I am saying all this especially for you Gentiles.
God has appointed me as the apostle to the Gentiles.
I stress this, 14 for I want somehow to make the people of Israel jealous of what you Gentiles have, so I
might save some of them. 15 For since their rejection
meant that God offered salvation to the rest of the
world, their acceptance will be even more wonderful. It will be life for those who were dead! 16 And
since Abraham and the other patriarchs were holy,
their descendants will also be holy—just as the entire
batch of dough is holy because the portion given as
an offering is holy. For if the roots of the tree are holy,
the branches will be, too.
17 But some of these branches from Abraham's
tree—some of the people of Israel—have been broken off. And you Gentiles, who were branches from a
wild olive tree, have been grafted in. So now you also
receive the blessing God has promised Abraham and
his children, sharing in the rich nourishment from
the root of God's special olive tree. 18 But you must
not brag about being grafted in to replace the
branches that were broken off. You are just a branch,
not the root.
19 "Well," you may say, "those branches were broken off to make room for me." 20 Yes, but remember—those branches were broken off because they
didn't believe in Christ, and you are there because
you do believe. So don't think highly of yourself, but
fear what could happen. 21 For if God did not spare
the original branches, he won't* spare you either.

11:8 Isa 29:10; Deut 29:4. **11:9-10** Ps 69:22-23 (Greek version).
11:21 Some manuscripts read *perhaps he won't*.

KING JAMES VERSION

22Behold therefore the goodness and severity of
God: on them which fell, severity; but toward thee,
goodness, if thou continue in *his* goodness: otherwise thou also shalt be cut off.
23And they also, if they abide not still in unbelief,
shall be graffed in: for God is able to graff them in
again.
24For if thou wert cut out of the olive tree which is
wild by nature, and wert graffed contrary to nature
into a good olive tree: how much more shall these,
which be the natural *branches,* be graffed into their
own olive tree?

25For I would not, brethren, that ye should be ignorant of this mystery, lest ye should be wise in your
own conceits; that blindness in part is happened to
Israel, until the fulness of the Gentiles be come in.
26And so all Israel shall be saved: as it is written,
There shall come out of Sion the Deliverer, and shall
turn away ungodliness from Jacob:
27For this *is* my covenant unto them, when I shall
take away their sins.
28As concerning the gospel, *they are* enemies for
your sakes: but as touching the election, *they are*
beloved for the fathers' sakes.
29For the gifts and calling of God *are* without
repentance.
30For as ye in times past have not believed God, yet
have now obtained mercy through their unbelief:
31Even so have these also now not believed, that
through your mercy they also may obtain mercy.
32For God hath concluded them all in unbelief,
that he might have mercy upon all.
33O the depth of the riches both of the wisdom
and knowledge of God! how unsearchable *are* his
judgments, and his ways past finding out!
34For who hath known the mind of the Lord? or
who hath been his counsellor?
35Or who hath first given to him, and it shall be
recompensed unto him again?
36For of him, and through him, and to him, *are* all
things: to whom *be* glory for ever. Amen.

12 1I beseech you therefore, brethren, by the
mercies of God, that ye present your bodies a
living sacrifice, holy, acceptable unto God, *which is*
your reasonable service.

NEW LIVING TRANSLATION

22Notice how God is both kind and severe. He is
severe toward those who disobeyed, but kind to you
if you continue to trust in his kindness. But if you
stop trusting, you also will be cut off. 23And if the
people of Israel turn from their unbelief, they will be
grafted in again, for God has the power to graft them
back into the tree. 24You, by nature, were a branch
cut from a wild olive tree. So if God was willing to do
something contrary to nature by grafting you into his
cultivated tree, he will be far more eager to graft the
original branches back into the tree where they
belong.

God's Mercy Is for Everyone

25I want you to understand this mystery, dear brothers and sisters,* so that you will not feel proud about
yourselves. Some of the people of Israel have hard
hearts, but this will last only until the full number of
Gentiles comes to Christ. 26And so all Israel will be
saved. As the Scriptures say,

"The one who rescues will come from
Jerusalem,*
and he will turn Israel* away from ungodliness.
27 And this is my covenant with them,
that I will take away their sins."*

28Many of the people of Israel are now enemies of
the Good News, and this benefits you Gentiles. Yet
they are still the people he loves because he chose
their ancestors Abraham, Isaac, and Jacob. 29For
God's gifts and his call can never be withdrawn.
30Once, you Gentiles were rebels against God, but
when the people of Israel rebelled against him, God
was merciful to you instead. 31Now they are the rebels, and God's mercy has come to you so that they,
too, will share* in God's mercy. 32For God has imprisoned everyone in disobedience so he could have
mercy on everyone.
33Oh, how great are God's riches and wisdom and
knowledge! How impossible it is for us to understand his decisions and his ways!

34 For who can know the LORD's thoughts?
Who knows enough to give him advice?*
35 And who has given him so much
that he needs to pay it back?*

36For everything comes from him and exists by his
power and is intended for his glory. All glory to him
forever! Amen.

A Living Sacrifice to God

12 And so, dear brothers and sisters,* I plead
with you to give your bodies to God because
of all he has done for you. Let them be a living and
holy sacrifice—the kind he will find acceptable. This

11:25 Greek *brothers.* **11:26a** Greek *from Zion.* **11:26b** Greek *Jacob.* **11:26-27** Isa 59:20-21; 27:9 (Greek version). **11:31** Other manuscripts read *will now share;* still others read *will someday share.* **11:34** Isa 40:13 (Greek version). **11:35** See Job 41:11. **12:1a** Greek *brothers.*

KING JAMES VERSION

2And be not conformed to this world: but be ye transformed by the renewing of your mind, that ye may prove what *is* that good, and acceptable, and perfect, will of God.

3For I say, through the grace given unto me, to every man that is among you, not to think *of himself* more highly than he ought to think; but to think soberly, according as God hath dealt to every man the measure of faith.

4For as we have many members in one body, and all members have not the same office:

5So we, *being* many, are one body in Christ, and every one members one of another.

6Having then gifts differing according to the grace that is given to us, whether prophecy, *let us prophesy* according to the proportion of faith;

7Or ministry, *let us wait* on *our* ministering: or he that teacheth, on teaching;

8Or he that exhorteth, on exhortation: he that giveth, *let him do it* with simplicity; he that ruleth, with diligence; he that sheweth mercy, with cheerfulness.

9*Let* love be without dissimulation. Abhor that which is evil; cleave to that which is good.

10*Be* kindly affectioned one to another with brotherly love; in honour preferring one another;

11Not slothful in business; fervent in spirit; serving the Lord;

12Rejoicing in hope; patient in tribulation; continuing instant in prayer;

13Distributing to the necessity of saints; given to hospitality.

14Bless them which persecute you: bless, and curse not.

15Rejoice with them that do rejoice, and weep with them that weep.

16*Be* of the same mind one toward another. Mind not high things, but condescend to men of low estate. Be not wise in your own conceits.

17Recompense to no man evil for evil. Provide things honest in the sight of all men.

18If it be possible, as much as lieth in you, live peaceably with all men.

19Dearly beloved, avenge not yourselves, but *rather* give place unto wrath: for it is written, Vengeance *is* mine; I will repay, saith the Lord.

20Therefore if thine enemy hunger, feed him; if he thirst, give him drink: for in so doing thou shalt heap coals of fire on his head.

21Be not overcome of evil, but overcome evil with good.

NEW LIVING TRANSLATION

is truly the way to worship him.* 2Don't copy the behavior and customs of this world, but let God transform you into a new person by changing the way you
think. Then you will learn to know God's will for you,
which is good and pleasing and perfect.
3Because of the privilege and authority* God has
given me, I give each of you this warning: Don't think
you are better than you really are. Be honest in your
evaluation of yourselves, measuring yourselves by
the faith God has given us.* 4Just as our bodies have
many parts and each part has a special function, 5so
it is with Christ's body. We are many parts of one
body, and we all belong to each other.
6In his grace, God has given us different gifts for
doing certain things well. So if God has given you the
ability to prophesy, speak out with as much faith as
God has given you. 7If your gift is serving others, serve
them well. If you are a teacher, teach well. 8If your gift
is to encourage others, be encouraging. If it is giving,
give generously. If God has given you leadership ability, take the responsibility seriously. And if you have
a gift for showing kindness to others, do it gladly.
9Don't just pretend to love others. Really love them.
Hate what is wrong. Hold tightly to what is good. 10Love
each other with genuine affection,* and take delight in
honoring each other. 11Never be lazy, but work hard
and serve the Lord enthusiastically.* 12Rejoice in our
confident hope. Be patient in trouble, and keep on
praying. 13When God's people are in need, be ready to
help them. Always be eager to practice hospitality.
14Bless those who persecute you. Don't curse
them; pray that God will bless them. 15Be happy with
those who are happy, and weep with those who weep.
16Live in harmony with each other. Don't be too
proud to enjoy the company of ordinary people. And
don't think you know it all!
17Never pay back evil with more evil. Do things in
such a way that everyone can see you are honorable.
18Do all that you can to live in peace with everyone.
19Dear friends, never take revenge. Leave that to
the righteous anger of God. For the Scriptures say,

"I will take revenge;
I will pay them back,"*
says the LORD.

20Instead,

"If your enemies are hungry, feed them.
If they are thirsty, give them something
to drink.
In doing this, you will heap
burning coals of shame on their heads."*

21Don't let evil conquer you, but conquer evil by doing good.

12:1b Or *This is your spiritual worship;* or *This is your reasonable service.* **12:3a** Or *Because of the grace;* compare 1:5. **12:3b** Or *by the faith God has given you;* or *by the standard of our God-given faith.* **12:10** Greek *with brotherly love.* **12:11** Or *but serve the Lord with a zealous spirit;* or *but let the Spirit excite you as you serve the Lord.* **12:19** Deut 32:35. **12:20** Prov 25:21-22.

KING JAMES VERSION

13

[1]Let every soul be subject unto the higher powers. For there is no power but of God: the powers that be are ordained of God.

[2]Whosoever therefore resisteth the power, resisteth the ordinance of God: and they that resist shall receive to themselves damnation.

[3]For rulers are not a terror to good works, but to the evil. Wilt thou then not be afraid of the power? do that which is good, and thou shalt have praise of the same:

[4]For he is the minister of God to thee for good. But if thou do that which is evil, be afraid; for he beareth not the sword in vain: for he is the minister of God, a revenger to *execute* wrath upon him that doeth evil.

[5]Wherefore *ye* must needs be subject, not only for wrath, but also for conscience sake.

[6]For for this cause pay ye tribute also: for they are God's ministers, attending continually upon this very thing.

[7]Render therefore to all their dues: tribute to whom tribute *is due;* custom to whom custom; fear to whom fear; honour to whom honour.

[8]Owe no man any thing, but to love one another: for he that loveth another hath fulfilled the law.

[9]For this, Thou shalt not commit adultery, Thou shalt not kill, Thou shalt not steal, Thou shalt not bear false witness, Thou shalt not covet; and if *there be* any other commandment, it is briefly comprehended in this saying, namely, Thou shalt love thy neighbour as thyself.

[10]Love worketh no ill to his neighbour: therefore love *is* the fulfilling of the law.

[11]And that, knowing the time, that now *it is* high time to awake out of sleep: for now *is* our salvation nearer than when we believed.

[12]The night is far spent, the day is at hand: let us therefore cast off the works of darkness, and let us put on the armour of light.

[13]Let us walk honestly, as in the day; not in rioting and drunkenness, not in chambering and wantonness, not in strife and envying.

[14]But put ye on the Lord Jesus Christ, and make not provision for the flesh, to *fulfil* the lusts *thereof.*

14

[1]Him that is weak in the faith receive ye, *but* not to doubtful disputations.

[2]For one believeth that he may eat all things: another, who is weak, eateth herbs.

[3]Let not him that eateth despise him that eateth

NEW LIVING TRANSLATION

Respect for Authority

13

Everyone must submit to governing authorities. For all authority comes from God, and those in positions of authority have been placed there by God. [2]So anyone who rebels against authority is rebelling against what God has instituted, and they will be punished. [3]For the authorities do not strike fear in people who are doing right, but in those who are doing wrong. Would you like to live without fear of the authorities? Do what is right, and they will honor you. [4]The authorities are God's servants, sent for your good. But if you are doing wrong, of course you should be afraid, for they have the power to punish you. They are God's servants, sent for the very purpose of punishing those who do what is wrong. [5]So you must submit to them, not only to avoid punishment, but also to keep a clear conscience.

[6]Pay your taxes, too, for these same reasons. For government workers need to be paid. They are serving God in what they do. [7]Give to everyone what you owe them: Pay your taxes and government fees to those who collect them, and give respect and honor to those who are in authority.

Love Fulfills God's Requirements

[8]Owe nothing to anyone—except for your obligation to love one another. If you love your neighbor, you will fulfill the requirements of God's law. [9]For the commandments say, "You must not commit adultery. You must not murder. You must not steal. You must not covet."* These—and other such commandments—are summed up in this one commandment: "Love your neighbor as yourself."* [10]Love does no wrong to others, so love fulfills the requirements of God's law.

[11]This is all the more urgent, for you know how late it is; time is running out. Wake up, for our salvation is nearer now than when we first believed. [12]The night is almost gone; the day of salvation will soon be here. So remove your dark deeds like dirty clothes, and put on the shining armor of right living. [13]Because we belong to the day, we must live decent lives for all to see. Don't participate in the darkness of wild parties and drunkenness, or in sexual promiscuity and immoral living, or in quarreling and jealousy. [14]Instead, clothe yourself with the presence of the Lord Jesus Christ. And don't let yourself think about ways to indulge your evil desires.

The Danger of Criticism

14

Accept other believers who are weak in faith, and don't argue with them about what they think is right or wrong. [2]For instance, one person believes it's all right to eat anything. But another believer with a sensitive conscience will eat only vegetables. [3]Those who feel free to eat anything

13:9a Exod 20:13-15, 17. **13:9b** Lev 19:18.

KING JAMES VERSION

not; and let not him which eateth not judge him that eateth: for God hath received him.

4 Who art thou that judgest another man's servant? to his own master he standeth or falleth. Yea, he shall be holden up: for God is able to make him stand.

5 One man esteemeth one day above another: another esteemeth every day *alike*. Let every man be fully persuaded in his own mind.

6 He that regardeth the day, regardeth *it* unto the Lord; and he that regardeth not the day, to the Lord he doth not regard *it*. He that eateth, eateth to the Lord, for he giveth God thanks; and he that eateth not, to the Lord he eateth not, and giveth God thanks.

7 For none of us liveth to himself, and no man dieth to himself.

8 For whether we live, we live unto the Lord; and whether we die, we die unto the Lord: whether we live therefore, or die, we are the Lord's.

9 For to this end Christ both died, and rose, and revived, that he might be Lord both of the dead and living.

10 But why dost thou judge thy brother? or why dost thou set at nought thy brother? for we shall all stand before the judgment seat of Christ.

11 For it is written, *As* I live, saith the Lord, every knee shall bow to me, and every tongue shall confess to God.

12 So then every one of us shall give account of himself to God.

13 Let us not therefore judge one another any more: but judge this rather, that no man put a stumblingblock or an occasion to fall in *his* brother's way.

14 I know, and am persuaded by the Lord Jesus, that *there is* nothing unclean of itself: but to him that esteemeth any thing to be unclean, to him *it is* unclean.

15 But if thy brother be grieved with *thy* meat, now walkest thou not charitably. Destroy not him with thy meat, for whom Christ died.

16 Let not then your good be evil spoken of:

17 For the kingdom of God is not meat and drink; but righteousness, and peace, and joy in the Holy Ghost.

18 For he that in these things serveth Christ *is* acceptable to God, and approved of men.

19 Let us therefore follow after the things which make for peace, and things wherewith one may edify another.

20 For meat destroy not the work of God. All things indeed *are* pure; but *it is* evil for that man who eateth with offence.

21 *It is* good neither to eat flesh, nor to drink wine, nor *any thing* whereby thy brother stumbleth, or is offended, or is made weak.

22 Hast thou faith? have *it* to thyself before God. Happy *is* he that condemneth not himself in that thing which he alloweth.

NEW LIVING TRANSLATION

must not look down on those who don't. And those
who don't eat certain foods must not condemn
those who do, for God has accepted them. 4 Who are
you to condemn someone else's servants? Their own
master will judge whether they stand or fall. And
with the Lord's help, they will stand and receive his
approval.

5 In the same way, some think one day is more holy
than another day, while others think every day is
alike. You should each be fully convinced that
whichever day you choose is acceptable. 6 Those who
worship the Lord on a special day do it to honor him.
Those who eat any kind of food do so to honor the
Lord, since they give thanks to God before eating.
And those who refuse to eat certain foods also want
to please the Lord and give thanks to God. 7 For we
don't live for ourselves or die for ourselves. 8 If we
live, it's to honor the Lord. And if we die, it's to honor
the Lord. So whether we live or die, we belong to the
Lord. 9 Christ died and rose again for this very purpose—to be Lord both of the living and of the dead.

10 So why do you condemn another believer*?
Why do you look down on another believer? Remember, we will all stand before the judgment seat
of God. 11 For the Scriptures say,

"'As surely as I live,' says the LORD,
'every knee will bend to me,
and every tongue will confess and
give praise to God.*'"

12 Yes, each of us will give a personal account to God.
13 So let's stop condemning each other. Decide instead to live in such a way that you will not cause
another believer to stumble and fall.

14 I know and am convinced on the authority of the
Lord Jesus that no food, in and of itself, is wrong to
eat. But if someone believes it is wrong, then for that
person it is wrong. 15 And if another believer is distressed by what you eat, you are not acting in love if
you eat it. Don't let your eating ruin someone for
whom Christ died. 16 Then you will not be criticized
for doing something you believe is good. 17 For the
Kingdom of God is not a matter of what we eat or
drink, but of living a life of goodness and peace and
joy in the Holy Spirit. 18 If you serve Christ with this
attitude, you will please God, and others will approve
of you, too. 19 So then, let us aim for harmony in the
church and try to build each other up.

20 Don't tear apart the work of God over what you
eat. Remember, all foods are acceptable, but it is
wrong to eat something if it makes another person
stumble. 21 It is better not to eat meat or drink wine or
do anything else if it might cause another believer to
stumble. 22 You may believe there's nothing wrong
with what you are doing, but keep it between yourself
and God. Blessed are those who don't feel guilty for

14:10 Greek *your brother;* also in 14:10b, 13, 15, 21. **14:11** Or *confess allegiance to God.* Isa 49:18; 45:23 (Greek version).

KING JAMES VERSION

23And he that doubteth is damned if he eat, because *he eateth* not of faith: for whatsoever *is* not of faith is sin.

15

1We then that are strong ought to bear the infirmities of the weak, and not to please ourselves.

2Let every one of us please *his* neighbour for *his* good to edification.

3For even Christ pleased not himself; but, as it is written, The reproaches of them that reproached thee fell on me.

4For whatsoever things were written aforetime were written for our learning, that we through patience and comfort of the scriptures might have hope.

5Now the God of patience and consolation grant you to be likeminded one toward another according to Christ Jesus:

6That ye may with one mind *and* one mouth glorify God, even the Father of our Lord Jesus Christ.

7Wherefore receive ye one another, as Christ also received us to the glory of God.

8Now I say that Jesus Christ was a minister of the circumcision for the truth of God, to confirm the promises *made* unto the fathers:

9And that the Gentiles might glorify God for *his* mercy; as it is written, For this cause I will confess to thee among the Gentiles, and sing unto thy name.

10And again he saith, Rejoice, ye Gentiles, with his people.

11And again, Praise the Lord, all ye Gentiles; and laud him, all ye people.

12And again, Esaias saith, There shall be a root of Jesse, and he that shall rise to reign over the Gentiles; in him shall the Gentiles trust.

13Now the God of hope fill you with all joy and peace in believing, that ye may abound in hope, through the power of the Holy Ghost.

14And I myself also am persuaded of you, my brethren, that ye also are full of goodness, filled with all knowledge, able also to admonish one another.

NEW LIVING TRANSLATION

doing something they have decided is right. 23But if you have doubts about whether or not you should eat something, you are sinning if you go ahead and do it. For you are not following your convictions. If you do anything you believe is not right, you are sinning.

Living to Please Others

15

We who are strong must be considerate of those who are sensitive about things like this. We must not just please ourselves. 2We should help others do what is right and build them up in the Lord. 3For even Christ didn't live to please himself. As the Scriptures say, "The insults of those who insult you, O God, have fallen on me."* 4Such things were written in the Scriptures long ago to teach us. And the Scriptures give us hope and encouragement as we wait patiently for God's promises to be fulfilled.

5May God, who gives this patience and encouragement, help you live in complete harmony with each other, as is fitting for followers of Christ Jesus. 6Then all of you can join together with one voice, giving praise and glory to God, the Father of our Lord Jesus Christ.

7Therefore, accept each other just as Christ has accepted you so that God will be given glory. 8Remember that Christ came as a servant to the Jews* to show that God is true to the promises he made to their ancestors. 9He also came so that the Gentiles might give glory to God for his mercies to them. That is what the psalmist meant when he wrote:

"For this, I will praise you among the Gentiles;
I will sing praises to your name."*

10And in another place it is written,

"Rejoice with his people,
you Gentiles."*

11And yet again,

"Praise the LORD, all you Gentiles.
Praise him, all you people of the earth."*

12And in another place Isaiah said,

"The heir to David's throne* will come,
and he will rule over the Gentiles.
They will place their hope on him."*

13I pray that God, the source of hope, will fill you completely with joy and peace because you trust in him. Then you will overflow with confident hope through the power of the Holy Spirit.

Paul's Reason for Writing

14I am fully convinced, my dear brothers and sisters,* that you are full of goodness. You know these things so well you can teach each other all about them.

15:3 Greek *who insult you have fallen on me.* Ps 69:9. **15:8** Greek *servant of circumcision.* **15:9** Ps 18:49. **15:10** Deut 32:43. **15:11** Ps 117:1. **15:12a** Greek *The root of Jesse.* David was the son of Jesse. **15:12b** Isa 11:10 (Greek version). **15:14** Greek *brothers;* also in 15:30.

KING JAMES VERSION

15 Nevertheless, brethren, I have written the more boldly unto you in some sort, as putting you in mind, because of the grace that is given to me of God,

16 That I should be the minister of Jesus Christ to the Gentiles, ministering the gospel of God, that the offering up of the Gentiles might be acceptable, being sanctified by the Holy Ghost.

17 I have therefore whereof I may glory through Jesus Christ in those things which pertain to God.

18 For I will not dare to speak of any of those things which Christ hath not wrought by me, to make the Gentiles obedient, by word and deed,

19 Through mighty signs and wonders, by the power of the Spirit of God; so that from Jerusalem, and round about unto Illyricum, I have fully preached the gospel of Christ.

20 Yea, so have I strived to preach the gospel, not where Christ was named, lest I should build upon another man's foundation:

21 But as it is written, To whom he was not spoken of, they shall see: and they that have not heard shall understand.

22 For which cause also I have been much hindered from coming to you.

23 But now having no more place in these parts, and having a great desire these many years to come unto you;

24 Whensoever I take my journey into Spain, I will come to you: for I trust to see you in my journey, and to be brought on my way thitherward by you, if first I be somewhat filled with your *company*.

25 But now I go unto Jerusalem to minister unto the saints.

26 For it hath pleased them of Macedonia and Achaia to make a certain contribution for the poor saints which are at Jerusalem.

27 It hath pleased them verily; and their debtors they are. For if the Gentiles have been made partakers of their spiritual things, their duty is also to minister unto them in carnal things.

28 When therefore I have performed this, and have sealed to them this fruit, I will come by you into Spain.

29 And I am sure that, when I come unto you, I shall come in the fulness of the blessing of the gospel of Christ.

30 Now I beseech you, brethren, for the Lord Jesus Christ's sake, and for the love of the Spirit, that ye strive together with me in *your* prayers to God for me;

31 That I may be delivered from them that do not believe in Judaea; and that my service which *I have* for Jerusalem may be accepted of the saints;

NEW LIVING TRANSLATION

15 Even so, I have been bold enough to write about some of these points, knowing that all you need is this reminder. For by God's grace, 16 I am a special messenger from Christ Jesus to you Gentiles. I bring you the Good News so that I might present you as an acceptable offering to God, made holy by the Holy Spirit. 17 So I have reason to be enthusiastic about all Christ Jesus has done through me in my service to God. 18 Yet I dare not boast about anything except what Christ has done through me, bringing the Gentiles to God by my message and by the way I worked among them. 19 They were convinced by the power of miraculous signs and wonders and by the power of God's Spirit.* In this way, I have fully presented the Good News of Christ from Jerusalem all the way to Illyricum.*

20 My ambition has always been to preach the Good News where the name of Christ has never been heard, rather than where a church has already been started by someone else. 21 I have been following the plan spoken of in the Scriptures, where it says,

"Those who have never been told about him
will see,
and those who have never heard of him
will understand."*

22 In fact, my visit to you has been delayed so long because I have been preaching in these places.

Paul's Travel Plans

23 But now I have finished my work in these regions, and after all these long years of waiting, I am eager to visit you. 24 I am planning to go to Spain, and when I do, I will stop off in Rome. And after I have enjoyed your fellowship for a little while, you can provide for my journey.

25 But before I come, I must go to Jerusalem to take a gift to the believers* there. 26 For you see, the believers in Macedonia and Achaia* have eagerly taken up an offering for the poor among the believers in Jerusalem. 27 They were glad to do this because they feel they owe a real debt to them. Since the Gentiles received the spiritual blessings of the Good News from the believers in Jerusalem, they feel the least they can do in return is to help them financially. 28 As soon as I have delivered this money and completed this good deed of theirs, I will come to see you on my way to Spain. 29 And I am sure that when I come, Christ will richly bless our time together.

30 Dear brothers and sisters, I urge you in the name of our Lord Jesus Christ to join in my struggle by praying to God for me. Do this because of your love for me, given to you by the Holy Spirit. 31 Pray that I will be rescued from those in Judea who refuse to obey God. Pray also that the believers there will be willing to accept the donation* I am taking to Jerusalem.

15:19a Other manuscripts read *the Spirit;* still others read *the Holy Spirit.* **15:19b** *Illyricum* was a region northeast of Italy. **15:21** Isa 52:15 (Greek version). **15:25** Greek *God's holy people;* also in 15:26, 31. **15:26** *Macedonia* and *Achaia* were the northern and southern regions of Greece. **15:31** Greek *the ministry;* other manuscripts read *the gift.*

KING JAMES VERSION

32 That I may come unto you with joy by the will of God, and may with you be refreshed.

33 Now the God of peace *be* with you all. Amen.

16

1 I commend unto you Phebe our sister, which is a servant of the church which is at Cenchrea:

2 That ye receive her in the Lord, as becometh saints, and that ye assist her in whatsoever business she hath need of you: for she hath been a succourer of many, and of myself also.

3 Greet Priscilla and Aquila my helpers in Christ Jesus:

4 Who have for my life laid down their own necks: unto whom not only I give thanks, but also all the churches of the Gentiles.

5 Likewise *greet* the church that is in their house. Salute my wellbeloved Epaenetus, who is the firstfruits of Achaia unto Christ.

6 Greet Mary, who bestowed much labour on us.

7 Salute Andronicus and Junia, my kinsmen, and my fellowprisoners, who are of note among the apostles, who also were in Christ before me.

8 Greet Amplias my beloved in the Lord.

9 Salute Urbane, our helper in Christ, and Stachys my beloved.

10 Salute Apelles approved in Christ. Salute them which are of Aristobulus' *household*.

11 Salute Herodion my kinsman. Greet them that be of the *household* of Narcissus, which are in the Lord.

12 Salute Tryphena and Tryphosa, who labour in the Lord. Salute the beloved Persis, which laboured much in the Lord.

13 Salute Rufus chosen in the Lord, and his mother and mine.

14 Salute Asyncritus, Phlegon, Hermas, Patrobas, Hermes, and the brethren which are with them.

15 Salute Philologus, and Julia, Nereus, and his sister, and Olympas, and all the saints which are with them.

16 Salute one another with an holy kiss. The churches of Christ salute you.

17 Now I beseech you, brethren, mark them which cause divisions and offences contrary to the doctrine which ye have learned; and avoid them.

18 For they that are such serve not our Lord Jesus Christ, but their own belly; and by good words and fair speeches deceive the hearts of the simple.

19 For your obedience is come abroad unto all *men*. I am glad therefore on your behalf: but yet I would

NEW LIVING TRANSLATION

32 Then, by the will of God, I will be able to come to you with a joyful heart, and we will be an encouragement to each other.

33 And now may God, who gives us his peace, be with you all. Amen.*

Paul Greets His Friends

16

I commend to you our sister Phoebe, who is a deacon in the church in Cenchrea. 2 Welcome her in the Lord as one who is worthy of honor among God's people. Help her in whatever she needs, for she has been helpful to many, and especially to me.

3 Give my greetings to Priscilla and Aquila, my co-workers in the ministry of Christ Jesus. 4 In fact, they once risked their lives for me. I am thankful to them, and so are all the Gentile churches. 5 Also give my greetings to the church that meets in their home.

Greet my dear friend Epenetus. He was the first person from the province of Asia to become a follower of Christ. 6 Give my greetings to Mary, who has worked so hard for your benefit. 7 Greet Andronicus and Junia,* my fellow Jews,* who were in prison with me. They are highly respected among the apostles and became followers of Christ before I did. 8 Greet Ampliatus, my dear friend in the Lord. 9 Greet Urbanus, our co-worker in Christ, and my dear friend Stachys.

10 Greet Apelles, a good man whom Christ approves. And give my greetings to the believers from the household of Aristobulus. 11 Greet Herodion, my fellow Jew.* Greet the Lord's people from the household of Narcissus. 12 Give my greetings to Tryphena and Tryphosa, the Lord's workers, and to dear Persis, who has worked so hard for the Lord. 13 Greet Rufus, whom the Lord picked out to be his very own; and also his dear mother, who has been a mother to me.

14 Give my greetings to Asyncritus, Phlegon, Hermes, Patrobas, Hermas, and the brothers and sisters* who meet with them. 15 Give my greetings to Philologus, Julia, Nereus and his sister, and to Olympas and all the believers* who meet with them. 16 Greet each other in Christian love.* All the churches of Christ send you their greetings.

Paul's Final Instructions

17 And now I make one more appeal, my dear brothers and sisters. Watch out for people who cause divisions and upset people's faith by teaching things contrary to what you have been taught. Stay away from them. 18 Such people are not serving Christ our Lord; they are serving their own personal interests. By smooth talk and glowing words they deceive innocent people. 19 But everyone knows that you are

15:33 Some manuscripts do not include *Amen.* One very early manuscript places 16:25-27 here. **16:7a** *Junia* is a feminine name. Some late manuscripts accent the word so it reads *Junias,* a masculine name; still others read *Julia* (feminine). **16:7b** Or *compatriots;* also in 16:21. **16:11** Or *compatriot.* **16:14** Greek *brothers;* also in 16:17. **16:15** Greek *all of God's holy people.* **16:16** Greek *with a sacred kiss.*

KING JAMES VERSION

have you wise unto that which is good, and simple concerning evil.

[20]And the God of peace shall bruise Satan under your feet shortly. The grace of our Lord Jesus Christ *be* with you. Amen.

[21]Timotheus my workfellow, and Lucius, and Jason, and Sosipater, my kinsmen, salute you.

[22]I Tertius, who wrote *this* epistle, salute you in the Lord.

[23]Gaius mine host, and of the whole church, saluteth you. Erastus the chamberlain of the city saluteth you, and Quartus a brother.

[24]The grace of our Lord Jesus Christ *be* with you all. Amen.

[25]Now to him that is of power to stablish you according to my gospel, and the preaching of Jesus Christ, according to the revelation of the mystery, which was kept secret since the world began,

[26]But now is made manifest, and by the scriptures of the prophets, according to the commandment of the everlasting God, made known to all nations for the obedience of faith:

[27]To God only wise, *be* glory through Jesus Christ for ever. Amen.

NEW LIVING TRANSLATION

obedient to the Lord. This makes me very happy. I want you to be wise in doing right and to stay innocent of any wrong. [20]The God of peace will soon crush Satan under your feet. May the grace of our Lord Jesus* be with you.

[21]Timothy, my fellow worker, sends you his greetings, as do Lucius, Jason, and Sosipater, my fellow Jews.

[22]I, Tertius, the one writing this letter for Paul, send my greetings, too, as one of the Lord's followers.

[23]Gaius says hello to you. He is my host and also serves as host to the whole church. Erastus, the city treasurer, sends you his greetings, and so does our brother Quartus.*

[25]Now all glory to God, who is able to make you strong, just as my Good News says. This message about Jesus Christ has revealed his plan for you Gentiles, a plan kept secret from the beginning of time. [26]But now as the prophets* foretold and as the eternal God has commanded, this message is made known to all Gentiles everywhere, so that they too might believe and obey him. [27]All glory to the only wise God, through Jesus Christ, forever. Amen.

16:20 Some manuscripts read *Lord Jesus Christ.* **16:23** Some manuscripts add verse 24, *May the grace of our Lord Jesus Christ be with you all. Amen.* Still others add this sentence after verse 27. **16:26** Greek *the prophetic writings.*

1 Corinthians

KING JAMES VERSION

1 1 Paul, called *to be* an apostle of Jesus Christ through the will of God, and Sosthenes *our* brother,

2 Unto the church of God which is at Corinth, to them that are sanctified in Christ Jesus, called *to be* saints, with all that in every place call upon the name of Jesus Christ our Lord, both theirs and ours:

3 Grace *be* unto you, and peace, from God our Father, and *from* the Lord Jesus Christ.

4 I thank my God always on your behalf, for the grace of God which is given you by Jesus Christ;

5 That in every thing ye are enriched by him, in all utterance, and *in* all knowledge;

6 Even as the testimony of Christ was confirmed in you:

7 So that ye come behind in no gift; waiting for the coming of our Lord Jesus Christ:

8 Who shall also confirm you unto the end, *that ye may be* blameless in the day of our Lord Jesus Christ.

9 God *is* faithful, by whom ye were called unto the fellowship of his Son Jesus Christ our Lord.

10 Now I beseech you, brethren, by the name of our Lord Jesus Christ, that ye all speak the same thing, and *that* there be no divisions among you; but *that* ye be perfectly joined together in the same mind and in the same judgment.

11 For it hath been declared unto me of you, my brethren, by them *which are of the house* of Chloe, that there are contentions among you.

12 Now this I say, that every one of you saith, I am of Paul; and I of Apollos; and I of Cephas; and I of Christ.

13 Is Christ divided? was Paul crucified for you? or were ye baptized in the name of Paul?

14 I thank God that I baptized none of you, but Crispus and Gaius;

15 Lest any should say that I had baptized in mine own name.

NEW LIVING TRANSLATION

Greetings from Paul

1 This letter is from Paul, chosen by the will of God to be an apostle of Christ Jesus, and from our brother Sosthenes.

2 I am writing to God's church in Corinth,* to you who have been called by God to be his own holy people. He made you holy by means of Christ Jesus,* just as he did for all people everywhere who call on the name of our Lord Jesus Christ, their Lord and ours.

3 May God our Father and the Lord Jesus Christ give you grace and peace.

Paul Gives Thanks to God

4 I always thank my God for you and for the gracious gifts he has given you, now that you belong to Christ Jesus. 5 Through him, God has enriched your church in every way—with all of your eloquent words and all of your knowledge. 6 This confirms that what I told you about Christ is true. 7 Now you have every spiritual gift you need as you eagerly wait for the return of our Lord Jesus Christ. 8 He will keep you strong to the end so that you will be free from all blame on the day when our Lord Jesus Christ returns. 9 God will do this, for he is faithful to do what he says, and he has invited you into partnership with his Son, Jesus Christ our Lord.

Divisions in the Church

10 I appeal to you, dear brothers and sisters,* by the authority of our Lord Jesus Christ, to live in harmony with each other. Let there be no divisions in the church. Rather, be of one mind, united in thought and purpose. 11 For some members of Chloe's household have told me about your quarrels, my dear brothers and sisters. 12 Some of you are saying, "I am a follower of Paul." Others are saying, "I follow Apollos," or "I follow Peter,*" or "I follow only Christ."

13 Has Christ been divided into factions? Was I, Paul, crucified for you? Were any of you baptized in the name of Paul? Of course not! 14 I thank God that I did not baptize any of you except Crispus and Gaius, 15 for now no one can say they were baptized in my

1:2a *Corinth* was the capital city of Achaia, the southern region of the Greek peninsula. **1:2b** Or *because you belong to Christ Jesus.* **1:10** Greek *brothers;* also in 1:11, 26. **1:12** Greek *Cephas.*

KING JAMES VERSION

16And I baptized also the household of Stephanas: besides, I know not whether I baptized any other.

17For Christ sent me not to baptize, but to preach the gospel: not with wisdom of words, lest the cross of Christ should be made of none effect.

18For the preaching of the cross is to them that perish foolishness; but unto us which are saved it is the power of God.

19For it is written, I will destroy the wisdom of the wise, and will bring to nothing the understanding of the prudent.

20Where *is* the wise? where *is* the scribe? where *is* the disputer of this world? hath not God made foolish the wisdom of this world?

21For after that in the wisdom of God the world by wisdom knew not God, it pleased God by the foolishness of preaching to save them that believe.

22For the Jews require a sign, and the Greeks seek after wisdom:

23But we preach Christ crucified, unto the Jews a stumblingblock, and unto the Greeks foolishness;

24But unto them which are called, both Jews and Greeks, Christ the power of God, and the wisdom of God.

25Because the foolishness of God is wiser than men; and the weakness of God is stronger than men.

26For ye see your calling, brethren, how that not many wise men after the flesh, not many mighty, not many noble, *are called:*

27But God hath chosen the foolish things of the world to confound the wise; and God hath chosen the weak things of the world to confound the things which are mighty;

28And base things of the world, and things which are despised, hath God chosen, *yea,* and things which are not, to bring to nought things that are:

29That no flesh should glory in his presence.

30But of him are ye in Christ Jesus, who of God is made unto us wisdom, and righteousness, and sanctification, and redemption:

31That, according as it is written, He that glorieth, let him glory in the Lord.

2 1And I, brethren, when I came to you, came not with excellency of speech or of wisdom, declaring unto you the testimony of God.

2For I determined not to know any thing among you, save Jesus Christ, and him crucified.

3And I was with you in weakness, and in fear, and in much trembling.

4And my speech and my preaching *was* not with enticing words of man's wisdom, but in demonstration of the Spirit and of power:

NEW LIVING TRANSLATION

name. 16(Oh yes, I also baptized the household of Stephanas, but I don't remember baptizing anyone else.) 17For Christ didn't send me to baptize, but to preach the Good News—and not with clever speech, for fear that the cross of Christ would lose its power.

The Wisdom of God

18The message of the cross is foolish to those who are headed for destruction! But we who are being saved know it is the very power of God. 19As the Scriptures say,

"I will destroy the wisdom of the wise
and discard the intelligence of the
intelligent."*

20So where does this leave the philosophers, the scholars, and the world's brilliant debaters? God has made the wisdom of this world look foolish. 21Since God in his wisdom saw to it that the world would never know him through human wisdom, he has used our foolish preaching to save those who believe. 22It is foolish to the Jews, who ask for signs from heaven. And it is foolish to the Greeks, who seek human wisdom. 23So when we preach that Christ was crucified, the Jews are offended and the Gentiles say it's all nonsense.

24But to those called by God to salvation, both Jews and Gentiles,* Christ is the power of God and the wisdom of God. 25This foolish plan of God is wiser than the wisest of human plans, and God's weakness is stronger than the greatest of human strength.

26Remember, dear brothers and sisters, that few of you were wise in the world's eyes or powerful or wealthy* when God called you. 27Instead, God chose things the world considers foolish in order to shame those who think they are wise. And he chose things that are powerless to shame those who are powerful. 28God chose things despised by the world,* things counted as nothing at all, and used them to bring to nothing what the world considers important. 29As a result, no one can ever boast in the presence of God.

30God has united you with Christ Jesus. For our benefit God made him to be wisdom itself. Christ made us right with God; he made us pure and holy, and he freed us from sin. 31Therefore, as the Scriptures say, "If you want to boast, boast only about the LORD."*

Paul's Message of Wisdom

2 When I first came to you, dear brothers and sisters,* I didn't use lofty words and impressive wisdom to tell you God's secret plan.* 2For I decided that while I was with you I would forget everything except Jesus Christ, the one who was crucified. 3I came to you in weakness—timid and trembling. 4And my message and my preaching were very plain. Rather than using clever and persuasive speeches, I

1:19 Isa 29:14. **1:24** Greek *and Greeks.* **1:26** Or *high born.* **1:28** Or *God chose those who are low born.* **1:31** Jer 9:24. **2:1a** Greek *brothers.* **2:1b** Greek *God's mystery;* other manuscripts read *God's testimony.*

KING JAMES VERSION

5That your faith should not stand in the wisdom of men, but in the power of God.

6Howbeit we speak wisdom among them that are perfect: yet not the wisdom of this world, nor of the princes of this world, that come to nought:

7But we speak the wisdom of God in a mystery, *even* the hidden *wisdom*, which God ordained before the world unto our glory:

8Which none of the princes of this world knew: for had they known *it*, they would not have crucified the Lord of glory.

9But as it is written, Eye hath not seen, nor ear heard, neither have entered into the heart of man, the things which God hath prepared for them that love him.

10But God hath revealed *them* unto us by his Spirit: for the Spirit searcheth all things, yea, the deep things of God.

11For what man knoweth the things of a man, save the spirit of man which is in him? even so the things of God knoweth no man, but the Spirit of God.

12Now we have received, not the spirit of the world, but the spirit which is of God; that we might know the things that are freely given to us of God.

13Which things also we speak, not in the words which man's wisdom teacheth, but which the Holy Ghost teacheth; comparing spiritual things with spiritual.

14But the natural man receiveth not the things of the Spirit of God: for they are foolishness unto him: neither can he know *them*, because they are spiritually discerned.

15But he that is spiritual judgeth all things, yet he himself is judged of no man.

16For who hath known the mind of the Lord, that he may instruct him? But we have the mind of Christ.

3 1And I, brethren, could not speak unto you as unto spiritual, but as unto carnal, *even* as unto babes in Christ.

2I have fed you with milk, and not with meat: for hitherto ye were not able *to bear it*, neither yet now are ye able.

3For ye are yet carnal: for whereas *there is* among you envying, and strife, and divisions, are ye not carnal, and walk as men?

NEW LIVING TRANSLATION

relied only on the power of the Holy Spirit. 5I did this so you would trust not in human wisdom but in the power of God.

6Yet when I am among mature believers, I do speak with words of wisdom, but not the kind of wisdom that belongs to this world or to the rulers of this world, who are soon forgotten. 7No, the wisdom we speak of is the mystery of God*—his plan that was previously hidden, even though he made it for our ultimate glory before the world began. 8But the rulers of this world have not understood it; if they had, they would not have crucified our glorious Lord. 9That is what the Scriptures mean when they say,

"No eye has seen, no ear has heard,
  and no mind has imagined
what God has prepared
  for those who love him."*

10But* it was to us that God revealed these things by his Spirit. For his Spirit searches out everything and shows us God's deep secrets. 11No one can know a person's thoughts except that person's own spirit, and no one can know God's thoughts except God's own Spirit. 12And we have received God's Spirit (not the world's spirit), so we can know the wonderful things God has freely given us.

13When we tell you these things, we do not use words that come from human wisdom. Instead, we speak words given to us by the Spirit, using the Spirit's words to explain spiritual truths.* 14But people who aren't spiritual* can't receive these truths from God's Spirit. It all sounds foolish to them and they can't understand it, for only those who are spiritual can understand what the Spirit means. 15Those who are spiritual can evaluate all things, but they themselves cannot be evaluated by others. 16For,

"Who can know the LORD's thoughts?
  Who knows enough to teach him?"*

But we understand these things, for we have the mind of Christ.

Paul and Apollos, Servants of Christ

3 Dear brothers and sisters,* when I was with you I couldn't talk to you as I would to spiritual people.* I had to talk as though you belonged to this world or as though you were infants in the Christian life.* 2I had to feed you with milk, not with solid food, because you weren't ready for anything stronger. And you still aren't ready, 3for you are still controlled by your sinful nature. You are jealous of one another and quarrel with each other. Doesn't that prove you are controlled by your sinful nature?

2:7 Greek *But we speak God's wisdom in a mystery.* **2:9** Isa 64:4. **2:10** Some manuscripts read *For.* **2:13** Or *explaining spiritual truths in spiritual language,* or *explaining spiritual truths to spiritual people.* **2:14** Or *who don't have the Spirit;* or *who have only physical life.* **2:16** Isa 40:13 (Greek version). **3:1a** Greek *Brothers.* **3:1b** Or *to people who have the Spirit.* **3:1c** Greek *in Christ.*

KING JAMES VERSION

4 For while one saith, I am of Paul; and another, I *am* of Apollos; are ye not carnal?

5 Who then is Paul, and who *is* Apollos, but ministers by whom ye believed, even as the Lord gave to every man?

6 I have planted, Apollos watered; but God gave the increase.

7 So then neither is he that planteth any thing, neither he that watereth; but God that giveth the increase.

8 Now he that planteth and he that watereth are one: and every man shall receive his own reward according to his own labour.

9 For we are labourers together with God: ye are God's husbandry, *ye are* God's building.

10 According to the grace of God which is given unto me, as a wise masterbuilder, I have laid the foundation, and another buildeth thereon. But let every man take heed how he buildeth thereupon.

11 For other foundation can no man lay than that is laid, which is Jesus Christ.

12 Now if any man build upon this foundation gold, silver, precious stones, wood, hay, stubble;

13 Every man's work shall be made manifest: for the day shall declare it, because it shall be revealed by fire; and the fire shall try every man's work of what sort it is.

14 If any man's work abide which he hath built thereupon, he shall receive a reward.

15 If any man's work shall be burned, he shall suffer loss: but he himself shall be saved; yet so as by fire.

16 Know ye not that ye are the temple of God, and *that* the Spirit of God dwelleth in you?

17 If any man defile the temple of God, him shall God destroy; for the temple of God is holy, which *temple* ye are.

18 Let no man deceive himself. If any man among you seemeth to be wise in this world, let him become a fool, that he may be wise.

19 For the wisdom of this world is foolishness with God. For it is written, He taketh the wise in their own craftiness.

20 And again, The Lord knoweth the thoughts of the wise, that they are vain.

21 Therefore let no man glory in men. For all things are yours;

22 Whether Paul, or Apollos, or Cephas, or the world, or life, or death, or things present, or things to come; all are yours;

23 And ye are Christ's; and Christ *is* God's.

4 1 Let a man so account of us, as of the ministers of Christ, and stewards of the mysteries of God.

NEW LIVING TRANSLATION

Aren't you living like people of the world? 4 When
one of you says, "I am a follower of Paul," and another
says, "I follow Apollos," aren't you acting just like
people of the world?

5 After all, who is Apollos? Who is Paul? We are
only God's servants through whom you believed the
Good News. Each of us did the work the Lord gave us.
6 I planted the seed in your hearts, and Apollos watered it, but it was God who made it grow. 7 It's not
important who does the planting, or who does the
watering. What's important is that God makes the
seed grow. 8 The one who plants and the one who
waters work together with the same purpose. And
both will be rewarded for their own hard work. 9 For
we are both God's workers. And you are God's field.
You are God's building.

10 Because of God's grace to me, I have laid the
foundation like an expert builder. Now others are
building on it. But whoever is building on this foundation must be very careful. 11 For no one can lay any
foundation other than the one we already have—
Jesus Christ.

12 Anyone who builds on that foundation may use a
variety of materials—gold, silver, jewels, wood, hay, or
straw. 13 But on the judgment day, fire will reveal what
kind of work each builder has done. The fire will
show if a person's work has any value. 14 If the work
survives, that builder will receive a reward. 15 But if
the work is burned up, the builder will suffer great
loss. The builder will be saved, but like someone
barely escaping through a wall of flames.

16 Don't you realize that all of you together are the
temple of God and that the Spirit of God lives in*
you? 17 God will destroy anyone who destroys this
temple. For God's temple is holy, and you are that
temple.

18 Stop deceiving yourselves. If you think you are
wise by this world's standards, you need to become a
fool to be truly wise. 19 For the wisdom of this world
is foolishness to God. As the Scriptures say,

"He traps the wise
in the snare of their own cleverness."*

20 And again,

"The Lord knows the thoughts of the wise;
he knows they are worthless."*

21 So don't boast about following a particular
human leader. For everything belongs to you—
22 whether Paul or Apollos or Peter,* or the world, or
life and death, or the present and the future. Everything belongs to you, 23 and you belong to Christ, and
Christ belongs to God.

Paul's Relationship with the Corinthians

4 So look at Apollos and me as mere servants of Christ who have been put in charge of explaining

3:16 Or *among.* **3:19** Job 5:13. **3:20** Ps 94:11. **3:22** Greek *Cephas.*

KING JAMES VERSION

2 Moreover it is required in stewards, that a man be found faithful.

3 But with me it is a very small thing that I should be judged of you, or of man's judgment: yea, I judge not mine own self.

4 For I know nothing by myself; yet am I not hereby justified: but he that judgeth me is the Lord.

5 Therefore judge nothing before the time, until the Lord come, who both will bring to light the hidden things of darkness, and will make manifest the counsels of the hearts: and then shall every man have praise of God.

6 And these things, brethren, I have in a figure transferred to myself and *to* Apollos for your sakes; that ye might learn in us not to think *of men* above that which is written, that no one of you be puffed up for one against another.

7 For who maketh thee to differ *from another?* and what hast thou that thou didst not receive? now if thou didst receive *it,* why dost thou glory, as if thou hadst not received *it?*

8 Now ye are full, now ye are rich, ye have reigned as kings without us: and I would to God ye did reign, that we also might reign with you.

9 For I think that God hath set forth us the apostles last, as it were appointed to death: for we are made a spectacle unto the world, and to angels, and to men.

10 We *are* fools for Christ's sake, but ye *are* wise in Christ; we *are* weak, but ye *are* strong; ye *are* honourable, but we *are* despised.

11 Even unto this present hour we both hunger, and thirst, and are naked, and are buffeted, and have no certain dwellingplace;

12 And labour, working with our own hands: being reviled, we bless; being persecuted, we suffer it:

13 Being defamed, we intreat: we are made as the filth of the world, *and are* the offscouring of all things unto this day.

14 I write not these things to shame you, but as my beloved sons I warn *you.*

15 For though ye have ten thousand instructors in Christ, yet *have ye* not many fathers: for in Christ Jesus I have begotten you through the gospel.

16 Wherefore I beseech you, be ye followers of me.

17 For this cause have I sent unto you Timotheus, who is my beloved son, and faithful in the Lord, who shall bring you into remembrance of my ways which be in Christ, as I teach every where in every church.

18 Now some are puffed up, as though I would not come to you.

19 But I will come to you shortly, if the Lord will, and will know, not the speech of them which are puffed up, but the power.

20 For the kingdom of God *is* not in word, but in power.

NEW LIVING TRANSLATION

God's mysteries.
2 Now, a person who is put in charge as
a manager must be faithful.
3 As for me, it matters very
little how I might be evaluated by you or by any human
authority. I don't even trust my own judgment on this
point.
4 My conscience is clear, but that doesn't prove
I'm right. It is the Lord himself who will examine me
and decide.

5 So don't make judgments about anyone ahead of
time—before the Lord returns. For he will bring our
darkest secrets to light and will reveal our private
motives. Then God will give to each one whatever
praise is due.

6 Dear brothers and sisters,* I have used Apollos
and myself to illustrate what I've been saying. If you
pay attention to what I have quoted from the Scriptures,* you won't be proud of one of your leaders at
the expense of another.
7 For what gives you the right
to make such a judgment? What do you have that
God hasn't given you? And if everything you have is
from God, why boast as though it were not a gift?

8 You think you already have everything you need.
You think you are already rich. You have begun to
reign in God's kingdom without us! I wish you really
were reigning already, for then we would be reigning
with you.
9 Instead, I sometimes think God has put us
apostles on display, like prisoners of war at the end
of a victor's parade, condemned to die. We have become a spectacle to the entire world—to people and
angels alike.

10 Our dedication to Christ makes us look like
fools, but you claim to be so wise in Christ! We are
weak, but you are so powerful! You are honored, but
we are ridiculed.
11 Even now we go hungry and
thirsty, and we don't have enough clothes to keep
warm. We are often beaten and have no home.
12 We
work wearily with our own hands to earn our living.
We bless those who curse us. We are patient with
those who abuse us.
13 We appeal gently when evil
things are said about us. Yet we are treated like the
world's garbage, like everybody's trash—right up to
the present moment.

14 I am not writing these things to shame you, but
to warn you as my beloved children.
15 For even if you
had ten thousand others to teach you about Christ,
you have only one spiritual father. For I became your
father in Christ Jesus when I preached the Good
News to you.
16 So I urge you to imitate me.

17 That's why I have sent Timothy, my beloved and
faithful child in the Lord. He will remind you of how
I follow Christ Jesus, just as I teach in all the churches
wherever I go.

18 Some of you have become arrogant, thinking I
will not visit you again.
19 But I will come—and soon—
if the Lord lets me, and then I'll find out whether
these arrogant people just give pretentious speeches
or whether they really have God's power.
20 For the
Kingdom of God is not just a lot of talk; it is living by

4:6a Greek *Brothers.* **4:6b** Or *If you learn not to go beyond "what is written."*

KING JAMES VERSION

[21]What will ye? shall I come unto you with a rod, or in love, and *in* the spirit of meekness?

5

[1]It is reported commonly *that there is* fornication among you, and such fornication as is not so much as named among the Gentiles, that one should have his father's wife.

[2]And ye are puffed up, and have not rather mourned, that he that hath done this deed might be taken away from among you.

[3]For I verily, as absent in body, but present in spirit, have judged already, as though I were present, *concerning* him that hath so done this deed,

[4]In the name of our Lord Jesus Christ, when ye are gathered together, and my spirit, with the power of our Lord Jesus Christ,

[5]To deliver such an one unto Satan for the destruction of the flesh, that the spirit may be saved in the day of the Lord Jesus.

[6]Your glorying *is* not good. Know ye not that a little leaven leaveneth the whole lump?

[7]Purge out therefore the old leaven, that ye may be a new lump, as ye are unleavened. For even Christ our passover is sacrificed for us:

[8]Therefore let us keep the feast, not with old leaven, neither with the leaven of malice and wickedness; but with the unleavened *bread* of sincerity and truth.

[9]I wrote unto you in an epistle not to company with fornicators:

[10]Yet not altogether with the fornicators of this world, or with the covetous, or extortioners, or with idolaters; for then must ye needs go out of the world.

[11]But now I have written unto you not to keep company, if any man that is called a brother be a fornicator, or covetous, or an idolater, or a railer, or a drunkard, or an extortioner; with such an one no not to eat.

[12]For what have I to do to judge them also that are without? do not ye judge them that are within?

[13]But them that are without God judgeth. Therefore put away from among yourselves that wicked person.

6

[1]Dare any of you, having a matter against another, go to law before the unjust, and not before the saints?

[2]Do ye not know that the saints shall judge the world? and if the world shall be judged by you, are ye unworthy to judge the smallest matters?

NEW LIVING TRANSLATION

God's power. [21]Which do you choose? Should I come with a rod to punish you, or should I come with love and a gentle spirit?

Paul Condemns Spiritual Pride

5

I can hardly believe the report about the sexual immorality going on among you—something that even pagans don't do. I am told that a man in your church is living in sin with his stepmother.* [2]You are so proud of yourselves, but you should be mourning in sorrow and shame. And you should remove this man from your fellowship.

[3]Even though I am not with you in person, I am with you in the Spirit.* And as though I were there, I have already passed judgment on this man [4]in the name of the Lord Jesus. You must call a meeting of the church.* I will be present with you in spirit, and so will the power of our Lord Jesus. [5]Then you must throw this man out and hand him over to Satan so that his sinful nature will be destroyed* and he himself* will be saved on the day the Lord* returns.

[6]Your boasting about this is terrible. Don't you realize that this sin is like a little yeast that spreads through the whole batch of dough? [7]Get rid of the old "yeast" by removing this wicked person from among you. Then you will be like a fresh batch of dough made without yeast, which is what you really are. Christ, our Passover Lamb, has been sacrificed for us.* [8]So let us celebrate the festival, not with the old bread* of wickedness and evil, but with the new bread* of sincerity and truth.

[9]When I wrote to you before, I told you not to associate with people who indulge in sexual sin. [10]But I wasn't talking about unbelievers who indulge in sexual sin, or are greedy, or cheat people, or worship idols. You would have to leave this world to avoid people like that. [11]I meant that you are not to associate with anyone who claims to be a believer* yet indulges in sexual sin, or is greedy, or worships idols, or is abusive, or is a drunkard, or cheats people. Don't even eat with such people.

[12]It isn't my responsibility to judge outsiders, but it certainly is your responsibility to judge those inside the church who are sinning. [13]God will judge those on the outside; but as the Scriptures say, "You must remove the evil person from among you."*

Avoiding Lawsuits with Christians

6

When one of you has a dispute with another believer, how dare you file a lawsuit and ask a secular court to decide the matter instead of taking it to other believers*! [2]Don't you realize that someday we believers will judge the world? And since you are going to judge the world, can't you decide even these

5:1 Greek *his father's wife.* **5:3** Or *in spirit.* **5:4** Or *In the name of the Lord Jesus, you must call a meeting of the church.* **5:5a** Or *so that his body will be destroyed;* Greek reads *for the destruction of the flesh.* **5:5b** Greek *and the spirit.* **5:5c** Other manuscripts read *the Lord Jesus;* still others read *our Lord Jesus Christ.* **5:7** Greek *has been sacrificed.* **5:8a** Greek *not with old leaven.* **5:8b** Greek *but with unleavened [bread].* **5:11** Greek *a brother.* **5:13** Deut 17:7. **6:1** Greek *God's holy people;* also in 6:2.

KING JAMES VERSION

3 Know ye not that we shall judge angels? how
much more things that pertain to this life?
4 If then ye have judgments of things pertaining to
this life, set them to judge who are least esteemed in
the church.
5 I speak to your shame. Is it so, that there is not a
wise man among you? no, not one that shall be able
to judge between his brethren?
6 But brother goeth to law with brother, and that
before the unbelievers.
7 Now therefore there is utterly a fault among you,
because ye go to law one with another. Why do ye not
rather take wrong? why do ye not rather *suffer yourselves to* be defrauded?
8 Nay, ye do wrong, and defraud, and that *your*
brethren.
9 Know ye not that the unrighteous shall not inherit the kingdom of God? Be not deceived: neither
fornicators, nor idolaters, nor adulterers, nor effeminate, nor abusers of themselves with mankind,
10 Nor thieves, nor covetous, nor drunkards, nor
revilers, nor extortioners, shall inherit the kingdom
of God.
11 And such were some of you: but ye are washed,
but ye are sanctified, but ye are justified in the name
of the Lord Jesus, and by the Spirit of our God.

12 All things are lawful unto me, but all things are
not expedient: all things are lawful for me, but I will
not be brought under the power of any.
13 Meats for the belly, and the belly for meats: but
God shall destroy both it and them. Now the body *is*
not for fornication, but for the Lord; and the Lord for
the body.
14 And God hath both raised up the Lord, and will
also raise up us by his own power.
15 Know ye not that your bodies are the members of
Christ? shall I then take the members of Christ, and
make *them* the members of an harlot? God forbid.
16 What? know ye not that he which is joined to an
harlot is one body? for two, saith he, shall be one
flesh.
17 But he that is joined unto the Lord is one spirit.
18 Flee fornication. Every sin that a man doeth is
without the body; but he that committeth fornication sinneth against his own body.
19 What? know ye not that your body is the temple
of the Holy Ghost *which is* in you, which ye have of
God, and ye are not your own?
20 For ye are bought with a price: therefore glorify
God in your body, and in your spirit, which are God's.

7 1 Now concerning the things whereof ye wrote
unto me: *It is* good for a man not to touch a
woman.

NEW LIVING TRANSLATION

little things among yourselves? 3 Don't you realize
that we will judge angels? So you should surely be
able to resolve ordinary disputes in this life. 4 If you
have legal disputes about such matters, why go to
outside judges who are not respected by the church?
5 I am saying this to shame you. Isn't there anyone in
all the church who is wise enough to decide these issues? 6 But instead, one believer* sues another—right
in front of unbelievers!
7 Even to have such lawsuits with one another is a
defeat for you. Why not just accept the injustice and
leave it at that? Why not let yourselves be cheated?
8 Instead, you yourselves are the ones who do wrong
and cheat even your fellow believers.*
9 Don't you realize that those who do wrong will
not inherit the Kingdom of God? Don't fool yourselves. Those who indulge in sexual sin, or who
worship idols, or commit adultery, or are male prostitutes, or practice homosexuality, 10 or are thieves, or
greedy people, or drunkards, or are abusive, or cheat
people—none of these will inherit the Kingdom of
God. 11 Some of you were once like that. But you were
cleansed; you were made holy; you were made right
with God by calling on the name of the Lord Jesus
Christ and by the Spirit of our God.

Avoiding Sexual Sin

12 You say, "I am allowed to do anything"—but not
everything is good for you. And even though "I am
allowed to do anything," I must not become a slave
to anything. 13 You say, "Food was made for the stomach, and the stomach for food." (This is true, though
someday God will do away with both of them.) But
you can't say that our bodies were made for sexual
immorality. They were made for the Lord, and the
Lord cares about our bodies. 14 And God will raise us
from the dead by his power, just as he raised our
Lord from the dead.
15 Don't you realize that your bodies are actually
parts of Christ? Should a man take his body, which is
part of Christ, and join it to a prostitute? Never!
16 And don't you realize that if a man joins himself
to a prostitute, he becomes one body with her? For
the Scriptures say, "The two are united into one."*
17 But the person who is joined to the Lord is one spirit
with him.
18 Run from sexual sin! No other sin so clearly affects the body as this one does. For sexual immorality
is a sin against your own body. 19 Don't you realize that
your body is the temple of the Holy Spirit, who lives in
you and was given to you by God? You do not belong
to yourself, 20 for God bought you with a high price. So
you must honor God with your body.

Instruction on Marriage

7 Now regarding the questions you asked in
your letter. Yes, it is good to abstain from sexual

6:6 Greek *one brother.* **6:8** Greek *even the brothers.* **6:16** Gen 2:24.

KING JAMES VERSION

2Nevertheless, *to avoid* fornication, let every man have his own wife, and let every woman have her own husband.

3Let the husband render unto the wife due benevolence: and likewise also the wife unto the husband.

4The wife hath not power of her own body, but the husband: and likewise also the husband hath not power of his own body, but the wife.

5Defraud ye not one the other, except *it be* with consent for a time, that ye may give yourselves to fasting and prayer; and come together again, that Satan tempt you not for your incontinency.

6But I speak this by permission, *and* not of commandment.

7For I would that all men were even as I myself. But every man hath his proper gift of God, one after this manner, and another after that.

8I say therefore to the unmarried and widows, It is good for them if they abide even as I.

9But if they cannot contain, let them marry: for it is better to marry than to burn.

10And unto the married I command, *yet* not I, but the Lord, Let not the wife depart from *her* husband:

11But and if she depart, let her remain unmarried, or be reconciled to *her* husband: and let not the husband put away *his* wife.

12But to the rest speak I, not the Lord: If any brother hath a wife that believeth not, and she be pleased to dwell with him, let him not put her away.

13And the woman which hath an husband that believeth not, and if he be pleased to dwell with her, let her not leave him.

14For the unbelieving husband is sanctified by the wife, and the unbelieving wife is sanctified by the husband: else were your children unclean; but now are they holy.

15But if the unbelieving depart, let him depart. A brother or a sister is not under bondage in such *cases:* but God hath called us to peace.

16For what knowest thou, O wife, whether thou shalt save *thy* husband? or how knowest thou, O man, whether thou shalt save *thy* wife?

17But as God hath distributed to every man, as the Lord hath called every one, so let him walk. And so ordain I in all churches.

18Is any man called being circumcised? let him not become uncircumcised. Is any called in uncircumcision? let him not be circumcised.

19Circumcision is nothing, and uncircumcision is nothing, but the keeping of the commandments of God.

NEW LIVING TRANSLATION

relations.* 2But because there is so much sexual immorality, each man should have his own wife, and each woman should have her own husband.

3The husband should fulfill his wife's sexual needs, and the wife should fulfill her husband's needs. 4The wife gives authority over her body to her husband, and the husband gives authority over his body to his wife.

5Do not deprive each other of sexual relations, unless you both agree to refrain from sexual intimacy for a limited time so you can give yourselves more completely to prayer. Afterward, you should come together again so that Satan won't be able to tempt you because of your lack of self-control. 6I say this as a concession, not as a command. 7But I wish everyone were single, just as I am. Yet each person has a special gift from God, of one kind or another.

8So I say to those who aren't married and to widows—it's better to stay unmarried, just as I am. 9But if they can't control themselves, they should goahead and marry. It's better to marry than to burn with lust.

10But for those who are married, I have a command that comes not from me, but from the Lord.* A wife must not leave her husband. 11But if she does leave him, let her remain single or else be reconciled to him. And the husband must not leave his wife.

12Now, I will speak to the rest of you, though I do not have a direct command from the Lord. If a Christian man* has a wife who is not a believer and she is willing to continue living with him, he must not leave her. 13And if a Christian woman has a husband who is not a believer and he is willing to continue living with her, she must not leave him. 14For the Christian wife brings holiness to her marriage, and the Christian husband* brings holiness to his marriage. Otherwise, your children would not be holy, but now they are holy. 15(But if the husband or wife who isn't a believer insists on leaving, let them go. In such cases the Christian husband or wife* is no longer bound to the other, for God has called you* to live in peace.) 16Don't you wives realize that your husbands might be saved because of you? And don't you husbands realize that your wives might be saved because of you?

17Each of you should continue to live in whatever situation the Lord has placed you, and remain as you were when God first called you. This is my rule for all the churches. 18For instance, a man who was circumcised before he became a believer should not try to reverse it. And the man who was uncircumcised when he became a believer should not be circumcised now. 19For it makes no difference whether or not a man has been circumcised. The important thing is to keep God's commandments.

7:1 Or *to live a celibate life;* Greek reads *It is good for a man not to touch a woman.* **7:10** See Matt 5:32; 19:9; Mark 10:11-12; Luke 16:18. **7:12** Greek *a brother.* **7:14** Greek *the brother.* **7:15a** Greek *the brother or sister.* **7:15b** Some manuscripts read *us.*

KING JAMES VERSION

20Let every man abide in the same calling wherein
he was called.
21Art thou called *being* a servant? care not for it:
but if thou mayest be made free, use *it* rather.
22For he that is called in the Lord, *being* a servant,
is the Lord's freeman: likewise also he that is called,
being free, is Christ's servant.
23Ye are bought with a price; be not ye the servants
of men.
24Brethren, let every man, wherein he is called,
therein abide with God.
25Now concerning virgins I have no commandment of the Lord: yet I give my judgment, as one that
hath obtained mercy of the Lord to be faithful.
26I suppose therefore that this is good for the present distress, *I say,* that *it is* good for a man so to be.
27Art thou bound unto a wife? seek not to be
loosed. Art thou loosed from a wife? seek not a wife.
28But and if thou marry, thou hast not sinned; and
if a virgin marry, she hath not sinned. Nevertheless
such shall have trouble in the flesh: but I spare you.
29But this I say, brethren, the time *is* short: it remaineth, that both they that have wives be as though
they had none;
30And they that weep, as though they wept not;
and they that rejoice, as though they rejoiced not;
and they that buy, as though they possessed not;
31And they that use this world, as not abusing *it:*
for the fashion of this world passeth away.
32But I would have you without carefulness. He
that is unmarried careth for the things that belong to
the Lord, how he may please the Lord:
33But he that is married careth for the things that
are of the world, how he may please *his* wife.
34There is difference *also* between a wife and a
virgin. The unmarried woman careth for the things
of the Lord, that she may be holy both in body and in
spirit: but she that is married careth for the things of
the world, how she may please *her* husband.
35And this I speak for your own profit; not that I
may cast a snare upon you, but for that which is
comely, and that ye may attend upon the Lord without distraction.
36But if any man think that he behaveth himself
uncomely toward his virgin, if she pass the flower of
her age, and need so require, let him do what he will,
he sinneth not: let them marry.
37Nevertheless he that standeth stedfast in his
heart, having no necessity, but hath power over his
own will, and hath so decreed in his heart that he will
keep his virgin, doeth well.
38So then he that giveth *her* in marriage doeth well;
but he that giveth *her* not in marriage doeth better.
39The wife is bound by the law as long as her husband liveth; but if her husband be dead, she is at liberty to be married to whom she will; only in the Lord.

NEW LIVING TRANSLATION

20Yes, each of you should remain as you were when
God called you. 21Are you a slave? Don't let that worry
you—but if you get a chance to be free, take it. 22And
remember, if you were a slave when the Lord called
you, you are now free in the Lord. And if you were
free when the Lord called you, you are now a slave of
Christ. 23God paid a high price for you, so don't be
enslaved by the world.* 24Each of you, dear brothers
and sisters,* should remain as you were when God
first called you.
25Now regarding your question about the young
women who are not yet married. I do not have a command from the Lord for them. But the Lord in his
mercy has given me wisdom that can be trusted, and
I will share it with you. 26Because of the present cri-
sis,* I think it is best to remain as you are. 27If you
have a wife, do not seek to end the marriage. If you
do not have a wife, do not seek to get married. 28But if
you do get married, it is not a sin. And if a young
woman gets married, it is not a sin. However, those
who get married at this time will have troubles, and I
am trying to spare you those problems.
29But let me say this, dear brothers and sisters: The
time that remains is very short. So from now on, those
with wives should not focus only on their marriage.
30Those who weep or who rejoice or who buy things
should not be absorbed by their weeping or their joy
or their possessions. 31Those who use the things of
the world should not become attached to them. For
this world as we know it will soon pass away.
32I want you to be free from the concerns of this
life. An unmarried man can spend his time doing the
Lord's work and thinking how to please him. 33But a
married man has to think about his earthly responsibilities and how to please his wife. 34His interests are
divided. In the same way, a woman who is no longer
married or has never been married can be devoted
to the Lord and holy in body and in spirit. But a married woman has to think about her earthly responsibilities and how to please her husband. 35I am saying
this for your benefit, not to place restrictions on you.
I want you to do whatever will help you serve the
Lord best, with as few distractions as possible.
36But if a man thinks that he's treating his fiancée
improperly and will inevitably give in to his passion,
let him marry her as he wishes. It is not a sin. 37But if
he has decided firmly not to marry and there is no
urgency and he can control his passion, he does well
not to marry. 38So the person who marries his
fiancée does well, and the person who doesn't marry
does even better.
39A wife is bound to her husband as long as he
lives. If her husband dies, she is free to marry anyone

7:23 Greek *don't become slaves of people.* **7:24** Greek *brothers;* also in 7:29. **7:26** Or *the pressures of life.*

KING JAMES VERSION

40But she is happier if she so abide, after my judgment: and I think also that I have the Spirit of God.

8

1Now as touching things offered unto idols, we
know that we all have knowledge. Knowledge
puffeth up, but charity edifieth.
2And if any man think that he knoweth any thing,
he knoweth nothing yet as he ought to know.
3But if any man love God, the same is known of
him.
4As concerning therefore the eating of those
things that are offered in sacrifice unto idols, we
know that an idol *is* nothing in the world, and that
there is none other God but one.
5For though there be that are called gods, whether
in heaven or in earth, (as there be gods many, and
lords many,)
6But to us *there is but* one God, the Father, of
whom *are* all things, and we in him; and one Lord
Jesus Christ, by whom *are* all things, and we by him.
7Howbeit *there is* not in every man that knowledge: for some with conscience of the idol unto this
hour eat *it* as a thing offered unto an idol; and their
conscience being weak is defiled.
8But meat commendeth us not to God: for neither,
if we eat, are we the better; neither, if we eat not, are
we the worse.
9But take heed lest by any means this liberty of
yours become a stumblingblock to them that are
weak.
10For if any man see thee which hast knowledge
sit at meat in the idol's temple, shall not the conscience of him which is weak be emboldened to eat
those things which are offered to idols;
11And through thy knowledge shall the weak
brother perish, for whom Christ died?
12But when ye sin so against the brethren, and
wound their weak conscience, ye sin against Christ.
13Wherefore, if meat make my brother to offend, I
will eat no flesh while the world standeth, lest I make
my brother to offend.

9

1Am I not an apostle? am I not free? have I not
seen Jesus Christ our Lord? are not ye my work
in the Lord?
2If I be not an apostle unto others, yet doubtless I
am to you: for the seal of mine apostleship are ye in
the Lord.
3Mine answer to them that do examine me is this,
4Have we not power to eat and to drink?

NEW LIVING TRANSLATION

she wishes, but only if he loves the Lord.* 40But in my
opinion it would be better for her to stay single, and
I think I am giving you counsel from God's Spirit
when I say this.

Food Sacrificed to Idols

8

Now regarding your question about food that
has been offered to idols. Yes, we know that
"we all have knowledge" about this issue. But while
knowledge makes us feel important, it is love that
strengthens the church. 2Anyone who claims to
know all the answers doesn't really know very much.
3But the person who loves God is the one whom God
recognizes.*
4So, what about eating meat that has been offered
to idols? Well, we all know that an idol is not really a
god and that there is only one God. 5There may be
so-called gods both in heaven and on earth, and
some people actually worship many gods and many
lords. 6But we know that there is only one God, the
Father, who created everything, and we live for him.
And there is only one Lord, Jesus Christ, through
whom God made everything and through whom we
have been given life.
7However, not all believers know this. Some are
accustomed to thinking of idols as being real, so
when they eat food that has been offered to idols,
they think of it as the worship of real gods, and their
weak consciences are violated. 8It's true that we can't
win God's approval by what we eat. We don't lose
anything if we don't eat it, and we don't gain anything
if we do.
9But you must be careful so that your freedom
does not cause others with a weaker conscience to
stumble. 10For if others see you—with your "superior
knowledge"—eating in the temple of an idol, won't
they be encouraged to violate their conscience by
eating food that has been offered to an idol? 11So because of your superior knowledge, a weak believer*
for whom Christ died will be destroyed. 12And when
you sin against other believers* by encouraging
them to do something they believe is wrong, you are
sinning against Christ. 13So if what I eat causes another believer to sin, I will never eat meat again as
long as I live—for I don't want to cause another believer to stumble.

Paul Gives Up His Rights

9

Am I not as free as anyone else? Am I not an
apostle? Haven't I seen Jesus our Lord with my
own eyes? Isn't it because of my work that you belong to the Lord? 2Even if others think I am not an
apostle, I certainly am to you. You yourselves are
proof that I am the Lord's apostle.
3This is my answer to those who question my
authority.* 4Don't we have the right to live in your

7:39 Greek *but only in the Lord.* **8:3** Some manuscripts read *the person who loves has full knowledge.* **8:11** Greek *brother;* also in 8:13. **8:12** Greek *brothers.* **9:3** Greek *those who examine me.*

KING JAMES VERSION

5 Have we not power to lead about a sister, a wife,
as well as other apostles, and *as* the brethren of the
Lord, and Cephas?
6 Or I only and Barnabas, have not we power to
forbear working?
7 Who goeth a warfare any time at his own
charges? who planteth a vineyard, and eateth not of
the fruit thereof? or who feedeth a flock, and eateth
not of the milk of the flock?
8 Say I these things as a man? or saith not the law
the same also?
9 For it is written in the law of Moses, Thou shalt
not muzzle the mouth of the ox that treadeth out the
corn. Doth God take care for oxen?
10 Or saith he *it* altogether for our sakes? For our
sakes, no doubt, *this* is written: that he that ploweth
should plow in hope; and that he that thresheth in
hope should be partaker of his hope.
11 If we have sown unto you spiritual things, *is it* a
great thing if we shall reap your carnal things?
12 If others be partakers of *this* power over you, *are*
not we rather? Nevertheless we have not used this
power; but suffer all things, lest we should hinder
the gospel of Christ.
13 Do ye not know that they which minister about
holy things live *of the things* of the temple? and they
which wait at the altar are partakers with the altar?
14 Even so hath the Lord ordained that they which
preach the gospel should live of the gospel.
15 But I have used none of these things: neither
have I written these things, that it should be so done
unto me: for *it were* better for me to die, than that
any man should make my glorying void.
16 For though I preach the gospel, I have nothing to
glory of: for necessity is laid upon me; yea, woe is
unto me, if I preach not the gospel!
17 For if I do this thing willingly, I have a reward:
but if against my will, a dispensation *of the gospel* is
committed unto me.
18 What is my reward then? *Verily* that, when I
preach the gospel, I may make the gospel of Christ
without charge, that I abuse not my power in the
gospel.
19 For though I be free from all *men,* yet have I
made myself servant unto all, that I might gain the
more.
20 And unto the Jews I became as a Jew, that I might
gain the Jews; to them that are under the law, as
under the law, that I might gain them that are under
the law;
21 To them that are without law, as without law, (being not without law to God, but under the law to
Christ,) that I might gain them that are without law.
22 To the weak became I as weak, that I might gain

NEW LIVING TRANSLATION

homes and share your meals? 5 Don't we have the
right to bring a Christian wife with us as the other
apostles and the Lord's brothers do, and as Peter*
does? 6 Or is it only Barnabas and I who have to work
to support ourselves?
7 What soldier has to pay his own expenses? What
farmer plants a vineyard and doesn't have the right
to eat some of its fruit? What shepherd cares for a
flock of sheep and isn't allowed to drink some of the
milk? 8 Am I expressing merely a human opinion,
or does the law say the same thing? 9 For the law of
Moses says, "You must not muzzle an ox to keep
it from eating as it treads out the grain."* Was God
thinking only about oxen when he said this?
10 Wasn't he actually speaking to us? Yes, it was written for us, so that the one who plows and the one
who threshes the grain might both expect a share of
the harvest.
11 Since we have planted spiritual seed among you,
aren't we entitled to a harvest of physical food and
drink? 12 If you support others who preach to you,
shouldn't we have an even greater right to be supported? But we have never used this right. We would
rather put up with anything than be an obstacle to
the Good News about Christ.
13 Don't you realize that those who work in the
temple get their meals from the offerings brought to
the temple? And those who serve at the altar get a
share of the sacrificial offerings. 14 In the same way,
the Lord ordered that those who preach the Good
News should be supported by those who benefit
from it. 15 Yet I have never used any of these rights.
And I am not writing this to suggest that I want to
start now. In fact, I would rather die than lose my
right to boast about preaching without charge. 16 Yet
preaching the Good News is not something I can
boast about. I am compelled by God to do it. How
terrible for me if I didn't preach the Good News!
17 If I were doing this on my own initiative, I would
deserve payment. But I have no choice, for God has
given me this sacred trust. 18 What then is my pay? It
is the opportunity to preach the Good News without
charging anyone. That's why I never demand my
rights when I preach the Good News.
19 Even though I am a free man with no master, I
have become a slave to all people to bring many to
Christ. 20 When I was with the Jews, I lived like a Jew
to bring the Jews to Christ. When I was with those
who follow the Jewish law, I too lived under that law.
Even though I am not subject to the law, I did this so I
could bring to Christ those who are under the law.
21 When I am with the Gentiles who do not follow the
Jewish law,* I too live apart from that law so I can
bring them to Christ. But I do not ignore the law of
God; I obey the law of Christ.
22 When I am with those who are weak, I share

9:5 Greek *Cephas.* **9:9** Deut 25:4. **9:21** Greek *those without the law.*

KING JAMES VERSION

the weak: I am made all things to all *men,* that I might by all means save some.

[23]And this I do for the gospel's sake, that I might be partaker thereof with *you.*

[24]Know ye not that they which run in a race run all, but one receiveth the prize? So run, that ye may obtain.

[25]And every man that striveth for the mastery is temperate in all things. Now they *do it* to obtain a corruptible crown; but we an incorruptible.

[26]I therefore so run, not as uncertainly; so fight I, not as one that beateth the air:

[27]But I keep under my body, and bring *it* into subjection: lest that by any means, when I have preached to others, I myself should be a castaway.

10 [1]Moreover, brethren, I would not that ye should be ignorant, how that all our fathers were under the cloud, and all passed through the sea;

[2]And were all baptized unto Moses in the cloud and in the sea;

[3]And did all eat the same spiritual meat;

[4]And did all drink the same spiritual drink: for they drank of that spiritual Rock that followed them: and that Rock was Christ.

[5]But with many of them God was not well pleased: for they were overthrown in the wilderness.

[6]Now these things were our examples, to the intent we should not lust after evil things, as they also lusted.

[7]Neither be ye idolaters, as *were* some of them; as it is written, The people sat down to eat and drink, and rose up to play.

[8]Neither let us commit fornication, as some of them committed, and fell in one day three and twenty thousand.

[9]Neither let us tempt Christ, as some of them also tempted, and were destroyed of serpents.

[10]Neither murmur ye, as some of them also murmured, and were destroyed of the destroyer.

[11]Now all these things happened unto them for ensamples: and they are written for our admonition, upon whom the ends of the world are come.

[12]Wherefore let him that thinketh he standeth take heed lest he fall.

[13]There hath no temptation taken you but such as is common to man: but God *is* faithful, who will not suffer you to be tempted above that ye are able; but will with the temptation also make a way to escape, that ye may be able to bear *it.*

[14]Wherefore, my dearly beloved, flee from idolatry.

[15]I speak as to wise men; judge ye what I say.

[16]The cup of blessing which we bless, is it not the communion of the blood of Christ? The bread which we break, is it not the communion of the body of Christ?

[17]For we *being* many are one bread, *and* one body: for we are all partakers of that one bread.

NEW LIVING TRANSLATION

their weakness, for I want to bring the weak to Christ. Yes, I try to find common ground with everyone, doing everything I can to save some. [23]I do everything to spread the Good News and share in its blessings.

[24]Don't you realize that in a race everyone runs, but only one person gets the prize? So run to win! [25]All athletes are disciplined in their training. They do it to win a prize that will fade away, but we do it for an eternal prize. [26]So I run with purpose in every step. I am not just shadowboxing. [27]I discipline my body like an athlete, training it to do what it should. Otherwise, I fear that after preaching to others I myself might be disqualified.

Lessons from Israel's Idolatry

10 I don't want you to forget, dear brothers and sisters,* about our ancestors in the wilderness long ago. All of them were guided by a cloud that moved ahead of them, and all of them walked through the sea on dry ground. [2]In the cloud and in the sea, all of them were baptized as followers of Moses. [3]All of them ate the same spiritual food, [4]and all of them drank the same spiritual water. For they drank from the spiritual rock that traveled with them, and that rock was Christ. [5]Yet God was not pleased with most of them, and their bodies were scattered in the wilderness.

[6]These things happened as a warning to us, so that we would not crave evil things as they did, [7]or worship idols as some of them did. As the Scriptures say, "The people celebrated with feasting and drinking, and they indulged in pagan revelry."* [8]And we must not engage in sexual immorality as some of them did, causing 23,000 of them to die in one day.

[9]Nor should we put Christ* to the test, as some of them did and then died from snakebites. [10]And don't grumble as some of them did, and then were destroyed by the angel of death. [11]These things happened to them as examples for us. They were written down to warn us who live at the end of the age.

[12]If you think you are standing strong, be careful not to fall. [13]The temptations in your life are no different from what others experience. And God is faithful. He will not allow the temptation to be more than you can stand. When you are tempted, he will show you a way out so that you can endure.

[14]So, my dear friends, flee from the worship of idols. [15]You are reasonable people. Decide for yourselves if what I am saying is true. [16]When we bless the cup at the Lord's Table, aren't we sharing in the blood of Christ? And when we break the bread, aren't we sharing in the body of Christ? [17]And though we are many, we all eat from one loaf of bread, showing

10:1 Greek *brothers.* **10:7** Exod 32:6. **10:9** Some manuscripts read *the Lord.*

KING JAMES VERSION

18 Behold Israel after the flesh: are not they which eat of the sacrifices partakers of the altar?

19 What say I then? that the idol is any thing, or that which is offered in sacrifice to idols is any thing?

20 But *I say,* that the things which the Gentiles sacrifice, they sacrifice to devils, and not to God: and I would not that ye should have fellowship with devils.

21 Ye cannot drink the cup of the Lord, and the cup of devils: ye cannot be partakers of the Lord's table, and of the table of devils.

22 Do we provoke the Lord to jealousy? are we stronger than he?

23 All things are lawful for me, but all things are not expedient: all things are lawful for me, but all things edify not.

24 Let no man seek his own, but every man another's *wealth.*

25 Whatsoever is sold in the shambles, *that* eat, asking no question for conscience sake:

26 For the earth *is* the Lord's, and the fulness thereof.

27 If any of them that believe not bid you *to a feast,* and ye be disposed to go; whatsoever is set before you, eat, asking no question for conscience sake.

28 But if any man say unto you, This is offered in sacrifice unto idols, eat not for his sake that shewed it, and for conscience sake: for the earth *is* the Lord's, and the fulness thereof:

29 Conscience, I say, not thine own, but of the other: for why is my liberty judged of another *man's* conscience?

30 For if I by grace be a partaker, why am I evil spoken of for that for which I give thanks?

31 Whether therefore ye eat, or drink, or whatsoever ye do, do all to the glory of God.

32 Give none offence, neither to the Jews, nor to the Gentiles, nor to the church of God:

33 Even as I please all *men* in all *things,* not seeking mine own profit, but the *profit* of many, that they may be saved.

11 1 Be ye followers of me, even as I also *am* of Christ.

2 Now I praise you, brethren, that ye remember me in all things, and keep the ordinances, as I delivered *them* to you.

3 But I would have you know, that the head of every man is Christ; and the head of the woman *is* the man; and the head of Christ *is* God.

4 Every man praying or prophesying, having *his* head covered, dishonoureth his head.

5 But every woman that prayeth or prophesieth with *her* head uncovered dishonoureth her head: for that is even all one as if she were shaven.

6 For if the woman be not covered, let her also be

NEW LIVING TRANSLATION

that we are one body. 18 Think about the people of
Israel. Weren't they united by eating the sacrifices
at the altar?
19 What am I trying to say? Am I saying that food
offered to idols has some significance, or that idols
are real gods? 20 No, not at all. I am saying that these
sacrifices are offered to demons, not to God. And I
don't want you to participate with demons. 21 You
cannot drink from the cup of the Lord and from the
cup of demons, too. You cannot eat at the Lord's
Table and at the table of demons, too. 22 What? Do
we dare to rouse the Lord's jealousy? Do you think we
are stronger than he is?
23 You say, "I am allowed to do anything"*—but not
everything is good for you. You say, "I am allowed to
do anything"—but not everything is beneficial.
24 Don't be concerned for your own good but for the
good of others.
25 So you may eat any meat that is sold in the
marketplace without raising questions of conscience. 26 For "the earth is the LORD's, and everything in it."*
27 If someone who isn't a believer asks you home
for dinner, accept the invitation if you want to. Eat
whatever is offered to you without raising questions
of conscience. 28 (But suppose someone tells you,
"This meat was offered to an idol." Don't eat it, out of
consideration for the conscience of the one who told
you. 29 It might not be a matter of conscience for you,
but it is for the other person.) For why should my
freedom be limited by what someone else thinks?
30 If I can thank God for the food and enjoy it, why
should I be condemned for eating it?
31 So whether you eat or drink, or whatever you do,
do it all for the glory of God. 32 Don't give offense to
Jews or Gentiles* or the church of God. 33 I, too, try
to please everyone in everything I do. I don't just
do what is best for me; I do what is best for others so
that many may be saved. 11:1 And you should imitate
me, just as I imitate Christ.

Instructions for Public Worship

11 2 I am so glad that you always keep me in your
thoughts, and that you are following the teachings I passed on to you. 3 But there is one thing I want
you to know: The head of every man is Christ, the head
of woman is man, and the head of Christ is God.* 4 A
man dishonors his head* if he covers his head while
praying or prophesying. 5 But a woman dishonors her
head* if she prays or prophesies without a covering
on her head, for this is the same as shaving her head.
6 Yes, if she refuses to wear a head covering, she
should cut off all her hair! But since it is shameful for

10:23 Greek *All things are lawful;* also in 10:23b. **10:26** Ps 24:1. **10:32** Greek *or Greeks.* **11:3** Or *to know: The source of every man is Christ, the source of woman is man, and the source of Christ is God.* Or *to know: Every man is responsible to Christ, a woman is responsible to her husband, and Christ is responsible to God.* **11:4** Or *dishonors Christ.* **11:5** Or *dishonors her husband.*

KING JAMES VERSION

shorn: but if it be a shame for a woman to be shorn or shaven, let her be covered.

7 For a man indeed ought not to cover *his* head, forasmuch as he is the image and glory of God: but the woman is the glory of the man.

8 For the man is not of the woman; but the woman of the man.

9 Neither was the man created for the woman; but the woman for the man.

10 For this cause ought the woman to have power on *her* head because of the angels.

11 Nevertheless neither is the man without the woman, neither the woman without the man, in the Lord.

12 For as the woman *is* of the man, even so *is* the man also by the woman; but all things of God.

13 Judge in yourselves: is it comely that a woman pray unto God uncovered?

14 Doth not even nature itself teach you, that, if a man have long hair, it is a shame unto him?

15 But if a woman have long hair, it is a glory to her: for *her* hair is given her for a covering.

16 But if any man seem to be contentious, we have no such custom, neither the churches of God.

17 Now in this that I declare *unto you* I praise *you* not, that ye come together not for the better, but for the worse.

18 For first of all, when ye come together in the church, I hear that there be divisions among you; and I partly believe it.

19 For there must be also heresies among you, that they which are approved may be made manifest among you.

20 When ye come together therefore into one place, *this* is not to eat the Lord's supper.

21 For in eating every one taketh before *other* his own supper: and one is hungry, and another is drunken.

22 What? have ye not houses to eat and to drink in? or despise ye the church of God, and shame them that have not? What shall I say to you? shall I praise you in this? I praise *you* not.

23 For I have received of the Lord that which also I delivered unto you, That the Lord Jesus the *same* night in which he was betrayed took bread:

24 And when he had given thanks, he brake *it,* and said, Take, eat: this is my body, which is broken for you: this do in remembrance of me.

25 After the same manner also *he took* the cup, when he had supped, saying, This cup is the new testament in my blood: this do ye, as oft as ye drink *it,* in remembrance of me.

26 For as often as ye eat this bread, and drink this cup, ye do shew the Lord's death till he come.

27 Wherefore whosoever shall eat this bread, and

NEW LIVING TRANSLATION

a woman to have her hair cut or her head shaved, she should wear a covering.*

7 A man should not wear anything on his head when worshiping, for man is made in God's image and reflects God's glory. And woman reflects man's glory. 8 For the first man didn't come from woman, but the first woman came from man. 9 And man was not made for woman, but woman was made for man. 10 For this reason, and because the angels are watching, a woman should wear a covering on her head to show she is under authority.*

11 But among the Lord's people, women are not independent of men, and men are not independent of women. 12 For although the first woman came from man, every other man was born from a woman, and everything comes from God.

13 Judge for yourselves. Is it right for a woman to pray to God in public without covering her head? 14 Isn't it obvious that it's disgraceful for a man to have long hair? 15 And isn't long hair a woman's pride and joy? For it has been given to her as a covering. 16 But if anyone wants to argue about this, I simply say that we have no other custom than this, and neither do God's other churches.

Order at the Lord's Supper

17 But in the following instructions, I cannot praise you. For it sounds as if more harm than good is done when you meet together. 18 First, I hear that there are divisions among you when you meet as a church, and to some extent I believe it. 19 But, of course, there must be divisions among you so that you who have God's approval will be recognized!

20 When you meet together, you are not really interested in the Lord's Supper. 21 For some of you hurry to eat your own meal without sharing with others. As a result, some go hungry while others get drunk. 22 What? Don't you have your own homes for eating and drinking? Or do you really want to disgrace God's church and shame the poor? What am I supposed to say? Do you want me to praise you? Well, I certainly will not praise you for this!

23 For I pass on to you what I received from the Lord himself. On the night when he was betrayed, the Lord Jesus took some bread 24 and gave thanks to God for it. Then he broke it in pieces and said, "This is my body, which is given for you.* Do this to remember me." 25 In the same way, he took the cup of wine after supper, saying, "This cup is the new covenant between God and his people—an agreement confirmed with my blood. Do this to remember me as often as you drink it." 26 For every time you eat this bread and drink this cup, you are announcing the Lord's death until he comes again.

27 So anyone who eats this bread or drinks this cup of the Lord unworthily is guilty of sinning against*

11:6 Or *should have long hair.* **11:10** Greek *should have an authority on her head.* **11:24** Greek *which is for you;* other manuscripts read *which is broken for you.* **11:27** Or *is responsible for.*

KING JAMES VERSION

drink *this* cup of the Lord, unworthily, shall be guilty of the body and blood of the Lord.

28 But let a man examine himself, and so let him eat of *that* bread, and drink of *that* cup.

29 For he that eateth and drinketh unworthily, eateth and drinketh damnation to himself, not discerning the Lord's body.

30 For this cause many *are* weak and sickly among you, and many sleep.

31 For if we would judge ourselves, we should not be judged.

32 But when we are judged, we are chastened of the Lord, that we should not be condemned with the world.

33 Wherefore, my brethren, when ye come together to eat, tarry one for another.

34 And if any man hunger, let him eat at home; that ye come not together unto condemnation. And the rest will I set in order when I come.

12 1 Now concerning spiritual *gifts,* brethren, I would not have you ignorant.

2 Ye know that ye were Gentiles, carried away unto these dumb idols, even as ye were led.

3 Wherefore I give you to understand, that no man speaking by the Spirit of God calleth Jesus accursed: and *that* no man can say that Jesus is the Lord, but by the Holy Ghost.

4 Now there are diversities of gifts, but the same Spirit.

5 And there are differences of administrations, but the same Lord.

6 And there are diversities of operations, but it is the same God which worketh all in all.

7 But the manifestation of the Spirit is given to every man to profit withal.

8 For to one is given by the Spirit the word of wisdom; to another the word of knowledge by the same Spirit;

9 To another faith by the same Spirit; to another the gifts of healing by the same Spirit;

10 To another the working of miracles; to another prophecy; to another discerning of spirits; to another *divers* kinds of tongues; to another the interpretation of tongues:

11 But all these worketh that one and the selfsame Spirit, dividing to every man severally as he will.

12 For as the body is one, and hath many members, and all the members of that one body, being many, are one body: so also *is* Christ.

13 For by one Spirit are we all baptized into one body, whether *we be* Jews or Gentiles, whether *we be*

NEW LIVING TRANSLATION

the body and blood of the Lord. 28 That is why you
should examine yourself before eating the bread and
drinking the cup. 29 For if you eat the bread or drink
the cup without honoring the body of Christ,* you
are eating and drinking God's judgment upon yourself.
30 That is why many of you are weak and sick and
some have even died.
31 But if we would examine ourselves, we would
not be judged by God in this way. 32 Yet when we are
judged by the Lord, we are being disciplined so that
we will not be condemned along with the world.
33 So, my dear brothers and sisters,* when you
gather for the Lord's Supper, wait for each other. 34 If
you are really hungry, eat at home so you won't bring
judgment upon yourselves when you meet together.
I'll give you instructions about the other matters
after I arrive.

Spiritual Gifts

12 Now, dear brothers and sisters,* regarding
your question about the special abilities the
Spirit gives us. I don't want you to misunderstand this.
2 You know that when you were still pagans, you were
led astray and swept along in worshiping speechless
idols. 3 So I want you to know that no one speaking by
the Spirit of God will curse Jesus, and no one can say
Jesus is Lord, except by the Holy Spirit.
4 There are different kinds of spiritual gifts, but
the same Spirit is the source of them all. 5 There are
different kinds of service, but we serve the same
Lord. 6 God works in different ways, but it is the same
God who does the work in all of us.
7 A spiritual gift is given to each of us so we can
help each other. 8 To one person the Spirit gives the
ability to give wise advice*; to another the same
Spirit gives a message of special knowledge.* 9 The
same Spirit gives great faith to another, and to someone
else the one Spirit gives the gift of healing. 10 He
gives one person the power to perform miracles, and
another the ability to prophesy. He gives someone
else the ability to discern whether a message is from
the Spirit of God or from another spirit. Still another
person is given the ability to speak in unknown languages,*
while another is given the ability to interpret
what is being said. 11 It is the one and only Spirit
who distributes all these gifts. He alone decides
which gift each person should have.

One Body with Many Parts

12 The human body has many parts, but the many
parts make up one whole body. So it is with the body
of Christ. 13 Some of us are Jews, some are Gentiles,*
some are slaves, and some are free. But we have all

11:29 Greek *the body;* other manuscripts read *the Lord's body.* **11:33** Greek *brothers.* **12:1** Greek *brothers.* **12:8a** Or *gives a word of wisdom.* **12:8b** Or *gives a word of knowledge.* **12:10** Or *in various tongues;* also in 12:28, 30. **12:13a** Greek *some are Greeks.*

KING JAMES VERSION

bond or free; and have been all made to drink into one Spirit.

14 For the body is not one member, but many.

15 If the foot shall say, Because I am not the hand, I am not of the body; is it therefore not of the body?

16 And if the ear shall say, Because I am not the eye, I am not of the body; is it therefore not of the body?

17 If the whole body *were* an eye, where *were* the hearing? If the whole *were* hearing, where *were* the smelling?

18 But now hath God set the members every one of them in the body, as it hath pleased him.

19 And if they were all one member, where *were* the body?

20 But now *are they* many members, yet but one body.

21 And the eye cannot say unto the hand, I have no need of thee: nor again the head to the feet, I have no need of you.

22 Nay, much more those members of the body, which seem to be more feeble, are necessary:

23 And those *members* of the body, which we think to be less honourable, upon these we bestow more abundant honour; and our uncomely *parts* have more abundant comeliness.

24 For our comely *parts* have no need: but God hath tempered the body together, having given more abundant honour to that *part* which lacked:

25 That there should be no schism in the body; but *that* the members should have the same care one for another.

26 And whether one member suffer, all the members suffer with it; or one member be honoured, all the members rejoice with it.

27 Now ye are the body of Christ, and members in particular.

28 And God hath set some in the church, first apostles, secondarily prophets, thirdly teachers, after that miracles, then gifts of healings, helps, governments, diversities of tongues.

29 *Are* all apostles? *are* all prophets? *are* all teachers? *are* all workers of miracles?

30 Have all the gifts of healing? do all speak with tongues? do all interpret?

31 But covet earnestly the best gifts: and yet shew I unto you a more excellent way.

13 1 Though I speak with the tongues of men and of angels, and have not charity, I am become *as* sounding brass, or a tinkling cymbal.

2 And though I have *the gift of* prophecy, and understand all mysteries, and all knowledge; and

NEW LIVING TRANSLATION

been baptized into one body by one Spirit, and we all
share the same Spirit.*
14 Yes, the body has many different parts, not just
one part. 15 If the foot says, "I am not a part of the
body because I am not a hand," that does not make it
any less a part of the body. 16 And if the ear says, "I am
not part of the body because I am not an eye," would
that make it any less a part of the body? 17 If the
whole body were an eye, how would you hear? Or if
your whole body were an ear, how would you smell
anything?
18 But our bodies have many parts, and God has put
each part just where he wants it. 19 How strange a
body would be if it had only one part! 20 Yes, there are
many parts, but only one body. 21 The eye can never
say to the hand, "I don't need you." The head can't say
to the feet, "I don't need you."
22 In fact, some parts of the body that seem weakest
and least important are actually the most necessary.
23 And the parts we regard as less honorable are those
we clothe with the greatest care. So we carefully protect those parts that should not be seen, 24 while the
more honorable parts do not require this special care.
So God has put the body together such that extra
honor and care are given to those parts that have less
dignity. 25 This makes for harmony among the members, so that all the members care for each other. 26 If
one part suffers, all the parts suffer with it, and if one
part is honored, all the parts are glad.
27 All of you together are Christ's body, and each of
you is a part of it. 28 Here are some of the parts God
has appointed for the church:

first are apostles,
second are prophets,
third are teachers,
then those who do miracles,
those who have the gift of healing,
those who can help others,
those who have the gift of leadership,
those who speak in unknown languages.

29 Are we all apostles? Are we all prophets? Are we
all teachers? Do we all have the power to do miracles?
30 Do we all have the gift of healing? Do we all have
the ability to speak in unknown languages? Do we all
have the ability to interpret unknown languages? Of
course not! 31 So you should earnestly desire the most
helpful gifts.

But now let me show you a way of life that is best of all.

Love Is the Greatest

13 If I could speak all the languages of earth and
of angels, but didn't love others, I would only
be a noisy gong or a clanging cymbal. 2 If I had the gift
of prophecy, and if I understood all of God's secret

12:13b Greek *we were all given one Spirit to drink.*

KING JAMES VERSION

though I have all faith, so that I could remove mountains, and have not charity, I am nothing.
3And though I bestow all my goods to feed *the*
poor, and though I give my body to be burned, and
have not charity, it profiteth me nothing.
4Charity suffereth long, *and* is kind; charity envi-
eth not; charity vaunteth not itself, is not puffed up,
5Doth not behave itself unseemly, seeketh not her
own, is not easily provoked, thinketh no evil;
6Rejoiceth not in iniquity, but rejoiceth in the
truth;
7Beareth all things, believeth all things, hopeth all
things, endureth all things.
8Charity never faileth: but whether *there be*
prophecies, they shall fail; whether *there be* tongues,
they shall cease; whether *there be* knowledge, it shall
vanish away.
9For we know in part, and we prophesy in part.
10But when that which is perfect is come, then that
which is in part shall be done away.
11When I was a child, I spake as a child, I understood as a child, I thought as a child: but when I became a man, I put away childish things.
12For now we see through a glass, darkly; but then
face to face: now I know in part; but then shall I know
even as also I am known.
13And now abideth faith, hope, charity, these
three; but the greatest of these *is* charity.

14 1Follow after charity, and desire spiritual *gifts,*
but rather that ye may prophesy.
2For he that speaketh in an *unknown* tongue
speaketh not unto men, but unto God: for no man
understandeth *him;* howbeit in the spirit he speaketh mysteries.
3But he that prophesieth speaketh unto men *to*
edification, and exhortation, and comfort.
4He that speaketh in an *unknown* tongue edifieth
himself; but he that prophesieth edifieth the church.
5I would that ye all spake with tongues, but rather
that ye prophesied: for greater *is* he that prophesieth
than he that speaketh with tongues, except he interpret, that the church may receive edifying.
6Now, brethren, if I come unto you speaking with
tongues, what shall I profit you, except I shall speak
to you either by revelation, or by knowledge, or by
prophesying, or by doctrine?
7And even things without life giving sound,
whether pipe or harp, except they give a distinction
in the sounds, how shall it be known what is piped or
harped?

NEW LIVING TRANSLATION

plans and possessed all knowledge, and if I had such
faith that I could move mountains, but didn't love
others, I would be nothing. 3If I gave everything I have
to the poor and even sacrificed my body, I could boast
about it;* but if I didn't love others, I would have
gained nothing.
4Love is patient and kind. Love is not jealous or
boastful or proud 5or rude. It does not demand its
own way. It is not irritable, and it keeps no record of
being wronged. 6It does not rejoice about injustice
but rejoices whenever the truth wins out. 7Love
never gives up, never loses faith, is always hopeful,
and endures through every circumstance.
8Prophecy and speaking in unknown languages*
and special knowledge will become useless. But love
will last forever! 9Now our knowledge is partial and
incomplete, and even the gift of prophecy reveals
only part of the whole picture! 10But when the time
of perfection comes, these partial things will become useless.
11When I was a child, I spoke and thought and
reasoned as a child. But when I grew up, I put away
childish things. 12Now we see things imperfectly,
like puzzling reflections in a mirror, but then we will
see everything with perfect clarity.* All that I know
now is partial and incomplete, but then I will know
everything completely, just as God now knows me
completely.
13Three things will last forever—faith, hope, and
love—and the greatest of these is love.

Tongues and Prophecy

14 Let love be your highest goal! But you should
also desire the special abilities the Spirit
gives—especially the ability to prophesy. 2For if you
have the ability to speak in tongues,* you will be talking only to God, since people won't be able to understand you. You will be speaking by the power of the
Spirit,* but it will all be mysterious. 3But one who
prophesies strengthens others, encourages them, and
comforts them. 4A person who speaks in tongues is
strengthened personally, but one who speaks a word
of prophecy strengthens the entire church.
5I wish you could all speak in tongues, but even
more I wish you could all prophesy. For prophecy is
greater than speaking in tongues, unless someone
interprets what you are saying so that the whole
church will be strengthened.
6Dear brothers and sisters,* if I should come to
you speaking in an unknown language,* how would
that help you? But if I bring you a revelation or some
special knowledge or prophecy or teaching, that will
be helpful. 7Even lifeless instruments like the flute
or the harp must play the notes clearly, or no one

13:3 Some manuscripts read *sacrificed my body to be burned.* **13:8** Or *in tongues.* **13:12** Greek *see face to face.* **14:2a** Or *in unknown languages;* also in 14:4, 5, 13, 14, 18, 22, 26, 27, 28, 39. **14:2b** Or *speaking in your spirit.* **14:6a** Greek *brothers;* also in 14:20, 26, 39. **14:6b** Or *in tongues;* also in 14:19, 23.

KING JAMES VERSION

8For if the trumpet give an uncertain sound, who
shall prepare himself to the battle?
9So likewise ye, except ye utter by the tongue
words easy to be understood, how shall it be known
what is spoken? for ye shall speak into the air.
10There are, it may be, so many kinds of voices in
the world, and none of them *is* without signification.
11Therefore if I know not the meaning of the voice,
I shall be unto him that speaketh a barbarian, and he
that speaketh *shall be* a barbarian unto me.
12Even so ye, forasmuch as ye are zealous of spiritual *gifts,* seek that ye may excel to the edifying of
the church.
13Wherefore let him that speaketh in an *unknown* tongue pray that he may interpret.
14For if I pray in an *unknown* tongue, my spirit
prayeth, but my understanding is unfruitful.
15What is it then? I will pray with the spirit, and I
will pray with the understanding also: I will sing with
the spirit, and I will sing with the understanding also.
16Else when thou shalt bless with the spirit, how
shall he that occupieth the room of the unlearned
say Amen at thy giving of thanks, seeing he understandeth not what thou sayest?
17For thou verily givest thanks well, but the other
is not edified.
18I thank my God, I speak with tongues more than
ye all:
19Yet in the church I had rather speak five words
with my understanding, that *by my voice* I might
teach others also, than ten thousand words in an
unknown tongue.
20Brethren, be not children in understanding:
howbeit in malice be ye children, but in understanding be men.
21In the law it is written, With *men of* other
tongues and other lips will I speak unto this people;
and yet for all that will they not hear me, saith the
Lord.
22Wherefore tongues are for a sign, not to them
that believe, but to them that believe not: but prophesying *serveth* not for them that believe not, but for
them which believe.
23If therefore the whole church be come together
into one place, and all speak with tongues, and there
come in *those that are* unlearned, or unbelievers,
will they not say that ye are mad?
24But if all prophesy, and there come in one that
believeth not, or *one* unlearned, he is convinced of
all, he is judged of all:
25And thus are the secrets of his heart made manifest; and so falling down on *his* face he will worship
God, and report that God is in you of a truth.

NEW LIVING TRANSLATION

will recognize the melody. 8And if the bugler doesn't
sound a clear call, how will the soldiers know they
are being called to battle?
9It's the same for you. If you speak to people in
words they don't understand, how will they know
what you are saying? You might as well be talking
into empty space.
10There are many different languages in the world,
and every language has meaning. 11But if I don't
understand a language, I will be a foreigner to someone who speaks it, and the one who speaks it will be a
foreigner to me. 12And the same is true for you. Since
you are so eager to have the special abilities the
Spirit gives, seek those that will strengthen the
whole church.
13So anyone who speaks in tongues should pray
also for the ability to interpret what has been said.
14For if I pray in tongues, my spirit is praying, but I
don't understand what I am saying.
15Well then, what shall I do? I will pray in the
spirit,* and I will also pray in words I understand. I
will sing in the spirit, and I will also sing in words I
understand. 16For if you praise God only in the spirit,
how can those who don't understand you praise
God along with you? How can they join you in giving
thanks when they don't understand what you are
saying? 17You will be giving thanks very well, but it
won't strengthen the people who hear you.
18I thank God that I speak in tongues more than
any of you. 19But in a church meeting I would rather
speak five understandable words to help others than
ten thousand words in an unknown language.
20Dear brothers and sisters, don't be childish in
your understanding of these things. Be innocent as
babies when it comes to evil, but be mature in understanding matters of this kind. 21It is written in the
Scriptures*:

"I will speak to my own people
through strange languages
and through the lips of foreigners.
But even then, they will not listen to me,"*
says the LORD.

22So you see that speaking in tongues is a sign, not
for believers, but for unbelievers. Prophecy, however, is for the benefit of believers, not unbelievers.
23Even so, if unbelievers or people who don't understand these things come into your church meeting
and hear everyone speaking in an unknown language, they will think you are crazy. 24But if all of you
are prophesying, and unbelievers or people who
don't understand these things come into your meeting, they will be convicted of sin and judged by what
you say. 25As they listen, their secret thoughts will be
exposed, and they will fall to their knees and worship God, declaring, "God is truly here among you."

14:15 Or *in the Spirit;* also in 14:15b, 16. **14:21a** Greek *in the law.*
14:21b Isa 28:11-12.

KING JAMES VERSION

26 How is it then, brethren? when ye come together, every one of you hath a psalm, hath a doctrine, hath a tongue, hath a revelation, hath an interpretation. Let all things be done unto edifying.

27 If any man speak in an *unknown* tongue, *let it be* by two, or at the most *by* three, and *that* by course; and let one interpret.

28 But if there be no interpreter, let him keep silence in the church; and let him speak to himself, and to God.

29 Let the prophets speak two or three, and let the other judge.

30 If *any thing* be revealed to another that sitteth by, let the first hold his peace.

31 For ye may all prophesy one by one, that all may learn, and all may be comforted.

32 And the spirits of the prophets are subject to the prophets.

33 For God is not *the author* of confusion, but of peace, as in all churches of the saints.

34 Let your women keep silence in the churches: for it is not permitted unto them to speak; but *they are commanded* to be under obedience, as also saith the law.

35 And if they will learn any thing, let them ask their husbands at home: for it is a shame for women to speak in the church.

36 What? came the word of God out from you? or came it unto you only?

37 If any man think himself to be a prophet, or spiritual, let him acknowledge that the things that I write unto you are the commandments of the Lord.

38 But if any man be ignorant, let him be ignorant.

39 Wherefore, brethren, covet to prophesy, and forbid not to speak with tongues.

40 Let all things be done decently and in order.

15 1 Moreover, brethren, I declare unto you the gospel which I preached unto you, which also ye have received, and wherein ye stand;

2 By which also ye are saved, if ye keep in memory what I preached unto you, unless ye have believed in vain.

3 For I delivered unto you first of all that which I also received, how that Christ died for our sins according to the scriptures;

4 And that he was buried, and that he rose again the third day according to the scriptures:

5 And that he was seen of Cephas, then of the twelve:

6 After that, he was seen of above five hundred

NEW LIVING TRANSLATION

A Call to Orderly Worship

26 Well, my brothers and sisters, let's summarize. When you meet together, one will sing, another will teach, another will tell some special revelation God has given, one will speak in tongues, and another will interpret what is said. But everything that is done must strengthen all of you.

27 No more than two or three should speak in tongues. They must speak one at a time, and someone must interpret what they say. 28 But if no one is present who can interpret, they must be silent in your church meeting and speak in tongues to God privately.

29 Let two or three people prophesy, and let the others evaluate what is said. 30 But if someone is prophesying and another person receives a revelation from the Lord, the one who is speaking must stop. 31 In this way, all who prophesy will have a turn to speak, one after the other, so that everyone will learn and be encouraged. 32 Remember that people who prophesy are in control of their spirit and can take turns. 33 For God is not a God of disorder but of peace, as in all the meetings of God's holy people.*

34 Women should be silent during the church meetings. It is not proper for them to speak. They should be submissive, just as the law says. 35 If they have any questions, they should ask their husbands at home, for it is improper for women to speak in church meetings.*

36 Or do you think God's word originated with you Corinthians? Are you the only ones to whom it was given? 37 If you claim to be a prophet or think you are spiritual, you should recognize that what I am saying is a command from the Lord himself. 38 But if you do not recognize this, you yourself will not be recognized.*

39 So, my dear brothers and sisters, be eager to prophesy, and don't forbid speaking in tongues. 40 But be sure that everything is done properly and in order.

The Resurrection of Christ

15 Let me now remind you, dear brothers and sisters,* of the Good News I preached to you before. You welcomed it then, and you still stand firm in it. 2 It is this Good News that saves you if you continue to believe the message I told you—unless, of course, you believed something that was never true in the first place.*

3 I passed on to you what was most important and what had also been passed on to me. Christ died for our sins, just as the Scriptures said. 4 He was buried, and he was raised from the dead on the third day, just as the Scriptures said. 5 He was seen by Peter* and then by the Twelve. 6 After that, he was seen by

14:33 The phrase *as in all the meetings of God's holy people* could instead be joined to the beginning of 14:34. **14:35** Some manuscripts place verses 34-35 after 14:40. **14:38** Some manuscripts read *If you are ignorant of this, stay in your ignorance.* **15:1** Greek *brothers;* also in 15:31, 50, 58. **15:2** Or *unless you never believed it in the first place.* **15:5** Greek *Cephas.*

KING JAMES VERSION

brethren at once; of whom the greater part remain unto this present, but some are fallen asleep.

7 After that, he was seen of James; then of all the apostles.

8 And last of all he was seen of me also, as of one born out of due time.

9 For I am the least of the apostles, that am not meet to be called an apostle, because I persecuted the church of God.

10 But by the grace of God I am what I am: and his grace which *was bestowed* upon me was not in vain; but I laboured more abundantly than they all: yet not I, but the grace of God which was with me.

11 Therefore whether *it were* I or they, so we preach, and so ye believed.

12 Now if Christ be preached that he rose from the dead, how say some among you that there is no resurrection of the dead?

13 But if there be no resurrection of the dead, then is Christ not risen:

14 And if Christ be not risen, then *is* our preaching vain, and your faith *is* also vain.

15 Yea, and we are found false witnesses of God; because we have testified of God that he raised up Christ: whom he raised not up, if so be that the dead rise not.

16 For if the dead rise not, then is not Christ raised:

17 And if Christ be not raised, your faith *is* vain; ye are yet in your sins.

18 Then they also which are fallen asleep in Christ are perished.

19 If in this life only we have hope in Christ, we are of all men most miserable.

20 But now is Christ risen from the dead, *and* become the firstfruits of them that slept.

21 For since by man *came* death, by man *came* also the resurrection of the dead.

22 For as in Adam all die, even so in Christ shall all be made alive.

23 But every man in his own order: Christ the firstfruits; afterward they that are Christ's at his coming.

24 Then *cometh* the end, when he shall have delivered up the kingdom to God, even the Father; when he shall have put down all rule and all authority and power.

25 For he must reign, till he hath put all enemies under his feet.

26 The last enemy *that* shall be destroyed *is* death.

27 For he hath put all things under his feet. But when he saith all things are put under *him, it is* manifest that he is excepted, which did put all things under him.

28 And when all things shall be subdued unto him, then shall the Son also himself be subject unto him that put all things under him, that God may be all in all.

NEW LIVING TRANSLATION

more than 500 of his followers* at one time, most of
whom are still alive, though some have died. 7 Then
he was seen by James and later by all the apostles.
8 Last of all, as though I had been born at the wrong
time, I also saw him. 9 For I am the least of all the
apostles. In fact, I'm not even worthy to be called an
apostle after the way I persecuted God's church.
10 But whatever I am now, it is all because God
poured out his special favor on me—and not without
results. For I have worked harder than any of the
other apostles; yet it was not I but God who was working through me by his grace. 11 So it makes no difference whether I preach or they preach, for we all
preach the same message you have already believed.

The Resurrection of the Dead

12 But tell me this—since we preach that Christ rose
from the dead, why are some of you saying there will
be no resurrection of the dead? 13 For if there is no
resurrection of the dead, then Christ has not been
raised either. 14 And if Christ has not been raised,
then all our preaching is useless, and your faith is
useless. 15 And we apostles would all be lying about
God—for we have said that God raised Christ from
the grave. But that can't be true if there is no resurrection of the dead. 16 And if there is no resurrection
of the dead, then Christ has not been raised. 17 And if
Christ has not been raised, then your faith is useless
and you are still guilty of your sins. 18 In that case, all
who have died believing in Christ are lost! 19 And if
our hope in Christ is only for this life, we are more to
be pitied than anyone in the world.
20 But in fact, Christ has been raised from the dead.
He is the first of a great harvest of all who have died.
21 So you see, just as death came into the world
through a man, now the resurrection from the dead
has begun through another man. 22 Just as everyone
dies because we all belong to Adam, everyone who
belongs to Christ will be given new life. 23 But there is
an order to this resurrection: Christ was raised as the
first of the harvest; then all who belong to Christ will
be raised when he comes back.
24 After that the end will come, when he will turn
the Kingdom over to God the Father, having destroyed every ruler and authority and power. 25 For
Christ must reign until he humbles all his enemies
beneath his feet. 26 And the last enemy to be destroyed is death. 27 For the Scriptures say, "God has
put all things under his authority."* (Of course, when
it says "all things are under his authority," that does
not include God himself, who gave Christ his authority.) 28 Then, when all things are under his authority,
the Son will put himself under God's authority, so
that God, who gave his Son authority over all things,
will be utterly supreme over everything everywhere.

15:6 Greek *the brothers.* **15:27** Ps 8:6.

KING JAMES VERSION

29 Else what shall they do which are baptized for the dead, if the dead rise not at all? why are they then baptized for the dead?

30 And why stand we in jeopardy every hour?

31 I protest by your rejoicing which I have in Christ Jesus our Lord, I die daily.

32 If after the manner of men I have fought with beasts at Ephesus, what advantageth it me, if the dead rise not? let us eat and drink; for tomorrow we die.

33 Be not deceived: evil communications corrupt good manners.

34 Awake to righteousness, and sin not; for some have not the knowledge of God: I speak *this* to your shame.

35 But some *man* will say, How are the dead raised up? and with what body do they come?

36 *Thou* fool, that which thou sowest is not quickened, except it die:

37 And that which thou sowest, thou sowest not that body that shall be, but bare grain, it may chance of wheat, or of some other *grain:*

38 But God giveth it a body as it hath pleased him, and to every seed his own body.

39 All flesh *is* not the same flesh: but *there is* one *kind of* flesh of men, another flesh of beasts, another of fishes, *and* another of birds.

40 *There are* also celestial bodies, and bodies terrestrial: but the glory of the celestial *is* one, and the *glory* of the terrestrial *is* another.

41 *There is* one glory of the sun, and another glory of the moon, and another glory of the stars: for *one* star differeth from *another* star in glory.

42 So also *is* the resurrection of the dead. It is sown in corruption; it is raised in incorruption:

43 It is sown in dishonour; it is raised in glory: it is sown in weakness; it is raised in power:

44 It is sown a natural body; it is raised a spiritual body. There is a natural body, and there is a spiritual body.

45 And so it is written, The first man Adam was made a living soul; the last Adam *was made* a quickening spirit.

46 Howbeit that *was* not first which is spiritual, but that which is natural; and afterward that which is spiritual.

47 The first man *is* of the earth, earthy: the second man *is* the Lord from heaven.

48 As *is* the earthy, such *are* they also that are earthy: and as *is* the heavenly, such *are* they also that are heavenly.

49 And as we have borne the image of the earthy, we shall also bear the image of the heavenly.

50 Now this I say, brethren, that flesh and blood

NEW LIVING TRANSLATION

29 If the dead will not be raised, what point is there
in people being baptized for those who are dead?
Why do it unless the dead will someday rise again?
30 And why should we ourselves risk our lives hour
by hour? 31 For I swear, dear brothers and sisters, that
I face death daily. This is as certain as my pride in
what Christ Jesus our Lord has done in you. 32 And
what value was there in fighting wild beasts—those
people of Ephesus*—if there will be no resurrection
from the dead? And if there is no resurrection, "Let's
feast and drink, for tomorrow we die!"* 33 Don't be
fooled by those who say such things, for "bad company corrupts good character." 34 Think carefully
about what is right, and stop sinning. For to your
shame I say that some of you don't know God at all.

The Resurrection Body

35 But someone may ask, "How will the dead be
raised? What kind of bodies will they have?" 36 What
a foolish question! When you put a seed into the
ground, it doesn't grow into a plant unless it dies
first. 37 And what you put in the ground is not the
plant that will grow, but only a bare seed of wheat
or whatever you are planting. 38 Then God gives it the
new body he wants it to have. A different plant grows
from each kind of seed. 39 Similarly there are different kinds of flesh—one kind for humans, another for
animals, another for birds, and another for fish.
40 There are also bodies in the heavens and bodies
on the earth. The glory of the heavenly bodies is different from the glory of the earthly bodies. 41 The sun
has one kind of glory, while the moon and stars each
have another kind. And even the stars differ from
each other in their glory.
42 It is the same way with the resurrection of the
dead. Our earthly bodies are planted in the ground
when we die, but they will be raised to live forever.
43 Our bodies are buried in brokenness, but they will
be raised in glory. They are buried in weakness, but
they will be raised in strength. 44 They are buried as
natural human bodies, but they will be raised as spiritual bodies. For just as there are natural bodies,
there are also spiritual bodies.
45 The Scriptures tell us, "The first man, Adam,
became a living person."* But the last Adam—that is,
Christ—is a life-giving Spirit. 46 What comes first is
the natural body, then the spiritual body comes later.
47 Adam, the first man, was made from the dust of
the earth, while Christ, the second man, came from
heaven. 48 Earthly people are like the earthly man,
and heavenly people are like the heavenly man.
49 Just as we are now like the earthly man, we will
someday be like* the heavenly man.
50 What I am saying, dear brothers and sisters, is
that our physical bodies cannot inherit the Kingdom

15:32a Greek *fighting wild beasts in Ephesus.* **15:32b** Isa 22:13. **15:45** Gen 2:7. **15:49** Some manuscripts read *let us be like.*

KING JAMES VERSION

cannot inherit the kingdom of God; neither doth
corruption inherit incorruption.
51 Behold, I shew you a mystery; We shall not all
sleep, but we shall all be changed,
52 In a moment, in the twinkling of an eye, at the
last trump: for the trumpet shall sound, and the dead
shall be raised incorruptible, and we shall be
changed.
53 For this corruptible must put on incorruption,
and this mortal *must* put on immortality.
54 So when this corruptible shall have put on
incorruption, and this mortal shall have put on immortality, then shall be brought to pass the saying
that is written, Death is swallowed up in victory.
55 O death, where *is* thy sting? O grave, where *is* thy
victory?
56 The sting of death *is* sin; and the strength of sin
is the law.
57 But thanks *be* to God, which giveth us the victory
through our Lord Jesus Christ.
58 Therefore, my beloved brethren, be ye stedfast,
unmoveable, always abounding in the work of the
Lord, forasmuch as ye know that your labour is not in
vain in the Lord.

16 1 Now concerning the collection for the saints,
as I have given order to the churches of Galatia, even so do ye.
2 Upon the first *day* of the week let every one of
you lay by him in store, as *God* hath prospered him,
that there be no gatherings when I come.
3 And when I come, whomsoever ye shall approve
by *your* letters, them will I send to bring your liberality unto Jerusalem.
4 And if it be meet that I go also, they shall go
with me.

5 Now I will come unto you, when I shall pass
through Macedonia: for I do pass through Macedonia.
6 And it may be that I will abide, yea, and winter
with you, that ye may bring me on my journey
whithersoever I go.
7 For I will not see you now by the way; but I trust to
tarry a while with you, if the Lord permit.
8 But I will tarry at Ephesus until Pentecost.
9 For a great door and effectual is opened unto me,
and *there are* many adversaries.
10 Now if Timotheus come, see that he may be
with you without fear: for he worketh the work of
the Lord, as I also *do*.
11 Let no man therefore despise him: but conduct
him forth in peace, that he may come unto me: for I
look for him with the brethren.

NEW LIVING TRANSLATION

of God. These dying bodies cannot inherit what will
last forever.
51 But let me reveal to you a wonderful secret. We
will not all die, but we will all be transformed! 52 It will
happen in a moment, in the blink of an eye, when the
last trumpet is blown. For when the trumpet sounds,
those who have died will be raised to live forever.
And we who are living will also be transformed. 53 For
our dying bodies must be transformed into bodies
that will never die; our mortal bodies must be transformed into immortal bodies.
54 Then, when our dying bodies have been transformed into bodies that will never die,* this Scripture will be fulfilled:

"Death is swallowed up in victory.*
55 O death, where is your victory?
O death, where is your sting?*"

56 For sin is the sting that results in death, and the law
gives sin its power. 57 But thank God! He gives us victory over sin and death through our Lord Jesus Christ.
58 So, my dear brothers and sisters, be strong and
immovable. Always work enthusiastically for the
Lord, for you know that nothing you do for the Lord
is ever useless.

The Collection for Jerusalem

16 Now regarding your question about the
money being collected for God's people in
Jerusalem. You should follow the same procedure I
gave to the churches in Galatia. 2 On the first day of
each week, you should each put aside a portion of the
money you have earned. Don't wait until I get there
and then try to collect it all at once. 3 When I come, I
will write letters of recommendation for the messengers you choose to deliver your gift to Jerusalem. 4 And
if it seems appropriate for me to go along, they can
travel with me.

Paul's Final Instructions

5 I am coming to visit you after I have been to Macedonia,* for I am planning to travel through Macedonia. 6 Perhaps I will stay awhile with you, possibly all
winter, and then you can send me on my way to my
next destination. 7 This time I don't want to make
just a short visit and then go right on. I want to come
and stay awhile, if the Lord will let me. 8 In the meantime, I will be staying here at Ephesus until the Festival of Pentecost. 9 There is a wide-open door for a
great work here, although many oppose me.
10 When Timothy comes, don't intimidate him. He
is doing the Lord's work, just as I am. 11 Don't let anyone treat him with contempt. Send him on his way
with your blessing when he returns to me. I expect
him to come with the other believers.*

15:54a Some manuscripts add *and our mortal bodies have been transformed into immortal bodies.* **15:54b** Isa 25:8. **15:55** Hos 13:14 (Greek version). **16:5** *Macedonia* was in the northern region of Greece. **16:11** Greek *with the brothers;* also in 16:12.

KING JAMES VERSION

12 As touching *our* brother Apollos, I greatly desired him to come unto you with the brethren: but
his will was not at all to come at this time; but he will
come when he shall have convenient time.
13 Watch ye, stand fast in the faith, quit you like
men, be strong.
14 Let all your things be done with charity.
15 I beseech you, brethren, (ye know the house of
Stephanas, that it is the firstfruits of Achaia, and *that*
they have addicted themselves to the ministry of the
saints,)
16 That ye submit yourselves unto such, and to
every one that helpeth with *us*, and laboureth.
17 I am glad of the coming of Stephanas and For-
tunatus and Achaicus: for that which was lacking on
your part they have supplied.
18 For they have refreshed my spirit and yours:
therefore acknowledge ye them that are such.

19 The churches of Asia salute you. Aquila and
Priscilla salute you much in the Lord, with the
church that is in their house.
20 All the brethren greet you. Greet ye one another
with an holy kiss.
21 The salutation of *me* Paul with mine own hand.
22 If any man love not the Lord Jesus Christ, let him
be Anathema Maran-atha.
23 The grace of our Lord Jesus Christ *be* with you.
24 My love *be* with you all in Christ Jesus. Amen.

NEW LIVING TRANSLATION

12 Now about our brother Apollos—I urged him to
visit you with the other believers, but he was not willing to go right now. He will see you later when he has
the opportunity.
13 Be on guard. Stand firm in the faith. Be courageous.* Be strong. 14 And do everything with love.
15 You know that Stephanas and his household
were the first of the harvest of believers in Greece,*
and they are spending their lives in service to God's
people. I urge you, dear brothers and sisters,* 16 to
submit to them and others like them who serve with
such devotion. 17 I am very glad that Stephanas, For-
tunatus, and Achaicus have come here. They have
been providing the help you weren't here to give me.
18 They have been a wonderful encouragement to me,
as they have been to you. You must show your appreciation to all who serve so well.

Paul's Final Greetings

19 The churches here in the province of Asia* send
greetings in the Lord, as do Aquila and Priscilla* and
all the others who gather in their home for church
meetings. 20 All the brothers and sisters here send
greetings to you. Greet each other with Christian
love.*
21 HERE IS MY GREETING IN MY OWN HANDWRITING—
PAUL.
22 If anyone does not love the Lord, that person is
cursed. Our Lord, come!*
23 May the grace of the Lord Jesus be with you.
24 My love to all of you in Christ Jesus.*

16:13 Greek *Be men.* **16:15a** Greek *in Achaia,* the southern region of the Greek peninsula. **16:15b** Greek *brothers;* also in 16:20. **16:19a** *Asia* was a Roman province in what is now western Turkey. **16:19b** Greek *Prisca.* **16:20** Greek *with a sacred kiss.* **16:22** From Aramaic, *Marana tha.* Some manuscripts read *Maran atha, "Our Lord has come."* **16:24** Some manuscripts add *Amen.*

2 Corinthians

KING JAMES VERSION

1 1Paul, an apostle of Jesus Christ by the will of God, and Timothy *our* brother, unto the church of God which is at Corinth, with all the saints which are in all Achaia:

2Grace *be* to you and peace from God our Father, and *from* the Lord Jesus Christ.

3Blessed *be* God, even the Father of our Lord Jesus Christ, the Father of mercies, and the God of all comfort;

4Who comforteth us in all our tribulation, that we may be able to comfort them which are in any trouble, by the comfort wherewith we ourselves are comforted of God.

5For as the sufferings of Christ abound in us, so our consolation also aboundeth by Christ.

6And whether we be afflicted, *it is* for your consolation and salvation, which is effectual in the enduring of the same sufferings which we also suffer: or whether we be comforted, *it is* for your consolation and salvation.

7And our hope of you *is* stedfast, knowing, that as ye are partakers of the sufferings, so *shall ye be* also of the consolation.

8For we would not, brethren, have you ignorant of our trouble which came to us in Asia, that we were pressed out of measure, above strength, insomuch that we despaired even of life:

9But we had the sentence of death in ourselves, that we should not trust in ourselves, but in God which raiseth the dead:

10Who delivered us from so great a death, and doth deliver: in whom we trust that he will yet deliver *us;*

11Ye also helping together by prayer for us, that for the gift *bestowed* upon us by the means of many persons thanks may be given by many on our behalf.

12For our rejoicing is this, the testimony of our conscience, that in simplicity and godly sincerity, not with fleshly wisdom, but by the grace of God, we have

NEW LIVING TRANSLATION

Greetings from Paul

1 This letter is from Paul, chosen by the will of God to be an apostle of Christ Jesus, and from our brother Timothy.

I am writing to God's church in Corinth and to all of his holy people throughout Greece.*

2May God our Father and the Lord Jesus Christ give you grace and peace.

God Offers Comfort to All

3All praise to God, the Father of our Lord Jesus Christ.
God is our merciful Father and the source of all comfort.
4He comforts us in all our troubles so that we
can comfort others. When they are troubled, we will
be able to give them the same comfort God has given
us. 5For the more we suffer for Christ, the more God
will shower us with his comfort through Christ.
6Even when we are weighed down with troubles, it is
for your comfort and salvation! For when we ourselves are comforted, we will certainly comfort you.
Then you can patiently endure the same things we
suffer. 7We are confident that as you share in our
sufferings, you will also share in the comfort God
gives us.

8We think you ought to know, dear brothers and
sisters,* about the trouble we went through in the
province of Asia. We were crushed and overwhelmed
beyond our ability to endure, and we thought we
would never live through it. 9In fact, we expected to
die. But as a result, we stopped relying on ourselves
and learned to rely only on God, who raises the dead.
10And he did rescue us from mortal danger, and he
will rescue us again. We have placed our confidence
in him, and he will continue to rescue us. 11And you
are helping us by praying for us. Then many people
will give thanks because God has graciously answered
so many prayers for our safety.

Paul's Change of Plans

12We can say with confidence and a clear conscience that we have lived with a God-given holiness* and sincerity in all our dealings. We have

1:1 Greek *Achaia,* the southern region of the Greek peninsula. **1:8** Greek *brothers.* **1:12** Some manuscripts read *honesty.*

KING JAMES VERSION

had our conversation in the world, and more abundantly to you-ward.

[13]For we write none other things unto you, than what ye read or acknowledge; and I trust ye shall acknowledge even to the end;

[14]As also ye have acknowledged us in part, that we are your rejoicing, even as ye also *are* ours in the day of the Lord Jesus.

[15]And in this confidence I was minded to come unto you before, that ye might have a second benefit;

[16]And to pass by you into Macedonia, and to come again out of Macedonia unto you, and of you to be brought on my way toward Judaea.

[17]When I therefore was thus minded, did I use lightness? or the things that I purpose, do I purpose according to the flesh, that with me there should be yea yea, and nay nay?

[18]But *as* God *is* true, our word toward you was not yea and nay.

[19]For the Son of God, Jesus Christ, who was preached among you by us, *even* by me and Silvanus and Timotheus, was not yea and nay, but in him was yea.

[20]For all the promises of God in him *are* yea, and in him Amen, unto the glory of God by us.

[21]Now he which stablisheth us with you in Christ, and hath anointed us, *is* God;

[22]Who hath also sealed us, and given the earnest of the Spirit in our hearts.

[23]Moreover I call God for a record upon my soul, that to spare you I came not as yet unto Corinth.

[24]Not for that we have dominion over your faith, but are helpers of your joy: for by faith ye stand.

2

[1]But I determined this with myself, that I would not come again to you in heaviness.

[2]For if I make you sorry, who is he then that maketh me glad, but the same which is made sorry by me?

[3]And I wrote this same unto you, lest, when I came, I should have sorrow from them of whom I ought to rejoice; having confidence in you all, that my joy is *the joy* of you all.

[4]For out of much affliction and anguish of heart I wrote unto you with many tears; not that ye should be grieved, but that ye might know the love which I have more abundantly unto you.

[5]But if any have caused grief, he hath not grieved me, but in part: that I may not overcharge you all.

[6]Sufficient to such a man *is* this punishment, which *was inflicted* of many.

NEW LIVING TRANSLATION

depended on God's grace, not on our own human wisdom. That is how we have conducted ourselves before the world, and especially toward you. [13]Our letters have been straightforward, and there is nothing written between the lines and nothing you can't understand. I hope someday you will fully understand us, [14]even if you don't understand us now. Then on the day when the Lord Jesus* returns, you will be proud of us in the same way we are proud of you.

[15]Since I was so sure of your understanding and trust, I wanted to give you a double blessing by visiting you twice—[16]first on my way to Macedonia and again when I returned from Macedonia.* Then you could send me on my way to Judea.

[17]You may be asking why I changed my plan. Do you think I make my plans carelessly? Do you think I am like people of the world who say "Yes" when they really mean "No"? [18]As surely as God is faithful, our word to you does not waver between "Yes" and "No." [19]For Jesus Christ, the Son of God, does not waver between "Yes" and "No." He is the one whom Silas,* Timothy, and I preached to you, and as God's ultimate "Yes," he always does what he says. [20]For all of God's promises have been fulfilled in Christ with a resounding "Yes!" And through Christ, our "Amen" (which means "Yes") ascends to God for his glory.

[21]It is God who enables us, along with you, to stand firm for Christ. He has commissioned us, [22]and he has identified us as his own by placing the Holy Spirit in our hearts as the first installment that guarantees everything he has promised us.

[23]Now I call upon God as my witness that I am telling the truth. The reason I didn't return to Corinth was to spare you from a severe rebuke. [24]But that does not mean we want to dominate you by telling you how to put your faith into practice. We want to work together with you so you will be full of joy, for it is by your own faith that you stand firm.

2

So I decided that I would not bring you grief with another painful visit. [2]For if I cause you grief, who will make me glad? Certainly not someone I have grieved. [3]That is why I wrote to you as I did, so that when I do come, I won't be grieved by the very ones who ought to give me the greatest joy. Surely you all know that my joy comes from your being joyful. [4]I wrote that letter in great anguish, with a troubled heart and many tears. I didn't want to grieve you, but I wanted to let you know how much love I have for you.

Forgiveness for the Sinner

[5]I am not overstating it when I say that the man who caused all the trouble hurt all of you more than he hurt me. [6]Most of you opposed him, and that was

1:14 Some manuscripts read *our Lord Jesus.* 1:16 *Macedonia* was in the northern region of Greece. 1:19 Greek *Silvanus.*

KING JAMES VERSION

7So that contrariwise ye *ought* rather to forgive *him,* and comfort *him,* lest perhaps such a one should be swallowed up with overmuch sorrow.

8Wherefore I beseech you that ye would confirm *your* love toward him.

9For to this end also did I write, that I might know the proof of you, whether ye be obedient in all things.

10To whom ye forgive any thing, I *forgive* also: for if I forgave any thing, to whom I forgave *it,* for your sakes *forgave I it* in the person of Christ;

11Lest Satan should get an advantage of us: for we are not ignorant of his devices.

12Furthermore, when I came to Troas to *preach* Christ's gospel, and a door was opened unto me of the Lord,

13I had no rest in my spirit, because I found not Titus my brother: but taking my leave of them, I went from thence into Macedonia.

14Now thanks *be* unto God, which always causeth us to triumph in Christ, and maketh manifest the savour of his knowledge by us in every place.

15For we are unto God a sweet savour of Christ, in them that are saved, and in them that perish:

16To the one *we are* the savour of death unto death; and to the other the savour of life unto life. And who *is* sufficient for these things?

17For we are not as many, which corrupt the word of God: but as of sincerity, but as of God, in the sight of God speak we in Christ.

3 1Do we begin again to commend ourselves? or need we, as some *others,* epistles of commendation to you, or *letters* of commendation from you?

2Ye are our epistle written in our hearts, known and read of all men:

3*Forasmuch as ye are* manifestly declared to be the epistle of Christ ministered by us, written not with ink, but with the Spirit of the living God; not in tables of stone, but in fleshly tables of the heart.

4And such trust have we through Christ to Godward:

5Not that we are sufficient of ourselves to think any thing as of ourselves; but our sufficiency *is* of God;

6Who also hath made us able ministers of the new testament; not of the letter, but of the spirit: for the letter killeth, but the spirit giveth life.

NEW LIVING TRANSLATION

punishment enough. 7Now, however, it is time to forgive and comfort him. Otherwise he may be overcome by discouragement. 8So I urge you now to
reaffirm your love for him.
9I wrote to you as I did to test you and see if you
would fully comply with my instructions. 10When
you forgive this man, I forgive him, too. And when I
forgive whatever needs to be forgiven, I do so with
Christ's authority for your benefit, 11so that Satan
will not outsmart us. For we are familiar with his evil
schemes.
12When I came to the city of Troas to preach the
Good News of Christ, the Lord opened a door of opportunity for me. 13But I had no peace of mind because my dear brother Titus hadn't yet arrived with
a report from you. So I said good-bye and went on to
Macedonia to find him.

Ministers of the New Covenant

14But thank God! He has made us his captives and
continues to lead us along in Christ's triumphal procession. Now he uses us to spread the knowledge of
Christ everywhere, like a sweet perfume. 15Our lives
are a Christ-like fragrance rising up to God. But this
fragrance is perceived differently by those who are
being saved and by those who are perishing. 16To
those who are perishing, we are a dreadful smell of
death and doom. But to those who are being saved,
we are a life-giving perfume. And who is adequate for
such a task as this?
17You see, we are not like the many hucksters*
who preach for personal profit. We preach the word
of God with sincerity and with Christ's authority,
knowing that God is watching us.

3 Are we beginning to praise ourselves again? Are
we like others, who need to bring you letters
of recommendation, or who ask you to write such
letters on their behalf? Surely not! 2The only letter
of recommendation we need is you yourselves. Your
lives are a letter written in our* hearts; everyone can
read it and recognize our good work among you.
3Clearly, you are a letter from Christ showing the result of our ministry among you. This "letter" is written not with pen and ink, but with the Spirit of the
living God. It is carved not on tablets of stone, but on
human hearts.
4We are confident of all this because of our great
trust in God through Christ. 5It is not that we think
we are qualified to do anything on our own. Our
qualification comes from God. 6He has enabled us to
be ministers of his new covenant. This is a covenant
not of written laws, but of the Spirit. The old written
covenant ends in death; but under the new covenant,
the Spirit gives life.

2:17 Some manuscripts read *the rest of the hucksters.* **3:2** Some manuscripts read *your.*

KING JAMES VERSION

7 But if the ministration of death, written *and* engraven in stones, was glorious, so that the children of Israel could not stedfastly behold the face of Moses for the glory of his countenance; which *glory* was to be done away:

8 How shall not the ministration of the spirit be rather glorious?

9 For if the ministration of condemnation *be* glory, much more doth the ministration of righteousness exceed in glory.

10 For even that which was made glorious had no glory in this respect, by reason of the glory that excelleth.

11 For if that which is done away *was* glorious, much more that which remaineth *is* glorious.

12 Seeing then that we have such hope, we use great plainness of speech:

13 And not as Moses, *which* put a veil over his face, that the children of Israel could not stedfastly look to the end of that which is abolished:

14 But their minds were blinded: for until this day remaineth the same veil untaken away in the reading of the old testament; which *veil* is done away in Christ.

15 But even unto this day, when Moses is read, the veil is upon their heart.

16 Nevertheless when it shall turn to the Lord, the veil shall be taken away.

17 Now the Lord is that Spirit: and where the Spirit of the Lord *is,* there *is* liberty.

18 But we all, with open face beholding as in a glass the glory of the Lord, are changed into the same image from glory to glory, *even* as by the Spirit of the Lord.

4 1 Therefore seeing we have this ministry, as we have received mercy, we faint not;

2 But have renounced the hidden things of dishonesty, not walking in craftiness, nor handling the word of God deceitfully; but by manifestation of the truth commending ourselves to every man's conscience in the sight of God.

3 But if our gospel be hid, it is hid to them that are lost:

4 In whom the god of this world hath blinded the minds of them which believe not, lest the light of the glorious gospel of Christ, who is the image of God, should shine unto them.

5 For we preach not ourselves, but Christ Jesus the Lord; and ourselves your servants for Jesus' sake.

6 For God, who commanded the light to shine out of darkness, hath shined in our hearts, to *give* the light of the knowledge of the glory of God in the face of Jesus Christ.

NEW LIVING TRANSLATION

The Glory of the New Covenant

7 The old way,* with laws etched in stone, led to
death, though it began with such glory that the
people of Israel could not bear to look at Moses' face.
For his face shone with the glory of God, even though
the brightness was already fading away. 8 Shouldn't
we expect far greater glory under the new way, now
that the Holy Spirit is giving life? 9 If the old way,
which brings condemnation, was glorious, how
much more glorious is the new way, which makes us
right with God! 10 In fact, that first glory was not glorious at all compared with the overwhelming glory of
the new way. 11 So if the old way, which has been replaced, was glorious, how much more glorious is the
new, which remains forever!

12 Since this new way gives us such confidence, we
can be very bold. 13 We are not like Moses, who put a
veil over his face so the people of Israel would not
see the glory, even though it was destined to fade
away. 14 But the people's minds were hardened, and
to this day whenever the old covenant is being read,
the same veil covers their minds so they cannot understand the truth. And this veil can be removed only
by believing in Christ. 15 Yes, even today when they
read Moses' writings, their hearts are covered with
that veil, and they do not understand.

16 But whenever someone turns to the Lord, the
veil is taken away. 17 For the Lord is the Spirit, and
wherever the Spirit of the Lord is, there is freedom.
18 So all of us who have had that veil removed can see
and reflect the glory of the Lord. And the Lord—who
is the Spirit—makes us more and more like him as we
are changed into his glorious image.

Treasure in Fragile Clay Jars

4 Therefore, since God in his mercy has given
us this new way,* we never give up. 2 We reject
all shameful deeds and underhanded methods. We
don't try to trick anyone or distort the word of God.
We tell the truth before God, and all who are honest
know this.

3 If the Good News we preach is hidden behind a
veil, it is hidden only from people who are perishing.
4 Satan, who is the god of this world, has blinded the
minds of those who don't believe. They are unable to
see the glorious light of the Good News. They don't
understand this message about the glory of Christ,
who is the exact likeness of God.

5 You see, we don't go around preaching about ourselves. We preach that Jesus Christ is Lord, and we
ourselves are your servants for Jesus' sake. 6 For God,
who said, "Let there be light in the darkness," has
made this light shine in our hearts so we could know
the glory of God that is seen in the face of Jesus
Christ.

3:7 Or *ministry;* also in 3:8, 9, 10, 11, 12. 4:1 Or *ministry.*

KING JAMES VERSION

7 But we have this treasure in earthen vessels, that the excellency of the power may be of God, and not of us.

8 *We are* troubled on every side, yet not distressed; *we are* perplexed, but not in despair;

9 Persecuted, but not forsaken; cast down, but not destroyed;

10 Always bearing about in the body the dying of the Lord Jesus, that the life also of Jesus might be made manifest in our body.

11 For we which live are alway delivered unto death for Jesus' sake, that the life also of Jesus might be made manifest in our mortal flesh.

12 So then death worketh in us, but life in you.

13 We having the same spirit of faith, according as it is written, I believed, and therefore have I spoken; we also believe, and therefore speak;

14 Knowing that he which raised up the Lord Jesus shall raise up us also by Jesus, and shall present *us* with you.

15 For all things *are* for your sakes, that the abundant grace might through the thanksgiving of many redound to the glory of God.

16 For which cause we faint not; but though our outward man perish, yet the inward *man* is renewed day by day.

17 For our light affliction, which is but for a moment, worketh for us a far more exceeding *and* eternal weight of glory;

18 While we look not at the things which are seen, but at the things which are not seen: for the things which are seen *are* temporal; but the things which are not seen *are* eternal.

5 1 For we know that if our earthly house of *this* tabernacle were dissolved, we have a building of God, an house not made with hands, eternal in the heavens.

2 For in this we groan, earnestly desiring to be clothed upon with our house which is from heaven:

3 If so be that being clothed we shall not be found naked.

4 For we that are in *this* tabernacle do groan, being burdened: not for that we would be unclothed, but clothed upon, that mortality might be swallowed up of life.

5 Now he that hath wrought us for the selfsame thing *is* God, who also hath given unto us the earnest of the Spirit.

6 Therefore *we are* always confident, knowing that, whilst we are at home in the body, we are absent from the Lord:

7 (For we walk by faith, not by sight:)

8 We are confident, *I say,* and willing rather to be absent from the body, and to be present with the Lord.

9 Wherefore we labour, that, whether present or absent, we may be accepted of him.

NEW LIVING TRANSLATION

7 We now have this light shining in our hearts, but
we ourselves are like fragile clay jars containing this
great treasure.* This makes it clear that our great
power is from God, not from ourselves.
8 We are pressed on every side by troubles, but we
are not crushed. We are perplexed, but not driven to
despair. 9 We are hunted down, but never abandoned
by God. We get knocked down, but we are not destroyed. 10 Through suffering, our bodies continue to
share in the death of Jesus so that the life of Jesus
may also be seen in our bodies.
11 Yes, we live under constant danger of death because we serve Jesus, so that the life of Jesus will be
evident in our dying bodies. 12 So we live in the face
of death, but this has resulted in eternal life for you.
13 But we continue to preach because we have the
same kind of faith the psalmist had when he said,
"I believed in God, so I spoke."* 14 We know that God,
who raised the Lord Jesus,* will also raise us with Jesus
and present us to himself together with you. 15 All of
this is for your benefit. And as God's grace reaches
more and more people, there will be great thanksgiving, and God will receive more and more glory.
16 That is why we never give up. Though our bodies are dying, our spirits are* being renewed every
day. 17 For our present troubles are small and won't
last very long. Yet they produce for us a glory that
vastly outweighs them and will last forever! 18 So we
don't look at the troubles we can see now; rather, we
fix our gaze on things that cannot be seen. For the
things we see now will soon be gone, but the things
we cannot see will last forever.

New Bodies

5 For we know that when this earthly tent we live
in is taken down (that is, when we die and leave
this earthly body), we will have a house in heaven, an
eternal body made for us by God himself and not by
human hands. 2 We grow weary in our present bodies, and we long to put on our heavenly bodies like
new clothing. 3 For we will put on heavenly bodies; we
will not be spirits without bodies.* 4 While we live in
these earthly bodies, we groan and sigh, but it's not
that we want to die and get rid of these bodies that
clothe us. Rather, we want to put on our new bodies
so that these dying bodies will be swallowed up by
life. 5 God himself has prepared us for this, and as a
guarantee he has given us his Holy Spirit.
6 So we are always confident, even though we know
that as long as we live in these bodies we are not at
home with the Lord. 7 For we live by believing and not
by seeing. 8 Yes, we are fully confident, and we would
rather be away from these earthly bodies, for then we
will be at home with the Lord. 9 So whether we are
here in this body or away from this body, our goal is

4:7 Greek *We now have this treasure in clay jars.* **4:13** Ps 116:10. **4:14** Some manuscripts read *who raised Jesus.* **4:16** Greek *our inner being is.* **5:3** Greek *we will not be naked.*

KING JAMES VERSION

10 For we must all appear before the judgment seat of Christ; that every one may receive the things *done* in *his* body, according to that he hath done, whether *it be* good or bad.

11 Knowing therefore the terror of the Lord, we persuade men; but we are made manifest unto God; and I trust also are made manifest in your consciences.

12 For we commend not ourselves again unto you, but give you occasion to glory on our behalf, that ye may have somewhat to *answer* them which glory in appearance, and not in heart.

13 For whether we be beside ourselves, *it is* to God: or whether we be sober, *it is* for your cause.

14 For the love of Christ constraineth us; because we thus judge, that if one died for all, then were all dead:

15 And *that* he died for all, that they which live should not henceforth live unto themselves, but unto him which died for them, and rose again.

16 Wherefore henceforth know we no man after the flesh: yea, though we have known Christ after the flesh, yet now henceforth know we *him* no more.

17 Therefore if any man *be* in Christ, *he is* a new creature: old things are passed away; behold, all things are become new.

18 And all things *are* of God, who hath reconciled us to himself by Jesus Christ, and hath given to us the ministry of reconciliation;

19 To wit, that God was in Christ, reconciling the world unto himself, not imputing their trespasses unto them; and hath committed unto us the word of reconciliation.

20 Now then we are ambassadors for Christ, as though God did beseech *you* by us: we pray *you* in Christ's stead, be ye reconciled to God.

21 For he hath made him *to be* sin for us, who knew no sin; that we might be made the righteousness of God in him.

6

1 We then, *as* workers together *with him,* beseech *you* also that ye receive not the grace of God in vain.

2 (For he saith, I have heard thee in a time accepted, and in the day of salvation have I succoured thee: behold, now *is* the accepted time; behold, now *is* the day of salvation.)

3 Giving no offence in any thing, that the ministry be not blamed:

4 But in all *things* approving ourselves as the ministers of God, in much patience, in afflictions, in necessities, in distresses,

NEW LIVING TRANSLATION

to please him. 10 For we must all stand before Christ to be judged. We will each receive whatever we deserve for the good or evil we have done in this earthly body.

We Are God's Ambassadors

11 Because we understand our fearful responsibility to the Lord, we work hard to persuade others. God knows we are sincere, and I hope you know this, too.
12 Are we commending ourselves to you again? No, we are giving you a reason to be proud of us,* so you can answer those who brag about having a spectacular ministry rather than having a sincere heart. 13 If it seems we are crazy, it is to bring glory to God. And if we are in our right minds, it is for your benefit.
14 Either way, Christ's love controls us.* Since we believe that Christ died for all, we also believe that we have all died to our old life.* 15 He died for everyone so that those who receive his new life will no longer live for themselves. Instead, they will live for Christ, who died and was raised for them.

16 So we have stopped evaluating others from a human point of view. At one time we thought of Christ merely from a human point of view. How differently we know him now! 17 This means that anyone who belongs to Christ has become a new person. The old life is gone; a new life has begun!

18 And all of this is a gift from God, who brought us back to himself through Christ. And God has given us this task of reconciling people to him. 19 For God was in Christ, reconciling the world to himself, no longer counting people's sins against them. And he gave us this wonderful message of reconciliation.
20 So we are Christ's ambassadors; God is making his appeal through us. We speak for Christ when we plead, "Come back to God!" 21 For God made Christ, who never sinned, to be the offering for our sin,* so that we could be made right with God through Christ.

6

As God's partners,* we beg you not to accept this marvelous gift of God's kindness and then ignore it. 2 For God says,

"At just the right time, I heard you.
On the day of salvation, I helped you."*

Indeed, the "right time" is now. Today is the day of salvation.

Paul's Hardships

3 We live in such a way that no one will stumble because of us, and no one will find fault with our ministry. 4 In everything we do, we show that we are true ministers of God. We patiently endure troubles and

5:12 Some manuscripts read *proud of yourselves.* 5:14a Or *urges us on.* 5:14b Greek *Since one died for all, then all died.* 5:21 Or *to become sin itself.* 6:1 Or *As we work together.* 6:2 Isa 49:8 (Greek version).

KING JAMES VERSION

5In stripes, in imprisonments, in tumults, in labours, in watchings, in fastings;

6By pureness, by knowledge, by longsuffering, by kindness, by the Holy Ghost, by love unfeigned,

7By the word of truth, by the power of God, by the armour of righteousness on the right hand and on the left,

8By honour and dishonour, by evil report and good report: as deceivers, and *yet* true;

9As unknown, and *yet* well known; as dying, and, behold, we live; as chastened, and not killed;

10As sorrowful, yet alway rejoicing; as poor, yet making many rich; as having nothing, and *yet* possessing all things.

11O *ye* Corinthians, our mouth is open unto you, our heart is enlarged.

12Ye are not straitened in us, but ye are straitened in your own bowels.

13Now for a recompence in the same, (I speak as unto *my* children,) be ye also enlarged.

14Be ye not unequally yoked together with unbelievers: for what fellowship hath righteousness with unrighteousness? and what communion hath light with darkness?

15And what concord hath Christ with Belial? or what part hath he that believeth with an infidel?

16And what agreement hath the temple of God with idols? for ye are the temple of the living God; as God hath said, I will dwell in them, and walk in *them;* and I will be their God, and they shall be my people.

17Wherefore come out from among them, and be ye separate, saith the Lord, and touch not the unclean *thing;* and I will receive you,

18And will be a Father unto you, and ye shall be my sons and daughters, saith the Lord Almighty.

7 1Having therefore these promises, dearly beloved, let us cleanse ourselves from all filthiness of the flesh and spirit, perfecting holiness in the fear of God.

2Receive us; we have wronged no man, we have corrupted no man, we have defrauded no man.

3I speak not *this* to condemn *you:* for I have said before, that ye are in our hearts to die and live with *you.*

NEW LIVING TRANSLATION

hardships and calamities of every kind. 5We have
been beaten, been put in prison, faced angry mobs,
worked to exhaustion, endured sleepless nights, and
gone without food. 6We prove ourselves by our purity,
our understanding, our patience, our kindness, by the
Holy Spirit within us,* and by our sincere love. 7We
faithfully preach the truth. God's power is working in
us. We use the weapons of righteousness in the right
hand for attack and the left hand for defense. 8We
serve God whether people honor us or despise us,
whether they slander us or praise us. We are honest,
but they call us impostors. 9We are ignored, even
though we are well known. We live close to death, but
we are still alive. We have been beaten, but we have
not been killed. 10Our hearts ache, but we always have
joy. We are poor, but we give spiritual riches to others.
We own nothing, and yet we have everything.

11Oh, dear Corinthian friends! We have spoken
honestly with you, and our hearts are open to you.
12There is no lack of love on our part, but you have
withheld your love from us. 13I am asking you to respond
as if you were my own children. Open your
hearts to us!

The Temple of the Living God

14Don't team up with those who are unbelievers.
How can righteousness be a partner with wickedness?
How can light live with darkness? 15What harmony
can there be between Christ and the devil*?
How can a believer be a partner with an unbeliever?
16And what union can there be between God's
temple and idols? For we are the temple of the living
God. As God said:

"I will live in them
and walk among them.
I will be their God,
and they will be my people.*
17 Therefore, come out from among unbelievers,
and separate yourselves from them, says
the LORD.
Don't touch their filthy things,
and I will welcome you.*
18 And I will be your Father,
and you will be my sons and daughters,
says the LORD Almighty.*"

7 Because we have these promises, dear friends,
let us cleanse ourselves from everything that
can defile our body or spirit. And let us work toward
complete holiness because we fear God.

2Please open your hearts to us. We have not done
wrong to anyone, nor led anyone astray, nor taken
advantage of anyone. 3I'm not saying this to condemn
you. I said before that you are in our hearts,

6:6 Or *by our holiness of spirit.* **6:15** Greek *Beliar;* various other manuscripts render this proper name of the devil as *Belian, Beliab,* or *Belial.* **6:16** Lev 26:12; Ezek 37:27. **6:17** Isa 52:11; Ezek 20:34 (Greek version). **6:18** 2 Sam 7:14.

KING JAMES VERSION

4Great *is* my boldness of speech toward you, great *is* my glorying of you: I am filled with comfort, I am exceeding joyful in all our tribulation.

5For, when we were come into Macedonia, our flesh had no rest, but we were troubled on every side; without *were* fightings, within *were* fears.

6Nevertheless God, that comforteth those that are cast down, comforted us by the coming of Titus;

7And not by his coming only, but by the consolation wherewith he was comforted in you, when he told us your earnest desire, your mourning, your fervent mind toward me; so that I rejoiced the more.

8For though I made you sorry with a letter, I do not repent, though I did repent: for I perceive that the same epistle hath made you sorry, though *it were* but for a season.

9Now I rejoice, not that ye were made sorry, but that ye sorrowed to repentance: for ye were made sorry after a godly manner, that ye might receive damage by us in nothing.

10For godly sorrow worketh repentance to salvation not to be repented of: but the sorrow of the world worketh death.

11For behold this selfsame thing, that ye sorrowed after a godly sort, what carefulness it wrought in you, yea, *what* clearing of yourselves, yea, *what* indignation, yea, *what* fear, yea, *what* vehement desire, yea, *what* zeal, yea, *what* revenge! In all *things* ye have approved yourselves to be clear in this matter.

12Wherefore, though I wrote unto you, *I did it* not for his cause that had done the wrong, nor for his cause that suffered wrong, but that our care for you in the sight of God might appear unto you.

13Therefore we were comforted in your comfort: yea, and exceedingly the more joyed we for the joy of Titus, because his spirit was refreshed by you all.

14For if I have boasted any thing to him of you, I am not ashamed; but as we spake all things to you in truth, even so our boasting, which *I made* before Titus, is found a truth.

15And his inward affection is more abundant toward you, whilst he remembereth the obedience of you all, how with fear and trembling ye received him.

16I rejoice therefore that I have confidence in you in all *things*.

8 1Moreover, brethren, we do you to wit of the grace of God bestowed on the churches of Macedonia;

2How that in a great trial of affliction the abundance of their joy and their deep poverty abounded unto the riches of their liberality.

3For to *their* power, I bear record, yea, and beyond *their* power *they were* willing of themselves;

NEW LIVING TRANSLATION

and we live or die together with you. 4I have the
highest confidence in you, and I take great pride in
you. You have greatly encouraged me and made me
happy despite all our troubles.

Paul's Joy at the Church's Repentance

5When we arrived in Macedonia, there was no rest
for us. We faced conflict from every direction, with
battles on the outside and fear on the inside. 6But
God, who encourages those who are discouraged, encouraged us by the arrival of Titus. 7His presence was
a joy, but so was the news he brought of the encouragement he received from you. When he told us how
much you long to see me, and how sorry you are for
what happened, and how loyal you are to me, I was
filled with joy!

8I am not sorry that I sent that severe letter to you,
though I was sorry at first, for I know it was painful to
you for a little while. 9Now I am glad I sent it, not because it hurt you, but because the pain caused you
to repent and change your ways. It was the kind of
sorrow God wants his people to have, so you were
not harmed by us in any way. 10For the kind of sorrow
God wants us to experience leads us away from sin
and results in salvation. There's no regret for that
kind of sorrow. But worldly sorrow, which lacks repentance, results in spiritual death.

11Just see what this godly sorrow produced in you!
Such earnestness, such concern to clear yourselves,
such indignation, such alarm, such longing to see
me, such zeal, and such a readiness to punish wrong.
You showed that you have done everything necessary
to make things right. 12My purpose, then, was not to
write about who did the wrong or who was wronged.
I wrote to you so that in the sight of God you could
see for yourselves how loyal you are to us. 13We have
been greatly encouraged by this.

In addition to our own encouragement, we were
especially delighted to see how happy Titus was
about the way all of you welcomed him and set his
mind* at ease. 14I had told him how proud I was of
you—and you didn't disappoint me. I have always
told you the truth, and now my boasting to Titus has
also proved true! 15Now he cares for you more than
ever when he remembers the way all of you obeyed
him and welcomed him with such fear and deep respect. 16I am very happy now because I have complete confidence in you.

A Call to Generous Giving

8 Now I want you to know, dear brothers and
sisters,* what God in his kindness has done
through the churches in Macedonia. 2They are being
tested by many troubles, and they are very poor. But
they are also filled with abundant joy, which has
overflowed in rich generosity.

3For I can testify that they gave not only what they

7:13 Greek *his spirit.* 8:1 Greek *brothers.*

KING JAMES VERSION

4 Praying us with much intreaty that we would receive the gift, and *take upon us* the fellowship of the ministering to the saints.

5 And *this they did,* not as we hoped, but first gave their own selves to the Lord, and unto us by the will of God.

6 Insomuch that we desired Titus, that as he had begun, so he would also finish in you the same grace also.

7 Therefore, as ye abound in every *thing, in* faith, and utterance, and knowledge, and *in* all diligence, and *in* your love to us, *see* that ye abound in this grace also.

8 I speak not by commandment, but by occasion of the forwardness of others, and to prove the sincerity of your love.

9 For ye know the grace of our Lord Jesus Christ, that, though he was rich, yet for your sakes he became poor, that ye through his poverty might be rich.

10 And herein I give *my* advice: for this is expedient for you, who have begun before, not only to do, but also to be forward a year ago.

11 Now therefore perform the doing *of it;* that as *there was* a readiness to will, so *there may be* a performance also out of that which ye have.

12 For if there be first a willing mind, *it is* accepted according to that a man hath, *and* not according to that he hath not.

13 For *I mean* not that other men be eased, and ye burdened:

14 But by an equality, *that* now at this time your abundance *may be a supply* for their want, that their abundance also may be *a supply* for your want: that there may be equality:

15 As it is written, He that *had gathered* much had nothing over; and he that *had gathered* little had no lack.

16 But thanks *be* to God, which put the same earnest care into the heart of Titus for you.

17 For indeed he accepted the exhortation; but being more forward, of his own accord he went unto you.

18 And we have sent with him the brother, whose praise *is* in the gospel throughout all the churches;

19 And not *that* only, but who was also chosen of the churches to travel with us with this grace, which is administered by us to the glory of the same Lord, and *declaration of* your ready mind:

20 Avoiding this, that no man should blame us in this abundance which is administered by us:

21 Providing for honest things, not only in the sight of the Lord, but also in the sight of men.

NEW LIVING TRANSLATION

could afford, but far more. And they did it of their own free will. 4 They begged us again and again for the privilege of sharing in the gift for the believers in Jerusalem.* 5 They even did more than we had hoped, for their first action was to give themselves to the Lord and to us, just as God wanted them to do.

6 So we have urged Titus, who encouraged your giving in the first place, to return to you and encourage you to finish this ministry of giving. 7 Since you excel in so many ways—in your faith, your gifted speakers, your knowledge, your enthusiasm, and your love from us*—I want you to excel also in this gracious act of giving.

8 I am not commanding you to do this. But I am testing how genuine your love is by comparing it with the eagerness of the other churches.

9 You know the generous grace of our Lord Jesus Christ. Though he was rich, yet for your sakes he became poor, so that by his poverty he could make you rich.

10 Here is my advice: It would be good for you to finish what you started a year ago. Last year you were the first who wanted to give, and you were the first to begin doing it. 11 Now you should finish what you started. Let the eagerness you showed in the beginning be matched now by your giving. Give in proportion to what you have. 12 Whatever you give is acceptable if you give it eagerly. And give according to what you have, not what you don't have. 13 Of course, I don't mean your giving should make life easy for others and hard for yourselves. I only mean that there should be some equality. 14 Right now you have plenty and can help those who are in need. Later, they will have plenty and can share with you when you need it. In this way, things will be equal. 15 As the Scriptures say,

"Those who gathered a lot had nothing left over,
and those who gathered only a little had
enough."*

Titus and His Companions

16 But thank God! He has given Titus the same enthusiasm for you that I have. 17 Titus welcomed our request that he visit you again. In fact, he himself was very eager to go and see you. 18 We are also sending another brother with Titus. All the churches praise him as a preacher of the Good News. 19 He was appointed by the churches to accompany us as we take the offering to Jerusalem*—a service that glorifies the Lord and shows our eagerness to help.

20 We are traveling together to guard against any criticism for the way we are handling this generous gift. 21 We are careful to be honorable before the Lord, but we also want everyone else to see that we are honorable.

8:4 Greek *for God's holy people.* **8:7** Some manuscripts read *your love for us.* **8:15** Exod 16:18. **8:19** See 1 Cor 16:3-4.

KING JAMES VERSION

[22]And we have sent with them our brother, whom we have oftentimes proved diligent in many things, but now much more diligent, upon the great confidence which *I have* in you.

[23]Whether *any do inquire* of Titus, *he is* my partner and fellowhelper concerning you: or our brethren *be inquired of, they are* the messengers of the churches, *and* the glory of Christ.

[24]Wherefore shew ye to them, and before the churches, the proof of your love, and of our boasting on your behalf.

9 [1]For as touching the ministering to the saints, it is superfluous for me to write to you:

[2]For I know the forwardness of your mind, for which I boast of you to them of Macedonia, that Achaia was ready a year ago; and your zeal hath provoked very many.

[3]Yet have I sent the brethren, lest our boasting of you should be in vain in this behalf; that, as I said, ye may be ready:

[4]Lest haply if they of Macedonia come with me, and find you unprepared, we (that we say not, ye) should be ashamed in this same confident boasting.

[5]Therefore I thought it necessary to exhort the brethren, that they would go before unto you, and make up before hand your bounty, whereof ye had notice before, that the same might be ready, as *a matter of* bounty, and not as *of* covetousness.

[6]But this *I say,* He which soweth sparingly shall reap also sparingly; and he which soweth bountifully shall reap also bountifully.

[7]Every man according as he purposeth in his heart, *so let him give;* not grudgingly, or of necessity: for God loveth a cheerful giver.

[8]And God *is* able to make all grace abound toward you; that ye, always having all sufficiency in all *things,* may abound to every good work:

[9](As it is written, He hath dispersed abroad; he hath given to the poor: his righteousness remaineth for ever.

[10]Now he that ministereth seed to the sower both minister bread for *your* food, and multiply your seed sown, and increase the fruits of your righteousness;)

[11]Being enriched in every thing to all bountifulness, which causeth through us thanksgiving to God.

[12]For the administration of this service not only supplieth the want of the saints, but is abundant also by many thanksgivings unto God;

NEW LIVING TRANSLATION

[22]We are also sending with them another of our brothers who has proven himself many times and has shown on many occasions how eager he is. He is now even more enthusiastic because of his great confidence in you. [23]If anyone asks about Titus, say that he is my partner who works with me to help you. And the brothers with him have been sent by the churches,* and they bring honor to Christ. [24]So show them your love, and prove to all the churches that our boasting about you is justified.

The Collection for Christians in Jerusalem

9 I really don't need to write to you about this ministry of giving for the believers in Jerusalem.* [2]For I know how eager you are to help, and I have been boasting to the churches in Macedonia that you in Greece* were ready to send an offering a year ago. In fact, it was your enthusiasm that stirred up many of the Macedonian believers to begin giving.

[3]But I am sending these brothers to be sure you really are ready, as I have been telling them, and that your money is all collected. I don't want to be wrong in my boasting about you. [4]We would be embarrassed—not to mention your own embarrassment—if some Macedonian believers came with me and found that you weren't ready after all I had told them! [5]So I thought I should send these brothers ahead of me to make sure the gift you promised is ready. But I want it to be a willing gift, not one given grudgingly.

[6]Remember this—a farmer who plants only a few seeds will get a small crop. But the one who plants generously will get a generous crop. [7]You must each decide in your heart how much to give. And don't give reluctantly or in response to pressure. "For God loves a person who gives cheerfully."* [8]And God will generously provide all you need. Then you will always have everything you need and plenty left over to share with others. [9]As the Scriptures say,

"They share freely and give generously
to the poor.
Their good deeds will be remembered
forever."*

[10]For God is the one who provides seed for the farmer and then bread to eat. In the same way, he will provide and increase your resources and then produce a great harvest of generosity* in you.

[11]Yes, you will be enriched in every way so that you can always be generous. And when we take your gifts to those who need them, they will thank God. [12]So two good things will result from this ministry of giving—the needs of the believers in Jerusalem* will be met, and they will joyfully express their thanks to God.

8:23 Greek *are apostles of the churches.* **9:1** Greek *about the offering for God's holy people.* **9:2** Greek *in Achaia,* the southern region of the Greek peninsula. *Macedonia* was in the northern region of Greece. **9:7** See footnote on Prov 22:8. **9:9** Ps 112:9. **9:10** Greek *righteousness.* **9:12** Greek *of God's holy people.*

KING JAMES VERSION

13 While by the experiment of this ministration
they glorify God for your professed subjection unto
the gospel of Christ, and for *your* liberal distribution
unto them, and unto all *men;*
14 And by their prayer for you, which long after you
for the exceeding grace of God in you.
15 Thanks *be* unto God for his unspeakable gift.

10 1 Now I Paul myself beseech you by the
meekness and gentleness of Christ, who in
presence *am* base among you, but being absent am
bold toward you:
2 But I beseech *you*, that I may not be bold when I
am present with that confidence, wherewith I think
to be bold against some, which think of us as if we
walked according to the flesh.
3 For though we walk in the flesh, we do not war
after the flesh:
4 (For the weapons of our warfare *are* not carnal,
but mighty through God to the pulling down of
strong holds;)
5 Casting down imaginations, and every high thing
that exalteth itself against the knowledge of God,
and bringing into captivity every thought to the
obedience of Christ;
6 And having in a readiness to revenge all disobedience, when your obedience is fulfilled.
7 Do ye look on things after the outward appearance? If any man trust to himself that he is Christ's,
let him of himself think this again, that, as he *is*
Christ's, even so *are* we Christ's.
8 For though I should boast somewhat more of our
authority, which the Lord hath given us for edification, and not for your destruction, I should not be
ashamed:
9 That I may not seem as if I would terrify you by
letters.
10 For *his* letters, say they, *are* weighty and powerful; but *his* bodily presence *is* weak, and *his* speech
contemptible.
11 Let such an one think this, that, such as we are in
word by letters when we are absent, such *will we be*
also in deed when we are present.
12 For we dare not make ourselves of the number,
or compare ourselves with some that commend
themselves: but they measuring themselves by
themselves, and comparing themselves among
themselves, are not wise.
13 But we will not boast of things without *our* measure, but according to the measure of the rule which
God hath distributed to us, a measure to reach even
unto you.
14 For we stretch not ourselves beyond *our measure*, as though we reached not unto you: for we are
come as far as to you also in *preaching* the gospel of
Christ:
15 Not boasting of things without *our* measure,

NEW LIVING TRANSLATION

13 As a result of your ministry, they will give glory to
God. For your generosity to them and to all believers
will prove that you are obedient to the Good News of
Christ. 14 And they will pray for you with deep
affection because of the overflowing grace God has
given to you. 15 Thank God for this gift* too wonderful for words!

Paul Defends His Authority

10 Now I, Paul, appeal to you with the gentleness and kindness of Christ—though I realize you think I am timid in person and bold only
when I write from far away. 2 Well, I am begging you
now so that when I come I won't have to be bold with
those who think we act from human motives.
3 We are human, but we don't wage war as humans
do. 4* We use God's mighty weapons, not worldly
weapons, to knock down the strongholds of human
reasoning and to destroy false arguments. 5 We destroy every proud obstacle that keeps people from
knowing God. We capture their rebellious thoughts
and teach them to obey Christ. 6 And after you have
become fully obedient, we will punish everyone who
remains disobedient.
7 Look at the obvious facts.* Those who say they
belong to Christ must recognize that we belong to
Christ as much as they do. 8 I may seem to be boasting too much about the authority given to us by
the Lord. But our authority builds you up; it doesn't
tear you down. So I will not be ashamed of using my
authority.
9 I'm not trying to frighten you by my letters. 10 For
some say, "Paul's letters are demanding and forceful,
but in person he is weak, and his speeches are worthless!" 11 Those people should realize that our actions
when we arrive in person will be as forceful as what
we say in our letters from far away.
12 Oh, don't worry; we wouldn't dare say that we are
as wonderful as these other men who tell you how
important they are! But they are only comparing
themselves with each other, using themselves as the
standard of measurement. How ignorant!
13 We will not boast about things done outside our
area of authority. We will boast only about what has
happened within the boundaries of the work God
has given us, which includes our working with you.
14 We are not reaching beyond these boundaries
when we claim authority over you, as if we had never
visited you. For we were the first to travel all the way
to Corinth with the Good News of Christ.
15 Nor do we boast and claim credit for the work

9:15 Greek *his gift.* **10:4** English translations divide verses 4 and 5 in various ways. **10:7** Or *You look at things only on the basis of appearance.*

KING JAMES VERSION

that is, of other men's labours; but having hope, when your faith is increased, that we shall be enlarged by you according to our rule abundantly,

16To preach the gospel in the *regions* beyond you, *and* not to boast in another man's line of things made ready to our hand.

17But he that glorieth, let him glory in the Lord.

18For not he that commendeth himself is approved, but whom the Lord commendeth.

11 1Would to God ye could bear with me a little in *my* folly: and indeed bear with me.

2For I am jealous over you with godly jealousy: for I have espoused you to one husband, that I may present *you as* a chaste virgin to Christ.

3But I fear, lest by any means, as the serpent beguiled Eve through his subtilty, so your minds should be corrupted from the simplicity that is in Christ.

4For if he that cometh preacheth another Jesus, whom we have not preached, or *if* ye receive another spirit, which ye have not received, or another gospel, which ye have not accepted, ye might well bear with *him.*

5For I suppose I was not a whit behind the very chiefest apostles.

6But though *I be* rude in speech, yet not in knowledge; but we have been throughly made manifest among you in all things.

7Have I committed an offence in abasing myself that ye might be exalted, because I have preached to you the gospel of God freely?

8I robbed other churches, taking wages *of them,* to do you service.

9And when I was present with you, and wanted, I was chargeable to no man: for that which was lacking to me the brethren which came from Macedonia supplied: and in all *things* I have kept myself from being burdensome unto you, and *so* will I keep *myself.*

10As the truth of Christ is in me, no man shall stop me of this boasting in the regions of Achaia.

11Wherefore? because I love you not? God knoweth.

12But what I do, that I will do, that I may cut off occasion from them which desire occasion; that wherein they glory, they may be found even as we.

13For such *are* false apostles, deceitful workers, transforming themselves into the apostles of Christ.

14And no marvel; for Satan himself is transformed into an angel of light.

15Therefore *it is* no great thing if his ministers also be transformed as the ministers of righteousness; whose end shall be according to their works.

NEW LIVING TRANSLATION

someone else has done. Instead, we hope that your faith will grow so that the boundaries of our work among you will be extended. 16Then we will be able to go and preach the Good News in other places far beyond you, where no one else is working. Then there will be no question of our boasting about work done in someone else's territory. 17As the Scriptures say, "If you want to boast, boast only about the LORD."*

18When people commend themselves, it doesn't count for much. The important thing is for the Lord to commend them.

Paul and the False Apostles

11 I hope you will put up with a little more of my foolishness. Please bear with me. 2For I am jealous for you with the jealousy of God himself. I promised you as a pure bride* to one husband—Christ. 3But I fear that somehow your pure and undivided devotion to Christ will be corrupted, just as Eve was deceived by the cunning ways of the serpent. 4You happily put up with whatever anyone tells you, even if they preach a different Jesus than the one we preach, or a different kind of Spirit than the one you received, or a different kind of gospel than the one you believed.

5But I don't consider myself inferior in any way to these "super apostles" who teach such things. 6I may be unskilled as a speaker, but I'm not lacking in knowledge. We have made this clear to you in every possible way.

7Was I wrong when I humbled myself and honored you by preaching God's Good News to you without expecting anything in return? 8I "robbed" other churches by accepting their contributions so I could serve you at no cost. 9And when I was with you and didn't have enough to live on, I did not become a financial burden to anyone. For the brothers who came from Macedonia brought me all that I needed. I have never been a burden to you, and I never will be. 10As surely as the truth of Christ is in me, no one in all of Greece* will ever stop me from boasting about this. 11Why? Because I don't love you? God knows that I do.

12But I will continue doing what I have always done. This will undercut those who are looking for an opportunity to boast that their work is just like ours. 13These people are false apostles. They are deceitful workers who disguise themselves as apostles of Christ. 14But I am not surprised! Even Satan disguises himself as an angel of light. 15So it is no wonder that his servants also disguise themselves as servants of righteousness. In the end they will get the punishment their wicked deeds deserve.

10:17 Jer 9:24. **11:2** Greek *a virgin.* **11:10** Greek *Achaia,* the southern region of the Greek peninsula.

KING JAMES VERSION

[16]I say again, Let no man think me a fool; if otherwise, yet as a fool receive me, that I may boast myself a little.

[17]That which I speak, I speak *it* not after the Lord, but as it were foolishly, in this confidence of boasting.

[18]Seeing that many glory after the flesh, I will glory also.

[19]For ye suffer fools gladly, seeing ye *yourselves* are wise.

[20]For ye suffer, if a man bring you into bondage, if a man devour *you*, if a man take *of you*, if a man exalt himself, if a man smite you on the face.

[21]I speak as concerning reproach, as though we had been weak. Howbeit whereinsoever any is bold, (I speak foolishly,) I am bold also.

[22]Are they Hebrews? so *am* I. Are they Israelites? so *am* I. Are they the seed of Abraham? so *am* I.

[23]Are they ministers of Christ? (I speak as a fool) I *am* more; in labours more abundant, in stripes above measure, in prisons more frequent, in deaths oft.

[24]Of the Jews five times received I forty *stripes* save one.

[25]Thrice was I beaten with rods, once was I stoned, thrice I suffered shipwreck, a night and a day I have been in the deep;

[26]*In* journeyings often, *in* perils of waters, *in* perils of robbers, *in* perils by *mine own* countrymen, *in* perils by the heathen, *in* perils in the city, *in* perils in the wilderness, *in* perils in the sea, *in* perils among false brethren;

[27]In weariness and painfulness, in watchings often, in hunger and thirst, in fastings often, in cold and nakedness.

[28]Beside those things that are without, that which cometh upon me daily, the care of all the churches.

[29]Who is weak, and I am not weak? who is offended, and I burn not?

[30]If I must needs glory, I will glory of the things which concern mine infirmities.

[31]The God and Father of our Lord Jesus Christ, which is blessed for evermore, knoweth that I lie not.

[32]In Damascus the governor under Aretas the king kept the city of the Damascenes with a garrison, desirous to apprehend me:

[33]And through a window in a basket was I let down by the wall, and escaped his hands.

12 [1]It is not expedient for me doubtless to glory. I will come to visions and revelations of the Lord.

[2]I knew a man in Christ above fourteen years ago, (whether in the body, I cannot tell; or whether out of the body, I cannot tell: God knoweth;) such an one caught up to the third heaven.

[3]And I knew such a man, (whether in the body, or out of the body, I cannot tell: God knoweth;)

[4]How that he was caught up into paradise, and

NEW LIVING TRANSLATION

Paul's Many Trials

[16]Again I say, don't think that I am a fool to talk like this. But even if you do, listen to me, as you would to a foolish person, while I also boast a little. [17]Such boasting is not from the Lord, but I am acting like a fool. [18]And since others boast about their human achievements, I will, too. [19]After all, you think you are so wise, but you enjoy putting up with fools! [20]You put up with it when someone enslaves you, takes everything you have, takes advantage of you, takes control of everything, and slaps you in the face. [21]I'm ashamed to say that we've been too "weak" to do that!

But whatever they dare to boast about—I'm talking like a fool again—I dare to boast about it, too. [22]Are they Hebrews? So am I. Are they Israelites? So am I. Are they descendants of Abraham? So am I. [23]Are they servants of Christ? I know I sound like a madman, but I have served him far more! I have worked harder, been put in prison more often, been whipped times without number, and faced death again and again. [24]Five different times the Jewish leaders gave me thirty-nine lashes. [25]Three times I was beaten with rods. Once I was stoned. Three times I was shipwrecked. Once I spent a whole night and a day adrift at sea. [26]I have traveled on many long journeys. I have faced danger from rivers and from robbers. I have faced danger from my own people, the Jews, as well as from the Gentiles. I have faced danger in the cities, in the deserts, and on the seas. And I have faced danger from men who claim to be believers but are not.* [27]I have worked hard and long, enduring many sleepless nights. I have been hungry and thirsty and have often gone without food. I have shivered in the cold, without enough clothing to keep me warm.

[28]Then, besides all this, I have the daily burden of my concern for all the churches. [29]Who is weak without my feeling that weakness? Who is led astray, and I do not burn with anger?

[30]If I must boast, I would rather boast about the things that show how weak I am. [31]God, the Father of our Lord Jesus, who is worthy of eternal praise, knows I am not lying. [32]When I was in Damascus, the governor under King Aretas kept guards at the city gates to catch me. [33]I had to be lowered in a basket through a window in the city wall to escape from him.

Paul's Vision and His Thorn in the Flesh

12 This boasting will do no good, but I must go on. I will reluctantly tell about visions and revelations from the Lord. [2]I* was caught up to the third heaven fourteen years ago. Whether I was in my body or out of my body, I don't know—only God knows. [3]Yes, only God knows whether I was in my body or outside my body. But I do know [4]that I was

11:26 Greek *from false brothers.* **12:2** Greek *I know a man in Christ who.*

KING JAMES VERSION

heard unspeakable words, which it is not lawful for a
man to utter.
5 Of such an one will I glory: yet of myself I will not
glory, but in mine infirmities.
6 For though I would desire to glory, I shall not be a
fool; for I will say the truth: but *now* I forbear, lest any
man should think of me above that which he seeth
me *to be*, or *that* he heareth of me.
7 And lest I should be exalted above measure
through the abundance of the revelations, there was
given to me a thorn in the flesh, the messenger of
Satan to buffet me, lest I should be exalted above
measure.
8 For this thing I besought the Lord thrice, that it
might depart from me.
9 And he said unto me, My grace is sufficient for
thee: for my strength is made perfect in weakness.
Most gladly therefore will I rather glory in my infirmities, that the power of Christ may rest upon me.
10 Therefore I take pleasure in infirmities, in reproaches, in necessities, in persecutions, in distresses for Christ's sake: for when I am weak, then am
I strong.

11 I am become a fool in glorying; ye have compelled me: for I ought to have been commended of
you: for in nothing am I behind the very chiefest
apostles, though I be nothing.
12 Truly the signs of an apostle were wrought
among you in all patience, in signs, and wonders, and
mighty deeds.
13 For what is it wherein ye were inferior to other
churches, except *it be* that I myself was not burdensome to you? forgive me this wrong.
14 Behold, the third time I am ready to come to you;
and I will not be burdensome to you: for I seek not
yours, but you: for the children ought not to lay up
for the parents, but the parents for the children.
15 And I will very gladly spend and be spent for you;
though the more abundantly I love you, the less I be
loved.
16 But be it so, I did not burden you: nevertheless,
being crafty, I caught you with guile.
17 Did I make a gain of you by any of them whom I
sent unto you?
18 I desired Titus, and with *him* I sent a brother.
Did Titus make a gain of you? walked we not in the
same spirit? *walked we* not in the same steps?
19 Again, think ye that we excuse ourselves unto
you? we speak before God in Christ: but *we do* all
things, dearly beloved, for your edifying.
20 For I fear, lest, when I come, I shall not find you
such as I would, and *that* I shall be found unto you
such as ye would not: lest *there be* debates, envyings,
wraths, strifes, backbitings, whisperings, swellings,
tumults:
21 *And* lest, when I come again, my God will humble

NEW LIVING TRANSLATION

caught up* to paradise and heard things so astounding that they cannot be expressed in words, things no
human is allowed to tell.
5 That experience is worth boasting about, but I'm
not going to do it. I will boast only about my weaknesses. 6 If I wanted to boast, I would be no fool in
doing so, because I would be telling the truth. But I
won't do it, because I don't want anyone to give me
credit beyond what they can see in my life or hear in
my message, 7 even though I have received such wonderful revelations from God. So to keep me from becoming proud, I was given a thorn in my flesh, a
messenger from Satan to torment me and keep me
from becoming proud.
8 Three different times I begged the Lord to take it
away. 9 Each time he said, "My grace is all you need.
My power works best in weakness." So now I am glad
to boast about my weaknesses, so that the power of
Christ can work through me. 10 That's why I take pleasure in my weaknesses, and in the insults, hardships,
persecutions, and troubles that I suffer for Christ.
For when I am weak, then I am strong.

Paul's Concern for the Corinthians

11 You have made me act like a fool—boasting like
this.* You ought to be writing commendations for me,
for I am not at all inferior to these "super apostles,"
even though I am nothing at all. 12 When I was with
you, I certainly gave you proof that I am an apostle. For
I patiently did many signs and wonders and miracles
among you. 13 The only thing I failed to do, which I do
in the other churches, was to become a financial burden to you. Please forgive me for this wrong!
14 Now I am coming to you for the third time, and I
will not be a burden to you. I don't want what you
have—I want you. After all, children don't provide for
their parents. Rather, parents provide for their children. 15 I will gladly spend myself and all I have for
you, even though it seems that the more I love you,
the less you love me.
16 Some of you admit I was not a burden to you. But
others still think I was sneaky and took advantage of
you by trickery. 17 But how? Did any of the men I sent
to you take advantage of you? 18 When I urged Titus
to visit you and sent our other brother with him, did
Titus take advantage of you? No! For we have the
same spirit and walk in each other's steps, doing
things the same way.
19 Perhaps you think we're saying these things just
to defend ourselves. No, we tell you this as Christ's
servants, and with God as our witness. Everything we
do, dear friends, is to strengthen you. 20 For I am
afraid that when I come I won't like what I find, and
you won't like my response. I am afraid that I will
find quarreling, jealousy, anger, selfishness, slander,
gossip, arrogance, and disorderly behavior. 21 Yes, I

12:3-4 Greek *But I know such a man, 4that he was caught up.* **12:11** Some manuscripts do not include *boasting like this.*

KING JAMES VERSION

me among you, and *that* I shall bewail many which have sinned already, and have not repented of the uncleanness and fornication and lasciviousness which they have committed.

13 1This *is* the third *time* I am coming to you. In the mouth of two or three witnesses shall every word be established.

2I told you before, and foretell you, as if I were present, the second time; and being absent now I write to them which heretofore have sinned, and to all other, that, if I come again, I will not spare:

3Since ye seek a proof of Christ speaking in me, which to you-ward is not weak, but is mighty in you.

4For though he was crucified through weakness, yet he liveth by the power of God. For we also are weak in him, but we shall live with him by the power of God toward you.

5Examine yourselves, whether ye be in the faith; prove your own selves. Know ye not your own selves, how that Jesus Christ is in you, except ye be reprobates?

6But I trust that ye shall know that we are not reprobates.

7Now I pray to God that ye do no evil; not that we should appear approved, but that ye should do that which is honest, though we be as reprobates.

8For we can do nothing against the truth, but for the truth.

9For we are glad, when we are weak, and ye are strong: and this also we wish, *even* your perfection.

10Therefore I write these things being absent, lest being present I should use sharpness, according to the power which the Lord hath given me to edification, and not to destruction.

11Finally, brethren, farewell. Be perfect, be of good comfort, be of one mind, live in peace; and the God of love and peace shall be with you.

12Greet one another with an holy kiss.

13All the saints salute you.

14The grace of the Lord Jesus Christ, and the love of God, and the communion of the Holy Ghost, *be* with you all. Amen.

NEW LIVING TRANSLATION

am afraid that when I come again, God will humble me in your presence. And I will be grieved because many of you have not given up your old sins. You have not repented of your impurity, sexual immorality, and eagerness for lustful pleasure.

Paul's Final Advice

13 This is the third time I am coming to visit you (and as the Scriptures say, "The facts of every case must be established by the testimony of two or three witnesses"*). 2I have already warned those who had been sinning when I was there on my second visit. Now I again warn them and all others, just as I did before, that next time I will not spare them.

3I will give you all the proof you want that Christ speaks through me. Christ is not weak when he deals with you; he is powerful among you. 4Although he was crucified in weakness, he now lives by the power of God. We, too, are weak, just as Christ was, but when we deal with you we will be alive with him and will have God's power.

5Examine yourselves to see if your faith is genuine. Test yourselves. Surely you know that Jesus Christ is among you*; if not, you have failed the test of genuine faith. 6As you test yourselves, I hope you will recognize that we have not failed the test of apostolic authority.

7We pray to God that you will not do what is wrong by refusing our correction. I hope we won't need to demonstrate our authority when we arrive. Do the right thing before we come—even if that makes it look like we have failed to demonstrate our authority. 8For we cannot oppose the truth, but must always stand for the truth. 9We are glad to seem weak if it helps show that you are actually strong. We pray that you will become mature.

10I am writing this to you before I come, hoping that I won't need to deal severely with you when I do come. For I want to use the authority the Lord has given me to strengthen you, not to tear you down.

Paul's Final Greetings

11Dear brothers and sisters,* I close my letter with these last words: Be joyful. Grow to maturity. Encourage each other. Live in harmony and peace. Then the God of love and peace will be with you.

12Greet each other with Christian love.* 13All of God's people here send you their greetings.

14*May the grace of the Lord Jesus Christ, the love of God, and the fellowship of the Holy Spirit be with you all.

13:1 Deut 19:15. **13:5** Or *in you.* **13:11** Greek *Brothers.* **13:12** Greek *with a sacred kiss.* **13:14** Some English translations include verse 13 as part of verse 12, and then verse 14 becomes verse 13.

Galatians

KING JAMES VERSION

1 1 Paul, an apostle, (not of men, neither by man, but by Jesus Christ, and God the Father, who raised him from the dead;)

2 And all the brethren which are with me, unto the churches of Galatia:

3 Grace *be* to you and peace from God the Father, and *from* our Lord Jesus Christ,

4 Who gave himself for our sins, that he might deliver us from this present evil world, according to the will of God and our Father:

5 To whom *be* glory for ever and ever. Amen.

6 I marvel that ye are so soon removed from him that called you into the grace of Christ unto another gospel:

7 Which is not another; but there be some that trouble you, and would pervert the gospel of Christ.

8 But though we, or an angel from heaven, preach any other gospel unto you than that which we have preached unto you, let him be accursed.

9 As we said before, so say I now again, If any *man* preach any other gospel unto you than that ye have received, let him be accursed.

10 For do I now persuade men, or God? or do I seek to please men? for if I yet pleased men, I should not be the servant of Christ.

11 But I certify you, brethren, that the gospel which was preached of me is not after man.

12 For I neither received it of man, neither was I taught *it,* but by the revelation of Jesus Christ.

13 For ye have heard of my conversation in time past in the Jews' religion, how that beyond measure I persecuted the church of God, and wasted it:

14 And profited in the Jews' religion above many my equals in mine own nation, being more exceedingly zealous of the traditions of my fathers.

NEW LIVING TRANSLATION

Greetings from Paul

1 This letter is from Paul, an apostle. I was not appointed by any group of people or any human authority, but by Jesus Christ himself and by God the Father, who raised Jesus from the dead.

2 All the brothers and sisters* here join me in sending this letter to the churches of Galatia.

3 May God our Father and the Lord Jesus Christ* give you grace and peace. 4 Jesus gave his life for our sins, just as God our Father planned, in order to rescue us from this evil world in which we live. 5 All glory to God forever and ever! Amen.

There Is Only One Good News

6 I am shocked that you are turning away so soon from God, who called you to himself through the loving mercy of Christ.* You are following a different way that pretends to be the Good News 7 but is not the Good News at all. You are being fooled by those who deliberately twist the truth concerning Christ.

8 Let God's curse fall on anyone, including us or even an angel from heaven, who preaches a different kind of Good News than the one we preached to you. 9 I say again what we have said before: If anyone preaches any other Good News than the one you welcomed, let that person be cursed.

10 Obviously, I'm not trying to win the approval of people, but of God. If pleasing people were my goal, I would not be Christ's servant.

Paul's Message Comes from Christ

11 Dear brothers and sisters, I want you to understand that the gospel message I preach is not based on mere human reasoning. 12 I received my message from no human source, and no one taught me. Instead, I received it by direct revelation from Jesus Christ.*

13 You know what I was like when I followed the Jewish religion—how I violently persecuted God's church. I did my best to destroy it. 14 I was far ahead of my fellow Jews in my zeal for the traditions of my ancestors.

1:2 Greek *brothers;* also in 1:11. **1:3** Some manuscripts read *God the Father and our Lord Jesus Christ.* **1:6** Some manuscripts read *through loving mercy.* **1:12** Or *by the revelation of Jesus Christ.*

KING JAMES VERSION

15 But when it pleased God, who separated me from my mother's womb, and called *me* by his grace,

16 To reveal his Son in me, that I might preach him among the heathen; immediately I conferred not with flesh and blood:

17 Neither went I up to Jerusalem to them which were apostles before me; but I went into Arabia, and returned again unto Damascus.

18 Then after three years I went up to Jerusalem to see Peter, and abode with him fifteen days.

19 But other of the apostles saw I none, save James the Lord's brother.

20 Now the things which I write unto you, behold, before God, I lie not.

21 Afterwards I came into the regions of Syria and Cilicia;

22 And was unknown by face unto the churches of Judaea which were in Christ:

23 But they had heard only, That he which persecuted us in times past now preacheth the faith which once he destroyed.

24 And they glorified God in me.

2 1 Then fourteen years after I went up again to Jerusalem with Barnabas, and took Titus with *me* also.

2 And I went up by revelation, and communicated unto them that gospel which I preach among the Gentiles, but privately to them which were of reputation, lest by any means I should run, or had run, in vain.

3 But neither Titus, who was with me, being a Greek, was compelled to be circumcised:

4 And that because of false brethren unawares brought in, who came in privily to spy out our liberty which we have in Christ Jesus, that they might bring us into bondage:

5 To whom we gave place by subjection, no, not for an hour; that the truth of the gospel might continue with you.

6 But of these who seemed to be somewhat, (whatsoever they were, it maketh no matter to me: God accepteth no man's person:) for they who seemed *to be somewhat* in conference added nothing to me:

7 But contrariwise, when they saw that the gospel of the uncircumcision was committed unto me, as *the gospel* of the circumcision *was* unto Peter;

8 (For he that wrought effectually in Peter to the apostleship of the circumcision, the same was mighty in me toward the Gentiles:)

9 And when James, Cephas, and John, who seemed to be pillars, perceived the grace that was given unto me, they gave to me and Barnabas the right hands of

NEW LIVING TRANSLATION

15 But even before I was born, God chose me and called me by his marvelous grace. Then it pleased him 16 to reveal his Son to me* so that I would proclaim the Good News about Jesus to the Gentiles.

When this happened, I did not rush out to consult with any human being.* 17 Nor did I go up to Jerusalem to consult with those who were apostles before I was. Instead, I went away into Arabia, and later I returned to the city of Damascus.

18 Then three years later I went to Jerusalem to get to know Peter,* and I stayed with him for fifteen days. 19 The only other apostle I met at that time was James, the Lord's brother. 20 I declare before God that what I am writing to you is not a lie.

21 After that visit I went north into the provinces of Syria and Cilicia. 22 And still the Christians in the churches in Judea didn't know me personally. 23 All they knew was that people were saying, "The one who used to persecute us is now preaching the very faith he tried to destroy!" 24 And they praised God because of me.

The Apostles Accept Paul

2 Then fourteen years later I went back to Jerusalem again, this time with Barnabas; and Titus came along, too. 2 I went there because God revealed to me that I should go. While I was there I met privately with those considered to be leaders of the church and shared with them the message I had been preaching to the Gentiles. I wanted to make sure that we were in agreement, for fear that all my efforts had been wasted and I was running the race for nothing. 3 And they supported me and did not even demand that my companion Titus be circumcised, though he was a Gentile.*

4 Even that question came up only because of some so-called Christians there—false ones, really*—who were secretly brought in. They sneaked in to spy on us and take away the freedom we have in Christ Jesus. They wanted to enslave us and force us to follow their Jewish regulations. 5 But we refused to give in to them for a single moment. We wanted to preserve the truth of the gospel message for you.

6 And the leaders of the church had nothing to add to what I was preaching. (By the way, their reputation as great leaders made no difference to me, for God has no favorites.) 7 Instead, they saw that God had given me the responsibility of preaching the gospel to the Gentiles, just as he had given Peter the responsibility of preaching to the Jews. 8 For the same God who worked through Peter as the apostle to the Jews also worked through me as the apostle to the Gentiles.

9 In fact, James, Peter,* and John, who were known as pillars of the church, recognized the gift God had given me, and they accepted Barnabas and me as their

1:16a Or *in me.* **1:16b** Greek *with flesh and blood.* **1:18** Greek *Cephas.* **2:3** Greek *a Greek.* **2:4** Greek *some false brothers.* **2:9** Greek *Cephas;* also in 2:11, 14.

KING JAMES VERSION

fellowship; that we *should go* unto the heathen, and they unto the circumcision.

10 Only *they would* that we should remember the poor; the same which I also was forward to do.

11 But when Peter was come to Antioch, I withstood him to the face, because he was to be blamed.

12 For before that certain came from James, he did eat with the Gentiles: but when they were come, he withdrew and separated himself, fearing them which were of the circumcision.

13 And the other Jews dissembled likewise with him; insomuch that Barnabas also was carried away with their dissimulation.

14 But when I saw that they walked not uprightly according to the truth of the gospel, I said unto Peter before *them* all, If thou, being a Jew, livest after the manner of Gentiles, and not as do the Jews, why compellest thou the Gentiles to live as do the Jews?

15 We *who are* Jews by nature, and not sinners of the Gentiles,

16 Knowing that a man is not justified by the works of the law, but by the faith of Jesus Christ, even we have believed in Jesus Christ, that we might be justified by the faith of Christ, and not by the works of the law: for by the works of the law shall no flesh be justified.

17 But if, while we seek to be justified by Christ, we ourselves also are found sinners, *is* therefore Christ the minister of sin? God forbid.

18 For if I build again the things which I destroyed, I make myself a transgressor.

19 For I through the law am dead to the law, that I might live unto God.

20 I am crucified with Christ: nevertheless I live; yet not I, but Christ liveth in me: and the life which I now live in the flesh I live by the faith of the Son of God, who loved me, and gave himself for me.

21 I do not frustrate the grace of God: for if righteousness *come* by the law, then Christ is dead in vain.

3 1 O foolish Galatians, who hath bewitched you, that ye should not obey the truth, before whose eyes Jesus Christ hath been evidently set forth, crucified among you?

2 This only would I learn of you, Received ye the Spirit by the works of the law, or by the hearing of faith?

NEW LIVING TRANSLATION

co-workers. They encouraged us to keep preaching
to the Gentiles, while they continued their work
with the Jews. 10 Their only suggestion was that we
keep on helping the poor, which I have always been
eager to do.

Paul Confronts Peter

11 But when Peter came to Antioch, I had to oppose
him to his face, for what he did was very wrong.
12 When he first arrived, he ate with the Gentile
Christians, who were not circumcised. But afterward,
when some friends of James came, Peter wouldn't eat
with the Gentiles anymore. He was afraid of criticism
from these people who insisted on the necessity of
circumcision. 13 As a result, other Jewish Christians
followed Peter's hypocrisy, and even Barnabas was
led astray by their hypocrisy.

14 When I saw that they were not following the
truth of the gospel message, I said to Peter in front
of all the others, "Since you, a Jew by birth, have discarded the Jewish laws and are living like a Gentile,
why are you now trying to make these Gentiles follow
the Jewish traditions?

15 "You and I are Jews by birth, not 'sinners' like
the Gentiles. 16 Yet we know that a person is made
right with God by faith in Jesus Christ, not by obeying the law. And we have believed in Christ Jesus, so
that we might be made right with God because of
our faith in Christ, not because we have obeyed the
law. For no one will ever be made right with God by
obeying the law."*

17 But suppose we seek to be made right with God
through faith in Christ and then we are found guilty
because we have abandoned the law. Would that
mean Christ has led us into sin? Absolutely not!
18 Rather, I am a sinner if I rebuild the old system
of law I already tore down. 19 For when I tried to keep
the law, it condemned me. So I died to the law—I
stopped trying to meet all its requirements—so that I
might live for God. 20 My old self has been crucified
with Christ.* It is no longer I who live, but Christ lives
in me. So I live in this earthly body by trusting in the
Son of God, who loved me and gave himself for me.
21 I do not treat the grace of God as meaningless. For
if keeping the law could make us right with God, then
there was no need for Christ to die.

The Law and Faith in Christ

3 Oh, foolish Galatians! Who has cast an evil spell
on you? For the meaning of Jesus Christ's death
was made as clear to you as if you had seen a picture
of his death on the cross. 2 Let me ask you this one
question: Did you receive the Holy Spirit by obeying
the law of Moses? Of course not! You received the
Spirit because you believed the message you heard

2:16 Some translators hold that the quotation extends through verse 14; others through verse 16; and still others through verse 21. **2:20** Some English translations put this sentence in verse 19.

KING JAMES VERSION

3 Are ye so foolish? having begun in the Spirit, are ye now made perfect by the flesh?

4 Have ye suffered so many things in vain? if *it be* yet in vain.

5 He therefore that ministereth to you the Spirit, and worketh miracles among you, *doeth he it* by the works of the law, or by the hearing of faith?

6 Even as Abraham believed God, and it was accounted to him for righteousness.

7 Know ye therefore that they which are of faith, the same are the children of Abraham.

8 And the scripture, foreseeing that God would justify the heathen through faith, preached before the gospel unto Abraham, *saying,* In thee shall all nations be blessed.

9 So then they which be of faith are blessed with faithful Abraham.

10 For as many as are of the works of the law are under the curse: for it is written, Cursed *is* every one that continueth not in all things which are written in the book of the law to do them.

11 But that no man is justified by the law in the sight of God, *it is* evident: for, The just shall live by faith.

12 And the law is not of faith: but, The man that doeth them shall live in them.

13 Christ hath redeemed us from the curse of the law, being made a curse for us: for it is written, Cursed *is* every one that hangeth on a tree:

14 That the blessing of Abraham might come on the Gentiles through Jesus Christ; that we might receive the promise of the Spirit through faith.

15 Brethren, I speak after the manner of men; Though *it be* but a man's covenant, yet *if it be* confirmed, no man disannulleth, or addeth thereto.

16 Now to Abraham and his seed were the promises made. He saith not, And to seeds, as of many; but as of one, And to thy seed, which is Christ.

17 And this I say, *that* the covenant, that was confirmed before of God in Christ, the law, which was four hundred and thirty years after, cannot disannul, that it should make the promise of none effect.

18 For if the inheritance *be* of the law, *it is* no more of promise: but God gave *it* to Abraham by promise.

NEW LIVING TRANSLATION

about Christ. 3 How foolish can you be? After starting your Christian lives in the Spirit, why are you now trying to become perfect by your own human effort? 4 Have you experienced* so much for nothing? Surely it was not in vain, was it?

5 I ask you again, does God give you the Holy Spirit and work miracles among you because you obey the law? Of course not! It is because you believe the message you heard about Christ.

6 In the same way, "Abraham believed God, and God counted him as righteous because of his faith."* 7 The real children of Abraham, then, are those who put their faith in God.

8 What's more, the Scriptures looked forward to this time when God would declare the Gentiles to be righteous because of their faith. God proclaimed this good news to Abraham long ago when he said, "All nations will be blessed through you."* 9 So all who put their faith in Christ share the same blessing Abraham received because of his faith.

10 But those who depend on the law to make them right with God are under his curse, for the Scriptures say, "Cursed is everyone who does not observe and obey all the commands that are written in God's Book of the Law."* 11 So it is clear that no one can be made right with God by trying to keep the law. For the Scriptures say, "It is through faith that a righteous person has life."* 12 This way of faith is very different from the way of law, which says, "It is through obeying the law that a person has life."*

13 But Christ has rescued us from the curse pronounced by the law. When he was hung on the cross, he took upon himself the curse for our wrongdoing. For it is written in the Scriptures, "Cursed is everyone who is hung on a tree."* 14 Through Christ Jesus, God has blessed the Gentiles with the same blessing he promised to Abraham, so that we who are believers might receive the promised* Holy Spirit through faith.

The Law and God's Promise

15 Dear brothers and sisters,* here's an example from everyday life. Just as no one can set aside or amend an irrevocable agreement, so it is in this case. 16 God gave the promises to Abraham and his child.* And notice that the Scripture doesn't say "to his children,*" as if it meant many descendants. Rather, it says "to his child"—and that, of course, means Christ. 17 This is what I am trying to say: The agreement God made with Abraham could not be canceled 430 years later when God gave the law to Moses. God would be breaking his promise. 18 For if the inheritance could be received by keeping the law, then it would not be the result of accepting God's promise. But God graciously gave it to Abraham as a promise.

3:4 Or *Have you suffered.* **3:6** Gen 15:6. **3:8** Gen 12:3; 18:18; 22:18. **3:10** Deut 27:26. **3:11** Hab 2:4. **3:12** Lev 18:5. **3:13** Deut 21:23 (Greek version). **3:14** Some manuscripts read *the blessing of the.* **3:15** Greek *Brothers.* **3:16a** Greek *seed;* also in 3:16c, 19. See notes on Gen 12:7 and 13:15. **3:16b** Greek *seeds.*

KING JAMES VERSION

19 Wherefore then *serveth* the law? It was added because of transgressions, till the seed should come to whom the promise was made; *and it was* ordained by angels in the hand of a mediator.

20 Now a mediator is not *a mediator* of one, but God is one.

21 *Is* the law then against the promises of God? God forbid: for if there had been a law given which could have given life, verily righteousness should have been by the law.

22 But the scripture hath concluded all under sin, that the promise by faith of Jesus Christ might be given to them that believe.

23 But before faith came, we were kept under the law, shut up unto the faith which should afterwards be revealed.

24 Wherefore the law was our schoolmaster *to bring us* unto Christ, that we might be justified by faith.

25 But after that faith is come, we are no longer under a schoolmaster.

26 For ye are all the children of God by faith in Christ Jesus.

27 For as many of you as have been baptized into Christ have put on Christ.

28 There is neither Jew nor Greek, there is neither bond nor free, there is neither male nor female: for ye are all one in Christ Jesus.

29 And if ye *be* Christ's, then are ye Abraham's seed, and heirs according to the promise.

4

1 Now I say, *That* the heir, as long as he is a child, differeth nothing from a servant, though he be lord of all;

2 But is under tutors and governors until the time appointed of the father.

3 Even so we, when we were children, were in bondage under the elements of the world:

4 But when the fulness of the time was come, God sent forth his Son, made of a woman, made under the law,

5 To redeem them that were under the law, that we might receive the adoption of sons.

6 And because ye are sons, God hath sent forth the Spirit of his Son into your hearts, crying, Abba, Father.

7 Wherefore thou art no more a servant, but a son; and if a son, then an heir of God through Christ.

NEW LIVING TRANSLATION

19 Why, then, was the law given? It was given alongside the promise to show people their sins. But the law was designed to last only until the coming of the child who was promised. God gave his law through angels to Moses, who was the mediator between God and the people. 20 Now a mediator is helpful if more than one party must reach an agreement. But God, who is one, did not use a mediator when he gave his promise to Abraham.

21 Is there a conflict, then, between God's law and God's promises?* Absolutely not! If the law could give us new life, we could be made right with God by obeying it. 22 But the Scriptures declare that we are all prisoners of sin, so we receive God's promise of freedom only by believing in Jesus Christ.

God's Children through Faith

23 Before the way of faith in Christ was available to us, we were placed under guard by the law. We were kept in protective custody, so to speak, until the way of faith was revealed.

24 Let me put it another way. The law was our guardian until Christ came; it protected us until we could be made right with God through faith. 25 And now that the way of faith has come, we no longer need the law as our guardian.

26 For you are all children* of God through faith in Christ Jesus. 27 And all who have been united with Christ in baptism have put on Christ, like putting on new clothes.* 28 There is no longer Jew or Gentile,* slave or free, male and female. For you are all one in Christ Jesus. 29 And now that you belong to Christ, you are the true children* of Abraham. You are his heirs, and God's promise to Abraham belongs to you.

4

Think of it this way. If a father dies and leaves an inheritance for his young children, those children are not much better off than slaves until they grow up, even though they actually own everything their father had. 2 They have to obey their guardians until they reach whatever age their father set. 3 And that's the way it was with us before Christ came. We were like children; we were slaves to the basic spiritual principles* of this world.

4 But when the right time came, God sent his Son, born of a woman, subject to the law. 5 God sent him to buy freedom for us who were slaves to the law, so that he could adopt us as his very own children.* 6 And because we* are his children, God has sent the Spirit of his Son into our hearts, prompting us to call out, "Abba, Father."* 7 Now you are no longer a slave but God's own child.* And since you are his child, God has made you his heir.

3:21 Some manuscripts read *and the promises?* **3:26** Greek *sons.* **3:27** Greek *have put on Christ.* **3:28** Greek *Jew or Greek.* **3:29** Greek *seed.* **4:3** Or *powers;* also in 4:9. **4:5** Greek *sons;* also in 4:6. **4:6a** Greek *you.* **4:6b** *Abba* is an Aramaic term for "father." **4:7** Greek *son;* also in 4:7b.

KING JAMES VERSION

8 Howbeit then, when ye knew not God, ye did service unto them which by nature are no gods.

9 But now, after that ye have known God, or rather are known of God, how turn ye again to the weak and beggarly elements, whereunto ye desire again to be in bondage?

10 Ye observe days, and months, and times, and years.

11 I am afraid of you, lest I have bestowed upon you labour in vain.

12 Brethren, I beseech you, be as I *am;* for I *am* as ye *are:* ye have not injured me at all.

13 Ye know how through infirmity of the flesh I preached the gospel unto you at the first.

14 And my temptation which was in my flesh ye despised not, nor rejected; but received me as an angel of God, *even* as Christ Jesus.

15 Where is then the blessedness ye spake of? for I bear you record, that, if *it had been* possible, ye would have plucked out your own eyes, and have given them to me.

16 Am I therefore become your enemy, because I tell you the truth?

17 They zealously affect you, *but* not well; yea, they would exclude you, that ye might affect them.

18 But *it is* good to be zealously affected always in *a* good *thing,* and not only when I am present with you.

19 My little children, of whom I travail in birth again until Christ be formed in you,

20 I desire to be present with you now, and to change my voice; for I stand in doubt of you.

21 Tell me, ye that desire to be under the law, do ye not hear the law?

22 For it is written, that Abraham had two sons, the one by a bondmaid, the other by a freewoman.

23 But he *who was* of the bondwoman was born after the flesh; but he of the freewoman *was* by promise.

24 Which things are an allegory: for these are the two covenants; the one from the mount Sinai, which gendereth to bondage, which is Agar.

25 For this Agar is mount Sinai in Arabia, and answereth to Jerusalem which now is, and is in bondage with her children.

26 But Jerusalem which is above is free, which is the mother of us all.

27 For it is written, Rejoice, *thou* barren that

NEW LIVING TRANSLATION

Paul's Concern for the Galatians

8 Before you Gentiles knew God, you were slaves to so-
called gods that do not even exist. 9 So now that you
know God (or should I say, now that God knows you),
why do you want to go back again and become slaves
once more to the weak and useless spiritual principles of this world? 10 You are trying to earn favor with
God by observing certain days or months or seasons
or years. 11 I fear for you. Perhaps all my hard work
with you was for nothing. 12 Dear brothers and sisters,* I plead with you to live as I do in freedom from
these things, for I have become like you Gentiles—
free from those laws.

You did not mistreat me when I first preached to
you. 13 Surely you remember that I was sick when I
first brought you the Good News. 14 But even though
my condition tempted you to reject me, you did not
despise me or turn me away. No, you took me in and
cared for me as though I were an angel from God or
even Christ Jesus himself. 15 Where is that joyful and
grateful spirit you felt then? I am sure you would
have taken out your own eyes and given them to me
if it had been possible. 16 Have I now become your
enemy because I am telling you the truth?

17 Those false teachers are so eager to win your favor, but their intentions are not good. They are trying
to shut you off from me so that you will pay attention
only to them. 18 If someone is eager to do good things
for you, that's all right; but let them do it all the time,
not just when I'm with you.

19 Oh, my dear children! I feel as if I'm going
through labor pains for you again, and they will continue until Christ is fully developed in your lives. 20 I
wish I were with you right now so I could change my
tone. But at this distance I don't know how else to
help you.

Abraham's Two Children

21 Tell me, you who want to live under the law, do you
know what the law actually says? 22 The Scriptures
say that Abraham had two sons, one from his slave
wife and one from his freeborn wife.* 23 The son of
the slave wife was born in a human attempt to bring
about the fulfillment of God's promise. But the son of
the freeborn wife was born as God's own fulfillment
of his promise.

24 These two women serve as an illustration of
God's two covenants. The first woman, Hagar, represents Mount Sinai where people received the law
that enslaved them. 25 And now Jerusalem is just like
Mount Sinai in Arabia,* because she and her children live in slavery to the law. 26 But the other
woman, Sarah, represents the heavenly Jerusalem.
She is the free woman, and she is our mother. 27 As
Isaiah said,

4:12 Greek *brothers;* also in 4:28, 31. **4:22** See Gen 16:15; 21:2-3.
4:25 Greek *And Hagar, which is Mount Sinai in Arabia, is now like Jerusalem;* other manuscripts read *And Mount Sinai in Arabia is now like Jerusalem.*

KING JAMES VERSION

bearest not; break forth and cry, thou that travailest
not: for the desolate hath many more children than
she which hath an husband.

28 Now we, brethren, as Isaac was, are the children
of promise.

29 But as then he that was born after the flesh persecuted him *that was born* after the Spirit, even so
it is now.

30 Nevertheless what saith the scripture? Cast out
the bondwoman and her son: for the son of the bondwoman shall not be heir with the son of the
freewoman.

31 So then, brethren, we are not children of the
bondwoman, but of the free.

5 1 Stand fast therefore in the liberty wherewith
Christ hath made us free, and be not entangled
again with the yoke of bondage.

2 Behold, I Paul say unto you, that if ye be circumcised, Christ shall profit you nothing.

3 For I testify again to every man that is circumcised, that he is a debtor to do the whole law.

4 Christ is become of no effect unto you, whosoever of you are justified by the law; ye are fallen from
grace.

5 For we through the Spirit wait for the hope of
righteousness by faith.

6 For in Jesus Christ neither circumcision availeth
any thing, nor uncircumcision; but faith which
worketh by love.

7 Ye did run well; who did hinder you that ye
should not obey the truth?

8 This persuasion *cometh* not of him that calleth
you.

9 A little leaven leaveneth the whole lump.

10 I have confidence in you through the Lord, that
ye will be none otherwise minded: but he that
troubleth you shall bear his judgment, whosoever
he be.

11 And I, brethren, if I yet preach circumcision, why
do I yet suffer persecution? then is the offence of the
cross ceased.

12 I would they were even cut off which trouble
you.

13 For, brethren, ye have been called unto liberty;
only *use* not liberty for an occasion to the flesh, but
by love serve one another.

NEW LIVING TRANSLATION

"Rejoice, O childless woman,
you who have never given birth!
Break into a joyful shout,
you who have never been in labor!
For the desolate woman now has more children
than the woman who lives with her husband!"*

28 And you, dear brothers and sisters, are children
of the promise, just like Isaac. 29 But you are now being persecuted by those who want you to keep the
law, just as Ishmael, the child born by human effort,
persecuted Isaac, the child born by the power of the
Spirit.

30 But what do the Scriptures say about that? "Get
rid of the slave and her son, for the son of the slave
woman will not share the inheritance with the free
woman's son."* 31 So, dear brothers and sisters, we
are not children of the slave woman; we are children
of the free woman.

Freedom in Christ

5 So Christ has truly set us free. Now make sure
that you stay free, and don't get tied up again in
slavery to the law.

2 Listen! I, Paul, tell you this: If you are counting on
circumcision to make you right with God, then Christ
will be of no benefit to you. 3 I'll say it again. If you are
trying to find favor with God by being circumcised,
you must obey every regulation in the whole law of
Moses. 4 For if you are trying to make yourselves right
with God by keeping the law, you have been cut off
from Christ! You have fallen away from God's grace.

5 But we who live by the Spirit eagerly wait to receive by faith the righteousness God has promised
to us. 6 For when we place our faith in Christ Jesus,
there is no benefit in being circumcised or being
uncircumcised. What is important is faith expressing itself in love.

7 You were running the race so well. Who has held
you back from following the truth? 8 It certainly isn't
God, for he is the one who called you to freedom.
9 This false teaching is like a little yeast that spreads
through the whole batch of dough! 10 I am trusting
the Lord to keep you from believing false teachings.
God will judge that person, whoever he is, who has
been confusing you.

11 Dear brothers and sisters,* if I were still preaching that you must be circumcised—as some say I
do—why am I still being persecuted? If I were no longer preaching salvation through the cross of Christ,
no one would be offended. 12 I just wish that those
troublemakers who want to mutilate you by circumcision would mutilate themselves.*

13 For you have been called to live in freedom, my
brothers and sisters. But don't use your freedom to
satisfy your sinful nature. Instead, use your freedom

4:27 Isa 54:1. **4:30** Gen 21:10. **5:11** Greek *Brothers;* similarly in 5:13.
5:12 Or *castrate themselves,* or *cut themselves off from you;* Greek reads *cut themselves off.*

KING JAMES VERSION

14 For all the law is fulfilled in one word, *even* in this; Thou shalt love thy neighbour as thyself.

15 But if ye bite and devour one another, take heed that ye be not consumed one of another.

16 *This* I say then, Walk in the Spirit, and ye shall not fulfil the lust of the flesh.

17 For the flesh lusteth against the Spirit, and the Spirit against the flesh: and these are contrary the one to the other: so that ye cannot do the things that ye would.

18 But if ye be led of the Spirit, ye are not under the law.

19 Now the works of the flesh are manifest, which are *these;* Adultery, fornication, uncleanness, lasciviousness,

20 Idolatry, witchcraft, hatred, variance, emulations, wrath, strife, seditions, heresies,

21 Envyings, murders, drunkenness, revellings, and such like: of the which I tell you before, as I have also told *you* in time past, that they which do such things shall not inherit the kingdom of God.

22 But the fruit of the Spirit is love, joy, peace, longsuffering, gentleness, goodness, faith,

23 Meekness, temperance: against such there is no law.

24 And they that are Christ's have crucified the flesh with the affections and lusts.

25 If we live in the Spirit, let us also walk in the Spirit.

26 Let us not be desirous of vain glory, provoking one another, envying one another.

6 1 Brethren, if a man be overtaken in a fault, ye which are spiritual, restore such an one in the spirit of meekness; considering thyself, lest thou also be tempted.

2 Bear ye one another's burdens, and so fulfil the law of Christ.

3 For if a man think himself to be something, when he is nothing, he deceiveth himself.

4 But let every man prove his own work, and then shall he have rejoicing in himself alone, and not in another.

5 For every man shall bear his own burden.

6 Let him that is taught in the word communicate unto him that teacheth in all good things.

7 Be not deceived; God is not mocked: for whatsoever a man soweth, that shall he also reap.

8 For he that soweth to his flesh shall of the flesh reap corruption; but he that soweth to the Spirit shall of the Spirit reap life everlasting.

NEW LIVING TRANSLATION

to serve one another in love. 14 For the whole law can
be summed up in this one command: "Love your
neighbor as yourself."* 15 But if you are always biting
and devouring one another, watch out! Beware of
destroying one another.

Living by the Spirit's Power

16 So I say, let the Holy Spirit guide your lives. Then
you won't be doing what your sinful nature craves.
17 The sinful nature wants to do evil, which is just the
opposite of what the Spirit wants. And the Spirit
gives us desires that are the opposite of what the sinful nature desires. These two forces are constantly
fighting each other, so you are not free to carry out
your good intentions. 18 But when you are directed
by the Spirit, you are not under obligation to the law
of Moses.

19 When you follow the desires of your sinful nature, the results are very clear: sexual immorality, impurity, lustful pleasures, 20 idolatry, sorcery, hostility,
quarreling, jealousy, outbursts of anger, selfish ambition, dissension, division, 21 envy, drunkenness, wild
parties, and other sins like these. Let me tell you
again, as I have before, that anyone living that sort of
life will not inherit the Kingdom of God.

22 But the Holy Spirit produces this kind of fruit in
our lives: love, joy, peace, patience, kindness, goodness, faithfulness, 23 gentleness, and self-control.
There is no law against these things!

24 Those who belong to Christ Jesus have nailed
the passions and desires of their sinful nature to his
cross and crucified them there. 25 Since we are living
by the Spirit, let us follow the Spirit's leading in every
part of our lives. 26 Let us not become conceited, or
provoke one another, or be jealous of one another.

We Harvest What We Plant

6 Dear brothers and sisters, if another believer*
is overcome by some sin, you who are godly*
should gently and humbly help that person back
onto the right path. And be careful not to fall into the
same temptation yourself. 2 Share each other's burdens, and in this way obey the law of Christ. 3 If you
think you are too important to help someone, you are
only fooling yourself. You are not that important.

4 Pay careful attention to your own work, for then
you will get the satisfaction of a job well done, and
you won't need to compare yourself to anyone else.
5 For we are each responsible for our own conduct.

6 Those who are taught the word of God should
provide for their teachers, sharing all good things
with them.

7 Don't be misled—you cannot mock the justice of
God. You will always harvest what you plant. 8 Those
who live only to satisfy their own sinful nature
will harvest decay and death from that sinful nature.
But those who live to please the Spirit will harvest

5:14 Lev 19:18. 6:1a Greek *Brothers, if a man.* 6:1b Greek *spiritual.*

KING JAMES VERSION

9 And let us not be weary in well doing: for in due
season we shall reap, if we faint not.
10 As we have therefore opportunity, let us do good
unto all *men,* especially unto them who are of the
household of faith.

11 Ye see how large a letter I have written unto you
with mine own hand.
12 As many as desire to make a fair shew in the
flesh, they constrain you to be circumcised; only lest
they should suffer persecution for the cross of
Christ.
13 For neither they themselves who are circumcised keep the law; but desire to have you circumcised, that they may glory in your flesh.
14 But God forbid that I should glory, save in the
cross of our Lord Jesus Christ, by whom the world is
crucified unto me, and I unto the world.
15 For in Christ Jesus neither circumcision availeth
any thing, nor uncircumcision, but a new creature.
16 And as many as walk according to this rule,
peace *be* on them, and mercy, and upon the Israel of
God.
17 From henceforth let no man trouble me: for I
bear in my body the marks of the Lord Jesus.
18 Brethren, the grace of our Lord Jesus Christ *be*
with your spirit. Amen.

NEW LIVING TRANSLATION

everlasting life from the Spirit. 9 So let's not get tired
of doing what is good. At just the right time we will
reap a harvest of blessing if we don't give up.
10 Therefore, whenever we have the opportunity, we
should do good to everyone—especially to those in
the family of faith.

Paul's Final Advice

11 NOTICE WHAT LARGE LETTERS I USE AS I WRITE THESE
CLOSING WORDS IN MY OWN HANDWRITING.
12 Those who are trying to force you to be circumcised want to look good to others. They don't want to
be persecuted for teaching that the cross of Christ
alone can save. 13 And even those who advocate circumcision don't keep the whole law themselves.
They only want you to be circumcised so they can
boast about it and claim you as their disciples.
14 As for me, may I never boast about anything except the cross of our Lord Jesus Christ. Because of
that cross,* my interest in this world has been crucified, and the world's interest in me has also died. 15 It
doesn't matter whether we have been circumcised
or not. What counts is whether we have been transformed into a new creation. 16 May God's peace and
mercy be upon all who live by this principle; they are
the new people of God.*
17 From now on, don't let anyone trouble me with
these things. For I bear on my body the scars that
show I belong to Jesus.
18 Dear brothers and sisters,* may the grace of our
Lord Jesus Christ be with your spirit. Amen.

6:14 Or *Because of him.* **6:16** Greek *this principle, and upon the Israel of God.* **6:18** Greek *Brothers.*

Ephesians

KING JAMES VERSION

1 1Paul, an apostle of Jesus Christ by the will of God, to the saints which are at Ephesus, and to the faithful in Christ Jesus:

2Grace *be* to you, and peace, from God our Father, and *from* the Lord Jesus Christ.

3Blessed *be* the God and Father of our Lord Jesus Christ, who hath blessed us with all spiritual blessings in heavenly *places* in Christ:

4According as he hath chosen us in him before the foundation of the world, that we should be holy and without blame before him in love:

5Having predestinated us unto the adoption of children by Jesus Christ to himself, according to the good pleasure of his will,

6To the praise of the glory of his grace, wherein he hath made us accepted in the beloved.

7In whom we have redemption through his blood, the forgiveness of sins, according to the riches of his grace;

8Wherein he hath abounded toward us in all wisdom and prudence;

9Having made known unto us the mystery of his will, according to his good pleasure which he hath purposed in himself:

10That in the dispensation of the fulness of times he might gather together in one all things in Christ, both which are in heaven, and which are on earth; *even* in him:

11In whom also we have obtained an inheritance, being predestinated according to the purpose of him who worketh all things after the counsel of his own will:

12That we should be to the praise of his glory, who first trusted in Christ.

13In whom ye also *trusted,* after that ye heard the word of truth, the gospel of your salvation: in whom also after that ye believed, ye were sealed with that holy Spirit of promise,

14Which is the earnest of our inheritance until the redemption of the purchased possession, unto the praise of his glory.

NEW LIVING TRANSLATION

Greetings from Paul

1 This letter is from Paul, chosen by the will of God to be an apostle of Christ Jesus.

I am writing to God's holy people in Ephesus,* who are faithful followers of Christ Jesus.

2May God our Father and the Lord Jesus Christ give you grace and peace.

Spiritual Blessings

3All praise to God, the Father of our Lord Jesus Christ, who has blessed us with every spiritual blessing in the heavenly realms because we are united with Christ. 4Even before he made the world, God loved us and chose us in Christ to be holy and without fault in his eyes. 5God decided in advance to adopt us into his own family by bringing us to himself through Jesus Christ. This is what he wanted to do, and it gave him great pleasure. 6So we praise God for the glorious grace he has poured out on us who belong to his dear Son.* 7He is so rich in kindness and grace that he purchased our freedom with the blood of his Son and forgave our sins. 8He has showered his kindness on us, along with all wisdom and understanding.

9God has now revealed to us his mysterious plan regarding Christ, a plan to fulfill his own good pleasure. 10And this is the plan: At the right time he will bring everything together under the authority of Christ—everything in heaven and on earth. 11Furthermore, because we are united with Christ, we have received an inheritance from God,* for he chose us in advance, and he makes everything work out according to his plan.

12God's purpose was that we Jews who were the first to trust in Christ would bring praise and glory to God. 13And now you Gentiles have also heard the truth, the Good News that God saves you. And when you believed in Christ, he identified you as his own* by giving you the Holy Spirit, whom he promised long ago. 14The Spirit is God's guarantee that he will give us the inheritance he promised and that he has purchased us to be his own people. He did this so we would praise and glorify him.

1:1 The most ancient manuscripts do not include *in Ephesus.* **1:6** Greek *to us in the beloved.* **1:11** Or *we have become God's inheritance.* **1:13** Or *he put his seal on you.*

KING JAMES VERSION

15 Wherefore I also, after I heard of your faith in the Lord Jesus, and love unto all the saints,
16 Cease not to give thanks for you, making mention of you in my prayers;
17 That the God of our Lord Jesus Christ, the Father of glory, may give unto you the spirit of wisdom and revelation in the knowledge of him:
18 The eyes of your understanding being enlightened; that ye may know what is the hope of his calling, and what the riches of the glory of his inheritance in the saints,

19 And what *is* the exceeding greatness of his power to us-ward who believe, according to the working of his mighty power,
20 Which he wrought in Christ, when he raised him from the dead, and set *him* at his own right hand in the heavenly *places*,
21 Far above all principality, and power, and might, and dominion, and every name that is named, not only in this world, but also in that which is to come:
22 And hath put all *things* under his feet, and gave him *to be* the head over all *things* to the church,

23 Which is his body, the fulness of him that filleth all in all.

2 1 And you *hath he quickened,* who were dead in trespasses and sins:

2 Wherein in time past ye walked according to the course of this world, according to the prince of the power of the air, the spirit that now worketh in the children of disobedience:
3 Among whom also we all had our conversation in times past in the lusts of our flesh, fulfilling the desires of the flesh and of the mind; and were by nature the children of wrath, even as others.
4 But God, who is rich in mercy, for his great love wherewith he loved us,
5 Even when we were dead in sins, hath quickened us together with Christ, (by grace ye are saved;)

6 And hath raised *us* up together, and made *us* sit together in heavenly *places* in Christ Jesus:

7 That in the ages to come he might shew the exceeding riches of his grace in *his* kindness toward us through Christ Jesus.
8 For by grace are ye saved through faith; and that not of yourselves: *it is* the gift of God:
9 Not of works, lest any man should boast.

10 For we are his workmanship, created in Christ Jesus unto good works, which God hath before ordained that we should walk in them.

NEW LIVING TRANSLATION

Paul's Prayer for Spiritual Wisdom

15 Ever since I first heard of your strong faith in the Lord Jesus and your love for God's people everywhere,* 16 I have not stopped thanking God for you. I pray for you constantly, 17 asking God, the glorious Father of our Lord Jesus Christ, to give you spiritual wisdom* and insight so that you might grow in your knowledge of God. 18 I pray that your hearts will be flooded with light so that you can understand the confident hope he has given to those he called—his holy people who are his rich and glorious inheritance.*

19 I also pray that you will understand the incredible greatness of God's power for us who believe him. This is the same mighty power 20 that raised Christ from the dead and seated him in the place of honor at God's right hand in the heavenly realms. 21 Now he is far above any ruler or authority or power or leader or anything else—not only in this world but also in the world to come. 22 God has put all things under the authority of Christ and has made him head over all things for the benefit of the church. 23 And the church is his body; it is made full and complete by Christ, who fills all things everywhere with himself.

Made Alive with Christ

2 Once you were dead because of your disobedience and your many sins. 2 You used to live in sin, just like the rest of the world, obeying the devil—the commander of the powers in the unseen world.* He is the spirit at work in the hearts of those who refuse to obey God. 3 All of us used to live that way, following the passionate desires and inclinations of our sinful nature. By our very nature we were subject to God's anger, just like everyone else.

4 But God is so rich in mercy, and he loved us so much, 5 that even though we were dead because of our sins, he gave us life when he raised Christ from the dead. (It is only by God's grace that you have been saved!) 6 For he raised us from the dead along with Christ and seated us with him in the heavenly realms because we are united with Christ Jesus. 7 So God can point to us in all future ages as examples of the incredible wealth of his grace and kindness toward us, as shown in all he has done for us who are united with Christ Jesus.

8 God saved you by his grace when you believed. And you can't take credit for this; it is a gift from God. 9 Salvation is not a reward for the good things we have done, so none of us can boast about it. 10 For we are God's masterpiece. He has created us anew in Christ Jesus, so we can do the good things he planned for us long ago.

1:15 Some manuscripts read *your faithfulness to the Lord Jesus and to God's people everywhere.* **1:17** Or *to give you the Spirit of wisdom.* **1:18** Or *called, and the rich and glorious inheritance he has given to his holy people.* **2:2** Greek *obeying the commander of the power of the air.*

KING JAMES VERSION

11 Wherefore remember, that ye *being* in time past Gentiles in the flesh, who are called Uncircumcision by that which is called the Circumcision in the flesh made by hands;

12 That at that time ye were without Christ, being aliens from the commonwealth of Israel, and strangers from the covenants of promise, having no hope, and without God in the world:

13 But now in Christ Jesus ye who sometimes were far off are made nigh by the blood of Christ.

14 For he is our peace, who hath made both one, and hath broken down the middle wall of partition *between us;*

15 Having abolished in his flesh the enmity, *even* the law of commandments *contained* in ordinances; for to make in himself of twain one new man, *so* making peace;

16 And that he might reconcile both unto God in one body by the cross, having slain the enmity thereby:

17 And came and preached peace to you which were afar off, and to them that were nigh.

18 For through him we both have access by one Spirit unto the Father.

19 Now therefore ye are no more strangers and foreigners, but fellowcitizens with the saints, and of the household of God;

20 And are built upon the foundation of the apostles and prophets, Jesus Christ himself being the chief corner *stone;*

21 In whom all the building fitly framed together groweth unto an holy temple in the Lord:

22 In whom ye also are builded together for an habitation of God through the Spirit.

3 1 For this cause I Paul, the prisoner of Jesus Christ for you Gentiles,

2 If ye have heard of the dispensation of the grace of God which is given me to you-ward:

3 How that by revelation he made known unto me the mystery; (as I wrote afore in few words,

4 Whereby, when ye read, ye may understand my knowledge in the mystery of Christ)

5 Which in other ages was not made known unto the sons of men, as it is now revealed unto his holy apostles and prophets by the Spirit;

6 That the Gentiles should be fellowheirs, and of the same body, and partakers of his promise in Christ by the gospel:

NEW LIVING TRANSLATION

Oneness and Peace in Christ

11 Don't forget that you Gentiles used to be outsiders.
You were called "uncircumcised heathens" by the
Jews, who were proud of their circumcision, even
though it affected only their bodies and not their
hearts. 12 In those days you were living apart from
Christ. You were excluded from citizenship among
the people of Israel, and you did not know the covenant promises God had made to them. You lived in
this world without God and without hope. 13 But now
you have been united with Christ Jesus. Once you
were far away from God, but now you have been
brought near to him through the blood of Christ.

14 For Christ himself has brought peace to us. He
united Jews and Gentiles into one people when, in
his own body on the cross, he broke down the wall of
hostility that separated us. 15 He did this by ending
the system of law with its commandments and regulations. He made peace between Jews and Gentiles
by creating in himself one new people from the two
groups. 16 Together as one body, Christ reconciled
both groups to God by means of his death on the
cross, and our hostility toward each other was put to
death.

17 He brought this Good News of peace to you
Gentiles who were far away from him, and peace to
the Jews who were near. 18 Now all of us can come to
the Father through the same Holy Spirit because of
what Christ has done for us.

A Temple for the Lord

19 So now you Gentiles are no longer strangers and
foreigners. You are citizens along with all of God's
holy people. You are members of God's family. 20 Together, we are his house, built on the foundation of
the apostles and the prophets. And the cornerstone is
Christ Jesus himself. 21 We are carefully joined together in him, becoming a holy temple for the Lord.
22 Through him you Gentiles are also being made part
of this dwelling where God lives by his Spirit.

God's Mysterious Plan Revealed

3 When I think of all this, I, Paul, a prisoner of
Christ Jesus for the benefit of you Gentiles* . . .
2 assuming, by the way, that you know God gave me
the special responsibility of extending his grace to
you Gentiles. 3 As I briefly wrote earlier, God himself
revealed his mysterious plan to me. 4 As you read
what I have written, you will understand my insight
into this plan regarding Christ. 5 God did not reveal it
to previous generations, but now by his Spirit he has
revealed it to his holy apostles and prophets.

6 And this is God's plan: Both Gentiles and Jews who
believe the Good News share equally in the riches
inherited by God's children. Both are part of the
same body, and both enjoy the promise of blessings

3:1 Paul resumes this thought in verse 14: "When I think of all this, I fall to my knees and pray to the Father."

KING JAMES VERSION

7 Whereof I was made a minister, according to the gift of the grace of God given unto me by the effectual working of his power.

8 Unto me, who am less than the least of all saints, is this grace given, that I should preach among the Gentiles the unsearchable riches of Christ;

9 And to make all *men* see what *is* the fellowship of the mystery, which from the beginning of the world hath been hid in God, who created all things by Jesus Christ:

10 To the intent that now unto the principalities and powers in heavenly *places* might be known by the church the manifold wisdom of God,

11 According to the eternal purpose which he purposed in Christ Jesus our Lord:

12 In whom we have boldness and access with confidence by the faith of him.

13 Wherefore I desire that ye faint not at my tribulations for you, which is your glory.

14 For this cause I bow my knees unto the Father of our Lord Jesus Christ,

15 Of whom the whole family in heaven and earth is named,

16 That he would grant you, according to the riches of his glory, to be strengthened with might by his Spirit in the inner man;

17 That Christ may dwell in your hearts by faith; that ye, being rooted and grounded in love,

18 May be able to comprehend with all saints what *is* the breadth, and length, and depth, and height;

19 And to know the love of Christ, which passeth knowledge, that ye might be filled with all the fulness of God.

20 Now unto him that is able to do exceeding abundantly above all that we ask or think, according to the power that worketh in us,

21 Unto him *be* glory in the church by Christ Jesus throughout all ages, world without end. Amen.

4 1 I therefore, the prisoner of the Lord, beseech you that ye walk worthy of the vocation wherewith ye are called,

2 With all lowliness and meekness, with longsuffering, forbearing one another in love;

3 Endeavouring to keep the unity of the Spirit in the bond of peace.

4 *There is* one body, and one Spirit, even as ye are called in one hope of your calling;

5 One Lord, one faith, one baptism,

6 One God and Father of all, who *is* above all, and through all, and in you all.

7 But unto every one of us is given grace according to the measure of the gift of Christ.

8 Wherefore he saith, When he ascended up on

NEW LIVING TRANSLATION

because they belong to Christ Jesus.*
7 By God's grace and mighty power, I have been given the privilege of serving him by spreading this Good News.

8 Though I am the least deserving of all God's people, he graciously gave me the privilege of telling the Gentiles about the endless treasures available to them in Christ.
9 I was chosen to explain to everyone* this mysterious plan that God, the Creator of all things, had kept secret from the beginning.

10 God's purpose in all this was to use the church to display his wisdom in its rich variety to all the unseen rulers and authorities in the heavenly places.
11 This was his eternal plan, which he carried out through Christ Jesus our Lord.

12 Because of Christ and our faith in him,* we can now come boldly and confidently into God's presence.
13 So please don't lose heart because of my trials here. I am suffering for you, so you should feel honored.

Paul's Prayer for Spiritual Growth

14 When I think of all this, I fall to my knees and pray to the Father,*
15 the Creator of everything in heaven and on earth.*
16 I pray that from his glorious, unlimited resources he will empower you with inner strength through his Spirit.
17 Then Christ will make his home in your hearts as you trust in him. Your roots will grow down into God's love and keep you strong.
18 And may you have the power to understand, as all God's people should, how wide, how long, how high, and how deep his love is.
19 May you experience the love of Christ, though it is too great to understand fully. Then you will be made complete with all the fullness of life and power that comes from God.

20 Now all glory to God, who is able, through his mighty power at work within us, to accomplish infinitely more than we might ask or think.
21 Glory to him in the church and in Christ Jesus through all generations forever and ever! Amen.

Unity in the Body

4 Therefore I, a prisoner for serving the Lord, beg you to lead a life worthy of your calling, for you have been called by God.
2 Always be humble and gentle. Be patient with each other, making allowance for each other's faults because of your love.
3 Make every effort to keep yourselves united in the Spirit, binding yourselves together with peace.
4 For there is one body and one Spirit, just as you have been called to one glorious hope for the future.
5 There is one Lord, one faith, one baptism,
6 and one God and Father, who is over all and in all and living through all.

7 However, he has given each one of us a special gift* through the generosity of Christ.
8 That is why the Scriptures say,

3:6 Or *because they are united with Christ Jesus.* **3:9** Some manuscripts do not include *to everyone.* **3:12** Or *Because of Christ's faithfulness.* **3:14** Some manuscripts read *the Father of our Lord Jesus Christ.* **3:15** Or *from whom every family in heaven and on earth takes its name.* **4:7** Greek *a grace.*

KING JAMES VERSION

high, he led captivity captive, and gave gifts unto men.

9 (Now that he ascended, what is it but that he also descended first into the lower parts of the earth?

10 He that descended is the same also that ascended up far above all heavens, that he might fill all things.)

11 And he gave some, apostles; and some, prophets; and some, evangelists; and some, pastors and teachers;

12 For the perfecting of the saints, for the work of the ministry, for the edifying of the body of Christ:

13 Till we all come in the unity of the faith, and of the knowledge of the Son of God, unto a perfect man, unto the measure of the stature of the fulness of Christ:

14 That we *henceforth* be no more children, tossed to and fro, and carried about with every wind of doctrine, by the sleight of men, *and* cunning craftiness, whereby they lie in wait to deceive;

15 But speaking the truth in love, may grow up into him in all things, which is the head, *even* Christ:

16 From whom the whole body fitly joined together and compacted by that which every joint supplieth, according to the effectual working in the measure of every part, maketh increase of the body unto the edifying of itself in love.

17 This I say therefore, and testify in the Lord, that ye henceforth walk not as other Gentiles walk, in the vanity of their mind,

18 Having the understanding darkened, being alienated from the life of God through the ignorance that is in them, because of the blindness of their heart:

19 Who being past feeling have given themselves over unto lasciviousness, to work all uncleanness with greediness.

20 But ye have not so learned Christ;

21 If so be that ye have heard him, and have been taught by him, as the truth is in Jesus:

22 That ye put off concerning the former conversation the old man, which is corrupt according to the deceitful lusts;

23 And be renewed in the spirit of your mind;

24 And that ye put on the new man, which after God is created in righteousness and true holiness.

25 Wherefore putting away lying, speak every man truth with his neighbour: for we are members one of another.

26 Be ye angry, and sin not: let not the sun go down upon your wrath:

27 Neither give place to the devil.

28 Let him that stole steal no more: but rather let him labour, working with *his* hands the thing which is good, that he may have to give to him that needeth.

29 Let no corrupt communication proceed out of

NEW LIVING TRANSLATION

"When he ascended to the heights,
he led a crowd of captives
and gave gifts to his people."*

9 Notice that it says "he ascended." This clearly means
that Christ also descended to our lowly world.*
10 And the same one who descended is the one who
ascended higher than all the heavens, so that he
might fill the entire universe with himself.
11 Now these are the gifts Christ gave to the church:
the apostles, the prophets, the evangelists, and the
pastors and teachers. 12 Their responsibility is to
equip God's people to do his work and build up the
church, the body of Christ. 13 This will continue until
we all come to such unity in our faith and knowledge
of God's Son that we will be mature in the Lord, measuring up to the full and complete standard of Christ.
14 Then we will no longer be immature like children. We won't be tossed and blown about by every
wind of new teaching. We will not be influenced
when people try to trick us with lies so clever they
sound like the truth. 15 Instead, we will speak the
truth in love, growing in every way more and more
like Christ, who is the head of his body, the church.
16 He makes the whole body fit together perfectly. As
each part does its own special work, it helps the
other parts grow, so that the whole body is healthy
and growing and full of love.

Living as Children of Light

17 With the Lord's authority I say this: Live no longer
as the Gentiles do, for they are hopelessly confused.
18 Their minds are full of darkness; they wander far
from the life God gives because they have closed
their minds and hardened their hearts against him.
19 They have no sense of shame. They live for lustful
pleasure and eagerly practice every kind of impurity.
20 But that isn't what you learned about Christ.
21 Since you have heard about Jesus and have learned
the truth that comes from him, 22 throw off your old
sinful nature and your former way of life, which is
corrupted by lust and deception. 23 Instead, let the
Spirit renew your thoughts and attitudes. 24 Put on
your new nature, created to be like God—truly righteous and holy.
25 So stop telling lies. Let us tell our neighbors the
truth, for we are all parts of the same body. 26 And
"don't sin by letting anger control you."* Don't let the
sun go down while you are still angry, 27 for anger
gives a foothold to the devil.
28 If you are a thief, quit stealing. Instead, use your
hands for good hard work, and then give generously
to others in need. 29 Don't use foul or abusive language. Let everything you say be good and helpful, so

4:8 Ps 68:18. **4:9** Or *to the lowest parts of the earth.* **4:26** Ps 4:4.

your mouth, but that which is good to the use of edifying, that it may minister grace unto the hearers.
30 And grieve not the holy Spirit of God, whereby
ye are sealed unto the day of redemption.
31 Let all bitterness, and wrath, and anger, and
clamour, and evil speaking, be put away from you,
with all malice:
32 And be ye kind one to another, tenderhearted,
forgiving one another, even as God for Christ's sake
hath forgiven you.

5 1 Be ye therefore followers of God, as dear
children;
2 And walk in love, as Christ also hath loved us, and
hath given himself for us an offering and a sacrifice
to God for a sweetsmelling savour.
3 But fornication, and all uncleanness, or covetousness, let it not be once named among you, as becometh saints;
4 Neither filthiness, nor foolish talking, nor jesting,
which are not convenient: but rather giving of thanks.
5 For this ye know, that no whoremonger, nor unclean person, nor covetous man, who is an idolater,
hath any inheritance in the kingdom of Christ and
of God.
6 Let no man deceive you with vain words: for because of these things cometh the wrath of God upon
the children of disobedience.
7 Be not ye therefore partakers with them.
8 For ye were sometimes darkness, but now *are ye*
light in the Lord: walk as children of light:
9 (For the fruit of the Spirit *is* in all goodness and
righteousness and truth;)
10 Proving what is acceptable unto the Lord.
11 And have no fellowship with the unfruitful
works of darkness, but rather reprove *them*.
12 For it is a shame even to speak of those things
which are done of them in secret.
13 But all things that are reproved are made manifest by the light: for whatsoever doth make manifest
is light.
14 Wherefore he saith, Awake thou that sleepest,
and arise from the dead, and Christ shall give thee
light.
15 See then that ye walk circumspectly, not as fools,
but as wise,
16 Redeeming the time, because the days are evil.
17 Wherefore be ye not unwise, but understanding
what the will of the Lord *is*.
18 And be not drunk with wine, wherein is excess;
but be filled with the Spirit;
19 Speaking to yourselves in psalms and hymns
and spiritual songs, singing and making melody in
your heart to the Lord;
20 Giving thanks always for all things unto God and
the Father in the name of our Lord Jesus Christ;

that your words will be an encouragement to those
who hear them.
30 And do not bring sorrow to God's Holy Spirit by
the way you live. Remember, he has identified you as
his own,* guaranteeing that you will be saved on the
day of redemption.
31 Get rid of all bitterness, rage, anger, harsh
words, and slander, as well as all types of evil behavior. 32 Instead, be kind to each other, tenderhearted,
forgiving one another, just as God through Christ has
forgiven you.

Living in the Light

5 Imitate God, therefore, in everything you do,
because you are his dear children. 2 Live a life
filled with love, following the example of Christ. He
loved us* and offered himself as a sacrifice for us,
a pleasing aroma to God.
3 Let there be no sexual immorality, impurity, or
greed among you. Such sins have no place among
God's people. 4 Obscene stories, foolish talk, and
coarse jokes—these are not for you. Instead, let there
be thankfulness to God. 5 You can be sure that no immoral, impure, or greedy person will inherit the
Kingdom of Christ and of God. For a greedy person
is an idolater, worshiping the things of this world.
6 Don't be fooled by those who try to excuse these
sins, for the anger of God will fall on all who disobey
him. 7 Don't participate in the things these people do.
8 For once you were full of darkness, but now you
have light from the Lord. So live as people of light!
9 For this light within you produces only what is good
and right and true.
10 Carefully determine what pleases the Lord.
11 Take no part in the worthless deeds of evil and
darkness; instead, expose them. 12 It is shameful even
to talk about the things that ungodly people do in secret. 13 But their evil intentions will be exposed when
the light shines on them, 14 for the light makes everything visible. This is why it is said,

"Awake, O sleeper,
rise up from the dead,
and Christ will give you light."

Living by the Spirit's Power

15 So be careful how you live. Don't live like fools, but
like those who are wise. 16 Make the most of every opportunity in these evil days. 17 Don't act thoughtlessly,
but understand what the Lord wants you to do.
18 Don't be drunk with wine, because that will ruin
your life. Instead, be filled with the Holy Spirit,
19 singing psalms and hymns and spiritual songs
among yourselves, and making music to the Lord in
your hearts. 20 And give thanks for everything to God
the Father in the name of our Lord Jesus Christ.

4:30 Or *has put his seal on you.* **5:2** Some manuscripts read *loved you.*

KING JAMES VERSION

21 Submitting yourselves one to another in the fear of God.

22 Wives, submit yourselves unto your own husbands, as unto the Lord.

23 For the husband is the head of the wife, even as Christ is the head of the church: and he is the saviour of the body.

24 Therefore as the church is subject unto Christ, so *let* the wives *be* to their own husbands in every thing.

25 Husbands, love your wives, even as Christ also loved the church, and gave himself for it;

26 That he might sanctify and cleanse it with the washing of water by the word,

27 That he might present it to himself a glorious church, not having spot, or wrinkle, or any such thing; but that it should be holy and without blemish.

28 So ought men to love their wives as their own bodies. He that loveth his wife loveth himself.

29 For no man ever yet hated his own flesh; but nourisheth and cherisheth it, even as the Lord the church:

30 For we are members of his body, of his flesh, and of his bones.

31 For this cause shall a man leave his father and mother, and shall be joined unto his wife, and they two shall be one flesh.

32 This is a great mystery: but I speak concerning Christ and the church.

33 Nevertheless let every one of you in particular so love his wife even as himself; and the wife *see* that she reverence *her* husband.

6 1 Children, obey your parents in the Lord: for this is right.

2 Honour thy father and mother; which is the first commandment with promise;

3 That it may be well with thee, and thou mayest live long on the earth.

4 And, ye fathers, provoke not your children to wrath: but bring them up in the nurture and admonition of the Lord.

5 Servants, be obedient to them that are *your* masters according to the flesh, with fear and trembling, in singleness of your heart, as unto Christ;

6 Not with eyeservice, as menpleasers; but as the servants of Christ, doing the will of God from the heart;

7 With good will doing service, as to the Lord, and not to men:

8 Knowing that whatsoever good thing any man doeth, the same shall he receive of the Lord, whether *he be* bond or free.

9 And, ye masters, do the same things unto them, forbearing threatening: knowing that your Master

NEW LIVING TRANSLATION

Spirit-Guided Relationships: Wives and Husbands

21 And further, submit to one another out of reverence for Christ.

22 For wives, this means submit to your husbands as to the Lord. 23 For a husband is the head of his wife as Christ is the head of the church. He is the Savior of his body, the church. 24 As the church submits to Christ, so you wives should submit to your husbands in everything.

25 For husbands, this means love your wives, just as Christ loved the church. He gave up his life for her 26 to make her holy and clean, washed by the cleansing of God's word.* 27 He did this to present her to himself as a glorious church without a spot or wrinkle or any other blemish. Instead, she will be holy and without fault. 28 In the same way, husbands ought to love their wives as they love their own bodies. For a man who loves his wife actually shows love for himself. 29 No one hates his own body but feeds and cares for it, just as Christ cares for the church. 30 And we are members of his body.

31 As the Scriptures say, "A man leaves his father and mother and is joined to his wife, and the two are united into one."* 32 This is a great mystery, but it is an illustration of the way Christ and the church are one. 33 So again I say, each man must love his wife as he loves himself, and the wife must respect her husband.

Children and Parents

6 Children, obey your parents because you belong to the Lord,* for this is the right thing to do. 2 "Honor your father and mother." This is the first commandment with a promise: 3 If you honor your father and mother, "things will go well for you, and you will have a long life on the earth."*

4 Fathers, do not provoke your children to anger by the way you treat them. Rather, bring them up with the discipline and instruction that comes from the Lord.

Slaves and Masters

5 Slaves, obey your earthly masters with deep respect and fear. Serve them sincerely as you would serve Christ. 6 Try to please them all the time, not just when they are watching you. As slaves of Christ, do the will of God with all your heart. 7 Work with enthusiasm, as though you were working for the Lord rather than for people. 8 Remember that the Lord will reward each one of us for the good we do, whether we are slaves or free.

9 Masters, treat your slaves in the same way. Don't

5:26 Greek *washed by water with the word.* **5:31** Gen 2:24. **6:1** Or *Children, obey your parents who belong to the Lord;* some manuscripts read simply *Children, obey your parents.* **6:2-3** Exod 20:12; Deut 5:16.

KING JAMES VERSION

also is in heaven; neither is there respect of persons with him.

10 Finally, my brethren, be strong in the Lord, and in the power of his might.

11 Put on the whole armour of God, that ye may be able to stand against the wiles of the devil.

12 For we wrestle not against flesh and blood, but against principalities, against powers, against the rulers of the darkness of this world, against spiritual wickedness in high *places*.

13 Wherefore take unto you the whole armour of God, that ye may be able to withstand in the evil day, and having done all, to stand.

14 Stand therefore, having your loins girt about with truth, and having on the breastplate of righteousness;

15 And your feet shod with the preparation of the gospel of peace;

16 Above all, taking the shield of faith, wherewith ye shall be able to quench all the fiery darts of the wicked.

17 And take the helmet of salvation, and the sword of the Spirit, which is the word of God:

18 Praying always with all prayer and supplication in the Spirit, and watching thereunto with all perseverance and supplication for all saints;

19 And for me, that utterance may be given unto me, that I may open my mouth boldly, to make known the mystery of the gospel,

20 For which I am an ambassador in bonds: that therein I may speak boldly, as I ought to speak.

21 But that ye also may know my affairs, *and* how I do, Tychicus, a beloved brother and faithful minister in the Lord, shall make known to you all things:

22 Whom I have sent unto you for the same purpose, that ye might know our affairs, and *that* he might comfort your hearts.

23 Peace *be* to the brethren, and love with faith, from God the Father and the Lord Jesus Christ.

24 Grace *be* with all them that love our Lord Jesus Christ in sincerity. Amen.

NEW LIVING TRANSLATION

threaten them; remember, you both have the same Master in heaven, and he has no favorites.

The Whole Armor of God

10 A final word: Be strong in the Lord and in his
mighty power. 11 Put on all of God's armor so that you
will be able to stand firm against all strategies of the
devil. 12 For we* are not fighting against flesh-and-
blood enemies, but against evil rulers and authorities
of the unseen world, against mighty powers in this
dark world, and against evil spirits in the heavenly
places.

13 Therefore, put on every piece of God's armor so
you will be able to resist the enemy in the time of
evil. Then after the battle you will still be standing
firm. 14 Stand your ground, putting on the belt of
truth and the body armor of God's righteousness.
15 For shoes, put on the peace that comes from the
Good News so that you will be fully prepared.* 16 In
addition to all of these, hold up the shield of faith to
stop the fiery arrows of the devil.* 17 Put on salvation
as your helmet, and take the sword of the Spirit,
which is the word of God.

18 Pray in the Spirit at all times and on every occasion. Stay alert and be persistent in your prayers for all believers everywhere.*

19 And pray for me, too. Ask God to give me the
right words so I can boldly explain God's mysterious
plan that the Good News is for Jews and Gentiles
alike.* 20 I am in chains now, still preaching this message as God's ambassador. So pray that I will keep
on speaking boldly for him, as I should.

Final Greetings

21 To bring you up to date, Tychicus will give you a full
report about what I am doing and how I am getting
along. He is a beloved brother and faithful helper in
the Lord's work. 22 I have sent him to you for this very
purpose—to let you know how we are doing and to
encourage you.

23 Peace be with you, dear brothers and sisters,*
and may God the Father and the Lord Jesus Christ
give you love with faithfulness. 24 May God's grace be
eternally upon all who love our Lord Jesus Christ.

6:12 Some manuscripts read *you.* **6:15** Or *For shoes, put on the readiness to preach the Good News of peace with God.* **6:16** Greek *the evil one.* **6:18** Greek *all of God's holy people.* **6:19** Greek *explain the mystery of the Good News;* some manuscripts read simply *explain the mystery.*

Philippians

KING JAMES VERSION

1 1Paul and Timotheus, the servants of Jesus Christ, to all the saints in Christ Jesus which are at Philippi, with the bishops and deacons:

2Grace *be* unto you, and peace, from God our Father, and *from* the Lord Jesus Christ.

3I thank my God upon every remembrance of you,

4Always in every prayer of mine for you all making request with joy,

5For your fellowship in the gospel from the first day until now;

6Being confident of this very thing, that he which hath begun a good work in you will perform *it* until the day of Jesus Christ:

7Even as it is meet for me to think this of you all, because I have you in my heart; inasmuch as both in my bonds, and in the defence and confirmation of the gospel, ye all are partakers of my grace.

8For God is my record, how greatly I long after you all in the bowels of Jesus Christ.

9And this I pray, that your love may abound yet more and more in knowledge and *in* all judgment;

10That ye may approve things that are excellent; that ye may be sincere and without offence till the day of Christ;

11Being filled with the fruits of righteousness, which are by Jesus Christ, unto the glory and praise of God.

12But I would ye should understand, brethren, that the things *which happened* unto me have fallen out rather unto the furtherance of the gospel;

13So that my bonds in Christ are manifest in all the palace, and in all other *places;*

14And many of the brethren in the Lord, waxing

NEW LIVING TRANSLATION

Greetings from Paul

1 This letter is from Paul and Timothy, slaves of Christ Jesus.

I am writing to all of God's holy people in Philippi who belong to Christ Jesus, including the elders* and deacons.

2May God our Father and the Lord Jesus Christ give you grace and peace.

Paul's Thanksgiving and Prayer

3Every time I think of you, I give thanks to my God.
4Whenever I pray, I make my requests for all of you
with joy, 5for you have been my partners in spreading
the Good News about Christ from the time you first
heard it until now. 6And I am certain that God, who
began the good work within you, will continue his
work until it is finally finished on the day when
Christ Jesus returns.

7So it is right that I should feel as I do about all of
you, for you have a special place in my heart. You
share with me the special favor of God, both in my
imprisonment and in defending and confirming
the truth of the Good News. 8God knows how much I
love you and long for you with the tender compassion of Christ Jesus.

9I pray that your love will overflow more and
more, and that you will keep on growing in knowledge and understanding. 10For I want you to understand what really matters, so that you may live pure
and blameless lives until the day of Christ's return.
11May you always be filled with the fruit of your salvation—the righteous character produced in your
life by Jesus Christ*—for this will bring much glory
and praise to God.

Paul's Joy That Christ Is Preached

12And I want you to know, my dear brothers and sisters,* that everything that has happened to me here
has helped to spread the Good News. 13For everyone
here, including the whole palace guard,* knows that I
am in chains because of Christ. 14And because of my
imprisonment, most of the believers* here have

1:1 Or *overseers;* or *bishops.* **1:11** Greek *with the fruit of righteousness through Jesus Christ.* **1:12** Greek *brothers.* **1:13** Greek *including all the Praetorium.* **1:14a** Greek *brothers in the Lord.*

KING JAMES VERSION

confident by my bonds, are much more bold to speak the word without fear.

15 Some indeed preach Christ even of envy and strife; and some also of good will:

16 The one preach Christ of contention, not sincerely, supposing to add affliction to my bonds:

17 But the other of love, knowing that I am set for the defence of the gospel.

18 What then? notwithstanding, every way, whether in pretence, or in truth, Christ is preached; and I therein do rejoice, yea, and will rejoice.

19 For I know that this shall turn to my salvation through your prayer, and the supply of the Spirit of Jesus Christ,

20 According to my earnest expectation and *my* hope, that in nothing I shall be ashamed, but *that* with all boldness, as always, *so* now also Christ shall be magnified in my body, whether *it be* by life, or by death.

21 For to me to live *is* Christ, and to die *is* gain.

22 But if I live in the flesh, this *is* the fruit of my labour: yet what I shall choose I wot not.

23 For I am in a strait betwixt two, having a desire to depart, and to be with Christ; which is far better:

24 Nevertheless to abide in the flesh *is* more needful for you.

25 And having this confidence, I know that I shall abide and continue with you all for your furtherance and joy of faith;

26 That your rejoicing may be more abundant in Jesus Christ for me by my coming to you again.

27 Only let your conversation be as it becometh the gospel of Christ: that whether I come and see you, or else be absent, I may hear of your affairs, that ye stand fast in one spirit, with one mind striving together for the faith of the gospel;

28 And in nothing terrified by your adversaries: which is to them an evident token of perdition, but to you of salvation, and that of God.

29 For unto you it is given in the behalf of Christ, not only to believe on him, but also to suffer for his sake;

30 Having the same conflict which ye saw in me, and now hear *to be* in me.

2 1 If *there be* therefore any consolation in Christ, if any comfort of love, if any fellowship of the Spirit, if any bowels and mercies,

2 Fulfil ye my joy, that ye be likeminded, having the same love, *being* of one accord, of one mind.

NEW LIVING TRANSLATION

gained confidence and boldly speak God's message* without fear.

15 It's true that some are preaching out of jealousy and rivalry. But others preach about Christ with pure motives. 16 They preach because they love me, for they know I have been appointed to defend the Good News. 17 Those others do not have pure motives as they preach about Christ. They preach with selfish ambition, not sincerely, intending to make my chains more painful to me. 18 But that doesn't matter. Whether their motives are false or genuine, the message about Christ is being preached either way, so I rejoice. And I will continue to rejoice. 19 For I know that as you pray for me and the Spirit of Jesus Christ helps me, this will lead to my deliverance.

Paul's Life for Christ

20 For I fully expect and hope that I will never be ashamed, but that I will continue to be bold for Christ, as I have been in the past. And I trust that my life will bring honor to Christ, whether I live or die. 21 For to me, living means living for Christ, and dying is even better. 22 But if I live, I can do more fruitful work for Christ. So I really don't know which is better. 23 I'm torn between two desires: I long to go and be with Christ, which would be far better for me. 24 But for your sakes, it is better that I continue to live.

25 Knowing this, I am convinced that I will remain alive so I can continue to help all of you grow and experience the joy of your faith. 26 And when I come to you again, you will have even more reason to take pride in Christ Jesus because of what he is doing through me.

Live as Citizens of Heaven

27 Above all, you must live as citizens of heaven, conducting yourselves in a manner worthy of the Good News about Christ. Then, whether I come and see you again or only hear about you, I will know that you are standing together with one spirit and one purpose, fighting together for the faith, which is the Good News. 28 Don't be intimidated in any way by your enemies. This will be a sign to them that they are going to be destroyed, but that you are going to be saved, even by God himself. 29 For you have been given not only the privilege of trusting in Christ but also the privilege of suffering for him. 30 We are in this struggle together. You have seen my struggle in the past, and you know that I am still in the midst of it.

Have the Attitude of Christ

2 Is there any encouragement from belonging to Christ? Any comfort from his love? Any fellowship together in the Spirit? Are your hearts tender and compassionate? 2 Then make me truly happy by agreeing wholeheartedly with each other, loving one another, and working together with one mind and purpose.

1:14b Some manuscripts read *speak the message.*

KING JAMES VERSION

[3]*Let* nothing *be done* through strife or vainglory;
but in lowliness of mind let each esteem other better
than themselves.
[4]Look not every man on his own things, but every
man also on the things of others.
[5]Let this mind be in you, which was also in Christ
Jesus:
[6]Who, being in the form of God, thought it not
robbery to be equal with God:
[7]But made himself of no reputation, and took
upon him the form of a servant, and was made in the
likeness of men:
[8]And being found in fashion as a man, he humbled
himself, and became obedient unto death, even the
death of the cross.
[9]Wherefore God also hath highly exalted him, and
given him a name which is above every name:
[10]That at the name of Jesus every knee should
bow, of *things* in heaven, and *things* in earth, and
things under the earth;
[11]And *that* every tongue should confess that Jesus
Christ *is* Lord, to the glory of God the Father.

[12]Wherefore, my beloved, as ye have always
obeyed, not as in my presence only, but now much
more in my absence, work out your own salvation
with fear and trembling.
[13]For it is God which worketh in you both to will
and to do of *his* good pleasure.
[14]Do all things without murmurings and disputings:
[15]That ye may be blameless and harmless, the
sons of God, without rebuke, in the midst of a
crooked and perverse nation, among whom ye shine
as lights in the world;
[16]Holding forth the word of life; that I may rejoice
in the day of Christ, that I have not run in vain, neither laboured in vain.
[17]Yea, and if I be offered upon the sacrifice and
service of your faith, I joy, and rejoice with you all.
[18]For the same cause also do ye joy, and rejoice
with me.

[19]But I trust in the Lord Jesus to send Timotheus
shortly unto you, that I also may be of good comfort,
when I know your state.
[20]For I have no man likeminded, who will naturally
care for your state.
[21]For all seek their own, not the things which are
Jesus Christ's.
[22]But ye know the proof of him, that, as a son with
the father, he hath served with me in the gospel.
[23]Him therefore I hope to send presently, so soon
as I shall see how it will go with me.

NEW LIVING TRANSLATION

[3]Don't be selfish; don't try to impress others. Be
humble, thinking of others as better than yourselves.
[4]Don't look out only for your own interests, but take
an interest in others, too.
[5]You must have the same attitude that Christ Jesus
had.

6 Though he was God,*
he did not think of equality with God
as something to cling to.
7 Instead, he gave up his divine privileges*;
he took the humble position of a slave*
and was born as a human being.
When he appeared in human form,*
8 he humbled himself in obedience to God
and died a criminal's death on a cross.

9 Therefore, God elevated him to the place
of highest honor
and gave him the name above all other names,
10 that at the name of Jesus every knee should bow,
in heaven and on earth and under the earth,
11 and every tongue confess that Jesus Christ
is Lord,
to the glory of God the Father.

Shine Brightly for Christ

[12]Dear friends, you always followed my instructions
when I was with you. And now that I am away, it is
even more important. Work hard to show the results
of your salvation, obeying God with deep reverence
and fear. [13]For God is working in you, giving you the
desire and the power to do what pleases him.
[14]Do everything without complaining and arguing, [15]so that no one can criticize you. Live clean, innocent lives as children of God, shining like bright
lights in a world full of crooked and perverse people.
[16]Hold firmly to the word of life; then, on the day of
Christ's return, I will be proud that I did not run the
race in vain and that my work was not useless. [17]But I
will rejoice even if I lose my life, pouring it out like a
liquid offering to God,* just like your faithful service
is an offering to God. And I want all of you to share
that joy. [18]Yes, you should rejoice, and I will share
your joy.

Paul Commends Timothy

[19]If the Lord Jesus is willing, I hope to send Timothy
to you soon for a visit. Then he can cheer me up by
telling me how you are getting along. [20]I have no one
else like Timothy, who genuinely cares about your
welfare. [21]All the others care only for themselves and
not for what matters to Jesus Christ. [22]But you know
how Timothy has proved himself. Like a son with his
father, he has served with me in preaching the Good
News. [23]I hope to send him to you just as soon as I

2:6 Or *Being in the form of God.* **2:7a** Greek *he emptied himself.* **2:7b** Or *the form of a slave.* **2:7c** Some English translations put this phrase in verse 8. **2:17** Greek *I will rejoice even if I am to be poured out as a liquid offering.*

KING JAMES VERSION

24But I trust in the Lord that I also myself shall come shortly.

25Yet I supposed it necessary to send to you Epaphroditus, my brother, and companion in labour, and fellowsoldier, but your messenger, and he that ministered to my wants.

26For he longed after you all, and was full of heaviness, because that ye had heard that he had been sick.

27For indeed he was sick nigh unto death: but God had mercy on him; and not on him only, but on me also, lest I should have sorrow upon sorrow.

28I sent him therefore the more carefully, that, when ye see him again, ye may rejoice, and that I may be the less sorrowful.

29Receive him therefore in the Lord with all gladness; and hold such in reputation:

30Because for the work of Christ he was nigh unto death, not regarding his life, to supply your lack of service toward me.

3 1Finally, my brethren, rejoice in the Lord. To write the same things to you, to me indeed *is* not grievous, but for you *it is* safe.

2Beware of dogs, beware of evil workers, beware of the concision.

3For we are the circumcision, which worship God in the spirit, and rejoice in Christ Jesus, and have no confidence in the flesh.

4Though I might also have confidence in the flesh. If any other man thinketh that he hath whereof he might trust in the flesh, I more:

5Circumcised the eighth day, of the stock of Israel, *of* the tribe of Benjamin, an Hebrew of the Hebrews; as touching the law, a Pharisee;

6Concerning zeal, persecuting the church; touching the righteousness which is in the law, blameless.

7But what things were gain to me, those I counted loss for Christ.

8Yea doubtless, and I count all things *but* loss for the excellency of the knowledge of Christ Jesus my Lord: for whom I have suffered the loss of all things, and do count them *but* dung, that I may win Christ,

9And be found in him, not having mine own righteousness, which is of the law, but that which is through the faith of Christ, the righteousness which is of God by faith:

10That I may know him, and the power of his

NEW LIVING TRANSLATION

find out what is going to happen to me here.
24And I have confidence from the Lord that I myself will come to see you soon.

Paul Commends Epaphroditus

25Meanwhile, I thought I should send Epaphroditus back to you. He is a true brother, co-worker, and fellow soldier. And he was your messenger to help me
in my need.
26I am sending him because he has been longing to see you, and he was very distressed that
you heard he was ill.
27And he certainly was ill; in fact, he almost died. But God had mercy on him—and also on me, so that I would not have one sorrow after another.

28So I am all the more anxious to send him back to you, for I know you will be glad to see him, and then I will not be so worried about you.
29Welcome him with Christian love* and with great joy, and give him the honor that people like him deserve.
30For he risked his life for the work of Christ, and he was at the point of death while doing for me what you couldn't do from far away.

The Priceless Value of Knowing Christ

3 Whatever happens, my dear brothers and sisters,* rejoice in the Lord. I never get tired of telling you these things, and I do it to safeguard your faith.

2Watch out for those dogs, those people who do evil, those mutilators who say you must be circumcised to be saved.
3For we who worship by the Spirit of God* are the ones who are truly circumcised. We rely on what Christ Jesus has done for us. We put no confidence in human effort,
4though I could have confidence in my own effort if anyone could. Indeed, if others have reason for confidence in their own efforts, I have even more!

5I was circumcised when I was eight days old. I am a pure-blooded citizen of Israel and a member of the tribe of Benjamin—a real Hebrew if there ever was one! I was a member of the Pharisees, who demand the strictest obedience to the Jewish law.
6I was so zealous that I harshly persecuted the church. And as for righteousness, I obeyed the law without fault.

7I once thought these things were valuable, but now I consider them worthless because of what
Christ has done.
8Yes, everything else is worthless when compared with the infinite value of knowing Christ Jesus my Lord. For his sake I have discarded everything else, counting it all as garbage, so that I
could gain Christ
9and become one with him. I no longer count on my own righteousness through obeying the law; rather, I become righteous through faith in Christ.* For God's way of making us right
with himself depends on faith.
10I want to know

2:29 Greek *in the Lord.* **3:1** Greek *brothers;* also in 3:13, 17. **3:3** Some manuscripts read *worship God in spirit;* one early manuscript reads *worship in spirit.* **3:9** Or *through the faithfulness of Christ.*

KING JAMES VERSION

resurrection, and the fellowship of his sufferings, being made conformable unto his death;

11 If by any means I might attain unto the resurrection of the dead.

12 Not as though I had already attained, either were already perfect: but I follow after, if that I may apprehend that for which also I am apprehended of Christ Jesus.

13 Brethren, I count not myself to have apprehended: but *this* one thing *I do,* forgetting those things which are behind, and reaching forth unto those things which are before,

14 I press toward the mark for the prize of the high calling of God in Christ Jesus.

15 Let us therefore, as many as be perfect, be thus minded: and if in any thing ye be otherwise minded, God shall reveal even this unto you.

16 Nevertheless, whereto we have already attained, let us walk by the same rule, let us mind the same thing.

17 Brethren, be followers together of me, and mark them which walk so as ye have us for an ensample.

18 (For many walk, of whom I have told you often, and now tell you even weeping, *that they are* the enemies of the cross of Christ:

19 Whose end *is* destruction, whose God *is their* belly, and *whose* glory *is* in their shame, who mind earthly things.)

20 For our conversation is in heaven; from whence also we look for the Saviour, the Lord Jesus Christ:

21 Who shall change our vile body, that it may be fashioned like unto his glorious body, according to the working whereby he is able even to subdue all things unto himself.

4

1 Therefore, my brethren, dearly beloved and longed for, my joy and crown, so stand fast in the Lord, *my* dearly beloved.

2 I beseech Euodias, and beseech Syntyche, that they be of the same mind in the Lord.

3 And I intreat thee also, true yokefellow, help those women which laboured with me in the gospel, with Clement also, and *with* other my fellowlabourers, whose names *are* in the book of life.

4 Rejoice in the Lord alway: *and* again I say, Rejoice.

5 Let your moderation be known unto all men. The Lord *is* at hand.

6 Be careful for nothing; but in every thing by prayer and supplication with thanksgiving let your requests be made known unto God.

NEW LIVING TRANSLATION

Christ and experience the mighty power that raised him from the dead. I want to suffer with him, sharing in his death, 11 so that one way or another I will experience the resurrection from the dead!

Pressing toward the Goal

12 I don't mean to say that I have already achieved these things or that I have already reached perfection. But I press on to possess that perfection for which Christ Jesus first possessed me. 13 No, dear brothers and sisters, I have not achieved it,* but I focus on this one thing: Forgetting the past and looking forward to what lies ahead, 14 I press on to reach the end of the race and receive the heavenly prize for which God, through Christ Jesus, is calling us.

15 Let all who are spiritually mature agree on these things. If you disagree on some point, I believe God will make it plain to you. 16 But we must hold on to the progress we have already made.

17 Dear brothers and sisters, pattern your lives after mine, and learn from those who follow our example. 18 For I have told you often before, and I say it again with tears in my eyes, that there are many whose conduct shows they are really enemies of the cross of Christ. 19 They are headed for destruction. Their god is their appetite, they brag about shameful things, and they think only about this life here on earth. 20 But we are citizens of heaven, where the Lord Jesus Christ lives. And we are eagerly waiting for him to return as our Savior. 21 He will take our weak mortal bodies and change them into glorious bodies like his own, using the same power with which he will bring everything under his control.

4

Therefore, my dear brothers and sisters,* stay true to the Lord. I love you and long to see you, dear friends, for you are my joy and the crown I receive for my work.

Words of Encouragement

2 Now I appeal to Euodia and Syntyche. Please, because you belong to the Lord, settle your disagreement. 3 And I ask you, my true partner,* to help these two women, for they worked hard with me in telling others the Good News. They worked along with Clement and the rest of my co-workers, whose names are written in the Book of Life.

4 Always be full of joy in the Lord. I say it again—rejoice! 5 Let everyone see that you are considerate in all you do. Remember, the Lord is coming soon.

6 Don't worry about anything; instead, pray about everything. Tell God what you need, and thank him

3:13 Some manuscripts read *not yet achieved it.* **4:1** Greek *brothers;* also in 4:8. **4:3** Or *loyal Syzygus.*

KING JAMES VERSION

7 And the peace of God, which passeth all understanding, shall keep your hearts and minds through
Christ Jesus.
8 Finally, brethren, whatsoever things are true,
whatsoever things *are* honest, whatsoever things *are*
just, whatsoever things *are* pure, whatsoever things
are lovely, whatsoever things *are* of good report; if
there be any virtue, and if *there be* any praise, think
on these things.
9 Those things, which ye have both learned, and received, and heard, and seen in me, do: and the God of
peace shall be with you.

10 But I rejoiced in the Lord greatly, that now at the
last your care of me hath flourished again; wherein
ye were also careful, but ye lacked opportunity.
11 Not that I speak in respect of want: for I have
learned, in whatsoever state I am, *therewith* to be
content.
12 I know both how to be abased, and I know how to
abound: every where and in all things I am instructed
both to be full and to be hungry, both to abound and
to suffer need.
13 I can do all things through Christ which strengtheneth me.
14 Notwithstanding ye have well done, that ye did
communicate with my affliction.
15 Now ye Philippians know also, that in the beginning of the gospel, when I departed from Macedonia,
no church communicated with me as concerning
giving and receiving, but ye only.
16 For even in Thessalonica ye sent once and again
unto my necessity.
17 Not because I desire a gift: but I desire fruit that
may abound to your account.
18 But I have all, and abound: I am full, having received of Epaphroditus the things *which were sent*
from you, an odour of a sweet smell, a sacrifice acceptable, wellpleasing to God.
19 But my God shall supply all your need according
to his riches in glory by Christ Jesus.
20 Now unto God and our Father *be* glory for ever
and ever. Amen.
21 Salute every saint in Christ Jesus. The brethren
which are with me greet you.
22 All the saints salute you, chiefly they that are of
Caesar's household.
23 The grace of our Lord Jesus Christ *be* with you
all. Amen.

NEW LIVING TRANSLATION

for all he has done. 7 Then you will experience God's
peace, which exceeds anything we can understand.
His peace will guard your hearts and minds as you
live in Christ Jesus.
8 And now, dear brothers and sisters, one final
thing. Fix your thoughts on what is true, and honorable, and right, and pure, and lovely, and admirable.
Think about things that are excellent and worthy of
praise. 9 Keep putting into practice all you learned
and received from me—everything you heard from
me and saw me doing. Then the God of peace will be
with you.

Paul's Thanks for Their Gifts

10 How I praise the Lord that you are concerned about
me again. I know you have always been concerned for
me, but you didn't have the chance to help me. 11 Not
that I was ever in need, for I have learned how to be
content with whatever I have. 12 I know how to live on
almost nothing or with everything. I have learned the
secret of living in every situation, whether it is with
a full stomach or empty, with plenty or little. 13 For I
can do everything through Christ,* who gives me
strength. 14 Even so, you have done well to share with
me in my present difficulty.
15 As you know, you Philippians were the only ones
who gave me financial help when I first brought you
the Good News and then traveled on from Macedonia. No other church did this. 16 Even when I was in
Thessalonica you sent help more than once. 17 I don't
say this because I want a gift from you. Rather, I want
you to receive a reward for your kindness.
18 At the moment I have all I need—and more! I am
generously supplied with the gifts you sent me with
Epaphroditus. They are a sweet-smelling sacrifice
that is acceptable and pleasing to God. 19 And this
same God who takes care of me will supply all your
needs from his glorious riches, which have been
given to us in Christ Jesus.
20 Now all glory to God our Father forever and ever!
Amen.

Paul's Final Greetings

21 Give my greetings to each of God's holy people—all
who belong to Christ Jesus. The brothers who are
with me send you their greetings. 22 And all the rest of
God's people send you greetings, too, especially those
in Caesar's household.
23 May the grace of the Lord Jesus Christ be with
your spirit.

4:13 Greek *through the one.*

Colossians

KING JAMES VERSION

1 [1]Paul, an apostle of Jesus Christ by the will of
God, and Timotheus *our* brother,
[2]To the saints and faithful brethren in Christ
which are at Colosse: Grace *be* unto you, and peace,
from God our Father and the Lord Jesus Christ.

[3]We give thanks to God and the Father of our Lord
Jesus Christ, praying always for you,
[4]Since we heard of your faith in Christ Jesus, and
of the love *which ye have* to all the saints,
[5]For the hope which is laid up for you in heaven,
whereof ye heard before in the word of the truth of
the gospel;
[6]Which is come unto you, as *it is* in all the world;
and bringeth forth fruit, as *it doth* also in you, since
the day ye heard *of it,* and knew the grace of God in
truth:
[7]As ye also learned of Epaphras our dear
fellowservant, who is for you a faithful minister of
Christ;
[8]Who also declared unto us your love in the Spirit.
[9]For this cause we also, since the day we heard *it,*
do not cease to pray for you, and to desire that ye
might be filled with the knowledge of his will in all
wisdom and spiritual understanding;
[10]That ye might walk worthy of the Lord unto all
pleasing, being fruitful in every good work, and increasing in the knowledge of God;
[11]Strengthened with all might, according to his
glorious power, unto all patience and longsuffering
with joyfulness;
[12]Giving thanks unto the Father, which hath made
us meet to be partakers of the inheritance of the
saints in light:
[13]Who hath delivered us from the power of darkness, and hath translated *us* into the kingdom of his
dear Son:

NEW LIVING TRANSLATION

Greetings from Paul

1 This letter is from Paul, chosen by the will of
God to be an apostle of Christ Jesus, and from
our brother Timothy.
[2]We are writing to God's holy people in the city
of Colosse, who are faithful brothers and sisters* in
Christ.
May God our Father give you grace and peace.

Paul's Thanksgiving and Prayer

[3]We always pray for you, and we give thanks to God,
the Father of our Lord Jesus Christ. [4]For we have
heard of your faith in Christ Jesus and your love for
all of God's people, [5]which come from your confident hope of what God has reserved for you in
heaven. You have had this expectation ever since you
first heard the truth of the Good News.
[6]This same Good News that came to you is going
out all over the world. It is bearing fruit everywhere
by changing lives, just as it changed your lives from
the day you first heard and understood the truth
about God's wonderful grace.
[7]You learned about the Good News from Epaphras, our beloved co-worker. He is Christ's faithful
servant, and he is helping us on your behalf.* [8]He has
told us about the love for others that the Holy Spirit
has given you.
[9]So we have not stopped praying for you since we
first heard about you. We ask God to give you complete knowledge of his will and to give you spiritual
wisdom and understanding. [10]Then the way you live
will always honor and please the Lord, and your lives
will produce every kind of good fruit. All the while,
you will grow as you learn to know God better and
better.
[11]We also pray that you will be strengthened with
all his glorious power so you will have all the endurance and patience you need. May you be filled with
joy,* [12]always thanking the Father. He has enabled
you to share in the inheritance that belongs to his
people, who live in the light. [13]For he has rescued us
from the kingdom of darkness and transferred us

1:2 Greek *faithful brothers.* **1:7** Or *he is ministering on your behalf;* some manuscripts read *he is ministering on our behalf.* **1:11** Or *all the patience and endurance you need with joy.*

KING JAMES VERSION

14 In whom we have redemption through his
blood, *even* the forgiveness of sins:

15 Who is the image of the invisible God, the firstborn of every creature:

16 For by him were all things created, that are in
heaven, and that are in earth, visible and invisible,
whether *they be* thrones, or dominions, or principalities, or powers: all things were created by him, and
for him:

17 And he is before all things, and by him all things
consist.

18 And he is the head of the body, the church: who
is the beginning, the firstborn from the dead; that
in all *things* he might have the preeminence.

19 For it pleased *the Father* that in him should
all fulness dwell;

20 And, having made peace through the blood of
his cross, by him to reconcile all things unto himself;
by him, *I say,* whether *they be* things in earth, or
things in heaven.

21 And you, that were sometime alienated and enemies in *your* mind by wicked works, yet now hath he
reconciled

22 In the body of his flesh through death, to present
you holy and unblameable and unreproveable in his
sight:

23 If ye continue in the faith grounded and settled,
and *be* not moved away from the hope of the gospel,
which ye have heard, *and* which was preached to
every creature which is under heaven; whereof I Paul
am made a minister;

24 Who now rejoice in my sufferings for you,
and fill up that which is behind of the afflictions
of Christ in my flesh for his body's sake, which is
the church:

25 Whereof I am made a minister, according to the
dispensation of God which is given to me for you, to
fulfil the word of God;

26 *Even* the mystery which hath been hid from ages
and from generations, but now is made manifest to
his saints:

27 To whom God would make known what *is* the
riches of the glory of this mystery among the
Gentiles; which is Christ in you, the hope of glory:

NEW LIVING TRANSLATION

into the Kingdom of his dear Son, 14 who purchased
our freedom* and forgave our sins.

Christ Is Supreme

15 Christ is the visible image of the invisible God.
He existed before anything was created and
is supreme over all creation,*
16 for through him God created everything
in the heavenly realms and on earth.
He made the things we can see
and the things we can't see—
such as thrones, kingdoms, rulers, and authorities
in the unseen world.
Everything was created through him
and for him.
17 He existed before anything else,
and he holds all creation together.
18 Christ is also the head of the church,
which is his body.
He is the beginning,
supreme over all who rise from the dead.*
So he is first in everything.
19 For God in all his fullness
was pleased to live in Christ,
20 and through him God reconciled
everything to himself.
He made peace with everything in heaven
and on earth
by means of Christ's blood on the cross.

21 This includes you who were once far away from
God. You were his enemies, separated from him by
your evil thoughts and actions. 22 Yet now he has reconciled you to himself through the death of Christ in
his physical body. As a result, he has brought you into
his own presence, and you are holy and blameless as
you stand before him without a single fault.

23 But you must continue to believe this truth and
stand firmly in it. Don't drift away from the assurance you received when you heard the Good News.
The Good News has been preached all over the
world, and I, Paul, have been appointed as God's servant to proclaim it.

Paul's Work for the Church

24 I am glad when I suffer for you in my body, for I am
participating in the sufferings of Christ that continue for his body, the church. 25 God has given me
the responsibility of serving his church by proclaiming his entire message to you. 26 This message was
kept secret for centuries and generations past, but
now it has been revealed to God's people. 27 For God
wanted them to know that the riches and glory of
Christ are for you Gentiles, too. And this is the secret:
Christ lives in you. This gives you assurance of sharing his glory.

1:14 Some manuscripts add *with his blood.* **1:15** Or *He is the firstborn of all creation.* **1:18** Or *the firstborn from the dead.*

KING JAMES VERSION

28Whom we preach, warning every man, and
teaching every man in all wisdom; that we may present every man perfect in Christ Jesus:
29Whereunto I also labour, striving according to
his working, which worketh in me mightily.

2 1For I would that ye knew what great conflict I
have for you, and *for* them at Laodicea, and *for*
as many as have not seen my face in the flesh;
2That their hearts might be comforted, being knit
together in love, and unto all riches of the full assurance of understanding, to the acknowledgment of
the mystery of God, and of the Father, and of Christ;
3In whom are hid all the treasures of wisdom and
knowledge.
4And this I say, lest any man should beguile you
with enticing words.
5For though I be absent in the flesh, yet am I with
you in the spirit, joying and beholding your order,
and the stedfastness of your faith in Christ.

6As ye have therefore received Christ Jesus the
Lord, *so* walk ye in him:
7Rooted and built up in him, and stablished in the
faith, as ye have been taught, abounding therein with
thanksgiving.
8Beware lest any man spoil you through philosophy and vain deceit, after the tradition of men, after
the rudiments of the world, and not after Christ.
9For in him dwelleth all the fulness of the Godhead bodily.
10And ye are complete in him, which is the head of
all principality and power:
11In whom also ye are circumcised with the circumcision made without hands, in putting off the
body of the sins of the flesh by the circumcision of
Christ:
12Buried with him in baptism, wherein also ye are
risen with *him* through the faith of the operation of
God, who hath raised him from the dead.
13And you, being dead in your sins and the
uncircumcision of your flesh, hath he quickened together with him, having forgiven you all trespasses;
14Blotting out the handwriting of ordinances that
was against us, which was contrary to us, and took it
out of the way, nailing it to his cross;
15*And* having spoiled principalities and powers,
he made a shew of them openly, triumphing over
them in it.
16Let no man therefore judge you in meat, or in
drink, or in respect of an holyday, or of the new
moon, or of the sabbath *days:*
17Which are a shadow of things to come; but the
body *is* of Christ.

NEW LIVING TRANSLATION

28So we tell others about Christ, warning everyone
and teaching everyone with all the wisdom God has
given us. We want to present them to God, perfect*
in their relationship to Christ. 29That's why I work
and struggle so hard, depending on Christ's mighty
power that works within me.

2 I want you to know how much I have agonized
for you and for the church at Laodicea, and for
many other believers who have never met me personally. 2I want them to be encouraged and knit
together by strong ties of love. I want them to have
complete confidence that they understand God's
mysterious plan, which is Christ himself. 3In him lie
hidden all the treasures of wisdom and knowledge.
4I am telling you this so no one will deceive you
with well-crafted arguments. 5For though I am far
away from you, my heart is with you. And I rejoice
that you are living as you should and that your faith
in Christ is strong.

Freedom from Rules and New Life in Christ

6And now, just as you accepted Christ Jesus as your
Lord, you must continue to follow him. 7Let your
roots grow down into him, and let your lives be built
on him. Then your faith will grow strong in the truth
you were taught, and you will overflow with thankfulness.
8Don't let anyone capture you with empty philosophies and high-sounding nonsense that come from
human thinking and from the spiritual powers* of
this world, rather than from Christ. 9For in Christ lives
all the fullness of God in a human body.* 10So you also
are complete through your union with Christ, who is
the head over every ruler and authority.
11When you came to Christ, you were "circumcised," but not by a physical procedure. Christ performed a spiritual circumcision—the cutting away of
your sinful nature.* 12For you were buried with
Christ when you were baptized. And with him you
were raised to new life because you trusted the
mighty power of God, who raised Christ from the
dead.
13You were dead because of your sins and because
your sinful nature was not yet cut away. Then God
made you alive with Christ, for he forgave all our sins.
14He canceled the record of the charges against us
and took it away by nailing it to the cross. 15In this
way, he disarmed* the spiritual rulers and authorities. He shamed them publicly by his victory over
them on the cross.
16So don't let anyone condemn you for what you
eat or drink, or for not celebrating certain holy days
or new moon ceremonies or Sabbaths. 17For these
rules are only shadows of the reality yet to come. And

1:28 Or *mature.* **2:8** Or *the spiritual principles;* also in 2:20. **2:9** Or *in him dwells all the completeness of the Godhead bodily.* **2:11** Greek *the cutting away of the body of the flesh.* **2:15** Or *he stripped off.*

KING JAMES VERSION

18 Let no man beguile you of your reward in a voluntary humility and worshipping of angels, intrud-
ing into those things which he hath not seen, vainly
puffed up by his fleshly mind,
19 And not holding the Head, from which all the
body by joints and bands having nourishment ministered, and knit together, increaseth with the increase
of God.
20 Wherefore if ye be dead with Christ from the
rudiments of the world, why, as though living in the
world, are ye subject to ordinances,
21 (Touch not; taste not; handle not;
22 Which all are to perish with the using;) after the
commandments and doctrines of men?
23 Which things have indeed a shew of wisdom
in will worship, and humility, and neglecting of the
body; not in any honour to the satisfying of the flesh.

3 1 If ye then be risen with Christ, seek those
things which are above, where Christ sitteth on
the right hand of God.
2 Set your affection on things above, not on things
on the earth.
3 For ye are dead, and your life is hid with Christ
in God.
4 When Christ, *who is* our life, shall appear, then
shall ye also appear with him in glory.
5 Mortify therefore your members which are upon
the earth; fornication, uncleanness, inordinate affection, evil concupiscence, and covetousness, which is
idolatry:
6 For which things' sake the wrath of God cometh
on the children of disobedience:
7 In the which ye also walked some time, when ye
lived in them.
8 But now ye also put off all these; anger, wrath,
malice, blasphemy, filthy communication out of your
mouth.
9 Lie not one to another, seeing that ye have put off
the old man with his deeds;
10 And have put on the new *man*, which is renewed
in knowledge after the image of him that created
him:
11 Where there is neither Greek nor Jew, circumcision nor uncircumcision, Barbarian, Scythian, bond
nor free: but Christ *is* all, and in all.
12 Put on therefore, as the elect of God, holy and beloved, bowels of mercies, kindness, humbleness
of mind, meekness, longsuffering;
13 Forbearing one another, and forgiving one another, if any man have a quarrel against any: even as
Christ forgave you, so also *do* ye.
14 And above all these things *put on* charity, which
is the bond of perfectness.
15 And let the peace of God rule in your hearts, to
the which also ye are called in one body; and be ye
thankful.

NEW LIVING TRANSLATION

Christ himself is that reality. 18 Don't let anyone
condemn you by insisting on pious self-denial or
the worship of angels,* saying they have had visions
about these things. Their sinful minds have made
them proud, 19 and they are not connected to Christ,
the head of the body. For he holds the whole body together with its joints and ligaments, and it grows as
God nourishes it.
20 You have died with Christ, and he has set you
free from the spiritual powers of this world. So why
do you keep on following the rules of the world, such
as, 21 "Don't handle! Don't taste! Don't touch!"? 22 Such
rules are mere human teachings about things that
deteriorate as we use them. 23 These rules may seem
wise because they require strong devotion, pious
self-denial, and severe bodily discipline. But they
provide no help in conquering a person's evil desires.

Living the New Life

3 Since you have been raised to new life with
Christ, set your sights on the realities of heaven,
where Christ sits in the place of honor at God's right
hand. 2 Think about the things of heaven, not the
things of earth. 3 For you died to this life, and your real
life is hidden with Christ in God. 4 And when Christ,
who is your* life, is revealed to the whole world, you
will share in all his glory.
5 So put to death the sinful, earthly things lurking
within you. Have nothing to do with sexual immorality, impurity, lust, and evil desires. Don't be greedy,
for a greedy person is an idolater, worshiping the
things of this world. 6 Because of these sins, the anger of God is coming.* 7 You used to do these things
when your life was still part of this world. 8 But now is
the time to get rid of anger, rage, malicious behavior,
slander, and dirty language. 9 Don't lie to each other,
for you have stripped off your old sinful nature and
all its wicked deeds. 10 Put on your new nature, and be
renewed as you learn to know your Creator and
become like him. 11 In this new life, it doesn't matter
if you are a Jew or a Gentile,* circumcised or uncircumcised, barbaric, uncivilized,* slave, or free.
Christ is all that matters, and he lives in all of us.
12 Since God chose you to be the holy people he
loves, you must clothe yourselves with tenderhearted mercy, kindness, humility, gentleness, and
patience. 13 Make allowance for each other's faults,
and forgive anyone who offends you. Remember, the
Lord forgave you, so you must forgive others.
14 Above all, clothe yourselves with love, which binds
us all together in perfect harmony. 15 And let the
peace that comes from Christ rule in your hearts. For
as members of one body you are called to live in
peace. And always be thankful.

2:18 Or *or worshiping with angels.* **3:4** Some manuscripts read *our.* **3:6** Some manuscripts read *is coming on all who disobey him.* **3:11a** Greek *a Greek.* **3:11b** Greek *Barbarian, Scythian.*

KING JAMES VERSION

16 Let the word of Christ dwell in you richly in all
wisdom; teaching and admonishing one another in
psalms and hymns and spiritual songs, singing with
grace in your hearts to the Lord.
17 And whatsoever ye do in word or deed, *do* all in
the name of the Lord Jesus, giving thanks to God and
the Father by him.

18 Wives, submit yourselves unto your own husbands, as it is fit in the Lord.
19 Husbands, love *your* wives, and be not bitter
against them.
20 Children, obey *your* parents in all things: for this
is well pleasing unto the Lord.
21 Fathers, provoke not your children *to anger*, lest
they be discouraged.
22 Servants, obey in all things *your* masters according to the flesh; not with eyeservice, as menpleasers;
but in singleness of heart, fearing God:
23 And whatsoever ye do, do *it* heartily, as to the
Lord, and not unto men;
24 Knowing that of the Lord ye shall receive the reward of the inheritance: for ye serve the Lord Christ.
25 But he that doeth wrong shall receive for the
wrong which he hath done: and there is no respect of
persons.

4 1 Masters, give unto *your* servants that which is
just and equal; knowing that ye also have a
Master in heaven.

2 Continue in prayer, and watch in the same with
thanksgiving;
3 Withal praying also for us, that God would open
unto us a door of utterance, to speak the mystery of
Christ, for which I am also in bonds:
4 That I may make it manifest, as I ought to speak.
5 Walk in wisdom toward them that are without,
redeeming the time.
6 Let your speech *be* alway with grace, seasoned
with salt, that ye may know how ye ought to answer
every man.

7 All my state shall Tychicus declare unto you, *who
is* a beloved brother, and a faithful minister and
fellowservant in the Lord:
8 Whom I have sent unto you for the same purpose,
that he might know your estate, and comfort your
hearts;
9 With Onesimus, a faithful and beloved brother,
who is *one* of you. They shall make known unto you
all things which *are done* here.
10 Aristarchus my fellowprisoner saluteth you, and
Marcus, sister's son to Barnabas, (touching whom ye
received commandments: if he come unto you, receive him;)
11 And Jesus, which is called Justus, who are of the

NEW LIVING TRANSLATION

16 Let the message about Christ, in all its richness,
fill your lives. Teach and counsel each other with all
the wisdom he gives. Sing psalms and hymns and
spiritual songs to God with thankful hearts. 17 And
whatever you do or say, do it as a representative of
the Lord Jesus, giving thanks through him to God
the Father.

Instructions for Christian Households

18 Wives, submit to your husbands, as is fitting for
those who belong to the Lord.
19 Husbands, love your wives and never treat them
harshly.
20 Children, always obey your parents, for this
pleases the Lord. 21 Fathers, do not aggravate your
children, or they will become discouraged.
22 Slaves, obey your earthly masters in everything
you do. Try to please them all the time, not just when
they are watching you. Serve them sincerely because
of your reverent fear of the Lord. 23 Work willingly
at whatever you do, as though you were working for
the Lord rather than for people. 24 Remember that
the Lord will give you an inheritance as your reward,
and that the Master you are serving is Christ.* 25 But
if you do what is wrong, you will be paid back for the
wrong you have done. For God has no favorites.

4 Masters, be just and fair to your slaves. Remember that you also have a Master—in heaven.

An Encouragement for Prayer

2 Devote yourselves to prayer with an alert mind and a
thankful heart. 3 Pray for us, too, that God will give us
many opportunities to speak about his mysterious
plan concerning Christ. That is why I am here in
chains. 4 Pray that I will proclaim this message as
clearly as I should.
5 Live wisely among those who are not believers,
and make the most of every opportunity. 6 Let your
conversation be gracious and attractive* so that you
will have the right response for everyone.

Paul's Final Instructions and Greetings

7 Tychicus will give you a full report about how I am
getting along. He is a beloved brother and faithful
helper who serves with me in the Lord's work. 8 I have
sent him to you for this very purpose—to let you
know how we are doing and to encourage you. 9 I am
also sending Onesimus, a faithful and beloved
brother, one of your own people. He and Tychicus
will tell you everything that's happening here.
10 Aristarchus, who is in prison with me, sends you
his greetings, and so does Mark, Barnabas's cousin.
As you were instructed before, make Mark welcome
if he comes your way. 11 Jesus (the one we call Justus)
also sends his greetings. These are the only Jewish

3:24 Or *and serve Christ as your Master.* **4:6** Greek *and seasoned with salt.*

KING JAMES VERSION

circumcision. These only *are my* fellowworkers unto the kingdom of God, which have been a comfort unto me.

[12]Epaphras, who is *one* of you, a servant of Christ, saluteth you, always labouring fervently for you in prayers, that ye may stand perfect and complete in all the will of God.

[13]For I bear him record, that he hath a great zeal for you, and them *that are* in Laodicea and them in Hierapolis.

[14]Luke, the beloved physician, and Demas, greet you.

[15]Salute the brethren which are in Laodicea, and Nymphas, and the church which is in his house.

[16]And when this epistle is read among you, cause that it be read also in the church of the Laodiceans; and that ye likewise read the *epistle* from Laodicea.

[17]And say to Archippus, Take heed to the ministry which thou hast received in the Lord, that thou fulfil it.

[18]The salutation by the hand of me Paul. Remember my bonds. Grace *be* with you. Amen.

NEW LIVING TRANSLATION

believers among my co-workers; they are working with me here for the Kingdom of God. And what a comfort they have been!

[12]Epaphras, a member of your own fellowship and a servant of Christ Jesus, sends you his greetings. He always prays earnestly for you, asking God to make you strong and perfect, fully confident that you are following the whole will of God. [13]I can assure you that he prays hard for you and also for the believers in Laodicea and Hierapolis.

[14]Luke, the beloved doctor, sends his greetings, and so does Demas. [15]Please give my greetings to our brothers and sisters* at Laodicea, and to Nympha and the church that meets in her house.

[16]After you have read this letter, pass it on to the church at Laodicea so they can read it, too. And you should read the letter I wrote to them.

[17]And say to Archippus, "Be sure to carry out the ministry the Lord gave you."

[18]HERE IS MY GREETING IN MY OWN HANDWRITING—PAUL.

Remember my chains.
May God's grace be with you.

4:15 Greek *brothers.*

1 Thessalonians

KING JAMES VERSION

1 1Paul, and Silvanus, and Timotheus, unto the
church of the Thessalonians *which is* in God the
Father and *in* the Lord Jesus Christ: Grace *be* unto
you, and peace, from God our Father, and the Lord
Jesus Christ.

2We give thanks to God always for you all, making
mention of you in our prayers;
3Remembering without ceasing your work of
faith, and labour of love, and patience of hope in our
Lord Jesus Christ, in the sight of God and our Father;
4Knowing, brethren beloved, your election of God.
5For our gospel came not unto you in word only,
but also in power, and in the Holy Ghost, and in much
assurance; as ye know what manner of men we were
among you for your sake.
6And ye became followers of us, and of the Lord,
having received the word in much affliction, with joy
of the Holy Ghost:
7So that ye were ensamples to all that believe in
Macedonia and Achaia.
8For from you sounded out the word of the Lord
not only in Macedonia and Achaia, but also in every
place your faith to God-ward is spread abroad; so
that we need not to speak any thing.
9For they themselves shew of us what manner of
entering in we had unto you, and how ye turned to
God from idols to serve the living and true God;
10And to wait for his Son from heaven, whom he
raised from the dead, *even* Jesus, which delivered us
from the wrath to come.

2 1For yourselves, brethren, know our entrance in
unto you, that it was not in vain:
2But even after that we had suffered before, and
were shamefully entreated, as ye know, at Philippi,

NEW LIVING TRANSLATION

Greetings from Paul

1 This letter is from Paul, Silas,* and Timothy.
We are writing to the church in Thessalonica, to
you who belong to God the Father and the Lord Jesus
Christ.
May God give you grace and peace.

The Faith of the Thessalonian Believers

2We always thank God for all of you and pray for you
constantly. 3As we pray to our God and Father about
you, we think of your faithful work, your loving
deeds, and the enduring hope you have because of
our Lord Jesus Christ.
4We know, dear brothers and sisters,* that God
loves you and has chosen you to be his own people.
5For when we brought you the Good News, it was not
only with words but also with power, for the Holy
Spirit gave you full assurance* that what we said was
true. And you know of our concern for you from the
way we lived when we were with you. 6So you received the message with joy from the Holy Spirit in
spite of the severe suffering it brought you. In this
way, you imitated both us and the Lord. 7As a result,
you have become an example to all the believers in
Greece—throughout both Macedonia and Achaia.*
8And now the word of the Lord is ringing out from
you to people everywhere, even beyond Macedonia
and Achaia, for wherever we go we find people telling us about your faith in God. We don't need to tell
them about it, 9for they keep talking about the wonderful welcome you gave us and how you turned
away from idols to serve the living and true God.
10And they speak of how you are looking forward to
the coming of God's Son from heaven—Jesus, whom
God raised from the dead. He is the one who has rescued us from the terrors of the coming judgment.

Paul Remembers His Visit

2 You yourselves know, dear brothers and sisters,* that our visit to you was not a failure. 2You
know how badly we had been treated at Philippi just

1:1 Greek *Silvanus,* the Greek form of the name. **1:4** Greek *brothers.*
1:5 Or *with the power of the Holy Spirit, so you can have full assurance.*
1:7 *Macedonia* and *Achaia* were the northern and southern regions of Greece. **2:1** Greek *brothers;* also in 2:9, 14, 17.

KING JAMES VERSION

we were bold in our God to speak unto you the gospel of God with much contention.

3For our exhortation *was* not of deceit, nor of uncleanness, nor in guile:

4But as we were allowed of God to be put in trust with the gospel, even so we speak; not as pleasing men, but God, which trieth our hearts.

5For neither at any time used we flattering words, as ye know, nor a cloak of covetousness; God *is* witness:

6Nor of men sought we glory, neither of you, nor *yet* of others, when we might have been burdensome, as the apostles of Christ.

7But we were gentle among you, even as a nurse cherisheth her children:

8So being affectionately desirous of you, we were willing to have imparted unto you, not the gospel of God only, but also our own souls, because ye were dear unto us.

9For ye remember, brethren, our labour and travail: for labouring night and day, because we would not be chargeable unto any of you, we preached unto you the gospel of God.

10Ye *are* witnesses, and God *also,* how holily and justly and unblameably we behaved ourselves among you that believe:

11As ye know how we exhorted and comforted and charged every one of you, as a father *doth* his children,

12That ye would walk worthy of God, who hath called you unto his kingdom and glory.

13For this cause also thank we God without ceasing, because, when ye received the word of God which ye heard of us, ye received *it* not *as* the word of men, but as it is in truth, the word of God, which effectually worketh also in you that believe.

14For ye, brethren, became followers of the churches of God which in Judaea are in Christ Jesus: for ye also have suffered like things of your own countrymen, even as they *have* of the Jews:

15Who both killed the Lord Jesus, and their own prophets, and have persecuted us; and they please not God, and are contrary to all men:

16Forbidding us to speak to the Gentiles that they might be saved, to fill up their sins alway: for the wrath is come upon them to the uttermost.

17But we, brethren, being taken from you for a short time in presence, not in heart, endeavoured the more abundantly to see your face with great desire.

18Wherefore we would have come unto you, even I Paul, once and again; but Satan hindered us.

NEW LIVING TRANSLATION

before we came to you and how much we suffered
there. Yet our God gave us the courage to declare his
Good News to you boldly, in spite of great opposition.
3So you can see we were not preaching with any deceit or impure motives or trickery.

4For we speak as messengers approved by God to
be entrusted with the Good News. Our purpose is to
please God, not people. He alone examines the motives of our hearts. 5Never once did we try to win you
with flattery, as you well know. And God is our witness that we were not pretending to be your friends
just to get your money! 6As for human praise, we have
never sought it from you or anyone else.

7As apostles of Christ we certainly had a right to
make some demands of you, but instead we were like
children* among you. Or we were like a mother feeding and caring for her own children. 8We loved you
so much that we shared with you not only God's
Good News but our own lives, too.

9Don't you remember, dear brothers and sisters,
how hard we worked among you? Night and day we
toiled to earn a living so that we would not be a burden to any of you as we preached God's Good News
to you. 10You yourselves are our witnesses—and so is
God—that we were devout and honest and faultless
toward all of you believers. 11And you know that we
treated each of you as a father treats his own children. 12We pleaded with you, encouraged you, and
urged you to live your lives in a way that God would
consider worthy. For he called you to share in his
Kingdom and glory.

13Therefore, we never stop thanking God that
when you received his message from us, you didn't
think of our words as mere human ideas. You accepted what we said as the very word of God—which,
of course, it is. And this word continues to work in
you who believe.

14And then, dear brothers and sisters, you suffered
persecution from your own countrymen. In this way,
you imitated the believers in God's churches in Judea
who, because of their belief in Christ Jesus, suffered
from their own people, the Jews. 15For some of the
Jews killed the prophets, and some even killed the
Lord Jesus. Now they have persecuted us, too. They
fail to please God and work against all humanity 16as
they try to keep us from preaching the Good News of
salvation to the Gentiles. By doing this, they continue
to pile up their sins. But the anger of God has caught
up with them at last.

Timothy's Good Report about the Church

17Dear brothers and sisters, after we were separated
from you for a little while (though our hearts never
left you), we tried very hard to come back because of
our intense longing to see you again. 18We wanted
very much to come to you, and I, Paul, tried again and

2:7 Some manuscripts read *we were gentle.*

KING JAMES VERSION

19For what *is* our hope, or joy, or crown of rejoicing? *Are* not even ye in the presence of our Lord Jesus
Christ at his coming?
20For ye are our glory and joy.

3 1Wherefore when we could no longer forbear,
we thought it good to be left at Athens alone;
2And sent Timotheus, our brother, and minister
of God, and our fellowlabourer in the gospel of
Christ, to establish you, and to comfort you concerning your faith:
3That no man should be moved by these afflictions:
for yourselves know that we are appointed thereunto.
4For verily, when we were with you, we told you
before that we should suffer tribulation; even as it
came to pass, and ye know.
5For this cause, when I could no longer forbear, I
sent to know your faith, lest by some means the
tempter have tempted you, and our labour be in vain.
6But now when Timotheus came from you unto
us, and brought us good tidings of your faith and
charity, and that ye have good remembrance of us always, desiring greatly to see us, as we also *to see* you:
7Therefore, brethren, we were comforted over you
in all our affliction and distress by your faith:
8For now we live, if ye stand fast in the Lord.
9For what thanks can we render to God again for
you, for all the joy wherewith we joy for your sakes
before our God;
10Night and day praying exceedingly that we
might see your face, and might perfect that which
is lacking in your faith?
11Now God himself and our Father, and our Lord
Jesus Christ, direct our way unto you.
12And the Lord make you to increase and abound
in love one toward another, and toward all *men,* even
as we *do* toward you:
13To the end he may stablish your hearts unblameable in holiness before God, even our Father, at the
coming of our Lord Jesus Christ with all his saints.

4 1Furthermore then we beseech you, brethren,
and exhort *you* by the Lord Jesus, that as ye
have received of us how ye ought to walk and to
please God, *so* ye would abound more and more.
2For ye know what commandments we gave you
by the Lord Jesus.
3For this is the will of God, *even* your sanctification, that ye should abstain from fornication:
4That every one of you should know how to possess his vessel in sanctification and honour;
5Not in the lust of concupiscence, even as the
Gentiles which know not God:
6That no *man* go beyond and defraud his brother
in *any* matter: because that the Lord *is* the avenger of
all such, as we also have forewarned you and testified.

NEW LIVING TRANSLATION

again, but Satan prevented us. 19After all, what gives
us hope and joy, and what will be our proud reward
and crown as we stand before our Lord Jesus when he
returns? It is you! 20Yes, you are our pride and joy.

3 Finally, when we could stand it no longer, we
decided to stay alone in Athens, 2and we sent
Timothy to visit you. He is our brother and God's co-
worker* in proclaiming the Good News of Christ. We
sent him to strengthen you, to encourage you in your
faith, 3and to keep you from being shaken by the
troubles you were going through. But you know that
we are destined for such troubles. 4Even while we
were with you, we warned you that troubles would
soon come—and they did, as you well know. 5That is
why, when I could bear it no longer, I sent Timothy to
find out whether your faith was still strong. I was
afraid that the tempter had gotten the best of you
and that our work had been useless.
6But now Timothy has just returned, bringing us
good news about your faith and love. He reports that
you always remember our visit with joy and that you
want to see us as much as we want to see you. 7So we
have been greatly encouraged in the midst of our
troubles and suffering, dear brothers and sisters,*
because you have remained strong in your faith. 8It
gives us new life to know that you are standing firm
in the Lord.
9How we thank God for you! Because of you we
have great joy as we enter God's presence. 10Night
and day we pray earnestly for you, asking God to let
us see you again to fill the gaps in your faith.
11May God our Father and our Lord Jesus bring us
to you very soon. 12And may the Lord make your love
for one another and for all people grow and overflow,
just as our love for you overflows. 13May he, as a result, make your hearts strong, blameless, and holy as
you stand before God our Father when our Lord
Jesus comes again with all his holy people. Amen.

Live to Please God

4 Finally, dear brothers and sisters,* we urge you
in the name of the Lord Jesus to live in a way
that pleases God, as we have taught you. You live this
way already, and we encourage you to do so even
more. 2For you remember what we taught you by the
authority of the Lord Jesus.
3God's will is for you to be holy, so stay away from
all sexual sin. 4Then each of you will control his own
body* and live in holiness and honor—5not in lustful
passion like the pagans who do not know God and
his ways. 6Never harm or cheat a Christian brother
in this matter by violating his wife,* for the Lord
avenges all such sins, as we have solemnly warned

3:2 Other manuscripts read *and God's servant;* still others read *and a co-worker,* or *and a servant and co-worker for God,* or *and God's servant and our co-worker.* **3:7** Greek *brothers.* **4:1** Greek *brothers;* also in 4:10, 13. **4:4** Or *will know how to take a wife for himself;* or *will learn to live with his own wife;* Greek reads *will know how to possess his own vessel.* **4:6** Greek *Never harm or cheat a brother in this matter.*

KING JAMES VERSION

7 For God hath not called us unto uncleanness, but unto holiness.

8 He therefore that despiseth, despiseth not man, but God, who hath also given unto us his holy Spirit.

9 But as touching brotherly love ye need not that I write unto you: for ye yourselves are taught of God to love one another.

10 And indeed ye do it toward all the brethren which are in all Macedonia: but we beseech you, brethren, that ye increase more and more;

11 And that ye study to be quiet, and to do your own business, and to work with your own hands, as we commanded you;

12 That ye may walk honestly toward them that are without, and *that* ye may have lack of nothing.

13 But I would not have you to be ignorant, brethren, concerning them which are asleep, that ye sorrow not, even as others which have no hope.

14 For if we believe that Jesus died and rose again, even so them also which sleep in Jesus will God bring with him.

15 For this we say unto you by the word of the Lord, that we which are alive *and* remain unto the coming of the Lord shall not prevent them which are asleep.

16 For the Lord himself shall descend from heaven with a shout, with the voice of the archangel, and with the trump of God: and the dead in Christ shall rise first:

17 Then we which are alive *and* remain shall be caught up together with them in the clouds, to meet the Lord in the air: and so shall we ever be with the Lord.

18 Wherefore comfort one another with these words.

5 1 But of the times and the seasons, brethren, ye have no need that I write unto you.

2 For yourselves know perfectly that the day of the Lord so cometh as a thief in the night.

3 For when they shall say, Peace and safety; then sudden destruction cometh upon them, as travail upon a woman with child; and they shall not escape.

4 But ye, brethren, are not in darkness, that that day should overtake you as a thief.

5 Ye are all the children of light, and the children of the day: we are not of the night, nor of darkness.

6 Therefore let us not sleep, as *do* others; but let us watch and be sober.

7 For they that sleep sleep in the night; and they that be drunken are drunken in the night.

8 But let us, who are of the day, be sober, putting on

NEW LIVING TRANSLATION

you before. 7 God has called us to live holy lives, not
impure lives. 8 Therefore, anyone who refuses to live
by these rules is not disobeying human teaching but
is rejecting God, who gives his Holy Spirit to you.
9 But we don't need to write to you about the importance of loving each other,* for God himself has
taught you to love one another. 10 Indeed, you already
show your love for all the believers* throughout
Macedonia. Even so, dear brothers and sisters, we
urge you to love them even more.
11 Make it your goal to live a quiet life, minding
your own business and working with your hands, just
as we instructed you before. 12 Then people who are
not Christians will respect the way you live, and you
will not need to depend on others.

The Hope of the Resurrection

13 And now, dear brothers and sisters, we want you to
know what will happen to the believers who have
died* so you will not grieve like people who have no
hope. 14 For since we believe that Jesus died and was
raised to life again, we also believe that when Jesus
returns, God will bring back with him the believers
who have died.
15 We tell you this directly from the Lord: We who
are still living when the Lord returns will not meet
him ahead of those who have died.* 16 For the Lord
himself will come down from heaven with a commanding shout, with the voice of the archangel, and
with the trumpet call of God. First, the Christians
who have died* will rise from their graves. 17 Then,
together with them, we who are still alive and remain
on the earth will be caught up in the clouds to meet
the Lord in the air. Then we will be with the Lord forever. 18 So encourage each other with these words.

5 Now concerning how and when all this will happen, dear brothers and sisters,* we don't really
need to write you. 2 For you know quite well that the
day of the Lord's return will come unexpectedly, like
a thief in the night. 3 When people are saying, "Everything is peaceful and secure," then disaster will fall
on them as suddenly as a pregnant woman's labor
pains begin. And there will be no escape.
4 But you aren't in the dark about these things, dear
brothers and sisters, and you won't be surprised
when the day of the Lord comes like a thief.* 5 For
you are all children of the light and of the day; we
don't belong to darkness and night. 6 So be on your
guard, not asleep like the others. Stay alert and be
clearheaded. 7 Night is the time when people sleep
and drinkers get drunk. 8 But let us who live in the
light be clearheaded, protected by the armor of faith

4:9 Greek *about brotherly love.* **4:10** Greek *the brothers.* **4:13** Greek *those who have fallen asleep;* also in 4:14. **4:15** Greek *those who have fallen asleep.* **4:16** Greek *the dead in Christ.* **5:1** Greek *brothers;* also in 5:4, 12, 14, 25, 26, 27. **5:4** Some manuscripts read *comes upon you as if you were thieves.*

KING JAMES VERSION

the breastplate of faith and love; and for an helmet,
the hope of salvation.
9 For God hath not appointed us to wrath, but to
obtain salvation by our Lord Jesus Christ,
10 Who died for us, that, whether we wake or sleep,
we should live together with him.
11 Wherefore comfort yourselves together, and
edify one another, even as also ye do.

12 And we beseech you, brethren, to know them
which labour among you, and are over you in the
Lord, and admonish you;
13 And to esteem them very highly in love for their
work's sake. *And* be at peace among yourselves.
14 Now we exhort you, brethren, warn them that
are unruly, comfort the feebleminded, support the
weak, be patient toward all *men.*
15 See that none render evil for evil unto any *man;*
but ever follow that which is good, both among yourselves, and to all *men.*
16 Rejoice evermore.
17 Pray without ceasing.
18 In every thing give thanks: for this is the will of
God in Christ Jesus concerning you.
19 Quench not the Spirit.
20 Despise not prophesyings.
21 Prove all things; hold fast that which is good.
22 Abstain from all appearance of evil.

23 And the very God of peace sanctify you wholly;
and *I pray God* your whole spirit and soul and body
be preserved blameless unto the coming of our Lord
Jesus Christ.
24 Faithful *is* he that calleth you, who also will do *it.*
25 Brethren, pray for us.
26 Greet all the brethren with an holy kiss.
27 I charge you by the Lord that this epistle be read
unto all the holy brethren.
28 The grace of our Lord Jesus Christ *be* with you.
Amen.

NEW LIVING TRANSLATION

and love, and wearing as our helmet the confidence
of our salvation.
9 For God chose to save us through our Lord Jesus
Christ, not to pour out his anger on us. 10 Christ died
for us so that, whether we are dead or alive when he
returns, we can live with him forever. 11 So encourage
each other and build each other up, just as you are
already doing.

Paul's Final Advice

12 Dear brothers and sisters, honor those who are your
leaders in the Lord's work. They work hard among
you and give you spiritual guidance. 13 Show them
great respect and wholehearted love because of their
work. And live peacefully with each other.
14 Brothers and sisters, we urge you to warn those
who are lazy. Encourage those who are timid. Take
tender care of those who are weak. Be patient with
everyone.
15 See that no one pays back evil for evil, but always
try to do good to each other and to all people.
16 Always be joyful. 17 Never stop praying. 18 Be
thankful in all circumstances, for this is God's will for
you who belong to Christ Jesus.
19 Do not stifle the Holy Spirit. 20 Do not scoff at
prophecies, 21 but test everything that is said. Hold
on to what is good. 22 Stay away from every kind
of evil.

Paul's Final Greetings

23 Now may the God of peace make you holy in every
way, and may your whole spirit and soul and body be
kept blameless until our Lord Jesus Christ comes
again. 24 God will make this happen, for he who calls
you is faithful.
25 Dear brothers and sisters, pray for us.
26 Greet all the brothers and sisters with Christian
love.*
27 I command you in the name of the Lord to read
this letter to all the brothers and sisters.
28 May the grace of our Lord Jesus Christ be with
you.

5:26 Greek *with a holy kiss.*

2 Thessalonians

KING JAMES VERSION

1 1 Paul, and Silvanus, and Timotheus, unto the church of the Thessalonians in God our Father and the Lord Jesus Christ:

2 Grace unto you, and peace, from God our Father and the Lord Jesus Christ.

3 We are bound to thank God always for you, brethren, as it is meet, because that your faith groweth exceedingly, and the charity of every one of you all toward each other aboundeth;

4 So that we ourselves glory in you in the churches of God for your patience and faith in all your persecutions and tribulations that ye endure:

5 *Which is* a manifest token of the righteous judgment of God, that ye may be counted worthy of the kingdom of God, for which ye also suffer:

6 Seeing *it is* a righteous thing with God to recompense tribulation to them that trouble you;

7 And to you who are troubled rest with us, when the Lord Jesus shall be revealed from heaven with his mighty angels,

8 In flaming fire taking vengeance on them that know not God, and that obey not the gospel of our Lord Jesus Christ:

9 Who shall be punished with everlasting destruction from the presence of the Lord, and from the glory of his power;

10 When he shall come to be glorified in his saints, and to be admired in all them that believe (because our testimony among you was believed) in that day.

11 Wherefore also we pray always for you, that our God would count you worthy of *this* calling, and fulfil all the good pleasure of *his* goodness, and the work of faith with power:

12 That the name of our Lord Jesus Christ may be glorified in you, and ye in him, according to the grace of our God and the Lord Jesus Christ.

NEW LIVING TRANSLATION

Greetings from Paul

1 This letter is from Paul, Silas,* and Timothy.
We are writing to the church in Thessalonica,
to you who belong to God our Father and the Lord
Jesus Christ.

2 May God our Father* and the Lord Jesus Christ
give you grace and peace.

Encouragement during Persecution

3 Dear brothers and sisters,* we can't help but thank
God for you, because your faith is flourishing and
your love for one another is growing. 4 We proudly
tell God's other churches about your endurance and
faithfulness in all the persecutions and hardships
you are suffering. 5 And God will use this persecution
to show his justice and to make you worthy of his
Kingdom, for which you are suffering. 6 In his justice
he will pay back those who persecute you.

7 And God will provide rest for you who are being
persecuted and also for us when the Lord Jesus appears from heaven. He will come with his mighty angels,
8 in flaming fire, bringing judgment on those
who don't know God and on those who refuse to
obey the Good News of our Lord Jesus. 9 They will be
punished with eternal destruction, forever separated
from the Lord and from his glorious power. 10 When
he comes on that day, he will receive glory from his
holy people—praise from all who believe. And this
includes you, for you believed what we told you
about him.

11 So we keep on praying for you, asking our God to
enable you to live a life worthy of his call. May he
give you the power to accomplish all the good things
your faith prompts you to do. 12 Then the name of
our Lord Jesus will be honored because of the way
you live, and you will be honored along with him.
This is all made possible because of the grace of our
God and Lord, Jesus Christ.*

1:1 Greek *Silvanus,* the Greek form of the name. **1:2** Some manuscripts read *God the Father.* **1:3** Greek *Brothers.* **1:12** Or *of our God and our Lord Jesus Christ.*

KING JAMES VERSION

2 1Now we beseech you, brethren, by the coming of our Lord Jesus Christ, and *by* our gathering together unto him,

2That ye be not soon shaken in mind, or be troubled, neither by spirit, nor by word, nor by letter as from us, as that the day of Christ is at hand.

3Let no man deceive you by any means: for *that day shall not come,* except there come a falling away first, and that man of sin be revealed, the son of perdition;

4Who opposeth and exalteth himself above all that is called God, or that is worshipped; so that he as God sitteth in the temple of God, shewing himself that he is God.

5Remember ye not, that, when I was yet with you, I told you these things?

6And now ye know what withholdeth that he might be revealed in his time.

7For the mystery of iniquity doth already work: only he who now letteth *will let,* until he be taken out of the way.

8And then shall that Wicked be revealed, whom the Lord shall consume with the spirit of his mouth, and shall destroy with the brightness of his coming: 9*Even him,* whose coming is after the working of Satan with all power and signs and lying wonders,

10And with all deceivableness of unrighteousness in them that perish; because they received not the love of the truth, that they might be saved.

11And for this cause God shall send them strong delusion, that they should believe a lie:

12That they all might be damned who believed not the truth, but had pleasure in unrighteousness.

13But we are bound to give thanks alway to God for you, brethren beloved of the Lord, because God hath from the beginning chosen you to salvation through sanctification of the Spirit and belief of the truth:

14Whereunto he called you by our gospel, to the obtaining of the glory of our Lord Jesus Christ.

15Therefore, brethren, stand fast, and hold the traditions which ye have been taught, whether by word, or our epistle.

16Now our Lord Jesus Christ himself, and God, even our Father, which hath loved us, and hath given *us* everlasting consolation and good hope through grace,

17Comfort your hearts, and stablish you in every good word and work.

3 1Finally, brethren, pray for us, that the word of the Lord may have *free* course, and be glorified, even as *it is* with you:

NEW LIVING TRANSLATION

Events prior to the Lord's Second Coming

2 Now, dear brothers and sisters,* let us clarify some things about the coming of our Lord Jesus Christ and how we will be gathered to meet him. 2Don't be so easily shaken or alarmed by those who say that the day of the Lord has already begun. Don't believe them, even if they claim to have had a spiritual vision, a revelation, or a letter supposedly from us. 3Don't be fooled by what they say. For that day will not come until there is a great rebellion against God and the man of lawlessness* is revealed—the one who brings destruction.* 4He will exalt himself and defy everything that people call god and every object of worship. He will even sit in the temple of God, claiming that he himself is God.

5Don't you remember that I told you about all this when I was with you? 6And you know what is holding him back, for he can be revealed only when his time comes. 7For this lawlessness is already at work secretly, and it will remain secret until the one who is holding it back steps out of the way. 8Then the man of lawlessness will be revealed, but the Lord Jesus will kill him with the breath of his mouth and destroy him by the splendor of his coming.

9This man will come to do the work of Satan with counterfeit power and signs and miracles. 10He will use every kind of evil deception to fool those on their way to destruction, because they refuse to love and accept the truth that would save them. 11So God will cause them to be greatly deceived, and they will believe these lies. 12Then they will be condemned for enjoying evil rather than believing the truth.

Believers Should Stand Firm

13As for us, we can't help but thank God for you, dear brothers and sisters loved by the Lord. We are always thankful that God chose you to be among the first* to experience salvation—a salvation that came through the Spirit who makes you holy and through your belief in the truth. 14He called you to salvation when we told you the Good News; now you can share in the glory of our Lord Jesus Christ.

15With all these things in mind, dear brothers and sisters, stand firm and keep a strong grip on the teaching we passed on to you both in person and by letter.

16Now may our Lord Jesus Christ himself and God our Father, who loved us and by his grace gave us eternal comfort and a wonderful hope, 17comfort you and strengthen you in every good thing you do and say.

Paul's Request for Prayer

3 Finally, dear brothers and sisters,* we ask you to pray for us. Pray that the Lord's message will spread rapidly and be honored wherever it goes, just

2:1 Greek *brothers;* also in 2:13, 15. **2:3a** Some manuscripts read *the man of sin.* **2:3b** Greek *the son of destruction.* **2:13** Some manuscripts read *chose you from the very beginning.* **3:1** Greek *brothers;* also in 3:6, 13.

KING JAMES VERSION

2And that we may be delivered from unreasonable
and wicked men: for all *men* have not faith.
3But the Lord is faithful, who shall stablish you,
and keep *you* from evil.
4And we have confidence in the Lord touching
you, that ye both do and will do the things which we
command you.
5And the Lord direct your hearts into the love of
God, and into the patient waiting for Christ.

6Now we command you, brethren, in the name of
our Lord Jesus Christ, that ye withdraw yourselves
from every brother that walketh disorderly, and not
after the tradition which he received of us.
7For yourselves know how ye ought to follow us:
for we behaved not ourselves disorderly among you;
8Neither did we eat any man's bread for nought;
but wrought with labour and travail night and day,
that we might not be chargeable to any of you:
9Not because we have not power, but to make
ourselves an ensample unto you to follow us.
10For even when we were with you, this we commanded
you, that if any would not work, neither
should he eat.
11For we hear that there are some which walk
among you disorderly, working not at all, but are
busybodies.
12Now them that are such we command and exhort
by our Lord Jesus Christ, that with quietness
they work, and eat their own bread.
13But ye, brethren, be not weary in well doing.
14And if any man obey not our word by this epistle,
note that man, and have no company with him, that
he may be ashamed.
15Yet count *him* not as an enemy, but admonish
him as a brother.
16Now the Lord of peace himself give you peace
always by all means. The Lord *be* with you all.
17The salutation of Paul with mine own hand,
which is the token in every epistle: so I write.
18The grace of our Lord Jesus Christ *be* with you
all. Amen.

NEW LIVING TRANSLATION

as when it came to you. 2Pray, too, that we will be
rescued from wicked and evil people, for not everyone
is a believer. 3But the Lord is faithful; he will
strengthen you and guard you from the evil one.*
4And we are confident in the Lord that you are doing
and will continue to do the things we commanded
you. 5May the Lord lead your hearts into a full understanding
and expression of the love of God and the
patient endurance that comes from Christ.

An Exhortation to Proper Living

6And now, dear brothers and sisters, we give you this
command in the name of our Lord Jesus Christ: Stay
away from all believers* who live idle lives and don't
follow the tradition they received* from us. 7For you
know that you ought to imitate us. We were not idle
when we were with you. 8We never accepted food
from anyone without paying for it. We worked hard
day and night so we would not be a burden to any of
you. 9We certainly had the right to ask you to feed us,
but we wanted to give you an example to follow.
10Even while we were with you, we gave you this command:
"Those unwilling to work will not get to eat."
11Yet we hear that some of you are living idle lives,
refusing to work and meddling in other people's
business. 12We command such people and urge
them in the name of the Lord Jesus Christ to settle
down and work to earn their own living. 13As for the
rest of you, dear brothers and sisters, never get tired
of doing good.
14Take note of those who refuse to obey what we
say in this letter. Stay away from them so they will be
ashamed. 15Don't think of them as enemies, but
warn them as you would a brother or sister.*

Paul's Final Greetings

16Now may the Lord of peace himself give you his
peace at all times and in every situation. The Lord be
with you all.
17HERE IS MY GREETING IN MY OWN HANDWRITING—
PAUL. I DO THIS IN ALL MY LETTERS TO PROVE THEY ARE
FROM ME.
18May the grace of our Lord Jesus Christ be with
you all.

3:3 Or *from evil.* **3:6a** Greek *from every brother.* **3:6b** Some manuscripts
read *you received.* **3:15** Greek *as a brother.*

1 Timothy

KING JAMES VERSION

1 [1]Paul, an apostle of Jesus Christ by the commandment of God our Saviour, and Lord Jesus Christ, *which is* our hope;

[2]Unto Timothy, *my* own son in the faith: Grace, mercy, *and* peace, from God our Father and Jesus Christ our Lord.

[3]As I besought thee to abide still at Ephesus, when I went into Macedonia, that thou mightest charge some that they teach no other doctrine,

[4]Neither give heed to fables and endless genealogies, which minister questions, rather than godly edifying which is in faith: *so do.*

[5]Now the end of the commandment is charity out of a pure heart, and *of* a good conscience, and *of* faith unfeigned:

[6]From which some having swerved have turned aside unto vain jangling;

[7]Desiring to be teachers of the law; understanding neither what they say, nor whereof they affirm.

[8]But we know that the law *is* good, if a man use it lawfully;

[9]Knowing this, that the law is not made for a righteous man, but for the lawless and disobedient, for the ungodly and for sinners, for unholy and profane, for murderers of fathers and murderers of mothers, for manslayers,

[10]For whoremongers, for them that defile themselves with mankind, for menstealers, for liars, for perjured persons, and if there be any other thing that is contrary to sound doctrine;

[11]According to the glorious gospel of the blessed God, which was committed to my trust.

[12]And I thank Christ Jesus our Lord, who hath enabled me, for that he counted me faithful, putting me into the ministry;

[13]Who was before a blasphemer, and a persecutor, and injurious: but I obtained mercy, because I did *it* ignorantly in unbelief.

NEW LIVING TRANSLATION

Greetings from Paul

1 This letter is from Paul, an apostle of Christ Jesus, appointed by the command of God our Savior and Christ Jesus, who gives us hope.

[2]I am writing to Timothy, my true son in the faith. May God the Father and Christ Jesus our Lord give you grace, mercy, and peace.

Warnings against False Teachings

[3]When I left for Macedonia, I urged you to stay there in Ephesus and stop those whose teaching is contrary to the truth. [4]Don't let them waste their time in endless discussion of myths and spiritual pedigrees. These things only lead to meaningless speculations,* which don't help people live a life of faith in God.*

[5]The purpose of my instruction is that all believers would be filled with love that comes from a pure heart, a clear conscience, and genuine faith. [6]But some people have missed this whole point. They have turned away from these things and spend their time in meaningless discussions. [7]They want to be known as teachers of the law of Moses, but they don't know what they are talking about, even though they speak so confidently.

[8]We know that the law is good when used correctly. [9]For the law was not intended for people who do what is right. It is for people who are lawless and rebellious, who are ungodly and sinful, who consider nothing sacred and defile what is holy, who kill their father or mother or commit other murders. [10]The law is for people who are sexually immoral, or who practice homosexuality, or are slave traders,* liars, promise breakers, or who do anything else that contradicts the wholesome teaching [11]that comes from the glorious Good News entrusted to me by our blessed God.

Paul's Gratitude for God's Mercy

[12]I thank Christ Jesus our Lord, who has given me strength to do his work. He considered me trustworthy and appointed me to serve him, [13]even though I used to blaspheme the name of Christ. In my insolence, I persecuted his people. But God had

1:4a Greek *in myths and endless genealogies, which cause speculation.*
1:4b Greek *a stewardship of God in faith.* **1:10** Or *kidnappers.*

KING JAMES VERSION

14 And the grace of our Lord was exceeding abundant with faith and love which is in Christ Jesus.
15 This *is* a faithful saying, and worthy of all acceptation, that Christ Jesus came into the world to save
sinners; of whom I am chief.
16 Howbeit for this cause I obtained mercy, that
in me first Jesus Christ might shew forth all longsuffering, for a pattern to them which should hereafter believe on him to life everlasting.
17 Now unto the King eternal, immortal, invisible,
the only wise God, *be* honour and glory for ever and
ever. Amen.

18 This charge I commit unto thee, son Timothy,
according to the prophecies which went before on
thee, that thou by them mightest war a good warfare;
19 Holding faith, and a good conscience; which
some having put away concerning faith have made
shipwreck:
20 Of whom is Hymenaeus and Alexander; whom I
have delivered unto Satan, that they may learn not to
blaspheme.

2 1 I exhort therefore, that, first of all, supplications, prayers, intercessions, *and* giving of
thanks, be made for all men;
2 For kings, and *for* all that are in authority; that we
may lead a quiet and peaceable life in all godliness
and honesty.
3 For this *is* good and acceptable in the sight of God
our Saviour;
4 Who will have all men to be saved, and to come
unto the knowledge of the truth.
5 For *there is* one God, and one mediator between
God and men, the man Christ Jesus;
6 Who gave himself a ransom for all, to be testified
in due time.
7 Whereunto I am ordained a preacher, and an
apostle, (I speak the truth in Christ, *and* lie not;) a
teacher of the Gentiles in faith and verity.
8 I will therefore that men pray every where, lifting
up holy hands, without wrath and doubting.
9 In like manner also, that women adorn themselves in modest apparel, with shamefacedness and
sobriety; not with broided hair, or gold, or pearls, or
costly array;
10 But (which becometh women professing godliness) with good works.
11 Let the woman learn in silence with all subjection.
12 But I suffer not a woman to teach, nor to usurp
authority over the man, but to be in silence.
13 For Adam was first formed, then Eve.

NEW LIVING TRANSLATION

mercy on me because I did it in ignorance and unbelief. 14 Oh, how generous and gracious our Lord
was! He filled me with the faith and love that come
from Christ Jesus.
15 This is a trustworthy saying, and everyone
should accept it: "Christ Jesus came into the world to
save sinners"—and I am the worst of them all. 16 But
God had mercy on me so that Christ Jesus could use
me as a prime example of his great patience with
even the worst sinners. Then others will realize that
they, too, can believe in him and receive eternal life.
17 All honor and glory to God forever and ever! He is
the eternal King, the unseen one who never dies; he
alone is God. Amen.

Timothy's Responsibility

18 Timothy, my son, here are my instructions for you,
based on the prophetic words spoken about you earlier. May they help you fight well in the Lord's battles.
19 Cling to your faith in Christ, and keep your conscience clear. For some people have deliberately
violated their consciences; as a result, their faith has
been shipwrecked. 20 Hymenaeus and Alexander are
two examples. I threw them out and handed them
over to Satan so they might learn not to blaspheme
God.

Instructions about Worship

2 I urge you, first of all, to pray for all people. Ask
God to help them; intercede on their behalf,
and give thanks for them. 2 Pray this way for kings
and all who are in authority so that we can live peaceful and quiet lives marked by godliness and dignity.
3 This is good and pleases God our Savior, 4 who
wants everyone to be saved and to understand the
truth. 5 For there is only one God and one Mediator
who can reconcile God and humanity—the man
Christ Jesus. 6 He gave his life to purchase freedom
for everyone. This is the message God gave to the
world at just the right time. 7 And I have been chosen
as a preacher and apostle to teach the Gentiles this
message about faith and truth. I'm not exaggerat-
ing—just telling the truth.
8 In every place of worship, I want men to pray
with holy hands lifted up to God, free from anger and
controversy.
9 And I want women to be modest in their appearance.* They should wear decent and appropriate
clothing and not draw attention to themselves by the
way they fix their hair or by wearing gold or pearls or
expensive clothes. 10 For women who claim to be devoted to God should make themselves attractive by
the good things they do.
11 Women should learn quietly and submissively.
12 I do not let women teach men or have authority
over them.* Let them listen quietly. 13 For God made

2:9 Or *to pray in modest apparel.* **2:12** Or *teach men or usurp their authority.*

KING JAMES VERSION

14And Adam was not deceived, but the woman being deceived was in the transgression.
15Notwithstanding she shall be saved in childbearing, if they continue in faith and charity and
holiness with sobriety.

3 1This *is* a true saying, If a man desire the office
of a bishop, he desireth a good work.
2A bishop then must be blameless, the husband of
one wife, vigilant, sober, of good behaviour, given to
hospitality, apt to teach;
3Not given to wine, no striker, not greedy of filthy
lucre; but patient, not a brawler, not covetous;
4One that ruleth well his own house, having his
children in subjection with all gravity;
5(For if a man know not how to rule his own house,
how shall he take care of the church of God?)
6Not a novice, lest being lifted up with pride he fall
into the condemnation of the devil.
7Moreover he must have a good report of them
which are without; lest he fall into reproach and the
snare of the devil.
8Likewise *must* the deacons *be* grave, not double-
tongued, not given to much wine, not greedy of filthy
lucre;
9Holding the mystery of the faith in a pure conscience.
10And let these also first be proved; then let them
use the office of a deacon, being *found* blameless.
11Even so *must their* wives *be* grave, not slander-
ers, sober, faithful in all things.
12Let the deacons be the husbands of one wife,
ruling their children and their own houses well.
13For they that have used the office of a deacon
well purchase to themselves a good degree, and great
boldness in the faith which is in Christ Jesus.

14These things write I unto thee, hoping to come
unto thee shortly:
15But if I tarry long, that thou mayest know how
thou oughtest to behave thyself in the house of God,
which is the church of the living God, the pillar and
ground of the truth.
16And without controversy great is the mystery of
godliness: God was manifest in the flesh, justified in

NEW LIVING TRANSLATION

Adam first, and afterward he made Eve. 14And it was
not Adam who was deceived by Satan. The woman
was deceived, and sin was the result. 15But women
will be saved through childbearing,* assuming they
continue to live in faith, love, holiness, and modesty.

Leaders in the Church

3 This is a trustworthy saying: "If someone as-
pires to be an elder,* he desires an honorable
position." 2So an elder must be a man whose life is
above reproach. He must be faithful to his wife.* He
must exercise self-control, live wisely, and have a
good reputation. He must enjoy having guests in his
home, and he must be able to teach. 3He must not be
a heavy drinker* or be violent. He must be gentle, not
quarrelsome, and not love money. 4He must manage
his own family well, having children who respect and
obey him. 5For if a man cannot manage his own
household, how can he take care of God's church?
6An elder must not be a new believer, because he
might become proud, and the devil would cause him
to fall.* 7Also, people outside the church must speak
well of him so that he will not be disgraced and fall
into the devil's trap.
8In the same way, deacons must be well respected
and have integrity. They must not be heavy drinkers
or dishonest with money. 9They must be committed
to the mystery of the faith now revealed and must
live with a clear conscience. 10Before they are appointed as deacons, let them be closely examined.
If they pass the test, then let them serve as deacons.
11In the same way, their wives* must be respected
and must not slander others. They must exercise
self-control and be faithful in everything they do.
12A deacon must be faithful to his wife, and he
must manage his children and household well.
13Those who do well as deacons will be rewarded
with respect from others and will have increased
confidence in their faith in Christ Jesus.

The Truths of Our Faith

14I am writing these things to you now, even though I
hope to be with you soon, 15so that if I am delayed, you
will know how people must conduct themselves in the
household of God. This is the church of the living God,
which is the pillar and foundation of the truth.
16Without question, this is the great mystery of
our faith*:

Christ* was revealed in a human body
and vindicated by the Spirit.*
He was seen by angels
and announced to the nations.

2:15 Or *will be saved by accepting their role as mothers,* or *will be saved by the birth of the Child.* **3:1** Or *an overseer,* or *a bishop;* also in 3:2, 6. **3:2** Or *must have only one wife,* or *must be married only once;* Greek reads *must be the husband of one wife;* also in 3:12. **3:3** Greek *must not drink too much wine;* similarly in 3:8. **3:6** Or *he might fall into the same judgment as the devil.* **3:11** Or *the women deacons.* The Greek word can be translated *women* or *wives.* **3:16a** Or *of godliness.* **3:16b** Greek *He who;* other manuscripts read *God.* **3:16c** Or *in his spirit.*

KING JAMES VERSION

the Spirit, seen of angels, preached unto the Gentiles, believed on in the world, received up into glory.

4

1 Now the Spirit speaketh expressly, that in the latter times some shall depart from the faith, giving heed to seducing spirits, and doctrines of devils;

2 Speaking lies in hypocrisy; having their conscience seared with a hot iron;

3 Forbidding to marry, *and commanding* to abstain from meats, which God hath created to be received with thanksgiving of them which believe and know the truth.

4 For every creature of God *is* good, and nothing to be refused, if it be received with thanksgiving:

5 For it is sanctified by the word of God and prayer.

6 If thou put the brethren in remembrance of these things, thou shalt be a good minister of Jesus Christ, nourished up in the words of faith and of good doctrine, whereunto thou hast attained.

7 But refuse profane and old wives' fables, and exercise thyself *rather* unto godliness.

8 For bodily exercise profiteth little: but godliness is profitable unto all things, having promise of the life that now is, and of that which is to come.

9 This *is* a faithful saying and worthy of all acceptation.

10 For therefore we both labour and suffer reproach, because we trust in the living God, who is the Saviour of all men, specially of those that believe.

11 These things command and teach.

12 Let no man despise thy youth; but be thou an example of the believers, in word, in conversation, in charity, in spirit, in faith, in purity.

13 Till I come, give attendance to reading, to exhortation, to doctrine.

14 Neglect not the gift that is in thee, which was given thee by prophecy, with the laying on of the hands of the presbytery.

15 Meditate upon these things; give thyself wholly to them; that thy profiting may appear to all.

16 Take heed unto thyself, and unto the doctrine; continue in them: for in doing this thou shalt both save thyself, and them that hear thee.

5

1 Rebuke not an elder, but intreat *him* as a father; *and* the younger men as brethren;

2 The elder women as mothers; the younger as sisters, with all purity.

3 Honour widows that are widows indeed.

NEW LIVING TRANSLATION

He was believed in throughout the world
and taken to heaven in glory.

Warnings against False Teachers

4

Now the Holy Spirit tells us clearly that in the last times some will turn away from the true faith; they will follow deceptive spirits and teachings that come from demons. 2 These people are hypocrites and liars, and their consciences are dead.*

3 They will say it is wrong to be married and wrong to eat certain foods. But God created those foods to be eaten with thanks by faithful people who know the truth. 4 Since everything God created is good, we should not reject any of it but receive it with thanks. 5 For we know it is made acceptable* by the word of God and prayer.

A Good Servant of Christ Jesus

6 If you explain these things to the brothers and sisters,* Timothy, you will be a worthy servant of Christ Jesus, one who is nourished by the message of faith and the good teaching you have followed. 7 Do not waste time arguing over godless ideas and old wives' tales. Instead, train yourself to be godly. 8 "Physical training is good, but training for godliness is much better, promising benefits in this life and in the life to come." 9 This is a trustworthy saying, and everyone should accept it. 10 This is why we work hard and continue to struggle,* for our hope is in the living God, who is the Savior of all people and particularly of all believers.

11 Teach these things and insist that everyone learn them. 12 Don't let anyone think less of you because you are young. Be an example to all believers in what you say, in the way you live, in your love, your faith, and your purity. 13 Until I get there, focus on reading the Scriptures to the church, encouraging the believers, and teaching them.

14 Do not neglect the spiritual gift you received through the prophecy spoken over you when the elders of the church laid their hands on you. 15 Give your complete attention to these matters. Throw yourself into your tasks so that everyone will see your progress. 16 Keep a close watch on how you live and on your teaching. Stay true to what is right for the sake of your own salvation and the salvation of those who hear you.

Advice about Widows, Elders, and Slaves

5

Never speak harshly to an older man,* but appeal to him respectfully as you would to your own father. Talk to younger men as you would to your own brothers. 2 Treat older women as you would your mother, and treat younger women with all purity as you would your own sisters.

3 Take care of* any widow who has no one else

4:2 Greek *are seared.* **4:5** Or *made holy.* **4:6** Greek *brothers.* **4:10** Some manuscripts read *continue to suffer.* **5:1** Or *an elder.* **5:3** Or *Honor.*

KING JAMES VERSION

4 But if any widow have children or nephews, let them learn first to shew piety at home, and to requite their parents: for that is good and acceptable before God.

5 Now she that is a widow indeed, and desolate, trusteth in God, and continueth in supplications and prayers night and day.

6 But she that liveth in pleasure is dead while she liveth.

7 And these things give in charge, that they may be blameless.

8 But if any provide not for his own, and specially for those of his own house, he hath denied the faith, and is worse than an infidel.

9 Let not a widow be taken into the number under threescore years old, having been the wife of one man,

10 Well reported of for good works; if she have brought up children, if she have lodged strangers, if she have washed the saints' feet, if she have relieved the afflicted, if she have diligently followed every good work.

11 But the younger widows refuse: for when they have begun to wax wanton against Christ, they will marry;

12 Having damnation, because they have cast off their first faith.

13 And withal they learn *to be* idle, wandering about from house to house; and not only idle, but tattlers also and busybodies, speaking things which they ought not.

14 I will therefore that the younger women marry, bear children, guide the house, give none occasion to the adversary to speak reproachfully.

15 For some are already turned aside after Satan.

16 If any man or woman that believeth have widows, let them relieve them, and let not the church be charged; that it may relieve them that are widows indeed.

17 Let the elders that rule well be counted worthy of double honour, especially they who labour in the word and doctrine.

18 For the scripture saith, Thou shalt not muzzle the ox that treadeth out the corn. And, The labourer *is* worthy of his reward.

19 Against an elder receive not an accusation, but before two or three witnesses.

20 Them that sin rebuke before all, that others also may fear.

21 I charge *thee* before God, and the Lord Jesus Christ, and the elect angels, that thou observe these things without preferring one before another, doing nothing by partiality.

22 Lay hands suddenly on no man, neither be partaker of other men's sins: keep thyself pure.

NEW LIVING TRANSLATION

to care for her. 4 But if she has children or grandchildren, their first responsibility is to show godliness at home and repay their parents by taking care of them. This is something that pleases God.

5 Now a true widow, a woman who is truly alone in this world, has placed her hope in God. She prays night and day, asking God for his help. 6 But the widow who lives only for pleasure is spiritually dead even while she lives. 7 Give these instructions to the church so that no one will be open to criticism.

8 But those who won't care for their relatives, especially those in their own household, have denied the true faith. Such people are worse than unbelievers.

9 A widow who is put on the list for support must be a woman who is at least sixty years old and was faithful to her husband.* 10 She must be well respected by everyone because of the good she has done. Has she brought up her children well? Has she been kind to strangers and served other believers humbly?* Has she helped those who are in trouble? Has she always been ready to do good?

11 The younger widows should not be on the list, because their physical desires will overpower their devotion to Christ and they will want to remarry. 12 Then they would be guilty of breaking their previous pledge. 13 And if they are on the list, they will learn to be lazy and will spend their time gossiping from house to house, meddling in other people's business and talking about things they shouldn't. 14 So I advise these younger widows to marry again, have children, and take care of their own homes. Then the enemy will not be able to say anything against them. 15 For I am afraid that some of them have already gone astray and now follow Satan.

16 If a woman who is a believer has relatives who are widows, she must take care of them and not put the responsibility on the church. Then the church can care for the widows who are truly alone.

17 Elders who do their work well should be respected and paid well,* especially those who work hard at both preaching and teaching. 18 For the Scripture says, "You must not muzzle an ox to keep it from eating as it treads out the grain." And in another place, "Those who work deserve their pay!"*

19 Do not listen to an accusation against an elder unless it is confirmed by two or three witnesses. 20 Those who sin should be reprimanded in front of the whole church; this will serve as a strong warning to others.

21 I solemnly command you in the presence of God and Christ Jesus and the highest angels to obey these instructions without taking sides or showing favoritism to anyone.

22 Never be in a hurry about appointing a church leader.* Do not share in the sins of others. Keep yourself pure.

5:9 Greek *was the wife of one husband.* **5:10** Greek *and washed the feet of God's holy people?* **5:17** Greek *should be worthy of double honor.* **5:18** Deut 25:4; Luke 10:7. **5:22** Greek *about the laying on of hands.*

KING JAMES VERSION

23 Drink no longer water, but use a little wine for
thy stomach's sake and thine often infirmities.
24 Some men's sins are open beforehand, going before to judgment; and some *men* they follow after.
25 Likewise also the good works *of some* are manifest beforehand; and they that are otherwise cannot
be hid.

6

1 Let as many servants as are under the yoke
count their own masters worthy of all honour,
that the name of God and *his* doctrine be not blasphemed.
2 And they that have believing masters, let them
not despise *them,* because they are brethren; but
rather do *them* service, because they are faithful and
beloved, partakers of the benefit. These things teach
and exhort.
3 If any man teach otherwise, and consent not to
wholesome words, *even* the words of our Lord Jesus
Christ, and to the doctrine which is according to
godliness;
4 He is proud, knowing nothing, but doting about
questions and strifes of words, whereof cometh envy,
strife, railings, evil surmisings,
5 Perverse disputings of men of corrupt minds,
and destitute of the truth, supposing that gain is
godliness: from such withdraw thyself.
6 But godliness with contentment is great gain.
7 For we brought nothing into *this* world, *and it is*
certain we can carry nothing out.
8 And having food and raiment let us be therewith
content.
9 But they that will be rich fall into temptation and
a snare, and *into* many foolish and hurtful lusts,
which drown men in destruction and perdition.
10 For the love of money is the root of all evil: which
while some coveted after, they have erred from the
faith, and pierced themselves through with many
sorrows.

11 But thou, O man of God, flee these things; and
follow after righteousness, godliness, faith, love,
patience, meekness.
12 Fight the good fight of faith, lay hold on eternal
life, whereunto thou art also called, and hast professed a good profession before many witnesses.
13 I give thee charge in the sight of God, who
quickeneth all things, and *before* Christ Jesus, who
before Pontius Pilate witnessed a good confession;
14 That thou keep *this* commandment without
spot, unrebukeable, until the appearing of our Lord
Jesus Christ:

NEW LIVING TRANSLATION

23 Don't drink only water. You ought to drink a
little wine for the sake of your stomach because you
are sick so often.
24 Remember, the sins of some people are obvious,
leading them to certain judgment. But there are others whose sins will not be revealed until later. 25 In
the same way, the good deeds of some people are
obvious. And the good deeds done in secret will
someday come to light.

6

All slaves should show full respect for their
masters so they will not bring shame on the
name of God and his teaching. 2 If the masters are
believers, that is no excuse for being disrespectful.
Those slaves should work all the harder because
their efforts are helping other believers* who are
well loved.

False Teaching and True Riches

Teach these things, Timothy, and encourage everyone to obey them. 3 Some people may contradict our
teaching, but these are the wholesome teachings
of the Lord Jesus Christ. These teachings promote a
godly life. 4 Anyone who teaches something different
is arrogant and lacks understanding. Such a person
has an unhealthy desire to quibble over the meaning
of words. This stirs up arguments ending in jealousy,
division, slander, and evil suspicions. 5 These people
always cause trouble. Their minds are corrupt, and
they have turned their backs on the truth. To them, a
show of godliness is just a way to become wealthy.
6 Yet true godliness with contentment is itself
great wealth. 7 After all, we brought nothing with us
when we came into the world, and we can't take anything with us when we leave it. 8 So if we have enough
food and clothing, let us be content.
9 But people who long to be rich fall into temptation and are trapped by many foolish and harmful
desires that plunge them into ruin and destruction.
10 For the love of money is the root of all kinds of evil.
And some people, craving money, have wandered
from the true faith and pierced themselves with
many sorrows.

Paul's Final Instructions

11 But you, Timothy, are a man of God; so run from all
these evil things. Pursue righteousness and a godly
life, along with faith, love, perseverance, and gentleness. 12 Fight the good fight for the true faith. Hold
tightly to the eternal life to which God has called you,
which you have confessed so well before many witnesses. 13 And I charge you before God, who gives life
to all, and before Christ Jesus, who gave a good testimony before Pontius Pilate, 14 that you obey this
command without wavering. Then no one can find
fault with you from now until our Lord Jesus Christ

6:2 Greek *brothers.*

KING JAMES VERSION

[15]Which in his times he shall shew, *who is* the blessed and only Potentate, the King of kings, and Lord of lords;

[16]Who only hath immortality, dwelling in the light which no man can approach unto; whom no man hath seen, nor can see: to whom *be* honour and power everlasting. Amen.

[17]Charge them that are rich in this world, that they be not highminded, nor trust in uncertain riches, but in the living God, who giveth us richly all things to enjoy;

[18]That they do good, that they be rich in good works, ready to distribute, willing to communicate;

[19]Laying up in store for themselves a good foundation against the time to come, that they may lay hold on eternal life.

[20]O Timothy, keep that which is committed to thy trust, avoiding profane *and* vain babblings, and oppositions of science falsely so called:

[21]Which some professing have erred concerning the faith. Grace *be* with thee. Amen.

NEW LIVING TRANSLATION

comes again. [15]For at just the right time Christ will
be revealed from heaven by the blessed and only
almighty God, the King of all kings and Lord of all
lords. [16]He alone can never die, and he lives in light
so brilliant that no human can approach him. No human eye has ever seen him, nor ever will. All honor and power to him forever! Amen.

[17]Teach those who are rich in this world not to be
proud and not to trust in their money, which is so unreliable. Their trust should be in God, who richly
gives us all we need for our enjoyment. [18]Tell them to
use their money to do good. They should be rich in good works and generous to those in need, always
being ready to share with others. [19]By doing this they
will be storing up their treasure as a good foundation for the future so that they may experience true life.

[20]Timothy, guard what God has entrusted to you.
Avoid godless, foolish discussions with those who
oppose you with their so-called knowledge. [21]Some
people have wandered from the faith by following such foolishness.

May God's grace be with you all.

2 Timothy

KING JAMES VERSION

1 1 Paul, an apostle of Jesus Christ by the will of God, according to the promise of life which is in Christ Jesus,

2 To Timothy, *my* dearly beloved son: Grace, mercy, *and* peace, from God the Father and Christ Jesus our Lord.

3 I thank God, whom I serve from *my* forefathers with pure conscience, that without ceasing I have remembrance of thee in my prayers night and day;

4 Greatly desiring to see thee, being mindful of thy tears, that I may be filled with joy;

5 When I call to remembrance the unfeigned faith that is in thee, which dwelt first in thy grandmother Lois, and thy mother Eunice; and I am persuaded that in thee also.

6 Wherefore I put thee in remembrance that thou stir up the gift of God, which is in thee by the putting on of my hands.

7 For God hath not given us the spirit of fear; but of power, and of love, and of a sound mind.

8 Be not thou therefore ashamed of the testimony of our Lord, nor of me his prisoner: but be thou partaker of the afflictions of the gospel according to the power of God;

9 Who hath saved us, and called *us* with an holy calling, not according to our works, but according to his own purpose and grace, which was given us in Christ Jesus before the world began,

10 But is now made manifest by the appearing of our Saviour Jesus Christ, who hath abolished death, and hath brought life and immortality to light through the gospel:

11 Whereunto I am appointed a preacher, and an apostle, and a teacher of the Gentiles.

12 For the which cause I also suffer these things: nevertheless I am not ashamed: for I know whom I have believed, and am persuaded that he is able to keep that which I have committed unto him against that day.

NEW LIVING TRANSLATION

Greetings from Paul

1 This letter is from Paul, chosen by the will of God to be an apostle of Christ Jesus. I have been sent out to tell others about the life he has promised through faith in Christ Jesus.

2 I am writing to Timothy, my dear son.

May God the Father and Christ Jesus our Lord give you grace, mercy, and peace.

Encouragement to Be Faithful

3 Timothy, I thank God for you—the God I serve with a clear conscience, just as my ancestors did. Night and day I constantly remember you in my prayers. 4 I long to see you again, for I remember your tears as we parted. And I will be filled with joy when we are together again.

5 I remember your genuine faith, for you share the faith that first filled your grandmother Lois and your mother, Eunice. And I know that same faith continues strong in you. 6 This is why I remind you to fan into flames the spiritual gift God gave you when I laid my hands on you. 7 For God has not given us a spirit of fear and timidity, but of power, love, and self-discipline.

8 So never be ashamed to tell others about our Lord. And don't be ashamed of me, either, even though I'm in prison for him. With the strength God gives you, be ready to suffer with me for the sake of the Good News. 9 For God saved us and called us to live a holy life. He did this, not because we deserved it, but because that was his plan from before the beginning of time—to show us his grace through Christ Jesus. 10 And now he has made all of this plain to us by the appearing of Christ Jesus, our Savior. He broke the power of death and illuminated the way to life and immortality through the Good News. 11 And God chose me to be a preacher, an apostle, and a teacher of this Good News.

12 That is why I am suffering here in prison. But I am not ashamed of it, for I know the one in whom I trust, and I am sure that he is able to guard what I have entrusted to him* until the day of his return.

1:12 Or *what has been entrusted to me.*

KING JAMES VERSION

13Hold fast the form of sound words, which thou hast heard of me, in faith and love which is in Christ Jesus.

14That good thing which was committed unto thee keep by the Holy Ghost which dwelleth in us.

15This thou knowest, that all they which are in Asia be turned away from me; of whom are Phygellus and Hermogenes.

16The Lord give mercy unto the house of Onesiphorus; for he oft refreshed me, and was not ashamed of my chain:

17But, when he was in Rome, he sought me out very diligently, and found *me*.

18The Lord grant unto him that he may find mercy of the Lord in that day: and in how many things he ministered unto me at Ephesus, thou knowest very well.

2 1Thou therefore, my son, be strong in the grace that is in Christ Jesus.

2And the things that thou hast heard of me among many witnesses, the same commit thou to faithful men, who shall be able to teach others also.

3Thou therefore endure hardness, as a good soldier of Jesus Christ.

4No man that warreth entangleth himself with the affairs of *this* life; that he may please him who hath chosen him to be a soldier.

5And if a man also strive for masteries, *yet* is he not crowned, except he strive lawfully.

6The husbandman that laboureth must be first partaker of the fruits.

7Consider what I say; and the Lord give thee understanding in all things.

8Remember that Jesus Christ of the seed of David was raised from the dead according to my gospel:

9Wherein I suffer trouble, as an evil doer, *even* unto bonds; but the word of God is not bound.

10Therefore I endure all things for the elect's sakes, that they may also obtain the salvation which is in Christ Jesus with eternal glory.

11*It is* a faithful saying: For if we be dead with *him,* we shall also live with *him:*

12If we suffer, we shall also reign with *him:* if we deny *him,* he also will deny us:

13If we believe not, *yet* he abideth faithful: he cannot deny himself.

14Of these things put *them* in remembrance, charging *them* before the Lord that they strive not about words to no profit, *but* to the subverting of the hearers.

NEW LIVING TRANSLATION

13Hold on to the pattern of wholesome teaching you learned from me—a pattern shaped by the faith and love that you have in Christ Jesus. 14Through the power of the Holy Spirit who lives within us, carefully guard the precious truth that has been entrusted to you.

15As you know, everyone from the province of Asia has deserted me—even Phygelus and Hermogenes.

16May the Lord show special kindness to Onesiphorus and all his family because he often visited and encouraged me. He was never ashamed of me because I was in chains. 17When he came to Rome, he searched everywhere until he found me. 18May the Lord show him special kindness on the day of Christ's return. And you know very well how helpful he was in Ephesus.

A Good Soldier of Christ Jesus

2 Timothy, my dear son, be strong through the grace that God gives you in Christ Jesus. 2You have heard me teach things that have been confirmed by many reliable witnesses. Now teach these truths to other trustworthy people who will be able to pass them on to others.

3Endure suffering along with me, as a good soldier of Christ Jesus. 4Soldiers don't get tied up in the affairs of civilian life, for then they cannot please the officer who enlisted them. 5And athletes cannot win the prize unless they follow the rules. 6And hardworking farmers should be the first to enjoy the fruit of their labor. 7Think about what I am saying. The Lord will help you understand all these things.

8Always remember that Jesus Christ, a descendant of King David, was raised from the dead. This is the Good News I preach. 9And because I preach this Good News, I am suffering and have been chained like a criminal. But the word of God cannot be chained. 10So I am willing to endure anything if it will bring salvation and eternal glory in Christ Jesus to those God has chosen.

11This is a trustworthy saying:

If we die with him,
    we will also live with him.
12 If we endure hardship,
    we will reign with him.
If we deny him,
    he will deny us.
13 If we are unfaithful,
    he remains faithful,
    for he cannot deny who he is.

14Remind everyone about these things, and command them in God's presence to stop fighting over words. Such arguments are useless, and they can ruin those who hear them.

KING JAMES VERSION

15 Study to shew thyself approved unto God, a
workman that needeth not to be ashamed, rightly
dividing the word of truth.

16 But shun profane *and* vain babblings: for they
will increase unto more ungodliness.

17 And their word will eat as doth a canker: of
whom is Hymenaeus and Philetus;

18 Who concerning the truth have erred, saying
that the resurrection is past already; and overthrow
the faith of some.

19 Nevertheless the foundation of God standeth
sure, having this seal, The Lord knoweth them that
are his. And, Let every one that nameth the name of
Christ depart from iniquity.

20 But in a great house there are not only vessels of
gold and of silver, but also of wood and of earth; and
some to honour, and some to dishonour.

21 If a man therefore purge himself from these, he
shall be a vessel unto honour, sanctified, and meet
for the master's use, *and* prepared unto every good
work.

22 Flee also youthful lusts: but follow righteousness, faith, charity, peace, with them that call on the
Lord out of a pure heart.

23 But foolish and unlearned questions avoid,
knowing that they do gender strifes.

24 And the servant of the Lord must not strive; but
be gentle unto all *men,* apt to teach, patient,

25 In meekness instructing those that oppose
themselves; if God peradventure will give them repentance to the acknowledging of the truth;

26 And *that* they may recover themselves out of
the snare of the devil, who are taken captive by him
at his will.

3

1 This know also, that in the last days perilous
times shall come.

2 For men shall be lovers of their own selves, covetous, boasters, proud, blasphemers, disobedient to
parents, unthankful, unholy,

3 Without natural affection, trucebreakers, false
accusers, incontinent, fierce, despisers of those that
are good,

4 Traitors, heady, highminded, lovers of pleasures
more than lovers of God;

5 Having a form of godliness, but denying the
power thereof: from such turn away.

6 For of this sort are they which creep into houses,
and lead captive silly women laden with sins, led
away with divers lusts,

7 Ever learning, and never able to come to the
knowledge of the truth.

NEW LIVING TRANSLATION

An Approved Worker

15 Work hard so you can present yourself to God and
receive his approval. Be a good worker, one who does
not need to be ashamed and who correctly explains
the word of truth. 16 Avoid worthless, foolish talk that
only leads to more godless behavior. 17 This kind of
talk spreads like cancer,* as in the case of Hymenaeus and Philetus. 18 They have left the path of truth,
claiming that the resurrection of the dead has already occurred; in this way, they have turned some
people away from the faith.

19 But God's truth stands firm like a foundation
stone with this inscription: "The LORD knows those
who are his,"* and "All who belong to the LORD must
turn away from evil."*

20 In a wealthy home some utensils are made of
gold and silver, and some are made of wood and clay.
The expensive utensils are used for special occasions,
and the cheap ones are for everyday use. 21 If you keep
yourself pure, you will be a special utensil for honorable use. Your life will be clean, and you will be ready
for the Master to use you for every good work.

22 Run from anything that stimulates youthful
lusts. Instead, pursue righteous living, faithfulness,
love, and peace. Enjoy the companionship of those
who call on the Lord with pure hearts.

23 Again I say, don't get involved in foolish, ignorant arguments that only start fights. 24 A servant of
the Lord must not quarrel but must be kind to everyone, be able to teach, and be patient with difficult
people. 25 Gently instruct those who oppose the
truth. Perhaps God will change those people's
hearts, and they will learn the truth. 26 Then they will
come to their senses and escape from the devil's
trap. For they have been held captive by him to do
whatever he wants.

The Dangers of the Last Days

3

You should know this, Timothy, that in the last
days there will be very difficult times. 2 For
people will love only themselves and their money.
They will be boastful and proud, scoffing at God, disobedient to their parents, and ungrateful. They will
consider nothing sacred. 3 They will be unloving and
unforgiving; they will slander others and have no
self-control. They will be cruel and hate what is good.
4 They will betray their friends, be reckless, be puffed
up with pride, and love pleasure rather than God.
5 They will act religious, but they will reject the power
that could make them godly. Stay away from people
like that!

6 They are the kind who work their way into
people's homes and win the confidence of* vulnerable women who are burdened with the guilt of sin
and controlled by various desires. 7 (Such women are
forever following new teachings, but they are never

2:17 Greek *gangrene.* **2:19a** Num 16:5. **2:19b** See Isa 52:11.
3:6 Greek *and take captive.*

KING JAMES VERSION

8 Now as Jannes and Jambres withstood Moses, so do these also resist the truth: men of corrupt minds, reprobate concerning the faith.
9 But they shall proceed no further: for their folly shall be manifest unto all *men,* as theirs also was.
10 But thou hast fully known my doctrine, manner of life, purpose, faith, longsuffering, charity, patience,
11 Persecutions, afflictions, which came unto me at Antioch, at Iconium, at Lystra; what persecutions I endured: but out of *them* all the Lord delivered me.
12 Yea, and all that will live godly in Christ Jesus shall suffer persecution.
13 But evil men and seducers shall wax worse and worse, deceiving, and being deceived.
14 But continue thou in the things which thou hast learned and hast been assured of, knowing of whom thou hast learned *them;*
15 And that from a child thou hast known the holy scriptures, which are able to make thee wise unto salvation through faith which is in Christ Jesus.
16 All scripture *is* given by inspiration of God, and *is* profitable for doctrine, for reproof, for correction, for instruction in righteousness:
17 That the man of God may be perfect, throughly furnished unto all good works.

4 1 I charge *thee* therefore before God, and the Lord Jesus Christ, who shall judge the quick and the dead at his appearing and his kingdom;
2 Preach the word; be instant in season, out of season; reprove, rebuke, exhort with all longsuffering and doctrine.
3 For the time will come when they will not endure sound doctrine; but after their own lusts shall they heap to themselves teachers, having itching ears;
4 And they shall turn away *their* ears from the truth, and shall be turned unto fables.
5 But watch thou in all things, endure afflictions, do the work of an evangelist, make full proof of thy ministry.
6 For I am now ready to be offered, and the time of my departure is at hand.
7 I have fought a good fight, I have finished *my* course, I have kept the faith:
8 Henceforth there is laid up for me a crown of righteousness, which the Lord, the righteous judge, shall give me at that day: and not to me only, but unto all them also that love his appearing.

NEW LIVING TRANSLATION

able to understand the truth.) 8 These teachers oppose the truth just as Jannes and Jambres opposed
Moses. They have depraved minds and a counterfeit
faith. 9 But they won't get away with this for long.
Someday everyone will recognize what fools they
are, just as with Jannes and Jambres.

Paul's Charge to Timothy

10 But you, Timothy, certainly know what I teach, and
how I live, and what my purpose in life is. You know
my faith, my patience, my love, and my endurance.
11 You know how much persecution and suffering I
have endured. You know all about how I was persecuted in Antioch, Iconium, and Lystra—but the Lord
rescued me from all of it. 12 Yes, and everyone who
wants to live a godly life in Christ Jesus will suffer
persecution. 13 But evil people and impostors will
flourish. They will deceive others and will themselves be deceived.
14 But you must remain faithful to the things you
have been taught. You know they are true, for you
know you can trust those who taught you. 15 You
have been taught the holy Scriptures from childhood, and they have given you the wisdom to receive the salvation that comes by trusting in Christ
Jesus. 16 All Scripture is inspired by God and is useful to teach us what is true and to make us realize
what is wrong in our lives. It corrects us when we
are wrong and teaches us to do what is right. 17 God
uses it to prepare and equip his people to do every
good work.

4 I solemnly urge you in the presence of God
and Christ Jesus, who will someday judge the
living and the dead when he appears to set up his
Kingdom: 2 Preach the word of God. Be prepared,
whether the time is favorable or not. Patiently correct, rebuke, and encourage your people with good
teaching.
3 For a time is coming when people will no longer
listen to sound and wholesome teaching. They will
follow their own desires and will look for teachers
who will tell them whatever their itching ears want
to hear. 4 They will reject the truth and chase after
myths.
5 But you should keep a clear mind in every situation. Don't be afraid of suffering for the Lord. Work
at telling others the Good News, and fully carry out
the ministry God has given you.
6 As for me, my life has already been poured out as
an offering to God. The time of my death is near. 7 I
have fought the good fight, I have finished the race,
and I have remained faithful. 8 And now the prize
awaits me—the crown of righteousness, which the
Lord, the righteous Judge, will give me on the day of
his return. And the prize is not just for me but for all
who eagerly look forward to his appearing.

KING JAMES VERSION

9 Do thy diligence to come shortly unto me:
10 For Demas hath forsaken me, having loved this
present world, and is departed unto Thessalonica;
Crescens to Galatia, Titus unto Dalmatia.
11 Only Luke is with me. Take Mark, and bring him
with thee: for he is profitable to me for the ministry.
12 And Tychicus have I sent to Ephesus.
13 The cloak that I left at Troas with Carpus, when
thou comest, bring *with thee*, and the books, *but*
especially the parchments.
14 Alexander the coppersmith did me much evil:
the Lord reward him according to his works:
15 Of whom be thou ware also; for he hath greatly
withstood our words.
16 At my first answer no man stood with me, but all
men forsook me: *I pray God* that it may not be laid
to their charge.
17 Notwithstanding the Lord stood with me, and
strengthened me; that by me the preaching might be
fully known, and *that* all the Gentiles might hear:
and I was delivered out of the mouth of the lion.
18 And the Lord shall deliver me from every evil
work, and will preserve *me* unto his heavenly kingdom: to whom *be* glory for ever and ever. Amen.
19 Salute Prisca and Aquila, and the household of
Onesiphorus.
20 Erastus abode at Corinth: but Trophimus have I
left at Miletum sick.
21 Do thy diligence to come before winter. Eubulus
greeteth thee, and Pudens, and Linus, and Claudia,
and all the brethren.
22 The Lord Jesus Christ *be* with thy spirit. Grace
be with you. Amen.

NEW LIVING TRANSLATION

Paul's Final Words

9 Timothy, please come as soon as you can.
10 Demas has deserted me because he loves the things of this
life and has gone to Thessalonica. Crescens has
gone to Galatia, and Titus has gone to Dalmatia.
11 Only Luke is with me. Bring Mark with you when
you come, for he will be helpful to me in my ministry.
12 I sent Tychicus to Ephesus.
13 When you come, be
sure to bring the coat I left with Carpus at Troas. Also
bring my books, and especially my papers.*
14 Alexander the coppersmith did me much harm,
but the Lord will judge him for what he has done.
15 Be careful of him, for he fought against everything
we said.
16 The first time I was brought before the judge, no
one came with me. Everyone abandoned me. May it
not be counted against them.
17 But the Lord stood
with me and gave me strength so that I might preach
the Good News in its entirety for all the Gentiles to
hear. And he rescued me from certain death.*
18 Yes,
and the Lord will deliver me from every evil attack
and will bring me safely into his heavenly Kingdom.
All glory to God forever and ever! Amen.

Paul's Final Greetings

19 Give my greetings to Priscilla and Aquila and those
living in the household of Onesiphorus.
20 Erastus
stayed at Corinth, and I left Trophimus sick at
Miletus.
21 Do your best to get here before winter. Eubulus
sends you greetings, and so do Pudens, Linus, Claudia, and all the brothers and sisters.*
22 May the Lord be with your spirit. And may his
grace be with all of you.

4:13 Greek *especially the parchments.* **4:17** Greek *from the mouth of a lion.* **4:21** Greek *brothers.*

Titus

KING JAMES VERSION

1 1Paul, a servant of God, and an apostle of Jesus Christ, according to the faith of God's elect, and the acknowledging of the truth which is after godliness;

2In hope of eternal life, which God, that cannot lie, promised before the world began;

3But hath in due times manifested his word through preaching, which is committed unto me according to the commandment of God our Saviour;

4To Titus, *mine* own son after the common faith: Grace, mercy, *and* peace, from God the Father and the Lord Jesus Christ our Saviour.

5For this cause left I thee in Crete, that thou shouldest set in order the things that are wanting, and ordain elders in every city, as I had appointed thee:

6If any be blameless, the husband of one wife, having faithful children not accused of riot or unruly.

7For a bishop must be blameless, as the steward of God; not selfwilled, not soon angry, not given to wine, no striker, not given to filthy lucre;

8But a lover of hospitality, a lover of good men, sober, just, holy, temperate;

9Holding fast the faithful word as he hath been taught, that he may be able by sound doctrine both to exhort and to convince the gainsayers.

10For there are many unruly and vain talkers and deceivers, specially they of the circumcision:

11Whose mouths must be stopped, who subvert whole houses, teaching things which they ought not, for filthy lucre's sake.

12One of themselves, *even* a prophet of their own, said, The Cretians *are* alway liars, evil beasts, slow bellies.

NEW LIVING TRANSLATION

Greetings from Paul

1 This letter is from Paul, a slave of God and an apostle of Jesus Christ. I have been sent to proclaim faith to* those God has chosen and to teach them to know the truth that shows them how to live godly lives. 2This truth gives them confidence that they have eternal life, which God—who does not lie—promised them before the world began. 3And now at just the right time he has revealed this message, which we announce to everyone. It is by the command of God our Savior that I have been entrusted with this work for him.

4I am writing to Titus, my true son in the faith that we share.

May God the Father and Christ Jesus our Savior give you grace and peace.

Titus's Work in Crete

5I left you on the island of Crete so you could complete our work there and appoint elders in each town as I instructed you. 6An elder must live a blameless life. He must be faithful to his wife,* and his children must be believers who don't have a reputation for being wild or rebellious. 7An elder* is a manager of God's household, so he must live a blameless life. He must not be arrogant or quick-tempered; he must not be a heavy drinker,* violent, or dishonest with money.

8Rather, he must enjoy having guests in his home, and he must love what is good. He must live wisely and be just. He must live a devout and disciplined life. 9He must have a strong belief in the trustworthy message he was taught; then he will be able to encourage others with wholesome teaching and show those who oppose it where they are wrong.

10For there are many rebellious people who engage in useless talk and deceive others. This is especially true of those who insist on circumcision for salvation. 11They must be silenced, because they are turning whole families away from the truth by their false teaching. And they do it only for money. 12Even one of their own men, a prophet from Crete, has said about them, "The people of Crete are all liars, cruel

1:1 Or *to strengthen the faith of.* **1:6** Or *must have only one wife,* or *must be married only once;* Greek reads *must be the husband of one wife.* **1:7a** Or *An overseer,* or *A bishop.* **1:7b** Greek *must not drink too much wine.*

KING JAMES VERSION

13 This witness is true. Wherefore rebuke them sharply, that they may be sound in the faith;

14 Not giving heed to Jewish fables, and commandments of men, that turn from the truth.

15 Unto the pure all things *are* pure: but unto them that are defiled and unbelieving *is* nothing pure; but even their mind and conscience is defiled.

16 They profess that they know God; but in works they deny *him*, being abominable, and disobedient, and unto every good work reprobate.

2 1 But speak thou the things which become sound doctrine:

2 That the aged men be sober, grave, temperate, sound in faith, in charity, in patience.

3 The aged women likewise, that *they be* in behaviour as becometh holiness, not false accusers, not given to much wine, teachers of good things;

4 That they may teach the young women to be sober, to love their husbands, to love their children,

5 *To be* discreet, chaste, keepers at home, good, obedient to their own husbands, that the word of God be not blasphemed.

6 Young men likewise exhort to be sober minded.

7 In all things shewing thyself a pattern of good works: in doctrine *shewing* uncorruptness, gravity, sincerity,

8 Sound speech, that cannot be condemned; that he that is of the contrary part may be ashamed, having no evil thing to say of you.

9 *Exhort* servants to be obedient unto their own masters, *and* to please *them* well in all *things;* not answering again;

10 Not purloining, but shewing all good fidelity; that they may adorn the doctrine of God our Saviour in all things.

11 For the grace of God that bringeth salvation hath appeared to all men,

12 Teaching us that, denying ungodliness and worldly lusts, we should live soberly, righteously, and godly, in this present world;

13 Looking for that blessed hope, and the glorious appearing of the great God and our Saviour Jesus Christ;

14 Who gave himself for us, that he might redeem us from all iniquity, and purify unto himself a peculiar people, zealous of good works.

15 These things speak, and exhort, and rebuke with all authority. Let no man despise thee.

NEW LIVING TRANSLATION

animals, and lazy gluttons."* 13 This is true. So reprimand them sternly to make them strong in the faith. 14 They must stop listening to Jewish myths and the commands of people who have turned away from the truth.

15 Everything is pure to those whose hearts are pure. But nothing is pure to those who are corrupt and unbelieving, because their minds and consciences are corrupted. 16 Such people claim they know God, but they deny him by the way they live. They are detestable and disobedient, worthless for doing anything good.

Promote Right Teaching

2 As for you, Titus, promote the kind of living that reflects wholesome teaching. 2 Teach the older men to exercise self-control, to be worthy of respect, and to live wisely. They must have sound faith and be filled with love and patience.

3 Similarly, teach the older women to live in a way that honors God. They must not slander others or be heavy drinkers.* Instead, they should teach others what is good. 4 These older women must train the younger women to love their husbands and their children, 5 to live wisely and be pure, to work in their homes,* to do good, and to be submissive to their husbands. Then they will not bring shame on the word of God.

6 In the same way, encourage the young men to live wisely. 7 And you yourself must be an example to them by doing good works of every kind. Let everything you do reflect the integrity and seriousness of your teaching. 8 Teach the truth so that your teaching can't be criticized. Then those who oppose us will be ashamed and have nothing bad to say about us.

9 Slaves must always obey their masters and do their best to please them. They must not talk back 10 or steal, but must show themselves to be entirely trustworthy and good. Then they will make the teaching about God our Savior attractive in every way.

11 For the grace of God has been revealed, bringing salvation to all people. 12 And we are instructed to turn from godless living and sinful pleasures. We should live in this evil world with wisdom, righteousness, and devotion to God, 13 while we look forward with hope to that wonderful day when the glory of our great God and Savior, Jesus Christ, will be revealed. 14 He gave his life to free us from every kind of sin, to cleanse us, and to make us his very own people, totally committed to doing good deeds.

15 You must teach these things and encourage the believers to do them. You have the authority to correct them when necessary, so don't let anyone disregard what you say.

1:12 This quotation is from Epimenides of Knossos. **2:3** Greek *be enslaved to much wine.* **2:5** Some manuscripts read *to care for their homes.*

KING JAMES VERSION

3

1Put them in mind to be subject to principalities and powers, to obey magistrates, to be ready to every good work,

2To speak evil of no man, to be no brawlers, *but* gentle, shewing all meekness unto all men.

3For we ourselves also were sometimes foolish, disobedient, deceived, serving divers lusts and pleasures, living in malice and envy, hateful, *and* hating one another.

4But after that the kindness and love of God our Saviour toward man appeared,

5Not by works of righteousness which we have done, but according to his mercy he saved us, by the washing of regeneration, and renewing of the Holy Ghost;

6Which he shed on us abundantly through Jesus Christ our Saviour;

7That being justified by his grace, we should be made heirs according to the hope of eternal life.

8*This is* a faithful saying, and these things I will that thou affirm constantly, that they which have believed in God might be careful to maintain good works. These things are good and profitable unto men.

9But avoid foolish questions, and genealogies, and contentions, and strivings about the law; for they are unprofitable and vain.

10A man that is an heretic after the first and second admonition reject;

11Knowing that he that is such is subverted, and sinneth, being condemned of himself.

12When I shall send Artemas unto thee, or Tychicus, be diligent to come unto me to Nicopolis: for I have determined there to winter.

13Bring Zenas the lawyer and Apollos on their journey diligently, that nothing be wanting unto them.

14And let ours also learn to maintain good works for necessary uses, that they be not unfruitful.

15All that are with me salute thee. Greet them that love us in the faith. Grace *be* with you all. Amen.

NEW LIVING TRANSLATION

Do What Is Good

3

Remind the believers to submit to the government and its officers. They should be obedient,
always ready to do what is good. 2They must not slan-
der anyone and must avoid quarreling. Instead, they
should be gentle and show true humility to everyone.
3Once we, too, were foolish and disobedient. We
were misled and became slaves to many lusts and
pleasures. Our lives were full of evil and envy, and we
hated each other.
4But—"When God our Savior revealed his kindness and love, 5he saved us, not because of the righteous things we had done, but because of his mercy.
He washed away our sins, giving us a new birth and
new life through the Holy Spirit.* 6He generously
poured out the Spirit upon us through Jesus Christ
our Savior. 7Because of his grace he declared us righteous and gave us confidence that we will inherit
eternal life." 8This is a trustworthy saying, and I want
you to insist on these teachings so that all who trust
in God will devote themselves to doing good. These
teachings are good and beneficial for everyone.
9Do not get involved in foolish discussions about
spiritual pedigrees* or in quarrels and fights about
obedience to Jewish laws. These things are useless
and a waste of time. 10If people are causing divisions
among you, give a first and second warning. After
that, have nothing more to do with them. 11For people
like that have turned away from the truth, and their
own sins condemn them.

Paul's Final Remarks and Greetings

12I am planning to send either Artemas or Tychicus
to you. As soon as one of them arrives, do your best to
meet me at Nicopolis, for I have decided to stay there
for the winter. 13Do everything you can to help Zenas
the lawyer and Apollos with their trip. See that they
are given everything they need. 14Our people must
learn to do good by meeting the urgent needs of
others; then they will not be unproductive.
15Everybody here sends greetings. Please give my
greetings to the believers—all who love us.
May God's grace be with you all.

3:5 Greek *He saved us through the washing of regeneration and renewing of the Holy Spirit.* **3:9** Or *spiritual genealogies.*

Philemon

KING JAMES VERSION

1 Paul, a prisoner of Jesus Christ, and Timothy *our*
brother, unto Philemon our dearly beloved, and
fellowlabourer,
2 And to *our* beloved Apphia, and Archippus our
fellowsoldier, and to the church in thy house:
3 Grace to you, and peace, from God our Father and
the Lord Jesus Christ.

4 I thank my God, making mention of thee always
in my prayers,
5 Hearing of thy love and faith, which thou hast
toward the Lord Jesus, and toward all saints;
6 That the communication of thy faith may become effectual by the acknowledging of every good
thing which is in you in Christ Jesus.
7 For we have great joy and consolation in thy love,
because the bowels of the saints are refreshed by
thee, brother.

8 Wherefore, though I might be much bold in
Christ to enjoin thee that which is convenient,
9 Yet for love's sake I rather beseech *thee,* being
such an one as Paul the aged, and now also a prisoner
of Jesus Christ.
10 I beseech thee for my son Onesimus, whom I
have begotten in my bonds:
11 Which in time past was to thee unprofitable, but
now profitable to thee and to me:
12 Whom I have sent again: thou therefore receive
him, that is, mine own bowels:
13 Whom I would have retained with me, that in
thy stead he might have ministered unto me in the
bonds of the gospel:
14 But without thy mind would I do nothing; that
thy benefit should not be as it were of necessity, but
willingly.
15 For perhaps he therefore departed for a season,
that thou shouldest receive him for ever;

NEW LIVING TRANSLATION

Greetings from Paul

This letter is from Paul, a prisoner for preaching the
Good News about Christ Jesus, and from our brother
Timothy.
I am writing to Philemon, our beloved co-worker,
2 and to our sister Apphia, and to our fellow soldier
Archippus, and to the church that meets in your*
house.
3 May God our Father and the Lord Jesus Christ
give you grace and peace.

Paul's Thanksgiving and Prayer

4 I always thank my God when I pray for you, Philemon, 5 because I keep hearing about your faith in the
Lord Jesus and your love for all of God's people. 6 And
I am praying that you will put into action the generosity that comes from your faith as you understand
and experience all the good things we have in Christ.
7 Your love has given me much joy and comfort, my
brother, for your kindness has often refreshed the
hearts of God's people.

Paul's Appeal for Onesimus

8 That is why I am boldly asking a favor of you. I could
demand it in the name of Christ because it is the
right thing for you to do. 9 But because of our love,
I prefer simply to ask you. Consider this as a request
from me—Paul, an old man and now also a prisoner
for the sake of Christ Jesus.*
10 I appeal to you to show kindness to my child,
Onesimus. I became his father in the faith while here
in prison. 11 Onesimus* hasn't been of much use to
you in the past, but now he is very useful to both of
us. 12 I am sending him back to you, and with him
comes my own heart.
13 I wanted to keep him here with me while I am in
these chains for preaching the Good News, and he
would have helped me on your behalf. 14 But I didn't
want to do anything without your consent. I wanted
you to help because you were willing, not because
you were forced. 15 It seems you lost Onesimus for a
little while so that you could have him back forever.

2 Throughout this letter, *you* and *your* are singular except in verses 3, 22, and 25. **9** Or *a prisoner of Christ Jesus.* **11** *Onesimus* means "useful."

KING JAMES VERSION

16 Not now as a servant, but above a servant, a
brother beloved, specially to me, but how much
more unto thee, both in the flesh, and in the Lord?
17 If thou count me therefore a partner, receive
him as myself.
18 If he hath wronged thee, or oweth *thee* aught,
put that on mine account;
19 I Paul have written *it* with mine own hand, I will
repay *it:* albeit I do not say to thee how thou owest
unto me even thine own self besides.
20 Yea, brother, let me have joy of thee in the Lord:
refresh my bowels in the Lord.
21 Having confidence in thy obedience I wrote
unto thee, knowing that thou wilt also do more than
I say.
22 But withal prepare me also a lodging: for I trust
that through your prayers I shall be given unto you.

23 There salute thee Epaphras, my fellowprisoner
in Christ Jesus;
24 Marcus, Aristarchus, Demas, Lucas, my fellowlabourers.
25 The grace of our Lord Jesus Christ *be* with your
spirit. Amen.

NEW LIVING TRANSLATION

16 He is no longer like a slave to you. He is more than
a slave, for he is a beloved brother, especially to me.
Now he will mean much more to you, both as a man
and as a brother in the Lord.
17 So if you consider me your partner, welcome
him as you would welcome me. 18 If he has wronged
you in any way or owes you anything, charge it to me.
19 I, PAUL, WRITE THIS WITH MY OWN HAND: I WILL REPAY
IT. AND I WON'T MENTION THAT YOU OWE ME YOUR VERY
SOUL!
20 Yes, my brother, please do me this favor* for the
Lord's sake. Give me this encouragement in Christ.
21 I am confident as I write this letter that you will
do what I ask and even more! 22 One more thing—
please prepare a guest room for me, for I am hoping
that God will answer your prayers and let me return
to you soon.

Paul's Final Greetings

23 Epaphras, my fellow prisoner in Christ Jesus, sends
you his greetings. 24 So do Mark, Aristarchus, Demas,
and Luke, my co-workers.
25 May the grace of the Lord Jesus Christ be with
your spirit.

20 Greek *onaimen,* a play on the name Onesimus.

Hebrews

KING JAMES VERSION

1 [1]God, who at sundry times and in divers manners spake in time past unto the fathers by the prophets,
[2]Hath in these last days spoken unto us by *his* Son,
whom he hath appointed heir of all things, by whom
also he made the worlds;
[3]Who being the brightness of *his* glory, and the
express image of his person, and upholding all
things by the word of his power, when he had by
himself purged our sins, sat down on the right hand
of the Majesty on high;
[4]Being made so much better than the angels, as he
hath by inheritance obtained a more excellent name
than they.
[5]For unto which of the angels said he at any time,
Thou art my Son, this day have I begotten thee? And
again, I will be to him a Father, and he shall be to me
a Son?
[6]And again, when he bringeth in the firstbegotten
into the world, he saith, And let all the angels of God
worship him.
[7]And of the angels he saith, Who maketh his angels spirits, and his ministers a flame of fire.
[8]But unto the Son *he saith,* Thy throne, O God, *is*
for ever and ever: a sceptre of righteousness *is* the
sceptre of thy kingdom.
[9]Thou hast loved righteousness, and hated iniquity; therefore God, *even* thy God, hath anointed thee
with the oil of gladness above thy fellows.

NEW LIVING TRANSLATION

Jesus Christ Is God's Son

1 Long ago God spoke many times and in many ways to our ancestors through the prophets.
[2]And now in these final days, he has spoken to us
through his Son. God promised everything to the Son
as an inheritance, and through the Son he created the
universe. [3]The Son radiates God's own glory and expresses the very character of God, and he sustains
everything by the mighty power of his command.
When he had cleansed us from our sins, he sat down
in the place of honor at the right hand of the majestic
God in heaven. [4]This shows that the Son is far greater
than the angels, just as the name God gave him is
greater than their names.

The Son Is Greater Than the Angels

[5]For God never said to any angel what he said to
Jesus:

"You are my Son.
Today I have become your Father.*"

God also said,

"I will be his Father,
and he will be my Son."*

[6]And when he brought his supreme* Son into the
world, God said,*

"Let all of God's angels worship him."*

[7]Regarding the angels, he says,

"He sends his angels like the winds,
his servants like flames of fire."*

[8]But to the Son he says,

"Your throne, O God, endures forever and ever.
You rule with a scepter of justice.
[9] You love justice and hate evil.
Therefore, O God, your God has anointed you,
pouring out the oil of joy on you more than
on anyone else."*

1:5a Or *Today I reveal you as my Son.* Ps 2:7. **1:5b** 2 Sam 7:14. **1:6a** Or *firstborn.* **1:6b** Or *when he again brings his supreme Son* [or *firstborn Son*] *into the world, God will say.* **1:6c** Deut 32:43. **1:7** Ps 104:4 (Greek version). **1:8-9** Ps 45:6-7.

KING JAMES VERSION

10 And, Thou, Lord, in the beginning hast laid the
foundation of the earth; and the heavens are the
works of thine hands:

11 They shall perish; but thou remainest; and they
all shall wax old as doth a garment;

12 And as a vesture shalt thou fold them up, and
they shall be changed: but thou art the same, and thy
years shall not fail.

13 But to which of the angels said he at any time, Sit
on my right hand, until I make thine enemies thy
footstool?

14 Are they not all ministering spirits, sent forth to
minister for them who shall be heirs of salvation?

2 1 Therefore we ought to give the more earnest
heed to the things which we have heard, lest at
any time we should let *them* slip.

2 For if the word spoken by angels was stedfast,
and every transgression and disobedience received
a just recompense of reward;

3 How shall we escape, if we neglect so great salvation; which at the first began to be spoken by the
Lord, and was confirmed unto us by them that heard
him;

4 God also bearing *them* witness, both with signs
and wonders, and with divers miracles, and gifts of
the Holy Ghost, according to his own will?

5 For unto the angels hath he not put in subjection
the world to come, whereof we speak.

6 But one in a certain place testified, saying, What
is man, that thou art mindful of him? or the son of
man, that thou visitest him?

7 Thou madest him a little lower than the angels;
thou crownedst him with glory and honour, and
didst set him over the works of thy hands:

8 Thou hast put all things in subjection under his
feet. For in that he put all in subjection under him,
he left nothing *that is* not put under him. But now
we see not yet all things put under him.

9 But we see Jesus, who was made a little lower
than the angels for the suffering of death, crowned
with glory and honour; that he by the grace of God
should taste death for every man.

10 For it became him, for whom *are* all things, and
by whom *are* all things, in bringing many sons unto
glory, to make the captain of their salvation perfect
through sufferings.

11 For both he that sanctifieth and they who are

NEW LIVING TRANSLATION

10 He also says to the Son,

"In the beginning, Lord, you laid the foundation
of the earth
and made the heavens with your hands.
11 They will perish, but you remain forever.
They will wear out like old clothing.
12 You will fold them up like a cloak
and discard them like old clothing.
But you are always the same;
you will live forever."*

13 And God never said to any of the angels,

"Sit in the place of honor at my right hand
until I humble your enemies,
making them a footstool under your feet."*

14 Therefore, angels are only servants—spirits sent to
care for people who will inherit salvation.

A Warning against Drifting Away

2 So we must listen very carefully to the truth we
have heard, or we may drift away from it. 2 For
the message God delivered through angels has always stood firm, and every violation of the law and
every act of disobedience was punished. 3 So what
makes us think we can escape if we ignore this great
salvation that was first announced by the Lord Jesus
himself and then delivered to us by those who heard
him speak? 4 And God confirmed the message by giving signs and wonders and various miracles and gifts
of the Holy Spirit whenever he chose.

Jesus, the Man

5 And furthermore, it is not angels who will control
the future world we are talking about. 6 For in one
place the Scriptures say,

"What are mere mortals that you should think
about them,
or a son of man* that you should care for him?
7 Yet you made them only a little lower than
the angels
and crowned them with glory and honor.*
8 You gave them authority over all things."*

Now when it says "all things," it means nothing is left
out. But we have not yet seen all things put under
their authority. 9 What we do see is Jesus, who was
given a position "a little lower than the angels"; and
because he suffered death for us, he is now "crowned
with glory and honor." Yes, by God's grace, Jesus
tasted death for everyone. 10 God, for whom and
through whom everything was made, chose to bring
many children into glory. And it was only right that he
should make Jesus, through his suffering, a perfect
leader, fit to bring them into their salvation.

11 So now Jesus and the ones he makes holy have the

1:10-12 Ps 102:25-27. **1:13** Ps 110:1. **2:6** Or *the Son of Man.*
2:7 Some manuscripts add *You gave them charge of everything you made.*
2:6-8 Ps 8:4-6 (Greek version).

KING JAMES VERSION

sanctified *are* all of one: for which cause he is not
ashamed to call them brethren,
12 Saying, I will declare thy name unto my brethren, in the midst of the church will I sing praise unto
thee.
13 And again, I will put my trust in him. And again,
Behold I and the children which God hath given me.
14 Forasmuch then as the children are partakers of
flesh and blood, he also himself likewise took part of
the same; that through death he might destroy him
that had the power of death, that is, the devil;
15 And deliver them who through fear of death
were all their lifetime subject to bondage.
16 For verily he took not on *him the nature of* angels; but he took on *him* the seed of Abraham.
17 Wherefore in all things it behoved him to be
made like unto *his* brethren, that he might be a merciful and faithful high priest in things *pertaining*
to God, to make reconciliation for the sins of the
people.
18 For in that he himself hath suffered being
tempted, he is able to succour them that are tempted.

3 1 Wherefore, holy brethren, partakers of the
heavenly calling, consider the Apostle and
High Priest of our profession, Christ Jesus;
2 Who was faithful to him that appointed him, as
also Moses *was faithful* in all his house.
3 For this *man* was counted worthy of more glory
than Moses, inasmuch as he who hath builded the
house hath more honour than the house.
4 For every house is builded by some *man;* but he
that built all things *is* God.
5 And Moses verily *was* faithful in all his house, as a
servant, for a testimony of those things which were
to be spoken after;
6 But Christ as a son over his own house; whose
house are we, if we hold fast the confidence and the
rejoicing of the hope firm unto the end.
7 Wherefore (as the Holy Ghost saith, Today if ye
will hear his voice,
8 Harden not your hearts, as in the provocation, in
the day of temptation in the wilderness:
9 When your fathers tempted me, proved me, and
saw my works forty years.

NEW LIVING TRANSLATION

same Father. That is why Jesus is not ashamed to call
them his brothers and sisters.* 12 For he said to God,

"I will proclaim your name to my
brothers and sisters.
I will praise you among your
assembled people."*

13 He also said,

"I will put my trust in him,"
that is, "I and the children God has given me."*

14 Because God's children are human beings—
made of flesh and blood—the Son also became flesh
and blood. For only as a human being could he die,
and only by dying could he break the power of the
devil, who had* the power of death. 15 Only in this
way could he set free all who have lived their lives as
slaves to the fear of dying.
16 We also know that the Son did not come to help
angels; he came to help the descendants of Abraham.
17 Therefore, it was necessary for him to be made in
every respect like us, his brothers and sisters,* so that
he could be our merciful and faithful High Priest before God. Then he could offer a sacrifice that would
take away the sins of the people. 18 Since he himself
has gone through suffering and testing, he is able to
help us when we are being tested.

Jesus Is Greater Than Moses

3 And so, dear brothers and sisters who belong to
God and* are partners with those called to
heaven, think carefully about this Jesus whom we
declare to be God's messenger* and High Priest. 2 For
he was faithful to God, who appointed him, just as
Moses served faithfully when he was entrusted with
God's entire* house.
3 But Jesus deserves far more glory than Moses,
just as a person who builds a house deserves more
praise than the house itself. 4 For every house has a
builder, but the one who built everything is God.
5 Moses was certainly faithful in God's house as a
servant. His work was an illustration of the truths
God would reveal later. 6 But Christ, as the Son, is
in charge of God's entire house. And we are God's
house, if we keep our courage and remain confident
in our hope in Christ.*
7 That is why the Holy Spirit says,

"Today when you hear his voice,
8 don't harden your hearts
as Israel did when they rebelled,
when they tested me in the wilderness.
9 There your ancestors tested and tried my patience,
even though they saw my miracles for
forty years.

2:11 Greek *brothers;* also in 2:12. **2:12** Ps 22:22. **2:13** Isa 8:17-18.
2:14 Or *has.* **2:17** Greek *like the brothers.* **3:1a** Greek *And so, holy
brothers who.* **3:1b** Greek *God's apostle.* **3:2** Some manuscripts do not
include *entire.* **3:6** Some manuscripts add *faithful to the end.*

KING JAMES VERSION

[10]Wherefore I was grieved with that generation, and said, They do alway err in *their* heart; and they have not known my ways.

[11]So I sware in my wrath, They shall not enter into my rest.)

[12]Take heed, brethren, lest there be in any of you an evil heart of unbelief, in departing from the living God.

[13]But exhort one another daily, while it is called Today; lest any of you be hardened through the deceitfulness of sin.

[14]For we are made partakers of Christ, if we hold the beginning of our confidence stedfast unto the end;

[15]While it is said, To day if ye will hear his voice, harden not your hearts, as in the provocation.

[16]For some, when they had heard, did provoke: howbeit not all that came out of Egypt by Moses.

[17]But with whom was he grieved forty years? *was it* not with them that had sinned, whose carcases fell in the wilderness?

[18]And to whom sware he that they should not enter into his rest, but to them that believed not?

[19]So we see that they could not enter in because of unbelief.

4 [1]Let us therefore fear, lest, a promise being left *us* of entering into his rest, any of you should seem to come short of it.

[2]For unto us was the gospel preached, as well as unto them: but the word preached did not profit them, not being mixed with faith in them that heard *it*.

[3]For we which have believed do enter into rest, as he said, As I have sworn in my wrath, if they shall enter into my rest: although the works were finished from the foundation of the world.

[4]For he spake in a certain place of the seventh *day* on this wise, And God did rest the seventh day from all his works.

[5]And in this *place* again, If they shall enter into my rest.

[6]Seeing therefore it remaineth that some must enter therein, and they to whom it was first preached entered not in because of unbelief:

[7]Again, he limiteth a certain day, saying in David, To day, after so long a time; as it is said, To day if ye will hear his voice, harden not your hearts.

NEW LIVING TRANSLATION

[10] So I was angry with them, and I said,
'Their hearts always turn away from me.
They refuse to do what I tell them.'
[11] So in my anger I took an oath:
'They will never enter my place of rest.'"*

[12]Be careful then, dear brothers and sisters.* Make sure that your own hearts are not evil and unbelieving, turning you away from the living God. [13]You must warn each other every day, while it is still "today," so that none of you will be deceived by sin and hardened against God. [14]For if we are faithful to the end, trusting God just as firmly as when we first believed, we will share in all that belongs to Christ. [15]Remember what it says:

"Today when you hear his voice,
don't harden your hearts
as Israel did when they rebelled."*

[16]And who was it who rebelled against God, even though they heard his voice? Wasn't it the people Moses led out of Egypt? [17]And who made God angry for forty years? Wasn't it the people who sinned, whose corpses lay in the wilderness? [18]And to whom was God speaking when he took an oath that they would never enter his rest? Wasn't it the people who disobeyed him? [19]So we see that because of their unbelief they were not able to enter his rest.

Promised Rest for God's People

4 God's promise of entering his rest still stands, so we ought to tremble with fear that some of you might fail to experience it. [2]For this good news—that God has prepared this rest—has been announced to us just as it was to them. But it did them no good because they didn't share the faith of those who listened to God.* [3]For only we who believe can enter his rest. As for the others, God said,

"In my anger I took an oath:
'They will never enter my place of rest,'"*

even though this rest has been ready since he made the world. [4]We know it is ready because of the place in the Scriptures where it mentions the seventh day: "On the seventh day God rested from all his work."* [5]But in the other passage God said, "They will never enter my place of rest."*

[6]So God's rest is there for people to enter, but those who first heard this good news failed to enter because they disobeyed God. [7]So God set another time for entering his rest, and that time is today. God announced this through David much later in the words already quoted:

"Today when you hear his voice,
don't harden your hearts."*

3:7-11 Ps 95:7-11. **3:12** Greek *brothers*. **3:15** Ps 95:7-8. **4:2** Some manuscripts read *they didn't combine what they heard with faith*. **4:3** Ps 95:11. **4:4** Gen 2:2. **4:5** Ps 95:11. **4:7** Ps 95:7-8.

KING JAMES VERSION

8For if Jesus had given them rest, then would he not afterward have spoken of another day.

9There remaineth therefore a rest to the people of God.

10For he that is entered into his rest, he also hath ceased from his own works, as God *did* from his.

11Let us labour therefore to enter into that rest, lest any man fall after the same example of unbelief.

12For the word of God *is* quick, and powerful, and sharper than any twoedged sword, piercing even to the dividing asunder of soul and spirit, and of the joints and marrow, and *is* a discerner of the thoughts and intents of the heart.

13Neither is there any creature that is not manifest in his sight: but all things *are* naked and opened unto the eyes of him with whom we have to do.

14Seeing then that we have a great high priest, that is passed into the heavens, Jesus the Son of God, let us hold fast *our* profession.

15For we have not an high priest which cannot be touched with the feeling of our infirmities; but was in all points tempted like as *we are, yet* without sin.

16Let us therefore come boldly unto the throne of grace, that we may obtain mercy, and find grace to help in time of need.

5 1For every high priest taken from among men is ordained for men in things *pertaining* to God, that he may offer both gifts and sacrifices for sins:

2Who can have compassion on the ignorant, and on them that are out of the way; for that he himself also is compassed with infirmity.

3And by reason hereof he ought, as for the people, so also for himself, to offer for sins.

4And no man taketh this honour unto himself, but he that is called of God, as *was* Aaron.

5So also Christ glorified not himself to be made an high priest; but he that said unto him, Thou art my Son, today have I begotten thee.

6As he saith also in another *place,* Thou *art* a priest for ever after the order of Melchisedec.

7Who in the days of his flesh, when he had offered up prayers and supplications with strong crying and tears unto him that was able to save him from death, and was heard in that he feared;

8Though he were a Son, yet learned he obedience by the things which he suffered;

9And being made perfect, he became the author of eternal salvation unto all them that obey him;

10Called of God an high priest after the order of Melchisedec.

NEW LIVING TRANSLATION

8Now if Joshua had succeeded in giving them this rest, God would not have spoken about another day of rest still to come. 9So there is a special rest* still waiting for the people of God. 10For all who have entered into God's rest have rested from their labors, just as God did after creating the world. 11So let us do our best to enter that rest. But if we disobey God, as the people of Israel did, we will fall.

12For the word of God is alive and powerful. It is sharper than the sharpest two-edged sword, cutting between soul and spirit, between joint and marrow. It exposes our innermost thoughts and desires. 13Nothing in all creation is hidden from God. Everything is naked and exposed before his eyes, and he is the one to whom we are accountable.

Christ Is Our High Priest

14So then, since we have a great High Priest who has entered heaven, Jesus the Son of God, let us hold firmly to what we believe. 15This High Priest of ours understands our weaknesses, for he faced all of the same testings we do, yet he did not sin. 16So let us come boldly to the throne of our gracious God. There we will receive his mercy, and we will find grace to help us when we need it most.

5 Every high priest is a man chosen to represent other people in their dealings with God. He presents their gifts to God and offers sacrifices for their sins. 2And he is able to deal gently with ignorant and wayward people because he himself is subject to the same weaknesses. 3That is why he must offer sacrifices for his own sins as well as theirs.

4And no one can become a high priest simply because he wants such an honor. He must be called by God for this work, just as Aaron was. 5That is why Christ did not honor himself by assuming he could become High Priest. No, he was chosen by God, who said to him,

"You are my Son.
Today I have become your Father."*

6And in another passage God said to him,

"You are a priest forever in the order of
Melchizedek."*

7While Jesus was here on earth, he offered prayers and pleadings, with a loud cry and tears, to the one who could rescue him from death. And God heard his prayers because of his deep reverence for God. 8Even though Jesus was God's Son, he learned obedience from the things he suffered. 9In this way, God qualified him as a perfect High Priest, and he became the source of eternal salvation for all those who obey him. 10And God designated him to be a High Priest in the order of Melchizedek.

4:9 Or *a Sabbath rest.* **5:5** Or *Today I reveal you as my Son.* Ps 2:7. **5:6** Ps 110:4.

KING JAMES VERSION

11Of whom we have many things to say, and hard to be uttered, seeing ye are dull of hearing.

12For when for the time ye ought to be teachers, ye have need that one teach you again which *be* the first principles of the oracles of God; and are become such as have need of milk, and not of strong meat.

13For every one that useth milk *is* unskilful in the word of righteousness: for he is a babe.

14But strong meat belongeth to them that are of full age, *even* those who by reason of use have their senses exercised to discern both good and evil.

6 1Therefore leaving the principles of the doctrine of Christ, let us go on unto perfection; not laying again the foundation of repentance from dead works, and of faith toward God,

2Of the doctrine of baptisms, and of laying on of hands, and of resurrection of the dead, and of eternal judgment.

3And this will we do, if God permit.

4For *it is* impossible for those who were once enlightened, and have tasted of the heavenly gift, and were made partakers of the Holy Ghost,

5And have tasted the good word of God, and the powers of the world to come,

6If they shall fall away, to renew them again unto repentance; seeing they crucify to themselves the Son of God afresh, and put *him* to an open shame.

7For the earth which drinketh in the rain that cometh oft upon it, and bringeth forth herbs meet for them by whom it is dressed, receiveth blessing from God:

8But that which beareth thorns and briers *is* rejected, and *is* nigh unto cursing; whose end *is* to be burned.

9But, beloved, we are persuaded better things of you, and things that accompany salvation, though we thus speak.

10For God *is* not unrighteous to forget your work and labour of love, which ye have shewed toward his name, in that ye have ministered to the saints, and do minister.

11And we desire that every one of you do shew the same diligence to the full assurance of hope unto the end:

12That ye be not slothful, but followers of them who through faith and patience inherit the promises.

13For when God made promise to Abraham, because he could swear by no greater, he sware by himself,

NEW LIVING TRANSLATION

A Call to Spiritual Growth

11There is much more we would like to say about this, but it is difficult to explain, especially since you are spiritually dull and don't seem to listen. 12You have been believers so long now that you ought to be teaching others. Instead, you need someone to teach you again the basic things about God's word.* You are like babies who need milk and cannot eat solid food. 13For someone who lives on milk is still an infant and doesn't know how to do what is right. 14Solid food is for those who are mature, who through training have the skill to recognize the difference between right and wrong.

6 So let us stop going over the basic teachings about Christ again and again. Let us go on instead and become mature in our understanding. Surely we don't need to start again with the fundamental importance of repenting from evil deeds* and placing our faith in God. 2You don't need further instruction about baptisms, the laying on of hands, the resurrection of the dead, and eternal judgment. 3And so, God willing, we will move forward to further understanding.

4For it is impossible to bring back to repentance those who were once enlightened—those who have experienced the good things of heaven and shared in the Holy Spirit, 5who have tasted the goodness of the word of God and the power of the age to come—6and who then turn away from God. It is impossible to bring such people back to repentance; by rejecting the Son of God, they themselves are nailing him to the cross once again and holding him up to public shame.

7When the ground soaks up the falling rain and bears a good crop for the farmer, it has God's blessing. 8But if a field bears thorns and thistles, it is useless. The farmer will soon condemn that field and burn it.

9Dear friends, even though we are talking this way, we really don't believe it applies to you. We are confident that you are meant for better things, things that come with salvation. 10For God is not unjust. He will not forget how hard you have worked for him and how you have shown your love to him by caring for other believers,* as you still do. 11Our great desire is that you will keep on loving others as long as life lasts, in order to make certain that what you hope for will come true. 12Then you will not become spiritually dull and indifferent. Instead, you will follow the example of those who are going to inherit God's promises because of their faith and endurance.

God's Promises Bring Hope

13For example, there was God's promise to Abraham. Since there was no one greater to swear by, God took an oath in his own name, saying:

6:1 Greek *from dead works.* **5:12** Or *about the oracles of God.* **6:10** Greek *for God's holy people.*

KING JAMES VERSION

14 Saying, Surely blessing I will bless thee, and
multiplying I will multiply thee.
15 And so, after he had patiently endured, he obtained the promise.
16 For men verily swear by the greater: and an oath
for confirmation *is* to them an end of all strife.
17 Wherein God, willing more abundantly to shew
unto the heirs of promise the immutability of his
counsel, confirmed *it* by an oath:
18 That by two immutable things, in which *it was*
impossible for God to lie, we might have a strong
consolation, who have fled for refuge to lay hold
upon the hope set before us:
19 Which *hope* we have as an anchor of the soul,
both sure and stedfast, and which entereth into that
within the veil;
20 Whither the forerunner is for us entered, *even*
Jesus, made an high priest for ever after the order of
Melchisedec.

7 1 For this Melchisedec, king of Salem, priest of
the most high God, who met Abraham returning from the slaughter of the kings, and blessed him;
2 To whom also Abraham gave a tenth part of all;
first being by interpretation King of righteousness,
and after that also King of Salem, which is, King of
peace;
3 Without father, without mother, without descent, having neither beginning of days, nor end of
life; but made like unto the Son of God; abideth a
priest continually.
4 Now consider how great this man *was,* unto
whom even the patriarch Abraham gave the tenth of
the spoils.
5 And verily they that are of the sons of Levi, who
receive the office of the priesthood, have a commandment to take tithes of the people according to
the law, that is, of their brethren, though they come
out of the loins of Abraham:
6 But he whose descent is not counted from them
received tithes of Abraham, and blessed him that
had the promises.
7 And without all contradiction the less is blessed
of the better.
8 And here men that die receive tithes; but there he
receiveth them, of whom it is witnessed that he
liveth.
9 And as I may so say, Levi also, who receiveth
tithes, payed tithes in Abraham.
10 For he was yet in the loins of his father, when
Melchisedec met him.
11 If therefore perfection were by the Levitical

NEW LIVING TRANSLATION

14 "I will certainly bless you,
and I will multiply your descendants
beyond number."*

15 Then Abraham waited patiently, and he received
what God had promised.
16 Now when people take an oath, they call on
someone greater than themselves to hold them to it.
And without any question that oath is binding.
17 God also bound himself with an oath, so that those
who received the promise could be perfectly sure
that he would never change his mind. 18 So God has
given both his promise and his oath. These two
things are unchangeable because it is impossible for
God to lie. Therefore, we who have fled to him for
refuge can have great confidence as we hold to the
hope that lies before us. 19 This hope is a strong and
trustworthy anchor for our souls. It leads us through
the curtain into God's inner sanctuary. 20 Jesus has
already gone in there for us. He has become our
eternal High Priest in the order of Melchizedek.

Melchizedek Is Greater Than Abraham

7 This Melchizedek was king of the city of Salem
and also a priest of God Most High. When
Abraham was returning home after winning a great
battle against the kings, Melchizedek met him and
blessed him. 2 Then Abraham took a tenth of all he
had captured in battle and gave it to Melchizedek.
The name Melchizedek means "king of justice," and
king of Salem means "king of peace." 3 There is no
record of his father or mother or any of his ancestors—no beginning or end to his life. He remains a
priest forever, resembling the Son of God.
4 Consider then how great this Melchizedek was.
Even Abraham, the great patriarch of Israel, recognized this by giving him a tenth of what he had taken
in battle. 5 Now the law of Moses required that the
priests, who are descendants of Levi, must collect a
tithe from the rest of the people of Israel,* who are
also descendants of Abraham. 6 But Melchizedek,
who was not a descendant of Levi, collected a tenth
from Abraham. And Melchizedek placed a blessing
upon Abraham, the one who had already received
the promises of God. 7 And without question, the person who has the power to give a blessing is greater
than the one who is blessed.
8 The priests who collect tithes are men who die, so
Melchizedek is greater than they are, because we are
told that he lives on. 9 In addition, we might even say
that these Levites—the ones who collect the tithe—
paid a tithe to Melchizedek when their ancestor
Abraham paid a tithe to him. 10 For although Levi
wasn't born yet, the seed from which he came was in
Abraham's body when Melchizedek collected the
tithe from him.
11 So if the priesthood of Levi, on which the law

6:14 Gen 22:17. **7:5** Greek *from their brothers.*

KING JAMES VERSION

priesthood, (for under it the people received the law,) what further need *was there* that another priest should rise after the order of Melchisedec, and not be called after the order of Aaron?

12For the priesthood being changed, there is made of necessity a change also of the law.

13For he of whom these things are spoken pertaineth to another tribe, of which no man gave attendance at the altar.

14For *it is* evident that our Lord sprang out of Judah; of which tribe Moses spake nothing concerning priesthood.

15And it is yet far more evident: for that after the similitude of Melchisedec there ariseth another priest,

16Who is made, not after the law of a carnal commandment, but after the power of an endless life.

17For he testifieth, Thou *art* a priest for ever after the order of Melchisedec.

18For there is verily a disannulling of the commandment going before for the weakness and unprofitableness thereof.

19For the law made nothing perfect, but the bringing in of a better hope *did;* by the which we draw nigh unto God.

20And inasmuch as not without an oath *he was made priest:*

21(For those priests were made without an oath; but this with an oath by him that said unto him, The Lord sware and will not repent, Thou *art* a priest for ever after the order of Melchisedec:)

22By so much was Jesus made a surety of a better testament.

23And they truly were many priests, because they were not suffered to continue by reason of death:

24But this *man,* because he continueth ever, hath an unchangeable priesthood.

25Wherefore he is able also to save them to the uttermost that come unto God by him, seeing he ever liveth to make intercession for them.

26For such an high priest became us, *who is* holy, harmless, undefiled, separate from sinners, and made higher than the heavens;

27Who needeth not daily, as those high priests, to offer up sacrifice, first for his own sins, and then for the people's: for this he did once, when he offered up himself.

28For the law maketh men high priests which have infirmity; but the word of the oath, which was since the law, *maketh* the Son, who is consecrated for evermore.

NEW LIVING TRANSLATION

was based, could have achieved the perfection God intended, why did God need to establish a different priesthood, with a priest in the order of Melchizedek instead of the order of Levi and Aaron?*

12And if the priesthood is changed, the law must
also be changed to permit it. 13For the priest we are
talking about belongs to a different tribe, whose
members have never served at the altar as priests.
14What I mean is, our Lord came from the tribe of
Judah, and Moses never mentioned priests coming
from that tribe.

Jesus Is like Melchizedek

15This change has been made very clear since a different priest, who is like Melchizedek, has appeared.
16Jesus became a priest, not by meeting the physical
requirement of belonging to the tribe of Levi, but by
the power of a life that cannot be destroyed. 17And
the psalmist pointed this out when he prophesied,

"You are a priest forever in the order
of Melchizedek."*

18Yes, the old requirement about the priesthood was
set aside because it was weak and useless. 19For the
law never made anything perfect. But now we have
confidence in a better hope, through which we draw
near to God.

20This new system was established with a solemn
oath. Aaron's descendants became priests without
such an oath, 21but there was an oath regarding
Jesus. For God said to him,

"The LORD has taken an oath and will not
break his vow:
'You are a priest forever.'"*

22Because of this oath, Jesus is the one who guarantees this better covenant with God.

23There were many priests under the old system,
for death prevented them from remaining in office.
24But because Jesus lives forever, his priesthood lasts
forever. 25Therefore he is able, once and forever, to
save* those who come to God through him. He lives
forever to intercede with God on their behalf.

26He is the kind of high priest we need because he
is holy and blameless, unstained by sin. He has been
set apart from sinners and has been given the highest
place of honor in heaven.* 27Unlike those other high
priests, he does not need to offer sacrifices every day.
They did this for their own sins first and then for the
sins of the people. But Jesus did this once for all when
he offered himself as the sacrifice for the people's
sins. 28The law appointed high priests who were limited by human weakness. But after the law was given,
God appointed his Son with an oath, and his Son has
been made the perfect High Priest forever.

7:11 Greek *the order of Aaron?* 7:17 Ps 110:4. 7:21 Ps 110:4.
7:25 Or *is able to save completely.* 7:26 Or *has been exalted higher than the heavens.*

KING JAMES VERSION

8

1 Now of the things which we have spoken *this is* the sum: We have such an high priest, who is set on the right hand of the throne of the Majesty in the heavens;

2 A minister of the sanctuary, and of the true tabernacle, which the Lord pitched, and not man.

3 For every high priest is ordained to offer gifts and sacrifices: wherefore *it is* of necessity that this man have somewhat also to offer.

4 For if he were on earth, he should not be a priest, seeing that there are priests that offer gifts according to the law:

5 Who serve unto the example and shadow of heavenly things, as Moses was admonished of God when he was about to make the tabernacle: for, See, saith he, *that* thou make all things according to the pattern shewed to thee in the mount.

6 But now hath he obtained a more excellent ministry, by how much also he is the mediator of a better covenant, which was established upon better promises.

7 For if that first *covenant* had been faultless, then should no place have been sought for the second.

8 For finding fault with them, he saith, Behold, the days come, saith the Lord, when I will make a new covenant with the house of Israel and with the house of Judah:

9 Not according to the covenant that I made with their fathers in the day when I took them by the hand to lead them out of the land of Egypt; because they continued not in my covenant, and I regarded them not, saith the Lord.

10 For this *is* the covenant that I will make with the house of Israel after those days, saith the Lord; I will put my laws into their mind, and write them in their hearts: and I will be to them a God, and they shall be to me a people:

11 And they shall not teach every man his neighbour, and every man his brother, saying, Know the Lord: for all shall know me, from the least to the greatest.

12 For I will be merciful to their unrighteousness, and their sins and their iniquities will I remember no more.

13 In that he saith, A new *covenant,* he hath made the first old. Now that which decayeth and waxeth old *is* ready to vanish away.

9

1 Then verily the first *covenant* had also ordinances of divine service, and a worldly sanctuary.

NEW LIVING TRANSLATION

Christ Is Our High Priest

8

Here is the main point: We have a High Priest who sat down in the place of honor beside the throne of the majestic God in heaven. 2 There he ministers in the heavenly Tabernacle,* the true place of worship that was built by the Lord and not by human hands.

3 And since every high priest is required to offer gifts and sacrifices, our High Priest must make an offering, too. 4 If he were here on earth, he would not even be a priest, since there already are priests who offer the gifts required by the law. 5 They serve in a system of worship that is only a copy, a shadow of the real one in heaven. For when Moses was getting ready to build the Tabernacle, God gave him this warning: "Be sure that you make everything according to the pattern I have shown you here on the mountain."*

6 But now Jesus, our High Priest, has been given a ministry that is far superior to the old priesthood, for he is the one who mediates for us a far better covenant with God, based on better promises.

7 If the first covenant had been faultless, there would have been no need for a second covenant to replace it. 8 But when God found fault with the people, he said:

"The day is coming, says the LORD,
when I will make a new covenant
with the people of Israel and Judah.
9 This covenant will not be like the one
I made with their ancestors
when I took them by the hand
and led them out of the land of Egypt.
They did not remain faithful to my covenant,
so I turned my back on them, says the LORD.
10 But this is the new covenant I will make
with the people of Israel on that day,* says
the LORD:
I will put my laws in their minds,
and I will write them on their hearts.
I will be their God,
and they will be my people.
11 And they will not need to teach their neighbors,
nor will they need to teach their relatives,*
saying, 'You should know the LORD.'
For everyone, from the least to the greatest,
will know me already.
12 And I will forgive their wickedness,
and I will never again remember their sins."*

13 When God speaks of a "new" covenant, it means he has made the first one obsolete. It is now out of date and will soon disappear.

Old Rules about Worship

9

That first covenant between God and Israel had regulations for worship and a place of worship

8:2 Or *tent;* also in 8:5. **8:5** Exod 25:40; 26:30. **8:10** Greek *after those days.* **8:11** Greek *their brother.* **8:8-12** Jer 31:31-34.

KING JAMES VERSION

2For there was a tabernacle made; the first, wherein *was* the candlestick, and the table, and the shewbread; which is called the sanctuary.

3And after the second veil, the tabernacle which is called the Holiest of all;

4Which had the golden censer, and the ark of the covenant overlaid round about with gold, wherein *was* the golden pot that had manna, and Aaron's rod that budded, and the tables of the covenant;

5And over it the cherubims of glory shadowing the mercyseat; of which we cannot now speak particularly.

6Now when these things were thus ordained, the priests went always into the first tabernacle, accomplishing the service *of God.*

7But into the second *went* the high priest alone once every year, not without blood, which he offered for himself, and *for* the errors of the people:

8The Holy Ghost this signifying, that the way into the holiest of all was not yet made manifest, while as the first tabernacle was yet standing:

9Which *was* a figure for the time then present, in which were offered both gifts and sacrifices, that could not make him that did the service perfect, as pertaining to the conscience;

10*Which stood* only in meats and drinks, and divers washings, and carnal ordinances, imposed *on them* until the time of reformation.

11But Christ being come an high priest of good things to come, by a greater and more perfect tabernacle, not made with hands, that is to say, not of this building;

12Neither by the blood of goats and calves, but by his own blood he entered in once into the holy place, having obtained eternal redemption *for us.*

13For if the blood of bulls and of goats, and the ashes of an heifer sprinkling the unclean, sanctifieth to the purifying of the flesh:

14How much more shall the blood of Christ, who through the eternal Spirit offered himself without spot to God, purge your conscience from dead works to serve the living God?

15And for this cause he is the mediator of the new testament, that by means of death, for the redemption of the transgressions *that were* under the first testament, they which are called might receive the promise of eternal inheritance.

16For where a testament *is,* there must also of necessity be the death of the testator.

NEW LIVING TRANSLATION

here on earth. 2There were two rooms in that Tabernacle.* In the first room were a lampstand, a table, and sacred loaves of bread on the table. This room was called the Holy Place. 3Then there was a curtain, and behind the curtain was the second room* called the Most Holy Place. 4In that room were a gold incense altar and a wooden chest called the Ark of the Covenant, which was covered with gold on all sides. Inside the Ark were a gold jar containing manna, Aaron's staff that sprouted leaves, and the stone tablets of the covenant. 5Above the Ark were the cherubim of divine glory, whose wings stretched out over the Ark's cover, the place of atonement. But we cannot explain these things in detail now.

6When these things were all in place, the priests regularly entered the first room* as they performed their religious duties. 7But only the high priest ever entered the Most Holy Place, and only once a year. And he always offered blood for his own sins and for the sins the people had committed in ignorance. 8By these regulations the Holy Spirit revealed that the entrance to the Most Holy Place was not freely open as long as the Tabernacle* and the system it represented were still in use.

9This is an illustration pointing to the present time. For the gifts and sacrifices that the priests offer are not able to cleanse the consciences of the people who bring them. 10For that old system deals only with food and drink and various cleansing ceremonies—physical regulations that were in effect only until a better system could be established.

Christ Is the Perfect Sacrifice

11So Christ has now become the High Priest over all the good things that have come.* He has entered that greater, more perfect Tabernacle in heaven, which was not made by human hands and is not part of this created world. 12With his own blood—not the blood of goats and calves—he entered the Most Holy Place once for all time and secured our redemption forever.

13Under the old system, the blood of goats and bulls and the ashes of a young cow could cleanse people's bodies from ceremonial impurity. 14Just think how much more the blood of Christ will purify our consciences from sinful deeds* so that we can worship the living God. For by the power of the eternal Spirit, Christ offered himself to God as a perfect sacrifice for our sins. 15That is why he is the one who mediates a new covenant between God and people, so that all who are called can receive the eternal inheritance God has promised them. For Christ died to set them free from the penalty of the sins they had committed under that first covenant.

16Now when someone leaves a will,* it is necessary to prove that the person who made it is dead.*

9:2 Or *tent;* also in 9:11, 21. **9:3** Greek *second tent.* **9:6** Greek *first tent.* **9:8** Or *the first room;* Greek reads *the first tent.* **9:11** Some manuscripts read *that are about to come.* **9:14** Greek *from dead works.* **9:16a** Or *covenant;* also in 9:17. **9:16b** Or *Now when someone makes a covenant, it is necessary to ratify it with the death of a sacrifice.*

KING JAMES VERSION

17 For a testament *is* of force after men are dead: otherwise it is of no strength at all while the testator liveth.

18 Whereupon neither the first *testament* was dedicated without blood.

19 For when Moses had spoken every precept to all the people according to the law, he took the blood of calves and of goats, with water, and scarlet wool, and hyssop, and sprinkled both the book, and all the people,

20 Saying, This *is* the blood of the testament which God hath enjoined unto you.

21 Moreover he sprinkled with blood both the tabernacle, and all the vessels of the ministry.

22 And almost all things are by the law purged with blood; and without shedding of blood is no remission.

23 *It was* therefore necessary that the patterns of things in the heavens should be purified with these; but the heavenly things themselves with better sacrifices than these.

24 For Christ is not entered into the holy places made with hands, *which are* the figures of the true; but into heaven itself, now to appear in the presence of God for us:

25 Nor yet that he should offer himself often, as the high priest entereth into the holy place every year with blood of others;

26 For then must he often have suffered since the foundation of the world: but now once in the end of the world hath he appeared to put away sin by the sacrifice of himself.

27 And as it is appointed unto men once to die, but after this the judgment:

28 So Christ was once offered to bear the sins of many; and unto them that look for him shall he appear the second time without sin unto salvation.

10 1 For the law having a shadow of good things to come, *and* not the very image of the things, can never with those sacrifices which they offered year by year continually make the comers thereunto perfect.

2 For then would they not have ceased to be offered? because that the worshippers once purged should have had no more conscience of sins.

3 But in those *sacrifices there is* a remembrance again *made* of sins every year.

4 For *it is* not possible that the blood of bulls and of goats should take away sins.

5 Wherefore when he cometh into the world, he

NEW LIVING TRANSLATION

17 The will goes into effect only after the person's
death. While the person who made it is still alive,
the will cannot be put into effect.
18 That is why even the first covenant was put into
effect with the blood of an animal. 19 For after Moses
had read each of God's commandments to all the
people, he took the blood of calves and goats,* along
with water, and sprinkled both the book of God's law
and all the people, using hyssop branches and scarlet
wool. 20 Then he said, "This blood confirms the covenant God has made with you."* 21 And in the same
way, he sprinkled blood on the Tabernacle and on
everything used for worship. 22 In fact, according to
the law of Moses, nearly everything was purified
with blood. For without the shedding of blood, there
is no forgiveness.
23 That is why the Tabernacle and everything in it,
which were copies of things in heaven, had to be
purified by the blood of animals. But the real things
in heaven had to be purified with far better sacrifices than the blood of animals.
24 For Christ did not enter into a holy place made
with human hands, which was only a copy of the true
one in heaven. He entered into heaven itself to appear now before God on our behalf. 25 And he did not
enter heaven to offer himself again and again, like
the high priest here on earth who enters the Most
Holy Place year after year with the blood of an animal. 26 If that had been necessary, Christ would have
had to die again and again, ever since the world
began. But now, once for all time, he has appeared at
the end of the age* to remove sin by his own death as
a sacrifice.
27 And just as each person is destined to die once
and after that comes judgment, 28 so also Christ died
once for all time as a sacrifice to take away the sins of
many people. He will come again, not to deal with
our sins, but to bring salvation to all who are eagerly
waiting for him.

Christ's Sacrifice Once for All

10 The old system under the law of Moses was
only a shadow, a dim preview of the good
things to come, not the good things themselves. The
sacrifices under that system were repeated again and
again, year after year, but they were never able to provide perfect cleansing for those who came to worship.
2 If they could have provided perfect cleansing, the
sacrifices would have stopped, for the worshipers
would have been purified once for all time, and their
feelings of guilt would have disappeared.
3 But instead, those sacrifices actually reminded
them of their sins year after year. 4 For it is not possible for the blood of bulls and goats to take away sins.
5 That is why, when Christ* came into the world, he
said to God,

9:19 Some manuscripts do not include *and goats.* **9:20** Exod 24:8.
9:26 Greek *the ages.* **10:5** Greek *he;* also in 10:8.

KING JAMES VERSION

saith, Sacrifice and offering thou wouldest not, but a
body hast thou prepared me:

6 In burnt offerings and *sacrifices* for sin thou hast
had no pleasure.

7 Then said I, Lo, I come (in the volume of the book
it is written of me,) to do thy will, O God.

8 Above when he said, Sacrifice and offering and
burnt offerings and *offering* for sin thou wouldest
not, neither hadst pleasure *therein;* which are offered by the law;

9 Then said he, Lo, I come to do thy will, O God. He
taketh away the first, that he may establish the
second.

10 By the which will we are sanctified through the
offering of the body of Jesus Christ once *for all.*

11 And every priest standeth daily ministering and
offering oftentimes the same sacrifices, which can
never take away sins:

12 But this man, after he had offered one sacrifice
for sins for ever, sat down on the right hand of God;

13 From henceforth expecting till his enemies be
made his footstool.

14 For by one offering he hath perfected for ever
them that are sanctified.

15 *Whereof* the Holy Ghost also is a witness to us:
for after that he had said before,

16 This *is* the covenant that I will make with them
after those days, saith the Lord, I will put my laws
into their hearts, and in their minds will I write them;

17 And their sins and iniquities will I remember
no more.

18 Now where remission of these *is, there is* no
more offering for sin.

19 Having therefore, brethren, boldness to enter
into the holiest by the blood of Jesus,

20 By a new and living way, which he hath consecrated for us, through the veil, that is to say, his flesh;

21 And *having* an high priest over the house of
God;

22 Let us draw near with a true heart in full assurance of faith, having our hearts sprinkled from an
evil conscience, and our bodies washed with pure
water.

23 Let us hold fast the profession of *our* faith without wavering; (for he *is* faithful that promised;)

24 And let us consider one another to provoke unto
love and to good works:

NEW LIVING TRANSLATION

"You did not want animal sacrifices or sin
offerings.
But you have given me a body to offer.
6 You were not pleased with burnt offerings
or other offerings for sin.
7 Then I said, 'Look, I have come to do your will,
O God—
as is written about me in the Scriptures.'"*

8 First, Christ said, "You did not want animal sacrifices or sin offerings or burnt offerings or other
offerings for sin, nor were you pleased with them"
(though they are required by the law of Moses).
9 Then he said, "Look, I have come to do your will." He
cancels the first covenant in order to put the second
into effect. 10 For God's will was for us to be made
holy by the sacrifice of the body of Jesus Christ, once
for all time.

11 Under the old covenant, the priest stands and
ministers before the altar day after day, offering the
same sacrifices again and again, which can never
take away sins. 12 But our High Priest offered himself
to God as a single sacrifice for sins, good for all time.
Then he sat down in the place of honor at God's right
hand. 13 There he waits until his enemies are humbled and made a footstool under his feet. 14 For by
that one offering he forever made perfect those who
are being made holy.

15 And the Holy Spirit also testifies that this is so.
For he says,

16 "This is the new covenant I will make
with my people on that day,* says the LORD:
I will put my laws in their hearts,
and I will write them on their minds."*

17 Then he says,
"I will never again remember
their sins and lawless deeds."*

18 And when sins have been forgiven, there is no need
to offer any more sacrifices.

A Call to Persevere

19 And so, dear brothers and sisters,* we can boldly
enter heaven's Most Holy Place because of the blood
of Jesus. 20 By his death,* Jesus opened a new and life-
giving way through the curtain into the Most Holy
Place. 21 And since we have a great High Priest who
rules over God's house, 22 let us go right into the presence of God with sincere hearts fully trusting him.
For our guilty consciences have been sprinkled with
Christ's blood to make us clean, and our bodies have
been washed with pure water.

23 Let us hold tightly without wavering to the hope
we affirm, for God can be trusted to keep his promise. 24 Let us think of ways to motivate one another to

10:5-7 Ps 40:6-8 (Greek version). **10:16a** Greek *after those days.* **10:16b** Jer 31:33a. **10:17** Jer 31:34b. **10:19** Greek *brothers.* **10:20** Greek *Through his flesh.*

KING JAMES VERSION

25Not forsaking the assembling of ourselves together, as the manner of some *is;* but exhorting *one another:* and so much the more, as ye see the day approaching.

26For if we sin wilfully after that we have received the knowledge of the truth, there remaineth no more sacrifice for sins,

27But a certain fearful looking for of judgment and fiery indignation, which shall devour the adversaries.

28He that despised Moses' law died without mercy under two or three witnesses:

29Of how much sorer punishment, suppose ye, shall he be thought worthy, who hath trodden under foot the Son of God, and hath counted the blood of the covenant, wherewith he was sanctified, an unholy thing, and hath done despite unto the Spirit of grace?

30For we know him that hath said, Vengeance *belongeth* unto me, I will recompense, saith the Lord. And again, The Lord shall judge his people.

31*It is* a fearful thing to fall into the hands of the living God.

32But call to remembrance the former days, in which, after ye were illuminated, ye endured a great fight of afflictions;

33Partly, whilst ye were made a gazingstock both by reproaches and afflictions; and partly, whilst ye became companions of them that were so used.

34For ye had compassion of me in my bonds, and took joyfully the spoiling of your goods, knowing in yourselves that ye have in heaven a better and an enduring substance.

35Cast not away therefore your confidence, which hath great recompense of reward.

36For ye have need of patience, that, after ye have done the will of God, ye might receive the promise.

37For yet a little while, and he that shall come will come, and will not tarry.

38Now the just shall live by faith: but if *any man* draw back, my soul shall have no pleasure in him.

39But we are not of them who draw back unto perdition; but of them that believe to the saving of the soul.

11 1Now faith is the substance of things hoped for, the evidence of things not seen.

2For by it the elders obtained a good report.

NEW LIVING TRANSLATION

acts of love and good works. 25And let us not neglect
our meeting together, as some people do, but encourage one another, especially now that the day of
his return is drawing near.
26Dear friends, if we deliberately continue sinning
after we have received knowledge of the truth, there
is no longer any sacrifice that will cover these sins.
27There is only the terrible expectation of God's
judgment and the raging fire that will consume his
enemies. 28For anyone who refused to obey the law
of Moses was put to death without mercy on the testimony of two or three witnesses. 29Just think how
much worse the punishment will be for those who
have trampled on the Son of God, and have treated
the blood of the covenant, which made us holy, as if it
were common and unholy, and have insulted and
disdained the Holy Spirit who brings God's mercy to
us. 30For we know the one who said,

> "I will take revenge.
> I will pay them back."*

He also said,

> "The LORD will judge his own people."*

31It is a terrible thing to fall into the hands of the living God.
32Think back on those early days when you first
learned about Christ.* Remember how you remained faithful even though it meant terrible suffering. 33Sometimes you were exposed to public
ridicule and were beaten, and sometimes you helped
others who were suffering the same things. 34You
suffered along with those who were thrown into jail,
and when all you owned was taken from you, you accepted it with joy. You knew there were better things
waiting for you that will last forever.
35So do not throw away this confident trust in the
Lord. Remember the great reward it brings you!
36Patient endurance is what you need now, so that
you will continue to do God's will. Then you will
receive all that he has promised.

> 37 "For in just a little while,
> the Coming One will come and not delay.
> 38 And my righteous ones will live by faith.*
> But I will take no pleasure in anyone who
> turns away."*

39But we are not like those who turn away from God
to their own destruction. We are the faithful ones,
whose souls will be saved.

Great Examples of Faith

11 Faith is the confidence that what we hope for
will actually happen; it gives us assurance
about things we cannot see. 2Through their faith, the
people in days of old earned a good reputation.

10:30a Deut 32:35. **10:30b** Deut 32:36. **10:32** Greek *when you were first enlightened.* **10:38** Or *my righteous ones will live by their faithfulness;* Greek reads *my righteous one will live by faith.* **10:37-38** Hab 2:3-4.

KING JAMES VERSION

3 Through faith we understand that the worlds were framed by the word of God, so that things which are seen were not made of things which do appear.

4 By faith Abel offered unto God a more excellent sacrifice than Cain, by which he obtained witness that he was righteous, God testifying of his gifts: and by it he being dead yet speaketh.

5 By faith Enoch was translated that he should not see death; and was not found, because God had translated him: for before his translation he had this testimony, that he pleased God.

6 But without faith *it is* impossible to please *him:* for he that cometh to God must believe that he is, and that he is a rewarder of them that diligently seek him.

7 By faith Noah, being warned of God of things not seen as yet, moved with fear, prepared an ark to the saving of his house; by the which he condemned the world, and became heir of the righteousness which is by faith.

8 By faith Abraham, when he was called to go out into a place which he should after receive for an inheritance, obeyed; and he went out, not knowing whither he went.

9 By faith he sojourned in the land of promise, as *in* a strange country, dwelling in tabernacles with Isaac and Jacob, the heirs with him of the same promise:

10 For he looked for a city which hath foundations, whose builder and maker *is* God.

11 Through faith also Sara herself received strength to conceive seed, and was delivered of a child when she was past age, because she judged him faithful who had promised.

12 Therefore sprang there even of one, and him as good as dead, *so many* as the stars of the sky in multitude, and as the sand which is by the sea shore innumerable.

13 These all died in faith, not having received the promises, but having seen them afar off, and were persuaded of *them,* and embraced *them,* and confessed that they were strangers and pilgrims on the earth.

14 For they that say such things declare plainly that they seek a country.

15 And truly, if they had been mindful of that *country* from whence they came out, they might have had opportunity to have returned.

16 But now they desire a better *country,* that is, an heavenly: wherefore God is not ashamed to be called their God: for he hath prepared for them a city.

17 By faith Abraham, when he was tried, offered up Isaac: and he that had received the promises offered up his only begotten *son,*

18 Of whom it was said, That in Isaac shall thy seed be called:

19 Accounting that God *was* able to raise *him* up,

NEW LIVING TRANSLATION

3 By faith we understand that the entire universe was formed at God's command, that what we now see did not come from anything that can be seen.

4 It was by faith that Abel brought a more acceptable offering to God than Cain did. Abel's offering gave evidence that he was a righteous man, and God showed his approval of his gifts. Although Abel is long dead, he still speaks to us by his example of faith.

5 It was by faith that Enoch was taken up to heaven without dying—"he disappeared, because God took him."* For before he was taken up, he was known as a person who pleased God. 6 And it is impossible to please God without faith. Anyone who wants to come to him must believe that God exists and that he rewards those who sincerely seek him.

7 It was by faith that Noah built a large boat to save his family from the flood. He obeyed God, who warned him about things that had never happened before. By his faith Noah condemned the rest of the world, and he received the righteousness that comes by faith.

8 It was by faith that Abraham obeyed when God called him to leave home and go to another land that God would give him as his inheritance. He went without knowing where he was going. 9 And even when he reached the land God promised him, he lived there by faith—for he was like a foreigner, living in tents. And so did Isaac and Jacob, who inherited the same promise. 10 Abraham was confidently looking forward to a city with eternal foundations, a city designed and built by God.

11 It was by faith that even Sarah was able to have a child, though she was barren and was too old. She believed* that God would keep his promise. 12 And so a whole nation came from this one man who was as good as dead—a nation with so many people that, like the stars in the sky and the sand on the seashore, there is no way to count them.

13 All these people died still believing what God had promised them. They did not receive what was promised, but they saw it all from a distance and welcomed it. They agreed that they were foreigners and nomads here on earth. 14 Obviously people who say such things are looking forward to a country they can call their own. 15 If they had longed for the country they came from, they could have gone back. 16 But they were looking for a better place, a heavenly homeland. That is why God is not ashamed to be called their God, for he has prepared a city for them.

17 It was by faith that Abraham offered Isaac as a sacrifice when God was testing him. Abraham, who had received God's promises, was ready to sacrifice his only son, Isaac, 18 even though God had told him, "Isaac is the son through whom your descendants will be counted."* 19 Abraham reasoned that if Isaac

11:5 Gen 5:24. **11:11** Or *It was by faith that he [Abraham] was able to have a child, even though Sarah was barren and he was too old. He believed.* **11:18** Gen 21:12.

even from the dead; from whence also he received
him in a figure.
20By faith Isaac blessed Jacob and Esau concerning things to come.
21By faith Jacob, when he was a dying, blessed
both the sons of Joseph; and worshipped, *leaning*
upon the top of his staff.
22By faith Joseph, when he died, made mention of
the departing of the children of Israel; and gave
commandment concerning his bones.
23By faith Moses, when he was born, was hid three
months of his parents, because they saw *he was* a
proper child; and they were not afraid of the king's
commandment.
24By faith Moses, when he was come to years, refused to be called the son of Pharaoh's daughter;
25Choosing rather to suffer affliction with the
people of God, than to enjoy the pleasures of sin for a
season;
26Esteeming the reproach of Christ greater riches
than the treasures in Egypt: for he had respect unto
the recompense of the reward.
27By faith he forsook Egypt, not fearing the wrath
of the king: for he endured, as seeing him who is
invisible.
28Through faith he kept the passover, and the
sprinkling of blood, lest he that destroyed the firstborn should touch them.
29By faith they passed through the Red sea as by
dry *land:* which the Egyptians assaying to do were
drowned.
30By faith the walls of Jericho fell down, after they
were compassed about seven days.
31By faith the harlot Rahab perished not with
them that believed not, when she had received the
spies with peace.
32And what shall I more say? for the time would
fail me to tell of Gedeon, and *of* Barak, and *of* Samson, and *of* Jephthae; *of* David also, and Samuel, and
of the prophets:
33Who through faith subdued kingdoms, wrought
righteousness, obtained promises, stopped the
mouths of lions,
34Quenched the violence of fire, escaped the edge
of the sword, out of weakness were made strong,
waxed valiant in fight, turned to flight the armies of
the aliens.
35Women received their dead raised to life again:
and others were tortured, not accepting deliverance;
that they might obtain a better resurrection:
36And others had trial of *cruel* mockings and
scourgings, yea, moreover of bonds and imprisonment:
37They were stoned, they were sawn asunder, were

died, God was able to bring him back to life again.
And in a sense, Abraham did receive his son back
from the dead.
20It was by faith that Isaac promised blessings for
the future to his sons, Jacob and Esau.
21It was by faith that Jacob, when he was old and
dying, blessed each of Joseph's sons and bowed in
worship as he leaned on his staff.
22It was by faith that Joseph, when he was about to
die, said confidently that the people of Israel would
leave Egypt. He even commanded them to take his
bones with them when they left.
23It was by faith that Moses' parents hid him for
three months when he was born. They saw that God
had given them an unusual child, and they were not
afraid to disobey the king's command.
24It was by faith that Moses, when he grew up, refused to be called the son of Pharaoh's daughter.
25He chose to share the oppression of God's people
instead of enjoying the fleeting pleasures of sin.
26He thought it was better to suffer for the sake of
Christ than to own the treasures of Egypt, for he was
looking ahead to his great reward. 27It was by faith
that Moses left the land of Egypt, not fearing the
king's anger. He kept right on going because he kept
his eyes on the one who is invisible. 28It was by faith
that Moses commanded the people of Israel to keep
the Passover and to sprinkle blood on the doorposts
so that the angel of death would not kill their firstborn sons.
29It was by faith that the people of Israel went
right through the Red Sea as though they were on dry
ground. But when the Egyptians tried to follow, they
were all drowned.
30It was by faith that the people of Israel marched
around Jericho for seven days, and the walls came
crashing down.
31It was by faith that Rahab the prostitute was not
destroyed with the people in her city who refused to
obey God. For she had given a friendly welcome to
the spies.
32How much more do I need to say? It would take
too long to recount the stories of the faith of Gideon,
Barak, Samson, Jephthah, David, Samuel, and all the
prophets. 33By faith these people overthrew kingdoms, ruled with justice, and received what God had
promised them. They shut the mouths of lions,
34quenched the flames of fire, and escaped death by
the edge of the sword. Their weakness was turned to
strength. They became strong in battle and put
whole armies to flight. 35Women received their
loved ones back again from death.
But others were tortured, refusing to turn from
God in order to be set free. They placed their hope in
a better life after the resurrection. 36Some were
jeered at, and their backs were cut open with whips.
Others were chained in prisons. 37Some died by

KING JAMES VERSION

tempted, were slain with the sword: they wandered
about in sheepskins and goatskins; being destitute,
afflicted, tormented;
38(Of whom the world was not worthy:) they wandered in deserts, and *in* mountains, and *in* dens and
caves of the earth.
39And these all, having obtained a good report
through faith, received not the promise:
40God having provided some better thing for us,
that they without us should not be made perfect.

12 1Wherefore seeing we also are compassed
about with so great a cloud of witnesses, let us
lay aside every weight, and the sin which doth so easily
beset *us*, and let us run with patience the race that is
set before us,
2Looking unto Jesus the author and finisher of
our faith; who for the joy that was set before him
endured the cross, despising the shame, and is set
down at the right hand of the throne of God.
3For consider him that endured such contradiction of sinners against himself, lest ye be wearied
and faint in your minds.
4Ye have not yet resisted unto blood, striving
against sin.
5And ye have forgotten the exhortation which
speaketh unto you as unto children, My son, despise
not thou the chastening of the Lord, nor faint when
thou art rebuked of him:
6For whom the Lord loveth he chasteneth, and
scourgeth every son whom he receiveth.
7If ye endure chastening, God dealeth with you as
with sons; for what son is he whom the father
chasteneth not?
8But if ye be without chastisement, whereof all are
partakers, then are ye bastards, and not sons.
9Furthermore we have had fathers of our flesh
which corrected *us*, and we gave *them* reverence:
shall we not much rather be in subjection unto the
Father of spirits, and live?
10For they verily for a few days chastened *us* after
their own pleasure; but he for *our* profit, that *we*
might be partakers of his holiness.
11Now no chastening for the present seemeth to
be joyous, but grievous: nevertheless afterward it
yieldeth the peaceable fruit of righteousness unto
them which are exercised thereby.
12Wherefore lift up the hands which hang down,
and the feeble knees;
13And make straight paths for your feet, lest that
which is lame be turned out of the way; but let it
rather be healed.

NEW LIVING TRANSLATION

stoning, some were sawed in half,* and others were
killed with the sword. Some went about wearing
skins of sheep and goats, destitute and oppressed
and mistreated. 38They were too good for this world,
wandering over deserts and mountains, hiding in
caves and holes in the ground.
39All these people earned a good reputation because of their faith, yet none of them received all that
God had promised. 40For God had something better
in mind for us, so that they would not reach perfection without us.

God's Discipline Proves His Love

12 Therefore, since we are surrounded by such a
huge crowd of witnesses to the life of faith, let
us strip off every weight that slows us down, especially
the sin that so easily trips us up. And let us run with
endurance the race God has set before us. 2We do this
by keeping our eyes on Jesus, the champion who
initiates and perfects our faith.* Because of the joy*
awaiting him, he endured the cross, disregarding its
shame. Now he is seated in the place of honor beside
God's throne. 3Think of all the hostility he endured
from sinful people;* then you won't become weary
and give up. 4After all, you have not yet given your lives
in your struggle against sin.
5And have you forgotten the encouraging words
God spoke to you as his children?* He said,

"My child,* don't make light of the LORD's
discipline,
and don't give up when he corrects you.
6 For the LORD disciplines those he loves,
and he punishes each one he accepts as
his child."*

7As you endure this divine discipline, remember that
God is treating you as his own children. Who ever
heard of a child who is never disciplined by its father? 8If God doesn't discipline you as he does all of
his children, it means that you are illegitimate and
are not really his children at all. 9Since we respected
our earthly fathers who disciplined us, shouldn't we
submit even more to the discipline of the Father of
our spirits, and live forever?*
10For our earthly fathers disciplined us for a few
years, doing the best they knew how. But God's discipline is always good for us, so that we might share
in his holiness. 11No discipline is enjoyable while it is
happening—it's painful! But afterward there will be
a peaceful harvest of right living for those who are
trained in this way.
12So take a new grip with your tired hands and
strengthen your weak knees. 13Mark out a straight
path for your feet so that those who are weak and
lame will not fall but become strong.

11:37 Some manuscripts add *some were tested.* **12:2a** Or *Jesus, the originator and perfecter of our faith.* **12:2b** Or *Instead of the joy.* **12:3** Some manuscripts read *Think of how people hurt themselves by opposing him.* **12:5a** Greek *sons;* also in 12:7, 8. **12:5b** Greek *son;* also in 12:6, 7. **12:5-6** Prov 3:11-12 (Greek version). **12:9** Or *and really live?*

14Follow peace with all *men,* and holiness, without which no man shall see the Lord:

15Looking diligently lest any man fail of the grace of God; lest any root of bitterness springing up trouble *you,* and thereby many be defiled;

16Lest there *be* any fornicator, or profane person, as Esau, who for one morsel of meat sold his birthright.

17For ye know how that afterward, when he would have inherited the blessing, he was rejected: for he found no place of repentance, though he sought it carefully with tears.

18For ye are not come unto the mount that might be touched, and that burned with fire, nor unto blackness, and darkness, and tempest,

19And the sound of a trumpet, and the voice of words; which *voice* they that heard intreated that the word should not be spoken to them any more:

20(For they could not endure that which was commanded, And if so much as a beast touch the mountain, it shall be stoned, or thrust through with a dart:

21And so terrible was the sight, *that* Moses said, I exceedingly fear and quake:)

22But ye are come unto mount Sion, and unto the city of the living God, the heavenly Jerusalem, and to an innumerable company of angels,

23To the general assembly and church of the firstborn, which are written in heaven, and to God the Judge of all, and to the spirits of just men made perfect,

24And to Jesus the mediator of the new covenant, and to the blood of sprinkling, that speaketh better things than *that of* Abel.

25See that ye refuse not him that speaketh. For if they escaped not who refused him that spake on earth, much more *shall not* we *escape,* if we turn away from him that *speaketh* from heaven:

26Whose voice then shook the earth: but now he hath promised, saying, Yet once more I shake not the earth only, but also heaven.

27And this *word,* Yet once more, signifieth the removing of those things that are shaken, as of things that are made, that those things which cannot be shaken may remain.

28Wherefore we receiving a kingdom which cannot be moved, let us have grace, whereby we may serve God acceptably with reverence and godly fear:

29For our God *is* a consuming fire.

13 1Let brotherly love continue.

2Be not forgetful to entertain strangers: for thereby some have entertained angels unawares.

3Remember them that are in bonds, as bound with

A Call to Listen to God

14Work at living in peace with everyone, and work at living a holy life, for those who are not holy will not see the Lord. 15Look after each other so that none of you fails to receive the grace of God. Watch out that no poisonous root of bitterness grows up to trouble you, corrupting many. 16Make sure that no one is immoral or godless like Esau, who traded his birthright as the firstborn son for a single meal. 17You know that afterward, when he wanted his father's blessing, he was rejected. It was too late for repentance, even though he begged with bitter tears.

18You have not come to a physical mountain,* to a place of flaming fire, darkness, gloom, and whirlwind, as the Israelites did at Mount Sinai. 19For they heard an awesome trumpet blast and a voice so terrible that they begged God to stop speaking. 20They staggered back under God's command: "If even an animal touches the mountain, it must be stoned to death."* 21Moses himself was so frightened at the sight that he said, "I am terrified and trembling."*

22No, you have come to Mount Zion, to the city of the living God, the heavenly Jerusalem, and to countless thousands of angels in a joyful gathering. 23You have come to the assembly of God's firstborn children, whose names are written in heaven. You have come to God himself, who is the judge over all things. You have come to the spirits of the righteous ones in heaven who have now been made perfect. 24You have come to Jesus, the one who mediates the new covenant between God and people, and to the sprinkled blood, which speaks of forgiveness instead of crying out for vengeance like the blood of Abel.

25Be careful that you do not refuse to listen to the One who is speaking. For if the people of Israel did not escape when they refused to listen to Moses, the earthly messenger, we will certainly not escape if we reject the One who speaks to us from heaven! 26When God spoke from Mount Sinai his voice shook the earth, but now he makes another promise: "Once again I will shake not only the earth but the heavens also."* 27This means that all of creation will be shaken and removed, so that only unshakable things will remain.

28Since we are receiving a Kingdom that is unshakable, let us be thankful and please God by worshiping him with holy fear and awe. 29For our God is a devouring fire.

Concluding Words

13 Keep on loving each other as brothers and sisters.* 2Don't forget to show hospitality to strangers, for some who have done this have entertained angels without realizing it! 3Remember those in prison, as if you were there yourself. Remember

12:18 Greek *to something that can be touched.* **12:20** Exod 19:13. **12:21** Deut 9:19. **12:26** Hag 2:6. **13:1** Greek *Continue in brotherly love.*

them; *and* them which suffer adversity, as being yourselves also in the body.

4 Marriage *is* honourable in all, and the bed undefiled: but whoremongers and adulterers God will judge.

5 *Let your* conversation *be* without covetousness; *and be* content with such things as ye have: for he hath said, I will never leave thee, nor forsake thee.

6 So that we may boldly say, The Lord *is* my helper, and I will not fear what man shall do unto me.

7 Remember them which have the rule over you, who have spoken unto you the word of God: whose faith follow, considering the end of *their* conversation.

8 Jesus Christ the same yesterday, and today, and for ever.

9 Be not carried about with divers and strange doctrines. For *it is* a good thing that the heart be established with grace; not with meats, which have not profited them that have been occupied therein.

10 We have an altar, whereof they have no right to eat which serve the tabernacle.

11 For the bodies of those beasts, whose blood is brought into the sanctuary by the high priest for sin, are burned without the camp.

12 Wherefore Jesus also, that he might sanctify the people with his own blood, suffered without the gate.

13 Let us go forth therefore unto him without the camp, bearing his reproach.

14 For here have we no continuing city, but we seek one to come.

15 By him therefore let us offer the sacrifice of praise to God continually, that is, the fruit of *our* lips giving thanks to his name.

16 But to do good and to communicate forget not: for with such sacrifices God is well pleased.

17 Obey them that have the rule over you, and submit yourselves: for they watch for your souls, as they that must give account, that they may do it with joy, and not with grief: for that *is* unprofitable for you.

18 Pray for us: for we trust we have a good conscience, in all things willing to live honestly.

19 But I beseech *you* the rather to do this, that I may be restored to you the sooner.

20 Now the God of peace, that brought again from the dead our Lord Jesus, that great shepherd of the sheep, through the blood of the everlasting covenant,

21 Make you perfect in every good work to do his will, working in you that which is wellpleasing in his

also those being mistreated, as if you felt their pain in your own bodies.

4 Give honor to marriage, and remain faithful to one another in marriage. God will surely judge people who are immoral and those who commit adultery.

5 Don't love money; be satisfied with what you have. For God has said,

"I will never fail you.
I will never abandon you."*

6 So we can say with confidence,

"The LORD is my helper,
so I will have no fear.
What can mere people do to me?"*

7 Remember your leaders who taught you the word of God. Think of all the good that has come from their lives, and follow the example of their faith.

8 Jesus Christ is the same yesterday, today, and for-
ever. 9 So do not be attracted by strange, new ideas. Your strength comes from God's grace, not from rules about food, which don't help those who follow them.

10 We have an altar from which the priests in the
Tabernacle* have no right to eat. 11 Under the old
system, the high priest brought the blood of animals into the Holy Place as a sacrifice for sin, and the bodies of the animals were burned outside the camp.
12 So also Jesus suffered and died outside the city gates to make his people holy by means of his own
blood. 13 So let us go out to him, outside the camp,
and bear the disgrace he bore. 14 For this world is not
our permanent home; we are looking forward to a home yet to come.

15 Therefore, let us offer through Jesus a continual sacrifice of praise to God, proclaiming our allegiance
to his name. 16 And don't forget to do good and to
share with those in need. These are the sacrifices that please God.

17 Obey your spiritual leaders, and do what they say. Their work is to watch over your souls, and they are accountable to God. Give them reason to do this with joy and not with sorrow. That would certainly not be for your benefit.

18 Pray for us, for our conscience is clear and we
want to live honorably in everything we do. 19 And especially pray that I will be able to come back to you soon.

20 Now may the God of peace—
who brought up from the dead our Lord Jesus,
the great Shepherd of the sheep,
and ratified an eternal covenant with his blood—
21 may he equip you with all you need
for doing his will.
May he produce in you,*
through the power of Jesus Christ,

13:5 Deut 31:6, 8. **13:6** Ps 118:6. **13:10** Or *tent.* **13:21** Some manuscripts read *in us.*

KING JAMES VERSION

sight, through Jesus Christ; to whom *be* glory for ever
and ever. Amen.
22 And I beseech you, brethren, suffer the word of
exhortation: for I have written a letter unto you in
few words.
23 Know ye that *our* brother Timothy is set at liberty; with whom, if he come shortly, I will see you.
24 Salute all them that have the rule over you, and
all the saints. They of Italy salute you.
25 Grace *be* with you all. Amen.

NEW LIVING TRANSLATION

every good thing that is pleasing to him.
All glory to him forever and ever! Amen.

22 I urge you, dear brothers and sisters,* to pay
attention to what I have written in this brief exhortation.
23 I want you to know that our brother Timothy has
been released from jail. If he comes here soon, I will
bring him with me to see you.
24 Greet all your leaders and all the believers there.*
The believers from Italy send you their greetings.
25 May God's grace be with you all.

13:22 Greek *brothers.* **13:24** Greek *all of God's holy people.*

James

KING JAMES VERSION

1 1James, a servant of God and of the Lord Jesus Christ, to the twelve tribes which are scattered abroad, greeting.

2My brethren, count it all joy when ye fall into divers temptations;

3Knowing *this,* that the trying of your faith worketh patience.

4But let patience have *her* perfect work, that ye may be perfect and entire, wanting nothing.

5If any of you lack wisdom, let him ask of God, that giveth to all *men* liberally, and upbraideth not; and it shall be given him.

6But let him ask in faith, nothing wavering. For he that wavereth is like a wave of the sea driven with the wind and tossed.

7For let not that man think that he shall receive any thing of the Lord.

8A double minded man *is* unstable in all his ways.

9Let the brother of low degree rejoice in that he is exalted:

10But the rich, in that he is made low: because as the flower of the grass he shall pass away.

11For the sun is no sooner risen with a burning heat, but it withereth the grass, and the flower thereof falleth, and the grace of the fashion of it perisheth: so also shall the rich man fade away in his ways.

12Blessed *is* the man that endureth temptation: for when he is tried, he shall receive the crown of life, which the Lord hath promised to them that love him.

13Let no man say when he is tempted, I am tempted of God: for God cannot be tempted with evil, neither tempteth he any man:

14But every man is tempted, when he is drawn away of his own lust, and enticed.

15Then when lust hath conceived, it bringeth forth sin: and sin, when it is finished, bringeth forth death.

16Do not err, my beloved brethren.

NEW LIVING TRANSLATION

Greetings from James

1 This letter is from James, a slave of God and of the Lord Jesus Christ.

I am writing to the "twelve tribes"—Jewish believers scattered abroad.

Greetings!

Faith and Endurance

2Dear brothers and sisters,* when troubles come your way, consider it an opportunity for great joy. 3For you know that when your faith is tested, your endurance has a chance to grow. 4So let it grow, for when your endurance is fully developed, you will be perfect and complete, needing nothing.

5If you need wisdom, ask our generous God, and he will give it to you. He will not rebuke you for asking. 6But when you ask him, be sure that your faith is in God alone. Do not waver, for a person with divided loyalty is as unsettled as a wave of the sea that is blown and tossed by the wind. 7Such people should not expect to receive anything from the Lord. 8Their loyalty is divided between God and the world, and they are unstable in everything they do.

9Believers who are* poor have something to boast about, for God has honored them. 10And those who are rich should boast that God has humbled them. They will fade away like a little flower in the field. 11The hot sun rises and the grass withers; the little flower droops and falls, and its beauty fades away. In the same way, the rich will fade away with all of their achievements.

12God blesses those who patiently endure testing and temptation. Afterward they will receive the crown of life that God has promised to those who love him. 13And remember, when you are being tempted, do not say, "God is tempting me." God is never tempted to do wrong,* and he never tempts anyone else. 14Temptation comes from our own desires, which entice us and drag us away. 15These desires give birth to sinful actions. And when sin is allowed to grow, it gives birth to death.

16So don't be misled, my dear brothers and sisters.

1:2 Greek *brothers;* also in 1:16, 19. **1:9** Greek *The brother who is.*
1:13 Or *God should not be put to a test by evil people.*

KING JAMES VERSION

17Every good gift and every perfect gift is from
above, and cometh down from the Father of lights,
with whom is no variableness, neither shadow of
turning.
18Of his own will begat he us with the word of
truth, that we should be a kind of firstfruits of his
creatures.

19Wherefore, my beloved brethren, let every man
be swift to hear, slow to speak, slow to wrath:
20For the wrath of man worketh not the righteousness of God.
21Wherefore lay apart all filthiness and super-
fluity of naughtiness, and receive with meekness the
engrafted word, which is able to save your souls.
22But be ye doers of the word, and not hearers
only, deceiving your own selves.
23For if any be a hearer of the word, and not a doer,
he is like unto a man beholding his natural face in a
glass:
24For he beholdeth himself, and goeth his way, and
straightway forgetteth what manner of man he was.
25But whoso looketh into the perfect law of liberty, and continueth *therein,* he being not a forgetful
hearer, but a doer of the work, this man shall be
blessed in his deed.
26If any man among you seem to be religious, and
bridleth not his tongue, but deceiveth his own heart,
this man's religion *is* vain.
27Pure religion and undefiled before God and the
Father is this, To visit the fatherless and widows in
their affliction, *and* to keep himself unspotted from
the world.

2 1My brethren, have not the faith of our Lord
Jesus Christ, *the Lord* of glory, with respect of
persons.
2For if there come unto your assembly a man with
a gold ring, in goodly apparel, and there come in also
a poor man in vile raiment;
3And ye have respect to him that weareth the gay
clothing, and say unto him, Sit thou here in a good
place; and say to the poor, Stand thou there, or sit
here under my footstool:
4Are ye not then partial in yourselves, and are
become judges of evil thoughts?
5Hearken, my beloved brethren, Hath not God
chosen the poor of this world rich in faith, and heirs
of the kingdom which he hath promised to them
that love him?
6But ye have despised the poor. Do not rich men
oppress you, and draw you before the judgment
seats?
7Do not they blaspheme that worthy name by the
which ye are called?
8If ye fulfil the royal law according to the scripture,
Thou shalt love thy neighbour as thyself, ye do well:

NEW LIVING TRANSLATION

17Whatever is good and perfect comes down to us
from God our Father, who created all the lights in the
heavens.* He never changes or casts a shifting
shadow.* 18He chose to give birth to us by giving us
his true word. And we, out of all creation, became his
prized possession.*

Listening and Doing

19Understand this, my dear brothers and sisters: You
must all be quick to listen, slow to speak, and slow
to get angry. 20Human anger* does not produce the
righteousness* God desires. 21So get rid of all the filth
and evil in your lives, and humbly accept the word
God has planted in your hearts, for it has the power to
save your souls.
22But don't just listen to God's word. You must do
what it says. Otherwise, you are only fooling yourselves. 23For if you listen to the word and don't obey,
it is like glancing at your face in a mirror. 24You see
yourself, walk away, and forget what you look like.
25But if you look carefully into the perfect law that
sets you free, and if you do what it says and don't
forget what you heard, then God will bless you for
doing it.
26If you claim to be religious but don't control your
tongue, you are fooling yourself, and your religion
is worthless. 27Pure and genuine religion in the sight
of God the Father means caring for orphans and
widows in their distress and refusing to let the world
corrupt you.

A Warning against Prejudice

2 My dear brothers and sisters,* how can you
claim to have faith in our glorious Lord Jesus
Christ if you favor some people over others?
2For example, suppose someone comes into your
meeting* dressed in fancy clothes and expensive
jewelry, and another comes in who is poor and
dressed in dirty clothes. 3If you give special attention
and a good seat to the rich person, but you say to the
poor one, "You can stand over there, or else sit on the
floor"—well, 4doesn't this discrimination show that
your judgments are guided by evil motives?
5Listen to me, dear brothers and sisters. Hasn't
God chosen the poor in this world to be rich in faith?
Aren't they the ones who will inherit the Kingdom he
promised to those who love him? 6But you dishonor
the poor! Isn't it the rich who oppress you and drag
you into court? 7Aren't they the ones who slander
Jesus Christ, whose noble name* you bear?
8Yes indeed, it is good when you obey the royal law
as found in the Scriptures: "Love your neighbor as

1:17a Greek *from above, from the Father of lights.* **1:17b** Some manuscripts read *He never changes, as a shifting shadow does.* **1:18** Greek *we became a kind of firstfruit of his creatures.* **1:20a** Greek *A man's anger.* **1:20b** Or *the justice.* **2:1** Greek *brothers;* also in 2:5, 14. **2:2** Greek *your synagogue.* **2:7** Greek *slander the noble name.*

KING JAMES VERSION

9 But if ye have respect to persons, ye commit sin,
and are convinced of the law as transgressors.
10 For whosoever shall keep the whole law, and yet
offend in one *point,* he is guilty of all.
11 For he that said, Do not commit adultery, said
also, Do not kill. Now if thou commit no adultery,
yet if thou kill, thou art become a transgressor of
the law.
12 So speak ye, and so do, as they that shall be
judged by the law of liberty.
13 For he shall have judgment without mercy, that
hath shewed no mercy; and mercy rejoiceth against
judgment.

14 What *doth it* profit, my brethren, though a man
say he hath faith, and have not works? can faith
save him?
15 If a brother or sister be naked, and destitute of
daily food,
16 And one of you say unto them, Depart in peace,
be *ye* warmed and filled; notwithstanding ye give
them not those things which are needful to the body;
what *doth it* profit?
17 Even so faith, if it hath not works, is dead, being
alone.
18 Yea, a man may say, Thou hast faith, and I have
works: shew me thy faith without thy works, and I
will shew thee my faith by my works.
19 Thou believest that there is one God; thou doest
well: the devils also believe, and tremble.
20 But wilt thou know, O vain man, that faith without works is dead?
21 Was not Abraham our father justified by works,
when he had offered Isaac his son upon the altar?
22 Seest thou how faith wrought with his works,
and by works was faith made perfect?
23 And the scripture was fulfilled which saith, Abraham believed God, and it was imputed unto him for
righteousness: and he was called the Friend of God.
24 Ye see then how that by works a man is justified,
and not by faith only.
25 Likewise also was not Rahab the harlot justified
by works, when she had received the messengers,
and had sent *them* out another way?
26 For as the body without the spirit is dead, so
faith without works is dead also.

3 1 My brethren, be not many masters, knowing
that we shall receive the greater condemnation.
2 For in many things we offend all. If any man offend not in word, the same *is* a perfect man, *and* able
also to bridle the whole body.

NEW LIVING TRANSLATION

yourself."* 9 But if you favor some people over
others, you are committing a sin. You are guilty of
breaking the law.
10 For the person who keeps all of the laws except
one is as guilty as a person who has broken all of
God's laws. 11 For the same God who said, "You must
not commit adultery," also said, "You must not murder."* So if you murder someone but do not commit
adultery, you have still broken the law.
12 So whatever you say or whatever you do, remember that you will be judged by the law that sets you
free. 13 There will be no mercy for those who have not
shown mercy to others. But if you have been merciful, God will be merciful when he judges you.

Faith without Good Deeds Is Dead

14 What good is it, dear brothers and sisters, if you say
you have faith but don't show it by your actions? Can
that kind of faith save anyone? 15 Suppose you see a
brother or sister who has no food or clothing, 16 and
you say, "Good-bye and have a good day; stay warm
and eat well"—but then you don't give that person
any food or clothing. What good does that do?
17 So you see, faith by itself isn't enough. Unless it
produces good deeds, it is dead and useless.
18 Now someone may argue, "Some people have
faith; others have good deeds." But I say, "How can
you show me your faith if you don't have good deeds?
I will show you my faith by my good deeds."
19 You say you have faith, for you believe that there
is one God.* Good for you! Even the demons believe
this, and they tremble in terror. 20 How foolish! Can't
you see that faith without good deeds is useless?
21 Don't you remember that our ancestor Abraham
was shown to be right with God by his actions when he
offered his son Isaac on the altar? 22 You see, his faith
and his actions worked together. His actions made his
faith complete. 23 And so it happened just as the Scriptures say: "Abraham believed God, and God counted
him as righteous because of his faith."* He was even
called the friend of God.* 24 So you see, we are shown to
be right with God by what we do, not by faith alone.
25 Rahab the prostitute is another example. She
was shown to be right with God by her actions when
she hid those messengers and sent them safely away
by a different road. 26 Just as the body is dead without
breath,* so also faith is dead without good works.

Controlling the Tongue

3 Dear brothers and sisters,* not many of you
should become teachers in the church, for we
who teach will be judged more strictly. 2 Indeed, we
all make many mistakes. For if we could control our
tongues, we would be perfect and could also control
ourselves in every other way.

2:8 Lev 19:18. **2:11** Exod 20:13-14; Deut 5:17-18. **2:19** Some manuscripts read *that God is one;* see Deut 6:4. **2:23a** Gen 15:6. **2:23b** See Isa 41:8. **2:26** Or *without spirit.* **3:1** Greek *brothers;* also in 3:10.

3Behold, we put bits in the horses' mouths, that they may obey us; and we turn about their whole body.

4Behold also the ships, which though *they be* so great, and *are* driven of fierce winds, yet are they turned about with a very small helm, whithersoever the governor listeth.

5Even so the tongue is a little member, and boasteth great things. Behold, how great a matter a little fire kindleth!

6And the tongue *is* a fire, a world of iniquity: so is the tongue among our members, that it defileth the whole body, and setteth on fire the course of nature; and it is set on fire of hell.

7For every kind of beasts, and of birds, and of serpents, and of things in the sea, is tamed, and hath been tamed of mankind:

8But the tongue can no man tame; *it is* an unruly evil, full of deadly poison.

9Therewith bless we God, even the Father; and therewith curse we men, which are made after the similitude of God.

10Out of the same mouth proceedeth blessing and cursing. My brethren, these things ought not so to be.

11Doth a fountain send forth at the same place sweet *water* and bitter?

12Can the fig tree, my brethren, bear olive berries? either a vine, figs? so *can* no fountain both yield salt water and fresh.

13Who *is* a wise man and endued with knowledge among you? let him shew out of a good conversation his works with meekness of wisdom.

14But if ye have bitter envying and strife in your hearts, glory not, and lie not against the truth.

15This wisdom descendeth not from above, but *is* earthly, sensual, devilish.

16For where envying and strife *is*, there *is* confusion and every evil work.

17But the wisdom that is from above is first pure, then peaceable, gentle, *and* easy to be intreated, full of mercy and good fruits, without partiality, and without hypocrisy.

18And the fruit of righteousness is sown in peace of them that make peace.

4 1From whence *come* wars and fightings among you? *come they* not hence, *even* of your lusts that war in your members?

2Ye lust, and have not: ye kill, and desire to have, and cannot obtain: ye fight and war, yet ye have not, because ye ask not.

3Ye ask, and receive not, because ye ask amiss, that ye may consume *it* upon your lusts.

3We can make a large horse go wherever we want
by means of a small bit in its mouth. 4And a small
rudder makes a huge ship turn wherever the pilot
chooses to go, even though the winds are strong. 5In
the same way, the tongue is a small thing that makes
grand speeches.

But a tiny spark can set a great forest on fire. 6And
the tongue is a flame of fire. It is a whole world of
wickedness, corrupting your entire body. It can set
your whole life on fire, for it is set on fire by hell
itself.*

7People can tame all kinds of animals, birds, reptiles, and fish, 8but no one can tame the tongue. It is
restless and evil, full of deadly poison. 9Sometimes it
praises our Lord and Father, and sometimes it curses
those who have been made in the image of God.
10And so blessing and cursing come pouring out of
the same mouth. Surely, my brothers and sisters, this
is not right! 11Does a spring of water bubble out with
both fresh water and bitter water? 12Does a fig tree
produce olives, or a grapevine produce figs? No, and
you can't draw fresh water from a salty spring.*

True Wisdom Comes from God

13If you are wise and understand God's ways, prove it
by living an honorable life, doing good works with
the humility that comes from wisdom. 14But if you
are bitterly jealous and there is selfish ambition in
your heart, don't cover up the truth with boasting
and lying. 15For jealousy and selfishness are not
God's kind of wisdom. Such things are earthly, un-
spiritual, and demonic. 16For wherever there is jealousy and selfish ambition, there you will find
disorder and evil of every kind.

17But the wisdom from above is first of all pure. It
is also peace loving, gentle at all times, and willing to
yield to others. It is full of mercy and good deeds.
It shows no favoritism and is always sincere. 18And
those who are peacemakers will plant seeds of peace
and reap a harvest of righteousness.*

Drawing Close to God

4 What is causing the quarrels and fights among
you? Don't they come from the evil desires at
war within you? 2You want what you don't have, so
you scheme and kill to get it. You are jealous of what
others have, but you can't get it, so you fight and
wage war to take it away from them. Yet you don't
have what you want because you don't ask God for it.
3And even when you ask, you don't get it because
your motives are all wrong—you want only what will
give you pleasure.

3:6 Or *for it will burn in hell* (Greek *Gehenna*). **3:12** Greek *from salt.*
3:18 Or *of good things*, or *of justice.*

KING JAMES VERSION

4 Ye adulterers and adulteresses, know ye not that the friendship of the world is enmity with God? whosoever therefore will be a friend of the world is the enemy of God.

5 Do ye think that the scripture saith in vain, The spirit that dwelleth in us lusteth to envy?

6 But he giveth more grace. Wherefore he saith, God resisteth the proud, but giveth grace unto the humble.

7 Submit yourselves therefore to God. Resist the devil, and he will flee from you.

8 Draw nigh to God, and he will draw nigh to you. Cleanse *your* hands, *ye* sinners; and purify *your* hearts, *ye* double minded.

9 Be afflicted, and mourn, and weep: let your laughter be turned to mourning, and *your* joy to heaviness.

10 Humble yourselves in the sight of the Lord, and he shall lift you up.

11 Speak not evil one of another, brethren. He that speaketh evil of *his* brother, and judgeth his brother, speaketh evil of the law, and judgeth the law: but if thou judge the law, thou art not a doer of the law, but a judge.

12 There is one lawgiver, who is able to save and to destroy: who art thou that judgest another?

13 Go to now, ye that say, To day or to morrow we will go into such a city, and continue there a year, and buy and sell, and get gain:

14 Whereas ye know not what *shall be* on the morrow. For what *is* your life? It is even a vapour, that appeareth for a little time, and then vanisheth away.

15 For that ye *ought* to say, If the Lord will, we shall live, and do this, or that.

16 But now ye rejoice in your boastings: all such rejoicing is evil.

17 Therefore to him that knoweth to do good, and doeth *it* not, to him it is sin.

5 1 Go to now, *ye* rich men, weep and howl for your miseries that shall come upon *you*.

2 Your riches are corrupted, and your garments are motheaten.

3 Your gold and silver is cankered; and the rust of them shall be a witness against you, and shall eat your flesh as it were fire. Ye have heaped treasure together for the last days.

4 Behold, the hire of the labourers who have reaped down your fields, which is of you kept back by fraud,

NEW LIVING TRANSLATION

4 You adulterers!* Don't you realize that friendship with the world makes you an enemy of God? I
say it again: If you want to be a friend of the world,
you make yourself an enemy of God. 5 What do you
think the Scriptures mean when they say that the
spirit God has placed within us is filled with envy?*
6 But he gives us even more grace to stand against
such evil desires. As the Scriptures say,

"God opposes the proud
but favors the humble."*

7 So humble yourselves before God. Resist the
devil, and he will flee from you. 8 Come close to God,
and God will come close to you. Wash your hands,
you sinners; purify your hearts, for your loyalty is divided between God and the world. 9 Let there be tears
for what you have done. Let there be sorrow and deep
grief. Let there be sadness instead of laughter, and
gloom instead of joy. 10 Humble yourselves before the
Lord, and he will lift you up in honor.

Warning against Judging Others

11 Don't speak evil against each other, dear brothers
and sisters.* If you criticize and judge each other,
then you are criticizing and judging God's law. But
your job is to obey the law, not to judge whether it
applies to you. 12 God alone, who gave the law, is the
Judge. He alone has the power to save or to destroy.
So what right do you have to judge your neighbor?

Warning about Self-Confidence

13 Look here, you who say, "Today or tomorrow we are
going to a certain town and will stay there a year. We
will do business there and make a profit." 14 How do
you know what your life will be like tomorrow? Your
life is like the morning fog—it's here a little while,
then it's gone. 15 What you ought to say is, "If the Lord
wants us to, we will live and do this or that." 16 Otherwise you are boasting about your own plans, and all
such boasting is evil.

17 Remember, it is sin to know what you ought to
do and then not do it.

Warning to the Rich

5 Look here, you rich people: Weep and groan
with anguish because of all the terrible troubles ahead of you. 2 Your wealth is rotting away, and
your fine clothes are moth-eaten rags. 3 Your gold
and silver have become worthless. The very wealth
you were counting on will eat away your flesh like
fire. This treasure you have accumulated will stand
as evidence against you on the day of judgment. 4 For
listen! Hear the cries of the field workers whom you
have cheated of their pay. The wages you held back
cry out against you. The cries of those who harvest

4:4 Greek *You adulteresses!* **4:5** Or *that God longs jealously for the human spirit he has placed within us?* or *that the Holy Spirit, whom God has placed within us, opposes our envy?* **4:6** Prov 3:34 (Greek version). **4:11** Greek *brothers.*

KING JAMES VERSION

crieth: and the cries of them which have reaped are entered into the ears of the Lord of sabaoth.

5 Ye have lived in pleasure on the earth, and been wanton; ye have nourished your hearts, as in a day of slaughter.

6 Ye have condemned *and* killed the just; *and* he doth not resist you.

7 Be patient therefore, brethren, unto the coming of the Lord. Behold, the husbandman waiteth for the precious fruit of the earth, and hath long patience for it, until he receive the early and latter rain.

8 Be ye also patient; stablish your hearts: for the coming of the Lord draweth nigh.

9 Grudge not one against another, brethren, lest ye be condemned: behold, the judge standeth before the door.

10 Take, my brethren, the prophets, who have spoken in the name of the Lord, for an example of suffering affliction, and of patience.

11 Behold, we count them happy which endure. Ye have heard of the patience of Job, and have seen the end of the Lord; that the Lord is very pitiful, and of tender mercy.

12 But above all things, my brethren, swear not, neither by heaven, neither by the earth, neither by any other oath: but let your yea be yea; and *your* nay, nay; lest ye fall into condemnation.

13 Is any among you afflicted? let him pray. Is any merry? let him sing psalms.

14 Is any sick among you? let him call for the elders of the church; and let them pray over him, anointing him with oil in the name of the Lord:

15 And the prayer of faith shall save the sick, and the Lord shall raise him up; and if he have committed sins, they shall be forgiven him.

16 Confess *your* faults one to another, and pray one for another, that ye may be healed. The effectual fervent prayer of a righteous man availeth much.

17 Elias was a man subject to like passions as we are, and he prayed earnestly that it might not rain: and it rained not on the earth by the space of three years and six months.

18 And he prayed again, and the heaven gave rain, and the earth brought forth her fruit.

19 Brethren, if any of you do err from the truth, and one convert him;

20 Let him know, that he which converteth the sinner from the error of his way shall save a soul from death, and shall hide a multitude of sins.

NEW LIVING TRANSLATION

your fields have reached the ears of the LORD of Heaven's Armies.

5 You have spent your years on earth in luxury, satisfying your every desire. You have fattened yourselves for the day of slaughter. 6 You have condemned and killed innocent people,* who do not resist you.*

Patience and Endurance

7 Dear brothers and sisters,* be patient as you wait for the Lord's return. Consider the farmers who patiently wait for the rains in the fall and in the spring. They eagerly look for the valuable harvest to ripen. 8 You, too, must be patient. Take courage, for the coming of the Lord is near.

9 Don't grumble about each other, brothers and sisters, or you will be judged. For look—the Judge is standing at the door!

10 For examples of patience in suffering, dear brothers and sisters, look at the prophets who spoke in the name of the Lord. 11 We give great honor to those who endure under suffering. For instance, you know about Job, a man of great endurance. You can see how the Lord was kind to him at the end, for the Lord is full of tenderness and mercy.

12 But most of all, my brothers and sisters, never take an oath, by heaven or earth or anything else. Just say a simple yes or no, so that you will not sin and be condemned.

The Power of Prayer

13 Are any of you suffering hardships? You should pray. Are any of you happy? You should sing praises. 14 Are any of you sick? You should call for the elders of the church to come and pray over you, anointing you with oil in the name of the Lord. 15 Such a prayer offered in faith will heal the sick, and the Lord will make you well. And if you have committed any sins, you will be forgiven.

16 Confess your sins to each other and pray for each other so that you may be healed. The earnest prayer of a righteous person has great power and produces wonderful results. 17 Elijah was as human as we are, and yet when he prayed earnestly that no rain would fall, none fell for three and a half years! 18 Then, when he prayed again, the sky sent down rain and the earth began to yield its crops.

Restore Wandering Believers

19 My dear brothers and sisters, if someone among you wanders away from the truth and is brought back, 20 you can be sure that whoever brings the sinner back will save that person from death and bring about the forgiveness of many sins.

5:6a Or *killed the Righteous One.* **5:6b** Or *Don't they resist you?* or *Doesn't God oppose you?* or *Aren't they now accusing you before God?* **5:7** Greek *brothers;* also in 5:9, 10, 12, 19.

1 Peter

KING JAMES VERSION

1 1Peter, an apostle of Jesus Christ, to the strangers scattered throughout Pontus, Galatia, Cappadocia, Asia, and Bithynia,

2Elect according to the foreknowledge of God the Father, through sanctification of the Spirit, unto obedience and sprinkling of the blood of Jesus Christ: Grace unto you, and peace, be multiplied.

3Blessed *be* the God and Father of our Lord Jesus Christ, which according to his abundant mercy hath begotten us again unto a lively hope by the resurrection of Jesus Christ from the dead,

4To an inheritance incorruptible, and undefiled, and that fadeth not away, reserved in heaven for you,

5Who are kept by the power of God through faith unto salvation ready to be revealed in the last time.

6Wherein ye greatly rejoice, though now for a season, if need be, ye are in heaviness through manifold temptations:

7That the trial of your faith, being much more precious than of gold that perisheth, though it be tried with fire, might be found unto praise and honour and glory at the appearing of Jesus Christ:

8Whom having not seen, ye love; in whom, though now ye see *him* not, yet believing, ye rejoice with joy unspeakable and full of glory:

9Receiving the end of your faith, *even* the salvation of *your* souls.

10Of which salvation the prophets have inquired and searched diligently, who prophesied of the grace *that should come* unto you:

11Searching what, or what manner of time the Spirit of Christ which was in them did signify, when

NEW LIVING TRANSLATION

Greetings from Peter

1 This letter is from Peter, an apostle of Jesus Christ.

I am writing to God's chosen people who are living as foreigners in the provinces of Pontus, Galatia, Cappadocia, Asia, and Bithynia.* 2God the Father knew you and chose you long ago, and his Spirit has made you holy. As a result, you have obeyed him and have been cleansed by the blood of Jesus Christ.

May God give you more and more grace and peace.

The Hope of Eternal Life

3All praise to God, the Father of our Lord Jesus Christ. It is by his great mercy that we have been born again, because God raised Jesus Christ from the dead. Now we live with great expectation, 4and we have a priceless inheritance—an inheritance that is kept in heaven for you, pure and undefiled, beyond the reach of change and decay. 5And through your faith, God is protecting you by his power until you receive this salvation, which is ready to be revealed on the last day for all to see.

6So be truly glad.* There is wonderful joy ahead, even though you have to endure many trials for a little while. 7These trials will show that your faith is genuine. It is being tested as fire tests and purifies gold—though your faith is far more precious than mere gold. So when your faith remains strong through many trials, it will bring you much praise and glory and honor on the day when Jesus Christ is revealed to the whole world.

8You love him even though you have never seen him. Though you do not see him now, you trust him; and you rejoice with a glorious, inexpressible joy. 9The reward for trusting him will be the salvation of your souls.

10This salvation was something even the prophets wanted to know more about when they prophesied about this gracious salvation prepared for you. 11They wondered what time or situation the Spirit of Christ within them was talking about when he told

1:1 *Pontus, Galatia, Cappadocia, Asia,* and *Bithynia* were Roman provinces in what is now Turkey. 1:6 Or *So you are truly glad.*

KING JAMES VERSION

it testified beforehand the sufferings of Christ, and the glory that should follow.

12 Unto whom it was revealed, that not unto themselves, but unto us they did minister the things, which are now reported unto you by them that have preached the gospel unto you with the Holy Ghost sent down from heaven; which things the angels desire to look into.

13 Wherefore gird up the loins of your mind, be sober, and hope to the end for the grace that is to be brought unto you at the revelation of Jesus Christ;

14 As obedient children, not fashioning yourselves according to the former lusts in your ignorance:

15 But as he which hath called you is holy, so be ye holy in all manner of conversation;

16 Because it is written, Be ye holy; for I am holy.

17 And if ye call on the Father, who without respect of persons judgeth according to every man's work, pass the time of your sojourning *here* in fear:

18 Forasmuch as ye know that ye were not redeemed with corruptible things, *as* silver and gold, from your vain conversation *received* by tradition from your fathers;

19 But with the precious blood of Christ, as of a lamb without blemish and without spot:

20 Who verily was foreordained before the foundation of the world, but was manifest in these last times for you,

21 Who by him do believe in God, that raised him up from the dead, and gave him glory; that your faith and hope might be in God.

22 Seeing ye have purified your souls in obeying the truth through the Spirit unto unfeigned love of the brethren, *see that ye* love one another with a pure heart fervently:

23 Being born again, not of corruptible seed, but of incorruptible, by the word of God, which liveth and abideth for ever.

24 For all flesh *is* as grass, and all the glory of man as the flower of grass. The grass withereth, and the flower thereof falleth away:

25 But the word of the Lord endureth for ever. And this is the word which by the gospel is preached unto you.

2 1 Wherefore laying aside all malice, and all guile, and hypocrisies, and envies, and all evil speakings,

2 As newborn babes, desire the sincere milk of the word, that ye may grow thereby:

3 If so be ye have tasted that the Lord *is* gracious.

NEW LIVING TRANSLATION

them in advance about Christ's suffering and his great glory afterward.

12 They were told that their messages were not for themselves, but for you. And now this Good News has been announced to you by those who preached in the power of the Holy Spirit sent from heaven. It is all so wonderful that even the angels are eagerly watching these things happen.

A Call to Holy Living

13 So think clearly and exercise self-control. Look forward to the gracious salvation that will come to you when Jesus Christ is revealed to the world. 14 So you must live as God's obedient children. Don't slip back into your old ways of living to satisfy your own desires. You didn't know any better then. 15 But now you must be holy in everything you do, just as God who chose you is holy. 16 For the Scriptures say, "You must be holy because I am holy."*

17 And remember that the heavenly Father to whom you pray has no favorites. He will judge or reward you according to what you do. So you must live in reverent fear of him during your time as "foreigners in the land." 18 For you know that God paid a ransom to save you from the empty life you inherited from your ancestors. And the ransom he paid was not mere gold or silver. 19 It was the precious blood of Christ, the sinless, spotless Lamb of God. 20 God chose him as your ransom long before the world began, but he has now revealed him to you in these last days.

21 Through Christ you have come to trust in God. And you have placed your faith and hope in God because he raised Christ from the dead and gave him great glory.

22 You were cleansed from your sins when you obeyed the truth, so now you must show sincere love to each other as brothers and sisters.* Love each other deeply with all your heart.*

23 For you have been born again, but not to a life that will quickly end. Your new life will last forever because it comes from the eternal, living word of God. 24 As the Scriptures say,

"People are like grass;
  their beauty is like a flower in the field.
The grass withers and the flower fades.
25 But the word of the Lord remains forever."*

And that word is the Good News that was preached to you.

2 So get rid of all evil behavior. Be done with all deceit, hypocrisy, jealousy, and all unkind speech. 2 Like newborn babies, you must crave pure spiritual milk so that you will grow into a full experience of salvation. Cry out for this nourishment, 3 now that you have had a taste of the Lord's kindness.

1:16 Lev 11:44-45; 19:2; 20:7. **1:22a** Greek *must have brotherly love.* **1:22b** Some manuscripts read *with a pure heart.* **1:24-25** Isa 40:6-8.

KING JAMES VERSION

4 To whom coming, *as unto* a living stone, disallowed indeed of men, but chosen of God, *and* precious,

5 Ye also, as lively stones, are built up a spiritual house, an holy priesthood, to offer up spiritual sacrifices, acceptable to God by Jesus Christ.

6 Wherefore also it is contained in the scripture, Behold, I lay in Sion a chief corner stone, elect, precious: and he that believeth on him shall not be confounded.

7 Unto you therefore which believe *he is* precious: but unto them which be disobedient, the stone which the builders disallowed, the same is made the head of the corner,

8 And a stone of stumbling, and a rock of offence, *even to them* which stumble at the word, being disobedient: whereunto also they were appointed.

9 But ye *are* a chosen generation, a royal priesthood, an holy nation, a peculiar people; that ye should shew forth the praises of him who hath called you out of darkness into his marvellous light:

10 Which in time past *were* not a people, but *are* now the people of God: which had not obtained mercy, but now have obtained mercy.

11 Dearly beloved, I beseech *you* as strangers and pilgrims, abstain from fleshly lusts, which war against the soul;

12 Having your conversation honest among the Gentiles: that, whereas they speak against you as evildoers, they may by *your* good works, which they shall behold, glorify God in the day of visitation.

13 Submit yourselves to every ordinance of man for the Lord's sake: whether it be to the king, as supreme;

14 Or unto governors, as unto them that are sent by him for the punishment of evildoers, and for the praise of them that do well.

15 For so is the will of God, that with well doing ye may put to silence the ignorance of foolish men:

16 As free, and not using *your* liberty for a cloak of maliciousness, but as the servants of God.

17 Honour all *men*. Love the brotherhood. Fear God. Honour the king.

NEW LIVING TRANSLATION

Living Stones for God's House

4 You are coming to Christ, who is the living cornerstone of God's temple. He was rejected by people, but he was chosen by God for great honor.

5 And you are living stones that God is building into his spiritual temple. What's more, you are his holy priests.* Through the mediation of Jesus Christ, you offer spiritual sacrifices that please God. 6 As the Scriptures say,

"I am placing a cornerstone in Jerusalem,*
chosen for great honor,
and anyone who trusts in him
will never be disgraced."*

7 Yes, you who trust him recognize the honor God has given him. But for those who reject him,

"The stone that the builders rejected
has now become the cornerstone."*

8 And,

"He is the stone that makes people stumble,
the rock that makes them fall."*

They stumble because they do not obey God's word, and so they meet the fate that was planned for them.

9 But you are not like that, for you are a chosen people. You are royal priests,* a holy nation, God's very own possession. As a result, you can show others the goodness of God, for he called you out of the darkness into his wonderful light.

10 "Once you had no identity as a people;
now you are God's people.
Once you received no mercy;
now you have received God's mercy."*

11 Dear friends, I warn you as "temporary residents and foreigners" to keep away from worldly desires that wage war against your very souls. 12 Be careful to live properly among your unbelieving neighbors. Then even if they accuse you of doing wrong, they will see your honorable behavior, and they will give honor to God when he judges the world.*

Respecting People in Authority

13 For the Lord's sake, respect all human authority—whether the king as head of state, 14 or the officials he has appointed. For the king has sent them to punish those who do wrong and to honor those who do right.

15 It is God's will that your honorable lives should silence those ignorant people who make foolish accusations against you. 16 For you are free, yet you are God's slaves, so don't use your freedom as an excuse to do evil. 17 Respect everyone, and love your Christian brothers and sisters.* Fear God, and respect the king.

2:5 Greek *holy priesthood.* **2:6a** Greek *in Zion.* **2:6b** Isa 28:16 (Greek version). **2:7** Ps 118:22. **2:8** Isa 8:14. **2:9** Greek *a royal priesthood.* **2:10** Hos 1:6, 9; 2:23. **2:12** Or *on the day of visitation.* **2:17** Greek *love the brotherhood.*

KING JAMES VERSION

18 Servants, *be* subject to *your* masters with all fear; not only to the good and gentle, but also to the froward.

19 For this *is* thankworthy, if a man for conscience toward God endure grief, suffering wrongfully.

20 For what glory *is it,* if, when ye be buffeted for your faults, ye shall take it patiently? but if, when ye do well, and suffer *for it,* ye take it patiently, this *is* acceptable with God.

21 For even hereunto were ye called: because Christ also suffered for us, leaving us an example, that ye should follow his steps:

22 Who did no sin, neither was guile found in his mouth:

23 Who, when he was reviled, reviled not again; when he suffered, he threatened not; but committed *himself* to him that judgeth righteously:

24 Who his own self bare our sins in his own body on the tree, that we, being dead to sins, should live unto righteousness: by whose stripes ye were healed.

25 For ye were as sheep going astray; but are now returned unto the Shepherd and Bishop of your souls.

3 1 Likewise, ye wives, *be* in subjection to your own husbands; that, if any obey not the word, they also may without the word be won by the conversation of the wives;

2 While they behold your chaste conversation *coupled* with fear.

3 Whose adorning let it not be that outward *adorning* of plaiting the hair, and of wearing of gold, or of putting on of apparel;

4 But *let it be* the hidden man of the heart, in that which is not corruptible, *even the ornament* of a meek and quiet spirit, which is in the sight of God of great price.

5 For after this manner in the old time the holy women also, who trusted in God, adorned themselves, being in subjection unto their own husbands:

6 Even as Sara obeyed Abraham, calling him lord: whose daughters ye are, as long as ye do well, and are not afraid with any amazement.

7 Likewise, ye husbands, dwell with *them* according to knowledge, giving honour unto the wife, as unto the weaker vessel, and as being heirs together of the grace of life; that your prayers be not hindered.

NEW LIVING TRANSLATION

Slaves

18 You who are slaves must accept the authority of
your masters with all respect.* Do what they tell
you—not only if they are kind and reasonable, but
even if they are cruel. 19 For God is pleased with you
when you do what you know is right and patiently
endure unfair treatment. 20 Of course, you get no
credit for being patient if you are beaten for doing
wrong. But if you suffer for doing good and endure it
patiently, God is pleased with you.

21 For God called you to do good, even if it means
suffering, just as Christ suffered* for you. He is your
example, and you must follow in his steps.

22 He never sinned,
  nor ever deceived anyone.*
23 He did not retaliate when he was insulted,
  nor threaten revenge when he suffered.
He left his case in the hands of God,
  who always judges fairly.
24 He personally carried our sins
  in his body on the cross
so that we can be dead to sin
  and live for what is right.
By his wounds
  you are healed.
25 Once you were like sheep
  who wandered away.
But now you have turned to your Shepherd,
  the Guardian of your souls.

Wives

3 In the same way, you wives must accept the
authority of your husbands. Then, even if some
refuse to obey the Good News, your godly lives will
speak to them without any words. They will be won
over 2 by observing your pure and reverent lives.

3 Don't be concerned about the outward beauty
of fancy hairstyles, expensive jewelry, or beautiful
clothes. 4 You should clothe yourselves instead with
the beauty that comes from within, the unfading
beauty of a gentle and quiet spirit, which is so precious to God. 5 This is how the holy women of old
made themselves beautiful. They trusted God and
accepted the authority of their husbands. 6 For instance, Sarah obeyed her husband, Abraham, and
called him her master. You are her daughters when
you do what is right without fear of what your husbands might do.

Husbands

7 In the same way, you husbands must give honor to
your wives. Treat your wife with understanding as
you live together. She may be weaker than you are,
but she is your equal partner in God's gift of new life.
Treat her as you should so your prayers will not be
hindered.

2:18 Or *because you fear God.* **2:21** Some manuscripts read *died.*
2:22 Isa 53:9.

KING JAMES VERSION

8 Finally, *be ye* all of one mind, having compassion one of another, love as brethren, *be* pitiful, *be* courteous:

9 Not rendering evil for evil, or railing for railing: but contrariwise blessing; knowing that ye are thereunto called, that ye should inherit a blessing.

10 For he that will love life, and see good days, let him refrain his tongue from evil, and his lips that they speak no guile:

11 Let him eschew evil, and do good; let him seek peace, and ensue it.

12 For the eyes of the Lord *are* over the righteous, and his ears *are open* unto their prayers: but the face of the Lord *is* against them that do evil.

13 And who *is* he that will harm you, if ye be followers of that which is good?

14 But and if ye suffer for righteousness' sake, happy *are ye:* and be not afraid of their terror, neither be troubled;

15 But sanctify the Lord God in your hearts: and *be* ready always to *give* an answer to every man that asketh you a reason of the hope that is in you with meekness and fear:

16 Having a good conscience; that, whereas they speak evil of you, as of evildoers, they may be ashamed that falsely accuse your good conversation in Christ.

17 For *it is* better, if the will of God be so, that ye suffer for well doing, than for evil doing.

18 For Christ also hath once suffered for sins, the just for the unjust, that he might bring us to God, being put to death in the flesh, but quickened by the Spirit:

19 By which also he went and preached unto the spirits in prison;

20 Which sometime were disobedient, when once the longsuffering of God waited in the days of Noah, while the ark was a preparing, wherein few, that is, eight souls were saved by water.

21 The like figure whereunto *even* baptism doth also now save us (not the putting away of the filth of the flesh, but the answer of a good conscience toward God,) by the resurrection of Jesus Christ:

22 Who is gone into heaven, and is on the right hand of God; angels and authorities and powers being made subject unto him.

NEW LIVING TRANSLATION

All Christians

8 Finally, all of you should be of one mind. Sympathize with each other. Love each other as brothers and sisters.* Be tenderhearted, and keep a humble attitude. 9 Don't repay evil for evil. Don't retaliate with insults when people insult you. Instead, pay them back with a blessing. That is what God has called you to do, and he will bless you for it. 10 For the Scriptures say,

"If you want to enjoy life
  and see many happy days,
keep your tongue from speaking evil
  and your lips from telling lies.
11 Turn away from evil and do good.
  Search for peace, and work to maintain it.
12 The eyes of the Lord watch over those who
    do right,
  and his ears are open to their prayers.
But the Lord turns his face
  against those who do evil."*

Suffering for Doing Good

13 Now, who will want to harm you if you are eager to do good? 14 But even if you suffer for doing what is right, God will reward you for it. So don't worry or be afraid of their threats. 15 Instead, you must worship Christ as Lord of your life. And if someone asks about your Christian hope, always be ready to explain it. 16 But do this in a gentle and respectful way.* Keep your conscience clear. Then if people speak against you, they will be ashamed when they see what a good life you live because you belong to Christ. 17 Remember, it is better to suffer for doing good, if that is what God wants, than to suffer for doing wrong!

18 Christ suffered* for our sins once for all time. He never sinned, but he died for sinners to bring you safely home to God. He suffered physical death, but he was raised to life in the Spirit.*

19 So he went and preached to the spirits in prison—20 those who disobeyed God long ago when God waited patiently while Noah was building his boat. Only eight people were saved from drowning in that terrible flood.* 21 And that water is a picture of baptism, which now saves you, not by removing dirt from your body, but as a response to God from* a clean conscience. It is effective because of the resurrection of Jesus Christ.

22 Now Christ has gone to heaven. He is seated in the place of honor next to God, and all the angels and authorities and powers accept his authority.

3:8 Greek *Show brotherly love.* **3:10-12** Ps 34:12-16. **3:16** Some English translations put this sentence in verse 15. **3:18a** Some manuscripts read *died.* **3:18b** Or *in spirit.* **3:20** Greek *saved through water.* **3:21** Or *as an appeal to God for.*

KING JAMES VERSION

4

1 Forasmuch then as Christ hath suffered for us in the flesh, arm yourselves likewise with the same mind: for he that hath suffered in the flesh hath ceased from sin;

2 That he no longer should live the rest of *his* time in the flesh to the lusts of men, but to the will of God.

3 For the time past of *our* life may suffice us to have wrought the will of the Gentiles, when we walked in lasciviousness, lusts, excess of wine, revellings, banquetings, and abominable idolatries:

4 Wherein they think it strange that ye run not with *them* to the same excess of riot, speaking evil of *you:*

5 Who shall give account to him that is ready to judge the quick and the dead.

6 For for this cause was the gospel preached also to them that are dead, that they might be judged according to men in the flesh, but live according to God in the spirit.

7 But the end of all things is at hand: be ye therefore sober, and watch unto prayer.

8 And above all things have fervent charity among yourselves: for charity shall cover the multitude of sins.

9 Use hospitality one to another without grudging.

10 As every man hath received the gift, *even so* minister the same one to another, as good stewards of the manifold grace of God.

11 If any man speak, *let him speak* as the oracles of God; if any man minister, *let him do it* as of the ability which God giveth: that God in all things may be glorified through Jesus Christ, to whom be praise and dominion for ever and ever. Amen.

12 Beloved, think it not strange concerning the fiery trial which is to try you, as though some strange thing happened unto you:

13 But rejoice, inasmuch as ye are partakers of Christ's sufferings; that, when his glory shall be revealed, ye may be glad also with exceeding joy.

14 If ye be reproached for the name of Christ, happy *are ye;* for the spirit of glory and of God resteth upon you: on their part he is evil spoken of, but on your part he is glorified.

15 But let none of you suffer as a murderer, or *as* a thief, or *as* an evildoer, or as a busybody in other men's matters.

16 Yet if *any man suffer* as a Christian, let him not be ashamed; but let him glorify God on this behalf.

17 For the time *is come* that judgment must begin at the house of God: and if *it* first *begin* at us, what shall the end *be* of them that obey not the gospel of God?

NEW LIVING TRANSLATION

Living for God

4

So then, since Christ suffered physical pain, you must arm yourselves with the same attitude he had, and be ready to suffer, too. For if you have suffered physically for Christ, you have finished with sin.* 2 You won't spend the rest of your lives chasing your own desires, but you will be anxious to do the will of God. 3 You have had enough in the past of the evil things that godless people enjoy—their immorality and lust, their feasting and drunkenness and wild parties, and their terrible worship of idols.

4 Of course, your former friends are surprised when you no longer plunge into the flood of wild and destructive things they do. So they slander you. 5 But remember that they will have to face God, who will judge everyone, both the living and the dead. 6 That is why the Good News was preached to those who are now dead*—so although they were destined to die like all people,* they now live forever with God in the Spirit.*

7 The end of the world is coming soon. Therefore, be earnest and disciplined in your prayers. 8 Most important of all, continue to show deep love for each other, for love covers a multitude of sins. 9 Cheerfully share your home with those who need a meal or a place to stay.

10 God has given each of you a gift from his great variety of spiritual gifts. Use them well to serve one another. 11 Do you have the gift of speaking? Then speak as though God himself were speaking through you. Do you have the gift of helping others? Do it with all the strength and energy that God supplies. Then everything you do will bring glory to God through Jesus Christ. All glory and power to him forever and ever! Amen.

Suffering for Being a Christian

12 Dear friends, don't be surprised at the fiery trials you are going through, as if something strange were happening to you. 13 Instead, be very glad—for these trials make you partners with Christ in his suffering, so that you will have the wonderful joy of seeing his glory when it is revealed to all the world.

14 So be happy when you are insulted for being a Christian,* for then the glorious Spirit of God* rests upon you.* 15 If you suffer, however, it must not be for murder, stealing, making trouble, or prying into other people's affairs. 16 But it is no shame to suffer for being a Christian. Praise God for the privilege of being called by his name! 17 For the time has come for judgment, and it must begin with God's household. And if judgment begins with us, what terrible

4:1 Or *For the one* [or *One*] *who has suffered physically has finished with sin.* **4:6a** Greek *preached even to the dead.* **4:6b** Or *so although people had judged them worthy of death.* **4:6c** Or *in spirit.* **4:14a** Greek *for the name of Christ.* **4:14b** Or *for the glory of God, which is his Spirit.* **4:14c** Some manuscripts add *On their part he is blasphemed, but on your part he is glorified.*

KING JAMES VERSION

18And if the righteous scarcely be saved, where shall the ungodly and the sinner appear?

19Wherefore let them that suffer according to the will of God commit the keeping of their souls *to him* in well doing, as unto a faithful Creator.

5 1The elders which are among you I exhort, who am also an elder, and a witness of the sufferings of Christ, and also a partaker of the glory that shall be revealed:

2Feed the flock of God which is among you, taking the oversight *thereof,* not by constraint, but willingly; not for filthy lucre, but of a ready mind;

3Neither as being lords over *God's* heritage, but being ensamples to the flock.

4And when the chief Shepherd shall appear, ye shall receive a crown of glory that fadeth not away.

5Likewise, ye younger, submit yourselves unto the elder. Yea, all *of you* be subject one to another, and be clothed with humility: for God resisteth the proud, and giveth grace to the humble.

6Humble yourselves therefore under the mighty hand of God, that he may exalt you in due time:

7Casting all your care upon him; for he careth for you.

8Be sober, be vigilant; because your adversary the devil, as a roaring lion, walketh about, seeking whom he may devour:

9Whom resist stedfast in the faith, knowing that the same afflictions are accomplished in your brethren that are in the world.

10But the God of all grace, who hath called us unto his eternal glory by Christ Jesus, after that ye have suffered a while, make you perfect, stablish, strengthen, settle *you.*

11To him *be* glory and dominion for ever and ever. Amen.

12By Silvanus, a faithful brother unto you, as I suppose, I have written briefly, exhorting, and testifying that this is the true grace of God wherein ye stand.

13The *church that is* at Babylon, elected together with *you,* saluteth you; and *so doth* Marcus my son.

14Greet ye one another with a kiss of charity. Peace *be* with you all that are in Christ Jesus. Amen.

NEW LIVING TRANSLATION

fate awaits those who have never obeyed God's Good News? 18And also,

"If the righteous are barely saved,
what will happen to godless sinners?"*

19So if you are suffering in a manner that pleases God, keep on doing what is right, and trust your lives to the God who created you, for he will never fail you.

Advice for Elders and Young Men

5 And now, a word to you who are elders in the churches. I, too, am an elder and a witness to the sufferings of Christ. And I, too, will share in his glory when he is revealed to the whole world. As a fellow elder, I appeal to you: 2Care for the flock that God has entrusted to you. Watch over it willingly, not grudgingly—not for what you will get out of it, but because you are eager to serve God. 3Don't lord it over the people assigned to your care, but lead them by your own good example. 4And when the Great Shepherd appears, you will receive a crown of never-ending glory and honor.

5In the same way, you younger men must accept the authority of the elders. And all of you, serve each other in humility, for

"God opposes the proud
but favors the humble."*

6So humble yourselves under the mighty power of God, and at the right time he will lift you up in honor. 7Give all your worries and cares to God, for he cares about you.

8Stay alert! Watch out for your great enemy, the devil. He prowls around like a roaring lion, looking for someone to devour. 9Stand firm against him, and be strong in your faith. Remember that your Christian brothers and sisters* all over the world are going through the same kind of suffering you are.

10In his kindness God called you to share in his eternal glory by means of Christ Jesus. So after you have suffered a little while, he will restore, support, and strengthen you, and he will place you on a firm foundation. 11All power to him forever! Amen.

Peter's Final Greetings

12I have written and sent this short letter to you with the help of Silas,* whom I commend to you as a faithful brother. My purpose in writing is to encourage you and assure you that what you are experiencing is truly part of God's grace for you. Stand firm in this grace.

13Your sister church here in Babylon* sends you greetings, and so does my son Mark. 14Greet each other with Christian love.*

Peace be with all of you who are in Christ.

4:18 Prov 11:31 (Greek version). **5:5** Prov 3:34 (Greek version). **5:9** Greek *your brothers.* **5:12** Greek *Silvanus.* **5:13** Greek *The elect one in Babylon.* Babylon was probably symbolic for Rome. **5:14** Greek *with a kiss of love.*

2 Peter

KING JAMES VERSION

1 1 Simon Peter, a servant and an apostle of Jesus
Christ, to them that have obtained like precious
faith with us through the righteousness of God and
our Saviour Jesus Christ:
2 Grace and peace be multiplied unto you through
the knowledge of God, and of Jesus our Lord,

3 According as his divine power hath given unto
us all things that *pertain* unto life and godliness,
through the knowledge of him that hath called us to
glory and virtue:
4 Whereby are given unto us exceeding great and
precious promises: that by these ye might be partakers of the divine nature, having escaped the corruption that is in the world through lust.
5 And beside this, giving all diligence, add to your
faith virtue; and to virtue knowledge;
6 And to knowledge temperance; and to temperance patience; and to patience godliness;
7 And to godliness brotherly kindness; and to
brotherly kindness charity.
8 For if these things be in you, and abound, they
make *you that ye shall* neither *be* barren nor unfruitful in the knowledge of our Lord Jesus Christ.
9 But he that lacketh these things is blind, and
cannot see afar off, and hath forgotten that he was
purged from his old sins.
10 Wherefore the rather, brethren, give diligence to
make your calling and election sure: for if ye do these
things, ye shall never fall:
11 For so an entrance shall be ministered unto you
abundantly into the everlasting kingdom of our Lord
and Saviour Jesus Christ.

NEW LIVING TRANSLATION

Greetings from Peter

1 This letter is from Simon* Peter, a slave and
apostle of Jesus Christ.
I am writing to you who share the same precious
faith we have. This faith was given to you because
of the justice and fairness* of Jesus Christ, our God
and Savior.
2 May God give you more and more grace and
peace as you grow in your knowledge of God and
Jesus our Lord.

Growing in Faith

3 By his divine power, God has given us everything we
need for living a godly life. We have received all of this
by coming to know him, the one who called us to himself by means of his marvelous glory and excellence.
4 And because of his glory and excellence, he has given
us great and precious promises. These are the promises that enable you to share his divine nature and escape the world's corruption caused by human desires.
5 In view of all this, make every effort to respond
to God's promises. Supplement your faith with a
generous provision of moral excellence, and moral
excellence with knowledge, 6 and knowledge with
self-control, and self-control with patient endurance, and patient endurance with godliness, 7 and
godliness with brotherly affection, and brotherly
affection with love for everyone.
8 The more you grow like this, the more productive
and useful you will be in your knowledge of our Lord
Jesus Christ. 9 But those who fail to develop in this
way are shortsighted or blind, forgetting that they
have been cleansed from their old sins.
10 So, dear brothers and sisters,* work hard to
prove that you really are among those God has called
and chosen. Do these things, and you will never fall
away. 11 Then God will give you a grand entrance into
the eternal Kingdom of our Lord and Savior Jesus
Christ.

1:1a Greek *Symeon.* **1:1b** Or *to you in the righteousness.* **1:10** Greek *brothers.*

KING JAMES VERSION

12 Wherefore I will not be negligent to put you always in remembrance of these things, though ye know *them,* and be established in the present truth.

13 Yea, I think it meet, as long as I am in this tabernacle, to stir you up by putting *you* in remembrance;

14 Knowing that shortly I must put off *this* my tabernacle, even as our Lord Jesus Christ hath shewed me.

15 Moreover I will endeavour that ye may be able after my decease to have these things always in remembrance.

16 For we have not followed cunningly devised fables, when we made known unto you the power and coming of our Lord Jesus Christ, but were eyewitnesses of his majesty.

17 For he received from God the Father honour and glory, when there came such a voice to him from the excellent glory, This is my beloved Son, in whom I am well pleased.

18 And this voice which came from heaven we heard, when we were with him in the holy mount.

19 We have also a more sure word of prophecy; whereunto ye do well that ye take heed, as unto a light that shineth in a dark place, until the day dawn, and the day star arise in your hearts:

20 Knowing this first, that no prophecy of the scripture is of any private interpretation.

21 For the prophecy came not in old time by the will of man: but holy men of God spake *as they were* moved by the Holy Ghost.

2 1 But there were false prophets also among the people, even as there shall be false teachers among you, who privily shall bring in damnable heresies, even denying the Lord that bought them, and bring upon themselves swift destruction.

2 And many shall follow their pernicious ways; by reason of whom the way of truth shall be evil spoken of.

3 And through covetousness shall they with feigned words make merchandise of you: whose judgment now of a long time lingereth not, and their damnation slumbereth not.

4 For if God spared not the angels that sinned, but cast *them* down to hell, and delivered *them* into chains of darkness, to be reserved unto judgment;

5 And spared not the old world, but saved Noah the eighth *person,* a preacher of righteousness, bringing in the flood upon the world of the ungodly;

6 And turning the cities of Sodom and Gomorrha into ashes condemned *them* with an overthrow, making *them* an ensample unto those that after should live ungodly;

NEW LIVING TRANSLATION

Paying Attention to Scripture

12 Therefore, I will always remind you about these things—even though you already know them and are standing firm in the truth you have been taught.
13 And it is only right that I should keep on reminding you as long as I live.* 14 For our Lord Jesus Christ has shown me that I must soon leave this earthly life,*
15 so I will work hard to make sure you always remember these things after I am gone.

16 For we were not making up clever stories when we told you about the powerful coming of our Lord Jesus Christ. We saw his majestic splendor with our own eyes 17 when he received honor and glory from God the Father. The voice from the majestic glory of God said to him, "This is my dearly loved Son, who brings me great joy."* 18 We ourselves heard that voice from heaven when we were with him on the holy mountain.

19 Because of that experience, we have even greater confidence in the message proclaimed by the prophets. You must pay close attention to what they wrote, for their words are like a lamp shining in a dark place—until the Day dawns, and Christ the Morning Star shines* in your hearts. 20 Above all, you must realize that no prophecy in Scripture ever came from the prophet's own understanding,* 21 or from human initiative. No, those prophets were moved by the Holy Spirit, and they spoke from God.

The Danger of False Teachers

2 But there were also false prophets in Israel, just as there will be false teachers among you. They will cleverly teach destructive heresies and even deny the Master who bought them. In this way, they will bring sudden destruction on themselves. 2 Many will follow their evil teaching and shameful immorality. And because of these teachers, the way of truth will be slandered. 3 In their greed they will make up clever lies to get hold of your money. But God condemned them long ago, and their destruction will not be delayed.

4 For God did not spare even the angels who sinned. He threw them into hell,* in gloomy pits of darkness,* where they are being held until the day of judgment. 5 And God did not spare the ancient world—except for Noah and the seven others in his family. Noah warned the world of God's righteous judgment. So God protected Noah when he destroyed the world of ungodly people with a vast flood. 6 Later, God condemned the cities of Sodom and Gomorrah and turned them into heaps of ashes. He made them an example of what will happen to

1:13 Greek *as long as I am in this tent* [or *tabernacle*]. **1:14** Greek *I must soon put off my tent* [or *tabernacle*]. **1:17** Matt 17:5; Mark 9:7; Luke 9:35. **1:19** Or *rises.* **1:20** Or *is a matter of one's own interpretation.* **2:4a** Greek *Tartarus.* **2:4b** Some manuscripts read *in chains of gloom.*

KING JAMES VERSION

7And delivered just Lot, vexed with the filthy conversation of the wicked:

8(For that righteous man dwelling among them, in seeing and hearing, vexed *his* righteous soul from day to day with *their* unlawful deeds;)

9The Lord knoweth how to deliver the godly out of temptations, and to reserve the unjust unto the day of judgment to be punished:

10But chiefly them that walk after the flesh in the lust of uncleanness, and despise government. Presumptuous *are they,* selfwilled, they are not afraid to speak evil of dignities.

11Whereas angels, which are greater in power and might, bring not railing accusation against them before the Lord.

12But these, as natural brute beasts, made to be taken and destroyed, speak evil of the things that they understand not; and shall utterly perish in their own corruption;

13And shall receive the reward of unrighteousness, *as* they that count it pleasure to riot in the day time. Spots *they are* and blemishes, sporting themselves with their own deceivings while they feast with you;

14Having eyes full of adultery, and that cannot cease from sin; beguiling unstable souls: an heart they have exercised with covetous practices; cursed children:

15Which have forsaken the right way, and are gone astray, following the way of Balaam *the son* of Bosor, who loved the wages of unrighteousness;

16But was rebuked for his iniquity: the dumb ass speaking with man's voice forbad the madness of the prophet.

17These are wells without water, clouds that are carried with a tempest; to whom the mist of darkness is reserved for ever.

18For when they speak great swelling *words* of vanity, they allure through the lusts of the flesh, *through much* wantonness, those that were clean escaped from them who live in error.

19While they promise them liberty, they themselves are the servants of corruption: for of whom a man is overcome, of the same is he brought in bondage.

20For if after they have escaped the pollutions of the world through the knowledge of the Lord and Saviour Jesus Christ, they are again entangled therein, and overcome, the latter end is worse with them than the beginning.

21For it had been better for them not to have known the way of righteousness, than, after they have known *it,* to turn from the holy commandment delivered unto them.

22But it is happened unto them according to the true proverb, The dog *is* turned to his own vomit again; and the sow that was washed to her wallowing in the mire.

NEW LIVING TRANSLATION

ungodly people. 7But God also rescued Lot out of Sodom because he was a righteous man who was sick of the shameful immorality of the wicked people around him. 8Yes, Lot was a righteous man who was tormented in his soul by the wickedness he saw and heard day after day. 9So you see, the Lord knows how to rescue godly people from their trials, even while keeping the wicked under punishment until the day of final judgment. 10He is especially hard on those who follow their own twisted sexual desire, and who despise authority.

These people are proud and arrogant, daring even to scoff at supernatural beings* without so much as trembling. 11But the angels, who are far greater in power and strength, do not dare to bring from the Lord* a charge of blasphemy against those supernatural beings.

12These false teachers are like unthinking animals, creatures of instinct, born to be caught and destroyed. They scoff at things they do not understand, and like animals, they will be destroyed. 13Their destruction is their reward for the harm they have done. They love to indulge in evil pleasures in broad daylight. They are a disgrace and a stain among you. They delight in deception* even as they eat with you in your fellowship meals. 14They commit adultery with their eyes, and their desire for sin is never satisfied. They lure unstable people into sin, and they are well trained in greed. They live under God's curse. 15They have wandered off the right road and followed the footsteps of Balaam son of Beor,* who loved to earn money by doing wrong. 16But Balaam was stopped from his mad course when his donkey rebuked him with a human voice.

17These people are as useless as dried-up springs or as mist blown away by the wind. They are doomed to blackest darkness. 18They brag about themselves with empty, foolish boasting. With an appeal to twisted sexual desires, they lure back into sin those who have barely escaped from a lifestyle of deception. 19They promise freedom, but they themselves are slaves of sin and corruption. For you are a slave to whatever controls you. 20And when people escape from the wickedness of the world by knowing our Lord and Savior Jesus Christ and then get tangled up and enslaved by sin again, they are worse off than before. 21It would be better if they had never known the way to righteousness than to know it and then reject the command they were given to live a holy life. 22They prove the truth of this proverb: "A dog returns to its vomit."* And another says, "A washed pig returns to the mud."

2:10 Greek *at glorious ones,* which are probably evil angels. **2:11** Other manuscripts read *to the Lord;* still others do not include this phrase at all. **2:13** Some manuscripts read *in fellowship meals.* **2:15** Some manuscripts read *Bosor.* **2:22** Prov 26:11.

KING JAMES VERSION

3 1 This second epistle, beloved, I now write unto you; in *both* which I stir up your pure minds by way of remembrance:

2 That ye may be mindful of the words which were spoken before by the holy prophets, and of the commandment of us the apostles of the Lord and Saviour:

3 Knowing this first, that there shall come in the last days scoffers, walking after their own lusts,

4 And saying, Where is the promise of his coming? for since the fathers fell asleep, all things continue as *they were* from the beginning of the creation.

5 For this they willingly are ignorant of, that by the word of God the heavens were of old, and the earth standing out of the water and in the water:

6 Whereby the world that then was, being overflowed with water, perished:

7 But the heavens and the earth, which are now, by the same word are kept in store, reserved unto fire against the day of judgment and perdition of ungodly men.

8 But, beloved, be not ignorant of this one thing, that one day *is* with the Lord as a thousand years, and a thousand years as one day.

9 The Lord is not slack concerning his promise, as some men count slackness; but is longsuffering to us-ward, not willing that any should perish, but that all should come to repentance.

10 But the day of the Lord will come as a thief in the night; in the which the heavens shall pass away with a great noise, and the elements shall melt with fervent heat, the earth also and the works that are therein shall be burned up.

11 *Seeing* then *that* all these things shall be dissolved, what manner *of persons* ought ye to be in *all* holy conversation and godliness,

12 Looking for and hasting unto the coming of the day of God, wherein the heavens being on fire shall be dissolved, and the elements shall melt with fervent heat?

13 Nevertheless we, according to his promise, look for new heavens and a new earth, wherein dwelleth righteousness.

14 Wherefore, beloved, seeing that ye look for such things, be diligent that ye may be found of him in peace, without spot, and blameless.

15 And account *that* the longsuffering of our Lord *is* salvation; even as our beloved brother Paul also according to the wisdom given unto him hath written unto you;

16 As also in all *his* epistles, speaking in them of these things; in which are some things hard to be understood, which they that are unlearned and unstable wrest, as *they do* also the other scriptures, unto their own destruction.

NEW LIVING TRANSLATION

The Day of the Lord Is Coming

3 This is my second letter to you, dear friends, and in both of them I have tried to stimulate your wholesome thinking and refresh your memory. 2 I want you to remember what the holy prophets said long ago and what our Lord and Savior commanded through your apostles.

3 Most importantly, I want to remind you that in the last days scoffers will come, mocking the truth and following their own desires. 4 They will say, "What happened to the promise that Jesus is coming again? From before the times of our ancestors, everything has remained the same since the world was first created."

5 They deliberately forget that God made the heavens by the word of his command, and he brought the earth out from the water and surrounded it with water. 6 Then he used the water to destroy the ancient world with a mighty flood. 7 And by the same word, the present heavens and earth have been stored up for fire. They are being kept for the day of judgment, when ungodly people will be destroyed.

8 But you must not forget this one thing, dear friends: A day is like a thousand years to the Lord, and a thousand years is like a day. 9 The Lord isn't really being slow about his promise, as some people think. No, he is being patient for your sake. He does not want anyone to be destroyed, but wants everyone to repent. 10 But the day of the Lord will come as unexpectedly as a thief. Then the heavens will pass away with a terrible noise, and the very elements themselves will disappear in fire, and the earth and everything on it will be found to deserve judgment.*

11 Since everything around us is going to be destroyed like this, what holy and godly lives you should live, 12 looking forward to the day of God and hurrying it along. On that day, he will set the heavens on fire, and the elements will melt away in the flames. 13 But we are looking forward to the new heavens and new earth he has promised, a world filled with God's righteousness.

14 And so, dear friends, while you are waiting for these things to happen, make every effort to be found living peaceful lives that are pure and blameless in his sight.

15 And remember, our Lord's patience gives people time to be saved. This is what our beloved brother Paul also wrote to you with the wisdom God gave him—16 speaking of these things in all of his letters. Some of his comments are hard to understand, and those who are ignorant and unstable have twisted his letters to mean something quite different, just as they do with other parts of Scripture. And this will result in their destruction.

3:10 Other manuscripts read *will be burned up;* still others read *will be found destroyed.*

KING JAMES VERSION

17 Ye therefore, beloved, seeing ye know *these*
things before, beware lest ye also, being led away
with the error of the wicked, fall from your own
stedfastness.
18 But grow in grace, and *in* the knowledge of our
Lord and Saviour Jesus Christ. To him *be* glory both
now and for ever. Amen.

NEW LIVING TRANSLATION

Peter's Final Words

17 I am warning you ahead of time, dear friends. Be
on guard so that you will not be carried away by the
errors of these wicked people and lose your own
secure footing. 18 Rather, you must grow in the grace
and knowledge of our Lord and Savior Jesus Christ.
All glory to him, both now and forever! Amen.

1 John

KING JAMES VERSION

1 1 That which was from the beginning, which we have heard, which we have seen with our eyes, which we have looked upon, and our hands have handled, of the Word of life;

2 (For the life was manifested, and we have seen *it*, and bear witness, and shew unto you that eternal life, which was with the Father, and was manifested unto us;)

3 That which we have seen and heard declare we unto you, that ye also may have fellowship with us: and truly our fellowship *is* with the Father, and with his Son Jesus Christ.

4 And these things write we unto you, that your joy may be full.

5 This then is the message which we have heard of him, and declare unto you, that God is light, and in him is no darkness at all.

6 If we say that we have fellowship with him, and walk in darkness, we lie, and do not the truth:

7 But if we walk in the light, as he is in the light, we have fellowship one with another, and the blood of Jesus Christ his Son cleanseth us from all sin.

8 If we say that we have no sin, we deceive ourselves, and the truth is not in us.

9 If we confess our sins, he is faithful and just to forgive us *our* sins, and to cleanse us from all unrighteousness.

10 If we say that we have not sinned, we make him a liar, and his word is not in us.

2 1 My little children, these things write I unto you, that ye sin not. And if any man sin, we have an advocate with the Father, Jesus Christ the righteous:

2 And he is the propitiation for our sins: and not for ours only, but also for *the sins of* the whole world.

3 And hereby we do know that we know him, if we keep his commandments.

4 He that saith, I know him, and keepeth not his commandments, is a liar, and the truth is not in him.

5 But whoso keepeth his word, in him verily is the love of God perfected: hereby know we that we are in him.

NEW LIVING TRANSLATION

Introduction

1 We proclaim to you the one who existed from the beginning,* whom we have heard and seen. We saw him with our own eyes and touched him with our own hands. He is the Word of life. 2 This one who is life itself was revealed to us, and we have seen him. And now we testify and proclaim to you that he is the one who is eternal life. He was with the Father, and then he was revealed to us. 3 We proclaim to you what we ourselves have actually seen and heard so that you may have fellowship with us. And our fellowship is with the Father and with his Son, Jesus Christ. 4 We are writing these things so that you may fully share our joy.*

Living in the Light

5 This is the message we heard from Jesus* and now declare to you: God is light, and there is no darkness in him at all. 6 So we are lying if we say we have fellowship with God but go on living in spiritual darkness; we are not practicing the truth. 7 But if we are living in the light, as God is in the light, then we have fellowship with each other, and the blood of Jesus, his Son, cleanses us from all sin.

8 If we claim we have no sin, we are only fooling ourselves and not living in the truth. 9 But if we confess our sins to him, he is faithful and just to forgive us our sins and to cleanse us from all wickedness. 10 If we claim we have not sinned, we are calling God a liar and showing that his word has no place in our hearts.

2 My dear children, I am writing this to you so that you will not sin. But if anyone does sin, we have an advocate who pleads our case before the Father. He is Jesus Christ, the one who is truly righteous. 2 He himself is the sacrifice that atones for our sins—and not only our sins but the sins of all the world.

3 And we can be sure that we know him if we obey his commandments. 4 If someone claims, "I know God," but doesn't obey God's commandments, that person is a liar and is not living in the truth. 5 But those who obey God's word truly show how completely they love him. That is how we know we are

1:1 Greek *What was from the beginning.* **1:4** Or *so that our joy may be complete;* some manuscripts read *your joy.* **1:5** Greek *from him.*

KING JAMES VERSION

[6]He that saith he abideth in him ought himself also so to walk, even as he walked.

[7]Brethren, I write no new commandment unto you, but an old commandment which ye had from the beginning. The old commandment is the word which ye have heard from the beginning.

[8]Again, a new commandment I write unto you, which thing is true in him and in you: because the darkness is past, and the true light now shineth.

[9]He that saith he is in the light, and hateth his brother, is in darkness even until now.

[10]He that loveth his brother abideth in the light, and there is none occasion of stumbling in him.

[11]But he that hateth his brother is in darkness, and walketh in darkness, and knoweth not whither he goeth, because that darkness hath blinded his eyes.

[12]I write unto you, little children, because your sins are forgiven you for his name's sake.

[13]I write unto you, fathers, because ye have known him *that is* from the beginning. I write unto you, young men, because ye have overcome the wicked one. I write unto you, little children, because ye have known the Father.

[14]I have written unto you, fathers, because ye have known him *that is* from the beginning. I have written unto you, young men, because ye are strong, and the word of God abideth in you, and ye have overcome the wicked one.

[15]Love not the world, neither the things *that are* in the world. If any man love the world, the love of the Father is not in him.

[16]For all that *is* in the world, the lust of the flesh, and the lust of the eyes, and the pride of life, is not of the Father, but is of the world.

[17]And the world passeth away, and the lust thereof: but he that doeth the will of God abideth for ever.

[18]Little children, it is the last time: and as ye have heard that antichrist shall come, even now are there many antichrists; whereby we know that it is the last time.

[19]They went out from us, but they were not of us; for if they had been of us, they would *no doubt* have

NEW LIVING TRANSLATION

living in him. [6]Those who say they live in God should live their lives as Jesus did.

A New Commandment

[7]Dear friends, I am not writing a new commandment for you; rather it is an old one you have had from the very beginning. This old commandment—to love one another—is the same message you heard before. [8]Yet it is also new. Jesus lived the truth of this commandment, and you also are living it. For the darkness is disappearing, and the true light is already shining.

[9]If anyone claims, "I am living in the light," but hates a Christian brother or sister,* that person is still living in darkness. [10]Anyone who loves another brother or sister* is living in the light and does not cause others to stumble. [11]But anyone who hates another brother or sister is still living and walking in darkness. Such a person does not know the way to go, having been blinded by the darkness.

[12] I am writing to you who are God's children
because your sins have been forgiven through Jesus.*
[13] I am writing to you who are mature in the faith*
because you know Christ, who existed from the beginning.
I am writing to you who are young in the faith
because you have won your battle with the evil one.
[14] I have written to you who are God's children
because you know the Father.
I have written to you who are mature in the faith
because you know Christ, who existed from the beginning.
I have written to you who are young in the faith
because you are strong.
God's word lives in your hearts,
and you have won your battle with the evil one.

Do Not Love This World

[15]Do not love this world nor the things it offers you, for when you love the world, you do not have the love of the Father in you. [16]For the world offers only a craving for physical pleasure, a craving for everything we see, and pride in our achievements and possessions. These are not from the Father, but are from this world. [17]And this world is fading away, along with everything that people crave. But anyone who does what pleases God will live forever.

Warning about Antichrists

[18]Dear children, the last hour is here. You have heard that the Antichrist is coming, and already many such antichrists have appeared. From this we know that the last hour has come. [19]These people left our churches, but they never really belonged with us;

2:9 Greek *hates his brother;* similarly in 2:11. **2:10** Greek *loves his brother.* **2:12** Greek *through his name.* **2:13** Or *to you fathers;* also in 2:14.

KING JAMES VERSION

continued with us: but *they went out,* that they might be made manifest that they were not all of us.

20But ye have an unction from the Holy One, and ye know all things.

21I have not written unto you because ye know not the truth, but because ye know it, and that no lie is of the truth.

22Who is a liar but he that denieth that Jesus is the Christ? He is antichrist, that denieth the Father and the Son.

23Whosoever denieth the Son, the same hath not the Father: [*but*] *he that acknowledgeth the Son hath the Father also.*

24Let that therefore abide in you, which ye have heard from the beginning. If that which ye have heard from the beginning shall remain in you, ye also shall continue in the Son, and in the Father.

25And this is the promise that he hath promised us, *even* eternal life.

26These *things* have I written unto you concerning them that seduce you.

27But the anointing which ye have received of him abideth in you, and ye need not that any man teach you: but as the same anointing teacheth you of all things, and is truth, and is no lie, and even as it hath taught you, ye shall abide in him.

28And now, little children, abide in him; that, when he shall appear, we may have confidence, and not be ashamed before him at his coming.

29If ye know that he is righteous, ye know that every one that doeth righteousness is born of him.

3 1Behold, what manner of love the Father hath bestowed upon us, that we should be called the sons of God: therefore the world knoweth us not, because it knew him not.

2Beloved, now are we the sons of God, and it doth not yet appear what we shall be: but we know that, when he shall appear, we shall be like him; for we shall see him as he is.

3And every man that hath this hope in him purifieth himself, even as he is pure.

4Whosoever committeth sin transgresseth also the law: for sin is the transgression of the law.

5And ye know that he was manifested to take away our sins; and in him is no sin.

6Whosoever abideth in him sinneth not: whosoever sinneth hath not seen him, neither known him.

7Little children, let no man deceive you: he that doeth righteousness is righteous, even as he is righteous.

8He that committeth sin is of the devil; for the devil sinneth from the beginning. For this purpose the Son of God was manifested, that he might destroy the works of the devil.

9Whosoever is born of God doth not commit sin;

NEW LIVING TRANSLATION

otherwise they would have stayed with us. When they left, it proved that they did not belong with us.

20But you are not like that, for the Holy One has given you his Spirit,* and all of you know the truth. 21So I am writing to you not because you don't know the truth but because you know the difference between truth and lies. 22And who is a liar? Anyone who says that Jesus is not the Christ.* Anyone who denies the Father and the Son is an antichrist.* 23Anyone who denies the Son doesn't have the Father, either. But anyone who acknowledges the Son has the Father also.

24So you must remain faithful to what you have been taught from the beginning. If you do, you will remain in fellowship with the Son and with the Father. 25And in this fellowship we enjoy the eternal life he promised us.

26I am writing these things to warn you about those who want to lead you astray. 27But you have received the Holy Spirit,* and he lives within you, so you don't need anyone to teach you what is true. For the Spirit* teaches you everything you need to know, and what he teaches is true—it is not a lie. So just as he has taught you, remain in fellowship with Christ.

Living as Children of God

28And now, dear children, remain in fellowship with Christ so that when he returns, you will be full of courage and not shrink back from him in shame.

29Since we know that Christ is righteous, we also know that all who do what is right are God's children.

3 See how very much our Father loves us, for he calls us his children, and that is what we are! But the people who belong to this world don't recognize that we are God's children because they don't know him. 2Dear friends, we are already God's children, but he has not yet shown us what we will be like when Christ appears. But we do know that we will be like him, for we will see him as he really is. 3And all who have this eager expectation will keep themselves pure, just as he is pure.

4Everyone who sins is breaking God's law, for all sin is contrary to the law of God. 5And you know that Jesus came to take away our sins, and there is no sin in him. 6Anyone who continues to live in him will not sin. But anyone who keeps on sinning does not know him or understand who he is.

7Dear children, don't let anyone deceive you about this: When people do what is right, it shows that they are righteous, even as Christ is righteous. 8But when people keep on sinning, it shows that they belong to the devil, who has been sinning since the beginning. But the Son of God came to destroy the works of the devil. 9Those who have been born into God's family

2:20 Greek *But you have an anointing from the Holy One.* **2:22a** Or *not the Messiah.* **2:22b** Or *the antichrist.* **2:27a** Greek *the anointing from him.* **2:27b** Greek *the anointing.*

KING JAMES VERSION

for his seed remaineth in him: and he cannot sin, because he is born of God.

[10]In this the children of God are manifest, and the children of the devil: whosoever doeth not righteousness is not of God, neither he that loveth not his brother.

[11]For this is the message that ye heard from the beginning, that we should love one another.

[12]Not as Cain, *who* was of that wicked one, and slew his brother. And wherefore slew he him? Because his own works were evil, and his brother's righteous.

[13]Marvel not, my brethren, if the world hate you.

[14]We know that we have passed from death unto life, because we love the brethren. He that loveth not *his* brother abideth in death.

[15]Whosoever hateth his brother is a murderer: and ye know that no murderer hath eternal life abiding in him.

[16]Hereby perceive we the love *of God,* because he laid down his life for us: and we ought to lay down *our* lives for the brethren.

[17]But whoso hath this world's good, and seeth his brother have need, and shutteth up his bowels *of compassion* from him, how dwelleth the love of God in him?

[18]My little children, let us not love in word, neither in tongue; but in deed and in truth.

[19]And hereby we know that we are of the truth, and shall assure our hearts before him.

[20]For if our heart condemn us, God is greater than our heart, and knoweth all things.

[21]Beloved, if our heart condemn us not, *then* have we confidence toward God.

[22]And whatsoever we ask, we receive of him, because we keep his commandments, and do those things that are pleasing in his sight.

[23]And this is his commandment, That we should believe on the name of his Son Jesus Christ, and love one another, as he gave us commandment.

[24]And he that keepeth his commandments dwelleth in him, and he in him. And hereby we know that he abideth in us, by the Spirit which he hath given us.

4

[1]Beloved, believe not every spirit, but try the spirits whether they are of God: because many false prophets are gone out into the world.

[2]Hereby know ye the Spirit of God: Every spirit that confesseth that Jesus Christ is come in the flesh is of God:

[3]And every spirit that confesseth not that Jesus Christ is come in the flesh is not of God: and this is

NEW LIVING TRANSLATION

do not make a practice of sinning, because God's life* is in them. So they can't keep on sinning, because they are children of God. [10]So now we can tell who are children of God and who are children of the devil. Anyone who does not live righteously and does not love other believers* does not belong to God.

Love One Another

[11]This is the message you have heard from the beginning: We should love one another. [12]We must not be like Cain, who belonged to the evil one and killed his brother. And why did he kill him? Because Cain had been doing what was evil, and his brother had been doing what was righteous. [13]So don't be surprised, dear brothers and sisters,* if the world hates you.

[14]If we love our Christian brothers and sisters,* it proves that we have passed from death to life. But a person who has no love is still dead. [15]Anyone who hates another brother or sister* is really a murderer at heart. And you know that murderers don't have eternal life within them.

[16]We know what real love is because Jesus gave up his life for us. So we also ought to give up our lives for our brothers and sisters. [17]If someone has enough money to live well and sees a brother or sister* in need but shows no compassion—how can God's love be in that person?

[18]Dear children, let's not merely say that we love each other; let us show the truth by our actions. [19]Our actions will show that we belong to the truth, so we will be confident when we stand before God. [20]Even if we feel guilty, God is greater than our feelings, and he knows everything.

[21]Dear friends, if we don't feel guilty, we can come to God with bold confidence. [22]And we will receive from him whatever we ask because we obey him and do the things that please him.

[23]And this is his commandment: We must believe in the name of his Son, Jesus Christ, and love one another, just as he commanded us. [24]Those who obey God's commandments remain in fellowship with him, and he with them. And we know he lives in us because the Spirit he gave us lives in us.

Discerning False Prophets

4

Dear friends, do not believe everyone who claims to speak by the Spirit. You must test them to see if the spirit they have comes from God. For there are many false prophets in the world. [2]This is how we know if they have the Spirit of God: If a person claiming to be a prophet* acknowledges that Jesus Christ came in a real body, that person has the Spirit of God. [3]But if someone claims to be a prophet and does not acknowledge the truth about Jesus, that

3:9 Greek *because his seed.* **3:10** Greek *does not love his brother.* **3:13** Greek *brothers.* **3:14** Greek *the brothers;* similarly in 3:16. **3:15** Greek *hates his brother.* **3:17** Greek *sees his brother.* **4:2** Greek *If a spirit;* similarly in 4:3.

KING JAMES VERSION

that *spirit* of antichrist, whereof ye have heard that it
should come; and even now already is it in the world.
4 Ye are of God, little children, and have overcome
them: because greater is he that is in you, than he
that is in the world.
5 They are of the world: therefore speak they of the
world, and the world heareth them.
6 We are of God: he that knoweth God heareth us;
he that is not of God heareth not us. Hereby know we
the spirit of truth, and the spirit of error.

7 Beloved, let us love one another: for love is of
God; and every one that loveth is born of God, and
knoweth God.
8 He that loveth not knoweth not God; for God is
love.
9 In this was manifested the love of God toward us,
because that God sent his only begotten Son into the
world, that we might live through him.
10 Herein is love, not that we loved God, but that he
loved us, and sent his Son *to be* the propitiation for
our sins.
11 Beloved, if God so loved us, we ought also to love
one another.
12 No man hath seen God at any time. If we love
one another, God dwelleth in us, and his love is perfected in us.
13 Hereby know we that we dwell in him, and he in
us, because he hath given us of his Spirit.
14 And we have seen and do testify that the Father
sent the Son *to be* the Saviour of the world.
15 Whosoever shall confess that Jesus is the Son of
God, God dwelleth in him, and he in God.
16 And we have known and believed the love that
God hath to us. God is love; and he that dwelleth in
love dwelleth in God, and God in him.
17 Herein is our love made perfect, that we may
have boldness in the day of judgment: because as he
is, so are we in this world.
18 There is no fear in love; but perfect love casteth
out fear: because fear hath torment. He that feareth
is not made perfect in love.
19 We love him, because he first loved us.
20 If a man say, I love God, and hateth his brother,
he is a liar: for he that loveth not his brother whom
he hath seen, how can he love God whom he hath
not seen?
21 And this commandment have we from him, That
he who loveth God love his brother also.

5 1 Whosoever believeth that Jesus is the Christ is
born of God: and every one that loveth him that
begat loveth him also that is begotten of him.

NEW LIVING TRANSLATION

person is not from God. Such a person has the spirit
of the Antichrist, which you heard is coming into the
world and indeed is already here.
4 But you belong to God, my dear children. You
have already won a victory over those people, because the Spirit who lives in you is greater than the
spirit who lives in the world. 5 Those people belong
to this world, so they speak from the world's view-
point, and the world listens to them. 6 But we belong
to God, and those who know God listen to us. If they
do not belong to God, they do not listen to us. That is
how we know if someone has the Spirit of truth or
the spirit of deception.

Loving One Another

7 Dear friends, let us continue to love one another, for
love comes from God. Anyone who loves is a child of
God and knows God. 8 But anyone who does not love
does not know God, for God is love.
9 God showed how much he loved us by sending
his one and only Son into the world so that we might
have eternal life through him. 10 This is real love—not
that we loved God, but that he loved us and sent his
Son as a sacrifice to take away our sins.
11 Dear friends, since God loved us that much, we
surely ought to love each other. 12 No one has ever
seen God. But if we love each other, God lives in us,
and his love is brought to full expression in us.
13 And God has given us his Spirit as proof that we
live in him and he in us. 14 Furthermore, we have seen
with our own eyes and now testify that the Father
sent his Son to be the Savior of the world. 15 All who
confess that Jesus is the Son of God have God living
in them, and they live in God. 16 We know how much
God loves us, and we have put our trust in his love.
God is love, and all who live in love live in God, and
God lives in them. 17 And as we live in God, our love
grows more perfect. So we will not be afraid on the
day of judgment, but we can face him with confidence because we live like Jesus here in this world.
18 Such love has no fear, because perfect love expels
all fear. If we are afraid, it is for fear of punishment,
and this shows that we have not fully experienced his
perfect love. 19 We love each other* because he loved
us first.
20 If someone says, "I love God," but hates a Christian brother or sister,* that person is a liar; for if we
don't love people we can see, how can we love God,
whom we cannot see? 21 And he has given us this
command: Those who love God must also love their
Christian brothers and sisters.*

Faith in the Son of God

5 Everyone who believes that Jesus is the Christ*
has become a child of God. And everyone who

4:19 Greek *We love.* Other manuscripts read *We love God;* still others read *We love him.* **4:20** Greek *hates his brother.* **4:21** Greek *The one who loves God must also love his brother.* **5:1** Or *the Messiah.*

KING JAMES VERSION

2 By this we know that we love the children of God, when we love God, and keep his commandments.

3 For this is the love of God, that we keep his commandments: and his commandments are not grievous.

4 For whatsoever is born of God overcometh the world: and this is the victory that overcometh the world, *even* our faith.

5 Who is he that overcometh the world, but he that believeth that Jesus is the Son of God?

6 This is he that came by water and blood, *even* Jesus Christ; not by water only, but by water and blood. And it is the Spirit that beareth witness, because the Spirit is truth.

7 For there are three that bear record in heaven, the Father, the Word, and the Holy Ghost: and these three are one.

8 And there are three that bear witness in earth, the Spirit, and the water, and the blood: and these three agree in one.

9 If we receive the witness of men, the witness of God is greater: for this is the witness of God which he hath testified of his Son.

10 He that believeth on the Son of God hath the witness in himself: he that believeth not God hath made him a liar; because he believeth not the record that God gave of his Son.

11 And this is the record, that God hath given to us eternal life, and this life is in his Son.

12 He that hath the Son hath life; *and* he that hath not the Son of God hath not life.

13 These things have I written unto you that believe on the name of the Son of God; that ye may know that ye have eternal life, and that ye may believe on the name of the Son of God.

14 And this is the confidence that we have in him, that, if we ask any thing according to his will, he heareth us:

15 And if we know that he hear us, whatsoever we ask, we know that we have the petitions that we desired of him.

16 If any man see his brother sin a sin *which is* not unto death, he shall ask, and he shall give him life for them that sin not unto death. There is a sin unto death: I do not say that he shall pray for it.

17 All unrighteousness is sin: and there is a sin not unto death.

18 We know that whosoever is born of God sinneth not; but he that is begotten of God keepeth himself, and that wicked one toucheth him not.

19 *And* we know that we are of God, and the whole world lieth in wickedness.

20 And we know that the Son of God is come, and hath given us an understanding, that we may know him that is true, and we are in him that is true, *even* in his Son Jesus Christ. This is the true God, and eternal life.

21 Little children, keep yourselves from idols. Amen.

NEW LIVING TRANSLATION

loves the Father loves his children, too. 2 We know we
love God's children if we love God and obey his
commandments. 3 Loving God means keeping his
commandments, and his commandments are not
burdensome. 4 For every child of God defeats this evil
world, and we achieve this victory through our faith.
5 And who can win this battle against the world? Only
those who believe that Jesus is the Son of God.
6 And Jesus Christ was revealed as God's Son by his
baptism in water and by shedding his blood on the
cross*—not by water only, but by water and blood.
And the Spirit, who is truth, confirms it with his testimony. 7 So we have these three witnesses*—8 the
Spirit, the water, and the blood—and all three agree.
9 Since we believe human testimony, surely we can
believe the greater testimony that comes from God.
And God has testified about his Son. 10 All who believe in the Son of God know in their hearts that this
testimony is true. Those who don't believe this are
actually calling God a liar because they don't believe
what God has testified about his Son.
11 And this is what God has testified: He has given
us eternal life, and this life is in his Son. 12 Whoever
has the Son has life; whoever does not have God's
Son does not have life.

Conclusion

13 I have written this to you who believe in the name of
the Son of God, so that you may know you have eternal
life. 14 And we are confident that he hears us whenever
we ask for anything that pleases him. 15 And since we
know he hears us when we make our requests, we also
know that he will give us what we ask for.
16 If you see a Christian brother or sister* sinning
in a way that does not lead to death, you should pray,
and God will give that person life. But there is a sin
that leads to death, and I am not saying you should
pray for those who commit it. 17 All wicked actions
are sin, but not every sin leads to death.
18 We know that God's children do not make a
practice of sinning, for God's Son holds them securely, and the evil one cannot touch them. 19 We
know that we are children of God and that the world
around us is under the control of the evil one.
20 And we know that the Son of God has come, and
he has given us understanding so that we can know the
true God.* And now we live in fellowship with the true
God because we live in fellowship with his Son, Jesus
Christ. He is the only true God, and he is eternal life.
21 Dear children, keep away from anything that
might take God's place in your hearts.*

5:6 Greek *This is he who came by water and blood.* **5:7** A few very late manuscripts add *in heaven—the Father, the Word, and the Holy Spirit, and these three are one. And we have three witnesses on earth.* **5:16** Greek *a brother.* **5:20** Greek *the one who is true.* **5:21** Greek *keep yourselves from idols.*

2 John

KING JAMES VERSION

1The elder unto the elect lady and her children,
whom I love in the truth; and not I only, but also all
they that have known the truth;
2For the truth's sake, which dwelleth in us, and
shall be with us for ever.
3Grace be with you, mercy, *and* peace, from God
the Father, and from the Lord Jesus Christ, the Son of
the Father, in truth and love.

4I rejoiced greatly that I found of thy children
walking in truth, as we have received a commandment from the Father.
5And now I beseech thee, lady, not as though I
wrote a new commandment unto thee, but that
which we had from the beginning, that we love one
another.
6And this is love, that we walk after his commandments. This is the commandment, That, as ye have
heard from the beginning, ye should walk in it.
7For many deceivers are entered into the world,
who confess not that Jesus Christ is come in the
flesh. This is a deceiver and an antichrist.
8Look to yourselves, that we lose not those things
which we have wrought, but that we receive a full
reward.
9Whosoever transgresseth, and abideth not in the
doctrine of Christ, hath not God. He that abideth in
the doctrine of Christ, he hath both the Father and
the Son.
10If there come any unto you, and bring not this
doctrine, receive him not into *your* house, neither
bid him God speed:
11For he that biddeth him God speed is partaker of
his evil deeds.
12Having many things to write unto you, I would
not *write* with paper and ink: but I trust to come unto
you, and speak face to face, that our joy may be full.
13The children of thy elect sister greet thee.
Amen.

NEW LIVING TRANSLATION

Greetings

1This letter is from John, the elder.*
I am writing to the chosen lady and to her children,* whom I love in the truth—as does everyone
else who knows the truth—
2because the truth lives
in us and will be with us forever.
3Grace, mercy, and peace, which come from God the
Father and from Jesus Christ—the Son of the Father—
will continue to be with us who live in truth and love.

Live in the Truth

4How happy I was to meet some of your children and
find them living according to the truth, just as the
Father commanded.
5I am writing to remind you, dear friends,* that we
should love one another. This is not a new commandment, but one we have had from the beginning.
6Love means doing what God has commanded us,
and he has commanded us to love one another, just
as you heard from the beginning.
7I say this because many deceivers have gone out
into the world. They deny that Jesus Christ came* in
a real body. Such a person is a deceiver and an
antichrist.
8Watch out that you do not lose what we*
have worked so hard to achieve. Be diligent so that you
receive your full reward.
9Anyone who wanders away
from this teaching has no relationship with God. But
anyone who remains in the teaching of Christ has a
relationship with both the Father and the Son.
10If anyone comes to your meeting and does not
teach the truth about Christ, don't invite that person
into your home or give any kind of encouragement.
11Anyone who encourages such people becomes a
partner in their evil work.

Conclusion

12I have much more to say to you, but I don't want to
do it with paper and ink. For I hope to visit you soon
and talk with you face to face. Then our joy will be
complete.
13Greetings from the children of your sister,* chosen by God.

1a Greek *From the elder.* **1b** Or *the church God has chosen and its members.* **5** Greek *I urge you, lady.* **7** Or *will come.* **8** Some manuscripts read *you.* **13** Or *from the members of your sister church.*

3 John

KING JAMES VERSION

[1]The elder unto the wellbeloved Gaius, whom I
love in the truth.
[2]Beloved, I wish above all things that thou mayest
prosper and be in health, even as thy soul prospereth.
[3]For I rejoiced greatly, when the brethren came
and testified of the truth that is in thee, even as thou
walkest in the truth.
[4]I have no greater joy than to hear that my children walk in truth.

[5]Beloved, thou doest faithfully whatsoever thou
doest to the brethren, and to strangers;
[6]Which have borne witness of thy charity before
the church: whom if thou bring forward on their
journey after a godly sort, thou shalt do well:
[7]Because that for his name's sake they went forth,
taking nothing of the Gentiles.
[8]We therefore ought to receive such, that we
might be fellowhelpers to the truth.
[9]I wrote unto the church: but Diotrephes, who
loveth to have the preeminence among them,
receiveth us not.
[10]Wherefore, if I come, I will remember his deeds
which he doeth, prating against us with malicious
words: and not content therewith, neither doth he
himself receive the brethren, and forbiddeth them
that would, and casteth *them* out of the church.
[11]Beloved, follow not that which is evil, but that
which is good. He that doeth good is of God: but he
that doeth evil hath not seen God.
[12]Demetrius hath good report of all *men,* and of
the truth itself: yea, and we *also* bear record; and ye
know that our record is true.

NEW LIVING TRANSLATION

Greetings

This letter is from John, the elder.*
I am writing to Gaius, my dear friend, whom I love
in the truth.
[2]Dear friend, I hope all is well with you and that
you are as healthy in body as you are strong in spirit.
[3]Some of the traveling teachers* recently returned
and made me very happy by telling me about your
faithfulness and that you are living according to the
truth. [4]I could have no greater joy than to hear that
my children are following the truth.

Caring for the Lord's Workers

[5]Dear friend, you are being faithful to God when you
care for the traveling teachers who pass through,
even though they are strangers to you. [6]They have
told the church here of your loving friendship.
Please continue providing for such teachers in a
manner that pleases God. [7]For they are traveling for
the Lord,* and they accept nothing from people who
are not believers.* [8]So we ourselves should support
them so that we can be their partners as they teach
the truth.
[9]I wrote to the church about this, but Diotrephes,
who loves to be the leader, refuses to have anything
to do with us. [10]When I come, I will report some of
the things he is doing and the evil accusations he is
making against us. Not only does he refuse to welcome the traveling teachers, he also tells others not
to help them. And when they do help, he puts them
out of the church.
[11]Dear friend, don't let this bad example influence
you. Follow only what is good. Remember that those
who do good prove that they are God's children, and
those who do evil prove that they do not know God.*
[12]Everyone speaks highly of Demetrius, as does
the truth itself. We ourselves can say the same for
him, and you know we speak the truth.

1 Greek *From the elder.* **3** Greek *the brothers;* also in verses 5 and 10.
7a Greek *They went out on behalf of the Name.* **7b** Greek *from Gentiles.*
11 Greek *they have not seen God.*

KING JAMES VERSION

13I had many things to write, but I will not with ink
and pen write unto thee:
14But I trust I shall shortly see thee, and we shall
speak face to face. Peace *be* to thee. *Our* friends
salute thee. Greet the friends by name.

NEW LIVING TRANSLATION

Conclusion

13I have much more to say to you, but I don't want
to write it with pen and ink. 14For I hope to see you
soon, and then we will talk face to face.
15*Peace be with you.
Your friends here send you their greetings. Please
give my personal greetings to each of our friends
there.

15 Some English translations combine verses 14 and 15 into verse 14.

Jude

KING JAMES VERSION

1 Jude, the servant of Jesus Christ, and brother of James, to them that are sanctified by God the Father, and preserved in Jesus Christ, *and* called:

2 Mercy unto you, and peace and love, be multiplied.

3 Beloved, when I gave all diligence to write unto you of the common salvation, it was needful for me to write unto you, and exhort *you* that ye should earnestly contend for the faith which was once delivered unto the saints.

4 For there are certain men crept in unawares, who were before of old ordained to this condemnation, ungodly men, turning the grace of our God into lasciviousness, and denying the only Lord God, and our Lord Jesus Christ.

5 I will therefore put you in remembrance, though ye once knew this, how that the Lord, having saved the people out of the land of Egypt, afterward destroyed them that believed not.

6 And the angels which kept not their first estate, but left their own habitation, he hath reserved in everlasting chains under darkness unto the judgment of the great day.

7 Even as Sodom and Gomorrha, and the cities about them in like manner, giving themselves over to fornication, and going after strange flesh, are set forth for an example, suffering the vengeance of eternal fire.

8 Likewise also these *filthy* dreamers defile the flesh, despise dominion, and speak evil of dignities.

9 Yet Michael the archangel, when contending with the devil he disputed about the body of Moses, durst not bring against him a railing accusation, but said, The Lord rebuke thee.

NEW LIVING TRANSLATION

Greetings from Jude

This letter is from Jude, a slave of Jesus Christ and a brother of James.

I am writing to all who have been called by God the Father, who loves you and keeps you safe in the care of Jesus Christ.*

2 May God give you more and more mercy, peace, and love.

The Danger of False Teachers

3 Dear friends, I had been eagerly planning to write to you about the salvation we all share. But now I find that I must write about something else, urging you to defend the faith that God has entrusted once for all time to his holy people. 4 I say this because some ungodly people have wormed their way into your churches, saying that God's marvelous grace allows us to live immoral lives. The condemnation of such people was recorded long ago, for they have denied our only Master and Lord, Jesus Christ.

5 So I want to remind you, though you already know these things, that Jesus* first rescued the nation of Israel from Egypt, but later he destroyed those who did not remain faithful. 6 And I remind you of the angels who did not stay within the limits of authority God gave them but left the place where they belonged. God has kept them securely chained in prisons of darkness, waiting for the great day of judgment. 7 And don't forget Sodom and Gomorrah and their neighboring towns, which were filled with immorality and every kind of sexual perversion. Those cities were destroyed by fire and serve as a warning of the eternal fire of God's judgment.

8 In the same way, these people—who claim authority from their dreams—live immoral lives, defy authority, and scoff at supernatural beings.* 9 But even Michael, one of the mightiest of the angels,* did not dare accuse the devil of blasphemy, but simply said, "The Lord rebuke you!" (This took place when Michael was arguing with the devil about Moses'

1 Or *keeps you for Jesus Christ.* **5** As in the best manuscripts; various other manuscripts read *[the] Lord,* or *God,* or *Christ;* one reads *God Christ.* **8** Greek *at glorious ones,* which are probably evil angels. **9** Greek *Michael, the archangel.*

KING JAMES VERSION

[10]But these speak evil of those things which they know not: but what they know naturally, as brute beasts, in those things they corrupt themselves.

[11]Woe unto them! for they have gone in the way of Cain, and ran greedily after the error of Balaam for reward, and perished in the gainsaying of Core.

[12]These are spots in your feasts of charity, when they feast with you, feeding themselves without fear: clouds *they are* without water, carried about of winds; trees whose fruit withereth, without fruit, twice dead, plucked up by the roots;

[13]Raging waves of the sea, foaming out their own shame; wandering stars, to whom is reserved the blackness of darkness for ever.

[14]And Enoch also, the seventh from Adam, prophesied of these, saying, Behold, the Lord cometh with ten thousands of his saints,

[15]To execute judgment upon all, and to convince all that are ungodly among them of all their ungodly deeds which they have ungodly committed, and of all their hard *speeches* which ungodly sinners have spoken against him.

[16]These are murmurers, complainers, walking after their own lusts; and their mouth speaketh great swelling *words,* having men's persons in admiration because of advantage.

[17]But, beloved, remember ye the words which were spoken before of the apostles of our Lord Jesus Christ;

[18]How that they told you there should be mockers in the last time, who should walk after their own ungodly lusts.

[19]These be they who separate themselves, sensual, having not the Spirit.

[20]But ye, beloved, building up yourselves on your most holy faith, praying in the Holy Ghost,

[21]Keep yourselves in the love of God, looking for the mercy of our Lord Jesus Christ unto eternal life.

[22]And of some have compassion, making a difference:

[23]And others save with fear, pulling *them* out of the fire; hating even the garment spotted by the flesh.

NEW LIVING TRANSLATION

body.) [10]But these people scoff at things they do not understand. Like unthinking animals, they do whatever their instincts tell them, and so they bring about their own destruction. [11]What sorrow awaits them! For they follow in the footsteps of Cain, who killed his brother. Like Balaam, they deceive people for money. And like Korah, they perish in their rebellion.

[12]When these people eat with you in your fellowship meals commemorating the Lord's love, they are like dangerous reefs that can shipwreck you.* They are like shameless shepherds who care only for themselves. They are like clouds blowing over the land without giving any rain. They are like trees in autumn that are doubly dead, for they bear no fruit and have been pulled up by the roots. [13]They are like wild waves of the sea, churning up the foam of their shameful deeds. They are like wandering stars, doomed forever to blackest darkness.

[14]Enoch, who lived in the seventh generation after Adam, prophesied about these people. He said, "Listen! The Lord is coming with countless thousands of his holy ones [15]to execute judgment on the people of the world. He will convict every person of all the ungodly things they have done and for all the insults that ungodly sinners have spoken against him."*

[16]These people are grumblers and complainers, living only to satisfy their desires. They brag loudly about themselves, and they flatter others to get what they want.

A Call to Remain Faithful

[17]But you, my dear friends, must remember what the apostles of our Lord Jesus Christ said. [18]They told you that in the last times there would be scoffers whose purpose in life is to satisfy their ungodly desires. [19]These people are the ones who are creating divisions among you. They follow their natural instincts because they do not have God's Spirit in them.

[20]But you, dear friends, must build each other up in your most holy faith, pray in the power of the Holy Spirit,* [21]and await the mercy of our Lord Jesus Christ, who will bring you eternal life. In this way, you will keep yourselves safe in God's love.

[22]And you must show mercy to* those whose faith is wavering. [23]Rescue others by snatching them from the flames of judgment. Show mercy to still others,* but do so with great caution, hating the sins that contaminate their lives.*

12 Or *they are contaminants among you;* or *they are stains.* **14-15** The quotation comes from intertestamental literature: Enoch 1:9. **20** Greek *pray in the Holy Spirit.* **22** Some manuscripts read *must reprove.* **22-23a** Some manuscripts have only two categories of people: (1) those whose faith is wavering and therefore need to be snatched from the flames of judgment, and (2) those who need to be shown mercy. **23b** Greek *with fear, hating even the clothing stained by the flesh.*

KING JAMES VERSION

24 Now unto him that is able to keep you from falling, and to present *you* faultless before the presence
of his glory with exceeding joy,
25 To the only wise God our Saviour, *be* glory and
majesty, dominion and power, both now and for ever.
Amen.

NEW LIVING TRANSLATION

A Prayer of Praise

24 Now all glory to God, who is able to keep you from
falling away and will bring you with great joy into
his glorious presence without a single fault. 25 All
glory to him who alone is God, our Savior through
Jesus Christ our Lord. All glory, majesty, power, and
authority are his before all time, and in the present,
and beyond all time! Amen.

Revelation

KING JAMES VERSION

1 1 The Revelation of Jesus Christ, which God gave unto him, to shew unto his servants things which must shortly come to pass; and he sent and signified *it* by his angel unto his servant John:

2 Who bare record of the word of God, and of the testimony of Jesus Christ, and of all things that he saw.

3 Blessed *is* he that readeth, and they that hear the words of this prophecy, and keep those things which are written therein: for the time *is* at hand.

4 John to the seven churches which are in Asia: Grace *be* unto you, and peace, from him which is, and which was, and which is to come; and from the seven Spirits which are before his throne;

5 And from Jesus Christ, *who is* the faithful witness, *and* the first begotten of the dead, and the prince of the kings of the earth. Unto him that loved us, and washed us from our sins in his own blood,

6 And hath made us kings and priests unto God and his Father; to him *be* glory and dominion for ever and ever. Amen.

7 Behold, he cometh with clouds; and every eye shall see him, and they *also* which pierced him: and all kindreds of the earth shall wail because of him. Even so, Amen.

8 I am Alpha and Omega, the beginning and the ending, saith the Lord, which is, and which was, and which is to come, the Almighty.

9 I John, who also am your brother, and companion in tribulation, and in the kingdom and patience of Jesus Christ, was in the isle that is called Patmos, for the word of God, and for the testimony of Jesus Christ.

NEW LIVING TRANSLATION

Prologue

1 This is a revelation from* Jesus Christ, which God gave him to show his servants the events that must soon* take place. He sent an angel to present this revelation to his servant John, 2 who faithfully reported everything he saw. This is his report of the word of God and the testimony of Jesus Christ.

3 God blesses the one who reads the words of this prophecy to the church, and he blesses all who listen to its message and obey what it says, for the time is near.

John's Greeting to the Seven Churches

4 This letter is from John to the seven churches in the province of Asia.*

Grace and peace to you from the one who is, who always was, and who is still to come; from the sevenfold Spirit* before his throne; 5 and from Jesus Christ. He is the faithful witness to these things, the first to rise from the dead, and the ruler of all the kings of the world.

All glory to him who loves us and has freed us from our sins by shedding his blood for us. 6 He has made us a Kingdom of priests for God his Father. All glory and power to him forever and ever! Amen.

7 Look! He comes with the clouds of heaven.
  And everyone will see him—
  even those who pierced him.
And all the nations of the world
  will mourn for him.
Yes! Amen!

8 "I am the Alpha and the Omega—the beginning and the end,"* says the Lord God. "I am the one who is, who always was, and who is still to come—the Almighty One."

Vision of the Son of Man

9 I, John, am your brother and your partner in suffering and in God's Kingdom and in the patient endurance to which Jesus calls us. I was exiled to the island of Patmos for preaching the word of God and

1:1a Or *of.* **1:1b** Or *suddenly,* or *quickly.* **1:4a** *Asia* was a Roman province in what is now western Turkey. **1:4b** Greek *the seven spirits.* **1:8** Greek *I am the Alpha and the Omega,* referring to the first and last letters of the Greek alphabet.

KING JAMES VERSION

10 I was in the Spirit on the Lord's day, and heard behind me a great voice, as of a trumpet,

11 Saying, I am Alpha and Omega, the first and the last: and, What thou seest, write in a book, and send *it* unto the seven churches which are in Asia; unto Ephesus, and unto Smyrna, and unto Pergamos, and unto Thyatira, and unto Sardis, and unto Philadelphia, and unto Laodicea.

12 And I turned to see the voice that spake with me. And being turned, I saw seven golden candlesticks;

13 And in the midst of the seven candlesticks *one* like unto the Son of man, clothed with a garment down to the foot, and girt about the paps with a golden girdle.

14 His head and *his* hairs *were* white like wool, as white as snow; and his eyes *were* as a flame of fire;

15 And his feet like unto fine brass, as if they burned in a furnace; and his voice as the sound of many waters.

16 And he had in his right hand seven stars: and out of his mouth went a sharp twoedged sword: and his countenance *was* as the sun shineth in his strength.

17 And when I saw him, I fell at his feet as dead. And he laid his right hand upon me, saying unto me, Fear not; I am the first and the last:

18 I *am* he that liveth, and was dead; and, behold, I am alive for evermore, Amen; and have the keys of hell and of death.

19 Write the things which thou hast seen, and the things which are, and the things which shall be hereafter;

20 The mystery of the seven stars which thou sawest in my right hand, and the seven golden candlesticks. The seven stars are the angels of the seven churches: and the seven candlesticks which thou sawest are the seven churches.

2 1 Unto the angel of the church of Ephesus write; These things saith he that holdeth the seven stars in his right hand, who walketh in the midst of the seven golden candlesticks;

2 I know thy works, and thy labour, and thy patience, and how thou canst not bear them which are evil: and thou hast tried them which say they are apostles, and are not, and hast found them liars:

3 And hast borne, and hast patience, and for my name's sake hast laboured, and hast not fainted.

4 Nevertheless I have *somewhat* against thee, because thou hast left thy first love.

5 Remember therefore from whence thou art fallen, and repent, and do the first works; or else I will come unto thee quickly, and will remove thy candlestick out of his place, except thou repent.

NEW LIVING TRANSLATION

for my testimony about Jesus. 10 It was the Lord's Day, and I was worshiping in the Spirit.* Suddenly, I heard behind me a loud voice like a trumpet blast. 11 It said, "Write in a book* everything you see, and send it to the seven churches in the cities of Ephesus, Smyrna, Pergamum, Thyatira, Sardis, Philadelphia, and Laodicea."

12 When I turned to see who was speaking to me, I saw seven gold lampstands. 13 And standing in the middle of the lampstands was someone like the Son of Man.* He was wearing a long robe with a gold sash across his chest. 14 His head and his hair were white like wool, as white as snow. And his eyes were like flames of fire. 15 His feet were like polished bronze refined in a furnace, and his voice thundered like mighty ocean waves. 16 He held seven stars in his right hand, and a sharp two-edged sword came from his mouth. And his face was like the sun in all its brilliance.

17 When I saw him, I fell at his feet as if I were dead. But he laid his right hand on me and said, "Don't be afraid! I am the First and the Last. 18 I am the living one. I died, but look—I am alive forever and ever! And I hold the keys of death and the grave.*

19 "Write down what you have seen—both the things that are now happening and the things that will happen.* 20 This is the meaning of the mystery of the seven stars you saw in my right hand and the seven gold lampstands: The seven stars are the angels* of the seven churches, and the seven lampstands are the seven churches.

The Message to the Church in Ephesus

2 "Write this letter to the angel* of the church in Ephesus. This is the message from the one who holds the seven stars in his right hand, the one who walks among the seven gold lampstands:

2 "I know all the things you do. I have seen your
hard work and your patient endurance. I know
you don't tolerate evil people. You have examined
the claims of those who say they are apostles but
are not. You have discovered they are liars. 3 You
have patiently suffered for me without quitting.
4 "But I have this complaint against you. You
don't love me or each other as you did at first!*
5 Look how far you have fallen! Turn back to me
and do the works you did at first. If you don't
repent, I will come and remove your lampstand

1:10 Or *in spirit.* **1:11** Or *on a scroll.* **1:13** Or *like a son of man.* See Dan 7:13. "Son of Man" is a title Jesus used for himself. **1:18** Greek *and Hades.* **1:19** Or *what you have seen and what they mean—the things that have already begun to happen.* **1:20** Or *the messengers.* **2:1** Or *the messenger;* also in 2:8, 12, 18. **2:4** Greek *You have lost your first love.*

KING JAMES VERSION

6 But this thou hast, that thou hatest the deeds of the Nicolaitanes, which I also hate.

7 He that hath an ear, let him hear what the Spirit saith unto the churches; To him that overcometh will I give to eat of the tree of life, which is in the midst of the paradise of God.

8 And unto the angel of the church in Smyrna write; These things saith the first and the last, which was dead, and is alive;

9 I know thy works, and tribulation, and poverty, (but thou art rich) and *I know* the blasphemy of them which say they are Jews, and are not, but *are* the synagogue of Satan.

10 Fear none of those things which thou shalt suffer: behold, the devil shall cast *some* of you into prison, that ye may be tried; and ye shall have tribulation ten days: be thou faithful unto death, and I will give thee a crown of life.

11 He that hath an ear, let him hear what the Spirit saith unto the churches; He that overcometh shall not be hurt of the second death.

12 And to the angel of the church in Pergamos write; These things saith he which hath the sharp sword with two edges;

13 I know thy works and where thou dwellest, *even* where Satan's seat *is:* and thou holdest fast my name, and hast not denied my faith, even in those days wherein Antipas *was* my faithful martyr, who was slain among you, where Satan dwelleth.

14 But I have a few things against thee, because thou hast there them that hold the doctrine of Balaam, who taught Balac to cast a stumblingblock before the children of Israel, to eat things sacrificed unto idols, and to commit fornication.

15 So hast thou also them that hold the doctrine of the Nicolaitanes, which thing I hate.

16 Repent; or else I will come unto thee quickly, and will fight against them with the sword of my mouth.

17 He that hath an ear, let him hear what the Spirit saith unto the churches; To him that overcometh will I give to eat of the hidden manna, and will give him a white stone, and in the stone a new name written, which no man knoweth saving he that receiveth *it.*

NEW LIVING TRANSLATION

from its place among the churches. 6 But this
is in your favor: You hate the evil deeds of the
Nicolaitans, just as I do.

7 "Anyone with ears to hear must listen to the
Spirit and understand what he is saying to the
churches. To everyone who is victorious I will
give fruit from the tree of life in the paradise
of God.

The Message to the Church in Smyrna

8 "Write this letter to the angel of the church in
Smyrna. This is the message from the one who is the
First and the Last, who was dead but is now alive:

9 "I know about your suffering and your poverty—
but you are rich! I know the blasphemy of those
opposing you. They say they are Jews, but they are
not, because their synagogue belongs to Satan.
10 Don't be afraid of what you are about to suffer.
The devil will throw some of you into prison to
test you. You will suffer for ten days. But if you
remain faithful even when facing death, I will
give you the crown of life.

11 "Anyone with ears to hear must listen to the
Spirit and understand what he is saying to the
churches. Whoever is victorious will not be
harmed by the second death.

The Message to the Church in Pergamum

12 "Write this letter to the angel of the church in
Pergamum. This is the message from the one with
the sharp two-edged sword:

13 "I know that you live in the city where Satan
has his throne, yet you have remained loyal to me.
You refused to deny me even when Antipas, my
faithful witness, was martyred among you there
in Satan's city.

14 "But I have a few complaints against you. You
tolerate some among you whose teaching is like
that of Balaam, who showed Balak how to trip
up the people of Israel. He taught them to sin by
eating food offered to idols and by committing
sexual sin. 15 In a similar way, you have some
Nicolaitans among you who follow the same
teaching. 16 Repent of your sin, or I will come to
you suddenly and fight against them with the
sword of my mouth.

17 "Anyone with ears to hear must listen to the
Spirit and understand what he is saying to the
churches. To everyone who is victorious I will
give some of the manna that has been hidden
away in heaven. And I will give to each one a
white stone, and on the stone will be engraved
a new name that no one understands except the
one who receives it.

KING JAMES VERSION

18And unto the angel of the church in Thyatira
write; These things saith the Son of God, who hath
his eyes like unto a flame of fire, and his feet *are* like
fine brass;
19I know thy works, and charity, and service, and
faith, and thy patience, and thy works; and the last *to*
be more than the first.
20Notwithstanding I have a few things against
thee, because thou sufferest that woman Jezebel,
which calleth herself a prophetess, to teach and to
seduce my servants to commit fornication, and to eat
things sacrificed unto idols.
21And I gave her space to repent of her fornication; and she repented not.
22Behold, I will cast her into a bed, and them that
commit adultery with her into great tribulation, except they repent of their deeds.
23And I will kill her children with death; and all the
churches shall know that I am he which searcheth
the reins and hearts: and I will give unto every one of
you according to your works.
24But unto you I say, and unto the rest in Thyatira,
as many as have not this doctrine, and which have
not known the depths of Satan, as they speak; I will
put upon you none other burden.
25But that which ye have *already* hold fast till I
come.
26And he that overcometh, and keepeth my works
unto the end, to him will I give power over the
nations:
27And he shall rule them with a rod of iron; as the
vessels of a potter shall they be broken to shivers:
even as I received of my Father.
28And I will give him the morning star.
29He that hath an ear, let him hear what the Spirit
saith unto the churches.

3 1And unto the angel of the church in Sardis
write; These things saith he that hath the seven
Spirits of God, and the seven stars; I know thy works,
that thou hast a name that thou livest, and art dead.
2Be watchful, and strengthen the things which remain, that are ready to die: for I have not found thy
works perfect before God.
3Remember therefore how thou hast received and
heard, and hold fast, and repent. If therefore thou
shalt not watch, I will come on thee as a thief, and
thou shalt not know what hour I will come upon
thee.

NEW LIVING TRANSLATION

The Message to the Church in Thyatira

18"Write this letter to the angel of the church in Thyatira. This is the message from the Son of God, whose
eyes are like flames of fire, whose feet are like polished bronze:

19"I know all the things you do. I have seen your
love, your faith, your service, and your patient
endurance. And I can see your constant
improvement in all these things.
20"But I have this complaint against you. You
are permitting that woman—that Jezebel who
calls herself a prophet—to lead my servants
astray. She teaches them to commit sexual sin
and to eat food offered to idols. 21I gave her time
to repent, but she does not want to turn away
from her immorality.
22"Therefore, I will throw her on a bed of
suffering,* and those who commit adultery with
her will suffer greatly unless they repent and
turn away from her evil deeds. 23I will strike her
children dead. Then all the churches will know
that I am the one who searches out the thoughts
and intentions of every person. And I will give to
each of you whatever you deserve.
24"But I also have a message for the rest of
you in Thyatira who have not followed this false
teaching ('deeper truths,' as they call them—
depths of Satan, actually). I will ask nothing more
of you 25except that you hold tightly to what you
have until I come. 26To all who are victorious,
who obey me to the very end,

To them I will give authority over all the
nations.
27 They will rule the nations with an iron rod
and smash them like clay pots.*

28They will have the same authority I received
from my Father, and I will also give them the
morning star!
29"Anyone with ears to hear must listen to the
Spirit and understand what he is saying to the
churches.

The Message to the Church in Sardis

3 "Write this letter to the angel* of the church in
Sardis. This is the message from the one who
has the sevenfold Spirit* of God and the seven stars:

"I know all the things you do, and that you have
a reputation for being alive—but you are dead.
2Wake up! Strengthen what little remains, for
even what is left is almost dead. I find that your
actions do not meet the requirements of my God.
3Go back to what you heard and believed at first;
hold to it firmly. Repent and turn to me again.
If you don't wake up, I will come to you suddenly,
as unexpected as a thief.

2:22 Greek *a bed.* **2:26-27** Ps 2:8-9 (Greek Version). **3:1a** Or *the messenger;* also in 3:7, 14. **3:1b** Greek *the seven spirits.*

KING JAMES VERSION

4 Thou hast a few names even in Sardis which have not defiled their garments; and they shall walk with me in white: for they are worthy.

5 He that overcometh, the same shall be clothed in white raiment; and I will not blot out his name out of the book of life, but I will confess his name before my Father, and before his angels.

6 He that hath an ear, let him hear what the Spirit saith unto the churches.

7 And to the angel of the church in Philadelphia write; These things saith he that is holy, he that is true, he that hath the key of David, he that openeth, and no man shutteth; and shutteth, and no man openeth;

8 I know thy works: behold, I have set before thee an open door, and no man can shut it: for thou hast a little strength, and hast kept my word, and hast not denied my name.

9 Behold, I will make them of the synagogue of Satan, which say they are Jews, and are not, but do lie; behold, I will make them to come and worship before thy feet, and to know that I have loved thee.

10 Because thou hast kept the word of my patience, I also will keep thee from the hour of temptation, which shall come upon all the world, to try them that dwell upon the earth.

11 Behold, I come quickly: hold that fast which thou hast, that no man take thy crown.

12 Him that overcometh will I make a pillar in the temple of my God, and he shall go no more out: and I will write upon him the name of my God, and the name of the city of my God, *which is* new Jerusalem, which cometh down out of heaven from my God: and *I will write upon him* my new name.

13 He that hath an ear, let him hear what the Spirit saith unto the churches.

14 And unto the angel of the church of the Laodiceans write; These things saith the Amen, the faithful and true witness, the beginning of the creation of God;

15 I know thy works, that thou art neither cold nor hot: I would thou wert cold or hot.

16 So then because thou art lukewarm, and neither cold nor hot, I will spue thee out of my mouth.

17 Because thou sayest, I am rich, and increased with goods, and have need of nothing; and knowest not that thou art wretched, and miserable, and poor, and blind, and naked:

NEW LIVING TRANSLATION

4 "Yet there are some in the church in Sardis
who have not soiled their clothes with evil. They
will walk with me in white, for they are worthy.
5 All who are victorious will be clothed in white.
I will never erase their names from the Book of
Life, but I will announce before my Father and
his angels that they are mine.
6 "Anyone with ears to hear must listen to the
Spirit and understand what he is saying to the
churches.

The Message to the Church in Philadelphia

7 "Write this letter to the angel of the church in
Philadelphia.

This is the message from the one who is holy
and true,
the one who has the key of David.
What he opens, no one can close;
and what he closes, no one can open:*

8 "I know all the things you do, and I have opened
a door for you that no one can close. You have
little strength, yet you obeyed my word and did
not deny me. 9 Look, I will force those who belong
to Satan's synagogue—those liars who say they
are Jews but are not—to come and bow down at
your feet. They will acknowledge that you are the
ones I love.
10 "Because you have obeyed my command to
persevere, I will protect you from the great time
of testing that will come upon the whole world
to test those who belong to this world. 11 I am
coming soon.* Hold on to what you have, so that
no one will take away your crown. 12 All who are
victorious will become pillars in the Temple of
my God, and they will never have to leave it. And
I will write on them the name of my God, and they
will be citizens in the city of my God—the new
Jerusalem that comes down from heaven from my
God. And I will also write on them my new name.
13 "Anyone with ears to hear must listen to the
Spirit and understand what he is saying to the
churches.

The Message to the Church in Laodicea

14 "Write this letter to the angel of the church in
Laodicea. This is the message from the one who is
the Amen—the faithful and true witness, the beginning* of God's new creation:

15 "I know all the things you do, that you are neither
hot nor cold. I wish that you were one or the other!
16 But since you are like lukewarm water, neither
hot nor cold, I will spit you out of my mouth! 17 You
say, 'I am rich. I have everything I want. I don't
need a thing!' And you don't realize that you are
wretched and miserable and poor and blind and

3:7 Isa 22:22. **3:11** Or *suddenly*, or *quickly*. **3:14** Or *the ruler*, or *the source*.

KING JAMES VERSION

18 I counsel thee to buy of me gold tried in the fire, that thou mayest be rich; and white raiment, that thou mayest be clothed, and *that* the shame of thy nakedness do not appear; and anoint thine eyes with eyesalve, that thou mayest see.

19 As many as I love, I rebuke and chasten: be zealous therefore, and repent.

20 Behold, I stand at the door, and knock: if any man hear my voice, and open the door, I will come in to him, and will sup with him, and he with me.

21 To him that overcometh will I grant to sit with me in my throne, even as I also overcame, and am set down with my Father in his throne.

22 He that hath an ear, let him hear what the Spirit saith unto the churches.

4 1 After this I looked, and, behold, a door *was* opened in heaven: and the first voice which I heard *was* as it were of a trumpet talking with me; which said, Come up hither, and I will shew thee things which must be hereafter.

2 And immediately I was in the spirit; and, behold, a throne was set in heaven, and *one* sat on the throne.

3 And he that sat was to look upon like a jasper and a sardine stone: and *there was* a rainbow round about the throne, in sight like unto an emerald.

4 And round about the throne *were* four and twenty seats: and upon the seats I saw four and twenty elders sitting, clothed in white raiment; and they had on their heads crowns of gold.

5 And out of the throne proceeded lightnings and thunderings and voices: and *there were* seven lamps of fire burning before the throne, which are the seven Spirits of God.

6 And before the throne *there was* a sea of glass like unto crystal: and in the midst of the throne, and round about the throne, *were* four beasts full of eyes before and behind.

7 And the first beast *was* like a lion, and the second beast like a calf, and the third beast had a face as a man, and the fourth beast *was* like a flying eagle.

8 And the four beasts had each of them six wings about *him;* and *they were* full of eyes within: and they rest not day and night, saying, Holy, holy, holy, Lord God Almighty, which was, and is, and is to come.

9 And when those beasts give glory and honour and thanks to him that sat on the throne, who liveth for ever and ever,

10 The four and twenty elders fall down before him that sat on the throne, and worship him that liveth for ever and ever, and cast their crowns before the throne, saying,

11 Thou art worthy, O Lord, to receive glory and

NEW LIVING TRANSLATION

naked. 18 So I advise you to buy gold from me—gold that has been purified by fire. Then you will be rich. Also buy white garments from me so you will not be shamed by your nakedness, and ointment for your eyes so you will be able to see. 19 I correct and discipline everyone I love. So be diligent and turn from your indifference.

20 "Look! I stand at the door and knock. If you hear my voice and open the door, I will come in, and we will share a meal together as friends. 21 Those who are victorious will sit with me on my throne, just as I was victorious and sat with my Father on his throne.

22 "Anyone with ears to hear must listen to the Spirit and understand what he is saying to the churches."

Worship in Heaven

4 Then as I looked, I saw a door standing open in heaven, and the same voice I had heard before spoke to me like a trumpet blast. The voice said, "Come up here, and I will show you what must happen after this." 2 And instantly I was in the Spirit,* and I saw a throne in heaven and someone sitting on it. 3 The one sitting on the throne was as brilliant as gemstones—like jasper and carnelian. And the glow of an emerald circled his throne like a rainbow. 4 Twenty-four thrones surrounded him, and twenty-four elders sat on them. They were all clothed in white and had gold crowns on their heads. 5 From the throne came flashes of lightning and the rumble of thunder. And in front of the throne were seven torches with burning flames. This is the sevenfold Spirit* of God. 6 In front of the throne was a shiny sea of glass, sparkling like crystal.

In the center and around the throne were four living beings, each covered with eyes, front and back. 7 The first of these living beings was like a lion; the second was like an ox; the third had a human face; and the fourth was like an eagle in flight. 8 Each of these living beings had six wings, and their wings were covered all over with eyes, inside and out. Day after day and night after night they keep on saying,

"Holy, holy, holy is the Lord God, the Almighty—
the one who always was, who is, and who is
still to come."

9 Whenever the living beings give glory and honor and thanks to the one sitting on the throne (the one who lives forever and ever), 10 the twenty-four elders fall down and worship the one sitting on the throne (the one who lives forever and ever). And they lay their crowns before the throne and say,

11 "You are worthy, O Lord our God,
to receive glory and honor and power.
For you created all things,

4:2 Or *in spirit.* 4:5 Greek *They are the seven spirits.*

KING JAMES VERSION

honour and power: for thou hast created all things, and for thy pleasure they are and were created.

5

1 And I saw in the right hand of him that sat on the throne a book written within and on the backside, sealed with seven seals.

2 And I saw a strong angel proclaiming with a loud voice, Who is worthy to open the book, and to loose the seals thereof?

3 And no man in heaven, nor in earth, neither under the earth, was able to open the book, neither to look thereon.

4 And I wept much, because no man was found worthy to open and to read the book, neither to look thereon.

5 And one of the elders saith unto me, Weep not: behold, the Lion of the tribe of Judah, the Root of David, hath prevailed to open the book, and to loose the seven seals thereof.

6 And I beheld, and, lo, in the midst of the throne and of the four beasts, and in the midst of the elders, stood a Lamb as it had been slain, having seven horns and seven eyes, which are the seven Spirits of God sent forth into all the earth.

7 And he came and took the book out of the right hand of him that sat upon the throne.

8 And when he had taken the book, the four beasts and four *and* twenty elders fell down before the Lamb, having every one of them harps, and golden vials full of odours, which are the prayers of saints.

9 And they sung a new song, saying, Thou art worthy to take the book, and to open the seals thereof: for thou wast slain, and hast redeemed us to God by thy blood out of every kindred, and tongue, and people, and nation;

10 And hast made us unto our God kings and priests: and we shall reign on the earth.

11 And I beheld, and I heard the voice of many angels round about the throne and the beasts and the elders: and the number of them was ten thousand times ten thousand, and thousands of thousands;

12 Saying with a loud voice, Worthy is the Lamb that was slain to receive power, and riches, and wisdom, and strength, and honour, and glory, and blessing.

13 And every creature which is in heaven, and on the earth, and under the earth, and such as are in the sea, and all that are in them, heard I saying, Blessing, and honour, and glory, and power, *be* unto him that sitteth upon the throne, and unto the Lamb for ever and ever.

NEW LIVING TRANSLATION

and they exist because you created what
you pleased."

The Lamb Opens the Scroll

5 Then I saw a scroll* in the right hand of the one
who was sitting on the throne. There was writing on the inside and the outside of the scroll, and it was sealed with seven seals.
2 And I saw a strong angel, who shouted with a loud voice: "Who is worthy to break the seals on this scroll and open it?"
3 But no one in heaven or on earth or under the earth was able to open the scroll and read it.

4 Then I began to weep bitterly because no one was found worthy to open the scroll and read it.
5 But one of the twenty-four elders said to me, "Stop weeping! Look, the Lion of the tribe of Judah, the heir to David's throne,* has won the victory. He is worthy to open the scroll and its seven seals."

6 Then I saw a Lamb that looked as if it had been slaughtered, but it was now standing between the throne and the four living beings and among the twenty-four elders. He had seven horns and seven eyes, which represent the sevenfold Spirit* of God that is sent out into every part of the earth.
7 He stepped forward and took the scroll from the right hand of the one sitting on the throne.
8 And when he took the scroll, the four living beings and the twenty-four elders fell down before the Lamb. Each one had a harp, and they held gold bowls filled with incense, which are the prayers of God's people.
9 And they sang a new song with these words:

"You are worthy to take the scroll
and break its seals and open it.
For you were slaughtered, and your blood has
ransomed people for God
from every tribe and language and people
and nation.
10 And you have caused them to become
a Kingdom of priests for our God.
And they will reign* on the earth."

11 Then I looked again, and I heard the voices of thousands and millions of angels around the throne and of the living beings and the elders.
12 And they sang in a mighty chorus:

"Worthy is the Lamb who was slaughtered—
to receive power and riches
and wisdom and strength
and honor and glory and blessing."

13 And then I heard every creature in heaven and on earth and under the earth and in the sea. They sang:

"Blessing and honor and glory and power
belong to the one sitting on the throne
and to the Lamb forever and ever."

5:1 Or *book;* also in 5:2, 3, 4, 5, 7, 8, 9. 5:5 Greek *the root of David.* See Isa 11:10. 5:6 Greek *which are the seven spirits.* 5:10 Some manuscripts read *they are reigning.*

KING JAMES VERSION

[14]And the four beasts said, Amen. And the four *and* twenty elders fell down and worshipped him that liveth for ever and ever.

6 [1]And I saw when the Lamb opened one of the seals, and I heard, as it were the noise of thunder, one of the four beasts saying, Come and see.

[2]And I saw, and behold a white horse: and he that sat on him had a bow; and a crown was given unto him: and he went forth conquering, and to conquer.

[3]And when he had opened the second seal, I heard the second beast say, Come and see.

[4]And there went out another horse *that was* red: and *power* was given to him that sat thereon to take peace from the earth, and that they should kill one another: and there was given unto him a great sword.

[5]And when he had opened the third seal, I heard the third beast say, Come and see. And I beheld, and lo a black horse; and he that sat on him had a pair of balances in his hand.

[6]And I heard a voice in the midst of the four beasts say, A measure of wheat for a penny, and three measures of barley for a penny; and *see* thou hurt not the oil and the wine.

[7]And when he had opened the fourth seal, I heard the voice of the fourth beast say, Come and see.

[8]And I looked, and behold a pale horse: and his name that sat on him was Death, and Hell followed with him. And power was given unto them over the fourth part of the earth, to kill with sword, and with hunger, and with death, and with the beasts of the earth.

[9]And when he had opened the fifth seal, I saw under the altar the souls of them that were slain for the word of God, and for the testimony which they held:

[10]And they cried with a loud voice, saying, How long, O Lord, holy and true, dost thou not judge and avenge our blood on them that dwell on the earth?

[11]And white robes were given unto every one of them; and it was said unto them, that they should rest yet for a little season, until their fellowservants also and their brethren, that should be killed as they *were*, should be fulfilled.

[12]And I beheld when he had opened the sixth seal, and, lo, there was a great earthquake; and the sun became black as sackcloth of hair, and the moon became as blood;

[13]And the stars of heaven fell unto the earth, even as a fig tree casteth her untimely figs, when she is shaken of a mighty wind.

[14]And the heaven departed as a scroll when it is rolled together; and every mountain and island were moved out of their places.

[15]And the kings of the earth, and the great men, and the rich men, and the chief captains, and the mighty men, and every bondman, and every free

NEW LIVING TRANSLATION

[14]And the four living beings said, "Amen!" And the twenty-four elders fell down and worshiped the Lamb.

The Lamb Breaks the First Six Seals

6 As I watched, the Lamb broke the first of the seven seals on the scroll.* Then I heard one of the four living beings say with a voice like thunder, "Come!" [2]I looked up and saw a white horse standing there. Its rider carried a bow, and a crown was placed on his head. He rode out to win many battles and gain the victory.

[3]When the Lamb broke the second seal, I heard the second living being say, "Come!" [4]Then another horse appeared, a red one. Its rider was given a mighty sword and the authority to take peace from the earth. And there was war and slaughter everywhere.

[5]When the Lamb broke the third seal, I heard the third living being say, "Come!" I looked up and saw a black horse, and its rider was holding a pair of scales in his hand. [6]And I heard a voice from among the four living beings say, "A loaf of wheat bread or three loaves of barley will cost a day's pay.* And don't waste* the olive oil and wine."

[7]When the Lamb broke the fourth seal, I heard the fourth living being say, "Come!" [8]I looked up and saw a horse whose color was pale green. Its rider was named Death, and his companion was the Grave.* These two were given authority over one-fourth of the earth, to kill with the sword and famine and disease* and wild animals.

[9]When the Lamb broke the fifth seal, I saw under the altar the souls of all who had been martyred for the word of God and for being faithful in their testimony. [10]They shouted to the Lord and said, "O Sovereign Lord, holy and true, how long before you judge the people who belong to this world and avenge our blood for what they have done to us?" [11]Then a white robe was given to each of them. And they were told to rest a little longer until the full number of their brothers and sisters*—their fellow servants of Jesus who were to be martyred—had joined them.

[12]I watched as the Lamb broke the sixth seal, and there was a great earthquake. The sun became as dark as black cloth, and the moon became as red as blood. [13]Then the stars of the sky fell to the earth like green figs falling from a tree shaken by a strong wind. [14]The sky was rolled up like a scroll, and all of the mountains and islands were moved from their places.

[15]Then everyone—the kings of the earth, the rulers, the generals, the wealthy, the powerful, and

6:1 Or *book.* **6:6a** Greek *A choinix* [1 quart or 1 liter] *of wheat for a denarius, and 3 choinix of barley for a denarius.* A denarius was equivalent to a laborer's full day's wage. **6:6b** Or *harm.* **6:8a** Greek *was Hades.* **6:8b** Greek *death.* **6:11** Greek *their brothers.*

KING JAMES VERSION

man, hid themselves in the dens and in the rocks of
the mountains;
16 And said to the mountains and rocks, Fall on us,
and hide us from the face of him that sitteth on the
throne, and from the wrath of the Lamb:
17 For the great day of his wrath is come; and who
shall be able to stand?

7 1 And after these things I saw four angels standing on the four corners of the earth, holding the
four winds of the earth, that the wind should not
blow on the earth, nor on the sea, nor on any tree.
2 And I saw another angel ascending from the east,
having the seal of the living God: and he cried with a
loud voice to the four angels, to whom it was given to
hurt the earth and the sea,
3 Saying, Hurt not the earth, neither the sea, nor
the trees, till we have sealed the servants of our God
in their foreheads.
4 And I heard the number of them which were
sealed: *and there were* sealed an hundred *and* forty
and four thousand of all the tribes of the children of
Israel.
5 Of the tribe of Judah *were* sealed twelve thousand.
Of the tribe of Reuben *were* sealed twelve thousand.
Of the tribe of Gad *were* sealed twelve thousand.
6 Of the tribe of Aser *were* sealed twelve thousand.
Of the tribe of Nephthalim *were* sealed twelve thousand. Of the tribe of Manasses *were* sealed twelve
thousand.
7 Of the tribe of Simeon *were* sealed twelve thousand. Of the tribe of Levi *were* sealed twelve thousand. Of the tribe of Issachar *were* sealed twelve
thousand.
8 Of the tribe of Zabulon *were* sealed twelve thousand. Of the tribe of Joseph *were* sealed twelve thousand. Of the tribe of Benjamin *were* sealed twelve
thousand.
9 After this I beheld, and, lo, a great multitude,
which no man could number, of all nations, and kindreds, and people, and tongues, stood before the
throne, and before the Lamb, clothed with white
robes, and palms in their hands;
10 And cried with a loud voice, saying, Salvation to
our God which sitteth upon the throne, and unto
the Lamb.
11 And all the angels stood round about the throne,
and *about* the elders and the four beasts, and fell before the throne on their faces, and worshipped God,
12 Saying, Amen: Blessing, and glory, and wisdom,
and thanksgiving, and honour, and power, and might,
be unto our God for ever and ever. Amen.

NEW LIVING TRANSLATION

every slave and free person—all hid themselves in
the caves and among the rocks of the mountains.
16 And they cried to the mountains and the rocks,
"Fall on us and hide us from the face of the one who
sits on the throne and from the wrath of the Lamb.
17 For the great day of their wrath has come, and who
is able to survive?"

God's People Will Be Preserved

7 Then I saw four angels standing at the four corners of the earth, holding back the four winds
so they did not blow on the earth or the sea, or even
on any tree. 2 And I saw another angel coming up
from the east, carrying the seal of the living God. And
he shouted to those four angels, who had been given
power to harm land and sea, 3 "Wait! Don't harm the
land or the sea or the trees until we have placed the
seal of God on the foreheads of his servants."
4 And I heard how many were marked with the seal
of God—144,000 were sealed from all the tribes of
Israel:

5 from Judah 12,000
from Reuben 12,000
from Gad 12,000
6 from Asher 12,000
from Naphtali 12,000
from Manasseh. 12,000
7 from Simeon 12,000
from Levi 12,000
from Issachar. 12,000
8 from Zebulun. 12,000
from Joseph. 12,000
from Benjamin 12,000

Praise from the Great Crowd

9 After this I saw a vast crowd, too great to count, from
every nation and tribe and people and language,
standing in front of the throne and before the Lamb.
They were clothed in white robes and held palm
branches in their hands. 10 And they were shouting
with a great roar,

"Salvation comes from our God who sits
on the throne
and from the Lamb!"

11 And all the angels were standing around the
throne and around the elders and the four living beings. And they fell before the throne with their faces
to the ground and worshiped God. 12 They sang,

"Amen! Blessing and glory and wisdom
and thanksgiving and honor
and power and strength belong to our God
forever and ever! Amen."

KING JAMES VERSION

13 And one of the elders answered, saying unto me,
What are these which are arrayed in white robes?
and whence came they?
14 And I said unto him, Sir, thou knowest. And he
said to me, These are they which came out of great
tribulation, and have washed their robes, and made
them white in the blood of the Lamb.
15 Therefore are they before the throne of God, and
serve him day and night in his temple: and he that
sitteth on the throne shall dwell among them.
16 They shall hunger no more, neither thirst any
more; neither shall the sun light on them, nor any
heat.
17 For the Lamb which is in the midst of the throne
shall feed them, and shall lead them unto living
fountains of waters: and God shall wipe away all tears
from their eyes.

8 1 And when he had opened the seventh seal,
there was silence in heaven about the space of
half an hour.
2 And I saw the seven angels which stood before
God; and to them were given seven trumpets.
3 And another angel came and stood at the altar,
having a golden censer; and there was given unto
him much incense, that he should offer *it* with the
prayers of all saints upon the golden altar which was
before the throne.
4 And the smoke of the incense, *which came* with
the prayers of the saints, ascended up before God out
of the angel's hand.
5 And the angel took the censer, and filled it with
fire of the altar, and cast *it* into the earth: and there
were voices, and thunderings, and lightnings, and
an earthquake.

6 And the seven angels which had the seven trumpets prepared themselves to sound.
7 The first angel sounded, and there followed hail
and fire mingled with blood, and they were cast
upon the earth: and the third part of trees was burnt
up, and all green grass was burnt up.
8 And the second angel sounded, and as it were a
great mountain burning with fire was cast into the
sea: and the third part of the sea became blood;
9 And the third part of the creatures which were in
the sea, and had life, died; and the third part of the
ships were destroyed.
10 And the third angel sounded, and there fell a
great star from heaven, burning as it were a lamp, and
it fell upon the third part of the rivers, and upon the
fountains of waters;

NEW LIVING TRANSLATION

13 Then one of the twenty-four elders asked me,
"Who are these who are clothed in white? Where did
they come from?"
14 And I said to him, "Sir, you are the one who
knows."
Then he said to me, "These are the ones who died
in* the great tribulation.* They have washed their
robes in the blood of the Lamb and made them
white.

15 "That is why they stand in front of God's throne
and serve him day and night in his Temple.
And he who sits on the throne
will give them shelter.
16 They will never again be hungry or thirsty;
they will never be scorched by the heat |
of the sun.
17 For the Lamb on the throne*
will be their Shepherd.
He will lead them to springs of life-giving water.
And God will wipe every tear from their eyes."

The Lamb Breaks the Seventh Seal

8 When the Lamb broke the seventh seal on the
scroll,* there was silence throughout heaven
for about half an hour. 2 I saw the seven angels
who stand before God, and they were given seven
trumpets.
3 Then another angel with a gold incense burner
came and stood at the altar. And a great amount of
incense was given to him to mix with the prayers of
God's people as an offering on the gold altar before
the throne. 4 The smoke of the incense, mixed with
the prayers of God's holy people, ascended up to God
from the altar where the angel had poured them out.
5 Then the angel filled the incense burner with fire
from the altar and threw it down upon the earth; and
thunder crashed, lightning flashed, and there was a
terrible earthquake.

The First Four Trumpets

6 Then the seven angels with the seven trumpets prepared to blow their mighty blasts.
7 The first angel blew his trumpet, and hail and fire
mixed with blood were thrown down on the earth.
One-third of the earth was set on fire, one-third of
the trees were burned, and all the green grass was
burned.
8 Then the second angel blew his trumpet, and a
great mountain of fire was thrown into the sea. One-
third of the water in the sea became blood, 9 one-
third of all things living in the sea died, and one-third
of all the ships on the sea were destroyed.
10 Then the third angel blew his trumpet, and a
great star fell from the sky, burning like a torch. It
fell on one-third of the rivers and on the springs of

7:14a Greek *who came out of.* **7:14b** Or *the great suffering.* **7:17** Greek *on the center of the throne.* **8:1** Or *book.*

KING JAMES VERSION

11And the name of the star is called Wormwood:
and the third part of the waters became wormwood;
and many men died of the waters, because they were
made bitter.

12And the fourth angel sounded, and the third part
of the sun was smitten, and the third part of the
moon, and the third part of the stars; so as the third
part of them was darkened, and the day shone not for
a third part of it, and the night likewise.

13And I beheld, and heard an angel flying through
the midst of heaven, saying with a loud voice, Woe,
woe, woe, to the inhabiters of the earth by reason of
the other voices of the trumpet of the three angels,
which are yet to sound!

9 1And the fifth angel sounded, and I saw a star
fall from heaven unto the earth: and to him was
given the key of the bottomless pit.

2And he opened the bottomless pit; and there
arose a smoke out of the pit, as the smoke of a great
furnace; and the sun and the air were darkened by
reason of the smoke of the pit.

3And there came out of the smoke locusts upon
the earth: and unto them was given power, as the
scorpions of the earth have power.

4And it was commanded them that they should
not hurt the grass of the earth, neither any green
thing, neither any tree; but only those men which
have not the seal of God in their foreheads.

5And to them it was given that they should not kill
them, but that they should be tormented five
months: and their torment *was* as the torment of a
scorpion, when he striketh a man.

6And in those days shall men seek death, and shall
not find it; and shall desire to die, and death shall flee
from them.

7And the shapes of the locusts *were* like unto
horses prepared unto battle; and on their heads *were*
as it were crowns like gold, and their faces *were* as
the faces of men.

8And they had hair as the hair of women, and their
teeth were as *the teeth* of lions.

9And they had breastplates, as it were breastplates
of iron; and the sound of their wings *was* as the
sound of chariots of many horses running to battle.

10And they had tails like unto scorpions, and there
were stings in their tails: and their power *was* to hurt
men five months.

11And they had a king over them, *which is* the angel of the bottomless pit, whose name in the Hebrew
tongue *is* Abaddon, but in the Greek tongue hath *his*
name Apollyon.

12One woe is past; *and,* behold, there come two
woes more hereafter.

13And the sixth angel sounded, and I heard a voice
from the four horns of the golden altar which is
before God,

NEW LIVING TRANSLATION

water. 11The name of the star was Bitterness.* It
made one-third of the water bitter, and many people
died from drinking the bitter water.

12Then the fourth angel blew his trumpet, and
one-third of the sun was struck, and one-third of the
moon, and one-third of the stars, and they became
dark. And one-third of the day was dark, and also
one-third of the night.

13Then I looked, and I heard a single eagle crying
loudly as it flew through the air, "Terror, terror, terror to all who belong to this world because of what
will happen when the last three angels blow their
trumpets."

The Fifth Trumpet Brings the First Terror

9 Then the fifth angel blew his trumpet, and I
saw a star that had fallen to earth from the sky,
and he was given the key to the shaft of the bottomless pit.* 2When he opened it, smoke poured out as
though from a huge furnace, and the sunlight and air
turned dark from the smoke.

3Then locusts came from the smoke and descended on the earth, and they were given power to
sting like scorpions. 4They were told not to harm the
grass or plants or trees, but only the people who did
not have the seal of God on their foreheads. 5They
were told not to kill them but to torture them for five
months with pain like the pain of a scorpion sting.
6In those days people will seek death but will not
find it. They will long to die, but death will flee from
them!

7The locusts looked like horses prepared for
battle. They had what looked like gold crowns on
their heads, and their faces looked like human faces.
8They had hair like women's hair and teeth like the
teeth of a lion. 9They wore armor made of iron, and
their wings roared like an army of chariots rushing
into battle. 10They had tails that stung like scorpions,
and for five months they had the power to torment
people. 11Their king is the angel from the bottomless
pit; his name in Hebrew is *Abaddon,* and in Greek,
Apollyon—the Destroyer.

12The first terror is past, but look, two more
terrors are coming!

The Sixth Trumpet Brings the Second Terror

13Then the sixth angel blew his trumpet, and I heard
a voice speaking from the four horns of the gold altar

8:11 Greek *Wormwood.* **9:1** Or *the abyss,* or *the underworld;* also in 9:11.

KING JAMES VERSION

[14]Saying to the sixth angel which had the trumpet, Loose the four angels which are bound in the great river Euphrates.

[15]And the four angels were loosed, which were prepared for an hour, and a day, and a month, and a year, for to slay the third part of men.

[16]And the number of the army of the horsemen *were* two hundred thousand thousand: and I heard the number of them.

[17]And thus I saw the horses in the vision, and them that sat on them, having breastplates of fire, and of jacinth, and brimstone: and the heads of the horses *were* as the heads of lions; and out of their mouths issued fire and smoke and brimstone.

[18]By these three was the third part of men killed, by the fire, and by the smoke, and by the brimstone, which issued out of their mouths.

[19]For their power is in their mouth, and in their tails: for their tails *were* like unto serpents, and had heads, and with them they do hurt.

[20]And the rest of the men which were not killed by these plagues yet repented not of the works of their hands, that they should not worship devils, and idols of gold, and silver, and brass, and stone, and of wood: which neither can see, nor hear, nor walk:

[21]Neither repented they of their murders, nor of their sorceries, nor of their fornication, nor of their thefts.

10 [1]And I saw another mighty angel come down from heaven, clothed with a cloud: and a rainbow *was* upon his head, and his face *was* as it were the sun, and his feet as pillars of fire:

[2]And he had in his hand a little book open: and he set his right foot upon the sea, and *his* left *foot* on the earth,

[3]And cried with a loud voice, as *when* a lion roareth: and when he had cried, seven thunders uttered their voices.

[4]And when the seven thunders had uttered their voices, I was about to write: and I heard a voice from heaven saying unto me, Seal up those things which the seven thunders uttered, and write them not.

[5]And the angel which I saw stand upon the sea and upon the earth lifted up his hand to heaven,

[6]And sware by him that liveth for ever and ever, who created heaven, and the things that therein are, and the earth, and the things that therein are, and the sea, and the things which are therein, that there should be time no longer:

[7]But in the days of the voice of the seventh angel, when he shall begin to sound, the mystery of God should be finished, as he hath declared to his servants the prophets.

[8]And the voice which I heard from heaven spake unto me again, and said, Go *and* take the little book which is open in the hand of the angel which standeth upon the sea and upon the earth.

NEW LIVING TRANSLATION

that stands in the presence of God. [14]And the voice said to the sixth angel who held the trumpet, "Release the four angels who are bound at the great Euphrates River." [15]Then the four angels who had been prepared for this hour and day and month and year were turned loose to kill one-third of all the people on earth. [16]I heard the size of their army, which was 200 million mounted troops.

[17]And in my vision, I saw the horses and the riders sitting on them. The riders wore armor that was fiery red and dark blue and yellow. The horses had heads like lions, and fire and smoke and burning sulfur billowed from their mouths. [18]One-third of all the people on earth were killed by these three plagues—by the fire and smoke and burning sulfur that came from the mouths of the horses. [19]Their power was in their mouths and in their tails. For their tails had heads like snakes, with the power to injure people.

[20]But the people who did not die in these plagues still refused to repent of their evil deeds and turn to God. They continued to worship demons and idols made of gold, silver, bronze, stone, and wood—idols that can neither see nor hear nor walk! [21]And they did not repent of their murders or their witchcraft or their sexual immorality or their thefts.

The Angel and the Small Scroll

10 Then I saw another mighty angel coming down from heaven, surrounded by a cloud, with a rainbow over his head. His face shone like the sun, and his feet were like pillars of fire. [2]And in his hand was a small scroll* that had been opened. He stood with his right foot on the sea and his left foot on the land. [3]And he gave a great shout like the roar of a lion. And when he shouted, the seven thunders answered.

[4]When the seven thunders spoke, I was about to write. But I heard a voice from heaven saying, "Keep secret* what the seven thunders said, and do not write it down."

[5]Then the angel I saw standing on the sea and on the land raised his right hand toward heaven. [6]He swore an oath in the name of the one who lives forever and ever, who created the heavens and everything in them, the earth and everything in it, and the sea and everything in it. He said, "There will be no more delay. [7]When the seventh angel blows his trumpet, God's mysterious plan will be fulfilled. It will happen just as he announced it to his servants the prophets."

[8]Then the voice from heaven spoke to me again: "Go and take the open scroll from the hand of the angel who is standing on the sea and on the land."

10:2 Or *book;* also in 10:8, 9, 10. **10:4** Greek *Seal up.*

KING JAMES VERSION

9 And I went unto the angel, and said unto him, Give me the little book. And he said unto me, Take *it,* and eat it up; and it shall make thy belly bitter, but it shall be in thy mouth sweet as honey.

10 And I took the little book out of the angel's hand, and ate it up; and it was in my mouth sweet as honey: and as soon as I had eaten it, my belly was bitter.

11 And he said unto me, Thou must prophesy again before many peoples, and nations, and tongues, and kings.

11 1 And there was given me a reed like unto a rod: and the angel stood, saying, Rise, and measure the temple of God, and the altar, and them that worship therein.

2 But the court which is without the temple leave out, and measure it not; for it is given unto the Gentiles: and the holy city shall they tread under foot forty *and* two months.

3 And I will give *power* unto my two witnesses, and they shall prophesy a thousand two hundred *and* threescore days, clothed in sackcloth.

4 These are the two olive trees, and the two candlesticks standing before the God of the earth.

5 And if any man will hurt them, fire proceedeth out of their mouth, and devoureth their enemies: and if any man will hurt them, he must in this manner be killed.

6 These have power to shut heaven, that it rain not in the days of their prophecy: and have power over waters to turn them to blood, and to smite the earth with all plagues, as often as they will.

7 And when they shall have finished their testimony, the beast that ascendeth out of the bottomless pit shall make war against them, and shall overcome them, and kill them.

8 And their dead bodies *shall lie* in the street of the great city, which spiritually is called Sodom and Egypt, where also our Lord was crucified.

9 And they of the people and kindreds and tongues and nations shall see their dead bodies three days and an half, and shall not suffer their dead bodies to be put in graves.

10 And they that dwell upon the earth shall rejoice over them, and make merry, and shall send gifts one to another; because these two prophets tormented them that dwelt on the earth.

11 And after three days and an half the Spirit of life from God entered into them, and they stood upon their feet; and great fear fell upon them which saw them.

12 And they heard a great voice from heaven saying unto them, Come up hither. And they ascended up to heaven in a cloud; and their enemies beheld them.

13 And the same hour was there a great earthquake, and the tenth part of the city fell, and in the earthquake were slain of men seven thousand: and the remnant were affrighted, and gave glory to the God of heaven.

NEW LIVING TRANSLATION

9 So I went to the angel and told him to give me the small scroll. "Yes, take it and eat it," he said. "It will be sweet as honey in your mouth, but it will turn sour in your stomach!" 10 So I took the small scroll from the hand of the angel, and I ate it! It was sweet in my mouth, but when I swallowed it, it turned sour in my stomach.

11 Then I was told, "You must prophesy again about many peoples, nations, languages, and kings."

The Two Witnesses

11 Then I was given a measuring stick, and I was told, "Go and measure the Temple of God and the altar, and count the number of worshipers. 2 But do not measure the outer courtyard, for it has been turned over to the nations. They will trample the holy city for 42 months. 3 And I will give power to my two witnesses, and they will be clothed in burlap and will prophesy during those 1,260 days."

4 These two prophets are the two olive trees and the two lampstands that stand before the Lord of all the earth. 5 If anyone tries to harm them, fire flashes from their mouths and consumes their enemies. This is how anyone who tries to harm them must die. 6 They have power to shut the sky so that no rain will fall for as long as they prophesy. And they have the power to turn the rivers and oceans into blood, and to strike the earth with every kind of plague as often as they wish.

7 When they complete their testimony, the beast that comes up out of the bottomless pit* will declare war against them, and he will conquer them and kill them. 8 And their bodies will lie in the main street of Jerusalem,* the city that is figuratively called "Sodom" and "Egypt," the city where their Lord was crucified. 9 And for three and a half days, all peoples, tribes, languages, and nations will stare at their bodies. No one will be allowed to bury them. 10 All the people who belong to this world will gloat over them and give presents to each other to celebrate the death of the two prophets who had tormented them.

11 But after three and a half days, God breathed life into them, and they stood up! Terror struck all who were staring at them. 12 Then a loud voice from heaven called to the two prophets, "Come up here!" And they rose to heaven in a cloud as their enemies watched.

13 At the same time there was a terrible earthquake that destroyed a tenth of the city. Seven thousand people died in that earthquake, and everyone else was terrified and gave glory to the God of heaven.

11:7 Or *the abyss, or the underworld.* **11:8** Greek *the great city.*

KING JAMES VERSION

14 The second woe is past; *and,* behold, the third woe cometh quickly.

15 And the seventh angel sounded; and there were great voices in heaven, saying, The kingdoms of this world are become *the kingdoms* of our Lord, and of his Christ; and he shall reign for ever and ever.

16 And the four and twenty elders, which sat before God on their seats, fell upon their faces, and worshipped God,

17 Saying, We give thee thanks, O Lord God Almighty, which art, and wast, and art to come; because thou hast taken to thee thy great power, and hast reigned.

18 And the nations were angry, and thy wrath is come, and the time of the dead, that they should be judged, and that thou shouldest give reward unto thy servants the prophets, and to the saints, and them that fear thy name, small and great; and shouldest destroy them which destroy the earth.

19 And the temple of God was opened in heaven, and there was seen in his temple the ark of his testament: and there were lightnings, and voices, and thunderings, and an earthquake, and great hail.

12

1 And there appeared a great wonder in heaven; a woman clothed with the sun, and the moon under her feet, and upon her head a crown of twelve stars:

2 And she being with child cried, travailing in birth, and pained to be delivered.

3 And there appeared another wonder in heaven; and behold a great red dragon, having seven heads and ten horns, and seven crowns upon his heads.

4 And his tail drew the third part of the stars of heaven, and did cast them to the earth: and the dragon stood before the woman which was ready to be delivered, for to devour her child as soon as it was born.

5 And she brought forth a man child, who was to rule all nations with a rod of iron: and her child was caught up unto God, and *to* his throne.

6 And the woman fled into the wilderness, where she hath a place prepared of God, that they should feed her there a thousand two hundred *and* threescore days.

7 And there was war in heaven: Michael and his angels fought against the dragon; and the dragon fought and his angels,

NEW LIVING TRANSLATION

14 The second terror is past, but look, the third terror is coming quickly.

The Seventh Trumpet Brings the Third Terror

15 Then the seventh angel blew his trumpet, and there were loud voices shouting in heaven:

"The world has now become the Kingdom of
our Lord and of his Christ,*
and he will reign forever and ever."

16 The twenty-four elders sitting on their thrones before God fell with their faces to the ground and worshiped him. 17 And they said,

"We give thanks to you, Lord God, the Almighty,
the one who is and who always was,
for now you have assumed your great power
and have begun to reign.
18 The nations were filled with wrath,
but now the time of your wrath has come.
It is time to judge the dead
and reward your servants the prophets,
as well as your holy people,
and all who fear your name,
from the least to the greatest.
It is time to destroy
all who have caused destruction on the earth."

19 Then, in heaven, the Temple of God was opened and the Ark of his covenant could be seen inside the Temple. Lightning flashed, thunder crashed and roared, and there was an earthquake and a terrible hailstorm.

The Woman and the Dragon

12

Then I witnessed in heaven an event of great significance. I saw a woman clothed with the sun, with the moon beneath her feet, and a crown of twelve stars on her head. 2 She was pregnant, and she cried out because of her labor pains and the agony of giving birth.

3 Then I witnessed in heaven another significant event. I saw a large red dragon with seven heads and ten horns, with seven crowns on his heads. 4 His tail swept away one-third of the stars in the sky, and he threw them to the earth. He stood in front of the woman as she was about to give birth, ready to devour her baby as soon as it was born.

5 She gave birth to a son who was to rule all nations with an iron rod. And her child was snatched away from the dragon and was caught up to God and to his throne. 6 And the woman fled into the wilderness, where God had prepared a place to care for her for 1,260 days.

7 Then there was war in heaven. Michael and his angels fought against the dragon and his angels.

11:15 Or *his Messiah.*

KING JAMES VERSION

8 And prevailed not; neither was their place found any more in heaven.

9 And the great dragon was cast out, that old serpent, called the Devil, and Satan, which deceiveth the whole world: he was cast out into the earth, and his angels were cast out with him.

10 And I heard a loud voice saying in heaven, Now is come salvation, and strength, and the kingdom of our God, and the power of his Christ: for the accuser of our brethren is cast down, which accused them before our God day and night.

11 And they overcame him by the blood of the Lamb, and by the word of their testimony; and they loved not their lives unto the death.

12 Therefore rejoice, *ye* heavens, and ye that dwell in them. Woe to the inhabiters of the earth and of the sea! for the devil is come down unto you, having great wrath, because he knoweth that he hath but a short time.

13 And when the dragon saw that he was cast unto the earth, he persecuted the woman which brought forth the man *child.*

14 And to the woman were given two wings of a great eagle, that she might fly into the wilderness, into her place, where she is nourished for a time, and times, and half a time, from the face of the serpent.

15 And the serpent cast out of his mouth water as a flood after the woman, that he might cause her to be carried away of the flood.

16 And the earth helped the woman, and the earth opened her mouth, and swallowed up the flood which the dragon cast out of his mouth.

17 And the dragon was wroth with the woman, and went to make war with the remnant of her seed, which keep the commandments of God, and have the testimony of Jesus Christ.

13 1 And I stood upon the sand of the sea, and saw a beast rise up out of the sea, having seven heads and ten horns, and upon his horns ten crowns, and upon his heads the name of blasphemy.

2 And the beast which I saw was like unto a leopard, and his feet were as *the feet* of a bear, and his mouth as the mouth of a lion: and the dragon gave him his power, and his seat, and great authority.

3 And I saw one of his heads as it were wounded to death; and his deadly wound was healed: and all the world wondered after the beast.

NEW LIVING TRANSLATION

8 And the dragon lost the battle, and he and his angels were forced out of heaven. 9 This great dragon—the ancient serpent called the devil, or Satan, the one deceiving the whole world—was thrown down to the earth with all his angels.

10 Then I heard a loud voice shouting across the heavens,

"It has come at last—
salvation and power
and the Kingdom of our God,
and the authority of his Christ.*
For the accuser of our brothers and sisters*
has been thrown down to earth—
the one who accuses them
before our God day and night.
11 And they have defeated him by the blood
of the Lamb
and by their testimony.
And they did not love their lives so much
that they were afraid to die.
12 Therefore, rejoice, O heavens!
And you who live in the heavens, rejoice!
But terror will come on the earth and the sea,
for the devil has come down to you in
great anger,
knowing that he has little time."

13 When the dragon realized that he had been thrown down to the earth, he pursued the woman who had given birth to the male child. 14 But she was given two wings like those of a great eagle so she could fly to the place prepared for her in the wilderness. There she would be cared for and protected from the dragon* for a time, times, and half a time.

15 Then the dragon tried to drown the woman with a flood of water that flowed from his mouth. 16 But the earth helped her by opening its mouth and swallowing the river that gushed out from the mouth of the dragon. 17 And the dragon was angry at the woman and declared war against the rest of her children—all who keep God's commandments and maintain their testimony for Jesus.

18 Then the dragon took his stand* on the shore beside the sea.

The Beast out of the Sea

13 Then I saw a beast rising up out of the sea. It had seven heads and ten horns, with ten crowns on its horns. And written on each head were names that blasphemed God. 2 This beast looked like a leopard, but it had the feet of a bear and the mouth of a lion! And the dragon gave the beast his own power and throne and great authority.

3 I saw that one of the heads of the beast seemed wounded beyond recovery—but the fatal wound was healed! The whole world marveled at this miracle and

12:10a Or *his Messiah.* **12:10b** Greek *brothers.* **12:14** Greek *the serpent;* also in 12:15. See 12:9. **12:18** Greek *Then he took his stand;* some manuscripts read *Then I took my stand.* Some translations put this entire sentence into 13:1.

KING JAMES VERSION

4 And they worshipped the dragon which gave
power unto the beast: and they worshipped the
beast, saying, Who *is* like unto the beast? who is able
to make war with him?
5 And there was given unto him a mouth speaking
great things and blasphemies; and power was given
unto him to continue forty *and* two months.
6 And he opened his mouth in blasphemy against
God, to blaspheme his name, and his tabernacle, and
them that dwell in heaven.
7 And it was given unto him to make war with the
saints, and to overcome them: and power was given
him over all kindreds, and tongues, and nations.
8 And all that dwell upon the earth shall worship
him, whose names are not written in the book of life
of the Lamb slain from the foundation of the world.
9 If any man have an ear, let him hear.
10 He that leadeth into captivity shall go into captivity: he that killeth with the sword must be killed
with the sword. Here is the patience and the faith of
the saints.

11 And I beheld another beast coming up out of the
earth; and he had two horns like a lamb, and he spake
as a dragon.
12 And he exerciseth all the power of the first beast
before him, and causeth the earth and them which
dwell therein to worship the first beast, whose
deadly wound was healed.
13 And he doeth great wonders, so that he maketh
fire come down from heaven on the earth in the
sight of men,
14 And deceiveth them that dwell on the earth by
the means of those miracles which he had power to
do in the sight of the beast; saying to them that dwell
on the earth, that they should make an image to the
beast, which had the wound by a sword, and did live.
15 And he had power to give life unto the image of
the beast, that the image of the beast should both
speak, and cause that as many as would not worship
the image of the beast should be killed.
16 And he causeth all, both small and great, rich
and poor, free and bond, to receive a mark in their
right hand, or in their foreheads:
17 And that no man might buy or sell, save he that
had the mark, or the name of the beast, or the number of his name.
18 Here is wisdom. Let him that hath understanding count the number of the beast: for it is the
number of a man; and his number *is* Six hundred
threescore *and* six.

NEW LIVING TRANSLATION

gave allegiance to the beast. 4 They worshiped the
dragon for giving the beast such power, and they also
worshiped the beast. "Who is as great as the beast?"
they exclaimed. "Who is able to fight against him?"
5 Then the beast was allowed to speak great blasphemies against God. And he was given authority to
do whatever he wanted for forty-two months. 6 And
he spoke terrible words of blasphemy against God,
slandering his name and his dwelling—that is, those
who dwell in heaven.* 7 And the beast was allowed
to wage war against God's holy people and to conquer them. And he was given authority to rule over
every tribe and people and language and nation.
8 And all the people who belong to this world worshiped the beast. They are the ones whose names
were not written in the Book of Life before the world
was made—the Book that belongs to the Lamb who
was slaughtered.*

9 Anyone with ears to hear
should listen and understand.
10 Anyone who is destined for prison
will be taken to prison.
Anyone destined to die by the sword
will die by the sword.

This means that God's holy people must endure persecution patiently and remain faithful.

The Beast out of the Earth

11 Then I saw another beast come up out of the earth.
He had two horns like those of a lamb, but he spoke
with the voice of a dragon. 12 He exercised all the authority of the first beast. And he required all the
earth and its people to worship the first beast, whose
fatal wound had been healed. 13 He did astounding
miracles, even making fire flash down to earth from
the sky while everyone was watching. 14 And with all
the miracles he was allowed to perform on behalf
of the first beast, he deceived all the people who belong to this world. He ordered the people to make a
great statue of the first beast, who was fatally
wounded and then came back to life. 15 He was then
permitted to give life to this statue so that it could
speak. Then the statue of the beast commanded that
anyone refusing to worship it must die.
16 He required everyone—small and great, rich and
poor, free and slave—to be given a mark on the right
hand or on the forehead. 17 And no one could buy or
sell anything without that mark, which was either
the name of the beast or the number representing
his name. 18 Wisdom is needed here. Let the one with
understanding solve the meaning of the number of
the beast, for it is the number of a man.* His number
is 666.*

13:6 Some manuscripts read *and his dwelling and all who dwell in heaven.* **13:8** Or *not written in the Book of Life that belongs to the Lamb who was slaughtered before the world was made.* **13:18a** Or *of humanity.* **13:18b** Some manuscripts read *616.*

KING JAMES VERSION

14 1And I looked, and, lo, a Lamb stood on the mount Sion, and with him an hundred forty *and* four thousand, having his Father's name written in their foreheads.

2And I heard a voice from heaven, as the voice of many waters, and as the voice of a great thunder: and I heard the voice of harpers harping with their harps:

3And they sung as it were a new song before the throne, and before the four beasts, and the elders: and no man could learn that song but the hundred *and* forty *and* four thousand, which were redeemed from the earth.

4These are they which were not defiled with women; for they are virgins. These are they which follow the Lamb whithersoever he goeth. These were redeemed from among men, *being* the firstfruits unto God and to the Lamb.

5And in their mouth was found no guile: for they are without fault before the throne of God.

6And I saw another angel fly in the midst of heaven, having the everlasting gospel to preach unto them that dwell on the earth, and to every nation, and kindred, and tongue, and people,

7Saying with a loud voice, Fear God, and give glory to him; for the hour of his judgment is come: and worship him that made heaven, and earth, and the sea, and the fountains of waters.

8And there followed another angel, saying, Babylon is fallen, is fallen, that great city, because she made all nations drink of the wine of the wrath of her fornication.

9And the third angel followed them, saying with a loud voice, If any man worship the beast and his image, and receive *his* mark in his forehead, or in his hand,

10The same shall drink of the wine of the wrath of God, which is poured out without mixture into the cup of his indignation; and he shall be tormented with fire and brimstone in the presence of the holy angels, and in the presence of the Lamb:

11And the smoke of their torment ascendeth up for ever and ever: and they have no rest day nor night, who worship the beast and his image, and whosoever receiveth the mark of his name.

12Here is the patience of the saints: here *are* they that keep the commandments of God, and the faith of Jesus.

13And I heard a voice from heaven saying unto me, Write, Blessed *are* the dead which die in the Lord from henceforth: Yea, saith the Spirit, that they may rest from their labours; and their works do follow them.

14And I looked, and behold a white cloud, and upon the cloud *one* sat like unto the Son of man, having on his head a golden crown, and in his hand a sharp sickle.

NEW LIVING TRANSLATION

The Lamb and the 144,000

14 Then I saw the Lamb standing on Mount Zion, and with him were 144,000 who had his name and his Father's name written on their foreheads. 2And I heard a sound from heaven like the roar of mighty ocean waves or the rolling of loud thunder. It was like the sound of many harpists playing together.

3This great choir sang a wonderful new song in front of the throne of God and before the four living beings and the twenty-four elders. No one could learn this song except the 144,000 who had been redeemed from the earth. 4They have kept themselves as pure as virgins,* following the Lamb wherever he goes. They have been purchased from among the people on the earth as a special offering* to God and to the Lamb. 5They have told no lies; they are without blame.

The Three Angels

6And I saw another angel flying through the sky, carrying the eternal Good News to proclaim to the people who belong to this world—to every nation, tribe, language, and people. 7"Fear God," he shouted. "Give glory to him. For the time has come when he will sit as judge. Worship him who made the heavens, the earth, the sea, and all the springs of water."

8Then another angel followed him through the sky, shouting, "Babylon is fallen—that great city is fallen—because she made all the nations of the world drink the wine of her passionate immorality."

9Then a third angel followed them, shouting, "Anyone who worships the beast and his statue or who accepts his mark on the forehead or on the hand 10must drink the wine of God's anger. It has been poured full strength into God's cup of wrath. And they will be tormented with fire and burning sulfur in the presence of the holy angels and the Lamb. 11The smoke of their torment will rise forever and ever, and they will have no relief day or night, for they have worshiped the beast and his statue and have accepted the mark of his name."

12This means that God's holy people must endure persecution patiently, obeying his commands and maintaining their faith in Jesus.

13And I heard a voice from heaven saying, "Write this down: Blessed are those who die in the Lord from now on. Yes, says the Spirit, they are blessed indeed, for they will rest from their hard work; for their good deeds follow them!"

The Harvest of the Earth

14Then I saw a white cloud, and seated on the cloud was someone like the Son of Man.* He had a gold crown on his head and a sharp sickle in his hand.

14:4a Greek *They are virgins who have not defiled themselves with women.* **14:4b** Greek *as firstfruits.* **14:14** Or *like a son of man.* See Dan 7:13. "Son of Man" is a title Jesus used for himself.

KING JAMES VERSION

15 And another angel came out of the temple, crying with a loud voice to him that sat on the cloud, Thrust in thy sickle, and reap: for the time is come for thee to reap; for the harvest of the earth is ripe.

16 And he that sat on the cloud thrust in his sickle on the earth; and the earth was reaped.

17 And another angel came out of the temple which is in heaven, he also having a sharp sickle.

18 And another angel came out from the altar, which had power over fire; and cried with a loud cry to him that had the sharp sickle, saying, Thrust in thy sharp sickle, and gather the clusters of the vine of the earth; for her grapes are fully ripe.

19 And the angel thrust in his sickle into the earth, and gathered the vine of the earth, and cast *it* into the great winepress of the wrath of God.

20 And the winepress was trodden without the city, and blood came out of the winepress, even unto the horse bridles, by the space of a thousand *and* six hundred furlongs.

15 1 And I saw another sign in heaven, great and marvellous, seven angels having the seven last plagues; for in them is filled up the wrath of God.

2 And I saw as it were a sea of glass mingled with fire: and them that had gotten the victory over the beast, and over his image, and over his mark, *and* over the number of his name, stand on the sea of glass, having the harps of God.

3 And they sing the song of Moses the servant of God, and the song of the Lamb, saying, Great and marvellous *are* thy works, Lord God Almighty; just and true *are* thy ways, thou King of saints.

4 Who shall not fear thee, O Lord, and glorify thy name? for *thou* only *art* holy: for all nations shall come and worship before thee; for thy judgments are made manifest.

5 And after that I looked, and, behold, the temple of the tabernacle of the testimony in heaven was opened:

6 And the seven angels came out of the temple, having the seven plagues, clothed in pure and white linen, and having their breasts girded with golden girdles.

7 And one of the four beasts gave unto the seven angels seven golden vials full of the wrath of God, who liveth for ever and ever.

8 And the temple was filled with smoke from the glory of God, and from his power; and no man was able to enter into the temple, till the seven plagues of the seven angels were fulfilled.

NEW LIVING TRANSLATION

15 Then another angel came from the Temple and
shouted to the one sitting on the cloud, "Swing the
sickle, for the time of harvest has come; the crop on
earth is ripe." 16 So the one sitting on the cloud
swung his sickle over the earth, and the whole earth
was harvested.

17 After that, another angel came from the Temple
in heaven, and he also had a sharp sickle. 18 Then another angel, who had power to destroy with fire,
came from the altar. He shouted to the angel with
the sharp sickle, "Swing your sickle now to gather
the clusters of grapes from the vines of the earth, for
they are ripe for judgment." 19 So the angel swung his
sickle over the earth and loaded the grapes into the
great winepress of God's wrath. 20 The grapes were
trampled in the winepress outside the city, and blood
flowed from the winepress in a stream about
180 miles* long and as high as a horse's bridle.

The Song of Moses and of the Lamb

15 Then I saw in heaven another marvelous
event of great significance. Seven angels
were holding the seven last plagues, which would
bring God's wrath to completion. 2 I saw before me
what seemed to be a glass sea mixed with fire. And
on it stood all the people who had been victorious
over the beast and his statue and the number representing his name. They were all holding harps that
God had given them. 3 And they were singing the
song of Moses, the servant of God, and the song of
the Lamb:

"Great and marvelous are your works,
O Lord God, the Almighty.
Just and true are your ways,
O King of the nations.*
4 Who will not fear you, Lord,
and glorify your name?
For you alone are holy.
All nations will come and worship before you,
for your righteous deeds have been revealed."

The Seven Bowls of the Seven Plagues

5 Then I looked and saw that the Temple in heaven,
God's Tabernacle, was thrown wide open. 6 The
seven angels who were holding the seven plagues
came out of the Temple. They were clothed in spotless white linen* with gold sashes across their
chests. 7 Then one of the four living beings handed
each of the seven angels a gold bowl filled with
the wrath of God, who lives forever and ever. 8 The
Temple was filled with smoke from God's glory and
power. No one could enter the Temple until the
seven angels had completed pouring out the seven
plagues.

14:20 Greek *1,600 stadia* [296 kilometers]. **15:3** Some manuscripts read *King of the ages.* **15:6** Other manuscripts read *white stone;* still others read *white [garments] made of linen.*

KING JAMES VERSION

16 1 And I heard a great voice out of the temple
saying to the seven angels, Go your ways, and
pour out the vials of the wrath of God upon the earth.
2 And the first went, and poured out his vial upon
the earth; and there fell a noisome and grievous sore
upon the men which had the mark of the beast, and
upon them which worshipped his image.
3 And the second angel poured out his vial upon
the sea; and it became as the blood of a dead *man;*
and every living soul died in the sea.
4 And the third angel poured out his vial upon the
rivers and fountains of waters; and they became
blood.
5 And I heard the angel of the waters say, Thou art
righteous, O Lord, which art, and wast, and shalt be,
because thou hast judged thus.
6 For they have shed the blood of saints and prophets, and thou hast given them blood to drink; for they
are worthy.
7 And I heard another out of the altar say, Even
so, Lord God Almighty, true and righteous *are* thy
judgments.
8 And the fourth angel poured out his vial upon the
sun; and power was given unto him to scorch men
with fire.
9 And men were scorched with great heat, and
blasphemed the name of God, which hath power
over these plagues: and they repented not to give
him glory.
10 And the fifth angel poured out his vial upon the
seat of the beast; and his kingdom was full of darkness; and they gnawed their tongues for pain,
11 And blasphemed the God of heaven because of
their pains and their sores, and repented not of their
deeds.
12 And the sixth angel poured out his vial upon the
great river Euphrates; and the water thereof was
dried up, that the way of the kings of the east might
be prepared.
13 And I saw three unclean spirits like frogs *come*
out of the mouth of the dragon, and out of the mouth
of the beast, and out of the mouth of the false
prophet.
14 For they are the spirits of devils, working miracles, *which* go forth unto the kings of the earth and
of the whole world, to gather them to the battle of
that great day of God Almighty.
15 Behold, I come as a thief. Blessed *is* he that
watcheth, and keepeth his garments, lest he walk
naked, and they see his shame.
16 And he gathered them together into a place
called in the Hebrew tongue Armageddon.

NEW LIVING TRANSLATION

16 Then I heard a mighty voice from the Temple
say to the seven angels, "Go your ways and
pour out on the earth the seven bowls containing
God's wrath."
2 So the first angel left the Temple and poured out
his bowl on the earth, and horrible, malignant sores
broke out on everyone who had the mark of the beast
and who worshiped his statue.
3 Then the second angel poured out his bowl on
the sea, and it became like the blood of a corpse. And
everything in the sea died.
4 Then the third angel poured out his bowl on the
rivers and springs, and they became blood.
5 And I
heard the angel who had authority over all water
saying,

"You are just, O Holy One, who is and who
always was,
because you have sent these judgments.
6 Since they shed the blood
of your holy people and your prophets,
you have given them blood to drink.
It is their just reward."

7 And I heard a voice from the altar,* saying,

"Yes, O Lord God, the Almighty,
your judgments are true and just."

8 Then the fourth angel poured out his bowl on the
sun, causing it to scorch everyone with its fire.
9 Everyone was burned by this blast of heat, and they
cursed the name of God, who had control over all
these plagues. They did not repent of their sins and
turn to God and give him glory.
10 Then the fifth angel poured out his bowl on the
throne of the beast, and his kingdom was plunged
into darkness. His subjects ground their teeth in anguish,
11 and they cursed the God of heaven for their
pains and sores. But they did not repent of their evil
deeds and turn to God.
12 Then the sixth angel poured out his bowl on the
great Euphrates River, and it dried up so that the
kings from the east could march their armies toward
the west without hindrance.
13 And I saw three evil*
spirits that looked like frogs leap from the mouths of
the dragon, the beast, and the false prophet.
14 They
are demonic spirits who work miracles and go out to
all the rulers of the world to gather them for battle
against the Lord on that great judgment day of God
the Almighty.

15 "Look, I will come as unexpectedly as a thief!
Blessed are all who are watching for me, who keep
their clothing ready so they will not have to walk
around naked and ashamed."

16 And the demonic spirits gathered all the rulers
and their armies to a place with the Hebrew name
*Armageddon.**

16:7 Greek *I heard the altar.* **16:13** Greek *unclean.* **16:16** Or *Harmagedon.*

KING JAMES VERSION

[17]And the seventh angel poured out his vial into the air; and there came a great voice out of the temple of heaven, from the throne, saying, It is done.

[18]And there were voices, and thunders, and lightnings; and there was a great earthquake, such as was not since men were upon the earth, so mighty an earthquake, *and* so great.

[19]And the great city was divided into three parts, and the cities of the nations fell: and great Babylon came in remembrance before God, to give unto her the cup of the wine of the fierceness of his wrath.

[20]And every island fled away, and the mountains were not found.

[21]And there fell upon men a great hail out of heaven, *every stone* about the weight of a talent: and men blasphemed God because of the plague of the hail; for the plague thereof was exceeding great.

17 [1]And there came one of the seven angels which had the seven vials, and talked with me, saying unto me, Come hither; I will shew unto thee the judgment of the great whore that sitteth upon many waters:

[2]With whom the kings of the earth have committed fornication, and the inhabitants of the earth have been made drunk with the wine of her fornication.

[3]So he carried me away in the spirit into the wilderness: and I saw a woman sit upon a scarlet coloured beast, full of names of blasphemy, having seven heads and ten horns.

[4]And the woman was arrayed in purple and scarlet colour, and decked with gold and precious stones and pearls, having a golden cup in her hand full of abominations and filthiness of her fornication:

[5]And upon her forehead *was* a name written, MYSTERY, BABYLON THE GREAT, THE MOTHER OF HARLOTS AND ABOMINATIONS OF THE EARTH.

[6]And I saw the woman drunken with the blood of the saints, and with the blood of the martyrs of Jesus: and when I saw her, I wondered with great admiration.

[7]And the angel said unto me, Wherefore didst thou marvel? I will tell thee the mystery of the woman, and of the beast that carrieth her, which hath the seven heads and ten horns.

[8]The beast that thou sawest was, and is not; and shall ascend out of the bottomless pit, and go into perdition: and they that dwell on the earth shall wonder, whose names were not written in the book of life from the foundation of the world, when they behold the beast that was, and is not, and yet is.

[9]And here *is* the mind which hath wisdom. The seven heads are seven mountains, on which the woman sitteth.

[10]And there are seven kings: five are fallen, and one is, *and* the other is not yet come; and when he cometh, he must continue a short space.

NEW LIVING TRANSLATION

[17]Then the seventh angel poured out his bowl into the air. And a mighty shout came from the throne in the Temple, saying, "It is finished!" [18]Then the thunder crashed and rolled, and lightning flashed. And a great earthquake struck—the worst since people were placed on the earth. [19]The great city of Babylon split into three sections, and the cities of many nations fell into heaps of rubble. So God remembered all of Babylon's sins, and he made her drink the cup that was filled with the wine of his fierce wrath. [20]And every island disappeared, and all the mountains were leveled. [21]There was a terrible hailstorm, and hailstones weighing as much as seventy-five pounds* fell from the sky onto the people below. They cursed God because of the terrible plague of the hailstorm.

The Great Prostitute

17 One of the seven angels who had poured out the seven bowls came over and spoke to me. "Come with me," he said, "and I will show you the judgment that is going to come on the great prostitute, who rules over many waters. [2]The kings of the world have committed adultery with her, and the people who belong to this world have been made drunk by the wine of her immorality."

[3]So the angel took me in the Spirit* into the wilderness. There I saw a woman sitting on a scarlet beast that had seven heads and ten horns, and blasphemies against God were written all over it. [4]The woman wore purple and scarlet clothing and beautiful jewelry made of gold and precious gems and pearls. In her hand she held a gold goblet full of obscenities and the impurities of her immorality. [5]A mysterious name was written on her forehead: "Babylon the Great, Mother of All Prostitutes and Obscenities in the World." [6]I could see that she was drunk—drunk with the blood of God's holy people who were witnesses for Jesus. I stared at her in complete amazement.

[7]"Why are you so amazed?" the angel asked. "I will tell you the mystery of this woman and of the beast with seven heads and ten horns on which she sits. [8]The beast you saw was once alive but isn't now. And yet he will soon come up out of the bottomless pit* and go to eternal destruction. And the people who belong to this world, whose names were not written in the Book of Life before the world was made, will be amazed at the reappearance of this beast who had died.

[9]"This calls for a mind with understanding: The seven heads of the beast represent the seven hills where the woman rules. They also represent seven kings. [10]Five kings have already fallen, the sixth now reigns, and the seventh is yet to come, but his reign will be brief.

16:21 Greek *1 talent* [34 kilograms]. **17:3** Or *in spirit.* **17:8** Or *the abyss,* or *the underworld.*

KING JAMES VERSION

11 And the beast that was, and is not, even he is the eighth, and is of the seven, and goeth into perdition.

12 And the ten horns which thou sawest are ten kings, which have received no kingdom as yet; but receive power as kings one hour with the beast.

13 These have one mind, and shall give their power and strength unto the beast.

14 These shall make war with the Lamb, and the Lamb shall overcome them: for he is Lord of lords, and King of kings: and they that are with him *are* called, and chosen, and faithful.

15 And he saith unto me, The waters which thou sawest, where the whore sitteth, are peoples, and multitudes, and nations, and tongues.

16 And the ten horns which thou sawest upon the beast, these shall hate the whore, and shall make her desolate and naked, and shall eat her flesh, and burn her with fire.

17 For God hath put in their hearts to fulfil his will, and to agree, and give their kingdom unto the beast, until the words of God shall be fulfilled.

18 And the woman which thou sawest is that great city, which reigneth over the kings of the earth.

18 1 And after these things I saw another angel come down from heaven, having great power; and the earth was lightened with his glory.

2 And he cried mightily with a strong voice, saying, Babylon the great is fallen, is fallen, and is become the habitation of devils, and the hold of every foul spirit, and a cage of every unclean and hateful bird.

3 For all nations have drunk of the wine of the wrath of her fornication, and the kings of the earth have committed fornication with her, and the merchants of the earth are waxed rich through the abundance of her delicacies.

4 And I heard another voice from heaven, saying, Come out of her, my people, that ye be not partakers of her sins, and that ye receive not of her plagues.

5 For her sins have reached unto heaven, and God hath remembered her iniquities.

6 Reward her even as she rewarded you, and double unto her double according to her works: in the cup which she hath filled fill to her double.

7 How much she hath glorified herself, and lived deliciously, so much torment and sorrow give her:

NEW LIVING TRANSLATION

11 "The scarlet beast that was, but is no longer, is the eighth king. He is like the other seven, and he, too, is headed for destruction. 12 The ten horns of the beast are ten kings who have not yet risen to power. They will be appointed to their kingdoms for one brief moment to reign with the beast. 13 They will all agree to give him their power and authority. 14 Together they will go to war against the Lamb, but the Lamb will defeat them because he is Lord of all lords and King of all kings. And his called and chosen and faithful ones will be with him."

15 Then the angel said to me, "The waters where the prostitute is ruling represent masses of people of every nation and language. 16 The scarlet beast and his ten horns all hate the prostitute. They will strip her naked, eat her flesh, and burn her remains with fire. 17 For God has put a plan into their minds, a plan that will carry out his purposes. They will agree to give their authority to the scarlet beast, and so the words of God will be fulfilled. 18 And this woman you saw in your vision represents the great city that rules over the kings of the world."

The Fall of Babylon

18 After all this I saw another angel come down from heaven with great authority, and the earth grew bright with his splendor. 2 He gave a mighty shout:

"Babylon is fallen—that great city is fallen!
She has become a home for demons.
She is a hideout for every foul* spirit,
a hideout for every foul vulture
and every foul and dreadful animal.*
3 For all the nations have fallen*
because of the wine of her passionate immorality.
The kings of the world
have committed adultery with her.
Because of her desires for extravagant luxury,
the merchants of the world have grown rich."

4 Then I heard another voice calling from heaven,

"Come away from her, my people.
Do not take part in her sins,
or you will be punished with her.
5 For her sins are piled as high as heaven,
and God remembers her evil deeds.
6 Do to her as she has done to others.
Double her penalty* for all her evil deeds.
She brewed a cup of terror for others,
so brew twice as much* for her.
7 She glorified herself and lived in luxury,
so match it now with torment and sorrow.
She boasted in her heart,
'I am queen on my throne.

18:2a Greek *unclean;* also in each of the two following phrases. **18:2b** Some manuscripts condense the last two lines to read *a hideout for every foul [unclean] and dreadful vulture.* **18:3** Some manuscripts read *have drunk.* **18:6a** Or *Give her an equal penalty.* **18:6b** Or *brew just as much.*

KING JAMES VERSION

for she saith in her heart, I sit a queen, and am no widow, and shall see no sorrow.

8 Therefore shall her plagues come in one day, death, and mourning, and famine; and she shall be utterly burned with fire: for strong *is* the Lord God who judgeth her.

9 And the kings of the earth, who have committed fornication and lived deliciously with her, shall bewail her, and lament for her, when they shall see the smoke of her burning,

10 Standing afar off for the fear of her torment, saying, Alas, alas, that great city Babylon, that mighty city! for in one hour is thy judgment come.

11 And the merchants of the earth shall weep and mourn over her; for no man buyeth their merchandise any more:

12 The merchandise of gold, and silver, and precious stones, and of pearls, and fine linen, and purple, and silk, and scarlet, and all thyine wood, and all manner vessels of ivory, and all manner vessels of most precious wood, and of brass, and iron, and marble,

13 And cinnamon, and odours, and ointments, and frankincense, and wine, and oil, and fine flour, and wheat, and beasts, and sheep, and horses, and chariots, and slaves, and souls of men.

14 And the fruits that thy soul lusted after are departed from thee, and all things which were dainty and goodly are departed from thee, and thou shalt find them no more at all.

15 The merchants of these things, which were made rich by her, shall stand afar off for the fear of her torment, weeping and wailing,

16 And saying, Alas, alas, that great city, that was clothed in fine linen, and purple, and scarlet, and decked with gold, and precious stones, and pearls!

17 For in one hour so great riches is come to nought. And every shipmaster, and all the company in ships, and sailors, and as many as trade by sea, stood afar off,

18 And cried when they saw the smoke of her burning, saying, What *city is* like unto this great city!

19 And they cast dust on their heads, and cried, weeping and wailing, saying, Alas, alas, that great city, wherein were made rich all that had ships in the sea by reason of her costliness! for in one hour is she made desolate.

NEW LIVING TRANSLATION

I am no helpless widow,
and I have no reason to mourn.'
8 Therefore, these plagues will overtake her
in a single day—
death and mourning and famine.
She will be completely consumed by fire,
for the Lord God who judges her is mighty."

9 And the kings of the world who committed adultery with her and enjoyed her great luxury will
mourn for her as they see the smoke rising from
her charred remains. 10 They will stand at a distance,
terrified by her great torment. They will cry out,

"How terrible, how terrible for you,
O Babylon, you great city!
In a single moment
God's judgment came on you."

11 The merchants of the world will weep and
mourn for her, for there is no one left to buy their
goods. 12 She bought great quantities of gold, silver,
jewels, and pearls; fine linen, purple, silk, and scarlet
cloth; things made of fragrant thyine wood, ivory
goods, and objects made of expensive wood; and
bronze, iron, and marble. 13 She also bought cinnamon, spice, incense, myrrh, frankincense, wine, olive
oil, fine flour, wheat, cattle, sheep, horses, chariots,
and bodies—that is, human slaves.

14 "The fancy things you loved so much
are gone," they cry.
"All your luxuries and splendor
are gone forever,
never to be yours again."

15 The merchants who became wealthy by selling her these things will stand at a distance, terrified by her great torment. They will weep and cry out,

16 "How terrible, how terrible for that great city!
She was clothed in finest purple and
scarlet linens,
decked out with gold and precious stones
and pearls!
17 In a single moment
all the wealth of the city is gone!"

And all the captains of the merchant ships and
their passengers and sailors and crews will stand at a
distance. 18 They will cry out as they watch the smoke
ascend, and they will say, "Where is there another
city as great as this?" 19 And they will weep and throw
dust on their heads to show their grief. And they will
cry out,

"How terrible, how terrible for that great city!
The shipowners became wealthy
by transporting her great wealth on the seas.
In a single moment it is all gone."

KING JAMES VERSION

20 Rejoice over her, *thou* heaven, and *ye* holy
apostles and prophets; for God hath avenged you
on her.
21 And a mighty angel took up a stone like a great
millstone, and cast *it* into the sea, saying, Thus with
violence shall that great city Babylon be thrown
down, and shall be found no more at all.
22 And the voice of harpers, and musicians, and of
pipers, and trumpeters, shall be heard no more at all
in thee; and no craftsman, of whatsoever craft *he be*,
shall be found any more in thee; and the sound of a
millstone shall be heard no more at all in thee;
23 And the light of a candle shall shine no more at
all in thee; and the voice of the bridegroom and of
the bride shall be heard no more at all in thee: for thy
merchants were the great men of the earth; for by thy
sorceries were all nations deceived.
24 And in her was found the blood of prophets, and
of saints, and of all that were slain upon the earth.

19 1 And after these things I heard a great voice
of much people in heaven, saying, Alleluia;
Salvation, and glory, and honour, and power, unto the
Lord our God:
2 For true and righteous *are* his judgments: for he
hath judged the great whore, which did corrupt
the earth with her fornication, and hath avenged the
blood of his servants at her hand.
3 And again they said, Alleluia. And her smoke rose
up for ever and ever.
4 And the four and twenty elders and the four
beasts fell down and worshipped God that sat on the
throne, saying, Amen; Alleluia.
5 And a voice came out of the throne, saying, Praise
our God, all ye his servants, and ye that fear him, both
small and great.

NEW LIVING TRANSLATION

20 Rejoice over her fate, O heaven
and people of God and apostles and prophets!
For at last God has judged her
for your sakes.

21 Then a mighty angel picked up a boulder the
size of a huge millstone. He threw it into the ocean
and shouted,

"Just like this, the great city Babylon
will be thrown down with violence
and will never be found again.
22 The sound of harps, singers, flutes, and trumpets
will never be heard in you again.
No craftsmen and no trades
will ever be found in you again.
The sound of the mill
will never be heard in you again.
23 The light of a lamp
will never shine in you again.
The happy voices of brides and grooms
will never be heard in you again.
For your merchants were the greatest in
the world,
and you deceived the nations with
your sorceries.
24 In your* streets flowed the blood of the prophets
and of God's holy people
and the blood of people slaughtered all over
the world."

Songs of Victory in Heaven

19 After this, I heard what sounded like a vast
crowd in heaven shouting,

"Praise the LORD!*
Salvation and glory and power belong
to our God.
2 His judgments are true and just.
He has punished the great prostitute
who corrupted the earth with her immorality.
He has avenged the murder of his servants."

3 And again their voices rang out:

"Praise the LORD!
The smoke from that city ascends forever
and ever!"

4 Then the twenty-four elders and the four living
beings fell down and worshiped God, who was sitting
on the throne. They cried out, "Amen! Praise the
LORD!"
5 And from the throne came a voice that said,

"Praise our God,
all his servants,
all who fear him,
from the least to the greatest."

18:24 Greek *her.* **19:1** Greek *Hallelujah;* also in 19:3, 4, 6. *Hallelujah* is the transliteration of a Hebrew term that means "Praise the LORD."

KING JAMES VERSION

6 And I heard as it were the voice of a great multitude, and as the voice of many waters, and as the
voice of mighty thunderings, saying, Alleluia: for the
Lord God omnipotent reigneth.
7 Let us be glad and rejoice, and give honour to
him: for the marriage of the Lamb is come, and his
wife hath made herself ready.
8 And to her was granted that she should be arrayed in fine linen, clean and white: for the fine linen
is the righteousness of saints.
9 And he saith unto me, Write, Blessed *are* they
which are called unto the marriage supper of the
Lamb. And he saith unto me, These are the true sayings of God.
10 And I fell at his feet to worship him. And he said
unto me, See *thou do it* not: I am thy fellowservant,
and of thy brethren that have the testimony of Jesus:
worship God: for the testimony of Jesus is the spirit
of prophecy.

11 And I saw heaven opened, and behold a white
horse; and he that sat upon him *was* called Faithful
and True, and in righteousness he doth judge and
make war.
12 His eyes *were* as a flame of fire, and on his head
were many crowns; and he had a name written, that
no man knew, but he himself.
13 And he *was* clothed with a vesture dipped in
blood: and his name is called The Word of God.
14 And the armies *which were* in heaven followed
him upon white horses, clothed in fine linen, white
and clean.
15 And out of his mouth goeth a sharp sword, that
with it he should smite the nations: and he shall rule
them with a rod of iron: and he treadeth the winepress of the fierceness and wrath of Almighty God.
16 And he hath on *his* vesture and on his thigh a
name written, KING OF KINGS, AND LORD OF
LORDS.
17 And I saw an angel standing in the sun; and he
cried with a loud voice, saying to all the fowls that fly
in the midst of heaven, Come and gather yourselves
together unto the supper of the great God;
18 That ye may eat the flesh of kings, and the flesh of
captains, and the flesh of mighty men, and the flesh of
horses, and of them that sit on them, and the flesh
of all *men, both* free and bond, both small and great.
19 And I saw the beast, and the kings of the earth,
and their armies, gathered together to make war
against him that sat on the horse, and against his
army.

NEW LIVING TRANSLATION

6 Then I heard again what sounded like the shout
of a vast crowd or the roar of mighty ocean waves or
the crash of loud thunder:

"Praise the LORD!
For the Lord our God,* the Almighty, reigns.
7 Let us be glad and rejoice,
and let us give honor to him.
For the time has come for the wedding feast
of the Lamb,
and his bride has prepared herself.
8 She has been given the finest of pure white linen
to wear."
For the fine linen represents the good deeds
of God's holy people.

9 And the angel said to me, "Write this: Blessed are
those who are invited to the wedding feast of the
Lamb." And he added, "These are true words that
come from God."
10 Then I fell down at his feet to worship him, but
he said, "No, don't worship me. I am a servant of God,
just like you and your brothers and sisters* who testify about their faith in Jesus. Worship only God. For
the essence of prophecy is to give a clear witness
for Jesus.*"

The Rider on the White Horse

11 Then I saw heaven opened, and a white horse was
standing there. Its rider was named Faithful and
True, for he judges fairly and wages a righteous war.
12 His eyes were like flames of fire, and on his head
were many crowns. A name was written on him that
no one understood except himself. 13 He wore a robe
dipped in blood, and his title was the Word of God.
14 The armies of heaven, dressed in the finest of pure
white linen, followed him on white horses. 15 From
his mouth came a sharp sword to strike down the
nations. He will rule them with an iron rod. He will
release the fierce wrath of God, the Almighty, like
juice flowing from a winepress. 16 On his robe at his
thigh* was written this title: King of all kings and
Lord of all lords.
17 Then I saw an angel standing in the sun, shouting to the vultures flying high in the sky: "Come!
Gather together for the great banquet God has prepared. 18 Come and eat the flesh of kings, generals,
and strong warriors; of horses and their riders; and
of all humanity, both free and slave, small and great."
19 Then I saw the beast and the kings of the world
and their armies gathered together to fight against

19:6 Some manuscripts read *the Lord God.* **19:10a** Greek *brothers.* **19:10b** Or *is the message confirmed by Jesus.* **19:16** Or *On his robe and thigh.*

KING JAMES VERSION

20 And the beast was taken, and with him the false
prophet that wrought miracles before him, with
which he deceived them that had received the mark
of the beast, and them that worshipped his image.
These both were cast alive into a lake of fire burning
with brimstone.
21 And the remnant were slain with the sword of
him that sat upon the horse, which *sword* proceeded
out of his mouth: and all the fowls were filled with
their flesh.

20 1 And I saw an angel come down from
heaven, having the key of the bottomless
pit and a great chain in his hand.
2 And he laid hold on the dragon, that old serpent,
which is the Devil, and Satan, and bound him a thousand years,
3 And cast him into the bottomless pit, and shut
him up, and set a seal upon him, that he should deceive the nations no more, till the thousand years
should be fulfilled: and after that he must be loosed
a little season.
4 And I saw thrones, and they sat upon them, and
judgment was given unto them: and *I saw* the souls
of them that were beheaded for the witness of Jesus,
and for the word of God, and which had not worshipped the beast, neither his image, neither had
received *his* mark upon their foreheads, or in their
hands; and they lived and reigned with Christ a thousand years.
5 But the rest of the dead lived not again until
the thousand years were finished. This *is* the first
resurrection.
6 Blessed and holy *is* he that hath part in the first
resurrection: on such the second death hath no
power, but they shall be priests of God and of Christ,
and shall reign with him a thousand years.
7 And when the thousand years are expired, Satan
shall be loosed out of his prison,
8 And shall go out to deceive the nations which are
in the four quarters of the earth, Gog and Magog, to
gather them together to battle: the number of whom
is as the sand of the sea.
9 And they went up on the breadth of the earth, and
compassed the camp of the saints about, and the beloved city: and fire came down from God out of
heaven, and devoured them.
10 And the devil that deceived them was cast into
the lake of fire and brimstone, where the beast and
the false prophet *are,* and shall be tormented day
and night for ever and ever.

11 And I saw a great white throne, and him that sat
on it, from whose face the earth and the heaven fled
away; and there was found no place for them.

NEW LIVING TRANSLATION

the one sitting on the horse and his army. 20 And the
beast was captured, and with him the false prophet
who did mighty miracles on behalf of the beast—
miracles that deceived all who had accepted the
mark of the beast and who worshiped his statue.
Both the beast and his false prophet were thrown
alive into the fiery lake of burning sulfur. 21 Their entire army was killed by the sharp sword that came
from the mouth of the one riding the white horse.
And the vultures all gorged themselves on the dead
bodies.

The Thousand Years

20 Then I saw an angel coming down from
heaven with the key to the bottomless pit*
and a heavy chain in his hand. 2 He seized the
dragon—that old serpent, who is the devil, Satan—
and bound him in chains for a thousand years. 3 The
angel threw him into the bottomless pit, which he
then shut and locked so Satan could not deceive the
nations anymore until the thousand years were finished. Afterward he must be released for a little
while.
4 Then I saw thrones, and the people sitting on
them had been given the authority to judge. And I
saw the souls of those who had been beheaded for
their testimony about Jesus and for proclaiming the
word of God. They had not worshiped the beast or
his statue, nor accepted his mark on their forehead
or their hands. They all came to life again, and they
reigned with Christ for a thousand years.
5 This is the first resurrection. (The rest of the dead
did not come back to life until the thousand years had
ended.) 6 Blessed and holy are those who share in the
first resurrection. For them the second death holds
no power, but they will be priests of God and of Christ
and will reign with him a thousand years.

The Defeat of Satan

7 When the thousand years come to an end, Satan will
be let out of his prison. 8 He will go out to deceive the
nations—called Gog and Magog—in every corner of
the earth. He will gather them together for battle—a
mighty army, as numberless as sand along the seashore. 9 And I saw them as they went up on the broad
plain of the earth and surrounded God's people and
the beloved city. But fire from heaven came down on
the attacking armies and consumed them.
10 Then the devil, who had deceived them, was
thrown into the fiery lake of burning sulfur, joining
the beast and the false prophet. There they will be
tormented day and night forever and ever.

The Final Judgment

11 And I saw a great white throne and the one sitting
on it. The earth and sky fled from his presence, but

20:1 Or *the abyss,* or *the underworld;* also in 20:3.

KING JAMES VERSION

12 And I saw the dead, small and great, stand before God; and the books were opened: and another book was opened, which is *the book* of life: and the dead were judged out of those things which were written in the books, according to their works.

13 And the sea gave up the dead which were in it; and death and hell delivered up the dead which were in them: and they were judged every man according to their works.

14 And death and hell were cast into the lake of fire. This is the second death.

15 And whosoever was not found written in the book of life was cast into the lake of fire.

21 1 And I saw a new heaven and a new earth: for the first heaven and the first earth were passed away; and there was no more sea.

2 And I John saw the holy city, new Jerusalem, coming down from God out of heaven, prepared as a bride adorned for her husband.

3 And I heard a great voice out of heaven saying, Behold, the tabernacle of God *is* with men, and he will dwell with them, and they shall be his people, and God himself shall be with them, *and be* their God.

4 And God shall wipe away all tears from their eyes; and there shall be no more death, neither sorrow, nor crying, neither shall there be any more pain: for the former things are passed away.

5 And he that sat upon the throne said, Behold, I make all things new. And he said unto me, Write: for these words are true and faithful.

6 And he said unto me, It is done. I am Alpha and Omega, the beginning and the end. I will give unto him that is athirst of the fountain of the water of life freely.

7 He that overcometh shall inherit all things; and I will be his God, and he shall be my son.

8 But the fearful, and unbelieving, and the abominable, and murderers, and whoremongers, and sorcerers, and idolaters, and all liars, shall have their part in the lake which burneth with fire and brimstone: which is the second death.

9 And there came unto me one of the seven angels which had the seven vials full of the seven last plagues, and talked with me, saying, Come hither, I will shew thee the bride, the Lamb's wife.

10 And he carried me away in the spirit to a great and high mountain, and shewed me that great city, the holy Jerusalem, descending out of heaven from God,

11 Having the glory of God: and her light *was* like unto a stone most precious, even like a jasper stone, clear as crystal;

12 And had a wall great and high, *and* had twelve gates, and at the gates twelve angels, and names written thereon, which are *the names* of the twelve tribes of the children of Israel:

13 On the east three gates; on the north three gates; on the south three gates; and on the west three gates.

14 And the wall of the city had twelve foundations,

NEW LIVING TRANSLATION

they found no place to hide. 12 I saw the dead, both great and small, standing before God's throne. And the books were opened, including the Book of Life. And the dead were judged according to what they had done, as recorded in the books. 13 The sea gave up its dead, and death and the grave* gave up their dead. And all were judged according to their deeds. 14 Then death and the grave were thrown into the lake of fire. This lake of fire is the second death. 15 And anyone whose name was not found recorded in the Book of Life was thrown into the lake of fire.

The New Jerusalem

21 Then I saw a new heaven and a new earth, for the old heaven and the old earth had disappeared. And the sea was also gone. 2 And I saw the holy city, the new Jerusalem, coming down from God out of heaven like a bride beautifully dressed for her husband.

3 I heard a loud shout from the throne, saying, "Look, God's home is now among his people! He will live with them, and they will be his people. God himself will be with them.* 4 He will wipe every tear from their eyes, and there will be no more death or sorrow or crying or pain. All these things are gone forever."

5 And the one sitting on the throne said, "Look, I am making everything new!" And then he said to me, "Write this down, for what I tell you is trustworthy and true." 6 And he also said, "It is finished! I am the Alpha and the Omega—the Beginning and the End. To all who are thirsty I will give freely from the springs of the water of life. 7 All who are victorious will inherit all these blessings, and I will be their God, and they will be my children.

8 "But cowards, unbelievers, the corrupt, murderers, the immoral, those who practice witchcraft, idol worshipers, and all liars—their fate is in the fiery lake of burning sulfur. This is the second death."

9 Then one of the seven angels who held the seven bowls containing the seven last plagues came and said to me, "Come with me! I will show you the bride, the wife of the Lamb."

10 So he took me in the Spirit* to a great, high mountain, and he showed me the holy city, Jerusalem, descending out of heaven from God. 11 It shone with the glory of God and sparkled like a precious stone—like jasper as clear as crystal. 12 The city wall was broad and high, with twelve gates guarded by twelve angels. And the names of the twelve tribes of Israel were written on the gates. 13 There were three gates on each side—east, north, south, and west. 14 The wall of the city had twelve foundation stones,

20:13 Greek *and Hades;* also in 20:14. **21:3** Some manuscripts read *God himself will be with them, their God.* **21:10** Or *in spirit.*

KING JAMES VERSION

and in them the names of the twelve apostles of the Lamb.

15 And he that talked with me had a golden reed to measure the city, and the gates thereof, and the wall thereof.

16 And the city lieth foursquare, and the length is as large as the breadth: and he measured the city with the reed, twelve thousand furlongs. The length and the breadth and the height of it are equal.

17 And he measured the wall thereof, an hundred *and* forty *and* four cubits, *according to* the measure of a man, that is, of the angel.

18 And the building of the wall of it was *of* jasper: and the city *was* pure gold, like unto clear glass.

19 And the foundations of the wall of the city *were* garnished with all manner of precious stones. The first foundation *was* jasper; the second, sapphire; the third, a chalcedony; the fourth, an emerald;

20 The fifth, sardonyx; the sixth, sardius; the seventh, chrysolyte; the eighth, beryl; the ninth, a topaz; the tenth, a chrysoprasus; the eleventh, a jacinth; the twelfth, an amethyst.

21 And the twelve gates *were* twelve pearls: every several gate was of one pearl: and the street of the city *was* pure gold, as it were transparent glass.

22 And I saw no temple therein: for the Lord God Almighty and the Lamb are the temple of it.

23 And the city had no need of the sun, neither of the moon, to shine in it: for the glory of God did lighten it, and the Lamb *is* the light thereof.

24 And the nations of them which are saved shall walk in the light of it: and the kings of the earth do bring their glory and honour into it.

25 And the gates of it shall not be shut at all by day: for there shall be no night there.

26 And they shall bring the glory and honour of the nations into it.

27 And there shall in no wise enter into it any thing that defileth, neither *whatsoever* worketh abomination, or *maketh* a lie: but they which are written in the Lamb's book of life.

22 1 And he shewed me a pure river of water of life, clear as crystal, proceeding out of the throne of God and of the Lamb.

2 In the midst of the street of it, and on either side of the river, *was there* the tree of life, which bare twelve *manner of* fruits, *and* yielded her fruit every month: and the leaves of the tree *were* for the healing of the nations.

3 And there shall be no more curse: but the throne of God and of the Lamb shall be in it; and his servants shall serve him:

4 And they shall see his face; and his name *shall be* in their foreheads.

5 And there shall be no night there; and they need no candle, neither light of the sun; for the Lord God giveth them light: and they shall reign for ever and ever.

NEW LIVING TRANSLATION

and on them were written the names of the twelve apostles of the Lamb.

15 The angel who talked to me held in his hand a gold measuring stick to measure the city, its gates, and its wall. 16 When he measured it, he found it was a square, as wide as it was long. In fact, its length and width and height were each 1,400 miles.* 17 Then he measured the walls and found them to be 216 feet thick* (according to the human standard used by the angel).

18 The wall was made of jasper, and the city was pure gold, as clear as glass. 19 The wall of the city was built on foundation stones inlaid with twelve precious stones:* the first was jasper, the second sapphire, the third agate, the fourth emerald, 20 the fifth onyx, the sixth carnelian, the seventh chrysolite, the eighth beryl, the ninth topaz, the tenth chrysoprase, the eleventh jacinth, the twelfth amethyst.

21 The twelve gates were made of pearls—each gate from a single pearl! And the main street was pure gold, as clear as glass.

22 I saw no temple in the city, for the Lord God Almighty and the Lamb are its temple. 23 And the city has no need of sun or moon, for the glory of God illuminates the city, and the Lamb is its light. 24 The nations will walk in its light, and the kings of the world will enter the city in all their glory. 25 Its gates will never be closed at the end of day because there is no night there. 26 And all the nations will bring their glory and honor into the city. 27 Nothing evil* will be allowed to enter, nor anyone who practices shameful idolatry and dishonesty—but only those whose names are written in the Lamb's Book of Life.

22 Then the angel showed me a river with the water of life, clear as crystal, flowing from the throne of God and of the Lamb. 2 It flowed down the center of the main street. On each side of the river grew a tree of life, bearing twelve crops of fruit,* with a fresh crop each month. The leaves were used for medicine to heal the nations.

3 No longer will there be a curse upon anything. For the throne of God and of the Lamb will be there, and his servants will worship him. 4 And they will see his face, and his name will be written on their foreheads. 5 And there will be no night there—no need for lamps or sun—for the Lord God will shine on them. And they will reign forever and ever.

21:16 Greek *12,000 stadia* [2,220 kilometers]. **21:17** Greek *144 cubits* [65 meters]. **21:19** The identification of some of these gemstones is uncertain. **21:27** Or *ceremonially unclean.* **22:2** Or *twelve kinds of fruit.*

KING JAMES VERSION

6 And he said unto me, These sayings *are* faithful and true: and the Lord God of the holy prophets sent his angel to shew unto his servants the things which must shortly be done.

7 Behold, I come quickly: blessed *is* he that keepeth the sayings of the prophecy of this book.

8 And I John saw these things, and heard *them*. And when I had heard and seen, I fell down to worship before the feet of the angel which shewed me these things.

9 Then saith he unto me, See *thou do it* not: for I am thy fellowservant, and of thy brethren the prophets, and of them which keep the sayings of this book: worship God.

10 And he saith unto me, Seal not the sayings of the prophecy of this book: for the time is at hand.

11 He that is unjust, let him be unjust still: and he which is filthy, let him be filthy still: and he that is righteous, let him be righteous still: and he that is holy, let him be holy still.

12 And, behold, I come quickly; and my reward *is* with me, to give every man according as his work shall be.

13 I am Alpha and Omega, the beginning and the end, the first and the last.

14 Blessed *are* they that do his commandments, that they may have right to the tree of life, and may enter in through the gates into the city.

15 For without *are* dogs, and sorcerers, and whoremongers, and murderers, and idolaters, and whosoever loveth and maketh a lie.

16 I Jesus have sent mine angel to testify unto you these things in the churches. I am the root and the offspring of David, *and* the bright and morning star.

17 And the Spirit and the bride say, Come. And let him that heareth say, Come. And let him that is athirst come. And whosoever will, let him take the water of life freely.

18 For I testify unto every man that heareth the words of the prophecy of this book, If any man shall add unto these things, God shall add unto him the plagues that are written in this book:

19 And if any man shall take away from the words of the book of this prophecy, God shall take away his part out of the book of life, and out of the holy city, and *from* the things which are written in this book.

20 He which testifieth these things saith, Surely I come quickly. Amen. Even so, come, Lord Jesus.

21 The grace of our Lord Jesus Christ *be* with you all. Amen.

NEW LIVING TRANSLATION

6 Then the angel said to me, "Everything you have heard and seen is trustworthy and true. The Lord God, who inspires his prophets,* has sent his angel to tell his servants what will happen soon.*"

Jesus Is Coming

7 "Look, I am coming soon! Blessed are those who
obey the words of prophecy written in this book.*"

8 I, John, am the one who heard and saw all these things. And when I heard and saw them, I fell down to worship at the feet of the angel who showed them to me. 9 But he said, "No, don't worship me. I am a servant of God, just like you and your brothers the prophets, as well as all who obey what is written in this book. Worship only God!"

10 Then he instructed me, "Do not seal up the prophetic words in this book, for the time is near. 11 Let the one who is doing harm continue to do harm; let the one who is vile continue to be vile; let the one who is righteous continue to live righteously; let the one who is holy continue to be holy."

12 "Look, I am coming soon, bringing my reward
with me to repay all people according to their
deeds. 13 I am the Alpha and the Omega, the First
and the Last, the Beginning and the End."

14 Blessed are those who wash their robes. They will be permitted to enter through the gates of the city and eat the fruit from the tree of life. 15 Outside the city are the dogs—the sorcerers, the sexually immoral, the murderers, the idol worshipers, and all who love to live a lie.

16 "I, Jesus, have sent my angel to give you this
message for the churches. I am both the source
of David and the heir to his throne.* I am the
bright morning star."

17 The Spirit and the bride say, "Come." Let anyone who hears this say, "Come." Let anyone who is thirsty come. Let anyone who desires drink freely from the water of life. 18 And I solemnly declare to everyone who hears the words of prophecy written in this book: If anyone adds anything to what is written here, God will add to that person the plagues described in this book. 19 And if anyone removes any of the words from this book of prophecy, God will remove that person's share in the tree of life and in the holy city that are described in this book.

20 He who is the faithful witness to all these things says, "Yes, I am coming soon!"

Amen! Come, Lord Jesus!

21 May the grace of the Lord Jesus be with God's holy people.*

22:6a Or *The Lord, the God of the spirits of the prophets.* **22:6b** Or *suddenly*, or *quickly;* also in 22:7, 12, 20. **22:7** Or *scroll;* also in 22:9, 10, 18, 19. **22:16** Greek *I am the root and offspring of David.* **22:21** Other manuscripts read *be with all;* still others read *be with all of God's holy people.* Some manuscripts add *Amen.*

TABLE OF WEIGHTS AND MEASURES

WEIGHT	*talent* (60 *minas*)	75	pounds	34	kilograms
	mina (50 *shekels*)	1.25	pounds	600	grams
	shekel	0.4	ounces	11.4	grams
	pim (⅔ *shekel*)	0.25	ounces	8	grams
	beka (½ *shekel*)	0.2	ounces	5.7	grams
	gerah (1/20 *shekel*)	0.02	ounces	0.6	grams
	litra	12	ounces	327	grams
LENGTH	*long cubit*	21	inches	53	centimeters
	cubit	18	inches	45	centimeters
	span	9	inches	23	centimeters
	fathom	6	inches	15	centimeters
	handbreadth	3	inches	8	centimeters
	schoinos (33 *stadia*)	3.8	miles	6.1	kilometers
	stadion	205	yards	187	meters
CAPACITY					
Dry Measure	*cor/homer* (10 *ephahs*)	5	bushels	182	liters
	lethek (5 *ephahs*)	2.5	bushels	91	liters
	ephah	0.5	bushels	18	liters
	seah (⅓ *ephah*)	5	quarts	6	liters
	omer (1/10 *ephah*)	2	quarts	2	liters
	cab (½ *omer*)	1	quart	1.3	liters
Liquid Measure	*bath*	5.5	gallons	21	liters
	hin (1/6 *bath*)	1	gallon	3.8	liters
	log (1/72 *bath*)	0.3	quarts	0.3	liters